Oxford Dictionary of Pronunciation for Current English

Clive Upton
William A. Kretzschmar, Jr
Rafal Konopka

OXFORD
UNIVERSITY PRESS

OXFORD

UNIVERSITY PRESS

Great Clarendon Street, Oxford OX2 6DP

Oxford University Press is a department of the University of Oxford.
It furthers the University's objective of excellence in research, scholarship,
and education by publishing worldwide in

Oxford New York

Auckland Bangkok Buenos Aires Cape Town Chennai
Dar es Salaam Delhi Hong Kong Istanbul Karachi Kolkata
Kuala Lumpur Madrid Melbourne Mexico City Mumbai Nairobi
São Paulo Shanghai Taipei Tokyo Toronto

Oxford is a registered trade mark of Oxford University Press
in the UK and in certain other countries

Published in the United States
by Oxford University Press Inc., New York

British Library Cataloguing in Publication Data
Data available

Library of Congress Cataloging in Publication Data
Data available
ISBN 0-19-860772-5

10 9 8 7 6 5 4 3 2 1

Typeset in Nimrod and Arial
by Selwood Systems
Printed in Great Britain by
T. J. International Ltd.
Padstow, Cornwall

OXFORD DICTIONARY OF PRONUNCIATION
FOR CURRENT ENGLISH

421.52
UPT

Contents

Dictionary team

Clive Upton
William A. Kretzschmar, Jr
Rafal Konopka

Oxford University Press

Editors
Susan Wilkin
Judith Scott

Editorial assistants
Alison Curr
Phil Gerrish
Anne McConnell

Foreign language consultants

Afrikaans
Penny Silva, *formerly*
Managing editor,
*Dictionary of South
African English on
Historical Principles*,
Oxford University Press

Brazilian Portuguese
Lixia Xavier, freelance
lexicographer and
translator

Lusitanian Portuguese
Lia Correia-Raitt, Sub-
Faculty of Portuguese,
Modern Languages,
Oxford University

Czech
Dr Jaromír Málek,
Griffith Institute,
Ashmolean Museum,
Oxford

Danish
Britt-Katrin Keson, The
Society for Danish
Language and Literature,
Copenhagen, Denmark

Dutch & Flemish
Susan Wilkin, Oxford
Dictionary Department

French
Isabelle Stables, *formerly*
Oxford French
Dictionaries

German
Dr Michael Clark,
Projects Manager,
Bilingual Dictionaries,
Oxford University Press

Hungarian
Dr Gábor Bátonyi,
University of Bradford

Irish Gaelic
Mary O'Neill, Managing
Editor, Language
Engineering, Oxford
University Press

Italian
Francesca Logi, freelance
lexicographer and
translator

Norwegian
Dr Olav Veka,
Brumunddal, Norway

Polish
Danuta Padley, Oxford
English Dictionary

Russian
Dr Della Thompson,
Projects Manager,
Bilingual Dictionaries,
Oxford University Press

Spanish
Ana Cristina Llompart,
freelance lexicographer
and translator

Swedish
Susanne Charlett, Oxford
English Dictionary

Turkish
Helen Liebeck, *formerly*
Oxford Dictionary
Department

Welsh
Dr Hywel Wyn Owen,
University of Wales,
Bangor

Preface

In this dictionary we present fresh information on how some 100,000 words are pronounced with both a British and an American accent. In a procedure that is unique in a pronouncing dictionary, every word is given separate British and American transcriptions, however closely it might be pronounced in the two accents, so that users particularly interested in one of the accents need be in no doubt as to where to direct their attention. Any alternative pronunciations within the British and American varieties are also given where appropriate. Inflection transcriptions provide information on the pronunciation of such grammatical variants as plurals, comparative and superlative adjectives, and verb tenses.

The model accents through which British and American pronunciations are described have been chosen because we judge them to be most widely representative in their respective locations. They are not accents which anyone will regard as being pretentious or the property of remote or aristocratic minorities. Nor are they accents which are tied to narrowly-defined geographical regions. All the pronunciations can be expected to be widely heard in the United Kingdom or in the United States, being used by many and approximated closely by even more people in populations that are increasingly mobile and well educated. Selected as they have been for their modernity, and for the fact that they are not rarified in any way, the model accents differ in some small but important ways from those which have previously been described as representative of speech in the two communities.

The transcribed words include both the unusual and the everyday, so that the dictionary will be of value to the fully accomplished user of English, whether a native or a non-native speaker, and also to the learner of English. The expert speaker will find in the unusually large headword list many words which they might expect to encounter only rarely and for which pronunciations might not be immediately apparent. They should also find the pronunciation models informative and even reassuring, since the two accents described are in some details more familiar in the everyday experience of residents of Britain and America than those offered as models elsewhere. The learner will, of course, find here two accents on which they can reliably fashion their own, confident that, if they faithfully reproduce the sounds according to phonetic principles, their pronunciation will not be judged to be quaint, affected, ill-educated, or narrowly regional. Once the model accent itself has been mastered, learners will, like the expert English-user, have at their disposal the largest-available list of pronunciation transcriptions, for both commonplace and more unusual words.

It has been our aim, then, to create the most serviceable pronunciation models possible for the two major international varieties of English, British and American, and to present these side by side, with no bias towards either one. Speakers can use our pronunciations confident both that they will be understood and will attract no adverse judgements. We are conscious that, although vital to the accurate presentation of pronunciations, phonetic script is not a user-friendly medium for many readers, and it has also been our aim to create an uncomplicated book. Consequently alternative pronunciations are shown in full rather than being abbreviated to include only their variant parts, and grammatically inflected forms of words are given separately for each accent. Furthermore because the headword list is tied closely to the lists of all the major dictionaries of Oxford University Press, users can expect ready access to the meanings of the words that are featured here, should those meanings be unclear.

We have developed our British and American models not as incremental improve-

ments on some prior practice, but as the product of our long research experience as students of language variation. We believe that our familiarity with facts of variation gives us standing to create pronunciation models which avoid slavish imitation of the dictates of self-appointed arbiters of taste or style in language, in favour of patterns which reflect the actual speech of real people. But of course, linguists do not operate outside a tradition, even when they are bringing a fresh perspective to bear to meet modern needs. We have greatly profited from the research and scholarship on English pronunciation of those who have come before us. We cannot but admire the achievements of Daniel Jones and A. C. Gimson in Britain, or of John Kenyon and Edward Artin in America. We must acknowledge our great debt to the speakers, field workers, and our predecessors as editors of the two great national surveys of speech in Britain and American, the Survey of English Dialects and the American Linguistic Atlas Project. And we must also offer our gratitude to our colleagues in lexicography, dialectology, sociolinguistics, and other branches of the study of the English language, whether cited in the front matter or not, without whose observations and insights we could not have assessed the facts of current English pronunciation and compiled our lists.

We would also like to make a few more individual acknowledgements. We would like to thank Eric Rochester for his invaluable technical assistance. Clive Upton owes a great debt of gratitude to John Widdowson, and before him to Harold Orton and David Parry, who taught him to listen attentively and work independently; and to Lesley Upton, who herself listened and made all the right noises. William A. Kretzschmar, Jr would like to thank three people for their contributions toward this work: Virginia McDavid, for her judgement and support over many years; Lee Pederson, whose unmatched knowledge of American pronunciation, and whose friendship, provided inspiration; and Claudia Kretzschmar, who not only endured and helped to brighten the extended work on transcriptions but contributed herself, on many occasions, to their quality. Rafal Konopka would like to thank his teachers at the Jagiellonian University in Krakow, Poland, where the adventure with English began; his mentors and colleagues at the University of Georgia, without whom the adventure would not have evolved into fascination; and his family for their patience, support, and active interest.

Finally, we appeal to our readers, the living speakers of contemporary English, whether native or later acquired, to listen to the pronunciation of English around them and to revel in the endless variety of English voices and accents that they will hear. We have in this volume ascertained particular models of British and American pronunciation, and we assert their essential value for native speakers and for learners alike. Yet we will join you, our readers, in the appreciation of the multitude of accents and voices which we have not included here, and assert as well their own great value for the subtlety and richness of our English language.

CLIVE UPTON · WILLIAM A. KRETZSCHMAR, JR · RAFAL KONOPKA
September 2003

Introduction

Use of the dictionary

This dictionary presents the pronunciations of a large body of words in both British English (BR) and United States American English (AM) varieties. It is intended for use both by fluent English speakers and by learners of the language. On the one hand, it will provide those possessing a high degree of competence in English with a guide to the pronunciation of those uncommon words with which they may be unfamiliar and whose pronunciation may not immediately be apparent. On the other hand, it will give the English-language learner a comprehensive guide to the pronunciation of the core vocabulary of the two principal international English varieties.

It would of course be both impracticable and confusing to attempt to present transcriptions for even a fraction of the variety of regional and social accents which characterize British and American English. For both pragmatic and pedagogic reasons model accents have to be sought, transcriptions of which may be generally accepted as embodying the major elements of the pronunciation-types under consideration. Descriptions of the BR and AM models which have been decided upon are given on pp. xii–xviii, and a summary of the pronunciation models is given on p. xxi. In each case the choice has been for that model which, if reproduced by users of this dictionary in accordance with the principles of the International Phonetic Association, will enable them to be understood by native speakers of English without being categorized as belonging to any narrow class, age, or regional grouping.

The text of this dictionary has been so designed that reference can be made to it without careful study of a set of complicated conventions. For example, British and American pronunciations are introduced by 'BR' and 'AM' rather than by symbols. Again, when more than one transcription of a headword is thought to be necessary in either variety, complete transcriptions rather than abbreviated transcriptions are given for each alternative pronunciation. Nevertheless, given below is an explanation of the arrangement of entries for anyone wishing to study it prior to detailed use of the dictionary.

The text explained

1. Headwords

Headwords are arranged in alphabetical order.

If a word can be spelt in two or more ways, the variants are given at their respective places in the alphabetical listing. Although spelling differences are sometimes associated with written British and American English, no indication is given in this dictionary as to which spelling may be most characteristic of which accent: it is not always possible cat-egorically to make a statement on this, and this dictionary concerns pronunciation rather than spelling. Separate headwords are created for variant spellings, regardless of whether they occupy consecutive places in the alphabetical run or are separated by other headwords.

2. The basic entry

A most basic entry consists of a headword in bold type and identical transcriptions for BR and AM:

ablaze
BR ə'bleɪz
AM ə'bleɪz

This indicates that the headword has the same pronunciations for both BR and AM, and that no derived forms need to be considered.

A simple development of this occurs when the BR and AM pronunciations differ in some way but there are still no derived forms:

afloat
BR ə'fləʊt
AM ə'floʊt

3. Several pronunciations: use of comma and plus sign

Where more than one pronunciation is shown for one variety (BR or AM), those pronunciations are separated by a comma or commas:

cast
BR kɑːst, kast

digitization
AM ˌdɪdʒədə'zeɪʃən,
ˌdɪdʒə,taɪ'zeɪʃən

The ordering of variant pronunciations does not imply that one form is more desirable or 'correct' than another.

Commas are also used to separate transcriptions of inflectional endings: see section 6 below.

When elements of an open compound have variant pronunciations, only the variant elements are freshly transcribed, a plus sign being used to avoid repetition:

fer de lance
BR ˌfɛː də 'lɑːns, + 'lans

In addition to the first form shown, this allows the creation of a variant [ˌfɛː də 'lans].

dramatis personae
AM drə,mɑdəs pər'soʊni,
ˌdrɑmədəs +, + pər'soʊnaɪ

This creates a total of four possible forms: the original [drə,mɑdəs pər'soʊni], and the variants [ˌdrɑmədəs pər'soʊni], [drə,mɑdəs pər'soʊnaɪ], and [ˌdrɑmədəs pər'soʊnaɪ].

4. Added elements in transcriptions: use of parentheses

Parentheses within a phonetic transcription have two functions:

(i) they enclose optional elements in a pronunciation, the presence or absence of which will not affect the acceptability of a pronunciation.

winter
AM 'wɪn(t)ər

(ii) in BR transcriptions they enclose linking (orthographic) /r/ or intrusive (non-orthographic) /r/. See below, p. xiii. Linking /r/ is shown in ordinary roman script; intrusive /r/ is italicized.

danger
BR 'deɪndʒə(r)

balsa
BR 'bɔːlsə(*r*)

5. Creation of transcriptions for derived forms: use of vertical bar

A vertical bar in a transcription denotes the place at which it should be broken in order that an inflectional ending (for example plural -s, verbal -ing) may be added (see section 6 below).

6. Inflectional form: use of comma and reverse oblique stroke

The transcription of a first or an only inflectional ending is shown immediately after transcriptions of the headword form, preceded by a hyphen and separated from the headword transcription by a comma. Such endings are to be added either to the full headword-transcription form:

dale
deɪl, -z
(gives plural [deɪlz])

or to that part of the headword-transcription form which precedes the vertical bar, should one be in place:

eatery
BR 'iːtər|i, -ɪz
(gives plural ['iːtərɪz])

eat
AM iːt, -ts, -dɪŋ
(gives inflections [its], [idɪŋ])

Endings which frequently occur in this position are:

nominal plural and verbal -(e)s
verbal -ing, -ed
comparative -er, and agent nominal
-er(s)
superlative -est

Transcriptions of different endings are separated from each other by commas. Alternative forms of inflections are

denoted by the use of the reverse oblique stroke (\):

> **spell**
> BR spɛl, -z, -ɪŋ, -d\-t
> AM spɛl, -z, -ɪŋ, -d

In order to keep the presentation of entries as plain as possible, the presence of endings is not signalled at the headword nor elsewhere in the alphabetical listing. A user requiring information on a word which is derived from a headword, and which does not itself have headword-status, should seek it at the end of the entry for its base form.

7. The composite symbols [ɨ] and [ʉ] (see also pp. xiv and xviii)

[ɪ] and [ʊ], when they occur in unstressed or weakly stressed syllables, are regularly reduced to [ə] by many RP (Received Pronunciation) speakers. The reduced vowel [ə] is even more a feature of AM in certain contexts for [ɪ], though less so for [ʊ]. The IPA convention of barring to signify centralization of high vowels and retraction of front vowels is a convenient way of showing this, and has been adopted for this feature. Whenever the barred symbols are used it is to be taken that both [ɪ] and [ə] for [ɨ], or [ʊ] and [ə] for [ʉ], are acceptable.

Technical discussion: transcription sets

Transcriptions in the text are broadly phonetic. That is, the transcriptions represent actual pronunciations, often with several variant forms per headword, not abstract sound units which include and hide potential variation. For instance, both [ru:m~rum] and [rʊm] are possible pronunciations of *room*, both [ɛks-] and [ɛgz-] are presented for some words beginning with ex- + vowel. A limited symbol set results in broad transcriptions, and may suggest de facto phonemicization to some readers, but our intention is always to indicate actual sounds to be produced.

No single set of vowel and consonant phonemes can represent all varieties; the following sets are appropriate to the BR and AM models used:

Vowels (BR):

	Front	Central	Back
High	i(:)		u:
	ɪ		ʊ
	e	ə(:)	
Mid			
	ɛ(:)	ʌ	ɔ:
Low	a	ɑ:	ɒ

diphthongs: eɪ, ʌɪ, ɔɪ, aʊ, əʊ
nasality (superscript diacritic): ˜

Vowels (AM):

	Front	Central	Back
High	i		u
	ɪ	ʊ	
	e		o
Mid		ə	
	ɛ		ɔ
	æ		
Low	a	ɑ	

diphthongs: eɪ, aɪ, ɔɪ, aʊ, oʊ

Consonants (BR and AM):

Stops: p, b, t, d, k, g
Click: ǀ
Fricatives: f, v, θ, ð, s, z, ʃ, ʒ, x, h
Lateral fricative: ɬ (=Welsh ll)
Affricates: tʃ, dʒ
Nasals: m, n, ŋ
Liquids: l, r
Semivowels: j, w

syllabic consonants: m̩-, n̩-, l̩- (the syllabic diacritic is only used in situations where ambiguity would otherwise occur)

Pronunciation models

The British English (BR) pronunciation model

An obvious model for British English pronunciation is that which is usually termed Received Pronunciation (normally abbreviated to RP), this being 'a standard of pronunciation which is generally considered correct and is also used as a model for the teaching of English to foreigners' (Upton et al., p. 4). A model labelled 'RP' has long been the norm in British English pronouncing and general dictionaries and in language-teaching classrooms. In this regard transcribers of BR, with access to a generally agreed model for description, may be considered to be more fortunate than transcribers of AM, for which no nationwide model can readily be identified (p. xiv below).

However, problems for the transcriber of BR begin rather than end with the choice of RP as the model: it is not possible to justify the choice of model for British English pronunciation simply by claiming that one has chosen RP. As Daniel Jones, like many other commentators, has made clear, RP is not and was not formerly one monolithic accent: there are variations between the pronunciations of individuals who can legitimately lay claim to an RP accent (Jones, p. 13, note 5).

Within a range of RP accents two essential trends, which have been termed 'U-RP' and 'mainstream RP' (by Wells) or 'marked' and 'unmarked' (by Honey), are to be distinguished. The one variety ('U' or 'marked') is an accent which, when heard by most native speakers of BR, leads to the user being judged old-fashioned, affected, or pretentious. The other ('mainstream' or 'unmarked') is an accent which, for native-speakers, carries connotations of education and sophistication but no especially narrow regional overtones and certainly no serious negative judgements. With obvious idiolectal variations, it is the accent we hear used by most national radio and television newsreaders and by very many middle-aged and younger professional people. It might loosely be labelled

'broadcast RP' if yet another label were to be thought desirable: it is reasonable to maintain, however, that since it is 'mainstream' and 'unmarked' it can legitimately lay claim to the RP label without qualification. This variety of the accent contrasts strongly with the 'U' or 'marked' accent of the previous generation of newsreaders and of conservative (often older) RP speakers generally.

In spite of the acknowledged existence of broadly based and more restricted RP varieties, it is the latter which have tended to characterize many descriptions of RP. Rather than being regarded as referring to a universal standard to which a large number of speakers around the country can claim at least partial access, the RP label has undeniably come to be associated restrictively with a small group of older middle- and upper-class speakers possessing close links with the south-east of England.

To correct a situation where the BR model is the possession of a small minority restricted in terms of age, class, and region, a younger, unmarked RP is that which provides the model in this dictionary. The intention is to describe for the user that accent which will be most widely acceptable, as well as most intelligible, to native BR speakers, and to which the speech of very many of them will in turn approximate closely. The model is an accent which is not regionally centred or redolent of class. Unlike the model more usually described, speech conforming to this new model can be heard spoken by a wide range of natives of many parts of the country, with a wide variety of professional backgrounds (though generally with a higher than average level of education). Note that the linking of accent to the concept of social class is avoided here. 'Class', when considered from a linguistic point of view, has rightly been described as 'a proxy variable covering distinctions in life-style, attitude and belief, as well as differential access to wealth, power and prestige' (Milroy, p. 101). Assigning social class according to accent is an increasingly unreliable

procedure in Britain.

Implicit in the British English model presented here, then, is the view that a larger group of people can lay claim to possession of an RP accent than has often hitherto been acknowledged. Each word transcribed has been considered with this in mind, and each transcription is descriptive of a pronunciation which would be judged to be unexceptionable by native speakers of British English generally. As a result of this policy, certain regularly-occurring pronunciation features which have to date been ignored or marked prescriptively are allowed where they are now judged to be established features of RP. Notable examples of such features are [-tʃ-] in place of [-tj-] and [-dʒ-] in place of [-dj-] in such words as *destitute* and *reduce*: since it is considered that these are very frequent in RP, both [tʃ] and [tj], [dʒ] and [dj] transcriptions are given.

Another very significant feature judged worthy of inclusion in the model is that of 'intrusive' <r>. Intrusive <r> is a 'linking' <r> which is unhistorical and which is therefore not supported by orthography. For example, *law* in the phrase *law and order* is in BR frequently [lɔːr] (i.e. [lɔːr an(d) ɔːdə]). Long condemned by teachers of pronunciation, this is nevertheless a firmly established feature of today's mainstream RP: it is indicated in transcriptions by means of a convention similar to that for linking <r>, that is by parentheses, so that *law* is transcribed [lɔː(*r*)], but with [r] italicized. Wells (pp. 284–85) makes the point that avoidance of intrusive <r> is a feature of 'speech-conscious adoptive-RP', that is the RP of those who, not being native RP-speakers, self-consciously attempt the accent and in consequence produce a mannered and somewhat artificial variety.

The range of pronunciations 'allowable' in the description of RP presented in this dictionary is therefore somewhat greater than that in the transcriptions of more prescriptive pronouncing and general dictionaries, the criterion for inclusion being what is heard used by educated, non-regionally-marked

speakers rather than what is 'allowed' by a preconceived model. In addition to requiring the inclusion of some hitherto rejected variants, this policy of recording a modern model has necessitated changes being made to existing RP transcription conventions. The principal regular points of departure from traditional RP transcription practice are discussed below.

[a] is the vowel sound in *had*, *hand*, the BR vowel having in recent years come to be articulated in a more open position than the [æ] commonly (though not universally) used by phoneticians for the RP phoneme (MacCarthy, p. 92). The use of the more open vowel is an RP change which, it has been pointed out (Wells, pp. 291–92), is carrying BR further away from AM (where [æ] is generally found).

[a] is also shown as a variant of /ɑː/, representing <a> before a voiceless fricative [s], [f], and [θ] (*brass*, *staff*, *bath*), and before a nasal [n] and [m] + consonant (*dance*, *sample*). Possession of this variant is often the one significant factor distinguishing a north-British RP speaker from her or his south-British counterpart, and RP is not to be considered as exclusively a southern-British phenomenon. This [a] is the one specifically 'northern' BR feature which has regularly been incorporated into the transcription system.

The more open /a/ can be seen to be related to our transcribing RP /e/ as [ɛ], as this reflects the lowering of this RP sound also. Gimson (p. 106) argues that /e/ once tended to be the close variety, [e], this maintaining a marked qualitative distinction between the /a/ and /e/ phonemes at a time when /a/ was [æ]. As /a/ has become lowered from the higher [æ] to the lower [a], so /e/ as [ɛ], long an acknowledged variant, has come to be the norm.

[ʌɪ] is the diphthong of *nice*, *try*. The start-point for the unmarked BR diphthong is judged to be now characteristically in the area of the vowel of *but* (half-open, back centralized), rather than the low front position [a]. The notation

[ʌɪ] is that first used for RP by MacCarthy.

[ɛ:] is the vowel sound of *square, hair*. The mainstream sound is normally monophthongal, although it is sometimes attended by an off-glide, giving [ɛ:ᵊ], particularly in a stressed final syllable. A full diphthong [ɛə] in this position should now be taken to be especially a feature of a marked variety of RP. The diphthong is even more rarely heard in a compound such as *hairpiece* than it is in the simplex *hair*.

Final [-i] is the vowel of *-y* in *happy*. This symbol, as used in this dictionary, is intended to imply both greater tension that the [ɪ] commonly used for BR in this position and also greater length. It should be noted that the shorter, less tense [ɪ] occurs in BR when, for example, the suffix *-er* is added, and this is signalled in the transcriptions, thus:

happy
BR hap|i, -ɪə(r)

In addition to these transcriptions of recent developments in RP, the two composite symbols, [ɪ] and [ʊ], are used to represent [ɪ] or [ə] and [ʊ] or [ə] respectively (see p. xi above and the discussion of vowel reduction below, p. xviii). The following are some of the major situations in which the composite symbols are used to show the possible RP choices:

-ity	[-ɪti]	as in *falsity, responsibility*
-ily	[-ɪli]	as in *happily*
-ible	[-ɪbl]	as in *responsible*
-ibly	[-ɪbli]	as in *terribly*
-ical	[-ɪkl]	as in *theatrical*
-ace	[-ɪs]	as in *pinnace, palace*
-is	[-ɪs]	as in *appendicitis*
-ist	[-ɪst]	as in *pianist*
-ful	[-fʊl]	as in *beautiful*
-ed	[-ɪd]	as in *noted*
-es	[-ɪz]	as in *rises, houses*

It should be noted that in the transcriptions the endings *-ed* and *-es* are for convenience regularly transcribed as [-ɪd] and [-ɪz] when they occur as derived forms under a base headword. However, although AM pronunciations are normally [-əd] and [-əz], BR pronunciations are more normally [-ɪd] and [-ɪz]. BR usage is due at least in part to the fact that pronunciations with [ə] can in cer-

tain contexts create confusing homophones in BR in such pairs as *halted* and *haltered, poses* and *posers* (whereas rhoticity prevents homophones being created in such pairs in AM, the <r> being pronounced in the second of each pair in that accent).

The American English (AM) pronunciation model

Unlike British English, English in the United States has no obvious standard spoken model (that is, no identifiable variety widely spoken by well-educated, cultivated residents). Education is the prime consideration in the formation of American standards, and historically different spoken standards have obtained for different regions of the country. Regional varieties of pronunciation show few signs of giving way before the mobility of the population and the omnipresence of national broadcast media. Many educated speakers from New England and from the Coastal South have accents readily identified by speakers from other parts of the country, yet speakers from the Pacific Coast also have their regional pronunciation habits, even if these are not often recognized by the public. Broadcasters with network ambitions traditionally have tried to limit the regionalisms of their accents, but the present anchorman on one network's news has achieved a certain notoriety for his preservation of certain Canadian pronunciations, and local reporters and weather forecasters often retain their regional accents. While there are indeed dialect coaches who help actors and some other people tone down their regional accents, many Americans take pride in their regional speech as a marker of cultural identity.

Since the mid 20th Century, however, there has been a trend among educated speakers, especially those of the younger generation, towards limitation of the use of marked regional features while speaking in formal settings. It is common for college students, for example, to speak without much influence of regional pronunciation in the classroom, but to use regionally marked pronunciations

among friends in the hallway. Some younger educated speakers show little influence of regional speech even in informal conversation. Thus it is possible to hear a variety of voices in every American city or town. The pronunciation model adopted here follows the trend among younger educated speakers of exclusion of regional features. This model is quite similar to what one hears in the national broadcast media, since broadcasters have long participated in the more general trend of younger educated speakers.

Areas often mentioned as having regional varieties include Eastern New England (as far west as the Connecticut River valley), the Inland North (western New England to Wisconsin along the northernmost tier of states), the North Midland (the mid-Atlantic Coast through Pennsylvania to the Mississippi River, north of the Ohio River), the South Midland (the highlands extending southwest from Pennsylvania south of the Ohio River, as far as the Mississippi River and across it to Arkansas), the Coastal South (the area formerly of plantation agriculture from tidewater Virginia south through the Carolinas and Georgia and as far west as East Texas). The Western United States is variously divided: the Great Plains and Upper Midwest show a greater degree of dialect mixture owing to recent settlement; further west, the Southwest (West Texas, New Mexico, and Arizona), the Pacific Coast (California), and the Northwest (Washington, Oregon, and northern California) are often distinguished. The accents of these areas are generally not mutually exclusive in their component pronunciation features; particular features like absence of postvocalic <r> (pronunciation of an <r> sound after a vowel, before a consonant or pause) are often shared by different regions, in this case Eastern New England and the Coastal South. Rather, it is the special combination and distribution of features that distinguish a regional variety. Further, since individual speakers show idiolectal variation, the combination and distribution of features in a region are matters of statistical probabil-

ities, not strict rules. Our AM model avoids as far as possible those pronunciation features that are strongly marked by region or are heard in only a few regions.

Canadian English preserves some differences from the speech of the United States in its eastern provinces, while the pronunciation of its western provinces is generally quite similar to what one might hear in the western states. Pronunciations which are distinctively Canadian are not included here. While Canadians would be quite right to ask that their speech not be subsumed by a model based on the speech of their southern neighbours, it is still the case that the American pronunciation model presented here will offer a fair description of Canadian English as well as that of the English of the United States.

James Hartman, author of the 'Guide to Pronunciation' for the *Dictionary of American Regional English*, classifies major regional variants under four headings: postvocalic <r>, weakened variants of diphthongs, diphthongized variants of monophthongs, and vowel alternations (Cassidy et al., pp. lviii–lxi):

Postvocalic <r> is generally not pronounced in Eastern New England and the Coastal South; the AM transcriptions always include postvocalic <r> because the various pronunciations without it (lengthening of the preceding vowel, replacement by [ə], or varying degrees of weak constriction) are regionally marked.

Weakened variants of diphthongs, whether the second element is weakly realized, e.g. [aɪz] in *eyes*, or is absent with lengthening of the first element, e.g. [aːs] in *ice*, are characteristic of the Coastal South, the South Midland, and large parts of the Great Plains and Southwest. They are also possible for many other speakers in rapid speech. These variants are not included in the transcriptions, both because of regional marking and because this volume seeks to present pronunciations typical of the model adopted in slow to moderate speech, not all possible pronunciations.

Diphthongized variants of monoph-

thongs, e.g. [pɪət] for *pit*, [lɑɔft] for *loft*, are possible in many regions but characteristic of the Coastal South and South Midland. According to Bronstein, it is common in all regions to realize /u/ as [ʊu] (p. 171) and /i/ as [ɪi] (p. 147), especially when positionally lengthened or under stress. These variants are not offered in the transcriptions. Possible diphthongization of vowels before <r> is shown by an optional mid-central vowel, as in [faɪ(ə)r] for *fire*, except for /ɔ/, for which no diphthongization is offered (only a weakly realized diphthong is likely for /ɔ/, e.g. [fɔ⁽ᵊ⁾r] for *four*). /e/ and /o/, however, are always represented by [eɪ] and [oʊ] in the transcriptions, since these stressed vowels are rarely heard in AM as monophthongs unless in rapid speech (see Bronstein, pp. 152, 167–68), or from Upper Midwestern speakers.

Some vowel alternations are shown in the transcription, some not.

/ɛ/ ~ /æ/ ~ /a/ – In words spelled with <a> or <e> before <r>, whether or not followed by another vowel, as in *care, carry, marry, merry, Mary*, the AM transcriptions present [ɛ], as [kɛr, kɛri, mɛri, mɛri, mɛri]. Kurath and McDavid suggest characteristic use of [ɛ] before r in the North Midland but divided usage in the Inland North and other regions (p. 16). Bronstein reports that in the Coastal South it is possible to hear *Mary* realized with [eɪ], and there and along the Atlantic Coast *carry, marry* can be realized with [æ] (pp. 152–53). We judge the pronunciations with [eɪ] and [æ] now to be recessive and regionally marked, and we do not offer them in transcriptions. In Eastern New England /æ/ is realized as [a] (or retracted to [ɑ]) before voiceless fricatives, as in *ask, path, half*, and before nasal + consonant, as in *aunt*. Outside of New England, a minority of cultivated speakers, who may view it as a prestige pronunciation, realize the vowel with [ɑ] in particular words such as *aunt* or *ask*, though not systematically. These pronunciations have not been included, because of regional and social marking. Hartman (Cassidy et al., p. lx) and Bronstein (pp. 155–56) report that /æ/ may be raised towards [ɛ] in several environments in

different regions, but these pronunciations are not shown here.

/ɑ/ ~ /ɔ/ – The contrast between these sounds deserves a long historical treatment that is not possible here. There is high variability and ongoing change in the realization of the stressed vowels of words historically containing either [ɑ] or [ɔ] (see Labov for detailed analysis of the regional status for merger of these sounds). We represent the merger of the two sounds in all words of the historical [ɔ] classes. Rather than present both realizations for all words with historical [ɑ], which would sanction marked regionalisms for some word classes, we have observed the following practices, though with exceptions for particular headwords: 1) short <o> words like *cot, lot* are transcribed with [ɑ]; 2) words with short <o> before <r>, with [ɔ]; 3) words with short <o> before <g, ng, nk> with [ɔ]; 4) <wa-> words like *water, wash, watch*, with [ɑ] and [ɔ]. For commentary, see Hartman in Cassidy et al., pp. lx–lxi, and Bronstein, pp. 162–67.

/o/ ~ /ɔ/ – When it occurs before <r>, this sound is indicated consistently as [ɔ] in the transcriptions, as in [fɔr], [fɔrəst] for *four, forest*. Our transcriptions thus will not distinguish between such potentially (but recessively) contrastive pairs as *horse/hoarse* or *morning/mourning*. Kurath and McDavid indicate characteristic use of [ɔ] before <r> in the North Midland but not in the Inland North or other regions (p. 16); Bronstein reports increasing use of [ɔ] before <r> (pp. 167, 169); and Hartman's later evidence indicates wide use of [ɔ] before <r> except in the Coastal South. In some words, like *forest*, the stressed vowel can sometimes be realized as [ɑ], but these pronunciations are not represented in the transcriptions.

It is quite normal in AM to simplify consonant clusters in particular environments. For example, when *-nt-* occurs intervocalically and a syllable boundary with stress does not split the cluster, it is more frequent for the <t> to be dropped than for it to be pronounced, as in ['twɛn(t)i], ['mæn(t)l] for *twenty, mantle*, but [kən'teɪn] for *contain*. Clusters are

often simplified in word-final position, especially with addition of suffixes: *asked* is normally pronounced [æst], not [æskt], though *ask* is pronounced [æsk]. Substitution of [-ɪn] for [-ɪŋ] in the ending -*ing* is often thought to be characteristic of the Coastal South and South Midland, but it occurs with some frequency in the speech of all regions. It is not represented in the transcriptions.

Another normal practice in AM is to pronounce many words according to how they are spelled, even if such a pronunciation has no historical justification. Words like *calm, palm* often acquire an [l] sound in this manner, and even *sword* sometimes gains a [w]. Unfamiliar words are routinely pronounced as they are spelled, including many learned words and foreign words and names. Common spelling pronunciations are represented here as optional, as in *palm* [pɑ(l)m].

Vowel length is not marked in the AM transcriptions. It is only rarely minimally distinctive (e.g. *have* vs *halve*), and in AM is best considered as being environmentally conditioned. Some lengthening of vowels typically occurs before voiced consonants (*grade* vs *grate*) and before juncture, including phrase-final position.

Several variations from common transcription practices among American linguists are employed here. The schwa symbol ([ə]) has been used for both stressed and unstressed vowels. As a stressed vowel, /ə/ includes pronunciations written with [ʌ] by some American linguists, e.g. *sun* [sʌn], here transcribed [sən]; use of /ʌ/ in BR represents a more retracted and somewhat lowered sound. The [ɜ] symbol, often used to indicate a mid-central stressed vowel with r-colouring, as in *bird* [bɜd], is not used here, and neither is the symbol for a mid-central unstressed vowel with r-colouring, as in *father* [fɑðə]; rather, r-colouring and syllabic <r> pronunciations are always indicated by a combination of vowel + <r>, as in [bərd], [fɑðər]. The phonemes /t/ and /r/ include rather wide ranges of possible allophones, but the AM transcriptions offer only the following options: 1) intervocalic /t/, as in *latter*, is often realized as a flap [ɾ] or voiced t [t], but is transcribed

here as [d], so that *latter* and *ladder* have identical transcriptions; 2) final <t> is often realized as a glottal stop [ʔ] or is unreleased, but is transcribed here as [t]; 3) /r/ may be realized as a trill or flap, or with varying degrees of constriction, but all allophones of /r/ are here transcribed [r]. We have not employed diacritical marks, except those for stress and syllabicity. All of these variations contribute to ease of use of the dictionary by limiting the symbol set that readers must know to read the transcriptions, without undue sacrifice in accuracy.

We have created a consistent AM model, in the absence of any actual general standard, according to the editorial policies described. The model grants us a systematic means to decide what transcriptions among many regional variants should be presented. However, we have reviewed every headword independently, and we have occasionally included pronunciations that do not fit the model when they are warranted by widespread use. If any regional or idiolectal bias can be detected among our choices for transcriptions, it is that of Kretzschmar, an Inland Northern speaker.

BR and AM stress marking

As a general rule the standard IPA stress-marking system is employed in this volume, for both primary stress (') and secondary stress (ˌ). Marks precede the stressed syllable. Absence of a mark indicates weak or tertiary stress.

BR transcriptions simply conform to this usage. AM, however, has a heavier stressing pattern than BR, with disyllabic compounds for example exhibiting both primary and secondary stress when BR characteristically exhibits only primary and weak (or tertiary) stress. Thus AM may receive two stress marks when BR exhibits only one:

baseball
BR 'beɪsbɔːl
AM 'beɪsˌbɔl

AM is also characterized by the use of secondary stress on syllables with unreduced vowels or diphthongs, where BR has an unstressed reduced vowel or an elided syllable. Thus ['dɪkʃəˌnɛri] is the

characteristic AM pronunciation of *dictionary*, rather than BR ['dɪkʃnri].

Variability of the stress pattern in polysyllabic words is also characteristic of AM. To represent this fact most efficiently, we have borrowed the notation used in *Webster's Third New International Dictionary*, whereby a variably stressed syllable is marked by a combination of both stress markings (ˌ). In those instances where two syllables receive variable stress markings, e.g. *overbearing* [ˌouvərˈbɛrɪŋ], only three of the four stress permutations are possible when the word is pronounced: primary-primary, primary-secondary, and secondary-primary. Each word must have primary stress for at least one syllable.

BR and AM vowel reduction

Stress patterns exert considerable influence on the quality of unstressed vowels. In the system adopted here, there are four vowels used in unstressed syllables, [ɪ], [ə], [ɨ], and, for BR though seldom for AM, [ʊ]. The alternations of these merit explanation. Even within the limits of our models the linguistic realities do not readily lend themselves to clearly statable rules. We have, however, chosen certain principles as most representative of BR and AM:

[ɪ] is used invariably in those syllables where it precedes word-final [k], [ʃ], [dʒ], [v] in derivational suffixes, and in the participial/gerundive suffix [-ɪŋ], as in *conic, breakage, dragging*.

Similarly, [ə] is used in the suffix [-ə(r)~-ər] as in *leader*, and for AM in [-ʃ(ə)n] and [-ʒ(ə)n], as in *relation, equation*.

[ʊ], representing a free choice between [ʊ] and [ə], is a vowel transcription in BR adjectival ending *-ful*.

For the vowel of the inflectional suffixes plural and third-person present tense *-es*, past tense *-ed*, and superlative *-est*, and for the derivational suffix *-ist*, [ɨ] is regularly used. In these suffixes, BR usually, though not necessarily, exhibits [ɪ]. For AM, environmental factors are decisive in the selection of the unstressed variant: if the preceding syllable contains a high front vowel or a diphthong ending in a high front vowel, [ɪ] is the norm; otherwise there is a free choice in AM between [ɪ] and [ə]. The same environmental factors frequently govern the choice of vowel-sound for both varieties in the derivational suffixes *-ness* and, especially for BR, *-less*.

It must be emphasized that, while all our practices regarding unstressed vowels are generally valid, many speakers of both BR and AM alternate between the variants [ɪ] and [ə] in the environments we have considered.

Bibliography

Bronstein, Arthur J. *The Pronunciation of American English*. Englewood Cliffs, NJ: Prentice-Hall, 1960.

Cassidy, Frederic G., et al., eds. *Dictionary of American Regional English*, Vol. 1. Cambridge, Massachusetts: Belknap/Harvard Univ. Press, 1985.

Fudge, Erik. *English Word-Stress*. London: George Allen and Unwin, 1984.

Gimson, A.C. *An Introduction to the Pronunciation of English*. 4th ed., revised by Susan Ramsaran. London: Edward Arnold, 1989.

Honey, John. *Does Accent Matter?: The Pygmalion Factor*. London: Faber & Faber, 1989.

Jones, Daniel. *An Outline of English Phonetics*. 9th ed. Cambridge: Heffer, 1969.

Kurath, Hans, and Raven I. McDavid, Jr. *The*

Pronunciation of English in the Atlantic States. Tuscaloosa: Univ. of Alabama Press, 1961, reprinted 1982.

Labov, William. 'The Three Dialects of English'. In P. Eckert, ed., *New Ways of Analyzing Sound Change*. San Diego: Academic Press, 1991, pp. 1–44.

MacCarthy, Peter. *The Teaching of Pronunciation*. Cambridge: Cambridge Univ. Press, 1978.

Milroy, Lesley. *Observing and Analysing Natural Language*. Oxford: Basil Blackwell, 1987.

Upton, Clive, Stewart Sanderson, and John Widdowson. *Word Maps: A Dialect Atlas of England*. London: Croom Helm, 1987.

Wells, J. C. *Accents of English*. 3 Vols. Cambridge: Cambridge Univ. Press, 1982.

Foreign pronunciations

When given in native form, a limited number of foreign headwords also have native pronunciations based on current national standards, but only where these differ significantly from the anglicized pronunciations. Foreign headwords falling within specific subject fields, e.g. culinary and musical terminology, have not been given native pronunciations. Neither have words such as 'Guignolesque' and phrases such as 'au grand sérieux', because although they contain French elements they are in fact of English coinage.

Vowels

	Front	Central	Back
High	y:		u
	ʏ		
	e(:) ø		o
Mid			
			ɔ
	œ		
		ɐ	
Low	a(:)		ɑ

/aː/	Dutch/Flemish	Waal
	German	Aachen
	Irish	Dáil, Tánaiste

/ɑ/	Danish	Dagmar
	Dutch/Flemish	Breda
	Portuguese	Beira, Carajás

| /ɐ/ | German | Hannover |

/œ/	Danish	Ertebølle, Helsingør
	French	Verdun
	German	Götterdämmerung
	Hungarian	Fertő Tó
	Norwegian	øre

/ɔ/	Czech	Brno
	Dutch/Flemish	Concertgebouw
	French	Aix-en-Provence
	German	Worms
	Greek	Ayios Nikólaos
	Hungarian	Balaton, Magyar

/e/	Danish	Blixen
	Greek	Seféris
	Irish	feiseanna
	Norwegian	Lofoten
	Russian	Comintern
	Spanish	Algeciras
	Welsh	Betws-y-Coed

/eː/	Czech	háler
	Danish	Petersen
	Dutch/Flemish	Breda, Vermeer, Zeebrugge
	German	Dresden
	Irish	Dáil Eireann
	Swedish	Alfvén

| /ø/ | Dutch/Flemish | Leuven |
| | French | Montreux |

/o/	Danish	Odense
	Dutch/Flemish	Groningen, Oostende
	French	Aubusson, Utrillo
	Italian/Spanish	mid vowel
	Brazilian Portuguese	Belo Horizonte, Estoril
	Lusitanian Portuguese	Belo Horizonte, Douro

| /oː/ | Norwegian | Bokmål |
| | Swedish | Bofors |

| /ɤ/ | German | Baden-Württemberg, Duisburg |

/y/	Afrikaans	krugerrand
	Dutch/Flemish	Rijksmuseum
	French	Althusser

| /yː/ | German | Zürich |
| | Norwegian | Nynorsk |

/u/	Spanish	Murillo
	Norwegian	Oslo
	Portuguese	Rio de Janeiro
	Russian	Godunov

Introduction

Diphthongs

Dutch/Flemish	/ɛi/	Rijksmuseum
	/ɔu/	Gouda
	/œy/	Huygens
German	/ɔy/	Löwenbräu

Semivowels

/ɥ/	French	Guyenne

Consonants

Fricatives:	/β/	Spanish	Iberia
	/ʑ/	Hungarian	Magyar
	/ç/	German	Leipzig
		Polish	Łódź
	/ɤ/	Spanish	Segovia

Nasals

/ɲ/	French	Boulogne
	Spanish	Muñoz

Liquids

/ʀ/	Danish	Brahe
	Lusitanian Portuguese	Rio de Janeiro
/ʎ/	Italian	Gigli

Diacritics

~	nasality	French	Verdun
ʲ	palatalization	Irish	Dun Laoghaire
			Fianna Fáil
		Russian	Yekaterinburg
ʼ	no audible release	Danish	Aarhus

Summary of the Pronunciation Models

A. *The British and American vowels*

BR	AM	
i:	i	f<u>ee</u>t, b<u>ea</u>m
i	i	cit<u>y</u>, hand<u>y</u>
ɪ	ɪ	f<u>i</u>t, l<u>i</u>mp
ɛ	ɛ	s<u>e</u>t, b<u>e</u>ll
a	æ	h<u>a</u>t, b<u>a</u>g
a	ɛ	ch<u>a</u>rity, m<u>a</u>rry
ɑ:	ɑ	f<u>a</u>ther, ch<u>a</u>rm
ɒ	ɑ	l<u>o</u>t, b<u>o</u>ther
ɔ:	ɔ, ɑ	h<u>a</u>wk, b<u>ou</u>ght
ɔ:	ɔ	f<u>o</u>rge, m<u>o</u>rning
ʌ	ə	f<u>u</u>n, h<u>u</u>rry
ʊ	ʊ	p<u>u</u>ll, b<u>u</u>tcher
u:	u	m<u>oo</u>n, s<u>ou</u>p
ə	ə	<u>a</u>lpha, fath<u>er</u>
ə:	ər	g<u>er</u>m, f<u>ir</u>m
ɪə	ɪ(ə)r	h<u>e</u>re, f<u>ea</u>r
ɛ:	ɛ(ə)r	d<u>a</u>re, h<u>ai</u>r
eɪ	eɪ	r<u>ei</u>n, g<u>a</u>me
ʌɪ	aɪ	f<u>i</u>ne, v<u>i</u>tal
ɔɪ	ɔɪ	b<u>oy</u>, s<u>oi</u>l
aʊ	aʊ	h<u>ou</u>se
əʊ	oʊ	g<u>o</u>, h<u>o</u>me

B. *The Consonants* (both models)

p	<u>p</u>ut, <u>p</u>a<u>p</u>er
b	<u>b</u>eat, <u>b</u>ar<u>b</u>er
t	<u>t</u>ake, <u>t</u>arge<u>t</u>
d	<u>d</u>ive, <u>d</u>ivi<u>d</u>e
k	<u>c</u>ake, <u>c</u>on<u>c</u>ord
g	gate, sugar
f	<u>f</u>un, <u>f</u>an<u>f</u>are
v	<u>v</u>ain, <u>v</u>i<u>v</u>a
θ	<u>th</u>ick, wrea<u>th</u>
ð	<u>th</u>is, wrea<u>th</u>e
s	<u>s</u>un, <u>s</u>au<u>c</u>er
z	<u>z</u>oo, ro<u>s</u>e
ʃ	<u>sh</u>oe, ru<u>sh</u>
ʒ	re<u>g</u>ime
x	lo<u>ch</u> (Scots)
h	<u>h</u>igh, a<u>h</u>ead
ɫ	L<u>l</u>ane<u>ll</u>i (Welsh)
tʃ	<u>ch</u>in, <u>ch</u>ur<u>ch</u>
dʒ	<u>j</u>oke, ju<u>dg</u>e
m	<u>m</u>e, <u>m</u>ur<u>m</u>er
n	<u>n</u>ow, <u>n</u>oo<u>n</u>
ŋ	wro<u>ng</u>, si<u>ng</u>er
l	<u>l</u>imp, <u>l</u>i<u>l</u>y
r	<u>r</u>ope, <u>r</u>oa<u>r</u>ing
j	<u>y</u>ellow, <u>y</u>o<u>y</u>o
w	<u>w</u>ish, <u>wh</u>ite<u>w</u>ash

Abbreviations used in the dictionary

AFK	Afrikaans	IR	Irish
AM	US English	IT	Italian
B PORT	Brazilian Portuguese	L PORT	Lusitanian Portuguese
BR	British English	NO	Norwegian
CZ	Czech	POL	Polish
DAN	Danish	PORT	Brazilian and Lusitanian Portuguese
DU	Dutch		
FL	Flemish	RUS	Russian
FR	French	SP	Spanish
GER	German	SW	Swedish
GR	Greek	TU	Turkish
HU	Hungarian	WE	Welsh

Note on trademarks and proprietary status

This dictionary includes some words which have, or are asserted to have, proprietary status as trademarks or otherwise. Their inclusion does not imply that they have acquired for legal purposes a non-proprietary or general significance, nor any other judgement concerning their legal status. In cases where the editorial staff have some evidence that a word has proprietary status this is indicated in the entry for that word by the symbol ®, but no judgement concerning the legal status of such words is made or implied thereby.

Aa

a¹
indefinite article,
strong form
BR eɪ
AM eɪ

a²
indefinite article,
weak form
BR ə(r)
AM ə

a³
letter
BR eɪ, -z
AM eɪ, -z

Aachen
BR 'ɑːk(ə)n
AM 'ɑkən
GER 'aːxn

aah
BR ɑː(r), -z, -ɪŋ, -d
AM ɑ, -z, -ɪŋ, -d

Aalborg
BR 'ɑːlbɔːg
AM 'ɔl,bɔrg, 'ɑl,bɔrg
DAN 'ʌl,bɔ:'

aardvark
BR 'ɑːdvɑːk, -s
AM 'ɑrd,vɑrk, -s

aardwolf
BR 'ɑːdwʊlf
AM 'ɑrd,wʊlf

aardwolves
BR 'ɑːdwʊlvz
AM 'ɑrd,wʊlvz

Aargau
BR 'ɑːgaʊ
AM 'ɑr,gaʊ

aargh
BR ɑː(r)
AM arg

Aarhus
BR 'ɑːhuːs
AM 'ɔr,(h)us, 'ɑr,(h)us
DAN 'ɔːhuː's

Aaron
BR 'ɛːrən, 'ɛːrn̩
AM 'ɛrən

aasvogel
BR 'ɑːs,fəʊgl, -z
AM 'ɑs,foʊgəl, -z

ab
BR ab
AM æb

aba
BR 'ɑbə(r), -z
AM 'ɑbɑ, ə'bɑ, -z

abaca
BR 'abəkə(r), -z
AM 'æbəkɑ, -z

abaci
BR 'abəsʌɪ, 'abəkʌɪ

aback
BR ə'bak
AM ə'bæk

abacus
BR 'abəkəs, -ɪz
AM 'æbəkəs, -əz

Abadan
BR ,abə'dɑːn, ,abə'dan
AM ,abə'dɑn,
,æbə'dæn

Abaddon
BR ə'badn
AM ə'bædən

abaft
BR ə'bɑːft, ə'baft
AM ə'bæft

abalone
BR ,abə'ləʊn|i, -iz
AM 'æbə,loʊni, -z

abandon
BR ə'band|(ə)n, -(ə)nz,
-ənɪŋ \-n̩ɪŋ, -(ə)nd
AM ə'bændən, -z, -ɪŋ, -d

abandonee
BR ə,bandə'niː, -z
AM ə,bændə'ni, -z

abandoner
BR ə'bandənə(r),
ə'bandnə(r), -z
AM ə'bændənər, -z

abandonment
BR ə'band(ə)nm(ə)nt,
-s
AM ə'bændənmənt, -s

abase
BR ə'beɪs, -ɪz, -ɪŋ, -t
AM ə'beɪs, -ɪz, -ɪŋ, -t

abasement
BR ə'beɪsm(ə)nt
AM ə'beɪsmənt

abash
BR ə'baʃ, -ɪz, -ɪŋ, -t
AM ə'bæʃ, -əz, -ɪŋ, -t

abashment
BR ə'baʃm(ə)nt
AM ə'bæʃmənt

abask
BR ə'bɑːsk, ə'bask
AM ə'bæsk

abatable
BR ə'beɪtəbl
AM ə'beɪdəbəl

abate
BR ə'beɪt, -s, -ɪŋ, -ɪd
AM ə'beɪ|t, -ts, -dɪŋ, -dɪd

abatement
BR ə'beɪtm(ə)nt, -s
AM ə'beɪtmənt, -s

abatis¹
singular
BR 'abətɪs
AM 'æbə,ti, 'æbədəs

abatis²
plural
BR 'abəti:z, 'abətɪsɪz

AM 'æbə,sʌɪ, 'æbə,kʌɪ

aback
BR ə'bak
AM ə'bæk

AM 'æbə,tiz,
'æbədəsəz

abatised
BR 'abətɪst
AM 'æbə,tid, 'æbədəst

abatises
BR 'abətɪsɪz
AM 'æbədəsəz

abattis¹
singular
BR ə'batɪs
AM 'æbə,ti, 'æbədəs

abattis²
plural
BR ə'bati:z, ə'batɪsɪz
AM 'æbə,tiz,
'æbədəsəz

abattised
BR ə'batɪst
AM 'æbə,tid, 'æbədəst

abattises
BR ə'batɪsɪz
AM 'æbədəsəz

abattoir
BR 'abətwɑː(r), -z
AM 'æbə,twar, -z

abaxial
BR ab'aksɪəl
AM æ'bæksɪəl

abaya
BR ə'beɪ(j)ə(r), -z
AM ə'bɑ(ɪ)jə, -z

abba
BR ə'bə(r), -z
AM 'ɑbə, ə'bɑ, -z

abbacy
BR 'abəs|i, -ɪz
AM 'æbəsi, -z

Abbas
BR 'abəs
AM 'æbəs

Abbasid
BR ə'basɪd, 'abəsɪd
AM ə'bæsɪd, 'æbəsɪd

abbatial
BR ə'beɪʃl
AM ə'beɪʃəl

abbé
BR 'abeɪ, -z
AM 'æ,'beɪ, -z

abbess
BR 'abɪs, 'abɛs, -ɪz
AM 'æbəs, -əz

Abbeville
BR 'ab(ɪ)vɪl
AM 'æbi,vɪl

Abbevillian
BR ab'vɪlɪən,
,abɪ'vɪlɪən
AM æb'vɪljən,
,æbə'vɪljən,
æb'vɪlɪən, ,æbə'vɪlɪən

abbey
BR 'ab|i, -ɪz
AM 'æbi, -z

abbot
BR 'abət, -s

AM 'æbət, -s

abbotship
BR 'abətʃɪp, -s
AM 'æbət,ʃɪp, -s

Abbott
BR 'abət
AM 'æbət

abbreviate
BR ə'briːvɪeɪt, -s, -ɪŋ,
-ɪd
AM ə'brivi,eɪ|t, -ts, -dɪŋ,
-dɪd

abbreviation
BR ə,briːvɪ'eɪʃn, -z
AM ə,brivi'eɪʃən, -z

abbreviatory
BR ə'briːvɪət(ə)ri
AM ə'briviə,tɔri

Abby
BR 'abi
AM 'æbi

Abdela
BR ab'dɛlə(r)
AM æb'dɛlə

abdicable
BR 'abdɪkəbl
AM 'æbdəkəbəl

abdicant
BR 'abdɪk(ə)nt, -s
AM 'æbdəkənt, -s

abdicate
BR 'abdɪkeɪt, -s, -ɪŋ, -ɪd
AM 'æbdə,keɪ|t, -ts,
-dɪŋ, -dɪd

abdication
BR ,abdɪ'keɪʃn, -z
AM ,æbdə'keɪʃən, -z

abdicator
BR 'abdɪkeɪtə(r), -z
AM 'æbdə,keɪdər, -z

abdomen
BR 'abdəmən,
ab'dəʊmən, -z
AM 'æbdəmən, -z

abdominal
BR ab'dɒmɪnl,
əb'dɒmɪnl
AM æb'dɑmənəl,
əb'dɑmənəl

abdominally
BR ab'dɒmɪnl̩i,
əb'dɒmɪnəli,
əb'dɒmɪnl̩i,
əb'dɒmɪnəli
AM æb'dɑmənəli,
əb'dɑmənəli

abdominous
BR ab'dɒmɪnəs,
əb'dɒmɪnəs
AM æb'dɑmənəs,
əb'dɑmənəs

abduct
BR əb'dʌkt, -s, -ɪŋ, -ɪd
AM əb'dʌk|(t),
æb'dək|(t), -(t)s, -tɪŋ,
-təd

abduction
BR əb'dʌkʃn, -z

AM əb'dəkʃən,
æb'dəkʃən, -z
abductor
BR əb'dʌktə(r),
ab'dʌktə(r), -z
AM əb'dəktər,
æb'dəktər, -z
Abdul
BR 'abdʊl
AM ˌab'dʊl, ˌæb'dʊl
Abdullah
BR ab'dʌlə(r),
əb'dʌlə(r), ab'dʊlə(r),
əb'dʊlə(r)
AM ɑb'dʊlə, æb'dʊlə
Abe
BR eɪb
AM eɪb
abeam
BR ə'biːm
AM ə'bim
abecedarian
BR ˌeɪbiːsiː'deːrɪən, -z
AM ˌeɪbisi'dɛrɪən, -z
abed
BR ə'bɛd
AM ə'bɛd
Abednego
BR ˌabed'niːgəʊ,
ə'bɛdnɪgəʊ
AM ə'bɛdnəˌgoʊ
Abel
BR 'eɪbl
AM 'eɪbəl
Abelard
BR 'abɪlɑːd, 'abl̩ɑːd
AM 'æbəˌlɑrd
abele
BR ə'biːl, 'eɪbl, -z
AM ə'bil, ə'beɪl, -z
abelia
BR ə'biːlɪə(r), -z
AM ə'biljə, ə'biliə , -z
abelian
BR ə'biːlɪən
AM ə'biljən, ə'biliən
Aberaeron
BR ˌabər'ʌɪrən,
ˌabər'ʌɪrn̩
AM ˌæbər'ɛrən
WE ˌaber'eɪrɒn
Aberavon
BR ˌabə(r)'avn
AM ˌæbər'eɪvən
Abercrombie
BR 'abəkrʌmbi,
'abəkrɒmbi
AM 'æbərˌkrɑmbi
Aberdare
BR ˌabə'dɛː(r)
AM ˌæbər'dɛ(ə)r
Aberdaron
BR ˌabə'darən,
ˌabə'darn̩
AM ˌæbər'dɛrən
Aberdeen¹
place in UK
BR ˌabə'diːn

AM ˌæbər'din
Aberdeen²
place in USA
BR 'abədiːn
AM 'æbərˌdin
Aberdonian
BR ˌabə'dəʊnɪən, -z
AM ˌæbər'doʊnɪən, -z
Aberdovey
BR ˌabə'dʌvi
AM ˌæbər'dəvi
Aberfan
BR ˌabə'van
AM ˌæbər'væn
WE ˌaber'van
Abergavenny
BR ˌabəgə'vɛni
AM ˌæbərgə'vɛni
Abergele
BR ˌabə'gɛli
AM ˌæbər'gɛli
Abernathy
BR ˌabə'naθl̩i, -ɪz
AM ˌæbərˌnæθi, -z
Abernethy
BR ˌabə'nɛθl̩i,
ˌabə'niːθl̩i, -ɪz
AM ˌæbərˌnɛθi, -z
Aberporth
BR 'abəpɔːθ, ˌabə'pɔːθ
AM 'æbərˌpɔ(ə)rθ
aberrance
BR ə'bɛrəns, ə'bɛrn̩s
AM 'æbərəns, ə'bɛrəns
aberrancy
BR ə'bɛrənsi, ə'bɛrn̩si
AM 'æbərənsi,
ə'bɛrənsi
aberrant
BR ə'bɛrənt, ə'bɛrn̩t
AM 'æbərənt, ə'bɛrənt
aberrate
BR 'abəreɪt, -s, -ɪŋ, -ɪd
AM 'æbəˌreɪ|t, -ts, -dɪŋ,
-dɪd
aberration
BR ˌabə'reɪʃn, -z
AM ˌæbə'reɪʃən, -z
Abersoch
BR ˌabə'səʊk, ˌabə'sɒk
AM 'æbər'sak
Abersychan
BR ˌabə'sʌk(ə)n
AM 'æbər'sak(ə)n
WE ˌaber'sʌxan
Abertillery
BR ˌabətɪ'leːri
AM ˌæbərtə'ləri
Aberystwyth
BR ˌabə'rɪstwɪθ
AM ˌæbə'rɪstwɪθ
WE ˌaber'ʌstwɪθ
abet
BR ə'bɛt, -s, -ɪŋ, -ɪd
AM ə'bɛ|t, -ts, -dɪŋ, -dəd
abetment
BR ə'bɛtm(ə)nt

AM ə'bɛtmənt
abetter
BR ə'bɛtə(r), -z
AM ə'bɛdər, -z
abettor
BR ə'bɛtə(r), -z
AM ə'bɛdər, -z
abeyance
BR ə'beɪəns
AM ə'beɪəns
abeyant
BR ə'beɪənt
AM ə'beɪənt
abhor
BR əb'hɔː(r), ə'bɔː(r),
-z, -ɪŋ, -d
AM əb'hɔ(ə)r,
æb'hɔ(ə)r, -z, -ɪŋ, -d
abhorrence
BR əb'hɒrəns,
əb'hɒrn̩s, ə'bɒrəns,
ə'bɒrn̩s
AM əb'hɔrəns,
æb'hɔrəns
abhorrent
BR əb'hɒrənt,
əb'hɒrn̩t, ə'bɒrənt,
ə'bɒrn̩t
AM əb'hɔrənt,
æb'hɔrənt
abhorrently
BR əb'hɒrəntli,
əb'hɒrn̩tli, ə'bɒrəntli,
ə'bɒrn̩tli
AM əb'hɔrən(t)li,
æb'hɔrən(t)li
abhorrer
BR əb'hɔːrə(r),
ə'bɔːrə(r), -z
AM əb'hɔrər,
æb'hɔrər, -z
abidance
BR ə'bʌɪd(ə)ns
AM ə'baɪdns
abide
BR ə'bʌɪd, -z, -ɪŋ, -ɪd
AM ə'baɪd, -z, -ɪŋ, -ɪd
abidingly
BR ə'bʌɪdɪŋli
AM ə'baɪdɪŋli
Abidjan
BR ˌabɪ'dʒɑːn,
ˌabɪ'dʒan
AM ˌæbə'dʒɑn
Abigail
BR 'abɪgeɪl
AM 'æbəˌgeɪl
Abilene
BR 'abɪliːn, 'abl̩iːn
AM 'æbəˌlin
ability
BR ə'bɪlɪt|i, -ɪz
AM ə'bɪlɪdi, -z
Abingdon
BR 'abɪŋd(ə)n
AM 'æbɪŋdən
ab initio
BR ˌab ɪ'nɪʃɪəʊ

AM ˌæb ə'nɪʃioʊ
abiogenesis
BR ˌeɪbʌɪə(ʊ)'dʒɛnɪsɪs
AM ˌeɪˌbaɪoʊ'dʒɛnəsəs
abiogenic
BR ˌeɪbʌɪəʊ'dʒɛnɪk
AM ˌeɪˌbaɪoʊ'dʒɛnɪk
abiogenically
BR ˌeɪbʌɪəʊ'dʒɛnɪkli
AM ˌeɪˌbaɪoʊ'dʒɛnək(ə)li
abiogenist
BR ˌeɪbʌɪ'ɒdʒɪnɪst, -s
AM ˌeɪˌbaɪ'ɑdʒənəst, -s
Abiola
BR ˌabɪ'əʊlə(r)
AM ˌabi'oʊlə
abiotic
BR ˌeɪbʌɪ'ɒtɪk
AM ˌeɪˌbaɪ'ɑdɪk
abject
BR 'abdʒɛkt
AM 'æb|dʒɛk(t)
abjection
BR əb'dʒɛkʃn
AM æb'dʒɛkʃən
abjectly
BR 'abdʒɛktli
AM 'æb|dʒɛk(t)li
abjectness
BR 'abdʒɛk(t)nəs
AM 'æb|dʒɛk(t)nəs
abjuration
BR ˌabdʒʊ'reɪʃn
AM ˌæbdʒə'reɪʃən
abjure
BR əb'dʒʊə(r),
əb'dʒɔː(r), -z, -ɪŋ, -d
AM æb'dʒʊ(ə)r,
əb'dʒʊ(ə)r, -z, -ɪŋ, -d
Abkhaz
BR ab'kaz, ab'kɑːz
AM ab'kaz
RUS ab'xas
Abkhazi
BR ab'kɑːz|i, -ɪz
AM ab'kazi, -z
Abkhazia
BR ab'kɑːzɪə(r)
AM ab'kaziə
RUS ab'xazʲijə
Abkhazian
BR ab'kɑːzɪən, -z
AM ab'kaziən, -z
ablate
BR ə'bleɪt, -s, -ɪŋ, -ɪd
AM ə'bleɪ|t, -ts, -dɪŋ,
-dɪd
ablation
BR ə'bleɪʃn
AM ə'bleɪʃən
ablatival
BR ˌablə'tʌɪvl
AM ˌæblə'taɪvəl
ablative
BR 'ablətɪv, -z
AM 'æblədɪv, ə'bleɪdɪv,
-z

ablatively
BR 'ablətɪvli
AM 'æblədɪvli,
ə'bleɪdɪvli

ablaut
BR 'ablaʊt, -s
AM 'æˌblaʊt, -s

ablaze
BR ə'bleɪz
AM ə'bleɪz

able
BR 'eɪbl̩, -ə(r), -ɪst, -d
AM 'eɪbəl, -ər, -əst, -d

ableism
BR 'eɪbl̩ɪz(ə)m
AM 'eɪbəˌlɪzəm

abloom
BR ə'bluːm
AM ə'blum

ablush
BR ə'blʌʃ
AM ə'blʃ

ablution
BR ə'bluːʃn, -z
AM ə'bluʃən, -z

ablutionary
BR ə'bluːʃn̩(ə)ri
AM ə'bluʃəˌnɛri

ably
BR 'eɪbli
AM 'eɪbli, 'eɪbl̩i

abnegate
BR 'abnɪgeɪt, -s, -ɪŋ, -ɪd
AM 'æbnəˌgeɪ|t, -ts, -dɪŋ, -dɪd

abnegation
BR ˌabnɪ'geɪʃn
AM ˌæbnə'geɪʃən

abnegator
BR 'abnɪgeɪtə(r), -z
AM 'æbnəˌgeɪdər, -z

Abner
BR 'abnə(r)
AM 'æbnər

abnormal
BR ab'nɔːml, əb'nɔːml
AM æb'nɔrməl, əb'nɔrməl

abnormality
BR ˌabnə'malɪt|i, ˌabnɔː'malɪt|i, -ɪz
AM ˌæbnər'mælədi, ˌæbˌnɔr'mælədi, -z

abnormally
BR ab'nɔːml̩i, ab'nɔːməli, əb'nɔːml̩i, əb'nɔːməli
AM æb'nɔrməli, əb'nɔrməli

abnormity
BR ab'nɔːmɪt|i, əb'nɔːmɪt|i, -ɪz
AM æb'nɔrmədi, əb'nɔrmədi, -z

abo
BR 'abəʊ, -z
AM 'aboʊ, -z

aboard
BR ə'bɔːd
AM ə'bɔ(ə)rd

abode
BR ə'bəʊd, -z
AM ə'boʊd, -z

abolish
BR ə'bɒl|ɪʃ, -ɪʃɪz, -ɪʃɪŋ, -ɪʃt
AM ə'balɪʃ, -ɪz, -ɪŋ, -t

abolishable
BR ə'bɒlɪʃəbl
AM ə'baləʃəbəl

abolisher
BR ə'bɒlɪʃə(r), -z
AM ə'balɪʃər, -z

abolishment
BR ə'bɒlɪʃm(ə)nt
AM ə'balɪʃmənt

abolition
BR ˌabə'lɪʃn
AM ˌæbə'lɪʃən

abolitionism
BR ˌabə'lɪʃn̩ɪz(ə)m, ˌabə'lɪʃənɪz(ə)m
AM ˌæbə'lɪʃəˌnɪzəm

abolitionist
BR ˌabə'lɪʃn̩ɪst, ˌabə'lɪʃənɪst, -s
AM ˌæbə'lɪʃənəst, -s

abomasa
BR ˌabə(ʊ)'meɪsə(r)
AM ˌæbə'meɪsə

abomasum
BR ˌabə(ʊ)'meɪsəm
AM ˌæbə'meɪsəm

abominable
BR ə'bɒm(ɪ)nəbl
AM ə'bam(ə)nəbəl

abominableness
BR ə'bɒm(ɪ)nəblnəs
AM ə'bam(ə)nəbəlnəs

abominably
BR ə'bɒm(ɪ)nəbli
AM ə'bam(ə)nəbli

abominate
BR ə'bɒmɪneɪt, -s, -ɪŋ, -ɪd
AM ə'baməˌneɪ|t, -ts, -dɪŋ, -dɪd

abomination
BR ə,bɒmɪ'neɪʃn, -z
AM ə,bamə'neɪʃən, -z

abominator
BR ə'bɒmɪneɪtə(r), -z
AM ə'baməˌneɪdər, -z

aboral
BR ab'ɔːrəl, ab'ɔːrl̩
AM æb'ɔrəl

aboriginal
BR ˌabə'rɪdʒɪnl, -z
AM ˌæbə'rɪdʒənl, ˌæbə'rɪdʒnəl, -z

aboriginality
BR ˌabəˌrɪdʒɪ'nalɪti
AM ˌæbəˌrɪdʒə'nælədi

aboriginally
BR ˌabə'rɪdʒɪnəli, ˌabə'rɪdʒɪnl̩i
AM ˌæbə'rɪdʒ(ə)nəli

aborigine
BR ˌabə'rɪdʒɪn|i, -ɪz
AM ˌæbə'rɪdʒəni, -z

aborning
BR ə'bɔːnɪŋ
AM ə'bɔrnɪŋ

abort
BR ə'bɔːt, -s, -ɪŋ, -ɪd
AM ə'bɔ(ə)rt, -ts, -'bɔrdɪŋ, -'bɔrdəd

abortifacient
BR ə,bɔːtɪ'feɪʃnt, ə,bɔːtɪ'feɪʃɪənt, -s
AM ə,bɔrdə'feɪʃənt, -s

abortion
BR ə'bɔːʃn, -z
AM ə'bɔrʃən, -z

abortionist
BR ə'bɔːʃn̩ɪst, ə'bɔːʃənɪst, -s
AM ə'bɔrʃənəst, -s

abortive
BR ə'bɔːtɪv
AM ə'bɔrdɪv

abortively
BR ə'bɔːtɪvli
AM ə'bɔrdɪvli

abortiveness
BR ə'bɔːtɪvnɪs
AM ə'bɔrdɪvnɪs

Aboukir Bay
BR ˌabuːkɪə 'beɪ
AM ˌabu'kɪ(ə)r 'beɪ

aboulia
BR ə'buːlɪə(r)
AM ə'buljə, ə'buliə

aboulic
BR ə'buːlɪk
AM ə'bulɪk

abound
BR ə'baʊnd, -z, -ɪŋ, -ɪd
AM ə'baʊnd, -z, -ɪŋ, -əd

about
BR ə'baʊt
AM ə'baʊt

above
BR ə'bʌv
AM ə'bəv

aboveboard
BR ə'bʌvbɔːd, ə,bʌv'bɔːd
AM ə'bəv,bɔ(ə)rd

aboveground
BR ə'bʌvgraʊnd, ə,bʌv'graʊnd
AM ə'bəv'graʊnd

ab ovo
BR ,ab 'əʊvəʊ
AM æ'boʊ,voʊ

abracadabra
BR ˌabrəkə'dabrə(r)
AM ˌæbrəkə'dæbrə

abrade
BR ə'breɪd, -z, -ɪŋ, -ɪd
AM ə'breɪd, -z, -ɪŋ, -ɪd

abrader
BR ə'breɪdə(r), -z
AM ə'breɪdər, -z

Abraham
BR 'eɪbrəham
AM 'eɪbrəˌhæm

Abrahams
BR 'eɪbrəhamz
AM 'eɪbrəˌhæmz

Abram¹
name
BR 'eɪbrəm
AM 'eɪbrəm

Abram²
place in UK
BR 'abrəm, 'abram
AM 'eɪbrəm

Abrams
BR 'eɪbrəmz
AM 'eɪbrəmz

abrasion
BR ə'breɪʒn, -z
AM ə'breɪʒən, -z

abrasive
BR ə'breɪsɪv, ə'breɪzɪv, -z
AM ə'breɪsɪv, ə'breɪzɪv, -z

abrasively
BR ə'breɪsɪvli, ə'breɪzɪvli
AM ə'breɪsɪvli, ə'breɪzɪvli

abrasiveness
BR ə'breɪsɪvnɪs, ə'breɪzɪvnɪs
AM ə'breɪsɪvnɪs, ə'breɪzɪvnɪs

abraxus
BR ə'braksəs
AM ə'bræksəs

abreact
BR ˌabrɪ'akt, -s, -ɪŋ, -ɪd
AM ˌæbri'æk|(t), -(t)s, -tɪŋ, -təd

abreaction
BR ˌabrɪ'akʃn
AM ˌæbri'ækʃən

abreactive
BR ˌabrɪ'aktɪv
AM ˌæbri'æktɪv

abreast
BR ə'brɛst
AM ə'brɛst

abridgable
BR ə'brɪdʒəbl
AM ə'brɪdʒəbəl

abridge
BR ə'brɪdʒ, -ɪz, -ɪŋ, -d
AM ə'brɪdʒ, -z, -ɪŋ, -d

abridgement
BR ə'brɪdʒm(ə)nt, -s
AM ə'brɪdʒmənt, -s

abridger
BR ə'brɪdʒə(r), -z

AM əˈbrɪdʒər, -z
abroach
BR əˈbrəʊtʃ
AM əˈbroʊtʃ
abroad
BR əˈbrɔːd
AM əˈbrɔd, əˈbrɑd
abrogate¹
adjective
BR ˈæbrəgət
AM ˈæbrəgət
abrogate²
verb
BR ˈæbrəgeɪt, -s, -ɪŋ, -ɪd
AM ˈæbrəˌgeɪ|t, -ts, -dɪŋ, -dɪd
abrogation
BR ˌæbrəˈgeɪʃn
AM ˌæbrəˈgeɪʃən
abrogator
BR ˈæbrəgeɪtə(r), -z
AM ˈæbrəˌgeɪdər, -z
abrupt
BR əˈbrʌpt
AM əˈbrəpt
abruption
BR əˈbrʌpʃn
AM əˈbrəpʃən
abruptly
BR əˈbrʌptli
AM əˈbrəp(t)li
abruptness
BR əˈbrʌp(t)nəs
AM əˈbrəp(t)nəs
Abruzzi
BR əˈbrʊtsi
AM əˈbrutsi
Absalom
BR ˈæbsələm, ˈæbsl̩əm
AM ˈæbsəˌlɑm
abscess
BR ˈæbsɪs, ˈæbsɛs, -ɪz, -t
AM ˈæbˌsɛs, -əz, -t
abscisic acid
BR əbˌsɪsɪk ˈæsɪd, abˌsɪsɪk +
AM æbˈsɪsɪk ˈæsəd
abscissa
BR əbˈsɪsə(r), abˈsɪsə(r), -z
AM æbˈsɪsə, -z
abscissae
BR əbˈsɪsiː, abˈsɪsiː
AM æbˈsɪsi, æbˈsɪˌsaɪ
abscission
BR əbˈsɪʃn, abˈsɪʃn, -z
AM æbˈsɪʒən, -z
abscond
BR əbˈskɒnd, abˈskɒnd, -z, -ɪŋ, -ɪd
AM æbˈskɑnd, əbˈskɑnd, -z, -ɪŋ, -ɪd
absconder
BR əbˈskɒndə(r), abˈskɒndə(r), -z
AM æbˈskɑndər, əbˈskɑndər, -z

Abse
BR ˈabzi
AM ˈæbsi
abseil
BR ˈabseɪl, ˈapseɪl, ˈabsʌɪl, ˈapsʌɪl, -z, -ɪŋ, -d
AM ˈæbˌseɪl, -z, -ɪŋ, -d
abseiler
BR ˈabseɪlə(r), ˈapseɪlə(r), ˈabsʌɪlə(r), ˈapsʌɪlə(r), -z
AM ˈæbˌseɪlər, -z
absence
BR ˈabs(ə)ns, -ɪz
AM ˈæbsəns, -əz
absent¹
adjective
BR ˈabs(ə)nt
AM ˈæbsənt
absent²
verb
BR əbˈsɛnt, abˈsɛnt, -s, -ɪŋ, -ɪd
AM æbˈsɛn|t, -ts, -(t)ɪŋ, -(t)əd
absentee
BR ˌabs(ə)nˈtiː, -z
AM ˌæbsənˈti, -z
absenteeism
BR ˌabs(ə)nˈtiːɪz(ə)m
AM ˌæbsənˈtiˌɪzəm
absently
BR ˈabs(ə)ntli
AM ˈæbsən(t)li
absentness
BR ˈabs(ə)ntnəs
AM ˈæbsən(t)nəs
absinth
BR ˈabsɪnθ, -s
AM ˈæbˌsɪnθ, -s
absinthe
BR ˈabsɪnθ, -s
AM ˈæbˌsɪnθ, -s
absit omen
BR ˌabsɪt ˈəʊmɛn
AM ˌæbsə ˈdoʊmən
absolute
BR ˈabsəluːt, ˌabsəˈluːt, -s
AM ˈæbsəˌl(j)ut, -s
absolutely
BR ˈabsəluːtli, ˌabsəˈluːtli
AM ˈæbsəˌl(j)utli
absoluteness
BR ˈabsəluːtnəs, ˌabsəˈluːtnəs
AM ˈæbsəˌl(j)utnəs
absolution
BR ˌabsəˈluːʃn, -z
AM ˌæbsəˈl(j)uʃən, -z
absolutism
BR ˈabsəluːtɪz(ə)m, ˌabsəˈluːtɪz(ə)m
AM ˈæbsəˌl(j)uˌtɪzəm, ˈæbsəˌl(j)udɪzəm

absolutist
BR ˈabsəluːtɪst, ˌabsəˈluːtɪst, -s
AM ˈæbsəˌl(j)udəst, -s
absolve
BR əbˈzɒlv, -z, -ɪŋ, -d
AM əbˈzɑlv, æbˈzɒlv, əbˈsɒlv, æbˈsɒlv, əbˈzɑlv, æbˈzɑlv, əbˈsɑlv, æbˈsɑlv, -z, -ɪŋ, -d
absolver
BR əbˈzɒlvə(r), -z
AM əbˈzɑlvər, æbˈzɑlvər, əbˈsɒlvər, æbˈsɒlvər, əbˈzɑlvər, əbˈzɑlvər, æbˈsɑlvər, əbˈsɑlvər, -z
absorb
BR əbˈzɔːb, əbˈsɔːb, -z, -ɪŋ, -d
AM əbˈzɔ(ə)rb, æbˈzɔ(ə)rb, əbˈsɔ(ə)rb, æbˈsɔ(ə)rb, -z, -ɪŋ, -d
absorbability
BR əbˌzɔːbəˈbɪlɪti, əbˌsɔːbəˈbɪlɪti
AM əbˌzɔrbəˈbɪlɪdi, æbˌzɔrbəˈbɪlɪdi, əbˌsɔrbəˈbɪlɪdi, æbˌsɔrbəˈbɪlɪdi
absorbable
BR əbˈzɔːbəbl, əbˈsɔːbəbl
AM əbˈzɔrbəbəl, æbˈzɔrbəbəl, əbˈsɔrbəbəl, æbˈsɔrbəbəl
absorbance
BR əbˈzɔːb(ə)ns, əbˈsɔːb(ə)ns
AM əbˈzɔrbəns, æbˈzɔrbəns, əbˈsɔrbəns, æbˈsɔrbəns
absorbedly
BR əbˈzɔːbɪdli, əbˈsɔːbɪdli
AM əbˈzɔrbədli, æbˈzɔrbədli, əbˈsɔrbədli, æbˈsɔrbədli
absorbency
BR əbˈzɔːb(ə)nsi, əbˈsɔːb(ə)nsi
AM əbˈzɔrbənsi, æbˈzɔrbənsi, əbˈsɔrbənsi, æbˈsɔrbənsi
absorbent
BR əbˈzɔːb(ə)nt, əbˈsɔːb(ə)nt
AM əbˈzɔrbənt, æbˈzɔrbənt, əbˈsɔrbənt, æbˈsɔrbənt

absorbently
BR əbˈzɔːb(ə)ntli, əbˈsɔːb(ə)ntli
AM əbˈzɔrbən(t)li, æbˈzɔrbən(t)li, əbˈsɔrbən(t)li, æbˈsɔrbən(t)li
absorber
BR əbˈzɔːbə(r), əbˈsɔːbə(r), -z
AM əbˈzɔrbər, æbˈzɔrbər, əbˈsɔrbər, æbˈsɔrbər, -z
absorbingly
BR əbˈzɔːbɪŋli, əbˈsɔːbɪŋli
AM əbˈzɔrbɪŋli, æbˈzɔrbɪŋli, əbˈsɔrbɪŋli, æbˈsɔrbɪŋli
absorption
BR əbˈzɔːpʃn, əbˈsɔːpʃn
AM əbˈzɔrpʃən, æbˈzɔrpʃən, əbˈsɔrpʃən, æbˈsɔrpʃən
absorptive
BR əbˈzɔːptɪv, əbˈsɔːptɪv
AM əbˈzɔrptɪv, æbˈzɔrptɪv, əbˈsɔrptɪv, æbˈsɔrptɪv
absorptiveness
BR əbˈzɔːptɪvnɪs, əbˈsɔːptɪvnɪs
AM əbˈzɔrptɪvnɪs, æbˈzɔrptɪvnɪs, əbˈsɔrptɪvnɪs, æbˈsɔrptɪvnɪs
absorptivity
BR ˌabzɔːpˈtɪvɪti, ˌabsɔːpˈtɪvɪti
AM ˌæbzɔrpˈtɪvɪdi, ˌæbzɔrpˈtɪvɪdi, ˌæbsɔrpˈtɪvɪdi, ˌæbsɔrpˈtɪvɪdi
absquatulate
BR əbˈskwɒtjʊleɪt, əbˈskwɒtʃʊleɪt, -s, -ɪŋ, -ɪd
AM əbˈskwɑtʃəˌleɪt, ˌæbˈskwɑtʃəˌleɪt, -ts, -dɪŋ, -dɪd
abstain
BR əbˈsteɪn, -z, -ɪŋ, -d
AM əbˈsteɪn, æbˈsteɪn, -z, -ɪŋ, -d
abstainer
BR əbˈsteɪnə(r)
ab'steɪnə(r), -z
AM əbˈsteɪnər, æbˈsteɪnər, -z
abstemious
BR əbˈstiːmɪəs
AM æbˈstimɪəs, əbˈstimɪəs

abstemiously
BR əbˈstiːmɪəsli
AM æbˈstimiəsli,
əbˈstimiəsli

abstemiousness
BR əbˈstiːmɪəsnəs
AM æbˈstimiəsnəs,
əbˈstimiəsnəs

abstention
BR əbˈstɛnʃn, -z
AM əbˈstɛn(t)ʃən,
æbˈstɛn(t)ʃən, -z

abstentionism
BR əbˈstɛnʃnɪz(ə)m,
əbˈstɛnʃənɪz(ə)m
AM əbˈstɛn(t)ʃəˌnɪzəm,
æbˈstɛn(t)ʃəˌnɪzəm

abstergent
BR əbˈstɜːdʒ(ə)nt,
əbˈstɜːdʒ(ə)nt, -s
AM əbˈstɜrdʒənt,
æbˈstɜrdʒənt, -s

abstersion
BR əbˈstɜːʃn,
əbˈstɜːʃn, -z
AM əbˈstɜrʒən,
æbˈstɜrʒən, -z

abstersive
BR əbˈstɜːsɪv,
əbˈstɜːsɪv
AM əbˈstɜrzɪv,
æbˈstɜrzɪv

abstersively
BR əbˈstɜːsɪvli,
əbˈstɜːsɪvli
AM əbˈstɜrzɪvli,
æbˈstɜrzɪvli

abstinence
BR ˈabstɪnəns
AM ˈæbstənəns

abstinency
BR ˈabstɪnənsi
AM ˈæbstənənsi

abstinent
BR ˈabstɪnənt
AM ˈæbstənənt

abstinently
BR ˈabstɪnəntli
AM ˈæbstənən(t)li

abstract¹
adjective
BR ˈabstrakt
AM əbˈstræk(t),
ˌæbˈstræk(t)

abstract²
noun
BR ˈabstrakt, -s
AM ˈæbˌstræk(t), -s

abstract³
verb
BR əbˈstrakt, -s, -ɪŋ, -ɪd
AM əbˈstræk(t),
ˌæbˈstræk|(t), -(t)s,
-tɪŋ, -təd

abstractedly
BR əbˈstraktɪdli
AM əbˈstræktədli,
æbˈstræktədli

abstractedness
BR əbˈstraktɪdnɪs
AM əbˈstræktədnəs,
æbˈstræktədnəs

abstraction
BR əbˈstrakʃn, -z
AM əbˈstrækʃən,
æbˈstrækʃən, -z

abstractionism
BR əbˈstrakʃnɪz(ə)m,
əbˈstrakʃənɪz(ə)m
AM əbˈstrækʃəˌnɪzəm,
æbˈstrækʃəˌnɪzəm

abstractionist
BR əbˈstrakʃnɪst,
əbˈstrakʃənɪst, -s
AM əbˈstrækʃənəst,
æbˈstrækʃənəst, -s

abstractive
BR əbˈstraktɪv
AM əbˈstræktɪv,
æbˈstræktɪv

abstractly
BR ˈabstrak(t)li
AM əbˈstræk(t)li,
æbˈstræk(t)li

abstractness
BR əbˈstrak(t)nəs
AM əbˈstræk(t)nəs,
æbˈstræk(t)nəs

abstractor
BR əbˈstraktə(r), -z
AM əbˈstræktər,
æbˈstræktər, -z

abstruse
BR əbˈstruːs
AM əbˈstrus, æbˈstrus

abstrusely
BR əbˈstruːsli
AM əbˈstrusli,
æbˈstrusli

abstruseness
BR əbˈstruːsnəs
AM əbˈstrusnəs,
æbˈstrusnəs

absurd
BR əbˈsəːd, əbˈzəːd
AM əbˈsərd, æbˈsərd,
əbˈzərd, æbˈzərd

absurdism
BR əbˈsəːdɪz(ə)m,
əbˈzəːdɪz(ə)m
AM əbˈsərdˌɪzəm,
æbˈsərdˌɪzəm,
əbˈzərdˌɪzəm,
æbˈzərdˌɪzəm

absurdist
BR əbˈsəːdɪst,
əbˈzəːdɪst, -s
AM əbˈsərdəst,
əbˈzərdəst,
æbˈzərdəst, -s

absurdity
BR əbˈsəːdɪt|i,
əbˈzəːdɪti, -ɪz
AM əbˈsərdədi,
æbˈsərdədi,

abstractedness
əbˈzərdədi,
æbˈzərdədi, -z

absurdly
BR əbˈsəːdli, əbˈzəːdli
AM əbˈsərdli,
æbˈsərdli, əbˈzərdli,
æbˈzərdli

absurdness
BR əbˈsəːdnəs,
əbˈzəːdnəs
AM əbˈsərdnəs,
æbˈsərdnəs,
əbˈzərdnəs,
æbˈzərdnəs

ABTA
BR ˈabtə(r)
AM ˌeɪˌbiˌtiˈeɪ, ˈæbdə

Abu Dhabi
BR ˌabu: ˈdɑːbi
AM ˌɑbu ˈdɑbi

Abuja
BR əˈbuːdʒə(r)
AM əˈbudʒə

Abukir Bay
BR ˌabəkɪə ˈbeɪ
AM ˌɑbuˈkɪ(ə)r ˈbeɪ

abulia
BR əˈb(j)uːlɪə(r)
AM əˈbuljə, əˈbuliə

Abu Musa
BR əˈbuː ˈmuːsə(r)
AM ˌɑbu ˈmusə

abundance
BR əˈbʌnd(ə)ns
AM əˈbənd(ə)ns

abundant
BR əˈbʌnd(ə)nt
AM əˈbəndənt

abundantly
BR əˈbʌnd(ə)ntli
AM əˈbəndən(t)li

abuse¹
noun
BR əˈbjuːs, -ɪz
AM əˈbjus, -əz

abuse²
verb
BR əˈbjuːz, -ɪz, -ɪŋ, -d
AM əˈbjuz, -əz, -ɪŋ, -d

abuser
BR əˈbjuːzə(r), -z
AM əˈbjuzər, -z

Abu Simbel
BR ˌabu: ˈsɪmbl
AM ˌɑbu ˈsɪmbəl

abusive
BR əˈbjuːsɪv, əˈbjuːzɪv
AM əˈbjusɪv, əˈbjuzɪv

abusively
BR əˈbjuːsɪvli,
əˈbjuːzɪvli
AM əˈbjusɪvli,
əˈbjuzɪvli

abusiveness
BR əˈbjuːsɪvnɪs,
əˈbjuːzɪvnɪs
AM əˈbjusɪvnəs,
əˈbjuzɪvnɪs

abut
BR əˈbʌt, -s, -ɪŋ, -ɪd
AM əˈbə|t, -ts, -dɪŋ, -dəd

abutilon
BR əˈbjuːtɪlən,
əˈbjuːtɪlɒn, -z
AM əˈbjudlˌɑn, -z

abutment
BR əˈbʌtm(ə)nt, -s
AM əˈbətmənt, -s

abuttal
BR əˈbʌtl
AM əˈbədl

abutter
BR əˈbʌtə(r), -z
AM əˈbədər, -z

abuzz
BR əˈbʌz
AM əˈbəz

Abydos
BR əˈbaɪdɒs
AM əˈbaɪˌdɒs, əˈbaɪˌdɑs

abysm
BR əˈbɪz(ə)m
AM əˈbɪz(ə)m

abysmal
BR əˈbɪzml
AM əˈbɪzməl

abysmally
BR əˈbɪzmˌli, əˈbɪzməli
AM əˈbɪzməli

abyss
BR əˈbɪs, -ɪz
AM əˈbɪs, -ɪz

abyssal
BR əˈbɪsl
AM əˈbɪsəl

Abyssinia
BR ˌabɪˈsɪnɪə(r)
AM ˌæbəˈsɪniə

abzyme
BR ˈabzʌɪm, -z
AM ˈæbˌzaɪm, -z

a/c
BR əˈkaʊnt, -s
AM əˈkaʊnt, -s

acacia
BR əˈkeɪʃə(r), -z
AM əˈkeɪʃə, -z

academe
BR ˈakədiːm
AM ˈækəˌdim

academia
BR ˌakəˈdiːmɪə(r)
AM ˌækəˈdimiə

academic
BR ˌakəˈdɛmɪk, -s
AM ˌækəˈdɛmɪk, -s

academical
BR ˌakəˈdɛmɪkl, -z
AM ˌækəˈdɛməkəl, -z

academically
BR ˌakəˈdɛmɪkli
AM ˌækəˈdɛmək(ə)li

academician
BR əˌkadəˈmɪʃn,
ˌakədəˈmɪʃn, -z

AM ˌækədəˈmɪʃən,
əˌkædəˈmɪʃən, -z

academicism
BR ˌakəˈdɛmɪsɪz(ə)m
AM ˌækəˈdɛməˌsɪzəm

academism
BR əˈkadəmɪz(ə)m
AM əˈkædəˌmɪzəm

academy
BR əˈkadəm|i, -ɪz
AM əˈkædəmi, -z

Acadia
BR əˈkeɪdɪə(r)
AM əˈkeɪdiə

Acadian
BR əˈkeɪdɪən, -z
AM əˈkeɪdiən, -z

acaemia
BR əˈsiːmɪə(r)
AM əˈsimjə, əˈsimiə

acajau
BR ˈakaʒuː, -z
AM ˈɑkəʒu, -z

acanthi
BR əˈkanθʌɪ
AM əˈkænˌθaɪ

acanthine
BR əˈkanθʌɪn
AM əˈkænθən,
əˈkænˌθaɪn

acanthus
BR əˈkanθəs, -ɪz
AM əˈkænθəs, -əz

a capella
BR ˌa kəˈpɛlə(r), ˌɑ: +
AM ˌɑ kəˈpɛlə

a cappella
BR ˌa kəˈpɛlə(r), ˌɑ: +
AM ˌɑ kəˈpɛlə

Acapulco
BR ˌakəˈpʊlkəʊ
AM ˌɑkəˈpʊlkoʊ,
ˌɑkəˈpoʊkoʊ

acaricide
BR ˈakərɪsʌɪd,
əˈkarɪsʌɪd, -z
AM əˈkɛrəˌsaɪd, -z

acarid
BR ˈakərɪd, -z
AM ˈakərəd, -z

acaroid
BR ˈakərɔɪd
AM ˈækəˌrɔɪd

acarology
BR ˌakəˈrɒlədʒi
AM ˌækəˈrɑlədʒi

acarpous
BR ˌeɪˈkɑːpəs
AM eɪˈkarpəs

ACAS
BR ˈeɪkas
AM ˈeɪˌkæs

acatalectic
BR əˌkatəˈlɛktɪk,
ˌeɪkatəˈlɛktɪk
AM ˌeɪˌkædlˈɛktɪk,
əˌkædlˈɛktɪk

acatalepsy
BR əˈkatəlɛpsi,
(ˌ)eɪˈkatəlɛpsi
AM eɪˈkædlˌɛpsi

acataleptic
BR əˌkatəˈlɛptɪk,
ˌeɪkatəˈlɛptɪk
AM ˈeɪˌkædlˈɛptɪk,
əˌkædlˈɛptɪk

acaudal
BR (ˌ)eɪˈkɔːdl

acaudate
BR (ˌ)eɪˈkɔːdeɪt
AM eɪˈkɔˌdeɪt,
eɪˈkɑˌdeɪt

acausal
BR (ˌ)eɪˈkɔːzl
AM eɪˈkɔzəl, eɪˈkɑzəl

Accadian
BR əˈkeɪdɪən, -z
AM əˈkeɪdiən, -z

accaroid
BR ˈakərɔɪd
AM ˈækəˌrɔɪd

accede
BR əkˈsiːd, akˈsiːd, -z,
-ɪŋ, -ɪd
AM ækˈsid, ə(k)ˈsid, -z,
-ɪŋ, -ɪd

accelerando
BR əkˌsɛləˈrandəʊ,
akˌsɛləˈrandəʊ,
əˌtʃɛləˈrandəʊ
AM ɑkˌsɛləˈrɑndoʊ,
ɑˌtʃɛləˈrɑndoʊ

accelerant
BR əkˈsɛlərənt,
əkˈsɛlərn̩t, -s
AM əkˈsɛlərənt,
ækˈsɛlərənt, -s

accelerate
BR əkˈsɛləreɪt,
akˈsɛləreɪt, -s, -ɪŋ, -ɪd
AM əkˈsɛləˌreɪ|t,
ækˈsɛləˌreɪ|t, -ts, -dɪŋ,
-dɪd

acceleration
BR əkˌsɛləˈreɪʃn
AM əkˌsɛləˈreɪʃən,
ækˌsɛləˈreɪʃən

accelerative
BR əkˈsɛl(ə)rətɪv
AM əkˈsɛlərədɪv,
ækˈsɛlərədɪv,
əkˈsɛləˌreɪdɪv,
ækˈsɛləˌreɪdɪv

accelerator
BR əkˈsɛləreɪtə(r)
akˈsɛləreɪtə(r), -z
AM əkˈsɛləˌreɪdər,
ækˈsɛləˌreɪdər, -z

accelerometer
BR əkˌsɛləˈrɒmɪtə(r)
akˌsɛləˈrɒmɪtə(r), -z
AM əkˌsɛləˈrɑmədər,
ækˌsɛləˈrɑmədər, -z

accent¹
noun
BR ˈaks(ə)nt, -s
AM ˈækˌsɛnt, -s

accent²
verb
BR əkˈsɛnt, akˈsɛnt, -s,
-ɪŋ, -ɪd
AM ˈækˈsɛn|t, -ts, -(t)ɪŋ,
-(t)əd

accentor
BR əkˈsɛntə(r),
akˈsɛntə(r), -z
AM ˈæksɛn(t)ər, -z

accentual
BR əkˈsɛn(t)ʃʊəl,
əkˈsɛn(t)ʃ(ʊ)l,
akˈsɛn(t)ʃʊəl,
akˈsɛn(t)ʃ(ʊ)l,
əkˈsɛntjʊəl,
əkˈsɛntjʊl,
akˈsɛntjʊəl,
akˈsɛntjʊl,
AM ækˈsɛn(t)ʃ(əw)əl,
əkˈsɛn(t)ʃ(əw)əl

accentually
BR əkˈsɛn(t)ʃʊəli,
əkˈsɛn(t)ʃʊli,
əkˈsɛn(t)ʃli,
akˈsɛn(t)ʃʊəli,
akˈsɛn(t)ʃʊli,
akˈsɛn(t)ʃli,
əkˈsɛntjʊəli,
əkˈsɛntjʊli,
akˈsɛntjʊəli,
akˈsɛntjʊli
AM ækˈsɛn(t)ʃ(əw)əli,
əkˈsɛn(t)ʃ(əw)əli

accentuate
BR əkˈsɛn(t)ʃʊeɪt,
akˈsɛn(t)ʃʊeɪt,
əkˈsɛntjʊeɪt,
akˈsɛntjʊeɪt, -s, -ɪŋ, -ɪd
AM ækˈsɛn(t)ʃə,weɪ|t,
əkˈsɛn(t)ʃə,weɪ|t, -ts,
-dɪŋ, -dɪd

accentuation
BR əkˌsɛn(t)ʃʊˈeɪʃn,
akˌsɛn(t)ʃʊˈeɪʃn,
əkˌsɛntjʊˈeɪʃn,
akˌsɛntjʊˈeɪʃn,
AM ækˌsɛn(t)ʃəˈweɪʃən,
əkˌsɛn(t)ʃəˈweɪʃən

accept
BR əkˈsɛpt, akˈsɛpt, -s,
-ɪŋ, -ɪd
AM əkˈsɛpt, ækˈsɛpt, -s,
-ɪŋ, -əd

acceptability
BR əkˌsɛptəˈbɪlɪti,
akˌsɛptəˈbɪlɪti,
AM əkˌsɛptəˈbɪlɪdi,
ækˌsɛptəˈbɪlɪdi

acceptable
BR əkˈsɛptəbl,
akˈsɛptəbl
AM əkˈsɛptəbəl,
ækˈsɛptəbəl

acceptableness
BR əkˈsɛptəblnəs,
akˈsɛptəblnəs
AM əkˈsɛptəbəlnəs,
ækˈsɛptəbəlnəs

acceptably
BR əkˈsɛptəbli,
akˈsɛptəbli
AM əkˈsɛptəbli,
ækˈsɛptəbli

acceptance
BR əkˈsɛpt(ə)ns,
akˈsɛpt(ə)ns, -ɪz
AM əkˈsɛpt(ə)ns,
ækˈsɛpt(ə)ns, -əz

acceptant
BR əkˈsɛpt(ə)nt,
akˈsɛpt(ə)nt, -s
AM əkˈsɛptənt,
ækˈsɛptənt, -s

acceptation
BR ˌaksɛpˈteɪʃn,
ˌaksəpˈteɪʃn, -z
AM ˌækˌsɛpˈteɪʃən, -z

accepter
BR əkˈsɛptə(r),
akˈsɛptə(r), -z
AM əkˈsɛptər,
ækˈsɛptər, -z

acceptor
BR əkˈsɛptə(r),
akˈsɛptə(r), -z
AM əkˈsɛptər,
ækˈsɛptər, -z

access¹
noun
BR ˈaksɛs, -ɪz
AM ˈækˌsɛs, -əz

access²
verb
BR ˈaksɛs, əkˈsɛs, -ɪz,
-ɪŋ, -t
AM ˈækˌsɛs, -əz, -ɪŋ, -t

accessary
BR əkˈsɛs(ə)r|i,
akˈsɛs(ə)r|i, -ɪz
AM əkˈsɛs(ə)ri,
ækˈsɛs(ə)ri, -z

accessibility
BR əkˌsɛsɪˈbɪlɪti,
akˌsɛsɪˈbɪlɪti
AM əkˌsɛsəˈbɪlɪdi,
ækˌsɛsəˈbɪlɪdi

accessible
BR əkˈsɛsɪbl, akˈsɛsɪbl
AM əkˈsɛsəbəl,
ækˈsɛsəbəl

accessibly
BR əkˈsɛsɪbli,
akˈsɛsɪbli
AM əkˈsɛsəbli,
ækˈsɛsəbli

accession
BR əkˈsɛʃn, akˈsɛʃn
AM əkˈsɛʃən, ækˈsɛʃən

accessit
BR akˈsɛsɪt
AM ækˈsɛsət

accessorial
BR ˌakse'sɔːriəl
AM ˌæksə'sɔriəl

accessorise
BR ək'sɛsərʌɪz
ak'sɛsərʌɪz, -ɪz, -ɪŋ, -d
AM ək'sɛsəˌraɪz,
æk'sɛsəˌraɪz, -ɪz, -ɪŋ,
-d

accessorize
BR ək'sɛsərʌɪz
ak'sɛsərʌɪz, -ɪz, -ɪŋ, -d
AM ək'sɛsəˌraɪz,
æk'sɛsəˌraɪz, -ɪz, -ɪŋ,
-d

accessory
BR ək'sɛs(ə)r|i,
ak'sɛs(ə)r|i, -ɪz
AM ək'sɛs(ə)ri,
æk'sɛs(ə)ri, -z

acciaccatura
BR əˌtʃakə'tʊərə(r)
AM ɑˌtʃakə'tʊrə

accidence
BR 'aksɪd(ə)ns
AM 'æksəd(ə)ns

accident
BR 'aksɪd(ə)nt, -s
AM 'æksədnt, -s

accidental
BR ˌaksɪ'dɛntl
AM ˌæksə'dɛn(t)l

accidentally
BR ˌaksɪ'dɛntḷi,
ˌaksɪ'dɛntli
AM ˌæksə'dɛn(t)li

accidie
BR 'aksɪdi
AM 'æksədi

accipiter
BR ak'sɪpɪtə(r), -z
AM æ(k)'sɪpədər, -z

acclaim
BR ə'kleɪm, -z, -ɪŋ, -d
AM ə'kleɪm, -z, -ɪŋ, -d

acclaimer
BR ə'kleɪmə(r), -z
AM ə'kleɪmər, -z

acclamation
BR ˌaklə'meɪʃn, -z
AM ˌæklə'meɪʃən, -z

acclamatory
BR ə'klamət(ə)ri
AM ə'klæməˌtɔri

acclimatation
BR əˌklaɪmə'teɪʃn
AM əˌklaɪmə'teɪʃən

acclimate
BR 'aklɪmeɪt, -s, -ɪŋ, -ɪd
AM 'æklə,meɪ|t, -ts,
-dɪŋ, -dɪd

acclimation
BR ˌaklɪ'meɪʃn
AM ˌæklə'meɪʃən

acclimatisation
BR əˌklʌɪmətʌɪ'zeɪʃn
AM əˌklaɪmədə'zeɪʃən,
əˌklaɪmə,taɪ'zeɪʃən

acclimatise
BR ə'klʌɪmətʌɪz, -ɪz,
-ɪŋ, -d
AM ə'klaɪmə,taɪz, -ɪz,
-ɪŋ, -d

acclimatization
BR əˌklʌɪmətʌɪ'zeɪʃn
AM əˌklaɪmədə'zeɪʃən,
əˌklaɪmə,taɪ'zeɪʃən

acclimatize
BR ə'klʌɪmətʌɪz, -ɪz,
-ɪŋ, -d
AM ə'klaɪmə,taɪz, -ɪz,
-ɪŋ, -d

acclivitous
BR ə'klɪvɪtəs
AM ə'klɪvədəs

acclivity
BR ə'klɪvɪt|i, -ɪz
AM ə'klɪvɪdi, -z

accolade
BR 'akəleɪd, ˌakə'leɪd,
-z
AM 'ækə,leɪd, -z

accommodate
BR ə'kɒmədeɪt, -s, -ɪŋ,
-ɪd
AM ə'kɑmə,deɪ|t, -ts,
-dɪŋ, -dɪd

accommodatingly
BR ə'kɒmədeɪtɪŋli
AM ə'kɑmə,deɪdɪŋli

accommodation
BR əˌkɒmə'deɪʃn, -z
AM əˌkɑmə'deɪʃən, -z

accommodationist
BR əˌkɒmə'deɪʃnɪst,
əˌkɒmə'deɪʃənɪst, -s
AM əˌkɑmə'deɪʃənəst,
-s

accompaniment
BR ə'kʌmp(ə)nɪm(ə)nt,
-s
AM ə'kəmp(ə)nimənt,
ə'kəmp(ə)nəmənt, -s

accompanist
BR ə'kʌmpənɪst,
ə'kʌmpnɪst, -s
AM ə'kəmpənəst, -s

accompany
BR ə'kʌmp(ə)n|i,
ə'kʌmpn|i, -ɪz, -ɪɪŋ, -ɪd
AM ə'kəmp(ə)ni, -z, -ɪŋ,
-d

accompanyist
BR ə'kʌmpənɪɪst,
ə'kʌmpnɪɪst
AM ə'kəmp(ə)niəst

accomplice
BR ə'kʌmplɪs,
ə'kɒmplɪs, -ɪz
AM ə'kɑmpləs, -əz

accomplish
BR ə'kʌmpl|ɪʃ,
ə'kɒmpl|ɪʃ, -ɪʃɪz, -ɪʃɪŋ,
-ɪʃt
AM ə'kɑmplɪʃ, -ɪz, -ɪŋ, -t

accomplishment
BR ə'kʌmplɪʃm(ə)nt,
ə'kɒmplɪʃm(ə)nt, -s
AM ə'kɑmplɪʃmənt, -s

accompt
BR ə'kaʊnt, -s
AM ə'kaʊnt, -s

accord
BR ə'kɔːd, -z, -ɪŋ, -ɪd
AM ə'kɔ(ə)rd, -z, -ɪŋ, -əd

accordance
BR ə'kɔːdns
AM ə'kɔrdns

accordant
BR ə'kɔːdnt
AM ə'kɔrdnt

accordantly
BR ə'kɔːdntli
AM ə'kɔrdn(t)li

according
BR ə'kɔːdɪŋ
AM ə'kɔrdɪŋ

accordingly
BR ə'kɔːdɪŋli
AM ə'kɔrdɪŋli

accordion
BR ə'kɔːdɪən, -z
AM ə'kɔrdiən, -z

accordionist
BR ə'kɔːdɪənɪst, -s
AM ə'kɔrdiənəst, -s

accost
BR ə'kɒst, -s, -ɪŋ, -ɪd
AM ə'kɔst, ə'kɑst, -s,
-ɪŋ, -əd

accouchement
BR ə'kuːʃmɒ̃, -z
AM ˌaku'ʃ'mant,
ə'kuʃmənt, -s

accoucheur
BR ˌaku:'ʃə:(r), -z
AM ˌaku'ʃər, -z

accoucheuse
BR ˌaku:'ʃə:z, -ɪz
AM ˌaku'ʃəz, -əz

account
BR ə'kaʊnt, -s, -ɪŋ, -ɪd
AM ə'kaʊn|t, -ts, -(t)ɪŋ,
-(t)əd

accountability
BR əˌkaʊntə'bɪlɪti
AM əˌkaʊn(t)ə'bɪlɪdi

accountable
BR ə'kaʊntəbl
AM ə'kaʊn(t)əbəl

accountableness
BR ə'kaʊntəblnəs
AM ə'kaʊn(t)əbəlnəs

accountably
BR ə'kaʊntəbli
AM ə'kaʊn(t)əbli

accountancy
BR ə'kaʊnt(ə)nsi
AM ə'kaʊn(t)nsi

accountant
BR ə'kaʊnt(ə)nt, -s
AM ə'kaʊn(t)ənt, -s

accounting
BR ə'kaʊntɪŋ
AM ə'kaʊn(t)ɪŋ

accouter
BR ə'ku:t|ə(r), -əz,
-(ə)rɪŋ, -əd
AM ə'kudər, -z, -ɪŋ, -d

accouterment
BR ə'ku:trɪm(ə)nt,
ə'ku:təm(ə)nt, -s
AM ə'kudərmənt, -s

accoutre
BR ə'ku:t|ə(r), -əz,
-(ə)rɪŋ, -əd
AM ə'kudər, -z, -ɪŋ, -d

accoutrement
BR ə'ku:trɪm(ə)nt,
ə'ku:təm(ə)nt, -s
AM ə'kudərmənt, -s

Accra
BR ə'krɑ:(r)
AM 'ækrə

accredit
BR ə'krɛd|ɪt, -ɪts, -ɪtɪŋ,
-ɪtɪd
AM ə'krɛdə|t, -ts, -dɪŋ,
-dəd

accreditation
BR əˌkrɛdɪ'teɪʃn
AM əˌkrɛdə'deɪʃən

accrete
BR ə'kri:t, -s, -ɪŋ, -ɪd
AM ə'kri|t, -ts, -dɪŋ, -dɪd

accretion
BR ə'kri:ʃn, -z
AM ə'kriʃən, -z

accretive
BR ə'kri:tɪv
AM ə'kridɪv

Accrington
BR 'akrɪŋt(ə)n
AM 'ækrɪŋtən

accrual
BR ə'kru:əl, -z
AM ə'kruəl, -z

accrue
BR ə'kru:, -z, -ɪŋ, -d
AM ə'kru, -z, -ɪŋ, -d

acct
BR ə'kaʊnt, -s
AM ə'kaʊnt, -s

acculturate
BR ə'kʌltʃʊreɪt, -s, -ɪŋ,
-ɪd
AM ə'kəltʃəˌreɪ|t, -ts,
-dɪŋ, -dɪd

acculturation
BR əˌkʌltʃə'reɪʃn
AM əˌkəltʃə'reɪʃən

acculturative
BR ə'kʌltʃ(ə)rətɪv
AM ə'kəltʃ(ə)rədɪv,
ə'kəltʃəˌreɪdɪv

accumulable
BR ə'kju:mjələbl
AM ə'kjum(j)ələbəl

accumulate
BR əˈkjuːmjʊleɪt, -s,
-ɪŋ, -ɪd
AM əˈkjuːm(j)əˌleɪ|t, -ts,
-dɪŋ, -dɪd

accumulation
BR əˌkjuːmjʊˈleɪʃn, -z
AM əˌkjuːm(j)əˈleɪʃən,
-z

accumulative
BR əˈkjuːmjʊlətɪv
AM əˈkjuːm(j)ələdɪv,
əˈkjuːm(j)əˌleɪdɪv

accumulatively
BR əˈkjuːmjʊlətɪvli
AM əˈkjuːm(j)ələdɪvli,
əˈkjuːm(j)əˌleɪdɪvli

accumulator
BR əˈkjuːmjʊleɪtə(r),
-z
AM əˈkjuːm(j)əˌleɪdər,
-z

accuracy
BR ˈakjʊrəsi
AM ˈækjərəsi

accurate
BR ˈakjʊrət
AM ˈækjərət

accurately
BR ˈakjʊrətli
AM ˈækjərətli

accurateness
BR ˈakjʊrətnəs
AM ˈækjərətnəs

Accurist®
BR ˈakjʊrɪst
AM ˈækjʊrəst

accursed
BR əˈkɜːst, əˈkɜːsɪd
AM əˈkɜrst, əˈkɜrsəd

accursedly
BR əˈkɜːsɪdli
AM əˈkɜrsədli

accusal
BR əˈkjuːzl, -z
AM əˈkjuzəl, -z

accusation
BR ˌakjʊˈzeɪʃn, -z
AM ˌækjʊˈzeɪʃən,
ˌækjuˈzeɪʃən, -z

accusatival
BR əˌkjuːzəˈtaɪvl
AM əˌkjuzəˈtaɪvəl

accusative
BR əˈkjuːzətɪv, -z
AM əˈkjuzədɪv, -z

accusatively
BR əˈkjuːzətɪvli
AM əˈkjuzədɪvli

accusatorial
BR əˌkjuːzəˈtɔːriəl
AM əˌkjuzəˈtoriəl

accusatory
BR əˈkjuːzət(ə)ri,
ˌakjʊˈzeɪt(ə)ri
AM əˈkjuzəˌtori

accuse
BR əˈkjuːz, -ɪz, -ɪŋ, -d

accuser
AM əˈkjuz, -əz, -ɪŋ, -d

accuser
BR əˈkjuːzə(r), -z
AM əˈkjuzər, -z

accusingly
BR əˈkjuːzɪŋli
AM əˈkjuzɪŋli

accustom
BR əˈkʌstəm, -z, -ɪŋ, -d
AM əˈkəstəm, -z, -ɪŋ, -d

ace
BR eɪs, -ɪz, -ɪŋ, -t
AM eɪs, -ɪz, -ɪŋ, -t

acedia
BR əˈsiːdɪə(r)
AM əˈsidiə

Aceldama
BR əˈkɛldəmə(r),
əˈsɛldəmə(r)
AM əˈsɛldəmə,
əˈkɛldəmə

acellular
BR (ˌ)eɪˈsɛljʊlə(r)
AM eɪˈsɛljələr

acephalous
BR (ˌ)eɪˈsɛfələs,
(ˌ)eɪˈsɛfləs,
(ˌ)eɪˈkɛfələs,
(ˌ)eɪˈkɛfləs
AM eɪˈsɛfələs

acer
BR ˈeɪsə(r), -z
AM ˈeɪsər, -z

acerb
BR əˈsɜːb
AM əˈsɜrb

acerbic
BR əˈsɜːbɪk
AM əˈsɜrbɪk

acerbically
BR əˈsɜːbɪkli
AM əˈsɜrbək(ə)li

acerbity
BR əˈsɜːbɪti
AM əˈsɜrbədi

acescence
BR əˈsɛsns
AM əˈsɛsəns

acescent
BR əˈsɛsnt
AM əˈsɛsənt

acetabula
BR ˌasɪˈtabjʊlə(r)
AM ˌæsəˈtæbjələ

acetabulum
BR ˌasɪˈtabjʊləm
AM ˌæsəˈtæbjələm

acetal
BR ˈasɪtal
AM ˈæsədl, ˈæsəˌtæl

acetaldehyde
BR ˌasɪˈtaldɪhʌɪd
AM ˌæsɪˈtældəˌhaɪd

acetaminophen
BR əˌsiːtəˈmɪnəfɛn,
əˌsɛtəˈmɪnəfɛn,
AM əˌsɪdəˈmɪnəfən

acetanilide
BR ˌasɪˈtanɪlʌɪd
AM ˌæsəˈtænəˌlaɪd

acetate
BR ˈasɪteɪt, -s
AM ˈæsəˌteɪt, -s

acetic
BR əˈsiːtɪk, əˈsɛtɪk
AM əˈsidɪk

acetification
BR əˌsiːtɪfɪˈkeɪʃn,
əˌsɛtɪfɪˈkeɪʃn
AM əˌsidəfəˈkeɪʃən,
əˌsɛdəfəˈkeɪʃən

acetify
BR əˈsiːtɪfʌɪ, əˈsɛtɪfʌɪ,
-z, -ɪŋ, -d
AM əˈsidəˌfaɪ,
əˈsɛdəˌfaɪ, -z, -ɪŋ, -d

acetone
BR ˈasɪtəʊn
AM ˈæsəˌtoʊn

acetose
BR ˈasɪtəʊs
AM ˈæsəˌtoʊs,
ˈæsəˌtoʊz

acetous
BR əˈsiːtəs, ˈasɪtəs
AM əˈsidəs, ˈæsədəs

acetyl
BR ˈasɪtʌɪl, ˈasɪtɪl
AM əˈsidl, ˈæsədl

acetylcholine
BR ˌasɪtʌɪlˈkəʊliːn,
ˌasɪtʌɪlˈkəʊlɪn,
ˌasɪtɪlˈkəʊlɪn
AM əˌsidlˈkoʊˌlin,
ˌæsədlˈkoʊˌlaɪn

acetylene
BR əˈsɛtɪliːn, əˈsɛtɪˈiːn
AM əˈsɛdlən, əˈsɛdəˌlin

acetylide
BR əˈsɛtɪlʌɪd, əˈsɛtɭʌɪd
AM əˈsɛdlˌaɪd

acetylsalicylic
BR ˌasɪtʌɪlˌsalɪˈsɪlɪk,
ˌasɪtɪlˌsalɪˈsɪlɪk
AM əˌsidlˌsæləˈsɪlɪk

acey-deucey
BR ˌeɪsɪˈdjuːsi,
ˌeɪsɪˈdʒuːsi
AM ˌeɪsɪˈd(j)usi

acey-deucy
BR ˌeɪsɪˈdjuːsi,
ˌeɪsɪˈdʒuːsi
AM ˌeɪsɪˈd(j)usi

Achaea
BR əˈkiːə(r)
AM əˈkiə, əˈkeɪə

Achaean
BR əˈkiːən, -z
AM əˈkiən, əˈkeɪən, -z

Achaemenid
BR əˈkiːmənɪd, -z
AM əˈkimənəd, -z

acharnement
BR aˈʃaːnmō

acetanilide — AM əˌʃɑːnəˈmɑn(t)

Achates
BR əˈkeɪtiːz
AM əˈkeɪdiz

ache
BR eɪk, -s, -ɪŋ, -t
AM eɪk, -s, -ɪŋ, -t

Achebe
BR əˈtʃeɪbi
AM əˈtʃeɪbeɪ

achene
BR əˈkiːn, -z
AM əˈkin, -z

Acheron
BR ˈak(ə)rən, ˈak(ə)rn,
ˈakərɒn
AM ˈækəˌrɑn,
ˈætˌʃəˌrɑn

Acheson
BR ˈatʃɪs(ə)n
AM ˈætʃəsən

Acheulean
BR əˈ(t)ʃuːliən, -z
AM əˈʃuliən, -z

Acheulian
BR əˈ(t)ʃuːliən, -z
AM əˈʃuljən, əˈʃuliən,
-z

achievable
BR əˈtʃiːvəbl
AM əˈtʃivəbəl

achieve
BR əˈtʃiːv, -z, -ɪŋ, -d
AM əˈtʃiv, -z, -ɪŋ, -d

achievement
BR əˈtʃiːvm(ə)nt, -s
AM əˈtʃivmənt, -s

achiever
BR əˈtʃiːvə(r), -z
AM əˈtʃivər, -z

achillea
BR ˌakɪˈliːə(r),
əˈkɪliə(r)
AM əˈkɪliə

Achilles
BR əˈkɪliːz
AM əˈkɪliz

Achinese
BR ˌatʃɪˈniːz
AM ˌætʃəˈniz, ˌatʃəˈniz

achingly
BR ˈeɪkɪŋli
AM ˈeɪkɪŋli

achiral
BR eɪˈkʌɪrəl, eɪˈkʌɪrɭ
AM eɪˈkaɪrəl

achondroplasia
BR əˌkɒndrəˈpleɪzɪə(r),
ˌeɪkɒndrəˈpleɪzɪə(r),
əˌkɒndrəˈpleɪʒə(r),
ˌeɪkɒndrəˈpleɪʒə(r)
AM ˌeɪˌkɑndrəˈpleɪʒ(i)ə,
ˌeɪˌkɑndrəˈpleɪzɪə

achondroplasic
BR əˌkɒndrəˈpleɪzɪk,
ˌeɪkɒndrəˈpleɪzɪk, -s
AM ˌeɪˌkɑndrəˈpleɪʒɪk,
ˌeɪˌkɑndrəˈpleɪzɪk-s

achondroplastic
BR əˌkɒndrəˈplastɪk,
ˌeɪkɒndrəˈplastɪk, -s
AM ˌeɪˌkɑndrəˈplæstɪk,
-s

achoo
BR əˈtʃuː
AM əˈtʃu

achromat
BR ˈakrə(ʊ)mat, -s
AM ˈækrəˌmæt, -s

achromatic
BR ˌakrə(ʊ)ˈmatɪk,
ˌeɪkrə(ʊ)ˈmatɪk
AM ˌækrəˈmædɪk,
ˌeɪkrəˈmædɪk

achromatically
BR ˌakrə(ʊ)ˈmatɪkli,
ˌeɪkrə(ʊ)ˈmatɪkli
AM ˌækrəˈmædək(ə)li,
ˌeɪkrəˈmædək(ə)li

achromaticity
BR əˌkrəʊməˈtɪsɪti,
ˌeɪkrəʊməˈtɪsɪti
AM eɪˌkrəʊməˈtɪsɪdi,
æˌkrəʊməˈtɪsɪdi

achromatism
BR əˈkrəʊmətɪz(ə)m,
(ˌ)eɪˈkrəʊmətɪz(ə)m
AM eɪˈkrəʊməˌtɪzəm,
æˈkrəʊməˌtɪzəm

achromatize
BR əˈkrəʊmətʌɪz,
(ˌ)eɪˈkrəʊmətʌɪz, -z,
-ɪŋ, -d
AM eɪˈkrəʊməˌtaɪz,
æˈkrəʊməˌtaɪz, -ɪz,
-ɪŋ, -d

achronical
BR (ˌ)eɪˈkrɒnɪkl
AM eɪˈkrɒnəkəl

achy
BR ˈeɪki
AM ˈeɪki

acicula
BR əˈsɪkjʉlə(r)
AM əˈsɪkjələ

acicular
BR əˈsɪkjʉlə(r)
AM əˈsɪkjələr

acid
BR ˈasɪd, -z
AM ˈæsəd, -z

acidic
BR əˈsɪdɪk
AM əˈsɪdɪk, æˈsɪdɪk

acidification
BR əˌsɪdɪfɪˈkeɪʃn
AM əˌsɪdəfəˈkeɪʃən,
æˌsɪdəfəˈkeɪʃən

acidify
BR əˈsɪdɪfʌɪ, -z, -ɪŋ, -d
AM əˈsɪdəˌfaɪ,
æˈsɪdəˌfaɪ, -z, -ɪŋ, -d

acidimeter
BR ˌasɪˈdɪmɪtə(r), -z
AM ˌæsəˈdɪmədər, -z

acidimetry
BR ˌasɪˈdɪmɪtri
AM ˌæsəˈdɪmɪtri

acidity
BR əˈsɪdɪti
AM əˈsɪdɪdi, æˈsɪdɪdi

acidly
BR ˈasɪdli
AM ˈasədli

acidness
BR ˈasɪdnɪs
AM ˈæsədnəs

acidophilic
BR ˌasɪdə(ʊ)ˈfɪlɪk
AM ˌæsədoʊˈfɪlɪk,
ˌæsədəˈfɪlɪk

acidophilus
BR ˌasɪˈdɒfɪləs
AM ˌæsəˈdɑfələs

acidosis
BR ˌasɪˈdəʊsɪs
AM ˌæsəˈdoʊsəs

acidotic
BR ˌasɪˈdɒtɪk
AM ˌæsəˈdɑdɪk

acidulate
BR əˈsɪdjʉleɪt,
əˈsɪdʒʉleɪt, -s, -ɪŋ, -ɪd
AM əˈsɪdʒəˌleɪ|t, -ts,
-dɪŋ, -dɪd

acidulation
BR əˌsɪdjʉˈleɪʃn,
əˌsɪdʒʉˈleɪʃn
AM əˌsɪdʒəˈleɪʃən

acidulous
BR əˈsɪdjʉləs,
əˈsɪdʒʉləs
AM əˈsɪdʒələs

acini
BR ˈasɪnʌɪ
AM ˈæsəˌnaɪ

acinus
BR ˈasɪnəs
AM ˈæsənəs

ack
BR ak
AM æk

ack-ack
BR ˈakak
AM ˈækˌæk

ackee
BR ˈak|i, -ɪz
AM ˈæˌki, -z

ack emma
BR ˌak ˈɛmə(r)
AM ˌæk ˈɛmə

Ackerman
BR ˈakəmən
AM ˈækərmən

acknowledge
BR əkˈnɒlɪdʒ, -ɪdʒɪz,
-ɪdʒɪŋ, -ɪdʒd
AM əkˈnɑlədʒ,
ækˈnɑlədʒ, -əz, -ɪŋ, -d

acknowledgeable
BR əkˈnɒlɪdʒəbl
AM əkˈnɑlədʒəbəl,
ækˈnɑlədʒəbəl

acknowledgement
BR əkˈnɒlɪdʒm(ə)nt, -s
AM əkˈnɑlədʒmənt,
ækˈnɑlədʒmənt, -s

Ackroyd
BR ˈakrɔɪd, ˈeɪkrɔɪd
AM ˈækrɔɪd

aclinic
BR əˈklɪnɪk
AM eɪˈklɪnɪk

acme
BR ˈakm|i, -ɪz
AM ˈækmi, -z

acne
BR ˈakn|i, -ɪd
AM ˈækni, -d

acolyte
BR ˈakəlʌɪt, -s
AM ˈækəˌlaɪt, -s

Aconcagua
BR ˌak(ə)nˈkagwə(r),
ˌakɒnˈkagwə(r),
ˌak(ə)nˈkɑːgwə(r),
ˌakɒnˈkɑːgwə(r)
AM ˌækənˈkagwə,
ˌakənˈkagwə
SP ˌakoŋˈkaʏwa

aconite
BR ˈakənʌɪt, -s
AM ˈækəˌnaɪt, -s

aconitic
BR ˌakəˈnɪtɪk
AM ˌækəˈnɪdɪk

aconitine
BR əˈkɒnɪtiːn
AM əˈkanətin,
əˈkanədən

acorn
BR ˈeɪkɔːn, -z
AM ˈeɪˌkɔ(ə)rn, -z

acotyledon
BR əˌkɒtɪˈliːd(ə)n,
ˌeɪkɒtɪˈliːd(ə)n, -z
AM ˌeɪˌkɑdlˈidən, -z

acotyledonous
BR əˌkɒtɪˈliːdɪnəs,
əˌkɒtɪˈliːdnəs,
ˌeɪkɒtɪˈliːdɪnəs,
ˌeɪkɒtɪˈliːdnəs,
AM ˌeɪˌkɑdlˈidnəs

acoustic
BR əˈkuːstɪk, -s
AM əˈkustɪk, -s

acoustical
BR əˈkuːstɪkl
AM əˈkustəkəl

acoustically
BR əˈkuːstɪkli
AM əˈkustək(ə)li

acoustician
BR əˌkuːˈstɪʃn,
ˌakuːˈstɪʃn, -z
AM əˌkuːˈstɪʃən,
ˌæˌkuːˈstɪʃən, -z

acquaint
BR əˈkweɪnt, -s, -ɪŋ, -ɪd
AM əˈkweɪn|t, -ts, -(t)ɪŋ,
-(t)ɪd

acquaintance
BR əˈkweɪnt(ə)ns, -ɪz
AM əˈkweɪn(t)ns, -əz

acquaintanceship
BR əˈkweɪnt(ə)n(s)ʃɪp,
-s
AM əˈkweɪnt(ə)n(s)ˌʃɪp,
-s

acquest
BR əˈkwɛst, -s
AM əˈkwɛst, -s

acquiesce
BR ˌakwiˈɛs, -ɪz, -ɪŋ, -t
AM ˌækwiˈɛs, -əz, -ɪŋ, -t

acquiescence
BR ˌakwiˈɛsns
AM ˌækwiˈɛsəns

acquiescent
BR ˌakwiˈɛsnt
AM ˌækwiˈɛsənt

acquiescingly
BR ˌakwiˈɛsɪŋli
AM ˌækwiˈɛsɪŋli

acquirable
BR əˈkwʌɪərəbl
AM əˈkwaɪ(ə)rəbəl

acquire
BR əˈkwʌɪə(r), -z, -ɪŋ, -d
AM əˈkwaɪ(ə)r, -z, -ɪŋ,
-d

acquirement
BR əˈkwʌɪəm(ə)nt
AM əˈkwaɪ(ə)rmənt

acquirer
BR əˈkwʌɪərə(r), -z
AM əˈkwaɪ(ə)rər, -z

acquisition
BR ˌakwɪˈzɪʃn, -z
AM ˌækwəˈzɪʃən, -z

acquisitive
BR əˈkwɪzɪtɪv
AM əˈkwɪzɪdɪv,
æˈkwɪzɪdɪv

acquisitively
BR əˈkwɪzɪtɪvli
AM əˈkwɪzɪdɪvli,
æˈkwɪzɪdɪvli

acquisitiveness
BR əˈkwɪzɪtɪvnɪs
AM əˈkwɪzɪdɪvnɪs,
æˈkwɪzɪdɪvnɪs

acquit
BR əˈkwɪt, -s, -ɪŋ, -ɪd
AM əˈkwɪ|t, -ts, -dɪŋ,
-dɪd

acquittal
BR əˈkwɪtl, -z
AM əˈkwɪdəl, -z

acquittance
BR əˈkwɪtns, -ɪz
AM əˈkwɪtns,
əˈkwɪdəns, -əz

Acre
BR ˈeɪkə(r), ˈɑːkə(r)
AM ˈeɪkər, ˈɑkər, ˈɑkrə

acre
BR ˈeɪkə(r), -z, -d
AM ˈeɪkər, -z, -d

acreage
BR 'eɪk(ə)r|ɪdʒ, -ɪdʒɪz
AM 'eɪk(ə)rɪdʒ, -ɪz

acrid
BR 'akrɪd
AM 'ækrəd

acridine
BR 'akrɪdiːn,
'akrɪdʌɪn
AM 'ækrəˌdin,
'ækrədən

acridity
BR ə'krɪdɪti
AM ə'krɪdɪdi,
æ'krɪdɪdi

acridly
BR 'akrɪdli
AM 'ækrədli

acridness
BR 'akrɪdnɪs
AM 'ækrədnəs

acriflavine
BR ˌakrɪ'fleɪvɪn,
ˌakrɪ'fleɪviːn
AM ˌækrə'fleɪvin

Acrilan®
BR 'akrɪlan
AM 'ækrəˌlæn

acrimonious
BR ˌakrɪ'məʊnɪəs
AM ˌækrə'moʊnɪəs

acrimoniously
BR ˌakrɪ'məʊnɪəsli
AM ˌækrə'moʊnɪəsli

acrimoniousness
BR ˌakrɪ'məʊnɪəsnəs
AM ˌækrə'moʊnɪəsnəs

acrimony
BR 'akrɪməni
AM 'ækrəˌmoʊni

acrobat
BR 'akrəbat, -s
AM 'ækrəˌbæt, -s

acrobatic
BR ˌakrə'batɪk, -s
AM ˌækrə'bædɪk, -s

acrobatically
BR ˌakrə'batɪkli
AM ˌækrə'bædək(ə)li

acrocyanosis
BR ˌakrəʊsʌɪə'nəʊsɪs
AM ˌækroʊˌsaɪə'noʊsɪs

acrogen
BR 'akrədʒ(ə)n, -z
AM 'ækrədʒən, -z

acrogenous
BR ə'krɒdʒɪnəs,
ə'krɒdʒnəs
AM ə'krɑdʒənəs

acrolect
BR 'akrəlɛkt, -s
AM 'ækrəˌlɛkt, -s

acromegalic
BR ˌakrə(ʊ)mɪ'galɪk, -s
AM ˌækroʊmə'gælɪk,
-s

acromegaly
BR ˌakrə(ʊ)'mɛgəli,
ˌakrə(ʊ)'mɛgli
AM ˌækroʊ'mɛgəli

acronycal
BR ə'krɒnɪkl
AM ə'kranəkəl,
æ'kranəkəl

acronycally
BR ə'krɒnɪkli
AM ə'kranək(ə)li,
æ'kranək(ə)li

acronychal
BR ə'krɒnɪkl
AM ə'kranəkəl,
æ'kranəkəl

acronychally
BR ə'krɒnɪkli
AM ə'kranək(ə)li,
æ'kranək(ə)li

acronym
BR 'akrənɪm, -z
AM 'ækrəˌnɪm, -z

acropetal
BR ə'krɒpɪtl
AM ə'krapɛdl,
æ'krapɛdl

acropetally
BR ə'krɒpɪtli
AM ə'krapɛdli,
æ'krapɛdli

acrophobia
BR ˌakrə(ʊ)'fəʊbɪə(r)
AM ˌækrə'foʊbɪə

acrophobic
BR ˌakrə(ʊ)'fəʊbɪk, -s
AM ˌækrə'foʊbɪk, -s

acropolis
BR ə'krɒpəlɪs,
ə'krɒplɪs, -ɪz
AM ə'krapələs, -əz

across
BR ə'krɒs
AM ə'krɔs, ə'kras

acrostic
BR ə'krɒstɪk, -s
AM ə'krastɪk,
ə'krastɪk, -s

acrylic
BR ə'krɪlɪk
AM ə'krɪlɪk, æ'krɪlɪk

acrylonitrate
BR ˌakrɪləʊ'nʌɪtreɪt
AM ˌækrəloʊ'naɪˌtreɪt

act
BR akt, -s, -ɪŋ, -ɪd
AM æk|(t), -(t)s, -tɪŋ,
-təd

acta
BR 'aktə(r)
AM 'æktə

actability
BR ˌaktə'bɪlɪti
AM ˌæktə'bɪlɪdi

actable
BR 'aktəbl
AM 'æktəbəl

Actaeon
BR ak'tiːən
AM æk'tiən, 'æktiˌɑn

actin
BR 'aktɪn
AM 'æktən

actinia
BR ak'tiːnɪə(r)
AM æk'tiniə

actiniae
BR ak'tiːniː
AM æk'tiniˌi,
æk'tiniˌaɪ

actinic
BR ak'tɪnɪk
AM æk'tɪnɪk

actinide
BR 'aktɪnʌɪd, -z
AM 'æktəˌnaɪd, -z

actinism
BR 'aktɪnɪz(ə)m
AM 'æktəˌnɪzəm

actinium
BR ak'tɪnɪəm
AM æk'tɪniəm

actinometer
BR ˌaktɪ'nɒmɪtə(r), -z
AM ˌæktə'namədər, -z

actinomorphic
BR ˌaktɪnə(ʊ)'mɔːfɪk
AM ˌæktənoʊ'mɔrfɪk

Actinomycetales
BR ˌaktɪnəʊˌmʌɪsɪ'teɪliːz
AM ˌæktənoʊˌmaɪsə'teɪliz

actinomycete
BR ˌaktɪnəʊ'mʌɪsiːt,
ˌaktɪnəʊˌmʌɪ'siːt, -s
AM ˌæktənoʊ'maɪˌsit,
ˌæktənoʊˌmaɪ'sit, -s

action
BR 'akʃn, -z
AM 'ækˌʃən, -z

actionable
BR 'akʃnəbl,
'akʃ(ə)nəbl
AM 'ækˌʃ(ə)nəbəl

actionably
BR 'akʃnəbli,
'akʃ(ə)nəbli
AM 'ækˌʃ(ə)nəbli

activate
BR 'aktɪveɪt, -s, -ɪŋ, -ɪd
AM 'æktəˌveɪ|t, -ts,
-dɪŋ, -dɪd

activation
BR ˌaktɪ'veɪʃn
AM ˌæktə'veɪʃən

activator
BR 'aktɪveɪtə(r), -z
AM 'æktəˌveɪdər, -z

active
BR 'aktɪv
AM 'æktɪv

actively
BR 'aktɪvli
AM 'æktɪvli

activeness
BR 'aktɪvnɪs
AM 'æktɪvnɪs

activism
BR 'aktɪvɪz(ə)m
AM 'æktəˌvɪzəm

activist
BR 'aktɪvɪst, -s
AM 'æktəvəst, -s

activity
BR ak'tɪvɪt|i, ək'tɪvɪt|i,
-ɪz
AM æk'tɪvɪdi, -z

acton
BR 'aktən, -z
AM 'æktən, -z

actor
BR 'aktə(r), -z
AM 'æktər, -z

actress
BR 'aktrɪs, -ɪz
AM 'æktrəs, -əz

actressy
BR 'aktrɪsi
AM 'æktrəsi

actual
BR 'ak(t)ʃʊəl,
'ak(t)ʃ(ə)l
AM 'æk(t)ʃ(əw)əl

actualisation
BR ˌak(t)ʃʊəlʌɪ'zeɪʃn,
ˌak(t)ʃəlʌɪ'zeɪʃn,
ˌak(t)ʃlʌɪ'zeɪʃn
AM ˌæk(t)ʃ(əw)əˌlaɪ'zeɪʃən,
ˌæk(t)ʃ(əw)ələ'zeɪʃən

actualise
BR 'ak(t)ʃʊəlʌɪz,
'ak(t)ʃəlʌɪz,
'ak(t)ʃlʌɪz, -ɪz, -ɪŋ, -d
AM 'æk(t)ʃ(əw)əˌlaɪz,
-ɪz, -ɪŋ, -d

actuality
BR ˌaktʃʊ'alɪti
AM ˌæk(t)ʃə'wælədi

actualization
BR ˌak(t)ʃʊəlʌɪ'zeɪʃn,
ˌak(t)ʃəlʌɪ'zeɪʃn,
ˌak(t)ʃlʌɪ'zeɪʃn
AM ˌæk(t)ʃ(əw)əˌlaɪ'zeɪʃən,
ˌæk(t)ʃ(əw)ələ'zeɪʃən

actualize
BR 'ak(t)ʃʊəlʌɪz,
'ak(t)ʃəlʌɪz,
'ak(t)ʃlʌɪz, -ɪz, -ɪŋ, -d
AM 'æk(t)ʃ(əw)əˌlaɪz,
-ɪz, -ɪŋ, -d

actually
BR 'ak(t)ʃʊəli,
'ak(t)ʃəli, 'ak(t)ʃli
AM 'æk(t)ʃ(əw)əli

actuarial
BR ˌaktʃʊ'ɛːrɪəl
AM ˌæk(t)ʃə'wɛriəl

actuarially
BR ˌaktʃʊ'ɛːrɪəli
AM ˌæk(t)ʃə'wɛriəli

actuary
BR 'aktʃʊər|i, 'aktʃʊr|i, -ız
AM 'æk(t)ʃə,wɛri, -z

actuate
BR 'aktʃʊeıt, -s, -ıŋ, -ıd
AM 'æk(t)ʃə,weı|t, -ts, -dıŋ, -dıd

actuation
BR ,aktʃʊ'eıʃn, -z
AM ,æk(t)ʃə'weıʃən, -z

actuator
BR 'aktʃʊeıtə(r), -z
AM 'æk(t)ʃə,weıdər, -z

acuity
BR ə'kju:ti
AM ə'kjuədi, æ'kjuədi

aculeate
BR ə'kju:lıət, -s
AM ə'kjuliət, ə'kjuli,eıt, -s

acumen
BR 'akjʊmən
AM ə'kjumən, æ'kjumən, 'ækjəmən, 'ækjə,mɛn

acuminate
BR ə'kju:mınət
AM ə'kjumənət, ə'kjumə,neıt

acupressure
BR 'akjʊ,prɛʃə(r)
AM 'ækjə,prəʃər, 'ækju,prəʃər

acupuncture
BR 'akjʊpʌŋ(k)tʃə(r)
AM 'ækjə,pəŋk(t)ʃər, 'ækju,pəŋk(t)ʃər

acupuncturist
BR 'akjʊpʌŋ(k)tʃ(ə)rıst, -s
AM 'ækjə,pəŋ(k)(t)ʃər-əst, 'ækju,pəŋ(k)(t)ʃərəst, -s

acushla
BR ə'kʊʃlə(r), -z
AM ə'kʊʃlə, -z

acute
BR ə'kju:t, -ə(r), -ıst
AM ə'kju|t, -dər, -dəst

acutely
BR ə'kju:tli
AM ə'kjutli

acuteness
BR ə'kju:tnəs
AM ə'kjutnəs

acyclic
BR (,)eı'sʌıklık
AM eı'saıklık

acyclovir
BR (,)eı'sʌıkləvıə(r)
AM eı'saıklə,vı(ə)r

acyl
BR 'eısʌıl, 'asıl
AM 'æsəl, 'æ,sıl

ad
BR ad

AM æd

Ada
BR 'eıdə(r)
AM 'eıdə

adage
BR 'ad|ıdʒ, -ıdʒız
AM 'ædıdʒ, -ız

adagio
BR ə'dɑ:dʒıəʊ, ə'dadʒıəʊ, -z
AM ə'dɑ(d)ʒioʊ, -z

Adam
BR 'adəm
AM 'ædəm

adamance
BR 'adəm(ə)ns
AM 'ædəməns

adamancy
BR 'adəm(ə)nsi
AM 'ædəmənsi

adamant
BR 'adəm(ə)nt
AM 'ædəmənt

adamantine
BR ,adə'mantʌın
AM ,ædə'mæn,taın, ,ædə'mæn,tin

adamantly
BR 'adəm(ə)ntli
AM 'ædəmən(t)li

Adamite
BR 'adəmʌıt, -s
AM 'ædə,maıt, -s

Adams
BR 'adəmz
AM 'ædəmz

Adamson
BR 'adəms(ə)n
AM 'ædəmsən

adapt
BR ə'dapt, -s, -ıŋ, -ıd
AM ə'dæpt, -s, -ıŋ, -əd

adaptability
BR ə,daptə'bılıti
AM ə,dæptə'bılıdi

adaptable
BR ə'daptəbl
AM ə'dæptəbəl

adaptableness
BR ə'daptəblnəs
AM ə'dæptəbəlnəs

adaptably
BR ə'daptəbli
AM ə'dæptəbli

adaptation
BR ,adəp'teıʃn, ,adap'teıʃn, -z
AM ,ædæp'teıʃən, ,ædəp'teıʃən, -z

adapter
BR ə'daptə(r), -z
AM ə'dæptər, -z

adaptive
BR ə'daptıv
AM ə'dæptıv

adaptively
BR ə'daptıvli
AM ə'dæptıvli

adaptiveness
BR ə'daptıvnıs
AM ə'dæptıvnıs

adaptogen
BR ə'daptədʒ(ə)n, -z
AM ə'dæptə,dʒɛn, ə'dæptəgən, -z

adaptogenic
BR ə,daptə'dʒɛnık
AM ə,dæptə'dʒɛnık

adaptor
BR ə'daptə(r), -z
AM ə'dæptər, -z

adat
BR 'adat
AM ɑ'dɑt

adaxial
BR a'daksıəl
AM æ'dæksıəl

ad captandum vulgus
BR ,ad kap,tandəm 'vʌlgəs
AM ,æd ,kæp,tændəm 'vəlgəs

Adcock
BR 'adkɒk
AM 'æd,kɑk

add
BR ad, -z, -ıŋ, -ıd
AM æd, -z, -ıŋ, -əd

Addams
BR 'adəmz
AM 'ædəmz

addax
BR 'adaks, -ız
AM 'æ,dæks, -əz

addenda
BR ə'dɛndə(r)
AM ə'dɛndə

addendum
BR ə'dɛndəm
AM ə'dɛndəm

adder
BR 'adə(r), -z
AM 'ædər, -z

addict¹
noun
BR 'adıkt, -s
AM 'ædık(t), -s

addict²
verb
BR ə'dıkt, -s, -ıŋ, -ıd
AM ə'dık(t), -s, -ıŋ, -ıd

addictedness
BR ə'dıktıdnıs
AM ə'dıktıdnıs

addiction
BR ə'dıkʃn, -z
AM ə'dıkʃən, -z

addictive
BR ə'dıktıv
AM ə'dıktıv

addictiveness
BR ə'dıktıvnıs
AM ə'dıktıvnıs

Addie
BR 'adi
AM 'ædi

Addington
BR 'adıŋt(ə)n
AM 'ædıŋtən

Addis Ababa
BR ,adıs 'ababə(r)
AM ,ædəs 'æbəbə, ,adəs 'ababə

Addison
BR 'adıs(ə)n
AM 'ædəsən

addition
BR ə'dıʃn
AM ə'dıʃən

additional
BR ə'dıʃn(ə)l, ə'dıʃən(ə)l
AM ə'dıʃənl, ə'dıʃnəl

additionality
BR ə,dıʃə'nalıti
AM ə,dıʃə'nælədi

additionally
BR ə'dıʃnəli, ə'dıʃn̩li, ə'dıʃənli, ə'dıʃ(ə)nəli
AM ə'dıʃ(ə)nəli

additive
BR 'adıtıv, -z
AM 'ædədıv, -z

addle
BR 'ad|l, -lz, -lıŋ \-lıŋ, -ld
AM 'æd|əl, -əlz, -(ə)lıŋ, -əld

address
BR ə'drɛs, -ız
AM ə'drɛs, 'æ,drɛs, -əz

addressable
BR ə'drɛsəbl
AM ə'drɛsəbəl

addressee
BR ,adrɛ'si:, ,adrə'si:, -z
AM ,æ,drɛ'si, ə,drɛ'si, -z

addresser
BR ə'drɛsə(r), -z
AM ə'drɛsər, æ'drɛsər, -z

Addressograph®
BR ə'drɛsəgrɑ:f, ə'drɛsəgraf, -s
AM ə'drɛsə,græf, -s

adduce
BR ə'dju:s, ə'dʒu:s, -ız, -ıŋ, -t
AM ə'd(j)us, -əz, -ıŋ, -t

adducible
BR ə'dju:sıbl, ə'dʒu:sıbl
AM ə'd(j)usəbəl

adduct
BR ə'dʌkt, -s, -ıŋ, -ıd

adduction
AM ə'dək|(t), -(t)s, -tɪŋ,
-təd

adduction
BR ə'dʌkʃn
AM ə'dəkʃən

adductive
BR ə'dʌktɪv
AM ə'dəktɪv

adductor
BR ə'dʌktə(r), -z
AM ə'dəktər, -z

Addy
BR 'adi
AM 'ædi

Adela
BR ə'deɪlə(r), 'adɪlə(r),
'ad|ə(r)
AM ə'dɛlə

Adelaide
BR 'adɪleɪd, 'ad|eɪd
AM 'ædl,eɪd

Adele
BR ə'dɛl
AM ə'dɛl

Adélie
BR ə'deɪli
AM ə'deɪli

Adelina
BR ,adɪ'li:nə(r),
,adl'i:nə(r)
AM ,ædɛ'linə

Adeline
BR 'adɪlʌɪn, 'adlʌɪn
AM 'ædl,aɪn

Aden
BR 'eɪdn
AM 'eɪdən

Adenauer
BR 'adənaʊə(r),
'ɑ:dənaʊə(r)
AM 'æd(ə)n,aʊər

Adeney
BR 'eɪdni
AM 'æd(ə)ni

adenine
BR 'adɪni:n, 'adɪnʌɪn
AM 'ædn,in, 'ædn,aɪn

adenocarcinoma
BR ,adɪnəʊ,ka:sɪ'nəʊ-
mə(r),
,adnəʊ,ka:sɪ'nəʊmə(r),
-z
AM ,ædnoʊ,kɑrsə'noʊ-
mə

adenoid
BR 'adɪnɔɪd, 'adnɔɪd, -z
AM 'ædn,ɔɪd, -z

adenoidal
BR ,adɪ'nɔɪdl,
,adn'ɔɪdl
AM ,ædn'ɔɪdəl

adenoidally
BR ,adɪ'nɔɪdˌli,
,adn'ɔɪdˌli
AM ,ædn'ɔɪd(ə)li

adenoids
BR 'adɪnɔɪdz, 'adnɔɪdz
AM 'ædn,ɔɪdz

adenoma
BR ,adɪ'nəʊmə(r),
,adn'əʊmə(r), -z
AM ,ædn'oʊmə, -z

adenomata
BR ,adɪ'nəʊmətə(r),
,adn'əʊmətə(r)
AM ,ædn'oʊmədə

adenopathy
BR ,adɪ'nɒpəθi,
,adn'ɒpəθi
AM ,ædn'ɑpəθi

adenosine
BR ə'dɛnə(ʊ)si:n
AM ə'dɛnə,sin,
ə'dɛnəsən

adept¹
adjective
BR 'adɛpt, ə'dɛpt
AM ə'dɛpt

adept²
noun
BR 'adɛpt, -s
AM ə'dɛpt, -s

adeptly
BR 'adɛptli, ə'dɛptli
AM ə'dɛp(t)li

adeptness
BR 'adɛp(t)nəs,
ə'dɛp(t)nəs
AM ə'dɛp(t)nəs

adequacy
BR 'adɪkwəsi
AM 'ædəkwəsi

adequate
BR 'adɪkwət
AM 'ædəkwət

adequately
BR 'adɪkwətli
AM 'ædəkwətli

adequateness
BR 'adɪkwətnəs
AM 'ædəkwətnəs

ad eundem
BR ,ad ɪ'ʌndəm
AM ,ædi 'əndəm

à deux
BR a 'dəː(r), ɑ: +
AM ,ɑ 'də

ad fin
BR ,ad 'fɪn
AM ,æd 'fɪn

adhere
BR əd'hɪə(r), ad'hɪə(r),
-z, -ɪŋ, -d
AM əd'hɪ(ə)r,
əd'hɪ(ə)r, -z, -ɪŋ, -d

adherence
BR əd'hɪərəns,
əd'hɪərn̩s, ad'hɪərəns,
ad'hɪərn̩s
AM æd'hɪrəns,
æd'hɛrəns, əd'hɪrəns,
əd'hɛrəns

adherent
BR əd'hɪərənt,
əd'hɪərn̩t, ad'hɪərənt,
ad'hɪərn̩t, -s

adenoma
AM æd'hɪrənt,
æd'hɛrənt, əd'hɪrənt,
əd'hɛrənt, -s

adhesion
BR əd'hi:ʒn, ad'hi:ʒn
AM æd'hiʒən, əd'hiʒən

adhesive
BR əd'hi:sɪv, əd'hi:zɪv,
ad'hi:sɪv, ad'hi:zɪv
AM æd'hizɪv, əd'hizɪv,
æd'hisɪv, əd'hisɪv

adhesively
BR əd'hi:sɪvli,
əd'hi:zɪvli,
ad'hi:sɪvli, ad'hi:zɪvli
AM æd'hizɪvli,
əd'hizɪvli, æd'hisɪvli,
əd'hisɪvli

adhesiveness
BR əd'hi:sɪvnɪs,
əd'hi:zɪvnɪs,
ad'hi:sɪvnɪs,
ad'hi:zɪvnɪs
AM æd'hizɪvnɪs,
əd'hizɪvnɪs,
æd'hisɪvnɪs,
əd'hisɪvnɪs

adhibit
BR əd'hɪb|ɪt, ad'hɪb|ɪt,
-ɪts, -ɪtɪŋ, -ɪtɪd
AM æd'hɪbə|t, -ts, -dɪŋ,
-dəd

adhibition
BR ,ad(h)ɪ'bɪʃn, -z
AM ,æd(h)ə'bɪʃən, -z

ad hoc
BR ,ad 'hɒk
AM ,æd 'hɑk, + 'hoʊk

adhocracy
BR ad'hɒkrəsi
AM ,æd'hɑkrəsi

ad hominem
BR ,ad 'hɒmɪnɛm
AM ,æd 'hɑmənəm

adiabatic
BR ,eɪdʌɪə'batɪk,
,adɪə'batɪk
AM ,eɪ,daɪə'bædɪk,
,ædɪə'bædɪk

adiabatically
BR ,eɪdʌɪə'batɪkli,
,adɪə'batɪkli
AM ,eɪ,daɪə'bædək(ə)li,
,ædɪə'bædək(ə)li

adiantum
BR ,adɪ'antəm, -z
AM ,ædi'æn(t)əm, -z

Adidas®
BR 'adɪdas, ə'di:das
AM ə'didəs

Adie
BR 'eɪdi
AM 'eɪdi

adieu
BR ə'dju:, ə'dʒu:, -z
AM ə'd(j)u, -z

adieux
BR ə'dju:z, ə'dʒu:z

ad'hɪrənt,
æd'hɛrənt, əd'hɪrənt,
əd'hɛrənt, -s

ad'd(j)u

Adi Granth
BR ,ɑ:dɪ 'grʌnt
AM ,ɑdi 'grɑnt

ad infinitum
BR ,ad ɪnfɪ'nʌɪtəm
AM ,æd ,ɪnfə'naɪdəm

ad initium
BR ,ad ɪn'ɪʃɪəm
AM ,æd ,ɪn'ɪʃiəm

ad interim
BR ,ad ɪnt(ə)rɪm
AM ,æd ,ɪn(t)ərəm

adiós
BR ,adɪ'ɒs, ,adɪ'ɒs
AM ,adi'oʊs, ,ædi'oʊs
SP a'ðjos

adipocere
BR ,adɪpə'sɪə(r)
AM ,ædəpoʊ'sɪ(ə)r

adipose
BR 'adɪpəʊs, 'adɪpəʊz
AM 'ædə,poʊs,
'ædə,poʊz

adiposity
BR ,adɪ'pɒsɪti
AM ,ædə'pɑsədi

Adirondack
BR ,adɪ'rɒndak, -s
AM ,ædə'rɑn,dæk, -s

adit
BR 'adɪt, -s
AM 'ædət, -s

Adivasi
BR ,ɑ:dɪ'vɑ:s|i, -ɪz
AM ,ædɪ'vɑsi, -z

adjacency
BR ə'dʒeɪs(ə)nsi
AM ə'dʒeɪsənsi

adjacent
BR ə'dʒeɪs(ə)nt
AM ə'dʒeɪsənt

adjacently
BR ə'dʒeɪs(ə)ntli
AM ə'dʒeɪsn(t)li

adjectival
BR ,adʒɪk'tʌɪvl
AM ,ædʒə(k)'taɪvəl

adjectivally
BR ,adʒɪk'tʌɪvˌli,
,adʒɪk'tʌɪvəli
AM ,ædʒə(k)'taɪvəli

adjective
BR 'adʒɪktɪv, -z
AM 'ædʒəktɪv, -z

adjoin
BR ə'dʒɔɪn, -z, -ɪŋ, -d
AM ə'dʒɔɪn, -z, -ɪŋ, -d

adjourn
BR ə'dʒəːn, -z, -ɪŋ, -d
AM ə'dʒərn, -z, -ɪŋ, -d

adjournment
BR ə'dʒəːnm(ə)nt, -s
AM ə'dʒərnmənt, -s

adjudge
BR ə'dʒʌdʒ, -ɪz, -ɪŋ, -d
AM ə'dʒədʒ, -əz, -ɪŋ, -d

adjudgement
BR əˈdʒʌdʒm(ə)nt, -s
AM əˈdʒədʒmənt, -s
adjudicate
BR əˈdʒuːdɪkeɪt, -s, -ɪŋ, -ɪd
AM əˈdʒudəˌkeɪ|t, -ts, -dɪŋ, -dɪd
adjudication
BR əˌdʒuːdɪˈkeɪʃn
AM əˌdʒudəˈkeɪʃən
adjudicative
BR əˈdʒuːdɪkətɪv
AM əˈdʒudəˌkeɪdɪv
adjudicator
BR əˈdʒuːdɪkeɪtə(r), -z
AM əˈdʒudəˌkeɪdər, -z
adjunct
BR ˈadʒʌŋ(k)t, -s
AM ˈæˌdʒəŋ(k)t, ˈæˌdʒəŋk(t), -s
adjunctive
BR əˈdʒʌŋ(k)tɪv, -z
AM əˈdʒəŋ(k)tɪv, æˈdʒəŋ(k)tɪv, -z
adjunctively
BR əˈdʒʌŋ(k)tɪvli
AM əˈdʒəŋ(k)tɪvli, æˈdʒəŋ(k)tɪvli
adjuration
BR ˌadʒʊˈreɪʃn
AM ˌædʒəˈreɪʃən
adjuratory
BR əˈdʒʊərət(ə)ri, əˈdʒɔːrət(ə)ri
AM əˈdʒʊrəˌtɔri, ˈædʒərəˌtɔri
adjure
BR əˈdʒʊə(r), əˈdʒɔː(r), -z, -ɪŋ, -d
AM əˈdʒʊ(ə)r, æˈdʒʊ(ə)r, -z, -ɪŋ, -d
adjust
BR əˈdʒʌst, -s, -ɪŋ, -ɪd
AM əˈdʒəst, -s, -ɪŋ, -əd
adjustability
BR əˌdʒʌstəˈbɪlɪti
AM əˌdʒəstəˈbɪlɪdi
adjustable
BR əˈdʒʌstəbl
AM əˈdʒəstəbəl
adjuster
BR əˈdʒʌstə(r), -z
AM əˈdʒəstər, -z
adjustment
BR əˈdʒʌs(t)m(ə)nt, -s
AM əˈdʒəs(t)mənt, -s
adjutage
BR ˈadʒʊtɪdʒ, əˈdʒuːtɪdʒ
AM ˈædʒədɪdʒ, əˈdʒudɪdʒ
adjutancy
BR ˈadʒʊt(ə)nsi
AM ˈædʒədənsi, ˈædʒətnsi
adjutant
BR ˈadʒʊt(ə)nt, -s

AM ˈædʒədənt, ˈædʒətnt, -s
adjuvant
BR ˈadʒʊv(ə)nt, -s
AM ˈædʒəvənt, -s
Adkins
BR ˈadkɪnz
AM ˈædkɪnz
Adlai
BR ˈadlʌɪ
AM ˈædˌlaɪ
Adler
BR ˈadlə(r)
AM ˈædlər
Adlerian
BR adˈlɪərɪən, -z
AM adˈlɪrɪən, ædˈlɛrɪən, -z
ad lib
BR ˌad ˈlɪb, -z, -ɪŋ, -d
AM ˌæd ˈlɪb, -z, -ɪŋ, -d
ad libitum
BR ˌad ˈlɪbɪtəm
AM ˌæd ˈlɪbədəm
ad litem
BR ˌad ˈlʌɪtəm
AM ˌæd ˈlaɪdəm
adman
BR ˈadman
AM ˈædˌmæn
admass
BR ˈadmas
AM ˈædˌmæs
admeasure
BR adˈmɛʒ|ə(r), -əz, -(ə)rɪŋ, -əd
AM ædˈmɛʒər, -z, -ɪŋ, -d
admeasurement
BR adˈmɛʒəm(ə)nt, -s
AM ædˈmɛʒərmənt, -s
admen
BR ˈadmɛn
AM ˈædˌmɛn
admin
BR ˈadmɪn
AM ˈædˌmɪn
adminicle
BR ədˈmɪnɪkl, -z
AM ædˈmɪnəkəl, ædˈmɪnəkəl, -z
adminicular
BR ˌadmɪˈnɪkjʊlə(r)
AM ˌædməˈnɪkjələr
administer
BR ədˈmɪnɪst|ə(r), -əz, -(ə)rɪŋ, -əd
AM ədˈmɪnɪst|ər, -ərz, -(ə)rɪŋ, -ərd
administrable
BR ədˈmɪnɪstrəbl
AM ədˈmɪnɪstrəbəl
administrant
BR ədˈmɪnɪstr(ə)nt, -s
AM ədˈmɪnɪstrənt, -s

administrate
BR ədˈmɪnɪstreɪt, -s, -ɪŋ, -ɪd
AM ədˈmɪnɪˌstreɪ|t, -ts, -dɪŋ, -dɪd
administration
BR ədˌmɪnɪˈstreɪʃn, -z
AM ədˌmɪnəˈstreɪʃən, -z
administrative
BR ədˈmɪnɪstrətɪv
AM ədˈmɪnəˌstreɪdɪv, ədˈmɪnəstrədɪv
administratively
BR ədˈmɪnɪstrətɪvli
AM ədˈmɪnəˌstreɪdɪvli
administrator
BR ədˈmɪnɪstreɪtə(r), -z
AM ədˈmɪnəˌstreɪdər, -z
administratorship
BR ədˈmɪnɪstreɪtəʃɪp, -s
AM ədˈmɪnəˌstreɪdərˌʃɪp, -s
administratrices
BR ədˌmɪnɪˈstreɪtrɪsiːz
AM ədˌmɪnəˈstreɪtrəˌsiz
administratrix
BR ədˈmɪnɪstreɪtrɪks, -ɪz
AM ədˈmɪnəˌstreɪtrɪks, -ɪz
admirable
BR ˈadm(ə)rəbl
AM ˈædm(ə)rəbəl
admirableness
BR ˈadm(ə)rəblnəs
AM ˈædm(ə)rəbəlnəss
admirably
BR ˈadm(ə)rəbli
AM ˈædm(ə)rəbli
admiral
BR ˈadm(ə)rəl, ˈadm(ə)r|, -z
AM ˈædm(ə)rəl, -z
admiralship
BR ˈadm(ə)rəlʃɪp, ˈadm(ə)r|ʃɪp, -s
AM ˈædm(ə)rəlˌʃɪp, -s
admiralty
BR ˈadm(ə)rəlt|i, ˈadm(ə)r|t|i, -z
AM ˈædm(ə)rəlti, -z
admiration
BR ˌadmɪˈreɪʃn
AM ˌædməˈreɪʃən
admire
BR ədˈmʌɪə(r), -z, -ɪŋ, -d
AM ədˈmaɪ(ə)r, -z, -ɪŋ, -d
admirer
BR ədˈmʌɪərə(r), -z
AM ədˈmaɪ(ə)rər, -z
admiringly
BR ədˈmʌɪərɪŋli

AM ədˈmaɪ(ə)rɪŋli
admissibility
BR ədˌmɪsɪˈbɪlɪti
AM ədˌmɪsəˈbɪlɪdi
admissible
BR ədˈmɪsɪbl
AM ədˈmɪsəbəl
admission
BR ədˈmɪʃn, -z
AM ədˈmɪʃən, -z
admissive
BR ədˈmɪsɪv
AM ədˈmɪsɪv
admit
BR ədˈmɪt, -s, -ɪŋ, -ɪd
AM ədˈmɪ|t, -ts, -dɪŋ, -dɪd
admittable
BR ədˈmɪtəbl
AM ədˈmɪdəbəl
admittance
BR ədˈmɪt(ə)ns
AM ədˈmɪtns
admittedly
BR ədˈmɪtɪdli
AM ədˈmɪdɪdli
admix
BR ədˈmɪks, adˈmɪks, -ɪz, -ɪŋ, -t
AM ædˈmɪks, -ɪz, -ɪŋ, -t
admixture
BR ədˈmɪkstʃə(r), adˈmɪkstʃə(r), -z
AM ædˈmɪkstʃər, -z
admonish
BR ədˈmɒnɪʃ, -ɪʃɪz, -ɪʃɪŋ, -ɪʃt
AM ədˈmɑnɪʃ, -ɪz, -ɪŋ, -t
admonishment
BR ədˈmɒnɪʃm(ə)nt, -s
AM ədˈmɑnɪʃmənt, -s
admonition
BR ˌadməˈnɪʃn, -z
AM ˌædməˈnɪʃən, -z
admonitory
BR ədˈmɒnɪt(ə)ri
AM ədˈmɑnəˌtɔri
adnate
BR ˈadneɪt
AM ˈædˌneɪt
ad nauseam
BR ˌad ˈnɔːzɪam
AM ˌæd ˈnɔzɪəm, +ˈnɑzɪəm
adnexa
BR adˈnɛksə(r)
AM ædˈnɛksə
adnexal
BR adˈnɛksl
AM ædˈnɛks(ə)l
adnominal
BR adˈnɒmɪnl
AM ædˈnɑmənəl
ado
BR əˈduː
AM əˈdu

adobe
BR ə'dəʊbi
AM ə'doʊbi

adolescence
BR ˌadə'lɛsns
AM ˌædl'ɛsəns

adolescent
BR ˌadə'lɛsnt, -s
AM ˌædl'ɛsənt, -s

adolescently
BR ˌadə'lɛsntli
AM ˌædl'ɛsn(t)li

Adonis
BR ə'dəʊnɪs, -ɪz
AM ə'dɑnəs, -əz

adopt
BR ə'dɒpt, -s, -ɪŋ, -ɪd
AM ə'dɑpt, -s, -ɪŋ, -əd

adoptee
BR ə,dɒp'tiː, -z
AM ə,dɑp'ti, -z

adopter
BR ə'dɒptə(r), -z
AM ə'dɑptər, -z

adoption
BR ə'dɒpʃn, -z
AM ə'dɑpʃən, -z

adoptive
BR ə'dɒptɪv
AM ə'dɑptɪv

adoptively
BR ə'dɒptɪvli
AM ə'dɑptɪvli

adorable
BR ə'dɔːrəbl
AM ə'dɔrəbəl

adorably
BR ə'dɔːrəbli
AM ə'dɔrəbli

adoral
BR ad'ɔːrəl ad'ɔːrl̩
AM æd'ɔrəl

adoration
BR ˌadə'reɪʃn
AM ˌædə'reɪʃən,
ˌædɔ'reɪʃən

adore
BR ə'dɔː(r), -z, -ɪŋ, -d
AM ə'dɔ(ə)r, -z, -ɪŋ, -d

adorer
BR ə'dɔːrə(r), -z
AM ə'dɔrər, -z

adoringly
BR ə'dɔːrɪŋli
AM ə'dɔrɪŋli

adorn
BR ə'dɔːn, -z, -ɪŋ, -d
AM ə'dɔ(ə)rn, -z, -ɪŋ, -d

adornment
BR ə'dɔːnm(ə)nt, -s
AM ə'dɔrnmənt, -s

adown
BR ə'daʊn
AM ə'daʊn

ad personam
BR ˌad pə'səʊnam
AM ˌæd pər'soʊnəm

ad rem
BR ˌad 'rɛm
AM ˌæd 'rɛm

adrenal
BR ə'driːnl
AM ə'drinəl

adrenalin
BR ə'drɛnəlɪn,
ə'drɛnlɪn
AM ə'drɛnlən

adrenaline
BR ə'drɛnəlɪn,
ə'drɛnlɪn
AM ə'drɛnlən

**adrenocortico-
trophic**
BR ə,driːnəʊˌkɔːtɪkə(ʊ)-
'trɒfɪk,
ə,drɛnəʊˌkɔːtɪkə(ʊ)-
'trəʊfɪk,
ə,drɛnəʊˌkɔːtɪkə(ʊ)-
'trɒfɪk,
ə,drɛnəʊˌkɔːtɪkə(ʊ)-
'trəʊfɪk
AM ə,drinoʊˌkɑrdəkoʊ-
'trɑfɪk

**adrenocortico-
trophin**
BR ə,driːnəʊˌkɔːtɪkə(ʊ)-
'trəʊfn̩,
ə,drɛnəʊˌkɔːtɪkə(ʊ)-
'trəʊfn̩
AM ə,drinoʊˌkɑrdəkoʊ-
'troʊfən

**adrenocortico-
tropic**
BR ə,driːnəʊˌkɔːtɪkə(ʊ)-
'trɒpɪk,
ə,driːnəʊˌkɔːtɪkə(ʊ)-
'trəʊpɪk,
ə,drɛnəʊˌkɔːtɪkə(ʊ)-
'trɒpɪk,
ə,drɛnəʊˌkɔːtɪkə(ʊ)-
'trəʊpɪk
AM ə,drinoʊˌkɑrdəkoʊ-
'trɑpɪk

Adrian
BR 'eɪdriən
AM 'eɪdriən

Adrianne
BR ˌadrɪ'an
AM ˌeɪdri'æn

Adriatic
BR ˌeɪdrɪ'atɪk
AM ˌeɪdri'ædɪk

Adrienne
BR ˌeɪdrɪ'ɛn, 'eɪdriən
AM ˌeɪdri'ɛn

adrift
BR ə'drɪft
AM ə'drɪft

adroit
BR ə'drɔɪt, -ɪst
AM ə'drɔɪ|t, -ɪst

adroitly
BR ə'drɔɪtli
AM ə'drɔɪtli

adroitness
BR ə'drɔɪtnɪs
AM ə'drɔɪtnɪs

adscititious
BR ˌadsɪ'tɪʃəs
AM ˌædsə'tɪʃəs

adsorb
BR ad'zɔːb, əd'zɔːb,
ad'sɔːb, əd'sɔːb
AM æd'zɔ(ə)rb,
æd'sɔ(ə)rb

adsorbable
BR ad'zɔːbəbl,
əd'zɔːbəbl, ad'sɔːbəbl,
əd'sɔːbəbl
AM æd'zɔrbəbəl,
æd'sɔrbəbəl

adsorbate
BR ad'zɔːbət, ad'sɔːbət,
ad'zɔːbeɪt, ad'sɔːbeɪt,
əd'zɔːbət, əd'sɔːbət,
əd'zɔːbeɪt, əd'sɔːbeɪt,
-s
AM æd'zɔrbət,
æd'sɔrbət,
æd'zɔr,beɪt,
æd'sɔr,beɪt, -s

adsorbent
BR ad'zɔːb(ə)nt,
əd'zɔːb(ə)nt,
ad'sɔːb(ə)nt,
əd'sɔːb(ə)nt
AM æd'zɔrbənt,
æd'sɔrbənt

adsorption
BR ad'zɔːpʃn,
əd'zɔːpʃn, ad'sɔːpʃn,
əd'sɔːpʃn
AM æd'zɔrbʃən,
æd'sɔrpʃən

adsorptive
BR ad'zɔːptɪv,
əd'zɔːptɪv, ad'sɔːptɪv,
əd'sɔːptɪv
AM æd'zɔrptɪv,
æd'sɔrptɪv

adsuki
BR ad'suːk|i, -ɪz
AM æd'suki, -z

adsum
BR 'adsʊm, 'adsʌm
AM 'æd,səm

adulate
BR 'adjʊleɪt, 'adʒʊleɪt,
-s, -ɪŋ, -ɪd
AM 'ædʒə,leɪ|t,
'ædjə,leɪ|t, -ts, -dɪŋ,
-dɪd

adulation
BR ˌadjʊ'leɪʃn,
ˌadʒʊ'leɪʃn
AM ˌædʒə'leɪʃən,
ˌædjə'leɪʃən

adulator
BR 'adjʊleɪtə(r)
'adʒʊleɪtə(r), -z
AM 'ædʒə,leɪdər,
'ædjə,leɪdər, -z

adulatory
BR ˌadjʊ'leɪt(ə)ri,
ˌadʒʊ'leɪt(ə)ri,
'adjʊlət(ə)ri,
'adʒʊlət(ə)ri
AM 'ædʒələˌtɔri,
'ædjələˌtɔri

Adullamite
BR ə'dʌləmʌɪt, -s
AM ə'dələˌmaɪt, -s

adult
BR 'adʌlt, ə'dʌlt, -s
AM ə'dəlt, 'æˌdəlt, -s

adulterant
BR ə'dʌlt(ə)rənt,
ə'dʌlt(ə)rn̩t, -s
AM ə'dəlt(ə)rənt, -s

adulterate
BR ə'dʌltəreɪt, -s, -ɪŋ,
-ɪd
AM ə'dəltəˌreɪ|t, -ts,
-dɪŋ, -dɪd

adulteration
BR ə,dʌltə'reɪʃn, -z
AM ə,dəltə'reɪʃən, -z

adulterator
BR ə'dʌltəreɪtə(r), -z
AM ə'dəltəˌreɪdər, -z

adulterer
BR ə'dʌlt(ə)rə(r), -z
AM ə'dəltərər, -z

adulteress
BR ə'dʌltrɪs, -ɪz
AM ə'dəltrəs, -əz

adulterine
BR ə'dʌlt(ə)rʌɪn,
AM ə'dəltərən,
ə'dəltəˌrin,
ə'dəltəˌraɪn

adulterous
BR ə'dʌlt(ə)rəs
AM ə'dəlt(ə)rəs

adulterously
BR ə'dʌlt(ə)rəsli
AM ə'dəlt(ə)rəsli

adulterousness
BR ə'dʌlt(ə)rəsnəs
AM ə'dəlt(ə)rəsnəs

adultery
BR ə'dʌlt(ə)r|i, -ɪz
AM ə'dəlt(ə)ri, -z

adulthood
BR 'adʌlthʊd,
ə'dʌlthʊd
AM ə'dəlt,(h)ʊd

adultly
BR 'adʌltli, ə'dʌltli
AM ə'dəltli

adultness
BR 'adʌltnəs,
ə'dʌltnəs
AM ə'dəltnəs

adumbrate
BR 'adʌmbreɪt,
'adəmbreɪt, -s, -ɪŋ, -ɪd
AM 'ædəm,breɪt,
ə'dəm,breɪ|t, -ts, -dɪŋ,
-dɪd

adumbration
BR ˌadʌm'breɪʃn,
ˌadəm'breɪʃn
AM ˌædəm'breɪʃən

adumbrative
BR 'adʌmbreɪtɪv,
'adəmbreɪtɪv
AM 'ædəmˌbreɪdɪv,
ə'dəmbrədɪv

ad valorem
BR ˌad və'lɔːrɛm
AM ˌæd və'lɔrəm

advance
BR əd'vɑːns, əd'vans,
-ɪz, -ɪŋ, -t
AM əd'væns, -əz, -ɪŋ, -t

advancement
BR əd'vɑːnsm(ə)nt,
əd'vansm(ə)nt, -s
AM əd'vænsmənt, -s

advancer
BR əd'vɑːnsə(r),
əd'vansə(r), -z
AM əd'vænsər, -z

advantage
BR əd'vɑːntˌɪdʒ,
əd'vantˌɪdʒ, -ɪdʒɪz,
-ɪdʒɪŋ, -ɪdʒd
AM əd'væn(t)ɪdʒ, -ɪz,
-ɪŋ, -d

advantageous
BR ˌadv(ə)n'teɪdʒəs,
ˌadvɑːn'teɪdʒəs,
ˌadvan'teɪdʒəs
AM ˌædˌvæn'teɪdʒəs,
ˌædvən'teɪdʒəs

advantageously
BR ˌadv(ə)n'teɪdʒəsli,
ˌadvɑːn'teɪdʒəsli,
ˌadvan'teɪdʒəsli
AM ˌædˌvæn'teɪdʒəsli,
ˌædvən'teɪdʒəsli

advantageousness
BR ˌadv(ə)n'teɪdʒəsnəs,
ˌadvɑːn'teɪdʒəsnəs,
ˌadvan'teɪdʒəsnəs
AM ˌædˌvæn'teɪdʒəsnəs,
ˌædvən'teɪdʒəsnəs

advect
BR ad'vɛkt, əd'vɛkt, -s,
-ɪŋ, -ɪd
AM æd'vɛk|(t), -(t)s,
-tɪŋ, -təd

advection
BR ad'vɛkʃn, əd'vɛkʃn
AM æd'vɛkʃən

advective
BR ad'vɛktɪv,
əd'vɛktɪv
AM æd'vɛktɪv

advent
BR 'adv(ə)nt, 'advɛnt,
-s
AM 'ædˌvɛnt, -s

Adventism
BR 'adv(ə)ntɪz(ə)m
AM 'ædˌvɛnˌtɪzəm

Adventist
BR 'adv(ə)ntɪst, -s
AM 'ædˌvɛn(t)əst, -s

adventitious
BR ˌadv(ə)n'tɪʃəs,
ˌadvɛn'tɪʃəs
AM ˌædˌvɛn'tɪʃəs

adventitiously
BR ˌadv(ə)n'tɪʃəsli,
ˌadvɛn'tɪʃəsli
AM ˌædˌvɛn'tɪʃəsli

adventure
BR əd'vɛn(t)ʃə(r), -z
AM əd'vɛn(t)ʃər, -z

adventurer
BR əd'vɛn(t)ʃ(ə)rə(r),
-z
AM əd'vɛn(t)ʃərər, -z

adventuresome
BR əd'vɛn(t)ʃəs(ə)m
AM əd'vɛn(t)ʃərsəm

adventuress
BR əd'vɛn(t)ʃ(ə)rɪs, -ɪz
AM əd'vɛn(t)ʃ(ə)rəs,
-əz

adventurism
BR əd'vɛn(t)ʃərɪz(ə)m,
-z
AM əd'vɛn(t)ʃəˌrɪzəm,
-z

adventurist
BR ad'vɛn(t)ʃ(ə)rɪst, -s
AM əd'vɛn(t)ʃəˌrɪst, -s

adventurous
BR əd'vɛn(t)ʃ(ə)rəs
AM əd'vɛn(t)ʃ(ə)rəs

adventurously
BR əd'vɛn(t)ʃ(ə)rəsli
AM əd'vɛn(t)ʃ(ə)rəsli

adventurousness
BR əd'vɛn(t)ʃ(ə)rəsnəs
AM əd'vɛn(t)ʃ(ə)rəsnəs

adverb
BR 'advəːb, -z
AM 'ædˌvərb, -z

adverbial
BR əd'vəːbɪəl,
ad'vəːbɪəl, -z
AM əd'vərbɪəl,
æd'vərbɪəl, -z

adverbially
BR əd'vəːbɪəli,
ad'vəːbɪəli
AM əd'vərbɪəli,
æd'vərbɪəli

ad verbum
BR ˌad 'vəːbəm
AM ˌæd 'vərbəm,
+ 'wɛrbəm

adversarial
BR ˌadvə'sɛːrɪəl
AM ˌædvər'sɛrɪəl

adversary
BR 'advəs(ə)r|i,
əd'vəːs(ə)r|i, -iz
AM 'ædvərˌsɛri, -z

adversative
BR əd'vəːsətɪv, -z

AM əd'vərsədɪv, -z

adversatively
BR əd'vəːsətɪvli
AM əd'vərsədɪvli

adverse
BR 'advəːs, əd'vəːs
AM 'ædˌvərs, əd'vərs

adversely
BR 'advəːsli, əd'vəːsli
AM 'ædˌvərsli,
əd'vərsli

adverseness
BR 'advəːsnəs,
əd'vəːsnəs
AM əd'vərsnəs,
əd'vərsnəs

adversity
BR əd'vəːsɪt|i, -ɪz
AM əd'vərsəd|i, -z

advert¹
advertisement
BR 'advəːt, -s
AM 'ædˌvərt, -s

advert²
verb
BR əd'vəːt, -s, -ɪŋ, -ɪd
AM əd'vər|t, əd'vər|t,
-ts, -dɪŋ, -dəd

advertence
BR əd'vəːt(ə)ns
AM æd'vərtns,
əd'vərtns

advertency
BR əd'vəːt(ə)nsi
AM æd'vərtnsi,
əd'vərtnsi

advertent
BR əd'vəːt(ə)nt
AM æd'vərtnt,
əd'vərtnt

advertently
BR əd'vəːt(ə)ntli
AM æd'vərtn(t)li,
əd'vərtn(t)li

advertise
BR 'advətʌɪz, -ɪz, -ɪŋ, -d
AM 'ædvərˌtaɪz, -ɪz, -ɪŋ,
-d

advertisement
BR əd'vəːtɪsm(ə)nt,
əd'vəːtɪzm(ə)nt, -s
AM 'ædvərˌtaɪzmənt,
əd'vərdəzmənt, -s

advertiser
BR 'advətʌɪzə(r), -z
AM 'ædvərˌtaɪzər, -z

advertize
BR 'advətʌɪz, -ɪz, -ɪŋ, -d
AM 'ædvərˌtaɪz, -ɪz, -ɪŋ,
-d

advertizer
BR 'advətʌɪzə(r), -z
AM 'ædvərˌtaɪzər, -z

advertorial
BR ˌadvə'tɔːrɪəl, -z
AM ˌædvər'tɔrɪəl, -z

advice
BR əd'vʌɪs
AM əd'vaɪs

advisability
BR əd,vʌɪzə'bɪlɪti
AM əd,vaɪzə'bɪlɪdi

advisable
BR əd'vʌɪzəbl
AM əd'vaɪzəbəl

advisableness
BR əd'vʌɪzəblnəs
AM əd'vaɪzəbəlnəs

advisably
BR əd'vʌɪzəbli
AM əd'vaɪzəbli

advise
BR əd'vʌɪz, -ɪz, -ɪŋ, -d
AM əd'vaɪz, -ɪz, -ɪŋ, -d

advisedly
BR əd'vʌɪzɪdli
AM əd'vaɪzɪdli

advisee
BR əd,vʌɪ'ziː, -z
AM əd,vaɪ'zi, -z

adviser
BR əd'vʌɪzə(r), -z
AM əd'vaɪzər, -z

advisor
BR əd'vʌɪzə(r), -z
AM əd'vaɪzər, -z

advisory
BR əd'vʌɪz(ə)ri
AM əd'vaɪzəri

advocaat
BR 'advəkɑː(r), -z
AM 'ædvoʊˌkɑ|(t),
-z\-ts

advocacy
BR 'advəkəsi
AM 'ædvəkəsi

advocate¹
noun
BR 'advəkət, -s
AM 'ædvəkət, -s

advocate²
verb
BR 'advəkeɪt, -s, -ɪŋ, -ɪd
AM 'ædvəˌkeɪ|t, -ts,
-dɪŋ, -dɪd

advocateship
BR 'advəkətˌʃɪp, -s
AM 'ædvəkətˌʃɪp, -s

advocation
BR ˌadvə'keɪʃn
AM ˌædvə'keɪʃən

advocatory
BR əd'vɒkət(ə)ri
AM æd'vəkəˌtɔri

advokaat
BR 'advəkɑː(r), -z
AM 'ædvoʊˌkɑ|(t),
-z\-ts

advowson
BR əd'vaʊzn, -z
AM əd'vaʊzn,
æd'vaʊzn, -z

advt.
BR əd'vɜːtɪsm(ə)nt,
əd'vɜːtɪzm(ə)nt
AM ˌædvərˈtaɪzmənt,
əd'vɜrdəzmənt

adyta
BR 'ædɪtə(r)
AM 'ædədə, 'ædətə

adytum
BR 'ædɪtəm
AM 'ædədəm,
'ædəˌtəm

adz
BR adz, -ɪz, -ɪŋ, -d
AM ædz, -əz, -ɪŋ, -d

adze
BR adz, -ɪz, -ɪŋ, -d
AM ædz, -əz, -ɪŋ, -d

adzuki
BR adˈzuːk|i, -ɪz
AM æd'zuki, -z

aedes
BR eɪˈiːdiːz
AM eɪˈidiz

aedile
BR 'iːdʌɪl, -z
AM 'iˌdaɪl, -z

aedileship
BR 'iːdʌɪlˌʃɪp, -s
AM 'iˌdaɪlˌʃɪp, -s

Aegean
BR ɪ'dʒiːən, ɪ'dʒiːən
AM ə'dʒiːən, eɪ'dʒiən

aegis
BR 'iːdʒɪs
AM 'idʒɪs, 'eɪdʒɪs

Aegisthus
BR ɪ'dʒɪsθəs
AM ə'dʒɪsθəs, ɪ'dʒɪsθəs

aegrotat
BR 'aɪɡrə(ʊ)tat,
'iːɡrə(ʊ)tat, -s
AM i'ɡroʊˌtɑt,
'iɡroʊˌtɑt, -s

aelectasis
BR ˌatɪˈlɛktəsɪs
AM ˌædəˈlɛktəsɪs

Aelfric
BR 'alfrɪk
AM 'ælfrɪk

Aeneas
BR iːˈniːəs, ɪ'niːəs
AM ə'niəs

Aeneid
BR 'iːnɪɪd, iːˈniːɪd,
ɪ'niːɪd
AM ə'niəd

aeolian
BR ɪ'əʊlɪən, eɪˈəʊlɪən
AM i'oʊljən, eɪˈoʊljən,
i'oʊlɪən, eɪˈoʊlɪən

Aeolic
BR ɪ'ɒlɪk, ɪ'əʊlɪk
AM i'oʊlɪk, eɪˈoʊlɪk

aeolotropy
BR ˌiːə(ʊ)'lɒtrəpi
AM ˌiə'lɑtrəpi

Aeolus
BR ɪ'əʊləs, 'iːələs
AM i'oʊləs, eɪˈoʊləs

aeon
BR 'iːən, 'iːɒn, -z
AM 'iən, 'iˌɑn, -z

aeonian
BR ɪ'əʊnɪən
AM i'oʊnɪən

aepyornis
BR ˌiːpɪˈɔːnɪs, -ɪz
AM ˌipi'ɔrnəs, -əz

aerate
BR ɛːˈreɪt, -s, -ɪŋ, -ɪd
AM 'ɛ,reɪ|t, -ts, -dɪŋ,-dɪd

aeration
BR ɛːˈreɪʃn
AM ɛ'reɪʃən

aerator
BR ɛːˈreɪtə(r), -z
AM 'ɛˌreɪdər, -z

aerenchyma
BR ɛːˈrɛŋkɪmə(r), -z
AM 'ɛˌrɛŋkəmə, -z

aerial
BR 'ɛːrɪəl, -z
AM 'ɛrɪəl, -z

aerialist
BR 'ɛːrɪəlɪst, -s
AM 'ɛrɪələst, -s

aeriality
BR ˌɛrɪ'alɪti
AM ˌɛri'ælədi

aerially
BR 'ɛːrɪəli
AM 'ɛrɪəli

aerie
BR 'ɪər|i, 'ɛːr|i, 'ʌɪr|i, -ɪz
AM 'ɛri, 'ɪri, 'iri, 'eɪri, -z

aeriform
BR 'ɛːrɪfɔːm
AM 'ɛrəˌfɔ(ə)rm

Aer Lingus®
BR ˌɛː 'lɪŋɡəs
AM 'ɛr 'lɪŋɡəs

aero
BR 'ɛːrəʊ, -z
AM 'ɛroʊ, -z

aerobatic
BR ˌɛːrə(ʊ)'batɪk, -s
AM ˌɛroʊ'bædɪk,
ˌɛrə'bædɪk, -s

aerobe
BR 'ɛːrəʊb, -z
AM 'ɛˌroʊb, -z

aerobic
BR ɛːˈrəʊbɪk, -s
AM ə'roʊbɪk, ɛ'roʊbɪk,
-s

aerobically
BR ɛːˈrəʊbɪkli
AM ə'roʊbəkli,
ɛ'roʊbəkli

aerobiologist
BR ˌɛːrə(ʊ)bʌɪ'ɒlədʒɪst,
-s

AM ˌɛroʊˌbaɪ'ɑlədʒəst,
ˌɛrəˌbaɪ'ɑlədʒəst, -s

aerobiology
BR ˌɛːrə(ʊ)bʌɪ'ɒlədʒi
AM ˌɛroʊˌbaɪ'ɑlədʒi,
ˌɛrəˌbaɪ'ɑlədʒi

aerodrome
BR 'ɛːrədrəʊm, -z
AM 'ɛroʊˌdroʊm,
'ɛrəˌdroʊm, -z

aerodynamic
BR ˌɛːrə(ʊ)dʌɪ'namɪk,
-s
AM ˌɛroʊˌdaɪ'næmɪk,
ˌɛrəˌdaɪ'næmɪk, -s

aerodynamically
BR ˌɛːrə(ʊ)dʌɪ'namɪkli
AM ˌɛroʊˌdaɪ'næmək-
(ə)li,
ˌɛrəˌdaɪ'næmək(ə)li

aerodynamicist
BR ˌɛːrə(ʊ)dʌɪ'namɪsɪst,
-s
AM ˌɛroʊˌdaɪ'næməsəst,
ˌɛrəˌdaɪ'næməsəst, -s

aerodyne
BR 'ɛːrə(ʊ)dʌɪn, -z
AM 'ɛroʊˌdaɪn,
'ɛrəˌdaɪn, -z

aero-engine
BR 'ɛːrəʊˌɛn(d)ʒ(ɪ)n, -z
AM 'ɛroʊˌɛndʒən,
'ɛrəˌɛndʒən, -z

Aeroflot®
BR 'ɛːrə(ʊ)flɒt
AM 'ɛroʊˌflɑt, 'ɛrəˌflɑt
RUS aira'flot

aerofoil
BR 'ɛːrə(ʊ)fɔɪl, -z
AM 'ɛroʊˌfɔɪl, 'ɛrəˌfɔɪl,
-z

aerogram
BR 'ɛːrə(ʊ)gram, -z
AM 'ɛroʊˌgræm,
'ɛrəˌgræm, -z

aerogramme
BR 'ɛːrə(ʊ)gram, -z
AM 'ɛroʊˌgræm,
'ɛrəˌgræm, -z

aerolite
BR 'ɛːrə(ʊ)lʌɪt, -s
AM 'ɛroʊˌlaɪt, 'ɛrəˌlaɪt,
-s

aerological
BR ˌɛːrə'lɒdʒɪkl
AM ˌɛroʊ'lɑdʒəkəl,
ˌɛrə'lɑdʒəkəl

aerologist
BR ɛːˈrɒlədʒɪst, -s
AM ɛ'rɑlədʒəst, -s

aerology
BR ɛːˈrɒlədʒi
AM ɛ'rɑlədʒi

aeromagnetic
BR ˌɛːrə(ʊ)mag'nɛtɪk
AM ˌɛroʊmæg'nɛdɪk,
ˌɛrəmæg'nɛdɪk

aeronaut
BR 'ɛːrə(ʊ)nɔːt, -s
AM 'ɛroʊˌnɔt, 'ɛrəˌnɔt,
'ɛroʊˌnɑt, 'ɛrəˌnɑt, -s

aeronautic
BR ˌɛːrə(ʊ)'nɔːtɪk, -s
AM ˌɛroʊ'nɔdɪk,
ˌɛrə'nɔdɪk,
ˌɛroʊ'nɑdɪk,
ˌɛrə'nɑdɪk, -s

aeronautical
BR ˌɛːrə(ʊ)'nɔːtɪkl
AM ˌɛroʊ'nɔdəkəl,
ˌɛrə'nɔdəkəl,
ˌɛroʊ'nɑdəkəl,
ˌɛrə'nɑdəkəl

aeronautically
BR ˌɛːrə(ʊ)'nɔːtɪkli
AM ˌɛroʊ'nɔdək(ə)li,
ˌɛrə'nɔdək(ə)li,
ˌɛroʊ'nɑdək(ə)li,
ˌɛrə'nɑdək(ə)li

aeronomy
BR ɛːˈrɒnəmi
AM ɛ'rɑnəmi

aeroplane
BR 'ɛːrəpleɪn, -z
AM 'ɛr(ə)ˌpleɪn,
'ɛroʊˌpleɪn, -z

aerosol
BR 'ɛːrəsɒl, -z
AM 'ɛrəˌsɔl, 'ɛrəˌsɑl, -z

aerospace
BR 'ɛːrə(ʊ)speɪs
AM 'ɛroʊˌspeɪs,
'ɛrəˌspeɪs

aerostat
BR 'ɛːrə(ʊ)stat, -s
AM 'ɛroʊˌstæt,
'ɛrəˌstæt, -s

aerostatic
BR ˌɛːrə(ʊ)'statɪk
AM ˌɛroʊ'stædɪk,
ˌɛrə'stædɪk

aerostatically
BR ˌɛːrə(ʊ)'statɪkli
AM ˌɛroʊ'stædək(ə)li,
ˌɛrə'stædək(ə)li

aerotow
BR 'ɛːrə(ʊ)təʊ, -z, -ɪŋ, -d
AM 'ɛroʊˌtoʊ, 'ɛrəˌtoʊ,
-z, -ɪŋ,-d

aerotrain
BR 'ɛːrə(ʊ)treɪn, -z
AM 'ɛroʊˌtreɪn,
'ɛrəˌtreɪn, -z

Aertex®
BR 'ɛːtɛks
AM 'ɛrˌtɛks

aeruginous
BR ɪəˈruːdʒɪnəs
AM ɪ'rudʒənəs

aery[1]
adjective
BR 'ɛːri
AM 'ɛri, 'ɪri, 'iri, 'eɪri

aery²
noun
BR 'ɪər|i, 'ɛːr|i, 'ʌɪr|i, -ɪz
AM 'ɛri, 'ɪri, 'iri, 'eɪri, -z
Aeschines
BR 'iːskɪniːz
AM 'ɛskəniz
Aeschylean
BR ˌiːskɪ'liːən
AM ˌɛskə'liən
Aeschylus
BR 'iːskɪləs, 'iːskļəs
AM 'ɛskələs
Aesculapian
BR ˌiːskjʊ'leɪpiən
AM ˌɛskə'leɪpiən
Aesop
BR 'iːsɒp
AM 'iˌsɑp, 'eɪˌsɑp
aesthete
BR 'iːsθiːt, -s
AM 'ɛsˌθit, -s
aesthetic
BR iːs'θɛtɪk, ɪs'θɛtɪk, ɛs'θɛtɪk, -s
AM ɛs'θɛdɪk, əs'θɛdɪk, -s
aesthetical
BR iːs'θɛtɪkl, ɪs'θɛtɪkl, ɛs'θɛtɪkl
AM ɛs'θɛdəkəl, əs'θɛdəkəl
aesthetically
BR iːs'θɛtɪkli, ɪs'θɛtɪkli, ɛs'θɛtɪkli
AM ɛs'θɛdək(ə)li, əs'θɛdək(ə)li
aesthetician
BR ˌiːsθɪ'tɪʃn, ˌɛsθɪ'tɪʃn
AM ˌɛsθə'tɪʃən
aestheticism
BR iːs'θɛtɪsɪz(ə)m, ɪs'θɛtɪsɪz(ə)m, ɛs'θɛtɪsɪz(ə)m
AM ɛs'θɛdəˌsɪzəm, əs'θɛdəˌsɪzəm
aestival
BR 'iːstɪvl, iːs'tʌɪvl, ɛs'tʌɪvl
AM 'ɛstəvəl, ɛs'taɪvəl
aestivate
BR 'iːstɪveɪt, 'ɛstɪveɪt, -s, -ɪŋ, ɪd
AM 'ɛstəˌveɪ|t, -ts, -dɪŋ, dɪd
aestivation
BR ˌiːstɪ'veɪʃn, ˌɛstɪ'veɪʃn
AM ˌɛstə'veɪʃən
aetatis
BR ʌɪ'tɑːtɪs, iː'teɪtɪs
AM aɪ'tadəs, i'tadəs
aether
BR 'iːθə(r)
AM 'iθər
aetiologic
BR ˌiːtɪə'lɒdʒɪk
AM ˌidiə'lɑdʒɪk

aetiological
BR ˌiːtɪə'lɒdʒɪkl
AM ˌidiə'lɑdʒəkəl
aetiologically
BR ˌiːtɪə'lɒdʒɪkli
AM ˌidiə'lɑdʒək(ə)li
aetiology
BR iːtɪ'ɒlədʒi
AM ˌidi'ɑlədʒi
Afar
African people
BR 'afɑː(r), -z
AM ə'fɑr, -z
afar
BR ə'fɑː(r)
AM ə'fɑr
afeard
BR ə'fɪəd
AM ə'fɪ(ə)rd
affability
BR ˌafə'bɪlɪti
AM ˌæfə'bɪlɪdi
affable
BR 'afəbl
AM 'æfəbəl
affably
BR 'afəbli
AM 'æfəbli
affair
BR ə'fɛː(r), -z
AM ə'fe(ə)r, -z
affaire
BR ə'fɛː(r), -z
AM ə'fe(ə)r, -z
affairé
BR ə'fɛːreɪ
AM əˌfɛ'reɪ
affaire de cœur
BR əˌfɛː də 'kəː(r)
AM əˌfɛr də 'kər
affaires de cœur
BR əˌfɛː(z) də 'kəː(r)
AM əˌfɛr(z) də 'kər
affect¹
noun
BR 'afɛkt, -s
AM 'æˌfɛk(t), ə'fɛk(t), -s
affect²
verb
BR ə'fɛkt, -s, -ɪŋ, -ɪd
AM ə'fɛk|(t), -(t)s, -tɪŋ, -təd
affectation
BR ˌafək'teɪʃn, ˌafɛk'teɪʃn, -z
AM ˌæˌfɛk'teɪʃən, -z
affectedly
BR ə'fɛktɪdli
AM ə'fɛktədli
affectingly
BR ə'fɛktɪŋli
AM ə'fɛktɪŋli
affection
BR ə'fɛkʃn, -z
AM ə'fɛkʃən, -z

affectional
BR ə'fɛkʃn(ə)l, ə'fɛkʃən(ə)l
AM ə'fɛkʃənl, ə'fɛkʃnəl
affectionally
BR ə'fɛkʃnəli, ə'fɛkʃnļi, ə'fɛkʃənļi
AM ə'fɛkʃ(ə)nəli
affectionate
BR ə'fɛkʃənət, ə'fɛkʃnət
AM ə'fɛkʃ(ə)nət
affectionately
BR ə'fɛkʃənətli, ə'fɛkʃnətli
AM ə'fɛkʃ(ə)nətli
affective
BR ə'fɛktɪv
AM ə'fɛktɪv, æ'fɛktɪv
affectively
BR ə'fɛktɪvli
AM ə'fɛktɪvli, æ'fɛktɪvli
affectiveness
BR ə'fɛktɪvnɪs
AM ə'fɛktɪvnɪs, æ'fɛktɪvnɪs
affectivity
BR əˌfɛk'tɪvɪti, ˌafɛk'tɪvɪti
AM əˌfɛk'tɪvɪdi, æˌfɛk'tɪvɪdi
affenpinscher
BR 'afnˌpɪn(t)ʃə(r), -z
AM 'ɑfənˌpɪn(t)ʃər, -z
afferent
BR 'af(ə)rənt, 'af(ə)rnt
AM 'æf(ə)rənt
affiance
BR ə'faɪəns, -ɪz, -ɪŋ, -t
AM ə'faɪəns, -əz, -ɪŋ, -t
affiant
BR ə'faɪənt, -s
AM ə'faɪənt, -s
affiche
BR ə'fiːʃ, -ɪz
AM ə'fiʃ, -ɪz
affidavit
BR ˌafɪ'deɪvɪt, -s
AM ˌæfə'deɪvɪt, -s
affiliate¹
noun
BR ə'fɪliət, -s
AM ə'fɪliət, -s
affiliate²
verb
BR ə'fɪlieɪt, -s, -ɪŋ, -ɪd
AM ə'fɪliˌeɪ|t, -ts, -dɪŋ, -dɪd
affiliation
BR əˌfɪlɪ'eɪʃn, -z
AM əˌfɪli'eɪʃən, -z
affined
BR ə'fʌɪnd
AM ə'faɪnd

affinity
BR ə'fɪnɪt|i, -ɪz
AM ə'fɪnɪdi, -z
affirm
BR ə'fəːm, -z, -ɪŋ, -d
AM ə'fərm, -z, -ɪŋ, -d
affirmable
BR ə'fəːməbl
AM ə'fərməbəl
affirmation
BR ˌafə'meɪʃn, -z
AM ˌæfər'meɪʃən, -z
affirmative
BR ə'fəːmətɪv
AM ə'fərmədɪv
affirmatively
BR ə'fəːmətɪvli
AM ə'fərmədɪvli
affirmatory
BR ə'fəːmət(ə)ri
AM ə'fərməˌtɔri
affirmer
BR ə'fəːmə(r), -z
AM ə'fərmər, -z
affix¹
noun
BR 'afɪks, -ɪz
AM 'æˌfɪks, -ɪz
affix²
verb
BR ə'fɪks, -ɪz, -ɪŋ, -t
AM ə'fɪks, -ɪz, -ɪŋ, -t
affixture
BR ə'fɪkstʃə(r), a'fɪkstʃə(r)
AM ə'fɪkstʃər
afflatus
BR ə'fleɪtəs
AM ə'fleɪdəs
afflict
BR ə'flɪkt, -s, -ɪŋ, -ɪd
AM ə'flɪk|(t), -(t)s, -tɪŋ, -tɪd
affliction
BR ə'flɪkʃn, -z
AM ə'flɪkʃən, -z
afflictive
BR ə'flɪktɪv
AM ə'flɪktɪv
afflictively
BR ə'flɪktɪvli
AM ə'flɪktɪvli
affluence
BR 'aflʊəns
AM 'æˌfluəns, ə'fluəns
affluent
BR 'aflʊənt
AM 'æˌfluənt, ə'fluənt
affluential
BR ˌaflʊ'ɛnʃl
AM ˌæflə'wɛn(t)ʃəl
affluently
BR 'aflʊəntli
AM 'æˌfluən(t)li, ə'fluən(t)li
afflux
BR 'aflʌks, -ɪz

afforce
AM ˈæˌflǝks, -ǝz

afforce
BR ǝˈfɔːs, -ɪz, -ɪŋ, -t
AM ǝˈfɔː(ǝ)rs, -ǝz, -ɪŋ, -t

afford
BR ǝˈfɔːd, -z, -ɪŋ, -ɪd
AM ǝˈfɔː(ǝ)rd, -z, -ɪŋ, -ǝd

affordability
BR ǝˌfɔːdǝˈbɪlɪti
AM ǝˌfɔrdǝˈbɪlɪdi

affordable
BR ǝˈfɔːdǝbl
AM ǝˈfɔrdǝbǝl

affordably
BR ǝˈfɔːdǝbli
AM ǝˈfɔrdǝbli

afforest
BR ǝˈfɒrɪst, -s, -ɪŋ, -ɪd
AM ǝˈfɔrǝst, -s, -ɪŋ, -ǝd

afforestation
BR ǝˌfɒrɪˈsteɪʃn
AM ǝˌfɔrǝsˈteɪʃǝn

affranchise
BR ǝˈfran(t)ʃʌɪz, -ɪz, -ɪŋ, -d
AM ǝˈfrænˌtʃaɪz, -ɪz, -ɪŋ, -d

affray
BR ǝˈfreɪ, -z
AM ǝˈfreɪ, -z

affreightment
BR ǝˈfreɪtm(ǝ)nt
AM ǝˈfreɪtmǝnt

affricate
BR ˈafrɪkǝt, -s
AM ˈæfrǝkǝt, -s

affrication
BR ˌafrɪˈkeɪʃn
AM ˌæfrǝˈkeɪʃǝn

affricative
BR ǝˈfrɪkǝtɪv, -z
AM ǝˈfrɪkǝdɪv, ˈæfrǝˌkeɪdɪv, -z

affright
BR ǝˈfrʌɪt, -s, -ɪŋ, -ɪd
AM ǝˈfraɪt, -ts, -dɪŋ, -dɪd

affront
BR ǝˈfrʌnt, -s, -ɪŋ, -ɪd
AM ǝˈfrǝnt, -ts, -ts, -(t)ɪŋ, -(t)ǝd

affusion
BR ǝˈfjuːʒn
AM ǝˈfjuʒǝn

Afghan
BR ˈafgan, -z
AM ˈæfˌgæn, -z

Afghani
BR afˈgɑːnǀi, afˈganǀi, -ɪz
AM ˌæfˈgɑni, ˌæfˈgæni, -z

Afghanistan
BR afˈganɪstɑːn, afˈganɪstan, afˌganɪˈstɑːn, afˌganɪˈstan
AM æfˈgænǝˌstæn

aficionado
BR ǝˌfɪʃ(j)ǝˈnɑːdǝʊ, ǝˌfɪsjǝˈnɑːdǝʊ, -z
AM ǝˌfɪʃǝˈnɑdǝʊ, ǝˌfɪsjǝˈnɑdǝʊ, -z

afield
BR ǝˈfiːld
AM ǝˈfild

afire
BR ǝˈfʌɪǝ(r)
AM ǝˈfaɪ(ǝ)r

aflame
BR ǝˈfleɪm
AM ǝˈfleɪm

aflatoxin
BR ˌaflǝˈtɒksɪn, -z
AM ˌæflǝˈtɑks(ǝ)n, -z

afloat
BR ǝˈflǝʊt
AM ǝˈfloʊt

aflutter
BR ǝˈflʌtǝ(r)
AM ǝˈflǝdǝr

afon
BR ˈav(ɒ)n
AM ˈæfǝn
WE ˈavɒn

afoot
BR ǝˈfʊt
AM ǝˈfʊt

afore
BR ǝˈfɔː(r)
AM ǝˈfɔ(ǝ)r

aforementioned
BR ǝˌfɔːˈmenʃnd, ǝˈfɔːˌmenʃnd
AM ǝˈfɔrˌmen(t)ʃǝnd

aforesaid
BR ǝˈfɔːsed
AM ǝˈfɔrˌsed

aforethought
BR ǝˈfɔːθɔːt
AM ǝˈfɔrˌθɔt, ǝˈfɔrˌθɑt

a fortiori
BR ˌeɪ ˌfɔːtɪˈɔːrʌɪ, + ˌfɔːtɪˈɔːri
AM ˌɑ ˌfɔrdiˈɔri, ˌeɪ ˌfɔrdiˈɔraɪ

afoul
BR ǝˈfaʊl
AM ǝˈfaʊl

afraid
BR ǝˈfreɪd
AM ǝˈfreɪd

afreet
BR ˈafriːt, -s
AM ˈæˌfrit, ǝˈfrit, -s

afresh
BR ǝˈfreʃ
AM ǝˈfreʃ

afric
BR ˈafrɪk
AM ˈæfrɪk

Africa
BR ˈafrɪkǝ(r)
AM ˈæfrǝkǝ

African
BR ˈafrɪk(ǝ)n, -z
AM ˈæfrǝkǝn, -z

Africana
BR ˌafrɪˈkɑːnǝ(r)
AM ˌæfrǝˈkænǝ

Africander
BR ˌafrɪˈkandǝ(r), -z
AM ˌæfrǝˈkændǝr, -z

africanisation
BR ˌafrɪkǝnʌɪˈzeɪʃn, ˌafrɪkʌnˈaɪˈzeɪʃn
AM ˌæfrǝkǝnǝˈzeɪʃǝn, ˌæfrǝkǝˌnaɪˈzeɪʃǝn

Africanise
BR ˈafrɪkǝnʌɪz, ˈafrɪkʌnˌaɪz, -ɪz, -ɪŋ, -d
AM ˈæfrǝkǝˌnaɪz, -ɪz, -ɪŋ, -d

Africanism
BR ˈafrɪkǝnɪz(ǝ)m, ˈafrɪkʌnɪz(ǝ)m
AM ˈæfrǝkǝˌnɪzǝm

Africanist
BR ˈafrɪkǝnɪst, ˈafrɪkʌnɪst, -s
AM ˈæfrǝkǝnǝst, -s

africanization
BR ˌafrɪkǝnʌɪˈzeɪʃn, ˌafrɪkʌnˈaɪˈzeɪʃn
AM ˌæfrǝkǝnǝˈzeɪʃǝn, ˌæfrǝkǝˌnaɪˈzeɪʃǝn

Africanize
BR ˈafrɪkǝnʌɪz, ˈafrɪkʌnˌaɪz, -ɪz, -ɪŋ, -d
AM ˈæfrǝkǝˌnaɪz, -ɪz, -ɪŋ, -d

Afrikaans
BR ˌafrɪˈkɑːns, ˌafrǝˈkɑːnz
AM ˌæfrǝˈkɑnz

Afrika Korps
BR ˈafrɪkǝ ˌkɔː(r)
AM ˈæfrikǝ ˌkɔ(ǝ)r

afrikander
BR ˌafrɪˈkandǝ(r), -z
AM ˌæfrǝˈkandǝr, -z

Afrikaner
BR ˌafrɪˈkɑːnǝ(r), -z
AM ˌæfrǝˈkɑnǝr, -z

afrit
BR ˈafrɪt, -s
AM ˈæˌfrit, ǝˈfrit, -s

Afro
BR ˈafrǝʊ
AM ˈæfroʊ

Afrocentric
BR ˌafrǝʊˈsentrɪk
AM ˌæfroʊˈsentrɪk

afrormosia
BR ˌafrɔːˈmǝʊzɪǝ(r)
AM ˌæfrɔrˈmoʊʒ(i)ǝ, ˌæfrɔrˈmoʊziǝ

AFSCME
BR ˈafsmi
AM ˈæfsmi

aft
BR ɑːft, aft

African
AM æft

after
BR ˈɑːftǝ(r), ˈaftǝ(r), -z
AM ˈæftǝr, -z

afterbirth
BR ˈɑːftǝbɜːθ, ˈaftǝbɜːθ, -s
AM ˈæftǝrˌbɜrθ, -s

afterburner
BR ˈɑːftǝˌbɜːnǝ(r), ˈaftǝˌbɜːnǝ(r), -z
AM ˈæftǝrˌbɜrnǝr, -z

aftercare
BR ˈɑːftǝkɛː(r), ˈaftǝkɛː(r)
AM ˈæftǝrˌkɛ(ǝ)r

afterdeck
BR ˈɑːftǝdɛk, ˈaftǝdɛk, -s
AM ˈæftǝrˌdɛk, -s

afterglow
BR ˈɑːftǝglǝʊ, ˈaftǝglǝʊ, -z
AM ˈæftǝrˌgloʊ, -z

aftergrass
BR ˈɑːftǝgrɑːs, ˈaftǝgras
AM ˈæftǝrˌgræs

afterlife
BR ˈɑːftǝlʌɪf, ˈaftǝlʌɪf
AM ˈæftǝrˌlaɪf

afterlight
BR ˈɑːftǝlʌɪt, ˈaftǝlʌɪt
AM ˈæftǝrˌlaɪt

afterlives
BR ˈɑːftǝlʌɪvz, ˈaftǝlʌɪvz
AM ˈæftǝrˌlaɪvz

aftermarket
BR ˈɑːftǝˌmɑːkɪt, ˈaftǝˌmɑːkɪt, -s
AM ˈæftǝrˌmɑrkǝt, -s

aftermath
BR ˈɑːftǝmaθ, ˈaftǝmaθ, -s
AM ˈæftǝrˌmæθ, -s

aftermost
BR ˈɑːftǝmǝʊst, ˈaftǝmǝʊst
AM ˈæftǝrˌmoʊst

afternoon
BR ˌɑːftǝˈnuːn, ˌaftǝˈnuːn, -z
AM ˌæftǝrˈnun, -z

afterpains
BR ˈɑːftǝpeɪnz, ˈaftǝpeɪnz
AM ˈæftǝrˌpeɪnz

afterpart
BR ˈɑːftǝpɑːt, ˈaftǝpɑːt, -s
AM ˈæftǝrˌpɑrt, -s

aftershave
BR ˈɑːftǝʃeɪv, ˈaftǝʃeɪv, -z
AM ˈæftǝrˌʃeɪv, -z

aftershock
BR 'ɑːftəʃɒk, 'aftəʃɒk,
-s
AM 'æftər,ʃɑk, -s

aftertaste
BR 'ɑːftəteɪst,
'aftəteɪst, -s
AM 'æftər,teɪst, -s

afterthought
BR 'ɑːftəθɔːt, 'aftəθɔːt,
-s
AM 'æftər,θɔt,
'æftər,θɑt, -s

afterward
BR 'ɑːftəwəd, 'aftəwəd,
-z
AM 'æftərwərd, -z

afterword
BR 'ɑːftəwəːd,
'aftəwəːd, -z
AM 'æftər,wərd, -z

afterworld
BR 'ɑːftəwəːld,
'aftəwəːld
AM 'æftər,wərld

Aga®
BR 'ɑːgə(r), -z
AM 'ɑgə, -z

Agadir
BR ,agə'dɪə(r)
AM ,ɑgə'dɪ(ə)r

Agag
BR 'eɪgag
AM 'ɑgæg

again
BR ə'gɛn, ə'geɪn
AM ə'gɛn

against
BR ə'gɛnst, ə'geɪnst
AM ə'gɛnst

Aga Khan
BR ,ɑːgə 'kɑːn
AM ,ɑgə 'kɑn

agama
BR 'agəmə(r), -z
AM ə'geɪmə, 'ægəmə, -z

Agamemnon
BR ,agə'mɛmnɒn,
,agə'mɛmnən
AM ,ægə'mɛm,nɑn

agamic
BR ə'gamɪk
AM eɪ'gæmɪk,
ə'gæmɪk

agamogenesis
BR ,agəmə'dʒɛnɪsɪs
AM ,eɪ,gæmə'dʒɛnəsəs,
,ægəmoʊ'dʒɛnəsəs

agamogenetic
BR ,agəmə(ʊ)dʒɪ'nɛtɪk
AM ,eɪ,gæmədʒə'nɛdɪk,
,ægəmoʊdʒə'nɛdɪk

agamospermy
BR 'agəmə,spəːmi
AM eɪ'gæmə,spərmi,
'ægəmoʊ,spərmi

agamous
BR 'agəməs

AM 'ægəməs

agapanthus
BR ,agə'panθəs, -ɪz
AM ,ægə'pænθəs, -əz

agape¹
adjective
BR ə'geɪp
AM ə'geɪp

agape²
noun
BR 'agəpeɪ, 'agəpiː, -z
AM ɑ'gɑ,peɪ, 'agə,peɪ, -z

agapemone
BR ,agə'piːməni,
,agə'piːmŋi,
,agə'pɛməni,
,agə'pɛmŋi
AM ,ægə'pɛməni

agar
BR 'eɪgə(r), 'eɪgɑː(r)
AM 'ɑ,gɑr, 'eɪ,gɑr

agaric
BR 'ag(ə)rɪk, -s
AM 'ægərɪk, ə'gɛrɪk, -s

agate
BR 'agɪt
AM 'ægət

Agatha
BR 'agəθə(r)
AM 'ægəθə

agave
BR ə'geɪvi, ə'gɑːvi,
'ageɪv,
ə'geɪvɪz\ə'gɑːvɪz
\'ageɪvz
AM ə'gɑvi, -z

agaze
BR ə'geɪz
AM ə'geɪz

agba
BR 'agbə(r), -z
AM 'ægbə, -z

age
BR eɪdʒ, -ɪz, -ɪŋ, -d
AM eɪdʒ, -ɪz, -ɪŋ, -d

aged¹
adjective
BR 'eɪdʒɪd
AM 'eɪdʒɪd

aged²
past tense of verb age
BR eɪdʒd
AM eɪdʒd

Agee
BR 'eɪdʒi
AM 'eɪdʒi

ageism
BR 'eɪdʒɪz(ə)m
AM 'eɪdʒ,ɪzəm

ageist
BR 'eɪdʒɪst, -s
AM 'eɪdʒɪst, -s

ageless
BR 'eɪdʒlɪs
AM 'eɪdʒlɪs

agelessness
BR 'eɪdʒlɪsnɪs
AM 'eɪdʒlɪsnɪs

agency
BR 'eɪdʒ(ə)ns|i, -ɪz
AM 'eɪdʒ(ə)nsi, -z

agenda
BR ə'dʒɛndə(r), -z
AM ə'dʒɛndə, -z

agendum
BR ə'dʒɛndəm
AM ə'dʒɛndəm

agent
BR 'eɪdʒ(ə)nt, -s
AM 'eɪdʒ(ə)nt, -s

agential
BR eɪ'dʒɛnʃl
AM eɪ'dʒɛn(t)ʃəl

agent provocateur
BR ,aʒɒ
prə,vɒkə'təː(r)
AM ,aʒɑn(t)
prə,vɒkə'tər

agents provocateurs
BR ,aʒɒ prə,vɒkə'təːz
AM ,aʒɑn(t)(s)
prə,vɒkə'tər(z)

ager
BR 'eɪdʒə(r), -z
AM 'eɪdʒər, -z

ageratum
BR ,adʒə'reɪtəm, -z
AM ,ædʒə'reɪdəm, -z

Agfa®
BR 'agfə(r)
AM 'ægfə

Aggie
BR 'agi
AM 'ægi

aggiornamento
BR ə,dʒɔːnə'mɛntəʊ
AM ə,dʒɔrnə'mɛn,(t)oʊ

agglomerate¹
noun, adjective
BR ə'glɒm(ə)rət, -s
AM ə'glɑmərət, -s

agglomerate²
verb
BR ə'glɒməreɪt, -s, -ɪŋ,
-ɪd
AM ə'glɑmə,reɪt, -ts,
-dɪŋ, -dɪd

agglomeration
BR ə,glɒmə'reɪʃn
AM ə,glɑmə'reɪʃən

agglomerative
BR ə'glɒm(ə)rətɪv
AM ə'glɑmə,reɪdɪv,
ə'glɑmərədɪv

agglutinate¹
adjective
BR ə'gluːtɪnət
AM ə'glutnət

agglutinate²
verb
BR ə'gluːtɪneɪt, -s, -ɪŋ,
-ɪd
AM ə'glutn,eɪ|t, -ts,
-dɪŋ, -dɪd

agglutination
BR ə,gluːtɪ'neɪʃn
AM ə,glutn'eɪʃən

agglutinative
BR ə'gluːtɪnətɪv
AM ə'glutnədɪv,
ə'glutn,eɪdɪv

agglutinin
BR ə'gluːtɪnɪn, -z
AM ə'glutnən, -z

aggrandise
BR ə'grandʌɪz, -ɪz, -ɪŋ,
-d
AM ə'græn,daɪz, -ɪz, -ɪŋ,
-d

aggrandisement
BR ə'grandɪzm(ə)nt,
ə'grandʌɪzm(ə)nt, -s
AM ə'græn,daɪzmənt,
-s

aggrandiser
BR ə'grandʌɪzə(r), -z
AM ə'græn,daɪzər, -z

aggrandize
BR ə'grandʌɪz, -ɪz, -ɪŋ,
-d
AM ə'græn,daɪz, -ɪz, -ɪŋ,
-d

aggrandizement
BR ə'grandɪzm(ə)nt,
ə'grandʌɪzm(ə)nt, -s
AM ə'græn,daɪzmənt,
-s

aggrandizer
BR ə'grandʌɪzə(r), -z
AM ə'græn,daɪzər, -z

aggravate
BR 'agrəveɪt, -s, -ɪŋ, -ɪd
AM 'ægrə,veɪ|t, -ts,
-dɪŋ, -dɪd

aggravatingly
BR 'agrəveɪtɪŋli
AM 'ægrə,veɪdɪŋli

aggravation
BR ,agrə'veɪʃn
AM ,ægrə'veɪʃən

aggregate¹
noun, adjective
BR 'agrɪgət, -s
AM 'ægrəgət, -s

aggregate²
verb
BR 'agrɪgeɪt, -s, -ɪŋ, -ɪd
AM 'ægrə,geɪ|t, -ts,
-dɪŋ, -dɪd

aggregation
BR ,agrɪ'geɪʃn
AM ,ægrə'geɪʃən

aggregative
BR 'agrɪgətɪv
AM 'ægrə,geɪdɪv

aggress
BR ə'grɛs, -ɪz, -ɪŋ, -t
AM ə'grɛs, -əz, -ɪŋ, -t

aggression
BR ə'grɛʃn
AM ə'grɛʃən

aggressive
BR əˈgresɪv
AM əˈgresɪv

aggressively
BR əˈgresɪvli
AM əˈgresɪvli

aggressiveness
BR əˈgresɪvnɪs
AM əˈgresɪvnɪs

aggressor
BR əˈgresə(r), -z
AM əˈgresər, -z

aggrieve
BR əˈgriːv, -z, -ɪŋ, -d
AM əˈgriv, -z, -ɪŋ, -d

aggrievedly
BR əˈgriːvɪdli
AM əˈgrivɪdli

aggro
BR ˈagrəʊ
AM ˈægroʊ

aghast
BR əˈgɑːst, əˈgast
AM əˈgæst

agile
BR ˈadʒʌɪl
AM ˈædʒəl

agilely
BR ˈadʒʌɪl(l)i
AM ˈædʒə(l)li

agility
BR əˈdʒɪlɪti
AM əˈdʒɪlɪdi

agin
BR əˈgɪn
AM əˈgɪn

Agincourt
BR ˈa(d)ʒɪnkɔː(r), ˈadʒɪnkɔːt
AM ˈædʒən,kɔ(ə)rt

aging
BR ˈeɪdʒɪŋ
AM ˈeɪdʒɪŋ

agio
BR ˈadʒɪəʊ, -z
AM ˈædʒioʊ, -z

agiotage
BR ˈadʒ(ɪ)ətɪdʒ, ˈadʒ(ɪ)ətɑːʒ
AM ˈædʒədɪdʒ

agism
BR ˈeɪdʒɪz(ə)m
AM ˈeɪˌdʒɪzəm

agist
BR ˈeɪdʒɪst, -s
AM ˈeɪdʒɪst, -s

agistment
BR əˈdʒɪs(t)m(ə)nt
AM ˈədʒɪs(t)mənt

agitate
BR ˈadʒɪteɪt, -s, -ɪŋ, -ɪd
AM ˈædʒə,teɪ|t, -ts, -dɪŋ, -dɪd

agitatedly
BR ˈadʒɪteɪtɪdli
AM ˈædʒə,teɪdɪdli

agitation
BR ˌadʒɪˈteɪʃn, -z
AM ˌædʒəˈteɪʃən, -z

agitato
BR ˌadʒɪˈtɑːtəʊ
AM ˌædʒəˈtɑdoʊ

agitator
BR ˈadʒɪteɪtə(r), -z
AM ˈædʒə,teɪdər, -z

agitprop
BR ˈadʒɪtprɒp
AM ˈædʒət,prɑp

agleam
BR əˈgliːm
AM əˈglim

aglet
BR ˈaglɪt, -s
AM ˈæglət, -s

agley
BR əˈgleɪ, əˈgliː; əˈglʌɪ
AM əˈgleɪ, əˈgli

aglow
BR əˈgləʊ
AM əˈgloʊ

agma
BR ˈagmə(r), -z
AM ˈægmə, -z

agnail
BR ˈagneɪl, -z
AM ˈæg,neɪl, -z

agnate
BR ˈagneɪt, -s
AM ˈæg,neɪt, -s

agnatic
BR agˈnatɪk, əgˈnatɪk
AM ægˈnædɪk

agnation
BR agˈneɪʃn, əgˈneɪʃn
AM ægˈneɪʃən

Agnes
BR ˈagnɪs
AM ˈægnəs

Agnew
BR ˈagnjuː
AM ˈægnu

Agni
BR ˈagni
AM ˈægni

agnomen
BR agˈnəʊmen
AM ægˈnoʊmən

agnosia
BR agˈnəʊzɪə(r), agˈnəʊsɪə(r)
AM ægˈnoʊʒə

agnostic
BR agˈnɒstɪk, əgˈnɒstɪk, -s
AM ægˈnɑstɪk, əgˈnɑstɪk, -s

agnosticism
BR agˈnɒstɪsɪz(ə)m, əgˈnɒstɪsɪz(ə)m
AM ægˈnɑstə,sɪzəm, əgˈnɑstə,sɪzəm

Agnus Dei
BR ˌagnʊs ˈdeɪiː

AM ˈag,nʊs ˈdeɪ,i, ˈæg,nʊs +, ˈagnəs +, ˈægnəs +

ago
BR əˈgəʊ
AM əˈgoʊ

agog
BR əˈgɒg
AM əˈgɑg

a-go-go
BR əˈgəʊgəʊ
AM əˈgoʊ,goʊ

agonic
BR eɪˈgɒnɪk, əˈgɒnɪk
AM eɪˈgɑnɪk, əˈgɑnɪk

agonise
BR ˈagənʌɪz, -ɪz, -ɪŋ, -d
AM ˈægə,naɪz, -ɪz, -ɪŋ, -d

agonisingly
BR ˈagənʌɪzɪŋli
AM ˈægə,naɪzɪŋli

agonist
BR ˈagənɪst, -s
AM ˈægənəst, -s

Agonistes
BR ˌagəˈnɪstiːz
AM ˌægəˈnɪstiz

agonistic
BR ˌagəˈnɪstɪk
AM ˌægəˈnɪstɪk

agonistically
BR ˌagəˈnɪstɪkli
AM ˌægəˈnɪstɪk(ə)li

agonize
BR ˈagənʌɪz, -ɪz, -ɪŋ, -d
AM ˈægə,naɪz, -ɪz, -ɪŋ, -d

agonizingly
BR ˈagənʌɪzɪŋli
AM ˈægə,naɪzɪŋli

agony
BR ˈagən|i, ˈagn|i, -ɪz
AM ˈægəni, -z

agoraphobe
BR ˈag(ə)rəfəʊb, -z
AM ˈæg(ə)rə,foʊb, -z

agoraphobia
BR ˌag(ə)rəˈfəʊbɪə(r)
AM ˌæg(ə)rəˈfoʊbiə

agoraphobic
BR ˌag(ə)rəˈfəʊbɪk, -s
AM ˌæg(ə)rəˈfoʊbɪk, -s

agouti
BR əˈguːt|i, -ɪz
AM əˈgudi, -z

Agra
BR ˈɑːgrə(r)
AM ˈɑgrə

agrapha
BR ˈagrəfə(r)
AM ˈægrəfə

agraphon
BR ˈagrəfɒn
AM ˈægrə,fɑn

agrarian
BR əˈgreːrɪən
AM əˈgrerɪən

agree
BR əˈgriː, -z, -ɪŋ, -d
AM əˈgri, -z, -ɪŋ, -d

agreeable
BR əˈgriːəbl
AM əˈgriəbəl

agreeableness
BR əˈgriːəblnəs
AM əˈgriəbəlnəs

agreeably
BR əˈgriːəbli
AM əˈgriəbli

agreement
BR əˈgriːm(ə)nt, -s
AM əˈgrimənt, -s

agribusiness
BR ˈagrɪ,bɪznɪs
AM ˈægrə,bɪznɪs

agribusinessman
BR ˈagrɪ,bɪznɪsmən
AM ˈægrə,bɪznɪs,mæn

agribusinessmen
BR ˈagrɪ,bɪznɪsmən
AM ˈægrə,bɪznɪs,men

agrichemical
BR ˌagrɪˈkemɪkl, -z
AM ˌægrəˈkeməkəl, -z

Agricola
BR əˈgrɪkələ(r)
AM əˈgrɪkələ

agricultural
BR ˌagrɪˈkʌltʃ(ə)rəl, ˌagrɪˈkaltʃ(ə)rl̩
AM ˌægrəˈkəltʃ(ə)rəl

agriculturalist
BR ˌagrɪˈkʌltʃ(ə)rəlɪst, ˌagrɪˈkaltʃ(ə)rl̩ɪst, -s
AM ˌægrəˈkəltʃ(ə)rələst, -s

agriculturally
BR ˌagrɪˈkʌltʃ(ə)rəli, ˌagrɪˈkaltʃ(ə)rl̩i
AM ˌægrəˈkəltʃ(ə)rəli

agriculture
BR ˈagrɪkʌltʃə(r)
AM ˈægrə,kəltʃər

agriculturist
BR ˌagrɪˈkʌltʃ(ə)rɪst, -s
AM ˌægrəˈkəltʃ(ə)rəst, -s

agrimony
BR ˈagrɪməni
AM ˈægrə,moʊni

Agrippa
BR əˈgrɪpə(r)
AM əˈgrɪpə

agrochemical
BR ˌagrə(ʊ)ˈkemɪkl, -z
AM ˌægroʊˈkeməkəl, ˌægrəˈkeməkəl, -z

agroforestry
BR ˌagrə(ʊ)ˈfɒrɪstri
AM ˌægroʊˈfɔrəstri, ˌægrəˈfɔrəstri

agro-industry
BR ˌagrəʊˈɪndəstri
AM ˌægroʊˈɪndəstri

agronomic
BR ˌagrəˈnɒmɪk, -s
AM ˌægrəˈnɑmɪk, -s

agronomical
BR ˌagrəˈnɒmɪkl
AM ˌægrəˈnɑmɪkəl

agronomically
BR ˌagrəˈnɒmɪkli
AM ˌægrəˈnɑmɪk(ə)li

agronomist
BR əˈgrɒnəmɪst, -s
AM əˈgrɑnəməst, -s

agronomy
BR əˈgrɒnəmi
AM əˈgrɑnəmi

aground
BR əˈgraʊnd
AM əˈgraʊnd

ague
BR ˈeɪgjuː, -z, -d
AM ˈeɪˌgju, -z, -d

Aguecheek
BR ˈeɪgjuːtʃiːk
AM ˈeɪˌgjuˌtʃik

Aguilar
BR ˌagwɪˈlɑː(r)
AM ˌagwiˈlar
SP ʌyiˈlar

aguish
BR ˈeɪgjʊʃ
AM ˈeɪˌgjəwɪʃ, ˈeɪˌgjuɪʃ

Agulhas
BR əˈgʌləs
AM əˈgələs

aguti
BR əˈguːt|i, -ɪz
AM əˈgudi, -z

Agutter
BR ˈagətə(r), əˈgʌtə(r)
AM əˈgədər

ah
BR ɑː(r)
AM ɑ

aha
BR ɑːˈhɑː(r), əˈhɑː(r)
AM əˈhɑ

Ahab
BR ˈeɪhab
AM ˈeɪhæb

Ahasuerus
BR əˌhazjʊˈɪərəs,
ˌeɪhazjʊˈɪərəs,
əˌhazjʊˈɛːrəs,
ˌeɪhazjʊˈɛːrəs
AM əˌhæzjuˈɛrəs,
əˌhæʒuˈɛrəs

ahead
BR əˈhɛd
AM əˈhɛd

ahem
BR əˈhɛm, əˈhm
AM əˈhɛm, əˈhm

Aherne
BR əˈhɜːn, ˈeɪhɜːn
AM ˈeɪhərn

ahimsa
BR əˈhɪmsɑː(r)

AM əˈhɪmˌsɑ

ahistoric
BR ˌeɪhɪˈstɒrɪk
AM ˌeɪhɪsˈtɔrɪk

ahistorical
BR ˌeɪhɪˈstɒrɪkl
AM ˌeɪhɪsˈtɔrəkəl

Ahmadabad
BR ˈɑːmədəbad,
ˈɑːmədəbɑːd
AM ˈɑmədəˌbɑd,
ˈɑmədəˌbæd

Ahmed
BR ˈɑː(k)mɛd, ˈɑːxmɛd
AM ˈɑmɛd

ahold
BR əˈhəʊld
AM əˈhoʊld

ahoy
BR əˈhɔɪ
AM əˈhɔɪ

ahull
BR əˈhʌl
AM əˈhəl

Ahura Mazda
BR əˌhʊərə ˈmazdə(r)
AM əˌhʊrə ˈmazdə

ai
BR ʌɪ, ˈɑːɪ, -z
AM ʌɪ, -z

aid
BR eɪd, -z, -ɪŋ, -ɪd
AM eɪd, -z, -ɪŋ, -ɪd

Aïda
BR ʌɪˈiːdə(r)
AM aɪˈidə

Aidan
BR ˈeɪdn
AM ˈeɪdən

aide
BR eɪd, -z
AM eɪd, -z

aide-de-camp
BR ˌeɪddəˈkɒ̃,
ˌeɪddəˈkɑ̃ː
AM ˌeɪddəˈkæmp

aide-mémoire
BR ˌeɪdmɛmˈwɑː(r),
ˌeɪdˈmɛmwɑː(r), -z
AM ˌeɪdˌmɛmˈwɑr, -z

aider
BR ˈeɪdə(r), -z
AM ˈeɪdər, -z

aides-de-camp
BR ˌeɪd(z)dəˈkɒ̃,
ˌeɪd(z)dəˈkɑ̃ː
AM ˌeɪdzdəˈkæmp

aides-mémoire
BR ˌeɪd(z)mɛmˈwɑː(r),
ˌeɪd(z)ˈmɛmwɑː(r)
AM ˌeɪd(z)ˌmɛmˈwɑr

aides-mémoires
BR ˌeɪd(z)mɛmˈwɑːz,
ˌeɪd(z)ˈmɛmwɑːz
AM ˌeɪd(z)ˌmɛmˈwɑr(z)

AIDS
BR eɪdz

AM əˈhɪmˌsɑ

aiglet
BR ˈeɪglɪt, -s
AM ˈeɪglət, -s

aigrette
BR ˈeɪgrɛt, erˈgrɛt, -s
AM erˈgrɛt, -s

Aigues-Mortes
BR ˌeɪgˈmɔːt
AM ɛgˈmɔ(ə)rt

aiguille
BR ˌeɪgwɪˈjɛt,
ˌeɪgwɪˈlɛt, -s
AM ˌeɪgwəˈlɛt, -s

aiguille
BR ˈeɪgwiː(l),
erˈgwiː(l), -z
AM erˈgwil, -z

aiguillette
BR ˌeɪgwɪˈjɛt,
ˌeɪgwɪˈlɛt, -s
AM ˌeɪgwəˈlɛt, -s

Aiken
BR ˈeɪk(ə)n
AM ˈeɪkɛn

aikido
BR ʌɪˈkiːdəʊ
AM aɪˈkidoʊ, ˌaɪkiˈdoʊ

ail
BR eɪl, -z, -ɪŋ, -d
AM eɪl, -z, -ɪŋ, -d

ailanthus
BR erˈlanθəs, -ɪz
AM erˈlænθəs, -əz

Aileen
BR ˈeɪliːn, ˈʌɪliːn
AM arˈlin

aileron
BR ˈeɪlərɒn, -z
AM ˈeɪləˌran, -z

ailment
BR ˈeɪlm(ə)nt, -s
AM ˈeɪlmənt, -s

Ailsa
BR ˈeɪlsə(r)
AM ˈeɪlsə

ailurophile
BR ʌɪˈl(j)ʊərə(ʊ)fʌɪl,
erˈl(j)ʊərə(ʊ)fʌɪl,
ˈeɪljərə(ʊ)fʌɪl, -z
AM arˈlʊrəˌfaɪl,
erˈlʊrəˌfaɪl, -z

ailurophobe
BR ʌɪˈl(j)ʊərə(ʊ)fəʊb,
erˈl(j)ʊərə(ʊ)fəʊb,
ˈeɪljərə(ʊ)fəʊb, -z
AM arˈlʊrəˌfoʊb,
erˈlʊrəˌfoʊb, -z

ailurophobia
BR ʌɪˌl(j)ʊərə(ʊ)ˈfəʊ-
bɪə(r),
erˌl(j)ʊərə(ʊ)ˈfəʊbɪə(r)
AM arˌlʊrəˈfoʊbiə,
erˌlʊrəˈfoʊbiə

aim
BR eɪm, -z, -ɪŋ, -d
AM eɪm, -z, -ɪŋ, -d

Aimée
BR ˈeɪmeɪ, ˈeɪmi
AM ɛˈmeɪ

aimless
BR ˈeɪmlɪs
AM ˈeɪmlɪs

aimlessly
BR ˈeɪmlɪsli
AM ˈeɪmlɪsli

aimlessness
BR ˈeɪmlɪsnɪs
AM ˈeɪmlɪsnɪs

ain
BR eɪn
AM eɪn

Ainsley
BR ˈeɪnzli
AM ˈeɪnzli

ain't
BR eɪnt
AM eɪnt

Aintree
BR ˈeɪntriː
AM ˈeɪntri

Ainu
BR ˈʌɪnuː, -z
AM ˈaɪˌnu, -z

aïoli
BR ʌɪˈəʊli, erˈəʊli
AM erˈoʊli

air
BR ɛː(r), -z, -ɪŋ, -d
AM ɛ(ə)r, -z, -ɪŋ, -d

airbag
BR ˈɛːbag, -z
AM ˈɛrˌbæg, -z

airbase
BR ˈɛːbeɪs, -ɪz
AM ˈɛrˌbeɪs, -ɪz

airbed
BR ˈɛːbɛd, -z
AM ˈɛrˌbɛd, -z

airborne
BR ˈɛːbɔːn
AM ˈɛrˌbɔ(ə)rn

airbrake
BR ˈɛːbreɪk, -s
AM ˈɛrˌbreɪk, -s

airbrick
BR ˈɛːbrɪk, -s
AM ˈɛrˌbrɪk, -s

airbrush
BR ˈɛːbrʌʃ, -ɪz, -ɪŋ, -t
AM ˈɛrˌbrəʃ, -əz, -ɪŋ, -t

airburst
BR ˈɛːbɜːst, -s
AM ˈɛrˌbərst, -s

airbus
BR ˈɛːbʌs, -ɪz
AM ˈɛrˌbəs, -əz

aircraft
BR ˈɛːkrɑːft, ˈɛːkraft
AM ˈɛrˌkræf(t)

aircraftman
BR ˈɛːkrɑːf(t)mən,
ˈɛːkraf(t)mən
AM ˈɛrˌkræf(t)mən

aircraftmen
BR 'ɛːkrɑːf(t)mən,
'ɛːkrɑːf(t)mən
AM 'ɛr,kræf(t)mən

aircraftsman
BR 'ɛːkrɑːf(t)smən,
'ɛːkrɑːf(t)smən
AM 'ɛr,kræf(t)smən

aircraftsmen
BR 'ɛːkrɑːf(t)smən,
'ɛːkrɑːf(t)smən
AM 'ɛr,kræf(t)smən

aircraftswoman
BR 'ɛːkrɑːf(t)s,wʊmən,
'ɛːkrɑːf(t)s,wʊmən
AM 'ɛr,kræf(t)s,wʊmən

aircraftswomen
BR 'ɛːkrɑːf(t)s,wɪmɪn,
'ɛːkrɑːf(t)s,wɪmɪn
AM 'ɛr,kræf(t)s,wɪmɪn

aircraftwoman
BR 'ɛːkrɑːf(t),wʊmən,
'ɛːkrɑːf(t),wʊmən
AM 'ɛr,kræf(t),wʊmən

aircraftwomen
BR 'ɛːkrɑːf(t),wɪmɪn,
'ɛːkrɑːf(t),wɪmɪn
AM 'ɛr,kræf(t),wɪmɪn

aircrew
BR 'ɛːkruː, -z
AM 'ɛr,kru, -z

airdate
BR 'ɛːdeɪt
AM 'ɛr,deɪt

Airdrie
BR 'ɛːdri
AM 'ɛrdri

airdrop
BR 'ɛːdrɒp, -s, -ɪŋ, -t
AM 'ɛr,drɑp, -s, -ɪŋ, -t

Airedale
BR 'ɛːdeɪl, -z
AM 'ɛr,deɪl, -z

airer
BR 'ɛːrə(r), -z
AM 'ɛrər, -z

airfare
BR 'ɛːfɛː(r), -z
AM 'ɛr,fɛ(ə)r, -z

airfield
BR 'ɛːfiːld, -z
AM 'ɛr,fild, -z

airflow
BR 'ɛːfləʊ, -z
AM 'ɛr,floʊ, -z

airfoil
BR 'ɛːfɔɪl, -z
AM 'ɛr,fɔɪl, -z

airframe
BR 'ɛːfreɪm, -z
AM 'ɛr,freɪm, -z

airfreight
BR 'ɛːfreɪt, -s, -ɪŋ, -ɪd
AM 'ɛr,freɪ|t, -ts, -dɪŋ,
-dɪd

airglow
BR 'ɛːgləʊ
AM 'ɛr,gloʊ

airgun
BR 'ɛːgʌn, -z
AM 'ɛr,gən, -z

airhead
BR 'ɛːhɛd, -z
AM 'ɛr,(h)ɛd, -z

airhole
BR 'ɛːhəʊl, -z
AM 'ɛr,(h)oʊl, -z

airily
BR 'ɛːrɪli
AM 'ɛrəli

airiness
BR 'ɛːrɪnɪs
AM 'ɛrɪnɪs

airing
BR 'ɛːrɪŋ, -z
AM 'ɛrɪŋ, -z

airlane
BR 'ɛːleɪn, -z
AM 'ɛr,leɪn, -z

airless
BR 'ɛːləs
AM 'ɛrləs

airlessly
BR 'ɛːləsli
AM 'ɛrləsli

airlessness
BR 'ɛːləsnəs
AM 'ɛrləsnəs

airlift
BR 'ɛːlɪft, -s
AM 'ɛr,lɪft, -s

airline
BR 'ɛːlaɪn, -z
AM 'ɛr,laɪn, -z

airliner
BR 'ɛːlaɪnə(r), -z
AM 'ɛr,laɪnər, -z

airlock
BR 'ɛːlɒk, -s
AM 'ɛr,lɑk, -s

airmail
BR 'ɛːmeɪl, -z, -ɪŋ, -d
AM 'ɛr,meɪl, -z, -ɪŋ, -d

airman
BR 'ɛːmən
AM 'ɛrmən

airmen
BR 'ɛːmən
AM 'ɛrmən

airmiss
BR 'ɛːmɪs, -ɪz
AM 'ɛr,mɪs, -ɪz

airmobile
BR 'ɛːmə(ʊ)biːl, -z
AM 'ɛr,moʊbəl, -z

airplane
BR 'ɛːpleɪn, -z
AM 'ɛr,pleɪn, -z

airplay
BR 'ɛːpleɪ, -z
AM 'ɛr,pleɪ, -z

airpocket
BR 'ɛːpɒkɪt, -s
AM 'ɛr,pɑkət, -s

airport
BR 'ɛːpɔːt, -s
AM 'ɛr,pɔ(ə)rt, -s

airscrew
BR 'ɛːskruː, -z
AM 'ɛr,skru, -z

airshaft
BR 'ɛːʃɑːft, 'ɛːʃaft, -s
AM 'ɛr,ʃæft, -s

airship
BR 'ɛːʃɪp, -s
AM 'ɛr,ʃɪp, -s

airsick
BR 'ɛːsɪk
AM 'ɛr,sɪk

airsickness
BR 'ɛːsɪknɪs
AM 'ɛr,sɪknɪs

airside
BR 'ɛːsaɪd
AM 'ɛr,said

airspace
BR 'ɛːspeɪs
AM 'ɛr,speɪs

airspeed
BR 'ɛːspiːd, -z
AM 'ɛr,spid, -z

airstream
BR 'ɛːstriːm, -z
AM 'ɛr,strim, -z

airstrip
BR 'ɛːstrɪp, -s
AM 'ɛr,strɪp, -s

airtight
BR 'ɛːtʌɪt
AM 'ɛr,tait

airtime
BR 'ɛːtʌɪm
AM 'ɛr,taim

airwave
BR 'ɛːweɪv, -z
AM 'ɛr,weɪv, -z

airway
BR 'ɛːweɪ, -z
AM 'ɛr,wei, -z

airwoman
BR 'ɛː,wʊmən
AM 'ɛr,wʊmən

airwomen
BR 'ɛː,wɪmɪn
AM 'ɛr,wɪmɪn

airworthiness
BR 'ɛː,wəːðɪnɪs
AM 'ɛr,wərðinɪs

airworthy
BR 'ɛː,wəːði
AM 'ɛr,wərði

airy
BR 'ɛːr|i, -ɪə(r), -ɪɪst
AM 'ɛri, -ər, -ɪst

aisle
BR ʌɪl, -z, -d
AM aɪl, -z, -d

ait
BR eɪt, -s
AM eɪt, -s

aitch
BR eɪtʃ, -ɪz
AM eɪtʃ, -ɪz

aitchbone
BR 'eɪtʃbəʊn, -z
AM 'eɪtʃboʊn, -z

Aitchison
BR 'eɪtʃɪs(ə)n
AM 'eɪtʃɪsən

Aitken
BR 'eɪ(t)kɪn
AM 'eɪ(t)kən

Aix-en-Provence
BR ,eɪksɒ̃prɒ̃'vɒ̃s
AM ,ɛksɑnprou'vɑns
FR ɛks ɑ̃ prɔvɑ̃s

Aix-la-Chapelle
BR ,eɪkslɑʃə'pɛl,
,eɪkslaʃə'pɛl
AM ,ɛkslɑʃɑ'pɛl
FR ɛks la ʃapɛl

Ajaccio
BR a'dʒaksɪəʊ
AM ɑ'jɑtʃ(i)ou
FR aʒaksjo

ajar
BR ə'dʒɑː(r)
AM ə'dʒɑr

Ajax
BR 'eɪdʒaks
AM 'eɪ,dʒæks

ajuga
BR ə'dʒuːgə(r)
AM ə'dʒugə

aka
BR ,eɪkeɪ'eɪ, 'eɪkə(r)
AM ,eɪ,keɪ'eɪ

Akai
BR 'akʌɪ
AM 'ɑkaɪ

akala
BR ɑː'kɑːlə(r), -z
AM ə'kɑlə, -z

Akbar
BR 'akbɑː(r)
AM 'ɑk,bɑr

akebia
BR ə'kiː,bɪə(r)
AM ə'kibiə

akee
BR 'akɪi, -ɪz
AM æ'ki, 'æ,ki, -z

akela
BR ɑː'keɪlə(r), -z
AM ə'kilə, -z

Akerman
BR 'akəmən, 'eɪkəmən
AM 'ækərmən

Akhenaten
BR ak'nɑːtn
AM ɑk'nɑtn

Akhetaten
BR ,akə'tɑːtn
AM ,akɛ'tɑtn

akimbo
BR ə'kɪmbəʊ
AM ə'kɪmboʊ

akin
BR əˈkɪn
AM əˈkɪn
Akins
BR ˈeɪkɪnz
AM ˈeɪkɪnz
Akita
BR ɑːˈkiːtə(r)
AM ɑˈkidə
Akkad
BR ˈakad
AM ˈæk͵æd, ˈɑk͵ɑd
Akkadian
BR əˈkeɪdɪən,
əˈkeɪdɪən, əˈkadɪən,
əˈkadɪən, -z
AM əˈkeɪdiən, -z
Akko
BR aˈkəʊ
AM ɑˈkoʊ
Akron
BR ˈakrɒn, ˈakr(ə)n
AM ˈækrən
Aksai Chin
BR ͵aksʌɪ ˈtʃɪn
AM ͵æk͵saɪ ˈtʃɪn
Aksum
BR ˈaksʊm
AM ˈɑk͵sʊm
Al
BR al
AM æl
à la
BR ͵a la(r), ͵ɑː ˈlɑː(r),
+ lə(r)
AM ͵ɑ lɑ, + lə
Alabama
BR ͵aləˈbamə(r)
AM ͵æləˈbæmə
Alabaman
BR ͵aləˈbamən, -z
AM ͵æləˈbæmən, -z
Alabamian
BR ͵aləˈbamiən, -z
AM ͵æləˈbæmiən, -z
alabaster
BR ˈaləbɑːstə(r),
ˈaləbastə(r)
AM ˈælə͵bæstər
alabastrine
BR ͵aləˈbɑːstrʌɪn,
͵aləˈbɑːstrɪn,
͵aləˈbastrʌɪn,
͵aləˈbastrɪn
AM ͵æləˈbæstrən
à la carte
BR ͵a la ˈkɑːt, ͵a lə +,
͵ɑː lɑː +
AM ͵ɑ lɑ ˈkɑrt, ͵a lə +
alack
BR əˈlak
AM əˈlæk
alacrity
BR əˈlakrɪti
AM əˈlækrədi
Aladdin
BR əˈladɪn
AM əˈlædən

Alaister
BR ˈalɪstə(r)
AM ˈæləstər,
ˈælə͵stɛ(ə)r
Alamein
BR ˈaləmeɪn, ͵aləˈmeɪn
AM ͵æləˈmeɪn
Alamo
BR ˈaləməʊ
AM ˈælə͵moʊ
à la mode
BR ͵a la ˈməʊd, ͵a lə +,
͵ɑː lɑː +
AM ͵ɑ lɑ ˈmoʊd
Alan
BR ˈalən
AM ˈælən
Alana
BR əˈlanə(r)
AM əˈlanə
alanine
BR ˈaləniːn, ˈalənʌɪn
AM ˈælə͵nin
Alar®
BR ˈeɪlɑː(r)
AM ˈeɪ͵lɑr
alar
BR ˈeɪlə(r), ˈeɪlɑː(r)
AM ˈeɪlər
Alaric
BR ˈalərɪk
AM ˈælərɪk
alarm
BR əˈlɑːm, -z, -ɪŋ, -d
AM əˈlɑrm, -z, -ɪŋ, -d
alarmingly
BR əˈlɑːmɪŋli
AM əˈlɑrmɪŋli
alarmism
BR əˈlɑːmɪz(ə)m
AM əˈlɑrm͵ɪzəm
alarmist
BR əˈlɑːmɪst, -s
AM əˈlɑrməst, -s
alarum
BR əˈlɑːrəm, -z
AM əˈlɑrəm, -z
alas
BR əˈlas, əˈlɑːs
AM əˈlæs
Alasdair
BR əˈlastə(r),
ˈaləstɛː(r)
AM ˈæləstər,
ˈælə͵stɛ(ə)r
Alaska
BR əˈlaskə(r)
AM əˈlæskə
Alaskan
BR əˈlaskən, -z
AM əˈlæskən, -z
Alastair
BR əˈlastə(r),
ˈaləstɛː(r)
AM ˈæləstər,
ˈælə͵stɛ(ə)r

Alastor
BR əˈlɑːstə(r),
əˈlastə(r), -z
AM əˈlæstər, -z
alate
BR ˈeɪleɪt, -s
AM ˈeɪ͵leɪt, -s
alb
BR alb, -z
AM ælb, -z
Alba
BR ˈalbə(r)
AM ˈælbə
Albacete
BR ͵albəˈseɪti
AM ͵ælbəˈseɪ͵di
SP ͵alβaˈθete,
alβaˈsete
albacore
BR ˈalbəkɔː(r), -z
AM ˈælbə͵kɔ(ə)r, -z
Alban
BR ˈɔːlbən, ˈɒlbən
AM ˈɑlbən
Albania
BR alˈbeɪnɪə(r)
AM ælˈbeɪniə,
alˈbeɪniə
Albanian
BR alˈbeɪnɪən, -z
AM ælˈbeɪniən,
alˈbeɪniən, -z
Albany
BR ˈɔːlbəni, ˈɒlbəni
AM ˈɔlbəni, ˈɑlbəni
albata
BR alˈbeɪtə(r)
AM ælˈbædə
albatross
BR ˈalbətrɒs, -ɪz
AM ˈælbə͵trɔs,
ˈælbə͵trɑs, -əz
albedo
BR alˈbiːdəʊ, -z
AM ælˈbidoʊ, -z
Albee
BR ˈɔːlbi, ˈalbi
AM ˈælbi
albeit
BR ɔːlˈbiːɪt
AM ælˈbiɪt, ɔlˈbiɪt,
alˈbiɪt
Albemarle
BR ˈalbəmɑːl
AM ˈælbə͵mɑr(ə)l
Albert
BR ˈalbət
AM ˈælbərt
Alberta
BR alˈbəːtə(r)
AM ælˈbərdə
Albertan
BR alˈbəːt(ə)n, -z
AM ælˈbərd(ə)n, -z
Alberti
BR alˈbəːti
AM alˈbərdi

Albertus Magnus
BR al͵bəːtəs ˈmagnəs
AM æl͵bərdəs
ˈmægnəs
albescence
BR alˈbɛsns
AM ælˈbɛsəns
albescent
BR alˈbɛsnt
AM ælˈbɛsənt
Albigenses
BR ͵albɪˈdʒɛnsiːz,
͵albɪˈgɛnsiːz
AM ͵ælbəˈdʒɛnsiz
Albigensian
BR ͵albɪˈdʒɛnsɪən,
͵albɪˈgɛnsɪən, -z
AM ͵ælbəˈdʒɛn(t)sɪən,
͵ælbəˈdʒɛn(t)ʃən, -z
albinism
BR ˈalbɪnɪz(ə)m
AM ˈælbə͵nɪzəm
albino
BR alˈbiːnəʊ, -z
AM ælˈbaɪ͵noʊ, -z
Albinoni
BR ͵albɪˈnəʊni
AM ͵ælbəˈnoʊni
albinotic
BR ͵albɪˈnɒtɪk
AM ͵ælbəˈnɑdɪk
Albion
BR ˈalbɪən
AM ˈælbiən
albite
BR ˈalbʌɪt
AM ˈæl͵baɪt
Ålborg
BR ˈɔːlbɔːg, ˈɑːlbɔːg
AM ˈɔl͵bɔrg, ˈɑl͵bɔrg
DAN ˈʌl͵bɒː
Albright
BR ˈɔːlbrʌɪt, ˈɒlbrʌɪt
AM ˈɔlbraɪt, ˈalbraɪt
album
BR ˈalbəm, -z
AM ˈælbəm, -z
albumen
BR ˈalbjʊmɪn
AM ˈælˈbjumən
albumin
BR ˈalbjʊmɪn
AM ˈælˈbjumən
albuminoid
BR alˈbjuːmɪnɔɪd, -z
AM ælˈbjuməˌnɔɪd, -z
albuminous
BR alˈbjuːmɪnəs
AM ælˈbjumənəs
albuminuria
BR al͵bjuːmɪˈnjʊərɪə(r)
AM æl͵bjuməˈnʊriə
Albuquerque
BR ˈalbəkəːki
AM ˈælbə͵kərki
alburnum
BR alˈbəːnəm

AM æl'bɜːnəm

Albury
BR 'ɔːlb(ə)ri, 'ɒlb(ə)ri
AM 'ɔːlbəri, 'ɑlbəri

Alcaeus
BR 'alsɪəs, al'siːəs
AM 'æl,siəs

alcahest
BR 'alkəhɛst
AM 'ælkə,hɛst

alcaic
BR al'keɪɪk
AM æl'keɪɪk

alcalde
BR al'kaldｊi, al'kɑːldｊi, -ɪz
AM al'kaldi, æl'kaldi, -z

Alcan®
BR 'alkan
AM 'ælkæn

Alcatraz
BR 'alkətraz, ,alkə'traz
AM 'ælkə,træz

Alcazar
BR ,alkə'zɑː(r), al'kazə(r)
AM ,alkə,zar, ,æl'kæzər

Alceste
BR al'sɛst
AM ɔl'sɛst, ɑl'sɛst

Alcester
BR 'ɔːlstə(r)
AM 'ɔlsɛstər, 'ɑlsɛstər

Alcestis
BR al'sɛstɪs
AM ɔl'sɛstəs, ɑl'sɛstəs

alchemic
BR al'kɛmɪk
AM æl'kɛmɪk

alchemical
BR al'kɛmɪkl
AM æl'kɛməkəl

alchemise
BR 'alkəmʌɪz, -ɪz, -ɪŋ, -d
AM 'ælkə,maɪz, -ɪz, -ɪŋ, -d

alchemist
BR 'alkəmɪst, -s
AM 'ælkəməst, -s

alchemize
BR 'alkəmʌɪz, -ɪz, -ɪŋ, -d
AM 'ælkə,maɪz, -ɪz, -ɪŋ, -d

alchemy
BR 'alkəmi
AM 'ælkəmi

alcheringa
BR ,altʃə'rɪŋgə(r)
AM ,æltʃə'rɪŋgə

Alcibiades
BR ,alsɪ'bʌɪədiːz
AM ,ælsə'baɪədiz

alcid
BR 'alsɪd, -z
AM 'ælsəd, -z

Alcock
BR 'ɔːlkɒk, 'alkɒk
AM 'ɔl,kak, 'al,kak

alcohol
BR 'alkəhɒl, -z
AM 'ælkə,hɔl, 'ælkə,hal, -z

alcoholic
BR ,alkə'hɒlɪk
AM ,ælkə'hɔlɪk, ,ælkə'halɪk

alcoholism
BR 'alkəhɒlɪz(ə)m, 'alkəhəlɪz(ə)m
AM 'ælkə,hɔ,lɪzəm, 'ælkə,ha,lɪzəm

alcoholometer
BR ,alkəhɒ'lɒmɪtə(r), -z
AM ,ælkə,hɔ'lamədər, ,ælkə,ha'lamədər, -z

alcoholometry
BR ,alkəhɒ'lɒmɪtri
AM ,ælkə,hɔ'lamətri, ,ælkə,ha'lamətri

Alconbury
BR 'ɔːlk(ə)nb(ə)ri, 'ɒlk(ə)nb(ə)ri
AM 'ɔlkənbəri, 'alkənbəri

Alcoran
BR ,alkə'rɑːn, 'alkəran
AM ,alkoʊ'ran

Alcott
BR 'ɔːlkət, 'ɔːlkɒt, 'ɒlkət, 'ɒlkɒt
AM 'æl,kat

alcove
BR 'alkəʊv, -z
AM 'æl,koʊv, -z

Alcuin
BR 'alkwɪn
AM 'ælkwən

Aldabra
BR al'dabrə(r)
AM æl'dæbrə

Aldebaran
BR al'dɛb(ə)rən, al'dɛb(ə)rn
AM æl'dɛbərən

Aldeburgh
BR 'ɔːl(d)b(ə)rə(r)
AM 'ɑl(d),bəroʊ

aldehyde
BR 'aldɪhʌɪd, -z
AM 'ældə,haɪd, -z

aldehydic
BR ,aldɪ'hɪdɪk
AM ,ældə'hɪdɪk

Alden
BR 'ɔːld(ə)n, 'ɒld(ə)n
AM 'ɔldən, 'aldən

al dente
BR al 'dɛnti, + 'dɛnteɪ
AM ,æl 'dɛn(t)eɪ, al +

alder
BR 'ɔːldə(r), 'ɒldə(r), -z
AM 'ɔldər, 'aldər, -z

Aldergrove
BR 'ɔːldəgrəʊv, 'ɒldəgrəʊv
AM 'ɔldər,groʊv, 'aldər,groʊv

alderman
BR 'ɔːldəmən, 'ɒldəmən
AM 'ɔldərmən, 'aldərmən

aldermanic
BR ,ɔːldə'manɪk, ,ɒldə'manɪk
AM ,ɔldər'mænɪk, ,aldər'mænɪk

aldermanry
BR 'ɔːldəmənri, 'ɒldəmənri
AM 'ɔldərmənri, 'aldərmənri

aldermanship
BR 'ɔːldəmənʃɪp, 'ɒldəmənʃɪp
AM 'ɔldərmən,ʃɪp, 'aldərmən,ʃɪp

Aldermaston
BR 'ɔːldəmɑːst(ə)n, 'ɔːldəmast(ə)n, 'ɒldəmɑːst(ə)n, 'ɒldəmast(ə)n
AM 'ɔldər,mæstən, 'aldər,mæstən

aldermen
BR 'ɔːldəmən, 'ɒldəmən
AM 'ɔldərmən, 'aldərmən

Alderney
BR 'ɔːldəni, 'ɒldəni
AM 'ɔldərni, 'aldərni

Aldersgate
BR 'ɔːldəzgeɪt, 'ɒldəzgeɪt
AM 'ɔldərs,geɪt, 'aldərs,geɪt

Aldershot
BR 'ɔːldəʃɒt, 'ɒldəʃɒt
AM 'ɔldər,ʃat, 'aldər,ʃat

Alderson
BR 'ɔːldəs(ə)n, 'ɒldəs(ə)n
AM 'ɔldərsən, 'aldərsən

Alderton
BR 'ɔːldət(ə)n, 'ɒldət(ə)n
AM 'ɔldərt(ə)n, 'aldərt(ə)n

alderwoman
BR 'ɔːldə,wʊmən, 'ɒldə,wʊmən
AM 'ɔldər,wʊmən, 'aldər,wʊmən

alderwomen
BR 'ɔːldə,wɪmɪn, 'ɒldə,wɪmɪn
AM 'ɔldər,wɪmɪn, 'aldər,wɪmɪn

Aldgate
BR 'ɔːl(d)geɪt, 'ɒl(d)geɪt, 'ɔːl(d)geɪt, 'ɒl(d)geɪt
AM 'ɔl(d),geɪt, 'al(d),geɪt

Aldine
BR 'ɔːldʌɪn, 'ɔːldiːn, 'ɒldʌɪn, 'ɒldiːn
AM 'ɔl,daɪn, 'ɔldin, 'al,daɪn, 'aldin

Aldis
BR 'ɔːldɪs, 'ɒldɪs
AM 'ɔldəs, 'aldəs

Aldiss
BR 'ɔːldɪs, 'ɒldɪs
AM 'ɔldəs, 'aldəs

aldol
BR 'aldɒl
AM 'æl,dɒl, 'æl,dal

aldosterone
BR al'dɒstərəʊn
AM ,æl'dastə,roʊn

Aldous
BR 'ɔːldəs, 'ɒldəs
AM 'ɔldəs, 'aldəs

Aldridge
BR 'ɔːldrɪdʒ, 'ɒldrɪdʒ
AM 'ɔldrɪdʒ, 'aldrɪdʒ

Aldrin
BR 'ɔːldrɪn, 'ɒldrɪn
AM 'ɔldrɪn, 'aldrɪn

Aldwych
BR 'ɔːldwɪtʃ, 'ɒldwɪtʃ
AM 'ɔldwɪtʃ, 'aldwɪtʃ

ale
BR eɪl, -z
AM eɪl, -z

aleatoric
BR ,eɪlɪə'tɒrɪk, ,alɪə'tɒrɪk
AM ,eɪlɪə'tɔrɪk, ,ælɪə'tɔrɪk

aleatory
BR ,eɪlɪ'eɪt(ə)ri, ,alɪ'eɪt(ə)ri, 'eɪlɪət(ə)ri, 'alɪət(ə)ri
AM ,eɪlɪə,tɔri, 'ælɪə,tɔri

Alec
BR 'alɪk
AM 'ælək

alecost
BR 'eɪlkɒst
AM 'eɪl,kast

alee
BR ə'liː
AM ə'li

alegar
BR 'eɪlɪgə(r), 'alɪgə(r)
AM 'æləgər, 'eɪləgər

alehouse
BR 'eɪlhaʊｓ, -zɪz
AM 'eɪl,(h)aʊｓ, -zəz

Aleksandrovsk
BR ˌalɪgzan'drɒfsk,
ˌalɪg'zandrɒfsk,
ˌalɪksan'drɒfsk,
ˌalɪk'sandrɒfsk
AM ˌæləg'zændrɒvsk,
ˌælək'sændrɒvsk,
ˌæləg'zændrɑvsk,
ˌælək'sændrɑvsk

alembic
BR ə'lɛmbɪk, -s
AM ə'lɛmbɪk, -s

alembicated
BR ə'lɛmbɪkeɪtɪd
AM ə'lɛmbəˌkeɪdɪd

alembication
BR əˌlɛmbɪ'keɪʃn
AM əˌlɛmbə'keɪʃən

aleph
BR 'alɛf, 'ɑːlɛf, 'alɪf,
'ɑːlɪf, -s
AM 'ɑlɛf, 'ɑləf, -s

Aleppo
BR ə'lɛpəʊ
AM ə'lɛpoʊ

alert
BR ə'ləːt, -s, -ɪŋ, -ɪd, -ɪst
AM ə'lɜr|t, -ts, -dɪŋ,
-dəd, -dəst

alertly
BR ə'ləːtli
AM ə'lɜrtli

alertness
BR ə'ləːtnəs
AM ə'lɜrtnəs

aleuron
BR 'aljʊrən
AM 'æljəˌroʊn,
ə'lʊroʊn

aleurone
BR 'aljʊrəʊn
AM 'æljəˌroʊn,
ə'lʊroʊn

Aleut
BR 'aljuːt, 'alɪuːt,
ə'l(j)uːt, -s
AM 'ælut, 'æliˌut, -s

Aleutian
BR ə'l(j)uːʃn, -z
AM ə'l(j)uʃən, -z

alewife
BR 'eɪlwʌɪf
AM 'eɪlˌwaɪf

alewives
BR 'eɪlwʌɪvz
AM 'eɪlˌwaɪvz

Alex
BR 'alɪks
AM 'ælɛks

Alexa
BR ə'lɛksə(r)
AM ə'lɛksə

Alexander
BR ˌalɪg'zɑːndə(r),
ˌalɪg'zandə(r)
AM ˌæləg'zændər

alexanders
BR ˌalɪg'zɑːndəz,
ˌalɪg'zandəz
AM ˌæləg'zændərz

Alexandra
BR ˌalɪg'zɑːndrə(r),
ˌalɪg'zandrə(r)
AM ˌæləg'zændrə

Alexandretta
BR ˌalɪgzɑːn'drɛtə(r),
ˌalɪgzan'drɛtə(r)
AM ˌæləgˌzæn'drɛdə

Alexandria
BR ˌalɪg'zɑːndrɪə(r),
ˌalɪg'zandrɪə(r)
AM ˌæləg'zændrɪə

Alexandrian
BR ˌalɪg'zɑːndrɪən,
ˌalɪg'zandrɪən, -z
AM ˌæləg'zændrɪən, -z

alexandrine
BR ˌalɪg'zɑːndrʌɪn,
ˌalɪg'zɑːndrɪn,
ˌalɪg'zandrʌɪn,
ˌalɪg'zandrɪn, -z
AM ˌæləg'zændrən,
ˌæləg'zænˌdrin,
ˌæləg'zænˌdraɪn, -z

alexandrite
BR ˌalɪg'zɑːndrʌɪt,
ˌalɪg'zandrʌɪt
AM ˌæləg'zænˌdraɪt

alexia
BR ə'lɛksɪə(r)
AM ə'lɛksɪə

alexin
BR ə'lɛksɪn
AM ə'lɛksən

alexine
BR ə'lɛksiːn
AM ə'lɛkˌsin

alexipharmic
BR əˌlɛksɪ'fɑːmɪk
AM əˌlɛksə'fɑrmɪk

Alexis
BR ə'lɛksɪs
AM ə'lɛksəs

alfa
BR 'alfə(r), -z
AM 'ælfə, -z

Alfa-Laval
BR ˌalfələ'val
AM ˌælfələ'vɑl

alfalfa
BR al'falfə(r)
AM æl'fælfə

Alfa Romeo®
BR ˌalfə rə(ʊ)'meɪəʊ,
+ 'rəʊmɪəʊ, -z
AM ˌælfə ˌroʊ'meɪoʊ, -z

al-Fatah
BR al'fatə(r),
ˌalfa'tɑː(r)
AM ˌɑlfa'tɑ

alfisol
BR 'alfɪsɒl
AM 'ælfəˌsɒl 'ælfəˌsɑl

Alfonso
BR al'fɒnzəʊ,
al'fɒnsəʊ
AM æl'fɑnˌzoʊ,
æl'fɑnˌsoʊ

Alford
BR 'ɔːlfəd, 'ɒlfəd
AM 'ɔlfərd, 'ælfərd,
'ɑlfərd

Alfred
BR 'alfrɪd
AM 'ælfrəd

Alfreda
BR al'friːdə(r)
AM æl'frɛdə

alfresco
BR al'frɛskəʊ
AM æl'frɛskoʊ,
ɑl'frɛskoʊ

Alfreton
BR 'alfrɪt(ə)n,
'ɔːlfrɪt(ə)n, 'ɒlfrɪt(ə)n
AM 'ɔlfrədən,
'ælfrədən, 'ɑlfrədən,
'ɔlfrətn, 'ælfrətn,
'ɑlfrətn

Alfvén
BR 'alfveɪn, 'alfvən
AM 'ɑlˌveɪn
sw al've:n

alga
BR 'algə(r)
AM 'ælgə

algae
BR 'aldʒiː, 'algiː
AM 'ælˌdʒi

algal
BR 'algl
AM 'ælgəl

Algarve
BR al'gɑːv
AM ɑl'gɑrv
B PORT 'awgarvi
L PORT al'garvə

algebra
BR 'aldʒɪbrə(r)
AM 'ældʒəbrə

algebraic
BR ˌaldʒɪ'breɪɪk
AM ˌældʒə'breɪɪk

algebraical
BR ˌaldʒɪ'breɪɪkl
AM ˌældʒə'breɪɪkəl

algebraically
BR ˌaldʒɪ'breɪɪkli
AM ˌældʒə'breɪɪk(ə)li

algebraist
BR 'aldʒɪbreɪɪst,
ˌaldʒɪ'breɪɪst, -s
AM 'ældʒəˌbreɪɪst,
ˌældʒə'breɪɪst, -s

Algeciras
BR ˌaldʒɪ'sɪərəs
AM ˌældʒə'sɪrəs
SP ˌalxe'θiras,
ˌalhe'siras

Algeo
BR 'aldʒɪəʊ

Alger
AM 'ældʒioʊ

Alger
BR 'aldʒə(r)
AM 'ældʒər

Algeria
BR al'dʒɪərɪə(r)
AM æl'dʒɪrɪə

Algerian
BR al'dʒɪərɪən, -z
AM æl'dʒɪrɪən, -z

Algernon
BR 'aldʒənən,
'aldʒnən, 'aldʒənɒn,
'aldʒnɒn
AM 'ældʒərˌnɑn

algicide
BR 'aldʒɪsʌɪd, -z
AM 'ældʒəˌsaɪd, -z

algid
BR 'aldʒɪd
AM 'ældʒɪd

algidity
BR al'dʒɪdɪti
AM æl'dʒɪdɪdi

Algie
BR 'aldʒi
AM 'ældʒi

Algiers
BR al'dʒɪəz
AM æl'dʒɪ(ə)rz

alginate
BR 'aldʒɪneɪt,
'aldʒɪnət, -s
AM 'ældʒəˌneɪt,
'ældʒənət, -s

alginic
BR al'dʒɪnɪk
AM æl'dʒɪnɪk

Algipan
BR 'aldʒɪpan
AM 'ældʒɪˌpæn

Algoa
BR al'gəʊə(r)
AM æl'goʊə

algoid
BR 'algɔɪd
AM 'ælˌgɔɪd

Algol
BR 'algɒl
AM 'ælˌgɒl, 'ælˌgɑl

algolagnia
BR ˌalgə(ʊ)'lagnɪə(r)
AM ˌælgoʊ'lægnɪə

algolagnic
BR ˌalgə(ʊ)'lagnɪk
AM ˌælgoʊ'lægnɪk

algological
BR ˌaldʒɪ'lɒdʒɪkl
AM ˌælgə'lɑdʒəkəl

algologist
BR al'gɒlədʒɪst, -s
AM æl'gɑlədʒəst, -s

algology
BR al'gɒlədʒi
AM æl'gɑlədʒi

Algonkian
BR al'gɒŋkɪən

AM æl'gɑŋkiən
Algonkin
BR al'gɒŋkɪn
AM æl'gɑŋkən
Algonquian
BR al'gɒŋk(w)iən
AM æl'gɑŋk(w)iən
Algonquin
BR al'gɒŋk(w)ɪn
AM æl'gɑŋkwən
algorithm
BR 'algərɪð(ə)m, -z
AM 'ælgə,rɪðəm, -z
algorithmic
BR ,algə'rɪðmɪk
AM ,ælgə'rɪðmɪk
algorithmically
BR ,algə'rɪðmɪkli
AM ,ælgə'rɪðmɪk(ə)li
alguacil
BR ,algwə'sɪl,
,algwə'si:l, 'algwəsɪl,
'algwəsi:l, -z
AM ,ælgwə'sɪl,
,ælgwə'sɪl, -z
alguaciles
BR ,algwə'si:leɪz
AM ,ælgwə'sileɪz
alguazil
BR ,algwə'zɪl,
,algwə'zi:l, -z
AM ,ælgwə'zil,
,ælgwə'zɪl, -z
alguaziles
BR ,algwə'zi:leɪz
AM ,ælgwə'zileɪz
Algy
BR 'aldʒi
AM 'ældʒi
Alhambra
BR al'hambrə(r),
ə'lambrə(r)
AM æl'hæmbrə
SP a'lambra
Alhambresque
BR ,alham'brɛsk,
,aləm'brɛsk
AM ,æl,(h)æm'brɛsk
Ali¹
BR 'ali 'ɑːli
AM 'ɑli
Ali²
Muhammed, boxer
BR 'alí, ɑː'liː
AM ɑ'li
alias
BR 'eɪliəs, -ɪz
AM 'eɪliəs, -əz
Ali Baba
BR ,alɪ 'bɑːbə(r)
AM ,ɑli 'bɑbə
alibi
BR 'alɪbʌɪ, -z
AM 'ælə,baɪ, -z
Alicante
BR ,alɪ'kanti
AM ,ælə'kæn(t)i,
,ɑlə'kɑn(t)i

SP ali'kante
Alice
BR 'alɪs
AM 'æləs
Alicia
BR ə'lɪʃ(ɪ)ə(r),
ə'lɪsɪə(r)
AM ə'lɪʃə
Alick
BR 'alɪk
AM 'ælək
alicyclic
BR ,alɪ'sʌɪklɪk
AM ,ælə'saɪklɪk
alidad
BR 'alɪdad, -z
AM 'ælə,dæd, -z
alidade
BR 'alɪdeɪd, -z
AM 'ælə,deɪd, -z
alien
BR 'eɪliən, -z
AM 'eɪliən, 'eɪljən, -z
alienability
BR ,eɪliənə'bɪlɪti
AM ,eɪliənə'bɪlɪdi,
,eɪljənə'bɪlɪdi
alienable
BR 'eɪliənəbl
AM 'eɪliənəbəl,
'eɪljənəbəl
alienage
BR 'eɪliənɪdʒ
AM 'eɪliənɪdʒ,
'eɪljənɪdʒ
alienate
BR 'eɪliəneɪt, -s, -ɪŋ, -ɪd
AM 'eɪliə,neɪt,
'eɪljə,neɪ|t, -ts, -dɪŋ,
-dɪd
alienation
BR ,eɪliə'neɪʃn
AM ,eɪliə'neɪʃən,
,eɪljə'neɪʃən
alienator
BR 'eɪliəneɪtə(r), -z
AM 'eɪliə,neɪdər,
'eɪljə,neɪdər, -z
alienism
BR 'eɪliənɪz(ə)m
AM 'eɪliə,nɪzəm,
'eɪljə,nɪzəm
alienist
BR 'eɪliənɪst, -s
AM 'eɪliənəst,
'eɪljənəst, -s
alienness
BR 'eɪliənnəs
AM 'eɪliə(n)nəs,
'eɪljə(n)nəs
aliform
BR 'eɪlɪfɔːm, 'alɪfɔːm
AM 'ælə,fɔ(ə)rm,
'eɪlə,fɔ(ə)rm
alight
BR ə'lʌɪt, -s, -ɪŋ, -ɪd
AM ə'laɪ|t, -ts, -dɪŋ, -dɪd

align
BR ə'lʌɪn, -z, -ɪŋ, -d
AM ə'laɪn, -z, -ɪŋ, -d
alignment
BR ə'lʌɪnm(ə)nt, -s
AM ə'laɪnmənt, -s
alike
BR ə'lʌɪk
AM ə'laɪk
aliment
BR 'alɪm(ə)nt, -s
AM 'æləmənt, -s
alimental
BR ,alɪ'mentl
AM ,ælə'mɛn(t)l
alimentary
BR ,alɪ'ment(ə)ri
AM ,ælə'mɛn(t)əri
alimentation
BR ,alɪmɛn'teɪʃn,
,alɪm(ə)n'teɪʃn
AM ,æləmən'teɪʃən
alimony
BR 'alɪmən|i, -ɪz
AM 'ælə,moʊni, -z
aline
BR ə'lʌɪn, -z, -ɪŋ, -d
AM ə'laɪn, -z, -ɪŋ, -d
alineation
BR ə,lɪnɪ'eɪʃn, -z
AM ə,lɪni'eɪʃən, -z
alinement
BR ə'lʌɪnm(ə)nt, -s
AM ə'laɪnmənt, -s
aliphatic
BR ,alɪ'fatɪk
AM ,ælə'fædɪk
aliquant
BR 'alɪkw(ə)nt
AM 'ælə,kwɑnt,
'æləkwənt
aliquot
BR 'alɪkwɒt
AM 'ælə,kwɑt,
'æləkwɑt
Alisdair
BR 'alɪstə(r), 'alɪstɛː(r)
AM 'æləstər,
'æləs,tɛ(ə)r
Alison
BR 'alɪs(ə)n
AM 'æləsən
Alissa
BR ə'lɪsə(r)
AM ə'lɪsə
Alistair
BR 'alɪstə(r), 'alɪstɛː(r)
AM 'æləstər,
'æləs,tɛ(ə)r
Alitalia®
BR ,alɪ'talɪə(r)
AM ,ɑlə'tɑljə,
,ælə'tæljə, ,ɑlə'tɑliə,
,ælə'tæliə
alive
BR ə'lʌɪv
AM ə'laɪv

aliveness
BR ə'lʌɪvnɪs
AM ə'laɪvnɪs
Alix
BR 'alɪks
AM 'æləks
aliyah
BR ə'li:ə(r)
AM ə'liə
alizarin
BR ə'lɪz(ə)rɪn
AM ə'lɪzərən
alizarine
BR ə'lɪz(ə)ri:n
AM ə'lɪzərən, ə'lɪzə,rin
alkahest
BR 'alkəhɛst
AM 'ælkə,hɛst
alkalescence
BR ,alkə'lɛsns
AM ,ælkə'lɛsəns
alkalescency
BR ,alkə'lɛsnsi
AM ,ælkə'lɛsənsi
alkalescent
BR ,alkə'lɛsnt
AM ,ælkə'lɛsənt
alkali
BR 'alkəlʌɪ, -z
AM 'ælkə,laɪ, -z
alkalify
BR al'kalɪfʌɪ,
'alkəlɪfʌɪ, -z, -ɪŋ, -d
AM 'ælkələ,faɪ, -z, -ɪŋ,
-d
alkalimeter
BR ,alkə'lɪmɪtə(r), -z
AM ,ælkə'lɪmədər, -z
alkalimetry
BR ,alkə'lɪmɪtri
AM ,ælkə'lɪmətri
alkaline
BR 'alkəlʌɪn
AM 'ælkələn,
'ælkə,laɪn
alkalinity
BR ,alkə'lɪnɪti
AM ,ælkə'lɪnɪdi
alkaloid
BR 'alkəlɔɪd, -z
AM 'ælkə,lɔɪd, -z
alkaloidal
BR ,alkə'lɔɪdl
AM ,ælkə'lɔɪdəl
alkaloses
BR ,alkə'ləusi:z
AM ,ælkə'lousiz
alkalosis
BR ,alkə'ləusɪs
AM ,ælkə'lousəs
alkane
BR 'alkeɪn, -z
AM 'æl,keɪn, -z
alkanet
BR 'alkənɛt, -s
AM 'ælkə,nɛt, -s

Alka-Seltzer®
BR ˌalkəˈsɛltsə(r),
'alkəˌsɛltsə(r), -z
AM 'ælkəˌsɛl(t)sər, -z

alkene
BR 'alkiːn, -z
AM 'ælˌkin, -z

alkyd
BR 'alkɪd
AM 'ælˌkɪd

alkyl
BR 'alkɪl, 'alkʌɪl, -z
AM 'ælˌkɪl, 'ælkəl, -z

alkylate
BR 'alkɪleɪt, -s, -ɪŋ, -ɪd
AM 'ælkəˌleɪ|t, -ts, -dɪŋ, -dɪd

alkyne
BR 'alkʌɪn, -z
AM 'ælkaɪn, -z

all
BR ɔːl
AM ɔl, ɑl

alla breve
BR ˌalə 'breɪvi, ˌɑːlə +, + 'brɛvi, + 'breɪveɪ
AM ˌɑlə 'brɛv(ə)

alla cappella
BR ˌalə kəˈpɛlə(r), ˌɑːlə +
AM ˌɑlə kəˈpɛlə

Allah
BR 'alə(r)
AM 'ɑlə, 'ælə

Allahabad
BR ˌaləhəˈbad, ˌaləhəˈbɑːd
AM ˌɑləhəˈbɑd, ˌæləhəˈbæd

allamanda
BR ˌaləˈmandə(r)
AM ˌæləˈmændə

Allan
BR 'alən
AM 'ælən

allanite
BR 'alənʌɪt
AM 'æləˌnaɪt

allantoic
BR ˌalənˈtəʊɪk
AM ˌælənˈtoʊɪk

allantoid
BR əˈlantɔɪd
AM əˈlæntɔɪd

allantoides
BR əˈlantəʊɪdiːz
AM ˈælənˈtɔɪdiz

allantoin
BR əˈlantəʊɪn
AM əˈlæntoʊən

allantois
BR əˈlantəʊɪs
AM əˈlæntəwəs

Allaun
BR əˈlɔːn
AM 'ælɔn, 'ælɑn

allay
BR əˈleɪ, -z, -ɪŋ, -d
AM əˈleɪ, æˈleɪ, -z, -ɪŋ, -d

Allbeury
BR ɔːlˈbjʊəri
AM 'ɔlbəri, 'ɑlbəri

allegation
BR ˌalɪˈgeɪʃn, -z
AM ˌæləˈgeɪʃən, -z

allege
BR əˈlɛdʒ, -ɪz, -ɪŋ, -d
AM əˈlɛdʒ, -əz, -ɪŋ, -d

alleged
BR əˈlɛdʒ(ɪ)d
AM əˈlɛdʒ(ə)d

allegedly
BR əˈlɛdʒɪdli
AM əˈlɛdʒədli

Alleghany
BR ˌalɪˈgeɪn|i, -ɪz
AM ˌæləˈgeɪni, -z

Allegheny
BR ˌalɪˈgeɪn|i, -ɪz
AM ˌæləˈgeɪni, -z

allegiance
BR əˈliːdʒ(ə)ns, -ɪz
AM əˈlidʒəns, -əz

allegiant
BR əˈliːdʒ(ə)nt
AM əˈlidʒənt

allegoric
BR ˌalɪˈgɒrɪk
AM ˌæləˈgɔrɪk

allegorical
BR ˌalɪˈgɒrɪkl
AM ˌæləˈgɔrəkəl

allegorically
BR ˌalɪˈgɒrɪkli
AM ˌæləˈgɔrək(ə)li

allegorisation
BR ˌalɪg(ə)rʌɪˈzeɪʃn
AM ˌæləˌgɔrəˈzeɪʃən, ˌæləgəˌraɪˈzeɪʃən

allegorise
BR ˌalɪg(ə)rʌɪz, -ɪz, -ɪŋ, -d
AM ˈæləˌgɔˌraɪz, ˈæləgəˌraɪz, -ɪz, -ɪŋ, -d

allegorist
BR ˈalɪg(ə)rɪst, -s
AM ˈæləgərəst, 'æləˌgɔrəst, -s

allegorization
BR ˌalɪg(ə)rʌɪˈzeɪʃn
AM ˌæləˌgɔrəˈzeɪʃən, ˌæləgəˌraɪˈzeɪʃən

allegorize
BR ˌalɪg(ə)rʌɪz, -ɪz, -ɪŋ, -d
AM ˈæləˌgɔˌraɪz, ˈæləgəˌraɪz, -ɪz, -ɪŋ, -d

allegory
BR ˈalɪg(ə)r|i, -ɪz
AM ˈæləˌgɔri, -z

allegretto
BR ˌalɪˈgrɛtəʊ, -z
AM ˌæləˈgrɛdoʊ, -z

allegro
BR əˈlɛgrəʊ, əˈleɪgrəʊ, -z
AM əˈlɛgroʊ, -z

allel
BR əˈlɛl, 'alɛl, -z
AM əˈlɛl, -z

allele
BR əˈliːl, 'aliːl, -z
AM əˈlil, -z

allelic
BR əˈliːlɪk, əˈlɛlɪk
AM əˈlilɪk, əˈlɛlɪk

allelomorph
BR əˈliːlə(ʊ)mɔːf, əˈlɛlə(ʊ)mɔːf, -s
AM əˈlɛləˌmɔ(ə)rf, əˈliləˌmɔ(ə)rf, -s

allelomorphic
BR əˌliːlə(ʊ)ˈmɔːfɪk, əˌlɛlə(ʊ)ˈmɔːfɪk
AM əˌlɛləˈmɔrfɪk, əˌliləˈmɔrfɪk

alleluia
BR ˌalɪˈluːjə(r), -z
AM ˌæləˈlujə, -z

allemande
BR ˈalɪmand, -z
AM ˈæləˌmænd, -z

Allen
BR 'alən
AM 'ælən

Allenby
BR 'alənbi
AM 'ælənbi

Allende
BR ʌ(j)ˈɛndeɪ, ʌ(j)ˈɛndi
AM ɑˈjɛnˌdeɪ
SP aˈjende, aˈʒende

Allentown
BR 'aləntaʊn
AM 'ælənˌtaʊn

allergen
BR 'alədʒɛn, 'alədʒ(ə)n
AM 'ælərˌdʒɛn, 'ælərdʒ(ə)n

allergenic
BR ˌaləˈdʒɛnɪk
AM ˌælərˈdʒɛnɪk

allergic
BR əˈləːdʒɪk
AM əˈlərdʒɪk

allergist
BR 'alədʒɪst, -s
AM 'ælərdʒəst, -s

allergy
BR 'alədʒ|i, -ɪz
AM 'ælərdʒi, -z

Allerton
BR 'alət(ə)n, 'ɒlət(ə)n
AM 'ælərt(ə)n

alleviate
BR əˈliːvɪeɪt, -s, -ɪŋ, -ɪd
AM əˈliviˌeɪ|t, -ts, -dɪŋ, -dɪd

alleviation
BR əˌliːvɪˈeɪʃn
AM əˌliviˈeɪʃən

alleviative
BR əˈliːvɪətɪv
AM əˈliviədɪv, əˈliviˌeɪdɪv

alleviator
BR əˈliːvɪeɪtə(r), -z
AM əˈliviˌeɪdər, -z

alleviatory
BR əˈliːvɪət(ə)ri
AM əˈliviəˌtɔri

alley
BR 'al|i, -ɪz
AM 'æli, -z

Alleyn
BR 'alɪn
AM 'ælən

Alleyne
BR aˈleɪn, aˈliːn, 'alɪn
AM əˈleɪn

alleyway
BR 'alɪweɪ, -z
AM 'æliˌweɪ, -z

alliaceous
BR ˌalɪˈeɪʃəs
AM ˌæliˈeɪʃəs

alliance
BR əˈlʌɪəns, -ɪz
AM əˈlaɪəns, -əz

allicin
BR 'alɪsɪn, -z
AM 'æləsən, -z

Allie
BR 'ali
AM 'æli

allied
BR 'alʌɪd
AM əˈlaɪd, 'æˌlaɪd

alligator
BR 'alɪgeɪtə(r), -z
AM 'æləˌgeɪdər, -z

allineation
BR əˌlɪnɪˈeɪʃn, -z
AM əˌliniˈeɪʃən, -z

Allinson
BR 'alɪns(ə)n
AM 'ɔlɪnsən, 'ɑlɪnsən

Allison
BR 'alɪs(ə)n
AM 'æləsən

alliterate
BR əˈlɪtəreɪt, -s, -ɪŋ, -ɪd
AM əˈlɪdəˌreɪ|t, -ts, -dɪŋ, -dɪd

alliteration
BR əˌlɪtəˈreɪʃn, -z
AM əˌlɪdəˈreɪʃən, -z

alliterative
BR əˈlɪt(ə)rətɪv
AM əˈlɪdərədɪv, əˈlɪdəˌreɪdɪv

allium
BR 'alɪəm, -z
AM 'æliəm, -z

all-nighter
BR ˌɔːlˈnʌɪtə(r), -z
AM ˌɔlˈnaɪdər,
ˌɑlˈnaɪdər, -z

Alloa
BR ˈaləʊə(r)
AM ɑˈloʊə

allocable
BR ˈaləkəbl
AM ˈæləkəbəl

allocate
BR ˈaləkeɪt, -s, -ɪŋ, -ɪd
AM ˈæləˌkeɪ|t, -ts, -dɪŋ, -dɪd

allocation
BR ˌaləˈkeɪʃn, -z
AM ˌæləˈkeɪʃən, -z

allocator
BR ˈaləkeɪtə(r), -z
AM ˈæləˌkeɪdər, -z

allochthonous
BR əˈlɒkθənəs
AM əˈlɑkθənəs,
æˈlɑkθənəs

allocution
BR ˌaləˈkjuːʃn
AM ˌæləˈkjuʃən

allodia
BR əˈləʊdɪə(r)
AM əˈloʊdiə

allodial
BR əˈləʊdɪəl, -z
AM əˈloʊdiəl, -z

allodium
BR əˈləʊdɪəm
AM əˈloʊdiəm

allogamy
BR əˈlɒgəmi
AM əˈlɑgəmi,
æˈlɑgəmi

allograft
BR ˈaləgrɑːft, ˈaləgraft, -s
AM ˈæləˌgræft, -s

allograph
BR ˈaləgrɑːf, ˈaləgraf, -s
AM ˈæləˌgræf, -s

allographic
BR ˌaləˈgrafɪk
AM ˌæləˈgræfɪk

allomorph
BR ˈaləmɔːf, -s
AM ˈæləˌmɔ(ə)rf, -s

allomorphic
BR ˌaləˈmɔːfɪk
AM ˌæləˈmɔrfɪk

allomorphically
BR ˌaləˈmɔːfɪkli
AM ˌæləˈmɔrfək(ə)li

allopath
BR ˈaləpaθ, -s
AM ˈæləˌpæθ, -s

allopathic
BR ˌaləˈpaθɪk
AM ˌæləˈpæθɪk

allopathist
BR əˈlɒpəθɪst, -s
AM əˈlɑpəθəst,
æˈlɑpəθəst, -s

allopathy
BR əˈlɒpəθi
AM əˈlɑpəθi, æˈlɑpəθi

allopatric
BR ˌaləˈpatrɪk,
ˌaləˈpeɪtrɪk
AM ˌæləˈpætrɪk,
ˌæləˈpeɪtrɪk

allophone
BR ˈaləfəʊn, -z
AM ˈæləfoʊn, -z

allophonic
BR ˌaləˈfɒnɪk
AM ˌæləˈfɑnɪk

allopolyploid
BR ˌaləˈpɒləplɔɪd, -z
AM ˌæləˈpɑləˌplɔɪd, -z

allot
BR əˈlɒt, -s, -ɪŋ, -ɪd
AM əˈlɑ|t, -ts, -dɪŋ, -təd

allotment
BR əˈlɒtm(ə)nt, -s
AM əˈlɑtmənt, -s

allotrope
BR ˈalətrəʊp, -s
AM ˈæləˌtroʊp, -s

allotropic
BR ˌaləˈtrɒpɪk,
ˌaləˈtrəʊpɪk
AM ˌæləˈtrɑpɪk

allotropical
BR ˌaləˈtrɒpɪkl
AM ˌæləˈtrɑpəkəl

allotropy
BR əˈlɒtrəpi
AM əˈlɑtrəpi

Allott
BR ˈalət
AM ˈælət

allottee
BR ˌaləˈtiː, -z
AM əˌlɑˈti, ˌæləˈti, -z

allow
BR əˈlaʊ, -z, -ɪŋ, -d
AM əˈlaʊ, -z, -ɪŋ, -d

allowable
BR əˈlaʊəbl
AM əˈlaʊəbəl

allowableness
BR əˈlaʊəblnəs
AM əˈlaʊəbəlnəs

allowably
BR əˈlaʊəbli
AM əˈlaʊəbli

allowance
BR əˈlaʊəns, -ɪz
AM əˈlaʊəns, -əz

Alloway
BR ˈaləweɪ
AM ˈæləˌweɪ

allowedly
BR əˈlaʊɪdli
AM əˈlaʊədli

alloy¹
noun
BR ˈalɔɪ, -z
AM ˈæˌlɔɪ, -z

alloy²
verb
BR əˈlɔɪ, -z, -ɪŋ, -d
AM ˈæˌlɔɪ, əˈlɔɪ, -z, -ɪŋ, -d

allseed
BR ˈɔːlsiːd
AM ˈɔlˌsid, ˈɑlˌsid

Allsop
BR ˈɔːlsɒp, ˈɒlsɒp
AM ˈɔlsap, ˈɑlsap

Allsopp
BR ˈɔːlsɒp, ˈɒlsɒp
AM ˈɔlsap, ˈɑlsap

allsorts
BR ˈɔːlsɔːts
AM ˈɔlˌsɔ(ə)rts,
ˈɑlˌsɔ(ə)rts

allspice
BR ˈɔːlspʌɪs
AM ˈɔlˌspaɪs, ˈɑlˌspaɪs

Allston
BR ˈɔːlst(ə)n, ˈɒlst(ə)n
AM ˈɔlstən, ˈɑlstən

allude
BR əˈl(j)uːd, -z, -ɪŋ, -ɪd
AM əˈlud, -z, -ɪŋ, -əd

allure
BR əˈl(j)ʊə(r), əˈljɔː(r), -z, -ɪŋ, -d
AM əˈlu(ə)r, æˈlu(ə)r, əˈlʊr, æˈlʊr, -z, -ɪŋ, -d

allurement
BR əˈl(j)ʊəm(ə)nt, əˈljɔːm(ə)nt, -s
AM əˈlʊrmənt, -s

allusion
BR əˈl(j)uːʒn, -z
AM əˈluʒən, æˈluʒən, -z

allusive
BR əˈl(j)uːsɪv
AM əˈlusɪv, æˈlusɪv, əˈluzɪv, æˈluzɪv

allusively
BR əˈl(j)uːsɪvli
AM əˈlusɪvli, æˈlusɪvli, əˈluzɪvli, æˈluzɪvli

allusiveness
BR əˈl(j)uːsɪvnɪs
AM əˈlusɪvnɪs, æˈlusɪvnɪs, əˈluzɪvnɪs, æˈluzɪvnɪs

alluvia
BR əˈl(j)uːvɪə(r)
AM əˈluviə

alluvial
BR əˈl(j)uːvɪəl
AM əˈluviəl

alluvion
BR əˈl(j)uːvɪən
AM əˈluviən

alluvium
BR əˈl(j)uːvɪəm
AM əˈluviəm

Ally
BR ˈali
AM ˈæli

ally¹
noun, friend
BR ˈalʌɪ, -z
AM ˈæˌlaɪ, əˈlaɪ, -z

ally²
noun, marble
BR ˈal|i, -ɪz
AM ˈæli, -z

ally³
verb
BR əˈlʌɪ, -z, -ɪŋ, -d
AM əˈlaɪ, æˈlaɪ, ˈæˌlaɪ, -z, -ɪŋ, -d

allyl
BR ˈalʌɪl, ˈalɪl, -z
AM ˈælɪl, -z

Alma
BR ˈalmə(r)
AM ˈælmə

Alma-Ata
BR ˌalˌmɑː(r)əˈtɑː(r)
AM ɑlˌmɑɑˈta
RUS alˈmaaˈta

Almagest
BR ˈalmədʒɛst
AM ˈælməˌdʒɛst

alma mater
BR ˌalmə ˈmɑːtə(r), + ˈmeɪtə(r), -z
AM ˌɑlmə ˈmɑdər, ˌælmə +, -z

almanac
BR ˈɔːlmənak, ˈɒlmənak, ˈalmənak, -s
AM ˈɔlməˌnæk, ˈælməˌnæk, ˈɑlməˌnæk, -s

almanack
BR ˈɔːlmənak, ˈɒlmənak, ˈalmənak, -s
AM ˈɔlməˌnæk, ˈælməˌnæk, ˈɑlməˌnæk, -s

almandine
BR ˈalmændiːn, ˈalmændʌɪn, -z
AM ˈɑ(l)mənˌdin, ˈæ(l)mənˌdin, -z

Alma-Tadema
BR ˈalməˈtadɪmə(r)
AM ˌɑlməˈtadəmə

Almería
BR ˌalməˈriːə(r)
AM ˌɑlməˈriə

almightily
BR ɔːlˈmʌɪtɪli, ɔːlˈmʌɪtli
AM ɔlˈmaɪdɪli, ɑlˈmaɪdɪli

almightiness
BR ɔːlˈmʌɪtɪnɪs
AM ɔlˈmaɪdɪnɪs, ɑlˈmaɪdɪnɪs

almighty
BR ɔːlˈmʌɪti
AM ɔlˈmaɪdi, alˈmaɪdi
almirah
BR alˈmʌɪrə(r), -z
AM ælˈmaɪrə, -z
almond
BR ˈɑː(l)mənd, ˈalmənd, ˈɒlmənd, -z
AM ˈɑ(l)mənd, ˈæ(l)mənd, -z
almoner
BR ˈɑː(l)mənə(r), ˈalmənə(r), ˈɒlmənə(r), -z
AM ˈæ(l)mənər, ˈɑ(l)mənər, -z
almonry
BR ˈɑː(l)mənri, ˈalmənri, ˈɒlmənri
AM ˈæ(l)mənri, ˈɑ(l)mənri
almost
BR ˈɔːlməʊst
AM ɔlˈmoʊst, ˈɔlmoʊst, alˈmoʊst, ˈalmoʊst
alms
BR ɑːmz
AM ɑ(l)mz
almshouse
BR ˈɑːmzhaʊ|s, -zɪz
AM ˈɑ(l)mz,(h)aʊ|s, -zəz
almsman
BR ˈɑːmzmən
AM ˈɑ(l)mzmən
almsmen
BR ˈɑːmzmən
AM ˈɑ(l)mzmən
almucantar
BR ˌalm(j)ʉˈkantə(r), -z
AM ˌælm(j)uˈkæn(t)ər, -z
Alne
BR ɔː(l)n, aln
AM ɔln, aln
Alnmouth
BR ˈalnmaʊθ
AM ˈɑlnməθ, ˈalnməθ
Alnwick
BR ˈanɪk
AM ˈɒlnwɪk, ˈalnwɪk
aloe
BR ˈaləʊ, -z
AM ˈæloʊ, -z
aloetic
BR ˌaləʊˈetɪk
AM ˌaloʊˈedɪk
aloe vera
BR ˌaləʊ ˈvɛrə(r), + ˈvɪərə(r)
AM ˌæloʊ ˈvɛrə
aloft
BR əˈlɒft
AM əˈlɔft, əˈlaft
alogical
BR eɪˈlɒdʒɪkl

AM eɪˈladʒəkəl
alogically
BR eɪˈlɒdʒɪkli
AM eɪˈladʒək(ə)li
aloha
BR əˈləʊ(h)ə(r)
AM əˈloʊˌ(h)ɑ
alone
BR əˈləʊn
AM əˈloʊn
aloneness
BR əˈləʊnnəs
AM əˈloʊ(n)nəs
along
BR əˈlɒŋ
AM əˈlɔŋ, əˈlaŋ
alongshore
BR əˈlɒŋˈʃɔː(r)
AM əˌlɒŋˈʃɔ(ə)r, əˌlaŋˈʃɔ(ə)r
alongside
BR əˈlɒŋsʌɪd, əˌlɒŋˈsʌɪd
AM əˌlɔŋˈsaɪd, əˌlaŋˈsaɪd
Alonzo
BR əˈlɒnzəʊ
AM əˈlanzoʊ
aloof
BR əˈluːf
AM əˈluf
aloofly
BR əˈluːfli
AM əˈlufli
aloofness
BR əˈluːfnəs
AM əˈlufnəs
alopecia
BR ˌaləˈpiːʃ(ɪ)ə(r)
AM ˌæləˈpiʃ(i)ə
aloud
BR əˈlaʊd
AM əˈlaʊd
alow
BR əˈləʊ
AM əˈloʊ
Aloysius
BR ˌaləʊˈɪʃəs
AM ˌæləˈwɪʃɪs
alp
BR alp, -s
AM ælp, -s
alpaca
BR alˈpakə(r), -z
AM ælˈpækə, -z
alpargata
BR ˌalpɑːˈgɑːtə(r), -z
AM ˌælpərˈgɑdə, -z
alpenglow
BR ˈalp(ə)ngləʊ
AM ˈælpənˌgloʊ
alpenhorn
BR ˈalp(ə)nhɔːn, -z
AM ˈælpənˌ(h)ɔ(ə)rn, -z
alpenstock
BR ˈalp(ə)nstɒk, -s

AM ˈælpənˌstak, -s
alpha
BR ˈalfə(r)
AM ˈælfə
alphabet
BR ˈalfəbet, -s
AM ˈælfəˌbet, -s
alphabetic
BR ˌalfəˈbetɪk
AM ˌælfəˈbedɪk
alphabetical
BR ˌalfəˈbetɪkl
AM ˌælfəˈbedəkəl
alphabetically
BR ˌalfəˈbetɪkli
AM ˌælfəˈbedək(ə)li
alphabetisation
BR ˌalfəbetʌɪˈzeɪʃn, ˌalfəbɪtʌɪˈzeɪʃn
AM ˌælfəbəˌtaɪˈzeɪʃən, ˌælfəˌbedəˈzeɪʃən
alphabetise
BR ˈalfəbətʌɪz, ˈalfəbɪtʌɪz, -ɪz, -ɪŋ, -d
AM ˈælfəbəˌtaɪz, -ɪz, -ɪŋ, -d
alphabetization
BR ˌalfəbetʌɪˈzeɪʃn, ˌalfəbɪtʌɪˈzeɪʃn
AM ˌælfəbəˌtaɪˈzeɪʃən, ˌælfəˌbedəˈzeɪʃən
alphabetize
BR ˈɑːlfəbetʌɪz, ˈalfəbətʌɪz, -ɪz, -ɪŋ, -d
AM ˈælfəbəˌtaɪz, -ɪz, -ɪŋ, -d
alphanumeric
BR ˌalfənjuːˈmerɪk, ˌalfənjʉˈmerɪk
AM ˌælfən(j)uˈmerɪk
alphanumerical
BR ˌalfənjuːˈmerɪkl, ˌalfənjʉˈmerɪkl
AM ˌælfən(j)uˈmerəkəl
alphanumerically
BR ˌalfənjuːˈmerɪkli, ˌalfənjʉˈmerɪkli
AM ˌælfən(j)uˈmerək-(ə)li
Alphege
BR ˈalfɪdʒ
AM ˈælfɪdʒ
Alphonso
BR alˈfɒnsəʊ, alˈfɒnzəʊ
AM ælˈfansoʊ, ælˈfanzoʊ
alphorn
BR ˈalphɔːn, -z
AM ˈalp,(h)ɔ(ə)rn, -z
alpine
BR ˈalpʌɪn
AM ˈælˌpaɪn
alpinism
BR ˈalpɪnɪz(ə)m
AM ˈælpəˌnɪzəm
alpinist
BR ˈalpɪnɪst, -s

AM ˈælpənˌstak, -s
Alport
BR ˈɔːlpɔːt
AM ˈɔlpɔ(ə)rt, ˈalpɔ(ə)rt
alprazolam
BR alˈpreɪzəlam
AM ælˈpreɪzəˌlæm
already
BR ɔːlˈrɛdi
AM ˌɔlˈrɛdi, ˌalˈrɛdi
Alresford
BR ˈɔːlzfəd
AM ˈɔlrɛsfɔ(ə)rd, ˈalrɛsfɔ(ə)rd
alright
BR ɔːlˈrʌɪt
AM ˌɔlˈraɪt, ˌalˈraɪt
Alsace
BR alˈsas
AM ˈælˈsæs, ˈalˈsæs, ˈælˈsas, ˈalˈsas
Alsager
BR ˈɔːlsədʒə(r), ɔːlˈseɪdʒə(r)
AM ˈɔlsɪdʒər, ˈalsɪdʒər
Alsatian
BR alˈseɪʃn, -z
AM ælˈseɪʃən, alˈseɪʃən, -z
alsike
BR ˈalsɪk
AM ˈælˌsɪk, ˈælˌsaɪk
also
BR ˈɔːlsəʊ, ˈɒlsəʊ
AM ˈɔlsoʊ, ˈalsoʊ
Alsop
BR ˈɔːlsɒp, ˈɒlsɒp
AM ˈɔlsap, ˈalsap
Alston
BR ˈɔːlst(ə)n, ˈɒlst(ə)n
AM ˈɔlstən, ˈalstən
alstroemeria
BR ˌalstrəˈmɪərɪə(r), -z
AM ˌælztrəˈmɪriə, ˌælstrəˈmɪriə, -z
alt
BR alt
AM alt
Altai
BR alˈtʌɪ, ɑːlˈtʌɪ
AM ˈælˌtaɪ, ˈalˌtaɪ
Altaic
BR alˈteɪɪk
AM ælˈteɪɪk, alˈteɪɪk
Altair
BR alˈtɛː(r), ˈaltɛː(r)
AM ˈælˌtɛ(ə)r, ˈalˌtɛ(ə)r
Altamira
BR ˌaltəˈmɪərə(r)
AM ˌaltəˈmɪrə
SP ˌalta'mira
B PORT ˌawta'mira
L PORT alta'mira
altar
BR ˈɔːltə(r), ˈɒltə(r), -z
AM ˈɔltər, ˈaltər, -z

Altarnun
BR ˌɔːltəˈnʌn,
ˌɒltəˈnʌn
AM ˈɔltərˌnən,
ˈɑltərˌnɑn
altarpiece
BR ˈɔːltəpiːs, ˈɒltəpiːs,
-ɪz
AM ˈɔltərˌpis,
ˈɑltərˌpis, -ɪz
altazimuth
BR alˈtazɪməθ, -s
AM ælˈtæzəməθ,
ɑlˈtæzəməθ, -s
Altdorfer
BR ˈaltˌdɔːfə(r)
AM ˈaltˌdɔrfər
alter
BR ˈɔːlt|ə(r), ˈɒlt|ə(r),
-əz, -(ə)rɪŋ, -əd
AM ˈɔlt|ər, ˈɑlt|ər, -ərz,
-(ə)rɪŋ, -ərd
alterable
BR ˈɔːlt(ə)rəbl,
ˈɒlt(ə)rəbl
AM ˈɔlt(ə)rəbəl,
ˈɑlt(ə)rəbəl
alteration
BR ˌɔːltəˈreɪʃn,
ˌɒltəˈreɪʃn, -z
AM ˌɔltəˈreɪʃən,
ˌɑltəˈreɪʃən, -z
alterative
BR ˈɔːlt(ə)rətɪv,
ˈɒlt(ə)rətɪv
AM ˈɔltəˌreɪdɪv,
ˈɔltərədɪv,
ˈɑltəˌreɪdɪv,
ˈɑltərədɪv
altercate
BR ˈɔːltəkeɪt, ˈɒltəkeɪt,
-s, -ɪŋ, -ɪd
AM ˈɔltərˌkeɪ|t,
ˈɑltərˌkeɪ|t, -ts, -dɪŋ,
-dɪd
altercation
BR ˌɔːltəˈkeɪʃn,
ˌɒltəˈkeɪʃn, -z
AM ˌɔltərˈkeɪʃən,
ˌɑltərˈkeɪʃən, -z
alter ego
BR ˌæltər ˈɛgəʊ,
ˌɔːltər +, ˌɒltə(r) +,
+ ˈiːgəʊ, -z
AM ˌɔltəˈrigoʊ,
ˌɑltəˈrigoʊ, -z
alternance
BR ˈɔːltənəns,
ˈɒltənəns, -ɪz
AM ˈɔltərnəns,
ˈɑltərnəns, -əz
alternant
BR ˈɔːltənənt,
ˈɒltənənt, -s
AM ˈɔltərnənt,
ˈɑltərnənt, -s

alternate¹
adjective
BR ɔːlˈtəːnɪt, ɒlˈtəːnɪt
AM ˈɔltərnət, ˈɑltərnət
alternate²
verb
BR ˈɔːltəneɪt, ˈɒltəneɪt,
-s, -ɪŋ, -ɪd
AM ˈɔltərˌneɪ|t,
ˈɑltərˌneɪ|t, -ts, -dɪŋ,
-dɪd
alternately
BR ɔːlˈtəːnɪtli,
ɒlˈtəːnɪtli
AM ˈɔltərnətli,
ˈɑltərnətli
alternation
BR ˌɔːltəˈneɪʃn,
ˌɒltəˈneɪʃn
AM ˌɔltərˈneɪʃən,
ˌɑltərˈneɪʃən
alternative
BR ɔːlˈtəːnətɪv,
ɒlˈtəːnətɪv, -z
AM ɔlˈtəːnədɪv,
ɑlˈtəːnədɪv, -z
alternatively
BR ɔːlˈtəːnətɪvli,
ɒlˈtəːnətɪvli
AM ɔlˈtəːnədɪvli,
ɑlˈtəːnədɪvli
alternator
BR ˈɔːltəneɪtə(r),
ˈɒltəneɪtə(r), -z
AM ˈɔltərˌneɪdər,
ˈɑltərˌneɪdər, -z
Althea
BR ˈalθɪə(r)
AM ælˈθɪə
althorn
BR ˈalt(h)ɔːn, -z
AM ˈælt,(h)ɔ(ə)rn, -z
although
BR ɔːlˈðəʊ, ɒlˈðəʊ
AM ɔlˈðoʊ, ɑlˈðoʊ
Althusser
BR ˌæltʊˈsɛː(r)
AM ˈalt,(h)usər
FR altysɛʀ
Althusserean
BR ˌæltʊˈsɛːrɪən, -z
AM ˌalt(h)ʊˈsɛrɪən, -z
Althusserian
BR ˌæltʊˈsɛːrɪən, -z
AM ˌalt(h)ʊˈsɛrɪən, -z
altimeter
BR ˈaltɪmiːtə(r),
ɔːlˈtɪmiːtə(r),
ˈɒltɪmiːtə(r), -z
AM ælˈtɪmədər,
ɑlˈtɪmədər, -z
altimetry
BR alˈtɪmɪtri,
ɔːlˈtɪmɪtri, ɒlˈtɪmɪtri
AM ælˈtɪmɪtri,
ɑlˈtɪmɪtri
Altiplano
BR ˌaltɪˈplɑːnəʊ,

ˌaltɪˈplanəʊ
AM ˌɔltɪˈplanoʊ,
ˌɑltɪˈplanoʊ
altissimo
BR alˈtɪsɪməʊ
AM ælˈtɪsɪmoʊ,
alˈtɪsɪmoʊ
altitude
BR ˈaltɪtjuːd,
ˈaltɪtʃuːd, -z
AM ˈældəˌt(j)ud, -z
altitudinal
BR ˈaltɪˌtjuːdɪn(ə)l,
ˈaltɪˌtjuːdn̩(ə)l,
ˈaltɪˌtʃuːdɪn(ə)l,
ˈaltɪˌtʃuːdn̩(ə)l
AM ˌældəˈt(j)udənl,
ˌældəˈt(j)udnəl
alto
BR ˈaltəʊ, -z
AM ˈæltoʊ, ˈɔltoʊ,
ˈɑltoʊ, -z
altocumulus
BR ˌaltəʊˈkjuːmjʊləs
AM ˌæltoʊˈkjumjələs,
ˌɔltoʊˈkjumjələs,
ˌɑltoʊˈkjumjələs
altogether
BR ˌɔːltəˈgɛðə(r)
AM ˌɔltəˈgɛðər,
ˈɑltəˈgɛðər
Alton
BR ˈɔːlt(ə)n, ˈɒlt(ə)n
AM ˈɔldən, ˈɑldən
Altoona
BR alˈtuːnə(r)
AM ælˈtunə
alto-relievo
BR ˌaltəʊriˈliːvəʊ
AM ˌæltoʊrəˈlivoʊ,
ˌɑltoʊrəˈlivoʊ
altostratus
BR ˌaltəʊˈstrɑːtəs,
ˌaltəʊˈstreɪtəs
AM ˌæltoʊˈstreɪdəs,
ˌæltoʊˈstrædəs,
ˌɔltoʊˈstreɪdəs,
ˌɔltoʊˈstrædəs,
ˌɑltoʊˈstreɪdəs,
ˌɑltoʊˈstrædəs
altricial
BR alˈtrɪʃl
AM ælˈtrɪʃəl
Altrincham
BR ˈɔːltrɪŋəm,
ˈɒltrɪŋəm
AM ˈɔltrɪn(t)ʃəm,
ˈɑltrɪn(t)ʃəm
altruism
BR ˈaltrʊɪz(ə)m
AM ˈæltrəˌwɪzəm,
ˈælˌtruˌɪzəm
altruist
BR ˈaltrʊɪst, -s
AM ˈæltrəwəst,
ˈælˌtruəst, -s
altruistic
BR ˌaltrʊˈɪstɪk

AM ˌæltrəˈwɪstɪk,
ˌælˌtruˈɪstɪk
altruistically
BR ˌaltrʊˈɪstɪkli
AM ˌæltrəˈwɪstɪk(ə)li,
ˌælˌtruˈɪstɪk(ə)li
aludel
BR ˈaljʊdɛl, -z
AM ˈæljəˌdɛl, -z
alum
BR ˈaləm, -z
AM ˈæləm, -z
alumina
BR əˈl(j)uːmɪnə(r)
AM əˈlumənə
aluminisation
BR əˌl(j)uːmɪnaɪˈzeɪʃn
AM əˌlumənəˈzeɪʃən,
əˌluməˌnaɪˈzeɪʃən
aluminise
BR əˈl(j)uːmɪnaɪz, -ɪz,
-ɪŋ, -d
AM əˈluməˌnaɪz, -ɪz, -ɪŋ,
-d
aluminium
BR ˌal(j)əˈmɪnɪəm
AM əˈlumənəm
aluminization
BR əˌl(j)uːmɪnaɪˈzeɪʃn
AM əˌlumənəˈzeɪʃən,
əˌluməˌnaɪˈzeɪʃən
aluminize
BR əˈl(j)uːmɪnaɪz, -ɪz,
-ɪŋ, -d
AM əˈluməˌnaɪz, -ɪz, -ɪŋ,
-d
aluminosilicate
BR əˌl(j)uːmɪnəʊˈsɪlɪkət,
-s
AM əˌlumənəˈsɪləkət,
-s
aluminous
BR əˈl(j)uːmɪnəs
AM əˈlumənəs
aluminum
BR əˈl(j)uːmɪnəm
AM əˈlumənəm
alumna
BR əˈlʌmnə(r)
AM əˈləmnə
alumnae
BR əˈlʌmniː
AM əˈləmˌnaɪ, əˈləmni
alumni
BR əˈlʌmnaɪ
AM əˈləmˌnaɪ
alumnus
BR əˈlʌmnəs
AM əˈləmnəs
Alun
BR ˈalɪn
AM ˈælən
Alvar
BR ˈalvɑː(r)
AM ˈalˌvɑr
Alvarez
BR alˈvɑːrɛz, ˈalvərɛz
AM ˈælvəˌrɛz

alveolar
BR ˌælvɪˈəʊlə(r),
alˈvɪələ(r),
ˈælvɪələ(r), -z
AM ælˈvi(ə)lər,
ˌælviˈoʊlər, -z

alveolarisation
BR ˌælvɪəʊlərʌɪˈzeɪʃn,
alˌvɪ ələrəˈzeɪʃn
AM ælˌvi(ə)lərəˈzeɪʃən,
ælˌvi(ə)ləˌraɪˈzeɪʃən

alveolarise
BR ˌælvɪˈəʊlərʌɪz,
alˈvɪələrʌɪz,
ˈælvɪələrʌɪz
AM ælˈvi(ə)ləˌraɪz

alveolarization
BR ˌælvɪə(ʊ)lərʌɪˈzeɪʃn,
alˌvɪələrəˈzeɪʃn
AM ælˌvi(ə)lərəˈzeɪʃən,
ælˌvi(ə)ləˌraɪˈzeɪʃən

alveolarize
BR ˌælvɪˈəʊlərʌɪz,
alˈvɪələrʌɪz,
ˈælvɪələrʌɪz
AM ælˈvi(ə)ləˌraɪz

alveolate
BR alˈvɪələt
AM ælˈvɪələt

alveole
BR ˈalvɪəʊl, -z
AM ˈælviˌoʊl, -z

alveoli
BR ˌælvɪˈəʊlʌɪ,
ˌalvɪˈəʊliː, alˈvɪəlʌɪ,
alˈvɪəliː, ˈalvɪəlʌɪ,
ˈalvɪəliː
AM ælˈviəˌlaɪ, ælˈviəˌli

alveolus
BR ˌalvɪˈəʊləs,
alˈvɪələs, ˈalvɪələs
AM ælˈvɪələs,
ˌælviˈoʊləs

Alvin
BR ˈalvɪn
AM ˈælvən

always
BR ˈɔːlweɪz, ˈɔːlwɪz
AM ˈɔlweɪz, ˈɔlˌweɪz,
ˈalweɪz, ˈalˌweɪz

Alwyn
BR ˈɔːlwɪn, ˈalwɪn
AM ˈɔlwɪn, ˈalwɪn

alyssum
BR ˈalɪs(ə)m, -z
AM əˈlɪsəm, -z

Alzheimer's
BR ˈaltshʌɪməz,
ˈɔːltshʌɪməz
AM ˈalts,(h)aɪmərz

am¹
strong form
BR am
AM æm

am²
weak form
BR əm, m

AM əm, m

a.m.
BR ˌeɪˈɛm
AM ˌeɪˈɛm

amadavat
BR ˈamədavat, -s
AM ˈæmədəˌvæt, -s

amadou
BR ˈaməduː
AM ˈaməˌdu

amah
BR ˈɑːmə(r), -z
AM ˈamə, -z

amain
BR əˈmeɪn
AM əˈmeɪn

Amal
BR əˈmɑːl, ˈamɑːl
AM ˈɑmɑl

Amalekite
BR əˈmaləkʌɪt
AM əˈmæləˌkaɪt

Amalfi
BR əˈmalfi
AM əˈmɑlfi, əˈmælfi

amalgam
BR əˈmalgəm, -z
AM əˈmælgəm, -z

amalgamate
BR əˈmalgəmeɪt, -s, -ɪŋ,
-ɪd
AM əˈmælgəˌmeɪt, -ts,
-dɪŋ, -dɪd

amalgamation
BR əˌmalgəˈmeɪʃn, -z
AM əˌmælgəˈmeɪʃən, -z

Amanda
BR əˈmandə(r)
AM əˈmændə

amanita
BR ˌaməˈnʌɪtə(r),
ˌaməˈniːtə(r), -z
AM ˌæməˈnaɪdə,
ˌæməˈnidə, -z

amanuenses
BR əˌmanjʊˈɛnsiːz
AM əˌmænjəˈwɛnˌsiz

amanuensis
BR əˌmanjʊˈɛnsɪs
AM əˌmænjəˈwɛnsəs

amaranth
BR ˈaməranθ, -s
AM ˈæməˌrænθ, -s

amaranthine
BR ˌaməˈranθʌɪn
AM ˌæməˈrænθən,
ˌæməˈrænˌθaɪn

amaretti
BR ˌaməˈrɛti
AM ˌæməˈrɛdi

amaretto
BR ˌaməˈrɛtəʊ
AM ˌæməˈrɛdoʊ

Amarillo
BR ˌaməˈrɪləʊ
AM ˌæməˈrɪloʊ

amaryllis
BR ˌaməˈrɪlɪs, -ɪz
AM ˌæməˈrɪlɪs, -ɪz

amass
BR əˈmas, -ɪz, -ɪŋ, -t
AM əˈmæs, -əz, -ɪŋ, -t

amasser
BR əˈmasə(r), -z
AM əˈmæsər, -z

amassment
BR əˈmasm(ə)nt
AM əˈmæsmənt

amateur
BR ˈamət(ʃ)ə(r),
ˌaməˈtə:(r), -z
AM ˈæmədər, ˈæməˌtər,
ˌæməˈt(j)ʊr, -z

amateurish
BR ˈamət(ə)rɪʃ,
ˈaməˌtʃərɪʃ,
ˌaməˈtə:rɪʃ
AM ˌæməˈtʃʊrɪʃ,
ˌæməˌtərɪʃ,
ˌæməˈt(j)ʊrɪʃ

amateurishly
BR ˈamət(ə)rɪʃli,
ˈaməˌtʃərɪʃli,
ˌaməˈtə:rɪʃli
AM ˌæməˈtʃʊrɪʃli,
ˌæməˌtərɪʃli,
ˌæməˈt(j)ʊrɪʃli

amateurishness
BR ˈamət(ə)rɪʃnɪs,
ˈaməˌtʃərɪʃnɪs,
ˌaməˈtə:rɪʃnɪs
AM ˌæməˈtʃʊrɪʃnɪs,
ˌæməˌtərɪʃnɪs,
ˌæməˈt(j)ʊrɪʃnɪs

amateurism
BR ˈamət(ʃ)ərɪz(ə)m,
ˌaməˈtə:rɪz(ə)m
AM ˈæməˌtʃʊˌrɪzəm,
ˈæmədəˌrɪzəm,
ˈæməˌt(j)ʊˌrɪzəm

Amati
BR əˈmɑːtʃi, əˈmɑːtʃi,
-ɪz
AM ɑˈmɑdi, -z

amative
BR ˈamətɪv
AM ˈæmədɪv

amativeness
BR ˈamətɪvnɪs
AM ˈæmədɪvnɪs

amatol
BR ˈamətɒl
AM ˈæməˌdɒl ˈæməˌdɑl

amatory
BR ˈamət(ə)ri
AM ˈæməˌtɔri

amauroses
BR ˌamɔːˈrəʊsiːz
AM ˌæmɔˈroʊsiz,
ˌæmɑˈroʊsiz

amaurosis
BR ˌamɔːˈrəʊsɪs
AM ˌæmɔˈroʊsəs,
ˌæmɑˈroʊsəs

amaurotic
BR ˌamɔːˈrɒtɪk
AM ˌæməˈrɑdɪk,
ˌæmɑˈradɪk

amaze
BR əˈmeɪz, -ɪz, -ɪŋ, -d
AM əˈmeɪz, -ɪz, -ɪŋ, -d

amazement
BR əˈmeɪzm(ə)nt
AM əˈmeɪzmənt

amazingly
BR əˈmeɪzɪŋli
AM əˈmeɪzɪŋli

amazingness
BR əˈmeɪzɪŋnɪs
AM əˈmeɪzɪŋnɪs

Amazon
BR ˈaməz(ə)n, -z
AM ˈæməˌzɑn,
ˈæməzən, -z

Amazonia
BR ˌaməˈzəʊnɪə(r)
AM ˌæməˈzoʊniə

Amazonian
BR ˌaməˈzəʊnɪən, -z
AM ˌæməˈzoʊniən, -z

Amazulu
BR ˌaməˈzuːluː
AM ˌæməˈzulu

ambages
BR ˈambɪdʒɪz,
amˈbeɪdʒɪz
AM ˈæmbɪdʒɪz,
æmˈbeɪdʒɪz

ambassador
BR amˈbasədə(r), -z
AM æmˈbæsədər,
əmˈbæsədər, -z

ambassadorial
BR amˌbasəˈdɔːrɪəl,
ˌambasəˈdɔːrɪəl
AM æmˌbæsəˈdɔriəl,
əmˌbæsəˈdɔriəl

ambassadorship
BR amˈbasədəʃɪp, -s
AM æmˈbæsədərˌʃɪp,
əmˈbæsədərˌʃɪp, -s

ambassadress
BR amˈbasədrɪs,
amˌbasəˈdrɛs, -ɪz
AM æmˈbæsədrəs,
əmˈbæsədrəs, -əz

ambatch
BR ˈambatʃ, -ɪz
AM ˈæmˌbætʃ, -əz

Ambato
BR amˈbɑːtəʊ
AM ɑmˈbɑdoʊ

amber
BR ˈambə(r)
AM ˈæmbər

ambergris
BR ˈambəgriːs
AM ˈæmbərˌgri(s),
ˈæmbərˌgrɪs

amberjack
BR ˈambədʒak, -s
AM ˈæmbərˌdʒæk, -s

ambiance
BR 'ambɪəns,
'ɒmbɪɒns, 'ɒbɪɒs, -ɪz
AM 'æmbiəns,
'æmbjɑns, -əz

ambidexter
BR ˌambɪ'dɛkstə(r), -z
AM ˌæmbə'dɛkstər, -z

ambidexterity
BR ˌambɪdɛk'stɛrɪti
AM ˌæmbəˌdɛks'tɛrədi

ambidextrous
BR ˌambɪ'dɛkstrəs
AM ˌæmbə'dɛkst(ə)rəs

ambidextrously
BR ˌambɪ'dɛkstrəsli
AM ˌæmbə'dɛkst(ə)rəsli

ambidextrousness
BR ˌambɪ'dɛkstrəsnəs
AM ˌæmbə'dɛkst(ə)rəs-
nəs

ambience
BR 'ambɪəns,
'ɒmbɪɒns, 'ɒbɪɒs, -ɪz
AM 'æmbiəns,
'æmbjɑns, -əz

ambient
BR 'ambɪənt
AM 'æmbiənt,
'æmbjənt

ambiguous
BR am'bɪɡjʊəs
AM æm'bɪɡjəwəs

ambiguously
BR am'bɪɡjʊəsli
AM æm'bɪɡjəwəsli

ambiguousness
BR am'bɪɡjʊəsnəs
AM æm'bɪɡjəwəsnəs

ambisonics
BR ˌambɪ'sɒnɪks
AM ˌæmbə'sɑnɪks

ambit
BR 'ambɪt, -s
AM 'æmbət, -s

ambition
BR am'bɪʃn, -z
AM æm'bɪʃən, -z

ambitious
BR am'bɪʃəs
AM æm'bɪʃəs

ambitiously
BR am'bɪʃəsli
AM æm'bɪʃəsli

ambitiousness
BR am'bɪʃəsnəs
AM æm'bɪʃəsnəs

ambivalence
BR am'bɪvələns,
am'bɪvəlns,
am'bɪvl̩(ə)ns
AM æm'bɪv(ə)ləns

ambivalency
BR am'bɪvələnsi,
am'bɪvəlnsi,
am'bɪvl̩(ə)nsi
AM æm'bɪv(ə)lənsi

ambivalent
BR am'bɪvələnt,
am'bɪvəlnt,
am'bɪvl̩(ə)nt
AM æm'bɪv(ə)lənt

ambivalently
BR am'bɪvələntli,
am'bɪvəlntli,
am'bɪvl̩(ə)ntli
AM æm'bɪvələn(t)li

ambiversion
BR ˌambɪ'vɜːʃn
AM ˌæmbi'vɜrʒən

ambivert
BR 'ambɪvɜːt, -s
AM 'æmbəˌvɜrt, -s

amble
BR 'ambl̩, -lz, -lɪŋ \-lɪŋ,
-ld
AM 'æmbl̩əl, -əlz,
-(ə)lɪŋ, -əld

ambler
BR 'amblə(r),
'amblə(r), -z
AM 'æmblər, -z

Ambleside
BR 'amblsʌɪd
AM 'æmbəlˌsaɪd

amblyopia
BR ˌamblɪ'əʊpɪə(r)
AM ˌæmblɪ'oʊpiə

amblyopic
BR ˌamblɪ'ɒpɪk
AM ˌæmblɪ'ɑpɪk

ambo
BR 'ambəʊ, -z
AM 'æmˌboʊ, -z

amboina
BR am'bɔɪnə(r)
AM æm'bɔɪnə

Amboinese
BR ˌambɔɪ'niːz
AM ˌæmˌbɔɪ'niːz

ambones
BR am'bəʊniːz
AM æm'boʊniːz

Ambonese
BR ˌambə(ʊ)'niːz
AM ˌæmbə'niːz

amboyna
BR am'bɔɪnə(r)
AM æm'bɔɪnə

Ambrose
BR 'ambrəʊz
AM 'æmˌbroʊz

ambrosia
BR am'brəʊzɪə(r)
AM æm'broʊʒə

ambrosial
BR am'brəʊzɪəl
AM æm'broʊʒ(i)əl

ambrosian
BR am'brəʊzɪən
AM æm'broʊʒən

ambry
BR 'ambr̩i, -ɪz
AM 'æmbri, -z

ambs-ace
BR 'eɪmzeɪs, 'amzeɪs,
ˌamz'eɪs
AM 'eɪmˌzeɪs, 'æmˌzeɪs

ambulance
BR 'ambjʊləns,
'ambjʊlns, -ɪz
AM 'æmbjələns, -əz

ambulanceman
BR 'ambjʊlənsˌman,
'ɑːmbjʊlnsˌman
AM 'æmbjələnsˌmæn

ambulancemen
BR 'ambjʊlənsˌmɛn,
'ambjʊlnsˌmɛn
AM 'æmbjələnsˌmɛn

ambulant
BR 'ambjʊlənt,
'ambjʊlnt
AM 'æmbjələnt

ambulate
BR 'ambjʊleɪt, -s, -ɪŋ,
-ɪd
AM 'æmbjəˌleɪt, -ts,
-dɪŋ, -dɪd

ambulation
BR ˌambjʊ'leɪʃn
AM ˌæmbjə'leɪʃən

ambulatory
BR 'ambjʊlət(ə)ri
AM 'æmbjələˌtɔri

ambuscade
BR ˌambə'skeɪd, -z
AM 'æmbəˌskeɪd,
ˌæmbə'skeɪd, -z

ambush
BR 'ambʊʃ, -ɪz, -ɪŋ, -t
AM 'æmbʊʃ, -əz, -ɪŋ, -t

ambystoma
BR am'bɪstəmə(r), -z
AM æm'bɪstəmə, -z

Amdahl
BR 'amdɑːl
AM 'æmdɑl

ameer
BR ə'mɪə(r), -z
AM ə'mɪ(ə)r, -z

Amelia
BR ə'miːlɪə(r)
AM ə'miljə, ə'miliə

ameliorate
BR ə'miːlɪəreɪt, -s, -ɪŋ,
-ɪd
AM ə'miljəˌreɪt,
ə'miljəˌreɪt, -ts, -dɪŋ,
-dɪd

amelioration
BR əˌmiːlɪə'reɪʃn
AM əˌmiliə'reɪʃən,
əˌmiljə'reɪʃən

ameliorative
BR ə'miːlɪərətɪv, -z
AM ə'miliərədɪv,
ə'miljərədɪv,
ə'miliəˌreɪdɪv,
ə'miljəˌreɪdɪv, -z

ameliorator
BR ə'miːlɪəreɪtə(r), -z

amenta
AM ə'miliəˌreɪdər,
ə'miljəˌreɪdər, -z

amen
BR ˌɑː'mɛn, ˌeɪ'mɛn, -z
AM ˌɑ'mɛn, ˌeɪ'mɛn, -z

amenability
BR əˌmiːnə'bɪlɪti
AM əˌminə'bɪlɪdi

amenable
BR ə'miːnəbl
AM ə'minəbəl

amenableness
BR ə'miːnəblnəs
AM ə'minəbəlnəs

amenably
BR ə'miːnəbli
AM ə'minəbli

amend
BR ə'mɛnd, -z, -ɪŋ, -ɪd
AM ə'mɛnd, -z, -ɪŋ, -əd

amendable
BR ə'mɛndəbl
AM ə'mɛndəbəl

amendatory
BR ə'mɛndət(ə)ri
AM ə'mɛndəˌtɔri

amende
honorable
BR əˌmɒd
ɒnə'rɑːbl(ə)(r), -z
AM ˌamɑnˌdɒnə'rɑbl,
-z

amender
BR ə'mɛndə(r), -z
AM ə'mɛndər, -z

amendment
BR ə'mɛn(d)m(ə)nt, -s
AM ə'mɛn(d)mənt, -s

Amenhotep
BR ˌamɛn'həʊtɛp,
a'mɛn(h)əʊtɛp
AM ˌæmən'hoʊtəp,
ˌamən'hoʊtəp

amenity
BR ə'miːnɪt|i,
ə'mɛnɪt|i, -ɪz
AM ə'mɛnədi, -z

amenorrhea
BR əˌmɛnə'riːə(r)
AM eɪˌmɛnə'riə,
ɑˌmɛnə'riə

amenorrhoea
BR əˌmɛnə'riːə(r)
AM eɪˌmɛnə'riə,
ɑˌmɛnə'riə

ament¹
catkin
BR ə'mɛnt, -s
AM 'eɪˌmɛnt, 'eɪmənt,
-s

ament²
person with amentia
BR 'eɪmɛnt, ə'mɛnt, -s
AM 'eɪˌmɛnt, 'eɪmənt,
-s

amenta
BR ə'mɛntə(r)
AM ə'mɛn(t)ə

amentia
BR eɪˈmenʃ(ɪ)ə(r),
əˈmenʃ(ɪ)ə(r)
AM eɪˈmen(t)ʃiə

amentum
BR əˈmentəm
AM əˈmen(t)əm

Amerasian
BR ˌaməˈreɪʃn,
ˌaməˈreɪʒn, -z
AM ˌæmərˈeɪʒən,
ˌæmərˈeɪʃən, -z

amerce
BR əˈmɜːs, -ɪz, -ɪŋ, -t
AM əˈmɜrs, -əz, -ɪŋ, -t

amercement
BR əˈmɜːsm(ə)nt, -s
AM əˈmɜrsmənt, -s

amerciable
BR əˈmɜːsɪəbl
AM əˈmɜrsiəbəl,
əˈmɜrʃəbəl

America
BR əˈmerɪkə(r), -z
AM əˈmerəkə, -z

American
BR əˈmerɪk(ə)n, -z
AM əˈmer(ə)kən, -z

Americana
BR əˌmerɪˈkɑːnə(r)
AM əˌmerəˈkɑnə,
əˌmerəˈkænə

Americanisation
BR əˌmerɪkənʌɪˈzeɪʃn,
əˌmerɪkn̩ʌɪˈzeɪʃn
AM əˌmerəkənəˈzeɪʃən,
əˌmerəkəˌnaɪˈzeɪʃən

Americanise
BR əˈmerɪkənʌɪz,
əˈmerɪkn̩ʌɪz, -ɪz, -ɪŋ, -d
AM əˈmerəkəˌnaɪz, -ɪz,
-ɪŋ, -d

Americanism
BR əˈmerɪkənɪz(ə)m,
əˈmerɪkn̩ɪz(ə)m, -z
AM əˈmerəkəˌnɪzəm, -z

americanist
BR əˈmerɪkənɪst,
əˈmerɪkn̩ɪst, -s
AM əˈmerəkənəst, -s

Americanization
BR əˈmerɪkənʌɪˈzeɪʃn,
əˌmerɪkn̩ʌɪˈzeɪʃn
AM əˌmerəkənəˈzeɪʃən,
əˌmerəkəˌnaɪˈzeɪʃən

Americanize
BR əˈmerɪkənʌɪz,
əˈmerɪkn̩ʌɪz, -ɪz, -ɪŋ, -d
AM əˈmerəkəˌnaɪz, -ɪz,
-ɪŋ, -d

americium
BR ˌaməˈrɪsɪəm,
ˌaməˈrɪʃɪəm
AM æməˈrisiəm,
æməˈriʃiəm

Amerind
BR ˈamərɪnd, -z
AM ˈæməˌrɪnd, -z

Amerindian
BR ˌaməˈrɪndiən, -z
AM ˌæməˈrɪndiən,
ˌæməˈrɪndjən, -z

Amerindic
BR ˌaməˈrɪndɪk
AM ˌæməˈrɪndɪk

Amersham
BR ˈaməʃ(ə)m
AM ˈæmərʃəm

Ames
BR eɪmz
AM eɪmz

Amesbury
BR ˈeɪmzb(ə)ri
AM ˈeɪmzbəri

Ameslan
BR ˈamɪslan
AM ˈam(ə),slæn

amethyst
BR ˈamɪθɪst, -s
AM ˈæməθəst, -s

amethystine
BR ˌamɪˈθɪstʌɪn
AM ˌæməˈθɪstən,
ˌæməˈθɪsˌtaɪn,
ˌæməˈθɪsˌtin

Amex®
BR ˈameks, ˈeɪmeks
AM ˈæˌmeks

Amharic
BR amˈharɪk
AM æmˈherɪk

Amherst
BR ˈam(h)əːst
AM ˈæm(h)ərst

amiability
BR ˌeɪmɪəˈbɪlɪti
AM ˌeɪmiəˈbɪlɪdi

amiable
BR ˈeɪmɪəbl
AM ˈeɪmiəbəl

amiableness
BR ˈeɪmɪəblnəs
AM ˈeɪmiəbəlnəs

amiably
BR ˈeɪmɪəbli
AM ˈeɪmiəbli

amianthus
BR ˌamɪˈanθəs
AM ˌæmiˈænθəs

amibiguity
BR ˌambɪˈgjuːɪt|i, -ɪz
AM ˌæmbəˈgjuwədi, -z

amicability
BR ˌamɪkəˈbɪlɪti
AM ˌæməkəˈbɪlɪdi

amicable
BR ˈamɪkəbl
AM ˈæməkəbəl

amicableness
BR ˈamɪkəblnəs
AM ˈæməkəbəlnəs

amicably
BR ˈamɪkəbli
AM ˈæməkəbli

amice
BR ˈam|ɪs, -ɪsɪz
AM ˈæməs, -əz

amicus curiae
BR əˌmʌɪkəs
ˈkjʊərɪʌɪ, əˈmiːkəs +,
aˈmʌɪkəs +,
aˈmiːkəs +,
+ ˈkjʊərriː,
+ ˈkjɔːrɪʌɪ, + ˈkjɔːrriː
AM əˌmikəs ˈk(j)ʊri,ʌɪ,
+ ˈk(j)ʊri,i

amid
BR əˈmɪd
AM əˈmɪd

amide
BR ˈamʌɪd, -z
AM ˈæˌmaɪd, ˈæmər, -z

Amidol®
BR ˈamɪdɒl
AM ˈæmədɔl, ˈæmədɑl

amidone
BR ˈamɪdəʊn
AM ˈæməˌdoʊn

amidships
BR əˈmɪdʃɪps
AM əˈmɪdˌʃɪps

amidst
BR əˈmɪdst
AM əˈmɪdst

Amiens
BR əˈmiɒ̃
AM ˈɑmiən
FR amjɛ̃

Amies
BR ˈeɪmɪz
AM ˈeɪmis

amigo
BR əˈmiːgəʊ, -z
AM əˈmigoʊ, -z

Amin
BR ɑːˈmiːn, aˈmiːn
AM ɑˈmin

amine
BR ˈamiːn, ˈamɪn,
əˈmiːn, -z
AM əˈmin, ˈæˌmin, -z

amino
BR əˈmiːnəʊ,
əˈmʌɪnəʊ, ˈamɪnəʊ
AM əˈminoʊ

amir
BR aˈmɪə(r), əˈmɪə(r),
-z
AM əˈmɪ(ə)r, -z

Amirante Islands
BR ˈamɪrant
ˌʌɪlən(d)z,
ˌamɪˈranti +
AM ˈæməˌrænt
ˈaɪlən(d)z

amirate
BR ˈamɪrət, ˈamɪərət,
aˈmɪərət, əˈmɪərət,
aˈmɪəreɪt, əˈmɪəreɪt,
-s
AM ˈɛmərət, -s

Amis
BR ˈeɪmɪs
AM ˈeɪmɪs

Amish
BR ˈɑːmɪʃ, ˈamɪʃ
AM ˈɑmɪʃ

amiss
BR əˈmɪs
AM əˈmɪs

amitosis
BR ˌeɪmʌɪˈtəʊsɪs,
ˌamɪˈtəʊsɪs
AM ˌeɪˌmaɪˈtoʊsəs,
ˌæməˈtoʊsəs

amitriptyline
BR ˌamɪˈtrɪptɪliːn
AM ˌæməˈtrɪptələn

amity
BR ˈamɪti
AM ˈæmədi

Amlwch
BR ˈamlʊx, ˈamlʊk
AM ˈæmlwɪtʃ

Amman¹
place in Jordan
BR əˈmɑːn, aˈmɑːn,
aˈman
AM ɑˈman

Amman²
river in Wales
BR ˈamən
AM ˈæmən

ammeter
BR ˈamiːtə(r),
ˈamˌmiːtə(r), -z
AM ˈæ(m)ˌmidər, -z

ammo
BR ˈaməʊ
AM ˈæmoʊ

Ammon
BR ˈamən
AM ˈæmən

ammonia
BR əˈməʊnɪə(r)
AM əˈmoʊnjə

ammoniac
BR əˈməʊnɪak
AM əˈmoʊniˌæk

ammoniacal
BR ˌamə(ʊ)ˈnʌɪəkl
AM ˌæməˈnaɪəkəl

ammoniated
BR əˈməʊnɪeɪtɪd
AM əˈmoʊniˌeɪdəd

ammonite
BR ˈamənʌɪt, -s
AM ˈæməˌnaɪt, -s

ammonium
BR əˈməʊnɪəm
AM əˈmoʊniəm

ammtrak
BR ˈamtrak, -s
AM ˈæmˌtræk, -s

ammunition
BR ˌamjʊˈnɪʃn
AM ˌæmjəˈnɪʃən

amnesia
BR am'niːzɪə(r),
am'niːʒə(r)
AM æm'niʒə

amnesiac
BR am'niːzɪak, -s
AM æm'nizi,æk, -s

amnesic
BR am'niːzɪk,
am'niːsɪk, -s
AM æm'nizɪk,
æm'nisɪk, -s

amnesty
BR 'amnɪstˌi, -ɪz
AM 'æmnəsti,
'æm,nɛsti, -z

amniocentesis
BR ,amnɪəʊsɛn'tiːsɪs
AM ,æmnioʊ,sɛn'tisɪs

amnion
BR 'amnɪən, -z
AM 'æmni,ɑn,
'æmnɪən, -z

amniote
BR 'amnɪəʊt, -s
AM 'æmni,oʊt, -s

amniotic
BR ,amnɪ'ɒtɪk
AM ,æmni'adɪk

Amoco®
BR 'aməkəʊ
AM 'æməkoʊ

amoeba
BR ə'miːbə(r), -z
AM ə'mibə, -z

amoebae
BR ə'miːbiː
AM ə'mibi

amoebean
BR ə'miːbɪən
AM ə'mibɪən

amoebic
BR ə'miːbɪk
AM ə'mibɪk

amoeboid
BR ə'miːbɔɪd
AM ə'mi,bɔɪd

amok
BR ə'mɒk, ə'mʌk
AM ə'mək, ə'mɑk

among
BR ə'mʌŋ
AM ə'məŋ

amongst
BR ə'mʌŋst
AM ə'məŋs(t)

amontillado
BR ə,mɒntɪ'lɑːdəʊ, -z
AM ə,mɑntə'lɑdoʊ,
ə,mɑntə'jɑdoʊ, -z

amoral
BR ,eɪ'mɒrəl, ,eɪ'mɒrl̩
AM ,eɪ'mɔrəl

amoralism
BR ,eɪ'mɒrəlɪz(ə)m,
,eɪ'mɒrˌlɪz(ə)m
AM ,eɪ'mɔrə,lɪzəm

amoralist
BR ,eɪ'mɒrəlɪst,
,eɪ'mɒrˌlɪst, -s
AM ,eɪ'mɔrələst, -s

amorality
BR ,eɪmə'ralɪti
AM ,eɪmə'rælədi

amorally
BR ,eɪ'mɒrəli,
,eɪ'mɒrl̩i
AM ,eɪ'mɔrəli

amoretti
BR ,amə'rɛti
AM ,æmə'rɛdi

amoretto
BR ,amə'rɛtəʊ
AM ,æmə'rɛdoʊ

amorist
BR 'amərɪst, -s
AM 'æmərəst, -s

Amorite
BR 'amərʌɪt, -s
AM 'æmə,raɪt, -s

amoroso
BR ,amə'rəʊsəʊ, -z
AM ,amə'roʊsoʊ,
,æmə'roʊsoʊ, -z

amorous
BR 'am(ə)rəs
AM 'æm(ə)rəs

amorously
BR 'am(ə)rəsli
AM 'æm(ə)rəsli

amorousness
BR 'am(ə)rəsnəs
AM 'æm(ə)rəsnəs

amorpha
BR ə'mɔːfə(r), -z
AM ə'mɔrfə, -z

amorphism
BR ə'mɔːfɪz(ə)m
AM ə'mɔr,fɪzəm,
eɪ'mɔr,fɪzəm

amorphous
BR ə'mɔːfəs
AM ə'mɔrfəs, eɪ'mɔrfəs

amorphously
BR ə'mɔːfəsli
AM ə'mɔrfəsli,
eɪ'mɔrfəsli

amorphousness
BR ə'mɔːfəsnəs
AM ə'mɔrfəsnəs,
eɪ'mɔrfəsnəs

amortisable
BR ə'mɔːtʌɪzəbl
AM 'æmər,taɪzəbəl

amortisation
BR ə,mɔːtʌɪ'zeɪʃn, -z
AM 'æmərdə'zeɪʃən,
'æmɔr,taɪ'zeɪʃən, -z

amortise
BR ə'mɔːtʌɪz, -ɪz, -ɪŋ, -d
AM 'æmər,taɪz, -ɪz, -ɪŋ,
-d

amortizable
BR ə'mɔːtʌɪzəbl
AM 'æmər,taɪzəbəl

amortization
BR ə,mɔːtʌɪ'zeɪʃn, -z
AM 'æmərdə'zeɪʃən,
'æmɔr,taɪ'zeɪʃən, -z

amortize
BR ə'mɔːtʌɪz, -ɪz, -ɪŋ, -d
AM 'æmər,taɪz, -ɪz, -ɪŋ,
-d

Amory
BR 'eɪm(ə)ri
AM 'eɪməri

Amos
BR 'eɪmɒs
AM 'eɪməs

amount
BR ə'maʊnt, -s, -ɪŋ, -ɪd
AM ə'maʊn|t, -ts, -(t)ɪŋ,
-(t)əd

amour
BR ə'mʊə(r), ə'mɔː(r),
-z
AM ə'mʊ(ə)r, ɑ'mʊ(ə)r,
-z

amourette
BR ,amə'rɛt, -s
AM ,æmə'rɛt, -s

amour propre
BR ,amʊə 'prɒpr(ər),
,amɔː +
AM ,amʊr 'prɒpr(ə)

Amoy
BR ə'mɔɪ
AM ɑ'mɔɪ

amp
BR amp, -s
AM æmp, -s

ampelopsis
BR ,ampɪ'lɒpsɪs
AM ,æmpə'lɑpsəs

amperage
BR 'amp(ə)rɪdʒ
AM 'æmp(ə)rɪdʒ

ampere
BR 'ampɛː(r), -z
AM 'æm,pɪ(ə)r,
'æm,pɛ(ə)r, -z

ampersand
BR 'ampəsand, -z
AM 'æmpər,sænd, -z

Ampex®
BR 'ampɛks
AM 'æmpɛks

amphetamine
BR am'fɛtəmiːn,
am'fɛtəmɪn, -z
AM æm'(p)fɛdə,min,
æm'(p)fɛdəmən, -z

amphibia
BR am'fɪbɪə(r)
AM æm'(p)fɪbiə

amphibian
BR am'fɪbɪən, -z
AM æm'(p)fɪbiən, -z

amphibiology
BR am,fɪbɪ'ɒlədʒi
AM æm,(p)fɪbi'ɑlədʒi

amphibious
BR am'fɪbɪəs

amphibiously
BR am'fɪbɪəsli
AM æm'(p)fɪbiəsli

amphibole
BR 'amfɪbəʊl, -z
AM 'æm(p)fə,boʊl, -z

amphibolite
BR am'fɪbəlʌɪt, -s
AM æm'(p)fɪbə,laɪt, -s

amphibology
BR ,amfɪ'bɒlədʒi, -ɪz
AM ,æm(p)fə'bɑlədʒi,
-z

amphibrach
BR 'amfɪbrak, -s
AM 'æm(p)fə,bræk, -s

amphibrachic
BR ,amfɪ'brakɪk
AM ,æm(p)fə'brækɪk

amphictyon
BR am'fɪktɪən, -z
AM æm'(p)fɪktiən, -z

amphictyonic
BR am,fɪktɪ'ɒnɪk
AM ,æm,(p)fɪkti'ɑnɪk

amphictyony
BR am'fɪktɪəni
AM æm'(p)fɪktiəni

amphigamous
BR am'fɪgəməs
AM æm'(p)fɪgəməs

amphigori
BR 'amfɪ,gɔːr|i,
'amfɪg(ə)r|i,
am'fɪg(ə)r|i, -ɪz
AM 'æm(p)fə,gɔri,
æm'(p)fɪgəri, -z

amphigouri
BR 'amfɪ,gʊər|i,
'amfɪg(ə)r|i,
am'fɪg(ə)r|i, -ɪz
AM 'æm(p)fə,guri,
æm'(p)fɪgəri, -z

amphimictic
BR ,amfɪ'mɪktɪk
AM ,æm(p)fə'mɪktɪk

amphimixes
BR ,amfɪ'mɪksiːz
AM ,æm(p)fə'mɪksiz

amphimixis
BR ,amfɪ'mɪksɪs
AM ,æm(p)fə'mɪksɪs

amphioxi
BR ,amfɪ'ɒksi
AM ,æm(p)fi'aksi

amphioxus
BR ,amfɪ'ɒksəs
AM ,æm(p)fi'aksəs

amphipathic
BR ,amfɪ'paθɪk
AM ,æm(p)fə'pæθɪk

amphipod
BR 'amfɪpɒd, -z
AM 'æm(p)fə,pɑd, -z

amphipoda
BR am'fɪpədə(r)

AM æm'(p)fɪpədə

amphiprostyle
BR ˌæmfɪ'prəʊstʌɪl, -z
AM ˌæm(p)fə'prəʊˌstaɪl, -z

amphisbaena
BR ˌæmfɪs'biːnə(r), -z
AM ˌæm(p)fəs'binə, -z

amphitheater
BR 'æmfɪθɪətə(r), -z
AM 'æm(p)fə,θiədər, -z

amphitheatre
BR 'æmfɪθɪətə(r), -z
AM 'æm(p)fə,θiədər, -z

Amphitrite
BR ˌæmfɪ'trʌɪti
AM ˌæm(p)fə'traɪdi

Amphitryon
BR am'fɪtrɪən
AM æm'(p)fɪtri,ɑn

amphora
BR 'æmf(ə)rə(r), -z
AM 'æm(p)fərə, æm(p)'fɔrə, -z

amphorae
BR 'amf(ə)riː
AM 'æm(p)fə,ri, æm(p)'fɔ,raɪ

amphoteric
BR ˌamfə(ʊ)'tɛrɪk
AM ˌæm(p)fə'tɛrɪk

amphotericin
BR ˌamfə(ʊ)'tɛrɪsɪn
AM ˌæm(p)fə'tɛrəsən

ampicillin
BR ˌampɪ'sɪlɪn
AM 'æmpəˌsɪlɪn

ample
BR 'ampl, -ə(r), -ɪst
AM 'æmpəl, -(ə)lər, -(ə)ləst

Ampleforth
BR 'amplfɔːθ
AM 'æmpəl,fɔ(ə)rθ

ampleness
BR 'amplnəs
AM 'æmpəlnəs

Amplex®
BR 'amplɛks
AM 'æmplɛks

amplexicaul
BR am'plɛksɪkɔːl
AM æm'plɛksəˌkɔl, æm'plɛksəˌkɑl

amplification
BR ˌamplɪfɪ'keɪʃn
AM ˌæmpləfə'keɪʃən

amplifier
BR 'amplɪfʌɪə(r), -z
AM 'æmplə,faɪər, -z

amplify
BR 'amplɪfʌɪ, -z, -ɪŋ, -d
AM 'æmplə,faɪ, -z, -ɪŋ, -d

amplitude
BR 'amplɪtjuːd, 'amplɪtʃuːd, -z

AM 'æmplə,t(j)ud, -z

amply
BR 'ampli
AM 'æmp(ə)li

Ampney
BR 'ampni
AM 'æmpni

ampoule
BR 'amp(j)uːl, -z
AM 'æm,pjul, -z

Ampthill
BR 'am(p)t(h)ɪl
AM 'æm(p)t(h)ɪl

ampule
BR 'amp(j)uːl, -z
AM 'æm,pjul, -z

ampulla
BR am'pʊlə(r)
AM æm'p(j)ʊlə, æm'pələ, 'æm,pjʊlə

ampullae
BR am'pʊliː
AM æm'p(j)ʊ,li, æm'pə,li

amputate
BR 'ampjʉteɪt, -s, -ɪŋ, -ɪd
AM 'æmpjə,teɪt, -ts, -dɪŋ, -dɪd

amputation
BR ˌampjʉ'teɪʃn, -z
AM ˌæmpjə'teɪʃən, -z

amputator
BR 'ampjʉteɪtə(r), -z
AM 'æmpjə,teɪdər, -z

amputee
BR ˌampjʉ'tiː, -z
AM ˌæmpjə'ti, -z

Amritsar
BR am'rɪtsə(r), am'rɪtsɑ:(r)
AM ɑm'rɪtsər

Amsterdam
BR ˌam(p)stə'dam, 'am(p)stədam
AM 'æm(p)stər,dæm

Amstrad®
BR 'amstrad
AM 'æmstræd

amtrac
BR 'amtrak, -s
AM 'æm,træk, -s

Amtrak®
BR 'amtrak
AM 'æm,træk

amuck
BR ə'mʌk
AM ə'mək

Amu Darya
BR ˌɑːmuː 'dɑːrɪə(r), a,mu: +
AM ˌɑmu 'dɑrjə
RUS a'mu da'r'ja

amulet
BR 'amjʉlət, -s
AM 'æmjələt, 'æmjə,lɛt, -s

Amundsen
BR 'amən(d)s(ə)n, 'amʊn(d)s(ə)n
AM 'æmən(d)sən
NO 'a:mʉnsen

Amur
BR a'muːə(r), 'amʊə(r)
AM ɑ'mu(ə)r

amuse
BR ə'mjuːz, -ɪz, -ɪŋ, -d
AM ə'mjuz, -əz, -ɪŋ, -d

amusement
BR ə'mjuːzm(ə)nt, -s
AM ə'mjuzmənt, -s

amusing
BR ə'mjuːzɪŋ
AM ə'mjuzɪŋ

amusingly
BR ə'mjuːzɪŋli
AM ə'mjuzɪŋli

amusive
BR ə'mjuːzɪv
AM ə'mjuzɪv

Amy
BR 'eɪmi
AM 'eɪmi

amygdala
BR ə'mɪgdələ(r), -z
AM ə'mɪgdələ, -z

amygdalae
BR ə'mɪgdəli:
AM ə'mɪgdəli, ə'mɪgdə,laɪ

amygdale
BR ə'mɪgdəli:
AM ə'mɪgdəli

amygdaloid
BR ə'mɪgdəlɔɪd
AM ə'mɪgdə,lɔɪd

amyl
BR 'am(ɪ)l, 'eɪmʌɪl
AM 'æməl

amylase
BR 'amɪleɪz
AM 'æmə,leɪs, 'æmə,leɪz

amyloid
BR 'amɪlɔɪd
AM 'æmə,lɔɪd

amylopsin
BR 'amɪlɒpsɪn, ,amɪ'lɒpsɪn
AM ,æmə'lɑpsən

amyotrophy
BR ,amɪ'ɒtrəfi
AM ,æmi'ɑtrəfi

Amytal®
BR 'amɪtal
AM 'æmə,tɔl, 'æmə,tal

an
strong form
BR an
AM æn

an²
weak form
BR ən, n
AM ən, n

ana
BR 'ɑ:nə(r), -z
AM 'ɑnə, -z

Anabaptism
BR ,anə'baptɪz(ə)m
AM ,ænə'bæp,tɪzəm

Anabaptist
BR ,anə'baptɪst, -s
AM ,ænə'bæptəst, -s

anabas
BR 'anəbas
AM 'ænəbas, 'ænə,bæs

anabases
BR ə'nabəsi:z
AM ə'næbə,siz

anabasis
BR ə'nabəsɪs
AM ə'næbəsəs

anabatic
BR ,anə'batɪk
AM ,ænə'bædɪk

anabioses
BR ,anəbaɪ'əʊsi:z
AM ,ænə,baɪ'ousiz

anabiosis
BR ,anəbaɪ'əʊsɪs
AM ,ænə,baɪ'ousəs

anabiotic
BR ,anəbaɪ'ɒtɪk
AM ,ænə,baɪ'ɑdɪk

anabolic
BR ,anə'bɒlɪk, -s
AM ,ænə'balɪk, -s

anabolism
BR ə'nabəlɪz(ə)m
AM ə'næbə,lɪzəm, æ'næbə,lɪzəm

anabranch
BR 'anəbra:n(t)ʃ, 'anəbran(t)ʃ, -z
AM 'ænə,bræŋk, -s

anachronic
BR ,anə'krɒnɪk
AM ,ænə'krɑnɪk

anachronism
BR ə'nakrənɪz(ə)m, -z
AM ə'nækrə,nɪzəm, -z

anachronistic
BR ə,nakrə'nɪstɪk
AM ə,nækrə'nɪstɪk

anachronistically
BR ə,nakrə'nɪstɪkli
AM ə,nækrə'nɪstək(ə)li

Anacin®
BR 'anəsɪn, -z
AM 'ænəsɪn, -z

anacolutha
BR ,anəkə'lu:θə(r)
AM ,ænəkə'luːθə

anacoluthic
BR ,anəkə'lu:θɪk
AM ,ænəkə'luːθɪk

anacoluthon
BR ,anəkə'lu:θ(ə)n, ,anəkə'lu:θɒn
AM ,ænəkə'luːˌθɑn

anaconda
BR ˌænəˈkɒndə(r), -z
AM ˌænəˈkɑndə, -z
Anacreon
BR əˈnækriən
AM əˈnækriən
anacreontic
BR əˌnækrɪˈɒntɪk
AM əˈnækriˈɑn(t)ɪk
anacruses
BR ˌænəˈkruːsiːz
AM ˌænəˈkruˌsiz
anacrusis
BR ˌænəˈkruːsɪs
AM ˌænəˈkrusəs
Anadin®
BR ˈænədɪn, -z
AM ˈænədɪn, -z
anadromous
BR əˈnædrəməs
AM əˈnædrəməs, æˈnædrəməs
anaemia
BR əˈniːmɪə(r)
AM əˈnimiə
anaemic
BR əˈniːmɪk, -s
AM əˈnimɪk, -s
anaerobe
BR ˈanərəʊb, -z
AM ˈænəˌroʊb, -z
anaerobic
BR ˌænəˈrəʊbɪk, ˌanɛːˈrəʊbɪk
AM ˌænˌɛˈroʊbɪk, ˌænəˈroʊbɪk
anaesthesia
BR ˌanɪsˈθiːzɪə(r), ˌanɪsˈθiːʒə(r)
AM ˌænəsˈθiʒə
anaesthesiologist
BR ˌanɪsθiːzɪˈɒlədʒɪst, -s
AM ˌænəsˌθiz;iˈɑlədʒəst, -s
anaesthesiology
BR ˌanɪsθiːzɪˈɒlədʒi
AM ˌænəsˌθizi ˈɑlədʒi
anaesthetic
BR ˌanɪsˈθɛtɪk, -s
AM ˌænəsˈθɛdɪk, -s
anaesthetical
BR ˌanɪsˈθɛtɪkl
AM ˌænəsˈθɛdəkəl
anaesthetically
BR ˌanɪsˈθɛtɪkli
AM ˌænəsˈθɛdək(ə)li
anaesthetisation
BR əˌniːsθɪtʌɪˈzeɪʃn
AM əˌnɛsθədəˈzeɪʃən, əˌnɛsθətaɪˈzeɪʃən
anaesthetise
BR əˈniːsθɪtʌɪz, -ɪz, -ɪŋ, -d
AM əˈnɛsθəˌtaɪz, -ɪz, -ɪŋ, -d
anaesthetist
BR əˈniːsθɪtɪst, -s

AM əˈnɛsθədəst, -s
anaesthetization
BR əˌniːsθɪtʌɪˈzeɪʃn
AM əˌnɛsθədəˈzeɪʃən, əˌnɛsθəˌtaɪˈzeɪʃən
anaesthetize
BR əˈniːsθɪtʌɪz, -ɪz, -ɪŋ, -d
AM əˈnɛsθəˌtaɪz, -ɪz, -ɪŋ, -d
anaglyph
BR ˈanəɡlɪf, -s
AM ˈænəˌɡlɪf, -s
anaglyphic
BR ˌanəˈɡlɪfɪk
AM ˌænəˈɡlɪfɪk
anaglypta
BR ˌanəˈɡlɪptə(r), -z
AM ˌænəˈɡlɪptə, -z
anagnorises
BR ˌanəɡˈnɒrɪsiːz
AM ˌæˌnæɡˈnɒrəsiz
anagnorisis
BR ˌanəɡˈnɒrɪsɪs
AM ˌæˌnæɡˈnɒrəsəs
anagoge
BR ˈanəɡɒdʒi, ˈanəɡəʊdʒi
AM ˈænəˌɡadʒi, ˈænəˌɡoʊdʒi
anagogic
BR ˌanəˈɡɒdʒɪk, -s
AM ˌænəˈɡadʒɪk, -s
anagogical
BR ˌanəˈɡɒdʒɪkl
AM ˌænəˈɡadʒəkəl
anagogically
BR ˌanəˈɡɒdʒɪkli
AM ˌænəˈɡadʒək(ə)li
anagogy
BR ˈanəɡɒdʒi, ˈanəɡəʊdʒi
AM ˈænəˌɡadʒi, ˈænəˌɡoʊdʒi
anagram
BR ˈanəɡram, -z
AM ˈænəˌɡræm, -z
anagrammatic
BR ˌanəɡrəˈmatɪk
AM ˌænəɡrəˈmædɪk
anagrammatical
BR ˌanəɡrəˈmatɪkl
AM ˌænəɡrəˈmædəkəl
anagrammatically
BR ˌanəɡrəˈmatɪkli
AM ˌænəɡrəˈmædək(ə)li
anagrammatise
BR ˌanəˈɡramətʌɪz, -ɪz, -ɪŋ, -d
AM ˌænəˈɡræməˌtaɪz, -ɪz, -ɪŋ, -d
anagrammatize
BR ˌanəˈɡramətʌɪz, -ɪz, -ɪŋ, -d
AM ˌænəˈɡræməˌtaɪz, -ɪz, -ɪŋ, -d
Anaheim
BR ˈanəhʌɪm

AM əˈnɛsθədəst, -s
anal
BR ˈeɪnl
AM ˈeɪnəl
analect
BR ˈanəlɛkt, -s
AM ˈænlˌɛk|(t), -(t)s
analecta
BR ˌanəˈlɛktə(r)
AM ˌænəˈlɛktə
analemma
BR ˌanəˈlɛmə(r)
AM ˌænəˈlɛmə
analemmatic
BR ˌanəlɛˈmatɪk
AM ˌanələˈmædɪk
analeptic
BR ˌanəˈlɛptɪk
AM ˌænəˈlɛptɪk
analgesia
BR ˌanlˈdʒiːzɪə(r)
AM ˌænlˈdʒiziə, ˌænlˈdʒiʒə
analgesic
BR ˌanlˈdʒiːzɪk, -s
AM ˌænlˈdʒizɪk, -s
anally
BR ˈeɪnl̩i, ˈeɪnəli
AM ˈeɪnəli
analog
BR ˈanəlɒɡ, ˈanlɒɡ, -z
AM ˈænlˌɔɡ, ˈænlˌɑɡ, -z
analogic
BR ˌanəˈlɒdʒɪk
AM ˌænəˈladʒɪk
analogical
BR ˌanəˈlɒdʒɪkl
AM ˌænəˈladʒəkəl
analogically
BR ˌanəˈlɒdʒɪkli
AM ˌænəˈladʒək(ə)li
analogise
BR əˈnalədʒʌɪz, -ɪz, -ɪŋ, -d
AM əˈnælədʒaɪz, -ɪz, -ɪŋ, -d
analogist
BR əˈnalədʒɪst, -s
AM əˈnælədʒəst, -s
analogize
BR əˈnalədʒʌɪz, -ɪz, -ɪŋ, -d
AM əˈnælədʒaɪz, -ɪz, -ɪŋ, -d
analogous
BR əˈnaləɡəs
AM əˈnæləɡəs
analogously
BR əˈnaləɡəsli
AM əˈnæləɡəsli
analogousness
BR əˈnaləɡəsnəs
AM əˈnæləɡəsnəs
analogue
BR ˈanəlɒɡ, ˈanlɒɡ, -z
AM ˈænlˌɔɡ, ˈænlˌɑɡ, -z

analogy
BR əˈnalədʒ|i, -ɪz
AM əˈnælədʒi, -z
analphabetic
BR ˌanalfəˈbɛtɪk
AM ˌæˌnælfəˈbɛdɪk
analphabetical
BR ˌanalfəˈbɛtɪkl
AM ˌæˌnælfəˈbɛdəkəl
analphabetically
BR ˌanalfəˈbɛtɪkli
AM ˌæˌnælfəˈbɛdək(ə)li
analysable
BR ˈanəlʌɪzəbl, ˈanlʌɪzəbl
AM ˌænəˈlaɪzəbəl
analysand
BR əˈnalɪsand, -z
AM əˈnælə ˌsænd, əˈnæləˌzænd, -z
analyse
BR ˈanəlʌɪz, ˈanlʌɪz, -ɪz, -ɪŋ, -d
AM ˈænl̩ˌaɪz, -ɪz, -ɪŋ, -d
analyser
BR ˈanəlʌɪzə(r), ˈanl̩ʌɪzə(r), -z
AM ˈænl̩ˌaɪzər, -z
analyses
BR əˈnalɪsiːz
AM əˈnæləˌsiz
analysis
BR əˈnalɪsɪs
AM əˈnæləsəs
analyst
BR ˈanəlɪst, ˈanl̩ɪst, -s
AM ˈænələst, -s
analytic
BR ˌanəˈlɪtɪk
AM ˌænəˈlɪdɪk
analytical
BR ˌanəˈlɪtɪkl
AM ˌænəˈlɪdɪkəl
analytically
BR ˌanəˈlɪtɪkli
AM ˌænəˈlɪdɪk(ə)li
analyzable
BR ˈanəlʌɪzəbl, ˈanl̩ʌɪzəbl
AM ˌænəˈlaɪzəbəl
analyze
BR ˈanəlʌɪz, ˈanl̩ʌɪz, -ɪz, -ɪŋ, -d
AM ˈænl̩ˌaɪz, -ɪz, -ɪŋ, -d
analyzer
BR ˈanəlʌɪzə(r), ˈanl̩ʌɪzə(r), -z
AM ˈænl̩ˌaɪzər, -z
anamnesis
BR ˌanəmˈniːsɪs
AM ˌænəmˈnisɪs
anamorphic
BR ˌanəˈmɔːfɪk
AM ˌænəˈmɔrfɪk
anamorphoses
BR ˌanəˈmɔːfəsiːz
AM ˌænəˈmɔrfəsiz

anamorphosis
BR ˌanəˈmɔːfəsɪs
AM ˌænəˈmɔrfəsəs
ananas
BR əˈnɑːnəs, ˈananəs,
əˈnanəs
AM ˌanaˈnɑs
anandrous
BR əˈnandrəs
AM əˈnændrəs
Ananias
BR ˌanəˈnʌɪəs
AM ˌænəˈnaɪəs
anapaest
BR ˈanəpiːst, ˈanapɛst,
-s
AM ˈænəˌpɛst, -s
anapaestic
BR ˌanəˈpiːstɪk,
ˌanəˈpɛstɪk
AM ˌænəˈpɛstɪk
anapest
BR ˈanəpiːst, ˈanapɛst,
-s
AM ˈænəˌpɛst, -s
anapestic
BR ˌanəˈpiːstɪk,
ˌanəˈpɛstɪk
AM ˌænəˈpɛstɪk
anaphase
BR ˈanəfeɪz, -ɪz
AM ˈænəˌfeɪz, -ɪz
anaphor
BR ˈanəfɔː(r)
AM ˈænəˌfɔ(ə)r
anaphora
BR əˈnaf(ə)rə(r)
AM əˈnæf(ə)rə
anaphoric
BR ˌanəˈfɒrɪk
AM ˌænəˈfɔrɪk
anaphrodisiac
BR əˌnafrəˈdɪzɪak, -s
AM ˌæˌnəfrəˈdɪzɪˌæk, -s
anaphylactic
BR ˌanəfɪˈlaktɪk
AM ˌænəfəˈlæktɪk
anaphylaxis
BR ˌanəfɪˈlaksɪs
AM ˌænəfəˈlæksəs
anaptyctic
BR ˌanəpˈtɪktɪk,
ˌanapˈtɪktɪk
AM ˌænəpˈtɪktɪk
anaptyxes
BR ˌanəpˈtɪksiːz,
ˌanapˈtɪksiːz
AM ˌænæpˈtɪksiz
anaptyxis
BR ˌanəpˈtɪksɪs,
ˌanapˈtɪksɪs
AM ˌænæpˈtɪksɪs
anarch
BR ˈanɑːk, -s
AM ˈæn,ɑrk, -s
anarchic
BR əˈnɑːkɪk

AM æˈnɑːkɪk,
əˈnærkɪk
anarchical
BR əˈnɑːkɪkl
AM æˈnɑrkəkəl,
əˈnɑrkəkəl
anarchically
BR əˈnɑːkɪkli
AM æˈnɑrkək(ə)li,
əˈnɑrkək(ə)li
anarchism
BR ˈanəkɪz(ə)m
AM ˈænərˌkɪzəm,
ˈæˌnɑrˌkɪzəm
anarchist
BR ˈanəkɪst, -s
AM ˈænərkəst, -s
anarchistic
BR ˌanəˈkɪstɪk
AM ˌænərˈkɪstɪk
anarchy
BR ˈanəki
AM ˈænərki
Anasazi
BR ˌanəˈsɑːzi, ˌanəˈsazi
AM ˌænəˈsɑzi
Anastasia
BR ˌanəˈsteɪzɪə(r),
ˌanəˈstɑːzɪə(r)
AM ˌænəˈsteɪʒə
RUS ənəstaˈsʲijə
anastigmat
BR anˈastɪgmat,
ənˈastɪgmat,
ˌanəˈstɪgmat, -s
AM ˌænəˈstɪgˌmæt, -s
anastigmatic
BR ˌanəstɪgˈmatɪk
AM ˌænəˌstɪgˈmædɪk
anastomose
BR əˈnastəməʊz,
aˈnastəməʊz, -ɪz, -ɪŋ,
-d
AM əˈnæstəˌmoʊz,
əˈnæstəˌmoʊs, -əz, -ɪŋ,
-d
anastomoses
BR əˌnastəˈməʊsiːz,
aˌnastəˈməʊsiːz,
ˌanəstəˈməʊsiːz
anastomosis
BR əˌnastəˈməʊsɪs,
aˌnastəˈməʊsɪs,
ˌanəstəˈməʊsɪs
AM əˌnæstəˈmoʊsəs
anastrophe
BR əˈnastrəfi,
aˈnastrəfi
AM əˈnæstrəfi
anathema
BR əˈnaθɪmə(r)
AM əˈnæθəmə
anathematisation
BR əˌnaθɪmətʌɪˈzeɪʃn
AM əˌnæθ(ə)mədəˈzeɪ-
ʃən,
əˌnæθ(ə)məˌtaɪˈzeɪʃən

anathematise
BR əˈnaθɪmətʌɪz, -ɪz,
-ɪŋ, -d
AM əˈnæθ(ə)məˌtaɪz,
-ɪz, -ɪŋ, -d
anathematization
BR əˌnaθɪmətʌɪˈzeɪʃn
AM əˌnæθ(ə)mədəˈzeɪ-
ʃən,
əˌnæθ(ə)məˌtaɪˈzeɪʃən
anathematize
BR əˈnaθɪmətʌɪz, -ɪz,
-ɪŋ, -d
AM əˈnæθ(ə)məˌtaɪz,
-ɪz, -ɪŋ, -d
Anatolia
BR ˌanəˈtəʊlɪə(r)
AM ˌænəˈtoʊljə,
ˌænəˈtoʊlɪə
Anatolian
BR ˌanəˈtəʊlɪən, -z
AM ˌænəˈtoʊljən,
ˌænəˈtoʊlɪən, -z
anatomic
BR ˌanəˈtɒmɪk
AM ˌænəˈtamɪk
anatomical
BR ˌanəˈtɒmɪkl
AM ˌænəˈtaməkəl
anatomically
BR ˌanəˈtɒmɪkli
AM ˌænəˈtamək(ə)li
anatomise
BR əˈnatəmʌɪz, -ɪz, -ɪŋ,
-d
AM əˈnædəˌmaɪz, -ɪz,
-ɪŋ, -d
anatomist
BR əˈnatəmɪst, -s
AM əˈnædəməst, -s
anatomize
BR əˈnatəmʌɪz, -ɪz, -ɪŋ,
-d
AM əˈnædəˌmaɪz, -ɪz,
-ɪŋ, -d
anatomy
BR əˈnatəm|i, -ɪz
AM əˈnædəmi, -z
anatta
BR əˈnatə(r)
AM əˈnɑdə
anatto
BR əˈnatəʊ
AM əˈnɑdoʊ
Anaxagoras
BR ˌanakˈsag(ə)rəs,
ˌanakˈsagərəs
AM ˌænəkˈsægərəs
Anaximander
BR əˌnaksɪˈmandə(r)
AM əˌnæksəˈmændər
Anaximenes
BR ˌanakˈsɪmɪniːz
AM ˌænəkˈsɪməniz
anbury
BR ˈanb(ə)r|i, -ɪz
AM ˈænbəri, -z

ancestor
BR ˈansɪstə(r),
ˈansɛstə(r), -z
AM ˈænˌsɛstər, -z
ancestral
BR anˈsɛstr(ə)l
AM ænˈsɛstrəl
ancestrally
BR anˈsɛstr|i,
anˈsɛstrəli
AM ænˈsɛstrəli
ancestress
BR ˈansɪstrɪs,
ˈansɛstrɪs, -ɪz
AM ˈænˌsɛstrəs, -əz
ancestry
BR ˈansɪstr|i,
ˈansɛstr|i, -ɪz
AM ˈænˌsɛstri, -z
Anchises
BR anˈkʌɪsiːz
AM æŋˈkaɪsiz
anchor
BR ˈaŋk|ə(r), -əz,
-(ə)rɪŋ, -əd
AM ˈæŋk|ər, -ərz,
-(ə)rɪŋ, -ərd
anchorage
BR ˈaŋk(ə)r|ɪdʒ, -ɪdʒɪz
AM ˈæŋk(ə)rɪdʒ, -ɪz
anchoress
BR ˈaŋk(ə)rɪs,
ˈaŋkərɛs, -ɪz
AM ˈæŋk(ə)rəs, -əz
anchoretic
BR ˌaŋkəˈrɛtɪk
AM ˌæŋkəˈrɛdɪk
anchorhold
BR ˈaŋkəhəʊld, -z
AM ˈæŋkər,(h)oʊld, -z
anchorite
BR ˈaŋkərʌɪt, -s
AM ˈæŋkəˌraɪt, -s
anchoritic
BR ˌaŋkəˈrɪtɪk
AM ˌæŋkəˈrɪdɪk
anchorman
BR ˈaŋkəman
AM ˈæŋkərˌmæn
anchormen
BR ˈaŋkəmɛn
AM ˈæŋkərˌmɛn
anchorperson
BR ˈaŋkəˌpəːsn, -z
AM ˈæŋkərˌpərsən, -z
anchorwoman
BR ˈaŋkəˌwʊmən
AM ˈæŋkərˌwʊmən
anchorwomen
BR ˈaŋkəˌwɪmɪn
AM ˈæŋkərˌwɪmɪn
anchoveta
BR ˌantʃ|ə(ʊ)ˈvetə(r), -z
AM ˌæntʃoʊˈvɛdə, -z
anchovy
BR ˈantʃəv|i, -ɪz
AM ˈænˌtʃoʊvi, -z

anchusa
BR aŋˈk(j)uːzə(r),
anˈtʃuːzə(r), -z
AM æŋˈkjuzə,
æŋˈkjusə, -z

anchylose
BR ˈaŋkɪləʊz,
ˈaŋkɪləʊs, -ɪz, -ɪŋ, -d\-t
AM ˈæŋkəˌloʊs,
ˈæŋkəˌloʊz, -əz, -ɪŋ,
-t\-d

ancien régime
BR ˌɒsiɑ̃ reɪˈʒiːm,
ˌɒnsiɑ̃ +, -z
AM ˌɑnsiɛn rəˈʒim, -z

ancient
BR ˈeɪnʃ(ə)nt, -s
AM ˈeɪn(t)ʃənt, -s

anciently
BR ˈeɪnʃ(ə)ntli
AM ˈeɪn(t)ʃən(t)li

ancientness
BR ˈeɪnʃ(ə)ntnəs
AM ˈeɪn(t)ʃən(t)nəs

ancillary
BR anˈsɪlər|i, -ɪz
AM ˈænsəˌlɛri, -z

ancipital
BR anˈsɪpɪtl
AM anˈsɪpədl

ancon
BR ˈaŋkɒn, ˈaŋk(ə)n, -z
AM ˈæŋˌkɑn, -z

ancones
BR aŋˈkəʊniːz
AM ˌæŋˈkoʊniz

Ancyra
BR anˈsʌɪrə(r)
AM ænˈsaɪrə

and¹
strong form
BR and
AM ænd

and²
weak form
BR (ə)n(d)
AM (ə)n(d)

Andalucía
BR ˌandəluːˈsiə(r)
AM ˌændəˈluʒə,
ˌændəˈluʃ(i)ə
SP ˌandaluˈθia,
ˌandaluˈsia

Andalusia
BR ˌandəˈluːsiə(r),
ˌandəluːˈsiːə(r)
AM ˌændəˈluʒə,
ˌændəˈluʃ(i)ə

Andalusian
BR ˌandəˈluːsiən,
ˌandəluːˈsiːən, -z
AM ˌændəˈluʒən,
ˌændəˈluʃən, -z

Andaman
BR ˈandəmən, -z
AM ˈændəmən, -z

Andamanese
BR ˌandəməˈniːz
AM ˌændəməˈniz

andante
BR anˈdant|i,
anˈdant|eɪ, -ɪz\-eɪz
AM ɑnˈdɑn(t)eɪ, -z

andantino
BR ˌandanˈtiːnəʊ, -z
AM ˌɑnˌdɑnˈtinoʊ, -z

Andean
BR ˈandɪən, anˈdiːən
AM ˈænˌdiən

Andersen
BR ˈandəs(ə)n
AM ˈændərsən

Anderson
BR ˈandəs(ə)n
AM ˈændərsən

Andes
BR ˈandiːz
AM ˈændiz

andesite
BR ˈandɪsʌɪt, ˈandɪzʌɪt
AM ˈændəˌzaɪt

Andhra Pradesh
BR ˌandrə prəˈdɛʃ
AM ˌɑndrə prəˈdɛʃ

andiron
BR ˈandʌɪən, -z
AM ˈænˌdaɪ(ə)rn, -z

Andorra
BR anˈdɔːrə(r),
anˈdɒrə(r)
AM ænˈdɔrə

Andorran
BR anˈdɔːrən, anˈdɔːrŋ,
anˈdɒrən, anˈdɒrŋ, -z
AM ænˈdɔrən, -z

André
BR ˈɒndreɪ, ˈandreɪ,
ˈɑːndreɪ
AM ˈɑnˌdreɪ

Andrea
BR ˈandrɪə(r)
AM ˈændriə, ænˈdreɪə

Andreas
BR anˈdreɪəs
AM ænˈdreɪəs

Andrew
BR ˈandruː
AM ˈænˌdru

Andrews
BR ˈandruːz
AM ˈænˌdruz

androcentric
BR ˌandrə(ʊ)ˈsɛntrɪk
AM ˌændroʊˈsɛntrɪk

androcentrism
BR ˌandrə(ʊ)ˈsɛntrɪ-
z(ə)m
AM ˌændroʊˈsɛnˌtrɪzm

Androcles
BR ˈandrəkliːz
AM ˈændrəˌkliz

androecia
BR anˈdriːsɪə(r)
AM ænˈdriʃ(i)ə

androecium
BR anˈdriːsɪəm
AM ænˈdriʃ(i)əm

androgen
BR ˈandrədʒ(ə)n,
ˈandrədʒɛn, -z
AM ˈændrədʒən, -z

androgenic
BR ˌandrə(ʊ)ˈdʒɛnɪk
AM ˌændrəˈdʒɛnɪk

androgyne
BR ˈandrədʒʌɪn, -z
AM ˈændrəˌdʒaɪn, -z

androgynous
BR anˈdrɒdʒɪnəs
AM ænˈdrɑdʒənəs

androgyny
BR anˈdrɒdʒɪni
AM ænˈdrɑdʒəni

android
BR ˈandrɔɪd, -z
AM ˈænˌdrɔɪd, -z

Andromache
BR anˈdrɒməki
AM ænˈdrɑməki

Andromeda
BR anˈdrɒmɪdə(r)
AM ænˈdrɑmədə

androstenedione
BR ˌandrɒstiːnˈdʌɪəʊn
AM ˌændrəstinˈdaɪoʊn

androsterone
BR ˌandrə(ʊ)ˈstɪərəʊn
anˈdrɒstərəʊn
AM ænˈdrɑstəˌroʊn

Andy
BR ˈandi
AM ˈændi

anear
BR əˈnɪə(r)
AM əˈni(ə)r

anecdotage
BR ˈanɪkdəʊtɪdʒ
AM ˈænəkˌdoʊdɪdʒ

anecdotal
BR ˌanɪkˈdəʊtl
AM ˌænəkˈdoʊdl

anecdotalist
BR ˌanɪkˈdəʊtlɪst, -s
AM ˌænəkˈdoʊdələst,
-s

anecdotally
BR ˌanɪkˈdəʊtli
AM ˌænəkˈdoʊdəli

anecdote
BR ˈanɪkdəʊt, -s
AM ˈænəkˌdoʊt, -s

anecdotic
BR ˌanɪkˈdɒtɪk
AM ˌænəkˈdɑdɪk

anechoic
BR ˌanɪˈkəʊɪk
AM ˌænəˈkoʊɪk

anele
BR əˈniːl, -z, -ɪŋ, -d
AM əˈni(ə)l, -z, -ɪŋ, -d

anemia
BR əˈniːmɪə(r)
AM əˈnimiə

anemic
BR əˈniːmɪk, -s
AM əˈnimɪk, -s

anemograph
BR əˈnɛməɡrɑːf,
əˈnɛməɡraf, -s
AM əˈnɛməˌɡræf, -s

anemographic
BR əˌnɛməˈɡrafɪk
AM əˌnɛməˈɡræfɪk

anemometer
BR ˌanɪˈmɒmɪtə(r), -z
AM ˌænəˈmɑmədər, -z

anemometric
BR ˌanɪməˈmɛtrɪk
AM ˌænəməˈmɛtrɪk

anemometry
BR ˌanɪˈmɒmɪtri
AM ˌænəˈmɑmətri

anemone
BR əˈnɛmən|i, -ɪz
AM əˈnɛməni, -z

anemophilous
BR ˌanɪˈmɒfɪləs,
ˌanɪˈmɒfləs
AM ˌænəˈmɑfələs

anencephalic
BR ˌanɛnsɪˈfalɪk,
ˌanɛŋkɛˈfalɪk
AM ˌænˌɛnsəˈfælɪk

anencephaly
BR ˌanɛnˈsɛfəli,
ˌanɛnˈsɛfli,
ˌanɛnˈkɛfəli,
ˌanɛnˈkɛfli
AM ˌænˌɛnˈsɛfəli

anent
BR əˈnɛnt
AM əˈnɛnt

aneroid
BR ˈanərɔɪd
AM ˈænəˌrɔɪd

anesthesia
BR ˌanɪsˈθiːzɪə(r),
ˌanɪsˈθiːʒə(r)
AM ˌænəsˈθiʒə

anesthesiologist
BR ˌanɪsθiːzɪˈɒlədʒɪst,
-s
AM ˌænəsˌθiziˈɑlədʒəst,
-s

anesthesiology
BR ˌanɪsθiːzɪˈɒlədʒi
AM ˌænəsˌθiziˈɑlədʒi

anesthetic
BR ˌanɪsˈθɛtɪk, -s
AM ˌænəsˈθɛdɪk, -s

anesthetical
BR ˌanɪsˈθɛtɪkl
AM ˌænəsˈθɛdəkəl

anesthetically
BR ˌanɪsˈθɛtɪkli

AM ˌænəs'θedək(ə)li

anesthetist
BR ə'niːsθɪtɪst, -s
AM ə'nɛsθədəst, -s

anesthetization
BR ə,niːsθɪtaɪ'zeɪʃn
AM ə,nɛsθədə'zeɪʃən,
ə,nɛsθə,taɪ'zeɪʃn

anesthetize
BR ə'niːsθɪtaɪz, -ɪz, -ɪŋ,
-d
AM ə'nɛsθə,taɪz, -ɪz, -ɪŋ,
-d

anestrous
BR (,)an'iːstrəs
AM æn'ɛstrəs

anestrus
BR (,)an'iːstrəs
AM æn'ɛstrəs

Aneurin
BR ə'nʌɪrɪn, ə'nʌɪrɪŋ
AM ə'njərən, 'ænjərən
WE an'eɪrɪn

aneurin
BR ə'njʊərɪn,
ə'njɔːrɪn, 'anjʊrɪn
AM 'ænjərən, ə'njərən

aneurism
BR 'anjʊrɪz(ə)m, -z
AM 'ænjə,rɪzəm, -z

aneurysm
BR 'anjʊrɪz(ə)m, -z
AM 'ænjə,rɪzəm, -z

aneurysmal
BR ,anjʊ'rɪzml
AM ,ænjə'rɪzməl

anew
BR ə'njuː
AM ə'n(j)u

Anfield
BR 'anfiːld
AM 'æn,fild

anfractuosity
BR ,anfraktjʊ'ɒsɪti,
,anfraktʃʊ'ɒsɪti
AM æn,fræktʃə'wɑsədi

anfractuous
BR an'fraktjʊəs,
an'fraktʃʊəs
AM æn'fræk(t)ʃ(əw)əs

angary
BR 'aŋg(ə)ri
AM 'æŋgəri

angel
BR 'eɪn(d)ʒ(ə)l, -z
AM 'eɪndʒəl, -z

Angela
BR 'an(d)ʒ(ɪ)lə(r)
AM 'ændʒələ

angeldust
BR 'eɪn(d)ʒ(ə)ldʌst
AM 'eɪndʒəl,dəst

angelfish
BR 'eɪn(d)ʒ(ə)lfɪʃ
AM 'eɪndʒəl,fɪʃ

angelic
BR an'dʒɛlɪk

AM æn'dʒɛlɪk

angelica
BR an'dʒɛlɪkə(r)
AM æn'dʒɛləkə

angelical
BR an'dʒɛlɪkl
AM æn'dʒɛləkəl

angelically
BR an'dʒɛlɪkli
AM æn'dʒɛlək(ə)li

Angelico
BR an'dʒɛlɪkəʊ
AM æn'dʒɛlə,koʊ

Angelina
BR ,an(d)ʒɪ'liːnə(r)
AM ,ændʒə'linə

Angelo
BR 'an(d)ʒɪləʊ
AM 'ændʒɛloʊ

Angelou
BR 'an(d)ʒəluː
AM 'ændʒəlu

angelus
BR 'an(d)ʒ(ɪ)ləs,
'an(d)ʒləs, -ɪz
AM 'ændʒələs, -əz

anger
BR 'aŋg|ə(r), -əz,
-(ə)rɪŋ, -əd
AM 'æŋg|ər, -ərz,
-(ə)rɪŋ, -ərd

Angers
BR ɒ̃'ʒeɪ
AM ɑn'ʒɛr(z)

Angevin
BR 'an(d)ʒɪvɪn, -z
AM 'ændʒəvən, -z
FR ɑ̃ʒvɛ̃

Angharad
BR aŋ'harəd
AM 'æŋgə,ræd
WE aŋ'harad

Angie
BR 'an(d)ʒi
AM 'ændʒi

angina
BR an'dʒʌɪnə(r)
AM æn'dʒaɪnə

angiogram
BR 'an(d)ʒɪə(ʊ)gram,
-z
AM 'ændʒioʊ,græm,
'ændʒ(i)ə,græm, -z

angiography
BR ,an(d)ʒɪ'ɒgrəfi
AM ,ændʒi'ɑgrəfi

angioma
BR ,an(d)ʒɪ'əʊmə(r), -z
AM ,ændʒi'oʊmə, -z

angiomata
BR ,an(d)ʒɪ'əʊmətə(r)
AM ,ændʒi'oʊmədə

angioplasty
BR 'an(d)ʒɪə(ʊ)plasti
AM 'ændʒiə,plæsti

angiosperm
BR 'an(d)ʒɪə(ʊ)spəːm,
-z
AM 'ændʒiə,spərm, -z

angiospermous
BR ,an(d)ʒɪə(ʊ)'spəːməs
AM ,ændʒiə'spərməs

Angkor
BR 'aŋkɔː(r)
AM 'æŋkɔ(ə)r

angle
BR 'aŋg|l, -lz, -lɪŋ \-lɪŋ,
-ld
AM 'æŋg|əl, -əlz,
-(ə)lɪŋ, -əld

angledozer
BR 'aŋgl,dəʊzə(r), -z
AM 'æŋgəl,doʊzər, -z

Anglepoise®
BR 'aŋglpɔɪz
AM 'æŋgəl,pɔɪz

angler
BR 'aŋglə(r), -z
AM 'æŋglər, -z

Anglesey
BR 'aŋglsi
AM 'æŋgəlsi

angleworm
BR 'aŋglwəːm, -z
AM 'æŋgəl,wərm, -z

Anglia
BR 'aŋglɪə(r)
AM 'æŋgliə

Anglian
BR 'aŋglɪən, -z
AM 'æŋgliən, -z

Anglican
BR 'aŋglɪk(ə)n, -z
AM 'æŋgləkən, -z

Anglicanism
BR 'aŋglɪkənɪz(ə)m,
'aŋglɪkŋɪz(ə)m
AM 'æŋgləkə,nɪzəm

anglice
BR 'aŋglɪsi
AM 'æŋgləsi

Anglicisation
BR ,aŋglɪsʌɪ'zeɪʃn
AM ,æŋgləsə'zeɪʃən,
,æŋglə,saɪ'zeɪʃən

Anglicise
BR 'aŋglɪsʌɪz, -ɪz, -ɪŋ, -d
AM 'æŋglə,saɪz, -ɪz, -ɪŋ,
-d

Anglicism
BR 'aŋglɪsɪz(ə)m, -z
AM 'æŋglə,sɪzəm, -z

Anglicist
BR 'aŋglɪsɪst, -s
AM 'æŋgləsəst, -s

Anglicization
BR ,aŋglɪsʌɪ'zeɪʃn
AM ,æŋgləsə'zeɪʃən,
,æŋglə,saɪ'zeɪʃən

Anglicize
BR 'aŋglɪsʌɪz, -ɪz, -ɪŋ, -d
AM 'æŋglə,saɪz, -ɪz, -ɪŋ,
-d

Anglist
BR 'aŋglɪst, -s
AM 'æŋgləst, -s

Anglistics
BR aŋ'glɪstɪks
AM æŋ'lɪstɪks

Anglo
BR 'aŋgləʊ, -z
AM 'æŋgloʊ, -z

Anglocentric
BR ,aŋglə(ʊ)'sɛntrɪk
AM ,æŋgloʊ'sɛntrɪk,
,æŋglə'sɛntrɪk

Anglomania
BR ,aŋglə(ʊ)'meɪnɪə(r)
AM ,æŋgloʊ'meɪniə,
,æŋglə'meɪniə

Anglomaniac
BR ,aŋgləʊ'meɪnɪak, -s
AM ,æŋgloʊ'meɪni,æk,
,æŋglə'meɪni,æk, -s

Anglophile
BR 'aŋglə(ʊ)fʌɪl, -z
AM 'æŋgloʊ,faɪl,
'æŋglə,faɪl, -z

Anglophilia
BR ,aŋglə(ʊ)'fɪlɪə(r)
AM ,æŋgloʊ'fɪljə,
,æŋglə'fɪljə,
,æŋgloʊ'fɪliə,
,æŋglə'fɪliə

Anglophobe
BR 'aŋglə(ʊ)fəʊb, -z
AM 'æŋgloʊ,foʊb,
'æŋglə,foʊb, -z

Anglophobia
BR ,aŋglə(ʊ)'fəʊbɪə(r)
AM ,æŋgloʊ'foʊbiə,
,æŋglə'foʊbiə

Anglophone
BR 'aŋgləfəʊn
AM 'æŋgloʊ,foʊn,
'æŋglə,foʊn

Angmering
BR 'aŋmərɪŋ
AM 'æŋ,mɛrɪŋ

Angola
BR aŋ'gəʊlə(r)
AM æŋ'goʊlə,
æn'goʊlə

Angolan
BR aŋ'gəʊlən, -z
AM æŋ'goʊlən,
æn'goʊlən, -z

angora
BR aŋ'gɔːrə(r), -z
AM æŋ'gɔrə, -z

Angostura
BR ,aŋgə'stjʊərə(r),
,aŋgə'stjɔːrə(r),
,aŋgə'stʃʊərə(r),
,aŋgə'stʃɔːrə(r)
AM ,æŋgə'st(j)ʊrə

Angoulême
BR ,ɒŋguː'lɛm
AM ,æŋgʊ'lɛm

angrily
BR 'aŋgrɪli

AM 'æŋgrəli

angry
BR 'aŋgr|i, -ɪə(r), -ɪɪst
AM 'æŋgri, -ər, -ɪst

angst
BR aŋ(k)st
AM æŋ(k)st, aŋ(k)st

angstrom
BR 'aŋstrəm,
'aŋstrʌm, 'aŋstrɒm,
-z
AM 'æŋstrəm, -z

Anguilla
BR aŋ'gwɪlə(r)
AM æŋ'gwɪlə

Anguillan
BR aŋ'gwɪlən, -z
AM æŋ'gwɪlən, -z

anguine
BR 'aŋgwɪn
AM 'æŋgwɪn

anguish
BR 'aŋgw|ɪʃ, -ɪʃɪz, -ɪʃɪŋ,
-ɪʃt
AM 'æŋgwɪʃ, -əz, -ɪŋ, -t

angular
BR 'aŋgjʊlə(r)
AM 'æŋgjələr

angularity
BR ˌaŋgjʊ'larɪt|i, -ɪz
AM ˌæŋgjʊ'lɛrədi, -z

angularly
BR 'aŋgjʊləli
AM 'æŋgjələrli

Angus
BR 'aŋgəs
AM 'æŋgəs

angwantibo
BR əŋ'gwɒntɪbəʊ, -z
AM æŋ'(g)wan(t)ə,bəʊ, -z

anharmonic
BR ˌanhɑː'mɒnɪk
AM ˌænhɑr'mɑnɪk

anhedral
BR an'hiːdr(ə)l, an'hɛdr(ə)l
AM æn'hidrəl

Anhui
BR 'ɑːn(h)wiː
AM 'ɑnˌ(h)wi

Anhwei
BR 'ɑːn(h)weɪ
AM 'ɑnˌ(h)weɪ

anhydride
BR an'hʌɪdrʌɪd, -z
AM æn'haɪˌdraɪd, -z

anhydrite
BR an'hʌɪdrʌɪt
AM æn'haɪˌdraɪt

anhydrous
BR an'hʌɪdrəs
AM æn'haɪdrəs

ani
BR 'ɑːn|i, -ɪz
AM 'ɑni, -z

aniconic
BR ˌanʌɪ'kɒnɪk
AM ˌæˌnaɪ'kɑnɪk

anicut
BR 'anɪkʌt, -s
AM 'ænəkət, -s

anigh
BR ə'nʌɪ
AM ə'naɪ

anil
BR 'an(ɪ)l
AM 'ænəl

anile
BR 'anʌɪl
AM 'æˌnaɪl, 'eɪˌnaɪl

aniline
BR 'anɪliːn, 'anⱼiːn, 'anɪln, 'anⱼln
AM 'ænələn

anilingus
BR ˌeɪnɪ'lɪŋgəs
AM ˌeɪnɪ'lɪŋgəs

anility
BR ə'nɪlɪti
AM ə'nɪlɪdi, æ'nɪlɪdi

anima
BR 'anɪmə(r)
AM 'ænəmə

animadversion
BR ˌanɪmad'vəːʃn, ˌanɪməd'vəːʃn, ˌanɪmad'vəːʒn, ˌanɪməd'vəːʒn-z
AM ˌænəmˌæd'vərʒən, -z

animadvert
BR ˌanɪmad'vəːt, ˌanɪməd'vəːt, -s, -ɪŋ, -ɪd
AM ˌænəmˌæd'vərⱼt, -ts, -dɪŋ, -dəd

animal
BR 'anɪml, -z
AM 'ænəməl, -z

animalcular
BR ˌanɪ'malkjʊlə(r)
AM ˌænə'mæ(l)kjələr

animalcule
BR ˌanɪ'malkjuːl, -z
AM ˌænə'mæl,kjul, -z

animalisation
BR ˌanɪmələʌɪ'zeɪʃn, ˌanɪmⱼʌɪ'zeɪʃn
AM ˌænəmələ'zeɪʃən, ˌænəməˌlaɪ'zeɪʃən

animalise
BR 'anɪmələʌɪz, 'anɪmⱼʌɪz, -ɪz, -ɪŋ, -d
AM 'ænəməˌlaɪz, -ɪz, -ɪŋ, -d

animalism
BR 'anɪmələɪz(ə)m, 'anɪmⱼɪz(ə)m
AM 'ænəməˌlɪzəm

animalist
BR 'anɪmələɪst, 'anɪmⱼɪst, -s
AM 'ænəmələst, -s

animalistic
BR ˌanɪmə'lɪstɪk, ˌanɪml'ɪstɪk
AM ˌænəmə'lɪstɪk

animality
BR ˌanɪ'malɪti
AM ˌænə'mæləɪ

animalization
BR ˌanɪmələʌɪ'zeɪʃn, ˌanɪmⱼʌɪ'zeɪʃn
AM ˌænəmələ'zeɪʃən, ˌænəməˌlaɪ'zeɪʃən

animalize
BR 'anɪmələʌɪz, 'anɪmⱼʌɪz, -ɪz, -ɪŋ, -d
AM 'ænəməˌlaɪz, -ɪz, -ɪŋ, -d

anima mundi
BR ˌanɪmə 'mʊndi
AM ˌænəmə 'mʊndi

animate¹
adjective
BR 'anɪmət
AM 'ænəmət

animate²
verb
BR 'anɪmeɪt, -s, -ɪŋ, -ɪd
AM 'ænəˌmeɪ|t, -ts, -dɪŋ, -dɪd

animatedly
BR 'anɪmeɪtɪdli
AM 'ænəˌmeɪdɪdli

animation
BR ˌanɪ'meɪʃn
AM ˌænə'meɪʃən

animator
BR 'anɪmeɪtə(r), -z
AM 'ænəˌmeɪdər, -z

animatron
BR 'anɪmətrɒn, -z
AM 'ænəməˌtran, -z

animatronic
BR ˌanɪmə'trɒnɪk, -s
AM ˌænəmə'tranɪk, -s

animé
BR 'anɪmeɪ
AM ˌænə'meɪ

animism
BR 'anɪmɪz(ə)m
AM 'ænəˌmɪzəm

animist
BR 'anɪmɪst, -s
AM 'ænəməst, -s

animistic
BR ˌanɪ'mɪstɪk
AM ˌænə'mɪstɪk

animosity
BR ˌanɪ'mɒsɪt|i, -ɪz
AM ˌænə'mɑsədi, -z

animus
BR 'anɪməs
AM 'ænəməs

anion
BR 'an,ʌɪən, -z
AM 'æn,aɪən, -z

anionic
BR ˌanʌɪ'ɒnɪk
AM ˌænaɪ'ɑnɪk

anis
BR a'niːs
AM ɑ'nis, ə'nis

anise
BR 'anɪs
AM 'ænəs

aniseed
BR 'anɪsiːd
AM 'ænə(s)ˌsid

anisette
BR ˌanɪ'zɛt, ˌanɪ'sɛt
AM ˌænə'sɛt, ˌænə'zɛt

anisogamy
BR ˌanʌɪ'sɒgəmi
AM ˌænˌaɪ'sɑgəmi

anisomorphic
BR anˌʌɪsə(ʊ)'mɔːfɪk, ˌanʌɪsə(ʊ)'mɔːfɪk
AM ˌænˌaɪsə'mɔrfɪk, ˌænˌaɪsə'mɔrfɪk

anisotropic
BR anˌʌɪsə(ʊ)'trɒpɪk, ˌanʌɪsə(ʊ)'trɒpɪk, anˌʌɪsə(ʊ)'trəʊpɪk, ˌanʌɪsə(ʊ)'trəʊpɪk
AM ˌænˌaɪsə'trapɪk, ˌænˌaɪsə'trapɪk

anisotropically
BR anˌʌɪsə(ʊ)'trɒpɪkli, ˌanʌɪsə(ʊ)'trɒpɪkli
AM ˌænˌaɪsə'trapək(ə)li, ˌænˌaɪsə'trapək(ə)li

anisotropy
BR anʌɪ'sɒtrəpi
AM ˌænˌaɪ'sɑtrəpi

Anita
BR ə'niːtə(r)
AM ə'nidə

Anjou
BR ˌɑːn'ʒuː, ˌɒ'ʒuː
AM 'ɑnʒu

Ankara
BR 'aŋk(ə)rə(r)
AM 'æŋkərə

anker
BR 'aŋkə(r), -z
AM 'æŋkər, -z

ankerite
BR 'aŋkərʌɪt
AM 'æŋkəˌraɪt

ankh
BR aŋk, -s
AM ɑŋk, -s

ankle
BR 'aŋkl, -z
AM 'æŋkəl, -z

anklet
BR 'aŋklɪt, -s
AM 'æŋklət, -s

ankylose
BR 'aŋkɪləʊz, 'aŋkɪləʊs
AM 'æŋkəˌloʊs, 'æŋkəˌloʊz, -əz, -ɪŋ, -t\-d

ankyloses
BR ˌaŋkɪ'ləʊsiːz
AM 'æŋkəˌloʊsiz

ankylosis
BR ˌaŋkɪˈləʊsɪs
AM ˌæŋkəˌloʊsəs

ankylotic
BR ˌaŋkɪˈlɒtɪk
AM ˌæŋkəˈladɪk

Anlaby
BR ˈanləbi
AM ˈænləbi

anlace
BR ˈanləs, -ɪz
AM ˈænləs, -əz

Ann
BR an
AM æn

Anna
BR ˈanə(r)
AM ˈænə

Annaba
BR əˈnɑːbə(r)
AM æ(n)ˈnɑbə

Annabel
BR ˈanəbɛl
AM ˈænəˌbɛl

Annabella
BR ˌanəˈbɛlə(r)
AM ˌænəˈbɛlə

annal
BR ˈanl̩, -z
AM ˈænəl, -z

annalist
BR ˈanəlɪst, ˈanl̩ɪst, -s
AM ˈænl̩əst, -s

annalistic
BR ˌanəˈlɪstɪk, ˌanl̩ˈɪstɪk
AM ˌænl̩ˈɪstɪk

annalistically
BR ˌanəˈlɪstɪkli, ˌanl̩ˈɪstɪkli
AM ˌænl̩ˈɪstɪk(ə)li

Annamarie
BR ˌanəməˈriː
AM ˌænəməˈri

Annamese
BR ˌanəˈmiːz
AM ˌænəˈmiz

Annapolis
BR əˈnapəlɪs, əˈnapl̩ɪs
AM əˈnæpəlɪs, ˌænˈæpəlɪs

Annapurna
BR ˌanəˈpəːnə(r)
AM ˌænəˈpərnə

annates
BR ˈaneɪts
AM ˈæˌneɪts, ˈænəts

annatto
BR əˈnɑːtəʊ
AM əˈnɑdoʊ

Anne
BR an
AM æn

anneal
BR əˈniːl, -z, -ɪŋ, -d
AM əˈni(ə)l, -z, -ɪŋ, -d

annealer
BR əˈniːlə(r), -z
AM əˈnilər, -z

annectent
BR əˈnɛkt(ə)nt
AM əˈnɛkt(ə)nt

Anneka
BR ˈanɪkə(r)
AM ˈænɛkə

annelid
BR ˈanəlɪd, ˈanl̩ɪd, -z
AM ˈænələd, ˈænəˌlɪd, -z

annelidan
BR əˈnɛlɪd(ə)n
AM əˈnɛlədən, æˈnɛlədən

Annemarie
BR ˌanməˈriː
AM ˌænməˈri

Annesley
BR ˈan(ɪ)zli
AM ˈænzli

Annette
BR əˈnɛt, aˈnɛt
AM əˈnet

annex¹
noun
BR ˈanɛks, -ɪz
AM ˈæˌnɛks, -əz

annex²
verb
BR əˈnɛks, ˈanɛks, -ɪz, -ɪŋ, -t
AM əˈnɛks, æˈnɛks, -əz, -ɪŋ, -t

annexation
BR ˌanɛkˈseɪʃn, ˌanəkˈseɪʃn, -z
AM ˌæˌnɛkˈseɪʃən, ˌænəkˈseɪʃən, -z

annexe
BR ˈanɛks, -ɪz
AM ˈæˌnɛks, -əz

annexure
BR ˈanɛkʃʊə(r), -z
AM ˈænɛkˌʃʊ(ə)r, -z

annicut
BR ˈanɪkʌt, -s
AM ˈænəkət, -s

Annie
BR ˈani
AM ˈæni

Annigoni
BR ˌanɪˈɡəʊni
AM ˌænəˈɡoni, ˌænəˈɡani

annihilate
BR əˈnʌɪəleɪt, -s, -ɪŋ, -ɪd
AM əˈnaɪəˌleɪt, -ts, -ɪŋ, -dɪd

annihilation
BR əˌnʌɪəˈleɪʃn
AM əˌnaɪəˈleɪʃən

annihilationism
BR əˌnʌɪəˈleɪʃnɪz(ə)m, əˌnʌɪəˈleɪʃ(ə)nɪz(ə)m
AM əˌnaɪəˈleɪʃəˌnɪzəm

annihilator
BR əˈnʌɪəleɪtə(r), -z
AM əˈnaɪəˌleɪdər, -z

anniversary
BR ˌanɪˈvəːs(ə)r|i, -ɪz
AM ˌænəˈvɜrs(ə)ri, -z

Anno Domini
BR ˌanəʊ ˈdɒmɪnʌɪ,
+ ˈdɒmɪni:
AM ˌænoʊ ˈdɑməni

annotatable
BR ˈanə(ʊ)teɪtəbl
AM ˈænəˌteɪdəbəl

annotate
BR ˈanə(ʊ)teɪt, -s, -ɪŋ, -ɪd
AM ˈænəˌteɪ|t, -ts, -dɪŋ, -dɪd

annotation
BR ˌanə(ʊ)ˈteɪʃn, -z
AM ˌænəˈteɪʃən, -z

annotative
BR ˈanə(ʊ)teɪtɪv
AM ˈænəˌteɪdɪv

annotator
BR ˈanə(ʊ)teɪtə(r), -z
AM ˈænəˌteɪdər, -z

announce
BR əˈnaʊns, -ɪz, -ɪŋ, -t
AM əˈnaʊns, -əz, -ɪŋ, -t

announcement
BR əˈnaʊnsm(ə)nt, -s
AM əˈnaʊnsmənt, -s

announcer
BR əˈnaʊnsə(r), -z
AM əˈnaʊnsər, -z

annoy
BR əˈnɔɪ, -z, -ɪŋ, -d
AM əˈnɔɪ, -z, -ɪŋ, -d

annoyance
BR əˈnɔɪəns, -ɪz
AM əˈnɔɪəns, -əz

annoyer
BR əˈnɔɪə(r), -z
AM əˈnɔɪər, -z

annoying
BR əˈnɔɪɪŋ
AM əˈnɔɪɪŋ

annoyingly
BR əˈnɔɪɪŋli
AM əˈnɔɪɪŋli

annoyingness
BR əˈnɔɪɪŋnɪs
AM əˈnɔɪɪŋnɪs

annual
BR ˈanjʊəl, ˈanjəl, -z
AM ˈænj(əw)əl, -z

annualise
BR ˈanjʊəlʌɪz, ˈanjəlʌɪz, -ɪz, -ɪŋ, -d
AM ˈænj(əw)əˌlaɪz, -ɪz, -ɪŋ, -d

annualize
BR ˈanjʊəlʌɪz, ˈanjəlʌɪz, -ɪz, -ɪŋ, -d
AM ˈænj(əw)əˌlaɪz, -ɪz, -ɪŋ, -d

annually
BR ˈanjʊəli, ˈanjəli
AM ˈænj(əw)əli

annuitant
BR əˈnjuːɪt(ə)nt, -s
AM əˈn(j)uədənt, əˈn(j)uətnt, -s

annuity
BR əˈnjuːɪt|i, -ɪz
AM əˈn(j)uədi, -z

annul
BR əˈnʌl, -z, -ɪŋ, -d
AM əˈnəl, -z, -ɪŋ, -d

annular
BR ˈanjʊlə(r)
AM ˈænjələr

annularly
BR ˈanjʊləli
AM ˈænjələrli

annulate
BR ˈanjʊleɪt, -s, -ɪŋ, -ɪd
AM ˈænjəˌleɪ|t, -ts, -dɪŋ, -dɪd

annulation
BR ˌanjʊˈleɪʃn
AM ˌænjəˈleɪʃən

annulet
BR ˈanjʊlɪt, -s
AM ˈænjələt, ˈænjəˌlɛt, -s

annuli
BR ˈanjʊlʌɪ
AM ˈænjəˌlaɪ

annulment
BR əˈnʌlm(ə)nt, -s
AM əˈnəlmənt, -s

annulus
BR ˈanjʊləs, -ɪz
AM ˈænjələs, -əz

annunciate
BR əˈnʌnsɪeɪt, əˈnʌnˌʃɪeɪt, -s, -ɪŋ, -ɪd
AM əˈnənsiˌeɪ|t, -ts, -dɪŋ, -dɪd

annunciation
BR əˌnʌnsɪˈeɪʃn, əˌnʌnˌʃɪˈeɪʃn, -z
AM əˌnənsiˈeɪʃən, -z

annunciator
BR əˈnʌnsɪeɪtə(r), əˈnʌnʃɪeɪtə(r), -z
AM əˈnənsiˌeɪdər, -z

annus
BR ˈanʊs
AM ˈænəs

annus horribilis
BR ˌanʊs hɒˈrɪbɪlɪs, + həˈrɪbɪlɪs
AM ˌænəs həˈrɪbələs

annus mirabilis
BR ˌanʊs mɪˈrɑːbɪlɪs
AM ˌænəs məˈrabələs

Anny
BR ˈani
AM ˈæni

anoa
BR əˈnəʊə(r), aˈnəʊə(r), -z

AM əˈnəʊə, -z

anodal
BR aˈnəʊdl
AM ˈænəʊdəl,
eɪˈnəʊdəl

anode
BR ˈanəʊd, -z
AM ˈænəʊd, -z

anodic
BR aˈnɒdɪk
AM ænˈɑdɪk

anodise
BR ˈanədʌɪz, -ɪz, -ɪŋ, -d
AM ˈænəˌdaɪz, -ɪz, -ɪŋ, -d

anodiser
BR ˈanədʌɪzə(r), -z
AM ˈænəˌdaɪzər, -z

anodize
BR ˈanədʌɪz, -ɪz, -ɪŋ, -d
AM ˈænəˌdaɪz, -ɪz, -ɪŋ, -d

anodizer
BR ˈanədʌɪzə(r), -z
AM ˈænəˌdaɪzər, -z

anodyne
BR ˈanədʌɪn, -z
AM ˈænəˌdaɪn, -z

anoeses
BR ˌanəʊˈiːsiːz
AM ˌænoʊˈisiz

anoesis
BR ˌanəʊˈiːsɪs
AM ˌænoʊˈisəs

anoetic
BR ˌanəʊˈɛtɪk
AM ˌænəˈwɛdɪk

anoint
BR əˈnɔɪnt, -s, -ɪŋ, -ɪd
AM əˈnɔɪn|t, -(t)s, -(t)ɪŋ, -(t)ɪd

anointer
BR əˈnɔɪntə(r), -z
AM əˈnɔɪn(t)ər, -z

anole
BR əˈnəʊl|i, -ɪz
AM əˈnoʊli, -z

anomalistic
BR əˌnɒməˈlɪstɪk
AM əˌnɑməˈlɪstɪk

anomalous
BR əˈnɒmələs,
əˈnɒmləs
AM əˈnɑmələs

anomalously
BR əˈnɒmələsli,
əˈnɒmləsli
AM əˈnɑmələsli

anomalousness
BR əˈnɒmələsnəs,
əˈnɒmləsnəs
AM əˈnɑmələsnəs

anomalure
BR əˈnɒməl(j)ʊə(r),
əˈnɒml(j)ʊə(r), -z
AM əˈnɑməˌlʊ(ə)r, -z

anomaly
BR əˈnɒməl|i,
əˈnɒml|i, -ɪz

AM əˈnaməli, -z

anomic
BR əˈnɒmɪk, aˈnɒmɪk,
əˈnəʊmɪk, aˈnəʊmɪk
AM əˈnamɪk, əˈnoʊmɪk

anomie
BR ˈanəmi
AM ˈænəmi, ˌænəˈmi

anomy
BR ˈanəmi
AM ˈænəmi, ˌænəˈmi

anon
BR əˈnɒn
AM əˈnan

Anona
BR əˈnəʊnə(r)
AM əˈnoʊnə

anonym
BR ˈanənɪm, -z
AM ˈænəˌnɪm, -z

anonymity
BR ˌanəˈnɪmɪti
AM ˌænəˈnɪmɪdi

anonymous
BR əˈnɒnɪməs
AM əˈnanəməs

anonymously
BR əˈnɒnɪməsli
AM əˈnanəməsli

anopheles
BR əˈnɒfɪli:z, əˈnɒfl̩i:z
AM əˈnafəliz

anophthalmia
BR ˌanɒfˈθalmɪə(r)
AM ˌænafˈθælmiə,
ˌænɑpˈθælmiə

anorak
BR ˈanərak, -s
AM ˈænəˌræk, -s

anorectic
BR ˌanəˈrɛktɪk, -s
AM ˌænəˈrɛktɪk, -s

anorexia
BR ˌanəˈrɛksɪə(r)
AM ˌænəˈrɛksiə

anorexia nervosa
BR ˌanərɛksɪə
nəːˈvəʊsə(r),
anəˈrɛksɪə +,
nəːˈvəʊzə(r)
AM ˌænəˈrɛksiə
nərˈvoʊsə,
+ nərˈvoʊzə

anorexic
BR ˌanəˈrɛksɪk, -s
AM ˌænəˈrɛksɪk, -s

anorexically
BR ˌanəˈrɛksɪkli
AM ˌænəˈrɛksək(ə)li

anorgasmia
BR ˌanɔːˈgazmɪə(r)
AM ˌænɔrˈgæzmiə

anorthite
BR əˈnɔːθʌɪt
AM əˈnɔrˌθaɪt

anorthosite
BR əˈnɔːθəsʌɪt

AM əˈnɔːθəˌsaɪt

anorthositic
BR əˌnɔːθəˈsɪtɪk
AM əˌnɔrθəˈsɪdɪk

anosmia
BR aˈnɒzmɪə(r),
aˈnɒsmɪə(r)
AM æˈnazmiə,
æˈnasmiə

anosmic
BR aˈnɒzmɪk,
aˈnɒsmɪk, -s
AM æˈnazmɪk,
æˈnasmɪk, -s

another
BR əˈnʌðə(r)
AM əˈnəðər

Anouilh
BR aˈnuːi:, ˌanuˈi:,
aˈnu:i
AM ɑˈnui, ɑˈnwi
FR anuj

anovulant
BR aˈnɒvjʊlənt,
aˈnɒvjʊl̩nt, -s
AM əˈnavjələnt, -s

anoxaemia
BR ˌanɒkˈsiːmɪə(r)
AM ˌæˌnɑkˈsimiə

anoxia
BR aˈnɒksɪə(r)
AM æˈnaksiə

anoxic
BR aˈnɒksɪk
AM æˈnaksɪk

Ansafone®
BR ˈɑːnsəfəʊn,
ˈansəfəʊn
AM ˈænsəˌfoʊn

Ansbacher
BR ˈanzbakə(r)
AM ˈænzˌbakər
GER ˈansbaxɛ

Anschluss
BR ˈanʃlʊs
AM ˈanˌʃlus

Anscombe
BR ˈanskəm, ˈanzkəm
AM ˈænskəmb

Ansell
BR ˈansl
AM ˈæns(ɛ)l

Anselm
BR ˈansɛlm
AM ˈænsəlm

anserine
BR ˈansərʌɪn
AM ˈænsəˌraɪn,
ˈænsərən, ˈænsəˌrin

Anshan
BR ˈanʃan
AM ˈænˌʃæn

Anson
BR ˈansn
AM ˈænsən

Anstey
BR ˈansti
AM ˈænsti

Anstruther¹
BR ˈanstrʌðə(r)
AM ˈænstrəðər

Anstruther²
traditional form
BR ˈanstə(r), ˈeɪnstə(r)
AM ˈænstər

Ansty
BR ˈansti
AM ˈænsti

answer
BR ˈɑːns|ə(r), ˈans|ə(r),
-əz, -(ə)rɪŋ, -əd
AM ˈæns|ər, -ərz,
-(ə)rɪŋ, -ərd

answerability
BR ˌɑːns(ə)rəˈbɪlɪti,
ˌans(ə)rəˈbɪlɪti
AM ˌæns(ə)rəˈbɪlɪdi

answerable
BR ˈɑːns(ə)rəbl,
ˈans(ə)rəbl
AM ˈæns(ə)rəbəl

answerably
BR ˈɑːns(ə)rəbli,
ˈans(ə)rəbli
AM ˈæns(ə)rəbli

answerphone
BR ˈɑːnsəfəʊn,
ˈansəfəʊn, -z
AM ˈænsərˌfoʊn, -z

ant
BR ant, -s
AM ænt, -s

antacid
BR ˌantˈasɪd, ˌanˈtasɪd,
-z
AM ˌæn(t)ˈæsəd, -z

Antaeus
BR anˈteɪəs
AM ænˈteɪəs

antagonisation
BR anˌtagənʌɪˈzeɪʃn,
anˌtagnʌɪˈzeɪʃn
AM ænˌtægənəˈzeɪʃən,
ænˌtægəˌnaɪˈzeɪʃən

antagonise
BR anˈtagənʌɪz,
anˈtagnʌɪz, -ɪz, -ɪŋ, -d
AM ænˈtægəˌnaɪz, -ɪz,
-ɪŋ, -d

antagonism
BR anˈtagənɪz(ə)m,
anˈtagnɪz(ə)m, -z
AM ænˈtægəˌnɪzəm, -z

antagonist
BR anˈtagənɪst,
anˈtagnɪst, -s
AM ænˈtægənəst, -s

antagonistic
BR anˌtagəˈnɪstɪk,
ˌantagəˈnɪstɪk
AM ænˌtægəˈnɪstɪk

antagonistically
BR anˌtagəˈnɪstɪkli,
ˌantagəˈnɪstɪkli
AM ˌænˌtægəˈnɪstɪk(ə)li

antagonization
BR anˌtagənʌɪˈzeɪʃn,
anˌtagn̩ʌɪˈzeɪʃn
AM ænˌtægənəˈzeɪʃən,
ænˌtægn̩ʌɪˈzeɪʃən

antagonize
BR anˈtagənʌɪz,
anˈtagn̩ʌɪz, -ɪz, -ɪŋ, -d
AM ænˈtægəˌnaɪz, -ɪz,
-ɪŋ, -d

Antakya
BR anˈtakjə(r)
AM ænˈtakjə
TU ʌnˈtʌkjʌ

antalkali
BR antˈalkəlʌɪ, -z
AM ænˈtælkəlaɪ, -z

Antalya
BR anˈtalɪə(r)
AM ænˈtɑlɪə
TU ʌnˈtʌljʌ

Antananarivo
BR ˌantənənəˈriːvəʊ
AM ˌɑn(t)əˌnɑnəˈrivoʊ,
ˌænθə,nænəˈrivoʊ

Antarctic
BR anˈtɑːktɪk
AM ænˈ(t)ɑrktɪk,
ænˈ(t)ɑrdɪk

Antarctica
BR anˈtɑːktɪkə(r)
AM ænˈ(t)ɑrktəkə
ænˈ(t)ɑrdəkə

Antares
BR anˈtɛːriːz, anˈtɑːriːz
AM ænˈtɛriz

ante
BR ˈanti
AM ˈæn(t)i

anteater
BR ˈantˌiːtə(r), -z
AM ˈæn(t),idər, -z

antebellum
BR ˌantɪˈbɛləm
AM ˌæn(t)iˈbɛləm,
ˌæn(t)əˈbɛləm

antecedence
BR ˌantɪˈsiːd(ə)ns,
ˈantɪˌsiːd(ə)ns
AM ˌæn(t)əˈsidns

antecedent
BR ˌantɪˈsiːd(ə)nt,
ˈantɪˌsiːd(ə)nt, -s
AM ˌæn(t)əˈsidnt, -s

antecedently
BR ˌantɪˈsiːd(ə)ntli,
ˈantɪˌsiːd(ə)ntli
AM ˌæn(t)əˈsidn(t)li

antechamber
BR ˈantɪˌtʃeɪmbə(r), -z
AM ˈæn(t)iˌtʃeɪmbər,
ˈæn(t)əˌtʃeɪmbər, -z

antechapel
BR ˈantɪˌtʃapl, -z
AM ˈæn(t)iˌtʃæpəl,
ˈæn(t)əˌtʃæpəl, -z

antedate
BR ˈantɪdeɪt, -s, -ɪŋ, -ɪd

AM ˈæn(t)əˌdeɪt,
ˈæn(t)iˌdeɪt, -ts, -dɪŋ,
-dɪd

antediluvial
BR ˌantɪdɪˈluːvɪəl
AM ˌæn(t)idəˈluviəl,
ˌæn(t)ədəˈluviəl

antediluvially
BR ˌantɪdɪˈluːvɪəli
AM ˌæn(t)idəˈluviəli,
ˌæn(t)ədəˈluviəli

antediluvian
BR ˌantɪdɪˈluːvɪən, -z
AM ˌæn(t)idəˈluviən,
ˌæn(t)ədəˈluviən, -z

antelope
BR ˈantɪləʊp, -s
AM ˈæn(t)əˌloʊp,
ˈæntlˌoʊp, -s

ante-mortem
BR ˌantɪˈmɔːtəm
AM ˌæn(t)iˈmɔrdəm,
ˌæn(t)əˈmɔrdəm

antemundane
BR ˌantɪmʌnˈdeɪn
AM ˌæn(t)iˌmənˈdeɪn,
ˌæn(t)əˌmənˈdeɪn

antenatal
BR ˌantɪˈneɪtl
AM ˌæn(t)iˈneɪdl,
ˌæn(t)əˈneɪdl

antenna
BR anˈtɛnə(r), -z
AM ænˈtɛnə, -z

antennae
BR anˈtɛniː, anˈtɛnʌɪ
AM ænˈtɛni, ænˈtɛˌnaɪ

antennal
BR anˈtɛnl
AM ænˈtɛnəl

antennary
BR anˈtɛn(ə)ri
AM ænˈtɛnəri

antennule
BR anˈtɛnjuːl, -z
AM ænˈtɛnjul, -z

antenuptial
BR ˌantɪˈnʌp(t)ʃ(ə)l
AM ˌæn(t)iˈnəpʃəl,
ˌæn(t)əˈnəpʃəl

antepartum
BR ˌantɪˈpɑːtəm
AM ˌæn(t)iˈpɑrdəm

antependia
BR ˌantɪˈpɛndɪə(r)
AM ˌæn(t)iˈpɛndiə,
ˌæn(t)əˈpɛndiə

antependium
BR ˌantɪˈpɛndɪəm
AM ˌæn(t)iˈpɛndiəm,
ˌæn(t)əˈpɛndiəm

antepenult
BR ˌantɪpɪˈnʌlt, -s
AM ˌæn(t)iˈpɛnəlt,
ˌæn(t)əˈpɛnəlt,
ˌæn(t)iˈpinəlt,
ˌæn(t)əˈpinəlt, -s

antepenultimate
BR ˌantɪpɪˈnʌltɪmət, -s
AM ˌæn(t)ipəˈnəltəmət,
ˌæn(t)əpəˈnəltəmət,
-s

anteprandial
BR ˌantɪˈprandɪəl
AM ˌæn(t)iˈprændiəl,
ˌæn(t)əˈprændiəl

anterior
BR anˈtɪərɪə(r)
AM ænˈtɪriər

anteriority
BR anˌtɪərɪˈɒrɪti
AM ænˌtɪriˈɔrədi

anteriorly
BR anˈtɪərɪəli
AM ænˈtɪriərli

anteriorness
BR anˈtɪərɪənəs
AM ænˈtɪriərnəs

anteroom
BR ˈantɪruːm,
ˈantrʊm, -z
AM ˈæn(t)iˌrum,
ˈæn(t)iˌrʊm,
ˈæn(t)əˌrum,
ˈæn(t)əˌrʊm, -z

Anthea
BR ˈanθɪə(r)
AM ænˈθiə

antheap
BR ˈanthiːp, -s
AM ˈæn(t),(h)ip, -s

anthelion
BR antˈhiːlɪən,
anˈθiːlɪən, -z
AM ænˈthiliən,
ænˈθiliən, -z

anthelminthic
BR ˌanθɛlˈmɪnθɪk
AM ˌæn,θɛlˈmɪnθɪk

anthelmintic
BR ˌanθɛlˈmɪntɪk
AM ˌæn,θɛlˈmɪntɪk

anthem
BR ˈanθəm, -z
AM ˈænθəm, -z

anthemia
BR anˈθiːmɪə(r)
AM ænˈθimiə

anthemion
BR anˈθiːmɪən
AM ænˈθimiən

anther
BR ˈanθə(r), -z
AM ˈænθər, -z

antheral
BR ˈanθ(ə)rəl,
ˈanθ(ə)r̩
AM ˈænθərəl

antheridia
BR ˌanθɪˈrɪdɪə(r)
AM ˌænθəˈrɪdiə

antheridium
BR ˌanθɪˈrɪdɪəm
AM ˌænθəˈrɪdiəm

anthill
BR ˈanthɪl, -z
AM ˈæn(t),(h)ɪl, -z

anthological
BR ˌanθəˈlɒdʒɪkl
AM ˌænθəˈlɑdʒəkəl

anthologise
BR anˈθɒlədʒʌɪz, -ɪz,
-ɪŋ, -d
AM ænˈθɑləˌdʒaɪz, -ɪz,
-ɪŋ, -d

anthologist
BR anˈθɒlədʒɪst, -s
AM ænˈθɑlədʒəst, -s

anthologize
BR anˈθɒlədʒʌɪz, -ɪz,
-ɪŋ, -d
AM ænˈθɑləˌdʒaɪz, -ɪz,
-ɪŋ, -d

anthology
BR anˈθɒlədʒli, -ɪz
AM ænˈθɑlədʒi, -z

Anthony
BR ˈantəni
AM ˈænθəni, ˈæntəni

anthozoan
BR ˌanθəˈzəʊən, -z
AM ˌænθəˈzoʊən, -z

anthracene
BR ˈanθrəsiːn
AM ˈænθrəˌsin

anthracic
BR anˈθrasɪk
AM ænˈθræsɪk

anthracite
BR ˈanθrəsʌɪt
AM ˈænθrəˌsaɪt

anthracitic
BR ˌanθrəˈsɪtɪk
AM ˌænθrəˈsɪdɪk

anthracnose
BR anˈθraknəʊs,
anˈθraknəʊz
AM ænˈθrækˌnoʊs,
ænˈθrækˌnoʊz

anthrax
BR ˈanθraks
AM ˈænˌθræks

anthropocentric
BR ˌanθrəpəˈsɛntrɪk
AM ˌænθrəˌpoʊˈsɛntrɪk,
ˌænθrəpəˈsɛntrɪk

anthropocentrically
BR ˌanθrəpəˈsɛntrɪkli
AM ˌænθrəˌpoʊˈsɛntrək(ə)li,
ˌænθrəpəˈsɛntrək(ə)li

anthropocentrism
BR ˌanθrəpə(ʊ)ˈsɛntrɪz(ə)m
AM ˌænθrəˌpoʊˈsɛnˌtrɪzəm,
ˌænθrəpəˈsɛnˌtrɪzəm

anthropogenesis
BR ˌanθrəpəˈdʒɛnɪsɪs
AM ˌænθrəˌpoʊˈdʒɛnəsəs,
ˌænθrəpəˈdʒɛnəsəs

anthropogenic
BR ˌanθrəpəˈdʒɛnɪk
AM ˌænθrəˌpoʊˈdʒɛnɪk,
ˌænθrəpəˈdʒɛnɪk

anthropogeny
BR ˌanθrəˈpɒdʒɪni,
ˌanθrəˈpɒdʒni
AM ˌænθrəˈpɑdʒəni
anthropography
BR ˌanθrəˈpɒgrəfi
AM ˌænθrəˈpɑgrəfi
anthropoid
BR ˈanθrəpɔɪd, -z
AM ˈænθrəˌpɔɪd, -z
anthropoidal
BR ˌanθrəˈpɔɪdl
AM ˌænθrəˈpɔɪdəl
anthropological
BR ˌanθrəpəˈlɒdʒɪkl
AM ˌænθrəpəˈlɑdʒəkəl
anthropologically
BR ˌanθrəpəˈlɒdʒɪkli
AM ˌænθrəpəˈlɑdʒək-
(ə)li
anthropologist
BR ˌanθrəˈpɒlədʒɪst, -s
AM ˌænθrəˈpɑlədʒəst,
-s
anthropology
BR ˌanθrəˈpɒlədʒi
AM ˌænθrəˈpɑlədʒi
anthropometric
BR ˌanθrəpəˈmɛtrɪk
AM ˌænθrəpəˈmɛtrɪk
anthropometry
BR ˌanθrəˈpɒmɪtri
AM ˌænθrəˈpɑmətri
anthropomorphic
BR ˌanθrəpəˈmɔːfɪk
AM ˌænθrəpəˈmɔrfɪk
**anthropomorphic-
ally**
BR ˌanθrəpəˈmɔːfɪkli
AM ˌænθrəpəˈmɔrfək-
(ə)li
anthropomorphise
BR ˌanθrəpəˈmɔːfʌɪz,
-ɪz, -ɪŋ, -d
AM ˌænθrəpəˈmɔrˌfaɪz,
-ɪz, -ɪŋ, -d
**anthropomorph-
ism**
BR ˌanθrəpəˈmɔːfɪz(ə)m
AM ˌænθrəpəˈmɔrˌfɪzəm
anthropomorphist
BR ˌanθrəpəˈmɔːfɪst, -s
AM ˌænθrəpəˈmɔrfəst,
-s
anthropomorphize
BR ˌanθrəpəˈmɔːfʌɪz,
-ɪz, -ɪŋ, -d
AM ˌænθrəpəˈmɔrˌfaɪz,
-ɪz, -ɪŋ, -d
**anthropomorph-
ous**
BR ˌanθrəpəˈmɔːfəs
AM ˌænθrəpəˈmɔrfəs
anthroponymy
BR ˌanθrəˈpɒnɪmi
AM ˌænθrəˈpɑnəmi
anthropophagi
BR ˌanθrəˈpɒfəgʌɪ

AM ˌænθrəˈpafədʒʌɪ,
ˌænθrəˈpɒfəgaɪ
anthropophagous
BR ˌanθrəˈpɒfəgəs
AM ˌænθrəˈpafəgəs
anthropophagus
BR ˌanθrəˈpɒfəgəs
AM ˌænθrəˈpafəgəs
anthropophagy
BR ˌanθrəˈpɒfədʒi
AM ˌænθrəˈpafədʒi
anti
BR ˈantｉi, -ɪz
AM ˈænˌtaɪ, ˈæn(t)i, -z
antibacterial
BR ˌantɪbakˈtɪərɪəl
AM ˌænˌtaɪˈbæktɪrɪəl,
ˌæn(t)iˈbæktɪrɪəl
Antibes
BR ɒnˈtiːb, ɒ̃ˈtiːb,
ɑːnˈtiːb, anˈtiːb
AM ɑnˈtib(z)
antibioses
BR ˌantɪbʌɪˈəʊsiːz
AM ˌæn(t)iˌbaɪˈoʊsiz
antibiosis
BR ˌantɪbʌɪˈəʊsɪs
AM ˌæn(t)iˌbaɪˈoʊsəs
antibiotic
BR ˌantɪbʌɪˈɒtɪk, -s
AM ˌæn(t)iˌbaɪˈɑdɪk, -s
antibiotically
BR ˌantɪbʌɪˈɒtɪkli
AM ˌæn(t)iˌbaɪˈɑdək(ə)li
antibody
BR ˈantɪˌbɒdｉi, -ɪz
AM ˈænˌtaɪˌbɑdi,
ˈæn(t)iˌbɑdi, -z
antic
BR ˈantɪk, -s
AM ˈæn(t)ɪk, -s
anticathode
BR ˌantɪˈkaθəʊd, -z
AM ˌæn(t)əˈkæˌθoʊd,
ˌæn(t)iˈkæˌθoʊd, -z
anticatholic
BR ˌantɪˈkaθ(ə)lɪk,
ˌantɪˈkaθlɪk, -s
AM ˌænˌtaɪˈkæθ(ə)lɪk,
ˌæn(t)iˈkæθ(ə)lɪk, -s
Antichrist
BR ˈantɪkrʌɪst, -s
AM ˈænˌtaɪˌkraɪst,
ˈæn(t)iˌkraɪst,
ˈæn(t)əˌkraɪst, -s
antichristian
BR ˌantɪˈkrɪstʃ(ə)n,
ˌantɪˈkrɪstən
AM ˌænˌtaɪˈkrɪstʃən,
ˈæn(t)iˈkrɪstʃən,
ˈæn(t)əˈkrɪstʃən
anticipant
BR anˈtɪsɪp(ə)nt, -s
AM ænˈtɪsəpənt, -s
anticipate
BR anˈtɪsɪpeɪt, -s, -ɪŋ,
-ɪd

AM ænˈtɪsəˌpeɪｔt, -ts,
-dɪŋ, -dɪd
anticipation
BR anˌtɪsɪˈpeɪʃn,
ˌantɪsɪˈpeɪʃn, -z
AM ænˌtɪsəˈpeɪʃən, -z
anticipative
BR anˈtɪsɪpətɪv
AM ænˈtɪsəˌpeɪdɪv,
ænˈtɪsəpədɪv
anticipator
BR anˈtɪsɪpeɪtə(r), -z
AM ænˈtɪsəˌpeɪdər, -z
anticipatory
BR anˈtɪsɪpət(ə)ri,
ˌantɪsɪˈpeɪt(ə)ri
AM ænˈtɪsəpəˌtɔri
anticlerical
BR ˌantɪˈklɛrɪkl
AM ˌænˌtaɪˈklɛrəkəl,
ˌæn(t)iˈklɛrəkəl,
ˌæn(t)əˈklɛrəkəl
anticlericalism
BR ˌantɪˈklɛrɪklɪz(ə)m,
ˌantɪˈklɛrɪkəlɪz(ə)m
AM ˌænˌtaɪˈklɛrəkə-
ˌlɪzəm,
ˌæn(t)iˈklɛrəkəˌlɪzəm,
ˌæn(t)əˈklɛrəkəˌlɪzəm
anticlimactic
BR ˌantɪklʌɪˈmaktɪk
AM ˌænˌtaɪklaɪˈmæktɪk,
ˌæn(t)iˌklaɪˈmæktɪk,
ˌæn(t)əˌklaɪˈmæktɪk,
ˌænˌtaɪˌklaɪˈmædɪk,
ˌæn(t)iˌklaɪˈmædɪk,
ˌæn(t)əˌklaɪˈmædɪk
anticlimactically
BR ˌantɪklʌɪˈmaktɪkli,
ˌantɪklɪˈmaktɪkli
AM ˌænˌtaɪklaɪˈmæktək-
(ə)li,
ˌæn(t)iˌklaɪˈmæktək-
(ə)li,
ˌæn(t)əˌklaɪˈmæktək-
(ə)li,
ˌænˌtaɪˌklaɪˈmædək-
(ə)li,
ˌæn(t)iˌklaɪˈmæd(ə)k-
(ə)li,
ˌæn(t)əˌklaɪˈmædək-
(ə)li
anticlimax
BR ˌantɪˈklʌɪmaks, -ɪz
AM ˌænˌtaɪˈklaɪˌmæks,
ˌæn(t)iˈklaɪˌmæks,
ˌæn(t)əˈklaɪˌmæks,
-əz
anticlinal
BR ˈantɪklʌɪnl
AM ˌænˌtaɪˈklaɪnl,
ˌæn(t)iˈklaɪnl,
ˌæn(t)əˈklaɪnl, -s
anticline
BR ˈantɪklʌɪn, -z
AM ˈænˌtaɪˌklaɪn,
ˈæn(t)iˌklaɪn,
ˈæn(t)əˌklaɪn, -z

anticlockwise
BR ˌantɪˈklɒkwʌɪz
AM ˌænˌtaɪˈklɑkˌwaɪz,
ˌæn(t)iˈklɑkˌwaɪz,
ˌæn(t)əˈklɑkˌwaɪz
anticoagulant
BR ˌantɪkəʊˈagjʊlənt,
ˌantɪkəʊˈagjʊln̩t, -s
AM ˌænˌtaɪkoʊˈægjələnt,
ˌæn(t)ikoʊˈægjələnt,
ˌæn(t)əkoʊˈægjələnt,
-s
anticodon
BR ˌantɪˈkəʊdɒn, -z
AM ˌænˌtaɪˈkoʊdən,
ˌæn(t)iˈkoʊdən,
ˌæn(t)əˈkoʊdən, -z
anticommunist
BR ˌantɪˈkɒmjʊnɪst, -s
AM ˌænˌtaɪˈkɑmjənəst,
ˌæn(t)iˈkɑmjənəst,
ˌæn(t)əˈkɑmjənəst, -s
anticonstitutional
BR ˌantɪˌkɒnstɪˈtjuː-
ʃn(ə)l,
ˌantɪˌkɒnstɪˈtjuːʃə-
n(ə)l,
ˌantɪˌkɒnstɪˈtʃuːʃə-
n(ə)l
AM ˌænˌtaɪˌkɑnstəˈt(j)u-
ʃ(ə)nəl,
ˌæn(t)iˌkɑnstəˈt(j)u-
ʃ(ə)nəl,
ˌæn(t)əˌkɑnstəˈt(j)u-
ʃ(ə)nəl
anticonvulsant
BR ˌantɪkənˈvʌls(ə)nt,
-s
AM ˌænˌtaɪkənˈvəlsənt,
ˌæn(t)ikənˈvəlsənt,
ˌæn(t)əkənˈvəlsənt, -s
anticyclone
BR ˌantɪˈsʌɪkləʊn, -z
AM ˌænˌtaɪˈsaɪˌkloʊn,
ˌæn(t)iˈsaɪˌkloʊn,
ˌæn(t)əˈsaɪˌkloʊn, -z
anticyclonic
BR ˌantɪsʌɪˈklɒnɪk
AM ˌænˌtaɪˌsaɪˈklɑnɪk,
ˌæn(t)iˌsaɪˈklɑnɪk,
ˌæn(t)əˌsaɪˈklɑnɪk
antidazzle
BR ˌantɪˈdazl
AM ˌænˌtaɪˈdæzəl,
ˌæn(t)iˈdæzəl,
ˌæn(t)əˈdæzəl
antidepressant
BR ˌantɪdɪˈprɛsnt, -s
AM ˌæn(t)ədəˈprɛsənt,
ˌænˌtaɪdəˈprɛsənt,
ˌæn(t)idəˈprɛsənt, -s
antidiuretic
BR ˌantɪˌdʌɪjəˈrɛtɪk, -s
AM ˌænˌtaɪˌdaɪəˈrɛdɪk,
ˌæn(t)iˌdaɪəˈrɛdɪk,
ˌæn(t)əˌdaɪəˈrɛdɪk, -s
antidotal
BR ˈantɪdəʊtl,
ˌantɪˈdəʊtl

AM ˌæn(t)ə'doʊdl
antidote
BR 'æntɪdəʊt, -s
AM 'æn(t)ə,doʊt, -s
antielectron
BR ˌæntɪ'lɛktrɒn
AM ˌæn(t)iə'lɛk,trɑn,
ˌæn,taɪə'lɛk,trɑn
anti-establishment
BR ˌæntɪ'stablɪʃm(ə)nt,
ˌæntɪɛs'tablɪʃm(ə)nt
AM ˌæn,taɪə'stæblɪʃ-mənt,
ˌæn(t)iə'stæblɪʃmənt,
ˌæn,taɪɛ'stæblɪʃmənt,
ˌæn(t)iɛ'stæblɪʃmənt
Antietam
BR an'ti:təm
AM æn'tidəm
anti-fascist
BR ˌæntɪ'faʃɪst, -s
AM ˌæn,taɪ'fæʃəst,
ˌæn(t)i'fæʃəst,
ˌæn(t)ə'fæʃəst, -s
antifebrile
BR ˌæntɪ'fi:brʌɪl,
ˌæntɪ'fɛbrʌɪl
AM ˌæn(t)ə'fɛbrəl,
ˌæn(t)ə'fɛ,braɪl
antifreeze
BR 'æntɪfri:z, -ɪz
AM 'æn(t)ə,friz,
'æn(t)i,friz,
ˌæn,taɪ'friz, -ɪz
anti-g
BR ˌæntɪ'dʒi:
AM ˌæn,taɪ'dʒi,
ˌæn(t)i'dʒi
antigen
BR 'æntɪdʒ(ə)n, -z
AM 'æn(t)ədʒən,
'æn(t)ə,dʒɛn, -z
antigenic
BR ˌæntɪ'dʒɛnɪk
AM ˌæn(t)ə'dʒɛnɪk
Antigone
BR an'tɪgəni, an'tɪgɲi
AM æn'tɪgəni
anti-government
BR ˌæntɪ'gʌv(ə)nm(ə)nt,
ˌæntɪ'gʌvəm(ə)nt
AM ˌæn,taɪ'gəvər(n)-mənt,
ˌæn(t)i'gəvər(n)mənt,
ˌæn(t)ə'gəvər(n)mənt
anti-gravity
BR ˌæntɪ'gravɪti
AM ˌæn,taɪ'grævədi,
ˌæn(t)i'grævədi,
ˌæn(t)ə'grævədi
Antigua
BR an'ti:g(w)ə(r)
AM æn'tig(w)ə
Antiguan
BR an'ti:g(w)ən, -z
AM æn'tig(w)ən, -z

antihero
BR 'antɪ,hɪərəʊ, -z
AM 'æn,taɪ,hiroʊ,
'æn(t)i,hiroʊ,
'æn(t)ə,hiroʊ, -z
antihistamine
BR ˌantɪ'hɪstəmi:n,
ˌantɪ'hɪstəmɪn
AM ˌæn(t)ə'hɪstəmən,
ˌæn,taɪ'hɪstəmən,
ˌæn(t)i'hɪstəmən,
ˌæn(t)ə'hɪstəmɪn,
ˌæn,taɪ'hɪstəmɪn,
ˌæn(t)i'hɪstəmɪn
anti-inflammatory
BR ˌantɪm'flamət(ə)r|i, -ɪz
AM ˌæn,taɪən'flæmə-,tɔri,
ˌæn(t)iən'flæmə,tɔri, -z
anti-inflation
BR ˌantɪm'fleɪʃn
AM ˌæn,taɪən'fleɪʃən,
ˌæn(t)iən'fleɪʃən
anti-intellectual
BR ˌantɪ,ɪntɪ'lɛktʃʊəl,
ˌantɪ,ɪntɪ'lɛktʃ(ʉ)l,
ˌantɪ,ɪntɪ'lɛktjʊəl,
ˌantɪ,ɪntɪ'lɛktjʉl, -z
AM ˌæn,taɪ,ɪn(t)ə'lɛk-(t)ʃ(əw)əl,
ˌæn(t)i,ɪn(t)ə'lɛk-(t)ʃ(əw)əl, -z
anti-Jacobin
BR ˌantɪ'dʒakəbɪn, -z
AM ˌæn,taɪ'dʒækəbən,
ˌæn(t)i'dʒækəbən,
ˌæn(t)ə'dʒækəbən, -z
antiknock
BR ˌantɪ'nɒk
AM ˌæn,taɪ'nak,
ˌæn(t)i'nak,
ˌæn(t)ə'nak
Antillean
BR an'tɪliən, -z
AM æn'tɪljən,
æn'tɪliən, -z
Antilles
BR an'tɪli:z
AM æn'tɪliz
antilog
BR 'antɪlɒg, -z
AM 'æn,taɪ,lɔg,
ˌæn(t)i,lɔg,
'æn(t)ə,lɔg,
'æn,taɪ,lɑg,
'æn(t)i,lɑg,
'æn(t)ə,lɑg, -z
antilogarithm
BR ˌantɪ'lɒgərɪð(ə)m, -z
AM ˌæn,taɪ'lɔgə,rɪðəm,
ˌæn(t)i'lɔgə,rɪðəm,
ˌæn(t)ə'lɔgə,rɪðəm,
ˌæn,taɪ'lagə,rɪðəm,
ˌæn(t)i'lagə,rɪðəm,
ˌæn(t)ə'lagə,rɪðəm, -z

antilogy
BR an'tɪlədʒ|i, -ɪz
AM æn'tɪlədʒi, -z
antimacassar
BR ˌantɪmə'kasə(r), -z
AM ˌæn(t)imə'kæsər,
ˌæn(t)əmə'kæsər, -z
antimalarial
BR ˌantɪmə'lɛ:rɪəl
AM ˌæn,taɪmə'lɛriəl,
ˌæn(t)imə'lɛriəl,
ˌæn(t)əmə'lɛriəl
antimasque
BR 'antɪmɑ:sk,
'antɪmask, -s
AM ˌæn(t)i'mæsk,
ˌæn(t)ə'mæsk, -s
antimatter
BR 'antɪ,matə(r)
AM 'æn,taɪ,mædər,
'æn(t)i,mædər
antimetabolite
BR ˌantɪmɪ'tabəlʌɪt,
ˌantɪmɪ'tablʌɪt, -s
AM ˌæn,taɪmə'tæbə,laɪt,
ˌæn(t)imə'tæbə,laɪt,
ˌæn(t)əmə'tæbə,laɪt, -s
antimonarchical
BR ˌantɪmə'nɑ:kɪkl
AM ˌæn,taɪmə'nɑrkə-kəl,
ˌæn(t)imə'nɑrkəkəl,
ˌæn(t)əmə'nɑrkəkəl
antimonial
AM ˌæn(t)ə'moʊniəl
antimonic
BR ˌantɪ'mɒnɪk
AM ˌæn(t)ə'mɑnɪk
antimonious
BR ˌantɪ'məʊnɪəs
AM ˌæn(t)ə'moʊniəs
antimony
BR 'antɪməni
AM 'æn(t)ə,moʊni
antinode
BR 'antməʊd, -z
AM 'æn(t)i,noʊd,
'æn(t)ə,noʊd, -z
antinomian
BR ˌantɪ'nəʊmiən, -z
AM ˌæn(t)i,noʊmiən,
ˌæn(t)ə,noʊmiən, -z
antinomianism
BR ˌantɪ'nəʊmɪənɪz(ə)m
AM ˌæn(t)i'noʊmiə,nɪ-zəm,
ˌæn(t)ə'noʊmiə,nɪzəm
antinomy
BR an'tɪnəm|i, -ɪz
AM æn'tɪnəmi, -z
antinovel
BR 'antɪ,nɒvl, -z
AM 'æn,taɪ,nɑvəl,
'æn(t)i,nɑvəl,
'æn(t)ə,nɑvəl, -z

anti-nuclear
BR ˌantɪ'n(j)u:klɪə(r)
AM ˌæn,taɪ'n(j)ʊklɪ(ə)r,
ˌæn(t)i'n(j)ʊklɪ(ə)r,
ˌæn(t)ə'n(j)ʊklɪ(ə)r
Antioch
BR 'antɪɒk
AM 'ɑn(t)i,ɑk
Antiochus
BR an'tʌɪəkəs
AM æn'taɪəkəs
antioxidant
BR ˌantɪ'ɒksɪd(ə)nt, -s
AM 'æn,taɪ'aksədnt,
ˌæn(t)i'aksədnt,
ˌæn(t)ə'aksədnt, -s
antiparticle
BR 'antɪ,pɑ:tɪkl, -z
AM 'æn,taɪ,pardəkəl,
'æn(t)i,pardəkəl,
'æn(t)ə,pardəkəl, -z
Antipas
BR 'antɪpas
AM 'æn(t)əpəs
antipasto
BR ˌantɪ'pastəʊ,
ˌantɪ'pɑ:stəʊ,
'antɪ,pastəʊ,
'antɪ,pɑ:stəʊ
AM ˌæn(t)ə'pastoʊ,
ˌæn(t)ə'pæstoʊ
antipathetic
BR ˌantɪpə'θɛtɪk,
an,tɪpə'θɛtɪk
AM ˌæn(t)əpə'θɛdɪk,
æn,tɪpə'θɛdɪk
antipathetical
BR ˌantɪpə'θɛtɪkl,
an,tɪpə'θɛtɪkl
AM ˌæn(t)əpə'θɛdəkəl,
æn,tɪpə'θɛdəkəl
antipathetically
BR ˌantɪpə'θɛtɪkli,
an,tɪpə'θɛtɪkli
AM ˌæn(t)əpə'θɛdək-(ə)li,
æn,tɪpə'θɛdək(ə)li
antipathic
BR ˌantɪ'paθɪk
AM ˌæn(t)ə'pæθɪk
antipathy
BR an'tɪpəθ|i, -ɪz
AM æn'tɪpəθi, -z
antipersonnel
BR ˌantɪpɑ:sə'nɛl,
ˌantɪpɑ:sn'ɛl
AM ˌæn,taɪ,pərsə'nɛl,
ˌæn(t)i,pərsə'nɛl,
ˌæn(t)ə,pərsə'nɛl
antiperspirant
BR ˌantɪ'pɜ:spɪrənt,
ˌantɪ'pɜ:spɪrn̩t, -s
AM ˌæn,taɪ'pərspərənt,
ˌæn,taɪ'pərspərənt,
ˌæn(t)i'pərspərənt, -s
antiphlogistic
BR ˌantɪflə'dʒɪstɪk
AM ˌæn(t)əflə'dʒɪstɪk

antiphon
BR 'antɪf(ə)n, 'antɪfɒn, -z
AM 'æn(t)ifən, 'æn(t)ə,fɑn, -z
antiphonal
BR an'tɪfn(ə)l, an'tɪfən(ə)l
AM æn'tɪfənəl
antiphonally
BR an'tɪfnəli, an'tɪfn̩li, an'tɪfənļi, an'tɪf(ə)n(ə)li
AM æn'tɪfənəli
antiphonary
BR an'tɪfnər|i, an'tɪf(ə)nər|i, -ɪz
AM æn'tɪfə,neri, -z
antiphony
BR an'tɪfn̩|i, an'tɪfən|i, -ɪz
AM æn'tɪfəni, -z
antiphrasis
BR an'tɪfrəsɪs
AM æn'tɪfrəsəs
antipodal
BR an'tɪpədl
AM æn'tɪpədəl
antipode
BR 'antɪpəʊd, -z
AM 'æn(t)ə,pəʊd, -z
antipodean
BR an,tɪpə'dɪən, ,antɪpə'dɪən, -z
AM æn,tɪpə'dian, -z
antipodes
BR an'tɪpədiːz
AM æn'tɪpədiz
antipole
BR 'antɪpəʊl, -z
AM ,æn,taɪ'pəʊl, ,æn(t)i'pəʊl, ,æn(t)ə'pəʊl, -z
antipope
BR 'antɪpəʊp, -s
AM ,æn,taɪ'pəʊp, ,æn(t)i'pəʊp, ,æn(t)ə'pəʊp, -s
antiproton
BR 'antɪ,prəʊtɒn, -z
AM ,æn,taɪ,proʊ,tɑn, 'æn(t)i,proʊ,tɑn, 'æn(t)ə,proʊ,tɑn, -z
antipruritic
BR ,antɪprʊə'rɪtɪk
AM ,æn,taɪprə'rɪdɪk, ,æn(t)i,prə'rɪdɪk, ,æn(t)ə,prə'rɪdɪk
antipyretic
BR ,antɪpʌɪ'rɛtɪk, -s
AM ,æn,taɪ,paɪ'rɛdɪk, ,æn(t)i,paɪ'rɛdɪk, ,æn(t)ə,paɪ'rɛdɪk, -s
antiquarian
BR ,antɪ'kwɛːrɪən, -z
AM ,æn(t)ə'kwɛːrɪən, -z
antiquarianism
BR ,antɪ'kwɛːrɪənɪz(ə)m

AM ,æn(t)ə'kwɛːriə-,nɪzəm
antiquary
BR 'antɪkwər|i, -ɪz
AM 'æn(t)ə,kwɛri, -z
antiquated
BR 'antɪkweɪtɪd
AM 'æn(t)ə,kweɪdɪd
antique
BR an'tiːk, -s, -ɪŋ, -t
AM 'æn'tik, -s, -ɪŋ, -t
antiquity
BR an'tɪkwɪt|i, -ɪz
AM æn'tɪkwɪdi, -z
anti-racism
BR ,antɪ'reɪsɪz(ə)m
AM ,æn,taɪ'reɪ,sɪzəm, ,æn(t)i'reɪ,sɪzəm, ,æn(t)ə'reɪ,sɪzəm
anti-racist
BR ,antɪ'reɪsɪst, -s
AM ,æn,taɪ'reɪsɪst, ,æn(t)i'reɪsɪst, ,æn(t)ə'reɪsɪst, -s
antirrhinum
BR ,antɪ'rʌɪnəm, -z
AM ,æn(t)ə'raɪnəm, ,æn(t)i'raɪnəm, -z
antisabbatarian
BR ,antɪ,sabə'tɛːrɪən, -z
AM ,æn,taɪ,sæbə'tɛrɪən, ,æn(t)i,sæbə'tɛrɪən, ,æn(t)ə,sæbə'tɛrɪən, -z
antiscorbutic
BR ,antɪskɔː'bjuːtɪk, -s
AM ,æn,taɪ,skɔr'bjudɪk, ,æn(t)i,skɔr'bjudɪk, ,æn(t)ə,skɔr'bjudɪk, -s
antiscriptural
BR ,antɪ'skrɪptʃ(ə)rəl, ,antɪ'skrɪptʃ(ə)rļ
AM ,æn,taɪ'skrɪp(t)ʃ(ə)-rəl, ,æn(t)i'skrɪp(t)ʃ(ə)rəl, ,æn(t)ə'skrɪp(t)ʃ(ə)rəl
antisepsis
BR ,antɪ'sɛpsɪs
AM ,æn(t)ə'sɛpsəs, ,æn(t)i'sɛpsəs, ,æn,taɪ'sɛpsəs
antiseptic
BR ,antɪ'sɛptɪk, -s
AM ,æn(t)ə'sɛptɪk, -s
antiseptically
BR ,antɪ'sɛptɪkli
AM ,æn(t)ə'sɛptək(ə)li
antisera
BR ,antɪ,sɪərə(r)
AM 'æn,taɪ,sɪrə, 'æn(t)i,sɪrə
antiserum
BR ,antɪ,sɪərəm, -z
AM 'æn,taɪ,sɪrəm, 'æn(t)i,sɪrəm, -z

antisocial
BR ,antɪ'səʊʃl
AM ,æn,taɪ'soʊʃəl, ,æn(t)i'soʊʃəl, ,æn(t)ə'soʊʃəl
antisocially
BR ,antɪ'səʊʃli, ,antɪ'səʊʃəli
AM ,æn,taɪ'soʊʃəli, ,æn(t)i'soʊʃəli, ,æn(t)ə'soʊʃəli
antispasmodic
BR ,antɪspaz'mɒdɪk, -s
AM ,æn,taɪ,spæz'madɪk, ,æn(t)i,spæz'madɪk, ,æn(t)ə'spæz'madɪk, -s
antistatic
BR ,antɪ'statɪk
AM ,æn,taɪ'stædɪk, ,æn(t)i'stædɪk, ,æn(t)ə'stædɪk
antistatically
BR ,antɪ'statɪkli
AM ,æn,taɪ'stædək(ə)li, ,æn(t)i'stædək(ə)li, ,æn(t)ə'stædək(ə)li
Antisthenes
BR an'tɪsθɪniːz
AM æn'tɪsθəniz
antistrophe
BR an'tɪstrəf|i, -ɪz
AM æn'tɪstrəfi, -z
antistrophic
BR ,antɪ'strɒfɪk
AM ,æn(t)ə'strɑfɪk
antitetanus
BR ,antɪ'tɛtənəs, ,antɪ'tɛtnəs
AM ,æn,taɪ'tɛtnəs, ,æn(t)i'tɛtnəs, ,æn(t)ə'tɛtnəs
antitheism
BR ,antɪ'θiːɪz(ə)m
AM ,æn,taɪ'θi,ɪzəm, ,æn(t)i'θi,ɪzəm, ,æn(t)ə'θi,ɪzəm
antitheist
BR ,antɪ'θiːɪst, -s
AM ,æn,taɪ'θiɪst, ,æn(t)i'θiɪst, ,æn(t)ə'θiɪst, -s
antitheses
BR an'tɪθɪsiːz
AM æn'tɪθəsəs
antithesis
BR an'tɪθɪsɪs
AM æn'tɪθəsəs
antithetic
BR ,antɪ'θɛtɪk
AM ,æn(t)ə'θɛdɪk
antithetical
BR ,antɪ'θɛtɪkl
AM ,æn(t)ə'θɛdəkəl
antithetically
BR ,antɪ'θɛtɪkli
AM ,æn(t)ə'θɛdək(ə)li

antitoxic
BR ,antɪ'tɒksɪk
AM ,æn,taɪ'taksɪk, ,æn(t)i'taksɪk, ,æn(t)ə'taksɪk
antitoxin
BR ,antɪ'tɒksɪn, -z
AM ,æn(t)i',taksən, ,æn(t)ə'taksən, -z
antitrade
BR ,antɪ'treɪd, -z
AM ,æn,taɪ'treɪd, ,æn(t)i'treɪd, ,æn(t)ə'treɪd, -z
antitrinitarian
BR ,antɪ,trɪnɪ'tɛːrɪən, -z
AM ,æn,taɪ,trɪnɪ'tɛrɪən, ,æn(t)i,trɪnɪ'tɛrɪən, ,æn(t)ə,trɪnɪ'tɛrɪən, -z
antitrust
BR ,antɪ'trʌst
AM ,æn,taɪ'trəst, ,æn(t)i'trəst, ,æn(t)ə'trəst
antitype
BR 'antɪtʌɪp, -s
AM ,æn,taɪ'taɪp, ,æn(t)i'taɪp, ,æn(t)ə'taɪp, -s
antitypical
BR ,antɪ'tɪpɪkl
AM ,æn,taɪ'tɪpɪkəl, ,æn(t)i'tɪpɪkəl, ,æn(t)ə'tɪpɪkəl
antivenene
BR ,antɪ'vɛniːn, -z
AM ,æn,taɪ'vɛnən, ,æn(t)i'vɛnən, ,æn,taɪ'vinɪn, ,æn(t)i'vinɪn, ,æn(t)ə'vinɪn, -z
antivenin
BR ,antɪ'vɛnɪn, -z
AM ,æn,taɪ'vɛnən, ,æn(t)i'vɛnən, ,æn(t)ə'vɛnən, -z
antiviral
BR ,antɪ'vʌɪrəl, ,antɪ'vʌɪrļ
AM ,æn,taɪ'vaɪrəl, ,æn(t)i'vaɪrəl, ,æn(t)ə'vaɪrəl
antivirus
BR 'antɪvʌɪrəs, -ɪz
AM ,æn,taɪ'vaɪrəs, ,æn(t)i'vaɪrəs, ,æn(t)ə'vaɪrəs, -əz
antivivisection
BR ,antɪ,vɪvɪ'sɛkʃn
AM ,æn,taɪ,vɪvə'sɛkʃən, ,æn(t)i,vɪvə'sɛkʃən, ,æn(t)ə,vɪvə'sɛkʃən
antivivisectionism
BR ,antɪ,vɪvɪ'sɛkʃn̩ɪz(ə)m, ,antɪ,vɪvɪ'sɛkʃənɪz(ə)m

AM ˌænˌtaɪˌvɪvəˈsɛkʃə-
ˌnɪzəm,
ˌæn(t)iˌvɪvəˈsɛkʃə-
ˌnɪzəm,
ˌæn(t)əˌvɪvəˈsɛkʃə-
ˌnɪzəm
antivivisectionist
BR ˌantɪˌvɪvɪˈsɛkʃn̩ɪst,
ˌantɪˌvɪvɪˈsɛkʃənɪst,
-s
AM ˌænˌtaɪˌvɪvəˈsɛkʃən-
əst
ˌæn(t)iˌvɪvəˈsɛkʃənəst,
ˌæn(t)əˌvɪvəˈsɛkʃənəst,
-s
antler
BR ˈantlə(r), -z, -d
AM ˈæntlər, -z, -d
antlike
BR ˈantlʌɪk
AM ˈæntˌlaɪk
antlion
BR ˈantˌlʌɪən, -z
AM ˈæntˌlaɪən, -z
Antofagasta
BR ˌantəfəˈgasta(r)
AM ˌantoʊfəˈgastə
Antoine
BR anˈtwaːn
AM ˌænˈtwɑn
Antoinette
BR ˌantwəˈnɛt
AM ˌæntwəˈnɛt
Anton
BR ˈantɒn
AM ˈænˌtɑn
Antonia
BR anˈtəʊniə(r)
AM ænˈtoʊniə
Antonine
BR ˈantənʌɪn, -z
AM ˈæntəˌnaɪn, -z
Antoninus
BR ˌantəˈnʌɪnəs
AM ˌæntəˈnaɪnəs
Antonio
BR anˈtəʊniəʊ
AM ænˈtoʊnioʊ
Antonioni
BR ˌantəʊniˈəʊni,
anˌtəʊniˈəʊni
AM ˌænˌtoʊniˈoʊni
Antonius
BR anˈtəʊniəs
AM ænˈtoʊniəs
antonomasia
BR ˌantənəˈmeɪziə(r)
AM ˌænˌtanəˈmeɪʒə
Antony
BR ˈantəni
AM ˈæntəni, ˈænθəni
antonym
BR ˈantənɪm, -z
AM ˈæntəˌnɪm, -z
antonymous
BR anˈtɒnɪməs
AM ænˈtanəməs

antonymy
BR anˈtɒnɪmi
AM ænˈtanəmi
antra
BR ˈantrə(r)
AM ˈæntrə
antral
BR ˈantr(ə)l
AM ˈæntrəl
Antrim
BR ˈantrɪm
AM ˈæntrəm
Antrobus
BR ˈantrəbəs
AM ˈæntrəbəs
antrum
BR ˈantrəm, -z
AM ˈæntrəm, -z
antsy
BR ˈan(t)si
AM ˈæn(t)si
Antwerp
BR ˈantwəːp
AM ˈæntwərp
Anubis
BR əˈnjuːbɪs
AM əˈnubis
anuran
BR əˈnjʊərən,
əˈnjʊərn̩, -z
AM əˈn(j)ʊrən, -z
anuresis
BR ˌanjʊˈriːsɪs
AM ˌænjəˈrisɪs
anus
BR ˈeɪnəs, -ɪz
AM ˈeɪnəs, -əz
Anvers
BR ɒ̃ˈvɛː(r)
AM ɑnˈvɛ(ə)r(z)
anvil
BR ˈanv(ɪ)l, -z
AM ˈænvəl, ˈænˌvɪl, -z
Anwar
BR ˈanwɑː(r)
AM ˈænwɑr
Anwen
BR ˈanwɛn, ˈanwɪn
AM ˈænwən
Anwyl
BR ˈanw(ɪ)l
AM ˈænwəl
anxiety
BR aŋˈzaɪɪt|i, -ɪz
AM æŋˈzaɪɪdi, -z
anxious
BR ˈaŋ(k)ʃəs
AM ˈæŋ(k)ʃəs
anxiously
BR ˈaŋ(k)ʃəsli
AM ˈæŋ(k)ʃəsli
anxiousness
BR ˈaŋ(k)ʃəsnəs
AM ˈæŋ(k)ʃəsnəs
any
BR ˈɛni
AM ˈɛni

anybody
BR ˈɛnɪbʊdi, ˈɛnɪbədi
AM ˈɛniˌbadi, ˈɛniˌbədi
anyhow
BR ˈɛnɪhaʊ
AM ˈɛniˌhaʊ
anymore
BR ˌɛnɪˈmɔː(r)
AM ˌɛniˈmɔ(ə)r
anyone
BR ˈɛnɪwʌn
AM ˈɛniˌwən
anyplace
BR ˈɛnɪpleɪs
AM ˈɛniˌpleɪs
anything
BR ˈɛnɪθɪŋ
AM ˈɛniˌθɪŋ
anytime
BR ˈɛnɪtʌɪm
AM ˈɛniˌtaɪm
anyway
BR ˈɛnɪweɪ, -z
AM ˈɛniˌweɪ, -z
anywhere
BR ˈɛnɪwɛː(r)
AM ˈɛniˌ(h)wɛ(ə)r
anywise
BR ˈɛnɪwʌɪz
AM ˈɛniˌwaɪz
Anzac
BR ˈanzak, -s
AM ˈænˌzæk, -s
Anzio
BR ˈanzɪəʊ
AM ˈænzioʊ
ANZUS
BR ˈanzəs
AM ˈænzəs
ao dai
BR ˌaʊ ˈdʌɪ, -z
AM ˈɔ ˌdaɪ, ˈoʊ +, -z
A-OK
BR ˌeɪəʊˈkeɪ
AM ˈeɪˌoʊˈkeɪ
A-okay
BR ˌeɪəʊˈkeɪ
AM ˈeɪˌoʊˈkeɪ
aorist
BR ˈeɪərɪst, ˈɛːrɪst, -s
AM ˈeɪərəst, -s
aoristic
BR ˌeɪəˈrɪstɪk, ˌɛːˈrɪstɪk
AM ˌeɪəˈrɪstɪk
aorta
BR eɪˈɔːtə(r), -z
AM eɪˈɔrdə, -z
aortal
BR eɪˈɔːtl
AM eɪˈɔrdl
aortic
BR eɪˈɔːtɪk
AM eɪˈɔrdɪk
aoudad
BR ˈɑːʊdad, ˈaʊdad, -z

anyday
AM ˈaʊˌdæd, ˈɑˌudæd,
-z
à outrance
BR ˌa uːˈtrɑːns, ˌɑː +
AM ˌɑ uˈtrans
apace
BR əˈpeɪs
AM əˈpeɪs
Apache
BR əˈpatʃ|i, -ɪz
AM əˈpætʃi, -z
apanage
BR ˈapən|ɪdʒ, ˈapn̩|ɪdʒ,
-ɪdʒɪz
AM ˈæpənɪdʒ, -ɪz
apart
BR əˈpaːt
AM əˈpart
apartheid
BR əˈpaːteɪt, əˈpaːtʌɪd,
əˈpaːtʌɪt
AM əˈparˌteɪt,
əˈparˌtaɪt
apartment
BR əˈpaːtm(ə)nt, -s
AM əˈpartmənt, -s
apartness
BR əˈpaːtnəs
AM əˈpartnəs
apathetic
BR ˌapəˈθɛtɪk
AM ˌæpəˈθɛdɪk
apathetical
BR ˌapəˈθɛtɪkl
AM ˌæpəˈθɛdəkəl
apathetically
BR ˌapəˈθɛtɪkli
AM ˌæpəˈθɛdək(ə)li
apathy
BR ˈapəθi
AM ˈæpəθi
apatite
BR ˈapətʌɪt, -s
AM ˈæpəˌtaɪt, -s
ape
BR eɪp, -s, -ɪŋ, -t
AM eɪp, -s, -ɪŋ, -t
apeak
BR əˈpiːk
AM əˈpik
Apeldoorn
BR ˈapldɔːn
AM ˈæpəlˌdɔ(ə)rn
apelike
BR ˈeɪplʌɪk
AM ˈeɪpˌlaɪk
Apelles
BR əˈpɛliːz
AM əˈpɛliz
apeman
BR ˈeɪpman
AM ˈeɪpˌmæn
apemen
BR ˈeɪpmɛn
AM ˈeɪpˌmɛn
Apennines
BR ˈapɪnʌɪnz

AM 'æpə‚naɪnz
aperçu
BR ‚apə:'s(j)u:, -z
AM ‚æpər'su,
‚ɑpɛr's(j)u, -z
aperient
BR ə'pɪərɪənt, -s
AM ə'pɪriənt, -s
aperiodic
BR ‚eɪpɪərɪ'ɒdɪk
AM ‚eɪ‚pɪri'ɑdɪk
aperiodicity
BR ‚eɪpɪərɪərɪə'dɪsɪti
AM ‚eɪ‚pɪriə'dɪsɪdi
aperitif
BR ə‚pɛrə'ti:f,
ə'pɛrəti:f, -s
AM ‚ɑ‚pɛrə'tif,
ə'pɛrə‚tif, -s
aperture
BR 'æpətʃə(r), -z
AM 'æpər‚tʃʊ(ə)r, -z
apery
BR 'eɪpər|i, -ɪz
AM 'eɪpəri, -z
apetalous
BR ‚eɪ'pɛtləs
AM ‚eɪ'pɛdləs
apex
BR 'eɪpɛks, -ɪz
AM 'eɪ‚pɛks, -əz
Apfelstrudel
BR 'apf(ə)l‚stru:dl,
'apf(ə)l‚ʃtru:dl, -z
AM ‚æpfəl'strudəl, -z
aphaeresis
BR ə'fɪərɪsɪs, a'fɪərɪsɪs
AM ə'fɛrəsəs,
æ'fɛrəsəs
aphasia
BR ə'feɪzɪə(r),
ə'feɪʒə(r)
AM ə'feɪʒiə
aphasic
BR ə'feɪzɪk
AM ə'feɪzɪk
aphelia
BR ə'fi:lɪə(r)
AM ə'filjə, ə'filiə
aphelion
BR ə'fi:lɪən, ap'hi:lɪən
AM ə'filjən, ə'filiən
apheresis
BR ə'fɪərɪsɪs, a'fɪərɪsɪs
AM ə'fɛrəsəs,
æ'fɛrəsəs
aphesis
BR 'afɪsɪs
AM 'æfəsəs
aphetic
BR ə'fɛtɪk
AM ə'fɛdɪk, æ'fɛdɪk
aphetically
BR ə'fɛtɪkli
AM ə'fɛdək(ə)li,
æ'fɛdək(ə)li

aphid
BR 'eɪfɪd, -z
AM 'eɪfɪd, -z
aphides
BR 'eɪfɪdi:z
AM 'eɪfɪ‚diz, 'æfə‚diz
aphis
BR 'eɪfɪs, -ɪz
AM 'eɪfɪs, 'æfəs, -ɪz
aphonia
BR eɪ'fəʊnɪə(r)
AM ‚eɪ'foʊniə, ə'foʊniə
aphonic
BR eɪ'fɒnɪk, ə'fɒnɪk
AM eɪ'fɑnɪk
aphony
BR 'afəni, 'afn̩i
AM 'æfəni
aphorise
BR 'afərʌɪz, -ɪz, -ɪŋ, -d
AM 'æfə‚raɪz, -ɪz, -ɪŋ, -d
aphorism
BR 'afərɪz(ə)m, -z
AM 'æfə‚rɪzəm, -z
aphorist
BR 'af(ə)rɪst, -s
AM 'æfərəst, -s
aphoristic
BR ‚afə'rɪstɪk
AM ‚æfə'rɪstɪk
aphoristically
BR ‚afə'rɪstɪkli
AM ‚æfə'rɪstɪk(ə)li
aphorize
BR 'afərʌɪz, -ɪz, -ɪŋ, -d
AM 'æfə‚raɪz, -ɪz, -ɪŋ, -d
Aphra
BR 'afrə(r)
AM 'æfrə
aphrodisiac
BR ‚afrə'dɪzɪak, -s
AM ‚æfrə'dɪzi‚æk,
‚æfrə'dizi‚æk,
‚æfrə'diʒi‚æk, -s
Aphrodisias
BR ‚afrə'dɪzɪas
AM ‚æfrə'dɪziəs,
‚æfrə'diziəs,
‚æfrə'diʒiəs
Aphrodite
BR ‚afrə'dʌɪti
AM ‚æfroʊ'daɪdi,
‚æfrə'daɪdi
aphtha
BR 'afθə(r)
AM 'æfθə
aphthous
BR 'afθəs
AM 'æfθəs
aphyllous
BR eɪ'fɪləs
AM eɪ'fɪləs
Apia
BR ɑ:'pi:ə(r), ə'pi:ə(r),
'apɪə(r)
AM 'ɑpiə

apian
BR 'eɪpɪən
AM 'eɪpiən
apiarian
BR ‚eɪpɪ'ɛ:rɪən
AM ‚æpi'ɛriən
apiarist
BR 'eɪpɪərɪst, -s
AM 'eɪpiərəst, -s
apiary
BR 'eɪpɪər|i, -ɪz
AM 'eɪpi‚ɛri, -z
apical
BR 'apɪkl, 'eɪpɪkl
AM 'æpəkəl, 'eɪpɪkəl
apically
BR 'apɪkli, 'eɪpɪkli
AM 'æpək(ə)li,
'eɪpɪk(ə)li
apices
BR 'eɪpɪsi:z
AM 'eɪpə‚siz, 'æpə‚siz
apicultural
BR ‚eɪpɪ'kʌltʃ(ə)rəl,
‚eɪpɪ'kʌltʃ(ə)r|
AM ‚eɪpə'kəltʃ(ə)rəl
apiculture
BR 'eɪpɪ‚kʌltʃə(r)
AM 'eɪpə‚kəltʃər
apiculturist
BR ‚eɪpɪ'kʌltʃ(ə)rɪst, -s
AM ‚eɪpə'kəltʃ(ə)rəst,
-s
apiece
BR ə'pi:s
AM ə'pis
apis
BR 'eɪpɪs
AM 'eɪpɪs
apish
BR 'eɪpɪʃ
AM 'eɪpɪʃ
apishly
BR 'eɪpɪʃli
AM 'eɪpɪʃli
apishness
BR 'eɪpɪʃnɪs
AM 'eɪpɪʃnɪs
aplanat
BR 'aplənət, -s
AM 'æplə‚næt, -s
aplanatic
BR ‚aplə'natɪk
AM ‚æplə'nædɪk
aplasia
BR ə'pleɪzɪə(r),
ə'pleɪʒə(r)
AM ə'pleɪʒiə
aplastic
BR ‚eɪ'plastɪk
AM ‚eɪ'plæstɪk
aplenty
BR ə'plɛnti
AM ə'plen(t)i
aplomb
BR ə'plɒm

AM ə'plɑm, ə'pləm,
ə'ploʊm
apnea
BR 'apnɪə(r)
AM 'æpniə
apnoea
BR 'apnɪə(r)
AM 'æpniə
apocalypse
BR ə'pɒkəlɪps, -ɪz
AM ə'pɑkə‚lɪps, -ɪz
apocalyptic
BR ə‚pɒkə'lɪptɪk
AM ə‚pɑkə'lɪptɪk
apocalyptical
BR ə‚pɒkə'lɪptɪkl
AM ə‚pɑkə'lɪptɪkəl
apocalyptically
BR ə‚pɒkə'lɪptɪkli
AM ə‚pɑkə'lɪptɪk(ə)li
apocarpous
BR ‚apə'kɑ:pəs
AM ‚æpə'kɑrpəs
apochromat
BR ‚apə'krəʊmat,
'apəkrə(ʊ)mat, -s
AM ‚æpə'kroʊmət, -s
apochromatic
BR ‚apəkrə(ʊ)'matɪk
AM ‚æpəkroʊ'mædɪk
apocope
BR ə'pɒkəp|i, -ɪz
AM ə'pɑkəpi, -z
apocrine
BR 'apəkrʌɪn,
'apəkrɪn
AM 'æpəkrən,
'æpə‚kraɪn,
'æpə‚krɪn
apocrypha
BR ə'pɒkrɪfə(r), -z
AM ə'pɑkrəfə, -z
apocryphal
BR ə'pɒkrɪfl
AM ə'pɑkrəfəl
apocryphally
BR ə'pɒkrɪfl̩i,
ə'pɒkrɪfəli
AM ə'pɑkrəfəli
apodal
BR 'apədl
AM eɪ'poʊdəl
apodeictic
BR ‚apə'dʌɪktɪk
AM ‚æpə'daɪktɪk
apodeictical
BR ‚apə'dʌɪktɪkl
AM ‚æpə'daɪktɪkəl
apodeictically
BR ‚apə'dʌɪktɪkli
AM ‚æpə'daɪktɪk(ə)li
apodictic
BR ‚apə'dɪktɪk
AM ‚æpə'dɪktɪk
apodictical
BR ‚apə'dɪktɪkl
AM ‚æpə'dɪktɪkəl

apodictically
BR ˌapəˈdɪktɪkli
AM ˌæpəˈdɪktɪk(ə)li

apodoses
BR əˈpɒdəsiːz
AM əˈpɑdəsiz

apodosis
BR əˈpɒdəsɪs
AM əˈpɑdəsəs

apogean
BR ˌapə(ʊ)ˈdʒiːən
AM ˌæpəˈdʒiən

apogee
BR ˈapədʒiː, -z
AM ˈæpədʒi, -z

apolaustic
BR ˌapəˈlɔːstɪk
AM ˌæpəˈlɒstɪk, ˌæpəˈlastɪk

apolitical
BR ˌeɪpəˈlɪtɪkl
AM ˌeɪpəˈlɪdəkəl

apolitically
BR ˌeɪpəˈlɪtɪkli
AM ˌeɪpəˈlɪdək(ə)li

Apollinaire
BR əˌpɒlɪˈnɛː(r)
AM əˌpɑləˈnɛːr

Apollinaris
BR əˌpɒlɪˈnɛːrɪs, əˌpɒlɪˈnɑːrɪs
AM əˌpɑləˈnɛrəs

Apollo
BR əˈpɒləʊ
AM əˈpɑloʊ

Apollonian
BR ˌapəˈləʊnɪən
AM ˌæpəˈloʊnɪən

Apollonius
BR ˌapəˈləʊnɪəs
AM ˌæpəˈloʊnɪəs

Apollyon
BR əˈpɒlɪən, əˈpɒlɪɒn
AM əˈpɑlɪən

apologetic
BR əˌpɒləˈdʒɛtɪk, -s
AM əˌpɑləˈdʒɛdɪk, -s

apologetical
BR əˌpɒləˈdʒɛtɪkl
AM əˌpɑləˈdʒɛdəkəl

apologetically
BR əˌpɒləˈdʒɛtɪkli
AM əˌpɑləˈdʒɛdək(ə)li

apologia
BR ˌapəˈləʊdʒ(ɪ)ə(r), -z
AM ˌæpəˈloʊdʒ(i)ə, əˌpoʊləˈdʒiə, -z

apologise
BR əˈpɒlədʒʌɪz, -ɪz, -ɪŋ, -d
AM əˈpɑləˌdʒaɪz, -ɪz, -ɪŋ, -d

apologist
BR əˈpɒlədʒɪst, -s
AM əˈpɑlədʒəst, -s

apologize
BR əˈpɒlədʒʌɪz, -ɪz, -ɪŋ, -d
AM əˈpɑləˌdʒaɪz, -ɪz, -ɪŋ, -d

apologue
BR ˈapəlɒg, -z
AM ˈæpəˌlɔg, ˈæpəˌlɑg, -z

apology
BR əˈpɒlədʒ|i, -ɪz
AM əˈpɑlədʒi, -z

apolune
BR ˈapəluːn, -z
AM ˈæpəˌlun, -z

apomictic
BR ˌapəˈmɪktɪk
AM ˌæpəˈmɪktɪk

apomixis
BR ˌapəˈmɪksɪs
AM ˌæpəˈmɪksɪs

apophatic
BR ˌapəˈfatɪk
AM ˌæpəˈfædɪk

apophthegm
BR ˈapəθɛm, -z
AM ˈæpəˌθɛm, -z

apophthegmatic
BR ˌapəθɛgˈmatɪk
AM ˌæpəθəˈmædɪk

apophthegmatic- ally
BR ˌapəθɛgˈmatɪkli
AM ˌæpəθəˈmædək(ə)li

apophyses
BR əˈpɒfɪsiːz
AM əˈpɑfəˌsiz

apophysis
BR əˈpɒfɪsɪs
AM əˈpɑfəsəs

apoplectic
BR ˌapəˈplɛktɪk
AM ˌæpəˈplɛktɪk

apoplectical
BR ˌapəˈplɛktɪkl
AM ˌæpəˈplɛktəkəl

apoplectically
BR ˌapəˈplɛktɪkli
AM ˌæpəˈplɛktək(ə)li

apoplexy
BR ˈapəplɛks|i, -ɪz
AM ˈæpəˌplɛksi, -z

aposematic
BR ˌapə(ʊ)sɪˈmatɪk
AM ˌæpəsɛˈmædɪk

aposiopeses
BR ˌapə(ʊ)sʌɪəˈpiːsiːz
AM ˌæpəˌsaɪəˈpisiz

aposiopesis
BR ˌapə(ʊ)sʌɪəˈpiːsɪs
AM ˌæpəˌsaɪəˈpisɪs

apostasy
BR əˈpɒstəs|i, -ɪz
AM əˈpɑstəsi, -z

apostate
BR əˈpɒsteɪt, -s

apostatic
BR ˌapəˈstatɪk
AM ˌæpəˈstædɪk

apostatical
BR ˌapəˈstatɪkl
AM ˌæpəˈstædəkəl

apostatically
BR ˌapəˈstatɪkli
AM ˌæpəˈstædək(ə)li

apostatise
BR əˈpɒstətʌɪz, -ɪz, -ɪŋ, -d
AM əˈpɑstəˌtaɪz, -ɪz, -ɪŋ, -d

apostatize
BR əˈpɒstətʌɪz, -ɪz, -ɪŋ, -d
AM əˈpɑstəˌtaɪz, -ɪz, -ɪŋ, -d

a posteriori
BR ˌeɪ pɒˌstɛrɪˈɔːrʌɪ, ˌɑː +, + pɒˌstɪərɪˈɔːrʌɪ
AM ˌɑ ˌpɑˌstɪriˈɔˌri, ˌeɪ ˌpɑˌstiriˈɔˌraɪ

apostigmat
BR ˈapəstɪgmat, -s
AM ˈæpəˌstɪgˌmæt, -s

apostil
BR əˈpɒstɪl, -z
AM əˈpɑstl, -z

apostille
BR əˈpɒstɪl, -z
AM əˈpɑstl, -z

apostle
BR əˈpɒsl, -z
AM əˈpɑsəl, -z

apostleship
BR əˈpɒslʃɪp, -s
AM əˈpɑsəlˌʃɪp, -s

apostolate
BR əˈpɒstəleɪt, əˈpɒstələt, -s
AM əˈpɑstəˌleɪt, əˈpɑstələt, -s

apostolic
BR ˌapəˈstɒlɪk
AM ˌæpəˈstɑlɪk

apostolical
BR ˌapəˈstɒlɪkl
AM ˌæpəˈstɑləkəl

apostolically
BR ˌapəˈstɒlɪkli
AM ˌæpəˈstɑlək(ə)li

apostrophe
BR əˈpɒstrəf|i, -ɪz
AM əˈpɑstrəfi, -z

apostrophic
BR ˌapəˈstrɒfɪk
AM ˌæpəˈstrɑfɪk

apostrophise
BR əˈpɒstrəfʌɪz, -ɪz, -ɪŋ, -d
AM əˈpɑstrəˌfaɪz, -ɪz, -ɪŋ, -d

apostrophize
BR əˈpɒstrəfʌɪz, -ɪz, -ɪŋ, -d
AM əˈpɑstrəˌfaɪz, -ɪz, -ɪŋ, -d

apothecary
BR əˈpɒθɪk(ə)r|i, -ɪz
AM əˈpɑθəˌkɛri, -z

apothegm
BR ˈapəθɛm, -z
AM ˈæpəˌθɛm, -z

apothem
BR ˈapəθɛm, -z
AM ˈæpəˌθɛm, -z

apotheoses
BR əˌpɒθɪˈəʊsiːz
AM əˌpaθiˈoʊˌsiz

apotheosis
BR əˌpɒθɪˈəʊsɪs
AM əˌpaθiˈoʊsəs

apotheosise
BR əˈpɒθɪəsʌɪz, -ɪz, -ɪŋ, -d
AM əˈpaθiəˌsaɪz, ˌæpəˈθiəˌsaɪz, -ɪz, -ɪŋ, -d

apotheosize
BR əˈpɒθɪəsʌɪz, -ɪz, -ɪŋ, -d
AM əˈpaθiəˌsaɪz, ˌæpəˈθiəˌsaɪz, -ɪz, -ɪŋ, -d

apotropaic
BR ˌapətrəˈpeɪk
AM ˌæpətrəˈpeɪk

appal
BR əˈpɔːl, -z, -ɪŋ, -d
AM əˈpɔl, əˈpɑl, -z, -ɪŋ, -d

Appalachia
BR ˌapəˈleɪ(t)ʃ(ɪ)ə(r)
AM ˌæpəˈleɪ(t)ʃ(i)ə, ˌæpəˈlæ(t)ʃ(i)ə

Appalachian
BR ˌapəˈleɪ(t)ʃən, ˌapəˈleɪtʃn, -z
AM ˌæpəˈleɪ(t)ʃ(i)ən, ˌæpəˈlæ(t)ʃ(i)ən, -z

appall
BR əˈpɔːl, -z, -ɪŋ, -d
AM əˈpɔl, əˈpɑl, -z, -ɪŋ, -d

appallingly
BR əˈpɔːlɪŋli
AM əˈpɔlɪŋli, əˈpɑlɪŋli

Appaloosa
BR ˌapəˈluːsə(r), -z
AM ˌæpəˈlusə, -z

appanage
BR ˈapən|ɪdʒ, ˈapn|ɪdʒ, -ɪdʒɪz
AM ˈæpənɪdʒ, -ɪz

apparat
BR ˌapəˈrɑːt, ˌapəˈrat, -s
AM ˌæpəˌræt, ˈapəˌrat, ˌæpəˌrat, -s

apparatchik
BR ˌapəˈra(t)tʃɪk, ˌapəˈrɑː(t)tʃɪk, -s

AM ˌæpəˈrætʃɪk, -s
apparatus
BR ˌæpəˈreɪtəs, -ɪz
AM ˌæpəˈrædəs,
ˌæpəˈreɪdəs, -əz
apparel
BR əˈpærəl, əˈparl, -z,
-ɪŋ, -d
AM əˈpɛrəl, -z, -ɪŋ, -d
apparent
BR əˈparənt, əˈparɲt
AM əˈpɛrənt
apparently
BR əˈparəntli,
əˈparɲtli
AM əˈpɛrən(t)li
apparentness
BR əˈparəntnəs,
əˈparɲtnəs
AM əˈpɛrən(t)nəs
apparition
BR ˌæpəˈrɪʃn, -z
AM ˌæpəˈrɪʃən, -z
apparitor
BR əˈparɪtə(r), -z
AM əˈpɛrədər, -z
appassionata
BR əˌpasjəˈnɑːtə(r)
AM əˌpɑsiəˈnɑdə,
əˌpæsiəˈnɑdə
appeal
BR əˈpiːl, -z, -ɪŋ, -d
AM əˈpil, -z, -ɪŋ, -d
appealable
BR əˈpiːləbl
AM əˈpiləbəl
appealer
BR əˈpiːlə(r), -z
AM əˈpilər, -z
appealing
BR əˈpiːlɪŋ
AM əˈpilɪŋ
appealingly
BR əˈpiːlɪŋli
AM əˈpilɪŋli
appear
BR əˈpɪə(r), -z, -ɪŋ, -d
AM əˈpɪ(ə)r, -z, -ɪŋ, -d
appearance
BR əˈpɪərəns, əˈpɪərns,
-ɪz
AM əˈpɪrəns, -əz
appease
BR əˈpiːz, -ɪz, -ɪŋ, -d
AM əˈpiz, -ɪz, -ɪŋ, -d
appeasement
BR əˈpiːzm(ə)nt
AM əˈpizmənt
appeaser
BR əˈpiːzə(r), -z
AM əˈpizər, -z
appellant
BR əˈpɛlənt, əˈpɛlɲt, -s
AM əˈpɛlənt, -s
appellate
BR əˈpɛlət
AM əˈpɛlət

appellation
BR ˌapəˈleɪʃn, -z
AM ˌæpəˈleɪʃən, -z
**appellation
contrôlée**
BR ˌapɛlasjɔ̃
ˌkɔ̃trəʊˈleɪ
AM ɑˌpɛlɑˈsiɔn
ˌkɔntrəˈleɪ
**appellation
d'origine
contrôlée**
BR ˌapɛlasjɔ̃ ˌdɒrɪˈʒiːn
ˌkɔ̃trəʊˈleɪ
AM ɑˌpɛlɑˈsiɔn
dɔriˌʒin ˌkɔntrəˈleɪ
appellative
BR əˈpɛlətɪv, -z
AM əˈpɛlədɪv, -z
appellatively
BR əˈpɛlətɪvli
AM əˈpɛlədɪvli
appellee
BR ˌapəˈliː, ˌapɛlˈiː, -z
AM ˌæpɛlˈi, -z
append
BR əˈpɛnd, -z, -ɪŋ, -ɪd
AM əˈpɛnd, -z, -ɪŋ, -əd
appendage
BR əˈpɛnd|ɪdʒ, -ɪdʒɪz
AM əˈpɛndɪdʒ, -ɪz
appendant
BR əˈpɛnd(ə)nt, -s
AM əˈpɛnd(ə)nt, -s
appendectomy
BR ˌapɛnˈdɛktəm|i,
ˌap(ə)nˈdɛktəm|i, -ɪz
AM ˌæpənˈdɛktəmi,
ˌæˌpɛnˈdɛktəmi, -z
appendicectomy
BR əˌpɛndɪˈsɛktəm|i,
-ɪz
AM əˌpɛndəˈsɛktəmi, -z
appendices
BR əˈpɛndɪsiːz
AM əˈpɛndəˌsiz
appendicitis
BR əˌpɛndɪˈsaɪtɪs
AM əˌpɛndəˈsaɪdɪs
appendix
BR əˈpɛnd|ɪks, -ɪksɪz
AM əˈpɛndɪks, -ɪz
apperceive
BR ˌapəˈsiːv, -z, -ɪŋ, -d
AM ˌæpərˈsiv, -z, -ɪŋ, -d
apperception
BR ˌapəˈsɛpʃn
AM ˌæpərˈsɛpʃən
apperceptive
BR ˌapəˈsɛptɪv
AM ˌæpərˈsɛptɪv
appertain
BR ˌapəˈteɪn, -z, -ɪŋ, -d
AM ˌæpərˈteɪn, -z, -ɪŋ, -d
appertinent
BR əˈpəːtɪnənt
AM əˈpərtnənt

appestat
BR ˈapɪstat, -s
AM ˈæpəˌstæt, -s
appetence
BR ˈapɪt(ə)ns
AM ˈæpədəns, ˈæpətns
appetency
BR ˈapɪt(ə)ns|i, -ɪz
AM ˈæpədənsi,
ˈæpətnsi, -z
appetent
BR ˈapɪt(ə)nt
AM ˈæpədənt, ˈæpətnt
appetise
BR ˈapɪtaɪz, -ɪz, -ɪŋ, -d
AM ˈæpəˌtaɪz, -ɪz, -ɪŋ, -d
appetiser
BR ˈapɪtaɪzə(r), -z
AM ˈæpəˌtaɪzər, -z
appetisingly
BR ˈapɪtaɪzɪŋli
AM ˈæpəˌtaɪzɪŋli
appetite
BR ˈapɪtaɪt, -s
AM ˈæpəˌtaɪt, -s
appetitive
BR əˈpɛtɪtɪv
AM ˈæpəˌtaɪdɪv,
əˈpədədɪv
appetize
BR ˈapɪtaɪz, -ɪz, -ɪŋ, -d
AM ˈæpəˌtaɪz, -ɪz, -ɪŋ, -d
appetizer
BR ˈapɪtaɪzə(r), -z
AM ˈæpəˌtaɪzər, -z
appetizing
BR ˈapɪtaɪzɪŋ
AM ˈæpəˌtaɪzɪŋ
appetizingly
BR ˈapɪtaɪzɪŋli
AM ˈæpəˌtaɪzɪŋli
Appian Way
BR ˌapɪən ˈweɪ
AM ˌæpiən ˈweɪ
applaud
BR əˈplɔːd, -z, -ɪŋ, -ɪd
AM əˈplɑd, əˈplad, -z,
-ɪŋ, -əd
applause
BR əˈplɔːz
AM əˈplɔz, əˈplɑz
apple
BR ˈapl, -z
AM ˈæpəl, -z
Appleby
BR ˈaplbi
AM ˈæpəlˌbi
applecart
BR ˈaplkɑːt, -s
AM ˈæpəlˌkɑrt, -s
Appledore
BR ˈapldɔː(r)
AM ˈæpəlˌdɔ(ə)r
applejack
BR ˈapldʒak
AM ˈæpəlˌdʒæk

Appleton
BR ˈaplt(ə)n
AM ˈæpəlt(ə)n
appliable
BR əˈplʌɪəbl
AM əˈplaɪəbəl
appliableness
BR əˈplʌɪəblnəs
AM əˈplaɪəbəlnəs
appliance
BR əˈplʌɪəns, -ɪz
AM əˈplaɪəns, -əz
applicability
BR əˌplɪkəˈbɪləti,
ˌaplɪkəˈbɪlɪti
AM ˌæplɪkəˈbɪlɪdi
applicable
BR əˈplɪkəbl, ˈaplɪkəbl
AM ˈæpləkəbəl
applicableness
BR əˈplɪkəblnəs,
ˈaplɪkəblnəs
AM ˈæpləkəbəlnəs
applicably
BR əˈplɪkəbli,
ˈaplɪkəbli
AM ˈæpləkəbli
applicant
BR ˈaplɪk(ə)nt, -s
AM ˈæpləkənt, -s
application
BR ˌaplɪˈkeɪʃn, -z
AM ˌæpləˈkeɪʃən, -z
applicator
BR ˈaplɪkeɪtə(r), -z
AM ˈæpləˌkeɪdər, -z
applied
BR əˈplʌɪd
AM əˈplaɪd
applier
BR əˈplʌɪə(r), -z
AM əˈplaɪər, -z
appliqué
BR əˈpliːkeɪ, -z, -ɪŋ, -d
AM ˌæpləˈkeɪ, -z, -ɪŋ, -d
apply
BR əˈplʌɪ, -z, -ɪŋ, -d
AM əˈplaɪ, -z, -ɪŋ, -d
appoggiatura
BR əˌpɒdʒ(ɪ)əˈt(j)ʊərə(r),
-z
AM əˌpɑdʒəˈtʊrə, -z
appoint
BR əˈpɔɪnt, -s, -ɪŋ, -ɪd
AM əˈpɔɪn|t, -ts, -(t)ɪŋ,
-(t)ɪd
appointee
BR əˌpɔɪnˈtiː, ˌapɔɪnˈtiː,
-z
AM əˌpɔɪnˈti, -z
appointer
BR əˈpɔɪntə(r), -z
AM əˈpɔɪn(t)ər, -z
appointive
BR əˈpɔɪntɪv
AM əˈpɔɪn(t)ɪv

appointment
BR ə'pɔɪntm(ə)nt, -s
AM ə'pɔɪntmənt, -s

Appomattox
BR ˌæpə'mætəks
AM ˌæpə'mædəks

apport
BR ə'pɔːt
AM ə'pɔ(ə)rt

apportion
BR ə'pɔːʃ|n, -nz,
-nɪŋ\-ənɪŋ, -nd
AM ə'pɔrʃ|ən, -ənz,
-(ə)nɪŋ, -ənd

apportionable
BR ə'pɔːʃnəbl,
ə'pɔːʃ(ə)nəbl
AM ə'pɔrʃ(ə)nəbəl

apportionment
BR ə'pɔːʃnm(ə)nt, -s
AM ə'pɔrʃənmənt, -s

appose
BR ə'pəʊz, -ɪz, -ɪŋ, -d
AM ə'pouz, -əz, -ɪŋ, -d

apposite
BR 'apəzɪt
AM 'æpəzət

appositely
BR 'apəzɪtli
AM 'æpəzətli

appositeness
BR 'apəzɪtnɪs
AM 'æpəzətnəs

apposition
BR ˌapə'zɪʃn, -z
AM ˌæpə'zɪʃən, -z

appositional
BR ˌapə'zɪʃ|n(ə)l,
ˌapə'zɪʃən(ə)l
AM ˌæpə'zɪʃ(ə)nəl

appositive
BR ə'pɒzɪtɪv
AM ə'pazədɪv

appositively
BR ə'pɒzɪtɪvli
AM ə'pazədɪvli

appraisable
BR ə'preɪzəbl
AM ə'preɪzəbəl

appraisal
BR ə'preɪzl, -z
AM ə'preɪzəl, -z

appraise
BR ə'preɪz, -ɪz, -ɪŋ, -d
AM ə'preɪz, -ɪz, -ɪŋ, -d

appraisee
BR ə'preɪ'ziː, -z
AM ə'preɪ'zi, -z

appraisement
BR ə'preɪzm(ə)nt, -s
AM ə'preɪzmənt, -s

appraiser
BR ə'preɪzə(r), -z
AM ə'preɪzər, -z

appraisingly
BR ə'preɪzɪŋli
AM ə'preɪzɪŋli

appraisive
BR ə'preɪzɪv
AM ə'preɪzɪv

appreciable
BR ə'priːʃ(ɪ)əbl
AM ə'priʃ(i)əbəl

appreciably
BR ə'priːʃ(ɪ)əbli
AM ə'priʃ(i)əbli

appreciate
BR ə'priːʃɪeɪt,
ə'priːsɪeɪt, -s, -ɪŋ, -ɪd
AM ə'priʃiˌeɪ|t, -ts, -dɪŋ,
-dɪd

appreciation
BR əˌpriːʃɪ'eɪʃn,
əˌpriːsɪ'eɪʃn, -z
AM əˌpriʃi'eɪʃən, -z

appreciative
BR ə'priːʃ(ɪ)ətɪv,
ə'priːsɪətɪv
AM ə'priʃ(i)ədɪv

appreciatively
BR ə'priːʃ(ɪ)ətɪvli,
ə'priːsɪətɪvli
AM ə'priʃ(i)ədɪvli

appreciativeness
BR ə'priːʃ(ɪ)ətɪvnɪs,
ə'priːsɪətɪvnɪs
AM ə'priʃ(i)ədɪvnɪs

appreciator
BR ə'priːʃɪeɪtə(r),
ə'priːsɪeɪtə(r), -z
AM ə'priʃiˌeɪdər, -z

appreciatory
BR ə'priːʃ(ɪ)ət(ə)ri,
ə'priːsɪət(ə)ri
AM ə'priʃ(i)əˌtɔri

apprehend
BR ˌapri'hɛnd, -z, -ɪŋ,
-ɪd
AM ˌæprə'hɛnd,
ˌæpri'hɛnd, -z, -ɪŋ, -əd

apprehensibility
BR ˌaprihɛnsɪ'bɪlɪti
AM ˌæprəˌhɛnsə'bɪlɪdi,
ˌæpriˌhɛnsə'bɪlɪdi

apprehensible
BR ˌapri'hɛnsɪbl
AM ˌæprə'hɛnsəbəl,
ˌæpri'hɛnsəbəl

apprehension
BR ˌapri'hɛnʃn, -z
AM ˌæprə'hɛn(t)ʃən,
ˌæpri'hɛn(t)ʃən, -z

apprehensive
BR ˌapri'hɛnsɪv
AM ˌæprə'hɛnsɪv,
ˌæpri'hɛnsɪv

apprehensively
BR ˌapri'hɛnsɪvli
AM ˌæprə'hɛnsɪvli,
ˌæpri'hɛnsɪvli

apprehensiveness
BR ˌaprɪ'hɛnsɪvnɪs
AM ˌæprə'hɛnsɪvnɪs,
ˌæpri'hɛnsɪvnɪs

apprentice
BR ə'prɛntɪs, -ɪz, -ɪŋ, -t
AM ə'prɛn(t)əs, -əz, -ɪŋ,
-t

apprenticeship
BR ə'prɛntɪ(s)ʃɪp, -s
AM ə'prɛn(t)əsˌʃɪp, -s

apprise
BR ə'praɪz, -ɪz, -ɪŋ, -d
AM ə'praɪz, -ɪz, -ɪŋ, -d

apprize
BR ə'praɪz, -ɪz, -ɪŋ, -d
AM ə'praɪz, -ɪz, -ɪŋ, -d

appro
BR 'aprəʊ
AM 'æproʊ

approach
BR ə'prəʊtʃ, -ɪz, -ɪŋ, -t
AM ə'proʊtʃ, -əz, -ɪŋ, -t

approachability
BR əˌprəʊtʃə'bɪlɪti
AM əˌproʊtʃə'bɪlɪdi

approachable
BR ə'prəʊtʃəbl
AM ə'proʊtʃəbəl

approbate
BR 'aprə(ʊ)beɪt, -s, -ɪŋ,
-ɪd
AM 'æprəˌbeɪ|t,
'æproʊˌbeɪ|t, -ts, -dɪŋ,
-dɪd

approbation
BR ˌaprə(ʊ)'beɪʃn
AM ˌæprə'beɪʃən

approbative
BR 'aprəbeɪtɪv
AM ˌæprə'beɪdɪv,
ə'proʊbədɪv

approbatory
BR ˌaprə(ʊ)'beɪt(ə)ri
AM 'æprəbəˌtɔri,
ə'proʊbəˌtɔri

appropriate¹
adjective
BR ə'prəʊprɪət
AM ə'proʊpriət

appropriate²
verb
BR ə'prəʊprɪeɪt, -s, -ɪŋ,
-ɪd
AM ə'proʊpriˌeɪ|t, -ts,
-dɪŋ, -dɪd

appropriately
BR ə'prəʊprɪətli
AM ə'proʊpriətli

appropriateness
BR ə'prəʊprɪətnəs
AM ə'proʊpriətnəs

appropriation
BR əˌprəʊprɪ'eɪʃn, -z
AM əˌproʊpri'eɪʃən, -z

appropriationist
BR əˌprəʊprɪ'eɪʃnɪst,
ə'prəʊprɪ'eɪʃənɪst, -s
AM əˌproʊpri'eɪʃənəst,
-s

appropriative
BR ə'prəʊprɪətɪv

appropriator
BR ə'prəʊprɪeɪtə(r), -z
AM ə'proʊpriˌeɪdər, -z

approval
BR ə'pruːvl, -z
AM ə'pruvəl, -z

approve
BR ə'pruːv, -z, -ɪŋ, -d
AM ə'pruv, -z, -ɪŋ, -d

approving
BR ə'pruːvɪŋ
AM ə'pruvɪŋ

approvingly
BR ə'pruːvɪŋli
AM ə'pruvɪŋli

approximant
BR ə'prɒksɪm(ə)nt, -s
AM ə'praksəmənt, -s

approximate¹
adjective
BR ə'prɒksɪmət
AM ə'praksəmət

approximate²
verb
BR ə'prɒksɪmeɪt, -s,
-ɪŋ, -ɪd
AM ə'praksəˌmeɪ|t, -ts,
-dɪŋ, -dɪd

approximately
BR ə'prɒksɪmətli
AM ə'praksəmətli

approximation
BR əˌprɒksɪ'meɪʃn, -z
AM əˌpraksə'meɪʃən,
-z

approximative
BR ə'prɒksɪmətɪv
AM ə'praksəˌmeɪdɪv

approximatively
BR ə'prɒksɪmətɪvli
AM ə'praksəˌmeɪdɪvli

appurtenance
BR ə'pɜːtɪnəns,
ə'pɜːtnəns, -ɪz
AM ə'pɜrtnəns, -əz

appurtenant
BR ə'pɜːtɪnənt,
ə'pɜːtnənt
AM ə'pɜrtnənt

apraxia
BR eɪ'praksɪə(r),
ə'praksɪə(r)
AM eɪ'præksiə

après-ski
BR ˌapreɪ'skiː
AM ˌɑpreɪ'ski

apricot
BR 'eɪprɪkɒt, -s
AM 'æprəˌkɑt,
'eɪprəˌkɑt, -s

April
BR 'eɪpr(ɪ)l, -z
AM 'eɪprəl, -z

a priori
BR ˌeɪ prɑɪ'ɔːrɑɪ, ˌɑː +,
+ prɑɪ'ɔːri, prɪ'ɔːri

apriorism
AM ˌɑ priˈɔːri, ˌeɪ priˈɔːri
apriorism
BR (ˌ)eɪˈprʌɪərɪz(ə)m
AM eɪˈpraɪəˌrɪzəm
aprioristic
BR ˌeɪprʌɪəˈrɪstɪk
AM ˌeɪˌpraɪəˈrɪstɪk
aprioristically
BR ˌeɪprʌɪəˈrɪstɪkli
AM ˌeɪˌpraɪəˈrɪstɪk(ə)li
apron
BR ˈeɪpr(ə)n, -z, -d
AM ˈeɪprən, -z, -d
apronful
BR ˈeɪpr(ə)nfʊl, -z
AM ˈeɪprənˌfʊl, -z
apropos
BR ˌaprəˈpəʊ, ˈaprəpəʊ
AM ˌæprəˈpoʊ
apse
BR aps, -ɪz
AM æps, -əz
apsidal
BR ˈapsɪdl
AM ˈæpsədəl
apsides
BR ˈapsɪdiːz
AM ˈæpsəˌdiz
apsis
BR ˈapsɪs
AM ˈæpsəs
Apsley
BR ˈapsli
AM ˈæpsli
apt
BR apt, -ə(r), -ɪst
AM æpt, -ər, -əst
Apted
BR ˈaptɪd
AM ˈæptəd
apterous
BR ˈapt(ə)rəs
AM ˈæptərəs
apteryx
BR ˈapt(ə)rɪks, -ɪz
AM ˈæptərɪks, -ɪz
aptitude
BR ˈaptɪtjuːd,
ˈaptɪtʃuːd, -z
AM ˈæptəˌt(j)ud, -z
aptly
BR ˈaptli
AM ˈæp(t)li
aptness
BR ˈap(t)nəs
AM ˈæp(t)nəs
Apuleius
BR ˌapjʉˈliːəs,
ˌapjʉˈleɪəs
AM ˌapjəˈliəs
Apulia
BR əˈpjuːlɪə(r)
AM əˈpjuljə, əˈpjuliə
Aqaba
BR ˈakəbə(r),
ˈakəbɑː(r)
AM ˈɑkəˌbɑ

aqua
BR ˈakwə(r)
AM ˈɑkwə, ˈækwə
aquaculture
BR ˈakwəˌkʌltʃə(r)
AM ˈɑkwəˌkəltʃər,
ˈækwəˌkəltʃər
aqua fortis
BR ˌakwə ˈfɔːtɪs
AM ˌakwə ˈfɔrdəs,
ˌækwə +
Aqua Libra®
BR ˌakwə ˈliːbrə(r)
AM ˌakwə ˈlɪbrə,
ˌækwə +
aqualung
BR ˈakwəlʌŋ, -z
AM ˈakwəˌləŋ,
ˈækwəˌləŋ, -z
aquamarine
BR ˌakwəməˈriːn, -z
AM ˌɑkwəməˈrin,
ˌækwəməˈrin, -z
aquanaut
BR ˈakwənɔːt, -s
AM ˈɑkwəˌnɔt,
ˈækwəˌnɔt, ˈɑkwəˌnɑt,
ˈækwəˌnɑt, -s
aquaphobia
BR ˌakwəˈfəʊbɪə(r)
AM ˌɑkwəˈfoʊbiə,
ˌækwəˈfoʊbiə
aquaplane
BR ˈakwəpleɪn, -z, -ɪŋ,
-d
AM ˈɑkwəˌpleɪn,
ˈækwəˌpleɪn, -z, -ɪŋ, -d
aqua regia
BR ˌakwə ˈrɛdʒɪə(r)
AM ˌakwə ˈrɛdʒiə,
ˌækwə +
aquarelle
BR ˌakwəˈrɛl, -z
AM ˌɑk(w)əˈrɛl,
ˌæk(w)əˈrɛl, -z
aquaria
BR əˈkwɛːrɪə(r)
AM əˈkwɛriə
Aquarian
BR əˈkwɛːrɪən, -z
AM əˈkwɛriən, -z
aquarist
BR ˈakwərɪst, -s
AM əˈkwɛrəst, -s
aquarium
BR əˈkwɛːrɪəm, -z
AM əˈkwɛriəm, -z
Aquarius
BR əˈkwɛːrɪəs
AM əˈkwɛriəs
Aquarobics®
BR ˌakwəˈrəʊbɪks
AM ˌɑkwəˈroʊbɪks,
ˌækwəˈroʊbɪks
Aquascutum®
BR ˌakwəˈskjuːtəm
AM ˌɑkwəˈskjudəm,
ˌækwəˈskjudəm

aquatic
BR əˈkwatɪk, -s
AM əˈkwɑdɪk,
əˈkwædɪk, -s
aquatint
BR ˈakwətɪnt, -s
AM ˈɑkwəˌtɪnt,
ˈækwəˌtɪnt, -s
aquavit
BR ˈakwəvɪt, ˈakwəviːt
AM ˈɑkwəˌvɪt,
ˈækwəˌvit
aqua vitae
BR ˌakwə ˈviːtʌɪ, ˈvʌɪtiː
AM ˌɑkwə ˈvaɪdi,
ˌækwə +, + ˈviˌtaɪ
aqueduct
BR ˈakwɪdʌkt, -s
AM ˈɑkwəˌdək|(t),
ˈækwəˌdək|(t), -(t)s
aqueous
BR ˈakwɪəs, ˈeɪkwɪəs
AM ˈɑkwiəs, ˈeɪkwiəs,
ˈækwiəs
aqueously
BR ˈakwɪəsli,
ˈeɪkwɪəsli
AM ˈɑkwiəsli,
ˈeɪkwiəsli, ˈækwiəsli
aquiculture
BR ˈakwɪˌkʌltʃə(r)
AM ˈɑkwəˌkəltʃər,
ˈækwəˌkəltʃər
aquifer
BR ˈakwɪfə(r), -z
AM ˈɑkwəfər,
ˈækwəfər, -z
Aquila
BR əˈkwɪlə(r)
AM əˈk(w)ɪlə, ˈækwələ
aquilegia
BR ˌakwɪˈliːdʒ(ɪ)ə(r),
-z
AM ˌækwəˈlidʒ(i)ə, -z
aquiline
BR ˈakwɪlʌɪn
AM ˈækwəˌlaɪn,
ˈækwələn
Aquinas
BR əˈkwʌɪnəs
AM əˈkwaɪnəs
Aquitaine
BR ˈakwɪteɪn
AM ˈækwəˌteɪn
FR akiten
Aquitania
BR ˌakwɪˈteɪnɪə(r)
AM ˌækwəˈteɪniə
aquiver
BR əˈkwɪvə(r)
AM əˈkwɪvər
Arab
BR ˈarəb, -z
AM ˈɛrəb, -z
Arabella
BR ˌarəˈbɛlə(r)
AM ˌɛrəˈbɛlə

arabesque
BR ˌarəˈbɛsk, -s
AM ˌɛrəˈbɛsk, -s
Arabia
BR əˈreɪbɪə(r)
AM əˈreɪbiə
Arabian
BR əˈreɪbɪən, -z
AM əˈreɪbjən, -z
Arabic
BR ˈarəbɪk
AM ˈɛrəbɪk
Arabicism
BR əˈrabɪsɪz(ə)m, -z
AM əˈræbəˌsɪzəm, -z
arabinose
BR əˈrabɪnəʊz,
əˈrabɪnəʊs
AM əˈræbəˌnoʊs,
əˈræbəˌnoʊz
arabis
BR ˈarəbɪs
AM ˈɛrəbəs
Arabism
BR ˈarəbɪz(ə)m
AM ˈɛrəˌbɪzəm
Arabist
BR ˈarəbɪst, -s
AM ˈɛrəbəst, -s
arable
BR ˈarəbl
AM ˈɛrəbəl
Araby
BR ˈarəbi
AM ˈɛrəbi
Arachne
BR əˈrakni
AM əˈrækni
arachnid
BR əˈraknɪd, -z
AM əˈræknəd, -z
arachnida
BR əˈraknɪdə(r)
AM əˈræknədə
arachnidae
BR əˈraknɪdiː
AM əˈræknəˌdi,
əˈræknəˌdaɪ,
əˈræknəˌdeɪ
arachnidan
BR əˈraknɪd(ə)n, -z
AM əˈræknədən, -z
arachnoid
BR əˈraknɔɪd, -z
AM əˈrækˌnɔɪd, -z
arachnologist
BR ˌarəkˈnɒlədʒɪst, -s
AM ˌɛˌrækˈnɑlədʒəst,
-s
arachnology
BR ˌarəkˈnɒlədʒi
AM ˌɛˌrækˈnɑlədʒi
Arafat
BR ˈarəfat
AM ˈɛrəˌfæt

Arafura
BR ˌarə'f(j)ʊərə(r),
ˌarə'fjɔːrə(r)
AM ˌɛrə'f(j)ʊrə

Aragon
BR 'arəg(ə)n
AM 'ɛrə,gan

arak
BR 'arək
AM 'ɛrək, 'ɛ,ræk

Arakan
BR ˌarə'kan
AM ˌɛrə'kan

Aral
BR 'arəl, 'arl̩
AM 'ɛrəl

Araldite®
BR 'arəldʌɪt, 'arl̩dʌɪt
AM 'ɛrəl,daɪt

Aramaic
BR ˌarə'meɪɪk
AM ˌɛrə'meɪɪk

Araminta
BR ˌarə'mɪntə(r)
AM ˌɛrə'mɪn(t)ə

Aran
BR 'arən, 'arn̩
AM 'ɛrən

Aranda
BR ə'randə(r), -z
AM ə'rændə, -z

Arapaho
BR ə'rapəhəʊ
AM ə'ræpə,hoʊ

arapaima
BR ˌarə'pʌɪmə(r), -z
AM ˌɛrə'paɪmə, -z

Ararat
BR 'arərat
AM 'ɛrə,ræt

arational
BR eɪ'raʃn̩(ə)l,
eɪ'raʃən(ə)l
AM eɪ'ræʃənl,
eɪ'ræʃnəl

Araucanian
BR ˌarɔː'keɪnɪən, -z
AM ˌɛ,rɔː'keɪnɪən,
ˌɛ,rɑ'keɪnɪən, -z

araucaria
BR ˌarɔː'kɛːrɪə(r),
ˌarə'kɛːrɪə(r), -z
AM ˌɛ,rɔː'kɛːrɪə,
ˌɛ,rɑ'kɛːrɪə, -z

Arawak
BR 'arəwak
AM 'ɛrə,wɑk

arb
BR ɑːb, -z
AM ɑrb, -z

arbalest
BR 'ɑːbəlɪst, 'ɑːbl̩ɪst,
'ɑːbəlɛst, 'ɑːbl̩ɛst, -s
AM 'ɑrbələst,
'ɑrbə,lɛst, -s

arbiter
BR 'ɑːbɪtə(r), -z
AM 'ɑrbədər, -z

arbitrage
BR 'ɑːbɪtrɑːʒ,
ˌɑːbɪ'trɑːʒ
AM 'ɑrbə,trɑʒ

arbitrager
BR 'ɑːbɪtrɑːʒə(r),
ˌɑːbɪ'trɑːʒə(r), -z
AM 'ɑrbə,trɑʒər, -z

arbitrageur
BR ˌɑːbɪtrɑː'ʒɜː(r), -z
AM ˌɑrbɑ,trɑ'ʒɜr, -z

arbitral
BR 'ɑːbɪtr(ə)l
AM 'ɑrbətrəl

arbitrament
BR ɑː'bɪtrəm(ə)nt, -s
AM ɑr'bɪtrəmənt, -s

arbitrarily
BR 'ɑːbɪt(rə)rɪli,
ˌɑːbɪ'trɛrɪli
AM ˌɑrbə'trɛrəli

arbitrariness
BR 'ɑːbɪt(rə)rɪnɪs
AM ˌɑrbə'trɛrɪnɪs

arbitrary
BR 'ɑːbɪt(rə)ri
AM 'ɑrbə,trɛri

arbitrate
BR 'ɑːbɪtreɪt, -s, -ɪŋ, -ɪd
AM 'ɑrbə,treɪ|t, -ts,
-dɪŋ, -dɪd

arbitration
BR ˌɑːbɪ'treɪʃn
AM ˌɑrbə'treɪʃən

arbitrator
BR 'ɑːbɪtreɪtə(r), -z
AM 'ɑrbə,treɪdər, -z

arbitratorship
BR 'ɑːbɪtreɪtəʃɪp, -s
AM 'ɑrbə,treɪdərˌʃɪp, -s

arbitress
BR 'ɑːbətrɪs, -ɪz
AM 'ɑrbətrəs, -əz

arblast
BR 'ɑːblɑːst, 'ɑːblast, -s
AM 'ɑrˌblæst, -s

arbor
BR 'ɑːbə(r), -z, -d
AM 'ɑrbər, -z, -d

arboraceous
BR ˌɑːbə'reɪʃəs
AM ˌɑrbə'reɪʃəs

arboreal
BR ɑː'bɔːrɪəl
AM ɑr'bɔrɪəl

arboreous
BR ɑː'bɔːrɪəs
AM ɑr'bɔrɪəs

arborescence
BR ˌɑːbə'rɛsns
AM ˌɑrbə'rɛsəns

arborescent
BR ˌɑːbə'rɛsnt
AM ˌɑrbə'rɛsənt

arboreta
BR ˌɑːbə'riːtə(r)
AM ˌɑrbə'ridə

arboretum
BR ˌɑːbə'riːtəm, -z
AM ˌɑrbə'ridəm, -z

arboricultural
BR ɑːˌbɔːrɪ'kʌltʃ(ə)rəl,
ɑːˌbɔːrɪ'kʌltʃ(ə)rl̩,
ˌɑːb(ə)rɪ'kʌltʃ(ə)rəl,
ˌɑːb(ə)rɪ'kʌltʃ(ə)rl̩
AM ˌɑrbərə'kəltʃ(ə)rəl,
ɑr'bɔrə,kəltʃ(ə)rəl

arboriculture
BR 'ɑːb(ə)rɪ,kʌltʃə(r),
ɑː'bɔːrɪ,kʌltʃə(r)
AM 'ɑrbərə,kəltʃər,
ɑr'bɔrə,kəltʃər

arboriculturist
BR ɑːˌbɔːrɪ'kʌltʃ(ə)rɪst,
ˌɑːb(ə)rɪ'kʌltʃ(ə)rɪst,
-s
AM ˌɑrbərə'kəltʃ(ə)rəst,
ɑr'bɔrə,kəltʃ(ə)rəst,
-s

arborisation
BR ˌɑːb(ə)rʌɪ'zeɪʃn
AM ˌɑrbərə'zeɪʃən,
ˌɑrbə,rɑr'zeɪʃən

arborization
BR ˌɑːb(ə)rʌɪ'zeɪʃn
AM ˌɑrbərə'zeɪʃən,
ˌɑrbə,rɑr'zeɪʃən

arbor vitae
BR ˌɑːbə 'vʌɪtiː,
+ 'viːtʌɪ
AM 'ɑrbər 'vaɪdi,
+ 'vi,taɪ

arbour
BR 'ɑːbə(r), -z, -d
AM 'ɑrbər, -z, -d

Arbus
BR 'ɑːbəs
AM 'ɑrbəs

Arbuthnot
BR ɑː'bʌθnət,
ɑː'bʌθnɒt
AM 'ɑrbəθnət,
'ɑrbəθ,nɑt

arbutus
BR ɑː'bjuːtəs, -ɪz
AM ɑr'bjudəs, -əz

arc
BR ɑːk, -s, -ɪŋ, -t
AM ɑrk, -s, -ɪŋ, -t

arcade
BR ɑː'keɪd, -z, -ɪd
AM ɑr'keɪd, -z, -ɪd

Arcadia
BR ɑː'keɪdɪə(r)
AM ɑr'keɪdiə

Arcadian
BR ɑː'keɪdɪən, -z
AM ɑr'keɪdiən, -z

Arcadianism
BR ɑː'keɪdɪənɪz(ə)m
AM ɑr'keɪdiə,nɪzəm

arcading
BR ɑː'keɪdɪŋ
AM ɑr'keɪdɪŋ

Arcady
BR 'ɑːkədi
AM 'ɑrkədi

arcana
BR ɑː'keɪnə(r),
ɑː'kɑːnə(r)
AM ɑr'keɪnə

arcane
BR ɑː'keɪn
AM ɑr'keɪn

arcanely
BR ɑː'keɪnli
AM ɑr'keɪnli

arcanum
BR ɑː'keɪnəm
AM ɑr'keɪnəm

Arc de Triomphe
BR ˌɑːk də 'trɪɒmf
AM 'ɑrk də ˌtri'ɔnf

arch
BR ɑːtʃ, -ɪz, -ɪŋ, -t, -ə(r),
-ɪst
AM ɑrtʃ, -əz, -ɪŋ, -t, -ər,
-əst

Archaean
BR ɑː'kiːən, -z
AM ɑr'kiən, -z

archaeologic
BR ˌɑːkɪə'lɒdʒɪk
AM ˌɑrkiə'lɑdʒɪk

archaeological
BR ˌɑːkɪə'lɒdʒɪkl
AM ˌɑrkiə'lɑdʒəkəl

archaeologically
BR ˌɑːkɪə'lɒdʒɪkli
AM ˌɑrkiə'lɑdʒək(ə)li

archaeologise
BR ɑː'kɪ'ɒlədʒʌɪz, -ɪz,
-ɪŋ, -d
AM ˌɑrki'ɑlə,dʒaɪz, -ɪz,
-ɪŋ, -d

archaeologist
BR ɑː'kɪ'ɒlədʒɪst, -s
AM ˌɑrki'ɑlədʒəst, -s

archaeologize
BR ɑː'kɪ'ɒlədʒʌɪz, -ɪz,
-ɪŋ, -d
AM ˌɑrki'ɑlə,dʒaɪz, -ɪz,
-ɪŋ, -d

archaeology
BR ˌɑːkɪ'ɒlədʒi
AM ˌɑrki'ɑlədʒi

archaeopteryx
BR ˌɑːkɪ'ɒpt(ə)r|ɪks,
-ɪksɪz
AM ˌɑrki'ɑptərɪks, -ɪz

archaic
BR ɑː'keɪɪk
AM ɑr'keɪɪk

archaically
BR ɑː'keɪɪkli
AM ɑr'keɪɪk(ə)li

archaise
BR 'ɑːkeɪʌɪz, 'ɑː'kɪʌɪz,
-ɪz, -ɪŋ, -d
AM 'ɑrki,aɪz,
'ɑrkeɪ,aɪz, -ɪz, -ɪŋ, -d

archaism
BR ˈɑːkeɪɪz(ə)m, -z
AM ˈɑːrkiˌɪzəm,
ˈɑːrkeɪˌɪzəm, -z

archaist
BR ˈɑːkeɪɪst, -s
AM ˈɑːrkiɪst, ˈɑːrkeɪɪst, -s

archaistic
BR ˌɑːkeɪˈɪstɪk
AM ˌɑːrkiˈɪstɪk, ˌɑːrkeɪˈɪstɪk

archaistically
BR ˌɑːkeɪˈɪstɪkli
AM ˌɑːrkiˈɪstɪk(ə)li, ˌɑːrkeɪˈɪstɪk(ə)li

archaize
BR ˈɑːkeɪʌɪz, ˈɑːkɪʌɪz, -ɪz, -ɪŋ, -d
AM ˈɑːrkiˌʌɪz, ˈɑːrkeɪˌʌɪz, -ɪz, -ɪŋ, -d

archangel
BR ˈɑːkeɪn(d)ʒ(ə)l, ˌɑːkˈeɪn(d)ʒ(ə)l, -z
AM ˈɑːrkˌeɪndʒəl, -z

archangelic
BR ˌɑːkanˈdʒɛlɪk
AM ˌɑːrkˌænˈdʒɛlɪk

archbishop
BR (ˌ)ɑːtʃˈbɪʃəp, -s
AM ˈɑːrtʃˈbɪʃəp, -s

archbishopric
BR (ˌ)ɑːtʃˈbɪʃəprɪk, -s
AM ˈɑːrtʃˈbɪʃəprɪk, -s

archdeacon
BR (ˌ)ɑːtʃˈdiːk(ə)n, -z
AM ˈɑːrtʃˈdikən, -z

archdeaconry
BR ˌɑːtʃˈdiːk(ə)nrˌi, -ɪz
AM ˈɑːrtʃˈdikənri, -z

archdeaconship
BR ˌɑːtʃˈdiːk(ə)nʃɪp, -s
AM ˈɑːrtʃˈdikənˌʃɪp, -s

archdiocesan
BR ˌɑːtʃdʌɪˈɒsɪsn
AM ˈɑːrtʃˌdaɪˈəsəsən

archdiocese
BR ˌɑːtʃˈdʌɪəsɪs, -ɪz
AM ˈɑːrtʃˈdaɪəsɪs, ˌɑːrtʃˈdaɪəˌsiz, -ɪz

archducal
BR ˌɑːtʃˈdjuːkl, ˌɑːtʃˈdʒuːkl
AM ˈɑːrtʃˈd(j)ukəl

archduchess
BR ˌɑːtʃˈdʌtʃɪs, -ɪz
AM ˈɑːrtʃˈdətʃəs, -əz

archduchy
BR ˌɑːtʃˈdʌtʃ|i, -ɪz
AM ˈɑːrtʃˈdətʃ|i, -z

archduke
BR ˌɑːtʃˈdjuːk, ˌɑːtʃˈdʒuːk, -s
AM ˈɑːrtʃˈd(j)uk, -s

archdukedom
BR ˌɑːtʃˈdjuːkdəm, ˌɑːtʃˈdʒuːkdəm, -z
AM ˌɑːrtʃˈd(j)ukdəm, -z

archegonia
BR ˌɑːkɪˈɡəʊnɪə(r)
AM ˌɑːrkəˈɡoʊnɪə

archegonium
BR ˌɑːkɪˈɡəʊnɪəm
AM ˌɑːrkəˈɡoʊnɪəm

Archelaus
BR ˌɑːkɪˈleɪəs
AM ˌɑːrkəˈleɪəs

arch-enemy
BR ˌɑːtʃˈɛnɪm|i, -ɪz
AM ˈɑːrtʃˌɛnəmi, -z

archeologic
BR ˌɑːkɪəˈlɒdʒɪk
AM ˌɑːrkiəˈlɑdʒɪk

archeological
BR ˌɑːkɪəˈlɒdʒɪkl
AM ˌɑːrkiəˈlɑdʒəkəl

archeologically
BR ˌɑːkɪəˈlɒdʒɪkli
AM ˌɑːrkiəˈlɑdʒək(ə)li

archeologist
BR ˌɑːkɪˈɒlədʒɪst, -s
AM ˌɑːrkiˈɑlədʒəst, -s

archeologize
BR ˌɑːkɪˈɒlədʒʌɪz, -ɪz, -ɪŋ, -d
AM ˌɑːrkiˈɑləˌdʒaɪz, -ɪz, -ɪŋ, -d

archeology
BR ˌɑːkɪˈɒlədʒi
AM ˌɑːrkiˈɑlədʒi

archeopteryx
BR ˌɑːkɪˈɒpt(ə)r|ɪks, -ɪksɪz
AM ˌɑːrkiˈɑptərɪks, -ɪz

archer
BR ˈɑːtʃə(r), -z
AM ˈɑːrtʃər, -z

archery
BR ˈɑːtʃ(ə)ri
AM ˈɑːrtʃ(ə)ri

archetypal
BR ˌɑːkɪˈtʌɪpl, ˈɑːkɪˌtʌɪpl
AM ˈɑːrk(ə)ˌtaɪpəl

archetypally
BR ˌɑːkɪˈtʌɪp|li, ˈɑːkɪˌtʌɪp|li, ˈɑːkɪˌtʌɪpəli
AM ˈɑːrk(ə)ˌtaɪpəli

archetype
BR ˈɑːkɪtʌɪp, -s
AM ˈɑːrk(ə)ˌtaɪp, -s

archetypical
BR ˌɑːkɪˈtɪpɪkl
AM ˌɑːrk(ə)ˈtɪpɪkəl

archetypically
BR ˌɑːkɪˈtɪpɪkli
AM ˌɑːrk(ə)ˈtɪpɪk(ə)li

Archibald
BR ˈɑːtʃɪbɔːld, ˈɑːtʃɪb(ə)ld
AM ˈɑːrtʃəˌbɔld, ˈɑːrtʃəˌbald

archidiaconal
BR ˌɑːkɪdʌɪˈakənl, ˌɑːkɪdʌɪˈaknl
AM ˌɑːrkəˌdaɪˈækənəl, ˌɑːrkəˌdiˈækənəl

archidiaconate
BR ˌɑːkɪdʌɪˈakəneɪt, ˌɑːkɪdʌɪˈakənɪt, ˌɑːkɪdʌɪˈakneɪt, ˌɑːkɪdʌɪˈaknɪt, ˌɑːkɪdɪˈakəneɪt, ˌɑːkɪdɪˈakənɪt, ˌɑːkɪdɪˈakneɪt, ˌɑːkɪdɪˈaknɪt, -s
AM ˌɑːrkəˌdaɪˈækənət, ˌɑːrkəˌdiˈækənət, -s

Archie
BR ˈɑːtʃi
AM ˈɑːrtʃi

archiepiscopacy
BR ˌɑːkɪˈpɪskəpəs|i, -ɪz
AM ˌɑːrkiəˈpɪskəpəsi, -z

archiepiscopal
BR ˌɑːkɪˈpɪskəpl
AM ˌɑːrkiəˈpɪskəpəl

archiepiscopate
BR ˌɑːkɪˈpɪskəpət, -s
AM ˌɑːrkiəˈpɪskəpət, -s

archil
BR ˈɑːkɪl, ˈɑːtʃɪl, -z
AM ˈɑːrtʃəl, -z

Archilochus
BR ɑːˈkɪˈləʊkəs
AM ɑːrˈkəˈloʊkəs

archimandrite
BR ˌɑːkɪˈmandrʌɪt, -s
AM ˌɑːrkəˈmænˌdraɪt, -s

Archimedean
BR ˌɑːkɪˈmiːdɪən, -z
AM ˌɑːrkəˈmidiən, -z

Archimedes
BR ˌɑːkɪˈmiːdiːz
AM ˌɑːrkəˈmidiz

archipelago
BR ˌɑːkɪˈpɛlɪɡəʊ, -z
AM ˌɑːrkəˈpɛləˌɡoʊ, ˌɑːrtʃəˈpɛləˌɡoʊ, -z

architect
BR ˈɑːkɪtɛkt, -s
AM ˈɑːrkəˌtɛk|(t), -(t)s

architectonic
BR ˌɑːkɪtɛkˈtɒnɪk, -s
AM ˌɑːrkəˌtɛkˈtɑnɪk, -s

architectural
BR ˌɑːkɪˈtɛktʃ(ə)rəl, ˌɑːkɪˈtɛktʃ(ə)rl
AM ˌɑːrkəˈtɛk(t)ʃ(ə)rəl

architecturally
BR ˌɑːkɪˈtɛktʃ(ə)rəli, ˌɑːkɪˈtɛktʃ(ə)r|li
AM ˌɑːrkəˈtɛk(t)ʃ(ə)rəli

architecture
BR ˈɑːkɪtɛktʃə(r)
AM ˈɑːrkəˌtɛk(t)ʃər

architrave
BR ˈɑːkɪtreɪv, -z

AM ˈɑːrkəˌtreɪv, -z

archival
BR ˈɑːkʌɪvl, ɑːˈkʌɪvl
AM ɑːrˈkaɪvəl

archive
BR ˈɑːkʌɪv, -z, -ɪŋ, -d
AM ˈɑːrˌkaɪv, -z, -ɪŋ, -d

archivist
BR ˈɑːkɪvɪst, -s
AM ˈɑːrkəvəst, ˈɑːrˌkaɪvɪst, -s

archivolt
BR ˈɑːkɪvəʊlt, -s
AM ˈɑːrkəˌvoʊlt, -s

archlute
BR ˈɑːtʃl(j)uːt, -s
AM ˈɑːrtʃˌlut, -s

archly
BR ˈɑːtʃli
AM ˈɑːrtʃli

archness
BR ˈɑːtʃnəs
AM ˈɑːrtʃnəs

archon
BR ˈɑːkɒn, ˈɑːk(ə)n, -z
AM ˈɑːrˌkɑn, -z

archonship
BR ˈɑːkɒnʃɪp, ˈɑːk(ə)nʃɪp, -s
AM ˈɑːrˌkɑnˌʃɪp, -s

archpriest
BR ˌɑːtʃˈpriːst, -s
AM ˈɑːrtʃˈprist, -s

arch-rival
BR ˌɑːtʃˈrʌɪvl, -z
AM ˈɑːrtʃˈraɪvəl, -z

archway
BR ˈɑːtʃweɪ, -z
AM ˈɑːrtʃˌweɪ, -z

Archy
BR ˈɑːtʃi
AM ˈɑːrtʃi

Arco
BR ˈɑːkəʊ
AM ˈɑːrkoʊ

arctic
BR ˈɑːktɪk
AM ˈɑːrktɪk, ˈɑːrdɪk

Arcturus
BR ɑːkˈtjʊərəs
AM ɑːrkˈt(j)ʊrəs

arcuate¹
adjective
BR ˈɑːkjʊət
AM ˈɑːrkjəwət, ˈɑːrkjəˌweɪt

arcuate²
verb
BR ˈɑːkjʊeɪt, -s, -ɪŋ, -ɪd
AM ˈɑːrkjəˌweɪ|t, -ts, -dɪŋ, -dɪd

arcus senilis
BR ˌɑːkəs sɪˈnʌɪlɪs
AM ˌɑːrkəs səˈnɪlɪs

Ardagh
BR ˈɑːdə(r), ˈɑːdɑː(r)
AM ˈɑːrdə

Ardèche
BR ɑːˈdɛʃ
AM ɑrˈdɛʃ

Arden
BR ˈɑːdn
AM ˈɑrdən

ardency
BR ˈɑːdnsi
AM ˈɑrdnsi

Ardennes
BR ɑːˈdɛn(z)
AM ɑrˈdɛn(z)

ardent
BR ˈɑːdnt
AM ˈɑrdnt

ardently
BR ˈɑːdntli
AM ˈɑrdn(t)li

Ardizzone
BR ˌɑːdɪˈzəʊni
AM ˌɑrdɪˈzəʊni

Ardmore
BR ɑːˈdmɔː(r)
AM ˈɑrdmɔ(ə)r

Ardnamurchan
BR ˌɑːdnəˈmɜːk(ə)n
AM ˌɑrdnəˈmɜrtʃən

ardor
BR ˈɑːdə(r), -z
AM ˈɑrdər, -z

ardour
BR ˈɑːdə(r), -z
AM ˈɑrdər, -z

Ardoyne
BR ɑːˈdɔɪn
AM ɑrˈdɔɪn

Ardrossan
BR ɑːˈdrɒsn
AM ˈɑrdrɒsən,
ˈɑrdrɑsən

Ards
BR ɑːdz
AM ɑrdz

arduous
BR ˈɑːdjʊəs, ˈɑːdʒʊəs
AM ˈɑrdʒəwəs

arduously
BR ˈɑːdjʊəsli,
ˈɑːdʒʊəsli
AM ˈɑrdʒəwəsli

arduousness
BR ˈɑːdjʊəsnəs,
ˈɑːdʒʊəsnəs
AM ˈɑrdʒəwəsnəs

are[1]
strong form
BR ɑː(r)
AM ɑr

are[2]
unit
BR ɑː(r), -z
AM ɑr, -z

are[3]
weak form
BR ə(r)
AM ər

area
BR ˈɛːrɪə(r), -z
AM ˈɛrɪə, -z

areal
BR ˈɛːrɪəl
AM ˈɛrɪəl

areaway
BR ˈɛːrɪəweɪ, -z
AM ˈɛrɪəˌweɪ, -z

areca
BR ˈarɪkə(r),
əˈriːkə(r), -z
AM əˈrikə, ˈɛrəkə, -z

areg
BR ˈɑːrɛg, ˈarɛg
AM ˈɑˌrɛg

arena
BR əˈriːnə(r), -z
AM əˈrinə, -z

arenaceous
BR ˌarɪˈneɪʃəs
AM ˌarəˈneɪʃəs

Arendt
BR ˈɑːrənt
AM ˈɑrənt

Arenig
BR əˈrɛnɪg, əˈrɛnɪg
AM ˈɛrənɪg

aren't
BR ɑːnt
AM ˈɑr(ə)nt

areola
BR əˈriːələ(r), -z
AM əˈriələ, -z

areolae
BR əˈriːəliː
AM əˈriəˌli, əˈriəˌlaɪ

areolar
BR əˈriːələ(r)
AM əˈriələr

areometer
BR ˌɛːrɪˈɒmɪtə(r),
ˌarɪˈɒmɪtə(r), -z
AM ˌɛriˈɑmədər, -z

Areopagi
BR ˌarɪˈɒpəgaɪ
AM ˌɛriˈɑpəgai

Areopagite
BR ˌarɪˈɒpəgaɪt, -s
AM ˌærɪˈɑpəˌgaɪt, -s

Areopagitica
BR ˌarɪɒpəˈdʒɪtɪkə(r)
AM ˌærɪˌɑpəˈdʒɪdɪkə

Areopagus
BR ˌarɪˈɒpəgəs
AM ˌɛriˈɑpəgəs

Arequipa
BR ˌarɪˈk(w)iːpə(r)
AM ˌɛrəˈk(w)ipə

Ares
BR ˈɛːriːz
AM ˈɛriz

arête
BR əˈrɛt, aˈrɛt, -s
AM əˈreɪt, -s

Aretha
BR əˈriːθə(r)

area
BR əˈriːθə
Arethusa
BR ˌarɪˈθjuːzə(r)
AM ˌɛrəˈθuzə

Arfon
BR ˈɑːv(ɒ)n
WE ˈarvɒn
AM ˈarfən

argala
BR ˈɑːgələ(r), ˈɑːglə(r),
-z
AM ˈargələ, -z

argali
BR ˈɑːgəli, ˈɑːgli
AM ˈargəli

argent
BR ˈɑːdʒ(ə)nt
AM ˈardʒənt

argentiferous
BR ˌɑːdʒ(ə)nˈtɪf(ə)rəs
AM ˌɑrdʒənˈtɪf(ə)rəs

Argentina
BR ˌɑːdʒ(ə)nˈtiːnə(r)
AM ˌɑrdʒənˈtinə
SP ˌarxenˈtina

Argentine
BR ˈɑːdʒəntaɪn,
ˈɑːdʒ(ə)ntiːn
AM ˈardʒənˌtin,
ˈardʒənˌtam

Argentinian
BR ˌɑːdʒ(ə)nˈtɪnɪən, -z
AM ˌɑrdʒənˈtɪnɪən, -z

Argie
BR ˈɑːdʒi, -ɪz
AM ˈardʒi, -z

argil
BR ˈɑːdʒɪl
AM ˈardʒəl

argilaceous
BR ˌɑːdʒɪˈleɪʃəs
AM ˌardʒəˈleɪʃəs

argillaceous
BR ˌɑːdʒɪˈleɪʃəs
AM ˌardʒəˈleɪʃəs

arginine
BR ˈɑːdʒmiːn,
ˈɑːdʒɪnaɪn
AM ˈardʒəˌnin,
ˈardʒəˌnam

Argive
BR ˈɑːgaɪv, ˈɑːdʒaɪv
AM ˈarˌgaɪv

argle-bargle
BR ˌɑːglˈbɑːgl
AM ˈargəlˈbargəl

Argo
BR ˈɑːgəʊ
AM ˈargoʊ

argol
BR ˈɑːgɒl, -z
AM ˈargəl, -z

argon
BR ˈɑːgɒn, ˈɑːg(ə)n
AM ˈarˌgan

Argonaut
BR ˈɑːgənɔːt, -s

Argus
AM ˈargəˌnɒt,
ˈargəˌnɑt, -s

Argos
BR ˈɑːgɒs
AM ˈargəs, ˈargɔs,
ˈargas

argosy
BR ˈɑːgəsɪi, -ɪz
AM ˈargəsi, -z

argot
BR ˈɑːgəʊ, -z
AM ˈarˌgou, ˈargət, -z

arguable
BR ˈɑːgjʊəbl
AM ˈargjəwəbəl

arguably
BR ˈɑːgjʊəbli
AM ˈargjəwəbli

argue
BR ˈɑːgjuː, -z, -ɪŋ, -d
AM ˈargju, -z, -ɪŋ, -d

arguer
BR ˈɑːgjʊə(r), -z
AM ˈargjəwər, -z

argufy
BR ˈɑːgjʊfʌɪ, -z, -ɪŋ, -d
AM ˈargjəˌfaɪ, -z, -ɪŋ, -d

argument
BR ˈɑːgjʊm(ə)nt, -s
AM ˈargjəmənt, -s

argumental
BR ˌɑːgjʊˈmɛntl
AM ˌargjəˈmɛn(t)l

argumentation
BR ˌɑːgjʊmɛnˈteɪʃn,
ˌɑːgjʊm(ə)nˈteɪʃn
AM ˌargjəmənˈteɪʃən,
ˌargjəˌmɛnˈteɪʃən

argumentative
BR ˌɑːgjʊˈmɛntətɪv
AM ˌargjəˈmɛn(t)ədɪv

argumentatively
BR ˌɑːgjʊˈmɛntətɪvli
AM ˌargjəˈmɛn(t)ədɪvli

argumentative-ness
BR ˌɑːgjʊˈmɛntətɪvnɪs
AM ˌargjəˈmɛn(t)ədɪv-nɪs

argumentum e silencio
BR ɑːgjʊˌmɛntəm eɪ
sɪˈlɛnsɪəʊ
+ sɪˈlɛnʃɪəʊ
AM ˌargjəˈmɛn(t)əm eɪ
sɪˈlɛnsɪoʊ

Argus
BR ˈɑːgəs, -ɪz
AM ˈargəs, -əz

argute
BR ɑːˈgjuːt
AM ɑrˈgjut

argutely
BR ɑːˈgjuːtli
AM ɑrˈgjutli

argy-bargy
BR ˌɑːdʒɪˈbɑːdʒi
AM ˈardʒiˈbardʒi

Argyle
BR ɑːˈgʌɪl
AM ˈɑrˌgaɪl
Argyll
BR ɑːˈgʌɪl
AM ˈɑrˌgaɪl
Argyllshire
BR ɑːˈgʌɪlʃ(ɪ)ə(r)
AM ˈɑrˌgaɪlˌʃɪ(ə)r
Århus
BR ˈɔːhuːs
AM ˈɔrˌ(h)us, ˈɑrˌ(h)us
DAN ˈɔːhuːˈs
aria
BR ˈɑːrɪə(r), -z
AM ˈɑriə, -z
Ariadne
BR ˌarɪˈadni
AM ˌɛriˈædni
Arian
BR ˈɛːrɪən, -z
AM ˈɛriən, -z
Ariane
BR ˌarɪˈan
AM ˌɛriˈæn
Arianism
BR ˈɛːrɪənɪz(ə)m
AM ˈɛriəˌnɪzəm
Arianna
BR ˌarɪˈanə(r)
AM ˌɛriˈænə
arid
BR ˈarɪd
AM ˈɛrəd
aridisol
BR əˈrɪdɪsɒl
AM əˈrɪdɪˌsɔl əˈrɪdɪˌsɑl
aridity
BR əˈrɪdɪti
AM əˈrɪdɪdi, ɛˈrɪdɪdi
aridly
BR ˈarɪdli
AM ˈɛrədli
aridness
BR ˈarɪdnɪs
AM ˈɛrədnəs
ariel
BR ˈɛːrɪəl, -z
AM ˈɛriəl, -z
Arielle
BR ˌarɪˈɛl
AM ˌɛriˈɛl
Aries
BR ˈɛːriːz
AM ˈɛˌriz, ˈeɪˌriz
arietta
BR ˌarɪˈɛtə(r)
AM ˌariˈɛdə, ˌɛriˈɛdə
aright
BR əˈrʌɪt
AM əˈraɪt
aril
BR ˈarɪl, ˈarl̩, -z
AM ˈɛrəl, -z
arillate
BR ˈarɪlət, ˈarɪleɪt
AM ˈɛrələt, ˈɛrəˌleɪt

Arimathaea
BR ˌarɪməˈθiːə(r)
AM ˌɛrəməˈθiə
Arimathea
BR ˌarɪməˈθiːə(r)
AM ˌɛrəməˈθiə
arioso
BR ˌarɪˈəʊzəʊ,
ˌɑːrɪˈəʊzəʊ, ˌarɪˈəʊsəʊ,
ˌɑːrɪˈəʊsəʊ, -z
AM ˌɑriˈoʊsoʊ,
ˌariˈoʊzoʊ, -z
Ariosto
BR ˌarɪˈɒstəʊ
AM ˌariˈɑstoʊ
arise
BR əˈrʌɪz, -ɪz, -ɪŋ
AM əˈraɪz, -ɪz, -ɪŋ
arisen
BR əˈrɪzn
AM əˈrɪzn
arisings
BR əˈrʌɪzɪŋz
AM əˈraɪzɪŋz
Aristarchus
BR ˌarɪˈstɑːkəs
AM ˌɛrəˈstɑrkəs
Aristides
BR ˌarɪˈstʌɪdiːz
AM ˌɛrəˈstaɪdiz
Aristippus
BR ˌarɪˈstɪpəs
AM ˌɛrəˈstɪpəs
aristocracy
BR ˌarɪˈstɒkrəsɪ, -ɪz
AM ˌɛrəˈstɑkrəsi, -z
aristocrat
BR ˈarɪstəkrat,
əˈrɪstəkrat, -s
AM əˈrɪstəˌkræt, -s
aristocratic
BR ˌarɪstəˈkratɪk,
əˌrɪstəˈkratɪk
AM əˌrɪstəˈkrædɪk
aristocratically
BR ˌarɪstəˈkratɪkli,
əˌrɪstəˈkratɪkli
AM əˌrɪstəˈkrædək(ə)li
Aristophanes
BR ˌarɪˈstɒfəniːz,
ˌarɪˈstɒfn̩iːz
AM ˌɛrəˈstɑfəniz
Aristotelian
BR ˌarɪstəˈtiːlɪən, -z
AM əˌrɪstəˈtil(i)jən,
ˌɛrəstəˈtil(i)jən, -z
Aristotle
BR ˈarɪstɒtl
AM ˈɛrəsˌtɑdəl
Arita
BR əˈriːtə(r)
AM əˈridə
arithmetic¹
adjective
BR ˌarɪθˈmɛtɪk
AM ˌɛriθˈmɛdɪk

arithmetic²
noun
BR əˈrɪθmətɪk
AM əˈrɪθməˌtɪk
arithmetical
BR ˌarɪθˈmɛtɪkl
AM ˌɛriθˈmɛdəkəl
arithmetically
BR ˌarɪθˈmɛtɪkli
AM ˌɛriθˈmɛdək(ə)li
arithmetician
BR ˌarɪθməˈtɪʃn,
əˌrɪθməˈtɪʃn, -z
AM əˌrɪθməˈtɪʃən, -z
Arius
BR ˈɛːrɪəs, əˈrʌɪəs
AM ˈɛriəs, əˈraɪəs
Arizona
BR ˌarɪˈzəʊnə(r)
AM ˌɛrəˈzoʊnə
Arizonan
BR ˌarɪˈzəʊnən, -z
AM ˌɛrəˈzoʊnən, -z
ark
BR ɑːk, -s
AM ɑrk, -s
Arkansas
BR ˈɑːk(ə)nsɔː(r)
AM ˈɑrkənˌsɑ
arkose
BR ˈɑːkəʊs, ˈɑːkəʊz
AM ˈɑrˌkoʊs, ˈɑrˌkoʊz
Arkwright
BR ˈɑːkrʌɪt
AM ˈɑrkˌraɪt
Arlene
BR ˈɑːliːn
AM ɑrˈlin
Arles
BR ˈɑːl(z)
AM ˈɑr(ə)l(z)
Arlette
BR ɑːˈlɛt
AM ɑrˈlɛt
Arlington
BR ˈɑːlɪŋt(ə)n
AM ˈɑrlɪŋtən
arm
BR ɑːm, -z, -ɪŋ, -d
AM ɑrm, -z, -ɪŋ, -d
armada
BR ɑːˈmɑːdə(r), -z
AM ɑrˈmɑdə, -z
Armadale
BR ˈɑːmədeɪl
AM ˈɑrməˌdeɪl
armadillo
BR ˌɑːməˈdɪləʊ, -z
AM ˌɑrməˈdɪloʊ, -z
Armageddon
BR ˌɑːməˈgɛdn
AM ˌɑrməˈgɛdən
Armagh
BR ˌɑːˈmɑː(r)
AM ɑrˈmɑ
Armagnac
BR ˈɑːmənjak, -s

Armalite®
AM ˈɑrmənˌjæk, -s
Armalite®
BR ˈɑːmələɪt, -s
AM ˈɑrməˌlaɪt, -s
armament
BR ˈɑːməm(ə)nt, -s
AM ˈɑrməmənt, -s
armamentaria
BR ˌɑːməmənˈtɛːrɪə(r),
ˌɑːməm(ə)nˈtɛːrɪə(r)
AM ˌɑrməmənˈtɛriə
armamentarium
BR ˌɑːməmənˈtɛːrɪəm,
ˌɑːməm(ə)nˈtɛːrɪəm
AM ˌɑrməmənˈtɛriəm
Armand
BR ˈɑːmənd
AM ˈɑrmənd
Armani
BR ɑːˈmɑːni
AM ɑrˈmɑni
Armatrading
BR ˌɑːməˈtreɪdɪŋ
AM ˌɑrməˌtreɪdɪŋ
armature
BR ˈɑːmətʃ(ʊ)ə(r),
ˈɑːmətjʊə(r), -z
AM ˈɑrmətˌʃər,
ˈɑrməˌtʃʊ(ə)r,
ˈɑrməˌt(j)ʊ(ə)r, -z
armband
BR ˈɑːmband, -z
AM ˈɑrmˌbænd, -z
armchair
BR ˈɑːmtʃɛː(r),
ˌɑːmˈtʃɛː(r), -z
AM ˈɑrmˌtʃɛ(ə)r, -z
arme blanche
BR ˌɑːm ˈblɒʃ
AM ˌɑrm ˈblɑnʃ
Armenia
BR ɑːˈmiːnɪə(r)
AM ɑrˈminiə
Armenian
BR ɑːˈmiːnɪən, -z
AM ɑrˈminiən, -z
Armentières
BR ˌɑːm(ə)nˈtɪəz,
ˈɑːm(ə)ntɪəz,
ˌɑːm(ə)ntɪˈɛː(r)
AM ɑrˌmɑntiˈɛr(z)
FR ɑrmɑ̃tjɛr
armeria
BR ɑːˈmɪərɪə(r)
AM ɑrˈmiriə
armes blanches
BR ˌɑːm(z) ˈblɒʃ
AM ˌɑrm(z)ˈblɑnʃ
Armfield
BR ˈɑːmfiːld
AM ˈɑrmˌfild
armful
BR ˈɑːmfʊl, -z
AM ˈɑrmˌfʊl, -z
armhole
BR ˈɑːmhəʊl, -z
AM ˈɑrmˌ(h)oʊl, -z

Armidale
BR ˈɑːmɪdeɪl
AM ˈɑrməˌdeɪl
armiger
BR ˈɑːmɪdʒə(r), -z
AM ˈɑrmədʒər, -z
armigerous
BR ɑːˈmɪdʒ(ə)rəs
AM ɑrˈmɪdʒ(ə)rəs
armillaria
BR ˌɑːmɪˈlɛːriə(r)
AM ˌɑrməˈlɛriə
armillary
BR ɑːˈmɪl(ə)rˌi,
ˈɑːmɪl(ə)rˌi, -ɪz
AM ˈɑrməˌlɛri, -z
Arminian
BR ɑːˈmɪniən, -z
AM ɑrˈmɪniən, -z
Arminianism
BR ɑːˈmɪniənɪz(ə)m
AM ɑrˈmɪniəˌnɪzəm
Arminius
BR ɑːˈmɪniəs
AM ɑrˈmɪniəs
Armistead
BR ˈɑːmɪstɛd,
ˈɑːmɪstɪd
AM ˈɑrməˌstɛd
armistice
BR ˈɑːmɪstɪs, -ɪz
AM ˈɑrməstəs, -əz
Armitage
BR ˈɑːmɪtɪdʒ
AM ˈɑrmədɪdʒ
armless
BR ˈɑːmləs
AM ˈɑrmləs
armlet
BR ˈɑːmlɪt, -s
AM ˈɑrmlət, -s
Armley
BR ˈɑːmli
AM ˈɑrmli
armload
BR ˈɑːmləʊd, -z
AM ˈɑrmˌloʊd, -z
armlock
BR ˈɑːmlɒk, -s, -ɪŋ, -t
AM ˈɑrmˌlɑk, -s, -ɪŋ, -t
armoire
BR ɑːˈmwɑː(r), -z
AM ɑrmˈwɑr, -z
armor
BR ˈɑːm|ə(r), -əz,
-(ə)rɪŋ, -əd
AM ˈɑrmər, -z, -ɪŋ, -d
armorer
BR ˈɑːm(ə)rə(r), -z
AM ˈɑrmərər, -z
armorial
BR ɑːˈmɔːriəl
AM ɑrˈmɔriəl
Armorica
BR ɑːˈmɒrɪkə(r)
AM ɑrˈmɔrəkə

armorist
BR ˈɑːm(ə)rɪst, -s
AM ˈɑrmərəst, -s
armory
BR ˈɑːm(ə)rˌi, -ɪz
AM ˈɑrm(ə)ri, -z
armour
BR ˈɑːm|ə(r), -əz,
-(ə)rɪŋ, -əd
AM ˈɑrmər, -z, -ɪŋ, -d
armourer
BR ˈɑːm(ə)rə(r), -z
AM ˈɑrmərər, -z
armoury
BR ˈɑːm(ə)rˌi, -ɪz
AM ˈɑrm(ə)ri, -z
armpit
BR ˈɑːmpɪt, -s
AM ˈɑrmˌpɪt, -s
armrest
BR ˈɑːmrɛst, -s
AM ˈɑrmˌrɛst, -s
Armstrong
BR ˈɑːmstrɒŋ
AM ˈɑrmˌstrɔŋ,
ˈɑrmˌstrɑŋ
army
BR ˈɑːm|i, -ɪz
AM ˈɑrmi, -z
Arndale
BR ˈɑːndeɪl
AM ˈɑrnˌdeɪl
Arne
BR ɑːn
AM ɑrn
Arnhem
BR ˈɑːnəm
AM ˈɑrnəm, ˈɑrnˌhɛm
arnica
BR ˈɑːnɪkə(r)
AM ˈɑrnəkə
Arno
BR ˈɑːnəʊ
AM ˈɑrˌnoʊ
Arnold
BR ˈɑːnld
AM ˈɑrnəld
aroid
BR ˈɛːrɔɪd, -z
AM ˈɛrɔɪd, -z
aroint
BR əˈrɔɪnt
AM əˈrɔɪnt
aroma
BR əˈrəʊmə(r), -z
AM əˈroʊmə, -z
aromatherapeutic
BR əˌrəʊməˌθɛrəˈpjuːtɪk
AM əˌroʊməˌθɛrəˈpjʊdɪk
aromatherapist
BR əˌrəʊməˈθɛrəpɪst,
əˈrəʊməˌθɛrəpɪst, -s
AM əˌroʊməˈθɛrəpəst,
-s
aromatherapy
BR əˌrəʊməˈθɛrəpi,
əˈrəʊməˌθɛrəpi

AM əˌroʊməˈθɛrəpi
aromatic
BR ˌarəˈmatɪk
AM ˌɛrəˈmædɪk,
ˌɛroʊˈmædɪk
aromatically
BR ˌarəˈmatɪkli
AM ˌɛrəˈmædək(ə)li,
ˌɛroʊˈmædək(ə)li
aromaticity
BR ˌarəməˈtɪsɪti
AM ˌɛrəməˈtɪsɪdi
aromatisation
BR əˌrəʊmətaɪˈzeɪʃn
AM əˌroʊmədəˈzeɪʃən,
əˌroʊməˌtarˈzeɪʃən
aromatise
BR əˌrəʊmətaɪz, -ɪz,
-ɪŋ, -d
AM əˈroʊməˌtaɪz, -ɪz,
-ɪŋ, -d
aromatization
BR əˌrəʊmətaɪˈzeɪʃn
AM əˌroʊmədəˈzeɪʃən,
əˌroʊməˌtarˈzeɪʃən
aromatize
BR əˌrəʊmətaɪz, -ɪz,
-ɪŋ, -d
AM əˈroʊməˌtaɪz, -ɪz,
-ɪŋ, -d
arose
BR əˈrəʊz
AM əˈroʊz
around
BR əˈraʊnd
AM əˈraʊnd
arousable
BR əˈraʊzəbl
AM əˈraʊzəbəl
arousal
BR əˈraʊzl
AM əˈraʊzəl
arouse
BR əˈraʊz, -ɪz, -ɪŋ, -d
AM əˈraʊz, -əz, -ɪŋ, -d
arouser
BR əˈraʊzə(r), -z
AM əˈraʊzər, -z
Arp
BR ɑːp
AM ɑrp
arpeggio
BR ɑːˈpɛdʒɪəʊ, -z
AM ɑrˈpɛdʒioʊ, -z
arquebus
BR ˈɑːkwɪbəs, -ɪz
AM ˈɑrk(w)əbəs, -əz
arquebusier
BR ˌɑːkwɪbəˈsiːə(r), -z
AM ˌɑrk(w)əbəˈsɪ(ə)r,
-z
arrack
BR ˈarək
AM ˈɛrək, ˈɛˌræk
arraign
BR əˈreɪn, -z, -ɪŋ, -d
AM əˈreɪn, -z, -ɪŋ, -d

arraignment
BR əˈreɪnm(ə)nt, -s
AM əˈreɪnmənt, -s
Arran
BR ˈarən, ˈarŋ
AM ˈɛrən
arrange
BR əˈreɪndʒ, -ɪz, -ɪŋ, -d
AM əˈreɪndʒ, -ɪz, -ɪŋ, -d
arrangeable
BR əˈreɪn(d)ʒəbl
AM əˈreɪndʒəbəl
arrangement
BR əˈreɪn(d)ʒm(ə)nt,
-s
AM əˈreɪndʒmənt, -s
arranger
BR əˈreɪn(d)ʒə(r), -z
AM əˈreɪndʒər, -z
arrant
BR ˈarənt, ˈarŋt
AM ˈɛrənt
arrantly
BR ˈarəntli, ˈarŋtli
AM ˈɛrən(t)li
Arras
BR ˈarəs
AM ˈɛrəs
arras
BR ˈarəs, -ɪz
AM ˈɛrəs, -əz
Arrau
BR əˈraʊ
AM əˈraʊ
array
BR əˈreɪ, -z, -ɪŋ, -d
AM əˈreɪ, -z, -ɪŋ, -d
arrear
BR əˈrɪə(r), -z
AM əˈrɪ(ə)r, -z
arrearage
BR əˈrɪərɪdʒ
AM əˈrɪrɪdʒ
arrest
BR əˈrɛst, -s, -ɪŋ, -ɪd
AM əˈrɛst, -s, -ɪŋ, -əd
arrestable
BR əˈrɛstəbl
AM əˈrɛstəbəl
arrestation
BR ˌarɛˈsteɪʃn
AM ˌɛrɛsˈteɪʃən
arrester
BR əˈrɛstə(r), -z
AM əˈrɛstər, -z
arresting
BR əˈrɛstɪŋ
AM əˈrɛstɪŋ
arrestingly
BR əˈrɛstɪŋli
AM əˈrɛstɪŋli
arrestment
BR əˈrɛs(t)m(ə)nt, -s
AM əˈrɛs(t)mənt, -s
arrhythmia
BR əˈrɪðmɪə(r),
eɪˈrɪðmɪə(r)

AM ə'rɪðmiə, eɪ'rɪðmiə

arrière-pensée
BR ˌarɪɛː'pɒnseɪ,
ˌarɪɛː'põseɪ,
ˌarɪɛː'pɒn'seɪ,
ˌarɪɛː'põ'seɪ
AM ˌarɪɛr,pɑn'seɪ

arrière-pensées
BR ˌarɪɛː'pɒnseɪ(z),
ˌarɪɛː'põseɪ(z),
ˌarɪɛː'pɒn'seɪ(z),
ˌarɪɛː'põ'seɪ(z)
AM ˌarɪɛr,pɑn'seɪ(z)

arris
BR 'arɪs, -ɪz
AM 'ɛrəs, -əz

arrival
BR ə'rʌɪvl, -z
AM ə'raɪvəl, -z

arrive
BR ə'rʌɪv, -z, -ɪŋ, -d
AM ə'raɪv, -z, -ɪŋ, -d

arrivederci
BR ˌarɪvə'dɛːtʃi,
AM ˌɛrəvə'dɛrtʃi,
ə,rivə'dɛrtʃi

arrivisme
BR ˌari:'vɪz(ə)m
AM ˌari'vizm(ə)

arriviste
BR ˌari:'vi:st, -s
AM ˌari'vist, -s

arrogance
BR 'arəg(ə)ns
AM 'ɛrəgəns

arrogancy
BR 'arəg(ə)nsi
AM 'ɛrəgənsi

arrogant
BR 'arəg(ə)nt
AM 'ɛrəgənt

arrogantly
BR 'arəg(ə)ntli
AM 'ɛrəgən(t)li

arrogate
BR 'arəgeɪt, -s, -ɪŋ, -ɪd
AM 'ɛrəˌgeɪlt, -ts, -dɪŋ,
-dɪd

arrogation
BR ˌarə'geɪʃn, -z
AM ˌɛrə'geɪʃən, -z

arrondissement
BR ə'rɒndɪsm(ə)nt,
ə,rõdi:'smõ
AM ə'randəsmənt,
ə'randɪˌsman

arrondissements
BR ə'rɒndɪsm(ə)nts,
ə,rõdi:'smõ(z)
AM ə'randəsmən(ts),
ə'randɪˌsman(z)

arrow
BR 'arəʊ, -z
AM 'ɛrəʊ, -z

arrowhead
BR 'arə(ʊ)hɛd, -z
AM 'ɛrəʊ,(h)ɛd, -z

arrowroot
BR 'arə(ʊ)ru:t
AM 'ɛrəʊ,rut

Arrowsmith
BR 'arə(ʊ)smɪθ
AM 'ɛrəʊ,smɪθ

arrowy
BR 'arəʊi
AM 'ɛrəwi

arroyo
BR ə'rɔɪəʊ, -z
AM ə'rɔɪ(j)oʊ, -z

arrythmia
BR ə'rɪðmɪə(r),
eɪ'rɪðmɪə(r)
AM ə'rɪðmiə, eɪ'rɪðmiə

arse
BR ɑːs, -ɪz
AM æs, ɑrs, -əz

arsehole
BR 'ɑːshəʊl, -z
AM 'æs,(h)oʊl, -z

arsenal
BR 'ɑːs(ə)nl, 'ɑːsn̩l, -z
AM 'ɑrs(ə)nəl, -z

arsenate
BR 'ɑːs(ɪ)neɪt, 'ɑːsn̩eɪt,
'ɑːs(ɪ)nɪt, 'ɑːsn̩ɪt, -s
AM 'ɑrs(ə)nət,
'ɑrs(ə),neɪt, -s

arsenic[1]
adjective
BR ɑː'sɛnɪk
AM ɑr'sɛnɪk

arsenic[2]
noun
BR 'ɑːs(ə)nɪk, 'ɑːsn̩ɪk
AM 'ɑrs(ə)nɪk

arsenical
BR ɑː'sɛnɪkl
AM ɑr'sɛnəkəl

arsenically
BR ɑː'sɛnɪkli
AM ɑr'sɛnək(ə)li

arsenicum
BR ɑː'sɛnɪkəm
AM ɑr'sɛnəkəm

arsenious
BR ɑː'si:nɪəs
AM ɑr'siniəs

arses[1]
plural of arse
BR 'ɑːsɪz
AM 'æsəz, 'ɑrsəz

arses[2]
plural of arsis
BR 'ɑːsi:z
AM 'ɑr,siz

arsine
BR 'ɑːsi:n
AM ˌɑr'sin

arsis
BR 'ɑːsɪs, -ɪz
AM 'ɑrsəs, -əz

arson
BR 'ɑːsn
AM 'ɑrsən

arsonist
BR 'ɑːsnɪst, 'ɑːsənɪst, -s
AM 'ɑrs(ə)nəst, -s

arsphenamine
BR ɑːs'fɛnəmiːn,
ɑːs'fɛnəmɪn
AM ɑr'sfɛnəmən,
ɑr'sfɛnə,min

arsy-versy
BR ˌɑːsɪ'vəːsi
AM ˌɑrsi'vərsi

art
BR ɑːt, -s
AM ɑrt, -s

Artaxerxes
BR ˌɑːtə'zəːksiːz
AM ˌɑrdə'zərksiz

art deco
BR ˌɑːt 'dɛkəʊ
AM ˌɑrt 'dɛkoʊ

artefact
BR 'ɑːtɪfakt, -s
AM 'ɑrdə,fæk(t), -(t)s

artefactual
BR ˌɑːtɪ'faktʃʊəl,
ˌɑːtɪ'faktʃ(ʊ)l
AM ˌɑrdə'fæk(t)ʃ(əw)əl

artel
BR ɑː'tɛl, -z
AM ɑr'tɛl, -z

Artemis
BR 'ɑːtɪmɪs
AM 'ɑrdəməs

artemisia
BR ˌɑːtɪ'mɪzɪə(r),
ˌɑːtɪ'miːziə(r), -z
AM ˌɑrdə'miʒ(i)ə,
ˌɑrdə'miziə , -z

Artemus
BR 'ɑːtɪməs
AM 'ɑrdəməs

arterial
BR ɑː'tɪərɪəl
AM ɑr'tɪriəl

arterialisation
BR ɑːˌtɪərɪəlʌɪ'zeɪʃn
AM ɑrˌtɪriələ'zeɪʃən,
ɑrˌtɪriəˌlaɪ'zeɪʃən

arterialise
BR ɑː'tɪərɪəlʌɪz, -ɪz, -ɪŋ,
-d
AM ɑr'tɪriəˌlaɪz, -ɪz, -ɪŋ,
-d

arterialization
BR ɑːˌtɪərɪəlʌɪ'zeɪʃn
AM ɑrˌtɪriələ'zeɪʃən,
ɑrˌtɪriəˌlaɪ'zeɪʃən

arterialize
BR ɑː'tɪərɪəlʌɪz, -ɪz, -ɪŋ,
-d
AM ɑr'tɪriəˌlaɪz, -ɪz, -ɪŋ,
-d

arteriogram
BR ɑː'tɪərɪə(ʊ)gram, -z
AM ɑr'tɪrioʊˌgræm, -z

arteriole
BR ɑː'tɪərɪəʊl, -z
AM ɑr'tɪriˌoʊl, -z

arterioscleroses
BR ɑːˌtɪərɪəʊsklə'rəʊsiːz,
ɑrˌtɪriəskləˈroʊsiz

arteriosclerosis
BR ɑːˌtɪərɪəʊsklə'rəʊsɪs
AM ɑːˌtɪrioʊsklɪˈroʊsəs,
ɑrˌtɪriəskləˈroʊsəs

arteriosclerotic
BR ɑːˌtɪərɪəʊsklə'rɒtɪk
AM ɑr'tɪriousklə'radɪk,
ɑr'tɪriəskləˈradɪk

arteritis
BR ˌɑːtə'rʌɪtɪs
AM ˌɑrdə'raɪdɪs

artery
BR 'ɑːt(ə)r|i, -ɪz
AM 'ɑrdəri, -z

artesian
BR ɑː'tiːzɪən, ɑː'tiːʒn
AM ɑr'tiʒən

artful
BR 'ɑːtf(ʊ)l
AM 'ɑrtfəl

artfully
BR 'ɑːtfʊli, 'ɑːtfli
AM 'ɑrtfəli

artfulness
BR 'ɑːtf(ʊ)lnəs
AM 'ɑrtfəlnəs

arthritic
BR ɑː'θrɪtɪk, -s
AM ɑr'θrɪdɪk, -s

arthritis
BR ɑː'θrʌɪtɪs
AM ɑr'θraɪdɪs

arthrodesis
BR ɑː'θrɒdɪsɪs
AM ˌɑr'θrɑdəsɪs

arthropod
BR 'ɑːθrəpɒd, -z
AM 'ɑrθrəˌpɑd, -z

arthroscope
BR 'ɑːθrəskəʊp, -s
AM 'ɑrθrəˌskoʊp, -s

arthroscopic
BR ˌɑːθrə'skɒpɪk
AM ˌɑrθrə'skɑpɪk

arthroscopy
BR ɑː'θrɒskəp|i, -ɪz
AM ɑr'θrɑskəpi, -z

Arthur
BR 'ɑːθə(r)
AM 'ɑrθər

Arthurian
BR ɑː'θjʊərɪən,
ɑː'θjɔːrɪən
AM ɑr'θ(j)ʊrian

artic
BR ɑː'tɪk, -s
AM ɑr'tɪk, -s

artichoke
BR 'ɑːtɪtʃəʊk, -s
AM 'ɑrdəˌtʃoʊk, -s

article
BR ˈɑːtɪk|l̩, -lz, -lɪŋ/-lɪŋ,
-ld
AM ˈɑrdəkəl, -z, -ɪŋ, -d

articulacy
BR ɑːˈtɪkjələsi
AM ɑrˈtɪkjələsi

articular
BR ɑːˈtɪkjələ(r)
AM ɑrˈtɪkjələr

articulate¹
adjective
BR ɑːˈtɪkjələt
AM ɑrˈtɪkjələt

articulate²
verb
BR ɑːˈtɪkjəleɪt, -s, -ɪŋ,
-ɪd
AM ɑrˈtɪkjəˌleɪ|t, -ts,
-dɪŋ, -dɪd

articulately
BR ɑːˈtɪkjələtli
AM ɑrˈtɪkjələtli

articulateness
BR ɑːˈtɪkjələtnəs
AM ɑrˈtɪkjələtnəs

articulation
BR ɑːˌtɪkjəˈleɪʃn, -z
AM ɑrˌtɪkjəˈleɪʃən, -z

articulator
BR ɑːˈtɪkjəleɪtə(r), -z
AM ɑrˈtɪkjəˌleɪdər, -z

articulatory
BR ɑːˈtɪkjələt(ə)ri,
ɑːˌtɪkjəˈleɪt(ə)ri
AM ɑrˈtɪkjələˌtɔri

artifact
BR ˈɑːtɪfakt, -s
AM ˈɑrdəˌfæk(t), -(t)s

artifactual
BR ˌɑːtɪˈfaktʃʊəl,
ˌɑːtɪˈfaktʃ(ʊ)l
AM ˌɑrdəˈfæk(t)ʃ(əw)əl

artifice
BR ˈɑːtɪfɪs, -ɪz
AM ˈɑrdəfəs, -əz

artificer
BR ɑːˈtɪfɪsə(r), -z
AM ɑrˈtɪfəsər,
ˈɑrdəˌfɪsər, -z

artificial
BR ˌɑːtɪˈfɪʃl
AM ˌɑrdəˈfɪʃəl

artificialise
BR ˌɑːtɪˈfɪʃəlʌɪz,
ˌɑːtɪˈfɪʃ|lʌɪz, -ɪz, -ɪŋ, -d
AM ˌɑrdəˈfɪʃəˌlaɪz, -ɪz,
-ɪŋ, -d

artificiality
BR ˌɑːtɪˌfɪʃɪˈalɪti
AM ˌɑrdəˌfɪʃiˈælədi

artificialize
BR ˌɑːtɪˈfɪʃəlʌɪz,
ˌɑːtɪˈfɪʃ|lʌɪz, -ɪz, -ɪŋ, -d
AM ˌɑrdəˈfɪʃəˌlaɪz, -ɪz,
-ɪŋ, -d

artificially
BR ˌɑːtɪˈfɪʃli,
ˌɑːtɪˈfɪʃəli
AM ˌɑrdəˈfɪʃəli

artillerist
BR ɑːˈtɪl(ə)rɪst, -s
AM ɑrˈtɪl(ə)rɪst, -s

artillery
BR ɑːˈtɪl(ə)r|i, -ɪz
AM ɑrˈtɪl(ə)ri, -z

artilleryman
BR ɑːˈtɪl(ə)rɪmən
AM ɑrˈtɪl(ə)rɪmən

artillerymen
BR ɑːˈtɪl(ə)rɪmən
AM ɑrˈtɪl(ə)rɪmən

artily
BR ˈɑːtɪli
AM ˈɑrdəli

artiness
BR ˈɑːtɪnɪs
AM ˈɑrdɪnɪs

artisan
BR ˌɑːtɪˈzan, -z
AM ˈɑrdəzn, ˈɑrdəˌzæn,
-z

artisanate
BR ˌɑːtɪˈzaneɪt
AM ˈɑrdəzəˌneɪt

artist
BR ˈɑːtɪst, -s
AM ˈɑrdəst, -s

artiste
BR ɑːˈtiːst, -s
AM ɑrˈtist, -s

artistic
BR ɑːˈtɪstɪk
AM ɑrˈtɪstɪk

artistical
BR ɑːˈtɪstɪkl
AM ɑrˈtɪstɪkəl

artistically
BR ɑːˈtɪstɪkli
AM ɑrˈtɪstɪk(ə)li

artistry
BR ˈɑːtɪstri
AM ˈɑrdəstri

artless
BR ˈɑːtləs
AM ˈɑrtləs

artlessly
BR ˈɑːtləsli
AM ˈɑrtləsli

artlessness
BR ˈɑːtləsnəs
AM ˈɑrtləsnəs

art nouveau
BR ˌɑː(t) nuːˈvəʊ,
+ nʊˈvəʊ
AM ˌɑr(t) ˌnuˈvoʊ

Artois
BR ɑːˈtwɑː(r)
AM ɑrˈtwɑ

artsy-craftsy
BR ˌɑːtsɪˈkrɑːf(t)si
AM ˌɑrtsiˈkræf(t)si

artwork
BR ˈɑːtwəːk
AM ˈɑrtˌwərk

arty
BR ˈɑːt|i, -ɪə(r), -ɪɪst
AM ˈɑrdi, -ər, -ɪst

arty-crafty
BR ˌɑːtɪˈkrɑːfti
AM ˌɑrdiˈkræfti

Aruba
BR əˈruːbə(r)
AM əˈrubə

arugula
BR əˈruːgjələ(r)
AM əˈrugələ

arum
BR ˈɛːrəm, -z
AM ˈɛrəm, -z

Arundel
BR ˈarəndl, ˈarn̩dl
AM əˈrəndəl, ˈɛrəndəl

Arunta
BR əˈrʌntə(r), -z
AM əˈrən(t)ə, -z

arvo
BR ˈɑːvəʊ, -z
AM ˈɑrˌvoʊ, -z

Arwel
BR ˈɑːwɛl
AM ˈɑrwəl

Arwyn
BR ˈɑːwɪn
AM ˈɑrwɪn

Aryan
BR ˈɛːrɪən, ˈɑːrɪən,
ˈarɪən, -z
AM ˈɛrɪən, -z

aryl
BR ˈarɪl, ˈarl̩, -z
AM ˈɛrəl, -z

arytenoid
BR ˌarɪˈtiːnɔɪd
AM əˈrɪdəˌnɔɪd,
əˈrɪtnɔɪd, ˌɛrəˈtiˌnɔɪd

as¹
strong form
BR az
AM æz

as²
weak form
BR əz
AM əz

Asa
BR ˈeɪsə(r), ˈeɪzə(r),
ˈɑːsə(r)
AM ˈeɪzə

asafoetida
BR ˌasəˈfɛtɪdə(r),
ˌasəˈfiːtɪdə(r)
AM ˌæsəˈfɛdədə,
ˌæsəˈfidədə

Asante
BR əˈsanti
AM əˈsɑn(t)i

Asaph
BR ˈasaf, ˈasəf
AM ˈæsəf

asbestine
BR asˈbɛstʌɪn,
azˈbɛstʌɪn
AM æsˈbɛsˌtɪn,
æzˈbɛsˌtɪn, əsˈbɛsˌtɪn,
əzˈbɛsˌtɪn

asbestos
BR asˈbɛstəs,
asˈbɛstɒs, azˈbɛstəs,
azˈbɛstɒs
AM æsˈbɛstəs,
æzˈbɛstəs, əsˈbɛstəs,
əzˈbɛstəs

asbestosine
BR asˈbɛstəsʌɪn,
azˈbɛstəsʌɪn
AM æsˈbɛstəˌsɪn,
æzˈbɛstəˌsɪn

asbestosis
BR ˌasbɛˈstəʊsɪs,
ˌazbɛˈstəʊsɪs
AM ˌæsˌbɛsˈtoʊsəs,
ˌæzˌbɛsˈtoʊsəs

Asbury
BR ˈasb(ə)ri
AM ˈæzbəri

Ascalon
BR ˈaskələn
AM ˈaskəˌlɑn

ASCAP
BR ˈaskap
AM ˈæskæp

ascarid
BR ˈaskərɪd, -z
AM ˈæskərɪd, -z

ascaris
BR ˈaskərɪs, -ɪz
AM ˈæskərəs, -əz

ascend
BR əˈsɛnd, -z, -ɪŋ, -ɪd
AM əˈsɛnd, -z, -ɪŋ, -əd

ascendance
BR əˈsɛnd(ə)ns
AM əˈsɛnd(ə)ns,
æˈsɛnd(ə)ns

ascendancy
BR əˈsɛnd(ə)nsi
AM əˈsɛnd(ə)nsi

ascendant
BR əˈsɛnd(ə)nt
AM əˈsɛnd(ə)nt

ascender
BR əˈsɛndə(r), -z
AM əˈsɛndər, -z

ascension
BR əˈsɛnʃn
AM əˈsɛn(t)ʃən

ascensional
BR əˈsɛnʃn(ə)l,
əˈsɛnʃən(ə)l
AM əˈsɛn(t)ʃ(ə)nəl

Ascensiontide
BR əˈsɛnʃ(ə)ntʌɪd
AM əˈsɛn(t)ʃənˌtaɪd

ascent
BR əˈsɛnt, -s
AM əˈsɛnt, -s

ascentionist
BR əˈsɛnʃɲɪst,
əˈsɛnʃ(ə)nɪst, -s
AM əˈsɛn(t)ʃənəst, -s

Ascentiontide
BR əˈsɛnʃntʌɪd
AM əˈsɛn(t)ʃənˌtaɪd

ascertain
BR ˌasəˈteɪn, -z, -ɪŋ, -d
AM ˌæsərˈteɪn, -z, -ɪŋ, -d

ascertainable
BR ˌasəˈteɪnəbl
AM ˌæsərˈteɪnəbəl

ascertainment
BR ˌasəˈteɪnm(ə)nt
AM ˌæsərˈteɪnmənt

asceses
BR əˈsiːsiːz
AM əˈsisiz, æˈsisiz

ascesis
BR əˈsiːsɪs
AM əˈsisɪs, æˈsisɪs

ascetic
BR əˈsɛtɪk
AM əˈsɛdɪk, æˈsɛdɪk

ascetically
BR əˈsɛtɪkli
AM əˈsɛdək(ə)li,
æˈsɛdək(ə)li

asceticism
BR əˈsɛtɪsɪz(ə)m
AM əˈsɛdəˌsɪzəm,
æˈsɛdəˌsɪzəm

Ascham
BR ˈaskəm
AM ˈæskəm

aschelminth
BR ˈaʃhɛlmɪnθ
ˈaskhɛlmɪnθ, -s
AM ˈæʃɛlˌmɪnθ
ˈæskɛlˌmɪnθ, -s

asci
BR ˈaskʌɪ, ˈaski
AM ˈæsˌkaɪ, ˈæski

ascidian
BR əˈsɪdɪən, -z
AM əˈsɪdiən, -z

ASCII
BR ˈaski
AM ˈæski

ascites
BR əˈsʌɪtiːz
AM əˈsaɪdiz

Asclepiad
BR əˈskliːpɪad, -z
AM əˈsklipiəd,
æˈsklipiəd, -z

Asclepius
BR əˈskliːpɪəs
AM əˈsklipiəs,
æˈsklipiəs

ascomycete
BR ˌaskəˈmʌɪsiːt
AM ˌæskəˈmaɪˌsit

ascomycetes
BR ˌaskəˈmʌɪsiːts
ˌaskəmʌɪˈsiːtiːz

AM ˌæskəˈmaɪˌsits,
ˌæskəˈmaɪˌsidiz

Ascona
BR aˈskəʊnə(r)
AM æsˈkoʊnə

ascorbic
BR əˈskɔːbɪk
AM əˈskɔrbɪk

ascot
BR ˈaskət, ˈaskɒt, -s
AM ˈæsˌkat, ˈæskət, -s

ascribable
BR əˈskrʌɪbəbl
AM əˈskraɪbəbəl

ascribe
BR əˈskrʌɪb, -z, -ɪŋ, -d
AM əˈskraɪb, -z, -ɪŋ, -d

ascription
BR əˈskrɪpʃn
AM əˈskrɪpʃən

ascus
BR ˈaskəs
AM ˈæskəs

Asda®
BR ˈazdə(r)
AM ˈæzdə

asdic
BR ˈazdɪk
AM ˈæzdɪk

ASEAN
BR ˈasɪan
AM əˈsiən

aseity
BR (ˌ)eɪˈsiːɪti, əˈsiːɪti
AM eɪˈsiɪdi, əˈsiɪdi

asepsis
BR (ˌ)eɪˈsɛpsɪs,
əˈsɛpsɪs, aˈsɛpsɪs
AM eɪˈsɛpsəs

aseptic
BR (ˌ)eɪˈsɛptɪk,
əˈsɛptɪk, aˈsɛptɪk
AM eɪˈsɛptɪk

aseptically
BR (ˌ)eɪˈsɛptɪkli,
əˈsɛptɪkli, aˈsɛptɪkli
AM eɪˈsɛptək(ə)li

asexual
BR (ˌ)eɪˈsɛkʃʊəl,
(ˌ)eɪˈsɛkʃ(ʉ)l,
(ˌ)eɪˈsɛksjʊ(ə)l
AM eɪˈsɛkʃ(əw)əl

asexuality
BR ˌeɪsɛkʃʊˈalɪti,
eɪˌsɛkʃʊˈalɪti,
ˌeɪsɛksjʊˈalɪti,
eɪˌsɛksjʊˈalɪti
AM eɪsɛkʃəˈwælədi

asexually
BR (ˌ)eɪˈsɛkʃʊəli,
(ˌ)eɪˈsɛkʃʉli,
(ˌ)eɪˈsɛkʃʲli,
(ˌ)eɪˈsɛksjʊ(ə)li
AM eɪˈsɛkʃ(əw)əli

Asgard
BR ˈasgɑːd, ˈazgɑːd
AM ˈæsˌgard, ˈæzˌgard

ash
BR aʃ, -ɪz
AM æʃ, -əz

ashamed
BR əˈʃeɪmd
AM əˈʃeɪmd

ashamedly
BR əˈʃeɪmɪdli
AM əˈʃeɪmɪdli

ashamedness
BR əˈʃeɪm(ɪ)dnɪs
AM əˈʃeɪmɪdnɪs,
əˈʃeɪm(d)nɪs

Ashanti
BR əˈʃanti
AM əˈʃan(t)i

ashbin
BR ˈaʃbɪn, -z
AM ˈæʃˌbɪn, -z

Ashby
BR ˈaʃbi
AM ˈæʃbi

Ashby-de-la-Zouch
BR ˌaʃbɪˌdələˈzuːʃ
AM ˌæʃˌbidələˈzuʃ

ashcan
BR ˈaʃkan, -z
AM ˈæʃˌkæn, -z

Ashcroft
BR ˈaʃkrɒft
AM ˈæʃˌkrɔft, ˈæʃˌkraft

Ashdod
BR ˈaʃdɒd
AM ˈæʃˌdad

Ashdown
BR ˈaʃdaʊn
AM ˈæʃˌdaʊn

Ashe
BR aʃ
AM æʃ

ashen
BR ˈaʃn
AM ˈæʃən

Asher
BR ˈaʃə(r)
AM ˈæʃər

ashet
BR ˈaʃɪt, -s
AM ˈæʃət, -s

Ashford
BR ˈaʃfəd
AM ˈæʃfərd

ashiness
BR ˈaʃɪnɪs
AM ˈæʃinɪs

Ashington
BR ˈaʃɪŋt(ə)n
AM ˈæʃɪŋtən

Ashkelon
BR ˈaʃkəlɒn
AM ˈæʃkəˌlɑn

Ashkenazi
BR ˌaʃkɪˈnaːzi
AM ˌæʃkəˈnazi

Ashkenazic
BR ˌaʃkɪˈnaːzɪk

AM ˌæʃkəˈnɑzɪk

Ashkenazim
BR ˌaʃkɪˈnaːzɪm
AM ˌæʃkəˈnazɪm

Ashkenazy
BR ˌaʃkɪˈnaːzi
AM ˌæʃkəˈnazi
RUS əʃkʲiˈnazʲi

Ashkhabad
BR ˈaʃkəbad,
ˈaʃkəbaːd
AM ˈaʃkəˌbad,
ˈaʃkəˌbæd
RUS əʃxaˈbat

ashlar
BR ˈaʃlə(r), ˈaʃlaː(r)
AM ˈæʃlər

ashlaring
BR ˈaʃlərɪŋ, ˈaʃlaːrɪŋ
AM ˈæʃlərɪŋ

Ashley
BR ˈaʃli
AM ˈæʃli

Ashmolean
BR aʃˈməʊliən
AM æʃˈmoʊliən

ashore
BR əˈʃɔː(r)
AM əˈʃɔ(ə)r

ashpan
BR ˈaʃpan, -z
AM ˈæʃˌpæn, -z

ashplant
BR ˈaʃplaːnt, ˈaʃplant,
-s
AM ˈæʃˌplænt, -s

Ashquelon
BR ˈaʃkəlɒn
AM ˈæʃkəˌlɑn,
ˈæskəˌlan

ashram
BR ˈaʃram, ˈaʃrəm, -z
AM ˈaʃrəm, -z

ashrama
BR ˈaʃrəmə(r), -z
AM ˈaʃrəmə, -z

Ash Shariqah
BR ˌaʃ ʃəˈriːkə(r)
AM ˌæʃ ʃəˈrikə

Ashton
BR ˈaʃt(ə)n
AM ˈæʃt(ə)n

Ashton-under-Lyne
BR ˌaʃt(ə)nˌʌndəˈlʌɪn
AM ˌæʃt(ə)nˌəndərˈlaɪn

ashtray
BR ˈaʃtreɪ, -z
AM ˈæʃˌtreɪ, -z

Ashur
BR ˈaʃə(r)
AM ˈæʃər

Ashurbanipal
BR ˌaʃʊəˈbanɪpal
AM ɑˌʃʊrˈbaniˌpal

ashwood
BR ˈaʃwʊd

AM 'æʃˌwʊd
Ashworth
BR 'aʃwə(:)θ
AM 'æʃˌwərθ
ashy
BR 'aʃ|i, -ɪə(r), -ɪɪst
AM 'æʃi, -ər, -ɪst
Asia
BR 'eɪʃə(r), 'eɪʒə(r)
AM 'eɪʒə
Asian
BR 'eɪʃ(ə)n, 'eɪʒ(ə)n, -z
AM 'eɪʒən, -z
Asiatic
BR ˌeɪzɪ'atɪk, ˌeɪsɪ'atɪk, ˌeɪʃɪ'atɪk, ˌeɪʒɪ'atɪk
AM ˌeɪʒi'ædɪk, ˌeɪzi'ædɪk
aside
BR ə'sʌɪd, -z
AM ə'saɪd, -z
Asimov
BR 'asɪmɒv, 'azɪmɒv
AM 'æzəˌmɔv, 'æzəˌmav
asinine
BR 'asɪnʌɪn
AM 'æsəˌnaɪn, 'æsnˌaɪn
asininity
BR ˌasɪ'nɪnɪt|i, -ɪz
AM ˌæsə'nɪnɪdi, -z
ask
BR ɑːsk, ask, -s, -ɪŋ, -t
AM æsk, -s, -ɪŋ, -t
askance
BR ə'skans, ə'skɑːns
AM ə'skæns
askari
BR ə'skɑːr|i, a'skɑːr|i, -ɪz
AM æ'skəri, ə'skɑri, -z
Askelon
BR 'askɪlɒn, 'askļɒn, 'askɪlən, 'askļən
AM 'æskɛˌlɑn, 'æʃkəˌlɑn
asker
BR 'ɑːskə(r), 'askə(r), -z
AM 'æskər, -z
askeses
BR ə'skɛsiːz
AM ə'skisiz
askesis
BR ə'skɛsɪs
AM ə'skisəs
Askew
surname
BR 'askjuː
AM 'æskju
askew
BR ə'skjuː
AM ə'skju
Askey
BR 'aski
AM 'æski

Askham
BR 'askəm
AM 'æskəm
Askrigg
BR 'askrɪg
AM 'æskrɪg
aslant
BR ə'slɑːnt, ə'slant
AM ə'slænt
asleep
BR ə'sliːp
AM ə'slip
ASLEF
BR 'azlɛf
AM 'æzˌlɛf
aslope
BR ə'sləʊp
AM ə'sloʊp
Asmara
BR ə'smɑːrə(r), as'mɑːrə(r), az'mɑːrə(r)
AM æs'mɛrə
asocial
BR eɪ'səʊʃl
AM eɪ'soʊʃəl
asocially
BR eɪ'səʊʃļi, eɪ'səʊʃəli
AM eɪ'soʊʃəli
Asoka
BR ə'səʊkə(r), ə'ʃəʊkə(r)
AM ə'soʊkə, ə'ʃoʊkə
asp
BR asp, -s
AM æsp, -s
asparagus
BR ə'sparəgəs
AM ə'spɛrəgəs
aspartame
BR ə'spɑːteɪm
AM 'æspɑrˌteɪm
aspartic
BR ə'spɑːtɪk
AM ə'spɑrdɪk
Aspatria
BR a'speɪtrɪə(r), ə'speɪtrɪə(r)
AM æ'speɪtrɪə
aspect
BR 'aspɛkt, -s
AM 'æˌspɛk|(t), -(t)s
aspected
BR a'spɛktɪd, 'aspɛktɪd
AM 'æsˌpɛktəd, æ'spɛktəd
aspectual
BR a'spɛktʃʊəl, a'spɛktʃ(ʉ)l, a'spɛktʃʊəl, a'spɛktjʉl
AM æ'spɛk(t)ʃ(əw)əl
aspectually
BR a'spɛktʃʊəli, a'spɛktʃʉli, a'spɛktʃʃļi,

a'spɛktjʊəli, a'spɛktjʉli
AM æ'spɛk(t)ʃ(əw)əli
Aspel
BR 'aspl
AM 'æspɛl
Aspell
BR 'aspl
AM 'æspɛl
aspen
BR 'aspən, -z
AM 'æspən, -z
asperge
BR ə'spəːdʒ, -ɪz, -ɪŋ, -d
AM ə'spərdʒ, -əz, -ɪŋ, -d
aspergill
BR 'aspədʒɪl, -z
AM 'æspərˌdʒɪl, -z
aspergilla
BR ˌaspə'dʒɪlə(r)
AM ˌæspər'dʒɪlə
aspergillum
BR ˌaspə'dʒɪləm, -z
AM ˌæspər'dʒɪləm, -z
asperity
BR ə'spɛrɪt|i, -ɪz
AM ə'spɛrədi, æ'spɛrədi, -z
asperse
BR ə'spəːs, -ɪz, -ɪŋ, -t
AM ə'spərs, æ'spərs, -əz, -ɪŋ, -t
aspersion
BR ə'spəːʃn, ə'spəːʒn, -z
AM ə'spərʒən, æ'spərʃən, -z
aspersoria
BR ˌaspə'sɔːrɪə(r)
AM ˌæspər'sɔriə
aspersorium
BR ˌaspə'sɔːrɪəm
AM ˌæspər'sɔriəm
asphalt
BR 'asfalt, 'aʃfalt, 'asfɔːlt, 'aʃfɔːlt, 'asfalt, 'aʃfalt
AM 'æsˌfɔlt, 'æsˌfalt
asphalter
BR 'asfɔːltə(r), 'aʃfɔːltə(r), 'asfəltə(r), 'aʃfəltə(r), -z
AM æs'fɔltər, æs'faltər, -z
asphaltic
BR as'faltɪk, aʃ'faltɪk
AM æs'fɔltɪk, æs'faltɪk
asphodel
BR 'asfədɛl, -z
AM 'æsfəˌdɛl, -z
asphyxia
BR əs'fɪksɪə(r)
AM æs'sfɪksɪə, ə'sfɪksiə
asphyxial
BR əs'fɪksɪəl
AM æ'sfɪksɪəl, ə'sfɪksɪəl

a'spɛktjʊəli, a'spɛktjʉli
a'spɛktjʉli
AM æ'spɛk(t)ʃ(əw)əli
Aspel

a'spɛktjuəli, a'spɛktjʉli,

a'spɛktjʊəli,

a'speʃktjʊəli,

asphyxiant
BR əs'fɪksɪənt, -s
AM æ'sfɪksiənt, ə'sfɪksiənt, -s
asphyxiate
BR əs'fɪksɪeɪt, -s, -ɪŋ, -ɪd
AM æ'sfɪksiˌeɪ|t, ə'sfɪksiˌeɪ|t, -ts, -dɪŋ, -dɪd
asphyxiation
BR əsˌfɪksɪ'eɪʃn
AM æˌsfɪksi'eɪʃən, əˌsfɪksi'eɪʃən
asphyxiator
BR əs'fɪksɪeɪtə(r), -z
AM æ'sfɪksiˌeɪdər, ə'sfɪksiˌeɪdər, -z
aspic
BR 'aspɪk
AM 'æspɪk
aspidistra
BR ˌaspɪ'dɪstrə(r), -z
AM ˌæspə'dɪstrə, -z
Aspinall
BR 'aspɪnl, 'aspɪnɔːl
AM 'æspəˌnɔl, 'æspəˌnɑl
aspirant
BR 'asp(ɪ)rənt, 'asp(ɪ)rņt, ə'spʌɪrənt, ə'spʌɪrņt, -s
AM 'æspərənt, ə'spaɪrənt, -s
aspirate¹
noun, adjective
BR 'asp(ɪ)rət, -s
AM 'æsp(ə)rət, -s
aspirate²
verb
BR 'aspɪreɪt, -s, -ɪŋ, -ɪd
AM 'æspəˌreɪ|t, -ts, -dɪŋ, -dɪd
aspiration
BR ˌaspɪ'reɪʃn, -z
AM ˌæspə'reɪʃən, -z
aspirational
BR ˌaspɪ'reɪʃn(ə)l, ˌaspɪ'reɪʃən(ə)l
AM ˌæspə'reɪʃ(ə)nəl
aspirator
BR 'aspɪreɪtə(r), -z
AM 'æspəˌreɪdər, -z
aspire
BR ə'spʌɪə(r), -z, -ɪŋ, -d
AM ə'spaɪ(ə)r, -z, -ɪŋ, -d
aspirin
BR 'asp(ɪ)n, -z
AM 'æsp(ə)rən, -z
asplenium
BR ə'spliːnɪəm, -z
AM ə'spliniəm, æ'spliniəm, -z
Aspro®
BR 'asprəʊ, -z
AM 'æsproʊ, -z
asquint
BR ə'skwɪnt

AM 'æskwɪnt
Asquith
BR 'askwɪθ
AM 'æskwəθ
ass
BR as, -ɪz
AM æs, -əz
Assad
BR a'sɑːd, a'sad
AM ɑ'sad, 'ɑ,sad
assagai
BR 'asəgʌɪ, -z
AM 'æsə'gaɪ, -z
assai
BR a'sʌɪ
AM ɑ'saɪ
assail
BR ə'seɪl, -z, -ɪŋ, -d
AM ə'seɪl, -z, -ɪŋ, -d
assailable
BR ə'seɪləbl
AM ə'seɪləbəl,
æ'seɪləbəl
assailant
BR ə'seɪlənt, ə'seɪl̩nt, -s
AM ə'seɪlənt, -s
Assam
BR ə'sam, a'sam
AM ə'sæm, æ'sæm,
'æ,sæm
Assamese
BR ,asə'miːz
AM ,æsə'miz
assassin
BR ə'sas(ɨ)n, -z
AM ə'sæsn̩, -z
assassinate
BR ə'sasɪneɪt, -s, -ɪŋ, -ɪd
AM ə'sæsn̩,eɪ|t, -ts,
-dɪŋ, -dɪd
assassination
BR ə,sasɪ'neɪʃn, -z
AM ə,sæsn̩'eɪʃən, -z
assassinator
BR ə'sasɪneɪtə(r), -z
AM ə'sæsn̩,eɪdər, -z
assault
BR ə'sɔːlt, ə'sɒlt, -s, -ɪŋ,
-ɪd
AM ə'sɒlt, ə'sɑlt, -s, -ɪŋ,
-əd
assaulter
BR ə'sɔːltə(r),
ə'sɒltə(r), -z
AM ə'sɒltər, ə'sɑltər, -z
assaultive
BR ə'sɔːltɪv, ə'sɒltɪv
AM ə'sɒltɪv, ə'sɑltɪv
assay
BR ə'seɪ, 'aseɪ, -z, -ɪŋ, -d
AM 'æ,seɪ, ə'seɪ, -z, -ɪŋ,
-d
assayable
BR a'seɪəbl, 'aseɪəbl, -z
AM 'æseɪəbəl, ə'seɪəbl,
-z

assayer
BR ə'seɪə(r), 'aseɪə(r),
-z
AM 'æseɪər, ə'seɪər, -z
assegai
BR 'asəgʌɪ, -z
AM 'æsə'gaɪ, -z
assemblage
BR ə'sembl|ɪdʒ, -ɪdʒɪz
AM ə'semblɪdʒ, -ɪz
assemble
BR ə'sembl|l, -lz,
-lɪŋ\-lɪŋ, -ld
AM ə'sembl|əl, -əlz,
-(ə)lɪŋ, -əld
assembler
BR ə'semblə(r), -z
AM ə'semblər, -z
assembly
BR ə'sembl|i, -ɪz
AM ə'sembli, -z
assemblyman
BR ə'semblɪmən
AM ə'semblimən
assemblymen
BR ə'semblɪmən
AM ə'semblimən
assent
BR ə'sent, -s, -ɪŋ, -ɪd
AM ə'sen|t, æ'sen|t, -ts,
-(t)ɪŋ, -(t)əd
assenter
BR ə'sentə(r), -z
AM ə'sen(t)ər,
æ'sen(t)ər, -z
assentient
BR ə'senʃ(ə)nt
AM ə'sen(t)ʃənt,
æ'sen(t)ʃənt
assentor
BR ə'sentə(r), -z
AM ə'sen(t)ər,
æ'sen(t)ər, -z
assert
BR ə'səːt, -s, -ɪŋ, -ɪd
AM ə'sər|t, -ts, -dɪŋ,
-dəd
asserter
BR ə'səːtə(r), -z
AM ə'sərdər, -z
assertion
BR ə'səː|ʃn, -z
AM ə'sər|ʃən, -z
assertive
BR ə'səːtɪv
AM ə'sərdɪv
assertively
BR ə'səːtɪvli
AM ə'sərdɪvli
assertiveness
BR ə'səːtɪvnɪs
AM ə'sərdɪvnɪs
assertor
BR ə'səːtə(r), -z
AM ə'sərdər, -z
assess
BR ə'sɛs, -ɪz, -ɪŋ, -t
AM ə'sɛs, -əz, -ɪŋ, -t

assessable
BR ə'sɛsəbl
AM ə'sɛsəbəl
assessment
BR ə'sɛsm(ə)nt, -s
AM ə'sɛsmənt, -s
assessor
BR ə'sɛsə(r), -z
AM ə'sɛsər, -z
assessorial
BR ,asɛ'sɔːrɪəl,
,asɛ'sɔːrɪəl
AM ,æ,sɛ'sɔrɪəl,
,æsə'sɔrɪəl
asset
BR 'asɛt, 'asɪt, -s
AM 'æ,sɛt, -s
assever
BR ə'sɛvə(r), -z, -ɪŋ, -d
AM ə'sɛvər, -z, -ɪŋ, -d
asseverate
BR ə'sɛvəreɪt, -s, -ɪŋ, -ɪd
AM ə'sɛvə,reɪ|t, -ts,
-dɪŋ, -dɪd
asseveration
BR ə,sɛvə'reɪʃn, -z
AM ə,sɛvə'reɪʃən, -z
asshole
BR 'ɑːshəʊl, -z
AM 'æs,(h)oʊl, -z
assibilate
BR ə'sɪbɪleɪt, -s, -ɪŋ, -ɪd
AM ə'sɪbə,leɪ|t, -ts, -dɪŋ,
-dɪd
assibilation
BR ə,sɪbɪ'leɪʃn
AM ə,sɪbə'leɪʃən
assiduity
BR ,asɪ'dju:ɪt|i,
,asɪ'dʒuːɪt|i, -ɪz
AM ,æsə'd(j)uədi, -z
assiduous
BR ə'sɪdjʊəs, ə'sɪdʒʊəs
AM ə'sɪdʒəwəs
assiduously
BR ə'sɪdjʊəsli,
ə'sɪdʒʊəsli
AM ə'sɪdʒ(ə)wəsli
assiduousness
BR ə'sɪdjʊəsnəs,
ə'sɪdʒʊəsnəs
AM ə'sɪdʒ(əw)əsnəs
assign
BR ə'sʌɪn, -z, -ɪŋ, -d
AM ə'saɪn, -z, -ɪŋ, -d
assignable
BR ə'sʌɪnəbl
AM ə'saɪnəbəl
assignat
BR 'asɪgnat,
,asɪ'nja:(r),
'asɪgnats\,asi:'njaːz
AM 'æsɪg,næt, -s
assignation
BR ,asɪg'neɪʃn, -z
AM ,æsɪg'neɪʃən, -z
assignee
BR ,asʌɪ'ni:, -z

assigner
BR ə'sʌɪnə(r), -z
AM ə'saɪnər, -z
assignment
BR ə'sʌɪnm(ə)nt, -s
AM ə'saɪnmənt, -s
assignor
BR ə'sʌɪnə(r), -z
AM ə'saɪnər, -z
assimilable
BR ə'sɪmɪləbl
AM ə'sɪmələbəl
assimilate
BR ə'sɪmɪleɪt, -s, -ɪŋ, -ɪd
AM ə'sɪmə,leɪ|t, -ts,
-dɪŋ, -dɪd
assimilation
BR ə,sɪmɪ'leɪʃn
AM ə,sɪmə'leɪʃən
assimilative
BR ə'sɪmɪlətɪv
AM ə'sɪmə,leɪdɪv,
ə'sɪmələdɪv
assimilator
BR ə'sɪmɪleɪtə(r), -z
AM ə'sɪmə,leɪdər, -z
assimilatory
BR ə'sɪmɪlət(ə)ri
AM ə'sɪmɪlə,tɔri
Assisi
BR ə'si:si, ə'si:zi
AM ə'sisi, ə'sizi
assist
BR ə'sɪst, -s, -ɪŋ, -ɪd
AM ə'sɪst, -s, -ɪŋ, -ɪd
assistance
BR ə'sɪst(ə)ns
AM ə'sɪst(ə)ns
assistant
BR ə'sɪst(ə)nt, -s
AM ə'sɪst(ə)nt, -s
assister
BR ə'sɪstə(r), -z
AM ə'sɪstər, -z
assize
BR ə'sʌɪz, -ɪz
AM ə'saɪz, -ɪz
ass-kicking
BR 'ɑːs,kɪkɪŋ
AM 'æs,kɪkɪŋ
ass-licking
BR 'ɑːs,lɪkɪŋ
AM 'æs,lɪkɪŋ
associability
BR ə,səʊʃ(ɪə)'bɪlɪti,
ə,səʊsɪə'bɪlɪti
AM ə,səʊʃ(i)ə'bɪlɪdi
associable
BR ə'səʊʃ(ɪ)bl,
ə'səʊsɪəbl
AM ə'səʊʃ(i)əbəl
associate[1]
noun
BR ə'səʊʃ(ɪ)ət,
ə'səʊsɪət, -s

AM əˈsoʊsiət,
əˈsoʊʃ(i)ət, -s

associate²
verb
BR əˈsəʊʃieɪt,
əˈsəʊsieɪt, -s, -ɪŋ, -ɪd
AM əˈsoʊsiˌeɪt,
əˈsoʊʃiˌeɪt, -ts, -dɪŋ,
-dɪd

associateship
BR əˈsəʊʃiətʃɪp,
əˈsəʊsiətʃɪp, -s
AM əˈsoʊsiətˌʃɪp,
əˈsoʊʃiətˌʃɪp, -s

association
BR əˌsəʊsɪˈeɪʃn̩,
əˌsəʊʃɪˈeɪʃn̩, -z
AM əˌsoʊsiˈeɪʃən,
əˌsoʊʃiˈeɪʃən, -z

associational
BR əˌsəʊsɪˈeɪʃn̩(ə)l,
əˌsəʊsɪˈeɪʃən(ə)l,
əˌsəʊʃrˈeɪʃn̩(ə)l,
əˌsəʊʃrˈeɪʃən(ə)l
AM əˌsoʊsiˈeɪʃ(ə)nəl,
əˌsoʊʃiˈeɪʃ(ə)nəl

associationist
BR əˌsəʊsɪˈeɪʃn̩ɪst,
əˌsəʊsɪˈeɪʃənɪst,
əˌsəʊʃrˈeɪʃn̩ɪst,
əˌsəʊʃrˈeɪʃənɪst, -s
AM əˌsoʊsiˈeɪʃənəst,
əˌsoʊʃiˈeɪʃənəst, -s

associative
BR əˈsəʊʃ(ɪ)ətɪv,
əˈsəʊsiətɪv
AM əˈsoʊʃədɪv,
əˈsoʊsiˌeɪdɪv,
əˈsoʊʃiˌeɪdɪv

associatively
BR əˈsəʊʃ(ɪ)ətɪvli,
əˈsəʊsiətɪvli
AM əˈsoʊsiədɪvli,
əˈsoʊʃədɪvli,
əˈsoʊsiˌeɪdɪvli,
əˈsoʊʃiˌeɪdɪvli

associativity
BR əˌsəʊʃ(ɪ)əˈtɪvɪti,
əˌsəʊsɪəˈtɪvɪti
AM əˌsoʊsɪəˈtɪvɪdi,
əˌsoʊʃ(i)əˈtɪvɪdi

associator
BR əˈsəʊʃɪeɪtə(r),
əˈsəʊsɪeɪtə(r), -z
AM əˈsoʊsiˌeɪdər,
əˈsoʊʃiˌeɪdər, -z

associatory
BR əˈsəʊʃ(ɪ)ət(ə)ri,
əˈsəʊsiət(ə)ri
AM əˈsoʊsiəˌtɔri,
əˈsoʊʃiəˌtɔri

assoil
BR əˈsɔɪl, -z, -ɪŋ, -d
AM əˈsɔɪl, -z, -ɪŋ, -d

assonance
BR ˈasənəns, ˈasn̩əns,
-ɪz

AM ˈæsn̩əns, -əz

assonant
BR ˈasənənt, ˈasn̩ənt
AM ˈæsn̩ənt

assonate
BR ˈasəneɪt, ˈasn̩eɪt, -s,
-ɪŋ, -ɪd
AM ˈæsəˌneɪt, -ts, -dɪŋ,
-dɪd

assort
BR əˈsɔːt, -s, -ɪŋ, -ɪd
AM əˈsɔ(ə)rt, -ts,
-ˈsɔrdɪŋ, -ˈsɔrdəd

assortative
BR əˈsɔːtətɪv
AM əˈsɔrdədɪv

assortment
BR əˈsɔːtm(ə)nt, -s
AM əˈsɔrtmənt, -s

assuage
BR əˈsweɪdʒ, -ɪz, -ɪŋ, -d
AM əˈsweɪdʒ, -ɪz, -ɪŋ, -d

assuagement
BR əˈsweɪdʒm(ə)nt
AM əˈsweɪdʒmənt

assuager
BR əˈsweɪdʒə(r), -z
AM əˈsweɪdʒər, -z

assuasive
BR əˈsweɪsɪv,
əˈsweɪzɪv
AM əˈsweɪsɪv,
əˈsweɪzɪv

assumable
BR əˈsjuːməbl
AM əˈsuːməbəl

assume
BR əˈsjuːm, -z, -ɪŋ, -d
AM əˈsum, -z, -ɪŋ, -d

assumedly
BR əˈsjuːmɪdli
AM əˈsuːmədli

assuming
BR əˈsjuːmɪŋ
AM əˈsumɪŋ

assumingly
BR əˈsjuːmɪŋli
AM əˈsumɪŋli

assumpsit
BR əˈsʌm(p)sɪt
AM əˈsəm(p)sət

assumption
BR əˈsʌm(p)ʃn̩, -z
AM əˈsəm(p)ʃən, -z

assumptive
BR əˈsʌm(p)tɪv
AM əˈsəm(p)tɪv

Assur
BR ˈasə(r)
AM ˈæsər

assurable
BR əˈʃʊərəbl, əˈʃɔːrəbl
AM əˈʃʊrəbəl

assurance
BR əˈʃʊərəns, əˈʃʊərn̩s,
əˈʃɔːrəns, əˈʃɔːrn̩s, -ɪz
AM əˈʃʊrəns, -əz

assure
BR əˈʃʊə(r), əˈʃɔː(r), -z,
-ɪŋ, -d
AM əˈʃʊ(ə)r, -z, -ɪŋ, -d

assuredly
BR əˈʃʊərɪdli,
əˈʃɔːrɪdli
AM əˈʃʊr(ə)dli

assuredness
BR əˈʃʊərɪdnɪs,
əˈʃɔːrɪdnɪs
AM əˈʃʊr(ə)dnəs

assurer
BR əˈʃʊərə(r),
əˈʃɔːrə(r), -z
AM əˈʃʊrər, -z

Assyria
BR əˈsɪrɪə(r)
AM əˈsɪriə

Assyrian
BR əˈsɪriən, -z
AM əˈsɪriən, -z

Assyriologist
BR əˌsɪriˈɒlədʒɪst, -s
AM əˌsɪriˈɑlədʒəst, -s

Assyriology
BR əˌsɪriˈɒlədʒi
AM əˌsɪriˈɑlədʒi

astable
BR eɪˈsterbl
AM eɪˈsterbəl

Astaire
BR əˈsteː(r)
AM əˈstɛ(ə)r

Astarte
BR əˈstɑːti, əˈstɑːti
AM əˈstardi

astatic
BR (ˌ)erˈstatɪk
AM eɪˈstædɪk

astatine
BR ˈastətiːn, ˈastətɪn
AM ˈæstəˌtin

Astbury
BR ˈas(t)b(ə)ri
AM ˈæs(t)bɛri

aster
BR ˈastə(r), -z
AM ˈæstər, -z

asterisk
BR ˈast(ə)rɪsk, -s, -ɪŋ, -t
AM ˈæstəˌrɪsk,
ˈæstəˌrɪks,
-sks\-ksɪz, -ɪŋ, -t

asterism
BR ˈast(ə)rɪz(ə)m, -z
AM ˈæstəˌrɪzəm, -z

Asterix
BR ˈastərɪks
AM ˈæstəˌrɪks

astern
BR əˈstəːn
AM əˈstərn

asteroid
BR ˈastərɔɪd, -z
AM ˈæstəˌrɔɪd, -z

asteroidal
BR ˌastəˈrɔɪdl
AM ˌæstəˈrɔɪdəl

asthenia
BR asˈθiːnɪə(r),
əsˈθiːnɪə(r)
AM æsˈθiniə, əsˈθiniə

asthenic
BR asˈθɛnɪk, əsˈθɛnɪk
AM æsˈθɛnɪk, əsˈθɛnɪk

asthenosphere
BR asˈθɛnə(ʊ)sfɪə(r),
əsˈθɛnə(ʊ)sfɪə(r)
AM æsˈθɛnəˌsfɪ(ə)r,
əsˈθɛnəˌsfɪ(ə)r

asthma
BR ˈasmə(r)
AM ˈæzmə

asthmatic
BR asˈmatɪk, -s
AM æzˈmædɪk, -s

asthmatical
BR asˈmatɪkl
AM æzˈmædəkəl

asthmatically
BR asˈmatɪkli
AM æzˈmædək(ə)li

Asti
BR ˈast|i, -ɪz
AM ˈɑsti, -z

astigmatic
BR ˌastɪɡˈmatɪk
AM ˌæstɪɡˈmædɪk

astigmatism
BR əˈstɪɡmətɪz(ə)m
AM əˈstɪɡməˌtɪzəm

astilbe
BR əˈstɪlb|i, -ɪz
AM əˈstɪlbi, -z

astir
BR əˈstəː(r)
AM əˈstər

Asti spumante
BR ˌasti spjəˈmanti
AM ˌasti spʊˈman(t)i

Astley
BR ˈastli
AM ˈæs(t)li

Aston
BR ˈast(ə)n
AM ˈæst(ə)n

astonish
BR əˈstɒnɪʃ, -ɪʃɪz,
-ɪʃɪŋ, -ɪʃt
AM əˈstɑnɪʃ, -ɪz, -ɪŋ, -t

astonishingly
BR əˈstɒnɪʃɪŋli
AM əˈstɑnɪʃɪŋli

astonishment
BR əˈstɒnɪʃm(ə)nt, -s
AM əˈstɑnɪʃmənt, -s

Astor
BR ˈastə(r)
AM ˈæstər

Astoria
BR əˈstɔːrɪə(r),
əˈstɔːrɪə(r)

AM ə'stɔːriə
astound
BR ə'staʊnd, -z, -ɪŋ, -ɪd
AM ə'staʊnd, -z, -ɪŋ, -əd
astoundingly
BR ə'staʊndɪŋli
AM ə'staʊndɪŋli
astra
BR 'astrə(r)
AM 'æstrə
astraddle
BR ə'stradl
AM ə'strædəl
astragal
BR 'astrəg(ə)l, -z
AM 'æstrəgəl, -z
astragali
BR ə'stragəlʌɪ,
ə'straglʌɪ
AM ə'stræɡə,laɪ
astragalus
BR ə'stragələs,
ə'straɡləs
AM ə'stræɡələs
astrakhan
BR ,astrə'kan
AM 'astrə,kan,
'æstrə,kæn
astral
BR 'astr(ə)l
AM 'æstrəl
astrally
BR 'astrəli, 'astr̩li
AM 'æstrəli
astrantia
BR ə'strantɪə(r)
AM ə'stræn(t)ɪə
astray
BR ə'streɪ
AM ə'streɪ
Astrid
BR 'astrɪd
AM 'æstrəd
astride
BR ə'strʌɪd
AM ə'straɪd
astringency
BR ə'strɪn(d)ʒ(ə)nsi
AM ə'strɪndʒənsi
astringent
BR ə'strɪn(d)ʒ(ə)nt, -s
AM ə'strɪndʒənt, -s
astringently
BR ə'strɪn(d)ʒ(ə)ntli
AM ə'strɪndʒən(t)li
astrobiology
BR ,astrəʊbʌɪ'ɒlədʒi
AM ,æstroʊ,baɪ'ɑlədʒi
astrobotany
BR ,astrəʊ'bɒtəni,
,astrəʊ'bɒtn̩i
AM ,æstroʊ'batn̩i
astrochemistry
BR ,astrəʊ'kɛmɪstri
AM ,æstroʊ'kɛməstri
astrodome
BR 'astrə(ʊ)dəʊm, -z

AM 'æstrə,doʊm, -z
astrohatch
BR 'astrə(ʊ)hatʃ, -ɪz
AM 'æstrə,hætʃ,
'æstroʊ,hætʃ, -əz
astrolabe
BR 'astrə(ʊ)leɪb, -z
AM 'æstrə,leɪb,
'æstrə,læb, -z
astrologer
BR ə'strɒlədʒə(r), -z
AM ə'strɑlədʒər, -z
astrologic
BR ,astrə'lɒdʒɪk
AM ,æstrə'lɑdʒɪk
astrological
BR ,astrə'lɒdʒɪkl
AM ,æstrə'lɑdʒəkəl
astrologically
BR ,astrə'lɒdʒɪkli
AM ,æstrə'lɑdʒək(ə)li
astrology
BR ə'strɒlədʒi
AM ə'strɑlədʒi
åstrom
BR 'ɔːstrəm, 'ɑːstrəm,
-z
AM 'ɒstrəm, 'astrəm, -z
astronaut
BR 'astrənɔːt, -s
AM 'æstrə,nɒt,
'æstrə,nɑt, -s
astronautical
BR ,astrə'nɔːtɪkl
AM ,æstrə'nɒdəkəl,
,æstrə'nɑdəkəl
astronautically
BR ,astrə'nɔːtɪkli
AM ,æstrə'nɒdək(ə)li,
,æstrə'nɑdək(ə)li
astronautics
BR ,astrə'nɔːtɪks
AM ,æstrə'nɑdɪks
astronomer
BR ə'strɒnəmə(r), -z
AM ə'strɑnəmər, -z
astronomic
BR ,astrə'nɒmɪk
AM ,æstrə'namɪk
astronomical
BR ,astrə'nɒmɪkl
AM ,æstrə'naməkəl
astronomically
BR ,astrə'nɒmɪkli
AM ,æstrə'namək(ə)li
astronomy
BR ə'strɒnəmi
AM ə'strɑnəmi
astrophysical
BR ,astrəʊ'fɪzɪkl
AM ,æstroʊ'fɪzəkəl
astrophysicist
BR ,astrəʊ'fɪzɪsɪst, -s
AM ,æstroʊ'fɪzəsəst, -s
astrophysics
BR ,astrəʊ'fɪzɪks
AM 'æstroʊ'fɪzɪks

Astroturf®
BR 'astrəʊtəːf
AM 'æstrə,tɝf,
'æstroʊ,tɝf
Asturias
BR a'st(j)ʊərɪas,
ə'st(j)ʊərɪas,
a'st(j)ʊərɪas,
ə'st(j)ʊərɪəs
AM æ'st(j)ʊərɪəs,
ə'st(j)ʊərɪəs
astute
BR ə'stjuːt, ə'stʃuːt,
-ə(r), -ɪst
AM ə'st(j)u|t, -dər,
-dəst
astutely
BR ə'stjuːtli, ə'stʃuːtli
AM ə'st(j)utli
astuteness
BR ə'stjuːtnəs,
ə'stʃuːtnəs
AM ə'st(j)utnəs
Astyanax
BR a'stʌɪənaks,
ə'stʌɪənaks
AM ə'staɪə,næks
Asunción
BR a,sʊn(t)sɪ'ɒn
AM æ,sʊn(t)si'ɑn,
æ,sʊn(t)si'ɔn
SP asun'θjon,
asun'sjon
asunder
BR ə'sʌndə(r)
AM ə'səndər
Asur
BR 'asə(r)
AM 'æsər
Aswad
BR 'azwɒd, 'aswɒd
AM 'æswɑd
Aswan
BR ,as'wɑːn, ,as'wan,
'aswɑːn, 'aswan
AM 'æz|wɑn
asylum
BR ə'sʌɪləm, -z
AM ə'saɪləm, -z
asymmetric
BR ,eɪsɪ'mɛtrɪk,
,asɪ'mɛtrɪk
AM ,eɪsə'mɛtrɪk
asymmetrical
BR ,eɪsɪ'mɛtrɪkl,
,asɪ'mɛtrɪkl
AM ,eɪsə'mɛtrəkəl
asymmetrically
BR ,eɪsɪ'mɛtrɪkli,
,asɪ'mɛtrɪkli
AM ,eɪsə'mɛtrək(ə)li
asymmetry
BR eɪ'sɪmɪtri
AM eɪ'sɪmətri
asymptomatic
BR ,eɪsɪm(p)tə'matɪk
AM ,eɪ,sɪm(p)tə'mædɪk

asymptote
BR 'asɪm(p)təʊt, -s
AM 'æsəm(p),toʊt, -s
asymptotic
BR ,asɪm'tɒtɪk
AM ,æsəm(p)'tɑdɪk
asymptotically
BR ,asɪm'tɒtɪkli
AM ,æsəm(p)'tɑdək(ə)li
asynchronous
BR eɪ'sɪŋkrənəs
AM eɪ'sɪŋkrənəs
asynchronously
BR eɪ'sɪŋkrənəsli
AM eɪ'sɪŋkrənəsli
asyndetic
BR ,asɪn'dɛtɪk,
,eɪsɪn'dɛtɪk
AM ,æsn'dɛdɪk
asyndeton
BR ə'sɪndɪt(ə)n
AM ə'sɪndə,tan,
eɪ'sɪndə,tan
at¹
strong form
BR at
AM æt
at²
weak form
BR ət
AM ət
Atabrine®
BR 'atəbriːn, 'atəbrɪn
AM 'ædəbrən,
'ædə,brin
Atacama
BR ,atə'kɑːmə(r)
AM ,adə'kɑmə
Atack
BR 'eɪtak
AM 'eɪtæk
Atahualpa
BR ,atə'(h)wɑːlpə(r),
,atə'(h)walpə(r)
AM ,atə'(h)wɑlpə
Atalanta
BR ,atə'lantə(r)
AM ,ædə'læn(t)ə
ataractic
BR ,atər'aktɪk
AM ,ædə'ræktɪk
ataraxia
BR ,atər'aksɪə(r)
AM ,ædə'ræksɪə
ataraxic
BR ,atər'aksɪk
AM ,ædə'ræksɪk
ataraxy
BR ,atəraksi
AM ,ædə,ræksi
Atari®
BR ə'tɑːri
AM ɑ'tɑri
Atatürk
BR 'atətəːk
AM 'ædə,tɝk
TU ʌtʌ'tyrk

atavism
BR 'atəvɪz(ə)m
AM 'ædə,vɪzəm
atavistic
BR ,atə'vɪstɪk
AM ,ædə'vɪstɪk
atavistically
BR ,atə'vɪstɪkli
AM ,ædə'vɪstək(ə)li
ataxia
BR ə'taksɪə(r),
a'taksɪə(r)
AM ə'tæksɪə, eɪ'tæksɪə
ataxic
BR ə'taksɪk, -s
AM ə'tæksɪk, -s
ataxy
BR ə'taksi
AM ə'tæksi
Atchison
BR 'atʃɪs(ə)n
AM 'ætʃɪsən
atchoo
BR ə'tʃuː
AM ə'tʃu
Atco®
BR 'atkəʊ
AM 'ætkoʊ
ate
BR ɛt, eɪt
AM eɪt
Atebrin®
BR 'atɪbriːn, 'atɪbrɪn
AM 'ædəbrən,
'ædə,brin
atelier
BR ə'tɛlɪeɪ, -z
AM ,ædl'jeɪ, ə'tɛl,jeɪ, -z
a tempo
BR ,ɑː 'tɛmpəʊ
AM ,ɑ 'tɛmpoʊ
atemporal
BR eɪ'tɛmp(ə)rəl,
eɪ'tɛmp(ə)rl̩
AM eɪ,tɛm'pɔrəl,
eɪ'tɛmp(ə)rəl
Aten
BR 'ɑːt(ə)n
AM 'ɑtn
Athabasca
BR ,aθə'baskə(r)
AM ,æθə'bæskə
Athabascan
BR ,aθə'bask(ə)n, -z
AM ,æθə'bæskən, -z
Athanasian
BR ,aθə'neɪʃn,
,aθə'neɪʒn,
,aθə'neɪsɪən,
,aθə'neɪzɪən
AM ,æθə'neɪʒən
Athanasius
BR ,aθə'neɪʃəs,
,aθə'neɪʒəs,
,aθə'neɪsɪəs,
,aθə'neɪzɪəs
AM ,æθə'neɪʃ(i)əs,
,æθə'neɪʒ(i)əs

Athapaskan
BR ,aθə'pask(ə)n, -z
AM ,æθə'pæskən, -z
atheism
BR 'eɪθɪɪz(ə)m
AM 'eɪθi,ɪzəm
atheist
BR 'eɪθɪɪst, -s
AM 'eɪθiɪst, -s
atheistic
BR ,eɪθɪ'ɪstɪk
AM ,eɪθi'ɪstɪk
atheistical
BR ,eɪθɪ'ɪstɪkl
AM ,eɪθi'ɪstɪkəl
atheistically
BR ,eɪθɪ'ɪstɪkli
AM ,eɪθi'ɪstɪk(ə)li
atheling
BR 'aθəlɪŋ, 'aθl̩ɪŋ, -z
AM 'æθ(ə)lɪŋ, -z
Athelstan
BR 'aθəlst(ə)n,
'aθlst(ə)n, 'aθəlstan,
'aθl̩stan
AM 'æθəl,stæn
athematic
BR ,aθiː'matɪk,
,eɪθiː'matɪk,
,aθɪ'matɪk,
,eɪθɪ'matɪk
AM ,æθi'mædɪk,
,eɪθi'mædɪk
Athena
BR ə'θiːnə(r)
AM ə'θinə
athenaeum
BR ,aθɪ'niːəm, -z
AM ,æθə'niəm, -z
Athene
BR ə'θiːni
AM ə'θini
atheneum
BR ,aθɪ'niːəm, -z
AM ,æθə'niəm, -z
Athenian
BR ə'θiːnɪən, -z
AM ə'θiniən, -z
Athens
BR 'aθ(ɪ)nz
AM 'æθənz
atheoretical
BR ,eɪθɪə'rɛtɪkl
AM eɪ,θiə'rɛdəkəl
atheroma
BR ,aθə'rəʊmə(r), -z
AM ,æθə'roʊmə, -z
atheromata
BR ,aθə'rəʊmətə(r)
AM ,æθə'roʊmədə
atheroscleroses
BR ,aθ(ə)rəʊsklɪ'rəʊ-
siːz,
,aθ(ə)rəʊsklɛ'rəʊsiːz
AM ,æθə,rəʊsklə'roʊsiz
atherosclerosis
BR ,aθ(ə)rəʊsklɪ'rəʊsɪs,
,aθ(ə)rəʊsklɛ'rəʊsɪs

AM ,æθə,rəʊsklə'roʊsəs
atherosclerotic
BR ,aθ(ə)rəʊsklɪ'rɒtɪk
AM ,æθə,rəʊsklə'rɑdɪk
Atherstone
BR 'aθəst(ə)n
AM 'æðər,stoʊn
Atherton
BR 'aθət(ə)n
AM 'æðərt(ə)n
athetosis
BR ,aθɪ'təʊsɪs
AM ,æθə'toʊsɪs
athirst
BR ə'θəːst
AM ə'θərst
athlete
BR 'aθliːt, -s
AM 'æθ(ə),lit, -s
athletic
BR aθ'lɛtɪk, əθ'lɛtɪk
AM æθ(ə)'lɛdɪk
athletically
BR aθ'lɛtɪkli, əθ'lɛtɪkli
AM æθ(ə)'lɛdək(ə)li
athleticism
BR aθ'lɛtɪsɪz(ə)m,
əθ'lɛtɪsɪz(ə)m
AM æθ(ə)'lɛdə,sɪzəm
Athlone
BR (,)aθ'ləʊn
AM 'æθloʊn
Athol
BR 'aθɒl
AM 'æθɒl, 'æθɑl
Atholl
BR 'aθ(ɒ)l
AM 'æθɒl, 'æθɑl
Athos
BR 'aθɒs, 'eɪθɒs
AM 'aθ,ɑs, 'eɪ,θɑs
athwart
BR ə'θwɔːt
AM ə'θwɔ(ə)rt
atilt
BR ə'tɪlt
AM ə'tɪlt
atingle
BR ə'tɪŋgl
AM ə'tɪŋgəl
atishoo
BR ə'tɪʃuː
AM ə'tɪʃu
Ativan®
BR 'atɪvan
AM 'ædɪvæn
Atkin
BR 'atkɪn
AM 'ætkɪn
Atkins
BR 'atkɪnz
AM 'ætkɪnz
Atkinson
BR 'atkɪns(ə)n
AM 'ætkɪnsən
Atlanta
BR ət'lantə(r)

AM ə(t)'læn(t)ə
Atlantean
BR ət'lantɪən, -z
AM ,æt'læn(t)iən, -z
atlantes
BR ət'lantiːz
AM ət'læntiz,
æt'læntiz
Atlantic
BR ət'lantɪk
AM ət'læn(t)ɪk
Atlanticism
BR ət'lantɪsɪz(ə)m
AM ət'læn(t)ə,sɪzəm
Atlanticist
BR ət'lantɪsɪst, -s
AM ət'læn(t)əsəst, -s
Atlantis
BR ət'lantɪs, at'lantɪs
AM ət'læn(t)əs
atlantosaurus
BR ət,lantə'sɔːrəs, -ɪz
AM ət,læn(t)ə'sɔrəs,
-əz
atlas
BR 'atləs, -ɪz
AM 'ætləs, -əz
atman
BR 'ɑːtmən
AM 'ɑtmən
atmosphere
BR 'atməsfɪə(r), -z
AM 'ætmə,sfɪ(ə)r, -z
atmospheric
BR ,atməs'fɛrɪk, -s
AM ,ætmə'sfɪrɪk, -s
atmospherical
BR ,atməs'fɛrɪkl
AM ,ætmə'sfɪrɪkəl
atmospherically
BR ,atməs'fɛrɪkli
AM ,ætmə'sfɪrɪk(ə)li
atoll
BR 'atɒl, -z
AM 'æ,tɒl, 'æ,tɑl, -z
atom
BR 'atəm, -z
AM 'ædəm, -z
atomic
BR ə'tɒmɪk
AM ə'tɑmɪk
atomically
BR ə'tɒmɪkli
AM ə'tɑmək(ə)li
atomicity
BR ,atə'mɪsɪti
AM ,ædə'mɪsɪdi
atomisation
BR ,atəmʌɪ'zeɪʃn
AM ,ædəmə'zeɪʃən,
,ædə,maɪ'zeɪʃən
atomise
BR 'atəmʌɪz, -ɪz, -ɪŋ, -d
AM 'ædə,maɪz, -ɪz, -ɪŋ,
-d
atomiser
BR 'atəmʌɪzə(r), -z

AM 'ædə,maɪzər, -z
atomism
BR 'atəmɪz(ə)m
AM 'ædə,mɪzəm
atomist
BR 'atəmɪst, -s
AM 'ædəməst, -s
atomistic
BR ,atə'mɪstɪk
AM ,ædə'mɪstɪk
atomistically
BR ,atə'mɪstɪkli
AM ,ædə'mɪstɪk(ə)li
atomization
BR ,atəmaɪ'zeɪʃn
AM ,ædəmə'zeɪʃən,
,ædə,maɪ'zeɪʃən
atomize
BR 'atəmaɪz, -ɪz, -ɪŋ, -d
AM 'ædə,maɪz, -ɪz, -ɪŋ,
-d
atomizer
BR 'atəmaɪzə(r), -z
AM 'ædə,maɪzər, -z
atomy
BR 'atəm|i, -ɪz
AM 'ædəmi, -z
atonal
BR (,)eɪ'təʊnl
AM eɪ'toʊnəl, æ'toʊnəl
atonality
BR ,eɪtə(ʊ)'nalɪti
AM ,eɪtoʊ'næcədi,
,ætoʊ'næcədi
atonally
BR (,)eɪ'təʊnḷi,
(,)eɪ'təʊnəli
AM eɪ'toʊnəli
atone
BR ə'təʊn, -z, -ɪŋ, -d
AM ə'toʊn, -z, -ɪŋ, -d
atonement
BR ə'təʊnm(ə)nt, -s
AM ə'toʊnmənt, -s
atonic
BR (,)eɪ'tɒnɪk
AM eɪ'tɑnɪk
atony
BR 'atəni
AM 'ætn̩i
atop
BR ə'tɒp
AM ə'tɑp
Atora®
BR ə'tɔːrə(r)
AM ə'tɔrə
atrabilious
BR ,atrə'bɪliəs
AM ,ætrə'bɪliəs
atrabiliousness
BR ,atrə'bɪliəsnəs
AM ,ætrə'bɪliəsnəs
Atreus
BR 'eɪtriəs, 'eɪtrɪuːs
AM 'eɪtriəs
atria
BR 'eɪtriə(r)

AM 'eɪtriə
atrial
BR 'eɪtrɪəl
AM 'eɪtrɪəl
atrium
BR 'eɪtriəm, -z
AM 'eɪtriəm, -z
atrocious
BR ə'trəʊʃəs
AM ə'troʊʃəs
atrociously
BR ə'trəʊʃəsli
AM ə'troʊʃəsli
atrociousness
BR ə'trəʊʃəsnəs
AM ə'troʊʃəsnəs
atrocity
BR ə'trɒsɪt|i, -ɪz
AM ə'trɑsədi, -z
atrophic
BR ə'trɒfɪk, (,)eɪ'trɒfɪk
AM ə'trɑfɪk
atrophy
BR 'atrəf|i, -ɪz, -ɪŋ, -ɪd
AM 'ætrəfi, -z, -ɪŋ, -d
atropine
BR 'atrəpiːn, 'atrəpɪn
AM 'ætrə,pin
Atropos
BR 'atrəpɒs, 'atrəpəs
AM 'ætrə,pɑs,
'ætrə,pəs, 'ætrə,pɑs
attaboy
BR 'atəbɔɪ
AM ,ædə'bɔɪ
attach
BR ə'tatʃ, -ɪz, -ɪŋ, -t
AM ə'tætʃ, -əz, -ɪŋ, -t
attachable
BR ə'tatʃəbl
AM ə'tætʃəbəl
attaché
BR ə'taʃeɪ, -z
AM ,ædə'ʃeɪ, æ,tæ'ʃeɪ,
-z
attacher
BR ə'tatʃə(r), -z
AM ə'tætʃər, -z
attachment
BR ə'tatʃm(ə)nt, -s
AM ə'tætʃmənt, -s
attack
BR ə'tak, -s, -ɪŋ, -t
AM ə'tæk, -s, -ɪŋ, -t
attacker
BR ə'takə(r), -z
AM ə'tækər, -z
attain
BR ə'teɪn, -z, -ɪŋ, -d
AM ə'teɪn, -z, -ɪŋ, -d
attainability
BR ə,teɪnə'bɪlɪti
AM ə,teɪnə'bɪlɪdi
attainable
BR ə'teɪnəbl
AM ə'teɪnəbəl

attainableness
BR ə'teɪnəblnəs
AM ə'teɪnəbəlnəs
attainder
BR ə'teɪndə(r), -z
AM ə'teɪndər, -z
attainment
BR ə'teɪnm(ə)nt, -s
AM ə'teɪnmənt, -s
attaint
BR ə'teɪnt, -s, -ɪŋ, -ɪd
AM ə'teɪn|t, -ts, -(t)ɪŋ,
-(t)ɪd
Attalid
BR 'atəlɪd, -z
AM 'ædl̩,ɪd, -z
attar
BR 'atə(r), 'ataː(r)
AM 'ædər, 'æ,tɑr
attemper
BR ə'tɛmp|ə(r), -əz,
-(ə)rɪŋ, -əd
AM ə'tɛmp|ər, -ərz,
-(ə)rɪŋ, -ərd
attempt
BR ə'tɛm(p)t, -s, -ɪŋ, -ɪd
AM ə'tɛm(p)t, -s, -ɪŋ, -əd
attemptable
BR ə'tɛm(p)təbl
AM ə'tɛm(p)təbəl
Attenborough
BR 'atnb(ə)rə(r)
AM 'ætn̩,bərə
attend
BR ə'tɛnd, -z, -ɪŋ, -ɪd
AM ə'tɛnd, -z, -ɪŋ, -əd
attendance
BR ə'tɛnd(ə)ns, -ɪz
AM ə'tɛnd(ə)ns, -əz
attendant
BR ə'tɛnd(ə)nt, -s
AM ə'tɛnd(ə)nt, -s
attendee
BR ə,tɛn'diː, ,atɛn'diː,
-z
AM ə,tɛn'di, ,ætɛn'di, -z
attender
BR ə'tɛndə(r), -z
AM ə'tɛndər, -z
attention
BR ə'tɛnʃn, -z
AM ə'tɛn(t)ʃən, -z
attentional
BR ə'tɛnʃn̩(ə)l,
ə'tɛnʃən(ə)l
AM ə'tɛn(t)ʃ(ə)nəl
attentive
BR ə'tɛntɪv
AM ə'tɛn(t)ɪv
attentively
BR ə'tɛntɪvli
AM ə'tɛn(t)ɪvli
attentiveness
BR ə'tɛntɪvnɪs
AM ə'tɛn(t)ɪvnɪs

attenuate¹
adjective
BR ə'tɛnjʊət
AM ə'tɛnjəwət
attenuate²
verb
BR ə'tɛnjʊeɪt, -s, -ɪŋ, -ɪd
AM ə'tɛnjə,weɪ|t, -ts,
-dɪŋ, -dɪd
attenuation
BR ə,tɛnjʊ'eɪʃn
AM ə,tɛnjə'weɪʃən
attenuator
BR ə'tɛnjʊeɪtə(r), -z
AM ə'tɛnjə,weɪdər, -z
attest
BR ə'tɛst, -s, -ɪŋ, -ɪd
AM ə'tɛst, -s, -ɪŋ, -əd
attestable
BR ə'tɛstəbl
AM ə'tɛstəbəl
attestation
BR ,atɛ'steɪʃn,
,atə'steɪʃn, -z
AM ,æ,tɛ'steɪʃən,
,ædə'steɪʃən, -z
attestor
BR ə'tɛstə(r), -z
AM ə'tɛstər, -z
attic
BR 'atɪk, -s
AM 'ædɪk, -s
Attica
BR 'atɪkə(r)
AM 'ædəkə
Atticism
BR 'atɪsɪz(ə)m, -z
AM 'ædə,sɪzəm, -z
Attila
BR ə'tɪlə(r)
AM ə'tɪlə
attire
BR ə'tʌɪə(r), -z, -ɪŋ, -d
AM ə'taɪ(ə)r, -z, -ɪŋ, -d
Attis
BR 'atɪs
AM 'ædəs
attitude
BR 'atɪtjuːd, 'atɪtʃuːd,
-z
AM 'ædə,t(j)ud, -z
attitudinal
BR ,atɪ'tjuːdɪnl,
,atɪ'tʃuːdɪnl
AM ,ædə't(j)udn̩əl
attitudinise
BR ,atɪ'tjuːdɪnʌɪz,
,atɪ'tʃuːdɪnʌɪz, -ɪz, -ɪŋ,
-d
AM ,ædə't(j)udn̩,aɪz,
-ɪz, -ɪŋ, -d
attitudinize
BR ,atɪ'tjuːdɪnʌɪz,
,atɪ'tʃuːdɪnʌɪz, -ɪz, -ɪŋ,
-d
AM ,ædə't(j)udn̩,aɪz,
-ɪz, -ɪŋ, -d

Attlee
BR 'atli
AM 'ætli
attorney
BR ə'tɜːn|i, -ɪz
AM ə'tɜrni, -z
attorneyship
BR ə'tɜːnɪʃɪp, -s
AM ə'tɜrni‚ʃɪp, -s
attract
BR ə'trakt, -s, -ɪŋ, -ɪd
AM ə'træk(t), -(t)s, -tɪŋ, -təd
attractability
BR ə‚traktə'bɪlɪti
AM ə‚træktə'bɪlɪdi
attractable
BR ə'traktəbl
AM ə'træktəbəl
attractant
BR ə'trakt(ə)nt, -s
AM ə'træktnt, -s
attraction
BR ə'trakʃn, -z
AM ə'trækʃən, -z
attractive
BR ə'traktɪv
AM ə'træktɪv
attractively
BR ə'traktɪvli
AM ə'træktɪvli
attractiveness
BR ə'traktɪvnɪs
AM ə'træktɪvnɪs
attractor
BR ə'traktə(r), -z
AM ə'træktər, -z
attributable
BR ə'trɪbjʊtəbl
AM ə'trɪbjədəbəl
attributableness
BR ə'trɪbjʊtəblnəs
AM ə'trɪbjədəbəlnəs
attributably
BR ə'trɪbjʊtəbli
AM ə'trɪbjədəbli
attribute¹
noun
BR 'atrɪbjuːt, -s
AM 'ætrə‚bjut, -s
attribute²
verb
BR ə'trɪbj|uːt, -uːts, -ʊtɪŋ, -ʊtɪd
AM ə'trɪbj|ət, ə'trɪ‚bj|ut, -əts \ -uts, -ədɪŋ, -ədəd
attribution
BR ‚atrɪ'bjuːʃn, -z
AM ‚ætrə'bjuʃən, -z
attributive
BR ə'trɪbjʊtɪv
AM ə'trɪbjədɪv
attributively
BR ə'trɪbjʊtɪvli
AM ə'trɪbjədɪvli

attrition
BR ə'trɪʃn
AM ə'trɪʃən
attritional
BR ə'trɪʃn̩(ə)l,
ə'trɪʃən(ə)l
AM ə'trɪʃ(ə)nəl
attune
BR ə'tjuːn, ə'tʃuːn, -z, -ɪŋ, -d
AM ə't(j)un, -z, -ɪŋ, -d
Atwell
BR 'atwɛl
AM 'ætwɛl
atwitter
BR ə'twɪtə(r)
AM ə'twɪdər
Atwood
BR 'atwʊd
AM 'æt‚wʊd
atypical
BR (‚)eɪ'tɪpɪkl
AM ‚eɪ'tɪpɪkəl
atypically
BR (‚)eɪ'tɪpɪkli
AM ‚eɪ'tɪpɪk(ə)li
aubade
BR əʊ'bɑːd, -z
AM oʊ'bɑd, -z
auberge
BR əʊ'bɛːʒ, 'əʊbɛːʒ, -ɪz
AM oʊ'bɛrʒ, -ɪz
aubergine
BR 'əʊbəʒiːn, -z
AM 'oʊbər‚ʒin, -z
Auberon
BR 'ɔːb(ə)rən, 'ɔːb(ə)rɒn, 'ɔːb(ə)rɒn, 'əʊb(ə)rən, 'əʊb(ə)rɒn, 'əʊb(ə)rɒn
AM 'oʊbə‚rɑn
Aubrey
BR 'ɔːbri
AM 'ɔbri, 'ɑbri
aubrietia
BR ɔː'briːʃə(r), -z
AM ɔ'briʃ(i)ə, ɑ'briʃ(i)ə, -z
auburn
BR 'ɔːbən
AM 'ɔbərn, 'ɑbərn
Aubusson
BR 'əʊbjʊsɒn, -z
AM 'oʊbə‚sɒn, 'oʊbə‚san, -z
FR obysɔ̃
Auchinleck
BR 'ɔːk(ɪ)nlɛk
AM 'ɔkɪn‚lɛk, 'æflək, 'ɑkɪn‚lɛk
Auchtermuchty
BR ‚ɒxtə'mʊxti, ‚ɒktə'mʌkti, ‚ɔːktə'mʌkti
AM 'ɔktər‚məkti, 'ɑktər‚məkti
Auckland
BR 'ɔːkland
AM 'ɔːklənd

AM 'ɒklənd, 'ɑklənd
au contraire
BR ‚əʊ kɒn'trɛː(r)
AM ‚oʊ ‚kɑn'trɛ(ə)r
au courant
BR ‚əʊ kʊ'rɒ̃
AM ‚oʊ 'kʊrant
auction
BR 'ɔːkʃ|n, 'ɒkʃ|n, -nz, -nɪŋ \ -ənɪŋ, -nd
AM 'ɔkʃən, 'ɑkʃən, -ənz, -(ə)nɪŋ, -ənd
auctioneer
BR ‚ɔːkʃə'nɪə(r), ‚ɒkʃə'nɪə(r), -z
AM ‚ɔkʃə'nɪ(ə)r, ‚ɑkʃə'nɪ(ə)r, -z
auctioneering
BR ‚ɔːkʃə'nɪərɪŋ, ‚ɒkʃə'nɪərɪŋ
AM ‚ɔkʃə'nɪrɪŋ, ‚ɑkʃə'nɪrɪŋ
auctorial
BR ɔː'ktɔːrɪəl
AM ɔk'tɔriəl, ɑk'tɔriəl
audacious
BR ɔː'deɪʃəs
AM ɔ'deɪʃəs, ɑ'deɪʃəs
audaciously
BR ɔː'deɪʃəsli
AM ɔ'deɪʃəsli, ɑ'deɪʃəsli
audaciousness
BR ɔː'deɪʃəsnəs
AM ɔ'deɪʃəsnəs, ɑ'deɪʃəsnəs
audacity
BR ɔː'dasɪti
AM ɔ'dæsədi, ɑ'dæsədi
Auden
BR 'ɔːdn
AM 'ɔdən, 'ɑdən
Audi®
BR 'aʊd|i, -ɪz
AM 'aʊdi, -z
audibility
BR ‚ɔːdɪ'bɪlɪti
AM ‚ɑdə'bɪlɪdi, ‚ɔdə'bɪlɪdi
audible
BR 'ɔːdɪbl
AM 'ɔdəbəl, 'ɑdəbəl
audibleness
BR 'ɔːdɪblnəs
AM 'ɔdəbəlnəs, 'ɑdəbəlnəs
audibly
BR 'ɔːdɪbli
AM 'ɔdəbli, 'ɑdəbli
Audie
BR 'ɔːdi
AM 'ɔdi, 'ɑdi
audience
BR 'ɔːdɪəns, -ɪz
AM 'ɔdiəns, 'ɑdiəns, -əz
audile
BR 'ɔːdʌɪl, -z
AM 'ɔ‚daɪl, 'ɑ‚daɪl, -z

audio
BR 'ɔːdɪəʊ, -z
AM 'ɔdioʊ, 'ɑdioʊ, -z
audiocassette
BR 'ɔːdɪəʊkə‚sɛt, -s
AM ‚ɔdioʊkə'sɛt, ‚adioʊkə'sɛt, -s
audiolingual
BR ‚ɔːdɪəʊ'lɪŋgw(ə)l
AM ‚ɔdioʊ'lɪŋgwəl, ‚adioʊ'lɪŋgwəl
audiological
BR ‚ɔːdɪə'lɒdʒɪkl
AM ‚ɔdiə'ladʒəkəl, ‚adiə'ladʒəkəl
audiologist
BR ‚ɔːdɪ'ɒlədʒɪst, -s
AM ‚ɔdi'alədʒəst, ‚adi'alədʒəst, -s
audiology
BR ‚ɔːdɪ'ɒlədʒi
AM ‚ɔdi'alədʒi, ‚adi'alədʒi
audiometer
BR ‚ɔːdɪ'ɒmɪtə(r), -z
AM ‚ɔdi'amədər, ‚adi'amədər, -z
audiometry
BR ‚ɔːdɪ'ɒmɪtri
AM ‚ɔdi'amətri, ‚adi'amətri
audiophile
BR 'ɔːdɪə(ʊ)fʌɪl, -z
AM 'ɔdioʊ‚faɪl, 'adioʊ‚faɪl, -z
audiotape
BR 'ɔːdɪəʊ‚teɪp, -s
AM 'ɔdioʊ‚teɪp, 'adioʊ‚teɪp, -s
audiotyping
BR 'ɔːdɪəʊ‚taɪpɪŋ
AM 'ɔdioʊ‚taɪpɪŋ, 'adioʊ‚taɪpɪŋ
audiotypist
BR 'ɔːdɪəʊ‚taɪpɪst, -s
AM 'ɔdioʊ‚taɪpɪst, 'adioʊ‚taɪpɪst, -s
audio-visual
BR ‚ɔːdɪəʊ'vɪʒʊ(ə)l, ‚ɔːdɪəʊ'vɪzjʊ(ə)l, ‚ɔːdɪəʊ'vɪʒ(ʊ)l, ‚ɔːdɪəʊ'vɪzj(ʊ)l
AM ‚ɔdioʊ'vɪʒ(ə)wəl, ‚ɑdioʊ'vɪʒəl, ‚adioʊ'vɪʒ(ə)wəl, ‚adioʊ'vɪʒəl
audit
BR ɔː'd|ɪt, -ɪts, -ɪtɪŋ, -ɪtɪd
AM 'ɔdə|t, 'ɑdə|t, -ts, -dɪŋ, -dəd
audition
BR ɔː'dɪʃ|n, -nz, -nɪŋ \ -ənɪŋ, -nd
AM ɔ'dɪʃ|ən, ɑ'dɪʃ|ən, -ənz, -(ə)nɪŋ, -ənd
auditive
BR 'ɔːdɪtɪv

AM 'ɔdədɪv, 'ɑdədɪv

auditor
BR 'ɔːdɪtə(r), -z
AM 'ɔdədər, 'ɑdədər, -z

auditoria
BR ˌɔːdɪ'tɔːrɪə(r)
AM ˌɔdə'tɔriə, ˌɑdə'tɔriə

auditorial
BR ˌɔːdɪ'tɔːrɪəl
AM ˌɔdə'tɔriəl, ˌɑdə'tɔriəl

auditorium
BR ˌɔːdɪ'tɔːrɪəm, -z
AM ˌɔdə'tɔriəm, ˌɑdə'tɔriəm, -z

auditory
BR 'ɔːdɪt(ə)ri
AM 'ɔdəˌtɔri, 'ɑdəˌtɔri

Audlem
BR 'ɔːdləm
AM 'ɔdləm, 'ɑdləm

Audley
BR 'ɔːdli
AM 'ɔdli, 'ɑdli

Audra
BR 'ɔːdrə(r)
AM 'ɔdrə, 'ɑdrə

Audrey
BR 'ɔːdri
AM 'ɔdri, 'ɑdri

Audubon
BR 'ɔːdəbɒn
AM 'ɔdəˌbɑn, 'ɑdəˌbɑn

au fait
BR ˌəʊ 'feɪ
AM ˌoʊ 'feɪ

au fond
BR ˌəʊ 'fɒ̃
AM ˌoʊ 'fɔnd

Augean
BR ɔː'dʒiːən
AM ɔ'dʒiən, ˌɔˌgiən, ɑ'dʒiən, 'ɑgiən

auger
BR 'ɔːgə(r), -z
AM 'ɔgər, 'ɑgər, -z

aught
BR ɔːt
AM ɔt, ɑt

augite
BR 'ɔːdʒaɪt
AM 'ɔˌdʒaɪt, 'ɔgaɪt, 'ɑˌdʒaɪt, 'ɑgaɪt

augment
BR ɔːg'mɛnt, -s, -ɪŋ, -ɪd
AM ɔg'mɛn|t, ɑg'mɛn|t, -ts, -(t)ɪŋ, -(t)əd

augmentation
BR ˌɔːgmɛn'teɪʃn, ˌɔːgm(ə)n'teɪʃn
AM ˌɔgmən'teɪʃən, ˌɔgˌmɛn'teɪʃən, ˌɑgmən'teɪʃən, ˌɑgˌmɛn'teɪʃən

augmentative
BR ɔːg'mɛntətɪv

AM ɔg'mɛn(t)ədɪv, ɑg'mɛn(t)ədɪv

augmenter
BR ɔːg'mɛntə(r), -z
AM ɔg'mɛn(t)ər, ɑg'mɛn(t)ər, -z

au grand sérieux
BR əʊ ˌgrɒ̃ ˌsɛrɪ'əː(z)
AM ˌoʊ ˌgrɑn ˌsɛri'ə

au gratin
BR əʊ 'gratã, + 'gratan
AM ˌoʊ 'grɑtn, + 'grætn

Augsburg
BR 'aʊgzbəːg
AM 'ɔgzbəːg, 'aʊgz,bəːg, 'ɑgz,bəːg
GER 'aʊksbʊrk

augur
BR 'ɔːgə(r), -z, -ɪŋ, -d
AM 'ɔgər, 'ɑgər, -z, -ɪŋ, -d

augural
BR 'ɔːgjʊrəl, 'ɔːgjʊr|
AM 'ɔg(j)ərəl, 'ɑg(j)ərəl

augury
BR 'ɔːgjʊr|i, -ɪz
AM 'ɔg(j)əri, 'ɑg(j)əri, -z

August[1]
forename
BR 'aʊgʊst
AM 'ɔgəst, 'ɑgəst

August[2]
month
BR 'ɔːgəst, -s
AM 'ɔgəst, 'ɑgəst, -s

august[1]
adjective
BR ɔː'gʌst, -ɪst
AM ɔ'gəst, ɑ'gəst, -əst

august[2]
clown
BR 'aʊgʊst, -s
AM 'ɔgəst, 'ɑgəst, -s

Augusta
BR ɔː'gʌstə(r), ə'gʌstə(r)
AM ə'gəstə

Augustan
BR ə'gʌst(ə)n, ɔː'gʌst(ə)n, -z
AM ɔ'gəstən, ə'gəstən, ɑ'gəstən, -z

Augustine
BR 'ɔːgəstiːn, 'ɔːgəstʌɪn, -z
AM 'ɔgə,stin, 'ɑgə,stin, ə'gəstən, -z

Augustinian
BR ˌɔːgə'stɪnɪən, -z
AM ˌɔgə'stɪniən, ˌɑgə'stɪniən, -z

augustly
BR ɔː'gʌstli
AM ɔ'gəs(t)li, ɑ'gəs(t)li

augustness
BR ɔː'gʌs(t)nəs

AM ɔː'gəs(t)nəs, ɑ'gəs(t)nəs

Augustus
BR ɔː'gʌstəs, ə'gʌstəs
AM ə'gəstəs

au jus
BR əʊ 'ʒuː(s)
AM oʊ 'ʒu(s)

auk
BR ɔːk, -s
AM ɔk, ɑk, -s

auklet
BR 'ɔːklɪt, -s
AM 'ɔklət, 'ɑklət, -s

auld lang syne
BR ˌɔːld laŋ 'zʌɪn, ˌəʊld +, + 'sʌɪn
AM ˌoʊ(l) ˌlæŋ 'zaɪn, ˌoʊl ˌdlæŋ +

aulic
BR 'ɔːlɪk
AM 'ɔlɪk, 'ɑlɪk

aumbry
BR 'ɔːmbr|i, -ɪz
AM 'ɔmbri, 'ɑmbri, -z

au naturel
BR əʊ ˌnatʃə'rɛl, + ˌnatjə'rɛl
AM ˌoʊ ˌnætʃə'rɛl

aunt
BR ɑːnt, -s
AM ænt, -s

auntie
BR 'ɑːnt|i, -ɪz
AM 'æn(t)i, -z

aunty
BR 'ɑːnt|i, -ɪz
AM 'æn(t)i, -z

au pair
BR ˌəʊ 'pɛː(r), -z
AM ˌoʊ 'pɛ(ə)r, -z

aura
BR 'ɔːrə(r), -z
AM 'ɔrə, -z

aural
BR 'ɔːrl, 'ɔːrəl
AM 'ɔrəl

aurally
BR 'ɔːr|i, 'ɔːrəli
AM 'ɔrəli

Aurangzeb
BR ˌɔːraŋ'zɛb
AM ˌɔˌræŋ'zɛb, ɑˌræŋ'zɛb

aureate
BR 'ɔːreɪt, 'ɔːriət
AM 'ɔriət, 'ɔri,eɪt

Aurelia
BR ɔː'riːlɪə(r)
AM ɔ'riliə, ɑ'riliə, ɔ'rɪljə, ɑ'rɪljə

Aurelian[1]
BR ɔː'riːlɪən
AM ɔ'riliən

Aurelian[2]
BR ɔː'riːlɪən

AM ɔ'rilɪən, ɑ'rilɪən, ɔ'rɪljən, ɑ'rɪljən

Aurelius
BR ɔː'riːlɪəs
AM ɔ'rilɪəs, ɑ'rilɪəs

aureola
BR ɔː'riːələ(r), ˌɔːrɪ'əʊlə(r), -z
AM ɔ'riələ, ɑ'riələ, -z

aureole
BR 'ɔːrɪəʊl, -z
AM 'ɔri,oʊl, -z

aureomycin
BR ˌɔːrɪə(ʊ)'mʌɪsɪn
AM ˌɔrioʊ'maɪsɪn

au revoir
BR ˌəʊ rɪ'vwɑː(r), ˌɔː +
AM ˌɔ rə'vwɑr, ˌoʊ +

auric
BR 'ɔːrɪk
AM 'ɔrɪk

auricle
BR 'ɔːrɪkl, 'ɒrɪkl, -z
AM 'ɔrəkəl, -z

auricula
BR ɔː'rɪkjələ(r), -z
AM ɔ'rɪkjələ, ɑ'rɪkjələ, -z

auricular
BR ɔː'rɪkjələ(r)
AM ɔ'rɪkjələr, ɑ'rɪkjələr

auricularly
BR ɔː'rɪkjələli
AM ɔ'rɪkjələrli, ɑ'rɪkjələrli

auriculate[1]
adjective
BR ɔː'rɪkjələt
AM ɔ'rɪkjələt, ɑ'rɪkjələt

auriculate[2]
verb
BR ɔː'rɪkjəleɪt, -s, -ɪŋ, -ɪd
AM ɔ'rɪkjə,leɪt, ɑ'rɪkjə,leɪt, -ts, -dɪŋ, -dɪd

auriferous
BR ɔː'rɪf(ə)rəs
AM ɔ'rɪfərəs, ɑ'rɪfərəs

Auriga
BR ɔː'rʌɪgə(r)
AM ɔ'raɪgə, ɑ'raɪgə

Aurignacian
BR ˌɔːrɪ'njeɪʃn, ˌɔːrɪg'neɪʃn, -z
AM ˌɔrə'gneɪʃən, -z

auriscope
BR 'ɔːrɪskəʊp, -s
AM 'ɔrə,skoʊp, -s

aurist
BR 'ɔːrɪst, -s
AM 'ɔrəst, -s

aurochs
BR 'ɔːrɒks
AM 'aʊ,rɑks, 'ɔ,rɑks, 'ɑ,raks

aurora
BR ə'rɔːrə(r),
ɔː'rɔːrə(r)
AM ə'rɔrə, ɔ'rɔrə,
α'rɔrə
aurora australis
BR ə,rɔːrə(r)ɔː'strɑːlɪs,
ɔː,rɔːrə(r)+,
+ ɔː'streɪlɪs,
+ ɒ'strɑːlɪs,
+ ɒ'streɪlɪs
AM ə'rɔrə ɔ'streɪlɪs,
ɔ'rɔrə +, α'rɔrə +
aurora borealis
BR ə,rɔːrə ,bɔːrɪ'eɪlɪs,
ɔː,rɔːrə +,
+ ,bɔːrɪ'ɑːlɪs
AM ə'rɔrə ,bɔri'æləs,
ɔ'rɔrə +, α'rɔrə +
auroral
BR ə'rɔːrəl, ə'rɒːrl̩,
ɔː'rɔːrəl, ɔː'rɒːrl̩
AM ə'rɔrəl, ɔ'rɔrəl,
α'rɔrəl
Auschwitz
BR 'auʃwɪts, 'auʃvɪts
AM 'auʃwɪts, 'auʃvɪts
auscultate
BR 'ɔːsk(ə)lteɪt,
'ɔːskʌlteɪt, -s, -ɪŋ, -ɪd
AM 'ɔskəl,teɪ|t,
'αskəl,teɪ|t, -ts, -dɪŋ,
-dɪd
auscultation
BR ,ɔːsk(ə)l'teɪʃn,
,ɔːskʌl'teɪʃn, -z
AM ,ɔskəl'teɪʃən,
,αskəl'teɪʃən, -z
auscultatory
BR ɔː'skʌltət(ə)ri
AM ɔ'skʌltə,tɔri,
α'skʌltə,tɔri
au sérieux
BR ,əʊ sɛrɪ'əː(z)
AM ,oʊ ,sɛri'ə
auspicate
BR 'ɔːspɪkeɪt, -s, -ɪŋ, -ɪd
AM 'ɔspə,keɪ|t,
'αspə,keɪ|t, -ts, -dɪŋ,
-dɪd
auspice
BR 'ɔːsp|ɪs, -ɪsɪz\-ɪsiːz
AM 'ɔspəs, 'αspəs, -əz
auspicious
BR ɔː'spɪʃəs
AM ɔ'spɪʃəs, α'spɪʃəs
auspiciously
BR ɔː'spɪʃəsli
AM ɔ'spɪʃəsli,
α'spɪʃəsli
auspiciousness
BR ɔː'spɪʃəsnəs
AM ɔ'spɪʃəsnəs,
α'spɪʃəsnəs
Aussie
BR 'ɒz|i, -ɪz
AM 'ɔsi, 'αsi, -z

Aust
BR ɔːst
AM ɔst, αst
Austell
BR 'ɔːstl̩, 'ɒstl̩
AM 'ɒs'tɛl, ,αs'tɛl
Austen
BR 'ɒstɪn, 'ɔːstɪn
AM 'ɔstən, 'αstən
austere
BR ɔː'stɪə(r), ɒ'stɪə(r),
-ə(r), -ɪst
AM ɔː'stɪ(ə)r, α'stɪ(ə)r,
-ər, -ɪst
austerely
BR ɔː'stɪəli, ɒ'stɪəli
AM ɔ'stɪrli, α'stɪrli
austereness
BR ɔː'stɪənəs,
ɒ'stɪənəs
AM ɔ'stɪrnɪs, α'stɪrnɪs
austerity
BR ɔː'stɛrɪti, ɒ'stɛrɪt|i,
-ɪz
AM ɔ'stɛrədi,
α'stɛrədi, -z
Austerlitz
BR 'austəlɪts, 'ɔːstəlɪts
AM 'ɔstər,lɪts,
'austər,lɪts, 'αstər,lɪts
Austick
BR 'ɔːstɪk, 'ɒstɪk
AM 'ɔstɪk, 'αstɪk
Austin
BR 'ɒstɪn, 'ɔːstɪn
AM 'ɔstən, 'αstən
austral
BR 'ɔːstr(ə)l, 'ɒstr(ə)l
AM 'ɔstrəl, 'αstrəl
Australasia
BR ,ɒstrə'leɪʒə(r),
,ɒstrə'leɪʃə(r),
ɔː'strə'leɪʒə(r),
ɔː'strə'leɪʃə(r)
AM ,ɔstrə'leɪʒə,
,ɔstrə'leɪʃə,
,αstrə'leɪʒə,
,αstrə'leɪʃə
Australasian
BR ,ɒstrə'leɪʒn,
,ɒstrə'leɪʃn,
ɔː'strə'leɪʒn,
ɔː'strə'leɪʃn, -z
AM ,ɔstrə'leɪʒən,
,ɔstrə'leɪʃən,
,αstrə'leɪʒən,
,αstrə'leɪʃən, -z
Australia
BR ɒ'streɪlɪə(r),
ɔː'streɪlɪə(r),
ə'streɪlɪə(r)
AM ɔ'streɪljə,
ɔ'streɪliə, α'streɪljə,
α'streɪliə
Australian
BR ɒ'streɪlɪən,
ɔː'streɪlɪən, -z

AM ɔ'streɪljən,
ɔ'streɪliən,
α'streɪljən,
α'streɪliən, -z
Australianise
BR ɒ'streɪlɪənʌɪz,
ɔː'streɪlɪənʌɪz, -ɪz, -ɪŋ,
-d
AM ɔ'streɪljə,naɪz,
ɔ'streɪliə,naɪz,
α'streɪljə,naɪz,
α'streɪliə,naɪz, -ɪz, -ɪŋ,
-d
Australianism
BR ɒ'streɪlɪənɪz(ə)m,
ɔː'streɪlɪənɪz(ə)m, -z
AM ɔ'streɪljə,nɪzəm,
ɔ'streɪliə,nɪzəm,
α'streɪljə,nɪzəm,
α'streɪliə,nɪzəm, -z
Australianize
BR ɒ'streɪlɪənʌɪz,
ɔː'streɪlɪənʌɪz, -ɪz, -ɪŋ,
-d
AM ɔ'streɪljə,naɪz,
ɔ'streɪliə,naɪz,
α'streɪljə,naɪz,
α'streɪliə,naɪz, -ɪz, -ɪŋ,
-d
Australoid
BR 'ɒstrəlɔɪd,
'ɔːstrəlɔɪd, -z
AM 'ɔstrə,lɔɪd,
'αstrə,lɔɪd, -z
australopithecine
BR ,ɒstrələʊ'pɪθɪsiːn,
,ɒstrələʊ'pɪθɪsʌɪn,
,ɔːstrələʊ'pɪθɪsiːn,
,ɔːstrələʊ'pɪθɪsʌɪn, -z
AM ,ɔstrəloʊ'pɪθə,sin,
,αstrəloʊ'pɪθə,sin, -z
Australopithecus[1]
BR ,ɒstrələʊ'pɪθɪkəs,
,ɔːstrələʊ'pɪθɪkəs
AM ,ɔstrəloʊ'pɪθəkəs,
,αstrəʊ'pɪθəkəs
Australopithecus[2]
BR ,ɒstrələʊ'pɪθɪkəs,
,ɔːstrələʊ'pɪθɪkəs
AM ,ɔstrəloʊ'pɪθəkəs,
,αstrəloʊ'pɪθəkəs
Austria
BR 'ɒstrɪə(r),
'ɔːstrɪə(r)
AM 'ɔstriə, 'αstriə
Austrian
BR 'ɒstrɪən, 'ɔːstrɪən,
-z
AM 'ɔstriən, 'αstriən,
-z
Austro-
BR 'ɒstrəʊ, 'ɔːstrəʊ
AM 'ɔstroʊ, 'αstroʊ
Austronesian
BR ,ɒstrə'niːzj(ə)n,
,ɔːstrə'niːzj(ə)n,
,ɒstrə'niːʒn,
,ɔːstrə'niːʒn, -z

AM ,ɔstroʊ'niːʒən,
,ɔstroʊ'niːʃən,
,αstroʊ'niːʒən,
,αstroʊ'niːʃən, -z
Austyn
BR 'ɒstɪn, 'ɔːstɪn
AM 'ɔstən, 'αstən
autarchic
BR ɔː'tɑːkɪk
AM ɔ'tɑrkɪk, α'tɑrkɪk
autarchical
BR ɔː'tɑːkɪkl̩
AM ɔ'tɑrkəkəl,
α'tɑrkəkəl
autarchy
BR 'ɔːtɑːk|i, -ɪz
AM 'ɔ,tɑrki, 'α,tɑrki, -z
autarkic
BR ɔː'tɑːkɪk
AM ɔ'tɑrkɪk, α'tɑrkɪk
autarkical
BR ɔː'tɑːkɪkl̩
AM ɔ'tɑrkəkəl,
α'tɑrkəkəl
autarkist
BR ɔː'tɑːkɪst, -s
AM 'ɔ,tɑrkəst,
'α,tɑrkəst, -s
autarky
BR 'ɔːtɑːk|i, -ɪz
AM 'ɔ,tɑrki, 'α,tɑrki, -z
auteur
BR ɔː'təː(r), əʊ'təː(r), -z
AM oʊ'tər, ɔ'tər, α'tər,
-z
auteurism
BR ɔː'təːrɪz(ə)m,
əʊ'təːrɪz(ə)m
AM oʊ'tə,rɪzəm,
ɔ'tə,rɪzəm, α'tə,rɪzəm
auteurist
BR ɔː'təːrɪst, əʊ'təːrɪst
AM oʊ'tərəst, ɔ'tərəst,
α'tərəst
authentic
BR ɔː'θɛntɪk
AM ə'θɛn(t)ɪk,
ɔ'θɛn(t)ɪk, α'θɛn(t)ɪk
authentically
BR ɔː'θɛntɪkli
AM ə'θɛn(t)ək(ə)li,
ɔ'θɛn(t)ək(ə)li,
α'θɛn(t)ək(ə)li
authenticate
BR ɔː'θɛntɪkeɪt, -s, -ɪŋ,
-ɪd
AM ə'θɛn(t)ə,keɪ|t,
ɔ'θɛn(t)ə,keɪ|t,
α'θɛn(t)ə,keɪ|t , -ts,
-dɪŋ, -dɪd
authentication
BR ɔː,θɛntɪ'keɪʃn
AM ə,θɛn(t)ə'keɪʃən,
ɔ'θɛn(t)ə'keɪʃən,
α'θɛn(t)ə'keɪʃən
authenticator
BR ɔː'θɛntɪkeɪtə(r), -z

AM ə'θen(t)ə,keɪdər,
ɔ'θen(t)ə,keɪdər,
a'θen(t)ə,keɪdər, -z
authenticity
BR ,ɔ:θen'tɪsɪti
AM ,ɔ,θen'tɪsɪdi,
,ɔθən'tɪsɪdi,
,a,θen'tɪsɪdi,
,aθən'tɪsɪdi
author
BR 'ɔ:θə(r), -z, -ɪŋ, -d
AM 'ɔθər, 'aθər, -z, -ɪŋ,
-d
authoress
BR 'ɔ:θ(ə)rɪs, ,ɔ:θə'res,
-ɪz
AM 'ɔθ(ə)rəs, 'aθ(ə)rəs,
-əz
authorial
BR ɔ:'θɔ:rɪəl
AM ɔ'θɔriəl, a'θɔriəl
authorisation
BR ,ɔ:θ(ə)raɪ'zeɪʃn,
,ɔ:θ(ə)rɪ'zeɪʃn, -z
AM ,ɔθərə'zeɪʃən,
,ɔθə,raɪ'zeɪʃən,
,aθərə'zeɪʃən,
,aθə,raɪ'zeɪʃən, -z
authorise
BR 'ɔ:θəraɪz, -ɪz, -ɪŋ, -d
AM 'ɔθə,raɪz, 'aθə,raɪz,
-ɪz, -ɪŋ, -d
authoritarian
BR ɔ:,θɒrɪ'te:rɪən,
,ɔ:θɒrɪ'te:rɪən, -z
AM ə,θɔrə'teriən,
ə,θɔrə'teriən,
a,θɔrə'teriən, -z
authoritarianism
BR ɔ:,θɒrɪ'te:rɪənɪz(ə)m,
,ɔ:θɒrɪ'te:rɪənɪz(ə)m
AM ə,θɔrə'teriə,nɪzəm,
ə,θɔrə'teriə,nɪzəm,
a,θɔrə'teriə,nɪzəm
authoritative
BR ɔ:'θɒrɪtətɪv
AM ɔ'θɔrə,teɪdɪv,
ə'θɔrə,teɪdɪv,
a'θɔrə,teɪdɪv
authoritatively
BR ɔ:'θɒrɪtətɪvli
AM ɔ'θɔrə,teɪdɪvli,
ə'θɔrə,teɪdɪvli,
a'θɔrə,teɪdɪvli
authoritativeness
BR ɔ:'θɒrɪtətɪvnɪs
AM ɔ'θɔrə,teɪdɪvnɪs,
ə'θɔrə,teɪdɪvnɪs,
a'θɔrə,teɪdɪvnɪs
authority
BR ɔ:'θɒrɪt|i, -ɪz
AM ɔ'θɔrədi, ə'θɔrədi,
a'θɔrədi, -z
authorization
BR ,ɔ:θəraɪ'zeɪʃn, -z
AM ,ɔθərə'zeɪʃən,
,ɔθə,raɪ'zeɪʃən,

,aθərə'zeɪʃən,
,aθə,raɪ'zeɪʃən, -z
authorize
BR 'ɔ:θəraɪz, -ɪz, -ɪŋ, -d
AM 'ɔθə,raɪz, 'aθə,raɪz,
-ɪz, -ɪŋ, -d
authorship
BR 'ɔ:θəʃɪp
AM 'ɔθər,ʃɪp, 'aθər,ʃɪp
autism
BR 'ɔ:tɪz(ə)m
AM 'ɔ,tɪzəm, 'a,tɪzəm
autistic
BR ɔ:'tɪstɪk
AM ɔ'tɪstɪk, a'tɪstɪk
auto
BR 'ɔ:təu, -z
AM 'ɔdou, 'adou, -z
Autobahn
BR 'ɔ:təba:n, -z
AM 'ɔdə,ban,
'ɔdou,ban, 'adə,ban,
'adou,ban, -z
GER 'autoba:n
autobiographer
BR ,ɔ:tə(u)bʌɪ'ɒgrəfə(r),
-z
AM ,ɔdə,baɪ'agrəfər,
,ɔdou,baɪ'agrəfər,
,adə,baɪ'agrəfər,
,adou,baɪ'agrəfər, -z
autobiographic
BR ,ɔ:tə(u)bʌɪə'grafɪk
AM ,ɔdə,baɪə'græfɪk,
,ɔdou,baɪə'græfɪk,
,adə,baɪə'græfɪk,
,adou,baɪə'græfɪk
autobiographical
BR ,ɔ:tə(u)bʌɪə'grafɪkl
AM ,ɔdə,baɪə'græfəkəl,
,ɔdou,baɪə'græfəkəl,
,adə,baɪə'græfəkəl,
,adou,baɪə'græfəkəl
**autobiographic-
ally**
BR ,ɔ:tə(u)bʌɪə'grafɪkli
AM ,ɔdə,baɪə'græfək-
(ə)li,
,ɔdou,baɪə'græfək(ə)li,
,adə,baɪə'græfək(ə)li,
,adou,baɪə'græfək(ə)li
autobiography
BR ,ɔ:tə(u)bʌɪ'ɒgrəf|i,
-ɪz
AM ,ɔdə,baɪ'agrəf|i,
,ɔdou,baɪ'agrəfi,
,adə,baɪ'agrəf|i,
,adou,baɪ'agrəfi, -z
autocade
BR 'ɔ:təkeɪd, -z
AM 'ɔdə,keɪd,
'ɔdou,keɪd, 'adə,keɪd,
'adou,keɪd, -z
autocar
BR 'ɔ:tə(u)ka:(r), -z
AM 'ɔdə,kar, 'ɔdou,kar,
'adə,kar, 'adou,kar, -z

autocatalyst
BR ,ɔ:təu'katəlɪst,
,ɔ:təu'katlɪst, -s
AM ,ɔdə'kædələst,
,ɔdou'kædələst,
,adə'kædələst,
,adou'kædələst, -s
autocephalous
BR ,ɔ:tə'sef(ə)ləs,
,ɔ:tə'sefləs,
,ɔ:tə'kef(ə)ləs,
,ɔ:tə'kefləs
AM ,ɔdə'sefələs,
,ɔdou'sefələs,
,adə'sefələs,
,adou'sefələs
autochange
BR 'ɔ:tə(u)tʃeɪm(d)ʒ,
-ɪz
AM ,ɔdə,tʃeɪmdʒ,
'ɔdou,tʃeɪmdʒ,
'adə,tʃeɪmdʒ,
'adou,tʃeɪmdʒ, -ɪz
autochanger
BR 'ɔ:tə(u),tʃeɪm(d)ʒ-
ə(r), -z
AM 'ɔdə,tʃeɪmdʒər,
'ɔdou,tʃeɪmdʒər,
'adə,tʃeɪmdʒər,
'adou,tʃeɪmdʒər, -z
autochthon
BR ɔ:'tɒkθ(ə)n,
ɔ:'tɒkθɒn, -z
AM ɔ'takθən,
ɔ'tak,θan, a'takθən,
a'tak,θan, -z
autochthonal
BR ɔ:'tɒkθənl,
ɔ:'tɒkθɒnl
AM ɔ'takθənəl,
a'takθənəl
autochthonic
BR ,ɔ:tɒk'θɒnɪk
AM ,ɔ,tak'θanɪk,
,a,tak'θanɪk
autochthonous
BR ɔ:'tɒkθənəs,
ɔ:'tɒkθɒnəs
AM ɔ'takθənəs,
a'takθənəs
autoclave
BR 'ɔ:tə(u)kleɪv, -z
AM 'ɔdə,kleɪv,
'ɔdou,kleɪv,
'adə,kleɪv,
'adou,kleɪv, -z
autocode
BR 'ɔ:tə(u)kəud, -z
AM 'ɔdə,koud,
'ɔdou,koud,
'adə,koud,
'adou,koud, -z
autocracy
BR ɔ:'tɒkrəs|i, -ɪz
AM ɔ'takrəsi,
a'takrəsi, -z
autocrat
BR 'ɔ:təkrat, -s

AM 'ɔdə,kræt,
'ɔdou,kræt, 'adə,kræt,
'adou,kræt, -s
autocratic
BR ,ɔ:tə'kratɪk
AM ,ɔdə'krædɪk,
,ɔdou'krædɪk,
,adə'krædɪk,
,adou'krædɪk
autocratical
BR ,ɔ:tə'kratɪkl
AM ,ɔdə'krædəkəl,
,ɔdou'krædəkəl,
,adə'krædəkəl,
,adou'krædəkəl
autocratically
BR ,ɔ:tə'kratɪkli
AM ,ɔdə'krædək(ə)li,
,ɔdou'krædək(ə)li,
,adə'krædək(ə)li,
,adou'krædək(ə)li
autocross
BR 'ɔ:təukrɒs
AM 'ɔdou,krɔs,
'ɔdə,krɔs, 'adou,kras,
'adə,kras
Autocue®
BR 'ɔ:tə(u)kju:, -z
AM 'ɔdou,kju, 'ɔdə,kju
'adou,kju, 'adə,kju, -z
autocycle
BR 'ɔ:tə(u),sʌɪkl, -z
AM 'ɔdə,saɪkəl,
'ɔdou,saɪkəl,
'adə,saɪkəl,
'adou,saɪkəl, -z
auto-da-fé
BR ,ɔ:tə(u)də'feɪ, -z
AM ,ɔdədə'feɪ,
,ɔ,toudə'feɪ,
,adədə'feɪ,
,a,toudə'feɪ, -z
autodestruct
BR ,ɔ:təudɪ'strʌkt, -s,
-ɪŋ, -ɪd
AM ,ɔdədə'strək|(t),
,ɔdədi'strək|(t),
,ɔdoudə'strək|(t),
,ɔdoudi'strək|(t),
,adədə'strək|(t),
,adədi'strək|(t),
,adoudə'strək|(t),
,adoudi'strək|(t),
-(t)s, -tɪŋ, -təd
autodidact
BR ,ɔ:təu'dʌɪdakt, -s
AM ,ɔdə'daɪ,dæk(t),
,ɔdou'daɪ,dæk(t),
,adə'daɪ,dæk(t),
,adou'daɪ,dæk(t), -s
autodidactic
BR ,ɔ:tə(u)dʌɪ'daktɪk
AM ,ɔdədə'dæktɪk,
,ɔdə,dar'dæktɪk,
,ɔdoudə'dæktɪk,
,ɔdou,dar'dæktɪk,
,adədə'dæktɪk,
,adə,dar'dæktɪk,

,ɑdoʊðə'dæktɪk,
,ɑdoʊ,daɪ'dæktɪk

autoerotic
BR ,ɔ:təʊɪ'rɒtɪk
AM ,ɒdoʊə'rɑdɪk,
,ɑdoʊə'rɑdɪk

autoeroticism
BR ,ɔ:təʊɪ'rɒtɪsɪz(ə)m
AM ,ɒdoʊə'rɑdə,sɪzəm,
,ɑdoʊə'rɑdə,sɪzəm

autofocus
BR 'ɔ:tə(ʊ),fəʊkəs
AM 'ɒdə,foʊkəs,
'ɒdoʊ,foʊkəs,
'ɑdə,foʊkəs,
'ɑdoʊ,foʊkəs

autogamous
BR ɔ:'tɒgəməs
AM ɔ'tɑgəməs,
ə'tɑgəməs, ɑ'tɑgəməs

autogamy
BR ɔ:'tɒgəmi
AM ɔ'tɑgəmi, ə'tɑgəmi,
ɑ'tɑgəmi

autogenic
BR ,ɔ:tə(ʊ)'dʒɛnɪk
AM ,ɒdə'dʒɛnɪk,
,ɒdoʊ'dʒɛnɪk,
,ɑdə'dʒɛnɪk,
,ɑdoʊ'dʒɛnɪk

autogenous
BR ɔ:'tɒdʒɪnəs
AM ɔ'tɑdʒənəs,
ə'tɑdʒənəs,
ɑ'tɑdʒənəs

autogiro
BR ,ɔ:tə(ʊ)'dʒʌɪrəʊ,
'ɔ:tə(ʊ),dʒʌɪrəʊ, -z
AM ,ɒdoʊ'dʒaɪroʊ,
,ɒdə'dʒaɪroʊ,
,ɑdoʊ'dʒaɪroʊ,
,ɑdə'dʒaɪroʊ, -z

autograft
BR 'ɔ:tə(ʊ)grɑ:ft,
'ɔ:tə(ʊ)graft, -s
AM 'ɒdə,græft,
'ɒdoʊ,græft,
'ɑdə,græft,
'ɑdoʊ,græft, -s

autograph
BR 'ɔ:təgrɑ:f, 'ɔ:təgraf,
-s, -ɪŋ, -t
AM 'ɒdə,græf,
'ɒdoʊ,græf, 'ɑdə,græf,
'ɑdoʊ,græf, -s, -ɪŋ, -t

autographic
BR ,ɔ:tə'grafɪk
AM ,ɒdə'græfɪk,
,ɒdoʊ'græfɪk,
,ɑdə'græfɪk,
,ɑdoʊ'græfɪk

autography
BR ɔ:'tɒgrəfi
AM ɔ'tɑgrəfi, ɑ'tɑgrəfi

autogyro
BR ,ɔ:tə(ʊ)'dʒʌɪrəʊ,
'ɔ:tə(ʊ),dʒʌɪrəʊ, -z

AM ,ɒdoʊ'dʒaɪroʊ,
,ɒdə'dʒaɪroʊ,
,ɑdoʊ'dʒaɪroʊ,
,ɑdə'dʒaɪroʊ, -z

autoharp
BR 'ɔ:təʊhɑ:p, -s
AM 'ɒdə,hɑrp,
'ɒdoʊ,hɑrp,
'ɑdə,hɑrp,
'ɑdoʊ,hɑrp, -s

autoimmune
BR ,ɔ:təʊɪ'mju:n
AM ,ɒdoʊə'mjun,
,ɑdoʊə'mjun

autoimmunity
BR ,ɔ:təʊɪ'mju:nɪti
AM ,ɒdoʊə'mjunədi,
,ɑdoʊə'mjunədi, -z

autointoxication
BR ,ɔ:təʊɪn,tɒksɪ'keɪʃn
AM ,ɒdoʊən,taksə'keɪ-
ʃən,
,ɑdoʊən,taksə'keɪʃən

autologous
BR ɔ:'tɒləgəs
AM ɔ'taləgəs, ɑ'taləgəs

Autolycus
BR ɔ:'tɒlɪkəs
AM ɔ'taləkəs,
ɑ'taləkəs

autolyses
BR ɔ:'tɒlɪsi:z
AM ɔ'taləsiz, ɑ'taləsiz

autolysis
BR ɔ:'tɒlɪsɪs
AM ɔ'taləsəs, ɑ'taləsəs

autolytic
BR ,ɔ:tə(ʊ)'lɪtɪk
AM ,ɒdl'ɪdɪk, ,ɑdl'ɪdɪk

automaker
BR 'ɔ:təʊ,meɪkə(r), -z
AM 'ɒdə,meɪkər,
'ɑdoʊ,meɪkər,
'ɑdə,meɪkər, -z

automat
BR 'ɔ:təmat, -s
AM 'ɒdə,mæt,
'ɒdoʊ,mæt, 'ɑdə,mæt,
'ɑdoʊ,mæt, -s

automata
BR ɔ:'tɒmətə(r)
AM ɔ'tɑmədə,
ɑ'tɑmədə

automate
BR 'ɔ:təmeɪt, -s, -ɪŋ, -ɪd
AM 'ɒdə,meɪt,
'ɒdoʊ,meɪt,
'ɑdə,meɪt,
'ɑdoʊ,meɪt, -ts, -dɪŋ,
-dɪd

automatic
BR ,ɔ:tə'matɪk
AM ,ɒdə'mædɪk,
,ɒdoʊ'mædɪk,
,ɑdə'mædɪk,
,ɑdoʊə'mædɪk

automatically
BR ,ɔ:tə'matɪkli
AM ,ɒdə'mædək(ə)li,
,ɒdoʊ'mædək(ə)li,
,ɑdə'mædək(ə)li,
,ɑdoʊ'mædək(ə)li

automaticity
BR ,ɔ:təmə'tɪsɪti
AM ,ɒdəmə'tɪsɪdi,
,ɑdəmə'tɪsɪdi

automation
BR ,ɔ:tə'meɪʃn
AM ,ɒdə'meɪʃən,
,ɒdoʊ'meɪʃən,
,ɑdə'meɪʃən,
,ɑdoʊ'meɪʃən

automatisation
BR ,ɔ:təmatʌɪ'zeɪʃn
AM ɔ,tamədə'zeɪʃən,
ɔ,tamə,taɪ'zeɪʃən,
ə,tamədə'zeɪʃən,
ɑ,tamədə'zeɪʃən,
ɑ,tamə,taɪ'zeɪʃən

automatise
BR 'ɔ:təmətʌɪz, -ɪz, -ɪŋ,
-d
AM ɔ'tamə,taɪz,
ə'tamə,taɪz,
ɑ'tamə,taɪz, -ɪz, -ɪŋ, -d

automatism
BR ɔ:'tɒmətɪz(ə)m
AM ɔ'tamə,tɪzəm,
ə'tamə,tɪzəm,
ɑ'tamə,tɪzəm

automatist
BR ɔ:'tɒmətɪst, -s
AM ɔ'tamədəst,
ə'tamədəst,
ɑ'tamədəst, -s

automatization
BR ,ɔ:təmatʌɪ'zeɪʃn
AM ɔ,tamədə'zeɪʃən,
ɔ,tamə,taɪ'zeɪʃən,
ə,tamədə'zeɪʃən,
ɑ,tamədə'zeɪʃən,
ɑ,tamə,taɪ'zeɪʃən

automatize
BR 'ɔ:təmətʌɪz, -ɪz, -ɪŋ,
-d
AM ɔ'tamə,taɪz,
ə'tamə,taɪz,
ɑ'tamə,taɪz, -ɪz, -ɪŋ, -d

automaton
BR ɔ:'tɒmət(ə)n, -z
AM ɔ'tɑmədən,
ɑ'tɑmədən,
ɔ:tamə,tan,
ɑ'tamə,tan, -z

automobile
BR 'ɔ:təmə(ʊ)bi:l, -z
AM ,ɒdəmoʊ'bil,
'ɔ:doʊmoʊ'bil,
'ɑdəmoʊ'bil,
'ɑdoʊmoʊ'bil, -z

automotive
BR ,ɔ:tə'məʊtɪv
AM ,ɒdə'moʊdɪv,
,ɒdoʊ'moʊdɪv,

,ɑdə'moʊdɪv,
,ɑdoʊ'moʊdɪv

autonomic
BR ,ɔ:tə'nɒmɪk
AM ,ɒdə'nɑmɪk,
,ɒdoʊ'namɪk,
,ɑdə'namɪk,
,ɑdoʊ'namɪk

autonomist
BR ɔ:'tɒnəmɪst, -s
AM ɔ'tanəməst,
ə'tanəməst,
ɑ'tanəməst, -s

autonomous
BR ɔ:'tɒnəməs
AM ɔ'tanəməs,
ə'tanəməs,
ɑ'tanəməs

autonomously
BR ɔ:'tɒnəməsli
AM ɔ'tanəməsli,
ə'tanəməsli,
ɑ'tanəməsli

autonomy
BR ɔ:'tɒnəm‖i, -ɪz
AM ɔ'tanəmi,
ə'tanəmi, ɑ'tanəmi, -z

autopilot
BR 'ɔ:tə(ʊ),pʌɪlət, -s
AM 'ɒdə,paɪlət,
'ɑdoʊ,paɪlət,
'ɑdə,paɪlət, -s

autopista
BR 'ɔ:tə(ʊ),pi:stə(r), -z
AM 'ɒdoʊ,pistə,
'ɑdoʊ,pistə, -z

autopolyploid
BR ,ɔ:təʊ'pɒlɪplɔɪd, -z
AM ,ɒdoʊ'pɑlə,plɔɪd,
,ɒdə'palə,plɔɪd,
,ɑdoʊ'palə,plɔɪd,
,ɑdə'palə,plɔɪd, -z

autopolyploidy
BR ,ɔ:təʊ'pɒlɪplɔɪdi
AM ,ɒdoʊ'palə,plɔɪdi,
,ɒdə'palə,plɔɪdi,
,ɑdoʊ'palə,plɔɪdi,
,ɑdə'palə,plɔɪdi

autopsy
BR 'ɔ:tɒps‖i, -ɪz
AM 'ɔ:,tapsi, 'ɑ,tapsi, -z

autoradiograph
BR ,ɔ:təʊ'reɪdɪə(ʊ)grɑ:f,
,ɔ:təʊ'reɪdɪə(ʊ)graf
AM ,ɒdə'reɪdɪə,græf,
,ɒdoʊ'reɪdɪə,græf,
,ɑdə'reɪdɪə,græf,
,ɑdoʊ'reɪdɪə,græf

autoradiographic
BR ,ɔ:təʊ,reɪdɪə'grafɪk
AM ,ɒdə,reɪdɪə'græfɪk,
,ɒdoʊ,reɪdɪə'græfɪk,
,ɑdə,reɪdɪə'græfɪk,
,ɑdoʊ,reɪdɪə'græfɪk

autoradiography
BR ,ɔ:təʊ,reɪdɪ'ɒgrəfi

AM ˌɔdəˌreɪdiˈɑgrəfi,
ˌɔdouˌreɪdiˈɑgrəfi,
ˌadəˌreɪdiˈɑgrəfi,
ˌadouˌreɪdiˈɑgrəfi

autorotation
BR ˌɔːtəʊrə(ʊ)ˈteɪʃn, -z
AM ˌɔdouˌrouˈteɪʃən,
ˌadouˌrouˈteɪʃən, -z

autoroute
BR ˈɔːtəʊruːt, -s
AM ˈɔdouˌrut,
ˈadouˌrut, ˈɔdouˌrʊt,
ˈadouˌrʊt, ˈɔdouˌraʊt,
ˈadouˌraʊt, -s

autostrada
BR ˈɔːtə(ʊ)ˌstrɑːdə(r),
-z
AM ˈɔdouˌstrɑdə,
ˈɔdəˌstrɑdə,
ˈadouˌstrɑdə,
ˈadəˌstrɑdə, -z
IT autoˈstrada

autostrade
BR ˈɔːtə(ʊ)ˌstrɑːdi
AM ˈɔdouˌstrɑdi,
ˈɔdəˌstrɑdi,
ˈadouˌstrɑdi,
ˈadəˌstrɑdi
IT autoˈstrade

autotelic
BR ˌɔːtə(ʊ)ˈtelɪk
AM ˌɔdouˈtɛlɪk,
ˌɔdəˈtɛlɪk, ˌadouˈtɛlɪk,
ˌadəˈtɛlɪk

autotomy
BR ɔːˈtɒtəmi
AM ɔˈtɑdəmi, ɑˈtɑdəmi

autotoxic
BR ˌɔːtəʊˈtɒksɪk
AM ˌɔdouˈtaksɪk,
ˌɔdəˈtaksɪk,
ˌadouˈtaksɪk,
ˌadəˈtaksɪk

autotoxin
BR ˈɔːtə(ʊ)ˌtɒksɪn, -z
AM ˈɔdouˌtaksən,
ˈɔdəˌtaksən,
ˈadouˌtaksən,
ˈadəˌtaksən, -z

autotrophic
BR ˌɔːtə(ʊ)ˈtrɒfɪk,
ˌɔːtə(ʊ)ˈtrəʊfɪk
AM ˌɔdouˈtrafɪk,
ˌɔdəˈtrafɪk,
ˌadouˈtrafɪk,
ˌadəˈtrafɪk

autotype
BR ˈɔːtə(ʊ)ˌtaɪp, -s, -ɪŋ, -t
AM ˈɔdouˌtaɪp,
ˈɔdəˌtaɪp, ˈadouˌtaɪp,
ˈadəˌtaɪp, -s, -ɪŋ, -t

autotypography
BR ˌɔːtə(ʊ)tʌɪˈpɒgrəfi
AM ˌɔdouˌtaɪˈpɑgrəfi,
ˌɔdəˌtaɪˈpɑgrəfi,
ˌadouˌtaɪˈpɑgrəfi,
ˌadəˌtaɪˈpɑgrəfi

autoworker
BR ˈɔːtəʊˌwɜːkə(r), -z
AM ˈɔdəˌwɜrkər,
ˈɔdouˌwɜrkər,
ˈadəˌwɜrkər,
ˈadouˌwɜrkər, -z

autoxidation
BR ˌɔːtəʊˌɒksɪˈdeɪʃn
AM ˌɔdəˌaksəˈdeɪʃən,
ˌɔdouˌaksəˈdeɪʃən,
ˌadəˌaksəˈdeɪʃən,
ˌadouˌaksəˈdeɪʃən

autumn
BR ˈɔːtəm, -z
AM ˈɔdəm, ˈadəm, -z

autumnal
BR ɔːˈtʌmn(ə)l
AM ɔˈtəmnəl, ɑˈtəmnəl

autumnally
BR ɔːˈtʌmnˌli,
ɔːˈtʌmnəli
AM ɔˈtəmnəli,
ɑˈtəmnəli

Auty
BR ˈɔːti
AM ˈɔdi, ˈɑdi

Auvergne
BR əʊˈvɛːn, əʊˈvəːn
AM ouˈvɛ(ə)rn,
ouˈvərn
FR OVƐRɲ

auxanometer
BR ˌɔːksəˈnɒmɪtə(r), -z
AM ˌɔgzəˈnɑmədər,
ˌɔksəˈnamədər,
ˌagzəˈnamədər,
ˌaksəˈnamədər, -z

auxiliary
BR ɔːgˈzɪlɪərˌi,
ɒgˈzɪlɪərˌi, -ɪz
AM ɔgˈzɪl(ə)ri,
əgˈzɪl(ə)ri, ɑgˈzɪl(ə)ri,
ɔgˈzɪljəri, əgˈzɪljəri,
ɑgˈzɪljəri, -z

auxin
BR ˈɔːksɪn, -z
AM ˈɔksən, ˈaksən, -z

Ava
BR ˈeɪvə(r)
AM ˈeɪvə

avadavat
BR ˈavədəvat, -s
AM ˈævədəˌvæt, -s

avail
BR əˈveɪl, -z, -ɪŋ, -d
AM əˈveɪl, -z, -ɪŋ, -d

availability
BR əˌveɪləˈbɪlɪti
AM əˌveɪləˈbɪlɪdi

available
BR əˈveɪləbl
AM əˈveɪləbəl

availableness
BR əˈveɪləblnəs
AM əˈveɪləbəlnəs

availably
BR əˈveɪləbli
AM əˈveɪlɪbli

avalanche
BR ˈavəlɑːn(t)ʃ,
ˈavəlan(t)ʃ, -ɪz, -ɪŋ, -t
AM ˈævəˌlæn(t)ʃ, -əz,
-ɪŋ, -t

Avalon
BR ˈavəlɒn
AM ˈævəˌlan

avant-garde
BR ˌavɒˈgɑːd,
ˌavɒŋˈgaːd
AM ˌɑˌvɑnˈgard,
əˌvan(t)ˈgard

avant-gardism
BR ˌavɒˈgɑːdɪz(ə)m,
ˌavɒŋˈgaːdɪz(ə)m
AM ˌɑˌvɑnˈgarˌdɪzəm,
əˌvan(t)ˈgarˌdɪzəm

avant-gardist
BR ˌavɒˈgɑːdɪst,
ˌavɒŋˈgaːdɪst, -s
AM ˌɑˌvɑnˈgardəst,
əˌvan(t)ˈgardəst, -s

Avar
BR ˈavɑː(r), -z
AM ˈɑvɑr, -z

avarice
BR ˈav(ə)rɪs
AM ˈævərəs

avaricious
BR ˌavəˈrɪʃəs
AM ˌævəˈrɪʃəs

avariciously
BR ˌavəˈrɪʃəsli
AM ˌævəˈrɪʃəsli

avariciousness
BR ˌavəˈrɪʃəsnəs
AM ˌævəˈrɪʃəsnəs

avast
BR əˈvɑːst, əˈvast
AM əˈvæst

avatar
BR ˈavətɑː(r),
ˌavəˈtɑː(r), -z
AM ˈævəˌtɑr, ˌævəˈtɑr,
-z

avaunt
BR əˈvɔːnt
AM əˈvɔnt, əˈvɑnt

ave
prayer
BR ˈɑːvˌi, ˈɑːvˌeɪ,
-ɪz\-eɪz
AM ˈɑˌveɪ, ˈɑˌvi, -z

Avebury
BR ˈeɪvb(ə)ri
AM ˈeɪvbəri

avenge
BR əˈvɛn(d)ʒ, -ɪz, -ɪŋ, -d
AM əˈvɛndʒ, -əz, -ɪŋ, -d

avenger
BR əˈvɛn(d)ʒə(r), -z
AM əˈvɛndʒər, -z

avens
BR ˈeɪv(ɪ)nz, ˈav(ɪ)nz
AM ˈævənz

aventurine
BR əˈvɛntʃʊrʌɪn

Avesta
BR əˈvɛstə(r)
AM əˈvɛstə

avenue
BR ˈavɪnjuː, -z
AM ˈævəˌn(j)u, -z

aver
BR əˈvɜː(r), -z, -ɪŋ, -d
AM əˈvər, -z, -ɪŋ, -d

average
BR ˈav(ə)rˌɪdʒ, -ɪdʒɪz,
-ɪdʒɪŋ, -ɪdʒd
AM ˈæv(ə)rɪdʒ, -ɪz, -ɪŋ,
-d

averagely
BR ˈav(ə)rɪdʒli
AM ˈæv(ə)rɪdʒli

avermectin
BR ˌeɪvəˈmɛktɪn
AM ˌeɪvərˈmɛktɪn

averment
BR əˈvəːm(ə)nt
AM əˈvərmənt

Avernus
BR əˈvəːnəs
AM əˈvərnəs

Averroës
BR əˈvɛrəʊiːz,
ˌavəˈrəʊiːz
AM əˈvɛrouˌiz,
əˈvɛrəwiz

averse
BR əˈvəːs
AM əˈvərs

aversely
BR əˈvəːsli
AM əˈvərsli

averseness
BR əˈvəːsnəs
AM əˈvərsnəs

aversion
BR əˈvəːʃn, -z
AM əˈvərʒən, -z

aversive
BR əˈvəːsɪv, əˈvəːzɪv
AM əˈvərsɪv, əˈvərzɪv

aversively
BR əˈvəːsɪvli,
əˈvəːzɪvli
AM əˈvərsɪvli,
əˈvərzɪvli

avert
BR əˈvəːt, -s, -ɪŋ, -ɪd
AM əˈvər|t, æˈvər|t, -ts,
-dɪŋ, -dəd

avertable
BR əˈvəːtəbl
AM əˈvərdəbəl

avertible
BR əˈvəːtɪbl
AM əˈvərdəbəl

Avery
BR ˈeɪv(ə)ri
AM ˈeɪvəri

Avesta
BR əˈvɛstə(r)
AM əˈvɛstə

Avestan
BR ə'vɛst(ə)n, -z
AM ə'vɛstən, -z

Avestic
BR ə'vɛstɪk, -s
AM ə'vɛstɪk, -s

avgolemono
BR ˌavgə(ʊ)'lɛmənəʊ
AM ˌavgə'lɛmənoʊ

Avia®
BR 'eɪvɪə(r)
AM 'avɪə

avian
BR 'eɪvɪən
AM 'eɪvɪən

aviary
BR 'eɪvɪərǀi, -ɪz
AM 'eɪvɪˌɛri, -z

aviate
BR 'eɪvɪeɪt, -s, -ɪŋ, -ɪd
AM 'eɪviˌeɪǀt, -ts, -dɪŋ, -dɪd

aviation
BR ˌeɪvɪ'eɪʃn
AM ˌeɪvi'eɪʃən

aviator
BR 'eɪvɪeɪtə(r), -z
AM 'eɪviˌeɪdər, -z

aviatrices
BR ˌeɪvɪ'eɪtrɪsiːz
AM ˌeɪvɪ'eɪtrɪˌsiz

aviatrix
BR 'eɪvɪətrɪks, -ɪz
AM ˌeɪvɪ'eɪtrɪks, 'eɪvɪəˌtrɪks, -ɪz

Avicenna
BR ˌavɪ'sɛnə(r)
AM ˌævə'sɛnə

aviculture
BR 'eɪvɪˌkʌltʃə(r)
AM 'eɪvəˌkʌltʃər, 'ævəˌkəltʃər

aviculturist
BR 'eɪvɪˌkʌltʃ(ə)rɪst, -s
AM 'eɪvəˌkəltʃ(ə)rəst, 'ævəˌkəltʃ(ə)rəst, -s

avid
BR 'avɪd
AM 'ævəd

avidity
BR ə'vɪdɪti
AM ə'vɪdɪdi

avidly
BR 'avɪdli
AM 'ævədli

Aviemore
BR ˌavɪ'mɔː(r), 'avɪmɔː(r)
AM 'ævɪˌmɔ(ə)r

avifauna
BR 'eɪvɪˌfɔːnə(r)
AM ˌeɪvɪ'fɔnə, ˌævɪ'fɔnə, ˌeɪvɪ'fɑnə, ˌævɪ'fɑnə

Avignon
BR 'aviːnjɒ̃, 'av(ɪ)njɒ̃
AM ˌævən'jɒn, ˌævən'jɑn

Ávila
BR 'avɪlə(r), 'avḻə(r)
AM 'avilə

avionic
BR ˌeɪvɪ'ɒnɪk, -s
AM ˌeɪvi'ɑnɪk, -s

Avis®
BR 'eɪvɪs
AM 'eɪvɪs

avitaminoses
BR eɪˌvɪtəmɪ'nəʊsiːz, eɪˌvʌɪtəmɪ'nəʊsiːz
AM ˌeɪˌvaɪdəmə'noʊsiz

avitaminosis
BR eɪˌvɪtəmɪ'nəʊsɪs, eɪˌvʌɪtəmɪ'nəʊsɪs
AM ˌeɪˌvaɪdəmə'noʊsəs

avizandum
BR ˌavɪ'zandəm
AM ˌævɪ'zændəm

Avoca
BR ə'vəʊkə(r)
AM ə'voʊkə

avocado
BR ˌavə'kɑːdəʊ, -z
AM ˌævə'kadoʊ, ˌavə'kadoʊ, -z

avocation
BR ˌavə'keɪʃn, -z
AM ˌævə'keɪʃən, -z

avocet
BR 'avəsɛt, -s
AM 'ævəˌsɛt, -s

Avogadro
BR ˌavə(ʊ)'gadrəʊ, ˌavə(ʊ)'gɑːdrəʊ
AM ˌavə'gadroʊ

avoid
BR ə'vɔɪd, -z, -ɪŋ, -ɪd
AM ə'vɔɪd, -z, -ɪŋ, -ɪd

avoidable
BR ə'vɔɪdəbl
AM ə'vɔɪdəbəl

avoidably
BR ə'vɔɪdəbli
AM ə'vɔɪdəbli

avoidance
BR ə'vɔɪd(ə)ns, -ɪz
AM ə'vɔɪd(ə)ns, -ɪz

avoider
BR ə'vɔɪdə(r), -z
AM ə'vɔɪdər, -z

avoirdupois
BR ˌavədə'pɔɪz, ˌavwəd(j)uː'pwɑː(r)
AM ˌavərdə'pɔɪz, 'avərdəˌpɔɪz

Avon¹
Devon river
BR 'avn
AM 'eɪˌvan

Avon²
English county, English Midland river
BR 'eɪvn
AM 'eɪˌvan

Avon³
Scottish loch and river
BR ɑːn
AM 'eɪˌvan

Avon⁴
tradename
BR 'eɪvɒn
AM 'eɪˌvan

Avonmouth
BR 'eɪvnmaʊθ
AM 'eɪˌvanˌmaʊθ

avouch
BR ə'vaʊtʃ, -ɪz, -ɪŋ, -t
AM ə'vaʊtʃ, -əz, -ɪŋ, -t

avouchment
BR ə'vaʊtʃm(ə)nt, -s
AM ə'vaʊtʃmənt, -s

avow
BR ə'vaʊ, -z, -ɪŋ, -d
AM ə'vaʊ, -z, -ɪŋ, -d

avowable
BR ə'vaʊəbl
AM ə'vaʊəbəl

avowal
BR ə'vaʊəl, -z
AM ə'vaʊ(ə)l, -z

avowedly
BR ə'vaʊwɪdli
AM ə'vaʊədli

Avril
BR 'avrɪl
AM 'ævrəl

avulsion
BR ə'vʌlʃn
AM ə'vəlʃən

avuncular
BR ə'vʌŋkjʊlə(r)
AM ə'vəŋkjələr

AWACS
BR 'eɪwaks
AM 'eɪˌwæks

await
BR ə'weɪt, -s, -ɪŋ, -ɪd
AM ə'weɪǀt, -ts, -dɪŋ, -dɪd

awake
BR ə'weɪk, -s, -ɪŋ
AM ə'weɪk, -s, -ɪŋ

awaken
BR ə'weɪk|(ə)n, -(ə)nz, -(ə)nɪŋ \-nɪŋ, -(ə)nd
AM ə'weɪkǀən, -ənz, -(ə)nɪŋ, -ənd

award
BR ə'wɔːd, -z, -ɪŋ, -ɪd
AM ə'wɔ(ə)rd, -z, -ɪŋ, -əd

awarder
BR ə'wɔːdə(r), -z
AM ə'wɔrdər, -z

aware
BR ə'wɛː(r)
AM ə'wɛ(ə)r

awareness
BR ə'wɛːnəs, -ɪz
AM ə'wɛrnəs, -əz

awash
BR ə'wɒʃ
AM ə'wɔʃ, ə'waʃ

away
BR ə'weɪ
AM ə'weɪ

awe
BR ɔː(r), -z, -ɪŋ, -d
AM ɔ, ɑ, -z, -ɪŋ, -d

aweary
BR ə'wɪəri
AM ə'wɪri

aweigh
BR ə'weɪ
AM ə'weɪ

aweless
BR 'ɔːləs
AM 'ɔləs, 'aləs

awelessness
BR 'ɔːləsnəs
AM 'ɔləsnəs, 'aləsnəs

awesome
BR 'ɔːs(ə)m
AM 'ɔsəm, 'asəm

awesomely
BR 'ɔːs(ə)mli
AM 'ɔsəmli, 'asəmli

awesomeness
BR 'ɔːs(ə)mnəs
AM 'ɔsəmnəs, 'asəmnəs

awestricken
BR 'ɔːˌstrɪk(ə)n
AM 'ɔˌstrɪkən, 'aˌstrɪkən

awestruck
BR 'ɔːstrʌk
AM 'ɔˌstrək, 'aˌstrək

awful
BR 'ɔːf(ʊ)l
AM 'ɔfəl, 'afəl

awfully¹
horribly
BR 'ɔːfʊli, 'ɔːfḻi
AM 'ɔf(ə)li, 'af(ə)li

awfully²
very
BR 'ɔːfli, 'ɔːfḻi
AM 'ɔf(ə)li, 'af(ə)li

awfulness
BR 'ɔːf(ʊ)lnəs
AM 'ɔfəlnəs, 'afəlnəs

awheel
BR ə'wiːl
AM ə'(h)wil

awhile
BR ə'wʌɪl
AM ə'(h)waɪl

awkward
BR 'ɔːkwəd
AM 'ɔkwərd, 'akwərd

awkwardly
BR 'ɔːkwədli
AM 'ɔkwərdli, 'akwərdli

awkwardness
BR 'ɔːkwədnəs, -ɪz

AM ˈɔkwərdnəs,
ˈɑkwərdnəs, -əz
awl
BR ɔːl, -z
AM ɒl, ɑl, -z
awn
BR ɔːn, -z, -d
AM ɒn, ɑn, -z, -d
awning
BR ˈɔːnɪŋ, -z
AM ˈɒnɪŋ, ˈɑnɪŋ, -z
awoke
BR əˈwəʊk
AM əˈwoʊk
awoken
BR əˈwəʊk(ə)n
AM əˈwoʊkən
AWOL
BR ˈeɪwɒl
AM ˈeɪˌwɒl, ˈeɪˌwɑl
awry
BR əˈrʌɪ
AM əˈraɪ
ax
BR aks, -ɪz, -ɪŋ, -t
AM æks, -əz, -ɪŋ, -t
axe
BR aks, -ɪz, -ɪŋ, -t
AM æks, -əz, -ɪŋ, -t
axel
BR ˈaksl, -z
AM ˈæksəl, -z
axeman
BR ˈaksmən, ˈaksman
AM ˈæksˌmæn
axemen
BR ˈaksmən, ˈaksmɛn
AM ˈæksˌmɛn
axes[1]
plural of axis
BR ˈaksiːz
AM ˈækˌsiz
axes[2]
plural of ax, axe
BR ˈaksɪz
AM ˈæksəz
Axholme
BR ˈakshəʊm
AM ˈæksˌ(h)oʊm
axial
BR ˈaksɪəl
AM ˈæksiəl
axiality
BR ˌaksɪˈalɪti
AM ˌæksiˈælədi
axially
BR ˈaksɪəli
AM ˈæksiəli
axil
BR ˈaks(ɪ)l, -z
AM ˈæksəl, -z
axilla
BR akˈsɪlə(r)
AM ækˈsɪlə
axillae
BR akˈsɪliː
AM ækˈsɪli, ækˈsɪˌlaɪ

axillary
BR akˈsɪl(ə)ri
AM ˈæksɪləri
axiological
BR ˌaksɪəˈlɒdʒɪkl
AM ˌæksiəˈlɑdʒəkəl
axiologist
BR ˌaksɪˈɒlədʒɪst, -s
AM ˌæksiˈɑlədʒəst, -s
axiology
BR ˌaksɪˈɒlədʒi
AM ˌæksiˈɑlədʒi
axiom
BR ˈaksɪəm, -z
AM ˈæksiəm, -z
axiomatic
BR ˌaksɪəˈmatɪk
AM ˌæksiəˈmædɪk
axiomatically
BR ˌaksɪəˈmatɪkli
AM ˌæksiəˈmædək(ə)li
axis
BR ˈaksɪs
AM ˈæksəs
axle
BR ˈaksl, -z, -d
AM ˈæksəl, -z, -d
axman
BR ˈaksmən, ˈaksman
AM ˈæksˌmæn
axmen
BR ˈaksmən, ˈaksmɛn
AM ˈæksˌmɛn
Axminster
BR ˈaksˌmɪnstə(r), -z
AM ˈæksˌmɪnstər, -z
axolotl
BR ˌaksəˈlɒtl,
ˈaksəlɒtl, -z
AM ˈæksəˈlɑdl, -z
axon
BR ˈaksɒn, -z
AM ˈækˌsɑn, -z
axonometric
BR ˌaksənə(ʊ)ˈmɛtrɪk,
ˌaksŋə(ʊ)ˈmɛtrɪk
AM ˌæksənəˈmɛtrɪk
axonometrically
BR ˌaksənə(ʊ)ˈmɛtrɪkli,
ˌaksŋə(ʊ)ˈmɛtrɪkli
AM ˌæksənəˈmɛtrək(ə)li
Axum
BR ˈaksʌm
AM ˈɑkˌsʊm
ay
yes
BR ʌɪ, -z
AM aɪ, -z
Ayacucho
BR ˌʌɪ(j)əˈkuːtʃəʊ
AM ˌaɪəˈkutʃoʊ
ayah
BR ˈʌɪ(j)ə(r), -z
AM ˈaɪə, -z
ayatollah
BR ˌʌɪ(j)əˈtɒlə(r), -z
AM ˌaɪəˈtoʊlə, -z

Ayckbourn
BR ˈeɪkbɔːn
AM ˈaɪkˌbɔ(ə)rn
Aycliffe
BR ˈeɪklɪf
AM ˈaɪklɪf
aye[1]
always
BR eɪ, ʌɪ
AM eɪ
aye[2]
yes
BR ʌɪ, -z
AM aɪ, -z
aye-aye
noun
BR ˈʌɪʌɪ, -z
AM ˈaɪˈaɪ, -z
aye aye
interjection
BR ˌʌɪ ˈʌɪ
AM ˌaɪ ˈaɪ
Ayer
BR ɛː(r)
AM ɛ(ə)r
Ayers
BR ɛːz
AM ɛ(ə)rz
Áyios Nikólaos
BR ˌʌɪ(j)ɒs ˌnɪkəˈleɪɒs
AM ˌaɪəs ˌnɪkəˈleɪəs
GR ˌaɪɒs niːˈkɔlaɔs
Aylesbury
BR ˈeɪlzb(ə)r|i, -ɪz
AM ˈeɪlzbəri, -z
Aylesham
BR ˈeɪlʃ(ə)m
AM ˈeɪlˌʃæm, ˈeɪlʃəm
Aylmer
BR ˈeɪlmə(r)
AM ˈeɪlmər
Aylsham
BR ˈeɪlʃ(ə)m
AM ˈeɪlˌʃæm, ˈeɪlʃəm
Aylward
BR ˈeɪlwəd, ˈeɪlwɔːd
AM ˈeɪlwɔ(ə)rd
Aymara
BR ˈʌɪmərɑː(r), -z
AM ˈaɪmɑrɑ, -z
Aynho
BR ˈeɪnhəʊ
AM ˈeɪnhoʊ
Ayot
BR ˈeɪət
AM ˈeɪɑt
Ayr
BR ɛː(r)
AM ɛ(ə)r
Ayrshire
BR ˈɛːʃ(ɪ)ə(r)
AM ˈɛrˌʃi(ə)r
Ayrton
BR ˈɛːt(ə)n
AM ˈɛrt(ə)n
Aysgarth
BR ˈeɪzgɑːθ

AM ˈaɪsgɑrθ
Ayto
BR ˈeɪtəʊ
AM ˈeɪtu
Ayub Khan
BR ʌɪˌjuːb ˈkɑːn,
ˌʌɪjuːb +
AM ˌɑˈjub ˈkɑn
azalea
BR əˈzeɪlɪə(r), -z
AM əˈzeɪljə, əˈzeɪliə, -z
Azania
BR əˈzeɪnɪə(r)
AM əˈzeɪniə
Azanian
BR əˈzeɪnɪən
AM əˈzeɪniən
azeotrope
BR ˈeɪzɪətrəʊp,
əˈziːətrəʊp, -s
AM eɪˈziəˌtroʊp, -s
azeotropic
BR ˌeɪzɪəˈtrɒpɪk,
ˌeɪzɪəˈtrəʊpɪk,
əˌziːəˈtrɒpɪk,
əˌziːəˈtrəʊpɪk
AM ˌeɪˌziəˈtrɑpɪk
Azerbaijan
BR ˌazəbʌɪˈ(d)ʒɑːn
AM ˌæzərˌbaɪˈ(d)ʒɑn,
ˌæʒər-ˌbaɪˈ(d)ʒɑn
Azerbaijani
BR ˌazəbʌɪˈ(d)ʒɑːn|i,
-ɪz
AM ˌæzərˌbaɪˈ(d)ʒɑni,
ˌæʒərˌbaɪˈ(d)ʒɑni, -z
Azeri
BR əˈzɛːr|i, -ɪz
AM əˈzɛri, -z
azide
BR ˈeɪzʌɪd, -z
AM ˈeɪˌzaɪd, -z
Azilian
BR əˈzɪliən
AM əˈzɪljən, əˈzɪliən
azimuth
BR ˈazɪməθ, -s
AM ˈæzəməθ, -s
azimuthal
BR ˌazɪˈmʌθl,
ˌazɪˈmjuːθl
AM ˌæzəˈməθəl
azine
BR ˈeɪziːn, -z
AM ˈæˌzin, ˈeɪˌzin, -z
Aziz
BR əˈziːz, əˈziːz, əˈzɪz
əˈzɪz
AM əˈziz
Aznavour
BR ˈaznəvʊə(r),
ˈaznəvɔː(r)
AM ˈæznəˌvɔ(ə)r
azobenzine
BR ˌeɪzəʊˈbɛnziːn,
ˌazəʊˈbɛnziːn
AM ˌeɪzoʊˈbɛnzin,
ˌæzoʊˈbɛnzin

azoic
BR eɪˈzəʊɪk, əˈzəʊɪk
AM eɪˈzoʊɪk, əˈzɪk
Azores
BR əˈzɔːz
AM ˈeɪˌzɔːz(ə)z
Azov
BR ˈazɒv, ˈɑːzɒv, ˈeɪzɒv
AM ˈæzɒv, ˈæzəv

Aztec
BR ˈaztɛk, -s
AM ˈæztɛk, -s
Aztecan
BR ˈaztɛk(ə)n,
azˈtɛk(ə)n
AM ˈæzˌtɛkən
azuki
BR əˈzuːk|i, -ɪz

AM əˈzuki, -z
azure
BR ˈaʒə(r), ˈaʒj(ʊ)ə(r),
ˈazj(ʊ)ə(r), ˈeɪʒə(r),
ˈeɪʒj(ʊ)ə(r),
ˈeɪzj(ʊ)ə(r)
AM ˈæʒər
azurite
BR ˈaʒʊraɪt

ˈaʒj(ʊ)ərʌɪt,
ˈazj(ʊ)ərʌɪt,
ˈeɪʒərʌɪt,
ˈeɪʒj(ʊ)ərʌɪt,
ˈeɪzj(ʊ)ərʌɪt
AM ˈæʒəˌraɪt
azygous
BR ˈazɪgəs
AM ˌeɪˈzaɪgəs

Bb

b
BR biː, -z
AM bi, -z

baa
BR bɑː(r), -z, -ɪŋ, -d
AM bɑ, -z, -ɪŋ, -d

Baader-Meinhof
BR ˌbɑːdəˈmʌɪnhʊf
AM ˌbɑdərˈmaɪnˌ(h)ɔf,
ˌbɑdərˈmaɪnˌ(h)ɑf

Baal
BR ˈbeɪ(ə)l, bɑːl
AM ˈbeɪ(ə)l, bɑl

Baalbek
BR ˈbɑːlbɛk
AM ˈbɑlˌbɛk

Baalim
BR ˈbeɪlɪm, ˈbɑːlɪm
AM ˈbeɪlɪm

Baalism
BR ˈbeɪlɪz(ə)m,
ˈbɑːlɪz(ə)m
AM ˈbeɪˌlɪzəm

baas
BR bɑːs, -ɪz
AM bɑs, -əz

baasskap
BR ˈbɑːskap, ˈbɑːskɑːp,
ˈbaskap
AM ˈbɑsˌkæp,
ˈbæsˌkæp

Baath
BR bɑːθ
AM bɑs, bɑθ

Ba'ath
BR bɑːθ
AM bɑs, bɑθ

Baathist
BR ˈbɑːθɪst, -s
AM ˈbɑθəst, -s

baba
BR bɑːbɑːˈ(r),
ˈbɑːbə(r), -z
AM ˈbɑˌbɑ, -z

babacoote
BR ˈbabəkuːt,
ˈbɑːbəkuːt, -s
AM ˈbɑbəˌkut, -s

Babbage
BR ˈbabɪdʒ
AM ˈbæbɪdʒ

Babbitt
BR ˈbabɪt
AM ˈbæbət

Babbittry
BR ˈbabɪtri
AM ˈbæbətri

babble
BR ˈbab|l, -lz, -ḷɪŋ \-lɪŋ,
-ld

babble
AM ˈbæb|əl, -əlz, -(ə)lɪŋ,
-əld

babblement
BR ˈbablm(ə)nt
AM ˈbæbəlmənt

babbler
BR ˈbablə(r),
ˈbablə(r), -z
AM ˈbæb(ə)lər, -z

babbling
BR ˈbabḷɪŋ, ˈbablɪŋ, -z
AM ˈbæb(ə)lɪŋ, -z

Babcock
BR ˈbabkɒk
AM ˈbæbˌkɑk

babe
BR beɪb, -z
AM beɪb, -z

Babel
BR ˈbeɪbl, -z
AM ˈbeɪbəl, ˈbæbəl, -z

babesiasis
BR ˌbɑːbɪˈzaɪəsɪs
AM ˌbæbəˈzaɪəsɪs

babesiosis
BR bəˌbiːziˈəʊsɪs
AM ˌbæbəˈzaɪəsɪs

Babi
BR ˈbɑːb|i, -ɪz
AM ˈbɑbi, -z

babiche
BR bəˈbiːʃ
AM bəˈbiʃ

Babington
BR ˈbabɪŋt(ə)n
AM ˈbæbɪŋtən

babirusa
BR ˌbɑːbɪˈruːsə(r), -z
AM ˌbɑbəˈrusə, -z

Babism
BR ˈbɑːbɪz(ə)m
AM ˈbɑˌbɪzəm

Babist
BR ˈbɑːbɪst, -s
AM ˈbɑbəst, -s

baboo
BR ˈbɑːbuː, -z
AM ˈbɑˌbu, -z

baboon
BR bəˈbuːn, -z
AM bæˈbun, -z

Babs
BR babz
AM bæbz

babu
BR ˈbɑːbuː, -z
AM ˈbɑˌbu, -z

babushka
BR bəˈbuːʃkə(r),
baˈbuːʃkə(r),
bəˈbʊʃkə(r),
baˈbʊʃkə(r), -z
AM bəˈbʊʃkə, -z
RUS ˈbabuʃkə

baby
BR ˈbeɪb|i, -ɪz, -ɪɪŋ, -ɪd
AM ˈbeɪbi, -z, -ɪŋ, -d

Babycham®
BR ˈbeɪbɪʃam, -z
AM ˈbeɪbɪˌʃam, -z

Babygro®
BR ˈbeɪbɪɡrəʊ, -z
AM ˈbeɪbɪˌɡroʊ, -z

babyhood
BR ˈbeɪbɪhʊd
AM ˈbeɪbiˌ(h)ʊd

babyish
BR ˈbeɪbɪɪʃ
AM ˈbeɪbɪʃ

babyishly
BR ˈbeɪbɪɪʃli
AM ˈbeɪbɪʃli

babyishness
BR ˈbeɪbɪɪʃnɪs
AM ˈbeɪbɪɪʃnɪs

Babylon
BR ˈbabɪlɒn, ˈbabɪlən,
ˈbablən
AM ˈbæbəˌlɑn

Babylonia
BR ˌbabɪˈləʊnɪə(r)
AM ˌbæbəˈloʊnɪə

Babylonian
BR ˌbabɪˈləʊnɪən, -z
AM ˌbæbəˈloʊnɪən, -z

babysat
BR ˈbeɪbɪsat
AM ˈbeɪbiˌsæt

babysit
BR ˈbeɪbɪsɪt, -s, -ɪŋ
AM ˈbeɪbiˌsɪ|t, -ts, -dɪŋ

babysitter
BR ˈbeɪbɪˌsɪtə(r), -z
AM ˈbeɪbiˌsɪdər, -z

Bacall
BR bəˈkɔːl
AM bəˈkɔl, bəˈkɑl

Bacardi®
BR bəˈkɑːd|i, -ɪz
AM bəˈkɑrdi, -z

baccalaureate
BR ˌbakəˈlɔːrɪət, -s
AM ˌbækəˈlɔriət, -s

baccara
BR ˈbakərɑː(r),
ˌbakəˈrɑː(r)
AM ˈbakəˌrɑ, ˈbækəˌrɑ

baccarat
BR ˈbakərɑː(r),
ˌbakəˈrɑː(r)
AM ˈbakəˌrɑ, ˈbækəˌrɑ

baccate
BR ˈbakeɪt
AM ˈbæˌkeɪt

Bacchae
BR ˈbakiː, ˈbakʌɪ
AM ˈbakˌi, ˈbakˌaɪ,
ˈbækˌi, ˈbækˌaɪ

bacchanal
BR ˌbakəˈnal,
ˈbakənəl, ˈbakən(ə)l,
ˈbakṇl, -z
AM ˌbakəˈnal,
ˌbækəˈnæl, -z

bacchanalia
BR ˌbakəˈneɪlɪə(r)
AM ˌbakəˈneɪljə,
ˌbækəˈneɪljə,
ˌbakəˈneɪlɪə,
ˌbækəˈneɪlɪə

bacchanalian
BR ˌbakəˈneɪlɪən, -z
AM ˌbakəˈneɪljən,
ˌbækəˈneɪljən,
ˌbakəˈneɪlɪən,
ˌbækəˈneɪlɪən, -z

bacchant
BR ˈbak(ə)nt, -s
AM bəˈkant, bəˈkænt,
-s

bacchante
BR bəˈkant|i, bəˈkant,
-ɪz \-s
AM bəˈkɑn(t)i,
bəˈkæn(t)i, -z

bacchantic
BR bəˈkantɪk
AM bəˈkɑn(t)ɪk,
bəˈkæn(t)ɪk

bacchic
BR ˈbakɪk
AM ˈbakɪk, ˈbækɪk

Bacchus
BR ˈbakəs
AM ˈbakəs, ˈbækəs

bacciferous
BR bakˈsɪf(ə)rəs
AM bakˈsɪf(ə)rəs,
bækˈsɪf(ə)rəs

baccy
BR ˈbaki
AM ˈbaki, ˈbæki

Bach
BR bɑːk, bɑːx
AM bɑk

Bacharach
BR ˈbakərak
AM ˈbækəˌræk,
ˈbakəˌrɑk

bachelor
BR ˈbatʃ(ə)lə(r),
ˈbatʃlə(r), -z
AM ˈbætʃ(ə)lər, -z

bachelorhood
BR ˈbatʃ(ə)ləhʊd,
ˈbatʃləhʊd
AM ˈbætʃ(ə)lər,(h)ʊd

bachelorship
BR ˈbatʃ(ə)ləʃɪp,
ˈbatʃləʃɪp
AM ˈbætʃ(ə)lərˌʃɪp

bacillar
BR bəˈsɪlə(r),
ˈbasɪlə(r)
AM bəˈsɪlər, ˈbæsələr

bacillary
BR bəˈsɪl(ə)ri,
ˈbasɪl(ə)ri, ˈbasḷ(ə)ri
AM ˈbæsəˌlɛri

bacilli
BR bəˈsɪlʌɪ
AM bəˈsɪˌlaɪ

bacilliform
BR bə'sɪlɪfɔːm
AM bə'sɪlə͵fɔ(ə)rm
bacillus
BR bə'sɪləs
AM bə'sɪləs
bacitracin
BR ͵basɪ'treɪsɪn
AM ͵bæ(k)sə'treɪsɪn
back
BR bak, -s, -ɪŋ, -t
AM bæk, -s, -ɪŋ, -t
backache
BR 'bakeɪk, -s
AM 'bæk͵eɪk, -s
backbench
BR ͵bak'bɛn(t)ʃ, -ɪz
AM ͵bæk'bɛn(t)ʃ, -əz
backbencher
BR 'bak͵bɛn(t)ʃə(r),
͵bak'bɛn(t)ʃə(r), -z
AM ͵bæk'bɛn(t)ʃər, -z
backbit
BR 'bakbɪt
AM 'bæk͵bɪt
backbite
BR 'bakbʌɪt, -s, -ɪŋ
AM 'bæk͵baɪ|t, -ts, -dɪŋ
backbiter
BR 'bak͵bʌɪtə(r), -z
AM 'bæk͵baɪdər, -z
backbitten
BR 'bak͵bɪtn
AM 'bæk͵bɪtn
backblocks
BR 'bakblɒks
AM 'bæk͵blɑks
backboard
BR 'bakbɔːd, -z
AM 'bæk͵bɔ(ə)rd, -z
backbone
BR 'bakbəʊn, -z
AM 'bæk͵boʊn, -z
backbreaking
BR 'bak͵breɪkɪŋ
AM 'bæk͵breɪkɪŋ
backchat
BR 'baktʃat
AM 'bæk͵tʃæt
backcloth
BR 'bakklɒ|θ, -θs\-ðz
AM 'bæk͵klɔ|θ,
'bæk͵klɑ|θ, -θs\-ðz
backcomb
BR 'bakkəʊm, -z, -ɪŋ, -d
AM 'bæk͵koʊm, -z, -ɪŋ,
-d
backcourt
BR 'bakkɔːt, -s
AM 'bæk͵kɔ(ə)rt, -s
backdate
BR ͵bak'deɪt, -s, -ɪŋ, -ɪd
AM 'bæk͵deɪ|t, -ts, -dɪŋ,
-dɪd
backdraft
BR 'bakdrɑːft,
'bakdraft, -s

backdrop
BR 'bakdrɒp, -s
AM 'bæk͵drɑp, -s
backer
BR 'bakə(r), -z
AM 'bækər, -z
backfield
BR 'bakfiːld, -z
AM 'bæk͵fild, -z
back-fill
BR 'bakfɪl, -z, -ɪŋ, -d
AM 'bæk͵fɪl, -z, -ɪŋ, -d
backfire¹
noun
BR 'bak͵fʌɪə(r), -z
AM 'bæk͵faɪ(ə)r, -z
backfire²
verb
BR ͵bak'fʌɪə(r), -z, -ɪŋ,
-d
AM 'bæk͵faɪ(ə)r, -z, -ɪŋ,
-d
backgammon
BR 'bak͵gamən
AM 'bæk͵gæmən
background
BR 'bakgraʊnd, -z
AM 'bæk͵graʊnd, -z
backhand
BR 'bakhand, -z
AM 'bæk͵(h)ænd, -z
backhanded
BR ͵bak'handɪd
AM 'bæk͵(h)ændəd
backhandedly
BR ͵bak'handɪdli
AM 'bæk͵(h)ændədli
backhander
BR 'bak͵handə(r),
͵bak'handə(r), -z
AM 'bæk͵(h)ændər, -z
Backhouse
BR 'bakhaʊs
AM 'bæk͵(h)aʊs
backing
BR 'bakɪŋ, -z
AM 'bækɪŋ, -z
backlash
BR 'baklaʃ, -ɪz
AM 'bæk͵læʃ, -əz
backless
BR 'bakləs
AM 'bækləs
backlighting
BR ͵bak'lʌɪtɪŋ,
'bak͵lʌɪtɪŋ
AM 'bæk͵laɪdɪŋ
backlist
BR 'baklɪst, -s
AM 'bæk͵lɪst, -s
backlit
BR ͵bak'lɪt, 'baklɪt
AM 'bæk͵lɪt
backlog
BR 'baklɒg, -z

backmost
AM 'bæk͵lɒg, 'bæk͵lɑg,
-z
backmarker
BR 'bak͵mɑːkə(r), -z
AM 'bæk͵mɑrkər, -z
backmost
BR 'bakməʊst
AM 'bæk͵moʊst
backpack
BR 'bakpak, -s, -ɪŋ, -t
AM 'bæk͵pæk, -s, -ɪŋ, -t
backpacker
BR 'bak͵pakə(r), -z
AM 'bæk͵pækər, -z
backpedal
BR ͵bak'pɛd|l, -lz,
-lɪŋ\-lɪŋ, -ld
AM 'bæk͵pɛd|əl, -əlz,
-(ə)lɪŋ, -əld
backrest
BR 'bakrɛst, -s
AM 'bæk͵rɛst, -s
backroom
BR ͵bak'ruːm,
͵bak'rʊm, 'bakruːm,
'bakrʊm, -z
AM 'bæk͵rum,
'bæk͵rʊm, -z
Backs
BR baks
AM bæks
backscratcher
BR 'bak͵skratʃə(r), -z
AM 'bæk͵skrætʃər, -z
backscratching
BR 'bak͵skratʃɪŋ
AM 'bæk͵skrætʃɪŋ
backsheesh
BR 'bakʃiːʃ, ͵bak'ʃiːʃ
AM 'bæk͵ʃɪʃ
backside
BR 'baksʌɪd, ͵bak'sʌɪd,
-z
AM 'bæk͵saɪd, -z
backsight
BR 'baksʌɪt, -s
AM 'bæk͵saɪt, -s
backslapping
BR 'bak͵slapɪŋ, -z
AM 'bæk͵slæpɪŋ, -z
backslash
BR 'bakslaʃ, -ɪz
AM 'bæk͵slæʃ, -əz
backslid
BR 'bak'slɪd
AM 'bæk͵slɪd
backslide
BR ͵bak'slʌɪd, -z, -ɪŋ
AM 'bæk͵slaɪd, -z, -ɪŋ
backslider
BR 'bak͵slʌɪdə(r),
͵bak'slʌɪdə(r), -z
AM 'bæk͵slaɪdər, -z
backspace¹
noun
BR 'bakspeɪs, -ɪz
AM 'bæk͵speɪs, -ɪz

backspace²
verb
BR ͵bak'speɪs, -ɪz, -ɪŋ, -t
AM 'bæk͵speɪs, -ɪz, -ɪŋ,
-t
backspin
BR 'bakspɪn, -z
AM 'bæk͵spɪn, -z
backstage
BR ͵bak'steɪdʒ
AM ͵bæk'steɪdʒ
backstair
adjective
BR ͵bak'stɛː(r)
AM ͵bæk'stɛ(ə)r
backstairs
BR ͵bak'stɛːz
AM ͵bæk'stɛ(ə)rz
backstay
BR 'baksteɪ, -z
AM 'bæk͵steɪ, -z
backstitch
BR 'bakstɪtʃ, -ɪz, -ɪŋ, -t
AM 'bæk͵stɪtʃ, -ɪz, -ɪŋ, -t
backstop
BR 'bakstɒp, -s
AM 'bæk͵stɑp, -s
backstrap
BR 'bakstrap, -s
AM 'bæk͵stræp, -s
backstreet
BR 'bakstriːt, -s
AM 'bæk͵strit, -s
backstretch
BR 'bakstrɛtʃ
AM 'bæk͵strɛtʃ
backstroke
BR 'bakstrəʊk
AM 'bæk͵stroʊk
backtalk
BR 'baktɔːk
AM 'bæk͵tɔk, 'bæk͵tak
backtrack
BR 'baktrak, -s, -ɪŋ, -t
AM 'bæk͵træk, -s, -ɪŋ, -t
backtracker
BR 'bak͵trakə(r), -z
AM 'bæk͵trækər, -z
backup
BR 'bakʌp, -s
AM 'bæk͵əp, -s
backveld
BR 'bakvɛlt, -s
AM 'bæk͵vɛlt, -s
backvelder
BR 'bak͵vɛltə(r),
'bak͵vɛldə(r), -z
AM 'bæk͵vɛldər, -z
backward
BR 'bakwəd
AM 'bækwərd
backwardation
BR ͵bakwə'deɪʃn
AM ͵bækwər'deɪʃən
backwardly
BR 'bakwədli
AM 'bækwərdli

backwardness
BR ˈbakwədnəs
AM ˈbækwərdnəs

backwards
BR ˈbakwədz
AM ˈbækwərdz

backwash
BR ˈbakwɒʃ
AM ˈbækˌwɔʃ, ˈbækˌwɑʃ

backwater
BR ˈbakˌwɔːtə(r), -z
AM ˈbækˌwɔdər, ˈbækˌwɑdər, -z

backwoods
BR ˈbakwʊdz
AM ˈbækˈwʊdz

backwoodsman
BR ˈbakˌwʊdzmən
AM ˌbækˈwʊdzmən

backwoodsmen
BR ˈbakˌwʊdzmən
AM ˈbækˈwʊdzmən

backy
BR ˈbaki
AM ˈbæki

backyard
BR ˌbakˈjɑːd, -z
AM ˌbækˈjɑrd, -z

Bacofoil
BR ˈbeɪkə(ʊ)fɔɪl
AM ˈbækəˌfɔɪl

Bacolod
BR bəˈkəʊlɒd
AM bəˈkoʊˌlɑd

bacon
BR ˈbeɪk(ə)n
AM ˈbeɪkən

Baconian
BR beɪˈkəʊnɪən, bəˈkəʊnɪən, -z
AM bəˈkoʊnɪən, beɪˈkoʊnɪən, -z

bacteraemia
BR ˌbaktəˈriːmɪə(r)
AM ˌbæktəˈrimɪə

bacteremia
BR ˌbaktəˈriːmɪə(r)
AM ˌbæktəˈrimɪə

bacteria
BR bakˈtɪərɪə(r)
AM bækˈtɪrɪə

bacterial
BR bakˈtɪərɪəl
AM bækˈtɪrɪəl

bactericidal
BR bakˌtɪərɪˈsʌɪdl
AM bækˌtɪriˈsaɪdəl

bactericide
BR bakˈtɪərɪsʌɪd, -z
AM bækˈtɪriˌsaɪd, -z

bacteriological
BR bakˌtɪərɪəˈlɒdʒɪkl
AM bækˌtɪrɪəˈlɑdʒəkəl

bacteriologically
BR bakˌtɪərɪəˈlɒdʒɪkli
AM bækˌtɪrɪəˈlɑdʒək(ə)li

bacteriologist
BR bakˌtɪərɪˈɒlədʒɪst, -s
AM bækˌtɪriˈɑlədʒəst, -s

bacteriology
BR bakˌtɪərɪˈɒlədʒi
AM bækˌtɪriˈɑlədʒi

bacteriolyses
BR bakˌtɪərɪˈɒlɪsiːz
AM bækˌtɪriˈɑləsiz

bacteriolysis
BR bakˌtɪərɪˈɒlɪsɪs
AM bækˌtɪriˈɑləsəs

bacteriolytic
BR bakˌtɪərɪəˈlɪtɪk
AM bækˌtɪriəˈlɪdɪk

bacteriophage
BR bakˈtɪərɪəˌfeɪdʒ, -ɪz
AM bækˈtɪriəˌfeɪdʒ, -ɪz

bacteriostases
BR bakˌtɪərɪəʊˈsteɪsiːz
AM bækˌtɪriəʊˈsteɪsiz, bækˌtɪriəʊˈstæsiz, bækˌtɪriˈastəsiz

bacteriostasis
BR bakˌtɪərɪəʊˈsteɪsɪs
AM bækˌtɪriəʊˈsteɪsɪs, bækˌtɪriəʊˈstæsəs, bækˌtɪriˈastəsəs

bacteriostatic
BR bakˌtɪərɪə(ʊ)ˈstatɪk
AM bækˌtɪriəˈstædɪk

bacterium
BR bakˈtɪərɪəm
AM bækˈtɪriəm

Bactria
BR ˈbaktrɪə(r)
AM ˈbæktriə

Bactrian
BR ˈbaktrɪən, -z
AM ˈbæktriən, -z

bad
BR bad
AM bæd

badass
BR ˈbadɑːs, -ɪz
AM ˈbædˌæs, -əz

Baddesley
BR ˈbad(ɪ)zli
AM ˈbæd(ə)zli

baddish
BR ˈbadɪʃ
AM ˈbædɪʃ

baddy
BR ˈbad|i, -ɪz
AM ˈbædi, -z

bade
BR bad, beɪd
AM beɪd, bæd

Badedas®
BR bəˈdeɪdəs, bəˈdeɪdas, ˈbɑːdɪdas, ˈbadidas
AM ˈbædədəs

Badel
BR bəˈdɛl
AM ˈbeɪdəl, ˈbædəl

Baden[1]
English surname
BR ˈbeɪdn
AM ˈbeɪdən

Baden[2]
German placename
BR ˈbɑːdn
AM ˈbɑdən

Baden-Baden
BR ˌbɑːdnˈbɑːdn
AM ˈbɑdənˈbɑdən

Baden-Powell
BR ˌbeɪdnˈpaʊ(ə)l
AM ˈbɑdnˈpaʊəl

Baden-Württemberg
BR ˌbɑːdnˈwəːtəmbəːg
AM ˌbɑdnˈwərtəmˌbərg
GER ˌbaːdnˈvʏrtəmbɛrk

Bader
BR ˈbɑːdə(r)
AM ˈbeɪdər

badge
BR badʒ, -ɪz, -ɪŋ, -d
AM bædʒ, -əz, -ɪŋ, -d

badger
BR ˈbadʒ|ə(r), -əz, -(ə)rɪŋ, -əd
AM ˈbædʒər, -z, -ɪŋ, -d

Badian
BR ˈbeɪdɪən, -z
AM ˈbɑdiən, -z

badinage
BR ˈbadɪnɑːʒ, ˌbadɪˈnɑːʒ
AM ˌbædnˈɑʒ

badlands
BR ˈbadlandz
AM ˈbædˌlændz

badly
BR ˈbadli
AM ˈbædli

badminton
BR ˈbadmɪnt(ə)n
AM ˈbædˌmɪtn, ˈbædˌmɪn(t)ən

bad-mouth
BR ˈbadmaʊθ, ˈbadmaʊð, ˈbadmaʊð, -θs\-ðz, -θɪŋ\-ðɪŋ, -θt\-ðd
AM ˈbædˌmaʊθ, -θs\-ðz, -θɪŋ\-ðɪŋ, -θt\-ðd

badness
BR ˈbadnəs
AM ˈbædnəs

Badon
BR ˈbeɪdn
AM ˈbeɪdən

Baedeker
BR ˈbeɪdɪkə(r), ˈbeɪˌdɛkə(r), -z
AM ˈbeɪdəkər, ˈbeɪˌdɛkə(r), -z

Baerlein
BR ˈbɛːlʌɪn

Baden[1]
English surname
BR ˈbeɪdn
AM ˈbeɪdən

Baez
BR ˈbʌɪ(ɛ)z
AM baɪˈɛz

Baffin
BR ˈbafɪn
AM ˈbæfən

baffle
BR ˈbaf|l, -lz, -lɪŋ\-lɪŋ, -ld
AM ˈbæf|əl, -əlz, -(ə)lɪŋ, -əld

baffleboard
BR ˈbaflbɔːd, -z
AM ˈbæfəlˌbɔ(ə)rd, -z

bafflement
BR ˈbaflm(ə)nt
AM ˈbæfəlmənt

baffle-plate
BR ˈbaflpleɪt, -s
AM ˈbæfəlˌpleɪt, -s

baffler
BR ˈbaflə(r), ˈbaflə(r), -z
AM ˈbæf(ə)lər, -z

bafflingly
BR ˈbaflɪŋli, ˈbaflɪŋli
AM ˈbæf(ə)lɪŋli

BAFTA
BR ˈbaftə(r)
AM ˈbæftə

bag
BR bag, -z, -ɪŋ, -d
AM bæg, -z, -ɪŋ, -d

Baganda
BR bəˈgandə(r)
AM bəˈgɑndə

Bagandan
BR bəˈgandən, -z
AM bəˈgɑndən, -z

bagarre
BR bəˈgɑː(r), baˈgɑː(r), -z
AM bəˈgɑr, -z

bagasse
BR bəˈgas, baˈgas, bəˈgɑːs, baˈgɑːs
AM bəˈgɑs

bagatelle
BR ˌbagəˈtɛl
AM ˌbægəˈtɛl

Bagdad
BR ˌbagˈdad
AM ˈbægˌdæd

Bagehot
BR ˈbadʒət
AM ˈbædʒət

bagel
BR ˈbeɪgl, -z
AM ˈbeɪgəl, -z

bagful
BR ˈbagfʊl, -z
AM ˈbægˌfʊl, -z

baggage
BR ˈbagɪdʒ
AM ˈbægɪdʒ

baggily
BR ˈbagɪli
AM ˈbægəli

bagginess
BR ˈbagɪnɪs
AM ˈbæginɪs

baggy
BR ˈbagǀi, -ɪə(r), -ɪɪst
AM ˈbægi, -ər, -ɪst

Baghdad
BR ˌbagˈdad
AM ˈbæɡ.dæd

bagman
BR ˈbagman
AM ˈbæɡˌmæn

bagmen
BR ˈbagmɛn
AM ˈbæɡˌmɛn

Bagnall
BR ˈbagnl
AM ˈbægnl

Bagnell
BR ˈbagnl
AM ˈbægnl

bagnio
BR ˈbanjəʊ, ˈbɑːnjəʊ, -z
AM ˈbænˌjoʊ, -z

bagpipe
BR ˈbagpʌɪp, -s, -ɪŋ, -t
AM ˈbæɡˌpaɪp, -s, -ɪŋ, -t

bagpiper
BR ˈbagˌpʌɪpə(r), -z
AM ˈbæɡˌpaɪpər, -z

Bagshaw
BR ˈbagʃɔː(r)
AM ˈbæɡˌʃɔ

Bagshot
BR ˈbagʃɒt
AM ˈbæɡˌʃɑt

baguet
BR baˈɡɛt, -s
AM bæˈɡɛt, -s

baguette
BR baˈɡɛt, -s
AM bæˈɡɛt, -s

Baguley
BR ˈbagəli, ˈbagǀi
AM ˈbægəli

bagwash
BR ˈbagwɒʃ, -ɪz
AM ˈbæɡˌwɔʃ,
ˈbæɡˌwaʃ, -əz

bah
BR bɑː(r)
AM bɑ

Bahai
BR bəˈhʌɪ, bɑːˈhʌɪ, -z
AM bɑˈhaɪ, -z

Baha'i
BR bəˈhʌɪ, bɑːˈhʌɪ, -z
AM bɑˈhaɪ, -z

Baha'ism
BR bəˈhʌɪɪz(ə)m,
bɑːˈhʌɪɪz(ə)m
AM bɑˈhaɪˌɪzəm

Baha'ist
BR bəˈhʌɪɪst,
bɑːˈhʌɪɪst, -s
AM bɑˈhaɪɪst, -s

Baha'ite
BR bɑːhəʌɪt, -s
AM ˈbɑhaɪˌaɪt, -s

Bahamas
BR bəˈhɑːməz
AM bəˈhaməs

Bahamian
BR bəˈheɪmɪən,
bəˈhɑːmɪən, -z
AM bəˈhamiən,
bəˈheɪmiən, -z

Bahasa
BR bəˈhɑːsə(r)
AM bəˈhasə

Baha Ullah
BR ˌbɑːhɑː ˈʊlɑː(r),
+ ˈʊlə(r), bəˌhɑː(r)
ʊˈlɑː(r)
AM ˌbɑhɑ ˈʊlɑ

Bahawalpur
BR bəˌhɑːˈw(ə)lˈpʊə(r)
AM bɑˌhawəlˈpʊ(ə)r

Bahía
BR bəˈhiːə(r)
AM bɑˈ(h)iə

Bahrain
BR bɑːˈreɪn
AM bɑˈreɪn

Bahraini
BR bɑːˈreɪnǀi, -ɪz
AM bɑˈreɪni, -z

Bahrein
BR bɑːˈreɪn
AM bɑˈreɪn

Bahreini
BR bɑːˈreɪnǀi, -ɪz
AM bɑˈreɪni, -z

baht
BR bɑːt, -s
AM bɑt, -s

baignoire
BR ˈbeɪnwɑː(r), -z
AM ˌbeɪnˈwɑr, -z

Baikal
BR bʌɪˈkɑːl, bʌɪˈkal
AM baɪˈkɑl

bail
BR beɪl, -z, -ɪŋ, -d
AM beɪl, -z, -ɪŋ, -d

bailable
BR ˈbeɪləbl
AM ˈbeɪləbəl

Baildon
BR ˈbeɪld(ə)n
AM ˈbeɪldən

Baile Átha Cliath
BR ˌblɑː ˌɑθə ˈkliə(r)
AM ˌbal ˌæθə ˈkliə
IR ˌblʲaː ˈkʲlʲiə

bailee
BR ˌbeɪˈliː, ˈbeɪliː, -z
AM beɪˈli, -z

bailer
BR ˈbeɪlə(r), -z
AM ˈbeɪlər, -z

bailey
BR ˈbeɪlǀi, -ɪz
AM ˈbeɪli, -z

bailie
BR ˈbeɪlǀi, -ɪz
AM ˈbeɪli, -z

bailiff
BR ˈbeɪlɪf, -s
AM ˈbeɪlɪf, -s

bailiwick
BR ˈbeɪlɪwɪk, -s
AM ˈbeɪliˌwɪk,
ˈbeɪlɪˌwɪk, -s

Baillie
BR ˈbeɪli
AM ˈbeɪli

Bailly
BR ˈbeɪli
AM ˈbeɪli

bailment
BR ˈbeɪlm(ə)nt
AM ˈbeɪlmənt

bailor
BR ˈbeɪlə(r), -z
AM ˈbeɪlər, -z

bailout
BR ˈbeɪlaʊt
AM ˈbeɪˌlaʊt

bailsman
BR ˈbeɪlzmən
AM ˈbeɪlzmən

bailsmen
BR ˈbeɪlzmən
AM ˈbeɪlzmən

Bain
BR beɪn
AM beɪn

Bainbridge
BR ˈbeɪnbrɪdʒ
AM ˈbeɪnˌbrɪdʒ

Baines
BR beɪnz
AM beɪnz

bain-marie
BR ˌbanməˈriː,
ˌba(m)məˈriː, -z
AM ˌbænməˈri,
ˌbæ(m)məˈri

bains-marie
BR ˌbanməˈriː,
ˌba(m)məˈriː, -z
AM ˌbænməˈri,
ˌbæ(m)məˈri, -z

Bairam
BR bʌɪˈrɑːm
AM baɪˈrɑm

Baird
BR bɛːd
AM bɛ(ə)rd

bairn
BR bɛːn, -z
AM bɛ(ə)rn, -z

Bairstow
BR ˈbɛːstəʊ

Balaclava
AM ˈbɛrstoʊ

bait
BR beɪt, -s, -ɪŋ, -ɪd
AM beɪǀt, -ts, -dɪŋ, -dɪd

baize
BR beɪz
AM beɪz

Baja California
BR ˌbɑːhə
ˌkalɪˈfɔːnɪə(r)
AM ˌbɑhɑ ˌkæləˈfɔrniə

Bajan
BR ˈbeɪdʒ(ə)n, -z
AM ˈbahən, -z

bajra
BR ˈbɑːdʒrɑː(r)
AM ˈbadʒrə

bake
BR beɪk, -s, -ɪŋ, -t
AM beɪk, -s, -ɪŋ, -t

bakehouse
BR ˈbeɪkhaʊǀs, -zɪz
AM ˈbeɪkˌ(h)aʊǀs, -zəz

Bakelite®
BR ˈbeɪkəlʌɪt
AM ˈbeɪkˌə)ˌlaɪt

baker
BR ˈbeɪkə(r), -z
AM ˈbeɪkər, -z

Bakerloo
BR ˌbeɪkəˈluː
AM ˌbeɪkərˈlu

bakery
BR ˈbeɪkˌ(ə)rǀi, -ɪz
AM ˈbeɪkəri, -z

Bakewell
BR ˈbeɪkw(ɛ)l
AM ˈbeɪkˌwɛl

Bakhtin
BR bakˈtiːn
AM ˌbakˈtin, ˌbækˈtin
RUS baxˈtʲin

baklava
BR ˈbakləvə(r)
AM ˌbakləˈva
TU bʌklʌˈvʌ

baksheesh
BR ˈbakʃiːʃ, ˌbakˈʃiːʃ
AM ˈbækˈʃiʃ

Bakst
BR bakst
AM bækst

Baku
BR bɑːˌkuː, bɑːˈkuː
AM bɑˈku

Bakunin
BR bəˈkuːnɪn,
baˈkuːnɪn
AM bəˈkunɪn

Bala
BR ˈbalə(r), ˈbɑːlə(r)
AM ˈbalə

Balaam
BR ˈbeɪləm
AM ˈbeɪləm

balaclava
BR ˌbaləˈklɑːvə(r), -z

AM ˌbæləˈklɑvə,
ˌbaləˈklɑvə, -z
balafon
BR ˈbaləfɒn, -z
AM ˈbæləˌfɑn, -z
balalaika
BR ˌbaləˈlʌɪkə(r), -z
AM ˌbaləˈlaɪkə,
ˌbæləˈlaɪkə, -z
balance
BR ˈbaləns, ˈbaln̩s, -ɪz,
-ɪŋ, -t
AM ˈbæləns, -əz, -ɪŋ, -t
balanceable
BR ˈbalənsəbl,
ˈbaln̩səbl
AM ˈbælənsəbəl
balancer
BR ˈbalənsə(r),
ˈbaln̩sə(r), -z
AM ˈbælənsər, -z
Balanchine
BR ˈbalən(t)ʃiːn,
ˌbalənˈ(t)ʃiːn
AM ˈbalænˌ(t)ʃin
balas-ruby
BR ˈbaləsˌruːb|i, -ɪz
AM ˈbæləsˌrubi, -z
balata
BR ˈbalətə(r),
bəˈlɑːtə(r), -z
AM bəˈladə, ˈbælədə, -z
Balaton
BR ˈbalətɒn
AM ˈbaləˌtɑn
HU ˌbɒlɔˈtɒn
Balboa
BR balˈbəʊə(r)
AM bælˈboʊə
Balbriggan
BR balˈbrɪg(ə)n
AM bælˈbrɪgən
Balchin
BR ˈbɔːl(t)ʃɪn,
ˈbɒl(t)ʃɪn
AM ˈbɔːltʃɪn, ˈbaltʃɪn
Balcomb
BR ˈbɔːlkəm, ˈbɒlkəm
AM ˈbɔlkəmb,
ˈbalkəmb
Balcombe
BR ˈbɔːlkəm, ˈbɒlkəm
AM ˈbɔlkəmb,
ˈbalkəmb
Balcon
BR ˈbɔːlk(ə)n,
ˈbɒlk(ə)n
AM ˈbælkən
balcony
BR ˈbalkən|i, ˈbalkn̩|i,
-ɪz, -ɪd
AM ˈbælkəni, -z, -d
bald
BR bɔːld, -z, -ɪŋ, -ɪd,
-ə(r), -ɪst
AM bɔld, bald, -ər, -əst,
-z, -ɪŋ, -əd

baldachin
BR ˈbɔːldəkɪn, -z
AM ˈbɒldəkən,
ˈbaldəkən, -z
baldaquin
BR ˈbɔːldəkɪn, -z
AM ˈbɒldəkən,
ˈbaldəkən, -z
Balder
BR ˈbɔːldə(r), ˈbɒldə(r)
AM ˈbɔldər, ˈbaldər
balderdash
BR ˈbɔːldədaʃ
AM ˈbɔldərˌdæʃ,
ˈbaldərˌdæʃ
baldhead
BR ˈbɔːldhɛd, -z
AM ˈbɒldˌ(h)ɛd,
ˈbaldˌ(h)ɛd, -z
baldheaded
BR ˌbɔːldˈhɛdɪd
AM ˈbɒldˈhɛdəd,
ˈbaldˈhɛdəd
baldie
BR ˈbɔːld|i, -ɪz
AM ˈbɒldi, ˈbaldi, -z
baldish
BR ˈbɔːldɪʃ
AM ˈbɔldɪʃ, ˈbaldɪʃ
baldly
BR ˈbɔːldli
AM ˈbɔl(d)li, ˈbal(d)li
baldmoney
BR ˈbɔːldˌmʌn|i, -ɪz
AM ˈbɒl(d)ˌməni,
ˈbal(d)ˌməni, -z
baldness
BR ˈbɔːldnəs
AM ˈbɔl(d)nəs,
ˈbal(d)nəs
Baldock
BR ˈbɔːldɒk, ˈbɒldɒk
AM ˈbɔldak, ˈbaldak
baldpate
BR ˈbɔːldpeɪt, -s
AM ˈbɔl(d)ˌpeɪt,
ˈbal(d)ˌpeɪt, -s
baldric
BR ˈbɔːldrɪk, -s
AM ˈbɔldˌrɪk, ˈbaldˌrɪk,
-s
Baldry
BR ˈbɔːldri, ˈbɒldri
AM ˈbɔldri, ˈbaldri
Baldwin
BR ˈbɔːldwɪn
AM ˈbɔldwən,
ˈbaldwən
baldy
BR ˈbɔːld|i, -ɪz
AM ˈbɔldi, ˈbaldi, -z
bale
BR beɪl, -z, -ɪŋ, -d
AM beɪl, -z, -ɪŋ, -d
Balearic
BR ˌbalɪˈarɪk,
bəˈlɪərɪk, bəˈlɛːrɪk, -s
AM ˌbæliˈɛrɪk, -s

baleen
BR bəˈliːn
AM bəˈlin
baleful
BR ˈbeɪlf(ʊ)l
AM ˈbeɪlfəl
balefully
BR ˈbeɪlfəli, ˈbeɪlf̩li
AM ˈbeɪlfəli
balefulness
BR ˈbeɪlf(ʊ)lnəs
AM ˈbeɪlfəlnəs
Balenciaga
BR bəˌlɛnsɪˈɑːgə(r)
AM bəˈlɛnsiˈagə
SP ˌbalenˈθjaɣa,
ˌbalenˈsjaɣa
baler
BR ˈbeɪlə(r), -z
AM ˈbeɪlər, -z
Balfour
BR ˈbalfə(r), ˈbalfɔː(r),
ˌbalˈfɔː(r)
AM ˈbælˌfɔ(ə)r
Balham
BR ˈbaləm
AM ˈbɒləm, ˈbaləm
Bali
BR ˈbɑːli
AM ˈbɑˌli
Balinese
BR ˌbɑːlɪˈniːz
AM ˌbaləˈniz, ˌbæləˈniz
Baliol
BR ˈbeɪlɪəl
AM ˈbeɪliəl
balk
BR ˈbɔː(l)k, -s, -ɪŋ, -t
AM bɔ(l)k, bɑ(l)k, -s,
-ɪŋ, -t
Balkan
BR ˈbɔːlk(ə)n,
ˈbɒlk(ə)n, -z
AM ˈbɔlkən, ˈbalkən, -z
Balkanisation
BR ˌbɔːlkənʌɪˈzeɪʃn,
ˌbɔːlkn̩ʌɪˈzeɪʃn,
ˌbɒlkənʌɪˈzeɪʃn,
ˌbɒlkn̩ʌɪˈzeɪʃn
AM ˌbɔlkənəˈzeɪʃən,
ˌbɒlkəˌnaɪˈzeɪʃən,
ˌbalkənəˈzeɪʃən,
ˌbalkəˌnaɪˈzeɪʃən
Balkanise
BR ˈbɔːlkənʌɪz,
ˈbɔːlkn̩ʌɪz,
ˈbɒlkənʌɪz, ˈbɒlkn̩ʌɪz,
-ɪz, -ɪŋ, -d
AM ˈbɔlkəˌnaɪz,
ˈbalkəˌnaɪz, -ɪz, -ɪŋ, -d
Balkanization
BR ˌbɔːlkənʌɪˈzeɪʃn,
ˌbɔːlkn̩ʌɪˈzeɪʃn,
ˌbɒlkənʌɪˈzeɪʃn,
ˌbɒlkn̩ʌɪˈzeɪʃn
AM ˌbɔlkənəˈzeɪʃən,
ˌbɒlkəˌnaɪˈzeɪʃən,

ˌbɔlkənəˈzeɪʃən,
ˌbalkəˌnaɪˈzeɪʃən
Balkanize
BR ˈbɔːlkənʌɪz,
ˈbɔːlkn̩ʌɪz,
ˈbɒlkənʌɪz, ˈbɒlkn̩ʌɪz,
-ɪz, -ɪŋ, -d
AM ˈbɔlkəˌnaɪz,
ˈbalkəˌnaɪz, -ɪz, -ɪŋ, -d
Balkhash
BR ˈbalkaʃ
AM ˈbælˌkæʃ
RUS balˈxaʃ
balky
BR ˈbɔːk|i, -ɪə(r), -ɪɪst
AM ˈbɔki, ˈbaki, -ər, -ɪst
ball
BR bɔːl, -z, -ɪŋ, -d
AM bɔl, bal, -z, -ɪŋ, -d
Ballachulish
BR ˌbaləˈhuːlɪʃ
AM ˌbæləˈtʃulɪʃ
ballad
BR ˈbaləd, -z
AM ˈbæləd, -z
ballade
BR bəˈlɑːd, baˈlɑːd, -z
AM bəˈlad, -z
balladeer
BR ˌbaləˈdɪə(r), -z
AM ˌbæləˈdɪ(ə)r, -z
balladry
BR ˈbalədr|i, -ɪz
AM ˈbælədri, -z
Ballantine
BR ˈbaləntʌɪn
AM ˈbælənˌtaɪn
Ballantrae
BR ˌbalənˈtreɪ
AM ˈbæləntri
Ballantyne
BR ˈbaləntʌɪn
AM ˈbælənˌtaɪn
Ballarat
BR ˈbalarat, ˌbaləˈrat
AM ˈbæləˌræt
Ballard
BR ˈbalɑːd
AM ˈbælərd
ballast
BR ˈbaləst
AM ˈbæləst
Ballater
BR ˈbalətə(r)
AM ˈbælədər
ballbearing
BR ˌbɔːlˈbɛːrɪŋ, -z
AM ˈbɔlˌbɛrɪŋ,
ˈbalˌbɛrɪŋ, -z
ballboy
BR ˈbɔːlbɔɪ, -z
AM ˈbɔlˌbɔɪ, ˈbalˌbɔɪ, -z
ballcock
BR ˈbɔːlkɒk, -s
AM ˈbɔlˌkak, ˈbalˌkak,
-s

ballerina
BR ˌbæləˈriːnə(r), -z
AM ˌbæləˈriːnə, -z
Ballesteros
BR ˌbalɪˈstɛːrɒs
AM ˌbæləˈstɛˌroʊs, ˌbaɪjəsˈteroʊs
SP ˌbajesˈteros
ballet
BR ˈbaleɪ, -z
AM bæˈleɪ, -z
balletic
BR bəˈlɛtɪk, baˈlɛtɪk
AM bæˈlɛdɪk, bəˈlɛdɪk
balletomane
BR ˈbalɪtə(ʊ)meɪn, bəˈlɛtə(ʊ)meɪn, baˈlɛtə(ʊ)meɪn, -z
AM bəˈlɛdəˌmeɪn, bæˈlɛdəˌmeɪn, -z
balletomania
BR ˌbalɪtə(ʊ)ˈmeɪnɪə(r), bəˌlɛtəˌmeɪnɪə(r), baˌlɛtəˌmeɪnɪə(r)
AM bəˌlɛdəˈmeɪnɪə, bæˌlɛdəˈmeɪnɪə
Ballets Russes
BR ˌbaleɪ ˈruːs
AM ˌbæˌleɪ ˈrus
ballgirl
BR ˈbɔːlgəːl, -z
AM ˈbɔlˌgərl, ˈbalˌgərl, -z
ballhandler
BR ˈbɔːlˌhandlə(r), ˈbɔːlˌhandlə(r), -z
AM ˈbɔlˌ(h)æn(də)lər, ˈbalˌ(h)æn(də)lər, -z
ballhawk
BR ˈbɔːlhɔːk, -s
AM ˈbɔlˌ(h)ɔk, ˈbalˌ(h)ɑk, -s
Balliol
BR ˈbeɪlɪəl
AM ˈbeɪlɪəl
ballista
BR bəˈlɪstə(r), -z
AM bəˈlɪstə, -z
ballistae
BR bəˈlɪstiː
AM bəˈlɪsti
ballistic
BR bəˈlɪstɪk, -s
AM bəˈlɪstɪk, -s
ballistically
BR bəˈlɪstɪkli
AM bəˈlɪstɪk(ə)li
ballock
BR ˈbɒlək, -s
AM ˈbɑlək, ˈbɑlək, -s
ballon d'essai
BR ˌbalõ dɛˈseɪ
AM bɑˌlɒn ˌdɛˈseɪ
ballons d'essai
BR ˌbalõ dɛˈseɪ
AM bɑˌlɒn ˌdɛˈseɪ
balloon
BR bəˈluːn, -z, -ɪŋ, -d

AM bəˈlun, -z, -ɪŋ, -d
balloonist
BR bəˈluːnɪst, -s
AM bəˈlunəst, -s
ballot
BR ˈbalət, -s, -ɪŋ, -ɪd
AM ˈbæləlt, -ts, -dɪŋ, -dɪd
ballpark
BR ˈbɔːlpɑːk, -s
AM ˈbɔlˌpɑrk, ˈbalˌpɑrk, -s
ballplayer
BR ˈbɔːlˌpleɪə(r), -z
AM ˈbɔlˌpleɪər, ˈbalˌpleɪər, -z
ballpoint
BR ˈbɔːlpɔɪnt, -s
AM ˈbɔlˌpɔɪnt, ˈbalˌpɔɪnt, -s
ballroom
BR ˈbɔːlruːm, ˈbɔːlrʊm, -z
AM ˈbɔlˌrum, ˈbɔlˌrʊm, ˈbalˌrum, ˈbalˌrʊm, -z
balls
verb
BR bɔːlz, -ɪz, -ɪŋ, -d
AM bɔlz, bɑlz, -əz, -ɪŋ, -d
ballsy
BR ˈbɔːlzi
AM ˈbɔlzi, ˈbalzi
bally
BR ˈbali
AM ˈbæli
Ballycastle
BR ˌbalɪˈkɑːsl, ˌbalɪˈkasl
AM ˈbæliˌkæsəl
ballyhoo
BR ˌbalɪˈhuː, -z
AM ˈbæliˌhu, -z
Ballymacarrett
BR ˌbalɪməˈkarət
AM ˌbælɪˈməˈkɛrət
Ballymena
BR ˌbalɪˈmiːnə(r)
AM ˌbæliˈminə
Ballymoney
BR ˌbalɪˈmʌni
AM ˌbæliˈməni
ballyrag
BR ˈbalɪrag, -z, -ɪŋ, -d
AM ˈbæliˌræg, -z, -ɪŋ, -d
balm
BR bɑːm, -z
AM bɑ(l)m, -z
Balmain
BR ˈbalmã
AM ˈbɒlmeɪn, ˈbalmeɪn
balmily
BR ˈbɑːmɪli
AM ˈbɑ(l)məli
balminess
BR ˈbɑːmɪnɪs
AM ˈbɑ(l)mɪnɪs

Balmoral
BR balˈmɒrəl, balˈmɒrl
AM bælˈmɔrəl
balmy
BR ˈbɑːm|i, -ɪə(r), -ɪɪst
AM ˈbɑ(l)mi, -ər, -ɪst
balneary
BR ˈbalnɪəri
AM ˈbælniˌɛri
balneological
BR ˌbalnɪəˈlɒdʒɪkl
AM ˌbælnɪəˈladʒəkəl
balneologist
BR ˌbalnɪˈɒlədʒɪst, -s
AM ˌbælniˈɑlədʒəst, -s
balneology
BR ˌbalnɪˈɒlədʒi
AM ˌbælniˈɑlədʒi
balniel
BR ˈbalnɪəl
AM ˈbælnɪəl
baloney
BR bəˈləʊni
AM bəˈloʊni
BALPA
BR ˈbalpə(r)
AM ˈbælpə
balsam
BR ˈbɔːls(ə)m, ˈbɒls(ə)m, -z
AM ˈbɒlsəm, ˈbalsəm, -z
balsamic
BR bɔːlˈsamɪk, bɒlˈsamɪk
AM bɒlˈsamɪk, balˈsamɪk, bɔlˈsæmɪk, balˈsæmɪk
balsamiferous
BR ˌbɔːlsəˈmɪf(ə)rəs, ˌbɒlsəˈmɪf(ə)rəs
AM ˌbɒlsəˈmɪf(ə)rəs, ˌbalsəˈmɪf(ə)rəs
balsa wood
BR ˈbɔːlsə wʊd, ˈbɒlsə +
AM ˈbɒlsə ˌwʊd, ˈbalsə ˌwʊd
Balt
BR bɔːlt, bɒlt, -s
AM bolt, balt, -s
Balthasar
BR balˈθazə(r), ˈbalθəzɑː(r), ˌbalθəˈzɑː(r)
AM bælˈθæzər, bɒlˈθæzər, balˈθæzər, ˈbɒlθəˌzar, ˈbalθəˌzar
Balthazar
BR balˈθazə(r), ˈbalθəzɑː(r), ˌbalθəˈzɑː(r)
AM bælˈθæzər, bɒlˈθæzər, balˈθæzər, ˈbɒlθəˌzar, ˈbalθəˌzar
balti
BR ˈbɔːlt|i, ˈbɒlt|i, -ɪz

Balmoral
AM ˈbælti, ˈbɒlti, ˈbalti, -z
Baltic
BR ˈbɔːltɪk, ˈbɒltɪk
AM ˈbɒltɪk, ˈbaltɪk
Baltimore
BR ˈbɔːltɪmɔː(r), ˈbɒltɪmɔː(r)
AM ˈbɒltəˌmɔ(ə)r, ˈbaltəˌmɔ(ə)r
Baltistan
BR ˌbɔːltɪˈstɑːn, ˌbɔːltɪˈstan, ˌbɒltɪˈstɑːn, ˌbɒltɪˈstan
AM ˈbɒltəˌstæn, ˈbaltəˌstæn
Baluchistan
BR bəˌluːtʃɪˈstɑːn, bəˌluːtʃɪˈstan
AM bəˈlutʃəˌstæn
balun
BR ˈbalʌn, -z
AM ˈbælən, -z
baluster
BR ˈbaləstə(r), -z, -d
AM ˈbæləstər, -z, -d
balustrade
BR ˌbaləˈstreɪd, -z, -ɪŋ, -ɪd
AM ˌbæləˌstreɪd, -z, -ɪŋ, -ɪd
Balzac
BR ˈbalzak
AM balˈzɑk, balˈzæk
Bamako
BR ˌbaməˈkəʊ, ˈbamakəʊ
AM bəˈmæˌkoʊ, bəˈmaˌkoʊ
bambini
BR bamˈbiːni
AM bæmˈbini
bambino
BR bamˈbiːnəʊ, -z
AM bæmˈbinoʊ, -z
bamboo
BR ˌbamˈbuː, -z
AM ˌbæmˈbu, -z
bamboozle
BR bamˈbuːz|l, -lz, -lɪŋ \ -lɪŋ, -ld
AM bæmˈbuz|əl, -əlz, -(ə)lɪŋ, -əld
bamboozlement
BR bamˈbuːzlm(ə)nt
AM bæmˈbuzlmənt
bamboozler
BR bamˈbuːzlə(r), bamˈbuːzlə(r), -z
AM bæmˈbuz(ə)lər, -z
Bamian
BR ˈbeɪmɪən
AM ˈbeɪmɪən
ban
BR ban, -z, -ɪŋ, -d
AM bæn, -z, -ɪŋ, -d

banal
BR bə'nɑːl, bə'nal
AM 'beɪnl, bə'næl,
bə'nɑl

banality
BR bə'nalɪt|i, -ɪz
AM bə'nælədi,
beɪ'nælədi, -z

banally
BR bə'nɑːlli
AM 'beɪnɪli

banana
BR bə'nɑːnə(r), -z
AM bə'nænə, -z

banausic
BR bə'nɔːzɪk, bə'nɔːsɪk
AM bə'nɔzɪk, bə'nɔsɪk,
bə'nɑzɪk, bə'nɑsɪk

Banbury
BR 'banb(ə)ri
AM 'bænbəri

banc
BR baŋk
AM bæŋk

Bancroft
BR 'bankrɒft,
'baŋkrʊft
AM 'bæn,krɒft,
'bæŋ,krɒft,
'bæn,krɑft,
'bæŋ,krɑft

band
BR band, -z, -ɪŋ, -ɪd
AM bænd, -z, -ɪŋ, -əd

Banda
BR 'bandə(r)
AM 'bændə

bandage
BR 'band|ɪdʒ, -ɪdʒɪz,
-ɪdʒɪŋ, -ɪdʒd
AM 'bænd|ɪdʒ, -ɪdʒɪz,
-ɪdʒɪŋ, -ɪdʒd

bandana
BR ban'danə(r), -z
AM bæn'dænə, -z

bandanna
BR ban'danə(r), -z
AM bæn'dænə, -z

Bandaranaike
BR ,band(ə)rə'nʌɪkə(r)
AM ,bændrə'niki

**Bandar Seri
Begawan**
BR ,bandɑː ,sɛri
bə'gɑːwən, ,bandə +
AM ,bændər ,sɛri
bə'gawən

bandbox
BR 'ban(d)bɒks, -ɪz
AM 'bæn(d),bɑks, -əz

bandeau
BR 'bandəʊ, -z
AM 'bæn,doʊ, -z

bandeaux
BR 'bandəʊz
AM 'bæn,doʊz

banderilla
BR ,bandə'rɪljə(r), -z

AM ,bændə'ri(j)ə, -z

banderol
BR 'bandərəʊl, -z
AM 'bændə,roʊl, -z

banderole
BR 'bandərəʊl, -z
AM 'bændə,roʊl, -z

bandicoot
BR 'bandɪkuːt, -s
AM 'bændi,kut, -s

bandit
BR 'bandɪt, -s
AM 'bændɪt, -s

bandito
BR ban'diːtəʊ, -z
AM bæn'didoʊ, -z

banditry
BR 'bandɪtri
AM 'bændɪtri

banditti
BR ban'dɪtiː
AM bæn'didi

bandleader
BR 'band,liːdə(r), -z
AM 'bæn(d),lidər, -z

bandmaster
BR 'band,mɑːstə(r),
'ban(d),mastə(r), -z
AM 'bæn(d),mæstər, -z

bandoleer
BR ,bandə'lɪə(r), -z
AM ,bændə'lɪ(ə)r, -z

bandolier
BR ,bandə'lɪə(r), -z
AM ,bændə'lɪ(ə)r, -z

bandore
BR ban'dɔː(r),
'bandɔː(r), -z
AM 'bæn,dɔ(ə)r, -z

bandsman
BR 'ban(d)zmən
AM 'bæn(d)zmən

bandsmen
BR 'ban(d)zmən
AM 'bæn(d)zmən

bandstand
BR 'ban(d)stand, -z
AM 'bæn(d),stænd, -z

Bandung
BR 'bandʊŋ, ban'dʊŋ
AM 'ban,dʊŋ, 'ban,dʊŋ

bandwagon
BR 'band,wag(ə)n, -z
AM 'bæn(d),wægən, -z

bandwidth
BR 'bandwɪdθ,
'bandwɪtθ
AM 'bæn(d),wɪdθ,
'bæn(d),wɪtθ

bandy
BR 'band|i, -ɪz, -ɪɪŋ, -ɪd,
-ɪə(r), -ɪɪst
AM 'bændi, -z, -ɪŋ, -d,
-ər, -ɪst

bane
BR beɪn
AM beɪn

baneberry
BR 'beɪnb(ə)r|i, -ɪz
AM 'beɪn,bɛri, -z

baneful
BR 'beɪnf(ʊ)l
AM 'beɪnfəl

banefully
BR 'beɪnfəli, 'beɪnfļi
AM 'beɪnfəli

banefulness
BR 'beɪnf(ʊ)lnəs
AM 'beɪnfəlnəs

Banff
BR banf
AM bænf

bang
BR baŋ, -z, -ɪŋ, -d
AM bæŋ, -z, -ɪŋ, -d

Bangalore
BR ,baŋgə'lɔː(r)
AM ,bæŋgə'lɔ(ə)r

banger
BR 'baŋə(r), -z
AM 'bæŋər, -z

Bangkok
BR ,baŋ'kɒk
AM 'bæŋkak

Bangladesh
BR ,baŋglə'dɛʃ
AM ,baŋglə'dɛʃ

Bangladeshi
BR ,baŋglə'dɛʃ|i, -ɪz
AM ,baŋglə'dɛʃi, -z

bangle
BR 'baŋgl, -z
AM 'bæŋgəl, -z

Bangor
BR 'baŋgə(r)
AM 'bæŋgər,
'bæŋ,gɔ(ə)r

bangtail
BR 'baŋteɪl, -z
AM 'bæŋ,teɪl, -z

Bangui
BR ,bɒŋ'giː, ,bɑː ŋ'giː,
'bɑːŋgi
AM 'bæŋgi

banian
BR 'banjan, 'banjən, -z
AM 'bænjən, -z

banish
BR 'ban|ɪʃ, -ɪʃɪz, -ɪʃɪŋ,
-ɪʃt
AM 'bænɪʃ, -ɪz, -ɪŋ, -t

banishment
BR 'banɪʃm(ə)nt
AM 'bænɪʃmənt

banister
BR 'banɪstə(r), -z
AM 'bænəstər, -z

banjax
BR 'bandʒaks, -t
AM 'bæn,dʒæks, -t

banjo
BR 'bandʒəʊ, -z
AM 'bændʒoʊ, -z

banjoist
BR 'bandʒəʊɪst, -s
AM 'bændʒəwəst, -s

Banjul
BR ban'dʒuːl
AM 'bæn,dʒul

bank
BR baŋ|k, -ks, -kɪŋ,
-(k)t
AM bæŋ|k, -ks, -kɪŋ,
-(k)t

bankability
BR ,baŋkə'bɪlɪti
AM ,bæŋkə'bɪlɪdi

bankable
BR 'baŋkəbl
AM 'bæŋkəbəl

bankbill
BR 'baŋkbɪl, -z
AM 'bæŋk,bɪl, -z

bankbook
BR 'baŋkbʊk, -s
AM 'bæŋk,bʊk, -s

banker
BR 'baŋkə(r), -z
AM 'bæŋkər, -z

banknote
BR 'baŋknəʊt, -s
AM 'bæŋk,noʊt, -s

bankroll
BR 'baŋkrəʊl, -z, -ɪŋ, -d
AM 'bæŋk,roʊl, -z, -ɪŋ,
-d

bankrupt
BR 'baŋk,rʌpt, -s, -ɪŋ,
-ɪd
AM 'bæŋk,rəpt, -s, -ɪŋ,
-əd

bankruptcy
BR 'baŋkrʌp(t)s|i, -ɪz
AM 'bæŋk,rəp(t)si, -z

banksia
BR 'baŋksɪə(r), -z
AM 'bæŋksiə, -z

banner
BR 'banə(r), -z, -d
AM 'bænər, -z, -d

banneret
BR 'banərɪt, ,banə'rɛt,
-s
AM 'bænərət,
,bænə'rɛt, -s

bannister
BR 'banɪstə(r), -z
AM 'bænəstər, -z

bannock
BR 'banək, -s
AM 'bænək, -s

Bannockburn
BR 'banəkbəːn
AM 'bænək,bərn

banns
BR banz
AM bænz

banquet
BR 'baŋkwɪt, -ɪts, -ɪtɪŋ,
-ɪtɪd

AM ˈbæŋkwɪ|t, -ts, -dɪŋ, -dɪd

banqueter
BR ˈbaŋkwɪtə(r), -z
AM ˈbæŋkwɪdər, -z

banquette
BR baŋˈkɛt, -s
AM bæŋˈkɛt, -s

banshee
BR ˈbanʃiː, -z
AM ˈbænʃi, -z

banshie
BR ˈbanʃiː, -z
AM ˈbænʃi, -z

bantam
BR ˈbantəm, -z
AM ˈbæn(t)əm, -z

bantamweight
BR ˈbantəmweɪt, -s
AM ˈbæn(t)əmˌweɪt, -s

banter
BR ˈbant|ə(r), -əz, -(ə)rɪŋ, -əd
AM ˈbæn(t)ər, -z, -ɪŋ, -d

banterer
BR ˈbant(ə)rə(r), -z
AM ˈbæn(t)ərər, -z

Banting
BR ˈbantɪŋ
AM ˈbæn(t)ɪŋ

Bantu
BR ˈbantuː, banˈtuː, -z
AM ˈbænˌtu, -z

Bantustan
BR ˌbantuːˈstɑːn, ˌbantuːˈstan, -z
AM ˈbænˌtuˌstæn, -z

banyan
BR ˈbanjan, ˈbanjən, -z
AM ˈbænjən, ˈbænˌjæn, -z

banzai
BR ˈbanzʌɪ
AM ˈbɑnˌzaɪ

baobab
BR ˈbeɪə(ʊ)bab, ˈbaʊbab, -z
AM ˈbaʊˌbæb, ˈbeɪəˌbæb, -z

bap
BR bap, -s
AM bæp, -s

baptise
BR bapˈtʌɪz, -ɪz, -ɪŋ, -d
AM ˈbæpˌtaɪz, ˈbæbˌtaɪz, -ɪz, -ɪŋ, -d

baptism
BR ˈbaptɪz(ə)m, -z
AM ˈbæpˌtɪzəm, ˈbæbˌtɪzəm, -z

baptismal
BR bapˈtɪzml
AM bæpˈtɪzməl, bæbˈtɪzməl

Baptist
BR ˈbaptɪst, -s
AM ˈbæptəst, ˈbæbtəst, -s

baptistery
BR ˈbaptɪst(ə)r|i, -ɪz
AM ˈbæptəstri, ˈbæbtəstri, -z

baptistry
BR ˈbaptɪstr|i, -ɪz
AM ˈbæptəstri, ˈbæbtəstri, -z

baptize
BR bapˈtʌɪz, -ɪz, -ɪŋ, -d
AM ˈbæpˌtaɪz, ˈbæbˌtaɪz, -ɪz, -ɪŋ, -d

bar
BR bɑː(r), -z, -ɪŋ, -d
AM bɑr, -z, -ɪŋ, -d

Barabbas
BR bəˈrabəs
AM bəˈræbəs

barathea
BR ˌbarəˈθiːə(r)
AM ˌbærəˈθiə

barb
BR bɑːb, -z, -ɪŋ, -d
AM bɑrb, -z, -ɪŋ, -d

Barbadian
BR bɑːˈbeɪdiən, bɑːˈbeɪdʒ(ə)n, -z
AM bɑrˈbeɪdiən, -z

Barbados
BR bɑːˈbeɪdəs, bɑːˈbeɪdɒs
AM bɑrˈbeɪdəs, bɑrˈbeɪˌdoʊs

Barbara
BR ˈbɑːb(ə)rə(r)
AM ˈbɑrb(ə)rə

barbarian
BR bɑːˈbɛːrɪən, -z
AM bɑrˈbɛrɪən, -z

barbaric
BR bɑːˈbarɪk
AM bɑrˈbɛrɪk

barbarically
BR bɑːˈbarɪkli
AM bɑrˈbɛrək(ə)li

barbarisation
BR ˌbɑːb(ə)rʌɪˈzeɪʃn
AM ˌbɑrbərəˈzeɪʃən, ˌbɑrbəˌraɪˈzeɪʃən

barbarise
BR ˈbɑːbərʌɪz, -ɪz, -ɪŋ, -d
AM ˈbɑrbəˌraɪz, -ɪz, -ɪŋ, -d

barbarism
BR ˈbɑːbərɪz(ə)m, -z
AM ˈbɑrbəˌrɪzəm, -z

barbarity
BR bɑːˈbarɪt|i, -ɪz
AM bɑrˈbɛrədi, -z

barbarization
BR ˌbɑːb(ə)rʌɪˈzeɪʃn
AM ˌbɑrbərəˈzeɪʃən, ˌbɑrbəˌraɪˈzeɪʃən

barbarize
BR ˈbɑːbərʌɪz, -ɪz, -ɪŋ, -d

AM ˈbɑːbəˌraɪz, -ɪz, -ɪŋ, -d

Barbarossa
BR ˌbɑːbəˈrɒsə(r)
AM ˌbɑrbəˈroʊsə, ˌbɑrbəˈrɒsə

barbarous
BR ˈbɑːb(ə)rəs
AM ˈbɑrbərəs

barbarously
BR ˈbɑːb(ə)rəsli
AM ˈbɑrbərəsli

barbarousness
BR ˈbɑːb(ə)rəsnəs
AM ˈbɑrbərəsnəs

Barbary
BR ˈbɑːb(ə)ri
AM ˈbɑrbəri

barbate
BR ˈbɑːbeɪt
AM ˈbɑrˌbeɪt

barbecue
BR ˈbɑːbɪkjuː, -z, -ɪŋ, -d
AM ˈbɑrbəˌkju, ˈbɑrbiˌkju, -z, -ɪŋ, -d

barbel
BR ˈbɑːbl, -z
AM ˈbɑrbəl, -z

barbell
BR ˈbɑːbɛl, -z
AM ˈbɑrˌbɛl, -z

barber
BR ˈbɑːbə(r), -z
AM ˈbɑrbər, -z

barberry
BR ˈbɑːb(ə)r|i, -ɪz
AM ˈbɑrˌbɛri, -z

barbershop
BR ˈbɑːbəʃɒp, -s
AM ˈbɑrbərˌʃɑp, -s

barbet
BR ˈbɑːbɪt, -s
AM ˈbɑrbət, -s

barbette
BR ˈbɑːbɛt, -s
AM ˈbɑrbɛt, -s

barbican
BR ˈbɑːbɪk(ə)n, -z
AM ˈbɑrbəkən, -z

Barbirolli
BR ˌbɑːbɪˈrɒli
AM ˌbɑrbəˈroʊli

barbital
BR ˈbɑːbɪtl
AM ˈbɑrbəˌtal, ˈbɑrbəˌtɔl

barbitone
BR ˈbɑːbɪtəʊn
AM ˈbɑrbəˌtoʊn

barbiturate
BR bɑːˈbɪtʃ(ʊ)rɪt, bɑːˈbɪtjʊrɪt, -s
AM bɑrˈbɪtʃərət, -s

barbituric
BR ˌbɑːbɪˈtʃʊərɪk, ˌbɑːbɪˈtjʊərɪk, AM ˌbɑrbəˈtʃʊrɪk

Barbizon
BR ˈbɑːbɪzɒn
AM ˈbɑrbəˌzan

barbless
BR ˈbɑːbləs
AM ˈbɑrbləs

barbola
BR bɑːˈbəʊlə(r)
AM bɑrˈboʊlə

Barbour®
BR ˈbɑːbə(r), -z
AM ˈbɑrbər, -z

Barbuda
BR bɑːˈbjuːdə(r)
AM bɑrˈbjudə

Barbudan
BR bɑːˈbjuːdn, -z
AM bɑrˈbjudən, -z

barbule
BR ˈbɑːbjuːl, -z
AM ˈbɑrˌbjul, -z

barbwire
BR ˌbɑːbˈwʌɪə(r)
AM ˌbɑrbˈwaɪ(ə)r

barcarole
BR ˌbɑːkəˈrəʊl, ˈbɑːkərəʊl, -z
AM ˈbɑrkəˌroʊl, -z

barcarolle
BR ˌbɑːkəˈrəʊl, ˈbɑːkərəʊl, -z
AM ˈbɑrkəˌroʊl, -z

Barcelona
BR ˌbɑːsɪˈləʊnə(r)
AM ˌbɑrsəˈloʊnə
SP ˌbarθeˈlona, ˌbarseˈlona

Barclay
BR ˈbɑːkli, ˈbɑːkleɪ
AM ˈbɑrkli

Bar-Cochba
BR ˌbɑːˈkɒtʃbə(r)
AM ˌbɑrˈkɒtʃbə, ˌbɑrˈkɒtʃbə

barcode
BR ˈbɑːkəʊd, -z, -ɪŋ, -ɪd
AM ˈbɑrˌkoʊd, -z, -ɪŋ, -əd

bard
BR bɑːd, -z
AM bɑrd, -z

bardic
BR ˈbɑːdɪk
AM ˈbɑrdɪk

Bardo
BR ˈbɑːdəʊ
AM ˈbɑrˌdoʊ

bardolater
BR bɑːˈdɒlətə(r), -z
AM bɑrˈdɑlədər, -z

bardolatry
BR bɑːˈdɒlətri
AM bɑrˈdɑlətri

Bardot
BR bɑːˈdəʊ
AM bɑrˈdoʊ

bardy
BR ˈbɑːd|i, -ɪz
AM ˈbɑrdi, -z
bare
BR bɛː(r), -ə(r), -ɪst, -z, -ɪŋ, -d
AM bɛ(ə)r, -ər, -əst, -z, -ɪŋ, -d
bareback
BR ˈbɛːbak
AM ˈbɛr,bæk
barebacked
BR ˌbɛːˈbakt
AM ˈbɛr,bækt
barebones
BR ˈbɛːbəʊnz
AM ˈbɛrˌboʊnz
barefaced
BR ˌbɛːˈfeɪst
AM ˈbɛrˌfeɪst
barefacedly
BR ˌbɛːˈfeɪstli, ˌbɛːˈfeɪsɪdli
AM ˈbɛrˌfeɪsɪdli, ˈbɛrˈfeɪstli
barefacedness
BR ˌbɛːˈfeɪstnɪs, ˌbɛːˈfeɪsɪdnɪs
AM ˈbɛrˈfeɪsɪdnɪs, ˈbɛrˈfeɪstnɪs
barefoot
BR ˈbɛːfʊt
AM ˈbɛrˌfʊt
barefooted
BR ˌbɛːˈfʊtɪd
AM ˈbɛrˌfʊdəd
barège
BR baˈrɛːʒ, -ɪz
AM bəˈrɛʒ, -əz
bareheaded
BR ˌbɛːˈhɛdɪd
AM ˈbɛrˌhɛdəd
barelegged
BR ˌbɛːˈlɛg(ɪ)d
AM ˈbɛrˌlɛg(ə)d
barely
BR ˈbɛːli
AM ˈbɛrli
bareness
BR ˈbɛːnəs
AM ˈbɛrnəs
Barents
BR ˈbarənts, ˈbarn̩ts
AM ˈbɛrən(t)s
barf
BR bɑːf, -s, -ɪŋ, -t
AM bɑrf, -s, -ɪŋ, -t
barfly
BR ˈbɑːflʌɪ, -z
AM ˈbɑrˌflaɪ, -z
bargain
BR ˈbɑːg|(ɪ)n, -(ɪ)nz, -ɪnɪŋ\-ŋɪŋ, -(ɪ)nd
AM ˈbɑrgən, -z, -ɪŋ, -d
bargainer
BR ˈbɑːgɪnə(r), ˈbɑːgnə(r), -z
AM ˈbɑrgənər, -z

barge
BR bɑːdʒ, -ɪz, -ɪŋ, -d
AM bɑrdʒ, -əz, -ɪŋ, -d
bargeboard
BR ˈbɑːdʒbɔːd, -z
AM ˈbɑrdʒˌbɔ(ə)rd, -z
bargee
BR bɑːˈdʒiː, -z
AM bɑrdʒi, -z
Bargello
BR bɑːˈdʒɛləʊ
AM bɑrˈ(d)ʒɛloʊ
bargeman
BR ˈbɑːdʒmən
AM ˈbɑrdʒmən
bargemen
BR ˈbɑːdʒmən
AM ˈbɑrdʒmən
bargepole
BR ˈbɑːdʒpəʊl, -z
AM ˈbɑrdʒˌpoʊl, -z
bargirl
BR ˈbɑːgəːl, -z
AM ˈbɑrˌgərl, -z
bargraph
BR ˈbɑːgrɑːf, ˈbɑːgraf, -s
AM ˈbɑrˌgræf, -s
Bari
BR ˈbɑːri
AM ˈbɑri, ˈbɛri
baric
BR ˈbɛːrɪk, ˈbarɪk
AM ˈbɛrɪk
barilla
BR bəˈrɪlə(r), -z
AM bəˈrɪlə, -z
Barisal
BR ˌbarɪˈsɑːl
AM ˈbɛrəˌsɔl, ˈbɛrəˌsal
barite
BR ˈbɑrʌɪt, ˈbɛːrʌɪt
AM ˈbɛˌraɪt
baritone
BR ˈbarɪtəʊn, -z
AM ˈbɛrəˌtoʊn, -z
barium
BR ˈbɛːrɪəm
AM ˈbɛriəm
bark
BR bɑːk, -s, -ɪŋ, -t
AM bɑrk, -s, -ɪŋ, -t
barkeep
BR ˈbɑːkiːp, -s
AM ˈbɑrˌkip, -s
barkeeper
BR ˈbɑːˌkiːpə(r), -z
AM ˈbɑrˌkipər, -z
barkentine
BR ˈbɑːk(ə)ntiːn
AM ˈbɑrkənˌtin
barker
BR ˈbɑːkə(r), -z
AM ˈbɑrkər, -z
Barkley
BR ˈbɑːkli
AM ˈbɑrkli

Barkly
BR ˈbɑːkli
AM ˈbɑrkli
barley
BR ˈbɑːli
AM ˈbɑrli
barleycorn
BR ˈbɑːlɪkɔːn, -z
AM ˈbɑrliˌkɔ(ə)rn, -z
barleymow
BR ˈbɑːlɪˈməʊ, -z
AM ˈbɑrliˌmoʊ, -z
Barlow
BR ˈbɑːləʊ
AM ˈbɑrloʊ
barm
BR bɑːm
AM bɑrm
barmaid
BR ˈbɑːmeɪd, -z
AM ˈbɑrˌmeɪd, -z
barman
BR ˈbɑːmən
AM ˈbɑrmən
barmbrack
BR ˈbɑːmbrak, -s
AM ˈbɑrmˌbræk, -s
barmecidal
BR ˌbɑːmɪˈsʌɪdl
AM ˌbɑrməˈsaɪdəl
Barmecide
BR ˈbɑːmɪsʌɪd, -z
AM ˈbɑrməˌsaɪd, -z
barmen
BR ˈbɑːmən
AM ˈbɑrmən
barmily
BR ˈbɑːmɪli
AM ˈbɑrməli
barminess
BR ˈbɑːmɪnɪs
AM ˈbɑrmɪnɪs
bar mitzvah
BR ˌbɑː ˈmɪtsvə(r), -z
AM ˈbɑr ˈmɪtsvə, -z
barmy
BR ˈbɑːm|i, -ɪə(r), -ɪɪst
AM ˈbɑrmi, -ər, -ɪst
barn
BR bɑːn, -z
AM bɑrn, -z
Barnabas
BR ˈbɑːnəbəs
AM ˈbɑrnəbəs
Barnaby
BR ˈbɑːnəbi
AM ˈbɑrnəbi
barnacle
BR ˈbɑːnəkl, -z, -d
AM ˈbɑrnəkəl, -z, -d
Barnard
BR ˈbɑːnɑːd
AM ˈbɑrˌnɑrd
Barnardo
BR bəˈnɑːdəʊ
AM bərˈnɑrdoʊ

barnbrack
BR ˈbɑːnbrak, -s
AM ˈbɑrnˌbræk, -s
Barnes
BR bɑːnz
AM bɑrnz
Barnett
BR ˈbɑːnɪt, bɑːˈnɛt
AM bɑrˈnɛt
Barney
BR ˈbɑːni
AM ˈbɑrni
barney
BR ˈbɑːn|i, -ɪz, -ɪɪŋ, -ɪd
AM ˈbɑrni, -z, -ɪŋ, -d
Barnsley
BR ˈbɑːnzli
AM ˈbɑrnzli
barnstorm
BR ˈbɑːnstɔːm, -z, -ɪŋ, -d
AM ˈbɑrnˌstɔ(ə)rm, -z, -ɪŋ, -d
barnstormer
BR ˈbɑːnˌstɔːmə(r), -z
AM ˈbɑrnˌstɔrmər, -z
Barnum
BR ˈbɑːnəm
AM ˈbɑrnəm
barnyard
BR ˈbɑːnjɑːd, -z
AM ˈbɑrnˌjɑrd, -z
Baroda
BR bəˈrəʊdə(r)
AM bəˈroʊdə
barograph
BR ˈbarəgrɑːf, ˈbarəgraf, -s
AM ˈbɛrəˌgræf, -s
barographic
BR ˌbarəˈgrafɪk
AM ˌbɛrəˈgræfɪk
barographical
BR ˌbarəˈgrafɪkl
AM ˌbɛrəˈgræfəkəl
barographically
BR ˌbarəˈgrafɪkli
AM ˌbɛrəˈgræfək(ə)li
barometer
BR bəˈrɒmɪtə(r), -z
AM bəˈramədər, -z
barometric
BR ˌbarəˈmɛtrɪk
AM ˌbɛrəˈmɛtrɪk
barometrical
BR ˌbɛrəˈmɛtrɪkl
AM ˌbɛrəˈmɛtrəkəl
barometrically
BR ˌbarəˈmɛtrɪkli
AM ˌbɛrəˈmɛtrək(ə)li
barometry
BR bəˈrɒmɪtri
AM bəˈramətri
baron
BR ˈbarən, ˈbarn̩, -z
AM ˈbɛrən, -z

baronage BR ˈbarən‖ɪdʒ, ˈbarn̩‖ɪdʒ, -ɪdʒɪz AM ˈbɛrənɪdʒ, -ɪz	**barramunda** BR ˌbarəˈmʌndə(r), -z AM ˌbɛrəˈməndə, -z	**barrister** BR ˈbarɪstə(r), -z AM ˈbɛrəstər, -z	**Barton** BR ˈbɑːtn AM ˈbɑrt(ə)n
baroness BR ˈbarənɪs, ˈbarn̩ɪs, ˈbarənɛs, ˈbarn̩ɛs, -ɪz AM ˈbɛrənəs, -əz	**barramundi** BR ˌbarəˈmʌndi AM ˌbɛrəˈməndi	**Barron** BR ˈbarən, ˈbarn̩ AM ˈbɛrən	**bartsia** BR ˈbɑːtsɪə(r), -z AM ˈbɑrtsɪə, -z
baronet BR ˈbarənɪt, ˈbarn̩ɪt, ˈbarənɛt, ˈbarn̩ɛt, AM ˈbɛrəˌnɛt, -s	**barrator** BR ˈbarətə(r), -z AM ˈbɛrədər, -z	**barrow** BR ˈbarəʊ, -z AM ˈbɛroʊ, -z	**Baruch** BR ˈbarək AM ˈbɑrək, bəˈruk
baronetage BR ˈbarənɪt‖ɪdʒ, ˈbarn̩ɪt‖ɪdʒ, ˈbarənɛt‖ɪdʒ, ˈbarn̩ɛt‖ɪdʒ, ˌbarˈnɛt‖ɪdʒ, -ɪdʒɪz AM ˈbɛrəˌnɛdɪdʒ, ˈbɛrənədɪdʒ, -ɪz	**barratrous** BR ˈbarətrəs AM ˈbɛrətrəs **barratry** BR ˈbarətri AM ˈbɛrətri **barre** BR bɑː(r), -z AM bɑr, -z	**Barrow-in-** **Furness** BR ˈbarəʊɪnˈfəːnɪs AM ˈbɛroʊənˈfərnəs **barrowload** BR ˈbarə(ʊ)ləʊd, -z AM ˈbɛroʊˌloʊd, -z	**baryon** BR ˈbarɪɒn, -z AM ˈbɛriˌɑn, -z **baryonic** BR ˌbarɪˈɒnɪk AM ˌbɛriˈɑnɪk
baronetcy BR ˈbarənɪts‖i, ˈbarn̩ɪts‖i, ˈbarənɛts‖i, ˈbarn̩ɛts‖i, -ɪz AM ˈbɛrənɛtsi, -z	**barré** BR ˈbareɪ AM bɑˈreɪ **barrel** BR ˈbarəl, ˈbarl̩, -z AM ˈbɛrəl, -z	**Barry** BR ˈbari AM ˈbɛri **Barrymore** BR ˈbarɪmɔː(r) AM ˈbɛriˌmɔ(ə)r	**Baryshnikov** BR bəˈrɪʃnɪkɒf, bəˈrɪʃnɪkɒv AM bəˈrɪʃnəˌkɔv, bəˈrɪʃnəˌkɔf, bəˈrɪʃnəˌkɑv, bəˈrɪʃnəˌkɑf
baronial BR bəˈrəʊnɪəl AM bəˈroʊnɪəl	**barrelful** BR ˈbarəlfʊl, ˈbarl̩fʊl, -z AM ˈbɛrəlˌfʊl, -z	**Barsac** BR ˈbɑːsak, -s AM ˈbɑrˌsæk, -s **Bart** BR bɑːt AM bɑrt	**barysphere** BR ˈbarɪsfɪə(r), -z AM ˈbɛrəˌsfɪ(ə)r, -z **baryta** BR bəˈrʌɪtə(r) AM bəˈraɪdə
barony BR ˈbarən‖i, ˈbarn̩‖i, -ɪz AM ˈbɛrəni, -z	**barrelhead** BR ˈbarəlhɛd, ˈbarl̩hed, -z AM ˈbɛrəl‖(h)ɛd, -z	**Bart.** *Baronet* BR ˈbarənɪt, ˈbarn̩ɪt, ˈbarənɛt, ˈbarn̩ɛt, ˌbarəˈnɛt AM ˈbɛrənət	**barytes** BR bəˈrʌɪtiːz AM bəˈraɪdiz **barytic** BR bəˈrɪtɪk AM bəˈrɪdɪk
baroque BR bəˈrɒk AM bəˈroʊk, bəˈrɑk	**barrelhouse** BR ˈbarəlhaʊ‖s, ˈbarl̩haʊ‖s, -zɪz AM ˈbɛrəl‖(h)aʊ‖s, -zəz	**bartender** BR ˈbɑːˌtɛndə(r), -z AM ˈbɑrˌtɛndər, -z	**barytone** BR ˈbarɪtəʊn, -z AM ˈbɛrəˌtoʊn, -z
barouche BR bəˈruːʃ, -ɪz AM bəˈruʃ, -əz	**barren** BR ˈbarən, ˈbarn̩, -ə(r), -ɪst AM ˈbɛrən, -ər, -əst	**barter** BR ˈbɑːtə‖(r), -əz, -(ə)rɪŋ, -əd AM ˈbɑrdər, -z, -ɪŋ, -d	**basal** BR ˈbeɪsl AM ˈbeɪsəl, ˈbeɪzəl
barquantine BR ˈbɑːk(ə)ntiːn, -z AM ˈbɑrkənˌtin, -z	**barrenly** BR ˈbarənli, ˈbarn̩li AM ˈbɛrənli	**barterer** BR ˈbɑːt(ə)rə(r), -z AM ˈbɑrdərər, -z	**basalt** BR ˈbasɔːlt, ˈbaslt AM bəˈsɔlt, ˈbæˌsɔlt, ˈbeɪˌsɔlt, bəˈsalt,
barque BR bɑːk, -s AM bɑrk, -s	**barrenness** BR ˈbarənnəs, ˈbarn̩nəs AM ˈbɛrə(n)nəs	**Barth** BR bɑːθ AM bɑrθ	ˈbæˌsalt, ˈbeɪˌsalt **basaltic** BR bəˈsɔːltɪk, bəˈsɒltɪk
barquentine BR ˈbɑːk(ə)ntiːn, -z AM ˈbɑrkənˌtin, -z	**barret** BR ˈbarɪt, -s AM ˈbɛrət, -s	**Barthes** BR bɑːt AM bɑrt	AM bəˈsɔltɪk, bəˈsɑltɪk **basan** BR ˈbaz(ə)n
Barr BR bɑː(r) AM bɑr	**barrette** BR bəˈrɛt, bɑːˈrɛt, baˈrɛt, -s AM bəˈrɛt, -s	**Bartholomew** BR bɑːˈθɒləmjuː AM bɑrˈθɑləˌmju	AM ˈbæsən, ˈbæzn **bascule** BR ˈbaskjuːl, -z AM ˈbæsˌkjul, -z
barrack BR ˈbarək, -s, -ɪŋ, -t AM ˈbɛrək, -s, -ɪŋ, -t	**barricade** BR ˌbarɪˈkeɪd, ˈbarɪkeɪd, -z, -ɪŋ, -ɪd AM ˈbɛrəˌkeɪd, -z, -ɪŋ, -ɪd	**bartizan** BR ˈbɑːtɪz(ə)n, ˌbɑːtɪˈzan, -z, -d AM ˈbɑrdəzən, ˈbɑrdəˌzæn, -z, -d	**base** BR beɪs, -ɪz, -ɪŋ, -t, -ə(r), -ɪst AM beɪs, -ɪz, -ɪŋ, -t, -ər, -ɪst
barracks BR ˈbarəks AM ˈbɛrəks	**Barrie** BR ˈbari AM ˈbɛri	**Bartlett** BR ˈbɑːtlɪt AM ˈbɑrtlət	**baseball** BR ˈbeɪsbɔːl, -z
barracoon BR ˌbarəˈkuːn, -z AM ˌbɛrəˈkun, -z	**barrier** BR ˈbarɪə(r), -z AM ˈbɛriər, -z	**Bartók** BR ˈbɑːtɒk AM ˈbɑrˌtɑk HU ˈbɒrtɔːk	AM ˈbeɪsˌbɔl, ˈbeɪsˌbɑl, -z
barracouta BR ˌbarəˈkuːtə(r), -z AM ˌbɛrəˈkudə, -z	**barrio** BR ˈbarɪəʊ, -z AM ˈbɑrioʊ, -z	**Bartolomeo** BR bɑːˌtɒləˈmeɪəʊ AM bɑrˌtɑləˈmeɪoʊ	**baseboard** BR ˈbeɪsbɔːd, -z AM ˈbeɪsˌbɔ(ə)rd, -z
barracuda BR ˌbarəˈk(j)uːdə(r), -z AM ˌbɛrəˈkudə, -z			
barrage BR ˈbarɑː(d)ʒ, -ɪz, -ɪŋ, -d AM bəˈrɑ(d)ʒ, -əz, -ɪŋ, -d			

baseborn
BR ˌbeɪsˈbɔːn,
ˈbeɪsbɔːn
AM ˈbeɪsˌbɔ(ə)rn
basehead
BR ˈbeɪshɛd, -z
AM ˈbeɪsˌ(h)ɛd, -z
Basel
BR ˈbɑːzl
AM ˈbɑzəl
baseless
BR ˈbeɪslɪs
AM ˈbeɪslɪs
baselessly
BR ˈbeɪslɪsli
AM ˈbeɪslɪsli
baselessness
BR ˈbeɪslɪsnɪs
AM ˈbeɪslɪsnɪs
baseline
BR ˈbeɪslʌɪn, -z
AM ˈbeɪˌslaɪn, -z
baseload
BR ˈbeɪsləʊd, -z
AM ˈbeɪsˌloʊd, -z
baseman
BR ˈbeɪsmən
AM ˈbeɪsmən
basemen
BR ˈbeɪsmən
AM ˈbeɪsmən
basement
BR ˈbeɪsm(ə)nt, -s
AM ˈbeɪsmənt, -s
baseness
BR ˈbeɪsnɪs
AM ˈbeɪsnɪs
basenji
BR bəˈsɛn(d)ʒi, -ɪz
AM bəˈsɛn(d)ʒi, -z
baseplate
BR ˈbeɪspleɪt, -s
AM ˈbeɪsˌpleɪt, -s
bases
plural of basis
BR ˈbeɪsiːz
AM ˈbeɪsiz
bash
BR baʃ, -ɪz, -ɪŋ, -t
AM bæʃ, -əz, -ɪŋ, -t
bashful
BR ˈbaʃf(ʊ)l
AM ˈbæʃfəl
bashfully
BR ˈbaʃfʊli, ˈbaʃfli
AM ˈbæʃfəli
bashfulness
BR ˈbaʃf(ʊ)lnəs
AM ˈbæʃfəlnəs
bashi-bazouk
BR ˌbaʃibəˈzuːk, -s
AM ˌbæʃibəˈzuk, -s
Bashkir
BR baʃˈkɪə(r), -z
AM bæʃˈkɪ(ə)r, -z
Bashkiria
BR baʃˈkɪərɪə(r)
AM bæʃˈkɪriə

basho
BR ˈbaʃəʊ, -z
AM ˈbaʃɔ, ˈbaʃoʊ, -z
basic
BR ˈbeɪsɪk, -s
AM ˈbeɪsɪk, -s
basically
BR ˈbeɪsɪkli
AM ˈbeɪsɪk(ə)li
basicity
BR beɪˈsɪsɪt̬i, -ɪz
AM beɪˈsɪsɪdi, -z
basidia
BR bəˈsɪdɪə(r)
AM bəˈsɪdiə
basidial
BR bəˈsɪdɪəl
AM bəˈsɪdiəl
basidium
BR bəˈsɪdɪəm
AM bəˈsɪdiəm
Basie
BR ˈbeɪsi, ˈbeɪzi
AM ˈbeɪsi
basil
BR ˈbazl
AM ˈbæzəl, ˈbeɪzəl
basilar
BR ˈbazɪlə(r),
ˈbazlə(r), ˈbasɪlə(r),
ˈbaslə(r)
AM ˈbæzələr, ˈbeɪsələr
basilect
BR ˈbazɪlɛkt,
ˈbeɪsɪlɛkt, -s
AM ˈbæzəˌlɛk|(t),
ˈbeɪsəˌlɛk|(t), -(t)s
basilectal
BR ˌbazɪˈlɛktl,
ˌbeɪsɪˈlɛktl
AM ˌbæzəˈlɛktəl,
ˌbeɪsəˈlɛktəl
basilectally
BR ˌbazɪˈlɛktļi,
ˌbeɪsɪˈlɛktəli
AM ˌbæzəˈlɛktəli,
ˌbeɪsəˈlɛktəli
basilica
BR bəˈzɪlɪkə(r),
bəˈsɪlɪkə(r), -z
AM bəˈsɪləkə,
bəˈzɪlɪkə, -z
basilican
BR bəˈzɪlɪk(ə)n,
bəˈsɪlɪk(ə)n
AM bəˈsɪləkən,
bəˈzɪləkən
basilisk
BR ˈbazɪlɪsk, ˈbasɪlɪsk,
-s
AM ˈbæsəˌlɪsk,
ˈbæzəˌlɪsk, -s
basin
BR ˈbeɪsn, -z
AM ˈbeɪsn, -z

basinet
BR ˌbasɪˈnɛt, ˈbasɪnɛt,
ˈbasɪnɪt, -s
AM ˌbæsəˈnɛt, -s
basinful
BR ˈbeɪsnfʊl, -z
AM ˈbeɪsnˌfʊl, -z
basipetal
BR beɪˈsɪpɪtl
AM beɪˈsɪpɪtl̩
basipetally
BR beɪˈsɪpɪtļi,
beɪˈsɪpɪtəli
AM beɪˈsɪpɪdļi
basis
BR ˈbeɪsɪs
AM ˈbeɪsəs
bask
BR bɑːsk, bask, -s, -ɪŋ,
-t
AM bæsk, -s, -ɪŋ, -t
Baskerville
BR ˈbaskəvɪl
AM ˈbæskərˌvɪl
basket
BR ˈbɑːskɪt, ˈbaskɪt, -s
AM ˈbæskət, -s
basketball
BR ˈbɑːskɪtbɔːl,
ˈbaskɪtbɔːl, -z
AM ˈbæskətˌbɔl,
ˈbæskətˌbal, -z
basketful
BR ˈbɑːskɪtfʊl,
ˈbaskɪtfʊl, -z
AM ˈbæskətˌfʊl, -z
basketry
BR ˈbɑːskɪtri, ˈbaskɪtri
AM ˈbæskətri
basketwork
BR ˈbɑːskɪtwəːk,
ˈbaskɪtwəːk
AM ˈbæskətˌwərk
Baskin
BR ˈbaskɪn
AM ˈbæskən
Basle
BR bɑːl, ˈbɑːzl
AM bal, ˈbazəl
basmati
BR basˈmɑːti,
bazˈmɑːti, basˈmati,
bazˈmati
AM ˌbasˈmadi,
ˌbazˈmadi
bas mitzvah
BR ˌbɑːs ˈmɪtsvə(r), -z
AM ˌbas ˈmɪtsvə, -z
basnet
BR ˈbasnɪt, -s
AM ˈbæsnət, -s
basophilic
BR ˌbeɪsə(ʊ)ˈfɪlɪk
AM ˌbeɪsəˈfɪlɪk
Basotho
BR bəˈsuːtu:
AM bəˈsoʊtoʊ,
bəˈsoʊθoʊ

Basotholand
BR bəˈsuːtuːland
AM bəˈsoʊdoʊˌlænd,
bəˈsoʊθoʊˌlænd
Basque
BR bask, bɑːsk, -s
AM bæsk, -s
Basra
BR ˈbazrə(r),
ˈbɑːzrə(r)
AM ˈbasrə
bas-relief
BR ˈbasrɪˌliːf, ˌbɑːrɪˈliːf,
ˌbasrɪˈliːf, -s
AM ˈbɑrəˌlif, -s
Bass
BR bas, -ɪz
AM bæs, -əz
bass¹
fish
BR bas, -ɪz
AM bæs, -əz
bass²
music
BR beɪs, -ɪz
AM beɪs, -ɪz
basset
BR ˈbasɪt, -s
AM ˈbæsət, -s
Bassey
BR ˈbasi
AM ˈbæsi
bassi
BR ˈbasi
AM ˈbæsi
bassinet
BR ˌbasɪˈnɛt, -s
AM ˌbæsəˈnɛt, -s
bassinette
BR ˌbasɪˈnɛt, -s
AM ˌbæsəˈnɛt, -s
bassi profondi
BR ˌbasi prəˈfɒndi
AM ˌbæsi prəˈfandi
bassi profundi
BR ˌbasi prəˈfʌndi
AM ˌbæsi prəˈfandi
bassist
BR ˈbeɪsɪst, -s
AM ˈbeɪsɪst, -s
basso
BR ˈbasəʊ
AM ˈbæsoʊ
bassoon
BR bəˈsuːn, -z
AM bəˈsun, -z
bassoonist
BR bəˈsuːnɪst, -s
AM bəˈsunəst, -s
basso profondo
BR ˌbasəʊ prəˈfɒndəʊ
AM ˌbæsoʊ prəˈfandoʊ
basso-relievo
BR ˌbasəʊrɪˈliːvəʊ,
ˌbasəʊriˈljeɪvəʊ, -z
AM ˌbæsoʊrəˈlivoʊ,
ˌbæsoʊriˈlivoʊ, -z

basswood
BR ˈbɑːswʊd
AM ˈbæsˌwʊd

bast
BR bɑːst
AM bæst

bastard
BR ˈbɑːstəd, ˈbastəd, -z
AM ˈbæstərd, -z

bastardisation
BR ˌbɑːstədʌɪˈzeɪʃn, ˌbastədʌɪˈzeɪʃn
AM ˌbæstərdəˈzeɪʃən, ˌbæstərˌdʌɪˈzeɪʃən

bastardise
BR ˈbɑːstədʌɪz, ˈbastədʌɪz, -ɪz, -ɪŋ, -d
AM ˈbæstərˌdʌɪz, -ɪz, -ɪŋ, -d

bastardization
BR ˌbɑːstədʌɪˈzeɪʃn, ˌbastədʌɪˈzeɪʃn
AM ˌbæstərdəˈzeɪʃən, ˌbæstərˌdʌɪˈzeɪʃən

bastardize
BR ˈbɑːstədʌɪz, ˈbastədʌɪz, -ɪz, -ɪŋ, -d
AM ˈbæstərˌdʌɪz, -ɪz, -ɪŋ, -d

bastardy
BR ˈbɑːstədi, ˈbastədi
AM ˈbæstərdi

baste
BR beɪst, -s, -ɪŋ, -ɪd
AM beɪst, -s, -ɪŋ, -ɪd

Bastet
BR ˈbastɪt
AM ˈbæstət

Bastia
BR ˈbastɪə(r)
AM ˈbastiə

Bastille
BR baˈstiːl
AM bæˈstil

bastinado
BR ˌbastɪˈnɑːdəʊ, ˌbastɪˈneɪdəʊ, -z
AM ˌbæstəˈneɪdoʊ, -z

bastion
BR ˈbastiən, -z
AM ˈbæstʃən, ˈbæstiən, -z

Bastogne
BR baˈstəʊn(jə(r))
AM bæˈstoʊn(jə)
FR bastɔŋ

basuco
BR bəˈsuːkəʊ
AM bəˈsukoʊ

Basuto
BR bəˈsuːtəʊ
AM bəˈsudoʊ

Basutoland
BR bəˈsuːtəʊland
AM bəˈsudoʊˌlænd

bat
BR bat, -s, -ɪŋ, -ɪd
AM bæ|t, -ts, -dɪŋ, -dəd

Bata
BR ˈbɑːtə(r)
AM ˈbɑdə

batata
BR bəˈtɑːtə(r), -z
AM bəˈtɑdə, -z

Batavia
BR bəˈteɪvɪə(r)
AM bəˈteɪviə

Batavian
BR bəˈteɪvɪən, -z
AM bəˈteɪviən, -z

batch
BR batʃ, -ɪz, -ɪŋ, -t
AM bætʃ, -əz, -ɪŋ, -t

Batdambang
BR ˌbat(ə)mˈbaŋ
AM ˌbædəmˈbæŋ

bate
BR beɪt, -s, -ɪŋ, -ɪd
AM beɪ|t, -ts, -dɪŋ, -dɪd

bateau
BR ˈbatəʊ, baˈtəʊ, -z
AM bæˈtoʊ, bəˈtoʊ, ˈbædoʊ, -z

bateaux
BR ˈbatəʊz, baˈtəʊz
AM bæˈtoʊ, bəˈtoʊ, ˈbædoʊ

bateleur
BR ˈbatələː(r), ˈbatlə(ː)(r), -z
AM ˌbædəˈlər, -z

Bates
BR beɪts
AM beɪts

Batesian mimicry
BR ˌbeɪtsɪən ˈmɪmɪkri
AM ˌbeɪtsiən ˈmɪməkri

Bateson
BR ˈbeɪtsn
AM ˈbeɪtsən

bath¹
noun
BR bɑːθ, baθ, bɑːðʒ\bɑːθs\baθs
AM bæ|θ, -ðz\-θs

bath²
verb
BR bɑːθ, baθ, -s, -ɪŋ, -t
AM bæθ, -s, -ɪŋ, -t

bathe
BR beɪð, -z, -ɪŋ, -d
AM beɪð, -z, -ɪŋ, -d

bather
BR ˈbeɪðə(r), -z
AM ˈbeɪðər, -z

bathetic
BR bəˈθɛtɪk
AM bəˈθɛdɪk

bathhouse
BR ˈbɑːθhaʊ|s, ˈbaθhaʊ|s, -zɪz
AM ˈbæθˌ(h)aʊ|s, -zəz

batholith
BR ˈbaθəlɪθ, -s
AM ˈbæθəˌlɪθ, -s

bathometer
BR bəˈθɒmɪtə(r), -z
AM bəˈθɑmədər, -z

bathos
BR ˈbeɪθɒs
AM ˈbeɪˌθɑs

bathotic
BR beɪˈθɒtɪk
AM beɪˈθɑdɪk

bathrobe
BR ˈbɑːθrəʊb, ˈbaθrəʊb, -z
AM ˈbæθˌroʊb, -z

bathroom
BR ˈbɑːθruːm, ˈbaθruːm, ˈbɑːθrʊm, -z
AM ˈbæθˌrum, ˈbæθˌrʊm, -z

Bathsheba
BR ˌbaθˈʃiːbə(r), ˈbaθʃɪbə(r)
AM ˌbæθˈʃibə

bathtub
BR ˈbɑːθtʌb, ˈbaθtʌb, -z
AM ˈbæθˌtəb, -z

Bathurst
BR ˈbaθəːst
AM ˈbæθərst

bathwater
BR ˈbɑːθˌwɔːtə(r), ˈbaθˌwɔːtə(r)
AM ˈbæθˌwɔdər, ˈbæθˌwadər

bathyal
BR ˈbaθɪəl
AM ˈbæθiəl

bathypelagic
BR ˌbaθɪpɪˈladʒɪk
AM ˌbæθəpəˈlædʒɪk

bathyscaphe
BR ˈbaθɪskaf, -s
AM ˈbæθəˌskæf, -s

bathysphere
BR ˈbaθɪsfɪə(r), -z
AM ˈbæθəˌsfɪ(ə)r, -z

batik
BR bəˈtiːk, baˈtiːk, ˈbatɪk, -s
AM bəˈtik, ˈbædɪk, -s

Batista
BR bəˈtiːstə(r), bəˈtiːstə(r)
AM bəˈtistə

batiste
BR baˈtiːst, bəˈtiːst, -s
AM bəˈtist, -s

Batman
cartoon and film hero
BR ˈbatman
AM ˈbætˌmæn

batman
army servant
BR ˈbatmən
AM ˈbætmən

batmen
army servants
BR ˈbatmən
AM ˈbætmən

baton
BR ˈbat(ə)n, ˈbatɒn, -z
AM bəˈtan, bæˈtan, -z

Baton Rouge
BR ˌbat(ə)n ˈruːʒ
AM ˌbædən ˈruʒ, ˌbætn ˈruʒ

batrachian
BR bəˈtreɪkɪən, -z
AM bəˈtreɪkiən, -z

batsman
BR ˈbatsmən
AM ˈbætsmən

batsmanship
BR ˈbatsmənʃɪp
AM ˈbætsmənˌʃɪp

batsmen
BR ˈbatsmən
AM ˈbætsmən

battalion
BR bəˈtalɪən, -z
AM bəˈtæljən, -z

Battambang
BR ˌbat(ə)mˈbaŋ
AM ˌbædəmˌbæŋ

batteau
BR ˈbatəʊ, baˈtəʊ, -z
AM bæˈtoʊ, bəˈtoʊ, ˈbædoʊ, -z

batteaux
BR ˈbatəʊz, baˈtəʊz
AM bæˈtoʊ, bəˈtoʊ, ˈbædoʊ

battels
BR ˈbatlz
AM ˈbædlz

batten
BR ˈbat|n, -nz, -nɪŋ\-nɪŋ, -nd
AM ˈbætn, -z, -ɪŋ, -d

Battenberg
BR ˈbatnbəːg, -z
AM ˈbætnˌbərg, -z

batter
BR ˈbatə(r), -əz, -(ə)rɪŋ, -əd
AM ˈbædər, -z, -ɪŋ, -d

batterer
BR ˈbat(ə)rə(r), -z
AM ˈbædərər, -z

Battersea
BR ˈbatəsi:
AM ˈbædərˌsi

battery
BR ˈbat(ə)r|i, -ɪz
AM ˈbædəri, -z

Batticaloa
BR ˌbatɪkəˈləʊə(r)
AM ˌbædəkəˈloʊə

battily
BR ˈbatɪli
AM ˈbædəli

battiness
BR ˈbatɪnɪs
AM ˈbædɪnɪs

battle
BR 'bæt|l, -lz, -|ɪŋ\-lɪŋ, -ld
AM 'bædəl, -z, -ɪŋ, -d
battleax
BR 'bætl,aks, -ɪz
AM 'bædl,æks, -əz
battleaxe
BR 'bætl,aks, -ɪz
AM 'bædl,æks, -əz
battlebus
BR 'bætlbʌs, -ɪz
AM 'bædl,bəs, -əz
battlecruiser
BR 'bætl,kruːzə(r), -z
AM 'bædl,kruzər, -z
battledore
BR 'bætldɔː(r), -z
AM 'bædl,dɔ(ə)r, -z
battledress
BR 'bætldrɛs
AM 'bædl,drɛs
battlefield
BR 'bætlfiːld, -z
AM 'bædl,fild, -z
battleground
BR 'bætlgraʊnd, -z
AM 'bædl,graʊnd, -z
battlegroup
BR 'bætlgruːp, -s
AM 'bædl,grup, -s
battlement
BR 'bætlm(ə)nt, -s, -ɪd
AM 'bædlmən|t, -ts, -(t)əd
battler
BR 'bætlə(r), 'batlə(r), -z
AM 'bætlər, 'bædələr, -z
battleship
BR 'bætlʃɪp, -s
AM 'bædl,ʃɪp, -s
battue
BR ba't(j)uː, -z
AM bæ'tu, -z
batty
BR 'bæt|i, -ɪə(r), -ɪɪst
AM 'bædi, -ər, -ɪst
batwing
BR 'bætwɪŋ, -z
AM 'bæt,wɪŋ, -z
batwoman
BR 'bæt,wʊmən
AM 'bæt,wʊmən
batwomen
BR 'bæt,wɪmɪn
AM 'bæt,wɪmɪn
bauble
BR 'bɔːbl, -z
AM 'bɔbəl, 'babəl, -z
baud
BR bɔːd, bəʊd, -z
AM bɔd, bad, -z
Baudelaire
BR 'bəʊdəlɛː(r), 'bəʊd]ɛː(r)

AM ,bəʊdə'lɛ(ə)r
Bauer
BR 'baʊə(r)
AM 'baʊər
Bauhaus
BR 'baʊhaʊs
AM 'baʊ,haʊs
baulk
BR bɔː(l)k, -s, -ɪŋ, -t
AM bɔk, bak, -s, -ɪŋ, -t
baulker
BR 'bɔː(l)kə(r), -z
AM 'bɔkər, 'bakər, -z
baulkiness
BR 'bɔː(l)kɪnɪs
AM 'bɔkɪnɪs, 'bakɪnɪs
baulky
BR 'bɔː(l)k|i, -ɪə(r), -ɪɪst
AM 'bɔki, 'baki, -ər, -ɪst
Baum
BR bɔːm, baʊm
AM bɔm, bam, baʊm
bauxite
BR 'bɔːksʌɪt
AM 'bak,saɪt, 'bɔk,saɪt
bauxitic
BR bɔːk'sɪtɪk
AM ,bak'sɪdɪk, ,bɔk'sɪdɪk
Bavaria
BR bə'vɛːrɪə(r)
AM bə'vɛrɪə
Bavarian
BR bə'vɛːrɪən, -z
AM bə'vɛrɪən, -z
bawbee
BR ,bɔː'b|iː, 'bɔːb|i, -iːz\-ɪz
AM 'bɔːbi, 'ba,bi, -z
bawd
BR bɔːd, -z
AM bɔd, bad, -z
bawdily
BR 'bɔːdɪli
AM 'bɔdəli, 'badəli
bawdiness
BR 'bɔːdɪnɪs
AM 'bɔdɪnɪs, 'badɪnɪs
bawdry
BR 'bɔːdri
AM 'bɔdri, 'badri
bawdy
BR 'bɔːd|i, -ɪə(r), -ɪɪst
AM 'bɔdi, 'badi, -ər, -ɪst
bawl
BR bɔːl, -z, -ɪŋ, -d
AM bɔl, bal, -z, -ɪŋ, -d
bawler
BR 'bɔːlə(r), -z
AM 'bɔlər, 'balər, -z
Bax
BR baks
AM bæks
Baxter
BR 'bakstə(r)
AM 'bækstər

bay
BR beɪ, -z, -ɪŋ, -d
AM beɪ, -z, -ɪŋ, -d
bayadère
BR ,bʌɪə'dɪə(r), ,bʌɪə'dɛː(r)
AM ,baɪə'dɛ(ə)r
Bayard
BR 'beɪɑːd
AM baɪ'ɑrd
bayberry
BR 'beɪb(ə)r|i, -ɪz
AM 'beɪ,bɛri, -z
Bayer
BR 'beɪə(r)
AM 'beɪər
Bayern
BR 'bʌɪə:n
AM 'baɪərn
Bayeux Tapestry
BR ,bʌɪə: 'tapɪstri, ,beɪə: +
AM bɑ,jə 'tæpəstri
Baylis
BR 'beɪlɪs
AM 'beɪlɪs
bayonet
BR 'beɪənɪt, 'beɪənɛt, ,beɪə'nɛt, -s, -ɪŋ, -ɪd
AM 'beɪə'nɛ|t, -ts, -dɪŋ, -dəd
Bayonne¹
place in France
BR bʌɪ'ɒn
AM ,ba'jɔn
Bayonne²
place in New Jersey
BR beɪ'əʊn
AM beɪ'joʊn
bayou
BR 'bʌɪuː, -z
AM 'baɪu, 'baɪoʊ, -z
Bayreuth
BR 'bʌɪrɔɪt, ,bʌɪ'rɔɪt
AM ,baɪ'rɔɪt
Baz
BR baz
AM bæz
bazaar
BR bə'zɑː(r), -z
AM bə'zɑr, -z
bazar
BR bə'zɑː(r), -z
AM bə'zɑr, -z
bazooka
BR bə'zuːkə(r), -z
AM bə'zukə, -z
bazuco
BR bə'zuːkəʊ
AM bə'zukoʊ
bdellium
BR 'dɛlɪəm
AM '(b)dɛlɪəm
be
BR biː, -ɪŋ
AM bi, -ɪŋ

Bea
BR biː
AM bi
beach
BR biːtʃ, -ɪz, -ɪŋ, -t
AM bitʃ, -ɪz, -ɪŋ, -t
beachcomber
BR 'biːtʃ,kəʊmə(r), -z
AM 'bitʃ,koʊmər, -z
beachfront
BR 'biːtʃfrʌnt, -s
AM 'bitʃ,frənt, -s
beachhead
BR 'biːtʃhɛd, -z
AM 'bitʃ,(h)ɛd, -z
Beach-la-mar
BR ,biːtʃlə'mɑː(r)
AM ,bitʃlə'mar
beachside
BR 'biːtʃsʌɪd
AM 'bitʃ,saɪd
beachwear
BR 'biːtʃwɛː(r)
AM 'bitʃ,wɛ(ə)r
Beachy Head
BR ,biːtʃi 'hɛd
AM ,bitʃi 'hɛd
beacon
BR 'biːk(ə)n, -z
AM 'bikən, -z
bead
BR biːd, -z, -ɪŋ, -ɪd
AM bid, -z, -ɪŋ, -ɪd
beadily
BR 'biːdɪli
AM 'bidɪli
beadiness
BR 'biːdɪnɪs
AM 'bidɪnɪs
beadle
BR 'biːdl, -z
AM 'bidəl, -z
beadleship
BR 'biːdlʃɪp, -s
AM 'bidl,ʃɪp, -s
beadsman
BR 'biːdzmən
AM 'bidzmən
beadsmen
BR 'biːdzmən
AM 'bidzmən
beadwork
BR 'biːdwəːk
AM 'bid,wərk
beady
BR 'biːd|i, -ɪə(r), -ɪɪst
AM 'bidi, -ər, -ɪst
beagle
BR 'biːg|l, -lz, -|ɪŋ\-lɪŋ, -ld
AM 'bigləl, -əlz, -(ə)lɪŋ, -əld
beagler
BR 'biːglə(r), 'biːglə(r), -z
AM 'big(ə)lər, -z

beak
BR biːk, -s, -t
AM bik, -s, -t

beaker
BR 'biːkə(r), -z
AM 'bikər, -z

beaky
BR 'biːki
AM 'biki

Beale
BR biːl
AM bil

beam
BR biːm, -z, -ɪŋ, -d
AM bim, -z, -ɪŋ, -d

beamer
BR 'biːmə(r), -z
AM 'bimər, -z

Beamon
BR 'biːmən
AM 'bimən

beamy
BR 'biːm|i, -ɪə(r), -ɪɪst
AM 'bimi, -ər, -ɪst

bean
BR biːn, -z
AM bin, -z

beanbag
BR 'biːnbag, -z
AM 'bin,bæg, -z

beanery
BR 'biːn(ə)r|i, -ɪz
AM 'binəri, -z

beanfeast
BR 'biːnfiːst, -s
AM 'bin,fist, -s

beanie
BR 'biːn|i, -ɪz
AM 'bini, -z

beano
BR 'biːnəʊ, -z
AM 'binoʊ, -z

beanpole
BR 'biːnpəʊl, -z
AM 'bin,poʊl, -z

beanshoot
BR 'biːnʃuːt, -s
AM 'bin,ʃut, -s

beansprout
BR 'biːnspraʊt, -s
AM 'bin,spraʊt, -s

beanstalk
BR 'biːnstɔːk, -s
AM 'bin,stɔk, 'bin,stɑk, -s

bear
BR bɛː(r), -z, -ɪŋ
AM bɛ(ə)r, -z, -ɪŋ

bearability
BR ,bɛːrə'bɪlɪti
AM ,bɛrə'bɪlɪdi

bearable
BR 'bɛːrəbl
AM 'bɛrəbəl

bearably
BR 'bɛːrəbli
AM 'bɛrəbli

bearcat
BR 'bɛːkat, -s
AM 'bɛr,kæt, -s

beard
BR bɪəd, -z, -ɪŋ, -ɪd
AM bɪ(ə)rd, -z, -ɪŋ, -ɪd

beardie
BR 'bɪəd|i, -ɪz
AM 'bɪrdi, -z

beardless
BR 'bɪədləs
AM 'bɪrdləs

beardlessness
BR 'bɪədləsnəs
AM 'bɪrdləsnəs

Beardsley
BR 'bɪədzli
AM 'bɪrdzli

bearer
BR 'bɛːrə(r), -z
AM 'bɛrər, -z

beargarden
BR 'bɛː,gɑːdn, -z
AM 'bɛr,gɑrdən, -z

bearing
BR 'bɛːrɪŋ, -z
AM 'bɛrɪŋ, -z

bearish
BR 'bɛːrɪʃ
AM 'bɛrɪʃ

bearishness
BR 'bɛːrɪʃnɪs
AM 'bɛrɪʃnəs

bearleader
BR 'bɛː,liːdə(r), -z
AM 'bɛr,lidər, -z

Béarnaise
BR ,bɛː'neɪz
AM ,bɛr'neɪz

bearpit
BR 'bɛː,pɪt, -s
AM 'bɛr,pɪt, -s

bearskin
BR 'bɛːskɪn, -z
AM 'bɛr,skɪn, -z

Beasley
BR 'biːzli
AM 'bizli

beast
BR biːst, -s
AM bist, -s

beastie
BR 'biːst|i, -ɪz
AM 'bisti, -z

beastings
BR 'biːstɪŋz
AM 'bistɪŋz

beastliness
BR 'biːs(t)lmɪs
AM 'bis(t)linɪs

beastly
BR 'biːs(t)l|i, -ɪə(r), -ɪɪst
AM 'bis(t)li, -ər, -ɪst

beat
BR biːt, -s, -ɪŋ
AM biɪt, -ts, -dɪŋ

beatable
BR 'biːtəbl
AM 'bidəbəl

beaten
BR 'biːtn
AM 'bitn

beater
BR 'biːtə(r), -z
AM 'bidər, -z

beatific
BR ,bɪə'tɪfɪk
AM ,bɪə'tɪfɪk

beatifically
BR ,bɪə'tɪfɪkli
AM ,bɪə'tɪfɪk(ə)li

beatification
BR bɪ,atɪfɪ'keɪʃn
AM bi,ædəfə'keɪʃən

beatify
BR bɪ'atɪfʌɪ, -z, -ɪŋ, -d
AM bi'ædə,faɪ, -z, -ɪŋ, -d

beating
BR 'biːtɪŋ, -z
AM 'bidɪŋ, -z

beatitude
BR bɪ'atɪtjuːd,
bɪ'atɪtʃuːd, -z
AM bi'ædə,t(j)ud, -z

Beatles
BR 'biːtlz
AM 'bidlz

beatnik
BR 'biːtnɪk, -s
AM 'bitnɪk, -s

Beaton
BR 'biːtn
AM 'bitn

Beatrice
BR 'bɪətrɪs
AM 'bɪətrɪs

Beatrix
BR 'bɪətrɪks
AM 'bɪətrɪks

Beatty
BR 'biːti, 'beɪti
AM 'bidi, 'beɪdi

beau
BR bəʊ, -z
AM boʊ, -z

Beaufort
BR 'bəʊfət, 'bəʊfɔːt
AM 'boʊfərt

beau geste
BR ,bəʊ 'ʒɛst
AM ,boʊ 'ʒɛst

beau idéal
BR ,bəʊ ʌɪ'dɪəl,
+ ,ɪdeɪ'ɑːl, -z
AM ,boʊ ɪdeɪ'ɑl, -z

Beaujolais
BR 'bəʊʒəleɪ
AM ,boʊʒə,leɪ

Beaujolais Nouveau
BR ,bəʊʒəleɪ nuː'vəʊ
AM ,boʊʒə,leɪ nu'voʊ

Beaumarchais
BR 'bəʊmɑːʃeɪ,
,bəʊmɑː'ʃeɪ
AM ,boʊ,mɑr'ʃeɪ

Beaumaris
BR ,bəʊ'marɪs
AM ,boʊ'mɛrəs

beau monde
BR ,bəʊ 'mɒnd
AM ,boʊ 'mɑnd

Beaumont
BR 'bəʊmɒnt
AM 'boʊ,mɑnt

Beaune
BR bəʊn, -z
AM boʊn, -z

beaut
BR bjuːt, -s
AM bjut, -s

beauteous
BR 'bjuːtɪəs
AM 'bjudiəs

beauteously
BR 'bjuːtɪəsli
AM 'bjudiəsli

beauteousness
BR 'bjuːtɪəsnəs
AM 'bjudiəsnəs

beautician
BR bju:'tɪʃn, -z
AM bju'tɪʃən, -z

beautification
BR ,bju:tɪfɪ'keɪʃn
AM ,bjudəfə'keɪʃən

beautifier
BR 'bju:tɪfʌɪə(r), -z
AM 'bjudə,faɪər, -z

beautiful
BR 'bju:tɪf(ʊ)l
AM 'bjudəfəl

beautifully
BR 'bju:tɪf(ʊ)li,
'bju:tɪfli
AM 'bjudəf(ə)li

beautify
BR 'bju:tɪfʌɪ, -z, -ɪŋ, -d
AM 'bjudə,faɪ, -z, -ɪŋ, -d

beauty
BR 'bju:t|i, -ɪz
AM 'bjudi, -z

Beauvais
BR bəʊ'veɪ
AM ,boʊ'veɪ

beaux
BR bəʊ(z)
AM boʊ

beaux-arts
BR ,bəʊ'zɑː(r)
AM ,boʊ'zɑr

beaver
BR 'biːv|ə(r), -əz,
-(ə)rɪŋ, -əd
AM 'bivər, -z, -ɪŋ, -d

Beaverboard
BR 'biːvəbɔːd
AM 'bivər,bɔ(ə)rd

Beaverbrook
BR ˈbiːvəbrʊk
AM ˈbiːvərˌbrʊk

bebop
BR ˈbiːbɒp
AM ˈbiːˌbɑp

bebopper
BR ˈbiːˌbɒpə(r), -z
AM ˈbiːˌbɑpər, -z

becalm
BR bɪˈkɑːm, -z, -ɪŋ, -d
AM bəˈkɑː(l)m,
bɪˈkɑː(l)m, -z, -ɪŋ, -d

became
BR bɪˈkeɪm
AM bəˈkeɪm, bɪˈkeɪm

becard
BR ˈbɛkəd, bəˈkɑːd, -z
AM bəˈkɑrd, ˈbɛkərd, -z

because
BR bɪˈkɒz, bɪˈkʌz
AM bəˈkəz, bɪˈkəz,
bəˈkɒz, bɪˈkɒz, bəˈkɑz,
bɪˈkɑz,

béchamel
BR ˌbeɪʃəˈmɛl
AM ˌbeɪʃəˈmɛl

bêche-de-mer
BR ˌbɛʃdəˈmɛː(r)
AM ˌbɛʃdəˈmɛ(ə)r

Bechstein
BR ˈbɛkstaɪn, -z
AM ˈbɛkˌstaɪn, -z

Bechuanaland
BR ˌbɛtʃʊˈɑːnəland
AM ˌbɛtʃˈwɑnəˌlænd

beck
BR bɛk, -s
AM bɛk, -s

Beckenbauer
BR ˈbɛk(ə)nbaʊə(r)
AM ˈbɛkənˌbaʊər

Becker
BR ˈbɛkə(r)
AM ˈbɛkər

Becket
BR ˈbɛkɪt
AM ˈbɛkət

Beckett
BR ˈbɛkɪt
AM ˈbɛkət

Beckford
BR ˈbɛkfəd
AM ˈbɛkfərd

Beckmann
BR ˈbɛkmən
AM ˈbɛkmən

beckon
BR ˈbɛk|(ə)n, -(ə)nz,
-ənɪŋ \-ɲɪŋ, -(ə)nd
AM ˈbɛk|ən, -ənz,
-(ə)nɪŋ, -ənd

Becky
BR ˈbɛki
AM ˈbɛki

becloud
BR bɪˈklaʊd, -z, -ɪŋ, -ɪd

AM bəˈklaʊd, bɪˈklaʊd,
-z, -ɪŋ, -əd

become
BR bɪˈkʌm, -z, -ɪŋ
AM bəˈkəm, bɪˈkəm, -z,
-ɪŋ

becoming
BR bɪˈkʌmɪŋ
AM bəˈkəmɪŋ,
bɪˈkəmɪŋ

becomingly
BR bɪˈkʌmɪŋli
AM bəˈkəmɪŋli,
bɪˈkəmɪŋli

becomingness
BR bɪˈkʌmɪŋnɪs
AM bəˈkəmɪŋnɪs,
bɪˈkəmɪŋnɪs

bed
BR bɛd, -z, -ɪŋ, -ɪd
AM bɛd, -z, -ɪŋ, -əd

bedabble
BR bɪˈdab|l, -lz,
-l̩ɪŋ \-l̩ɪŋ, -ld
AM bəˈdæb|əl,
bɪˈdæb|əl, -əlz, -(ə)lɪŋ,
-əld

bedad
BR bɪˈdad
AM bəˈdæd

bedaub
BR bɪˈdɔːb, -z, -ɪŋ, -d
AM bəˈdɔb, bɪˈdɔb,
bəˈdab, bɪˈdab, -z, -ɪŋ,
-d

bedazzle
BR bɪˈdaz|l, -lz,
-l̩ɪŋ \-l̩ɪŋ, -ld
AM bəˈdæz|əl,
bɪˈdæz|əl, -əlz, -(ə)lɪŋ,
-əld

bedazzlement
BR bɪˈdazlm(ə)nt
AM bəˈdæzlmənt,
bɪˈdæzlmənt

bedbug
BR ˈbɛdbʌg, -z
AM ˈbɛdˌbəg, -z

bedchamber
BR ˈbɛdˌtʃeɪmbə(r), -z
AM ˈbɛdˌtʃeɪmbər, -z

bedclothes
BR ˈbɛdkləʊ(ð)z
AM ˈbɛdˌkloʊ(ð)z

beddable
BR ˈbɛdəbl
AM ˈbɛdəbəl

bedder
BR ˈbɛdə(r), -z
AM ˈbɛdər, -z

Beddoes
BR ˈbɛdəʊz
AM ˈbɛdoʊz

Bede
BR biːd
AM bid

bedeck
BR bɪˈdɛk, -s, -ɪŋ, -t

AM bəˈdɛk, bɪˈdɛk, -s,
-ɪŋ, -t

bedeguar
BR ˈbɛdɪgɑː(r)
AM ˈbɛdəˌgɑr

bedel
BR ˈbiːdl, bɪˈdɛl, -z
AM ˈbidəl, -z

bedell
BR ˈbiːdl, -z
AM ˈbidəl, -z

bedevil
BR bɪˈdɛv|l, -lz,
-l̩ɪŋ \-l̩ɪŋ, -ld
AM bəˈdɛv|əl, bɪˈdɛv|əl,
-əlz, -(ə)lɪŋ, -əld

bedevilment
BR bɪˈdɛvlm(ə)nt
AM bəˈdɛvəlmənt,
bɪˈdevəlmənt

bedew
BR bɪˈdjuː, bɪˈdʒuː, -z,
-ɪŋ, -d
AM bəˈd(j)u, bɪˈd(j)u,
-z, -ɪŋ, -d

bedfast
BR ˈbɛdfɑːst, ˈbɛdfast
AM ˈbɛdˌfæst

bedfellow
BR ˈbɛdˌfɛləʊ, -z
AM ˈbɛdˌfɛloʊ, -z

Bedford
BR ˈbɛdfəd
AM ˈbɛdfərd

Bedfordshire
BR ˈbɛdfədʃ(ɪ)ə(r)
AM ˈbɛdfərdˌʃɪ(ə)r

bedframe
BR ˈbɛdfreɪm, -z
AM ˈbɛdˌfreɪm, -z

bedhead
BR ˈbɛdhɛd, -z
AM ˈbɛd(h)ɛd, -z

bedight
BR bɪˈdaɪt, -s, -ɪŋ, -ɪd
AM bəˈdaɪ|t, bɪˈdaɪ|t,
-ts, -dɪŋ, -dɪd

bedim
BR bɪˈdɪm, -z, -ɪŋ, -d
AM bəˈdɪm, bɪˈdɪm, -z,
-ɪŋ, -d

bedizen
BR bɪˈdʌɪz|(ə)n, -(ə)nz,
-ənɪŋ \-ɲɪŋ, -(ə)nd
AM bəˈdaɪzən, -z, -ɪŋ, -d

bedjacket
BR ˈbɛdˌdʒakɪt, -s
AM ˈbɛdˌdʒækət, -s

bedlam
BR ˈbɛdləm
AM ˈbɛdləm

bedlinen
BR ˈbɛdˌlɪnɪn
AM ˈbɛdˌlɪnɪn

Bedlington
BR ˈbɛdlɪŋtən, -z
AM ˈbɛdlɪŋtən, -z

bedmaker
BR ˈbɛdˌmeɪkə(r), -z
AM ˈbɛdˌmeɪkər, -z

Bedouin
BR ˈbɛduɪn, -z
AM ˈbɛd(ə)wən, -z

bedpan
BR ˈbɛdpan, -z
AM ˈbɛdˌpæn, -z

bedplate
BR ˈbɛdˌpleɪt, -s
AM ˈbɛdˌpleɪt, -s

bedpost
BR ˈbɛdpəʊst, -s
AM ˈbɛdˌpoʊst, -s

bedraggle
BR bɪˈdrag|l, -lz,
-l̩ɪŋ \-l̩ɪŋ, -ld
AM bəˈdræg|əl,
bɪˈdræg|əl, -əlz,
-(ə)lɪŋ, -əld

bedridden
BR ˈbɛdˌrɪdn
AM ˈbɛdˌrɪdən

bedrock
BR ˈbɛdrɒk
AM ˈbɛdˌrɑk

bedroll
BR ˈbɛdrəʊl, -z
AM ˈbɛdˌroʊl, -z

bedroom
BR ˈbɛdruːm, ˈbɛdrʊm,
-z
AM ˈbɛdˌrum,
ˈbɛdˌrʊm, -z

bedside
BR ˈbɛdsʌɪd
AM ˈbɛdˌsaɪd

bedsit
BR ˌbɛdˈsɪt, ˈbɛdsɪt, -s
AM ˈbɛdˌsɪt, -s

bedsitter
BR ˌbɛdˈsɪtə(r), -z
AM ˈbɛdˌsɪdər, -z

bed-sitting room
BR ˌbɛdˈsɪtɪŋ ruːm,
+ rʊm, -z
AM ˌbɛdˈsɪdɪŋ ˌrum
+ ˌrʊm, -z

bedsock
BR ˈbɛdsɒk, -s
AM ˈbɛdˌsɑk, -s

bedsore
BR ˈbɛdsɔː(r), -z
AM ˈbɛdˌsɔ(ə)r, -z

bedspread
BR ˈbɛdsprɛd, -z
AM ˈbɛdˌsprɛd, -z

bedstead
BR ˈbɛdstɛd, -z
AM ˈbɛdˌstɛd, -z

bedstraw
BR ˈbɛdstrɔː(r)
AM ˈbɛdˌstrɔ, ˈbɛdˌstrɑ

bedtable
BR ˈbɛdˌteɪbl, -z
AM ˈbɛdˌteɪbəl, -z

bedtime
BR 'bɛdtʌɪm, -z
AM 'bɛd,taɪm, -z

Beduin
BR 'bɛdʊɪn, -z
AM 'bɛd(ə)wən,
'bɛdə,wɪn, -z

bee
BR biː, -z
AM biː, -z

Beeb
BR biːb
AM biːb

Beebe
BR 'biːbi
AM 'bibi

beech
BR biːtʃ, -ɪz
AM bitʃ, -ɪz

Beecham
BR 'biːtʃəm
AM 'bitʃəm

beechmast
BR 'biːtʃmɑːst,
'biːtʃmast
AM 'bitʃmæst

beechnut
BR 'biːtʃnʌt, -s
AM 'bitʃnət, -s

beechwood
BR 'biːtʃwʊd
AM 'bitʃwʊd

beechy
BR 'biːtʃi
AM 'bitʃi

beef
BR biːf, -s, -ɪŋ, -t
AM bif, -s, -ɪŋ, -t

beefalo
BR 'biːfəlʊʊ, -z
AM 'bifə,loʊ, -z

beefburger
BR 'biːf,bəːgə(r), -z
AM 'bif,bərgər, -z

beefcake
BR 'biːfkeɪk, -s
AM 'bif,keɪk, -s

beefeater
BR 'biːf,iːtə(r), -z
AM 'bif,idər, -z

beefheart
BR 'biːfhɑːt
AM 'bif,(h)ɑrt

beefily
BR 'biːfɪli
AM 'bifɪli

beefiness
BR 'biːfɪnɪs
AM 'bifɪnɪs

beefsteak
BR 'biːfsteɪk, -s
AM 'bif,steɪk, -s

beefwood
BR 'biːfwʊd, -z
AM 'bif,wʊd, -z

beefy
BR 'biːf‖i, -ɪə(r), -ɪɪst

AM 'bifi, -ər, -ɪst

beehive
BR 'biːhʌɪv, -z
AM 'biː,(h)aɪv, -z

beeline
BR 'biːlʌɪn
AM 'biː,laɪn

Beelzebub
BR bɪ'ɛlzɪbʌb
AM bi'ɛlzəbəb

been
BR biːn
AM bin

beep
BR biːp, -s, -ɪŋ, -t
AM bip, -s, -ɪŋ, -t

beeper
BR 'biːpə(r), -z
AM 'bipər, -z

beer
BR bɪə(r), -z
AM bɪ(ə)r, -z

beerbelly
BR 'bɪə,bɛl‖i, -ɪz
AM 'bɪr,bɛli, -z

Beerbohm
BR 'bɪəbəʊm
AM 'bɪr,bam

beerhouse
BR 'bɪəhaʊ‖s, -zɪz
AM 'bɪr,(h)aʊ‖s, -zəz

beerily
BR 'bɪərɪli
AM 'bɪrɪli

beeriness
BR 'bɪərɪnɪs
AM 'bɪrɪnɪs

beermoney
BR 'bɪə,mʌni
AM 'bɪr,məni

beerpot
BR 'bɪəpʊt, -s
AM 'bɪr,pat, -s

Beersheba
BR ,bɪə'ʃiːbə(r)
AM ,bɪr'ʃibə

beery
BR 'bɪər‖i, -ɪə(r), -ɪɪst
AM 'bɪri, -ər, -ɪst

beestings
BR 'biːstɪŋz
AM 'bi,stɪŋz

beeswax
BR 'biːzwaks
AM 'biz,wæks

beeswing
BR 'biːzwɪŋ
AM 'biz,wɪŋ

beet
BR biːt, -s
AM bit, -s

Beethoven
BR 'beɪt(h)əʊvn
AM 'beɪ,toʊvən

beetle
BR 'biːt‖l, -lz, -lɪŋ \-lɪŋ,
-ld

AM 'bidəl, -z, -ɪŋ, -d

Beeton
BR 'biːtn
AM 'bitn

beetroot
BR 'biːtruːt, -s
AM 'bit,rut, -s

beeves
BR biːvz
AM bivz

befall
BR bɪ'fɔːl, -z, -ɪŋ
AM bə'fɔl, bi'fɔl, bə'fal,
bi'fal, -z, -ɪŋ

befallen
BR bɪ'fɔːlən
AM bə'fɔlən, bi'fɔlən,
bə'falən, bi'falən

befell
BR bɪ'fɛl
AM bə'fɛl, bi'fɛl

befit
BR bɪ'fɪt, -s, -ɪŋ, -ɪd
AM bə'fɪ‖t, bi'fɪ‖t, -ts,
-dɪŋ, -dɪd

befittingly
BR bɪ'fɪtɪŋli
AM bə'fɪdɪŋli,
bi'fɪdɪŋli

befog
BR bɪ'fʊg, -z, -ɪŋ, -d
AM bə'fag, bi'fag, -z, -ɪŋ,
-d

befool
BR bɪ'fuːl, -z, -ɪŋ, -d
AM bə'ful, bi'ful, -z, -ɪŋ,
-d

before
BR bɪ'fɔː(r)
AM bə'fɔ(ə)r, bi'fɔ(ə)r

beforehand
BR bɪ'fɔːhand
AM bə'fɔr,(h)ænd,
bi'fɔr,(h)ænd

beforetime
BR bɪ'fɔːtʌɪm
AM bə'fɔr,taɪm,
bi'fɔr,taɪm

befoul
BR bɪ'faʊl, -z, -ɪŋ, -d
AM bə'faʊl, bi'faʊl, -z,
-ɪŋ, -d

befriend
BR bɪ'frɛnd, -z, -ɪŋ, -ɪd
AM bə'frɛnd, bi'frɛnd,
-z, -ɪŋ, -əd

befuddle
BR bɪ'fʌd‖l, -lz,
-lɪŋ \-lɪŋ, -ld
AM bə'fəd‖əl, bi'fəd‖əl,
-əlz, -(ə)lɪŋ, -əld

befuddlement
BR bɪ'fʌdlm(ə)nt
AM bə'fədəlmənt,
bi'fədəlmənt

beg
BR bɛg, -z, -ɪŋ, -d
AM bɛg, -z, -ɪŋ, -d

begad
BR bɪ'gad
AM bə'gæd, bi'gæd

began
BR bɪ'gan
AM bə'gæn, bi'gæn

begat
BR bɪ'gat
AM bə'gæt, bi'gæt

beget
BR bɪ'gɛ‖t, -s, -ɪŋ
AM bə'gɛ‖t, bi'gɛ‖t, -ts,
-dɪŋ

begetter
BR bɪ'gɛtə(r), -z
AM bə'gɛdər, bi'gɛdər,
-z

beggar
BR 'bɛgə(r), -z, -ɪŋ, -d
AM 'bɛgər, -z, -ɪŋ, -d

beggarliness
BR 'bɛgəlɪnɪs
AM 'bɛgərlɪnɪs

beggarly
BR 'bɛgəli
AM 'bɛgərli

beggary
BR 'bɛgəri
AM 'bɛgəri

Begin
Menachem
BR 'beɪgɪn
AM 'beɪgɪn

begin
BR bɪ'gɪn, -z, -ɪŋ
AM bə'gɪn, bi'gɪn, -z, -ɪŋ

beginner
BR bɪ'gɪnə(r), -z
AM bə'gɪnər, bi'gɪnər,
-z

beginning
BR bɪ'gɪnɪŋ, -z
AM bə'gɪnɪŋ, bi'gɪnɪŋ,
-z

begird
BR bɪ'gəːd, -z, -ɪŋ
AM bə'gərd, bi'gərd, -z,
-ɪŋ

begirt
BR bɪ'gəːt
AM bə'gərt, bi'gərt

begone
BR bɪ'gʊn
AM bə'gɔn, bə'gɑn,
bi'gɔn, bi'gɑn

begonia
BR bɪ'gəʊnɪə(r), -z
AM bə'goʊnjə,
bi'goʊnjə, -z

begorra
BR bɪ'gʊrə(r)
AM bə'gɔrə, bi'gɔrə

begot
BR bɪ'gʊt
AM bə'gɑt, bi'gɑt

begotten
BR bɪ'gʊtn
AM bə'gɑtn, bi'gɑtn

begrime
BR bɪˈgrʌɪm, -z, -ɪŋ, -d
AM bəˈgraɪm,
biˈgraɪm, -z, -ɪŋ, -d

begrudge
BR bɪˈgrʌdʒ, -ɪz, -ɪŋ, -d
AM bəˈgrədʒ, biˈgrədʒ,
-əz, -ɪŋ, -d

begrudgingly
BR bɪˈgrʌdʒɪŋli
AM bəˈgrədʒɪŋli,
biˈgrədʒɪŋli

beguile
BR bɪˈgʌɪl, -z, -ɪŋ, -d
AM bəˈgaɪl, biˈgaɪl, -z,
-ɪŋ, -d

beguilement
BR bɪˈgʌɪlm(ə)nt
AM bəˈgaɪlmənt,
biˈgaɪlmənt

beguiler
BR bɪˈgʌɪlə(r), -z
AM bəˈgaɪlər, biˈgaɪlər,
-z

beguilingly
BR bɪˈgʌɪlɪŋli
AM bəˈgaɪlɪŋli,
biˈgaɪlɪŋli

beguine
BR bɪˈgiːn, -z
AM bəˈgin, -z

begum
BR ˈbiːgəm, ˈbeɪgəm, -z
AM ˈbigəm, ˈbeɪgəm, -z

begun
BR bɪˈgʌn
AM bəˈgən, biˈgən

behalf
BR bɪˈhɑːf
AM bəˈhæf, bəˈhɑf,
biˈhæf, biˈhɑf

Behan
BR ˈbiːən
AM ˈbiən

behave
BR bɪˈheɪv, -z, -ɪŋ, -d
AM bəˈheɪv, biˈheɪv, -z,
-ɪŋ, -d

behavior
BR bɪˈheɪvjə(r), -z
AM bəˈheɪvjər,
biˈheɪvjər, -z

behavioral
BR bɪˈheɪvjərəl,
bɪˈheɪvjər̩l
AM bəˈheɪvjərəl,
biˈheɪvjərəl

behavioralist
BR bɪˈheɪvjərəlɪst,
bɪˈheɪvjər̩lɪst, -s
AM bəˈheɪvjərəlɪst,
biˈheɪvjərəlɪst, -s

behaviorally
BR bɪˈheɪvjərəli,
bɪˈheɪvjər̩li
AM bəˈheɪvjərəli,
biˈheɪvjərəli

behaviorism
BR bɪˈheɪvjərɪz(ə)m
AM bəˈheɪvjəˌrɪzəm,
biˈheɪvjəˌrɪzəm

behaviorist
BR bɪˈheɪvjərɪst, -s
AM bəˈheɪvjərəst,
biˈheɪvjərəst, -s

behavioristic
BR bɪˌheɪvjəˈrɪstɪk
AM bəˌheɪvjəˈrɪstɪk,
biˌheɪvjəˈrɪstɪk

behavioristically
BR bɪˌheɪvjəˈrɪstɪkli
AM bəˌheɪvjəˈrɪstɪk(ə)li,
biˌheɪvjəˈrɪstɪk(ə)li

behaviour
BR bɪˈheɪvjə(r), -z
AM bəˈheɪvjər,
biˈheɪvjər, -z

behavioural
BR bɪˈheɪvjərəl,
bɪˈheɪvjər̩l
AM bəˈheɪvjərəl,
biˈheɪvjərəl

behaviouralist
BR bɪˈheɪvjərəlɪst,
bɪˈheɪvjər̩lɪst, -s
AM bəˈheɪvjərələst,
biˈheɪvjərələst, -s

behaviourally
BR bɪˈheɪvjərəli,
bɪˈheɪvjər̩li
AM bəˈheɪvjərəli,
biˈheɪvjərəli

behaviourism
BR bɪˈheɪvjərɪz(ə)m
AM bəˈheɪvjəˌrɪzəm,
biˈheɪvjəˌrɪzəm

behaviourist
BR bɪˈheɪvjərɪst, -s
AM bəˈheɪvjərɪst,
biˈheɪvjərɪst, -s

behaviouristic
BR bɪˌheɪvjəˈrɪstɪk
AM bəˌheɪvjəˈrɪstɪk,
biˌheɪvjəˈrɪstɪk

behaviouristically
BR bɪˌheɪvjəˈrɪstɪkli
AM bəˌheɪvjəˈrɪstɪk(ə)li,
biˌheɪvjəˈrɪstɪk(ə)li

behead
BR bɪˈhɛd, -z, -ɪŋ, -ɪd
AM bəˈhɛd, biˈhɛd, -z,
-ɪŋ, -əd

beheld
BR bɪˈhɛld
AM bəˈhɛld, biˈhɛld

behemoth
BR bɪˈhiːməθ,
bɪˈhiːmɒθ, -s
AM bɪˈhiməθ, biˈhiməθ,
ˈbiəməθ, -s

behest
BR bɪˈhɛst, -s
AM bəˈhɛst, biˈhɛst, -s

behind
BR bɪˈhʌɪnd, -z

AM bəˈhaɪnd, biˈhaɪnd,
-z

behindhand
BR bɪˈhʌɪndhand
AM bəˈhaɪnd(d),(h)ænd,
biˈhaɪn(d),(h)ænd

Behn
BR bɛn
AM beɪn

behold
BR bɪˈhəʊld, -z, -ɪŋ
AM bəˈhoʊld, biˈhoʊld,
-z, -ɪŋ

beholden
BR bɪˈhəʊld(ə)n
AM bəˈhoʊldən,
biˈhoʊldən

beholder
BR bɪˈhəʊldə(r), -z
AM bəˈhoʊldər,
biˈhoʊldər, -z

behoof
BR bɪˈhuːf
AM bəˈhuf, biˈhuf

behoove
BR bɪˈhuːv, -z, -ɪŋ, -d
AM bəˈhuv, biˈhuv, -z,
-ɪŋ, -d

behove
BR bɪˈhəʊv, -z, -ɪŋ, -d
AM bəˈhuv, biˈhuv, -z,
-ɪŋ, -d

Behrens
BR ˈbɛːrəns, ˈbɛːrənz
AM ˈbɛrəns

Behring
BR ˈbɛːrɪŋ
AM ˈbɛrɪŋ

Beiderbecke
BR ˈbʌɪdəbɛk
AM ˈbaɪdərˌbɛk

beige
BR beɪʒ
AM beɪʒ

beigel
BR ˈbeɪgl, -z
AM ˈbeɪgəl, -z

Beijing
BR ˌbeɪˈ(d)ʒɪŋ
AM ˌbeɪˈ(d)ʒɪŋ

being
BR ˈbiːɪŋ, -z
AM ˈbiɪŋ, -z

Beira
BR ˈbʌɪrə(r)
AM ˈbaɪrə
PORT ˈbejra

Beirut
BR ˌbeɪˈruːt
AM ˌbeɪˈrut

beisa
BR ˈbeɪzə(r)
AM ˈbeɪzə

bejabbers
BR bɪˈdʒabəz
AM bəˈdʒæbərz,
biˈdʒæbərz

bejabers
BR bɪˈdʒeɪbəz
AM bəˈdʒeɪbərz,
biˈdʒæbərz

bejewel
BR bɪˈdʒuː(ə)l, -z, -ɪŋ, -d
AM bəˈdʒuəl, biˈdʒuəl,
-z, -ɪŋ, -d

Bekaa
BR bɛˈkɑː(r), bɪˈkɑː(r)
AM bəˈkɑ

bel
BR bɛl, -z
AM bɛl, -z

belabor
BR bɪˈleɪbə(r), -əz,
-(ə)rɪŋ, -əd
AM bəˈleɪbər, biˈleɪbər,
-z, -ɪŋ, -d

belabour
BR bɪˈleɪb|ə(r), -əz,
-(ə)rɪŋ, -əd
AM bəˈleɪbər, biˈleɪbər,
-z, -ɪŋ, -d

Belafonte
BR ˌbɛləˈfɒnti
AM ˌbɛləˈfɑn(t)i

Belarus
BR ˌbɛləˈruːs, ˌbɛləˈrus
AM ˌbɛləˈrus

belated
BR bɪˈleɪtɪd
AM bəˈleɪdɪd, biˈleɪdɪd

belatedly
BR bɪˈleɪtɪdli
AM bəˈleɪtɪdli,
biˈleɪtɪdli

belatedness
BR bɪˈleɪtɪdnɪs
AM bəˈleɪtɪdnɪs,
biˈleɪtɪdnɪs

Belau
BR bɛˈlau, bɪˈlau
AM bəˈlau

belay[1]
noun
BR ˈbiːleɪ, -z
AM bəˈleɪ, biˈleɪ, -z

belay[2]
verb
BR bɪˈleɪ, -z, -ɪŋ, -d
AM bəˈleɪ, biˈleɪ, -z, -ɪŋ,
-d

bel canto
BR ˌbɛl ˈkantəʊ
AM ˌbɛl ˈkan(t)oʊ

belch
BR bɛltʃ, -ɪz, -ɪŋ, -t
AM bɛltʃ, -əz, -ɪŋ, -t

belcher
BR ˈbɛltʃə(r), -z
AM ˈbɛltʃər, -z

beldam
BR ˈbɛldəm, -z
AM ˈbɛldəm, -z

beldame
BR ˈbɛldəm, -z

AM 'bɛldəm, 'bɛlˌdeɪm, -z

beleaguer
BR bɪ'liːglə(r), -əz, -(ə)rɪŋ, -əd
AM bɪ'liːgər, bi'ligər, -z, -ɪŋ, -d

Belém
BR bɛ'lɛm
AM beɪ'lɛm, bɛ'lɛm

belemnite
BR 'bɛləmnaɪt, -s
AM 'bɛləmˌnaɪt, -s

bel esprit
BR ˌbɛl ɛ'spriː, -z
AM ˌbɛl ə'spriː, -z

Belfast
BR ˌbɛl'fɑːst, ˌbɛl'fast, 'bɛlfɑːst, 'belfast
AM 'bɛlˌfæst

belfry
BR 'bɛlfr|i, -ɪz
AM 'bɛlfri, -z

Belgae
BR 'bɛlgaɪ, 'bɛldʒiː, 'bɛlgi:
AM 'bɛldʒi, 'bɛlgi, 'bɛldʒaɪ

Belgian
BR 'bɛldʒ(ə)n, -z
AM 'bɛldʒən, -z

Belgic
BR 'bɛldʒɪk
AM 'bɛldʒɪk

Belgium
BR 'bɛldʒəm
AM 'bɛldʒəm

Belgrade
BR ˌbɛl'greɪd
AM 'bɛlˌgreɪd, 'bɛlˌgræd

Belgravia
BR bɛl'greɪvɪə(r)
AM ˌbɛl'greɪvɪə

Belgravian
BR bɛl'greɪvɪən, -z
AM ˌbɛl'greɪvɪən, -z

Belial
BR 'biːlɪəl
AM 'bilɪəl, 'bɛlɪəl

belie
BR bɪ'lʌɪ, -z, -ɪŋ, -d
AM bə'laɪ, bi'laɪ, -z, -ɪŋ, -d

belief
BR bɪ'liːf, -s
AM bə'lif, bi'lif, -s

believability
BR bɪ,liːvə'bɪlɪti
AM bə,livə'bɪlɪdi, bi,livə'bɪlɪdi

believable
BR bɪ'liːvəbl
AM bə'livəbəl, bi'livəbəl

believably
BR bɪ'liːvəbli

AM bə'livəbli, bi'livəbli

believe
BR bɪ'liːv, -z, -ɪŋ, -d
AM bə'liv, bi'liv, -z, -ɪŋ, -d

believer
BR bɪ'liːvə(r), -z
AM bə'livər, bi'livər, -z

belike
BR bɪ'lʌɪk
AM bə'laɪk, bi'laɪk

Belinda
BR bɪ'lɪndə(r)
AM bə'lɪndə

Belisarius
BR ˌbɛlɪ'sɛːrɪəs, ˌbɛlɪ'sɑːrɪəs
AM ˌbɛlə'sɛriəs

belittle
BR bɪ'lɪt|l, -lz, -lɪŋ \-lɪŋ, -ld
AM bə'lɪdəl, bi'lɪdəl-z, -ɪŋ, -d

belittlement
BR bɪ'lɪtlm(ə)nt
AM bə'lɪdlmənt, bi'lɪdlmənt

belittler
BR bɪ'lɪtlə(r), bɪ'lɪtlə(r), -z
AM bə'lɪdələr, bi'lɪdələr, -z

belittlingly
BR bɪ'lɪtlɪŋli, bɪ'lɪtlɪŋli
AM bə'lɪdəlɪŋli, bi'lɪdəlɪŋli

Belize
BR bɪ'liːz, bɛ'liːz
AM bə'liz

Belizean
BR bɪ'liːzɪən, bɛ'liːzɪən, -z
AM bə'lizɪən, bə'liʒən, -z

Belizian
BR bɪ'liːzɪən, bɛ'liːzɪən, -z
AM bə'lizɪən, bə'liʒən, -z

bell
BR bɛl, -z, -ɪŋ, -d
AM bɛl, -z, -ɪŋ, -d

Bella
BR 'bɛlə(r)
AM 'bɛlə

belladona
BR ˌbɛlə'dɒnə(r)
AM ˌbɛlə'danə

belladonna
BR ˌbɛlə'dɒnə(r)
AM ˌbɛlə'danə

Bellamy
BR 'bɛləmi
AM 'bɛləmi

Bellay
BR bə'leɪ

AM bə'leɪ

bellbird
BR 'bɛlbəːd, -z
AM 'bɛlˌbərd, -z

bellboy
BR 'bɛlbɔɪ, -z
AM 'bɛlˌbɔɪ, -z

belle
BR bɛl, -z
AM bɛl, -z

belle époque
BR ˌbɛl eɪ'pɒk, -s
AM ˌbɛl ə'pak, -s

belle laide
BR ˌbɛl 'leɪd, -z
AM ˌbɛl 'lɛd, -z

Bellerophon
BR bɪ'lɛrəfɒn, bɪ'lɛrəf(ə)n
AM bə'lɛrəˌfɑn, bə'lɛrəfən

belles-lettres
BR ˌbɛl'lɛtr(ər)
AM ˌbɛl'lɛtr(ə)

belletrism
BR ˌbɛl'lɛtrɪz(ə)m
AM ˌbɛl'lɛtrɪzəm

belletrist
BR ˌbɛl'lɛtrɪst, -s
AM ˌbɛl'lɛtrəst, -s

belletristic
BR ˌbɛlə'trɪstɪk
AM ˌbɛlə'trɪstɪk

bellettrist
BR ˌbɛl'lɛtrɪst, -s
AM ˌbɛl'lɛtrəst, -s

Bellevue
BR ˌbɛl'vjuː
AM ˌbɛlˌvju

bellflower
BR 'bɛlˌflaʊə(r), -z
AM 'bɛlˌflaʊ(ə)r, -z

bellhop
BR 'bɛlˌhɒp, -s
AM 'bɛlˌ(h)ap, -s

bellicose
BR 'bɛlɪkəʊs, 'bɛlɪkəʊz
AM 'bɛləˌkoʊs, 'bɛləˌkoʊz

bellicosely
BR 'bɛlɪkəʊsli, 'bɛlɪkəʊzli
AM 'bɛləˌkoʊsli, 'bɛləˌkoʊzli

bellicosity
BR ˌbɛlɪ'kɒsɪti
AM ˌbɛlə'kɑsədi

belligerence
BR bɪ'lɪdʒ(ə)rəns, bɪ'lɪdʒ(ə)rns
AM bə'lɪdʒ(ə)rəns

belligerency
BR bɪ'lɪdʒ(ə)rənsi, bɪ'lɪdʒ(ə)rnsi
AM bə'lɪdʒ(ə)rənsi

belligerent
BR bɪ'lɪdʒ(ə)rənt, bɪ'lɪdʒ(ə)rnt, -s
AM bə'lɪdʒ(ə)rənt, -s

belligerently
BR bɪ'lɪdʒ(ə)rəntli, bɪ'lɪdʒ(ə)rntli
AM bə'lɪdʒ(ə)rən(t)li

Bellini
BR bɛ'liːni, bə'liːni
AM bə'lini

bellman
BR 'bɛlmən
AM 'bɛlmən

bellmen
BR 'bɛlmən
AM 'bɛlmən

Belloc
BR 'bɛlɒk
AM bə'lɑk, bə'lak

bellow
BR 'bɛləʊ, -z, -ɪŋ, -d
AM 'bɛlˌoʊ, -oʊz, -əwɪŋ, -oʊd

bellpush
BR 'bɛlpʊʃ, -ɪz
AM 'bɛlˌpʊʃ, -əz

bellringer
BR 'bɛlˌrɪŋə(r), -z
AM 'bɛlˌrɪŋər, -z

bellringing
BR 'bɛlˌrɪŋɪŋ
AM 'bɛlˌrɪŋɪŋ

bellrope
BR 'bɛlrəʊp, -s
AM 'bɛlˌroʊp, -s

bellwether
BR 'bɛlˌwɛðə(r), -z
AM 'bɛlˌwɛðər, -z

belly
BR 'bɛl|i, -ɪz, -ɪɪŋ, -ɪd
AM 'bɛli, -z, -ɪŋ, -d

bellyache
BR 'bɛlɪeɪk, -s, -ɪŋ, -t
AM 'bɛliˌeɪk, -s, -ɪŋ, -t

bellyacher
BR 'bɛli ˌeɪkə(r), -z
AM 'bɛliˌeɪkər, -z

bellyband
BR 'bɛliband, -z
AM 'bɛliˌbænd, -z

bellyflop
BR 'bɛlɪflɒp, -s, -ɪŋ, -t
AM 'bɛliˌflap, -s, -ɪŋ, -t

bellyful
BR 'bɛlɪfʊl, -z
AM 'bɛliˌfʊl, -z

Belmondo
AM bɛl'mɒndəʊ, bɛl'mandoʊ

Belmont
BR 'bɛlmɒnt
AM 'bɛlmɑnt

Belmopan
BR ˌbɛlmə(ʊ)'pan
AM ˌbɛlməˌpæn

Belo Horizonte
BR ˌbeləʊ ˌhɒrɪˈzɒnteɪ
AM ˌbeloʊ
ˌhɔːrəˈzɒnˌteɪ, +
ˌhɔːrəˈzɑːnˌteɪ
B PORT ˌbelu orizõˈtʃi
L PORT ˌbelori'zõtə
belong
BR bɪˈlɒŋ, -z, -ɪŋ, -d
AM bəˈlɔːŋ, biˈlɔːŋ,
bəˈlɑːŋ, biˈlɑːŋ, -z, -ɪŋ, -d
belongingness
BR bɪˈlɒŋɪŋnɪs
AM bəˈlɔːŋɪŋnɪs,
biˈlɔːŋɪŋnɪs,
bəˈlɑːŋɪŋnɪs,
biˈlɑːŋɪŋnɪs
belongings
BR bɪˈlɒŋɪŋz
AM bəˈlɔːŋɪŋz,
biˈlɔːŋɪŋz, bəˈlɑːŋɪŋz,
biˈlɑːŋɪŋz
Belorussia
BR ˌbelə(ʊ)ˈrʌʃə(r),
ˌbelə(ʊ)ˈruːsɪə(r)
AM ˌbeloʊˈrəʃə
Belorussian
BR ˌbelə(ʊ)ˈrʌʃn,
ˌbelə(ʊ)ˈruːsɪən, -z
AM ˌbeloʊˈrəʃən, -z
beloved
BR bɪˈlʌv(ɪ)d
AM bəˈləv(ə)d,
biˈləv(ə)d
below
BR bɪˈləʊ
AM bəˈloʊ, biˈloʊ
Bel Paese®
BR ˌbel pɑːˈeɪzi
AM ˌbel pɑːˈeɪzi
Belsen
BR ˈbelsn
AM ˈbelsən
Belshazzar
BR belˈʃazə(r)
AM ˈbelʃəˌzar,
belˈʃæzər
belt
BR belt, -s, -ɪŋ, -ɪd
AM belt, -s, -ɪŋ, -əd
Beltane
BR ˈbelteɪn
AM ˈbelˌteɪn
belter
BR ˈbeltə(r), -z
AM ˈbeltər, -z
beltman
BR ˈbeltmən
AM ˈbeltmən
beltmen
BR ˈbeltmən
AM ˈbeltmən
beluga
BR bɪˈluːgə(r),
beˈluːgə(r), -z
AM bəˈlugə, -z

belvedere
BR ˈbelvɪdɪə(r),
ˌbelvɪˈdɪə(r), -z
AM ˌbelvəˈdɪ(ə)r, -z
Belvoir
BR ˈbiːvə(r)
AM ˈbel,vwɑr,
ˈbel,vɔ(ə)r
belying
BR bɪˈlaɪɪŋ
AM bəˈlaɪɪŋ, biˈlaɪɪŋ
bema
BR ˈbiːmə(r), -z
AM ˈbimə, -z
bemata
BR ˈbiːmətə(r)
AM ˈbimədə
Bemba
BR ˈbembə(r), -z
AM ˈbembə, -z
Bembridge
BR ˈbembrɪdʒ
AM ˈbem,brɪdʒ
bemedaled
BR bɪˈmedld
AM bəˈmedld,
biˈmedld
bemedalled
BR bɪˈmedld
AM bəˈmedld,
biˈmedld
bemire
BR bɪˈmaɪə(r), -z, -ɪŋ, -d
AM bəˈmaɪ(ə)r,
biˈmaɪ(ə)r, -z, -ɪŋ, -d
bemoan
BR bɪˈməʊn, -z, -ɪŋ, -d
AM bəˈmoʊn, biˈmoʊn,
-z, -ɪŋ, -d
bemuse
BR bɪˈmjuːz, -ɪz, -ɪŋ, -d
AM bəˈmjuz, biˈmjuz,
-əz, -ɪŋ, -d
bemusedly
BR bɪˈmjuːzɪdli
AM bəˈmjuzədli,
biˈmjuzədli
bemusement
BR bɪˈmjuːzm(ə)nt
AM bəˈmjuzmənt,
biˈmjuzmənt
Ben
BR ben
AM ben
Benares
BR bɪˈnɑːrɪz, beˈnɑːrɪz,
bɪˈnɑːriːz, beˈnɑːriːz
AM bəˈnɑriz
Benbecula
BR ˌbenˈbekjələ(r)
AM ˌbenˈbekjələ
Ben Bella
BR ˌben ˈbelə(r)
AM ˌben ˈbelə
bench
BR ben(t)ʃ, -ɪz, -ɪŋ, -t
AM ben(t)ʃ, -əz, -ɪŋ, -t

bencher
BR ben(t)ʃə(r), -z
AM ben(t)ʃər, -z
benchmark
BR ben(t)ʃmɑːk, -s
AM ben(t)ʃˌmɑrk, -s
bend
BR bend, -z, -ɪŋ, -ɪd
AM bend, -z, -ɪŋ, -əd
bendable
BR ˈbendəbl
AM ˈbendəbəl
bender
BR ˈbendə(r), -z
AM ˈbendər, -z
Bendigo
BR ˈbendɪgəʊ
AM ˈbendəˌgoʊ
bendiness
BR ˈbendɪnɪs
AM ˈbendɪnɪs
Bendix®
BR ˈbendɪks
AM ˈbendɪks
bendy
BR ˈbend|i, -ɪə(r), -ɪɪst
AM ˈbendi, -ər, -ɪst
beneath
BR bɪˈniːθ
AM bəˈniθ, biˈniθ
benedicite
BR ˌbenɪˈdʌɪsɪtʃi,
ˌbenɪˈdiːtʃɪtʃi, -ɪz
AM ˌbenəˈdɪsɪdi,
ˌbemerˈditʃɪˌteɪ, -z
Benedick
BR ˈbenɪdɪk
AM ˈbenəˌdɪk
Benedict
BR ˈbenɪdɪkt
AM ˈbenəˌdɪk(t)
Benedictine
BR ˌbenɪˈdɪktiːn, -z
AM ˌbenəˈdɪkˌtin, -z
benediction
BR ˌbenɪˈdɪkʃn, -z
AM ˌbenəˈdɪkʃən, -z
benedictory
BR ˌbenɪˈdɪkt(ə)ri
AM ˌbenəˈdɪktəri
Benedictus
BR ˌbenɪˈdɪktəs
AM ˌbenəˈdɪktəs
benefaction
BR ˌbenɪˈfakʃn, -z
AM ˌbenəˈfækʃən, -z
benefactor
BR ˈbenɪˌfaktə(r), -z
AM ˈbenəˌfæktər, -z
benefactress
BR ˈbenɪfaktrɪs, -ɪz
AM ˈbenəˌfæktrəs, -əz
benefic
BR bɪˈnefɪk
AM bəˈnefɪk
benefice
BR ˈbenɪfɪs, -ɪz, -t

beneficence
BR bɪˈnefɪs(ə)ns
AM bəˈnefəs(ə)ns
beneficent
BR bɪˈnefɪs(ə)nt
AM bəˈnefəs(ə)nt
beneficently
BR bɪˈnefɪs(ə)ntli
AM bəˈnefəsən(t)li
beneficial
BR ˌbenɪˈfɪʃl
AM ˌbenəˈfɪʃəl
beneficially
BR ˌbenɪˈfɪʃli,
ˌbenɪˈfɪʃəli
AM ˌbenəˈfɪʃəli
beneficiary
BR ˌbenɪˈfɪʃ(ə)r|i,
ˌbenɪˈfɪʃɪər|i, -ɪz
AM ˌbenəˈfɪʃiˌeri, -z
beneficiation
BR ˌbenɪfɪʃɪˈeɪʃn
AM ˌbenəˌfɪʃiˈeɪʃən
benefit
BR ˈbenɪfɪt, -s, -ɪtɪŋ,
-ɪtɪd
AM ˈbenəfɪ|t, -ts, -dɪŋ,
-dɪd
Benelux
BR ˈbenɪlʌks
AM ˈbenlˌəks,
ˈbenəˌleks
Benenden
BR ˈbenəndən
AM ˈbenəndən
Benetton®
BR ˈbenɪtɒn,
ˈbenɪt(ə)n
AM ˈbenəˌtan, ˈbenətn
benevolence
BR bɪˈnevələns,
bɪˈnevəlns,
bɪˈnevl(ə)ns
AM bəˈnevəl(ə)ns
benevolent
BR bɪˈnevələnt,
bɪˈnevəlnt,
bɪˈnevl(ə)nt
AM bəˈnevəl(ə)nt
benevolently
BR bɪˈnevələntli,
bɪˈnevəlntli,
bɪˈnevləntli
AM bəˈnevəl(ə)n(t)li
Benfleet
BR ˈbenfliːt
AM ˈbenˌflit
Bengal
BR ˌbenˈgɔːl, ˌbenˈgɔːl
AM ˈbenˌgal, ˈbenˌgɑl
Bengali
BR ˌbenˈgɔːl|i,
ˌbenˈgɔːl|i, -ɪz
AM ˌbenˈgali, ˌbenˈgali,
-z

Benghazi
BR ˌbenˈgɑːzi,
ˌbeŋˈgɑːzi
AM ˌbenˈgɑzi, ˌbeŋˈgɑzi

Benguela
BR ˌbenˈgweɪlə(r),
ˌbeŋˈgweɪlə(r),
ˌbenˈgwelə(r),
ˌbeŋˈgwelə(r)
AM ˌbenˈgwelə,
ˌbeŋˈgwelə
PORT bẽˈgelɐ

Ben-Gurion
BR ˌbenˈgʊəriən
AM ˌbenˈguriən

Benidorm
BR ˈbenɪdɔːm
AM ˈbenəˌdɔ(ə)rm
SP ˌbeniˈðor(m)

benighted
BR bɪˈnaɪtɪd
AM bəˈnaɪdɪd,
biˈnaɪdɪd

benightedly
BR bɪˈnaɪtɪdli
AM bəˈnaɪdɪdli,
biˈnaɪdɪdli

benightedness
BR bɪˈnaɪtɪdnɪs
AM bəˈnaɪdɪdnɪs,
biˈnaɪdɪdnɪs

benign
BR bɪˈnaɪn
AM bəˈnaɪn, biˈnaɪn

benignancy
BR bɪˈnɪgnənsi
AM bəˈnɪgnənsi

benignant
BR bɪˈnɪgnənt
AM bəˈnɪgnənt

benignantly
BR bɪˈnɪgnəntli
AM bəˈnɪgnən(t)li

benignity
BR bɪˈnɪgnɪti
AM bəˈnɪgnɪdi, -z

benignly
BR bɪˈnaɪnli
AM bəˈnaɪnli, biˈnaɪnli

Benin
BR bɪˈniːn, beˈniːn
AM bəˈnin

Beninese
BR ˌbenɪˈniːz,
bɪˌniːˈniːz, beˌniːˈniːz
AM ˌbenəˈniz

benison
BR ˈbenɪz(ə)n,
ˈbenɪs(ə)n, -z
AM ˈbenəsən, ˈbenəzn,
-z

Benito
BR bɪˈniːtəʊ, beˈniːtəʊ
AM bəˈnidoʊ

Benjamin
BR ˈben(d)ʒəmɪn
AM ˈbendʒəmən

Benlate
BR ˈbenleɪt
AM ˈbenˌleɪt

Benn
BR ben
AM ben

Bennett
BR ˈbenɪt
AM ˈbenət

Ben Nevis
BR ˌben ˈnevɪs
AM ˌben ˈnevəs

benni
BR ˈbeni
AM ˈbeni

Benny
BR ˈbeni
AM ˈbeni

Benson
BR ˈbensn
AM ˈbensən

bent
BR bent, -s
AM bent, -s

Bentham
BR ˈbenθəm, ˈbentəm
AM ˈbenθəm

Benthamism
BR ˈbenθəmɪz(ə)m,
ˈbentəmɪz(ə)m
AM ˈbenθəˌmɪzəm,
ˈben(t)əˌmɪzəm

Benthamite
BR ˈbenθəmaɪt,
ˈbentəmaɪt, -s
AM ˈbenθəˌmaɪt,
ˈben(t)əˌmaɪt, -s

benthic
BR ˈbenθɪk
AM ˈbenθɪk

benthos
BR ˈbenθɒs
AM ˈbenˌθɑs

Bentley
BR ˈbentlˌi, -ɪz
AM ˈbentli, -z

Benton
BR ˈbentən
AM ˈben(t)ən

bentonite
BR ˈbentənaɪt
AM ˈbentnˌaɪt

bentwood
BR ˈbentwʊd
AM ˈbentˌwʊd

Benue
BR ˈbenʊeɪ
AM ˈbeɪnwɑ

benumb
BR bɪˈnʌm, -z, -ɪŋ, -d
AM bəˈnəm, biˈnəm, -z,
-ɪŋ, -d

Benz
BR benz
AM benz

Benzedrine®
BR ˈbenzɪdriːn,
ˈbenzɪdrɪn
AM ˈbenzəˌdrin,
ˈbenzədrən

benzene
BR ˈbenziːn, benˈziːn
AM ˈbenˌzin

benzenoid
BR ˈbenzɪnɔɪd
AM ˈbenzəˌnɔɪd

Benzies
BR ˈbenjɪz
AM ˈbenziz

benzin
BR ˈbenzɪn, benˈzɪn
AM ˈbenˌzin, ˈbenzən

benzine
BR ˈbenziːn, benˈziːn
AM ˈbenˌzin, ˌbenˈzin

benzocaine
BR ˈbenzəkeɪn
AM ˈbenzəˌkeɪn

benzodiazepine
BR ˌbenzəʊdʌɪˈeɪzɪpiːn,
ˌbenzəʊdʌɪˈazɪpiːn, -z
AM ˌbenzəˌdaɪˈæzəˌpin,
-z

benzoic
BR benˈzəʊɪk
AM benˈzoʊɪk

benzoin
BR ˈbenzəʊɪn
AM ˈbenzəwən,
ˈbenzəˌwin

benzol
BR ˈbenzɒl
AM ˈbenˌzɔl, ˈbenˌzɑl

benzole
BR ˈbenzəʊl
AM ˈbenˌzoʊl

benzoyl
BR ˈbenzəʊɪl
AM ˈbenzəwəl

benzyl
BR ˈbenz(ɪ)l
AM ˈbenˌzil, ˈbenzəl

Beowulf
BR ˈbeɪə(ʊ)wʊlf
AM ˈbeɪəˌwʊlf

bequeath
BR bɪˈkwiːð, bɪˈkwiːθ,
-ðz\-θ , -ðɪŋ\-θɪŋ,
-ðd\-θt
AM bəˈkwiːð, bəˈkwiːθ,
biˈkwiːð, biˈkwiːθ,
-ðz\-θs, -ðɪŋ\-θɪŋ,
-ðd\-θt

bequeather
BR bɪˈkwiːðə(r),
bɪˈkwiːθə(r), -z
AM bəˈkwiðər,
bəˈkwiθər, biˈkwiðər,
biˈkwiθər, -z

bequest
BR bɪˈkwest, -s
AM bəˈkwest, biˈkwest,
-s

Bequia
BR ˈbekwi, ˈbekweɪ
AM ˈbɪkwiə

berate
BR bɪˈreɪt, -s, -ɪŋ, -ɪd
AM bəˈreɪ|t, bɪˈreɪ|t, -ts,
-dɪŋ, -dɪd

Berber
BR ˈbɜːbə(r), -z
AM ˈbərbər, -z

Berbera
BR ˈbɜːb(ə)rə(r)
AM ˈbərbərə

berberine
BR ˈbɜːbəriːn
AM ˈbərbəˌrin

berberis
BR ˈbɜːb(ə)rɪs
AM ˈbərbərəs

berceuse
BR bɜːˈsəːz, -ɪz
AM bɛrˈsəz, -əz

Bere
BR bɪə(r)
AM bɪ(ə)r

bereave
BR bɪˈriːv, -z, -ɪŋ, -d
AM bəˈriv, biˈriv, -z, -ɪŋ,
-d

bereavement
BR bɪˈriːvm(ə)nt
AM bəˈrivmənt,
biˈrivmənt

bereft
BR bɪˈreft
AM bəˈreft, biˈreft

Berengaria
BR ˌber(ə)ŋˈgeːrɪə(r)
AM ˌberəŋˈgeriə

Berenice
BR ˌberɪˈniːs,
ˌberɪˈnaɪsi,
ˌberɪˈniːtʃeɪ,
ˌberɪˈniːtʃi
AM ˌberəˈnis

Beresford
BR ˈberɪsfəd, ˈberɪzfəd
AM ˈberəsfərd

beret
BR ˈberˌeɪ, ˈberˌi,
-eɪz-ɪz
AM bəˈreɪ, beˈreɪ, -z

Berg
BR bɜːg
AM bərg

berg
BR bɜːg, -z
AM bərg, -z

bergamasque
BR ˈbɜːgəmɑːsk,
ˈbɜːgəmask, -s
AM ˈbərgəˌmæsk, -s

Bergamo
BR ˈbɜːgəməʊ,
ˈbɜːgəməʊ
AM ˈbərgəˌmoʊ

bergamot
BR ˈbɜːgəmɒt, -s

AM 'bɜrgə,mæt, -s
Bergen
BR 'bɜːg(ə)n, 'beːg(ə)n
AM 'bɜrgən
bergenia
BR bəˈgiːnɪə(r)
AM bərˈginiə
Berger
BR 'bɜːgə(r), 'bɜːdʒə(r)
AM 'bɜrgər
Bergerac
BR 'bɜːʒərak
AM 'bɜrʒə,ræk
Bergman
BR 'bɜːgmən
AM 'bɜrgmən
SW bɛrjˈman
bergschrund
BR 'bɜːgʃrʊnd,
'bɜːkʃrʊnt, -s
AM 'bɜrk,ʃrʊnt, -s
Bergson
BR 'bɜːgsn
AM 'bɜrgsən
beribboned
BR bɪˈrɪb(ə)nd
AM bəˈrɪbənd,
bɪˈrɪbənd
beriberi
BR ,bɛrɪˈbɛri
AM ,bɛriˈbɛri
Bering
BR 'bɜːrɪŋ
AM 'bɛrɪŋ
DAN 'beʌeŋ
berk
BR bɜːk, -s
AM bɜrk, -s
Berkeleian
BR bɑːˈkliːən, -z
AM 'bɜrkliən,
'bɑrkliən, -z
Berkeley[1]
places and names in Britain
BR 'bɑːkli
AM 'bɑrkli
Berkeley[2]
places and names in U.S.A.
BR 'bɜːkli
AM 'bɜrkli
berkelium
BR bɜːˈkiːlɪəm
AM 'bɜrk(i)liəm
Berkhampstead
BR 'bɜːkəmstɛd
AM 'bɜrkəm,stɛd
Berkley
BR 'bɜːkli
AM 'bɜrkli
Berks
abbreviation of English county
BR bɑːks
AM bɜrks
Berkshire
BR 'bɑːkʃ(ɪ)ə(r)

AM 'bɜrkʃɪ(ə)r
Berlei
BR 'bɜːli
AM 'bɜrli
Berlin
BR 'bɜːˈlɪn
AM bɜrˈlɪn
Berliner
BR bɜːˈlɪnə(r), -z
AM bɜrˈlɪnər, -z
Berlioz
BR 'bɛːlɪəʊz
AM 'bɜrli,oʊz
Berlitz
BR 'bɜːlɪts
AM ,bɜrˈlɪts
berm
BR bɜːm, -z
AM bɜrm, -z
berme
BR bɜːm, -z
AM bɜrm, -z
Bermondsey
BR 'bɜːmən(d)zi
AM 'bɜrmənzi
Bermuda
BR bəˈmjuːdə(r)
AM bərˈmjudə
Bermudan
BR bəˈmjuːdn, -z
AM bərˈmjudən, -z
Bermudas
BR bəˈmjuːdəz
AM bərˈmjudəz
Bermudian
BR bəˈmjuːdɪən, -z
AM bərˈmjudiən, -z
Bern
BR bɜːn, bɛːn
AM bɜrn, bɛrn
Bernadette
BR ,bɜːnəˈdɛt
AM ,bɜrnəˈdɛt
Bernadotte
BR ,bɜːnəˈdɒt
AM ,bɜrnəˈdɑt
Bernard[1]
British name
BR 'bɜːnəd
AM 'bɜrnərd
Bernard[2]
U.S. name
BR bəˈnɑːd
AM bərˈnɑrd
Bernardette
BR ,bɜːnəˈdɛt
AM ,bɜrnəˈdɛt
Berne
BR bɜːn, bɛːn
AM bɜrn, bɛrn
Berners
BR 'bɜːnəz
AM 'bɜrnərz
Bernese
BR ,bɜːˈniːz
AM ,bɜrˈniz

Bernhardt
BR 'bɜːnhɑːt
AM 'bɜrn,(h)ɑrt
Bernice
BR 'bɜːnɪs, bəˈniːs,
bəːˈniːs
AM bərˈnis
Bernini
BR bə(ː)ˈniːni
AM bərˈnini
Bernouilli
BR bə(ː)ˈnuːli
AM bərˈnuli
FR bɛrnuji
Bernstein
BR 'bɜːnstʌɪn,
'bɜːnstiːn
AM 'bɜrnstin,
'bɜrnstaɪn
Berol®
BR 'biːrɒl
AM 'bɛrəl
Berra
BR 'bɛrə(r)
AM 'bɛrə
Berridge
BR 'bɛrɪdʒ
AM 'bɛrɪdʒ
berry
BR 'bɛr|i, -ɪz, -ɪŋ, -ɪd
AM 'bɛri, -z, -ɪŋ, -d
berserk
BR bə(ː)ˈzɜːk,
bə(ː)ˈsɜːk
AM bərˈsɜrk, bərˈzɜrk
berserker
BR bə(ː)ˈzɜːkə(r),
bə(ː)ˈsɜːkə(r)
AM bərˈsɜrkər,
bərˈzɜrkər, -z
Bert
BR bɜːt
AM bɜrt
berth
BR bɜːθ, -s, -ɪŋ, -t
AM bɜrθ, -s, -ɪŋ, -t
Bertha
BR 'bɜːθə(r)
AM 'bɜrθə
Bertie
BR 'bɜːti
AM 'bɜrdi
Bertolucci
BR ,bɜːtəˈluːtʃi
AM ,bɜrdəˈlutʃi
Bertram
BR 'bɜːtrəm
AM 'bɜrtrəm
Bertrand
BR 'bɜːtr(ə)nd
AM 'bɜrtrən(d)
Berwick
BR 'bɛrɪk
AM 'bɛrɪk
Berwickshire
BR 'bɛrɪkʃ(ɪ)ə(r)
AM 'bɜr(w)ɪkʃɪ(ə)r

Berwyn
BR 'bɜːwɪn, 'bɜːwɪn
AM 'bɜrwən
beryl
BR 'bɛrɪl, 'bɛrḷ, -z
AM 'bɛrəl, -z
berylliosis
BR bɪ,rɪliˈəʊsɪs
AM bə,rɪliˈoʊsɪs
beryllium
BR bɪˈrɪlɪəm
AM bəˈrɪliəm
Berzelius
BR bəˈziːlɪəs,
bəˈzeɪlɪəs
AM bərˈzilɪəs
SW bɛrˈseːlɪəs
Bes
BR bɛs
AM bɛs
Besançon
BR 'bɛz(ə)nsɒn,
bɪˈzɒsɔ̃
AM ,bɛzənˈsɔn
Besant
BR 'bɛsnt, 'bɛznt
AM 'bɛsənt
beseech
BR bɪˈsiːtʃ, -ɪz, -ɪŋ, -t
AM bəˈsitʃ, bɪˈsitʃ, -ɪz,
-ɪŋ, -t
beseem
BR bɪˈsiːm, -z, -ɪŋ, -d
AM bəˈsim, bɪˈsim, -z,
-ɪŋ, -d
beset
BR bɪˈsɛt, -s, -ɪŋ
AM bəˈsɛ|t, bɪˈsɛ|t, -ts,
-dɪŋ
besetment
BR bɪˈsɛtm(ə)nt
AM bəˈsɛtmənt,
bɪˈsɛtmənt
beshrew
BR bɪˈʃruː, -z, -ɪŋ, -d
AM bəˈʃru, bɪˈʃru, -z,
-ɪŋ, -d
beside
BR bɪˈsʌɪd, -z
AM bəˈsaɪd, bɪˈsaɪd, -z
besiege
BR bɪˈsiːdʒ, -ɪz, -ɪŋ, -d
AM bəˈsidʒ, bɪˈsidʒ, -ɪz,
-ɪŋ, -d
besieger
BR bɪˈsiːdʒə(r), -z
AM bəˈsidʒər,
bɪˈsidʒər, -z
beslaver
BR bɪˈslav|ə(r),
bɪˈsleɪv|ə(r), -əz,
-(ə)rɪŋ, -əd
AM bəˈsleɪvər,
bɪˈsleɪvər, -z, -ɪŋ, -d
beslobber
BR bɪˈslɒb|ə(r), -əz,
-(ə)rɪŋ, -əd

AM bəˈslabər,
biˈslabər, -z, -ɪŋ, -d
besmear
BR bɪˈsmɪə(r), -z, -ɪŋ, -d
AM bəˈsmɪ(ə)r,
biˈsmɪ(ə)r, -z, -ɪŋ, -d
besmirch
BR bɪˈsmɜːtʃ, -ɪz, -ɪŋ, -t
AM bəˈsmɜrtʃ,
biˈsmɜrtʃ, -əz, -ɪŋ, -t
besom
BR ˈbiːz(ə)m, ˈbɪz(ə)m,
-z
AM ˈbizəm, ˈbɛzəm, -z
besotted
BR bɪˈsɒtɪd
AM bəˈsadəd, biˈsadəd
besottedly
BR bɪˈsɒtɪdli
AM bəˈsadədli,
biˈsadədli
besottedness
BR bɪˈsɒtɪdnɪs
AM bəˈsadədnəs,
biˈsadədnəs
besought
BR bɪˈsɔːt
AM bəˈsɔt, biˈsɔt,
bəˈsat, biˈsat
bespangle
BR bɪˈspæŋɡl̩, -lz,
-lɪŋ \-lɪŋ, -ld
AM bəˈspæŋɡləl,
biˈspæŋɡləl, -əlz,
-(ə)lɪŋ, -əld
bespatter
BR bɪˈspatlə(r), -əz,
-(ə)rɪŋ, -əd
AM bəˈspædər,
biˈspædər, -z, -ɪŋ, -d
bespeak
BR bɪˈspiːk, -s, -ɪŋ
AM bəˈspik, biˈspik, -s,
-ɪŋ
bespectacled
BR bɪˈspɛktəkld
AM bəˈspɛktəkəld,
biˈspɛktəkəld
bespoke
BR bɪˈspəʊk
AM bəˈspoʊk, biˈspoʊk
bespoken
BR bɪˈspəʊk(ə)n
AM bəˈspoʊkən,
biˈspoʊkən
besprinkle
BR bɪˈsprɪŋk|l̩, -lz,
-lɪŋ \-lɪŋ, -ld
AM bəˈsprɪŋk|əl,
biˈsprɪŋk|əl, -əlz,
-(ə)lɪŋ, -əld
Bess
BR bɛs
AM bɛs
Bessarabia
BR ˌbɛsəˈreɪbɪə(r)
AM ˌbɛsəˈreɪbɪə
RUS bʲisaˈrabʲijə

Bessarabian
BR ˌbɛsəˈreɪbɪən, -z
AM ˌbɛsəˈreɪbɪən, -z
Bessel
BR ˈbɛsl
AM ˈbɛsəl
Bessemer
BR ˈbɛsɪmə(r)
AM ˈbɛs(ə)mər
Bessie
BR ˈbɛsi
AM ˈbɛsi
best
BR bɛst, -s, -ɪŋ, -ɪd
AM bɛst, -s, -ɪŋ, -əd
bestial
BR ˈbɛstɪəl, ˈbɛstʃl
AM ˈbɪstʃəl, ˈbɪsdiəl,
ˈbɛstʃəl, ˈbɛsdiəl
bestialise
BR ˈbɛstɪəlʌɪz,
ˈbɛstʃl̩ʌɪz, -ɪz, -ɪŋ, -d
AM ˈbɪstʃə‚lʌɪz,
ˈbɪsdiə‚lʌɪz,
ˈbɛstʃə‚lʌɪz,
ˈbɛsdiə‚lʌɪz, -ɪz, -ɪŋ, -d
bestialism
BR ˈbɛstɪəliz(ə)m,
ˈbɛstʃlɪz(ə)m
AM ˈbɪstʃə‚lɪzəm,
ˈbɪsdiə‚lɪzəm,
ˈbɛstʃə‚lɪzəm,
ˈbɛsdiə‚lɪzəm
bestiality
BR ˌbɛstrˈalɪt|i,
ˌbɛstʃɪˈalɪt|i, -ɪz
AM ˌbɪstʃiˈæl ədi,
ˌbɪsdiˈæl ədi,
ˌbɛstʃiˈæl ədi,
ˌbɛsdiˈæl ədi, -z
bestialize
BR ˈbɛstɪəlʌɪz,
ˈbɛstʃl̩ʌɪz, -ɪz, -ɪŋ, -d
AM ˈbɛstʃə‚lʌɪz,
ˈbɪstʃə‚lʌɪz, -ɪz, -ɪŋ, -d
bestially
BR ˈbɛstɪəli, ˈbɛstʃli
AM ˈbɪstʃəli, ˈbɪsdiəli,
ˈbɛstʃəli, ˈbɛsdiəli
bestiary
BR ˈbɛstɪər|i,
ˈbɛstʃər|i, -ɪz
AM ˈbɪsdiˌɛri, ˈbɛsdiˌɛri,
ˈbɛstʃiˌɛri, -z
bestir
BR bɪˈstɜː(r), -z, -ɪŋ, -d
AM bəˈstər, biˈstər, -z,
-ɪŋ, -d
bestow
BR bɪˈstəʊ, -z, -ɪŋ, -d
AM bəˈstoʊ, biˈstoʊ, -z,
-ɪŋ, -d
bestowal
BR bɪˈstəʊəl
AM bəˈstoʊəl, biˈstoʊəl
bestowment
BR bɪˈstəʊm(ə)nt

AM bəˈstoʊmənt,
biˈstoʊmənt
bestrew
BR bɪˈstruː, -z, -ɪŋ, -d
AM bəˈstru, biˈstru, -z,
-ɪŋ, -d
bestrewn
BR bɪˈstruːn
AM bəˈstrun, biˈstrun
bestridden
BR bɪˈstrɪdn
AM bəˈstrɪdən,
biˈstrɪdən
bestride
BR bɪˈstrʌɪd, -z, -ɪŋ
AM bəˈstraɪd,
biˈstraɪd, -z, -ɪŋ
bestrode
BR bɪˈstrəʊd
AM bəˈstroʊd,
biˈstroʊd
bestseller
BR ˌbɛs(t)ˈsɛlə(r), -z
AM ˌbɛstˈsɛlər, -z
Beswick
BR ˈbɛzɪk
AM ˈbɛzwɪk
bet
BR bɛt, -s, -ɪŋ, -ɪd
AM bɛ|t, -ts, -dɪŋ, -dəd
beta
BR ˈbiːtə(r), -z
AM ˈbeɪdə, -z
betake
BR bɪˈteɪk, -s, -ɪŋ
AM bəˈteɪk, biˈteɪk, -s,
-ɪŋ
betaken
BR bɪˈteɪk(ə)n
AM bəˈteɪkən,
biˈteɪkən
Betamax®
BR ˈbiːtəmaks
AM ˈbeɪdəˌmæks
betatron
BR ˈbiːtətrɒn, -z
AM ˈbeɪdəˌtran, -z
betcha
BR ˈbɛtʃə(r)
AM ˈbɛtʃə
betel
BR ˈbiːtl
AM ˈbidl
Betelgeuse
BR ˈbiːtl(d)ʒɜːz,
ˈbɛtl(d)ʒəːz,
ˈbiːtldʒuːs
AM ˈbidlˌdʒus, ˈbidlˌdʒuz,
ˈbɛdlˌdʒuz
bête noire
BR ˌbɛt ˈnwɑː(r)
AM ˌbeɪt ˈnwɑr, ˌbɛt +
bêtes noires
BR ˌbɛt ˈnwɑː(r),
+ ˈnwɑːz
AM ˌbeɪt ˈnwɑrz, ˌbɛt +

Beth
BR bɛθ
AM bɛθ
Bethan
BR ˈbɛθ(ə)n
AM ˈbɛθən
Bethany
BR ˈbɛθəni, ˈbɛθn̩i
AM ˈbɛθəni
Bethel
BR ˈbɛθl, -z
AM ˈbɛθəl, -z
Bethesda
BR bɪˈθɛzdə(r),
bɛˈθɛzdə(r)
AM bəˈθɛzdə
bethink
BR bɪˈθɪŋk, -s, -ɪŋ
AM bəˈθɪŋk, biˈθɪŋk, -s,
-ɪŋ
Bethlehem
BR ˈbɛθlɪhɛm,
ˈbɛθlɪəm
AM ˈbɛθlə‚hɛm
Bethnal Green
BR ˌbɛθnl̩ ˈɡriːn
AM ˌbɛθnəl ˈɡrin
bethought
BR bɪˈθɔːt
AM bəˈθɔt, biˈθɔt,
bəˈθat, biˈθat
Bethune
BR ˈbiːtn, bɪˈθjuːn,
bɛˈθjuːn
AM bəˈθ(j)un
Béthune
place in France
BR bɪˈθjuːn, bɛˈθjuːn,
bɪˈt(j)uːn, bɛˈt(j)uːn
AM bəˈt(j)un
FR betyn
betide
BR bɪˈtʌɪd, -z
AM bəˈtaɪd, biˈtaɪd, -z
betimes
BR bɪˈtʌɪmz
AM bəˈtaɪmz, biˈtaɪmz
bêtise
BR beɪˈtiːz, -ɪz
AM beɪˈtiz, -ɪz
Betjeman
BR ˈbɛtʃɪmən
AM ˈbɛtʃəmən
betoken
BR bɪˈtəʊk|(ə)n, -(ə)nz,
-ənɪŋ \-n̩ɪŋ, -(ə)nd
AM bəˈtoʊkən,
biˈtoʊkən, -z, -ɪŋ, -d
betony
BR ˈbɛtəni, ˈbɛtn̩i
AM ˈbɛtn̩i
betook
BR bɪˈtʊk
AM bəˈtʊk, biˈtʊk
betray
BR bɪˈtreɪ, -z, -ɪŋ, -d

betrayal
BR bɪˈtreɪəl, -z
AM bəˈtreɪ(ə)l,
bɪˈtreɪ(ə)l, -z

betrayer
BR bɪˈtreɪə(r), -z
AM bəˈtreɪər, bɪˈtreɪər,
-z

betroth
BR bɪˈtrəʊ|ð, bɪˈtrəʊ|θ,
-ðz\-θs, -ðɪŋ\-θɪŋ,
-ðd\-θt
AM bəˈtrəʊ|ð, bəˈtrɔ|θ,
bəˈtrəʊ|θ, bɪˈtrəʊ|ð,
bɪˈtrɔ|θ, bɪˈtrəʊ|θ,
bəˈtra|θ, bɪˈtra|θ,
-θs\-ðz, -θɪŋ\-ðɪŋ,
-θt\-ðd

betrothal
BR bɪˈtrəʊðl, -z
AM bəˈtrəʊðəl,
bəˈtrɔθəl, bəˈtrəʊθəl,
bɪˈtrəʊðəl, bɪˈtrɔθəl,
bɪˈtrəʊθəl, bəˈtraθəl,
bɪˈtraθəl, -z

Betsy
BR ˈbetsi
AM ˈbetsi

Bette
BR bet
AM bet

better
BR ˈbetə(r), -əz,
-(ə)rɪŋ, -əd
AM ˈbedər, -z, -ɪŋ, -d

betterment
BR ˈbetəm(ə)nt
AM ˈbedərmənt

Betterton
BR ˈbetət(ə)n
AM ˈbedərt(ə)n

Betteshanger
BR ˈbet(ɪ)s,haŋ(g)ə(r)
AM ˈbedəs,(h)æŋər

Betti
BR ˈbeti
AM ˈbedi

Bettina
BR bɪˈtiːnə(r)
AM bəˈtinə

bettor
BR ˈbetə(r), -z
AM ˈbedər, -z

Betts
BR bets
AM bets

Bettws
BR ˈbetəs
AM ˈbedwz

Betty
BR ˈbeti
AM ˈbedi

between
BR bɪˈtwiːn
AM bəˈtwin, bɪˈtwin

betweentimes
BR bɪˈtwiːntʌɪmz
AM bəˈtwin,taɪmz,
bɪˈtwin,taɪmz

betwixt
BR bɪˈtwɪkst
AM bəˈtwɪkst,
bɪˈtwɪkst

Betws-y-Coed
BR ˌbet(ə)s ə ˈkɔɪd,
+ ˈkəʊɪd
AM ˌbedəs ə ˈkɔɪd
WE ˌbetʊs ʌ ˈkɔɪd

Beulah
BR ˈbjuːlə(r)
AM ˈbjʊlə

Bevan
BR ˈbevn
AM ˈbevən

bevatron
BR ˈbevətrɒn, -z
AM ˈbevəˌtran, -z

bevel
BR ˈbev|l, -lz,
-|ɪŋ\-əlɪŋ, -ld
AM ˈbev|əl, -əlz, -(ə)lɪŋ,
-əld

beverage
BR ˈbev(ə)r|ɪdʒ, -ɪdʒɪz
AM ˈbev(ə)rɪdʒ, -ɪz

Beveridge
BR ˈbev(ə)rɪdʒ
AM ˈbev(ə)rɪdʒ

Beverley
BR ˈbevəli
AM ˈbevərli

Beverly
BR ˈbevəli
AM ˈbevərli

Bevin
BR ˈbevɪn
AM ˈbevən

Bevis
BR ˈbevɪs, ˈbiːvɪs
AM ˈbivɪs

bevvy
BR ˈbev|i, -ɪz, -ɪd
AM ˈbevi, -z, -d

bevy
BR ˈbev|i, -ɪz
AM ˈbevi, -z

bewail
BR bɪˈweɪl, -z, -ɪŋ, -d
AM bəˈweɪl, bɪˈweɪl, -z,
-ɪŋ, -d

bewailer
BR bɪˈweɪlə(r), -z
AM bəˈweɪlər,
bɪˈweɪlər, -z

beware
BR bɪˈwɛː(r)
AM bəˈwɛ(ə)r,
ˌbiˈwɛ(ə)r

Bewdley
BR ˈbjuːdli
AM ˈbjudli

Bewes
BR bjuːz

bewhiskered
BR bɪˈwɪskəd
AM bəˈwɪskərd,
bɪˈwɪskərd

Bewick
BR ˈbjuːɪk, -s
AM ˈbiwɪk, -s

bewigged
BR bɪˈwɪgd
AM bəˈwɪgd, bɪˈwɪgd

bewilder
BR bɪˈwɪld|ə(r), -əz,
-(ə)rɪŋ, -əd
AM bəˈwɪldər,
bɪˈwɪldər, -z, -ɪŋ, -d

bewilderingly
BR bɪˈwɪld(ə)rɪŋli
AM bəˈwɪldərɪŋli,
bɪˈwɪldərŋli

bewilderment
BR bɪˈwɪldəm(ə)nt
AM bəˈwɪldərmənt,
bɪˈwɪldərmənt

bewitch
BR bɪˈwɪtʃ, -ɪz, -ɪŋ, -t
AM bəˈwɪtʃ, bɪˈwɪtʃ, -ɪz,
-ɪŋ, -t

bewitchingly
BR bɪˈwɪtʃɪŋli
AM bəˈwɪtʃɪŋli,
bɪˈwɪtʃɪŋli

Bexhill
BR ˌbeksˈhɪl
AM ˌbeksˈhɪl

Bexley
BR ˈbeksli
AM ˈbeksli

Bexleyheath
BR ˌbekslɪˈhiːθ
AM ˌbeksliˈhiθ

bey
BR beɪ, -z
AM beɪ, -z

Beynon
BR ˈbʌɪmən
AM ˈbaɪmən

beyond
BR bɪˈjɒnd
AM biˈ(j)ɑnd

bezant
BR ˈbez(ə)nt, -s
AM ˈbeznt, -s

bezel
BR ˈbezl, -z
AM ˈbezəl, -z

bezique
BR bɪˈziːk
AM bəˈzik

bezoar
BR ˈbiːzɔː(r), -z
AM ˈbiˌzɔ(ə)r, -z

Bhagavadgita
BR ˌbagəvədˈgiːtə(r),
ˌbʌgəvədˈgiːtə(r)
AM ˌbagəˌvadˈgidə

bhagwan
BR ˈbagwɑːn,
bʌˈgwɑːn, -z
AM ˈbag,wɑn, -z

bhaji
BR ˈbʌdʒ|i, ˈbɑːdʒ|i, -ɪz
AM ˈbadʒi, -z

bhakti
BR ˈbʌkti, ˈbɑːkti
AM ˈbakti

bhang
BR baŋ
AM bæŋ

bhangra
BR ˈbaŋgrə(r),
ˈbɑːŋgrə(r)
AM ˈbæŋ(g)rə

bharal
BR ˈbʌrəl, ˈbʌrɭ, -z
AM ˈbarəl, -z

Bhopal
BR bəˈ(ʊ)ˈpɑːl
AM boʊˈpal

Bhutan
BR ˌbuːˈtɑːn, bəˈtɑːn
AM ˌbuˈtan

Bhutanese
BR ˌbuːtəˈniːz
AM ˌbudəˈniz

Bhutto
BR ˈbuːtəʊ, ˈbʊtəʊ
AM ˈbudoʊ

bi
BR bʌɪ, -z
AM baɪ, -z

Biafra
BR bɪˈafrə(r)
AM biˈæfrə

Biafran
BR bɪˈafrən, -z
AM biˈæfrən, -z

bialy
BR bɪˈɑːl|i, -ɪz
AM biˈɑli, -z

Bianca
BR bɪˈaŋkə(r)
AM biˈaŋkə

biannual
BR (ˌ)bʌɪˈanjʊəl,
(ˌ)bʌɪˈanjəl
AM ˌbaɪˈænj(əw)əl

biannually
BR (ˌ)bʌɪˈanjʊəli,
(ˌ)bʌɪˈanjəli
AM ˌbaɪˈænj(əw)əli

Biarritz
BR ˌbɪəˈrɪts, ˈbɪərɪts
AM ˈbiəˌrɪts

bias
BR ˈbʌɪəs, -ɪz, -ɪŋ, -t
AM ˈbaɪəs, -əz, -ɪŋ, -t

biathlete
BR bʌɪˈaθliːt, -s
AM biˈæθ(ə)lit, -s

biathlon
BR bʌɪˈaθlən, -z
bʌɪˈaθlɒn, -z

AM baɪˈæθ‚lən, -z

biaxal
BR ‚bʌɪˈaksl
AM ‚baɪˈæksəl

biaxial
BR ‚bʌɪˈaksɪəl
AM ‚baɪˈæksiəl

bib
BR bɪb, -z
AM bɪb, -z

bibber
BR ˈbɪbə(r), -z
AM ˈbɪbər, -z

bibelot
BR ˈbɪb(ə)ləʊ, -z
AM ˈbɪb(ə)‚loʊ, -z

Bible
BR ˈbʌɪbl, -z
AM ˈbaɪbəl, -z

biblical
BR ˈbɪblɪkl
AM ˈbɪblɪkəl

biblically
BR ˈbɪblɪkli
AM ˈbɪblɪk(ə)li

bibliographer
BR ‚bɪblɪˈɒɡrəfə(r), -z
AM ‚bɪbliˈɑɡrəfər, -z

bibliographic
BR ‚bɪblɪəˈɡrafɪk
AM ‚bɪbliəˈɡræfɪk

bibliographical
BR ‚bɪblɪəˈɡrafɪkl
AM ‚bɪbliəˈɡræfəkəl

bibliographically
BR ‚bɪblɪəˈɡrafɪkli
AM ‚bɪbliəˈɡræfək(ə)li

bibliographise
BR ‚bɪblɪˈɒɡrəfʌɪz, -ɪz,
-ɪŋ, -d
AM ‚bɪbliˈɑɡrə‚faɪz, -ɪz,
-ɪŋ, -d

bibliographize
BR ‚bɪblɪˈɒɡrəfʌɪz, -ɪz,
-ɪŋ, -d
AM ‚bɪbliˈɑɡrə‚faɪz, -ɪz,
-ɪŋ, -d

bibliography
BR ‚bɪblɪˈɒɡrəf]i, -ɪz
AM ‚bɪbliˈɑɡrəfi, -z

bibliolater
BR ‚bɪblɪˈɒlətə(r), -z
AM ‚bɪbliˈɑlədər, -z

bibliolatry
BR ‚bɪblɪˈɒlətri
AM ‚bɪbliˈɑlətri

bibliomancy
BR ˈbɪblɪə‚mansi
AM ˈbɪbliə‚mænsi

bibliomania
BR ‚bɪblɪəˈmeɪnɪə(r)
AM ‚bɪbliəˈmeɪniə

bibliomaniac
BR ‚bɪblɪəˈmeɪnɪak
AM ‚bɪbliəˈmeɪni‚æk,
-s

bibliophil
BR ˈbɪblɪə(ʊ)fɪl, -z
AM ˈbɪbliə‚faɪl, -z

bibliophile
BR ˈbɪblɪə(ʊ)fʌɪl, -z
AM ˈbɪbliə‚faɪl, -z

bibliophilic
BR ‚bɪblɪəˈfɪlɪk
AM ‚bɪbliəˈfɪlɪk

bibliophily
BR ‚bɪblɪˈɒfɪli,
‚bɪblɪˈɒf]li
AM ‚bɪbliˈɑfəli

bibliopole
BR ˈbɪblɪə(ʊ)pəʊl, -z
AM ˈbɪbliə‚poʊl, -z

bibliopoly
BR ‚bɪblɪˈɒpəli,
‚bɪblɪˈɒp]i
AM ‚bɪbliˈɑpəli

bibulous
BR ˈbɪbjʉləs
AM ˈbɪbjələs

bibulousness
BR ˈbɪbjʉləsnəs
AM ˈbɪbjələsnəs

Bic®
BR bɪk, -s
AM bɪk, -s

bicameral
BR (‚)bʌɪˈkam(ə)rəl,
(‚)bʌɪˈkam(ə)r]
AM ‚baɪˈkæmərəl

bicameralism
BR (‚)bʌɪˈkam(ə)rəl-
ɪz(ə)m,
(‚)bʌɪˈkam(ə)r]ɪz(ə)m
AM ‚baɪˈkæmərə‚lɪzəm

bicarb
BR ˈbʌɪkɑːb
AM ˈbaɪ‚kɑrb

bicarbonate
BR (‚)bʌɪˈkɑːbənət,
(‚)bʌɪˈkɑːbn̩ət
AM ‚baɪˈkɑrbənət

bice
BR bʌɪs
AM baɪs

bicentenary
BR ‚bʌɪs(ɛ)nˈtiːnər]i,
‚bʌɪs(ɛ)nˈtɛnər]i, -ɪz
AM ‚baɪsɛnˈtɛnəri, -z

bicentennial
BR ‚bʌɪs(ɛ)nˈtɛnɪəl, -z
AM ‚baɪsɛnˈtɛniəl, -z

bicephalous
BR (‚)bʌɪˈsɛfələs,
(‚)bʌɪˈsɛf]əs,
(‚)bʌɪˈkɛf]əs
AM baɪˈsɛfələs

biceps
BR ˈbʌɪsɛps
AM ˈbaɪ‚sɛps

Bicester
BR ˈbɪstə(r)
AM ˈbɪ(sɛ)stər

bichir
BR ˈbɪʃɪə(r)
AM ˈbɪʃɪ(ə)r

bichloride
BR (‚)bʌɪˈklɔːrʌɪd, -z
AM baɪˈklɔ‚raɪd, -z

bichromate
BR (‚)bʌɪˈkrəʊmeɪt, -s
AM baɪˈkroʊ‚meɪt, -s

bicker
BR ˈbɪk]ə(r), -əz,
-(ə)rɪŋ, -əd
AM ˈbɪkər, -z, -ɪŋ, -d

bickerer
BR ˈbɪk(ə)rə(r), -z
AM ˈbɪkərər, -z

Bickerton
BR ˈbɪkət(ə)n
AM ˈbɪkərt(ə)n

bicolor
BR ˈbʌɪˈkʌlə(r), -z
AM ‚baɪˈkələr, -z

bicolored
BR ˈbʌɪˈkʌləd, -z
AM ‚baɪˈkələrd, -z

bicolour
BR ˈbʌɪˈkʌlə(r), -z
AM ‚baɪˈkələr, -z

bicoloured
BR ˈbʌɪˈkʌləd, -z
AM ‚baɪˈkələrd, -z

biconcave
BR (‚)bʌɪˈkɒŋkeɪv
AM baɪˈkɑnkeɪv

biconcavity
BR ‚bʌɪkɒnˈkavɪti,
‚bʌɪkɒŋˈkavɪti,
‚bʌɪkən̩ˈkavɪti,
‚bʌɪkən]ˈkavɪti
AM ‚baɪ‚kɑnˈkævədi

biconvex
BR (‚)bʌɪˈkɒnvɛks
AM baɪˈkɑnvɛks

biconvexity
BR ‚bʌɪkɒnˈvɛksɪti,
‚bʌɪk(ə)nˈvɛksɪti
AM ‚baɪ‚kɑnˈvɛksədi

bicultural
BR ‚bʌɪˈkʌltʃ(ə)rəl,
‚bʌɪˈkʌltʃ(ə)r]
AM baɪˈkəltʃ(ə)rəl

bicuspid
BR ‚bʌɪˈkʌspɪd, -z
AM baɪˈkəspəd, -z

bicuspidate
BR ‚bʌɪˈkʌspɪdeɪt
AM baɪˈkəspədət,
baɪˈkəspə‚deɪt

bicycle
BR ˈbʌɪsɪk]l, -lz,
-]ɪŋ \-lɪŋ, -ld
AM ˈbaɪsɪk]əl,
ˈbaɪ‚sɪk]əl, -əlz, -(ə)lɪŋ,
-əld

bicycler
BR ˈbʌɪsɪklə(r), -z
AM ˈbaɪsɪk(ə)lər,
ˈbaɪ‚sɪk(ə)lər, -z

bicyclist
BR ˈbʌɪsɪklɪst, -s
AM ˈbaɪ‚sɪk(ə)ləst,
ˈbaɪsɪkləst, -s

bid
BR bɪd, -z, -ɪŋ
AM bɪd, -z, -ɪŋ

biddability
BR ‚bɪdəˈbɪlɪti
AM ‚bɪdəˈbɪlɪdi

biddable
BR ˈbɪdəbl
AM ˈbɪdəbəl

Biddell
BR ˈbɪdl, bɪˈdɛl
AM ˈbɪdəl, bɪˈdɛl

bidden
BR ˈbɪdn
AM ˈbɪd(ə)n

bidder
BR ˈbɪdə(r), -z
AM ˈbɪdər, -z

Biddie
BR ˈbɪdi
AM ˈbɪdi

Biddle
BR ˈbɪdl
AM ˈbɪdəl

Biddulph
BR ˈbɪdʌlf
AM ˈbɪdəlf

biddy
BR ˈbɪd]i, -ɪz
AM ˈbɪdi, -z

bide
BR bʌɪd, -z, -ɪŋ, -ɪd
AM baɪd, -z, -ɪŋ, -ɪd

Bideford
BR ˈbɪdɪfəd
AM ˈbɪdəfərd

bidet
BR ˈbiːdeɪ, -z
AM bəˈdeɪ, biˈdeɪ, -z

bidialectal
BR ‚bʌɪdʌɪəˈlɛkt(ə)l
AM ‚baɪ‚daɪəˈlɛktəl

bidialectalism
BR ‚bʌɪdʌɪəˈlɛktəlɪz(ə)m,
‚bʌɪdʌɪəˈlɛkt]ɪz(ə)m
AM ‚baɪ‚daɪˈlɛktə‚lɪzəm

bidonville
BR ˈbɪdnvɪl, -z
AM ˈbaɪdn‚vɪl,
ˈbaɪdnvəl, -z

Biedermeier
BR ˈbiːdəmʌɪə(r)
AM ˈbiːdər‚maɪər

Bielefeld
BR ˈbiːləfɛld, ˈbiːləfɛlt
AM ˈbiːlə‚fɛld

biennia
BR bʌɪˈɛnɪə(r)
AM baɪˈɛniə

biennial
BR bʌɪˈɛnɪəl
AM baɪˈɛniəl

biennially
BR baɪˈenɪəli
AM barˈenɪəli

biennium
BR baɪˈenɪəm, -z
AM barˈenɪəm, -z

bier
BR bɪə(r), -z
AM bɪ(ə)r, -z

Bierce
BR bɪəs
AM bɪərs

bierwurst
BR ˈbɪəwə:st, ˈbɪəvə:st, ˈbɪəvʊəst
AM ˈbɪrˌwɜrst, ˈbɪrˌvʊrst

biff
BR bɪf, -s, -ɪŋ, -t
AM bɪf, -s, -ɪŋ, -t

Biffen
BR ˈbɪfɪn
AM ˈbɪfən

biffin
BR ˈbɪfɪn, -z
AM ˈbɪfɪn, -z

Biffo
BR ˈbɪfəʊ
AM ˈbɪfoʊ

bifid
BR ˈbaɪfɪd
AM ˈbaɪfɪd

bifida
BR ˈbɪfɪdə(r)
AM ˈbɪfɪdə

bifidly
BR ˈbaɪfɪdli
AM ˈbaɪfɪdli

bifocal
BR ˌbaɪˈfəʊkl, -z
AM ˌbaɪˈfoʊkəl, -z

bifoliate
BR ˌbaɪˈfəʊlɪeɪt, ˌbaɪˈfəʊlɪət
AM ˌbaɪˈfoʊliˌeɪt, ˌbaɪˈfoʊliət

bifurcate¹
adjective
BR ˌbaɪˈfə:keɪt, ˌbaɪˈfə:kɪt
AM baɪˈfərˌkeɪt, baɪˈfərkət

bifurcate²
verb
BR ˈbaɪfəkeɪt, -s, -ɪŋ, -ɪd
AM ˈbaɪfərˌkeɪ|t, -ts, -dɪŋ, -dɪd

bifurcation
BR ˌbaɪfəˈkeɪʃn, -z
AM ˌbaɪfərˈkeɪʃən, -z

big
BR bɪg, -ə(r), -ɪst
AM bɪg, -ər, -ɪst

bigamist
BR ˈbɪgəmɪst, -s
AM ˈbɪgəməst, -s

bigamous
BR ˈbɪgəməs

AM ˈbɪgəməs

bigamously
BR ˈbɪgəməsli
AM ˈbɪgəməsli

bigamy
BR ˈbɪgəmi
AM ˈbɪgəmi

Bigelow
BR ˈbɪgɪləʊ
AM ˈbɪgəˌloʊ

biggie
BR ˈbɪg|i, -ɪz
AM ˈbɪgi, -z

biggish
BR ˈbɪgɪʃ
AM ˈbɪgɪʃ

Biggles
BR ˈbɪglz
AM ˈbɪg(ə)lz

Biggleswade
BR ˈbɪglzweɪd
AM ˈbɪg(ə)lzˌweɪd

Biggs
BR bɪgz
AM bɪgz

bighead
BR ˈbɪghed, -z, -ɪd
AM ˈbɪgˌ(h)ed, -z, -əd

bigheadedness
BR ˈbɪgˈhedɪdnɪs
AM ˈbɪgˈhedədnəs

bighorn
BR ˈbɪghɔ:n, -z
AM ˈbɪgˌ(h)ɔ(ə)rn, -z

bight
BR baɪt, -s
AM baɪt, -s

bigmouth
BR ˈbɪgmaʊ|θ, -ðz
AM ˈbɪgˌmaʊ|θ, -ðz

bigness
BR ˈbɪgnɪs
AM ˈbɪgnɪs

bigot
BR ˈbɪgət, -s, -ɪd
AM ˈbɪgə|t, -ts, -dəd

bigotry
BR ˈbɪgətri
AM ˈbɪgətri

bigraph
BR ˈbaɪgrɑːf, ˈbaɪgraf, -s
AM ˈbaɪˌgræf, -s

bigwig
BR ˈbɪgwɪg, -z
AM ˈbɪgˌwɪg, -z

Bihar
BR bɪˈhɑː(r)
AM biˈhɑr

Bihari
BR bɪˈhɑːr|i, -ɪz
AM bəˈhɑri, -z

bijou
BR ˈbi:ʒu:, -z
AM ˈbiˌʒu, -z

bijouterie
BR ˌbi:ˈʒu:t(ə)ri

AM bi:ˌʒudəˈri

bijoux
BR ˈbi:ʒu:(z)
AM ˈbiˌʒu(z)

bike
BR baɪk, -s, -ɪŋ, -t
AM baɪk, -s, -ɪŋ, -t

biker
BR ˈbaɪkə(r), -z
AM ˈbaɪkər, -z

bikini
BR bɪˈki:n|i, -ɪz
AM bɪˈkini, -z

Biko
BR ˈbi:kəʊ
AM ˈbikoʊ

bilabial
BR ˌbaɪˈleɪbɪəl, -z
AM baɪˈleɪbɪəl, -z

bilabially
BR ˌbaɪˈleɪbɪəli
AM ˌbaɪˈleɪbɪəli

bilateral
BR ˌbaɪˈlat(ə)rəl, ˌbaɪˈlat(ə)rl̩
AM ˌbaɪˈlædərəl

bilateralism
BR ˌbaɪˈlat(ə)rəlɪz(ə)m, ˌbaɪˈlat(ə)rl̩ɪz(ə)m
AM ˌbaɪˈlædərəˌlɪzəm

bilaterally
BR ˌbaɪˈlat(ə)rəli, ˌbaɪˈlat(ə)rl̩i
AM ˌbaɪˈlædərəli

Bilbao
BR bɪlˈbaʊ
AM bɪlˈbaʊ

bilberry
BR ˈbɪlb(ə)r|i, -ɪz
AM ˈbɪlˌberi, -z

bilbo
BR ˈbɪlbəʊ, -z
AM ˈbɪlboʊ, -z

Bildungsroman
BR ˈbɪldʊŋsrə(ʊ)ˌmɑːn
AM ˈbɪldʊŋzˌroʊˌman

Bildungsromane
BR ˈbɪldʊŋsrə(ʊ)ˌmɑːnə(r)
AM ˈbɪldʊŋzˌroʊˌmanə

bile
BR baɪl
AM baɪl

bilge
BR bɪldʒ, -ɪz
AM bɪldʒ, -ɪz

bilgepump
BR ˈbɪldʒpʌmp, -s
AM ˈbɪldʒˌpəmp, -s

bilharzia
BR bɪlˈhɑːtsɪə(r), bɪlˈhɑːzɪə(r)
AM bɪlˈhɑrziə

bilharziasis
BR ˌbɪlhɑːˈtsaɪəsɪs, ˌbɪlhɑːˈzaɪəsɪs
AM ˌbɪlˌ(h)ɑrˈzaɪəsəs

biliary
BR ˈbɪlɪəri
AM ˈbɪliˌeri, ˈbɪljəri

bilingual
BR (ˌ)baɪˈlɪŋgw(ə)l
AM ˌbaɪˈlɪŋgwəl

bilingualism
BR (ˌ)baɪˈlɪŋgwəlɪz(ə)m, (ˌ)baɪˈlɪŋgwlɪz(ə)m
AM ˌbaɪˈlɪŋgwəˌlɪzəm

bilious
BR ˈbɪlɪəs
AM ˈbɪlɪəs, ˈbɪljəs

biliously
BR ˈbɪlɪəsli
AM ˈbɪlɪəsli, ˈbɪljəsli

biliousness
BR ˈbɪlɪəsnəs
AM ˈbɪlɪəsnəs, ˈbɪljəsnəs

bilirubin
BR ˌbɪlɪˈru:bɪn
AM ˈbɪliˌrubən

bilk
BR bɪlk, -s, -ɪŋ, -t
AM bɪlk, -s, -ɪŋ, -t

bilker
BR ˈbɪlkə(r), -z
AM ˈbɪlkər, -z

bill
BR bɪl, -z, -ɪŋ, -d
AM bɪl, -z, -ɪŋ, -d

billable
BR ˈbɪləbl
AM ˈbɪləbəl

billabong
BR ˈbɪləbɒŋ, -z
AM ˈbɪləˌbɔŋ, ˈbɪləˌbaŋ, -z

billboard
BR ˈbɪlbɔːd, -z
AM ˈbɪlˌbɔ(ə)rd, -z

Billericay
BR ˌbɪləˈrɪki
AM ˌbɪləˈrɪki

billet
BR ˈbɪlɪt, -s, -ɪŋ, -ɪd
AM ˈbɪlɪ|t, -ts, -dɪŋ, -dɪd

billet-doux
BR ˌbɪleɪˈduː, ˌbɪlɪˈduː
AM ˌbɪleɪˈdu

billetee
BR ˌbɪlɪˈtiː, -z
AM ˌbɪləˈti, -z

billeter
BR ˈbɪlɪtə(r), -z
AM ˈbɪlədər, -z

billets-doux
BR ˌbɪleɪˈduːz, ˌbɪlɪˈduːz
AM ˌbɪleɪˈduz

billfold
BR ˈbɪlfəʊld, -z
AM ˈbɪlˌfoʊld, -z

billhead
BR ˈbɪlhed, -z
AM ˈbɪlˌ(h)ed, -z

billhook
BR 'bɪlhʊk, -s
AM 'bɪl,(h)ʊk, -s
billiard
BR 'bɪljəd, -z
AM 'bɪljərd, -z
Billie
BR 'bɪli
AM 'bɪli
Billingham
BR 'bɪlɪŋəm
AM 'bɪlɪŋ,(h)æm
Billingsgate
BR 'bɪlɪŋzgeɪt
AM 'bɪlɪŋz,geɪt
Billingshurst
BR 'bɪlɪŋzhə:st
AM 'bɪlɪŋz,(h)ərst
billion
BR 'bɪljən, -z
AM 'bɪljən, -z
billionaire
BR ,bɪljə'neː(r), -z
AM ,bɪljə'nɛ(ə)r, -z
billionairess
BR ,bɪljə'neːrɪs,
,bɪljə'nɛːres, -ɪz
AM ,bɪljə'nɛrəs, -əz
billionth
BR 'bɪljənθ, -s
AM 'bɪljənθ, -s
billon
BR 'bɪlən
AM 'bɪlən
billow
BR 'bɪləʊ, -z, -ɪŋ, -d
AM 'bɪl|oʊ, -oʊz, -əwɪŋ, -oʊd
billowy
BR 'bɪləʊi
AM 'bɪləwi
billposter
BR 'bɪl,pəʊstə(r), -z
AM 'bɪl,poʊstər, -z
billposting
BR 'bɪl,pəʊstɪŋ
AM 'bɪl,poʊstɪŋ
billsticker
BR 'bɪl,stɪkə(r), -z
AM 'bɪl,stɪkər, -z
billy
BR 'bɪl|i, -ɪz
AM 'bɪli, -z
billybong
BR 'bɪlɪbɒŋ, -z
AM 'bɪlɪ,bɒŋ, 'bɪlɪ,bɑŋ, -z
billycan
BR 'bɪlɪkan, -z
AM 'bɪli,kæn, -z
billycock
BR 'bɪlɪkɒk, -s
AM 'bɪli,kɑk, -s
billy-o
BR 'bɪlɪəʊ
AM 'bɪli,oʊ

billy-oh
BR 'bɪlɪəʊ
AM 'bɪli,oʊ
bilobate
BR ,baɪ'ləʊbeɪt
AM baɪ'loʊ,beɪt
bilobed
BR ,baɪ'ləʊbd
AM baɪ'loʊbd
Biloxi
BR bɪ'lʌksi, bɪ'lɒksi
AM bə'ləksi
biltong
BR 'bɪltɒŋ
AM 'bɪl,tɒŋ, 'bɪl,tɑŋ
bimanal
BR (,)baɪ'meɪnl,
'bɪmənl
AM baɪ'meɪnl,
'bɪmənl
bimanous
BR 'bɪmənəs
AM 'bɪmənəs
bimbashi
BR bɪm'baʃ|i, -ɪz
AM bɪm'bæʃi, -z
bimbo
BR 'bɪmbəʊ, -z
AM 'bɪmboʊ, -z
bi-media
BR ,baɪ'miːdɪə(r)
AM ,baɪ'midɪə
bimetallic
BR ,baɪmɪ'talɪk,
,baɪmɛ'talɪk
AM ,baɪmə'tælɪk
bimetallism
BR ,baɪ'mɛtlɪz(ə)m
AM ,baɪ'mɛdl,ɪzəm
bimetallist
BR ,baɪ'mɛtlɪst, -s
AM ,baɪ'mɛdləst, -s
bimillenary
BR ,baɪmɪ'lɛn(ə)r|i,
,bAɪmɪ'liːn(ə)r|i,
,baɪ'mɪlɪn(ə)r|i, -ɪz
AM baɪ'mɪlə,nɛri, -z
bimodal
BR (,)baɪ'məʊdl
AM ,baɪ'moʊdəl
bimodality
BR ,baɪmə(ʊ)'dalɪti
AM ,baɪ,moʊ'dælədi
bimonthly
BR (,)baɪ'mʌnθl|i, -ɪz
AM ,baɪ'mənθli, -z
bin
BR bɪn, -z, -ɪŋ, -d
AM bɪn, -z, -ɪŋ, -d
binary
BR 'baɪn(ə)r|i, -ɪz
AM 'baɪnəri, 'baɪ,nɛri,
-z
binate
BR 'baɪneɪt
AM 'baɪ,neɪt

binaural
BR (,)baɪ'nɔːrəl,
(,)baɪ'nɔːrl
AM ,baɪ'nɔrəl
Binchy
BR 'bɪn(t)ʃi
AM 'bɪn(t)ʃi
bind
BR baɪnd, -z, -ɪŋ
AM baɪnd, -z, -ɪŋ
binder
BR 'baɪndə(r), -z
AM 'baɪndər, -z
bindery
BR 'baɪnd(ə)r|i, -ɪz
AM 'baɪnd(ə)ri, -z
bindi-eye
BR 'bɪndɪaɪ
AM 'bɪn(d)i,aɪ
binding
BR 'baɪndɪŋ, -z
AM 'baɪndɪŋ, -z
bindweed
BR 'baɪndwiːd
AM 'baɪn(d),wid
bine
BR baɪn, -z
AM baɪn, -z
bin-end
BR 'bɪnɛnd, -z
AM 'bɪn,ɛnd, -z
Binet
BR 'biːneɪ
AM bə'neɪ
bing
BR bɪŋ, -z
AM bɪŋ, -z
binge
BR bɪn(d)ʒ, -ɪz, -ɪŋ, -d
AM bɪndʒ, -ɪz, -ɪŋ, -d
Bingen
BR 'bɪŋən
AM 'bɪŋɛn
Bingham
BR 'bɪŋəm
AM 'bɪŋəm
Bingley
BR 'bɪŋli
AM 'bɪŋgli
bingo
BR 'bɪŋgəʊ
AM 'bɪŋgoʊ
binman
BR 'bɪnman
AM 'bɪn,mæn
binmen
BR 'bɪnmɛn
AM 'bɪn,mɛn
binnacle
BR 'bɪnəkl, -z
AM 'bɪnəkəl, -z
Binnie
BR 'bɪni
AM 'bɪni
Binns
BR bɪnz
AM bɪnz

binocular
adjective
BR (,)baɪ'nɒkjʊlə(r),
bɪ'nɒkjʊlə(r)
AM bə'nɑkjələr,
baɪ'nɑkjələr
binoculars
noun
BR bɪ'nɒkjʊləz
AM bə'nɑkjələrz
binomial
BR (,)baɪ'nəʊmɪəl
AM baɪ'noʊmɪəl
binomially
BR (,)baɪ'nəʊmɪəli
AM baɪ'noʊmɪəli
binominal
BR (,)baɪ'nɒmɪnl
AM baɪ'nɑmənəl
bint
BR bɪnt, -s
AM bɪnt, -s
Binyon
BR 'bɪnjən
AM 'bɪnjən
bio
BR 'baɪəʊ
AM 'baɪoʊ
bioceramic
BR ,baɪə(ʊ)sɪ'ramɪk, -s
AM ,baɪoʊsə'ræmɪk, -s
biochemical
BR ,baɪə(ʊ)'kɛmɪkl
AM ,baɪoʊ'kɛməkəl
biochemist
BR ,baɪə(ʊ)'kɛmɪst, -s
AM ,baɪoʊ'kɛməst,
,baɪə'kɛməst, -s
biochemistry
BR ,baɪə(ʊ)'kɛmɪstri
AM ,baɪoʊ'kɛməstri,
,baɪə'kɛməstri
biochip
BR 'baɪəʊtʃɪp, -s
AM 'baɪoʊ,tʃɪp, -s
biocoenology
BR ,baɪə(ʊ)sɪ'nɒlədʒi
AM ,baɪoʊsi'nɑlədʒi,
,baɪəsi'nɑlədʒi
biocoenoses
BR ,baɪə(ʊ)sɪ'nəʊsiːz
AM ,baɪoʊsə'noʊsiz,
,baɪəsə'noʊsiz
biocoenosis
BR ,baɪə(ʊ)sɪ'nəʊsɪs
AM ,baɪoʊsə'noʊsəs,
,baɪəsə'noʊsəs
biocoenotic
BR ,baɪə(ʊ)sɪ'nɒtɪk
AM ,baɪoʊsə'nɑdɪk,
,baɪəsə'nɑdɪk
biocompatibility
BR ,baɪəʊkəm,patɪ'bɪlɪti
AM ,baɪoʊkəm,pædə'bɪlɪdi,
,baɪəkəm,pædə'bɪlɪdi
biocompatible
BR ,baɪə(ʊ)kəm'patɪbl

AM ˌbaɪoʊkəm'pædəbəl,
ˌbaɪəkəm'pædəbəl
biocomputing
BR ˌbʌɪə(ʊ)kəm'pjuːtɪŋ
AM ˌbaɪoʊkəm'pjudɪŋ,
ˌbaɪəkəm'pjudɪŋ
biocontrol
BR ˌbʌɪəʊkən'trəʊl
AM ˌbaɪoʊkən'troʊl,
ˌbaɪəkən'troʊl
biodata
BR 'bʌɪə(ʊ)ˌdeɪtə(r)
AM 'baɪoʊˌdædə
biodegradability
BR ˌbʌɪə(ʊ)dɪˌɡreɪdə-
'bɪlɪti
AM ˌbaɪoʊdəˌɡreɪdə'bɪl-
ɪdi,
ˌbaɪoʊdiˌɡreɪdə'bɪlɪdi
biodegradable
BR ˌbʌɪə(ʊ)dɪ'ɡreɪdəbl
AM ˌbaɪoʊdə'ɡreɪdəbəl,
ˌbaɪoʊdi'ɡreɪdəbəl
biodegradation
BR ˌbʌɪə(ʊ)ˌdɛɡrə'deɪʃn
AM ˌbaɪoʊˌdɛɡrə'deɪʃən
biodiversity
BR ˌbʌɪə(ʊ)dʌɪ'vəːsɪti
AM ˌbaɪoʊdə'vɜrsədi,
ˌbaɪoʊˌdaɪ'vərsədi
bioenergetic
BR ˌbʌɪəʊˌɛnə'dʒɛtɪk
AM ˌbaɪoʊˌɛnər'dʒɛdɪk
bioenergy
BR ˌbʌɪəʊ'ɛnədʒi
AM ˌbaɪoʊ'ɛnərdʒi
bioengineer
BR ˌbʌɪəʊˌɛndʒɪ'nɪə(r),
-z, -ɪŋ
AM ˌbaɪoʊˌɛndʒəni(ə)r,
-z, -ɪŋ
bioethicist
BR ˌbʌɪəʊ'ɛθɪsɪst, -s
AM ˌbaɪoʊ'ɛθəsəst, -s
bioethics
BR ˌbʌɪəʊ'ɛθɪks
AM ˌbaɪoʊ'ɛθɪks
biofeedback
BR ˌbʌɪəʊ'fiːdbak
AM ˌbaɪoʊ'fidˌbæk
bioflavonoid
BR ˌbʌɪəʊ'fleɪvɪnɔɪd
AM ˌbaɪoʊ'fleɪvəˌnɔɪd
biogas
BR 'bʌɪə(ʊ)ɡas
AM 'baɪoʊˌɡæs
biogenesis
BR ˌbʌɪə(ʊ)'dʒɛnɪsɪs
AM ˌbaɪoʊ'dʒɛnəsəs
biogenetic
BR ˌbʌɪə(ʊ)dʒɪ'nɛtɪk
AM ˌbaɪoʊdʒə'nɛdɪk
biogenic
BR ˌbʌɪə(ʊ)'dʒɛnɪk
AM ˌbaɪoʊ'dʒɛnɪk
biogeographic
BR ˌbʌɪə(ʊ)ˌdʒɪə'ɡrafɪk
AM ˌbaɪoʊˌdʒiə'ɡræfɪk

biogeographical
BR ˌbʌɪə(ʊ)ˌdʒɪə'ɡrafɪkl
AM ˌbaɪoʊˌdʒiə'ɡræfəkəl
biogeography
BR ˌbʌɪə(ʊ)dʒɪ'ɒɡrəfi
AM ˌbaɪoʊdʒi'ɑɡrəfi
biograph
BR 'bʌɪə(ʊ)ɡrɑːf,
'bʌɪə(ʊ)ɡraf, -s
AM 'baɪəˌɡræf, -s
biographer
BR bʌɪ'ɒɡrəfə(r), -z
AM ˌbaɪ'ɑɡrəfər, -z
biographic
BR ˌbʌɪə'ɡrafɪk
AM ˌbaɪə'ɡræfɪk
biographical
BR ˌbʌɪə'ɡrafɪkl
AM ˌbaɪə'ɡræfəkəl
biographically
BR ˌbʌɪə'ɡrafɪkli
AM ˌbaɪə'ɡræfək(ə)li
biography
BR bʌɪ'ɒɡrəfji, -ɪz
AM baɪ'ɑɡrəfi, -z
biological
BR ˌbʌɪə'lɒdʒɪkl
AM ˌbaɪə'lɑdʒəkəl
biologically
BR ˌbʌɪə'lɒdʒɪkli
AM ˌbaɪə'lɑdʒək(ə)li
biologist
BR ˌbʌɪə'blədʒɪst, -s
AM baɪ'ɑlədʒəst, -s
biology
BR bʌɪ'ɒlədʒi
AM baɪ'ɑlədʒi
bioluminescence
BR ˌbʌɪəʊˌl(j)uːmɪ-
'nɛsns
AM ˌbaɪəˌlumə'nɛs(ə)ns
bioluminescent
BR ˌbʌɪəʊˌl(j)uːmɪ'nɛsnt
AM ˌbaɪəˌlumə'nɛs(ə)nt
biomass
BR ˌbʌɪə(ʊ)mas
AM 'baɪoʊˌmæs
biomaterial
BR ˌbʌɪə(ʊ)mə'tɪərɪəl,
-z
AM ˌbaɪəmə'tɪriəl, -z
biomathematics
BR ˌbʌɪə(ʊ)maθ(ɪ)'mat-
ɪks
AM ˌbaɪəˌmæθ'mædɪks
biome
BR 'bʌɪəʊm, -z
AM 'baɪˌoʊm, -z
biomechanics
BR ˌbʌɪə(ʊ)mɪ'kanɪks
AM ˌbaɪəmə'kænɪks
biomedical
BR ˌbʌɪə(ʊ)'mɛdɪkl
AM ˌbaɪə'mɛdəkəl
biomedicine
BR ˌbʌɪəʊ'mɛd(ɪ)s(ɪ)n
AM ˌbaɪə'mɛd(ə)sən

biometric
BR ˌbʌɪə(ʊ)'mɛtrɪk, -s
AM ˌbaɪoʊ'mɛtrɪk, -s
biometrical
BR ˌbʌɪə(ʊ)'mɛtrɪkl
AM ˌbaɪoʊ'mɛtrəkəl
biometrician
BR ˌbʌɪə(ʊ)mɪ'trɪʃn, -z
AM ˌbaɪoʊmə'trɪʃən, -z
biometry
BR bʌɪ'ɒmɪtri
AM baɪ'ɑmətri
biomorph
BR 'bʌɪə(ʊ)mɔːf, -s
AM 'baɪəˌmɔ(ə)rf, -s
biomorphic
BR ˌbʌɪə(ʊ)'mɔːfɪk
AM ˌbaɪə'mɔrfɪk
bionic
BR bʌɪ'ɒnɪk, -s
AM baɪ'ɑnɪk, -s
bionically
BR bʌɪ'ɒnɪkli
AM baɪ'ɑnək(ə)li
bionomic
BR ˌbʌɪə(ʊ)'nɒmɪk, -s
AM baɪ'nɑmɪk, -s
biophysic
BR ˌbʌɪə(ʊ)'fɪzɪk, -s
AM ˌbaɪoʊ'fɪzɪk, -s
biophysical
BR ˌbʌɪə(ʊ)'fɪzɪkl
AM ˌbaɪoʊ'fɪzɪkəl
biophysically
BR ˌbʌɪə(ʊ)'fɪzɪkli
AM ˌbaɪoʊ'fɪzɪkəl(ə)li
biophysicist
BR ˌbʌɪə(ʊ)'fɪzɪsɪst, -s
AM ˌbaɪoʊ'fɪzɪsɪst, -s
biopic
BR 'bʌɪə(ʊ)pɪk, -s
AM 'baɪoʊˌpɪk, -s
biopsy
BR 'bʌɪɒps|i, -ɪz
AM 'baɪˌɑpsi, -z
biorhythm
BR 'bʌɪə(ʊ)ˌrɪðm, -z
AM 'baɪoʊˌrɪðəm, -z
biorhythmic
BR ˌbʌɪə(ʊ)'rɪðmɪk
AM ˌbaɪoʊ'rɪðmɪk
biorhythmically
BR ˌbʌɪə(ʊ)'rɪðmɪkli
AM ˌbaɪoʊ'rɪðmɪk(ə)li
bioscope
BR 'bʌɪəskəʊp, -s
AM 'baɪəsˌkoʊp, -s
biosensor
BR 'bʌɪə(ʊ)ˌsɛnsə(r),
-z
AM 'baɪoʊˌsɛnsər,
'baɪəˌsɛnsər, -z
biosphere
BR 'bʌɪəsfɪə(r)
AM 'baɪəˌsfɪ(ə)r
biosyntheses
BR ˌbʌɪə(ʊ)'sɪnθɪsiːz

AM ˌbaɪoʊ'sɪnθəsiz
biosynthesis
BR ˌbʌɪə(ʊ)'sɪnθɪsɪs
AM ˌbaɪoʊ'sɪnθəsəs
biosynthetic
BR ˌbʌɪə(ʊ)sɪn'θɛtɪk
AM ˌbaɪoʊˌsɪn'θɛdɪk
biota
BR bʌɪ'əʊtə(r)
AM baɪ'oʊdə
biotechnologist
BR ˌbʌɪə(ʊ)tɛk'nɒlə-
dʒɪst, -s
AM ˌbaɪoʊˌtɛk'nɑlə-
dʒəst, -s
biotechnology
BR ˌbʌɪə(ʊ)tɛk'nɒlədʒi
AM ˌbaɪoʊˌtɛk'nɑlədʒi
biotic
BR bʌɪ'ɒtɪk
AM baɪ'adɪk
biotin
BR 'bʌɪətɪn, -z
AM 'baɪətn, -z
biotite
BR 'bʌɪətʌɪt, -s
AM 'baɪəˌtaɪt, -s
biparous
BR 'bɪp(ə)rəs
AM 'bɪpərəs
bipartisan
BR ˌbʌɪpɑː'tɪ'zan,
bʌɪ'pɑːtɪz(ə)n
AM baɪ'pɑrdəz(ə)n
bipartisanship
BR ˌbʌɪpɑː'tɪz(ə)nˌʃɪp,
bʌɪ'pɑːtɪz(ə)nˌʃɪp
AM baɪ'pɑrdəzənˌʃɪp
bipartite
BR (ˌ)bʌɪ'pɑːtʌɪt
AM baɪ'pɑrˌtaɪt
biped
BR 'bʌɪpɛd, -z
AM 'baɪˌpɛd, -z
bipedal
BR bʌɪ'piːdl, bʌɪ'pɛdl
AM ˌbaɪ'pɛdəl,
ˌbaɪ'pidəl
bipedalism
BR bʌɪ'piːdlɪz(ə)m,
ˌbʌɪ'pɛdlɪz(ə)m
AM baɪ'pɛdlˌɪzəm,
ˌbaɪ'pɛdlˌɪzəm
bipedality
BR ˌbʌɪpɛ'dalɪti,
ˌbʌɪpɪ'dalɪti
AM ˌbaɪpə'dælədi
biphenyl
BR ˌbʌɪ'fiːnʌɪl,
ˌbʌɪ'fɛnɪl, -z
AM baɪ'fɛnəl, -z
bipinnate
BR bʌɪ'pɪneɪt,
ˌbʌɪ'pɪnɪt
AM baɪ'pɪnɪt
biplane
BR 'bʌɪpleɪn, -z
AM 'baɪˌpleɪn, -z

bipolar
BR ˌbaɪˈpəʊlə(r)
AM baɪˈpoʊlər

bipolarity
BR ˌbaɪpə(ʊ)ˈlarɪti
AM ˌbaɪpoʊˈlærədi

biquadratic
BR ˌbaɪkwɒˈdratɪk,
ˌbaɪkwəˈdratɪk, -s
AM ˌbaɪkwɑˈdrædɪk,
ˌbaɪkwəˈdrædɪk, -s

birch
BR bəːtʃ, -ɪz, -ɪŋ, -t
AM bɜrtʃ, -əz, -ɪŋ, -t

birchen
BR ˈbəːtʃn
AM ˈbɜrtʃən

birchwood
BR ˈbəːtʃwʊd
AM ˈbɜrtʃˌwʊd

bird
BR bəːd, -z
AM bɜrd, -z

birdbath
BR ˈbəːd|bɑːθ,
ˈbəːd|baθ,
-bɑːðz\-bɑːθs\-baθs
AM ˈbɜrd,bæ|θ, -θs\-ðz

birdbrain
BR ˈbəːdbreɪn, -z, -d
AM ˈbɜrd,breɪn, -z, -d

birdcage
BR ˈbəːdkeɪdʒ, -ɪz
AM ˈbɜrd,keɪdʒ, -ɪz

birder
BR ˈbəːdə(r), -z
AM ˈbɜrdər, -z

birdie
BR ˈbəːd|i, -ɪz
AM ˈbɜrdi, -z

birdlime
BR ˈbəːdlaɪm
AM ˈbɜrd,laɪm

birdseed
BR ˈbəːdsiːd
AM ˈbɜrd,sid

Birdseye
BR ˈbəːdʒaɪ
AM ˈbɜrdz,aɪ

bird's-eye
BR ˈbəːdʒaɪ
AM ˈbɜrdz,aɪ

birdsong
BR ˈbəːdsɒŋ
AM ˈbɜrd,sɒŋ,
ˈbɜrd,sɑŋ

birdtable
BR ˈbəːd,teɪbl, -z
AM ˈbɜrd,teɪbəl, -z

birdwatcher
BR ˈbəːd,wɒtʃə(r), -z
AM ˈbɜrd,wɒtʃər,
ˈbɜrd,wɑtʃər, -z

birdwatching
BR ˈbəːd,wɒtʃɪŋ
AM ˈbɜrd,wɒtʃɪŋ,
ˈbɜrd,wɑtʃɪŋ

birefringence
BR ˌbaɪrɪˈfrɪn(d)ʒ(ə)ns
AM ˌbaɪrəˈfrɪndʒəns

birefringent
BR ˌbaɪrɪˈfrɪn(d)ʒ(ə)nt
AM ˌbaɪrəˈfrɪndʒənt

bireme
BR ˈbaɪriːm, -z
AM ˈbaɪˌrim, -z

biretta
BR bɪˈrɛtə(r), -z
AM bəˈrɛdə, -z

Birgitta
BR bɪəˈɡɪtə(r)
AM bərˈɡidə

biriani
BR ˌbɪrɪˈɑːn|i, -ɪz
AM ˌbɪriˈɑni, -z

Birkbeck
BR ˈbəːkbɛk
AM ˈbɜrkbɛk

Birkenhead
BR ˌbəːk(ə)nˈhɛd,
ˈbəːk(ə)nhɛd
AM ˈbɜrkən,(h)ɛd

Birkenshaw
BR ˈbəːk(ɪ)nʃɔː(r)
AM ˈbɜrk(ə)n,ʃɔ

Birkett
BR ˈbəːkɪt
AM ˈbɜrkət

birl
BR bəːl, -z, -ɪŋ, -d
AM bɜrl, -z, -ɪŋ, -d

Birmingham¹
place in England
BR ˈbəːmɪŋəm
AM ˈbɜrmɪŋ,(h)æm

Birmingham²
place in USA
BR ˈbəːmɪŋham
AM ˈbɜrmɪŋ,(h)æm

biro®
BR ˈbaɪrəʊ, -z
AM ˈbaɪroʊ, ˈbaɪroʊ, -z

Birobidzhan
BR ˌbɪrəbɪˈdʒɑːn,
ˌbɪrəbɪˈdʒan
AM ˌbɪroʊbəˈ(d)ʒan

birr
BR bəː(r), -z, -ɪŋ, -d
AM bɜr, -z, -ɪŋ, -d

Birt
BR bəːt
AM bɜrt

birth
BR bəːθ, -s, -ɪŋ, -t
AM bɜrθ, -s, -ɪŋ, -t

birthday
BR ˈbəːθdeɪ, -z
AM ˈbɜrθ,deɪ, -z

birthmark
BR ˈbəːθmɑːk, -s
AM ˈbɜrθ,mark, -s

birthplace
BR ˈbəːθpleɪs, -ɪz
AM ˈbɜrθ,pleɪs, -ɪz

birthrate
BR ˈbəːθreɪt, -s
AM ˈbɜrθ,reɪt, -s

birthright
BR ˈbəːθraɪt, -s
AM ˈbɜrθ,raɪt, -s

birthstone
BR ˈbəːθstəʊn, -z
AM ˈbɜrθ,stoʊn, -z

birthweight
BR ˈbəːθweɪt
AM ˈbɜrθ,weɪt

Birtwistle
BR ˈbəːtwɪsl
AM ˈbɜrt,wɪsəl

biryani
BR ˌbɪrɪˈɑːn|i, -ɪz
AM ˌbɪriˈɑni, -z

bis
BR bɪs
AM bɪs

Biscay
BR ˈbɪskeɪ
AM ˌbɪsˈkeɪ

Biscayne
BR bɪˈskeɪn
AM bɪsˈkeɪn

biscuit
BR ˈbɪskɪt, -s
AM ˈbɪskɪt, -s

biscuity
BR ˈbɪskɪti
AM ˈbɪskɪdi

bisect
BR baɪˈsɛkt, -s, -ɪŋ, -ɪd
AM ˌbaɪˈsɛk|(t), -(t)s,
-tɪŋ, -təd

bisection
BR baɪˈsɛkʃn
AM baɪˈsɛkʃən

bisector
BR baɪˈsɛktə(r), -z
AM baɪˈsɛktər, -z

bisexual
BR (ˌ)baɪˈsɛkʃʊəl,
(ˌ)baɪˈsɛkʃ(ʊ)l,
(ˌ)baɪˈsɛksju(ə)l, -z
AM ˌbaɪˈsɛkʃ(əw)əl, -z

bisexuality
BR ˌbaɪsɛkʃʊˈalɪti,
ˌbaɪsɛksjuˈalɪti
AM ˌbaɪˌsɛkʃəˈwælədi

bish
BR bɪʃ, -ɪz
AM bɪʃ, -ɪz

bishop
BR ˈbɪʃəp, -s
AM ˈbɪʃəp, -s

bishopric
BR ˈbɪʃəprɪk, -s
AM ˈbɪʃəprɪk, -s

Bishopsgate
BR ˈbɪʃəpsɡeɪt
AM ˈbɪʃəps,ɡeɪt

bisk
BR bɪsk, -s
AM bɪsk, -s

Bislama
BR ˈbɪʃləmɑː(r)
AM bɪsˈlamə

Bisley
BR ˈbɪzli
AM ˈbɪzli

Bismarck
BR ˈbɪzmɑːk
AM ˈbɪzmark

bismuth
BR ˈbɪzməθ
AM ˈbɪzməθ

bison
BR ˈbaɪsn, -z
AM ˈbaɪsən, -z

bisque
BR bɪsk, -s
AM bɪsk, -s

Bissau
BR bɪˈsaʊ
AM bɪˈsaʊ

Bissell
BR ˈbɪsl
AM ˈbɪsəl

bissextile
BR bɪˈsɛkstʌɪl
AM baɪˈsɛkstəl

bistable
BR ˌbaɪˈsteɪbl
AM baɪˈsteɪbəl

bister
BR ˈbɪstə(r), -d
AM ˈbɪstər, -d

Bisto®
BR ˈbɪstəʊ
AM ˈbɪstoʊ

bistort
BR ˈbɪstɔːt, -s
AM ˈbɪstɔ(ə)rt, -s

bistoury
BR ˈbɪst(ə)r|i, -ɪz
AM ˈbɪst(ə)ri, -z

bistre
BR ˈbɪstə(r), -d
AM ˈbɪstər, -d

bistro
BR ˈbɪstrəʊ, ˈbiːstrəʊ,
-z
AM ˈbɪstroʊ, ˈbistroʊ, -z

bisulfate
BR ˌbaɪˈsʌlfeɪt
AM baɪˈsəl,feɪt

bisulphate
BR ˌbaɪˈsʌlfeɪt
AM baɪˈsəl,feɪt

bisulphite
BR ˌbaɪˈsʌlfʌɪt
AM baɪˈsəl,faɪt

bit
BR bɪt, -s
AM bɪt, -s

bitch
BR bɪtʃ, -ɪz, -ɪŋ, -t
AM bɪtʃ, -ɪz, -ɪŋ, -t

bitchily
BR ˈbɪtʃɪli
AM ˈbɪtʃɪli

bitchiness
BR ˈbɪtʃɪnɪs
AM ˈbɪtʃɪnɪs

bitchy
BR ˈbɪtʃ|i, -ɪə(r), -ɪɪst
AM ˈbɪtʃi, -ər, -əst

bite
BR bʌɪt, -s, -ɪŋ
AM baɪ|t, -ts, -dɪŋ

biter
BR ˈbʌɪtə(r), -z
AM ˈbaɪdər, -z

Bithynia
BR bɪˈθɪnɪə(r)
AM bəˈθɪnɪə

bitingly
BR ˈbʌɪtɪŋli
AM ˈbaɪdɪŋli

bitmap
BR ˈbɪtmap, -s, -ɪŋ, -t
AM ˈbɪt,mæp, -s, -ɪŋ, -t

bitt
BR bɪt, -s
AM bɪt, -s

bitten
BR ˈbɪtn
AM ˈbɪtn

bitter
BR ˈbɪt|ə(r), -əz,
-(ə)rə(r), -(ə)rɪst
AM ˈbɪdər, -z, -ər, -əst

bitterling
BR ˈbɪtəlɪŋ, -z
AM ˈbɪdərlɪŋ, -z

bitterly
BR ˈbɪtəli
AM ˈbɪdərli

bittern
BR ˈbɪtn, ˈbɪtɔːn, -z
AM ˈbɪdərn, -z

bitterness
BR ˈbɪtənəs
AM ˈbɪdərnəs

bitterroot
BR ˈbɪtəruːt
AM ˈbɪdər,rut,
ˈbɪdər,rʊt

bittersweet¹
adjective
BR ˌbɪtəˈswiːt
AM ˈbɪdərˈswit

bittersweet²
noun
BR ˈbɪtəswiːt
AM ˈbɪdərˈswit

bittily
BR ˈbɪtɪli
AM ˈbɪdɪli

bittiness
BR ˈbɪtɪnɪs
AM ˈbɪdɪnɪs

bitty
BR ˈbɪt|i, -ɪə(r), -ɪɪst
AM ˈbɪdi, -ər, -ɪst

bitumen
BR ˈbɪtʃʉmɨn,
ˈbɪtjʉmɨn

AM baɪˈt(j)umən,
bəˈt(j)umən

bituminisation
BR bɪˌtjuːmɪnʌɪˈzeɪʃn,
bɪˌtʃuːmɪnʌɪˈzeɪʃn
AM baɪˌt(j)umənəˈzeɪ-
ʃən,
bəˌt(j)umənəˈzeɪʃən,
baɪˌt(j)uməˌnaɪˈzeɪʃən,
bəˌt(j)uməˌnaɪˈzeɪʃən

bituminise
BR bɪˈtjuːmɪnʌɪz,
bɪˈtʃuːmɪnʌɪz, -ɪz, -ɪŋ,
-d
AM baɪˈt(j)umən,aɪz,
bəˈt(j)umən,aɪz, -ɪz,
-ɪŋ, -d

bituminization
BR bɪˌtjuːmɪnʌɪˈzeɪʃn,
bɪˌtʃuːmɪnʌɪˈzeɪʃn
AM baɪˌt(j)umənəˈzeɪ-
ʃən,
bəˌt(j)umənəˈzeɪʃən,
baɪˌt(j)uməˌnaɪˈzeɪʃən,
bəˌt(j)uməˌnaɪˈzeɪʃən

bituminize
BR bɪˈtjuːmɪnʌɪz,
bɪˈtʃuːmɪnʌɪz, -ɪz, -ɪŋ,
-d
AM baɪˈt(j)umən,aɪz,
bəˈt(j)umən,aɪz, -ɪz,
-ɪŋ, -d

bituminous
BR bɪˈtjuːmɪnəs,
bɪˈtʃuːmɪnəs
AM baɪˈt(j)umənəs,
bəˈt(j)umənəs

bivalence
BR (ˌ)bʌɪˈveɪləns,
(ˌ)bʌɪˈveɪlns
AM ˌbaɪˈveɪləns

bivalency
BR (ˌ)bʌɪˈveɪlənsi,
(ˌ)bʌɪˈveɪlnsi
AM ˌbaɪˈveɪlənsi

bivalent
BR (ˌ)bʌɪˈveɪlənt,
ˌbʌɪˈveɪlnt
AM ˌbaɪˈveɪlənt

bivalve
BR ˈbʌɪvalv, -z
AM ˈbaɪ,vælv, -z

bivouac
BR ˈbɪvʊak, -s, -ɪŋ, -t
AM ˈbɪv(ə),wæk, -s, -ɪŋ,
-t

bivvy
BR ˈbɪv|i, -ɪz
AM ˈbɪvi, -z

biweekly
BR (ˌ)bʌɪˈwiːkl|i, -ɪz
AM ˌbaɪˈwikli, -z

biyearly
BR ˌbʌɪˈjɪəli, ˌbʌɪˈjɔːli
AM ˌbaɪˈjɪrli

biz
BR bɪz
AM bɪz

bizarre
BR bɪˈzɑː(r)
AM bəˈzɑr

bizarrely
BR bɪˈzɑːli
AM bəˈzɑrli

bizarreness
BR bɪˈzɑːnəs
AM bəˈzɑrnəs

bizarrerie
BR bɪˈzɑːrəri
AM bəˈzɑrəri,
bə,zɑrəˈri

Bizerta
BR bɪˈzəːtə(r)
AM bəˈzərdə

Bizerte
BR bɪˈzəːtə(r)
AM bəˈzərdə

Bizet
BR ˈbiːzeɪ
AM bɪˈzeɪ

Bjorn
BR bɪˈɔːn
AM bjɔ(ə)rn
sw bjəːrn

blab
BR blab, -z, -ɪŋ, -d
AM blæb, -z, -ɪŋ, -d

blabber
BR ˈblab|ə(r), -əz,
-(ə)rɪŋ, -əd
AM ˈblæbər, -z, -ɪŋ, -d

blabbermouth
BR ˈblabəmaʊ|θ, -ðz
AM ˈblæbər,maʊ|θ,
-θs\-ðz

Blaby
BR ˈbleɪbi
AM ˈblæbi

black
BR blak, -s, -ɪŋ, -t, -ə(r),
-ɪst
AM blæk, -s, -ɪŋ, -t, -ər,
-əst

blackamoor
BR ˈblakəmɔː(r), -z
AM ˈblækə,mɔ(ə)r, -z

blackball
BR ˈblakbɔːl, -z, -ɪŋ, -d
AM ˈblæk,bɔl,
ˈblæk,bɑl, -z, -ɪŋ, -d

blackbeetle
BR ˈblak,biːtl, -z
AM ˈblæk,bidəl, -z

blackberry
BR ˈblakb(ə)r|i, -ɪz
AM ˈblæk,bɛri, -z

blackberrying
BR ˈblak,bɛrɪɪŋ
AM ˈblæk,bɛrɪŋ

blackbird
BR ˈblakbəːd, -z
AM ˈblæk,bərd, -z

blackboard
BR ˈblakbɔːd, -z
AM ˈblæk,bɔ(ə)rd, -z

blackboy
BR ˈblakbɔɪ, -z
AM ˈblæk,bɔɪ, -z

blackbuck
BR ˈblakbʌk, -s
AM ˈblæk,bək, -s

Blackburn
BR ˈblakbəːn
AM ˈblækbərn

blackcap
BR ˈblakkap, -s
AM ˈblæk,kæp, -s

blackcock
BR ˈblakkɒk, -s
AM ˈblæk,kɑk, -s

blackcurrant
BR ˌblakˈkʌrənt,
ˌblakˈkʌrnt
AM ˈblækˈkərənt

blacken
BR ˈblak|(ə)n, -(ə)nz,
-ənɪŋ\-nɪŋ, -(ə)nd
AM ˈblæk|ən, -ənz,
-(ə)nɪŋ, -ənd

Blackett
BR ˈblakɪt
AM ˈblækət

Blackfeet
BR ˈblakfiːt
AM ˈblæk,fit

blackfellow
BR ˈblak,fɛləʊ, -z
AM ˈblæk,fɛloʊ, -z

blackfish
BR ˈblakfɪʃ
AM ˈblæk,fɪʃ

blackfly
BR ˈblakflʌɪ, -z
AM ˈblæk,flaɪ, -z

Blackfoot
BR ˈblakfʊt
AM ˈblæk,fʊt

Blackfriars
BR ˌblakˈfrʌɪəz,
ˈblak,frʌɪəz
AM ˈblæk,fraɪərz

blackguard
BR ˈblagɑːd, ˈblagəd, -z
AM ˈblægərd,
ˈblæ,gard, -z

blackguardly
BR ˈblagɑːdli,
ˈblagədli
AM ˈblæ,gərdli,
ˈblæ,gardli

blackhead
BR ˈblakhɛd, -z
AM ˈblæk,(h)ɛd, -z

Blackheath
BR ˌblakˈhiːθ
AM ˈblæk,(h)iθ

Blackie
BR ˈblaki, ˈbleɪki
AM ˈblæki

blacking
BR ˈblakɪŋ
AM ˈblækɪŋ

blackish
BR 'blakɪʃ
AM 'blækɪʃ
blackjack
BR 'blakdʒak
AM 'blæk͵dʒæk
blacklead
BR 'blaklɛd, -z, -ɪŋ, -ɪd
AM 'blæk͵lɛd, -z, -ɪŋ, -əd
blackleg
BR 'blaklɛg, -z
AM 'blæk͵lɛg, -z
blacklist
BR 'blaklɪst, -s, -ɪŋ, -ɪd
AM 'blæk͵lɪst, -s, -ɪŋ, -ɪd
blackly
BR 'blakli
AM 'blækli
blackmail
BR 'blakmeɪl, -z, -ɪŋ, -d
AM 'blæk͵meɪl, -z, -ɪŋ, -d
blackmailer
BR 'blak͵meɪlə(r), -z
AM 'blæk͵meɪlər, -z
Black Maria
BR ͵blak mə'rʌɪə(r), -z
AM ͵blæk mə'riə, -z
Blackmore
BR 'blakmɔː(r)
AM 'blæk͵mɔ(ə)r
blackness
BR 'blaknəs
AM 'blæknəs
blackout
BR 'blakaʊt, -s
AM 'blæk͵aʊt, -s
Blackpool
BR 'blakpuːl
AM 'blæk͵pul
Blackshirt
BR 'blakʃəːt, -s
AM 'blæk͵ʃərt, -s
blacksmith
BR 'blaksmɪθ, -s
AM 'blæk͵smɪθ, -s
blackspot
BR 'blakspɒt, -s
AM 'blæk͵spat, -s
Blackstone
BR 'blakstəʊn, 'blakst(ə)n
AM 'blæk͵stoʊn, 'blækstən
blackthorn
BR 'blakθɔːn, -z
AM 'blæk͵θɔ(ə)rn, -z
blacktop
BR 'blaktɒp, -s
AM 'blæk͵tap, -s
Blackwall
BR 'blakwɔːl
AM 'blæk͵wɔl, 'blæk͵wɑl
Blackwell
BR 'blakw(ɛ)l

AM 'blæk͵wɛl, 'blækwəl
Blackwood
BR 'blakwʊd
AM 'blæk͵wʊd
bladder
BR 'bladə(r), -z
AM 'blædər, -z
bladderwort
BR 'bladəwɔːt, -s
AM 'blædər͵wərt, 'blædər͵wɔ(ə)rt, -s
bladderwrack
BR 'bladərak
AM 'blædə(r)ræk
blade
BR bleɪd, -z, -ɪd
AM bleɪd, -z, -ɪd
bladebone
BR 'bleɪdbəʊn, -z
AM 'bleɪd͵boʊn, -z
Bladon
BR 'bleɪdn
AM 'bleɪdən
blaeberry
BR 'bleɪb(ə)r|i, -ɪz
AM 'bleɪ͵bɛri, -z
Blaenau Ffestiniog
BR ͵blʌɪnʌɪ fɛ'stɪnɪɒg
AM 'bleɪnaɪ fɛ'stɪnjɑg
WE ͵bleɪnaɪ fɛ'stɪnjʊg
blag
BR blag, -z, -ɪŋ, -d
AM blæg, -z, -ɪŋ, -d
blagger
BR 'blagə(r), -z
AM 'blægər, -z
blague
BR blag
AM blɑg
blagueur
BR bla'gəː(r), -z
AM 'blagər, blɑ'gər, -z
blah
BR blɑː(r)
AM blɑ
blah-blah
BR ͵blɑː'blɑː(r)
AM 'blɑ'blɑ
blain
BR bleɪn, -z
AM bleɪn, -z
Blair
BR blɛː(r)
AM blɛ(ə)r
Blairgowrie
BR ͵blɛː'gaʊri
AM ͵blɛr'gaʊri
Blaise
BR bleɪz
AM bleɪz
Blake
BR bleɪk
AM bleɪk
Blakemore
BR 'bleɪkmɔː(r)

AM 'bleɪk͵mɔ(ə)r
Blakeney
BR 'bleɪkni
AM 'bleɪkni
Blakey
BR 'bleɪk|i, -ɪz
AM 'bleɪki, -z
blamable
BR 'bleɪməbl
AM 'bleɪməbəl
blamably
BR 'bleɪməbli
AM 'bleɪməbli
blame
BR bleɪm, -z, -ɪŋ, -d
AM bleɪm, -z, -ɪŋ, -d
blameable
BR 'bleɪməbl
AM 'bleɪməbəl
blameably
BR 'bleɪməbli
AM 'bleɪməbli
blameful
BR 'bleɪmf(ʊ)l
AM 'bleɪmfəl
blamefully
BR 'bleɪmfʊli, 'bleɪmfli
AM 'bleɪmfəli
blameless
BR 'bleɪmlɪs
AM 'bleɪmlɪs
blamelessly
BR 'bleɪmlɪsli
AM 'bleɪmlɪsli
blamelessness
BR 'bleɪmlɪsnɪs
AM 'bleɪmlɪsnɪs
blameworthiness
BR 'bleɪm͵wəːðɪnɪs
AM 'bleɪm͵wərðɪnɪs
blameworthy
BR 'bleɪm͵wəːði
AM 'bleɪm͵wərði
blanc
BR blɑːŋk, blõ
AM blaŋk
blanch
BR blɑːn(t)ʃ, blan(t)ʃ, -ɪz, -ɪŋ, -t
AM blæn(t)ʃ, -əz, -ɪŋ, -t
Blanchard
BR 'blan(t)ʃəd, 'blan(t)ʃɑːd
AM 'blæn(t)ʃərd
Blanche
BR blɑːn(t)ʃ, blan(t)ʃ
AM blæn(t)ʃ
blancmange
BR blə'mɒn(d)ʒ, -ɪz
AM blə'mɑn(d)ʒ, -əz
blanco
BR 'blaŋkəʊ, -z, -ɪŋ, -d
AM 'blæŋkoʊ, -z, -ɪŋ, -d
bland
BR bland, -ə(r), -ɪst
AM blænd, -ər, -əst

Blandford
BR 'blan(d)fəd
AM 'blæn(d)fərd
blandish
BR 'blandɪʃ, -ɪʃɪz, -ɪʃɪŋ, -ɪʃt
AM 'blændɪʃ, -ɪz, -ɪŋ, -t
blandishment
BR 'blandɪʃm(ə)nt, -s
AM 'blændɪʃmənt, -s
blandly
BR 'blandli
AM 'blæn(d)li
blandness
BR 'blan(d)nəs
AM 'blæn(d)nəs
blank
BR blaŋ|k, -ks, -kɪŋ, -(k)t, -kə(r), -kɪst
AM blæŋ|k, -ks, -kɪŋ, -(k)t, -kər, -kəst
Blankenship
BR 'blaŋk(ə)nʃɪp
AM 'blæŋkɛn͵ʃɪp
blanket
BR 'blaŋk|ɪt, -ɪts, -ɪtɪŋ, -ɪtɪd
AM 'blæŋkə|t, -ts, -dɪŋ, -dəd
blanketweed
BR 'blaŋkɪtwiːd
AM 'blæŋkət͵wid
blankety
BR 'blaŋkɪti
AM 'blæŋkədi
blankness
BR 'blaŋknəs
AM 'blæŋknəs
blanky
BR 'blaŋki
AM 'blæŋki
blanquette
BR ͵blɒŋ'kɛt, ͵blaŋ'kɛt, -s
AM ͵blɑŋ'kɛt, -s
Blantyre
BR 'blantʌɪə(r)
AM 'blæn͵taɪ(ə)r
blare
BR blɛː(r), -z, -ɪŋ, -d
AM blɛ(ə)r, -z, -ɪŋ, -d
blarney
BR 'blɑːni
AM 'blɑrni
blasé
BR 'blɑːzeɪ
AM blɑ'zeɪ
blaspheme
BR blas'fiːm, blɑːs'fiːm, -z, -ɪŋ, -d
AM ͵blæs'fim, -z, -ɪŋ, -d
blasphemer
BR blas'fiːmə(r), blɑːs'fiːmə(r), -z
AM blæs'fimər, 'blæsfəmər, -z

blasphemous
BR 'blæsfəməs,
'blɑːsfəməs
AM 'blæsfəməs
blasphemously
BR 'blæsfəməsli,
'blɑːsfəməsli
AM 'blæsfəməsli
blasphemy
BR 'blæsfəm|i,
'blɑːsfəmi, -ɪz
AM 'blæsfəmi, -z
blast
BR blɑːst, blast, -s, -ɪŋ,
-ɪd
AM blæst, -s, -ɪŋ, -əd
blaster
BR 'blɑːstə(r),
'blastə(r), -z
AM 'blæstər, -z
blastula
BR 'blastjʊlə(r),
'blastʃʊlə(r), -z
AM 'blæstʃələ, -z
blastulae
BR 'blastjʊliː,
'blastʃʊliː
AM 'blæstʃəli,
'blæstʃə,laɪ
blatancy
BR 'bleɪtnsi
AM 'bleɪtnsi
blatant
BR 'bleɪtnt
AM 'bleɪtnt
blatantly
BR 'bleɪtntli
AM 'bleɪtn(t)li
Blatchford
BR 'blatʃfəd
AM 'blætʃfərd
blather
BR 'blaðə(r), -əz,
-(ə)rɪŋ, -əd
AM 'blæðər, -z, -ɪŋ, -d
blatherer
BR 'blað(ə)rə(r), -z
AM 'blæðərər, -z
blatherskite
BR 'blaðəskaɪt, -s
AM 'blæðər,skaɪt, -s
Blavatsky
BR blə'vatski
AM blə'vætski
Blawith¹
BR 'bleɪwɪθ
AM 'bleɪ,wɪθ
Blawith²
places in Cumbria,
UK
BR blɑːð
AM 'bleɪ,wɪθ
Blaydon
BR 'bleɪdn
AM 'bleɪdən
blaze
BR bleɪz, -ɪz, -ɪŋ, -d
AM bleɪz, -ɪz, -ɪŋ, -d

blazer
BR 'bleɪzə(r), -z
AM 'bleɪzər, -z
blazingly
BR 'bleɪzɪŋli
AM 'bleɪzɪŋli
blazon
BR 'bleɪzn̩, -z, -ɪŋ, -d
AM 'bleɪzən, -z, -ɪŋ, -d
blazonment
BR 'bleɪznm(ə)nt
AM 'bleɪzənmənt
blazonry
BR 'bleɪznri
AM 'bleɪzənri
Blea
BR bliː
AM bli
bleach
BR bliːtʃ, -ɪz, -ɪŋ, -t
AM blitʃ, -ɪz, -ɪŋ, -t
bleacher
BR 'bliːtʃə(r), -z
AM 'blitʃər, -z
bleak
BR bliːk, -ə(r), -ɪst
AM blik, -ər, -ɪst
bleakly
BR 'bliːkli
AM 'blikli
bleakness
BR 'bliːknɪs
AM 'bliknɪs
blear
BR blɪə(r)
AM blɪ(ə)r
blearily
BR 'blɪərɪli
AM 'blɪrɪli, 'blɪrɪli
bleariness
BR 'blɪərɪnɪs
AM 'blɪrɪnɪs, 'blɪrɪnɪs
bleary
BR 'blɪər|i, -ɪə(r), -ɪɪst
AM 'blɪri, 'bliri, -ər, -ɪst
Bleasdale
BR 'bliːzdeɪl
AM 'bliz,deɪl
bleat
BR bliːt, -s, -ɪŋ, -ɪd
AM bli|t, -ts, -ɪŋ, -dɪd
bleatingly
BR 'bliːtɪŋli
AM 'blidɪŋli
bleb
BR blɛb, -z
AM blɛb, -z
bled
BR blɛd
AM blɛd
Bleddyn
BR 'blɛðɪn
AM 'blɛdən
bleed
BR bliːd, -z, -ɪŋ
AM blid, -z, -ɪŋ

bleeder
BR 'bliːdə(r), -z
AM 'blidər, -z
bleep
BR bliːp, -s, -ɪŋ, -t
AM blip, -s, -ɪŋ, -t
bleeper
BR 'bliːpə(r), -z
AM 'blipər, -z
blemish
BR 'blɛm|ɪʃ, -ɪʃɪz, -ɪʃɪŋ,
-ɪʃt
AM 'blɛmɪʃ, -ɪz, -ɪŋ, -t
Blencathra
BR blɛn'kaθrə(r)
AM blɛn'kæθrə
blench
BR blɛn(t)ʃ, -ɪz, -ɪŋ, -t
AM blɛn(t)ʃ, -əz, -ɪŋ, -t
blend
BR blɛnd, -z, -ɪŋ, -ɪd
AM blɛnd, -z, -ɪŋ, -əd
blende
BR blɛnd, -z
AM blɛnd, -z
blender
BR 'blɛndə(r), -z
AM 'blɛndər, -z
Blenheim
BR 'blɛnɪm
AM 'blɛnəm
Blenkinsop
BR 'blɛŋkɪnsɒp
AM 'blɛŋkən,sɑp
Blennerhassett
BR ,blɛnə'hasɪt,
'blɛnəhasɪt
AM ,blɛnər',(h)æsət
blenny
BR 'blɛn|i, -ɪz
AM 'blɛni, -z
blent
BR blɛnt
AM blɛnt
blepharitis
BR ,blɛfə'raɪtɪs
AM ,blɛfə'raɪdɪs
Blériot
BR 'blɛ(ː)rɪəʊ
AM 'blɛrioʊ
blesbok
BR 'blɛsbɒk, -s
AM 'blɛs,bɑk, -s
blesbuck
BR 'blɛsbʌk, -s
AM 'blɛs,bək, -s
bless
BR blɛs, -ɪz, -ɪŋ, -t
AM blɛs, -əz, -ɪŋ, -t
blessed
adjective
BR blɛst, 'blɛsɪd
AM blɛst, 'blɛsəd
blessedly
BR 'blɛsɪdli
AM 'blɛsədli

blessedness
BR 'blɛsɪdnɪs
AM 'blɛsədnəs
blessing
BR 'blɛsɪŋ, -z
AM 'blɛsɪŋ, -z
Blessington
BR 'blɛsɪŋt(ə)n
AM 'blɛsɪŋtən
blest
BR blɛst
AM blɛst
Bletchley
BR 'blɛtʃli
AM 'blɛtʃli
blether
BR 'blɛðə(r), -əz,
-(ə)rɪŋ, -əd
AM 'blɛðər, -əz, -(ə)rɪŋ,
-əd
bletherskate
BR 'blɛðəskeɪt, -s
AM 'blɛðər,skeɪt, -s
Blevins
BR 'blɛvɪnz
AM 'blɛvənz
blew
BR bluː
AM blu
Blewett
BR 'bluːɪt
AM 'bluət
blewits
BR 'bluːɪts
AM 'bluəts
Blewitt
BR 'bluːɪt
AM 'bluət
Bligh
BR blaɪ
AM blaɪ
blight
BR blaɪt, -s, -ɪŋ, -ɪd
AM blaɪ|t, -ts, -dɪŋ, -dɪd
blighter
BR 'blaɪtə(r), -z
AM 'blaɪdər, -z
Blighty
BR 'blaɪti
AM 'blaɪdi
blimey
BR 'blaɪmi
AM 'blaɪmi
blimp
BR blɪmp, -s
AM blɪmp, -s
blimpery
BR 'blɪmp(ə)ri
AM 'blɪmp(ə)ri
blimpish
BR 'blɪmpɪʃ
AM 'blɪmpɪʃ
blind
BR blaɪn|d, -(d)z, -dɪŋ,
-dɪd, -də(r), -dɪst
AM blaɪn|d, -(d)z, -dɪŋ,
-dɪd, -ər, -dɪst

blinder
BR ˈblaɪndə(r), -z
AM ˈblaɪndər, -z
blindfold
BR ˈblaɪn(d)fəʊld, -z
AM ˈblaɪn(d)ˌfoʊld, -z
blindingly
BR ˈblaɪndɪŋli
AM ˈblaɪndɪŋli
blindly
BR ˈblaɪndli
AM ˈblaɪn(d)li
blindness
BR ˈblaɪn(d)nɪs
AM ˈblaɪn(d)nɪs
blindworm
BR ˈblaɪn(d)wəːm, -z
AM ˈblaɪn(d)ˌwɜːrm, -z
blini
BR ˈblɪn|i, -ɪz
AM ˈblɪni, -z
blink
BR ˈblɪŋ|k, -ks, -kɪŋ, -(k)t
AM ˈblɪŋ|k, -ks, -kɪŋ, -(k)t
blinker
BR ˈblɪŋk|ə(r), -əz, -(ə)rɪŋ, -əd
AM ˈblɪŋkər, -z, -ɪŋ, -d
blintz
BR ˈblɪn(t)s, -ɪz
AM ˈblɪn(t)s, -ɪz
blip
BR ˈblɪp, -s, -ɪŋ, -t
AM ˈblɪp, -s, -ɪŋ, -t
bliss
BR ˈblɪs, -ɪz, -ɪŋ, -t
AM ˈblɪs, -əz, -ɪŋ, -t
Blissett
BR ˈblɪsɪt
AM ˈblɪsɪt
blissful
BR ˈblɪsf(ʊ)l
AM ˈblɪsfəl
blissfully
BR ˈblɪsfəli, ˈblɪsfˌli
AM ˈblɪsfəli
blissfulness
BR ˈblɪsf(ʊ)lnəs
AM ˈblɪsfəlnəs
blister
BR ˈblɪst|ə(r), -əz, -(ə)rɪŋ, -əd
AM ˈblɪst|ər, -ərz, -(ə)rɪŋ, -ərd
blistery
BR ˈblɪst(ə)ri
AM ˈblɪst(ə)ri
blithe
BR ˈblaɪð, -ə(r), -ɪst
AM ˈblaɪð, -ər, -ɪst
blithely
BR ˈblaɪðli
AM ˈblaɪðli
blitheness
BR ˈblaɪðnɪs

blithering
BR ˈblɪð(ə)rɪŋ
AM ˈblɪðərɪŋ
blithesome
BR ˈblaɪðs(ə)m
AM ˈblaɪðsəm
blitz
BR blɪts, -ɪz, -ɪŋ, -t
AM blɪts, -ɪz, -ɪŋ, -t
Blitzkrieg
BR ˈblɪtskriːg, -z
AM ˈblɪtsˌkrig, -z
Blixen
BR ˈblɪksn
AM ˈblɪksən
DAN ˈblegsən
blizzard
BR ˈblɪzəd, -z
AM ˈblɪzərd, -z
bloat
BR bləʊt, -s, -ɪŋ, -ɪd
AM bloʊ|t, -ts, -dɪŋ, -dəd
bloater
BR ˈbləʊtə(r), -z
AM ˈbloʊdər, -z
blob
BR blɒb, -z, -ɪŋ, -d
AM blɑb, -z, -ɪŋ, -d
bloc
BR blɒk, -s
AM blɑk, -s
Bloch
BR blɒx, blɒk
AM blɑk
block
BR blɒk, -s, -ɪŋ, -t
AM blɑk, -s, -ɪŋ, -t
blockade
BR blɒˈkeɪd, bləˈkeɪd, -z, -ɪŋ, -ɪd
AM blɑˈkeɪd, -z, -ɪŋ, -ɪd
blockader
BR blɒˈkeɪdə(r), bləˈkeɪdə(r), -z
AM blɑˈkeɪdər, -z
blockage
BR ˈblɒk|ɪdʒ, -ɪdʒɪz
AM ˈblɑkɪdʒ, -ɪz
blockboard
BR ˈblɒkbɔːd, -z
AM ˈblɑkˌbɔ(ə)rd, -z
blockbuster
BR ˈblɒkˌbʌstə(r), -z
AM ˈblɑkˌbəstər, -z
blockbusting
BR ˈblɒkˌbʌstɪŋ
AM ˈblɑkˌbəstɪŋ
blocker
BR ˈblɒkə(r), -z
AM ˈblɑkər, -z
blockhead
BR ˈblɒkhɛd, -z
AM ˈblɑkˌ(h)ɛd, -z
blockheaded
BR ˌblɒkˈhɛdɪd
AM ˈblɑkˌ(h)ɛdəd

blockhouse
BR ˈblɒkhaʊ|s, -zɪz
AM ˈblɑkˌ(h)aʊ|s, -zəz
blockish
BR ˈblɒkɪʃ
AM ˈblɑkɪʃ
blockishly
BR ˈblɒkɪʃli
AM ˈblɑkɪʃli
blockishness
BR ˈblɒkɪʃnɪs
AM ˈblɑkɪʃnɪs
Blodwen
BR ˈblɒdwɪn, ˈblɒdwɛn
AM ˈblɑdwən
Bloemfontein
BR ˈbluːmfɒnteɪn, ˈbluːmf(ə)nteɪn
AM ˈblɒmˌfɑnteɪn, ˈblɑmˌfɑnteɪn
Blofeld
BR ˈbləʊfɛld
AM ˈbloʊˌfɛld
Blok
BR blɒk
AM blɑk
bloke
BR bləʊk, -s
AM bloʊk, -s
Blomfield
BR ˈblɒmfiːld, ˈbluːmfiːld
AM ˈblɑmˌfild
blond
BR blɒnd, -z, -ə(r), -ɪst
AM blɑnd, -z, -ər, -əst
blonde
BR blɒnd, -z, -ə(r), -ɪst
AM blɑnd, -z, -ər, -əst
Blondel
BR blɒnˈdɛl
AM ˌblɑnˈdɛl
blondie
BR ˈblɒnd|i, -ɪz
AM ˈblɑndi, -z
Blondin
BR ˈblɒndɪn
AM ˈblɑndən
blondness
BR ˈblɒn(d)nəs
AM ˈblɑn(d)nəs
blood
BR blʌd, -z, -ɪŋ, -ɪd
AM bləd, -z, -ɪŋ, -əd
bloodbath
BR ˈblʌd|bɑːθ, ˈblʌd|bɑθ, -bɑːðz\-bɑːθs\-bɑθs
AM ˈbləd|bæθ, -s, -ðz
bloodhound
BR ˈblʌdhaʊnd, -z
AM ˈbləd|(h)aʊnd, -z
bloodily
BR ˈblʌdɪli
AM ˈblədɪli
bloodiness
BR ˈblʌdɪnɪs

blockhouse (third col cont.)

bloodless
BR ˈblʌdləs
AM ˈblədləs
bloodlessly
BR ˈblʌdləsli
AM ˈblədləsli
bloodlessness
BR ˈblʌdləsnəs
AM ˈblədləsnəs
bloodletting
BR ˈblʌdˌlɛtɪŋ, -z
AM ˈblədˌlɛdɪŋ, -z
bloodline
BR ˈblʌdlaɪn, -z
AM ˈblədˌlaɪn, -z
bloodlust
BR ˈblʌdlʌst
AM ˈblədˌləst
bloodroot
BR ˈblʌdruːt
AM ˈblədˌrut, ˈblədˌrʊt
bloodshed
BR ˈblʌdʃɛd
AM ˈblədˌʃɛd
bloodshot
BR ˈblʌdʃɒt
AM ˈblədˌʃɑt
bloodstain
BR ˈblʌdsteɪn, -z, -d
AM ˈblədˌsteɪn, -z, -d
bloodstock
BR ˈblʌdstɒk
AM ˈblədˌstɑk
bloodstone
BR ˈblʌdstəʊn, -z
AM ˈblədˌstoʊn, -z
bloodstream
BR ˈblʌdstriːm, -z
AM ˈblədˌstrim, -z
bloodsucker
BR ˈblʌdˌsʌkə(r), -z
AM ˈblədˌsəkər, -z
bloodsucking
BR ˈblʌdˌsʌkɪŋ
AM ˈblədˌsəkɪŋ
bloodthirstily
BR ˈblʌdˌθəːstɪli
AM ˈblədˌθərstɪli
bloodthirstiness
BR ˈblʌdˌθəːstɪnɪs
AM ˈblədˌθərstɪnɪs
bloodthirsty
BR ˈblʌdˌθəːst|i, -ɪə(r), -ɪɪst
AM ˈblədˌθərsti, -ər, -ɪst
bloodworm
BR ˈblʌdwəːm, -z
AM ˈblədˌwɜːrm, -z
bloom
BR bluːm, -z, -ɪŋ, -d
AM blum, -z, -ɪŋ, -d
bloomer
BR ˈbluːmə(r), -z
AM ˈblumər, -z
bloomery
BR ˈbluːm(ə)r|i, -ɪz

AM 'blumǝri, -z
Bloomfield
BR 'blu:mfi:ld
AM 'blum̩fild
Bloomingdale's
BR 'blu:mɪŋdeɪlz
AM 'blumɪŋ͵deɪlz
Bloomsbury
BR 'blu:mzb(ǝ)ri
AM 'blumz͵bɛri,
  'blumzbǝri
bloop
BR blu:p, -s, -ɪŋ, -t
AM blup, -s, -ɪŋ, -t
blooper
BR 'blu:pǝ(r), -z
AM 'blupǝr, -z
blossom
BR 'blɒs|(ǝ)m, -(ǝ)mz,
  -(ǝ)mɪŋ \ -m̩ɪŋ, -(ǝ)md
AM 'blasǝm, -z, -ɪŋ, -d
blossomy
BR 'blɒsǝmi, 'blɒsm̩i
AM 'blasǝmi
blot
BR blɒt, -s, -ɪŋ, -ɪd
AM blɑ|t, -ts, -dɪŋ, -dǝd
blotch
BR blɒtʃ, -ɪz, -ɪŋ, -t
AM blatʃ, -ǝz, -ɪŋ, -t
blotchily
BR 'blɒtʃǝli
AM 'blatʃǝli
blotchiness
BR 'blɒtʃɪnɪs
AM 'blatʃɪnɪs
blotchy
BR 'blɒtʃ|i, -ɪǝ(r), -ɪɪst
AM 'blatʃi, -ǝr, -ɪst
blotter
BR 'blɒtǝ(r), -z
AM 'blɑdǝr, -z
blotto
BR 'blɒtǝʊ
AM 'bladoʊ
Blount
BR blʌnt, blaʊnt
AM blaʊnt, blɒnt
blouse
BR blaʊz, -ɪz, -ɪŋ, -d
AM blaʊs, blaʊz, -ǝz,
  -ɪŋ, -d
blouson
BR 'blaʊz(ʊ)n,
  'blu:z(ʊ)n, -z
AM 'blaʊzn, 'blaʊ͵zɑn,
  'blaʊsǝn, 'blaʊ͵sɑn, -z
blow
BR blǝʊ, -z, -ɪŋ
AM bloʊ, -z, -ɪŋ
blowback
BR 'blǝʊbak, -s
AM 'bloʊ͵bæk, -s
blowby
BR 'blǝʊbʌɪ
AM 'bloʊ͵baɪ

blowdry
BR 'blǝʊdrʌɪ,
  ͵blǝʊ'drʌɪ, -z, -ɪŋ, -d
AM 'bloʊ͵draɪ, -z, -ɪŋ, -d
blower
BR 'blǝʊǝ(r), -z
AM 'bloʊǝr, -z
blowfish
BR 'blǝʊfɪʃ
AM 'bloʊ͵fɪʃ
blowfly
BR 'blǝʊflʌɪ, -z
AM 'bloʊ͵flaɪ, -z
blowgun
BR 'blǝʊgʌn, -z
AM 'bloʊ͵gǝn, -z
blowhard
BR 'blǝʊhɑ:d, -z
AM 'bloʊ͵hard, -z
blowhole
BR 'blǝʊhǝʊl, -z
AM 'bloʊ͵hoʊl, -z
blowily
BR 'blǝʊɪli
AM 'bloʊǝli
blowiness
BR 'blǝʊɪnɪs
AM 'bloʊɪnɪs
blowlamp
BR 'blǝʊlamp, -s
AM 'bloʊ͵læmp, -s
blown
BR blǝʊn
AM bloʊn
blowout
BR 'blǝʊaʊt, -s
AM 'bloʊ͵aʊt, -s
blowpipe
BR 'blǝʊpʌɪp, -s
AM 'bloʊ͵paɪp, -s
blowsily
BR 'blaʊzɪli
AM 'blaʊzǝli
blowsiness
BR 'blaʊzɪnɪs
AM 'blaʊzɪnɪs
blowsy
BR 'blaʊz|i, -ɪǝ(r), -ɪɪst
AM 'blaʊzi, -ǝr, -ɪst
blowtorch
BR 'blǝʊtɔ:tʃ, -ɪz
AM 'bloʊ͵tɔ(ǝ)rtʃ, -ɪz
blowy
BR 'blǝʊ|i, -ɪǝ(r), -ɪɪst
AM 'bloʊi, -ǝr, -ɪst
blowzily
BR 'blaʊzɪli
AM 'blaʊzǝli
blowziness
BR 'blaʊzɪnɪs
AM 'blaʊzɪnɪs
blowzy
BR 'blaʊz|i, -ɪǝ(r), -ɪɪst
AM 'blaʊzi, -ǝr, -ɪst
blub
BR blʌb, -z, -ɪŋ, -d
AM blǝb, -z, -ɪŋ, -d

blubber
BR 'blʌb|ǝ(r), -ǝz,
  -(ǝ)rɪŋ, -ǝd
AM 'blǝbǝr, -ǝz, -(ǝ)rɪŋ,
  -ǝd
blubberer
BR 'blʌb(ǝ)rǝ(r), -z
AM 'blǝbǝrǝr, -z
blubberingly
BR 'blʌb(ǝ)rɪŋli
AM 'blǝbǝrɪŋli
blubbery
BR 'blʌb(ǝ)ri
AM 'blǝbǝri
Blücher
BR 'blu:kǝ(r),
  'blu:tʃǝ(r)
AM 'blutʃǝr, 'blukǝr
GER 'blʏçɐ
bluchers
BR 'blu:kǝz, 'blu:tʃǝz
AM 'blukǝrz, 'blutʃǝrz
bludge
BR blʌdʒ, -ɪz, -ɪŋ, -d
AM blǝdʒ, -ǝz, -ɪŋ, -d
bludgeon
BR 'blʌdʒ|(ǝ)n, -(ǝ)nz,
  -n̩ɪŋ \ -ǝnɪŋ, -(ǝ)nd
AM 'blǝdʒǝn, -z, -ɪŋ, -d
bludger
BR 'blʌdʒǝ(r), -z
AM 'blǝdʒǝr, -z
blue
BR blu:, -z, -ɪŋ, -d, -ǝ(r),
  -ɪst
AM blu, -z, -ɪŋ, -d, -ǝr,
  -ǝst
bluebag
BR 'blu:bag, -z
AM 'blu͵bæg, -z
bluebeard
BR 'blu:bɪǝd, -z
AM 'blu͵bɪ(ǝ)rd, -z
bluebell
BR 'blu:bɛl, -z
AM 'blu͵bɛl, -z
blueberry
BR 'blu:b(ǝ)r|i,
  'blu:͵bɛr|i, -ɪz
AM 'blu͵bɛri, -z
bluebird
BR 'blu:bɜ:d, -z
AM 'blu͵bɜrd, -z
bluebonnet
BR 'blu:͵bɒnɪt, -s
AM 'blu͵banǝt, -s
bluebottle
BR 'blu:͵bɒtl, -z
AM 'blu͵bɑdǝl, -z
bluecoat
BR 'blu:kǝʊt, -s
AM 'blu͵koʊt, -s
Bluecol
BR 'blu:kɒl
AM 'blu͵kɑl, 'blukɑl
Bluefields
BR 'blu:fi:ldz
AM 'blu͵fildz

bluefish
BR 'blu:fɪʃ
AM 'blu͵fɪʃ
bluegill
BR 'blu:gɪl, -z
AM 'blu͵gɪl, -z
bluegrass
BR 'blu:grɑ:s,
  'blu:gras
AM 'blu͵græs
bluegum
BR 'blu:gʌm
AM 'blu͵gǝm
blueish
BR 'blu:ɪʃ
AM 'bluɪʃ
bluejacket
BR 'blu:͵dʒakɪt, -s
AM 'blu͵dʒækǝt, -s
bluejay
BR 'blu:dʒeɪ, -z
AM 'blu͵dʒeɪ, -z
Bluemantle
BR 'blu:͵mantl
AM 'blu͵mæn(t)ǝl
blueness
BR 'blu:nǝs
AM 'blunǝs
blueprint
BR 'blu:prɪnt, -s
AM 'blu͵prɪnt, -s
blues
BR blu:z
AM bluz
bluestocking
BR 'blu:͵stɒkɪŋ, -z
AM 'blu͵stakɪŋ, -z
bluestone
BR 'blu:stǝʊn, -z
AM 'blu͵stoʊn, -z
bluesy
BR 'blu:zi
AM 'bluzi
bluet
BR 'blu:ɪt
AM 'bluǝt
bluethroat
BR 'blu:θrǝʊt, -s
AM 'blu͵θroʊt, -s
bluetit
BR 'blu:tɪt, -s
AM 'blu͵tɪt, -s
Bluett
BR 'blu:ɪt
AM 'bluǝt
Blue Vinney
BR ͵blu: 'vɪni
AM ͵blu 'vɪni
bluey
BR 'blu:|i, -ɪz
AM 'blui, -z
bluff
BR blʌf, -s, -ɪŋ, -t, -ɪst
AM blǝf, -s, -ɪŋ, -t, -ǝst
bluffer
BR 'blʌfǝ(r), -z
AM 'blǝfǝr, -z

bluffly
BR ˈblʌfli
AM ˈbləfli
bluffness
BR ˈblʌfnəs
AM ˈbləfnəs
bluing
BR ˈbluːɪŋ
AM ˈbluɪŋ
bluish
BR ˈbluːɪʃ
AM ˈbluɪʃ
Blum
BR bluːm
AM blum
Blumenbach
BR ˈbluːmənbak
AM ˈblumənˌbɑk
Blundell
BR ˈblʌndl
AM ˈbləndəl, blənˈdɛl
Blunden
BR ˈblʌndən
AM ˈbləndən
blunder
BR ˈblʌnd|ə(r), -əz,
-(ə)rɪŋ, -əd
AM ˈblənd|ər, -ərz,
-(ə)rɪŋ, -ərd
blunderbuss
BR ˈblʌndəbʌs, -ɪz
AM ˈbləndərˌbəs, -əz
blunderer
BR ˈblʌnd(ə)rə(r), -z
AM ˈbləndərər, -z
blunderingly
BR ˈblʌnd(ə)rɪŋli
AM ˈbləndərɪŋli
blunge
BR blʌn(d)ʒ, -ɪz, -ɪŋ, -d
AM blən(d)ʒ, -əz, -ɪŋ, -d
blunger
BR ˈblʌn(d)ʒə(r), -z
AM ˈblən(d)ʒər, -z
blunt
BR blʌnt, -s, -ɪŋ, -ɪd,
-ə(r), -ɪst
AM blənt, -s, -ɪŋ, -əd, -ər,
-əst
bluntly
BR ˈblʌntli
AM ˈblən(t)li
bluntness
BR ˈblʌntnəs
AM ˈblən(t)nəs
blur
BR bləː(r), -z, -ɪŋ, -d
AM blər, -z, -ɪŋ, -d
blurb
BR bləːb, -z
AM blərb, -z
blurry
BR ˈbləːr|i, -ɪə(r), -ɪɪst
AM ˈbləri, -ər, -ɪst
blurt
BR bləːt, -s, -ɪŋ, -ɪd
AM blər|t, -ts, -dɪŋ, -dəd

blush
BR blʌʃ, -ɪz, -ɪŋ, -t
AM bləʃ, -əz, -ɪŋ, -t
blusher
BR ˈblʌʃə(r), -z
AM ˈbləʃər, -z
blushful
BR ˈblʌʃf(ʊ)l
AM ˈbləʃfəl
bluster
BR ˈblʌst|ə(r), -əz,
-(ə)rɪŋ, -əd
AM ˈbləstər, -əz, -(ə)rɪŋ,
-əd
blusterous
BR ˈblʌst(ə)rəs
AM ˈbləst(ə)rəs
blusterously
BR ˈblʌst(ə)rəsli
AM ˈbləst(ə)rəsli
blustery
BR ˈblʌst(ə)ri
AM ˈbləstəri
Blu-Tack®
BR ˈbluːtak
AM ˈblutæk
Bly
BR blʌɪ
AM blaɪ
Blyth
BR blʌɪð, blʌɪθ, blʌɪ
AM blaɪθ, blaɪð
Blythe
BR blʌɪð
AM blaɪð
Blyton
BR ˈblʌɪtn
AM ˈblaɪtn
B.Mus.
Bachelor of Music
BR ˌbiː ˈmjuːz
AM ˌbi ˈmjuz
B'nai B'rith
BR bəˈneɪ bəˈriːθ,
+ ˈbrɪθ
AM bəˈneɪ ˈbrɪθ
bo
BR bəʊ, -z, -ɪŋ, -d
AM boʊ, -z, -ɪŋ, -d
boa
BR ˈbəʊə(r), -z
AM ˈboʊə, -z
Boadicea
BR ˌbəʊ(ə)dɪˈsiːə(r)
AM ˌboʊədəˈsiə
Boakes
BR bəʊks
AM boʊks
Boaks
BR bəʊks
AM boʊks
Boanerges
BR ˌbəʊəˈnəːdʒiːz,
bəʊˈanədʒiːz
AM ˌboʊəˈnərˌdʒiz
boar
BR bɔː(r), -z

AM bɔ(ə)r, -z
board
BR bɔːd, -z, -ɪŋ, -ɪd
AM bɔ(ə)rd, -z, -ɪŋ, -əd
boarder
BR ˈbɔːdə(r), -z
AM ˈbɔrdər, -z
boardroom
BR ˈbɔːdruːm,
ˈbɔːdrʊm, -z
AM ˈbɔrdˌrum,
ˈbɔrdˌrʊm, -z
boardsailer
BR ˈbɔːdˌseɪlə(r), -z
AM ˈbɔrdˌseɪlər, -z
boardsailing
BR ˈbɔːdˌseɪlɪŋ, -z
AM ˈbɔrdˌseɪlɪŋ, -z
boardsailor
BR ˈbɔːdˌseɪlə(r), -z
AM ˈbɔrdˌseɪlər, -z
boardwalk
BR ˈbɔːdwɔːk, -s
AM ˈbɔrdˌwɔk,
ˈbɔrdˌwɑk, -s
boart
BR bɔːt, -s
AM bɔ(ə)rt, -s
Boas
BR ˈbəʊaz
AM ˈboʊæz
boast
BR bəʊst, -s, -ɪŋ, -ɪd
AM boʊst, -s, -ɪŋ, -əd
boaster
BR ˈbəʊstə(r), -z
AM ˈboʊstər, -z
boastful
BR ˈbəʊs(t)f(ʊ)l
AM ˈboʊs(t)fəl
boastfully
BR ˈbəʊs(t)fʊli,
ˈbəʊstflɪ
AM ˈboʊs(t)fəli
boastfulness
BR ˈbəʊs(t)f(ʊ)lnəs
AM ˈboʊs(t)fəlnəs
boastingly
BR ˈbəʊstɪŋli
AM ˈboʊstɪŋli
boat
BR bəʊt, -s, -ɪŋ, -ɪd
AM boʊ|t, -ts, -dɪŋ, -dəd
boatbuilder
BR ˈbəʊtˌbɪldə(r), -z
AM ˈboʊtˌbɪldər, -z
boatel
BR ˌbəʊˈtɛl, -z
AM ˌboʊˈtɛl, -z
Boateng
BR ˈbwʌtɛŋ, ˈbəʊ(ə)tɛŋ
AM ˈbwɑˌtɛŋ,
ˈboʊ(ə)ˌtɛŋ
boater
BR ˈbəʊtə(r), -z
AM ˈboʊdər, -z

boatful
BR ˈbəʊtfʊl, -z
AM ˈboʊtˌfʊl, -z
boathouse
BR ˈbəʊthaʊ|s, -zɪz
AM ˈboʊtˌ(h)aʊ|s, -zəz
boatlift
BR ˈbəʊtlɪft, -s
AM ˈboʊtˌlɪft, -s
boatload
BR ˈbəʊtləʊd, -z
AM ˈboʊtˌloʊd, -z
boatman
BR ˈbəʊtmən
AM ˈboʊtmən
boatmen
BR ˈbəʊtmən
AM ˈboʊtmən
boatswain
BR ˈbəʊsn, -z
AM ˈboʊsn, -z
boatyard
BR ˈbəʊtjɑːd, -z
AM ˈboʊtˌjard, -z
Boaz
BR ˈbəʊaz
AM ˈboʊæz
bob
BR bɒb, -z, -ɪŋ, -d
AM bab, -z, -ɪŋ, -d
Bobbie
BR ˈbɒbi
AM ˈbabi
bobbin
BR ˈbɒbɪn, -z
AM ˈbabɪn, -z
bobbinet
BR ˈbɒbɪnɪt, -s
AM ˌbabəˈnɛt, -s
bobble
BR ˈbɒbl̩, -z, -ɪŋ, -d
AM ˈbabəl, -z, -ɪŋ, -d
bobbly
BR ˈbɒbl̩i
AM ˈbabli
bobby
BR ˈbɒb|i, -ɪz
AM ˈbabi, -z
bobbysox
BR ˈbɒbɪsɒks
AM ˈbabiˌsaks
bobbysoxer
BR ˈbɒbɪˌsɒksə(r), -z
AM ˈbabiˌsaksər, -z
bobcat
BR ˈbɒbkat, -s
AM ˈbabˌkæt, -s
bobolink
BR ˈbɒbəlɪŋk, -s
AM ˈbabəˌlɪŋk, -s
bobsled
BR ˈbɒbslɛd, -z, -ɪŋ, -ɪd
AM ˈbabˌslɛd, -z, -ɪŋ, -əd
bobsleigh
BR ˈbɒbsleɪ, -z, -ɪŋ, -d
AM ˈbabˌsleɪ, -z, -ɪŋ, -d

bobsleigher
BR ˈbɒbˌsleɪə(r), -z
AM ˈbabˌsleɪər, -z

bobstay
BR ˈbɒbsteɪ, -z
AM ˈbabˌsteɪ, -z

bobtail
BR ˈbɒbteɪl, -z, -d
AM ˈbabˌteɪl, -z, -d

bobwhite
BR ˈbɒbwʌɪt, -s
AM bab'(h)waɪt, -s

bocage
BR bəˈkɑːʒ, bɒˈkɑːʒ
AM boʊˈkɑʒ

Boca Raton
BR ˌbəʊkə rəˈtəʊn
AM ˌboʊkə rəˈtoʊn

Boccaccio
BR bəˈkɑːtʃɪəʊ,
bɒˈkɑːtʃɪəʊ,
bəˈkatʃɪəʊ,
bɒˈkatʃɪəʊ
AM bəˈkatʃioʊ

bocce
BR ˈbɒtʃiː
AM ˈbatʃi

Boccherini
BR ˌbɒkəˈriːni
AM ˌbakəˈrini

bocci
BR ˈbɒtʃiː
AM ˈbatʃi

Boche
BR bɒʃ, -ɪz
AM bɔʃ, baʃ, -əz

bock
BR bɒk, -s
AM bak, -s

bod
BR bɒd, -z
AM bad, -z

bodacious
BR bəˈdeɪʃəs
AM ˌboʊˈdeɪʃəs

bodaciously
BR bəˈdeɪʃəsli
AM ˌboʊˈdeɪʃəsli

bodaciousness
BR bəˈdeɪʃəsnəs
AM ˌboʊˈdeɪʃəsnəs

Boddington
BR ˈbɒdɪŋt(ə)n
AM ˈbadɪŋtən

bode
BR bəʊd, -z, -ɪŋ, -ɪd
AM boʊd, -z, -ɪŋ, -əd

bodeful
BR ˈbəʊdf(ʊ)l
AM ˈboʊdfəl

bodega
BR bəˈ(ʊ)diːgə(r), -z
AM boʊˈdeɪgə, -z
SP boˈdeɣa

bodement
BR ˈbəʊdm(ə)nt, -s
AM ˈboʊdmənt, -s

bodge
BR bɒdʒ, -ɪz, -ɪŋ, -d
AM badʒ, -z, -ɪŋ, -d

Bodiam
BR ˈbəʊdɪəm, ˈbɒdɪəm
AM ˈbadɪəm

bodice
BR ˈbɒdɪs, -ɪz
AM ˈbadəs, -əz

bodiless
BR ˈbɒdɪlɪs
AM ˈbadɪləs

bodily
BR ˈbɒdɪli
AM ˈbadəli

bodkin
BR ˈbɒdkɪn, -z
AM ˈbadkən, -z

Bodleian
BR ˈbɒdlɪən
AM ˈbadlɪən

Bodley
BR ˈbɒdli
AM ˈbadli

Bodmer
BR ˈbɒdmə(r)
AM ˈbadmər

Bodmin
BR ˈbɒdmɪn
AM ˈbadmən

Bodnant
BR ˈbɒdnant
AM ˈbadnənt

Bodoni
BR bəˈdəʊni
AM boʊˈdoʊni

body
BR ˈbɒd|i, -ɪz
AM ˈbadi, -z

bodybuilder
BR ˈbɒdɪˌbɪldə(r), -z
AM ˈbadiˌbɪldər, -z

bodybuilding
BR ˈbɒdɪˌbɪldɪŋ
AM ˈbadiˌbɪldɪŋ

bodyguard
BR ˈbɒdɪgɑːd, -z
AM ˈbadiˌgard, -z

bodyline
BR ˈbɒdɪlʌɪn
AM ˈbadiˌlaɪn

bodyliner
BR ˈbɒdɪˌlʌɪnə(r), -z
AM ˈbadiˌlaɪnər, -z

bodylining
BR ˈbɒdɪˌlʌɪnɪŋ, -z
AM ˈbadiˌlaɪnɪŋ, -z

bodysuit
BR ˈbɒdɪs(j)uːt, -s
AM ˈbadiˌsut, -s

bodywork
BR ˈbɒdɪwəːk
AM ˈbadiˌwərk

Boehm
BR ˈbəʊ(ə)m, bəːm
AM boʊm, bʊm

Boeing®
BR ˈbəʊɪŋ, -z
AM ˈboʊɪŋ, -z

Boeotia
BR bɪˈəʊʃə(r)
AM biˈoʊʃə

Boeotian
BR bɪˈəʊʃn, -z
AM biˈoʊʃən, -z

Boer
BR bɔː(r), ˈbəʊə(r),
bʊə(r), -z
AM ˈboʊ(ə)r, bɔ(ə)r, -z

Boethius
BR bəʊˈiːθɪəs
AM boʊˈiθɪəs

**boeuf
bourgignon**
BR ˌbəːf ˈbɔːgɪnjɒ̃
AM ˌbuf ˌbɛrgɪnˈjɒn

boff
BR bɒf, -s
AM baf, -s

boffin
BR ˈbɒfɪn, -z
AM ˈbafən, -z

boffo
BR ˈbɒfəʊ
AM ˈbafoʊ

boffola
BR bɒˈfəʊlə(r),
bəˈfəʊlə(r), -z
AM baˈfoʊlə, -z

Bofors
BR ˈbəʊfəz
AM ˈboʊfɔ(ə)rz
sw bɔːˈfɒʃ

bog
BR bɒg, -z, -ɪŋ, -d
AM bɔg, bag, -z, -ɪŋ, -d

Bogarde
BR ˈbəʊgɑːd
AM ˈboʊˌgard

Bogart
BR ˈbəʊgɑːt
AM ˈboʊˌgart

bogey
BR ˈbəʊg|i, -ɪz, -ɪŋ, -ɪd
AM ˈboʊgi, -z, -ɪŋ, -d

bogeyman
BR ˈbəʊgɪman
AM ˈboʊgiˌmæn,
ˈbʊgiˌmæn

bogeymen
BR ˈbəʊgɪmɛn
AM ˈboʊgiˌmɛn,
ˈbʊgiˌmɛn

bogginess
BR ˈbɒgɪnɪs
AM ˈbɑgɪnəs, ˈbagɪnɪs

Boggis
BR ˈbɒgɪs
AM ˈbagəs

boggle
BR ˈbɒg|l, -lz, -lɪŋ \ -lɪŋ,
-ld
AM ˈbag|əl, -əlz, -(ə)lɪŋ,
-əld

boggy
BR ˈbɒg|i, -ɪə(r), -ɪɪst
AM ˈbagi, ˈbagi, -ər, -ɪst

bogie
BR ˈbəʊg|i, -ɪz
AM ˈboʊgi, -z

bogle
BR ˈbəʊgl, -z
AM ˈboʊgəl, -z

Bognor
BR ˈbɒgnə(r)
AM ˈbagnər

bogong
BR ˈbəʊgɒŋ, -z
AM ˈboʊgaŋ, -z

Bogotá
BR ˌbɒgəˈtɑː(r)
AM ˈboʊgəˌta

bogus
BR ˈbəʊgəs
AM ˈboʊgəs

bogusness
BR ˈbəʊgəsnəs
AM ˈboʊgəsnəs

bogy
BR ˈbəʊg|i, -ɪz
AM ˈboʊgi, -z

bogyman
BR ˈbəʊgɪman
AM ˈboʊgiˌmæn,
ˈbʊgiˌmæn

bogymen
BR ˈbəʊgɪmɛn
AM ˈboʊgiˌmɛn,
ˈbʊgiˌmɛn

bohea
BR bəʊˈhi
AM boʊˈhi

Bohème
BR bəʊˈɛm, bəʊˈeɪm
AM boʊˈɛm

Bohemia
BR bəˈ(ʊ)hiːmɪə(r)
AM boʊˈhimɪə

Bohemian
BR bəˈ(ʊ)hiːmɪən, -z
AM boʊˈhimɪən, -z

Bohemianism
BR bəˈ(ʊ)hiːmɪənɪz(ə)m
AM boʊˈhimɪəˌnɪzəm

boho
BR ˈbəʊhəʊ, -z
AM ˈboʊˌhoʊ, -z

Bohr
BR bɔː(r)
AM bɔ(ə)r
DAN ˈboːˀʌ

bohunk
BR ˈbəʊhʌŋk, -s
AM ˈboʊˌhəŋk, -s

boil
BR bɔɪl, -z, -ɪŋ, -d
AM bɔɪl, -z, -ɪŋ, -d

Boileau
BR bwaˈləʊ, bwɑːˈləʊ
AM ˌbwaˈloʊ

boiler
BR ˈbɔɪlə(r), -z
AM ˈbɔɪlər, -z

boilermaker
BR ˈbɔɪləˌmeɪkə(r), -z
AM ˈbɔɪlərˌmeɪkər, -z

boing
BR bɔɪŋ
AM bɔɪŋ

boink
BR bɔɪŋk
AM bɔɪŋk

Boise
BR ˈbɔɪzi
AM ˈbɔɪzi

boisterous
BR ˈbɔɪst(ə)rəs
AM ˈbɔɪst(ə)rəs

boisterously
BR ˈbɔɪst(ə)rəsli
AM ˈbɔɪst(ə)rəsli

boisterousness
BR ˈbɔɪst(ə)rəsnəs
AM ˈbɔɪst(ə)rəsnəs

Bokhara
BR bɒˈkɑːrə(r),
bə(ʊ)ˈkɑːrə(r)
AM boʊˈkɑrə, boʊˈkɛrə
RUS buxaˈra

Bokmål
BR ˈbʊkmɔːl
AM ˈbʊkˌmɔl, ˈbʊkˌmal
NO ˈbuːkmɔːl

bola
BR ˈbəʊlə(r), -z
AM ˈboʊlə, -z

Bolam
BR ˈbəʊləm
AM ˈboʊləm

bolas
BR ˈbəʊləs, -ɪz
AM ˈboʊləs, -əz

bold
BR bəʊld, -ə(r), -ɪst
AM boʊld, -ər, -əst

boldface
BR ˈbəʊldfeɪs
AM ˈboʊl(d)ˌfeɪs

boldfaced
BR ˌbəʊldˈfeɪst
AM ˈboʊl(d)ˌfeɪst

boldly
BR ˈbəʊldli
AM ˈboʊl(d)li

boldness
BR ˈbəʊldnəs
AM ˈboʊl(d)nəs

Boldre
BR ˈbəʊldə(r)
AM ˈboʊldər

Boldrewood
BR ˈbəʊldəwʊd
AM ˈboʊldərˌwʊd

bole
BR bəʊl, -z
AM boʊl, -z

Boléat
BR ˈbəʊliat, ˈbəʊliət,
ˈbəʊliɑː(r)
AM ˈboʊliət

bolection
BR bə(ʊ)ˈlekʃn, -z
AM boʊˈlekʃən, -z

bolero¹
dance
BR bəˈlɛːrəʊ, -z
AM bəˈlɛroʊ, -z

bolero²
jacket
BR ˈbɒlərəʊ, -z
AM bəˈlɛroʊ, -z

boletus
BR bəˈliːtəs, -ɪz
AM boʊˈlidəs, -əz

Boleyn
BR bəˈlɪn, ˈbʊlɪn
AM bəˈlɪn, ˈbʊlən

bolide
BR ˈbəʊlʌɪd, ˈbəʊlɪd, -z
AM ˈboʊˌlaɪd, ˈboʊləd, -z

Bolingbroke
BR ˈbɒlɪŋbrʊk,
ˈbʊlɪŋbrʊk
AM ˈbɒlɪŋˌbrʊk,
ˈbʊlɪŋˌbrʊk

Bolinger
BR ˈbɒlɪn(d)ʒə(r)
AM ˈboʊlɪndʒər,
ˈbəlɪndʒər

Bolitho
BR bəˈlʌɪθəʊ
AM bəˈlaɪθoʊ

Bolívar
BR bɒlɪvɑː(r),
ˌbɒlɪˈvɑː(r)
AM ˈboʊləˌvɑr,
ˈbələˌvɑr

bolivar
BR ˈbɒlɪvɑː(r), -z
AM ˈboʊləˌvɑr,
ˈbələˌvɑr, -z

Bolivia
BR bəˈlɪvɪə(r)
AM bəˈlɪvɪə

Bolivian
BR bəˈlɪvɪən, -z
AM bəˈlɪvɪən, -z

boliviano
BR bəˌlɪvɪˈɑːnəʊ, -z
AM bəˌlɪvɪˈanoʊ, -z
SP ˌboliˈβjano

boll
BR bɒl, bəʊl, -z
AM bɑl, boʊl, -z

Bollandist
BR ˈbɒləndɪst
AM ˈbaləndəst,
ˈbələndəst

bollard
BR ˈbɒlɑːd, ˈbɒləd, -z
AM ˈbalərd, ˈbɑˌlard, -z

Bollin
BR ˈbɒlɪn

Bollinger®
BR ˈbɒlɪn(d)ʒə(r)
AM ˈbaləndʒər,
ˈbələndʒər

bollocking
BR ˈbɒləkɪŋ
AM ˈbaləkɪŋ, ˈbələkɪŋ

bollocks
BR ˈbɒləks
AM ˈbaləks, ˈbələks

bolo
BR ˈbəʊləʊ, -z
AM ˈboʊˌloʊ, -z

Bologna
BR bəˈlɒnjə(r)
AM bəˈloʊnjə

bologna
sausage
BR bəˈləʊni,
bəˈlɒnjə(r)
AM bəˈloʊni

Bolognese
BR ˌbɒləˈn(j)eɪz
AM ˌboʊləˈniz,
ˌboʊləˈneɪz

bolometer
BR bəˈlɒmɪtə(r), -z
AM boʊˈlamədər,
bəˈlamədər, -z

bolometric
BR ˌbɒləˈmɛtrɪk
AM ˌboʊloʊˈmɛtrɪk,
ˌboʊləˈmɛtrɪk

bolometry
BR bəˈlɒmɪtri
AM boʊˈlamɪtri,
bəˈlamətri

boloney
BR bəˈləʊni
AM bəˈloʊni

Bolshevik
BR ˈbɒlʃɪvɪk, -s
AM ˈboʊlʃəˌvɪk, -s

Bolshevism
BR ˈbɒlʃɪvɪz(ə)m
AM ˈboʊlʃəˌvɪzəm

Bolshevist
BR ˈbɒlʃɪvɪst, -s
AM ˈboʊlʃəvəst, -s

bolshie
BR ˈbɒlʃi, -ɪz
AM ˈboʊlʃi, -z

bolshily
BR ˈbɒlʃɪli
AM ˈboʊlʃəli

bolshiness
BR ˈbɒlʃɪnɪs
AM ˈboʊlʃinɪs

Bolshoi
BR ˌbɒlˈʃɔɪ, ˈbɒlʃɔɪ
AM ˈboʊlˌʃɔɪ

Bolshoy
BR ˌbɒlˈʃɔɪ, ˈbɒlʃɔɪ
AM ˈboʊlˌʃɔɪ

bolshy
BR ˈbɒlʃi, -ɪz, -ɪə(r),
-ɪɪst
AM ˈboʊlʃi, -z, -ər, -ɪst

Bolsover
BR ˈbɒlsəʊvə(r)
AM ˈboʊlˌsoʊvər

bolster
BR ˈbəʊlstlə(r), -əz,
-(ə)rɪŋ, -əd
AM ˈboʊlstər, -z, -ɪŋ, -d

bolsterer
BR ˈbəʊlst(ə)rə(r), -z
AM ˈboʊlstərər, -z

bolt
BR bəʊlt, -s, -ɪŋ, -ɪd
AM boʊlt, -s, -ɪŋ, -əd

bolter
BR ˈbəʊltə(r), -z
AM ˈboʊltər, -z

bolthole
BR ˈbəʊlthəʊl, -z
AM ˈboʊlt,(h)oʊl, -z

Bolton
BR ˈbəʊlt(ə)n
AM ˈboʊltən

Boltzmann
BR ˈbɒltsmən
AM ˈbɒltsmən,
ˈbaltsmən

bolus
BR ˈbəʊləs, -ɪz
AM ˈboʊləs, -əz

Bolzano
BR bɒlˈzɑːnəʊ,
bɒlˈtsɑːnəʊ
AM ˌbɔlˈzanoʊ,
ˌbalˈzanoʊ

bomb
BR bɒm, -z, -ɪŋ, -d
AM bam, -z, -ɪŋ, -d

bombard¹
noun
BR ˈbɒmbɑːd, -z
AM ˈbamˌbard, -z

bombard²
verb
BR bɒmˈbɑːd, -z, -ɪŋ, -ɪd
AM bamˈbard, -z, -ɪŋ,
-əd

bombarde
BR ˈbɒmbɑːd, -z
AM ˈbamˌbard, -z

bombardier
BR ˌbɒmbəˈdɪə(r), -z
AM ˌbambə(r)ˈdɪ(ə)r, -z

bombardment
BR bɒmˈbɑːdm(ə)nt, -s
AM bamˈbardmənt, -s

bombardon
BR ˈbɒmbədən, -z
AM ˈbambərdən,
bamˈbardən, -z

bombasine
BR ˈbɒmbəziːn
AM ˈbambəˌzin,
ˈbambəˌsin

bombast
BR ˈbɒmbast
AM ˈbɑmbæst
bombastic
BR bɒmˈbastɪk
AM bɑmˈbæstɪk
bombastically
BR bɒmˈbastɪkli
AM bɑmˈbæstək(ə)li
Bombay
BR ˌbɒmˈbeɪ
AM ˌbɑmˈbeɪ
bombazine
BR ˈbɒmbəziːn,
ˌbɒmbəˈziːn
AM ˈbɑmbəˌzin,
ˈbɑmbəˌsin
bombe
BR bɒm(b), bɔːb, -z
AM bɑm(b), -z
bomber
BR ˈbɒmə(r), -z
AM ˈbɑmər, -z
bombora
BR bɒmˈbɔːrə(r), -z
AM ˌbɑmˈbɔrə, -z
bombproof
BR ˈbɒmpruːf
AM ˈbɑmˌpruf
bombshell
BR ˈbɒmʃɛl, -z
AM ˈbɑmˌʃɛl, -z
bombsight
BR ˈbɒmsʌɪt, -s
AM ˈbɑmˌsaɪt, -s
bombsite
BR ˈbɒmsʌɪt, -s
AM ˈbɑmˌsaɪt, -s
bona fide
BR ˌbəʊnə ˈfʌɪdi
AM ˈboʊnə ˌfaɪd,
ˈbɑnə +, ˌboʊnə ˈfaɪdi
bona fides
BR ˌbəʊnə ˈfʌɪdiːz
AM ˈboʊnə ˌfaɪdz,
ˈbɑnə +, ˌboʊnə
ˈfaɪdiz
Bonaire
BR bɒnˈɛː(r)
AM bəˈnɛ(ə)r
Bonallack
BR bəˈnalək
AM bəˈnælək
bonanza
BR bəˈnanzə(r), -z
AM bəˈnænzə, -z
Bonaparte
BR ˈbəʊnəpɑːt
AM ˈboʊnəˌpɑrt
bona vacantia
BR ˌbəʊnə
vəˈkantɪə(r)
AM ˈboʊnə vəˈkɑn(t)iə
Bonaventura
BR ˌbɒnəvɛnˈtjʊərə(r),
ˌbɒnəvɛnˈtjɔːrə(r),
ˌbɒnəvɛnˈtʃʊərə(r),
ˌbɒnəvɛnˈtʃɔːrə(r)

AM ˌbɑnəvənˈtʃʊrə
Bonaventure
BR ˈbɒnəvɛn(t)ʃə(r),
ˌbɒnəˈvɛn(t)ʃə(r)
AM ˈbɑnəˌvən(t)ʃər
bon-bon
BR ˈbɒnbɒn, -z
AM ˈbɑnˌbɑn, -z
bonce
BR bɒns, -ɪz
AM bɑns, -əz
bond
BR bɒnd, -z, -ɪŋ, -ɪd
AM bɑnd, -z, -ɪŋ, -əd
bondage
BR ˈbɒndɪdʒ
AM ˈbɑndɪdʒ
bondager
BR ˈbɒndɪdʒə(r), -z
AM ˈbɑndɪdʒər, -z
bondholder
BR ˈbɒndˌhəʊldə(r), -z
AM ˈbɑnd(d),(h)oʊldər, -z
Bondi
BR ˈbɒndʌɪ
AM ˈbɑndi
bondman
BR ˈbɒndmən
AM ˈbɑn(d)mən
bondmen
BR ˈbɒndmən
AM ˈbɑn(d)mən
bondsman
BR ˈbɒn(d)zmən
AM ˈbɑn(d)zmən
bondsmen
BR ˈbɒn(d)zmən
AM ˈbɑn(d)zmən
bondstone
BR ˈbɒn(d)stəʊn, -z
AM ˈbɑn(d)ˌstoʊn, -z
bondswoman
BR ˈbɒn(d)zˌwʊmən
AM ˈbɑn(d)zˌwʊmən
bondswomen
BR ˈbɒn(d)zˌwɪmɪn
AM ˈbɑn(d)zˌwɪmɪn
bondwoman
BR ˈbɒndˌwʊmən
AM ˈbɑn(d)ˌwʊmən
bondwomen
BR ˈbɒndˌwɪmɪn
AM ˈbɑn(d)ˌwɪmɪn
bone
BR bəʊn, -z, -ɪŋ, -d
AM boʊn, -z, -ɪŋ, -d
bonefish
BR ˈbəʊnfɪʃ
AM ˈboʊnˌfɪʃ
bonehead
BR ˈbəʊnhɛd, -z
AM ˈboʊn,(h)ɛd, -z
boneheaded
BR ˌbəʊnˈhɛdɪd
AM ˈboʊn,(h)ɛdəd

boneless
BR ˈbəʊnləs
AM ˈboʊnləs
bonemeal
BR ˈbəʊnmiːl
AM ˈboʊnˌmil
boner
BR ˈbəʊnə(r), -z
AM ˈboʊnər, -z
boneshaker
BR ˈbəʊnˌʃeɪkə(r), -z
AM ˈboʊnˌʃeɪkər, -z
Bo'ness
BR ˌbəʊˈnɛs
AM boʊˈnɛs
bonfire
BR ˈbɒnfʌɪə(r), -z
AM ˈbɑnˌfaɪ(ə)r, -z
bong
BR bɒŋ, -z, -ɪŋ, -d
AM bɑŋ, -z, -ɪŋ, -d
bongo
BR ˈbɒŋgəʊ, -z
AM ˈbɑŋgoʊ, ˈbɑŋgoʊ, -z
Bonham
BR ˈbɒnəm
AM ˈbɑnəm
Bonhoeffer
BR ˈbɒnˌhɜːfə(r), ˈbɒnˌhʊfə(r)
AM ˈbɑn,(h)ɔfər, ˈbɑn,(h)ɑfər
bonhomie
BR ˈbɒnəmiː, ˈbɒnɒmiː
AM ˈbɑnəmi, ˌbɑnəˈmi
bonhomous
BR ˈbɒnəməs
AM ˈbɑnəməs
bonier
BR ˈbəʊnɪə(r)
AM ˈboʊniər
boniest
BR ˈbəʊnɪɪst
AM ˈboʊniɪst
Boniface
BR ˈbɒnɪfeɪs
AM ˈbɑnəfəs
boniness
BR ˈbəʊnɪnɪs
AM ˈboʊnɪnɪs
Bonington
BR ˈbɒnɪŋt(ə)n
AM ˈbɑnɪŋtən
Bonio
BR ˈbəʊnɪəʊ
AM ˈboʊnioʊ
bonism
BR ˈbəʊnɪz(ə)m
AM ˈboʊˌnɪzəm
bonist
BR ˈbəʊnɪst, -s
AM ˈboʊnəst, -s
Bonita
BR bəˈniːtə(r)
AM bəˈnidə

bonito
BR bəˈniːtəʊ, -z
AM bəˈnidoʊ, bəˈnidə, -z
bonk
BR bɒŋk, -ks, -kɪŋ, -(k)t
AM bɑŋk, -ks, -kɪŋ, -(k)t
bonker
BR ˈbɒŋkə(r), -z
AM ˈbɑŋkər, -z
bon mot
BR ˌbɒn ˈməʊ, ˌbɔ̃ +
AM ˌbɑn ˈmoʊ
Bonn
BR bɒn
AM bɑn
Bonnard
BR bɒˈnɑː(r)
AM bəˈnɑr, bɑˈnɑr
bonne bouche
BR ˌbɒn ˈbuːʃ, -ɪz
AM ˌbən ˈbuʃ, -əz
Bonner
BR ˈbɒnə(r)
AM ˈbɑnər
bonnes bouches
BR ˌbɒn ˈbuːʃ
AM ˌbən ˈbuʃ
bonnet
BR ˈbɒnɪt, -ɪts, -ɪtɪd
AM ˈbɑnəɪt, -ts, -dəd
bonnethead
BR ˈbɒnɪthɛd, -z
AM ˈbɑnət,(h)ɛd, -z
Bonneville
BR ˈbɒnəvɪl
AM ˈbɑnəˌvɪl
Bonnie
BR ˈbɒni
AM ˈbɑni
bonnily
BR ˈbɒnɪli
AM ˈbɑnəli
bonniness
BR ˈbɒnɪnɪs
AM ˈbɑnɪnɪs
bonny
BR ˈbɒn|i, -ɪə(r), -ɪɪst
AM ˈbɑni, -ər, -ɪst
bonsai
BR ˈbɒnsʌɪ
AM ˈbɑnˌsaɪ
Bonser
BR ˈbɒnsə(r)
AM ˈbɑnsər
bons mots
BR ˌbɒn ˈməʊ(z), ˌbɔ̃ +
AM ˌbɔn ˈmoʊz
Bonsor
BR ˈbɒnsə(r)
AM ˈbɑnsər
bonspiel
BR ˈbɒnspiːl, -z

AM 'bɑn,spil, 'bɑn,ʃpil,
-z
bons vivants
BR ,bõ viː'võz, ,bɒn
viː'vɒnz, ,bɒn
viː'vɒnts
AM ,bɑn vi'vɑn(t)s
bons viveurs
BR ,bõ viː'vəː, ,bɒn +
AM ,bɑn vi'vɚz
bontbok
BR 'bɒntbɒk, -s
AM 'bɑnt,bɑk, -s
bontebok
BR 'bɒntɪbɒk, -s
AM 'bɑn(t)i,bɑk, -s
bonus
BR 'bəʊnəs, -ɪz
AM 'boʊnəs, -ɪz
bon vivant
BR ,bõ viː'võ, ,bɒn
viː'vɒn(t), -ts\-z
AM ,bɑn vi'vɑnt, -s
bon viveur
BR ,bõ viː'vəː(r),
,bɒn +, -z
AM ,bɑn vi'vɚr, -z
bon voyage
BR ,bɒn vɔɪ'ɑːʒ
AM 'bɑn ,vɔɪ'ɑʒ,
'boʊn +
bonxie
BR 'bɒŋks|i, -z
AM 'bɑŋksi, -z
bony
BR 'bəʊn|i, -iə(r), -ɪst
AM 'boʊni, -ɚr, -ɪst
bonze
BR bɒnz, -ɪz
AM bɑnz, -əz
bonzer
BR 'bɒnzə(r)
AM 'bɑnzɚr
Bonzo
BR 'bɒnzəʊ
AM 'bɑnzoʊ
boo
BR buː, -z, -ɪŋ, -d
AM bu, -z, -ɪŋ, -d
boob
BR buːb, -z, -ɪŋ, -d
AM bub, -z, -ɪŋ, -d
booboisie
BR ,buː'bwɑː'ziː
AM ,bu,bwɑ'zi
booboo
BR 'buːbuː, -z
AM 'bu,bu, -z
boobook
BR 'buːbʊk, -s
AM 'bu,bʊk, -s
booby
BR 'buːb|i, -ɪz
AM 'bubi, -z
boobyish
BR 'buːbɪɪʃ
AM 'bubiɪʃ

boodle
BR 'buːdl
AM 'budəl
boogie
BR 'buːg|i, -ɪz, -ɪŋ, -ɪd
AM ,bʊgi, -z, -ɪŋ, -d
boogie-woogie
BR ,buː'gɪ'wuːgi
AM ,bʊgi'wʊgi
boohoo
BR ,buː'huː
AM ,bu'hu
book
BR bʊk, -s, -ɪŋ, -t
AM bʊk, -s, -ɪŋ, -t
bookable
BR 'bʊkəbl
AM 'bʊkəbəl
bookbinder
BR 'bʊk,baɪndə(r), -z
AM 'bʊk,baɪndɚr, -z
bookbinding
BR 'bʊk,baɪndɪŋ
AM 'bʊk,baɪndɪŋ
bookcase
BR 'bʊkkeɪs, -ɪz
AM 'bʊ(k),keɪs, -ɪz
bookend
BR 'bʊkɛnd, -z
AM 'bʊk,ɛnd, -z
booker
BR 'bʊkə(r), -z
AM 'bʊkɚr, -z
bookie
BR 'bʊk|i, -ɪz
AM 'bʊki, -z
booking
BR 'bʊkɪŋ, -z
AM 'bʊkɪŋ, -z
bookish
BR 'bʊkɪʃ
AM 'bʊkɪʃ
bookishly
BR 'bʊkɪʃli
AM 'bʊkɪʃli
bookishness
BR 'bʊkɪʃnɪs
AM 'bʊkɪʃnɪs
bookkeeper
BR 'bʊk,kiːpə(r), -z
AM 'bʊ(k),kipɚr, -z
bookkeeping
BR 'bʊk,kiːpɪŋ
AM 'bʊ(k),kipɪŋ
booklet
BR 'bʊklɪt, -s
AM 'bʊklɪt, -s
booklist
BR 'bʊklɪst, -s
AM 'bʊk,lɪst, -s
bookmaker
BR 'bʊk,meɪkə(r), -z
AM 'bʊk,meɪkɚr, -z
bookmaking
BR 'bʊk,meɪkɪŋ
AM 'bʊk,meɪkɪŋ

bookman
BR 'bʊkmən
AM 'bʊkmən
bookmark
BR 'bʊkmɑːk, -s
AM 'bʊk,mɑrk, -s
bookmarker
BR 'bʊk,mɑːkə(r), -z
AM 'bʊk,mɑrkɚr, -z
bookmen
BR 'bʊkmən
AM 'bʊkmən
bookmobile
BR 'bʊkmə(ʊ)biːl, -z
AM 'bʊkmoʊbil,
'bʊkmə,bil, -z
bookplate
BR 'bʊkpleɪt, -s
AM 'bʊk,pleɪt, -s
bookseller
BR 'bʊk,sɛlə(r), -z
AM 'bʊk,sɛlɚr, -z
bookshelf
BR 'bʊkʃelf
AM 'bʊk,ʃɛlf
bookshelves
BR 'bʊkʃɛlvz
AM 'bʊk,ʃɛlvz
bookshop
BR 'bʊkʃɒp, -s
AM 'bʊk,ʃɑp, -s
bookstall
BR 'bʊkstɔːl, -z
AM 'bʊk,stɔl, 'bʊk,stɑl,
-z
bookstand
BR 'bʊkstænd, -z
AM 'bʊk,stænd, -z
bookstore
BR 'bʊkstɔː(r), -z
AM 'bʊk,stɔ(ə)r, -z
booksy
BR 'bʊksi
AM 'bʊksi
bookwork
BR 'bʊkwəːk
AM 'bʊk,wɚrk
bookworm
BR 'bʊkwəːm, -z
AM 'bʊk,wɚrm, -z
Boole
BR buːl
AM bul
Boolean
BR 'buːliən
AM 'buliən
boom
BR buːm, -z, -ɪŋ, -d
AM bum, -z, -ɪŋ, -d
boomer
BR 'buːmə(r), -z
AM 'bumɚr, -z
boomerang
BR 'buːmərəŋ, -z, -ɪŋ, -d
AM 'bumə,ræŋ, -z, -ɪŋ,
-d

boomlet
BR 'buːmlɪt, -s
AM 'bumlət, -s
boomslang
BR 'buːmslaŋ, -z
AM 'bum,slæŋ, -z
boomtown
BR 'buːmtaʊn, -z
AM 'bum,taʊn, -z
boon
BR buːn, -z
AM bun, -z
boondock
BR 'buːndɒk, -s
AM 'bun,dɑk, -s
boondoggle
BR 'buːn,dɒg|l, -lz,
-lɪŋ \-lɪŋ, -ld
AM 'bun,dɑg|əl, -əlz,
-(ə)lɪŋ, -əld
Boone
BR buːn
AM bun
boonies
BR 'buːnɪz
AM 'buniz
boor
BR bʊə(r), bɔː(r), -z
AM bʊ(ə)r, -z
boorish
BR 'bʊərɪʃ, 'bɔːrɪʃ
AM 'bʊrɪʃ
boorishly
BR 'bʊərɪʃli, 'bɔːrɪʃli
AM 'bʊrɪʃli
boorishness
BR 'bʊərɪʃnɪs,
'bɔːrɪʃnɪs
AM 'bʊrɪʃnɪs
Boosey
BR 'buːzi
AM 'buzi
boost
BR buːst, -s, -ɪŋ, -ɪd
AM bust, -s, -ɪŋ, -ɪd
booster
BR 'buːstə(r), -z
AM 'bustɚr, -z
boot
BR buːt, -s, -ɪŋ, -ɪd
AM bu|t, -ts, -dɪŋ, -dəd
bootblack
BR 'buːtblak, -s
AM 'but,blæk, -s
bootboy
BR 'buːtbɔɪ, -z
AM 'but,bɔɪ, -z
bootee
BR 'buːtiː, 'buːtiː, -z
AM bu'ti, -z
Boötes
BR bəʊ'əʊtiːz
AM boʊ'oʊdiz
booth
BR buː|ð, buː|θ, -ðz
AM bu|θ, -ðz

Bootham
BR ˈbuːðəm
AM ˈbuðəm

Boothby
BR ˈbuːθbi
AM ˈbuθbi

Boothe
BR buːð, buːθ
AM buθ

Boothia
BR ˈbuːθɪə(r)
AM ˈbuθiə

Boothroyd
BR ˈbuːθrɔɪd
AM ˈbuθrɔɪd

bootie
BR ˈbuːtiː, ˈbuːtiː, -z
AM ˈbudi, -z

bootjack
BR ˈbuːtdʒak, -s
AM ˈbutˌdʒæk, -s

bootlace
BR ˈbuːtleɪs, -ɪz
AM ˈbutˌleɪs, -ɪz

Bootle
BR ˈbuːtl
AM ˈbudəl

bootleg
BR ˈbuːtlɛg, -z, -ɪŋ, -d
AM ˈbutˌlɛg, -z, -ɪŋ, -d

bootlegger
BR ˈbuːtˌlɛgə(r), -z
AM ˈbutˌlɛgər, -z

bootless
BR ˈbuːtləs
AM ˈbutləs

bootlicker
BR ˈbuːtˌlɪkə(r), -z
AM ˈbutˌlɪkər, -z

bootstrap
BR ˈbuːtstrap, -s, -ɪŋ, -t
AM ˈbutˌstræp, -s, -ɪŋ, -t

booty
BR ˈbuːti
AM ˈbudi

booze
BR buːz, -ɪz, -ɪŋ, -d
AM buz, -əz, -ɪŋ, -d

boozer
BR ˈbuːzə(r), -z
AM ˈbuzər, -z

boozily
BR ˈbuːzɪli
AM ˈbuzəli

booziness
BR ˈbuːzɪnɪs
AM ˈbuzɪnɪs

boozy
BR ˈbuːz|i, -ɪə(r), -ɪɪst
AM ˈbuzi, -ər, -ɪst

bop
BR bɒp, -s, -ɪŋ, -t
AM bɑp, -s, -ɪŋ, -t

Bophuthatswana
BR bəˌpuːtəˈtswɑːnə(r),
ˌbɒpuːtətˈswɑːnə(r)
AM ˌbouˌpʊdətˈswɑnə

bopper
BR ˈbɒpə(r), -z
AM ˈbɑpər, -z

bora
BR ˈbɔːrə(r), -z
AM ˈbɔrə, -z

Bora-Bora
BR ˌbɔːrəˈbɔːrə(r)
AM ˌbɔrəˈbɔrə

boracic
BR bəˈrasɪk
AM bəˈræsɪk

borage
BR ˈbɒrɪdʒ
AM ˈbɔrɪdʒ, ˈbɑrɪdʒ

borak
BR ˈbɔːrak
AM ˈbɔrək

borane
BR ˈbɔːreɪn, -z
AM ˈbɔˌreɪn, -z

borate
BR ˈbɔːreɪt, -s
AM ˈbɔˌreɪt, -s

borax
BR ˈbɔːraks
AM ˈbɔˌræks

borazon
BR ˈbɔːrəzɒn
AM ˈbɔrəˌzɑn

borborygmi
BR ˌbɔːbəˈrɪgmi
AM ˌbɔrbəˈrɪgmi

borborygmic
BR ˌbɔːbəˈrɪgmɪk
AM ˌbɔrbəˈrɪgmɪk

borborygmus
BR ˌbɔːbəˈrɪgməs
AM ˌbɔrbəˈrɪgməs

Bordeaux
BR bɔːˈdəʊ
AM ˌbɔrˈdou

bordel
BR bɔːˈdɛl, -z
AM ˈbɔrdəl, -z

bordello
BR bɔːˈdɛləʊ, -z
AM ˌbɔrˈdɛlou, -z

border
BR ˈbɔːd|ə(r), -əz,
-(ə)rɪŋ, -əd
AM ˈbɔrdər, -z, -ɪŋ, -d

bordereau
BR ˌbɔːdəˈrəʊ, -z
AM ˌbɔrdəˈrou, -z

bordereaux
BR ˌbɔːdəˈrəʊz
AM ˌbɔrdəˈrouz

borderer
BR ˈbɔːd(ə)rə(r), -z
AM ˈbɔrdərər, -z

borderland
BR ˈbɔːdəland, -z
AM ˈbɔrdərˌlænd, -z

borderline
BR ˈbɔːdəlʌɪn, -z
AM ˈbɔrdərˌlaɪn, -z

Bordet
BR bɔːˈdeɪ
AM bɔrˈdeɪ

bordone
BR bɔːˈdəʊni
AM bɔrˈdouni

bordure
BR ˈbɔːdjʊə(r), -z
AM ˈbɔrdʒər, -z

bore
BR bɔː(r), -z, -ɪŋ, -d
AM bɔː(ə)r, -z, -ɪŋ, -d

boreal
BR ˈbɔːrɪəl
AM ˈbɔrɪəl

borealis
BR ˌbɔːrɪˈeɪlɪs,
ˌbɔːrɪˈɑːlɪs
AM ˌbɔriˈæləs,
ˌbɔriˈeɪlɪs

boredom
BR ˈbɔːdəm
AM ˈbɔrdəm

Boreham
BR ˈbɔːrəm, ˈbɔːrm̩
AM ˈbɔrəm

borehole
BR ˈbɔːhəʊl, -z
AM ˈbɔrˌ(h)oʊl, -z

borer
BR ˈbɔːrə(r), -z
AM ˈbɔrər, -z

Borg
BR bɔːg
AM bɔ(ə)rg
SW bɔrj

Borges
BR ˈbɔːxɛs, ˈbɔːgəs
AM ˈbɔrˌhɛs, ˈbɔrgəs

Borgia
BR ˈbɔː(d)ʒ(ɪ)ə(r)
AM ˈbɔrʒə

boric
BR ˈbɔːrɪk, ˈbɒrɪk
AM ˈbɔrɪk

boring
BR ˈbɔːrɪŋ, -z
AM ˈbɔrɪŋ, -z

boringly
BR ˈbɔːrɪŋli
AM ˈbɔrɪŋli

boringness
BR ˈbɔːrɪŋnɪs
AM ˈbɔrɪŋnɪs

Boris
BR ˈbɒrɪs
AM ˈbɔrəs

Bork
BR bɔːk
AM bɔ(ə)rk

Bormann
BR ˈbɔːman
AM ˈbɔrmən

born
BR bɔːn
AM bɔ(ə)rn

borne
BR bɔːn
AM bɔ(ə)rn

borné
BR bɔːˈneɪ
AM bɔrˈneɪ

Bornean
BR ˈbɔːnɪən, -z
AM ˈbɔrniən, -z

Borneo
BR ˈbɔːnɪəʊ
AM ˈbɔrniou

Bornholm
BR ˈbɔːnhəʊm
AM ˈbɔrnˌ(h)oʊm
DAN ˌbɔːnˈhʌl'm

Borobudur
BR ˌbɒrəbəˈdʊə(r)
AM ˌbɒrəbəˈdʊ(ə)r

Borodin
BR ˈbɒrədɪn
AM ˈbɒrəˌdin
RUS bərʌˈdʲin

Borodino
BR ˌbɒrəˈdiːnəʊ
AM ˌbɒrəˈdinou
RUS bərədʲiˈno

borofluoride
BR ˌbɔːrə(ʊ)ˈflʊərʌɪd,
ˌbɔːrə(ʊ)ˈflɔːrʌɪd
AM ˌbɔrəˈfluˌraɪd,
ˌbɔrəˈflɔˌraɪd

boron
BR ˈbɔːrɒn
AM ˈbɔˌrɑn

boronia
BR bəˈrəʊnɪə(r), -z
AM bəˈrouniə, -z

borosilicate
BR ˌbɔːrə(ʊ)ˈsɪlɪkeɪt,
ˌbɔːrə(ʊ)ˈsɪlɪkət
AM ˌbɔrəˈsɪləkət

borough
BR ˈbʌrə(r), -z
AM ˈbərou, ˈbərə, -z

Borromini
BR ˌbɒrəˈmiːni
AM ˌbɒrəˈmini

borrow
BR ˈbɒrəʊ, -z, -ɪŋ, -d
AM ˈbɑr|oʊ, ˈbɔr|oʊ,
-oʊz, -əwɪŋ, -oʊd

Borrowdale
BR ˈbɒrə(ʊ)deɪl
AM ˈbɑrouˌdeɪl

borrower
BR ˈbɒrəʊə(r), -z
AM ˈbarəwər,
ˈbɔrəwər, -z

borrowing
BR ˈbɒrəʊɪŋ, -z
AM ˈbarəwɪŋ,
ˈbɔrəwɪŋ, -z

Borsalino®
BR ˌbɔːsəˈliːnəʊ, -z
AM ˌbɔrsəˈlinou, -z

borsch
BR bɔːʃ

AM bɔ(ə)rʃ
borscht
BR bɔːʃt
AM bɔ(ə)rʃt
borshcht
BR bɔːʃt
AM bɔ(ə)rʃt
Borstal
BR 'bɔːstl, -z
AM 'bɔ(ə)rstl, -z
bort
BR bɔːt
AM bɔ(ə)rt
Borth
BR bɔːθ
AM bɔ(ə)rθ
Borthwick
BR 'bɔːθwɪk
AM 'bɔrθwɪk
bortsch
BR bɔːtʃ
AM bɔ(ə)rtʃ
borzoi
BR 'bɔːzɔɪ, 'bɔːtsɔɪ, -z
AM 'bɔr,zɔɪ, -z
Bosanquet
BR 'bəʊznkɛt, 'bəʊŋkɛt
AM 'bouzən,kɛt
Bosc
BR bɒsk
AM bɑsk
boscage
BR 'bɒsk|ɪdʒ, -ɪdʒɪz
AM 'bɑskɪdʒ, -ɪz
Boscastle
BR 'bɒs,kɑːsl, 'bɒs,kɑsl
AM 'bɒz,kæsəl, 'bɑz,kæsəl
Boscawen¹
placename
BR 'bɒsk(ə)wɪn, 'bɒskwʌɪn
AM 'baskəwən
Boscawen²
surname
BR bɒ'skəʊən
AM bɑ'skaʊən
Bosch
BR bɒʃ
AM bɔʃ, bɑʃ
Boscobel
BR 'bɒskəbɛl
AM 'baskə,bɛl
Bose
BR bəʊz, bəʊs
AM bouz
bosh
BR bɒʃ
AM bɑʃ
bosie
BR 'bəʊz|i, -ɪz
AM 'bousi, -z
boskage
BR 'bɒsk|ɪdʒ, -ɪdʒɪz
AM 'baskɪdʒ, -ɪz

boskiness
BR 'bɒskɪnɪs
AM 'baskɪnɪs
Boskop
BR 'bɒskɒp
AM 'bas,kap
bosky
BR 'bɒski
AM 'baski
bos'n
BR 'bəʊsn, -z
AM 'bousn, -z
bo's'n
BR 'bəʊsn, -z
AM 'bousn, -z
Bosnia
BR 'bɒznɪə(r)
AM 'baznɪə, 'bɒznɪə
Bosnian
BR 'bɒznɪən, -z
AM 'baznɪən, 'bɒznɪən, -z
bosom
BR 'bʊz(ə)m, -z
AM 'bʊzəm, -z
bosomy
BR 'bʊzəmi, 'bʊzm̩i
AM 'bʊzəmi
boson
BR 'bəʊsɒn, 'bəʊzɒn
AM 'bou,san, 'bou,zan
Bosphorus
BR 'bɒsf(ə)rəs
AM 'basf(ə)rəs
Bosporus
BR 'bɒsp(ə)rəs
AM 'basp(ə)rəs
boss
BR bɒs, -ɪz, -ɪŋ, -t
AM bɔs, bas, -əz, -ɪŋ, -t
bossa nova
BR ,bɒsə 'nəʊvə(r), -z
AM ,basə 'nouvə, -z
bossily
BR 'bɒsɪli
AM 'bɔsəli, 'basəli
bossiness
BR 'bɒsɪnɪs
AM 'bɔsɪnɪs, 'basɪnɪs
bossy
BR 'bɒs|i, -ɪə(r), -ɪɪst
AM 'bɔsi, 'basi, -ər, -ɪɪst
Bostik®
BR 'bɒstɪk
AM 'bastɪk
Bostock
BR 'bɒstɒk
AM 'bastək
Boston
BR 'bɒst(ə)n
AM 'bɒstən, 'bastən
Bostonian
BR bɒ'stəʊnɪən, -z
AM bɔ'stounɪən, ba'stounɪən, -z
bosun
BR 'bəʊsn, -z

bo'sun
AM 'bousn, -z
bo'sun
BR 'bəʊsn, -z
AM 'bousn, -z
Boswell
BR 'bɒzw(ɛ)l
AM 'bazwəl
Bosworth
BR 'bɒzwə(:)θ
AM 'baz,wərθ
bot
BR bɒt, -s
AM bat, -s
botanic
BR bə'tanɪk
AM bə'tænɪk
botanical
BR bə'tanɪkl
AM bə'tænəkəl
botanically
BR bə'tanɪkli
AM bə'tænək(ə)li
botanise
BR 'bɒtənʌɪz, 'bɒtn̩ʌɪz, -ɪz, -ɪŋ, -d
AM 'batn̩,aɪz, -ɪz, -ɪŋ, -d
botanist
BR 'bɒtənɪst, 'bɒtn̩ɪst, -s
AM 'batn̩əst, -s
botanize
BR 'bɒtənʌɪz, 'bɒtn̩ʌɪz, -ɪz, -ɪŋ, -d
AM 'batn̩,aɪz, -ɪz, -ɪŋ, -d
botany
BR 'bɒtəni, 'bɒtn̩i
AM 'batn̩i
botargo
BR bə'tɑːgəʊ, -z
AM bou'targou, -z
botch
BR bɒtʃ, -ɪz, -ɪŋ, -t
AM batʃ, -əz, -ɪŋ, -t
botcher
BR 'bɒtʃə(r), -z
AM 'batʃər, -z
botel
BR ,bəʊ'tɛl, -z
AM ,bou'tɛl, -z
botfly
BR 'bɒtflʌɪ, -z
AM 'bat,flaɪ, -z
both
BR bəʊθ
AM bouθ
Botha
BR 'bəʊtə(r), 'bʊətə(r)
AM 'bouθə, 'boudə
AFK 'bʊətə
Botham
BR 'bəʊθəm
AM 'baðəm
bother
BR 'bɒð|ə(r), -əz, -(ə)rɪŋ, -əd
AM 'bað|ər, -ərz, -(ə)rɪŋ, -ərd

botheration
BR ,bɒðə'reɪʃn
AM ,baðə'reɪʃən
bothersome
BR 'bɒðəs(ə)m
AM 'baðərsəm
Bothnia
BR 'bɒθnɪə(r)
AM 'baθnɪə
Bothwell
BR 'bɒθw(ɛ)l
AM 'baθwəl
bothy
BR 'bɒθ|i, -ɪz
AM 'baθi, -z
Botolph
BR 'bɒtɒlf
AM 'badəlf
botryoid
BR 'bɒtrɪɔɪd
AM 'batri,ɔɪd
botryoidal
BR ,bɒtrɪ'ɔɪdl
AM ,batri'ɔɪdəl
Botswana
BR bɒt'swɑːnə(r)
AM bat'swanə
Botswanan
BR bɒt'swɑːnən, -z
AM bat'swanən, -z
bott
BR bɒt, -s
AM bat, -s
Botticelli
BR ,bɒtɪ'tʃɛli
AM ,badə'tʃɛli
bottle
BR 'bɒt|l, -lz, -lɪŋ \ -lɪŋ, -ld
AM 'badəl, -z, -ɪŋ, -d
bottleful
BR 'bɒtlfʊl, -z
AM 'badl,fʊl, -z
bottleneck
BR 'bɒtlnɛk, -s
AM 'badl,nɛk, -s
bottlenose
BR 'bɒtlnəʊz, -ɪz, -d
AM 'badl,nouz, -ɪz, -d
bottler
BR 'bɒtlə(r), 'bɒtlə(r), -z
AM 'badlər, 'badlər, -z
bottlewasher
BR 'bɒtl,wɒʃə(r), -z
AM 'badl,wɔʃər, 'badl,waʃər, -z
bottom
BR 'bɒtəm, -z, -ɪŋ, -d
AM 'badəm, -z, -ɪŋ, -d
bottomless
BR 'bɒtəmləs
AM 'badəmləs
bottomlessness
BR 'bɒtəmləsnəs
AM 'badəmləsnəs

Bottomley
BR ˈbɒtəmli
AM ˈbɑdəmli
bottommost
BR ˈbɒtə(m)məʊst
AM ˈbɑdə(m)ˌmoʊst
bottomry
BR ˈbɒtəmrˌli, -ɪz, -ɪŋ,
-ɪd
AM ˈbɑdəmri, -z, -ɪŋ, -d
botulinus
BR ˌbɒtjʊˈlʌɪnəs,
ˌbɒtʃʊˈlʌɪnəs
AM ˌbɑtʃəˈlaɪnəs
botulism
BR ˈbɒtjʊlɪz(ə)m,
ˈbɒtʃʊlɪz(ə)m
AM ˈbɑtʃəˌlɪzəm
Boucher
BR ˈbaʊtʃə(r), ˈbuːʃeɪ
AM buˈʃeɪ
bouclé
BR ˈbuːkleɪ
AM ˈbuːkleɪ
Boudicca
BR ˈbuːdɪkə(r)
AM buˈdɪkə
boudoir
BR ˈbuːdwɑː(r), -z
AM ˈbudˌwɑr, -z
bouffant
BR ˈbuːfɒ̃, ˈbuːfɒŋ,
ˈbuːfɒnt
AM ˌbuːfɑnt
bougainvillaea
BR ˌbuːg(ə)nˈvɪlɪə(r),
-z
AM ˌbugənˈvɪljə,
ˌbugənˈvɪliə, -z
Bougainville
BR ˈbuːg(ə)nvɪl
AM ˈbugənˌvɪl
bougainvillea
BR ˌbuːg(ə)nˈvɪlɪə(r),
-z
AM ˌbugənˈvɪljə,
ˌbugənˈvɪliə, -z
Bougainvillian
BR ˌbuːg(ə)nˈvɪlɪən, -z
AM ˌbugənˈvɪljən,
ˌbugənˈvɪliən, -z
bough
BR baʊ, -z
AM baʊ, -z
bought
BR bɔːt
AM bɔt, bɑt
boughten
BR ˈbɔːtn
AM ˈbɒtn, ˈbɑtn
bougie
BR ˈbuːʒˌli, -ɪz
AM ˈbu(d)ʒi, -z
bouillabaisse
BR ˌbuːjəˈbɛs,
ˌbuːjəˈbeɪs, ˈbuːjəbɛs,
ˈbuːjəbeɪs

AM ˌbu(l)jəˈbɛs,
ˌbu(l)jəˈbeɪs
bouilli
BR ˈbuːji
AM buˈji
bouillon
BR ˈbuːjɒ̃, ˈbuːjɒn,
ˈbwiːjɒ̃, ˈbwiːjɒn
AM ˈbu(l)ˌjɑn, ˈbəlˌjɑn
boulder
BR ˈbəʊldə(r), -z
AM ˈboʊldər, -z
bouldery
BR ˈbəʊld(ə)ri
AM ˈboʊldəri
boule[1]
Greek legislative body
BR ˈbuːlˌli, ˈbuːlˌleɪ,
-ɪz \ -eɪz
AM ˈbuli, -z
GR vuːˈli:
boule[2]
ornamental inlay
BR buːl, -z
AM bul, -z
boules
game
BR buːl
AM bul
boulevard
BR ˈbuːləvɑːd,
ˈbuːl(ə)vɑːd, -z
AM ˈbʊləˌvɑrd, -z
boulevardier
BR ˌbuːləvɑːˈdjeɪ, -z
AM ˌbʊlˌboʊvɑrˈdjeɪ, -z
Boulez
BR ˈbuːlɛz, ˈbuːleɪ
AM buˈlɛz
boulle
BR buːl
AM bul
Boulogne
BR bʊˈlɔɪn
AM buˈloʊn(jə)
FR bulɔn
boult
BR bəʊlt, -s, -ɪŋ, -ɪd
AM boʊlt, -s, -ɪŋ, -əd
Boulter
BR ˈbəʊltə(r)
AM ˈboʊldər
Boulting
BR ˈbəʊltɪŋ
AM ˈboʊltɪŋ
Boulton
BR ˈbəʊlt(ə)n
AM ˈboʊlt(ə)n
bounce
BR baʊns, -ɪz, -ɪŋ, -t
AM baʊns, -əz, -ɪŋ, -t
bouncer
BR ˈbaʊnsə(r), -z
AM ˈbaʊnsər, -z
bouncily
BR ˈbaʊnsɪli

AM ˈbaʊnsəli
bounciness
BR ˈbaʊnsɪnɪs
AM ˈbaʊnsinɪs
bouncy
BR ˈbaʊnsˌli, -ɪə(r), -ɪɪst
AM ˈbaʊnsi, -ər, -ɪst
bound
BR baʊnd, -z, -ɪŋ, -ɪd
AM baʊnd, -z, -ɪŋ, -əd
boundary
BR ˈbaʊnd(ə)rˌli, -ɪz
AM ˈbaʊnd(ə)ri, -z
bounden
BR ˈbaʊndən
AM ˈbaʊndən
bounder
BR ˈbaʊndə(r), -z
AM ˈbaʊndər, -z
boundless
BR ˈbaʊndləs
AM ˈbaʊn(d)ləs
boundlessly
BR ˈbaʊndləsli
AM ˈbaʊn(d)ləsli
boundlessness
BR ˈbaʊndləsnəs
AM ˈbaʊn(d)ləsnəs
bounteous
BR ˈbaʊntɪəs
AM ˈbaʊn(t)iəs
bounteously
BR ˈbaʊntɪəsli
AM ˈbaʊn(t)iəsli
bounteousness
BR ˈbaʊntɪəsnəs
AM ˈbaʊn(t)iəsnəs
bountiful
BR ˈbaʊntɪf(ʊ)l
AM ˈbaʊn(t)ifəl
bountifully
BR ˈbaʊntɪfʊli,
ˈbaʊntɪfli
AM ˈbaʊn(t)if(ə)li
bountifulness
BR ˈbaʊntɪf(ʊ)lnəs
AM ˈbaʊn(t)ifəlnəs
bounty
BR ˈbaʊntˌli, -ɪz
AM ˈbaʊn(t)i, -z
bouquet
BR bʊˈkeɪ, bəʊˈkeɪ, -z
AM boʊˈkeɪ, buˈkeɪ, -z
bouquet garni
BR ˌbʊkeɪ gɑːˈniː
AM ˌbʊkeɪ gɑrˈni,
ˌbukeɪ +
bouquetin
BR ˈbuːkətɪn, -z
AM ˌbukəˈtɛn, -z
bouquets garnis
BR ˌbʊkeɪ gɑːˈniː
AM ˌbʊkeɪ gɑrˈni,
ˌbukeɪ +

Bourbon
French royal family
BR ˈbɔːb(ə)n, ˈbɔːbɒn,
ˈbʊəb(ə)n, ˈbʊəbɒn
AM ˈbʊrbən
bourbon
whisky
BR ˈbəːb(ə)n
AM ˈbərbən
bourdon
BR ˈbʊəd(ə)n,
ˈbɔːd(ə)n, -z
AM ˈbʊrdən, -z
bourgeois[1]
middle class
BR ˈbʊəʒwɑː(r),
ˈbɔːʒwɑː(r)
AM ˌbʊrˈʒwɑ
bourgeois[2]
print
BR bəːˈdʒɔɪs
AM bərˈdʒɔɪs
bourgeoisie
BR ˌbʊəʒwɑːˈziː,
ˌbɔːʒwɑːˈzi:
AM ˌbʊrʒwɑˈzi
Bourguiba
BR bʊəˈgiːbə(r),
bɔːˈgiːbə(r)
AM bʊrˈgibə
Bourke
BR bəːk
AM bɔ(ə)rk
bourn
BR bɔːn, -z
AM bɔ(ə)rn, -z
bourne
BR bɔːn, -z
AM bɔ(ə)rn, -z
Bournemouth
BR ˈbɔːnməθ
AM ˈbɔrnməθ
Bournville
BR ˈbɔːnvɪl, ˌbɔːnˈvɪl
AM ˈbɔrnˌvɪl
Bournvita
BR ˌbɔːnˈviːtə(r)
AM ˌbɔrnˈvidə
bourrée
BR ˈbʊreɪ, ˈbʊəreɪ, -z
AM bʊˈreɪ, -z
bourse
BR bʊəs, bɔːs, -ɪz
AM bʊ(ə)rs, -əz
Bourton
BR ˈbɔːtn
AM ˈbɔrt(ə)n
boustrophedon
BR ˌbaʊstrəˈfiːdn,
ˌbuːstrəˈfiːdn
AM ˌbustrəˈfiˌdɑn,
ˌbustrəˈfidən
bout
BR baʊt, -s
AM baʊt, -s
boutique
BR buːˈtiːk, -s
AM buˈtik, -s

boutonnière
BR ˌbuːtɒnɪˈɛː(r),
ˌbuːtɒnˈjɛː(r), -z
AM ˌbuːtnˈɪ(ə)r, -z
Bouverie
BR ˈbuːvˈ(ə)ri
AM ˈbuvəri
Bouvet
BR ˈbuːveɪ
AM ˈbuˌveɪ
bouzouki
BR bʊˈzuːk|i, -ɪz
AM buˈzuki, bəˈzuki, -z
Bovary
BR ˈbəʊvˈ(ə)ri
AM ˈbouvəri
bovate
BR ˈbəʊveɪt, -s
AM ˈbouˌveɪt, -s
Bovey Tracy
BR ˌbʌvɪ ˈtreɪsi,
ˌbɒvɪ +
AM ˌbəvi ˈtreɪsi
bovid
BR ˈbəʊvɪd, -z
AM ˈbouvɪd, -z
bovine
BR ˈbəʊvʌɪn
AM ˈbouˌvaɪn
bovinely
BR ˈbəʊvʌɪnli
AM ˈbouˌvaɪnli
Bovingdon
BR ˈbɒvɪŋdən,
ˈbʌvɪŋdən
AM ˈbəvɪŋd(ə)n
Bovington
BR ˈbɒvɪŋt(ə)n
AM ˈbəvɪŋt(ə)n
Bovis
BR ˈbəʊvɪs
AM ˈbouvəs
Bovril®
BR ˈbɒvr(ɪ)l
AM ˈbavrəl
bovver
BR ˈbɒvə(r)
AM ˈbavər
Bow
BR bəʊ
AM bou
bow[1]
bend, submit
BR bau, -z, -ɪŋ, -d
AM bau, -z, -ɪŋ, -d
bow[2]
with violin, weapon,
knot
BR bəʊ, -z, -ɪŋ, -d
AM bou, -z, -ɪŋ, -d
Bowater
BR ˈbəʊˌwɔːtə(r)
AM ˈbouˌwɑdər,
ˈbouˌwɑdər
bow-compass
BR ˈbəʊˌkʌmpəs, -ɪz
AM ˈbouˌkʌmpəs, -əz

Bowden
BR ˈbaudn, ˈbəʊdn
AM ˈboudən, ˈbaudən
Bowdler
BR ˈbaudlə(r)
AM ˈbaudlər
bowdlerisation
BR ˌbaudlərʌɪˈzeɪʃn
AM ˌboudlərəˈzeɪʃən,
ˌboudləˌraɪˈzeɪʃən,
ˌbaudlərˈzeɪʃən,
ˌbaudləˌraɪˈzeɪʃən,
ˌbɒdlərəˈzeɪʃən,
ˌbɒdləˌraɪˈzeɪʃən,
ˌbɑdlərəˈzeɪʃən,
ˌbɑdləˌraɪˈzeɪʃən
bowdlerise
BR ˈbaudlərʌɪz, -ɪz, -ɪŋ,
-d
AM ˈboudləˌraɪz,
ˈbaudləˌraɪz,
ˈbɒdləˌraɪz,
ˈbɑdləˌraɪz, -ɪz, -ɪŋ, -d
bowdleriser
BR ˈbaudlərʌɪzə(r), -z
AM ˈboudləˌraɪzər,
ˈbaudləˌraɪzər,
ˈbɒdləˌraɪzər,
ˈbɑdləˌraɪzər, -z
bowdlerism
BR ˈbaudlərɪz(ə)m, -z
AM ˈboudləˌrɪzəm,
ˈbaudləˌrɪzəm,
ˈbɒdləˌrɪz(ə)m,
ˈbɑdləˌrɪz(ə)m, -z
bowdlerization
BR ˌbaudlərʌɪˈzeɪʃn
AM ˌboudlərəˈzeɪʃən,
ˌboudləˌraɪˈzeɪʃən,
ˌbaudlərəˈzeɪʃən,
ˌbaudləˌraɪˈzeɪʃən,
ˌbɒdlərəˈzeɪʃən,
ˌbɒdləˌraɪˈzeɪʃən,
ˌbɑdlərəˈzeɪʃən,
ˌbɑdləˌraɪˈzeɪʃən
bowdlerize
BR ˈbaudlərʌɪz, -ɪz, -ɪŋ,
-d
AM ˈboudləˌraɪz,
ˈbaudləˌraɪz,
ˈbɒdləˌraɪz,
ˈbɑdləˌraɪz, -ɪz, -ɪŋ, -d
bowdlerizer
BR ˈbaudlərʌɪzə(r), -z
AM ˈboudləˌraɪzər,
ˈbaudləˌraɪzər,
ˈbɒdləˌraɪzər,
ˈbɑdləˌraɪzər, -z
bowel
BR ˈbau(ə)l, -z
AM ˈbau(ə)l, -z
Bowen
BR ˈbəʊɪn
AM ˈbouən
bower
BR ˈbauə(r), -z
AM ˈbau(ə)r, -z

bowerbird
BR ˈbauəbəːd, -z
AM ˈbauərˌbərd, -z
Bowers
BR ˈbauəz
AM ˈbau(ə)rz
bowery
BR ˈbauər|i, -ɪz
AM ˈbau(ə)ri, -z
Bowes
BR bəʊz
AM bouz
bowfin
BR ˈbəʊfɪn, -z
AM ˈbouˌfɪn, -z
bowhead
BR ˈbəʊhed, -z
AM ˈbouˌ(h)ɛd, -z
bowie
BR ˈbau|i, ˈbəʊ|i, -ɪz
AM ˈboui, ˈbui, -z
bowie knife
BR ˈbəʊi naɪf, ˈbuːi +
AM ˈbui ˌnaɪf, ˈboui +
bowie knives
BR ˈbəʊi naɪvz, ˈbuːi +
AM ˈbui ˌnaɪvz, ˈboui +
Bowker
BR ˈbaukə(r)
AM ˈbaukər
bowl
BR bəʊl, -z, -ɪŋ, -d
AM boul, -z, -ɪŋ, -d
Bowlby
BR ˈbəʊlbi
AM ˈboulbi
bowler
BR ˈbəʊlə(r), -z
AM ˈboulər, -z
Bowles
BR bəʊlz
AM boulz
bowlful
BR ˈbəʊlfʊl, -z
AM ˈboulˌfʊl, -z
bowline
BR ˈbəʊlɪn, -z
AM ˈboulən, -z
Bowman
BR ˈbəʊmən
AM ˈboumən
bowman[1]
archer
BR ˈbəʊmən
AM ˈboumən
bowman[2]
on a boat
BR ˈbaumən
AM ˈbaumən
bowmen[1]
archers
BR ˈbəʊmən
AM ˈboumən
bowmen[2]
on a boat
BR ˈbaumən
AM ˈbaumən

Bowness
BR bəʊˈnɛs
AM ˈbounəs
Bowring
BR ˈbauərɪŋ
AM ˈbaurɪŋ, ˈbourɪŋ
bowsaw
BR ˈbəʊsɔː(r), -z
AM ˈbouˌsɔ, ˈbouˌsɑ, -z
bowser®
BR ˈbauzə(r), -z
AM ˈbauzər, -z
bowshot
BR ˈbəʊʃɒt, -s
AM ˈbouˌʃɑt, -s
bowsprit
BR ˈbəʊsprɪt, -s
AM ˈbauˌsprɪt,
ˈbouˌsprɪt, -s
bowstring
BR ˈbəʊstrɪŋ, -z
AM ˈbouˌstrɪŋ, -z
bow-wow[1]
a dog
BR ˈbauwau, -z
AM ˈbauˌwau, -z
bow-wow[2]
imitating a dog's
bark
BR ˌbauˈwau, -z
AM ˌbauˈwau, -z
bowyang
BR ˈbəʊjaŋ, -z
AM ˈbouˌjæŋ, -z
bowyer
BR ˈbəʊjə(r), -z
AM ˈboujər, -z
box
BR bɒks, -ɪz, -ɪŋ, -t
AM baks, -əz, -ɪŋ, -t
boxcalf
BR ˈbɒkskɑːf
AM ˈbaksˌkæ|f, -vz
boxcar
BR ˈbɒkskɑː(r), -z
AM ˈbaksˌkɑr, -z
boxer
BR ˈbɒksə(r), -z
AM ˈbaksər, -z
boxful
BR ˈbɒksfʊl, -z
AM ˈbaksˌfʊl, -z
boxroom
BR ˈbɒksruːm,
ˈbɒksrʊm, -z
AM ˈbaksˌrum,
ˈbaksˌrʊm, -z
boxwood
BR ˈbɒkswʊd
AM ˈbaksˌwʊd
boxy
BR ˈbɒks|i, -ɪə(r), -ɪɪst
AM ˈbaksi, -ər, -ɪst
boy
BR bɔɪ, -z
AM bɔɪ, -z

boyar
BR ˈbɔɪɑː(r), ˈbəʊjɑː(r),
bəʊˈjɑː(r), -z
AM bouˈjɑr, -z
Boyce
BR bɔɪs
AM bɔɪs
boycott
BR ˈbɔɪkɒt, -s, -ɪŋ, -ɪd
AM ˈbɔɪˌkɑ|t, -ts, -dɪŋ, -dəd
Boyd
BR bɔɪd
AM bɔɪd
Boyer
BR ˈbɔɪə(r)
AM ˈbɔɪər
boyfriend
BR ˈbɔɪfrɛnd, -z
AM ˈbɔɪˌfrɛnd, -z
boyhood
BR ˈbɔɪhʊd, -z
AM ˈbɔɪˌ(h)ʊd, -z
boyish
BR ˈbɔɪɪʃ
AM ˈbɔɪɪʃ
boyishly
BR ˈbɔɪɪʃli
AM ˈbɔɪɪʃli
boyishness
BR ˈbɔɪɪʃnɪs
AM ˈbɔɪɪʃnɪs
Boyle
BR bɔɪl
AM ˈbɔɪ(ə)l
Boyne
BR bɔɪn
AM bɔɪn
boyo
BR ˈbɔɪəʊ, -z
AM ˈbɔɪoʊ, -z
boysenberry
BR ˈbɔɪzn̩ˌbɛr|i, -ɪz
AM ˈbɔɪzənˌbɛri, -z
Boyson
BR ˈbɔɪsn
AM ˈbɔɪsən
Boz
BR bɒz
AM bɑz
bozo
BR ˈbəʊzəʊ, -z
AM ˈboʊˌzoʊ, -z
B.Phil.
BR ˌbiːˈfɪl, -z
AM ˌbiˈfɪl, -z
bra
BR brɑː(r), -z
AM brɑ, -z
braai
BR brɑɪ, -z, -ɪŋ, -d
AM brɑɪ, -z, -ɪŋ, -d
Brabant
BR brəˈbant
AM brəˈbænt
DU ˈbrɑːbant
FR bʀɑbɑ̃

Brabazon
BR ˈbrabəz(ə)n
AM ˈbræbəˌzɑn
Brabham
BR ˈbrabəm
AM ˈbrɑbəm
Brabin
BR ˈbreɪbɪn
AM ˈbreɪbɪn
Brabourne
BR ˈbreɪbɔːn,
ˈbreɪb(ə)n
AM ˈbreɪˌbərn
brace
BR breɪs, -ɪz, -ɪŋ, -t
AM breɪs, -ɪz, -ɪŋ, -t
Bracegirdle
BR ˈbreɪsˌgəːdl
AM ˈbreɪsˌgərdəl
bracelet
BR ˈbreɪslɪt, -s
AM ˈbreɪslət, -s
bracer
BR ˈbreɪsə(r), -z
AM ˈbreɪsər, -z
brach
BR bratʃ, -ɪz
AM brætʃ, -əz
brachial
BR ˈbreɪkɪəl
AM ˈbreɪkɪəl, ˈbrækɪəl
brachiate¹
adjective
BR ˈbreɪkɪeɪt, ˈbreɪkɪət
AM ˈbreɪkiˌeɪt,
ˈbreɪkiɪt
brachiate²
verb
BR ˈbreɪkɪeɪt, -s, -ɪŋ, -ɪd
AM ˈbreɪkiˌeɪ|t, -ts,
-dɪŋ, -dɪd
brachiation
BR ˌbreɪkɪˈeɪʃn
AM ˌbreɪkiˈeɪʃən
brachiator
BR ˈbreɪkɪeɪtə(r), -z
AM ˈbreɪkiˌeɪdər, -z
brachiopod
BR ˈbrakɪəpɒd,
ˈbreɪkɪəpɒd, -z
AM ˈbrækiəˌpɑd,
ˈbreɪkiəˌpɑd, -z
brachiosauri
BR ˌbrakɪə(ʊ)ˈsɔːrɑɪ
AM ˌbrækioʊˈsɔˌrɑɪ
brachiosaurus
BR ˌbrakɪəˈsɔːrəs, -ɪz
AM ˌbrækioʊˈsɔrəs, -əz
brachistochrone
BR brəˈkɪstəkrəʊn, -z
AM bræˈkɪstəˌkroʊn,
brəˈkɪstəˌkroʊn, -z
brachycephalic
BR ˌbrakɪsɪˈfalɪk,
ˌbrakɪkɛˈfalɪk
AM ˌbrækiˈsɛfəlɪk,
ˌbrækəˈsɛfəlɪk

brachycephalous
BR ˌbrakɪˈsɛfələs,
ˌbrakɪˈsɛfləs,
ˌbrakɪˈkɛfələs,
ˌbrakɪˈkɛfləs
AM ˌbræki ˈsɛfələs,
ˌbrækəˈsɛfələs
brachycephaly
BR ˌbrakɪˈsɛfəli,
ˌbrakɪˈsɛfli,
ˌbrakɪˈkɛfəli,
ˌbrakɪˈkɛfli
AM ˌbræki ˈsɛfəli,
ˌbrækəˈsɛfəli
brachylogy
BR brəˈkɪlədʒi, -z
AM brəˈkɪlədʒi,
brəˈkɪlədʒi, -z
bracing
BR ˈbreɪsɪŋ
AM ˈbreɪsɪŋ
bracingness
BR ˈbreɪsɪŋnɪs
AM ˈbreɪsɪŋnɪs
brack
BR brak, -s
AM bræk, -s
bracken
BR ˈbrak(ə)n
AM ˈbrækən
Brackenbury
BR ˈbrak(ə)nb(ə)ri
AM ˈbrækənˌbɛri,
ˈbrækənbəri
bracket
BR ˈbrak|ɪt, -ɪts, -ɪtɪŋ,
-ɪtɪd
AM ˈbræk|ət, -əts,
-ədɪŋ, -ədəd
brackish
BR ˈbrakɪʃ
AM ˈbrækɪʃ
brackishness
BR ˈbrakɪʃnɪs
AM ˈbrækɪʃnɪs
Bracknell
BR ˈbraknl
AM ˈbræknəl
braconid
BR ˈbrakənɪd, -z
AM ˈbrækəˌnɪd, -z
bract
BR brakt, -s
AM bræk|(t), -(t)s
bracteal
BR ˈbraktɪəl
AM ˈbræktɪəl
bracteate
BR ˈbraktɪət, -s
AM ˈbræktiɪt,
ˈbræktiˌeɪt, -s
brad
BR brad, -z
AM bræd, -z
bradawl
BR ˈbradɔːl, -z
AM ˈbrædˌɔl, ˈbrædˌɑl,
-z

Bradbury
BR ˈbradb(ə)ri
AM ˈbrædˌbɛri,
ˈbrædbəri
Braden
BR ˈbreɪdn
AM ˈbreɪdən
Bradford
BR ˈbradfəd
AM ˈbrædfərd
Bradley
BR ˈbradli
AM ˈbrædli
Bradman
BR ˈbradmən
AM ˈbrædmən
Bradshaw
BR ˈbradʃɔː(r), -z
AM ˈbrædˌʃɔ, ˈbrædˌʃɑ,
-z
Bradwell
BR ˈbradw(ɛ)l
AM ˈbrædˌwɛl
Brady
BR ˈbreɪdi
AM ˈbreɪdi
bradycardia
BR ˌbradɪˈkɑːdɪə(r)
AM ˌbrædəˈkɑrdɪə
bradykinin
BR ˌbradɪˈkʌɪnɪn
AM ˌbrædiˈkaɪnɪn
bradyseism
BR ˈbradɪsʌɪz(ə)m
AM ˈbrædəsɛˌɪzəm
brae
BR breɪ, -z
AM breɪ, -z
Braemar
BR ˌbreɪˈmɑː(r)
AM ˌbreɪˈmɑr
brag
BR brag, -z, -ɪŋ, -d
AM bræg, -z, -ɪŋ, -d
Braga
BR ˈbrɑːgə(r)
AM ˈbrɑgə
Braganza
BR brəˈganzə(r)
AM brəˈgɑnzə
Bragg
BR brag
AM bræg
braggadocio
BR ˌbragəˈdəʊtʃɪəʊ
AM ˌbrægəˈdoʊʃioʊ
braggart
BR ˈbragət, -s
AM ˈbrægərt, -s
bragger
BR ˈbragə(r), -z
AM ˈbrægər, -z
braggingly
BR ˈbragɪŋli
AM ˈbrægɪŋli
Brahe
BR ˈbrɑːhə(r), ˈbrɑːhi

AM 'brɑˌhi
DAN 'brɑːa
Brahma
BR 'brɑːmə(r), -z
AM 'brɑmə, -z
Brahman
BR 'brɑːmən, -z
AM 'brɑmən, -z
Brahmana
BR 'brɑːmənə(r)
AM 'brɑmənə
Brahmanic
BR brɑːˈmɑnɪk
AM brɑˈmænɪk
Brahmanical
BR brɑːˈmɑnɪkl
AM brɑˈmænəkəl
Brahmanism
BR 'brɑːmənɪz(ə)m
AM 'brɑməˌnɪzəm
Brahmaputra
BR ˌbrɑːməˈpuːtrə(r)
AM ˌbrɑməˈputrə
Brahmin
BR 'brɑːmɪn, -z
AM 'brɑmən, -z
Brahminism
BR 'brɑːmɪnɪz(ə)m
AM 'brɑməˌnɪzəm
Brahms
BR brɑːmz
AM brɑmz
braid
BR breɪd, -z, -ɪŋ, -ɪd
AM breɪd, -z, -ɪŋ, -ɪd
braider
BR 'breɪdə(r), -z
AM 'breɪdər, -z
brail
BR breɪl, -z
AM breɪl, -z
Braille
BR breɪl
AM breɪl
brain
BR breɪn, -z, -ɪŋ, -d
AM breɪn, -z, -ɪŋ, -d
brainbox
BR 'breɪnbɒks, -ɪz
AM 'breɪnˌbɑks, -əz
brainchild
BR 'breɪntʃaɪld
AM 'breɪnˌtʃaɪld
Braine
BR breɪn
AM breɪn
brainfag
BR 'breɪnfag
AM 'breɪnˌfæg
braininess
BR 'breɪnɪnɪs
AM 'breɪnɪnɪs
brainless
BR 'breɪnlɪs
AM 'breɪnlɪs
brainlessly
BR 'breɪnlɪsli

AM 'breɪnlɪsli
brainlessness
BR 'breɪnlɪsnɪs
AM 'breɪnlɪsnɪs
brainpan
BR 'breɪnpan, -z
AM 'breɪnˌpæn, -z
brainpower
BR 'breɪnˌpaʊə(r)
AM 'breɪnˌpaʊər
brainsick
BR 'breɪnsɪk
AM 'breɪnˌsɪk
brainstem
BR 'breɪnstɛm, -z
AM 'breɪnˌstɛm, -z
brainstorm
BR 'breɪnstɔːm, -z, -ɪŋ,
-d
AM 'breɪnˌstɔ(ə)rm, -z,
-ɪŋ, -d
Braintree
BR 'breɪntriː
AM 'breɪnˌtri
brainwash
BR 'breɪnwɒʃ, -ɪz, -ɪŋ, -t
AM 'breɪnˌwɒʃ,
'breɪnˌwɑʃ, -əz, -ɪŋ, -t
brainwave
BR 'breɪnweɪv, -z
AM 'breɪnˌweɪv, -z
brainwork
BR 'breɪnwəːk
AM 'breɪnˌwərk
brainy
BR 'breɪn|i, -ɪə(r), -ɪɪst
AM 'breɪni, -ər, -ɪst
braise
BR breɪz, -ɪz, -ɪŋ, -d
AM breɪz, -ɪz, -ɪŋ, -d
Braithwaite
BR 'breɪθweɪt
AM 'breɪθˌweɪt
brake
BR breɪk, -s, -ɪŋ, -t
AM breɪk, -s, -ɪŋ, -t
brakeless
BR 'breɪklɪs
AM 'breɪklɪs
brakeman
BR 'breɪkmən
AM 'breɪkmən
brakemen
BR 'breɪkmən
AM 'breɪkmən
brakesman
BR 'breɪksmən
AM 'breɪksmən
brakesmen
BR 'breɪksmən
AM 'breɪksmən
brakevan
BR 'breɪkvan, -z
AM 'breɪkˌvæn, -z
braless
BR 'brɑːləs
AM 'brɑləs

Bram
BR bram
AM bræm
Bramah
BR 'brɑːmə(r)
AM 'brɑmə
Bramante
BR brəˈmanti
AM brɑˈmɑn(t)i
bramble
BR 'brambl, -z
AM 'bræmbəl, -z
brambling
BR 'bramblɪŋ, -z
AM 'bræmblɪŋ, -z
brambly
BR 'brambli
AM 'bræmbli
Bramhope
BR 'bramhəʊp
AM 'bræmˌ(h)oʊp
Bramley
BR 'bramli, -z
AM 'bræmli, -z
Brampton
BR 'bram(p)tən
AM 'bræmt(ə)n
Bramwell
BR 'bramw(ɛ)l
AM 'bræmˌwɛl
bran
BR bran
AM bræn
Branagh
BR 'branə(r)
AM 'brænə
branch
BR brɑːn(t)ʃ, bran(t)ʃ,
-ɪz, -ɪŋ, -t
AM bræn(t)ʃ, -əz, -ɪŋ, -t
branchia
BR 'braŋkɪə(r)
AM 'braŋkɪə, 'bræŋkɪə
branchiae
BR 'braŋkiː
AM 'braŋki,i,
'bræŋki,i, 'braŋki,aɪ,
'bræŋki,aɪ
branchial
BR 'braŋkɪəl
AM 'braŋkɪəl,
'bræŋkɪəl
branchiate
BR 'braŋkɪeɪt,
'braŋkɪət
AM 'braŋkiːt,
'braŋki,ert,
'bræŋkiːt,
'bræŋki,ert
branchlet
BR 'brɑːn(t)ʃlɪt,
'bran(t)ʃlɪt, -s
AM 'bræn(t)ʃlət, -s
branchlike
BR 'brɑːn(t)ʃlaɪk,
'bran(t)ʃlaɪk
AM 'bræn(t)ʃˌlaɪk

branchy
BR 'brɑːn(t)ʃi,
'bran(t)ʃi
AM 'bræn(t)ʃi
brand
BR brand, -z, -ɪŋ, -ɪd
AM brænd, -z, -ɪŋ, -əd
Brandeis
BR 'brandʌɪs
AM 'brænˌdaɪs
Brandenburg
BR 'brand(ə)nbəːg
AM 'brændənˌbərg
brander
BR 'brandə(r), -z
AM 'brændər, -z
brandish
BR 'brand|ɪʃ, -ɪʃɪz,
-ɪʃɪŋ, -ɪʃt
AM 'brændɪʃ, -ɪz, -ɪŋ, -t
brandisher
BR 'brandɪʃə(r), -z
AM 'brændɪʃər, -z
brandling
BR 'brandlɪŋ, -z
AM 'bræn(d)lɪŋ, -z
Brando
BR 'brandəʊ
AM 'brændoʊ
Brandon
BR 'brandən
AM 'brændən
Brandreth
BR 'brandrɪθ,
'brandrɛθ
AM 'brændrəθ
Brands Hatch
BR ˌbran(d)z 'hatʃ
AM ˌbræn(d)z 'hætʃ
Brandt
BR brant
AM brænt
brandy
BR 'brand|i, -ɪz
AM 'brændi, -z
Brangwyn
BR 'braŋgwɪn
AM 'bræŋgwən
Braniff
BR 'branɪf
AM 'brænəf
Branigan
BR 'branɪg(ə)n
AM 'brænəgən
brank-ursine
BR ˌbraŋk'əːsʌɪn
AM ˌbræŋk'ərˌsaɪn
Brannigan
BR 'branɪg(ə)n
AM 'brænəgən
Branson
BR 'bransn
AM 'brænsən
Branston
BR 'branst(ə)n
AM 'brænstən

brant
BR brant
AM brænt
Braque
BR brɑːk, brak
AM brɑk
Brasenose
BR ˈbreɪznəʊz
AM ˈbreɪzˌnoʊz
brash
BR braʃ, -ə(r), -ɪst
AM bræʃ, -ər, -əst
Brasher
BR ˈbreɪʃə(r)
AM ˈbræʃər
brashly
BR ˈbraʃli
AM ˈbræʃli
brashness
BR ˈbraʃnəs
AM ˈbræʃnəs
brasier
BR ˈbreɪzɪə(r), ˈbreɪʒə(r), -z
AM ˈbreɪʒər, ˈbreɪˌziər, -z
Brasília
BR brəˈzɪlɪə(r)
AM brəˈzɪljə, brəˈzɪliə
brass
BR brɑːs, bras, -ɪz, -ɪŋ, -t
AM bræs, -əz, -ɪŋ, -t
brassage
BR ˈbrasɪdʒ
AM brəˈsɑʒ, ˈbræsɪdʒ
brassard
BR ˈbrasɑːd, -z
AM ˈbræˌsard, -z
brassbound
BR ˌbrɑːsˈbaʊnd, ˌbrasˈbaʊnd
AM ˈbræsˌbaʊnd
brasserie
BR ˈbras(ə)rˈli, -ɪz
AM ˌbræsəˈri, -z
FR brasʀi
Brassey
BR ˈbrasi
AM ˈbræsi
brassica
BR ˈbrasɪkə(r), -z
AM ˈbræsəkə, -z
brassie
BR ˈbrasi, -z
AM ˈbræsi, -z
brassiere
BR ˈbrazɪə(r), -z
AM brəˈzɪ(ə)r, -z
brassily
BR ˈbrɑːsɪli, ˈbrasɪli
AM ˈbræsəli
brassiness
BR ˈbrɑːsɪnɪs, ˈbrasɪnɪs
AM ˈbræsɪnɪs

Brasso®
BR ˈbrɑːsəʊ, ˈbrasəʊ
AM ˈbræsoʊ
brassware
BR ˈbrɑːswɛː(r), ˈbraswɛː(r)
AM ˈbræsˌwɛ(ə)r
brassy
BR ˈbrɑːsi, ˈbrasi
AM ˈbræsi
brat
BR brat, -s
AM bræt, -s
Bratislava
BR ˌbratɪˈslɑːvə(r)
AM ˌbrɑdəˈslavə
cz ˈbrʌtjslʌvʌ
brattice
BR ˈbrat|ɪs, -ɪsɪz
AM ˈbrædəs, -əz
bratty
BR ˈbrati
AM ˈbrædi
bratwurst
BR ˈbratwəːst, ˈbratvʊəst
AM ˈbrɑtˌwərst
Braun
BR brɔːn, braʊn
AM braʊn
Braunschweig
BR ˈbraʊnʃwʌɪg
AM ˈbraʊnˌʃwaɪg
braunschweiger
BR ˈbraʊnˌʃwʌɪgə(r)
AM ˈbraʊnˌʃwaɪgər
bravado
BR brəˈvɑːdəʊ
AM brəˈvɑˌdoʊ
brave
BR breɪv, -z, -ɪŋ, -d, -ə(r), -ɪst
AM breɪv, -z, -ɪŋ, -d, -ər, -ɪst
bravely
BR ˈbreɪvli
AM ˈbreɪvli
braveness
BR ˈbreɪvnɪs
AM ˈbreɪvnɪs
Bravington
BR ˈbravɪŋt(ə)n
AM ˈbreɪvɪŋt(ə)n
bravo! [1]
hooray!
BR (ˌ)brɑːˈvəʊ, -z
AM ˌbrɑˈvoʊ, -z
bravo [2]
letter B
BR ˈbrɑːvəʊ
AM ˈbravoʊ
bravura
BR brəˈvjʊərə(r), brəˈvjɔːrə(r)
AM brəˈv(j)ʊrə
braw
BR brɔː(r)
AM brɔ

Brawdy
BR ˈbrɔːdi
AM ˈbrɑdi, ˈbrɑdi
brawl
BR brɔːl, -z, -ɪŋ, -d
AM brɔl, brɑl, -z, -ɪŋ, -d
brawler
BR ˈbrɔːlə(r), -z
AM ˈbrɔlər, ˈbrɑlər, -z
brawn
BR brɔːn
AM brɔn, brɑn
brawniness
BR ˈbrɔːnɪnɪs
AM ˈbrɑnɪnɪs, ˈbrɑnɪnɪs
brawny
BR ˈbrɔːn|i, -ɪə(r), -ɪɪst
AM ˈbrɑni, ˈbrɑni, -ər, -ɪst
bray
BR breɪ, -z, -ɪŋ, -d
AM breɪ, -z, -ɪŋ, -d
braze
BR breɪz, -ɪz, -ɪŋ, -d
AM breɪz, -ɪz, -ɪŋ, -d
brazen
BR ˈbreɪzn
AM ˈbreɪzən
brazenly
BR ˈbreɪznli
AM ˈbreɪzənli
brazenness
BR ˈbreɪznnəs
AM ˈbreɪzə(n)nəs
brazer
BR ˈbreɪzə(r), -z
AM ˈbreɪzər, -z
brazier
BR ˈbreɪzɪə(r), ˈbreɪʒə(r), -z
AM ˈbreɪʒər, ˈbreɪˌziər, -z
braziery
BR ˈbreɪzɪəri, ˈbreɪʒəri, -z
AM ˈbreɪʒəri, ˈbreɪˌziəri, -z
Brazil
BR brəˈzɪl
AM brəˈzɪl
Brazilian
BR brəˈzɪlɪən, -z
AM brəˈzɪljən, brəˈzɪliən, -z
Brazzaville
BR ˈbrazəvɪl, ˈbrɑːzəvɪl
AM ˈbrɑzəˌvɪl
breach
BR briːtʃ, -ɪz, -ɪŋ, -t
AM britʃ, -ɪz, -ɪŋ, -t
bread
BR brɛd, -z, -ɪŋ, -ɪd
AM brɛd, -z, -ɪŋ, -əd
Breadalbane
BR brɪˈdɔːlb(ɪ)n, brɪˈdalb(ɪ)n

Brawdy
AM ˈbrɛdəlˌbeɪn
breadbasket
BR ˈbrɛdˌbɑːskɪt, ˈbrɛdˌbaskɪt, -s
AM ˈbrɛdˌbæskət, -s
breadboard
BR ˈbrɛdbɔːd, -z
AM ˈbrɛdˌbɔ(ə)rd, -z
breadbox
BR ˈbrɛdbɒks, -ɪz
AM ˈbrɛdˌbaks, -əz
breadcrumb
BR ˈbrɛdkrʌm, -z
AM ˈbrɛdˌkrəm, -z
breadfruit
BR ˈbrɛdfruːt, -s
AM ˈbrɛdˌfrut, -s
breadline
BR ˈbrɛdlʌɪn
AM ˈbrɛdˌlaɪn
breadth
BR brɛdθ, brɛtθ
AM brɛdθ, brɛtθ
breadthways
BR ˈbrɛdθweɪz, ˈbrɛtθweɪz
AM ˈbrɛdθˌweɪz, ˈbrɛtθˌweɪz
breadthwise
BR ˈbrɛdθwʌɪz, ˈbrɛtθwʌɪz
AM ˈbrɛdθˌwaɪz, ˈbrɛtθˌwaɪz
breadwinner
BR ˈbrɛdˌwɪnə(r), -z
AM ˈbrɛdˌwɪnər, -z
break
BR breɪk, -s, -ɪŋ
AM breɪk, -s, -ɪŋ
breakable
BR ˈbreɪkəbl, -z
AM ˈbreɪkəbəl, -z
breakage
BR ˈbreɪk|ɪdʒ, -ɪdʒɪz
AM ˈbreɪkɪdʒ, -ɪz
breakaway
BR ˈbreɪkəweɪ, -z
AM ˈbreɪkəˌweɪ, -z
breakdown
BR ˈbreɪkdaʊn, -z
AM ˈbreɪkˌdaʊn, -z
breaker
BR ˈbreɪkə(r), -z
AM ˈbreɪkər, -z
breakfast
BR ˈbrɛkfəst, -s, -ɪŋ, -ɪd
AM ˈbrɛkfəst, -s, -ɪŋ, -əd
breakfaster
BR ˈbrɛkfəstə(r), -z
AM ˈbrɛkfəstər, -z
breakneck
BR ˈbreɪknɛk
AM ˈbreɪkˌnɛk
breakout
BR ˈbreɪkaʊt, -s
AM ˈbreɪkˌaʊt, -s

breakpoint
BR ˈbreɪkpɔɪnt, -s
AM ˈbreɪkˌpɔɪnt, -s
Breakspear
BR ˈbreɪkspɪə(r)
AM ˈbreɪkˌspɪ(ə)r
breakthrough
BR ˈbreɪkθruː, -z
AM ˈbreɪkˌθru, -z
breakup
BR ˈbreɪkʌp, -s
AM ˈbreɪkˌəp, -s
breakwater
BR ˈbreɪkˌwɔːtə(r), -z
AM ˈbreɪkˌwɔdər,
ˈbreɪkˌwɑdər, -z
bream
BR briːm
AM brim
Brearley
BR ˈbrɪəli
AM ˈbrɪrli
breast
BR brɛst, -s, -ɪŋ, -ɪd
AM brɛst, -s, -ɪŋ, -əd
breastbone
BR ˈbrɛs(t)bəʊn, -z
AM ˈbrɛs(t)ˌboʊn, -z
breastfed
BR ˈbrɛs(t)fɛd
AM ˈbrɛs(t)ˌfɛd
breastfeed
BR ˈbrɛs(t)fiːd, -z, -ɪŋ
AM ˈbrɛs(t)ˌfid, -z, -ɪŋ
breastless
BR ˈbrɛstləs
AM ˈbrɛs(t)ləs
breastplate
BR ˈbrɛs(t)pleɪt, -s
AM ˈbrɛs(t)ˌpleɪt, -s
breaststroke
BR ˈbrɛs(t)strəʊk
AM ˈbrɛs(t)ˌstroʊk
breastsummer
BR ˈbrɛs(t)ˌsʌmə(r), -z
AM ˈbrɛs(t)ˌsəmər, -z
breastwork
BR ˈbrɛstwəːk, -s
AM ˈbrɛs(t)ˌwərk, -s
breath
BR brɛθ, -s
AM brɛθ, -s
breathable
BR ˈbriːðəbl
AM ˈbriðəbəl
breathalyse
BR ˈbrɛθəlaɪz,
ˈbrɛθˌlaɪz, -ɪz, -ɪŋ, -d
AM ˈbrɛθəˌlaɪz, -ɪz, -ɪŋ,
-d
breathalyze
BR ˈbrɛθəlaɪz,
ˈbrɛθˌlaɪz, -ɪz, -ɪŋ, -d
AM ˈbrɛθəˌlaɪz, -ɪz, -ɪŋ,
-d

Breathalyzer®
BR ˈbrɛθəlaɪzə(r),
ˈbrɛθˌlaɪzə(r), -z
AM ˈbrɛθəˌlaɪzər, -z
breathe
BR briːð, -z, -ɪŋ, -d
AM brið, -z, -ɪŋ, -d
breather
BR ˈbriːðə(r), -z
AM ˈbriðər, -z
breathily
BR ˈbrɛθɪli
AM ˈbrɛθɪli
breathiness
BR ˈbrɛθɪnɪs
AM ˈbrɛθɪnɪs
breathless
BR ˈbrɛθləs
AM ˈbrɛθləs
breathlessly
BR ˈbrɛθləsli
AM ˈbrɛθləsli
breathlessness
BR ˈbrɛθləsnəs
AM ˈbrɛθləsnəs
breathtaking
BR ˈbrɛθˌteɪkɪŋ
AM ˈbrɛθˌteɪkɪŋ
breathtakingly
BR ˈbrɛθˌteɪkɪŋli
AM ˈbrɛθˌteɪkɪŋli
breathy
BR ˈbrɛθ|i, -ɪə(r), -ɪɪst
AM ˈbrɛθi, -ər, -ɪst
breccia
BR ˈbrɛtʃ(ɪ)ə(r), -z
AM ˈbrɛ(t)ʃ(i)ə, -z
brecciate
BR ˈbrɛtʃɪeɪt, -s, -ɪŋ, -ɪd
AM ˈbrɛ(t)ʃ(i)ˌeɪ|t, -ts,
-dɪŋ, -dɪd
brecciation
BR ˌbrɛtʃɪˈeɪʃn
AM ˌbrɛ(t)ʃiˈeɪʃən
Brechin
BR ˈbriːkɪn, ˈbriːxɪn
AM ˈbrikɪn
Brecht
BR brɛxt, brɛkt
AM brɛkt
Brechtian
BR ˈbrɛxtɪən,
ˈbrɛktɪən
AM ˈbrɛktiən
Breckenridge
BR ˈbrɛk(ə)nrɪdʒ
AM ˈbrɛkənˌrɪdʒ
Breckland
BR ˈbrɛklənd
AM ˈbrɛklənd
Brecknock
BR ˈbrɛknɒk
AM ˈbrɛkˌnɑk
Brecknockshire
BR ˈbrɛknəkʃ(ɪ)ə(r)
AM ˈbrɛkˌnɑkˌʃɪ(ə)r

Brecon
BR ˈbrɛkn
AM ˈbrɛkən
Breconshire
BR ˈbrɛknʃ(ɪ)ə(r)
AM ˈbrɛkənˌʃɪ(ə)r
bred
BR brɛd
AM brɛd
Breda
BR ˈbriːdə(r),
ˈbreɪdə(r)
AM ˈbreɪdə
DU breːˈdɑ
Bredon
BR ˈbriːdn
AM ˈbridn
breech
of gun
BR briːtʃ, -ɪz, -ɪŋ, -t
AM britʃ, -ɪz, -ɪŋ, -t
breeches
trousers
BR ˈbrɪtʃɪz, ˈbriːtʃɪz
AM ˈbrɪtʃɪz, ˈbritʃɪz
breeches-buoy
BR ˌbrɪtʃɪzˈbɔɪ,
ˈbriːtʃɪzbɔɪ, -z
AM ˈbrɪtʃɪzˌbɔɪ,
ˈbritʃɪzˌbui, -z
breed
BR briːd, -z, -ɪŋ
AM brid, -z, -ɪŋ
breeder
BR ˈbriːdə(r), -z
AM ˈbridər, -z
breeks
BR briːks
AM briks
Breen
BR briːn
AM brin
breeze
BR briːz, -ɪz, -ɪŋ, -d
AM briz, -ɪz, -ɪŋ, -d
breezeblock
BR ˈbriːzblɒk, -s
AM ˈbrizˌblɑk, -s
breezeless
BR ˈbriːzlɪs
AM ˈbrizlɪs
breezeway
BR ˈbriːzweɪ, -z
AM ˈbrizˌweɪ, -z
breezily
BR ˈbriːzɪli
AM ˈbrizɪli
breeziness
BR ˈbriːzɪnɪs
AM ˈbrizɪnɪs
breezy
BR ˈbriːz|i, -ɪə(r), -ɪɪst
AM ˈbrizi, -ər, -ɪst
Bremen
BR ˈbreɪmən, ˈbrɛmən
AM ˈbreɪmən, ˈbrɛmən

Bremner
BR ˈbrɛmnə(r)
AM ˈbrɛmnər
bremsstrahlung
BR ˈbrɛmzˌʃtrɑːlʊŋ
AM ˈbrɛmˌʃtrɑləŋ
Bren
BR brɛn
AM brɛn
Brenda
BR ˈbrɛndə(r)
AM ˈbrɛndə
Brendan
BR ˈbrɛnd(ə)n
AM ˈbrɛndən
Brendel
BR ˈbrɛndl
AM ˈbrɛndəl
Brennan
BR ˈbrɛnən
AM ˈbrɛnən
Brenner Pass
BR ˌbrɛnəˈpɑːs, + ˈpas
AM ˈbrɛnərˈpæs
brent
BR brɛnt
AM brɛnt
Brentwood
BR ˈbrɛntwʊd
AM ˈbrɛntˌwʊd
Breslau
BR ˈbrɛslaʊ
AM ˈbrɛˌslaʊ
Bresson
BR ˈbrɛsn
AM ˈbrɛsən
FR brɛsɔ̃
Brest
BR brɛst
AM brɛst
Brest-Litovsk
BR ˌbrɛstlɪˈtɒfsk
AM ˌbrɛstˈlɪtəfsk
brethren
BR ˈbrɛðr(ɪ)n
AM ˈbrɛð(ə)rən
Breton
BR ˈbrɛt(ə)n, ˈbrɛtɒn,
-z
AM ˈbrɛtn, -z
Brett
BR brɛt
AM brɛt
Bretton
BR ˈbrɛtn
AM ˈbrɛtn
Breughel
BR ˈbrɔɪgl
AM ˈbrɔɪgəl
breve
BR briːv, -z
AM briv, brɛv, -z
brevet
BR ˈbrɛv|ɪt, -ɪts, -ɪtɪŋ,
-ɪtɪd
AM brəˈvɛ|t, -ts, -dɪŋ,
-dəd

breviary
BR ˈbrɛvɪə‖i,
ˈbriːvɪər‖i, -ɪz
AM ˈbriv(j)əri,
ˈbriviˌɛri, -z
breviate
BR ˈbriːvɪət, -s
AM ˈbriviət, -s
brevity
BR ˈbrɛvɪti
AM ˈbrɛvədi
brew
BR bruː, -z, -ɪŋ, -d
AM bru, -z, -ɪŋ, -d
brewer
BR ˈbruːə(r), -z
AM ˈbruər, -z
brewery
BR ˈbruːər‖i, -ɪz
AM ˈbru(ə)ri, -z
Brewis
BR ˈbruːɪs
AM ˈbruɪs
brewster
BR ˈbruːstə(r), -z
AM ˈbrustər, -z
Brezel
BR ˈbrɛtsl, -z
AM ˈbrɛtsəl, -z
Brezhnev
BR ˈbrɛʒnɛv, ˈbrɛʒnɛf
AM ˈbrɛʒˌnɛv, ˈbrɛʒˌnɛf
Brian
BR ˈbraɪən
AM ˈbraɪən
Brian Ború
BR ˌbraɪən bəˈruː
AM ˌbraɪən bəˈru
briar
BR ˈbraɪə(r), -z
AM ˈbraɪ(ə)r, -z
Briard
BR brɪˈɑːd, -z
AM briˈard, -z
briarwood
BR ˈbraɪəwʊd
AM ˈbraɪ(ə)rˌwʊd
bribable
BR ˈbraɪbəbl
AM ˈbraɪbəbəl
bribe
BR braɪb, -z, -ɪŋ, -d
AM braɪb, -z, -ɪŋ, -d
briber
BR ˈbraɪbə(r), -z
AM ˈbraɪbər, -z
bribery
BR ˈbraɪb(ə)ri
AM ˈbraɪb(ə)ri
bric-à-brac
BR ˈbrɪkəbrak
AM ˈbrɪkəˌbræk
Brice
BR brʌɪs
AM braɪs
brick
BR brɪk, -s, -ɪŋ, -t

AM brɪk, -s, -ɪŋ, -t
brickbat
BR ˈbrɪkbat, -s
AM ˈbrɪkˌbæt, -s
brickdust
BR ˈbrɪkdʌst
AM ˈbrɪkˌdəst
brickfield
BR ˈbrɪkfiːld, -z
AM ˈbrɪkˌfild, -z
brickfielder
BR ˈbrɪkˌfiːldə(r), -z
AM ˈbrɪkˌfildər, -z
brickie
BR ˈbrɪk‖i, -ɪz
AM ˈbrɪki, -z
bricklayer
BR ˈbrɪkˌleɪə(r), -z
AM ˈbrɪkˌleɪ(ə)r, -z
bricklaying
BR ˈbrɪkˌleɪɪŋ
AM ˈbrɪkˌleɪɪŋ
brickmaker
BR ˈbrɪkˌmeɪkə(r), -z
AM ˈbrɪkˌmeɪkər, -z
brickmaking
BR ˈbrɪkˌmeɪkɪŋ
AM ˈbrɪkˌmeɪkɪŋ
brickwork
BR ˈbrɪkwəːk, -s
AM ˈbrɪkˌwərk, -s
bricky
BR ˈbrɪki
AM ˈbrɪki
brickyard
BR ˈbrɪkjɑːd, -z
AM ˈbrɪkˌjard, -z
bridal
BR ˈbraɪdl
AM ˈbraɪdəl
bridally
BR ˈbraɪdl̩i
AM ˈbraɪdl̩i
bride
BR braɪd, -z
AM braɪd, -z
bridegroom
BR ˈbraɪdgruːm, -z
AM ˈbraɪdˌgrum, -z
Brideshead
BR ˈbraɪdzhɛd
AM ˈbraɪdzˌ(h)ɛd
bridesmaid
BR ˈbraɪdzmeɪd, -z
AM ˈbraɪdzˌmeɪd, -z
bridesman
BR ˈbraɪdzmən
AM ˈbraɪdzmən
bridesmen
BR ˈbraɪdzmən
AM ˈbraɪdzmən
bridewell
BR ˈbraɪdw(ɛ)l, -z
AM ˈbraɪdˌwɛl,
ˈbraɪdwəl, -z
bridge
BR brɪdʒ, -ɪz, -ɪŋ, -d

AM brɪdʒ, -ɪz, -ɪŋ, -d
bridgeable
BR ˈbrɪdʒəbl
AM ˈbrɪdʒəbəl
bridgehead
BR ˈbrɪdʒhɛd, -z
AM ˈbrɪdʒˌ(h)ɛd, -z
Bridgeman
BR ˈbrɪdʒmən
AM ˈbrɪdʒmən
Bridgend
BR ˌbrɪdʒˈɛnd
AM ˌbrɪdʒˌɛnd
Bridgeport
BR ˈbrɪdʒpɔːt
AM ˈbrɪdʒˌpɔ(ə)rt
Bridger
BR ˈbrɪdʒə(r)
AM ˈbrɪdʒər
Bridges
BR ˈbrɪdʒɪz
AM ˈbrɪdʒɪz
Bridget
BR ˈbrɪdʒɪt
AM ˈbrɪdʒət
Bridgetown
BR ˈbrɪdʒtaʊn
AM ˈbrɪdʒˌtaʊn
Bridgewater
BR ˈbrɪdʒwɔːtə(r)
AM ˈbrɪdʒˌwɔdər,
ˈbrɪdʒˌwɑdər
bridgework
BR ˈbrɪdʒwəːk
AM ˈbrɪdʒˌwərk
Bridgman
BR ˈbrɪdʒmən
AM ˈbrɪdʒmən
Bridgnorth
BR ˈbrɪdʒnɔːθ
AM ˈbrɪdʒˌnorθ
Bridgwater
BR ˈbrɪdʒwɔːtə(r)
AM ˈbrɪdʒˌwɔdər,
ˈbrɪdʒˌwɑdər
bridle
BR ˈbraɪdl̩, -lz,
-l̩ɪŋ\-lɪŋ, -ld
AM ˈbraɪdl̩əl, -əlz,
-(ə)lɪŋ, -əld
bridleway
BR ˈbraɪdlweɪ, -z
AM ˈbraɪdl̩ˌweɪ, -z
Bridlington
BR ˈbrɪdlɪŋt(ə)n
AM ˈbrɪdlɪŋt(ə)n
bridoon
BR brɪˈduːn, -z
AM brəˈdun, -z
Bridport
BR ˈbrɪdpɔːt
AM ˈbrɪdˌpɔ(ə)rt
Brie
BR briː
AM bri

brief
BR briːf, -s, -ɪŋ, -t, -ə(r),
-ɪst
AM brif, -s, -ɪŋ, -t, -ər,
-ɪst
briefcase
BR ˈbriːfkeɪs, -ɪz
AM ˈbrifˌkeɪs, -ɪz
briefless
BR ˈbriːflɪs
AM ˈbriflɪs
briefly
BR ˈbriːfli
AM ˈbrifli
briefness
BR ˈbriːfnɪs
AM ˈbrifnɪs
brier
BR ˈbrʌɪə(r), -z
AM ˈbraɪ(ə)r, -z
Brierley
BR ˈbrʌɪəli, ˈbrɪəli
AM ˈbraɪ(ə)rli
Brierly
BR ˈbrʌɪəli, ˈbrɪəli
AM ˈbraɪ(ə)rli
Briers
BR ˈbrʌɪəz
AM ˈbraɪ(ə)rz
brierwood
BR ˈbrʌɪəwʊd, -z
AM ˈbraɪ(ə)rˌwʊd, -z
briery
BR ˈbrʌɪəri
AM ˈbraɪ(ə)ri
brig
BR brɪg, -z
AM brɪg, -z
brigade
BR brɪˈgeɪd, -z
AM brəˈgeɪd, -z
brigadier
BR ˌbrɪgəˈdɪə(r), -z
AM ˌbrɪgəˈdɪ(ə)r, -z
Brigadoon
BR ˌbrɪgəˈduːn
AM ˌbrɪgəˈdun
brigalow
BR ˈbrɪgələʊ, -z
AM ˈbrɪgəˌloʊ, -z
brigand
BR ˈbrɪg(ə)nd, -z
AM ˈbrɪg(ə)nd, -z
brigandage
BR ˈbrɪg(ə)ndɪdʒ
AM ˈbrɪg(ə)ndɪdʒ
brigandine
BR ˈbrɪg(ə)ndiːn, -z
AM ˈbrɪgənˌdin, -z
brigandish
BR ˈbrɪg(ə)ndɪʃ
AM ˈbrɪgəndɪʃ
brigandism
BR ˈbrɪg(ə)ndɪz(ə)m
AM ˈbrɪgənˌdɪzəm
brigandry
BR ˈbrɪg(ə)ndri

AM 'brɪgəndri
brigantine
BR 'brɪg(ə)ntiːn, -z
AM 'brɪgənˌtiːn, -z
Brigg
BR brɪg
AM brɪg
Briggs
BR brɪgz
AM brɪgz
Brigham
BR 'brɪgəm
AM 'brɪgəm
Brighouse
BR 'brɪghaʊs
AM 'brɪg,(h)aʊs
bright
BR brʌɪt, -ə(r), -ɪst
AM brʌɪ|t, -dər, -dɪst
brighten
BR 'brʌɪt|n, -nz,
-ɳɪŋ \-nɪŋ, -nd
AM 'braɪtn, -z, -ɪŋ, -d
brightish
BR 'brʌɪtɪʃ
AM 'braɪdɪʃ
Brightlingsea
BR 'brʌɪtlɪŋsiː
AM 'braɪtlɪŋˌsi
brightly
BR 'brʌɪtli
AM 'braɪtli
brightness
BR 'brʌɪtnɪs
AM 'braɪtnɪs
Brighton
BR 'brʌɪtn
AM 'braɪtn
brightwork
BR 'brʌɪtwəːk
AM 'braɪtˌwərk
Brigid
BR 'brɪdʒɪd
AM 'brɪdʒəd
Brigit
BR 'brɪdʒɪt
AM 'brɪdʒət
Brigitte
BR 'brɪʒɪt, brɪ'ʒiːt
AM 'brɪdʒət
brill
BR brɪl
AM brɪl
brilliance
BR 'brɪlj(ə)ns,
'brɪlɪəns
AM 'brɪljəns
brilliancy
BR 'brɪlj(ə)nsi,
'brɪlɪənsi
AM 'brɪljənsi
brilliant
BR 'brɪlj(ə)nt,
'brɪlɪənt, -s
AM 'brɪljənt, -s
brilliantine
BR 'brɪlj(ə)ntiːn

AM 'brɪljənˌtiːn
brilliantly
BR 'brɪlj(ə)ntli,
'brɪlɪəntli
AM 'brɪljən(t)li
brilliantness
BR 'brɪlj(ə)ntnəs,
'brɪlɪəntnəs
AM 'brɪljən(t)nɪs
Brillo®
BR 'brɪləʊ
AM 'brɪloʊ
brim
BR brɪm, -z, -ɪŋ, -d
AM brɪm, -z, -ɪŋ, -d
Brimble
BR 'brɪmbl
AM 'brɪmbəl
brimful
BR ˌbrɪm'fʊl, 'brɪmfʊl
AM ˌbrɪmˈfʊl
brimless
BR 'brɪmlɪs
AM 'brɪmlɪs
brimstone
BR 'brɪmstən,
'brɪmstəʊn
AM 'brɪmzˌtoʊn,
'brɪmˌstoʊn
brimstony
BR 'brɪmstəni,
'brɪmstəʊni
AM 'brɪmzˌtoʊni,
'brɪmˌstoʊni
Brindisi
BR 'brɪndɪzi
AM 'brɪndɪzi
brindle
BR 'brɪndl, -d
AM 'brɪndəl, -d
Brindley
BR 'brɪndli
AM 'brɪm(d)li
brine
BR brʌɪn
AM braɪn
bring
BR brɪŋ, -z, -ɪŋ
AM brɪŋ, -z, -ɪŋ
bringer
BR 'brɪŋə(r), -z
AM 'brɪŋər, -z
brininess
BR 'brʌɪnɪnɪs
AM 'braɪnɪnɪs
brinjal
BR 'brɪn(d)ʒ(ə)l
AM 'brɪn(d)ʒəl
brink
BR brɪŋk, -s
AM brɪŋk, -s
brinkmanship
BR 'brɪŋkmənʃɪp
AM 'brɪŋkmənˌʃɪp
brinksmanship
BR 'brɪŋksmənʃɪp
AM 'brɪŋksmənˌʃɪp

Brinks-Mat®
BR 'brɪŋksmat
AM 'brɪŋksˌmæt
briny
BR 'brʌɪni
AM 'braɪni
bri-nylon
BR ˌbrʌɪ'nʌɪlɒn
AM ˌbraɪ'naɪlən
brio
BR 'briːəʊ
AM 'brioʊ
brioche
BR ˌbriːˈɒʃ, 'briːɒʃ,
ˌbriːˈəʊʃ, 'briːəʊʃ, -ɪz
AM bri'ɔʃ, bri'oʊʃ, -əz
briolette
BR ˌbriːə(ʊ)'lɛt, -s
AM ˌbriə'lɛt, -s
Briony
BR 'brʌɪəni
AM 'braɪəni
briquet
BR brɪ'kɛt, -s
AM brə'kɛt, -s
briquette
BR brɪ'kɛt, -s
AM brə'kɛt, -s
Brisbane
BR 'brɪzbən
AM 'brɪzbən, 'brɪzˌbeɪn
Brisco
BR 'brɪskəʊ
AM 'brɪskoʊ
Briscoe
BR 'brɪskəʊ
AM 'brɪskoʊ
brisk
BR brɪsk, -ə(r), -ɪst
AM brɪsk, -ər, -ɪst
brisken
BR 'brɪsk|(ə)n, -(ə)nz,
-ɳɪŋ \-ənɪŋ, -nd
AM 'brɪsk|n, -nz, -ɳɪŋ,
-nd
brisket
BR 'brɪskɪt, -s
AM 'brɪskɪt, -s
briskly
BR 'brɪskli
AM 'brɪskli
briskness
BR 'brɪsknɪs
AM 'brɪsknɪs
brisling
BR 'brɪzlɪŋ, 'brɪslɪŋ
AM 'brɪzlɪŋ, 'brɪslɪŋ
bristle
BR 'brɪs|l, -lz, -lɪŋ \-lɪŋ,
-ld
AM 'brɪs|əl, -əlz, -(ə)lɪŋ,
-əld
bristletail
BR 'brɪslteɪl, -z
AM 'brɪsəlˌteɪl, -z
bristleworm
BR 'brɪslwəːm, -z

AM 'brɪsəlˌwərm, -z
bristliness
BR 'brɪslɪnɪs
AM 'brɪslɪnɪs,
'brɪslɪnɪs
bristly
BR 'brɪsli
AM 'brɪsli, 'brɪsl̩i
Bristol
BR 'brɪstl
AM 'brɪstl
bristols
BR 'brɪstlz
AM 'brɪstlz
Bristow
BR 'brɪstəʊ
AM 'brɪstoʊ
Bristowe
BR 'brɪstəʊ
AM 'brɪstoʊ
Brit
BR brɪt, -s
AM brɪt, -s
Britain
BR 'brɪtn
AM 'brɪtn, 'brɪdn
Britannia
BR brɪ'tanjə(r)
AM brɪ'tænjə
Britannic
BR brɪ'tanɪk
AM brɪ'tænɪk
britches
BR 'brɪtʃɪz
AM 'brɪtʃɪz
Briticism
BR 'brɪtɪsɪz(ə)m, -z
AM 'brɪdəˌsɪzəm, -z
British
BR 'brɪtɪʃ
AM 'brɪdɪʃ
Britisher
BR 'brɪtɪʃə(r), -z
AM 'brɪdɪʃər, -z
Britishism
BR 'brɪtɪʃɪz(ə)m, -z
AM 'brɪdəˌʃɪzəm, -z
Britishness
BR 'brɪtɪʃnɪs
AM 'brɪdɪʃnɪs
Britoil
BR 'brɪtɔɪl
AM 'brɪdɔɪl
Briton
BR 'brɪtn, -z
AM 'brɪtn, -z
Britt
BR brɪt
AM brɪt
Brittain
BR 'brɪtn
AM 'brɪtn
Brittan
BR 'brɪtn
AM 'brɪtn
Brittany
BR 'brɪtəni, 'brɪtn̩i

AM ˈbrɪtn̩i
Britten
BR ˈbrɪtn
AM ˈbrɪtn
brittle
BR ˈbrɪtl̩, -ə(r), -ɪst
AM ˈbrɪdəl, -ər, -ɪst
brittlely
BR ˈbrɪtl̩li
AM ˈbrɪdl̩i
brittleness
BR ˈbrɪtlnəs
AM ˈbrɪdlnɪs
brittly
BR ˈbrɪtl̩i
AM ˈbrɪdl̩i
Britton
BR ˈbrɪtn
AM ˈbrɪtn
Britvic®
BR ˈbrɪtvɪk, -s
AM ˈbrɪtvɪk, -s
britzka
BR ˈbrɪtskə(r), -z
AM ˈbrɪtʃkə, ˈbrɪtskə, -z
Brixham
BR ˈbrɪks(ə)m
AM ˈbrɪksəm
Brize Norton
BR ˌbrʌɪz ˈnɔːtn
AM ˌbraɪz ˈnɔrtən
Brno
BR ˈbəːnəʊ, brəˈnəʊ
AM ˈbərˌnoʊ
cz ˈbrnɔ
bro
BR brəʊ
AM broʊ
broach
BR brəʊtʃ, -ɪz, -ɪŋ, -t
AM broʊtʃ, -əz, -ɪŋ, -t
broad
BR brɔːd, -z, -ə(r), -ɪst
AM brɔd, brad, -z, -ər, -əst
broadband
BR ˈbrɔːdband
AM ˈbrɔdˌbænd, ˈbradˌbænd
Broadbent
BR ˈbrɔːdbɛnt
AM ˈbrɔdˌbɛnt, ˈbradˌbɛnt
broadbrimmed
BR ˌbrɔːdˈbrɪmd
AM ˌbrɔdˌbrɪmd, ˌbradˈbrɪmd
broadcast
BR ˈbrɔːdkɑːst, ˈbrɔːdˌkast, -s, -ɪŋ
AM ˈbrɔdˌkæst, ˈbradˌkæst, -s, -ɪŋ
broadcaster
BR ˈbrɔːdˌkɑːstə(r), ˈbrɔːdˌkastə(r), -z
AM ˈbrɔdˌkæstər, ˈbradˌkæstər, -z

broadcloth
BR ˈbrɔːdklɒθ
AM ˈbrɔdˌklɔθ, ˈbradˌklaθ
broaden
BR ˈbrɔːdn̩, -nz, -n̩ɪŋ \ -nɪŋ, -nd
AM ˈbrɔdən, ˈbradən, -z, -ɪŋ, -d
Broadhead
BR ˈbrɔːdhɛd
AM ˈbrɔdˌ(h)ɛd, ˈbradˌ(h)ɛd
Broadhurst
BR ˈbrɔːdhəːst
AM ˈbrɔdˌ(h)ərst, ˈbradˌ(h)ərst
broadleaf
BR ˈbrɔːdliːf
AM ˈbrɔdˌliːf, ˈbradˌliːf
broadleaved
BR ˌbrɔːdˈliːvd
AM ˈbrɔdˌliːvd, ˈbradˌliːvd
broadloom
BR ˈbrɔːdluːm
AM ˈbrɔdˌlum, ˈbradˌlum
broadly
BR ˈbrɔːdli
AM ˈbrɔdli, ˈbradli
broadminded
BR ˌbrɔːdˈmʌɪndɪd
AM ˌbrɔdˈmaɪn(d)ɪd, ˌbradˈmaɪn(d)ɪd
broadmindedly
BR ˌbrɔːdˈmʌɪndɪdli
AM ˌbrɔdˈmaɪn(d)ɪdli, ˌbradˈmaɪn(d)ɪdli
broadmindedness
BR ˌbrɔːdˈmʌɪndɪdnɪs
AM ˌbrɔdˈmaɪn(d)ɪdnɪs, ˌbradˈmaɪn(d)ɪdnɪs
Broadmoor
BR ˈbrɔːdmɔː(r), ˈbrɔːdmʊə(r)
AM ˈbrɔdˌmɔ(ə)r, ˈbrɔdˌmʊ(ə)r, ˈbradˌmɔ(ə)r, ˈbradˌmʊ(ə)r
broadness
BR ˈbrɔːdnəs
AM ˈbrɔdnəs, ˈbradnəs
broadsheet
BR ˈbrɔːdʃiːt, -s
AM ˈbrɔdˌʃit, ˈbradˌʃit, -s
broadside
BR ˈbrɔːdsʌɪd, -z
AM ˈbrɔdˌsaɪd, ˈbradˌsaɪd, -z
broadspectrum
BR ˌbrɔːdˈspɛktrəm
AM ˌbrɔdˈspɛktrəm, ˌbradˈspɛktrəm
Broadstairs
BR ˈbrɔːdstɛːz

AM ˈbrɔdˌstɛrz, ˈbradˌstɛrz
broadsword
BR ˈbrɔːdsɔːd, -z
AM ˈbrɔdˌsɔ(ə)rd, ˈbradˌsɔ(ə)rd, -z
broadtail
BR ˈbrɔːdteɪl, -z
AM ˈbrɔdˌteɪ(ə)l, ˈbradˌteɪ(ə)l, -z
Broadway
BR ˈbrɔːdweɪ
AM ˈbrɔdˌweɪ, ˈbradˌweɪ
broadwise
BR ˈbrɔːdwʌɪz
AM ˈbrɔdˌwaɪz, ˈbradˌwaɪz
Broadwood
BR ˈbrɔːdwʊd
AM ˈbrɔdˌwʊd, ˈbradˌwʊd
Brobdingnag
BR ˈbrɒbdɪŋnag
AM ˈbrabdɪŋˌnæg
Brobdingnagian
BR ˌbrɒbdɪŋˈnagɪən, -z
AM ˌbrabdɪŋˈnægiən, -z
brocade
BR brəˈkeɪd, -z, -ɪd
AM broʊˈkeɪd, -z, -ɪd
brocatel
BR ˌbrɒkəˈtɛl
AM ˌbrakəˈtɛl
brocatelle
BR ˌbrɒkəˈtɛl
AM ˌbrakəˈtɛl
broccoli
BR ˈbrɒkəli
AM ˈbrak(ə)li
broch
BR brɒk, brɒx, -s
AM brak, -s
brochette
BR brɒˈʃɛt, -s
AM broʊˈʃɛt, -s
brochure
BR ˈbrəʊʃə(r), brəˈʃʊə(r), -z
AM broʊˈʃʊ(ə)r, -z
brock
BR brɒk, -s
AM brak, -s
Brockbank
BR ˈbrɒkbaŋk
AM ˈbrakˌbæŋk
Brocken
BR ˈbrɒk(ə)n
AM ˈbrakən
Brockenhurst
BR ˈbrɒk(ə)nhəːst
AM ˈbrakənˌ(h)ərst
brocket
BR ˈbrɒkɪt, -s
AM ˈbrakət, -s

Brocklebank
BR ˈbrɒklbaŋk
AM ˈbrakəlˌbæŋk
Broderick
BR ˈbrɒd(ə)rɪk
AM ˈbrad(ə)rɪk, ˈbrɒd(ə)rɪk
broderie anglaise
BR ˌbrəʊd(ə)rɪ ˌɒ̃ˈgleɪz, ˌbrɒd(ə)rɪ +, + ˈɒ̃gleɪz
AM ˌbroʊdəriˌɑ̃ˈglɛz
Brodie
BR ˈbrəʊdi
AM ˈbroʊdi
Brodsky
BR ˈbrɒdski
AM ˈbradski
Broederbond
BR ˈbruːdəbɒnd, ˈbruːdəbɒnd
AM ˈbroʊdərˌband
Brogan
BR ˈbrəʊg(ə)n
AM ˈbroʊgən
brogue
BR brəʊg, -z
AM broʊg, -z
broil
BR brɔɪl, -z, -ɪŋ, -d
AM brɔɪl, -z, -ɪŋ, -d
broiler
BR ˈbrɔɪlə(r), -z
AM ˈbrɔɪlər, -z
broke
BR brəʊk, -s, -ɪŋ, -t
AM broʊk, -s, -ɪŋ, -t
broken
BR ˈbrəʊk(ə)n
AM ˈbroʊk(ə)n
brokenly
BR ˈbrəʊk(ə)nli
AM ˈbroʊkənli
brokenness
BR ˈbrəʊk(ə)nnəs
AM ˈbroʊkə(n)nəs
broker
BR ˈbrəʊkə(r), -z
AM ˈbroʊkər, -z
brokerage
BR ˈbrəʊk(ə)rɪdʒ
AM ˈbroʊk(ə)rɪdʒ
Brolac
BR ˈbrəʊlak
AM ˈbroʊlak
brolga
BR ˈbrɒlgə(r), -z
AM ˈbralgə, -z
brolly
BR ˈbrɒli, -ɪz
AM ˈbrali, -z
bromate
BR ˈbrəʊmeɪt, -s
AM ˈbroʊˌmeɪt, -s
Bromberg
BR ˈbrɒmbəːg

brome · 125 · browbeaten

AM 'brɑmˌbərg
brome
BR brəʊm, -z
AM broʊm, -z
bromelia
BR brə(ʊ)'miːlɪə(r), -z
AM broʊ'mɪljə,
broʊ'mɛljə,
broʊ'mɪlɪə,
broʊ'mɛlɪə ,-z
bromeliad
BR brə(ʊ)'miːlɪad, -z
AM broʊ'mɪliˌæd,
broʊ'mɛlɪəd, -z
bromic
BR 'brəʊmɪk
AM 'broʊmɪk
bromide
BR 'brəʊmʌɪd, -z
AM 'broʊˌmaɪd, -z
bromine
BR 'brəʊmiːn
AM 'broʊˌmin
bromism
BR 'brəʊmɪz(ə)m
AM 'broʊˌmɪzəm
Bromley
BR 'brɒmli, 'brʌmli
AM 'brɑmli
bromoform
BR 'brəʊməfɔːm
AM 'broʊməˌfɔ(ə)rm
Brompton
BR 'brɒm(p)t(ə)n,
'brʌm(p)t(ə)n
AM 'brɑm(p)tən
Bromsgrove
BR 'brɒmzgrəʊv
AM 'brɑmzˌgroʊv
Bromwich
BR 'brɒmɪtʃ, 'brɒmɪdʒ
AM 'brɑmwɪtʃ
Bromyard
BR 'brɒmjɑːd
AM 'brɑmjərd,
'brɑmˌjɑrd
bronc
BR brɒŋk, -s
AM brɑŋk, -s
bronchi
BR 'brɒŋkʌɪ, 'brɒŋkiː
AM 'brɑŋˌkaɪ, 'brɑŋˌki
bronchia
BR 'brɒŋkɪə(r)
AM 'brɑŋkɪə
bronchiae
BR 'brɒŋkriː
AM 'brɑŋkiˌi,
'brɑŋkiˌaɪ
bronchial
BR 'brɒŋkɪəl
AM 'brɑŋkɪəl
bronchiolar
BR ˌbrɒŋkɪ'əʊlə(r),
'brɒŋkɪələ(r)
AM 'brɑŋkɪələr,
ˌbrɑŋki'oʊlər

bronchiole
BR 'brɒŋkɪəʊl, -z
AM 'brɑŋkiˌoʊl, -z
bronchitic
BR brɒŋ'kɪtɪk
AM brɑŋ'kɪdɪk
bronchitis
BR brɒŋ'kʌɪtɪs
AM brɑŋ'kaɪdɪs,
brɑn'kaɪdɪs
bronchocele
BR 'brɒŋkə(ʊ)siːl, -z
AM 'brɑŋkoʊˌsil, -z
bronchopneumonia
BR ˌbrɒŋkə(ʊ)nju:
-'məʊnɪə(r),
ˌbrɒŋkə(ʊ)njʊ'məʊ-
nɪə(r)
AM ˌbrɑŋkoʊn(j)ʊ-
'moʊnjə
bronchoscope
BR 'brɒŋkə(ʊ)skəʊp,
-s
AM 'brɑŋkəˌskoʊp, -s
bronchoscopy
BR brɒŋ'kɒskəp|i, -ɪz
AM ˌbrɑŋ'kɑskəpi, -z
bronchus
BR 'brɒŋkəs
AM 'brɑŋkəs
bronco
BR 'brɒŋkəʊ, -z
AM 'brɑŋkoʊ, -z
Bronski
BR 'brɒnski
AM 'brɑnski
Bronstein
BR 'brɒnstiːn
AM 'brɑnˌstin,
'brɑnˌstaɪn
Brontë
BR 'brɒnti
AM 'brɑn(t)i
brontosaur
BR 'brɒntəsɔː(r), -z
AM 'brɑn(t)əˌsɔ(ə)r, -z
brontosauri
BR ˌbrɒntə'sɔːrʌɪ
AM ˌbrɑn(t)ə'sɔraɪ
brontosaurus
BR ˌbrɒntə'sɔːrəs, -ɪz
AM ˌbrɑn(t)ə'sɔrəs, -əz
Bronwen
BR 'brɒnwən
AM 'brɑnwən
Bronx
BR brɒŋks
AM brɑŋks, brɑŋs
bronze
BR brɒnz, -ɪz, -ɪŋ, -d
AM brɑnz, -əz, -ɪŋ, -d
bronzy
BR 'brɒnzi
AM 'brɑnzi
brooch
BR brəʊtʃ, -ɪz
AM broʊtʃ, brutʃ, -əz

brood
BR bruːd, -z, -ɪŋ, -ɪd
AM brud, -z, -ɪŋ, -əd
brooder
BR 'bruːdə(r), -z
AM 'brudər, -z
broodily
BR 'bruːdɪli
AM 'brudəli
broodiness
BR 'bruːdɪnɪs
AM 'brudɪnɪs
broodingly
BR 'bruːdɪŋli
AM 'brudɪŋli
broody
BR 'bruːd|i, -ɪə(r), -ɪɪst
AM 'brudi, -ər, -ɪɪst
brook
BR brʊk, -s, -ɪŋ, -t
AM brʊk, -s, -ɪŋ, -t
Brooke
BR brʊk
AM brʊk
Brookes
BR brʊks
AM brʊks
Brookfield
BR 'brʊkfiːld
AM 'brʊkˌfild
Brooking
BR 'brʊkɪŋ
AM 'brʊkɪŋ
Brooklands
BR 'brʊklən(d)z
AM 'brʊklən(d)z
brooklet
BR 'brʊklɪt, -s
AM 'brʊklət, -s
brooklime
BR 'brʊklʌɪm
AM 'brʊkˌlaɪm
Brooklyn
BR 'brʊklɪn
AM 'brʊklən
Brookner
BR 'brʊknə(r)
AM 'brʊknər
Brooks
BR brʊks
AM brʊks
Brookside
BR 'brʊksʌɪd,
ˌbrʊk'sʌɪd
AM 'brʊkˌsaɪd
brookweed
BR 'brʊkwiːd
AM 'brʊkˌwid
Brookwood
BR 'brʊkwʊd
AM 'brʊkˌwʊd
broom
BR bruːm, -z
AM brum, -z
Broome
BR bruːm
AM brum

broomrape
BR 'bruːmreɪp
AM 'brumˌreɪp
broomstick
BR 'bruːmstɪk, -s
AM 'brumˌstɪk, -s
Brophy
BR 'brəʊfi
AM 'broʊfi
Bros
Brothers
BR brɒs, brɒz
AM 'brəðərz
brose
BR brəʊz
AM broʊz
Brosnahan
BR 'brɒznəhən
AM 'brɑznəˌhæn,
'brɑznən
broth
BR brɒθ, -s
AM brɔθ, brɑθ, -s
brothel
BR 'brɒθl, -z
AM 'brɑθəl, 'brɔθəl,
'brɑðəl, 'brɔðəl, -z
brother
BR 'brʌðə(r), -z
AM 'brəðər, -z
brotherhood
BR 'brʌðəhʊd, -z
AM 'brəðər,(h)ʊd, -z
brotherliness
BR 'brʌðəlinɪs
AM 'brəðərlinɪs
brotherly
BR 'brʌðəli
AM 'brəðərli
Brotherton
BR 'brʌðət(ə)n
AM 'brəðərt(ə)n
Brough
BR brʌf
AM brɒf
brougham
BR 'bruːəm, bruːm, -z
AM 'broʊ(ə)m,
'bru(ə)m, -z
brought
BR brɔːt
AM brɔt, brɑt
Broughton
BR 'brɔːtn, 'brʌft(ə)n,
'braʊtn
AM 'brɔtn, 'brɑtn
brouhaha
BR bruːhɑːhɑː(r)
AM 'bruˌhɑˌhɑ
brow
BR braʊ, -z, -d
AM braʊ, -z, -d
browbeat
BR 'braʊbiːt, -s, -ɪŋ
AM 'braʊˌbi|t, -ts, -dɪŋ
browbeaten
BR 'braʊˌbiːtn

AM 'braʊˌbitn
browbeater
BR 'braʊˌbiːtə(r), -z
AM 'braʊˌbidər, -z
brown
BR braʊn, -z, -ɪŋ, -d, -ə(r), -ɪst
AM braʊn, -z, -ɪŋ, -d, -ər, -əst
Browne
BR braʊn
AM braʊn
brownfield
BR 'braʊnfiːld
AM 'braʊnˌfild
Brownhills
BR 'braʊnhɪlz
AM 'braʊnˌ(h)ɪlz
Brownian
BR 'braʊnɪən, -z
AM 'braʊnjən, -z
brownie
BR 'braʊn|i, -ɪz
AM 'braʊni, -z
Browning
BR 'braʊnɪŋ
AM 'braʊnɪŋ
brownish
BR 'braʊnɪʃ
AM 'braʊnɪʃ
Brownjohn
BR 'braʊndʒɒn
AM 'braʊnˌdʒɑn
brownness
BR 'braʊnnəs
AM 'braʊ(n)nəs
brownout
BR 'braʊnaʊt, -s
AM 'braʊnˌaʊt, -s
Brownshirt
BR 'braʊnʃəːt, -s
AM 'braʊnˌʃərt, -s
brownstone
BR 'braʊnstəʊn, -z
AM 'braʊnˌstoʊn, -z
browny
BR 'braʊni
AM 'braʊni
browse
BR braʊz, -ɪz, -ɪŋ, -d
AM braʊz, -əz, -ɪŋ, -d
browser
BR 'braʊzə(r), -z
AM 'braʊzər, -z
browze
BR braʊz, -ɪz, -ɪŋ, -d
AM braʊz, -əz, -ɪŋ, -d
browzer
BR 'braʊzə(r), -z
AM 'braʊzər, -z
Broxbourne
BR 'brɒksbɔːn
AM 'brɑksˌbərn
Brubeck
BR 'bruːbɛk
AM 'bruːbɛk

Bruce
BR bruːs
AM brus
brucellosis
BR ˌbruːsɪ'ləʊsɪs
AM ˌbruːsə'loʊsəs
Bruch
BR brʊk
AM brʊk
GER brʊx
brucite
BR 'bruːsaɪt
AM 'bruːˌsaɪt
Bruckner
BR 'brʊknə(r)
AM 'brʊknər
Bruegel
BR 'brɔɪgl
AM 'brɔɪgəl
Brueghel
BR 'brɔɪgl
AM 'brɔɪgəl
Bruges
BR bruːʒ
AM bruʒ
bruin
BR 'bruːɪn, -z
AM 'bruən, -z
bruise
BR bruːz, -ɪz, -ɪŋ, -d
AM bruz, -əz, -ɪŋ, -d
bruiser
BR 'bruːzə(r), -z
AM 'bruːzər, -z
bruit
BR bruːt, -s, -ɪŋ, -ɪd
AM bru|t, -ts, -dɪŋ, -dəd
Brum
BR brʌm
AM brəm
brumby
BR 'brʌmb|i, -ɪz
AM 'brəmbi, -z
brume
BR bruːm
AM brum
Brummagem
BR 'brʌmədʒəm
AM 'brəmədʒəm
Brummell
BR 'brʌml
AM 'brəməl
Brummie
BR 'brʌm|i, -ɪz
AM 'brəmi, -z
Brummy
BR 'brʌm|i, -ɪz
AM 'brəmi, -z
brumous
BR 'bruːməs
AM 'brəməs
brunch
BR brʌn(t)ʃ, -ɪz, -ɪŋ, -t
AM brən(t)ʃ, -əz, -ɪŋ, -t
Brunei
BR 'bruːnʌɪ, brʊ'nʌɪ
AM ˌbruː'naɪ

Bruneian
BR 'bruːnʌɪən
brʊ'nʌɪən, -z
AM ˌbruː'naɪən, -z
Brunel
BR brʊ'nɛl
AM brə'nɛl
brunet
BR bruː'nɛt, brʊ'nɛt, -s
AM bruː'nɛt, -s
brunette
BR bruː'nɛt, brʊ'nɛt, -s
AM bruː'nɛt, -s
Brunhild
BR 'brʊnhɪld
AM 'brʊn,(h)ɪld
Brünhilde
BR ˌbrʊn'hɪldə(r), 'brʊnˌhɪldə(r)
AM ˌbrʊn'hɪldə
Bruno
BR 'bruːnəʊ
AM 'brunoʊ
Brunswick
BR 'brʌnzwɪk
AM 'brənzwɪk
brunt
BR brʌnt
AM brənt
Brunton
BR 'brʌnt(ə)n
AM 'brən(t)ən, 'brəntn
bruschetta
BR brʊ'skɛtə(r)
AM bru'skɛdə
brush
BR brʌʃ, -ɪz, -ɪŋ, -t
AM brəʃ, -əz, -ɪŋ, -t
brushfire
BR 'brʌʃfʌɪə(r), -z
AM 'brəʃˌfaɪ(ə)r, -z
brushless
BR 'brʌʃləs
AM 'brəʃləs
brushlike
BR 'brʌʃlaɪk
AM 'brəʃˌlaɪk
brushwood
BR 'brʌʃwʊd
AM 'brəʃˌwʊd
brushwork
BR 'brʌʃwəːk
AM 'brəʃˌwərk
brushy
BR 'brʌʃi
AM 'brəʃi
brusque
BR brʊsk, bruːsk,
brʌsk
AM brəsk
brusquely
BR 'bruːskli, 'bruːskli,
'brʌskli
AM 'brəskli

brusqueness
BR 'bruːsknəs,
'bruːsknəs,
'brʌsknəs
AM 'brəsknəs
brusquerie
BR 'bruːskəri,
'bruːskəri, 'brʌskəri
AM 'brəskəri
Brussels
BR 'brʌslz
AM 'brəsəlz
brut
BR bruːt
AM brut
brutal
BR 'bruːtl
AM 'brudl
brutalisation
BR ˌbruːtlʌɪ'zeɪʃn
AM ˌbrudlə'zeɪʃən,
'brudlˌaɪ'zeɪʃən
brutalise
BR 'bruːtlʌɪz, -ɪz, -ɪŋ, -d
AM 'brudlˌaɪz, -ɪz, -ɪŋ,
-d
brutalism
BR 'bruːtlɪz(ə)m
AM 'brudlɪzəm
brutalist
BR 'bruːtlɪst, -s
AM 'brudləst, -s
brutality
BR bruː'talɪt|i,
brʊ'talɪti, -ɪz
AM bruː'tælədi, -z
brutalization
BR ˌbruːtlʌɪ'zeɪʃn
AM 'brudlə'zeɪʃən,
'brudlˌaɪ'zeɪʃən
brutalize
BR 'bruːtlʌɪz, -ɪz, -ɪŋ, -d
AM 'brudlˌaɪz, -ɪz, -ɪŋ,
-d
brutally
BR 'bruːtli
AM 'brudli
brute
BR bruːt, -s
AM brut, -s
brutish
BR 'bruːtɪʃ
AM 'brudɪʃ
brutishly
BR 'bruːtɪʃli
AM 'brudɪʃli
brutishness
BR 'bruːtɪʃnɪs
AM 'brudɪʃnɪs
Brutus
BR 'bruːtəs
AM 'brudəs
bruxism
BR 'brʊksɪz(ə)m,
'brʌksɪz(ə)m
AM 'brəkˌsɪzəm

Bryan
BR ˈbrʌɪən
AM ˈbraɪən
Bryant
BR ˈbrʌɪənt
AM ˈbraɪənt
Bryce
BR brʌɪs
AM braɪs
Bryden
BR ˈbrʌɪdn
AM ˈbraɪd(ə)n
Brylcreem®
BR ˈbrɪlkriːm
AM ˈbrɪlˌkrim
Bryn
BR brɪn
AM brɪn
Brynley
BR ˈbrɪnli
AM ˈbrɪnli
Bryn Mawr
place in USA
BR ˌbrɪn ˈmɔː(r)
AM ˌbrɪn ˈmɔ(ə)r
Brynmawr
place in UK
BR ˌbrɪnˈmaʊə(r)
AM ˌbrɪnˈmaʊ(ə)r,
ˌbrɪnˈmɔ(ə)r
WE ˌbrɪn ˈmaʊr
Brynmor
BR ˈbrɪnmɔː(r)
AM ˈbrɪnmɔ(ə)r
Brynner
BR ˈbrɪnə(r)
AM ˈbrɪnər
bryological
BR ˌbrʌɪəˈlɒdʒɪkl
AM ˌbraɪəˈladʒəkəl
bryologist
BR brʌɪˈɒlədʒɪst, -s
AM braɪˈɑlədʒəst, -s
bryology
BR brʌɪˈɒlədʒi
AM braɪˈɑlədʒi
bryony
BR ˈbrʌɪəni
AM ˈbraɪəni
bryophyte
BR ˈbrʌɪəfʌɪt, -s
AM ˈbraɪəˌfaɪt, -s
bryophytic
BR ˌbrʌɪəˈfɪtɪk
AM ˌbraɪəˈfɪdɪk
bryozoan
BR ˌbrʌɪəˈzəʊən, -z
AM ˌbraɪəˈzoʊən, -z
bryozoology
BR ˌbrʌɪəʊzuːˈɒlədʒi,
ˌbrʌɪəʊzəʊˈɒlədʒi
AM ˌbraɪəzuˈɑlədʒi,
ˌbraɪəzəˈwɑlədʒi
Bryson
BR ˈbrʌɪsn
AM ˈbraɪs(ə)n

Brythonic
BR brɪˈθɒnɪk
AM braɪˈθɑnɪk
Brzezinski
BR brəˈʒɪnski
AM brəˈʒɪnski
BSc
BR ˌbiːɛsˈsiː, -z
AM ˌbiˌɛsˈsi, -z
bub
BR bʌb, -z
AM bəb, -z
bubal
BR ˈbjuːbl, -z
AM ˈbjubl, -z
bubble
BR ˈbʌbl̩, -lz, -lɪŋ \ -lɪŋ,
-ld
AM ˈbəbl̩, -lz, -lɪŋ, -ld
bubblegum
BR ˈbʌblɡʌm
AM ˈbəblˌɡəm
bubbler
BR ˈbʌblə(r),
ˈbʌblə(r), -z
AM ˈbəb(ə)lər, -z
bubbly
BR ˈbʌbl̩i, ˈbʌbli
AM ˈbəb(ə)li
bubbly-jock
BR ˈbʌblɪdʒɒk, -s
AM ˈbəb(ə)liˌdʒɑk, -s
Buber
BR ˈb(j)uːbə(r)
AM ˈbubər
bubo
BR ˈbjuːbəʊ, -z
AM ˈb(j)uˌboʊ, -z
bubonic
BR bjuːˈbɒnɪk
AM b(j)uˈbɑnɪk
bubonocele
BR bjuːˈbɒnəsiːl, -z
AM bjuˈbɑnəˌsil, -z
buccal
BR ˈbʌkl
AM ˈbəkəl
buccaneer
BR ˌbʌkəˈnɪə(r), -z, -ɪŋ
AM ˌbəkəˈnɪ(ə)r, -z, -ɪŋ
buccaneerish
BR ˌbʌkəˈnɪərɪʃ
AM ˌbəkəˈnɪrɪʃ
buccinator
BR ˈbʌksɪneɪtə(r), -z
AM ˈbəksəˌneɪdər, -z
Buccleugh
BR bəˈkluː
AM bəˈklu
Bucelas
BR bjuːˈsɛləs
AM b(j)uˈsɛləs
Bucephalus
BR bjuːˈsɛfələs,
bjuːˈsɛfl̩əs
AM bju ˈsɛfələs

Buchan
BR ˈbʌk(ə)n
AM ˈbəkən
Buchanan
BR bjuːˈkanən,
b(j)uˈkanən
AM bjuˈkænən
Bucharest
BR ˌb(j)uːkəˈrɛst
AM ˈbukəˌrɛst
Buchenwald
BR ˈbuːk(ə)nvald
AM ˈbukənˌwald
Buchmanism
BR ˈbʌkmənɪz(ə)m
AM ˈbəkməˌnɪzəm
Buchmanite
BR ˈbʌkmənʌɪt, -s
AM ˈbəkməˌnaɪt, -s
buchu
BR ˈbʌkuː
AM ˈbəku
buck
BR bʌk, -s, -ɪŋ, -t
AM bək, -s, -ɪŋ, -t
buckaroo
BR ˌbʌkəˈruː, -z
AM ˌbəkəˈru, -z
buckbean
BR ˈbʌkbiːn, -z
AM ˈbəkˌbin, -z
buckboard
BR ˈbʌkbɔːd, -z
AM ˈbəkˌbɔ(ə)rd, -z
Buckden
BR ˈbʌkd(ə)n
AM ˈbəkdən
bucker
BR ˈbʌkə(r), -z
AM ˈbəkər, -z
bucket
BR ˈbʌkɪt, -s
AM ˈbəkət, -s
bucketful
BR ˈbʌkɪtfʊl, -z
AM ˈbəkətˌfʊl, -z
buckeye
BR ˈbʌkʌɪ, -z
AM ˈbəkˌaɪ, -z
Buckfastleigh
BR ˌbʌkfɑːs(t)ˈliː
AM ˌbəkfəs(t)ˈli
Buckie
BR ˈbʌki
AM ˈbəki
Buckingham
BR ˈbʌkɪŋəm
AM ˈbəkɪŋ,(h)æm
Buckinghamshire
BR ˈbʌkɪŋəmʃ(ɪ)ə(r)
AM ˈbəkɪŋəmʃɪ(ə)r
Buckland
BR ˈbʌklənd
AM ˈbəklənd
buckle
BR ˈbʌkl̩, -lz, -lɪŋ \ -lɪŋ,
-ld

AM ˈbəkəl, -z, -ɪŋ, -d
buckler
BR ˈbʌklə(r), -z
AM ˈbək(ə)lər, -z
Buckley
BR ˈbʌkli
AM ˈbəkli
buckling
BR ˈbʌklɪŋ, -z
AM ˈbəklɪŋ, -z
Buckmaster
BR ˈbʌkmɑːstə(r),
ˈbʌkmastə(r)
AM ˈbəkˌmæstər
Buckminster
BR ˈbʌkmɪnstə(r)
AM ˈbəkˌmɪnstər
Bucknall
BR ˈbʌknl
AM ˈbəknəl
Bucknell
BR ˈbʌknl
AM ˌbəkˈnɛl
Buckner
BR ˈbʌknə(r)
AM ˈbəknər
bucko
BR ˈbʌkəʊ, -z
AM ˈbəkoʊ, -z
buckra
BR ˈbʌkrə(r), -z
AM ˈbəkrə, -z
buckram
BR ˈbʌkrəm
AM ˈbəkrəm
buck rarebit
BR ˌbʌk ˈrɛːbɪt, + ˈrabɪt
AM ˌbək ˈrɛrbɪt
Bucks.
Buckinghamshire
BR bʌks
AM bəks
bucksaw
BR ˈbʌksɔː(r), -z
AM ˈbəkˌsɔ, ˈbəkˌsɑ, -z
buckshee
BR ˌbʌkˈʃiː
AM ˌbəkˈʃi
buckshot
BR ˈbʌkʃɒt
AM ˈbəkˌʃɑt
buckskin
BR ˈbʌkskɪn, -z
AM ˈbəkˌskɪn, -z
buckteeth
BR ˌbʌkˈtiːθ
AM ˌbəkˈtiθ
buckthorn
BR ˈbʌkθɔːn, -z
AM ˈbəkˌθɔ(ə)rn, -z
Buckton
BR ˈbʌktən
AM ˈbəktən
bucktooth
BR ˌbʌkˈtuːθ, -t
AM ˈbəkˌtuθ, -t

buckwheat
BR ˈbʌkwiːt
AM ˈbək,(h)wit
bucolic
BR bjuːˈkɒlɪk,
bjʊˈkʊlɪk
AM bjuˈkɑlɪk
bucolically
BR bjuːˈkɒlɪkli,
bjʊˈkʊlɪkli
AM bjuˈkɑlək(ə)li
bud
BR bʌd, -z, -ɪŋ, -ɪd
AM bəd, -z, -ɪŋ, -əd
Budapest
BR ˌb(j)uːdəˈpɛst
AM ˈbudəˌpɛst,
ˈbudə,pɛʃt
HU ˈbudapɛʃt
Buddha
BR ˈbʊdə(r), -z
AM ˈbudə, ˈbʊdə, -z
Buddhism
BR ˈbʊdɪz(ə)m
AM ˈbu,dɪzəm,
ˈbʊ,dɪzəm
Buddhist
BR ˈbʊdɪst, -s
AM ˈbudəst, ˈbʊdəst, -s
Buddhistic
BR bʊˈdɪstɪk
AM buˈdɪstɪk,
bʊˈdɪstɪk
Buddhistical
BR bʊˈdɪstɪkl
AM buˈdɪstɪkəl,
bʊˈdɪstɪkəl
buddleia
BR ˈbʌdlɪə(r), -z
AM ˌbədˈliə, -z
buddy
BR ˈbʌd|i, -ɪz
AM ˈbədi, -z
Bude
BR bjuːd
AM bjud
budge
BR bʌdʒ, -ɪz, -ɪŋ, -d
AM bədʒ, -ɪz, -ɪŋ, -d
budgerigar
BR ˈbʌdʒ(ə)rɪgɑː(r), -z
AM ˈbədʒəriˌgɑr, -z
budget
BR ˈbʌdʒ|ɪt, -ɪts, -ɪtɪŋ, -ɪtɪd
AM ˈbədʒə|t, -ts, -dɪŋ, -dəd
budgetary
BR ˈbʌdʒɪt(ə)ri
AM ˈbədʒəˌtɛri
budgie
BR ˈbʌdʒ|i, -ɪz
AM ˈbədʒi, -z
Budleigh
BR ˈbʌdli
AM ˈbədli
Budweiser®
BR ˈbʌdwʌɪzə(r), -z

AM ˈbəd,waɪzər, -z
Buenos Aires
BR ˌbweɪnəs ˈʌɪ(ə)riːz,
ˌbwenəs +, + ˈɛːriːz
AM ˌbweɪnəs ˈɛrəs,
+ ˈaɪrəz
Buerk
BR bəːk
AM bərk
buff
BR bʌf, -s, -ɪŋ, -t
AM bəf, -s, -ɪŋ, -t
buffalo
BR ˈbʌfələʊ, ˈbʌfləʊ, -z
AM ˈbəf(ə),loʊ, -z
buffer
BR ˈbʌfə(r), -z
AM ˈbəfər, -z
buffet¹
food
BR ˈbʊfeɪ, -z
AM ˌbəˈfeɪ, -z
buffet²
hit
BR ˈbʌf|ɪt, -ɪts, -ɪtɪŋ, -ɪtɪd
AM ˈbəfə|t, -ts, -dɪŋ, -dəd
bufflehead
BR ˈbʌflhɛd, -z
AM ˈbəfl,(h)ɛd, -z
buffo
BR ˈbʊfəʊ, -z
AM ˈbufoʊ, -z
buffoon
BR bəˈfuːn, -z
AM bəˈfun, -z
buffoonery
BR bəˈfuːn(ə)r|i, -ɪz
AM bəˈfunəri, -z
buffoonish
BR bəˈfuːnɪʃ
AM bəˈfunɪʃ
Buffs
BR bʌfs
AM bəfs
bug
BR bʌg, -z, -ɪŋ, -d
AM bəg, -z, -ɪŋ, -d
bugaboo
BR ˈbʌgəbuː, -z
AM ˈbəgəˌbu, -z
Buganda
BR bʊˈgandə(r)
AM bəˈgændə
Bugandan
BR bʊˈgandən, -z
AM bəˈgændən, -z
Bugatti
BR b(j)ʊˈgat|i, -ɪz
AM b(j)ʊˈgadi, -z
bugbear
BR ˈbʌgbɛː(r), -z
AM ˈbəg,bɛ(ə)r, -z
bugger
BR ˈbʌg|ə(r), -əz, -(ə)rɪŋ, -əd

AM ˈbəg|ər, -əz, -(ə)rɪŋ, -əd
buggery
BR ˈbʌg(ə)ri
AM ˈbəgəri
buggy
BR ˈbʌg|i, -ɪz
AM ˈbəgi, -z
bughouse
BR ˈbʌghaʊ|s, -zɪz
AM ˈbəg,(h)aʊ|s, -zəz
bugjuice
BR ˈbʌgdʒuːs
AM ˈbəg,dʒus
bugle
BR ˈbjuːg|l, -lz,
-l̩ŋ \-lŋ, -ld
AM ˈbjugləl, -əlz,
-(ə)lŋ, -əld
bugler
BR ˈbjuːglə(r), -z
AM ˈbjuglər, -z
buglet
BR ˈbjuːglɪt, -s
AM ˈbjuglət, -s
bugloss
BR ˈbjuːglɒs, -ɪz
AM ˈbjuˌglɑs, -əz
Bugner
BR ˈbʌgnə(r),
ˈbʊgnə(r)
AM ˈbəgnər
bugrake
BR ˈbʌgreɪk, -s
AM ˈbəgˌreɪk, -s
buhl
BR buːl, -z
AM bul, -z
Buick®
BR ˈbjuːɪk, -s
AM ˈbjuɪk, -s
build
BR bɪld, -z, -ɪŋ
AM bɪld, -z, -ɪŋ
builder
BR ˈbɪldə(r), -z
AM ˈbɪldər, -z
building
BR ˈbɪldɪŋ, -z
AM ˈbɪldɪŋ, -z
built
BR bɪlt
AM bɪlt
Builth Wells
BR ˌbɪlθ ˈwɛlz
AM ˌbɪlθ ˈwɛlz
Buitoni®
BR bjʊˈtəʊni
AM bjuˈtoʊni
Bujumbura
BR ˌbʊdʒʊmˈbʊərə(r)
AM bu,dʒəmˈburə
Bukhara
BR bʊˈkɑːrə(r),
bʊˈxɑːrə(r)
AM buˈkɑrə
RUS buka'ra

Bukovina
BR ˌbʊkəˈviːnə(r)
AM ˌbukəˈvinə
Bukowski
BR bʊˈkɒfski,
bʊˈkɒvski
AM buˈkaʊski
Bukta
BR ˈbʌktə(r)
AM ˈbəktə
Bulawayo
BR ˌbʊləˈweɪəʊ
AM ˌbʊləˈweɪˌoʊ
bulb
BR bʌlb, -z
AM bəlb, -z
bulbaceous
BR bʌlˈbeɪʃəs
AM ˌbəlˈbeɪʃəs
bulbar
BR ˈbʌlbə(r)
AM ˈbəlbər
bulbil
BR ˈbʌlbɪl, -z
AM ˈbəlbəl, -z
bulbous
BR ˈbʌlbəs
AM ˈbəlbəs
bulbousness
BR ˈbʌlbəsnəs
AM ˈbəlbəsnəs
bulbul
BR ˈbʊlbʊl, -z
AM ˈbʊl,bʊl, -z
Bulgar
BR ˈbʌlgɑː(r),
ˈbʊlgɑ(r), -z
AM ˈbəlgər, -z
Bulgaria
BR bʌlˈgɛːrɪə(r),
bʊlˈgɛːrɪə(r)
AM ˌbəlˈgɛrɪə
Bulgarian
BR bʌlˈgɛːrɪən,
bʊlˈgɛrɪən, -z
AM ˌbəlˈgɛrɪən, -z
bulge
BR bʌldʒ, -ɪz, -ɪŋ, -d
AM bəldʒ, -əz, -ɪŋ, -d
bulghur
BR ˈbʌlgə(r)
AM ˈbəlgər
bulginess
BR ˈbʌldʒɪnɪs
AM ˈbəldʒɪnɪs
bulgur
BR ˈbʌlgə(r)
AM ˈbəlgər
bulgy
BR ˈbʌldʒi
AM ˈbəldʒi
bulimarexia
BR b(j)ʊˌlɪməˈrɛksɪə(r)
AM ˌbʊlimaˈrɛksɪə
bulimarexic
BR b(j)ʊˌlɪməˈrɛksɪk, -s

AM ˌbuːlimə'rɛksɪk, -s
bulimia
BR b(j)ʉ'lɪmɪə(r)
AM buː'limiə
bulimia nervosa
BR b(j)ʉ,lɪmɪə
nəː'vəʊsə(r),
+ nəː'vəʊzə(r)
AM buː'limiə
ˌnər'vəʊsə,
+ ˌnər'vəʊzə
bulimic
BR b(j)ʉ'lɪmɪk, -s
AM buː'limɪk, -s
bulk
BR bʌlk, -s, -ɪŋ, -t
AM bəlk, -s, -ɪŋ, -t
bulkhead
BR 'bʌlkhɛd, -z
AM 'bəlk,(h)ɛd, -z
bulkily
BR 'bʌlkɪli
AM 'bəlkəli
bulkiness
BR 'bʌlkɪnɪs
AM 'bəlkɪnɪs
bulkmail
BR 'bʌlkmeɪl
AM 'bəlk,meɪl
bulky
BR 'bʌlk|i, -ɪə(r), -ɪɪst
AM 'bəlki, -ər, -ɪst
bull
BR bʊl, -z, -ɪŋ, -d
AM bʊl, -z, -ɪŋ, -d
bulla
BR 'bʊlə(r), 'bʌlə(r)
AM 'bʊlə
bullace
BR 'bʊləs, -ɪz
AM 'bʊləs, -əz
bullae
BR 'bʊliː, 'bʌliː
AM 'bʊli, 'bʊˌlaɪ
bullate
BR 'bʊleɪt
AM 'bʊˌleɪt
bulldog
BR 'bʊldɒg, -z
AM 'bʊl,dɔg, 'bʊl,dɑg, -z
bulldoze
BR 'bʊldəʊz, -ɪz, -ɪŋ, -d
AM 'bʊl,doʊz, -əz, -ɪŋ, -d
bulldozer
BR 'bʊl,dəʊzə(r), -z
AM 'bʊl,doʊzər, -z
Bullen
BR 'bʊlɪn
AM 'bʊlən
Buller
BR 'bʊlə(r)
AM 'bʊlər
bullet
BR 'bʊlɪt, -s
AM 'bʊlət, -s

bulletin
BR 'bʊlɪtɪn, -z
AM 'bʊlətn, 'bʊlədən, -z
bulletproof
BR 'bʊlɪtpruːf
AM 'bʊlət,pruf
bullfight
BR 'bʊlfʌɪt, -s
AM 'bʊl,faɪt, -s
bullfighter
BR 'bʊl,fʌɪtə(r), -z
AM 'bʊl,faɪdər, -z
bullfighting
BR 'bʊl,fʌɪtɪŋ
AM 'bʊl,faɪdɪŋ
bullfinch
BR 'bʊlfɪn(t)ʃ, -ɪz
AM 'bʊl,fɪn(t)ʃ, -ɪz
bullfrog
BR 'bʊlfrɒg, -z
AM 'bʊl,frɔg, 'bʊl,frɑg, -z
bullhead
BR 'bʊlhɛd, -z
AM 'bʊl,(h)ɛd, -z
bullhorn
BR 'bʊlhɔːn, -z
AM 'bʊl,(h)ɔ(ə)rn, -z
bullion
BR 'bʊliən
AM 'bʊljən, 'bʊliən
bullish
BR 'bʊlɪʃ
AM 'bʊlɪʃ
bullishly
BR 'bʊlɪʃli
AM 'bʊlɪʃli
bullishness
BR 'bʊlɪʃnɪs
AM 'bʊlɪʃnɪs
bullnecked
BR 'bʊl'nɛkt
AM 'bʊl,nɛkt
bullock
BR 'bʊlək, -s
AM 'bʊlək, -s
bullocky
BR 'bʊlək|i, -ɪz
AM 'bʊləki, -z
Bullokar
BR 'bʊləkɑː(r), 'bʊləkə(r)
AM 'bʊləkər
Bullough
BR 'bʊləʊ
AM 'bʊloʊ
bullring
BR 'bʊlrɪŋ, -z
AM 'bʊl,rɪŋ, -z
bullshit
BR 'bʊlʃɪt, -s, -ɪŋ, -ɪd
AM 'bʊl,ʃɪ|t, -ts, -dɪŋ, -dɪd
bullshitter
BR 'bʊl,ʃɪtə(r), -z
AM 'bʊl,ʃɪdər, -z

bulltrout
BR 'bʊltraʊt, -s
AM 'bʊl,traʊt, -s
bullwhip
BR 'bʊlwɪp, -s, -ɪŋ, -t
AM 'bʊl,(h)wɪp, -s, -ɪŋ, -t
bully
BR 'bʊl|i, -ɪz, -ɪɪŋ, -ɪd
AM 'bʊli, -z, -ɪŋ, -d
bullyboy
BR 'bʊlɪbɔɪ, -z
AM 'bʊli,bɔɪ, -z
bullyrag
BR 'bʊlɪrag, -z, -ɪŋ, -d
AM 'bʊli,ræg, -z, -ɪŋ, -d
Bulmer
BR 'bʊlmə(r)
AM 'bʊlmər
bulrush
BR 'bʊlrʌʃ, -ɪz
AM 'bʊl,rəʃ, -əz
Bulstrode
BR 'bʊlstrəʊd
AM 'bʊl,stroʊd
Bultitude
BR 'bʌltɪtjuːd, 'bʌltɪtʃuːd
AM 'bʊldə,tud
bulwark
BR 'bʊlwək, 'bʌlwək, 'bʊlwəːk, 'bʌlwəːk, -s
AM 'bʊl,wərk, -s
Bulwer-Lytton
BR ˌbʊlwə'lɪtn
AM ˌbʊlwər'lɪtn
bum
BR bʌm, -z, -ɪŋ, -d
AM bəm, -z, -ɪŋ, -d
bumbag
BR 'bʌmbag, -z
AM 'bəm,bæg, -z
bumble
BR 'bʌmb|l, -lz, -lɪŋ \-lɪŋ, -ld
AM 'bəmb|əl, -əlz, -(ə)lɪŋ, -əld
bumblebee
BR 'bʌmblbiː, -z
AM 'bəmbəl,bi, -z
bumbledom
BR 'bʌmbldəm
AM 'bəmbəldəm
bumbler
BR 'bʌmblə(r), -z
AM 'bəmb(ə)lər, -z
bumboat
BR 'bʌmbəʊt, -s
AM 'bəm,boʊt, -s
bumf
BR bʌmf
AM bəmf
bumiputra
BR ˌbuːmɪ'puːtrə(r), -z
AM ˌbumi'putrə, -z
bumkin
BR 'bʌmkɪn, -z

AM 'bəmkən, -z
bummalo
BR 'bʌmələʊ
AM 'bəmə,loʊ
bummaree
BR ˌbʌmə'riː, -z
AM ˌbəmə'ri, -z
bummer
BR 'bʌmə(r), -z
AM 'bəmər, -z
bump
BR bʌm|p, -ps, -pɪŋ, -(p)t
AM bəmp, -s, -ɪŋ, -t
bumper
BR 'bʌmpə(r), -z
AM 'bəmpər, -z
bumph
BR bʌmf
AM bəmf
bumpily
BR 'bʌmpɪli
AM 'bəmpəli
bumpiness
BR 'bʌmpɪnɪs
AM 'bəmpɪnɪs
bumpkin
BR 'bʌm(p)kɪn, -z
AM 'bəm(p)kən, -z
bumptious
BR 'bʌm(p)ʃəs
AM 'bəm(p)ʃəs
bumptiously
BR 'bʌm(p)ʃəsli
AM 'bəm(p)ʃəsli
bumptiousness
BR 'bʌm(p)ʃəsnəs
AM 'bəm(p)ʃəsnəs
bumpy
BR 'bʌmp|i, -ɪə(r), -ɪɪst
AM 'bəmpi, -ər, -ɪst
bun
BR bʌn, -z
AM bən, -z
Buna
BR 'b(j)uːnə(r)
AM 'b(j)unə
Bunbury
BR 'bʌnb(ə)ri
AM 'bən,bɛri
bunch
BR bʌn(t)ʃ, -ɪz, -ɪŋ, -t
AM bən(t)ʃ, -əz, -ɪŋ, -t
bunchy
BR 'bʌn(t)ʃi
AM 'bən(t)ʃi
bunco
BR 'bʌŋkəʊ, -z, -ɪŋ, -d
AM 'bəŋk|oʊ, -oʊz, -əwɪŋ, -oʊd
buncombe
BR 'bʌŋkəm
AM 'bəŋkəm
bund
BR bʌnd, -z
AM bənd, -z

bunder
BR ˈbʌndə(r), -z
AM ˈbəndər, -z

Bundesbank
BR ˈbʊndəzbaŋk
AM ˈbʊndəsˌbæŋk

Bundesrat
BR ˈbʊndəzrɑːt
AM ˈbʊndəsˌrɑt

Bundestag
BR ˈbʊndəztɑːg
AM ˈbʊndəsˌtɑg,
ˈbʊndəˌstæg

bundle
BR ˈbʌnd|l̩, -lz,
-lɪŋ\-lɪŋ, -ld
AM ˈbən|dəl, -dəlz,
-(d)(ə)lɪŋ, -dəld

bundler
BR ˈbʌndlə(r), -z
AM ˈbən(də)lər, -z

bundobust
BR ˈbʌndəbʌst
AM ˈbəndəˌbəst

Bundy
BR ˈbʌndi
AM ˈbəndi

bung
BR bʌŋ, -z, -ɪŋ, -d
AM bəŋ, -z, -ɪŋ, -d

bungaloid
BR ˈbʌŋgəlɔɪd
AM ˈbəŋgəˌlɔɪd

bungalow
BR ˈbʌŋgələʊ, -z
AM ˈbəŋgəˌloʊ, -z

Bungay
BR ˈbʌŋgi
AM ˈbəŋgi

bungee
BR ˈbʌndʒ|i, -ɪz
AM ˈbəndʒi, -z

bunghole
BR ˈbʌŋhəʊl, -z
AM ˈbəŋˌ(h)oʊl, -z

bungle
BR ˈbʌŋg|l̩, -lz,
-lɪŋ\-lɪŋ, -ld
AM ˈbəŋg|əl, -əlz,
-(ə)lɪŋ, -əld

bungler
BR ˈbʌŋglə(r), -z
AM ˈbəŋg(ə)lər, -z

bunion
BR ˈbʌnjən, -z
AM ˈbənjən, -z

bunk
BR bʌŋ|k, -ks, -kɪŋ,
-(k)t
AM bəŋ|k, -ks, -kɪŋ,
-(k)t

bunker
BR ˈbʌŋkə(r), -z, -ɪŋ, -d
AM ˈbəŋkər, -z, -ɪŋ, -d

bunkhouse
BR ˈbʌŋkhaʊ|s, -zɪz
AM ˈbəŋkˌ(h)aʊ|s, -zəz

bunko
BR ˈbʌŋkəʊ, -z, -ɪŋ, -d
AM ˈbəŋkoʊ, -z, -ɪŋ, -d

bunkum
BR ˈbʌŋkəm
AM ˈbəŋkəm

bunny
BR ˈbʌn|i, -ɪz
AM ˈbəni, -z

Bunsen
BR ˈbʌnsn
AM ˈbənsən

bunt
BR bʌn|t, -(t)s, -tɪŋ, -tɪd
AM bən|t, -ts, -(t)ɪŋ,
-(t)əd

buntal
BR ˈbʌntl
AM bʊnˈtɑl, ˈbən(t)l

Bunter
BR ˈbʌntə(r)
AM ˈbən(t)ər

bunting
BR ˈbʌntɪŋ, -z
AM ˈbən(t)ɪŋ, -z

buntline
BR ˈbʌntlaɪn, -z
AM ˈbəntˌlam, -z

Bunty
BR ˈbʌnti
AM ˈbən(t)i

Buñuel
BR buːˈnjʊɛl, bʊnˈwɛl
AM ˈbʊnjəwəl,
ˌbʊnˈwɛl

bunya
BR ˈbʌnjə(r), -z
AM ˈbənjə, -z

Bunyan
BR ˈbʌnjən
AM ˈbənjən

Bunyanesque
BR ˌbʌnjəˈnɛsk
AM ˌbənjəˈnɛsk

bunyip
BR ˈbʌnjɪp, -s
AM ˈbənjɪp, -s

Buonaparte
BR ˈbəʊnəpɑːt
AM ˈboʊnəˌpɑrt

buoy
BR bɔɪ, -z, -ɪŋ, -d
AM buɪ, bɔɪ, -z, -ɪŋ, -d

buoyage
BR ˈbɔɪɪdʒ
AM ˈbɔɪɪdʒ, ˈbujɪdʒ

buoyancy
BR ˈbɔɪənsi
AM ˈbɔɪənsi, ˈbujənsi

buoyant
BR ˈbɔɪənt
AM ˈbɔɪənt, ˈbujənt

buoyantly
BR ˈbɔɪəntli
AM ˈbɔɪən(t)li,
ˈbujən(t)li

BUPA
BR ˈb(j)uːpə(r)
AM ˈb(j)upə

buppie
BR ˈbʌp|i, -ɪz
AM ˈbəpi, -z

bur
BR bə(r), -z
AM bər, -z

burb
BR bəːb, -z
AM bərb, -z

Burbage
BR ˈbəːbɪdʒ
AM ˈbərbɪdʒ

Burbank
BR ˈbəːbaŋk
AM ˈbərˌbæŋk

Burberry®
BR ˈbəːb(ə)r|i, -ɪz
AM ˈbərbəri, ˈbərˌbɛri,
-z

burble
BR ˈbəːb|l̩, -lz, -lɪŋ\-lɪŋ,
-ld
AM ˈbərb|əl, -əlz,
-(ə)lɪŋ, -əld

burbler
BR ˈbəːblə(r),
ˈbəːblə(r), -z
AM ˈbərb(ə)lər, -z

burbot
BR ˈbəːbət, -s
AM ˈbərbət, -s

Burch
BR bəːtʃ
AM bərtʃ

Burchfield
BR ˈbəːtʃfiːld
AM ˈbərtʃˌfild

Burckhardt
BR ˈbəːkhɑːt
AM ˈbərkˌ(h)ɑrt

Burco
BR ˈbəːkəʊ
AM ˈbərkoʊ

burden
BR ˈbəːd|n, -nz,
-nɪŋ\-nɪŋ, -nd
AM ˈbərdən, -z, -ɪŋ, -d

burdensome
BR ˈbəːdns(ə)m
AM ˈbərdnsəm

burdensomeness
BR ˈbəːdns(ə)mnəs
AM ˈbərdnsəmnəs

Burdett
BR ˈbəːdɛt, ˌbəːˈdɛt,
bəˈdɛt
AM bərˈdɛt

burdock
BR ˈbəːdɒk
AM ˈbərˌdɑk

Burdon
BR ˈbəːdn
AM ˈbərd(ə)n

bureau
BR ˈbjʊərəʊ, ˈbjɔːrəʊ, -z
AM ˈbjuroʊ, -z

bureaucracy
BR bjʊˈrɒkrəs|i,
bjɔːˈrɒkrəsi, -ɪz
AM bjʊˈrɑkrəsi, -z

bureaucrat
BR ˈbjʊərəkrat,
ˈbjɔːrəkrat, -s
AM ˈbjurəˌkræt, -s

bureaucratic
BR ˌbjʊərəˈkratɪk,
ˌbjɔːrəˈkratɪk
AM ˌbjurəˈkrædɪk

bureaucratically
BR ˌbjʊərəˈkratɪkli,
ˌbjɔːrəˈkratɪkli
AM ˌbjurəˈkrædək(ə)li

bureaucratisation
BR bjʊˌrɒkrətaɪˈzeɪʃn,
bjɔːˌrɒkrətaɪˈzeɪʃn
AM bjuˌrɑkrədəˈzeɪʃən,
bjuˌrɑkrəˌtaɪˈzeɪʃən

bureaucratise
BR bjʊˈrɒkrətaɪz,
bjɔːˈrɒkrətaɪz, -ɪz, -ɪŋ,
-d
AM bjuˈrɑkrəˌtaɪz, -ɪz,
-ɪŋ, -d

bureaucratization
BR bjʊˌrɒkrətaɪˈzeɪʃn,
bjɔːˌrɒkrətaɪˈzeɪʃn
AM bjuˌrɑkrədəˈzeɪʃən,
bjuˌrɑkrəˌtaɪˈzeɪʃən

bureaucratize
BR bjʊˈrɒkrətaɪz,
bjɔːˈrɒkrətaɪz, -ɪz, -ɪŋ,
-d
AM bjuˈrɑkrəˌtaɪz, -ɪz,
-ɪŋ, -d

bureaux
BR ˈbjʊərəʊ(z),
ˈbjɔːrəʊ(z)
AM ˈbjuroʊ

buret
BR bjʊˈrɛt, -s
AM bjʊˈrɛt, -s

burette
BR bjʊˈrɛt, -s
AM bjʊˈrɛt, -s

Burford
BR ˈbəːfəd
AM ˈbərfərd

burg
BR bəːg, -z
AM bərg, -z

burgage
BR ˈbəːg|ɪdʒ, -ɪdʒɪz
AM ˈbərgɪdʒ, -ɪz

Burgas
BR ˈbəːgəs
AM ˈbərgəs

Burge
BR bəːdʒ
AM bərdʒ

burgee
BR ˈbəːdʒiː, bəːˈdʒiː, -z

AM ˈbɜrˈdʒi, -z

burgeon
BR ˈbəːdʒ|(ə)n, -(ə)nz,
-ɳɪŋ \-ənɪŋ, -(ə)nd
AM ˈbɜrdʒən, -z, -ɪŋ, -d

burger
BR ˈbəːgə(r), -z
AM ˈbɜrgər, -z

burgess
BR ˈbəːdʒɪs, -ɪz
AM ˈbɜrdʒəs, -əz

burgh
BR ˈbʌrə(r), -z
AM bɜrg, ˈbɜroʊ, -z

burghal
BR ˈbəːgl
AM ˈbɜrgəl

burgher
BR ˈbəːgə(r), -z
AM ˈbɜrgər, -z

Burghley
BR ˈbəːli
AM ˈbɜrli

burglar
BR ˈbəːglə(r), -z
AM ˈbɜrglər, -z

burglarious
BR (ˌ)bəːˈglɛːrɪəs
AM ˌbɜrˈglɛrɪəs

burglariously
BR (ˌ)bəːˈglɛːrɪəsli
AM ˌbɜrˈglɛrɪəsli

burglarise
BR ˈbəːglərʌɪz, -ɪz, -ɪŋ, -d
AM ˈbɜrgləˌraɪz, -ɪz, -ɪŋ, -d

burglarize
BR ˈbəːglərʌɪz, -ɪz, -ɪŋ, -d
AM ˈbɜrgləˌraɪz, -ɪz, -ɪŋ, -d

burglary
BR ˈbəːglər|i, -ɪz
AM ˈbɜrgləri, -z

burgle
BR ˈbəːg|l, -lz, -lɪŋ \-lɪŋ, -ld
AM ˈbɜrg|əl, -əlz, -(ə)lɪŋ, -əld

burgomaster
BR ˈbəːgəˌmɑːstə(r), ˈbəːgəˌmaste(r), -z
AM ˈbɜrgəˌmæstər, -z

burgoo
BR ˈbəːguː, ˌbəːˈguː
AM ˌbɜrˈgu

Burgoyne
BR ˈbəːgɔɪn, bəːˈgɔɪn
AM ˌbɜrˈgɔɪn

burgrave
BR ˈbəːgreɪv, -z
AM ˈbɜrˌgreɪv, -z

Burgundian
BR bə(ː)ˈgʌndɪən
AM bɜrˈgɑndɪən

burgundy
BR ˈbəːg(ə)nd|i, -ɪz
AM ˈbɜrgəndi, -z

burhel
BR ˈbʌrəl, ˈbʌrḷ, -z
AM ˈbɜrəl, -z

burial
BR ˈbɛrɪəl, -z
AM ˈbɛrɪəl, -z

burin
BR ˈbjʊərɪn, ˈbjɔːrɪn, -z
AM ˈbjurən, -z

burk
BR bəːk, -s
AM bɜrk, -s

burka
BR ˈbəːkə(r), -z
AM ˈbɜrkə, -z

burke
BR bəːk, -s, -ɪŋ, -t
AM bɜrk, -s, -ɪŋ, -t

Burkina
BR bəːˈkiːnə(r)
AM bɜrˈkinə

Burkina Faso
BR bəːˌkiːnə ˈfasəʊ
AM bɜrˌkinə ˈfasoʊ

Burkinan
BR bəːˈkiːnən, -z
AM bɜrˈkinən, -z

Burkitt's lymphoma
BR ˌbəːkɪts lɪmˈfəʊmə(r)
AM ˌbɜrkəts lɪmˈfoʊmə

burl
BR bəːl, -z, -ɪŋ, -d
AM bɜrl, -z, -ɪŋ, -d

burlap
BR ˈbəːlap
AM ˈbɜrˌlæp

Burleigh
BR ˈbəːli
AM ˈbɜrli

burlesque
BR bəːˈlɛsk, -s, -ɪŋ, -t
AM ˌbɜrˈlɛsk, -s, -ɪŋ, -t

burlesquer
BR bəːˈlɛskə(r), -z
AM ˌbɜrˈlɛskər, -z

Burley
BR ˈbəːli
AM ˈbɜrli

burliness
BR ˈbəːlɪnɪs
AM ˈbɜrlinɪs

Burlington
BR ˈbəːlɪŋt(ə)n
AM ˈbɜrlɪŋt(ə)n

burly
BR ˈbəːl|i, -ɪə(r), -ɪɪst
AM ˈbɜrli, -ər, -ɪst

Burma
BR ˈbəːmə(r)
AM ˈbɜrmə

Burman
BR ˈbəːmən, -z
AM ˈbɜrmən, -z

Burmese
BR ˌbəːˈmiːz
AM ˌbɜrˈmiz

burn
BR bəːn, -z, -ɪŋ, -d
AM bɜrn, -z, -ɪŋ, -d

Burnaby
BR ˈbəːnəbi
AM ˈbɜrnəbi

Burnaston
BR ˈbəːnəst(ə)n
AM ˈbɜrnəst(ə)n

Burne
BR bəːn
AM bɜrn

burner
BR ˈbəːnə(r), -z
AM ˈbɜrnər, -z

burnet
BR ˈbəːnɪt, -s
AM bɜrˈnɛt, ˈbɜrnət, -s

Burnett
BR bə(ː)ˈnɛt, ˈbəːnɪt
AM bɜrˈnɛt

Burney
BR ˈbəːni
AM ˈbɜrni

Burnham
BR ˈbəːnəm
AM ˈbɜrnəm

burningly
BR ˈbəːnɪŋli
AM ˈbɜrnɪŋli

burnish
BR ˈbəːn|ɪʃ, -ɪʃɪz, -ɪʃɪŋ, -ɪʃt
AM ˈbɜrnɪʃ, -ɪz, -ɪŋ, -t

burnisher
BR ˈbəːnɪʃə(r), -z
AM ˈbɜrnɪʃər, -z

Burnley
BR ˈbəːnli
AM ˈbɜrnli

burnoose
BR bəːˈnuːs, -ɪz
AM bɜrˈnus, -əz

burnous
BR bəːˈnuːs, -ɪz
AM bɜrˈnus, -əz

burnouse
BR bəːˈnuːs, -ɪz
AM bɜrˈnus, -əz

Burns
BR bəːnz
AM bɜrnz

Burnside
BR ˈbəːnsʌɪd
AM ˈbɜrnˌsaɪd

burnt
BR bəːnt
AM bɜrnt

Burntisland
BR (ˌ)bəːntˈʌɪlənd
AM ˌbɜrn(t)ˈaɪlənd

burp
BR bəːp, -s, -ɪŋ, -t
AM bɜrp, -s, -ɪŋ, -t

burr
BR bəː(r), -z, -ɪŋ, -d
AM bɜr, -z, -ɪŋ, -d

Burra
BR ˈbʌrə(r)
AM ˈbɜrə

burrawang
BR ˈbʌrəwaŋ, -z
AM ˈbɜrəˌwæŋ, -z

Burrell
BR ˈbʌrəl, ˈbʌrḷ
AM ˈbɜrəl

Burren
BR ˈbʌrən, ˈbʌrɳ
AM ˈbɜrən

burrito
BR bʊˈriːtəʊ, bʌˈriːtəʊ, -z
AM bəˈridoʊ, -z

burro
BR ˈbʌrəʊ, ˈbʊrəʊ, -z
AM ˈbɜroʊ, ˈbʊroʊ, ˈbɜrə, -z

Burrough
BR ˈbʌrəʊ
AM ˈbɜroʊ

Burroughs
BR ˈbʌrəʊz
AM ˈbɜroʊz

burrow
BR ˈbʌrəʊ, -z, -ɪŋ, -d
AM ˈbɜr|oʊ, -oʊz, -əwɪŋ, -oʊd

burrower
BR ˈbʌrəʊə(r), -z
AM ˈbɜrəwər, -z

Burrows
BR ˈbʌrəʊz
AM ˈbɜroʊz

bursa
BR ˈbəːsə(r), -z
AM ˈbɜrsə, -z

bursae
BR ˈbəːsiː
AM ˈbɜrsi, ˈbɜrˌsaɪ

bursal
BR ˈbəːsl
AM ˈbɜrsəl

bursar
BR ˈbəːsə(r), -z
AM ˈbɜrsər, ˈbɜrˌsɑr, -z

bursarial
BR bəːˈsɛːrɪəl
AM bɜrˈsɛrɪəl

bursarship
BR ˈbəːsəʃɪp, -s
AM ˈbɜrsərˌʃɪp, -s

bursary
BR ˈbəːs(ə)r|i, -ɪz
AM ˈbɜrsəri, -z

burse
BR bəːs, -ɪz
AM bɜrs, -ɪz

bursitis BR bəˈsaɪtɪs AM bərˈsaɪdɪs	**bushcraft** BR ˈbʊʃkrɑːft, ˈbʊʃkraft AM ˈbʊʃˌkræft	**businessman** BR ˈbɪznɪsmən, ˈbɪznɪsˌman AM ˈbɪznɪsˌmæn,	**busyness** BR ˈbɪznɪs AM ˈbɪzinɪs
Burslem BR ˈbəːzləm AM ˈbərzləm	**bushel** BR ˈbʊʃl, -z AM ˈbʊʃəl, -z	ˈbɪznɪzˌmæn **businessmen** BR ˈbɪznɪsmən,	**busywork** BR ˈbɪzɪwəːk AM ˈbɪziˌwərk
burst BR bəːst, -s, -ɪŋ AM bərst, -s, -ɪŋ	**bushelful** BR ˈbʊʃlfʊl, -z AM ˈbʊʃəlˌfʊl, -z	ˈbɪznɪsˌmɛn AM ˈbɪznɪsˌmɛn, ˈbɪznɪzˌmɛn	**but**[1] *strong form* BR bʌt, -s, -ɪŋ, -ɪd
Burstall BR ˈbəːst(ɔː)l AM ˈbərˌstɔl, ˈbərˌstɑl	**Bushey** BR ˈbʊʃi AM ˈbʊʃi	**businesswoman** BR ˈbɪznɪsˌwʊmən AM ˈbɪznɪsˌwʊmən,	AM bəlt, -ts, -dɪŋ, -dəd **but**[2] *weak form*
burstproof BR ˈbəːs(t)pruːf AM ˈbərs(t)ˌprʊf	**bushfire** BR ˈbʊʃˌfʌɪə(r), -z AM ˈbʊʃˌfaɪ(ə)r, -z	ˈbɪznɪzˌwʊmən **businesswomen** BR ˈbɪznɪsˌwɪmɪn	BR bət, -s AM bət, -s **butadiene**
Burt BR bəːt AM bərt	**bushido** BR bʊˈʃiːdəʊ, ˌbʊʃɪˈdəʊ AM ˈbuʃiˌdoʊ	AM ˈbɪznɪsˌwɪmɪn, ˈbɪznɪzˌwɪmɪn	BR ˌbjuːtəˈdʌɪiːn AM ˌbjudəˈdaɪˌin **but and ben**
burthen BR ˈbəːðn, -z AM ˈbərðən, -z	**bushily** BR ˈbʊʃɪli AM ˈbuʃəli	**busk** BR bʌsk, -s, -ɪŋ, -t AM bəsk, -s, -ɪŋ, -t	BR ˌbʌt (ə)n(d) ˈbɛn AM ˌbəd ən ˈbɛn **butane**
burton BR ˈbəːtn, -z AM ˈbərtn, -z	**bushiness** BR ˈbʊʃɪnɪs AM ˈbuʃinɪs	**busker** BR ˈbʌskə(r), -z AM ˈbəskər, -z	BR ˈbjuːteɪn AM ˈbjuˌteɪn **butanoic**
Burtonwood BR ˈbəːtnˈwʊd AM ˈbərtnˌwʊd	**Bushman** BR ˈbʊʃmən AM ˈbʊʃmən	**buskin** BR ˈbʌskɪn, -z, -d AM ˈbəskən, -z, -d	BR ˌbjuːtəˈnəʊɪk AM ˌbjudəˈnoʊɪk **butanol**
Burundan BR bʊˈrʊndən, -z AM bəˈrʊndən, -z	**bushmaster** BR ˈbʊʃˌmɑːstə(r), ˈbʊʃˌmastə(r), -z AM ˈbʊʃˌmæstər, -z	**busman** BR ˈbʌsmən AM ˈbəsmən	BR ˈbjuːtənɒl AM ˈbjudəˌnɒl, ˈbjudəˌnɑl
Burundi BR bʊˈrʊndi AM bəˈrʊndi	**Bushmen** BR ˈbʊʃmən AM ˈbʊʃmən	**busmen** BR ˈbʌsmən AM ˈbəsmən	**butanone** BR ˈbjuːtənəʊn AM ˈbjudəˌnoʊn
Burundian BR bʊˈrʊndɪən, -z AM bəˈrʊndɪən, -z	**Bushnell** BR ˈbʊʃnl AM ˈbʊʃˌnɛl	**buss** BR bʌs, -ɪz, -ɪŋ, -t AM bəs, -əz, -ɪŋ, -t	**butch** BR bʊtʃ AM bʊtʃ
bury BR ˈbɛr|i, -ɪz, -ɪŋ, -ɪd AM ˈbɛri, -z, -ɪŋ, -d	**bushranger** BR ˈbʊʃˌreɪn(d)ʒə(r), -z AM ˈbʊʃˌreɪndʒər, -z	**bust** BR bʌst, -s, -ɪŋ, -ɪd AM bəst, -s, -ɪŋ, -ɪd	**butcher** BR ˈbʊtʃə(r), -z, -ɪŋ, -d AM ˈbʊtʃər, -z, -ɪŋ, -d
Bury St Edmunds BR ˌbɛrɪ snt ˈɛdmən(d)z AM ˌbɛri ˌseɪnt ˈɛdmən(d)z	**bushveld** BR ˈbʊʃvɛlt AM ˈbʊʃˌvɛlt	**bustard** BR ˈbʌstəd, -z AM ˈbəstərd, -z **bustee**	**butcherly** BR ˈbʊtʃəli AM ˈbʊtʃərli **butchery**
bus BR bʌs, -ɪz, -ɪŋ, -t AM bəs, -ɪz, -ɪŋ, -t	**bushwhack** BR ˈbʊʃwak, -s, -ɪŋ, -t AM ˈbʊʃˌ(h)wæk, -s, -ɪŋ, -t	BR ˈbʌstiː, -z AM bəsˈti, -z **buster**	BR ˈbʊtʃ(ə)r|i, -ɪz AM ˈbʊtʃəri, -z **Bute**
busbar BR ˈbʌsbɑː(r), -z AM ˈbəsˌbɑr, -z	**bushwhacker** BR ˈbʊʃˌwakə(r), -z AM ˈbʊʃˌ(h)wækər, -z	BR ˈbʌstə(r), -z AM ˈbəstər, -z **bustier**	BR bjuːt AM bjut **butene**
busboy BR ˈbʌsbɔɪ, -z AM ˈbəsˌbɔɪ, -z	**bushy** BR ˈbʊʃ|i, -ɪə(r), -ɪɪst AM ˈbʊʃi, -ər, -ɪst	BR ˈbʌstɪeɪ, ˈbʊstɪeɪ, -z AM ˈbəstɪər, -z **bustiness**	BR ˈbjuːtiːn AM ˈbjudin **Buthelezi**
busby BR ˈbʌzb|i, -ɪz AM ˈbəzbi, -z	**busily** BR ˈbɪzɪli AM ˈbɪzɪli	BR ˈbʌstɪnɪs AM ˈbəstinɪs **bustle**	BR ˌbuːtəˈleɪzi AM ˌbudəˈleɪzi **butle**
bush BR bʊʃ, -ɪz, -ɪŋ, -t AM bʊʃ, -ɪz, -ɪŋ, -t	**business** BR ˈbɪznɪs, -ɪz AM ˈbɪznɪs, ˈbɪznɪz, -əz	BR ˈbʌs|l, -lz, -lɪŋ \-lɪŋ, -ld AM ˈbəs|əl, -əlz, -(ə)lɪŋ, -əld	BR ˈbʌt|l, -lz, -lɪŋ \-lɪŋ, -ld AM ˈbədəl, -z, -ɪŋ, -d
bushbaby BR ˈbʊʃˌbeɪb|i, -ɪz AM ˈbʊʃˌbeɪbi, -z	**businesslike** BR ˈbɪznɪslʌɪk AM ˈbɪznɪsˌlaɪk, ˈbɪznɪzˌlaɪk	**busty** BR ˈbʌst|i, -ɪə(r), -ɪɪst AM ˈbəsti, -ər, -ɪst	**butler** BR ˈbʌtlə(r), -z AM ˈbətlər, -z
bushbuck BR ˈbʊʃbʌk, -s AM ˈbʊʃˌbək, -s		**busy** BR ˈbɪz|i, -ɪə(r), -ɪɪst AM ˈbɪzi, -ər, -ɪst	**Butlin's** BR ˈbʌtlɪnz AM ˈbətlənz
		busybody BR ˈbɪzɪˌbɒd|i, -ɪz AM ˈbɪziˌbɑdi, -z	**butt** BR bʌt, -s, -ɪŋ, -ɪd AM bəlt, -ts, -dɪŋ, -dəd

butte
BR bjuːt, -s
AM bjut, -s
butter
BR 'bʌt|ə(r), -əz,
-(ə)rɪŋ, -əd
AM 'bʌd|ər, -əz, -(ə)rɪŋ,
-əd
butterball
BR 'bʌtəbɔːl, -z
AM 'bʌdər,bɒl,
'bʌdər,bɑl, -z
butterbur
BR 'bʌtəbəː(r), -z
AM 'bʌdər,bər, -z
buttercream
BR 'bʌtəkriːm
AM 'bʌdər,krim
buttercup
BR 'bʌtəkʌp, -s
AM 'bʌdər,kəp, -s
butterdish
BR 'bʌtədɪʃ, -ɪz
AM 'bʌdər,dɪʃ, -ɪz
butterfat
BR 'bʌtəfat
AM 'bʌdər,fæt
Butterfield
BR 'bʌtəfiːld
AM 'bʌdər,fild
butterfingers
BR 'bʌtə,fɪŋgəz
AM 'bʌdər,fɪŋgərz
butterfish
BR 'bʌtəfɪʃ
AM 'bʌdər,fɪʃ
butterfly
BR 'bʌtəflʌɪ, -z
AM 'bʌdər,flaɪ, -z
butteriness
BR 'bʌt(ə)rɪnɪs
AM 'bʌdərinɪs
Butterkist®
BR 'bʌtəkɪst
AM 'bʌdər,kɪst
butterknife
BR 'bʌtənʌɪf
AM 'bʌdər,naɪf
butterknives
BR 'bʌtənʌɪvz
AM 'bʌdər,naɪvz
Buttermere
BR 'bʌtəmɪə(r)
AM 'bʌdər,mɪ(ə)r
buttermilk
BR 'bʌtəmɪlk
AM 'bʌdər,mɪlk
butternut
BR 'bʌtənʌt, -s
AM 'bʌdər,nət, -s
Butters
BR 'bʌtəz
AM 'bʌdərz
butterscotch
BR 'bʌtəskɒtʃ, -ɪz
AM 'bʌdər,skɑtʃ, -ɪz

butterwort
BR 'bʌtəwəːt, -s
AM 'bʌdər,wərt,
'bʌdər,wɔ(ə)rt, -s
Butterworth
BR 'bʌtəwəːθ
AM 'bʌdər,wərθ
buttery
BR 'bʌt(ə)r|i, -ɪz
AM 'bʌdəri, 'bʌtri, -z
buttle
BR 'bʌt|l, -lz, -|ɪŋ\-lɪŋ,
-ld
AM 'bʌdəl, -z, -ɪŋ, -d
buttock
BR 'bʌtək, -s
AM 'bʌdək, -s
button
BR 'bʌtn, -z, -ɪŋ, -d
AM 'bʌt|n, -nz, -(ə)nɪŋ,
-nd
buttonhole
BR 'bʌtnhəʊl, -z, -ɪŋ, -d
AM 'bʌtn,(h)oʊl, -z, -ɪŋ,
-d
buttonhook
BR 'bʌtnhʊk, -s
AM 'bʌtn,(h)ʊk, -s
buttonless
BR 'bʌtnləs
AM 'bʌtnləs
Buttons
BR 'bʌtnz
AM 'bʌtnz
buttonwood
BR 'bʌtnwʊd, -z
AM 'bʌtn,wʊd, -z
buttony
BR 'bʌtni
AM 'bʌtni
buttress
BR 'bʌtrɪs, -ɪz, -ɪŋ, -t
AM 'bʌtrəs, -əz, -ɪŋ, -t
butty
BR 'bʌt|i, -ɪz
AM 'bʌdi, -z
butyl
BR 'bjuːtʌɪl, 'bjuːtɪl
AM 'bjudl, 'bju,tɪl
butyrate
BR 'bjuːtɪreɪt
AM 'bjudə,reɪt
butyric
BR bjuː'tɪrɪk
AM bju'tɪrɪk
buxom
BR 'bʌks(ə)m
AM 'bʌksəm
buxomly
BR 'bʌks(ə)mli
AM 'bʌksəmli
buxomness
BR 'bʌks(ə)mnəs
AM 'bʌksəmnəs
Buxted
BR 'bʌkstɪd, 'bʌkstɛd
AM 'bək,stɛd

Buxtehude
BR ,bʊkstə'huːdə(r),
'bʊkstə,hu:də(r)
AM 'bəkstə,hudə
DAN ,bugsdə'hu:ðə
Buxton
BR 'bʌkstən
AM 'bəkstən
buy
BR bʌɪ, -z, -ɪŋ
AM baɪ, -z, -ɪŋ
buyable
BR 'bʌɪəbl
AM 'baɪəbəl
buyer
BR 'bʌɪə(r), -z
AM 'baɪər, -z
buyout
BR 'bʌɪaʊt, -s
AM 'baɪ,aʊt, -s
Buzby
BR 'bʌzbi
AM 'bəzbi
Buzfuz
BR 'bʌzfʌz
AM 'bəz,fəz
buzz
BR bʌz, -ɪz, -ɪŋ, -d
AM bəz, -əz, -ɪŋ, -d
buzzard
BR 'bʌzəd, -z
AM 'bəzərd, -z
buzzer
BR 'bʌzə(r), -z
AM 'bəzər, -z
buzzword
BR 'bʌzwəːd, -z
AM 'bəz,wərd, -z
bwana
BR 'bwɑːnə(r), -z
AM 'bwɑnə, -z
Bwlch
BR bʊlx, bʊlk
AM bʊlk
by
BR bʌɪ
AM baɪ
Byatt
BR 'bʌɪət
AM 'baɪət
Byblos
BR 'bɪblɒs
AM 'bɪblɑs
bye
BR bʌɪ, -z
AM baɪ, -z
bye-bye
goodbye
BR ,bʌɪ'bʌɪ, -z
AM ,baɪ'baɪ, -z
bye-byes
sleep
BR 'bʌɪbʌɪz
AM ,baɪ'baɪz
byelaw
BR 'bʌɪlɔː(r), -z
AM 'baɪ,lɔ, 'baɪ,lɑ, -z

Byelorussia
BR ,bjɛləʊ'rʌʃə(r),
bɪ,ɛləʊ'rʌʃə(r),
,bjɛləʊ'ru:sɪə(r),
bɪ,ɛləʊ'ru:sɪə(r)
AM ,bjɛlə'rəʃə
Byelorussian
BR ,bjɛləʊ'rʌʃn,
bɪ,ɛləʊ'rʌʃn,
,bjɛləʊ'ru:sɪən,
bɪ,ɛləʊ'ru:sɪən, -z
AM ,bjɛlə'rəʃən, -z
Byers
BR 'bʌɪəz
AM 'baɪərz
Byfield
BR 'bʌɪfiːld
AM 'baɪ,fild
Byfleet
BR 'bʌɪfliːt
AM 'baɪ,flit
bygone
BR 'bʌɪgɒn, -z
AM 'baɪ,gɔn, 'baɪ,gɑn,
-z
Bygraves
BR 'bʌɪgreɪvz
AM 'baɪ,greɪvz
Byker
BR 'bʌɪkə(r)
AM 'baɪkər
bylaw
BR 'bʌɪlɔː(r), -z
AM 'baɪ,lɔ, 'baɪ,lɑ, -z
byline
BR 'bʌɪlʌɪn, -z
AM 'baɪ,laɪn, -z
byname
BR 'bʌɪneɪm, -z
AM 'baɪ,neɪm, -z
Byng
BR bɪŋ
AM bɪŋ
bypass
BR 'bʌɪpɑːs, 'bʌɪpas,
-ɪz, -ɪŋ, -t
AM 'baɪ,pæs, -əz, -ɪŋ, -t
bypath
BR 'bʌɪpɑː|θ, 'bʌɪpa|θ,
-θs\-ðz
AM 'baɪ,pæ|θ, -θs\-ðz
byplay
BR 'bʌɪpleɪ
AM 'baɪ,pleɪ
Byrd
BR bəːd
AM bərd
Byrds
BR bəːdz
AM bərdz
byre
BR 'bʌɪə(r), -z
AM 'baɪ(ə)r, -z
Byrne
BR bəːn
AM bərn
byroad
BR 'bʌɪrəʊd, -z

AM 'baɪˌruːd, -z

Byron
BR 'baɪrən
AM 'baɪrən

Byronic
BR baɪ'rɒnɪk
AM baɪ'rɑnɪk

Byronically
BR baɪ'rɒnɪkli
AM baɪ'rɑnək(ə)li

Bysshe
BR bɪʃ
AM bɪʃ

byssi
BR 'bɪsaɪ
AM 'bɪˌsaɪ, 'bɪˌsi

byssinosis
BR ˌbɪsɪ'nəʊsɪs
AM ˌbɪsɪ'noʊsəs

byssus
BR 'bɪsəs, -ɪz
AM 'bɪsəs, -əz

bystander
BR 'baɪˌstandə(r), -z
AM 'baɪˌstændər, -z

byte
BR baɪt, -s

AM baɪt, -s

byway
BR 'baɪweɪ, -z
AM 'baɪˌweɪ, -z

byword
BR 'baɪwɜːd, -z
AM 'baɪˌwərd, -z

Byzantine
BR bɪ'zantaɪn,
baɪ'zantaɪn,
'bɪzntaɪn,
'bɪznti:n
AM 'bɪzənˌtin

Byzantinism
BR bɪ'zantɪnɪz(ə)m,
baɪ'zantɪnɪz(ə)m
AM bə'zæn(t)əˌnɪzəm

Byzantinist
BR bɪ'zantɪnɪst,
baɪ'zantɪnɪst, -s
AM bə'zæn(t)ənəst, -s

Byzantium
BR bɪ'zantɪəm,
baɪ'zantəm
AM bə'zæn(t)iəm,
baɪ'zæn(t)iəm

Cc

c
BR siː, -z
AM siː, -z

Caaba
BR 'kɑːbə(r), 'kɑbə(r)
AM 'kɑbə, 'kæbə

cab
BR kab, -z
AM kæb, -z

cabal
BR kə'bal, -z
AM kə'bɑl, kə'bæl, -z

cabala
BR kə'bɑːlə(r),
'kabələ(r), -z
AM kə'bɑlə, 'kæbələ, -z

cabalism
BR kə'bɑːlɪz(ə)m,
'kabəlɪz(ə)m
AM 'kæbə,lɪzəm

cabalist
BR kə'bɑːlɪst,
'kabəlɪst, -s
AM 'kæbələst, -s

cabalistic
BR ,kabə'lɪstɪk
AM ,kæbə'lɪstɪk

cabalistical
BR ,kabə'lɪstɪkl
AM ,kæbə'lɪstɪkəl

cabalistically
BR ,kabə'lɪstɪkli
AM ,kæbə'lɪstək(ə)li

caballero
BR ,kabə'lɛːrəʊ,
,kabə'jɛːrəʊ, -z
AM ,kæbə'jerəʊ,
,kæbl'ɛrəʊ,
,kabə'jerəʊ,
,kabl'ərəʊ, -z

cabana
BR kə'bɑːnə(r), -z
AM kə'bænə, -z

cabaret
BR 'kabəreɪ, -z
AM ,kæbə,reɪ, -z

cabbage
BR 'kab|ɪdʒ, -ɪdʒɪz
AM 'kæbɪdʒ, -ɪz

cabbagy
BR 'kabɪdʒi
AM 'kæbɪdʒi

cabbala
BR kə'bɑːlə(r),
'kabələ(r), -s
AM kə'bɑlə, 'kæbələ, -z

cabbalism
BR kə'bɑːlɪz(ə)m,
'kabəlɪz(ə)m
AM 'kæbə,lɪzəm

cabbalist
BR kə'bɑːlɪst,
'kabəlɪst, -s
AM 'kæbələst, -s

cabbalistic
BR ,kabə'lɪstɪk
AM ,kæbə'lɪstɪk

cabbalistical
BR ,kabə'lɪstɪkl
AM ,kæbə'lɪstɪkəl

cabbalistically
BR ,kabə'lɪstɪkli
AM ,kæbə'lɪstək(ə)li

cabbie
BR 'kab|i, -ɪz
AM 'kæbi, -z

cabby
BR 'kab|i, -ɪz
AM 'kæbi, -z

cabdriver
BR 'kab,drʌɪvə(r), -z
AM 'kæb,draɪvər, -z

caber
BR 'keɪbə(r), -z
AM 'kɑbər, 'keɪbər, -z

cabernet
BR 'kabəneɪ
AM ,kæbər'neɪ

Cabernet Franc
BR ,kabəneɪ 'frɒ̃
AM ,kæbər'neɪ 'frɑŋk

Cabernet Sauvignon
BR ,kabəneɪ ,səʊvɪ'njɒ̃
AM 'kæbər'neɪ
soʊvən'jɑn

cabin
BR 'kabɪn, -z
AM 'kæbən, -z

Cabinda
BR kə'bɪndə(r)
AM kə'bɪndə

cabinet
BR 'kabɪnɪt, 'kabn̩ɪt, -s
AM 'kæb(ə)nət, -s

cabinetmaker
BR 'kabɪnɪt,meɪkə(r),
'kabn̩ɪt,meɪkə(r), -z
AM 'kæb(ə)nət,meɪkər,
-z

cabinetmaking
BR 'kabɪnɪt,meɪkɪŋ,
'kabn̩ɪt,meɪkɪŋ
AM 'kæb(ə)nət,meɪkɪŋ

cabinetry
BR 'kabɪnɪtri,
'kabn̩ɪtri
AM 'kæb(ə)nətri

cable
BR 'keɪb|l, -lz, -l̩ŋ \ -lɪŋ,
-ld
AM 'keɪbəl, -əlz,
-(ə)lɪŋ, -əld

cablecar
BR 'keɪblkɑː(r), -z
AM 'keɪbəl,kɑr, -z

cablegram
BR 'keɪblgram, -z

AM 'keɪbəl,græm, -z

cableway
BR 'keɪblweɪ, -z
AM 'keɪbəl,weɪ, -z

cabman
BR 'kabmən
AM 'kæb,mæn,
'kæbmən

cabmen
BR 'kabmən
AM 'kæb,men,
'kæbmən

cabochon
BR 'kabəʃɒn
AM 'kæbə,ʃɑn

caboodle
BR kə'buːdl
AM kə'budəl

caboose
BR kə'buːs, -ɪz
AM kə,bus, -ɪz

Cabora Bassa
BR kə,bɔːrə 'basə(r)
AM kə,bɔrə 'basə

Caborn
BR 'keɪbɔːn
AM 'keɪ,bɔ(ə)rn

caboshed
BR kə'bɒʃt
AM kə'baʃt

Cabot
BR 'kabət
AM 'kæbət

cabotage
BR 'kabətɑːʒ,
'kabətɪdʒ
AM 'kæbə,taʒ,
'kæbədɪdʒ

cabotin
BR 'kabətɪn, -z
AM 'kæbətɪn, -z

cabotine
BR 'kabətiːn, -z
AM 'kæbə,tin, -z

cabriole
BR 'kabrɪəʊl,
,kabrɪ'əʊl, -z
AM 'kæbriəʊl,
'kæbriɔl, -z

cabriolet
BR 'kabrɪəleɪ, -z
AM ,kæbriə'leɪ, -z

ca'canny
BR ,kɑː'kani, ,kɑː'kɒni
AM kæ'kæni

cacao
BR kə'kaʊ, kə'kɑːəʊ,
kə'keɪəʊ, -z
AM kə'kaʊ, kə'kaʊʊ,
kə'keɪəʊ, -z

cacciatore
BR ,katʃə'tɔːri,
,kɑːtʃə'tɔːri,
,katʃə'tɔːreɪ,
,kɑːtʃə'tɔːreɪ
AM ,katʃə'tɔːri,
,kætʃə'tɔːri

cachalot
BR 'kaʃəlɒt, -s
AM 'kæʃə,lɑt, -s

cache
BR kaʃ, -ɪz, -ɪŋ, -t
AM kæʃ, -əz, -ɪŋ, -t

cachectic
BR kə'kɛktɪk
AM kə'kɛktɪk

cachepot
BR ,kaʃ'pəʊ, 'kaʃpɒt
AM 'kæʃ,pɑt, 'kæʃ,poʊ

cachet
BR 'kaʃeɪ, -z
AM kæ'ʃeɪ, -z

cachexia
BR ka'kɛksɪə(r),
kə'kɛksɪə(r)
AM kə'kɛksɪə

cachexy
BR ka'kɛksi, kə'kɛksi
AM kə'kɛksi

cachinnate
BR 'kakɪneɪt, -s, -ɪŋ, -ɪd
AM 'kækə,neɪt, -ts,
-dɪŋ, -dɪd

cachinnation
BR ,kakɪ'neɪʃn, -z
AM ,kækə'neɪʃən, -z

cachinnatory
BR ,kakɪ'neɪt(ə)ri
AM 'kækənə,tɔri

cacholong
BR 'kaʃəlɒŋ, -z
AM 'kaʃə,lɔŋ,
'kaʃə,lɑŋ, -z

cachou
BR 'kaʃuː, kə'ʃuː, -z
AM kæ'ʃu, kə'ʃu, -z

cachucha
BR kə'tʃuːtʃə(r), -z
AM kə'tʃutʃə, -z

cacique
BR ka'siːk, kə'siːk, -s
AM kə'sik, -s

caciquism
BR ka'siːkɪz(ə)m,
kə'siːkɪz(ə)m
AM kə'si,kɪzəm

cackle
BR 'kak|l, -lz, -l̩ŋ \ -lɪŋ,
-ld
AM 'kæk|əl, -əlz,
-(ə)lɪŋ, -əld

cackler
BR 'kaklə(r),
'kaklə(r), -z
AM 'kæk(ə)lər, -z

cacodaemon
BR ,kakə'diːmən, -z
AM ,kækə'dimən, -z

cacodemon
BR ,kakə'diːmən, -z
AM ,kækə'dimən, -z

cacodyl
BR 'kakədʌɪl, 'kakədɪl
AM 'kækə,dɪl

cacodylic
BR ˌkakəˈdɪlɪk
AM ˌkækəˈdɪlɪk
cacoepy
BR kaˈkəʊɪpi,
kəˈkəʊɪpi, ˈkakəʊpi
AM ˈkækəˌwɛpi,
kəˈkawəpi
cacoethes
BR ˌkakəʊˈiːθiːz
AM ˌkækəˈwiðiz
cacographer
BR kaˈkɒgrəfə(r),
kəˈkɒgrəfə(r), -z
AM kəˈkɑgrəfər, -z
cacographic
BR ˌkakəˈgrafɪk
AM ˌkækəˈgræfɪk
cacographical
BR ˌkakəˈgrafɪkl
AM ˌkækəˈgræfɪkəl
cacography
BR kaˈkɒgrəfi,
kəˈkɒgrəfi
AM kəˈkɑgræfi
cacology
BR kaˈkɒlədʒi,
kəˈkɒlədʒi
AM kəˈkalədʒi
cacomistle
BR ˈkakəˌmɪsl, -z
AM ˈkækəˌmɪsəl, -z
cacophonous
BR kəˈkɒfənəs,
kəˈkɒfnəs,
kaˈkɒfənəs, kaˈkɒfnəs
AM kəˈkafənəs
cacophony
BR kəˈkɒfən|i,
kəˈkɒfn̩|i, kaˈkɒfən|i,
kaˈkɒfn̩|i, -ɪz
AM kəˈkafəni, -z
cactaceous
BR kakˈteɪʃəs
AM kækˈteɪʃəs
cactal
BR ˈkaktl
AM ˈkæktl
cacti
BR ˈkaktaɪ
AM ˈkækˌtaɪ
cactus
BR ˈkaktəs, -ɪz
AM ˈkæktəs, -əz
cacuminal
BR kaˈkjuːmɪnl,
kəˈkjuːmɪnl
AM kəˈkjumənəl
cad
BR kad, -z
AM kæd, -z
cadastral
BR kəˈdastr(ə)l
AM kəˈdæstrəl
cadaver
BR kəˈdavə(r),
kəˈdɑːvə(r),
kəˈdeɪvə(r), -z

cadaveric
BR kəˈdav(ə)rɪk
AM kəˈdæv(ə)rɪk
cadaverous
BR kəˈdav(ə)rəs
AM kəˈdæv(ə)rəs
cadaverousness
BR kəˈdav(ə)rəsnəs
AM kəˈdæv(ə)rəsnəs
Cadbury
BR ˈkadb(ə)ri
AM ˈkædbəri
CAD-CAM
BR ˈkadkam
AM ˈkædˌkæm
caddie
BR ˈkad|i, -ɪz
AM ˈkædi, -z
caddis
BR ˈkadɪs
AM ˈkædəs
caddish
BR ˈkadɪʃ
AM ˈkædɪʃ
caddishly
BR ˈkadɪʃli
AM ˈkædɪʃli
caddishness
BR ˈkadɪʃnɪs
AM ˈkædɪʃnɪs
caddy
BR ˈkad|i, -ɪz
AM ˈkædi, -z
cade
BR keɪd, -z
AM keɪd, -z
Cadell
BR kəˈdɛl, ˈkadl
AM kəˈdɛl, ˈkædəl
cadence
BR ˈkeɪdns, -ɪz, -t
AM ˈkeɪdns, -ɪz, -t
cadency
BR ˈkeɪdns|i, -ɪz
AM ˈkeɪdnsi, -z
cadential
BR keɪˈdɛnʃl
AM ˌkeɪˈdɛn(t)ʃəl
cadenza
BR kəˈdɛnzə(r), -z
AM kəˈdɛnzə, -z
Cader Idris
BR ˌkadər ˈɪdrɪs
AM ˌkɑdər ˈɪdrɪs
cadet
BR kəˈdɛt, -s
AM kəˈdɛt, -s
cadetship
BR kəˈdɛtˌʃɪp, -s
AM kəˈdɛtˌʃɪp, -s
cadge
BR kadʒ, -ɪz, -ɪŋ, -d
AM kædʒ, -əz, -ɪŋ, -d
cadger
BR kadʒə(r), -z
AM kædʒər, -z

cadi
BR ˈkɑːd|i, -ɪz
AM ˈkɑdi, -z
Cadillac®
BR ˈkadɪlak, ˈkadlak,
-s
AM ˈkædəˌlæk, -s
Cadiz
BR kəˈdɪz
AM kəˈdiz, kəˈdɪz
Cadíz
BR kəˈdɪz
AM kəˈdiz, kəˈdɪz
Cadman
BR ˈkadmən
AM ˈkædmən
Cadmean
BR kadˈmiːən
AM kædˈmi(ə)n,
ˈkædmin
cadmic
BR ˈkadmɪk
AM ˈkædmɪk
cadmium
BR ˈkadmɪəm
AM ˈkædmiəm
Cadmus
BR ˈkadməs
AM ˈkædməs
Cadogan
BR kəˈdʌg(ə)n
AM kəˈdagən
cadre
BR ˈkɑːdə(r), -z
AM ˈkædˌreɪ, ˈkædri,
ˈkadri, ˈkadˌreɪ, -z
caducei
BR kəˈdjuːsɪʌɪ,
kəˈdjuːʃɪʌɪ,
kəˈdʒuːsɪʌɪ,
kəˈdʒuːʃɪʌɪ
AM kəˈd(j)uʃiˌaɪ,
kəˈd(j)usiˌaɪ
caduceus
BR kəˈdjuːsɪəs,
kəˈdjuːʃɪəs,
kəˈdʒuːsɪəs,
kəˈdʒuːʃɪəs
AM kəˈd(j)uːʃ(i)əs,
kəˈd(j)usiəs
caducity
BR kəˈdjuːsɪti,
kəˈdʒuːsɪti
AM kəˈd(j)usədi
caducous
BR kəˈdjuːkəs,
kəˈdʒuːkəs
AM kəˈd(j)ukəs
Cadwallader
BR kadˈwɒlədə(r)
AM ˌkædˈwalədər
caeca
BR ˈsiːkə(r)
AM ˈsikə

caecilian
BR sɪˈsɪliən, -z
AM siˈsɪljən, siˈsɪliən,
-z
caecitis
BR sɪˈsaɪtɪs
AM siˈsaɪdəs
caecum
BR ˈsiːk(ə)m
AM ˈsikəm
Caedmon
BR ˈkadmən
AM ˈkædmən
Caen
BR kɒ̃, kɑːn
AM kɑn
Caenozoic
BR ˌsiːnəˈzəʊɪk
AM ˌsinəˈzoʊɪk
Caernarfon
BR kəˈnɑːvn
AM kərˈnarvən
WE kaɪrˈnarvɒn
Caernarvonshire
BR kəˈnɑːvnʃ(ɪ)ə(r)
AM kərˈnarvənʃɪ(ə)r
Caesar
BR ˈsiːzə(r), -z
AM ˈsizər, -z
Caesarea
BR ˌsiːzəˈriːə(r)
AM sɪzəˈriə
caesarean
BR sɪˈzɛːrɪən, -z
AM sɪˈzɛriən, -z
caesarian
BR sɪˈzɛːrɪən, -z
AM sɪˈzɛriən, -z
caesious
BR ˈsiːzɪəs
AM ˈsiziəs
caesium
BR ˈsiːzɪəm
AM ˈsiziəm
caesura
BR sɪˈzjʊərə(r),
sɪˈʒʊərə(r),
sɪˈzjɔːrə(r), -z
AM sɪˈʒʊrə, sɪˈzʊrə, -z
caesural
BR sɪˈzjʊərəl,
sɪˈzjʊərl̩, sɪˈʒʊərəl,
sɪˈʒʊərl̩, sɪˈzjɔːrəl,
sɪˈzjɔːrl̩, sɪˈʒɔːrəl,
sɪˈʒɔːrl̩
AM sɪˈʒʊrəl, sɪˈzurəl
cafard
BR kaˈfɑː(r)
AM ˈkæfər
café
BR ˈkafeɪ, ˈkaf|i, -eɪ-ɪz
AM ˌkæˈfeɪ, kəˈfeɪ, -z
café au lait
BR ˌkafeɪ əʊ ˈleɪ, -z
AM ˈkæˌfeɪ oʊ ˈleɪ,
kəˈfeɪ oʊ ˈleɪ, -z

café noir
BR ˌkafeɪ ˈnwɑː(r), -z
AM ˌkæˌfeɪ ˈnwɑr, -z

cafeteria
BR ˌkafɪˈtɪərɪə(r), -z
AM ˌkæfəˈtɪriə, -z

cafetière
BR ˌkafˈtjɛː(r), -z
AM ˌkæfˈtjɛ(ə)r, -z

caff
BR kaf, -s
AM kæf, -s

caffeine
BR ˈkafiːn
AM kæˈfin

caftan
BR ˈkaftan, -z
AM ˈkæftən, ˈkæfˌtæn, -z

cage
BR keɪdʒ, -ɪz, -ɪŋ, -d
AM keɪdʒ, -ɪz, -ɪŋ, -d

cagebird
BR ˈkeɪdʒbəːd, -z
AM ˈkeɪdʒˌbərd, -z

cagey
BR ˈkeɪdʒ|i, -ɪə(r), -ɪɪst
AM ˈkeɪdʒi, -ər, -ɪɪst

cageyness
BR ˈkeɪdʒɪnɪs
AM ˈkeɪdʒɪnɪs

cagily
BR ˈkeɪdʒɪli
AM ˈkeɪdʒɪli

caginess
BR ˈkeɪdʒɪnɪs
AM ˈkeɪdʒɪnɪs

Cagliari
BR ˌkalɪˈɑːri
AM ˌkælˈjɑri

Cagney
BR ˈkagni
AM ˈkægni

cagoule
BR kəˈguːl, -z
AM kəˈgul, -z

Cahill
BR ˈkɑːhɪl, ˈkeɪhɪl
AM ˈkeɪhɪl

cahoots
BR kəˈhuːts
AM kəˈhuts

Caiaphas
BR ˈkʌɪəfas
AM ˈkaɪəfəs

Caicos
BR ˈkeɪkɒs, ˈkeɪkəs
AM ˈkeɪkɔs, ˈkeɪkəs, ˈkeɪkɑs

caiman
BR ˈkeɪmən, -z
AM ˈkeɪmən, -z

Cain
BR keɪn
AM keɪn

Caine
BR keɪn

Cainozoic
BR ˌkʌɪnəˈzəʊɪk
AM ˌkeɪnəˈzoʊɪk

caïque
BR kʌɪˈiːk, kɑːˈiːk, -s
AM kɑˈik, kaɪˈik, -s

cairn
BR kɛːn, -z
AM kɛ(ə)rn, -z

Cairncross
BR ˈkɛːnkrɒs
AM ˈkɛrnˌkrɔs, ˈkɛrnˌkrɑs

cairngorm
BR ˈkɛːngɔːm, -z
AM ˈkɛrnˌgɔ(ə)rm, -z

Cairngorms
BR ˈkɛːngɔːmz
AM ˈkɛrnˌgɔ(ə)rmz

Cairns
BR kɛːnz
AM kɛrnz

Cairo
BR ˈkʌɪrəʊ
AM ˈkaɪroʊ

caisson
BR ˈkeɪsn, ˈkeɪsɒn, kəˈsuːn, -z
AM ˈkeɪsɑn, ˈkeɪsən, -z

Caister
BR ˈkeɪstə(r)
AM ˈkeɪstər

Caistor
BR ˈkeɪstə(r)
AM ˈkeɪstər

Caithness
BR ˈkeɪθnɛs, ˈkeɪθnɪs, keɪθˈnɛs
AM ˈkeɪθnɪs

caitiff
BR ˈkeɪtɪf, -s
AM ˈkeɪdəf, -s

Caitlin
BR ˈkeɪtlɪn
AM ˈkeɪtˌlɪn

Caius[1]
Cambridge college
BR kiːz
AM kiz

Caius[2]
Roman name
BR ˈkʌɪəs
AM ˈkaɪəs, ˈkeɪəs

cajole
BR kəˈdʒəʊl, -z, -ɪŋ, -d
AM kəˈdʒoʊl, -z, -ɪŋ, -d

cajolement
BR kəˈdʒəʊlm(ə)nt
AM kəˈdʒoʊlmənt

cajoler
BR kəˈdʒəʊlə(r), -z
AM kəˈdʒoʊlər, -z

cajolery
BR kəˈdʒəʊl(ə)ri
AM kəˈdʒoʊləri

Cajun
BR ˈkeɪdʒ(ə)n, -z
AM ˈkeɪdʒən, -z

cake
BR keɪk, -s, -ɪŋ, -t
AM keɪk, -s, -ɪŋ, -t

cakewalk
BR ˈkeɪkwɔːk, -s
AM ˈkeɪkˌwɔk, ˈkeɪkˌwɑk, -s

Calabar
BR ˌkaləˈbɑː(r), ˈkaləbɑː(r)
AM ˌkæləˈbɑr

calabash
BR ˈkaləbaʃ, -ɪz
AM ˈkæləˌbæʃ, -ɪz

calaboose
BR ˈkaləbuːs, ˌkaləˈbuːs, -ɪz
AM ˈkæləˌbus, -ɪz

calabrese
BR ˈkaləbriːs, ˌkaləbriːz
AM ˈkæləˌbris, ˈkæləˌbriz

Calabria
BR kəˈlabrɪə(r)
AM kɑˈlabriə, kəˈleɪbriə

Calabrian
BR kəˈlabrɪən, -z
AM kɑˈlabriən, kəˈleɪbriən, -z

Calais
BR ˈkaleɪ, ˈkali
AM kæˈleɪ

calaloo
BR ˈkaləluː
AM ˈkæləˌlu

calalu
BR ˈkaləluː
AM ˈkæləˌlu

calamanco
BR ˌkaləˈmaŋkəʊ, -z
AM ˌkæləˈmæŋkoʊ, -z

calamander
BR ˈkaləmandə(r)
AM ˈkæləmændər

calamari
BR kaləˈmɑːri
AM ˌkɑləˈmɑri

calamary
BR ˈkaləmər|i, -ɪz
AM ˈkæləˌmɛri, -z

calami
BR ˈkaləmʌɪ
AM ˈkæləˌmaɪ

calamine
BR ˈkaləmʌɪn
AM ˈkæləˌmaɪn

calamint
BR ˈkaləmɪnt
AM ˈkæləˌmɪnt

calamitous
BR kəˈlamɪtəs
AM kəˈlæmədəs

calamitously
BR kəˈlamɪtəsli
AM kəˈlæmədəsli

calamitousness
BR kəˈlamɪtəsnəs
AM kəˈlæmədəsnəs

calamity
BR kəˈlamɪt|i, -ɪz
AM kəˈlæmədi, -z

calamus
BR ˈkaləməs
AM ˈkæləməs

calando
BR kəˈlandəʊ
AM kəˈlændoʊ

calash
BR kəˈlaʃ, -ɪz
AM kəˈlæʃ, -əz

calathea
BR ˌkaləˈθiːə(r)
AM ˌkæləˈθiə

calcanea
BR kalˈkeɪnɪə(r)
AM kælˈkeɪnɪə

calcaneal
BR kalˈkeɪnɪəl
AM kælˈkeɪnɪəl

calcanei
BR kalˈkeɪnɪʌɪ
AM kælˈkeɪnɪˌaɪ

calcaneum
BR kalˈkeɪnɪəm
AM kælˈkeɪnɪəm

calcaneus
BR kalˈkeɪnɪəs
AM kælˈkeɪnɪəs

calcareous
BR kalˈkɛːrɪəs
AM kælˈkɛriəs

calcareousness
BR kalˈkɛːrɪəsnəs
AM kælˈkɛriəsnəs

calceolaria
BR ˌkalsɪəˈlɛːrɪə(r), -z
AM ˌkælsiəˈlɛriə, -z

calceolate
BR ˈkalsɪələt
AM ˈkælsɪələt

calces
BR ˈkalsiːz
AM ˈkælsiz

calciferol
BR kalˈsɪfərɒl, -z
AM kælˈsɪf(ə)rəl, -z

calciferous
BR kalˈsɪf(ə)rəs
AM kælˈsɪf(ə)rəs

calcific
BR kalˈsɪfɪk
AM ˌkælˈsɪfɪk

calcification
BR ˌkalsɪfɪˈkeɪʃn
AM ˌkælsəfəˈkeɪʃən

calcifuge
BR ˈkalsɪfjuː(d)ʒ, -ɪz
AM ˈkælsəˌfjudʒ, -əz

calcify
BR ˈkalsɪfʌɪ, -z, -ɪŋ, -d
AM ˈkælsəˌfaɪ, -z, -ɪŋ, -d

calcination
BR ˌkalsɪˈneɪʃn
AM ˌkælsəˈneɪʃən

calcine
BR ˈkalsʌɪn, ˈkalsɪn, -z, -ɪŋ, -d
AM ˈkælˌsaɪn, ˈkælˌsɪn, -z, -ɪŋ, -d

calcite
BR ˈkalsʌɪt
AM ˈkælˌsaɪt

calcitic
BR kalˈsɪtɪk
AM kælˈsɪdɪk

calcium
BR ˈkalsɪəm
AM ˈkælsɪəm

Calcot
BR ˈkalkət, ˈkalkɒt, ˈkɔːlkət, ˈkɔːlkɒt, ˈkʊlkət, ˈkʊlkɒt
AM ˈkælkɑt, ˈkɑlkɑt, ˈkɔlkɑt

Calcott
BR ˈkalkət, ˈkalkɒt, ˈkɔːlkət, ˈkɔːlkɒt, ˈkʊlkət, ˈkʊlkɒt
AM ˈkælkɑt, ˈkɑlkɑt, ˈkɔlkɑt

calcrete
BR ˈkalkriːt, -s
AM ˈkælˌkrit, -s

calc-sinter
BR ˌkalkˈsɪntə(r)
AM ˈkælkˈsɪn(t)ər

calcspar
BR ˈkalkspɑː(r)
AM ˈkælkˌspɑr

calc-tuff
BR ˈkalktʌf
AM ˈkælkˌtəf

calculability
BR ˌkalkjʊləˈbɪlɪti
AM ˌkælkjələˈbɪlɪdi

calculable
BR ˈkalkjʊləbl
AM ˈkælkjələbəl

calculably
BR ˈkalkjʊləbli
AM ˈkælkjələbli

calculate
BR ˈkalkjʊleɪt, -s, -ɪŋ, -ɪd
AM ˈkælkjəˌleɪt, -ts, -dɪŋ, -dɪd

calculatedly
BR ˈkalkjʊleɪtɪdli
AM ˈkælkjəˌleɪdɪdli

calculatingly
BR ˈkalkjʊleɪtɪŋli
AM ˈkælkjəˌleɪdɪŋli

calculation
BR ˌkalkjʊˈleɪʃn, -z
AM ˌkælkjəˈleɪʃən, -z

calculative
BR ˈkalkjʊlətɪv
AM ˈkælkjəˌleɪdɪv

calculator
BR ˈkalkjʊleɪtə(r), -z
AM ˈkælkjəˌleɪdər, -z

calculi
BR ˈkalkjʊlʌɪ
AM ˈkælkjəˌlaɪ

calculous
BR ˈkalkjʊləs
AM ˈkælkjələs

calculus
BR ˈkalkjʊləs, -ɪz
AM ˈkælkjələs, -əz

Calcutta
BR kalˈkʌtə(r)
AM kælˈkədə

caldaria
BR kalˈdɛːrɪə(r)
AM kælˈdɛrɪə

caldarium
BR kalˈdɛːrɪəm, -z
AM kælˈdɛrɪəm, -z

Caldecote
BR ˈkɔːldɪkət, ˈkɔːldɪkɒt, ˈkɒldɪkət, ˈkʊldɪkɒt
AM ˈkɔldəˌkɑt, ˈkɑldəˌkɑt

Caldecott
BR ˈkɔːldɪkɒt, ˈkɔːldɪkət, ˈkʊldɪkɒt, ˈkʊldɪkət
AM ˈkɔldəˌkɑt, ˈkɑldəˌkɑt

Calder
BR ˈkɔːldə(r), ˈkɒldə(r)
AM ˈkɔldər, ˈkɑldər

caldera
BR kalˈdɛːrə(r), kɔːlˈdɛːrə(r), ˈkɔːld(ə)rə(r)
AM kɒlˈdɛrə, kɑlˈdɛrə, kælˈdɛrə

Calderdale
BR ˈkɔːldədeɪl, ˈkʊldədeɪl
AM ˈkɔldərˌdeɪl, ˈkɑldəˌdeɪl

Calderón
BR ˈkaldərɒn
AM ˈkɔldəˌrɔn, ˈkɑldəˌrɔn
SP ˌkaldeˈron

caldron
BR ˈkɔːldr(ə)n, ˈkʊldr(ə)n, -z
AM ˈkɔldrən, ˈkɑldrən, -z

Caldwell
BR ˈkɔːldwɛl, ˈkʊldwɛl
AM ˈkɔldwɛl, ˈkɑldwɛl

Caldy
BR ˈkɔːldi, ˈkʊldi
AM ˈkɔldi, ˈkɑldi

Caleb
BR ˈkeɪlɛb

AM ˈkeɪləb

calebrese
BR ˈkalɪbriːs
AM ˈkæləˌbris, ˈkæləˌbriz

Caledonian
BR ˌkalɪˈdəʊnɪən, -z
AM ˌkæləˈdoʊnɪən, -z

calefacient
BR ˌkalɪˈfeɪʃnt
AM ˌkæləˈfeɪʃənt

calefaction
BR ˌkalɪˈfakʃn
AM ˌkæləˈfækʃən

calefactory
BR ˌkalɪˈfakt(ə)r|i, -ɪz
AM ˌkæləˈfæktɔri, -z

calendar
BR ˈkalɪndə(r), -z
AM ˈkæləndər, -z

calender
BR ˈkalɪndə(r), -z
AM ˈkæləndər, -z

calendric
BR kəˈlɛndrɪk, kaˈlɛndrɪk
AM kəˈlɛndrɪk

calendrical
BR kəˈlɛndrɪkl, kaˈlɛndrɪkl
AM kəˈlɛndrəkəl

calends
BR ˈkalɛndz, ˈkalɪndz
AM ˈkalɛn(d)z, ˈkælɛn(d)z

calendula
BR kəˈlɛndjʊlə(r), kaˈlɛndjʊlə(r), kəˈlɛndʒʊlə(r), kaˈlɛndʒʊlə(r)
AM kəˈlɛndʒələ

calenture
BR ˈkalɪntjʊə(r), ˈkalɪntjʊə(r), ˈkalɪntʃə(r), ˈkalɪntʃə(r)
AM ˈkælən(t)ʃʊ(ə)r, ˈkælən(t)ʃər

calf
BR kɑːf
AM kæf

calfhood
BR ˈkɑːfhʊd
AM ˈkæfˌ(h)ʊd

calfish
BR ˈkɑːfɪʃ
AM ˈkæfɪʃ

calf-length
BR ˌkɑːfˈlɛŋ(k)θ, ˈkɑːfˌlɛŋ(k)θ
AM ˈkæfˌlɛŋθ

calflike
BR ˈkɑːflʌɪk
AM ˈkæfˌlaɪk

calfskin
BR ˈkɑːfskɪn, -z
AM ˈkæfˌskɪn, -z

Calgary
BR ˈkalg(ə)ri
AM ˈkælgəri

Calhoun
BR kalˈhuːn, kəˈhuːn
AM kælˈ(h)un

Cali
BR ˈkɑːli
AM ˈkɑli

Caliban
BR ˈkalɪban
AM ˈkæləˌbæn

caliber
BR ˈkalɪbə(r), -z, -d
AM ˈkæləbər, -z, -d

calibrate
BR ˈkalɪbreɪt, -s, -ɪŋ, -ɪd
AM ˈkæləbreɪt, -ts, -dɪŋ, -dɪd

calibration
BR ˌkalɪˈbreɪʃn
AM ˌkæləˈbreɪʃən

calibrator
BR ˈkalɪbreɪtə(r), -z
AM ˈkæləˌbreɪdər, -z

calibre
BR ˈkalɪbə(r), -z, -d
AM ˈkæləbər, -z, -d

calices
BR ˈkeɪlɪsiːz
AM ˈkæləsiz

caliche
BR kəˈliːtʃi
AM kəˈliʃ

calicle
BR ˈkalɪkl, -z
AM ˈkæləkəl, -z

calico
BR ˈkalɪkəʊ
AM ˈkæləˌkoʊ

Calicut
BR ˈkalɪkət, ˈkalɪkʌt
AM ˈkæləkət

calif
BR ˈkeɪlɪf, ˈkalɪf, kaˈliːf, -s
AM ˈkeɪləf, ˈkæləf, -s

California
BR ˌkalɪˈfɔːnɪə(r)
AM ˌkæləˈfɔrnjə, ˌkæləˈfɔrniə

Californian
BR ˌkalɪˈfɔːnɪən, -z
AM ˌkæləˈfɔrnjən, ˌkæləˈfɔrnɪən, -z

californium
BR ˌkalɪˈfɔːnɪəm
AM ˌkæləˈfɔrniəm

Caligula
BR kəˈlɪgjʊlə(r)
AM kəˈlɪg(j)ʊlə

calipash
BR ˈkalɪpaʃ, -ɪz
AM ˈkæləˌpæʃ, -əz

calipee
BR ˈkalɪpiː, -z
AM ˈkæləˌpi, -z

caliper
BR ˈkalɪpə(r), -z
AM ˈkæləpər, -z

caliph
BR ˈkeɪlɪf, ˈkalɪf, kaˈliːf, -s
AM ˈkeɪləf, ˈkæləf, -s

caliphate
BR ˈkalɪfeɪt, ˈkeɪlɪfeɪt, -s
AM ˈkeɪləˌfeɪt, ˈkælə‚feɪt, -s

calisthenic
BR ˌkalɪsˈθɛnɪk, -s
AM ˌkæləsˈθɛnɪk, -s

calix
BR ˈkeɪl|ɪks, -ɪksɪz
AM ˈkeɪlɪks, ˈkælɪks, -ɪz

calk
BR kɔːk, -s, -ɪŋ, -t
AM kɔk, kak, -s, -ɪŋ, -t

Calke
BR kɔːk
AM kɔk, kak

calkin
BR ˈkalkɪn, -z
AM ˈkɔkən, ˈkælkən, ˈkakən, -z

call
BR kɔːl, -z, -ɪŋ, -d
AM kɔl, kal, -z, -ɪŋ, -d

calla
BR ˈkalə(r), -z
AM ˈkælə, -z

Callaghan
BR ˈkaləhan, ˈkaləhən
AM ˈkæləˌhæn

Callahan
BR ˈkaləhan, ˈkaləhən
AM ˈkæləˌhæn

Callander
BR ˈkalandə(r)
AM ˈkæləndər

Callas
BR ˈkaləs
AM ˈkæləs

callback
BR ˈkɔːlbak, -s
AM ˈkɔlˌbæk, ˈkalˌbæk, -s

callboy
BR ˈkɔːlbɔɪ, -z
AM ˈkɔlˌbɔɪ, ˈkalˌbɔɪ, -z

Callenor
BR tˈʃalənə(r)
AM tˈʃælənər

caller
BR ˈkɔːlə(r), -z
AM ˈkɔlər, ˈkalər, -z

callgirl
BR ˈkɔːlgəːl, -z
AM ˈkɔlˌgərl, ˈkalˌgərl, -z

calligrapher
BR kəˈlɪgrəfə(r), -z
AM kəˈlɪgrəfər, -z

calligraphic
BR ˌkalɪˈgrafɪk
AM ˌkæləˈgræfɪk

calligraphical
BR ˌkalɪˈgrafɪkl
AM ˌkæləˈgræfəkəl

calligraphically
BR ˌkalɪˈgrafɪkli
AM ˌkæləˈgræfək(ə)li

calligraphist
BR kəˈlɪgrəfɪst, -s
AM kəˈlɪgrəfəst, -s

calligraphy
BR kəˈlɪgrəfi
AM kəˈlɪgrəfi

Callil
BR kəˈlɪl
AM kəˈlɪl

Callimachus
BR kəˈlɪməkəs
AM kəˈlɪməkəs, ˌkæləˈmakəs

calling
BR ˈkɔːlɪŋ, -z
AM ˈkɔlɪŋ, ˈkalɪŋ, -z

calliope
BR kəˈlʌɪəp|i, kaˈlʌɪəp|i, -ɪz
AM kəˈlaɪəpi, -z

calliper
BR ˈkalɪpə(r), -z
AM ˈkæləpər, -z

callipygian
BR ˌkalɪˈpɪdʒɪən
AM ˌkæləˈpɪdʒiən

callipygous
BR ˌkalɪˈpɪdʒɪəs
AM ˌkæləˈpɪdʒiəs

callisthenic
BR ˌkalɪsˈθɛnɪk, -s
AM ˌkæləsˈθɛnɪk, -s

Callisto
BR kəˈlɪstəʊ
AM kəˈlɪstoʊ

callop
BR ˈkaləp, -s
AM ˈkæləp, -s

callosity
BR kəˈlɒsɪt|i, -ɪz
AM kəˈlasədi, -z

callous
BR ˈkaləs, -ɪz
AM ˈkæləs, -əz

callously
BR ˈkaləsli
AM ˈkæləsli

callousness
BR ˈkaləsnəs
AM ˈkæləsnəs

callow
BR ˈkaləʊ, -ə(r), -ɪst
AM ˈkæl|oʊ, -əwər, -əwəst

callowly
BR ˈkaləʊli
AM ˈkæloʊli

callowness
BR ˈkaləʊnəs
AM ˈkæloʊnəs

Callum
BR ˈkaləm
AM ˈkæləm

calluna
BR kəˈluːnə(r), -z
AM kəˈl(j)uːnə, -z

callus
BR ˈkaləs, -ɪz
AM ˈkæləs, -ɪz

calm
BR ˌkaːm, -z, -ɪŋ, -d, -ə(r), -ɪst
AM kɑ(l)m, -z, -ɪŋ, -d, -ər, -əst

calmative
BR ˈkalmətɪv, ˈkaːmətɪv, -z
AM ˈkɑ(l)mədɪv, -z

calmly
BR kaːmli
AM kɑ(l)mli

calmness
BR ˈkaːmnəs
AM kɑ(l)mnəs

calmodulin
BR kalˈmɒdjʊlɪn
AM kælˈmadjələn

Calne
BR kaːn
AM kɑ(l)n

calomel
BR ˈkaləmɛl
AM ˈkæləməl

calor
BR ˈkalə(r)
AM ˈkælər

caloric
BR kaˈlɒrɪk, kəˈlɒrɪk, ˈkal(ə)rɪk
AM kəˈlɔrɪk, kəˈlarɪk, ˈkælərɪk

calorie
BR ˈkal(ə)r|i, -ɪz
AM ˈkæl(ə)ri, -z

calorific
BR ˌkaləˈrɪfɪk
AM ˌkæləˈrɪfɪk

calorifically
BR ˌkaləˈrɪfɪkli
AM ˌkæləˈrɪfɪk(ə)li

calorification
BR kəˌlɒrɪfɪˈkeɪʃn
AM kəˌlɔrəfəˈkeɪʃən

calorimeter
BR ˌkaləˈrɪmɪtə(r), -z
AM ˌkæləˈrɪmədər, -z

calorimetric
BR ˌkal(ə)rɪˈmɛtrɪk
AM ˌkælərəˈmɛtrɪk

calorimetry
BR ˌkaləˈrɪmɪtri
AM ˌkæləˈrɪmətri

calory
BR ˈkal(ə)r|i, -ɪz

Calvinise
AM ˈkæl(ə)ri, -z

calotte
BR kəˈlɒt, -s
AM kəˈlɑt, -s

Calpurnia
BR kalˈpəːnɪə(r)
AM kælˈpərniə

calque
BR kalk, -s
AM kælk, -s

Calthorpe
BR ˈkalθɔːp
AM ˈkælˌθɔ(ə)rp

caltrop
BR ˈkaltrəp, ˈkɔːltrəp, -s
AM ˈkæltrəp, -s

Calum
BR ˈkaləm
AM ˈkæləm

calumet
BR ˈkaljʊmɛt, -s
AM ˈkæljəˌmɛt, -s

calumniate
BR kəˈlʌmnɪeɪt, -s, -ɪŋ, -ɪd
AM kəˈləmniˌeɪ|t, -ts, -dɪŋ, -dɪd

calumniation
BR kəˌlʌmnɪˈeɪʃn, -z
AM kəˈləmniˈeɪʃən, -z

calumniator
BR kəˈlʌmnɪeɪtə(r), -z
AM kəˈləmniˌeɪdər, -z

calumniatory
BR kəˈlʌmnɪət(ə)ri
AM kəˈləmniəˌtɔri

calumnious
BR kəˈlʌmnɪəs
AM kəˈləmniəs

calumny
BR ˈkaləmn|i, -ɪz
AM ˈkæləmni, -z

Calvados
BR ˈkalvədɒs
AM ˈkælvəˌdoʊs

calvary
BR ˈkalv(ə)r|i, -ɪz
AM ˈkælv(ə)ri, -z

calve
BR kaːv, -z, -ɪŋ, -d
AM kæ(l)v, -z, -ɪŋ, -d

Calverley
BR ˈkalvəli, ˈkaːvəli
AM ˈkælvərli

Calvert
BR ˈkalvət, ˈkɔːlvət
AM ˈkælvərt

calves
BR kaːvz
AM kævz

Calvin
BR ˈkalvɪn
AM ˈkælvən

Calvinise
BR ˈkalvɪnaɪz, -ɪz, -ɪŋ, -d

AM ˈkælvəˌnaɪz, -ɪz, -ɪŋ,
-d
Calvinism
BR ˈkalvɪnɪz(ə)m
AM ˈkælvəˌnɪzəm
Calvinist
BR ˈkalvɪnɪst, -s
AM ˈkælvənəst, -s
Calvinistic
BR ˌkalvɪˈnɪstɪk
AM ˌkælvəˈnɪstɪk
Calvinistical
BR ˌkalvɪˈnɪstɪkl
AM ˌkælvəˈnɪstɪkəl
Calvinistically
BR ˌkalvɪˈnɪstɪkli
AM ˌkælvəˈnɪstɪk(ə)li
Calvinize
BR ˈkalvɪnʌɪz, -ɪz, -ɪŋ,
-d
AM ˈkælvəˌnaɪz, -ɪz, -ɪŋ,
-d
calx
BR kalks, -ɪz
AM kælks, -ɪz
calyces
BR ˈkeɪlɪsiːz
AM ˈkeɪləsiz
calypso
BR kəˈlɪpsəʊ, -z
AM kəˈlɪpsoʊ, -z
calyx
BR ˈkeɪlˌɪks, ˈkalˌɪks,
-ɪksɪz\-ɪksiːz
AM ˈkeɪlɪks, -ɪz
calzone
BR kalˈtsəʊnˌi, -ɪz
AM kælˈzoʊn(i), -z
calzoni
BR kalˈtsəʊni
AM kælˈzoʊni
cam
BR kam, -z
AM kæm, -z
camaraderie
BR ˌkaməˈrɑːd(ə)ri,
ˌkaməˈrad(ə)ri
AM ˌkɑm(ə)ˈrædəri,
ˌkæm(ə)ˈradəri
Camargue
BR kəˈmɑːg
AM kəˈmɑrg
camarilla
BR ˌkaməˈrɪlə(r),
ˌkaməˈrɪjə(r), -z
AM ˌkæməˈrɪlə, -z
camaron
BR ˌkaməˈraʊn,
ˈkam(ə)rən,
ˈkam(ə)rn̩, -z
AM ˈkæmərən, -z
camber
BR ˈkambə(r), -z
AM ˈkæmbər, -z
Camberwell
BR ˈkambəw(ε)l
AM ˈkæmbər‚wεl

cambia
BR ˈkambɪə(r)
AM ˈkæmbɪə
cambial
BR ˈkambɪəl
AM ˈkæmbɪəl
cambist
BR ˈkambɪst, -s
AM ˈkæmbəst, -s
cambium
BR ˈkambɪəm
AM ˈkæmbɪəm
Cambodia
BR kamˈbəʊdɪə(r)
AM kæmˈboʊdiə
Cambodian
BR kamˈbəʊdɪən, -z
AM kæmˈboʊdiən, -z
Camborne
BR ˈkambɔːn
AM ˈkæmˌbɔ(ə)rn
Cambria
BR ˈkambrɪə(r)
AM ˈkæmbriə
Cambrian
BR ˈkambrɪən, -z
AM ˈkæmbriən, -z
cambric
BR ˈkambrɪk
AM ˈkeɪmbrɪk
Cambridge
BR ˈkeɪmbrɪdʒ
AM ˈkeɪmˌbrɪdʒ
Cambridgeshire
BR ˈkeɪmbrɪdʒʃ(ɪ)ə(r)
AM ˈkeɪmˌbrɪdʒʃɪ(ə)r
Cambyses
BR kamˈbʌɪsiːz
AM kæmˈbaɪsiz
camcorder
BR ˈkamˌkɔːdə(r), -z
AM ˈkæmˌkɔrdər, -z
Camden Town
BR ˌkamdən ˈtaʊn
AM ˌkæmdən ˈtaʊn
came
BR keɪm
AM keɪm
camel
BR ˈkaml, -z
AM ˈkæməl, -z
camelback
BR ˈkamlbak
AM ˈkæməlˌbæk
cameleer
BR ˌkaməˈlɪə(r), -z
AM ˌkæməˈlɪ(ə)r, -z
Camelford
BR ˈkamlfəd
AM ˈkæmlfərd
camelhair
BR ˈkamlhεː(r)
AM ˈkæməlˌ(h)ε(ə)r
Camelia
BR kəˈmiːlɪə(r)
AM kəˈmiːljə, kəˈmiːliə

camellia
BR kəˈmiːlɪə(r),
kəˈmεlɪə(r), -z
AM kəˈmiljə, kəˈmiliə,
-z
camelopard
BR ˈkamɪlə(ʊ)pɑːd,
ˈkamlə(ʊ)pɑːd,
kəˈmεləpɑːd, -z
AM kəˈmεləpɑrd,
ˈkæməloʊˌpɑrd, -z
Camelot
BR ˈkamɪlɒt
AM ˈkæməlˌlɑt
camelry
BR ˈkamlrˌi, -ɪz
AM ˈkæməlri, -z
Camembert
BR ˈkaməmbεː(r)
AM ˌkæməmˈbε(ə)r
cameo
BR ˈkamɪəʊ, -z
AM ˈkæmioʊ, -z
camera
BR ˈkam(ə)rə(r), -z
AM ˈkæm(ə)rə, -z
cameraman
BR ˈkamrəman,
ˈkamrəmən
AM ˈkæm(ə)rəˌmæn,
ˈkæm(ə)rəmən
cameramen
BR ˈkamrəmεn,
ˈkamrəmən
AM ˈkæm(ə)rəmən
camera obscura
BR ˌkam(ə)rə(r)
əbˈskjʊərə(r),
+ ɒbˈskjʊərə(r),
əbˈskjɔːrə(r),
ɒbˈskjɔːrə(r), -z
AM ˌkæm(ə)rə
ˈɑbskjʊrə, -z
camerawork
BR ˈkam(ə)rəwəːk
AM ˈkæm(ə)rəˌwərk
camerlingo
BR ˌkaməˈlɪŋgəʊ, -z
AM ˌkæmərˈlɪŋgoʊ, -z
Cameron
BR ˈkam(ə)rən,
ˈkam(ə)rn̩
AM ˈkæm(ə)rən
Cameroon
BR ˌkaməˈruːn
AM ˌkæməˈrun
Cameroonian
BR ˌkaməˈruːnɪən, -z
AM ˌkæməˈruniən, -z
camiknickers
BR ˈkamɪˌnɪkəz
AM ˈkæməˌnɪkərz
Camilla
BR kəˈmɪlə(r)
AM kəˈmɪlə
Camille
BR kəˈmɪl, kəˈmiːl
AM kəˈmil

cami-nicks
BR ˈkamɪnɪks
AM ˈkæməˌnɪks
camion
BR ˈkamɪən, -z
AM ˈkæmjən, -z
camisole
BR ˈkamɪsəʊl, -z
AM ˈkæməˌsoʊl, -z
camomile
BR ˈkaməmʌɪl
AM ˈkæməˌmil,
ˈkæməˌmaɪl
Camorra
BR kəˈmɔːrə(r)
AM kəˈmɔrə
camouflage
BR ˈkaməflɑː(d)ʒ, -ɪz,
-ɪŋ, -d
AM ˈkæməˌflɑ(d)ʒ, -əz,
-ɪŋ, -d
camp
BR kamp, -s, -ɪŋ, -t
AM kæmp, -s, -ɪŋ, -t
campaign
BR kamˈpeɪn, -z, -ɪŋ, -d
AM kæmˈpeɪn, -z, -ɪŋ, -d
campaigner
BR kamˈpeɪnə(r), -z
AM kæmˈpeɪnər, -z
Campania
BR kamˈpanɪə(r)
AM kɑmˈpaniə
campanile
BR ˌkampəˈniːlˌi, -ɪz
AM ˌkæmpəˈnil(i), -z
campanologer
BR ˌkampəˈnɒlədʒə(r),
-z
AM ˌkæmpəˈnɑlədʒər,
-z
campanological
BR ˌkampənəˈlɒdʒɪkl,
ˌkampnəˈlɒdʒɪkl
AM ˌkæmpənəˈlɑdʒəkəl
campanologist
BR ˌkampəˈnɒlədʒɪst,
-s
AM ˌkæmpəˈnɑlədʒəst,
-s
campanology
BR ˌkampəˈnɒlədʒi
AM ˌkæmpəˈnɑlədʒi
campanula
BR kamˈpanjʉlə(r),
kəmˈpanjʉlə(r), -z
AM kæmˈpænjələ, -z
campanulate
BR kamˈpanjʉlət,
kəmˈpanjʉlət
AM kæmˈpænjələt,
kæmˈpænjəˌleɪt
Campari®
BR kamˈpɑːri
AM kɑmˈpɑri
Campbell
BR ˈkambl
AM ˈkæmbəl

**Campbell-
Bannerman**
BR ˈkambl̩ˈbanəmən
AM ˈkæmbəlˈbænər-
mən

Campden
BR ˈkam(p)dən
AM ˈkæm(p)dən

Campeachy
BR kamˈpiːtʃi
AM kæmˈpitʃi

Campeche
BR kamˈpiːtʃi
AM kæmˈpitʃi

camper
BR ˈkampə(r), -z
AM ˈkæmpər, -z

campesino
BR ˌkampɪˈsiːnəʊ
AM ˌkæmpəˈsinoʊ

campfire
BR ˈkampfʌɪə(r), -z
AM ˈkæmpˌfaɪ(ə)r, -z

campground
BR ˈkampgraʊnd, -z
AM ˈkæmpˌgraʊnd, -z

camphor
BR ˈkamfə(r)
AM ˈkæmfər

camphorate
BR ˈkamfəreɪt, -s, -ɪŋ,
-ɪd
AM ˈkæmfəˌreɪ|t, -ts,
-dɪŋ, -dɪd

camphoric
BR kamˈfɒrɪk
AM ˌkæmˈfɔrɪk

campily
BR ˈkampɪli
AM ˈkæmpɪli

campiness
BR ˈkampɪnɪs
AM ˈkæmpɪnɪs

camping
BR ˈkampɪŋ
AM ˈkæmpɪŋ

Campion
BR ˈkampɪən
AM ˈkæmpɪən

Campsie
BR ˈkam(p)si
AM ˈkæmpsi, ˈkæmpzi

campsite
BR ˈkampsʌɪt, -s
AM ˈkæmpˌsaɪt, -s

campus
BR ˈkampəs, -ɪz
AM ˈkæmpəs, -əz

campy
BR ˈkamp|i, -ɪə(r), -ɪɪst
AM ˈkæmp|i, -ər, -ɪst

campylobacter
BR ˈkampɪlə(ʊ)ˌbak-
tə(r), -z
AM ˈkæmpələˌbæktər,
kæmˈpɪləˌbæktər, -z

CAMRA
BR ˈkamrə(r)
AM ˈkæmrə

Camrose
BR ˈkamrəʊz
AM ˈkæmˌroʊz

camshaft
BR ˈkamʃɑːft,
ˈkamʃaft, -s
AM ˈkæmˌʃæft, -s

Camus
BR ˈkamuː, kaˈmuː
AM kaˈmu

camwood
BR ˈkamwʊd
AM ˈkæmˌwʊd

can¹
*auxiliary verb,
strong form*
BR kan
AM kæn

can²
*auxiliary verb, weak
form*
BR kən
AM kən

can³
*noun, verb, put in
cans*
BR kan, -z, -ɪŋ, -d
AM kæn, -z, -ɪŋ, -d

Cana
BR ˈkeɪnə(r)
AM ˈkeɪnə

Canaan
BR ˈkeɪnən
AM ˈkeɪnən

Canaanite
BR ˈkeɪnənʌɪt, -s
AM ˈkeɪnəˌnaɪt, -s

Canada
BR ˈkanədə(r)
AM ˈkænədə

Canadian
BR kəˈneɪdɪən, -z
AM kəˈneɪdɪən, -z

canaille
BR kəˈnɑːɪ
AM kəˈnaɪ, kəˈneɪl

canal
BR kəˈnal, -z
AM kəˈnæl, -z

Canaletto
BR ˌkanəˈlɛtəʊ
AM ˌkænəˈlɛdoʊ

canalisation
BR ˌkanəlʌɪˈzeɪʃn,
ˌkanlʌɪˈzeɪʃn
AM ˌkænələˈzeɪʃən,
kænəlˌʌɪˈzeɪʃən

canalise
BR ˈkanəlʌɪz,
ˈkanlʌɪz, -ɪz, -ɪŋ, -d
AM ˈkænəˌlaɪz, -ɪz, -ɪŋ,
-d

canalization
BR ˌkanəlʌɪˈzeɪʃn,
ˌkanlʌɪˈzeɪʃn

AM ˌkænələˈzeɪʃən,
kænəlˌʌɪˈzeɪʃən

canalize
BR ˈkanəlʌɪz,
ˈkanlʌɪz, -ɪz, -ɪŋ, -d
AM ˈkænəˌlaɪz, -ɪz, -ɪŋ,
-d

canalside
BR ˈkanəlsʌɪd
AM kəˈnælˌsaɪd

canapé
BR ˈkanəpeɪ, -z
AM ˈkænəpeɪ, ˈkænəpi,
-z

canard
BR kəˈnɑːd, kaˈnɑːd,
ˈkanɑːd, -z
AM kəˈnɑrd, -z

Canarese
BR ˌkanəˈriːz
AM ˌkɑnəˈriz

Canaries
BR kəˈnɛːrɪz
AM kəˈnɛriz

canary
BR kəˈnɛːr|i, -ɪz
AM kəˈnɛri, -z

canasta
BR kəˈnastə(r)
AM kəˈnæstə

canaster
BR kəˈnastə(r)
AM kəˈnæstər,
kəˈnæstər

Canavan
BR ˈkanəv(ə)n
AM ˈkænəvn

Canaveral
BR kəˈnav(ə)rəl,
kəˈnav(ə)rl̩
AM kəˈnæv(ə)rəl

Canberra
BR ˈkanb(ə)rə(r)
AM ˈkænˌbɛrə,
ˈkænbərə

cancan
BR ˈkankan, -z
AM ˈkænˌkæn, -z

cancel
BR ˈkans|l, -lz,
-lɪŋ\-əlɪŋ, -ld
AM ˈkænslə|l, -əlz,
-(ə)lɪŋ, -əld

cancelation
BR ˌkansɪˈleɪʃn, -z
AM ˌkænsəˈleɪʃən, -z

canceler
BR ˈkansɪlə(r),
ˈkanslə(r), -z
AM ˈkæns(ə)lər, -z

cancellation
BR ˌkansɪˈleɪʃn, -z
AM ˌkænsəˈleɪʃən, -z

canceller
BR ˈkansɪlə(r),
ˈkanslə(r), -z
AM ˈkæns(ə)lər, -z

cancellous
BR ˈkansɪləs, ˈkansləs
AM ˈkænsələs

cancer
BR ˈkansə(r), -z
AM ˈkænsər, -z

Cancerian
BR kanˈsɪərɪən,
kanˈsɛːrɪən, -z
AM kænˈsɛrɪən, -z

cancerous
BR ˈkans(ə)rəs
AM ˈkæns(ə)rəs

cancerously
BR ˈkans(ə)rəsli
AM ˈkæns(ə)rəsli

cancroid
BR ˈkaŋkrɔɪd, -z
AM ˈkæŋkrɔɪd, -z

Cancún
BR kaŋˈkuːn
AM kæŋˈkun

Candace
BR ˈkandɪs, kanˈdeɪsi
AM ˈkændəs

candela
BR kanˈdiːlə(r),
kanˈdɛlə(r),
ˈkandələ(r), -z
AM kænˈdɛlə,
kænˈdilə, -z

candelabra
BR ˌkandɪˈlɑːbrə(r), -z
AM ˌkændəˈlɑbrə, -z

candelabrum
BR ˌkandɪˈlɑːbrəm
AM ˌkændəˈlɑbrəm

Canderel®
BR ˈkandərɛl
AM ˈkændərɛl

candescence
BR kanˈdɛsns,
kənˈdɛsns
AM kænˈdɛsns,
kənˈdɛsəns

candescent
BR kanˈdɛsnt,
kənˈdɛsnt
AM kænˈdɛsnt,
kənˈdɛsənt

Candice
BR ˈkandɪs
AM ˈkændəs

candid
BR ˈkandɪd
AM ˈkændəd

Candida
BR ˈkandɪdə(r)
AM ˈkændɪdə,
kænˈdidə

candida
BR ˈkandɪdə(r), -z
AM ˈkændɪdə, -z

candidacy
BR ˈkandɪdəs|i, -ɪz
AM ˈkæn(d)ədəsi, -z

candidate
BR ˈkandɪdeɪt,
ˈkandɪdət, -s
AM ˈkæn(d)əˌdeɪt, -s

candidature
BR ˈkandɪdətʃə(r), -z
AM ˈkæn(d)ədəˌtʃʊ(ə)r,
ˈkæn(d)əˌdeɪtʃər, -z

Candide
BR (ˌ)kɒnˈdiːd, kɔ̃ˈdiːd
AM kænˈdid

candidiasis
BR ˌkandɪˈdʌɪəsɪs
AM ˌkændəˈdaɪəsəs

candidly
BR ˈkandɪdli
AM ˈkændədli

candidness
BR ˈkandɪdnɪs
AM ˈkændədnəs

candied
BR ˈkandɪd
AM ˈkændid

candiru
BR ˌkandɪˈruː, -z
AM ˌkændəˈruː, -z

candle
BR ˈkandl̩, -z
AM ˈkændəl, -z

candleholder
BR ˈkandl̩ˌhəʊldə(r), -z
AM ˈkændl̩ˌ(h)oʊldər, -z

candlelight
BR ˈkandl̩lʌɪt
AM ˈkændl̩ˌlaɪt

candlelit
BR ˈkandl̩lɪt
AM ˈkændl̩ˌlɪt

Candlemas
BR ˈkandl̩mas, ˈkandl̩məs
AM ˈkændl̩məs

candlepower
BR ˈkandl̩ˌpaʊə(r)
AM ˈkændl̩ˌpaʊ(ə)r

candler
BR ˈkandlə(r), -z
AM ˈkæn(də)lər, -z

candlestick
BR ˈkandlstɪk, -s
AM ˈkændl̩ˌstɪk, -s

candlewick
BR ˈkandlwɪk
AM ˈkændl̩ˌwɪk

Candlin
BR ˈkandlɪn
AM ˈkæn(d)lən

candor
BR ˈkandə(r)
AM ˈkændər

candour
BR ˈkandə(r)
AM ˈkændər

candy
BR ˈkandʲi, -ɪz, -ɪɪŋ, -ɪd
AM ˈkændi, -z, -ɪŋ, -d

candyfloss
BR ˈkandɪflɒs, -ɪz
AM ˈkændiˌflɔs,
ˈkændiˌflɑs, -əz

candytuft
BR ˈkandɪtʌft, -s
AM ˈkændiˌtəf(t), -s

cane
BR keɪn, -z, -ɪŋ, -d
AM keɪn, -z, -ɪŋ, -d

canebrake
BR ˈkeɪnbreɪk, -s
AM ˈkeɪnˌbreɪk, -s

canebreak
BR ˈkeɪnbreɪk, -s
AM ˈkeɪnˌbreɪk, -s

caner
BR ˈkeɪnə(r), -z
AM ˈkeɪnər, -z

Canes Venatici
BR ˌkeɪniːz vɪˈnatɪsʌɪ,
ˌkɑːniːz +, ˌkɑːneɪz +,
+ vɛˈnatɪsʌɪ
AM ˌkeɪniz vɛˈnadəsi

canicular
BR kəˈnɪkjʉlə(r)
AM kəˈnɪkjələr

canine
BR ˈkeɪnʌɪn, ˈkanʌɪn, -z
AM ˈkeɪˌnaɪn, -z

caning
BR ˈkeɪnɪŋ, -z
AM ˈkeɪnɪŋ, -z

Canis Major
BR ˌkanɪs ˈmeɪdʒə(r), ˌkeɪnɪs +
AM ˌkeɪnɪs ˈmeɪdʒər, ˌkænɪs +

Canis Minor
BR ˌkanɪs ˈmʌɪnə(r), ˌkeɪnɪs +
AM ˌkeɪnɪs ˈmaɪnər, ˌkænɪs +

canister
BR ˈkanɪstə(r), -z
AM ˈkænəstər, -z

canker
BR ˈkaŋk|ə(r), -əz, -(ə)rɪŋ, -əd
AM ˈkæŋkər, -z, -ɪŋ, -d

cankerous
BR ˈkaŋk(ə)rəs
AM ˈkæŋk(ə)rəs

cankerworm
BR ˈkaŋkəwəːm, -z
AM ˈkæŋkərˌwərm, -z

canna
BR ˈkanə(r), -z
AM ˈkænə, -z

cannabis
BR ˈkanəbɪs
AM ˈkænəbəs

Cannae
BR ˈkaniː
AM ˈkæni, ˈkæˌnaɪ

cannel
BR ˈkanl̩

AM ˈkænəl

cannellini
BR ˌkanəˈliːni, ˌkanlˈiːni
AM ˌkænəˈlini

cannelloni
BR ˌkanəˈləʊni, ˌkanlˈəʊni
AM ˌkænlˈoʊni

canneloni
BR ˌkanəˈləʊni, ˌkanlˈəʊni
AM ˌkænlˈoʊni

cannelure
BR ˈkanəljʉə(r), ˈkanljʉə(r), -z
AM ˈkænl̩ˌ(j)uər, -z

canner
BR ˈkanə(r), -z
AM ˈkænər, -z

cannery
BR ˈkan(ə)r|i, -ɪz
AM ˈkænəri, -z

Cannes
BR kan
AM kæn, kɑn

cannibal
BR ˈkanɪbl̩, -z
AM ˈkænəbəl, -z

cannibalisation
BR ˌkanɪbəlʌɪˈzeɪʃn̩, ˌkanɪbl̩ʌɪˈzeɪʃn̩
AM ˌkænəbələˈzeɪʃən, ˌkænəbəˌlaɪˈzeɪʃən

cannibalise
BR ˈkanɪbəlʌɪz, ˈkanɪbl̩ʌɪz, -ɪz, -ɪŋ, -d
AM ˈkænəbəˌlaɪz, -ɪz, -ɪŋ, -d

cannibalism
BR ˈkanɪbəlɪz(ə)m, ˈkanɪbl̩ɪz(ə)m
AM ˈkænəbəˌlɪzəm

cannibalistic
BR ˌkanɪbəˈlɪstɪk, ˌkanɪbl̩ˈɪstɪk
AM ˌkænəbəˈlɪstɪk

cannibalistically
BR ˌkanɪbəˈlɪstɪkli, ˌkanɪbl̩ˈɪstɪkli
AM ˌkænəbəˈlɪstɪk(ə)li

cannibalization
BR ˌkanɪbəlʌɪˈzeɪʃn̩, ˌkanɪbl̩ʌɪˈzeɪʃn̩
AM ˌkænəbələˈzeɪʃən, ˌkænəbəlˌaɪˈzeɪʃən

cannibalize
BR ˈkanɪbəlʌɪz, ˈkanɪbl̩ʌɪz, -ɪz, -ɪŋ, -d
AM ˈkænəbəˌlaɪz, -ɪz, -ɪŋ, -d

cannikin
BR ˈkanɪkɪn, -z
AM ˈkænəkən, -z

cannily
BR ˈkanɪli
AM ˈkænɪli

canniness
BR ˈkanɪnɪs
AM ˈkænɪnɪs

Canning
BR ˈkanɪŋ
AM ˈkænɪŋ

Cannizzaro
BR ˌkanɪˈzɑːrəʊ
AM ˌkænəˈzɑːroʊ, ˌkænəˈzɑroʊ

Cannock
BR ˈkanək
AM ˈkænək

cannoli
BR kəˈnəʊli
AM kəˈnoʊli

cannon
BR ˈkanən, -z, -ɪŋ, -d
AM ˈkænən, -z, -ɪŋ, -d

cannonade
BR ˌkanəˈneɪd, -z, -ɪŋ, -ɪd
AM ˌkænəˈneɪd, -z, -ɪŋ, -ɪd

cannonball
BR ˈkanənbɔːl, -z
AM ˈkænənˌbɔl, ˈkænənˌbɑl, -z

cannoneer
BR ˌkanəˈnɪə(r), -z
AM ˌkænəˈnɪ(ə)r, -z

cannonry
BR ˈkanənri
AM ˈkænənri

cannot
BR ˈkanɒt, ˈkanət, kaˈnɒt, kəˈnɒt
AM kəˈnat, ˈkæˌnat

cannula
BR ˈkanjʉlə(r), -z
AM ˈkænjələ, -z

cannulae
BR ˈkanjʉliː, ˈkanjʉlʌɪ
AM ˈkænjʉli, ˈkænjəˌlaɪ

cannulate
BR ˈkanjʉleɪt, -s, -ɪŋ, -ɪd
AM ˈkænjəˌleɪ|t, -ts, -dɪŋ, -dɪd

canny
BR ˈkanʲi, -ɪə(r), -ɪɪst
AM ˈkæni, -ər, -ɪst

canoe
BR kəˈnuː, -z, -ɪŋ, -d
AM kəˈnu, -z, -ɪŋ, -d

canoeist
BR kəˈnuːɪst, -s
AM kəˈnuəst, -s

canola
BR kəˈnəʊlə(r)
AM kəˈnoʊlə

canon
BR ˈkanən, -z
AM ˈkænən, -z

cañon
BR ˈkanjən, -z
AM ˈkænjən, -z

Canonbury
BR 'kanənb(ə)ri
AM 'kænən,bɛri,
'kænənbəri

canoness
BR ,kanə'nɛs, -ɪz
AM 'kænənəs, -əz

canonic
BR kə'nɒnɪk
AM kə'nɑnɪk

canonical
BR kə'nɒnɪkl, -z
AM kə'nɑnəkəl, -z

canonically
BR kə'nɒnɪkli
AM kə'nɑnək(ə)li

canonicate
BR kə'nɒnɪkət, -s
AM kə'nɑnə,kət, -s

canonicity
BR ,kanə'nɪsɪti
AM ,kænə'nɪsɪdi

canonisation
BR ,kanənʌɪ'zeɪʃn, -z
AM kænənə'zeɪʃn,
,kænə,naɪ'zeɪʃən, -z

canonise
BR 'kanənʌɪz, -ɪz, -ɪŋ,
-d
AM 'kænə,naɪz, -ɪz, -ɪŋ,
-d

canonist
BR 'kanənɪst, -s
AM 'kænənəst, -s

canonization
BR ,kanənʌɪ'zeɪʃn, -z
AM kænənə'zeɪʃn,
,kænə,naɪ'zeɪʃən, -z

canonize
BR 'kanənʌɪz, -ɪz, -ɪŋ,
-d
AM 'kænə,naɪz, -ɪz, -ɪŋ,
-d

canonry
BR 'kanənr|i, -ɪz
AM 'kænənri, -z

canoodle
BR kə'nu:d|l, -lz,
-|ɪŋ \-lɪŋ, -ld
AM kə'nud|əl, -əlz,
-(ə)lɪŋ, -əld

Canopic
BR kə'nəʊpɪk,
kə'nɒpɪk
AM kə'nɑpɪk

canopied
BR 'kanəpɪd
AM 'kænəpɪd

Canopus
BR kə'nəʊpəs
AM kə'noʊpəs

canopy
BR 'kanəp|i, -ɪz
AM 'kænəpi, -z

canorous
BR kə'nɔ:rəs
AM kə'nɔrəs

Canova
BR kə'nəʊvə(r)
AM kə'noʊvə

canst
BR kanst
AM kænst

cant
BR kant, -s, -ɪŋ, -ɪd
AM kænt, -s, -ɪŋ, -ɪd

can't
BR kɑːnt
AM kænt

Cantab.
BR 'kantab
AM 'kæntæb

cantabile
BR kan'tɑːbɪleɪ,
kan'tɑːbleɪ,
kan'tɑːbɪli,
kan'tɑːbli̥
AM kɑn'tɑbə,leɪ

Cantabria
BR kan'tabrɪə(r)
AM kən'teɪbrɪə

Cantabrian
BR kan'tabrɪən, -z
AM kən'teɪbrɪən, -z

Cantabrigian
BR ,kantə'brɪdʒɪən, -z
AM ,kæn(t)ə'brɪdʒɪən,
-z

cantal
BR 'kantɑːl
AM 'kɑn(t)l

cantaloup
BR 'kantəlu:p, -s
AM 'kæn(t)l,oʊp, -s

cantaloupe
BR 'kantəlu:p, -s
AM 'kæn(t)l,oʊp, -s

cantankerous
BR kan'taŋk(ə)rəs
AM kæn'tæŋk(ə)rəs

cantankerously
BR kan'taŋk(ə)rəsli
AM kæn'tæŋk(ə)rəsli

cantankerousness
BR kan'taŋk(ə)rəsnəs
AM kæn'tæŋk(ə)rəsnəs

cantata
BR kan'tɑːtə(r),
kən'tɑːtə(r), -z
AM kən'tɑdə, -z

cantatrice
BR 'kantətri:s, -ɪz
AM ,kɑn(t)ə'tris, -ɪz

canteen
BR kan'ti:n, -z
AM kæn'tin, -z

cantelope
BR 'kantəlu:p, -s
AM 'kæn(t)l,oʊp, -s

canter
BR 'kant|ə(r), -əz,
-(ə)rɪŋ, -əd
AM 'kæntər, -z, -ɪŋ, -d

Canterbury
BR 'kantəb(ə)ri
AM 'kæn(t)ər,bɛri,
'kæn(t)ərbəri

cantharides
BR kan'θarɪdi:z
AM kæn'θɛrədiz

canthi
BR 'kanθʌɪ
AM 'kæn,θaɪ

canthus
BR 'kanθəs
AM 'kænθəs

canticle
BR 'kantɪkl, -z
AM 'kæn(t)əkəl, -z

cantilena
BR ,kantɪ'leɪnə(r),
,kantɪ'li:nə(r), -z
AM ,kæn(t)ə'linə,
,kæn(t)ə'leɪnə, -z

cantilever
BR 'kantɪli:və(r),
'kantli:və(r), -z
AM 'kæn(t)ə),livər, -z

cantillate
BR 'kantɪleɪt,
'kantleɪt, -s, -ɪŋ, -ɪd
AM 'kæn(t)ə,leɪ|t, -ts,
-dɪŋ, -dɪd

cantillation
BR ,kantɪ'leɪʃn,
,kantl'eɪʃn
AM ,kæn(t)ə'leɪʃən

cantina
BR kan'ti:nə(r), -z
AM kæn'tinə, -z

cantle
BR 'kantl
AM 'kæn(t)əl

canto
BR 'kantəʊ, -z
AM 'kæn,toʊ,
'kæn(t)oʊ, -z

Canton¹
China
BR kan'tɒn
AM 'kæn,tɑn

Canton²
US, Wales
BR 'kantən
AM 'kæn(t)ən

canton
BR 'kantɒn, 'kantən, -z
AM 'kæn(t)ən,
'kæn,tɑn, -z

cantonal
BR kan'tɒnl, 'kantənl,
'kantn̩l
AM kæn'tɑnəl,
'kæn(t)ənəl,
'kænt(ə)nəl

Cantonese
BR ,kantə'ni:z
AM ,kæn(t)ə'niz

cantonment
BR kan'tu:nm(ə)nt,
kən'tu:nm(ə)nt, -s

AM kæn'toʊnmənt,
kæn'tɑnmənt, -s

cantor
BR 'kantɔ:(r),
'kantə(r), -z
AM 'kæn(t)ər,
'kæn,(t)ɔ(ə)r, -z

cantorial
BR kan'tɔ:rɪəl
AM kæn'tɔrɪəl

cantoris
BR kan'tɔ:rɪs
AM kæn'tɔrəs

cantrail
BR 'kantreɪl, -z
AM 'kæn,treɪl, -z

Cantrell
BR kan'trɛl
AM kæn'trɛl, 'kæntrəl

cantrip
BR 'kantrɪp, -s
AM 'kæn,trɪp, -s

Canuck
BR kə'nʌk, -s
AM kə'nək, -s

Canute
BR kə'nju:t
AM kə'n(j)ut

canvas
BR 'kanvəs, -ɪz
AM 'kænvəs, -əz

canvass
BR 'kanvəs, -ɪz, -ɪŋ, -t
AM 'kænvəs, -əz, -ɪŋ, -t

canvasser
BR 'kanvəsə(r), -z
AM 'kænvəsər, -z

Canvey
BR 'kanvi
AM 'kænvi

canyon
BR 'kanjən, -z
AM 'kænjən, -z

canzone
BR kan'tsəʊn|i,
kan'zəʊn|i, -ɪz
AM kɑn'zoʊneɪ,
kæn'zoʊni, -z

canzonet
BR ,kanzə'nɛt, -s
AM ,kænzə'nɛt, -s

canzonetta
BR ,kanzə'nɛtə(r), -z
AM ,kænzə'nɛdə, -z

caoutchouc
BR 'kaʊtʃʊk
AM kaʊ'tʃʊk

cap
BR kap, -s, -ɪŋ, -t
AM kæp, -s, -ɪŋ, -t

capability
BR ,keɪpə'bɪlɪt|i, -ɪz
AM ,keɪpə'bɪlɪdi, -z

Capablanca
BR 'kapə'blaŋkə(r)
AM ,kapə'blaŋkə

capable
BR ˈkeɪpəbl
AM ˈkeɪpəbəl
capableness
BR ˈkeɪpəblnəs
AM ˈkeɪpəbəlnəs
capably
BR ˈkeɪpəbli
AM ˈkeɪpəbli
capacious
BR kəˈpeɪʃəs
AM kəˈpeɪʃəs
capaciously
BR kəˈpeɪʃəsli
AM kəˈpeɪʃəsli
capaciousness
BR kəˈpeɪʃəsnəs
AM kəˈpeɪʃəsnəs
capacitance
BR kəˈpasɪt(ə)ns
AM kəˈpæsətns
capacitate
BR kəˈpasɪteɪt, -s, -ɪŋ, -ɪd
AM kəˈpæsəteɪ|t, -ts, -dɪŋ, -dɪd
capacitative
BR kəˈpasɪtətɪv
AM kəˈpæsəˌteɪdɪv
capacitive
BR kəˈpasɪtɪv
AM kəˈpæsədɪv
capacitor
BR kəˈpasɪtə(r), -z
AM kəˈpæsədər, -z
capacity
BR kəˈpasɪt|i, -ɪz
AM kəˈpæsədi, -z
cap-à-pie
BR ˌkapəˈpiː
AM ˌkapəˈpieɪ
caparison
BR kəˈparɪs(ə)n, -z, -ɪŋ, -d
AM kəˈpɛrəsən, -z, -ɪŋ, -d
cape
BR keɪp, -s
AM keɪp, -s
capelin
BR ˈkeɪplɪn, ˈkaplɪn, ˈkeɪplɪn
AM ˈkeɪpələn
Capella
BR kəˈpɛlə(r)
AM kəˈpɛlə
capellini
BR ˌkapəˈliːni, ˌkaplˈiːni
AM ˌkæpəˈlini
caper
BR ˈkeɪp|ə(r), -əz, -(ə)rɪŋ, -əd
AM ˈkeɪpər, -z, -ɪŋ, -d
capercaillie
BR ˌkapəˈkeɪl|i, -ɪz
AM ˌkæpərˈkeɪli, -z

capercailzie
BR ˌkapəˈkeɪl|i, -ɪz
AM ˌkæpərˈkeɪlzi, -z
caperer
BR ˈkeɪp(ə)rə(r), -z
AM ˈkeɪpərər, -z
Capernaum
BR kəˈpəːnɪəm
AM kəˈpərniəm
capeskin
BR ˈkeɪpskɪn
AM ˈkeɪpˌskɪn
Capet
BR ˈkapɪt
AM ˈkeɪpɪt, ˈkæpət
FR kapɛ
Capetian
BR kəˈpiːʃn, -z
AM kəˈpiʃən, -z
Cape Verde
BR ˌkeɪp ˈvəːd, + ˈvɛːd
AM ˌkeɪp ˈvərd(i)
Cape Verdean
BR ˌkeɪp ˈvəːdiən, + ˈvɛːdiən, -z
AM ˌkeɪp ˈvərdiən, -z
capful
BR ˈkapfʊl, -z
AM ˈkæpˌfʊl, -z
capias
BR ˈkeɪpɪəs
AM ˈkeɪpiəs
capillarity
BR ˌkapɪˈlarɪti
AM ˌkæpəˈlɛrədi
capillary
BR kəˈpɪl(ə)r|i, -ɪz
AM ˈkæpəˌlɛri, -z
Capistrano
BR ˌkapɪˈstrɑːnəʊ
AM ˌkæpəˈstrɑnoʊ
capital
BR ˈkapɪtl, -z
AM ˈkæpədl, -z
capitalisation
BR ˌkapɪtlʌɪˈzeɪʃn, ˌkapɪtəlʌɪˈzeɪʃn
AM ˌkæpədlˈəzeɪʃən, ˌkæpədlˌʌɪˈzeɪʃən
capitalise
BR ˈkapɪtlʌɪz, ˈkapɪtəlʌɪz, -ɪz, -ɪŋ, -d
AM ˈkæpədlˌʌɪz, -ɪz, -ɪŋ, -d
capitalism
BR ˈkapɪtlɪzm, ˈkapɪtəlɪzm
AM ˈkæpədlˌɪzəm
capitalist
BR ˈkapɪtlɪst, ˈkapɪtəlɪst, -s
AM ˈkæpədləst, -s
capitalistic
BR ˌkapɪtlˈɪstɪk, ˌkapɪtəˈlɪstɪk
AM ˌkæpədlˈɪstɪk

capitalistically
BR ˌkapɪtlˈɪstɪkli, ˌkapɪtəˈlɪstɪkli
AM ˌkæpədlˈɪstək(ə)li
capitalization
BR ˌkapɪtlʌɪˈzeɪʃn, ˌkapɪtəlʌɪˈzeɪʃn
AM ˌkæpədləˈzeɪʃən, ˌkæpədlˌʌɪˈzeɪʃən
capitalize
BR ˈkapɪtlʌɪz, ˈkapɪtəlʌɪz, -ɪz, -ɪŋ, -d
AM ˈkæpədlˌʌɪz, -ɪz, -ɪŋ, -d
capitally
BR ˈkapɪtlˌi
AM ˈkæpədlˌi
capitation
BR ˌkapɪˈteɪʃn, -z
AM ˌkæpəˈteɪʃən, -z
capitol
BR ˈkapɪt(ɒ)l, -z
AM ˈkæpədl, -z
capitolian
BR ˌkapɪˈtəʊliən
AM ˌkæpəˈtoʊljən, ˌkæpəˈtoʊliən
Capitoline
BR kəˈpɪtəlʌɪn, kəˈpɪtlʌɪn, ˈkapɪtəlʌɪn, ˈkapɪtlʌɪn
AM ˈkæpədəˌlaɪn
capitula
BR kəˈpɪtjʊlə(r), kəˈpɪtʃʊlə(r)
AM kəˈpɪtʃələ
capitular
BR kəˈpɪtjʊlə(r), kəˈpɪtʃʊlə(r)
AM kəˈpɪtʃələr
capitulary
BR kəˈpɪtjʊlər|i, kəˈpɪtʃʊlər|i, -ɪz
AM kəˈpɪtʃəˌlɛri, -z
capitulate
BR kəˈpɪtjʊleɪt, kəˈpɪtʃʊleɪt, -s, -ɪŋ, -ɪd
AM kəˈpɪtʃəˌleɪ|t, -ts, -dɪŋ, -dɪd
capitulation
BR kəˌpɪtjʊˈleɪʃn, kəˌpɪtʃʊˈleɪʃn
AM kəˌpɪtʃəˈleɪʃən
capitulator
BR kəˈpɪtjʊleɪtə(r), kəˈpɪtʃʊleɪtə(r), -z
AM kəˈpɪtʃəˌleɪdər, -z
capitulatory
BR kəˈpɪtjʊlət(ə)ri, kəˈpɪtʃʊlət(ə)ri
AM kəˈpɪtʃələˌtɔri
capitulum
BR kəˈpɪtjʊləm, kəˈpɪtʃʊləm
AM kəˈpɪtʃələm
Caplan
BR ˈkaplən

Caplet®
BR ˈkaplɪt
AM ˈkæplət
caplin
BR ˈkeɪplɪn, ˈkaplɪn, -z
AM ˈkæplən, -z
cap'n
captain
BR ˈkapn
AM ˈkæpn
capo
BR ˈkapəʊ, -z
AM ˈkeɪpoʊ, ˈkapoʊ, -z
Capo di Monte
BR ˌkapəʊ dɪ ˈmɒnti
AM ˌkapou di ˈman(t)i
capoeira
BR ˌkapʊˈeɪrə(r)
AM ˌkæpouˈeɪrə
capon
BR ˈkeɪpən, ˈkeɪpɒn, -z
AM ˈkeɪpɑn, ˈkeɪpən, -z
caponata
BR ˌkapə(ʊ)ˈnɑːtə(r)
AM ˌkæpəˈnɑdə
Capone
BR kəˈpəʊn
AM kəˈpoʊn
caponier
BR ˌkapəˈnɪə(r), -z
AM ˌkeɪpəˈnɪ(ə)r, -z
caponise
BR ˈkeɪpənʌɪz, ˈkeɪpnʌɪz, -ɪz, -ɪŋ, -d
AM ˈkeɪpəˌnaɪz, -ɪz, -ɪŋ, -d
caponize
BR ˈkeɪpənʌɪz, ˈkeɪpnʌɪz, -ɪz, -ɪŋ, -d
AM ˈkeɪpəˌnaɪz, -ɪz, -ɪŋ, -d
capot
BR kəˈpɒt, -s, -ɪŋ, -ɪd
AM kəˈpat, -z, -ɪŋ, -d
capo tasto
BR ˌkapəʊ ˈtastəʊ, -z
AM ˌkapou ˈtastoʊ, -z
Capote
BR kəˈpəʊti
AM kəˈpoʊdi
capote
BR kəˈpəʊt, -s
AM kəˈpoʊt, -s
Cappadocia
BR ˌkapəˈdəʊsɪə(r), ˌkapəˈdəʊʃ(ɪ)ə(r)
AM ˌkæpəˈdoʊʃə
Cappadocian
BR ˌkapəˈdəʊsɪən, ˌkapəˈdəʊʃɪən, -z
AM ˌkæpəˈdoʊʃən, -z
cappuccino
BR ˌkapəˈtʃiːnəʊ, -z
AM ˌkapəˈtʃinoʊ, ˌkæpəˈtʃinoʊ, -z

cappuchino
BR ‚kapʊ'tʃiːnəʊ, -z
AM ‚kapə'tʃinoʊ,
‚kæpə'tʃinoʊ, -z

Capra
BR 'kaprə(r)
AM 'kæprə

Capri
BR kə'priː, 'kapri
AM kə'pri, 'kæpri

capric
BR 'kaprɪk
AM 'kæprɪk

capriccio
BR kə'prɪtʃɪəʊ, -z
AM kə'prɪtʃioʊ, -z

capriccioso
BR kə‚prɪtʃɪ'əʊsəʊ
AM kə‚prɪtʃi'oʊsoʊ

caprice
BR kə'priːs, -ɪz
AM kə'pris, -ɪz

capricious
BR kə'prɪʃəs
AM kə'prɪʃəs,
kə'priʃəs

capriciously
BR kə'prɪʃəsli
AM kə'prɪʃəsli,
kə'priʃəsli

capriciousness
BR kə'prɪʃəsnəs
AM kə'prɪʃəsns,
kə'priʃəsnəs

Capricorn
BR 'kaprɪkɔːn
AM 'kæprə‚kɔ(ə)rn

Capricornian
BR ‚kaprɪ'kɔːnɪən, -z
AM ‚kæprə'kɔrnɪən, -z

Capricornus
BR ‚kaprɪ'kɔːnəs
AM ‚kæprə'kɔrnəs

caprine
BR 'kaprʌɪn
AM 'kæ‚praɪn

capriole
BR 'kaprɪəʊl, -z, -ɪŋ, -d
AM 'kæpri‚oʊl, -z, -ɪŋ, -d

caproic
BR kə'prəʊɪk, ka'prəʊɪk
AM kə'proʊɪk

caps.
capitals
BR kaps
AM kæps

Capsian
BR 'kapsɪən, -z
AM 'kæpsiən, -z

capsicum
BR 'kapsɪkəm, -z
AM 'kæpsəkəm, -z

capsid
BR 'kapsɪd, -z
AM 'kæpsəd, -z

capsizal
BR (‚)kap'sʌɪzl
AM 'kæp‚saɪzəl,
kæp'saɪzəl

capsize
BR (‚)kap'sʌɪz, -ɪz, -ɪŋ, -d
AM 'kæp‚saɪz,
kæp'saɪz, -ɪz, -ɪŋ, -d

capstan
BR 'kapstən, -z
AM 'kæpstən, -z

capstone
BR 'kapstəʊn, -z
AM 'kæp‚stoʊn, -z

capsular
BR 'kapsjʊlə(r)
AM 'kæps(j)ələr

capsulate
BR 'kapsjʊlət
AM 'kæps(j)ələt

capsule
BR 'kapsjuːl, 'kapsjʊl,
'kaps(ə)l, -z
AM 'kæpsəl,
'kæp‚s(j)ul, -z

capsulise
BR 'kapsjʊlʌɪz, -ɪz, -ɪŋ,
-d
AM 'kæps(j)ə‚laɪz, -ɪz,
-ɪŋ, -d

capsulize
BR 'kapsjʊlʌɪz, -ɪz, -ɪŋ,
-d
AM 'kæps(j)ə‚laɪz, -ɪz,
-ɪŋ, -d

captain
BR 'kapt(ɪ)n, -z, -ɪŋ, -d
AM 'kæpt(ə)n, -z, -ɪŋ, -d

captaincy
BR 'kapt(ɪ)ns|i, -ɪz
AM 'kæpt(ə)nsi, -z

captainship
BR 'kapt(ɪ)nʃɪp, -s
AM 'kæpt(ə)n‚ʃɪp, -s

caption
BR 'kapʃn, -z
AM 'kæpʃən, -z

captious
BR 'kapʃəs
AM 'kæpʃəs

captiously
BR 'kapʃəsli
AM 'kæpʃəsli

captiousness
BR 'kapʃəsnəs
AM 'kæpʃəsnəs

captivate
BR 'kaptɪveɪt, -s, -ɪŋ, -ɪd
AM 'kæptə‚veɪ|t, -ts,
-dɪŋ, -dɪd

captivatingly
BR 'kaptɪveɪtɪŋli
AM 'kæptə‚veɪdɪŋli

captivation
BR ‚kaptɪ'veɪʃn
AM ‚kæptə'veɪʃən

captive
BR 'kaptɪv, -z
AM 'kæptɪv, -z

captivity
BR kap'tɪvɪti
AM kæp'tɪvɪdi

captor
BR 'kaptə(r), -z
AM 'kæptər,
'kæp‚tɔ(ə)r, -z

capture
BR 'kaptʃə(r), -z, -ɪŋ, -d
AM 'kæp(t)ʃər, -z, -ɪŋ,
-d

capturer
BR 'kaptʃ(ə)rə(r), -z
AM 'kæp(t)ʃərər, -z

Capua
BR 'kapjʊə(r)
AM 'kæpjuə

capuche
BR kə'puː(t)ʃ, -ɪz
AM kə'pu(t)ʃ, -əz

Capuchin
BR 'kapjʊ(t)ʃɪn,
kə'puː(t)ʃɪn, -z
AM 'kæpjə(t)ʃən,
kə'p(j)u(t)ʃən, -z

Capulet
BR 'kapjʊlɪt
AM 'kæpjələt

capybara
BR ‚kapɪ'baːrə(r)
AM 'kæpə‚bɛrə

car
BR kaː(r), -z
AM kɑr, -z

Cara
BR 'kaːrə(r)
AM 'kɛrə

carabid
BR 'karəbɪd, -z
AM 'kərə‚bɪd, -z

carabineer
BR ‚karəbɪ'nɪə(r), -z
AM ‚kɛrəbə'nɪ(ə)r, -z

carabiner
BR ‚karə'biːnə(r), -z
AM ‚kɛrə'bɪnər, -z

carabiniere
BR ‚karəbɪ'njɛːri
AM ‚kɛrəbə'njɛri

carabinieri
BR ‚karəbɪ'njɛːri
AM ‚kɛrəbə'njɛri

caracal
BR 'karəkal, -z
AM 'karə‚kæl, -z

Caracalla
BR ‚karə'kalə(r)
AM ‚kɛrə'kalə

caracara
BR ‚karə'kaːrə(r), -z
AM ‚kɛrə'karə, -z

Caracas
BR kə'rakəs
AM kə'rakəs, kə'rækəs

caracole
BR 'karəkəʊl, -z
AM 'kɛrə‚koʊl, -z

Caractacus
BR kə'raktəkəs
AM kə'raktəkəs

caracul
BR 'karək(ʌ)l
AM 'kɛrəkəl

Caradoc
BR kə'radək, kə'radɒk
AM 'kɛrədak

Caradog
BR kə'radɒg
AM 'kɛrə‚dɒg,
'kɛrə‚dag

carafe
BR kə'raf, kə'raːf, -s
AM kə'ræf, -s

caragana
BR ‚karə'gaːnə(r)
AM ‚kɛrə'ganə

Carajás
BR kə'raːhəs
AM kə'rahəs
PORT kara'ʒaʃ

caramba
BR kə'rambə(r)
AM kə'rəmbə

carambola
BR ‚karəm'bəʊlə(r),
‚karm'bəʊlə(r), -z
AM ‚kɛrəm'boʊlə, -z

caramel
BR 'karəmɛl,
'karəm(ə)l, 'karm̩(ə)l,
-z
AM 'karməl, 'kɛrəməl,
'kɛrə‚mɛl, -z

caramelisation
BR ‚karəmɛlʌɪ'zeɪʃn,
‚karm̩əlʌɪ'zeɪʃn,
‚karm̩lʌɪ'zeɪʃn
AM ‚karmələ'zeɪʃən,
‚karmə‚laɪ'zeɪʃən

caramelise
BR 'karəmɛlʌɪz,
'karəml̩ʌɪz, -ɪz, -ɪŋ, -d
AM 'karmə‚laɪz, -ɪz, -ɪŋ,
-d

caramelization
BR ‚karəmɛlʌɪ'zeɪʃn,
‚karm̩əlʌɪ'zeɪʃn,
‚karm̩lʌɪ'zeɪʃn,
AM 'karmələ'zeɪʃən,
‚karmə‚laɪ'zeɪʃən

caramelize
BR 'karəmɛlʌɪz,
'karəml̩ʌɪz, -ɪz, -ɪŋ, -d
AM 'karmə‚laɪz, -ɪz, -ɪŋ,
-d

carangid
BR kə'randʒɪd, -z

AM kəˈrændʒəd,
kəˈræŋgəd, -z
carapace
BR ˈkarəpeɪs, -ɪz
AM ˈkɛrəˌpeɪs, -ɪz
carat
BR ˈkarət, -s
AM ˈkɛrət, -s
Caratacus
BR kəˈratəkəs
AM kəˈradəkəs
Caravaggio
BR ˌkarəˈvadʒɪəʊ
AM ˌkarəˈvadʒioʊ
caravan
BR ˈkarəvan, -z
AM ˈkɛrəˌvæn, -z
caravanette
BR ˌkarəvəˈnɛt,
ˌkarəvəˈnɛt, -s
AM ˌkɛrəvəˈnɛt, -s
caravanner
BR ˈkarəvanə(r), -z
AM ˈkɛrəˌvænər, -z
caravansary
BR ˌkarəˈvans(ə)r|i, -ɪz
AM ˌkɛrəˈvænsəri, -z
caravanserai
BR ˌkarəˈvan|sərʌɪ,
ˌkarəˈvan|s(ə)ri,
-sərʌɪz\-s(ə)riz
AM ˌkærəˈvænsəˌrʌɪ,
-z
caravansery
BR ˌkarəˈvans(ə)r|i, -ɪz
AM ˌkɛrəˈvænsəri, -z
caravel
BR ˈkarəvɛl, ˌkarəˈvɛl,
-z
AM ˈkɛrəvɛl, ˌkɛrəˈvɛl,
-z
caraway
BR ˈkarəweɪ, -z
AM ˈkɛrəˌweɪ, -z
carb
BR kɑːb, -z
AM kɑrb, -z
carbamate
BR ˈkɑːbəmeɪt
AM ˈkɑrbəˌmeɪt
carbazole
BR ˈkɑːbəzəʊl
AM ˈkɑrbəˌzoʊl
carbide
BR ˈkɑːbʌɪd, -z
AM ˈkɑrˌbaɪd, -z
carbine
BR ˈkɑːbʌɪn, -z
AM ˈkɑrˌbaɪn, kɑrbin,
-z
carbineer
BR ˌkɑːbɪˈnɪə(r), -z
AM ˌkɑrbəˈnɪ(ə)r, -z
carbohydrate
BR ˌkɑːbə(ʊ)ˈhʌɪdreɪt,
-s
AM ˌkɑrbəˈhaɪdˌreɪt, -s

carbolic
AM kɑːˈbɒlɪk
AM kɑrˈbɑlɪk
carbon
BR ˈkɑːbən, -z
AM ˈkɑrbən, -z
carbonaceous
BR ˌkɑːbəˈneɪʃəs
AM ˌkɑrbəˈneɪʃəs
carbonade
BR ˌkɑːbəˈneɪd,
ˌkɑːbəˈnɑːd, -z
AM ˌkɑrbəˈneɪd, -z
carbonado
BR ˌkɑːbəˈneɪdəʊ,
ˌkɑːbəˈnɑːdəʊ, -z
AM ˌkɑrbəˈneɪdoʊ, -z
carbonara
BR ˌkɑːbəˈnɑːrə(r)
AM ˌkɑrbəˈnɛrə
carbonate¹
noun
BR ˈkɑːbəneɪt,
ˈkɑːbənət, -s
AM ˈkɑrbənət, -s
carbonate²
verb
BR ˈkɑːbəneɪt, -s, -ɪŋ,
-ɪd
AM ˈkɑrbəˌneɪ|t, -ts,
-dɪŋ, -dɪd
carbonation
BR ˌkɑːbəˈneɪʃn
AM ˌkɑrbəˈneɪʃən
carbonatite
BR kɑːˈbɒnətʌɪt
AM ˈkɑrbənəˌtaɪt
carbonic
BR kɑːˈbɒnɪk
AM kɑrˈbɑnɪk
carboniferous
BR ˌkɑːbəˈnɪf(ə)rəs
AM ˌkɑrbəˈnɪf(ə)rəs
carbonisation
BR ˌkɑːbənʌɪˈzeɪʃn,
ˌkɑːbnʌɪˈzeɪʃn
AM ˌkɑrbənəˈzeɪʃən,
ˌkɑrbəˌnaɪˈzeɪʃən
carbonise
BR ˈkɑːbənʌɪz,
ˈkɑːbnʌɪz, -ɪz, -ɪŋ, -d
AM ˈkɑrbəˌnaɪz, -ɪz, -ɪŋ,
-d
carbonization
BR ˌkɑːbənʌɪˈzeɪʃn,
ˌkɑːbnʌɪˈzeɪʃn
AM ˌkɑrbənəˈzeɪʃən,
ˌkɑrbəˌnaɪˈzeɪʃən
carbonize
BR ˈkɑːbənʌɪz,
ˈkɑːbnʌɪz, -ɪz, -ɪŋ, -d
AM ˈkɑrbəˌnaɪz, -ɪz, -ɪŋ,
-d
carbon monoxide
BR ˌkɑːbən
məˈnɒksʌɪd,
+ mɒˈnɒksʌɪd

AM ˌkɑːbən
məˈnaksaɪd
carbonyl
BR ˈkɑːbənɪl,
ˈkɑːbənaɪl, -z
AM ˈkɑrbəˌnɪl, -z
Carborundum®
BR ˌkɑːbəˈrʌndəm
AM ˌkɑrbəˈrəndəm
carboxyl
BR kɑːˈbɒksɪl,
kɑːˈbɒksʌɪl, -z
AM kɑrˈbaksl, -z
carboxylase
BR kɑːˈbɒksɪleɪz
AM ˌkɑrˈbaksəˌleɪz
carboxylate
BR kɑːˈbɒksɪleɪt
AM ˌkɑrˈbaksəˌleɪt
carboxylic
BR ˌkɑːbɒkˈsɪlɪk
AM ˌkɑrˌbakˈsɪlɪk
carboy
BR ˈkɑːbɔɪ, -z
AM ˈkɑrˌbɔɪ, -z
carbuncle
BR ˈkɑːbʌŋkl, -z
AM ˈkɑrˌbəŋkəl, -z
carbuncular
BR kɑːˈbʌŋkjələ(r)
AM kɑrˈbəŋkjələr
carburant
BR ˈkɑːbjʊrənt,
ˈkɑːbjʊrnt, -s
AM ˈkɑrbərənt, -s
carburation
BR ˌkɑːbjʊˈreɪʃn,
ˌkɑːbəˈreɪʃn,
ˌkɑːbjʊˈreɪʃn
AM ˌkɑrb(j)əˈreɪʃən
carburet
BR ˈkɑːbjʊrət,
ˈkɑːbərət, -s, -ɪd
AM ˈkɑrbəˌret, -ts,
-dəd
carburetor
BR ˌkɑːbəˈrɛtə(r),
ˌkɑːbjʊˈrɛtə(r), -z
AM ˈkɑrbəˌreɪdər, -z
carburetter
BR ˌkɑːbəˈrɛtə(r),
ˌkɑːbjʊˈrɛtə(r), -z
AM ˈkɑrbəˌreɪdər, -z
carburettor
BR ˌkɑːbəˈrɛtə(r),
ˌkɑːbjʊˈrɛtə(r), -z
AM ˈkɑrbəˌreɪdər, -z
carcajou
BR ˈkɑːkə(d)ʒuː
AM ˈkɑrkə(d)ʒu
carcase
BR ˈkɑːkəs, -ɪz
AM ˈkɑrkəs, -əz
carcass
BR ˈkɑːkəs, -ɪz
AM ˈkɑrkəs, -əz
Carcassonne
BR ˌkɑːkəˈsɒn

AM ˌkɑrkəˈsɑn
Carchemish
BR ˈkɑːkəmɪʃ,
kɑːˈkɛmɪʃ, kɑːˈkiːmɪʃ
AM ˈkɑrkəˌmɪʃ
carcinogen
BR kɑːˈsɪnədʒ(ə)n,
ˈkɑːsɪnədʒ(ə)n,
ˈkɑːsnədʒ(ə)n, -z
AM ˈkɑrˈsɪnədʒən,
ˈkɑrsnəˌdʒɛn, -z
carcinogenesis
BR ˌkɑːs(ɪ)nəˈdʒɛnɪsɪs,
ˌkɑːsnəˈdʒɛnɪsɪs
AM ˌkɑrs(ə)nəˈdʒɛnəsəs,
ˈkɑrsnoʊˈdʒɛnəsəs
carcinogenic
BR ˌkɑːs(ɪ)nəˈdʒɛnɪk,
ˌkɑːsnəˈdʒɛnɪk,
kɑːˌsɪnəˈdʒɛnɪk
AM ˌkɑrs(ə)nəˈdʒɛnɪk,
ˈkɑrsnoʊˈdʒɛnɪk
carcinogenically
BR ˌkɑːs(ɪ)nəˈdʒɛnɪkli,
ˌkɑːsnəˈdʒɛnɪkli,
kɑːˌsɪnəˈdʒɛnɪkli
AM ˌkɑrs(ə)nəˈdʒɛnək(ə)li,
ˈkɑrsnoʊˈdʒɛnək(ə)li
carcinogenicity
BR ˌkɑːs(ɪ)nə(ʊ)dʒɛˈnɪsɪti,
ˌkɑːsnə(ʊ)dʒɛˈnɪsɪti,
kɑːˌsɪnə(ʊ)dʒɛˈnɪsɪti
AM ˌkɑrsnoʊdʒɛˈnɪsɪdi,
ˌkɑrs(ə)nədʒɛˈnɪsɪdi
carcinoma
BR ˌkɑːsɪˈnəʊmə(r),
ˌkɑːsnˈəʊmə(r), -z
AM ˌkɑrsəˈnoʊmə, -z
carcinomatous
BR ˌkɑːsɪˈnəʊmətəs,
ˌkɑːsnˈəʊmətəs
AM ˌkɑrsəˈnɑmədəs
card
BR kɑːd, -z, -ɪŋ, -ɪd
AM kɑrd, -z, -ɪŋ, -əd
cardamom
BR ˈkɑːdəməm
AM ˈkɑrdəməm
cardamum
BR ˈkɑːdəməm
AM ˈkɑrdəməm
cardboard
BR ˈkɑːdbɔːd
AM ˈkɑrdˌbɔ(ə)rd
carder
BR ˈkɑːdə(r), -z
AM ˈkɑrdər, -z
Cardew
BR ˈkɑːdjuː, ˈkɑːdʒuː
AM ˈkɑrdju, ˈkɑrdʒu
cardholder
BR ˈkɑːdˌhəʊldə(r), -z
AM ˈkɑrd,(h)oʊldər, -z
cardiac
BR ˈkɑːdɪak, -s
AM ˈkɑrdiˌæk, -s
cardiacal
BR kɑːˈdʌɪəkl

AM kɑr'daɪəkəl

cardie
BR 'kɑ:d|i, -ɪz
AM 'kɑrdi, -z

Cardiff
BR 'kɑ:dɪf
AM 'kɑrdəf

cardigan
BR 'kɑ:dɪg(ə)n, -z
AM 'kɑrdəgən, -z

Cardin
BR 'kɑ:dã, 'kɑ:dan
AM kɑr'dæn

cardinal
BR 'kɑ:dɪn(ə)l,
'kɑ:dŋ(ə)l, -z
AM 'kɑrdŋəl,
'kɑrdənəl, -z

cardinalate
BR 'kɑ:dɪnələt,
'kɑ:dɪŋlət, 'kɑ:dŋələt,
'kɑ:dŋlət, -s
AM 'kɑrdŋələt,
'kɑrdənələt, -s

cardinality
BR ,kɑ:dɪ'nalɪti
AM ,kɑrdə'nælədi,
,kɑrdn'ælədi

cardinally
BR 'kɑ:dɪŋli,
'kɑ:dɪnəli, 'kɑ:dŋli,
'kɑ:dŋəli
AM 'kɑrdŋəli,
'kɑrdənəli

cardinalship
BR 'kɑ:dɪn(ə)lʃɪp,
'kɑ:dŋ(ə)lʃɪp, -s
AM 'kɑrdŋəlˌʃɪp,
'kɑrdənəlˌʃɪp, -s

cardiogram
BR 'kɑ:dɪə(ʊ)gram, -z
AM 'kɑrdioʊˌgræm,
'kɑrdiəˌgræm, -z

cardiograph
BR 'kɑ:dɪə(ʊ)grɑ:f,
'kɑ:dɪə(ʊ)graf, -s
AM 'kɑrdioʊˌgræf,
'kɑrdiəˌgræf, -s

cardiographer
BR ˌkɑ:dɪ'ɒgrəfə(r), -z
AM ˌkɑrdi'ɑgrəfər, -z

cardiography
BR ˌkɑ:dɪ'ɒgrəfi
AM ˌkɑrdi'ɑgrəfi

cardiologist
BR ˌkɑ:dɪ'ɒlədʒɪst, -s
AM ˌkɑrdi'ɑlədʒəst, -s

cardiology
BR ˌkɑ:dɪ'ɒlədʒi
AM ˌkɑrdi'ɑlədʒi

cardiometer
BR ˌkɑ:dɪ'ɒmɪtə(r), -z
AM ˌkɑrdi'ɑmədər, -z

cardiopulmonary
BR 'kɑ:dɪəʊ'pʊlmən(ə)ri
AM ˌkɑrdioʊ'pʊlməˌnɛri

cardiovascular
BR ˌkɑ:dɪəʊ'vaskjʉlə(r)

AM ˌkɑrdioʊ'væskjələr,
ˌkɑrdiə'væskjələr

cardoon
BR ˌkɑ:'du:n, -z
AM ˌkɑr'dun, -z

cardphone
BR 'kɑ:dfəʊn, -z
AM 'kɑrdˌfoʊn, -z

cardpunch
BR 'kɑ:dpʌn(t)ʃ, -ɪz
AM 'kɑrdˌpən(t)ʃ, -əz

cardsharp
BR 'kɑ:dʃɑ:p, -s
AM 'kɑrdˌʃɑrp, -s

Cardus
BR 'kɑ:dəs
AM 'kɑrdəs

Cardwell
BR 'kɑ:dw(ɛ)l
AM 'kɑrdˌwɛl

cardy
BR 'kɑ:d|i, -ɪz
AM 'kɑrdi, -z

care
BR kɛ:(r), -z, -ɪŋ, -d
AM kɛ(ə)r, -z, -ɪŋ, -d

careen
BR kə'ri:n, -z, -ɪŋ, -d
AM kə'rin, -z, -ɪŋ, -d

careenage
BR kə'ri:nɪdʒ
AM kə'rinɪdʒ

career
BR kə'rɪə(r), -z, -ɪŋ, -d
AM kə'rɪ(ə)r, -z, -ɪŋ, -d

careerism
BR kə'rɪərɪz(ə)m
AM kə'rɪ(ə)ˌrɪzəm

careerist
BR kə'rɪərɪst, -s
AM kə'rɪrəst, -s

carefree
BR 'kɛ:fri:, ˌkɛ:'fri:
AM ˌkɛr'fri

carefreely
BR 'kɛ:fri:li, ˌkɛ:'fri:li
AM ˌkɛr'frili

carefreeness
BR 'kɛ:fri:nɪs,
ˌkɛ:'fri:nɪs
AM ˌkɛr'frinɪs

careful
BR 'kɛ:|f(ʊ)l,
-f(ʉ)lɪst\-fˌlɪst
AM 'kɛrfəl, -əst

carefully
BR 'kɛ:f(ʉ)li, 'kɛ:fˌli
AM 'kɛrf(ə)li

carefulness
BR 'kɛ:f(ʉ)lnəs
AM 'kɛrfəlnəs

careless
BR 'kɛ:ləs
AM 'kɛrləs

carelessly
BR 'kɛ:ləsli
AM 'kɛrləsli

carelessness
BR 'kɛ:ləsnəs
AM 'kɛrləsnəs

carer
BR 'kɛ:rə(r), -z
AM 'kɛrər, -z

caress
BR kə'rɛs, -ɪz, -ɪŋ, -t
AM kə'rɛs, -əz, -ɪŋ, -t

caressingly
BR kə'rɛsɪŋli
AM kə'rɛsɪŋli

caret
BR 'karɪt, -s
AM 'kɛrət, -s

caretake
BR 'kɛ:teɪk, -s, -ɪŋ
AM 'kɛrˌteɪk, -s, -ɪŋ

caretaker
BR 'kɛ:ˌteɪkə(r), -z
AM 'kɛrˌteɪkər, -z

Carew
BR kə'ru:, 'kɛ:ri
AM kə'ru, 'kɛru

careworn
BR 'kɛ:wɔ:n
AM 'kɛrˌwɔ(ə)rn

Carey
BR 'kɛ:ri
AM 'kɛri

carezza
BR kə'rɛtsə(r)
AM kə'rɛtsə, kə'rɛzə

carfare
BR 'kɑ:fɛ:(r)
AM 'kɑrˌfɛ(ə)r

carfax
BR 'kɑ:faks, -ɪz
AM 'kɑrˌfæks, -əz

carferry
BR 'kɑ:ˌfer|i, -ɪz
AM 'kɑrˌfɛri, -z

carful
BR 'kɑ:fʊl, -z
AM 'kɑrˌfʊl, -z

Cargill
BR 'kɑ:gɪl, kɑ:'gɪl
AM 'kɑrˌgɪl, 'kɑrgəl

cargo
BR 'kɑ:gəʊ, -z
AM 'kɑrgoʊ, -z

carhop
BR 'kɑ:hɒp, -s
AM 'kɑrˌ(h)ɑp, -s

Caria
BR 'kɛ:rɪə(r)
AM 'kɛriə

cariama
BR ˌkarɪ'ɑ:mə(r), -z
AM ˌkɛri'ɑmə, -z

Carian
BR 'karɪən, -z
AM 'kɛriən, -z

Carib
BR 'karɪb, -z
AM 'kɛrəb, -z

Caribbean
BR ˌkarɪ'bi:ən,
kə'rɪbɪən
AM ˌkɛrə'biən,
kə'rɪbɪən

Caribbean Sea
BR ˌkarɪbi:ən 'si:,
kəˌrɪbɪən +
AM ˌkɛrə'biən 'si,
kə'rɪbɪən +

caribou
BR 'karɪbu:, -z
AM 'kɛrəˌbu, -z

caricatural
BR ˌkarɪkə'tʃʊərəl,
ˌkarɪkə'tjʊərəl,
ˌkarɪkə'tjʊərl,
ˌkarɪkə'tʃɔ:rəl,
ˌkarɪkə'tʃɔ:rl,
ˌkarɪkə'tjɔ:rəl,
ˌkarɪkə'tjɔ:rl
AM ˌkɛrəkə'tʃʊrəl,
'kɛrəkətʃərəl

caricature
BR 'karɪkətʃʊə(r),
'karɪkətjʊə(r),
'karɪkətʃɔ:(r),
'karɪkətjɔ:(r), -z, -ɪŋ,
-d
AM 'kɛrəkəˌtʃʊ(ə)r,
'kɛrəkətʃər, -z, -ɪŋ, -d

caricaturist
BR 'karɪkətʃʊərɪst,
'karɪkətjʊərɪst,
'karɪkətʃɔ:rɪst,
'karɪkətjɔ:rɪst, -s
AM 'kɛrəkəˌtʃʊrəst, -s

CARICOM
BR 'karɪkɒm
AM 'kɛrəˌkɑm

caries
BR 'kɛ:ri:z
AM 'kɛriz

carillon
BR 'karɪljən, 'kɑrˌljən,
'karɪlɒn, 'kɑrˌlɒn,
kə'rɪljən, kə'rɪljɒn, -z
AM 'kɛrəˌlɑn, 'kɛrələn,
-z

carina
BR kə'ri:nə(r),
kə'rʌɪnə(r), -z
AM kə'rinə, kə'rʌɪnə,
-z

carinae
BR kə'ri:ni:, kə'ri:nʌɪ,
kə'rʌɪni:, kə'rʌɪnʌɪ
AM kə'rini, kə'rʌɪnaɪ,
kə'raɪni, kə'raɪˌnaɪ

carinal
BR kə'ri:nl, kə'rʌɪnl
AM kə'rinəl, kə'raɪnəl

carinate¹
adjective
BR 'karɪneɪt, 'karɪnət
AM 'kɛrənət, 'kɛrəˌneɪt

carinate²
verb
BR ˈkarɪneɪt, -s, -ɪŋ, -ɪd
AM ˈkɛrəˌneɪ|t, -ts, -dɪŋ, -dɪd

caring
BR ˈkɛːrɪŋ
AM ˈkɛrɪŋ

Carinthia
BR kəˈrɪnθɪə(r)
AM kəˈrɪnθɪə

carioca
BR ˌkarɪˈəʊkə(r)
AM ˌkɛriˈoʊkə

cariogenic
BR ˌkarɪəˈdʒɛnɪk
AM ˌkɛriəˈdʒɛnɪk, ˌkɛrioʊˈdʒɛnɪk

carious
BR ˈkɛːrɪəs
AM ˈkɛrɪəs

Carisbrooke
BR ˈkarɪzbrʊk, ˈkarɪsbrʊk
AM ˈkɛrəsˌbrʊk

carking
BR ˈkɑːkɪŋ
AM ˈkɑrkɪŋ

Carl
BR kɑːl
AM kɑrl

Carla
BR ˈkɑːlə(r)
AM ˈkɑrlə

Carleton
BR ˈkɑːlt(ə)n
AM ˈkɑrltən

Carlin
BR ˈkɑːlɪn
AM ˈkɑrlɪn

carline
BR ˈkɑːlʌɪn, ˈkɑːlɪn, -z
AM ˈkɑrˌlaɪn, -z

Carlisle
BR (ˌ)kɑːˈlʌɪl, ˈkɑːlʌɪl
AM ˈkɑrˌlaɪl

Carlo
BR ˈkɑːləʊ
AM ˈkɑrloʊ

carload
BR ˈkɑːləʊd, -z
AM ˈkɑrˌloʊd, -z

Carlovingian
BR ˌkɑːlə(ʊ)ˈvɪn(d)ʒɪən, ˌkɑːlə(ʊ)ˈvɪn(d)ʒ(i)ən, -z
AM ˌkɑrlə'vɪnd͡ʒ(i)ən, -z

Carlow
BR ˈkɑːləʊ
AM ˈkɑrloʊ

Carlsbad
BR ˈkɑːlzbad
AM ˈkɑrlzˌbæd, ˈkɑrlzˌbad

Carlsberg®
BR ˈkɑːlzbəːg
AM ˈkɑrlzˌbɜrg

Carlson
BR ˈkɑːlsn
AM ˈkɑrlsən

Carlton
BR ˈkɑːlt(ə)n
AM ˈkɑrltən

Carly
BR ˈkɑːli
AM ˈkɑrli

Carlyle
BR (ˌ)kɑːˈlʌɪl
AM ˈkɑrˌlaɪl

carmaker
BR ˈkɑːˌmeɪkə(r), -z
AM ˈkɑrˌmeɪkər, -z

Carman
BR ˈkɑːmən
AM ˈkɑrmən

carman
BR ˈkɑːmən
AM ˈkɑrmən

Carmarthen
BR kəˈmɑːðən
AM ˌkɑrˈmɑrðən

Carmel
BR ˈkɑːml, ˈkɑːmɛl, (ˌ)kɑːˈmɛl
AM kɑrˈmɛl

Carmelite
BR ˈkɑːmɪlʌɪt, ˈkɑːmlʌɪt, -s
AM ˈkɑrməˌlaɪt, -s

Carmen
BR ˈkɑːmən, ˈkɑːmɛn
AM ˈkɑrmən

carmen
BR ˈkɑːmən
AM ˈkɑrmən

Carmichael
BR kɑːˈmʌɪkl, ˈkɑːmʌɪkl
AM ˈkɑrˌmaɪkl

Carmina Burana
BR kɑːˌmiːnə bəˈrɑːnə(r)
AM ˌkɑrˌminə b(j)uˈrɑnə

carminative
BR ˈkɑːmɪnətɪv, ˈkɑːmˌnətɪv, -z
AM kɑrˈmɪnədɪv, ˈkɑrməˌneɪdɪv, -z

carmine
BR ˈkɑːmʌɪn
AM ˈkɑrmaɪn

Carnaby Street
BR ˈkɑːnəbɪ striːt
AM ˈkɑrnəbiˌstrɪt

Carnac
BR ˈkɑːnak
AM ˈkɑrˌnæk

carnage
BR ˈkɑːnɪdʒ
AM ˈkɑrnɪdʒ

carnal
BR ˈkɑːnl
AM ˈkɑrnəl

carnalise
BR ˈkɑːnəlʌɪz, ˈkɑːnlˌʌɪz, -ɪz, -ɪŋ, -d
AM ˈkɑrnəˌlaɪz, -ɪz, -ɪŋ, -d

carnality
BR kɑːˈnalɪti
AM kɑrˈnælədi

carnalize
BR ˈkɑːnəlʌɪz, ˈkɑːnlˌʌɪz, -ɪz, -ɪŋ, -d
AM ˈkɑrnəˌlaɪz, -ɪz, -ɪŋ, -d

carnally
BR ˈkɑːnəli, ˈkɑːnlˌi
AM ˈkɑrnəli

Carnap
BR ˈkɑːnap
AM ˈkɑrnæp

Carnarvon
BR kəˈnɑːvn
AM kəˈnɑrvn

carnassial
BR kɑːˈnasɪəl, -z
AM kɑrˈnæsɪəl, -z

Carnatic
BR kɑːˈnatɪk
AM kɑrˈnædɪk

carnation
BR kɑːˈneɪʃn, -z
AM kɑrˈneɪʃən, -z

carnauba
BR kɑːˈnɔːbə(r), kɑːˈnaʊbə(r)
AM kɑrˈnɔbə, kɑrˈnabə

Carné
BR kɑːˈneɪ
AM kɑrˈneɪ

Carnegie
BR kɑːˈniːgi
AM ˈkɑrnəgi, kɑrˈneɪgi

carnelian
BR kɑːˈniːlɪən, -z
AM kɑrˈnilɪən, -z

carnet
BR ˈkɑːneɪ, -z
AM kɑrˈneɪ, -z

Carney
BR ˈkɑːni
AM ˈkɑrni

Carnforth
BR ˈkɑːnfɔːθ
AM ˈkɑrnˌfɔ(ə)rθ

carnival
BR ˈkɑːnɪvl, -z
AM ˈkɑrnəvəl, -z

Carnivora
BR kɑːˈnɪv(ə)rə(r)
AM kɑrˈnɪv(ə)rə

carnivore
BR ˈkɑːnɪvɔː(r), -z
AM ˈkɑrnəˌvɔ(ə)r, -z

carnivorous
BR kɑːˈnɪv(ə)rəs
AM kɑrˈnɪv(ə)rəs

carnivorously
BR kɑːˈnɪv(ə)rəsli
AM kɑrˈnɪv(ə)rəsli

carnivorousness
BR kɑːˈnɪv(ə)rəsnəs
AM kɑrˈnɪv(ə)rəsnəs

Carnot
BR ˈkɑːnəʊ
AM kɑrˈnoʊ

Carnoustie
BR kɑːˈnuːsti
AM kɑrˈnusdi

carny
BR ˈkɑːni
AM ˈkɑrni

carob
BR ˈkarəb, -z
AM ˈkɛrəb, -z

carol
BR ˈkarəl, ˈkarl̩, -z, -ɪŋ, -d
AM ˈkɛrəl, -z, -ɪŋ, -d

Carole
BR ˈkarəl, ˈkarl̩
AM ˈkɛrəl

Carolean
BR ˌkarəˈliːən, -z
AM ˈkɛrəˌlin, -z

caroler
BR ˈkarələ(r), ˈkarl̩ə(r), -z
AM ˈkɛrələr, -z

Carolina
BR ˌkarəˈlʌɪnə(r), -z
AM ˌkɛrəˈlaɪnə, -z

Caroline
BR ˈkarəlʌɪn, ˈkarəlɪn, ˈkarl̩ɪn
AM ˈkɛrəˌlaɪn, ˈkɛrələn

Carolingian
BR ˌkarəˈlɪŋgɪən, ˌkarəˈlɪn(d)ʒɪən, -z
AM ˌkɛrəˈlɪn(d)ʒ(i)ən, -z

caroller
BR ˈkarələ(r), ˈkarl̩ə(r), -z
AM ˈkɛrələr, -z

carolus
BR ˈkarələs, -ɪz
AM ˈkɛrələs, -əz

Carolyn
BR ˈkarəlɪn, ˈkarl̩ɪn
AM ˈkɛrələn

carom
BR ˈkarəm, ˈkarm̩, -z, -ɪŋ, -d
AM ˈkɛrəm, -z, -ɪŋ, -d

Caron
BR ˈkarən, ˈkarn̩, kəˈrɒn
AM ˈkɛrən

carotene
BR ˈkarətiːn
AM ˈkɛrəˌtin

carotenoid
BR kəˈrɒtɪnɔɪd
AM kəˈratnˌɔɪd

Carothers
BR kə'rʌðəz
AM kə'rəðərz
carotid
BR kə'rɒtɪd
AM kə'radəd
carousal
BR kə'raʊzl̩, -z
AM kə'raʊzəl, -z
carouse
BR kə'raʊz, -ɪz, -ɪŋ, -d
AM kə'raʊz, -əz, -ɪŋ, -d
carousel
BR ˌkarə'sɛl, -z
AM ˌkɛrə'sɛl, -z
carouser
BR kə'raʊzə(r), -z
AM kə'raʊzər, -z
carp
BR kɑːp, -s, -ɪŋ, -t
AM kɑrp, -s, -ɪŋ, -t
Carpaccio
BR kɑː'patʃɪəʊ
AM kɑr'patʃ(i)oʊ
carpal
BR 'kɑːpl̩, -z
AM 'kɑrpəl, -z
carpark
BR 'kɑːpɑːk, -s, -ɪŋ
AM 'kɑrˌpɑrk, -s, -ɪŋ
Carpathian
BR kɑː'peɪθɪən, -z
AM kɑr'peɪθɪən, -z
carpe diem
BR ˌkɑːpɪ 'diːɛm
AM ˌkɑrpə di'ɛm
carpel
BR 'kɑːpl̩, -z
AM 'kɑrpəl, -z
carpellary
BR 'kɑːpəl(ə)ri, 'kɑːpl̩(ə)ri
AM 'kɑrpəˌlɛri
Carpentaria
BR ˌkɑːp(ə)n'tɛːrɪə(r), ˌkɑːpɛn'tɛːrɪə(r)
AM ˌkɑrpən'tɛrɪə
carpenter
BR 'kɑːp(ɪ)ntə(r), -z
AM 'kɑrpən(t)ər, -z
carpentry
BR 'kɑːp(ɪ)ntri
AM 'kɑrpəntri
carper
BR 'kɑːpə(r), -z
AM 'kɑrpər, -z
carpet
BR 'kɑːpɪt, -ɪts, -ɪtɪŋ, -ɪtɪd
AM 'kɑrpə|t, -ts, -dɪŋ, -dəd
carpetbag
BR 'kɑːpɪtbag, -z, -ɪŋ
AM 'kɑrpətˌbæg, -z, -ɪŋ
carpetbagger
BR 'kɑːpɪtˌbagə(r), -z
AM 'kɑrpətˌbægər, -z

carpeting
BR 'kɑːpɪtɪŋ, -z
AM 'kɑrpədɪŋ, -z
carphology
BR kɑː'fɒlədʒi
AM kɑr'fɑlədʒi
carpi
BR 'kɑːpʌɪ
AM 'kɑrˌpaɪ
carpology
BR kɑː'pɒlədʒi
AM kɑr'pɑlədʒi
carport
BR 'kɑːpɔːt, -s
AM 'kɑrˌpɔ(ə)rt, -s
carpus
BR 'kɑːpəs
AM 'kɑrpəs
Carr
BR kɑː(r)
AM kɑr
carrack
BR 'karək, -s
AM 'kɛrək, -s
carrageen
BR 'karəgiːn, ˌkarə'giːn
AM ˌkarə'giːn, 'kɛrəˌgin
carragheen
BR 'karəgiːn, ˌkarə'giːn
AM ˌkarə'giːn, 'kɛrəˌgin
Carrara
BR kə'rɑːrə(r)
AM kə'rɑrə, kə'rɛrə
carraway
BR 'karəweɪ, -z
AM 'kɛrəˌweɪ, -z
carrel
BR 'karəl, 'karl̩, -z
AM 'kɛrəl, -z
Carreras
BR kə'rɛːrəs
AM kə'rɛrəs
carriage
BR 'karɪdʒ, -ɪdʒɪz
AM 'kɛrɪdʒ, -ɪz
carriageway
BR 'karɪdʒweɪ, -z
AM 'kɛrɪdʒˌweɪ, -z
carrick
BR 'karɪk
AM 'kɛrɪk
Carrickfergus
BR ˌkarɪk'fəːgəs
AM ˌkɛrək'fərgəs
Carrie
BR 'kari
AM 'kɛri
carrier
BR 'karɪə(r), -z
AM 'kɛrɪər, -z
Carrington
BR 'karɪŋt(ə)n
AM 'kɛrɪŋtən
carriole
BR 'karɪəʊl, -z

carrion
BR 'karɪən
AM 'kɛrɪən
Carroll
BR 'karəl, 'karl̩
AM 'kɛrəl
Carron
BR 'karən, 'karn̩
AM 'kɛrən
carronade
BR ˌkarə'neɪd, -z
AM ˌkɛrə'neɪd, -z
carrot
BR 'karət, -s
AM 'kɛrət, -s
carroty
BR 'karəti
AM 'kɛrədi
carrousel
BR ˌkarə'sɛl, -z
AM ˌkɛrə'sɛl, -z
Carruthers
BR kə'rʌðəz, 'krɪðəz
AM kə'rəðərz
carry
BR 'kar|i, -ɪz, -ɪŋ, -ɪd
AM 'kɛri, -z, -ɪŋ, -d
carryall
BR 'karɪɔːl, -z
AM 'kɛriˌɔl, 'kɛriˌɑl, -z
carrycot
BR 'karɪkɒt, -s
AM 'kɛriˌkat, -s
carse
BR kɑːs, -ɪz
AM kɑrs, -əz
Carshalton
BR kɑː'ʃɔːlt(ə)n
AM kɑr'ʃɔltən, kɑr'ʃɑltən
carsick
BR 'kɑːsɪk
AM 'kɑrˌsɪk
carsickness
BR 'kɑːsɪknɪs
AM 'kɑrˌsɪknɪs
Carson
BR 'kɑːsn̩
AM 'kɑrsən
Carstairs
BR 'kɑːstɛːz
AM 'kɑrˌstɛrz
cart
BR kɑːt, -s, -ɪŋ, -ɪd
AM kɑr|t, -ts, -dɪŋ, -dəd
cartage
BR 'kɑːtɪdʒ
AM 'kɑrdɪdʒ
Cartagena
BR ˌkɑːtə'dʒiːnə(r), ˌkɑːtə'heɪmə(r)
AM ˌkɑrtə'heɪmə, ˌkɑrdə'ginə
carte
BR kɑːt
AM kɑrt

carte blanche
BR ˌkɑːt 'blɒ̃ʃ,
+ 'blɑːn(t)ʃ
AM 'kɑrt 'blɑn(t)ʃ
carte-de-visite
BR ˌkɑːtdəvɪ'ziːt
AM ˌkɑrtdəvɪ'zit
cartel
BR kɑː'tɛl, -z
AM kɑr'tɛl, -z
cartelisation
BR ˌkɑːtələɪ'zeɪʃn, ˌkɑːtlʌɪ'zeɪʃn
AM ˌkɑrˌtɛlə'zeɪʃən, 'kɑrdəˌlaɪ'zeɪʃən
cartelise
BR 'kɑːtəlʌɪz, 'kɑːtl̩ʌɪz, -ɪz, -ɪŋ, -d
AM 'kɑrdəˌlaɪz, -ɪz, -ɪŋ, -d
cartelization
BR ˌkɑːtələɪ'zeɪʃn, ˌkɑːtlʌɪ'zeɪʃn
AM ˌkɑrˌtɛlə'zeɪʃən, 'kɑrdəˌlaɪ'zeɪʃən
cartelize
BR 'kɑːtəlʌɪz, 'kɑːtl̩ʌɪz, -ɪz, -ɪŋ, -d
AM 'kɑrdəˌlaɪz, -ɪz, -ɪŋ, -d
carter
BR 'kɑːtə(r), -z
AM 'kɑrdər, -z
Carteret
BR 'kɑːtərɪt, 'kɑːtərɛt
AM 'kɑrdərət, ˌkɑrdər'ɛt
cartes blanches
BR ˌkɑːts 'blɒ̃ʃ,
+ 'blɑːn(t)ʃ
AM 'kɑrts 'blɑn(t)ʃ
cartes de visite
BR ˌkɑːt də vɪ'ziːt
AM ˌkɑrt də vɪ'zit
Cartesian
BR kɑː'tiːzɪən, kɑː'tiːʒn,
AM kɑr'tiʒən, -z
Cartesianism
BR kɑː'tiːzɪənɪz(ə)m
AM kɑr'tiʒəˌnɪzəm
cartful
BR 'kɑːtfʊl, -z
AM 'kɑrt,fʊl, -z
Carthage
BR 'kɑːθɪdʒ
AM 'kɑrθədʒ
Carthaginian
BR ˌkɑːθə'dʒɪnɪən, -z
AM ˌkɑrθə'dʒɪnɪən, -z
carthorse
BR 'kɑːthɔːs, -ɪz
AM 'kɑrt,(h)ɔ(ə)rs, -ɪz
Carthusian
BR kɑː'θjuːzɪən, -z
AM kɑr'θ(j)uʒən, -z
Cartier
BR 'kɑːtɪeɪ

AM ˈkɑːdiˌeɪ
Cartier-Bresson
BR ˌkɑːtɪeɪˈbresɒ̃
AM ˌkɑːdiˌeɪbrəˈsɔn,
ˌkɑːdiˌeɪbrəˈsɑn
cartilage
BR ˈkɑːtɪl|ɪdʒ,
ˈkɑːt|lɪdʒ, -ɪdʒɪz
AM ˈkɑːrdlɪdʒ, -ɪz
cartilaginoid
BR ˌkɑːtɪˈladʒɪnɔɪd,
ˌkɑːtlˈadʒɪnɔɪd,
ˌkɑːtɪˈladʒɪnɔɪd,
ˌkɑːtlˈadʒnɔɪd
AM ˌkɑːrdlˈædʒənɔɪd
cartilaginous
BR ˌkɑːtɪˈladʒɪnəs,
ˌkɑːtlˈadʒɪnəs,
ˌkɑːtɪˈladʒnəs,
ˌkɑːtlˈadʒnəs
AM ˌkɑːrdlˈædʒənəs
Cartland
BR ˈkɑːtlənd
AM ˈkɑːrtlənd
cartload
BR ˈkɑːtləʊd, -z
AM ˈkɑːrtˌloʊd, -z
Cartmel
BR ˈkɑːtm(ə)l,
ˈkɑːtmel
AM ˈkɑːrtˌmel
cartogram
BR ˈkɑːtəgram, -z
AM ˈkɑːrdəˌgræm, -z
cartographer
BR kɑːˈtɒgrəfə(r), -z
AM kɑːrˈtɑgrəfər, -z
cartographic
BR ˌkɑːtəˈfrafɪk
AM ˌkɑːrdəˈgræfɪk
cartographical
BR ˌkɑːtəˈfrafɪkl
AM ˌkɑːrdəˈgræfəkəl
cartographically
BR ˌkɑːtəˈfrafɪkli
AM ˌkɑːrdəˈgræfək(ə)li
cartography
BR kɑːˈtɒgrəfi
AM kɑːrˈtɑgrəfi
cartomancy
BR ˈkɑːtə(ʊ)mansi
AM ˈkɑːrdəˌmænsi
carton
BR ˈkɑːtn, -z
AM ˈkɑːrtn, -z
cartoon
BR kɑːˈtuːn, -z, -ɪŋ
AM kɑːrˈtuːn, -z, -ɪŋ
cartoonish
BR kɑːˈtuːnɪʃ
AM kɑːrˈtuːnɪʃ
cartoonist
BR kɑːˈtuːnɪst, -s
AM kɑːrˈtuːnəst, -s
cartoony
BR kɑːˈtuːni
AM kɑːrˈtuːni

cartophilist
BR kɑːˈtɒfɪlɪst,
kɑːˈtɒflɪst, -s
AM kɑːrˈtafələst, -s
cartophily
BR kɑːˈtɒfɪli, kɑːˈtɒflˌi
AM kɑːrˈtafəli
cartouche
BR kɑːˈtuːʃ, -ɪz
AM kɑːrˈtuːʃ, -ɪz
FR kaʁtuʃ
cartridge
BR ˈkɑːtr|ɪdʒ, -ɪdʒɪz
AM ˈkɑːrtrɪdʒ, -ɪz
cartulary
BR ˈkɑːtjʊləri,
ˈkɑːtʃʊləri
AM ˈkɑːrtʃəˌleri
cartwheel
BR ˈkɑːtwiːl, -z, -ɪŋ, -d
AM ˈkɑːrt,(h)wiːl, -z, -ɪŋ,
-d
cartwright
BR ˈkɑːtrʌɪt, -s
AM ˈkɑːrtˌraɪt, -s
caruncle
BR kəˈrʌŋkl, -z
AM kəˈrəŋkəl, -z
caruncular
BR kəˈrʌŋkjʊlə(r)
AM kəˈrəŋkjələr
Caruso
BR kəˈruːsəʊ,
kəˈruːzəʊ
AM kəˈrusoʊ
Caruthers
BR kəˈrʌðəz, ˈkrɪðəz
AM kəˈrəðərz
carve
BR kɑːv, -z, -ɪŋ, -d
AM kɑːrv, -z, -ɪŋ, -d
carvel
BR ˈkɑːv(ɛ)l, -z
AM ˈkɑːrvəl, -z
carven
BR ˈkɑːvn
AM ˈkɑːrvən
carver
BR ˈkɑːvə(r), -z
AM ˈkɑːrvər, -z
carvery
BR ˈkɑːvə(ə)r|i, -ɪz
AM ˈkɑːrv(ə)ri, -z
carve-up
BR ˈkɑːvʌp
AM ˈkɑːrvəp
carving
BR ˈkɑːvɪŋ, -z
AM ˈkɑːrvɪŋ, -z
carwash
BR ˈkɑːwɒʃ, -ɪz
AM ˈkɑːrˌwɒʃ, ˈkɑːrˌwɑʃ,
-əz
Cary[1]
forename
BR ˈkari
AM ˈkɛri

Cary[2]
surname
BR ˈkɛːri
AM ˈkɛri
caryatid
BR ˌkarɪˈatɪd, -z
AM ˌkɛriˈædəd,
ˈkɛriəˌtɪd, -z
Caryl
BR ˈkarɪl, ˈkarl
AM ˈkɛrəl
caryopsis
BR ˌkarɪˈɒpsɪs, -ɪz
AM ˌkɛriˈɑpsəs, -əz
carzey
BR ˈkɑːz|i, -ɪz
AM ˈkɑːrzi, -z
casa
BR ˈkɑːsə(r), ˈkasə(r),
-z
AM ˈkɑːzə, ˈkɑːsə, -z
Casablanca
BR ˌkasəˈblaŋkə(r)
AM ˌkɑːsəˈblɑŋkə,
ˌkæsəˈblæŋkə
Casals
BR kəˈsalz
AM kəˈsɑls
Casanova
BR ˌkasəˈnəʊvə(r), -z
AM ˌkæzəˈnoʊvə,
ˌkæsəˈnoʊvə, -z
casbah
BR ˈkazbɑː(r), -z
AM ˈkæs,bɑ, ˈkæz,bɑ, -z
cascabel
BR ˈkaskəb(ə)l, -z
AM ˈkæskəbəl, -z
cascade
BR kəˈskeɪd, kəˈskeɪd,
-z, -ɪŋ, -ɪd
AM kæˈskeɪd, -z, -ɪŋ, -ɪd
cascara
BR kaˈskɑːrə(r),
kəˈskɑːrə(r)
AM kæˈskɛrə
cascarilla
BR ˌkaskəˈrɪlə(r)
AM ˌkæskəˈrɪlə
case
BR keɪs, -ɪz, -ɪŋ, -t
AM keɪs, -ɪz, -ɪŋ, -t
caseation
BR ˌkeɪsɪˈeɪʃn
AM ˌkeɪsiˈeɪʃən
casebook
BR ˈkeɪsbʊk, -s
AM ˈkeɪs,bʊk, -s
casebound
BR ˈkeɪsbaʊnd
AM ˈkeɪs,baʊnd
casein
BR ˈkeɪsiːn, ˈkeɪsiːn
AM ˈkeɪsɪn, ˈkeɪsin
caseinogen
BR keɪˈsiːnədʒ(ə)n,
ˌkeɪsɪˈnədʒ(ə)n

Cary[2] (cont.)
AM keɪˈseɪmədʒən,
ˌkeɪsɪˈɪnədʒən
caseload
BR ˈkeɪsləʊd, -z
AM ˈkeɪs,loʊd, -z
casemate
BR ˈkeɪsmeɪt, -s
AM ˈkeɪs,meɪt, -s
casement
BR ˈkeɪsm(ə)nt, -s
AM ˈkeɪsmənt, -s
caseous
BR ˈkeɪsɪəs
AM ˈkeɪsiəs
casern
BR kəˈzəːn, -z
AM kəˈzərn, -z
casework
BR ˈkeɪswəːk
AM ˈkeɪs,wərk
caseworker
BR ˈkeɪs,wəːkə(r), -z
AM ˈkeɪs,wərkər, -z
Casey
BR ˈkeɪsi
AM ˈkeɪsi
cash
BR kaʃ, -ɪz, -ɪŋ, -t
AM kæʃ, -əz, -ɪŋ, -t
cashable
BR ˈkaʃəbl
AM ˈkæʃəbəl
cashbook
BR ˈkaʃbʊk, -s
AM ˈkæʃ,bʊk, -s
cashbox
BR ˈkaʃbɒks, -ɪz
AM ˈkæʃ,baks, -əz
cashew
BR ˈkaʃuː, kaˈʃuː,
kəˈʃuː, -z
AM ˈkæˌʃu, -z
cashflow
BR ˈkaʃfləʊ
AM ˈkæʃˌfloʊ
cashier
BR kəˈʃɪə(r), kaˈʃɪə(r),
-z, -ɪŋ, -d
AM kæˈʃɪ(ə)r, -z, -ɪŋ, -d
cashless
BR ˈkaʃləs
AM ˈkæʃləs
Cashman
BR ˈkaʃmən
AM ˈkæʃmən
cashmere
BR ˈkaʃmɪə(r),
ˌkaʃˈmɪə(r)
AM ˈkæʒmɪ(ə)r,
ˈkæʃmɪ(ə)r,
kæʒˈmɪ(ə)r,
kæʃˈmɪ(ə)r
cashpoint
BR ˈkaʃpɔɪnt, -s
AM ˈkæʃˌpɔɪnt, -s
casing
BR ˈkeɪsɪŋ, -z

AM 'keɪsɪŋ, -z

casino
BR kə'si:nəʊ, -z
AM kə'sinoʊ, -z

Casio®
BR 'kasɪəʊ
AM 'kæsioʊ

cask
BR kɑ:sk, kask, -s
AM kæsk, -s

casket
BR 'kɑ:skɪt, 'kaskɪt, -s
AM 'kæskət, -s

Caslon
BR 'kazlɒn
AM 'kæslən

Caspar
BR 'kaspə(r)
AM 'kæspər

Casper
BR 'kaspə(r)
AM 'kæspər

Caspian Sea
BR ˌkaspɪən 'si:
AM ˌkæspiən 'si

casque
BR kask, kɑ:sk, -s
AM kæsk, -s

Cassandra
BR kə'sandrə(r), -z
AM kə'sændrə, -z

cassareep
BR 'kasəri:p
AM 'kæsəˌrip

cassata
BR kə'sɑ:tə(r)
AM kə'sɑdə

cassation
BR kə'seɪʃn, kə'seɪʃn, -z
AM kə'seɪʃən, kæ'seɪʃən, -z

cassava
BR kə'sɑ:və(r)
AM kə'sɑvə

Cassegrain
BR ˌkasɪ'greɪn
AM ˌkæsəˌgreɪn

Cassel
BR 'kasl
AM 'kæsəl

Cassell
BR 'kasl
AM 'kæsəl

casserole
BR 'kasərəʊl, -z
AM 'kæsəˌroʊl, -z

cassette
BR kə'sɛt, -s
AM kə'sɛt, -s

cassia
BR 'kasɪə(r)
AM 'kæʃə

Cassidy
BR 'kasɪdi
AM 'kæsədi

Cassie
BR 'kasi
AM 'kæsi

Cassiopeia
BR ˌkasɪə(ʊ)'pi:ə(r)
AM ˌkæsiə'piə

cassis
BR ka'si:s, kə'si:s, 'kasi:s
AM ka'sis, kə'sis

cassiterite
BR kə'sɪtərʌɪt
AM kə'sɪdəˌraɪt

Cassius
BR 'kasɪəs
AM 'kæsiəs

Cassivelaunus
BR ˌkasɪvɪ'lɔ:nəs
AM ˌkæsəvə'lɔnəs, ˌkæsəvə'lanəs

cassock
BR 'kasək, -s, -t
AM 'kæsək, -s, -t

Casson
BR 'kasn
AM 'kæsən

cassoulet
BR ˌkasʊ'leɪ, 'kasʊleɪ, -z
AM ˌkæsə'leɪ, ˌkæsʊ'leɪ, -z

cassowary
BR 'kasəwərˌi, 'kasəwɛrˌri, -ɪz
AM 'kæsəwɛri, -z

cast
BR kɑ:st, kast, -s, -ɪŋ
AM kæst, -s, -ɪŋ

Castalia
BR ka'steɪlɪə(r)
AM ka'steɪljə, kə'steɪliə

Castalian
BR ka'steɪlɪən
AM ka'steɪljən, kə'steɪliən

castanet
BR ˌkastə'nɛt, -s
AM ˌkæstə'nɛt, -s

castaway
BR 'kɑ:stəweɪ, 'kastəweɪ, -z
AM 'kæstəˌweɪ, -z

caste
BR kɑ:st, kast, -s
AM kæst, -s

casteism
BR 'kɑ:stɪz(ə)m, 'kastɪz(ə)m
AM 'kæstˌɪzəm

castelan
BR 'kastələn, -z
AM 'kæstələn, 'kæstəˌlæn, -z

Castel Gandolfo
BR ˌkast(ɛ)l gan'dɒlfəʊ

AM ˌkæstəl gan'dɔlfoʊ, ˌkæstəl gan'dalfoʊ

castellan
BR 'kastələn, -z
AM 'kæstələn, 'kæstəˌlæn, -z

castellated
BR 'kastɪleɪtɪd, 'kastˌleɪtɪd
AM 'kæs(t)əˌleɪdɪd

castellation
BR ˌkastɪ'leɪʃn, ˌkastl'eɪʃn, -z
AM ˌkæs(t)ə'leɪʃən, -z

caster
BR 'kɑ:stə(r), 'kastə(r), -z
AM 'kæstər, -z

Casterbridge
BR 'kɑ:stəbrɪdʒ, 'kastəbrɪdʒ
AM 'kæstərˌbrɪdʒ

castigate
BR 'kastɪgeɪt, -s, -ɪŋ, -ɪd
AM 'kæstəˌgeɪ|t, -ts, -dɪŋ, -dɪd

castigation
BR ˌkastɪ'geɪʃn
AM ˌkæstə'geɪʃən

castigator
BR 'kastɪgeɪtə(r), -z
AM 'kæstəˌgeɪdər, -z

castigatory
BR 'kastɪgeɪt(ə)ri, 'kastɪgət(ə)ri
AM 'kæstəgəˌtɔri

Castile
BR ka'sti:l, kə'sti:l
AM kæ'stil

Castilian
BR ka'stɪlɪən, kə'stɪliən, -z
AM kæ'stɪljən, kə'stɪljən, kæ'stɪliən, kə'stɪliən, -z

Castillo
BR ka'sti:(j)əʊ
AM kæ'sti(j)oʊ

castle
BR 'kɑ:s|l, 'kas|l, -lz, -ɪ|ŋ \-lɪŋ, -ld
AM 'kæsəl, -z, -ɪŋ, -d

Castlebar
BR ˌkɑ:sl'bɑ:(r), ˌkasl'bɑ:(r)
AM ˌkæsəl'bɑr

Castleford
BR 'kaslfəd, 'kɑ:slfəd
AM 'kæsəlfərd

Castlemaine
BR 'kɑ:slmeɪn, 'kaslmeɪn
AM 'kæsəlˌmeɪn

Castlereagh
BR 'kɑ:slreɪ, 'kaslreɪ
AM 'kæsəlreɪ

Castleton
BR 'kaslt(ə)n, 'kɑ:slt(ə)n
AM 'kæsəltən

Castlewellan
BR ˌkɑ:sl'wɛlən, ˌkasl'wɛlən
AM ˌkæsəl'wɛlən

castor
BR 'kɑ:stə(r), 'kastə(r), -z
AM 'kæstər, -z

castrate
BR ka'streɪt, kə'streɪt, -s, -ɪŋ, -ɪd
AM 'kæˌstreɪ|t, -ts, -dɪŋ, -dɪd

castrati
BR ka'strɑ:ti:, kə'strɑ:ti
AM kæ'strɑdi

castration
BR ka'streɪʃn, kə'streɪʃn, -z
AM kæ'streɪʃən, -z

castrative
BR ka'streɪtɪv, kə'streɪtɪv
AM kæ'streɪdɪv

castrato
BR ka'strɑ:təʊ, kə'strɑ:təʊ
AM kæ'strɑdoʊ

castrator
BR ka'streɪtə(r), kə'streɪtə(r), -z
AM 'kæˌstreɪdər, -z

castratory
BR ka'streɪt(ə)ri, kə'streɪt(ə)ri
AM 'kæstrəˌtɔri

Castries
BR ka'stri:z, ka'stri:s
AM ˌkæsˌtriz

Castro
BR 'kastrəʊ
AM 'kæstroʊ

Castroism
BR 'kastrəʊɪz(ə)m
AM 'kæstrəˌwɪzəm

Castrol®
BR 'kastrɒl, 'kastr(ə)l
AM 'kæsˌtrɒl, 'kæsˌtrɑl

casual
BR 'kaʒʊ(ə)l, 'kaʒjʊl, 'kaʒ(ʊ)l, 'kaʒjʊ(ə)l, kazj(ʊ)l
AM 'kæʒuəl

casually
BR 'kaʒʊəli, 'kaʒjʊli, 'kaʒli, 'kazjʊli, 'kazjli
AM 'kæʒ(əw)əli

casualness
BR 'kaʒʊəlnəs, 'kaʒjʊlnəs, 'kaʒlnəs, 'kazjʊlnəs, 'kazjlnəs
AM 'kæʒ(əw)əlnəs

casualty
BR ˈkaʒ(j)ʊlt|i, -ɪz
AM ˈkæʒ(əw)əlti, -z

casuarina
BR ˌkazjʊəˈriːnə(r),
ˌkaʒjʊəˈriːnə(r),
ˌkaʒʊˈriːnə(r),
ˌkazjʊəˈrʌɪnə(r),
ˌkaʒjʊəˈrʌɪnə(r),
ˌkaʒʊˈrʌɪnə(r), -z
AM ˌkæʒʊəˈrinə,
ˌkæʒʊəˈraɪnə, -z

casuist
BR ˈkazjʊɪst, ˈkaʒʊɪst,
-s
AM ˈkæʒəwəst, -s

casuistic
BR ˌkazjʊˈɪstɪk,
ˌkaʒʊˈɪstɪk
AM ˌkæʒəˈwɪstɪk

casuistical
BR ˌkazjʊˈɪstɪkl,
ˌkaʒʊˈɪstɪkl
AM ˌkæʒəˈwɪstɪkəl

casuistically
BR ˌkazjʊˈɪstɪkli,
ˌkaʒʊˈɪstɪkli
AM ˌkæʒəˈwɪstɪk(ə)li

casuistry
BR ˈkazjʊɪstri,
ˈkaʒʊɪstri
AM ˈkæʒəwəstri

casus belli
BR ˌkɑːsəs ˈbɛliː,
ˌkeɪsəs ˈbɛlʌɪ
AM ˌkɑsəs ˈbɛli,
ˌkeɪsəs +

Casy
BR ˈkeɪsi
AM ˈkeɪsi

cat
BR kat, -s
AM kæt, -s

catabolic
BR ˌkatəˈbɒlɪk
AM ˌkædəˈbɒlɪk,
ˌkædəˈbɑlɪk

catabolically
BR ˌkatəˈbɒlɪkli
AM ˌkædəˈbɒlək(ə)li,
ˌkædəˈbɑlək(ə)li

catabolism
BR kəˈtabəlɪz(ə)m
AM kəˈtæbəˌlɪzəm

catabolize
BR kəˈtabəlʌɪz, -ɪz, -ɪŋ,
-d
AM kəˈtæbəˌlaɪz, -ɪz,
-ɪŋ, -d

catechesis
BR ˌkatəˈkiːsɪs
AM ˌkædəˈkisɪs

catachresis
BR ˌkatəˈkriːsɪs
AM ˌkædəˈkrisɪs

catachrestic
BR ˌkatəˈkrɛstɪk
AM ˌkædəˈkrɛstɪk

catachrestical
BR ˌkatəˈkrɛstɪkl
AM ˌkædəˈkrɛstəkəl

cataclasis
BR ˌkatəˈkleɪsɪs, -ɪz
AM ˌkædəˈkleɪsɪs, -ɪz

cataclasm
BR ˈkatəˌklaz(ə)m, -z
AM ˈkædəˌklæzəm, -z

cataclastic
BR ˌkatəˈklastɪk
AM ˌkædəˈklæstɪk

cataclysm
BR ˈkatəklɪz(ə)m, -z
AM ˈkædəˌklɪzəm, -z

cataclysmal
BR ˌkatəˈklɪzml
AM ˌkædəˈklɪzməl

cataclysmic
BR ˌkatəˈklɪzmɪk
AM ˌkædəˈklɪzmɪk

cataclysmically
BR ˌkatəˈklɪzmɪkli
AM ˌkædəˈklɪzmɪk(ə)li

catacomb
BR ˈkatəkuːm, -z
AM ˈkædəˌkoʊm, -z

catadioptric
BR ˌkatədʌɪˈɒptrɪk
AM ˌkædəˌdaɪˈɑptrɪk

catadromous
BR kəˈtadrəməs
AM kəˈtædrəməs

catafalque
BR ˈkatəfalk, -s
AM ˈkædəˌfælk, -s

Catalan
BR ˈkatəlan, ˈkatⱡan, -z
AM ˈkædⱡˌæn,
ˈkædələn, -z

catalase
BR ˈkatəleɪz, ˈkatⱡeɪz,
-ɪz
AM ˈkædⱡˌeɪs,
ˈkædⱡˌeɪz, -ɪz

catalectic
BR ˌkatəˈlɛktɪk,
ˈkatⱡɛktɪk
AM ˌkædəˈlɛktɪk

catalepsy
BR ˈkatəlɛpsi,
ˈkatⱡɛpsi
AM ˈkædⱡˌɛpsi

cataleptic
BR ˌkatəˈlɛptɪk,
ˈkatⱡɛptɪk
AM ˈkædⱡˌɛptɪk

Catalina
BR ˌkatəˈliːnə(r)
AM ˌkædəˈlinə

catalog
BR ˈkatəlɒg, ˈkatⱡɒg, -z,
-ɪŋ, -d
AM ˈkædⱡˌɔg, ˈkædⱡˌɑg,
-z, -ɪŋ, -d

catalogue
BR ˈkatəlɒg, ˈkatⱡɒg, -z,
-ɪŋ, -d

cataloguer
BR ˈkatəlɒgə(r),
ˈkatⱡɒgə(r), -z
AM ˈkædⱡˌɔgər,
ˈkædⱡˌɑgər, -z

catalogue raisonné
BR ˌkatəlɒg ˌreɪzɒˈneɪ,
ˈkatⱡɒg +
AM ˌkædⱡˌɔg rɛzəˈneɪ,
ˌkædⱡˌɑg rɛzəˈneɪ

catalogues raisonnés
BR ˌkatəlɒg
ˌreɪzɒˈneɪz, ˈkatⱡɒg +
AM ˌkædⱡˌɔg rɛzəˈneɪz,
ˌkædⱡˌɑg rɛzəˈneɪz

Catalonia
BR ˌkatəˈləʊnɪə(r),
ˈkatⱡˈəʊnɪə(r)
AM ˌkædⱡˈoʊniə

Catalonian
BR ˌkatəˈləʊnɪən,
ˈkatⱡˈəʊnɪən, -z
AM ˌkædⱡˈoʊnɪən, -z

catalpa
BR kəˈtalpə(r)
AM kəˈtælpə

catalyse
BR ˈkatəlʌɪz, ˈkatⱡʌɪz,
-ɪz, -ɪŋ, -d
AM ˈkædⱡˌaɪz, -ɪz, -ɪŋ, -d

catalyser
BR ˈkatəlʌɪzə(r),
ˈkatⱡʌɪzə(r)
AM ˈkædⱡˌaɪzər

catalysis
BR kəˈtalɪsɪs
AM kəˈtæləsəs

catalyst
BR ˈkatəlɪst, ˈkatⱡɪst, -s
AM ˈkædⱡˌəst, -s

catalytic
BR ˌkatəˈlɪtɪk
AM ˌkædəˈlɪdɪk

catalyze
BR ˈkatəlʌɪz, ˈkatⱡʌɪz,
-ɪz, -ɪŋ, -d
AM ˈkædⱡˌaɪz, -ɪz, -ɪŋ, -d

catamaran
BR ˈkatəməˌran,
ˌkatəməˈran, -z
AM ˈkædəməˈræn, -z

catamite
BR ˈkatəmʌɪt, -s
AM ˈkædəˌmaɪt, -s

catamount
BR ˈkatəmaʊnt, -s
AM ˈkædəˌmaʊnt, -s

catamountain
BR ˌkatəˌmaʊntn, -z
AM ˌkædəˌmaʊntn, -z

catananche
BR ˌkatəˈnaŋk|i, -ɪz
AM ˌkædəˈnæŋki, -z

Catania
BR kəˈtanɪə(r)
AM kəˈtaniə, kəˈteɪniə

cataphora
BR kəˈtaf(ə)rə(r)
AM kəˈtæf(ə)rə

cataphoresis
BR ˌkatəfəˈriːsɪs
AM ˌkædəfəˈrisɪs

cataphoretic
BR ˌkatəfəˈrɛtɪk
AM ˌkædəfəˈrɛdɪk

cataphoretically
BR ˌkatəfəˈrɛtɪkli
AM ˌkædəfəˈrɛdək(ə)li

cataplasm
BR ˈkatəˌplaz(ə)m, -z
AM ˈkædəˌplæzəm, -z

cataplectic
BR ˌkatəˈplɛktɪk
AM ˌkædəˈplɛktɪk

cataplexy
BR ˈkatəˌplɛks|i, -ɪz
AM ˈkædəˌplɛksi, -z

catapult
BR ˈkatəpʌlt,
ˈkatəpʊlt, -s, -ɪŋ, -ɪd
AM ˈkædəpəlt,
ˈkædəˌpʊlt, -s, -ɪŋ, -ɪd

cataract
BR ˈkatərakt, -s
AM ˈkædəˌræk|(t), -(t)s

catarrh
BR kəˈtɑː(r), -z
AM kəˈtɑr, -z

catarrhal
BR kəˈtɑːrəl, kəˈtɑːrⱡ
AM kəˈtɑrəl

catarrhine
BR ˈkatərʌɪn
AM ˈkædəˌraɪn

catastrophe
BR kəˈtastrəf|i, -ɪz
AM kəˈtæstrəfi, -z

catastrophic
BR ˌkatəˈstrɒfɪk
AM ˌkædəˈstrɑfɪk

catastrophically
BR ˌkatəˈstrɒfɪkli
AM ˌkædəˈstrɑfək(ə)li

catastrophism
BR kəˈtastrəˌfɪz(ə)m
AM kəˈtæstrəˌfɪzəm

catastrophist
BR kəˈtastrəfɪst, -s
AM kəˈtæstrəfəst, -s

catatonia
BR ˌkatəˈtəʊnɪə(r)
AM ˌkædəˈtoʊniə

catatonic
BR ˌkatəˈtɒnɪk
AM ˌkædəˈtɑnɪk

catawba
BR kəˈtɔːbə(r), -z
AM kəˈtɔbə, kəˈtɑbə, -z

catbird
BR ˈkatbəːd, -z

catboat
AM 'kæt͵bɔrd, -z

catboat
BR 'katbəʊt, -s
AM 'kæt͵bʊt, -s

catcall
BR 'katkɔːl, -z, -ɪŋ, -d
AM 'kæt͵kɔl, 'kæt͵kɑl, -z, -ɪŋ, -d

catch
BR katʃ, -ɪz, -ɪŋ
AM kɛtʃ, -əz, -ɪŋ

catchable
BR 'katʃəbl
AM 'kɛtʃəbəl

catchall
BR 'katʃɔːl, -z
AM 'kɛtʃ͵ɔl, 'kɛtʃ͵ɑl, -z

catcher
BR 'katʃə(r), -z
AM 'kɛtʃər, -z

catchfly
BR 'katʃflʌɪ, -z
AM 'kɛtʃ͵flaɪ, -z

catchily
BR 'katʃɪli
AM 'kɛtʃəli

catchiness
BR 'katʃɪnɪs
AM 'kɛtʃinɪs

catchline
BR 'katʃlʌɪn, -z
AM 'kɛtʃ͵laɪn, -z

catchment
BR 'katʃm(ə)nt, -s
AM 'kɛtʃmənt, -s

catchpenny
BR 'katʃ͵pɛn|i, -ɪz
AM 'kɛtʃ͵pɛni, -z

catchphrase
BR 'katʃfreɪz, -ɪz
AM 'kɛtʃ͵freɪz, -ɪz

catchpole
BR 'katʃpəʊl, -z
AM 'kɛtʃ͵pʊl, -z

catchup
BR 'kɛtʃʌp
AM 'kɛtʃəp

catchweight
BR 'katʃweɪt, -s
AM 'kætʃ͵weɪt, -s

catchword
BR 'katʃwəːd, -z
AM 'kætʃ͵wərd, -z

catchy
BR 'katʃ|i, -ɪə(r), -ɪɪst
AM 'kɛtʃi, -ər, -ɪst

cate
BR keɪt, -s
AM keɪt, -s

catechetic
BR ͵katɪ'kɛtɪk, -s
AM ͵kædə'kɛdɪk, -s

catechetical
BR ͵katɪ'kɛtɪkl
AM ͵kædə'kɛdəkəl

catechetically
BR ͵katɪ'kɛtɪkli

AM ͵kædə'kɛdək(ə)li

catechise
BR 'katɪkʌɪz, -ɪz, -ɪŋ, -d
AM 'kædə͵kaɪz, -ɪz, -ɪŋ, -d

catechiser
BR 'katɪkʌɪzə(r), -z
AM 'kædə͵kaɪzər, -z

catechism
BR 'katɪkɪz(ə)m, -z
AM 'kædə͵kɪzəm, -z

catechismal
BR ͵katɪ'kɪzml
AM ͵kædə'kɪzməl

catechist
BR 'katɪkɪst, -s
AM 'kædəkəst, -s

catechize
BR 'katɪkʌɪz, -ɪz, -ɪŋ, -d
AM 'kædə͵kaɪz, -ɪz, -ɪŋ, -d

catechizer
BR 'katɪkʌɪzə(r), -z
AM 'kædə͵kaɪzər, -z

catechol
BR 'katɪtʃɒl, 'katɪkɒl
AM 'kædə͵kɒl, 'kædə͵kal, 'kædə͵kʊl

catecholamine
BR ͵katɪ'kəʊləmiːn
AM ͵kædə'kəʊlə͵min

catechu
BR 'katɪ(t)ʃuː
AM 'kædə͵tʃu, 'kædə͵kju

catechumen
BR ͵katɪ'kjuːmɪn, ͵katɪ'kjuːmɛn, -z
AM ͵kædə'kjumən, -z

categorial
BR ͵katɪ'ɡɔːrɪəl
AM ͵kædə'ɡɔrɪəl

categoric
BR ͵katɪ'ɡɒrɪk
AM ͵kædə'ɡɒrɪk

categorical
BR ͵katɪ'ɡɒrɪkl
AM ͵kædə'ɡɒrəkəl

categorically
BR ͵katɪ'ɡɒrɪkli
AM ͵kædə'ɡɒrək(ə)li

categorisation
BR ͵katɪɡ(ə)rʌɪ'zeɪʃn
AM ͵kædəɡ(ə)rə'zeɪʃən, ͵kædəɡə͵raɪ'zeɪʃən

categorise
BR 'katɪɡərʌɪz, -ɪz, -ɪŋ, -d
AM 'kædəɡə͵raɪz, 'kædəɡɔ͵raɪz, -ɪz, -ɪŋ, -d

categorization
BR ͵katɪɡ(ə)rʌɪ'zeɪʃn
AM ͵kædəɡ(ə)rə'zeɪʃən, ͵kædəɡə͵raɪ'zeɪʃən

categorize
BR 'katɪɡərʌɪz, -ɪz, -ɪŋ, -d

AM ͵kædə'kɛdək(ə)li

category
BR 'katɪɡ(ə)r|i, -ɪz
AM 'kædə͵ɡɔri, -z

catena
BR kə'tiːnə(r)
AM kə'tinə

catenae
BR kə'tiːni:
AM kə'tini, kə'ti͵naɪ

catenary
BR kə'tiːn(ə)r|i, -ɪz
AM 'kædə͵nɛri, 'kædn͵ɛri, -z

catenate
BR 'katɪneɪt, -s, -ɪŋ, -ɪd
AM 'kædə͵neɪt, 'kædn͵eɪ|t, -ts, -dɪŋ, -dɪd

catenation
BR ͵katɪ'neɪʃn
AM ͵kædə'neɪʃən, ͵kædn'eɪʃən

cater
BR 'keɪt|ə(r), -əz, -(ə)rɪŋ, -əd
AM 'keɪdər, -z, -ɪŋ, -d

cateran
BR 'kat(ə)rən, 'kat(ə)rŋ, -z
AM 'kædərən, -z

cater-cornered
BR ͵keɪtə'kɔːnəd, ͵katə'kɔːnəd, 'keɪtə͵kɔːnəd, 'katə͵kɔːnəd
AM 'kædi͵kɔrnərd, 'kædə͵kɔrnər(d), 'kɪdi͵kɔrnər(d)

caterer
BR 'keɪt(ə)rə(r), -z
AM 'keɪdərər, -z

Caterham
BR 'keɪt(ə)rəm, 'keɪt(ə)rm̩
AM 'keɪdərəm

Caterina
BR ͵katə'riːnə(r)
AM ͵kædə'rinə

caterpillar
BR 'katəpɪlə(r), -z
AM 'kædər͵pɪlər, -z

caterwaul
BR 'katəwɔːl, -z, -ɪŋ, -d
AM 'kædər͵wɔl, 'kædər͵wal, -z, -ɪŋ, -d

Catesby
BR 'keɪtsbi
AM 'keɪtsbi

catfish
BR 'katfɪʃ, -ɪz
AM 'kæt͵fɪʃ, -ɪz

catfood
BR 'katfuːd
AM 'kæt͵fud

catheterise
BR ͵kædə'kɛdək(ə)li
AM 'kædəɡə͵raɪz

Catford
BR 'katfəd
AM 'kætfərd

catgut
BR 'katɡʌt
AM 'kæt͵ɡət

Cath
BR kaθ
AM kæθ

Cathar
BR 'kaθɑː(r), -z
AM 'kæθɑr, -z

Catharine
BR 'kaθ(ə)rɪn, 'kaθ(ə)rn̩
AM 'kæθ(ə)rən

Catharism
BR 'kaθərɪz(ə)m, 'kaθɑːrɪz(ə)m
AM 'kæθərɪzm

Catharist
BR 'kaθərɪst, 'kaθɑːrɪst, -s
AM 'kæθərəst, -s

catharsis
BR kə'θɑːsɪs
AM kə'θɑrsəs

cathartic
BR kə'θɑːtɪk
AM kə'θɑrdɪk

cathartically
BR kə'θɑːtɪkli
AM kə'θɑrdək(ə)li

Cathay
BR (͵)ka'θeɪ, kə'θeɪ
AM kæ'θeɪ

Cathays
BR kə'teɪz
AM kə'teɪz

Cathcart
BR 'kaθkɑːt, ͵kaθ'kɑːt
AM 'kæθ͵kɑrt

cathead
BR 'kathɛd, -z
AM 'kæt͵(h)ɛd, -z

cathectic
BR kə'θɛktɪk
AM kə'θɛktɪk

cathedra
BR kə'θiːdrə(r)
AM kə'θidrə

cathedral
BR kə'θiːdr(ə)l, -z
AM kə'θidrəl, -z

Cather
BR 'kaθə(r)
AM 'kæθər

Catherine
BR 'kaθ(ə)rɪn, 'kaθ(ə)rn̩
AM 'kæθ(ə)rɪn

catheter
BR 'kaθɪtə(r), -z
AM 'kæθədər, -z

catheterise
BR 'kaθɪtərʌɪz, -ɪz, -ɪŋ, -d

AM ˈkæθədəˌraɪz, -ɪz, -ɪŋ, -d

catheterization
BR ˌkaθɪtərʌɪˈzeɪʃn
AM ˌkæθədərəˈzeɪʃən, ˌkæθədəˌraɪˈzeɪʃən

catheterize
BR ˈkaθɪtərʌɪz, -ɪz, -ɪŋ, -d
AM ˈkæθədəˌraɪz, -ɪz, -ɪŋ, -d

cathetometer
BR ˌkaθɪˈtɒmɪtə(r), -z
AM ˌkæθəˈtamədər, -z

cathexis
BR kəˈθɛksɪs
AM kəˈθɛksəs

Cathie
BR ˈkaθi
AM ˈkæθi

Cathleen
BR ˈkaθliːn
AM ˌkæθˈlin

cathodal
BR kaˈθəʊdl̩, kəˈθəʊdl̩
AM kəˈθoʊdəl

cathode
BR ˈkaθəʊd, -z
AM ˈkæˌθoʊd, -z

cathodic
BR kaˈθɒdɪk, kəˈθɒdɪk
AM kəˈθɑdɪk

Catholic
BR ˈkaθ(ə)lɪk, -s
AM ˈkæθ(ə)lɪk, -s

catholic
BR ˈkaθ(ə)lɪk, -s
AM ˈkæθ(ə)lɪk, -s

catholically
BR ˈkaθ(ə)lɪkli
AM ˈkæθ(ə)lək(ə)li

Catholicise
BR kəˈθɒlɪsʌɪz, -ɪz, -ɪŋ, -d
AM kəˈθɑləˌsaɪz, -ɪz, -ɪŋ, -d

Catholicism
BR kəˈθɒlɪsɪz(ə)m
AM kəˈθɑləˌsɪzəm

Catholicity
BR ˌkaθəˈlɪsɪti
AM ˌkæθəˈlɪsɪdi

Catholicize
BR kəˈθɒlɪsʌɪz, -ɪz, -ɪŋ, -d
AM kəˈθɑləˌsaɪz, -ɪz, -ɪŋ, -d

catholicly
BR ˈkaθ(ə)lɪkli
AM ˈkæθ(ə)lək(ə)li

catholicon
BR kəˈθɒlɪkɒn, -z
AM kəˈθɑləkɑn, -z

cathouse
BR ˈkathaʊ|s, -zɪz
AM ˈkæt,(h)aʊ|s, -zɪz

Cathryn
BR ˈkaθr(ɪ)n
AM ˈkæθrɪn

Cathy
BR ˈkaθi
AM ˈkæθi

Catiline
BR ˈkatɪlʌɪn, ˈkatlʌɪn
AM ˈkædəˌlaɪn

cation
BR ˈkat,ʌɪən, -z
AM ˈkæd,aɪən, ˈkæd,aɪ,ɑn, -z

cationic
BR ˌkatʌɪˈɒnɪk
AM ˌkædaɪˈɑnɪk

catkin
BR ˈkatkɪn, -z
AM ˈkætkən, -z

catlick
BR ˈkatlɪk, -s
AM ˈkætlɪk, -s

catlike
BR ˈkatlʌɪk
AM ˈkæt,laɪk

Catling
BR ˈkatlɪŋ
AM ˈkætlɪŋ

catmint
BR ˈkatmɪnt
AM ˈkæt,mɪnt

catnap
BR ˈkatnap, -s, -ɪŋ, -t
AM ˈkæt,næp, -s, -ɪŋ, -t

catnip
BR ˈkatnɪp
AM ˈkæt,nɪp

Cato
BR ˈkeɪtəʊ
AM ˈkeɪdoʊ

cat-o'-nine-tails
BR ˌkatəˈnʌɪnteɪlz
AM ˌkædəˈnaɪn,teɪlz

catoptric
BR kaˈtɒptrɪk, kəˈtɒptrɪk, -s
AM kəˈtaptrɪk, -s

Catrin
BR ˈkatrɪn
AM ˈkætrɪn

Catrina
BR kəˈtriːnə(r)
AM kəˈtrinə

Catrine
BR ˈkatriːn
AM ˈkætrən, kəˈtrin(ə)

Catriona
BR kaˈtriː(ə)nə(r), kəˈtriː(ə)nə(r), ˌkatrɪˈəʊnə(r)
AM kæˈtrioʊnə, ˌkætriˈounə

CAT scan
BR ˈkat skan, -z
AM ˈkæt ˌskæn, -z

Catskill
BR ˈkatskɪl

AM ˈkætˌskɪl

catsuit
BR ˈkatsuːt, -s
AM ˈkætˌsut, -s

catsup
BR ˈkatsəp, ˈkatsʌp, ˈkatʃəp, ˈkatʃʌp
AM ˈkɛtʃəp, ˈkætsəp, ˈkætʃəp

cattail
BR ˈkatteɪl
AM ˈkæ(t),teɪl

Catterick
BR ˈkat(ə)rɪk
AM ˈkædərɪk

cattery
BR ˈkat(ə)r|i, -ɪz
AM ˈkædəri, -z

cattily
BR ˈkatɪli
AM ˈkædəli

cattiness
BR ˈkatɪnɪs
AM ˈkædinɪs

cattish
BR ˈkatɪʃ
AM ˈkædɪʃ

cattishly
BR ˈkatɪʃli
AM ˈkædɪʃli

cattishness
BR ˈkatɪʃnɪs
AM ˈkædɪʃnɪs

cattle
BR ˈkatl̩
AM ˈkædəl

cattleman
BR ˈkatlmən
AM ˈkædlmən

cattlemen
BR ˈkatlmən
AM ˈkædlmən

cattlepen
BR ˈkatlpɛn, -z
AM ˈkædl,pɛn, -z

cattleya
BR ˈkatlɪə(r)
AM ˈkætliə, kætˈleɪə, kætˈliə

Catto
BR ˈkatəʊ
AM ˈkædoʊ

Catton
BR ˈkatn
AM ˈkætn

catty
BR ˈkat|i, -ɪə(r), -ɪɪst
AM ˈkædi, -ər, -ɪɪst

Catullus
BR kəˈtʌləs
AM kəˈtələs

catwalk
BR ˈkatwɔːk, -s
AM ˈkæt,wɔk, ˈkæt,wak, -s

Caucasian
BR kɔːˈkeɪzɪən, kɔːˈkeɪʒn, -z
AM kɔˈkeɪʒən, kɑˈkeɪʒən, -z

Caucasoid
BR ˈkɔːkəsɔɪd, -z
AM ˈkɔkə,sɔɪd, ˈkɑkə,sɔɪd, -z

Caucasus
BR ˈkɔːkəsəs
AM ˈkɔkəsəs, ˈkakəsəs

caucus
BR ˈkɔːkəs, -ɪz
AM ˈkɔkəs, ˈkakəs, -əz

caudal
BR ˈkɔːdl̩
AM ˈkɔdəl, ˈkadəl

caudally
BR ˈkɔːdl̩i
AM ˈkɔdəli, ˈkadəli

caudate
BR ˈkɔːdeɪt
AM ˈkɔ,deɪt, ˈka,deɪt

caudillo
BR kɔːˈdiːljəʊ, kɔːˈdiːləʊ, kaʊˈdiːjəʊ, -z
AM kaʊˈdijoʊ, -z

Caughey
BR ˈkahi
AM ˈkahi

caught
BR kɔːt
AM kɔt, kat

caul
BR kɔːl, -z
AM kɔl, kal, -z

cauldron
BR ˈkɔːldr(ə)n, ˈkɒldr(ə)n, -z
AM ˈkɔldrən, ˈkaldrən, -z

Caulfield
BR ˈkɔː(l)fiːld
AM ˈkɔl,fild, ˈkal,fild

cauliflower
BR ˈkɒlɪflaʊə(r), -z
AM ˈkɔlə,flaʊər, ˈkalə,flaʊər, ˈkoli,flaʊər, ˈkali,flaʊər, -z

caulk
BR ˈkɔːk, -s, -ɪŋ, -t
AM kɔk, kak, -s, -ɪŋ, -t

caulker
BR ˈkɔːkə(r), -z
AM ˈkɔkər, ˈkakər, -z

Caunce
BR kɔːns
AM kɔns, kans

causable
BR ˈkɔːzəbl̩
AM ˈkɔzəbəl, ˈkazəbəl

causal
BR ˈkɔːzl̩
AM ˈkɔzəl, ˈkazəl

causality
BR kɔːˈzalɪti
AM kɔːˈzælədi,
kaˈzælədi

causally
BR ˈkɔːzl̩i, ˈkɔːzəli
AM ˈkɔzəli, ˈkazəli

causation
BR kɔːˈzeɪʃn
AM kɔːˈzeɪʃən,
kaˈzeɪʃən

causative
BR ˈkɔːzətɪv, -z
AM ˈkɔzədɪv, ˈkazədɪv,
-z

causatively
BR ˈkɔːzətɪvli
AM ˈkɔzədɪvli,
ˈkazədɪvli

cause
BR kɔːz, -ɪz, -ɪŋ, -d
AM kɔz, kaz, -əz, -ɪŋ, -d

'cause
because
BR kəz
AM kəz

cause célèbre
BR ˌkɔːz sɪˈlɛːbr(ər),
+ sɛˈlɛːbr(ər)
AM ˌkouz səˈlɛbr,
ˌkɔz +

causeless
BR ˈkɔːzləs
AM ˈkɔzləs, ˈkazləs

causelessly
BR ˈkɔːzləsli
AM ˈkɔzləsli, ˈkazləsli

causer
BR ˈkɔːzə(r), -z
AM ˈkɔzər, ˈkazər, -z

causerie
BR ˈkəuz(ə)rl̩i, -ɪz
AM ˌkouz(ə)ˈri,
ˈkouzəri, -z

causes célèbres
BR ˌkɔːz sɪˈlɛːbr(ər),
ˌkɔːz sɛˈlɛːbr(ər)
AM ˌkouz səˈlɛbr, ˌkɔz
səˈlɛbr

causeway
BR ˈkɔːzweɪ, -z
AM ˈkɔzˌweɪ, ˈkazˌweɪ,
-z

causey
BR ˈkɔːzl̩i, ˈkɔːsl̩i, -ɪz
AM ˈkɔzi, ˈkazi, -z

caustic
BR ˈkɔːstɪk, ˈkɒstɪk
AM ˈkɔstɪk, ˈkastɪk

caustically
BR ˈkɔːstɪkli, ˈkɒstɪkli
AM ˈkɔstək(ə)li,
ˈkastək(ə)li

causticise
BR ˈkɔːstɪsʌɪz,
ˈkɒstɪsʌɪz, -ɪz, -ɪŋ, -d
AM ˈkɔstəˌsaɪz,
ˈkastəˌsaɪz, -ɪz, -ɪŋ, -d

causticity
BR kɔːˈstɪsɪti,
kɒˈstɪsɪti
AM kɔːˈstɪsɪdi,
kaˈstɪsɪdi

causticize
BR ˈkɔːstɪsʌɪz,
ˈkɒstɪsʌɪz, -ɪz, -ɪŋ, -d
AM ˈkɔstəˌsaɪz,
ˈkastəˌsaɪz, -ɪz, -ɪŋ, -d

Caute
BR kəʊt
AM kɔt, kat

cauterisation
BR ˌkɔːt(ə)rʌɪˈzeɪʃn
AM ˌkɔdərəˈzeɪʃən,
ˌkɔdəˌraɪˈzeɪʃən,
ˌkadərəˈzeɪʃən,
ˌkadəˌraɪˈzeɪʃən

cauterise
BR ˈkɔːtərʌɪz, -ɪz, -ɪŋ, -d
AM ˈkɔdəˌraɪz,
ˈkadəˌraɪz, -ɪz, -ɪŋ, -d

cauterization
BR ˌkɔːt(ə)rʌɪˈzeɪʃn
AM ˌkɔdərəˈzeɪʃən,
ˌkɔdəˌraɪˈzeɪʃən,
ˌkadərəˈzeɪʃən,
ˌkadəˌraɪˈzeɪʃən

cauterize
BR ˈkɔːtərʌɪz, -ɪz, -ɪŋ, -d
AM ˈkɔdəˌraɪz,
ˈkadəˌraɪz, -ɪz, -ɪŋ, -d

cautery
BR ˈkɔːt(ə)r̩i, -ɪz
AM ˈkɔdəri, ˈkadəri, -z

Cauthen
BR ˈkɔːθn
AM ˈkɔθən, ˈkaθən

caution
BR ˈkɔːʃ|(ə)n, -(ə)nz,
-ɪŋ \ -ənɪŋ, -(ə)nd
AM ˈkɔʃ|ən, ˈkaʃ|ən,
-ənz, -(ə)nɪŋ, -ənd

cautionary
BR ˈkɔːʃn̩(ə)ri,
ˈkɔːʃən(ə)ri
AM ˈkɔʃəˌnɛri,
ˈkaʃəˌnɛri

cautious
BR ˈkɔːʃəs
AM ˈkɔʃəs, ˈkaʃəs

cautiously
BR ˈkɔːʃəsli
AM ˈkɔʃəsli, ˈkaʃəsli

cautiousness
BR ˈkɔːʃəsnəs
AM ˈkɔʃəsnəs,
ˈkaʃəsnəs

Cavafy
BR kaˈvɑːfi
AM kaˈvafi

cavalcade
BR ˌkavlˈkeɪd,
ˈkavlkeɪd, -z
AM ˌkævəlˈkeɪd, -z

cavalier
BR ˌkavəˈlɪə(r), -z

cavalierly
BR ˌkavəˈlɪəli
AM ˌkævəˈlɪrli

cavalry
BR ˈkavlr̩i, -ɪz
AM ˈkævəlri, -z

cavalryman
BR ˈkavlrɪmən
AM ˈkævəlrimən

cavalrymen
BR ˈkavlrɪmən
AM ˈkævəlrimən

Cavan
BR ˈkavn
AM ˈkævən

Cavanagh
BR ˈkavənə(r),
ˈkavnə(r), kəˈvanə(r)
AM ˈkævəˌnɔ, ˈkævəˌnɑ

cavatina
BR ˌkavəˈtiːnə(r), -z
AM ˌkævəˈtinə, -z

Cave
BR keɪv
AM keɪv

cave¹
beware!
BR ˈkeɪvi
AM ˈkeɪvi

cave²
noun, verb
BR keɪv, -z, -ɪŋ, -d
AM keɪv, -z, -ɪŋ, -d

caveat
BR ˈkavɪat, -s
AM ˈkæviˌat, -s

caveat emptor
BR ˌkavɪat
ˈɛm(p)tɔː(r)
AM ˈkæviˌat
ˈɛm(p)ˌtɔ(ə)r

cavelike
BR ˈkeɪvlʌɪk
AM ˈkeɪvˌlaɪk

Cavell
BR ˈkavl, kəˈvɛl
AM ˈkævəl, kəˈvɛl

caveman
BR ˈkeɪvman
AM ˈkeɪvˌmæn

cavemen
BR ˈkeɪvmɛn
AM ˈkeɪvmən,
ˈkeɪvˌmɛn

Cavendish
BR ˈkavndɪʃ
AM ˈkævndɪʃ

caver
BR ˈkeɪvə(r), -z
AM ˈkeɪvər, -z

cavern
BR ˈkavn, -z, -d
AM ˈkævərn, -z, -d

cavernous
BR ˈkavənəs, ˈkavn̩əs
AM ˈkævərnəs

cavernously
BR ˈkavənəsli,
ˈkavn̩əsli
AM ˈkævərnəsli

Caversham
BR ˈkavəʃ(ə)m
AM ˈkævərʃəm

cavesson
BR ˈkavɪsn, -z
AM ˈkævəsən, -z

cavetti
BR kəˈvɛti
AM kəˈvɛdi

cavetto
BR kəˈvɛtəu
AM kəˈvɛdou

caviar
BR ˈkavɪɑː(r)
AM ˈkæviˌɑr

caviare
BR ˈkavɪɑː(r)
AM ˈkæviˌɑr

cavil
BR ˈkavl̩, ˈkavɪl, -z, -ɪŋ,
-d
AM ˈkævl̩əl, -əlz,
-(ə)lɪŋ, -əld

caviller
BR ˈkavlə(r), -z
AM ˈkævələr, -z

cavitation
BR ˌkavɪˈteɪʃn
AM ˌkævəˈteɪʃən

cavity
BR ˈkavɪt|i, -ɪz
AM ˈkævədi, -z

cavort
BR kəˈvɔːt, -s, -ɪŋ, -ɪd
AM kəˈvɔ(ə)rt, -ts,
-ˈvɔrdɪŋ, -ˈvɔrdəd

Cavour
BR kəˈvuə(r), kəˈvɔː(r)
AM kəˈvʊ(ə)r

cavy
BR ˈkeɪv|i, -ɪz
AM ˈkeɪvvi, -z

caw
BR kɔː(r), -z, -ɪŋ, -d
AM kɔ, kɑ, -z, -ɪŋ, -d

Cawdor
BR ˈkɔːdɔː(r), ˈkɔːdə(r)
AM ˈkɔdɔ(ə)r,
ˈkadɔ(ə)r

Cawdrey
BR ˈkɔːdri
AM ˈkɔdri, ˈkadri

Cawley
BR ˈkɔːli
AM ˈkɔli, ˈkɑli

Cawnpore
BR ˌkɔːnˈpɔː(r)
AM ˈkɔnˌpɔ(ə)r,
ˈkɑnˌpɔ(ə)r

Cawood
BR ˈkeɪwʊd
AM ˈkeɪˌwʊd

Caxton
BR ˈkakst(ə)n
AM ˈkækstən

cay
BR kiː, keɪ, -z
AM ki, keɪ, -z

cayenne
BR (ˌ)keɪˈɛn, (ˌ)kʌɪˈɛn
AM ˌkaɪˈ(j)ɛn,
ˌkeɪˈ(j)ɛn

Cayley
BR ˈkeɪli
AM ˈkeɪli

cayman
BR ˈkeɪmən, -z
AM ˈkeɪmən, -z

cayuse
BR ˈkʌɪ(j)uːs, -ɪz
AM ˈkaɪˌ(j)us, -əz

Cazenove
BR ˈkazɪnəʊv
AM ˈkæzəˌnoʊv

cc
BR ˌsiːˈsiː, -z
AM ˌsiˈsi, -z

CD-ROM
BR ˌsiːdiːˈrɒm, -z
AM ˌsiˌdiˈrɑm, -z

ceanothus
BR ˌsiːəˈnəʊθəs, -ɪz
AM ˌsiəˈnoʊθəs, -əz

cease
BR siːs, -ɪz, -ɪŋ, -t
AM sis, -ɪz, -ɪŋ, -t

ceasefire
BR ˈsiːsfʌɪə(r),
ˌsiːsˈfʌɪə(r), -z
AM ˈsisˌfaɪ(ə)r, -z

ceaseless
BR ˈsiːslɪs
AM ˈsislɪs

ceaselessly
BR ˈsiːslɪsli
AM ˈsislɪsli

ceaselessness
BR ˈsiːslɪsnɪs
AM ˈsislɪsnɪs

ceca
BR ˈsiːkə(r)
AM ˈsikə

cecal
BR ˈsiːkl
AM ˈsikəl

Cecil
BR ˈsɛs(ɪ)l, ˈsɪs(ɪ)l,
ˈsiːs(ɪ)l
AM ˈsisəl, ˈsɛsəl

Cecile
BR sɪˈsiːl, sɛˈsiːl, ˈsɛsiːl
AM səˈsil

Cecilia
BR sɪˈsiːliə(r)
AM səˈsiljə, səˈsiliə

Cecily
BR ˈsɛsɪli, ˈsɛsˌli
AM ˈsɛsəli

cecitis
BR sɪˈsʌɪtɪs
AM siˈsaɪdɪs

cecity
BR ˈsiːsɪti
AM ˈsisɪdi

cecum
BR ˈsiːkəm
AM ˈsikəm

cedar
BR ˈsiːdə(r), -z
AM ˈsidər, -z

cedarn
BR ˈsiːdən
AM ˈsidərn

cedarwood
BR ˈsiːdəwʊd, -z
AM ˈsidərˌwʊd, -z

cede
BR siːd, -z, -ɪŋ, -ɪd
AM sid, -z, -ɪŋ, -ɪd

cedi
BR ˈsiːdˌi, -ɪz
AM ˈseɪdi, -z

cedilla
BR sɪˈdɪlə(r), -z
AM səˈdɪlə, -z

Cedric
BR ˈsɛdrɪk, ˈsiːdrɪk
AM ˈsidrɪk

Ceefax®
BR ˈsiːfaks
AM ˈsiˌfæks

ceili
BR ˈkeɪlˌi, -ɪz
AM ˈkeɪli, -z

ceilidh
BR ˈkeɪlˌi, -ɪz
AM ˈkeɪli, -z

ceiling
BR ˈsiːlɪŋ, -z
AM ˈsilɪŋ, -z

Ceinwen
BR ˈkʌɪnwɛn,
ˈkʌɪnwɪn
AM ˈkaɪnwən
WE ˈkeɪnwen

celadon
BR ˈsɛlədən
AM ˈsɛləˌdɑn

celandine
BR ˈsɛləndʌɪn, -z
AM ˈsɛlənˌdin,
ˈsɛlənˌdaɪn, -z

Celanese®
BR ˌsɛləˈniːz
AM ˌsɛləˈniz

celeb
BR sɪˈlɛb, -z
AM səˈlɛb, -z

Celebes
BR sɪˈliːbɪz, sɛˈliːbiːz,
ˈsɛlɪbiːz
AM ˈsɛləˌbiz

celebrant
BR ˈsɛlɪbr(ə)nt, -s
AM ˈsɛləbrənt, -s

celebrate
BR ˈsɛlɪbreɪt, -s, -ɪŋ, -ɪd
AM ˈsɛləˌbreɪlt, -ts, -dɪŋ,
-dɪd

celebration
BR ˌsɛlɪˈbreɪʃn, -z
AM ˌsɛləˈbreɪʃən, -z

celebrator
BR ˈsɛlɪbreɪtə(r), -z
AM ˈsɛləˌbreɪdər, -z

celebratory
BR ˌsɛlɪˈbreɪt(ə)ri,
ˈsɛlɪbrət(ə)ri
AM səˈlɛbrəˌtɔri,
ˈsɛləbrəˌtɔri

celebrity
BR sɪˈlɛbrɪtˌi, -ɪz
AM səˈlɛbrədi, -z

celeriac
BR sɪˈlɛrɪak
AM səˈlɛriˌæk

celerity
BR sɪˈlɛrɪti
AM səˈlɛrədi

celery
BR ˈsɛləri
AM ˈsɛl(ə)ri

celesta
BR sɪˈlɛstə(r)
AM səˈlɛstə

celeste
BR sɪˈlɛst, -s
AM səˈlɛst, -s

celestial
BR sɪˈlɛstɪəl
AM səˈlɛstʃəl,
səˈlɛsˌdiəl

celestially
BR sɪˈlɛstɪəli
AM səˈlɛstʃəli

celestine
BR ˈsɛlɪstʌɪn, ˈsɛlɪstiːn
AM ˌsɛləˈstin

Celia
BR ˈsiːlɪə(r)
AM ˈsiljə, ˈsiliə

celiac
BR ˈsiːlɪak
AM ˈsiliˌæk

celibacy
BR ˈsɛlɪbəsi
AM ˈsɛləbəsi

celibate
BR ˈsɛlɪbət, -s
AM ˈsɛləbət, -s

cell
BR sɛl, -z, -d
AM sɛl, -z, -d

cellar
BR ˈsɛlə(r), -z
AM ˈsɛlər, -z

cellarage
BR ˈsɛl(ə)rɪdʒ
AM ˈsɛlərɪdʒ

cellarer
BR ˈsɛl(ə)rə(r), -z
AM ˈsɛlərər, -z

cellaret
BR ˈsɛl(ə)rɪt, -s
AM ˈsɛlərət, -s

cellarman
BR ˈsɛləmən
AM ˈsɛlərmən

cellarmen
BR ˈsɛləmən
AM ˈsɛlərən

Cellini
BR tʃɛˈliːni, tʃɪˈliːni
AM ˈtʃɛlmi

cellist
BR ˈtʃɛlɪst, -s
AM ˈtʃɛləst, -s

Cellnet®
BR ˈsɛlnɛt
AM ˈsɛlˌnɛt

cello
BR ˈtʃɛləʊ, -z
AM ˈtʃɛloʊ, -z

Cellophane®
BR ˈsɛləfeɪn
AM ˈsɛləˌfeɪn

cellphone
BR ˈsɛlfəʊn, -z
AM ˈsɛlˌfoʊn, -z

cellular
BR ˈsɛljʊlə(r)
AM ˈsɛljələr

cellularity
BR ˌsɛljʊˈlarɪti
AM ˌsɛljəˈlɛrədi

cellulase
BR ˈsɛljʊleɪz
AM ˈsɛljəˌleɪz

cellulate
BR ˈsɛljʊleɪt, -s, -ɪŋ, -ɪd
AM ˈsɛljəˌleɪlt, -ts, -dɪŋ,
-dɪd

cellulation
BR ˌsɛljʊˈleɪʃn
AM ˌsɛljəˈleɪʃən

cellule
BR ˈsɛljuːl, -z
AM ˈsɛlˌjul, -z

cellulite
BR ˈsɛljʊlʌɪt
AM ˈsɛljəˌlaɪt

cellulitis
BR ˌsɛljʊˈlʌɪtɪs
AM ˌsɛljəˈlaɪdɪs

celluloid
BR ˈsɛljʊlɔɪd
AM ˈsɛljəˌlɔɪd

cellulose
BR ˈsɛljʊləʊs,
ˈsɛljʊləʊz
AM ˈsɛljəˌloʊs,
ˈsɛljəˌloʊz

cellulosic
BR ˌsɛljʊˈlɒsɪk
AM ˌsɛljəˈlɑsɪk

cellulous
BR ˈsɛljʊləs
AM ˈsɛljələs

celom
BR ˈsiːləm
AM ˈsiləm

Celsius
BR ˈsɛlsɪəs
AM ˈsɛlsɪəs, ˈsɛlʃəs

Celt
BR kɛlt, -s
AM kɛlt, sɛlt, -s

Celtic¹
noun, adjective,
language
BR ˈkɛltɪk
AM ˈkɛltɪk

Celtic²
noun, soccer team
BR ˈsɛltɪk
AM ˈsɛltɪk

Celticism
BR ˈkɛltɪsɪz(ə)m, -z
AM ˈkɛltəˌsɪzəm,
ˈsɛltəˌsɪzəm, -z

Celtics
basketball team
BR ˈsɛltɪks
AM ˈsɛltɪks

Cemaes
BR ˈkɛmʌɪs, kɪˈmʌɪs
AM ˈkɛmaɪs

cembalo
BR ˈtʃɛmbələʊ, -z
AM ˈtʃɛmbəˌloʊ, -z

cement
BR sɪˈmɛnt, -s, -ɪŋ, -ɪd
AM səˈmɛnt, -s, -ɪŋ, -əd

cementation
BR ˌsiːmɛnˈteɪʃn
AM ˌsimɛnˈteɪʃən

cementer
BR sɪˈmɛntə(r), -z
AM səˈmɛn(t)ər, -z

cementite
BR sɪˈmɛntʌɪt
AM səˈmɛnˌtaɪt

cementitious
BR ˌsiːmɛnˈtɪʃəs
AM ˌsimɛnˈtɪʃəs

cementium
BR sɪˈmɛntɪəm,
sɪˈmɛnʃɪəm
AM sɪˈmɛn(t)iəm

cementum
BR sɪˈmɛntəm
AM səˈmɛn(t)əm

cemetery
BR ˈsɛmɪt(ə)r|i, -ɪz
AM ˈsɛməˌtɛr|i, -z

Cemmaes
BR ˈkɛmʌɪs, kɪˈmʌɪs
AM ˈkɛmaɪs

cenacle
BR ˈsɛnəkl, -z
AM ˈsɛnək(ə)l, -z

cenobite
BR ˈsiːnəbʌɪt, -s
AM ˈsɛnəˌbaɪt, -s

cenotaph
BR ˈsɛnətɑːf, ˈsɛnətaf,
-s
AM ˈsɛnəˌtæf, -s

cenote
BR sɪˈnəʊti, sɪˈnəʊteɪ
AM sɪˈnoʊdi

Cenozoic
BR ˌsiːnəˈzəʊɪk
AM ˌsinəˈzoʊɪk,
ˌsɛnəˈzoʊɪk

cense
BR sɛns, -ɪz, -ɪŋ, -t
AM sɛns, -əz, -ɪŋ, -t

censer
BR ˈsɛnsə(r), -z
AM ˈsɛnsər, -z

censor
BR ˈsɛns|ə(r), -əz,
-(ə)rɪŋ, -əd
AM ˈsɛns|ər, -ərz,
-(ə)rɪŋ, -ərd

censorial
BR sɛnˈsɔːrɪəl
AM sɛnˈsɔriəl

censorially
BR sɛnˈsɔːrɪəli
AM sɛnˈsɔriəli

censorian
BR sɛnˈsɔːrɪən
AM sɛnˈsɔriən

censorious
BR sɛnˈsɔːrɪəs
AM sɛnˈsɔriəs

censoriously
BR sɛnˈsɔːrɪəsli
AM sɛnˈsɔriəsli

censoriousness
BR sɛnˈsɔːrɪəsnəs
AM sɛnˈsɔriəsnəs

censorship
BR ˈsɛnsəʃɪp
AM ˈsɛnsərˌʃɪp

censurable
BR ˈsɛnʃ(ə)rəbl
AM ˈsɛn(t)ʃ(ə)rəbəl

censure
BR ˈsɛnʃ|ə(r), -əz,
-(ə)rɪŋ, -əd
AM ˈsɛn(t)ʃər, -z, -ɪŋ, -d

census
BR ˈsɛnsəs, -ɪz
AM ˈsɛnsəs, -əz

cent
BR sɛnt, -s
AM sɛnt, -s

cental
BR ˈsɛntl, -z
AM ˈsɛn(t)l, -z

centaur
BR ˈsɛntɔː(r), -z
AM ˈsɛnˌtɔ(r), -z

Centaurus
BR sɛnˈtɔːrəs
AM sɛnˈtɔrəs

centaury
BR ˈsɛntɔːri

AM ˈsɛn(t)ɔːri

centavo
BR sɛnˈtɑːvəʊ, -z
AM sɛnˈtɑvoʊ, -z

centenarian
BR ˌsɛntɪˈnɛːrɪən, -z
AM ˌsɛn(t)əˈnɛriən, -z

centenary
BR sɛnˈtiːn(ə)r|i,
s(ə)nˈtiːn(ə)r|i,
sɛnˈtɛn(ə)r|i,
s(ə)nˈtɛn(ə)r|i, -ɪz
AM sɛnˈtɛnəri,
ˈsɛntnˌɛri, -z

centennial
BR sɛnˈtɛnɪəl,
s(ə)nˈtɛnɪəl, -z
AM sɛnˈtɛniəl,
sənˈtɛniəl, -z

center
BR ˈsɛnt|ə(r), -əz,
-(ə)rɪŋ, -əd
AM ˈsɛnt|ər, -ərz,
-(ə)rɪŋ, -ərd

centerboard
BR ˈsɛntəbɔːd, -z
AM ˈsɛn(t)ərˌbɔ(ə)rd,
-z

centerfold
BR ˈsɛntəfəʊld, -z
AM ˈsɛn(t)ərˌfoʊld, -z

centerline
BR ˈsɛntəlʌɪn, -z
AM ˈsɛn(t)ərˌlaɪn, -z

centermost
BR ˈsɛntəməʊst
AM ˈsɛn(t)ərˌmoʊst

centerpiece
BR ˈsɛntəpiːs, -ɪz
AM ˈsɛn(t)ərˌpis, -ɪz

centesimal
BR sɛnˈtɛsɪml
AM sɛnˈtɛsəməl

centesimally
BR sɛnˈtɛsɪmlˌi,
sɛnˈtɛsɪməli
AM sɛnˈtɛs(ə)məli

centigrade
BR ˈsɛntɪɡreɪd
AM ˈsɛn(t)əˌɡreɪd

centigram
BR ˈsɛntɪɡram, -z
AM ˈsɛn(t)əˌɡræm, -z

centigramme
BR ˈsɛntɪɡram, -z
AM ˈsɛn(t)əˌɡræm, -z

centiliter
BR ˈsɛntɪˌliːtə(r), -z
AM ˈsɛn(t)əˌlidər, -z

centilitre
BR ˈsɛntɪˌliːtə(r), -z
AM ˈsɛn(t)əˌlidər, -z

centime
BR ˈsɒntiːm, ˈsɑːntiːm,
-z
AM ˈsɑnˌtim, ˈsɑnˈtim,
-z

centi(m)eter
BR ˈsɛntɪˌmiːtə(r), -z
AM ˈsɛn(t)əˌmidər, -z

centimetre
BR ˈsɛntɪˌmiːtə(r), -z
AM ˈsɛn(t)əˌmidər, -z

centimo
BR ˈsɛntɪməʊ, -z
AM ˈsɛn(t)əmoʊ, -z

centipede
BR ˈsɛntɪpiːd, -z
AM ˈsɛn(t)əˌpid, -z

centner
BR ˈsɛntnə(r), -z
AM ˈsɛntnər, -z

cento
BR ˈsɛntəʊ, -z
AM ˈsɛnˌtoʊ, -z

centra
BR ˈsɛntrə(r)
AM ˈsɛntrə

central
BR ˈsɛntr(ə)l
AM ˈsɛntrəl

centralisation
BR ˌsɛntrəlʌɪˈzeɪʃn,
ˌsɛntrlʌɪˈzeɪʃn
AM ˌsɛntrələˈzeɪʃən,
ˌsɛntrəˌlaɪˈzeɪʃən

centralise
BR ˈsɛntrəlʌɪz,
ˈsɛntrlʌɪz, -ɪz, -ɪŋ, -d
AM ˈsɛntrəˌlaɪz, -ɪz, -ɪŋ,
-d

centralism
BR ˈsɛntrəlɪz(ə)m,
ˈsɛntrlɪz(ə)m
AM ˈsɛntrəˌlɪzəm

centralist
BR ˈsɛntrəlɪst,
ˈsɛntrlɪst
AM ˈsɛntrələst

centrality
BR sɛnˈtralɪti
AM sɛnˈtræləti

centralization
BR ˌsɛntrəlʌɪˈzeɪʃn,
ˌsɛntrlʌɪˈzeɪʃn
AM ˌsɛntrələˈzeɪʃən,
ˌsɛntrəˌlaɪˈzeɪʃən

centralize
BR ˈsɛntrəlʌɪz,
ˈsɛntrlʌɪz, -ɪz, -ɪŋ, -d
AM ˈsɛntrəˌlaɪz, -ɪz, -ɪŋ,
-d

centrally
BR ˈsɛntrəli, ˈsɛntrlˌi
AM ˈsɛntrəli

centre
BR ˈsɛnt|ə(r), -əz,
-(ə)rɪŋ, -əd
AM ˈsɛnt|ər, -ərz,
-(ə)rɪŋ, -əd

centreboard
BR ˈsɛntəbɔːd, -z
AM ˈsɛn(t)ərˌbɔ(ə)rd,
-z

centrefold
BR ˈsɛntəfəʊld, -z
AM ˈsɛn(t)ərˌfoʊld, -z

centreline
BR ˈsɛntəlaɪn, -z
AM ˈsɛn(t)ərˌlaɪn, -z

centremost
BR ˈsɛntəməʊst
AM ˈsɛn(t)ərˌmoʊst

centrepiece
BR ˈsɛntəpiːs, -ɪz
AM ˈsɛn(t)ərˌpiːs, -ɪz

centric
BR ˈsɛntrɪk
AM ˈsɛntrɪk

centrical
BR ˈsɛntrɪkl
AM ˈsɛntrəkəl

centricity
BR sɛnˈtrɪsɪti
AM ˌsɛnˈtrɪsɪdi

centrifugal
BR ˌsɛntrɪˈfjuːgl,
sɛnˈtrɪfjʊgl,
s(ə)nˈtrɪfjʊgl̩
AM sɛnˈtrɪf(j)əgəl

centrifugally
BR ˌsɛntrɪˈfjuːgḷi,
sɛnˈtrɪfjʊgḷi,
s(ə)nˈtrɪfjʊgḷi
AM sɛnˈtrɪf(j)əg(ə)li

centrifugation
BR ˌsɛntrɪfjəˈgeɪʃn
AM ˌsɛntrəˌfjuˈgeɪʃən

centrifuge
BR ˈsɛntrɪfjuː(d)ʒ, -ɪz
AM ˈsɛntrəˌfjudʒ, -əz

centriole
BR ˈsɛntrəʊl, -z
AM ˈsɛntriˌoʊl, -z

centripetal
BR ˌsɛntrɪˈpiːtl,
sɛnˈtrɪpɪtl,
s(ə)nˈtrɪpɪtl
AM sɛnˈtrɪpɪdl

centripetally
BR ˌsɛntrɪˈpiːtḷi,
sɛnˈtrɪpɪtḷi,
s(ə)nˈtrɪpɪtḷi
AM sɛnˈtrɪpədɪli

centrism
BR ˈsɛntrɪz(ə)m
AM ˈsɛntˌrɪzəm

centrist
BR ˈsɛntrɪst, -s
AM ˈsɛntrəst, -s

centroid
BR ˈsɛntrɔɪd, -z
AM ˈsɛntrɔɪd, -z

centromere
BR ˈsɛntrə(ʊ)mɪə(r), -z
AM ˈsɛntrəˌmɪ(ə)r, -z

centrosome
BR ˈsɛntrə(ʊ)səʊm, -z
AM ˈsɛntrəˌsoʊm, -z

centrum
BR ˈsɛntrəm
AM ˈsɛntrəm

centum
BR ˈkɛntəm
AM ˈkɛn(t)əm

centumvirate
BR sɛnˈtʌmvɪrət, -s
AM sɛnˈtəmvərət, -s

centuple
BR ˈsɛntjʊpl, ˈsɛntʃʊpl
AM sɛnˈt(j)upəl,
ˈsɛntəpəl

centurion
BR sɛnˈtjʊəriən,
sɛnˈtʃʊəriən,
sɛnˈtʃɔːriən, -z
AM sɛnˈt(j)ʊriən, -z

century
BR ˈsɛntʃ(ʊ)r|i, -ɪz
AM ˈsɛn(t)ʃ(ə)ri, -z

ceorl
BR tʃəːl, -z
AM tʃərl, -z

cep
BR sɛp, -s
AM sɛp, -s

cephalic
BR sɪˈfalɪk, kɛˈfalɪk
AM səˈfælɪk

Cephalonia
BR ˌkɛfəˈləʊniə(r),
ˌsɛfəˈləʊniə(r)
AM ˌsɛfəˈloʊniə

cephalopod
BR ˈkɛf(ə)ləpɒd,
ˈkɛfˌləpɒd,
ˈsɛf(ə)ləpɒd,
ˈsɛfˌləpɒd, -z
AM ˈsɛfələˌpɑd, -z

cephalopoda
BR ˌkɛfəˈlɒpədə(r),
ˌsɛfəˈlɒpədə(r)
AM sɛfəˈlɑpədə

cephalothorax
BR ˌkɛf(ə)ləʊˈθɔːraks,
ˌkɛfləʊˈθɔːraks,
ˌsɛf(ə)ləʊˈθɔːraks,
ˌsɛfləʊˈθɔːraks, -ɪz
AM sɛfələˈθɔræks, -əz

cephalothoraxes
BR ˌkɛfələʊˈθɔːraksɪz,
ˌkɛfləʊˈθɔːraksɪz,
ˌsɛf(ə)ləʊˈθɔːraksɪz,
ˌsɛfləʊˈθɔːraksɪz
AM ˌsɛfələˈθɔræksiz

Cephas
BR ˈsiːfas
AM ˈsifəs

cepheid
BR ˈsiːfiɪd, ˈsɛfiɪd, -z
AM ˈsifiəd, ˈsɛfiəd, -z

Cepheus
BR ˈsiːfiəs
AM ˈsifiəs

ceramic
BR sɪˈramɪk, -s
AM səˈræmɪk, -s

ceramicist
BR sɪˈramɪsɪst, -s

AM səˈræməsəst, -s

ceramist
BR sɪˈramɪst, -s
AM səˈræməst, -s

cerastes
BR sɪˈrastiːz, -ɪz
AM səˈræstiz, -ɪz

cerastium
BR sɪˈrastɪəm, -z
AM səˈræstiəm, -z

Cerberus
BR ˈsəːb(ə)rəs
AM ˈsɜrbərəs

cercaria
BR səˈkɛːrɪə(r)
AM sərˈkɛriə

cercariae
BR səːˈkɛːriː
AM sərˈkɛrii

cerci
BR ˈsəːkaɪ
AM ˈsɜrkaɪ, ˈsɜrsaɪ

cercopithecine
BR ˌsəːkə(ʊ)ˈpɪθɪsiːn
AM ˌsɜrkəˈpɪθɪˌsin

cercopithecoid
BR ˌsəːkə(ʊ)ˈpɪθɪkɔɪd
AM ˌsɜrkəˈpɪθɪˌkɔɪd

cercus
BR ˈsəːkəs
AM ˈsɜrkəs

cere
BR sɪə(r), -z
AM sɪ(ə)r, -z

cereal
BR ˈsɪərɪəl, -z
AM ˈsɪriəl, -z

cerebella
BR ˌsɛrɪˈbɛlə(r)
AM ˌsɛrəˈbɛlə

cerebellar
BR ˌsɛrɪˈbɛlə(r)
AM ˌsɛrəˈbɛlər

cerebellum
BR ˌsɛrɪˈbɛləm, -z
AM ˌsɛrəˈbɛləm, -z

Cerebos®
BR ˈsɛrɪbɒs
AM ˈsɛrəbɒs, ˈsɛrəbɑs

cerebra
BR sɪˈriːbrə(r),
ˈsɛrɪbrə(r)
AM səˈribrə, ˈsɛrəbrə

cerebral
BR sɪˈriːbr(ə)l,
ˈsɛrɪbr(ə)l
AM səˈribrəl, ˈsɛrəbrəl

cerebrally
BR sɪˈriːbrḷi,
sɪˈriːbrəli, ˈsɛrɪbrḷi,
ˈsɛrɪbrəli
AM səˈribrəli,
ˈsɛr(ə)brəli

cerebrate
BR ˈsɛrɪbreɪt, -s, -ɪŋ, -ɪd
AM ˈsɛrəˌbreɪ|t, -ts,
-dɪŋ, -dɪd

cerebration
BR ˌsɛrɪˈbreɪʃn
AM ˌsɛrəˈbreɪʃən

cerebroside
BR ˈsɛrɪbrəsʌɪd, -z
AM ˈsɛrəbrəˌsaɪd,
səˈribrəˌsaɪd, -z

cerebrospinal
BR ˌsɛrɪbrəʊˈspʌɪnl,
sɪˌriːbrəʊˈspʌɪnl
AM səˌribroʊˈspaɪnəl,
ˈsɛrəbroʊˈspaɪnəl

cerebrovascular
BR ˌsɛrɪbrəʊˈvaskjʊlə(r),
sɪˌriːbrəʊˈvaskjʊlə(r)
AM səˌribroʊˈvæskjələr,
ˈsɛrəbroʊˈvæskjələr

cerebrum
BR sɪˈriːbrəm,
ˈsɛrɪbrəm
AM səˈribrəm,
ˈsɛrəbrəm

cerecloth
BR ˈsɪəklɒθ, -s\-ðz
AM ˈsɪrˌklɑ|θ, ˈsɪrˌklɑθ,
-θs\-ðz

Ceredigion
BR ˌkɛrɪˈdɪgɪɒn
AM ˌkɛrəˈdɪgiən
WE ˌkere'dɪgjɒn

cerement
BR ˈsɪəm(ə)nt,
ˈsɛrɪm(ə)nt, -s
AM ˈsɪrmənt, -s

ceremonial
BR ˌsɛrɪˈməʊnɪəl
AM ˌsɛrəˈmoʊniəl

ceremonialism
BR ˌsɛrɪˈməʊnɪəlɪz(ə)m
AM ˌsɛrəˈmoʊniəˌlɪzəm

ceremonialist
BR ˌsɛrɪˈməʊnɪəlɪst, -s
AM ˌsɛrəˈmoʊniələst,
-s

ceremonially
BR ˌsɛrɪˈməʊnɪəli
AM ˌsɛrəˈmoʊniəli

ceremonious
BR ˌsɛrɪˈməʊnɪəs
AM ˌsɛrəˈmoʊniəs

ceremoniously
BR ˌsɛrɪˈməʊnɪəsli
AM ˌsɛrəˈmoʊniəsli

ceremoniousness
BR ˌsɛrɪˈməʊnɪəsnəs
AM ˌsɛrəˈmoʊniəsnəs

ceremony
BR ˈsɛrɪmən|i, -ɪz
AM ˈsɛrəˌmoʊni, -z

Cerenkov
BR tʃɪˈrɛŋkɒf,
tʃɪˈrɛŋkɒv
AM tʃəˈrɛŋkɒv,
tʃəˈrɛŋkɔf,
tʃəˈrɛŋkɑv,
tʃəˈrɛŋkɑf

Ceres
BR ˈsɪəriːz

AM 'sɪrɪz

ceresin
BR 'serɪsɪn
AM 'serəsən

Ceri
BR 'keri
AM 'keri

cerif
BR 'serɪf, -s
AM 'serɪf, -s

cerise
BR sɪ'riːz, sɪ'riːs
AM sə'riːs, sə'riz

cerium
BR 'sɪəriəm
AM 'sɪriəm

cermet
BR 'sɜːmet
AM 'sɜr‚met

CERN
BR sɜːn
AM sɜrn

Cerne Abbas
BR ‚sɜːn 'æbəs
AM ‚sɜrn 'æbəs

cerography
BR sɪ'rɒgrəfi
AM sə'ragrəfi

ceroplastic
BR ‚sɪərəʊ'plastɪk
AM ‚sɪroʊ'plæstɪk,
‚seroʊ'plæstɪk

cert
BR sɜːt, -s
AM sɜrt, -s

certain
BR 'sɜːt(ɪ)n
AM 'sɜrtn

certainly
BR 'sɜːt(ɪ)nli
AM 'sɜrtnli

certainty
BR 'sɜːt(ɪ)nt|i, -ɪz
AM 'sɜrtn(t)i, -z

Cert.Ed.
BR ‚sɜːt'ed, -z
AM ‚sɜrt'ed, -z

certes
BR 'sɜːti:z, 'sɜːtɪz
AM 'sɜrdiz

certifiable
BR ‚sɜːtɪ'faɪəbl,
'sɜːtɪfaɪəbl
AM ‚sɜrdə'faɪəbəl

certifiably
BR ‚sɜːtɪ'faɪəbli,
'sɜːtɪfaɪəbli
AM ‚sɜrdə'faɪəbli

certificate[1]
noun
BR sə'tɪfɪkət, -s
AM sɜr'tɪfəkət, -s

certificate[2]
verb
BR sə'tɪfɪkeɪt, -s, -ɪŋ, -ɪd
AM ‚sɜr'tɪfəkeɪ|t, -ts,
-dɪŋ, -dɪd

certification
BR ‚sɜːtɪfɪ'keɪʃn, -z
AM ‚sɜrdəfə'keɪʃən, -z

certificatory
BR sə'tɪfɪkət(ə)ri
AM sɜr'tɪfəkə‚tɔri

certify
BR 'sɜːtɪfaɪ, -z, -ɪŋ, -d
AM 'sɜrdə‚faɪ, -z, -ɪŋ, -d

certiorari
BR ‚sɜːtiə'rɜːraɪ,
‚sə:[ʃ]ə'rɜːraɪ,
‚sə:[ʃ]ə'rɑːri
AM ‚sɜrʃ(i)ə'rɛri

certitude
BR 'sɜːtɪtjuːd,
'sɜːtɪtʃuːd
AM 'sɜrdə‚t(j)ud

cerulean
BR sɪ'ruːliən
AM sə'ruliən

cerumen
BR sɪ'ruːmen,
sɪ'ruːmɪn
AM sə'rumən

ceruminous
BR sɪ'ruːmɪnəs
AM sə'rumənəs

ceruse
BR 'sɪəruːs, sɪ'ruːs
AM sə'rus, 'sɪrus

Cervantes
BR sɜː'vantiːz,
sə:'vantɪz
AM sɜr'vanteɪs

cervelat
BR 'sɜːvəlat,
'sɜːvəlɑː(r), ‚sɜːvə'lat,
‚sɜːvə'lɑː(r)
AM 'sɜrvələt

cervical
BR sɜː(:)'vaɪkl, 'sɜːvɪkl
AM 'sɜrvɪkəl

cervices
BR 'sɜːvɪsiːz
AM 'sɜrvə‚siz

cervine
BR 'sɜːvaɪn
AM 'sɜr‚vaɪn

cervix
BR 'sɜːv|ɪks, -ɪksɪz
AM 'sɜr‚vɪks, -ɪz

Cesar
BR 'seɪzɑː(r)
AM 'sizər, 'seɪzɑr

César
BR 'seɪzɑː(r)
AM 'seɪzɑr

cesarean
BR sɪ'zɛːriən, -z
AM sə'zɛriən, -z

Cesarewitch
BR sɪ'zarɪwɪtʃ
AM sə'zarəwɪtʃ

cesarian
BR sɪ'zɛːriən, -z
AM sə'zɛriən, -z

cesium
BR 'siːzɪəm
AM 'sizɪəm

cess
BR ses, -ɪz
AM ses, -əz

cessation
BR se'seɪʃn, sɪ'seɪʃn, -z
AM se'seɪʃən,
sə'seɪʃən, -z

cesser
BR 'sesə(r)
AM 'sesər

cession
BR 'seʃn, -z
AM 'seʃən, -z

cessionary
BR 'seʃən(ə)r|i,
'seʃn(ə)r|i, -ɪz
AM 'seʃə‚neri, -z

Cessna®
BR 'sesnə(r), -z
AM 'sesnə, -z

cesspit
BR 'sespɪt, -s
AM 'ses‚pɪt, -s

cesspool
BR 'sespuːl, -z
AM 'ses‚pul, -z

cesta
BR 'sestə(r), -z
AM 'sestə, -z

cesti
BR 'sestʌɪ, 'sestiː
AM 'ses‚taɪ, 'sesti

c'est la vie
BR ‚seɪ lɑː 'viː, + lə +
AM ‚seɪ lɑ 'vi

cestode
BR 'sestəʊd, -z
AM 'ses‚toʊd, -z

cestoid
BR 'sestɔɪd, -z
AM 'ses‚tɔɪd, -z

cestus
BR 'sestəs
AM 'sestəs

cetacea
BR sɪ'teɪʃə(r)
AM sə'teɪʃiə

cetacean
BR sɪ'teɪʃn
AM sə'teɪʃən

cetaceous
BR sɪ'teɪʃəs
AM sə'teɪʃəs

cetane
BR 'siːteɪn
AM 'si‚teɪn

ceteris paribus
BR ‚kert(ə)rɪs
'parɪbəs, ‚ket(ə)rɪs +,
+ 'pɑːrɪbəs,
+ 'parɪbʊs,
+ 'pɑːrɪbʊs
AM ‚keɪdərəs 'perəbəs,
'seɪdərəs +,
'sedərəs +

cetological
BR ‚siːtə'lɒdʒɪkl
AM ‚sidə'ladʒəkəl

cetologist
BR sɪ'tɒlədʒɪst,
siː'tɒlədʒɪst, -s
AM sə'talədʒəst,
si'talədʒəst, -s

cetology
BR sɪ'tɒlədʒi
AM sə'talədʒi,
si'talədʒi

Cetshwayo
BR ketʃ'wʌɪəʊ
AM ketʃ'waɪoʊ

Cetus
BR 'siːtəs
AM 'sidəs

Ceuta
BR 's(j)uːtə(r)
AM 'seɪudə

Cévennes
BR se'ven
AM sə'ven

Ceylon
BR sɪ'lɒn
AM seɪ'lɑn, sə'lɑn

Ceylonese
BR ‚selə'niːz
AM ‚selə'niz, ‚seɪlə'niz

Cézanne
BR sɪ'zan, seɪ'zan
AM seɪ'zɑn

cha
BR tʃɑː(r)
AM tʃɑ

Chablis
BR 'ʃabliː
AM ʃɑ'bli, ʃə'bli

Chabrier
BR 'ʃabrɪeɪ, 'ʃɑːbrɪeɪ
AM 'ʃabri‚eɪ

Chabrol
BR ʃa'brɒl, ʃə'brɒl
AM ʃɑ'broʊl

cha-cha
BR 'tʃɑːtʃɑː(r), -z, -ɪŋ
AM 'tʃɑ‚tʃɑ, -z, -ɪŋ

cha-cha-cha
BR ‚tʃɑːtʃɑː'tʃɑː(r)
AM ‚tʃɑ‚tʃɑ'tʃɑ,
'tʃɑ'tʃɑ'tʃɑ

chacma
BR 'tʃakmə(r), -z
AM 'tʃakmə, -z

chaconne
BR ʃə'kɒn, ʃa'kɒn, -z
AM ʃɑ'kɑn, ʃɑ'kɑn,
ʃə'kɑn, ʃə'kɑn, -z

Chad
BR tʃad
AM tʃæd

chadar
BR 'tʃɑːdə(r), -z
AM 'tʃɑdər, -z

Chadian
BR 'tʃadɪən, -z
AM 'tʃædiən, -z

Chadic
BR 'tʃadɪk
AM 'tʃædɪk

chador
BR 'tʃɑːdɔː(r),
'tʃʌdə(r)
AM 'tʃɑˌdɔ(ə)r

Chadwick
BR 'tʃadwɪk
AM 'tʃædˌwɪk

chaeta
BR 'kiːtə(r)
AM 'kidə

chaetae
BR 'kiːtiː
AM 'kidi

chaetognath
BR 'kiːtənaθ, -s
AM 'kidɑɡˌnaθ, -s

chaetopod
BR 'kiːtəpɒd, -z
AM 'kidəˌpɑd, -z

chafe
BR tʃeɪf, -s, -ɪŋ, -t
AM tʃeɪf, -s, -ɪŋ, -t

chafer
BR 'tʃeɪfə(r), -z
AM 'tʃeɪfər, -z

chaff
BR tʃɑːf, tʃaf, -s, -ɪŋ, -t
AM tʃæf, -s, -ɪŋ, -t

chaffer
BR 'tʃaflə(r), -əz,
-(ə)rɪŋ, -əd
AM 'tʃæfər, -z, -ɪŋ, -d

chafferer
BR 'tʃaf(ə)rə(r), -z
AM 'tʃæfərər, -z

chaffinch
BR 'tʃafɪn(t)ʃ, -ɪz
AM 'tʃæˌfɪntʃ, -ɪz

chaffiness
BR 'tʃɑːfɪnɪs, 'tʃafɪnɪs
AM 'tʃæfɪnɪs

chaffy
BR 'tʃɑːfi, 'tʃafi
AM 'tʃæfi

Chagall
BR ʃa'ɡal, ʃə'ɡal,
ʃa'ɡɑːl, ʃə'ɡɑːl
AM ʃə'ɡɑl

Chagas' disease
BR 'ʃɑːɡəs dɪˌziːz
AM 'ʃaɡəs dəˌziz,
+ dɪˌziz

Chagos Archipelago
BR 'ʃɑːɡəs
ˌɑːkɪ'peləɡəʊ
AM 'ʃaɡəs
ˌɑrkə'peləɡoʊ,
+ ˌɑrtʃɪ'peləɡoʊ

chagrin
BR 'ʃaɡr(ɪ)n, -z, -ɪŋ, -d
AM ʃə'ɡrɪn, -z, -ɪŋ, -d

Chaim
BR XʌIm, hʌIm
AM kaɪ(ə)m

chain
BR tʃeɪn, -z, -ɪŋ, -d
AM tʃeɪn, -z, -ɪŋ, -d

chaingang
BR 'tʃeɪŋɡaŋ, -z
AM 'tʃeɪnˌɡæŋɡ, -z

chainless
BR 'tʃeɪnlɪs
AM 'tʃeɪnləs

chainmail
BR ˌtʃeɪn'meɪl,
'tʃeɪnmeɪl
AM 'tʃeɪnˌmeɪl

chainsaw
BR 'tʃeɪnsɔː(r), -z
AM 'tʃeɪnˌsɔ, 'tʃeɪnˌsɑ,
-z

chainwork
BR 'tʃeɪnwəːk
AM 'tʃeɪnˌwərk

chair
BR tʃɛː(r), -z, -ɪŋ, -d
AM tʃɛ(ə)r, -z, -ɪŋ, -d

chairlady
BR 'tʃɛːˌleɪd|i, -ɪz
AM 'tʃɛrˌleɪdi, -z

chairlift
BR 'tʃɛːlɪft, -s
AM 'tʃɛrˌlɪft, -s

chairman
BR 'tʃɛːmən
AM 'tʃɛrmən

chairmanship
BR 'tʃɛːmənʃɪp, -s
AM 'tʃɛrmənˌʃɪp, -s

chairmen
BR 'tʃɛːmən
AM 'tʃɛrmən

chairperson
BR 'tʃɛːˌpəːsn, -z
AM 'tʃɛrˌpərsən, -z

chairwoman
BR 'tʃɛːˌwʊmən
AM 'tʃɛrˌwʊmən

chairwomen
BR 'tʃɛːˌwɪmɪn
AM 'tʃɛrˌwɪmɪn

chaise
BR ʃeɪz, -ɪz
AM ʃeɪz, -ɪz

chaise longue
BR ˌʃeɪz 'lɒŋ, -z
AM ˌʃeɪz 'lɔŋ, + 'laʊndʒ,
ˌʃeɪz 'lɑŋ, -z

chakra
BR 'tʃʌkrə(r),
'tʃakrə(r), 'tʃɑːkrə(r),
-z
AM 'tʃɑkrə, -z

chalaza
BR kə'leɪzə(r), -z
AM kə'leɪzə, -z

chalazae
BR kə'leɪzi:

AM kə'leɪzi, kə'leɪˌzaɪ

Chalcedon
BR 'kalsɪdɒn,
'kalsɪd(ə)n
AM 'kælsəˌdɑn,
kæl'siːdɒn

Chalcedonian
BR ˌkalsɪ'dəʊnɪən, -z
AM ˌkælsə'doʊniən, -z

chalcedonic
BR ˌkalsɪ'dɒnɪk
AM ˌkælsə'dɑnɪk

chalcedony
BR kal'sɛdən|i,
kal'sɛdn|i, -ɪz
AM kæl'sɛdn̩i,
tʃæl'sɛdn̩i,
'kælsəˌdoʊni,
'tʃælsəˌdoʊni, -z

Chalcidice
BR kal'sɪdɪsi
AM kæl'sɪdɪsi

Chalcis
BR 'kalsɪs
AM 'kælsəs

chalcolithic
BR ˌkalkə'lɪθɪk
AM ˌkælkə'lɪθɪk

chalcopyrite
BR ˌkalkə(ʊ)'pʌɪrʌɪt
AM ˌkælkə'paɪˌraɪt

Chaldea
BR kal'diːə(r)
AM kæl'diə

Chaldean
BR kal'diːən, -z
AM kæl'dion, -z

Chaldee
BR 'kaldiː, -z
AM 'kældi, -z

chaldron
BR 'tʃɔːldr(ə)n, -z
AM 'tʃɔldrən,
'tʃɑldrən, -z

chalet
BR 'ʃal|eɪ, 'ʃal|i,
-eɪz\-ɪz
AM ˌʃæ'leɪ, -z

Chalfont
BR 'tʃalf(ɒ)nt
AM 'tʃælfɑnt

Chaliapin
BR ʃal'jɑːpɪn
AM ˌʃal'jɑˌpɪn

chalice
BR 'tʃalɪs, -ɪz
AM 'tʃæləs, -əz

chalk
BR tʃɔːk, -s, -ɪŋ, -t
AM tʃɔk, tʃɑk, -s, -ɪŋ, -t

chalkboard
BR 'tʃɔːkbɔːd, -z
AM 'tʃɔkˌbɔ(ə)rd,
'tʃɑkˌbɔ(ə)rd, -z

Chalker
BR 'tʃɔːkə(r)
AM tʃɔkər, tʃɑkər

chalkily
BR 'tʃɔːkɪli
AM 'tʃɔkəli, 'tʃɑkəli

chalkiness
BR 'tʃɔːkɪnɪs
AM 'tʃɔkɪnɪs, 'tʃɑkɪnɪs

chalky
BR 'tʃɔːk|i, -ɪə(r), -ɪst
AM 'tʃɔki, 'tʃɑki, -ər,
-ɪst

challah
BR 'hɑːlə(r), xɑː'lɑː(r),
-z
AM 'hɑlə, -z

challenge
BR 'tʃalɪn(d)ʒ, -ɪz, -ɪŋ,
-d
AM 'tʃæləndʒ, -əz, -ɪŋ,
-d

challengeable
BR 'tʃalɪn(d)ʒəbl
AM 'tʃæləndʒəbəl

challenger
BR 'tʃalɪn(d)ʒə(r), -z
AM 'tʃæləndʒər, -z

challengingly
BR 'tʃalɪn(d)ʒɪŋli
AM 'tʃæləndʒɪŋli

Challes
BR 'tʃalɪs
AM 'tʃæləs

challis
BR 'ʃalɪs, 'ʃali
AM 'ʃali, 'ʃæləs

Challoner
BR 'tʃalənə(r)
AM 'tʃælənər

Chalmers
BR 'tʃɑːməz
AM 'tʃalmərz,
'tʃælmərz

chalumeau
BR 'ʃalʊməʊ
AM 'ʃæləˌmoʊ

chalumeaux
BR 'ʃalʊməʊ(z)
AM 'ʃæləˌmoʊ(z)

chalybeate
BR kə'lɪbɪət
AM kə'lɪbiət

cham
BR kam, -z
AM kæm, -z

chamaephyte
BR 'kamɪfʌɪt, -s
AM 'kæməˌfaɪt, -s

chamber
BR 'tʃeɪmbə(r), -z, -d
AM 'tʃeɪmbər, -z, -d

chamberlain
BR 'tʃeɪmbəlɪn, -z
AM 'tʃeɪmbərlən, -z

chamberlainship
BR 'tʃeɪmbəlɪnˌʃɪp
AM 'tʃeɪmbərlənˌʃɪp

chambermaid
BR 'tʃeɪmbəmeɪd, -z

Chambers
AM 'tʃeɪmbərˌmeɪd, -z
Chambers
BR 'tʃeɪmbəz
AM 'tʃeɪmbərz
Chambertin
BR 'ʃɒbətã, -z
AM ˌʃambər'tɛn, -z
Chambourcy®
BR ʃam'bʊəsi
AM ʃæm'bʊrsi
chambray
BR 'ʃɒmbreɪ, 'ʃambreɪ
AM 'ʃæmˌbreɪ
chambré
BR 'ʃɒmbreɪ, 'ʃambreɪ
AM 'ʃæmˌbreɪ
chameleon
BR kə'mi:lɪən, -z
AM kə'miljən,
kə'miliən, -z
chameleonic
BR kəˌmi:lɪ'ɒnɪk
AM kəˌmili'anɪk
chamfer
BR '(t)ʃamfʃə(r), -əz,
-(ə)rɪŋ, -əd
AM '(t)ʃæmfər, -z, -ɪŋ,
-d
chammy
BR 'ʃam|i, -ɪz, -ɪɪŋ, -ɪd
AM 'ʃæmi, -z, -ɪŋ, -d
chamois¹
animal
BR 'ʃamwɑ:(r), -z
AM 'ʃæmi, ʃæm'wɑ, -z
chamois²
leather
BR 'ʃam|i, -ɪz, -ɪɪŋ, -ɪd
AM 'ʃæmi, -z, -ɪŋ, -d
chamomile
BR 'kaməmʌɪl
AM 'kæməˌmil,
'kæməˌmaɪl
Chamonix
BR 'ʃaməni:, 'ʃamɒni:
AM ʃamə'ni
champ
BR tʃamp, -s, -ɪŋ, -t
AM tʃæmp, -s, -ɪŋ, -t
champagne
BR ˌʃam'peɪn, -z
AM ˌʃæm'peɪn, -z
champaign
BR ˌʃam'peɪn, -z
AM ˌʃæm'peɪn, -z
champenoise
BR ˌʃampə'nwɑ:z
AM ˌʃæmpə'nwaz
champers
BR 'ʃampəz
AM 'ʃæmpərz
champertous
BR 'tʃampətəs
AM 'tʃæmpərdəs
champerty
BR 'tʃampət|i, -ɪz
AM 'tʃæmpərdi, -z

champion
BR 'tʃampɪən, -z, -ɪŋ, -d
AM 'tʃæmpiən, -z, -ɪŋ, -d
championship
BR 'tʃampɪənʃɪp, -s
AM 'tʃæmpiənˌʃɪp, -s
Champlain
BR ʃam'pleɪn
AM ʃæm'pleɪn
champlevé
BR 'ʃampləveɪ
AM ˌʃɑm(p)lə'veɪ
Champneys
BR 'tʃampnɪz
AM 'tʃæmpnɪz
Champs-Élysées
BR ˌʃɒzə'li:zeɪ
AM ˌʃanzəli'zeɪ
Chan
BR tʃan
AM tʃæn
chance
BR tʃɑ:ns, tʃans, -ɪz,
-ɪŋ, -t
AM tʃæns, -əz, -ɪŋ, -t
chancel
BR 'tʃɑ:nsl, 'tʃansl, -z
AM 'tʃænsəl, -z
chancellery
BR 'tʃɑ:ns(ə)l(ə)r|i,
'tʃɑ:nsl(ə)r|i,
'tʃans(ə)l(ə)r|i,
'tʃansl(ə)r|i, -ɪz
AM 'tʃæns(ə)ləri, -z
chancellor
BR 'tʃɑ:ns(ə)lə(r),
'tʃɑ:nslə(r),
'tʃans(ə)lə(r),
'tʃanslə(r), -z
AM 'tʃæns(ə)lər, -z
chancellorship
BR 'tʃɑ:ns(ə)ləʃɪp,
'tʃɑ:nsləʃɪp,
'tʃans(ə)ləʃɪp,
'tʃansləʃɪp, -s
AM 'tʃæns(ə)lərˌʃɪp, -s
chance-medley
BR ˌtʃɑ:ns'mɛdl|i,
ˌtʃans'mɛdl|i, -ɪz
AM ˌtʃæns'mɛdli, -z
chancer
BR 'tʃɑ:nsə(r),
'tʃansə(r), -z
AM 'tʃænsər, -z
chancery
BR 'tʃɑ:ns(ə)r|i,
'tʃans(ə)r|i, -ɪz
AM 'tʃæns(ə)ri, -z
chancily
BR 'tʃɑ:nsɪli, 'tʃansɪli
AM 'tʃænsəli
chanciness
BR 'tʃɑ:nsɪnɪs,
'tʃansɪnɪs
AM 'tʃænsɪnɪs
chancre
BR 'ʃaŋkə(r), -z

AM 'kæŋkər, 'ʃæŋkər,
-z
chancroid
BR 'ʃaŋkrɔɪd
AM 'kæŋkˌrɔɪd,
'ʃæŋkˌrɔɪd
Chanctonbury
BR 'tʃaŋ(k)t(ə)nb(ə)ri
AM 'tʃæŋktən,bɛri,
'tʃæŋktənbəri
chancy
BR 'tʃɑ:ns|i, 'tʃans|i,
-ɪə(r), -ɪɪst
AM 'tʃænsi, -ər, -ɪst
chandelier
BR ˌʃandə'lɪə(r), -z
AM ˌʃændə'lɪ(ə)r, -z
chandelle
BR ʃan'dɛl, ʃɑ:n'dɛl
AM ʃan'dɛl, ʃæn'dɛl
Chandigarh
BR ˌtʃandɪ'gə:(r),
ˌtʃandɪ'ga:(r)
AM 'tʃəndəgər,
ˌtʃəndə'gər
chandler
BR 'tʃɑ:ndlə(r),
'tʃandlə(r), -z
AM 'tʃæn(d)lər, -z
chandlery
BR 'tʃɑ:ndləri,
'tʃandləri
AM 'tʃæn(d)ləri
Chandos
BR '(t)ʃandɒs
AM 'tʃændɒs, 'tʃændɑs
Chandrasekhar
BR ˌtʃandrə'seɪkə(r)
AM ˌʃandrə'seɪkər
Chanel
BR ʃə'nɛl
AM ʃə'nɛl
Chaney
BR 'tʃeɪni
AM 'tʃeɪni
Chang
BR tʃaŋ
AM tʃæŋ
Changchun
BR 'tʃaŋ'tʃu:n
AM ˌtʃæŋ'tʃun
chancer
BR 'tʃɑ:nsə(r),
'tʃansə(r), -z
AM 'tʃænsər, -z
change
BR tʃeɪn(d)ʒ, -ɪz, -ɪŋ, -d
AM tʃeɪndʒ, -ɪz, -ɪŋ, -d
changeability
BR ˌtʃeɪn(d)ʒə'bɪlɪti
AM ˌtʃeɪndʒə'bɪlɪdi
changeable
BR 'tʃeɪn(d)ʒəbl
AM 'tʃeɪndʒəbəl
changeableness
BR 'tʃeɪn(d)ʒəbəlnəs
AM 'tʃeɪndʒəbəlnəs
changeably
BR 'tʃeɪn(d)ʒəbli
AM 'tʃeɪndʒəbli

changeful
BR 'tʃeɪn(d)ʒf(ʊ)l
AM 'tʃeɪndʒfəl
changefulness
BR 'tʃeɪn(d)ʒf(ʊ)lnəs
AM 'tʃeɪndʒəfəlnəs
changeless
BR 'tʃeɪn(d)ʒlɪs
AM 'tʃeɪndʒlɪs
changelessly
BR 'tʃeɪn(d)ʒlɪsli
AM 'tʃeɪndʒlɪsli
changelessness
BR 'tʃeɪn(d)ʒlɪsnɪs
AM 'tʃeɪndʒlɪsnɪs
changeling
BR 'tʃeɪn(d)ʒlɪŋ, -z
AM 'tʃeɪndʒlɪŋ, -z
changeover
BR 'tʃeɪn(d)ʒˌəʊvə(r),
-z
AM 'tʃeɪndʒˌoʊvər, -z
changer
BR 'tʃeɪn(d)ʒə(r), -z
AM 'tʃeɪndʒər, -z
changeround
BR 'tʃeɪn(d)ʒraʊnd
AM 'tʃeɪndʒˌraʊnd
Changi
BR 'tʃaŋgi
AM 'tʃæŋ(g)i
Changsha
BR ˌtʃaŋ'ʃɑ:(r)
AM 'tʃæŋ'ʃa
channel
BR 'tʃanl, -z, -ɪŋ, -d
AM 'tʃænəl, -z, -ɪŋ, -d
channelise
BR 'tʃanlˌʌɪz, -ɪz, -ɪŋ, -d
AM 'tʃænlˌaɪz, -ɪz, -ɪŋ,
-d
channelize
BR 'tʃanlˌʌɪz, -ɪz, -ɪŋ, -d
AM 'tʃænlˌaɪz, -ɪz, -ɪŋ,
-d
Channing
BR 'tʃanɪŋ
AM 'tʃænɪŋ
Channon
BR 'tʃanən
AM 'tʃænən
chanson
BR 'ʃɒsɒ̃, 'ʃɒnsɒ̃,
'ʃɒnsɒn, -z
AM ʃan'sɒn, ʃan'san +,
-z
chanson de geste
BR ˌʃɒsɒ̃ də 'ʒɛst,
ˌʃɒnsɒ̃ +, ˌʃɒnsɒn +
AM ʃan'sɒn də 'ʒɛst,
ʃan'san +
chansons de geste
BR ˌʃɒsɒ̃(z) də 'ʒɛst,
ˌʃɒnsɒ̃(z) +,
ˌʃɒnsɒn(z) +

AM ʃanˈsɔn(z) də ˈʒɛst, ʃanˈsan(z) +

chant
BR tʃɑːnt, tʃant, -s, -ɪŋ, -ɪd
AM tʃænt, -z, -ɪŋ, -əd

Chantal
BR ˌʃɒnˈtal, ˌʃɑːnˈtal, ˌʃanˈtal, ˌʃɒnˈtɑːl, ˌʃɑːnˈtɑːl, ˌʃanˈtɑːl
AM ˌʃænˈtal, ʃanˈtal

chanter
BR tʃɑːntə(r), ˈtʃantə(r), -z
AM ˈtʃæn(t)ər, -z

chanterelle
BR ˌʃɑːntəˈrɛl, ˌʃantəˈrɛl, -z
AM ˌʃæn(t)əˈrɛl, ˌʃan(t)əˈrɛl, -z

chanteur
BR ˌʃɒnˈtəː(r), ˌʃɑːnˈtəː(r)
AM ˌʃanˈtər

chanteurs
BR ˌʃɒnˈtəːz, ˌʃɑːnˈtəːz
AM ˌʃanˈtərz

chanteuse
BR ˌʃɒnˈtəːz, ˌʃɑːnˈtəːz
AM ˌʃanˈtʊz

chanteuses
BR ˌʃɒnˈtəːz, ˌʃɒnˈtəːzɪz, ˌʃɑːnˈtəːz, ˌʃɑːnˈtəːzɪz
AM ˌʃanˈtʊz, ˌʃanˈtʊzəz

chantey
BR ˈʃantʲi, -ɪz
AM ˈʃæn(t)i, -z

chanticleer
BR ˈʃɑːntɪklɪə(r), ˈʃɒntɪklɪə(r), ˈʃantɪklɪə(r), ˈtʃɑːntɪklɪə(r), ˈtʃantɪklɪə(r), -z
AM ˈtʃæn(t)əˌklɪ(ə)r, -z

Chantilly
BR ʃanˈtɪli
AM ˌʃænˈtɪli

chantry
BR ˈtʃɑːntrʲi, ˈtʃantrʲi, -ɪz
AM ˈtʃæntri, -z

chanty
BR ˈʃantʲi, -ɪz
AM ˈʃæn(t)i, -z

Chanukkah
BR ˈhanʊkə(r), ˈxanʊkə(r), ˈhɑːnʊkə(r), ˈxɑːnʊkə(r)
AM ˈhanʊkə

chaology
BR keɪˈɒlədʒi
AM keɪˈɑːlədʒi

chaos
BR ˈkeɪɒs
AM ˈkeɪˌɑs, ˈkeɪˌɔs

chaotic
BR keɪˈɒtɪk
AM keɪˈɑːdɪk

chaotically
BR keɪˈɒtɪkli
AM keɪˈɑːdək(ə)li

chap
BR tʃap, -s, -ɪŋ, -t
AM tʃæp, -s, -ɪŋ, -t

chaparejos
BR ˌ(t)ʃapəˈreɪhəʊs
AM ˌʃæpəˈreɪəs

chaparral
BR ˌʃapəˈral
AM ˌʃæpəˈræl

chapati
BR tʃəˈpɑːtʲi, tʃəˈpatʲi, -ɪz
AM tʃəˈpɑdi, -z

chapatti
BR tʃəˈpɑːtʲi, tʃəˈpatʲi, -ɪz
AM tʃəˈpɑdi, -z

chapbook
BR ˈtʃapbʊk, -s
AM ˈtʃæpˌbʊk, -s

chape
BR ˈtʃeɪp, -s
AM ˈtʃeɪp, -s

chapeau-bras
BR ˌʃapəʊˈbrɑː(r), -z
AM ˌʃapoʊˈbrɑ, -z

chapel
BR ˈtʃapl, -z
AM ˈtʃæpəl, -z

Chapel-en-le-Frith
BR ˌtʃaplˌɛnləˈfrɪθ, ˌtʃaplˌɒnləˈfrɪθ
AM ˈtʃæpələnðəˈfrɪθ

chapelry
BR ˈtʃaplrʲi, -ɪz
AM ˈtʃæpəlri, -z

chaperon
BR ˈʃapərəʊn, -z, -ɪŋ, -d
AM ˈʃæpəˌroʊn, -z, -ɪŋ, -d

chaperonage
BR ˈʃapərəʊnɪdʒ
AM ˈʃæpəˌroʊnɪdʒ, ˌʃæpəˈroʊnɪdʒ

chaperone
BR ˈʃapərəʊn, -z, -ɪŋ, -d
AM ˈʃæpəˌroʊn, -z, -ɪŋ, -d

chapfallen
BR ˈtʃapˌfɔːlən
AM ˈtʃæpˌfɔlən, ˈtʃæpˌfɑlən

chaplain
BR ˈtʃaplɪn, -z
AM ˈtʃæplən, -z

chaplaincy
BR ˈtʃaplɪnsʲi, -ɪz
AM ˈtʃæplənsi, -z

chaplet
BR ˈtʃaplɪt, -s, -ɪd
AM ˈtʃæplət, -s, -əd

Chaplin
BR ˈtʃæplɪn
AM ˈtʃæplən

chapman
BR ˈtʃapmən
AM ˈtʃæpmən

chapmen
BR ˈtʃapmən
AM ˈtʃæpmən

chappal
BR ˈtʃapl, -z
AM ˈtʃæpəl, -z

Chappell
BR ˈtʃapl
AM ˈtʃæpəl

chappie
BR ˈtʃapʲi, -ɪz
AM ˈtʃæpi, -z

chappy
BR ˈtʃapʲi, -ɪz
AM ˈtʃæpi, -z

chapter
BR ˈtʃaptə(r), -z
AM ˈtʃæptər, -z

char
BR tʃɑː(r), -z, -ɪŋ, -d
AM ʃɑr, -z, -ɪŋ, -d

charabanc
BR ˈʃarəbaŋ, -z
AM ˈʃɛrəˌbæŋk, -z

char à bancs
BR ˈʃarəbaŋ
AM ˈʃɛrəˌbæŋk

characin
BR ˈkarəsɪn, -z
AM ˈkɛrəsən, -z

character
BR ˈkarɪktə(r), -z
AM ˈkɛr(ə)ktər, -z

characterful
BR ˈkarɪktəf(ʊ)l
AM ˈkɛr(ə)ktərfəl

characterfully
BR ˈkarɪktəf(ʊ)li, ˈkarɪktəfli
AM ˈkɛr(ə)ktərfəli

characterisation
BR ˌkarɪkt(ə)rʌɪˈzeɪʃn, -z
AM ˌkɛr(ə)ktərəˈzeɪʃən, ˌkɛr(ə)ktəˌrarˈzeɪʃən, -z

characterise
BR ˈkarɪktərʌɪz, -ɪz, -ɪŋ, -d
AM ˈkɛr(ə)ktəˌraɪz, -ɪz, -ɪŋ, -d

characteristic
BR ˌkarɪktəˈrɪstɪk, -s
AM ˌkɛr(ə)ktəˈrɪstɪk, -s

characteristically
BR ˌkarɪktəˈrɪstɪkli
AM ˌkɛr(ə)ktəˈrɪstək(ə)li

characterization
BR ˌkarɪkt(ə)rʌɪˈzeɪʃn, -z

Chaplin (AM) ˌkɛr(ə)ktərəˈzeɪʃən, ˌkɛr(ə)ktəˌrarˈzeɪʃən, -z

characterize
BR ˈkarɪktərʌɪz, -ɪz, -ɪŋ, -d
AM ˈkɛr(ə)ktəˌraɪz, -ɪz, -ɪŋ, -d

characterless
BR ˈkarɪktələs
AM ˈkɛr(ə)ktərˌləs

characterology
BR ˌkarɪktəˈrɒlədʒi
AM ˌkɛr(ə)ktəˈrɑlədʒi

charade
BR ʃəˈrɑːd, -z
AM ʃəˈreɪd, -z

charango
BR tʃəˈraŋgəʊ, -z
AM tʃəˈræŋgoʊ, -z

charas
BR ˈtʃɑːrəs
AM ˈtʃarəs

charbroil
BR ˈtʃɑːbrɔɪl, -z, -ɪŋ, -d
AM ˈtʃɑrˌbrɔɪl, -z, -ɪŋ, -d

charcoal
BR ˈtʃɑːkəʊl
AM ˈtʃɑrˌkoʊl

charcuterie
BR ʃɑːˈkuːt(ə)riː
AM ˌʃɑrˌkudəˈri

chard
BR tʃɑːd, -z
AM tʃɑrd, -z

Chardonnay
BR ˈʃɑːdəneɪ
AM ˈʃɑrdnˌeɪ

chare
BR tʃɛː(r), -z, -ɪŋ, -d
AM tʃɛ(ə)r, -z, -ɪŋ, -d

charge
BR tʃɑːdʒ, -ɪz, -ɪŋ, -d
AM tʃɑrdʒ, -əz, -ɪŋ, -d

chargeable
BR ˈtʃɑːdʒəbl
AM ˈtʃɑrdʒəbəl

chargeableness
BR ˈtʃɑːdʒəblnəs
AM ˈtʃɑrdʒəbəlnəs

chargeably
BR ˈtʃɑːdʒəbli
AM ˈtʃɑrdʒəbli

chargé d'affaires
BR ˌʃɑːʒeɪ daˈfɛː(r), + dəˈfɛː(r)
AM ˌʃɑrʒeɪ daˈfɛ(ə)r

chargehand
BR ˈtʃɑːdʒhand, -z
AM ˈtʃɑrdʒˌ(h)ænd, -z

charger
BR ˈtʃɑːdʒə(r), -z
AM ˈtʃɑrdʒər, -z

chargés d'affaires
BR ˌʃɑːʒeɪ daˈfɛːz, + dəˈfɛːz

AM ˌʃɑːrʒeɪ(z) dɑːˈfɛr(z)

charily
BR ˈtʃɛːrɪli
AM ˈtʃɛrəli

chariness
BR ˈtʃɛːrɪnɪs
AM ˈtʃɛrɪnɪs

Charing Cross
BR ˌtʃɑrɪŋ ˈkrɒs,
ˌtʃɛːrɪŋ +
AM ˌtʃɛrɪŋ ˈkrɔs,
ˌtʃɛrɪŋ ˈkrɑs

chariot
BR ˈtʃærɪət, -s
AM ˈtʃɛrɪət, -s

charioteer
BR ˌtʃærɪəˈtɪə(r), -z
AM ˌtʃɛrɪəˈtɪ(ə)r, -z

charisma
BR kəˈrɪzmə(r)
AM kəˈrɪzmə

charismatic
BR ˌkærɪzˈmatɪk
AM ˌkɛrəzˈmædɪk

charismatically
BR ˌkærɪzˈmatɪkli
AM ˌkɛrəzˈmædək(ə)li

Charisse
BR ʃəˈriːs
AM ʃəˈris

charitable
BR ˈtʃærɪtəbl
AM ˈtʃɛrədəbəl

charitableness
BR ˈtʃærɪtəblnəs
AM ˈtʃɛr(ə)dəbəlnəs

charitably
BR ˈtʃærɪtəbli
AM ˈtʃɛr(ə)dəbli

charity
BR ˈtʃærɪt|i, -ɪz
AM ˈtʃɛrədi, -z

charivari
BR ˌʃærɪˈvɑːr|i, -ɪz
AM ˌʃɪvəˈri, -z

charivaria
BR ˌʃærɪˈvɑːrɪə(r)
AM ˌʃɪvəˈrɪə

charlady
BR ˈtʃɑːˌleɪd|i, -ɪz
AM ˈtʃɑrˌleɪdi, -z

charlatan
BR ˈʃɑːlət(ə)n, -z
AM ˈʃɑrlədən, ˈʃɑrlətn, -z

charlatanism
BR ˈʃɑːlətənɪz(ə)m, ˈʃɑːlətn̩ɪz(ə)m
AM ˈʃɑrlədəˌnɪzəm, ˈʃɑrlətn̩ˌɪzəm

charlatanry
BR ˈʃɑːlət(ə)nri
AM ˈʃɑrlədənri, ˈʃɑrlətnri

Charlecote
BR ˈtʃɑːlkəʊt, ˈtʃɑːlkət
AM ˈtʃɑrl(ə)ˌkoʊt

Charlemagne
BR ˈʃɑːləmeɪn
AM ˈʃɑrləˌmeɪn

Charlene
BR ˈʃɑːliːn
AM ˈʃɑrˈlin

Charles
BR tʃɑːlz
AM tʃɑrlz

Charleston
BR ˈtʃɑːlst(ə)n, -z
AM ˈtʃɑrlstən, -z

charley horse
BR ˈtʃɑːli hɔːs
AM ˈtʃɑrli ˌhɔ(ə)rs

Charlie
BR ˈtʃɑːli
AM ˈtʃɑrli

charlie
BR ˈtʃɑːl|i, -ɪz
AM ˈtʃɑrli, -z

charlock
BR ˈtʃɑːlək, ˈtʃɑːlɒk
AM ˈtʃɑrˌlak, ˈtʃɑrlək

charlotte
BR ˈʃɑːlət, -s
AM ˈʃɑrlət, -s

Charlottenburg
BR ˈʃɑːˈlɒtnbəːg
AM ˈʃɑrˈladənˌbərg

charlotte russe
BR ˌʃɑːlət ˈruːs
AM ˌʃɑrˌlat ˈrus

charlottes russes
BR ˌʃɑːlət ˈruːs
AM ˌʃɑrˌlat ˈrus

Charlottetown
BR ˈʃɑːləttaʊn
AM ˈʃɑrlə(t)ˌtaʊn

Charlton
BR ˈtʃɑːlt(ə)n
AM ˈtʃɑrltən

charm
BR tʃɑːm, -z, -ɪŋ, -d
AM tʃɑrm, -z, -ɪŋ, -d

Charmaine
BR (ˌ)ʃɑːˈmeɪn
AM ˌʃɑrˈmeɪn

charmer
BR ˈtʃɑːmə(r), -z
AM ˈtʃɑrmər, -z

charmeuse
BR ʃɑːˈməːz
AM ˌʃɑrˈm(j)ʊz

Charmian
BR ˈʃɑːmɪən
AM ˈʃɑrmɪən

charming
BR ˈtʃɑːmɪŋ
AM ˈtʃɑrmɪŋ

charmingly
BR ˈtʃɑːmɪŋli
AM ˈtʃɑrmɪŋli

charmless
BR ˈtʃɑːmləs
AM ˈtʃɑrmləs

charmlessly
BR ˈtʃɑːmləsli
AM ˈtʃɑrmləsli

charmlessness
BR ˈtʃɑːmləsnəs
AM ˈtʃɑrmləsnəs

charnel
BR ˈtʃɑːnl, -z
AM ˈtʃɑrnəl, -z

Charnock
BR ˈtʃɑːnɒk, ˈtʃɑːnək
AM ˈtʃɑrnək

Charolais
BR ˈʃærəleɪ, -z
AM ˌʃɛrəˈleɪ, -z

Charollais
BR ˈʃærəleɪ, -z
AM ˌʃɛrəˈleɪ, -z

Charon
BR ˈkɛːrən, ˈkɛːrn̩, ˈkɛːrɒn
AM ˈkɛrən

charpoy
BR ˈtʃɑːpɔɪ, -z
AM ˈtʃɑrˌpɔɪ, -z

charr
BR tʃɑː(r)
AM tʃɑr

Charrington
BR ˈtʃɑrɪŋt(ə)n
AM ˈtʃɛrɪŋtən

charro
BR ˈtʃɑːrəʊ, -z
AM ˈtʃɑroʊ, -z

chart
BR tʃɑːt, -s, -ɪŋ, -ɪd
AM tʃɑr|t, -ts, -dɪŋ, -dəd

chartbuster
BR ˈtʃɑːtˌbʌstə(r), -z
AM ˈtʃɑrtˌbəstər, -z

charter
BR ˈtʃɑːt|ə(r), -əz, -(ə)rɪŋ, -əd
AM ˈtʃɑrdər, -z, -ɪŋ, -d

charterer
BR ˈtʃɑːt(ə)rə(r), -z
AM ˈtʃɑrdərər, -z

Charterhouse
BR ˈtʃɑːtəhaʊs
AM ˈtʃɑrdər,(h)aʊs

Charteris
BR ˈtʃɑːtərɪs, ˈtʃɑːtəz
AM ˈtʃɑrdərəs

Chartism
BR ˈtʃɑːtɪz(ə)m
AM ˈtʃɑrdɪzəm

Chartist
BR ˈtʃɑːtɪst, -s
AM ˈtʃɑrdəst, -s

Chartres
BR ˈʃɑːtr(ər)
AM ˈʃɑrt(rə)

chartreuse
BR ʃɑːˈtrəːz, -ɪz
AM ʃɑrˈtruz, ʃɑrˈtrus, -əz

Chartwell
BR ˈtʃɑːtw(ɛ)l
AM ˈtʃɑrt,wɛl

charwoman
BR ˈtʃɑːˌwʊmən
AM ˈtʃɑrˌwʊmən

charwomen
BR ˈtʃɑːˌwɪmɪn
AM ˈtʃɑrˌwɪmɨn

chary
BR ˈtʃɛːr|i, -ɪə(r), -ɪɪst
AM ˈtʃɛri, -ər, -ɪst

Charybdis
BR kəˈrɪbdɪs
AM kəˈrɪbdɪs, tʃəˈrɪbdɪs,

chase
BR tʃeɪs, -ɪz, -ɪŋ, -t
AM tʃeɪs, -ɪz, -ɪŋ, -t

chaser
BR ˈtʃeɪsə(r), -z
AM ˈtʃeɪsər, -z

Chasid
BR ˈhasɪd, ˈxasɪd
AM ˈhasɪd

Chasidim
BR ˈhasɪdɪm, ˈxasɪdɪm
AM ˈhasɪdɪm

Chasidism
BR ˈhasɪdɪz(ə)m, ˈxasɪdɪz(ə)m
AM ˈhasɪˌdɪzəm

chasm
BR ˈkaz(ə)m, -z
AM ˈkæzəm, -z

chasmic
BR ˈkazmɪk
AM ˈkæzmɪk

chasse
BR ʃas, ʃɑːs, -ɪz
AM ʃɑs, -əz

chassé
BR ʃaˈseɪ, ˈʃaseɪ, -z, -ɪŋ, -d
AM ʃɑˈseɪ, -z, -ɪŋ, -d

chasseur
BR ʃaˈsəː(r), -z
AM ʃɑˈsər, -z

chassis[1]
singular
BR ˈʃasi
AM ˈʃæsi, ˈʃæsi

chassis[2]
plural
BR ˈʃasɪz
AM ˈtʃæsiz, ˈʃæsiz

chaste
BR tʃeɪst
AM tʃeɪst

chastely
BR ˈtʃeɪstli
AM ˈtʃeɪs(t)li

chasten
BR ˈtʃeɪs|n, -nz, -nɪŋ \ -nɪŋ, -nd
AM ˈtʃeɪs|n, -nz, -(ə)nɪŋ, -nd

chastener
BR 'tʃeɪsnə(r), -z
AM 'tʃeɪsənər, -z
chasteness
BR 'tʃeɪstnɪs
AM tʃeɪs(t)nɪs
chastise
BR tʃa'staɪz, tʃə'staɪz, -ɪz, -ɪŋ, -d
AM 'tʃæs,taɪz, tʃæs'taɪz, -ɪz, -ɪŋ, -d
chastisement
BR tʃa'staɪzm(ə)nt, tʃə'staɪzm(ə)nt, 'tʃastɪzm(ə)nt, -s
AM tʃæs'taɪzmənt, 'tʃæs,taɪzmənt, -s
chastiser
BR tʃa'staɪzə(r), tʃə'staɪzə(r), -z
AM 'tʃæstaɪzər, -z
chastity
BR 'tʃastɪti
AM 'tʃæstədi
chasuble
BR 'tʃazjʊbl, -z
AM 'tʃæzəbəl, 'tʃæsəbəl, -z
chat
BR tʃat, -s, -ɪŋ, -ɪd
AM 'tʃæ|t, -ts, -dɪŋ, -dəd
Chataway
BR 'tʃatəweɪ
AM 'tʃædəweɪ
chateau
BR 'ʃatəʊ, -z
AM ʃæ'toʊ, -z
chateaubriand
BR ˌʃatəʊbrɪ'ɒn(d), ˌʃatəʊbrɪ'ɒ̃, -z
AM ʃæˌtoʊbri'ɒn, ʃæˌtoʊbrɪ̃'ɑn, -z
chateaux
BR 'ʃatəʊ(z)
AM ʃæ'toʊ(z)
châtelaine
BR 'ʃatəleɪn, 'ʃatļeɪn, -z
AM ˌʃædl'ɛn, 'ʃædlˌeɪn, -z
Chater
BR 'tʃeɪtə(r)
AM 'tʃeɪdər
Chatham
BR 'tʃatəm
AM 'tʃædəm
chatline
BR 'tʃatlʌɪn, -z
AM 'tʃæt,laɪn, -z
chatshow
BR 'tʃat-ʃəʊ, -z
AM 'tʃæt,ʃoʊ, -z
Chattanooga
BR ˌtʃatn'uːgə(r), ˌtʃatə'nuːgə(r)
AM ˌtʃætn'ugə
chattel
BR 'tʃatl, -z

AM 'tʃædl, -z
chatter
BR 'tʃatlə(r), -əz, -(ə)rɪŋ, -əd
AM 'tʃædər, -z, -ɪŋ, -d
chatterbox
BR 'tʃatəbɒks, -ɪz
AM 'tʃædər,bɑks, -əz
chatterer
BR 'tʃat(ə)rə(r), -z
AM 'tʃædərər, -z
Chatterjee
BR 'tʃatədʒiː
AM 'tʃædər,dʒi
Chatterji
BR 'tʃatədʒiː
AM 'tʃædər,dʒi
Chatterley
BR 'tʃatəli
AM 'tʃædərli
Chatterton
BR 'tʃatət(ə)n
AM 'tʃædərtən
chattery
BR 'tʃat(ə)ri
AM 'tʃædəri
chattily
BR 'tʃatɪli
AM 'tʃædəli
chattiness
BR 'tʃatmɪs
AM 'tʃædinɪs
Chatto
BR 'tʃatəʊ
AM 'tʃædoʊ
chatty
BR 'tʃat|i, -ɪə(r), -ɪɪst
AM 'tʃædi, -ər, -ɪst
Chatwin
BR 'tʃatwɪn
AM 'tʃæt,wɪn
Chaucer
BR 'tʃɔːsə(r)
AM 'tʃɔsər, 'tʃɑsər
Chaucerian
BR tʃɔː'sɪərɪən
AM tʃɔ'sɛrɪən, tʃɔ'sɪrɪən, tʃɑ'sɛrɪən, tʃɑ'sɪrɪən
chaud-froid
BR 'ʃəʊfrwɑː(r), ˌʃəʊ'frwɑː(r), -z
AM ˌʃoʊ'frwɑ, -z
Chaudhury
BR 'tʃaʊd(ə)ri
AM 'tʃaʊdəri
chaudron
BR 'tʃɔːdrən, -z
AM 'tʃɑdrən, 'tʃɔdrən, -z
chauds-froids
BR 'ʃəʊfrwɑː(r)z, ˌʃəʊ'frwɑː(r)z
AM 'ʃoʊ'frwɑz
chauffeur
BR 'ʃəʊfə(r), -z, -ɪŋ, -d

AM 'ʃoʊfər, ʃoʊ'fər, -z, -ɪŋ, -d
chauffeuse
BR ʃəʊ'fəːz, -ɪz
AM ˌʃoʊ'fəz, -əz
chaulmoogra
BR tʃɔːl'muːgrə(r), -z
AM tʃɔl'mugrə, tʃɑl'mugrə, -z
chausses
BR ʃəʊs
AM ʃoʊs
chautauqua
BR ʃə'tɔːkwə(r), -z
AM ʃə'tɔkwə, ʃə'takwə, -z
chauvinism
BR 'ʃəʊvɪnɪz(ə)m
AM 'ʃoʊvəˌnɪzəm
chauvinist
BR 'ʃəʊvɪnɪst, -s
AM 'ʃoʊvənəst, -s
chauvinistic
BR ˌʃəʊvɪ'nɪstɪk
AM ˌʃoʊvə'nɪstɪk
chauvinistically
BR ˌʃəʊvɪ'nɪstɪkli
AM ˌʃoʊvə'nɪstɪk(ə)li
Chavasse
BR ʃə'vas
AM ʃə'vɑs
Chavez
BR 'ʃavɛz
AM ˌʃɑ'vɛz
chaw
BR tʃɔː(r), -z, -ɪŋ, -d
AM tʃɔ, tʃɑ, -z, -ɪŋ, -d
chayote
BR tʃʌɪ'əʊt|i, -ɪz
AM tʃaɪ'oʊdi, tʃi'joʊdi, -z
Chaz
BR tʃaz
AM tʃæz
Che
BR tʃeɪ
AM (t)ʃeɪ
Cheadle
BR 'tʃiːdl
AM 'tʃidəl
Cheam
BR tʃiːm
AM tʃim
cheap
BR tʃiːp, -ə(r), -ɪst
AM tʃip, -ər, -ɪst
cheapen
BR 'tʃiːp|ə(n)n, -(ə)nz, -ənɪŋ\-nɪŋ, -(ə)nd
AM 'tʃip|ən, -ənz, -(ə)nɪŋ, -ənd
cheapie
BR 'tʃiːp|i, -ɪz
AM 'tʃipi, -z
cheapish
BR 'tʃiːpɪʃ
AM 'tʃipɪʃ

cheapjack
BR 'tʃiːpdʒak, -s
AM 'tʃip,dʒæk, -s
cheaply
BR 'tʃiːpli
AM 'tʃipli
cheapness
BR 'tʃiːpnɪs
AM 'tʃipnɪs
cheapo
BR 'tʃiːpəʊ, -z
AM 'tʃipoʊ, -z
Cheapside
BR 'tʃiːpsʌɪd
AM 'tʃip,saɪd
cheapskate
BR 'tʃiːpskeɪt, -s
AM 'tʃip,skeɪt, -s
cheat
BR tʃiːt, -s, -ɪŋ, -ɪd
AM tʃi|t, -ts, -dɪŋ, -dɪd
cheater
BR tʃiːtə(r), -z
AM tʃidər, -z
cheatingly
BR tʃiːtɪŋli
AM tʃidɪŋli
Chechen
BR 'tʃɛtʃɛn, -z
AM 'tʃɛtʃɛn, -z
Chechnya
BR 'tʃɛtʃnjɑː(r), ˌtʃɛtʃ'njɑː(r)
AM 'tʃɛtʃnɪə
check
BR tʃɛk, -s, -ɪŋ, -t
AM tʃɛk, -s, -ɪŋ, -t
checkable
BR 'tʃɛkəbl
AM 'tʃɛkəbəl
checkbook
BR 'tʃɛkbʊk, -s
AM 'tʃɛk,bʊk, -s
checker
BR 'tʃɛkə(r), -z
AM 'tʃɛkər, -z
checkerberry
BR 'tʃɛkəˌbɛr|i, -ɪz
AM 'tʃɛkərˌbɛri, -z
checkerboard
BR 'tʃɛkəbɔːd, -z
AM 'tʃɛkərˌbɔ(ə)rd, -z
checkerman
BR 'tʃɛkəmən
AM 'tʃɛkərmən
checkermen
BR 'tʃɛkəmən
AM 'tʃɛkərmən
Checkland
BR 'tʃɛklənd
AM 'tʃɛklənd
Checkley
BR 'tʃɛkli
AM 'tʃɛkli
checklist
BR 'tʃɛklɪst, -s
AM 'tʃɛkˌlɪst, -s

checkmark
BR ˈtʃɛkmɑːk, -s
AM ˈtʃɛkˌmɑrk, -s

checkmate
BR ˈtʃɛkmeɪt,
ˌtʃɛkˈmeɪt, -s, -ɪŋ, -ɪd
AM ˈtʃɛkˌmeɪt, -ts, -dɪŋ,
-dɪd

checkout
BR ˈtʃɛkaʊt, -s
AM ˈtʃɛkˌaʊt, -s

checkpoint
BR ˈtʃɛkpɔɪnt, -s
AM ˈtʃɛkˌpɔɪnt, -s

checkrail
BR ˈtʃɛkreɪl, -z
AM ˈtʃɛkˌreɪl, -z

checkrein
BR ˈtʃɛkreɪn, -z
AM ˈtʃɛkˌreɪn, -z

checkroom
BR ˈtʃɛkruːm,
ˈtʃɛkrʊm, -z
AM ˈtʃɛkˌrum,
ˈtʃɛkˌrʊm, -z

checkup
BR ˈtʃɛkʌp, -s
AM ˈtʃɛkˌəp, -s

check-valve
BR ˈtʃɛkvalv, -z
AM ˈtʃɛkˌvælv, -z

checkweighman
BR ˈtʃɛkweɪmən
AM ˈtʃɛkˌweɪmən

checkweighmen
BR ˈtʃɛkweɪmən
AM ˈtʃɛkˌweɪmən

cheddar
BR ˈtʃɛdə(r), -z
AM ˈtʃɛdər, -z

Chedzoy
BR ˈtʃɛdzɔɪ
AM ˈtʃɛdzɔɪ

cheek
BR tʃiːk, -s, -ɪŋ, -t
AM tʃik, -s, -ɪŋ, -t

cheekbone
BR ˈtʃiːkbəʊn, -z
AM ˈtʃikˌboʊn, -z

cheekily
BR ˈtʃiːkɪli
AM ˈtʃikɪli

cheekiness
BR ˈtʃiːkɪnɪs
AM ˈtʃikɪnɪs

cheeky
BR ˈtʃiːkǀi, -ɪə(r), -ɪɪst
AM ˈtʃiki, -ər, -ɪst

cheep
BR tʃiːp, -s, -ɪŋ, -t
AM tʃip, -s, -ɪŋ, -t

cheer
BR tʃɪə(r), -z, -ɪŋ, -d
AM tʃɪ(ə)r, -z, -ɪŋ, -d

cheerful
BR ˈtʃɪəf(ʊ)l
AM ˈtʃɪrfəl

cheerfully
BR ˈtʃɪəfʊli, ˈtʃɪəfǀi
AM ˈtʃɪrfəli

cheerfulness
BR ˈtʃɪəf(ʊ)lnəs
AM ˈtʃɪrfəlnəs

cheerily
BR ˈtʃɪərɪli
AM ˈtʃɪrɪli

cheeriness
BR ˈtʃɪərɪnɪs
AM ˈtʃɪrɪnɪs

cheerio
BR ˌtʃɪərɪˈəʊ
AM ˌtʃɪriˈoʊ

cheerleader
BR ˈtʃɪəˌliːdə(r), -z
AM ˈtʃɪrˌlidər, -z

cheerless
BR ˈtʃɪələs
AM ˈtʃɪrlɪs

cheerlessly
BR ˈtʃɪələsli
AM ˈtʃɪrlɪsli

cheerlessness
BR ˈtʃɪələsnəs
AM ˈtʃɪrlɪsnɪs

cheerly
BR ˈtʃɪəli
AM ˈtʃɪrli

cheers
BR tʃɪəz
AM tʃɪ(ə)rz

cheery
BR ˈtʃɪərǀi, -ɪɪst
AM ˈtʃɪri, -ɪst

cheese
BR tʃiːz, -ɪz, -d
AM tʃiz, -ɪz, -d

cheeseboard
BR ˈtʃiːzbɔːd, -z
AM ˈtʃizˌbɔːrd, -z

cheeseburger
BR ˈtʃiːzˌbəːgə(r), -z
AM ˈtʃizˌbɜrgər, -z

cheesecake
BR ˈtʃiːzkeɪk, -s
AM ˈtʃizˌkeɪk, -s

cheesecloth
BR ˈtʃiːzklɒǀθ, -θs\-ðz
AM ˈtʃizˌklɔǀθ,
ˈtʃizˌklɑǀθ, -θs\-ðz

cheesemaker
BR ˈtʃiːzˌmeɪkə(r), -z
AM ˈtʃizˌmeɪkər, -z

cheesemaking
BR ˈtʃiːzˌmeɪkɪŋ
AM ˈtʃizˌmeɪkɪŋ

Cheeseman
BR ˈtʃiːzmən
AM ˈtʃizmən

cheesemonger
BR ˈtʃiːzˌmʌŋgə(r), -z
AM ˈtʃizˌmɑŋgər,
ˈtʃizˌməngər, -z

cheeseparing
BR ˈtʃiːzˌpɛːrɪŋ, -z

AM ˈtʃiːzˌpɛrɪŋ, -z

cheesewood
BR ˈtʃiːzwʊd, -z
AM ˈtʃizˌwʊd, -z

Cheesewright
BR ˈtʃiːzraɪt
AM ˈtʃizˌraɪt

cheesily
BR ˈtʃiːzɪli
AM ˈtʃizɪli

cheesiness
BR ˈtʃiːzɪnɪs
AM ˈtʃizɪnɪs

cheesy
BR ˈtʃiːzi
AM ˈtʃizi

cheetah
BR ˈtʃiːtə(r), -z
AM ˈtʃidə, -z

Cheetham
BR ˈtʃiːtəm
AM ˈtʃidəm

chef
BR ʃɛf, -s
AM ʃɛf, -s

chef-d'œuvre
BR ˌʃeɪˈdəːv(rər), -z
AM ˌʃɛfˈdəvr(ə), -z

chefs-d'œuvre
BR ˌʃeɪˈdəːv(rər), -z
AM ˌʃɛf ˈdəvr(ə), -z

Chegwin
BR ˈtʃɛgwɪn
AM ˈtʃɛgwən

Cheka
BR ˈtʃɛkə(r)
AM ˈtʃɛkə
RUS tʃʲiˈka

Cheke
BR tʃiːk
AM tʃik

Chekhov
BR ˈtʃɛkɒf, ˈtʃɛkɒv
AM ˈtʃɛkɔv, ˈtʃɛkɔf,
ˈtʃɛkɑv, ˈtʃɛkɑf

Chekhovian
BR tʃɛˈkəʊvɪən
AM tʃɛˈkoʊviən

chela[1]
claw
BR ˈkiːlə(r)
AM ˈkilə

chela[2]
disciple
BR ˈtʃeɪlə(r), -z
AM ˈtʃeɪˌlɑ, -z

chelae
BR ˈkiːliː
AM ˈkili, ˈkiˌlaɪ

chelate
BR ˈkiːleɪt, -s
AM ˈkiˌleɪt, -s

chelation
BR kiːˈleɪʃn
AM kiˈleɪʃən

chelicera
BR kəˈlɪs(ə)rə(r)

AM kəˈlɪsərə

chelicerae
BR kəˈlɪs(ə)riː
AM kəˈlɪsəri

Chelicerata
BR kəˌlɪsəˈreɪtə(r)
AM kəˌlɪsəˈrɑdə

Chellean
BR ˈʃɛlɪən
AM ˈʃɛliən

Chellian
BR ˈʃɛlɪən
AM ˈʃɛliən

Chelmer
BR ˈtʃɛlmə(r)
AM ˈtʃɛlmər

Chelmsford
BR ˈtʃɛlmzfəd
AM ˈtʃɛlmsfərd

chelonian
BR kɪˈləʊnɪən, -z
AM kəˈloʊniən, -z

Chelsea
BR ˈtʃɛlsi
AM ˈtʃɛlsi

Cheltenham
BR ˈtʃɛltnəm,
ˈtʃɛltnəm
AM ˈtʃɛltnˌhæm,
ˈtʃɛltnəm

Chelyabinsk
BR ˌtʃɛljəˈbɪnsk
AM ˌtʃəˈljɑbɪnsk
RUS tʃʲiˈlʲiˈabʲinsk

chemical
BR ˈkɛmɪkl, -z
AM ˈkɛməkəl, -z

chemically
BR ˈkɛmɪkli
AM ˈkɛmək(ə)li

chemilumines-
cence
BR ˌkɛmɪˌluːmɪˈnɛsns
AM ˌkɛmiˌluməˈnɛsns

chemiluminescent
BR ˌkɛmɪˌluːmɪˈnɛsnt
AM ˌkɛmiˌluməˈnɛsnt

chemin de fer
BR ʃəˌman də ˈfɛː(r)
AM ʃəˌmɑn də ˈfɛ(ə)r

chemins de fer
BR ʃəˌman də ˈfɛː(r)
AM ʃəˌman(z) də
ˈfɛ(ə)r

chemise
BR ʃəˈmiːz, -ɪz
AM ʃəˈmiz, -ɪz

chemisorption
BR ˌkɛmɪˈsɔːpʃn
AM ˌkɛmiˈsɔrpʃən

chemist
BR ˈkɛmɪst, -s
AM ˈkɛməst, -s

chemistry
BR ˈkɛmɪstri
AM ˈkɛməstri

Chemnitz
BR ˈkɛmnɪts
AM ˈkɛmnɪts

chemosyntheses
BR ˌkiːmə(ʊ)ˈsɪnθɪsiːz,
ˌkɛmə(ʊ)sɪnθɪsiːz
AM ˌkimoʊˈsɪnθəsiz,
ˌkɛmoʊˈsɪnθəsiz

chemosynthesis
BR ˌkiːmə(ʊ)ˈsɪnθɪsɪs,
ˌkɛmə(ʊ)sɪnθɪsɪs
AM ˌkimoʊˈsɪnθəsəs,
ˌkɛmoʊˈsɪnθəsəs

chemotaxis
BR ˌkiːmə(ʊ)ˈtaksɪs,
ˌkɛmə(ʊ)taksɪs
AM ˌkimoʊˈtæksɪs,
ˌkɛmoʊˈtæksɪs

chemotherapist
BR ˌkiːmə(ʊ)ˈθɛrəpɪst,
ˌkɛmə(ʊ)θɛrəpɪst, -s
AM ˌkimoʊˈθɛrəpəst,
ˌkɛmoʊˈθɛrəpəst, -s

chemotherapy
BR ˌkiːmə(ʊ)ˈθɛrəpi,
ˌkɛmə(ʊ)θɛrəpi
AM ˌkimoʊˈθɛrəpi,
ˌkɛmoʊˈθɛrəpi

chemurgic
BR kɛˈmaːdʒɪk
AM kəˈmərdʒɪk

chemurgy
BR ˈkɛməːdʒi
AM ˈkɛmərdʒi

Chenevix
BR ˈ(t)ʃenəvɪks
AM ˈ(t)ʃenəvɪks

Cheney
BR ˈtʃeɪni, ˈtʃiːni
AM ˈtʃeɪni, ˈtʃini

chenille
BR ʃəˈniːl
AM ʃəˈnil

cheongsam
BR ˌtʃɒŋˈsam,
tʃɪˌɒŋˈsam, -z
AM ˌtʃɒŋˈsam,
ˈtʃaŋˌsam, -z

Cheops
BR ˈkiːɒps
AM ˈkiˌɑps

Chepstow
BR ˈtʃɛpstəʊ
AM ˈtʃɛpstoʊ

cheque
BR tʃɛk, -s
AM tʃɛk, -s

chequebook
BR ˈtʃɛkbʊk, -s
AM ˈtʃɛkˌbʊk, -s

chequer
BR ˈtʃɛkə(r), -z, -d
AM ˈtʃɛkər, -z, -d

chequerboard
BR ˈtʃɛkəbɔːd
AM ˈtʃɛkərˌbɔ(ə)rd

Chequers
BR ˈtʃɛkəz

AM ˈtʃɛkərz

Cher
BR ʃɛː(r)
AM ʃɛ(ə)r

Cherbourg
BR ˈʃəːbɔːg, ˈʃɛːbɔːg,
ˈʃəːbʊəg, ˈʃɛːbʊəg
AM ˈ(t)ʃɛrˌbʊ(ə)rg

Cherenkov
BR tʃɪˈrɛŋkɒf,
tʃɪˈrɛŋkɒv
AM tʃəˈrɛŋˌkɒv,
tʃəˈrɛŋˌkɔf,
tʃəˈrɛŋˌkɑv,
tʃəˈrɛŋˌkɑf

Chérie
BR ʃəˈriː, ʃɛˈriː
AM ʃəˈri, ˈʃɛri

cherish
BR ˈtʃɛr|ɪʃ, -ɪʃɪz, -ɪʃɪŋ,
-ɪʃt
AM ˈtʃɛrəʃ, -əz, -ɪŋ, -t

cherishable
BR ˈtʃɛrɪʃəbl
AM ˈtʃɛrəʃəbəl

Chernobyl
BR tʃəˈnɒbl, tʃəˈnəʊbl,
ˈtʃəːnə(ʊ)bɪl
AM tʃərˈnoʊbəl,
tʃɛrˈnoʊbəl

chernozem
BR ˈtʃəːnə(ʊ)zɛm
AM ˈtʃɛrnəˌzɛm

Cherokee
BR ˈtʃɛrəkiː, ˌtʃɛrəˈkiː,
-z
AM ˈtʃɛrəki, -z

cheroot
BR ʃəˈruːt, -s
AM ʃəˈrut, -s

cherry
BR ˈtʃɛr|i, -ɪz
AM ˈtʃɛri, -z

cherrystone
BR ˈtʃɛrɪstəʊn
AM ˈtʃɛriˌstoʊn

cherrywood
BR ˈtʃɛrɪwʊd
AM ˈtʃɛriˌwʊd

chersonese
BR ˈkəːsəniːs,
ˌkəːsəˈniːs, ˈkəːsəniːz,
ˌkəːsəˈniːz
AM ˈkɛrsəˌniz,
ˈkɛrsəˌnis

chert
BR tʃəːt, -s
AM tʃɛ(ə)rt, -s

Chertsey
BR ˈtʃəːtsi
AM ˈtʃərtsi

cherty
BR ˈtʃəːti
AM ˈtʃɛrdi

cherub
BR ˈtʃɛrəb, -z
AM ˈtʃɛrəb, -z

cherubic
BR tʃɪˈruːbɪk,
tʃɛˈruːbɪk, tʃɪˈrubɪk,
tʃɛˈrubɪk
AM tʃəˈrubɪk,
tʃɛˈrubɪk

cherubically
BR tʃɪˈruːbɪkli,
tʃɛˈruːbɪkli,
tʃɪˈrubɪkli,
tʃɛˈrubɪkli
AM tʃəˈrubək(ə)li,
tʃɛˈrubək(ə)li

cherubim
BR ˈtʃɛrəbɪm
AM ˈtʃɛrəbɪm

Cherubini
BR ˌkɛrʊˈbiːni
AM ˌkərəˈbini

chervil
BR ˈtʃəːv(ɪ)l
AM ˈtʃərvəl

Cherwell
BR ˈtʃɑːw(ɛ)l
AM ˈtʃɛrˌwɛl

Cheryl
BR ˈ(t)ʃɛrɪl, ˈ(t)ʃɛrl̩
AM ˈʃɛrəl

Chesapeake
BR ˈtʃɛsəpiːk
AM ˈtʃɛsəˌpik

Chesham
BR ˈtʃɛʃ(ə)m
AM ˈtʃɛʃəm

Cheshire
BR ˈtʃɛʃ(ɪ)ə(r)
AM ˈtʃɛʃər

Cheshunt
BR ˈtʃɛsnt
AM ˈtʃɛsnt

Chesil Beach
BR ˌtʃɛzl ˈbiːtʃ
AM ˌtʃɛzəl ˈbitʃ

Chesney
BR ˈtʃɛzni, ˈtʃɛsni
AM ˈtʃɛzni, ˈtʃɛsni

chess
BR tʃɛs
AM tʃɛs

chessboard
BR ˈtʃɛsbɔːd, -z
AM ˈtʃɛsˌbɔ(ə)rd, -z

chessel
BR ˈtʃɛsl, -z
AM ˈtʃɛsəl, -z

chessman
BR ˈtʃɛsman, ˈtʃɛsmən
AM ˈtʃɛsˌmæn,
ˈtʃɛsmən

chessmen
BR ˈtʃɛsmɛn, ˈtʃɛsmən
AM ˈtʃɛsmɛn, ˈtʃɛsmən

chest
BR tʃɛst, -s
AM tʃɛst, -s

Chester
BR ˈtʃɛstə(r)
AM ˈtʃɛstər

cherubic
BR tʃɪˈruːbɪk,

chesterfield
BR ˈtʃɛstəfiːld, -z
AM ˈtʃɛstərˌfild, -z

**Chester-le-
Street**
BR ˌtʃɛstəlɪˈstriːt
AM ˌtʃɛstərləˈstrit

Chesterton
BR ˈtʃɛstət(ə)n
AM ˈtʃɛstərtən

chestily
BR ˈtʃɛstɪli
AM ˈtʃɛstəli

chestiness
BR ˈtʃɛstɪnɪs
AM ˈtʃɛstɪnɪs

chestnut
BR ˈtʃɛs(t)nʌt, -s
AM ˈtʃɛs(t)ˌnət, -s

chesty
BR ˈtʃɛst|i, -ɪə(r), -ɪɪst
AM ˈtʃɛsti, -ər, -ɪst

Chetham
BR ˈtʃiːtəm, ˈtʃɛtəm
AM ˈtʃɛdəm, ˈtʃidəm

Chetnik
BR ˈtʃɛtnɪk, -s
AM ˈtʃɛtnɪk, -s

Chetwode
BR ˈtʃɛtwʊd
AM ˈtʃɛtˌwʊd

Chetwyn
BR ˈtʃɛtwɪn
AM ˈtʃɛtwən

Chetwynd
BR ˈtʃɛtwɪnd
AM ˈtʃɛtwənd

chevalet
BR ˌʃɛvəˈleɪ
AM ˌʃɛvəˈleɪ, ʃəˈvæleɪ

cheval glass
BR ʃəˈval glɑːs, + glas,
-ɪz
AM ʃəˈvæl ˌglæs, -ɪz

Chevalier
surname
BR ʃɪˈvalɪeɪ
AM ʃəˈvælˌjeɪ,
ʃəˌvælˈjeɪ

chevalier
BR ˌʃɛvəˈlɪə(r), -z
AM ˌʃɛvəˈlɪ(ə)r, -z

Chevening
BR ˈtʃiːvnɪŋ
AM ˈtʃiv(ə)nɪŋ

chevet
BR ʃəˈveɪ, -z
AM ʃəˈveɪ, -z

Chevette®
BR ʃəˈvɛt, -s
AM ʃəˈvɛt, -s

Chevington
BR ˈtʃɛvɪŋt(ə)n
AM ˈtʃɛvɪŋtən

Cheviot
BR ˈtʃiːvɪət, ˈtʃɛvɪət, -s
AM ˈʃɛviət, -s

cheviot
BR 'tʃiːviət, 'tʃɛvɪət
AM 'ʃɛviət

chèvre
BR 'ʃɛvrə(r), -z
AM 'ʃɛvrə, -z

Chevrolet®
BR 'ʃɛvrəleɪ, -z
AM ,ʃɛvrə'leɪ, -z

chevron
BR 'ʃɛvr(ə)n, -z
AM 'ʃɛvrən, -z

chevrotain
BR 'ʃɛvrəteɪn, -z
AM 'ʃɛvrə,teɪn, -z

Chevy
Chevrolet
BR 'ʃɛv|i, -ɪz
AM 'ʃɛvi, -z

chevy
chivvy
BR 'tʃɛv|i, -ɪz, -ɪɪŋ, -ɪd
AM 'tʃɪvi, -z, -ɪŋ, -d

chew
BR tʃuː, -z, -ɪŋ, -d
AM tʃu, -z, -ɪŋ, -d

chewable
BR 'tʃuːəbl
AM 'tʃuəbəl

chewer
BR 'tʃuːə(r), -z
AM 'tʃuər, -z

chewiness
BR 'tʃuːɪnɪs
AM 'tʃuinɪs

chewy
BR 'tʃuː|i, -ɪə(r), -ɪɪst
AM 'tʃui, -ər, -ɪɪst

Cheyenne
BR (,)ʃʌɪ'an
AM ,ʃaɪ'æn, ,ʃaɪ'ɛn

Cheyne
BR 'tʃeɪni
AM 'tʃeɪni

Cheyne-Stokes
BR ,tʃeɪn'stəʊks
AM ,tʃeɪn(i)'stoʊks

chez
BR ʃeɪ
AM ʃeɪ

chez nous
BR ,ʃeɪ 'nuː
AM ,ʃeɪ 'nu

chi
BR kʌɪ, -z
AM kaɪ, -z

chiack
BR 'tʃʌɪak, -s, -ɪŋ, -t
AM 'tʃaɪək, -s, -ɪŋ, -t

Chiang Kai-shek
BR ,tʃaŋ kʌɪ'ʃɛk
AM ,(t)ʃæŋ ,kaɪ'ʃɛk

Chiangmai
BR tʃɪ,aŋ'mʌɪ
AM ,(t)ʃ(i)æŋ'maɪ

Chianti
BR kɪ'anti

AM ki'an(t)i

Chiapas
BR tʃɪ'apəs
AM tʃi'apəs, 'tʃapəs

chiaroscuro
BR kɪ,aːrə'sk(j)ʊərəʊ, -z
AM kjarə'skʊroʊ, -z

chiasma
BR kʌɪ'azmə(r)
AM kaɪ'æzmə

chiasmus
BR kʌɪ'azməs
AM kaɪ'æzməs

chiastic
BR kʌɪ'astɪk
AM kaɪ'æstɪk

Chibcha
BR 'tʃɪbtʃə(r), -z
AM 'tʃɪbtʃə, -z

Chibchan
BR 'tʃɪbtʃən
AM 'tʃɪbtʃən

chibouk
BR tʃɪ'buːk, -s
AM ʃə'buk, ʃə'bʊk, -s

chic
BR ʃiːk
AM ʃik

Chicago
BR ʃɪ'kaːgəʊ
AM ʃɪ'kɔgoʊ, ʃɪ'kagoʊ

Chicagoan
BR ʃɪ'kaːgəʊən
AM ʃɪ'kɔgəwən, ʃɪ'kagəwən

chicana
BR (t)ʃɪ'kaːnə(r), -z
AM tʃɪ'kanɑ, -z

chicane
BR ʃɪ'keɪn, -z
AM ʃə'keɪn, -z

chicanery
BR ʃɪ'keɪn(ə)r|i, -ɪz
AM ʃə'keɪn(ə)ri, -z

chicano
BR (t)ʃɪ'kaːnəʊ, -z
AM (t)ʃɪ'kanoʊ, -z

Chichén Itzá
BR ,tʃɪtʃ(ə)n 'ɪtsə(r)
AM tʃi,tʃɛn it'sa

Chichester
BR 'tʃɪtʃɪstə(r)
AM 'tʃɪtʃəstər

Chichewa
BR tʃɪ'tʃeɪwə(r)
AM tʃə'tʃeɪwə

chichi
BR 'ʃiː'ʃi
AM 'tʃi,tʃi

Chichimec
BR 'tʃiː,tʃɪmɛk
AM 'tʃitʃə,mɛk

chick
BR tʃɪk, -s
AM tʃɪk, -s

chickabiddy
BR 'tʃɪkə,bɪd|i, -ɪz
AM 'tʃɪkə,bɪdi, -z

chickadee
BR 'tʃɪkədiː, -z
AM 'tʃɪkɪdi, -z

chickaree
BR 'tʃɪkəriː, -z
AM 'tʃɪkəri, -z

Chickasaw
BR 'tʃɪkəsɔː(r)
AM 'tʃɪkə,sɔ, 'tʃɪkə,sa

chicken
BR 'tʃɪk|(ɪ)n, -(ɪ)nz, -ɲɪŋ\-ɪnɪŋ, -(ɪ)nd
AM 'tʃɪkən, -z

chickenfeed
BR 'tʃɪk(ɪ)nfiːd
AM 'tʃɪkən,fid

chickenpox
BR 'tʃɪk(ɪ)npɒks
AM 'tʃɪkən,paks

chickling
BR 'tʃɪklɪŋ, -z
AM 'tʃɪklɪŋ, -z

chickpea
BR 'tʃɪkpiː, -z
AM 'tʃɪk,pi, -z

chickweed
BR 'tʃɪkwiːd
AM 'tʃɪk,wid

chicle
BR 'tʃɪkl
AM 'tʃɪkəl

chicly
BR 'ʃiːkli
AM 'ʃikli

chicness
BR 'ʃiːknɪs
AM 'ʃiknɪs

chicory
BR 'tʃɪk(ə)ri
AM 'tʃɪkəri

chid
BR tʃɪd
AM tʃɪd

chide
BR tʃʌɪd, -z, -ɪŋ, -ɪd
AM tʃaɪd, -z, -ɪŋ, -ɪd

chider
BR 'tʃʌɪdə(r), -z
AM 'tʃaɪdər, -z

chidingly
BR 'tʃʌɪdɪŋli
AM 'tʃaɪdɪŋli

chief
BR tʃiːf, -s
AM tʃif, -s

chiefdom
BR 'tʃiːfdəm, -z
AM 'tʃifdəm, -z

chiefly
BR 'tʃiːfli
AM 'tʃifli

chieftain
BR 'tʃiːft(ə)n, -z
AM 'tʃiftən, -z

chieftaincy
BR 'tʃiːft(ə)ns|i, -ɪz
AM 'tʃiftənsi, -z

chieftainship
BR 'tʃiːft(ə)nʃɪp, -s
AM 'tʃiftən,ʃɪp, -s

chiffchaff
BR 'tʃɪft,ʃaf, -s
AM 'tʃɪf,tʃæf, -s

chiffon
BR 'ʃɪfɒn
AM ʃɪ'fan, 'ʃɪ,fan

chiffonier
BR ,ʃɪfə'nɪə(r), -z
AM ,ʃɪfə'nɪ(ə)r, -z

chiffonnier
BR ,ʃɪfə'nɪə(r), -z
AM ,ʃɪfə'nɪ(ə)r, -z

chifforobe
BR 'ʃɪfərəʊb, -z
AM 'ʃɪfə,roʊb, -z

chigger
BR 'tʃɪgə(r), -z
AM 'tʃɪgər, -z

chignon
BR 'ʃiːnjɒ, 'ʃiːnjɒn, -z
AM 'ʃɪnjan, 'ʃɪn'jan, -z

chigoe
BR 'tʃɪgəʊ, -z
AM 'tʃɪgoʊ, -z

Chigwell
BR 'tʃɪgw(ə)l
AM 'tʃɪg,wɛl

Chihuahua
BR tʃɪ'waːwə(r), -z
AM tʃə'wawə

chihuahua
BR tʃɪ'waːwə(r), -z
AM tʃə'wawə, -z

chikungunya
BR ,tʃɪk(ə)n'gʌnjə(r)
AM ,tʃɪkən'gənjə

chilblain
BR 'tʃɪlbleɪn, -z, -d
AM 'tʃɪl,bleɪn, -z, -d

child
BR tʃʌɪld
AM tʃaɪld

childbearing
BR 'tʃʌɪl(d),bɛːrɪŋ
AM 'tʃaɪl(d),bɛrɪŋ

childbed
BR 'tʃʌɪl(d)bɛd
AM 'tʃaɪl(d),bɛd

childbirth
BR 'tʃʌɪl(d)bəːθ
AM 'tʃaɪl(d),bərθ

childcare
BR 'tʃʌɪl(d)kɛː(r)
AM 'tʃaɪl(d),kɛ(ə)r

Childe
BR tʃʌɪld
AM tʃaɪld

Childermas
BR 'tʃɪldəmas
AM 'tʃɪldər,mæs

Childers
BR 'tʃɪldəz
AM 'tʃɪldərz

childhood
BR 'tʃʌɪldhʊd, -z
AM 'tʃaɪl(d),(h)ʊd, -z

childish
BR 'tʃʌɪldɪʃ
AM 'tʃaɪldɪʃ

childishly
BR 'tʃʌɪldɪʃli
AM 'tʃaɪldɪʃli

childishness
BR 'tʃʌɪldɪʃnɪs
AM 'tʃaɪldɪʃnɪs

childless
BR 'tʃʌɪl(d)lɪs
AM 'tʃaɪl(d)lɪs

childlessly
BR 'tʃʌɪl(d)lɪsli
AM 'tʃaɪl(d)lɪsli

childlessness
BR 'tʃʌɪl(d)lɪsnɪs
AM 'tʃaɪl(d)lɪsnɪs

childlike
BR 'tʃʌɪl(d)lʌɪk
AM 'tʃaɪl(d),laɪk

childminder
BR 'tʃʌɪl(d),mʌɪndə(r),
-z
AM 'tʃaɪl(d),maɪndər,
-z

childproof
BR 'tʃʌɪl(d)pruːf
AM 'tʃaɪl(d),pruf

child-rearing
BR 'tʃʌɪld,rɪərɪŋ
AM 'tʃaɪl(d),rɪrɪŋ

children
BR 'tʃɪldr(ə)n
AM 'tʃɪldr(ə)n

Childs
BR tʃʌɪldz
AM tʃaɪldz

Childwall
BR 'tʃɪl(d)wɔːl
AM tʃaɪld,wɔl,
tʃaɪld,wɑl

Chile
BR 'tʃɪli
AM 'tʃɪli

chile
BR 'tʃɪl|i, -ɪz
AM 'tʃɪli, -z

Chilean
BR 'tʃɪliən, -z
AM 'tʃɪliən, tʃəˈleɪən,
-z

chili
BR 'tʃɪl|i, -ɪz
AM 'tʃɪli, -z

chiliad
BR 'kɪliad, 'kɪliəd, -z
AM 'kɪli,æd, -z

chiliasm
BR 'kɪliaz(ə)m
AM 'kɪli,æzəm

chiliast
BR 'kɪliast, -s
AM 'kɪli,æst, -s

chiliastic
BR ,kɪli'astɪk
AM ,kɪli'æstɪk

chill
BR tʃɪl, -z, -ɪŋ, -d
AM tʃɪl, -z, -ɪŋ, -d

chiller
BR 'tʃɪlə(r), -z
AM 'tʃɪlər, -z

chilli
BR 'tʃɪl|i, -ɪz
AM 'tʃɪli, -z

chilliness
BR 'tʃɪlɪnɪs
AM 'tʃɪlɪnɪs

chillingly
BR 'tʃɪlɪŋli
AM 'tʃɪlɪŋli

chillness
BR 'tʃɪlnɪs
AM 'tʃɪlnɪs

chillsome
BR 'tʃɪls(ə)m
AM 'tʃɪlsəm

chillum
BR 'tʃɪləm
AM 'tʃɪləm

chilly
BR 'tʃɪl|i, -ɪə(r), -ɪɪst
AM 'tʃɪli, -ər, -ɪst

Chilpruf
BR 'tʃɪlpruːf
AM 'tʃɪl,pruf

Chiltern
BR 'tʃɪlt(ə)n, -z
AM 'tʃɪltərn, -z

Chilton
BR 'tʃɪlt(ə)n
AM 'tʃɪltən

chimaera
BR kʌɪ'mɪərə(r),
kɪ'mɪərə(r), -z
AM kaɪ'mɪrə, kə'mɪrə,
-z

Chimborazo
BR ,tʃɪmbə'rɑːzəʊ
AM ,tʃɪmbə'rɑzoʊ

chime
BR tʃʌɪm, -z, -ɪŋ, -d
AM tʃaɪm, -z, -ɪŋ, -d

chimer
BR 'tʃɪmə(r), -z
AM 'tʃɪmər, -z

chimera
BR kʌɪ'mɪərə(r),
kɪ'mɪərə(r), -z
AM kaɪ'mɪrə, kə'mɪrə,
-z

chimere
BR tʃɪ'mɪə(r), -z
AM (t)ʃə'mɪ(ə)r, -z

chimeric
BR kʌɪ'mɛrɪk,
kɪ'mɛrɪk

AM kaɪ'mɛrɪk,
kə'mɛrɪk

chimerical
BR kʌɪ'mɛrɪkl,
kɪ'mɛrɪkl
AM kaɪ'mɛrəkəl,
kə'mɛrəkəl

chimerically
BR kʌɪ'mɛrɪkli,
kɪ'mɛrɪkli
AM kaɪ'mɛrək(ə)li,
kə'mɛrək(ə)li

chimney
BR 'tʃɪmn|i, -ɪz
AM 'tʃɪmni, -z

chimneybreast
BR 'tʃɪmnɪbrɛst, -s
AM 'tʃɪmni,brɛst, -s

chimneypiece
BR 'tʃɪmnɪpiːs, -ɪz
AM 'tʃɪmni,pis, -ɪz

chimneypot
BR 'tʃɪmnɪpɒt, -s
AM 'tʃɪmni,pɑt, -s

chimneystack
BR 'tʃɪmnɪstak, -s
AM 'tʃɪmni,stæk, -s

chimneysweep
BR 'tʃɪmnɪswiːp, -s
AM 'tʃɪmni,swip, -s

chimp
BR tʃɪmp, -s
AM tʃɪmp, -s

chimpanzee
BR ,tʃɪmpan'ziː,
,tʃɪmpən'ziː, -z
AM ,tʃɪm,pæn'zi,
,tʃɪm'pæn,zi, -z

chin
BR tʃɪn, -z
AM tʃɪn, -z

china
BR 'tʃʌɪnə(r), -z
AM 'tʃaɪnə, -z

Chinagraph
BR 'tʃʌɪnəgrɑːf,
'tʃʌɪnəgraf, -s
AM 'tʃaɪnə,græf, -s

Chinaman
BR 'tʃʌɪnəmən
AM 'tʃaɪnəmən

Chinamen
BR 'tʃʌɪnəmən
AM 'tʃaɪnəmən

Chinatown
BR 'tʃʌɪnətaʊn, -z
AM 'tʃaɪnə,taʊn, -z

chinaware
BR 'tʃʌɪnəwɛː(r)
AM 'tʃaɪnə,wɛ(ə)r

chinch
BR tʃɪn(t)ʃ, -ɪz
AM tʃɪn(t)ʃ, -ɪz

chincherinchee
BR ,tʃɪn(t)ʃɪrɪn'tʃiː, -z
AM ,tʃɪntʃərɪn'tʃi, -z

chinchilla
BR tʃɪn'tʃɪlə(r), -z
AM tʃɪn'tʃɪlə, -z

chin-chin
BR ,tʃɪn'tʃɪn
AM ,tʃɪn'tʃɪn

Chindit
BR 'tʃɪndɪt, -s
AM 'tʃɪndɪt, -s

Chindwin
BR 'tʃɪndwɪn
AM 'tʃɪndwən

chine
BR tʃʌɪn, -z, -ɪŋ, -d
AM tʃaɪn, -z, -ɪŋ, -d

chiné
BR ʃiː'neɪ
AM ʃə'neɪ

Chinese
BR ,tʃʌɪ'niːz
AM ,tʃaɪ'niz

Chingford
BR 'tʃɪŋfəd
AM 'tʃɪŋfərd

chink
BR tʃɪŋk, -s
AM tʃɪŋk, -s

Chinky
BR 'tʃɪŋk|i, -ɪz
AM 'tʃɪŋki, -z

chinless
BR 'tʃɪnlɪs
AM 'tʃɪnlɪs

chinlessness
BR 'tʃɪnlɪsnɪs
AM 'tʃɪnlɪsnɪs

chino
BR '(t)ʃiːnəʊ, -z
AM 'tʃɪnoʊ, -z

chinoiserie
BR ʃɪn'wɑːz(ə)ri,
ʃiːn'wɑːz(ə)ri,
ʃɪn,wɑːzə'riː
AM ,ʃin,wɑzə'ri,
,ʃin'wɑzəri

Chinook
BR tʃɪ'nʊk, tʃɪ'nuːk, -s
AM (t)ʃə'nʊk, -s

chinstrap
BR 'tʃɪnstrap, -s
AM 'tʃɪn,stræp, -s

chintz
BR tʃɪn(t)s
AM tʃɪn(t)s

chintzily
BR 'tʃɪn(t)sɪli
AM 'tʃɪn(t)sɪli

chintziness
BR 'tʃɪn(t)sɪnɪs
AM 'tʃɪn(t)sinɪs

chintzy
BR 'tʃɪn(t)s|i, -ɪə(r),
-ɪɪst
AM 'tʃɪn(t)si, -ər, -ɪst

chinwag
BR 'tʃɪnwag, -z
AM 'tʃɪn,wæg, -z

chionodoxa
BR ˌkaɪənə'dɒksə(r),
kaɪˌɒnə'dɒksə(r), -z
AM ˌkaɪənoʊ'daksə,
ˌkaɪˌɑnə'daksə, -z

Chios
BR 'kaɪɒs, 'kiːɒs
AM 'kiˌɒs, 'kiˌɑs

chip
BR tʃɪp, -s, -ɪŋ, -t
AM tʃɪp, -s, -ɪŋ, -t

chipboard
BR 'tʃɪpbɔːd
AM 'tʃɪpˌbɔ(ə)rd

chipmunk
BR 'tʃɪpmʌŋk, -s
AM 'tʃɪpˌməŋk, -s

chipolata
BR ˌtʃɪpə'lɑːtə(r), -z
AM ˌtʃɪpə'lɑdə, -z

Chippendale
BR 'tʃɪp(ə)ndeɪl
AM 'tʃɪpənˌdeɪl

Chippenham
BR 'tʃɪpənəm,
'tʃɪpŋəm
AM 'tʃɪpənəm,
'tʃɪpənˌhæm

chipper
BR 'tʃɪpə(r), -z
AM 'tʃɪpər, -z

Chippewa
BR 'tʃɪpɪwɑː(r),
'tʃɪpɪwə(r), -z
AM 'tʃɪpəwɑ, -z

chippie
BR 'tʃɪp|i, -ɪz
AM 'tʃɪpi, -z

chippiness
BR 'tʃɪpɪnɪs
AM 'tʃɪpɪnɪs

chipping
BR 'tʃɪpɪŋ, -z
AM 'tʃɪpɪŋ, -z

chippy
BR 'tʃɪp|i, -ɪz
AM 'tʃɪpi, -z

Chips
BR tʃɪps
AM tʃɪps

chipshot
BR 'tʃɪpˌʃɒt, -s
AM 'tʃɪpˌʃɑt, -s

chiral
BR 'kaɪrəl, 'kaɪrļ
AM 'kaɪrəl

chirality
BR kaɪ'ralɪti
AM kaɪ'rælədi

chi-rho
BR 'kʌɪˌrəʊ
AM 'kaɪˌroʊ

Chirk
BR tʃəːk
AM tʃərk

chirograph
BR 'kaɪrəgrɑːf,
'kaɪrəgraf, -s
AM 'kaɪrəˌgræf, -s

chirographer
BR ˌkaɪ'rɒgrəfə(r), -z
AM ˌkaɪ'rɑgrəfər, -z

chirographic
BR ˌkaɪrə'grafɪk
AM ˌkaɪrə'græfɪk

chirographist
BR ˌkaɪ'rɒgrəfɪst, -s
AM ˌkaɪ'rɑgrəfəst, -s

chirography
BR ˌkaɪ'rɒgrəfi
AM ˌkaɪ'rɑgrəfi

chiromancer
BR ˌkaɪrəˌmansə(r), -z
AM 'kaɪrəˌmænsər, -z

chiromancy
BR 'kaɪrəˌmansi
AM 'kaɪrəˌmænsi

Chiron
BR 'kaɪrən
AM 'kaɪrən

chiropodist
BR kɪ'rɒpədɪst,
ʃɪ'rɒpədɪst, -s
AM kə'rɑpədəst, -s

chiropody
BR kɪ'rɒpədi,
ʃɪ'rɒpədi
AM kə'rɑpədi

chiropractic
BR ˌkaɪrə'praktɪk,
'kaɪrəˌpraktɪk
AM ˌkaɪrə'præktɪk

chiropractor
BR 'kaɪrəˌpraktə(r), -z
AM 'kaɪrəˌpræktər, -z

chiropteran
BR kaɪ'rɒpt(ə)rən,
kaɪ'rɒpt(ə)rŋ, -z
AM kaɪ'raptərən, -z

chiropterous
BR kaɪ'rɒpt(ə)rəs
AM kaɪ'raptərəs

chirp
BR tʃəːp, -s, -ɪŋ, -t
AM tʃərp, -s, -ɪŋ, -t

chirper
BR 'tʃəːpə(r), -z
AM 'tʃərpər, -z

chirpily
BR 'tʃəːpɪli
AM 'tʃərpəli

chirpiness
BR 'tʃəːpɪnɪs
AM 'tʃərpɪnɪs

chirpy
BR 'tʃəːp|i, -ɪə(r), -ɪɪst
AM 'tʃərpi, -ər, -ɪst

chirr
BR tʃəː(r), -z, -ɪŋ, -d
AM tʃər, -z, -ɪŋ, -d

chirrup
BR 'tʃɪrʌp, -s, -ɪŋ, -t

AM 'tʃɪrəp, -s, -ɪŋ, -t

chirrupy
BR 'tʃɪrʌpi
AM 'tʃɪrəpi

chiru
BR 'tʃɪruː, -z
AM 'tʃɪru, -z

chisel
BR 'tʃɪz|l, -lz, -ļɪŋ \-lɪŋ,
-ld
AM 'tʃɪz|əl, -əlz, -(ə)lɪŋ,
-əld

chiseler
BR 'tʃɪzlə(r), 'tʃɪzlə(r),
-z
AM 'tʃɪz(ə)lər, -z

chiseller
BR 'tʃɪzlə(r), 'tʃɪzlə(r),
-z
AM 'tʃɪz(ə)lər, -z

Chisholm
BR 'tʃɪz(ə)m
AM 'tʃɪzəm

Chislehurst
BR 'tʃɪzlhəːst
AM 'tʃɪzlˌ(h)ərst

chi-square
BR 'kaɪskwɛː(r), -d
AM ˌkaɪˌskwɛ(ə)r, -d

Chiswick
BR 'tʃɪzɪk
AM 'tʃɪzˌwɪk, 'tʃɪzɪk

chit
BR tʃɪt, -s
AM tʃɪt, -s

chital
BR 'tʃiːtl
AM 'tʃɪdl

chitchat
BR 'tʃɪttʃat
AM 'tʃɪˌtʃæt

chitin
BR 'kʌɪt(ɪ)n
AM 'kaɪtn

chitinous
BR 'kʌɪtɪnəs, 'kaɪtŋəs
AM 'kaɪtnəs

chitlins
BR 'tʃɪtlɪnz
AM 'tʃɪtlɪnz

chiton
BR 'kʌɪt(ɒ)n
AM 'kaɪˌtɑn, 'kaɪtn

Chittagong
BR 'tʃɪtəgɒŋ
AM 'tʃɪdəˌgɒŋ,
'tʃɪdəˌgɑŋ

chitterling
BR 'tʃɪtlɪŋ, 'tʃɪt(ə)lɪŋ,
-z
AM 'tʃɪtlɪŋ, -z

chitty
BR 'tʃɪt|i, -ɪz
AM 'tʃɪdi, -z

chiv
BR (t)ʃɪv, -z
AM (t)ʃɪv, -z

chivalric
BR ʃɪ'valrɪk
AM ʃə'vælrɪk

chivalrous
BR 'ʃɪvlrəs
AM 'ʃɪvəlrəs

chivalrously
BR 'ʃɪvlrəsli
AM 'ʃɪvəlrəsli

chivalrousness
BR 'ʃɪvlrəsnəs
AM 'ʃɪvəlrəsnəs

chivalry
BR 'ʃɪvlri
AM 'ʃɪvəlri

Chivas
BR 'ʃɪvas, 'ʃɪvəs,
'ʃiːvəs
AM 'ʃɪvəs

chive
BR tʃʌɪv, -z
AM tʃaɪv, -z

Chivers
BR 'tʃɪvəz
AM 'tʃɪvərz

chivvy
BR 'tʃɪv|i, -ɪz, -ɪŋ, -ɪd
AM 'tʃɪvi, -z, -ɪŋ, -d

chiz
BR tʃɪz
AM tʃɪz

chizz
BR tʃɪz
AM tʃɪz

chlamydia
BR klə'mɪdɪə(r)
AM klə'mɪdɪə

chlamydial
BR klə'mɪdɪəl
AM klə'mɪdɪəl

chlamydomonas
BR ˌklamɪdə'məʊnəs
AM ˌklæmə'dɑmənəs

Chloë
BR 'kləʊi
AM 'kloʊi

chloracne
BR klɔːr'akni
AM klɔr'ækni

chloral
BR 'klɔːrəl, 'klɔːrļ
AM 'klɔrəl

chlorambucil
BR klɔːr'ambjʊsɪl
AM klɔr'æmbjəˌsɪl

chloramine
BR 'klɔːrəmiːn
AM 'klɔrəˌmin

chloramphenicol
BR ˌklɔːram'fɛnɪkɒl,
ˌklɔːrəm'fɛnɪkɒl, -z
AM ˌklɔræm'fɛnəˌkɔl,
ˌklɔrəm'fɛnəˌkɑl, -z

chlorate
BR 'klɔːreɪt, -s
AM 'klɔˌreɪt, -s

chlordane
BR ˈklɔːdeɪn
AM ˈklɔrˌdeɪn
chlorella
BR kləˈrelə(r), -z
AM kləˈrelə, -z
chloric
BR ˈklɔːrɪk, ˈklɒrɪk
AM ˈklɔrɪk
chloride
BR ˈklɔːraɪd, -z
AM ˈklɔˌraɪd, -z
chlorinate
BR ˈklɔːrɪneɪt,
ˈklɒrɪneɪt, -s, -ɪŋ, -ɪd
AM ˈklɔːrəˌneɪ|t, -ts,
-dɪŋ, -dɪd
chlorination
BR ˌklɔːrɪˈneɪʃn,
ˌklɒrɪˈneɪʃn
AM ˌklɔːrəˈneɪʃən
chlorinator
BR ˈklɔːrɪneɪtə(r),
ˈklɒrɪneɪtə(r), -z
AM ˈklɔːrəˌneɪdər, -z
chlorine
BR ˈklɔːriːn
AM ˈklɔːrin
chlorite
BR ˈklɔːrʌɪt
AM ˈklɔˌraɪt
chloritic
BR klɔːˈrɪtɪk, klɒˈrɪtɪk,
kləˈrɪtɪk
AM klɔːˈrɪdɪk, kləˈrɪdɪk
chlorodyne
BR ˈklɔːrə(ʊ)dʌɪn,
ˈklɒrə(ʊ)dʌɪn
AM ˈklɔːrəˌdaɪn
**chlorofluoro-
carbon**
BR ˌklɔːrəʊˌflʊərəʊ-
ˈkɑːb(ə)n,
ˌklɔːrəʊˌflɔːrəʊ-
ˈkɑːb(ə)n,
ˌklɒrəˌflʊərəˈkɑːb(ə)n,
ˌklɒrəʊˌflɔːrəʊ-
ˈkɑːb(ə)n
AM ˌklɔːrəˈflɔːrəˌkɑːbən,
ˈklɔːrəˈflʊərəˌkɑːbən
chloroform
BR ˈklɒrəfɔːm, -z, -ɪŋ, -d
AM ˈklɔːrəˌfɔ(ə)rm, -z,
-ɪŋ, -d
Chloromycetin®
BR ˌklɔːrəʊmʌɪˈsiːtɪn,
ˌklɒrəʊmʌɪˈsiːtɪn
AM ˌklɔːrəˌmaɪˈsitn
chlorophyll
BR ˈklɒrəfɪl
AM ˈklɔːrəˌfɪl
chlorophyllous
BR ˌklɒrəʊˈfɪləs
AM ˌklɔːrəˈfɪləs
chloroplast
BR ˈklɔːrə(ʊ)plast,
ˈklɒrə(ʊ)plast, -s
AM ˈklɔːrəˌplæst, -s

chloroquine
BR ˈklɔːrəkwɪn,
ˈklɒrəkwɪn
AM ˈklɔːrəˌkwaɪn
chlorosis
BR kləˈrəʊsɪs,
klɔːˈrəʊsɪs
AM klɔˈrousəs
chlorotic
BR klɔːˈrɒtɪk,
kləˈrɒtɪk
AM kləˈrɑdɪk,
klɔːˈrɑdɪk
chlorous acid
BR ˌklɔːrəs ˈasɪd
AM ˌklɔːrəs ˈæsəd
chlorpromazine
BR ˌklɔːˈprəʊməziːn,
ˌklɔːˈprɒməziːn
AM ˌklɔːrˈprɑməˌzin
Chobham
BR ˈtʃɒb(ə)m
AM ˈtʃɑbəm
choc
BR tʃɒk, -s
AM tʃɑk, -s
choc-a-bloc
BR ˌtʃɒkəˈblɒk
AM ˌtʃɑkəˈblɑk
chocaholic
BR ˌtʃɒkəˈhɒlɪk
AM ˌtʃɑkəˈhɔlɪk,
ˌtʃɑkəˈhɑlɪk
choccy
BR ˈtʃɒk|i, -ɪz
AM ˈtʃɑki, -z
chocho
BR ˈtʃəʊtʃəʊ, -z
AM ˈtʃouˌtʃou, -z
choc-ice
BR ˌtʃɒkˈʌɪs, ˈtʃɒkʌɪs,
-ɪz
AM ˈtʃɔkˌaɪs, ˈtʃɑkˌaɪs,
-ɪz
chock
BR tʃɒk, -s, -ɪŋ, -t
AM tʃɑk, -s, -ɪŋ, -t
chock-a-block
BR ˌtʃɒkəˈblɒk
AM ˌtʃɑkəˈblɑk
chocker
BR ˈtʃɒkə(r), -z
AM ˈtʃɑkər, -z
chockstone
BR ˈtʃɒkstəʊn
AM ˈtʃɑkˌstoun
chocoholic
BR ˌtʃɒkəˈhɒlɪk, -s
AM ˌtʃɑkəˈhɑlɪk,
ˌtʃɑkəˈhalɪk, -s
chocolate
BR ˈtʃɒk(ə)lət, -s
AM ˈtʃɔk(ə)lət,
ˈtʃɑk(ə)lət, -s
chocolatey
BR ˈtʃɒk(ə)ləti
AM ˈtʃɔk(ə)lədi,
ˈtʃɑk(ə)lədi

Choctaw
BR ˈtʃɒktɔː(r), -z
AM ˈtʃɔkˌtɔ, ˈtʃɑkˌtɔ, -z
choice
BR tʃɔɪs, -ɪz, -ə(r), -ɪst
AM tʃɔɪs, -ɪz, -ər, -ɪst
choicely
BR ˈtʃɔɪsli
AM ˈtʃɔɪsli
choiceness
BR ˈtʃɔɪsnɪs
AM ˈtʃɔɪsnɪs
choir
BR ˈkwʌɪə(r), -z
AM ˈkwaɪər, -z
choirboy
BR ˈkwʌɪəbɔɪ, -z
AM ˈkwaɪ(ə)rˌbɔɪ, -z
choirgirl
BR ˈkwʌɪəgəːl, -z
AM ˈkwaɪ(ə)rˌgərl, -z
choirmaster
BR ˈkwʌɪəˌmɑːstə(r),
ˈkwʌɪəˌmɑstə(r), -z
AM ˈkwaɪ(ə)rˌmæstər,
-z
choke
BR tʃəʊk, -s, -ɪŋ, -t
AM tʃouk, -s, -ɪŋ, -t
chokeberry
BR ˈtʃəʊkb(ə)r|i, -ɪz
AM ˈtʃoukˌberi, -z
chokecherry
BR ˈtʃəʊkˌtʃɛr|i, -ɪz
AM ˈtʃoukˌtʃɛri, -z
choker
BR ˈtʃəʊkə(r), -z
AM ˈtʃoukər, -z
chokey
BR ˈtʃəʊki
AM ˈtʃouki
chokily
BR ˈtʃəʊkɪli
AM ˈtʃoukəli
chokiness
BR ˈtʃəʊkɪnɪs
AM ˈtʃoukɪnɪs
choko
BR ˈtʃəʊkəʊ, -z
AM ˈtʃoukou, -z
choky
BR ˈtʃəʊk|i, -ɪz, -ɪə(r),
-ɪɪst
AM ˈtʃouki, -z, -ər, -ɪst
cholangiography
BR ˌkɒlan(d)ʒɪˈɒɡrəfi
AM ˌkoʊˌlændʒiˈaɡrəfi
cholecalciferol
BR ˌkɒlɪkalˈsɪf(ə)rɒl
AM ˌkoʊləˌkælˈsɪfəˌrɒl,
ˌkoʊləˌkælˈsɪfəˌral
cholecystectomy
BR ˌkɒlɪsɪstˈɛktəm|i,
-ɪz
AM ˌkoʊləˌsɪsˈtɛktəmi,
-z

cholecystography
BR ˌkɒlɪsɪstˈɒɡrəfi
AM ˌkoʊləˌsɪsˈtɑɡrəfi
choler
BR ˈkɒlə(r)
AM ˈkɑlər
cholera
BR ˈkɒl(ə)rə(r)
AM ˈkɑlərə
choleraic
BR ˌkɒləˈreɪɪk
AM ˌkɑləˈreɪɪk
choleric
BR ˈkɒl(ə)rɪk, kɒˈlɛrɪk
AM ˈkɑlərɪk, kəˈlɛrɪk
cholerically
BR ˈkɒl(ə)rɪkli,
kɒˈlɛrɪkli
AM ˈkɑlərək(ə)li,
kəˈlɛrək(ə)li
cholesterol
BR kəˈlɛst(ə)rɒl,
kɒˈlɛst(ə)rɒl,
kəˈlɛstr(ə)l,
kɒˈlɛstr(ə)l
AM kəˈlɛstəˌrɒl,
kəˈlɛstəˌral
choli
BR ˈtʃəʊl|i, -ɪz
AM ˈkoʊli, -z
choliamb
BR ˈkəʊlɪam(b), -z
AM ˈkoʊliˌæm(b), -z
choliambic
BR ˌkəʊlɪˈambɪk
AM ˌkoʊliˈæmbɪk
cholic
BR ˈkɒlɪk
AM ˈkoʊlɪk, ˈkalɪk
choline
BR ˈkəʊliːn
AM ˈkoʊlin
cholinergic
BR ˌkəʊlɪˈnəːdʒɪk,
ˌkɒlɪˈnəːdʒɪk
AM ˌkoʊləˈnərdʒɪk
Cholmeley
BR ˈtʃʌmli
AM ˈtʃəmli
Cholmondeley
BR ˈtʃʌmli
AM ˈtʃəmli
chomp
BR tʃɒmp, -s, -ɪŋ, -t
AM tʃɑmp, tʃamp, -s,
-ɪŋ, -t
Chomskian
BR ˈtʃɒmskɪən, -z
AM ˈtʃamskiən, -z
Chomsky
BR ˈtʃɒmski
AM ˈtʃamski
chondrite
BR ˈkɒndrʌɪt, -s
AM ˈkanˌdraɪt, -s
chondrocranium
BR ˌkɒndrəʊˈkreɪnɪəm,
-z

AM ˌkɑndroʊˈkreɪnɪəm,
ˌkɑndrəˈkreɪnɪəm, -z
chondroma
BR kɒnˈdrəʊmə(r), -z
AM kɑnˈdroʊmə, -z
chondromata
BR kɒnˈdrəʊmətə(r)
AM kɑnˈdroʊmədə
choochoo
BR ˈtʃuːtʃuːˌ, -z
AM ˈtʃuˌtʃu, -z
chook
BR tʃʊk, -s
AM tʃʊk, -s
choose
BR tʃuːz, -ɪz, -ɪŋ
AM tʃuz, -əz, -ɪŋ
chooser
BR ˈtʃuːzə(r), -z
AM ˈtʃuzər, -z
choosey
BR ˈtʃuːz|i, -ɪə(r), -ɪɪst
AM ˈtʃuzi, -ər, -ɪst
choosily
BR ˈtʃuːzɪli
AM ˈtʃuzəli
choosiness
BR ˈtʃuːzɪnɪs
AM ˈtʃuzinɪs
choosy
BR ˈtʃuːz|i, -ə(r), -ɪst
AM ˈtʃuzi, -ər, -ɪst
chop
BR tʃɒp, -s, -ɪŋ, -t
AM tʃɑp, -s, -ɪŋ, -t
chopfallen
BR ˈtʃɒpˌfɔːlən
AM ˈtʃɑpˌfɔlən,
ˈtʃɑpˌfɑlən
chophouse
BR ˈtʃɒphaʊ|s, -zɪz
AM ˈtʃɑp,(h)aʊ|s, -zəz
Chopin
BR ˈʃɒpæ̃, ˈʃəʊpæ̃,
ˈʃəʊpɑn
AM ˈʃoʊˌpæn
chopper
BR ˈtʃɒpə(r), -z
AM ˈtʃɑpər, -z
choppily
BR ˈtʃɒpɪli
AM ˈtʃɑpəli
choppiness
BR ˈtʃɒpɪnɪs
AM ˈtʃɑpɪnɪs
choppy
BR ˈtʃɒp|i, -ɪə(r), -ɪɪst
AM ˈtʃɑpi, -ər, -ɪst
chopstick
BR ˈtʃɒpstɪk, -s
AM ˈtʃɑpˌstɪk, -s
chop suey
BR ˌtʃɒp ˈsuː|i, -ɪz
AM ˌtʃɑp ˈsui, -z
choral
BR ˈkɔːrəl, ˈkɔːrl̩, -z
AM ˈkɔrəl, -z

chorale
BR kɒˈrɑːl, kɔːˈrɑːl, -z
AM kəˈræl, kəˈrɑl,
kɔːˈræl, kɔːˈrɑl, -z
chorally
BR ˈkɔːrəli, ˈkɔːrl̩i
AM ˈkɔrəli
chord
BR kɔːd, -z, -ɪŋ
AM kɔ(ə)rd, -z, -ɪŋ
chordal
BR ˈkɔːdl̩
AM ˈkɔrdəl
chordate
BR ˈkɔːdeɪt, ˈkɔːdət, -s
AM ˈkɔrdət, ˈkɔrˌdeɪt, -s
chore
BR tʃɔː(r), -z
AM tʃɔ(ə)r, -z
chorea
BR kɔːˈrɪə(r),
kɒˈrɪə(r). kəˈrɪə(r)
AM kəˈriə
choreograph
BR ˈkɒrɪəgrɑːf,
ˈkɒrɪəgraf, -s, -ɪŋ, -t
AM ˈkɔriəˌgræf, -s, -ɪŋ,
-t
choreographer
BR ˌkɒrɪˈɒgrəfə(r), -z
AM ˌkɔriˈɑgrəfər, -z
choreographic
BR ˌkɒrɪəˈgrafɪk
AM ˌkɔriəˈgræfɪk
choreographical
BR ˌkɒrɪəˈgrafɪkl̩
AM ˌkɔriəˈgræfəkəl
choreographically
BR ˌkɒrɪəˈgrafɪkli
AM ˌkɔriəˈgræfək(ə)li
choreography
BR ˌkɒrɪˈɒgrəfi
AM ˌkɔriˈɑgrəfi
choreologist
BR ˌkɒrɪˈɒlədʒɪst, -s
AM ˌkɔriˈɑlədʒəst, -s
choreology
BR ˌkɒrɪˈɒlədʒi
AM ˌkɔriˈɑlədʒi
choriamb
BR ˈkɒrɪamb, -z
AM ˈkoʊriəm(b), -z
choriambi
BR ˌkɒrɪˈambʌi
AM ˌkoʊriˈæmˌbaɪ
choriambic
BR ˌkɒrɪˈambɪk
AM ˌkoʊriˈæmbɪk
choriambus
BR ˌkɒrɪˈambəs
AM ˌkoʊriˈæmbəs
choric
BR ˈkɒrɪk
AM ˈkɔrɪk
chorine
BR ˈkɔːriːn, -z
AM ˈkɔrən, ˈkɔrin, -z

chorion
BR ˈkɔːrɪən, ˈkɔːrɪɒn, -z
AM ˈkɔriˌɑn, -z
chorionic
BR ˌkɔːrɪˈɒnɪk
AM ˌkoʊriˈɑnɪk
chorister
BR ˈkɒrɪstə(r), -z
AM ˈkɔrəstər, -z
Chorley
BR ˈtʃɔːli
AM ˈtʃɔrli
Chorlton
BR ˈtʃɔːlt(ə)n
AM ˈtʃɔrltən
**Chorlton-cum-
Hardy**
BR ˌtʃɔːlt(ə)nkʌmˈhɑːdi
AM ˌtʃɔrltnkəmˈhardi
chorographer
BR kɔːˈrɒgrəfə(r), -z
AM kəˈragrəfər, -z
chorographic
BR ˌkɔːrəˈgrafɪk,
ˌkɒrəˈgrafɪk
AM ˌkoʊrəˈgræfɪk
chorographically
BR ˌkɔːrəˈgrafɪkli,
ˌkɒrəˈgrafɪkli
AM ˌkoʊrəˈgræfək(ə)li
chorography
BR kɔːˈrɒgrəfi
AM kəˈragəfi
choroid
BR ˈkɔːrɔɪd, ˈkɒrɔɪd
AM ˈkɔrɔɪd
chorological
BR ˌkɒrəˈlɒdʒɪkl̩
AM ˌkoʊrəˈladʒəkəl
chorologically
BR ˌkɒrəˈlɒdʒɪkli
AM ˌkoʊrəˈladʒək(ə)li
chorologist
BR kɔːˈrɒlədʒɪst, -s
AM kəˈralədʒəst, -s
chorology
BR kɔːˈrɒlədʒi
AM kəˈralədʒi
chorten
BR ˈtʃɔːt(ə)n, -z
AM ˈtʃɔrt(ə)n, -z
chortle
BR ˈtʃɔːt|l̩, -lz, -l̩ɪŋ \ -lɪŋ,
-ld
AM ˈtʃɔrdəl, -z, -ɪŋ, -d
chorus
BR ˈkɔːrəs, -ɪz, -ɪŋ, -t
AM ˈkɔrəs, -əz, -ɪŋ, -t
chose
BR tʃəʊz
AM tʃoʊz
chosen
BR ˈtʃəʊzn̩
AM ˈtʃoʊzn̩
chota
BR ˈtʃəʊtə(r)
AM ˈtʃoʊdə

choucroute
BR ˈʃuːkruːt
AM ˌʃuˈkrut
chough
BR tʃʌf, -s
AM tʃəf, -s
choux
BR ʃuː
AM ʃu
chow
BR tʃaʊ, -z
AM tʃaʊ, -z
chowder
BR ˈtʃaʊdə(r)
AM ˈtʃaʊdər
chowkidar
BR ˈtʃəʊkɪdɑː(r), -z
AM ˈtʃoʊkəˌdar, -z
chow mein
BR ˌtʃaʊ ˈmeɪn, + ˈmiːn
AM ˌtʃaʊ ˈmeɪn
chrematistic
BR ˌkrɛməˈtɪstɪk, -s
AM ˌkrɛməˈtɪstɪk, -s
chrestomathy
BR krɛˈstɒməθ|i, -ɪz
AM krɛˈstaməθi, -z
Chris
BR krɪs
AM krɪs
chrism
BR ˈkrɪz(ə)m
AM ˈkrɪzəm
chrisom
BR ˈkrɪz(ə)m, -z
AM ˈkrɪzəm, -z
Chrissie
BR ˈkrɪsi
AM ˈkrɪsi
Chrissy
BR ˈkrɪsi
AM ˈkrɪsi
Christ
BR krʌɪst, -s
AM kraɪst, -s
Christabel
BR ˈkrɪstəbəl
AM ˈkrɪstəˌbɛl
Christadelphian
BR ˌkrɪstəˈdɛlfɪən, -z
AM ˌkrɪstəˈdɛlfiən, -z
Christchurch
BR ˈkrʌɪs(t)tʃəːtʃ
AM ˈkrɪs(t)ˌtʃərtʃ
christen
BR ˈkrɪs|n̩, -nz,
-n̩ɪŋ \ -nɪŋ, -nd
AM ˈkrɪsn̩, -z, -ɪŋ, -d
Christendom
BR ˈkrɪsndəm
AM ˈkrɪsndəm
christener
BR ˈkrɪsnə(r),
ˈkrɪsnə(r), -z
AM ˈkrɪs(ə)nər, -z

christening
BR ˈkrɪsn̩ɪŋ, ˈkrɪsnɪŋ, -z
AM ˈkrɪs(ə)nɪŋ, -z

Christensen
BR ˈkrɪst(ə)ns(ə)n
AM ˈkrɪstənsən

Christhood
BR ˈkrʌɪsthʊd
AM ˈkraɪst,(h)ʊd

Christi
BR ˈkrɪsti
AM ˈkrɪsti

Christian
BR ˈkrɪstʃ(ə)n, -z
AM ˈkrɪstʃən, -z

Christiana
BR ˌkrɪst(ʃ)ɪˈɑːnə(r)
AM ˌkrɪstiˈænə

Christiania
BR ˌkrɪst(ʃ)ɪˈɑːnɪə(r)
AM ˌkrɪstiˈæniə, ˌkrɪstʃiˈæniə

Christianisation
BR ˌkrɪstʃənʌɪˈzeɪʃn, ˌkrɪstʃn̩ʌɪˈzeɪʃn
AM ˌkrɪstʃənəˈzeɪʃən, ˌkrɪstʃən,ʌɪˈzeɪʃən

Christianise
BR ˈkrɪstʃənʌɪz, ˈkrɪstʃn̩ʌɪz, -ɪz, -ɪŋ, -d
AM ˈkrɪstʃə,naɪz, -ɪz, -ɪŋ, -d

Christianity
BR ˌkrɪst(ʃ)ɪˈanɪti
AM ˌkrɪstʃiˈænədi

Christianization
BR ˌkrɪstʃənʌɪˈzeɪʃn, ˌkrɪstʃn̩ʌɪˈzeɪʃn
AM ˌkrɪstʃənəˈzeɪʃən, ˌkrɪstʃən,ʌɪˈzeɪʃən

Christianize
BR ˈkrɪstʃənʌɪz, ˈkrɪstʃn̩ʌɪz, -ɪz, -ɪŋ, -d
AM ˈkrɪstʃə,naɪz, -ɪz, -ɪŋ, -d

Christianly
BR ˈkrɪstʃ(ə)nli
AM ˈkrɪstʃənli

Christie
BR ˈkrɪst|i, -ɪz
AM ˈkrɪsti, -z

Christina
BR krɪsˈtiːnə(r)
AM krɪsˈtinə

Christine
BR ˈkrɪstiːn, krɪsˈtiːn
AM krɪsˈtin

Christingle
BR ˈkrɪstɪŋgl, -z
AM ˈkrɪstɪŋgəl, -z

Christlike
BR ˈkrʌɪs(t)lʌɪk
AM ˈkraɪs(t),laɪk

Christly
BR ˈkrʌɪs(t)li
AM ˈkraɪs(t)li

Christmas
BR ˈkrɪsməs, -ɪz
AM ˈkrɪsməs, -əz

Christmassy
BR ˈkrɪsməsi
AM ˈkrɪsməsi

Christmastide
BR ˈkrɪsməstʌɪd
AM ˈkrɪsməs,taɪd

Christmastime
BR ˈkrɪsməstʌɪm
AM ˈkrɪsməs,taɪm

Christobel
BR ˈkrɪstəbel
AM ˈkrɪstə,bel

Christolatry
BR krɪˈstɒlətri
AM krɪsˈtɑlətri

Christological
BR ˌkrɪstəˈlɒdʒɪkl
AM ˌkrɪstəˈlɑdʒəkəl

Christology
BR krɪˈstɒlədʒi
AM krɪsˈtɑlədʒi

Christophany
BR krɪˈstɒfəni, krɪˈstɒfn̩i
AM krɪsˈtɑfəni

Christopher
BR ˈkrɪstəfə(r)
AM ˈkrɪstəfər

Christy
BR ˈkrɪsti
AM ˈkrɪsti

chroma
BR ˈkrəʊmə(r)
AM ˈkroʊmə

chromate
BR ˈkrəʊmeɪt, -s
AM ˈkroʊ,meɪt, -s

chromatic
BR krə(ʊ)ˈmatɪk
AM krəˈmædɪk, krəˈmædɪk

chromatically
BR krə(ʊ)ˈmatɪkli
AM kroʊˈmædək(ə)li, krəˈmædək(ə)li

chromaticism
BR krə(ʊ)ˈmatɪsɪz(ə)m
AM kroʊˈmædə,sɪzəm

chromaticity
BR ˌkrəʊməˈtɪsɪti
AM ˌkroʊməˈtɪsɪdi

chromatid
BR ˈkrəʊmətɪd, -z
AM ˈkroʊmə,tɪd, -z

chromatin
BR ˈkrəʊmətɪn
AM ˈkroʊmədən

chromatism
BR ˈkrəʊmətɪz(ə)m
AM ˈkroʊmə,tɪzəm

chromatogram
BR krə(ʊ)ˈmatəgram, -z

chromatograph
BR krə(ʊ)ˈmatəgrɑːf, krə(ʊ)ˈmatəgraf, -s
AM kroʊˈmædə,græf, -s

chromatographic
BR krə(ʊ),matəˈgrafɪk
AM kroʊ,mædəˈgræfɪk

chromatographically
BR krə(ʊ),matəˈgrafɪkli
AM kroʊ,mædəˈgræfək(ə)li

chromatography
BR ˌkrəʊməˈtɒgrəfi
AM ˌkroʊməˈtɑgrəfi

chromatopsia
BR ˌkrəʊməˈtɒpsɪə(r)
AM ˌkroʊməˈtɑpsiə

chrome
BR krəʊm
AM kroʊm

chromic
BR ˈkrəʊmɪk
AM ˈkroʊmɪk

chrominance
BR ˈkrəʊmɪnəns
AM ˈkroʊmənəns

chromite
BR ˈkrəʊmʌɪt, -s
AM ˈkroʊ,maɪt, -s

chromium
BR ˈkrəʊmɪəm
AM ˈkroʊmiəm

chromium-plate
BR ˌkrəʊmɪəmˈpleɪt, -s, -ɪŋ, -ɪd
AM ˌkroʊmiəmˈpleɪ|t, -ts, -dɪŋ, -dɪd

chromo
BR ˈkrəʊməʊ, -z
AM ˈkroʊ,moʊ, -z

chromolithograph
BR ˌkrəʊməʊˈlɪθəgrɑːf, ˌkrəʊməʊˈlɪθəgraf, -s
AM ˌkroʊmoʊˈlɪθə,græf, -s

chromolithographer
BR ˌkrəʊməʊlɪˈθɒgrəfə(r), -z
AM ˌkroʊmoʊlɪˈθɑgrəfər, -z

chromolithographic
BR ˌkrəʊməʊˌlɪθəˈgrafɪk
AM ˌkroʊmoʊˌlɪθəˈgræfɪk

chromolithography
BR ˌkrəʊməʊlɪˈθɒgrəfi
AM ˌkroʊmoʊlɪˈθɑgrəfi

chromoly
BR ˈkrəʊmɒli, ˌkrəʊmˈɒli
AM ˈkroʊˈmɑli

chromosomal
BR ˌkrəʊməˈsəʊml
AM ˌkroʊməˈsoʊməl

chromosome
BR ˈkrəʊməsəʊm, -z
AM ˈkroʊmə,soʊm, -z

chromosphere
BR ˈkrəʊmə(ʊ)sfɪə(r), -z
AM ˈkroʊmə,sfɪ(ə)r, -z

chromospheric
BR ˌkrəʊmə(ʊ)ˈsfɛrɪk
AM ˌkroʊməˈsfɛrɪk

chroneme
BR ˈkrəʊniːm, -z
AM ˈkroʊnim, -z

chronemic
BR krə(ʊ)ˈniːmɪk
AM kroʊˈnimɪk

chronic
BR ˈkrɒnɪk
AM ˈkrɑnɪk

chronically
BR ˈkrɒnɪkli
AM ˈkrɑnək(ə)li

chronicity
BR krɒˈnɪsəti
AM krɑˈnɪsɪdi

chronicle
BR ˈkrɒnɪk|l, -lz, -ḷɪŋ\-lɪŋ, -ld
AM ˈkrɑnək|əl, -əlz, -(ə)lɪŋ, -əld

chronicler
BR ˈkrɒnɪklə(r), ˈkrɒnɪklə(r), -z
AM ˈkrɑnəklər, -z

chronogram
BR ˈkrɒnəgram, -z
AM ˈkrɑnə,græm, -z

chronogrammatic
BR ˌkrɒnəgrəˈmatɪk
AM ˌkrɑnəgrəˈmædɪk

chronograph
BR ˈkrɒnəgrɑːf, ˈkrɒnəgraf, -s
AM ˈkrɑnə,græf, -s

chronographic
BR ˌkrɒnəˈgrafɪk
AM ˌkrɑnəˈgræfɪk

chronologer
BR krəˈnɒlədʒə(r), -z
AM krəˈnɑlədʒər, -z

chronologic
BR ˌkrɒnəˈlɒdʒɪk
AM ˌkrɑnəˈlɑdʒɪk

chronological
BR ˌkrɒnəˈlɒdʒɪkl
AM ˌkrɑnəˈlɑdʒəkəl

chronologically
BR ˌkrɒnəˈlɒdʒɪkli
AM ˌkrɑnəˈlɑdʒək(ə)li

chronologisation
BR krə,nɒlədʒʌɪˈzeɪʃn
AM ˌkrɑnə,lɑdʒəˈzeɪʃən, ˌkrɑnə,lɑ,dʒaɪˈzeɪʃən

chronologise
BR krə'nɒlədʒʌɪz, -ɪz,
-ɪŋ, -d
AM krə'nɑlə,dʒaɪz, -ɪz,
-ɪŋ, -d

chronologist
BR krə'nɒlədʒɪst, -s
AM krə'nɑlədʒəst, -s

chronologization
BR krə,nɒlədʒʌɪ'zeɪʃn
AM ,krɑnə,lɑdʒə'zeɪʃən,
,krɑnə,lɑ,dʒaɪ'zeɪʃən

chronologize
BR krə'nɒlədʒʌɪz, -ɪz,
-ɪŋ, -d
AM krə'nɑlə,dʒaɪz, -ɪz,
-ɪŋ, -d

chronology
BR krə'nɒlədʒ|i, -ɪz
AM krə'nɑlədʒi, -z

chronometer
BR krə'nɒmɪtə(r), -z
AM krə'nɑmədər, -z

chronometric
BR ,krɒnə'mɛtrɪk
AM ,krɑnə'mɛtrɪk

chronometrical
BR ,krɒnə'mɛtrɪkl
AM ,krɑnə'mɛtrəkəl

chronometrically
BR ,krɒnə'mɛtrɪkli
AM ,krɑnə'mɛtrək(ə)li

chronometry
BR krə'nɒmɪtri
AM krə'nɑmətri

chronoscope
BR 'krɒnəskəʊp, -s
AM 'krɑnə,skoʊp, -s

chrysalid
BR 'krɪsəlɪd, 'krɪsḷɪd,
-z
AM 'krɪsə,lɪd, -z

chrysalides
BR krɪ'salɪdiːz
AM krə'sælə,diz

chrysalis
BR 'krɪsəlɪs, 'krɪsḷɪs,
-ɪz
AM 'krɪsələs, -ɪz

chrysanth
BR krɪ'sanθ, -s
AM krə'sænθ, -s

chrysanthemum
BR krɪ'sanθɪməm, -z
AM krɪ'sænθəməm, -z

chryselephantine
BR ,krɪsɛlɪ'fantʌm
AM ,krɪs,ɛlə'fæn,tin,
,krɪs,ɛlə'fæn,taɪn

Chrysler®
BR 'krʌɪzlə(r), -z
AM 'kraɪslər, -z

chrysoberyl
BR ,krɪsə'bɛrɪl,
,krɪsə'bɛrḷ
AM 'krɪsə,bɛrəl

chrysolite
BR 'krɪsəlʌɪt, -s

AM 'krɪsə,laɪt, -s

chrysoprase
BR 'krɪsəpreɪz, -ɪz
AM 'krɪsə,preɪz, -ɪz

Chrysostom
BR 'krɪsəstəm
AM 'krɪsəstəm

Chrystal
BR 'krɪstl
AM 'krɪstl

chthonian
BR '(k)θəʊnɪən
AM 'θoʊnɪən

chthonic
BR '(k)θɒnɪk
AM 'θɑnɪk

chub
BR tʃʌb, -z
AM tʃəb, -z

Chubb®
BR tʃʌb
AM tʃəb

chubbily
BR 'tʃʌbɪli
AM 'tʃəbəli

chubbiness
BR 'tʃʌbɪnɪs
AM 'tʃəbɪnɪs

chubby
BR 'tʃʌb|i, -ɪə(r), -ɪɪst
AM 'tʃəbi, -ər, -ɪst

chuck
BR tʃʌk, -s, -ɪŋ, -t
AM tʃək, -s, -ɪŋ, -t

chucker-out
BR ,tʃʌkər'aʊt
AM 'tʃəkər'aʊt

chuckers-out
BR ,tʃʌkəz'aʊt
AM 'tʃəkərz'aʊt

chuckhole
BR 'tʃʌkhəʊl, -z
AM 'tʃək,(h)oʊl, -z

chuckle
BR 'tʃʌk|l, -lz, -lɪŋ \ -lɪŋ,
-ld
AM 'tʃək|əl, -əlz, -(ə)lɪŋ,
-əld

chucklehead
BR 'tʃʌklhɛd, -z
AM 'tʃəkəl,(h)ɛd, -z

chuckleheaded
BR ,tʃʌkl'hɛdɪd
AM 'tʃʌkəl,(h)ɛdəd

chuckler
BR 'tʃʌk|ə(r),
'tʃʌklə(r), -z
AM 'tʃək(ə)lər, -z

chuddar
BR 'tʃʌdə(r), -z
AM 'tʃədər, -z

chufa
BR 'tʃuːfə(r)
AM 'tʃufə

chuff
BR tʃʌf, -s, -ɪŋ, -t
AM tʃəf, -s, -ɪŋ, -t

chug
BR tʃʌg, -z, -ɪŋ, -d
AM tʃəg, -z, -ɪŋ, -d

chugalug
BR 'tʃʌgəlʌg, -z, -ɪŋ, -d
AM 'tʃəgə'ləg, -z, -ɪŋ, -d

chukar
BR 'tʃʊkɑː(r), -z
AM 'tʃəkər, -z

chukka
BR 'tʃʌkə(r), -z
AM 'tʃəkə, -z

chukker
BR 'tʃʌkə(r), -z
AM 'tʃəkər, -z

chum
BR tʃʌm, -z, -ɪŋ, -d
AM tʃəm, -z, -ɪŋ, -d

chummily
BR 'tʃʌmɪli
AM 'tʃəməli

chumminess
BR 'tʃʌmɪnɪs
AM 'tʃəmɪnɪs

chummy
BR 'tʃʌm|i, -ɪə(r), -ɪɪst
AM 'tʃəmi, -ər, -ɪst

chump
BR tʃʌmp, -s
AM tʃəmp, -s

chunder
BR 'tʃʌnd|ə(r), -əz,
-(ə)rɪŋ, -əd
AM 'tʃənd|ər, -ərz,
-(ə)rɪŋ, -ərd

Chungking
BR ,tʃʌŋ'kɪŋ
AM ,tʃəŋ'kɪŋ

chunk
BR tʃʌŋk, -s
AM tʃəŋk, -s

chunkily
BR 'tʃʌŋkɪli
AM 'tʃəŋkəli

chunkiness
BR 'tʃʌŋkɪnɪs
AM 'tʃəŋkɪnɪs

chunky
BR 'tʃʌŋk|i, -ɪə(r), -ɪɪst
AM 'tʃəŋki, -ər, -ɪst

Chunnel
BR 'tʃʌnl
AM 'tʃənəl

chunter
BR 'tʃʌnt|ə(r), -əz,
-(ə)rɪŋ, -əd
AM 'tʃən(t)ər, -z, -ɪŋ, -d

chupatty
BR tʃə'pɑːt|i, tʃə'pat|i,
-ɪz
AM tʃə'pædi, tʃə'pɑdi,
-z

church
BR tʃəːtʃ, -ɪz, -ɪŋ, -t
AM tʃərtʃ, -əz, -ɪŋ, -t

Churchdown
BR 'tʃəːtʃdaʊn

AM 'tʃərtʃ,daʊn

churchgoer
BR 'tʃəːtʃ,gəʊə(r), -z
AM 'tʃərtʃ,goʊər, -z

churchgoing
BR 'tʃəːtʃ,gəʊɪŋ
AM 'tʃərtʃ,goʊɪŋ

Churchill
BR 'tʃəːtʃ(ɪ)l
AM 'tʃərtʃəl

Churchillian
BR tʃəː'tʃɪlɪən
AM tʃər'tʃɪljən,
tʃər'tʃɪlɪən

churchily
BR 'tʃəːtʃɪli
AM 'tʃərtʃəli

churchiness
BR 'tʃəːtʃɪnɪs
AM 'tʃərtʃɪnɪs

churching
BR 'tʃəːtʃɪŋ, -z
AM 'tʃərtʃɪŋ, -z

churchman
BR 'tʃəːtʃmən
AM 'tʃərtʃmən

churchmanship
BR 'tʃəːtʃmən,ʃɪp
AM 'tʃərtʃmən,ʃɪp

churchmen
BR 'tʃəːtʃmən
AM 'tʃərtʃmən

churchwarden
BR 'tʃəːtʃ,wɔːdn, -z
AM 'tʃərtʃ,wɔrdən, -z

churchwoman
BR 'tʃəːtʃ,wʊmən
AM 'tʃərtʃ,wʊmən

churchwomen
BR 'tʃəːtʃ,wɪmɪn
AM 'tʃərtʃ,wɪmɪn

churchy
BR 'tʃəːtʃ|i, -ɪə(r), -ɪɪst
AM 'tʃərtʃi, -ər, -ɪst

churchyard
BR 'tʃəːtʃjɑːd, -z
AM 'tʃərtʃ,jard, -z

churinga
BR tʃʌ'rɪŋgə(r), -z
AM tʃə'rɪŋgə, -z

churl
BR tʃəːl, -z
AM tʃərl, -z

churlish
BR 'tʃəːlɪʃ
AM 'tʃərlɪʃ

churlishly
BR 'tʃəːlɪʃli
AM 'tʃərlɪʃli

churlishness
BR 'tʃəːlɪʃnɪs
AM 'tʃərlɪʃnɪs

churn
BR 'tʃəːn, -z, -ɪŋ, -d
AM 'tʃərn, -z, -ɪŋ, -d

churr
BR tʃəː(r), -z, -ɪŋ, -d

AM tʃər, -z, -ɪŋ, -d
churrasco
BR tʃəˈraskəʊ, -z
AM tʃəˈrɑskoʊ, -z
Churrigueresque
BR ˌtʃʊrɪgəˈresk
AM ˌtʃʊrɪgəˈresk
chute
BR ʃuːt, -s
AM ʃut, -s
chutist
BR ʃuːtɪst, -s
AM ʃudəst, -s
chutnee
BR tʃʌtn|i, -ɪz
AM tʃətni, -z
chutney
BR tʃʌtn|i, -ɪz
AM tʃətni, -z
chutzpah
BR ˈhʊtspə(r),
ˈxʊtspə(r)
AM ˈhʊtspə
Chuzzlewit
BR tʃʌzlwɪt
AM tʃəzl,wɪt
chyack
BR tʃʌɪak, -s, -ɪŋ, -t
AM tʃaɪək, -s, -ɪŋ, -t
chyle
BR kʌɪl
AM kaɪl
chylous
BR kʌɪləs
AM kaɪləs
chyme
BR kʌɪm
AM kaɪm
chymotrypsin
BR ˌkʌɪmə(ʊ)ˈtrɪpsɪn
AM ˌkaɪmoʊˈtrɪps(ə)n
chymous
BR kʌɪməs
AM kaɪməs
chypre
BR ʃiːprə(r)
AM ʃiprə
CIA
BR ˌsiːʌɪˈeɪ
AM ˌsi,aɪˈeɪ
ciabatta
BR tʃəˈbaːtə(r), -z
AM tʃɪˈbɑdə, -z
ciabatte
BR tʃəˈbaːtiː
AM tʃɪˈbɑdi
ciao
BR tʃaʊ
AM tʃaʊ
Ciba
BR siːbə(r)
AM siːbə
Cibachrome
BR ˌsiːbəkrəʊm, -z
AM ˌsiːbə,kroʊm, -z

Ciba-Geigy®
BR ˌsiːbəˈgʌɪgi
AM ˌsiːbəˈgaɪgi
ciboria
BR sɪˈbɔːrɪə(r)
AM səˈbɔriə
ciborium
BR sɪˈbɔːrɪəm
AM səˈbɔriəm
cicada
BR sɪˈkaːdə(r), -z
AM səˈkeɪdə, səˈkɑdə, -z
cicala
BR sɪˈkaːlə(r), -z
AM səˈkɑlə, -z
cicatrices
BR sɪkəˈtrʌɪsiː:z
AM sɪkəˈtraɪsiz, səˈkertrəsiz
cicatricial
BR sɪkəˈtrɪʃl
AM sɪkəˈtrɪʃəl
cicatrisation
BR ˌsɪkətrʌɪˈzeɪʃn
AM ˌsɪkətrəˈzeɪʃən, ˌsɪkə,traɪˈzeɪʃən
cicatrise
BR ˈsɪkətrʌɪz, -ɪz, -ɪŋ, -d
AM ˈsɪkə,traɪz, -ɪz, -ɪŋ, -d
cicatrix
BR ˈsɪkətrɪks, -ɪz
AM ˈsɪkə,trɪks, -ɪz
cicatrization
BR ˌsɪkətrʌɪˈzeɪʃn
AM ˌsɪkətrəˈzeɪʃən, ˌsɪkə,traɪˈzeɪʃən
cicatrize
BR ˈsɪkətrʌɪz, -ɪz, -ɪŋ, -d
AM ˈsɪkə,traɪz, -ɪz, -ɪŋ, -d
Cicely
BR sɪsɪli
AM sɪsɪli
cicely
BR sɪsɪl|i, -ɪz
AM sɪsɪli, -z
Cicero
BR sɪsərəʊ
AM sɪsəroʊ
cicerone
BR ˌtʃɪtʃəˈrəʊn|i, ˌsɪsəˈrəʊn|i, -ɪz
AM ˌsɪsəˈroʊni, -z
ciceroni
BR ˌtʃɪtʃəˈrəʊni, ˌsɪsəˈrəʊni
AM ˌsɪsəˈroʊni
Ciceronian
BR ˌsɪsəˈrəʊnɪən
AM ˌsɪsəˈroʊnɪən
cichlid
BR sɪklɪd, -z
AM sɪklɪd, -z
cicisbei
BR ˌtʃɪtʃɪzˈbeiː
AM ˌtʃɪtʃɪzˈbeiː

cicisbeo
BR ˌtʃɪtʃɪzˈbeiəʊ, -z
AM ˌtʃɪtʃɪzˈbeioʊ, -z
Cid, El
BR ɛl sɪd
AM ɛl sɪd
cider
BR sʌɪdə(r), -z
AM saɪdər, -z
ci-devant
BR ˌsiːdəˈvɒ̃
AM ˌsidəˈvɑnt
cig
BR sɪg, -z
AM sɪg, -z
cigala
BR sɪˈgaːlə(r), -z
AM səˈgalə, -z
cigar
BR sɪˈgaː(r), -z
AM səˈgɑr, -z
cigaret
BR ˌsɪgəˈret, -s
AM ˌsɪgəˈret, ˈsɪgə,ret, -s
cigarette
BR ˌsɪgəˈret, -s
AM ˌsɪgəˈret, ˈsɪgə,ret, -s
cigarillo
BR ˌsɪgəˈrɪləʊ, -z
AM ˌsɪgəˈrɪloʊ, -z
ciggie
BR sɪg|i, -ɪz
AM sɪgi, -z
ciggy
BR sɪg|i, -ɪz
AM sɪgi, -z
ciguatera
BR ˌsɪgwəˈtɛːrə(r)
AM ˌsigwəˈterə, ˌsɪgwəˈterə
cilantro
BR sɪˈlantrəʊ
AM sɪˈlæn,troʊ, sɪˈlan,troʊ
cilia
BR sɪlɪə(r)
AM sɪljə, sɪlɪə
ciliary
BR sɪlɪəri
AM sɪlɪəri
ciliate
BR sɪlɪeɪt
AM sɪli,eɪt, sɪliət
ciliated
BR sɪlɪeɪtɪd
AM sɪlieɪdɪd
ciliation
BR sɪlɪˈeɪʃn
AM sɪliˈeɪʃən
cilice
BR sɪl|ɪs, -ɪsɪz
AM sɪləs, -əz

Cilicia
BR sʌɪˈlɪsɪə(r), sɪˈlɪsɪə(r), sʌɪˈlɪʃɪə(r), sɪˈlɪʃɪə(r)
AM səˈlɪʃə
Cilician
BR sʌɪˈlɪsɪən, sɪˈlɪsɪən, sʌɪˈlɪʃɪən, sɪˈlɪʃɪən
AM səˈlɪʃən
cilium
BR sɪlɪəm
AM sɪlɪəm
cill
BR sɪl, -z
AM sɪl, -z
Cilla
BR sɪlə(r)
AM sɪlə
Cimabue
BR ˌtʃɪmaˈbuːeɪ, ˌtʃɪmaˈbuːi
AM ˌtʃɪmaˈbuei
cimbalom
BR sɪmbələm, ˈsɪmbləm, -z
AM sɪmbələm, -z
cimetadine
BR sʌɪˈmetədiːn
AM saɪˈmetə,din
Cimmerian
BR sɪˈmɪərɪən, sɪˈmɛrɪən, -z
AM səˈmɪrɪən, səˈmɛrɪən, -z
cinch
BR sɪn(t)ʃ, -ɪz, -ɪŋ, -t
AM sɪntʃ, -ɪz, -ɪŋ, -t
cinchona
BR sɪŋˈkəʊnə(r), -z
AM sɪŋˈkoʊnə, -z
cinchonic
BR sɪŋˈkɒnɪk
AM sɪŋˈkɑnɪk
cinchonine
BR sɪŋkənɪːn
AM sɪŋkə,nin, ˈʃɪŋkənən
Cincinnati
BR ˌsɪnsɪˈnati
AM ˌsɪn(t)səˈnædi
cincture
BR sɪn(k)tʃə(r), -z
AM sɪŋ(kt)ʃər, -z
cinder
BR sɪndə(r), -z
AM sɪndər, -z
Cinderella
BR ˌsɪndəˈrelə(r)
AM ˌsɪndəˈrelə
cindery
BR sɪnd(ə)ri
AM sɪndəri
Cindy
BR sɪndi
AM sɪndi
cine
BR sɪni
AM sɪni

cineaste
BR 'sɪneɪast, 'sɪnɪast,
-s
AM 'smɪˌæst, 'sɪnɪəst,
-s

cinecamera
BR 'sɪnɪˌkam(ə)rə(r),
-z
AM 'sɪnɪˌkæm(ə)rə, -z

cinefilm
BR 'sɪnɪfɪlm, -z
AM 'sɪnəˌfɪlm, -z

cinema
BR 'sɪnɪmə(r), -z
AM 'sɪnəmə, -z

CinemaScope®
BR 'sɪnɪməskəʊp
AM 'sɪnəməˌskoʊp

cinematheque
BR ˌsɪnɪmə'tɛk, -s
AM 'sɪnəməˌtɛk, -s

cinematic
BR ˌsɪnɪ'matɪk
AM ˌsɪnə'mædɪk

cinematically
BR ˌsɪnɪ'matɪkli
AM ˌsɪnə'mædək(ə)li

cinematograph
BR ˌsɪnɪ'matəgrɑːf,
ˌsɪnɪ'matəgraf, -s
AM ˌsɪnə'mædəgræf, -s

cinematographer
BR ˌsɪnɪmə'tɒgrəfə(r),
-z
AM ˌsɪnəmə'tɑgrəfər,
-z

cinematographic
BR ˌsɪnɪˌmatə'grafɪk
AM ˌsɪnəˌmædə'græfɪk

cinematographic-ally
BR ˌsɪnɪˌmatə'grafɪkli
AM ˌsɪnəˌmædə'græfək-(ə)li

cinematography
BR ˌsɪnɪmə'tɒgrəfi
AM ˌsɪnəmə'tɑgrəfi

cinéma-vérité
BR ˌsɪnɪmə'vɛrɪteɪ,
ˌsɪnɪmɑː'vɛrɪteɪ
AM ˌsɪnəməˌvɛri'teɪ

cinephile
BR 'sɪnɪfʌɪl, -z
AM 'sɪnəˌfaɪl, -z

Cinerama®
BR ˌsɪnɪ'rɑːmə(r)
AM ˌsɪnə'ræmə

cineraria
BR ˌsɪnə'rɛːrɪə(r)
AM ˌsɪnə'rɛriə

cinerarium
BR ˌsɪnə'rɛːrɪəm, -z
AM ˌsɪnə'rɛriəm, -z

cinerary
BR 'sɪn(ə)rəri
AM 'sɪnəˌrɛri

cinereous
BR sɪ'nɪərɪəs

AM sə'nɪrɪəs

Cingalese
BR ˌsɪŋgə'liːz
AM ˌsɪŋgə'liːz

cingula
BR 'sɪŋgjʊlə(r)
AM 'sɪŋgjələ

cingulum
BR 'sɪŋgjʊləm
AM 'sɪŋgjələm

cinnabar
BR 'sɪnəbɑː(r)
AM 'sɪnəˌbɑr

cinnamon
BR 'sɪnəmən
AM 'sɪnəmən

cinq
BR sɪŋk
AM sɪŋk, sæŋk

cinque
BR sɪŋk
AM sɪŋk, sæŋk

cinquecentist
BR ˌtʃɪŋkwɪ'tʃɛntɪst, -s
AM ˌsɪŋkwə'(t)ʃɛn(t)əst, -s

cinquecento
BR ˌtʃɪŋkwɪ'tʃɛntəʊ
AM ˌsɪŋkwə'(t)ʃɛnoʊ

cinquefoil
BR 'sɪŋkfɔɪl, -z
AM 'sɪŋkˌfɔɪl, 'sæŋkˌfɔɪl, -z

Cinque Ports
BR ˌsɪŋk 'pɔːts
AM 'sɪŋk 'pɔ(ə)rts, 'sæŋk +

Cinzano®
BR tʃɪn'zɑːnəʊ, tʃɪn(t)'sɑːnəʊ, -z
AM tʃɪn'zɑnoʊ, sɪn'zɑnoʊ, -z

cion
BR 'sʌɪən, -z
AM 'saɪən, -z

cipher
BR 'sʌɪfə(r), -əz, -(ə)rɪŋ, -əd
AM 'saɪf]ər, -ərz, -(ə)rɪŋ, -ərd

cipolin
BR 'sɪpəlɪn
AM 'sɪpələn

Cipriani
BR ˌsɪprɪ'ɑːni
AM ˌsɪpri'ɑni

circa
BR 'sə:kə(r)
AM 'sɜrkə

circadian
BR sə:'keɪdɪən
AM sɜr'keɪdiən

Circassian
BR sə'kasɪən, sə:'kasɪən, -z
AM sɜr'kæsɪən, -z

Circe
BR 'sə:si
AM 'sɜrsi

Circean
BR sə:'siːən
AM 'sɜrsiən

circinate
BR 'sə:sɪneɪt, 'sə:sɪnət
AM 'sɜrsəˌneɪt, 'sɜrsənət

circiter
BR 'sə:sɪtə(r)
AM 'sɜrsədər

circle
BR 'sə:k|l, -lz, -lɪŋ\-lɪŋ, -ld
AM 'sɜrkəl, -əlz, -(ə)lɪŋ, -əld

circler
BR 'sə:klə(r), -z
AM 'sɜrk(ə)lər, -z

circlet
BR 'sə:klɪt, -s
AM 'sɜrklət, -s

circlip
BR 'sə:klɪp, -s
AM 'sɜrklɪp, -s

circs
BR sə:ks
AM sɜrks

circuit
BR 'sə:k|ɪt, -ɪts, -ɪtɪŋ, -ɪtɪd
AM 'sɜrkə|t, -ts, -dɪŋ, -dəd

circuition
BR ˌsə:kjʊ'ɪʃn
AM ˌsɜrkjə'wɪʃən

circuitous
BR sə(:)'kjuːɪtəs
AM sɜr'kjuədəs

circuitously
BR sə(:)'kjuːɪtəsli
AM sɜr'kjuədəsli

circuitousness
BR sə(:)'kjuːɪtəsnəs
AM sɜr'kjuədəsnəs

circuitry
BR 'sə:kɪtri
AM 'sɜrkətri

circuity
BR sə(:)'kjuːti
AM sɜr'kjuədi

circular
BR 'sə:kjʊlə(r), -z
AM 'sɜrkjələr, -z

circularisation
BR ˌsə:kjʊlərʌɪ'zeɪʃn
AM ˌsɜrkjələrə'zeɪʃən, ˌsɜrkjələˌraɪ'zeɪʃən

circularise
BR 'sə:kjʊlərʌɪz, -ɪz, -ɪŋ, -d
AM 'sɜrkjələˌraɪz, -ɪz, -ɪŋ, -d

circularity
BR ˌsə:kjʊ'larɪti
AM ˌsɜrkjə'lɛrədi

circularization
BR ˌsə:kjʊlərʌɪ'zeɪʃn
AM ˌsɜrkjələrə'zeɪʃən, ˌsɜrkjələˌraɪ'zeɪʃən

circularize
BR 'sə:kjʊlərʌɪz, -ɪz, -ɪŋ, -d
AM 'sɜrkjələˌraɪz, -ɪz, -ɪŋ, -d

circularly
BR 'sə:kjʊləli
AM 'sɜrkjələrli

circulate
BR 'sə:kjʊleɪt, -s, -ɪŋ, -ɪd
AM 'sɜrkjəleɪ|t, -ts, -dɪŋ, -dɪd

circulation
BR ˌsə:kjʊ'leɪʃn, -z
AM ˌsɜrkjə'leɪʃən, -z

circulative
BR 'sə:kjʊlətɪv
AM 'sɜrkjələdɪv, 'sɜrkjəˌleɪdɪv

circulator
BR 'sə:kjʊleɪtə(r), -z
AM 'sɜrkjəˌleɪdər, -z

circulatory
BR 'sə:kjʊlət(ə)ri, ˌsə:kjʊ'leɪt(ə)ri
AM 'sɜrkjələˌtɔri

circumambience
BR ˌsə:kəm'ambɪəns
AM ˌsɜrkəm'æmbɪəns

circumambiency
BR ˌsə:kəm'ambɪənsi
AM ˌsɜrkəm'æmbɪənsi

circumambient
BR ˌsə:kəm'ambɪənt
AM ˌsɜrkəm'æmbɪənt

circumambulate
BR ˌsə:kəm'ambjʊleɪt, -s, -ɪŋ, -ɪd
AM ˌsɜrkəm'æmbjəˌleɪ|t, -ts, -dɪŋ, -dɪd

circumambulation
BR ˌsə:kəmˌambjʊ'leɪʃn, -z
AM ˌsɜrkəmˌæmbjə'leɪʃən, -z

circumambulatory
BR ˌsə:kəm'ambjʊlə-t(ə)ri
AM ˌsɜrkəm'æmbjələ-ˌtɔri

circumcircle
BR 'sə:kəmsə:k|l, -z
AM 'sɜrkəmˌsɜrkəl, -z

circumcise
BR 'sə:kəmsʌɪz, -ɪz, -ɪŋ, -d
AM 'sɜrkəmˌsaɪz, -ɪz, -ɪŋ, -d

circumcision
BR ˌsə:kəm'sɪʒn, -z
AM ˌsɜrkəm'sɪʒən, -z

circumference
BR sə'kʌmf(ə)rəns,
sə'kʌmf(ə)rn̩s, -ɪz
AM sər'kəmf(ə)rəns,
-əz

circumferential
BR sə‚kʌmfə'rɛnʃl
AM sər‚kəmfə'rɛn(t)ʃəl

circumferentially
BR sə‚kʌmfə'rɛnʃli,
sə‚kʌmfə'rɛnʃəli
AM sər‚kəmfə'rɛn(t)ʃəli

circumflex
BR 'sɜːkəmflɛks, -ɪz
AM 'sɜrkəm‚flɛks, -əz

circumfluence
BR sə'kʌmflʊəns
AM sər'kəmfluəns

circumfluent
BR sə'kʌmflʊənt
AM sər'kəmfləwənt

circumfuse
BR 'sɜːkəmfjuːz, -ɪz
AM 'sɜrkəm‚fjuz, -əz

circumjacent
BR ‚sɜːkəm'dʒeɪsnt
AM ‚sɜrkəm'dʒeɪsənt

circumlittoral
BR ‚sɜːkəm'lɪt(ə)rəl,
‚sɜːkəm'lɪt(ə)rl̩
AM ‚sɜrkəm'lɪdərəl

circumlocution
BR ‚sɜːkəmlə'kjuːʃn, -z
AM ‚sɜrkəm‚loʊ'kjuʃən,
-z

circumlocutional
BR ‚sɜːkəmlə'kjuːʃn̩(ə)l,
‚sɜːkəmlə'kjuːʃən(ə)l
AM ‚sɜrkəm‚loʊ'kju-
ʃ(ə)nəl

circumlocutionary
BR ‚sɜːkəmlə'kjuːʃn̩-
(ə)ri
AM ‚sɜrkəm‚loʊ'kjuʃə-
‚nɛri

circumlocutionist
BR ‚sɜːkəmlə'kjuːʃn̩ɪst,
‚sɜːkəmlə'kjuːʃənɪst,
-s
AM ‚sɜrkəm‚loʊ'kju-
ʃ(ə)nəst, -s

circumlocutory
BR ‚sɜːkəmlə'kjuːt(ə)ri
AM ‚sɜrkəm'lɑkjə‚tɔri

circumlunar
BR ‚sɜːkəm'l(j)uːnə(r)
AM ‚sɜrkəm'lunər

circumnavigate
BR ‚sɜːkəm'navɪɡeɪt,
-s, -ɪŋ, -ɪd
AM ‚sɜrkəm'nævə‚ɡeɪ|t,
-ts, -dɪŋ, -dɪd

circumnavigation
BR ‚sɜːkəm‚navɪ'ɡeɪʃn,
-z
AM ‚sɜrkəm‚nævə'ɡeɪ-
ʃən, -z

circumnavigator
BR ‚sɜːkəm'navɪɡeɪ-
tə(r), -z
AM ‚sɜrkəm'nævə-
‚ɡeɪdər, -z

circumpolar
BR ‚sɜːkəm'pəʊlə(r)
AM ‚sɜrkəm'poʊlər

circumscribable
BR 'sɜːkəmskrʌɪbəbl,
‚sɜːkəm'skrʌɪbəbl
AM ‚sɜrkəm'skraɪbəbəl

circumscribe
BR 'sɜːkəmskrʌɪb, -z,
-ɪŋ, -d
AM 'sɜrkəm‚skraɪb, -z,
-ɪŋ, -d

circumscriber
BR 'sɜːkəmskrʌɪbə(r),
-z
AM 'sɜrkəm‚skraɪbər,
-z

circumscription
BR ‚sɜːkəm'skrɪpʃn, -z
AM ‚sɜrkəm'skrɪpʃən,
-z

circumsolar
BR ‚sɜːkəm'səʊlə(r)
AM ‚sɜrkəm'soʊlər

circumspect
BR 'sɜːkəmspɛkt
AM 'sɜrkəm‚spɛk(t)

circumspection
BR ‚sɜːkəm'spɛkʃn
AM ‚sɜrkəm'spɛkʃən

circumspectly
BR 'sɜːkəmspɛktli
AM 'sɜrkəm‚spɛk(t)li

circumspectness
BR 'sɜːkəmspɛk(t)nəs
AM 'sɜrkəm‚spɛk(t)nəs

circumstance
BR 'sɜːkəmst(ə)ns,
'sɜːkəmstɑːns,
'sɜːkəmstans, -ɪz, -t
AM 'sɜrkəm‚stæns, -əz,
-t

circumstantial
BR ‚sɜːkəm'stanʃl
AM ‚sɜrkəm'stæn(t)ʃəl

circumstantiality
BR ‚sɜːkəm‚stanʃɪ'alɪti
AM ‚sɜrkəm‚stæn(t)ʃi-
'ælədi

circumstantially
BR ‚sɜːkəm'stanʃl̩i,
‚sɜːkəm'stanʃəli
AM ‚sɜrkəm'stæn(t)ʃəli

circumstantiate
BR ‚sɜːkəm'stanʃɪeɪt,
-s, -ɪŋ, -ɪd
AM ‚sɜrkəm'stæn-
(t)ʃi‚eɪ|t, -ts, -dɪŋ, -dɪd

circumterrestrial
BR ‚sɜːkəmtɪ'rɛstrɪəl
AM ‚sɜrkəmtə'rɛstriəl,
‚sɜrkəmtə'rɛstʃəl

circumvallate
BR ‚sɜː'əm'valeɪt, -s, -ɪŋ,
-ɪd
AM ‚sɜrkəm'væ‚leɪ|t,
-ts, -dɪŋ, -dɪd

circumvallation
BR ‚sɜːkəmvə'leɪʃn,
‚sɜːkəmva'leɪʃn, -z
AM ‚sɜrkəmvæ'leɪʃən,
-z

circumvent
BR ‚sɜːkəm'vɛnt,
'sɜːkəmvɛnt, -s, -ɪŋ, -ɪd
AM ‚sɜrkəm'vɛn|t, -ts,
-(t)ɪŋ, -(t)əd

circumvention
BR ‚sɜːkəm'vɛnʃn, -z
AM ‚sɜrkəm'vɛn(t)ʃən,
-z

circumvolution
BR ‚sɜːkəmvə'l(j)uːʃn,
-z
AM ‚sɜrkəmvə'luʃən,
-z

circus
BR 'sɜːkəs, -ɪz
AM 'sɜrkəs, -əz

ciré
BR 'siːreɪ
AM sə'reɪ

Cirencester
BR 'sʌɪrən‚sɛstə(r),
'sʌɪrn̩‚sɛstə(r),
'sɪsɪtə(r)
AM 'saɪrɛn‚sɛstər

cire perdue
BR ‚sɪə pɜː'djuː
AM 'sɪr ‚pɜr'd(j)u

cirque
BR sɜːk, -s
AM sɜrk, -s

cirrhosis
BR sɪ'rəʊsɪs
AM sə'roʊsəs

cirrhotic
BR sɪ'rɒtɪk
AM sə'rɑdɪk

cirri
BR 'sɪrʌɪ
AM 'sɪ‚raɪ

cirriped
BR 'sɪrɪpɛd, -z
AM 'sɪrə‚pɛd, -z

cirrocumulus
BR ‚sɪrə(ʊ)'kjuːmjʉləs
AM ‚sɪroʊ'kjumjələs

cirrose
BR 'sɪrəʊs
AM 'sɪroʊs

cirrostratus
BR ‚sɪrə(ʊ)'strɑːtəs,
‚sɪrə(ʊ)'streɪtəs
AM ‚sɪroʊ'strædəs,
‚sɪroʊ'streɪdəs

cirrous
BR 'sɪrəs
AM 'sɪrəs

cirrus
BR 'sɪrəs
AM 'sɪrəs

cisalpine
BR (‚)sɪs'alpʌɪn
AM sɪs'ælpaɪn

cisatlantic
BR ‚sɪsət'lantɪk
AM ‚sɪsət'læn(t)ɪk

cisco
BR 'sɪskəʊ, -z
AM 'sɪskoʊ, -z

Ciskei
BR ‚sɪs'kʌɪ, 'sɪskʌɪ
AM 'sɪs‚kaɪ

cislunar
BR ‚sɪs'l(j)uːnə(r)
AM sɪs'lunər

cispontine
BR ‚sɪs'pɒntʌɪn
AM sɪs'pɑn‚tin,
sɪs'pɑn‚taɪn

Cissie
BR 'sɪsi
AM 'sɪsi

cissoid
BR 'sɪsɔɪd, -z
AM 'sɪsɔɪd, -z

Cissy
BR 'sɪsi
AM 'sɪsi

cist
BR sɪst, -s
AM sɪst, -s

Cistercian
BR sɪ'stɜːʃn, -z
AM sɪ'stɜrʃən, -z

cistern
BR 'sɪstən, -z
AM 'sɪstɜrn, -z

cistron
BR 'sɪstrɒn, 'sɪstrən, -z
AM 'sɪs‚trɑn, -z

cistus
BR 'sɪstəs
AM 'sɪstəs

citable
BR 'sʌɪtəbl
AM 'saɪdəbəl

citadel
BR 'sɪtəd(ə)l, 'sɪtəd‚ɛl,
-z
AM 'sɪdədəl, 'sɪdə‚dɛl,
-z

citation
BR sʌɪ'teɪʃn, -z
AM saɪ'teɪʃən, -z

citatory
BR sʌɪ'teɪt(ə)ri,
'sʌɪtət(ə)ri
AM 'saɪdə‚tɔri

cite
BR sʌɪt, -s, -ɪŋ, -ɪd
AM saɪ|t, -ts, -dɪŋ, -dɪd

CITES
BR 'sʌɪtiːz
AM 'saɪdiz

cithara
BR ˈsɪθ(ə)rə(r), -z
AM ˈsɪθ(ə)rə, -z
cither
BR ˈsɪθə(r), -z
AM ˈsɪθər, -z
Citibank®
BR ˈsɪtɪbæŋk
AM ˈsɪdiˌbæŋk
Citicorp
BR ˈsɪtɪkɔːp
AM ˈsɪdiˌkɔː(ə)rp
citify
BR ˈsɪtɪfaɪ, -z, -ɪŋ, -d
AM ˈsɪdɪˌfaɪ, -z, -ɪŋ, -d
citizen
BR ˈsɪtɪz(ə)n, -z
AM ˈsɪdɪzən, ˈsɪdɪsən, -z
citizenhood
BR ˈsɪtɪz(ə)nhʊd
AM ˈsɪdɪzən,(h)ʊd,
ˈsɪdɪsən,(h)ʊd
citizenly
BR ˈsɪtɪz(ə)nli
AM ˈsɪdɪzɪnli, ˈsɪdɪsɪnli
citizenry
BR ˈsɪtɪz(ə)nri
AM ˈsɪdɪzɪnri,
ˈsɪdɪsɪnri
citizenship
BR ˈsɪtɪz(ə)nʃɪp
AM ˈsɪdɪzən,ʃɪp,
ˈsɪdɪsən,ʃɪp
citole
BR ˈsɪtəʊl, -z
AM ˈsɪˌtoʊl, -z
citral
BR ˈsɪtr(ə)l, ˈsɪtral
AM ˈsɪtrəl
citrate
BR ˈsɪtreɪt, -s
AM ˈsɪˌtreɪt, -s
citric
BR ˈsɪtrɪk
AM ˈsɪtrɪk
citrin
BR ˈsɪtrɪn
AM ˈsɪtrən
citrine
BR ˈsɪtriːn, ˈsɪtrɪn
AM ˈsɪtrin, ˈsɪtrən,
ˈsɪtraɪn
Citroën®
BR ˈsɪtrəʊən, ˈsɪtr(ə)n,
-z
AM ˈsɪtrən, -z
citron
BR ˈsɪtr(ə)n, -z
AM ˈsɪtrən, -z
citronella
BR ˌsɪtrəˈnɛlə(r)
AM ˌsɪtrəˈnɛlə
citrous
BR ˈsɪtrəs
AM ˈsɪtrəs
citrus
BR ˈsɪtrəs

AM ˈsɪtrəs
cittern
BR ˈsɪtɜːn, -z
AM ˈsɪdɜrn, -z
city
BR ˈsɪt|i, -ɪz
AM ˈsɪdi, -z
cityfied
BR ˈsɪtɪfaɪd
AM ˈsɪdɪfaɪd
cityscape
BR ˈsɪtɪskeɪp, -s
AM ˈsɪdiˌskeɪp, -s
cityward
BR ˈsɪtɪwəd, -z
AM ˈsɪdiˌwərd, -z
Ciudad
BR ˈθjuːdad, θjʊˈdad,
ˌθiuːˈdad, ˈθjuːdɑːd,
θjʊˈdɑːd, ˌθiuːˈdɑːd
AM ˈsiuˌdæd
civet
BR ˈsɪvɪt, -s
AM ˈsɪvət, -s
civic
BR ˈsɪvɪk, -s
AM ˈsɪvɪk, -s
civically
BR ˈsɪvɪkli
AM ˈsɪvɪk(ə)li
civies
BR ˈsɪvɪz
AM ˈsɪvɪz
civil
BR ˈsɪvl
AM ˈsɪvɪl
civilian
BR sɪˈvɪliən, -z
AM səˈvɪljən, səˈvɪliən,
-z
civilianisation
BR sɪˌvɪljənʌɪˈzeɪʃn
AM səˌvɪljənəˈzeɪʃən,
səˌvɪljəˌnaɪˈzeɪʃən
civilianise
BR sɪˈvɪljənʌɪz, -ɪz, -ɪŋ,
-d
AM səˈvɪljəˌnaɪz, -ɪz,
-ɪŋ, -d
civilianization
BR sɪˌvɪljənʌɪˈzeɪʃn
AM səˌvɪljənəˈzeɪʃən,
səˌvɪljəˌnaɪˈzeɪʃən
civilianize
BR sɪˈvɪljənʌɪz, -ɪz, -ɪŋ,
-d
AM səˈvɪljəˌnaɪz, -ɪz,
-ɪŋ, -d
civilisable
BR ˈsɪvlʌɪzəbl,
ˈsɪvɪlʌɪzəbl
AM ˈsɪvəˌlaɪzəbəl
civilisation
BR ˌsɪvlʌɪˈzeɪʃn,
ˌsɪvɪlʌɪˈzeɪʃn, -z
AM ˌsɪvələˈzeɪʃən,
ˌsɪvəˌlaɪˈzeɪʃən, -z

civilise
BR ˈsɪvlʌɪz, ˈsɪvɪlʌɪz,
-ɪz, -ɪŋ, -d
AM ˈsɪvəˌlaɪz, -ɪz, -ɪŋ, -d
civiliser
BR ˈsɪvlʌɪzə(r),
ˈsɪvɪlʌɪzə(r), -z
AM ˈsɪvəˌlaɪzər, -z
civility
BR sɪˈvɪlɪt|i, -ɪz
AM səˈvɪlɪdi, -z
civilizable
BR ˈsɪvlʌɪzəbl,
ˈsɪvɪlʌɪzəbl
AM ˈsɪvəˌlaɪzəbəl
civilization
BR ˌsɪvlʌɪˈzeɪʃn,
ˌsɪvɪlʌɪˈzeɪʃn, -z
AM ˌsɪvələˈzeɪʃən,
ˌsɪvəˌlaɪˈzeɪʃən, -z
civilize
BR ˈsɪvlʌɪz, ˈsɪvɪlʌɪz,
-ɪz, -ɪŋ, -d
AM ˈsɪvəˌlaɪz, -ɪz, -ɪŋ, -d
civilizer
BR ˈsɪvlʌɪzə(r),
ˈsɪvɪlʌɪzə(r), -z
AM ˈsɪvəˌlaɪzər, -z
civilly
BR ˈsɪvļi, ˈsɪvɪli
AM ˈsɪvɪ(l)li
civvies
BR ˈsɪvɪz
AM ˈsɪvɪz
civvy
BR ˈsɪv|i, -ɪz
AM ˈsɪvi, -z
clachan
BR ˈklax(ə)n,
ˈklak(ə)n
AM ˈklækən
clack
BR klak, -s, -ɪŋ, -t
AM klæk, -s, -ɪŋ, -t
clacker
BR ˈklakə(r), -z
AM ˈklækər, -z
Clackmannan
BR klak'manən
AM klæk'mænən
Clacton
BR ˈklaktən
AM ˈklæktən
clad
BR klad
AM klæd
clade
BR kleɪd, -z
AM kleɪd, -z
cladism
BR ˈkleɪdɪz(ə)m
AM ˈkleɪˌdɪzəm
cladistics
BR kləˈdɪstɪks,
klaˈdɪstɪks
AM kləˈdɪstɪks
cladode
BR ˈkleɪdəʊd, -z

AM ˈklæˌdoʊd, -z
Claiborne
BR ˈkleɪbɔːn
AM ˈkleɪˌbɔ(ə)rn
claim
BR kleɪm, -z, -ɪŋ, -d
AM kleɪm, -z, -ɪŋ, -d
claimable
BR ˈkleɪməbl
AM ˈkleɪməbəl
claimant
BR ˈkleɪm(ə)nt, -s
AM ˈkleɪmənt, -s
claimer
BR ˈkleɪmə(r), -z
AM ˈkleɪmər, -z
Clair
BR klɛː(r)
AM klɛ(ə)r
clairaudience
BR ˌklɛːrˈɔːdɪəns
AM ˌklɛˈrɔdiəns,
ˌklɛˈradiəns
clairaudient
BR ˌklɛːrˈɔːdɪənt, -s
AM ˌklɛˈrɔdiənt,
ˌklɛˈradiənt, -s
Claire
BR klɛː(r)
AM klɛ(ə)r
clairvoyance
BR klɛːˈvɔɪəns
AM ˌklɛrˈvɔɪəns
clairvoyant
BR klɛːˈvɔɪənt, -s
AM ˌklɛrˈvɔɪənt, -s
clairvoyantly
BR klɛːˈvɔɪəntli
AM ˌklɛrˈvɔɪən(t)li
clam
BR klam, -z, -ɪŋ, -d
AM klæm, -z, -ɪŋ, -d
clamant
BR ˈkleɪm(ə)nt,
ˈklam(ə)nt
AM ˈkleɪmənt
clamantly
BR ˈkleɪm(ə)ntli,
ˈklam(ə)ntli
AM ˈkleɪmən(t)li
clambake
BR ˈklambeɪk, -s
AM ˈklæmˌbeɪk, -s
clamber
BR ˈklambļə(r), -əz,
-(ə)rɪŋ, -əd
AM ˈklæmbər, -z, -ɪŋ, -d
clammily
BR ˈklamɪli
AM ˈklæməli
clamminess
BR ˈklamɪnɪs
AM ˈklæmɪnɪs
clammy
BR ˈklam|i, -ɪə(r), -ɪɪst
AM ˈklæmi, -ər, -ɪst

clamor
BR ˈklæm|ə(r), -əz, -(ə)rɪŋ, -əd
AM ˈklæmər, -z, -ɪŋ, -d

clamorous
BR ˈklæm(ə)rəs
AM ˈklæmərəs

clamorously
BR ˈklæm(ə)rəsli
AM ˈklæm(ə)rəsli

clamorousness
BR ˈklæm(ə)rəsnəs
AM ˈklæm(ə)rəsnəs

clamour
BR ˈklæm|ə(r), -əz, -(ə)rɪŋ, -əd
AM ˈklæmər, -z, -ɪŋ, -d

clamp
BR klæmp, -s, -ɪŋ, -t
AM klæmp, -s, -ɪŋ, -t

clampdown
BR ˈklæmpdaʊn, -z
AM ˈklæmp͵daʊn, -z

clamshell
BR ˈklæmʃɛl, -z
AM ˈklæm͵ʃɛl, -z

clan
BR klæn, -z
AM klæn, -z

Clancarty
BR klanˈkɑːti
AM klænˈkɑrdi

Clancey
BR ˈklænsi
AM ˈklænsi

Clancy
BR ˈklænsi
AM ˈklænsi

clandestine
BR klanˈdɛstɪn, klanˈdɛstʌɪn, ˈklandɪstɪn, ˈklandɪstʌɪn
AM klænˈdɛstən, ˈklændəs͵tin

clandestinely
BR klanˈdɛstɪnli, klanˈdɛstʌɪnli, ˈklandɪstɪnli, ˈklandɪstʌɪnli
AM klænˈdɛstənli, ˈklændəs͵tinli

clandestinity
BR ͵klandɛˈstɪnɪti, ͵klandɪˈstɪnɪti
AM ͵klændɛsˈtɪnɪdi

clang
BR klæŋ, -z, -ɪŋ, -d
AM klæŋ, -z, -ɪŋ, -d

clanger
BR ˈklæŋə(r), -z
AM ˈklæŋər, -z

clangor
BR ˈklæŋgə(r)
AM ˈklæŋər

clangorous
BR ˈklæŋg(ə)rəs
AM ˈklæŋərəs

clangorously
BR ˈklæŋg(ə)rəsli
AM ˈklæŋərəsli

clangour
BR ˈklæŋgə(r)
AM ˈklæŋər

clangourous
BR ˈklæŋg(ə)rəs
AM ˈklæŋərəs

clangourously
BR ˈklæŋg(ə)rəsli
AM ˈklæŋərəsli

clank
BR klæŋ|k, -ks, -kɪŋ, -(k)t
AM klæŋ|k, -ks, -kɪŋ, -(k)t

clankingly
BR ˈklæŋkɪŋli
AM ˈklæŋkɪŋli

clannish
BR ˈklanɪʃ
AM ˈklænɪʃ

clannishly
BR ˈklanɪʃli
AM ˈklænɪʃli

clannishness
BR ˈklanɪʃnɪs
AM ˈklænɪʃnɪs

clanship
BR ˈklanʃɪp
AM ˈklæn͵ʃɪp

clansman
BR ˈklanzmən
AM ˈklænzmən

clansmen
BR ˈklanzmən
AM ˈklænzmən

clanswoman
BR ˈklanzˌwʊmən
AM ˈklænzˌwʊmən

clanswomen
BR ˈklanzˌwɪmɪn
AM ˈklænzˌwɪmɪn

clap
BR klap, -s, -ɪŋ, -t
AM klæp, -s, -ɪŋ, -t

clapboard
BR ˈklapbɔːd
AM ˈklæpˌbɔ(ə)rd, ˈklæbərd

Clapham
BR ˈklap(ə)m
AM ˈklæpəm

clapper
BR ˈklapə(r), -z
AM ˈklæpər, -z

clapperboard
BR ˈklapəbɔːd, -z
AM ˈklæpərˌbɔ(ə)rd, -z

Clapton
BR ˈklaptən
AM ˈklæptən

claptrap
BR ˈklaptrap
AM ˈklæp͵træp

claque
BR klak, -s
AM klæk, -s

claqueur
BR ˈklakə(r), -z
AM ˈklæ͵kər, -z

Clara
BR ˈklɛːrə(r)
AM ˈklɛrə

Clarabella
BR ͵klarəˈbɛlə(r), -z
AM ͵klɛrəˈbɛlə, -z

Clarabelle
BR ˈklarəbɛl, -z
AM ˈklɛrəˌbɛl, -z

Clare
BR klɛː(r)
AM klɛ(ə)r

Claremont
BR ˈklɛːmɒnt, ˈklɛːm(ə)nt
AM ˈklɛr͵mɑnt

clarence
BR ˈklarəns, ˈklarn̩s, -ɪz
AM ˈklɛrəns, -əz

Clarenceux
BR ˈklarəns(j)uː, ˈklarn̩s(j)uː, ˈklarənsəʊ, ˈklarn̩səʊ
AM ͵klɛrənˈsoʊ

Clarendon
BR ˈklarəndən, ˈklarn̩dən
AM ˈklɛrəndən

claret
BR ˈklarət, -s
AM ˈklɛrət, -s

Clarges
BR ˈklɑːdʒɪz
AM ˈklɑrdʒəs

Clarice
BR ˈklarɪs
AM ˈklɛrɪs, kləˈris

Claridge's
BR ˈklarɪdʒɪz
AM ˈklɛrɪdʒɪz

clarification
BR ͵klarɪfɪˈkeɪʃn
AM ͵klɛrəfəˈkeɪʃn

clarificatory
BR ͵klarɪfɪˈkeɪt(ə)ri, ˈklarɪfɪkət(ə)ri
AM ˈklɛrəfəkəˌtɔri

clarifier
BR ˈklarɪfʌɪə(r), -z
AM ˈklɛrəˌfaɪər, -z

clarify
BR ˈklarɪfʌɪ, -z, -ɪŋ, -d
AM ˈklɛrəˌfaɪ, -z, -ɪŋ, -d

Clarinda
BR kləˈrɪndə(r)
AM kləˈrɪndə

clarinet
BR ͵klarɪˈnɛt, -s
AM ͵klɛrəˈnɛt, -s

clarinetist
BR ͵klarɪˈnɛtɪst, -s

clarinettist
BR ͵klarɪˈnɛtɪst, -s
AM ͵klɛrəˈnɛdəst, -s

clarion
BR ˈklarɪən, -z
AM ˈklɛrɪən, -z

Clarissa
BR kləˈrɪsə(r)
AM kləˈrɪsə

clarity
BR ˈklarɪti
AM ˈklɛrədi

Clark
BR klɑːk
AM klɑrk

Clarke
BR klɑːk
AM klɑrk

clarkia
BR ˈklɑːkɪə(r), -z
AM ˈklɑrkɪə, -z

Clarkson
BR ˈklɑːksn̩
AM ˈklɑrksən

Clarrie
BR ˈklari
AM ˈklɛri

clart
BR klɑːt, -s
AM klɑrt, -s

clarty
BR ˈklɑːti
AM ˈklɑrdi

clary
BR ˈklɛːr|i, -ɪz
AM ˈklɛri, -z

clash
BR klaʃ, -ɪz, -ɪŋ, -t
AM klæʃ, -əz, -ɪŋ, -t

clasher
BR ˈklaʃə(r), -z
AM ˈklæʃər, -z

clasp
BR klɑːsp, klasp, -s, -ɪŋ, -t
AM klæsp, -s, -ɪŋ, -t

clasper
BR ˈklɑːspə(r), ˈklaspə(r), -z
AM ˈklæspər, -z

class
BR klɑːs, klas, -ɪz, -ɪŋ, -t
AM klæs, -əz, -ɪŋ, -t

classable
BR ˈklɑːsəbl, ˈklasəbl
AM ˈklæsəbəl

classic
BR ˈklasɪk, -s
AM ˈklæsɪk, -s

classical
BR ˈklasɪkl
AM ˈklæsəkəl

classicalism
BR ˈklasɪklɪz(ə)m
AM ˈklæsəkəˌlɪzəm

classicalist
BR ˈklasɪkl̩ɪst, -s
AM ˈklæsəkələst, -s

classicality
BR ˌklasɪˈkalɪti
AM ˌklæsəˈkælədi

classically
BR ˈklasɪkl̩i, ˈklasɪkli
AM ˈklæsək(ə)li

classicalness
BR ˈklasɪklnəs
AM ˈklæsəkəlnəs

classicise
BR ˈklasɪsʌɪz, -ɪz, -ɪŋ, -d
AM ˈklæsəˌsaɪz, -ɪz, -ɪŋ, -d

classicism
BR ˈklasɪsɪz(ə)m, -z
AM ˈklæsəˌsɪzəm, -z

classicist
BR ˈklasɪsɪst, -s
AM ˈklæsəsəst, -s

classicize
BR ˈklasɪsʌɪz, -ɪz, -ɪŋ, -d
AM ˈklæsəˌsaɪz, -ɪz, -ɪŋ, -d

classicus
BR ˈklasɪkəs
AM ˈklæsəkəs

classifiable
BR ˈklasɪfʌɪəbl
AM ˌklæsəˈfaɪəbəl

classifiably
BR ˈklasɪfʌɪəbli
AM ˌklæsəˈfaɪəbli

classification
BR ˌklasɪfɪˈkeɪʃn, -z
AM ˌklæsəfəˈkeɪʃən, -z

classificatory
BR ˌklasɪfɪˈkeɪt(ə)ri, ˈklasɪfɪkət(ə)ri
AM ˈklæsəfəkəˌtɔri

classifieds
BR ˈklasɪfʌɪdz
AM ˈklæsəˌfaɪdz

classifier
BR ˈklasɪfʌɪə(r), -z
AM ˈklæsəˌfaɪər, -z

classify
BR ˈklasɪfʌɪ, -z, -ɪŋ, -d
AM ˈklæsəˌfaɪ, -z, -ɪŋ, -d

classily
BR ˈklɑːsɪli, ˈklasɪli
AM ˈklæsəli

classiness
BR ˈklɑːsɪnɪs, ˈklasɪnɪs
AM ˈklæsɪnɪs

classism
BR ˈklɑːsɪz(ə)m, ˈklasɪz(ə)m
AM ˈklæˌsɪzəm

classist
BR ˈklɑːsɪst, ˈklasɪst, -s
AM ˈklæsəst, -s

classless
BR ˈklɑːsləs, ˈklasləs
AM ˈklæsləs

classlessness
BR ˈklɑːsləsnəs, ˈklasləsnəs
AM ˈklæsləsnəs

classmate
BR ˈklɑːsmeɪt, ˈklasmeɪt, -s
AM ˈklæsˌmeɪt, -s

classroom
BR ˈklɑːsruːm, ˈklɑːsrʊm, ˈklasruːm, -z
AM ˈklæsˌrum, ˈklæsˌrʊm, -z

classy
BR ˈklɑːs|i, ˈklas|i, -ɪə(r), -ɪɪst
AM ˈklæsi, -ər, -ɪst

clastic
BR ˈklastɪk
AM ˈklæstɪk

clathrate
BR ˈklaθreɪt, -s
AM ˈklæθˌreɪt, -s

clatter
BR ˈklat|ə(r), -əz, -(ə)rɪŋ, -əd
AM ˈklædər, -z, -ɪŋ, -d

Claud
BR klɔːd
AM klɔd, klɑd

Claude
BR klɔːd
AM klɔd, klɑd

Claudette
BR (ˌ)klɔːˈdet
AM ˌklɔːˈdet, ˌklɑˈdet

Claudia
BR ˈklɔːdɪə(r)
AM ˈklɔdɪə, ˈklɑdɪə

Claudian
BR ˈklɔːdɪən
AM ˈklɔdiən, ˈklɑdiən

claudication
BR ˌklɔːdɪˈkeɪʃn
AM ˌklɔdəˈkeɪʃən, ˌklɑdəˈkeɪʃən

Claudine
BR (ˌ)klɔːˈdiːn, ˈklɔːdiːn
AM ˌklɔˈdin, ˌklɑˈdin

Claudius
BR ˈklɔːdɪəs
AM ˈklɔdiəs, ˈklɑdiəs

clausal
BR ˈklɔːzl
AM ˈklɔzəl, ˈklɑzəl

clausally
BR ˈklɔːzl̩i, ˈklɔːzəli
AM ˈklɔzəli, ˈklɑzəli

clause
BR klɔːz, -ɪz
AM klɔz, klɑz, -əz

Clausewitz
BR ˈklaʊzəvɪts
AM ˈklaʊzəˌvɪts

claustral
BR ˈklɔːstr(ə)l

claustrophobe
BR ˈklɔːstrəfəʊb, ˈklɒstrəfəʊb, -z
AM ˈklɔstrəˌfoʊb, ˈklastrəˌfoʊb, -z

claustrophobia
BR ˌklɔːstrəˈfəʊbɪə(r), ˌklɒstrəˈfəʊbɪə(r)
AM ˌklɔstrəˈfoʊbiə, ˌklastrəˈfoʊbiə

claustrophobic
BR ˌklɔːstrəˈfəʊbɪk, ˌklɒstrəˈfəʊbɪk
AM ˌklɔstrəˈfoʊbɪk, ˌklastrəˈfoʊbɪk

claustrophobically
BR ˌklɔːstrəˈfəʊbɪkli, ˌklɒstrəˈfəʊbɪkli
AM ˌklɔstrəˈfoʊbək(ə)li, ˌklastrəˈfoʊbək(ə)li

clavate
BR ˈkleɪveɪt
AM ˈkleɪˌveɪt

clave
BR kleɪv, -z
AM kleɪv, -z

Claverhouse
BR ˈkleɪvəhaʊs
AM ˈkleɪvər̩(h)aʊs

Clavering
BR ˈkleɪv(ə)rɪŋ, ˈklav(ə)rɪŋ
AM ˈkleɪvərɪŋ, ˈklævərɪŋ

Claverton
BR ˈklavət(ə)n
AM ˈklævərtən

clavicembalo
BR ˌklavɪˈtʃembələʊ, -z
AM ˌklævəˈtʃembəloʊ, -z

clavichord
BR ˈklavɪkɔːd, -z
AM ˈklævəˌkɔ(ə)rd, -z

clavicle
BR ˈklavɪkl, -z
AM ˈklævəkəl, -z

clavicular
BR kləˈvɪkjələ(r), kləˈvɪkjələ(r)
AM kləˈvɪkjələr

clavier
BR kləˈvɪə(r), ˈklavɪə(r), -z
AM kləˈvɪ(ə)r, -z

claviform
BR ˈklavɪfɔːm
AM ˈklævəˌfɔ(ə)rm

claw
BR klɔː(r), -z, -ɪŋ, -d
AM klɔ, klɑ, -z, -ɪŋ, -d

clawback
BR ˈklɔːbak, -s
AM ˈklɔˌbæk, ˈklɑˌbæk, -s

clawer
BR ˈklɔː(r)ə(r), -z

clawless
BR ˈklɔːləs
AM ˈklɔləs, ˈklɑləs

clay
BR kleɪ, -z
AM kleɪ, -z

clayey
BR ˈkleɪi
AM ˈkleɪi

clayiness
BR ˈkleɪɪnɪs
AM ˈkleɪɪnɪs

clayish
BR ˈkleɪɪʃ
AM ˈkleɪɪʃ

claylike
BR ˈkleɪlʌɪk
AM ˈkleɪˌlaɪk

claymore
BR ˈkleɪmɔː(r), -z
AM ˈkleɪˌmɔ(ə)r, -z

claypan
BR ˈkleɪpan, -z
AM ˈkleɪˌpæn, -z

Clayton
BR ˈkleɪtn
AM ˈkleɪtn

clean
BR kliːn, -z, -ɪŋ, -d, -ə(r), -ɪst
AM klin, -z, -ɪŋ, -d, -ər, -ɪst

cleanable
BR ˈkliːnəbl
AM ˈklinəbəl

cleaner
BR ˈkliːnə(r), -z
AM ˈklinər, -z

cleanish
BR ˈkliːnɪʃ
AM ˈklinɪʃ

cleanlily
BR ˈklɛnlɪli
AM ˈklɛnlɪli

cleanliness
BR ˈklɛnlɪnɪs
AM ˈklɛnlinɪs

cleanly¹
adjective
BR ˈklɛnl|i, -ɪə(r), -ɪɪst
AM ˈklɛnli, -ər, -ɪst

cleanly²
adverb
BR ˈkliːnli
AM ˈklinli

cleanse
BR klɛnz, -ɪz, -ɪŋ, -d
AM klɛnz, -əz, -ɪŋ, -d

cleanser
BR ˈklɛnzə(r), -z
AM ˈklɛnzər, -z

cleanskin
BR ˈkliːnskɪn, -z
AM ˈklinˌskɪn, -z

Cleanthes
BR klɪˈanθiːz

cleanup AM kliˈænθiz
cleanup
  BR ˈkliːnʌp, -s
  AM ˈklinˌəp, -s
clear
  BR klɪə(r), -z, -ɪŋ, -d, -ə(r), -ɪst
  AM klɪ(ə)r, -z, -ɪŋ, -d, -ər, -ɪst
clearable
  BR ˈklɪərəbl
  AM ˈklɪrəbəl
clearance
  BR ˈklɪərəns, ˈklɪərn̩s, -ɪz
  AM ˈklɪrəns, -əz
Clearasil®
  BR ˈklɪərəsɪl
  AM ˈklɪrəˌsɪl
clearcole
  BR ˈklɪəkəʊl
  AM ˈklɪrˌkoʊl
clearer
  BR ˈklɪərə(r), -z
  AM ˈklɪrər, -z
clearing
  BR ˈklɪərɪŋ, -z
  AM ˈklɪrɪŋ, -z
clearinghouse
  BR ˈklɪərɪŋhaʊ|s, -zɪz
  AM ˈklɪrɪŋˌ(h)aʊ|s, -əz
clearly
  BR ˈklɪəli
  AM ˈklɪrli
clearness
  BR ˈklɪənəs
  AM ˈklɪrnɪs
clearout
  BR ˈklɪəraʊt, -s
  AM ˈklɪrˌaʊt, -s
clearsighted
  BR ˌklɪəˈsʌɪtɪd
  AM ˌklɪrˈsaɪdɪd
clearsightedly
  BR ˌklɪəˈsʌɪtɪdli
  AM ˌklɪrˈsaɪdɪdli
clearsightedness
  BR ˌklɪəˈsʌɪtɪdnɪs
  AM ˌklɪrˈsaɪdɪdnɪs
clearstory
  BR ˈklɪəˌstɔːr|i, ˈklɪəst(ə)r|i, -ɪz
  AM ˈklɪrˌstɔri, -z
clearup
  BR ˈklɪərʌp, -s
  AM ˈklɪrˌəp, -s
clearway
  BR ˈklɪəweɪ, -z
  AM ˈklɪrˌweɪ, -z
Cleary
  BR ˈklɪəri
  AM ˈklɪri
cleat
  BR kliːt, -s
  AM klit, -s
cleavable
  BR ˈkliːvəbl

AM ˈklivəbəl
cleavage
  BR ˈkliːv|ɪdʒ, -ɪdʒɪz
  AM ˈklivɪdʒ, -ɪz
cleave
  BR kliːv, -z, -ɪŋ, -d
  AM kliv, -z, -ɪŋ, -d
cleaver
  BR ˈkliːvə(r), -z
  AM ˈklivər, -z
cleavers
  BR ˈkliːvəz
  AM ˈklivərz
Cleckheaton
  BR (ˌ)klɛkˈhiːtn̩
  AM ˈklɛkˈhitn̩
Cleddau
  BR ˈklɛðaɪ
  AM ˈklɛðaɪ
Cledwyn
  BR ˈklɛdwɪn
  AM ˈklɛdwən
cleek
  BR kliːk, -s
  AM klik, -s
Cleese
  BR kliːz
  AM kliz
Cleethorpes
  BR ˈkliːθɔːps
  AM ˈkliθɔ(ə)rps
clef
  BR klɛf, -s
  AM klɛf, -s
cleft
  BR klɛft, -s
  AM klɛft, -s
cleg
  BR klɛg, -z
  AM klɛg, -z
Clegg
  BR klɛg
  AM klɛg
Cleisthenes
  BR ˈklʌɪsθɪniːz
  AM ˈklaɪsθəˌniz
cleistogamic
  BR ˌklʌɪstəˈgamɪk
  AM ˌklaɪstəˈgæmɪk
cleistogamically
  BR ˌklʌɪstəˈgamɪkli
  AM ˌklaɪstəˈgæmək(ə)li
cleistogamy
  BR klʌɪˈstɒgəmi
  AM klaɪˈstagəmi
Cleland
  BR ˈklɛlənd, ˈkliːlənd
  AM ˈkliːlənd, ˈklɛlənd
Clem
  BR klɛm
  AM klɛm
clematis
  BR ˈklɛmətɪs, klɪˈmeɪtɪs
  AM ˈklɛmədəs, kləˈmædəs

Clemence
  BR ˈklɛməns
  AM ˈklɛməns
clemency
  BR ˈklɛm(ə)nsi
  AM ˈklɛmənsi
Clemens
  BR ˈklɛmənz
  AM ˈklɛməns
clement
  BR ˈklɛm(ə)nt
  AM ˈklɛmənt
Clementina
  BR ˌklɛm(ə)nˈtiːnə(r)
  AM ˌklɛmənˈtinə
clementine
  BR ˈklɛm(ə)ntʌɪn, -z
  AM ˈklɛmənˌtaɪn, ˈklɛmənˌtin, -z
clemently
  BR ˈklɛm(ə)ntli
  AM ˈklɛmən(t)li
Clements
  BR ˈklɛm(ə)n(t)s
  AM ˈklɛmən(t)s
Clemmie
  BR ˈklɛmi
  AM ˈklɛmi
clenbuterol
  BR klɛnˈbjuːtərɒl
  AM klɛnˈbjudəˌrɑl
clench
  BR klɛn(t)ʃ, -ɪz, -ɪŋ, -t
  AM klɛn(t)ʃ, -əz, -ɪŋ, -t
Cleo
  BR ˈkliəʊ
  AM ˈklioʊ
Cleobury¹
  placename
  BR ˈkliːb(ə)ri, ˈklɪb(ə)ri
  AM ˈklibəri
Cleobury²
  surname
  BR ˈkliːb(ə)ri, ˈkləʊb(ə)ri
  AM ˈklibəri
Cleopatra
  BR ˌkliːəˈpatrə(r), ˌkliːəˈpɑːtrə(r)
  AM ˌkliəˈpætrə
clepsydra
  BR ˈklɛpsɪdrə(r), klɛpˈsɪdrə(r), -z
  AM ˈklɛpsədrə, -z
clerestory
  BR ˈklɪəˌstɔːr|i, ˈklɪəst(ə)r|i, -ɪz
  AM ˈklɪrˌstɔri, -z
clergy
  BR ˈkləːdʒi
  AM ˈklərdʒi
clergyman
  BR ˈkləːdʒɪmən
  AM ˈklərdʒimən
clergymen
  BR ˈkləːdʒɪmən
  AM ˈklərdʒimən

cleric
  BR ˈklɛrɪk, -s
  AM ˈklɛrɪk, -s
clerical
  BR ˈklɛrɪkl, -z
  AM ˈklɛrəkəl, -z
clericalism
  BR ˈklɛrɪkəlɪz(ə)m, ˈklɛrɪk|ɪz(ə)m
  AM ˈklɛrəkəlˌɪzəm
clericalist
  BR ˈklɛrɪkəlɪst, ˈklɛrɪk|ɪst, -s
  AM ˈklɛrəkələst, -s
clericality
  BR ˌklɛrɪˈkalɪti
  AM ˌklɛrəˈkælədi
clerically
  BR ˈklɛrɪkli
  AM ˈklɛrək(ə)li
clerihew
  BR ˈklɛrɪhjuː, -z
  AM ˈklɛrəˌhju, -z
clerisy
  BR ˈklɛrɪsi
  AM ˈklɛrəsi
clerk
  BR klɑːk, -s, -ɪŋ, -t
  AM klərk, -s, -ɪŋ, -t
clerkdom
  BR ˈklɑːkdəm, -z
  AM ˈklərkdəm, -z
Clerkenwell
  BR ˈklɑːk(ə)nw(ɛ)l
  AM ˈklərkənˌwɛl
clerkess
  BR ˈklɑːkɪs, ˈklɑːkɛs, ˌklɑːkˈɛs, -ɪz
  AM ˈklərkəs, -əz
clerkish
  BR ˈklɑːkɪʃ
  AM ˈklərkɪʃ
clerkly
  BR ˈklɑːkli
  AM ˈklərkli
clerkship
  BR ˈklɑːkʃɪp, -s
  AM ˈklərkˌʃɪp, -s
Clermont
  BR ˈklɛːmɒnt, ˈkləːmɒnt
  AM ˈklɛrˌmɑnt
Clery
  BR ˈklɪəri
  AM ˈklɪri, ˈklɛri
Clevedon
  BR ˈkliːvdən
  AM ˈklivdən
Cleveland
  BR ˈkliːvlənd
  AM ˈklivlən(d)
clever
  BR ˈklɛv|ə(r), -(ə)rə(r), -(ə)rɪst
  AM ˈklɛvər, -ər, -əst
cleverly
  BR ˈklɛvəli

AM ˈklevərli

cleverness
BR ˈklevənəs
AM ˈklevərnəs

clevis
BR ˈklev|ɪs, -ɪsɪz
AM ˈklevəs, -ɪz

clew
BR kluː, -z, -ɪŋ, -d
AM klu, -z, -ɪŋ, -d

Clewes
BR kluːz
AM kluz

Clews
BR kluːz
AM kluz

Cley
BR kleɪ, klʌɪ
AM kleɪ

clianthus
BR klʌɪˈanθəs, klɪˈanθəs
AM kliˈænθəs

Clibborn
BR ˈklɪb(ə)n
AM ˈklɪbərn

Cliburn
BR ˈklʌɪbəːn
AM ˈklaɪbərn

cliché
BR ˈkliːʃeɪ, -z, -d
AM kliˈʃeɪ, ˈkliˌʃeɪ, -z, -d

click
BR klɪk, -s, -ɪŋ, -t
AM klɪk, -s, -ɪŋ, -t

click-clack
BR ˈklɪklak, -s, -ɪŋ, -t
AM ˈklɪ(k)ˈklæk, -s, -ɪŋ, -t

clicker
BR ˈklɪkə(r), -z
AM ˈklikər, -z

clickety-click
BR ˌklɪkɪtɪˈklɪk
AM ˈklɪkɪdiˈklɪk

client
BR ˈklʌɪənt, -s
AM ˈklaɪənt, -s

clientele
BR ˌkliːɒnˈtɛl, ˌkliːɑːnˈtɛl, ˌkliːənˈtɛl, -z
AM ˌklaɪənˈtɛl, ˌkliənˈtɛl, -z

clientship
BR ˈklʌɪəntʃɪp, -s
AM ˈklaɪən(t)ˌʃɪp, -s

cliff
BR klɪf, -s
AM klɪf, -s

Cliffe
BR klɪf
AM klɪf

cliffhanger
BR ˈklɪfˌhaŋə(r), -z
AM ˈklɪfˌ(h)æŋər, -z

cliffhanging
BR ˈklɪfˌhaŋɪŋ
AM ˈklɪfˌ(h)æŋɪŋ

cliffiness
BR ˈklɪfɪnɪs
AM ˈklɪfinɪs

clifflike
BR ˈklɪflʌɪk
AM ˈklɪfˌlaɪk

Clifford
BR ˈklɪfəd
AM ˈklɪfərd

cliffside
BR ˈklɪfsʌɪd
AM ˈklɪfˌsaɪd

clifftop
BR ˈklɪftɒp, -s
AM ˈklɪfˌtɑp, -s

cliffy
BR ˈklɪf]i, -ɪə(r), -ɪɪst
AM ˈklɪfi, -ər, -ɪst

Clifton
BR ˈklɪft(ə)n
AM ˈklɪftən

Cliftonville
BR ˈklɪft(ə)nvɪl
AM ˈklɪftənˌvɪl

climacteric
BR ˌklʌɪmakˈtɛrɪk, klʌɪˈmakt(ə)rɪk
AM klaɪˈmæktərɪk, ˌklaɪˌmækˈtɛrɪk

climacterical
BR ˌklʌɪmakˈtɛrɪkl
AM ˌklaɪˌmækˈtɛrəkəl

climactic
BR klʌɪˈmaktɪk
AM klaɪˈmæktɪk

climactical
BR klʌɪˈmaktɪkl
AM klaɪˈmæktəkəl

climactically
BR klʌɪˈmaktɪkli
AM klaɪˈmæktək(ə)li

climate
BR ˈklʌɪmɪt, -s
AM ˈklaɪmɪt, -s

climatic
BR klʌɪˈmatɪk
AM klaɪˈmædɪk

climatical
BR klʌɪˈmatɪkl
AM klaɪˈmædəkəl

climatically
BR klʌɪˈmatɪkli
AM klaɪˈmædək(ə)li

climatologic
BR ˌklʌɪmətəˈlɒdʒɪk
AM ˌklaɪmədəˈlɑdʒɪk

climatological
BR ˌklʌɪmətəˈlɒdʒɪkl
AM ˌklaɪmədəˈlɑdʒəkəl

climatologically
BR ˌklʌɪmətəˈlɒdʒɪkli
AM ˌklaɪmədəˈlɑdʒək-(ə)li

climatologist
BR ˌklʌɪməˈtɒlədʒɪst, -s
AM ˌklaɪməˈtɑlədʒəst, -s

climatology
BR ˌklʌɪməˈtɒlədʒi
AM ˌklaɪməˈtɑlədʒi

climax
BR ˈklʌɪmaks, -ɪz, -ɪŋ, -t
AM ˈklaɪˌmæks, -əz, -ɪŋ, -t

climb
BR klʌɪm, -z, -ɪŋ, -d
AM klaɪm, -z, -ɪŋ, -d

climbable
BR ˈklʌɪməbl
AM ˈklaɪməbəl

climbdown
BR ˈklʌɪmdaʊn, -z
AM ˈklaɪmˌdaʊn, -z

climber
BR ˈklʌɪmə(r), -z
AM ˈklaɪmər, -z

clime
BR klʌɪm, -z
AM klaɪm, -z

clinal
BR ˈklʌɪnl
AM ˈklaɪnl

clinch
BR klɪn(t)ʃ, -ɪz, -ɪŋ, -t
AM klɪn(t)ʃ, -ɪz, -ɪŋ, -t

clincher
BR ˈklɪn(t)ʃə(r), -z
AM ˈklɪn(t)ʃər, -z

cline
BR klʌɪn, -z
AM klaɪn, -z

cling
BR klɪŋ, -z, -ɪŋ
AM klɪŋ, -z, -ɪŋ

clinger
BR ˈklɪŋə(r), -z
AM ˈklɪŋər, -z

clingfilm
BR ˈklɪŋfɪlm
AM ˈklɪŋˌfɪlm

clingfoil
BR ˈklɪŋfɔɪl
AM ˈklɪŋˌfɔɪl

clinginess
BR ˈklɪŋɪnɪs
AM ˈklɪŋinɪs

clingingly
BR ˈklɪŋɪli
AM ˈklɪŋɪli

clingstone
BR ˈklɪŋstəʊn
AM ˈklɪŋˌstoʊn

clingy
BR ˈklɪŋ]i, -ɪə(r), -ɪɪst
AM ˈklɪŋi, -ər, -ɪst

clinic
BR ˈklɪnɪk, -s
AM ˈklɪnɪk, -s

clinical
BR ˈklɪnɪkl
AM ˈklɪnəkəl

clinically
BR ˈklɪnɪkli
AM ˈklɪnək(ə)li

clinician
BR klɪˈnɪʃn, -z
AM kləˈnɪʃən, -z

clink
BR klɪŋ|k, -ks, -kɪŋ, -(k)t
AM klɪŋ|k, -ks, -kɪŋ, -(k)t

clinker
BR ˈklɪŋkə(r), -z
AM ˈklɪŋkər, -z

clinkstone
BR ˈklɪŋkstəʊn, -z
AM ˈklɪŋkˌstoʊn, -z

clinometer
BR klɪˈnɒmɪtə(r), klʌɪˈnɒmɪtə(r), -z
AM klaɪˈnɑmədər, -z

clinometric
BR ˌklʌɪnəˈmɛtrɪk
AM ˌklaɪnəˈmɛtrɪk

clinometry
BR klɪˈnɒmɪtri, klʌɪˈnɒmɪtri
AM klaɪˈnɑmətri

clint
BR klɪnt, -s
AM klɪnt, -s

Clinton
BR ˈklɪntən
AM ˈklɪn(t)ən

Clio
BR ˈkliːəʊ, ˈklʌɪəʊ
AM ˈklaɪoʊ, ˈklioʊ

cliometric
BR ˌklʌɪə(ʊ)ˈmɛtrɪk, -s
AM ˌklaɪəˈmɛtrɪk, -s

clip
BR klɪp, -s, -ɪŋ, -t
AM klɪp, -s, -ɪŋ, -t

clipboard
BR ˈklɪpbɔːd, -z
AM ˈklɪpˌbɔ(ə)rd, -z

clip-clop
BR ˈklɪpklɒp, -s, -ɪŋ, -t
AM ˈklɪpˌklɑp, -s, -ɪŋ, -t

clippable
BR ˈklɪpəbl
AM ˈklɪpəbəl

clipper
BR ˈklɪpə(r), -z
AM ˈklɪpər, -z

clippie
BR ˈklɪp|i, -ɪz
AM ˈklɪpi, -z

clipping
BR ˈklɪpɪŋ, -z
AM ˈklɪpɪŋ, -z

Clipstone
BR ˈklɪpstəʊn
AM ˈklɪpˌstoʊn

clique
BR kliːk, -s
AM klik, -s

cliquey
BR 'kliːk|i, -ɪə(r), -ɪɪst
AM 'kliki, -ər, -ɪst

cliqueyness
BR 'kliːkɪnɪs
AM 'klikinɪs

cliquish
BR 'kliːkɪʃ
AM 'klikɪʃ

cliquishness
BR 'kliːkɪʃnɪs
AM 'klikɪʃnɪs

cliquism
BR 'kliːkɪz(ə)m
AM 'klikɪzəm

cliquy
BR 'kliːki
AM 'kliki

Clissold
BR 'klɪsəʊld
AM 'klɪsoʊld

Clitheroe
BR 'klɪðərəʊ
AM 'klɪðərou

clitic
BR 'klɪtɪk, -s
AM 'klɪdik, -s

cliticisation
BR ˌklɪtɪsʌɪ'zeɪʃn
AM ˌklɪdəsə'zeɪʃən, ˌklɪdəˌsaɪ'zeɪʃən

cliticization
BR ˌklɪtɪsʌɪ'zeɪʃn
AM ˌklɪdəsə'zeɪʃən, ˌklɪdəˌsaɪ'zeɪʃən

cliticize
BR 'klɪtɪsʌɪz, -ɪz, -ɪŋ, -d
AM 'klɪdəˌsaɪz, -ɪz, -ɪŋ, -d

clitoral
BR 'klɪt(ə)rəl, 'klɪt(ə)r|l
AM 'klɪdər(ə)l, klə'tɔrəl

clitoridectomy
BR ˌklɪt(ə)rɪ'dɛktəm|i, -ɪz
AM ˌklɪdərə'dɛktəmi, -z

clitoris
BR 'klɪt(ə)rɪs, -ɪz
AM 'klɪdərəs, klə'tɔrəs, -əz

Clive
BR klʌɪv
AM klaɪv

Cliveden
BR 'klɪvd(ə)n
AM 'klɪvdən

clivers
BR 'klɪvəz
AM 'klɪvərz

cloaca
BR kləʊ'eɪkə(r), -z
AM klou'eɪkə, -z

cloacae
BR kləʊ'eɪkiː
AM klouˈeɪˌki, klouˈeɪˌkaɪ

cloacal
BR kləʊ'eɪkl
AM klou'eɪkəl

cloak
BR kləʊk, -s, -ɪŋ, -t
AM klouk, -s, -ɪŋ, -t

cloakroom
BR 'kləʊkruːm, 'kləʊkrʊm, -z
AM 'kloukˌrum, 'koukˌrʊm, -z

clobber
BR 'klɒb|ə(r), -əz, -(ə)rɪŋ, -əd
AM 'klɑbər, -z, -ɪŋ, -d

cloche
BR klɒʃ, -ɪz
AM klouʃ, klɑʃ, klɔʃ, -əz

clock
BR klɒk, -s, -ɪŋ, -t
AM klɑk, -s, -ɪŋ, -t

clockmaker
BR 'klɒkˌmeɪkə(r), -z
AM 'klakˌmeɪkər, -z

clockmaking
BR 'klɒkˌmeɪkɪŋ
AM 'klakˌmeɪkɪŋ

clockwise
BR 'klɒkwʌɪz
AM 'klakˌwaɪz

clockwork
BR 'klɒkwəːk
AM 'klakˌwərk

clod
BR klɒd, -z
AM klad, -z

Clodagh
BR 'kləʊdə(r)
AM 'kloudə

cloddish
BR 'klɒdɪʃ
AM 'kladɪʃ

cloddishly
BR 'klɒdɪʃli
AM 'kladɪʃli

cloddishness
BR 'klɒdɪʃnɪs
AM 'kladɪʃnɪs

cloddy
BR 'klɒdi
AM 'kladi

clodhopper
BR 'klɒdˌhɒpə(r), -z
AM 'kladˌ(h)ɑpər, -z

clodhopping
BR 'klɒdˌhɒpɪŋ
AM 'kladˌ(h)ɑpɪŋ

clodpoll
BR 'klɒdpɒl, -z
AM 'kladˌpɑl, -z

clog
BR klɒg, -z, -ɪŋ, -d

AM klag, -z, -ɪŋ, -d

cloggily
BR 'klɒgɪli
AM 'klagəli

clogginess
BR 'klɒgɪnɪs
AM 'klagɪnɪs

cloggy
BR 'klɒg|i, -ɪə(r), -ɪɪst
AM 'klagi, -ər, -ɪst

Clogher
BR 'klɒxə(r), 'klɒhə(r)
AM 'klɔhər, 'klahər

cloisonné
BR klwɑː'zɒneɪ
AM ˌklɔɪzn'eɪ

cloister
BR 'klɔɪst|ə(r), -əz, -(ə)rɪŋ, -əd
AM 'klɔɪstər, -z, -ɪŋ, -d

cloistral
BR 'klɔɪstr(ə)l
AM 'klɔɪstrəl

clomiphene
BR 'kləʊmɪfiːn
AM 'kloʊməˌfin

clomp
BR klɒmp, -s, -ɪŋ, -t
AM klamp, -s, -ɪŋ, -t

clonal
BR 'kləʊnl
AM 'kloʊnəl

clone
BR kləʊn, -z, -ɪŋ, -d
AM kloʊn, -z, -ɪŋ, -d

Clones
BR 'kləʊnɪs
AM 'kloʊnəs

clonic
BR 'klɒnɪk
AM 'klanɪk

clonk
BR klɒŋ|k, -ks, -kɪŋ, -(k)t
AM klaŋ|k, -ks, -kɪŋ, -(k)t

Clonmel
BR klɒn'mɛl
AM klan'mɛl

clonus
BR 'kləʊnəs, -ɪz
AM 'kloʊnəs, -əz

clop
BR klɒp, -s, -ɪŋ, -t
AM klap, -s, -ɪŋ, -t

cloqué
BR 'kləʊkeɪ
AM klou'keɪ

closable
BR 'kləʊzəbl
AM 'kloʊzəbəl

Close
BR kləʊs
AM klous, klouz

close¹
noun enclosure, adjective
BR kləʊs, -ɪz, -ə(r), -ɪst
AM klous, -əz, -ər, -əst

close²
noun end, verb
BR kləʊz, -ɪz, -ɪŋ, -d
AM klouz, -əz, -ɪŋ, -d

closedown
BR 'kləʊzdaʊn, -z
AM 'klouzˌdaʊn, -z

closely
BR 'kləʊsli
AM 'klousli

closeness
BR 'kləʊsnəs
AM 'kloʊsnəs

closeout
BR 'kləʊzaʊt, -s
AM 'klouzˌaʊt, -s

closet
BR 'klɒz|ɪt, -ɪts, -ɪtɪŋ, -ɪtɪd
AM 'klazə|t, -ts, -dɪŋ, -dəd

closish
BR 'kləʊsɪʃ
AM 'klousɪʃ

clostridia
BR klɒ'strɪdɪə(r)
AM klɔ'strɪdɪə, klɑ'strɪdɪə

clostridium
BR klɒ'strɪdɪəm
AM klɔ'strɪdɪəm, klɑ'strɪdɪəm

closure
BR 'kləʊʒə(r), -z
AM 'klouʒər, -z

clot
BR klɒt, -s, -ɪŋ, -ɪd
AM kla|t, -ts, -dɪŋ, -dəd

clotbur
BR 'klɒtbəː(r)
AM 'klatˌbər

cloth
BR klɒ|θ, -θs \ -ðz
AM klɔ|θ, klɑ|θ, -θs \ -ðz

clothbound
BR 'klɒθbaʊnd
AM 'klɔθˌbaʊnd, 'klaθˌbaʊnd

clothe
BR kləʊð, -z, -ɪŋ, -d
AM klouð, -z, -ɪŋ, -d

clothes
noun
BR kləʊðz
AM klou(ð)z

clothesbasket
BR 'kləʊ(ð)zˌbɑːskɪt, 'kləʊ(ð)zˌbaskɪt, -s
AM 'klou(ð)zˌbæskət, -s

clothesbrush
BR 'kləʊ(ð)zbrʌʃ, -ɪz
AM 'klou(ð)zˌbrəʃ, -ɪz

clotheshorse
BR ˈkləʊ(ð)zhɔːs, -ɪz
AM ˈkloʊ(ð)z,(h)ɔ(ə)rs,
-əz

clothesline
BR ˈkləʊ(ð)zlʌɪn, -z
AM ˈkloʊ(ð)z,laɪn, -z

clothespeg
BR ˈkləʊ(ð)zpɛg, -z
AM ˈkloʊ(ð)z,pɛg, -z

clothespin
BR ˈkləʊ(ð)zpɪn, -z
AM ˈkloʊ(ð)z,pɪn, -z

clothier
BR ˈkləʊðɪə(r), -z
AM ˈkloʊðjər,
ˈkloʊðiər, -z

clothing
BR ˈkləʊðɪŋ
AM ˈkloʊðɪŋ

Clotho
BR ˈkləʊθəʊ
AM ˈkloʊ,θoʊ

cloths
BR klɒðs, klɒðz
AM klɔːðz, klɒθs, klɑðz,
klɑθs

cloture
BR ˈkləʊtʃə(r), -z
AM ˈkloʊtʃər, -z

clou
BR kluː, -z
AM klu, -z

cloud
BR klaʊd, -z, -ɪŋ, -ɪd
AM klaʊd, -z, -ɪŋ, -əd

cloudbank
BR ˈklaʊdbaŋk, -s
AM ˈklaʊd,bæŋk, -s

cloudberry
BR ˈklaʊdb(ə)r|i, -ɪz
AM ˈklaʊd,beri, -z

cloudburst
BR ˈklaʊdbəːst, -s
AM ˈklaʊd,bɜrst, -s

Cloudesley
BR ˈklaʊdzli
AM ˈklaʊdzli

cloudily
BR ˈklaʊdɪli
AM ˈklaʊdəli

cloudiness
BR ˈklaʊdɪnɪs
AM ˈklaʊdɪnɪs

cloudland
BR ˈklaʊdland
AM ˈklaʊd,lænd

cloudless
BR ˈklaʊdləs
AM ˈklaʊdləs

cloudlessly
BR ˈklaʊdləsli
AM ˈklaʊdlɪsli

cloudlessness
BR ˈklaʊdləsnəs
AM ˈklaʊdləsnəs

cloudlet
BR ˈklaʊdlɪt, -s
AM ˈklaʊdlət, -s

cloudscape
BR ˈklaʊdskeɪp, -s
AM ˈklaʊd,skeɪp, -s

cloudy
BR ˈklaʊd|i, -ɪə(r), -ɪɪst
AM ˈklaʊdi, -ər, -ɪst

Clough
place in Ireland
BR klɒx
AM klɑk

clough
BR klʌf, -s
AM klʌf, kloʊ,
kləfs\kloʊz

clout
BR klaʊt, -s, -ɪŋ, -ɪd
AM klaʊ|t, -ts, -dɪŋ, -dəd

Clouzot
BR ˈkluːzəʊ
AM ˈkluˈzoʊ

clove
BR kləʊv, -z
AM kloʊv, -z

Clovelly
BR kləˈvɛli
AM ˈkləvəli

cloven
BR ˈkləʊvn
AM ˈkloʊvən

clover
BR ˈkləʊvə(r), -z
AM ˈkloʊvər, -z

cloverleaf
BR ˈkləʊvəliːf, -s
AM ˈkloʊvər,lif, -s

cloverleaves
BR ˈkləʊvəliːvz
AM ˈkloʊvər,livz

Clovis
BR ˈkləʊvɪs
AM ˈkloʊvəs

Clowes
BR klaʊz, kləʊz, kluːz
AM klaʊz, kloʊz, kluz

clown
BR klaʊn, -z, -ɪŋ, -d
AM klaʊn, -z, -ɪŋ, -d

clownery
BR ˈklaʊn(ə)ri
AM ˈklaʊnəri

clownish
BR ˈklaʊnɪʃ
AM ˈklaʊnɪʃ

clownishly
BR ˈklaʊnɪʃli
AM ˈklaʊnɪʃli

clownishness
BR ˈklaʊnɪʃnɪs
AM ˈklaʊnɪʃnɪs

cloy
BR klɔɪ, -z, -ɪŋ, -d
AM klɔɪ, -z, -ɪŋ, -d

cloyingly
BR ˈklɔɪɪŋli

AM ˈklɔɪɪŋli

clozapine
BR ˈkləʊzəpiːn
AM ˈkloʊzə,pin

cloze
BR kləʊz
AM kloʊz

club
BR klʌb, -z, -ɪŋ, -d
AM kləb, -z, -ɪŋ, -d

clubbability
BR ,klʌbəˈbɪlɪti
AM ,kləbəˈbɪlɪdi

clubbable
BR ˈklʌbəbl
AM ˈkləbəbəl

clubbableness
BR ˈklʌbəblnəs
AM ˈkləbəbəlnəs

clubbably
BR ˈklʌbəbli
AM ˈkləbəbli

clubber
BR ˈklʌbə(r), -z
AM ˈkləbər, -z

clubby
BR ˈklʌb|i, -ɪə(r), -ɪɪst
AM ˈkləbi, -ər, -əst

clubfeet
BR ,klʌbˈfiːt
AM ˈkləb,fit

clubfoot
BR ,klʌbˈfʊt
AM ˈkləb,fʊt

clubfooted
BR ,klʌbˈfʊtɪd
AM ˈkləb,fʊdəd

clubhouse
BR ˈklʌbhaʊ|s, -zɪz
AM ˈkləb,(h)aʊ|s, -zəz

clubland
BR ˈklʌbland
AM ˈkləb,lænd

clubman
BR ˈklʌbmən
AM ˈkləbmən

clubmen
BR ˈklʌbmən
AM ˈkləbmən

clubmoss
BR ˈklʌbmɒs, -ɪz
AM ˈkləb,mɔs,
ˈkləb,mɑs, -əz

clubroom
BR ˈklʌbruːm,
ˈklʌbrʊm, -z
AM ˈkləb,rum,
ˈkləb,rʊm, -z

clubroot
BR ˈklʌbruːt
AM ˈkləb,rut, ˈkləb,rʊt

clubwoman
BR ˈklʌb,wʊmən
AM ˈkləb,wʊmən

clubwomen
BR ˈklʌb,wɪmɪn
AM ˈkləb,wɪmɪn

cluck
BR klʌk, -s, -ɪŋ, -t
AM klək, -s, -ɪŋ, -t

cluckily
BR ˈklʌkɪli
AM ˈkləkəli

cluckiness
BR ˈklʌkɪnɪs
AM ˈkləkinɪs

clucky
BR ˈklʌk|i, -ɪə(r), -ɪɪst
AM ˈkləki, -ər, -əst

cludge
BR klʌdʒ, kluːdʒ, -ɪz
AM klədʒ, kludʒ, -əz

clue
BR kluː, -z, -ɪŋ, -d
AM klu, -z, -ɪŋ, -d

clueless
BR ˈkluːləs
AM ˈkluləs

cluelessly
BR ˈkluːləsli
AM ˈkluləsli

cluelessness
BR ˈkluːləsnəs
AM ˈkluləsnəs

Cluj
BR kluːʒ
AM kluʒ

clump
BR klʌm|p, -ps, -pɪŋ,
-(p)t
AM kləmp, -s, -ɪŋ, -t

clumpy
BR ˈklʌmp|i, -ə(r), -ɪɪst
AM ˈkləmpi, -ər, -əst

clumsily
BR ˈklʌmzɪli
AM ˈkləmzəli

clumsiness
BR ˈklʌmzɪnɪs
AM ˈkləmzɪnɪs

clumsy
BR ˈklʌmz|i, -ɪə(r), -ɪɪst
AM ˈkləmzi, -ər, -ɪst

Clun
BR klʌn
AM klən

Clunes
BR kluːnz
AM klunz

clung
BR klʌŋ
AM kləŋ

Cluniac
BR ˈkluːnɪak, -s
AM ˈkluni,æk, -s

Clunie
BR ˈkluːni
AM ˈkluni

Clunies
BR ˈkluːnɪz
AM ˈkluniz

clunk
BR klʌŋ|k, -ks, -kɪŋ,
-(k)t

AM klən|k, -ks, -kıŋ, -(k)t

Cluny
BR 'kluːni
AM 'kluni

clupeid
BR 'kluːpɪɪd
AM 'klupiɪd

clupeoid
BR 'kluːpɪɔɪd
AM 'klupiˌɔɪd

cluster
BR 'klʌst|ə(r), -əz, -(ə)rɪŋ, -əd
AM 'kləst|ər, -ərz, -(ə)rɪŋ, -ərd

clutch
BR klʌtʃ, -ɪz, -ɪŋ, -t
AM klətʃ, -əz, -ɪŋ, -t

clutter
BR 'klʌt|ə(r), -əz, -(ə)rɪŋ, -əd
AM 'kləd|ər, -ərz, -(ə)rɪŋ, -ərd

Clutterbuck
BR 'klʌtəbʌk
AM 'klədərˌbək

Clutton
BR 'klʌtn
AM 'klətn

Clwyd
BR 'kluːɪd
AM 'kluəd
WE klwɪd

Clwydian
BR 'klʊ'ɪdɪən
AM klə'wɪdɪən

Clydach
BR 'klɪdəx, 'klɪdək
AM 'klɪdək
WE 'klʌdax

Clyde
BR klʌɪd
AM klaɪd

Clydebank
BR 'klʌɪdbaŋk
AM 'klaɪdˌbæŋk

Clydella
BR klʌɪ'dɛlə(r)
AM klaɪ'dɛlə

Clydesdale
BR 'klʌɪdzdeɪl, -z
AM 'klaɪdzˌdeɪl, -z

Clyne
BR klʌɪn
AM klaɪn

clypeal
BR 'klɪpɪəl
AM 'klɪpɪəl

clypeate
BR 'klɪpɪət
AM 'klɪpɪət

clypei
BR 'klɪpɪʌɪ
AM 'klɪpiˌaɪ

clypeus
BR 'klɪpɪəs

AM 'klɪpɪəs

Clyro
BR 'klʌɪrəʊ
AM 'klaɪroʊ

clyster
BR 'klɪstə(r), -z
AM 'klɪstər, -z

Clytemnestra
BR ˌklʌɪtɪm'nɛstrə(r), ˌklʌɪtɪm'nɛstrə(r)
AM ˌklaɪdəm'nɛstrə

Cnut
BR kə'njuːt
AM kə'nut

CO
Commanding Officer
BR ˌsiː'əʊ, -z
AM ˌsi'oʊ, -z

Co.
Company, County
BR kəʊ
AM koʊ

c/o
BR ˌkɛːr'ɒv, ˌsiː'əʊ
AM 'kɛr'əv, ˌsi'oʊ

co-accused
BR ˌkəʊə'kjuːzd
AM ˌkoʊə'kjuzd

coacervate
BR ˌkəʊə'səːveɪt, -s
AM ˌkoʊə'sərvət, koʊ'æsərˌveɪt, -s

coacervation
BR kəʊˌasə'veɪʃn
AM koʊˌæsər'veɪʃən

coach
BR kəʊtʃ, -ɪz, -ɪŋ, -t
AM koʊtʃ, -əz, -ɪŋ, -t

coachbuilder
BR 'kəʊtʃˌbɪldə(r), -z
AM 'koʊtʃˌbɪldər, -z

coachhouse
BR 'kəʊtʃhaʊ|s, -zɪz
AM 'koʊtʃˌ(h)aʊ|s, -zəz

coachload
BR 'kəʊtʃləʊd, -z
AM 'koʊtʃˌloʊd, -z

coachman
BR 'kəʊtʃmən
AM 'koʊtʃmən

coachmen
BR 'kəʊtʃmən
AM 'koʊtʃmən

coachwood
BR 'kəʊtʃwʊd
AM 'koʊtʃˌwʊd

coachwork
BR 'kəʊtʃwəːk
AM 'koʊtʃˌwərk

coaction
BR kəʊ'akʃn
AM koʊ'ækʃən

coactive
BR kəʊ'aktɪv
AM koʊ'æktɪv

coadjacent
BR ˌkəʊə'dʒeɪsnt

AM ˌkoʊə'dʒeɪsənt

coadjutant
BR kəʊ'adʒʊtənt
AM ˌkoʊ'ædʒətənt

coadjutor
BR kəʊ'adʒʊtə(r), -z
AM koʊ'ædʒədər, ˌkoʊə'dʒudər, -z

coadministrator
BR ˌkəʊəd'mɪnɪstreɪt-ə(r), -z
AM ˌkoʊəd'mɪnəˌstreɪd-ər, -z

coagula
BR kəʊ'agjʊlə(r)
AM koʊ'ægjələ

coagulable
BR kəʊ'agjʊləbl
AM koʊ'ægjələbəl

coagulant
BR kəʊ'agjʊlənt, kəʊ'agjʊlnt, -s
AM koʊ'ægjələnt, -s

coagulate
BR kəʊ'agjʊleɪt, -s, -ɪŋ, -ɪd
AM koʊ'ægjəˌleɪ|t, -ts, -dɪŋ, -dɪd

coagulation
BR kəʊˌagjʊ'leɪʃn
AM koʊˌægjə'leɪʃən

coagulative
BR kəʊ'agjʊlətɪv
AM koʊ'ægjəˌleɪdɪv

coagulator
BR kəʊ'agjʊleɪtə(r), -z
AM koʊ'ægjəˌleɪdər, -z

coagulatory
BR kəʊ'agjʊlət(ə)ri
AM koʊ'ægjələˌtori

coagulum
BR kəʊ'agjʊləm
AM koʊ'ægjələm

Coahuila
BR ˌkəʊə'wiːlə(r)
AM ˌkoʊə'wilɑ

coal
BR kəʊl, -z, -ɪŋ, -d
AM koʊl, -z, -ɪŋ, -d

Coalbrookdale
BR 'kəʊlbrʊkdeɪl, ˌkəʊlbrʊk'deɪl
AM 'koʊlbrʊkˌdeɪl, ˌkoʊlbrʊk'deɪl

coalbunker
BR 'kəʊlˌbʌŋkə(r), -z
AM 'koʊlˌbəŋkər, -z

coaler
BR 'kəʊlə(r), -z
AM 'koʊlər, -z

coalesce
BR ˌkəʊə'lɛs, -ɪz, -ɪŋ, -t
AM ˌkoʊə'lɛs, -əz, -ɪŋ, -t

coalescence
BR ˌkəʊə'lɛsns
AM ˌkoʊə'lɛsəns

AM ˌkoʊə'dʒeɪsənt

coalescent
BR ˌkəʊə'lɛsnt
AM ˌkoʊə'lɛsənt

coalface
BR 'kəʊlfeɪs, -ɪz
AM 'koʊlˌfeɪs, -ɪz

coalfield
BR 'kəʊlfiːld, -z
AM 'koʊlˌfild, -z

coalfish
BR 'kəʊlfɪʃ
AM 'koʊlˌfɪʃ

coalheaver
BR 'kəʊlˌhiːvə(r), -z
AM 'koʊlˌ(h)ivər, -z

coalhole
BR 'kəʊlhəʊl, -z
AM 'koʊlˌ(h)oʊl, -z

coalhouse
BR 'kəʊlhaʊ|s, -zɪz
AM 'koʊlˌ(h)aʊ|s, -zəz

Coalisland
BR (ˌ)kəʊl'ʌɪlənd
AM ˌkoʊl'aɪlənd

Coalite®
BR 'kəʊlʌɪt
AM 'koʊlaɪt

coalition
BR ˌkəʊə'lɪʃn, -z
AM ˌkoʊə'lɪʃən, -z

coalitionist
BR ˌkəʊə'lɪʃnɪst, -s
AM ˌkoʊə'lɪʃənəst, -s

coalman
BR 'kəʊlmən
AM 'koʊlmən

coalmen
BR 'kəʊlmən
AM 'koʊlmən

coalmice
BR 'kəʊlmʌɪs
AM 'koʊlˌmaɪs

coalmine
BR 'kəʊlmʌɪn, -z
AM 'koʊlˌmaɪn, -z

coalminer
BR 'kəʊlˌmʌɪnə(r), -z
AM 'koʊlˌmaɪnər, -z

coalmouse
BR 'kəʊlmaʊs
AM 'koʊlˌmaʊs

coaloil
BR 'kəʊlɔɪl
AM 'koʊlˌɔɪl

coalowner
BR 'kəʊlˌəʊnə(r), -z
AM 'koʊlˌoʊnər, -z

Coalport
BR 'kəʊlpɔːt
AM 'koʊlˌpɔ(ə)rt

coalsack
BR 'kəʊlsak, -s
AM 'koʊlˌsæk, -s

coalscuttle
BR 'kəʊlˌskʌtl, -z
AM 'koʊlˌskədəl, -z

coaly
BR 'kəʊli
AM 'koʊli

coaming
BR 'kəʊmɪŋ, -z
AM 'koʊmɪŋ, -z

coaptation
BR ˌkəʊapˈteɪʃn
AM ˌkoʊæpˈteɪʃən

coarctation
BR ˌkəʊɑːkˈteɪʃn
AM ˌkoʊɑːrkˈteɪʃən

coarse
BR kɔːs, -ə(r), -ɪst
AM kɔː(ə)rs, -ər, -əst

coarsely
BR 'kɔːsli
AM 'kɔrsli

coarsen
BR 'kɔːs|n, -nz,
-nɪŋ \-nɪŋ, -nd
AM 'kɔrsən, -z, -ɪŋ, -d

coarseness
BR 'kɔːsnəs
AM 'kɔrsnəs

coarsish
BR 'kɔːsɪʃ
AM 'kɔrsɪʃ

coast
BR kəʊst, -s, -ɪŋ, -ɪd
AM koʊst, -s, -ɪŋ, -əd

coastal
BR 'kəʊstl
AM 'koʊstəl

coaster
BR 'kəʊstə(r), -z
AM 'koʊstər, -z

coastguard
BR 'kəʊs(t)gɑːd, -z
AM 'koʊs(t)ˌgɑrd, -z

coastguardsman
BR 'kəʊs(t)gɑːdzmən
AM 'koʊs(t)ˌgɑrdzmən

coastguardsmen
BR 'kəʊs(t)gɑːdzmən
AM 'koʊs(t)ˌgɑrdzmən

coastland
BR 'kəʊs(t)land, -z
AM 'koʊs(t)ˌlænd, -z

coastline
BR 'kəʊs(t)laɪn, -z
AM 'koʊs(t)ˌlaɪn, -z

coastwise
BR 'kəʊstwaɪz
AM 'koʊs(t)ˌwaɪz

coat
BR kəʊt, -s, -ɪŋ, -ɪd
AM koʊt, -ts, -dɪŋ, -dəd

Coatbridge
BR 'kəʊtbrɪdʒ
AM 'koʊtˌbrɪdʒ

coatee
BR 'kəʊtiː, ˌkəʊ'tiː, -z
AM ˌkoʊ'ti, -z

Coates
BR kəʊts
AM koʊts

coati
BR kəʊ'ɑːt|i, -ɪz
AM koʊ'ɑdi, -z

coatimundi
BR kəʊˌɑːtɪ'mʌnd|i, -ɪz
AM koʊˌɑdi'məndi, -z

coating
BR 'kəʊtɪŋ, -z
AM 'koʊdɪŋ, -z

coatless
BR 'kəʊtləs
AM 'koʊtləs

Coats
BR kəʊts
AM koʊts

coax
BR kəʊks, -ɪz, -ɪŋ, -t
AM koʊks, -əz, -ɪŋ, -t

co-ax
cable
BR 'kəʊaks
AM 'koʊˌæks

coaxer
BR 'kəʊksə(r), -z
AM 'koʊksər, -z

coaxial
BR kəʊ'aksɪəl
AM koʊ'æksɪəl

coaxially
BR kəʊ'aksɪəli
AM koʊ'æksɪəli

coaxingly
BR 'kəʊksɪŋli
AM koʊksɪŋli

cob
BR kɒb, -z
AM kɑb, -z

cobalt
BR 'kəʊbɔːlt, 'kəʊbɒlt,
'kəʊb(ə)lt
AM 'koʊˌbɔlt, 'koʊˌbalt

cobaltic
BR kəʊ'bɔːltɪk,
kəʊ'bɒltɪk
AM koʊ'bɔldɪk,
koʊ'baldɪk

cobaltous
BR kəʊ'bɔːltəs,
kəʊ'bɒltəs
AM koʊ'bɔldəs,
koʊ'baldəs

Cobb
BR kɒb
AM kab

cobber
BR 'kɒbə(r), -z
AM 'kabər, -z

Cobbett
BR 'kɒbɪt
AM 'kabət

cobble
BR 'kɒb|l, -lz, -]lɪŋ \-lɪŋ,
-ld
AM 'kab|əl, -əlz, -(ə)lɪŋ,
-əld

cobbler
BR 'kɒblə(r), -z
AM 'kablər, -z

cobblestone
BR 'kɒblstəʊn, -z
AM 'kabəlˌstoʊn, -z

Cobbold
BR 'kɒbəʊld
AM 'kaboʊld

Cobden
BR 'kɒbd(ə)n
AM 'kabdən

Cobdenism
BR 'kɒbdənɪz(ə)m
AM 'kabdəˌnɪzəm

Cobham
BR 'kɒb(ə)m
AM 'kabəm

coble
BR 'kəʊbl, -z
AM 'koʊbəl, 'kabəl, -z

cobnut
BR 'kɒbnʌt, -s
AM 'kabnət, -s

COBOL
BR 'kəʊbɒl
AM 'koʊˌbal

cobra
BR 'kəʊbrə(r),
'kɒbrə(r), -z
AM 'koʊbrə, -z

coburg
BR 'kəʊbɜːg
AM 'koʊˌbɜrg

cobweb
BR 'kɒbwɛb, -z, -d
AM 'kabˌwɛb, -z, -d

cobwebby
BR 'kɒbwɛbi
AM 'kabˌwɛbi

coca
BR 'kəʊkə(r)
AM 'koʊkə(r)

Coca-Cola®
BR ˌkəʊkə'kəʊlə(r), -z
AM ˌkoʊkə'koʊlə, -z

cocaine
BR kə(ʊ)'keɪn
AM koʊ'keɪn,
'koʊˌkeɪn

cocainism
BR kə(ʊ)'keɪnɪz(ə)m
AM koʊ'keɪˌnɪzəm,
'koʊˌkeɪˌnɪzəm

coccal
BR 'kɒkl
AM 'kakəl

cocci
BR 'kɒk(s)ʌɪ
AM 'kaˌkaɪ

coccidiosis
BR ˌkɒksɪdɪ'əʊsɪs,
kɒkˌsɪdi'əʊsɪs
AM ˌkakˌsɪdi'oʊsəs

coccoid
BR 'kɒk(s)ɔɪd
AM 'kaˌkɔɪd

coccolith
BR 'kɒkəlɪθ, 'kɒkˌlɪθ, -s
AM 'kakəˌlɪθ, -s

coccolithophore
BR ˌkɒkə(ʊ)'lɪθəfɔː(r),
-z
AM ˌkakə'lɪθəˌfɔ(ə)r, -z

coccus
BR 'kɒkəs
AM 'kakəs

coccygeal
BR kɒk'sɪdʒɪəl
AM kak'sɪdʒɪəl

coccyx
BR 'kɒks|ɪks, -ɪksɪz
AM 'kakˌsɪks, -ɪz

Coch
in Welsh placenames
BR kɒx, kɒk
AM kak

Cochabamba
BR ˌkəʊtʃə'bambə(r)
AM ˌkoʊtʃə'bambə
SP kotʃa'βamba

cochair
BR ˌkəʊ'tʃɛː(r), -z
AM ˌkoʊ'tʃɛ(ə)r, -z

co-chairman
BR ˌkəʊ'tʃɛːmən
AM ˌkoʊ'tʃɛrmən

co-chairmen
BR ˌkəʊ'tʃɛːmən
AM ˌkoʊ'tʃɛrmən

Cochin
BR 'kəʊtʃɪn, 'kɒtʃɪn
AM 'koʊtʃɪn, 'katʃɪn

Cochin-China
BR ˌkəʊtʃɪn'tʃʌɪnə(r),
ˌkɒtʃɪn'tʃʌɪnə(r)
AM ˌkoʊtʃɪn'tʃaɪnə,
'katʃɪn'tʃaɪnə

cochineal
BR ˌkɒtʃɪ'niːl,
'kɒtʃɪniːl
AM 'katʃəˌniəl

Cochise
BR kəʊ'tʃiːs
AM koʊ'tʃis

cochlea
BR 'kɒklɪə(r), -z
AM 'kaklɪə, -z

cochleae
BR 'kɒklɪiː
AM 'kakli,i, 'kakli,aɪ

cochlear
BR 'kɒklɪə(r)
AM 'kakliər

Cochran
BR 'kɒkr(ə)n,
'kɒxr(ə)n
AM 'kakrən

Cochrane
BR 'kɒkr(ə)n,
'kɒxr(ə)n
AM 'kakrən

cock
BR kɒk, -s, -ɪŋ, -t
AM kak, -s, -ɪŋ, -t

cockade
BR kə'keɪd, kɒ'keɪd, -z,
-ɪd

cock-a-doodle-doo
AM kɑ'keɪd, -z, -ɪd

cock-a-doodle-doo
BR ˌkɒkə'duːdl'duː, -z
AM ˌkakə'dudəl'du, -z

cock-a-hoop
BR ˌkɒkə'huːp
AM ˌkakə'hup

cock-a-leekie
BR ˌkɒkə'liːki
AM ˌkakə'liki

cockalorum
BR ˌkɒkə'lɔːrəm, -z
AM ˌkakə'lɔrəm, -z

cockamamie
BR ˌkɒkə'meɪmi
AM ˌkakəˌmeɪmi

cockamamy
BR ˌkɒkə'meɪmi
AM ˌkakəˌmeɪmi

cock-and-bull
BR ˌkɒk(ə)n(d)'bʊl
AM 'kakən'bʊl

cockateel
BR ˌkɒkə'tiːl, -z
AM 'kakə,til, -z

cockatiel
BR ˌkɒkə'tiːl, -z
AM 'kakə,til, -z

cockatoo
BR ˌkɒkə'tuː, -z
AM 'kakə,tu, -z

cockatrice
BR 'kɒkətrʌɪs,
'kɒkətrɪs, -ɪz
AM 'kakətrəs,
'kakə,traɪs, -ɪz

cockboat
BR 'kɒkbəʊt, -s
AM 'kak,boʊt, -s

Cockburn
BR 'kəʊb(ə)n, 'kəʊbəːn
AM 'kak,bərn

cockchafer
BR 'kɒkˌtʃeɪfə(r), -z
AM 'kak,tʃeɪfər, -z

Cockcroft
BR 'kɒkrɒft
AM 'kakrɔft, 'kakraft

cockcrow
BR 'kɒkkrəʊ, -z
AM 'kak,kroʊ, -z

cocker
BR 'kɒkə(r), -z
AM 'kakər, -z

cockerel
BR 'kɒkr(ə)l, -z
AM 'kak(ə)rəl, -z

Cockerell
BR 'kɒkr(ə)l
AM 'kak(ə)rəl

Cockermouth
BR 'kɒkəmaʊθ
AM 'kakər,maʊθ

cockeyed
BR ˌkɒk'ʌɪd
AM 'kɑ,kaɪd

cockfight
BR 'kɒkfʌɪt, -s, -ɪŋ
AM 'kak,faɪt, -ts, -dɪŋ

Cockfosters
BR 'kɒkfɒstəz,
ˌkɒk'fɒstəz
AM ˌkak'fastərz,
ˌkak'fɒstərz

cockhorse
BR ˌkɒk'hɔːs, -ɪz
AM ˌkak'(h)ɔ(ə)rs, -əz

cockie-leekie
BR ˌkɒkɪ'liːki
AM ˌkakə'liki

cockily
BR 'kɒkɪli
AM 'kakəli

cockiness
BR 'kɒkɪnɪs
AM 'kakɪnɪs

cockle
BR 'kɒk|l, -lz, -ḷɪŋ\-lɪŋ,
-ld
AM 'kak|əl, -əlz, -(ə)lɪŋ,
-əld

cocklebur
BR 'kɒklbəː(r)
AM 'kakəl,bər

cockleshell
BR 'kɒklʃɛl, -z
AM 'kakəl,ʃɛl, -z

Cockney
BR 'kɒkn|i, -ɪz
AM 'kakni, -z

cockneyism
BR 'kɒknɪɪz(ə)m, -z
AM 'kakni,ɪzəm, -z

cockpit
BR 'kɒkpɪt, -s
AM 'kak,pɪt, -s

cockroach
BR 'kɒkrəʊtʃ
AM 'kak,roʊtʃ

Cockroft
BR 'kɒkrɒft, 'kəʊkrɒft
AM 'kakrɔft, 'kakraft

cockscomb
BR 'kɒkskəʊm, -z
AM 'kak,skoʊm, -z

cocksfoot
BR 'kɒksfʊt, -s
AM 'kaks,fʊt, -s

cockshy
BR 'kɒkʃʌɪ, -z
AM 'kak,ʃaɪ, -z

cocksucker
BR 'kɒk,sʌkə(r), -z
AM 'kak,səkər, -z

cocksure
BR ˌkɒk'ʃɔː(r),
ˌkɒk'ʃʊə(r)
AM ˌkak'ʃʊ(ə)r

cocksurely
BR ˌkɒk'ʃʊəli,
ˌkɒk'ʃɔːli
AM ˌkak'ʃʊrli

cocksureness
BR ˌkɒk'ʃɔːnəs,
ˌkɒk'ʃʊənəs
AM ˌkak'ʃʊrnəs

cockswain
BR 'kɒksn, -z
AM 'kaksən,
'kak,sweɪn, -z

cocktail
BR 'kɒkteɪl, -z
AM 'kak,teɪl, -z

cock-up
BR 'kɒkʌp, -s
AM 'kakəp, -s

cocky
BR 'kɒk|i, -ɪə(r), -ɪɪst
AM 'kaki, -ər, -ɪst

cocky-leeky
BR ˌkɒkɪ'liːki
AM ˌkakə'liki

coco
BR 'kəʊkəʊ, -z
AM 'koʊkoʊ, -z

cocoa
BR 'kəʊkəʊ, -z
AM 'koʊkoʊ, -z

cocoanut
BR 'kəʊkənʌt, -s
AM 'koʊkə,nət, -s

Cocom
BR 'kəʊkɒm
AM 'koʊ,kam

coconut
BR 'kəʊkənʌt, -s
AM 'koʊkə,nət, -s

cocoon
BR kə'kuːn, -z, -ɪŋ, -d
AM kə'kun, -z, -ɪŋ, -d

cocoonery
BR kə'kuːn(ə)ri
AM kə'kunəri

Cocos Islands
BR 'kəʊkəs ˌʌɪlən(d)z,
'kəʊkɒs +
AM ˌkoʊkəs 'aɪlən(d)z

cocotte
BR kə(ʊ)'kɒt, kɒ'kɒt, -s
AM koʊ'kat, kə'kat, -s

Cocteau
BR 'kɒktəʊ
AM kak'toʊ

cod
BR kɒd, -z
AM ˌkad, -z

coda
BR 'kəʊdə(r), -z
AM 'koʊdə(r), -z

coddle
BR 'kɒd|l, -lz, -ḷɪŋ\-lɪŋ,
-ld
AM 'kad|əl, -əlz, -(ə)lɪŋ,
-əld

coddler
BR 'kɒdlə(r), -z
AM 'kad(ə)lər, -z

code
BR kəʊd, -z, -ɪŋ, -ɪd

codeine
BR 'kəʊdiːn
AM 'koʊˌdin

codependency
BR ˌkəʊdɪ'pɛnd(ə)nsi
AM ˌkoʊdə'pɛnd(ə)nsi

codependent
BR ˌkəʊdɪ'pɛnd(ə)nt,
-s
AM ˌkoʊdə'pɛnd(ə)nt,
-s

coder
BR 'kəʊdə(r), -z
AM 'koʊdər, -z

codeword
BR 'kəʊdwəːd, -z
AM 'koʊd,wərd, -z

codex
BR 'kəʊdɛks, -ɪz
AM 'koʊˌdɛks, -əz

codfish
BR 'kɒdfɪʃ, -ɪz
AM 'kad,fɪʃ, -ɪz

codger
BR 'kɒdʒə(r), -z
AM 'kadʒər, -z

codices
BR 'kəʊdɪsiːz,
'kɒdɪsiːz
AM 'koʊdəsiz, 'kadəsiz

codicil
BR 'kəʊdɪsɪl, 'kɒdɪsɪl,
-z
AM 'kadə,səl, -z

codicillary
BR ˌkəʊdɪ'sɪləri,
ˌkɒdɪ'sɪləri
AM ˌkadə'sɪləri

codicological
BR ˌkəʊdɪkə'lɒdʒɪkl,
ˌkɒdɪkə'lɒdʒɪkl
AM ˌkadəkə'ladʒəkəl

codicologically
BR ˌkəʊdɪkə'lɒdʒɪkli,
ˌkɒdɪkə'lɒdʒɪkli
AM ˌkadəkə'ladʒəkəl

codicology
BR ˌkəʊdɪ'kɒlədʒi,
ˌkɒdɪ'kɒlədʒi
AM ˌkadə'kalədʒi

codification
BR ˌkəʊdɪfɪ'keɪʃn
AM ˌkadəfə'keɪʃən,
ˌkoʊdəfə'keɪʃən

codifier
BR 'kəʊdɪfʌɪə(r), -z
AM 'kadə,faɪər,
'koʊdə,faɪər, -z

codify
BR 'kəʊdɪfʌɪ, -z, -ɪŋ, -d
AM 'kadə,faɪ,
'koʊdə,faɪ, -z, -ɪŋ, -d

codlin
BR 'kɒdlɪn, -z
AM 'kadlən, -z

codling
BR 'kɒdlɪŋ, -z

AM ˈkɑdlɪŋ, -z
codliver oil
BR ˌkɒdlɪvər ˈɔɪl
AM ˈkɑdˌlɪvər ˈɔɪ
codomain
BR ˌkəʊdə(ʊ)ˈmeɪn
AM ˌkoʊdəˈmeɪn,
ˌkoʊˌdoʊˈmeɪn
codon
BR ˈkəʊdɒn, -z
AM ˈkoʊdɑn, -z
codpiece
BR ˈkɒdpiːs, -ɪz
AM ˈkɑdˌpis, -ɪz
codriver
BR ˈkəʊˌdrʌɪvə(r), -z
AM ˈkoʊˌdraɪvər, -z
codswallop
BR ˈkɒdzˌwɒləp
AM ˈkɑdzˌwɑləp
Cody
BR ˈkəʊdi
AM ˈkoʊdi
Coe
BR kəʊ
AM koʊ
coecilian
BR sɪˈsɪliən, -z
AM siˈsɪljən, səˈsɪljən,
sɪˈsɪliən, səˈsɪliən, -z
Coed
in Welsh placenames
BR kɔɪd
AM kɔɪd
coed
BR ˌkəʊˈɛd, -z
AM ˈkoʊˌɛd, -z
co-editor
BR ˈkəʊˌɛdɪtə(r), -z
AM ˈkoʊˌɛdədər, -z
coeducation
BR ˌkəʊɛdjʊˈkeɪʃn,
ˌkəʊɛdʒʊˈkeɪʃn
AM ˌkoʊˌɛdʒəˈkeɪʃən
coeducational
BR ˌkəʊɛdjʊˈkeɪʃn̩(ə)l,
ˌkəʊɛdjʊˈkeɪʃən(ə)l,
ˌkəʊɛdʒʊˈkeɪʃn̩(ə)l,
ˌkəʊɛdʒʊˈkeɪʃən(ə)l
AM ˌkoʊˌɛdʒəˈkeɪʃ(ə)nəl
coefficient
BR ˌkəʊɪˈfɪʃnt
AM ˌkoʊəˈfɪʃənt
coelacanth
BR ˈsiːləkanθ, -s
AM ˈsiləˌkænθ, -s
coelenterate
BR sɪˈlɛntəreɪt,
sɪˈlɛnt(ə)rət, -s
AM ˌsiˈlɛntəˌreɪt, -s
coeliac
BR ˈsiːlɪak
AM ˈsiliˌæk
coelom
BR ˈsiːləm
AM ˈsiləm

coelomate
BR ˈsiːlə(ʊ)meɪt
AM ˈsiləˌmeɪt
coelostat
BR ˈsiːlə(ʊ)stat, -s
AM ˈsiləˌstæt, -s
coemption
BR kəʊˈɛm(p)ʃn
AM ˈkoʊˈɛmpʃən
Coen
BR kəʊn
AM koʊn
coenobite
BR ˈsiːnə(ʊ)bʌɪt, -s
AM ˈsinəˌbaɪt,
ˈsɛnəˌbaɪt, -s
coenobitic
BR ˌsiːnəˈbɪtɪk
AM ˌsinəˈbɪdɪk,
ˌsɛnəˈbɪdɪk
coenobitical
BR ˌsiːnəˈbɪtɪkl
AM ˌsinəˈbɪdɪkl,
ˌsɛnəˈbɪdəkəl
coequal
BR (ˌ)kəʊˈiːkw(ə)l, -z
AM ˈkoʊˈikwəl, -z
coequality
BR ˌkəʊɪˈkwɒlɪti
AM ˌkoʊəˈkwɑlədi,
ˌkoʊiˈkwɒlədi,
ˌkoʊiˈkwɒlədi
coerce
BR kəʊˈəːs, -ɪz, -ɪŋ, -t
AM koʊˈərs, -əz, -ɪŋ, -t
coercer
BR kəʊˈəːsə(r), -z
AM koʊˈərsər, -z
coercible
BR kəʊˈəːsɪbl
AM koʊˈərsəbəl
coercibly
BR kəʊˈəːsɪbli
AM koʊˈərsəbli
coercion
BR kəʊˈəːʃn
AM koʊˈərʃən,
koʊˈərʒən
coercive
BR kəʊˈəːsɪv
AM koʊˈərsɪv
coercively
BR kəʊˈəːsɪvli
AM koʊˈərsɪvli
coerciveness
BR kəʊˈəːsɪvnɪs
AM koʊˈərsɪvnɪs
coessential
BR ˌkəʊɪˈsɛnʃl
AM ˌkoʊəˈsɛn(t)ʃəl
coeternal
BR ˌkəʊɪˈtəːnl
AM ˌkoʊəˈtərnəl
coeternally
BR ˌkəʊɪˈtəːnl̩i,
ˌkəʊɪˈtəːnəli
AM ˌkoʊəˈtərnəli

Coetzee
BR kuːtˈsɪə(r), kuːtˈsi:
AM ˈkoʊtsi
Coeur d'Alene
BR ˌkɔː dəˈleɪn, + dlˈeɪn
AM ˌkər dəˈleɪn
Cœur de Lion
BR ˌkə: də ˈliːõ, + ˈliːɒn,
+ ˈliːən
AM ˌkər də ˈliɒn
coeval
BR ˌkəʊˈiːvl
AM ˌkoʊˈivəl
coevality
BR ˌkəʊiːˈvalɪti
AM ˌkoʊiˈvælədi
coevally
BR ˌkəʊˈiːvl̩i
AM ˌkoʊˈivɪli
coexist
BR ˌkəʊɪɡˈzɪst, -s, -ɪŋ,
-ɪd
AM ˌkoʊəɡˈzɪst, -s, -ɪŋ,
-ɪd
coexistence
BR ˌkəʊɪɡˈzɪst(ə)ns
AM ˌkoʊəɡˈzɪstns
coexistent
BR ˌkəʊɪɡˈzɪst(ə)nt
AM ˌkoʊəɡˈzɪstənt
coextend
BR ˌkəʊɪkˈstɛnd, -z, -ɪŋ,
-ɪd
AM ˌkoʊəkˈstɛnd, -z,
-ɪŋ, -əd
coextension
BR ˌkəʊɪkˈstɛnʃn, -z
AM ˌkoʊəkˈstɛn(t)ʃən,
-z
coextensive
BR ˌkəʊɪkˈstɛnsɪv
AM ˌkoʊəkˈstɛnsɪv
C of E
BR ˌsiː əv ˈi:
AM ˌsi əv ˈi
coffee
BR ˈkɒfl̩i, -ɪz
AM ˈkɔfi, ˈkɑfi, -z
coffeecake
BR ˈkɒfɪkeɪk, -s
AM ˈkɔfiˌkeɪk,
ˈkɑfiˌkeɪk, -s
coffee klatch
BR ˈkɒfi klatʃ, -ɪz
AM ˈkɔfi ˌklatʃ, ˈkɑfi +,
-əz
coffer
BR ˈkɒfə(r), -z, -d
AM ˈkɔfər, ˈkɑfər, -z, -d
cofferdam
BR ˈkɒfədam, -z
AM ˈkɔfərˌdæm,
ˈkɑfərˌdæm, -z
Coffey
BR ˈkɒfi
AM ˈkɑfi
coffin
BR ˈkɒfɪn, -z

AM ˈkɒfən, ˈkɑfən, -z
coffle
BR ˈkɒfl, -z
AM ˈkɔfəl, ˈkɑfəl, -z
cog
BR kɒɡ, -z, -d
AM kɑɡ, -z, -d
Cogan
BR ˈkəʊɡ(ə)n
AM ˈkoʊɡən
cogency
BR ˈkəʊdʒ(ə)nsi
AM ˈkoʊdʒənsi
cogent
BR ˈkəʊdʒ(ə)nt
AM ˈkoʊdʒənt
cogently
BR ˈkəʊdʒ(ə)ntli
AM ˈkoʊdʒən(t)li
Coggeshall
BR ˈkɒɡɪʃl, ˈkɒksl
AM ˈkɑɡzˌ(h)ɔl,
ˈkɑɡzˌ(h)ɑl
Coghill
BR ˈkɒɡ(h)ɪl
AM ˈkɑɡ(h)ɪl
cogitable
BR ˈkɒdʒɪtəbl
AM ˈkɑdʒədəbəl
cogitate
BR ˈkɒdʒɪteɪt, -s, -ɪŋ, -ɪd
AM ˈkɑdʒəˌteɪ|t, -ts,
-dɪŋ, -dɪd
cogitation
BR ˌkɒdʒɪˈteɪʃn
AM ˌkɑdʒəˈteɪʃən
cogitative
BR ˈkɒdʒɪtətɪv
AM ˈkɑdʒəˌteɪdɪv
cogitator
BR ˈkɒdʒɪteɪtə(r), -z
AM ˈkɑdʒəˌteɪdər, -z
cogito
BR ˈkɒɡɪtəʊ
AM ˈkɑɡədoʊ
cogito ergo sum
BR ˌkɒɡɪtəʊ ˌəːɡəʊ
ˈsʊm, + ˈsʌm
AM ˌkɑɡədoʊ ˌərɡoʊ
ˈsəm
cognac
BR ˈkɒnjak, -s
AM ˈkoʊnˌjæk,
ˈkɑnˌjæk, -s
cognate
BR ˈkɒɡneɪt, -s
AM ˈkɑɡˌneɪt, -s
cognately
BR ˈkɒɡneɪtli
AM ˈkɑɡˌneɪtli
cognateness
BR ˈkɒɡneɪtnɪs
AM ˈkɑɡˌneɪtnɪs
cognatic
BR kɒɡˈnatɪk
AM ˌkɑɡˈnædɪk

cognation
BR kɒgˈneɪʃn
AM ˌkɑgˈneɪʃən
cognisable
BR ˈkɒg(g)nɪzəbl,
kɒgˈnaɪzəbl
AM ˈkɑgnəzəbəl,
ˌkɑgˈnaɪzəbəl
cognisably
BR ˈkɒg(g)nɪzəbli,
kɒgˈnaɪzəbli
AM ˈkɑgnəzəbli,
ˌkɑgˈnaɪzəbli
cognisance
BR ˈkɒg(g)nɪz(ə)ns,
kɒgˈnaɪz(ə)ns
AM ˈkɑgnəzns
cognisant
BR ˈkɒg(g)nɪz(ə)nt,
kɒgˈnaɪz(ə)nt
AM ˈkɑgnəznt
cognise
BR ˈkɒgnʌɪz, -ɪz, -ɪŋ, -d
AM ˈkɑgˌnaɪz, -ɪz, -ɪŋ, -d
cognition
BR kɒgˈnɪʃn
AM ˌkɑgˈnɪʃən
cognitional
BR kɒgˈnɪʃn(ə)l,
kɒgˈnɪʃən(ə)l
AM ˌkɑgˈnɪʃ(ə)nəl
cognitive
BR ˈkɒgnɪtɪv
AM ˈkɑgnədɪv
cognitively
BR ˈkɒgnɪtɪvli
AM ˈkɑgnədɪvli
cognitivism
BR ˈkɒgnɪtɪvɪz(ə)m
AM ˈkɑgnədɪˌvɪzəm
cognitivist
BR ˈkɒgnɪtɪvɪst, -s
AM ˈkɑgnədɪvɪst, -s
cognizable
BR ˈkɒg(g)nɪzəbl,
kɒgˈnaɪzəbl
AM ˈkɑgnəzəbəl,
ˌkɑgˈnaɪzəbəl
cognizably
BR ˈkɒg(g)nɪzəbli,
kɒgˈnaɪzəbli
AM ˈkɑgnəzəbli,
ˌkɑgˈnaɪzəbli
cognizance
BR ˈkɒg(g)nɪz(ə)ns,
kɒgˈnaɪz(ə)ns
AM ˈkɑgnəzns
cognizant
BR ˈkɒg(g)nɪz(ə)nt,
kɒgˈnaɪz(ə)nt
AM ˈkɑgnəznt
cognize
BR ˈkɒgnʌɪz, kɒgˈnʌɪz,
-ɪz, -ɪŋ, -d
AM ˈkɑgˌnaɪz, -ɪz, -ɪŋ, -d
cognomen
BR ˌkɒgˈnəʊmɛn,
ˌkɒgˈnəʊmən, -z

AM ˌkɑgˈnoʊmən,
ˈkɑgnəmən, -z
cognominal
BR ˌkɒgˈnɒmɪnl
AM ˌkɑgˈnɑmənəl
cognoscente
BR ˌkɒgnəˈʃɛnti,
ˌkɒnjəˈʃɛnti
AM ˌkɑgnəˈʃɛn(t)i,
ˌkɑnjoʊˈʃɛn(t)i
cognoscenti
BR ˌkɒgnəˈʃɛnti(:),
ˌkɒnjəˈʃɛnti(:)
AM ˌkɑgnəˈʃɛn(t)i,
ˌkɑnjoʊˈʃɛn(t)i
cogwheel
BR ˈkɒgwiːl, -z
AM ˈkɑg,(h)wil, -z
cohabit
BR (ˌ)kəʊˈhab|ɪt, -ɪts,
-ɪtɪŋ, -ɪtɪd
AM ˌkoʊˈhæbə|t, -ts,
-dɪŋ, -dəd
cohabitant
BR (ˌ)kəʊˈhabɪt(ə)nt,
-s
AM ˌkoʊˈhæbədənt, -s
cohabitation
BR ˌkəʊhabɪˈteɪʃn,
kə(ʊ)ˌhabɪˈteɪʃn
AM ˌkoʊˌhæbəˈteɪʃən
cohabitee
BR ˌkəʊhabɪˈtiː,
kə(ʊ)ˌhabɪˈtiː, -z
AM ˌkoʊhæbəˈti, -z
cohabiter
BR (ˌ)kəʊˈhabɪtə(r), -z
AM ˌkoʊˈhæbədər, -z
Cohan
BR ˈkəʊhan
AM ˈkoʊˌhæn, ˈkoʊ(ə)n
Cohen
BR ˈkəʊɪn
AM ˈkoʊ(ə)n
cohere
BR kə(ʊ)ˈhɪə(r), -z, -ɪŋ,
-d
AM koʊˈhɪ(ə)r, -z, -ɪŋ, -d
coherence
BR kə(ʊ)ˈhɪərəns,
kə(ʊ)ˈhɪərn̩s
AM koʊˈhɪrəns
coherency
BR kə(ʊ)ˈhɪərənsi,
kə(ʊ)ˈhɪərn̩si
AM koʊˈhɪrənsi
coherent
BR kə(ʊ)ˈhɪərənt,
kə(ʊ)ˈhɪərn̩t
AM koʊˈhɪrənt
coherently
BR kə(ʊ)ˈhɪərəntli,
kə(ʊ)ˈhɪərn̩tli
AM koʊˈhɪrən(t)li
coherer
BR kə(ʊ)ˈhɪərə(r), -z
AM koʊˈhɪrər, -z

cohesion
BR kə(ʊ)ˈhiːʒn
AM koʊˈhiʒən
cohesive
BR kə(ʊ)ˈhiːsɪv
AM koʊˈhisɪv
cohesively
BR kə(ʊ)ˈhiːsɪvli
AM koʊˈhisɪvli
cohesiveness
BR kə(ʊ)ˈhiːsɪvnɪs
AM koʊˈhisɪvnɪs
Cohn
BR kəʊn
AM koʊn
coho
BR ˈkəʊhəʊ, -z
AM ˈkoʊˌhoʊ, -z
cohort
BR ˈkəʊhɔːt, -s
AM ˈkoʊˌhɔ(ə)rt, -s
cohosh
BR kəˈhɒʃ
AM ˈkoʊˌhɑʃ
COHSE
BR ˈkəʊzi
AM ˈkoʊzi
cohune
BR kəˈhuːn, -z
AM kəˈhun, -z
coif[1]
noun
BR kɔɪf, -s
AM kɔɪf, -s
coif[2]
verb
BR kwaːf, kwɒf, -s, -ɪŋ,
-t
AM kwɑf, -s, -ɪŋ, -t
coiffeur
BR kwaːˈfəː(r),
kwɒˈfəː(r), -z
AM kwɑˈfər, -z
coiffeurs
BR kwaːˈfəːz, kwɒˈfəːz
AM kwɑˈfərz
coiffeuse
BR kwaːˈfəːz, kwɒˈfəːz
AM kwɑˈfʊz
coiffeuses
BR kwaːˈfəːz, kwɒˈfəːz
AM kwɑˈfʊz
coiffure
BR kwaːˈfjʊə(r),
kwɒˈfjʊə(r),
kwəˈfjʊə(r), -z
AM kwɑˈfjʊ(ə)r, -z
coign
BR kɔɪn, -z
AM kɔɪn, -z
coil
BR kɔɪl, -z, -ɪŋ, -d
AM kɔɪl, -z, -ɪŋ, -d
Coimbra
BR ˈkwɪmbrə(r)
AM kuˈɪmbrə

coin
BR kɔɪn, -z, -ɪŋ, -d
AM kɔɪn, -z, -ɪŋ, -d
coinage
BR ˈkɔɪn|ɪdʒ, -ɪdʒɪz
AM ˈkɔɪnɪdʒ, -ɪz
coincide
BR ˌkəʊɪnˈsʌɪd, -z, -ɪŋ,
-ɪd
AM ˌkoʊənˈsaɪd, -z, -ɪŋ,
-ɪd
coincidence
BR kəʊˈɪnsɪd(ə)ns, -ɪz
AM koʊˈɪnsədns, -ɪz
coincident
BR kəʊˈɪnsɪd(ə)nt
AM koʊˈɪnsədnt,
koʊˈɪnsəˌdɛnt
coincidental
BR kəʊˌɪnsɪˈdɛntl
AM koʊˌɪnsəˈdɛn(t)l
coincidentally
BR kəʊˌɪnsɪˈdɛntl̩i
AM koʊˌɪnsəˈdɛn(t)əli
coincidently
BR kəʊˌɪnsɪˈdɛntli
AM koʊˌɪnsəˈdɛn(t)li
coiner
BR ˈkɔɪnə(r), -z
AM ˈkɔɪnər, -z
co-inheritor
BR ˌkəʊɪnˈhɛrɪtə(r), -z
AM ˌkoʊənˈhɛrədər, -z
coin-op
BR ˈkɔɪnɒp, -s
AM ˈkɔɪnˌɑp, -s
cointreau
BR ˈkwɒntrəʊ,
ˈkwaːntrəʊ,
ˈkwantrəʊ, -z
AM kwɑnˈtroʊ, -z
coir
BR ˈkɔɪə(r)
AM ˈkɔɪ(ə)r
coit
BR kɔɪt
AM kɔɪt
coital
BR ˈkəʊɪtl, ˈkɔɪ(ɪ)tl
AM ˈkoʊədl, ˈkɔɪdl
coition
BR kəʊˈɪʃn
AM koʊˈɪʃən
coitus
BR ˈkəʊɪtəs, ˈkɔɪ(ɪ)təs
AM ˈkoʊədəs, ˈkɔɪdəs
coitus
interruptus
BR ˌkəʊɪtəs
ˌɪntəˈrʌptəs,
ˌkɔɪ(ɪ)təs +
AM ˌkoʊədəs
ɪn(t)əˈrəptəs,
ˌkɔɪdəs +
cojones
BR kəˈhəʊneɪz
AM koʊˈhoʊneɪz
kəˈhoʊneɪz

Coke[1]®
Coca-Cola
BR kəʊk, -s
AM koʊk, -s
Coke[2]
surname
BR kʊk, kəʊk
AM koʊk
coke
BR kəʊk, -s, -ɪŋ, -t
AM koʊk, -s, -ɪŋ, -t
Coker
BR ˈkəʊkə(r)
AM ˈkoʊkər
col
BR kɒl, -z
AM kɑl, -z
cola
BR ˈkəʊlə(r), -z
AM ˈkoʊlə, -z
colander
BR ˈkʌləndə(r), -z
AM ˈkɑləndər,
ˈkələndər, -z
Colbert[1]
French surname
BR ˈkɒlbɛː(r)
AM ˌkɔlˈbɛ(ə)r
Colbert[2]
English surname
BR ˈkəʊlbəːt
AM ˈkoʊlbərt
Colby
BR ˈkɒlbi
AM ˈkoʊlbi
colcannon
BR kɒlˈkanən,
kəlˈkanən
AM kəlˈkænən
Colchester
BR ˈkɒltʃɪstə(r),
ˈkɒlˌtʃɛstər
AM ˈkoʊlˌtʃɛstər
colchicine
BR ˈkɒltʃɪsiːn,
ˈkɒlkɪsiːn, -z
AM ˈkɑltʃəˌsin,
ˈkɑlkəˌsin, -z
colchicum
BR ˈkɒltʃɪkəm,
ˈkɒlkɪkəm
AM ˈkɑltʃəkəm
Colchis
BR ˈkɒlkɪs
AM ˈkɑlkəs, ˈkɑlkəs
cold
BR kəʊld, -z, -ə(r), -ɪst
AM koʊld, -z, -ər, -əst
cold-blooded
BR ˌkəʊl(d)ˈblʌdɪd
AM ˌkoʊl(d)ˈblədəd
cold-bloodedly
BR ˌkəʊl(d)ˈblʌdɪdli
AM ˌkoʊl(d)ˈblədədli
cold-
bloodedness
BR ˌkəʊl(d)ˈblʌdɪdnɪs
AM ˌkoʊl(d)ˈblədədnəs

coldish
BR ˈkəʊldɪʃ
AM ˈkoʊldɪʃ
Colditz
BR ˈkəʊldɪts, ˈkɒldɪts
AM ˈkoʊldɪts
coldly
BR ˈkəʊldli
AM ˈkoʊl(d)li
coldness
BR ˈkəʊldnəs
AM ˈkoʊl(d)nəs
coldstore
BR ˈkəʊl(d)stɔː(r), -z
AM ˈkoʊl(d)ˌstɔ(ə)r, -z
Coldstream
BR ˈkəʊl(d)striːm
AM ˈkoʊl(d)ˌstrim
Cole
BR kəʊl
AM koʊl
Colebrook
BR ˈkəʊlbrʊk
AM ˈkoʊlˌbrʊk
Coleclough
BR ˈkəʊlklʌf
AM ˈkoʊlkləf
colectomy
BR kə(ʊ)ˈlɛktəmǀi, -ɪz
AM kəˈlɛktəmi,
koʊˈlɛktəmi, -z
Coleford
BR ˈkəʊlfəd
AM ˈkoʊlfərd
Coleman
BR ˈkəʊlmən
AM ˈkoʊlmən
colemice
BR ˈkəʊlmʌɪs
AM ˈkoʊlˌmaɪs
colemouse
BR ˈkəʊlmaʊs
AM ˈkoʊlˌmaʊs
Colenso
BR kəˈlɛnzəʊ,
kəˈlɛnsəʊ
AM kəˈlɛnsoʊ
Coleoptera
BR ˌkɒlɪˈɒpt(ə)rə(r)
AM ˌkɑliˈɑpt(ə)rə
coleopteran
BR ˌkɒlɪˈɒpt(ə)rən, -z
AM ˌkɑliˈɑpt(ə)rən, -z
coleopterist
BR ˌkɒlɪˈɒpt(ə)rɪst, -s
AM ˌkɑliˈɑpt(ə)rəst, -s
coleopterous
BR ˌkɒlɪˈɒpt(ə)rəs
AM ˌkɑliˈɑpt(ə)rəs
coleoptile
BR ˌkɒlɪˈɒptʌɪl, -z
AM ˌkɑliˈɑpˌtaɪl, -z
Coleraine
BR ˌkəʊlˈreɪn
AM ˈkoʊlˌreɪn,
ˌkoʊlˈreɪn

Coleridge
BR ˈkəʊl(ə)rɪdʒ
AM ˈkoʊl(ə)rɪdʒ
Coles
BR kəʊlz
AM koʊlz
coleseed
BR ˈkəʊlsiːd
AM ˈkoʊlˌsid
coleslaw
BR ˈkəʊlslɔː(r)
AM ˈkoʊlˌslɔ
Colet
BR ˈkɒlɪt
AM ˈkɑlət
Colette
BR kɒˈlɛt, kəˈlɛt
AM kəˈlɛt
coleus
BR ˈkəʊlɪəs
AM ˈkoʊliəs
coley
BR ˈkəʊlǀi, -ɪz
AM ˈkoʊli, -z
Colgate®
BR ˈkəʊlgeɪt, ˈkɒlgeɪt
AM ˈkoʊlˌgeɪt
colic
BR ˈkɒlɪk
AM ˈkɑlɪk
colicky
BR ˈkɒlɪki
AM ˈkɑləki
coliform
BR ˈkəʊlɪfɔːm,
ˈkɒlɪfɔːm
AM ˈkoʊliˌfɔ(ə)rm
Colima
BR kɒˈliːmə(r),
kəˈliːmə(r)
AM kɔˈlimə, kəˈlimə,
kɑˈlimə
Colin
BR ˈkɒlɪn
AM ˈkɑlən
coliseum
BR ˌkɒlɪˈsiːəm, -z
AM ˌkɑləˈsiəm, -z
colitis
BR kəˈlʌɪtɪs, kɒˈlʌɪtɪs
AM kəˈlaɪdəs
Coll
BR kɒl
AM kɒl, kɑl
collaborate
BR kəˈlabəreɪt, -s, -ɪŋ, -ɪd
AM kəˈlæbəˌreɪǀt, -ts, -dɪŋ, -dɪd
collaboration
BR kəˌlabəˈreɪʃn
AM kəˌlæbəˈreɪʃən
collaborationist
BR kəˌlabəˈreɪʃnɪst, kəˌlabəˈreɪʃənɪst, -s
AM kəˌlæbəˈreɪʃənəst, -s

collaborative
BR kəˈlab(ə)rətɪv
AM kəˈlæbərədɪv
collaboratively
BR kəˈlab(ə)rətɪvli
AM kəˈlæbərədɪvli
collaborator
BR kəˌlabəreɪtə(r), -z
AM kəˈlæbəˌreɪdər, -z
collage
BR ˈkɒlɑːʒ, kɒˈlɑːʒ, kəˈlɑːʒ, -ɪz
AM kəˈlɑʒ, -ɪz
collagen
BR ˈkɒladʒ(ə)n
AM ˈkɑlədʒən
collagist
BR ˈkɒlɑːʒɪst, kɒˈlɑːʒɪst, kəˈlɑːʒɪst, -s
AM ˈkɑlədʒəst, -s
collapsar
BR kəˈlapsɑː(r), -z
AM kəˈlæpsər, -z
collapse
BR kəˈlaps, -ɪz, -ɪŋ, -t
AM kəˈlæps, -əz, -ɪn, -t
collapsibility
BR kəˌlapsɪˈbɪlɪti
AM kəˌlæpsəˈbɪlɪdi
collapsible
BR kəˈlapsɪbl
AM kəˈlæpsəbəl
collar
BR ˈkɒlə(r), -z, -ɪŋ, -d
AM ˈkɑlər, -z, -ɪŋ, -d
collarbone
BR ˈkɒləbəʊn, -z
AM ˈkɑlərˌboʊn, -z
collard
BR ˈkɒləd, -z
AM ˈkɑlərd, -z
collarette
BR ˌkɒləˈrɛt, -s
AM ˌkɑləˈrɛt, -s
collarless
BR ˈkɒlələs
AM ˈkɑlərləs
collate
BR kəˈleɪt, kɒˈleɪt, -s, -ɪŋ, -ɪd
AM ˈkoʊˌleɪǀt, ˈkɑˌleɪǀt, -ts, -dɪŋ, -dɪd
collateral
BR kəˈlat(ə)rəl, kəˈlat(ə)rl
AM kəˈlædərəl, kəˈlætrəl
collateralize
BR kəˈlat(ə)rəlʌɪz, kəˈlat(ə)rlʌɪz, -ɪz, -ɪŋ, -d
AM kəˈlædərəˌlaɪz, kəˈlætrəˌlaɪz, -ɪz, -ɪŋ, -d
collaterality
BR kəˌlatəˈralɪti
AM kəˌlædəˈrælədi

collateralize
BR kəˈlat(ə)rəlʌɪz, kəˈlat(ə)r|ʌɪz, -ɪz, -ɪŋ, -d
AM kəˈlædərəˌlaɪz, kəˈlætrəˌlaɪz, -ɪz, -ɪŋ, -d

collaterally
BR kəˈlat(ə)rəli, kəˈlat(ə)r|i
AM kəˈlædərəli, kəˈlætrəli

collation
BR kəˈleɪʃn, kɒˈleɪʃn
AM kəˈleɪʃən

collator
BR kəˈleɪtə(r), kɒˈleɪtə(r), -z
AM ˈkoʊˌleɪdər, ˈkɑˌleɪdər, -z

colleague
BR ˈkɒliːg, -z
AM ˈkɑlig, -z

collect¹
noun, prayer
BR ˈkɒlɛkt, -s
AM ˈkɑlɛk(t), -s

collect²
verb, gather together
BR kəˈlɛkt, -s, -ɪŋ, -ɪd
AM kəˈlɛk|(t), -(t)s, -tɪŋ, -təd

collectability
BR kəˌlɛktəˈbɪlɪti
AM kəˈlɛktəbɪlɪdi

collectable
BR kəˈlɛktəbl, -z
AM kəˈlɛktəbəl, -z

collectanea
BR ˌkɒlɛkˈteɪnɪə(r)
AM ˌkɑlɛkˈteɪnɪə

collectedly
BR kəˈlɛktɪdli
AM kəˈlɛktədli

collecteness
BR kəˈlɛktɪdnɪs
AM kəˈlɛktədnəs

collectible
BR kəˈlɛktəbl, -z
AM kəˈlɛktəbəl, -z

collection
BR kəˈlɛkʃn, -z
AM kəˈlɛkʃən, -z

collective
BR kəˈlɛktɪv, -z
AM kəˈlɛktɪv, -z

collectively
BR kəˈlɛktɪvli
AM kəˈlɛktɪvli

collectiveness
BR kəˈlɛktɪvnɪs
AM kəˈlɛktɪvnɪs

collectivisation
BR kəˌlɛktɪvʌɪˈzeɪʃn
AM kəˌlɛktəvəˈzeɪʃən, kəˌlɛktəˌvaɪˈzeɪʃən

collectivise
BR kəˈlɛktɪvʌɪz, -ɪz, -ɪŋ, -d
AM kəˈlɛktəˌvaɪz, -ɪz, -ɪŋ, -d

collectivism
BR kəˈlɛktɪvɪz(ə)m
AM kəˈlɛktəˌvɪzəm

collectivist
BR kəˈlɛktɪvɪst, -s
AM kəˈlɛktəvəst, -s

collectivistic
BR kəˌlɛktɪˈvɪstɪk
AM kəˌlɛktəˈvɪstɪk

collectivity
BR ˌkɒlɛkˈtɪvɪti
AM kəˌlɛkˈtɪvɪdi, ˌkɑlɛkˈtɪvɪdi

collectivization
BR kəˌlɛktɪvʌɪˈzeɪʃn
AM kəˌlɛktəvəˈzeɪʃən, kəˌlɛktəˌvaɪˈzeɪʃən

collectivize
BR kəˈlɛktɪvʌɪz, -ɪz, -ɪŋ, -d
AM kəˈlɛktəˌvaɪz, -ɪz, -ɪŋ, -d

collector
BR kəˈlɛktə(r), -z
AM kəˈlɛktər, -z

colleen
BR ˈkɒliːn, kɒˈliːn, kəˈliːn, -z
AM kəˈlin, ˈkɑlin, -z

college
BR ˈkɒl|ɪdʒ, -ɪdʒɪz
AM ˈkɑlɪdʒ, -ɪz

colleger
BR ˈkɒlɪdʒə(r)
AM ˈkɑlɪdʒər

collegia
BR kəˈliːdʒɪə(r), kəˈlɛgɪə(r)
AM kəˈlɛgɪə

collegial
BR kəˈliːdʒɪəl
AM kəˈlidʒ(i)əl

collegiality
BR kəˌliːdʒɪˈalɪti
AM kəˌlidgiˈælədi

collegian
BR kəˈliːdʒɪən, -z
AM kəˈlidʒən, -z

collegiate
BR kəˈliːdʒɪət
AM kəˈlidʒ(i)ət

collegiately
BR kəˈliːdʒɪətli
AM kəˈlidʒ(i)ətli

collegium
BR kəˈliːdʒɪəm, kəˈlɛgɪəm, -z
AM kəˈlɛgiəm, -z

collenchyma
BR kəˈlɛŋkɪmə(r)
AM kəˈlɛŋkəmə

collet
BR ˈkɒlɪt, -s

collectivise
AM kəˈlɛktɪvʌɪz, -ɪz, -ɪŋ, -d
AM kəˈlɛktəˌvaɪz, -ɪz, -ɪŋ, -d

Collette
BR kɒˈlɛt, kəˈlɛt
AM kəˈlɛt

Colley
BR ˈkɒli
AM ˈkɑli

collide
BR kəˈlʌɪd, -z, -ɪŋ, -ɪd
AM kəˈlaɪd, -z, -ɪŋ, -ɪd

collider
BR kəˈlʌɪdə(r), -z
AM kəˈlaɪdər, -z

collie
BR ˈkɒl|i, -ɪz
AM ˈkɑli, -z

collier
BR ˈkɒlɪə(r), -z
AM ˈkɑljər, -z

colliery
BR ˈkɒljər|i, -ɪz
AM ˈkɑljəri, -z

colligate
BR ˈkɒlɪgeɪt, -s, -ɪŋ, -ɪd
AM ˈkɑləˌgeɪ|t, -ts, -dɪŋ, -dɪd

colligation
BR ˌkɒlɪˈgeɪʃn, -z
AM ˌkɑləˈgeɪʃən, -z

colligative
BR kəˈlɪgətɪv
AM ˈkɑləˌgeɪdɪv

collimate
BR ˈkɒlɪmeɪt, -s, -ɪŋ, -ɪd
AM ˈkɑləˌmeɪ|t, -ts, -dɪŋ, -dɪd

collimation
BR ˌkɒlɪˈmeɪʃn, -z
AM ˌkɑləˈmeɪʃən, -z

collimator
BR ˈkɒlɪmeɪtə(r), -z
AM ˈkɑləˌmeɪdər, -z

collinear
BR kɒˈlɪnɪə(r), kə(ʊ)ˈlɪnɪə(r)
AM kəˈlɪnɪər

collinearity
BR kɒˌlɪnɪˈarɪti, kəˌlɪnɪˈarɪti
AM kəˌlɪnɪˈɛrədi

collinearly
BR kɒˈlɪnɪəli, kəˈlɪnɪəli
AM kəˈlɪnɪərli

Collinge
BR ˈkɒlɪn(d)ʒ
AM ˈkɑlɪŋ, ˈkɑləndʒ

Collingham
BR ˈkɒlɪŋəm
AM ˈkɑlɪŋ,(h)æm

Collingwood
BR ˈkɒlɪŋwʊd
AM ˈkɑlɪŋˌwʊd

collins
BR ˈkɒlɪnz, -ɪz
AM ˈkɑlənz, -əz

Collinson
BR ˈkɒlɪns(ə)n
AM ˈkɑlənsən

Collis
BR ˈkɒlɪs
AM ˈkɑləs

collision
BR kəˈlɪʒn, -z
AM kəˈlɪʒən, -z

collisional
BR kəˈlɪʒn(ə)l, kəˈlɪʒən(ə)l
AM kəˈlɪʒənl, kəˈlɪʒnəl

collocate¹
noun
BR ˈkɒləkət, -s
AM ˈkɑləkət, -s

collocate²
verb
BR ˈkɒləkeɪt, -s, -ɪŋ, -ɪd
AM ˈkɑləˌkeɪ|t, -ts, -dɪŋ, -dɪd

collocation
BR ˌkɒləˈkeɪʃn, -z
AM ˌkɑləˈkeɪʃən, -z

collocutor
BR kə(ʊ)ˈlɒkjətə(r), ˈkɒləkjuːtə(r), -z
AM kəˈlɑkjədər, -z

collodion
BR kəˈləʊdɪən
AM kəˈloʊdɪən

collodium
BR kəˈləʊdɪəm
AM kəˈloʊdɪəm

collogue
BR kɒˈləʊg, kəˈləʊg, -z, -ɪŋ, -d
AM kəˈloʊg, -z, -ɪŋ, -d

colloid
BR ˈkɒlɔɪd, -z
AM ˈkɑˌlɔɪd, -z

colloidal
BR kɒˈlɔɪdl, kəˈlɔɪdl
AM kəˈlɔɪdəl

collop
BR ˈkɒləp, -s
AM ˈkɑləp, -s

colloquia
BR kəˈləʊkwɪə(r)
AM kəˈloʊkwiə

colloquial
BR kəˈləʊkwɪəl
AM kəˈloʊkwɪəl

colloquialism
BR kəˈləʊkwɪəlɪz(ə)m, -z
AM kəˈloʊkwiəˌlɪzəm, -z

colloquially
BR kəˈləʊkwɪəli
AM kəˈloʊkwiəli

colloquium
BR kəˈləʊkwɪəm, -z
AM kəˈloʊkwiəm, -z

colloquy
BR ˈkɒləkw|i, -ɪz
AM ˈkɑləˌkwi, -z

collotype
BR ˈkɒlətʌɪp, -s
AM ˈkɑlə̩tɑɪp, -s

collude
BR kəˈl(j)uːd, -z, -ɪŋ, -ɪd
AM kəˈlud, -z, -ɪŋ, -əd

colluder
BR kəˈl(j)uːdə(r), -z
AM kəˈludər, -z

collusion
BR kəˈl(j)uːʒn
AM kəˈluʒən

collusive
BR kəˈl(j)uːsɪv
AM kəˈlusɪv

collusively
BR kəˈl(j)uːsɪvli
AM kəˈlusɪvli

collusiveness
BR kəˈl(j)uːsɪvnɪs
AM kəˈlusɪvnɪs

colluvia
BR kəˈl(j)uːvɪə(r)
AM kəˈluviə

colluvium
BR kəˈl(j)uːvɪəm, -z
AM kəˈluviəm, -z

colly
BR kɒli
AM ˈkɑli

collyria
BR kəˈlɪrɪə(r)
AM kəˈlɪriə

collyrium
BR kəˈlɪrɪəm
AM kəˈlɪriəm

collywobbles
BR ˈkɒlɪ̩wɒblz
AM ˈkɑlɪ̩wɑblz

Colman
BR ˈkəʊlmən, ˈkɒlmən
AM ˈkoʊlmən

Colnbrook
BR ˈkəʊ(l)nbrʊk
AM ˈkoʊ(l)n̩brʊk

Colne
BR kəʊ(l)n
AM koʊ(l)n

colobus
BR ˈkɒləbəs, -ɪz
AM ˈkɑləbəs, -əz

colocynth
BR ˈkɒləsɪnθ, -s
AM ˈkɑlə̩sɪnθ, -s

Cologne
BR kəˈləʊn
AM kəˈloʊn

Colombia
BR kəˈlʌmbɪə(r)
AM kəˈləmbiə

Colombian
BR kəˈlʌmbɪən, -z
AM kəˈləmbiən, -z

Colombo
BR kəˈlʌmbəʊ
AM kəˈləmboʊ

Colón
BR kɒˈlɒn, kəˈlɒn
AM kəˈloʊn

colon[1]
colonial settler
BR kɒˈlɒn, kəˈlɒn, -z
AM kəˈloʊn, -z

colon[2]
*large intestine,
punctuation mark*
BR ˈkəʊlən, ˈkəʊlɒn, -z
AM ˈkoʊlən, -z

colonel
BR ˈkɜːnl, -z
AM ˈkɜrnəl, -z

colonelcy
BR ˈkɜːnls̩li, -ɪz
AM ˈkɜrnlsi, -z

colonial
BR kəˈləʊnɪəl, -z
AM kəˈloʊnjəl,
kəˈloʊniəl, -z

colonialism
BR kəˈləʊnɪəlɪz(ə)m
AM kəˈloʊniə̩lɪzəm,
kəˈloʊnjə̩lɪzəm

colonialist
BR kəˈləʊnɪəlɪst, -s
AM kəˈloʊniələst,
kəˈloʊnjələst, -s

colonially
BR kəˈləʊnɪəli
AM kəˈloʊniəli,
kəˈloʊnjəli

colonic
BR kəˈlɒnɪk
AM koʊˈlɑnɪk,
kəˈlɑnɪk

colonisation
BR ˌkɒlənʌɪˈzeɪʃn
AM ˌkɑlənəˈzeɪʃən,
ˌkɑlə̩nɑɪˈzeɪʃən

colonise
BR ˈkɒlənʌɪz, -ɪz, -ɪŋ, -d
AM ˈkɑlə̩nɑɪz, -ɪz, -ɪŋ,
-d

coloniser
BR ˈkɒlənʌɪzə(r), -z
AM ˈkɑlə̩nɑɪzər, -z

colonist
BR ˈkɒlənɪst, -s
AM ˈkɑlənəst, -s

colonization
BR ˌkɒlənʌɪˈzeɪʃn
AM ˌkɑlənəˈzeɪʃən,
ˌkɑlə̩nɑɪˈzeɪʃən

colonize
BR ˈkɒlənʌɪz, -ɪz, -ɪŋ, -d
AM ˈkɑlə̩nɑɪz, -ɪz, -ɪŋ,
-d

colonizer
BR ˈkɒlənʌɪzə(r), -z
AM ˈkɑlə̩nɑɪzər, -z

colonnade
BR ˌkɒləˈneɪd, -z, -ɪd
AM ˌkɑləˈneɪd, -z, -ɪd

colonoscopy
BR ˌkɒləˈnɒskəps̩li, -ɪz

AM ˌkoʊləˈnɑskəpi, -z

Colonsay
BR ˈkɒlənzeɪ,
ˈkɒlənseɪ
AM ˈkɑlənzeɪ,
ˈkɑlənseɪ

colony
BR ˈkɒlən̩li, -ɪz
AM ˈkɑləni, -z

colophon
BR ˈkɒləfən, ˈkɒləfɒn,
-z
AM ˈkɑləfən, ˈkɑlə̩fɑn,
-z

colophony
BR kɒˈlɒfəni, kɒˈlɒfn̩i,
kəˈlɒfəni, kəˈlɒfn̩i
AM kəˈlɑfəni,
ˈkɑlə̩fɑni

coloquintida
BR ˌkɒləˈkwɪntɪdə(r)
AM ˌkɑləˈkwɪn(t)ədə

color
BR ˈkʌlə(r), -əz,
-(ə)rɪŋ, -əd
AM ˈkələr, -z, -ɪŋ, -d

colorable
BR ˈkʌl(ə)rəbl
AM ˈkələrəbəl

colorably
BR ˈkʌl(ə)rəbli
AM ˈkələrəbli

Coloradan
BR ˌkɒləˈrɑːd(ə)n, -z
AM ˌkɑləˈrad(ə)n, -z

Colorado
BR ˌkɒləˈrɑːdəʊ
AM ˌkɑləˈradoʊ

colorant
BR ˈkʌl(ə)rənt,
ˈkʌl(ə)rn̩t, -s
AM ˈkələrənt, -s

coloration
BR ˌkʌləˈreɪʃn
AM ˌkələˈreɪʃən

coloratura
BR ˌkɒl(ə)rəˈt(j)ʊərə(r),
ˌkɒl(ə)rəˈtʃʊərə(r), -z
AM ˌkələrəˈtʊrə, -z

colorblind
BR ˈkʌləblʌɪnd
AM ˈkələr̩blaɪnd

colorblindness
BR ˈkʌlə̩blʌɪn(d)nɪs
AM ˈkələr̩blaɪn(d)nɪs

colorectal
BR ˌkəʊləʊˈrɛktl
AM ˌkoʊloʊˈrɛktl

Colored
BR ˈkʌləd, -z
AM ˈkələrd, -z

colorfast
BR ˈkʌləfɑːst, ˈkʌləfast
AM ˈkələr̩fæst

colorfastness
BR ˈkʌlə̩fɑːs(t)nəs,
ˈkʌlə̩fas(t)nəs
AM ˈkələr̩fæs(t)nəs

colorful
BR ˈkʌləf(ʊ)l
AM ˈkələrfəl

colorfully
BR ˈkʌləfʊli, ˈkʌləfl̩i
AM ˈkələrf(ə)li

colorfulness
BR ˈkʌləf(ʊ)lnəs
AM ˈkələrfəlnəs

colorific
BR ˌkʌləˈrɪfɪk
AM ˌkələˈrɪfɪk

colorimeter
BR ˌkʌləˈrɪmɪtə(r), -z
AM ˌkələˈrɪmədər, -z

colorimetric
BR ˌkʌlərəˈmɛtrɪk
AM ˌkələrəˈmɛtrɪk

colorimetry
BR ˌkʌləˈrɪmɪtri
AM ˌkələˈrɪmətri

colorist
BR ˈkʌl(ə)rɪst, -s
AM ˈkələrəst, -s

colorize
BR ˈkʌlərʌɪz, -ɪz, -ɪŋ, -d
AM ˈkələ̩rɑɪz, -ɪz, -ɪŋ, -d

colorless
BR ˈkʌlələs
AM ˈkələrləs

colorlessly
BR ˈkʌlələsli
AM ˈkələrləsli

Coloroll®
BR ˈkʌlərəʊl
AM ˈkələroʊl

colorway
BR ˈkʌləweɪ, -z
AM ˈkələr̩weɪ, -z

colory
BR ˈkʌl(ə)ri
AM ˈkəl(ə)ri

colossal
BR kəˈlɒsl
AM kəˈlɑsəl

colossally
BR kəˈlɒsl̩i
AM kəˈlɑsəli

colosseum
BR ˌkɒləˈsiːəm, -z
AM ˌkɑləˈsiəm, -z

colossi
BR kəˈlɒsʌɪ
AM kəˈlɑ̩saɪ

Colossians
BR kəˈlɒʃ̩nz,
kəˈlɒsɪənz
AM kəˈlɑʃiənz

colossus
BR kəˈlɒsəs
AM kəˈlɑsəs

colostomy
BR kəˈlɒstəm̩li, -ɪz
AM kəˈlɑstəmi, -z

colostrum
BR kəˈlɒstrəm
AM kəˈlɑstrəm

colotomy
BR kəˈlɒtəm|i, -ɪz
AM kəˈlɑdəmi, -z

colour
BR ˈkʌl|ə(r), -əz,
-(ə)rɪŋ, -əd
AM ˈkələr, -z, -ɪŋ, -d

colourable
BR ˈkʌl(ə)rəbl
AM ˈkələrəbəl

colourably
BR ˈkʌl(ə)rəbli
AM ˈkələrəbli

colourant
BR ˈkʌl(ə)rənt,
ˈkʌl(ə)rn t̩, -s
AM ˈkələrənt, -s

colouration
BR ˌkʌləˈreɪʃn
AM ˌkələˈreɪʃən

colourblind
BR ˈkʌləblʌɪnd
AM ˈkələrˌblaɪn(d)

colourblindness
BR ˈkʌləˌblʌɪn(d)nɪs
AM ˈkələrˌblaɪn(d)nɪs

Coloured
BR ˈkʌləd, -z
AM ˈkələrd, -z

colourfast
BR ˈkʌləfɑːst, ˈkʌləfast
AM ˈkələrˌfæst

colourfastness
BR ˈkʌləfɑːs(t)nəs,
ˈkʌləfas(t)nəs
AM ˈkələrˌfæs(t)nəs

colourful
BR ˈkʌləf(ʊ)l
AM ˈkələrfəl

colourfully
BR ˈkʌləfʊli, ˈkʌləfʃi
AM ˈkələrfəli

colourfulness
BR ˈkʌləf(ʊ)lnəs
AM ˈkələrfəlnəs

colourise
BR ˈkʌlərʌɪz, -ɪz, -ɪŋ, -d
AM ˈkələˌraɪz, -ɪz, -ɪŋ, -d

colourist
BR ˈkʌl(ə)rɪst, -s
AM ˈkələrəst, -s

colourless
BR ˈkʌlələs
AM ˈkələrləs

colourlessly
BR ˈkʌlələsli
AM ˈkələrləsli

colourwash
BR ˈkʌləwɒʃ, -ɪz, -ɪŋ, -t
AM ˈkələrˌwɒʃ,
ˈkələrˌwɑʃ, -əz, -ɪŋ, -t

colourway
BR ˈkʌləweɪ, -z
AM ˈkələrˌweɪ, -z

coloury
BR ˈkʌl(ə)ri
AM ˈkəl(ə)ri

colpitis
BR kɒlˈpʌɪtɪs
AM kɑlˈpaɪdɪs

colporteur
BR ˈkɒlˌpɔːtə(r), -z
AM ˈkɑlˌpɔrdər,
ˈkɔlˌpɔrdər, -z

colposcope
BR ˈkɒlpəskəʊp, -s
AM ˈkɑlpəˌskoʊp, -s

colposcopy
BR kɒlˈpɒskəp|i, -ɪz
AM kɑlˈpaskəpi, -z

colpotomy
BR kɒlˈpɒtəm|i, -ɪz
AM kɑlˈpɑdəmi, -z

Colquhoun
BR kəˈhuːn
AM kəˈhun

Colson
BR ˈkəʊlsn
AM ˈkoʊlsən

Colston
BR ˈkəʊlst(ə)n
AM ˈkoʊlstən

colt
BR kəʊlt, -s
AM koʊlt, -s

colter
BR ˈkəʊltə(r), -z
AM ˈkoʊltər, -z

colthood
BR ˈkəʊlthʊd, -z
AM ˈkoʊlt,(h)ʊd, -z

coltish
BR ˈkəʊltɪʃ
AM ˈkoʊltɪʃ

coltishly
BR ˈkəʊltɪʃli
AM ˈkoʊltɪʃli

coltishness
BR ˈkəʊltɪʃnɪs
AM ˈkoʊltɪʃnɪs

Coltrane
BR kɒlˈtreɪn
AM ˈkoʊl,treɪn

coltsfoot
BR ˈkəʊltsfʊt
AM ˈkoʊlts,fʊt

colubrine
BR ˈkɒljʊbrʌɪn
AM ˈkɑl(j)əˌbraɪn,
ˈkɑl(j)əbrən

Colum
BR ˈkɒləm
AM ˈkɑləm

Columba
BR kəˈlʌmbə(r)
AM kəˈləmbə

columbaria
BR ˌkɒləmˈbɛːrɪə(r)
AM ˌkɑləmˈbɛrɪə

columbarium
BR ˌkɒləmˈbɛːrɪəm
AM ˌkɑləmˈbɛrɪəm

Columbia
BR kəˈlʌmbɪə(r)

AM kəˈlæmbɪə

Columbian
BR kəˈlʌmbɪən, -z
AM kəˈləmbɪən, -z

columbine
BR ˈkɒləmbʌɪn, -z
AM ˈkɑləmˌbaɪn, -z

columbite
BR kəˈlʌmbʌɪt,
ˈkɒləmbʌɪt
AM ˈkɑləmˌbaɪt

columbium
BR kəˈlʌmbɪəm
AM kəˈləmbɪəm

Columbus
BR kəˈlʌmbəs
AM kəˈləmbəs

column
BR ˈkɒləm, -z, -d
AM ˈkɑləm, -z, -d

columnar
BR kəˈlʌmnə(r),
ˈkɒləmnə(r)
AM kəˈləmnər

columnated
BR ˈkɒləmneɪtɪd
AM ˈkɑləmˌneɪdɪd

columnist
BR ˈkɒləm(n)ɪst, -s
AM ˈkɑləm(n)əst, -s

colure
BR kəˈl(j)ʊə(r),
ˈkəʊl(j)ʊə(r), -z
AM kəˈlʊ(ə)r, -z

Colville
BR ˈkɒlvɪl
AM ˈkoʊlˌvɪl

Colvin
BR ˈkɒlvɪn
AM ˈkɔlvən, ˈkɑlvən

Colwyn
BR ˈkɒlwɪn
AM ˈkɔlwən, ˈkɑlwən

Colyer
BR ˈkɒljə(r)
AM ˈkɑljər, ˈkɑliər

Colyton
BR ˈkɒlɪt(ə)n
AM ˈkɑlətn

colza
BR ˈkɒlzə(r)
AM ˈkɑlzə, ˈkoʊlzə

coma
BR ˈkəʊmə(r), -z
AM ˈkoʊmə, -z

Comanche
BR kəˈman(t)ʃ|i, -ɪz
AM kəˈmæn(t)ʃi, -z

comatose
BR ˈkəʊmətəʊs,
ˈkəʊmətəʊz
AM ˈkoʊməˌtoʊs,
ˈkɑmə,toʊz

comatosely
BR ˈkəʊmətəʊsli,
ˈkəʊmətəʊzli

AM ˈkoʊmə,toʊsli,
ˈkɑmə,toʊsli

comb
BR kəʊm, -z, -ɪŋ, -d
AM koʊm, -z, -ɪŋ, -d

combat¹
noun
BR ˈkɒmbat, ˈkʌmbat,
-s
AM ˈkɑm,bæt, -s

combat²
verb
BR ˈkɒmbat, ˈkʌmbat,
kəmˈbat, -s, -ɪŋ, -ɪd
AM kəmˈbæ|t,
ˈkɑm,bæ|t, -ts, -dɪŋ,
-dəd

combatant
BR ˈkɒmbət(ə)nt,
ˈkʌmbət(ə)nt,
kəmˈbat(ə)nt, -s
AM kəmˈbætnt,
kəmˈbædənt, -s

combative
BR ˈkɒmbətɪv,
ˈkʌmbətɪv, kəmˈbatɪv
AM kəmˈbædɪv

combatively
BR ˈkɒmbətɪvli,
ˈkʌmbətɪvli,
kəmˈbatɪvli
AM kəmˈbædɪvli

combativeness
BR ˈkɒmbətɪvnɪs,
ˈkʌmbətɪvnɪs,
kəmˈbatɪvnɪs
AM kəmˈbædɪvnɪs

combe
BR kuːm, -z
AM kum, koʊm, -z

comber
BR ˈkəʊmə(r), -z
AM ˈkoʊmər, -z

combinable
BR kəmˈbʌɪnəbl
AM ˈkɑmbənəbəl

combination
BR ˌkɒmbɪˈneɪʃn, -z
AM ˌkɑmbəˈneɪʃən, -z

combinational
BR ˌkɒmbɪˈneɪʃn(ə)l,
ˌkɒmbɪˈneɪʃən(ə)l
AM ˌkɑmbəˈneɪʃənl,
ˌkɑmbəˈneɪʃnəl

combinative
BR ˈkɒmbɪnətɪv,
ˈkɒmbnətɪv
AM ˈkɑmbəˌneɪdɪv,
kəmˈbaɪnədɪv,
ˈkɑmbənədɪv

combinatorial
BR ˌkɒmbɪnəˈtɔːrɪəl,
ˌkɒmbnəˈtɔːrɪəl
AM ˌkɑmbənəˈtɔrɪəl

combinatory
BR ˈkɒmbɪnət(ə)ri,
ˈkɒmbnət(ə)ri
AM ˈkɑmbənəˌtɔri

combine¹
noun
BR 'kɒmbʌɪn, -z
AM 'kɑm‚bɑɪn, -z

combine²
verb
BR kəm'bʌɪn, -z, -ɪŋ, -d
AM kəm'bɑɪn, -z, -ɪŋ, -d

combings
BR 'kəʊmɪŋz
AM 'koʊmɪŋz

combo
BR 'kɒmbəʊ, -z
AM 'kɑmboʊ, -z

Combs
BR kuːmz
AM kumz

combust
BR kəm'bʌst, -s, -ɪŋ, -ɪd
AM kəm'bəst, -s, -ɪn, -əd

combustibility
BR kəm‚bʌstɪ'bɪlɪti
AM kəm‚bəstə'bɪlɪdi

combustible
BR kəm'bʌstɪbl, -z
AM kəm'bəstəbəl, -z

combustibly
BR kəm'bʌstɪbli
AM kəm'bəstəbli

combustion
BR kəm'bʌstʃ(ə)n
AM kəm'bəstʃən

combustive
BR kəm'bʌstɪv
AM kə'bəstɪv

come
BR kʌm, -z, -ɪŋ
AM kəm, -z, -ɪŋ

come-all-ye
BR ‚kʌmɔːl'jiː, -z
AM ‚kəm‚ɔl'ji, ‚kəm‚ɑl'ji, -z

come-at-able
BR kʌm'atəbl
AM ‚kəm'ædəbəl

comeback
BR 'kʌmbak, -s
AM 'kəm‚bæk, -s

Comecon
BR 'kɒmɪkɒn
AM 'kɑmə‚kɑn

comedian
BR kə'miːdɪən, -z
AM kə'midiən, -z

comedic
BR kə'miːdɪk
AM kə'midɪk

comedically
BR kə'miːdɪkli
AM kə'midɪk(ə)li

comedienne
BR kə‚miːdɪ'ɛn, -z
AM kə'midi‚ɛn, kə‚midi'ɛn, -z

comedist
BR 'kɒmɪdɪst, -s
AM 'kɑmədəst, -s

comedo
BR 'kɒmɪdəʊ, kə'miːdəʊ, -z
AM 'kɑmə‚doʊ, -z

comedown
BR 'kʌmdaʊn, -z
AM 'kəm‚daʊn, -z

comedy
BR 'kɒmɪd|i, -ɪz
AM 'kɑmədi, -z

comeliness
BR 'kʌmlɪnɪs
AM 'kəmlinɪs

comely
BR 'kʌml|i, -ɪə(r), -ɪɪst
AM 'kəmli, -ər, -ɪst

Comenius
BR kə'meɪnɪəs, kə'miːnɪəs, kə'mɛnɪəs
AM kə'meɪniəs

comer
BR 'kʌmə(r), -z
AM 'kəmər, -z

comestible
BR kə'mɛstɪbl, -z
AM kə'mɛstəbəl, -z

comet
BR 'kɒmɪt, -s
AM 'kɑmət, -s

cometary
BR 'kɒmɪt(ə)ri
AM 'kɑmə‚tɛri

comeuppance
BR ‚kʌm'ʌp(ə)ns, -ɪz
AM kə'məpəns, -əz

comfily
BR 'kʌmfɪli
AM 'kəmfəli

comfiness
BR 'kʌmfɪnɪs
AM 'kəmfinɪs

comfit
BR 'kʌmfɪt, 'kɒmfɪt, -s
AM 'kəmfət, 'kamfət, -s

comfort
BR 'kʌmfət, -s, -ɪŋ, -ɪd
AM 'kəmfər|t, -ts, -dɪŋ, -dəd

comfortable
BR 'kʌmf(ə)təbl
AM 'kəmfərdəbəl, 'kəmftərbəl

comfortableness
BR 'kʌmf(ə)təblnəs
AM 'kəmfərdəbəlnəs, 'kəmftərbəlnəs

comfortably
BR 'kʌmf(ə)təbli
AM 'kəmfərdəbli, 'kəmftərbli

comforter
BR 'kʌmfətə(r), -z
AM 'kəmfərdər, -z

comfortingly
BR 'kʌmfətɪŋli
AM 'kəmfərdɪŋli

comfortless
BR 'kʌmfətləs
AM 'kəmfərtləs

comfrey
BR 'kʌmfri
AM 'kəmfri

comfy
BR 'kʌmfi
AM 'kəmfi

comic
BR 'kɒmɪk, -s
AM 'kɑmɪk, -s

comical
BR 'kɒmɪkl
AM 'kɑməkl

comicality
BR ‚kɒmɪ'kalɪti
AM ‚kɑmə'kælədi

comically
BR 'kɒmɪkli
AM 'kɑmək(ə)li

Cominform
BR 'kɒmɪnfɔːm
AM 'kɑmən‚fɔ(ə)rm

coming
BR 'kʌmɪŋ, -z
AM 'kəmɪŋ, -z

Comino
BR kə'miːnəʊ
AM kə'minoʊ

Comintern
BR 'kɒmɪntəːn
AM 'kɑmən‚tərn
RUS kəmj'in'tern

comitadji
BR ‚kɒmɪ'tadʒ|i, -ɪz
AM ‚kɑmə'tadʒi, -z

comity
BR 'kɒmɪt|i, -ɪz
AM 'kɑmədi, -z

comma
BR 'kɒmə(r), -z
AM 'kɑmə, -z

command
BR kə'mɑːnd, kə'mand, -z, -ɪŋ, -ɪd
AM kə'mænd, -z, -ɪŋ, -əd

commandant
BR 'kɒməndant, 'kɒməndənt, 'kɒməndɑːnt, ‚kɒmən'dant, ‚kɒmən'dɑːnt, -s
AM 'kɑmən‚dænt, ‚kɑmən'dɑnt, -s

commandeer
BR ‚kɒmən'dɪə(r), -z, -ɪŋ, -d
AM ‚kɑmən'dɪ(ə)r, -z, -ɪŋ, -d

commander
BR kə'mɑːndə(r), kə'mandə(r), -z
AM kə'mændər, -z

commandership
BR kə'mɑːndəʃɪp, kə'mandəʃɪp, -s

AM kə'mændər‚ʃɪp, -s

commandingly
BR kə'mɑːndɪŋli, kə'mandɪŋli
AM kə'mændɪŋli

commandment
BR kə'mɑːn(d)m(ə)nt, kə'man(d)m(ə)nt, -s
AM kə'mæn(d)mənt, -s

commando
BR kə'mɑːndəʊ, kə'mandəʊ, -z
AM kə'mæn‚doʊ, -z

comme ci, comme ça
BR kɒm ‚siː: kɒm 'sɑː:(r), + + +'sɑ(r)
AM kəm 'si kəm'sɑ

commedia dell'arte
BR kɒ'mɛdɪə dɛl'ɑːteɪ
AM kə'meɪdiə də'lɑrdi

comme il faut
BR ‚kɒm iːl 'fəʊ
AM ‚kəm il 'foʊ

commemorate
BR kə'mɛməreɪt, -s, -ɪŋ, -ɪd
AM kə'mɛmə‚reɪ|t, -ts, -dɪŋ, -dɪd

commemoration
BR kə‚mɛmə'reɪʃn, -z
AM kə‚mɛmə'reɪʃən, -z

commemorative
BR kə'mɛm(ə)rətɪv
AM kə'mɛm(ə)rədɪv, kə'mɛmə‚reɪdɪv

commemoratively
BR kə'mɛm(ə)rətɪvli
AM kə'mɛm(ə)rədɪvli, kə'mɛmə‚reɪdɪvli

commemorator
BR kə'mɛmə‚reɪtə(r), -z
AM kə'mɛmə‚reɪdər, -z

commence
BR kə'mɛns, -ɪz, -ɪŋ, -t
AM kə'mɛns, -əz, -ɪŋ, -t

commencement
BR kə'mɛnsm(ə)nt, -s
AM kə'mɛnsmənt, -s

commend
BR kə'mɛnd, -z, -ɪŋ, -ɪd
AM kə'mɛnd, -z, -ɪŋ, -əd

commendable
BR kə'mɛndəbl
AM kə'mɛndəbəl

commendably
BR kə'mɛndəbli
AM kə'mɛndəbli

commendation
BR ‚kɒm(ə)n'deɪʃn, -z
AM ‚kɑmən'deɪʃən, -z

commendatory
BR ‚kɒm(ə)n'deɪt(ə)ri
AM kə'mɛndə‚tori

commensal
BR kə'mɛnsl

AM kə'mɛnsəl

commensalism
BR kə'mɛns|ɪz(ə)m
AM kə'mɛnsə,lɪzəm

commensality
BR ,kɒmɛn'salɪt|i, -ɪz
AM ,kɑ,mɛn'sælədi, -z

commensally
BR kə'mɛns|i,
kə'mɛnsəli
AM kə'mɛnsəli

commensurability
BR kə,mɛnʃ(ə)rə'bɪlɪti,
kə,mɛns(ə)rə'bɪlɪti,
kə,mɛnsjʊrə'bɪlɪti
AM kə,mɛns(ə)rə'bɪlɪdi,
kə,mɛn(t)ʃ(ə)rə'bɪlɪdi

commensurable
BR kə'mɛnʃ(ə)rəbl,
kə'mɛns(ə)rəbl,
kə'mɛnsjʊrəbl
AM kə'mɛns(ə)rəbəl,
kə'mɛn(t)ʃ(ə)rəbəl

**commensurable-
ness**
BR kə'mɛnʃ(ə)rəblnəs,
kə'mɛns(ə)rəblnəs,
kə'mɛnsjʊrəblnəs
AM kə'mɛns(ə)rəbəlnəs,
kə'mɛn(t)ʃ(ə)rəbəlnəs

commensurably
BR kə'mɛnʃ(ə)rəbli,
kə'mɛns(ə)rəbli,
kə'mɛnsjʊrəbli
AM kə'mɛns(ə)rəbli,
kə'mɛn(t)ʃ(ə)rəbli

commensurate
BR kə'mɛnʃ(ə)rət,
kə'mɛns(ə)rət,
kə'mɛnsjʊrət
AM kə'mɛns(ə)rət,
kə'mɛn(t)ʃ(ə)rət

commensurately
BR kə'mɛnʃ(ə)rətli,
kə'mɛns(ə)rətli,
kə'mɛnsjʊrətli
AM kə'mɛns(ə)rətli,
kə'mɛn(t)ʃ(ə)rətli

**commensurate-
ness**
BR kə'mɛnʃ(ə)rətnəs,
kə'mɛns(ə)rətnəs,
kə'mɛnsjʊrətnəs
AM kə'mɛns(ə)rətnəs,
kə'mɛn(t)ʃ(ə)rətnəs

comment
BR 'kɒmɛnt, -s, -ɪŋ, -ɪd
AM 'kɑ,mɛnt, -s, -ɪŋ, -əd

commentary
BR 'kɒm(ə)nt(ə)r|i, -ɪz
AM 'kɑmən,tɛri, -z

commentate
BR 'kɒm(ə)nteɪt, -s, -ɪŋ,
-ɪd
AM 'kɑmən,teɪ|t, -ts,
-dɪŋ, -dɪd

commentator
BR 'kɒm(ə)nteɪtə(r), -z

AM 'kɑmən,teɪdər, -z

commenter
BR 'kɒmɛntə(r), -z
AM 'kɑ,mɛn(t)ər, -z

commerce
BR 'kɒmə:s
AM 'kɑmərs

commercial
BR kə'mə:ʃl, -z
AM kə'mərʃəl, -z

commercialisation
BR kə,mə:ʃəlʌɪ'zeɪʃn,
kə,mə:ʃlʌɪ'zeɪʃn
AM kə,mərʃələ'zeɪʃən,
kə,mərʃə,lɑɪ'zeɪʃən

commercialise
BR kə'mə:ʃəlʌɪz,
kə'mə:ʃl,ʌɪz, -ɪz, -ɪŋ, -d
AM kə'mərʃə,lʌɪz, -ɪz,
-ɪŋ, -d

commercialism
BR kə'mə:ʃəlɪz(ə)m,
kə'mə:ʃ|ɪz(ə)m
AM kə'mərʃə,lɪzəm

commerciality
BR kə,mə:ʃɪ'alɪti
AM kə,mərʃi'alədi

commercialization
BR kə,mə:ʃəlʌɪ'zeɪʃn,
kə,mə:ʃlʌɪ'zeɪʃn
AM kə,mərʃələ'zeɪʃən,
kə,mərʃə,lɑɪ'zeɪʃən

commercialize
BR kə'mə:ʃəlʌɪz,
kə'mə:ʃl,ʌɪz, -ɪz, -ɪŋ, -d
AM kə'mərʃə,lʌɪz, -ɪz,
-ɪŋ, -d

commercially
BR kə'mə:ʃəli,
kə'mə:ʃli
AM kə'mərʃəli

commère
BR 'kɒmɛ:(r), -z
AM 'kam,mɛ(ə)r, -z

commie
BR 'kɒm|i, -ɪz
AM 'kɑmi, -z

commination
BR ,kɒmɪ'neɪʃn, -z
AM ,kɑmə'neɪʃən, -z

comminatory
BR 'kɒmɪnət(ə)ri
AM 'kɑmənə,tɔri,
kə'mɪnə,tɔri

commingle
BR kɒ'mɪŋg|l,
kə'mɪŋg|l, -lz,
-lɪŋ \-lɪŋ, -ld
AM kə'mɪŋg|əl,
kɑ'mɪŋg|əl, -əlz,
-(ə)lɪŋ, -əld

comminute
BR 'kɒmɪnju:t, -s, -ɪŋ,
-ɪd
AM 'kɑmə(j)u|t, -ts,
-dɪŋ, -dəd

comminution
BR ,kɒmɪ'nju:ʃn

AM ,kɑmə'n(j)uʃən

commis
BR 'kɒmɪs, 'kɒmi
AM kə'mi
FR kɔmi

commiserate
BR kə'mɪzəreɪt, -s, -ɪŋ,
-ɪd
AM kə'mɪzə,reɪt, -ts,
-dɪŋ, -dɪd

commiseration
BR kə,mɪzə'reɪʃn
AM kə,mɪzə'reɪʃən

commiserative
BR kə'mɪz(ə)rətɪv,
kə'mɪzəreɪtɪv
AM kə'mɪzərədɪv,
kə'mɪzə,reɪdɪv

commiserator
BR kə'mɪzəreɪtə(r), -z
AM kə'mɪzə,reɪdər, -z

commissar
BR ,kɒmɪ'sɑ:(r),
'kɒmɪsɑ:(r), -z
AM 'kɑməsɑr, -z

commissarial
BR ,kɒmɪ'sɛ:rɪəl
AM ,kɑmə'sɛrɪəl

commissariat
BR ,kɒmɪ'sɛ:rɪət, -s
AM ,kɑmə'sɛrɪət, -s

commissary
BR 'kɒmɪs(ə)r|i, -ɪz
AM 'kɑmə,sɛri, -z

commissaryship
BR 'kɒmɪs(ə)rɪʃɪp
AM 'kɑmə,sɛri,ʃɪp

commission
BR kə'mɪʃ|n, -nz,
-ɳɪŋ \-nɪŋ, -nd
AM kə'mɪʃən, -z, -ɪŋ, -d

commissionaire
BR kə,mɪʃə'nɛ:(r), -z
AM kə,mɪʃə'nɛ(ə)r, -z

commissional
BR kə'mɪʃn(ə)l,
kə'mɪʃən(ə)l
AM kə'mɪʃ(ə)nəl

commissionary
BR kə'mɪʃn(ə)ri
AM kə'mɪʃə,nɛri

commissioner
BR kə'mɪʃnə(r),
kə'mɪʃ(ə)nə(r), -z
AM kə'mɪʃənər, -z

commissural
BR ,kɒmɪ'sjuərəl,
,kɒmɪ'sjuərl,
,kɒmɪ'sjɔ:rəl,
,kɒmɪ'sjɔ:r|,
,kɒmɪ'ʃuərəl,
,kɒmɪ'ʃuərl,
,kɒmɪ'ʃɔ:rəl,
,kɒmɪ'ʃɔ:r|
AM kə'mɪʃʊrəl,
,kɑmə'ʃʊrəl

AM ,kɑmə'n(j)uʃən

commis
BR 'kɒmɪs, 'kɒmi
AM kə'mi
FR kɔmi

commissure
BR 'kɒmɪsjuə(r),
'kɒmɪ,ʃʊə(r), -z
AM 'kɑmə,ʃʊ(ə)r, -z

commit
BR kə'mɪt, -s, -ɪŋ, -ɪd
AM kə'mɪ|t, -ts, -dɪŋ,
-dɪd

commitment
BR kə'mɪtm(ə)nt, -s
AM kə'mɪtmənt, -s

committable
BR kə'mɪtəbl
AM kə'mɪdəbəl

committal
BR kə'mɪtl, -z
AM kə'mɪdl, -z

committee
BR kə'mɪt|i:, -ɪz
AM kə'mɪdi, -z

committeeman
BR kə'mɪtman
AM kə'mɪdimən

committeemen
BR kə'mɪtmɛn
AM kə'mɪdimən

committeewoman
BR kə'mɪti,wʊmən
AM kə'mɪdi,wʊmən

committeewomen
BR kə'mɪti,wɪmɪn
AM kə'mɪdi,wɪmɪn

committer
BR kə'mɪtə(r), -z
AM kə'mɪdər, -z

commix
BR kɒ'mɪks, kə'mɪks,
-ɪz, -ɪŋ, -t
AM kə'mɪks, -ɪz, -ɪŋ, -t

commixture
BR kə'mɪkstʃə(r)
AM kə'mɪk(st)ʃər

commo
BR 'kɒməʊ, -z
AM 'kɑmoʊ, -z

commode
BR kə'məʊd, -z
AM kə'moʊd, -z

commodification
BR kə,mɒdɪfɪ'keɪʃn
AM kə,mɑdəfə'keɪʃən

commodify
BR kə'mɒdɪfʌɪ, -z, -ɪŋ,
-d
AM kə'mɑdə,faɪ, -z, -ɪŋ,
-d

commodious
BR kə'məʊdɪəs
AM kə'moʊdɪəs

commodiously
BR kə'məʊdɪəsli
AM kə'moʊdɪəsli

commodiousness
BR kə'məʊdɪəsnəs
AM kə'moʊdɪəsnəs

commodity
BR kə'mɒdɪt|i, -ɪz

AM kə'madədi, -z

commodore
BR 'kɒmədɔ:(r), -z
AM 'kɑmə,dɔ(ə)r, -z

common
BR 'kɒmən, -z, -ə(r),
-ɪst
AM 'kɑmən, -z, -ər, -əst

commonable
BR 'kɒmənəbl
AM 'kɑmənəbəl

commonage
BR 'kɒmənɪdʒ
AM 'kɑmənɪdʒ

commonality
BR ,kɒmə'nalɪti
AM 'kɑmən,ælədi

commonalty
BR 'kɒmənlti
AM 'kɑmənəlti

commoner
BR 'kɒmənə(r), -z
AM 'kɑmənər, -z

commonhold
BR 'kɒmənhəʊld
AM 'kɑmən,(h)oʊld

commonholder
BR 'kɒmən,həʊldə(r)
AM 'kɑmən,(h)oʊldər

commonly
BR 'kɒmənli
AM 'kɑmənli

commonness
BR 'kɒmənnəs
AM 'kɑmə(n)nəs

commonplace
BR 'kɒmənpleɪs
AM 'kɑmən,pleɪs

commonplaceness
BR 'kɒmənpleɪsnɪs
AM 'kɑmən,pleɪsnɪs

commonroom
BR 'kɒmənruːm,
'kɒmənrʊm, -z
AM 'kɑmən,rum,
'kɑmən,rʊm, -z

commons
BR 'kɒmənz
AM 'kɑmənz

commonsense
BR ,kɒmən'sɛns
AM ,kɑmən'sɛns

commonsensical
BR ,kɒmən'sɛnsɪkl
AM ,kɑmən'sɛnsəkəl

commonwealth
BR 'kɒmənwɛlθ, -s
AM 'kɑmən,wɛlθ, -s

commotion
BR kə'məʊʃn, -z
AM kə'moʊʃən, -z

commotional
BR kə'məʊʃn̩(ə)l,
kə'məʊʃən(ə)l
AM kə'moʊʃ(ə)nəl

comms
BR kɒmz

AM kɑmz

communal
BR 'kɒmjʊnl,
kə'mju:nl
AM kə'mjunəl

communalisation
BR ,kɒmjʊnəlʌɪ'zeɪʃn,
,kɒmjʊnl̩ʌɪ'zeɪʃn,
kə,mju:nəlʌɪ'zeɪʃn,
kə,mju:nl̩ʌɪ'zeɪʃn
AM kə,mjunələ'zeɪʃən,
kə,mjunə,lɑɪ'zeɪʃən

communalise
BR 'kɒmjʊnəlʌɪz,
'kɒmjʊnl̩ʌɪz,
kə'mju:nəlʌɪz,
kə'mju:nl̩ʌɪz, -ɪz, -ɪŋ,
-d
AM kə'mjunl̩,ʌɪz, -ɪz,
-ɪŋ, -d

communalism
BR 'kɒmjʊnəlɪz(ə)m,
'kɒmjʊnl̩ɪz(ə)m,
kə'mju:nəlɪz(ə)m,
kə'mju:nl̩ɪz(ə)m
AM kə'mjunl̩,ɪzəm

communalist
BR 'kɒmjʊnəlɪst,
'kɒmjʊnl̩ɪst,
kə'mju:nəlɪst,
kə'mju:nl̩ɪst, -s
AM kə'mjunl̩əst, -s

communalistic
BR ,kɒmjʊnə'lɪstɪk,
,kɒmjʊnl̩'ɪstɪk,
kə,mju:nə'lɪstɪk,
kə,mju:nl̩'ɪstɪk
AM kə,mjunə'lɪstɪk

communalistically
BR ,kɒmjʊnə'lɪstɪkli,
,kɒmjʊnl̩'ɪstɪkli,
kə,mju:nə'lɪstɪkli,
kə,mju:nl̩'ɪstɪkli
AM kə,mjunə'lɪstɪk(ə)li

communality
BR ,kɒmjʊ'nalɪti
AM ,kɑmjə'nælədi

communalization
BR ,kɒmjʊnəlʌɪ'zeɪʃn,
,kɒmjʊnl̩ʌɪ'zeɪʃn,
kə,mju:nəlʌɪ'zeɪʃn,
kə,mju:nl̩ʌɪ'zeɪʃn
AM kə,mjunələ'zeɪʃən,
kə,mjunə,lɑɪ'zeɪʃən

communalize
BR 'kɒmjʊnəlʌɪz,
'kɒmjʊnl̩ʌɪz,
kə'mju:nəlʌɪz,
kə'mju:nl̩ʌɪz, -ɪz, -ɪŋ,
-d
AM kə'mjunl̩,ʌɪz, -ɪz,
-ɪŋ, -d

communally
BR 'kɒmjʊnli,
'kɒmjʊnəli,
kə'mju:nl̩i,
kə'mju:nəli
AM kə'mjunəli

communard
BR 'kɒmjʊnɑːd, -z
AM 'kɑmjə,nɑrd, -z

commune¹
noun
BR 'kɒmju:n, -z
AM 'kɑ,mjun, -z

commune²
verb
BR kə'mju:n, -z, -ɪŋ, -d
AM kə'mjun, -z, -ɪŋ, -d

communicability
BR kə,mju:nɪkə'bɪlɪti
AM kə,mjunəkə'bɪlɪdi

communicable
BR kə'mju:nɪkəbl
AM kə'mjunəkəbəl

communicably
BR kə'mju:nɪkəbli
AM kə'mjunəkəbli

communicant
BR kə'mju:nɪk(ə)nt, -s
AM kə'mjunəkənt, -s

communicate
BR kə'mju:nɪkeɪt, -s,
-ɪŋ, -ɪd
AM kə'mjunə,keɪ|t, -ts,
-dɪŋ, -dɪd

communication
BR kə,mju:nɪ'keɪʃn, -z
AM kə,mjunə'keɪʃən,
-z

communicational
BR kə,mju:nɪ'keɪʃn(ə)l,
kə,mju:nɪ'keɪʃən(ə)l
AM kə,mjunə'keɪʃ(ə)nəl

communicative
BR kə'mju:nɪkətɪv
AM kə'mjunə,keɪdɪv,
kə'mjunəkədɪv

communicatively
BR kə'mju:nɪkətɪvli
AM kə'mjunə,keɪdɪvli,
kə'mjunəkədɪvli

**communicative-
ness**
BR kə'mju:nɪkətɪvnɪs
AM kə'mjunə,keɪdɪvnɪs,
kə'mjunəkədɪvnɪs

communicator
BR kə'mju:nɪkeɪtə(r),
-z
AM kə'mjunə,keɪdər,
-z

communicatory
BR kə'mju:nɪkət(ə)ri,
kə'mju:nɪkeɪt(ə)ri
AM kə'mjunəkə,tɔri

communion
BR kə'mju:nɪən, -z
AM kə'mjunjən, -z

communiqué
BR kə'mju:nɪkeɪ, -z
AM kə'mjunə'keɪ,
kə'mjunə,keɪ, -z

communisation
BR ,kɒmjʊnʌɪ'zeɪʃn

AM ,kɑmjənə'zeɪʃən,
,kɑmjə,nər'zeɪʃən

communise
BR 'kɒmjʊnʌɪz, -ɪz, -ɪŋ,
-d
AM 'kɑmjə,nɑɪz, -ɪz,
-ɪŋ, -d

communism
BR 'kɒmjʊnɪz(ə)m
AM 'kɑmjə,nɪzəm

communist
BR 'kɒmjʊnɪst, -s
AM 'kɑmjənəst, -s

communistic
BR ,kɒmjʊ'nɪstɪk
AM ,kɑmjə'nɪstɪk

communistically
BR ,kɒmjʊ'nɪstɪkli
AM ,kɑmjə'nɪstɪk(ə)li

communitarian
BR kə,mju:nɪ'tɛːrɪən,
-z
AM kə,mjunə'tɛrɪən, -z

community
BR kə'mju:nɪt|i, -ɪz
AM kə'mjunədi, -z

communization
BR ,kɒmjʊnʌɪ'zeɪʃn
AM ,kɑmjənə'zeɪʃən,
,kɑmjə,nər'zeɪʃən

communize
BR 'kɒmjʊnʌɪz, -ɪz, -ɪŋ,
-d
AM 'kɑmjə,nɑɪz, -ɪz,
-ɪŋ, -d

commutability
BR kə,mju:tə'bɪlɪti
AM kə,mjudə'bɪlɪdi

commutable
BR kə'mju:təbl
AM kə'mjudəbəl

commutate
BR 'kɒmjʊteɪt, -s, -ɪŋ,
-ɪd
AM 'kɑmju,teɪ|t, -ts,
-dɪŋ, -dɪd

commutation
BR ,kɒmjʊ'teɪʃn, -z
AM ,kɑmjə'teɪʃən, -z

commutative
BR kə'mju:tətɪv,
'kɒmjʊtətɪv,
'kɒmjʊteɪtɪv
AM 'kɑmjə,teɪdɪv,
kə'mjudədɪv

commutator
BR 'kɒmjʊteɪtə(r), -z
AM 'kɑmjə,teɪdər, -z

commute
BR kə'mju:t, -s, -ɪŋ, -ɪd
AM kə'mju|t, -ts, -dɪŋ,
-dəd

commuter
BR kə'mju:tə(r), -z
AM kə'mjudər, -z

Como
BR 'kəʊməʊ
AM 'koʊmoʊ

Comorin
BR 'kɒmərɪn
AM 'kɑmərən
Comoro
BR 'kɒmərəʊ
AM 'kɑməroʊ
comose
BR 'kəʊməʊs
AM 'koʊˌmoʊs,
'koʊˌmoʊz
comp
BR kɒmp, -s
AM kɑmp, -s
compact¹
noun
BR 'kɒmpakt, -s
AM 'kɑmˌpæk(t), -s
compact²
verb, adjective
BR kəm'pakt, -s, -ɪŋ, -ɪd
AM kəm'pæk|(t),
'kɑmˌpæk|(t), -(t)s,
-tɪŋ, -təd
compaction
BR kəm'pakʃn
AM kəm'pækʃən
compactly
BR kəm'paktli
AM kəm'pæk(t)li,
'kɑmˌpæk(t)li
compactness
BR kəm'pak(t)nəs
AM kəm'pæk(t)nəs,
'kɑmˌpæk(t)nəs
compactor
BR kəm'paktə(r), -z
AM 'kɑmˌpæktər, -z
compadre
BR kəm'pɑːdr|i, -iz
AM kəm'pɑdreɪ, -z
compages
BR kəm'peɪdʒiːz
AM kəm'peɪdʒɪz
compander
BR kəm'pandə(r), -z
AM kəm'pændər, -z
companion
BR kəm'panjən, -z
AM kəm'pænjən, -z
companionable
BR kəm'panjənəbl
AM kəm'pænjənəbəl
companionableness
BR kəm'panjənəblnəs
AM kəm'pænjənəbəlnəs
companionably
BR kəm'panjənəbli
AM kəm'pænjənəbli
companionate
BR kəm'panjənət
AM kəm'pænjənət
companionship
BR kəm'panjənʃɪp
AM kəm'pænjənˌʃɪp
companionway
BR kəm'panjənweɪ, -z

AM kəm'pænjənˌweɪ, -z
company
BR 'kʌmp(ə)n|i,
'kʌmpn̩|i, -ɪz
AM 'kʌmp(ə)ni, -z
Compaq
BR 'kɒmpak
AM 'kɑmpæk
comparability
BR ˌkɒmp(ə)rə'bɪlɪti
AM ˌkɑmp(ə)rə'bɪlɪdi
comparable
BR 'kɒmp(ə)rəbl
AM 'kɑmp(ə)rəbəl
comparableness
BR 'kɒmp(ə)rəblnəs
AM 'kɑmp(ə)rəbəlnəs
comparably
BR 'kɒmp(ə)rəbli
AM 'kɑmp(ə)rəbli
comparatist
BR kəm'parətɪst, -s
AM kəm'pɛrədəst, -s
comparative
BR kəm'parətɪv, -z
AM kəm'pɛrədɪv, -z
comparatively
BR kəm'parətɪvli
AM kəm'pɛrədɪvli
comparator
BR kəm'parətə(r), -z
AM kəm'pɛrədər, -z
compare
BR kəm'pɛː(r), -z, -ɪŋ, -d
AM kəm'pɛ(ə)r, -z, -ɪŋ, -d
comparison
BR kəm'parɪs(ə)n, -z
AM kəm'pɛrəsən, -z
compartment
BR kəm'pɑːtm(ə)nt, -s
AM kəm'pɑrtmənt, -s
compartmental
BR ˌkɒmpɑː't'mentl
AM kəmˌpɑrt'mɛn(t)l
compartmentalisation
BR ˌkɒmpɑːtˌmentl̩ʌɪ'zeɪʃn
AM kəmˌpɑrtˌmɛn(t)ələ'zeɪʃən,
kəmˌpɑrtˌmɛn(t)əlˌaɪ'zeɪʃən
compartmentalise
BR ˌkɒmpɑːt'mentl̩ʌɪz,
-ɪz, -ɪŋ, -d
AM kəmˌpɑrt'mɛn(t)l̩ˌaɪz, -ɪz, -ɪŋ, -d
compartmentalization
BR ˌkɒmpɑːtˌmentl̩ʌɪ'zeɪʃn
AM kəmˌpɑrtˌmɛn(t)ələ'zeɪʃən,
kəmˌpɑrtˌmɛn(t)əlˌaɪ'zeɪʃən

AM kəm'pænjənˌweɪ, -z
compartmentalize
BR ˌkɒmpɑːt'mentl̩ʌɪz, -ɪz, -ɪŋ, -d
AM kəmˌpɑrt'mɛn(t)l̩ˌaɪz, -ɪz, -ɪŋ, -d
compartmentally
BR ˌkɒmpɑːt'mentl̩i
AM kəmˌpɑrt'mɛn(t)l̩i
compartmentation
BR ˌkɒmpɑːtmen'teɪʃn
AM kəmˌpɑrtˌmɛn'teɪʃən
compass
BR 'kʌmpəs, -ɪz, -ɪŋ, -t
AM 'kʌmpəs, -əz, -ɪŋ, -t
compassable
BR 'kʌmpəsəbl
AM 'kʌmpəsəbəl
compassion
BR kəm'paʃn, -z
AM kəm'pæʃən, -z
compassionate
BR kəm'paʃnət, kəm'paʃənət
AM kəm'pæʃ(ə)nət
compassionately
BR kəm'paʃənətli, kəm'paʃnətli
AM kəm'pæʃ(ə)nətli
compass-saw
BR 'kʌmpəsɔː(r), -z
AM 'kʌmpəsˌsɔ, 'kɑmpəsˌsɑ, -z
compatibility
BR kəmˌpatɪ'bɪlɪti
AM kəmˌpædə'bɪlɪdi
compatible
BR kəm'patɪbl
AM kəm'pædəbəl
compatibly
BR kəm'patɪbli
AM kəm'pædəbli
compatriot
BR kəm'patrɪət, -s
AM kəm'peɪtriət, -s
compatriotic
BR kəmˌpatrɪ'ɒtɪk
AM kəmˌpeɪtri'ɑdɪk
compeer
BR 'kɒmpɪə(r), -z
AM 'kɑmpɪ(ə)r, kəm'pɪ(ə)r, -z
compel
BR kəm'pɛl, -z, -ɪŋ, -d
AM kəm'pɛl, -z, -ɪŋ, -d
compellable
BR kəm'pɛləbl
AM kəm'pɛləbəl
compellingly
BR kəm'pɛlɪŋli
AM kəm'pɛlɪŋli
compendia
BR kəm'pɛndɪə(r)
AM kəm'pɛndiə
compendious
BR kəm'pɛndɪəs
AM kəm'pɛndiəs

compendiously
BR kəm'pɛndɪəsli
AM kəm'pɛndiəsli
compendiousness
BR kəm'pɛndɪəsnəs
AM kəm'pɛndiəsnəs
compendium
BR kəm'pɛndɪəm, -z
AM kəm'pɛndiəm, -z
compensate
BR 'kɒmp(ə)nseɪt, 'kɒmpɛnseɪt, -s, -ɪŋ, -ɪd
AM 'kɑmpənˌseɪ|t, -ts, -dɪŋ, -dɪd
compensation
BR ˌkɒmp(ə)n'seɪʃn, ˌkɒmpɛn'seɪʃn
AM ˌkɑmpən'seɪʃən
compensational
BR ˌkɒmp(ə)n'seɪʃn̩(ə)l, ˌkɒmp(ə)n'seɪʃən(ə)l, ˌkɒmpɛn'seɪʃn̩(ə)l, ˌkɒmpɛn'seɪʃən(ə)l
AM ˌkɑmpən'seɪʃ(ə)nəl
compensative
BR kəm'pɛnsɪtɪv, 'kɒmp(ə)nseɪtɪv, 'kɒmpɛnseɪtɪv
AM kəm'pɛnsədɪv, 'kɑmpənˌseɪdɪv
compensator
BR 'kɒmp(ə)nseɪtə(r), 'kɒmpɛnseɪtə(r), -z
AM 'kɑmpənˌseɪdər, -z
compensatory
BR kəm'pɛnsət(ə)ri, ˌkɒmp(ə)n'seɪt(ə)ri, ˌkɒmpɛn'seɪt(ə)ri
AM kəm'pɛnsəˌtɔri
compère
BR 'kɒmpɛː(r), -z, -ɪŋ, -d
AM 'kɑmˌpɛ(ə)r, -z, -ɪŋ, -d
compete
BR kəm'piːt, -s, -ɪŋ, -ɪd
AM kəm'pi|t, -ts, -dɪŋ, -dɪd
competence
BR 'kɒmpɪt(ə)ns
AM 'kɑmpəd(ə)ns
competency
BR 'kɒmpɪt(ə)nsi
AM 'kɑmpəd(ə)nsi
competent
BR 'kɒmpɪt(ə)nt
AM 'kɑmpəd(ə)nt
competently
BR 'kɒmpɪt(ə)ntli
AM 'kɑmpədən(t)li
competition
BR ˌkɒmpɪ'tɪʃn, -z
AM ˌkɑmpə'tɪʃən, -z
competitive
BR kəm'pɛtɪtɪv
AM kəm'pɛdədɪv

competitively
BR kəmˈpɛtɪtɪvli
AM kəmˈpɛdədɪvli

competitiveness
BR kəmˈpɛtɪtɪvnɪs
AM kəmˈpɛdədɪvnɪs

competitor
BR kəmˈpɛtɪtə(r), -z
AM kəmˈpɛdədər, -z

compilation
BR ˌkɒmpɪˈleɪʃn, -z
AM ˌkɑmpəˈleɪʃən, -z

compile
BR kəmˈpaɪl, -z, -ɪŋ, -d
AM kəmˈpaɪl, -z, -ɪŋ, -d

compiler
BR kəmˈpaɪlə(r), -z
AM kəmˈpaɪlər, -z

complacence
BR kəmˈpleɪsns
AM kəmˈpleɪsəns

complacency
BR kəmˈpleɪsnsi
AM kəmˈpleɪsənsi

complacent
BR kəmˈpleɪsnt
AM kəmˈpleɪsənt

complacently
BR kəmˈpleɪsntli
AM kəmˈpleɪsn(t)li

complain
BR kəmˈpleɪn, -z, -ɪŋ, -d
AM kəmˈpleɪn, -z, -ɪŋ, -d

complainant
BR kəmˈpleɪnənt, -s
AM kəmˈpleɪnənt, -s

complainer
BR kəmˈpleɪnə(r), -z
AM kəmˈpleɪnər, -z

complainingly
BR kəmˈpleɪnɪŋli
AM kəmˈpleɪnɪŋli

complaint
BR kəmˈpleɪnt, -s
AM kəmˈpleɪnt, -s

complaisance
BR kəmˈpleɪzns
AM kəmˈpleɪsəns,
kəmˈpleɪzns

complaisant
BR kəmˈpleɪznt
AM kəmˈpleɪsənt

complaisantly
BR kəmˈpleɪzntli
AM kəmˈpleɪsn(t)li,
kəmˈpleɪzn(t)li

compleat
BR kəmˈpliːt
AM kəmˈplit

complected
BR kəmˈplɛktɪd
AM kəmˈplɛktəd

complement
BR ˈkɒmplɪm(ə)nt, -s,
-ɪŋ, -ɪd
AM ˈkɑmpləmən|t, -ts,
-(t)ɪŋ, -(t)əd

complemental
BR ˌkɒmplɪˈmɛntl
AM ˌkɑmpləˈmɛn(t)l

complementarily
BR ˌkɒmplɪˈmɛnt(ə)rɪli
AM ˌkɑmpləmɛnˈtɛrəli

**complementari-
ness**
BR ˌkɒmplɪˈmɛnt(ə)rɪ-
nɪs
AM ˌkɑmpləmɛnˈtɛri-
nɪs

complementarity
BR ˌkɒmplɪmɛnˈtarɪti,
ˌkɒmplɪm(ə)nˈtarɪti
AM ˌkɑmpləmənˈtɛrədi

complementary
BR ˌkɒmplɪˈmɛnt(ə)ri
AM ˌkɑmpləˈmɛn(t)əri,
ˌkɑmpləˈmɛntri

complementation
BR ˌkɒmplɪmɛnˈteɪʃn,
ˌkɒmplɪm(ə)nˈteɪʃn
AM ˌkɑmpləmənˈteɪʃən

complementizer
BR ˈkɒmplɪmɛntʌɪzə(r),
ˈkɒmplɪm(ə)ntʌɪzə(r),
-z
AM ˈkɑmpləmənˌtaɪzər,
ˈkɑmpləmənˌtaɪzər,
-z

complete
BR kəmˈpliːt, -s, -ɪŋ, -ɪd
AM kəmˈpli|t, -ts, -dɪŋ,
-dɪd

completely
BR kəmˈpliːtli
AM kəmˈplitli

completeness
BR kəmˈpliːtnɪs
AM kəmˈplitnɪs

completion
BR kəmˈpliːʃn, -z
AM kəmˈpliʃən, -z

completist
BR kəmˈpliːtɪst, -s
AM kəmˈplidɪst, -s

completive
BR kəmˈpliːtɪv
AM kəmˈplidɪv

complex¹
adjective
BR ˈkɒmplɛks
AM ˌkɑmˈplɛks

complex²
noun
BR ˈkɒmplɛks, -ɪz
AM ˈkɑmplɛks, -əz

complexation
BR ˌkɒmplɛkˈseɪʃn
AM kɑmˌplɛkˈseɪʃən

complexion
BR kəmˈplɛkʃn, -z, -d
AM kəmˈplɛkʃən, -z, -d

complexionless
BR kəmˈplɛkʃnləs
AM kəmˈplɛkʃənləs

complexity
BR kəmˈplɛksɪt|i, -ɪz
AM kəmˈplɛksədi, -z

complexly
BR ˈkɒmplɛksli
AM ˌkɑmˈplɛksli

compliance
BR kəmˈplʌɪəns
AM kəmˈplaɪəns

compliancy
BR kəmˈplʌɪənsi
AM kəmˈplaɪənsi

compliant
BR kəmˈplʌɪənt
AM kəmˈplaɪənt

compliantly
BR kəmˈplʌɪəntli
AM kəmˈplaɪən(t)li

complicacy
BR ˈkɒmplɪkəs|i, -ɪz
AM ˈkɑmpləkəsi, -z

complicate
BR ˈkɒmplɪkeɪt, -s, -ɪŋ,
-ɪd
AM ˈkɑmpləˌkeɪ|t, -ts,
-dɪŋ, -dɪd

complicatedly
BR ˈkɒmplɪkeɪtɪdli
AM ˈkɑmpləˌkeɪdɪdli

complicatedness
BR ˈkɒmplɪkeɪtɪdnɪs
AM ˈkɑmpləˌkeɪdɪdnɪs

complication
BR ˌkɒmplɪˈkeɪʃn, -z
AM ˌkɑmpləˈkeɪʃən, -z

complicit
BR kəmˈplɪsɪt
AM kəmˈplɪsɪt

complicity
BR kəmˈplɪsɪti
AM kəmˈplɪsɪdi

compliment¹
noun
BR ˈkɒmplɪm(ə)nt, -s
AM ˈkɑmpləmənt, -s

compliment²
verb
BR ˈkɒmplɪmɛnt, -s,
-ɪŋ, -ɪd
AM ˈkɑmpləˌmɛn|t, -ts,
-(t)ɪŋ, -(t)ɪd

complimentarily
BR ˌkɒmplɪˈmɛnt(ə)rɪli
AM ˌkɑmpləˌmɛnˈtɛrəli

complimentary
BR ˌkɒmplɪˈmɛnt(ə)r|i,
-ɪz
AM ˌkɑmpləˈmɛn(t)əri,
ˌkɑmpləˈmɛntri, -ɪz

complin
BR ˈkɒmplɪn, -z
AM ˈkɑmplɪn, -z

compline
BR ˈkɒmplɪn, -z
AM ˈkɑmplɪn, -z

comply
BR kəmˈplʌɪ, -z, -ɪŋ, -d
AM kəmˈplaɪ, -z, -ɪŋ, -d

compo
BR ˈkɒmpəʊ, -z
AM ˈkɑmˌpoʊ, -z

component
BR kəmˈpəʊnənt, -s
AM kəmˈpoʊnənt, -s

componential
BR ˌkɒmpə(ʊ)ˈnɛnʃl
AM ˌkɑmpəˈnɛn(t)ʃəl

comport
BR kəmˈpɔːt, -s, -ɪŋ, -ɪd
AM kəmˈpɔ(ə)rt, -ts,

comportment
BR kəmˈpɔːtm(ə)nt
AM kəmˈpɔrtmənt

compose
BR kəmˈpəʊz, -ɪz, -ɪŋ, -d
AM kəmˈpoʊz, -əz, -ɪŋ,
-d

composedly
BR kəmˈpəʊzɪdli
AM kəmˈpoʊzədli

composer
BR kəmˈpəʊzə(r), -z
AM kəmˈpoʊzər, -z

composite
BR ˈkɒmpəzɪt,
ˈkɒmpəzʌɪt,
ˈkɒmpəsʌɪt, -s
AM kəmˈpazət,
ˌkɑmˈpazət, -s

compositely
BR ˈkɒmpəzɪtli,
ˈkɒmpəzʌɪtli,
ˈkɒmpəsʌɪtli
AM kəmˈpazətli,
ˌkɑmˈpazətli

compositeness
BR ˈkɒmpəzɪtnɪs,
ˈkɒmpəzʌɪtnɪs,
ˈkɒmpəsʌɪtnɪs
AM kəmˈpazətnəs,
ˌkɑmˈpazətnəs

composition
BR ˌkɒmpəˈzɪʃn, -z
AM ˌkɑmpəˈzɪʃən, -z

compositional
BR ˌkɒmpəˈzɪʃn(ə)l,
ˌkɒmpəˈzɪʃən(ə)l
AM ˌkɑmpəˈzɪʃ(ə)nəl

compositionally
BR ˌkɒmpəˈzɪʃnəli,
ˌkɒmpəˈzɪʃn̩li,
ˌkɒmpəˈzɪʃən̩li,
ˌkɒmpəˈzɪʃ(ə)nəli
AM ˌkɑmpəˈzɪʃ(ə)nəli

compositor
BR kəmˈpɒzɪtə(r), -z
AM kəmˈpazədər, -z

compos mentis
BR ˌkɒmpəs ˈmɛntɪs,
ˌkɒmpɒs +
AM ˌkɑmpəs ˈmɛn(t)əs

compossible
BR kəmˈpɒsɪbl
AM kəmˈpasəbəl,
ˌkɑmˈpasəbəl

compost
BR 'kɒmpɒst, -s, -ɪŋ, -ɪd
AM 'kam,poʊst, -s, -ɪŋ, -əd

composure
BR kəm'pəʊʒə(r)
AM kəm'poʊʒər

compote
BR 'kɒmpəʊt, 'kɒmpɒt,
AM 'kam,poʊt, -s

compound¹
noun, adjective
BR 'kɒmpaʊnd, -z
AM 'kam,paʊnd, -z

compound²
verb
BR kəm'paʊnd, -z, -ɪŋ, -ɪd
AM kəm'paʊnd, -z, -ɪŋ, -əd

compoundable
BR kəm'paʊndəbl
AM kəm'paʊndəbəl

compounder
BR kəm'paʊndə(r), -z
AM kəm'paʊndər, -z

comprador
BR ,kɒmprə'dɔː(r), -z
AM ,kamprə'dɔ(ə)r, -z

compradore
BR ,kɒmprə'dɔː(r), -z
AM ,kamprə'dɔ(ə)r, -z

comprehend
BR ,kɒmprɪ'hɛnd, -z, -ɪŋ, -ɪd
AM ,kamprə'hɛnd, -z, -ɪŋ, -ɪd

comprehensibility
BR ,kɒmprɪ,hɛnsɪ'bɪlɪti
AM ,kamprə,hɛnsə'bɪl-ɪdi

comprehensible
BR ,kɒmprɪ'hɛnsɪbl
AM ,kamprə'hɛnsəbəl

comprehensible-ness
BR ,kɒmprɪ'hɛnsɪblnəs
AM ,kamprə'hɛnsəbəl-nəs

comprehensibly
BR ,kɒmprɪ'hɛnsɪbli
AM ,kamprə'hɛnsəbli

comprehension
BR ,kɒmprɪ'hɛnʃn, -z
AM ,kamprə'hɛn(t)ʃən, -z

comprehensive
BR ,kɒmprɪ'hɛnsɪv, -z
AM ,kamprə'hɛnsɪv, -z

comprehensively
BR ,kɒmprɪ'hɛnsɪvli
AM ,kamprə'hɛnsɪvli

comprehensive-ness
BR ,kɒmprɪ'hɛnsɪvnɪs
AM ,kamprə'hɛnsɪvnɪs

comprehensivis-ation
BR ,kɒmprɪhɛnsɪvaɪ-'zeɪʃn
AM ,kamprə,hɛnsəvə-'zeɪʃən, ,kamprə,hɛnsə,vaɪ-'zeɪʃən

comprehensivise
BR ,kɒmprɪ'hɛnsɪvaɪz, -ɪz, -ɪŋ, -d
AM ,kamprə'hɛnsə,vaɪz, -ɪz, -ɪŋ, -d

comprehensiviz-ation
BR ,kɒmprɪhɛnsɪvaɪ-'zeɪʃn
AM ,kamprə,hɛnsəvə-'zeɪʃən, ,kamprə,hɛnsə,vaɪ-'zeɪʃən

comprehensivize
BR ,kɒmprɪ'hɛnsɪvaɪz, -ɪz, -ɪŋ, -d
AM ,kamprə'hɛnsə,vaɪz, -ɪz, -ɪŋ, -d

compress¹
noun
BR 'kɒmprɛs, -ɪz
AM 'kam,prɛs, -əz

compress²
verb
BR kəm'prɛs, -ɪz, -ɪŋ, -t
AM kəm'prɛs, -əz, -ɪŋ, -t

compressibility
BR kəm,prɛsɪ'bɪlɪti
AM kəm,prɛsə'bɪlɪdi

compressible
BR kəm'prɛsɪbl
AM kəm'prɛsəbəl

compression
BR kəm'prɛʃn
AM kəm'prɛʃən

compressive
BR kəm'prɛsɪv
AM kəm'prɛsɪv

compressor
BR kəm'prɛsə(r), -z
AM kəm'prɛsər, -z

comprisable
BR kəm'praɪzəbl
AM kəm'praɪzəbəl

comprise
BR kəm'praɪz, -ɪz, -ɪŋ, -d
AM kəm'praɪz, -ɪz, -ɪŋ, -d

compromise
BR 'kɒmprəmaɪz, -ɪz, -ɪŋ, -d
AM 'kamprə,maɪz, -ɪz, -ɪŋ, -d

compromiser
BR 'kɒmprəmaɪzə(r), -z
AM 'kamprə,maɪzər, -z

compromisingly
BR 'kɒmprəmaɪzɪŋli

compte rendu
BR ,kɒt rɒ̃'duː
AM ,kɔnt ,rãn'd(j)u

comptes rendus
BR ,kɒt rɒ̃'duː(z)
AM ,kɔnt ,rãn'd(j)u(z)

comptometer
BR ,kɒm(p)'tɒmɪtə(r), -z
AM ,kam(p)'tamədər, -z

Compton
BR 'kɒm(p)t(ə)n, 'kʌm(p)t(ə)n
AM 'kam(p)tən

comptroller
BR kən'trəʊlə(r), kəmp'trəʊlə(r), ,kɒmp'trəʊlə(r), -z
AM kən'troʊlər, ,kam(p)'troʊlər, -z

compulsion
BR kəm'pʌlʃn, -z
AM kəm'pəlʃən, -z

compulsive
BR kəm'pʌlsɪv
AM kəm'pəlsɪv

compulsively
BR kəm'pʌlsɪvli
AM kəm'pəlsɪvli

compulsiveness
BR kəm'pʌlsɪvnɪs
AM kəm'pəlsɪvnɪs

compulsorily
BR kəm'pʌls(ə)rɪli
AM kəm'pəlsərəli

compulsoriness
BR kəm'pʌls(ə)rɪnɪs
AM kəm'pəlsərɪnɪs

compulsory
BR kəm'pʌls(ə)ri
AM kəm'pəlsəri

compunction
BR kəm'pʌŋ(k)ʃn
AM kəm'pəŋ(k)ʃən

compunctious
BR kəm'pʌŋ(k)ʃəs
AM kəm'pəŋ(k)ʃəs

compunctiously
BR kəm'pʌŋ(k)ʃəsli
AM kəm'pəŋ(k)ʃəsli

compurgate
BR 'kɒmpəːgeɪt, -s, -ɪŋ, -ɪd
AM 'kampər,geɪt, -ts, -dɪŋ, -dɪd

compurgation
BR ,kɒmpəː'geɪʃn
AM ,kampər'geɪʃən

compurgator
BR 'kɒmpəːgeɪtə(r), -z
AM 'kampər,geɪdər, -z

compurgatory
BR kəm'pəːgət(ə)ri
AM kəm'pərgə,tɔri

computability
BR kəm,pju:tə'bɪlɪti
AM kəm,pjudə'bɪlɪdi

computable
BR kəm'pju:təbl
AM kəm'pjudəbəl

computably
BR kəm'pju:təbli
AM kəm'pjudəbli

computation
BR ,kɒmpjʊ'teɪʃn, -z
AM ,kampjə'teɪʃən, -z

computational
BR ,kɒmpjʊ'teɪʃn(ə)l, ,kɒmpjʊ'teɪʃən(ə)l
AM ,kampjə'teɪʃ(ə)nəl

computationally
BR ,kɒmpjʊ'teɪʃn(ə)li, ,kɒmpjʊ'teɪʃn̩li, ,kɒmpjʊ'teɪʃənli, ,kɒmpjʊ'teɪʃ(ə)nəli
AM ,kampjə'teɪʃ(ə)nəli

compute
BR kəm'pju:t, -s, -ɪŋ, -ɪd
AM kəm'pju|t, -ts, -dɪŋ, -dəd

computer
BR kəm'pju:tə(r), -z
AM kəm'pjudər, -z

computerese
BR kəm,pju:tər'i:z
AM kəm,pjudər'iz

computerisation
BR kəm,pju:təraɪ'zeɪʃn
AM kəm,pjudərə'zeɪʃən, kəm,pjudə,raɪ'zeɪʃən

computerise
BR kəm'pju:təraɪz, -ɪz, -ɪŋ, -d
AM kəm'pjudə,raɪz, -ɪz, -ɪŋ, -d

computerization
BR kəm,pju:təraɪ'zeɪʃn
AM kəm,pjudərə'zeɪʃən, kəm,pjudə,raɪ'zeɪʃən

computerize
BR kəm'pju:təraɪz, -ɪz, -ɪŋ, -d
AM kəm'pjudə,raɪz, -ɪz, -ɪŋ, -d

comrade
BR 'kɒmreɪd, 'kɒmrəd, -z
AM 'kam,ræd, 'kamrəd, -z

comradely
BR 'kɒmreɪdli, 'kɒmrədli
AM 'kamrədli

comradeship
BR 'kɒmreɪdʃɪp, 'kɒmrədʃɪp
AM 'kamræd,ʃɪp, 'kamrəd,ʃɪp

Comrie
BR 'kɒmri
AM 'kamri

coms
BR kɒmz
AM kɑmz
Comsat®
BR ˈkɒmsat
AM ˈkɑmˌsæt
Comstock
BR ˈkɒmstɒk
AM ˈkɑmˌstak
Comte
BR kɒnt, kɔːnt
AM kɒnt, kɔmt, kɑnt, kɑmt
Comtism
BR ˈkɒmtɪz(ə)m
AM ˈkɑm(p)ˌtɪzəm
Comtist
BR ˈkɒmtɪst, -s
AM ˈkɑm(p)təst, -s
con
BR kɒn, -z, -ɪŋ, -d
AM kɑn, -z, -ɪŋ, -d
conacre
BR ˈkɒnˌeɪkə(r), -z
AM ˈkɑˌneɪkər, -z
Conakry
BR ˈkɒnəkri
AM ˈkɑnəkri
con amore
BR ˌkɒn əˈmɔːreɪ,
+ aˈmɔːreɪ
AM ˌkɑn əˈmɔˌreɪ
Conan
BR ˈkəʊnən
AM ˈkoʊnən
conation
BR kə(ʊ)ˈneɪʃn
AM koʊˈneɪʃən
conative
BR ˈkəʊnətɪv
AM ˈkoʊnədɪv, ˈkɑnədɪv
con brio
BR ˌkɒn ˈbriːəʊ
AM ˌkɑn ˈbrioʊ
Concannon
BR kɒnˈkanən
AM kənˈkænən
concatenate
BR kənˈkatɪneɪt, kənˈkatɪneɪt, (ˌ)kɒnˈkatɪneɪt, (ˌ)kɒnˈkatɪneɪt, -s, -ɪŋ, -ɪd
AM kənˈkædəˌneɪ|t, -ts, -dɪŋ, -dɪd
concatenation
BR kənˌkatɪˈneɪʃn, kənˌkatɪˈneɪʃn, kɒnˌkatɪˈneɪʃn, kɒŋˌkatɪˈneɪʃn, ˌkɒŋkatɪˈneɪʃn, ˌkɒŋkatɪˈneɪʃn, -z
AM kənˌkædəˈneɪʃən, -z
concatenative
BR kənˈkatənətɪv, kəŋˈkatənətɪv,

kənˈkatṇətɪv, kəŋˈkatṇətɪv, kɒnˈkatɪnətɪv, kɒŋˈkatɪnətɪv, kɒnˈkatṇətɪv, kɒŋˈkatṇətɪv
AM kənˈkædəˌneɪdɪv, kənˈkædṇˌeɪdɪv, kənˈkæd(ə)nədɪv
concave¹
adjective
BR ˌkɒnˈkeɪv, ˌkɒŋˈkeɪv
AM ˌkɑnˈkeɪv, ˌkɑŋˈkeɪv
concave²
noun
BR ˈkɒnkeɪv, ˈkɒŋkeɪv, -z
AM ˈkɑnˌkeɪv, ˈkɑŋˌkeɪv, -z
concavely
BR ˌkɒnˈkeɪvli, ˌkɒŋˈkeɪvli, ˈkɒnkeɪvli, ˈkɒŋkeɪvli
AM ˌkɑnˈkeɪvli, ˌkɑŋˈkeɪvli
concavity
BR kɒnˈkavɪti, kɒŋˈkavɪti, kənˈkavɪti, kəŋˈkavɪti
AM ˌkɑnˈkævədi, ˌkɑŋˈkavədi
conceal
BR kənˈsiːl, -z, -ɪŋ, -d
AM kənˈsil, -z, -ɪŋ, -d
concealer
BR kənˈsiːlə(r), -z
AM kənˈsilər, -z
concealment
BR kənˈsiːlm(ə)nt, -s
AM kənˈsilmənt, -s
concede
BR kənˈsiːd, -z, -ɪŋ, -ɪd
AM kənˈsid, -z, -ɪŋ, -ɪd
conceder
BR kənˈsiːdə(r), -z
AM kənˈsidər, -z
conceit
BR kənˈsiːt, -s
AM kənˈsit, -s
conceited
BR kənˈsiːtɪd
AM kənˈsidɪd
conceitedly
BR kənˈsiːtɪdli
AM kənˈsidɪdli
conceitedness
BR kənˈsiːtɪdnɪs
AM kənˈsidɪdnɪs
conceivability
BR kənˌsiːvəˈbɪlɪti
AM kənˌsivəˈbɪlɪdi
conceivable
BR kənˈsiːvəbl
AM kənˈsivəbəl

conceivably
BR kənˈsiːvəbli
AM kənˈsivəbli
conceive
BR kənˈsiːv, -z, -ɪŋ, -d
AM kənˈsiv, -z, -ɪŋ, -d
concelebrant
BR ˌkɒnˈsɛlɪbr(ə)nt, -s
AM ˌkɑnˈsɛləbrənt, -s
concelebrate
BR ˌkɒnˈsɛlɪbreɪt, -s, -ɪŋ, -ɪd
AM ˌkɑnˈsɛləˌbreɪ|t, -ts, -dɪŋ, -dɪd
concelebrating
BR ˌkɒnˈsɛləˈbreɪtɪŋ
AM ˌkɑnˈsɛləˌbreɪdɪŋ
concelebration
BR kɒnˌsɛləˈbreɪʃn, -z
AM ˌkɑnˌsɛləˈbreɪʃən, -z
concentrate
BR ˈkɒns(ɛ)ntreɪt, -s, -ɪŋ, -ɪd
AM ˈkɑnsənˌtreɪ|t, -ts, -dɪŋ, -dɪd
concentratedly
BR ˈkɒns(ɛ)ntreɪtɪdli
AM ˈkɑnsənˌtreɪdɪdli
concentration
BR ˌkɒns(ɛ)nˈtreɪʃn
AM ˌkɑnsənˈtreɪʃən
concentrative
BR ˈkɒns(ɛ)ntreɪtɪv
AM ˈkɑnsənˌtreɪdɪv
concentrator
BR ˈkɒns(ɛ)ntreɪtə(r), -z
AM ˈkɑnsənˌtreɪdər, -z
concentre
BR kənˈsɛnt|ə(r), ˌkɒnˈsɛnt|ə(r), -əz, -(ə)rɪŋ, -əd
AM kənˈsɛn(t)ər, -z, -ɪŋ, -d
concentric
BR kənˈsɛntrɪk, ˌkɒnˈsɛntrɪk
AM kənˈsɛntrɪk
concentrically
BR kənˈsɛntrɪkli, ˌkɒnˈsɛntrɪkli
AM kənˈsɛntrək(ə)li
concentricity
BR ˌkɒnsɛnˈtrɪsɪti
AM ˌkɑnˌsɛnˈtrɪsɪdi
Concepción
BR ˌkɒnsɛpˈsjɒn
AM ˌkɑnˌsɛpsiˈoʊn
SP ˌkonθepˈθjon, ˌkonsepˈsjon
concept
BR ˈkɒnsɛpt, -s
AM ˈkɑnˌsɛpt, -s
conception
BR kənˈsɛpʃn, -z
AM kənˈsɛpʃən, -z

conceptional
BR kənˈsɛpʃn̩(ə)l, kənˈsɛpʃən(ə)l
AM kənˈsɛpʃ(ə)nəl
conceptionally
BR kənˈsɛpʃn̩əli, kənˈsɛpʃn̩li, kənˈsɛpʃənli, kənˈsɛpʃ(ə)nəli
AM kənˈsɛpʃ(ə)nəli
conceptive
BR kənˈsɛptɪv
AM kənˈsɛptɪv
conceptual
BR kənˈsɛptʃʊəl, kənˈsɛptʃ(ʊ)l, kənˈsɛptjʊəl, kənˈsɛptjʊl
AM kənˈsɛp(t)ʃ(əw)əl
conceptualisation
BR kənˌsɛptʃʊəlʌɪˈzeɪʃn, kənˌsɛptʃʊəlʌɪˈzeɪʃn, kənˌsɛptʃʌɪˈzeɪʃn, kənˌsɛptjʊəlʌɪˈzeɪʃn, kənˌsɛptjʊəlʌɪˈzeɪʃn
AM kənˌsɛp(t)ʃ(əw)ələˈzeɪʃən, kənˌsɛp(t)ʃ(əw)əˌlʌɪˈzeɪʃən
conceptualise
BR kənˈsɛptʃʊəlʌɪz, kənˈsɛptʃʊəlʌɪz, kənˈsɛptʃʌɪz, kənˈsɛptjʊəlʌɪz, kənˈsɛptjʊəlʌɪz, -ɪz, -ɪŋ, -d
AM kənˈsɛp(t)ʃ(əw)əˌlʌɪz, -ɪz, -ɪŋ, -d
conceptualism
BR kənˈsɛptʃʊəlɪz(ə)m, kənˈsɛptʃʊəlɪz(ə)m, kənˈsɛptʃɪz(ə)m, kənˈsɛptjʊəlɪz(ə)m, kənˈsɛptjʊəlɪz(ə)m
AM kənˈsɛp(t)ʃ(əw)əˌlɪzəm
conceptualist
BR kənˈsɛptʃʊəlɪst, kənˈsɛptʃʊəlɪst, kənˈsɛptʃɪst, kənˈsɛptjʊəlɪst, kənˈsɛptjʊəlɪst, -s
AM kənˈsɛp(t)ʃ(əw)əlˌəst, -s
conceptualization
BR kənˌsɛptʃʊəlʌɪˈzeɪʃn, kənˌsɛptʃʊəlʌɪˈzeɪʃn, kənˌsɛptʃʌɪˈzeɪʃn, kənˌsɛptjʊəlʌɪˈzeɪʃn, kənˌsɛptjʊəlʌɪˈzeɪʃn
AM kənˌsɛp(t)ʃ(əw)ələˈzeɪʃən, kənˌsɛp(t)ʃ(əw)əˌlʌɪˈzeɪʃən
conceptualize
BR kənˈsɛptʃʊəlʌɪz, kənˈsɛptʃʊəlʌɪz, kənˈsɛptʃʌɪz,

kən'sɛptjʊəlʌɪz,
kən'sɛptjʊlʌɪz, -ɪz,
-ɪŋ, -d
AM kən'sɛp(t)ʃ(əw)ə-
ˌlaɪz, -ɪz, -ɪŋ, -d

conceptually
BR kən'sɛptʃʊəli,
kən'sɛptʃʊli,
kən'sɛptʃli,
kən'sɛptjʊəli,
kən'sɛptjʊli
AM kən'sɛp(t)ʃ(əw)əli

conceptus
BR kən'sɛptəs
AM kən'sɛptəs

concern
BR kən'sɜːn, -z, -ɪŋ, -d
AM kən'sɜrn, -z, -ɪŋ, -d

concernedly
BR kən'sɜːnɪdli
AM kən'sɜrnədli

concernedness
BR kən'sɜːnɪdnɪs
AM kən'sɜrnədnəs

concerningly
BR kən'sɜːnɪŋli
AM kən'sɜrnɪŋli

concernment
BR kən'sɜːnm(ə)nt, -s
AM kən'sɜrnmənt, -s

concert[1]
noun, agreement
BR 'kɒnsəːt
AM 'kɑnsərt

concert[2]
*noun, musical
performance*
BR 'kɒnsət, -s
AM 'kɑnˌsərt, -s

concert[3]
verb
BR kən'sɜːt, -s, -ɪŋ, -ɪd
AM kən'sɜr|t, -ts, -dɪŋ,
-dəd

concertante
BR ˌkɒntʃə'tanteɪ,
ˌkɒntʃə'tanti
AM ˌkɑntʃər'tan,teɪ,
ˌkɑnsər'tan,teɪ,
ˌkɑntʃər'tan,teɪ,
ˌkɑnsər'tan,teɪ

concerted
BR kən'sɜːtɪd
AM kən'sɜrdəd

concertedly
BR kən'sɜːtɪdli
AM kən'sɜrdədli

Concertgebouw
BR kən'sɜːtgɪ,baʊ
AM kən'sɜrtgə,baʊ
DU kɒn'sɛrtxə,bɔʊ

concertgoer
BR 'kɒnsət,gəʊə(r), -z
AM kən'sɜrt,gʊʊər, -z

concerti grossi
BR kənˌtʃɛːti: 'grɒsi:,
kənˌtʃɜːti: +

AM kənˌtʃɛrˌdi 'grɔsi,
kənˌsɛrˌdi +

concertina
BR ˌkɒnsə'ti:nə(r), -z,
-ɪŋ, -d
AM ˌkɑnsər'tinə, -z, -ɪŋ,
-d

concertino
BR ˌkɒn(t)ʃə'ti:nəʊ, -z
AM ˌkɑn(t)ʃər'tinoʊ,
ˌkɑnsər'tinoʊ , -z

concertmaster
BR 'kɒnsət,mɑːstə(r),
'kɒnsət,mastə(r), -z
AM 'kɑnsərt,mæstər,
-z

concerto
BR kən'tʃɛːtəʊ,
kən'tʃəːtəʊ, -z
AM kən'(t)ʃɛrdoʊ, -z

concerto grosso
BR kənˌtʃɛːtəʊ
'grɒsəʊ,
kənˌtʃəːtəʊ +, -z
AM kənˌ(t)ʃɛrˌdoʊ
'groʊsoʊ, -z

concession
BR kən'sɛʃn, -z
AM kən'sɛʃən, -z

concessionaire
BR kənˌsɛʃə'nɛː(r),
kənˌsɛʃn'ɛː(r), -z
AM kənˌsɛʃə'nɛ(ə)r, -z

concessionary
BR kən'sɛʃn(ə)ri
AM kən'sɛʃə,nɛri

concessive
BR kən'sɛsɪv
AM kən'sɛsɪv

conch
BR kɒn(t)ʃ, kɒŋk
AM kɑntʃ, kɑŋk

concha
BR 'kɒŋkə(r)
AM 'kɑŋkə

conchae
BR 'kɒŋki:
AM 'kɑŋki, 'kɑŋ,kaɪ

conches
BR 'kɒn(t)ʃɪz, kɒŋks
AM 'kɑn(t)ʃəz, kɑŋks

conchie
BR 'kɒnʃli, -ɪz
AM 'kɑn(t)ʃi, -z

conchoid
BR 'kɒŋkɔɪd, -z
AM 'kɑŋ,kɔɪd, -z

conchoidal
BR kɒŋ'kɔɪdl
AM 'kɑŋ'kɔɪdəl

conchological
BR ˌkɒŋkə'lɒdʒɪkl
AM ˌkɑŋkə'lɑdʒəkəl

conchologically
BR ˌkɒŋkə'lɒdʒɪkli
AM ˌkɑŋkə'lɑdʒək(ə)li

conchologist
BR kɒŋ'kɒlədʒɪst, -s

AM kənˌtʃɛrˌdi 'grɔsi, -s

conchology
BR kɒŋ'kɒlədʒi
AM ˌkɑŋ'kɑlədʒi

conchy
BR 'kɒnʃli, -ɪz
AM 'kɑn(t)ʃi, -z

concierge
BR 'kɒnsɪɛːʒ, 'kɒsɪɛːʒ,
ˌkɒnsɪ'ɛːʒ, ˌkɒsɪ'ɛːʒ, -ɪz
AM ˌkɑn'sɪɛr(d)ʒ, -əz

conciliar
BR kən'sɪlɪə(r)
AM kən'sɪlɪər

conciliate
BR kən'sɪlɪeɪt, -s, -ɪŋ,
-ɪd
AM kən'sɪliˌeɪ|t, -ts,
-dɪŋ, -dɪd

conciliation
BR kənˌsɪlɪ'eɪʃn
AM kənˌsɪli'eɪʃən

conciliative
BR kən'sɪlɪətɪv,
kən'sɪlɪeɪtɪv
AM kən'sɪliədɪv,
kən'sɪliˌeɪdɪv

conciliator
BR kən'sɪlɪeɪtə(r), -z
AM kən'sɪliˌeɪdər, -z

conciliatoriness
BR kən'sɪlɪətrɪnɪs
AM kən'sɪliəˌtɔrɪnɪs

conciliatory
BR kən'sɪlɪət(ə)ri
AM kən'sɪliəˌtɔri

concinnity
BR kən'sɪnɪti
AM kən'sɪnɪdi

concinnous
BR kən'sɪnəs
AM kən'sɪnəs

concise
BR kən'sʌɪs
AM kən'saɪs

concisely
BR kən'sʌɪsli
AM kən'saɪsli

conciseness
BR kən'sʌɪsnɪs
AM kən'saɪsnɪs

concision
BR kən'sɪʒn
AM kən'sɪʒən

conclave
BR 'kɒŋkleɪv, -z
AM 'kɑn,kleɪv,
'kɑŋ,kleɪv, -z

conclude
BR kən'klu:d,
kəŋ'klu:d, -z, -ɪŋ, -ɪd
AM kən'klud, -z, -ɪŋ, -əd

conclusion
BR kən'klu:ʒn,
kəŋ'klu:ʒn, -z
AM kən'klu:ʒən, -z

conclusive
BR kən'klu:sɪv,
kəŋ'klu:sɪv
AM kən'klusɪv

conclusively
BR kən'klu:sɪvli,
kəŋ'klu:sɪvli
AM kən'klusɪvli

conclusiveness
BR kən'klu:sɪvnɪs,
kəŋ'klu:sɪvnɪs
AM kən'klusɪvnɪs

concoct
BR kən'kɒkt,
kəŋ'kɒkt, -s, -ɪŋ, -ɪd
AM kən'kak|(t), -(t)s,
-tɪŋ, -təd

concocter
BR kən'kɒktə(r),
kəŋ'kɒktə(r), -z
AM kən'kaktər, -z

concoction
BR kən'kɒkʃn,
kəŋ'kɒkʃn, -z
AM kən'kakʃən, -z

concoctor
BR kən'kɒktə(r),
kəŋ'kɒktə(r), -z
AM kən'kaktər, -z

concomitance
BR kəŋ'kɒmɪt(ə)ns,
kəŋ'kɒmɪt(ə)ns
AM kən'kɑmədəns

concomitancy
BR kəŋ'kɒmɪt(ə)nsi,
kəŋ'kɒmɪt(ə)nsi
AM kən'kɑmədənsi

concomitant
BR kəŋ'kɒmɪt(ə)nt,
kəŋ'kɒmɪt(ə)nt
AM kən'kɑmədənt

concomitantly
BR kəŋ'kɒmɪt(ə)ntli,
kəŋ'kɒmɪt(ə)ntli
AM kən'kɑmədən(t)li

concord
BR 'kɒŋkɔːd, 'kɒnkɔːd
AM 'kɑŋkərd

concordance
BR kən'kɔːd(ə)ns,
kəŋ'kɔːd(ə)ns, -ɪz
AM kən'kɔrdns, -əz

concordant
BR kən'kɔːd(ə)nt,
kəŋ'kɔːd(ə)nt
AM kən'kɔrdnt

concordantly
BR kən'kɔːd(ə)ntli,
kəŋ'kɔːd(ə)ntli
AM kən'kɔrdn(t)li

concordat
BR kɒn'kɔːdat,
kɒŋ'kɔːdat,
kən'kɔːdat,
kəŋ'kɔːdat, -s

AM kən'kɔrˌdæt, -z

Concorde
BR 'kɒŋkɔːd, -z

AM ˈkɒŋˌkɔ(ə)rd,
ˈkɑnˌkɔ(ə)rd, -z
concourse
BR ˈkɒŋkɔːs, -ɪz
AM ˈkɒŋˌkɔ(ə)rs,
ˈkɑnˌkɔ(ə)rs, -əz
concrescence
BR kən'krɛsns,
kəŋ'krɛsns
AM kən'krɛsəns
concrescent
BR kən'krɛsnt,
kəŋ'krɛsnt
AM kən'krɛsənt
concrete
BR ˈkɒŋkriːt
AM ˌkɑnˈkriːt, ˌkɑŋˈkriːt
concretely
BR ˈkɒŋkriːtli
AM ˌkɑnˈkriːtli,
ˌkɑŋˈkriːtli
concreteness
BR ˈkɒŋkriːtnɪs
AM ˌkɑnˈkriːtnɪs,
ˌkɑŋˈkriːtnɪs
concretion
BR kən'kriːʃn,
kəŋ'kriːʃn, -z
AM kən'kriːʃən, -z
concretionary
BR kən'kriːʃn(ə)ri,
kəŋ'kriːʃn(ə)ri
AM kən'kriːʃəˌneri
concretisation
BR ˌkɒŋkriːtʌɪ'zeɪʃn,
ˌkɒŋkrɪtʌɪ'zeɪʃn
AM ˌkɑŋkrəˌtaɪ'zeɪʃən,
ˌkɑŋkrədə'zeɪʃən,
ˌkɑŋkrədə'zeɪʃən,
ˌkɑŋkrəˌtaɪ'zeɪʃən
concretise
BR ˈkɒŋkriːtʌɪz,
ˈkɒŋkrɪtʌɪz, -ɪz, -ɪŋ, -d
AM ˈkɑŋkrəˌtaɪz,
ˈkɑŋkrəˌtaɪz, -ɪz, -ɪŋ,
-d
concretization
BR ˌkɒŋkriːtʌɪ'zeɪʃn,
ˌkɒŋkrɪtʌɪ'zeɪʃn
AM ˌkɑŋkrəˌtaɪ'zeɪʃən,
ˌkɑŋkrədə'zeɪʃən,
ˌkɑŋkrədə'zeɪʃən,
ˌkɑŋkrəˌtaɪ'zeɪʃən
concretize
BR ˈkɒŋkriːtʌɪz,
ˈkɒŋkrɪtʌɪz, -ɪz, -ɪŋ, -d
AM ˈkɑŋkrəˌtaɪz,
ˈkɑŋkrəˌtaɪz, -ɪz, -ɪŋ,
-d
concubinage
BR kɒn'kjuːbɪnɪdʒ,
kɒŋ'kjuːbɪnɪdʒ,
kən'kjuːbɪnɪdʒ,
kəŋ'kjuːbɪnɪdʒ
AM kən'kjubənɪdʒ
concubinary
BR kɒn'kjuːbɪn(ə)ri,
kɒŋ'kjuːbɪn(ə)ri,

kən'kjuːbɪn(ə)ri,
kəŋ'kjuːbɪn(ə)ri
AM kən'kjubəˌneri
concubine
BR ˈkɒŋkjəbʌɪn, -z
AM ˈkɑŋkjəˌbaɪn,
ˈkɑnkjəˌbaɪn, -z
concupiscence
BR kən'kjuːpɪs(ə)ns,
kəŋ'kjuːpɪs(ə)ns
AM kɑn'kjupəsəns,
ˌkɑŋ'kjupəsəns
concupiscent
BR kən'kjuːpɪs(ə)nt,
kəŋ'kjuːpɪs(ə)nt
AM kɑn'kjupəsənt,
ˌkɑŋ'kjupəsənt
concur
BR kən'kəː(r),
kəŋ'kəː(r), -z, -ɪŋ, -d
AM kən'kər, -z, -ɪŋ, -d
concurrence
BR kən'kʌrəns,
kən'kʌrŋs,
kəŋ'kʌrəns,
kəŋ'kʌrŋs
AM kən'kərəns
concurrent
BR kən'kʌrənt,
kən'kʌrŋt,
kəŋ'kʌrənt,
kəŋ'kʌrŋt
AM kən'kərənt
concurrently
BR kən'kʌrəntli,
kən'kʌrŋtli,
kəŋ'kʌrəntli,
kəŋ'kʌrŋtli
AM kən'kərən(t)li
concuss
BR kən'kʌs, kəŋ'kʌs,
-ɪz, -ɪŋ, -t
AM kən'kəs, -əz, -ɪŋ, -t
concussion
BR kən'kʌʃn,
kəŋ'kʌʃn
AM kən'kəʃən
concussive
BR kən'kʌsɪv,
kəŋ'kʌsɪv
AM kən'kəsɪv
condemn
BR kən'dɛm, -z, -ɪŋ, -d
AM kən'dɛm, -z, -ɪŋ, -d
condemnable
BR kən'dɛmnəbl
AM kən'dɛm(n)əbəl
condemnation
BR ˌkɒndɛm'neɪʃn,
ˌkɒndəm'neɪʃn
AM ˌkɑndɛm'neɪʃən
condemnatory
BR kən'dɛmnət(ə)ri,
ˌkɒndəm'neɪt(ə)ri,
ˌkɒndəm'neɪt(ə)ri
AM ˌkɑndɛmnəˌtɔri
condensable
BR kən'dɛnsəbl

AM kən'dɛnsəbəl
condensate
BR ˈkɒndɛnseɪt,
ˈkɒnd(ə)nseɪt,
kən'dɛnseɪt, -s
AM kən'dɛnˌseɪt, -s
condensation
BR ˌkɒndɛn'seɪʃn,
ˌkɒnd(ə)n'seɪʃn
AM ˌkɑndɛn'seɪʃən
condense
BR kən'dɛns, -ɪz, -ɪŋ, -t
AM kən'dɛns, -əz, -ɪŋ, -t
condenser
BR kən'dɛnsə(r), -z
AM kən'dɛnsər, -z
condensery
BR kən'dɛns(ə)r|i, -ɪz
AM kən'dɛns(ə)ri, -z
condescend
BR ˌkɒndɪ'sɛnd, -z, -ɪŋ,
-ɪd
AM ˌkɑndə'sɛnd, -z, -ɪŋ,
-əd
condescendingly
BR ˌkɒndɪ'sɛndɪŋli
AM ˌkɑndə'sɛndɪŋli
condescension
BR ˌkɒndɪ'sɛnʃn
AM ˌkɑndə'sɛn(t)ʃən
condign
BR kən'dʌɪn, 'kɒndʌɪn
AM kən'daɪn,
'kɑnˌdaɪn
condignly
BR kən'dʌɪnli,
'kɒndʌɪnli
AM kən'daɪnli,
'kɑnˌdaɪnli
condiment
BR ˈkɒndɪm(ə)nt, -s
AM ˈkɑndəmənt, -s
condition
BR kən'dɪʃn, -nz,
-ŋɪŋ \-nɪŋ, -nd
AM kən'dɪʃ|ən, -nz,
-(ə)nɪŋ, -nd
conditional
BR kən'dɪʃŋ(ə)l,
kən'dɪʃən(ə)l
AM kən'dɪʃ(ə)nəl
conditionality
BR kən'dɪʃə'nalɪti
AM kən'dɪʃə'nælədi
conditionally
BR kən'dɪʃŋəli,
kən'dɪʃŋli,
kən'dɪʃənli,
kən'dɪʃ(ə)nəli
AM kən'dɪʃ(ə)nəli
conditioner
BR kən'dɪʃŋə(r),
kən'dɪʃ(ə)nə(r), -z
AM kən'dɪʃ(ə)nər, -z
condo
BR ˈkɒndəʊ, -z
AM ˈkɑndoʊ, -z

condolatory
BR kən'dəʊlət(ə)ri
AM kən'doʊləˌtɔri
condole
BR kən'dəʊl, -z, -ɪŋ, -d
AM kən'doʊl, -z, -ɪŋ, -d
condolence
BR kən'dəʊləns,
kən'dəʊlŋs, -ɪz
AM kən'doʊləns, -əz
condom
BR ˈkɒndəm,
ˈkɒndɒm, -z
AM ˈkɑndəm, -z
condominium
BR ˌkɒndə'mɪnɪəm, -z
AM ˌkɑndə'mɪniəm, -z
condonation
BR ˌkɒndə(ʊ)'neɪʃn
AM ˌkɑndoʊ'neɪʃən
condone
BR kən'dəʊn, -z, -ɪŋ, -d
AM kən'doʊn, -z, -ɪŋ, -d
condoner
BR kən'dəʊnə(r), -z
AM kən'doʊnər, -z
condor
BR ˈkɒndɔː(r), -z
AM ˈkɑnˌdɔ(ə)r, -z
condottiere
BR ˌkɒndɒtɪ'ɛːreɪ,
ˌkɒndɒtɪ'ɛːri
AM ˌkɑnˌdadi'ɛri
condottieri
BR ˌkɒndɒtɪ'ɛːri:
AM ˌkɑnˌdadi'ɛri
conduce
BR kən'djuːs,
kən'dʒuːs, -ɪz, -ɪŋ, -t
AM kən'd(j)us, -əz, -ɪŋ,
-t
conducement
BR kən'djuːsm(ə)nt,
kən'dʒuːsm(ə)nt, -s
AM kən'd(j)usmənt, -s
conducive
BR kən'djuːsɪv,
kən'dʒuːsɪv
AM kən'd(j)usɪv
conducively
BR kən'djuːsɪvli,
kən'dʒuːsɪvli
AM kən'd(j)usɪvli
conduciveness
BR kən'djuːsɪvnɪs,
kən'dʒuːsɪvnɪs
AM kən'd(j)usɪvnɪs
conduct¹
noun
BR ˈkɒndʌkt, ˈkɒndəkt
AM ˈkɑnˌdək(t)
conduct²
verb
BR kən'dʌkt, -s, -ɪŋ, -ɪd
AM kən'dək|(t), -(t)s,
-tɪŋ, -təd
conductance
BR kən'dʌkt(ə)ns

AM kənˈdəktns

conducti
BR kənˈdʌktʌɪ
AM kənˈdək͵taɪ

conductibility
BR kən͵dʌktɪˈbɪlɪti
AM kən͵dəktəˈbɪlɪdi

conductible
BR kənˈdʌktɪbl
AM kənˈdəktəbəl

conduction
BR kənˈdʌkʃn
AM kənˈdəkʃən

conductive
BR kənˈdʌktɪv
AM kənˈdəktɪv

conductively
BR kənˈdʌktɪvli
AM kənˈdəktɪvli

conductivity
BR ͵kɒndʌkˈtɪvɪti
AM ͵kɑndəkˈtɪvɪdi

conductor
BR kənˈdʌktə(r), -z
AM kənˈdəktər, -z

conductorship
BR kənˈdʌktəʃɪp
AM kənˈdəktərˌʃɪp

conductress
BR kənˈdʌktrɪs, -ɪz
AM kənˈdəktrəs, -əz

conductus
BR kənˈdʌktəs
AM kənˈdəktəs

conduit
BR ˈkɒnd(w)ɪt, ˈkɒndjʊɪt, ˈkʌndɪt, -s
AM ˈkɑnˌduət, ˈkɑndwət, -s

condylar
BR ˈkɒndɪlə(r)
AM ˈkɑndələr

condylarth
BR ˈkɒndɪlɑːθ, -s
AM ˈkɑndəˌlɑrθ, -s

condyle
BR ˈkɒndʌɪl, ˈkɒndɪl, -z
AM ˈkɑnˌdaɪl, -z

condyloid
BR ˈkɒndɪlɔɪd
AM ˈkɑndəˌlɔɪd

condyloma
BR ͵kɒndɪˈləʊmə(r), -z
AM ͵kɑndəˈloʊmə, -z

condylomata
BR ͵kɒndɪˈləʊmətə(r)
AM ͵kɑndəˈloʊmədə

cone
BR kəʊn, -z, -ɪŋ, -d
AM koʊn, -z, -ɪŋ, -d

conestoga
BR ͵kɒnɪˈstəʊgə(r), -z
AM ͵kɑnəˈstoʊgə, -z

coney
BR ˈkəʊn|i, -ɪz

confab[1]
noun
BR ˈkɒnfab, -z
AM ˈkɑnfæb, -z

confab[2]
verb
BR kənˈfab, -z, -ɪŋ, -d
AM kənˈfæb, -z, -ɪŋ, -d

confabulate
BR kənˈfabjʊleɪt, -s, -ɪŋ, -ɪd
AM kənˈfæbjəˌleɪt, -ts, -dɪŋ, -dɪd

confabulation
BR kən͵fabjʊˈleɪʃn, -z
AM kən͵fæbjəˈleɪʃən, -z

confabulatory
BR kənˈfabjʊlət(ə)ri
AM kənˈfæbjələˌtɔri

confect
BR kənˈfɛkt, -s, -ɪŋ, -ɪd
AM kənˈfɛk|t, -s, -tɪŋ, -təd

confection
BR kənˈfɛkʃn, -z
AM kənˈfɛkʃən, -z

confectionary
BR kənˈfɛkʃn(ə)r|i, kənˈfɛkʃnər|i, -ɪz
AM kənˈfɛkʃəˌnɛri, -z

confectioner
BR kənˈfɛkʃnə(r), -z
AM kənˈfɛkʃənər, -z

confectionery
BR kənˈfɛkʃn(ə)r|i, kənˈfɛkʃnər|i, -ɪz
AM kənˈfɛkʃəˌnɛri, -z

confederacy
BR kənˈfɛd(ə)rəs|i, -ɪz
AM kənˈfɛd(ə)rəsi, -z

confederate[1]
noun, adjective
BR kənˈfɛd(ə)rət, -s
AM kənˈfɛd(ə)rət, -s

confederate[2]
verb
BR kənˈfɛdəreɪt, -s, -ɪŋ, -ɪd
AM kənˈfɛdəˌreɪ|t, -ts, -dɪŋ, -dɪd

confederation
BR kən͵fɛdəˈreɪʃn, -z
AM kən͵fɛdəˈreɪʃən, -z

confer
BR kənˈfɜː(r), -z, -ɪŋ, -d
AM kənˈfər, -z, -ɪŋ, -d

conferee
BR ͵kɒnfə(ː)ˈriː, -z
AM ͵kɑnfəˈri, -z

conference
BR ˈkɒnf(ə)rəns, ˈkɒnf(ə)rns, -ɪz, -ɪŋ
AM ˈkɑnf(ə)rəns, -əz, -ɪŋ

conferential
BR ͵kɒnfəˈrɛnʃl

AM ͵kɑnfəˈrɛn(t)ʃəl

conferment
BR kənˈfɜːm(ə)nt, -s
AM kənˈfərmənt, -s

conferrable
BR kənˈfɜːrəbl
AM kənˈfərəbəl

conferral
BR kənˈfɜːr|, -z
AM kənˈfərəl, -z

confess
BR kənˈfɛs, -ɪz, -ɪŋ, -t
AM kənˈfɛs, -əz, -ɪn, -t

confessant
BR kənˈfɛsnt, -s
AM kənˈfɛsənt, -s

confessedly
BR kənˈfɛsɪdli
AM kənˈfɛsədli

confession
BR kənˈfɛʃn, -z
AM kənˈfɛʃən, -z

confessional
BR kənˈfɛʃn(ə)l, kənˈfɛʃən(ə)l, -z
AM kənˈfɛʃ(ə)nəl, -z

confessionary
BR kənˈfɛʃn(ə)ri
AM kənˈfɛʃəˌnɛri

confessor
BR kənˈfɛsə(r), -z
AM kənˈfɛsər, kənˈfɛˌsɔ(ə)r, -z

confetti
BR kənˈfɛti
AM kənˈfɛdi

confidant
BR ˈkɒnfɪdant, ͵kɒnfrˈdant, -s
AM ˈkɑnfəˌdænt, ˈkɑnfəˌdant, -s

confidante
BR ˈkɒnfɪdant, ͵kɒnfrˈdant, -s
AM ˈkɑnfəˌdænt, ˈkɑnfəˌdant, -s

confide
BR kənˈfʌɪd, -z, -ɪŋ, -ɪd
AM kənˈfaɪd, -z, -ɪŋ, -ɪd

confidence
BR ˈkɒnfɪd(ə)ns, -ɪz
AM ˈkɑnfədns, -ɪz

confident
BR ˈkɒnfɪd(ə)nt
AM ˈkɑnfədnt

confidential
BR ͵kɒnfrˈdɛnʃl
AM ͵kɑnfəˈdɛn(t)ʃəl

confidentiality
BR ͵kɒnfɪ͵dɛnʃɪˈalɪt|i, -ɪz
AM ͵kɑnfəˌdɛn(t)ʃiˈæl-ədi, -z

confidentially
BR ͵kɒnfrˈdɛnʃli, ͵kɒnfrˈdɛnʃəli
AM ͵kɑnfəˈdɛn(t)ʃəli

confidently
BR ˈkɒnfɪd(ə)ntli
AM ˈkɑnfədən(t)li

confiding
BR kənˈfʌɪdɪŋ
AM kənˈfaɪdɪŋ

confidingly
BR kənˈfʌɪdɪŋli
AM kənˈfaɪdɪŋli

configuration
BR kən͵fɪgəˈreɪʃn, kən͵fɪgjʊˈreɪʃn, -z
AM kən͵fɪg(j)əˈreɪʃən, -z

configurational
BR kən͵fɪgəˈreɪʃn(ə)l, kən͵fɪgəˈreɪʃən(ə)l, kən͵fɪgjʊˈreɪʃn(ə)l, kən͵fɪgjʊˈreɪʃən(ə)l
AM kən͵fɪg(j)əˈreɪʃ(ə)nəl

configure
BR kənˈfɪg|ə(r), -əz, -(ə)rɪŋ, -əd
AM kənˈfɪgjər, -z, -ɪŋ, -d

confine
verb
BR kənˈfʌɪn, -z, -ɪŋ, -d
AM kənˈfaɪn, -z, -ɪŋ, -d

confinement
BR kənˈfʌɪnm(ə)nt, -s
AM kənˈfaɪnmənt, -s

confines
noun
BR ˈkɒnfʌɪnz
AM ˈkɑnˌfaɪnz

confirm
BR kənˈfɜːm, -z, -ɪŋ, -d
AM kənˈfərm, -z, -ɪŋ, -d

confirmand
BR ˈkɒnfəmand, ͵kɒnfəˈmand, -z
AM ͵kɑnfərˈmænd, -z

confirmation
BR ͵kɒnfəˈmeɪʃn, -z
AM ͵kɑnfərˈmeɪʃən, -z

confirmative
BR kənˈfɜːmətɪv
AM kənˈfərmədɪv

confirmatory
BR kənˈfɜːmət(ə)ri, ͵kɒnfəˈmeɪt(ə)ri
AM kənˈfərməˌtɔri

confiscable
BR ˈkɒnfɪskəbl
AM ˈkɑnfəskəbəl

confiscate
BR ˈkɒnfɪskeɪt, -s, -ɪŋ, -ɪd
AM ˈkɑnfəˌskeɪ|t, -ts, -dɪŋ, -dɪd

confiscation
BR ͵kɒnfɪˈskeɪʃn, -z
AM ͵kɑnfəˈskeɪʃən, -z

confiscator
BR ˈkɒnfɪskeɪtə(r), -z
AM ˈkɑnfəˌskeɪdər, -z

confiscatory
BR kən'fɪskət(ə)ri,
ˌkɒnfɪ'skeɪt(ə)ri
AM kən'fɪskəˌtɔri
confiture
BR 'kɒnfɪtjʊə(r),
'kɒnfɪtʃə(r), -z
AM 'kɑnfətʃər, -z
conflagration
BR ˌkɒnflə'greɪʃn, -z
AM ˌkɑnflə'greɪʃən, -z
conflate
BR kən'fleɪt, -s, -ɪŋ, -ɪd
AM kən'fleɪ|t, -ts, -dɪŋ,
-dɪd
conflation
BR kən'fleɪʃn, -z
AM kən'fleɪʃən, -z
conflict[1]
noun
BR 'kɒnflɪkt, -s
AM 'kɑnˌflɪk(t), -s
conflict[2]
verb
BR kən'flɪkt, -s, -ɪŋ, -ɪd
AM kən'flɪk|(t), -(t)s,
-tɪŋ, -tɪd
confliction
BR kən'flɪkʃn, -z
AM kən'flɪkʃən, -z
conflictual[1]
BR kən'flɪktʃʊəl,
kən'flɪktʃ(ʊ)l,
kən'flɪktjʊəl,
kən'flɪktjʊl
AM kən'flɪk(t)ʃ(əw)əl
conflictual[2]
BR kən'flɪktʃʊəl,
kən'flɪktʃ(ʊ)l,
kən'flɪktjʊəl,
kən'flɪktjʊl
AM kən'flɪk(t)ʃ(əw)əl
confluence
BR 'kɒnflʊəns, -ɪz
AM 'kɑnˌflʊəns,
kən'flʊəns, -əz
confluent
BR 'kɒnflʊənt
AM 'kɑnˌflʊənt,
kən'flʊənt
conflux
BR 'kɒnflʌks, -ɪz
AM 'kɑnˌfləks, -əz
conform
BR kən'fɔːm, -z, -ɪŋ, -d
AM kən'fɔ(ə)rm, -z, -ɪŋ,
-d
conformability
BR kən'fɔːmə'bɪlɪti
AM kən'fɔrməbɪlɪdi
conformable
BR kən'fɔːməbl
AM kən'fɔrməbəl
conformably
BR kən'fɔːməbli
AM kən'fɔrməbli
conformal
BR kən'fɔːml

conformer
AM kən'fɔːml
conformally
BR kən'fɔːmli,
kən'fɔːməli
AM kən'fɔrməli
conformance
BR kən'fɔːməns
AM kən'fɔrməns
conformation
BR ˌkɒnfɔː'meɪʃn,
ˌkɒnfə'meɪʃn
AM ˌkɑnfər'meɪʃən,
ˌkɑnfor'meɪʃən
conformer
BR kən'fɔːmə(r), -z
AM kən'fɔrmər, -z
conformism
BR kən'fɔːmɪz(ə)m
AM kən'fɔrˌmɪzəm
conformist
BR kən'fɔːmɪst, -s
AM kən'fɔrməst, -s
conformity
BR kən'fɔːmɪti
AM kən'fɔrmədi
confound
BR kən'faʊnd, -z, -ɪŋ,
-ɪd
AM kən'faʊnd, -z, -ɪŋ,
-əd
confoundedly
BR kən'faʊndɪdli
AM kən'faʊndədli
confraternity
BR ˌkɒnfrə'tɜːnɪt|i, -ɪz
AM ˌkɑnfrə'tɜrnədi, -z
confrère
BR 'kɒnfrɛː(r), -z
AM 'kɑnˌfrɛ(ə)r, -z
confront
BR kən'frʌnt, -s, -ɪŋ, -ɪd
AM kən'frən|t, -ts,
-(t)ɪŋ, -(t)əd
confrontation
BR ˌkɒnfrʌn'teɪʃn,
ˌkɒnfrən'teɪʃn, -z
AM ˌkɑnfrən'teɪʃən, -z
confrontational
BR ˌkɒnfrʌn'teɪʃn(ə)l,
ˌkɒnfrʌn'teɪʃən(ə)l,
ˌkɒnfrən'teɪʃn(ə)l,
ˌkɒnfrən'teɪʃən(ə)l
AM ˌkɑnfrən'teɪʃ(ə)nəl
confrontationally
BR ˌkɒnfrʌn'teɪʃnəli,
ˌkɒnfrʌn'teɪʃnəli,
ˌkɒnfrʌn'teɪʃ(ə)nəli,
ˌkɒnfrən'teɪʃnəli,
ˌkɒnfrən'teɪʃn̩li,
ˌkɒnfrən'teɪʃn̩li,
ˌkɒnfrən'teɪʃ(ə)nəli
AM ˌkɑnfrən'teɪʃ(ə)nəli
Confucian
BR kən'fjuːʃn, -z
AM kən'fjuʃən, -z
Confucianism
BR kən'fjuːʃn̩ɪz(ə)m

congeneric
AM kən'fjuʃənˌɪzəm
Confucianist
BR kən'fjuːʃnɪst, -s
AM kən'fjuʃənəst, -s
Confucius
BR kən'fjuːʃəs
AM kən'fjuʃəs
confusability
BR kən'fjuːzə'bɪlɪti
AM kən'fjuzə'bɪlɪdi
confusable
BR kən'fjuːzəbl
AM kən'fjuzəbəl
confusably
BR kən'fjuːzəbli
AM kən'fjuzəbli
confuse
BR kən'fjuːz, -ɪz, -ɪŋ, -d
AM kən'fjuz, -əz, -ɪŋ, -d
confusedly
BR kən'fjuːzɪdli
AM kən'fjuzədli
confusible
BR kən'fjuːzɪbl, -z
AM kən'fjuzəbəl, -z
confusing
BR kən'fjuːzɪŋ
AM kən'fjuzɪŋ
confusingly
BR kən'fjuːzɪŋli
AM kən'fjuzɪŋli
confusion
BR kən'fjuːʒn
AM kən'fjuʒən
confutable
BR kən'fjuːtəbl
AM kən'fjudəbəl
confutation
BR ˌkɒnfjʊ'teɪʃn, -z
AM ˌkɑnfjə'teɪʃən, -z
confute
BR kən'fjuːt, -s, -ɪŋ, -ɪd
AM kən'fju|t, -ts, -dɪŋ,
-dəd
conga
BR 'kɒŋgə(r), -z
AM 'kɑŋgə, -z
congé
BR 'kɒnʒeɪ, 'kɒ̃ʒeɪ, -z
AM 'kɑnˌdʒeɪ, 'kɔnˌʒeɪ,
-z
congeal
BR kən'dʒiːl, -z, -ɪŋ, -d
AM kən'dʒil, -z, -ɪŋ, -d
congealable
BR kən'dʒiːləbl
AM kən'dʒiləbəl
congealment
BR kən'dʒiːlm(ə)nt
AM kən'dʒilmənt
congelation
BR ˌkɒndʒɪ'leɪʃn, -z
AM ˌkɑndʒə'leɪʃən, -z
congener
BR kən'dʒiːnə(r), -z
AM kən'dʒinər, -z

congeneric
BR ˌkɒndʒɪ'nɛrɪk
AM ˌkɑndʒə'nɛrɪk
congenerous
BR kən'dʒɛn(ə)rəs,
ˌkɒn'dʒɛn(ə)rəs
AM kən'dʒɛnərəs,
kən'dʒinərəs
congenerousness
BR kən'dʒɛn(ə)rəsnəs,
ˌkɒn'dʒɛn(ə)rəsnəs
AM kən'dʒɛnərəsnəs,
kən'dʒinərəsnəs
congenial
BR kən'dʒiːnɪəl
AM kən'dʒinjəl,
kən'dʒiniəl
congeniality
BR kən'dʒiːnɪ'ælɪti
AM kən'dʒini'æmədi
congenially
BR kən'dʒiːnɪəli
AM kən'dʒinjəli,
kən'dʒiniəli
congenital
BR kən'dʒɛnɪtl
AM kən'dʒɛnədl
congenitally
BR kən'dʒɛnɪt̩li,
kən'dʒɛnɪtəli
AM kən'dʒɛnədl̩i,
kən'dʒɛnədəli
conger
BR 'kɒŋgə(r), -z
AM 'kɑŋgər, -z
congeries
BR 'kɒn(d)ʒ(ə)riz
AM 'kɑndʒəriz
congest
BR kən'dʒɛst, -s, -ɪŋ, -ɪd
AM kən'dʒɛst, -s, -ɪŋ,
-əd
congestion
BR kən'dʒɛstʃn
AM kən'dʒɛstʃən
congestive
BR kən'dʒɛstɪv
AM kən'dʒɛstɪv
congii
BR 'kɒndʒɪaɪ
AM 'kɑndʒiaɪ
congius
BR 'kɒndʒɪəs
AM 'kɑndʒiəs
conglomerate[1]
noun, adjective
BR kən'glɒm(ə)rət,
kəŋ'glɒm(ə)rət, -s
AM kən'glam(ə)rət, -s
conglomerate[2]
verb
BR kən'glɒməreɪt,
kəŋ'glɒməreɪt, -s, -ɪŋ,
-ɪd
AM kən'glaməˌreɪ|t,
-ts, -dɪŋ, -dɪd

conglomeration
BR kənˌglɒməˈreɪʃn,
kənˌglɒməˈreɪʃn, -z
AM kənˌglɑməˈreɪʃən,
-z
Congo
BR ˈkɒŋgəʊ
AM ˈkɑŋgoʊ
Congolese
BR ˌkɒŋgəˈliːz
AM ˌkɑŋgəˈliz
congou
BR ˈkɒŋguː, ˈkɒŋgəʊ
AM ˈkɑŋgoʊ, ˈkɑŋgu
congrats
BR kənˈgrats,
kəŋˈgrats
AM kənˈgræts
congratulant
BR kənˈgratʃʊlənt,
kənˈgratʃʊlṇt,
kəŋˈgratʃʊlənt,
kəŋˈgratʃʊlṇt,
kənˈgratjʊlənt,
kənˈgratjʊlṇt,
kəŋˈgratjʊlənt,
kəŋˈgratjʊlṇt, -s
AM kənˈgrætʃələnt, -s
congratulate
BR kənˈgratʃʊleɪt,
kəŋˈgratʃʊleɪt,
kənˈgratjʊleɪt,
kəŋˈgratjʊleɪt, -s, -ɪŋ,
-ɪd
AM kənˈgrætʃəˌleɪt,
-ts, -dɪŋ, -dɪd
congratulation
BR kənˌgratʃʊˈleɪʃn,
kəŋˌgratʃʊˈleɪʃn,
kənˌgratjʊˈleɪʃn,
kəŋˌgratjʊˈleɪʃn, -z
AM kənˌgrætʃəˈleɪʃən,
-z
congratulative
BR kənˈgratʃʊlətɪv,
kəŋˈgratʃʊlətɪv,
kənˈgratjʊlətɪv,
kəŋˈgratjʊlətɪv
AM kənˈgrætʃələdɪv
congratulator
BR kənˈgratʃʊleɪtə(r),
kəŋˈgratʃʊleɪtə(r),
kənˈgratjʊleɪtə(r),
kəŋˈgratjʊleɪtə(r), -z
AM kənˈgrætʃəˌleɪdər,
-z
congratulatory
BR kənˌgratʃʊˈleɪt(ə)ri,
kəŋˌgratʃʊˈleɪt(ə)ri,
kənˌgratjʊˈleɪt(ə)ri,
kəŋˌgratjʊˈleɪt(ə)ri,
kənˈgratʃʊlət(ə)ri,
kəŋˈgratʃʊlət(ə)ri,
kənˈgratjʊlət(ə)ri,
kəŋˈgratʃʊlət(ə)ri
AM kənˈgrætʃələˌtɔri
congregant
BR ˈkɒŋgrɪg(ə)nt, -s
AM ˈkɑŋgrəgənt, -s

congregate
BR ˈkɒŋgrɪgeɪt, -s, -ɪŋ,
-ɪd
AM ˈkɑŋgrəˌgeɪ|t, -ts,
-dɪŋ, -dɪd
congregation
BR ˌkɒŋgrɪˈgeɪʃn, -z
AM ˌkɑŋgrəˈgeɪʃən, -z
congregational
BR ˌkɒŋgrɪˈgeɪʃṇ(ə)l,
ˌkɒŋgrɪˈgeɪʃən(ə)l
AM ˌkɑŋgrəˈgeɪʃ(ə)nəl
**Congregational-
ism**
BR ˌkɒŋgrɪˈgeɪʃnəl-
ɪz(ə)m,
ˌkɒŋgrɪˈgeɪʃṇ̩ɪz(ə)m,
ˌkɒŋgrɪˈgeɪʃ(ə)nəl-
ɪz(ə)m
AM ˌkɑŋgrəˈgeɪʃənl-
ˌɪzəm,
ˌkɑŋgrəˈgeɪʃnəˌlɪzəm
Congregationalist
BR ˌkɒŋgrɪˈgeɪʃnəlɪst,
ˌkɒŋgrɪˈgeɪʃṇ̩lɪst,
ˌkɒŋgrɪˈgeɪʃənlɪst,
ˌkɒŋgrɪˈgeɪʃ(ə)nəlɪst,
-s
AM ˌkɑŋgrəˈgeɪʃənlˌəst,
ˌkɑŋgrəˈgeɪʃnəˌləst,
-s
congress
BR ˈkɒŋgrɛs, ˈkɒŋgrɪs,
-ɪz
AM ˈkɑŋgrəs, -əz
congressional
BR kənˈgrɛʃṇ(ə)l,
kənˈgrɛʃən(ə)l,
kəŋˈgrɛʃṇ(ə)l,
kəŋˈgrɛʃən(ə)l
AM kənˈgrɛʃ(ə)nəl,
ˌkɑŋˈgrɛʃ(ə)nəl
congressman
BR ˈkɒŋgrɪsmən
AM ˈkɑŋgrəsmən
congressmen
BR ˈkɒŋgrɪsmən
AM ˈkɑŋgrəsmən
congresswoman
BR ˈkɒŋgrɪsˌwʊmən
AM ˈkɑŋgrəsˌwʊmən
congresswomen
BR ˈkɒŋgrɪsˌwɪmɪn
AM ˈkɑŋgrəsˌwɪmɪn
Congreve
BR ˈkɒŋgriːv
AM ˈkɑŋˌgriv
congruence
BR kənˈgruːəns, -ɪz
AM kənˈgruəns,
ˈkɑŋgrəwəns, -əz
congruency
BR kənˈgruːəns|i, -ɪz
AM kənˈgruənsi,
ˈkɑŋgrəwənsi, -z
congruent
BR ˈkɒŋgruənt

AM kənˈgruənt,
ˈkɑŋgrəwənt
congruential
BR ˌkɒŋgruˈɛnʃl
AM ˌkɑŋgruˈɛn(t)ʃəl
congruently
BR ˈkɒŋgruəntli
AM kənˈgruən(t)li,
ˈkɑŋgrəwən(t)li
congruity
BR kənˈgruːɪti,
kəŋˈgruːɪt|i,
(ˌ)kɒnˈgruːɪti,
(ˌ)kɒŋˈgruːɪti, -ɪz
AM kənˈgruədi,
kəŋˈgruədi, -z
congruous
BR ˈkɒŋgruəs
AM ˈkɑŋgrəwəs
congruously
BR ˈkɒŋgruəsli
AM ˈkɑŋgrəwəsli
congruousness
BR ˈkɒŋgruəsnəs
AM ˈkɑŋgrəwəsnəs
conic
BR ˈkɒnɪk, -s
AM ˈkɑnɪk, -s
conical
BR ˈkɒnɪkl
AM ˈkɑnəkəl
conically
BR ˈkɒnɪkli
AM ˈkɑnək(ə)li
conidia
BR kə(ʊ)ˈnɪdɪə(r)
AM kəˈnɪdiə
conidial
BR kə(ʊ)ˈnɪdɪəl
AM kəˈnɪdiəl
conidium
BR kə(ʊ)ˈnɪdɪəm
AM kəˈnɪdiəm
conifer
BR ˈkɒnɪfə(r),
ˈkəʊnɪfə(r), -z
AM ˈkɑnəfər, -z
coniferous
BR kəˈnɪf(ə)rəs
AM kəˈnɪf(ə)rəs
coniform
BR ˈkɒnɪfɔːm
AM ˈkoʊnəˌfɔ(ə)rm,
ˈkɑnəˌfɔ(ə)rm
coniine
BR ˈkəʊniːn
AM ˈkoʊniən,
ˈkoʊniˌin
Coningsby
BR ˈkɒnɪŋzbi
AM ˈkɑnɪŋzbi
Conisborough
BR ˈkɒnɪsb(ə)rə(r)
AM ˈkɑnəsˌbəroʊ
Conisbrough
BR ˈkɒnɪsbrə(r)
AM ˈkɑnəsbrə

Coniston
BR ˈkɒnɪst(ə)n
AM ˈkɑnəstən
conium
BR ˈkəʊnɪəm
AM ˈkoʊniəm
conjecturable
BR kənˈdʒɛktʃ(ə)rəbl
AM kənˈdʒɛk(t)ʃ(ə)rəbəl
conjecturably
BR kənˈdʒɛktʃ(ə)rəbli
AM kənˈdʒɛk(t)ʃ(ə)rəbli
conjectural
BR kənˈdʒɛktʃ(ə)rəl,
kənˈdʒɛktʃ(ə)r|
AM kənˈdʒɛk(t)ʃ(ə)rəl
conjecturally
BR kənˈdʒɛktʃ(ə)rəli,
kənˈdʒɛktʃ(ə)r|i
AM kənˈdʒɛk(t)ʃ(ə)rəli
conjecture
BR kənˈdʒɛktʃə(r),
-əz, -(ə)rɪŋ, -əd
AM kənˈdʒɛk(t)ʃər, -z,
-ɪŋ, -d
conjoin
BR kənˈdʒɔɪn,
(ˌ)kɒnˈdʒɔɪn, -z, -ɪŋ, -d
AM kənˈdʒɔɪn, -z, -ɪŋ, -d
conjoint
BR kənˈdʒɔɪnt,
(ˌ)kɒnˈdʒɔɪnt
AM kənˈdʒɔɪnt,
ˌkɑnˈdʒɔɪnt
conjointly
BR kənˈdʒɔɪntli,
(ˌ)kɒnˈdʒɔɪntli
AM kənˈdʒɔɪn(t)li,
ˌkɑnˈdʒɔɪn(t)li
conjugal
BR ˈkɒndʒʊgḷ
AM ˈkɑndʒəgəl
conjugality
BR ˌkɒndʒʊˈgalɪti
AM ˌkɑndʒəˈgælədi
conjugally
BR ˈkɒndʒʊgḷi,
ˈkɒndʒʊgəli
AM ˈkɑndʒəg(ə)li
conjugate¹
adjective
BR ˈkɒndʒʊgət
AM ˈkɑndʒəgət
conjugate²
verb
BR ˈkɒndʒʊgeɪt, -s, -ɪŋ,
-ɪd
AM ˈkɑndʒəˌgeɪ|t, -ts,
-dɪŋ, -dɪd
conjugately
BR ˈkɒndʒʊgətli
AM ˈkɑndʒəgətli
conjugation
BR ˌkɒndʒʊˈgeɪʃn, -z
AM ˌkɑndʒəˈgeɪʃən, -z
conjugational
BR ˌkɒndʒʊˈgeɪʃṇ(ə)l,
ˌkɒndʒʊˈgeɪʃən(ə)l

AM ˌkʌndʒəˈgeɪʃ(ə)nəl

conjunct[1]
adjective
BR kənˈdʒʌŋ(k)t
AM kənˈdʒəŋk(t)

conjunct[2]
noun
BR ˈkɒndʒʌŋ(k)t, -s
AM ˈkɑːndʒəŋ(k)t, -s

conjunction
BR kənˈdʒʌŋ(k)ʃn, -z
AM kənˈdʒəŋ(k)ʃən, -z

conjunctional
BR kənˈdʒʌŋ(k)ʃn̩(ə)l,
kənˈdʒʌŋ(k)ʃən(ə)l
AM kənˈdʒəŋ(k)ʃ(ə)nəl

conjunctionally
BR kənˈdʒʌŋ(k)ʃn̩əli,
kənˈdʒʌŋ(k)ʃn̩l̩i,
kənˈdʒʌŋ(k)ʃən̩l̩i,
kənˈdʒʌŋ(k)ʃ(ə)nəli
AM kənˈdʒəŋ(k)ʃ(ə)nəli

conjunctiva
BR ˌkɒndʒʌŋ(k)ˈtaɪ-
və(r), -z
AM ˌkɑːndʒəŋ(k)ˈtaɪvə,
-z

conjunctivae
BR ˌkɒndʒʌŋ(k)ˈtaɪviː
AM ˌkɑːndʒəŋ(k)ˈtaɪvi,
kənˈdʒəŋ(k)təˌvaɪ

conjunctival
BR ˌkɒndʒʌŋ(k)ˈtaɪvl
AM ˌkɑːndʒəŋ(k)ˈtaɪvəl

conjunctive
BR kənˈdʒʌŋ(k)tɪv
AM kənˈdʒəŋ(k)tɪv

conjunctively
BR kənˈdʒʌŋ(k)tɪvli
AM kənˈdʒəŋ(k)tɪvli

conjunctivitis
BR kənˌdʒʌŋ(k)tɪˈvʌɪtɪs
AM kənˌjəŋ(k)təˈvaɪdəs

conjuncture
BR kənˈdʒʌŋ(k)tʃə(r),
-z
AM kənˈdʒəŋ(kt)ʃər, -z

conjuration
BR ˌkɒndʒʊˈreɪʃn, -z
AM ˌkɑːndʒəˈeɪʃən, -z

conjure[1]
command, charge
BR kənˈdʒʊə(r), -z, -ɪŋ,
-d
AM kənˈdʒʊ(ə)r, -z, -ɪŋ,
-d

conjure[2]
invoke, use magic
BR ˈkʌn(d)ʒ|ə(r), -əz,
-(ə)rɪŋ, -əd
AM ˈkʌndʒər, -z, -ɪŋ, -d

conjurer
BR ˈkʌn(d)ʒ(ə)rə(r), -z
AM ˈkʌndʒərər, -z

conjuror
BR ˈkʌn(d)ʒ(ə)rə(r), -z
AM ˈkʌndʒərər, -z

conk
BR kɒŋ|k, -ks, -kɪŋ,
-(k)t
AM kɑŋ|k, kɔŋ|k, -ks,
-kɪŋ, -(k)t

conker
BR ˈkɒŋkə(r), -z
AM ˈkɑŋkər, ˈkɔŋkər, -z

Conley
BR ˈkɒnli
AM ˈkɑnli

Conlon
BR ˈkɒnlən
AM ˈkɑnlən

conman
BR ˈkɒnman
AM ˈkɑnˌmæn

conmen
BR ˈkɒnmɛn
AM ˈkɑnˌmɛn

con moto
BR ˌkɒn ˈməʊtəʊ
AM ˌkɑn ˈmoʊdoʊ

conn
BR kɒn, -z, -ɪŋ, -d
AM kɑn, -z, -ɪŋ, -d

Connacht
BR ˈkɒnɔːt, ˈkɒnət
AM ˈkɑnət

Connah
BR ˈkɒnə(r)
AM ˈkɑnə

connate
BR ˈkɒneɪt, kɒˈneɪt,
kəˈneɪt
AM ˈkɑneɪt, kəˈneɪt

connatural
BR kəˈnatʃ(ə)rəl,
kəˈnatʃ(ə)r|
AM kəˈnætʃ(ə)rəl

connaturally
BR kəˈnatʃ(ə)rəli,
kəˈnatʃ(ə)r|i
AM kəˈnætʃ(ə)rəli

Connaught
BR ˈkɒnɔːt, ˈkɒnət
AM ˈkɑnət

connect
BR kəˈnɛkt, -s, -ɪŋ, -ɪd
AM kəˈnɛk|t, -(t)s,
-tɪŋ, -təd

connectable
BR kəˈnɛktəbl
AM kəˈnɛktəbəl

connectedly
BR kəˈnɛktɪdli
AM kəˈnɛktədli

connectedness
BR kəˈnɛktɪdnɪs
AM kəˈnɛktədnəs

connecter
BR kəˈnɛktə(r), -z
AM kəˈnɛktər, -z

connectible
BR kəˈnɛktɪbl
AM kəˈnɛktəbəl

Connecticut
BR kəˈnɛtɪkət
AM kəˈnɛdəkət

connection
BR kəˈnɛkʃn, -z
AM kəˈnɛkʃən, -z

connectional
BR kəˈnɛkʃn̩(ə)l,
kəˈnɛkʃən(ə)l
AM kəˈnɛkʃ(ə)nəl

connectionism
BR kəˈnɛkʃn̩ɪz(ə)m,
kəˈnɛkʃənɪz(ə)m
AM kəˈnɛkʃəˌnɪzəm

connectionist
BR kəˈnɛkʃn̩ɪst,
kəˈnɛkʃənɪst, -s
AM kəˈnɛkʃənəst, -s

connective
BR kəˈnɛktɪv
AM kəˈnɛktɪv

connectivity
BR ˌkɒnɛkˈtɪvɪti,
kəˌnɛkˈtɪvɪti
AM kəˌnɛkˈtɪvɪdi,
ˌkɑnɛkˈtɪvɪdi

connector
BR kəˈnɛktə(r), -z
AM kəˈnɛktər, -z

Connell
BR ˈkɒnl, kəˈnɛl
AM ˈkɑnəl

Connemara
BR ˌkɒnɪˈmɑːrə(r)
AM ˌkɑnəˈmɑrə

Conner
BR ˈkɒnə(r)
AM ˈkɑn(ə)r

Connery
BR ˈkɒn(ə)ri
AM ˈkɑn(ə)ri

connexion
BR kəˈnɛkʃn, -z
AM kəˈnɛkʃən, -z

connexional
BR kəˈnɛkʃn̩(ə)l,
kəˈnɛkʃən(ə)l
AM kəˈnɛkʃ(ə)nəl

Connie
BR ˈkɒni
AM ˈkɑni

conniption
BR kəˈnɪpʃ(ə)n, -z
AM kəˈnɪpʃ(ə)n, -z

connivance
BR kəˈnʌɪvns
AM kəˈnaɪvəns

connive
BR kəˈnʌɪv, -z, -ɪŋ, -d
AM kəˈnaɪv, -z, -ɪŋ, -d

conniver
BR kəˈnʌɪvə(r), -z
AM kəˈnaɪvər, -z

connoisseur
BR ˌkɒnəˈsəː(r), -z
AM ˌkɑnəˈsər, -z

connoisseurship
BR ˌkɒnəˈsəːʃɪp
AM ˌkɑnəˈsərˌʃɪp

Connolly
BR ˈkɒnəli, ˈkɒnl̩i
AM ˈkɑn(ə)li

Connor
BR ˈkɒnə(r)
AM ˈkɑnər

Connors
BR ˈkɒnəz
AM ˈkɑnərz

connotation
BR ˌkɒnəˈteɪʃn, -z
AM ˌkɑnəˈteɪʃən, -z

connotative
BR ˈkɒnəteɪtɪv
AM ˈkɑnəˌteɪdɪv

connotatively
BR ˈkɒnəteɪtɪvli
AM ˈkɑnəˌteɪdɪvli

connote
BR kəˈnəʊt, -s, -ɪŋ, -ɪd
AM kəˈnoʊ|t, -ts, -dɪŋ,
-dəd

connubial
BR kəˈnjuːbɪəl
AM kəˈnubiəl

connubiality
BR kəˌnjuːbɪˈalɪti
AM kəˌnubiˈælədi

connubially
BR kəˈnjuːbɪəli
AM kəˈnubiəli

conodont
BR ˈkəʊnədɒnt, -s
AM ˈkoʊnəˌdɑnt,
ˈkɑnəˌdɑnt, -s

conoid
BR ˈkəʊnɔɪd, -z
AM ˈkoʊˌnɔɪd, -z

conoidal
BR kəˈ(ʊ)ˈnɔɪdl
AM kəˈnɔɪdəl

Conor
BR ˈkɒnə(r)
AM ˈkɑnər

conquer
BR ˈkɒŋk|ə(r), -əz,
-(ə)rɪŋ, -əd
AM ˈkɑŋkər, -z, -ɪŋ, -d

conquerable
BR ˈkɒŋk(ə)rəbl
AM ˈkɑŋk(ə)rəbəl

conqueror
BR ˈkɒŋk(ə)rə(r), -z
AM ˈkɑŋkərər, -z

conquest
BR ˈkɒŋkwɛst, -s
AM ˈkɑnˌkwɛst,
ˈkɑŋˌkwɛst, -s

conquistador
BR kɒnˈk(w)ɪstədɔː(r),
kɒŋˈk(w)ɪstədɔː(r),
kənˈk(w)ɪstədɔː(r),
kəŋˈk(w)ɪstədɔː(r), -z
AM ˌkɑnˈk(w)ɪstəˈdɔ(ə)r,
kənˈk(w)ɪstəˈdɔ(ə)r,

ˌkɒŋˈk(w)ɪstəˈdɔ(ə)r,
ˌkɒnˈk(w)ɪstəˈdɔ(ə)r,
kənˈk(w)ɪstəˈdɔ(ə)r,
ˌkɒŋˈk(w)ɪstəˈdɔ(ə)r,
-z

conquistadores
BR kɒnˌk(w)ɪstəˈdɔːr-
eɪz,
kɒŋˌk(w)ɪstəˈdɔːreɪz,
kənˌk(w)ɪstəˈdɔːreɪz,
kɒŋˌk(w)ɪstəˈdɔːreɪz
AM ˌkɑnˈk(w)ɪstəˈdɔr-
eɪz,
kənˈk(w)ɪstəˈdɔreɪz,
ˌkɑŋˈk(w)ɪstəˈdɔreɪz,
ˌkɑnˈk(w)ɪstəˈdɔreɪz,
kənˈk(w)ɪstəˈdɔreɪz,
ˌkɑŋˈk(w)ɪstəˈdɔreɪz

Conrad
BR ˈkɒnrad
AM ˈkɑnˌræd

Conran
BR ˈkɒnrən
AM ˈkɑnrən

con-rod
BR ˈkɒnrɒd, -z
AM ˈkɑnˌrɑd, -z

Conroy
BR ˈkɒnrɔɪ
AM ˈkɑnˌrɔɪ

consanguineous
BR ˌkɒnsəŋˈgwɪniəs
AM ˌkɑnsæŋˈgwɪniəs

consanguineously
BR ˌkɒnsəŋˈgwɪniəsli
AM ˌkɑnsæŋˈgwɪniəsli

consanguinity
BR ˌkɒnsəŋˈgwɪnɪti
AM ˌkɑnsæŋˈgwɪnɪdi

conscience
BR ˈkɒnʃns, -ɪz
AM ˈkɑnʃəns, -əz

conscienceless
BR ˈkɒnʃnsləs
AM ˈkɑnʃənsləs

conscientious
BR ˌkɒnʃɪˈɛnʃəs
AM ˌkɑntʃiˈɛn(t)ʃəs

conscientiously
BR ˌkɒnʃɪˈɛnʃəsli
AM ˌkɑntʃiˈɛn(t)ʃəsli

conscientiousness
BR ˌkɒnʃɪˈɛnʃəsnəs
AM ˌkɑntʃiˈɛn(t)ʃəsnəs

conscionable
BR ˈkɒnʃənəbl,
ˈkɒnʃn̩əbl
AM ˈkɑnʃ(ə)nəbəl

conscious
BR ˈkɒnʃəs
AM ˈkɑnʃəs

consciously
BR ˈkɒnʃəsli
AM ˈkɑnʃəsli

consciousness
BR ˈkɒnʃəsnəs
AM ˈkɑnʃəsnəs

conscribe
BR kənˈskrʌɪb, -z, -ɪŋ,
-d
AM kənˈskraɪb, -z, -ɪŋ,
-d

conscript[1]
noun
BR ˈkɒnskrɪpt, -s
AM ˈkɑnˌskrɪpt, -s

conscript[2]
verb
BR kənˈskrɪpt, -s, -ɪŋ,
-ɪd
AM kənˈskrɪp|t, -ts,
-dɪŋ, -dɪd

conscription
BR kənˈskrɪpʃn
AM kənˈskrɪpʃən

consecrate
BR ˈkɒnsɪkreɪt, -s, -ɪŋ,
-ɪd
AM ˈkɑnsəˌkreɪ|t, -ts,
-dɪŋ, -dɪd

consecration
BR ˌkɒnsɪˈkreɪʃn, -z
AM ˌkɑnsəˈkreɪʃən, -z

consecrator
BR ˈkɒnsɪkreɪtə(r), -z
AM ˈkɑnsəˌkreɪdər, -z

consecratory
BR ˌkɒnsɪˈkreɪt(ə)ri
AM ˈkɑnsəkrəˌtori

consecution
BR ˌkɒnsɪˈkjuːʃn, -z
AM ˌkɑnsəˈkjuʃən, -z

consecutive
BR kənˈsɛkjʊtɪv
AM kənˈsɛkjədɪv

consecutively
BR kənˈsɛkjʊtɪvli
AM kənˈsɛkjədɪvli

consecutiveness
BR kənˈsɛkjʊtɪvnɪs
AM kənˈsɛkjədɪvnɪs

consensual
BR kənˈsɛnsjʊəl,
kənˈsɛnsj(ʊ)l,
kənˈsɛnʃʊəl,
kənˈsɛnʃ(ʊ)l,
(ˌ)kɒnˈsɛnsjʊəl,
(ˌ)kɒnˈsɛnsj(ʊ)l,
(ˌ)kɒnˈsɛnʃʊəl,
(ˌ)kɒnˈsɛnʃ(ʊ)l
AM kənˈsɛnʃ(əw)əl

consensually
BR kənˈsɛnsjʊəli,
kənˈsɛnsjʊli,
kənˈsɛnʃʊəli,
kənˈsɛnʃʊli,
(ˌ)kɒnˈsɛnsjʊəli,
(ˌ)kɒnˈsɛnsjʊli,
(ˌ)kɒnˈsɛnʃʊəli,
(ˌ)kɒnˈsɛnʃʊli,
(ˌ)kɒnˈsɛnʃli
AM kənˈsɛnʃ(əw)əli

consensus
BR kənˈsɛnsəs

AM kənˈsɛnsəs

consent
BR kənˈsɛnt, -s, -ɪŋ, -ɪd
AM kənˈsɛn|t, -ts, -(t)ɪŋ,
-(t)əd

consentaneous
BR ˌkɒns(ɛ)nˈteɪnɪəs
AM ˌkɑnsənˈteɪnɪəs

consentient
BR kənˈsɛnʃ(ə)nt
AM kənˈsɛnʃənt

consequence
BR ˈkɒnsɪkw(ə)ns, -ɪz
AM ˈkɑnsəkwəns,
ˈkɑnsəˌkwɛns, -əz

consequent
BR ˈkɒnsɪkw(ə)nt
AM ˈkɑnsəkwənt

consequential
BR ˌkɒnsɪˈkwɛnʃl
AM ˌkɑnsəˈkwɛnʃəl

consequentialism
BR ˌkɒnsɪˈkwɛnʃl-
ɪz(ə)m,
ˌkɒnsɪˈkwɛnʃəlɪz(ə)m
AM ˌkɑnsəˈkwɛnʃəlɪzm

consequentialist
BR ˌkɒnsɪˈkwɛnʃlɪst,
ˌkɒnsɪˈkwɛnʃəlɪst, -s
AM ˌkɑnsəˈkwɛnʃələst,
-s

consequentiality
BR ˌkɒnsɪˌkwɛnʃɪˈalɪti
AM ˌkɑnsəˌkwɛnʃiˈæl-
ədi

consequentially
BR ˌkɒnsɪˈkwɛnʃli,
ˌkɒnsɪˈkwɛnʃəli
AM ˌkɑnsəˈkwɛnʃəli

consequently
BR ˈkɒnsɪkw(ə)ntli
AM ˈkɑnsəkwən(t)li

conservancy
BR kənˈsəːvns|i, -ɪz
AM kənˈsərvənsi, -z

conservation
BR ˌkɒnsəˈveɪʃn
AM ˌkɑnsərˈveɪʃən

conservational
BR ˌkɒnsəˈveɪʃn(ə)l,
ˌkɒnsəˈveɪʃən(ə)l
AM ˌkɑnsərˈveɪʃ(ə)nəl

conservationist
BR ˌkɒnsəˈveɪʃnɪst,
ˌkɒnsəˈveɪʃənɪst, -s
AM ˌkɑnsərˈveɪʃənəst,
-s

conservatism
BR kənˈsəːvətɪz(ə)m
AM kənˈsərvədɪzəm,
kənˈsərvəˌtɪzəm

conservative
BR kənˈsəːvətɪv, -z
AM kənˈsərvədɪv, -z

conservatively
BR kənˈsəːvətɪvli
AM kənˈsərvədɪvli

conservativeness
BR kənˈsəːvətɪvnɪs
AM kənˈsərvədɪvnɪs

conservatoire
BR kənˈsəːvətwɑː(r),
-z
AM kənsərvəˈtwɑr, -z

conservator
BR kənˈsəːvətə(r),
ˈkɒnsəveɪtə(r), -z
AM kənˈsərvədər, -z

conservatoria
BR kənˌsəːvəˈtɔːrɪə(r)
AM kənˌsərvəˈtɔriə

conservatorium
BR kənˌsəːvəˈtɔːrɪəm,
-z
AM kənˌsərvəˈtɔriəm,
-z

conservatory
BR kənˈsəːvət(ə)r|i, -ɪz
AM kənˈsərvəˌtɔri, -ɪz

conserve[1]
noun
BR ˈkɒnsəːv, kənˈsəːv,
-z
AM ˈkɑnsərv, kənˈsərv,
-z

conserve[2]
verb
BR kənˈsəːv, -z, -ɪŋ, -d
AM kənˈsərv, -z, -ɪŋ, -d

consessional
BR kənˈsɛʃn(ə)l,
kənˈsɛʃən(ə)l
AM kənˈsɛʃ(ə)nəl

Consett
BR ˈkɒnsɪt, ˈkɒnsɛt
AM ˈkɑnˌsɛt

consider
BR kənˈsɪd|ə(r), -əz,
-(ə)rɪŋ, -əd
AM kənˈsɪdər, -z, -ɪŋ, -d

considerable
BR kənˈsɪd(ə)rəbl
AM kənˈsɪdərəbəl

considerably
BR kənˈsɪd(ə)rəbli
AM kənˈsɪdər(ə)bli

considerate
BR kənˈsɪd(ə)rət
AM kənˈsɪdərət

considerately
BR kənˈsɪd(ə)rətli
AM kənˈsɪdərətli

consideration
BR kənˌsɪdəˈreɪʃn, -z
AM kənˌsɪdərˈeɪʃən, -z

Considine
BR ˈkɒnsɪdʌɪn
AM ˈkɑnsəˌdaɪn

consign
BR kənˈsaɪn, -z, -ɪŋ, -d
AM kənˈsaɪn, -z, -ɪŋ, -d

consignee
BR ˌkɒnsʌɪˈniː, -z
AM ˌkɑnsaɪˈni, -z

consignment
BR kən'sʌɪm(ə)nt, -s
AM kən'saɪnmənt, -s

consignor
BR kən'sʌɪnə(r),
ˌkɒnsʌɪ'nɔː(r),
kən,sʌɪ'nɔː(r), -z
AM kən'saɪnər, -z

consilience
BR kən'sɪlɪəns
AM kən'sɪlɪəns

consist
BR kən'sɪst, -s, -ɪŋ, -ɪd
AM kən'sɪs|t, -ts, -dɪŋ, -dɪd

consistence
BR kən'sɪst(ə)ns
AM kən'sɪstns

consistency
BR kən'sɪst(ə)ns|i, -ɪz
AM kən'sɪstnsi, -z

consistent
BR kən'sɪst(ə)nt
AM kən'sɪstənt

consistently
BR kən'sɪst(ə)ntli
AM kən'sɪstən(t)li

consistorial
BR ˌkɒnsɪ'stɔːrɪəl
AM ˌkɒnsə'stɔrɪəl

consistory
BR kən'sɪst(ə)r|i, -ɪz
AM kən'sɪstəri, -z

consociate
BR kɒn'səʊʃɪeɪt,
kɒn'səʊsɪeɪt, -s, -ɪŋ, -ɪd
AM ˌkɒn'səʊʃɪeɪ|t, -ts, -dɪŋ, -dɪd

consociation
BR kən,səʊʃɪ'eɪʃn, kən,səʊsɪ'eɪʃn, -z
AM ˌkɒn,səʊʃi'eɪʃən, -z

consolable
BR kən'səʊləbl
AM kən'səʊləbəl

consolation
BR ˌkɒnsə'leɪʃn, -z
AM ˌkɒnsə'leɪʃən, -z

consolatory
BR kən'sɒlət(ə)ri, kən'səʊlət(ə)ri
AM kən'səʊlə,tɔri

console¹
noun
BR 'kɒnsəʊl, -z
AM 'kɒn,səʊl, -z

console²
verb
BR kən'səʊl, -z, -ɪŋ, -d
AM kən'səʊl, -z, -ɪŋ, -d

consoler
BR kən'səʊlə(r), -z
AM kən'səʊlər, -z

consolidate
BR kən'sɒlɪdeɪt, -s, -ɪŋ, -ɪd

AM kən'sɒlədeɪ|t, -ts, -dɪŋ, -dɪd

consolidation
BR kən,sɒlɪ'deɪʃn, -z
AM kən,sɒlə'deɪʃən, -z

consolidator
BR kən'sɒlɪdeɪtə(r), -z
AM kən'sɒlə,deɪdər, -z

consolidatory
BR kən,sɒlɪ'deɪt(ə)ri
AM kən'sɒlədə,tɔri

consolingly
BR kən'səʊlɪŋli
AM kən'səʊlɪŋli

consols
BR 'kɒns(ɒ)lz, kən'sɒlz
AM 'kɒnsəlz, kən'sɑlz

consommé
BR kɒn'sɒmeɪ, kən'sɒmeɪ, 'kɒnsəmeɪ, -z
AM ˌkɒnsə'meɪ, 'kɒnsə,meɪ, -z

consonance
BR 'kɒnsənəns, 'kɒnsn̩əns
AM 'kɒnsənəns

consonant
BR 'kɒnsənənt, 'kɒnsn̩ənt, -s
AM 'kɒnsənənt, -s

consonantal
BR ˌkɒnsə'nantl
AM ˌkɒnsə'nɑn(t)l

consonantly
BR ˌkɒnsə'nantli, ˌkɒnsə'nantəli
AM ˌkɒnsə'nɑn(t)əli, 'kɒnsənən(t)li

con sordino
BR ˌkɒn sɔː'diːnəʊ, + 'sɔːdɪnəʊ
AM ˌkɑn ˌsɔr'dinoʊ

consort¹
noun
BR 'kɒnsɔːt, -s
AM 'kɒnsɔ(ə)rt, -s

consort²
verb
BR kən'sɔːt, -s, -ɪŋ, -ɪd
AM kən'sɔ(ə)rt, -ts, -sɔrdɪŋ, -sɔrdɪd

consortia
BR kən'sɔːtɪə(r), kən'sɔː'ʃə(r)
AM kən'sɔrdiə, kən'sɔrʃ(i)ə

consortium
BR kən'sɔːtɪəm, kən'sɔːʃɪəm, -z
AM kən'sɔrdiəm, kən'sɔrʃ(i)əm, -z

conspecific
BR ˌkɒnspɪ'sɪfɪk
AM ˌkɒnspə'sɪfɪk

conspectus
BR kən'spɛktəs, -ɪz
AM kən'spɛktəs, -əz

conspicuous
BR kən'spɪʃəs
AM kən'spɪkjəwəs

conspicuously
BR kən'spɪʃəsli
AM kən'spɪkjəwəsli

conspicuousness
BR kən'spɪkjʊəsnəs
AM kən'spɪkjəwəsnəs

conspiracy
BR kən'spɪrəs|i, -ɪz
AM kən'spɪrɪsi, -z

conspirator
BR kən'spɪrətə(r), -z
AM kən'spɪrədər, -z

conspiratorial
BR kən,spɪrə'tɔːrɪəl, ˌkɒnspɪrə'tɔːrɪəl
AM kən,spɪrə'tɔrɪəl

conspiratorially
BR kən,spɪrə'tɔːrɪəli, ˌkɒnspɪrə'tɔːrɪəli
AM kən,spɪrə'tɔrɪəli

conspire
BR kən'spʌɪə(r), -z, -ɪŋ, -d
AM kən'spaɪ(ə)r, -z, -ɪŋ, -d

constable¹
BR 'kʌnstəbl, 'kɒnstəbl, -z
AM 'kɑnstəbl, -z

constable²
BR 'kʌnstəbl, 'kɒnstəbl, -z
AM 'kɑnstəbəl, -z

constabulary
BR kən'stabjələr|i, -ɪz
AM kən'stæbjə,lɛri, -z

Constance
BR 'kɒnst(ə)ns
AM 'kɑnstəns

constancy
BR 'kɒnst(ə)nsi
AM 'kɑnstnsi

constant
BR 'kɒnst(ə)nt, -s
AM 'kɑnstənt, -s

constantan
BR 'kɒnst(ə)ntan
AM 'kɑnstəntən

Constantine
BR 'kɒnst(ə)ntʌɪn
AM 'kɑnstən,tin

Constantinople
BR ˌkɒnstantɪ'nəʊpl
AM ˌkɑn,stæn(t)ə'noʊpl

constantly
BR 'kɒnst(ə)ntli
AM 'kɑnstən(t)li

Constanza
BR kən'stanzə(r), kɒn'stanzə(r)
AM kən'stænzə

constatation
BR ˌkɒnstə'teɪʃn, -z
AM ˌkɑnstə'teɪʃən, -z

constellate
BR 'kɒnstɪleɪt, -s, -ɪŋ, -ɪd
AM 'kɑnstəleɪ|t, -ts, -dɪŋ, -dɪd

constellation
BR ˌkɒnstɪ'leɪʃn, -z
AM ˌkɑnstə'leɪʃən, -z

consternate
BR 'kɒnstəneɪt, -s, -ɪŋ, -ɪd
AM 'kɑnstər,neɪ|t, -ts, -dɪŋ, -dɪd

consternation
BR ˌkɒnstə'neɪʃn
AM ˌkɑnstər'neɪʃən

constipate
BR 'kɒnstɪpeɪt, -s, -ɪŋ, -ɪd
AM 'kɑnstə,peɪ|t, -ts, -dɪŋ, -dɪd

constipation
BR ˌkɒnstɪ'peɪʃn
AM ˌkɑnstə'peɪʃən

constituency
BR kən'stɪtjʊəns|i, kən'stɪtʃʊəns|i, -ɪz
AM kən'stɪtʃʊənsi, -ɪz

constituent
BR kən'stɪtjʊənt, kən'stɪtʃʊənt, -s
AM kən'stɪtʃʊənt, -s

constitute
BR 'kɒnstɪtjuːt, 'kɒnstɪtʃuːt, -s, -ɪŋ, -ɪd
AM 'kɑnstə,t(j)u|t, -ts, -dɪŋ, -dɪd

constitution
BR ˌkɒnstɪ'tju:ʃn, ˌkɒnstɪ'tʃu:ʃn, -z
AM ˌkɑnstə't(j)uʃən, -z

constitutional
BR ˌkɒnstɪ'tju:ʃn(ə)l, ˌkɒnstɪ'tju:ʃən(ə)l, ˌkɒnstɪ'tʃu:ʃn(ə)l, ˌkɒnstɪ'tʃu:ʃən(ə)l
AM ˌkɑnstə't(j)uʃ(ə)nəl

constitutionalise
BR ˌkɒnstɪ'tju:ʃnəlʌɪz, ˌkɒnstɪ'tju:ʃn̩lʌɪz, ˌkɒnstɪ'tju:ʃənlʌɪz, ˌkɒnstɪ'tju:ʃ(ə)nəlʌɪz, ˌkɒnstɪ'tʃu:ʃnəlʌɪz, ˌkɒnstɪ'tʃu:ʃn̩lʌɪz, ˌkɒnstɪ'tʃu:ʃ(ə)nəlʌɪz, -ɪz, -ɪŋ, -d
AM ˌkɑnstə't(j)uʃnə,laɪz, ˌkɑnstə't(j)uʃənlaɪz, -ɪz, -ɪŋ, -d

constitutionalism
BR ˌkɒnstɪ'tju:ʃnəl-ɪz(ə)m, ˌkɒnstɪ'tju:ʃn̩lɪz(ə)m, ˌkɒnstɪ'tju:ʃənlɪz(ə)m, ˌkɒnstɪ'tʃu:ʃ(ə)nəlɪz(ə)m, ˌkɒnstɪ'tʃu:ʃnəlɪz(ə)m,

ˌkɒnstɪˈtʃuːʃn̩l
ɪz(ə)m,
ˌkɒnstɪˈtʃuːʃənl
ɪz(ə)m,
ˌkɒnstɪˈtʃuːʃ(ə)nəl-
ɪz(ə)m
AM ˌkænstəˈt(j)uʃnə-
ˌlɪzm,
ˌkænstəˈt(j)uʃən̩ɪzm

constitutionalist
BR ˌkɒnstɪˈtjuːʃn̩lɪst,
ˌkɒnstɪˈtjuːʃn̩lɪst,
ˌkɒnstɪˈtjuːʃənl̩ɪst,
ˌkɒnstɪˈtʃuː(ə)nəlɪst,
ˌkɒnstɪˈtʃuːʃn̩ɪst,
ˌkɒnstɪˈtʃuːʃən̩lɪst,
ˌkɒnstɪˈtʃuːʃ(ə)nəlɪst,
-s
AM ˌkænstəˈt(j)uʃnəl-
əst,
ˌkænstəˈt(j)uʃən̩ləst,
-s

constitutionality
BR ˌkɒnstɪˌtjuːʃəˈnalɪti,
ˌkɒnstɪˌtʃuːʃəˈnalɪti
AM ˌkænstəˌt(j)uʃə-
ˈnælədi

constitutionalize
BR ˌkɒnstɪˈtjuːʃn̩əlʌɪz,
ˌkɒnstɪˈtjuːʃn̩lʌɪz,
ˌkɒnstɪˈtjuːʃənl̩ʌɪz,
ˌkɒnstɪˈtʃuː(ə)nəlʌɪz,
ˌkɒnstɪˈtʃuːʃn̩lʌɪz,
ˌkɒnstɪˈtʃuːʃən̩lʌɪz,
ˌkɒnstɪˈtʃuːʃ(ə)nəlʌɪz,
-ɪz, -ɪŋ, -d
AM ˌkænstəˈt(j)uʃnə-
ˌlaɪz,
ˌkænstəˈt(j)uʃən̩laɪz,
-ɪz, -ɪŋ, -d

constitutionally
BR ˌkɒnstɪˈtjuːʃn̩əli,
ˌkɒnstɪˈtjuːʃn̩li,
ˌkɒnstɪˈtjuːʃən̩li,
ˌkɒnstɪˈtjuːʃ(ə)nəli,
ˌkɒnstɪˈtʃuːʃn̩əli,
ˌkɒnstɪˈtʃuːʃn̩li,
ˌkɒnstɪˈtʃuːʃən̩li,
ˌkɒnstɪˈtʃuːʃ(ə)nəli
AM ˌkænstəˈt(j)uʃ(ə)n-
əli

constitutive
BR kənˈstɪtjʊtɪv,
kənˈstɪtʃʊtɪv,
ˈkɒnstɪtjuːtɪv,
ˈkɒnstɪtʃuːtɪv
AM ˈkænstəˌt(j)udɪv

constitutively
BR kənˈstɪtjʊtɪvli,
kənˈstɪtʃʊtɪvli,
ˈkɒnstɪtjuːtɪvli,
ˈkɒnstɪtʃuːtɪvli
AM ˈkænstəˌt(j)udɪvli

constitutor
BR ˈkɒnstɪtjuːtə(r),
ˈkɒnstɪtʃuːtə(r)
AM ˈkænstəˌt(j)udər

constrain
BR kənˈstreɪn, -z, -ɪŋ, -d
AM kənˈstreɪn, -z, -ɪŋ,
-d

constrainedly
BR kənˈstreɪnɪdli
AM kənˈstreɪnɪdli

constraint
BR kənˈstreɪnt, -s
AM kənˈstreɪnt, -s

constrict
BR kənˈstrɪkt, -s, -ɪŋ,
-ɪd
AM kənˈstrɪk|(t), -(t)s,
-tɪŋ, -tɪd

constriction
BR kənˈstrɪkʃn̩, -z
AM kənˈstrɪkʃən, -z

constrictive
BR kənˈstrɪktɪv
AM kənˈstrɪktɪv

constrictor
BR kənˈstrɪktə(r), -z
AM kənˈstrɪktər, -z

construable
BR kənˈstruːəbl
AM kənˈstruəbəl

construal
BR kənˈstruːəl
AM kənˈstruəl

construct[1]
noun
BR ˈkɒnstrʌkt, -s
AM ˈkɑnˌstrək(t), -s

construct[2]
BR kənˈstrʌkt, -s, -ɪŋ,
-ɪd
AM kənˈstrək|(t), -(t)s,
-tɪŋ, -tɪd

construction
BR kənˈstrʌkʃn̩, -z
AM kənˈstrəkʃən, -z

constructional
BR kənˈstrʌkʃn̩(ə)l,
kənˈstrʌkʃən(ə)l
AM kənˈstrəkʃ(ə)nəl

constructionally
BR kənˈstrʌkʃn̩əli,
kənˈstrʌkʃn̩li,
kənˈstrʌkʃən̩li,
kənˈstrʌkʃ(ə)nəli
AM kənˈstrəkʃ(ə)nəli

constructionism
BR kənˈstrʌʃnɪz(ə)m,
kənˈstrʌkʃənɪz(ə)m
AM kənˈstrəkʃənɪzm

constructionist
BR kənˈstrʌʃnɪst,
kənˈstrʌkʃənɪst, -s
AM kənˈstrəkʃənəst, -s

constructive
BR kənˈstrʌtɪv
AM kənˈstrəktɪv

constructively
BR kənˈstrʌktɪvli
AM kənˈstrəktɪvli

constructiveness
BR kənˈstrʌtɪvnɪs

AM kənˈstrəktɪvnɪs

constructivism
BR kənˈstrʌktɪvɪz(ə)m
AM kənˈstrəktɪvɪzm

constructivist
BR kənˈstrʌktɪvɪst, -s
AM kənˈstrəktɪvɪst, -s

constructor
BR kənˈstrʌtə(r), -z
AM kənˈstrəktər, -z

construe
BR kənˈstruː, -z, -ɪŋ, -d
AM kənˈstru, -z, -ɪŋ, -d

consubstantial
BR ˌkɒnsəbˈstanʃl,
ˌkɒnsəbˈstɑːnʃl
AM ˌkænsəbˈstænʃl

consubstantiality
BR ˌkɒnsəbˌstanʃɪˈalɪti,
ˌkɒnsəbˌstɑːnʃɪˈalɪti
AM ˌkænsəbˌstænʃiˈæl-
ədi

consubstantiate
BR ˌkɒnsəbˈstansɪeɪt,
ˌkɒnsəbˈstɑːnʃɪeɪt,
ˌkɒnsəbˈstɑːnsɪeɪt, -s,
-ɪŋ, -ɪd
AM ˌkænsəbˈstænʃiˌeɪ|t,
-ts, -dɪŋ, -dɪd

consubstantiation
BR ˌkɒnsəbˌstanʃɪˈeɪʃn,
ˌkɒnsəbˌstansɪˈeɪʃn,
ˌkɒnsəbˌstɑːnʃɪˈeɪʃn,
ˌkɒnsəbˌstɑːnsɪˈeɪʃn
AM ˌkænsəbˌstænʃiˈeɪ-
ʃən

consuetude
BR ˈkɒnswɪtjuːd,
ˈkɒnswɪtʃuːd
AM ˈkænswəˌt(j)ud

consuetudinary
BR ˌkɒnswɪˈtjuːdɪn(ə)ri,
ˌkɒnswɪˈtʃuːdɪn(ə)ri
AM ˌkænswəˈt(j)udən-
ˌɛri

consul
BR ˈkɒnsl, -z
AM ˈkænsəl, -z

consular
BR ˈkɒnsjʊlə(r)
AM ˈkæns(j)ələr

consulate
BR ˈkɒnsjʊlət, -s
AM ˈkænsələt, -s

consulship
BR ˈkɒnslʃɪp, -s
AM ˈkænsəlʃɪp, -s

consult
BR kənˈsʌlt, -s, -ɪŋ, -ɪd
AM kənˈsəl|t, -ts, -dɪŋ,
-dɪd

consultancy
BR kənˈsʌlt(ə)nsi
AM kənˈsəltnsi

consultant
BR kənˈsʌlt(ə)nt, -s
AM kənˈsəltnt, -s

consultation
BR ˌkɒnslˈteɪʃn,
ˌkɒnsʌlˈteɪʃn, -z
AM ˌkænsəlˈteɪʃən, -z

consultative
BR kənˈsʌltətɪv
AM kənˈsəltədɪv

consultee
BR ˌkɒnsʌlˈtiː, -z
AM ˌkʌn̩səlˈti, -z

consumable
BR kənˈsjuːməbl, -z
AM kənˈs(j)uməbəl, -z

consume
BR kənˈsjuːm, -z, -ɪŋ, -d
AM kənˈs(j)um, -z, -ɪŋ,
-d

consumer
BR kənˈsjuːmə(r), -z
AM kənˈs(j)umər, -z

consumerism
BR kənˈsjuːmərɪz(ə)m
AM kənˈs(j)umərˌɪzm

consumerist
BR kənˈsjuːmərɪst, -s
AM kənˈs(j)umərəst, -s

consumingly
BR kənˈsjuːmɪŋli
AM kənˈs(j)umɪŋli

consummate[1]
adjective
BR kənˈsʌmət
AM ˈkænsəmət,
kənˈsəmət

consummate[2]
verb
BR ˈkɒnsjʊmeɪt, -s, -ɪŋ,
-ɪd
AM ˈkænsəˌmeɪ|t, -ts,
-dɪŋ, -dɪd

consummately
BR kənˈsʌmətli
AM ˈkænsəmətli,
kənˈsəmətli

consummation
BR ˌkɒnsjʊˈmeɪʃn
AM ˌkænsəˈmeɪʃən

consummative
BR ˈkɒnsəmeɪtɪv,
ˈkɒnsjʊmeɪtɪv,
kənˈsʌmətɪv
AM ˈkænsəˌmeɪdɪv,
kənˈsəmədɪv

consummator
BR ˈkɒnsjʊmeɪtə(r), -z
AM ˈkænsəˌmeɪdər, -z

consumption
BR kənˈsʌm(p)ʃn
AM kənˈsəm(p)ʃən

consumptive
BR kənˈsʌm(p)tɪv
AM kənˈsəm(p)tɪv

consumptively
BR kənˈsʌm(p)tɪvli
AM kənˈsəm(p)tɪvli

Contac
BR ˈkɒntak
AM ˈkɑntæk

contact
BR 'kɒntakt, -s, -ɪŋ, -ɪd
AM 'kɑntæk|(t), -(t)s,
-tɪŋ, -tɪd
contactable
BR 'kɒntaktəbl,
kən'taktəbl
AM 'kɑntæktəbəl
Contadora
BR ,kɒntə'dɔːrə(r)
AM ,kɑn(t)ə'dɔrə
contagion
BR kən'teɪdʒ(ə)n, -z
AM kən'teɪdʒən, -z
contagious
BR kən'teɪdʒəs
AM kən'teɪdʒəs
contagiously
BR kən'teɪdʒəsli
AM kən'teɪdʒəsli
contagiousness
BR kən'teɪdʒəsnəs
AM kən'teɪdʒəsnəs
contain
BR kən'teɪn, -z, -ɪŋ, -d
AM kən'teɪn, -z, -ɪŋ, -d
containable
BR kən'teɪnəbl
AM kən'teɪnəbəl
container
BR kən'teɪnə(r), -z
AM kən'teɪnər, -z
containerisation
BR kən,teɪnərʌɪ'zeɪʃn
AM kən,teɪnərə'zeɪʃən,
kən,teɪnə,raɪ'zeɪʃən
containerise
BR kən'teɪnərʌɪz, -ɪz,
-ɪŋ, -d
AM kən,teɪnə,raɪz, -ɪz,
-ɪŋ, -d
containerization
BR kən,teɪnərʌɪ'zeɪʃn
AM kən,teɪnərə'zeɪʃən,
kən,teɪnə,raɪ'zeɪʃən
containerize
BR kən'teɪnərʌɪz, -ɪz,
-ɪŋ, -d
AM kən'teɪnə,raɪz, -ɪz,
-ɪŋ, -d
containment
BR kən'teɪnm(ə)nt
AM kən'teɪnmənt
contaminant
BR kən'tamɪnənt, -s
AM kən'tæmənənt, -s
contaminate
BR kən'tamɪneɪt, -s,
-ɪŋ, -ɪd
AM kən'tæməneɪ|t, -ts,
-dɪŋ, -dɪd
contamination
BR kən,tamɪ'neɪʃn
AM kən,tæmə'neɪʃən
contaminator
BR kən'tamɪneɪtə(r),
-z

AM kən'tæmə,neɪdər,
-z
contango
BR kən'taŋgəʊ,
kɒn'taŋgəʊ, -z
AM kən'tæŋgoʊ, -z
conte
BR kɒnt, -s
AM kɔnt, -s
Conteh
BR 'kɒnteɪ, 'kɒnti
AM 'kɑnteɪ
contemn
BR kən'tɛm, -z, -ɪŋ, -d
AM kən'tɛm, -z, -ɪŋ, -d
contemner
BR kən'tɛmə(r), -z
AM kən'tɛmər, -z
contemplate
BR 'kɒntəmpleɪt,
'kɒntɛmpleɪt, -s, -ɪŋ,
-ɪd
AM 'kɑn(t)əm,pleɪ|t,
-ts, -dɪŋ, -dɪd
contemplation
BR ,kɒntəm'pleɪʃn,
,kɒntɛm'pleɪʃn
AM ,kɑn(t)əm'pleɪʃən
contemplative
BR kən'tɛmplətɪv, -z
AM kən'tɛmplədɪv,
'kɑn(t)əm,pleɪdɪv, -z
contemplatively
BR kən'tɛmplətɪvli
AM kən'tɛmplədɪvli
contemplator
BR 'kɒntəmpleɪtə(r),
'kɒntɛmpleɪtə(r), -z
AM 'kɑn(t)əm,pleɪdər,
-z
contemporaneity
BR kən,tɛmp(ə)rə'niːɪti,
kən,tɛmp(ə)rə'neɪɪti
AM kən,tɛmpərə'niːɪdi,
kən,tɛmpərə'neɪɪdi
contemporaneous
BR kən,tɛmpə'reɪnɪəs
AM kən,tɛmpə'reɪnɪəs
contemporaneous-ly
BR kən,tɛmpə'reɪnɪəsli
AM kən,tɛmpə'reɪnɪəsli
contemporaneous-ness
BR kən,tɛmpə'reɪnɪəs-nəs
AM kən,tɛmpə'reɪnɪəs-nəs
contemporarily
BR kən'tɛmp(ə)r(ər)ɪli
AM kən,tɛmpə'rɛrəli
contemporariness
BR kən'tɛmp(ə)r(ər)ɪ-nɪs
AM kən'tɛmpə,rɛrɪnɪs
contemporary
BR kən'tɛmp(ə)r(ər)i
AM kən'tɛmpə,rɛri

contemporise
BR kən'tɛmp(ə)rʌɪz,
-ɪz, -ɪŋ, -d
AM kən'tɛmpə,raɪz, -ɪz,
-ɪŋ, -d
contemporize
BR kən'tɛmp(ə)rʌɪz,
-ɪz, -ɪŋ, -d
AM kən'tɛmpə,raɪz, -ɪz,
-ɪŋ, -d
contempt
BR kən'tɛm(p)t, -s
AM kən'tɛm(p)t, -s
contemptibility
BR kən,tɛm(p)tɪ'bɪlɪti
AM kən,tɛm(p)tə'bɪlɪdi
contemptible
BR kən'tɛm(p)tɪbl
AM kən'tɛm(p)təbəl
contemptibly
BR kən'tɛm(p)tɪbli
AM kən'tɛm(p)təbli
contemptuous
BR kən'tɛm(p)tjʊəs,
kən'tɛm(p)tʃʊəs
AM kən'tɛm(pt)ʃ(ʊ)əs
contemptuously
BR kən'tɛm(p)tjʊəsli,
kən'tɛm(p)tʃʊəsli
AM kən'tɛm(pt)ʃ(ʊ)əsli
contemptuous-ness
BR kən'tɛm(p)tjʊəsnəs,
kən'tɛm(p)tʃʊəsnəs
AM kən'tɛm(pt)ʃ(ʊ)əs-nəs
contend
BR kən'tɛnd, -z, -ɪŋ, -ɪd
AM kən'tɛnd, -z, -ɪŋ, -ɪd
contender
BR kən'tɛndə(r), -z
AM kən'tɛndər, -z
content¹
adjective
BR kən'tɛnt
AM kən'tɛnt
content²
noun
BR 'kɒntɛnt, -s
AM 'kɑntɛnt, -s
contentedly
BR kən'tɛntɪdli
AM kən'ten(t)ədli
contentedness
BR kən'tɛntɪdnɪs
AM kən'ten(t)ədnəs
contention
BR kən'tɛnʃn, -z
AM kən'tɛnʃən, -z
contentious
BR kən'tɛnʃəs
AM kən'tɛnʃəs
contentiously
BR kən'tɛnʃəsli
AM kən'tɛnʃəsli
contentiousness
BR kən'tɛnʃəsnəs
AM kən'tɛnʃəsnəs

contentment
BR kən'tɛntm(ə)nt
AM kən'tɛntmənt
conterminous
BR kɒn'təːmɪnəs,
kən'təːmɪnəs
AM ,kɑn'tərmənəs
conterminously
BR kɒn'təːmɪnəsli,
kən'təːmɪnəsli
AM ,kɑn'tərmənəsli
contessa
BR kɒn'tɛsə(r), -z
AM kən'tɛsə, -z
contest¹
noun
BR 'kɒntɛst, -s
AM 'kɑn,tɛst, -s
contest²
verb
BR kən'tɛst, 'kɒntɛst,
-s, -ɪŋ, -ɪd
AM kən'tɛs|t, -ts, -dɪŋ,
-dɪd
contestable
BR kən'tɛstəbl,
'kɒntɛstəbl
AM kən'tɛstəbəl
contestant
BR kən'tɛst(ə)nt, -s
AM kən'tɛstənt, -s
contestation
BR ,kɒntɛ'steɪʃn
AM ,kɑn(t)ə'steɪʃən,
kɑn,tɛs'teɪʃən
contester
BR kən'tɛstə(r),
'kɒntɛstə(r), -z
AM kən'tɛstər, -z
context
BR 'kɒntɛkst, -s
AM 'kɑntɛkst, -s
contextual
BR kən'tɛkstʃʊəl,
kən'tɛkstʃ(ʊ)l,
kən'tɛkstjʊəl,
kən'tɛkstjʊl
AM kən'tɛks(t)ʃ(əw)əl
contextualisation
BR kən,tɛkstjʊəlʌɪ'zeɪʃn,
kən,tɛkstjʊlʌɪ'zeɪʃn,
kən,tɛkstʃʊəlʌɪ'zeɪʃn,
kən,tɛkstʃʊlʌɪ'zeɪʃn,
kən,tɛkstʃʌɪ'zeɪʃn
AM kən,tɛks(t)ʃ(əw)ələ-
'zeɪʃən,
kən,tɛks(t)ʃ(əw)ə,laɪ-
'zeɪʃən
contextualise
BR kən'tɛkstjʊəlʌɪz,
kən'tɛkstjʊlʌɪz,
kən'tɛkstʃʊəlʌɪz,
kən'tɛkstʃʊlʌɪz,
kən'tɛkstʃʌɪz, -ɪz, -ɪŋ,
-d
AM kən'tɛks(t)ʃ(əw)ə-
,laɪz, -ɪz, -ɪŋ, -d

contextualist
BR kən'tɛkstjʊəlɪst,
kən'tɛkstjəlɪst,
kən'tɛkstʃʊəlɪst,
kən'tɛkstʃəlɪst,
kən'tɛkstʃɪst
AM kən'tɛks(t)ʃ(əw)əl-əst

contextuality
BR kən͵tɛkstjʊ'alɪti,
kən͵tɛkstʃʊ'alɪti
AM kən͵tɛks(t)ʃ(əw)-'ælədi

contextualization
BR kən͵tɛkstjʊəlʌɪ-'zeɪʃn,
kən͵tɛkstjəlʌɪ'zeɪʃn,
kən͵tɛkstʃʊəlʌɪ'zeɪʃn,
kən͵tɛkstʃəlʌɪ'zeɪʃn,
kən͵tɛkstʃʌɪ'zeɪʃn
AM kən͵tɛks(t)ʃ(əw)ələ-'zeɪʃən,
kən͵tɛks(t)ʃ(əw)ə͵laɪ-'zeɪʃən

contextualize
BR kən'tɛkstjʊəlʌɪz,
kən'tɛkstjəlʌɪz,
kən'tɛkstʃʊəlʌɪz,
kən'tɛkstʃəlʌɪz,
kən'tɛkstʃʌɪz, -ɪz, -ɪŋ,
-d
AM kən'tɛks(t)ʃ(əw)ə-͵laɪz, -ɪz, -ɪŋ, -d

contextually
BR kən'tɛkstjʊəli,
kən'tɛkstjəli,
kən'tɛkstʃʊəli,
kən'tɛkstʃəli,
kən'tɛkstʃli
AM kən'tɛks(t)ʃ(əw)əli

Contiboard
BR 'kɒntɪbɔːd
AM 'kɑn(t)ə͵bɔ(ə)rd

contiguity
BR ͵kɒntɪ'gjuːti
AM ͵kɑn(t)ə'gjuədi

contiguous
BR kən'tɪgjʊəs
AM kən'tɪgjuəs

contiguously
BR kən'tɪgjʊəsli
AM kən'tɪgjuəsli

contiguousness
BR kən'tɪgjʊəsnəs
AM kən'tɪgjuəsnəs

continence
BR 'kɒntɪnəns
AM 'kɑnt(ə)nəns,
'kɑn(t)ənəns

continent
BR 'kɒntɪnənt, -s
AM 'kɑnt(ə)nənt, -s

continental
BR ͵kɒntɪ'nɛntl
AM ͵kɑntə'nɛn(t)əl

continentally
BR ͵kɒntɪ'nɛntʃli
AM ͵kɑn(t)ə'nɛn(t)əli

continently
BR 'kɒntɪnəntli
AM 'kɑnt(ə)nən(t)li,
'kɑn(t)ənən(t)li

contingency
BR kən'tɪn(d)ʒ(ə)ns|i,
-ɪz
AM kən'tɪndʒənsi, -ɪz

contingent
BR kən'tɪn(d)ʒ(ə)nt, -s
AM kən'tɪndʒənt, -s

contingently
BR kən'tɪn(d)ʒ(ə)ntli
AM kən'tɪndʒən(t)li

continua
BR kən'tɪnjʊə(r)
AM kən'tɪnjuə

continuable
BR kən'tɪnjʊəbl
AM kən'tɪnjuəbəl

continual
BR kən'tɪnjʊəl,
kən'tɪnj(ʊ)l
AM kən'tɪnj(ʊ)əl

continually
BR kən'tɪnjʊəli,
kən͵tɪnjəli
AM kən'tɪnj(ʊ)əli

continuance
BR kən'tɪnjʊəns
AM kən'tɪnj(ʊ)əns

continuant
BR kən'tɪnjʊənt, -s
AM kən'tɪnj(ʊ)ənt, -s

continuation
BR kən͵tɪnjʊ'eɪʃn, -z
AM kən͵tɪnjʊ'eɪʃən, -z

continuative
BR kən'tɪnjʊətɪv
AM kən'tɪnjʊədɪv

continuator
BR kən'tɪnjʊeɪtə(r), -z
AM kən'tɪnjʊ͵eɪdər, -z

continue
BR kən'tɪnjuː, -z, -ɪŋ, -d
AM kən'tɪnju, -z, -ɪŋ, -d

continuer
BR kən'tɪnjʊə(r), -z
AM kən'tɪnjʊər, -z

continuity
BR ͵kɒntɪ'njuːti
AM ͵kɑn(t)ə'n(j)uədi,
͵kɑnt'n(j)uədi

continuo
BR kən'tɪnjʊəʊ, -z
AM kən'tɪnjuoʊ, -z

continuous
BR kən'tɪnjʊəs
AM kən'tɪnjuəs

continuously
BR kən'tɪnjʊəsli
AM kən'tɪnjuəsli

continuousness
BR kən'tɪnjʊəsnəs
AM kən'tɪnjuəsnəs

continuum
BR kən'tɪnjʊəm, -z

contort
BR kən'tɔːt, -s, -ɪŋ, -ɪd
AM kən'tɔ(ə)rt, -ts,
-'tɔrdɪŋ, -'tɔrdɪd

contortion
BR kən'tɔːʃn, -z
AM kən'tɔrʃən, -z

contortionist
BR kən'tɔːʃnɪst,
kən'tɔːʃənɪst, -s
AM kən'tɔrʃənəst, -s

contour
BR 'kɒntʊə(r),
'kɒntɔː(r), -z
AM 'kɑntʊ(ə)r, -z

contra
BR 'kɒntrə(r), -z
AM 'kɑntrə, -z

contraband
BR 'kɒntrəband
AM 'kɑntrə͵bænd

contrabandist
BR 'kɒntrəbandɪst, -s
AM 'kɑntrə͵bændəst,
-s

contrabass
BR ͵kɒntrə'beɪs,
'kɒntrəbeɪs
AM ͵kɑntrə'beɪs

contraception
BR ͵kɒntrə'sɛpʃn
AM ͵kɑntrə'sɛpʃən

contraceptive
BR ͵kɒntrə'sɛptɪv, -z
AM ͵kɑntrə'sɛptɪv, -z

contract¹
noun
BR 'kɒntrakt, -s
AM 'kɑntrækt, -s

contract²
verb, become smaller
BR kən'trakt, -s, -ɪŋ, -ɪd
AM kən'træk|(t), -(t)s,
-tɪŋ, -tɪd

contract³
verb, make an agreement
BR 'kɒntrakt,
kən'trakt, -s, -ɪŋ, -ɪd
AM 'kɑntræk|(t),
kən'træk|(t), -(t)s,
-tɪŋ, -tɪd

contractable
BR kən'traktəbl
AM kən'træktəbəl

contractible
BR kən'traktɪbl
AM kən'træktəbəl

contractile
BR kən'traktʌɪl
AM kən'træktəl

contractility
BR ͵kɒntrak'tɪlɪti
AM ͵kɑn͵træk'tɪlɪdi

contraction
BR kən'trakʃn, -z
AM kən'trækʃən, -z

contractive
BR kən'traktɪv
AM kən'træktɪv

contractor
BR kən'traktə(r),
'kɒntraktə(r), -z
AM 'kɑntræktər, -z

contractual
BR kən'traktʃʊəl,
kən'traktʃ(ə)l,
kən'traktjʊəl,
kən'traktjəl
AM kən'træk(t)ʃ(əw)əl

contractually
BR kən'traktʃʊəli,
kən'traktʃəli,
kən'traktʃli,
kən'traktjʊəli,
kən'traktjəli
AM kən'træk(t)ʃ(əw)əli

contradict
BR ͵kɒntrə'dɪkt, -s, -ɪŋ,
-ɪd
AM ͵kɑntrə'dɪk|(t),
-(t)s, -tɪŋ, -tɪd

contradictable
BR ͵kɒntrə'dɪktəbl
AM ͵kɑntrə'dɪktəbəl

contradiction
BR ͵kɒntrə'dɪkʃn, -z
AM ͵kɑntrə'dɪkʃən, -z

contradictious
BR ͵kɒntrə'dɪkʃəs
AM ͵kɑntrə'dɪkʃəs

contradictor
BR ͵kɒntrə'dɪktə(r), -z
AM ͵kɑntrə'dɪktər, -z

contradictorily
BR ͵kɒntrə'dɪkt(ə)rɪli
AM ͵kɑntrə'dɪktərəli

contradictoriness
BR ͵kɒntrə'dɪkt(ə)rmɪs
AM ͵kɑntrə'dɪktərɪnɪs

contradictory
BR ͵kɒntrə'dɪkt(ə)ri
AM ͵kɑntrə'dɪktəri

contradistinction
BR ͵kɒntrədɪ'stɪŋ(k)ʃn
AM ͵kɑntrədə'stɪŋ(k)ʃən

contradistinguish
BR ͵kɒntrədɪ'stɪŋgwɪʃ,
-ɪʃɪz, -ɪʃɪŋ, -ɪʃt
AM ͵kɑntrədə'stɪŋgwɪʃ,
-ɪz, -ɪŋ, -t

contraflow
BR 'kɒntrəfləʊ, -z
AM 'kɑntrə͵floʊ, -z

contrail
BR 'kɒntreɪl, -z
AM 'kɑn͵treɪl, -z

contraindicate
BR ͵kɒntrə'ɪndɪkeɪt, -s,
-ɪŋ, -ɪd
AM ͵kɑntrə'ɪndɪ͵keɪt,
-ts, -dɪŋ, -dɪd

contraindication
BR ͵kɒntrə͵ɪndɪ'keɪʃn,
-z

AM ˌkɑntrəˌɪndɪˈkeɪʃən, -z

contralto
BR kənˈtrɑːltəʊ, kənˈtraltəʊ, -z
AM kənˈtræltoʊ, -z

contraposition
BR ˌkɒntrəpəˈzɪʃn, -z
AM ˌkɑntrəpəˈzɪʃən, -z

contrapositive
BR ˌkɒntrəˈpɒzɪtɪv
AM ˌkɑntrəˈpɑzədɪv

contraption
BR kənˈtrapʃn, -z
AM kənˈtræpʃən, -z

contrapuntal
BR ˌkɒntrəˈpʌntl
AM ˌkɑntrəˈpən(t)əl

contrapuntally
BR ˌkɒntrəˈpʌntl̩i
AM ˌkɑntrəˈpən(t)əli

contrapuntist
BR ˌkɒntrəˈpʌntɪst, ˈkɒntrəˌpʌntɪst, -s
AM ˌkɑntrəˈpən(t)əst, -s

contrarian
BR kənˈtreːrɪən, -z
AM kənˈtreərɪən, ˌkɑnˈtreərɪən, -z

contrariety
BR ˌkɒntrəˈrʌɪɪti, -ɪz
AM ˌkɑntrəˈraɪdi, -z

contrarily
BR kənˈtreːrɪli
AM ˈkɑntrɛrəli, kənˈtrɛrəli

contrariness
BR kənˈtreːrɪnɪs
AM ˈkɑntrɛrinəs, kənˈtrɛrinəs

contrariwise
BR kənˈtreːrɪwʌɪz
AM ˈkɑntrɛriˌwaɪz, kənˈtreriˌwaɪz

contrary¹
opposite
BR ˈkɒntrəri
AM ˈkɑntrɛri

contrary²
perverse
BR kənˈtreːri
AM ˈkɑntrɛri, kənˈtreri

contrast¹
noun
BR ˈkɒntrɑːst, ˈkɒntrast, -s
AM ˈkɑnˌtræst, -s

contrast²
verb
BR kənˈtrɑːst, kənˈtrast, ˈkɒntrɑːst, ˈkɒntrast, -s, -ɪŋ, -ɪd
AM ˈkɑnˌtræst, kənˈtræst, -s, -ɪŋ, -ɪd

contrastingly
BR kənˈtrɑːstɪŋli, kənˈtrastɪŋli, ˈkɒntrɑːstɪŋli, ˈkɒntrastɪŋli
AM ˈkɑnˌtræstɪŋli, kənˈtræstɪŋli

contrastive
BR kənˈtrɑːstɪv, kənˈtrastɪv, ˈkɒntrɑːstɪv, ˈkɒntrastɪv
AM kənˈtræstɪv, ˈkɑnˌtræstɪv

contrasty
BR ˈkɒntrɑːsti, ˈkɒntrasti
AM ˈkɑnˌtræsti, kənˈtræsti

contravene
BR ˌkɒntrəˈviːn, -z, -ɪŋ, -d
AM ˌkɑntrəˈvin, -z, -ɪŋ, -d

contravener
BR ˌkɒntrəˈviːnə(r), -z
AM ˌkɑntrəˈvinər, -z

contravention
BR ˈkɒntrəˈvɛnʃn, -z
AM ˌkɑntrəˈvɛnʃən, -z

contretemps
BR ˈkɒntrətɒ̃, ˈkɒ̃trətɒ̃, -z
AM ˈkɑntrəˌtɑm(p), ˈkɑntrəˌtam(p), -z

contribute
BR kənˈtrɪbjuːt, ˈkɒntrɪbjuːt, -s, -ɪŋ, -ɪd
AM kənˈtrɪbjuːt, -ts, -dɪŋ, -dɪd

contribution
BR ˌkɒntrɪˈbjuːʃn, -z
AM ˌkɑntrəˈbjuːʃən, -z

contributive
BR kənˈtrɪbjətɪv
AM kənˈtrɪbjʊdɪv

contributor
BR kənˈtrɪbjətə(r), ˈkɒntrɪbjuːtə(r), -z
AM kənˈtrɪbjudər, -z

contributory
BR kənˈtrɪbjət(ə)ri, ˌkɒntrɪˈbjuːt(ə)ri
AM kənˈtrɪbjəˌtori

con-trick
BR ˈkɒntrɪk, -s
AM ˈkɑnˌtrɪk, -s

contrite
BR ˈkɒntrʌɪt, kənˈtrʌɪt
AM kənˈtraɪt

contritely
BR ˈkɒntrʌɪtli, kənˈtrʌɪtli
AM kənˈtraɪtli

contrition
BR kənˈtrɪʃn
AM kənˈtrɪʃən

contrivable
BR kənˈtrʌɪvəbl
AM kənˈtraɪvəbəl

contrivance
BR kənˈtrʌɪvns, -ɪz
AM kənˈtraɪvəns, -ɪz

contrive
BR kənˈtrʌɪv, -z, -ɪŋ, -d
AM kənˈtraɪv, -z, -ɪŋ, -d

contriver
BR kənˈtrʌɪvə(r), -z
AM kənˈtraɪvər, -z

control
BR kənˈtrəʊl, -z, -ɪŋ, -d
AM kənˈtroʊl, -z, -ɪŋ, -d

controllability
BR kənˌtrəʊləˈbɪlɪti
AM kənˌtroʊləˈbɪlɪdi

controllable
BR kənˈtrəʊləbl
AM kənˈtroʊləbəl

controllably
BR kənˈtrəʊləbli
AM kənˈtroʊləbli

controller
BR kənˈtrəʊlə(r), -z
AM kənˈtroʊlər, -z

controllership
BR kənˈtrəʊləʃɪp
AM kənˈtroʊlərˌʃɪp

controversial
BR ˌkɒntrəˈvɜːʃl, ˌkɑntrəˈvɜrsiəl, ˌkɑntrəˈvɜrʃəl
AM ˌkɑntrəˈvɜrsiəl, ˌkɑntrəˈvɜrʃəl

controversialism
BR ˌkɒntrəˈvɜːʃɪz(ə)m, ˌkɒntrəˈvɜːʃəlɪz(ə)m
AM ˌkɑntrəˈvɜrsiəlɪzm, ˌkɑntrəˈvɜrʃəlɪzm

controversialist
BR ˌkɒntrəˈvɜːʃlɪst, ˌkɒntrəˈvɜːʃəlɪst, -s
AM ˌkɑntrəˈvɜrsiələst, ˌkɑntrəˈvɜrʃələst, -s

controversially
BR ˌkɒntrəˈvɜːʃli, ˌkɒntrəˈvɜːʃəli
AM ˌkɑntrəˈvɜrsiəli, ˌkɑntrəˈvɜrʃəli

controversy
BR ˈkɒntrəˈvɜːs|i, kənˈtrɒvəs|i, -ɪz
AM ˈkɑntrəˌvɜrsi, -ɪz

controvert
BR ˈkɒntrəvɜːt, ˈkɒntrəvɜːt, -s, -ɪŋ, -ɪd
AM ˌkɑntrəˈvɜr|t, -ts, -dɪŋ, -dɪd

controvertible
BR ˌkɒntrəˈvɜːtɪbl
AM ˌkɑntrəˈvɜrdəbəl

contumacious
BR ˌkɒntjʊˈmeɪʃəs, ˌkɒntʃʊˈmeɪʃəs
AM ˌkɑnt(j)ʊˈmeɪʃəs

contumaciously
BR ˌkɒntjʊˈmeɪʃəsli, ˌkɒntʃʊˈmeɪʃəsli

AM ˌkɑnt(j)ʊˈmeɪʃəsli

contumacy
BR ˈkɒntjʊməsi, ˈkɒntʃʊməsi
AM ˈkɑnt(j)ʊməsi

contumelious
BR ˌkɒntjʊˈmiːlɪəs, ˌkɒntʃʊˈmiːlɪəs
AM ˌkɑnt(j)ʊˈmiːliəs

contumeliously
BR ˌkɒntjʊˈmiːlɪəsli, ˌkɒntʃʊˈmiːliəsli
AM ˌkɑnt(j)ʊˈmiːliəsli

contumely
BR ˈkɒntjuːm(ɪ)li, ˈkɒntjʊm(ɪ)li, ˈkɒntʃʊm(ɪ)li
AM ˈkɑnt(j)ʊm(ə)li, ˈkɑntəmli

contuse
BR kənˈtjuːz, kənˈtʃuːz, -ɪz, -ɪŋ, -d
AM kənˈtuz, -ɪz, -ɪŋ, -d

contusion
BR kənˈtjuːʒn, kənˈtʃuːʒn, -z
AM kənˈtuʒən, -z

conundrum
BR kəˈnʌndrəm, -z
AM kəˈnəndrəm, -z

conurbation
BR ˌkɒnə(ː)ˈbeɪʃn, -z
AM ˌkɑnərˈbeɪʃən, -z

conure
BR ˈkɒnjʊə(r), -z
AM ˈkɑn(j)ʊ(ə)r, -z

Convair
BR ˈkɒnvɛː(r)
AM ˈkɑnˌvɛ(ə)r

convalesce
BR ˌkɒnvəˈlɛs, -ɪz, -ɪŋ, -t
AM ˌkɑnvəˈlɛs, -ɪz, -ɪŋ, -t

convalescence
BR ˌkɒnvəˈlɛsns, -ɪz
AM ˌkɑnvəˈlɛsəns, -ɪz

convalescent
BR ˌkɒnvəˈlɛsnt, -s
AM ˌkɑnvəˈlɛsənt, -s

convection
BR kənˈvɛkʃn
AM kənˈvɛkʃən

convectional
BR kənˈvɛkʃn(ə)l, kənˈvɛkʃən(ə)l
AM kənˈvɛkʃ(ə)nəl

convective
BR kənˈvɛktɪv
AM kənˈvɛktɪv

convector
BR kənˈvɛktə(r), -z
AM kənˈvɛktər, -z

convenable
BR kənˈviːnəbl
AM kənˈvinəbəl

convenance
BR ˈkɒnvənɑːns, -ɪz
AM ˈkɑnvənəns, -ɪz

convene
BR kən'vi:n, -z, -ɪŋ, -d
AM kən'vin, -z, -ɪŋ, -d

convener
BR kən'vi:nə(r), -z
AM kən'vinər, -z

convenience
BR kən'vi:nɪəns, -ɪz
AM kən'vinjəns, -ɪz

convenient
BR kən'vi:nɪənt
AM kən'vinjənt

conveniently
BR kən'vi:nɪəntli
AM kən'vinjən(t)li

convenor
BR kən'vi:nə(r), -z
AM kən'vinər, -z

convent
BR 'kɒnv(ə)nt, -s
AM 'kɑn,vɛnt, -s

conventicle
BR kən'vɛntɪkl, -z
AM kən'vɛn(t)əkl, -z

convention
BR kən'vɛnʃn, -z
AM kən'vɛn(t)ʃən, -z

conventional
BR kən'vɛnʃn(ə)l
kən'vɛnʃən(ə)l
AM kən'vɛn(t)ʃ(ə)nəl

conventionalise
BR kən'vɛnʃn̩əlʌɪz,
kən'vɛnʃn̩ʌɪz,
kən'vɛnʃənlʌɪz,
kən'vɛnʃ(ə)nəlʌɪz,
-ɪz, -ɪŋ, -d
AM kən'vɛn(t)ʃənl,ʌɪz,
kən'vɛn(t)ʃnəl,ʌɪz,
-ɪz, -ɪŋ, -d

conventionalism
BR kən'vɛnʃn̩əlɪz(ə)m,
kən'vɛnʃn̩lɪz(ə)m,
kən'vɛnʃənlɪz(ə)m,
kən'vɛnʃ(ə)nəlɪz(ə)m
AM kən'vɛn(t)ʃənl,ɪzəm,
kən'vɛn(t)ʃnəl,ɪzəm

conventionalist
BR kən'vɛnʃn̩əlɪst,
kən'vɛnʃn̩lɪst,
kən'vɛnʃənlɪst,
kən'vɛnʃ(ə)nəlɪst, -s
AM kən'vɛn(t)ʃənləst,
kən'vɛn(t)ʃnələst, -s

conventionality
BR kən,vɛnʃə'nalɪt|i,
-ɪz
AM kən,vɛn(t)ʃə'næl|ədi,
-z

conventionalize
BR kən'vɛnʃn̩əlʌɪz,
kən'vɛnʃn̩lʌɪz,
kən'vɛnʃənlʌɪz,
kən'vɛnʃ(ə)nəlʌɪz,
-ɪz, -ɪŋ, -d

AM kən'vɛn(t)ʃənl,ʌɪz,
kən'vɛn(t)ʃnəl,ʌɪz,
-ɪz, -ɪŋ, -d

conventionally
BR kən'vɛnʃnəli,
kən'vɛnʃn̩li,
kən'vɛnʃənli,
kən'vɛnʃ(ə)nəli
AM kən'vɛn(t)ʃ(ə)nəli

conventioneer
BR kən,vɛnʃə'nɪə(r),
-z
AM kən'vɛn(t)ʃə,nɪ(ə)r,
-z

conventual
BR kən'vɛn(t)ʃʊəl,
kəm'vɛn(t)ʃ(ʊ)l,
kən'vɛntjʊəl,
kən'vɛntjʊl, -z
AM kən'vɛn(t)ʃ(əw)əl,
-z

converb
BR 'kɒnvə:b, -z
AM 'kɑn,vərb, -z

converge
BR kən'və:dʒ, -ɪz, -ɪŋ, -d
AM kən'vərdʒ, -ɪz, -ɪŋ,
-d

convergence
BR kən'və:dʒ(ə)ns, -ɪz
AM kən'vərdʒəns, -əz

convergency
BR kən'və:dʒ(ə)nsi
AM kən'vərdʒənsi

convergent
BR kən'və:dʒ(ə)nt
AM kən'vərdʒənt

conversance
BR kən'və:sns
AM kən'vərsəns

conversancy
BR kən'və:snsi
AM kən'vərsənsi

conversant
BR kən'və:snt
AM kən'vərsənt

conversation
BR ,kɒnvə'seɪʃn, -z
AM ,kɑnvər'seɪʃən, -z

conversational
BR kən'və:seɪʃn(ə)l,
,kɒnvə'seɪʃən(ə)l
AM ,kɑnvər'seɪʃ(ə)nəl

conversationalist
BR kən'və:seɪʃnəlɪst,
,kɒnvə'seɪʃn̩lɪst,
,kɒnvə'seɪʃənlɪst,
,kɒnvə'seɪʃ(ə)nəlɪst,
-s
AM ,kɑnvər'seɪʃənləst,
,kɑnvər'seɪʃnələst, -s

conversationally
BR ,kɒnvə'seɪʃnəli,
,kɒnvə'seɪʃn̩li,
,kɒnvə'seɪʃənli,
,kɒnvə'seɪʃ(ə)nəli
AM ,kɑnvər'seɪʃ(ə)nəli

conversationist
BR ,kɒnvə'seɪʃnɪst,
,kɒnvə'seɪʃənɪst, -s
AM ,kɑnvər'seɪʃənəst,
-s

conversazione
BR ,kɒnvəsatzɪ'əʊn|i,
-ɪz
AM ,kɑnvər,satsi'oʊni,
-z

conversazioni
BR ,kɒnvəsatzɪ'əʊni:
AM ,kɑnvər,satsi'oʊni

converse[1]
adjective
BR 'kɒnvə:s, kən'və:s
AM 'kɑn,vərs,
kən'vərs

converse[2]
noun
BR 'kɒnvə:s
AM 'kɑn,vərs

converse[3]
verb
BR kən'və:s, -ɪz, -ɪŋ, -t
AM kən'vərs, -əz, -ɪŋ, -t

conversely
BR 'kɒnvə:sli,
kən'və:sli
AM 'kɑn,vərsli,
kən'vərsli

converser
BR kən'və:sə(r), -z
AM kən'vərsər, -z

conversion
BR kən'və:ʃn, -z
AM kən'vərʒən, -z

convert[1]
noun
BR 'kɒnvə:t, -s
AM 'kɑn,vərt, -s

convert[2]
verb
BR kən'və:t, -s, -ɪŋ, -ɪd
AM kən'vər|t, -ts, -dɪŋ,
-dəd

converter
BR kən'və:tə(r), -z
AM kən'vərdər, -z

convertibility
BR kən,və:tɪ'bɪlɪti
AM kən,vərdə'bɪlɪdi

convertible
BR kən'və:tɪbl, -z
AM kən'vərdəbəl, -z

convertibly
BR kən'və:tɪbli
AM kən'vərdəbli

convertor
BR kən'və:tə(r), -z
AM kən'vərdər, -z

convex
BR ,kɒn'vɛks,
'kɒnvɛks
AM ,kɑn'vɛks

convexity
BR kən'vɛksɪt|i, -ɪz
AM kən'vɛksədi, -z

convexly
BR ,kɒn'vɛksli,
'kɒnvɛksli
AM ,kɑn'vɛksli

convey
BR kən'veɪ, -z, -ɪŋ, -d
AM kən'veɪ, -z, -ɪŋ, -d

conveyable
BR kən'veɪəbl
AM kən'veɪəbəl

conveyance
BR kən'veɪəns, -ɪz, -ɪŋ,
-t
AM kən'veɪəns, -ɪz, -ɪŋ,
-t

conveyancer
BR kən'veɪənsə(r), -z
AM kən'veɪənsər, -z

conveyancing
BR kən'veɪənsɪŋ
AM kən'veɪənsɪŋ

conveyer
BR kən'veɪə(r), -z
AM kən'veɪər, -z

conveyor
BR kən'veɪə(r), -z
AM kən'veɪər, -z

convict[1]
noun
BR 'kɒnvɪkt, -s
AM 'kɑn,vɪk(t), -s

convict[2]
verb
BR kən'vɪkt, -s, -ɪŋ, -ɪd
AM kən'vɪk|(t), -(t)s,
-dɪŋ, -dɪd

conviction
BR kən'vɪkʃn, -z
AM kən'vɪkʃən, -z

convictive
BR kən'vɪktɪv
AM kən'vɪktɪv

convince
BR kən'vɪns, -ɪz, -ɪŋ, -t
AM kən'vɪns, -ɪz, -ɪŋ, -t

convincement
BR kən'vɪnsm(ə)nt
AM kən'vɪnsmənt

convincer
BR kən'vɪnsə(r), -z
AM kən'vɪnsər, -z

convincible
BR kən'vɪnsɪbl
AM kən'vɪnsəbəl

convincibly
BR kən'vɪnsɪbli
AM kən'vɪnsəbli

convincingly
BR kən'vɪnsɪŋli
AM kən'vɪnsɪŋli

convivial
BR kən'vɪvɪəl
AM kən'vɪvɪəl,
kən'vɪvjəl

conviviality
BR kən,vɪvɪ'alɪti
AM kən,vɪvi'ælədi

convivially
BR kən'vɪvɪəli
AM kən'vɪviəli,
kən'vɪvjəli

convocation
BR ˌkɒnvə'keɪʃn
AM ˌkɑnvə'keɪʃən

convocational
BR ˌkɒnvə'keɪʃn̩(ə)l,
ˌkɒnvə'keɪʃən(ə)l
AM ˌkɑnvə'keɪʃ(ə)nəl

convoke
BR kən'vəʊk, -s, -ɪŋ, -t
AM kən'voʊk, -s, -ɪŋ, -t

convoluted
BR 'kɒnvəl(j)uːtɪd,
ˌkɒnvə'l(j)uːtɪd
AM 'kɑnvəˌludəd

convolutedly
BR 'kɒnvəl(j)uːtɪdli,
ˌkɒnvə'l(j)uːtɪdli
AM 'kɑnvəˌludədli

convolution
BR ˌkɒnvə'l(j)uːʃn, -z
AM ˌkɑnvə'luʃən, -z

convolutional
BR ˌkɒnvə'l(j)uːʃn̩(ə)l,
ˌkɒnvə'l(j)uːʃən(ə)l
AM ˌkɑnvə'luʃ(ə)nəl

convolve
BR kən'vɒlv, -z, -ɪŋ, -d
AM kən'vɑlv, -z, -ɪŋ, -d

convolvulus
BR kən'vɒlvjʊləs,
kən'vɑlvjʊləs, -ɪz
AM kən'vɑlvjəˌləs, -əz

convoy
BR 'kɒnvɔɪ, -z, -ɪŋ, -d
AM 'kɑnˌvɔɪ, -z, -ɪŋ, -d

convulsant
BR kən'vʌlsnt, -s
AM kən'vəlsənt, -s

convulse
BR kən'vʌls, -ɪz, -ɪŋ, -t
AM kən'vəlz, -əz, -ɪŋ, -d

convulsion
BR kən'vʌlʃn, -z
AM kən'vəlʃən, -z

convulsionary
BR kən'vʌlʃn̩(ə)ri
AM kən'vəlʃəˌneri

convulsive
BR kən'vʌlsɪv
AM kən'vəlsɪv

convulsively
BR kən'vʌlsɪvli
AM kən'vəlsɪvli

Conway
BR 'kɒnweɪ
AM 'kɑnweɪ

Conwy
BR 'kɒnwi
AM 'kɑnwi

cony
BR 'kəʊn|i, -ɪz
AM 'koʊni, -z

Conybeare
BR 'kɒnɪbɪə(r),
'kʌnɪbɪə(r)
AM 'kɑniˌbɛ(ə)r

coo
BR kuː, -z, -ɪŋ, -d
AM ku, -z, -ɪŋ, -d

Coober Pedy
BR ˌkuːbə 'piːdi
AM ˌkubər 'pidi

co-occur
BR ˌkəʊə'kəː(r), -z, -ɪŋ,
-d
AM ˌkoʊə'kər, -z, -ɪŋ, -d

co-occurrence
BR ˌkəʊə'kʌrəns,
ˌkəʊə'kʌrn̩s, -ɪz
AM ˌkoʊə'kərəns, -əz

Cooder
BR 'kuːdə(r)
AM 'kudər

cooee
BR 'kuːiː, ˌkuː'iː, -z, -ɪŋ,
-d
AM 'kuˌi, ˌku'i, -z, -ɪŋ, -d

cooey
BR 'kuːiː, ˌkuː'iː, -z, -ɪŋ,
-d
AM 'kuˌi, ˌku'i, -z, -ɪŋ, -d

cooingly
BR 'kuːɪŋli
AM 'kuːŋli

cook
BR kʊk, -s, -ɪŋ, -t
AM kʊk, -s, -ɪŋ, -t

cookability
BR ˌkʊkə'bɪlɪti
AM ˌkʊkə'bɪlɪdi

cookable
BR 'kʊkəbl
AM 'kʊkəbəl

cookbook
BR 'kʊkbʊk, -s
AM 'kʊkˌbʊk, -s

cookchill
BR ˌkʊk'tʃɪl
AM ˌkʊkˌtʃɪl

Cooke
BR kʊk
AM kʊk

cooker
BR 'kʊkə(r), -z
AM 'kʊkər, -z

cookery
BR 'kʊk(ə)ri
AM 'kʊk(ə)ri

cookhouse
BR 'kʊkhaʊ|s, -zɪz
AM 'kʊkˌ(h)aʊ|s, -zəz

cookie
BR 'kʊk|i, -ɪz
AM 'kʊki, -z

cookout
BR 'kʊkaʊt, -s
AM 'kʊkˌaʊt, -s

cookshop
BR 'kʊkʃɒp, -s

Cookson
AM 'kʊkˌʃɑp, -s

Cookson
BR 'kʊksn
AM 'kʊksən

cookstone
BR 'kʊkstəʊn, -z
AM 'kʊkˌstoʊn, -z

cookware
BR 'kʊkwɛː(r), -z
AM 'kʊkˌwe(ə)r, -z

cooky
BR 'kʊk|i, -ɪz
AM 'kʊki, -z

cool
BR kuːl, -z, -ɪŋ, -d
AM kul, -z, -ɪŋ, -d

coolabah
BR 'kuːləbɑː(r), -z
AM 'kuləˌbɑ, -z

coolant
BR 'kuːlənt, -s
AM 'kulənt, -s

cooler
BR 'kuːlə(r), -z
AM 'kulər, -z

Cooley
BR 'kuːli
AM 'kuli

Coolgardie
BR kuːl'gɑːdi
AM ˌkul'gɑrdi

coolibah
BR 'kuːlɪbɑː(r), -z
AM 'kuləˌbɑ, -z

coolibar
BR 'kuːlɪbɑː(r), -z
AM 'kuləˌbɑr, -z

Coolidge
BR 'kuːlɪdʒ
AM 'kulɪdʒ

coolie
BR 'kuːl|i, -ɪz
AM 'kuli, -z

coolish
BR 'kuːlɪʃ, -z
AM 'kulɪʃ, -z

coolly
BR 'kuːl(l)i
AM 'ku(l)li

coolness
BR 'kuːlnəs
AM 'kulnəs

coolth
BR kuːlθ
AM kulθ

coomb
BR kuːm, -z
AM kum, -z

coombe
BR kuːm, -z
AM kum, -z

Coombes
BR kuːmz
AM kumz

Coombs
BR kuːmz
AM kumz

Coomes
BR kuːmz
AM kumz

coon
BR kuːn, -z
AM kun, -z

Cooney
BR 'kuːni
AM 'kuni

coonskin
BR 'kuːnskɪn, -z
AM 'kunˌskɪn, -z

coop
BR kuːp, -s, -ɪŋ, -t
AM kup, -s, -ɪŋ, -t

co-op
BR 'kəʊɒp, -s
AM 'koʊˌɑp, -s

Coope
BR kuːp
AM kup

cooper
BR 'kuːpə(r), -z
AM 'kupər, -z

cooperage
BR 'kuːp(ə)rɪdʒ
AM 'kup(ə)rɪdʒ

cooperant
BR kəʊ'ɒp(ə)rənt,
kəʊ'ɒp(ə)rn̩t
AM koʊ'ɑpərənt

cooperate
BR kəʊ'ɒpəreɪt, -s, -ɪŋ,
-ɪd
AM koʊ'ɑpəˌreɪ|t, -ts,
-dɪŋ, -dɪd

cooperation
BR kəʊˌɒpə'reɪʃn, -z
AM koʊˌɑpə'reɪʃən, -z

cooperative
BR kəʊ'ɒp(ə)rətɪv, -z
AM koʊ'ɑp(ə)rədɪv, -z

cooperatively
BR kəʊ'ɒp(ə)rətɪvli
AM koʊ'ɑp(ə)rədɪvli

cooperativeness
BR kəʊ'ɒp(ə)rətɪvnɪs
AM koʊ'ɑp(ə)rədɪvnɪs

cooperator
BR kəʊ'ɒpəreɪtə(r), -z
AM koʊ'ɑpəˌreɪdər, -z

Cooperstown
BR 'kuːpəztaʊn
AM 'kupərzˌtaʊn

coopt
BR ˌkəʊ'ɒpt, -s, -ɪŋ, -ɪd
AM ˌkoʊ'ɑpt, -s, -ɪŋ, -ɪd

cooptation
BR ˌkəʊɒp'teɪʃn
AM ˌkoʊˌɑp'teɪʃən

cooption
BR ˌkəʊ'ɒpʃn, -z
AM ˌkoʊ'ɑpʃən, -z

cooptive
BR ˌkəʊ'ɒptɪv
AM ˌkoʊ'ɑptɪv

coordinate¹
noun, adjective
BR kəʊˈɔːdɪnət, -s
AM koʊˈɔrdənət, -s
coordinate²
verb
BR kəʊˈɔːdɪneɪt, -s, -ɪŋ, -ɪd
AM koʊˈɔrdəˌneɪ|t, -ts, -dɪŋ, -dɪd
coordinately
BR kəʊˈɔːdɪnətli
AM koʊˈɔrdənətli
coordination
BR kəʊˌɔːdɪˈneɪʃn, -z
AM koʊˌɔrdəˈneɪʃən, -z
coordinative
BR kəʊˈɔːdɪnətɪv
AM koʊˈɔrdəˌneɪdɪv, koʊˈɔrdənədɪv
coordinator
BR kəʊˈɔːdɪneɪtə(r), -z
AM koʊˈɔrdəˌneɪdər, -z
Coors®
BR kɔːz
AM kʊ(ə)rz, kɔ(ə)rz
coot
BR kuːt, -s
AM kut, -s
Coote
BR kuːt
AM kut
cootie
BR ˈkuːt|i, -ɪz
AM ˈkudi, -z
co-own
BR ˌkəʊˈəʊn, -z, -ɪŋ, -d
AM ˌkoʊˈoʊn, -z, -ɪŋ, -d
co-owner
BR ˌkəʊˈəʊnə(r), -z
AM ˌkoʊˈoʊnər, -z
co-ownership
BR ˌkəʊˈəʊnəʃɪp
AM ˌkoʊˈoʊnərˌʃɪp
cop
BR kɒp, -s, -ɪŋ, -t
AM kɑp, -s, -ɪŋ, -t
Copacabana
BR ˌkəʊpəkəˈbanə(r), ˌkəʊpəkəˈbaːnə(r)
AM ˌkoʊpəkəˈbænə
copacetic
BR ˌkəʊpəˈsɛtɪk, ˌkəʊpəˈsiːtɪk
AM ˌkoʊpəˈsɛdɪk, ˌkoʊpəˈsidɪk
copaiba
BR kəˈ(ʊ)paɪbə(r)
AM koʊˈpaɪbə
copal
BR ˈkəʊpl
AM ˈkoʊpəl
cope
BR kəʊp, -s, -ɪŋ, -t
AM koʊp, -s, -ɪŋ, -t
copeck
BR ˈkəʊpɛk, -s

AM ˈkoʊˌpɛk, -s
Copeland
BR ˈkəʊplənd
AM ˈkoʊplən(d)
Copenhagen
BR ˌkəʊp(ə)nˈheɪg(ə)n, ˌkəʊp(ə)nˈhaːg(ə)n
AM ˈkoʊpən,(h)agən, ˈkoʊpən,(h)eɪgən
copepod
BR ˈkəʊpɪpɒd, -z
AM ˈkoʊpəˌpad, -z
coper
BR ˈkəʊpə(r), -z
AM ˈkoʊpər, -z
Copernican
BR kəˈpɜːnɪk(ə)n
AM kəˈpɜrnəkən
Copernicus
BR kəˈpɜːnɪkəs
AM kəˈpɜrnəkəs
Copestake
BR ˈkəʊpsteɪk
AM ˈkoʊpˌsteɪk
copestone
BR ˈkəʊpstəʊn, -z
AM ˈkoʊpˌstoʊn, -z
copiable
BR ˈkɒpɪəbl
AM ˈkɑpiəbəl
copier
BR ˈkɒpɪə(r), -z
AM ˈkɑpiər, -z
copilot
BR ˈkəʊˌpaɪlət, -s
AM ˈkoʊˌpaɪlət, -s
coping
BR ˈkəʊpɪŋ, -z
AM ˈkoʊpɪŋ, -z
copingstone
BR ˈkəʊpɪŋstəʊn, -z
AM ˈkoʊpɪŋˌstoʊn, -z
copious
BR ˈkəʊpɪəs
AM ˈkoʊpiəs
copiously
BR ˈkəʊpɪəsli
AM ˈkoʊpiəsli
copiousness
BR ˈkəʊpɪəsnəs
AM ˈkoʊpiəsnəs
copita
BR kɒˈ(ʊ)ˈpiːtə(r), -z
AM koʊˈpidə, -z
coplanar
BR kəʊˈpleɪnə(r)
AM ˌkoʊˈpleɪnar
coplanarity
BR ˌkəʊpleɪˈnarɪti
AM ˌkoʊˌpleɪˈnɛrədi
Copland
BR ˈkəʊplənd
AM ˈkoʊplən(d)
Copley
BR ˈkɒpli
AM ˈkoʊpli

copolymer
BR ˌkəʊˈpɒlɪmə(r), -z
AM ˌkoʊˈpaləmər, -z
copolymerisation
BR ˌkəʊˌpɒlɪmərʌɪˈzeɪʃn
AM ˌkoʊˌpaləmərəˈzeɪʃən, ˌkoʊpəˌlɪmərəˈzeɪʃən, ˌkoʊpəˌlɪməˌraɪˈzeɪʃən, ˌkoʊpəˌlɪməˌraɪˈzeɪʃən
copolymerise
BR ˌkəʊˈpɒlɪmərʌɪz, -ɪz, -ɪŋ, -d
AM ˌkoʊˈpaləməˌraɪz, ˌkoʊpəˈlɪməˌraɪz, -ɪz, -ɪŋ, -d
copolymerization
BR ˌkəʊˌpɒlɪmərʌɪˈzeɪʃn
AM ˌkoʊˈpaləmərəˈzeɪʃən, ˌkoʊpəˌlɪmərəˈzeɪʃən, ˌkoʊpəˌlɪməˌraɪˈzeɪʃən, ˌkoʊpəˌlɪməˌraɪˈzeɪʃən
copolymerize
BR ˌkəʊˈpɒlɪmərʌɪz, -ɪz, -ɪŋ, -d
AM ˌkoʊˈpaləməˌraɪz, ˌkoʊpəˈlɪməˌraɪz, -ɪz, -ɪŋ, -d
copout
BR ˈkɒpaʊt, -s
AM ˈkɑpˌaʊt, -s
copper
BR ˈkɒpə(r), -z
AM ˈkɑpər, -z
copperas
BR ˈkɒp(ə)rəs
AM ˈkɑp(ə)rəs
Copperbelt
BR ˈkɒpəbɛlt
AM ˈkɑpərˌbɛlt
Copperfield
BR ˈkɒpəfiːld
AM ˈkɑpərˌfild
copperhead
BR ˈkɒpəhɛd, -z
AM ˈkɑpərˌ(h)ɛd, -z
coppermine
BR ˈkɒpəmʌɪn, -z
AM ˈkɑpərˌmaɪn, -z
copperplate
BR ˈkɒpəpleɪt
AM ˈkɑpərˌpleɪt
coppersmith
BR ˈkɒpəsmɪθ, -s
AM ˈkɑpərˌsmɪθ, -s
coppery
BR ˈkɒp(ə)ri
AM ˈkɑpəri
coppice
BR ˈkɒp|ɪs, -ɪsɪz, -ɪsɪŋ, -ɪst
AM ˈkɑpəs, -əz, -ɪŋ, -t
Coppola
BR ˈkɒpələ(r)
AM ˈkɑpələ

copra
BR ˈkɒprə(r)
AM ˈkɑprə
coprocessor
BR ˌkəʊˈprəʊsɛsə(r), ˈkəʊˌprəʊsɛsə(r), -z
AM ˌkoʊˈprasɛsər, -z
coprolite
BR ˈkɒprəlʌɪt
AM ˈkɑprəˌlaɪt
coprology
BR kɒˈprɒlədʒi, kəˈprɒlədʒi
AM kəˈprɑlədʒi
coprophagous
BR kɒˈprɒfəgəs, kəˈprɒfəgəs
AM kəˈprɑfəgəs
coprophilia
BR ˌkɒprəˈfɪlɪə(r)
AM ˌkɑprəˈfɪljə, ˌkɑprəˈfɪliə
coprophiliac
BR ˌkɒprəˈfɪliak, -s
AM ˌkɑprəˈfɪliˌæk, ˌkɑprəˈfɪliˌæk, -s
coprosma
BR kəˈprɒzmə(r), -z
AM kəˈprɑzmə, -z
copse
BR kɒps, -ɪz
AM kɑps, -əz
copsewood
BR ˈkɒpswʊd
AM ˈkɑpsˌwʊd
copsy
BR ˈkɒpsi
AM ˈkɑpsi
Copt
BR kɒpt, -s
AM kɑpt, -s
'copter
BR ˈkɒptə(r), -z
AM ˈkɑptər, -z
Coptic
BR ˈkɒptɪk
AM ˈkɑptɪk
copula
BR ˈkɒpjʊlə(r), -z
AM ˈkɑpjələ, ˈkoʊpjələ, -z
copular
BR ˈkɒpjʊlə(r)
AM ˈkɑpjələr, ˈkoʊpjələr
copulate
BR ˈkɒpjʊleɪt, -s, -ɪŋ, -ɪd
AM ˈkɑpjəˌleɪ|t, ˈkoʊpjəˌleɪ|t, -ts, -dɪŋ, -dɪd
copulation
BR ˌkɒpjʊˈleɪʃn, ˌkɑpjəˈleɪʃən, ˌkoʊpjəˈleɪʃən
copulative
BR ˈkɒpjʊlətɪv, -z

copulatively
AM ˈkɒpjələdɪv,
ˈkoʊpjələdɪv,
ˈkɑpjəˌleɪdɪv,
ˈkoʊpjəˌleɪdɪv, -z

copulatively
BR ˈkɒpjʊlətɪvli
AM ˈkɑpjəˌleɪdɪvli,
ˈkoʊpjəˌleɪdɪvli,
ˈkɑpjələdɪvli,
ˈkoʊpjələdɪvli

copulatory
BR ˈkɒpjʊlət(ə)ri
AM ˈkɑpjələˌtɔri,
ˈkoʊpjələˌtɔri

copy
BR ˈkɒp|i, -ɪz, -ɪŋ, -ɪd
AM ˈkɑpi, -z, -ɪŋ, -d

copybook
BR ˈkɒpɪbʊk, -s
AM ˈkɑpiˌbʊk, -s

copyboy
BR ˈkɒpɪbɔɪ, -z
AM ˈkɑpiˌbɔɪ, -z

copycat
BR ˈkɒpɪkat, -s
AM ˈkɑpiˌkæt, -s

copydesk
BR ˈkɒpɪdesk, -s
AM ˈkɑpiˌdesk, -s

Copydex®
BR ˈkɒpɪdeks
AM ˈkɑpiˌdeks

copyhold
BR ˈkɒpɪhəʊld, -z
AM ˈkɑpi,(h)oʊld, -z

copyholder
BR ˈkɒpɪˌhəʊldə(r), -z
AM ˈkɑpi,(h)oʊldər, -z

copyist
BR ˈkɒpɪɪst, -s
AM ˈkɑpiəst, -s

copyread
BR ˈkɒpɪriːd, -z, -ɪŋ
AM ˈkɑpiˌrid, -z, -ɪŋ

copyreader
BR ˈkɒpɪˌriːdə(r), -z
AM ˈkɑpiˌridər, -z

copyright
BR ˈkɒpɪrʌɪt, -s, -ɪŋ, -ɪd
AM ˈkɑpiˌraɪ|t, -ts, -dɪŋ, -dɪd

copywriter
BR ˈkɒpɪˌrʌɪtə(r), -z
AM ˈkɑpiˌraɪdər, -z

copywriting
BR ˈkɒpɪˌrʌɪtɪŋ
AM ˈkɑpiˌraɪdɪŋ

coq au vin
BR ˌkɒk əʊ ˈvã, + ˈvan
AM ˌkɑk oʊ ˈvæn

coquet
BR kɒˈket, kəˈket, -s, -ɪŋ, -ɪd
AM koʊˈkeɪt, -ts, -dɪŋ, -dəd

coquetry
BR ˈkɒkɪtri
AM ˈkoʊkətri

coquette
BR kɒˈket, kəˈket, -s
AM koʊˈket, -s

coquettish
BR kɒˈketɪʃ, kəˈketɪʃ
AM koʊˈkedɪʃ

coquettishly
BR kɒˈketɪʃli, kəˈketɪʃli
AM koʊˈkedɪʃli

coquettishness
BR kɒˈketɪʃnɪs, kəˈketɪʃnɪs
AM koʊˈkedɪʃnɪs

coquille
BR kɒˈkiː
AM koʊˈki(l)

coquilles
BR kɒˈkiː
AM koʊˈki(l)

coquina
BR kəʊˈkiːnə(r)
AM koʊˈkinə

coquito
BR kə(ʊ)ˈkiːtəʊ, -z
AM koʊˈkidoʊ, -z

cor
BR kɔː(r)
AM kɔ(ə)r

Cora
BR ˈkɔːrə(r)
AM ˈkɔrə

coracle
BR ˈkɒrəkl, -z
AM ˈkɔrəkl, ˈkɑrəkl, -z

coracoid
BR ˈkɒrəkɔɪd, -z
AM ˈkɔrəˌkɔɪd, -z

coral
BR ˈkɒrəl, ˈkɒrl̩, -z
AM ˈkɔrəl, -z

Coralie
BR ˈkɔːrəli
AM ˈkɔrəli

coralline
BR ˈkɒrəlʌɪn, -z
AM ˈkɔrələn, ˈkɔrəˌlin, -z

corallita
BR ˌkɒrəˈliːtə(r)
AM ˌkɔrəˈlidə

corallite
BR ˈkɒrəlʌɪt, -s
AM ˈkɔrəˌlaɪt, -s

coralloid
BR ˈkɒrəlɔɪd, -z
AM ˈkɔrəˌlɔɪd, -z

Coram
BR ˈkɔːrəm
AM ˈkɔrəm

coram populo
BR ˌkɔːrəm ˈpɒpjʊləʊ
AM ˌkoʊrəm ˈpapjəloʊ

cor anglais
BR ˌkɔːr ˈɑːŋgleɪ, + ˈɒŋgleɪ
AM ˌkɔ(ə)r ɒŋˈgleɪ

corbel
BR ˈkɔːb(ə)l, -z
AM ˈkɔrbl, -z

Corbet
BR ˈkɔːbɪt
AM ˈkɔrbət

Corbett
BR ˈkɔːbɪt
AM ˈkɔrbət

corbicula
BR kɔːˈbɪkjələ(r)
AM ˌkɔrˈbɪkjələ

corbiculae
BR kɔːˈbɪkjəliː
AM ˌkɔrˈbɪkjəli

corbie
BR ˈkɔːb|i, -ɪz
AM ˈkɔrbi, -z

Corbin
BR ˈkɔːbɪn
AM ˈkɔrbɪn

Corbishley
BR ˈkɔːbɪʃli
AM ˈkɔrbɪʃli

cor blimey!
BR ˌkɔː ˈblʌɪmi
AM ˌkɔ(ə)r ˈblaɪmi

Corbridge
BR ˈkɔːbrɪdʒ
AM ˈkɔrˌbrɪdʒ

Corby
BR ˈkɔːbi
AM ˈkɔrbi

Corcoran
BR ˈkɔːk(ə)rən, ˈkɔːk(ə)rn̩
AM ˈkɔrk(ə)rən

Corcyra
BR kɔːˈsʌɪrə(r)
AM ˈkɔrˈsɪrə

cord
BR kɔːd, -z, -ɪŋ
AM kɔ(ə)rd, -z, -ɪŋ

cordage
BR ˈkɔːdɪdʒ
AM ˈkɔrdɪdʒ

cordate
BR ˈkɔːdeɪt
AM ˈkɔrˌdeɪt

Corday
BR ˈkɔːdeɪ
AM kɔrˈdeɪ

Cordelia
BR kɔːˈdiːlɪə(r)
AM ˌkɔrˈdiljə, ˌkɔrˈdiliə

Cordelier
BR ˌkɔːdɪˈlɪə(r), -z
AM ˌkɔrdəˈlɪ(ə)r, -z

Cordell
BR ˌkɔːˈdel
AM ˌkɔrˈdel

cordial
BR ˈkɔːdɪəl
AM ˈkɔrdʒəl

cordiality
BR ˌkɔːdɪˈalɪti

co-referential
AM ˌkɔːdʒiˈæledi

cordially
BR ˈkɔːdɪəli
AM ˈkɔrdʒəli

cordillera
BR ˌkɔːdɪˈljeːrə(r)
AM ˌkɔrdl̩ˈ(j)ɛrə

cordite
BR ˈkɔːdʌɪt
AM ˈkɔrˌdaɪt

cordless
BR ˈkɔːdləs
AM ˈkɔrdləs

cordlessness
BR ˈkɔːdləsnəs
AM ˈkɔrdləsnəs

cordlike
BR ˈkɔːdlʌɪk
AM ˈkɔrˌlaɪk

Córdoba
BR ˈkɔːdəbə(r)
AM ˈkɔrdəbə, kɔrˈdoʊbə

cordon
BR ˈkɔːdn̩, -z, -ɪŋ, -d
AM ˈkɔrdən, -z, -ɪŋ, -d

cordon-bleu
BR ˌkɔːdɒn ˈblɜː(r), ˌkɔːdɜ̃ +
AM ˌkɔrdɒn ˈblə, ˌkɔrdn̩ ˈblu

cordon sanitaire
BR ˌkɔːdɒn ˌsanɪˈtɛː(r), ˌkɔːdɜ̃ +, -z
AM ˌkɔrdɒn ˌsɑniˈtɛ(ə)r, -z

Cordova
BR ˈkɔːdəvə(r)
AM ˈkɔrdəvə, kɔrˈdoʊvə

cordovan
BR ˈkɔːdəvn̩
AM ˈkɔrdəvən

corduroy
BR ˈkɔːdərɔɪ, ˈkɔːdjʊrɔɪ, ˈkɔːdʒʊrɔɪ, -z
AM ˈkɔrdəˌrɔɪ, -z

cordwain
BR ˈkɔːdweɪn
AM ˈkɔrdˌweɪn

cordwainer
BR ˈkɔːdˌweɪnə(r), -z
AM ˈkɔrdˌweɪnər, -z

cordwood
BR ˈkɔːdwʊd
AM ˈkɔrdˌwʊd

CORE
BR ˈkɔː(r)
AM kɔ(ə)r

core
BR kɔː(r), -z, -ɪŋ, -d
AM kɔ(ə)r, -z, -ɪŋ, -d

co-referential
BR ˌkəʊrefəˈrenʃl
AM ˌkoʊrefəˈrenʃəl

corelation
BR ˌkɒrɪˈleɪʃn, -z
AM ˌkɔːrəˈleɪʃən, -z
co-religionist
BR ˌkəʊrɪˈlɪdʒənɪst,
ˌkəʊrɪˈlɪdʒnɪst, -s
AM ˌkoʊrəˈlɪdʒənəst, -s
corella
BR kəˈrelə(r),
kɒˈrelə(r), -z
AM kəˈrelə, -z
Corelli
BR kəˈreli, kɒˈreli
AM kəˈreli
Coren
BR ˈkɔːrən, ˈkɔːrn̩
AM ˈkɔːrən
coreopsis
BR ˈkɒrɪˈɒpsɪs
AM ˌkɔːriˈɑpsəs
corer
BR ˈkɔːrə(r), -z
AM ˈkɔːrər, -z
co-respondent
BR ˌkəʊrɪˈspɒnd(ə)nt,
-s
AM ˌkoʊrəˈspɑndənt,
-s
Corey
BR ˈkɔːri
AM ˈkɔːri
corf
BR kɔːf, -s
AM kɔː(ə)rf, -s
Corfe
BR kɔːf
AM kɔː(ə)rf
Corfu
BR ˌkɔːˈf(j)uː
AM kɔːrˈfu, ˈkɔːrf(j)u
corgi
BR ˈkɔːgˌi, -ɪz
AM ˈkɔːrgi, -z
coria
BR ˈkɔːrɪə(r)
AM ˈkɔːriə
coriaceous
BR ˌkɒrɪˈeɪʃəs
AM ˌkɔːriˈeɪʃəs
coriander
BR ˌkɒrɪˈandə(r),
ˈkɒriandə(r)
AM ˈkɔːriˌændər
Corin
BR ˈkɒrɪn
AM ˈkɔːrən
Corinna
BR kəˈrɪnə(r)
AM kəˈrɪnə
Corinne
BR kəˈrɪn
AM kəˈrɪn
Corinth
BR ˈkɒr(ɪ)nθ
AM ˈkɔːrənθ
Corinthian
BR kəˈrɪnθɪən, -z

AM kəˈrɪnθɪən, -z
Coriolanus
BR ˌkɒrɪəˈleɪnəs
AM ˌkɔːriəˈleɪnəs
Coriolis
BR ˌkɒrɪˈəʊlɪs
AM ˌkɔːriˈoʊləs
corium
BR ˈkɔːrɪəm
AM ˈkɔːriəm
cork
BR kɔːk, -s, -ɪŋ, -t
AM kɔː(ə)rk, -s, -ɪŋ, -t
corkage
BR ˈkɔːkɪdʒ
AM ˈkɔːrkɪdʒ
corker
BR ˈkɔːkə(r), -z
AM ˈkɔːrkər, -z
corkiness
BR ˈkɔːkɪnɪs
AM ˈkɔːrkɪnɪs
corklike
BR ˈkɔːklʌɪk
AM ˈkɔːrkˌlaɪk
corkscrew
BR ˈkɔːkskruː, -z
AM ˈkɔːrkˌskru, -z
corkwood
BR ˈkɔːkwʊd
AM ˈkɔːrkˌwʊd
corky
BR ˈkɔːk|i, -ɪə(r), -ɪɪst
AM ˈkɔːrki, -ər, -ɪɪst
Corley
BR ˈkɔːli
AM ˈkɔːrli
corm
BR kɔːm, -z
AM kɔː(ə)rm, -z
Cormac
BR ˈkɔːmak, ˈkɔːmək
AM ˈkɔːrmək
cormorant
BR ˈkɔːm(ə)rənt,
ˈkɔːm(ə)rn̩t, -s
AM ˈkɔːrmərənt, -s
corn
BR kɔːn, -z, -d
AM kɔː(ə)rn, -z, -d
cornball
BR ˈkɔːnbɔːl, -z
AM ˈkɔːrnˌbɔl, -z
cornbrash
BR ˈkɔːnbraʃ
AM ˈkɔːrnˌbræʃ
cornbread
BR ˈkɔːnbred
AM ˈkɔːrnˌbred
corncob
BR ˈkɔːnkɒb, -z
AM ˈkɔːrnˌkɑb, -z
corncockle
BR ˈkɔːnkɒkl, -z
AM ˈkɔːrnˌkɑkəl, -z
corncrake
BR ˈkɔːnkreɪk, -s

AM ˈkɔːrnˌkreɪk, -s
corncrib
BR ˈkɔːnkrɪb, -z
AM ˈkɔːrnˌkrɪb, -z
cornea
BR ˈkɔːnɪə(r),
kɔːˈniːə(r), -z
AM ˈkɔːrniə, -z
corneal
BR ˈkɔːnɪəl, kɔːˈniːəl
AM ˈkɔːrniəl
cornel
BR ˈkɔːnl, -z
AM ˈkɔːrnəl, -z
Cornelia
BR kɔːˈniːlɪə(r)
AM kɔːrˈniljə, kɔːrˈniliə
cornelian
BR kɔːˈniːlɪən, -z
AM kɔːrˈniljən,
kɔːrˈniliən, -z
Cornelius
BR kɔːˈniːlɪəs
AM kɔːrˈniljəs,
kɔːrˈniliəs
Cornell
BR kɔːˈnel
AM kɔːrˈnel
corneous
BR ˈkɔːnɪəs
AM ˈkɔːrniəs
corner
BR ˈkɔːn|ə(r), -əz,
-(ə)rɪŋ, -əd
AM ˈkɔːrnər, -z, -ɪŋ, -d
cornerback
BR ˈkɔːnəbak, -s
AM ˈkɔːrnərˌbæk, -s
cornerstone
BR ˈkɔːnəstəʊn, -z
AM ˈkɔːrnərˌstoʊn, -z
cornerways
BR ˈkɔːnəweɪz
AM ˈkɔːrnərˌweɪz
cornerwise
BR ˈkɔːnəwʌɪz
AM ˈkɔːrnərˌwaɪz
cornet
BR ˈkɔːnɪt, -s
AM ˌkɔːrˈnet, -s
cornetcy
BR ˈkɔːnɪtsi
AM ˌkɔːrˈnetsi
cornetist
BR kɔːˈnetɪst, -s
AM ˌkɔːrˈnedəst, -s
cornett
BR ˈkɔːnɪt, -s
AM ˌkɔːrˈnet, -s
cornetti
BR kɔːˈneti:
AM kɔːrˈnedi
cornettist
BR kɔːˈnetɪst, -s
AM ˌkɔːrˈnedəst, -s
cornetto
BR kɔːˈnetəʊ, -z

AM ˈkɔːrnˌkreɪk, -s
cornfield
BR ˈkɔːnfiːld, -z
AM ˈkɔːrnˌfild, -z
cornflake
BR ˈkɔːnfleɪk, -s
AM ˈkɔːrnˌfleɪk, -s
cornflour
BR ˈkɔːnˌflaʊə(r)
AM ˈkɔːrnˌflaʊər
cornflower
BR ˈkɔːnˌflaʊə(r), -z
AM ˈkɔːrnˌflaʊər, -z
Cornhill
BR ˌkɔːnˈhɪl, ˈkɔːnhɪl
AM ˈkɔːrn(h)ɪl
cornhusk
BR ˈkɔːnhask, -s
AM ˈkɔːrn(h)əsk, -s
cornice
BR ˈkɔːnˌɪs, -ɪsɪz, -ɪst
AM ˈkɔːrnɪs, -ɪz, -ɪst
corniced
BR ˈkɔːnɪst
AM ˈkɔːrnɪst
corniche
BR ˈkɔːniːʃ, (ˌ)kɔːˈniːʃ,
-ɪz
AM kɔːrˈniʃ, kɔːrˈniʃ, -ɪz
cornily
BR ˈkɔːnɪli
AM ˈkɔːrnəli
corniness
BR ˈkɔːnɪnɪs
AM ˈkɔːrnɪnɪs
Corning
BR ˈkɔːnɪŋ
AM ˈkɔːrnɪŋ
Cornish
BR ˈkɔːnɪʃ
AM ˈkɔːrnɪʃ
Cornishman
BR ˈkɔːnɪʃmən
AM ˈkɔːrnɪʃmən
Cornishmen
BR ˈkɔːnɪʃmən
AM ˈkɔːrnɪʃmən
Cornishwoman
BR ˈkɔːnɪʃˌwʊmən
AM ˈkɔːrnɪʃˌwʊmən
Cornishwomen
BR ˈkɔːnɪʃˌwɪmɪn
AM ˈkɔːrnɪʃˌwɪmɪn
cornmeal
BR ˈkɔːnmiːl
AM ˈkɔːrnˌmil
cornrows
BR ˈkɔːnrəʊz
AM ˈkɔːrnˌroʊz
cornstalk
BR ˈkɔːnstɔːk, -s
AM ˈkɔːrnˌstɔk,
ˈkɔːrnˌstak, -s
cornstarch
BR ˈkɔːnstɑːtʃ
AM ˈkɔːrnˌstɑrtʃ

cornstone
BR 'kɔːnstəʊn
AM 'kɔrn,stoʊn

cornucopia
BR ,kɔːnjʊ'kəʊpiə(r),
-z
AM ,kɔrn(j)ə'koʊpiə, -z

cornucopian
BR ,kɔːnjʊ'kəʊpiən
AM ,kɔrn(j)ə'koʊpiən

Cornwall
BR 'kɔːnwɔːl,
'kɔːnw(ə)l
AM 'kɔrn,wɔl,
'kɔrn,wal

Cornwallis
BR (,)kɔːn'wɒlɪs
AM ,kɔrn'wɑləs

corny
BR 'kɔːn|i, -ɪə(r), -ɪɪst
AM 'kɔrni, -ər, -ɪst

corolla
BR kə'rɒlə(r), -z
AM kə'rɑlə, kə'roʊlə, -z

corollary
BR kə'rɒl(ə)r|i, -ɪz
AM 'kɔrə,lɛri,
'karə,lɛri, -z

Coromandel
BR ,kɒrə(ʊ)'mandl
AM ,kɔrə'mændəl

corona
BR kə'rəʊnə(r), -z
AM kə'roʊnə, -z

Corona Borealis
BR kə,rəʊnə
,bɔːrɪ'eɪlɪs,
+ ,bɔːrɪ'ɑːlɪs
AM kə'roʊnə
borɪ'æləs,
+ ,borɪ'eɪlɪs

coronach
BR 'kɒrənəx,
'kɒrənək, -s
AM 'kɔrənək, -s

coronae
BR kə'rəʊniː
AM kə'roʊni,
kə'roʊ,naɪ

coronagraph
BR kə'rəʊnəgrɑːf,
kə'rəʊnəgraf, -s
AM kə'roʊnə,græf, -s

coronal
BR 'kɒrənl, 'kɒrn̩l
AM 'kɔrənəl, kə'roʊnəl

coronary
BR 'kɒrən(ə)r|i,
'kɒrn̩(ə)r|i, -ɪz
AM 'kɔrə,nɛri, -z

coronation
BR ,kɒrə'neɪʃn, -z
AM ,kɒrə'neɪʃən, -z

coroner
BR 'kɒrənə(r),
'kɒrn̩ə(r), -z
AM 'kɔrənər, -z

coronership
BR 'kɒrənəʃɪp,
'kɒrn̩əʃɪp
AM 'kɔrənər,ʃɪp

coronet
BR 'kɒrənɪt, 'kɒrənɛt,
,kɒrə'nɛt, -s, -ɪd
AM ,kɔrə'nɛ|t, -ts, -dəd

Corot
BR 'kɒrəʊ
AM kə'roʊ

corozo
BR kə'rəʊzəʊ, -z
AM kə'roʊzoʊ, -z

Corp.
BR kɔːp
AM kɔrp

corpora
BR 'kɔːp(ə)rə(r)
AM 'kɔrp(ə)rə

corpora delicti
BR ,kɔːp(ə)rə dɪ'lɪktʌɪ
AM ,kɔrpərə də'lɪk,taɪ

corporal
BR 'kɔːp(ə)rəl,
'kɔːp(ə)rl̩, -z
AM 'kɔrp(ə)rəl, -z

corporality
BR ,kɔːpə'ralɪti
AM ,kɔrpə'rælədi

corporally
BR 'kɔːp(ə)rəli,
'kɔːp(ə)rl̩i
AM 'kɔrp(ə)rəli

corpora lutea
BR ,kɔːpərə 'luːtɪə(r)
AM ,kɔrpərə 'ludiə

corporate
BR 'kɔːp(ə)rət
AM 'kɔrp(ə)rət

corporately
BR 'kɔːp(ə)rətli
AM 'kɔrp(ə)rətli

corporateness
BR 'kɔːp(ə)rətnəs
AM 'kɔrp(ə)rətnəs

corporation
BR ,kɔːpə'reɪʃn, -z
AM ,kɔrpə'reɪʃən, -z

corporatism
BR 'kɔːp(ə)rətɪz(ə)m
AM 'kɔrp(ə)rə,tɪzəm

corporatist
BR 'kɔːp(ə)rətɪst
AM 'kɔrp(ə)rədəst

corporative
BR 'kɔːp(ə)rətɪv
AM 'kɔrp(ə)rədɪv

corporativism
BR 'kɔːp(ə)rətɪvɪz(ə)m
AM 'kɔrp(ə)rədə,vɪzəm

corporativist
BR 'kɔːp(ə)rətɪvɪst
AM 'kɔrp(ə)rədəvəst,
-s

corporeal
BR kɔː'pɔːrɪəl

AM kɔr'pɔːrɪəl

corporeality
BR kɔː,pɔːrɪ'alɪti
AM kɔr,pɔri'ælədi

corporeally
BR kɔː'pɔːrɪəli
AM kɔr'pɔːrɪəli

corporeity
BR ,kɔː,pə'riːɪti,
,kɔː,pə'reɪti
AM kɔrpə'riːdi,
kɔrpə'reɪdi

corposant
BR 'kɔːp(ə)snt, -s
AM 'kɔrpə,sænt,
'kɔrpəsənt, -s

corps
BR kɔː(r), -z
AM kɔ(ə)r, -z

corps de ballet
BR ,kɔː də 'baleɪ
AM ,kɔr də bæ'leɪ

corps d'élite
BR ,kɔː deɪ'liːt
AM ,kɔr der'lit

corps diplomatique
BR ,kɔː ,dɪpləmə'tiːk
AM ,kɔr ,dɪpləmə'tik

corpse
BR kɔːps, -ɪz
AM kɔ(ə)rps, -əz

corpulence
BR 'kɔːpjʊləns
AM 'kɔrpjələns

corpulency
BR 'kɔːpjʊlənsi
AM 'kɔrpjələnsi

corpulent
BR 'kɔːpjʊlənt,
'kɔːpjʊlnt
AM 'kɔrpjələnt

corpus
BR 'kɔːpəs, -ɪz
AM 'kɔrpəs, -əz

Corpus Christi
BR ,kɔːpəs 'krɪsti
AM ,kɔrpəs 'krɪsti

corpuscle
BR 'kɔːpʌsl, -z
AM 'kɔr,pʌsəl, -z

corpuscular
BR kɔː'pʌskjʊlə(r)
AM kɔr'pəskjələr

corpus delicti
BR ,kɔːpəs dɪ'lɪktʌɪ
AM ,kɔrpəs də'lɪktaɪ

corpus luteum
BR ,kɔːpəs 'luːtɪəm
AM ,kɔrpəs 'ludiəm

corral
BR kə'rɑːl, kə'ral, -z,
-ɪŋ, -d
AM kə'ræl, -z, -ɪŋ, -d

corrasion
BR kə'reɪʒn
AM kə'reɪʒən

correct
BR kə'rɛkt, -s, -ɪŋ, -ɪd
AM kə'rɛk|(t), -(t)s,
-dɪŋ, -dəd

correction
BR kə'rɛkʃn, -z
AM kə'rɛkʃən, -z

correctional
BR kə'rɛkʃn(ə)l,
kə'rɛkʃən(ə)l
AM kə'rɛkʃ(ə)nəl

correctitude
BR kə'rɛktɪtjuːd,
kə'rɛktɪtʃuːd
AM kə'rɛktə,tud

corrective
BR kə'rɛktɪv
AM kə'rɛktɪv

correctively
BR kə'rɛktɪvli
AM kə'rɛktɪvli

correctly
BR kə'rɛktli
AM kə'rɛk(t)li

correctness
BR kə'rɛk(t)nəs
AM kə'rɛk(t)nəs

corrector
BR kə'rɛktə(r), -z
AM kə'rɛktər, -z

Correggio
BR kə'rɛdʒɪəʊ
AM kə'rɛdʒioʊ

correlate[1]
noun
BR 'kɒrɪleɪt, 'kɒrɪlət,
'kɒrl̩ət, -s
AM 'kɔrələt, -s

correlate[2]
verb
BR 'kɒrɪleɪt, -s, -ɪŋ, -ɪd
AM 'kɔrə,leɪ|t, -ts, -dɪŋ,
-dɪd

correlation
BR ,kɒrɪ'leɪʃn
AM ,kɔrə'leɪʃən

correlational
BR ,kɒrɪ'leɪʃn(ə)l,
,kɒrɪ'leɪʃənəl
AM ,kɔrə'leɪʃ(ə)nəl

correlative
BR kə'rɛlətɪv, -z
AM kə'rɛlədɪv, -z

correlatively
BR kə'rɛlətɪvli
AM kə'rɛlədɪvli

correlativity
BR kə,rɛlə'tɪvɪti
AM kə,rɛlə'tɪvɪdi

correspond
BR ,kɒrɪ'spɒnd, -z, -ɪŋ,
-ɪd
AM ,kɔrə'spɑnd, -z, -ɪŋ,
-əd

correspondence
BR ,kɒrɪ'spɒnd(ə)ns,
-ɪz

AM ˌkɒrə'spɒnd(ə)ns, -əz

correspondent
BR ˌkɒrɪ'spɒnd(ə)nt, -s
AM ˌkɔrə'spɑndənt, -s

correspondently
BR ˌkɒrɪ'spɒnd(ə)ntli
AM ˌkɔrə'spɑndən(t)li

corresponding
BR ˌkɒrɪ'spɒndɪŋ
AM ˌkɔrə'spɑndɪŋ

correspondingly
BR ˌkɒrɪ'spɒndɪŋli
AM ˌkɔrə'spɑndɪŋli

corrida
BR kɒ'riːdə(r), kə'riːdə(r), -z
AM kɔ'ridə, -z

corridor
BR 'kɒrɪdɔː(r), -z
AM 'kɔrədər, 'kɔrə,dɔ(ə)r, -z

corrie
BR 'kɒr|i, -ɪz
AM 'kɔri, 'kɑri, -z

Corrigan
BR 'kɒrɪg(ə)n
AM 'kɔrəgən

corrigenda
BR ˌkɒrɪ'dʒendə(r), ˌkɒrɪ'gendə(r)
AM ˌkɔrə'dʒendə, ˌkɔrə'gendə

corrigendum
BR ˌkɒrɪ'dʒendəm, ˌkɒrɪ'gendəm
AM ˌkɔrə'dʒendəm, ˌkɔrə'gendəm

corrigible
BR 'kɒrɪdʒɪbl
AM 'kɔrədʒəbəl

corrigibly
BR 'kɒrɪdʒɪbli
AM 'kɔrədʒəbli

Corris
BR 'kɒrɪs
AM 'kɔrəs

corroborate
BR kə'rɒbəreɪt, -s, -ɪŋ, -ɪd
AM kə'rɑbə,reɪ|t, -ts, -dɪŋ, -dɪd

corroboration
BR kə,rɒbə'reɪʃn
AM kə,rɑbə'reɪʃən

corroborative
BR kə'rɒb(ə)rətɪv
AM kə'rɑbər(ə)dɪv

corroborator
BR kə'rɒbəreɪtə(r), -z
AM kə'rɑbə,reɪdər, -z

corroboratory
BR kə'rɒb(ə)rət(ə)ri
AM kə'rɑb(ə)rə,tɔri

corroboree
BR kə'rɒbəriː, kə,rɒbə'riː, -z
AM kə,rɑbə'ri, -z

corrode
BR kə'rəʊd, -z, -ɪŋ, -ɪd
AM kə'roʊd, -z, -ɪŋ, -əd

corrodible
BR kə'rəʊdɪbl
AM kə'roʊdəbəl

corrosion
BR kə'rəʊʒn
AM kə'roʊʒən

corrosive
BR kə'rəʊsɪv
AM 'kɔrslət, -s

corrosively
BR kə'rəʊsɪvli
AM kə'roʊsɪvli

corrosiveness
BR kə'rəʊsɪvnɪs
AM kə'roʊsɪvnɪs

corrugate
BR 'kɒrəgeɪt, -s, -ɪŋ, -ɪd
AM 'kɔrə,geɪ|t, -ts, -dɪŋ, -dɪd

corrugation
BR ˌkɒrə'geɪʃn, -z
AM ˌkɔrə'geɪʃən, -z

corrugator
BR 'kɒrəgeɪtə(r), -z
AM 'kɔrə,geɪdər, -z

corrupt
BR kə'rʌpt, -s, -ɪŋ, -ɪd
AM kə'rəpt, -s, -ɪŋ, -əd

corrupter
BR kə'rʌptə(r), -z
AM kə'rəptər, -z

corruptibility
BR kə,rʌptɪ'bɪlɪti
AM kə,rəptə'bɪlɪdi

corruptible
BR kə'rʌptɪbl
AM kə'rəptəbəl

corruptibleness
BR kə'rʌptɪblnəs
AM kə'rəptəbəlnəs

corruptibly
BR kə'rʌptɪbli
AM kə'rəptəbli

corruption
BR kə'rʌpʃn, -z
AM kə'rəpʃən, -z

corruptive
BR kə'rʌptɪv
AM kə'rʌptɪv

corruptly
BR kə'rʌptli
AM kə'rʌptli

corruptness
BR kə'rʌptnəs
AM kə'rəp(t)nəs

corsac
BR 'kɔːsak, -s
AM 'kɔr,sæk, kɔr'sæk, -s

corsage
BR 'kɔːsɑːʒ, -ɪz
AM kɔr'sɑʒ, -əz

corsair
BR 'kɔːsɛː(r), -z

AM 'kɔr,sɛ(ə)r, -z

corsak
BR 'kɔːsak, -s
AM 'kɔr,sæk, -s

corse
BR kɔːs, -ɪz
AM kɔ(ə)rs, -əz

corselet
BR 'kɔːslɪt, -s
AM 'kɔrslət, -s

corselette
BR 'kɔːslɪt, -s
AM 'kɔrslət, -s

corset
BR 'kɔːs|ɪt, -ɪts, -ɪtɪd
AM 'kɔrsət, -s, -əd

corsetière
BR ˌkɔːsɪ'tɪə(r), -z
AM ˌkɔrsə'tɪ(ə)r, -z

corsetry
BR 'kɔːsɪtri
AM 'kɔrsətri

Corsica
BR 'kɔːsɪkə(r)
AM 'kɔrsəkə

Corsican
BR 'kɔːsɪkən, -z
AM 'kɔrsəkən, -z

corslet
BR 'kɔːslɪt, -s
AM 'kɔrslət, -s

Corstorphine
BR kə'stɔːfɪn
AM kər'stɔrfən

Cort
BR kɔːt
AM kɔ(ə)rt

cortège
BR (ˌ)kɔː'teɪʒ, (ˌ)kɔː'teʒ, 'kɔːteɪʒ, 'kɔːteʒ, -ɪz
AM kɔr'teʒ, -əz

Cortes
parliament
BR 'kɔːtez, 'kɔːtes, 'kɔːtɪz
AM 'kɔrtez

Cortés
Hernando
BR 'kɔːtez, kɔː'tez
AM kɔr'tez

cortex
BR 'kɔːteks, -ɪz
AM 'kɔr,teks, -əz

Corti
BR 'kɔːti
AM 'kɔrdi

cortical
BR 'kɔːtɪkl
AM 'kɔrdəkl

corticate
BR 'kɔːtɪkeɪt
AM 'kɔrdə,keɪt, 'kɔrdəkət

corticated
BR 'kɔːtɪkeɪtɪd
AM 'kɔrdə,keɪdɪd

cortices
BR 'kɔːtɪsiːz
AM 'kɔrdə,siz

corticotrophic
BR ˌkɔːtɪkə(ʊ)'trɒfɪk, ˌkɔːtɪkə(ʊ)'trəʊfɪk
AM ˌkɔrdə,koʊ'trɑfɪk

corticotrophin
BR ˌkɔːtɪkə(ʊ)'trəʊfɪn
AM ˌkɔrdə,koʊ'troʊfən

corticotropic
BR ˌkɔːtɪkə(ʊ)'trɒpɪk, ˌkɔːtɪkə(ʊ)'trəʊpɪk
AM ˌkɔrdə,koʊ'trɑpɪk

corticotropin
BR ˌkɔːtɪkə(ʊ)'trəʊpɪn
AM ˌkɔrdə,koʊ'troʊpən

Cortina®
BR kɔː'tiːnə(r)
AM kɔr'tinə

cortisone
BR 'kɔːtɪzəʊn
AM 'kɔrdə,soʊn

Corton
BR 'kɔːtn
AM 'kɔrtən

corundum
BR kə'rʌndəm
AM kə'rəndəm

Corunna
BR kə'rʌnə(r)
AM kə'rʌnə

coruscate
BR 'kɒrəskeɪt, -s, -ɪŋ, -ɪd
AM 'kɔrə,skeɪ|t, -ts, -dɪŋ, -dɪd

coruscation
BR ˌkɒrə'skeɪʃn, -z
AM ˌkɔrə'skeɪʃən, -z

corvée
BR 'kɔːveɪ, -z
AM 'kɔr,veɪ, -z

corves
BR kɔːvz
AM kɔrvz

corvette
BR kɔː'vet, -s
AM kɔr'vet, -s

corvine
BR 'kɔːvaɪn
AM 'kɔr,vaɪn

Corwen
BR 'kɔːwɛn, 'kɔːwən
AM 'kɔrwən

Cory
BR 'kɔːri
AM 'kɔri

corybant
BR 'kɒrɪbant, -s
AM 'kɔrə,bænt, -s

corybantic
BR ˌkɒrɪ'bantɪk
AM ˌkɔrə'bæn(t)ɪk

Corydon
BR 'kɒrɪd(ə)n
AM 'kɔrəd(ə)n

corymb
BR ˈkɒrɪm(b)
AM ˈkɔːrɪm(b),
ˈkarɪm(b)

corymbose
BR ˈkɒrɪmbəʊs
AM ˈkɔːrɪmˌboʊs,
ˈkarɪmˌboʊs,
kəˈrɪmboʊs

corynebacteria
BR ˌkɒrɪnɪbakˈtɪərɪə(r),
kəˌrɪnɪbakˈtɪərɪə(r)
AM ˌkɔːrənɪbækˈtɪrɪə,
kəˌrɪnəbækˈtɪrɪə

corynebacterium
BR ˌkɒrɪnɪbakˈtɪərɪəm,
kəˌrɪnɪbakˈtɪərɪəm
AM ˌkɔːrənɪbækˈtɪrɪəm,
kəˌrɪnəbækˈtɪrɪəm

coryphaei
BR ˌkɒrɪˈfiːʌɪ
AM ˌkɔːrəˈfiˌaɪ

coryphaeus
BR ˌkɒrɪˈfiːəs
AM ˌkɔːrəˈfiəs

coryphée
BR ˈkɒrɪfeɪ, -z
AM ˌkɔːrəˈfeɪ, ˈkarəˌfeɪ,
-z

Coryton
BR ˈkɒrɪt(ə)n
AM ˈkɔːrət(ə)n

coryza
BR kəˈrʌɪzə(r)
AM kəˈraɪzə

Cos
BR kɒs
AM kas, kɔs

cos¹
cosine
BR kɒz, kɒs
AM kɔs

cos²
lettuce
BR kɒs
AM kas

'cos
because
BR kəz
AM kəz

Cosa Nostra
BR ˌkəʊzə ˈnɒstrə(r)
AM ˌkoʊsə ˈnoʊstrə,
ˌkoʊzə +

cosec
cosecant
BR ˈkəʊsɛk, -s
AM ˈkoʊsɛk, -s

cosecant
BR ˌkəʊˈsiːk(ə)nt, -s
AM koʊˈsikənt, -s

coseismal
BR kəʊˈseɪzml, -z
AM koʊˈsaɪsməl, -z

coset
BR ˈkəʊsɛt, -s
AM ˈkoʊˌsɛt, -s

Cosford
BR ˈkɒsfəd
AM ˈkasfərd, ˈkɔsfərd

Cosgrave
BR ˈkɒzgreɪv
AM ˈkazˌgreɪv,
ˈkɔzˌgreɪv

cosh¹
weapon, hit
BR kɒʃ, -ɪz, -ɪŋ, -t
AM kaʃ, -əz, -ɪŋ, -t

cosh²
hyperbolic cosine
BR kɒʃ, kɒsˈeɪtʃ
AM kɔs, kaʃ, kɔsˈeɪtʃ,
kasˈeɪtʃ

cosher
BR ˈkɒʃə(r), -z
AM ˈkaʃər, -z

cosies
BR ˈkəʊziz
AM ˈkoʊziz

Così Fan Tutte
BR ˌkəʊsɪ ˌfan ˈtʊti
AM ˌkoʊzi ˌfan ˈtudi

cosignatory
BR ˌkəʊˈsɪgnət(ə)r|i,
-ɪz
AM koʊˈsɪgnəˌtɔri, -z

cosigner
BR ˈkəʊˌsʌɪnə(r), -z
AM ˈkoʊˌsaɪnər, -z

cosily
BR ˈkəʊzɪli
AM ˈkoʊzəli

cosine
BR ˈkəʊsʌɪn
AM ˈkoʊˌsaɪn

cosiness
BR ˈkəʊzɪnɪs
AM ˈkoʊzɪnɪs

CoSIRA
BR kəˈ(ʊ)ˈsʌɪrə(r)
AM kəˈsaɪrə

cosmea
BR ˈkɒzmɪə(r)
AM ˈkazmɪə

cosmetic
BR kɒzˈmɛtɪk, -s
AM kazˈmɛdɪk, -s

cosmetically
BR kɒzˈmɛtɪkli
AM kazˈmɛdək(ə)li

cosmetician
BR ˌkɒzmɪˈtɪʃn, -z
AM ˌkazməˈtɪʃən, -z

cosmetologist
BR ˌkɒzmɪˈtɒlədʒɪst, -s
AM ˌkazməˈtalədʒəst,
-s

cosmetology
BR ˌkɒzmɪˈtɒlədʒi
AM ˌkazməˈtalədʒi

cosmic
BR ˈkɒzmɪk
AM ˈkazmɪk

cosmical
BR ˈkɒzmɪkl
AM ˈkazməkəl

cosmically
BR ˈkɒzmɪkli
AM ˈkazmək(ə)li

Cosmo
BR ˈkɒzməʊ
AM ˈkazmoʊ

cosmogonic
BR ˌkɒzməˈgɒnɪk
AM ˌkazməˈganɪk

cosmogonical
BR ˌkɒzməˈgɒnɪkl
AM ˌkazməˈganəkəl

cosmogonist
BR kɒzˈmɒgənɪst,
kɒzˈmɒgnɪst, -s
AM kazˈmagənəst, -s

cosmogony
BR kɒzˈmɒgəni,
kɒzˈmɒgni
AM kazˈmagəni

cosmographer
BR kɒzˈmɒgrəfə(r), -z
AM kazˈmagrəfər, -z

cosmographic
BR ˌkɒzməˈgrafɪk
AM ˌkazməˈgræfɪk

cosmographical
BR ˌkɒzməˈgrafɪkl
AM ˌkazməˈgræfəkəl

cosmography
BR kɒzˈmɒgrəfi
AM kazˈmagrəfi

cosmological
BR ˌkɒzməˈlɒdʒɪkl
AM ˌkazməˈladʒəkəl

cosmologist
BR kɒzˈmɒlədʒɪst, -s
AM kazˈmalədʒəst, -s

cosmology
BR kɒzˈmɒlədʒi
AM kazˈmalədʒi

cosmonaut
BR ˈkɒzmənɔːt, -s
AM ˈkazməˌnɔt,
ˈkazməˌnat, -s

cosmopolis
BR kɒzˈmɒpəlɪs
AM kazˈmapələs

cosmopolitan
BR ˌkɒzməˈpɒlɪt(ə)n,
-z
AM ˌkazməˈpalətn,
ˌkazməˈpalədən, -z

cosmopolitanise
BR ˌkɒzməˈpɒlɪtənʌɪz,
ˌkɒzməˈpɒlɪtnʌɪz, -ɪz,
-ɪŋ, -d
AM ˌkazməˈpalətnˌaɪz,
ˌkazməˈpalədəˌnaɪz,
-ɪz, -ɪŋ, -d

cosmopolitanism
BR ˌkɒzməˈpɒlɪtənɪz-
(ə)m,
ˌkɒzməˈpɒlɪtnɪz(ə)m
AM ˌkazməˈpalətnˌɪzəm,
ˌkazməˈpalədəˌnɪzəm

cosmopolitanize
BR ˌkɒzməˈpɒlɪtənʌɪz,
ˌkɒzməˈpɒlɪtnʌɪz, -ɪz,
-ɪŋ, -d
AM ˌkazməˈpalətn ˌaɪz,
ˌkazməˈpalədəˌnaɪz,
-ɪz, -ɪŋ, -d

cosmopolite
BR kɒzˈmɒpəlʌɪt,
kɒzˈmɒplʌɪt, -s
AM kazˈmapəˌlaɪt, -s

cosmos
BR ˈkɒzmɒs, -ɪz
AM ˈkazməs,
ˈkazˌmoʊs, -əz

co-sponsor
BR ˌkəʊˈspɒns|ə(r), -əz,
-(ə)rɪŋ, -əd
AM ˌkoʊˈspans|ər, -ərz,
-(ə)rɪŋ, -ərd

Cossack
BR ˈkɒsak, -s
AM ˈkɔsæk, ˈkasæk, -s

cosset
BR ˈkɒs|ɪt, -ɪts, -ɪtɪŋ,
-ɪtɪd
AM ˈkasə|t, -ts, -dɪŋ,
-dəd

cossie
BR ˈkɒz|i, -ɪz
AM ˈkazi, -z

cost
BR kɒst, -s, -ɪŋ
AM kɔst, kast, -s, -ɪŋ

Costa
BR ˈkɒstə(r)
AM ˈkɔstə, ˈkastə

Costa Blanca
BR ˌkɒstə ˈblaŋkə(r)
AM ˌkɔstə ˈblæŋkə,
ˌkastə ˈblæŋkə

Costa Brava
BR ˌkɒstə ˈbrɑːvə(r)
AM ˌkɔstə ˈbrɑvə,
ˌkastə ˈbrɑvə

Costa del Sol
BR ˌkɒstə dɛl ˈsɒl
AM ˌkɔstə ˌdɛl ˈsoʊl,
ˌkastə ˌdɛl ˈsoʊl

Costain
BR ˈkɒsteɪn, kɒˈsteɪn
AM ˈkasteɪn

costal
BR ˈkɒstl
AM ˈkastəl

co-star
BR ˈkəʊstɑː(r), -z, -ɪŋ, -d
AM ˈkoʊˌstɑr, -z, -ɪŋ, -d

costard
BR ˈkɒstəd, ˈkʌstəd, -z
AM ˈkastərd, -z

Costa Rica
BR ˌkɒstə ˈriːkə(r)
AM ˌkoʊstə ˈrikə,
ˌkɔstə +, ˌkastə +

Costa Rican
BR ˌkɒstə ˈriːkən, -z

costate
AM ˌkoʊstə'rikən,
ˌkɒstə +, ˌkʌstə +, -z
BR 'kɒsteɪt
AM 'kɑˌsteɪt

Costello
BR kɒ'stɛləʊ, 'kɒstɪləʊ,
'kɒstˌləʊ
AM ˌkɑs'tɛloʊ

coster
BR 'kɒstə(r), -z
AM 'kɑstər, -z

costermonger
BR 'kɒstəˌmʌŋgə(r), -z
AM 'kɑstərˌmɑŋgər,
'kɑstərˌməŋgər, -z

costing
BR 'kɒstɪŋ, -z
AM 'kɑstɪŋ, -z

costive
BR 'kɒstɪv
AM 'kɑstɪv

costively
BR 'kɒstɪvli
AM 'kɑstɪvli

costiveness
BR 'kɒstɪvnɪs
AM 'kɑstɪvnɪs

costliness
BR 'kɒs(t)lɪnɪs
AM 'kɒs(t)linɪs,
'kɑs(t)linɪs

costly
BR 'kɒs(t)l|i, -ɪə(r),
-ɪɪst
AM 'kɒs(t)li, 'kɑs(t)li,
-ər, -ɪst

costmary
BR 'kɒstˌmɛːr|i, -ɪz
AM 'kɒs(t)ˌmɛri,
'kɑs(t)ˌmɛri, -z

Costner
BR 'kɒs(t)nə(r)
AM 'kɒs(t)nər,
'kɑs(t)nər

costume
BR 'kɒstju:m,
'kɒstʃu:m, -z
AM 'kɑsˌt(j)u:m, -z

costumier
BR kɒ'stju:mɪə(r),
kə'stju:mɪə(r),
kɒ'stʃu:mɪə(r),
kə'stʃu:mɪə(r), -z
AM ˌkɑstəm'jeɪ,
kɑ'st(j)uˌmɪ(ə)r, -z

cosy
BR 'kəʊz|i, -ɪz, -ɪə(r),
-ɪɪst
AM 'koʊzi, -z, -ər, -ɪst

cot
BR kɒt
AM kɑt

cotangent
BR kəʊ'tan(d)ʒ(ə)nt, -s
AM ˌkoʊ'tændʒənt, -s

cote
BR kəʊt, -s

Côte d'Azur
BR ˌkəʊt də'zjʊə(r),
+ da'zjʊə(r)
AM ˌkoʊt də'zʊ(ə)r

coterie
BR 'kəʊt(ə)r|i, -ɪz
AM 'koʊdəri, -z

coterminous
BR (ˌ)kəʊ'tə:mɪnəs
AM koʊ'tɜrmənəs

coterminously
BR (ˌ)kəʊ'tə:mɪnəsli
AM koʊ'tɜrmənəsli

coth
hyperbolic cotangent
BR kɒθ, ˌkɒt'eɪtʃ
AM kɑθ

cotherni
BR kə(ʊ)'θə:nʌɪ
AM koʊ'θərˌnaɪ

cothernus
BR kə(ʊ)'θə:nəs
AM koʊ'θərnəs

Cothi
BR 'kɒθi
AM 'kɑθi

cotillion
BR kə(ʊ)'tɪlɪən,
kʊ'tɪlɪən, -z
AM kə'tɪljən, -z

Cotman
BR 'kɒtmən
AM 'kɑtmən

Coton
BR 'kəʊtn
AM 'koʊtn

cotoneaster
BR kəˌtəʊnɪ'astə(r), -z
AM kə'toʊniˌæstər, -z

Cotopaxi
BR ˌkəʊtə'paksi
AM ˌkoʊdə'pæksi

Cotswold
BR 'kɒtswəʊld, -z
AM 'kɑtsˌwoʊld, -z

cotta
BR 'kɒtə(r), -z
AM 'kɑdə, -z

cottage
BR 'kɒt|ɪdʒ, -ɪdʒɪz
AM 'kɑdɪdʒ, -ɪz

cottager
BR 'kɒtɪdʒə(r), -z
AM 'kɑdɪdʒər, -z

cottagey
BR 'kɒtɪdʒi
AM 'kɑdɪdʒi

cottaging
BR 'kɒtɪdʒɪŋ
AM 'kɑdɪdʒɪŋ

cottar
BR 'kɒtə(r), -z
AM 'kɑdər, -z

Cottbus
BR 'kɒtbʊs
AM 'kɑtˌbʊs

cotter
BR 'kɒtə(r), -z
AM 'kɑdər, -z

Cotterell
BR 'kɒt(ə)rɪl, 'kɒtr̩l
AM 'kɑdərəl

Cotterill
BR 'kɒt(ə)rɪl, 'kɒtr̩l
AM 'kɑdərəl

Cottesloe
BR 'kɒt(ɪ)sləʊ,
'kɒtɪzləʊ
AM 'kɑdəsloʊ

Cottesmore
BR 'kɒtsmɔ:(r)
AM 'kɑdəsˌmɔ(ə)r

cottier
BR 'kɒtɪə(r), -z
AM 'kɑdiər, -z

cottise
BR 'kɒt|ɪs, -ɪsɪz
AM 'kɑdəs, -əz

Cottle
BR 'kɒtl
AM 'kɑdəl

cotton
BR 'kɒtn̩, -z, -ɪŋ, -d
AM 'kɑtn, -z, -ɪŋ, -d

cottonseed
BR 'kɒtnsi:d, -z
AM 'kɑtnˌsid, -z

cottontail
BR 'kɒtnteɪl, -z
AM 'kɑtnˌteɪl, -z

cottonwood
BR 'kɒtnwʊd, -z
AM 'kɑtnˌwʊd, -z

cottony
BR 'kɒtni
AM 'kɑtn̩i

Cottrell
BR 'kɒtr(ə)l
AM kə'trɛl

cotyledon
BR ˌkɒtɪ'li:dn, -z
AM ˌkɑdə'lidən, -z

cotyledonary
BR ˌkɒtɪ'li:dn(ə)ri
AM ˌkɑdə'lidn̩ˌɛri

cotyledonous
BR ˌkɒtɪ'li:dn̩əs
AM ˌkɑdə'lidn̩əs

coucal
BR 'ku:kl, 'kʊkɑ:l, -z
AM 'kukəl, -z

Couch
BR ku:tʃ
AM kaʊtʃ

couch[1]
*sofa, lie down, choice
of words*
BR kaʊtʃ, -ɪz, -ɪŋ, -t
AM kaʊtʃ, -əz, -ɪŋ, -t

couch[2]
grass
BR kaʊtʃ, ku:tʃ
AM kaʊtʃ, kʊtʃ

couchant
BR 'kaʊtʃ(ə)nt, 'ku:ʃnt
AM 'kaʊtʃənt, 'kuʃnt

couchette
BR ku:'ʃɛt, -s
AM ku'ʃɛt, -s

coudé
BR ku:'deɪ, -z
AM ku'deɪ, -z

Coué
BR 'ku:eɪ
AM ku'eɪ

Couéism
BR 'ku:eɪɪz(ə)m
AM ku'eɪˌɪzəm

cougar
BR 'ku:gə(r),
'ku:gɑ:(r), -z
AM 'kugər, -z

cough
BR kɒf, -s, -ɪŋ, -t
AM kɔf, kɑf, -s, -ɪŋ, -t

cougher
BR 'kɒfə(r), -z
AM 'kɔfər, 'kɑfər, -z

Coughlan
BR 'kɒxlən, 'kɒklən,
'kɒflən
AM 'kɔflən, 'kɑflən

Coughton
BR 'kəʊtn, 'kaʊtn,
'kɔ:tn
AM 'kɔdən, 'kɑdən,
'kɔtn

could[1]
strong form
BR kʊd
AM kʊd

could[2]
weak form
BR kəd
AM kəd

couldn't
BR kʊdnt
AM kʊdnt

couldst
BR kʊdst
AM kʊdst

coulée
BR 'ku:l|i, 'ku:l|eɪ,
-ɪz\-eɪz
AM 'ku:l|eɪ, -z

coulisse
BR ku:'li:s, -ɪz
AM ku'lis, -ɪz

couloir
BR 'ku:lwɑː(r), -z
AM ˌkul'wɑr, -z

coulomb
BR 'ku:lɒm, -z
AM 'kuˌlɑm, 'kuˌloʊm,
-z

coulometric
BR ˌku:lə'mɛtrɪk
AM ˌkulə'mɛtrɪk

coulometry
BR ku:'lɒmɪtri
AM ku'lɑmətri

Coulsdon
BR ˈkuːlzd(ə)n,
ˈkəʊlzd(ə)n
AM ˈkulzdən

Coulson
BR ˈkuːlsn, ˈkəʊlsn
AM ˈkoʊlsən

Coulston
BR ˈkuːlst(ə)n
AM ˈkoʊlstən

coulter
BR ˈkəʊltə(r), -z
AM ˈkoʊltər, -z

Coulthard
BR ˈkuːltɑːd, ˈkuːlθɑːd
AM ˈkoʊltɑrd,
ˈkoʊlθɑrd

coumarin
BR ˈkuːm(ə)rɪn
AM ˈkumərən

coumarone
BR ˈkuːmərəʊn
AM ˈkuməˌroʊn

council
BR ˈkaʊnsl, -z
AM ˈkaʊnsəl, -z

councillor
BR ˈkaʊns(ɪ)lə(r), -z
AM ˈkaʊns(ə)lər, -z

councillorship
BR ˈkaʊns(ɪ)ləʃɪp
AM ˈkaʊns(ə)lərˌʃɪp

councilman
BR ˈkaʊnslmən
AM ˈkaʊnsəlmən

councilmen
BR ˈkaʊnslmən
AM ˈkaʊnsəlmən

councilwoman
BR ˈkaʊnslˌwʊmən
AM ˈkaʊnsəlˌwəmən

councilwomen
BR ˈkaʊnslˌwɪmɪn
AM ˈkaʊnsəlˌwɪmɪn

counsel
BR ˈkaʊnsl, -lz,
- lɪŋ \ -əlɪŋ, -ld
AM ˈkaʊnsəl, -əlz,
-(ə)lɪŋ, -əld

counsellor
BR ˈkaʊns(ɪ)lə(r), -z
AM ˈkaʊns(ə)lər, -z

counselor
BR ˈkaʊns(ɪ)lə(r), -z
AM ˈkaʊns(ə)lər, -z

count
BR kaʊnt, -s, -ɪŋ, -ɪd
AM kaʊn|t, -ts, -(t)ɪŋ,
-(t)əd

countable
BR ˈkaʊntəbl
AM ˈkaʊn(t)əbəl

countdown
BR ˈkaʊntdaʊn, -z
AM ˈkaʊn(t)ˌdaʊn, -z

countenance
BR ˈkaʊntɪnəns,
ˈkaʊntnəns, -ɪz, -ɪŋ, -t
AM ˈkaʊnt(ə)nəns,
ˈkaʊn(t)ənəns, -əz,
-ɪŋ, -t

counter
BR ˈkaʊnt|ə(r), -əz,
-(ə)rɪŋ, -əd
AM ˈkaʊn(t)ər, -z, -ɪŋ, -d

counteract
BR ˌkaʊntərˈakt, -s, -ɪŋ,
-ɪd
AM ˌkaʊn(t)ərˈæk|(t),
-(t)s, -tɪŋ, -təd

counteraction[1]
action taken in reply
BR ˌkaʊntərˈakʃn, -z
AM ˌkaʊn(t)ərˈækʃən,
-z

counteraction[2]
counteracting
BR ˈkaʊntərˈakʃn, -z
AM ˈkaʊn(t)ərˈækʃən,
-z

counteractive
BR ˌkaʊntərˈaktɪv
AM ˌkaʊn(t)ərˈæktɪv

counterattack
BR ˈkaʊnt(ə)rəˌtak,
ˌkaʊnt(ə)rəˈtak, -s,
-ɪŋ, -t
AM ˈkaʊn(t)ərəˌtæk, -s,
-ɪŋ, -t

counterattraction
BR ˈkaʊnt(ə)rəˌtrakʃn,
ˌkaʊnt(ə)rəˈtrakʃn, -z
AM ˌkaʊn(t)ərəˈtræk-
ʃən, -z

counterbalance[1]
noun
BR ˈkaʊntəˌbaləns, -ɪz
AM ˈkaʊn(t)ərˌbæləns,
-əz

counterbalance[2]
verb
BR ˌkaʊntəˈbaləns, -ɪz,
-ɪŋ, -t
AM ˌkaʊn(t)ərˈbæləns,
-əz, -ɪŋ, -t

counterblast
BR ˈkaʊntəblɑːst,
ˈkaʊntəblast, -s
AM ˈkaʊn(t)ərˌblæst,
-s

counterblow
BR ˈkaʊntəbləʊ, -z
AM ˈkaʊn(t)ərˌbloʊ, -z

counterchange
BR ˌkaʊntəˈtʃeɪn(d)ʒ,
-ɪz, -ɪŋ, -d
AM ˌkaʊn(t)ərˈtʃeɪndʒ,
-ɪz, -ɪŋ, -d

countercharge
BR ˈkaʊntətʃɑːdʒ, -ɪz
AM ˈkaʊn(t)ərˌtʃɑrdʒ,
-əz

countercheck
BR ˌkaʊntəˈtʃɛk, -s, -ɪŋ,
-t
AM ˌkaʊn(t)ərˈtʃɛk, -s,
-ɪŋ, -t

counterclaim
noun
BR ˈkaʊntəkleɪm, -z
AM ˈkaʊn(t)ərˌkleɪm,
-z

counter-claim
verb
BR ˌkaʊntəˈkleɪm, -z,
-ɪŋ, -d
AM ˌkaʊn(t)ərˈkleɪm,
-z, -ɪŋ, -d

counterclockwise
BR ˌkaʊntəˈklɒkwʌɪz
AM ˌkaʊn(t)ərˈklɑk-
ˌwaɪz

counterculture
BR ˈkaʊntəˌkʌltʃə(r),
-z
AM ˈkaʊn(t)ərˌkəltʃər,
-z

counterespionage
BR ˌkaʊntərˈɛspɪənɑːʒ
AM ˌkaʊn(t)ərˈɛspɪəˌnɑʒ

counterfeit
BR ˈkaʊntəfɪt,
ˈkaʊntəfiːt, -s, -ɪŋ, -ɪd
AM ˈkaʊn(t)ərˌfɪ|t, -ts,
-dɪŋ, -dɪd

counterfeiter
BR ˈkaʊntəfɪtə(r),
ˈkaʊntəfiːtə(r), -z
AM ˈkaʊn(t)ərˌfɪdər, -z

counterfoil
BR ˈkaʊntəfɔɪl, -z
AM ˈkaʊn(t)ərˌfɔɪl, -z

**counterinsurgen-
cy**
BR ˌkaʊnt(ə)rɪnˈsəː-
dʒ(ə)nsi
AM ˌkaʊn(t)ərɪnˈsər-
dʒənsi

**counterintelli-
gence**
BR ˌkaʊnt(ə)rɪnˈtɛlɪ-
dʒ(ə)ns
AM ˌkaʊn(t)ərɪnˈtɛlə-
dʒəns

counterirritant
BR ˌkaʊntərˈɪrɪt(ə)nt,
-s
AM ˌkaʊn(t)ərˈɪrədnt,
-s

counterirritation
BR ˌkaʊntərˌɪrɪˈteɪʃn
AM ˌkaʊn(t)ərˌɪrəˈteɪʃən

countermand
BR ˈkaʊntəmɑːnd,
ˈkaʊntəmand,
ˌkaʊntəˈmɑːnd,
ˌkaʊntəˈmand, -z, -ɪŋ,
-ɪd

countermarch
BR ˈkaʊntəmɑːtʃ, -ɪz,
-ɪŋ, -t
AM ˈkaʊn(t)ərˌmɑrtʃ,
-əz, -ɪŋ, -t

countermeasure
BR ˈkaʊntəˌmɛʒə(r), -z
AM ˈkaʊn(t)ərˌmɛʒər,
-z

countermine
BR ˈkaʊntəmʌɪn, -z,
-ɪŋ, -d
AM ˈkaʊn(t)ərˌmaɪn,
-z, -ɪŋ, -d

countermove
BR ˈkaʊntəmuːv, -z, -ɪŋ,
-d
AM ˈkaʊn(t)ərˌmuv, -z,
-ɪŋ, -d

countermovement
BR ˈkaʊntəˌmuːvm(ə)nt,
-s
AM ˈkaʊn(t)ərˌmuvmənt,
-s

counteroffensive
BR ˈkaʊnt(ə)rəˌfɛnsɪv,
-z
AM ˈkaʊn(t)ərəˌfɛnsɪv,
-z

counteroffer
BR ˈkaʊntərˌɒfə(r), -z
AM ˈkaʊn(t)ərˌɔfər,
ˈkaʊn(t)ərˌɑfər, -z

counterpane
BR ˈkaʊntəpeɪn, -z
AM ˈkaʊn(t)ərˌpeɪn, -z

counterpart
BR ˈkaʊntəpɑːt, -s
AM ˈkaʊn(t)ərˌpɑrt, -s

counterplot
BR ˈkaʊntəplɒt, -s, -ɪŋ,
-ɪd
AM ˈkaʊn(t)ərˌplɑ|t,
-ts, -dɪŋ, -dəd

counterpoint
BR ˈkaʊntəpɔɪnt, -s
AM ˈkaʊn(t)ərˌpɔɪnt, -s

counterpoise
BR ˈkaʊntəpɔɪz, -ɪz, -ɪŋ,
-d
AM ˈkaʊn(t)ərˌpɔɪz, -ɪz,
-ɪŋ, -d

counterproductive
BR ˌkaʊntəprəˈdʌktɪv
AM ˌkaʊn(t)ərprəˈdəktɪv

**counterproduct-
ively**
BR ˌkaʊntəprəˈdʌktɪvli
AM ˌkaʊn(t)ərprəˈdəkt-
ɪvli

**counterproductive-
ness**
BR ˌkaʊntəprəˈdʌktɪvnɪs
AM ˌkaʊn(t)ərprəˈdəktɪv-
nɪs

counter-proposal
BR ˈkaʊntəprəˌpəʊzl, -z
AM ˈkaʊn(t)ərprəˌpouzəl, -z

counterpunch
BR ˈkaʊntəpʌn(t)ʃ, -ɪz
AM ˈkaʊn(t)ərˌpən(t)ʃ, -əz

counterrevolution
BR ˌkaʊntəˌrevəˈl(j)uː-ʃn, -z
AM ˌkaʊn(t)ərˌrevəˈlu-ʃən, -z

counterrevolutionary
BR ˌkaʊntəˌrevəˈl(j)uː-ʃn(ə)r|i, -ɪz
AM ˌkaʊn(t)ərˌrevəˈlu-ʃəˌneri, -z

countersank
BR ˈkaʊntəsaŋk
AM ˈkaʊn(t)ərˌsæŋk

counterscarp
BR ˈkaʊntəskɑːp, -s
AM ˈkaʊn(t)ərˌskɑrp, -s

countershaft
BR ˈkaʊntəʃɑːft, ˈkaʊntəʃaft, -s
AM ˈkaʊn(t)ərˌʃaft, -s

countersign
BR ˈkaʊntəsaɪn, -z, -ɪŋ, -d
AM ˈkaʊn(t)ərˌsaɪn, -z, -ɪŋ, -d

countersignature
BR ˈkaʊntəˌsɪgnətʃə(r), -z
AM ˌkaʊn(t)ərˈsɪgnə-ˌtʃʊ(ə)r, ˌkaʊn(t)ərˈsɪgnətʃər, -z

countersigner
BR ˈkaʊntəsaɪnə(r), -z
AM ˈkaʊn(t)ərˌsaɪnər, -z

countersink
BR ˈkaʊntəsɪŋk, -s, -ɪŋ
AM ˈkaʊn(t)ərˌsɪŋk, -s, -ɪŋ

counterspy
BR ˈkaʊntəspʌɪ, -z
AM ˈkaʊn(t)ərˌspaɪ, -z

counterstroke
BR ˈkaʊntəstrəʊk, -s
AM ˈkaʊn(t)ərˌstroʊk, -s

countersunk
BR ˈkaʊntəsʌŋk
AM ˈkaʊn(t)ərˌsəŋk

countertenor
BR ˈkaʊntəˌtenə(r), -z
AM ˈkaʊn(t)ərˌtenər, -z

countertransference
BR ˈkaʊntəˌtransf(ə)r-əns,

ˈkaʊntəˌtransf(ə)rns, ˈkaʊntəˌtrɑːnsf(ə)rəns, ˈkaʊntəˌtrɑːnsf(ə)rns, ˈkaʊntəˌtranzf(ə)rəns, ˈkaʊntəˌtranzf(ə)rns, ˈkaʊntəˌtrɑːnzf(ə)rəns, ˈkaʊntəˌtrɑːnzf(ə)rns
AM ˈkaʊn(t)ərˌtræns-f(ə)rəns

countervail
BR ˌkaʊntəˈveɪl, -z, -ɪŋ, -d
AM ˌkaʊn(t)ərˈveɪl, -z, -ɪŋ, -d

countervalue
BR ˈkaʊntəˌvaljuː, -z
AM ˈkaʊn(t)ərˌvælju, -z

counterweight
BR ˈkaʊntəweɪt, -s
AM ˈkaʊn(t)ərˌweɪt, -s

countess
BR ˈkaʊntɪs, ˈkaʊntes, ˌkaʊnˈtes, -ɪz
AM ˈkaʊn(t)əs, -əz

countinghouse
BR ˈkaʊntɪŋhaʊ|s, -zɪz
AM ˈkaʊn(t)ɪŋˌ(h)aʊ|s, -zəz

countless
BR ˈkaʊntləs
AM ˈkaʊn(t)ləs

countrified
BR ˈkʌntrɪfʌɪd
AM ˈkəntriˌfaɪd

country
BR ˈkʌntr|i, -ɪz
AM ˈkəntri, -z

countryfied
BR ˈkʌntrɪfʌɪd
AM ˈkəntrəˌfaɪd

countryfolk
BR ˈkʌntrɪfəʊk
AM ˈkəntriˌfoʊk

countryman
BR ˈkʌntrɪmən
AM ˈkəntrimən

countrymen
BR ˈkʌntrɪmən
AM ˈkəntrimən

countryside
BR ˈkʌntrɪsʌɪd
AM ˈkəntriˌsaɪd

countrywoman
BR ˈkʌntrɪˌwʊmən
AM ˈkəntriˌwʊmən

countrywomen
BR ˈkʌntrɪˌwɪmɪn
AM ˈkəntriˌwɪmɪn

countship
BR ˈkaʊntʃɪp, -s
AM ˈkaʊntˌʃɪp, -s

county
BR ˈkaʊnt|i, -ɪz
AM ˈkaʊn(t)i, -z

coup
BR kuː, -z
AM ku, -z

coup de grâce
BR ˌkuː də ˈɡrɑːs, + ˈɡras
AM ˌku də ˈɡras

coup de main
BR ˌkuː də ˈmeɪn
AM ˌku də ˈmeɪn

coup d'état
BR ˌkuː deɪˈtɑː(r)
AM ku'rant, -s

coup de théâtre
BR ˌkuː də teɪˈɑːtr, + teɪˈɑːtrə(r)
AM ˌku də ˌteɪˈætr(ə), + ˌteɪˈatr(ə)

coupé
BR ˈkuːpeɪ, -z
AM kuˈpeɪ, -z

Couper
BR ˈkuːpə(r)
AM ˈkupər

Couperin
BR ˈkuːpərən, ˈkuːpərã
AM ˈkupəˈrɛn

Coupland
BR ˈkuːplənd, ˈkəʊplənd
AM ˈkup/lənd, ˈkoʊplən(d)

couple
BR ˈkʌp|l, -lz, -lɪŋ \-lɪŋ, -ld
AM ˈkəp|əl, -əlz, -(ə)lɪŋ, -əld

coupler
BR ˈkʌplə(r), -z
AM ˈkəplər, -z

couplet
BR ˈkʌplɪt, -s
AM ˈkəplət, -s

coupling
BR ˈkʌplɪŋ, -z
AM ˈkəplɪŋ, -z

coupon
BR ˈkuːpɒn, -z
AM ˈk(j)uˌpɑn, -z

coups de grâce
BR ˌkuː də ˈɡrɑːs, + ˈɡras
AM ˌku də ˈɡras

coups de main
BR ˌkuː də ˈmeɪn
AM ˌku də ˈmeɪn

coups d'état
BR ˌkuː deɪˈtɑː(r)
AM ˌku də ˈtɑːta

coups de théâtre
BR ˌkuː də teɪˈɑːtr, + teɪˈɑːtrə(r)
AM ˌku də ˌteɪˈætr(ə), + ˌteɪˈatr(ə)

courage
BR ˈkʌrɪdʒ
AM ˈkərɪdʒ

courageous
BR kəˈreɪdʒəs
AM kəˈreɪdʒəs

courageously
BR kəˈreɪdʒəsli
AM kəˈreɪdʒəsli

courageousness
BR kəˈreɪdʒəsnəs
AM kəˈreɪdʒəsnəs

courante
BR kʊˈrɑːnt, -s
AM kuˈrant, -s

courgette
BR (ˌ)kɔːˈʒɛt, (ˌ)kʊəˈʒɛt, -s
AM ˌkʊrˈʒɛt, -s

courier
BR ˈkʊrɪə(r), ˈkʌrɪə(r), -z
AM ˈkʊriər, ˈkəriər, -z

courlan
BR ˈkʊələn, -z
AM ˈkʊrlən, kʊrˈlɑn, -z

Courland
BR ˈkʊələnd
AM ˈkʊrlənd

Courrèges
BR kʊˈrɛʒ, kʊˈreɪʒ
AM kʊˈreʒ

course
BR kɔːs, -ɪz, -ɪŋ, -t
AM kɔ(ə)rs, -əz, -ɪŋ, -t

courser
BR ˈkɔːsə(r), -z
AM ˈkɔrsər, -z

coursework
BR ˈkɔːswɜːk
AM ˈkɔrsˌwərk

court
BR kɔːt, -s, -ɪŋ, -ɪd
AM kɔ(ə)r|t, -ts, -dɪŋ, -dəd

Courtauld
BR ˈkɔːtəʊld
AM kɔrˈtoʊld

court-bouillon
BR ˌkɔːt ˈbuː(l)jɒn, ˌkʊə buː(l)ˈjõ
AM ˈkʊr ˌbʊ(l)jɔn, ˈkɔr(t) ˌbʊ(l)jɔn

Courtelle®
BR (ˌ)kɔːˈtɛl
AM kɔrˈtɛl

courteous
BR ˈkɜːtɪəs
AM ˈkərdiəs

courteously
BR ˈkɜːtɪəsli
AM ˈkərdiəsli

courteousness
BR ˈkɜːtɪəsnɪs
AM ˈkərdiəsnəs

courtesan
BR ˌkɔːtɪˈzan, ˈkɔːtɪzan, -z
AM ˈkɔrdəˌzæn, ˈkɔrdəzn, -z

courtesy
BR ˈkɜːtɪs|i, -ɪz
AM ˈkərdəsi, -z

courthouse
BR 'kɔ:thaʊ|s, -zɪz
AM 'kɔrt,(h)aʊ|s, -zəz

courtier
BR 'kɔ:tɪə(r), 'kɔ:tjə(r),
-z
AM 'kɔrdiər, -z

courtliness
BR 'kɔ:tlɪnɪs
AM 'kɔrtlinɪs

courtly
BR 'kɔ:tl|i, -ɪə(r), -ɪɪst
AM 'kɔrtli, -ər, -ɪst

court-martial
BR ,kɔ:t'mɑ:ʃ|l, -lz,
-lɪŋ|-əlɪŋ, -ld
AM 'kɔrt,mɑrʃ|əl, -əlz,
-(ə)lɪŋ, -əld

Courtney
BR 'kɔ:tni
AM 'kɔrtni

courtroom
BR 'kɔ:tru:m,
'kɔ:trʊm, -z
AM 'kɔrt,rum,
'kɔrt,rʊm, -z

courts-bouillons
BR ,kɔ:t 'bu:(l)jɒn,
,kʊə bu:(l)'jɒ̃
AM 'kʊr ,bʊ(l)jɒn,
'kɔr(t) ,bʊ(l)jɒn

courtship
BR 'kɔ:tʃɪp, -s
AM 'kɔrt,ʃɪp, -s

courts-martial
BR ,kɔ:ts'mɑ:ʃl
AM ,kɔrts'mɑrʃəl

courtyard
BR 'kɔ:tjɑ:d, -z
AM 'kɔrt,jɑrd, -z

Courvoisier®
BR (,)kʊə'vwɑzɪeɪ,
(,)kʊə'vwɒzɪeɪ,
(,)kɔ:'vwɑzɪeɪ,
(,)kɔ:'vwɒzɪeɪ
AM kər,vwɑzi'eɪ

couscous
BR 'ku:sku:s
AM 'kus,kus

cousin
BR kʌzn, -z
AM kəzn, -z

cousinhood
BR 'kʌznhʊd
AM 'kəzn,(h)ʊd

cousinly
BR 'kʌznli
AM 'kʌznli

Cousins
BR 'kʌznz
AM 'kəzənz

cousinship
BR 'kʌznʃɪp
AM 'kəzn,ʃɪp

Cousteau
BR 'ku:stəʊ, ku:'stəʊ
AM ku'stoʊ

couth
BR ku:θ
AM kuθ

couture
BR kʊ'tjʊə(r),
kʊ'tʃʊə(r)
AM ku'tʊ(ə)r

couturier
BR kʊ'tjʊərɪeɪ,
kʊ'tʃʊərɪeɪ,
kʊ'tjʊərɪə(r),
kʊ'tʃʊərɪə(r), -z
AM kʊ'tʊriər,
ku'tʊri,eɪ, -z

couturière
BR kʊ'tjʊərɪɛː(r),
kʊ'tʃʊərɪɛː(r),
kʊ'tjʊərɪə(r),
kʊ'tʃʊərɪə(r), -z
AM ku'tʊriər,
ku'tʊri,ɛ(ə)r, -z

couvade
BR (,)ku:'vɑ:d, -z
AM ku'vɑd, -z

couvert
BR (,)ku:'vɛː(r), -z
AM ku'vɛ(ə)r, -z

couverture
BR ku:'vətjʊə(r),
'ku:vətʃʊə(r),
'ku:vətʃə(r), -z
AM 'kuvər,tʃ(ʊ)ər, -z

covalence
BR ,kəʊ'veɪləns,
,kəʊ'veɪlns
AM ,koʊ'veɪləns

covalency
BR ,kəʊ'veɪlns|i,
,kəʊ'veɪlnsi, -ɪz
AM ,koʊ'veɪlnsi, -z

covalent
BR ,kəʊ'veɪlənt,
,kəʊ'veɪlnt
AM ,koʊ'veɪlənt

covalently
BR ,kəʊ'veɪləntli,
kəʊ'veɪlntli
AM ,koʊ'veɪlən(t)li

covariance
BR ,kəʊ'vɛːrɪəns
AM ,koʊ'vɛrɪəns

cove
BR kəʊv, -z
AM koʊv, -z

covellite
BR kəʊ'vɛlaɪt
AM koʊ'vɛ,laɪt,
'koʊvə,laɪt

coven
BR 'kʌvn, -z
AM 'kəvən, -z

covenant
BR 'kʌvənənt,
'kʌvnənt, -s, -ɪŋ, -ɪd
AM 'kəvənənt, -s, -ɪŋ,
-əd

covenantal
BR ,kʌvə'nɑntl

AM ,kəvə'nən(t)l

covenanter
BR 'kʌv(ə)nəntə(r),
'kʌvnəntə(r), -z
AM 'kəvənən(t)ər, -z

covenantor
BR 'kʌv(ə)nəntə(r),
'kʌvnəntə(r), -z
AM 'kəvənən(t)ər, -z

Covent Garden
BR ,kɒvnt 'gɑ:dn,
,kʌvnt +
AM ,kəvən(t) 'gɑrdən

Coventry
BR 'kɒvntri, 'kʌvntri
AM 'kəvəntri

cover
BR 'kʌv|ə(r), -əz,
-(ə)rɪŋ, -əd
AM 'kəv|ər, -ərz,
-(ə)rɪŋ, -ərd

coverable
BR 'kʌv(ə)rəbl
AM 'kəv(ə)rəbəl

Coverack
BR 'kʌvərak
AM 'kəværæk

coverage
BR 'kʌv(ə)rɪdʒ
AM 'kəv(ə)rɪdʒ

coverall
BR 'kʌvərɔːl, -z
AM 'kəvər,ɔl, 'kəvər,ɑl,
-z

covercharge
BR 'kʌvərʃɑːdʒ, -ɪz
AM 'kəvər,tʃɑrdʒ, -əz

Coverdale
BR 'kʌvədeɪl
AM 'kəvər,deɪl

coverer
BR 'kʌv(ə)rə(r), -z
AM 'kəv(ə)rər, -z

covering
BR 'kʌv(ə)rɪŋ, -z
AM 'kəv(ə)rɪŋ, -z

coverlet
BR 'kʌvəlɪt, -s
AM 'kəvərlət, -s

Coverley
BR 'kʌvəli
AM 'kəvərli

covert¹
secret
BR 'kʌvət, 'kəʊvəːt
AM ,koʊ'vərt

covert²
undergrowth
BR 'kʌvət, -s
AM 'kəvərt, -s

covertly
BR 'kʌvətli, 'kəʊvəːtli
AM ,koʊ'vərtli

covertness
BR 'kʌvətnəs,
'kəʊvəːtnəs
AM ,koʊ'vərtnəs

coverture
BR 'kʌvətjʊə(r),
'kʌvətʃʊə(r),
'kʌvətʃə(r), -z
AM 'kəvər,tʃ(ʊ)ər,
'kəvərtʃər, -z

covet
BR 'kʌvɪt, -s, -ɪŋ, -ɪd
AM 'kəvə|t, -ts, -dɪŋ,
-dəd

covetable
BR 'kʌvɪtəbl
AM 'kəvədəbəl

covetous
BR 'kʌvɪtəs
AM 'kəvədəs

covetously
BR 'kʌvɪtəsli
AM 'kəvədəsli

covetousness
BR 'kʌvɪtəsnəs
AM 'kəvədəsnəs

covey
BR 'kʌv|i, -ɪz
AM 'kəvi, -z

covin
BR 'kʌvɪn, -z
AM 'kəvən, 'koʊvən, -z

coving
BR 'kəʊvɪŋ
AM 'koʊvɪŋ

cow
BR kaʊ, -z, -ɪŋ, -d
AM kaʊ, -z, -ɪŋ, -d

cowage
BR 'kaʊɪdʒ
AM 'kaʊɪdʒ

Cowan
BR 'kaʊən
AM 'kaʊən

coward
BR 'kaʊəd, -z
AM 'kaʊərd, -z

cowardice
BR 'kaʊədɪs
AM 'kaʊərdəs

cowardliness
BR 'kaʊədlɪnɪs
AM 'kaʊərdlinɪs

cowardly
BR 'kaʊədli
AM 'kaʊərdli

cowbane
BR 'kaʊbeɪn
AM 'kaʊ,beɪn

cowbell
BR 'kaʊbɛl, -z
AM 'kaʊ,bɛl, -z

cowberry
BR 'kaʊb(ə)r|i, -ɪz
AM 'kaʊ,bɛri, -z

cowbird
BR 'kaʊbəːd, -z
AM 'kaʊ,bərd, -z

cowboy
BR 'kaʊbɔɪ, -z
AM 'kaʊ,bɔɪ, -z

Cowbridge	**cowmen**	**coxswain**	**crabgrass**
BR ˈkaʊbrɪdʒ	BR ˈkaʊmən	BR ˈkɒksn, -z	BR ˈkræbgrɑːs,
AM ˈkaʊˌbrɪdʒ	AM ˈkaʊmən	AM ˈkɑksn, -z	ˈkræbgras
cowcatcher	**cowpat**	**coxswainship**	AM ˈkræbˌgræs
BR ˈkaʊˌkatʃə(r), -z	BR ˈkaʊpat, -s	BR ˈkɒksnʃɪp	**crablike**
AM ˈkaʊˌkɛtʃər, -z	AM ˈkaʊˌpæt, -s	AM ˈkɑksnˌʃɪp	BR ˈkrablʌɪk
Cowdenbeath	**cowpea**	**coy**	AM ˈkræbˌlaɪk
BR ˌkaʊdnˈbiːθ	BR ˈkaʊpiː, -z	BR kɔɪ	**crabmeat**
AM ˈkaʊdənˌbiθ	AM ˈkaʊˌpi, -z	AM kɔɪ	BR ˈkrabmiːt
Cowdray	**Cowper**	**coyly**	AM ˈkræbˌmit
BR ˈkaʊdri, ˈkaʊdreɪ	BR ˈkuːpə(r),	BR ˈkɔɪli	**Crabtree**
AM ˈkaʊdri, ˈkaʊdreɪ	ˈkaʊpə(r)	AM ˈkɔɪli	BR ˈkrabtriː
Cowdrey	AM ˈkaʊpər, ˈkupər	**coyness**	AM ˈkræbˌtri
BR ˈkaʊdri, ˈkaʊdreɪ	**cowpoke**	BR ˈkɔɪnɪs	**crabways**
AM ˈkaʊdri, ˈkaʊdreɪ	BR ˈkaʊpəʊk, -s	AM ˈkɔɪnɪs	BR ˈkrabweɪz
Cowell	AM ˈkaʊˌpoʊk, -s	**coyote**	AM ˈkræbˌweɪz
BR ˈkaʊ(ə)l	**cowpox**	BR kɔɪˈəʊt|i, kʌɪˈəʊt|i,	**crabwise**
AM ˈkaʊəl	BR ˈkaʊpɒks	-ɪz	BR ˈkrabwʌɪz
Cowen	AM ˈkaʊˌpɑks	AM ˈkaɪˌoʊt, kaɪˈoʊdi,	AM ˈkræbˌwaɪz
BR ˈkaʊɪn, ˈkəʊɪn	**cowpuncher**	ˈkaɪˌoʊts\kaɪˈoʊdiz	**crack**
AM ˈkaʊən, ˈkoʊən	BR ˈkaʊˌpʌn(t)ʃə(r), -z	**coypu**	BR krak, -s, -ɪŋ, -t
cower	AM ˈkaʊˌpən(t)ʃər, -z	BR ˈkɔɪp(j)uː, -z	AM kræk, -s, -ɪŋ, -t
BR ˈkaʊə(r), -z, -ɪŋ, -d	**cowrie**	AM ˈkɔɪˌpu, -z	**crackbrained**
AM ˈkaʊər, -z, -ɪŋ, -d	BR ˈkaʊr|i, -ɪz	**coz**	BR ˈkrakbreɪnd
Cowes	AM ˈkaʊri, -z	BR kʌz	AM ˈkrækˌbreɪn(d)
BR kaʊz	**cowry**	AM kəz	**crackdown**
AM kaʊz	BR ˈkaʊr|i, -ɪz	**cozen**	BR ˈkrakdaʊn, -z
Cowgill	AM ˈkaʊri, -z	BR ˈkʌzn̩, -z, -ɪŋ, -d	AM ˈkrækˌdaʊn, -z
BR ˈkaʊgɪl	**cowshed**	AM ˈkəzən, -z, -ɪŋ, -d	**cracker**
AM ˈkaʊˌgɪl	BR ˈkaʊʃɛd, -z	**cozenage**	BR ˈkrakə(r), -z
cowgirl	AM ˈkaʊˌʃɛd, -z	BR ˈkʌzn̩ɪdʒ	AM ˈkrækər, -z
BR ˈkaʊgəːl, -z	**cowslip**	AM ˈkəzənədʒ	**cracker-barrel**
AM ˈkaʊˌgərl, -z	BR ˈkaʊslɪp, -s	**Cozens**	BR ˈkrakəˌbarəl,
cowhage	AM ˈkaʊˌslɪp, -s	BR ˈkʌznz	ˈkrakəˌbarl, -z
BR ˈkaʊɪdʒ	**cowtown**	AM ˈkəzənz	AM ˈkrækərˌberəl, -z
AM ˈkaʊɪdʒ	BR ˈkaʊtaʊn, -z	**Cozumel**	**crackerjack**
cowhand	AM ˈkaʊˌtaʊn, -z	BR ˈkəʊzʊmel	BR ˈkrakədʒak, -s
BR ˈkaʊhand, -z	**cox**	AM ˈkoʊzʊˌmɛl	AM ˈkrækərˌdʒæk, -s
AM ˈkaʊˌ(h)ænd, -z	BR kɒks, -ɪz, -ɪŋ, -t	SP ˌkoθuˈmel,	**crackiness**
cowheel	AM kɑks, -əz, -ɪŋ, -t	ˌkosuˈmel	BR ˈkrakɪnɪs
BR ˌkaʊˈhiːl, ˈkaʊhiːl,	**coxa**	**cozy**	AM ˈkrækɪnɪs
-z	BR ˈkɒksə(r)	BR ˈkəʊz|i, -ɪə(r), -ɪɪst	**crack-jaw**
AM ˈkaʊˌ(h)il, -z	AM ˈkɑksə	AM ˈkoʊzi, -ər, -ɪst	BR ˈkrakdʒɔː(r)
cowherd	**coxae**	**cozzie**	AM ˈkrækˌdʒɔ
BR ˈkaʊhəːd, -z	BR ˈkɒksiː	BR ˈkɒz|i, -ɪz	**crackle**
AM ˈkaʊˌ(h)ərd, -z	AM ˈkɑksi, ˈkɑkˌsaɪ	AM ˈkɑzi, -z	BR ˈkrak|l̩, -lz,
cowhide	**coxal**	**crab**	-l̩ɪŋ\-l̩ɪŋ, -l̩d
BR ˈkaʊhʌɪd	BR ˈkɒksl	BR krab, -z, -ɪŋ, -d	AM ˈkræk|əl, -əlz,
AM ˈkaʊˌ(h)aɪd	AM ˈkɑksəl	AM kræb, -z, -ɪŋ, -d	-(ə)lɪŋ, -əld
Cowie	**coxalgia**	**Crabbe**	**crackling**
BR ˈkaʊi	BR kɒkˈsaldʒ(ɪ)ə(r)	BR krab	*noun*
AM ˈkaʊi	AM kɑkˈsældʒ(i)ə	AM kræb	BR ˈkraklɪŋ, -z
cowl	**coxcomb**	**crabbedly**	AM ˈkræk(ə)lɪŋ, -z
BR kaʊl, -z, -d	BR ˈkɒkskəʊm, -z	BR ˈkrabɪdli	**crackly**
AM kaʊl, -z, -d	AM ˈkɑksˌkoʊm, -z	AM ˈkræbədli	BR ˈkrakli
Cowley	**coxcombry**	**crabbedness**	AM ˈkræk(ə)li
BR ˈkaʊli	BR ˈkɒkskəʊmr|i, -ɪz	BR ˈkrabɪdnɪs	**cracknel**
AM ˈkaʊli	AM ˈkɑksˌkoʊmri, -z	AM ˈkræb(əd)nəs	BR ˈkraknl, -z
cowlick	**Coxe**	**crabbily**	AM ˈkræknəl, -z
BR ˈkaʊlɪk, -s	BR kɒks	BR ˈkrabɪli	**crackpot**
AM ˈkaʊlɪk, -s	AM kɑks	AM ˈkræbəli	BR ˈkrakpɒt, -s
cowling	**coxless**	**crabbiness**	AM ˈkrækˌpɑt, -s
BR ˈkaʊlɪŋ, -z	BR ˈkɒksləs	BR ˈkrabɪnɪs	**cracksman**
AM ˈkaʊlɪŋ, -z	AM ˈkɑksləs	AM ˈkræbɪnɪs	AM ˈkræksmən
cowman	**Coxsackie**	**crabby**	**cracksmen**
BR ˈkaʊmən	BR kɒkˈsaki, kʊkˈsaki	BR ˈkrab|i, -ɪə(r), -ɪɪst	BR ˈkraksmən
AM ˈkaʊmən	AM kɑkˈsæki	AM ˈkræbi, -ər, -ɪst	

AM ˈkræksmən

crackup
BR ˈkrakʌp, -s
AM ˈkræk̩əp, -s

cracky
BR ˈkraki
AM ˈkræki

Cracow
BR ˈkrakɒf, ˈkrakɒv,
ˈkrakaʊ
AM ˈkrɑkaʊ, ˈkrakɒf,
ˈkrakɑf

Craddock
BR ˈkradək
AM ˈkrædək

cradle
BR ˈkreɪd|l, -lz,
-l̩ɪŋ\-lɪŋ, -ld
AM ˈkreɪd|əl, -əlz,
-(ə)lɪŋ, -əld

Cradley
BR ˈkreɪdli, ˈkradli
AM ˈkrædli

craft
BR krɑːft, kraft, -s, -ɪŋ,
-ɪd
AM kræft, -s, -ɪŋ, -əd

craftily
BR ˈkrɑːftɪli, ˈkraftɪli
AM ˈkræftəli

craftiness
BR ˈkrɑːftɪnɪs,
ˈkraftɪnɪs
AM ˈkræftɪnɪs

craftsman
BR ˈkrɑːf(t)smən,
ˈkraf(t)smən
AM ˈkræf(t)smən

craftsmanship
BR ˈkrɑːf(t)smənʃɪp,
ˈkraf(t)smənʃɪp
AM ˈkræf(t)smənˌʃɪp

craftsmen
BR ˈkrɑːf(t)smən,
ˈkraf(t)smən
AM ˈkræf(t)smən

craftspeople
plural noun
BR ˈkrɑːf(t)sˌpiːpl,
ˈkraf(t)sˌpiːpl
AM ˈkræf(t)sˌpipl

craftsperson
BR ˈkrɑːf(t)sˌpəːsn,
ˈkraf(t)sˌpəːsn
AM ˈkræf(t)sˌpərsən

craftswoman
BR ˈkrɑːf(t)sˌwʊmən,
ˈkraf(t)sˌwʊmən
AM ˈkræf(t)sˌwʊmən

craftswomen
BR ˈkrɑːf(t)sˌwɪmɪn,
ˈkraf(t)sˌwɪmɪn
AM ˈkræf(t)sˌwɪmɪn

craftwork
BR ˈkrɑːftwəːk,
ˈkraftwəːk
AM ˈkræf(t)ˌwɜrk

craftworker
BR ˈkrɑːftˌwəːkə(r),
ˈkraftˌwəːkə(r), -z
AM ˈkræf(t)ˌwɜrkər, -z

crafty
BR ˈkrɑːft|i, ˈkraft|i,
-ɪə(r), -ɪɪst
AM ˈkræfti, -ər, -ɪst

crag
BR krag, -z
AM kræg, -z

craggily
BR ˈkragɪli
AM ˈkrægəli

cragginess
BR ˈkragɪnɪs
AM ˈkrægɪnɪs

craggy
BR ˈkrag|i, -ɪə(r), -ɪɪst
AM ˈkrægi, -ər, -ɪst

cragsman
BR ˈkragzmən
AM ˈkrægzmən

cragsmen
BR ˈkragzmən
AM ˈkrægzmən

cragswoman
BR ˈkragzˌwʊmən
AM ˈkrægzˌwʊmən

cragswomen
BR ˈkragzˌwɪmɪn
AM ˈkrægzˌwɪmɪn

Craig
BR kreɪg
AM kreɡ

Craigie
BR ˈkreɪgi
AM ˈkreɪgi

crake
BR kreɪk, -s
AM kreɪk, -s

cram
BR kram, -z, -ɪŋ, -d
AM kræm, -z, -ɪŋ, -d

crambo
BR ˈkrambəʊ
AM ˈkræmboʊ

Cramden
BR ˈkramd(ə)n
AM ˈkræmd(ə)n

Cramer
BR ˈkreɪmə(r)
AM ˈkreɪmər

crammer
BR ˈkramə(r), -z
AM ˈkræmər, -z

cramp
BR kramp, -s, -ɪŋ, -t
AM kræmp, -s, -ɪŋ, -t

crampon
BR ˈkrampɒn,
ˈkrampən, -z
AM ˈkræmˌpɑn, -z

cran
BR kran, -z
AM kræn, -z

cranage
BR ˈkreɪnɪdʒ
AM ˈkreɪnɪdʒ

cranberry
BR ˈkranb(ə)r|i, -ɪz
AM ˈkrænˌbɛri, -z

Cranborne
BR ˈkranbɔːn
AM ˈkrænˌbɔ(ə)rn

Cranbourn
BR ˈkranbɔːn
AM ˈkrænˌbɔ(ə)rn

Cranbourne
BR ˈkranbɔːn
AM ˈkrænˌbɔ(ə)rn

Cranbrook
BR ˈkranbrʊk
AM ˈkrænˌbrʊk

crane
BR kreɪn, -z, -ɪŋ, -d
AM kreɪn, -z, -ɪŋ, -d

cranesbill
BR ˈkreɪnzbɪl, -z
AM ˈkreɪnzˌbɪl, -z

Cranfield
BR ˈkranfiːld
AM ˈkrænˌfild

crania
BR ˈkreɪnɪə(r)
AM ˈkreɪnɪə

cranial
BR ˈkreɪnɪəl
AM ˈkreɪnɪəl

cranially
BR ˈkreɪnɪəli
AM ˈkreɪnɪəli

craniate
BR ˈkreɪnɪət, -s
AM ˈkreɪnɪəˌeɪt
ˈkreɪnɪət, -s

craniological
BR ˌkreɪnɪəˈlɒdʒɪkl
AM ˌkreɪniˈɑlədʒəkəl

craniologist
BR ˌkreɪnɪˈɒlədʒɪst, -s
AM ˌkreɪniˈɑlədʒəst, -s

craniology
BR ˌkreɪnɪˈɒlədʒi
AM ˌkreɪniˈɑlədʒi

craniometric
BR ˌkreɪnɪəˈmɛtrɪk
AM ˌkreɪnɪəˈmɛtrɪk

craniometry
BR ˌkreɪnɪˈɒmɪtri
AM ˌkreɪniˈɑmətri

craniotomy
BR ˌkreɪnɪˈɒtəmi, -ɪz
AM ˌkreɪniˈɑdəmi, -z

cranium
BR ˌkreɪnɪəm, -z
AM ˈkreɪniəm, -z

crank
BR kraŋ|k, -ks, -kɪŋ,
-(k)t
AM kræŋ|k, -ks, -kɪŋ,
-(k)t

crankcase
BR ˈkraŋkkeɪs, -ɪz
AM ˈkræŋˌkeɪs, -ɪz

crankily
BR ˈkraŋkɪli
AM ˈkræŋkəli

crankiness
BR ˈkraŋkɪnɪs
AM ˈkræŋkinɪs

crankpin
BR ˈkraŋkpɪn, -z
AM ˈkræŋkˌpɪn, -z

crankshaft
BR ˈkraŋkʃɑːft,
ˈkraŋkʃaft, -s
AM ˈkræŋkˌʃæft, -s

cranky
BR ˈkraŋk|i, -ɪə(r), -ɪɪst
AM ˈkræŋki, -ər, -ɪst

Cranleigh
BR ˈkranli
AM ˈkrænli

Cranley
BR ˈkranli
AM ˈkrænli

Cranmer
BR ˈkranmə(r)
AM ˈkrænmər

crannied
BR ˈkranid
AM ˈkrænid, ˈkrænəd

crannog
BR ˈkranəg, -z
AM ˈkrænəg, -z

cranny
BR ˈkran|i, -ɪz
AM ˈkræni, -z

Cranston
BR ˈkranst(ə)n
AM ˈkrænstən

Cranwell
BR ˈkranw(ɛ)l
AM ˈkrænˌwɛl

crap
BR krap, -s, -ɪŋ, -t
AM kræp, -s, -ɪŋ, -t

crape
BR kreɪp, -s
AM kreɪp, -s

crapper
BR ˈkrapə(r), -z
AM ˈkræpər, -z

crappie
BR ˈkrap|i, -ɪz
AM ˈkrɑpi, ˈkræpi, -z

crappily
BR ˈkrapɪli
AM ˈkræpəli

crappiness
BR ˈkrapɪnɪs
AM ˈkræpinɪs

crappy
BR ˈkrap|i, -ɪə(r), -ɪɪst
AM ˈkræpi, -ər, -ɪst

craps
BR kraps
AM kræps

crapshooter
BR ˈkrap.ʃuːtə(r), -z
AM ˈkræp.ʃudər, -z
crapulence
BR ˈkrapjələns,
ˈkrapjəlns
AM ˈkræpjələns
crapulent
BR ˈkrapjələnt,
ˈkrapjəlnt
AM ˈkræpjələnt
crapulently
BR ˈkrapjələntli,
ˈkrapjəlntli
AM ˈkræpjələn(t)li
crapulous
BR ˈkrapjələs
AM ˈkræpjələs
crapy
BR ˈkreɪpi
AM ˈkreɪpi
craquelure
BR ˈkrak|(j)ʊə(r)
AM ˈkrækə.lʊ(ə)r
crases
BR ˈkreɪsiːz
AM ˈkreɪsiz
crash
BR kraʃ, -ɪz, -ɪŋ, -t
AM kræʃ, -ɪz, -ɪŋ, -t
Crashaw
BR ˈkraʃɔː(r)
AM ˈkræʃɔ, ˈkreɪʃɔ,
ˈkræʃɑ, ˈkreɪʃɑ
crash-dove
BR ˈkraʃdəʊv,
ˌkraʃˈdəʊv
AM ˈkræʃˌdoʊv
crasis
BR ˈkreɪsɪs
AM ˈkreɪsɪs
crass
BR kras
AM kræs
crassitude
BR ˈkrasɪtjuːd,
ˈkrasɪtʃuːd
AM ˈkræsə.t(j)ud
crassly
BR ˈkrasli
AM ˈkræsli
crassness
BR ˈkrasnəs
AM ˈkræsnəs
Crassus
BR ˈkrasəs
AM ˈkræsəs
cratch
BR kratʃ, -ɪz
AM krætʃ, -əz
Cratchit
BR ˈkratʃɪt
AM ˈkrætʃət
crate
BR kreɪt, -s, -ɪŋ, -ɪd
AM kreɪ|t, -ts, -dɪŋ, -dɪd

crateful
BR ˈkreɪtfʊl, -z
AM ˈkreɪt.fʊl, -z
crater
BR ˈkreɪt|ə(r), -əz,
-(ə)rɪŋ, -əd
AM ˈkreɪdər, -z, -ɪŋ, -d
craterous
BR ˈkreɪt(ə)rəs
AM ˈkreɪdərəs
Crathorn
BR ˈkreɪθɔːn
AM ˈkreɪˌθɔ(ə)rn
Crathorne
BR ˈkreɪθɔːn
AM ˈkreɪˌθɔ(ə)rn
cravat
BR krəˈvat, -s
AM krəˈvæt, -s
cravatted
BR krəˈvatɪd
AM krəˈvædəd
crave
BR kreɪv, -z, -ɪŋ, -d
AM kreɪv, -z, -ɪŋ, -d
craven
BR ˈkreɪv(ə)n
AM ˈkreɪvən
cravenly
BR ˈkreɪv(ə)nli
AM ˈkreɪvənli
cravenness
BR ˈkreɪv(ə)nnəs
AM ˈkreɪvə(n)nəs
craver
BR ˈkreɪvə(r), -z
AM ˈkreɪvər, -z
craving
BR ˈkreɪvɪŋ, -z
AM ˈkreɪvɪŋ, -z
craw
BR krɔː(r), -z
AM krɔ, krɑ, -z
crawdad
BR ˈkrɔːdad, -z
AM ˈkrɔˌdæd,
ˈkrɑˌdæd, -z
crawfish
BR ˈkrɔːfɪʃ, -ɪz
AM ˈkrɔˌfɪʃ, ˈkrɑˌfɪʃ, -ɪz
Crawford
BR ˈkrɔːfəd
AM ˈkrɔfərd, ˈkrɑfərd
crawl
BR krɔːl, -z, -ɪŋ, -d
AM krɔl, krɑl, -z, -ɪŋ, -d
crawler
BR ˈkrɔːlə(r), -z
AM ˈkrɔlər, ˈkrɑlər, -z
crawlingly
BR ˈkrɔːlɪŋli
AM ˈkrɔlɪŋli, ˈkrɑlɪŋli
crawly
BR ˈkrɔːl|i, -ɪz
AM ˈkrɔli, ˈkrɑli, -z
Crawshaw
BR ˈkrɔːʃɔː(r)

crateful
AM ˈkrɔʃə, ˈkrɑʃɑ
Crawshay
BR ˈkrɔːʃeɪ
AM ˈkrɔʃeɪ, ˈkrɑʃeɪ
Cray
BR kreɪ, -z
AM kreɪ, -z
crayfish
BR ˈkreɪfɪʃ, -ɪz
AM ˈkreɪˌfɪʃ, -ɪz
Crayford
BR ˈkreɪfəd
AM ˈkreɪfərd
Crayola®
BR kreɪˈəʊlə(r)
AM kreɪˈoʊlə
crayon
BR ˈkreɪɒn, ˈkreɪən, -z,
-ɪŋ, -d
AM ˈkreɪˌɑn, -z, -ɪŋ, -d
craze
BR kreɪz, -ɪz, -ɪŋ, -d
AM kreɪz, -ɪz, -ɪŋ, -d
crazily
BR ˈkreɪzɪli
AM ˈkreɪzɪli
craziness
BR ˈkreɪzɪnɪs
AM ˈkreɪzinɪs
crazy
BR ˈkreɪz|i, -ɪə(r), -ɪɪst
AM ˈkreɪzi, -ər, -ɪst
creak
BR kriːk, -s, -ɪŋ, -t
AM krik, -s, -ɪŋ, -t
creakily
BR ˈkriːkɪli
AM ˈkrikɪli
creakiness
BR ˈkriːkɪnɪs
AM ˈkrikinɪs
creakingly
BR ˈkriːkɪŋli
AM ˈkrikɪŋli
creaky
BR ˈkriːk|i, -ɪə(r), -ɪɪst
AM ˈkriki, -ər, -ɪst
cream
BR kriːm, -z, -ɪŋ, -d
AM krim, -z, -ɪŋ, -d
creamer
BR ˈkriːmə(r), -z
AM ˈkrimər, -z
creamery
BR ˈkriːm(ə)r|i, -ɪz
AM ˈkrim(ə)ri, -z
creamily
BR ˈkriːmɪli
AM ˈkrimɪli
creaminess
BR ˈkriːmɪnɪs
AM ˈkriminɪs
creamware
BR ˈkriːmwɛː(r)
AM ˈkrimˌwɛ(ə)r
creamy
BR ˈkriːm|i, -ɪə(r), -ɪɪst

crateful
AM ˈkrɔʃə, ˈkrɑʃə
creance
BR ˈkriːəns, -ɪz
AM ˈkriəns, -əz
crease
BR kriːs, -ɪz, -ɪŋ, -t
AM kris, -ɪz, -ɪŋ, -t
Creasey
BR ˈkriːsi
AM ˈkrisi
Creasy
BR ˈkriːsi
AM ˈkrisi
creatable
BR krɪˈeɪtəbl
AM kriˈeɪdəbəl
create
BR krɪˈeɪt, -s, -ɪŋ, -ɪd
AM kriˈeɪ|t, -ts, -dɪŋ,
-dɪd
creatine
BR ˈkriːətiːn
AM ˈkriəˌtin, ˈkriədən
creation
BR krɪˈeɪʃn, -z
AM kriˈeɪʃən, -z
creationism
BR krɪˈeɪʃnɪz(ə)m,
krɪˈeɪʃənɪz(ə)m
AM kriˈeɪʃəˌnɪzəm
creationist
BR krɪˈeɪʃnɪst,
krɪˈeɪʃənɪst, -s
AM kriˈeɪʃənəst, -s
creative
BR krɪˈeɪtɪv
AM kriˈeɪdɪv
creatively
BR krɪˈeɪtɪvli
AM kriˈeɪdɪvli
creativeness
BR krɪˈeɪtɪvnɪs
AM kriˈeɪdɪvnɪs
creativity
BR ˌkriːeɪˈtɪvɪti
AM ˌkrieɪˈtɪvɪdi
creator
BR krɪˈeɪtə(r), -z
AM kriˈeɪdər, -z
creatrices
BR krɪˈeɪtrɪsiːz
AM kriˈeɪtrɪsiz
creatrix
BR krɪˈeɪtrɪks, -ɪz
AM kriˈeɪtrɪks, -ɪz
creature
BR ˈkriːtʃə(r), -z
AM ˈkritʃər, -z
creaturely
BR ˈkriːtʃəli
AM ˈkritʃərli
crèche
BR kreɪʃ, krɛʃ, -ɪz
AM krɛʃ, -əz
Crecy
BR ˈkrɛsi
AM ˈkrɛsi

Crécy
BR ˈkresi
AM ˈkreɪsi

cred
BR krɛd
AM krɛd

Creda®
BR ˈkriːdə(r)
AM ˈkridə

credal
BR ˈkriːdl
AM ˈkridəl

credence
BR ˈkriːdns
AM ˈkridns

credential
BR krɪˈdɛnʃl, -z
AM krəˈdɛn(t)ʃəl, -z

credenza
BR krɪˈdɛnzə(r), -z
AM krəˈdɛnzə, -z

credibility
BR ˌkrɛdɪˈbɪlɪti
AM ˌkrɛdəˈbɪlɪdi

credible
BR ˈkrɛdɪbl
AM ˈkrɛdəbəl

credibly
BR ˈkrɛdɪbli
AM ˈkrɛdəbli

credit
BR ˈkrɛd|ɪt, -ɪts, -ɪtɪŋ, -ɪtɪd
AM ˈkrɛdə|t, -ts, -dɪŋ, -dɪd

creditability
BR ˌkrɛdɪtəˈbɪlɪti
AM ˌkrɛdədəˈbɪlɪdi

creditable
BR ˈkrɛdɪtəbl
AM ˈkrɛdədəbəl

creditably
BR ˈkrɛdɪtəbli
AM ˈkrɛdədəbli

Crediton
BR ˈkrɛdɪt(ə)n
AM ˈkrɛdət(ə)n

creditor
BR ˈkrɛdɪtə(r), -z
AM ˈkrɛdədər, -z

creditworthiness
BR ˈkrɛdɪtˌwəːðɪnɪs
AM ˈkrɛdətˌwərðɪnɪs

creditworthy
BR ˈkrɛdɪtˌwəːði
AM ˈkrɛdətˌwərði

credo
BR ˈkriːdəʊ, ˈkreɪdəʊ, -z
AM ˈkriˌdoʊ, ˈkreɪˌdoʊ, -z

credulity
BR krɪˈdjuːlɪti, krɪˈdʒuːlɪti
AM krəˈd(j)ulədi

credulous
BR ˈkrɛdjʊləs, ˈkrɛdʒʊləs
AM ˈkrɛdʒələs

credulously
BR ˈkrɛdjʊləsli, ˈkrɛdʒʊləsli
AM ˈkrɛdʒələsli

credulousness
BR ˈkrɛdjʊləsnəs, ˈkrɛdʒʊləsnəs
AM ˈkrɛdʒələsnəs

Cree
BR kriː, -z
AM kri, -z

creed
BR kriːd, -z
AM krid, -z

creedal
BR ˈkriːdl
AM ˈkridəl

creek
BR kriːk, -s
AM krik, krɪk, -s

creel
BR kriːl, -z
AM kril, -z

Creeley
BR ˈkriːli
AM ˈkrili

creep
BR kriːp, -s, -ɪŋ
AM krip, -s, -ɪŋ

creeper
BR ˈkriːpə(r), -z
AM ˈkripər, -z

creepie
BR ˈkriːp|i, -ɪə(r), -ɪɪst
AM ˈkripi, -ər, -ɪst

creepily
BR ˈkriːpɪli
AM ˈkripəli

creepiness
BR ˈkriːpɪnɪs
AM ˈkripinɪs

creepy
BR ˈkriːp|i, -ɪə(r), -ɪɪst
AM ˈkripi, -ər, -ɪst

creepy-crawly
BR ˌkriːpɪˈkrɔːl|i, -ɪz
AM ˌkripiˈkrɔli, -z

creese
BR kriːs, -ɪz
AM kris, -ɪz

Creighton
BR ˈkrʌɪtn, ˈkreɪtn
AM ˈkreɪtn

cremate
BR krɪˈmeɪt, -s, -ɪŋ, -ɪd
AM ˈkriˌmeɪ|t, -ts, -dɪŋ, -dɪd

cremation
BR krɪˈmeɪʃn, -z
AM kriˈmeɪʃən, krəˈmeɪʃən, -z

cremator
BR krɪˈmeɪtə(r), -z
AM ˈkriˌmeɪdər, -z

crematoria
BR ˌkrɛməˈtɔːrɪə(r)
AM ˌkriməˈtɔriə

crematorium
BR ˌkrɛməˈtɔːrɪəm, -z
AM ˌkriməˈtɔriəm, -z

crematory
BR ˈkrɛmət(ə)r|i, -ɪz
AM ˈkriməˌtɔri, -z

crème brûlée
BR ˌkrɛm bruːˈleɪ
AM ˌkrɛm bruˈleɪ

crème caramel
BR ˌkrɛm ˌkarəˈmɛl, -z
AM ˌkrɛm ˌkɛrəˈmɛl, -z

crème de cassis
BR ˌkrɛm də kaˈsiːs
AM ˌkrɛm də kəˈsi(s)

crème de la crème
BR ˌkrɛm də la ˈkrɛm
AM ˌkrɛm də lə ˈkrɛm

crème de menthe
BR ˌkrɛm də ˈmɒnθ
AM ˌkrim də ˈmɛnθ

crème fraîche
BR ˌkrɛm ˈfrɛʃ
AM ˌkrɛm ˈfrɛʃ

crèmes brûlées
BR ˌkrɛm bruːˈleɪz
AM ˌkrɛm bruˈleɪz

Cremona
BR krɪˈməʊnə(r)
AM krəˈmoʊnə

crenate
BR ˈkriːneɪt, -ɪd
AM ˈkriˌneɪ|t, -dɪd

crenation
BR krɪˈneɪʃn
AM kriˈneɪʃən, krɛˈneɪʃən, krəˈneɪʃən

crenature
BR ˈkrɛnətjʊə(r), ˈkriːnətjʊə(r), ˈkrɛnətʃʊə(r), ˈkriːnətʃʊə(r), ˈkrɛnətʃə(r), ˈkriːnətʃə(r)
AM ˈkrɛnətʃər, ˈkrinətʃər

crenel
BR ˈkrɛnl, -z
AM ˈkrɛnəl, -z

crenelate
BR ˈkrɛnəleɪt, ˈkrɛnleɪt, -s, -ɪŋ, -ɪd
AM ˈkrɛnəˌleɪ|t, -ts, -dɪŋ, -dɪd

crenelation
BR ˌkrɛnəˈleɪʃn, ˌkrɛnlˈeɪʃn, -z
AM ˌkrɛnəˈleɪʃən, -z

crenellate
BR ˈkrɛnəleɪt, ˈkrɛnleɪt, -s, -ɪŋ, -ɪd
AM ˈkrɛnəˌleɪ|t, -ts, -dɪŋ, -dɪd

crenellation
BR ˌkrɛnəˈleɪʃn, ˌkrɛnlˈeɪʃn, -z
AM ˌkrɛnəˈleɪʃən, -z

crenelle
BR krɪˈnɛl, -z
AM krəˈnɛl, -z

Creole
BR ˈkriːəʊl, -z
AM ˈkriˌoʊl, -z

creole
BR ˈkriːəʊl, -z
AM ˈkriˌoʊl, -z

creolisation
BR ˌkriːələˈzeɪʃn
AM ˌkriələˈzeɪʃən, ˌkriəˌlaɪˈzeɪʃən

creolise
BR ˈkriːəlʌɪz, -ɪz, -ɪŋ, -d
AM ˈkriəˌlaɪz, -ɪz, -ɪŋ, -d

creolization
BR ˌkriːələˈzeɪʃn
AM ˌkriələˈzeɪʃən, ˌkriəˌlaɪˈzeɪʃən

creolize
BR ˈkriːəlʌɪz, -ɪz, -ɪŋ, -d
AM ˈkriəˌlaɪz, -ɪz, -ɪŋ, -d

Creon
BR ˈkriːɒn, ˈkriːən
AM ˈkriˌɑn

creosote
BR ˈkriːəsəʊt
AM ˈkriəˌsoʊt

crêpe
BR kreɪp, krɛp, -s
AM kreɪp, krɛp, -s

crêpe de Chine
BR ˌkreɪp də ˈʃiːn, ˌkrɛp +
AM ˌkreɪp də ˈʃin

crêpes suzette
BR ˌkreɪp(s) sʊˈzɛt, ˌkrɛp(s) +
AM ˌkreɪps suˈzɛt

crêpe suzette
BR ˌkreɪp sʊˈzɛt, ˌkrɛp +
AM ˌkreɪp suˈzɛt

crêpey
BR ˈkreɪpi
AM ˈkreɪpi

crepitant
BR ˈkrɛpɪtnt
AM ˈkrɛpədnt

crepitate
BR ˈkrɛpɪteɪt, -s, -ɪŋ, -ɪd
AM ˈkrɛpəˌteɪ|t, -ts, -dɪŋ, -dɪd

crepitation
BR ˌkrɛpɪˈteɪʃn, -z
AM ˌkrɛpəˈteɪʃən, -z

crepitus
BR ˈkrɛpɪtəs

crept
AM ˈkrɛpədəs
crept
BR krɛpt
AM krɛpt
crepuscular
BR krɪˈpʌskjʊlə(r)
AM krəˈpəskjələr
crêpy
BR ˈkreɪpi
AM ˈkreɪpi
crescendo
BR krɪˈʃɛndəʊ, -z
AM krəˈʃɛndoʊ, -z
crescent¹
increasing
BR ˈkrɛsnt
AM ˈkrɛs(ə)nt
crescent²
shape
BR ˈkrɛznt, ˈkrɛsnt, -s
AM ˈkrɛs(ə)nt, -s
crescentic
BR krɪˈsɛntɪk
AM krəˈsɛn(t)ɪk
cresol
BR ˈkriːsɒl
AM ˈkriˌsɔl, ˈkriˌsɑl
cress
BR krɛs
AM krɛs
cresset
BR ˈkrɛsɪt, -s
AM ˈkrɛsət, -s
Cressida
BR ˈkrɛsɪdə(r)
AM ˈkrɛsədə
Cresswell
BR ˈkrɛsw(ɛ)l,
ˈkrɛzw(ɛ)l
AM ˈkrɛsˌwɛl, ˈkrɛzˌwɛl
crest
BR krɛst, -s, -ɪd
AM krɛst, -s, -əd
crestfallen
BR ˈkrɛstˌfɔːlən
AM ˈkrɛs(t)ˌfɔlən,
ˈkrɛs(t)ˌfɑlən
crestless
BR ˈkrɛstləs
AM ˈkrɛs(t)ləs
Creswell
BR ˈkrɛsw(ɛ)l,
ˈkrɛzw(ɛ)l
AM ˈkrɛsˌwɛl, ˈkrɛzˌwɛl
cresyl
BR ˈkriːsʌɪl, ˈkriːsɪl
AM ˈkrɛsəl, ˈkrisəl
Cretaceous
BR krɪˈteɪʃəs
AM krəˈteɪʃəs
Cretan
BR ˈkriːtn, -z
AM ˈkritn, -z
Crete
BR kriːt
AM krit

cretic
BR ˈkriːtɪk, -s
AM ˈkridɪk, -s
cretin
BR ˈkrɛt(ɪ)n, -z
AM ˈkritn, -z
cretinise
BR ˈkrɛtɪnʌɪz,
ˈkrɛt̩ʌɪz, -ɪz, -ɪŋ, -d
AM ˈkritn̩ˌaɪz, -ɪz, -ɪŋ, -d
cretinism
BR ˈkrɛtɪnɪz(ə)m,
ˈkrɛtn̩ɪz(ə)m
AM ˈkritn̩ˌɪzəm
cretinize
BR ˈkrɛtɪnʌɪz,
ˈkrɛtn̩ʌɪz, -ɪz, -ɪŋ, -d
AM ˈkritn̩ˌaɪz, -ɪz, -ɪŋ, -d
cretinous
BR ˈkrɛtɪnəs, ˈkrɛtn̩əs
AM ˈkritn̩əs
cretinously
BR ˈkrɛtɪnəsli,
ˈkrɛtn̩əsli
AM ˈkritn̩əsli
cretonne
BR krɪˈtɒn, krɛˈtɒn,
ˈkrɛtɒn, -z
AM ˈkriˌtɑn, krəˈtɑn, -z
Creutzfeldt-
Jakob disease
BR ˌkrɔɪtsfeltˈjakɒb
dɪˌziːz
AM ˌkrɔɪtsˌfɛldˈdʒɑkəb
dəˌziz
crevasse
BR krɪˈvas, -ɪz
AM krəˈvæs, -əz
crevice
BR ˈkrɛv|ɪs, -ɪsɪz
AM ˈkrɛvəs, -əz
crew
BR kruː, -z, -ɪŋ, -d
AM kru, -z, -ɪŋ, -d
crewcut
BR ˈkruːkʌt, -s
AM ˈkruˌkət, -s
Crewe
BR kruː
AM kru
crewel
BR ˈkruːəl, -z
AM ˈkruwəl, -z
crewelwork
BR ˈkruːəlwəːk
AM ˈkruwəlˌwərk
Crewkerne
BR ˈkruːkəːn
AM ˈkruˌkərn
crewman
BR ˈkruːmən
AM ˈkrumən
crewmen
BR ˈkruːmən
AM ˈkrumən
cri
BR kriː
AM kri

crib
BR krɪb, -z, -ɪŋ, -d
AM krɪb, -z, -ɪŋ, -d
cribbage
BR ˈkrɪbɪdʒ
AM ˈkrɪbɪdʒ
cribber
BR ˈkrɪbə(r), -z
AM ˈkrɪbər, -z
cribella
BR krɪˈbɛlə(r)
AM krəˈbɛlə
cribellum
BR krɪˈbɛləm
AM krəˈbɛləm
cribo
BR ˈkriːbəʊ, -z
AM ˈkriˌboʊ, -z
cribriform
BR ˈkrɪbrɪfɔːm
AM ˈkrɪbrəˌfɔ(ə)rm
cribwork
BR ˈkrɪbwəːk
AM ˈkrɪbˌwərk
Criccieth
BR ˈkrɪkɪəθ, ˈkrɪkɪɛθ
AM ˈkrɪkiəθ
Crich
BR krʌɪtʃ
AM kraɪtʃ
Crichton
BR ˈkrʌɪtn
AM ˈkraɪtn
crick
BR krɪk, -s, -ɪŋ, -t
AM krɪk, -s, -ɪŋ, -t
cricket
BR ˈkrɪkɪt, -s
AM ˈkrɪkɪt, -s
cricketer
BR ˈkrɪkɪtə(r), -z
AM ˈkrɪkədər, -z
Crickhowell
BR krɪkˈhaʊ(ə)l
AM krɪkˈhaʊəl
cricoid
BR ˈkrʌɪkɔɪd, -z
AM ˈkraɪˌkɔɪd, -z
cri de cœur
BR ˌkriː də ˈkəː(r)
AM ˌkri də ˈkər
cried
BR krʌɪd
AM kraɪd
Crieff
BR kriːf
AM krif
crier
BR ˈkrʌɪə(r), -z
AM ˈkraɪər, -z
crikey!
BR ˈkrʌɪki
AM ˈkraɪki
crim
BR krɪm, -z
AM krɪm, -z

crime
BR krʌɪm, -z
AM kraɪm, -z
Crimea
BR krʌɪˈmɪə(r)
AM kraɪˈmiə
Crimean
BR krʌɪˈmɪən, -z
AM kraɪˈmiən, -z
crime passionnel
BR ˌkriːm ˌpasjəˈnɛl, -z
AM ˌkrim ˌpæsjəˈnɛl, -z
crimes
passionnels
BR ˌkriːm ˌpasjəˈnɛlz
AM ˌkrim
ˌpæsjəˈnɛl(z)
criminal
BR ˈkrɪmɪnl
AM ˈkrɪmənl, ˈkrɪmnəl
criminalisation
BR ˌkrɪmɪnəlʌɪˈzeɪʃn,
ˌkrɪmɪnl̩ʌɪˈzeɪʃn
AM ˌkrɪm(ə)nələˈzeɪʃən,
ˌkrɪm(ə)nəˌlaɪˈzeɪʃən
criminalise
BR ˈkrɪmɪnəlʌɪz,
ˈkrɪmɪnl̩ʌɪz, -ɪz, -ɪŋ, -d
AM ˈkrɪm(ə)nəˌlaɪz,
-ɪŋ, -d
criminalistic
BR ˌkrɪmɪnəˈlɪstɪk,
ˌkrɪmɪnl̩ˈɪstɪk, -s
AM ˌkrɪm(ə)nəˈlɪstɪk,
-s
criminality
BR ˌkrɪmɪˈnalɪti
AM ˌkrɪməˈnælədi
criminalization
BR ˌkrɪmɪnəlʌɪˈzeɪʃn,
ˌkrɪmɪnl̩ʌɪˈzeɪʃn
AM ˌkrɪm(ə)nələˈzeɪʃən,
ˌkrɪm(ə)nəˌlaɪˈzeɪʃən
criminalize
BR ˈkrɪmɪnəlʌɪz,
ˈkrɪmɪnl̩ʌɪz, -ɪz, -ɪŋ, -d
AM ˈkrɪm(ə)nəˌlaɪz, -ɪz,
-ɪŋ, -d
criminally
BR ˈkrɪmɪnl̩i,
ˈkrɪmɪnəli
AM ˈkrɪm(ə)nəli
criminate
BR ˈkrɪmɪneɪt, -s, -ɪŋ,
-ɪd
AM ˈkrɪməˌneɪ|t, -ts,
-dɪŋ, -dɪd
crimination
BR ˌkrɪmɪˈneɪʃn, -z
AM ˌkrɪməˈneɪʃən, -z
criminative
BR ˈkrɪmɪnətɪv, -z
AM ˈkrɪməˌneɪdɪv, -z
criminatory
BR ˈkrɪmɪnət(ə)ri
AM ˈkrɪmənəˌtɔri
criminological
BR ˌkrɪmɪnəˈlɒdʒɪkl

AM ˌkrɪmənəˈlɑdʒəkəl
criminologist
BR ˌkrɪmɪˈnɒlədʒɪst, -s
AM ˌkrɪməˈnɑlədʒəst,
-s
criminology
BR ˌkrɪmɪˈnɒlədʒi
AM ˌkrɪməˈnɑlədʒi
Crimond
BR ˈkrɪmənd
AM ˈkrɪmənd
crimp
BR krɪm|p, -ps, -pɪŋ,
-(p)t
AM krɪm|p, -ps, -pɪŋ,
-(p)t
crimper
BR ˈkrɪmpə(r), -z
AM ˈkrɪmpər, -z
crimpily
BR ˈkrɪmpɨli
AM ˈkrɪmpɨli
crimpiness
BR ˈkrɪmpɪnɪs
AM ˈkrɪmpɪnɪs
crimplene®
BR ˈkrɪmpliːn
AM ˈkrɪmpˌlin
crimpy
BR ˈkrɪmpi
AM ˈkrɪmpi
crimson
BR ˈkrɪmzn̩, -z, -ɪŋ, -d
AM ˈkrɪmzn, -z, -ɪŋ, -d
cringe
BR krɪn(d)ʒ, -ɪz, -ɪŋ, -d
AM krɪndʒ, -ɪz, -ɪŋ, -d
cringer
BR ˈkrɪn(d)ʒə(r), -z
AM ˈkrɪndʒər, -z
cringle
BR ˈkrɪŋgl, -z
AM ˈkrɪŋgəl, -z
crinkle
BR ˈkrɪŋk|l, -lz,
-l̩ŋ \-lŋ, -ld
AM ˈkrɪŋk|əl, -əlz,
-(ə)lɪŋ, -əld
crinkliness
BR ˈkrɪŋklɪnɪs
AM ˈkrɪŋk(ə)linɨs
crinkly
BR ˈkrɪŋkl|i, -ɪə(r),
-ɪɪst
AM ˈkrɪŋk(ə)li, -ər, -ɪst
crinoid
BR ˈkrʌɪnɔɪd, ˈkrɪnɔɪd
AM ˈkraɪˌnɔɪd,
ˈkrɪˌnɔɪd
crinoidal
BR krʌɪˈnɔɪdl,
krɪˈnɔɪdl
AM ˌkraɪˈnɔɪdəl,
ˌkrɪˈnɔɪdəl
crinoline
BR ˈkrɪnəlɪn, ˈkrɪnl̩ɪn,
-z

AM ˈkrɪn(ə)lɪn,
ˈkrɪn(ə)ˌlin, -z
criolla
BR krɪˈəʊlə(r), -z
AM kriˈoʊlə, -z
criollo
BR krɪˈəʊləʊ, -z
AM kriˈoʊˌloʊ, -z
cripes!
BR krʌɪps
AM kraɪps
Crippen
BR ˈkrɪp(ɪ)n
AM ˈkrɪpən
cripple
BR ˈkrɪp|l, -lz, -l̩ŋ \-lŋ,
-ld
AM ˈkrɪp|əl, -əlz,
-(ə)lɪŋ, -əld
crippledom
BR ˈkrɪpldəm
AM ˈkrɪpəldəm
cripplehood
BR ˈkrɪplhʊd
AM ˈkrɪpəl,(h)ʊd
crippler
BR ˈkrɪplə(r),
ˈkrɪpl̩ə(r), -z
AM ˈkrɪp(ə)lər, -z
cripplingly
BR ˈkrɪplɪŋli
AM ˈkrɪp(ə)lɪŋli
Cripps
BR krɪps
AM krɪps
Cris
BR kriːs, -ɪz
AM krɪs, -ɪz
cris de coeur
BR ˌkri: də ˈkə:(r)
AM ˌkri də ˈkər
crises
BR ˈkrʌɪsi:z
AM ˈkraɪˌsiz
crisis
BR ˈkrʌɪsɪs
AM ˈkraɪsɨs
crisp
BR krɪsp, -s, -ɪŋ, -t, -ə(r),
-ɪst
AM krɪsp, -s, -ɪŋ, -t, -ər,
-ɪst
crispate
BR ˈkrɪspeɪt
AM ˈkrɪsˌpeɪt
crispbread
BR ˈkrɪspbrɛd, -z
AM ˈkrɪs(p)ˌbrɛd, -z
crisper
BR ˈkrɪspə(r), -z
AM ˈkrɪspər, -z
Crispian
BR ˈkrɪspɪən
AM ˈkrɪspiən

Crispin
BR ˈkrɪspɪn
AM ˈkrɪspən
crispiness
BR ˈkrɪspɪnɪs
AM ˈkrɪspinɪs
crisply
BR ˈkrɪspli
AM ˈkrɪs(p)li
crispness
BR ˈkrɪspnɪs
AM ˈkrɪs(p)nɪs
crispy
BR ˈkrɪspi
AM ˈkrɪspi
crisscross
BR ˈkrɪskrɒs, -ɪz, -ɪŋ, -t
AM ˈkrɪsˌkrɔs,
ˈkrɪsˌkrɑs, -əz, -ɪŋ, -t
crista
BR ˈkrɪstə(r)
AM ˈkrɪstə
cristae
BR ˈkrɪsti:
AM ˈkrɪsˌteɪ, ˈkrɪsˌtaɪ,
ˈkrɪsti
cristate
BR ˈkrɪsteɪt
AM ˈkrɪˌsteɪt
cristobalite
BR krɪˈstəʊbəlʌɪt
AM krɪˈstoʊbəˌlaɪt
crit
BR krɪt, -s
AM krɪt, -s
Critchley
BR ˈkrɪtʃli
AM ˈkrɪtʃli
criteria
BR krʌɪˈtɪərɪə(r)
AM kraɪˈtɪriə
criterial
BR krʌɪˈtɪərɪəl
AM kraɪˈtɪriəl
criterion
BR krʌɪˈtɪərɪən, -z
AM kraɪˈtɪriən, -z
critic
BR ˈkrɪtɪk, -s
AM ˈkrɪdɪk, -s
critical
BR ˈkrɪtɪkl
AM ˈkrɪdəkəl
criticality
BR ˌkrɪtɨˈkalɪt|i, -ɪz
AM ˌkrɪdəˈkælədi, -z
critically
BR ˈkrɪtɪk(ə)li,
ˈkrɪtɪkli
AM ˈkrɪdək(ə)li
criticalness
BR ˈkrɪtɪklnəs
AM ˈkrɪdəkəlnəs
criticaster
BR ˌkrɪtɨˈkastə(r),
ˈkrɪtɪkastə(r), -z
AM ˈkrɪdəˌkæstər, -z

criticisable
BR ˈkrɪtɪsʌɪzəbl
AM ˈkrɪdəˌsaɪzəbəl
criticise
BR ˈkrɪtɪsʌɪz, -ɪz, -ɪŋ, -d
AM ˈkrɪdəˌsaɪz, -ɪz, -ɪŋ,
-d
criticiser
BR ˈkrɪtɪsʌɪzə(r), -z
AM ˈkrɪdəˌsaɪzər, -z
criticism
BR ˈkrɪtɪsɪz(ə)m, -z
AM ˈkrɪdəˌsɪzəm, -z
criticizable
BR ˈkrɪtɪsʌɪzəbl
AM ˈkrɪdəˌsaɪzəbəl
criticize
BR ˈkrɪtɪsʌɪz, -ɪz, -ɪŋ, -d
AM ˈkrɪdəˌsaɪz, -ɪz, -ɪŋ,
-d
criticizer
BR ˈkrɪtɪsʌɪzə(r), -z
AM ˈkrɪdəˌsaɪzər, -z
critique
BR krɪˈti:k, -s
AM krɪˈtik, -s
Crittall
BR ˈkrɪtɔːl
AM ˈkrɪdɔl, ˈkrɪdɑl
critter
BR ˈkrɪtə(r), -z
AM ˈkrɪdər, -z
croak
BR ˈkrəʊk, -s, -ɪŋ, -t
AM kroʊk, -s, -ɪŋ, -t
croaker
BR ˈkrəʊkə(r), -z
AM ˈkroʊkər, -z
croakily
BR ˈkrəʊkɨli
AM ˈkroʊkəli
croakiness
BR ˈkrəʊkɪnɪs
AM ˈkroʊkinɪs
croaky
BR ˈkrəʊk|i, -ɪə(r), -ɪɪst
AM ˈkroʊki, -ər, -ɪst
Croat
BR ˈkrəʊat, -s
AM ˈkroʊˌɑt, -s
Croatia
BR krəʊˈeɪʃə(r)
AM kroʊˈeɪʃə
Croatian
BR krəʊˈeɪʃn, -z
AM kroʊˈeɪʃən, -z
croc
BR krɒk, -s
AM krɑk, -s
Croce
BR ˈkrəʊtʃeɪ
AM ˈkroʊtʃeɪ
croceate
BR ˈkrəʊsɪeɪt
AM ˈkroʊtʃiət
crochet
BR ˈkrəʊʃeɪ, -z, -ɪŋ, -d

AM kroʊˈʃeɪ, -z, -ɪŋ, -d
crocheter
BR ˈkrəʊʃeɪə(r), -z
AM kroʊˈʃeɪər, -z
croci
BR ˈkrəʊkʌɪ, ˈkrəʊkiː
AM ˈkroʊˌsaɪ, ˈkroʊki
crocidolite
BR krə(ʊ)ˈsɪdəlʌɪt
AM kroʊˈsɪdəˌlaɪt
crock
BR krɒk, -s
AM krɑk, -s
Crocker
BR ˈkrɒkə(r)
AM ˈkrɑkər
crockery
BR ˈkrɒk(ə)ri
AM ˈkrɑk(ə)ri
crocket
BR ˈkrɒkɪt, -s
AM ˈkrɑkət, -s
Crockett
BR ˈkrɒkɪt
AM ˈkrɑkət
Crockford
BR ˈkrɒkfəd
AM ˈkrɑkfərd
crocodile
BR ˈkrɒkədʌɪl, -z
AM ˈkrɑkəˌdaɪl, -z
crocodilian
BR ˌkrɒkəˈdɪlɪən, -z
AM ˌkrɑkəˈdɪljən, ˌkrɑkəˈdɪliən, -z
crocus
BR ˈkrəʊkəs, -ɪz
AM ˈkroʊkəs, -ɪz
Croesus
BR ˈkriːsəs
AM ˈkrisəs
croft¹
BR krɒft, -s
AM krɔft, -s
croft²
BR krɒft, -s
AM krɔft, krɑft, -s
crofter
BR ˈkrɒftə(r), -z
AM ˈkrɔftər, ˈkrɑftər, -z
Crofton
BR ˈkrɒft(ə)n
AM ˈkrɑft(ə)n
Crohn's disease
BR ˈkrəʊnz dɪˌziːz
AM ˈkroʊnz dəˌziz
croissant
BR ˈk(r)wasɒ̃, ˈk(r)wɑːsɒ̃, -z
AM ˌk(r)wɑˈsɑn(t), -z
Croker
BR ˈkrəʊkə(r)
AM ˈkroʊkər
Cro-Magnon
BR krəʊˈmanjɒ̃, krəʊˈmanjɒn, krəʊˈmagnən

AM kroʊˈmægnən, kroʊˈmænjən
Cromartie
BR ˈkrɒməti
AM ˌkroʊˈmɑrdi
Cromarty
BR ˈkrɒməti
AM ˌkroʊˈmɑrdi
crombec
BR ˈkrɒmbɛk, -s
AM ˈkrɑmˌbɛk, -s
Crombie
BR ˈkrɒmbi, ˈkrʌmbi
AM ˈkrɑmbi
Crome
BR krəʊm
AM kroʊm
Cromer
BR ˈkrəʊmə(r)
AM ˈkroʊmər
Cromford
BR ˈkrɒmfəd
AM ˈkrɑmfərd
cromlech
BR ˈkrɒmləx, ˈkrɒmlək, -s
AM ˈkrɑmˌlɛk, -s
Crompton
BR ˈkrɒm(p)t(ə)n, ˈkrʌm(p)t(ə)n
AM ˈkramtən
Cromwell
BR ˈkrɒmw(ɛ)l
AM ˈkramwəl, ˈkram,wɛl
Cromwellian
BR krɒmˈwɛlən
AM ˌkramˈwɛljən, ˌkramˈwɛliən
crone
BR krəʊn, -z
AM kroʊn, -z
Cronenberg
BR ˈkrɒnənbəːg
AM ˈkranənˌbərg
Cronin
BR ˈkrəʊnɪn
AM ˈkroʊnən
cronk
BR krɒŋk
AM kraŋk
Cronus
BR ˈkrəʊnəs
AM ˈkroʊnəs
crony
BR ˈkrəʊn|i, -ɪz
AM ˈkroʊni, -z
cronyism
BR ˈkrəʊnɪɪz(ə)m
AM ˈkroʊniˌɪzəm
crook
BR krʊk, -s, -ɪŋ, -t
AM krʊk, -s, -ɪŋ, -t
crookback
BR ˈkrʊkbak, -s
AM ˈkrʊkˌbæk, -s

Crooke
BR krʊk
AM krʊk
crooked
adjective
BR ˈkrʊkɪd, -ə(r), -ɪst
AM ˈkrʊkəd, -ər, -əst
crookedly
BR ˈkrʊkɪdli
AM ˈkrʊkədli
crookedness
BR ˈkrʊkɪdnɪs
AM ˈkrʊkədnəs
crookery
BR ˈkrʊk(ə)ri
AM ˈkrʊkəri
Crookes
BR krʊks
AM krʊks
Croom
BR kruːm
AM krum
Croome
BR kruːm
AM krum
croon
BR kruːn, -z, -ɪŋ, -d
AM krun, -z, -ɪŋ, -d
crooner
BR ˈkruːnə(r), -z
AM ˈkrunər, -z
crop
BR krɒp, -s, -ɪŋ, -t
AM krɑp, -s, -ɪŋ, -t
cropper
BR ˈkrɒpə(r), -z
AM ˈkrɑpər, -z
croquet
BR ˈkrəʊkeɪ, ˈkrəʊki
AM ˌkroʊˈkeɪ
croquette
BR krɒˈkɛt, krəˈkɛt, -s
AM ˌkroʊˈkɛt, -s
crore
BR krɔː(r), -z
AM krɔ(ə)r, -z
Crosbie
BR ˈkrɒzbi
AM ˈkrɔzbi, ˈkrazbi
Crosby
BR ˈkrɒzbi, ˈkrɒsbi
AM ˈkrɔzbi, ˈkrazbi
crosier
BR ˈkrəʊzɪə(r), ˈkrəʊʒə(r), -z
AM ˈkroʊʒər, -z
Crosland
BR ˈkrɒslənd
AM ˈkrɔslənd, ˈkraslənd
cross
BR krɒs, -ɪz, -ɪŋ, -t
AM krɔs, kras, -əs, -ɪŋ, -t
crossbar
BR ˈkrɒsbɑː(r), -z

AM ˈkrɔsˌbar, ˈkrasˌbar, -z
crossbeam
BR ˈkrɒsbiːm, -z
AM ˈkrɔsˌbim, ˈkrasˌbim, -z
crossbench
BR ˈkrɒsbɛn(t)ʃ, -ɪz
AM ˈkrɔsˌbɛn(t)ʃ, ˈkrasˌbɛn(t)ʃ, -əz
cross-bencher
BR ˈkrɒsˌbɛn(t)ʃə(r), -z
AM ˈkrɔsˌbɛn(t)ʃər, ˈkrasˌbɛn(t)ʃər, -z
crossbill
BR ˈkrɒsbɪl, -z
AM ˈkrɔsˌbɪl, ˈkrasˌbɪl, -z
crossbones
BR ˈkrɒsbəʊnz
AM ˈkrɔsˌboʊnz, ˈkrasˌboʊnz
crossbow
BR ˈkrɒsbəʊ, -z
AM ˈkrɔsˌboʊ, ˈkrasˌboʊ, -z
crossbowman
BR ˈkrɒsbəʊmən
AM ˈkrɔsˌboʊmən, ˈkrasˌboʊmən
crossbowmen
BR ˈkrɒsbəʊmən
AM ˈkrɔsˌboʊmən, ˈkrasˌboʊmən
crossbred
BR ˌkrɒsˈbrɛd, ˈkrɒsbrɛd
AM ˌkrɔsˈbrɛd, ˌkrasˈbrɛd
crossbreed
BR ˈkrɒsbriːd, -z, -ɪŋ
AM ˈkrɔsˌbrid, ˈkrasˌbrid, -z, -ɪŋ
crosscheck
BR ˌkrɒsˈtʃɛk, ˈkrɒstʃɛk, -s, -ɪŋ, -t
AM ˈkrɔsˌtʃɛk, ˈkrasˌtʃɛk, -s, -ɪŋ, -t
crosscurrent
BR ˈkrɒsˌkʌrənt, ˈkrɒsˌkʌrnt, -s
AM ˈkrɔsˌkərənt, ˈkrasˌkərənt, -s
crosscut¹
adjective, verb
BR ˈkrɒskʌt, ˌkrɒsˈkʌt, -s, -ɪŋ
AM ˌkrɔsˈkəʃt, ˈkrasˈkəʃt, -ts, -dɪŋ
crosscut²
noun
BR ˈkrɒskʌt, -s
AM ˈkrɔsˌkət, ˈkrasˌkət, -s
crosse
BR krɒs, -ɪz
AM krɔs, kras, -əz

crossfield
BR ˌkrɒsˈfiːld
AM ˈkrɔːsˌfiːld,
ˈkrɑːsˌfild

crossfire
BR ˈkrɒsfaɪə(r)
AM ˈkrɔːsˌfaɪ(ə)r,
ˈkrɑːsˌfaɪ(ə)r

crosshatch[1]
noun
BR ˈkrɒshatʃ, -ɪz
AM ˈkrɔːsˌ(h)ætʃ,
ˈkrɑːsˌ(h)ætʃ, -əz

crosshatch[2]
verb
BR ˌkrɒsˈhatʃ, -ɪz, -ɪŋ, -t
AM ˈkrɔːsˌ(h)ætʃ,
ˈkrɑːsˌ(h)ætʃ, -əz, -ɪŋ, -t

crossing
BR ˈkrɒsɪŋ, -z
AM ˈkrɔːsɪŋ, ˈkrɑːsɪŋ, -z

Crossland
BR ˈkrɒslənd
AM ˈkrɔːslənd,
ˈkrɑːslənd

cross-legged
BR ˌkrɒsˈlɛg(ɪ)d
AM ˈkrɔːsˌlɛg(ə)d

Crossley
BR ˈkrɒsli
AM ˈkrɔːsli, ˈkrɑːsli

crossly
BR ˈkrɒsli
AM ˈkrɔːsli, ˈkrɑːsli

Crossmaglen
BR ˌkrɒsməˈglɛn
AM ˌkrɔːsməˈglɛn,
ˌkrɑːsməˈglɛn

Crossman
BR ˈkrɒsmən
AM ˈkrɔːsmən,
ˈkrɑːsmən

crossmatch
BR ˌkrɒsˈmatʃ, -ɪz, -ɪŋ, -t
AM ˈkrɔːsˌmætʃ,
ˈkrɑːsˌmætʃ, -əz, -ɪŋ, -t

crossness
BR ˈkrɒsnəs
AM ˈkrɔːsnəs, ˈkrɑːsnəs

crossover
BR ˈkrɒsəʊvə(r), -z
AM ˈkrɔːsˌoʊvər,
ˈkrɑːsˌoʊvər, -z

crosspatch
BR ˈkrɒspatʃ, -ɪz
AM ˈkrɔːsˌpætʃ,
ˈkrɑːsˌpætʃ, -əz

crosspiece
BR ˈkrɒspiːs, -ɪz
AM ˈkrɔːsˌpis, ˈkrɑːsˌpis, -ɪz

crossply
BR ˈkrɒsplʌɪ, -z
AM ˈkrɔːsˌplaɪ, ˈkrɑːsˌplaɪ, -z

crossrail
BR ˈkrɒsreɪl, -z

AM ˈkrɔːsˌreɪl,
ˈkrɑːsˌreɪl, -z

crossroad
BR ˈkrɒsrəʊd, -z
AM ˈkrɔːsˌroʊd,
ˈkrɑːsˌroʊd, -z

crosstab
BR ˈkrɒstab, -z
AM ˈkrɔːsˌtæb,
ˈkrɑːsˌtæb, -z

crosstalk
BR ˈkrɒstɔːk
AM ˈkrɔːsˌtɔk, ˈkrɑːsˌtɑk

crosstie
BR ˈkrɒstʌɪ, -z
AM ˈkrɔːsˌtaɪ, ˈkrɑːsˌtaɪ, -z

crosstown
BR ˌkrɒsˈtaʊn
AM ˈkrɔːsˌtaʊn,
ˈkrɑːsˌtaʊn

crosstree
BR ˈkrɒstriː, -z
AM ˈkrɔːsˌtri, ˈkrɑːsˌtri, -z

crosswalk
BR ˈkrɒswɔːk, -s
AM ˈkrɔːsˌwɔk,
ˈkrɑːsˌwak, -s

crossways
BR ˈkrɒsweɪz
AM ˈkrɔːsˌweɪz,
ˈkrɑːsˌweɪz

crosswind
BR ˈkrɒswɪnd, -z
AM ˈkrɔːsˌwɪnd,
ˈkrɑːsˌwɪnd, -z

crosswise
BR ˈkrɒswʌɪz
AM ˈkrɔːsˌwaɪz,
ˈkrɑːsˌwaɪz

crossword
BR ˈkrɒswəːd, -z
AM ˈkrɔːsˌwərd,
ˈkrɑːsˌwərd, -z

crotch
BR ˈkrɒtʃ, -ɪz
AM ˈkratʃ, -əz

crotchet
BR ˈkrɒtʃɪt, -s
AM ˈkratʃət, -s

crotchetiness
BR ˈkrɒtʃɪtɪnɪs
AM ˈkratʃədɪnɪs

crotchety
BR ˈkrɒtʃɪti
AM ˈkratʃədi

croton
BR ˈkrəʊtn, -z
AM ˈkroʊtn, -z

crouch
BR ˈkraʊtʃ, -ɪz, -ɪŋ, -t
AM ˈkraʊtʃ, -əz, -ɪŋ, -t

croup
BR ˈkruːp, -s
AM ˈkrup, -s

croupier
BR ˈkruːpɪeɪ,
ˈkruːpɪə(r), -z
AM ˈkrupiˌeɪ, ˈkrupiər, -z

croupy
BR ˈkruːpi
AM ˈkrupi

croustade
BR kruˈstɑːd, -z
AM ˌkruˈstɑd, -z

croûton
BR ˈkruːtɒn, -z
AM ˈkruˌtɑn, -z

crow
BR krəʊ, -z, -ɪŋ, -d
AM kroʊ, -z, -ɪŋ, -d

crowbar
BR ˈkrəʊbɑː(r), -z
AM ˈkroʊˌbar, -z

crowberry
BR ˈkrəʊb(ə)r|i, -ɪz
AM ˈkroʊˌbɛri, -z

Crowborough
BR ˈkrəʊb(ə)rə(r)
AM ˈkroʊˌbəroʊ,
ˈkroʊbərə

crowd
BR kraʊd, -z, -ɪŋ, -ɪd
AM kraʊd, -z, -ɪŋ, -əd

crowdedness
BR ˈkraʊdɪdnɪs
AM ˈkraʊdədnɪs

crowd-pleaser
BR ˈkraʊdˌpliːzə(r), -z
AM ˈkroʊdˌplizər, -z

Crowe
BR krəʊ
AM kroʊ

crowfoot
BR ˈkrəʊfʊt, -s
AM ˈkroʊˌfʊt, -s

Crowley
BR ˈkrəʊli
AM ˈkraʊli

crown
BR kraʊn, -z, -ɪŋ, -d
AM kraʊn, -z, -ɪŋ, -d

crownpiece
BR ˈkraʊnpiːs, -ɪz
AM ˈkraʊnˌpis, -ɪz

Crowther
BR ˈkraʊðə(r)
AM ˈkraʊðər

Crowthorne
BR ˈkrəʊθɔːn
AM ˈkroʊˌθɔ(ə)rn

Croydon
BR ˈkrɔɪdn
AM ˈkrɔɪdən

crozier
BR ˈkrəʊzɪə(r),
ˈkrəʊzə(r), -z
AM ˈkroʊʒər, -z

cru
BR kruː, -z
AM kru, -z

cruces
BR ˈkruːsiːz
AM ˈkrusiz

crucial
BR ˈkruːʃl
AM ˈkruʃəl

cruciality
BR ˌkruːʃɪˈalɪti
AM ˌkruʃiˈælədi

crucially
BR ˈkruːʃli, ˈkruːʃəli
AM ˈkruʃəli

crucian
BR ˈkruːʃn
AM ˈkruʃən

cruciate
BR ˈkruːʃɪət, ˈkruːʃɪeɪt
AM ˈkruʃ(i)ət,
ˈkruʃieɪt

crucible
BR ˈkruːsɪbl, -z
AM ˈkrusəbəl, -z

crucifer
BR ˈkruːsɪfə(r), -z
AM ˈkrusəfər, -z

cruciferous
BR kruːˈsɪf(ə)rəs
AM kruˈsɪf(ə)rəs

crucifier
BR ˈkruːsɪfʌɪə(r), -z
AM ˈkrusəˌfaɪər, -z

crucifix
BR ˈkruːsɪfɪks, -ɪz
AM ˈkrusəˌfɪks, -ɪz

crucifixion
BR ˌkruːsɪˈfɪkʃn, -z
AM ˌkrusəˈfɪkʃən, -z

cruciform
BR ˈkruːsɪfɔːm
AM ˈkrusəˌfɔ(ə)rm

crucify
BR ˈkruːsɪfʌɪ, -z, -ɪŋ, -d
AM ˈkrusəˌfaɪ, -z, -ɪŋ, -d

cruck
BR krʌk, -s
AM krək, -s

crud
BR krʌd
AM krəd

cruddy
BR ˈkrʌd|i, -ɪə(r), -ɪɪst
AM ˈkrədi, -ər, -ɪst

crude
BR kruːd, -ə(r), -ɪst
AM krud, -ər, -əst

crudely
BR ˈkruːdli
AM ˈkrudli

crudeness
BR ˈkruːdnəs
AM ˈkrudnəs

crudités
BR ˌkruːdɪˈteɪ
AM ˈkrudəˌteɪ

crudity
BR ˈkruːdɪt|i, -ɪz
AM ˈkrudədi, -z

cruel
BR 'kru:(ə)l, -ə(r), -ɪst
AM 'kru(ə)l, -ər, -əst
cruelly
BR 'kru:(ə)li
AM 'kru(ə)li
cruelness
BR 'kru:(ə)lnəs
AM 'kru(ə)lnəs
cruelty
BR 'kru:(ə)ltǀi, -ɪz
AM 'kru(ə)lti, -z
cruet
BR 'kru:ɪt, -s
AM 'kruət, -s
Crufts
BR krʌfts
AM krəf(t)s
Cruikshank
BR 'krʊkʃaŋk
AM 'krʊkˌʃæŋk
cruise
BR kru:z, -ɪz, -ɪŋ, -d
AM kruz, -əz, -ɪn, -d
cruiser
BR 'kru:zə(r), -z
AM 'kruzər, -z
cruiserweight
BR 'kru:zəweɪt, -s
AM 'kruzərˌweɪt, -s
cruiseway
BR 'kru:zweɪ, -z
AM 'kruzˌweɪ, -z
cruller
BR 'krʌlə(r), -z
AM 'krələr, -z
crumb
BR krʌm, -z
AM krəm, -z
crumble
BR 'krʌmbǀl, -lz,
-ǀɪŋ \-l̩ŋ, -ld
AM 'krəmbǀəl, -əlz,
-(ə)lŋ, -əld
crumbliness
BR 'krʌmblɪnɪs
AM 'krəmblinɪs
crumbly
BR 'krʌmbli
AM 'krəmbli
crumby
BR 'krʌmǀi, -ɪə(r), -ɪɪst
AM 'krəmi, -ər, -ɪst
crumhorn
BR 'krʌmhɔːn, -z
AM 'krəm,(h)ɔ(ə)rn, -z
Crumlin
BR 'krʌmlɪn
AM 'krəmlən
crummily
BR 'krʌmɪli
AM 'krəməli
crumminess
BR 'krʌmɪnɪs
AM 'krəminɪs
crummy
BR 'krʌmǀi, -ɪə(r), -ɪɪst

AM 'krəmi, -ər, -ɪst
crump
BR 'krʌmǀp, -ps, -pɪŋ,
-(p)t
AM 'krəmǀp, -ps, -pɪŋ,
-(p)t
crumpet
BR 'krʌmpɪt, -s
AM 'krəmpət, -s
crumple
BR 'krʌmpǀl, -lz,
-ǀɪŋ \-lŋ, -ld
AM 'krəmpǀəl, -əlz,
-(ə)lŋ, -əld
crumply
BR 'krʌmplǀi, -ɪə(r),
-ɪɪst
AM 'krəmp(ə)li, -ər,
-ɪst
crunch
BR krʌn(t)ʃ, -ɪz, -ɪŋ, -t
AM krən(t)ʃ, -əz, -ɪŋ, -t
cruncher
BR 'krʌn(t)ʃə(r), -z
AM 'krən(t)ʃər, -z
Crunchie®
BR 'krʌn(t)ʃǀi, -ɪz
AM 'krən(t)ʃi, -z
crunchily
BR 'krʌn(t)ʃɪli
AM 'krən(t)ʃəli
crunchiness
BR 'krʌn(t)ʃɪnɪs
AM 'krən(t)ʃinɪs
crunchy
BR 'krʌn(t)ʃǀi, -ɪə(r),
-ɪɪst
AM 'krən(t)ʃi, -ər, -ɪst
crupper
BR 'krʌpə(r), -z
AM 'krəpər, -z
crural
BR 'krʊərəl, 'krʊərl̩
AM 'krʊrəl
crusade
BR kru:'seɪd, -z, -ɪŋ, -ɪd
AM kru'seɪd, -z, -ɪŋ, -ɪd
crusader
BR kru:'seɪdə(r), -z
AM kru'seɪdər, -z
cruse
BR kru:z, -ɪz
AM kruz, -əz
crush
BR krʌʃ, -ɪz, -ɪŋ, -t
AM krəʃ, -əz, -ɪŋ, -t
crushable
BR 'krʌʃəbl
AM 'krəʃəbəl
crusher
BR 'krʌʃə(r), -z
AM 'krəʃər, -z
crushingly
BR 'krʌʃɪŋli
AM 'krəʃɪŋli
Crusoe
BR 'kru:səʊ

AM 'krusoʊ
crust
BR krʌst, -s
AM krəst, -s
crustacea
BR krʌ'steɪʃə(r)
AM krə'steɪʃə
crustacean
BR krʌ'steɪʃn, -z
AM krə'steɪʃən, -z
crustaceology
BR krʌˌsteɪʃɪ'ɒlədʒi
AM krəˌsteɪʃi'ɑlədʒi
crustaceous
BR krʌ'steɪʃəs
AM krə'steɪʃəs
crustal
BR 'krʌstl
AM 'krəstəl
crustily
BR 'krʌstɪli
AM 'krəstəli
crustiness
BR 'krʌstɪnɪs
AM 'krəstinɪs
crustose
BR 'krʌstəʊs
AM 'krəsˌtoʊs
crusty
BR 'krʌstǀi, -ɪə(r), -ɪɪst
AM 'krəsti, -ər, -ɪst
crutch
BR krʌtʃ, -ɪz
AM krətʃ, -əz
Cruttenden
BR 'krʌtndən
AM 'krətnd(ə)n
crux
BR krʌks, -ɪz
AM krəks, -əz
Cruyff
BR krɔɪf
AM krɔɪf
DU krœyf
Cruz
BR kru:z
AM kruz
cruzado
BR krʊ'zɑːdəʊ, -z
AM krʊ'zɑdoʊ, -z
cruzeiro
BR krʊ'zeːrəʊ, -z
AM krʊ'zeroʊ, -z
cry
BR krʌɪ, -z, -ɪŋ, -d
AM kraɪ, -z, -ɪŋ, -d
crybaby
BR 'krʌɪˌbeɪbǀi, -ɪz
AM 'kraɪˌbeɪbi, -z
cryer
BR 'krʌɪə(r), -z
AM 'kraɪ(ə)r, -z
cryobiological
BR ˌkrʌɪəʊˌbʌɪə'lɒdʒɪkl
AM ˌkraɪoʊˌbaɪə'lɑdʒək-
əl

cryobiologist
BR ˌkrʌɪəʊbʌɪ'ɒlədʒɪst,
-s
AM ˌkraɪoʊˌbaɪ'ɑlədʒəst,
-s
cryobiology
BR ˌkrʌɪəʊbʌɪ'ɒlədʒi
AM ˌkraɪoʊˌbaɪ'ɑlədʒi
cryogen
BR 'krʌɪə(ʊ)dʒ(ə)n,
'krʌɪə(ʊ)dʒen, -z
AM 'kraɪədʒən, -z
cryogenic
BR ˌkrʌɪə(ʊ)'dʒɛnɪk, -s
AM ˌkraɪoʊ'dʒɛnɪk, -s
cryolite
BR 'krʌɪə(ʊ)lʌɪt
AM 'kraɪəˌlaɪt
cryonics
BR krʌɪ'ɒnɪks
AM ˌkraɪ'ɑnɪks
cryopump
BR 'krʌɪə(ʊ)pʌmp, -s
AM 'kraɪəˌpəmp, -s
cryostat
BR 'krʌɪə(ʊ)stat, -s
AM 'kraɪəˌstæt, -s
cryosurgery
BR ˌkrʌɪəʊ'sɜːdʒ(ə)ri
AM ˌkraɪoʊ'sərdʒ(ə)ri
crypt
BR krɪpt, -s
AM krɪpt, -s
cryptanalysis
BR ˌkrɪptə'nalɪsɪs
AM ˌkrɪptə'næləsəs
cryptanalyst
BR ˌkrɪpt'analɪst, -s
AM ˌkrɪpt'ænələst, -s
cryptanalytic
BR ˌkrɪptə'lɪtɪk
AM ˌkrɪptˌænə'lɪdɪk
cryptanalytical
BR ˌkrɪptə'lɪtɪkl
AM ˌkrɪptˌænə'lɪdəkəl
cryptic
BR 'krɪptɪk
AM 'krɪptɪk
cryptically
BR 'krɪptɪkli
AM 'krɪptək(ə)li
crypto
BR 'krɪptəʊ, 'krɪptə(r),
-z
AM 'krɪpˌtoʊ, -z
cryptocrystalline
BR ˌkrɪptəʊ'krɪstəlʌɪn,
ˌkrɪptəʊ'krɪstl̩ʌɪn
AM ˌkrɪpˌtoʊ'krɪstəˌlaɪn,
ˌkrɪptə'krɪstəˌlaɪn,
ˌkrɪpˌtoʊ'krɪstələn,
ˌkrɪptə'krɪstələn
cryptogam
BR 'krɪptəgam, -z
AM 'krɪptəˌgæm, -z
cryptogamic
BR ˌkrɪptə'gamɪk
AM ˌkrɪptə'gæmɪk

cryptogamous
BR krɪpˈtɒɡəməs
AM krɪpˈtɑɡəməs
cryptogram
BR ˈkrɪptəgram, -z
AM ˈkrɪptəˌgræm, -z
cryptographer
BR krɪpˈtɒɡrəfə(r)
AM krɪpˈtɑgrəfər
cryptographic
BR ˌkrɪptəˈgrafɪk
AM ˌkrɪptəˈgræfɪk
cryptographically
BR ˌkrɪptəˈgrafɪkli
AM ˌkrɪptəˈgræfək(ə)li
cryptography
BR krɪpˈtɒɡrəfi
AM krɪpˈtɑgrəfi
cryptologist
BR krɪpˈtɒlədʒɪst, -s
AM krɪpˈtɑlədʒəst, -s
cryptology
BR krɪpˈtɒlədʒi
AM krɪpˈtɑlədʒi
cryptomeria
BR ˌkrɪptəˈmɪərɪə(r),
-z
AM ˌkrɪptəˈmɪrɪə, -z
cryptosporidia
BR ˌkrɪptəʊspəˈrɪdɪə(r)
AM ˌkrɪptəspəˈrɪdɪə
cryptosporidium
BR ˌkrɪptəʊspəˈrɪdɪəm
AM ˌkrɪptəspəˈrɪdɪəm
cryptozoic
BR ˌkrɪptə(ʊ)ˈzəʊɪk
AM ˌkrɪptəˈzoʊɪk
crystal
BR ˈkrɪstl, -z
AM ˈkrɪstl, -z
crystalline
BR ˈkrɪstəlʌɪn,
ˈkrɪstlʌɪn
AM ˈkrɪstələn,
ˈkrɪstəˌlaɪn
crystallinity
BR ˌkrɪstəˈlɪnɪti
AM ˌkrɪstəˈlɪnɪdi
crystallisable
BR ˈkrɪstəlʌɪzəbl,
ˈkrɪstlʌɪzəbl
AM ˌkrɪstəˈlaɪzəbəl
crystallisation
BR ˌkrɪstəlʌɪˈzeɪʃn,
ˌkrɪstlʌɪˈzeɪʃn
AM ˌkrɪstələˈzeɪʃən,
ˌkrɪstəˌlaɪˈzeɪʃən
crystallise
BR ˈkrɪstəlʌɪz,
ˈkrɪstlʌɪz, -ɪz, -ɪŋ, -d
AM ˈkrɪstəˌlaɪz, -ɪz, -ɪŋ,
-d
crystallite
BR ˈkrɪstəlʌɪt,
ˈkrɪstlʌɪt, -s
AM ˈkrɪstəˌlaɪt, -s

crystallizable
BR ˈkrɪstəlʌɪzəbl,
ˈkrɪstlʌɪzəbl
AM ˌkrɪstəˈlaɪzəbəl
crystallization
BR ˌkrɪstəlʌɪˈzeɪʃn,
ˌkrɪstlʌɪˈzeɪʃn
AM ˌkrɪstələˈzeɪʃən,
ˌkrɪstəˌlaɪˈzeɪʃən
crystallize
BR ˈkrɪstəlʌɪz,
ˈkrɪstlʌɪz, -ɪz, -ɪŋ, -d
AM ˈkrɪstəˌlaɪz, -ɪz, -ɪŋ,
-d
crystallographer
BR ˌkrɪstəˈlɒɡrəfə(r),
ˌkrɪstlˈɒɡrəfə(r)
AM ˌkrɪstəˈlɑgrəfər, -z
crystallographic
BR ˌkrɪstələˈgrafɪk,
ˌkrɪstləˈgrafɪk
AM ˌkrɪstələˈgræfɪk
crystallography
BR ˌkrɪstəˈlɒɡrəfi,
ˈkrɪstlˈɒɡrəfi
AM ˌkrɪstəˈlɑgrəfi
crystalloid
BR ˈkrɪstələɔɪd,
ˈkrɪstlɔɪd, -z
AM ˈkrɪstəˌlɔɪd, -z
csárdás
BR ˈtʃɑːdaʃ, -ɪz
AM ˈtʃɑrdɑʃ, -əz
HU ˈtʃɑːrdɑːʃ
ctenoid
BR ˈtiːnɔɪd, ˈtenɔɪd
AM ˈtiˌnɔɪd, ˈtɛˌnɔɪd
ctenophore
BR ˈtiːnəfɔː(r),
ˈtɛnəfɔː(r), -z
AM ˈtɛnəˌfɔ(ə)r, -z
Ctesiphon
BR ˈtɛsɪfɒn
AM ˈtɛsəˌfɑn
cuadrilla
BR kwɒˈdriː(l)jə(r), -z
AM kwəˈdri(l)jə, -z
cub
BR kʌb, -z, -ɪŋ, -d
AM kəb, -z, -ɪŋ, -d
Cuba
BR ˈkjuːbə(r)
AM ˈkjubə
Cuban
BR ˈkjuːbən, -z
AM ˈkjubən, -z
Cubango
BR kjuːˈbaŋgəʊ
AM kjuˈbæŋgoʊ
cubby
BR ˈkʌbˌi, -ɪz
AM ˈkəbi, -z
cubbyhole
BR ˈkʌbɪhəʊl, -z
AM ˈkəbiˌ(h)oʊl, -z
cube
BR kjuːb, -z, -ɪŋ, -d
AM kjub, -z, -ɪŋ, -d

cubeb
BR ˈkjuːbɛb, -z
AM ˈkjuˌbɛb, -z
cuber
BR ˈkjuːbə(r), -z
AM ˈkjubər, -z
cubhood
BR ˈkʌbhʊd
AM ˈkəbˌ(h)ʊd
cubic
BR ˈkjuːbɪk
AM ˈkjubɪk
cubical
BR ˈkjuːbɪkl
AM ˈkjubəkəl
cubically
BR ˈkjuːbɪkli
AM ˈkjubək(ə)li
cubicle
BR ˈkjuːbɪkl, -z
AM ˈkjubəkəl, -z
cubiform
BR ˈkjuːbɪfɔːm
AM ˈkjubəˌfɔ(ə)rm
cubism
BR ˈkjuːbɪz(ə)m
AM ˈkjuˌbɪzəm
cubist
BR ˈkjuːbɪst, -s
AM ˈkjubəst, -s
cubit
BR ˈkjuːbɪt, -s
AM ˈkjubət, -s
cubital
BR ˈkjuːbɪtl
AM ˈkjubədl
Cubitt
BR ˈkjuːbɪt
AM ˈkjubɪt
cuboid
BR ˈkjuːbɔɪd
AM ˈkjuˌbɔɪd
cuboidal
BR kjuːˈbɔɪdl
AM kjuˈbɔɪdəl
cuce
cucumber
BR ˈkjuːk, -s
AM ˈkjuk, -s
Cúchulainn
BR kuːˈkʌlən,
kuːˈxʌlən
AM kuˈkələn
IR kuːˈxulˈən
Cuckfield
BR ˈkʌkfiːld
AM ˈkəkˌfild
cucking-stool
BR ˈkʌkɪŋstuːl, -z
AM ˈkəkɪŋˌstul, -z
Cuckney
BR ˈkʌkni
AM ˈkəkni
cuckold
BR ˈkʌkəʊld,
ˈkʌk(ə)ld, -z, -ɪŋ, -ɪd
AM ˈkəkəld, -z, -ɪŋ, -əd

cuckoldry
BR ˈkʌk(ə)ldri
AM ˈkəkəldri
cuckoo
BR ˈkʊkuː, -z
AM ˈkuˌku, ˈkʊˌku, -z
cuckoo-spit
BR ˈkʊkuːspɪt
AM ˈkukuˌspɪt,
ˈkʊkuˌspɪt
cucumber
BR ˈkjuːkʌmbə(r), -z
AM ˈkjuˌkəmbər, -z
cucurbit
BR kjuːˈkəːbɪt, -s
AM kjuˈkərbət, -s
cucurbitaceous
BR kjuːˌkəːbɪˈteɪʃəs
AM kjuˌkərbəˈteɪʃəs
cud
BR kʌd
AM kəd
cudbear
BR ˈkʌdbɛː(r)
AM ˈkədˌbɛ(ə)r
cuddle
BR ˈkʌdl, -lz, -lɪŋ \-lɪŋ,
-ld
AM ˈkəd|əl, -əlz, -(ə)lɪŋ,
-əld
cuddlesome
BR ˈkʌdls(ə)m
AM ˈkədlsəm
cuddliness
BR ˈkʌdlɪnɪs
AM ˈkəd(ə)lɪnɪs
cuddly
BR ˈkʌdl|i, -ɪə(r), -ɪɪst
AM ˈkəd(ə)li, -ər, -ɪst
cuddy
BR ˈkʌdi
AM ˈkədi
cudgel
BR ˈkʌdʒ|(ə)l, -(ə)lz,
-lɪŋ \-əlɪŋ, -(ə)ld
AM ˈkədʒ|əl, -əlz,
-(ə)lɪŋ, -əld
Cudlipp
BR ˈkʌdlɪp
AM ˈkədˌlɪp
cudweed
BR ˈkʌdwiːd
AM ˈkədˌwid
cue
BR kjuː, -z, -ɪŋ, -d
AM kju, -z, -ɪŋ, -d
cueball
BR ˈkjuːbɔːl, -z
AM ˈkjuˌbɔl, ˈkjuˌbɑl, -z
cueist
BR ˈkjuːɪst, -s
AM ˈkjuəst, -s
Cuenca
BR ˈkwɛŋkə(r)
AM ˈkwɛŋkə
cuesta
BR ˈkwɛstə(r), -z

AM 'kwɛstə, -z

cuff
BR kʌf, -s, -ɪŋ, -t
AM kəf, -s, -ɪŋ, -t

Cuffley
BR 'kʌfli
AM 'kʌfli

cufflink
BR 'kʌflɪŋk, -s
AM 'kʌf‚lɪŋk, -s

Cufic
BR 'kjuːfɪk
AM 'k(j)ufɪk

cui bono?
BR ‚kuːi 'bəʊnəʊ, ‚kwiː +
AM ‚kwi 'boʊnoʊ

Cuillin
BR 'kuːlɪn, -z
AM 'kulən, -z

cuirass
BR kwɪ'ras, kjʊ'ras, -ɪz
AM kwɪ'ræs, kwi'ræs, -əz

cuirassier
BR ‚kwɪrə'sɪə(r), ‚kjʊrə'sɪə(r), -z
AM ‚kwɪrə'sɪ(ə)r, ‚kjʊrə'sɪ(ə)r, -z

cuish
BR kwɪʃ, -ɪz
AM kwɪʃ, -ɪz

cuisine
BR kwɪ'ziːn
AM kwə'zin, kwi'zin

cuisse
BR kwɪs, -ɪz
AM kwɪs, -ɪz

Culbertson
BR 'kʌlbəts(ə)n
AM 'kəlbərts(ə)n

Culceth
BR 'kʌltʃɪθ
AM 'kəltʃəθ

Culdees
BR 'kʌldiːz
AM 'kəl‚diz

cul-de-sac
BR 'kʌldəsak, 'kʊldəsak, -s
AM ‚kəldə'sæk, -s

culinarily
BR 'kʌlɪn(ə)rɪli
AM ‚kələ'nɛrəli, ‚kjulə'nɛrəli

culinary
BR 'kʌlɪn(ə)ri
AM 'kələ‚nɛri, 'kjulə‚nɛri

cull
BR kʌl, -z, -ɪŋ, -d
AM kʌl, -z, -ɪŋ, -d

Cullen
BR 'kʌlɪn
AM 'kələn

cullender
BR 'kʌlɪndə(r), -z

AM 'kələndər, -z

culler
BR 'kʌlə(r), -z
AM 'kələr, -z

cullet
BR 'kʌlɪt
AM 'kələt

Cullinan
BR 'kʌlɪnən
AM 'kələnən

Culloden
BR kə'lɒdn
AM kə'ladən

Cullompton
BR kə'lʌm(p)t(ə)n
AM kə'ləm(p)tən

culm
BR kʌlm
AM kəlm

culmiferous
BR kʌl'mɪf(ə)rəs
AM kəl'mɪf(ə)rəs

culminant
BR 'kʌlmɪnənt
AM 'kəlmənənt

culminate
BR 'kʌlmɪneɪt, -s, -ɪŋ, -ɪd
AM 'kəlmə‚neɪ|t, -ts, -dɪŋ, -dɪd

culmination
BR ‚kʌlmɪ'neɪʃn, -z
AM ‚kəlmə'neɪʃən, -z

culminative
BR 'kʌlmɪnətɪv
AM 'kəlmə‚neɪdɪv, 'kəlmənədɪv

culminatively
BR 'kʌlmɪnətɪvli
AM 'kəlmə‚neɪdɪvli, 'kəlmənədɪvli

culotte
BR kjʊ'lɒt, kjuː'lɒt, -s
AM 'k(j)ʊ‚lat, -s

culpability
BR ‚kʌlpə'bɪlɪti
AM ‚kəlpə'bɪlɪdi

culpable
BR 'kʌlpəbl
AM 'kəlpəbəl

culpably
BR 'kʌlpəbli
AM 'kəlpəbli

Culpeper
BR 'kʌl‚pɛpə(r)
AM 'kəl‚pɛpər

Culpepper
BR 'kʌl‚pɛpə(r)
AM 'kəl‚pɛpər

culprit
BR 'kʌlprɪt, -s
AM 'kəlprət, -s

cult
BR kʌlt, -s
AM kəlt, -s

cultic
BR 'kʌltɪk

cultigen
BR 'kʌltɪdʒɛn, 'kʌltɪdʒ(ə)n, -z
AM 'kəltə‚dʒɛn, 'kəltɪdʒən, -z

cultism
BR 'kʌltɪz(ə)m
AM 'kəl‚tɪzəm

cultist
BR 'kʌltɪst, -s
AM 'kəltəst, -s

cultivable
BR 'kʌltɪvəbl
AM 'kəltəvəbəl

cultivar
BR 'kʌltɪvɑː(r), -z
AM 'kəltə‚vɑr, -z

cultivatable
BR 'kʌltɪveɪtəbl
AM 'kəltə‚veɪdəbəl

cultivate
BR 'kʌltɪveɪt, -s, -ɪŋ, -ɪd
AM 'kəltə‚veɪ|t, -ts, -dɪŋ, -dɪd

cultivation
BR ‚kʌltɪ'veɪʃn
AM ‚kəltə'veɪʃən

cultivator
BR 'kʌltɪveɪtə(r), -z
AM 'kəltə‚veɪdər, -z

cultural
BR 'kʌltʃ(ə)rəl, 'kʌltʃ(ə)rl̩
AM 'kəltʃ(ə)rəl

culturalism
BR 'kʌltʃ(ə)rəlɪz(ə)m, 'kʌltʃ(ə)rl̩ɪz(ə)m
AM 'kəltʃ(ə)rə‚lɪzəm

culturalist
BR 'kʌltʃ(ə)rəlɪst, 'kʌltʃ(ə)rl̩ɪst, -s
AM 'kəltʃ(ə)rələst, -s

culturally
BR 'kʌltʃ(ə)rəli, 'kʌltʃ(ə)rl̩i
AM 'kəltʃ(ə)rəli

culture
BR 'kʌltʃə(r), -z, -d
AM 'kəltʃər, -z, -d

cultus
BR 'kʌltəs, -ɪz
AM 'kəltəs, -əz

Culver
BR 'kʌlvə(r)
AM 'kəlvər

culverin
BR 'kʌlv(ə)rɪn, -z
AM 'kəlv(ə)rən, -z

culvert
BR 'kʌlvət, -s, -ɪŋ, -ɪd
AM 'kəlvər|t, -ts, -dɪŋ, -dəd

cum
BR kʌm
AM kəm

cumber
BR 'kʌmb|ə(r), -əz, -(ə)rɪŋ, -əd
AM 'kəmbər, -z, -ɪŋ, -d

Cumberland
BR 'kʌmbələnd
AM 'kəmbərlənd

Cumberledge
BR 'kʌmbəlɪdʒ, 'kʌmbələdʒ
AM 'kəmbərlədʒ

Cumbernauld
BR 'kʌmbənɔːld, ‚kʌmbə'nɔːld
AM 'kəmbər‚nɔld, 'kəmbər‚nald

cumbersome
BR 'kʌmbəs(ə)m
AM 'kəmbərsəm

cumbersomely
BR 'kʌmbəs(ə)mli
AM 'kəmbərsəmli

cumbersomeness
BR 'kʌmbəs(ə)mnəs
AM 'kəmbərsəmnəs

cumbia
BR 'kʊmbɪə(r)
AM 'kəmbiə

Cumbria
BR 'kʌmbrɪə(r)
AM 'kəmbriə

Cumbrian
BR 'kʌmbrɪən, -z
AM 'kəmbriən, -z

cumbrous
BR 'kʌmbrəs
AM 'kəmbrəs

cumbrously
BR 'kʌmbrəsli
AM 'kəmbrəsli

cumbrousness
BR 'kʌmbrəsnəs
AM 'kəmbrəsnəs

cum grano salis
BR kʌm ‚grɑːnəʊ 'seɪlɪs, kʊm +, + ‚greɪnəʊ +, + 'sɑːlɪs, + 'salɪs
AM ‚kəm ‚granoʊ 'seɪlɪs, + 'sæləs

cumin
BR 'kʌmɪn, 'k(j)uːmɪn
AM 'kəmən, 'k(j)umən

cummerbund
BR 'kʌməbʌnd, -z
AM 'kəmər‚bənd, -z

cummin
BR 'kʌmɪn
AM 'kəmən

Cumming
BR 'kʌmɪŋ
AM 'kəmɪŋ

Cummings
BR 'kʌmɪŋz
AM 'kəmɪŋz

Cummins
BR 'kʌmɪnz
AM 'kəmənz

Cumnock
BR 'kʌmnək
AM 'kəmnək
Cumnor
BR 'kʌmnə(r)
AM 'kəmnər
cumquat
BR 'kʌmkwɒt, -s
AM 'kəm,kwɑt, -s
cumulate
BR 'kju:mjʊleɪt, -s, -ɪŋ,
-ɪd
AM 'kjumjə,leɪ|t, -ts,
-dɪŋ, -dɪd
cumulation
BR ,kju:mjʊ'leɪʃn, -z
AM ,kjumjə'leɪʃən, -z
cumulative
BR 'kju:mjʊlətɪv
AM 'kjumjələdɪv,
'kjumjə,leɪdɪv
cumulatively
BR 'kju:mjʊlətɪvli
AM 'kjumjələdɪvli,
'kjumjə,leɪdɪvli
cumulativeness
BR 'kju:mjʊlətɪvnɪs
AM 'kjumjələdɪvnɪs,
'kjumjə,leɪdɪvnɪs
cumulonimbus
BR ,kju:mjʊləʊ'nɪmbəs
AM ,kjumjəloʊ'nɪmbəs
cumulostratus
BR ,kju:jʊləʊ'strɑ:təs,
,kju:mjʊləʊ'streɪtəs
AM ,kjumjəloʊ'streɪdəs,
,kjumjəloʊ'strædəs
cumulous
BR 'kju:mjʊləs
AM 'kjumjələs
cumulus
BR 'kju:mjʊləs
AM 'kjumjələs
Cunard
BR kju:'nɑ:d, kjʊ'nɑ:d,
'kju:nɑ:d
AM kju'nɑrd
cunctation
BR ,kʌŋ(k)'teɪʃn, -z
AM ,kəŋk'teɪʃən, -z
cunctator
BR 'kʌŋ(k)teɪtə(r), -z
AM 'kəŋ(k),teɪdər, -z
cuneal
BR 'kju:nɪəl
AM 'kjunɪəl
cuneate
BR 'kju:nɪeɪt, 'kju:nɪət
AM 'kjuni,eɪt, 'kjuniət
cuneiform
BR 'kju:nɪfɔ:m
AM 'kju'niə,fɔ(ə)rm,
'kjuniə,fɔ(ə)rm,
'kjunə,fɔ(ə)rm
Cunene
BR ku:'neɪnə(r)
AM ku'neɪnə

Cuningham
BR 'kʌnɪŋəm
AM 'kənɪŋ,(h)æm
Cuninghame
BR 'kʌnɪŋəm
AM 'kənɪŋ,(h)æm
cunjevoi
BR 'kʌn(d)ʒɪvɔɪ, -z
AM 'kʌndʒə,vɔɪ, -z
cunnilinctus
BR ,kʌnɪ'lɪŋ(k)təs
AM ,kənə'lɪŋ(k)təs
cunnilingus
BR ,kʌnɪ'lɪŋgəs
AM ,kənə'lɪŋgəs
cunning
BR 'kʌnɪŋ
AM 'kənɪŋ
Cunningham
BR 'kʌnɪŋəm
AM 'kənɪŋ,(h)æm
cunningly
BR 'kʌnɪŋli
AM 'kənɪŋli
cunningness
BR 'kʌnɪŋnɪs
AM 'kənɪŋnɪs
Cunobelinus
BR ,kju:nə(ʊ)bɪ'laɪnəs,
,kju:nə(ʊ)bɪ'li:nəs
AM ,kjunoʊbə'linəs
cunt
BR kʌnt, -s
AM kən|t, -(t)s
cup
BR kʌp, -s, -ɪŋ, -t
AM kəp, -s, -ɪŋ, -t
Cupar
BR 'ku:pə(r)
AM 'kju)upər
cupbearer
BR 'kʌp,beːrə(r), -z
AM 'kəp,bɛrər, -z
cupboard
BR 'kʌbəd, -z
AM 'kəbərd, -z
cupcake
BR 'kʌpkeɪk, -s
AM 'kəp,keɪk, -s
cupel
BR 'kju:pl, -z
AM kju'pɛl, 'kjupəl, -z
cupellation
BR ,kju:pɪ'leɪʃn
AM ,kjupə'leɪʃən
cupful
BR 'kʌpfʊl, -z
AM 'kəp,fʊl, -z
Cupid
BR 'kju:pɪd
AM 'kjupəd
cupid
BR 'kju:pɪd, -z
AM 'kjupəd, -z
cupidity
BR kju:'pɪdɪti,
kjʊ'pɪdɪti

AM kju'pɪdɪdi
Cupit
BR 'kju:pɪt
AM 'kjupɪt
Cupitt
BR 'kju:pɪt
AM 'kjupɪt
cupola
BR 'kju:pələ(r),
'kju:plə(r), -z, -d
AM 'k(j)upələ, 'kəpələ,
-z, -d
cupola-furnace
BR 'kju:pələ,fə:nɪs,
'kju:plə,fə:nɪs, -ɪz
AM 'k(j)upələ,fərnəs,
'kəpələ,fərnəs, -əz
cuppa
BR 'kʌpə(r), -z
AM 'kəpə, -z
cuprammonium
BR ,kju:prə'məʊniəm
AM ,k(j)uprə'moʊniəm
cupreous
BR 'kju:prɪəs
AM 'k(j)uprɪəs
cupric
BR 'kju:prɪk
AM 'k(j)uprɪk
cupriferous
BR kju:'prɪf(ə)rəs
AM k(j)u'prɪf(ə)rəs
Cuprinol®
BR 'kju:prɪnɒl
AM 'k(j)upri,nɑl
cupronickel
BR ,kju:prəʊ'nɪkl
AM ,k(j)uproʊ'nɪkəl
cuprous
BR 'kju:prəs
AM 'k(j)uprəs
cupule
BR 'kju:pju:l, -z
AM 'kjupjul, -z
cur
BR kə:(r), -z
AM kər, -z
curability
BR ,kjʊərə'bɪlɪti,
,kjɔ:rə'bɪlɪti
AM ,kjʊrə'bɪlɪdi
curable
BR 'kjʊərəbl, 'kjɔ:rəbl
AM 'kjʊrəbəl
curably
BR 'kjʊərəbli,
'kjɔ:rəbli
AM 'kjʊrəbli
Curacao
BR 'kjʊərəsəʊ,
'kjɔ:rəsəʊ,
,kjʊərə'səʊ,
,kjɔ:rə'səʊ
AM 'k(j)ʊrə,saʊ,
'k(j)ʊrə,soʊ
Curaçao
BR 'kjʊərəsəʊ,
'kjɔ:rəsəʊ,

,kjʊərə'səʊ,
,kjɔ:rə'səʊ
AM 'k(j)ʊrə,saʊ,
'k(j)ʊrə,soʊ
curacy
BR 'kjʊərəs|i,
'kjɔ:rəs|i, -ɪz
AM 'kjʊrəsi, -z
curare
BR kjʊ'rɑ:ri
AM kjʊ'rɑri
curari
BR kjʊ'rɑ:ri
AM kjʊ'rɑri
curarine
BR 'kjʊərəri:n,
'kjɔ:rəri:n,
kjʊ'rɑ:ri:n,
AM kjʊ'rɑ,rin,
'kjʊrərən
curarise
BR 'kjʊərərʌɪz,
'kjɔ:rərʌɪz, -ɪz, -ɪŋ, -d
AM 'kjʊrə,rʌɪz, -ɪz, -ɪŋ,
-d
curarize
BR 'kjʊərərʌɪz,
'kjɔ:rərʌɪz, -ɪz, -ɪŋ, -d
AM 'kjʊrə,rʌɪz, -ɪz, -ɪŋ,
-d
curassow
BR 'kjʊərəsəʊ,
'kjɔ:rəsəʊ, -z
AM 'k(j)ʊrə,saʊ,
'k(j)ʊrə,soʊ, -z
curate
BR 'kjʊərət, 'kjɔ:rət, -s
AM 'kjʊrət, -s
curation
BR kjʊ'reɪʃn
AM kjə'reɪʃən
curative
BR 'kjʊərətɪv,
'kjɔ:rətɪv
AM 'kjʊrədɪv
curator
BR kjʊ'reɪtə(r), -z
AM 'kjʊ,reɪdər, -z
curatorial
BR ,kjʊərə'tɔ:rɪəl,
,kjɔ:rə'tɔ:rɪəl
AM ,kjʊrə'tɔrɪəl
curatorship
BR kjʊ'reɪtəʃɪp, -s
AM 'kjʊ,reɪdər,ʃɪp, -s
curb
BR kə:b, -z, -ɪŋ, -d
AM kərb, -z, -ɪŋ, -d
curbside
BR 'kə:bsʌɪd
AM 'kərb,saɪd
curbstone
BR 'kə:bstəʊn, -z
AM 'kərb,stoʊn, -z
curcuma
BR 'kə:kjʊmə(r), -z
AM 'kərkjəmə, -z

curd
BR kəːd, -z
AM kɜrd, -z

curdle
BR 'kəːd|l, -lz, -l̩ŋ\-lɪŋ,
-ld
AM 'kɜrd|əl, -əlz,
-(ə)lɪŋ, -əld

curdler
BR 'kəːdlə(r), -z
AM 'kɜrd(ə)lər, -z

curdy
BR 'kəːdi
AM 'kɜrdi

cure
BR 'kjʊə(r), kjɔː(r), -z,
-ɪŋ, -d
AM 'kjʊ(ə)r, -z, -ɪŋ, -d

curé
BR 'kjʊəreɪ, 'kjɔːreɪ, -z
AM kjə'reɪ, kjʊ'reɪ, -z

curer
BR 'kjʊərə(r),
'kjɔːrə(r), -z
AM 'kjʊrər, -z

curettage
BR kjʊ'retɪdʒ,
ˌkjʊəriˈtɑːʒ,
ˌkjɔːriˈtɑːʒ
AM ˌkjʊrəˈtɑʒ

curette
BR kjʊ'ret, -s
AM kjʊ'ret, -s

curfew
BR 'kəːfjuː, -z
AM 'kɜrˌfju, -z

curia
BR 'kjʊəriə(r),
'kjɔːriə(r)
AM 'kjʊriə

Curial
BR 'kjʊəriəl, 'kjɔːriəl
AM 'kjʊriəl

curie
BR 'kjʊər|i, 'kjɔːr|i, -ɪz
AM 'kjʊri, -z

curio
BR 'kjʊəriəʊ, 'kjɔːriəʊ,
-z
AM 'kjʊrioʊ, -z

curiosa
BR ˌkjʊəriˈəʊsə(r),
ˌkjʊəriˈəʊzə(r),
ˌkjɔːrɪˈəʊzə(r),
ˌkjɔːrɪˈəʊzə(r)
AM ˌkjʊriˈoʊsə,
ˌkjʊriˈoʊzə

curiosity
BR ˌkjʊərɪˈɒsɪt|i,
ˌkjɔːrɪˈɒsɪt|i, -ɪz
AM ˌkjʊriˈɑsədi, -z

curious
BR 'kjʊəriəs, 'kjɔːriəs
AM 'kjʊriəs

curiously
BR 'kjʊəriəsli,
'kjɔːriəsli
AM 'kjʊriəsli

curiousness
BR 'kjʊəriəsnəs,
'kjɔːriəsnəs
AM 'kjʊriəsnəs

Curitiba
BR ˌkjʊərɪˈtiːbə(r),
ˌkjɔːrɪˈtiːbə(r)
AM ˌkjuriˈtibə

curium
BR 'kjʊəriəm,
'kjɔːriəm
AM 'kjʊriəm

curl
BR kəːl, -z, -ɪŋ, -d
AM kɜrl, -z, -ɪŋ, -d

curler
BR 'kəːlə(r), -z
AM 'kɜrlər, -z

curlew
BR 'kəːl(j)uː, -z
AM 'kɜrˌlu, -z

Curley
BR 'kəːli
AM 'kɜrli

curlicue
BR 'kəːlɪkjuː, -z
AM 'kɜrliˌkju, -z

curliness
BR 'kəːlɪnɪs
AM 'kɜrlinɪs

curly
BR 'kəːl|li, -iə(r), -ɪɪst
AM 'kɜrli, -ər, -ɪst

curlycue
BR 'kəːlɪkjuː, -z
AM 'kɜrliˌkju, -z

curmudgeon
BR kəˈmʌdʒ(ə)n, -z
AM kər'mədʒən, -z

curmudgeonly
BR kəˈmʌdʒ(ə)nli
AM kər'mədʒənli

curmugeon
BR kəˈmʌdʒ(ə)n, -z
AM kər'mədʒən, -z

currach
BR 'kʌrə(r), 'kʌrəx,
'kʌrəz\'kʌrəxs
AM 'kʌrə(k), -z

curragh
BR 'kʌrə(r), 'kʌrəx
AM 'kʌrə(k), -z

currajong
BR 'kʌrədʒɒŋ, -z
AM 'kʌrəˌdʒɑŋ, -z

Curran
BR 'kʌrən, 'kʌrn̩
AM 'kʌrən

currant
BR 'kʌrənt, 'kʌrn̩t, -s
AM 'kʌrənt, -s

currawong
BR 'kʌrəwɒŋ, -z
AM 'kʌrəˌwɑŋ, -z

currency
BR 'kʌrəns|i, 'kʌrn̩s|i,
-ɪz

AM 'kʌrənsi, -z

current
BR 'kʌrənt, 'kʌrn̩t, -s
AM 'kɜrənt, -s

currently
BR 'kʌrəntli, 'kʌrn̩tli
AM 'kɜrən(t)li

currentness
BR 'kʌrəntnəs,
'kʌrn̩tnəs
AM 'kɜrən(t)nəs

curricle
BR 'kʌrɪkl, -z
AM 'kɜrəkəl, -z

curricula
BR kəˈrɪkjələ(r)
AM kəˈrɪkjələ

curricular
BR kəˈrɪkjələ(r)
AM kəˈrɪkjələr

curriculum
BR kəˈrɪkjələm, -z
AM kəˈrɪkjələm, -z

curriculum vitae
BR kəˌrɪkjələm 'viːtaɪ
AM kəˌrɪkjələm 'viˌtaɪ,
+ 'vaɪˌdi

Currie
BR 'kʌri
AM 'kɜri

currier
BR 'kʌrɪə(r), -z
AM 'kɜriər, -z

currish
BR 'kəːrɪʃ
AM 'kɜrɪʃ

currishly
BR 'kəːrɪʃli
AM 'kɜrɪʃli

currishness
BR 'kəːrɪʃnɪs
AM 'kɜrɪʃnɪs

curry
BR 'kʌr|i, -ɪz, -ɪɪŋ, -ɪd
AM 'kɜri, -z, -ɪŋ, -d

curse
BR kəːs, -ɪz, -ɪŋ, -t
AM kɜrs, -əz, -ɪn, -t

cursed
adjective
BR 'kəːsɪd, kəːst
AM 'kɜrsəd, kɜrst

cursedly
BR 'kəːsɪdli
AM 'kɜrsədli

cursedness
BR 'kəːsɪdnɪs
AM 'kɜrsədnəs

curser
BR 'kəːsə(r), -z
AM 'kɜrsər, -z

cursillo
BR kʊəˈsiː(l)jəʊ, -z
AM kər'sɪloʊ, -z

cursive
BR 'kəːsɪv
AM 'kɜrsɪv

cursively
BR 'kəːsɪvli
AM 'kɜrsɪvli

cursiveness
BR 'kəːsɪvnɪs
AM 'kɜrsɪvnɪs

cursor
BR 'kəːsə(r), -z
AM 'kɜrsər, -z

cursorial
BR kəːˈsɔːriəl
AM kər'sɔriəl

cursorily
BR 'kəːs(ə)rəli
AM 'kɜrs(ə)rəli

cursoriness
BR 'kəːs(ə)rɪnɪs
AM 'kɜrs(ə)rɪnɪs

cursory
BR 'kəːs(ə)ri
AM 'kɜrs(ə)ri

curst
BR kəːst
AM kɜrst

curt
BR kəːt
AM kɜrt

curtail
BR kəː(ˈ)teɪl, -z, -ɪŋ, -d
AM kər'teɪl, -z, -ɪŋ, -d

curtailment
BR kəː(ˈ)teɪlm(ə)nt, -s
AM kər'teɪlmɪnt, -s

curtain
BR 'kəːtn, -z, -ɪŋ, -d
AM 'kɜrtn̩, -z, -ɪŋ, -d

curtain wall
BR ˌkəːtn 'wɔːl, -z
AM 'kɜrtn̩ˌwɔl,
'kɜrtn̩ˌwal, -z

curtana
BR kəːˈtɑːnə(r),
kəːˈteɪnə(r), -z
AM kər'tɑnə, -z

curtilage
BR 'kəːtɪlɪdʒ, 'kəːtlɪdʒ,
-ɪz
AM 'kɜrdlɪdʒ, -ɪz

Curtin
BR 'kəːt(ɪ)n
AM 'kɜrtn̩

Curtis
BR 'kəːtɪs
AM 'kɜrdəs

Curtiss
BR 'kəːtɪs
AM 'kɜrdəs

curtly
BR 'kəːtli
AM 'kɜrtli

curtness
BR 'kəːtnəs
AM 'kɜrtnəs

curtsey
BR 'kəːts|i, -ɪz, -ɪɪŋ, -ɪd
AM 'kɜrtsi, -z, -ɪŋ, -d

curtsy
BR ˈkɜːts‖i, -ɪz, -ɪŋ, -ɪd
AM ˈkɝtsi, -z, -ɪŋ, -d

curule
BR ˈkjʊər(j)uːl
AM ˈkjuˌrul

curvaceous
BR kəˈveɪʃəs
AM kərˈveɪʃəs

curvaceously
BR kəˈveɪʃəsli
AM kərˈveɪʃəsli

curvacious
BR kəˈveɪʃəs
AM kərˈveɪʃəs

curvaciously
BR kəˈveɪʃəsli
AM kərˈveɪʃəsli

curvature
BR ˈkɜːvətʃə(r),
ˈkɜːvətjʊə(r), -z
AM ˈkɝvətʃər,
ˈkɝvəˌtʃʊ(ə)r, -z

curve
BR kɜːv, -z, -ɪŋ, -d
AM kɝv, -z, -ɪŋ, -d

curvet
BR kəˈvɛt, -s, -ɪŋ, -ɪd
AM kərˌve‖t, -ts, -dɪŋ,
-dəd

curvifoliate
BR ˌkɜːvɪˈfəʊliət
AM ˌkɝvəˈfoʊliət

curviform
BR ˈkɜːvɪfɔːm
AM ˈkɝvəˌfɔ(ə)rm

curvilinear
BR ˌkɜːvɪˈlɪnɪə(r)
AM ˌkɝvəˈlɪniər

curvilinearly
BR ˌkɜːvɪˈlɪnɪəli
AM ˌkɝvəˈlɪniərli

curviness
BR ˈkɜːvɪnɪs
AM ˈkɝvinɪs

curvirostral
BR ˌkɜːvɪˈrɒstr(ə)l
AM ˌkɝvəˈrɑstrəl

curvy
BR ˈkɜːv‖i, -ɪə(r), -ɪɪst
AM ˈkɝvi, -ər, -ɪst

Curzon
BR ˈkɜːzn
AM ˈkɝzən, ˈkərˌzɑn

Cusack
BR ˈkjuːsak, ˈkjuːzak
AM ˈkjusæk, ˈkjuzæk

cuscus
BR ˈkʌskʌs, -ɪz
AM ˈkʊskʊs, ˈkəskəs,
-əz

cusec
BR ˈkjuːsɛk, -s
AM ˈkjuˌsɛk, -s

cush
BR kʊʃ, -ɪz
AM kʊʃ, -əz

cushat
BR ˈkʊʃət, -s
AM ˈkʊʃət, -s

cush-cush
BR ˈkʊʃkʊʃ, -ɪz
AM ˈkʊʃˌkʊʃ, -əz

cushily
BR ˈkʊʃɪli
AM ˈkʊʃəli

cushiness
BR ˈkʊʃmɪs
AM ˈkʊʃinɪs

Cushing
BR ˈkʊʃɪŋ
AM ˈkʊʃɪŋ

cushion
BR ˈkʊʃ‖n, -nz,
-nɪŋ \-(ə)nɪŋ, -nd
AM ˈkʊʃ‖ən, -ənz,
-(ə)nɪŋ, -ənd

cushiony
BR ˈkʊʃ̬ni, ˈkʊʃəni
AM ˈkʊʃəni

Cushitic
BR kʊˈʃɪtɪk
AM kəˈʃɪdɪk

cushy
BR ˈkʊʃ‖i, -ɪə(r), -ɪɪst
AM ˈkʊʃi, -ər, -ɪst

cusp
BR kʌsp, -s, -t
AM kəsp, -s, -t

cuspate
BR ˈkʌspeɪt
AM ˈkəspət, ˈkəsˌpeɪt

cuspid
BR ˈkʌspɪd, -z
AM ˈkəspəd, -z

cuspidal
BR ˈkʌspɪdl
AM ˈkəspədəl

cuspidate
BR ˈkʌspɪdeɪt
AM ˈkəspəˌdeɪt

cuspidor
BR ˈkʌspɪdɔː(r), -z
AM ˈkəspəˌdɔ(ə)r, -z

cuss
BR kʌs, -ɪz, -ɪŋ, -t
AM kəs, -əz, -ɪŋ, -t

cussed
adjective
BR ˈkʌsɪd
AM ˈkəsəd

cussedly
BR ˈkʌsɪdli
AM ˈkəsədli

cussedness
BR ˈkʌsɪdnɪs
AM ˈkəsədnəs

Cusson
BR ˈkʌsn
AM ˈkəsən

custard
BR ˈkʌstəd, -z
AM ˈkəstərd, -z

Custer
BR ˈkʌstə(r)
AM ˈkəstər

custodial
BR kʌˈstəʊdɪəl,
kəˈstəʊdɪəl
AM kəsˈtoʊdiəl

custodian
BR kʌˈstəʊdɪən,
kəˈstəʊdɪən, -z
AM kəsˈtoʊdiən, -z

custodianship
BR kʌˈstəʊdɪənʃɪp,
kəˈstəʊdɪənʃɪp
AM kəsˈtoʊdiənˌʃɪp

custody
BR ˈkʌstədi
AM ˈkəstədi

custom
BR ˈkʌstəm, -z
AM ˈkəstəm, -z

customable
BR ˈkʌstəməbl
AM ˈkəstəməbəl

customarily
BR ˈkʌstəm(ə)rɪli,
ˈkʌstəm(ə)r‖i
AM ˌkəstəˈmɛrəli

customariness
BR ˈkʌstəm(ə)rɪnɪs
AM ˈkəstəˌmɛrinəs

customary
BR ˈkʌstəm(ə)ri
AM ˈkəstəˌmɛri

customer
BR ˈkʌstəmə(r), -z
AM ˈkəstəmər, -z

customise
BR ˈkʌstəmʌɪz, -ɪz, -ɪŋ,
-d
AM ˈkəstəˌmaɪz, -ɪz, -ɪŋ,
-d

customize
BR ˈkʌstəmʌɪz, -ɪz, -ɪŋ,
-d
AM ˈkəstəˌmaɪz, -ɪz, -ɪŋ,
-d

cut
BR kʌt, -s, -ɪŋ
AM kə‖t, -ts, -dɪŋ

cutaneous
BR kjuːˈteɪnɪəs
AM kjuˈteɪniəs

cutaway
BR ˈkʌtəweɪ, -z
AM ˈkədəˌweɪ, -z

cutback
BR ˈkʌtbak, -s
AM ˈkətˌbæk, -s

cutch
BR kʌtʃ
AM kətʃ

cutdown
BR ˌkʌtˈdaʊn
AM ˈkətˌdaʊn

cute
BR kjuːt, -ə(r), -ɪst
AM kju‖t, -dər, -dəst

cutely
BR ˈkjuːtli
AM ˈkjutli

cuteness
BR ˈkjuːtnəs
AM ˈkjutnəs

Cutex
BR ˈkjuːtɛks
AM ˈkjuˌtɛks

cutey
BR ˈkjuːt‖i, -ɪz
AM ˈkjudi, -z

Cutforth
BR ˈkʌtfɔːθ, ˈkʌtfəθ
AM ˈkətˌfɔ(ə)rθ

Cuthbert
BR ˈkʌθbət
AM ˈkəθbərt

Cuthbertson
BR ˈkʌθbəts(ə)n
AM ˈkəθbərtsən

cuticle
BR ˈkjuːtɪkl, -z
AM ˈkjudəkəl, -z

cuticular
BR kjuːˈtɪkjʊlə(r)
AM kjuˈdɪkjələr

Cuticura®
BR ˌkjuːtɪˈkjʊərə(r),
ˌkjuːtɪˈkjɔːrə(r)
AM ˌkjudəˈkjʊrə

cutie
BR ˈkjuːt‖i, -z
AM ˈkjudi, -z

cutis
BR ˈkjuːtɪs
AM ˈkjudəs

cutlass
BR ˈkʌtləs, -ɪz
AM ˈkətləs, -ɪz

cutler
BR ˈkʌtlə(r), -z
AM ˈkətlər, -z

cutlery
BR ˈkʌtləri
AM ˈkətləri

cutlet
BR ˈkʌtlɪt, -s
AM ˈkətlət, -s

cutoff
BR ˈkʌtɒf, -s
AM ˈkədˌɔf, ˈkədˌɑf, -s

cutout
BR ˈkʌtaʊt, -s
AM ˈkədˌaʊt, -s

cutpurse
BR ˈkʌtpɜːs, -ɪz
AM ˈkətˌpərs, -ɪz

cutter
BR ˈkʌtə(r), -z
AM ˈkədər, -z

cutthroat
BR ˈkʌtθrəʊt, -s
AM ˈkətˌθroʊt, -s

cutting
BR ˈkʌtɪŋ, -z
AM ˈkədɪŋ, -z

cuttingly
BR 'kʌtɪŋli
AM 'kədɪŋli
cuttle
BR 'kʌtl, -z
AM 'kədəl, -z
cuttlebone
BR 'kʌtlbəʊn, -z
AM 'kədl,boʊn, -z
cuttlefish
BR 'kʌtlfɪʃ
AM 'kədl,fɪʃ
cutty
BR 'kʌti, -ɪz
AM 'kədi, -z
Cutty Sark
BR ,kʌti 'sɑːk
AM ,kədi ,sɑrk
cutup
BR 'kʌtʌp, -s
AM 'kəd,əp, -s
cutwater
BR 'kʌt,wɔːtə(r), -z
AM 'kət,wɔdər, 'kət,wɑdər, -z
cutworm
BR 'kʌtwɜːm, -z
AM 'kət,wɜrm, -z
cuvée
BR kjuːˈveɪ, -z
AM k(j)uˈveɪ, -z
cuvette
BR kjuːˈvɛt, -s
AM kjuˈvɛt, -s
Cuvier
BR 'kjuːvɪeɪ
AM kuviˈeɪ
Cuxhaven
BR 'kʊks,hɑːvn
AM 'kʊks,(h)ɑvən
Cuyahoga
BR ,kʌɪəˈhəʊgə(r)
AM ,kaɪəˈhoʊgə
Cuzco
BR 'kʊskəʊ
AM 'kuskoʊ, 'kuzkoʊ
cwm
BR kʊm, -z
AM kʊm, -z
Cy
BR saɪ
AM saɪ
cyan
BR 'saɪən, 'saɪan
AM 'saɪən
cyanamid
BR saɪˈanəmɪd
AM saɪˈænəməd
cyanamide
BR saɪˈanəmʌɪd
AM saɪˈænə,maɪd
cyanic
BR saɪˈanɪk
AM saɪˈænɪk
cyanide
BR 'saɪənʌɪd
AM 'saɪə,naɪd

cyano
BR 'saɪənəʊ, saɪˈanəʊ
AM 'saɪə,noʊ
cyanobacteria
BR ,saɪənəʊ,bakˈtɪər-ɪə(r),
saɪ,anəʊbakˈtɪərɪə(r)
AM ,saɪənoʊ,bækˈtɪriə
cyanobacterium
BR ,saɪənəʊ,bakˈtɪə-rɪəm,
saɪ,anəʊbakˈtɪərɪəm
AM ,saɪənoʊ,bækˈtɪriəm
cyanocobalamin
BR ,saɪənəʊkəˈbaləmɪn,
saɪ,anəʊkəˈbaləmɪn, -z
AM ,saɪənoʊ,koʊˈbælə-mən,
,saɪənoʊ,koʊˈbælə,min, -z
cyanogen
BR saɪˈanədʒ(ə)n, -z
AM saɪˈænədʒən,
saɪˈænə,dʒɛn, -z
cyanogenic
BR ,saɪənəˈdʒɛnɪk
AM ,saɪənoʊˈdʒɛnɪk
cyanoses
BR ,saɪəˈnəʊsiːz
AM ,saɪəˈnoʊsiz
cyanosis
BR ,saɪəˈnəʊsɪs
AM ,saɪəˈnoʊsəs
cyanotic
BR ,saɪəˈnɒtɪk
AM ,saɪəˈnɑdɪk
Cybele
BR 'sɪbɪli, 'sɪbli
AM 'sɪbəli, 'sɪbəl
cybercafé
BR 'saɪbə,kafeɪ,
'saɪbə,kafli, -eɪz\-ɪz
AM 'saɪbər,kæ,feɪ, -z
cybernate
BR 'saɪbəneɪt, -s, -ɪŋ, -ɪd
AM 'saɪbər,neɪ|t, -ts, -dɪŋ, -dɪd
cybernation
BR ,saɪbəˈneɪʃn
AM ,saɪbərˈneɪʃən
cybernetic
BR ,saɪbəˈnɛtɪk, -s
AM ,saɪbərˈnɛdɪk, -s
cybernetician
BR ,saɪbənəˈtɪʃn, -z
AM ,saɪbərnəˈtɪʃən, -z
cyberneticist
BR ,saɪbəˈnɛtɪsɪst, -s
AM ,saɪbəˈnɛdəsəst, -s
cyberpunk
BR 'saɪbəpʌŋk, -s
AM 'saɪbər,pəŋk, -s
cyborg
BR 'saɪbɔːg, -z
AM 'saɪ,bɔrg, -z
cycad
BR 'saɪkad, 'saɪkəd, -z

AM 'saɪkəd, 'saɪ,kæd, -z
Cyclades
BR 'sɪklədiːz
AM 'sɪklə,diz
Cycladic
BR sɪˈkladɪk,
AM saɪˈkladɪk,
səˈkladɪk
cyclamate
BR 'sɪkləmeɪt,
'saɪkləmeɪt, -s
AM 'saɪklə,meɪt, -s
cyclamen
BR 'sɪkləmən
AM 'saɪkləmən,
'sɪkləmən
cycle
BR 'saɪkl, -z, -ɪŋ, -d
AM 'saɪk|əl, -əlz, -(ə)lɪŋ, -əld
cyclic
BR 'saɪklɪk, 'sɪklɪk
AM 'sɪklɪk, 'saɪklɪk
cyclical
BR 'sɪklɪkl, 'saɪklɪkl
AM 'sɪkləkəl, 'saɪkləkəl
cyclically
BR 'sɪklɪkli, 'saɪklɪkli
AM 'sɪklək(ə)li, 'saɪklək(ə)li
cyclist
BR 'saɪklɪst, -s
AM 'saɪkləst, -s
cycloalkane
BR ,saɪkləʊˈalkeɪn, -z
AM ,saɪkloʊˈæl,keɪn, -z
cyclo-cross
BR 'saɪklə(ʊ)krɒs
AM 'saɪkloʊ,krɔs,
'saɪkloʊ,krɑs
cyclodextrin
BR ,saɪkləʊˈdɛkstrɪn, -z
AM ,saɪkloʊˈdɛkstrən, -z
cyclograph
BR 'saɪklə(ʊ)grɑːf,
'saɪklə(ʊ)graf, -s
AM 'saɪkloʊ,græf,
'saɪklə,græf, -s
cyclohexane
BR ,saɪkləʊˈhɛksein, -z
AM ,saɪkloʊˈhɛk,sein, -z
cycloid
BR 'saɪklɔɪd, -z
AM 'saɪ,klɔɪd, -z
cycloidal
BR saɪˈklɔɪdl
AM saɪˈklɔɪdəl
cyclometer
BR saɪˈklɒmɪtə(r), -z
AM saɪˈklɑmədər, -z
cyclone
BR 'saɪkləʊn, -z
AM 'saɪ,kloʊn, -z

cyclonic
BR saɪˈklɒnɪk
AM saɪˈklɑnɪk
cyclonically
BR saɪˈklɒnɪkli
AM saɪˈklɑnək(ə)li
cyclopaedia
BR ,saɪklə(ʊ)ˈpiːdɪə(r), -z
AM ,saɪkləˈpidiə, -z
cyclopaedic
BR ,saɪklə(ʊ)ˈpiːdɪk
AM ,saɪkləˈpidɪk
cyclopaedically
BR ,saɪlə(ʊ)ˈpiːdɪkli
AM ,saɪkləˈpidɪk(ə)li
cycloparaffin
BR ,saɪkləʊˈparəfɪn
AM ,saɪkloʊˈpɛrəfən
Cyclopean
BR ,saɪklə(ʊ)ˈpiːən,
saɪˈkləʊpiən
AM ,saɪkləˈpiən,
saɪˈkloʊpiən
cyclopedia
BR ,saɪklə(ʊ)ˈpiːdɪə(r), -z
AM ,saɪkləˈpidiə, -z
cyclopedic
BR ,saɪklə(ʊ)ˈpiːdɪk
AM ,saɪkləˈpidɪk
cyclopedically
BR ,saɪlə(ʊ)ˈpiːdɪkli
AM ,saɪkləˈpidək(ə)li
cyclopropane
BR ,saɪkləʊˈprəʊpeɪn
AM ,saɪkloʊˈprou,peɪn
cyclopropyl
BR ,saɪkləʊˈprɒp(ɪ)l,
,saɪklə(ʊ)ˈprəʊp(ɪ)l
AM ,saɪkloʊˈproupəl
Cyclops
BR 'saɪklɒps
AM 'saɪ,klɑps
cyclorama
BR ,saɪkləˈrɑːmə(r), -z
AM ,saɪkləˈræmə, -z
cycloramic
BR ,saɪkləˈramɪk
AM ,saɪkləˈræmɪk
cyclosporin
BR ,saɪklə(ʊ)ˈspɔːrɪn
AM ,saɪkloʊˈsporən
cyclostomate
BR ,saɪklə(ʊ)ˈstəʊmeɪt
AM saɪˈklɑstəmət,
,saɪkloʊˈstoʊmət
cyclostome
BR 'saɪkləstəʊm, -z
AM 'saɪklə,stoʊm, -z
cyclostyle
BR 'saɪkləstʌɪl, -z, -ɪŋ, -d
AM 'saɪklə,staɪl, -z, -ɪŋ, -d
cyclothymia
BR ,saɪklə(ʊ)ˈθʌɪmɪə(r)
AM ,saɪkləˈθaɪmiə

cyclothymic
BR ˌsaɪklə(ʊ)'θaɪmɪk
AM ˌsaɪklə'θaɪmɪk

cyclotron
BR 'saɪklətrɒn, -z
AM 'saɪklə,trɑn, -z

cyder
BR 'saɪdə(r), -z
AM 'saɪdər, -z

cygnet
BR 'sɪgnɪt, -s
AM 'sɪgnət, -s

Cygnus
BR 'sɪgnəs
AM 'sɪgnəs

cylinder
BR 'sɪlɪndə(r), -z
AM 'sɪləndər, -z

cylindrical
BR sɪ'lɪndrɪkl
AM sə'lɪndrəkəl

cylindrically
BR sɪ'lɪndrɪkli
AM sə'lɪndrək(ə)li

cyma
BR 'saɪmə(r)
AM 'saɪmə

cymbal
BR 'sɪmbl, -z
AM 'sɪmbəl, -z

cymbalist
BR 'sɪmbl̩ɪst, -s
AM 'sɪmbələst, -s

cymbalo
BR 'sɪmbələʊ, -z
AM 'sɪmbə,loʊ, -z

Cymbeline
BR 'sɪmbɪli:n
AM 'sɪmbə,lin

cymbidium
BR ˌsɪm'bɪdɪəm, -z
AM ˌsɪm'bɪdɪəm, -z

cymbiform
BR 'sɪmbɪfɔːm
AM 'sɪmbə,fɔ(ə)rm

cyme
BR saɪm, -z
AM saɪm, -z

cymose
BR 'saɪməʊs
AM 'saɪˌmoʊs, 'saɪˌmoʊz

Cymric
BR 'kʌmrɪk, 'kɪmrɪk
AM 'kəmrɪk

Cymru
BR 'kʌmri, 'kʊmri
AM 'kəmri

Cynan
BR 'kʌnən
AM 'kənən

Cyncoed
BR kɪn'kɔɪd, kɪŋ'kɔɪd
AM ˌkɪŋ'kɔɪd

Cynewulf
BR 'kɪnɪwʊlf
AM 'kɪnə,wʊlf

cynghanedd
BR kʌŋ'hanəð
AM kəŋ'hanəð
WE kʌŋ'haneð

cynic
BR 'sɪnɪk, -s
AM 'sɪnɪk, -s

cynical
BR 'sɪnɪkl
AM 'sɪnəkəl

cynically
BR 'sɪnɪkli
AM 'sɪnək(ə)li

cynicism
BR 'sɪnɪsɪz(ə)m, -z
AM 'sɪnə,sɪzəm, -z

cynocephali
BR ˌsaɪnə(ʊ)'sɛfəlʌɪ,
ˌsɪnə(ʊ)'sɛfl̩ʌɪ
'saɪnə(ʊ)'kɛfəlʌɪ,
ˌsaɪnə(ʊ)'kɛfl̩ʌɪ
AM 'saɪnoʊ'sɛfə,laɪ,
'saɪnə'sɛfə,laɪ,
'saɪnoʊ'sɛfə,laɪ,
'saɪnə'sɛfə,laɪ

cynocephalus
BR ˌsaɪnə(ʊ)'sɛfələs,
ˌsɪnə(ʊ)'sɛfl̩əs,
'saɪnə(ʊ)'kɛfələs,
ˌsaɪnə(ʊ)'kɛfl̩əs
AM 'saɪnoʊ'sɛfələs,
'saɪnə'sɛfələs,
'saɪnoʊ'sɛfələs,
'saɪnə'sɛfələs

cynosure
BR 'saɪnəʃʊə(r),
'saɪnəzjʊə(r),
'saɪnəzʊə(r),
'sɪnəʃʊə(r),
'sɪnəzjʊə(r),
'sɪnəzʊə(r), -z
AM 'saɪnəˌʃʊ(ə)r, -z

Cynthia
BR 'sɪnθɪə(r)
AM 'sɪnθiə

cypher
BR 'saɪfl̩ə(r), -əz,
-(ə)rɪŋ, -əd
AM 'saɪfər, -z, -ɪŋ, -d

cy pres
BR ˌsi: 'preɪ
AM si 'preɪ

cypress
BR 'saɪprɪs, -ɪz
AM 'saɪprəs, -əz

Cyprian
BR 'sɪprɪən, -z
AM 'sɪprɪən, -z

cyprinoid
BR 'sɪprɪnɔɪd, -z
AM 'sɪprə,nɔɪd, -z

Cypriot
BR 'sɪprɪət, -s
AM 'sɪprɪət, 'sɪpri,ɑt, -s

cypripedium
BR ˌsɪprɪ'pi:dɪəm, -z
AM ˌsɪprə'pidɪəm, -z

Cyprus
BR 'saɪprəs
AM 'saɪprəs

cypsela
BR 'sɪpsɪlə(r)
AM 'sɪpsələ

cypselae
BR 'sɪpsɪli:
AM 'sɪpsə,li, 'sɪpsə,laɪ

Cyrano de Bergerac
BR ˌsɪrənəʊ də
'bə:ʒɛrak, sɪˌrɑːnəʊ +,
+ 'bɛːʒɛrak
AM ˌsɪrənoʊ də
'bərʒə,ræk

Cyrenaic
BR ˌsɪrɪ'neɪɪk, -s
AM ˌsɪrə'neɪɪk, -s

Cyrenaica
BR ˌsɪrɪ'neɪɪkə(r),
ˌsɪrɪ'nʌɪɪkə(r),
ˌsʌɪrɪ'neɪɪkə(r),
ˌsʌɪrɪ'nʌɪɪkə(r)
AM ˌsɪrə'neɪɪkə

Cyrene
BR sʌɪ'ri:ni
AM kaɪ'rini, saɪ'rini

Cyrenian
BR sʌɪ'ri:nɪən, -z
AM kaɪ'rinɪən,
saɪ'rinɪən, -z

Cyril
BR 'sɪrɪl, 'sɪrl̩
AM 'sɪrəl

Cyrillic
BR sɪ'rɪlɪk
AM sə'rɪlɪk

Cyrus
BR 'saɪrəs
AM 'saɪrəs

cyst
BR sɪst, -s
AM sɪst, -s

cystectomy
BR sɪ'stɛktəm|i, -ɪz
AM sɪs'tɛktəmi, -z

cysteine
BR 'sɪstɪi:n, 'sɪsteɪn
AM 'sɪˌstin

cystic
BR 'sɪstɪk
AM 'sɪstɪk

cystine
BR 'sɪstɪ:n
AM 'sɪˌstin

cystitis
BR sɪ'stʌɪtɪs
AM sɪs'taɪdəs

cystoscope
BR 'sɪstəskəʊp, -s
AM 'sɪstə,skoʊp, -s

cystoscopic
BR ˌsɪstə'skɒpɪk
AM ˌsɪstə'skɑpɪk

cystoscopy
BR sɪ'stɒskəp|i, -ɪz
AM sɪ'staskəpi, -z

cystotomy
BR sɪ'stɒtəm|i, -ɪz
AM sɪ'stɑdəmi, -z

Cythera
BR sɪ'θɪərə(r)
AM sə'θɪrə

Cytherea
BR ˌsɪθə'ri:ə(r)
AM sə'θɪriə

cytidine
BR 'sʌɪtɪdi:n
AM 'sɪdə,din

cytochrome
BR 'sʌɪtə(ʊ)krəʊm, -z
AM 'saɪdə,kroʊm, -z

cytogenetic
BR ˌsʌɪtə(ʊ)dʒɪ'nɛtɪk, -s
AM ˌsaɪdədʒə'nɛdɪk, -s

cytogenetical
BR ˌsʌɪtə(ʊ)dʒɪ'nɛtɪkl
AM ˌsaɪdədʒə'nɛdəkəl

cytogenetically
BR ˌsʌɪtə(ʊ)dʒɪ'nɛtɪkli
AM ˌsaɪdədʒə'nɛdək(ə)li

cytogeneticist
BR ˌsʌɪtə(ʊ)dʒɪ'nɛtɪsɪst, -s
AM ˌsaɪdədʒə'nɛdəsəst, -s

cytogenic
BR ˌsʌɪtə(ʊ)'dʒɛnɪk, -s
AM ˌsaɪdə'dʒɛnɪk, -s

cytological
BR ˌsʌɪtə'lɒdʒɪkl
AM ˌsaɪdə'lɑdʒəkəl

cytologically
BR ˌsʌɪtə'lɒdʒɪkli
AM ˌsaɪdə'lɑdʒək(ə)li

cytologist
BR sʌɪ'tɒlədʒɪst, -s
AM saɪ'talədʒəst, -s

cytology
BR sʌɪ'tɒlədʒi
AM saɪ'talədʒi

cytoplasm
BR 'sʌɪtə(ʊ)plaz(ə)m
AM 'saɪdə,plæzəm

cytoplasmic
BR ˌsʌɪtə(ʊ)'plazmɪk
AM ˌsaɪdə'plæzmɪk

cytosine
BR 'sʌɪtə(ʊ)si:n
AM 'saɪdə,sin

cytotoxic
BR ˌsʌɪtə(ʊ)'tɒksɪk
AM ˌsaɪdə'taksɪk

cytotoxin
BR ˌsʌɪtə(ʊ)'tɒksɪn, -z
AM ˌsaɪdə'taksən, -z

czar
BR zɑː(r), tsɑː(r), -z
AM zɑr, -z

czardas
BR 'tʃɑːdaʃ
AM 'tʃardaʃ

czarevich
BR 'zɑːrəvɪtʃ,
'tsɑːrəvɪtʃ, -ɪz
AM 'zɑrə͵vɪtʃ, -ɪz

czarevitch
BR 'zɑːrəvɪtʃ,
'tsɑːrəvɪtʃ, -ɪz
AM 'zɑrə͵vɪtʃ, -ɪz

czarevna
BR zɑːˈrɛvnə(r),
tsɑːˈrɛvnə(r), -z
AM zɑˈrɛvnə, -z

czarina
BR zɑːˈriːnə(r),
tsɑːˈriːnə(r), -z
AM zɑˈriːnə, -z

czarism
BR 'zɑːrɪz(ə)m,
'tsɑːrɪz(ə)m
AM 'zɑr͵ɪzəm

czarist
BR 'zɑːrɪst, 'tsɑːrɪst, -s
AM 'zɑrəst, -s

Czech
BR tʃɛk, -s
AM tʃɛk, -s

Czechoslovak
BR ͵tʃɛkəˈsləʊvak, -s
AM ͵tʃɛkəˈsloʊ͵væk,
͵tʃɛkoʊˈsloʊ͵væk,
͵tʃɛkəˈsloʊ͵vak,
͵tʃɛkoʊˈsloʊ͵vak, -s

Czechoslovakia
BR ͵tʃɛkəsləˈvakɪə(r),

͵tʃɛkəsləˈvaːkɪə(r)
AM ͵tʃɛkə͵sloʊˈvakɪə,
͵tʃɛkoʊ͵sloʊˈvakɪə

Czechoslovakian
BR ͵tʃɛkəsləˈvakɪən,
͵tʃɛkəsləˈvaːkɪən
AM ͵tʃɛkə͵sloʊˈvakɪən,
͵tʃɛkoʊ͵sloʊˈvakɪən

Czerny
BR 'tʃɜːni
AM 'tʃɜrni

Dd

d
BR diː, -z
AM di, -z

'd
had, would
BR d
AM d

DA
BR ˌdiːˈeɪ, -z
AM ˌdiˈeɪ, -z

dab
BR dæb, -z, -ɪŋ, -d
AM dæb, -z, -ɪŋ, -d

dabber
BR ˈdæbə(r), -z
AM ˈdæbər, -z

dabble
BR ˈdæb|l, -lz, -lɪŋ \ -lɪŋ, -ld
AM ˈdæb|əl, -əlz, -(ə)lɪŋ, -əld

dabbler
BR ˈdæb|ə(r), ˈdæblə(r), -z
AM ˈdæb(ə)lər, -z

dabbling
BR ˈdæb|lɪŋ, ˈdæblɪŋ, -z
AM ˈdæb(ə)lɪŋ, -z

dabchick
BR ˈdæbtʃɪk, -s
AM ˈdæb,tʃɪk, -s

dabster
BR ˈdæbstə(r), -z
AM ˈdæbstər, -z

da capo
BR ˌdɑː ˈkɑːpəʊ, də +
AM dɑ ˈkɑpoʊ, də +

Dacca
BR ˈdækɑː(r), ˈdækə(r)
AM ˈdækɑ

dace
BR deɪs, -ɪz
AM deɪs, -ɪz

dacha
BR ˈdatʃə(r), -z
AM ˈdɑ(t)ʃə, -z

Dachau
BR ˈdækaʊ, ˈdaxaʊ
AM ˈdɑkaʊ

dachshund
BR ˈdaks(ə)nd, -z
AM ˈdɑks,(h)ʊn|t, ˈdɑks,(h)ʊn|d, ˈdɑks,(h)aʊn|d, -ts \ -dz

Dacia
BR ˈdeɪsɪə(r), ˈdeɪʃə(r)
AM ˈdeɪʃə

Dacian
BR ˈdeɪsɪən, ˈdeɪʃ(ə)n, -z

dacite
BR ˈdeɪsʌɪt, -s
AM ˈdeɪˌsaɪt, -s

dacoit
BR dəˈkɔɪt, -s
AM dəˈkɔɪt, -s

Dacre
BR ˈdeɪkə(r)
AM ˈdeɪkər

Dacron®
BR ˈdakrɒn
AM ˈdeɪˌkrɑn, ˈdæˌkrɑn

dactyl
BR ˈdakt(ɪ)l, -z
AM ˈdæktl, -z

dactylic
BR dakˈtɪlɪk
AM dækˈtɪlɪk

dactylography
BR ˌdaktɪˈlɒgrəfi
AM ˌdæktəˈlɑgrəfi

dactylology
BR ˌdaktɪˈlɒlədʒi
AM ˌdæktəˈlɑlədʒi

dad
BR dad, -z
AM dæd, -z

Dada
BR ˈdɑːdɑː(r)
AM ˈdɑdɑ

Dadaism
BR ˈdɑːdɑː(r)ɪz(ə)m, ˈdɑːdə(r)ɪz(ə)m
AM ˈdɑdɑˌɪzəm

Dadaist
BR ˈdɑːdɑː(r)ɪst, ˈdɑːdə(r)ɪst, -s
AM ˈdɑdɑəst, -s

Dadaistic
BR ˌdɑːdɑː(r)ˈɪstɪk, ˌdɑːdə(r)ˈɪstɪk
AM ˌdɑdɑˈɪstɪk

daddie
BR ˈdad|i, -ɪz
AM ˈdædi, -z

daddy
BR ˈdad|i, -ɪz
AM ˈdædi, -z

daddy-long-legs
BR ˌdadɪˈlɒŋlɛgz, -ɪz
AM ˈdædiˈlɒŋˌlɛgz, ˈdædiˈlɑŋˌlɛgz, -əz

dado
BR ˈdeɪdəʊ, -z
AM ˈdeɪˌdoʊ, -z

Daedalian
BR dɪˈdeɪlɪən, -z
AM diˈdeɪljən, diˈdeɪlɪən, -z

Daedalus
BR ˈdiːdələs, ˈdiːdjləs
AM ˈdɛdələs

daemon
BR ˈdiːmən, -z
AM ˈdimən, -z

daemonic
BR dɪˈmɒnɪk
AM dəˈmɑnɪk, dɪˈmɑnɪk

daemonological
BR ˌdiːmənəˈlɒdʒɪkl
AM ˌdimənəˈlɑdʒəkəl

DAF®
BR daf, -s
AM dæf, ˌdiˌeɪˈɛf, -s

daff
BR daf, -s
AM dæf, -s

daffily
BR ˈdafɪli
AM ˈdæfəli

daffiness
BR ˈdafnɪs
AM ˈdæfinɪs

daffodil
BR ˈdafədɪl, -z
AM ˈdæfəˌdɪl, -z

daffy
BR ˈdaf|i, -ɪə(r), -ɪɪst
AM ˈdæfi, -ər, -ɪst

daft
BR dɑːft, daft, -ə(r), -ɪst
AM dæft, -ər, -əst

daftly
BR ˈdɑːftli, ˈdaftli
AM ˈdæf(t)li

daftness
BR ˈdɑːftnəs, ˈdaftnəs
AM ˈdæf(t)nəs

Dafydd
BR ˈdavið
AM ˈdævið

dag
BR dag, -z
AM dæg, -z

Dagenham
BR ˈdagən(ə)m, ˈdagn̩(ə)m
AM ˈdægənəm

Dagestan
BR ˌdagɪˈstaːn
AM ˈdagəˌstæn

dagga
BR ˈdɑːgə(r), ˈdagə(r), ˈdaxə(r), -z
AM ˈdægə, ˈdagə, -z

dagger
BR ˈdagə(r), -z
AM ˈdægər, -z

daggerboard
BR ˈdagəbɔːd, -z
AM ˈdægərˌbɔ(ə)rd, -z

daglock
BR ˈdaglɒk, -s
AM ˈdægˌlak, -s

Dagmar
BR ˈdagmɑː(r)
AM ˈdægmɑr
DAN ˈdɑwmɑ

dag-nab
BR ˈdagˈnab
AM ˈdægˈnæb

dago
BR ˈdeɪgəʊ, -z
AM ˈdeɪgoʊ, -z

Dagon
BR ˈdeɪgɒn
AM ˈdeɪˌgɑn

Daguerre
BR dəˈgɛː(r)
AM dəˈgɛ(ə)r

daguerreotype
BR dəˈgɛːrə(ʊ)tʌɪp, -s
AM dəˈgɛrəˌtaɪp, -s

daguerrotype
BR dəˈgɛːrə(ʊ)tʌɪp, -s
AM dəˈgɛrəˌtaɪp, -s

Dagwood
BR ˈdagwʊd
AM ˈdægˌwʊd

dah
BR dɑː(r)
AM dɑ

dahl
BR dɑːl
AM dɑl

dahlia[1]
BR ˈdeɪlɪə(r), -z
AM ˈdɑljə, ˈdæljə, -z

dahlia[2]
BR ˈdeɪlɪə(r), -z
AM ˈdɑljə, ˈdæljə, ˈdɑlɪə, ˈdælɪə, -z

Dahomey
BR dəˈhəʊmi
AM dəˈhoʊmi

Dahrendorf
BR ˈdarəndɔːf, ˈdarn̩dɔːf
AM ˈdarəndɔ(ə)rf

Dai
BR dʌɪ
AM daɪ

Daihatsu®
BR dʌɪˈhatsuː
AM daɪˈhatsu

Dáil
BR dɔɪl
AM dɔɪl
IR ˈdɑːlʲ

Dáil Eireann
BR ˌdɔɪl ˈɛːrən, + ˈɛːrn̩
AM ˌdɔɪl ˈɛrən
IR ˌdɑːlʲ ˈeːrʲən

Dailey
BR ˈdeɪli
AM ˈdeɪli

daily
BR ˈdeɪl|i, -ɪz
AM ˈdeɪli, -z

Daimler®
BR ˈdeɪmlə(r), -z
AM ˈdaɪmlər, -z

daimon
BR ˈdʌɪməʊn, -z
AM ˈdaɪˌmoʊn, -z

daimonic
BR dʌɪˈmɒnɪk, dʌɪˈməʊnɪk

AM daɪˈmoʊnɪk,
daɪˈmɑnɪk
daintily
BR ˈdeɪntɪli
AM ˈdeɪn(t)əli
daintiness
BR ˈdeɪntɪnɪs
AM ˈdeɪn(t)inɪs
dainty
BR ˈdeɪnt|i, -ɪz, -ɪə(r),
-ɪɪst
AM ˈdeɪn(t)i, -z, -ər, -ɪst
daiquiri
BR ˈdʌɪk(ɪ)r|i,
ˈdak(ɪ)r|i, -ɪz
AM ˈdækəri, -z
Dairen
BR dʌɪˈrɛn
AM daɪˈrɛn
dairy
BR ˈdɛ:r|i, -ɪz, -ɪɪŋ
AM ˈdɛri, -z, -ɪŋ
dairying
BR ˈdɛ:rɪɪŋ
AM ˈdɛriɪŋ
dairymaid
BR ˈdɛ:rɪmeɪd, -z
AM ˈdɛriˌmeɪd, -z
dairyman
BR ˈdɛ:rɪmən,
ˈdɛ:rɪman
AM ˈdɛrɪmən,
ˈdɛriˌmæn
dairymen
BR ˈdɛ:rɪmən,
ˈdɛ:rɪmɛn
AM ˈdɛrɪmən,
ˈdɛriˌmɛn
dais
BR ˈdeɪɪs, deɪs, -ɪz
AM ˈdeɪəs, ˈdaɪəs, -ɪz
daisy
BR ˈdeɪz|i, -ɪz
AM ˈdeɪzi, -z
Dakar
BR ˈdakɑ:(r), ˈdakə(r)
AM dɑˈkɑr
Dakin
BR ˈdeɪkɪn
AM ˈdeɪkɪn
Dakota
BR dəˈkəʊtə(r)
AM dəˈkoʊdə
Dakotan
BR dəˈkəʊt(ə)n, -z
AM dəˈkoʊtn, -z
DAKS
BR daks
AM dæks
dal
BR dɑ:l
AM dɑl
Dalai Lama
BR ˌdalaɪ ˈlɑ:mə(r), -z
AM ˈdɑˌlaɪ ˈlɑmə,
ˈdæˌlaɪ +, -z

dalasi
BR dəˈlɑ:si
AM dəˈlasi
dale
BR deɪl, -z
AM deɪl, -z
Dalek
BR ˈdɑ:lɛk, -s
AM ˈdɑlək, -s
dalesfolk
BR ˈdeɪlzfəʊk
AM ˈdeɪlzˌfoʊk
dalesman
BR ˈdeɪlzmən
AM ˈdeɪlzmən
daleswoman
BR ˈdeɪlzˌwʊmən
AM ˈdeɪlzˌwʊmən
daleswomen
BR ˈdeɪlzˌwɪmɪn
AM ˈdeɪlzˌwɪmɪn
daleth
BR ˈdɑ:lɪt
AM ˈdɑlɪt
Daley
BR ˈdeɪli
AM ˈdeɪli
Dalgetty
BR dalˈɡɛti
AM dælˈɡɛdi
Dalgleish
BR dalˈɡli:ʃ
AM dælˈɡliʃ
Dalglish
BR dalˈɡli:ʃ
AM dælˈɡliʃ
Dalhousie
BR dalˈhaʊzi, dalˈhu:zi
AM dælˈhuzi
Dali
BR ˈdɑ:li
AM ˈdɑli
Dalian
BR ˈdɑ:lɪən
AM ˈdaljən, ˈdaliən
Dalkeith
BR dalˈki:θ
AM dælˈkiθ
Dallapiccola
BR ˌdaləˈpɪkələ(r),
ˌdaləˈpɪklə(r)
AM ˌdaləˈpɪkələ
Dallas
BR ˈdaləs
AM ˈdæləs
dalliance
BR ˈdalɪəns
AM ˈdælɪəns, ˈdæljəns
dallier
BR ˈdalɪə(r), -z
AM ˈdælɪər, -z
dally
BR ˈdal|i, -ɪz, -ɪɪŋ, -ɪd
AM ˈdæli, -z, -ɪŋ, -d
Dalmatia
BR dalˈmeɪʃə(r)

AM dælˈmeɪʃə,
dalˈmeɪʃə
Dalmatian
BR dalˈmeɪʃ(ə)n, -z
AM dælˈmeɪʃən,
dalˈmeɪʃən, -z
dalmatic
BR dalˈmatɪk
AM dælˈmædɪk
Dalriada
BR ˌdalrɪˈɑ:də(r)
AM ˌdalriˈadə
Dalrymple
BR dalˈrɪmpl,
ˈdalrɪmpl
AM ˈdælˌrɪmpəl
dal segno
BR dal ˈseɪnjəʊ, dɑ:l +
AM ˌdal ˈseɪnjoʊ
Dalston
BR ˈdɔ:lst(ə)n,
ˈdɒlst(ə)n
AM ˈdɔlstən, ˈdalstən
Dalton
BR ˈdɔ:lt(ə)n, ˈdɒlt(ə)n
AM ˈdɔltən, ˈdaltən
Daltonise
BR ˈdɔ:ltənʌɪz,
ˈdɒltənʌɪz, ˈdɔ:ltn̩ʌɪz,
ˈdɒltn̩ʌɪz, -ɪz, -ɪŋ, -d
AM ˈdɔltəˌnaɪz,
ˈdaltəˌnaɪz, -ɪz, -ɪŋ, -d
daltonism
BR ˈdɔ:ltənɪz(ə)m,
ˈdɒltənɪz(ə)m,
ˈdɔ:ltn̩ɪz(ə)m,
ˈdɒltn̩ɪz(ə)m
AM ˈdɔltəˌnɪzəm,
ˈdaltəˌnɪzəm
Daltonize
BR ˈdɔ:ltənʌɪz,
ˈdɒltənʌɪz, ˈdɔ:ltn̩ʌɪz,
ˈdɒltn̩ʌɪz, -ɪz, -ɪŋ, -d
AM ˈdɔltəˌnaɪz,
ˈdaltəˌnaɪz, -ɪz, -ɪŋ, -d
Dalwhinnie
BR dalˈwɪni
AM dælˈwɪni
Daly
BR ˈdeɪli
AM deɪli
Dalyell
BR dɪˈɛl, dʌɪˈɛl,
ˈdalj(ə)l
AM ˈdælˌjɛl, daɪˈɛl
Dalzell
BR dɪˈɛl, dʌɪˈɛl, ˈdalzɛl
AM dælˈzɛl, daɪˈɛl
Dalziel
BR dɪˈɛl, dʌɪˈɛl, ˈdalzi:l
AM ˈdælzi(ə)l, daɪˈɛl
dam
BR dam, -z, -ɪŋ, -d
AM dæm, -z, -ɪŋ, -d
damage
BR ˈdam|ɪdʒ, -ɪdʒɪz,
-ɪdʒɪŋ, -ɪdʒd
AM ˈdæmɪdʒ, -ɪz, -ɪŋ, -d

damageable
BR ˈdamɪdʒəbl
AM ˈdæmədʒəbəl
damagingly
BR ˈdamɪdʒɪŋli
AM ˈdæmədʒɪŋli
Damara
BR dəˈmɑ:rə(r), -z
AM dəˈmɑrə, -z
Damaraland
BR dəˈmɑ:rələnd
AM ˈdamərəˌlænd,
dəˈmɑrəˌlænd
damascene
BR ˈdaməsi:n
AM ˈdæməˌsin,
ˌdæməˈsin
Damascus
BR dəˈmaskəs,
dəˈmɑ:skəs
AM dəˈmæskəs
damask
BR ˈdaməsk
AM ˈdæməsk
Dambuster
BR ˈdamˌbʌstə(r), -z
AM ˈdæmˌbəstər, -z
dame
BR deɪm, -z
AM deɪm, -z
Damian
BR ˈdeɪmɪən
AM ˈdeɪmiən
dammar
BR ˈdamə(r), -z
AM ˈdæmər, -z
dammit
BR ˈdamɪt
AM ˈdæmət
damn
BR dam, -z, -ɪŋ, -d
AM dæm, -z, -ɪŋ, -d
damna
BR ˈdamnə(r)
AM ˈdæmnə
damnable
BR ˈdamnəbl
AM ˈdæm(n)əbəl
damnably
BR ˈdamnəbli
AM ˈdæm(n)əbli
damnation
BR damˈneɪʃn
AM dæmˈneɪʃən
damnatory
BR ˈdamnət(ə)ri
AM ˈdæm(n)əˌtɔri
damnedest
BR ˈdamdɪst
AM ˈdæmdəst,
ˈdæmnəst
damn fool
adjective
BR ˌdam ˈfu:l
AM ˌdæm ˈful
damnification
BR ˌdamnɪfɪˈkeɪʃn

damnify
AM ˌdæm(n)əfəˈkeɪʃən, ˌdæmnəˌfaɪˈkeɪʃən
damnify
BR ˈdæmnɪfaɪ, -z, -ɪŋ, -d
AM ˈdæm(n)əˌfaɪ, -z, -ɪŋ, -d
damningly
BR ˈdamɪŋli
AM ˈdæmɪŋli
damnum
BR ˈdamnəm
AM ˈdæmnəm
Damocles
BR ˈdamǝkliːz
AM ˈdæməkliz
Damon
BR ˈdeɪmən
AM ˈdeɪmən
damosel
BR ˌdaməˈzɛl, -z
AM ˌdæm(ə)ˈzɛl, -z
damozel
BR ˌdaməˈzɛl, -z
AM ˌdæm(ə)ˈzɛl, -z
damp
BR damp, -ə(r), -ɪst
AM dæmp, -ər, -əst
dampen
BR ˈdamp|(ə)n, -(ə)nz, -ŋɪŋ\-nɪŋ, -(ə)nd
AM ˈdæmp|ən, -ənz, -(ə)nɪŋ, -ənd
dampener
BR ˈdamp(ə)nə(r), -z
AM ˈdæmpənər, -z
damper
BR ˈdampə(r), -z
AM ˈdæmpər, -z
Dampier
BR ˈdampɪə(r)
AM ˈdæmpɪ(ə)r
dampish
BR ˈdampɪʃ
AM ˈdæmpɪʃ
damply
BR ˈdampli
AM ˈdæmpli
dampness
BR ˈdampnəs
AM ˈdæmpnəs
damsel
BR ˈdamzl, -z
AM ˈdæmzəl, -z
damselfish
BR ˈdamzlfɪʃ, -ɪz
AM ˈdæmzəlˌfɪʃ, -ɪz
damselfly
BR ˈdamzlflaɪ, -z
AM ˈdæmzəlˌflaɪ, -z
damson
BR ˈdamzn, -z
AM ˈdæmzn, ˈdæmsən, -z
dan
BR dan, -z
AM dæn, -z

Dana
BR ˈdɑːnə(r), ˈdeɪnə(r)
AM ˈdeɪnə
Danae
BR ˈdaniː, ˈdaneɪiː
AM ˈdæneɪˌi, ˈdæˌnaɪ
Danaides
BR dəˈneɪdiːz
AM dəˈneɪəˌdiz
Dan-Air®
BR ˌdanˈɛː(r)
AM ˌdænˈɛ(ə)r
Danakil
BR ˈdanəkɪl
AM ˈdænəˌkɪl
Da Nang
BR ˌdɑːˈnaŋ
AM ˌdɑˈnæŋ
Danbury
BR ˈdanb(ə)ri
AM ˈdænˌbɛri
Danby
BR ˈdanbi
AM ˈdænbi
dance
BR dɑːns, dans, -ɪz, -ɪŋ, -t
AM dæns, -əz, -ɪŋ, -t
danceable
BR ˈdɑːnsəbl, ˈdansəbl
AM ˈdænsəbəl
dancer
BR ˈdɑːnsə(r), ˈdansə(r), -z
AM ˈdænsər, -z
dancewear
BR ˈdɑːnswɛː(r), ˈdanswɛː(r)
AM ˈdænsˌwɛ(ə)r
dandelion
BR ˈdandɪlaɪən, -z
AM ˈdændlˌaɪən, ˈdændiˌlaɪən, -z
dander
BR ˈdandə(r), -z
AM ˈdændər, -z
dandify
BR ˈdandɪfaɪ, -z, -ɪŋ, -d
AM ˈdændəˌfaɪ, -z, -ɪŋ, -d
Dandini
BR danˈdiːni
AM dænˈdini
dandle
BR ˈdandl, -z, -lɪŋ\-lɪŋ, -ld
AM ˈdændəl, -dəlz, -(d)əlɪŋ, -dəld
Dando
BR ˈdandəʊ
AM ˈdændoʊ
dandruff
BR ˈdandrʌf
AM ˈdændrəf
dandy
BR ˈdand|i, -ɪz
AM ˈdændi, -z

dandyish
BR ˈdandɪɪʃ
AM ˈdændiiʃ
dandyism
BR ˈdandɪɪz(ə)m
AM ˈdændiˌɪzəm
Dane
BR deɪn, -z
AM deɪn, -z
Danegeld
BR ˈdeɪngɛld
AM ˈdeɪnˌgɛld
Danelaugh
BR ˈdeɪnlɔː(r)
AM ˈdeɪnˌlɔ
Danelaw
BR ˈdeɪnlɔː(r)
AM ˈdeɪnˌlɔ
daneweed
BR ˈdeɪnwiːd
AM ˈdeɪnˌwid
danewort
BR ˈdeɪnwəːt
AM ˈdeɪnˌwərt, ˈdeɪnˌwɔ(ə)rt
dang
BR daŋ
AM dæŋ
danger
BR ˈdeɪn(d)ʒə(r), -z
AM ˈdeɪndʒər, -z
Dangerfield
BR ˈdeɪn(d)ʒəfiːld
AM ˈdeɪndʒərˌfild
dangerous
BR ˈdeɪn(d)ʒ(ə)rəs
AM ˈdeɪndʒ(ə)rəs
dangerously
BR ˈdeɪn(d)ʒ(ə)rəsli
AM ˈdeɪndʒ(ə)rəsli
dangerousness
BR ˈdeɪn(d)ʒ(ə)rəsnəs
AM ˈdeɪndʒ(ə)rəsnəs
dangle
BR ˈdaŋg|l, -lz, -lɪŋ\-lɪŋ, -ld
AM ˈdæŋgəl, -əlz, -(ə)lɪŋ, -əld
dangler
BR ˈdaŋglə(r), -z
AM ˈdæŋglər, -z
dangly
BR ˈdaŋgli
AM ˈdæŋgli
Daniel
BR ˈdanjəl
AM ˈdænjəl
Daniela
BR ˌdanɪˈɛlə(r), ˌdanˈjɛlə(r), ˌdænˈjɛlə
Daniell
BR ˈdanjəl
AM ˈdænjəl
Danielle
BR ˌdanɪˈɛl, ˌdanˈjɛl
AM ˌdænˈjɛl

Daniels
BR ˈdanjəlz
AM ˈdænjəlz
Danish
BR ˈdeɪnɪʃ
AM ˈdeɪnɪʃ
dank
BR daŋk, -ə(r), -ɪst
AM dæŋk, -ər, -əst
dankly
BR ˈdaŋkli
AM ˈdæŋkli
dankness
BR ˈdaŋknəs
AM ˈdæŋknəs
Dankworth
BR ˈdaŋkwə(ː)θ
AM ˈdæŋkˌwərθ
Dannimac
BR ˈdanɪmak
AM ˈdænəmæk
Danny
BR ˈdani
AM ˈdæni
danse macabre
BR ˌdɑːns məˈkɑːbr(ər), -z
AM ˈdɑns məˈkɑbr(ə), -z
danses macabres
BR ˌdɑːns məˈkɑːbr(ər)z
AM ˈdɑns məˈkɑbr(ə)z
Dansette
BR danˈsɛt, -s
AM dænˈsɛt, -s
danseur
BR dɒnˈsəː(r), dɑːnˈsəː(r), danˈsəː(r), -z
AM dænˈsər, -z
danseuse
BR dɒnˈsəːz, dɑːnˈsəːz, danˈsəːz, -z
AM dænˈsʊz, -z
Dante
BR ˈdanti, ˈdɑːnti, ˈdanteɪ, ˈdɑːnteɪ
AM ˈdɑnteɪ, ˈdænteɪ
Dantean
BR ˈdantɪən, ˈdɑːntɪən, danˈtiːən, dɑːnˈtiːən
AM ˈdɑn(t)iən, ˈdæn(t)iən
Dantesque
BR danˈtɛsk, dɑːnˈtɛsk
AM danˈtɛsk, dænˈtɛsk
danthonia
BR danˈθəʊnɪə(r)
AM dænˈθoʊniə
Danton
BR ˈdantɒn, dɒ̃ˈtɔ̃
AM ˈdæn(t)ən
Danube
BR ˈdanjuːb
AM ˈdænˌjub

Danubian
BR də'nju:bɪən,
də'nju:bɪən, -z
AM də'njubiən,-z
Danvers
BR 'dænvəz
AM 'dænvərz
Danzig
BR dɛ:nt
BR 'dan(t)zɪg
AM 'dæn(t)zɪg
Dão
BR daʊ, 'dɑ:əʊ
AM 'dɑ,oʊ, daʊ
PORT dãw
dap
BR dap, -s
AM dæp, -s
daphne
BR 'dafni
AM 'dæfni
daphnia
BR 'dafnɪə(r)
AM 'dæfniə
Daphnis
BR 'dafnɪs
AM 'dæfnəs
dapper
BR 'dap|ə(r), -(ə)rɪst
AM 'dæpər, -əst
dapperly
BR 'dapəli
AM 'dæpərli
dapperness
BR 'dapənəs
AM 'dæpərnəs
dapple
BR 'dap|l, -lz, -ļɪŋ \-lɪŋ,
-ld
AM 'dæpəl, -z, -ɪŋ, -d
dapsone
BR 'dapsəʊn
AM 'dæp,soʊn
daquiri
BR 'dak(ɪ)r|i, -ɪz
AM 'dækəri, -z
Darbishire
BR 'dɑ:bɪʃ(ɪ)ə(r)
AM 'dɑrbiʃɪ(ə)r
Darby
BR 'dɑ:bi
AM 'dərbi
Darcy
BR 'dɑ:si
AM 'dɑrsi
Dardanelles
BR ,dɑ:də'nɛlz,
,dɑ:dn'ɛlz
AM ,dɑrdn'ɛlz
dare
BR dɛ:(r), -z, -ɪŋ, -d
AM dɛ(ə)r, -z, -ɪŋ, -d
daredevil
BR 'dɛ:,dɛvl, -z
AM 'dɛr,dɛvəl, -z
daredevilry
BR 'dɛ:,dɛvlri
AM 'dɛr,dɛv(ə)lri

Darell
BR 'darəl, 'darļ
AM 'dɛrəl
Daren
BR 'darən, 'darņ
AM 'dɛrən
daren't
BR dɛ:nt
AM dɛr(ə)nt
darer
BR 'dɛ:rə(r), -z
AM 'dɛ(r)ər, -z
daresay
BR ,dɛ:'seɪ, 'dɛ:seɪ
AM 'dɛr,seɪ
Dar es Salaam
BR ,dɑ:r ɛs sə'lɑ:m,
+ ɪs +, + ɛz +, + ɪz +
AM ,dɑr ɛs sə'lɑm
Darfur
BR ,dɑ:'fɔ:(r)
AM 'dɑrfʊr
darg
BR dɑ:g, -z
AM dɑrg, -z
dargah
BR 'dɑ:gə(r), -z
AM 'dɑrgə, -z
Dari
BR 'dɛ:ri
AM 'dɛri
daric
BR 'darɪk, -s
AM 'dɛrɪk, -s
Darien
BR 'dɛ:rɪən, 'darɪən
AM ,dɛri'ɛn, 'dari,ɛn
Darin
BR 'darɪn, 'darən,
'darņ
AM 'dɛrən
daring
BR 'dɛ:rɪŋ
AM 'dɛrɪŋ
daringly
BR 'dɛ:rɪŋli
AM 'dɛrɪŋli
dariole
BR 'darɪəʊl, -z
AM 'dɛrioʊl, -z
Darius¹
forename
BR 'dɛ:rɪəs, 'darɪəs
AM 'dɛriəs
Darius²
Persian king
BR də'rʌɪəs
AM də'raɪəs, 'dɛriəs
Darjeeling
BR dɑ:'dʒi:lɪŋ
AM dɑr'dʒilɪŋ
dark
BR dɑ:k
AM dɑrk
darken
BR 'dɑ:k|(ə)n, -(ə)nz,
-ənɪŋ \-ņɪŋ, -(ə)nd

AM 'dɑrk|ən, -ənz,
-(ə)nɪŋ, -ənd
darkener
BR 'dɑ:k(ə)nə(r),
'dɑ:kŋə(r), -z
AM 'dɑrk(ə)nər, -z
darkey
BR 'dɑ:k|i, -ɪz
AM 'dɑrki, -z
darkie
BR 'dɑ:k|i, -ɪz
AM 'dɑrki, -z
darkish
BR 'dɑ:kɪʃ
AM 'dɑrkɪʃ
darkling
BR 'dɑ:klɪŋ
AM 'dɑrklɪŋ
darkly
BR 'dɑ:kli
AM 'dɑrkli
darkness
BR 'dɑ:knəs, -ɪz
AM 'dɑrknəs, -əz
darkroom
BR 'dɑ:kru:m,
'dɑ:krʊm, -z
AM 'dɑrk,rum,
'dɑrk,rʊm, -z
darksome
BR 'dɑ:ks(ə)m
AM 'dɑrksəm
darky
BR 'dɑ:k|i, -ɪz
AM 'dɑrki, -z
Darlene
BR 'dɑ:li:n
AM dɑr'lin
darling
BR 'dɑ:lɪŋ, -z
AM 'dɑrlɪŋ, -z
Darlington
BR 'dɑ:lɪŋt(ə)n
AM 'dɑrlɪŋtən
Darmstadt
BR 'dɑ:mstat,
'dɑ:mʃtat
AM 'dɑrm,stæt,
'dɑrm,ʃtæt
darn
BR dɑ:n, -z, -ɪŋ, -d
AM dɑrn, -z, -ɪŋ, -d
darnedest
BR 'dɑ:ndɪst
AM 'dɑrndəst
darnel
BR 'dɑ:nl, -z
AM 'dɑrnəl, -z
darner
BR 'dɑ:nə(r), -z
AM 'dɑrnər, -z
Darnley
BR 'dɑ:nli
AM 'dɑrnli
Darrell
BR 'darəl, 'darļ
AM 'dɛrəl

Darren
BR 'darən, 'darņ
AM 'dɛrən
Darrow
BR 'darəʊ
AM 'dɛroʊ
Darryl
BR 'darəl, 'darļ
AM 'dɛrəl
dart
BR dɑ:t, -s, -ɪŋ, -ɪd
AM dar|t, -ts, -dɪŋ, -dəd
d'Artagnan
BR dɑ:'tanjən
AM dɑr'tænjən
dartboard
BR 'dɑ:tbɔ:d, -z
AM 'dɑrt,bɔ(ə)rd, -z
darter
BR 'dɑ:tə(r), -z
AM 'dɑrdər, -z
Dartford
BR 'dɑ:tfəd
AM 'dɑrtfərd
Darth Vader
BR ,dɑ:θ 'veɪdə(r)
AM ,dɑrθ 'veɪdər
Dartmoor
BR 'dɑ:tmʊə(r),
'dɑ:tmɔ:(r)
AM 'dɑrt,mɔ(ə)r,
'dɑrt,mʊ(ə)r
Dartmouth
BR 'dɑ:tməθ
AM 'dɑrtməθ
dartre
BR 'dɑ:tə(r)
AM 'dɑrdər
Darwen
BR 'dɑ:wɪn
AM 'dɑrwən
Darwin
BR 'dɑ:wɪn
AM 'dɑrwən
Darwinian
BR dɑ:'wɪnɪən
AM dɑr'wɪniən
Darwinism
BR 'dɑ:wɪnɪz(ə)m
AM 'dɑrwən,ɪzəm
Darwinist
BR 'dɑ:wɪnɪst, -s
AM 'dɑrwənəst, -s
Daryl
BR 'darəl, 'darļ
AM 'dɛrəl
dash
BR daʃ, -ɪz, -ɪŋ, -t
AM dæʃ, -əz, -ɪŋ, -t
dashboard
BR 'daʃbɔ:d, -z
AM 'dæʃ,bɔ(ə)rd, -z
dashiki
BR da'ʃɪk|i, -ɪz, də:ʃɪki, -ɪz
AM də'ʃɪki, -z
dashing
BR 'daʃɪŋ

AM 'dæʃɪŋ
dashingly
BR 'dæʃɪŋli
AM 'dæʃɪŋli
dashingness
BR 'dæʃɪŋnɪs
AM 'dæʃɪŋnɪs
dashpot
BR 'dæʃpɒt, -s
AM 'dæʃˌpɑt, -s
dassie
BR 'dasˌi, -ɪz
AM 'dæsi, -z
dastard
BR 'dastəd, -z
AM 'dæstərd, -z
dastardliness
BR 'dastədlɪnɪs
AM 'dæstərdlɪnɪs
dastardly
BR 'dastədli
AM 'dæstərdli
dastur
BR da'stʊə(r), də'stʊə(r), -z
AM dæ'stʊ(ə)r, də'stʊ(ə)r, -z
dasyure
BR 'dasɪjʊə(r), -z
AM 'dæsiˌjʊ(ə)r, -z
data
BR 'deɪtə(r), 'dɑːtə(r)
AM 'dædə, 'deɪdə
databank
BR 'deɪtəbaŋk, 'dɑːtəbaŋk, -s
AM 'dædəˌbæŋk, 'deɪdəˌbæŋk, -s
database
BR 'deɪtəbeɪs, 'dɑːtəbeɪs, -ɪz
AM 'dædəˌbeɪs, 'deɪdəˌbeɪs, -ɪz
datable
BR 'deɪtəbl
AM 'deɪdəbəl
datafile
BR 'deɪtəfʌɪl, 'dɑːtəfʌɪl, -z
AM 'dædəˌfaɪl, 'deɪdəˌfaɪl, -z
Datapost®
BR 'deɪtəpəʊst, 'dɑːtəpəʊst
AM 'dædəˌpoʊst, 'deɪdəˌpoʊst
Datchet
BR 'datʃɪt
AM 'dætʃət
date
BR deɪt, -s, -ɪŋ, -ɪd
AM deɪt, -ts, -dɪŋ, -dɪd
dateless
BR 'deɪtlɪs
AM 'deɪtlɪs
dateline
BR 'deɪtlʌɪn, -z
AM 'deɪtˌlaɪn, -z

datival
BR deɪ'tʌɪvl
AM deɪ'taɪvəl, də'taɪvəl
datively
BR deɪ'tʌɪvəli, deɪ'tʌɪvˌli
AM deɪ'taɪvəli, də'taɪvəli
dative
BR 'deɪtɪv, -z
AM 'deɪdɪv, -z
Datsun®
BR 'dats(ə)n, -z
AM 'datsən, -z
datum
BR 'deɪtəm, 'dɑːtəm
AM 'dædəm, 'deɪdəm
datura
BR də'tjʊərə(r), də'tʃʊərə(r), -z
AM də't(j)ʊərə, də'tʃʊrə, -z
daub
BR dɔːb, -z, -ɪŋ, -d
AM dɑb, dab, -z, -ɪŋ, -d
daube
BR dəʊb, -z
AM doʊb, -z
dauber
BR 'dɔːbə(r), -z
AM 'dɔbər, 'dabər, -z
Daubigny
BR 'dɔːbɪnji
AM ˌdɔbi'nji, ˌdabi'nji
daubster
BR 'dɔːbstə(r), -z
AM 'dɔbstər, 'dabstər, -z
dauby
BR 'dɔːbi
AM 'dɔbi, 'dabi
Daudet
BR 'dəʊdeɪ
AM dɔ'deɪ, dɑ'deɪ
Daugherty
BR 'dɒkəti, 'dɒxəti
AM 'dɔrdi
daughter
BR 'dɔːtə(r), -z
AM 'dɔdər, 'dadər, -z
daughterhood
BR 'dɔːtəhʊd
AM 'dɔdərˌ(h)ʊd, 'dadərˌ(h)ʊd
daughterly
BR 'dɔːtəli
AM 'dɔdərli, 'dadərli
daunt
BR dɔːnt, -s, -ɪŋ, -ɪd
AM dɑn|t, dan|t, -ts, -(t)ɪŋ, -(t)əd
dauntingly
BR 'dɔːntɪŋli
AM 'dɑn(t)ɪŋli, 'dan(t)ɪŋli
dauntless
BR 'dɔːntləs

AM 'dɔn(t)ləs, 'dan(t)ləs
dauntlessly
BR 'dɔːntləsli
AM 'dɔn(t)ləsli, 'dan(t)ləsli
dauntlessness
BR 'dɔːntləsnəs
AM 'dɔn(t)ləsnəs, 'dan(t)ləsnəs
dauphin
BR 'dəʊfã, 'dɔːfɪn, -z
AM 'dɔfən, 'dafən, -z
dauphine
BR 'dəʊfiːn, 'dɔːfiːn, -z
AM 'dɔfin, 'dafin, -z
Dave
BR deɪv
AM deɪv
davenport
BR 'davnpɔːt, -s
AM 'dævənˌpɔ(ə)rt, -s
Daventry¹
older, local form
BR 'deɪntri
AM 'dævəntri
Daventry²
BR 'davntri
AM 'dævəntri
Davey
BR 'deɪvi
AM 'deɪvi
David
BR 'deɪvɪd
AM 'deɪvəd
Davidson
BR 'deɪvɪds(ə)n
AM 'deɪvɪdsən
Davie
BR 'deɪvi
AM 'deɪvi
Davies
BR 'deɪvɪs
AM 'deɪviz
da Vinci
BR də 'vɪn(t)ʃi
AM də 'vɪn(t)ʃi
Davis
BR 'deɪvɪs
AM 'deɪvəs
Davison
BR 'deɪvɪsn
AM 'deɪvɪsən
Davisson
BR 'deɪvɪsn
AM 'deɪvɪsən
davit
BR 'davɪt, -s
AM 'davɪt, 'dævət, -s
Davos
BR da'vəʊs
AM dɑ'voʊs
Davy
BR 'deɪvi
AM 'deɪvi
daw
BR dɔː(r), -z

AM dɔ, dɑ, -z
dawdle
BR 'dɔːd|l, -lz, -l̩ɪŋ \-lɪŋ, -ld
AM 'dɑd|əl, 'dad|əl, -əlz, -(ə)lɪŋ, -əld
dawdler
BR 'dɔːdlə(r), 'dɔːdlə(r), -z
AM 'dɑd(ə)lər, 'dad(ə)lər, -z
Dawe
BR dɔː(r)
AM dɔ
Dawes
BR dɔːz
AM dɔz, daz
Dawkins
BR 'dɔːkɪnz
AM 'dɔkənz, 'dakənz
Dawlish
BR 'dɔːlɪʃ
AM 'dɔləʃ, 'daləʃ
dawn
BR dɔːn, -z, -ɪŋ, -d
AM dɔn, dan, -z, -ɪŋ, -d
dawning
BR 'dɔːnɪŋ, -z
AM 'dɔnɪŋ, 'danɪŋ, -z
Dawson
BR 'dɔːsn
AM 'dɔsən, 'dasən
day
BR deɪ, -z
AM deɪ, -z
Dayak
BR 'dʌɪak, -s
AM 'daɪæk, -s
Dayan
BR dʌɪ'an, dʌɪ'ɑːn
AM dɑ'jan
daybed
BR 'deɪbɛd, -z
AM 'deɪˌbɛd, -z
daybook
BR 'deɪbʊk, -s
AM 'deɪˌbʊk, -s
daybreak
BR 'deɪbreɪk
AM 'deɪˌbreɪk
daydream
BR 'deɪdriːm, -z, -ɪŋ, -d
AM 'deɪˌdrim, -z, -ɪŋ, -d
daydreamer
BR 'deɪdriːmə(r), -z
AM 'deɪˌdrimər, -z
Day-Glo®
BR 'deɪgləʊ
AM 'deɪˌgloʊ
dayless
BR 'deɪlɪs
AM 'deɪlɪs
daylight
BR 'deɪlʌɪt
AM 'deɪˌlaɪt

dayroom
BR 'deɪruːm, 'deɪrʊm, -z
AM 'deɪˌrum, 'deɪˌrʊm, -z

daysack
BR 'deɪsak, -s
AM 'deɪˌsæk, -s

dayside
BR 'deɪsʌɪd
AM 'deɪˌsaɪd

daystar
BR 'deɪstɑː(r), -z
AM 'deɪˌstɑr, -z

daytime
BR 'deɪtʌɪm
AM 'deɪˌtaɪm

Daytona
BR deɪ'təʊnə(r)
AM deɪ'toʊnə

daywork
BR 'deɪwəːk
AM 'deɪˌwɜrk

Daz®
BR daz
AM dɑz

daze
BR deɪz, -ɪz, -ɪŋ, -d
AM deɪz, -ɪz, -ɪŋ, -d

dazedly
BR 'deɪzɪdli
AM 'deɪzɪdli

dazzle
BR 'daz|l, -lz, -lɪŋ\-lɪŋ, -ld
AM 'dæz|əl, -əlz, -(ə)lɪŋ, -əld

dazzlement
BR 'dazlm(ə)nt
AM 'dæzəlmənt

dazzler
BR 'dazlə(r), 'dazlə(r)
AM 'dæzlər

dazzlingly
BR 'dazlɪŋli, 'dazlɪŋli
AM 'dæz(ə)lɪŋli

dBase
BR 'diːbeɪs
AM 'diˌbeɪs

deaccession
BR ˌdiːək'seʃ|n, -nz, -ənɪŋ\-nɪŋ, -nd
AM ˌdiə(k)'sɛʃən, -z, -ɪŋ, -d

deacon
BR 'diːk(ə)n, -z
AM 'dikən, -z

deaconate
BR 'diːkənət, 'diːkn̩ət, -s
AM 'dikənət, -s

deaconess
BR ˌdiːkə'nɛs, -ɪz
AM 'dikənəs, -əz

deaconship
BR 'diːk(ə)nʃɪp, -s
AM 'dikənʃɪp, -s

deactivate
BR dɪ'aktɪveɪt, ˌdiː'aktɪvət, -s, -ɪŋ, -ɪd
AM diˈæktəˌveɪlt, -ts, -dɪŋ, -dɪd

deactivation
BR dɪˌaktɪ'veɪʃn, ˌdiː'aktɪ'veɪʃn
AM diˌæktə'veɪʃən

deactivator
BR dɪ'aktɪveɪtə(r), ˌdiː'aktɪveɪtə(r), -z
AM di'æktəˌveɪdər, -z

dead
BR dɛd, -ə(r), -ɪst
AM dɛd, -ər, -əst

deadbeat
noun
BR 'dɛdbiːt, -s
AM 'dɛdˌbit, -s

dead-beat
adjective
BR ˌdɛd'biːt
AM 'dɛd'bit

deadbolt
BR 'dɛdbəʊlt, -s
AM 'dɛdˌboʊlt, -s

deaden
BR 'dɛd|n, -nz, -n̩ɪŋ\-nɪŋ, -nd
AM 'dɛdən, -z, -ɪŋ, -d

deadener
BR 'dɛdnə(r), -z
AM 'dɛdnər, -z

deadeye
BR 'dɛdʌɪ
AM 'dɛdˌaɪ

deadfall
BR 'dɛdfɔːl, -z
AM 'dɛdˌfɔl, 'dɛdˌfɑl, -z

deadhead
BR 'dɛdhɛd, -z, -ɪŋ, -ɪd
AM 'dɛdˌ(h)ɛd, -z, -ɪŋ, -əd

deadlight
BR 'dɛdlʌɪt, -s
AM 'dɛdˌlaɪt, -s

deadline
BR 'dɛdlʌɪn, -z
AM 'dɛdˌlaɪn, -z

deadliness
BR 'dɛdlmɪs
AM 'dɛdlinɪs

deadlock
BR 'dɛdlɒk, -s, -t
AM 'dɛdˌlɑk, -s, -t

deadly
BR 'dɛdl|i, -ɪə(r), -ɪɪst
AM 'dɛdli, -ər, -ɪst

deadness
BR 'dɛdnəs
AM 'dɛdnəs

deadpan
BR 'dɛdpan
AM 'dɛdˌpæn

deadstock
BR 'dɛdstɒk
AM 'dɛdˌstɑk

de-aerate
BR ˌdiː'ɛːreɪt, -s, -ɪŋ, -ɪd
AM di'ɛˌreɪlt, -ts, -dɪŋ, -dɪd

de-aeration
BR ˌdiːɛː'reɪʃn
AM diˌɛr'eɪʃən

deaf
BR dɛf, -ə(r), -ɪst
AM dɛf, -ər, -əst

deafen
BR 'dɛf|n, -nz, -n̩ɪŋ\-nɪŋ, -nd
AM 'dɛf|ən, -ənz, -(ə)nɪŋ, -ənd

deafeningly
BR 'dɛfn̩ɪŋli, 'dɛfnɪŋli
AM 'dɛf(ə)nɪŋli

deafly
BR 'dɛfli
AM 'dɛfli

deafness
BR 'dɛfnəs
AM 'dɛfnəs

Deakin
BR 'diːkɪn
AM 'dikɪn

deal
BR diːl, -z, -ɪŋ
AM dil, -z, -ɪŋ

dealer
BR 'diːlə(r), -z
AM 'dilər, -z

dealership
BR 'diːləʃɪp, -s
AM 'dilərˌʃɪp, -s

dealing
BR 'diːlɪŋ, -z
AM 'dilɪŋ, -z

dealt
BR dɛlt
AM dɛlt

deambulation
BR dɪˌambjʊ'leɪʃn
AM ˌdiˌæmbjə'leɪʃən

deambulatory
BR dɪ'ambjələt(ə)ri
AM diˈæmbjələˌtɔri

deamination
BR dɪˌamɪ'neɪʃn
AM diˌæmə'neɪʃən

dean
BR diːn, -z
AM din, -z

deanery
BR 'diːn(ə)r|i, -ɪz
AM 'dinəri, -z

Deanna
BR dɪ'anə(r), 'diː'nə(r)
AM di'ænə, 'dinə

dear
BR dɪə(r), -z, -ə(r), -ɪst
AM dɪ(ə)r, -z, -ər, -ɪst

Deare
BR dɪə(r)
AM dɪ(ə)r

dearie
BR 'dɪər|i, -ɪz
AM 'diri, -z

dearly
BR 'dɪəli
AM 'dɪrli

Dearne
BR dəːn
AM dɜrn

dearness
BR 'dɪənəs
AM 'dɪrnɪs

dearth
BR dəːθ, -s
AM dɜrθ, -s

deary
BR 'dɪər|i, -ɪz
AM 'dɪri, -z

deasil
BR 'dɛsl, 'djɛʃl
AM 'dizəl

death
BR dɛθ, -s
AM dɛθ, -s

deathbed
BR 'dɛθbɛd, -z
AM 'dɛθˌbɛd, -z

deathblow
BR 'dɛθbləʊ, -z
AM 'dɛθˌbloʊ, -z

De'ath, DeAth
BR dɪ'aθ
AM di'ɑθ

deathless
BR 'dɛθləs
AM 'dɛθləs

deathlessly
BR 'dɛθləsli
AM 'dɛθləsli

deathlessness
BR 'dɛθləsnəs
AM 'dɛθləsnəs

deathlike
BR 'dɛθlʌɪk
AM 'dɛθˌlaɪk

deathliness
BR 'dɛθlmɪs
AM 'dɛθlinɪs

deathly
BR 'dɛθl|i, -ɪə(r), -ɪɪst
AM 'dɛθli, -ər, -ɪst

deathtrap
BR 'dɛθtrap, -s
AM 'dɛθˌtræp, -s

deathwatch
BR 'dɛθwɒtʃ
AM 'dɛθˌwɑtʃ, 'dɛθˌwɔtʃ

deattribute
BR ˌdiːə'trɪbjuːt, -s, -ɪŋ, -ɪd
AM ˌdiə'trɪbjuˌt, -ts, -dɪŋ, -dəd

deattribution
BR dɪˌatrɪ'bjuːʃn, ˌdiːatrɪ'bjuːʃn, -z
AM diˌætrə'bjuʃən, -z

Deauville
BR 'dəʊvɪl
AM 'doʊ,vɪl
deb
BR dɛb, -z
AM dɛb, -z
débâcle
BR deɪ'bɑːkl, dɪ'bɑːkl,
-z
AM də'bækəl,
də'bakəl, 'dɛbəkəl, -z
debag
BR ,diː'bag, -z, -ɪŋ, -d
AM di'bæg, -z, -ɪŋ, -d
debar
BR dɪ'bɑː(r),
(,)diː'bɑː(r), -z, -ɪŋ, -d
AM di'bɑr, -z, -ɪŋ, -d
debark
BR dɪ'bɑːk, ,diː'bɑːk, -s,
-ɪŋ, -t
AM di'bark, -s, -ɪŋ, -t
debarkation
BR ,diːbɑː'keɪʃn, -z
AM ,dibɑr'keɪʃən, -z
debarkment
BR dɪ'bɑːkm(ə)nt,
,diː'bɑːkm(ə)nt, -s
AM di'barkmənt, -s
debase
BR dɪ'beɪs, -ɪz, -ɪŋ, -t
AM di'beɪs, də'beɪs, -ɪz,
-ɪŋ, -t
debasement
BR dɪ'beɪsm(ə)nt
AM di'beɪsmənt,
də'beɪsmənt
debaser
BR dɪ'beɪsə(r), -z
AM di'beɪsər,
də'beɪsər, -z
debatable
BR dɪ'beɪtəbl
AM də'beɪdəbəl,
di'beɪdəbəl
debatably
BR dɪ'beɪtəbli
AM də'beɪdəbli,
di'beɪdəbli
debate
BR dɪ'beɪt, -s, -ɪŋ, -ɪd
AM də'beɪlt, di'beɪlt, -ts,
-dɪŋ, -dɪd
debater
BR dɪ'beɪtə(r), -z
AM də'beɪdər,
di'beɪdər, -z
debauch
BR dɪ'bɔːtʃ, -ɪz, -ɪŋ, -t
AM di'bɑtʃ, di'bɔtʃ,
di'batʃ, də'batʃ, -əz,
-ɪŋ, -t
debauchee
BR ,debɔː'(t)ʃiː,
,dɪbɔː'(t)ʃiː,
dɪ,bɔː'(t)ʃiː, -z
AM də,bɔ'tʃi, də,ba'tʃi,
di,bɔ'tʃi, di,bɔ'tʃi, -z

debaucher
BR dɪ'bɔːtʃə(r), -z
AM də'bɔtʃər,
di'bɔtʃər, di'batʃər,
də'batʃər, -z
debauchery
BR dɪ'bɔːtʃ(ə)r|i, -ɪz
AM də'bɔtʃəri,
di'bɔtʃ(ə)ri,
di'batʃ(ə)ri,
də'batʃəri, -z
Debbie
BR 'dɛbi
AM 'dɛbi
debeak
BR ,diː'biːk, -s, -ɪŋ, -t
AM di'bik, -s, -ɪŋ, -t
de Beauvoir
BR də ,bəʊv'wɑː(r)
AM də ,boʊv'wɑr
De Beers
BR də 'bɪəz
AM də 'bɪ(ə)rz
Debenhams
BR 'dɛbənəmz,
'dɛbnəmz
AM 'dɛbənəmz
debenture
BR dɪ'ben(t)ʃə(r), -z
AM də'bɛntʃər,
di'bɛntʃər, -z
debilitate
BR dɪ,bɪlɪteɪt, -s, -ɪŋ, -ɪd
AM də'bɪlə,teɪ|t,
di'bɪlə,teɪ|t, -ts, -dɪŋ,
-dɪd
debilitatingly
BR dɪ,bɪlɪteɪtɪŋli
AM də'bɪlə,teɪdɪŋli,
di'bɪlə,teɪdɪŋli
debilitation
BR dɪ,bɪlɪ'teɪʃn
AM də,bɪlə'teɪʃən,
di,bɪlə'teɪʃən
debilitative
BR dɪ'bɪlɪtətɪv
AM də'bɪlə,teɪdɪv,
di'bɪlə,teɪdɪv
debility
BR dɪ'bɪlɪt|i, -ɪz
AM də'bɪlɪdi, -z
debit
BR 'dɛb|ɪt, -ɪts, -ɪtɪŋ,
-ɪtɪd
AM 'dɛbɪ|t, -ts, -dɪŋ, -dɪd
debonair
BR ,dɛbə'nɛː(r)
AM ,dɛbə'nɛ(ə)r
debonaire
BR ,dɛbə'nɛː(r)
AM ,dɛbə'nɛ(ə)r
debonairly
BR ,dɛbə'nɛːli
AM ,dɛbə'nɛrli
de-bond
BR ,diː'bɒnd, -z, -ɪŋ, -ɪd
AM di'band, -z, -ɪŋ, -əd

de-bonder
BR ,diː'bɒndə(r), -z
AM di'bandər, -z
debone
BR ,diː'bəʊn, -z, -ɪŋ, -d
AM ,di'boʊn, -z, -ɪŋ, -d
Deborah
BR 'dɛb(ə)rə(r)
AM 'dɛb(ə)rə
debouch
BR dɪ'baʊtʃ, dɪ'buːʃ,
(,)diː'baʊtʃ, (,)diː'buːʃ,
-ɪz, -ɪŋ, -t
AM di'buʃ, di'buʃ,
də'baʊtʃ, di'baʊtʃ, -əz,
-ɪŋ, -t
debouchment
BR dɪ'baʊtʃm(ə)nt,
dɪ'buːʃm(ə)nt,
(,)diː'baʊtʃm(ə)nt,
(,)diː'buːʃm(ə)nt
AM də'buʃmənt,
di'buʃmənt,
də'baʊtʃmənt,
di'baʊtʃmənt
Debra
BR 'dɛbrə(r)
AM 'dɛbrə
Debrett
BR də'brɛt
AM də'brɛt
debridement
BR der'briːdmɒ̃,
dɪ'briːdm(ə)nt
AM də'bridmənt,
der'bridmənt
debrief
BR ,diː'briːf, -s, -ɪŋ, -t
AM di'brif, ,də'brif, -s,
-ɪŋ, -t
debriefing
BR ,diː'briːfɪŋ, -z
AM di'brifɪŋ,
,də'brifɪŋ, -z
débris
BR 'debriː, 'deɪbriː
AM də'bri, 'der'bri
debt
BR dɛt, -s
AM dɛt, -s
debtor
BR 'dɛtə(r), -z
AM 'dɛdər, -z
debug
BR ,diː'bʌg, -z, -ɪŋ, -d
AM ,di'bəg, -z, -ɪŋ, -d
debugger
BR ,diː'bʌgə(r), -z
AM ,di'bəgər, -z
debunk
BR (,)diː'bʌŋ|k, -ks,
-kɪŋ, -(k)t
AM ,di'bəŋ|k, -ks, -kɪŋ,
-(k)t
debunker
BR (,)diː'bʌŋkə(r), -z
AM ,di'bəŋkər, -z

debus
BR ,diː'bʌs, -ɪz, -ɪŋ, -t
AM də'bəs, di'bəs, -əz,
-ɪŋ, -t
Debussy
BR də'b(j)uːsi
AM ,dɛbjʊ'si
début
BR 'dɛbjuː, 'deɪbjuː, -z
-ɪŋ, -d
AM der'bju, 'der,bju, -z,
-ɪŋ, -d
débutant
BR 'dɛbjʊtɑːnt, -s
AM 'dɛbju,tant,
'dɛbjə,tant, -s
débutante
BR 'dɛbjʊtɑːnt, -s
AM 'dɛbju,tant,
'dɛbjə,tant, -s
DEC
BR dɛk
AM dɛk
decadal
BR 'dɛkədl
AM 'dɛkədəl
decade
BR 'dɛkeɪd, dɪ'keɪd, -z
AM 'dɛ,keɪd, -z
decadence
BR 'dɛkəd(ə)ns
AM 'dɛkədns
decadent
BR 'dɛkəd(ə)nt, -s
AM 'dɛkəd(ə)nt, -s
decadentism
BR 'dɛkəd(ə)ntɪz(ə)m
AM 'dɛkəd(ə)n,tɪzəm
decadently
BR 'dɛkəd(ə)ntli
AM 'dɛkəd(ə)ntli,
'dɛkədən(t)li
decadic
BR dɪ'kadɪk
AM də'kædɪk
decaf
BR 'diːkaf
AM 'di,kæf
decaffeinate
BR dɪ'kafɪneɪt,
dɪ'kafneɪt, -s, -ɪŋ, -ɪd
AM ,di'kæfə,neɪ|t,
də'kæfə,neɪ|t, -ts, -dɪŋ,
-dɪd
decagon
BR 'dɛkəg(ə)n,
'dɛkəgɒn, -z
AM 'dɛkə,gan, -z
decagonal
BR dɪ'kagənl, dɪ'kagn̩l
AM də'kægənəl
decagynous
BR dɪ'kadʒɪnəs,
dɛ'kadʒɪnəs
AM də'kædʒənəs
decahedra
BR ,dɛkə'hiːdrə(r)

AM ˌdɛkəˈhidrə

decahedral
BR ˌdɛkəˈhiːdr(ə)l
AM ˌdɛkəˈhidrəl

decahedron
BR ˌdɛkəˈhiːdr(ə)n, -z
AM ˌdɛkəˈhidrən, -z

decal
BR ˈdiːkal, dɪˈkal, -z
AM ˈdiˌkæl, dəˈkæl, -z

decalcification
BR diːˌkalsɪfɪˈkeɪʃn, diːˌkalsɪfrˈkeɪʃn
AM ˌdiˌkælsəfəˈkeɪʃən

decalcifier
BR diːˈkalsɪfʌɪə(r), -z, -ɪŋ, -d
AM ˌdiˈkælsəˌfaɪ(ə)r, -z, -ɪŋ, -d

decalcify
BR diːˈkalsɪfʌɪ, -z, -ɪŋ, -d
AM ˌdiˈkælsəˌfaɪ, -z, -ɪŋ, -d

decalcomania
BR ˌdiːkalkəˈmeɪnɪə(r), -z
AM ˌdiˌkælkəˈmeɪnɪə, -z

decaliter
BR ˈdɛkəˌliːtə(r), -z
AM ˈdɛkəˌlidər, -z

decalitre
BR ˈdɛkəˌliːtə(r), -z
AM ˈdɛkəˌlidər, -z

Decalogue
BR ˈdɛkəlɒg
AM ˈdɛkəˌlɔg, ˈdɛkəˌlag

Decameron
BR dɪˈkam(ə)rən, dɪˈkam(ə)rn,
AM dəˈkæmərən, dɪˈkæməˌran

decameter
BR ˈdɛkəˌmiːtə(r), -z
AM ˈdɛkəˌmidər, -z

decametre
BR ˈdɛkəˌmiːtə(r), -z
AM ˈdɛkəˌmidər, -z

decamp
BR diːˈkamp, dɪˈkamp, -s, -ɪŋ, -t
AM dɪˈkæmp, dəˈkæmp, -s, -ɪŋ, -t

decampment
BR diːˈkampm(ə)nt, dɪˈkampm(ə)nt
AM dɪˈkæmpmənt, dəˈkæmpmənt

decanal
BR dɪˈkeɪnl, ˈdɛkənl
AM ˌdəˈkeɪnəl, ˈdɛkənəl

decanally
BR dɪˈkeɪnļi, dɪˈkeɪnəli, ˈdɛkənļi, ˈdɛkənəli
AM ˌdəˈkeɪnəli, ˈdɛkənəli

decandrous
BR dɪˈkandrəs
AM dəˈkændrəs

decane
BR ˈdɛkeɪn
AM ˈdɛkeɪn

decani
BR dɪˈkeɪnʌɪ
AM dəˈkeɪˌnaɪ

decant
BR dɪˈkant, ˌdiːˈkant, -s, -ɪŋ, -ɪd
AM dəˈkæn|t, dɪˈkæn|t, -ts, -(t)ɪŋ, -(t)əd

decanter
BR dɪˈkantə(r), -z
AM dəˈkæn(t)ər, dɪˈkæn(t)ər, -z

decapitate
BR dɪˈkapɪteɪt, ˌ(ˌ)diːˈkapɪtert, -s, -ɪŋ, -ɪd
AM dəˈkæpəˌteɪ|t, dɪˈkæpəˌteɪ|t, -ts, -dɪŋ, -dɪd

decapitation
BR dɪˌkapɪˈteɪʃn, ˌdiːkapɪˈteɪʃn, -z
AM dəˌkæpəˈteɪʃən, dɪˌkæpəˈteɪʃən, -z

decapitator
BR dɪˈkapɪterrtə(r), ˌ(ˌ)diːˈkapɪterrtə(r), -z
AM dəˈkæpəˌteɪdər, dɪˈkæpəˌteɪdər, -z

decapod
BR ˈdɛkəpɒd, -z
AM ˈdɛkəˌpad, -z

decapodan
BR dɪˈkapəd(ə)n
AM dəˈkæpədən

decarbonisation
BR diːˌkɑːbənʌɪˈzeɪʃn, ˌdiːkɑːbˈnʌɪˈzeɪʃn
AM ˌdiˌkɑrbənəˈzeɪʃən, ˌdiˌkɑrbəˌnaɪˈzeɪʃən

decarbonise
BR ˌ(ˌ)diːˈkɑːbənʌɪz, ˌ(ˌ)diːˈkɑːbˌnʌɪz, -ɪz, -ɪŋ, -d
AM dɪˈkɑrbəˌnaɪz, -ɪz, -ɪŋ, -d

decarbonization
BR diːˌkɑːbənʌɪˈzeɪʃn, ˌdiːkɑːbˈnʌɪˈzeɪʃn, diːˌkɑːbənʌɪˈzeɪʃn, diːˌkɑːbˈnʌɪˈzeɪʃn
AM ˌdiˌkɑrbənəˈzeɪʃən, ˌdiˌkɑrbəˌnaɪˈzeɪʃən

decarbonize
BR ˌ(ˌ)diːˈkɑːbənʌɪz, ˌ(ˌ)diːˈkɑːbˌnʌɪz, -ɪz, -ɪŋ, -d
AM dɪˈkɑrbəˌnaɪz, -ɪz, -ɪŋ, -d

decastyle
BR ˈdɛkəstʌɪl, -z
AM ˈdɛkəˌstaɪl, -z

decasualisation
BR diːˌkaʒ(j)ʊəlʌɪˈzeɪʃn, ˌdiːkaʒ(j)ʊˈlʌɪˈzeɪʃn, ˌdiːkazjʊəlʌɪˈzeɪʃn, ˌdiːkazjʊˈlʌɪˈzeɪʃn, diːˌkaʒ(j)ʊəlʌɪˈzeɪʃn, diːˌkaʒ(j)ʊˈlʌɪˈzeɪʃn, diːˌkazjʊəlʌɪˈzeɪʃn, diːˌkazjʊˈlʌɪˈzeɪʃn
AM ˌdiˌkæʒ(ə)wˈ)ələˈzeɪʃən, ˌdiˌkæʒ(ə)wˈ)əˌlaɪˈzeɪʃən

decasualise
BR ˌ(ˌ)diːˈkaʒ(j)ʊəlʌɪz, ˌ(ˌ)diːˈkaʒ(j)ʊˈlʌɪz, ˌ(ˌ)diːˈkazjʊəlʌɪz, ˌ(ˌ)diːˈkazjʊˈlʌɪz, -ɪz, -ɪŋ, -d
AM ˌdiˈkæʒ(ə)wˈ)əˌlaɪz, -ɪz, -ɪŋ, -d

decasualization
BR diːˌkaʒ(j)ʊəlʌɪˈzeɪʃn, ˌdiːkaʒ(j)ʊˈlʌɪˈzeɪʃn, ˌdiːkazjʊəlʌɪˈzeɪʃn, diːˌkaʒ(j)ʊˈlʌɪˈzeɪʃn, diːˌkazjʊəlʌɪˈzeɪʃn, diːˌkazjʊˈlʌɪˈzeɪʃn
AM ˌdiˌkæʒ(ə)wˈ)ələˈzeɪʃən, ˌdiˌkæʒ(ə)wˈ)əˌlaɪˈzeɪʃən

decasualize
BR ˌ(ˌ)diːˈkaʒ(j)ʊəlʌɪz, ˌ(ˌ)diːˈkaʒ(j)ʊˈlʌɪz, ˌ(ˌ)diːˈkazjʊəlʌɪz, ˌ(ˌ)diːˈkazjʊˈlʌɪz, -ɪz, -ɪŋ, -d
AM ˌdiˈkæʒ(ə)wˈ)əˌlaɪz, -ɪz, -ɪŋ, -d

decasyllabic
BR ˌdɛkəsɪˈlabɪk
AM ˌdɛkəsɪˈlæbɪk

decasyllable
BR ˈdɛkəˌsɪləbl, ˌdɛkəˈsɪləbl, -z
AM ˈdɛkəˌsɪləbəl, -z

decathlete
BR dɪˈkaθliːt, -s
AM dəˈkæθ(ə)lit, dɪˈkæθ(ə)lit, -s

decathlon
BR dɪˈkaθlɒn, dɪˈkaθlən, -z
AM dəˈkæθ(ə)ˌlan, dɪˈkæθ(ə)ˌlan, dəˈkæθ(ə)lən, dɪˈkæθ(ə)lən, -z

Decatur
BR dɪˈkeɪtə(r)

AM dəˈkeɪdər, dɪˈkeɪdər

decay
BR dɪˈkeɪ, -z, -ɪŋ, -d
AM dəˈkeɪ, dɪˈkeɪ, -z, -ɪŋ, -d

decayable
BR dɪˈkeɪəbl
AM dəˈkeɪəbəl, dɪˈkeɪəbəl

Decca
BR ˈdɛkə(r)
AM ˈdɛkə

Deccan
BR ˈdɛk(ə)n
AM ˈdɛkən

decease
BR dɪˈsiːs, -ɪz, -ɪŋ, -t
AM dəˈsis, dɪˈsis, -ɪz, -ɪŋ, -t

decedent
BR dɪˈsiːdnt, -s
AM dəˈsidnt, dɪˈsidnt, -s

deceit
BR dɪˈsiːt
AM dəˈsit, dɪˈsit

deceitful
BR dɪˈsiːtf(ʊ)l
AM dəˈsitfəl, dɪˈsitfəl

deceitfully
BR dɪˈsiːtfəli, dɪˈsiːtfli
AM dəˈsitfəli, dɪˈsitfəli

deceitfulness
BR dɪˈsiːtf(ʊ)lnəs
AM dəˈsitfəlnəs, dɪˈsitfəlnəs

deceivable
BR dɪˈsiːvəbl
AM dəˈsivəbəl, dɪˈsivəbəl

deceive
BR dɪˈsiːv, -z, -ɪŋ, -d
AM dəˈsiv, dɪˈsiv, -z, -ɪŋ, -d

deceiver
BR dɪˈsiːvə(r), -z
AM dəˈsivər, dɪˈsivər, -z

decelerate
BR ˌdiːˈsɛlərert, dɪˈsɛlərert, -s, -ɪŋ, -ts, -dɪŋ, -dɪd
AM ˌdiˈsɛləˌreɪ|t, -ts, -dɪŋ, -dɪd

deceleration
BR ˌdiːsɛləˈreɪʃn, dɪˌsɛləˈreɪʃn
AM ˌdiˌsɛləˈreɪʃən, ˌdɪsɛləˈreɪʃən

decelerator
BR ˌdiːˈsɛlərertə(r), dɪˈsɛlərertə(r), -z
AM ˌdiˈsɛləˌreɪdər, -z

decelerometer
BR ˌdiːsɛləˈrɒmɪtə(r), -z
AM ˌdiˌsɛləˈramədər, -z

December
BR dɪˈsɛmbə(r), -z
AM dəˈsɛmbər,
di'sɛmbər, -z

Decembrist
BR dɪˈsɛmbrɪst, -s
AM dəˈsɛmbrəst,
di'sɛmbrəst, -s

decency
BR 'diːsn[s]i, -ɪz
AM 'disənsi, -z

decennia
BR dɪˈsɛnɪə(r)
AM dəˈsɛniə

decennial
BR dɪˈsɛnɪəl
AM dəˈsɛniəl

decennially
BR dɪˈsɛnɪəli
AM dəˈsɛniəli

decennium
BR dɪˈsɛnɪəm
AM dəˈsɛniəm

decent
BR 'diːsnt
AM 'disənt

decenter
BR diːˈsɛnt|ə(r), -əz,
-(ə)rɪŋ, -əd
AM diˈsɛn(t)ər, -z, -ɪŋ,
-d

decently
BR 'diːs(ə)ntli
AM 'disn(t)li

decentralisation
BR ˌdiːsɛntrəlAɪˈzeɪʃn,
ˌdiːsɛntrˌlAɪˈzeɪʃn,
diːˌsɛntrəlAɪˈzeɪʃn,
diːˌsɛntrˌlAɪˈzeɪʃn
AM 'diˌsɛntrələˈzeɪʃən,
'diˌsɛntrəˌlaɪˈzeɪʃən

decentralise
BR (ˌ)diːˈsɛntrəlAɪz,
(ˌ)diːˈsɛntrˌlAɪz, -ɪz,
-ɪŋ, -d
AM diˈsɛntrəˌlaɪz, -ɪz,
-ɪŋ, -d

decentralist
BR (ˌ)diːˈsɛntrəlɪst,
(ˌ)diːˈsɛntrˌlɪst, -s
AM diˈsɛntrələst, -s

decentralization
BR ˌdiːsɛntrəlAɪˈzeɪʃn,
ˌdiːsɛntrˌlAɪˈzeɪʃn,
diːˌsɛntrəlAɪˈzeɪʃn,
diːˌsɛntrˌlAɪˈzeɪʃn
AM 'diˌsɛntrələˈzeɪʃən,
'diˌsɛntrəˌlaɪˈzeɪʃən

decentralize
BR (ˌ)diːˈsɛntrəlAɪz,
(ˌ)diːˈsɛntrˌlAɪz, -ɪz,
-ɪŋ, -d
AM diˈsɛntrəˌlaɪz, -ɪz,
-ɪŋ, -d

decentre
BR ˌdiːˈsɛnt|ə(r), -əz,
-(ə)rɪŋ, -əd

AM ˌdiˈsɛn(t)|ər, -ərz,
-(ə)rɪŋ, -ərd

deception
BR dɪˈsɛpʃn, -z
AM dəˈsɛpʃən,
di'sɛpʃən, -z

deceptive
BR dɪˈsɛptɪv
AM dəˈsɛptɪv, di'sɛptɪv

deceptively
BR dɪˈsɛptɪvli
AM dəˈsɛptəvli,
di'sɛptəvli

deceptiveness
BR dɪˈsɛptɪvnɪs
AM dəˈsɛptɪvnɪs,
di'sɛptɪvnɪs

decerebrate
BR ˌdiːˈsɛrɪbreɪt, -s, -ɪŋ,
-ɪd
AM ˌdiˈsɛrəˌbreɪ|t, -ts,
-dɪŋ, -dɪd

decertify
BR (ˌ)diːˈsəːtɪfAɪ, -z, -ɪŋ,
-d
AM diˈsərdəˌfaɪ, -z, -ɪŋ,
-d

dechlorinate
BR (ˌ)diːˈklɒrɪneɪt, -s,
-ɪŋ, -ɪd
AM diˈklɔrəˌneɪ|t, -ts,
-dɪŋ, -dɪd

dechlorination
BR ˌdiːklɒrɪˈneɪʃn, -z
AM ˌdiˌklɔrəˈneɪʃən, -z

dechristianization
BR ˌdiːkrɪstʃənAɪˈzeɪʃn,
ˌdiːkrɪstʃˌnAɪˈzeɪʃn
AM diˌkrɪstʃənəˈzeɪ-
ʃən,
diˌkrɪstʃəˌnaɪˈzeɪʃən

dechristianize
BR (ˌ)diːˈkrɪstʃənAɪz,
(ˌ)diːˈkrɪstʃ ŋAɪz, -ɪz,
-ɪŋ, -d
AM diˈkrɪstʃəˌnaɪz, -ɪz,
-ɪŋ, -d

Decian
BR 'diːʃɪən
AM 'diʃ(i)ən

decibel
BR 'dɛsɪb(ɛ)l, -z
AM 'dɛsəbəl, 'dɛsəˌbɛl,
-z

decidable
BR dɪˈsAɪdəbl
AM dəˈsaɪdəbəl,
di'saɪdəbəl

decide
BR dɪˈsAɪd, -z, -ɪŋ, -ɪd
AM dəˈsaɪd, di'saɪd, -z,
-ɪŋ, -ɪd

decidedly
BR dɪˈsAɪdɪdli
AM dəˈsaɪdɪdli,
di'saɪdɪdli

decidedness
BR dɪˈsAɪdɪdnɪs

AM dəˈsaɪdɪdnɪs,
di'saɪdɪdnɪs

decider
BR dɪˈsAɪdə(r), -z
AM dəˈsaɪdər,
di'saɪdər, -z

deciduous
BR dɪˈsɪdjuəs,
dɪˈsɪdʒuəs
AM dɪˈsɪdʒəwəs,
di'sɪdʒəwəs

deciduousness
BR dɪˈsɪdjuəsnəs,
dɪˈsɪdʒuəsnəs
AM dɪˈsɪdʒəwəsnəs,
di'sɪdʒəwəsnəs

decigram
BR 'dɛsɪgram, -z
AM 'dɛsəˌgræm, -z

decigramme
BR 'dɛsɪgram, -z
AM 'dɛsəˌgræm, -z

decile
BR 'dɛsAɪl, 'dɛsɪl, -z
AM 'dɛˌsaɪl, -z

deciliter
BR 'dɛsɪˌliːtə(r), -z
AM 'dɛsɪˌlidər, -z

decilitre
BR 'dɛsɪˌliːtə(r), -z
AM 'dɛsəˌlidər, -z

decimal
BR 'dɛsɪml, -z
AM 'dɛs(ə)məl, -z

decimalisation
BR ˌdɛsɪməlAɪˈzeɪʃn,
ˌdɛsɪmlˌAɪˈzeɪʃn
AM ˌdɛs(ə)mələˈzeɪʃən,
ˌdɛs(ə)məˌlaɪˈzeɪʃən

decimalise
BR 'dɛsɪməlAɪz,
'dɛsɪmlˌAɪz, -ɪz, -ɪŋ, -d
AM 'dɛs(ə)məˌlaɪz, -ɪz,
-ɪŋ, -d

decimalization
BR ˌdɛsɪməlAɪˈzeɪʃn,
ˌdɛsɪmlˌAɪˈzeɪʃn
AM ˌdɛs(ə)mələˈzeɪʃən,
ˌdɛs(ə)məˌlaɪˈzeɪʃən

decimalize
BR 'dɛsɪməlAɪz,
'dɛsɪmlˌAɪz, -ɪz, -ɪŋ, -d
AM 'dɛsəməˌlaɪz, -ɪz,
-ɪŋ, -d

decimally
BR 'dɛsɪməli, 'dɛsɪmˌli
AM 'dɛsəməli

decimate
BR 'dɛsɪmeɪt, -s, -ɪŋ, -ɪd
AM 'dɛsəˌmeɪ|t, -ts,
-dɪŋ, -dɪd

decimation
BR ˌdɛsɪˈmeɪʃn
AM ˌdɛsəˈmeɪʃən

decimator
BR 'dɛsɪmeɪtə(r), -z
AM 'dɛsəˌmeɪdər, -z

decimeter
BR 'dɛsɪˌmiːtə(r), -z
AM 'dɛsəˌmidər, -z

decimetre
BR 'dɛsɪˌmiːtə(r), -z
AM 'dɛsəˌmidər, -z

Decimus
BR 'dɛsɪməs
AM 'dɛsəməs

decipher
BR dɪˈsAɪʃə(r), -əz,
-(ə)rɪŋ, -əd
AM dəˈsaɪʃər,
di'saɪfər, -ərz, -(ə)rɪŋ,
-ərd

decipherable
BR dɪˈsAɪf(ə)rəbl
AM dəˈsaɪf(ə)rəbəl,
di'saɪf(ə)rəbəl

decipherment
BR dɪˈsAɪfəm(ə)nt
AM dəˈsaɪfərmənt,
di'saɪfərmənt

decision
BR dɪˈsɪʒn, -z
AM dəˈsɪʒən, di'siʒən,
-z

decisive
BR dɪˈsAɪsɪv
AM dəˈsaɪsɪv, di'saɪsɪv

decisively
BR dɪˈsAɪsɪvli
AM dəˈsaɪsɪvli,
di'saɪsɪvli

decisiveness
BR dɪˈsAɪsɪvnɪs
AM dəˈsaɪsɪvnɪs,
di'saɪsɪvnɪs

deck
BR dɛk, -s, -ɪŋ, -t
AM dɛk, -s, -ɪŋ, -t

deckchair
BR 'dɛktʃɛː(r), -z
AM 'dɛkˌtʃɛ(ə)r, -z

decker
BR 'dɛkə(r), -z
AM 'dɛkər, -z

deckhand
BR 'dɛkhand, -z
AM 'dɛkˌ(h)ænd, -z

deckhouse
BR 'dɛkhaʊ|s, -zɪz
AM 'dɛkˌ(h)aʊ|s, -zəz

deckle
BR 'dɛkl, -d
AM 'dɛkəl, -d

declaim
BR dɪˈkleɪm, -z, -ɪŋ, -d
AM dəˈkleɪm, di'kleɪm,
-z, -ɪŋ, -d

declaimer
BR dɪˈkleɪmə(r), -z
AM dəˈkleɪmər,
di'kleɪmər, -z

declamation
BR ˌdɛkləˈmeɪʃn, -z
AM ˌdɛkləˈmeɪʃən, -z

declamatory
BR dɪˈklamət(ə)ri
AM dəˈklæməˌtori,
diˈklæməˌtori

Declan
BR ˈdɛklən
AM ˈdɛklən

declarable
BR dɪˈklɛːrəbl
AM dəˈklɛrəbəl,
diˈklɛrəbəl

declarant
BR dɪˈklɛːrənt,
dɪˈklɛːrn̩t, -s
AM dəˈklɛrənt,
diˈklɛrənt, -s

declaration
BR ˌdɛkləˈreɪʃn, -z
AM ˌdɛkləˈreɪʃən, -z

declarative
BR dɪˈklarətɪv, -z
AM dəˈklɛrədɪv, -z

declaratively
BR dɪˈklarətɪvli
AM dəˈklɛrədɪvli

declarativeness
BR dɪˈklarətɪvnɪs
AM dəˈklɛrədɪvnɪs

declaratory
BR dɪˈklarət(ə)ri
AM dəˈklɛrəˌtori

declare
BR dɪˈklɛː(r), -z, -ɪŋ, -d
AM dəˈklɛ(ə)r,
diˈklɛ(ə)r, -z, -ɪŋ, -d

declaredly
BR dɪˈklɛːrɪdli
AM dəˈklɛrədli

declarer
BR dɪˈklɛːrə(r), -z
AM dəˈklɛrər,
diˈklɛrər, -z

declass
BR (ˌ)diːˈklɑːs,
(ˌ)diːˈklas, -ɪz, -ɪŋ, -t
AM diˈklæs, dəˈklæs,
-əz, -ɪŋ, -t

déclassé
BR deɪˈklaseɪ,
ˌdeɪklaˈseɪ,
AM ˌdeɪklaˈseɪ

déclassée
BR deɪˈklaseɪ,
ˌdeɪklaˈseɪ
AM ˌdeɪklaˈseɪ

declassification
BR ˌdiːklasɪfɪˈkeɪʃn,
diːˌklasɪfɪˈkeɪʃn
AM diˌklæsəfəˈkeɪʃən

declassify
BR (ˌ)diːˈklasɪfʌɪ, -z,
-ɪŋ, -d
AM diˈklæsəˌfaɪ, -z, -ɪŋ,
-d

de-claw
BR ˌdiːˈklɔː(r), -z, -ɪŋ, -d
AM ˌdiˈklɔ, ˌdiˈklɑ, -z,
-ɪŋ, -d

declension
BR dɪˈklɛnʃn, -z
AM dəˈklɛn(t)ʃən,
diˈklɛn(t)ʃən, -z

declensional
BR dɪˈklɛnʃn(ə)l,
dɪˈklɛnʃən(ə)l
AM dəˈklɛn(t)ʃ(ə)nəl,
diˈklɛn(t)ʃ(ə)nəl

declinable
BR dɪˈklʌɪnəbl
AM dəˈklaɪnəbəl,
diˈklaɪnəbəl

declination
BR ˌdɛklɪˈneɪʃn, -z
AM ˌdɛkləˈneɪʃən, -z

declinational
BR ˌdɛklɪˈneɪʃn(ə)l,
ˌdɛklɪˈneɪʃən(ə)l
AM ˌdɛkləˈneɪʃ(ə)nəl

decline
BR dɪˈklʌɪn, -z, -ɪŋ, -d
AM dəˈklaɪn, diˈklaɪn,
-z, -ɪŋ, -d

decliner
BR dɪˈklʌɪnə(r), -z
AM dəˈklaɪnər,
diˈklaɪnər, -z

declinometer
BR ˌdɛklɪˈnɒmɪtə(r), -z
AM ˌdɛkləˈnamədər, -z

declivitous
BR dɪˈklɪvɪtəs
AM dəˈklɪvədəs

declivity
BR dɪˈklɪvɪt|i, -iz
AM dəˈklɪvɪdi, -z

declutch
BR (ˌ)diːˈklʌtʃ,
dɪˈklʌtʃ, -ɪz, -ɪŋ, -t
AM diˈklətʃ, -əz, -ɪŋ, -t

deco
BR ˈdɛkəʊ
AM ˈdɛkoʊ

decoct
BR dɪˈkɒkt, -s, -ɪŋ, -ɪd
AM dəˈkak|(t),
diˈkak|(t), -(t)s, -ɪŋ,
-ɪd

decoction
BR dɪˈkɒkʃn, -z
AM dəˈkakʃən,
diˈkakʃən, -z

decodable
BR (ˌ)diːˈkəʊdəbl,
dɪˈkəʊdəbl
AM diˈkoʊdəbəl,
dəˈkoʊdəbəl

decode
BR (ˌ)diːˈkəʊd, dɪˈkəʊd,
-z, -ɪŋ, -ɪd
AM ˌdiˈkoʊd, -z, -ɪŋ, -əd

decoder
BR (ˌ)diːˈkəʊdə(r),
dɪˈkəʊdə(r), -z
AM ˌdiˈkoʊdər,
dəˈkoʊdər, -z

decoke¹
noun
BR ˈdiːkəʊk, -s
AM ˈdiˌkoʊk, -s

decoke²
verb
BR ˌdiːˈkəʊk, dɪˈkəʊk,
-s, -ɪŋ, -t
AM ˌdiˈkoʊk, dəˈkoʊk,
-s, -ɪŋ, -t

decollate
BR ˈdɛkəleɪt, -s, -ɪŋ, -ɪd
AM ˈdɛkəˌleɪ|t, -ts, -dɪŋ,
-dɪd

decollation
BR ˌdɛkəˈleɪʃn, -z
AM ˌdɛkəˈleɪʃən, -z

décolletage
BR ˌdeɪkɒl(ɪ)ˈtɑːʒ,
deɪˈkɒltɑːʒ
AM deɪˈkɑləˌtɑʒ,
dɛˈkɑləˌtɑʒ,
deɪˈkɔləˌtɑʒ,
dɛˈkɔləˌtɑʒ

décolleté
BR deɪˈkɒl(ɪ)teɪ,
ˌdeɪkɒl(ɪ)ˈteɪ
AM deɪˈkɑləˈteɪ,
dɛˈkɑləˈteɪ,
deɪˈkɔləˈteɪ,
dɛˈkɔləˈteɪ

décolletée
BR deɪˈkɒl(ɪ)teɪ,
ˌdeɪkɒl(ɪ)ˈteɪ
AM deɪˈkɑləˈteɪ,
dɛˈkɑləˈteɪ,
deɪˈkɔləˈteɪ,
dɛˈkɔləˈteɪ

decolonisation
BR ˌdiːkɒlənʌɪˈzeɪʃn,
diːˌkɒlənʌɪˈzeɪʃn
AM diˌkalənəˈzeɪʃən,
diˌkaləˌnaɪˈzeɪʃən

decolonise
BR (ˌ)diːˈkɒlənʌɪz, -ɪz,
-ɪŋ, -d
AM diˈkaləˌnaɪz, -ɪz,
-ɪŋ, -d

decolonization
BR ˌdiːkɒlənʌɪˈzeɪʃn,
diːˌkɒlənʌɪˈzeɪʃn
AM diˌkalənəˈzeɪʃən,
diˌkaləˌnaɪˈzeɪʃən

decolonize
BR (ˌ)diːˈkɒlənʌɪz, -ɪz,
-ɪŋ, -d
AM diˈkaləˌnaɪz, -ɪz,
-ɪŋ, -d

decolorant
BR ˌdiːˈkʌl(ə)rənt,
ˌdiːˈkʌl(ə)rn̩t, -s
AM diˈkələrənt, -s

decolorisation
BR ˌdiːkʌlərʌɪˈzeɪʃn,
diːˌkʌlərʌɪˈzeɪʃn
AM diˌkələrəˈzeɪʃən,
diˌkələˌraɪˈzeɪʃən

decolorise
BR ˌdiːˈkʌlərʌɪz, -ɪz,
-ɪŋ, -d
AM diˈkələˌraɪz, -ɪz, -ɪŋ,
-d

decolorization
BR ˌdiːkʌlərʌɪˈzeɪʃn,
diːˌkʌlərʌɪˈzeɪʃn
AM diˌkələrəˈzeɪʃən,
diˌkələˌraɪˈzeɪʃən

decolorize
BR ˌdiːˈkʌlərʌɪz, -ɪz,
-ɪŋ, -d
AM diˈkələˌraɪz, -ɪz, -ɪŋ,
-d

decommission
BR ˌdiːkəˈmɪʃ|n, -nz,
-n̩ɪŋ \-n̩ŋ, -nd
AM ˌdikəˈmɪʃən, -z, -ɪŋ,
-d

decommunisation
BR ˌdiːkɒmjənʌɪˈzeɪʃn,
diːˌkɒmjənʌɪˈzeɪʃn
AM ˌdiˌkamjunəˈzeɪʃən,
ˌdiˌkamjuˌnaɪˈzeɪʃən

decommunise
BR ˌdiːˈkɒmjənʌɪz, -ɪz,
-ɪŋ, -d
AM ˌdiˈkamjuˌnaɪz, -ɪz,
-ɪŋ, -d

decommunization
BR ˌdiːkɒmjənʌɪˈzeɪʃn,
diːˌkɒmjənʌɪˈzeɪʃn
AM ˌdiˌkamjunəˈzeɪʃən,
ˌdiˌkamjuˌnaɪˈzeɪʃən

decommunize
BR ˌdiːˈkɒmjənʌɪz, -ɪz,
-ɪŋ, -d
AM ˌdiˈkamjuˌnaɪz, -ɪz,
-ɪŋ, -d

decomposable
BR ˌdiːkəmˈpəʊzəbl
AM ˌdikəmˈpoʊzəbəl

decompose
BR ˌdiːkəmˈpəʊz, -ɪz,
-ɪŋ, -d
AM ˌdikəmˈpoʊz, -əz,
-ɪŋ, -d

decomposition
BR ˌdiːkɒmpəˈzɪʃn, -z
AM ˌdiˌkampəˈzɪʃən, -z

decompound¹
noun
BR ˈdiːˌkɒmpaʊnd, -z
AM ˌdiˈkamˌpaʊnd, -z

decompound²
verb
BR ˌdiːkəmˈpaʊnd, -z,
-ɪŋ, -ɪd
AM ˌdikəmˈpaʊnd, -z,
-ɪŋ, -əd

decompress
BR ˌdiːkəmˈprɛs, -ɪz,
-ɪŋ, -t
AM ˌdikəmˈprɛs, -əz,
-ɪŋ, -t

decompression
BR ˌdiːkəmˈprɛʃn

AM ˈdiːkəmˈprɛʃən

decompressor
BR ˌdiːkəmˈprɛsə(r), -z
AM ˈdiːkəmˈprɛsər, -z

decongestant
BR ˌdiːk(ə)nˈdʒɛst(ə)nt, -s
AM ˌdiːkənˈdʒɛstənt, -s

deconsecrate
BR ˌdiːˈkɒnsɪkreɪt, -s, -ɪŋ, -ɪd
AM diːˈkɑːnsəˌkreɪt, -ts, -dɪŋ, -dɪd

deconsecration
BR ˌdiːkɒnsɪˈkreɪʃn, diːˌkɒnsɪˈkreɪʃn
AM ˌdiːkɑːnsəˈkreɪʃən

deconstruct
BR ˌdiːk(ə)nˈstrʌkt, -s, -ɪŋ, -ɪd
AM ˌdiːkənˈstrək|(t), -(t)s, -tɪŋ, -təd

deconstruction
BR ˌdiːk(ə)nˈstrʌkʃn
AM ˌdiːkənˈstrəkʃən

deconstructionism
BR ˌdiːk(ə)nˈstrʌkʃn-ɪz(ə)m, ˌdiːk(ə)nˈstrʌkʃən-ɪz(ə)m
AM ˌdiːk(ə)nˈstrəkʃə-ˌnɪzəm

deconstructionist
BR ˌdiːk(ə)nˈstrʌkʃnɪst, ˌdiːk(ə)nˈstrʌkʃənɪst, -s
AM ˌdiːkənˈstrəkʃənəst, -s

deconstructive
BR ˌdiːk(ə)nˈstrʌktɪv
AM ˌdiːkənˈstrəktɪv

decontaminate
BR ˌdiːk(ə)nˈtæmɪneɪt, -s, -ɪŋ, -ɪd
AM ˌdiːkənˈtæməˌneɪ|t, -ts, -dɪŋ, -dɪd

decontamination
BR ˌdiːk(ə)ntæmɪˈneɪʃn
AM ˈdiːkənˌtæməˈneɪʃən

decontextualise
BR ˌdiːk(ə)nˈtɛkstjʊəl-ʌɪz, ˌdiːk(ə)nˈtɛkstjəlʌɪz, ˌdiːk(ə)nˈtɛkstʃʊəlʌɪz, ˌdiːk(ə)nˈtɛkstʃəlʌɪz, ˌdiːk(ə)nˈtɛkstʃlʌɪz, -ɪz, -ɪŋ, -d
AM ˌdiːkənˈtɛks(t)ʃ(əw)-əˌlaɪz, -ɪz, -ɪŋ, -d

decontextualize
BR ˌdiːk(ə)nˈtɛkstjʊəl-ʌɪz, ˌdiːk(ə)nˈtɛkstjəlʌɪz, ˌdiːk(ə)nˈtɛkstʃʊəlʌɪz, ˌdiːk(ə)nˈtɛkstʃəlʌɪz, ˌdiːk(ə)nˈtɛkstʃlʌɪz, -ɪz, -ɪŋ, -d

AM ˌdiːkənˈtɛks(t)ʃ(əw)-əˌlaɪz, -ɪz, -ɪŋ, -d

decontrol
BR ˌdiːk(ə)nˈtrəʊl, -z, -ɪŋ, -d
AM ˌdiːkənˈtroʊl, -z, -ɪŋ, -d

décor
BR ˈdeɪkɔː(r), ˈdɛkɔː(r), -z
AM ˈdeɪˈkɔ(ə)r, deɪˈkɔ(ə)r, -z

decorate
BR ˈdɛkəreɪt, -s, -ɪŋ, -ɪd
AM ˈdɛkəˌreɪ|t, -ts, -dɪŋ, -dɪd

decoration
BR ˌdɛkəˈreɪʃn, -z
AM ˌdɛkəˈreɪʃən, -z

decorative
BR ˈdɛk(ə)rətɪv
AM ˈdɛk(ə)rədɪv, ˈdɛkəˌreɪdɪv

decoratively
BR ˈdɛk(ə)rətɪvli
AM ˈdɛk(ə)rədɪvnli, ˈdɛkəˌreɪdɪvli

decorativeness
BR ˈdɛk(ə)rətɪvnɪs
AM ˈdɛk(ə)rədɪvnɪs, ˈdɛkəˌreɪdɪvnɪs

decorator
BR ˈdɛkəreɪtə(r), -z
AM ˈdɛkəˌreɪdər, -z

decorous
BR ˈdɛk(ə)rəs
AM ˈdɛk(ə)rəs

decorously
BR ˈdɛk(ə)rəsli
AM ˈdɛk(ə)rəsli

decorousness
BR ˈdɛk(ə)rəsnəs
AM ˈdɛk(ə)rəsnəs

decorticate
BR ˌdiːˈkɔːtɪkeɪt, -s, -ɪŋ, -ɪd
AM diːˈkɔrdəˌkeɪ|t, dəˈkɔrdəˌkeɪ|t, -ts, -dɪŋ, -dɪd

decortication
BR ˌdiːkɔːtɪˈkeɪʃn
AM diːˌkɔrdəˈkeɪʃən

decorum
BR dɪˈkɔːrəm
AM dəˈkɔrəm, dɪˈkɔrəm

découpage
BR ˌdeɪkuːˈpɑːʒ, ˌdeɪkuːˈpɑːʒ
AM ˌdeɪkuːˈpɑʒ

decouple
BR (ˌ)diːˈkʌp|l, -lz, -l̩ŋ \-lɪŋ, -ld
AM diːˈkəpəl, -z, -ɪŋ, -d

De Courcy
BR də ˈkɔːsi, + ˈkəːsi, + ˈkʊəsi

AM də ˈkɜrsi

decoy¹
noun
BR ˈdiːkɔɪ, -z
AM ˈdiːˌkɔɪ, -z

decoy²
verb
BR dɪˈkɔɪ, -z, -ɪŋ, -d
AM dəˈkɔɪ, diːˈkɔɪ, -z, -ɪŋ, -d

decrease¹
noun
BR ˈdiːkriːs, -ɪz
AM dəˈkris, ˈdiˌkris, -ɪz

decrease²
verb
BR dɪˈkriːs, -ɪz, -ɪŋ, -t
AM dəˈkris, diˈkris, -ɪz, -ɪŋ, -t

decreasingly
BR dɪˈkriːsɪŋli
AM dəˈkrisɪŋli, diˈkrisɪŋli

decree
BR dɪˈkriː, -z, -ɪŋ, -d
AM dəˈkri, diˈkri, -z, -ɪŋ, -d

decrement¹
noun
BR ˈdɛkrɪm(ə)nt, -s
AM ˈdɛkrəmənt, -s

decrement²
verb
BR ˈdɛkrɪmɛnt, -s, -ɪŋ, -ɪd
AM ˈdɛkrəˌmen|t, -ts, -(t)ɪŋ, -(t)əd

decreolization
BR ˌdiːkriːəlʌɪˈzeɪʃn, diːˌkriːəlʌɪˈzeɪʃn
AM ˌdiˌkriːəˈzeɪʃən, ˌdiˌkriəˌlaɪˈzeɪʃən

decreolize
BR ˌdiːˈkriːəlʌɪz, -ɪz, -ɪŋ, -d
AM diːˈkriəˌlaɪz, -ɪz, -ɪŋ, -d

decrepit
BR dɪˈkrɛpɪt
AM dəˈkrɛpət, dɪˈkrəpət

decrepitate
BR dɪˈkrɛpɪteɪt, -s, -ɪŋ, -ɪd
AM dɪˈkrɛpəˌteɪ|t, -ts, -dɪŋ, -dɪd

decrepitation
BR dɪˌkrɛpɪˈteɪʃn
AM dəˌkrɛpəˈteɪʃən, dɪˌkrɛpəˈteɪʃən

decrepitness
BR dɪˈkrɛpɪtnɪs
AM dəˈkrɛpətnəs, dɪˈkrəpətnəs

decrepitude
BR dɪˈkrɛpɪtjuːd, dɪˈkrɛpɪtʃuːd

AM dəˈkrɛpəˌt(j)ud, dɪˈkrɛpəˌt(j)ud

decrescendo
BR ˌdiːkrɪˈʃendəʊ, -z
AM ˌdikrəˈʃendoʊ, -z

decrescent
BR dɪˈkrɛsnt
AM dəˈkrɛsənt, dɪˈkrɛsənt

decretal
BR dɪˈkriːtl
AM dəˈkridəl

decrial
BR dɪˈkrʌɪəl
AM dəˈkraɪəl, dɪˈkraɪəl

decrier
BR dɪˈkrʌɪə(r), -z
AM dəˈkraɪər, dɪˈkraɪər, -z

decriminalisation
BR diːˌkrɪmɪnəlʌɪˈzeɪʃn, ˌdiːkrɪmɪnlʌɪˈzeɪʃn, diːˌkrɪmɪnəlʌɪˈzeɪʃn, ˌdiːkrɪmɪnlʌɪˈzeɪʃn
AM ˌdiˌkrɪm(ə)nələˈzeɪʃən, ˌdiˌkrɪm(ə)nəˌlaɪˈzeɪʃən

decriminalise
BR (ˌ)diːˈkrɪmɪnəlʌɪz, (ˌ)diːˈkrɪmɪnl̩ʌɪz, -ɪz, -ɪŋ, -d
AM diːˈkrɪmənəlaɪz, -ɪz, -ɪŋ, -d

decriminalization
BR diːˌkrɪmɪnəlʌɪˈzeɪʃn, ˌdiːkrɪmɪnl̩ʌɪˈzeɪʃn, diːˌkrɪmɪnəlʌɪˈzeɪʃn, ˌdiːkrɪmɪnl̩ʌɪˈzeɪʃn
AM ˌdiˌkrɪm(ə)nələˈzeɪʃən, ˌdiˌkrɪm(ə)nəˌlaɪˈzeɪʃən

decriminalize
BR (ˌ)diːˈkrɪmɪnəlʌɪz, (ˌ)diːˈkrɪmɪnl̩ʌɪz, -ɪz, -ɪŋ, -d
AM diːˈkrɪmənəlaɪz, -ɪz, -ɪŋ, -d

decry
BR dɪˈkrʌɪ, -z, -ɪŋ, -d
AM dəˈkraɪ, diˈkraɪ, -z, -ɪŋ, -d

decrypt
BR (ˌ)diːˈkrɪpt, -s, -ɪŋ, -ɪd
AM diːˈkrɪpt, -s, -ɪŋ, -ɪd

decryption
BR (ˌ)diːˈkrɪpʃn
AM dəˈkrɪpʃən, dɪˈkrɪpʃən

decubitus
BR dɪˈkjuːbɪtəs
AM dəˈkjubədəs

decumbent
BR dɪˈkʌmb(ə)nt
AM dəˈkəmbənt, dɪˈkəmbənt

decuple
BR ˈdɛkjʊp|l, -lz, -lɪŋ \-lɪŋ, -ld

AM 'dɛkjəp|əl, -əlz,
-(ə)lɪŋ, -əld

decuplet
BR 'dɛkjʊplɪt, -s
AM 'dɛkjəplət, -s

decurvature
BR ˌdiːˈkəːvətʃə(r), -z
AM diˈkɚvətʃʊ(ə)r,
diˈkɚvətʃər, -z

decurve
BR ˌdiːˈkəːv, -z, -ɪŋ, -d
AM diˈkɚv, -z, -ɪŋ, -d

decussate
BR dɪˈkʌseɪt,
'dɛkəseɪt, -s, -ɪŋ, -ɪd
AM diˈkəsət,
'dɛkəˌseɪ|t, -ts, -dɪŋ,
-dɪd

decussation
BR ˌdɛkəˈseɪʃn
AM ˌdɛkəˈseɪʃən

dedans
BR dəˈdɒ̃, -z
AM dəˈdɑn(z), -z

dedicate
BR 'dɛdɪkeɪt, -s, -ɪŋ, -ɪd
AM 'dɛdəˌkeɪ|t, -ts, -dɪŋ,
-dɪd

dedicated
BR 'dɛdɪkeɪtɪd
AM 'dɛdəˌkeɪdɪd

dedicatedly
BR 'dɛdɪkeɪtɪdli
AM 'dɛdəˌkeɪdɪdli

dedicatee
BR ˌdɛdɪkəˈtiː, -z
AM ˌdɛdəkeɪˈti, -z

dedication
BR ˌdɛdɪˈkeɪʃn, -z
AM ˌdɛdəˈkeɪʃən, -z

dedicative
BR 'dɛdɪkətɪv
AM 'dɛdəkədɪv,
'dɛdəˌkeɪdɪv

dedicator
BR 'dɛdɪkeɪtə(r), -z
AM 'dɛdəˌkeɪdər, -z

dedicatory
BR 'dɛdɪkət(ə)ri,
'dɛdɪkeɪt(ə)ri
AM 'dɛdəkəˌtɔri

deduce
BR dɪˈdjuːs, dɪˈdʒuːs,
-ɪz, -ɪŋ, -t
AM dəˈd(j)us, diˈd(j)us,
-əz, -ɪŋ, -t

deducible
BR dɪˈdjuːsɪbl,
dɪˈdʒuːsɪbl
AM dəˈd(j)usəbəl,
diˈd(j)usəbəl

deduct
BR dɪˈdʌkt, -s, -ɪŋ, -ɪd
AM dəˈdək|(t),
diˈdək|(t), -(t)s, -tɪŋ,
-təd

deductibility
BR dɪˌdʌktɪˈbɪlɪti

AM dəˌdɛktəˈbɪlɪdi,
diˌdɛktəˈbɪlɪdi

deductible
BR dɪˈdʌktɪbl
AM dəˈdɛktəbəl,
diˈdɛktəbəl

deduction
BR dɪˈdʌkʃn, -z
AM dəˈdəkʃən,
diˈdəkʃən, -z

deductive
BR dɪˈdʌktɪv
AM dəˈdəktɪv,
diˈdəktɪv

deductively
BR dɪˈdʌktɪvli
AM dəˈdəktɪvli,
diˈdəktɪvli

Dee
BR diː
AM di

dee
BR diː, -z
AM di, -z

deed
BR diːd, -z
AM did, -z

deejay
BR ˌdiːˈdʒeɪ, -z
AM 'diˌdʒeɪ, -z

deem
BR diːm, -z, -ɪŋ, -d
AM dim, -z, -ɪŋ, -d

Deeming
BR 'diːmɪŋ
AM 'dimɪŋ

de-emphasise
BR ˌdiːˈɛmfəsaɪz, -ɪz,
-ɪŋ, -d
AM ˌdiˈɛmfəˌsaɪz, -ɪz,
-ɪŋ, -d

de-emphasize
BR ˌdiːˈɛmfəsaɪz, -ɪz,
-ɪŋ, -d
AM ˌdiˈɛmfəˌsaɪz, -ɪz,
-ɪŋ, -d

deemster
BR 'diːmstə(r), -z
AM 'dimstər, -z

deep
BR diːp, -ə(r), -ɪst
AM diːp, -ər, -əst

deepen
BR 'diːp|(ə)n, -(ə)nz,
-ənɪŋ \ -ŋ̩ɪŋ, -(ə)nd
AM 'dipən, -z, -ɪŋ, -d

deeping
BR 'diːpɪŋ
AM 'dipɪŋ

deeply
BR 'diːpli
AM 'dipli

deepness
BR 'diːpnɪs
AM 'dipnɪs

deer
BR dɪə(r)
AM dɪ(ə)r

Deere
BR dɪə(r)
AM dɪ(ə)r

deerfly
BR 'dɪəflʌɪ, -z
AM 'dɪrˌflaɪ, -z

deerhound
BR 'dɪəhaʊnd, -z
AM 'dɪrˌ(h)aʊnd, -z

deerskin
BR 'dɪəskɪn, -z
AM 'dɪrˌskɪn, -z

deerstalker
BR 'dɪəˌstɔːkə(r), -z
AM 'dɪrˌstɔkər,
'dɪrˌstakər, -z

de-escalate
BR (ˌ)diːˈeskəleɪt, -s,
-ɪŋ, -ɪd
AM ˌdiˈeskəˌleɪ|t, -ts,
-dɪŋ, -dɪd

de-escalation
BR (ˌ)diːˌeskəˈleɪʃn,
diːˌeskəˈleɪʃn
AM ˌdiˌeskəˈleɪʃən

Deeside
BR 'diːsʌɪd
AM 'diˌsaɪd

def
BR dɛf
AM dɛf

deface
BR dɪˈfeɪs, -ɪz, -ɪŋ, -t
AM dəˈfeɪs, diˈfeɪs, -ɪz,
-ɪŋ, -t

defaceable
BR dɪˈfeɪsəbl
AM dəˈfeɪsəbəl,
diˈfeɪsəbəl

defacement
BR dɪˈfeɪsm(ə)nt, -s
AM dəˈfeɪsmənt,
diˈfeɪsmənt, -s

defacer
BR dɪˈfeɪsə(r), -z
AM dəˈfeɪsər, diˈfeɪsər,
-z

de facto
BR ˌdeɪ ˈfaktəʊ
AM ˌdi ˈfæktoʊ, ˌdeɪ
ˈfæktoʊ, ˌdə ˈfæktoʊ

defalcate
BR 'diːfalkeɪt,
'diːfɔːlkeɪt, -s, -ɪŋ, -ɪd
AM dəˈfælˌkeɪ|t,
diˈfælˌkeɪ|t,
'diˌfælˌkeɪ|t,
dəˈfɔlˌkeɪ|t,
diˈfɔlˌkeɪ|t,
dəˈfalˌkeɪ|t,
'diˌfalˌkeɪ|t, -ts, -dɪŋ,
-dɪd

defalcation
BR ˌdiːfalˈkeɪʃn,
ˌdiːfɔːlˈkeɪʃn

AM di|fæl'keɪʃən,
dəˌfæl'keɪʃən,
diˌfɔl'keɪʃən,
dəˌfɔl'keɪʃən,
diˌfal'keɪʃən,
dəˌfal'keɪʃən

defalcator
BR 'diːfalkeɪtə(r),
'diːfɔːlkeɪtə(r), -z
AM dəˈfælˌkeɪdər,
diˈfælˌkeɪdər,
'diˌfælˌkeɪdər,
dəˈfɔlˌkeɪdər,
diˈfɔlˌkeɪdər,
'diˌfɔlˌkeɪdər,
dəˈfalˌkeɪdər,
diˈfalˌkeɪdər,
'diˌfalˌkeɪdər, -z

De Falla
BR də ˈfʌɪjə(r)
AM də ˈfaɪjə

defamation
BR ˌdɛfəˈmeɪʃn
AM ˌdɛfəˈmeɪʃən

defamatory
BR dɪˈfamət(ə)ri
AM dəˈfæməˌtɔri,
diˈfæməˌtɔri

defame
BR dɪˈfeɪm, -z, -ɪŋ, -d
AM dəˈfeɪm, diˈfeɪm, -z,
-ɪŋ, -d

defamer
BR dɪˈfeɪmə(r), -z
AM dəˈfeɪmər,
diˈfeɪmər, -z

defat
BR ˌdiːˈfat, -s, -ɪŋ, -ɪd
AM diˈfæ|t, -ts, -dɪŋ,
-dəd

default
BR dɪˈfɔːlt, -s, -ɪŋ, -ɪd
AM dəˈfɔlt, diˈfɔlt,
dəˈfalt, diˈfalt, -s, -ɪŋ,
-əd

defaulter
BR dɪˈfɔːltə(r), -z
AM dəˈfɔltər, diˈfɔltər,
dəˈfaltər, diˈfaltər, -z

defeasance
BR dɪˈfiːzns
AM dəˈfizns, diˈfizns

defeasibility
BR dɪˌfiːzɪˈbɪlɪti
AM dəˌfizəˈbɪlɪdi,
diˌfizəˈbɪlɪdi

defeasible
BR dɪˈfiːzɪbl
AM dəˈfizəbəl,
diˈfizəbəl

defeasibly
BR dɪˈfiːzɪbli
AM dəˈfizəbli,
diˈfizəbli

defeat
BR dɪˈfiːt, -s, -ɪŋ, -ɪd
AM dəˈfi|t, diˈfi|t, -ts,
-dɪŋ, -dɪd

defeatism
BR dɪˈfiːtɪz(ə)m
AM dəˈfidɪzəm,
diˈfidɪzəm

defeatist
BR dɪˈfiːtɪst, -s
AM dəˈfidəst, diˈfidəst,
-s

defecate
BR ˈdɛfɪkeɪt, ˈdiːfɪkeɪt,
-s, -ɪŋ, -ɪd
AM ˈdɛfəˌkeɪ|t, -ts, -dɪŋ,
-dɪd

defecation
BR ˌdɛfɪˈkeɪʃn,
ˌdiːfɪˈkeɪʃn
AM ˌdɛfəˈkeɪʃən

defecator
BR ˈdɛfɪkeɪtə(r),
ˈdiːfɪkeɪtə(r), -z
AM ˈdɛfəˌkeɪdər, -z

defect¹
noun
BR ˈdiːfɛkt, -s
AM ˈdifɛk(t), -s

defect²
verb
BR dɪˈfɛkt, -s, -ɪŋ, -ɪd
AM dəˈfɛk|(t),
diˈfɛk|(t), -(t)s, -tɪŋ,
-təd

defection
BR dɪˈfɛkʃn, -z
AM dəˈfɛkʃən,
diˈfɛkʃən, -z

defective
BR dɪˈfɛktɪv, -z
AM dəˈfɛktɪv, diˈfɛktɪv,
-z

defectively
BR dɪˈfɛktɪvli
AM dəˈfɛktɪvli,
diˈfɛktɪvli

defectiveness
BR dɪˈfɛktɪvnɪs
AM dəˈfɛktɪvnɪs,
diˈfɛktɪvnɪs

defector
BR dɪˈfɛktə(r), -z
AM dəˈfɛktər, diˈfɛktər,
-z

defence
BR dɪˈfɛns, -ɪz
AM dəˈfɛns, diˈfɛns,
ˈdiˌfɛns, -əz

defenceless
BR dɪˈfɛnsləs
AM dəˈfɛnsləs,
diˈfɛnsləs

defencelessly
BR dɪˈfɛnsləsli
AM dəˈfɛnsləsli,
diˈfɛnsləsli

defencelessness
BR dɪˈfɛnsləsnəs
AM dəˈfɛnsləsnəs,
diˈfɛnsləsnəs

defend
BR dɪˈfɛnd, -z, -ɪŋ, -ɪd
AM dəˈfɛnd, diˈfɛnd, -z,
-ɪŋ, -əd

defendable
BR dɪˈfɛndəbl
AM dəˈfɛndəbəl,
diˈfɛndəbəl

defendant
BR dɪˈfɛnd(ə)nt, -s
AM dəˈfɛndənt,
diˈfɛndənt, -s

defender
BR dɪˈfɛndə(r), -z
AM dəˈfɛndər,
diˈfɛndər, -z

defenestrate
BR (ˌ)diːˈfɛnɪstreɪt, -s,
-ɪŋ, -ɪd
AM diˈfɛnəˌstreɪ|t, -ts,
-dɪŋ, -dɪd

defenestration
BR ˌdiːfɛnɪˈstreɪʃn,
diːˌfɛnɪˈstreɪʃn
AM diˌfɛnəˈstreɪʃən

defense
BR dɪˈfɛns, -ɪz
AM dəˈfɛns, diˈfɛns,
ˈdiˌfɛns, -əz

defenseless
BR dɪˈfɛnsləs
AM dəˈfɛnsləs,
diˈfɛnsləs

defenselessly
BR dɪˈfɛnsləsli
AM dəˈfɛnsləsli,
diˈfɛnsləsli

defenselessness
BR dɪˈfɛnsləsnəs
AM dəˈfɛnsləsnəs,
diˈfɛnsləsnəs

defensibility
BR dɪˌfɛnsɪˈbɪlɪti
AM dəˌfɛnsəˈbɪlɪdi,
diˌfɛnsəˈbɪlɪdi

defensible
BR dɪˈfɛnsɪbl
AM dəˈfɛnsəbəl,
diˈfɛnsəbəl

defensibly
BR dɪˈfɛnsɪbli
AM dəˈfɛnsəbli,
diˈfɛnsəbli

defensive
BR dɪˈfɛnsɪv
AM dəˈfɛnsɪv, diˈfɛnsɪv

defensively
BR dɪˈfɛnsɪvli
AM dəˈfɛnsɪvli,
diˈfɛnsɪvli

defensiveness
BR dɪˈfɛnsɪvnɪs
AM dəˈfɛnsɪvnɪs,
diˈfɛnsɪvnɪs

defer
BR dɪˈfəː(r), -z, -ɪŋ, -d
AM dəˈfər, diˈfɛ(ə)r, -z,
-ɪŋ, -d

deference
BR ˈdɛf(ə)rəns,
ˈdɛf(ə)rn̩s
AM ˈdɛf(ə)rəns

deferens
BR ˈdɛfərɛnz
AM ˈdɛf(ə)rənz

deferent
BR ˈdɛf(ə)rənt,
ˈdɛf(ə)rn̩t
AM ˈdɛf(ə)rənt

deferential
BR ˌdɛfəˈrɛnʃl
AM ˌdɛfəˈrɛn(t)ʃəl

deferentially
BR ˌdɛfəˈrɛnʃəli,
ˌdɛfəˈrɛnʃli
AM ˌdɛfəˈrɛn(t)ʃəli

deferment
BR dɪˈfəː(m)(ə)nt, -s
AM dəˈfərmənt,
diˈfərmənt, -s

deferrable
BR dɪˈfəːrəbl
AM dəˈfərəbəl,
diˈfərəbəl

deferral
BR dɪˈfəːrəl, dɪˈfəːr], -z
AM dəˈfərəl, diˈfərəl, -z

deferrer
BR dɪˈfəːrə(r), -z
AM dəˈfərər, diˈfərər, -z

defiance
BR dɪˈfaɪəns
AM dəˈfaɪəns, diˈfaɪəns

defiant
BR dɪˈfaɪənt
AM dəˈfaɪənt, diˈfaɪənt

defiantly
BR dɪˈfaɪəntli
AM dəˈfaɪən(t)li,
diˈfaɪən(t)li

defibrillate
BR (ˌ)diːˈfɪbrɪleɪt, -s,
-ɪŋ, -ɪd
AM dəˈfɪbrəˌleɪ|t, -ts,
-dɪŋ, -dɪd

defibrillation
BR ˌdiːfɪbrɪˈleɪʃn,
diːˌfɪbrɪˈleɪʃn, -z
AM dəˌfɪbrəˈleɪʃən,
diˌfɪbrəˈleɪʃən, -z

defibrillator
BR (ˌ)diːˈfɪbrɪleɪtə(r),
-z
AM dəˈfɪbrəˌleɪdər,
diˈfɪbrəˌleɪdər, -z

deficiency
BR dɪˈfɪʃ(ə)ns|i, -ɪz
AM dəˈfɪʃənsi,
diˈfɪʃənsi, -z

deficient
BR dɪˈfɪʃ(ə)nt
AM dəˈfɪʃənt, diˈfɪʃənt

deficiently
BR dɪˈfɪʃ(ə)ntli
AM dəˈfɪʃən(t)li,
diˈfɪʃən(t)li

deficit
BR ˈdɛfɪsɪt, -s
AM ˈdɛfəsət, -s

defier
BR dɪˈfaɪə(r), -z
AM dəˈfaɪər, diˈfaɪər, -z

defilade
BR ˌdɛfɪˈleɪd, ˈdɛfɪleɪd,
-z, -ɪŋ, -ɪd
AM ˌdɛfəˈleɪd,
ˈdɛfəˌleɪd, -z, -ɪŋ, -ɪd

defile¹
noun
BR ˈdiːfaɪl, -z
AM ˈdiˌfaɪl, dəˈfaɪl, -z

defile²
verb
BR dɪˈfaɪl, -z, -ɪŋ, -d
AM dəˈfaɪl, diˈfaɪl, -z,
-ɪŋ, -d

defilement
BR dɪˈfaɪlm(ə)nt
AM dəˈfaɪlmənt,
diˈfaɪlmənt

defiler
BR dɪˈfaɪlə(r), -z
AM dəˈfaɪlər, diˈfaɪlər,
-z

definable
BR dɪˈfaɪnəbl
AM dəˈfaɪnəbəl,
diˈfaɪnəbəl

definably
BR dɪˈfaɪnəbli
AM dəˈfaɪnəbli,
diˈfaɪnəbli

define
BR dɪˈfaɪn, -z, -ɪŋ, -d
AM dəˈfaɪn, diˈfaɪn, -z,
-ɪŋ, -d

definer
BR dɪˈfaɪnə(r), -z
AM dəˈfaɪnər,
diˈfaɪnər, -z

definite
BR ˈdɛf(ɪ)nɪt
AM ˈdɛf(ə)nət

definitely
BR ˈdɛf(ɪ)nɪtli
AM ˈdɛf(ə)nətli

definiteness
BR ˈdɛf(ɪ)nɪtnɪs
AM ˈdɛf(ə)nətnəs

definition
BR ˌdɛfɪˈnɪʃn, -z
AM ˌdɛfəˈnɪʃən, -z

definitional
BR ˌdɛfɪˈnɪʃ(ə)l,
ˌdɛfɪˈnɪʃən(ə)l
AM ˌdɛfəˈnɪʃ(ə)nəl

definitionally
BR ˌdɛfɪˈnɪʃnəli,
ˌdɛfɪˈnɪʃn̩li,
ˌdɛfɪˈnɪʃən(ə)li
AM ˌdɛfəˈnɪʃ(ə)nəli

definitive
BR dɪˈfɪnɪtɪv

AM də'fɪnədɪv,
di'fɪnədɪv

definitively
BR dɪ'fɪnɪtɪvli
AM də'fɪnə,tɪvli,
di'fɪnə,tɪvli

definitiveness
BR dɪ'fɪnɪtɪvnɪs
AM də'fɪnədɪvnɪs,
di'fɪnədɪvnɪs

deflagrate
BR 'dɛfləgreɪt, -s, -ɪŋ,
-ɪd
AM 'dɛflə,greɪ|t, -ts,
-dɪŋ, -dɪd

deflagration
BR ,dɛflə'greɪʃn
AM ,dɛflə'greɪʃən

deflagrator
BR 'dɛfləgreɪtə(r), -z
AM 'dɛflə,greɪdər, -z

deflate
BR dɪ'fleɪt, -s, -ɪŋ, -ɪd
AM də'fleɪ|t, di'fleɪ|t,
-ts, -dɪŋ, -dɪd

deflation
BR ,di:'fleɪʃn, dɪ'fleɪʃn
AM də'fleɪʃən,
di'fleɪʃən

deflationary
BR ,di:'fleɪʃn(ə)ri,
,di:'fleɪʃən(ə)ri,
dɪ'fleɪʃn(ə)ri,
dɪ'fleɪʃən(ə)ri
AM də'fleɪʃə,nɛri,
də'fleɪʃə,nɛri

deflationist
BR ,di:'fleɪʃnɪst,
,di:'fleɪʃənɪst,
dɪ'fleɪʃnɪst,
dɪ'fleɪʃənɪst, -s
AM di'fleɪʃənəst,
də'fleɪʃənəst, -s

deflator
BR dɪ'fleɪtə(r), -z
AM di'fleɪdər,
də'fleɪdər, -z

deflect
BR dɪ'flɛkt, -s, -ɪŋ, -ɪd
AM də'flɛk|(t),
di'flɛk|(t), -(t)s, -tɪŋ,
-təd

deflection
BR dɪ'flɛkʃn, -z
AM də'flɛkʃən,
di'flɛkʃən, -z

deflector
BR dɪ'flɛktə(r), -z
AM də'flɛktər,
di'flɛktər, -z

deflexion
BR dɪ'flɛkʃn, -z
AM də'flɛkʃən,
di'flɛkʃən, -z

defloration
BR ,di:flɔː'reɪʃn,
,di:flə'reɪʃn,
,dɛflə'reɪʃn

AM ,dɛflə'reɪʃən

deflower
BR ,di:'flaʊə(r), -z, -ɪŋ,
-d
AM di'flaʊ(ə)r,
də'flaʊ(ə)r, -z, -ɪŋ, -d

defocus
BR ,di:'fəʊkəs, -ɪz, -ɪŋ, -t
AM di'foʊkəs, -əz, -ɪŋ, -t

defocussing
BR ,di:'fəʊkəsɪŋ
AM di'foʊkəsɪŋ

Defoe
BR dɪ'fəʊ
AM də'foʊ

defogger
BR ,di:'fɒgə(r), -z
AM də'fɔgər, di'fɔgər,
də'fɑgər, di'fɑgər, -z

defoliant
BR (,)di:'fəʊliənt, -s
AM di'foʊliənt, -s

defoliate
BR (,)di:'fəʊlieɪt, -s, -ɪŋ,
-ɪd
AM di'foʊli,eɪ|t, -ts,
-dɪŋ, -dɪd

defoliation
BR di:,fəʊli'eɪʃn,
,di:fəʊli'eɪʃn
AM di,foʊli'eɪʃən

defoliator
BR (,)di:'fəʊlieɪtə(r), -z
AM di'foʊli,eɪdər, -z

deforest
BR ,di:'fɒrɪst, -s, -ɪŋ, -ɪd
AM di'fɔrəst, -s, -ɪŋ, -əd

deforestation
BR ,di:fɒrɪ'steɪʃn,
di:,fɒrɪ'steɪʃn
AM ,di,fɔrə'steɪʃən

deform
BR dɪ'fɔːm, -z, -ɪŋ, -d
AM də'fɔ(ə)rm,
di'fɔ(ə)rm, -z, -ɪŋ, -d

deformable
BR dɪ'fɔːməbl
AM də'fɔrməbəl,
di'fɔrməbəl

deformation
BR ,di:fɔː'meɪʃn
AM ,di,fɔr'meɪʃən,
,dɛfər'meɪʃən

deformational
BR ,di:fɔː'meɪʃn(ə)l,
,di:fɔː'meɪʃən(ə)l
AM ,di,fɔr'meɪʃ(ə)nəl,
,dɛfər'meɪʃ(ə)nəl

deformity
BR dɪ'fɔːmɪt|i, -ɪz
AM də'fɔrmədi,
di'fɔrmədi, -z

defraud
BR dɪ'frɔːd, -z, -ɪŋ, -ɪd
AM də'frɔd, di'frɔd,
də'frɑd, di'frɑd, -z, -ɪŋ,
-əd

defrauder
BR dɪ'frɔːdə(r), -z
AM də'frɔdər,
di'frɔdər, də'frɑdər,
di'frɑdər, -z

defray
BR dɪ'freɪ, -z, -ɪŋ, -d
AM də'freɪ, di'freɪ, -z,
-ɪŋ, -d

defrayable
BR dɪ'freɪəbl
AM də'freɪəbəl,
di'freɪəbəl

defrayal
BR dɪ'freɪəl
AM də'freɪ(ə)l,
di'freɪ(ə)l

defrayment
BR dɪ'freɪm(ə)nt
AM də'freɪmənt,
di'freɪmənt

De Freitas
BR də 'freɪtəs
AM də 'fraɪdəs

defrock
BR ,di:'frɒk, -s, -ɪŋ, -t
AM di'frɑk, -s, -ɪŋ, -t

defrost
BR ,di:'frɒst, dɪ'frɒst,
-s, -ɪŋ, -ɪd
AM di'frɔst, di'frɑst,
də'frɔst, di'frɑst, -s,
-ɪŋ, -əd

defroster
BR ,di:'frɒstə(r),
dɪ'frɒstə(r), -z
AM di'frɔstər,
di'frɑstər, də'frɔstər,
di'frɑstər, -z

deft
BR dɛft, -ə(r), -ɪst
AM dɛft, -ər, -əst

deftly
BR 'dɛftli
AM 'dɛft(t)li

deftness
BR 'dɛf(t)nəs
AM 'dɛf(t)nəs

defumigate
BR ,di:'fju:mɪgeɪt, -s,
-ɪŋ, -ɪd
AM di'fjumə,geɪ|t, -ts,
-dɪŋ, -dɪd

defunct
BR dɪ'fʌŋ(k)t
AM də'fəŋ(k)t,
di'fəŋ(k)t, də'fʌŋk(t),
di'fʌŋk(t)

defunctness
BR dɪ'fʌŋ(k)tnəs,
dɪ'fʌŋk(t)nəs
AM də'fəŋk(t)nəs,
də'fəŋ(k)tnəs,
di'fəŋk(t)nəs,
di'fəŋ(k)tnəs

defuse
BR ,di:'fju:z, dɪ'fju:z,
-ɪz, -ɪŋ, -d

AM də'fjuz, di'fjuz, -əz,
-ɪŋ, -d

defy
BR dɪ'fʌɪ, -z, -ɪŋ, -d
AM də'faɪ, di'faɪ, -z, -ɪŋ,
-d

dégagé
BR ,deɪgɑː'ʒeɪ,
,deɪga'ʒeɪ
AM ,deɪgɑ'ʒeɪ

dégagée
BR ,deɪgɑː'ʒeɪ,
,deɪga'ʒeɪ
AM ,deɪgɑ'ʒeɪ

Deganwy
BR dɪ'ganwi
AM də'gænwi

Degas
BR 'deɪgɑː(r)
AM deɪ'gɑ

degas
BR ,di:'gas, -ɪz, -ɪŋ, -t
AM di'gæs, -əz, -ɪŋ, -t

de Gaulle
BR də 'gɔːl
AM də 'gɔl, də 'gɑl

degauss
BR ,di:'gaʊs, -ɪz, -ɪŋ, -t
AM di'gaʊs, -əz, -ɪŋ, -t

degausser
BR ,di:'gaʊsə(r), -z
AM di'gaʊsər, -z

degeminate
BR ,di:'dʒɛmɪneɪt, -s,
-ɪŋ, -ɪd
AM di'dʒɛmə,neɪ|t, -ts,
-dɪŋ, -dɪd

degemination
BR ,di:dʒɛmɪ'neɪʃn
AM di,dʒɛmə'neɪʃən

degeneracy
BR dɪ'dʒɛn(ə)rəsi
AM də'dʒɛn(ə)rəsi,
di'dʒɛn(ə)rəsi

degenerate[1]
noun, adjective
BR dɪ'dʒɛn(ə)rət, -s
AM də'dʒɛn(ə)rət,
di'dʒɛn(ə)rət, -s

degenerate[2]
verb
BR dɪ'dʒɛnəreɪt, -s, -ɪŋ,
-ɪd
AM də'dʒɛn(ə),reɪ|t,
di'dʒɛn(ə),reɪ|t, -ts,
-dɪŋ, -dɪd

degenerately
BR dɪ'dʒɛn(ə)rətli
AM də'dʒɛn(ə)rətli,
di'dʒɛn(ə)rətli

degeneration
BR dɪ,dʒɛnə'reɪʃn
AM də,dʒɛnə'reɪʃən,
di,dʒɛnə'reɪʃən

degenerative
BR dɪ'dʒɛn(ə)rətɪv
AM də'dʒɛnərədɪv,
di'dʒɛnərədɪv

deglaze
BR ˌdiːˈgleɪz, -ɪz, -ɪŋ, -d
AM diˈgleɪz, -ɪz, -ɪŋ, -d

degradability
BR dɪˌgreɪdəˈbɪlɪti
AM dəˌgreɪdəˈbɪlɪdi,
diˌgreɪdəˈbɪlɪdi

degradable
BR dɪˈgreɪdəbl
AM dəˈgreɪdəbəl,
diˈgreɪdəbəl

degradation
BR ˌdɛgrəˈdeɪʃn
AM ˌdɛgrəˈdeɪʃən

degradative
BR dɪˈgreɪdətɪv
AM dɛˈgreɪdədɪv,
ˈdɛgrəˌdeɪdɪv

degrade
BR dɪˈgreɪd, -z, -ɪŋ, -ɪd
AM dəˈgreɪd, diˈgreɪd,
-z, -ɪŋ, -ɪd

degrader
BR dɪˈgreɪdə(r), -z
AM dəˈgreɪdər,
diˈgreɪdər, -z

degradingly
BR dɪˈgreɪdɪŋli
AM dəˈgreɪdɪŋli,
diˈgreɪdɪŋli

degranulate
BR diˈgranjʊleɪt, -s,
-ɪŋ, -ɪd
AM diˈgrænjəˌleɪ|t, -ts,
-dɪŋ, -dɪd

degranulation
BR ˌdiˈgranjʊˈleɪʃn,
diˌgranjʊˈleɪʃn
AM diˌgrænjʊˈleɪʃən

degrease
BR ˌdiːˈgriːs, -ɪz, -ɪŋ, -t
AM diˈgris, -ɪz, -ɪŋ, -t

degreaser
BR ˌdiːˈgriːsə(r), -z
AM diˈgrisər, -z

degree
BR dɪˈgriː, -z
AM dəˈgri, diˈgri, -z

degreeless
BR dɪˈgriːlɪs
AM dəˈgrilɪs, diˈgrilɪs

degressive
BR dɪˈgrɛsɪv
AM dɪˈgrɛsɪv, diˈgrɛsɪv

degum
BR ˌdiːˈgʌm, -z, -ɪŋ, -d
AM diˈgəm, -z, -ɪŋ, -d

de haut en bas
BR də ˌəʊt ɒ̃ ˈbɑː
AM də ˌoʊt ɑn ˈbɑ

de Havilland
BR də ˈhavɪlənd,
+ ˈhavlənd
AM də ˈhævələn(d)

dehisce
BR dɪˈhɪs
AM dəˈhɪs, diˈhɪs

dehiscence
BR dɪˈhɪsns
AM dəˈhɪsns, diˈhɪsns

dehiscent
BR dɪˈhɪsnt
AM dəˈhɪsnt, diˈhɪsnt

dehistoricise
BR ˌdiːhɪˈstɒrɪsʌɪz, -ɪz,
-ɪŋ, -d
AM dɪˌhɪˈstɔrəˌsaɪz, -ɪz,
-ɪŋ, -d

dehistoricize
BR ˌdiːhɪˈstɒrɪsʌɪz, -ɪz,
-ɪŋ, -d
AM dɪˌhɪˈstɔrəˌsaɪz, -ɪz,
-ɪŋ, -d

dehorn
BR ˌdiːˈhɔːn, -z, -ɪŋ, -d
AM diˈhɔ(ə)rn, -z, -ɪŋ, -d

dehumanisation
BR ˌdiːhjuːmənʌɪˈzeɪʃn,
diːˌhjuːmənʌɪˈzeɪʃn
AM ˌdi,(h)jumənəˈzeɪ-
ʃən,
dəˌ(h)jumənəˈzeɪʃən,
ˈdi,(h)jumə,naɪˈzeɪʃən,
dəˌ(h)jumə,naɪˈzeɪʃən

dehumanise
BR (ˌ)diːˈhjuːmənʌɪz,
-ɪz, -ɪŋ, -d
AM diˈ(h)jumə,naɪz,
dəˈ(h)jumə,naɪz, -ɪz,
-ɪŋ, -d

dehumanization
BR ˌdiːhjuːmənʌɪˈzeɪʃn,
diːˌhjuːmənʌɪˈzeɪʃn
AM ˌdi,(h)jumənəˈzeɪ-
ʃən,
dəˌ(h)jumənəˈzeɪʃən,
ˈdi,(h)jumə,naɪˈzeɪʃən,
dəˌ(h)jumə,naɪˈzeɪʃən

dehumanize
BR (ˌ)diːˈhjuːmənʌɪz,
-ɪz, -ɪŋ, -d
AM diˈ(h)jumə,naɪz,
dəˈ(h)jumə,naɪz, -ɪz,
-ɪŋ, -d

dehumidification
BR ˌdiːhjuːˌmɪdɪfɪˈkeɪʃn
AM ˌdi(h)juˌmɪdəfəˈkeɪ-
ʃən

dehumidifier
BR ˌdiːhjuːˈmɪdɪfʌɪə(r),
-z
AM ˌdi(h)juˈmɪdəˌfaɪər,
-z

dehumidify
BR ˌdiːhjuːˈmɪdɪfʌɪ, -z,
-ɪŋ, -d
AM ˌdi(h)juˈmɪdəˌfaɪ,
-z, -ɪŋ, -d

dehydrate
BR ˌdiːˈhʌɪdreɪt, -s, -ɪŋ,
-ɪd
AM diˈhaɪˌdreɪ|t, -ts,
-dɪŋ, -dɪd

dehydration
BR ˌdiːhʌɪˈdreɪʃn

AM ˌdiˌhaɪˈdreɪʃən

dehydrator
BR ˌdiːhʌɪˈdreɪtə(r), -z
AM diˈhaɪˌdreɪdər, -z

dehydrogenate
BR ˌdiːhʌɪˈdrɒdʒɪneɪt,
-s, -ɪŋ, -ɪd
AM diˌhaɪˈdrɑdʒə,neɪ|t,
-ts, -dɪŋ, -dɪd

dehydrogenation
BR ˌdiːhʌɪdrɒdʒɪˈneɪʃn
AM ˌdihaɪˌdrɑdʒəˈneɪʃn

Deianira
BR ˌdeɪəˈnʌɪrə(r)
AM ˌdijəˈnaɪrə

de-ice
BR ˌdiːˈʌɪs, -ɪz, -ɪŋ, -t
AM ˌdiˈaɪs, -ɪz, -ɪŋ, -t

de-icer
BR ˌdiːˈʌɪsə(r), -z
AM ˌdiˈaɪsər, -z

deicide
BR ˈdeɪɪsʌɪd, ˈdiːɪsʌɪd,
-z
AM ˈdiə,saɪd, -z

deictic
BR ˈdʌɪktɪk, ˈdeɪktɪk
AM ˈdaɪktɪk

deification
BR ˌdeɪɪfɪˈkeɪʃn,
ˌdiːɪfɪˈkeɪʃn
AM ˌdiəfəˈkeɪʃən

deiform
BR ˈdeɪɪfɔːm, ˈdiːɪfɔːm
AM ˈdiə,fɔ(ə)rm

deify
BR ˈdeɪɪfʌɪ, ˈdiːɪfʌɪ, -z,
-ɪŋ, -d
AM ˈdiə,faɪ, -z, -ɪŋ, -d

Deighton
BR ˈdeɪtn
AM ˈdeɪtn

deign
BR deɪn, -z, -ɪŋ, -d
AM deɪn, -z, -ɪŋ, -d

Dei gratia
BR ˌdeɪiː ˈgraːtɪə(r),
ˌdiːʌɪ ˈgreɪʃɪə(r)
AM ˌdeɪi ˈgrɑtsiə

Deimos
BR ˈdeɪmɒs, ˈdʌɪmɒs
AM ˈdaɪ,mɑs

**de-
industrialisation**
BR ˌdiːm,dʌstriəlʌɪ-
ˈzeɪʃn
AM ˌdiːm,dəstriələˌzeɪ-
ʃən,
ˈdiːm,dəstriə,laɪˌzeɪʃən

**de-
industrialization**
BR ˌdiːm,dʌstriəlʌɪ-
ˈzeɪʃn
AM ˌdiːm,dəstriələˌzeɪʃən,
ˈdiːm,dəstriə,laɪˌzeɪʃən

deinonychus
BR dʌɪˈnɒnɪkəs, -ɪz
AM daɪˈnɑnəkəs, -əz

**deinstitutionalisa-
tion**
BR ˌdiːmstɪ,tjuːˈʃnəlʌɪˈzeɪʃn,
ˌdiːmstɪ,tjuːˈʃn̩lʌɪˈzeɪʃn,
ˌdiːmstɪ,tjuːˈʃənlʌɪˈzeɪʃn,
ˌdiːmstɪ,tjuːˈʃ(ə)nəlʌɪˈzeɪʃn,
ˌdiːmstɪ,tʃuːˈʃnəlʌɪˈzeɪʃn,
ˌdiːmstɪ,tʃuːˈʃn̩lʌɪˈzeɪʃn,
ˌdiːmstɪ,tʃuːˈʃənlʌɪˈzeɪʃn,
ˌdiːmstɪ,tʃuːˈʃ(ə)nəlʌɪˈzeɪʃn
AM ˈdi,mstə,t(j)uʃənləˈzeɪʃən,
ˈdi,mstə,t(j)uʃən̩,aɪˈzeɪʃən,
ˈdi,mstə,t(j)uʃnələˈzeɪʃən,
ˈdi,mstə,t(j)uʃənə,larˈzeɪʃən

deinstitutionalise
BR ˌdiːmstɪˈtjuːʃnəlʌɪz,
ˌdiːmstɪˈtjuːʃn̩lʌɪz,
ˌdiːmstɪˈtjuːʃənlʌɪz,
ˌdiːmstɪˈtjuːʃ(ə)nəlʌɪz,
ˌdiːmstɪˈtʃuːʃnəlʌɪz,
ˌdiːmstɪˈtʃuːʃn̩lʌɪz,
ˌdiːmstɪˈtʃuːʃənlʌɪz,
ˌdiːmstɪˈtʃuːʃ(ə)nəlʌɪz,
-ɪz, -ɪŋ, -d
AM ˈdi,mstəˈt(j)uʃənl,aɪz,
ˈdi,mstəˈt(j)uʃnə,laɪz,
-ɪz, -ɪŋ, -d

deinstitutionalization
BR ˌdiːmstɪ,tjuːˈʃnəlʌɪˈzeɪʃn,
ˌdiːmstɪ,tjuːˈʃn̩lʌɪˈzeɪʃn,
ˌdiːmstɪ,tjuːˈʃənlʌɪˈzeɪʃn,
ˌdiːmstɪ,tjuːˈʃ(ə)nəlʌɪˈzeɪʃn,
ˌdiːmstɪ,tʃuːˈʃnəlʌɪˈzeɪʃn,
ˌdiːmstɪ,tʃuːˈʃn̩lʌɪˈzeɪʃn,
ˌdiːmstɪ,tʃuːˈʃənlʌɪˈzeɪʃn,
ˌdiːmstɪ,tʃuːˈʃ(ə)nəlʌɪˈzeɪʃn
AM ˈdi,mstə,t(j)uʃənlə̍ˈzeɪʃən,
ˈdi,mstə,t(j)uʃənl,aɪˈzeɪʃən,
ˈdi,mstə,t(j)uʃnələˈzeɪʃən,
ˈdi,mstə,t(j)uʃənəlaɪˈzeɪʃən

deinstitutionalize
BR ˌdiːmstɪˈtjuːʃnəlʌɪz,
ˌdiːmstɪˈtjuːʃn̩lʌɪz,
ˌdiːmstɪˈtjuːʃənlʌɪz,
ˌdiːmstɪˈtjuːʃ(ə)nəlʌɪz,
ˌdiːmstɪˈtʃuːʃnəlʌɪz,
ˌdiːmstɪˈtʃuːʃn̩lʌɪz,
ˌdiːmstɪˈtʃuːʃ(ə)nəlʌɪz,
-ɪz, -ɪŋ, -d
AM ˈdi,mstəˈt(j)uʃənl,aɪz,
ˈdi,mstəˈt(j)uʃnə,laɪz,
-ɪz, -ɪŋ, -d

deionisation
BR ˌdiːʌɪənʌɪˈzeɪʃn,
diːˌʌɪənʌɪˈzeɪʃn
AM ˌdi,aɪənəˈzeɪʃən,
di,aɪə,naɪˈzeɪʃən

deionise
BR ˌdiːˈʌɪənʌɪz, -ɪz, -ɪŋ,
-d
AM diˈaɪə,naɪz, -ɪz, -ɪŋ,
-d

deioniser
BR ˌdiːˈʌɪənʌɪzə(r), -z
AM diˈaɪə,naɪzər, -z

deionization
BR ˌdiːʌɪənʌɪˈzeɪʃn,
diːˌʌɪənʌɪˈzeɪʃn

AM di͵aɪənəˈzeɪʃən,
di͵aɪə͵naɪˈzeɪʃən
deionize
BR ˌdiːˈʌɪənʌɪz, -ɪz, -ɪŋ,
-d
AM diˈaɪə͵naɪz, -ɪz, -ɪŋ,
-d
deionizer
BR ˌdiːˈʌɪənʌɪzə(r), -z
AM diˈaɪə͵naɪzər, -z
deipnosophist
BR daɪpˈnɒsəfɪst, -s
AM daɪpˈnɑsəfəst, -s
Deirdre
BR ˈdɪədri, ˈdɪədrə(r)
AM ˈdɪrˌdrə
deism
BR ˈdeɪɪz(ə)m,
ˈdiːɪz(ə)m
AM ˈdiˌɪzəm, ˈdeɪˌɪzəm
deist
BR ˈdeɪɪst, ˈdiːɪst, -s
AM ˈdiɪst, ˈdeɪɪst, -s
deistic
BR deɪˈɪstɪk, diːˈɪstɪk
AM diˈɪstɪk, deɪˈɪstɪk
deistical
BR deɪˈɪstɪkl, diːˈɪstɪkl
AM diˈɪstɪkəl,
deɪˈɪstɪkəl
deistically
BR deɪˈɪstɪkli,
diːˈɪstɪkli
AM diˈɪstɪk(ə)li,
deɪˈɪstɪk(ə)li
deity
BR ˈdeɪɪt|i, ˈdiːɪt|i, -ɪz
AM ˈdiədi, ˈdeɪɪdi, -z
deixis
BR ˈdʌɪksɪs, ˈdeɪksɪs
AM ˈdaɪksəs
déjà vu
BR ˌdeɪʒɑː ˈvuː
AM ˌdeɪʒɑ ˈv(j)u
deject
BR dɪˈdʒɛkt, -s, -ɪŋ, -ɪd
AM dəˈdʒɛk|(t),
diˈdʒɛk|(t), -(t)s, -tɪŋ,
-təd
dejectedly
BR dɪˈdʒɛktɪdli
AM dəˈdʒɛktədli,
diˈdʒɛktədli
dejection
BR dɪˈdʒɛkʃn
AM dəˈdʒɛkʃən,
diˈdʒɛkʃən
de jure
BR ˌdiː ˈdʒʊəri, ˌdeɪ
ˈjʊəreɪ
AM ˌdi ˈdʒʊri, deɪ ˈjʊˌreɪ
De Kalb
BR də ˈka(l)b
AM də ˈkæ(l)b
Dekker
BR ˈdɛkə(r)
AM ˈdɛkər

dekko
BR ˈdɛkəʊ, -z
AM ˈdɛkoʊ, -z
de Klerk
BR də ˈklɛːk
AM də ˈklɛrk
de Kooning
BR də ˈkuːnɪŋ
AM də ˈkunɪŋ
Delacourt
BR ˈdɛləkɔːt
AM ˈdɛlə͵kɔ(ə)rt
Delacroix
BR ˈdɛləkrwɑː(r),
ˌdɛləˈkrwɑː(r)
AM ˌdɛləˈk(r)wɑ
Delafield
BR ˈdɛləfiːld
AM ˈdɛlə͵fild
Delagoa
BR ˌdɛləˈgəʊə(r)
AM ˌdɛləˈgoʊə
Delahaye
BR ˈdɛləheɪ
AM ˈdɛlə͵heɪ
delaine
BR dɪˈleɪn
AM dəˈleɪn, diˈleɪn
de la Mare
BR də la ˈmɛː(r),
ˌdɛlə +
AM də lɑ ˈmɛ(ə)r
Delamere
BR ˈdɛləmɪə(r)
AM ˈdɛləmɪ(ə)r
Delaney
BR dɪˈleɪni
AM dəˈleɪni
de la Rue
BR də la ˈruː, ˌdɛlə +
AM də lɑ ˈru
delate
BR dɪˈleɪt, -s, -ɪŋ, -ɪd
AM dəˈleɪ|t, diˈleɪ|t, -ts,
-dɪŋ, -dɪd
delation
BR dɪˈleɪʃn
AM dəˈleɪʃən, diˈleɪʃən
delator
BR dɪˈleɪtə(r), -z
AM dəˈleɪdər, diˈleɪdər,
-z
Delaware
BR ˈdɛləwɛː(r)
AM ˈdɛlə͵wɛ(ə)r
delay
BR dɪˈleɪ, -z, -ɪŋ, -d
AM dəˈleɪ, diˈleɪ, -z, -ɪŋ,
-d
delayer
BR dɪˈleɪə(r), -z
AM dəˈleɪər, diˈleɪər, -z
Delbert
BR ˈdɛlbət
AM ˈdɛlbərt
Delbridge
BR ˈdɛlbrɪdʒ

AM ˈdɛl͵brɪdʒ
del credere
BR dɛl ˈkreɪdəri,
+ ˈkrɛdəri
AM dɛl ˈkreɪdəri
Delderfield
BR ˈdɛldəfiːld
AM ˈdɛldər͵fild
dele
BR ˈdiːl|i, -ɪz, -ɪŋ, -ɪd
AM ˈdili, -z, -ɪŋ, -d
delectability
BR dɪˌlɛktəˈbɪlɪti
AM dəˌlɛktəˈbɪlɪdi,
diˌlɛktəˈbɪlɪdi
delectable
BR dɪˈlɛktəbl
AM dəˈlɛktəbəl,
diˈlɛktəbəl
delectably
BR dɪˈlɛktəbli
AM dəˈlɛktəbli,
diˈlɛktəbli
delectation
BR ˌdiːlɛkˈteɪʃn
AM ˌdilɛkˈteɪʃən,
ˌdɪlɛkˈteɪʃən,
ˌdɛlɛkˈteɪʃən
delegable
BR ˈdɛlɪgəbl
AM ˈdɛləgəbəl
delegacy
BR ˈdɛlɪgəs|i, -ɪz
AM ˈdɛləgəsi, -z
delegate¹
noun
BR ˈdɛlɪgət, -s
AM ˈdɛləgət, ˈdɛlə͵geɪt,
-s
delegate²
verb
BR ˈdɛlɪgeɪt, -s, -ɪŋ, -ɪd
AM ˈdɛlə͵geɪ|t, -ts, -dɪŋ,
-dɪd
delegation
BR ˌdɛlɪˈgeɪʃn, -z
AM ˌdɛləˈgeɪʃən, -z
delegator
BR ˈdɛlɪgeɪtə(r), -z
AM ˈdɛlə͵geɪdər, -z
delete
BR dɪˈliːt, -s, -ɪŋ, -ɪd
AM dəˈli|t, diˈli|t, -ts,
-dɪŋ, -dɪd
deleterious
BR ˌdɛlɪˈtɪərɪəs
AM ˌdɛləˈtɪriəs
deleteriously
BR ˌdɛlɪˈtɪərɪəsli
AM ˌdɛləˈtɪriəsli
deleteriousness
BR ˌdɛlɪˈtɪərɪəsnəs
AM ˌdɛləˈtɪriəsnəs
deletion
BR dɪˈliːʃn, -z
AM dəˈliʃən, diˈliʃən, -z

AM dɛlˈfɑnt
Delft
BR dɛlft
AM dɛlft
delftware
BR ˈdɛlftwɛː(r)
AM ˈdɛlf(t)͵wɛ(ə)r
Delgado
BR dɛlˈgɑːdəʊ
AM delˈgɑdoʊ
Delhi
BR ˈdɛli
AM ˈdɛli
deli
BR ˈdɛl|i, -ɪz
AM ˈdɛli, -z
Delia
BR ˈdiːlɪə(r)
AM ˈdiljə, ˈdiliə
Delian
BR ˈdiːlɪən, -z
AM ˈdiliən, -z
deliberate¹
adjective
BR dɪˈlɪb(ə)rət
AM dəˈlɪb(ə)rət,
diˈlɪb(ə)rət
deliberate²
verb
BR dɪˈlɪbəreɪt, -s, -ɪŋ,
-ɪd
AM dəˈlɪbə͵reɪ|t,
dɪˈlɪbə͵reɪ|t, -ts, -dɪŋ,
-dɪd
deliberately
BR dɪˈlɪb(ə)rətli
AM dəˈlɪb(ə)rətli,
diˈlɪb(ə)rətli
deliberateness
BR dɪˈlɪb(ə)rətnəs
AM dəˈlɪb(ə)rətnəs,
diˈlɪb(ə)rətnəs
deliberation
BR dɪˌlɪbəˈreɪʃn, -z
AM də͵lɪbəˈreɪʃən,
di͵lɪbəˈreɪʃən, -z
deliberative
BR dɪˈlɪb(ə)rətɪv
AM dəˈlɪbərədɪv,
diˈlɪbərədɪv,
də͵lɪbə͵reɪdɪv,
di͵lɪbə͵reɪdɪv
deliberatively
BR dɪˈlɪb(ə)rətɪvli
AM dəˈlɪbərədɪvli,
diˈlɪbərədɪvli,
də͵lɪbə͵reɪdɪvli,
di͵lɪbə͵reɪdɪvli
deliberativeness
BR dɪˈlɪb(ə)rətɪvnɪs
AM dəˈlɪbərədɪvnɪs,
də͵lɪbə͵reɪdɪvnɪs,
di͵lɪbə͵reɪdɪvnɪs
deliberator
BR dɪˈlɪbəreɪtə(r), -z
AM də͵lɪbə͵reɪdər,
di͵lɪbə͵reɪdər, -z

Delibes
BR dɪˈliːb
AM dəˈlib

delicacy
BR ˈdɛlɪkəs|i, -ɪz
AM ˈdɛləkəsi, -z

delicate
BR ˈdɛlɪkət
AM ˈdɛlɪkət

delicately
BR ˈdɛlɪkətli
AM ˈdɛlɪkətli

delicateness
BR ˈdɛlɪkətnəs
AM ˈdɛlɪkətnəs

delicatessen
BR ˌdɛlɪkəˈtɛsn, -z
AM ˌdɛlɪkəˈtɛsən, -z

delicious
BR dɪˈlɪʃəs
AM dəˈlɪʃəs, dɪˈlɪʃəs

deliciously
BR dɪˈlɪʃəsli
AM dəˈlɪʃəsli, dɪˈlɪʃəsli

deliciousness
BR dɪˈlɪʃəsnəs
AM dəˈlɪʃəsnəs,
dɪˈlɪʃəsnəs

delict
BR dɪˈlɪkt, ˈdiːlɪkt, -s
AM dəˈlɪk|(t), dɪˈlɪk|(t),
-(t)s

delight
BR dɪˈlʌɪt, -s, -ɪŋ, -ɪd
AM dəˈlaɪ|t, dɪˈlaɪ|t, -ts,
-dɪŋ, -dɪd

delightedly
BR dɪˈlʌɪtɪdli
AM dəˈlaɪdɪdli,
dɪˈlaɪtɪdli

delightful
BR dɪˈlʌɪtf(ʊ)l
AM dəˈlaɪtfəl, dɪˈlaɪtfəl

delightfully
BR dɪˈlʌɪtfʊli,
dɪˈlʌɪtʃli
AM dəˈlaɪtfəli,
dɪˈlaɪtfəli

delightfulness
BR dɪˈlʌɪtf(ʊ)lnəs
AM dəˈlaɪtfəlnəs,
dɪˈlaɪtfəlnəs

Delilah
BR dɪˈlʌɪlə(r)
AM dəˈlaɪlə, dɪˈlaɪlə

delimit
BR ˌdiːˈlɪm|ɪt, dɪˈlɪm|ɪt,
-s, -ɪtɪŋ, -ɪdɪd
AM dəˈlɪmɪ|t, dɪˈlɪmɪ|t,
-ts, -dɪŋ, -dɪd

delimitate
BR dɪˈlɪmɪteɪt, -s, -ɪŋ,
-ɪd
AM dəˈlɪməˌteɪ|t,
dɪˈlɪməˌteɪ|t, -ts, -dɪŋ,
-dɪd

delimitation
BR dɪˌlɪmɪˈteɪʃn

AM dəˌlɪməˈteɪʃən,
dɪˌlɪməˈteɪʃən

delimitative
BR dɪˈlɪmɪtətɪv
AM dəˈlɪməˌteɪdɪv,
dəˈlɪmədədɪv,
dɪˈlɪməˌteɪdɪv,
dɪˈlɪmədədɪv

delimiter
BR ˌdiːˈlɪmɪtə(r),
dɪˈlɪmɪtə(r), -z
AM dəˈlɪmɪdər,
dɪˈlɪmɪdər, -z

delineate
BR dɪˈlɪnɪeɪt, -s, -ɪŋ, -ɪd
AM dəˈlɪniˌeɪ|t,
dɪˈlɪniˌeɪ|t, -ts, -dɪŋ,
-dɪd

delineation
BR dɪˌlɪnɪˈeɪʃn, -z
AM dəˌlɪniˈeɪʃən,
dɪˌlɪniˈeɪʃən, -z

delineator
BR dɪˈlɪnɪeɪtə(r), -z
AM dəˈlɪniˌeɪdər,
dɪˈlɪniˌeɪdər, -z

delinquency
BR dɪˈlɪŋkw(ə)ns|i, -ɪz
AM dəˈlɪŋkwənsi, -z

delinquent
BR dɪˈlɪŋkw(ə)nt, -s
AM dəˈlɪŋkwənt, -s

delinquently
BR dɪˈlɪŋkw(ə)ntli
AM dəˈlɪŋkwən(t)li

deliquesce
BR ˌdɛlɪˈkwɛs, -ɪz, -ɪŋ, -t
AM ˌdɛləˈkwɛs, -əz, -ɪŋ,
-t

deliquescence
BR ˌdɛlɪˈkwɛsns
AM ˌdɛləˈkwɛsəns

deliquescent
BR ˌdɛlɪˈkwɛsnt
AM ˌdɛləˈkwɛsənt

deliria
BR dɪˈlɪrɪə(r),
dɪˈlɪərɪə(r)
AM dəˈlɪrɪə

delirious
BR dɪˈlɪrɪəs, dɪˈlɪərɪəs
AM dəˈlɪrɪəs

deliriously
BR dɪˈlɪrɪəsli,
dɪˈlɪərɪəsli
AM dəˈlɪrɪəsli

delirium
BR dɪˈlɪrɪəm,
dɪˈlɪərɪəm
AM dəˈlɪrɪəm

delirium tremens
BR dɪˌlɪrɪəm ˈtrɛmɛnz,
dɪˌlɪərɪəm +
AM dɪˌlɪrɪəm ˈtrɛmənz

De Lisle
BR də ˈlʌɪl
AM də ˈlaɪl, + ˈlil

Delius
BR ˈdiːlɪəs
AM ˈdiːlɪəs

deliver
BR dɪˈlɪv|ə(r), -əz,
-(ə)rɪŋ, -əd
AM dəˈlɪv|ər, dɪˈlɪv|ər,
-ərz, -(ə)rɪŋ, -ərd

deliverable
BR dɪˈlɪv(ə)rəbl
AM dəˈlɪv(ə)rəbəl,
dɪˈlɪv(ə)rəbəl

deliverance
BR dɪˈlɪv(ə)rəns,
dɪˈlɪv(ə)rŋs
AM dəˈlɪv(ə)rəns,
dɪˈlɪv(ə)rəns

deliverer
BR dɪˈlɪv(ə)rə(r), -z
AM dəˈlɪv(ə)rər,
dɪˈlɪv(ə)rər, -z

delivery
BR dɪˈlɪv(ə)r|i, -ɪz
AM dəˈlɪv(ə)ri,
dɪˈlɪv(ə)ri, -z

deliveryman
BR dɪˈlɪv(ə)rɪˌman,
dɪˈlɪv(ə)rɪmən
AM dəˈlɪv(ə)rɪˌmæn,
dɪˈlɪv(ə)rɪˌmæn

deliverymen
BR dɪˈlɪv(ə)rɪˌmɛn,
dɪˈlɪv(ə)rɪmən
AM dəˈlɪv(ə)rɪˌmɛn,
dɪˈlɪv(ə)rɪˌmɛn

dell
BR dɛl, -z
AM dɛl, -z

Della
BR ˈdɛlə(r)
AM ˈdɛlə

Della Cruscan
BR ˌdɛlə ˈkrʌsk(ə)n, -z
AM ˌdɛlə ˈkruʃən, -z

Della Robbia
BR ˌdɛlə ˈrɒbɪə(r)
AM ˌdɛlə ˈroʊbɪə

delly
BR ˈdɛl|i, -ɪz
AM ˈdɛli, -z

Del Mar
BR dɛl ˈmɑː(r)
AM dɛl ˈmɑr

Del Monte
BR dɛl ˈmɒnti,
+ ˈmɒnteɪ
AM dɛl ˈmɑn(t)i

delocalisation
BR ˌdiːləʊkəlʌɪˈzeɪʃn,
ˌdiːˌləʊk|ʌɪˈzeɪʃn,
diːˌləʊkələʌɪˈzeɪʃn,
diːˌləʊkˌlʌɪˈzeɪʃn
AM dɪˌloʊkələˈzeɪʃən,
dɪˌloʊkəˌlaɪˈzeɪʃən

delocalise
BR (ˌ)diːˈləʊkəlʌɪz,
(ˌ)diːˈləʊkˌlʌɪz, -ɪz, -ɪŋ,
-d

Delius
AM dɪˈloʊkəˌlaɪz, -ɪz,
-ɪŋ, -d

delocalization
BR ˌdiːləʊkəlʌɪˈzeɪʃn,
ˌdiːˌləʊkˌlʌɪˈzeɪʃn,
diːˌləʊkələʌɪˈzeɪʃn,
diːˌləʊkˌlʌɪˈzeɪʃn
AM dɪˌloʊkələˈzeɪʃən,
dɪˌloʊkəˌlaɪˈzeɪʃən

delocalize
BR (ˌ)diːˈləʊkəlʌɪz,
(ˌ)diːˈləʊkˌlʌɪz, -ɪz, -ɪŋ,
-d
AM dɪˈloʊkəˌlaɪz, -ɪz,
-ɪŋ, -d

Delorean
BR dəˈlɔːrɪən, -z
AM də ˈlɔrɪən, -z

Delores
BR dəˈlɔːrɪz
AM dəˈlɔrəs

Delors
BR dəˈlɔː(r)
AM dəˈlɔ(ə)r

Delos
BR ˈdiːlɒs
AM ˈdilɑs

delouse
BR ˌdiːˈlaʊs, -ɪz, -ɪŋ, -t
AM dɪˈlaʊs, dəˈlaʊs, -əz,
-ɪŋ, -t

Delphi
BR ˈdɛlfʌɪ, ˈdɛlfi
AM ˈdɛlˌfaɪ

Delphian
BR ˈdɛlfɪən, -z
AM ˈdɛlfɪən, -z

Delphic
BR ˈdɛlfɪk
AM ˈdɛlfɪk

Delphine
BR ˈdɛlfiːn
AM ˈdɛlˌfin

delphinia
BR dɛlˈfɪnɪə(r)
AM dɛlˈfɪnɪə

delphinium
BR dɛlˈfɪnɪəm, -z
AM dɛlˈfɪnɪəm, -z

delphinoid
BR ˈdɛlfɪnɔɪd, -z
AM ˈdɛlfəˌnɔɪd, -z

Delphinus
BR dɛlˈfʌɪnəs
AM dɛlˈfaɪnəs

Delsey
BR ˈdɛlsi
AM ˈdɛlsi

delta
BR ˈdɛltə(r), -z
AM ˈdɛltə, -z

deltaic
BR dɛlˈteɪɪk
AM dɛlˈteɪɪk

deltiologist
BR ˌdɛltɪˈɒlədʒɪst, -s
AM ˌdɛltiˈɑlədʒəst, -s

deltiology
BR ˌdɛltɪˈɒlədʒi
AM ˌdɛltiˈɑlədʒi
deltoid
BR ˈdɛltɔɪd
AM ˈdɛlˌtɔɪd
delude
BR dɪˈl(j)uːd, -z, -ɪŋ, -ɪd
AM dəˈlud, diˈlud, -z, -ɪŋ, -əd
deluder
BR dɪˈl(j)uːdə(r), -z
AM dəˈludər, diˈludər, -z
deluge
BR ˈdɛljuː(d)ʒ, -ɪz, -ɪŋ, -d
AM ˈdɛlˌjudʒ, -əz, -ɪŋ, -d
delusion
BR dɪˈl(j)uːʒn, -z
AM dəˈluʒən, diˈluʒən, -z
delusional
BR dɪˈl(j)uːʒn(ə)l, dɪˈl(j)uːʒən(ə)l
AM dəˈluʒ(ə)nəl, diˈluʒ(ə)nəl
delusive
BR dɪˈl(j)uːsɪv
AM dəˈlusɪv, diˈlusɪv
delusively
BR dɪˈl(j)uːsɪvli
AM dəˈlusɪvli, diˈlusɪvli
delusiveness
BR dɪˈl(j)uːsɪvnɪs
AM dəˈlusɪvnɪs, diˈlusɪvnɪs
delusory
BR dɪˈl(j)uːs(ə)ri, dɪˈl(j)uːz(ə)ri
AM dəˈlus(ə)ri, diˈlus(ə)ri, dəˈluz(ə)ri, diˈluz(ə)ri
deluster
BR ˌdiːˈlʌstlə(r), -əz, -(ə)rɪŋ, -əd
AM dəˈləstər, diˈləstər, -z, -ɪŋ, -d
delustre
BR ˌdiːˈlʌstlə(r), -əz, -(ə)rɪŋ, -əd
AM dəˈləstər, diˈləstər, -z, -ɪŋ, -d
deluxe
BR dɪˈlʌks
AM dəˈləks, diˈləks
de luxe
BR dɪˈlʌks
AM dəˈləks, diˈləks
delve
BR dɛlv, -z, -ɪŋ, -d
AM dɛlv, -z, -ɪŋ, -d
delver
BR ˈdɛlvə(r), -z
AM ˈdɛlvər, -z

delving
BR ˈdɛlvɪŋ, -z
AM ˈdɛlvɪŋ, -z
Delwyn
BR ˈdɛlwɪn
AM ˈdɛlwən
Delyth
BR ˈdɛlɪθ
AM ˈdɛləθ
demagnetisation
BR ˌdiːmagnɪtʌɪˈzeɪʃn, diːˌmagnɪtʌɪˈzeɪʃn
AM ˌdiˌmægnədəˈzeɪʃən, ˌdiˌmægnəˌtaɪˈzeɪʃən
demagnetise
BR (ˌ)diːˈmagnɪtʌɪz, -ɪz, -ɪŋ, -d
AM diˈmægnəˌtaɪz, -ɪz, -ɪŋ, -d
demagnetiser
BR (ˌ)diːˈmagnɪtʌɪzə(r), -z
AM diˈmægnəˌtaɪzər, -z
demagnetization
BR ˌdiːmagnɪtʌɪˈzeɪʃn, diːˌmagnɪtʌɪˈzeɪʃn
AM ˌdiˌmægnədəˈzeɪʃən, ˌdiˌmægnəˌtaɪˈzeɪʃən
demagnetize
BR (ˌ)diːˈmagnɪtʌɪz, -ɪz, -ɪŋ, -d
AM diˈmægnəˌtaɪz, -ɪz, -ɪŋ, -d
demagnetizer
BR (ˌ)diːˈmagnɪtʌɪzə(r), -z
AM diˈmægnəˌtaɪzər, -z
demagogic
BR ˌdɛməˈgɒgɪk, ˌdɛməˈgɒdʒɪk
AM ˌdɛməˈgadʒɪk, ˌdɛməˈgagɪk
demagogical
BR ˌdɛməˈgɒgɪkl, ˌdɛməˈgɒdʒɪkl
AM ˌdɛməˈgadʒəkəl, ˌdɛməˈgagəkəl
demagogically
BR ˌdɛməˈgɒgɪkli, ˌdɛməˈgɒdʒɪkli
AM ˌdɛməˈgadʒək(ə)li, ˌdɛməˈgagək(ə)li
demagogue
BR ˈdɛməgɒg, -z
AM ˈdɛməˌgag, -z
demagoguery
BR ˈdɛməgɒg(ə)ri, ˌdɛməˈgɒg(ə)ri
AM ˈdɛməˌgag(ə)ri, ˌdɛməˈgag(ə)ri
demagogy
BR ˈdɛməgɒgi, ˈdɛməgɒdʒi
AM ˈdɛməˌgagi, ˈdɛməˌgagi

deman
BR ˌdiːˈman, -z, -ɪŋ, -d
AM diˈmæn, -z, -ɪŋ, -d
demand
BR dɪˈmɑːnd, dɪˈmand, -z, -ɪŋ, -ɪd
AM dəˈmænd, diˈmænd, -z, -ɪŋ, -əd
demandable
BR dɪˈmɑːndəbl, dɪˈmandəbl
AM dəˈmændəbəl, diˈmændəbəl
demandant
BR dɪˈmɑːnd(ə)nt, dɪˈmand(ə)nt, -s
AM dəˈmændnt, diˈmændnt, -s
demander
BR dɪˈmɑːndə(r), dɪˈmandə(r), -z
AM dəˈmændər, diˈmændər, -z
demandingly
BR dɪˈmɑːndɪŋli, dɪˈmandɪŋli
AM dəˈmændɪŋli, diˈmændɪŋli
demantoid
BR dɪˈmantɔɪd, -z
AM dəˈmænˌtɔɪd, diˈmænˌtɔɪd, -z
demarcate
BR ˈdiːmɑːkeɪt, -s, -ɪŋ, -ɪd
AM dəˈmɑrˌkeɪlt, diˈmɑrˌkeɪlt, ˈdimɑrˌkeɪlt, -ts, -dɪŋ, -dɪd
demarcation
BR ˌdiːmɑːˈkeɪʃn, -z
AM ˌdimɑrˈkeɪʃən, -z
demarcator
BR ˈdiːmɑːkeɪtə(r), -z
AM dəˈmɑrˌkeɪdər, diˈmɑrˌkeɪdər, ˈdimɑrˌkeɪdər, -z
démarche
BR deɪˈmɑːʃ, ˈdeɪmɑːʃ, -ɪz
AM deɪˈmɑrʃ, -əz
dematerialisation
BR ˌdiːməˌtɪərɪəlʌɪˈzeɪʃn
AM ˌdiˌmətɪriələˈzeɪʃən, ˌdimətɪriəˌlaɪˈzeɪʃən
dematerialise
BR ˌdiːməˈtɪərɪəlʌɪz, -ɪz, -ɪŋ, -d
AM ˌdiməˈtɪriəˌlaɪz, -ɪz, -ɪŋ, -d
dematerialization
BR ˌdiːməˌtɪərɪəlʌɪˈzeɪʃn
AM ˌdiˌmətɪriələˈzeɪʃən, ˌdimətɪriəˌlaɪˈzeɪʃən
dematerialize
BR ˌdiːməˈtɪərɪəlʌɪz, -ɪz, -ɪŋ, -d

deman
AM ˌdiməˈtɪriəˌlaɪz, -ɪz, -ɪŋ, -d
Demavend
BR ˈdɛməvɛnd
AM ˈdɛməˌvɛnd
deme
BR diːm, -z
AM dim, -z
demean
BR dɪˈmiːn, -z, -ɪŋ, -d
AM dəˈmin, diˈmin, -z, -ɪŋ, -d
demeanor
BR dɪˈmiːnə(r), -z
AM dəˈminər, diˈminər, -z
demeanour
BR dɪˈmiːnə(r), -z
AM dəˈminər, diˈminər, -z
Demelza
BR dəˈmɛlzə(r)
AM dəˈmɛlzə
dement
BR dɪˈmɛnt, -s, -ɪd
AM dəˈmɛn|t, diˈmən|t, -ts, -(t)əd
dementedly
BR dɪˈmɛntɪdli
AM dəˈmɛn(t)ədli, diˈmɛn(t)ədli
dementedness
BR dɪˈmɛntɪdnɪs
AM dəˈmɛn(t)ədnəs, diˈmɛn(t)ədnəs
démenti
BR ˌdeɪˈmɒtiː
AM ˌdeɪmɑnˈti
dementia
BR dɪˈmɛnʃə(r)
AM dəˈmɛn(t)ʃ(i)ə
dementia praecox
BR dɪˌmɛnʃə ˈpriːkɒks
AM dəˈmɛn(t)ʃ(i)ə ˈpriˌkaks
dementis
BR ˌdeɪˈmɒtiː(z)
AM ˌdeɪmɑnˈtiz
Demerara
BR ˌdɛməˈrɛːrə(r)
AM ˌdɛməˈrɛrə
demerge
BR ˌdiːˈməːdʒ, -ɪz, -ɪŋ, -d
AM ˌdiˈmərdʒ, -əz, -ɪŋ, -d
demerger
BR ˌdiːˈməːdʒə(r), -z
AM ˌdiˈmərdʒər, -z
demerit
BR (ˌ)diːˈmɛrɪt, -s
AM dəˈmɛrət, diˈmɛrət, -s
demeritorious
BR ˌdiːmɛrɪˈtɔːrɪəs
AM diˌmɛrəˈtɔriəs
demersal
BR dɪˈməːsl

demesne
AM də'mərsəl

demesne
BR dɪ'mem, -z
AM də'meɪn, -z

Demeter
BR dɪ'miːtə(r)
AM də'miːdər

Demetrius
BR dɪ'miːtrɪəs
AM də'mitriɪs

demigod
BR 'demɪgɒd, -z
AM 'demi,gad, -z

demigoddess
BR 'demɪ,gɒdɪs,
'demɪ,gɒdes, -ɪz
AM 'demi,gadəs, -əz

demijohn
BR 'demɪdʒɒn, -z
AM 'demi,dʒan, -z

demilitarisation
BR ,diːmɪlɪt(ə)rʌɪ'zeɪʃn,
diː,mɪlɪt(ə)rʌɪ'zeɪʃn
AM 'di,mɪlədərə'zeɪʃən,
də,mɪlədərə'zeɪʃən,
'di,mɪlədə,raɪ'zeɪʃən,
də,mɪlədə,raɪ'zeɪʃən

demilitarise
BR (,)diː'mɪlɪt(ə)rʌɪz,
-ɪz, -ɪŋ, -d
AM də'mɪlədə,raɪz,
di'mɪlədə,raɪz, -ɪz, -ɪŋ,
-d

demilitarization
BR ,diːmɪlɪt(ə)rʌɪ'zeɪʃn,
diː,mɪlɪt(ə)rʌɪ'zeɪʃn
AM 'di,mɪlədərə'zeɪʃən,
də,mɪlədərə'zeɪʃən,
'di,mɪlədə,raɪ'zeɪʃən,
də,mɪlədə,raɪ'zeɪʃən

demilitarize
BR (,)diː'mɪlɪt(ə)rʌɪz,
-ɪz, -ɪŋ, -d
AM də'mɪlədə,raɪz,
di'mɪlədə,raɪz, -ɪz, -ɪŋ,
-d

de Mille
BR də 'mɪl
AM də 'mɪl

demi-mondaine
BR ,demɪmɒn'deɪn, -z
AM 'demi,man'deɪn, -z

demi-monde
BR ,demɪ'mɒnd,
'demɪmɒnd
AM 'demi,'mand

demineralisation
BR ,diːmɪn(ə)rəlʌɪ'zeɪʃn,
,diːmɪn(ə)r[ʌɪ'zeɪʃn,
diː,mɪn(ə)rəlʌɪ'zeɪʃn,
diː,mɪn(ə)r[ʌɪ'zeɪʃn
AM di,mɪnərələ'zeɪʃən,
də,mɪnərələ'zeɪʃən,
di:,mɪnərə,laɪ'zeɪʃən,
də,mɪnərə,laɪ'zeɪʃn

demineralise
BR (,)diː'mɪn(ə)rəlʌɪz,
(,)diː'mɪn(ə)r[ʌɪz, -ɪz,
-ɪŋ, -d
AM də'mɪnərə,laɪz,
di'mɪnərə,laɪz, -ɪz, -ɪŋ,
-d

demineralization
BR ,diː'mɪn(ə)rəlʌɪ'zeɪʃn,
,diː:mɪn(ə)r[ʌɪ'zeɪʃn,
diː,mɪn(ə)rəlʌɪ'zeɪʃn,
diː:,mɪn(ə)r[ʌɪ'zeɪʃn
AM di,mɪnərələ'zeɪʃən,
də,mɪnərələ'zeɪʃən,
di:,mɪnərə,laɪ'zeɪʃən,
də,mɪnərə,laɪ'zeɪʃn

demineralize
BR (,)diː'mɪn(ə)rəlʌɪz,
(,)diː'mɪn(ə)r[ʌɪz, -ɪz,
-ɪŋ, -d
AM də'mɪnərə,laɪz,
di'mɪnərə,laɪz, -ɪz, -ɪŋ,
-d

demi-pension
BR ,demɪ'pɒsjō
AM ,demi'pɛn(t)ʃən

demirep
BR 'demɪrep, -s
AM ,demi'rep, -s

demise
BR dɪ'mʌɪz
AM də'maɪz, di'maɪz

demisemiquaver
BR 'demɪsemɪ,kweɪ-
və(r),
,demɪ'semɪkweɪvə(r),
-z
AM ,demɪ';semaɪ,kweɪ-
vər, -z

demission
BR dɪ'mɪʃn, -z
AM də'mɪʃən,
di'mɪʃən, -z

demist
BR di:'mɪst, dɪ'mɪst, -s,
-ɪŋ, -ɪd
AM di'mɪst, də'mɪst, -s,
-ɪŋ, -ɪd

demister
BR di:'mɪstə(r),
dɪ'mɪstə(r), -z
AM di'mɪstər,
də'mɪstər, -z

demit
BR ,di:'mɪt, dɪ'mɪt, -s,
-ɪŋ, -ɪd
AM di'mɪ|t, də'mɪ|t, -ts,
-dɪŋ, -dɪd

demitasse
BR 'demɪtas, 'demɪtɑ:s,
-ɪz
AM 'demi,tas,
'demi,tæs -əz

demiurge
BR 'demɪə:dʒ,
'di:mɪə:dʒ, -ɪz
AM 'demi,ərdʒ, -əz

demiurgic
BR ,demɪ'ə:dʒɪk,
,di:mɪ'ə:dʒɪk
AM ,demi'ərdʒɪk

demi-vierge
BR ,demɪvɪ'ə:ʒ, -z
AM ,demivi'ərʒ, -z

demo
BR 'deməʊ, -z
AM 'demoʊ, -z

demob
BR (,)diː'mɒb, dɪ'mɒb,
-z, -ɪŋ, -d
AM di'mab, də'mab, -z,
-ɪŋ, -d

demobilisation
BR dɪ,məʊbɪlʌɪ'zeɪʃn,
dɪ,məʊbl̩ʌɪ'zeɪʃn,
di:,məʊbɪlʌɪ'zeɪʃn,
di:,məʊbl̩ʌɪ'zeɪʃn,
,di:məʊbɪlʌɪ'zeɪʃn,
,di:məʊbl̩ʌɪ'zeɪʃn
AM di,moʊbələ'zeɪʃən,
də,moʊbələ'zeɪʃən,
di,moʊbə,laɪ'zeɪʃən,
də,moʊbə,laɪ'zeɪʃən

demobilise
BR dɪ'məʊbɪlʌɪz,
dɪ'məʊbl̩ʌɪz,
(,)diː'məʊbɪlʌɪz,
(,)diː'məʊbl̩ʌɪz, -ɪz,
-ɪŋ, -d
AM di'moʊbə,laɪz,
də'moʊbə,laɪz, -ɪz, -ɪŋ,
-d

demobilization
BR dɪ,məʊbɪlʌɪ'zeɪʃn,
dɪ,məʊbl̩ʌɪ'zeɪʃn,
di:,məʊbɪlʌɪ'zeɪʃn,
di:,məʊbl̩ʌɪ'zeɪʃn,
,di:məʊbɪlʌɪ'zeɪʃn,
,di:məʊbl̩ʌɪ'zeɪʃn
AM di,moʊbələ'zeɪʃən,
də,moʊbələ'zeɪʃən,
di,moʊbə,laɪ'zeɪʃən,
də,moʊbə,laɪ'zeɪʃən

demobilize
BR dɪ'məʊbɪlʌɪz,
dɪ'məʊbl̩ʌɪz,
(,)diː'məʊbɪlʌɪz,
(,)diː'məʊbl̩ʌɪz, -ɪz,
-ɪŋ, -d
AM di'moʊbə,laɪz,
də'moʊbə,laɪz, -ɪz, -ɪŋ,
-d

democracy
BR dɪ'mɒkrəs|i, -ɪz
AM də'mɑkrəsi, -ɪz

democrat
BR 'deməkrat, -s
AM 'demə,kræt, -s

democratic
BR ,demə'kratɪk
AM ,demə'krædɪk

democratically
BR ,demə'kratɪkli
AM ,demə'krædək(ə)li

democratisation
BR dɪ,mɒkrətʌɪ'zeɪʃn
AM də,makrədə'zeɪʃən,
di,makrədə'zeɪʃən,
də,makrə,taɪ'zeɪʃən,
di,makrə,taɪ'zeɪʃən

democratise
BR dɪ'mɒkrətʌɪz, -ɪz,
-ɪŋ, -d
AM də'makrə,taɪz,
di'makrə,taɪz, -ɪz, -ɪŋ,
-d

democratism
BR dɪ'mɒkrətɪz(ə)m
AM də'makrə,tɪzəm,
di'makrə,tɪzəm

democratization
BR dɪ,mɒkrətʌɪ'zeɪʃn
AM də,makrədə'zeɪʃən,
di,makrədə'zeɪʃən,
də,makrə,taɪ'zeɪʃən,
di,makrə,taɪ'zeɪʃən

democratize
BR dɪ'mɒkrətʌɪz, -ɪz,
-ɪŋ, -d
AM də'makrə,taɪz,
di'makrə,taɪz, -ɪz, -ɪŋ,
-d

Democritus
BR dɪ'mɒkrɪtəs
AM də'makrədəs,
di'makrədəs

démodé
BR ,deɪ'məʊdeɪ
AM ,deɪmoʊ'deɪ

demodectic
BR ,di'mə(ʊ)'dektɪk
AM ,dimə'dektɪk

demodulate
BR di:'mɒdjʊleɪt,
,di:'mɒdʒʊleɪt, -s, -ɪŋ,
-ɪd
AM di'madʒə,leɪ|t,
di'madjʊ,leɪ|t, -ts,
-dɪŋ, -dɪd

demodulation
BR ,di:mɒdjʊ'leɪʃn,
,di:mɒdʒʊ'leɪʃn
AM di,madʒə'leɪʃən

demodulator
BR ,di:'mɒdjʊleɪtə(r),
,di:'mɒdʒʊleɪtə(r), -z
AM di'madʒə,leɪdər, -z

demographer
BR dɪ'mɒgrəfə(r), -z
AM də'magrəfər, -z

demographic
BR ,demə'grafɪk, -s
AM ,demə'græfɪk, -s

demographical
BR ,demə'grafɪkl
AM ,demə'græfəkəl

demographically
BR ,demə'grafɪkli
AM ,demə'græfək(ə)li

demography
BR dɪ'mɒgrəfi
AM də'magrəfi

demoiselle
BR ˌdɛmwɑːˈzɛl,
ˌdɛm(w)əˈzɛl, -z
AM ˌdɛm(w)ɑˈzɛl, -z
demolish
BR dɪˈmɒl|ɪʃ, -ɪʃɪz,
-ɪʃɪŋ, -ɪʃt
AM dəˈmɑl|ɪʃ, dɪˈmɑl|ɪʃ,
-ɪz, -ɪŋ, -t
demolisher
BR dɪˈmɒlɪʃə(r), -z
AM dəˈmɑlɪʃər,
dɪˈmɑlɪʃər, -z
demolition
BR ˌdɛməˈlɪʃn, -z
AM ˌdɛməˈlɪʃən,
ˌdiːməˈlɪʃən, -z
demolitionist
BR ˌdɛməˈlɪʃnɪst,
ˌdɛməˈlɪʃənɪst, -s
AM ˌdɛməˈlɪʃənəst,
ˌdiːməˈlɪʃənəst, -s
demon
BR ˈdiːmən, -z
AM ˈdiːmən, -z
demonetisation
BR ˌdiːmʌnɪtʌɪˈzeɪʃn,
diːˌmʌnɪtʌɪˈzeɪʃn
AM diˌmɑnədəˈzeɪʃən,
diˌmɑnəˌtɑrˈzeɪʃən
demonetise
BR (ˌ)diːˈmʌnɪtʌɪz, -ɪz,
-ɪŋ, -d
AM diˈmɑnəˌtaɪz, -ɪz,
-ɪŋ, -d
demonetization
BR ˌdiːmʌnɪtʌɪˈzeɪʃn,
diːˌmʌnɪtʌɪˈzeɪʃn
AM diˌmɑnədəˈzeɪʃən,
diˌmɑnəˌtɑrˈzeɪʃən
demonetize
BR (ˌ)diːˈmʌnɪtʌɪz, -ɪz,
-ɪŋ, -d
AM diˈmɑnəˌtaɪz, -ɪz,
-ɪŋ, -d
demoniac
BR dɪˈməʊnɪak, -s
AM dəˈmoʊniˌæk,
ˌdiməˈnaɪək, -s
demoniacal
BR ˌdiːməˈnʌɪəkl
AM ˌdiməˈnaɪəkəl
demoniacally
BR ˌdiːməˈnʌɪəkli
AM ˌdiməˈnaɪək(ə)li
demonic
BR dɪˈmɒnɪk,
diːˈmɒnɪk
AM dəˈmɑnɪk,
dɪˈmɑnɪk
demonical
BR dɪˈmɒnɪkl,
diːˈmɒnɪkl
AM dəˈmɑnəkəl,
dɪˈmɑnəkəl
demonically
BR dɪˈmɒnɪkli,
diːˈmɒnɪkli

AM dəˈmanək(ə)li,
dɪˈmanək(ə)li
demonisation
BR ˌdiːmənʌɪˈzeɪʃn
AM ˌdimənəˈzeɪʃən,
ˌdiməˌnaɪˈzeɪʃən
demonise
BR ˈdiːmənʌɪz, -ɪz, -ɪŋ,
-d
AM ˈdiməˌnaɪz, -ɪz, -ɪŋ,
-d
demonism
BR ˈdiːmənɪz(ə)m
AM ˈdiməˌnɪzəm
demonization
BR ˌdiːmənʌɪˈzeɪʃn
AM ˌdimənəˈzeɪʃən,
ˌdiməˌnaɪˈzeɪʃən
demonize
BR ˈdiːmənʌɪz, -ɪz, -ɪŋ,
-d
AM ˈdiməˌnaɪz, -ɪz, -ɪŋ,
-d
demonolatry
BR ˌdiːməˈnɒlətri
AM ˌdiməˈnɑlətri
demonological
BR ˌdiːmənəˈlɒdʒɪkl
AM ˌdimənəˈlɑdʒəkəl
demonologist
BR ˌdiːməˈnɒlədʒɪst, -s
AM ˌdiməˈnɑlədʒəst, -s
demonology
BR ˌdiːməˈnɒlədʒi
AM ˌdiməˈnɑlədʒi
demonstrability
BR dɪˌmɒnstrəˈbɪlɪti
AM dəˌmɑnstrəˈbɪlɪdi
demonstrable
BR dɪˈmɒnstrəbl
AM dəˈmɑnstrəbəl,
dɪˈmɑnstrəbəl
demonstrably
BR dɪˈmɒnstrəbli
AM dəˈmɑnstrəbli,
dɪˈmɑnstrəbli
demonstrate
BR ˈdɛmənstreɪt, -s,
-ɪŋ, -ɪd
AM ˈdɛmənˌstreɪ|t, -ts,
-dɪŋ, -dɪd
demonstration
BR ˌdɛmənˈstreɪʃn, -z
AM ˌdɛmənˈstreɪʃən, -z
demonstrational
BR ˌdɛmənˈstreɪʃn(ə)l,
ˌdɛmənˈstreɪʃən(ə)l
AM ˌdɛmənˈstreɪʃ(ə)nəl
demonstrative
BR dɪˈmɒnstrətɪv, -z
AM dəˈmɑnstrədɪv,
dɪˈmɑnstrədɪv, -z
demonstratively
BR dɪˈmɒnstrətɪvli
AM dəˈmɑnstrədɪvli,
dɪˈmɑnstrədɪvli
demonstrativeness
BR dɪˈmɒnstrətɪvnɪs

AM dəˈmɑnstrədɪvnɪs,
dɪˈmɑnstrədɪvnɪs
demonstrator
BR ˈdɛmənstreɪtə(r),
-z
AM ˈdɛmənˌstreɪdər, -z
de Montfort
BR də ˈmɒntfət,
+ ˈmɒntfɔːt
AM də ˈman(t)fərt,
+ ˈman(t)ˌfɔ(ə)rt
demoralisation
BR dɪˌmɒrəlʌɪˈzeɪʃn,
dɪˌmɒrˌlʌɪˈzeɪʃn
AM dəˌmɔrələˈzeɪʃən,
dɪˌmɔrələˈzeɪʃən,
dəˌmɔrəˌlaɪˈzeɪʃən,
dɪˌmɔrəˌlaɪˈzeɪʃən
demoralise
BR dɪˈmɒrəlʌɪz,
dɪˈmɒrˌlʌɪz, -ɪz, -ɪŋ, -d
AM dəˈmɔrəˌlaɪz,
dɪˈmɔrəˌlaɪz, -ɪz, -ɪŋ, -d
demoralisingly
BR dɪˈmɒrəlʌɪzɪŋli,
dɪˈmɒrˌlʌɪzɪŋli
AM dəˈmɔrəˌlaɪzɪŋli,
dɪˈmɔrəˌlaɪzɪŋli
demoralization
BR dɪˌmɒrəlʌɪˈzeɪʃn,
dɪˈmɒrˌlʌɪˈzeɪʃn
AM dəˌmɔrələˈzeɪʃən,
dɪˌmɔrələˈzeɪʃən,
dəˌmɔrəˌlaɪˈzeɪʃən,
dɪˌmɔrəˌlaɪˈzeɪʃən
demoralize
BR dɪˈmɒrəlʌɪz,
dɪˈmɒrˌlʌɪz, -ɪz, -ɪŋ, -d
AM dəˈmɔrəˌlaɪz,
dɪˈmɔrəˌlaɪz, -ɪz, -ɪŋ, -d
demoralizingly
BR dɪˈmɒrəlʌɪzɪŋli,
dɪˈmɒrˌlʌɪzɪŋli
AM dəˈmɔrəˌlaɪzɪŋli,
dɪˈmɔrəˌlaɪzɪŋli
Demos
BR ˈdiːmɒs
AM ˈdiˌmas, ˈdiˌmɔs
Demosthenes
BR dɪˈmɒsθmiːz
AM dəˈmasθəˌniz
demote
BR dɪˈməʊt, ˌdiːˈməʊt,
-s, -ɪŋ, -ɪd
AM dəˈmoʊ|t, dɪˈmoʊ|t,
-ts, -dɪŋ, -dəd
demotic
BR dɪˈmɒtɪk
AM dəˈmadɪk
demotion
BR dɪˈməʊʃn,
ˌdiːˈməʊʃn, -z
AM dəˈmoʊʃən,
dɪˈmoʊʃən, -z
demotivate
BR ˌdiːˈməʊtɪveɪt, -s,
-ɪŋ, -ɪd

AM diˈmoʊdəˌveɪ|t, -ts,
-dɪŋ, -dɪd
demotivation
BR ˌdiːˈməʊtɪˈveɪʃn
AM diˌmoʊdəˈveɪʃən
demount
BR ˌdiːˈmaʊnt, -s, -ɪŋ,
-ɪd
AM diˈmaʊn|t, -ts,
-(t)ɪŋ, -(t)əd
demountable
BR ˌdiːˈmaʊntəbl
AM diˈmaʊn(t)əbəl
Dempsey
BR ˈdɛm(p)si
AM ˈdɛm(p)si
Dempster
BR ˈdɛm(p)stə(r)
AM ˈdɛm(p)stər
demulcent
BR dɪˈmʌlsnt, -s
AM dəˈməlsənt,
dɪˈməlsənt, -s
demur
BR dɪˈmɜː(r), -z, -ɪŋ, -d
AM dəˈmɜr, dɪˈmɜr, -z,
-ɪŋ, -d
demure
BR dɪˈmjʊə(r),
dɪˈmjɔː(r)
AM dəˈmjʊ(ə)r,
dɪˈmjʊ(ə)r
demurely
BR dɪˈmjʊəli, dɪˈmjɔːli
AM dəˈmjʊrli,
dɪˈmjʊrli
demureness
BR dɪˈmjʊənəs,
dɪˈmjɔːnəs
AM dəˈmjʊrnəs,
dɪˈmjʊrnəs
demurrable
BR dɪˈmɜːrəbl
AM dəˈmjʊrəbəl,
dɪˈmjʊrəbəl
demurrage
BR dɪˈmʌrɪdʒ
AM dəˈmɜrɪdʒ
demurral
BR dɪˈmʌrəl, dɪˈmʌrl̩
AM dəˈmɜrəl
demurrer[1]
dissent
BR dɪˈmʌrə(r), -z
AM dəˈmɜrər,
dɪˈmɜrər, -z
demurrer[2]
person who demurs
BR dɪˈmɜːrə(r), -z
AM dəˈmɜrər,
dɪˈmɜrər, -z
demy
BR dɪˈmʌɪ, -z
AM dɪˈmaɪ, -z
demystification
BR ˌdiːmɪstɪfrˈkeɪʃn,
diːˌmɪstɪfrˈkeɪʃn
AM ˌdiˌmɪstəfəˈkeɪʃən

demystify
BR (ˌ)diːˈmɪstɪfʌɪ, -z,
-ɪŋ, -d
AM diˈmɪstɪˌfaɪ, -z, -ɪŋ,
-d
demythologisation
BR ˌdiːmɪˌθɒlədʒʌɪˈzeɪʃn,
AM ˌdiməθæləədʒəˈzeɪʃən,
ˌdiməθaləˌdʒaɪˈzeɪʃən
demythologise
BR ˌdiːmɪˈθɒlədʒʌɪz,
-ɪz, -ɪŋ, -d
AM ˌdiˈmæˈθalə,dʒaɪz,
-ɪz, -ɪŋ, -d
demythologization
BR ˌdiːmɪˌθɒlədʒʌɪˈzeɪʃn
AM ˌdiməθæləədʒəˈzeɪʃən,
ˌdiməθaləˌdʒaɪˈzeɪʃən
demythologize
BR ˌdiːmɪˈθɒlədʒʌɪz,
-ɪz, -ɪŋ, -d
AM ˌdiˈmæˈθalə,dʒaɪz,
-ɪz, -ɪŋ, -d
den
BR dɛn, -z
AM dɛn, -z
denarii
BR dɪˈnɛːrɪʌɪ,
dɪˈnɛːriː, dɪˈnɑːrɪʌɪ,
dɪˈnɑːriː:
AM dəˈnɛri,i,
dəˈnariˌaɪ
denarius
BR dɪˈnɛːrɪəs,
dɪˈnɑːrɪəs
AM dəˈnɛriəs,
dəˈnariəs
denary
BR ˈdiːn(ə)ri, ˈdɛn(ə)ri
AM ˈdɛnəri, ˈdinəri
denationalisation
BR ˌdiːnaʃn̩əlʌɪˈzeɪʃn,
ˌdiːnaʃn̩ʌɪˈzeɪʃn,
ˌdiːnaʃən‌ʌɪˈzeɪʃn,
ˌdiːnaʃ(ə)nəlʌɪˈzeɪʃn,
diːnaʃn̩əlʌɪˈzeɪʃn,
diːnaʃn̩ʌɪˈzeɪʃn,
diːnaʃən‌ʌɪˈzeɪʃn,
diːnaʃ(ə)nəlʌɪˈzeɪʃn,
-z
AM ˌdinæʃ(ə)nələˈzeɪʃən,
ˌdinæʃ(ə)nəˌlaɪˈzeɪʃən,
dəˌnæʃ(ə)nəˌlaɪˈzeɪʃən,
dəˌnæʃ(ə)nələˈzeɪʃən,
-z
denationalise
BR (ˌ)diːˈnaʃn̩əlʌɪz,
(ˌ)diːˈnaʃn̩ʌɪz,
(ˌ)diːˈnaʃən‌ʌɪz,
(ˌ)diːˈnaʃ(ə)nələʌɪz,
-ɪz, -ɪŋ, -d
AM diˈnæʃ(ə)nə,laɪz,
dəˈnæʃ(ə)nəˌlaɪz, -ɪz,
-ɪŋ, -d
denationalization
BR ˌdiːnaʃn̩əlʌɪˈzeɪʃn,
ˌdiːnaʃn̩ʌɪˈzeɪʃn,
ˌdiːnaʃən‌ʌɪˈzeɪʃn,
ˌdiːnaʃ(ə)nəlʌɪˈzeɪʃn,

diˌnaʃn̩əlʌɪˈzeɪʃn,
diˌnaʃn̩ʌɪˈzeɪʃn,
diˌnaʃən‌ʌɪˈzeɪʃn,
diˌnaʃ(ə)nəlʌɪˈzeɪʃn,
-z
AM ˌdinæʃ(ə)nələˈzeɪʃən,
ˌdinæʃ(ə)nəˌlaɪˈzeɪʃən,
dəˌnæʃ(ə)nəˌlaɪˈzeɪʃən,
dəˌnæʃ(ə)nələˈzeɪʃən,
-z
denationalize
BR (ˌ)diːˈnaʃn̩əlʌɪz,
(ˌ)diːˈnaʃn̩ʌɪz,
(ˌ)diːˈnaʃən‌ʌɪz,
(ˌ)diːˈnaʃ(ə)nələʌɪz,
-ɪz, -ɪŋ, -d
AM diˈnæʃ(ə)nə,laɪz,
dəˈnæʃ(ə)nəˌlaɪz, -ɪz,
-ɪŋ, -d
denaturalisation
BR ˌdiːnatʃ(ə)rələʌɪ-
ˈzeɪʃn,
ˌdiːnatʃ(ə)rˌlʌɪˈzeɪʃn,
diːnatʃ(ə)rələʌɪˈzeɪʃn,
diːnatʃ(ə)rˌlʌɪˈzeɪʃn
AM diˌnætʃ(ə)rələ-
ˈzeɪʃən,
diˌnætʃ(ə)rəˌlaɪˈzeɪʃən
denaturalise
BR (ˌ)diːˈnatʃ(ə)rələʌɪz,
(ˌ)diːˈnatʃ(ə)rˌlʌɪz, -ɪz,
-ɪŋ, -d
AM diˈnætʃ(ə)rə,laɪz,
dəˈnætʃ(ə)rəˌlaɪz, -ɪz,
-ɪŋ, -d
denaturalization
BR ˌdiːnatʃ(ə)rələʌɪ-
ˈzeɪʃn,
diːnatʃ(ə)rˌlʌɪˈzeɪʃn,
diːnatʃ(ə)rələʌɪˈzeɪʃn,
diːnatʃ(ə)rˌlʌɪˈzeɪʃn
AM diˌnætʃ(ə)rələ-
ˈzeɪʃən,
diˌnætʃ(ə)rəˌlaɪˈzeɪʃən
denaturalize
BR (ˌ)diːˈnatʃ(ə)rələʌɪz,
(ˌ)diːˈnatʃ(ə)rˌlʌɪz, -ɪz,
-ɪŋ, -d
AM diˈnætʃ(ə)rə,laɪz,
dəˈnætʃ(ə)rəˌlaɪz, -ɪz,
-ɪŋ, -d
denaturant
BR ˌdiːˈneɪtʃ(ə)rənt,
ˌdiːˈneɪtʃ(ə)rn̩t, -s
AM diˈneɪtʃ(ə)rənt,
dəˈneɪtʃ(ə)rənt, -s
denaturation
BR ˌdiːneɪtʃəˈreɪʃn,
diːneɪtʃəˈreɪʃn
AM diˌneɪtʃəˈreɪʃən,
dəˌneɪtʃəˈreɪʃən
denature
BR ˌdiːˈneɪtʃə(r), -z, -ɪŋ,
-d
AM diˈneɪtʃər,
dəˈneɪtʃər, -z, -ɪŋ, -d
denazification
BR ˌdiːˌnɑːtsɪfɪˈkeɪʃn,
ˌdiːnɑːzɪfɪˈkeɪʃn,

diːˌnɑːtsɪfɪˈkeɪʃn,
diːˌnɑːzɪfɪˈkeɪʃn
AM diˌnɑtsəfəˈkeɪʃən
denazify
BR ˌdiːˈnɑːtsɪfʌɪ,
ˌdiːˈnɑːzɪfʌɪ, -z, -ɪŋ, -d
AM diˈnɑtsəˌfaɪ, -z, -ɪŋ,
-d
Denbigh
BR ˈdɛnbi
AM ˈdɛnbi
Denby
BR ˈdɛnbi
AM ˈdɛnbi
Dench
BR ˈdɛn(t)ʃ
AM ˈdɛn(t)ʃ
dendrite
BR ˈdɛndrʌɪt, -s
AM ˈdɛnˌdraɪt, -s
dendritic
BR dɛnˈdrɪtɪk
AM dɛnˈdrɪdɪk
dendritically
BR dɛnˈdrɪtɪkli
AM dɛnˈdrɪdɪk(ə)li
dendrochrono-
logical
BR ˌdɛndrəʊˌkrɒnə-
ˈlɒdʒɪkl
AM ˌdɛndroʊˌkranə-
ˈladʒəkəl
dendrochronolo-
gist
BR ˌdɛndrəʊkrəˈnɒlə-
dʒɪst, -s
AM ˌdɛndroʊkrəˈnalə-
dʒəst, -s
dendrochronology
BR ˌdɛndrəʊkrəˈnɒl-
ədʒi
AM ˌdɛndroʊkrəˈnal-
ədʒi
dendrogram
BR ˈdɛndrə(ʊ)gram, -z
AM ˈdɛndrəˌgræm, -z
dendroid
BR ˈdɛndrɔɪd
AM ˈdɛndrɔɪd
dendrological
BR ˌdɛndrəˈlɒdʒɪkl
AM ˌdɛndroʊˈladʒəkəl
dendrologist
BR dɛnˈdrɒlədʒɪst, -s
AM dɛnˈdralədʒəst, -s
dendrology
BR dɛnˈdrɒlədʒi
AM dɛnˈdralədʒi
Dene¹
North American
people
BR ˈdɛni, ˈdɛneɪ
AM ˈdɛneɪ
Dene²
surname
BR diːn
AM din

denigratory (continued right column)

dene
BR diːn, -z
AM din, -z
Deneb
BR ˈdɛnɛb
AM ˈdɛnˌɛb
de-net
BR ˌdiːˈnɛt, -s, -ɪŋ, -ɪd
AM diˈnɛ|t, -ts, -dɪŋ,
-dəd
Deneuve
BR dəˈnəːv
AM dəˈnʊv
dengue
BR ˈdɛŋgi
AM ˈdɛŋgi
Den Haag
BR dɛn ˈhɑːg
AM deɪn ˈhag
Denham
BR ˈdɛnəm
AM ˈdɛnəm
Denholm
BR ˈdɛnəm
AM ˈdɛnəm
Denholme¹
Yorkshire, England
BR ˈdɛnhɒlm
AM ˈdɛnhɔ(l)m,
ˈdɛnhoʊ(l)m
Denholme²
BR ˈdɛnəm
AM ˈdɛnəm
deniability
BR dɪˌnʌɪəˈbɪlɪti
AM dəˌnaɪbəˈbɪlɪdi
deniable
BR dɪˈnʌɪəbl
AM dəˈnaɪəbəl
deniably
BR dɪˈnʌɪəbli
AM dəˈnaɪəbli
denial
BR dɪˈnʌɪəl, -z
AM dəˈnaɪ(ə)l,
diˈnaɪ(ə)l, -z
denier¹
cloth, coin
BR ˈdɛnɪə(r), ˈdɛnɪeɪ
AM dəˈnɪ(ə)r, ˈdɛnjər
denier²
person or thing that
denies
BR dɪˈnʌɪə(r), -z
AM dəˈnaɪər, diˈnaɪər,
-z
denigrate
BR ˈdɛnɪgreɪt, -s, -ɪŋ, -ɪd
AM ˈdɛnəˌgreɪ|t, -ts,
-dɪŋ, -dɪd
denigration
BR ˌdɛnɪˈgreɪʃn
AM ˌdɛnəˈgreɪʃən
denigrator
BR ˈdɛnɪgreɪtə(r), -z
AM ˈdɛnəˌgreɪdər, -z
denigratory
BR ˌdɛnɪˈgreɪt(ə)ri

AM 'dɛnəgrə,tɔri

denim
BR 'dɛnɪm, -z
AM 'dɛnəm, -z

De Niro
BR də 'nɪərəʊ
AM də'nɪroʊ

Denis
BR 'dɛnɪs
AM 'dɛnəs

Denise
BR dɪ'ni:z, dɪ'ni:s
AM də'nis

denitrification
BR ˌdi:naɪtrɪfɪ'keɪʃn,
di:ˌnaɪtrɪfɪ'keɪʃn
AM də,naɪtrəfə'keɪʃən,
di,naɪtrəfə'keɪʃən

denitrify
BR (ˌ)di:'naɪtrɪfʌɪ, -z,
-ɪŋ, -d
AM də'naɪtrə,faɪ,
di'naɪtrə,faɪ, -z, -ɪŋ, -d

denizen
BR 'dɛnɪz(ə)n, -z
AM 'dɛnəzən, -z

Denmark
BR 'dɛnmɑːk
AM 'dɛnmɑrk

Denning
BR 'dɛnɪŋ
AM 'dɛnɪŋ

Dennis
BR 'dɛnɪs
AM 'dɛnəs

Dennison
BR 'dɛnɪs(ə)n
AM 'dɛnəsən

Denny
BR 'dɛni
AM 'dɛni

denominate
BR dɪ'nɒmɪneɪt, -s, -ɪŋ,
-ɪd
AM də'nɑmə,neɪ|t,
di'nɑmə,neɪ|t, -ts,
-dɪŋ, -dɪd

denomination
BR dɪ,nɒmɪ'neɪʃn, -z
AM də,nɑmə'neɪʃən,
di,nɑmə'neɪʃən, -z

denominational
BR dɪ,nɒmɪ'neɪʃn(ə)l,
dɪ,nɒmɪ'neɪʃən(ə)l
AM də,nɑmə'neɪʃ(ə)nəl,
di,nɑmə'neɪʃ(ə)nəl

**denominational-
ism**
BR dɪ,nɒmɪ'neɪʃnəl-
ɪz(ə)m,
dɪ,nɒmɪ'neɪʃn̩ɪz(ə)m,
dɪ,nɒmɪ'neɪʃən|ɪz(ə)m,
dɪ,nɒmɪ'neɪʃ(ə)nəl-
ɪz(ə)m
AM də,nɑmə'neɪʃənə-
,lɪzəm,
di,nɑmə'neɪʃənə,lɪzəm

denominationalist
BR dɪ,nɒmɪ'neɪʃnəlɪst,
dɪ,nɒmɪ'neɪʃn̩lɪst,
dɪ,nɒmɪ'neɪʃənlɪst,
dɪ,nɒmɪ'neɪʃ(ə)nəlɪst,
-s
AM də,nɑmə'neɪʃənəl-
əst,
di,nɑmə'neɪʃənələst,
-s

denominationally
BR dɪ,nɒmɪ'neɪʃn̩əli,
dɪ,nɒmɪ'neɪʃn̩li,
dɪ,nɒmɪ'neɪʃənli,
dɪ,nɒmɪ'neɪʃ(ə)nəli
AM də,nɑmə'neɪʃ(ə)n-
əli,
di,nɑmə'neɪʃ(ə)nəli

denominative
BR dɪ'nɒmɪnətɪv
AM də'nɑmə,neɪdɪv,
də'nɑmənədɪv,
di'nɑmə,neɪdɪv,
di'nɑmənədɪv

denominator
BR dɪ'nɒmɪneɪtə(r), -z
AM də'nɑmə,neɪdər,
di'nɑmə,neɪdər, -z

de nos jours
BR də ,nəʊ 'ʒʊə(r)
AM də ,noʊ 'ʒʊ(ə)r

denotation
BR ,di:nə(ʊ)'teɪʃn
AM ,dinoʊ'teɪʃən

denotative
BR dɪ'nəʊtətɪv,
'di:nə(ʊ)teɪtɪv
AM 'dinoʊ,teɪdɪv,
də'noʊdədɪv,
di'noʊdədɪv

denotatively
BR dɪ'nəʊtətɪvli,
'di:nə(ʊ)teɪtɪvli,
AM 'dinoʊ,teɪdɪvli,
də'noʊdədɪvli,
di'noʊdədɪvli

denote
BR dɪ'nəʊt, -s, -ɪŋ, -ɪd
AM də'noʊ|t, di'noʊ|t,
-ts, -dɪŋ, -dəd

dénouement
BR deɪ'n(j)u:mɒ̃, -z
AM ,deɪnu'mɑn, -z

denounce
BR dɪ'naʊns, -ɪz, -ɪŋ, -t
AM də'naʊns,
di'naʊns, -əz, -ɪŋ, -t

denouncement
BR dɪ'naʊnsm(ə)nt, -s
AM də'naʊnsmənt,
di'naʊnsmənt, -s

denouncer
BR dɪ'naʊnsə(r), -z
AM də'naʊnsər,
di'naʊnsər, -z

de nouveau
BR də ,nu:'vəʊ
AM də ,nu'voʊ

Denovo
BR dɪ'nəʊvəʊ
AM də'noʊvoʊ

de novo
BR deɪ 'nəʊvəʊ, di: +
AM də 'noʊvoʊ, di +

dense
BR dɛns, -ə(r), -ɪst
AM dɛns, -ər, -əst

densely
BR 'dɛnsli
AM 'dɛnsli

denseness
BR 'dɛnsnəs
AM 'dɛnsnəs

densitometer
BR ,dɛnsɪ'tɒmɪtə(r), -z
AM ,dɛnsə'tɑmədər, -z

density
BR 'dɛnsɪt|i, -ɪz
AM 'dɛnsədi, -z

dent
BR dɛnt, -s, -ɪŋ, -ɪd
AM dɛn|t, -(t)s, -(t)ɪŋ,
-(t)əd

dental
BR 'dɛntl
AM 'dɛn(t)l

dentalia
BR dɛn'teɪlɪə(r)
AM dɛn'teɪljə,
dɛn'teɪlɪə

dentalise
BR 'dɛntl̩ʌɪz,
'dɛntəlʌɪz, -ɪz, -ɪŋ, -d
AM 'dɛn(t)l̩,aɪz, -ɪz, -ɪŋ,
-d

dentalium
BR dɛn'teɪlɪəm
AM dɛn'teɪliəm

dentalize
BR 'dɛntl̩ʌɪz,
'dɛntəlʌɪz, -ɪz, -ɪŋ, -d
AM 'dɛn(t)l̩,aɪz, -ɪz, -ɪŋ,
-d

dentate
BR 'dɛnteɪt
AM 'dɛn,teɪt

denticle
BR 'dɛntɪkl, -z
AM 'dɛn(t)əkəl, -z

denticulate
BR dɛn'tɪkjələt,
dɛn'tɪkjəleɪt
AM dɛn'tɪkjələt

dentifrice
BR 'dɛntɪfrɪs, -ɪz
AM 'dɛn(t)əfrəs, -ɪz

dentil
BR 'dɛnt(ɪ)l, -z
AM 'dɛn(t)l, 'dɛn,tɪl, -z

dentilingual
BR ,dɛntɪ'lɪŋgwəl
AM 'dɛn(t)ə'lɪŋgwəl

dentin
BR 'dɛnti:n
AM 'dɛn,tɪn, dɛn'tɪn

dentinal
BR 'dɛntɪnl
AM dɛn'tinəl,
'dɛn(t)ənəl

dentine
BR 'dɛnti:n
AM 'dɛn,tin, dɛn'tin

dentist
BR 'dɛntɪst
AM 'dɛn(t)ɪst, -s

dentistry
BR 'dɛntɪstri
AM 'dɛn(t)ɪstri

dentition
BR dɛn'tɪʃn
AM dɛn'tɪʃən

Denton
BR 'dɛnt(ə)n
AM 'dɛn(t)ən

denture
BR 'dɛntʃə(r), -z
AM 'dɛn(t)ʃər, -z

denuclearisation
BR ,di:nju:klɪərʌɪ'zeɪʃn,
di:,nju:klɪərʌɪ'zeɪʃn
AM di,n(j)ukli(ə)rə'zeɪʃən,
di,n(j)ukli(ə),rar'zeɪʃən

denuclearise
BR ,di:'nju:klɪərʌɪz,
-ɪz, -ɪŋ, -d
AM di'n(j)uklɪə,raɪz,
-ɪz, -ɪŋ, -d

denuclearization
BR ,di:nju:klɪərʌɪ'zeɪʃn,
di:,nju:klɪərʌɪ'zeɪʃn
AM di,n(j)ukli(ə)rə'zeɪʃən,
di,n(j)ukli(ə),rar'zeɪʃən

denuclearize
BR ,di:'nju:klɪərʌɪz,
-ɪz, -ɪŋ, -d
AM di'n(j)uklɪə,raɪz,
-ɪz, -ɪŋ, -d

denudation
BR ,di:nju:'deɪʃn
AM ,din(j)u'deɪʃən,
,dɛnjə'deɪʃən

denudative
BR dɪ'nju:dətɪv
AM di'n(j)udədɪv

denude
BR dɪ'nju:d, -z, -ɪŋ, -ɪd
AM də'n(j)ud,
di'n(j)ud, -z, -ɪŋ, -əd

denumerability
BR dɪ,nju:m(ə)rə'bɪlɪti
AM di,n(j)umərə'bɪlɪdi

denumerable
BR dɪ'nju:m(ə)rəbl
AM di'n(j)um(ə)rəbəl

denumerably
BR dɪ'nju:m(ə)rəbli
AM di'n(j)um(ə)rəbli

denunciate
BR dɪ'nʌnsieɪt, -s, -ɪŋ,
-ɪd
AM də'nʌnsi,eɪ|t,
di'nənsi,eɪ|t, -ts, -dɪŋ,
-dɪd

denunciation
BR dɪˌnʌnsɪˈeɪʃn, -z
AM dəˌnənsiˈeɪʃən,
diˌnənsiˈeɪʃən, -z

denunciative
BR dɪˈnʌnsɪətɪv
AM dəˈnənsiˌeɪdɪv,
dəˈnənsiədɪv,
diˈnənsiˌeɪdɪv,
diˈnənsiədɪv

denunciator
BR dɪˈnʌnsɪeɪtə(r), -z
AM dəˈnənsiˌeɪdər,
diˈnənsiˌeɪdər, -z

denunciatory
BR dɪˈnʌnsɪət(ə)ri
AM dəˈnənsiəˌtɔri,
diˈnənsiəˌtɔri

Denver
BR ˈdɛnvə(r)
AM ˈdɛnvər

deny
BR dɪˈnʌɪ, -z, -ɪŋ, -d
AM dəˈnaɪ, diˈnaɪ, -z,
-ɪŋ, -d

Denys
BR ˈdɛnɪs
AM ˈdɛnəs

Denzil
BR ˈdɛnzl
AM ˈdɛnzəl

Deo
BR ˈdeɪəʊ
AM ˈdeɪoʊ

deoch an doris
BR ˌdɒx (ə)n ˈdɒrɪs,
ˌdɒk +
AM ˌd(j)akən'dɔrəs

deodand
BR ˈdiːə(ʊ)dand, -z
AM ˈdiəˌdænd, -z

deodar
BR ˈdɪə(ʊ)dɑː(r)
AM ˈdiəˌdɑr

deodorant
BR dɪˈəʊd(ə)rənt,
dɪˈəʊd(ə)rn̩t, -s
AM diˈoʊdərənt, -s

deodorisation
BR dɪˌəʊd(ə)rʌɪˈzeɪʃn
AM diˌoʊdərəˈzeɪʃən,
diˌoʊdəˌraɪˈzeɪʃən

deodorise
BR dɪˈəʊd(ə)rʌɪz, -ɪz,
-ɪŋ, -d
AM diˈoʊdəˌraɪz, -ɪz,
-ɪŋ, -d

deodoriser
BR dɪˈəʊd(ə)rʌɪzə(r)
AM diˈoʊdəˌraɪzər

deodorization
BR dɪˌəʊd(ə)rʌɪˈzeɪʃn
AM diˌoʊdərəˈzeɪʃən,
diˌoʊdəˌraɪˈzeɪʃən

deodorize
BR dɪˈəʊd(ə)rʌɪz, -ɪz,
-ɪŋ, -d

AM diˈoʊdəˌraɪz, -ɪz,
-ɪŋ, -d

deodorizer
BR dɪˈəʊd(ə)rʌɪzə(r),
-z
AM diˈoʊdəˌraɪzər, -z

Deo gratias
BR ˌdeɪəʊ ˈgrɑːtɪəs,
+ ˈgrɑːʃəs
AM ˈdeɪoʊ ˈgratsiəs

deontic
BR dɪˈɒntɪk
AM diˈɑn(t)ɪk

deontological
BR diːˌɒntəˈlɒdʒɪkl,
ˌdiːɒntəˈlɒdʒɪkl
AM diˌɑn(t)əˈlɑdʒəkəl

deontologist
BR diːˈɒntˈɒlədʒɪst, -s
AM diˌɑnˈtalədʒəst, -s

deontology
BR ˌdiːɒnˈtɒlədʒi
AM diˌɑnˈtalədʒi

Deo volente
BR ˌdeɪəʊ vɒˈlɛnteɪ
AM ˈdeɪoʊ vəˈlɛn(t)i

deoxygenate
BR diːˈɒksɪdʒəneɪt,
dɪˈɒksɪdʒəneɪt, -s, -ɪŋ,
-ɪd
AM diˈɑksədʒəˌneɪ|t,
-ts, -dɪŋ, -dɪd

deoxygenation
BR diːˌɒksɪdʒəˈneɪʃn,
dɪˌɒksɪdʒəˈneɪʃn
AM diˌaksədʒəˈneɪʃən

deoxyribonucleic
BR diˌɒksɪˌrʌɪbəʊnjuː-
ˈkliːɪk,
dɪˌɒksɪˌrʌɪbəʊnjuːˈkleɪ-
ɪk
AM diˌaksɪˌraɪboʊn(j)u-
ˈklik,
diˌaksɪˌraɪboʊˌn(j)u-
ˈkleɪk

depart
BR dɪˈpɑːt, -s, -ɪŋ, -ɪd
AM dəˈpɑr|t, diˈpɑr|t,
-ts, -dɪŋ, -dəd

department
BR dɪˈpɑːtm(ə)nt, -s
AM dəˈpɑrtmənt,
diˈpɑrtmənt, -s

departmental
BR ˌdiːpɑːˈmɛntl
AM dəˌpɑrtˈmɛn(t)l,
diˌpɑrtˈmɛn(t)l

**departmentalis-
ation**
BR ˌdiːpɑːtˌmɛntlʌɪ-
ˈzeɪʃn,
ˌdiːpɑːtˌmɛntəlʌɪˈzeɪʃn
AM dəˌpɑrtˌmɛn(t)lə-
ˈzeɪʃən,
diˌpɑrtˌmɛn(t)ləˈzeɪʃən,
dəˌpɑrtˌmɛn(t)lˌʌɪ-
ˈzeɪʃən,

diˌpɑrtˌmɛn(t)lˌʌɪ-
ˈzeɪʃən

departmentalise
BR ˌdiːpɑːtˈmɛntlʌɪz,
ˌdiːpɑːtˈmɛntəlʌɪz, -ɪz,
-ɪŋ, -d
AM dəˌpɑrtˈmɛn(t)lˌaɪz,
diˌpɑrtˈmɛn(t)lˌaɪz,
-ɪz, -ɪŋ, -d

departmentalism
BR ˌdiːpɑːtˈmɛntlɪz(ə)m,
ˌdiːpɑːtˈmɛntəlɪz(ə)m
AM dəˌpɑrtˈmɛn(t)l-
ˌɪzəm,
diˌpɑrtˈmɛn(t)lˌɪzəm

**departmentaliz-
ation**
BR ˌdiːpɑːtˌmɛntlʌɪ-
ˈzeɪʃn,
diˌpɑːtˌmɛntəlʌɪˈzeɪʃn
AM dəˌpɑrtˈmɛn(t)lə-
ˈzeɪʃən,
diˌpɑrtˌmɛn(t)ləˈzeɪʃən,
dəˌpɑrtˌmɛn(t)lˌʌɪ-
ˈzeɪʃən,
diˌpɑrtˌmɛn(t)lˌʌɪ-
ˈzeɪʃən

departmentalize
BR ˌdiːpɑːtˈmɛntlˌʌɪz,
ˌdiːpɑːtˈmɛntəlʌɪz, -ɪz,
-ɪŋ, -d
AM dəˌpɑrtˈmɛn(t)lˌaɪz,
diˌpɑrtˈmɛn(t)lˌaɪz,
-ɪz, -ɪŋ, -d

departmentally
BR ˌdiːpɑːtˈmɛntli,
ˌdiːpɑːtˈmɛntəli
AM dəˌpɑrtˈmɛn(t)li,
diˌpɑrtˈmɛn(t)li

departure
BR dɪˈpɑːtʃə(r), -z
AM dəˈpɑrtʃər,
diˈpɑrtʃər, -z

depasturage
BR diːˈpɑːstʃ(ə)rɪdʒ,
diːˈpastʃ(ə)rɪdʒ,
ˌdiːˈpɑːstjʊrɪdʒ,
ˌdiːˈpastjʊrɪdʒ
AM dəˈpastʃərɪdʒ,
diˈpastʃərɪdʒ

depasture
BR diːˈpɑːstʃ|ə(r),
diːˈpastʃ|ə(r), -əz,
-(ə)rɪŋ, -əd
AM dəˈpastʃər,
diˈpastʃər, -z, -ɪŋ, -d

dépaysé
BR ˌdeɪpeɪˈzeɪ
AM ˈdeɪˌpeɪˈzeɪ

dépaysée
BR ˌdeɪpeɪˈzeɪ
AM ˈdeɪˌpeɪˈzeɪ

depend
BR dɪˈpɛnd, -z, -ɪŋ, -ɪd
AM dəˈpɛnd, diˈpɛnd,
-z, -ɪŋ, -əd

dependability
BR dɪˌpɛndəˈbɪlɪti

AM dəˌpɛndəˈbɪlɪdi,
diˌpɛndəˈbɪlɪdi

dependable
BR dɪˈpɛndəbl
AM dəˈpɛndəbəl,
diˈpɛndəbəl

dependableness
BR dɪˈpɛndəblnəs
AM dəˈpɛndəblnəs,
diˈpɛndəblnəs

dependably
BR dɪˈpɛndəbli
AM dəˈpɛndəbli,
diˈpɛndəbli

dependant
BR dɪˈpɛnd(ə)nt, -s
AM dəˈpɛnd(ə)nt,
diˈpɛnd(ə)nt, -s

dependence
BR dɪˈpɛnd(ə)ns
AM dəˈpɛnd(ə)ns,
diˈpɛnd(ə)ns

dependency
BR dɪˈpɛnd(ə)ns|i, -ɪz
AM dəˈpɛnd(ə)nsi,
diˈpɛnd(ə)nsi, -z

dependent
BR dɪˈpɛnd(ə)nt
AM dəˈpɛnd(ə)nt,
diˈpɛnd(ə)nt

dependently
BR dɪˈpɛnd(ə)ntli
AM dəˈpɛnd(ə)n(t)li,
diˈpɛnd(ə)n(t)li

depersonalisation
BR ˌdiːpəˈsn̩əlʌɪˈzeɪʃn,
ˌdiːpəːs(ə)nəlʌɪˈzeɪʃn,
ˌdiːpəːsn̩lʌɪˈzeɪʃn
AM diˌpəːsn̩əlʌɪˈzeɪʃn,
diːˌpəːs(ə)nəlʌɪˈzeɪʃn,
diːˌpəːsn̩lʌɪˈzeɪʃn
AM dəˌpərsənəˌlaɪˈzeɪʃən,
diˌpərsənəˌlaɪˈzeɪʃən,
dəˌpərsənələˈzeɪʃən,
diˌpərsənələˈzeɪʃən

depersonalise
BR diːˈpəːsn̩əlʌɪz,
ˌdiːˈpəːs(ə)nəlʌɪz,
ˌdiːˈpəːsn̩lʌɪz, -ɪz, -ɪŋ,
-d
AM dəˈpərsənəˌlaɪz,
diˈpərsənəˌlaɪz, -ɪz,
-ɪŋ, -d

depersonalization
BR diːˈpəːsn̩əlʌɪˈzeɪʃn,
diːˈpəːs(ə)nəlʌɪˈzeɪʃn,
ˌdiːpəːsn̩lʌɪˈzeɪʃn,
diːˌpəːsn̩əlʌɪˈzeɪʃn,
ˌdiːpəːs(ə)nəlʌɪˈzeɪʃn,
ˌdiːpəːsn̩lʌɪˈzeɪʃn
AM dəˌpərsənəˌlaɪˈzeɪʃən,
diˌpərsənəˌlaɪˈzeɪʃən,
dəˌpərsənələˈzeɪʃən,
diˌpərsənələˈzeɪʃən

depersonalize
BR ˌdiːˈpəːsn̩əlʌɪz,
ˌdiːˈpəːs(ə)nəlʌɪz,

ˌdiːˈpəːsn̩ˌlaɪz, -ɪz, -ɪŋ,
-d
AM dəˈpəːsənəˌlaɪz,
diˈpəːsənəˌlaɪz, -ɪz,
-ɪŋ, -d

depict
BR dɪˈpɪkt, -s, -ɪŋ, -ɪd
AM dəˈpɪk|(t),
diˈpɪk|(t), -(t)s, -tɪŋ,
-tɪd

depicter
BR dɪˈpɪktə(r), -z
AM dəˈpɪktər,
diˈpɪktər, -z

depiction
BR dɪˈpɪkʃn
AM dəˈpɪkʃən,
diˈpɪkʃən

depictive
BR dɪˈpɪktɪv
AM dəˈpɪktɪv, diˈpɪktɪv

depictor
BR dɪˈpɪktə(r), -z
AM dəˈpɪktər,
diˈpɪktər, -z

depilate
BR ˈdepɪleɪt, -s, -ɪŋ, -ɪd
AM ˈdɛpəˌleɪ|t, -ts, -dɪŋ,
-dɪd

depilation
BR ˌdepɪˈleɪʃn
AM ˌdɛpəˈleɪʃən

depilatory
BR dɪˈpɪlət(ə)r|i, -ɪz
AM dəˈpɪləˌtɔːri,
diˈpɪləˌtɔːri, -z

deplane
BR ˌdiːˈpleɪn, -z, -ɪŋ, -d
AM diˈpleɪn, -z, -ɪŋ, -d

deplete
BR dɪˈpliːt, -s, -ɪŋ, -ɪd
AM dəˈpli|t, diˈpli|t, -ts,
-dɪŋ, -dɪd

depletion
BR dɪˈpliːʃn
AM dəˈpliːʃən
diˈplɪʃən

deplorable
BR dɪˈplɔːrəbl
AM dəˈplɔːrəbəl,
diˈplɔːrəbəl

deplorably
BR dɪˈplɔːrəbli
AM dəˈplɔːrəbli,
diˈplɔːrəbli

deplore
BR dɪˈplɔː|(r), -z, -rɪŋ, -d
AM dəˈplɔː(ə)r,
diˈplɔː(ə)r, -z, -rɪŋ, -d

deploringly
BR dɪˈplɔːrɪŋli
AM dəˈplɔːrɪŋli,
diˈplɔːrɪŋli

deploy
BR dɪˈplɔɪ, -z, -ɪŋ, -d
AM dəˈplɔɪ, diˈplɔɪ, -z,
-ɪŋ, -d

deployment
BR dɪˈplɔɪm(ə)nt, -s
AM dəˈplɔɪmənt,
diˈplɔɪmənt, -s

deplume
BR ˌdiːˈpluːm, -z, -ɪŋ, -d
AM diˈplum, -z, -ɪŋ, -d

depolarisation
BR ˌdiːpəʊlərʌɪˈzeɪʃn,
diːˌpəʊlərʌɪˈzeɪʃn
AM diˌpoʊlərəˈzeɪʃən,
diˌpoʊləˌraɪˈzeɪʃən,
dəˌpoʊləˌraɪˈzeɪʃən,
dəˌpoʊlərəˈzeɪʃən

depolarise
BR ˌdiːˈpəʊlərʌɪz, -ɪz,
-ɪŋ, -d
AM diˈpoʊləˌraɪz,
dəˈpoʊləˌraɪz, -ɪz, -ɪŋ,
-d

depolarization
BR ˌdiːpəʊlərʌɪˈzeɪʃn,
diːˌpəʊlərʌɪˈzeɪʃn
AM diˌpoʊlərəˈzeɪʃən,
diˌpoʊləˌraɪˈzeɪʃən,
dəˌpoʊləˌraɪˈzeɪʃən,
dəˌpoʊlərəˈzeɪʃən

depolarize
BR ˌdiːˈpəʊlərʌɪz, -ɪz,
-ɪŋ, -d
AM diˈpoʊləˌraɪz,
dəˈpoʊləˌraɪz, -ɪz, -ɪŋ,
-d

depoliticisation
BR ˌdiːpəˌlɪtɪsʌɪˈzeɪʃn
AM diˌpəˌlɪdəsəˈzeɪʃən,
diˌpəˌlɪdəˌsaɪˈzeɪʃən

depoliticise
BR ˌdiːpəˈlɪtɪsʌɪz, -ɪz,
-ɪŋ, -d
AM diˌpəˈlɪdəˌsaɪz, -əz,
-ɪŋ, -d

depoliticization
BR ˌdiːpəˌlɪtɪsʌɪˈzeɪʃn
AM diˌpəˌlɪdəsəˈzeɪʃən,
diˌpəˌlɪdəˌsaɪˈzeɪʃən

depoliticize
BR ˌdiːpəˈlɪtɪsʌɪz, -ɪz,
-ɪŋ, -d
AM diˌpəˈlɪdəˌsaɪz, -əz,
-ɪŋ, -d

depolymerisation
BR ˌdiːpɒlɪm(ə)rʌɪˈzeɪʃn,
diːˌpɒlɪm(ə)rʌɪˈzeɪʃn
AM diˌpaləˌmərəˈzeɪʃən,
diˌpaləmeˌraɪˈzeɪʃən

depolymerise
BR ˌdiːˈpɒlɪm(ə)rʌɪz,
-ɪz, -ɪŋ, -d
AM diˈpaləməˌraɪz, -ɪz,
-ɪŋ, -d

depolymerization
BR ˌdiːpɒlɪm(ə)rʌɪˈzeɪʃn,
diːˌpɒlɪm(ə)rʌɪˈzeɪʃn
AM diˌpaləˌmərəˈzeɪʃən,
diˌpaləmeˌraɪˈzeɪʃən

depolymerize
BR ˌdiːˈpɒlɪm(ə)rʌɪz,
-ɪz, -ɪŋ
AM diˈpaləməˌraɪz, -ɪz,
-ɪŋ

deponent
BR dɪˈpəʊnənt, -s
AM dəˈpoʊnənt,
diˈpoʊnənt, -s

Depo-Provera®
BR ˌdepəʊprə(ʊ)ˈvɪərə(r)
AM ˌdepoʊproʊˈvɪrə

depopulate
BR ˌdiːˈpɒpjʊleɪt, -s,
-ɪŋ, -ɪd
AM diˈpapjəˌleɪ|t, -ts,
-dɪŋ, -dɪd

depopulation
BR ˌdiːpɒpjʊˈleɪʃn
AM diˌpapjəˈleɪʃən

deport
BR dɪˈpɔːt, -s, -ɪŋ, -ɪd
AM dəˈpɔ(ə)rt,
diˈpɔ(ə)rt, -ts,
-ˈpɔrdɪŋ, -ˈpɔrdəd

deportable
BR dɪˈpɔːtəbl
AM dəˈpɔrdəbəl,
diˈpɔrdəbəl

deportation
BR ˌdiːpɔːˈteɪʃn, -z
AM ˌdiˌpɔrˈteɪʃən, -z

deportee
BR ˌdiːpɔːˈtiː, -z
AM ˌdiˌpɔrˈti, dəˌpɔrˈti,
-z

deportment
BR dɪˈpɔːtm(ə)nt
AM dəˈpɔrtmənt,
diˈpɔrtmənt

deposal
BR dɪˈpəʊzl, -z
AM dəˈpoʊzəl,
diˈpoʊzəl, -z

depose
BR dɪˈpəʊz, -ɪz, -ɪŋ, -d
AM dəˈpoʊz, diˈpoʊz,
-əz, -ɪŋ, -d

deposit
BR dɪˈpɒz|ɪt, -ɪts, -ɪtɪŋ,
-ɪtɪd
AM dəˈpazə|t, diˈpazə|t,
-ts, -dɪŋ, -dəd

depositary
BR dɪˈpɒzɪt(ə)ri, -ɪz
AM dəˈpazəˌteri, -z

deposition
BR ˌdepəˈzɪʃn,
ˌdiːpəˈzɪʃn, -z
AM ˌdepəˈzɪʃən,
ˌdipəˈzɪʃən, -z

depositional
BR ˌdepəˈzɪʃn(ə)l,
ˌdepəˈzɪʃnəl
AM diˌpəˈzɪʃn(ə)l,
ˌdiːpəˈzɪʃən(ə)l
AM ˌdɛpəˈzɪʃ(ə)nəl,
ˌdipəˈzɪʃ(ə)nəl

depositor
BR dɪˈpɒzɪtə(r), -z
AM dəˈpazədər, -z

depository
BR dɪˈpɒzɪt(ə)r|i, -ɪz
AM dəˈpazəˌtɔri, -z

depot
BR ˈdepəʊ, -z
AM ˈdɛˌpoʊ, ˈdiˌpoʊ, -z

depravation
BR ˌdɛprəˈveɪʃn
AM ˌdɛprəˈveɪʃən

deprave
BR dɪˈpreɪv, -z, -ɪŋ, -d
AM dəˈpreɪv, diˈpreɪv,
-z, -ɪŋ, -d

depravity
BR dɪˈprævɪt|i, -ɪz
AM dəˈprævədi,
diˈprævədi, -z

deprecate
BR ˈdeprɪkeɪt, -s, -ɪŋ, -ɪd
AM ˈdɛprəˌkeɪ|t, -ts,
-dɪŋ, -dɪd

deprecatingly
BR ˈdeprɪkeɪtɪŋli
AM ˈdɛprəˌkeɪdɪŋli

deprecation
BR ˌdeprɪˈkeɪʃn
AM ˌdeprəˈkeɪʃən

deprecative
BR ˈdeprɪkətɪv
AM ˈdeprəˌkeɪdɪv

deprecator
BR ˈdeprɪkeɪtə(r), -z
AM ˈdɛprəˌkeɪdər, -z

deprecatory
BR ˈdeprɪkət(ə)ri,
ˈdeprɪkeɪt(ə)ri,
ˌdeprɪˈkeɪt(ə)ri
AM ˈdeprəkəˌtɔri

depreciate
BR dɪˈpriːʃɪeɪt, -s, -ɪŋ,
-ɪd
AM dəˈpriʃiˌeɪ|t,
diˈpriʃiˌeɪ|t, -ts, -dɪŋ,
-dɪd

depreciatingly
BR dɪˈpriːʃɪeɪtɪŋli
AM dəˈpriʃiˌeɪdɪŋli,
diˈpriʃiˌeɪdɪŋli

depreciation
BR dɪˌpriːʃɪˈeɪʃn
AM dəˌpriʃiˈeɪʃən,
diˌpriʃiˈeɪʃən

depreciatory
BR dɪˈpriːʃ(ɪ)ət(ə)ri
AM dəˈpriʃ(i)əˌtɔri,
diˈpriʃ(i)əˌtɔri

depredate
BR ˈdɛprɪdeɪt, -s, -ɪŋ, -ɪd
AM ˈdɛprəˌdeɪ|t, -ts,
-dɪŋ, -dɪd

depredation
BR ˌdɛprɪˈdeɪʃn, -z
AM ˌdɛprəˈdeɪʃən, -z

depredator
BR ˈdɛprɪdeɪtə(r), -z

depredatory
AM 'dɛprə‚deɪdər, -z

depredatory
BR dɪ'prɛdət(ə)ri,
‚dɛprɪ'deɪt(ə)ri,
'dɛprɪdeɪt(ə)ri
AM də'prɛdə‚tɔri

depress
BR dɪ'prɛs, -ɪz, -ɪŋ, -t
AM də'prɛs, di'prɛs,
-əz, -ɪŋ, -t

depressant
BR dɪ'prɛsnt, -s
AM də'prɛsənt,
di'prɛsənt, -s

depressible
BR dɪ'prɛsɪbl
AM də'prɛsəbəl,
di'prɛsəbəl

depressing
BR dɪ'prɛsɪŋ
AM də'prɛsɪŋ,
di'prɛsɪŋ

depressingly
BR dɪ'prɛsɪŋli
AM də'prɛsɪŋli,
di'prɛsɪŋli

depression
BR dɪ'prɛʃn, -z
AM də'prɛʃən,
di'prɛʃən, -z

depressive
BR dɪ'prɛsɪv, -z
AM də'prɛsɪv,
di'prɛsɪv, -z

depressor
BR dɪ'prɛsə(r), -z
AM də'prɛsər,
di'prɛsər, -z

depressurisation
BR ‚di:prɛʃ(ə)rʌɪ'zeɪʃn,
di:‚prɛʃ(ə)rʌɪ'zeɪʃn
AM di‚prɛʃərə'zeɪʃən,
di‚prɛʃə‚raɪ'zeɪʃən

depressurise
BR (‚)di:'prɛʃərʌɪz, -ɪz,
-ɪŋ, -d
AM di'prɛʃə‚raɪz, -ɪz,
-ɪŋ, -d

depressurization
BR ‚di:prɛʃ(ə)rʌɪ'zeɪʃn,
di:‚prɛʃ(ə)rʌɪ'zeɪʃn
AM di‚prɛʃərə'zeɪʃən,
di‚prɛʃə‚raɪ'zeɪʃən

depressurize
BR (‚)di:'prɛʃərʌɪz, -ɪz,
-ɪŋ, -d
AM di'prɛʃə‚raɪz, -ɪz,
-ɪŋ, -d

deprivable
BR dɪ'prʌɪvəbl
AM də'praɪvəbəl,
di'praɪvəbəl

deprival
BR dɪ'prʌɪvl
AM də'praɪvəl,
di'praɪvəl

deprivation
BR ‚dɛprɪ'veɪʃn, -z

deprive
BR dɪ'prʌɪv, -z, -ɪŋ, -d
AM də'praɪv, di'praɪv,
-z, -ɪŋ, -d

de profundis
BR ‚deɪ prə'fʊndɪs
AM ‚deɪ prə'fʊndəs

deprogram
BR di:'prəʊgram, -z,
-ɪŋ, -d
AM di'proʊ‚græm, -z,
-ɪŋ, -d

Deptford
BR 'dɛtfəd
AM 'dɛtfərd

depth
BR dɛpθ, -s
AM dɛpθ, -s

depthless
BR 'dɛpθləs
AM 'dɛpθləs

depurate
BR 'dɛpjʊreɪt, -s, -ɪŋ,
-ɪd
AM 'dɛpjə‚reɪt, -ts,
-ɪŋ, -ɪd

depuration
BR ‚dɛpjʊ'reɪʃn
AM ‚dɛpjə'reɪʃən

depurative
BR dɪ'pjʊərətɪv,
dɪ'pjɔ:rətɪv, -z
AM də'pjərədɪv, -z

depurator
BR 'dɛpjʊreɪtə(r), -z
AM 'dɛpjə‚reɪdər, -z

deputation
BR ‚dɛpjʊ'teɪʃn, -z
AM ‚dɛpjə'teɪʃən, -z

depute
BR dɪ'pju:t, -s, -ɪŋ, -ɪd
AM də'pju:t, di'pju:t,
-ts, -ɪŋ, -dəd

deputise
BR 'dɛpjʊtʌɪz, -ɪz, -ɪŋ,
-d
AM 'dɛpjə‚taɪz, -ɪz, -ɪŋ,
-d

deputize
BR 'dɛpjʊtʌɪz, -ɪz, -ɪŋ,
-d
AM 'dɛpjə‚taɪz, -ɪz, -ɪŋ,
-d

deputy
BR 'dɛpjʊt|i, -ɪz
AM 'dɛpjədi, -z

deputyship
BR 'dɛpjʊtɪ‚ʃɪp, -s
AM 'dɛpjədi‚ʃɪp, -s

De Quincey
BR də 'kwɪnsi
AM də 'kwɪnsi

deracinate
BR dɪ'rasɪneɪt,
dɪ'rasneɪt, -s, -ɪŋ, -ɪd

AM də'ræsn‚eɪt,
di'ræsn‚eɪt, -ts, -dɪŋ,
-ɪd

deracination
BR dɪ‚rasɪ'neɪʃn,
dɪ‚rasn'eɪʃn
AM də‚ræsn'eɪʃən,
di‚ræsn'eɪʃən

derail
BR (‚)di:'reɪl, dɪ'reɪl, -z,
-ɪŋ, -d
AM də'reɪl, di'reɪl, -z,
-ɪŋ, -d

derailleur
BR dɪ'reɪl(j)ə(r)
AM də'reɪlər

derailment
BR (‚)di:'reɪlm(ə)nt,
dɪ'reɪlm(ə)nt, -s
AM də'reɪlmənt,
di'reɪlmənt, -s

derange
BR dɪ'reɪn(d)ʒ, -ɪz, -ɪŋ,
-d
AM də'reɪndʒ,
di'reɪndʒ, -ɪz, -ɪŋ, -d

derangement
BR dɪ'reɪn(d)ʒm(ə)nt
AM də'reɪndʒmənt

derate
BR di:'reɪt, -s, -ɪŋ, -ɪd
AM di'reɪt, -ts, -dɪŋ,
-ɪd

deration
BR di:'raʃ|n, -nz,
-nɪŋ \-nɪŋ, -nd
AM di'reɪʃ|ən, -ənz,
-(ə)nɪŋ, -ənd

derby
BR 'dɑ:b|i, -ɪz
AM 'dərbi, -z

Derbyshire
BR 'dɑ:bɪʃ(ɪ)ə(r)
AM 'dərbi‚ʃɪ(ə)r

derecognition
BR ‚di:rɛkəg'nɪʃn
AM ‚di‚rɛkəg'nɪʃən

deregister
BR ‚di:'rɛdʒɪstə(r), -əz,
-(ə)rɪŋ, -əd
AM ‚di'rɛdʒəst|ər, -ərz,
-(ə)rɪŋ, -ərd

deregistration
BR ‚di:rɛdʒɪ'streɪʃn, -z
AM ‚di‚rɛdʒə'streɪʃən,
-z

deregulate
BR ‚di:'rɛgjʊleɪt, -s, -ɪŋ,
-ɪd
AM də'rɛgjʊ‚leɪt,
di'rɛgjʊ‚leɪt, -ts, -dɪŋ,
-ɪd

deregulation
BR ‚di:rɛgjʊ'leɪʃn
AM də‚rɛgjʊ'leɪʃən,
di‚rɛgjʊ'leɪʃən

Dereham
BR 'dɪərəm

Derek
BR 'dɛrɪk
AM 'dɛrək

derelict
BR 'dɛrɪlɪkt, -s
AM 'dɛrə‚lɪk|(t), -(t)s

dereliction
BR ‚dɛrɪ'lɪkʃn, -z
AM ‚dɛrə'lɪkʃən, -z

derequisition
BR ‚di:rɛkwɪ'zɪʃn
AM di‚rɛkwə'zɪʃən

derestrict
BR ‚di:rɪ'strɪkt, -s, -ɪŋ,
-ɪd
AM di‚rə'strɪk|(t), -(t)s,
-tɪŋ, -tɪd

derestriction
BR ‚di:rɪ'strɪkʃn
AM di‚rə'strɪkʃən

deride
BR dɪ'rʌɪd, -z, -ɪŋ, -ɪd
AM də'raɪd, di'raɪd, -z,
-ɪŋ, -ɪd

derider
BR dɪ'rʌɪdə(r), -z
AM də'raɪdər,
di'raɪdər, -z

deridingly
BR dɪ'rʌɪdɪŋli
AM də'raɪdɪŋli,
di'raɪdɪŋli

de-rigging
BR ‚di:'rɪgɪŋ
AM di'rɪgɪŋ

de rigueur
BR də rɪ'gə:(r)
AM ‚də rɪ'gər

derisible
BR dɪ'rʌɪsəbl
AM də'raɪsəbəl,
di'raɪsəbəl

derision
BR dɪ'rɪʒn
AM də'rɪʒən, di'rɪʒən

derisive
BR dɪ'rʌɪsɪv, dɪ'rʌɪzɪv,
dɪ'rɪzɪv
AM də'raɪsɪv, di'raɪsɪv

derisively
BR dɪ'rʌɪsɪvli,
dɪ'rʌɪzɪvli, dɪ'rɪzɪvli
AM də'raɪsɪvli,
di'raɪsɪvli

derisiveness
BR dɪ'rʌɪsɪvnɪs,
dɪ'rʌɪzɪvnɪs,
dɪ'rɪzɪvnɪs
AM də'raɪsɪvnɪs,
di'raɪsɪvnɪs

derisorily
BR dɪ'rʌɪs(ə)rɪli,
dɪ'rʌɪz(ə)rɪli
AM də'raɪs(ə)rəli,
di'raɪs(ə)rəli,
də'rɪzərəli

derisory
BR dɪˈraɪs(ə)ri,
dɪˈraɪz(ə)ri
AM dəˈraɪs(ə)ri,
dɪˈraɪs(ə)ri, dəˈrɪzəri

derivable
BR dɪˈraɪvəbl
AM dəˈraɪvəbəl

derivation
BR ˌderɪˈveɪʃn
AM ˌderəˈveɪʃən

derivational
BR ˌderɪˈveɪʃn̩(ə)l,
ˌderɪˈveɪʃən(ə)l
AM ˌderəˈveɪʃ(ə)nəl

derivative
BR dɪˈrɪvətɪv, -z
AM dəˈrɪvədɪv, -z

derivatively
BR dɪˈrɪvətɪvli
AM dəˈrɪvədɪvli

derive
BR dɪˈraɪv, -z, -ɪŋ, -d
AM dəˈraɪv, dɪˈraɪv, -z,
-ɪŋ, -d

d'Erlanger
BR dɛːˈlɒ̃ʒeɪ
AM ˈdɜːˌlæŋər

derm
BR dɜːm
AM dɜrm

derma
BR ˈdɜːmə(r)
AM ˈdɜrmə

dermal
BR ˈdɜːml
AM ˈdɜrməl

Dermaptera
BR dɜːˈmæpt(ə)rə(r)
AM dɜrˈmæptərə

dermapteran
BR dɜːˈmæpt(ə)rən,
dɜːˈmæpt(ə)rn̩, -z
AM dɜrˈmæptərən, -z

dermapterous
BR dɜːˈmæpt(ə)rəs
AM dɜrˈmæptərəs

dermatitis
BR ˌdɜːməˈtaɪtɪs
AM ˌdɜrməˈtaɪdəs

dermatoglyphic
BR ˌdɜːmətəˈɡlɪfɪk, -s
AM ˌdɜrmədəˈɡlɪfɪk,
dɜrˌmædəˈɡlɪfɪk, -s

**dermatoglyphic-
ally**
BR ˌdɜːmətəˈɡlɪfɪkli
AM ˌdɜrmədəˈɡlɪfək(ə)li,
dɜrˌmædəˈɡlɪfək(ə)li

dermatoid
BR ˈdɜːmətɔɪd
AM ˈdɜrməˌtɔɪd

dermatological
BR ˌdɜːmətəˈlɒdʒɪkl
AM ˌdɜrmədəˈlɑdʒəkəl

dermatologically
BR ˌdɜːmətəˈlɒdʒɪkli

AM ˌdɜrmədəˈlɑdʒək-
(ə)li

dermatologist
BR ˌdɜːməˈtɒlədʒɪst, -s
AM ˌdɜrməˈtɑlədʒəst,
-s

dermatology
BR ˌdɜːməˈtɒlədʒi
AM ˌdɜrməˈtɑlədʒi

dermic
BR ˈdɜːmɪk
AM ˈdɜrmɪk

dermis
BR ˈdɜːmɪs
AM ˈdɜrməs

Dermot
BR ˈdɜːmət
AM ˈdɜrmət

Dermott
BR ˈdɜːmət
AM ˈdɜrmət

dernier cri
BR ˌdɛːnjeɪ ˈkriː,
ˌdəːnjeɪ +
AM ˌdɜrnˌjeɪ ˈkri

derogate
BR ˈderəɡeɪt, -s, -ɪŋ, -ɪd
AM ˈderəˌɡeɪt, -ts, -dɪŋ,
-dɪd

derogation
BR ˌderəˈɡeɪʃn
AM ˌderəˈɡeɪʃən

derogative
BR dɪˈrɒɡətɪv
AM dəˈraɡədɪv

derogatorily
BR dɪˈrɒɡət(ə)rɪli
AM dəˈraɡəˌtɔrəli,
dɪˈraɡəˌtɔrəli

derogatory
BR dɪˈrɒɡət(ə)ri
AM dəˈraɡəˌtɔri,
dɪˈraɡəˌtɔri

Deronda
BR dəˈrɒndə(r)
AM dəˈrandə

derrick
BR ˈdɛrɪk, -s
AM ˈdɛrɪk, -s

Derrida
BR dəˈriːdə(r)
AM dəriˈdɑ

Derridean
BR dəˈrɪdɪən
AM dəˈrɪdiən

derrière
BR ˌderɪˈɛː(r), -z
AM ˌderiˈe(ə)r, -z

derring-do
BR ˌderɪŋˈduː
AM ˌdɛrɪŋˈdu

derringer
BR ˈdɛrɪn(d)ʒə(r),
ˈdɜrn(d)ʒə(r), -z
AM ˈdɛrən(d)ʒər, -z

derris
BR ˈdɛrɪs

AM ˈdɜrəs

Derry
BR ˈderi
AM ˈdɛri

derv
BR dəːv
AM dərv

dervish
BR ˈdəːvɪʃ, -ɪʃɪz
AM ˈdɜrvɪʃ, -ɪz

Derwent
BR ˈdəːwənt
AM ˈdɜrwənt

Derwentwater
BR ˈdəːwəntˌwɔːtə(r)
AM ˈdɜrwəntˌwɔdər,
ˈdɜrwəntˌwadər

Deryck
BR ˈdɛrɪk
AM ˈdɛrək

Desai
BR dɪˈsaɪ, dɛˈsaɪ
AM dəˈsaɪ

desalinate
BR (ˌ)diːˈsalɪneɪt, -s,
-ɪŋ, -ɪd
AM diˈsælə͜neɪ|t, -ts,
-dɪŋ, -dɪd

desalination
BR ˌdiːsalɪˈneɪʃn
AM diˌsæləˈneɪʃən

desalinisation
BR diːsalɪnaɪˈzeɪʃn,
diːˌsalɪnaɪˈzeɪʃn
AM diˌsælənəˈzeɪʃən,
diˌsælənaɪˈzeɪʃən

desalinise
BR (ˌ)diːˈsalɪnaɪz, -ɪz,
-ɪŋ, -d
AM diˌsæləˌnaɪz, -ɪz,
-ɪŋ, -d

desalinization
BR diːsalɪnaɪˈzeɪʃn,
diːˌsalɪnaɪˈzeɪʃn
AM diˌsælənəˈzeɪʃən,
diˌsælənaɪˈzeɪʃən

desalinize
BR (ˌ)diːˈsalɪnaɪz, -ɪz,
-ɪŋ, -d
AM diˌsæləˌnaɪz, -ɪz,
-ɪŋ, -d

desalt
BR diːˈsɔːlt, diːˈsɒlt, -s,
-ɪŋ, -ɪd
AM diˈsɒlt, diˈsalt, -s,
-ɪŋ, -əd

desaparecido
BR ˌdɛsəpərəˈsiːdəʊ, -z
AM ˌdɛzəˌpɛrəˈsidoʊ, -z

descale
BR ˌdiːˈskeɪl, -z
AM diˈskeɪl, -z

descant
BR ˈdɛskant, -s, -ɪŋ, -ɪd
AM ˈdɛˌskænt, -s, -ɪŋ,
-əd

Descartes
BR ˈdeɪkɑːt, deɪˈkɑːt

AM deɪˈkɑrt

descend
BR dɪˈsend, -z, -ɪŋ, -ɪd-
AM dəˈsend, diˈsend, -z,
-ɪŋ, -əd

descendant
BR dɪˈsend(ə)nt, -s
AM dəˈsend(ə)nt,
diˈsend(ə)nt, -s

descendent
BR dɪˈsend(ə)nt
AM dəˈsend(ə)nt,
diˈsend(ə)nt

descender
BR dɪˈsendə(r), -z
AM dəˈsendər,
diˈsendər, -z

descendeur
BR dɪˈsendə(r), -z
AM dəˈsendər, -z

descendible
BR dɪˈsendɪbl
AM dəˈsendəbəl,
diˈsendəbəl

descent
BR dɪˈsent, -s
AM dəˈsent, diˈsent, -s

descramble
BR ˌdiːˈskrambl̩|l, -lz,
-lɪŋ\-lɪŋ, -ld
AM diˈskræmbləl, -əlz,
-(ə)lɪŋ, -əld

descrambler
BR ˌdiːˈskramblə(r),
ˌdiːˈskramblə(r), -z
AM diˈskræmb(ə)lər,
-z

describable
BR dɪˈskraɪbəbl
AM dəˈskraɪbəbəl,
diˈskraɪbəbəl

describe
BR dɪˈskraɪb, -z, -ɪŋ, -d
AM dəˈskraɪb,
diˈskraɪb, -z, -ɪŋ, -d

describer
BR dɪˈskraɪbə(r), -z
AM dəˈskraɪbər,
diˈskraɪbər, -z

description
BR dɪˈskrɪpʃn, -z
AM dəˈskrɪpʃən,
diˈskrɪpʃən, -z

descriptive
BR dɪˈskrɪptɪv
AM dəˈskrɪptɪv,
diˈskrɪptɪv

descriptively
BR dɪˈskrɪptɪvli
AM dəˈskrɪptɪvli,
diˈskrɪptɪvli

descriptiveness
BR dɪˈskrɪptɪvnɪs
AM dəˈskrɪptɪvnɪs,
diˈskrɪptɪvnɪs

descriptivism
BR dɪˈskrɪptɪvɪz(ə)m

AM dəˈskrɪptɪˌvɪzəm, diˈskrɪptɪˌvɪzəm

descriptor
BR dɪˈskrɪptə(r), -z
AM dəˈskrɪptər, diˈskrɪptər, -z

descry
BR dɪˈskrʌɪ, -z, -ɪŋ, -d
AM dəˈskraɪ, diˈskraɪ, -z, -ɪŋ, -d

Desdemona
BR ˌdɛzdɪˈməʊnə(r)
AM ˌdɛsdəˈmoʊnə

desecrate
BR ˈdɛsɪkreɪt, -s, -ɪŋ, -ɪd
AM ˈdɛsəˌkreɪ|t, -ts, -dɪŋ, -dɪd

desecration
BR ˌdɛsɪˈkreɪʃn
AM ˌdɛsəˈkreɪʃən

desecrator
BR ˈdɛsɪkreɪtə(r), -z
AM ˈdɛsəˌkreɪdər, -z

deseed
BR diˈsiːd, -z, -ɪŋ, -ɪd
AM diˈsid, -z, -ɪŋ, -ɪd

desegregate
BR (ˌ)diːˈsɛgrɪgeɪt, -s, -ɪŋ, -ɪd
AM ˈdiˈsɛgrəˌgeɪ|t, -ts, -dɪŋ, -dɪd

desegregation
BR ˌdiːsɛgrɪˈgeɪʃn
AM ˌdiˌsɛgrəˈgeɪʃən

deselect
BR ˌdiːsɪˈlɛkt, -s, -ɪŋ, -ɪd
AM ˌdisəˈlɛk|(t), -(t)s, -tɪŋ, -təd

deselection
BR ˌdiːsɪˈlɛkʃn
AM ˌdisəˈlɛkʃən

desensitisation
BR ˌdiːsɛnsɪtʌɪˈzeɪʃn, diːˌsɛnsɪtʌɪˈzeɪʃn
AM ˌdiˌsɛnsədəˈzeɪʃən, ˌdiˌsɛnsəˌtaɪˈzeɪʃən, dəˌsɛnsədəˈzeɪʃən, dəˌsɛnsəˌtaɪˈzeɪʃən

desensitise
BR (ˌ)diːˈsɛnsɪtʌɪz, -ɪz, -ɪŋ, -d
AM diˈsɛnsəˌtaɪz, dəˈsɛnsəˌtaɪz, -ɪz, -ɪŋ, -d

desensitiser
BR (ˌ)diːˈsɛnsɪtʌɪzə(r), -z
AM diˈsɛnsəˌtaɪzər, dəˈsɛnsəˌtaɪzər, -z

desensitization
BR ˌdiːsɛnsɪtʌɪˈzeɪʃn, diːˌsɛnsɪtʌɪˈzeɪʃn
AM ˌdiˌsɛnsədəˈzeɪʃən, ˌdiˌsɛnsəˌtaɪˈzeɪʃən, dəˌsɛnsədəˈzeɪʃən, dəˌsɛnsəˌtaɪˈzeɪʃən

desensitize
BR (ˌ)diːˈsɛnsɪtʌɪz, -ɪz, -ɪŋ, -d
AM diˈsɛnsəˌtaɪz, dəˈsɛnsəˌtaɪz, -ɪz, -ɪŋ, -d

desensitizer
BR (ˌ)diːˈsɛnsɪtʌɪzə(r), -z
AM diˈsɛnsəˌtaɪzər, dəˈsɛnsəˌtaɪzər, -z

desert[1]
noun
BR ˈdɛzət, -s
AM ˈdɛzɪrt, -s

desert[2]
verb
BR dɪˈzəːt, -s, -ɪŋ, -ɪd
AM dəˈzər|t, diˈzər|t, -ts, -dɪŋ, -dəd

deserter
BR dɪˈzəːtə(r), -z
AM dəˈzərdər, diˈzərdər, -z

desertification
BR dɪˌzəːtɪfɪˈkeɪʃn
AM dəˌzərdəfəˈkeɪʃən

desertion
BR dɪˈzəːʃn, -z
AM dəˈzərʃən, diˈzərʃən, -z

deserts
things deserved
BR dɪˈzəːts
AM dɪˈzərts, diˈzərts

deserve
BR dɪˈzəːv, -z, -ɪŋ, -d
AM dəˈzərv, diˈzərv, -z, -ɪŋ, -d

deservedly
BR dɪˈzəːvɪdli
AM dəˈzərvədli, diˈzərvədli

deservedness
BR dɪˈzəːvɪdnɪs
AM dəˈzərvədnəs, diˈzərvədnəs

deserver
BR dɪˈzəːvə(r), -z
AM dəˈzərvər, diˈzərvər, -z

deserving
BR dɪˈzəːvɪŋ
AM dəˈzərvɪŋ

deservingly
BR dɪˈzəːvɪŋli
AM dəˈzərvɪŋli

deservingness
BR dɪˈzəːvɪŋnɪs
AM dəˈzərvɪŋnɪs

desex
BR diˈsɛks, -ɪz, -ɪŋ, -t
AM diˈsɛks, -əz, -ɪn, -t

desexualisation
BR ˌdiːsɛkʃʊəlʌɪˈzeɪʃn, ˌdiːsɛkʃ ɛlʌɪˈzeɪʃn, ˌdiːsɛkʃ lʌɪˈzeɪʃn,

ˌdiːsɛksjʊ(ə)lʌɪˈzeɪʃn, diːˌsɛkʃʊəlʌɪˈzeɪʃn, diːˌsɛkʃ ɛlʌɪˈzeɪʃn, diːˌsɛkʃ lʌɪˈzeɪʃn, diːˌsɛksjʊ(ə)lʌɪˈzeɪʃn
AM diˌsɛkʃ(əw)ələˈzeɪʃən, diˌsɛkʃ(əw)əˌlaɪˈzeɪʃən

desexualise
BR ˌdiːˈsɛkʃʊəlʌɪz, ˌdiːˈsɛkʃ ɛlʌɪz, ˌdiːˈsɛkʃ lʌɪz, ˌdiːˈsɛksjʊ(ə)lʌɪz, -ɪz, -ɪŋ, -d
AM diˈsɛkʃ(əw)əˌlaɪz, -ɪz, -ɪŋ, -d

desexualization
BR ˌdiːsɛkʃʊəlʌɪˈzeɪʃn, ˌdiːsɛkʃ ɛlʌɪˈzeɪʃn, ˌdiːsɛkʃ lʌɪˈzeɪʃn, ˌdiːsɛksjʊ(ə)lʌɪˈzeɪʃn, diːˌsɛkʃʊəlʌɪˈzeɪʃn, diːˌsɛkʃ ɛlʌɪˈzeɪʃn, diːˌsɛkʃ lʌɪˈzeɪʃn, diːˌsɛksjʊ(ə)lʌɪˈzeɪʃn
AM diːsɛkʃ(əw)ələˈzeɪʃən, diˌsɛkʃ(əw)əˌlaɪˈzeɪʃən

desexualize
BR ˌdiːˈsɛkʃʊəlʌɪz, ˌdiːˈsɛkʃ ɛlʌɪz, ˌdiːˈsɛkʃ lʌɪz, ˌdiːˈsɛksjʊ(ə)lʌɪz, -ɪz, -ɪŋ, -d
AM diˈsɛkʃ(əw)əˌlaɪz, -ɪz, -ɪŋ, -d

déshabillé
BR ˌdɛzaˈbiːeɪ, ˌdeɪzaˈbiːeɪ, ˌdɛzəˈbiːl, ˌdeɪzəˈbiːl
AM ˌdeɪzabiˈeɪ

desiccant
BR ˈdɛsɪk(ə)nt, -s
AM ˈdɛsəkənt, -s

desiccate
BR ˈdɛsɪkeɪt, -s, -ɪŋ, -ɪd
AM ˈdɛsəˌkeɪ|t, -ts, -dɪŋ, -dɪd

desiccation
BR ˌdɛsɪˈkeɪʃn
AM ˌdɛsəˈkeɪʃən

desiccative
BR ˈdɛsɪkətɪv
AM ˈdɛsəˌkeɪdɪv

desiccator
BR ˈdɛsɪkeɪtə(r), -z
AM ˈdɛsəˌkeɪdər, -z

desiderata
BR dɪˌzɪdəˈrɑːtə(r)
AM dəˌzɪdəˈrɑdə

desiderate[1]
adjective, noun
BR dɪˈzɪd(ə)rət, dɪˈsɪd(ə)rət
AM dəˈzɪdərət, dəˈsɪdərət

desiderate[2]
verb
BR dɪˈzɪdəreɪt, dɪˈsɪdəreɪt, -s, -ɪŋ, -ɪd
AM dəˈzɪdəˌreɪ|t, dəˈsɪdəˌreɪ|t, -ts, -dɪŋ, -dɪd

desiderative
BR dɪˈzɪd(ə)rətɪv, dɪˈsɪd(ə)rətɪv
AM dəˈzɪdəˌr(ə)dɪv

desideratum
BR dɪˌzɪdəˈrɑːtəm
AM dəˌzɪdəˈrɑdəm

design
BR dɪˈzʌɪn, -z, -ɪŋ, -d
AM dəˈzaɪn, diˈzaɪn, -z, -ɪŋ, -d

designate[1]
adjective
BR ˈdɛzɪgnət, ˈdɛzɪgneɪt
AM ˈdɛzɪgˌneɪt, ˈdɛzɪgnət

designate[2]
verb
BR ˈdɛzɪgneɪt, -s, -ɪŋ, -ɪd
AM ˈdɛzɪgˌneɪ|t, -ts, -dɪŋ, -dɪd

designation
BR ˌdɛzɪgˈneɪʃn, -z
AM ˌdɛzɪgˈneɪʃən, -z

designator
BR ˈdɛzɪgneɪtə(r), -z
AM ˈdɛzɪgˌneɪdər, -z

designedly
BR dɪˈzʌɪnɪdli
AM dəˈzaɪnədli, diˈzaɪnədli

designer
BR dɪˈzʌɪnə(r), -z
AM dəˈzaɪnər, diˈzaɪnər, -z

designing
BR dɪˈzʌɪnɪŋ
AM dəˈzaɪnɪŋ, diˈzaɪnɪŋ

designingly
BR dɪˈzʌɪnɪŋli
AM dəˈzaɪnɪŋli, diˈzaɪnɪŋli

desinence
BR ˈdɛzɪnəns, ˈdɛznəns, ˈdɛsɪnəns, ˈdɛsnəns
AM ˈdɛsənəns, ˈdɛzənəns

desirability
BR dɪˌzʌɪərəˈbɪlɪti
AM dəˌzaɪrəˈbɪlɪdi

desirable
BR dɪˈzʌɪərəbl
AM dəˈzaɪrəbl

desirableness
BR dɪˈzʌɪərəblnəs
AM dəˈzaɪrəbəlnəs

desirably
BR dɪˈzʌɪərəbli

AM dəˈzaɪrəbli

desire
BR dɪˈzaɪə(r), -z, -ɪŋ, -d
AM dəˈzaɪ(ə)r,
di·ˈzaɪ(ə)r, -z, -ɪŋ, -d

Desirée
BR dɪˈzɪəreɪ, dɛˈzɪəreɪ
AM ˈdɛzəˌreɪ

desirous
BR dɪˈzaɪərəs
AM dəˈzaɪrəs

desist
BR dɪˈzɪst, dɪˈsɪst, -s, -ɪŋ, -ɪd
AM dəˈzɪst, dəˈsɪst, di·ˈzɪst, di·ˈsɪst, -s, -ɪŋ, -ɪd

desk
BR dɛsk, -s
AM dɛsk, -s

deskill
BR ˌdiːˈskɪl, -z, -ɪŋ, -d
AM ˌdiːˈskɪl, -z, -ɪŋ, -d

deskilled
BR ˌdiːˈskɪld
AM ˌdiːˈskɪld

deskilling
BR ˌdiːˈskɪlɪŋ
AM ˌdiːˈskɪlɪŋ

desktop
BR ˈdɛsktɒp, -s
AM ˈdɛs(k)ˌtɑp, -s

deskwork
BR ˈdɛskwəːk
AM ˈdɛs(k)ˌwərk

desman
BR ˈdɛzmən, -z
AM ˈdɛzmən, -z

desmid
BR ˈdɛzmɪd, -z
AM ˈdɛzmɪd, -z

Des Moines
BR də ˈmɔɪn
AM də ˈmɔɪn

Desmond
BR ˈdɛzm(ə)nd
AM ˈdɛzmən(d)

desolate¹
adjective
BR ˈdɛs(ə)lət
AM ˈdɛsələt, ˈdɛzələt

desolate²
verb
BR ˈdɛsəleɪt, -s, -ɪŋ, -ɪd
AM ˈdɛsəˌleɪ|t, -ts, -dɪŋ, -dɪd

desolately
BR ˈdɛs(ə)lətli
AM ˈdɛsələtli, ˈdɛzələtli

desolateness
BR ˈdɛs(ə)lətnəs
AM ˈdɛsələtnəs, ˈdɛzələtnəs

desolation
BR ˌdɛsəˈleɪʃn
AM ˌdɛzəˈleɪʃən, ˌdɛsəˈleɪʃən

desolator
BR ˈdɛsəleɪtə(r), -z
AM ˈdɛsəˌleɪdər, -z

desorb
BR ˌdiːˈsɔːb, -z, -ɪŋ, -d
AM diˈzɔ(ə)rb, -z, -ɪŋ, -d

desorbent
BR ˌdiːˈsɔːb(ə)nt, -s
AM diˈzɔrbənt, -s

desorption
BR ˌdiːˈsɔːpʃn, -z
AM diˈzɔrpʃən, -z

Desoutter
BR dɪˈsuːtə(r)
AM dəˈsudər

De Souza
BR də ˈsuːzə(r)
AM də ˈsuzə

despair
BR dɪˈspɛː(r), -z, -ɪŋ, -d
AM dəˈspɛ(ə)r, di·ˈspɛ(ə)r, -z, -ɪŋ, -d

despairingly
BR dɪˈspɛːrɪŋli
AM dəˈspɛrɪŋli, di·ˈspɛrɪŋli

despatch
BR dɪˈspatʃ, -ɪz, -ɪŋ, -t
AM dəˈspætʃ, -əz, -ɪŋ, -t

Despenser
BR dɪˈspɛnsə(r)
AM dəˈspɛnsər

desperado
BR ˌdɛspəˈrɑːdəʊ, -z
AM ˌdɛspəˈrɑdoʊ, -z

desperate
BR ˈdɛsp(ə)rət
AM ˈdɛsp(ə)rət

desperately
BR ˈdɛsp(ə)rətli
AM ˈdɛsp(ə)rətli

desperateness
BR ˈdɛsp(ə)rətnəs
AM ˈdɛsp(ə)rətnəs

desperation
BR ˌdɛspəˈreɪʃn
AM ˌdɛspəˈreɪʃən

despicability
BR dɪˌspɪkəˈbɪlɪti, ˌdɛspɪkəˈbɪlɪti
AM dəˌspɪkəˈbɪlɪdi, ˌdɛspəkəˈbɪlɪdi

despicable
BR dɪˈspɪkəbl, ˈdɛspɪkəbl
AM dəˈspɪkəbəl, ˈdɛspəkəbəl, diˈspɪkəbəl

despicably
BR dɪˈspɪkəbli, ˈdɛspɪkəbli
AM dəˈspɪkəbli, ˈdɛspəkəbli, diˈspɪkəbli

despise
BR dɪˈspʌɪz, -ɪz, -ɪŋ, -d
AM dəˈspaɪz, diˈspaɪz, -ɪz, -ɪŋ, -d

despiser
BR dɪˈspʌɪzə(r), -z
AM dəˈspaɪzər, diˈspaɪzər, -z

despite
BR dɪˈspʌɪt
AM dəˈspaɪt

despiteful
BR dɪˈspʌɪtf(ʊ)l
AM dəˈspaɪtfəl

despitefully
BR dɪˈspʌɪtfʊli, dɪˈspʌɪtfli
AM dəˈspaɪtfəli

despitefulness
BR dɪˈspʌɪtf(ʊ)lnəs
AM dəˈspaɪtfəlnəs

despoil
BR dɪˈspɔɪl, -z, -ɪŋ, -d
AM dəˈspɔɪl, diˈspɔɪl, -z, -ɪŋ, -d

despoiler
BR dɪˈspɔɪlə(r)
AM dəˈspɔɪlər, diˈspɔɪlər

despoilment
BR dɪˈspɔɪlm(ə)nt
AM dəˈspɔɪlmənt, diˈspɔɪlmənt

despoliation
BR dɪˌspəʊliˈeɪʃn
AM dəˌspoʊliˈeɪʃən, diˌspoʊliˈeɪʃən

despond
BR dɪˈspɒnd, -z, -ɪŋ, -ɪd
AM dəˈspɑnd, diˈspɑnd, -z, -ɪŋ, -əd

despondence
BR dɪˈspɒnd(ə)ns
AM dəˈspɑndəns, diˈspɑndns

despondency
BR dɪˈspɒnd(ə)nsi
AM dəˈspɑndənsi, diˈspɑndənsi

despondent
BR dɪˈspɒnd(ə)nt
AM dəˈspɑnd(ə)nt, diˈspɑnd(ə)nt

despondently
BR dɪˈspɒnd(ə)ntli
AM dəˈspɑndən(t)li, diˈspɑndən(t)li

despot
BR ˈdɛspɒt, -s
AM ˈdɛspət, ˈdɛsˌpɑt, -s

despotic
BR dɪˈspɒtɪk
AM dəˈspɑdɪk

despotically
BR dɪˈspɒtɪkli
AM dəˈspɑdək(ə)li

despotism
BR ˈdɛspətɪz(ə)m
AM ˈdɛspəˌtɪzəm

desquamate
BR ˈdɛskwəmeɪt, -s, -ɪŋ, -ɪd

AM ˈdɛskwəˌmeɪ|t, -ts, -dɪŋ, -dɪd

desquamation
BR ˌdɛskwəˈmeɪʃn
AM ˌdɛskwəˈmeɪʃən

desquamative
BR dɪˈskwamətɪv
AM dəˈskwɑmədɪv

desquamatory
BR dɪˈskwamət(ə)ri
AM dɛˈskwɑməˌtɔri

des res
BR ˌdɛz ˈrɛz, -ɪz
AM dəz ˈrɛz, -əz

Dessau
BR ˈdɛsaʊ
AM ˈdɛsaʊ

dessert
BR dɪˈzəːt, -s
AM dəˈzərt, diˈzərt, -s

dessertspoon
BR dɪˈzəːtspuːn, -z
AM dəˈzərtˌspun, diˈzərtˌspun, -z

dessertspoonful
BR dɪˈzəːtspuːnfʊl, -z
AM dəˈzərtˌspunˌfʊl, diˈzərtˌspunˌfəl, -z

destabilisation
BR ˌdiːsteɪblʌɪˈzeɪʃn, ˌdiːsteɪbəlʌɪˈzeɪʃn, diːˌsteɪblʌɪˈzeɪʃn, diːˌsteɪbəlʌɪˈzeɪʃn
AM diˌsteɪbələˈzeɪʃən, diˌsteɪbəˌlaɪˈzeɪʃən

destabilise
BR ˌdiːˈsteɪblʌɪz, ˌdiːˈsteɪbəlʌɪz, -ɪz, -ɪŋ, -d
AM diˈsteɪbəˌlaɪz, -ɪz, -ɪŋ, -d

destabilization
BR ˌdiːsteɪblʌɪˈzeɪʃn, ˌdiːsteɪbəlʌɪˈzeɪʃn, diːˌsteɪblʌɪˈzeɪʃn, diːˌsteɪbəlʌɪˈzeɪʃn
AM diˌsteɪbələˈzeɪʃən, diˌsteɪbəˌlaɪˈzeɪʃən

destabilize
BR ˌdiːˈsteɪblʌɪz, ˌdiːˈsteɪbəlʌɪz, -ɪz, -ɪŋ, -d
AM diˈsteɪbəˌlaɪz, -ɪz, -ɪŋ, -d

de-stalinisation
BR ˌdiːstɑːlɪnʌɪˈzeɪʃn, diːˌstɑːlɪnʌɪˈzeɪʃn
AM diˌstɑlɪnəˈzeɪʃən, diˌstɑləˌnaɪˈzeɪʃən

de-stalinization
BR ˌdiːstɑːlɪnʌɪˈzeɪʃn, diːˌstɑːlɪnʌɪˈzeɪʃn
AM diˌstɑlɪnəˈzeɪʃən, diˌstɑləˌnaɪˈzeɪʃən

De Stijl
BR də ˈstʌɪl
AM də ˈstaɪl

destination
BR ˌdestɪˈneɪʃn, -z
AM ˌdestəˈneɪʃən, -z

destine
BR ˈdestɪn, -z, -ɪŋ, -d
AM ˈdestɪn, -z, -ɪŋ, -d

destiny
BR ˈdestɪn|i, -ɪz
AM ˈdestɪni, -z

destitute
BR ˈdestɪtjuːt,
ˈdestɪtʃuːt
AM ˈdestəˌt(j)ut

destitution
BR ˌdestɪˈtjuːʃn,
ˌdestɪˈtʃuːʃn
AM ˌdestəˈt(j)uʃən

destock
BR ˌdiːˈstɒk, -s, -ɪŋ, -t
AM diˈstɑk, -s, -ɪŋ, -t

destrier
BR ˈdestrɪə(r),
deˈstriːə(r), -z
AM ˈdestriər, -z

destroy
BR dɪˈstrɔɪ, -z, -ɪŋ, -d
AM dəˈstrɔɪ, diˈstrɔɪ, -z,
-ɪŋ, -d

destroyable
BR dɪˈstrɔɪəbl
AM dəˈstrɔɪəbəl,
diˈstrɔɪəbəl

destroyer
BR dɪˈstrɔɪə(r), -z
AM dəˈstrɔɪər,
diˈstrɔɪər, -z

destruct
BR dɪˈstrʌkt, -s, -ɪŋ, -ɪd
AM dəˈstrʌk|(t),
diˈstrʌk|(t), -(t)s, -tɪŋ,
-təd

destructibility
BR dɪˌstrʌktɪˈbɪlɪti
AM dəˌstrʌktəˈbɪlɪdi,
diˌstrʌktəˈbɪlɪdi

destructible
BR dɪˈstrʌktɪbl
AM dəˈstrʌktəbəl,
diˈstrʌktəbəl

destruction
BR dɪˈstrʌkʃn
AM dəˈstrʌkʃən,
diˈstrʌkʃən

destructive
BR dɪˈstrʌktɪv
AM dəˈstrʌktɪv,
diˈstrʌktɪv

destructively
BR dɪˈstrʌktɪvli
AM dəˈstrʌktɪvli,
diˈstrʌktɪvli

destructiveness
BR dɪˈstrʌktɪvnɪs
AM dəˈstrʌktɪvnɪs,
diˈstrʌktɪvnɪs

destructor
BR dɪˈstrʌktə(r), -z

AM dəˈstrʌktər,
diˈstrʌktər, -z

Destry
BR ˈdestri
AM ˈdestri

desuetude
BR ˈdeswɪtjuːd,
ˈdeswɪtʃuːd,
dɪˈsjuːɪtjuːd,
dɪˈsjuːɪtʃuːd
AM ˈdeswiˌt(j)ud,
ˈdeswəˌt(j)ud,
dəˈs(j)uəˌt(j)ud

desulfurisation
BR ˌdiːsʌlf(ə)rʌɪˈzeɪʃn,
diːˌsʌlf(ə)rʌɪˈzeɪʃn
AM diˌsəlfərəˈzeɪʃən,
diˌsəlfəˌrʌɪˈzeɪʃən

desulfurization
BR ˌdiːsʌlf(ə)rʌɪˈzeɪʃn,
diːˌsʌlf(ə)rʌɪˈzeɪʃn
AM diˌsəlfərəˈzeɪʃən,
diˌsəlfəˌrʌɪˈzeɪʃən

desulphurisation
BR ˌdiːsʌlf(ə)rʌɪˈzeɪʃn,
diːˌsʌlf(ə)rʌɪˈzeɪʃn
AM diˌsəlfərəˈzeɪʃən,
diˌsəlfəˌrʌɪˈzeɪʃən

desulphurization
BR ˌdiːsʌlf(ə)rʌɪˈzeɪʃn,
diːˌsʌlf(ə)rʌɪˈzeɪʃn
AM diˌsəlfərəˈzeɪʃən,
diˌsəlfəˌrʌɪˈzeɪʃən

desultorily
BR ˈdes(ə)ltrɪli,
ˈdez(ə)ltrɪli
AM ˈdesəlˌtɔrəli

desultoriness
BR ˈdes(ə)ltrɪnɪs,
ˈdez(ə)ltrɪnɪs
AM ˈdesəlˌtɔrinɪs

desultory
BR ˈdes(ə)lt(ə)ri,
ˈdez(ə)lt(ə)ri
AM ˈdesəlˌtɔri,
dəˈsəltəri

detach
BR dɪˈtatʃ, -ɪz, -ɪŋ, -t
AM dəˈtætʃ, diˈtætʃ,
-əz, -ɪŋ, -t

detachable
BR dɪˈtatʃəbl
AM dəˈtætʃəbəl,
diˈtætʃəbəl

detachedly
BR dɪˈtatʃɪdli
AM dəˈtætʃədli,
diˈtætʃədli

detachment
BR dɪˈtatʃm(ə)nt, -s
AM dəˈtætʃmənt,
diˈtætʃmənt, -s

detail
BR ˈdiːteɪl, -z, -ɪŋ, -d
AM dəˈteɪl, ˈdiˌteɪl, -z,
-ɪŋ, -d

detain
BR dɪˈteɪn, -z, -ɪŋ, -d

AM dəˈteɪn, diˈteɪn, -z,
-ɪŋ, -d

Destry
BR ˈdestri
AM ˈdestri

detainee
BR ˌdiːteɪˈniː, dɪˌteɪˈniː,
-z
AM dəˈteɪˈni, diˈteɪˈni,
ˈdiˌteɪˈni, -z

detainer
BR dɪˈteɪnə(r), -z
AM dəˈteɪnər,
diˈteɪnər, -z

detainment
BR dɪˈteɪnm(ə)nt
AM dəˈteɪnmənt,
diˈteɪnmənt

detect
BR dɪˈtekt, -s, -ɪŋ, -ɪd
AM dəˈtek|(t),
diˈtek|(t), -(t)s, -tɪŋ,
-təd

detectable
BR dɪˈtektəbl
AM dəˈtektəbəl,
diˈtektəbəl

detectably
BR dɪˈtektəbli
AM dəˈtektəbli,
diˈtektəbli

detection
BR dɪˈtekʃn
AM dəˈtekʃən,
diˈtekʃən

detective
BR dɪˈtektɪv, -z
AM dəˈtektɪv, diˈtektɪv,
-z

detector
BR dɪˈtektə(r), -z
AM dəˈtektər,
diˈtektər, -z

detectorist
BR dɪˈtekt(ə)rɪst, -s
AM dəˈtektərɪst,
diˈtektərɪst, -s

detent
BR dɪˈtent, -s
AM dəˈtent, diˈtent, -s

détente
BR deɪˈtɑːnt, deɪˈtɒnt,
-s
AM deɪˈtɑnt, -s

detention
BR dɪˈtenʃn, -z
AM dəˈten(t)ʃən,
diˈten(t)ʃən, -z

deter
BR dɪˈtɜː(r), -z, -ɪŋ, -d
AM dəˈtɜr, diˈtɜr, -z, -ɪŋ,
-d

detergent
BR dɪˈtɜːdʒ(ə)nt, -s
AM dəˈtɜrdʒənt,
diˈtɜrdʒənt, -s

deteriorate
BR dɪˈtɪərɪəreɪt, -s, -ɪŋ,
-ɪd

AM dəˈteɪm, diˈteɪm, -z,
-ɪŋ, -d

AM dəˈteɪm, diˈteɪm, -z,
-ɪŋ, -d

deterioration
BR dɪˌtɪərɪəˈreɪʃn
AM dəˌtɪərɪəˈreɪʃən,
diˌtrɪəˈreɪʃən

deteriorative
BR dɪˈtɪərɪərətɪv
AM dəˈtɪərɪəˌreɪdɪv,
diˈtɪərɪəˌreɪdɪv

determent
BR dɪˈtɜːm(ə)nt
AM dəˈtɜrmənt,
diˈtɜrmənt

determinable
BR dɪˈtɜːmɪnəbl
AM dəˈtɜrmənəbəl,
diˈtɜrmənəbəl

determinacy
BR dɪˈtɜːmɪnəsi
AM dəˈtɜrmənəsi,
diˈtɜrmənəsi

determinant
BR dɪˈtɜːmɪnənt, -s
AM dəˈtɜrmənənt,
diˈtɜrmənənt, -s

determinate
BR dɪˈtɜːmɪnət
AM dəˈtɜrmənət,
diˈtɜrmənət

determinately
BR dɪˈtɜːmɪnətli
AM dəˈtɜrmənətli,
diˈtɜrmənətli

determinateness
BR dɪˈtɜːmɪnətnəs
AM dəˈtɜrmənətnəs,
diˈtɜrmənətnəs

determination
BR dɪˌtɜːmɪˈneɪʃn
AM dəˌtɜrməˈneɪʃən

determinative
BR dɪˈtɜːmɪnətɪv, -z
AM dəˈtɜrməˌneɪdɪv,
dəˈtɜrmənədɪv, -z

determinatively
BR dɪˈtɜːmɪnətɪvli
AM dəˈtɜrməˌneɪdɪvli,
dəˈtɜrmənədɪvli

determinativeness
BR dɪˈtɜːmɪnətɪvnɪs
AM dəˈtɜrməˌneɪdɪvnɪs,
dəˈtɜrmənədɪvnɪs

determine
BR dɪˈtɜːmɪn, -z, -ɪŋ, -d
AM dəˈtɜrm|ən,
diˈtɜrm|ən, -ənz,
-(ə)nɪŋ, -ənd

determinedly
BR dɪˈtɜːmɪndli
AM dəˈtɜrmɪndli,
diˈtɜrmɪndli

determinedness
BR dɪˈtɜːmɪn(d)nɪs
AM dəˈtɜrmən(d)nəs,
diˈtɜrmən(d)nəs

determiner
BR dɪˈtɜːmɪnə(r), -z
AM dəˈtɜːmənər,
di'tɜːmənər, -z

determinism
BR dɪˈtɜːmɪnɪz(ə)m
AM dəˈtɜːməˌnɪzəm,
di'tɜːməˌnɪzəm

determinist
BR dɪˈtɜːmɪnɪst, -s
AM dəˈtɜːmənəst,
di'tɜːmənəst, -s

deterministic
BR dɪˌtɜːmɪˈnɪstɪk
AM dəˌtɜːməˈnɪstɪk,
di'tɜːrməˈnɪstɪk

deterministically
BR dɪˌtɜːmɪˈnɪstɪkli
AM dəˈtɜːməˈnɪstək(ə)li,
di'tɜːrməˈnɪstək(ə)li

deterrence
BR dɪˈtɛrəns, dɪˈtɜːns
AM dəˈtɜːrəns,
di'tɜːrəns, dəˈtɛrəns,
di'tɛrəns

deterrent
BR dɪˈtɛrənt, dɪˈtɜːnt, -s
AM dəˈtɜːrənt,
di'tɜːrənt, dəˈtɛrənt,
di'tɛrənt, -s

detest
BR dɪˈtɛst, -s, -ɪŋ, -ɪd
AM dəˈtɛst, di'tɛst, -s,
-ɪŋ, -əd

detestable
BR dɪˈtɛstəbl
AM dəˈtɛstəbəl,
di'tɛstəbəl

detestably
BR dɪˈtɛstəbli
AM dəˈtɛstəbli,
di'tɛstəbli

detestation
BR ˌdiːtɛˈsteɪʃn
AM ˌdiːtɛˈsteɪʃən

detester
BR dɪˈtɛstə(r), -z
AM dəˈtɛstər, di'tɛstər,
-z

dethrone
BR ˌdiːˈθrəʊn,
dɪˈθrəʊn, -z, -ɪŋ, -d
AM dəˈθroʊn, di'θroʊn,
-z, -ɪŋ, -d

dethronement
BR dɪˈθrəʊnm(ə)nt,
ˌdiːˈθrəʊnm(ə)nt, -s
AM dəˈθroʊnmənt,
di'θroʊnmənt, -s

Detmold
BR ˈdɛtməʊld
AM ˈdɛtˌmoʊld

detonate
BR ˈdɛtəneɪt, ˈdɛtn̩eɪt,
-s, -ɪŋ, -ɪd

AM ˈdɛtn̩ˌeɪ|t,
ˈdɛdəˌneɪ|t, -ts, -dɪŋ,
-dɪd

detonation
BR ˌdɛtəˈneɪʃn,
ˌdɛtn̩ˈeɪʃn, -z
AM ˌdɛtn̩ˈeɪʃn,
ˌdɛdəˈneɪʃən, -z

detonative
BR ˈdɛtənətɪv,
ˈdɛtn̩ətɪv
AM ˈdɛtn̩ˌeɪdɪv,
ˈdɛtn̩ədɪv,
ˈdɛdəˌneɪdɪv,
ˈdɛdənədɪv

detonator
BR ˈdɛtəneɪtə(r),
ˈdɛtn̩eɪtə(r), -z
AM ˈdɛtn̩ˌeɪdər,
ˈdɛdəˌneɪdər, -z

detour
BR ˈdiːtʊə(r), ˈdiːtɔː(r),
ˈdeɪtʊə(r), ˈdeɪtɔː(r),
-z, -ɪŋ, -d
AM ˈdiːˌtʊ(ə)r, -z, -ɪŋ, -d

détour
BR ˈdiːtʊə(r), ˈdiːtɔː(r),
ˈdeɪtʊə(r), ˈdeɪtɔː(r),
-z, -ɪŋ, -d
AM ˈdiːˌtʊ(ə)r,
ˈdeɪˌtʊ(ə)r, -z, -ɪŋ, -d

detox
BR ˌdiːˈtɒks, -ɪz, -ɪŋ, -t
AM ˈdiːˌtaks, -əs, -ɪŋ, -t

detoxicate
BR ˌdiːˈtɒksɪkeɪt,
dɪˈtɒksɪkeɪt, -s, -ɪŋ, -ɪd
AM diˈtaksəˌkeɪ|t, -ts,
-dɪŋ, -dɪd

detoxication
BR ˌdiːtɒksɪˈkeɪʃn,
dɪˌtɒksɪˈkeɪʃn
AM diˌtaksəˈkeɪʃən,
di'taksəˈkeɪʃən

detoxification
BR ˌdiːtɒksɪfɪˈkeɪʃn,
diːˌtɒksɪfɪˈkeɪʃn,
dɪˌtɒksɪfɪˈkeɪʃn
AM dəˌtaksəfəˈkeɪʃən,
diˌtaksəfəˈkeɪʃən

detoxify
BR ˌdiːˈtɒksɪfʌɪ,
dɪˈtɒksɪfʌɪ, -z, -ɪŋ, -d
AM dəˈtaksəˌfaɪ,
di'taksəˌfaɪ, -z, -ɪŋ, -d

detract
BR dɪˈtrakt, -s, -ɪŋ, -ɪd
AM dəˈtræk|(t),
di'træk|(t), -(t)s, -tɪŋ,
-təd

detraction
BR dɪˈtrakʃn, -z
AM dəˈtrækʃən,
di'trækʃən, -z

detractive
BR dɪˈtraktɪv
AM dəˈtræktɪv,
di'træktɪv

detractor
BR dɪˈtraktə(r), -z
AM dəˈtræktər,
di'træktər, -z

detrain
BR ˌdiːˈtreɪn, -z, -ɪŋ, -d
AM ˌdiˈtreɪn, -z, -ɪŋ, -d

detrainment
BR ˌdiːˈtreɪnm(ə)nt
AM ˌdiˈtreɪnmənt

detribalisation
BR ˌdiːtrʌɪbəlʌɪˈzeɪʃn,
diːˌtrʌɪblʌɪˈzeɪʃn,
diːˌtrʌɪbəlʌɪˈzeɪʃn
diːˌtrʌɪblʌɪˈzeɪʃn
AM diˌtraɪbələˈzeɪʃən,
diˌtraɪbəˌlaɪˈzeɪʃən

detribalise
BR (ˌ)diːˈtrʌɪbəlʌɪz,
(ˌ)diːˈtrʌɪblʌɪz, -ɪz,
-ɪŋ, -d
AM diˈtraɪbəˌlaɪz, -ɪz,
-ɪŋ, -d

detribalization
BR ˌdiːtrʌɪbəlʌɪˈzeɪʃn,
diːˌtrʌɪblʌɪˈzeɪʃn,
diːˌtrʌɪbəlʌɪˈzeɪʃn
diːˌtrʌɪblʌɪˈzeɪʃn
AM diˌtraɪbələˈzeɪʃən,
diˌtraɪbəˌlaɪˈzeɪʃən

detribalize
BR (ˌ)diːˈtrʌɪbəlʌɪz,
(ˌ)diːˈtrʌɪblʌɪz, -ɪz,
-ɪŋ, -d
AM diˈtraɪbəˌlaɪz, -ɪz,
-ɪŋ, -d

detriment
BR ˈdɛtrɪm(ə)nt
AM ˈdɛtrɪm(ə)nt

detrimental
BR ˌdɛtrɪˈmɛntl
AM ˌdɛtrəˈmɛn(t)l

detrimentally
BR ˌdɛtrɪˈmɛntli,
ˌdɛtrɪˈmɛntəli
AM ˌdɛtrəˈmɛn(t)li

detrital
BR dɪˈtrʌɪtl
AM dəˈtraɪdəl,
di'traɪdəl

detrited
BR dɪˈtrʌɪtɪd
AM dəˈtraɪdɪd,
di'traɪdɪd

detrition
BR dɪˈtrɪʃn
AM dəˈtrɪʃən, di'trɪʃən

detritivore
BR dɪˈtrʌɪtvɔː(r), -z
AM dəˈtraɪdɪˌvɔ(ə)r, -z

detritus
BR dɪˈtrʌɪtəs
AM dəˈtraɪdəs,
di'traɪdəs, ˌdɛtrədəs

Detroit
BR dɪˈtrɔɪt
AM dəˈtrɔɪt, di'trɔɪt

de trop
BR də ˈtrəʊ, deɪ +
AM də ˈtroʊ

Dettol®
BR ˈdɛtɒl
AM ˈdɛdɑl

detumescence
BR ˌdiːtjuˈmɛsns,
ˌdiːtʃəˈmɛsns
AM ˌdit(j)uˈmɛsəns

detumescent
BR ˌdiːtjuˈmɛsnt,
ˌdiːtʃəˈmɛsnt
AM ˌdit(j)uˈmɛsənt

detune
BR ˌdiːˈtjuːn, ˌdiːˈtʃuːn,
-z, -ɪŋ, -d
AM dəˈt(j)un, di't(j)un,
-z, -ɪŋ, -d

Deucalion
BR djuˈkeɪlɪən
AM d(j)uˈkeɪliən

deuce
BR djuːs, dʒuːs, -ɪz
AM d(j)us, -əz

deuced
BR ˈdjuːsɪd, ˈdʒuːsɪd,
djuːst, dʒuːst
AM ˈd(j)usəd, d(j)ust

deucedly
BR ˈdjuːsɪdli,
ˈdʒuːsɪdli, djuːstli,
dʒuːstli
AM ˈd(j)usədli,
d(j)usˈt)li

deus ex machina
BR ˌdeɪəs ɛks
məˈʃiːnə(r),
+ ˈmakɪnə(r), -z
AM ˌdeɪəs ˌɛks
ˈmakənə, -z

deuteragonist
BR ˌdjuːtəˈragənɪst,
ˌdjuːtəˈragnɪst,
ˌdʒuːtəˈragənɪst,
ˌdʒuːtəˈragnɪst, -s
AM ˌd(j)udəˈrægənəst,
-s

deuterate
BR ˈdjuːtəreɪt,
ˈdʒuːtəreɪt, -s, -ɪŋ, -ɪd
AM ˈd(j)udəˌreɪ|t, -ts,
-dɪŋ, -dɪd

deuteration
BR ˌdjuːtəˈreɪʃn,
ˌdʒuːtəˈreɪʃn
AM ˌd(j)udəˈreɪʃən

deuteric
BR ˈdjuːt(ə)rɪk,
ˈdʒuːt(ə)rɪk
AM ˈd(j)udərɪk,
d(j)uˈtɛrɪk

deuterium
BR djuːˈtɪərɪəm,
dʒuːˈtɪərɪəm
AM d(j)uˈtɛriəm

Deutero-Isaiah
BR ,dju:tərəʊaɪ'zaɪə(r),
,dʒu:tərəʊaɪ'zaɪə(r)
AM 'd(j)udəroʊ,aɪ'zeɪə

deuteron
BR 'dju:tərɒn,
'dʒu:tərɒn, -z
AM 'd(j)udərən,
'd(j)udə,rɑn, -z

Deuteronomic
BR ,dju:t(ə)rə'nɒmɪk,
,dʒu:t(ə)rə'nɒmɪk
AM ,d(j)udərə'nɑmɪk

Deuteronomical
BR ,dju:t(ə)rə'nɒmɪkl,
,dʒu:t(ə)rə'nɒmɪkl
AM ,d(j)udərə'nɑməkəl

Deuteronomist
BR ,dju:tə'rɒnəmɪst,
,dʒu:tə'rɒnəmɪst, -s
AM ,d(j)udə'rɑnəməst,
-s

Deuteronomy
BR ,dju:tə'rɒnəmi,
,dʒu:tə'rɒnəmi
AM ,d(j)udə'rɑnəmi

deuteronope
BR 'dju:t(ə)rənəʊp,
'dʒu:t(ə)rənəʊp, -s
AM 'd(j)udərə,noʊp, -s

deuteronopia
BR ,dju:t(ə)rə'nəʊpɪə(r),
,dʒu:t(ə)rə'nəʊpɪə(r)
AM ,d(j)udərə'noʊpɪə

Deutschmark
BR 'dɔɪtʃmɑ:k, -s
AM 'dɔɪtʃ,mɑrk, -s

deutzia
BR 'dju:tsɪə(r),
'dɔɪtsɪə(r), -z
AM 'd(j)ʊtʃ(i)ə,
'dɔɪtsɪə, -z

deva
BR 'deɪvə(r), 'di:və(r),
-z
AM 'divə, 'deɪvə, -z

de Valera
BR ,də və'lɛ:rə(r), də +
AM də və'lɛrə

de Valois
BR də 'valwɑ:(r)
AM də vɑ'lwɑ, də
væ'lwɑ

devaluate
BR ,di:'valjʊeɪt, -s, -ɪŋ,
-ɪd
AM di'vælja,weɪt, -ts,
-dɪŋ, -dɪd

devaluation
BR ,di:valjʊ'eɪʃn,
dɪ,valjʊ'eɪʃn, -z
AM ,di:væljʊ'eɪʃən,
,di,vælja'weɪʃən, -z

devalue
BR ,di:'valju:, -z, -ɪŋ, -d
AM di'vælju, -z, -ɪŋ, -d

Devanagari
BR ,deɪvə'nɑ:g(ə)ri,
,devə'nɑ:g(ə)ri
AM ,deɪvə'nɑgəri

devastate
BR 'devəsteɪt, -s, -ɪŋ, -ɪd
AM 'devə,steɪ|t, -ts,
-dɪŋ, -dɪd

devastatingly
BR 'devəsteɪtɪŋli
AM 'devə,steɪdɪŋli

devastation
BR ,devə'steɪʃn
AM ,devə'steɪʃən

devastator
BR 'devəsteɪtə(r), -z
AM 'devə,steɪdər, -z

develop
BR dɪ'veləp, -s, -ɪŋ, -t
AM də'veləp, di'veləp,
-s, -ɪŋ, -t

developable
BR dɪ'veləpəbl
AM də'veləpəbəl,
di'veləpəbəl

developer
BR dɪ'veləpə(r), -z
AM də'veləpər,
di'veləpər, -z

development
BR dɪ'veləpm(ə)nt
AM də'veləpmənt,
di'veləpmənt

developmental
BR dɪ,veləp'mentl̩
AM də,veləp'mən(t)l,
di,veləp'mən(t)l

developmentally
BR dɪ,veləp'mentl̩i,
dɪ,veləp'mentəli
AM də,veləp'mən(t)l̩i,
di,veləp'mən(t)l̩i

De Vere
BR də 'vɪə(r)
AM də 'vɪ(ə)r

Devereux
BR 'dev(ə)rəʊ,
'dev(ə)rə(r),
'dev(ə)ru:,
'dev(ə)ru:ks
AM 'devəroʊ

Devi
BR 'deɪvi
AM 'deɪvi

deviance
BR 'di:vɪəns
AM 'divɪəns

deviancy
BR 'di:vɪəns|i, -ɪz
AM 'divɪənsi, -z

deviant
BR 'di:vɪənt
AM 'divɪənt

deviate
BR 'di:vɪeɪt, -s, -ɪŋ, -ɪd
AM 'divi,eɪ|t, -ts, -dɪŋ,
-dɪd

deviation
BR ,di:vɪ'eɪʃn, -z
AM ,divi'eɪʃən, -z

deviational
BR ,di:vɪ'eɪʃn(ə)l,
,di:vɪ'eɪʃən(ə)l
AM ,divi'eɪʃ(ə)nəl

deviationism
BR ,di:vɪ'eɪʃn̩ɪz(ə)m,
,di:vɪ'eɪʃənɪz(ə)m
AM ,divi'eɪʃə,nɪzəm

deviationist
BR ,di:vɪ'eɪʃn̩ɪst,
,di:v'eɪʃənɪst, -s
AM ,divi'eɪʃənəst, -s

deviator
BR 'di:vɪeɪtə(r), -z
AM 'divi,eɪdər, -z

deviatory
BR 'di:vɪət(ə)ri
AM 'divɪə,tɔri

device
BR dɪ'vaɪs, -ɪz
AM də'vaɪs, di'vaɪs, -ɪz

devil
BR 'devl, -z
AM 'devəl, -z

devildom
BR 'devldəm
AM 'devəldəm

devilfish
BR 'devlfɪʃ, -ɪz
AM 'devəl,fɪʃ, -ɪz

devilish
BR 'devlɪʃ, 'dev(ɪ)lɪʃ
AM 'devl(ə)lɪʃ

devilishly
BR 'devl̩ɪʃli,
'dev(ɪ)lɪʃli
AM 'dev(ə)lɪʃli

devilishness
BR 'devl̩ɪʃnɪs,
'dev(ɪ)lɪʃnɪs
AM 'dev(ə)lɪʃnɪs

devilism
BR 'devlɪz(ə)m,
'devɪlɪz(ə)m
AM 'devə,lɪzəm

devil-may-care
BR ,devlmeɪ'kɛ:(r),
'devlmeɪkɛ:(r)
AM ,devəl,meɪ'kɛ(ə)r

devilment
BR 'devlm(ə)nt
AM 'devlmənt

devilry
BR 'devlri
AM 'devəlri

deviltry
BR 'devltri
AM 'devəltri

Devine
BR dɪ'vʌɪn, dɪ'vi:n
AM də'vaɪn

devious
BR 'di:vɪəs
AM 'divɪəs, 'divjəs

deviously
BR 'di:vɪəsli
AM 'divɪəsli, 'divjəsli

deviousness
BR 'di:vɪəsnəs
AM 'divɪəsnəs,
'divjəsnəs

devisable
BR dɪ'vʌɪzəbl
AM də'vaɪzəbəl,
di'vaɪzəbəl

devise
BR dɪ'vʌɪz, -ɪz, -ɪŋ, -d
AM də'vaɪz, di'vaɪz, -ɪz,
-ɪŋ, -d

devisee
BR dɪ,vʌɪ'zi:, -z
AM də,vaɪ'zi, di,vaɪ'zi,
-z

deviser
BR dɪ'vʌɪzə(r), -z
AM də'vaɪzər,
di'vaɪzər, -z

devisor
BR dɪ'vʌɪzə(r), -z
AM də'vaɪzər,
di'vaɪzər, -z

devitalisation
BR di:vʌɪtl̩ʌɪ'zeɪʃn,
,di:vʌɪtələʌɪ'zeɪʃn,
di:,vʌɪtl̩ʌɪ'zeɪʃn,
di:,vʌɪtl̩ʌɪ'zeɪʃn
AM ,di,vaɪdlə'zeɪʃən,
,di,vaɪdl,aɪ'zeɪʃən

devitalise
BR (,)di:'vʌɪtl̩ʌɪz,
(,)di:'vʌɪtələʌɪz, -ɪz, -ɪŋ,
-d
AM di'vaɪdl̩aɪz, -ɪz, -ɪŋ,
-d

devitalization
BR ,di:vʌɪtl̩ʌɪ'zeɪʃn,
,di:vʌɪtələʌɪ'zeɪʃn,
di:,vʌɪtl̩ʌɪ'zeɪʃn,
di:,vʌɪtələʌɪ'zeɪʃn
AM ,di,vaɪdlə'zeɪʃən,
,di,vaɪdl,aɪ'zeɪʃən

devitalize
BR (,)di:'vʌɪtl̩ʌɪz,
(,)di:'vʌɪtələʌɪz, -ɪz, -ɪŋ,
-d
AM di'vaɪdl̩aɪz, -ɪz, -ɪŋ,
-d

devitrification
BR ,di:vɪtrɪfɪ'keɪʃn,
di:,vɪtrɪfɪ'keɪʃn
AM ,di,vɪtrəfə'keɪʃən

devitrify
BR (,)di:'vɪtrɪfʌɪ, -z, -ɪŋ,
-d
AM di'vɪtrə,faɪ, -z, -ɪŋ,
-d

Devizes
BR dɪ'vʌɪzɪz
AM də'vɪzɪz

Devlin
BR ˈdɛvlɪn
AM ˈdɛvlən

devoice
BR (ˌ)diːˈvɔɪs, -ɪz, -ɪŋ, -t
AM diːˈvɔɪs, -ɪz, -ɪŋ, -t

devoid
BR dɪˈvɔɪd
AM dəˈvɔɪd, dɪˈvɔɪd

devoir
BR dəˈvwɑː(r), -z
AM dəvˈwɑr, -z

devolute
BR ˈdiːvəl(j)uːt,
ˈdɛvəl(j)uːt, -s, -ɪŋ, -ɪd
AM ˈdɛvəˌl(j)u|t, -ts,
-dɪŋ, -dəd

devolution
BR ˌdiːvəˈl(j)uːʃn,
ˌdɛvəˈl(j)uːʃn
AM ˌdɛvəˈl(j)uʃən

devolutionary
BR ˌdiːvəˈl(j)uːʃn(ə)ri,
ˌdɛvəˈl(j)uːʃn(ə)ri
AM ˌdɛvəˈl(j)uʃəˌnɛri

devolutionist
BR ˌdiːvəˈl(j)uːʃnɪst,
ˌdiːvəˈl(j)uːʃənɪst,
ˌdɛvəˈl(j)uːʃnɪst,
ˌdɛvəˈl(j)uːʃənɪst, -s
AM ˌdɛvəˈl(j)uʃənəst,
-s

devolve
BR dɪˈvɒlv, -z, -ɪŋ, -d
AM dəˈvɑlv, dɪˈvɑlv, -z,
-ɪŋ, -d

devolvement
BR dɪˈvɒlvm(ə)nt, -s
AM dəˈvɑlvmənt,
dɪˈvɑlvmənt, -s

Devon
BR ˈdɛvn
AM ˈdɛvən

Devonian
BR dɪˈvəʊnɪən, -z
AM dəˈvoʊnɪən, -z

Devonport
BR ˈdɛvnpɔːt
AM ˈdɛvənˌpɔ(ə)rt

Devonshire
BR ˈdɛvnʃ(ɪ)ə(r)
AM ˈdɛvənˌʃɪ(ə)r

dévot
BR deɪˈvəʊ, -z
AM deɪˈvoʊ, -z

devote
BR dɪˈvəʊt, -s, -ɪŋ, -ɪd
AM dəˈvoʊ|t, dɪˈvoʊ|t,
-ts, -dɪŋ, -dəd

dévote
BR deɪˈvɒt, -s
AM deɪˈvoʊt, -s

devotedly
BR dɪˈvəʊtɪdli
AM dəˈvoʊdədli,
dɪˈvoʊdədli

devotedness
BR dɪˈvəʊtɪdnɪs
AM dəˈvoʊdədnəs,
dɪˈvoʊdədnəs

devotee
BR ˌdɛvəˈtiː, -z
AM ˌdɛvəˈti, ˈdɛvoʊˈti,
-z

devotement
BR dɪˈvəʊtm(ə)nt
AM dəˈvoʊtmənt,
dɪˈvoʊtmənt

devotion
BR dɪˈvəʊʃn, -z
AM dəˈvoʊʃən,
dɪˈvoʊʃən, -z

devotional
BR dɪˈvəʊʃn(ə)l,
dɪˈvəʊʃən(ə)l
AM dəˈvoʊʃ(ə)nəl,
dɪˈvoʊʃ(ə)nəl

devotionally
BR dɪˈvəʊʃnəli,
dɪˈvəʊʃn̩li,
dɪˈvəʊʃən̩li,
dɪˈvəʊʃ(ə)nəli
AM dəˈvoʊʃ(ə)nəli,
dɪˈvoʊʃ(ə)nəli

devour
BR dɪˈvaʊə(r), -z, -ɪŋ, -d
AM dəˈvaʊ(ə)r,
dɪˈvaʊ(ə)r, -z, -ɪŋ, -d

devourer
BR dɪˈvaʊərə(r), -z
AM dəˈvaʊrər,
dɪˈvaʊrər, -z

devouringly
BR dɪˈvaʊərɪŋli
AM dəˈvaʊrɪŋli,
dɪˈvaʊrɪŋli

devout
BR dɪˈvaʊt, -ə(r), -ɪst
AM dəˈvaʊ|t, dɪˈvaʊ|t,
-dər, -dəst

devoutly
BR dɪˈvaʊtli
AM dəˈvaʊtli, dɪˈvaʊtli

devoutness
BR dɪˈvaʊtnəs
AM dəˈvaʊtnəs,
dɪˈvaʊtnəs

de Vries
BR də ˈvriːs, + ˈvriːz
AM də ˈvris

dew
BR djuː
AM d(j)u

dewan
BR dɪˈwɑːn, -z
AM dəˈwɑn, -z

Dewar
BR ˈdjuːə(r)
AM ˈduwər

dewar
BR ˈdjuːə(r), -z
AM ˈduwər, -z

dewberry
BR ˈdjuːb(ə)r|i, -ɪz

dewclaw
BR ˈdjuːklɔː(r), -z
AM ˈd(j)uˌklɔ,
ˈd(j)uˌklɑ, -z

dewdrop
BR ˈdjuːdrɒp, -s
AM ˈd(j)uˌdrɑp, -s

Dewey
BR ˈdjuːi
AM ˈd(j)ui

dewfall
BR ˈdjuːfɔːl
AM ˈd(j)uˌfɔl, ˈd(j)uˌfɑl

Dewhurst
BR ˈdjuːhəːst,
ˈdʒuːhəːst
AM ˈd(j)uˌ(h)ərst

Dewi
BR ˈdɛwi
AM ˈdeɪwi
WE ˈdewi

dewily
BR ˈdjuːɪli
AM ˈd(j)uəli

dewiness
BR ˈdjuːɪnɪs
AM ˈd(j)uɪnɪs

dewlap
BR ˈdjuːlap, -s
AM ˈd(j)uˌlæp, -s

dewpoint
BR ˈdjuːpɔɪnt, -s
AM ˈd(j)uˌpɔɪnt, -s

dewpond
BR ˈdjuːpɒnd, -z
AM ˈd(j)uˌpɑnd, -z

Dewsbury
BR ˈdjuːzb(ə)ri,
ˈdʒuːzb(ə)ri
AM ˈd(j)uzˌbɛri

dewy
BR ˈdjuː|i, -ɪə(r), -ɪɪst
AM ˈd(j)ui, -ər, -ɪɪst

Dexedrine
BR ˈdɛksɪdriːn,
ˈdɛksədrɪn
AM ˈdɛksəˌdrin,
ˈdɛksədrən

dexter
BR ˈdɛkstə(r)
AM ˈdɛkstər

dexterity
BR dɛkˈstɛrɪti
AM dɛkˈstɛrədi

dexterous
BR ˈdɛkst(ə)rəs
AM ˈdɛkst(ə)rəs

dexterously
BR ˈdɛkst(ə)rəsli
AM ˈdɛkst(ə)rəsli

dexterousness
BR ˈdɛkst(ə)rəsnəs
AM ˈdɛkst(ə)rəsnəs

dextral
BR ˈdɛkstr(ə)l
AM ˈdɛkstrəl

dextrality
BR dɛkˈstralɪti
AM dɛkˈstrælədi

dextrally
BR ˈdɛkstrˌli,
ˈdɛkstrəli
AM ˈdɛkstrəli

dextran
BR ˈdɛkstrən, -z
AM ˈdɛkstrən, -z

dextrin
BR ˈdɛkstrɪn
AM ˈdɛkstrən

dextrorotation
BR ˌdɛkstrəʊrə(ʊ)ˈteɪʃn
AM ˌdɛkstrəˌroʊˈteɪʃən

dextrorotatory
BR ˌdɛkstrəʊˈrəʊtət(ə)ri
AM ˌdɛkstrəˈroʊdəˌtɔri

dextrorse
BR ˈdɛkstrɔːs
AM ˈdɛkstrɔ(ə)rs

dextrose
BR ˈdɛkstrəʊz,
ˈdɛkstrəʊs
AM ˈdɛkstroʊs

dextrous
BR ˈdɛkstrəs
AM ˈdɛkst(ə)rəs

dextrously
BR ˈdɛkstrəsli
AM ˈdɛkst(ə)rəsli

dextrousness
BR ˈdɛkstrəsnəs
AM ˈdɛkst(ə)rəsnəs

dey
BR deɪ, -z
AM deɪ, -z

Dhahran
BR ˌdɑːˈrɑːn, ˌdɑːˈran
AM ˌdɑˈran

Dhaka
BR ˈdakə(r)
AM ˈdɑkə

dhal
BR dɑːl
AM dɑl

dharma
BR ˈdɑːmə(r)
AM ˈdɑrmə

Dhekelia
BR dɪˈkeɪlɪə(r)
AM dəˈkeɪljə, dəˈkeɪlɪə

dhobi
BR ˈdəʊb|i, -ɪz
AM ˈdoʊbi, -z

Dhofar
BR ˌdəʊˈfɑː(r)
AM ˈdoʊˈfɑr

dhole
BR dəʊl, -z
AM doʊl, -z

dhoti
BR ˈdəʊt|i, -ɪz
AM ˈdoʊdi, -z

dhow
BR daʊ, -z

AM daʊ, -z

dhurrie
BR 'dʌr|i, -ɪz
AM 'dəri, -z

Di
BR dʌɪ
AM daɪ

diabetes
BR ˌdʌɪə'biːtiːz,
ˌdʌɪə'biːtɪs
AM ˌdaɪə'bidiz,
ˌdaɪə'bidɪs,
ˌdaɪə'biˌtiz

diabetic
BR ˌdʌɪə'bɛtɪk, -s
AM ˌdaɪə'bɛdɪk, -s

diablerie
BR dɪ'ɑːbləri, dɪ'ablɪri
AM di'ablɪri

diabolic
BR ˌdʌɪə'bɒlɪk
AM ˌdaɪə'bɑlɪk

diabolical
BR ˌdʌɪə'bɒlɪkl
AM ˌdaɪə'baləkəl

diabolically
BR ˌdʌɪə'bɒlɪkli
AM ˌdaɪə'balək(ə)li

diabolise
BR dʌɪ'abəlʌɪz, -ɪz, -ɪŋ,
-d
AM daɪ'æbəˌlaɪz, -ɪz,
-ɪŋ, -d

diabolism
BR dʌɪ'abəlɪz(ə)m
AM daɪ'æbəˌlɪzəm

diabolist
BR dʌɪ'abəlɪst, -s
AM daɪ'æbələst, -s

diabolize
BR dʌɪ'abəlʌɪz, -ɪz, -ɪŋ,
-d
AM daɪ'æbəˌlaɪz, -ɪz,
-ɪŋ, -d

diabolo
BR dɪ'abələʊ,
dʌɪ'abələʊ
AM di'ab(ə)loʊ

diachronic
BR ˌdʌɪə'krɒnɪk
AM ˌdaɪə'krɑnɪk

diachronically
BR ˌdʌɪə'krɒnɪkli
AM ˌdaɪə'kranək(ə)li

diachronism
BR dʌɪ'akrənɪz(ə)m
AM daɪ'krɑˌnɪzəm

diachronistic
BR ˌdʌɪəkrə'nɪstɪk
AM ˌdaɪəˌkrə'nɪstɪk

diachronous
BR dʌɪ'akrənəs
AM daɪ'ækrənəs

diachrony
BR dʌɪ'akrəni
AM daɪ'ækrəni

diaconal
BR dʌɪ'akənl, dʌɪ'akn̩l
AM daɪ'ækənəl,
di'ækənəl

diaconate
BR dʌɪ'akəneɪt,
dʌɪ'akn̩eɪt,
dʌɪ'akənət, dʌɪ'akn̩ət,
-s
AM daɪ'ækənət,
diˌækənət, -s

diacritic
BR ˌdʌɪə'krɪtɪk, -s
AM ˌdaɪəˈkrɪdɪk, -s

diacritical
BR ˌdʌɪə'krɪtɪkl
AM ˌdaɪəˈkrɪdɪkəl

diacritically
BR ˌdʌɪə'krɪtɪkli
AM ˌdaɪəˈkrɪdɪk(ə)li

diadelphous
BR ˌdʌɪə'dɛlfəs
AM ˌdaɪə'dɛlfəs

diadem
BR 'dʌɪədem, -z, -d
AM 'daɪəˌdɛm, -z, -d

Diadochi
BR dʌɪ'adəkʌɪ,
dʌɪ'adəki
AM daɪ'ædəˌki

diaereses
BR dʌɪ'ɪərɪsiːz,
dʌɪ'ɛrɪsiːz
AM daɪ'ɛrəˌsiz

diaeresis
BR dʌɪ'ɪərɪsɪs,
dʌɪ'ɛrɪsɪs
AM daɪ'ɛrəsəs

diageneses
BR ˌdʌɪə'dʒɛnɪsiːz
AM ˌdaɪə'dʒɛnəsiz

diagenesis
BR ˌdʌɪə'dʒɛnɪsɪs
AM ˌdaɪə'dʒɛnəsəs

Diaghilev
BR dɪ'agɪlɛf
AM di'agələv

diagnosable
BR ˌdʌɪəg'nəʊzəbl,
'dʌɪəgnəʊzəbl
AM ˌdaɪəg'noʊsəbəl,
ˌdaɪəg'noʊzəbəl

diagnose
BR ˌdʌɪəg'nəʊz,
'dʌɪəgnəʊz, -ɪz, -ɪŋ, -d
AM ˌdaɪəg'noʊz,
ˌdaɪəg'noʊs,
'daɪəgˌnoʊs,
'daɪəgˌnoʊz, -əz, -ɪŋ, -d

diagnoseable
BR ˌdʌɪəg'nəʊzəbl,
'dʌɪəgnəʊzəbl
AM ˌdaɪəg'noʊzəbəl,
ˌdaɪəg'noʊsəbəl

diagnoses
BR ˌdʌɪəg'nəʊsiːz
AM ˌdaɪəg'noʊˌsiz

diagnosis
BR ˌdʌɪəg'nəʊsɪs
AM ˌdaɪəg'noʊsəs

diagnostic
BR ˌdʌɪəg'nɒstɪk, -s
AM ˌdaɪəg'nɑstɪk, -s

diagnostically
BR ˌdʌɪəg'nɒstɪkli
AM ˌdaɪəg'nɑstək(ə)li

diagnostician
BR ˌdʌɪəgnɒ'stɪʃn, -z
AM ˌdaɪəgˌnɑs'tɪʃən, -z

diagonal
BR dʌɪ'ag(ə)nl,
dʌɪ'agn̩l, -z
AM daɪ'ægənəl, -z

diagonally
BR dʌɪ'ag(ə)n̩li,
dʌɪ'agn̩li,
dʌɪ'ag(ə)nəli,
dʌɪ'agn̩əli
AM daɪ'æg(ə)nəli

diagram
BR 'dʌɪəgram, -z
AM 'daɪəˌgræm, -z

diagrammatic
BR ˌdʌɪəgrə'matɪk
AM ˌdaɪəgrə'mædɪk

diagrammatically
BR ˌdʌɪəgrə'matɪkli
AM ˌdaɪəgrə'mædək(ə)li

diagrammatise
BR ˌdʌɪə'gramətʌɪz,
-ɪz, -ɪŋ, -d
AM ˌdaɪə'græməˌtaɪz,
-ɪz, -ɪŋ, -d

diagrammatize
BR ˌdʌɪə'gramətʌɪz,
-ɪz, -ɪŋ, -d
AM ˌdaɪə'græməˌtaɪz,
-ɪz, -ɪŋ, -d

diagrid
BR 'dʌɪəgrɪd, -z
AM 'daɪəˌgrɪd, -z

diakinesis
BR ˌdʌɪəkɪ'niːsɪs
AM ˌdaɪəkə'nisɪs

dial
BR 'dʌɪəl, -z, -ɪŋ, -d
AM 'daɪ(ə)l, -z, -ɪŋ, -d

dialect
BR 'dʌɪəlɛkt, -s
AM 'daɪəˌlɛk|(t), -(t)s

dialectal
BR ˌdʌɪə'lɛktl
AM ˌdaɪə'lɛkt(ə)l

dialectic
BR ˌdʌɪə'lɛktɪk, -s
AM ˌdaɪə'lɛktɪk, -s

dialectical
BR ˌdʌɪə'lɛktɪkl
AM ˌdaɪə'lɛktəkəl

dialectically
BR ˌdʌɪə'lɛktɪkli
AM ˌdaɪə'lɛktək(ə)li

dialectician
BR ˌdʌɪəlɛk'tɪʃn, -z
AM ˌdaɪlɛk'tɪʃən, -z

dialectologist
BR ˌdʌɪəlɛk'tɒlədʒɪst,
-s
AM ˌdaɪəlɛk'talədʒəst,
-s

dialectology
BR ˌdʌɪəlɛk'tɒlədʒi
AM ˌdaɪəlɛk'talədʒi

dialer
BR 'dʌɪələ(r), -z
AM 'daɪlər, -z

dialler
BR 'dʌɪələ(r), -z
AM 'daɪlər, -z

dialog
BR 'dʌɪəlɒg, -z
AM 'daɪəˌlɒg, 'daɪəˌlag,
-z

dialogic
BR ˌdʌɪə'lɒdʒɪk
AM ˌdaɪə'lɑdʒɪk

dialogist
BR dʌɪ'alədʒɪst, -s
AM daɪ'ælədʒəst,
'daɪəˌlɒgəst,
'daɪəˌlagəst, -s

dialogue
BR 'dʌɪəlɒg, -z
AM 'daɪəˌlɒg, 'daɪəˌlag,
-z

dialyse
BR 'dʌɪəlʌɪz, -ɪz, -ɪŋ, -d
AM 'daɪəˌlaɪz, -ɪz, -ɪŋ, -d

dialyses
pl of **dialysis**
BR dʌɪ'alɪsiːz
AM daɪ'æləsiz

dialysis
BR dʌɪ'alɪsɪs
AM daɪ'æləsəs

dialytic
BR ˌdʌɪə'lɪtɪk
AM ˌdaɪə'lɪdɪk

dialyze
BR 'dʌɪəlʌɪz, -ɪz, -ɪŋ, -d
AM 'daɪəˌlaɪz, -ɪz, -ɪŋ, -d

diamagnetic
BR ˌdʌɪəmag'nɛtɪk, -s
AM ˌdaɪəˌmæg'nɛdɪk,
-s

diamagnetically
BR ˌdʌɪəmag'nɛtɪkli
AM ˌdaɪəˌmæg'nɛdək(ə)li

diamagnetism
BR ˌdʌɪə'magnɪtɪz(ə)m
AM ˌdaɪə'mægnəˌtɪzəm

diamanté
BR dɪə'mɒnteɪ,
dʌɪə'mɒnteɪ,
dɪə'manti,
dʌɪə'manti
AM ˌdiəˌmɑn'teɪ

diamantiferous
BR ˌdʌɪəmən'tɪf(ə)rəs
AM ˌdaɪəmən'tɪfərəs

diamantine
BR ˌdʌɪə'mantiːn,
ˌdʌɪə'mantʌɪn

AM ˈdaɪəˈmænˌtaɪn, ˈdaɪəˈmænˌtin, ˈdaɪəˈmæntn

diameter
BR daɪˈamɪtə(r), -z
AM daɪˈæmədər, -z

diametral
BR daɪˈamɪtr(ə)l
AM daɪˈæmətrəl

diametric
BR ˌdaɪəˈmɛtrɪk
AM ˈdaɪəˈmetrɪk

diametrical
BR ˌdaɪəˈmɛtrɪkl
AM ˈdaɪəˈmɛtrəkəl

diametrically
BR ˌdaɪəˈmɛtrɪkli
AM ˈdaɪəˈmɛtrək(ə)li

diamond
BR ˈdaɪəmənd, -z
AM ˈdaɪ(ə)mən(d), -z

diamondback
BR ˈdaɪəmən(d)bak, -s
AM ˈdaɪmənˌbæk, -s

diamondiferous
BR ˌdaɪəmənˈdɪf(ə)rəs
AM ˌdaɪmənˈdɪfərəs

Diana
BR daɪˈanə(r)
AM daɪˈænə, diˈænə

diandrous
BR daɪˈandrəs
AM daɪˈændrəs

Diane
BR daɪˈan
AM daɪˈæn

Dianetics
BR ˌdaɪəˈnɛtɪks
AM ˌdaɪəˈnɛdɪks

dianthus
BR daɪˈanθəs, -ɪz
AM daɪˈænθəs, -əz

diapason
BR ˌdaɪəˈpeɪsn, ˌdaɪəˈpeɪzn, -z
AM ˌdaɪəˈpeɪzn, ˌdaɪəˈpeɪsən, -z

diapause
BR ˈdaɪəpɔːz, -ɪz
AM ˈdaɪəˌpɔz, ˈdaɪəˌpaz, -əz

diaper
BR ˈdaɪəpə(r), -z
AM ˈdaɪ(ə)pər, -z

diaphanous
BR daɪˈafənəs, daɪˈafnəs
AM daɪˈæfənəs

diaphanously
BR daɪˈafənəsli, daɪˈafnəsli
AM daɪˈæfənəsli

diaphone
BR ˈdaɪəfəʊn, -z
AM ˈdaɪəˌfoʊn, -z

diaphoneme
BR ˈdaɪəˌfəʊniːm, -z
AM ˈdaɪəˌfoʊnim, -z

diaphonemic
BR ˌdaɪəfəˈniːmɪk
AM ˌdaɪəfəˈnimɪk

diaphonemically
BR ˌdaɪəfəˈniːmɪkli
AM ˌdaɪəfəˈnimɪk(ə)li

diaphonic
BR ˌdaɪəˈfɒnɪk
AM ˌdaɪəˈfanɪk

diaphonically
BR ˌdaɪəˈfɒnɪkli
AM ˌdaɪəˈfanək(ə)li

diaphoreses
BR ˌdaɪəfəˈriːsiːz
AM ˌdaɪəfəˈrisiz

diaphoresis
BR ˌdaɪəfəˈriːsɪs
AM ˌdaɪəfəˈrisɪs

diaphoretic
BR ˌdaɪəfəˈrɛtɪk, -s
AM ˌdaɪəfəˈrɛdɪk, -s

diaphragm
BR ˈdaɪəfram, -z
AM ˈdaɪəˌfræm, -z

diaphragmatic
BR ˌdaɪəfrə(g)ˈmatɪk
AM ˌdaɪəfrə(g)ˈmædɪk

diapositive
BR ˌdaɪəˈpɒzɪtɪv, -z
AM ˌdaɪəˈpazədɪv, -z

diarchal
BR daɪˈɑːkl
AM daɪˈɑrkəl

diarchic
BR daɪˈɑːkɪk
AM daɪˈɑrkɪk

diarchy
BR ˈdaɪɑːk|i, -ɪz
AM ˈdaɪˌɑrki, -z

diarise
BR ˈdaɪərʌɪz, -ɪz, -ɪŋ, -d
AM ˈdaɪəˌraɪz, -ɪz, -ɪŋ, -d

diarist
BR ˈdaɪərɪst, -s
AM ˈdaɪərəst, -s

diaristic
BR ˌdaɪəˈrɪstɪk
AM ˌdaɪəˈrɪstɪk

diarize
BR ˈdaɪərʌɪz, -ɪz, -ɪŋ, -d
AM ˈdaɪəˌraɪz, -ɪz, -ɪŋ, -d

diarrhea
BR ˌdaɪəˈrɪə(r)
AM ˌdaɪəˈriə

diarrheal
BR ˌdaɪəˈrɪəl
AM ˌdaɪəˈriəl

diarrhoea
BR ˌdaɪəˈrɪə(r)
AM ˌdaɪəˈriə

diarrhoeal
BR ˌdaɪəˈrɪəl
AM ˌdaɪəˈriəl

diarrhoeic
BR ˌdaɪəˈrɪɪk
AM ˌdaɪəˈriɪk

diary
BR ˈdaɪər|i, -ɪz
AM ˈdaɪ(ə)ri, -z

diascope
BR ˈdaɪəskəʊp, -s
AM ˈdaɪəˌskoʊp, -s

Diaspora
BR daɪˈasp(ə)rə(r)
AM daɪˈæsp(ə)rə, diˈæsp(ə)rə

diaspore
BR ˈdaɪəspɔː(r)
AM ˈdaɪəˌspɔ(ə)r

diastalsis
BR ˌdaɪəˈstalsɪs
AM ˌdaɪəˈstalsəs

diastase
BR ˈdaɪəsteɪz
AM ˈdaɪəˌsteɪs, ˈdaɪəˌsteɪz

diastasic
BR ˌdaɪəˈsteɪsɪk
AM ˌdaɪəˈstæsɪk

diastatic
BR ˌdaɪəˈstatɪk
AM ˌdaɪəˈstædɪk

diastole
BR daɪˈastəli, daɪˈastli
AM daɪˈæstəli

diastolic
BR ˌdaɪəˈstɒlɪk
AM ˌdaɪəˈstalɪk

diatessaron
BR ˌdaɪəˈtɛs(ə)rɒn, -z
AM ˌdaɪəˈtɛsərən, ˌdaɪəˈtɛsəˌran, -z

diathermancy
BR ˌdaɪəˈθəːm(ə)nsi
AM ˌdaɪəˈθərmənsi

diathermanous
BR ˌdaɪəˈθəːmənəs
AM ˌdaɪəˈθərmənəs

diathermic
BR ˌdaɪəˈθəːmɪk
AM ˌdaɪəˈθərmɪk

diathermous
BR ˌdaɪəˈθəːməs
AM ˌdaɪəˈθərməs

diathermy
BR ˈdaɪəˌθəːmi
AM ˈdaɪəˌθərmi

diatheses
BR daɪˈaθɪsiːz
AM daɪˈæθəsiz

diathesis
BR daɪˈaθɪsɪs
AM daɪˈæθəsəs

diatom
BR ˈdaɪətəm, ˈdaɪətɒm, -z
AM ˈdaɪəˌtam, -z

diatomaceous
BR ˌdaɪətəˈmeɪʃəs
AM ˌdaɪədəˈmeɪʃəs

diatomic
BR ˌdaɪəˈtɒmɪk
AM ˌdaɪəˈtamɪk

diatomite
BR daɪˈatəmʌɪt
AM daɪˈædəˌmaɪt

diatonic
BR ˌdaɪəˈtɒnɪk
AM ˌdaɪəˈtanɪk

diatonically
BR ˌdaɪəˈtɒnɪkli
AM ˌdaɪəˈtanək(ə)li

diatribe
BR ˈdaɪətrʌɪb, -z
AM ˈdaɪəˌtraɪb, -z

Díaz
BR ˈdiːas, ˈdiːaθ
AM ˈdiˌæz, ˈdiəs

diazepam
BR daɪˈeɪzɪpam, daɪˈazɪpam
AM daɪˈæzəˌpæm

diazo
BR daɪˈazəʊ, daɪˈeɪzəʊ, -z
AM daɪˈazoʊ, daɪˈeɪzoʊ, -z

diazotype
BR daɪˈazə(ʊ)tʌɪp, daɪˈeɪzə(ʊ)tʌɪp, -s
AM daɪˈazoʊˌtaɪp, daɪˈeɪzoʊˌtaɪp, -s

dib
BR dɪb, -z
AM dɪb, -z

dibasic
BR daɪˈbeɪsɪk
AM daɪˈbeɪsɪk

dibatag
BR ˈdɪbətag, -z
AM ˈdɪbəˌtæg, -z

dibber
BR ˈdɪbə(r), -z
AM ˈdɪbər, -z

dibble
BR ˈdɪb|l, -lz, -lɪŋ \-lɪŋ, -ld
AM ˈdɪb|əl, -əlz, -(ə)lɪŋ, -əld

dice
BR daɪs, -ɪz, -ɪŋ, -t
AM daɪs, -ɪz, -ɪŋ, -t

dicentra
BR daɪˈsɛntrə(r)
AM daɪˈsɛntrə

dicentric
BR daɪˈsɛntrɪk
AM daɪˈsɛntrɪk

dicer
BR ˈdaɪsə(r), -z
AM ˈdaɪsər, -z

dicey
BR ˈdaɪs|i, -ɪə(r), -ɪɪst
AM ˈdaɪsi, -ər, -ɪst

dichotic
BR daɪˈkɒtɪk, dɪˈkɒtɪk
AM daɪˈkɑdɪk

dichotomic
BR ˌdaɪkəˈtɒmɪk
AM ˌdaɪkəˈtɑmɪk

dichotomise
BR dAɪ'kɒtəmʌɪz,
dɪ'kɒtəmʌɪz, -ɪz, -ɪŋ, -d
AM daɪ'kɑdə͵maɪz, -ɪz,
-ɪŋ, -d

dichotomize
BR dAɪ'kɒtəmʌɪz,
dɪ'kɒtəmʌɪz, -ɪz, -ɪŋ, -d
AM daɪ'kɑdə͵maɪz, -ɪz,
-ɪŋ, -d

dichotomous
BR dAɪ'kɒtəməs,
dɪ'kɒtəməs
AM daɪ'kɑdəməs

dichotomy
BR dAɪ'kɒtəm|i,
dɪ'kɒtəmi, -ɪz
AM daɪ'kɑdəmi, -z

dichroic
BR dAɪ'krəʊɪk
AM daɪ'krouɪk

dichroism
BR dAɪ'krəʊɪz(ə)m
AM daɪ'krou͵ɪzəm

dichromate
BR daɪ'krəʊmeɪt
AM daɪ'krou͵meɪt

dichromatic
BR ͵dʌɪkrə(ʊ)'matɪk
AM ͵daɪkrə'mædɪk,
͵daɪkroʊ'mædɪk

dichromatism
BR dAɪ'krəʊmətɪz(ə)m
AM daɪ'kroumə͵tɪzəm

dicily
BR 'dʌɪsɪli
AM 'daɪsɪli

diciness
BR 'dʌɪsɪnɪs
AM 'daɪsɪnɪs

dick
BR dɪk, -s
AM dɪk, -s

dickcissel
BR dɪk'sɪsl, 'dɪksɪsl, -z
AM dɪk'sɪsəl

dicken
BR 'dɪk(ɪ)n
AM 'dɪkən

Dickens
BR 'dɪkɪnz
AM 'dɪkənz

Dickensian
BR dɪ'kɛnzɪən, -z
AM də'kɛnzɪən, -z

Dickensianly
BR dɪ'kɛnzɪənli
AM də'kɛnzɪənli

dicker
BR 'dɪk|ə(r), -əz,
-(ə)rɪŋ, -əd
AM 'dɪk|ər, -ərz, -(ə)rɪŋ,
-ərd

dickerer
BR 'dɪk(ə)rə(r), -z
AM 'dɪk(ə)rər, -z

Dickerson
BR 'dɪkəs(ə)n

AM 'dɪkərsən

dickey
BR 'dɪk|i, -ɪz
AM 'dɪki, -z

dickhead
BR 'dɪkhɛd, -z
AM 'dɪk͵(h)ɛd, -z

Dickie
BR 'dɪki
AM 'dɪki

dickie
BR 'dɪk|i, -ɪz
AM 'dɪki, -z

Dickins
BR 'dɪkɪnz
AM 'dɪkɪnz

Dickinson
BR 'dɪkɪns(ə)n
AM 'dɪkənsən

Dickon
BR 'dɪk(ə)n
AM 'dɪkɪn

Dickson
BR 'dɪksn
AM 'dɪksən

Dicky
BR 'dɪki
AM 'dɪki

dicky
BR 'dɪk|i, -iə(r), -iɪst
AM 'dɪki, -ər, -ɪst

dickybird
BR 'dɪkɪbɑːd, -z
AM 'dɪki͵bərd, -z

dicot
BR 'dʌɪkɒt, -s
AM 'daɪ͵kɑt, -s

dicotyledon
BR ͵dʌɪkɒtɪ'liːdn, -z
AM ͵daɪ͵kɑdl'idn, -z

dicotyledonous
BR ͵dʌɪkɒtɪ'liːdnəs,
͵dʌɪkɒtɪ'liːdənəs,
dʌɪ͵kɒtɪ'liːdnəs,
dʌɪ͵kɒtɪ'liːdənəs
AM ͵daɪ͵kɑdl'idənəs

dicrotic
BR dʌɪ'krɒtɪk
AM daɪ'krɑdɪk

dicta
BR 'dɪktə(r)
AM 'dɪktə

dictaphone
BR 'dɪktəfəʊn, -z
AM 'dɪktə͵foun, -z

dictate¹
noun
BR 'dɪkteɪt, -s
AM 'dɪk͵teɪt, -s

dictate²
verb
BR dɪk'teɪt, -s, -ɪŋ, -ɪd
AM 'dɪk͵teɪ|t, -ts, -dɪŋ,
-dɪd

dictation
BR dɪk'teɪʃn
AM dɪk'teɪʃən

dictator
BR dɪk'teɪtə(r), -z
AM 'dɪk͵teɪdər, -z

dictatorial
BR ͵dɪktə'tɔːrɪəl
AM ͵dɪktə'tɔrɪəl

dictatorially
BR ͵dɪktə'tɔːrɪəli
AM ͵dɪktə'tɔrɪəli

dictatorship
BR dɪk'teɪtəʃɪp, -s
AM 'dɪkteɪdər͵ʃɪp,
dɪk'teɪdər͵ʃɪp, -s

diction
BR 'dɪkʃn
AM 'dɪkʃən

dictionary
BR 'dɪkʃn(ə)r|i,
'dɪkʃən(ə)r|i, -ɪz
AM 'dɪkʃə͵nɛri, -z

Dictograph®
BR 'dɪktəgraf
AM 'dɪktə͵græf

dictum
BR 'dɪktəm, -z
AM 'dɪktəm, -z

dicty
BR 'dɪkti
AM 'dɪkti

Dictyoptera
BR dɪktɪ'ɒpt(ə)rə(r)
AM ͵dɪkti'ɑptərə

dictyopteran
BR dɪktɪ'ɒpt(ə)rən, -z
AM ͵dɪkti'ɑptərən, -z

dictyopterous
BR dɪktɪ'ɒpt(ə)rəs
AM ͵dɪkti'ɑptərəs

dicynodont
BR dʌɪ'sɪnədɒnt, -s
AM daɪ'sɪnə͵dɑnt, -s

did
BR dɪd
AM dɪd

didactic
BR dʌɪ'daktɪk
AM də'dæktɪk,
daɪ'dæktɪk

didactically
BR dʌɪ'daktɪkli
AM də'dæktək(ə)li,
daɪ'dæktək(ə)li

didacticism
BR dʌɪ'daktɪsɪz(ə)m
AM də'dæktə͵sɪzəm,
daɪ'dæktə͵sɪzəm

didakai
BR 'dɪdəkʌɪ, -z
AM 'dɪdə͵kaɪ, -z

Didcot
BR 'dɪdkət, 'dɪdkɒt
AM 'dɪdkət

diddicoy
BR 'dɪdɪkɔɪ, -z
AM 'dɪdi͵kɔɪ, -z

diddle
BR 'dɪd|l, -lz, -lɪŋ \-lɪŋ,
-ld
AM 'dɪd|əl, -əlz, -(ə)lɪŋ,
-əld

diddler
BR 'dɪdlə(r), 'dɪdlə(r),
-z
AM 'dɪd(ə)lər, -z

diddly-squat
BR 'dɪdlɪskwɒt,
'dɪdlɪskwɒt
AM 'dɪdli͵skwɒt,
'dɪdlɪ͵skwɑt,
'dɪdli͵skwɑt,
'dɪdli͵skwɑt

diddums
BR 'dɪdəmz
AM 'dɪdəmz

diddy
BR 'dɪdi
AM 'dɪdi

Diderot
BR 'diːdərəʊ
AM 'dɪdə͵rou

didgeridoo
BR ͵dɪdʒərɪ'duː, -z
AM ͵dɪdʒəri'du, -z

didicoi
BR 'dɪdɪkɔɪ, -z
AM 'dɪdi͵kɔɪ, -z

didicoy
BR 'dɪdɪkɔɪ, -z
AM 'dɪdi͵kɔɪ, -z

didn't
BR dɪdnt
AM 'dɪdn(t)

Dido
BR 'dʌɪdəʊ
AM 'daɪdou

dido
BR 'dʌɪdəʊ, -z
AM 'daɪ͵dou, -z

didst
BR dɪdst
AM dɪdst

didy
BR 'dʌɪd|i, -ɪz
AM 'daɪdi, -z

didymium
BR dɪ'dɪmɪəm
AM daɪ'dɪmɪəm

die
BR dʌɪ, -z, -ɪŋ, -d
AM daɪ, -z, -ɪŋ, -d

dieback
BR 'dʌɪbak
AM 'daɪ͵bæk

dieffenbachia
BR ͵diːf(ə)n'bakɪə(r),
-z
AM ͵difən'bakɪə,
'difən͵bakɪə, -z

Diego
BR di'eɪgəʊ
AM di'eɪgou

diehard
BR 'dʌɪhɑːd, -z

AM 'daɪˌhɑːd, -z

Diekirch
BR 'dʌɪkəːk
AM 'daɪkɜrk
GER 'diːkɪrç

dieldrin
BR 'diːldr(ɪ)n
AM 'dildrən

dielectric
BR ˌdʌɪə'lɛktrɪk
AM ˌdaɪə'lɛktrɪk

dielectrically
BR ˌdʌɪə'lɛktrɪkli
AM ˌdaɪə'lɛktrək(ə)li

diene
BR 'dʌɪiːn
AM 'daɪˌin

Dieppe
BR dɪ'ɛp
AM di'ɛp

diereses
BR dʌɪ'ɪərɪsiːz,
dʌɪ'ɛrɪsiːz
AM daɪ'ɛrəˌsiz

dieresis
BR dʌɪ'ɪərɪsɪs,
dʌɪ'ɛrɪsɪs
AM daɪ'ɛrəsəs

diesel
BR 'diːzl, -z
AM 'dizəl, 'disəl, -z

dieselise
BR 'diːzlʌɪz, -ɪz, -ɪŋ, -d
AM 'dizəˌlaɪz,
'disəˌlaɪz, -ɪz, -ɪŋ, -d

dieselize
BR 'diːzlʌɪz, -ɪz, -ɪŋ, -d
AM 'dizəˌlaɪz,
'disəˌlaɪz, -ɪz, -ɪŋ, -d

Dies Irae
BR ˌdiːeɪz 'ɪəreɪ,
+ 'ɪərʌɪ
AM ˌdeɪs 'ɪreɪ

dies non
BR ˌdʌɪiːz 'nɒn
AM ˌdeɪs 'nɑn

diet
BR 'dʌɪət, -s, -ɪŋ, -ɪd
AM 'daɪə|t, -ts, -dɪŋ,
-dəd

dietary
BR 'dʌɪət(ə)ri
AM 'daɪəˌtɛri

Dieter
BR 'diːtə(r)
AM 'didər

dieter
BR 'dʌɪətə(r), -z
AM 'daɪədər, -z

dietetic
BR ˌdʌɪə'tɛtɪk, -s
AM ˌdaɪə'tɛdɪk, -s

dietetically
BR ˌdʌɪə'tɛtɪkli
AM ˌdaɪə'tɛdək(ə)li

diethyl
BR dʌɪ'iːθ(ɪ)l,
dʌɪ'ɛθ(ɪ)l
AM daɪ'ɛθəl

dietician
BR ˌdʌɪə'tɪʃn, -z
AM ˌdaɪə'tɪʃən, -z

dietitian
BR ˌdʌɪə'tɪʃn, -z
AM ˌdaɪə'tɪʃən, -z

Dietrich
BR 'diːtrɪk, 'diːtrɪx
AM 'ditrɪk

differ
BR 'dɪfə(r), -əz, -(ə)rɪŋ,
-əd
AM 'dɪf]ər, -ərz, -(ə)rɪŋ,
-ərd

difference
BR 'dɪf(ə)rəns,
'dɪf(ə)rn̩s, -ɪz
AM 'dɪf(ə)rəns,
'dɪfər(ə)ns, -əz

different
BR 'dɪf(ə)rənt,
'dɪf(ə)rn̩t
AM 'dɪf(ə)r(ə)nt,
'dɪfərnt

differentia
BR ˌdɪfə'rɛnʃ(ɪ)ə(r)
AM ˌdɪfə'rɛnʃ(i)ə

differentiae
BR ˌdɪfə'rɛnʃiː
AM ˌdɪfə'rɛnʃi,i,
ˌdɪfə'rɛnʃi,aɪ

differential
BR ˌdɪfə'rɛnʃl, -z
AM ˌdɪfə'rɛn(t)ʃəl, -z

differentially
BR ˌdɪfə'rɛnʃli,
ˌdɪfə'rɛnʃəli
AM ˌdɪfə'rɛn(t)ʃəli

differentiate
BR ˌdɪfə'rɛnʃɪeɪt, -s,
-ɪŋ, -ɪd
AM ˌdɪfə'rɛn(t)ʃi,eɪ|t,
-ts, -dɪŋ, -dɪd

differentiation
BR ˌdɪfərɛnʃɪ'eɪʃn
AM ˌdɪfəˌrɛn(t)ʃi'eɪʃən

differentiator
BR ˌdɪfə'rɛnʃɪeɪtə(r),
-z
AM ˌdɪfə'rɛn(t)ʃiˌeɪdər,
-z

differently
BR 'dɪf(ə)rn̩tli,
'dɪf(ə)rəntli
AM 'dɪf(ə)rən(t)li,
'dɪfərn̩(t)li

differentness
BR 'dɪf(ə)rn̩tnəs,
'dɪf(ə)rəntnəs
AM 'dɪf(ə)rən(t)nəs,
'dɪfərn̩(t)nəs

difficult
BR 'dɪfɪklt
AM 'dɪfəkəlt

difficultly
BR 'dɪfɪkltli
AM 'dɪfəkəltli

difficultness
BR 'dɪfɪkltnəs
AM 'dɪfəkəltnəs

difficulty
BR 'dɪfɪklt|i, -ɪz
AM 'dɪfəkəlti, -z

diffidence
BR 'dɪfɪd(ə)ns
AM 'dɪfəd(ə)ns

diffident
BR 'dɪfɪd(ə)nt
AM 'dɪfəd(ə)nt

diffidently
BR 'dɪfɪd(ə)ntli
AM 'dɪfəd(ə)n(t)li

diffract
BR dɪ'frakt, -s, -ɪŋ, -ɪd
AM də'fræk|(t), -(t)s,
-tɪŋ, -təd

diffraction
BR dɪ'frakʃn
AM də'frækʃən

diffractive
BR dɪ'fraktɪv
AM də'fræktɪv

diffractively
BR dɪ'fraktɪvli
AM də'fræktəvli

diffractometer
BR ˌdɪfrak'tɒmɪtə(r),
-z
AM ˌdɪfræk'tɑmədər,
-z

diffuse[1]
adjective
BR dɪ'fjuːs
AM də'fjus

diffuse[2]
verb
BR dɪ'fjuːz, -ɪz, -ɪŋ, -d
AM də'fjuz, -əz, -ɪŋ, -d

diffusely
BR dɪ'fjuːsli
AM də'fjusli

diffuseness
BR dɪ'fjuːsnəs
AM də'fjusnəs

diffuser
BR dɪ'fjuːzə(r), -z
AM də'fjuzər, -z

diffusible
BR dɪ'fjuːsɪbl
AM də'fjuzəbəl

diffusion
BR dɪ'fjuːʒn
AM də'fjuʒən

diffusionist
BR dɪ'fjuːʒn̩ɪst,
dɪ'fjuː'ʒənɪst, -s
AM də'fjuʒənəst, -s

diffusive
BR dɪ'fjuːsɪv
AM də'fjusɪv

diffusively
BR dɪ'fjuːsɪvli
AM də'fjusəvli

diffusiveness
BR dɪ'fjuːsɪvnɪs
AM də'fjusɪvnɪs

diffusivity
BR ˌdɪfju'sɪvɪti,
ˌdɪfjə'sɪvɪti
AM ˌdɪfju'sɪvɪdi

dig
BR dɪg, -z, -ɪŋ
AM dɪg, -z, -ɪŋ

Digambara
BR diː'gʌmb(ə)rə(r), -z
AM dɪ'gɑmbərə, -z

digamist
BR 'dɪgəmɪst, -s
AM 'dɪgəməst, -s

digamma
BR 'dʌɪˌgamə(r),
dʌɪ'gamə(r), -z
AM 'daɪˌgæmə, -z

digamous
BR 'dɪgəməs
AM 'dɪgəməs

digamy
BR 'dɪgəm|i, -ɪz
AM 'dɪgəmi, -z

digastric
BR dʌɪ'gastrɪk
AM daɪ'gæstrɪk

Digbeth
BR 'dɪgbəθ
AM 'dɪgbəθ

Digby
BR 'dɪgbi
AM 'dɪgbi

digest[1]
noun
BR 'dʌɪdʒɛst, -s
AM 'daɪˌdʒɛst, -s

digest[2]
verb
BR dʌɪ'dʒɛst, dɪ'dʒɛst,
-s, -ɪŋ, -ɪd
AM daɪ'dʒɛst, də'dʒɛst,
-s, -ɪŋ, -əd

digester
BR dʌɪ'dʒɛstə(r),
dɪ'dʒɛstə(r), -z
AM daɪ'dʒɛstər,
də'dʒɛstər, -z

digestibility
BR dʌɪˌdʒɛstɪ'bɪlɪti,
dɪˌdʒɛstɪ'bɪlɪti
AM dəˌdʒɛstə'bɪlɪdi,
daɪˌdʒɛstə'bɪlɪdi

digestible
BR dʌɪ'dʒɛstɪbl,
dɪ'dʒɛstɪbl
AM də'dʒɛstəbəl,
daɪ'dʒɛstəbəl

digestion
BR dʌɪ'dʒɛstʃ(ə)n,
dɪ'dʒɛstʃ(ə)n, -z
AM də'dʒɛstʃən,
daɪ'dʒɛstʃən, -z

digestive
BR dʌɪ'dʒɛstɪv,
dɪ'dʒɛstɪv, -z
AM də'dʒɛstɪv,
daɪ'dʒɛstɪv, -z

digestively
BR dʌɪ'dʒɛstɪvli,
dɪ'dʒɛstɪvli
AM də'dʒɛstəvli,
daɪ'dʒɛstəvli

digger
BR 'dɪgə(r), -z
AM 'dɪgər, -z

digging
BR 'dɪgɪŋ, -z
AM 'dɪgɪŋ, -z

dight
BR dʌɪt
AM daɪt

digit
BR 'dɪdʒɪt, -s
AM 'dɪdʒɪt, -s

digital
BR 'dɪdʒɪtl, -z
AM 'dɪdʒɪdl, -z

digitalin
BR ,dɪdʒɪ'teɪlɪn
AM ,dɪdʒɪ'tælən

digitalis
BR ,dɪdʒɪ'teɪlɪs
AM ,dɪdʒɪ'tæləs

digitalise
BR 'dɪdʒɪtlʌɪz,
'dɪdʒɪtəlʌɪz, -ɪz, -ɪŋ, -d
AM 'dɪdʒɪdl,aɪz, -ɪz, -ɪŋ,
-d

digitalize
BR 'dɪdʒɪtlʌɪz,
'dɪdʒɪtəlʌɪz, -ɪz, -ɪŋ, -d
AM 'dɪdʒɪdl,aɪz, -ɪz, -ɪŋ,
-d

digitally
BR 'dɪdʒɪtli, 'dɪdʒɪtəli
AM 'dɪdʒɪdʒi

digitate
BR 'dɪdʒɪteɪt, -s, -ɪŋ, -ɪd
AM 'dɪdʒɪ,teɪ|t, -ts, -dɪŋ,
-dɪd

digitately
BR 'dɪdʒɪtətli
AM 'dɪdʒɪ,teɪtli

digitation
BR ,dɪdʒɪ'teɪʃn
AM ,dɪdʒɪ'teɪʃən

digitigrade
BR 'dɪdʒɪtɪgreɪd, -z
AM 'dɪdʒɪdə,greɪd, -z

digitisation
BR ,dɪdʒɪtʌɪ'zeɪʃn
AM ,dɪdʒədə'zeɪʃən,
,dɪdʒə,taɪ'zeɪʃən

digitise
BR 'dɪdʒɪtʌɪz, -ɪz, -ɪŋ, -d
AM 'dɪdʒə,taɪz, -ɪz, -ɪŋ,
-d

digitization
BR ,dɪdʒɪtʌɪ'zeɪʃn

AM ,dɪdʒədə'zeɪʃən,
,dɪdʒə,taɪ'zeɪʃən

digitize
BR 'dɪdʒɪtʌɪz, -ɪz, -ɪŋ, -d
AM 'dɪdʒə,taɪz, -ɪz, -ɪŋ,
-d

diglossia
BR dʌɪ'glɒsɪə(r)
AM daɪ'glɔsɪə,
daɪ'glɑsɪə

diglossic
BR dʌɪ'glɒsɪk
AM daɪ'glɔsɪk,
daɪ'glɑsɪk

dignified
BR 'dɪgnɪfʌɪd
AM 'dɪgnə,faɪd

dignifiedly
BR 'dɪgnɪfʌɪdli
AM 'dɪgnə,faɪ(ə)dli

dignify
BR 'dɪgnɪfʌɪ, -z, -ɪŋ, -d
AM 'dɪgnə,faɪ, -z, -ɪŋ, -d

dignitary
BR 'dɪgnɪt(ə)r|i, -ɪz
AM 'dɪgnə,teri, -z

dignity
BR 'dɪgnɪt|i, -ɪz
AM 'dɪgnɪdi, -z

digraph
BR 'dʌɪgrɑːf, 'dʌɪgraf,
-s
AM 'daɪ,græf, -s

digraphic
BR dʌɪ'grafɪk
AM daɪ'græfɪk

digress
BR dʌɪ'grɛs, -ɪz, -ɪŋ, -t
AM daɪ'grɛs, -əz, -ɪŋ, -t

digresser
BR dʌɪ'grɛsə(r), -z
AM daɪ'grɛsər, -z

digression
BR dʌɪ'grɛʃn, -z
AM daɪ'grɛʃən, -z

digressive
BR dʌɪ'grɛsɪv
AM daɪ'grɛsɪv

digressively
BR dʌɪ'grɛsɪvli
AM daɪ'grɛsəvli

digressiveness
BR dʌɪ'grɛsɪvnɪs
AM daɪ'grɛsɪvnɪs

dihedral
BR dʌɪ'hiːdr(ə)l
AM daɪ'hidrəl

dihydric
BR dʌɪ'hʌɪdrɪk
AM daɪ'hidrɪk

Dijon
BR 'diːʒɒ̃
AM di'ʒɑn

dik-dik
BR 'dɪkdɪk, -s
AM 'dɪk,dɪk, -s

dike
BR dʌɪk, -s, -ɪŋ, -t
AM daɪk, -s, -ɪŋ, -t

diktat
BR 'dɪktat
AM dɪk'tat, 'dɪktat

dilapidate
BR dɪ'lapɪdeɪt, -s, -ɪŋ,
-ɪd
AM də'læpə,deɪ|t, -ts,
-dɪŋ, -dɪd

dilapidation
BR dɪ,lapɪ'deɪʃn, -z
AM də,læpə'deɪʃən, -z

dilatable
BR dʌɪ'leɪtəbl,
dɪ'leɪtəbl
AM 'daɪ,leɪdəbəl,
daɪ'leɪdəbəl,
də'leɪdəbəl

dilatation
BR ,dʌɪleɪ'teɪʃn,
,dʌɪlə'teɪʃn,
,dɪlə'teɪʃn
AM ,dɪlə'teɪʃən,
,daɪlə'teɪʃən

dilate
BR dʌɪ'leɪt, dɪ'leɪt, -s,
-ɪŋ, -ɪd
AM ,daɪ,leɪ|t, daɪ'leɪ|t,
də'leɪ|t, -ts, -dɪŋ, -dɪd

dilation
BR dʌɪ'leɪʃn, dɪ'leɪʃn
AM daɪ'leɪʃən,
də'leɪʃən

dilator
BR dʌɪ'leɪtə(r),
dɪ'leɪtə(r), -z
AM 'daɪ,leɪdər,
daɪ'leɪdər, də'leɪdər,
-z

dilatorily
BR 'dɪlət(ə)rɪli
AM ,dɪlə'tɔrəli

dilatoriness
BR 'dɪlət(ə)rɪnɪs
AM ,dɪlə,tɔrɪnɪs

dilatory
BR 'dɪlət(ə)ri
AM 'dɪlə,tɔri

dildo
BR 'dɪldəʊ, -z
AM 'dɪl,doʊ, -z

dildoe
BR 'dɪldəʊ, -z
AM 'dɪl,doʊ, -z

dilemma
BR dɪ'lɛmə(r), -z
AM də'lɛmə, daɪ'lɛmə,
-z

dilettante
BR ,dɪlɪ'tant|i, -ɪz
AM ,dɪlə,tant, -s

dilettanti
BR ,dɪlɪ'tanti
AM ,dɪlə'tan(t)i

dilettantism
BR ,dɪlɪ'tantɪz(ə)m

dike
AM 'dɪlə,tan(t)izəm

Dili
BR 'dɪli
AM 'dɪli

diligence
BR 'dɪlɪdʒ(ə)ns
AM 'dɪlədʒəns

diligent
BR 'dɪlɪdʒ(ə)nt
AM 'dɪlədʒənt

diligently
BR 'dɪlɪdʒ(ə)ntli
AM 'dɪlədʒən(t)li

Dilke
BR dɪlk
AM 'dɪlk(ə)

dill
BR dɪl
AM dɪl

Dillard
BR 'dɪlɑːd
AM 'dɪlərd

Dillon
BR 'dɪlən
AM 'dɪlɪn

Dillwyn
BR 'dɪlwɪn
AM 'dɪlwɪn

dilly
BR 'dɪl|i, -ɪz
AM 'dɪli, -z

dillybag
BR 'dɪlɪbag, -z
AM 'dɪli,bæg, -z

dilly-dally
BR ,dɪlɪ'dal|i,
'dɪlɪ,dal|i, -ɪz, -ɪɪŋ, -ɪd
AM 'dɪli,dæli, -z, -ɪŋ, -d

diluent
BR 'dɪljʊənt, -s
AM 'dɪljəwənt, -s

dilute
BR dʌɪ'l(j)uːt,
dɪ'l(j)uːt, -s, -ɪŋ, -ɪd
AM də'luːt, daɪ'luːt, -ts,
-dɪŋ, -dəd

dilutee
BR ,dʌɪl(j)uː'tiː, -z
AM də,luːti, daɪ'luːti, -z

diluter
BR dʌɪ'l(j)uːtə(r),
dɪ'l(j)uːtə(r), -z
AM də'ludər, daɪ'ludər,
-z

dilution
BR dʌɪ'l(j)uːʃn,
dɪ'l(j)uːʃn, -z
AM də'luʃən, daɪ'luʃn,
-z

diluvia
BR dʌɪ'l(j)uːvɪə(r),
dɪ'l(j)uːvɪə(r)
AM də'luvɪə

diluvial
BR dʌɪ'l(j)uːvɪəl,
dɪ'l(j)uːvɪəl
AM də'luvɪəl

diluvialist
BR dɑɪˈl(j)uːvɪəlɪst,
dɪˈl(j)uːvɪəlɪst, -s
AM dəˈluːvɪələst, -s

diluvian
BR dɑɪˈl(j)uːvɪən,
dɪˈl(j)uːvɪən
AM dəˈluːvɪən

diluvium
BR dɑɪˈl(j)uːvɪəm,
dɪˈl(j)uːvɪəm
AM dəˈluːvɪəm

Dilwyn
BR ˈdɪlwɪn
AM ˈdɪlwɪn

Dilys
BR ˈdɪlɪs
AM ˈdɪlɪs

dim
BR dɪm, -z, -ɪŋ, -d, -ə(r),
-əst
AM dɪm, -z, -ɪŋ, -d, -ər,
-ɪst

DiMaggio
BR dɪˈmɑdʒɪəʊ
AM diˈmædʒioʊ

Dimbleby
BR ˈdɪmblbi
AM ˈdɪmbəlbi

dime
BR dɑɪm, -z
AM dɑɪm, -z

dimension
BR dɑɪˈmɛnʃn,
dɪˈmɛnʃn, -z
AM dəˈmɛn(t)ʃən, -z

dimensional
BR dɑɪˈmɛnʃn(ə)l,
dɑɪˈmɛnʃən(ə)l,
dɪˈmɛnʃn(ə)l,
dɪˈmɛnʃən(ə)l
AM dəˈmɛn(t)ʃ(ə)nəl

dimensionality
BR dɑɪˌmɛnʃəˈnalɪti,
dɪˌmɛnʃəˈnalɪti
AM dəˌmɛn(t)ʃəˈnælədi,
dəˌmɛn(t)ʃnˈælədi,
dɑɪˌmɛn(t)ʃəˈnælədi,
dɑɪˌmɛn(t)ʃnˈælədi

dimensionally
BR dɑɪˈmɛnʃṇəli,
dɑɪˈmɛnʃṇ̩li,
dɑɪˈmɛnʃənḷi,
dɑɪˈmɛnʃ(ə)nəli,
dɪˈmɛnʃṇəli,
dɪˈmɛnʃṇ̩li,
dɪˈmɛnʃənḷi,
dɪˈmɛnʃ(ə)nəli
AM dəˈmɛn(t)ʃ(ə)nəli

dimensionless
BR dɑɪˈmɛnʃnləs,
dɑɪˈmɛnʃənləs,
dɪˈmɛnʃnləs,
dɪˈmɛnʃənləs
AM dəˈmɛn(t)ʃənləs

dimer
BR ˈdɑɪmə(r), -z
AM ˈdɑɪmər, -z

dimeric
BR dɑɪˈmɛrɪk
AM dɑɪˈmɛrɪk

dimerous
BR ˈdɪm(ə)rəs
AM ˈdɪm(ə)rəs

dimeter
BR ˈdɪmɪtə(r), -z
AM ˈdɪmədər, -z

dimidiate
BR dɪˈmɪdɪət
AM dəˈmɪdiˌeɪt

diminish
BR dɪˈmɪn|ɪʃ, -ɪʃɪz,
-ɪʃɪŋ, -ɪʃt
AM dəˈmɪnɪʃ, -ɪs, -ɪŋ, -t

diminishable
BR dɪˈmɪnɪʃəbl
AM dəˈmɪnəʃəbəl

diminuendo
BR dɪˌmɪnjuˈɛndəʊ, -z
AM dəˌmɪn(j)əˈwɛndoʊ,
-z

diminution
BR ˌdɪmɪˈnjuːʃn, -z
AM ˌdɪməˈn(j)uʃən, -z

diminutival
BR dɪˌmɪnjʊˈtɑɪvl
AM dəˌmɪnjəˈtɑɪvəl

diminutive
BR dɪˈmɪnjʊtɪv
AM dəˈmɪnjədɪv

diminutively
BR dɪˈmɪnjʊtɪvli
AM dəˈmɪnjədəvli

diminutiveness
BR dɪˈmɪnjʊtɪvnɪs
AM dəˈmɪnjədɪvnɪs

dimissory
BR ˈdɪmɪs(ə)ri
AM ˈdɪməˌsɔri

dimity
BR ˈdɪmɪti
AM ˈdɪmɪdi

dimly
BR ˈdɪmli
AM ˈdɪmli

dimmer
BR ˈdɪmə(r), -z
AM ˈdɪmər, -z

dimmish
BR ˈdɪmɪʃ
AM ˈdɪmɪʃ

Dimmock
BR ˈdɪmək
AM ˈdɪmək

dimness
BR ˈdɪmnɪs
AM ˈdɪmnɪs

dimorphic
BR dɑɪˈmɔːfɪk
AM dɑɪˈmɔrfɪk

dimorphism
BR dɑɪˈmɔːfɪz(ə)m
AM dɑɪˈmɔrfɪzəm

dimorphous
BR dɑɪˈmɔːfəs

AM dɑɪˈmɔrfəs

dimple
BR ˈdɪmpl, -z
AM ˈdɪmpəl, -z

Dimplex®
BR ˈdɪmplɛks
AM ˈdɪmˌplɛks

dimply
BR ˈdɪmpl|i, ˈdɪmpl|i,
-ɪə(r), -ɪɪst
AM ˈdɪmpli, -ər, -ɪst

Dimpna
BR ˈdɪmpnə(r)
AM ˈdɪm(p)nə

dim sum
BR ˌdɪm ˈsʌm, + ˈsʊm
AM ˌdɪm ˈsəm

dimwit
BR ˈdɪmwɪt, -s
AM ˈdɪmˌwɪt, -s

DIN
BR dɪn
AM dɪn, ˌdiˌaɪˈɛn

din
BR dɪn, -z, -ɪŋ, -d
AM dɪn, -z, -ɪŋ, -d

Dinah
BR ˈdɑɪnə(r)
AM ˈdɑɪnə

dinar
BR ˈdiːnɑː(r), -z
AM ˈdiˌnɑr, dəˈnɑr,
diˈnɑr, -z

Dinaric
BR dɪˌnarɪk
AM dəˈnɛrɪk

Dinas
BR ˈdiːnas
AM ˈdinɪs

dine
BR dɑɪn, -z, -ɪŋ, -d
AM dɑɪn, -z, -ɪŋ, -d

Dineen
BR dɪˈniːn
AM dɪˈnin

diner
BR ˈdɑɪnə(r), -z
AM ˈdɑɪnər, -z

dinero
BR dɪˈnɛːrəʊ
AM dəˈnɛroʊ

dinette
BR dɑɪˈnɛt, -s
AM dɑɪˈnɛt, -s

ding
BR dɪŋ, -z, -ɪŋ, -d
AM dɪŋ, -z, -ɪŋ, -d

Dingaan
BR ˈdɪŋɡɑːn
AM ˈdɪŋɡɪn

dingaling
BR ˌdɪŋəˈlɪŋ, ˈdɪŋəlɪŋ,
-z
AM ˈdɪŋəˌlɪŋ, -z

Ding an sich
BR ˌdɪŋ an ˈzɪk, + ˈzɪx
AM ˌdɪŋˌanˈsɪk

dingbat
BR ˈdɪŋbat, -s
AM ˈdɪŋˌbæt, -s

dingdong
BR ˈdɪŋdɒŋ, ˌdɪŋˈdɒŋ,
-z
AM ˈdɪŋˌdɔŋ, ˈdɪŋˌdɑŋ,
-z

dinge
BR dɪn(d)ʒ, -ɪz
AM dɪn(d)ʒ, -ɪz

dinghy
BR ˈdɪŋ(ɡ)|i, -ɪz
AM ˈdɪŋi, -z

dingily
BR ˈdɪn(d)ʒɪli
AM ˈdɪndʒɪli

dinginess
BR ˈdɪn(d)ʒɪnɪs
AM ˈdɪndʒɪnɪs

dingle
BR ˈdɪŋɡl, -z
AM ˈdɪŋɡəl, -z

Dingley
BR ˈdɪŋli
AM ˈdɪŋli

dingo
BR ˈdɪŋɡəʊ, -z
AM ˈdɪŋɡoʊ, -z

dingus
BR ˈdɪŋɡəs, -ɪz
AM ˈdɪŋɡəs, -əz

Dingwall
BR ˈdɪŋwɔːl, ˈdɪŋw(ə)l
AM ˈdɪŋˌwɔl, ˈdɪŋwəl,
ˈdɪŋˌwɑl

dingy
BR ˈdɪn(d)ʒ|i, -ɪə(r),
-ɪɪst
AM ˈdɪndʒi, -ər, -ɪst

dink
BR dɪŋk
AM dɪŋk

dinkily
BR ˈdɪŋkɪli
AM ˈdɪŋkɪli

dinkiness
BR ˈdɪŋkɪnɪs
AM ˈdɪŋkɪnɪs

dinkum
BR ˈdɪŋkəm
AM ˈdɪŋkəm

dinky
BR ˈdɪŋk|i, -ɪə(r), -ɪɪst
AM ˈdɪŋki, -ər, -ɪst

dinner
BR ˈdɪnə(r), -z
AM ˈdɪnər, -z

dinnertime
BR ˈdɪnətɑɪm, -z
AM ˈdɪnərˌtɑɪm, -z

dinnerware
BR ˈdɪnəwɛː(r)
AM ˈdɪnərˌwɛ(ə)r

Dinorwic
BR dɪˈnɔːwɪk
AM ˈdɪnərˌwɪk

WE dɪnˈɒrwɪg

dinosaur
BR ˈdaɪnəsɔː(r), -z
AM ˈdaɪnəˌsɔ(ə)r, -z

dinosaurian
BR ˌdaɪnəˈsɔːriən
AM ˌdaɪnəˈsɔriən

dinothere
BR ˈdaɪnə(ʊ)θɪə(r), -z
AM ˈdaɪnəˌθɪ(ə)r, -z

dint
BR dɪnt, -s
AM dɪnt, -s

Dinwiddie
BR dɪnˈwɪdi, ˈdɪnwɪdi
AM ˈdɪnˌwɪdi

Dinwiddy
BR dɪnˈwɪdi, ˈdɪnwɪdi
AM ˈdɪnˌwɪdi

diocesan
BR daɪˈɒsɪs(ə)n,
daɪˈɒsɪz(ə)n
AM daɪˈɑsəsən

diocese
BR ˈdaɪəsɪs, ˈdaɪəsiːz,
-ɪz
AM ˈdaɪəˌsiz, ˈdaɪəsəs,
-ɪz

Diocletian
BR ˌdaɪəˈkliːʃn
AM ˌdaɪəˈkliʃən

diode
BR ˈdaɪəʊd, -z
AM ˈdaɪˌoʊd, -z

dioecious
BR daɪˈiːʃəs
AM daɪˈiʃəs

dioeciously
BR daɪˈiːʃəsli
AM daɪˈiʃəsli

Diogenes
BR daɪˈɒdʒɪniːz
AM daɪˈɑdʒəniz

diol
BR ˈdaɪɒl, -z
AM ˈdaɪˌɔl, ˈdaɪˌɑl, -z

Diomede
BR ˈdaɪəmiːd
AM ˈdaɪəˌmid

Diomedes
BR ˌdaɪəˈmiːdiːz
AM ˌdaɪəˈmidiz

Dione
BR ˈdaɪəʊn, daɪˈəʊni
AM ˈdaɪˌoʊn

Dionysiac
BR ˌdaɪəˈnɪziak,
ˌdaɪəˈnɪsiak
AM ˌdaɪəˈnɪsiˌæk,
ˌdaɪəˈnɪziˌæk

Dionysian
BR ˌdaɪəˈnɪziən,
ˌdaɪəˈnɪsiən,
ˌdaɪəˈnaɪsiən
AM ˌdaɪəˈnɪsiən,
ˌdaɪəˈnɪziən,
ˌdaɪəˈnɪʒ(i)ən

Dionysius
BR ˌdaɪəˈnɪziəs,
ˌdaɪəˈnɪsiəs
AM ˌdaɪəˈnɪsiəs,
ˌdaɪəˈnɪziəs

Dionysus
BR ˌdaɪəˈnaɪsəs
AM ˌdaɪəˈnaɪsəs

Diophantine
BR ˌdaɪə(ʊ)ˈfantaɪn
AM ˌdaɪəˈfænˌtaɪn

Diophantus
BR ˌdaɪə(ʊ)ˈfantəs
AM ˌdaɪəˈfæn(t)əs

diopside
BR daɪˈɒpsaɪd
AM daɪˈɑpˌsaɪd

diopter
BR daɪˈɒptə(r),
ˈdaɪɒptə(r), -z
AM ˈdaɪˌɑptər, -z

dioptre
BR daɪˈɒptə(r),
ˈdaɪɒptə(r), -z
AM ˈdaɪˌɑptər, -z

dioptric
BR daɪˈɒptrɪk, -s
AM daɪˈɑptrɪk, -s

Dior
BR ˈdiːɔː(r), dɪˈɔː(r)
AM diˈɔ(ə)r

diorama
BR ˌdaɪəˈrɑːmə(r), -z
AM ˌdaɪəˈræmə,
ˌdaɪəˈrɑmə, -z

dioramic
BR ˌdaɪəˈramɪk
AM ˌdaɪəˈræmɪk,
ˌdaɪəˈramɪk

diorite
BR ˈdaɪərʌɪt
AM ˈdaɪəˌraɪt

dioritic
BR ˌdaɪəˈrɪtɪk
AM ˌdaɪəˈrɪdɪk,
ˌdaɪəˈrɪdɪk

Dioscuri
BR daɪˈɒskjʊri,
daɪˈɒskjərʌɪ,
ˌdaɪəˈskjʊəri,
ˌdaɪəˈskjʊərʌɪ
AM ˌdaɪəˈsk(j)ʊri

diotic
BR daɪˈɒtɪk, daɪˈəʊtɪk
AM daɪˈoʊdɪk, daɪˈɑdɪk

dioxan
BR daɪˈɒks(ə)n
AM daɪˈɑksən

dioxane
BR daɪˈɒkseɪn
AM daɪˈɑkˌseɪn

dioxide
BR daɪˈɒksaɪd, -z
AM daɪˈɑkˌsaɪd, -z

dioxin
BR daɪˈɒksɪn
AM daɪˈɑksən

DIP
BR dɪp
AM dɪp

dip
BR dɪp, -s, -ɪŋ, -t
AM dɪp, -s, -ɪŋ, -t

Dip. Ed.
Diploma in Education
BR ˌdɪp ˈɛd
AM ˌdɪp ˈɛd

dipeptide
BR daɪˈpɛptʌɪd, -z
AM daɪˈpɛpˌtaɪd, -z

diphone
BR ˈdaɪfəʊn, -z
AM ˈdaɪˌfoʊn, -z

diphtheria
BR dɪpˈθɪəriə(r),
dɪfˈθɪəriə(r)
AM dɪpˈθɪriə, dɪfˈθɪriə

diphtherial
BR dɪpˈθɪəriəl,
dɪfˈθɪəriəl
AM dɪpˈθɪriəl,
dɪfˈθɪriəl

diphtheric
BR dɪfˈθɛrɪk, dɪpˈθɛrɪk
AM dɪpˈθɪrɪk, dɪfˈθɪrɪk

diphtheritic
BR ˌdɪfθəˈrɪtɪk,
ˌdɪpθəˈrɪtɪk
AM ˌdɪpθəˈrɪdɪk,
ˌdɪfθəˈrɪdɪk

diphtheroid
BR ˈdɪfθərɔɪd,
ˈdɪpθərɔɪd
AM ˈdɪpθəˌrɔɪd,
ˈdɪfθəˌrɔɪd

diphthong
BR ˈdɪfθɒŋ, ˈdɪpθɒŋ, -z
AM ˈdɪpˌθɒŋ, ˈdɪfˌθɒŋ,
ˈdɪpˌθaŋ, ˈdɪfˌθaŋ, -z

diphthongal
BR dɪfˈθɒŋgl,
dɪpˈθɒŋgl
AM dɪpˈθɒŋ(g)əl,
dɪfˈθɒŋ(g)əl,
dɪpˈθaŋ(g)əl,
dɪfˈθaŋ(g)əl

diphthongally
BR dɪfˈθɒŋgli,
dɪfˈθɒŋgəli,
dɪpˈθɒŋgli,
dɪpˈθɒŋgəli,
dɪfˈθaŋ(g)əli,
dɪpˈθaŋ(g)əli,
dɪfˈθaŋ(g)əli

diphthongisation
BR ˌdɪfθɒŋgaɪˈzeɪʃn,
ˌdɪpθɒŋgaɪˈzeɪʃn
AM ˌdɪpθɒŋˌ(g)əˈzeɪʃən,
ˌdɪpθɒŋˌ(g)aɪˈzeɪʃən,
ˌdɪfθɒŋˌ(g)əˈzeɪʃən,
ˌdɪfθɒŋˌ(g)aɪˈzeɪʃən,
ˌdɪpθaŋˌ(g)əˈzeɪʃən,
ˌdɪpθaŋˌ(g)aɪˈzeɪʃən,

ˌdɪfθaŋˌ(g)əˈzeɪʃən,
ˌdɪfθaŋˌ(g)aɪˈzeɪʃən

diphthongise
BR ˈdɪfθɒŋgaɪz,
ˈdɪpθɒŋgaɪz, -ɪz, -ɪŋ, -d
AM ˈdɪpθɒŋˌ(g)aɪz,
ˈdɪfθɒŋˌ(g)aɪz,
ˈdɪpθaŋˌ(g)aɪz,
ˈdɪfθaŋˌ(g)aɪz, -ɪz, -ɪŋ,
-d

diphthongization
BR ˌdɪfθɒŋgaɪˈzeɪʃn,
ˌdɪpθɒŋgaɪˈzeɪʃn
AM ˌdɪpθɒŋˌ(g)əˈzeɪʃən,
ˌdɪfθɒŋˌ(g)əˈzeɪʃən,
ˌdɪfθaŋˌ(g)əˈzeɪʃən,
ˌdɪpθaŋˌ(g)əˈzeɪʃən,
ˌdɪpθaŋˌ(g)aɪˈzeɪʃən,
ˌdɪfθaŋˌ(g)əˈzeɪʃən,
ˌdɪfθaŋˌ(g)aɪˈzeɪʃən

diphthongize
BR ˈdɪfθɒŋgaɪz,
ˈdɪpθɒŋgaɪz, -ɪz, -ɪŋ, -d
AM ˈdɪpθɒŋˌ(g)aɪz,
ˈdɪfθɒŋˌ(g)aɪz,
ˈdɪpθaŋˌ(g)aɪz,
ˈdɪfθaŋˌ(g)aɪz, -ɪz, -ɪŋ,
-d

diphycercal
BR ˌdɪfɪˈsɜːkl
AM ˌdɪfɪˈsɜrkəl

Diplock
BR ˈdɪplɒk
AM ˈdɪpˌlɑk

diplococci
BR ˌdɪplə(ʊ)ˈkɒk(s)ʌɪ,
ˌdɪplə(ʊ)ˈkɒk(s)iː
AM ˌdɪploʊˈkɑˌkaɪ,
ˌdɪploʊˈkaki,
ˌdɪploʊˈkasaɪ,
ˌdɪploʊˈkaksi

diplococcus
BR ˌdɪplə(ʊ)ˈkɒkəs
AM ˌdɪploʊˈkɑkəs

diplodoci
BR dɪˈplɒdəkʌɪ,
ˌdɪplə(ʊ)ˈdəʊkʌɪ
AM dəˈpladəˌkaɪ

diplodocus
BR dɪˈplɒdəkəs,
ˌdɪplə(ʊ)ˈdəʊkəs, -ɪz
AM dəˈpladəkəs, -əz

diploid
BR ˈdɪplɔɪd, -z
AM ˈdɪplɔɪd, -z

diploidy
BR ˈdɪplɔɪdi
AM ˈdɪplɔɪdi

diploma
BR dɪˈpləʊmə(r), -z, -d
AM dəˈploʊmə, -z, -d

diplomacy
BR dɪˈpləʊməsi
AM dəˈploʊməsi

diplomat
BR ˈdɪpləmat, -s
AM ˈdɪpləˌmæt, -s

diplomate
BR ˈdɪpləmeɪt, -s
AM ˈdɪpləˌmeɪt, -s
diplomatic
BR ˌdɪpləˈmatɪk
AM ˌdɪpləˈmædɪk
diplomatically
BR ˌdɪpləˈmatɪkli
AM ˌdɪpləˈmædək(ə)li
diplomatise
BR dɪˈpləʊmətʌɪz, -ɪz,
-ɪŋ, -d
AM ˈdɪpləməˌtaɪz, -ɪz,
-ɪŋ, -d
diplomatist
BR dɪˈpləʊmətɪst, -s
AM dəˈpləʊmədəst, -s
diplomatize
BR dɪˈpləʊmətʌɪz, -ɪz,
-ɪŋ, -d
AM ˈdɪpləməˌtaɪz, -ɪz,
-ɪŋ, -d
diplont
BR ˈdɪplɒnt, -s
AM ˈdɪˌplɑnt, -s
Diplopoda
BR ˌdɪpləˈpəʊdə(r)
AM ˌdɪpləˈpoʊdə
diplotene
BR ˈdɪplə(ʊ)tiːn, -z
AM ˈdɪploʊˌtin, -z
dipolar
BR dʌɪˈpəʊlə(r)
AM daɪˈpoʊlər
dipole
BR ˈdʌɪpəʊl, -z
AM ˈdaɪˌpoʊl, -z
dipper
BR ˈdɪpə(r), -z
AM ˈdɪpər, -z
dippy
BR ˈdɪp|i, -ɪə(r), -ɪɪst
AM ˈdɪpi, -ər, -ɪst
dipso
BR ˈdɪpsəʊ, -z
AM ˈdɪpsoʊ, -z
dipsomania
BR ˌdɪpsə(ʊ)ˈmeɪnɪə(r)
AM ˌdɪpsəˈmeɪnɪə,
ˌdɪpsoʊˈmeɪnɪə
dipsomaniac
BR ˌdɪpsə(ʊ)ˈmeɪnɪak,
-s
AM ˌdɪpsəˈmeɪniˌæk,
ˌdɪpsoʊˈmeɪniˌæk, -s
dipstick
BR ˈdɪpstɪk, -s
AM ˈdɪpˌstɪk, -s
dipswitch
BR ˈdɪpswɪtʃ, -ɪz
AM ˈdɪpˌswɪtʃ, -ɪz
Diptera
BR ˈdɪpt(ə)rə(r)
AM ˈdɪpt(ə)rə
dipteral
BR ˈdɪpt(ə)rəl,
ˈdɪpt(ə)r̩l
AM ˈdɪpt(ə)rəl

dipteran
BR ˈdɪptərən, ˈdɪptər̩n,
ˈdɪptr(ə)n, -z
AM ˈdɪpt(ə)rən, -z
dipterist
BR ˈdɪpt(ə)rɪst, -s
AM ˈdɪpt(ə)rəst, -s
dipterous
BR ˈdɪpt(ə)rəs
AM ˈdɪpt(ə)rəs
diptych
BR ˈdɪptɪk, -s
AM ˈdɪptɪk, -s
Dirac
BR dɪˈrak
AM dəˈrɑk
dire
BR ˈdʌɪə(r), -ɪst
AM ˈdaɪ(ə)r, -ɪst
direct
BR dɪˈrɛkt, dʌɪˈrɛkt, -s,
-ɪŋ, -ɪd
AM dəˈrɛk|(t),
daɪˈrɛk|(t), -(t)s, -tɪŋ,
-təd
direction
BR dɪˈrɛkʃn,
dʌɪˈrɛkʃn, -z
AM dəˈrɛkʃən,
daɪˈrɛkʃən, -z
directional
BR dɪˈrɛkʃn̩(ə)l,
dɪˈrɛkʃən(ə)l,
dʌɪˈrɛkʃn̩(ə)l,
dʌɪˈrɛkʃən(ə)l
AM dəˈrɛkʃ(ə)nəl,
daɪˈrɛkʃ(ə)nəl
directionality
BR dɪˌrɛkʃəˈnalɪti,
dʌɪˌrɛkʃəˈnalɪti
AM dəˌrɛkʃəˈnælədi,
daɪˌrɛkʃəˈnælədi
directionally
BR dɪˈrɛkʃn̩əli,
dɪˈrɛkʃən̩li,
dɪˈrɛkʃ(ə)nəli,
dʌɪˈrɛkʃn̩əli,
dʌɪˈrɛkʃən̩li,
dʌɪˈrɛkʃ(ə)nəli
AM dəˈrɛkʃ(ə)nəli,
daɪˈrɛkʃ(ə)nəli
directionless
BR dɪˈrɛkʃnləs,
dʌɪˈrɛkʃnləs
AM dəˈrɛkʃənləs,
daɪˈrɛkʃənləs
directive
BR dɪˈrɛktɪv,
dʌɪˈrɛktɪv, -z
AM dəˈrɛktɪv, -z
directly
BR dɪˈrɛktli, dʌɪˈrɛktli
AM dəˈrɛk(t)li,
daɪˈrɛk(t)li

directness
BR dɪˈrɛk(t)nəs,
dʌɪˈrɛk(t)nəs
AM dəˈrɛk(t)nəs
Directoire
BR ˌdɪrɛkˈtwɑː(r),
ˌdiːrɛkˈtwɑː(r),
dɪˈrɛktwɑː(r)
AM dəˌrɛkˈtwɑr
director
BR dɪˈrɛktə(r),
dʌɪˈrɛktə(r), -z
AM dəˈrɛktər,
daɪˈrɛktər, -z
directorate
BR dɪˈrɛkt(ə)rət,
dʌɪˈrɛkt(ə)rət, -s
AM dəˈrɛkt(ə)rət, -s
directorial
BR ˌdʌɪrɛkˈtɔːrɪəl,
dɪˌrɛkˈtɔːrɪəl
AM dəˌrɛkˈtorɪəl,
ˌdaɪrɛkˈtorɪəl
directorship
BR dɪˈrɛktəʃɪp,
dʌɪˈrɛktəʃɪp, -s
AM dəˈrɛktərˌʃɪp, -s
directory
BR dɪˈrɛkt(ə)r|i,
dʌɪˈrɛkt(ə)r|i, -ɪz
AM dəˈrɛkt(ə)ri,
daɪˈrɛkt(ə)ri, -z
directress
BR dɪˈrɛktrɪs,
dʌɪˈrɛktrɪs, -ɪz
AM dəˈrɛktrəs,
daɪˈrɛktrəs, -əz
directrices
BR dɪˈrɛktrɪsiːz
AM dəˈrɛktrəˌsiz,
daɪˈrɛktrəˌsiz
directrix
BR dɪˈrɛktrɪks,
dʌɪˈrɛktrɪks, -ɪz
AM dəˈrɛktrɪks,
daɪˈrɛktrɪks, -ɪz
direful
BR ˈdʌɪəf(ʊ)l
AM ˈdaɪ(ə)rfəl
direfully
BR ˈdʌɪəfʊli, ˈdaɪəfʃli
AM ˈdaɪ(ə)rf(ə)li
direly
BR ˈdʌɪəli
AM ˈdaɪ(ə)rli
direness
BR ˈdʌɪənəs
AM ˈdaɪ(ə)rnəs
dirge
BR dəːdʒ, -ɪz
AM dərdʒ, -əz
dirgeful
BR ˈdəːdʒf(ʊ)l
AM ˈdərdʒfəl
dirham
BR ˈdɪəram, ˈdɪərəm, -z
AM ˈdɪrəm, -z

dirigible
BR ˈdɪrɪdʒɪbl, -z
AM dəˈrɪdʒəbəl,
ˈdɪrədʒəbəl, -z
dirigisme
BR ˈdɪrɪʒiːz(ə)m
AM ˌdiriˈʒizm
FR diriʒism
dirigiste
BR ˌdɪrɪˈʒiːst, -s
AM ˌdiriˈʒist, -s
FR diriʒist
diriment
BR ˈdɪrɪm(ə)nt
AM ˈdɪrəmənt
dirk
BR dəːk, -s
AM dərk, -s
dirndl
BR ˈdəːndl, -z
AM ˈdərndl, -z
dirt
BR dəːt
AM dərt
dirtily
BR ˈdəːtɪli
AM ˈdərdəli
dirtiness
BR ˈdəːtɪnɪs
AM ˈdərdinɪs
dirty
BR ˈdəːt|i, -ɪz, -ɪŋ, -ɪd,
-ɪə(r), -ɪɪst
AM ˈdərdi, -z, -ɪŋ, -d, -ər,
-ɪst
disability
BR ˌdɪsəˈbɪlɪt|i, -ɪz
AM ˌdɪsəˈbɪlɪdi, -z
disable
BR dɪsˈeɪb|l, -lz,
-l|ɪŋ \-l·ɪŋ, -ld
AM dəˈseɪb|əl, -əlz,
-(ə)lɪŋ, -əld
disablement
BR dɪsˈeɪblm(ə)nt, -s
AM dəˈseɪbəlmənt, -s
disablist
BR dɪˈseɪblɪst
AM dəˈseɪb(ə)ləst
disabuse
BR ˌdɪsəˈbjuːz, -ɪz, -ɪŋ,
-d
AM ˌdɪsəˌbjuz, -əz, -ɪŋ,
-d
disaccord
BR ˌdɪsəˈkɔːd, -z, -ɪŋ, -ɪd
AM ˌdɪsəˈkɔ(ə)rd, -z,
-ɪŋ, -əd
disaccustom
BR ˌdɪsəˈkʌstəm, -z, -ɪŋ,
-d
AM ˌdɪsəˈkəstəm, -z,
-ɪŋ, -d
disadvantage
BR ˌdɪsədˈvɑːnt|ɪdʒ,
ˌdɪsədˈvɑnt|ɪdʒ, -ɪdʒɪz
AM ˌdɪsədˈvæn(t)ɪdʒ,
-ɪz

disadvantageous
BR ˌdɪsædv(ə)nˈteɪdʒəs,
ˌdɪsædvanˈteɪdʒəs
AM ˌdɪsˌædvənˈteɪdʒəs

disadvantageously
BR ˌdɪsædv(ə)nˈteɪdʒəsli,
ˌdɪsædvanˈteɪdʒəsli
AM ˌdɪsˌædvənˈteɪdʒəsli

disadvantageous-ness
BR ˌdɪsædv(ə)nˈteɪdʒəs-nəs,
ˌdɪsædvanˈteɪdʒəsnəs
AM ˌdɪsˌædvənˈteɪdʒəs-nəs

disaffected
BR ˌdɪsəˈfɛktɪd
AM ˈdɪsəˈfɛktəd

disaffectedly
BR ˌdɪsəˈfɛktɪdli
AM ˈdɪsəˈfɛktədli

disaffection
BR ˌdɪsəˈfɛkʃn
AM ˈdɪsəˈfɛkʃən

disaffiliate
BR ˌdɪsəˈfɪlieɪt, -s, -ɪŋ, -ɪd
AM ˈdɪsəˈfɪlieɪ|t, -ts, -dɪŋ, -dɪd

disaffiliation
BR ˌdɪsəfɪlɪˈeɪʃn
AM ˈdɪsəˌfɪlɪˈeɪʃən

disaffirm
BR ˌdɪsəˈfəːm, -z, -ɪŋ, -d
AM ˈdɪsəˈfərm, -z, -ɪŋ, -d

disaffirmation
BR ˌdɪsafəˈmeɪʃn
AM ˈdɪsəˌfərˈmeɪʃən, ˈdɪsˌæfərˈmeɪʃən

disafforest
BR ˌdɪsəˈfɒrɪst, -s, -ɪŋ, -ɪd
AM ˌdɪsəˈfɔrəst, -s, -ɪŋ, -əd

disafforestation
BR ˌdɪsəfɒrɪˈsteɪʃn
AM ˈdɪsəˌfɔrəˈsteɪʃən

disaggregate
BR ˌdɪsˈagrɪgeɪt, -s, -ɪŋ, -ɪd
AM ˌdɪsˈægrəgeɪ|t, -ts, -dɪŋ, -dɪd

disaggregation
BR ˌdɪsagrɪˈgeɪʃn
AM ˌdɪsˌægrəˈgeɪʃən

disagree
BR ˌdɪsəˈgriː, -z, -ɪŋ, -d
AM ˈdɪsəˈgri, -z, -ɪŋ, -d

disagreeable
BR ˌdɪsəˈgriːəbl
AM ˈdɪsəˈgriəbəl

disagreeableness
BR ˌdɪsəˈgriːəblnəs
AM ˈdɪsəˈgriəbəlnəs

disagreeably
BR ˌdɪsəˈgriːəbli
AM ˈdɪsəˈgriəbli

disagreement
BR ˌdɪsəˈgriːm(ə)nt, -s
AM ˈdɪsəˈgrimənt, -s

disallow
BR ˌdɪsəˈlaʊ, -z, -ɪŋ, -d
AM ˈdɪsəˈlaʊ, -z, -ɪŋ, -d

disallowance
BR ˌdɪsəˈlaʊəns, -ɪz
AM ˈdɪsəˈlaʊəns, -əz

disambiguate
BR ˌdɪsamˈbɪgjʊeɪt, -s, -ɪŋ, -ɪd
AM ˌdɪsæmˈbɪgjəˌweɪ|t, -ts, -dɪŋ, -dɪd

disambiguation
BR ˌdɪsambɪgjʊˈeɪʃn
AM ˌdɪsamˌbɪgjəˈweɪʃən

disamenity
BR ˌdɪsəˈmiːnɪti, ˌdɪsəˈmɛnɪti, -ɪz
AM ˈdɪsəˈmɛnədi, -z

disannul
BR ˌdɪsəˈnʌl, -z, -ɪŋ, -d
AM ˈdɪsəˈnəl, -z, -ɪŋ, -d

disannulment
BR ˌdɪsəˈnʌlm(ə)nt
AM ˈdɪsəˈnəlmənt

disappear
BR ˌdɪsəˈpɪə(r), -z, -ɪŋ, -d
AM ˈdɪsəˈpɪ(ə)r, -z, -ɪŋ, -d

disappearance
BR ˌdɪsəˈpɪərəns, ˌdɪsəˈpɪərŋs, -ɪz
AM ˌdɪsəˈpɪrəns, -əz

disappoint
BR ˌdɪsəˈpɔɪnt, -s, -ɪŋ, -ɪd
AM ˌdɪsəˈpɔɪn|t, -ts, -(t)ɪŋ, -(t)əd

disappointedly
BR ˌdɪsəˈpɔɪntɪdli
AM ˌdɪsəˈpɔɪn(t)ədli

disappointing
BR ˌdɪsəˈpɔɪntɪŋ
AM ˌdɪsəˈpɔɪn(t)ɪŋ

disappointingly
BR ˌdɪsəˈpɔɪntɪŋli
AM ˌdɪsəˈpɔɪn(t)ɪŋli

disappointment
BR ˌdɪsəˈpɔɪntm(ə)nt, -s
AM ˌdɪsəˈpɔɪntmənt, -s

disapprobation
BR ˌdɪsaprəˈbeɪʃn, dɪsˌaprəˈbeɪʃn
AM ˌdɪsˌæprəˈbeɪʃən

disapprobative
BR ˌdɪsaprəˈbeɪtɪv, dɪsˌaprəˈbeɪtɪv
AM ˈdɪsəˈproʊbədɪv

disapprobatory
BR ˌdɪsaprəˈbeɪt(ə)ri
AM ˈdɪsəˈproʊbəˌtɔri

disapproval
BR ˌdɪsəˈpruːvl
AM ˈdɪsəˈpruvəl

disapprove
BR ˌdɪsəˈpruːv, -z, -ɪŋ, -d
AM ˈdɪsəˈpruv, -z, -ɪŋ, -d

disapprover
BR ˌdɪsəˈpruːvə(r), -z
AM ˈdɪsəˈpruvər, -z

disapprovingly
BR ˌdɪsəˈpruːvɪŋli
AM ˈdɪsəˈpruvɪŋli

disarm
BR dɪsˈɑːm, -z, -ɪŋ, -d
AM dɪsˈɑrm, -z, -ɪŋ, -d

disarmament
BR dɪsˈɑːməm(ə)nt
AM dɪsˈɑrməmənt

disarmer
BR dɪsˈɑːmə(r), -z
AM dɪsˈɑrmər, -z

disarming
BR dɪsˈɑːmɪŋ
AM dɪsˈɑrmɪŋ

disarmingly
BR dɪsˈɑːmɪŋli
AM dɪsˈɑrmɪŋli

disarrange
BR ˌdɪsəˈreɪn(d)ʒ, -ɪz, -ɪŋ, -d
AM ˈdɪsəˈreɪndʒ, -ɪz, -ɪŋ, -d

disarrangement
BR ˌdɪsəˈreɪn(d)ʒm(ə)nt
AM ˈdɪsəˈreɪndʒmənt

disarray
BR ˌdɪsəˈreɪ
AM ˈdɪsəˈreɪ

disarticulate
BR ˌdɪsɑːˈtɪkjʊleɪt, -s, -ɪŋ, -ɪd
AM ˈdɪsɑrˈtɪkjəˌleɪ|t, -ts, -dɪŋ, -dɪd

disarticulation
BR ˌdɪsɑːˈtɪkjəˈleɪʃn
AM ˌdɪsɑrˌtɪkjəˈleɪʃən

disassemble
BR ˌdɪsəˈsɛmb|l, -lz, -lɪŋ\-lɪŋ, -ld
AM ˈdɪsəˈsɛmb|əl, -əlz, -(ə)lɪŋ, -əld

disassembly
BR ˌdɪsəˈsɛmbli
AM ˌdɪsəˈsɛmbli

disassociate
BR ˌdɪsəˈsəʊʃieɪt, ˌdɪsəˈsəʊsieɪt, -s, -ɪŋ, -ɪd
AM ˈdɪsəˈsoʊʃiˌeɪ|t, ˈdɪsəˈsoʊsiˌeɪ|t, -ts, -dɪŋ, -dɪd

disassociation
BR ˌdɪsəsəʊʃɪˈeɪʃn, ˌdɪsəsəʊsiˈeɪʃn
AM ˈdɪsəˌsoʊʃiˈeɪʃən, ˈdɪsəˌsoʊsiˈeɪʃən

disaster
BR dɪˈzɑːstə(r), dɪˈzɑstə(r), -z
AM dəˈzæstər, -z

disastrous
BR dɪˈzɑːstrəs,
dɪˈzɑstrəs
AM dəˈzæstrəsli

disastrously
BR dɪˈzɑːstrəsli,
dɪˈzɑstrəsli
AM dəˈzæstrəs

disastrousness
BR dɪˈzɑːstrəsnəs,
dɪˈzɑstrəsnəs
AM dəˈzæstrəsnəs

disavow
BR ˌdɪsəˈvaʊ, -z, -ɪŋ, -d
AM ˈdɪsəˈvaʊ, -z, -ɪŋ, -d

disavowal
BR ˌdɪsəˈvaʊəl
AM ˈdɪsəˈvaʊ(ə)l

disband
BR dɪsˈband, -z, -ɪŋ, -ɪd
AM dɪsˈbænd, -z, -ɪn, -əd

disbandment
BR dɪsˈban(d)m(ə)nt
AM dɪsˈbæn(d)mənt

disbar
BR dɪsˈbɑː(r), -z, -ɪŋ, -d
AM dɪsˈbɑr, -z, -ɪŋ, -d

disbarment
BR dɪsˈbɑːm(ə)nt
AM dɪsˈbɑrmənt

disbelief
BR ˌdɪsbɪˈliːf
AM ˌdɪsbəˈlif

disbelieve
BR ˌdɪsbɪˈliːv, -z, -ɪŋ, -d
AM ˌdɪsbəˈliv, -z, -ɪŋ, -d

disbeliever
BR ˌdɪsbɪˈliːvə(r), -z
AM ˌdɪsbəˈlivər, -z

disbelievingly
BR ˌdɪsbɪˈliːvɪŋli
AM ˌdɪsbəˈlivɪŋli

disbenefit
BR dɪsˈbɛnfɪt, -s
AM dɪsˈbɛnəfɪt, -s

disbound
BR dɪsˈbaʊnd, -z, -ɪŋ, -ɪd
AM dɪsˈbaʊnd, -z, -ɪŋ, -əd

disbud
BR (ˌ)dɪsˈbʌd, -z, -ɪŋ, -ɪd
AM dɪsˈbəd, -z, -ɪŋ, -əd

disburden
BR dɪsˈbəːd|n, -nz, -nɪŋ\-nɪŋ, -nd
AM dɪsˈbərd|ən, -ənz, -(ə)nɪŋ, -ənd

disbursal
BR dɪsˈbəːsl
AM dɪsˈbərs(ə)l

disburse
BR dɪsˈbəːs, -ɪz, -ɪŋ, -t
AM dɪsˈbərs, -əz, -ɪŋ, -t

disbursement
BR dɪsˈbəːsm(ə)nt, -s
AM dɪsˈbərsmənt, -s

disburser
BR dɪsˈbəːsə(r), -z
AM dɪsˈbərsər, -z

disc
BR dɪsk, -s
AM dɪsk, -s

discalced
BR dɪsˈkalst
AM dəˈskælst

discard¹
noun
BR ˈdɪskɑːd, -z
AM ˈdɪsˌkɑrd, -z

discard²
verb
BR dɪsˈkɑːd, -z, -ɪŋ, -ɪd
AM dəˈskɑrd, -z, -ɪŋ, -ɪd

discardable
BR dɪsˈkɑːdəbl
AM dəˈskɑrdəbəl

discarnate
BR dɪsˈkɑːnət
AM dəˈskɑrnət,
dəˈskɑrˌneɪt

discern
BR dɪˈsəːn, -z, -ɪŋ, -d
AM dəˈsərn, -z, -ɪŋ, -d

discerner
BR dɪˈsəːnə(r), -z
AM dəˈsərnər, -z

discernible
BR dɪˈsəːnɪbl
AM dəˈsərnəbəl

discernibly
BR dɪˈsəːnɪbli
AM dəˈsərnəbli

discerning
BR dɪˈsəːnɪŋ
AM dəˈsərnɪŋ

discerningly
BR dɪˈsəːnɪŋli
AM dəˈsərnɪŋli

discernment
BR dɪˈsəːnm(ə)nt
AM dəˈsərnmənt

discerptibility
BR dɪˌsəːptɪˈbɪlɪti
AM dəˌsərptəˈbɪlɪdi

discerptible
BR dɪˈsəːptɪbl
AM dəˈsərptəbəl

discerption
BR dɪˈsəːpʃn, -z
AM dəˈsərpʃən, -z

discharge¹
noun
BR ˈdɪstʃɑːdʒ, -ɪz
AM ˈdɪsˌtʃɑrdʒ, -əz

discharge²
verb
BR dɪsˈtʃɑːdʒ, -ɪz, -ɪŋ, -d
AM dəsˈtʃɑrdʒ, -əz, -ɪŋ, -d

dischargeable
BR dɪsˈtʃɑːdʒəbl
AM dɪsˈtʃɑrdʒəbəl

discharger
BR dɪsˈtʃɑːdʒə(r), -z
AM dɪsˈtʃɑrdʒər, -z

dischuff
BR ˌdɪsˈtʃʌf, -s, -ɪŋ, -t
AM dəsˈtʃəf, -s, -ɪŋ, -t

disciple
BR dɪˈsʌɪpl, -z
AM dəˈsaɪpəl, -z

discipleship
BR dɪˈsʌɪplʃɪp
AM dəˈsaɪpəlˌʃɪp

disciplinable
BR ˈdɪsɪplɪnəbl
AM ˈdɪsɪˌplɪnəbəl

disciplinal
BR ˈdɪsɪplɪnl
AM ˈdɪsɪplɪnəl

disciplinarian
BR ˌdɪsɪplɪˈnɛːrɪən, -z
AM ˌdɪsəpləˈnɛrɪən, -z

disciplinary
BR ˌdɪsɪˈplɪn(ə)ri,
ˈdɪsɪplɪn(ə)ri
AM ˈdɪsəpləˌnɛri

discipline
BR ˈdɪsɪplɪn, -z, -ɪŋ, -d
AM ˈdɪsɪplɪn, -z, -ɪŋ, -d

discipular
BR dɪˈsɪpjʊlə(r)
AM dəˈsɪpjələr

disclaim
BR dɪsˈkleɪm, -z, -ɪŋ, -d
AM dɪsˈkleɪm, -z, -ɪŋ, -d

disclaimer
BR dɪsˈkleɪmə(r), -z
AM dɪsˈkleɪmər, -z

disclose
BR dɪsˈkləʊz, -ɪz, -ɪŋ, -d
AM dəˈsklouz, -əz, -ɪŋ, -d

discloser
BR dɪsˈkləʊzə(r), -z
AM dəˈsklouzər, -z

disclosure
BR dɪsˈkləʊʒə(r), -z
AM dəˈsklouʒər, -z

disco
BR ˈdɪskəʊ, -z
AM ˈdɪskou, -z

discoboli
BR dɪˈskɒbəlʌɪ,
dɪˈskɒblʌɪ,
dɪˈskɒbaliː, dɪˈskɒblʲiː
AM dəˈskabəˌlaɪ

discobolus
BR dɪˈskɒbələs,
dɪˈskɒbləs
AM dəˈskabələs

discographer
BR dɪsˈkɒɡrəfə(r), -z
AM dɪsˈkaɡrəfər, -z

discography
BR dɪsˈkɒɡrəfʲi, -ɪz
AM dɪsˈkaɡrəfi, -z

discoid
BR ˈdɪskɔɪd

AM ˈdɪsˌkɔɪd

discolor
BR dɪsˈkʌllə(r), -əz,
-(ə)rɪŋ, -əd

AM dɪsˈkələr, -z, -ɪŋ, -d

discoloration
BR dɪsˌkʌləˈreɪʃn,
ˌdɪskʌləˈreɪʃn
AM dɪsˌkələˈreɪʃən,
ˈdɪsˌkələˈreɪʃən

discolour
BR dɪsˈkʌlə(r), -z, -ɪŋ,
-d
AM dɪsˈkələr, -z, -ɪŋ, -d

discolouration
BR dɪsˌkʌləˈreɪʃn,
ˌdɪskʌləˈreɪʃn
AM dɪsˌkələˈreɪʃən,
ˈdɪsˌkələˈreɪʃən

discombobulate
BR ˌdɪskəmˈbɒbjʊleɪt,
-s, -ɪŋ, -ɪd
AM ˌdɪskəmˈbabjəˌleɪt,
-ts, -dɪŋ, -dɪd

discomfit
BR dɪsˈkʌmfɪt, -s, -ɪŋ,
-ɪd
AM dɪsˈkəmfəlt, -ts,
-dɪŋ, -dəd

discomfiture
BR dɪsˈkʌmfɪtʃə(r)
AM dɪsˈkəmfəˌtʃʊ(ə)r,
dɪsˈkəmfətʃər

discomfort
BR dɪsˈkʌmfət, -s
AM dɪsˈkəmfərt, -s

discommode
BR ˌdɪskəˈməʊd, -z, -ɪŋ,
-ɪd
AM ˈdɪskəˈmoud, -z, -ɪŋ,
-əd

discommodious
BR ˌdɪskəˈməʊdɪəs
AM ˌdɪskəˈmoudɪəs

discompose
BR ˌdɪskəmˈpəʊz, -ɪz,
-ɪŋ, -d
AM ˌdɪskəmˈpouz, -əz,
-ɪŋ, -d

discomposure
BR ˌdɪskəmˈpəʊʒə(r)
AM ˌdɪskəmˈpouʒər

disconcert
BR ˌdɪskənˈsəːt, -s, -ɪŋ,
-ɪd
AM ˌdɪskənˈsər|t, -ts,
-dɪŋ, -dəd

disconcertedly
BR ˌdɪskənˈsəːtɪdli
AM ˌdɪskənˈsərdədli

disconcerting
BR ˌdɪskənˈsəːtɪŋ
AM ˌdɪskənˈsərdɪŋ

disconcertingly
BR ˌdɪskənˈsəːtɪŋli
AM ˌdɪskənˈsərdɪŋli

disconcertion
BR ˌdɪskənˈsəːʃn

AM ˌdɪskənˈsərʃən

disconcertment
BR ˌdɪskənˈsəːtm(ə)nt
AM ˈdɪskənˈsərtmənt

disconfirm
BR ˌdɪskənˈfəːm, -z, -ɪŋ,
-d
AM ˈdɪskənˈfərm, -z,
-ɪŋ, -d

disconfirmation
BR ˌdɪskɒnfəːˈmeɪʃn
AM ˌdɪsˌkɒnfərˈmeɪʃən

disconformity
BR ˌdɪskənˈfɔːmɪt|i, -ɪz
AM ˌdɪskənˈfɔrmədi, -z

disconnect
BR ˌdɪskəˈnɛkt, -s, -ɪŋ,
-ɪd
AM ˈdɪskəˈnɛk|(t), -(t)s,
-tɪŋ, -təd

disconnected
BR ˌdɪskəˈnɛktɪd
AM ˌdɪskəˈnɛktəd

disconnectedly
BR ˌdɪskəˈnɛktɪdli
AM ˌdɪskəˈnɛktədli

disconnectedness
BR ˌdɪskəˈnɛktɪdnɪs
AM ˌdɪskəˈnɛktədnəs

disconnection
BR ˌdɪskəˈnɛkʃn, -z
AM ˌdɪskəˈnɛkʃən, -z

disconnexion
BR ˌdɪskəˈnɛkʃn, -z
AM ˌdɪskəˈnɛkʃən, -z

disconsolate
BR dɪsˈkɒnsələt,
dɪsˈkɒnslət
AM dɪsˈkɒnsə(ə)lət

disconsolately
BR dɪsˈkɒnsələtli,
dɪsˈkɒnslətli
AM dɪsˈkɑnsə(ə)lətli

disconsolateness
BR dɪsˈkɒnsələtnəs,
dɪsˈkɒnslətnəs
AM dɪsˈkɑnsə(ə)lətnəs

disconsolation
BR ˌdɪskɒnsəˈleɪʃn,
dɪˌskɒnsəˈleɪʃn
AM ˈdɪsˌkɑnsəˈleɪʃən

discontent
BR ˌdɪskənˈtɛnt, -s
AM ˌdɪskənˈtɛnt, -s

discontented
BR ˌdɪskənˈtɛntɪd
AM ˈdɪskənˈtɛn(t)əd

discontentedly
BR ˌdɪskənˈtɛntɪdli
AM ˈdɪskənˈtɛn(t)ədli

discontentedness
BR ˌdɪskənˈtɛntɪdnɪs
AM ˈdɪskənˈtɛn(t)ədnəs

discontently
BR ˌdɪskənˈtɛntli
AM ˈdɪskənˈtɛn(t)li

discontentment
BR ˌdɪskən'tɛntm(ə)nt, -s
AM 'dɪskən'tɛntmənt, -s

discontinuance
BR ˌdɪskən'tɪnjuəns
AM ˌdɪskən'tɪnjəwəns

discontinuation
BR ˌdɪskəntɪnju'eɪʃn
AM ˌdɪskən,tɪnjə'weɪʃən

discontinue
BR ˌdɪskən'tɪnjuː, -z, -ɪŋ, -d
AM ˌdɪskən'tɪnju, -z, -ɪŋ, -d

discontinuity
BR ˌdɪskɒntɪ'njuːɪti
AM 'dɪs,kɑntn̩(j)uədi, 'dɪs,kɑntə'n(j)uədi

discontinuous
BR ˌdɪskən'tɪnjuəs
AM ˌdɪskən'tɪnjəwəs

discontinuously
BR ˌdɪskən'tɪnjuəsli
AM ˌdɪskən'tɪnjəwəsli

discord
BR 'dɪskɔːd
AM 'dɪs,kɔ(ə)rd

discordance
BR dɪs'kɔːdns
AM 'dɪs'kɔrdəns

discordancy
BR dɪs'kɔːdns|i, -ɪz
AM 'dɪs'kɔrdənsi, -z

discordant
BR dɪs'kɔːdnt
AM 'dɪs'kɔrdənt

discordantly
BR dɪs'kɔːdntli
AM 'dɪs'kɔrdən(t)li

discothèque
BR 'dɪskətɛk, -s
AM 'dɪskə,tɛk, -s

discount¹
noun, verb, reduce price
BR 'dɪskaunt, -s, -ɪŋ, -ɪd
AM 'dɪs,kaun|t, -ts, -(t)ɪŋ, -(t)əd

discount²
verb, treat as untrue
BR dɪs'kaunt, -s, -ɪŋ, -ɪd
AM 'dɪs,kaun|t, -ts, -(t)ɪŋ, -(t)əd

discountable
adjective, to be treated as untrue
BR dɪs'kauntəbl
AM 'dɪs'kaun(t)əbəl

discountenance
BR dɪs'kauntɪnəns, -ɪz, -ɪŋ, -t
AM dɪs'kaunt(ə)nəns, dɪs'kaun(t)ənəns, -əz, -ɪŋ, -t

discounter
someone who treats something as untrue
BR dɪs'kauntə(r), -z
AM 'dɪs'kaun(t)ər, -z

discourage
BR dɪs'kʌr|ɪdʒ, dɪ'skʌr|ɪdʒ, -ɪdʒɪz, -ɪdʒɪŋ, -ɪdʒd
AM də'skærɪdʒ, -ɪz, -ɪŋ, -d

discouragement
BR dɪs'kʌrɪdʒm(ə)nt, dɪ'skʌrɪdʒm(ə)nt, -s
AM də'skærɪdʒmənt, -s

discouraging
BR dɪs'kʌrɪdʒɪŋ, dɪ'skʌrɪdʒɪŋ
AM də'skærɪdʒɪŋ

discouragingly
BR dɪs'kʌrɪdʒɪŋli, dɪ'skʌrɪdʒɪŋli
AM də'skærɪdʒɪŋli

discourse¹
noun
BR 'dɪskɔːs, -ɪz
AM 'dɪs,kɔ(ə)rs, -əz

discourse²
verb
BR dɪs'kɔːs, -ɪz, -ɪŋ, -t
AM dɪs'kɔ(ə)rs, -əz, -ɪŋ, -t

discourteous
BR dɪs'kɜːtɪəs
AM dɪs'kɜrdiəs

discourteously
BR dɪs'kɜːtɪəsli
AM dɪs'kɜrdiəsli

discourteousness
BR dɪs'kɜːtɪəsnəs
AM dɪs'kɜrdiəsnəs

discourtesy
BR dɪs'kɜːtəsi, -ɪz
AM dɪs'kɜrdəsi, -z

discover
BR dɪs'kʌv|ə(r), -əz, -(ə)rɪŋ, -əd
AM də'skʌv|ər, -ərz, -(ə)rɪŋ, -ərd

discoverable
BR dɪs'kʌv(ə)rəbl
AM də'skʌv(ə)rəbəl

discoverer
BR dɪs'kʌv(ə)rə(r), -z
AM də'skʌv(ə)rər, -z

discovery
BR dɪs'kʌv(ə)r|i, -ɪz
AM də'skʌv(ə)ri, -z

discredit
BR (ˌ)dɪs'krɛd|ɪt, -s, -ɪtɪŋ, -ɪtɪd
AM dɪs'krɛdə|t, -ts, -dɪŋ, -dəd

discreditable
BR (ˌ)dɪs'krɛdɪtəbl
AM dɪs'krɛdədəbəl

discreditably
BR (ˌ)dɪs'krɛdɪtəbli

discreet
BR dɪ'skriːt, -ɪst
AM də'skriːt, -dɪst

discreetly
BR dɪ'skriːtli
AM də'skriːtli

discreetness
BR dɪ'skriːtnɪs
AM də'skriːtnɪs

discrepancy
BR dɪ'skrɛpns|i, -ɪz
AM də'skrɛpənsi, -z

discrepant
BR dɪ'skrɛpnt
AM də'skrɛpənt

discrete
BR dɪ'skriːt
AM də'skriːt

discretely
BR dɪ'skriːtli
AM də'skriːtli

discreteness
BR dɪ'skriːtnɪs
AM də'skriːtnɪs

discretion
BR dɪ'skrɛʃn
AM də'skrɛʃən

discretionary
BR dɪ'skrɛʃn(ə)ri
AM də'skrɛʃə,nɛri

discriminant
BR dɪ'skrɪmɪnənt
AM də'skrɪm(ə)nənt

discriminate¹
adjective
BR dɪ'skrɪmɪnət
AM də'skrɪm(ə)nət

discriminate²
verb
BR dɪ'skrɪmɪneɪt, -s, -ɪŋ, -ɪd
AM də'skrɪmə,neɪ|t, -ts, -dɪŋ, -dɪd

discriminately
BR dɪ'skrɪmɪnətli
AM də'skrɪm(ə)nətli

discriminatingly
BR dɪ'skrɪmɪneɪtɪŋli
AM də'skrɪmə,neɪdɪŋli

discrimination
BR dɪˌskrɪmɪ'neɪʃn
AM dəˌskrɪmə'neɪʃən

discriminative
BR dɪ'skrɪmɪnətɪv
AM də'skrɪmə,neɪdɪv, də'skrɪmənədɪv

discriminator
BR dɪ'skrɪmɪneɪtə(r), -z
AM də'skrɪmə,neɪdər, -z

discriminatory
BR dɪ'skrɪmɪnət(ə)ri
AM də'skrɪmənə,tɔri

discursive
BR dɪs'kɜːsɪv

AM dɪs'krɛdədəbli

discursively
BR dɪs'kɜːsɪvli
AM də'skɜrsɪvli

discursiveness
BR dɪs'kɜːsɪvnɪs
AM də'skɜrsɪvnɪs

discus
BR 'dɪskəs, -ɪz
AM 'dɪskəs, -əz

discuss
BR dɪs'kʌs, -ɪz, -ɪŋ, -t
AM də'skʌs, -əz, -ɪŋ, -t

discussable
BR dɪ'skʌsəbl
AM də'skəsəbəl

discussant
BR dɪ'skʌsnt, -s
AM də'skəsənt, -s

discusser
BR dɪ'skʌsə(r), -z
AM də'skəsər, -z

discussible
BR dɪ'skʌsɪbl
AM də'skəsəbəl

discussion
BR dɪ'skʌʃn, -z
AM də'skəʃən, -z

disdain
BR dɪs'deɪn, -z, -ɪŋ, -d
AM dɪs'deɪn, -z, -ɪŋ, -d

disdainful
BR dɪs'deɪnf(ʊ)l
AM dɪs'deɪnfəl

disdainfully
BR dɪs'deɪnfʊli, dɪs'deɪnfli
AM dɪs'deɪnfəli

disdainfulness
BR dɪs'deɪnf(ʊ)lnəs
AM dɪs'deɪnfəlnəs

disease
BR dɪ'ziːz, -ɪz, -d
AM də'ziz, -ɪz, -d

diseconomy
BR ˌdɪsɪ'kɒnəmi
AM 'dɪsɪ'kɑnəmi

disembark
BR ˌdɪs(ɪ)m'bɑːk, ˌdɪsɛm'bɑːk, -s, -ɪŋ, -t
AM 'dɪsɛm'bɑrk, -s, -ɪŋ, -t

disembarkation
BR ˌdɪsɛmbɑː'keɪʃn, ˌdɪs(ɪ)mbɑː'keɪʃn
AM dɪs,ɛmbɑr'keɪʃən

disembarrass
BR ˌdɪs(ɪ)m'barəs, ˌdɪsɛm'barəs, -ɪz, -ɪŋ, -t
AM 'dɪsəm'bɛrəs, -əz, -ɪŋ, -t

disembarrassment
BR ˌdɪs(ɪ)m'barəsm(ə)nt, ˌdɪsɛm'barəsm(ə)nt
AM 'dɪsəm'bɛrəsmənt

disembodied
BR ˌdɪs(ɪ)mˈbɒdɪd,
ˌdɪsɛmˈbɒdɪd
AM ˈdɪsəmˈbɑdɪd

disembodiment
BR ˌdɪs(ɪ)mˈbɒdɪm(ə)nt,
ˌdɪsɛmˈbɒdɪm(ə)nt
AM ˈdɪsəmˈbɑdimənt

disembody
BR ˌdɪs(ɪ)mˈbɒd|i,
ˌdɪsɛmˈbɒd|i, -ɪz, -ɪɪŋ,
-ɪd
AM ˈdɪsəmˈbɑdi, -z, -ɪŋ,
-d

disembogue
BR ˌdɪs(ɪ)mˈbəʊg,
ˌdɪsɛmˈbəʊg, -z, -ɪŋ, -d
AM ˈdɪsəmˈboʊg, -z, -ɪŋ,
-d

disembowel
BR ˌdɪs(ɪ)mˈbaʊ(ə)l,
ˌdɪsɛmˈbaʊ(ə)l, -z, -ɪŋ,
-d
AM ˈdɪsəmˈbaʊ(ə)l, -z,
-ɪŋ, -d

disembowelment
BR ˌdɪs(ɪ)mˈbaʊ(ə)l-
m(ə)nt,
ˌdɪsɛmˈbaʊ(ə)lm(ə)nt
AM ˈdɪsəmˈbaʊlmənt

disembroil
BR ˌdɪs(ɪ)mˈbrɔɪl,
ˌdɪsɛmˈbrɔɪl, -z, -ɪŋ, -d
AM ˈdɪsəmˈbrɔɪl, -z, -ɪŋ,
-d

disempower
BR ˌdɪs(ɪ)mˈpaʊ|ə(r),
ˌdɪsɛmˈpaʊ|ə(r), -əz,
-(ə)rɪŋ, -əd
AM ˈdɪsəmˈpaʊ|(ə)r,
-ərd, -(ə)rɪŋ, -ərd

disenchant
BR ˌdɪs(ɪ)nˈtʃɑːnt,
ˌdɪs(ɪ)nˈtʃant,
ˌdɪsɛnˈtʃɑːnt,
ˌdɪsɛnˈtʃant, -s, -ɪŋ, -ɪd
AM ˈdɪsənˈtʃæn|t, -ts,
-(t)ɪŋ, -(t)əd

disenchantingly
BR ˌdɪs(ɪ)nˈtʃɑːntɪŋli,
ˌdɪs(ɪ)nˈtʃantɪŋli,
ˌdɪsɛnˈtʃɑːntɪŋli,
ˌdɪsɛnˈtʃantɪŋli
AM ˈdɪsənˈtʃæn(t)ɪŋli

disenchantment
BR ˌdɪs(ɪ)nˈtʃɑːntm(ə)nt,
ˌdɪs(ɪ)nˈtʃantm(ə)nt,
ˌdɪsɛnˈtʃɑːntm(ə)nt,
ˌdɪsɛnˈtʃantm(ə)nt, -s
AM ˈdɪsənˈtʃæntmənt,
-s

disencumber
BR ˌdɪs(ɪ)nˈkʌmb|ə(r),
ˌdɪsɛnˈkʌmb|ə(r), -əz,
-(ə)rɪŋ, -əd
AM ˈdɪsənˈkəmb|ər,
-ərd, -(ə)rɪŋ, -ərd

disendow
BR ˌdɪs(ɪ)nˈdaʊ,
ˌdɪsɛnˈdaʊ, -z, -ɪŋ, -d
AM ˈdɪsənˈdaʊ, -z, -ɪŋ, -d

disendowment
BR ˌdɪs(ɪ)nˈdaʊm(ə)nt,
ˌdɪsɛnˈdaʊm(ə)nt
AM ˈdɪsənˈdaʊmənt

disenfranchise
BR ˌdɪs(ɪ)nˈfrantʃʌɪz,
ˌdɪsɛnˈfrantʃʌɪz, -ɪz,
-ɪŋ, -d
AM ˈdɪsənˈfrænˌtʃaɪz,
-ɪz, -ɪŋ, -d

**disenfranchise-
ment**
BR ˌdɪs(ɪ)nˈfrantʃɪz-
m(ə)nt,
ˌdɪsɛnˈfrantʃɪzm(ə)nt
AM ˈdɪsənˈfrænˌtʃaɪz-
mənt,
ˈdɪsənˈfræntʃəz-
mənt

disengage
BR ˌdɪs(ɪ)nˈgeɪdʒ,
ˌdɪsɛnˈgeɪdʒ, -ɪz, -ɪŋ, -d
AM ˈdɪsənˈgeɪdʒ, -ɪz,
-ɪŋ, -d

disengagement
BR ˌdɪs(ɪ)nˈgeɪdʒm(ə)nt,
ˌdɪsɛnˈgeɪdʒm(ə)nt
AM ˈdɪsənˈgeɪdʒmənt

disentail
BR ˌdɪs(ɪ)nˈteɪl,
ˌdɪsɛnˈteɪl, -z, -ɪŋ, -d
AM ˈdɪsənˈteɪl, -z, -ɪŋ, -d

disentangle
BR ˌdɪs(ɪ)nˈtaŋg|l,
ˌdɪsɛnˈtaŋg|l, -lz,
-lɪŋ \-lɪŋ, -ld
AM ˈdɪsənˈtæŋg|əl, -əlz,
-(ə)lɪŋ, -əld

disentanglement
BR ˌdɪs(ɪ)nˈtaŋglm(ə)nt,
ˌdɪsɛnˈtaŋglm(ə)nt
AM ˈdɪsənˈtæŋgəlmənt

disenthral
BR ˌdɪs(ɪ)nˈθrɔːl,
ˌdɪsɛnˈθrɔːl, -z, -d
AM ˈdɪsənˈθrɔl,
ˈdɪsənˈθrɑl, -z, -d

disenthralment
BR ˌdɪs(ɪ)nˈθrɔːlm(ə)nt,
ˌdɪsɛnˈθrɔːlm(ə)nt
AM ˈdɪsənˈθrɔlmənt,
ˈdɪsənˈθrɑlmənt

disentitle
BR ˌdɪs(ɪ)nˈtʌɪt|l,
ˌdɪsɛnˈtʌɪt|l, -lz,
-lɪŋ \-lɪŋ, -ld
AM ˈdɪsənˈtaɪdəl, -z, -ɪŋ,
-d

disentitlement
BR ˌdɪs(ɪ)nˈtʌɪtlm(ə)nt,
ˌdɪsɛnˈtʌɪtlm(ə)nt
AM ˈdɪsənˈtaɪdlmənt

disentomb
BR ˌdɪs(ɪ)nˈtuːm,
ˌdɪsɛnˈtuːm, -z, -ɪŋ, -d
AM ˈdɪsənˈtum, -z, -ɪŋ,
-d

disentombment
BR ˌdɪs(ɪ)nˈtuːmm(ə)nt,
ˌdɪsɛnˈtuːmm(ə)nt
AM ˈdɪsənˈtu(m)mənt

disequilibria
BR ˌdɪsɛkwɪˈlɪbrɪə(r),
ˌdɪsiːkwɪˈlɪbrɪə(r)
AM ˌdɪsˌɛkwəˈlɪbriə,
ˌdɪsˌikwəˈlɪbriə

disequilibrium
BR ˌdɪsɛkwɪˈlɪbrɪəm,
ˌdɪsiːkwɪˈlɪbrɪəm
AM ˌdɪsˌɛkwəˈlɪbriəm,
ˌdɪsˌikwəˈlɪbriəm

disestablish
BR ˌdɪsɪˈstablɪ|ʃ,
ˌdɪsɛˈstablɪ|ʃ, -ɪʃɪz,
-ɪʃɪŋ, -ɪʃt
AM ˈdɪsəˈstæblɪʃ, -ɪz,
-ɪŋ, -t

disestablishment
BR ˌdɪsɪˈstablɪʃm(ə)nt,
ˌdɪsɛˈstablɪʃm(ə)nt
AM ˈdɪsəˈstæblɪʃmənt

disesteem
BR ˌdɪsɪˈstiːm,
ˌdɪsɛˈstiːm, -z, -ɪŋ, -d
AM ˈdɪsəˈstim, -z, -ɪŋ, -d

diseur
BR diːˈzəː(r), -z
AM diˈzər, -z

diseuse
BR diːˈzəːz, -ɪz
AM diˈzuz, -əz

disfavor
BR dɪsˈfeɪv|ə(r), -əz,
-(ə)rɪŋ, -əd
AM dɪsˈfeɪv|ər, -ərd,
-(ə)rɪŋ, -ərd

disfavour
BR dɪsˈfeɪv|ə(r), -əz,
-(ə)rɪŋ, -əd
AM dɪsˈfeɪv|ər, -ərd,
-(ə)rɪŋ, -ərd

disfigure
BR dɪsˈfɪg|ə(r), -əz,
-(ə)rɪŋ, -əd
AM dɪsˈfɪgjər, -z, -ɪŋ, -d

disfigurement
BR dɪsˈfɪgəm(ə)nt, -s
AM dɪsˈfɪgjərmənt, -s

disforest
BR dɪsˈfɒr|ɪst, -ɪsts,
-ɪstɪŋ, -ɪstɪd
AM dɪsˈfɔrəst, -s, -ɪŋ,
-əd

disforestation
BR ˌdɪsfɒrɪˈsteɪʃn,
ˌdɪsˌfɒrɪˈsteɪʃn
AM ˌdɪsˌfɔrəˈsteɪʃən,
ˈdɪsˌfɔrəˈsteɪʃən

disfranchise
BR dɪsˈfran(t)ʃʌɪz, -ɪz,
-ɪŋ, -d
AM dɪsˈfrænˌtʃaɪz, -ɪz,
-ɪŋ, -d

disfranchisement
BR dɪsˈfran(t)ʃɪzm(ə)nt
AM dɪsˈfrænˌtʃaɪzmənt

disfrock
BR dɪsˈfrɒk, -s, -ɪŋ, -t
AM dɪsˈfrɑk, -s, -ɪŋ, -t

disgorge
BR dɪsˈgɔːdʒ, -ɪz, -ɪŋ, -d
AM dɪsˈgɔrdʒ, -əz, -ɪŋ, -d

disgorgement
BR dɪsˈgɔːdʒm(ə)nt, -s
AM dɪsˈgɔrdʒmənt, -s

disgrace
BR dɪsˈgreɪs, dɪzˈgreɪs,
-ɪz, -ɪŋ, -t
AM dɪsˈgreɪs, -ɪz, -ɪŋ, -t

disgraceful
BR dɪsˈgreɪsf(ʊ)l,
dɪzˈgreɪsf(ʊ)l
AM dɪsˈgreɪsfəl

disgracefully
BR dɪsˈgreɪsf(ʊ)li,
dɪsˈgreɪsfli,
dɪzˈgreɪsf(ʊ)li,
dɪzˈgreɪsfli
AM dɪsˈgreɪsfəli

disgruntled
BR dɪsˈgrʌntld
AM dɪsˈgrəntld

disgruntlement
BR dɪsˈgrʌntlm(ə)nt
AM dɪsˈgrəntlmənt

disguise
BR dɪsˈgʌɪz, dɪzˈgʌɪz,
-ɪz, -ɪŋ, -d
AM dəˈskaɪz, dɪsˈgaɪz,
-ɪz, -ɪŋ, -d

disguisement
BR dɪsˈgʌɪzm(ə)nt,
dɪzˈgʌɪzm(ə)nt
AM dɪsˈgaɪzmənt

disgust
BR dɪsˈgʌst, dɪzˈgʌst
AM dəˈskəst, dɪsˈgəst

disgustedly
BR dɪsˈgʌstɪdli,
dɪzˈgʌstɪdli
AM dəˈskəstədli,
dɪsˈgəstədli

disgustful
BR dɪsˈgʌs(t)f(ʊ)l,
dɪzˈgʌs(t)f(ʊ)l
AM dəˈskəstfəl,
dɪsˈgəstfəl

disgusting
BR dɪsˈgʌstɪŋ,
dɪzˈgʌstɪŋ
AM dəˈskəstɪŋ,
dɪsˈgəstɪŋ

disgustingly
BR dɪsˈgʌstɪŋli,
dɪzˈgʌstɪŋli

AM də'skʌstɪŋli,
dɪs'gəstɪŋli
disgustingness
BR dɪs'gʌstɪŋnɪs,
dɪz'gʌstɪŋnɪs
AM də'skʌstɪŋnɪs,
dɪs'gəstɪŋnɪs
dish
BR dɪʃ, -ɪz, -ɪŋ, -t
AM dɪʃ, -ɪz, -ɪŋ, -t
dishabille
BR ˌdɪsə'biːl
AM ˌdɪsə'bi(ə)l
dishabituation
BR ˌdɪsəbɪtju'eɪʃn,
ˌdɪsəbɪtʃʊ'eɪʃn
AM ˌdɪsəˌbɪtʃə'weɪʃən
disharmonious
BR ˌdɪshɑː'məʊniəs
AM ˌdɪsˌ(h)ɑr'məʊniəs
disharmoniously
BR ˌdɪshɑː'məʊniəsli
AM ˌdɪsˌ(h)ɑr'məʊniəsli
disharmonise
BR (ˌ)dɪs'hɑːmənʌɪz,
-ɪz, -ɪŋ, -d
AM ˈdɪs'hɑːrməˌnaɪz,
-ɪz, -ɪŋ, -d
disharmonize
BR (ˌ)dɪs'hɑːmənʌɪz,
-ɪz, -ɪŋ, -d
AM ˈdɪs'hɑːrməˌnaɪz,
-ɪz, -ɪŋ, -d
disharmony
BR (ˌ)dɪs'hɑːməni
AM ˈdɪs'hɑːrməni
dishcloth
BR 'dɪʃklɒ|θ, -θs \ -ðz
AM 'dɪʃˌklɔ|θ, 'dɪʃˌklɑ|θ,
-θs \ -ðz
dishearten¹
BR dɪs'hɑːt|n, -nz,
-ŋɪŋ \ -nɪŋ, -nd
AM dɪs'hɑːtn̩, -z, -ɪŋ, -d
dishearten²
BR dɪs'hɑːt|n, -nz,
-ŋɪŋ \ -nɪŋ, -nd
AM dɪs'hɑːtn̩, -z, -ɪŋ, -d
dishearteningly
BR dɪs'hɑːtn̩ɪŋli
AM dɪs'hɑːrtn̩ɪŋli
disheartenment
BR dɪs'hɑːtnm(ə)nt, -s
AM dɪs'hɑːrtnmənt, -s
dishevel
BR dɪ'ʃevl, -z, -d
AM də'ʃevəl, -z, -d
dishevelment
BR dɪ'ʃevlm(ə)nt
AM də'ʃevəlmənt
Dishforth
BR 'dɪʃfəθ, 'dɪʃfɔːθ
AM 'dɪʃfərθ
dishful
BR 'dɪʃfʊl, -z
AM 'dɪʃfʊl, -z
dishily
BR 'dɪʃɪli

AM 'dɪʃɪli
dishiness
BR 'dɪʃmɪs
AM 'dɪʃinɪs
dishlike
BR 'dɪʃlʌɪk
AM 'dɪʃˌlaɪk
dishonest
BR dɪs'ɒnɪst
AM dɪs'ɑnəst
dishonestly
BR dɪs'ɒnɪstli
AM dɪs'ɑnəs(t)li
dishonesty
BR dɪs'ɒnɪsti
AM dɪs'ɑnəsti
dishonor
BR dɪs'ɒn|ə(r), -əz,
-(ə)rɪŋ, -əd
AM dɪs'ɑnər, -z, -ɪŋ, -d
dishonorable
BR dɪs'ɒn(ə)rəbl
AM dɪs'ɑn(ə)rəbəl
dishonorableness
BR dɪs'ɒn(ə)rəblnəs
AM dɪs'ɑn(ə)rəbəlnəs
dishonorably
BR dɪs'ɒn(ə)rəbli
AM dɪs'ɑn(ə)rəbli
dishonour
BR dɪs'ɒn|ə(r), -əz,
-(ə)rɪŋ, -əd
AM dɪs'ɑnər, -z, -ɪŋ, -d
dishonourable
BR dɪs'ɒn(ə)rəbl
AM dɪs'ɑn(ə)r(ə)bəl
dishonourableness
BR dɪs'ɒn(ə)rəblnəs
AM dɪs'ɑn(ə)rəbəlnəs
dishonourably
BR dɪs'ɒn(ə)rəbli
AM dɪs'ɑn(ə)rəbli
dishpan
BR 'dɪʃpan, -z
AM 'dɪʃˌpæn, -z
dishrag
BR 'dɪʃrag, -z
AM 'dɪʃˌræg, -z
dishwasher
BR 'dɪʃˌwɒʃə(r), -z
AM 'dɪʃˌwɔʃər,
'dɪʃˌwɑʃər, -z
dishwater
BR 'dɪʃˌwɔːtə(r)
AM 'dɪʃˌwɔdər,
'dɪʃˌwɑdər
dishy
BR 'dɪʃ|i, -ɪə(r), -ɪɪst
AM 'dɪʃi, -ər, -ɪst
disillusion
BR ˌdɪsɪ'l(j)uːʒ|n, -nz,
-ŋɪŋ \ -ənɪŋ, -nd
AM ˌdɪsə'luːʒən, -z, -ɪŋ,
-d

disillusionise
BR ˌdɪsɪ'l(j)uːʒn̩ʌɪz,
ˌdɪsɪ'l(j)uːʒənʌɪz, -ɪz,
-ɪŋ, -d
AM ˌdɪsə'luːʒəˌnaɪz, -ɪz,
-ɪŋ, -d
disillusionize
BR ˌdɪsɪ'l(j)uːʒn̩ʌɪz,
ˌdɪsɪ'l(j)uːʒənʌɪz, -ɪz,
-ɪŋ, -d
AM ˌdɪsə'luːʒəˌnaɪz, -ɪz,
-ɪŋ, -d
disillusionment
BR ˌdɪsɪ'l(j)uːʒnm(ə)nt,
-s
AM ˌdɪsə'luːʒənmənt, -s
disincentive
BR ˌdɪs(ɪ)n'sentɪv, -z
AM ˌdɪsən'sen(t)ɪv, -z
disinclination
BR ˌdɪsɪnklɪ'neɪʃn,
ˌdɪsɪŋklɪ'neɪʃn
AM ˌdɪsənklə'neɪʃən,
dɪsˌɪŋklə'neɪʃən
disincline
BR ˌdɪs(ɪ)n'klʌɪn,
ˌdɪsɪŋ'klʌɪn, -z, -ɪŋ, -d
AM ˌdɪsən'klaɪn, -z, -ɪŋ,
-d
disincorporate
BR ˌdɪs(ɪ)n'kɔːpəreɪt,
ˌdɪsɪŋ'kɔːpəreɪt, -s,
-ɪŋ, -ɪd
AM ˌdɪsən'kɔrpəˌreɪ|t,
-ts, -dɪŋ, -dɪd
disinfect
BR ˌdɪs(ɪ)n'fekt, -s, -ɪŋ,
-ɪd
AM ˌdɪsən'fek|(t), -(t)s,
-tɪŋ, -təd
disinfectant
BR ˌdɪs(ɪ)n'fekt(ə)nt,
-s
AM ˌdɪsən'fektnt, -s
disinfection
BR ˌdɪs(ɪ)n'fekʃn, -z
AM ˌdɪsən'fekʃən, -z
disinfest
BR ˌdɪs(ɪ)n'fest, -s, -ɪŋ,
-ɪd
AM ˌdɪsən'fest, -s, -ɪŋ,
-əd
disinfestation
BR ˌdɪs(ɪ)nfɛ'steɪʃn
AM ˌdɪsənˌfɛs'teɪʃən,
dɪsˌɪnfɛs'teɪʃən
disinflation
BR ˌdɪs(ɪ)n'fleɪʃn
AM ˌdɪsən'fleɪʃən
disinflationary
BR ˌdɪs(ɪ)n'fleɪʃn̩(ə)ri
AM ˌdɪsən'fleɪʃəˌneri
disinformation
BR ˌdɪsɪnfə'meɪʃn
AM ˌdɪsənfər'meɪʃən,
dɪsˌɪnfər'meɪʃən
disingenuous
BR ˌdɪs(ɪ)n'dʒenjʊəs

AM ˌdɪsən'dʒenjəwəs
disingenuously
BR ˌdɪs(ɪ)n'dʒenjʊəsli
AM ˌdɪsən'dʒenjəwəsli
disingenuousness
BR ˌdɪs(ɪ)n'dʒenjʊəsnəs
AM ˌdɪsən'dʒenjəwəsnəs
disinherit
BR ˌdɪs(ɪ)n'herɪt, -s,
-ɪŋ, -ɪd
AM ˌdɪsən'herɪ|t, -ts,
-dɪŋ, -dɪd
disinheritance
BR ˌdɪs(ɪ)n'herɪt(ə)ns
AM ˌdɪsən'herətns
disintegrate
BR dɪs'ɪntɪgreɪt, -s, -ɪŋ,
-ɪd
AM dɪs'ɪn(t)əˌgreɪ|t,
-ts, -dɪŋ, -dɪd
disintegration
BR dɪsˌɪntɪ'greɪʃn
AM dɪsˌɪn(t)ə'greɪʃən
disintegrative
BR dɪs'ɪntɪgrətɪv
AM dɪs'ɪn(t)əˌgreɪdɪv
disintegrator
BR dɪs'ɪntɪgreɪtə(r), -z
AM dɪs'ɪn(t)əˌgreɪdər,
-z
disinter
BR ˌdɪs(ɪ)n'təː(r), -z,
-ɪŋ, -d
AM ˌdɪsən'tər,
dɪsˌɪn'tər, -z, -ɪŋ, -d
disinterest
BR (ˌ)dɪs'ɪntrɪst,
(ˌ)dɪs'ɪnt(ə)rest, -ɪd
AM dɪs'ɪnt(ə)rəst, -əd
disinterestedly
BR (ˌ)dɪs'ɪntrɪstɪdli,
(ˌ)dɪs'ɪnt(ə)rɪstɪdli
AM dɪs'ɪnt(ə)rəstədli
disinterestedness
BR (ˌ)dɪs'ɪntrɪstɪdnɪs,
(ˌ)dɪs'ɪnt(ə)rɪstɪdnɪs
AM dɪs'ɪn(t)ə'rɪstədnəs,
dɪs'ɪn(t)əˌrestədnəs
disinterment
BR ˌdɪs(ɪ)n'təːm(ə)nt,
-s
AM ˌdɪsən'tərmənt,
dɪsˌɪn'tərmənt, -s
disinvest
BR ˌdɪs(ɪ)n'vest, -s, -ɪŋ,
-ɪd
AM ˌdɪsən'vest, -s, -ɪŋ,
-əd
disinvestment
BR ˌdɪs(ɪ)n'ves(t)m(ə)nt
AM ˌdɪsən'vestmənt
disjecta membra
BR dɪsˌdʒɛktə
'membrə
AM dəsˌdʒɛktə
'membrə
disjoin
BR dɪs'dʒɔɪn, -z, -ɪŋ, -d

AM dɪs'dʒɔɪn, -z, -ɪŋ, -d

disjoint
BR dɪs'dʒɔɪnt, -s, -ɪŋ, -ɪd
AM dɪs'dʒɔɪn|t, -ts, -(t)ɪŋ, -(t)ɪd

disjointedly
BR dɪs'jɔɪntɪdli
AM dɪs'dʒɔɪn(t)ɪdli

disjointedness
BR dɪs'jɔɪntɪdnɪs
AM dɪs'dʒɔɪn(t)ɪdnɪs

disjunct¹
adjective
BR dɪs'dʒʌŋ(k)t
AM dɪs'dʒəŋ(k)t

disjunct²
noun
BR dɪsdʒʌŋ(k)t, -s
AM 'dɪs,dʒəŋ(k)t, -s

disjunction
BR dɪs'dʒʌŋ(k)ʃn, -z
AM dɪs'dʒəŋ(k)ʃən, -z

disjunctive
BR dɪs'dʒʌŋ(k)tɪv
AM dɪs'dʒəŋ(k)tɪv

disjunctively
BR dɪs'dʒʌŋ(k)tɪvli
AM dɪs'dʒəŋ(k)təvli

disjuncture
BR dɪs'dʒʌŋ(k)tʃə(r), -z
AM dɪs'dʒəŋ(kt)ʃər, -z

disk
BR dɪsk, -s
AM dɪsk, -s

diskette
BR dɪ'skɛt, ,dɪsk'ɛt, -s
AM dɪs'kɛt, -s

diskless
BR 'dɪsklɪs
AM 'dɪskləs

Disko
BR 'dɪskəʊ
AM 'dɪskoʊ

Disley
BR 'dɪzli
AM 'dɪzli

dislikable
BR dɪs'laɪkəbl
AM dɪs'laɪkəbəl

dislike
BR dɪs'laɪk, -s, -ɪŋ, -t
AM dɪs'laɪk, -s, -ɪŋ, -t

dislikeable
BR dɪs'lʌɪkəbl
AM dɪs'laɪkəbəl

dislocate
BR 'dɪsləkeɪt, -s, -ɪŋ, -ɪd
AM dɪs'loʊ,keɪ|t, 'dɪslə,keɪ|t, -ts, -dɪŋ, -dɪd

dislocation
BR ,dɪslə'keɪʃn, -z
AM ,dɪsloʊ'keɪʃən, ,dɪslə'keɪʃən, -z

dislodge
BR dɪs'lɒdʒ, -ɪz, -ɪŋ, -d

dislodgement
BR dɪs'lɒdʒm(ə)nt
AM dɪs'ladʒmənt

disloyal
BR (,)dɪs'lɔɪ(ə)l
AM dɪs'lɔɪ(ə)l

disloyalist
BR (,)dɪs'lɔɪ(ə)lɪst, -s
AM dɪs'lɔɪ(ə)ləst, -s

disloyally
BR (,)dɪs'lɔɪ(ə)li
AM dɪs'lɔɪ(ə)li

disloyalty
BR (,)dɪs'lɔɪ(ə)lt|i, -ɪz
AM dɪs'lɔɪ(ə)lti, -z

dismal
BR 'dɪzm(ə)l
AM 'dɪzməl

dismally
BR 'dɪzm|li, 'dɪzməli
AM 'dɪzməli

dismalness
BR 'dɪzm(ə)lnəs
AM 'dɪzməlnəs

dismantle
BR dɪs'mant|l, -lz, -lɪŋ \ -lɪŋ, -ld
AM dɪs'mæn(t)əl, -z, -ɪŋ, -d

dismantlement
BR dɪs'mantlm(ə)nt
AM dɪs'mæn(t)lmənt

dismantler
BR dɪs'mantlə(r), dɪs'mantlə(r), -z
AM dɪs'mæn(t)lər, -z

dismast
BR ,dɪs'mɑːst, ,dɪs'mast, -s, -ɪŋ, -ɪd
AM dɪs'mæst, -s, -ɪŋ, -əd

dismay
BR dɪs'meɪ, -z, -ɪŋ, -d
AM də'smeɪ, -z, -ɪŋ, -d

dismember
BR (,)dɪs'mɛmbə(r), -əz, -(ə)rɪŋ, -əd
AM dɪs'mɛmb|ər, -ərd, -(ə)rɪŋ, -ərd

dismemberment
BR (,)dɪs'mɛmbəm(ə)nt, -s
AM dɪs'mɛmbərmənt, -s

dismiss
BR dɪs'mɪs, -ɪz, -ɪŋ, -t
AM də'smɪs, -ɪz, -ɪŋ, -t

dismissal
BR dɪs'mɪsl, -z
AM də'smɪsəl, -z

dismissible
BR dɪs'mɪsɪbl
AM də'smɪsəbəl

dismission
BR dɪs'mɪʃn
AM də'smɪʃən

dismissive
BR dɪs'mɪsɪv
AM də'smɪsɪv

dismissively
BR dɪs'mɪsɪvli
AM də'smɪsɪvli

dismissiveness
BR dɪs'mɪsɪvnɪs
AM də'smɪsɪvnɪs

dismount
BR (,)dɪs'maʊnt, -s, -ɪŋ, -ɪd
AM dɪs'maʊn|t, -ts, -(t)ɪŋ, -(t)əd

Disney
BR 'dɪzni
AM 'dɪzni

Disneyesque
BR ,dɪznɪ'ɛsk
AM 'dɪzni'ɛsk

Disneyland®
BR 'dɪznɪland
AM 'dɪzni,lænd

disobedience
BR ,dɪsə'biːdɪəns
AM ,dɪsə'bidɪəns

disobedient
BR ,dɪsə'biːdɪənt
AM 'dɪsə'bidiənt

disobediently
BR ,dɪsə'biːdɪəntli
AM 'dɪsə'bidiən(t)li

disobey
BR ,dɪsə'beɪ, -z, -ɪŋ, -d
AM 'dɪsə'beɪ, -z, -ɪŋ, -d

disobeyer
BR ,dɪsə'beɪə(r), -z
AM 'dɪsə'beɪər, -z

disoblige
BR ,dɪsə'blʌɪdʒ, -ɪz, -ɪŋ, -d
AM 'dɪsə'blaɪdʒ, -ɪz, -ɪŋ, -d

disobligingly
BR ,dɪsə'blʌɪdʒɪŋli
AM 'dɪsə'blaɪdʒɪŋli

disorder
BR dɪs'ɔːd|ə(r), -əz, -(ə)rɪŋ, -əd
AM dɪ'sɔrdər, -z, -ɪŋ, -d

disorderliness
BR dɪs'ɔːdəlɪnɪs
AM dɪ'sɔrdərlinɪs

disorderly
BR dɪs'ɔːdəli
AM dɪ'sɔrdərli

disorganisation
BR dɪs,ɔːgənʌɪ'zeɪʃn, dɪs,ɔːgnʌɪ'zeɪʃn
AM dɪ,sɔrg(ə)nə'zeɪʃən, dɪ,sɔrgə,naɪ'zeɪʃən

disorganise
BR dɪs'ɔːgənʌɪz, dɪs'ɔːgnʌɪz, -ɪz, -ɪŋ, -d
AM dɪ'sɔrgə,naɪz, -ɪz, -ɪŋ, -d

disorganization
BR dɪs,ɔːgənʌɪ'zeɪʃn, dɪs,ɔːgnʌɪ'zeɪʃn
AM dɪ,sɔrg(ə)nə'zeɪʃən, dɪ,sɔrgə,naɪ'zeɪʃən

disorganize
BR dɪs'ɔːgənʌɪz, dɪs'ɔːgnʌɪz, -ɪz, -ɪŋ, -d
AM dɪ'sɔrgə,naɪz, -ɪz, -ɪŋ, -d

disorient
BR (,)dɪs'ɔːrɪent, (,)dɪs'ɔːrɪənt, -s, -ɪŋ, -ɪd
AM dɪs'ɔrɪən|t, -ts, -(t)ɪŋ, -(t)əd

disorientate
BR (,)dɪs'ɔːrɪənteɪt, (,)dɪs'ɔːrɪenteɪt, -s, -ɪŋ, -ɪd
AM dɪs'ɔrɪən,teɪ|t, -ts, -dɪŋ, -dɪd

disorientation
BR dɪs,ɔːrɪən'teɪʃn, dɪs,ɔːrɪen'teɪʃn
AM dɪs,ɔrɪən'teɪʃən

disown
BR (,)dɪs'əʊn, -z, -ɪŋ, -d
AM də'soʊn, -z, -ɪŋ, -d

disowner
BR (,)dɪs'əʊnə(r), -z
AM də'soʊnər, -z

disparage
BR dɪ'spar|ɪdʒ, -ɪdʒɪz, -ɪdʒɪŋ, -ɪdʒd
AM də'sperɪdʒ, -ɪz, -ɪŋ, -d

disparagement
BR dɪ'sparɪdʒm(ə)nt
AM də'sperɪdʒmənt

disparagingly
BR dɪ'sparɪdʒɪŋli
AM də'sperɪdʒɪŋli

disparate
BR 'dɪsp(ə)rət
AM 'dɪspərət, də'sperət

disparately
BR 'dɪsp(ə)rətli
AM 'dɪspərətli, də'sperətli

disparateness
BR 'dɪsp(ə)rətnəs
AM 'dɪspərətnəs, də'sperətnəs

disparity
BR dɪ'spart|i, -ɪz
AM də'sperədi, -z

dispassionate
BR dɪs'paʃnət, dɪs'paʃənət
AM dɪs'pæʃ(ə)nət

dispassionately
BR dɪs'paʃnətli, dɪs'paʃənətli
AM dɪs'pæʃ(ə)nətli

dispassionateness
BR dɪsˈpaʃnətnəs,
dɪsˈpaʃənətnəs
AM dɪsˈpæʃ(ə)nətnəs

dispatch
BR dɪˈspatʃ, -ɪz, -ɪŋ, -t
AM dəˈspætʃ, -əz, -ɪŋ, -t

dispatcher
BR dɪˈspatʃə(r), -z
AM dəˈspætʃər, -z

dispel
BR dɪˈspɛl, -z, -ɪŋ, -d
AM dəˈspɛl, -z, -ɪŋ, -d

dispeller
BR dɪˈspɛlə(r), -z
AM dəˈspɛlər, -z

dispensability
BR dɪˌspɛnsəˈbɪlɪti
AM dəˈspɛnsəˈbɪlɪdi

dispensable
BR dɪˈspɛnsəbl
AM dəˈspɛnsəbəl

dispensary
BR dɪˈspɛns(ə)r|i, -ɪz
AM dəˈspɛns(ə)ri, -z

dispensation
BR ˌdɪsp(ə)nˈseɪʃn,
ˌdɪspɛnˈseɪʃn, -z
AM ˌdɪspənˈseɪʃən, -z

dispensational
BR ˌdɪsp(ə)nˈseɪʃn(ə)l,
ˌdɪsp(ə)nˈseɪʃən(ə)l,
ˌdɪspɛnˈseɪʃn(ə)l,
ˌdɪspɛnˈseɪʃən(ə)l
AM ˌdɪspənˈseɪʃ(ə)nəl

dispensatory
BR dɪˈspɛnsət(ə)ri
AM dəˈspɛnsəˌtɔri

dispense
BR dɪˈspɛns, -ɪz, -ɪŋ, -t
AM dəˈspɛns, -əz, -ɪŋ, -t

dispenser
BR dɪˈspɛnsə(r), -z
AM dəˈspɛnsər, -z

dispersable
BR dɪˈspɜːsəbl
AM dəˈspɜrsəbəl

dispersal
BR dɪˈspɜːsl, -z
AM dəˈspɜrsəl, -z

dispersant
BR dɪˈspɜːs(ə)nt, -s
AM dəˈspɜrsənt, -s

disperse
BR dɪˈspɜːs, -ɪz, -ɪŋ, -t
AM dəˈspɜrs, -əz, -ɪŋ, -t

disperser
BR dɪˈspɜːsə(r), -z
AM dəˈspɜrsər, -z

dispersible
BR dɪˈspɜːsɪbl
AM dəˈspɜrsəbəl

dispersion
BR dɪˈspɜːʃn
AM dəˈspɜrʒən,
dəˈspɜrʃən

dispersive
BR dɪˈspɜːsɪv
AM dəˈspɜrsɪv

dispirit
BR dɪˈspɪr|ɪt, -ɪts, -ɪtɪŋ,
-ɪtɪd
AM dəˈspɪr|ɪt, -ts, -dɪŋ,
-dɪd

dispiritedly
BR dɪˈspɪrɪtɪdli
AM dəˈspɪrɪdɪdli

dispiritedness
BR dɪˈspɪrɪtɪdnɪs
AM dəˈspɪrɪdɪdnɪs

dispiritingly
BR dɪˈspɪrɪtɪŋli
AM dəˈspɪrɪdɪŋli

displace
BR dɪsˈpleɪs, -ɪz, -ɪŋ, -t
AM dɪsˈpleɪs, -ɪz, -ɪŋ, -t

displacement
BR dɪsˈpleɪsm(ə)nt, -s
AM dɪsˈpleɪsmənt, -s

display
BR dɪsˈpleɪ, -z, -ɪŋ, -d
AM dəˈspleɪ, -z, -ɪŋ, -d

displayer
BR dɪsˈpleɪə(r), -z
AM dəˈspleɪər, -z

displease
BR (ˌ)dɪsˈpliːz, -ɪz, -ɪŋ,
-d
AM dəˈspliz, dɪˈspliz,
-ɪz, -ɪŋ, -d

displeasingly
BR (ˌ)dɪsˈpliːzɪŋli
AM dəˈsplizɪŋli,
dɪˈsplizɪŋli

displeasure
BR (ˌ)dɪsˈplɛʒə(r)
AM dɪsˈplɛʒər

disport
BR dɪˈspɔːt, -s, -ɪŋ, -ɪd
AM dəˈspɔ(ə)rt, -ts,
-ˈspɔrdɪŋ, -ˈspɔrdəd

disposability
BR dɪˌspəʊzəˈbɪlɪti
AM dəˌspoʊzəˈbɪlɪdi

disposable
BR dɪˈspəʊzəbl
AM dəˈspoʊzəbəl

disposal
BR dɪˈspəʊzl
AM dəˈspoʊzəl

dispose
BR dɪˈspəʊz, -ɪz, -ɪŋ, -d
AM dəˈspoʊz, -əz, -ɪŋ, -d

disposer
BR dɪˈspəʊzə(r), -z
AM dəˈspoʊzər, -z

disposition
BR ˌdɪspəˈzɪʃn, -z
AM ˌdɪspəˈzɪʃən, -z

dispossess
BR ˌdɪspəˈzɛs, -ɪz, -ɪŋ, -t
AM ˌdɪspəˈzɛs, -əz, -ɪŋ, -t

dispossession
BR ˌdɪspəˈzɛʃn
AM ˈdɪspəˈzɛʃən

dispraise
BR ˌdɪsˈpreɪz, -ɪz, -ɪŋ, -d
AM dɪsˈpreɪz, -ɪz, -ɪŋ, -d

Disprin®
BR ˈdɪsprɪn
AM ˈdɪsprɪn

disproof
BR (ˌ)dɪsˈpruːf
AM dɪsˈpruf

disproportion
BR ˌdɪsprəˈpɔːʃn
AM ˌdɪsprəˈpɔrʃən

disproportional
BR ˌdɪsprəˈpɔːʃn(ə)l,
ˌdɪsprəˈpɔːʃən(ə)l
AM ˌdɪsprəˈpɔrʃ(ə)nəl

disproportionally
BR ˌdɪsprəˈpɔːʃnəli,
ˌdɪsprəˈpɔːʃənli,
ˌdɪsprəˈpɔːʃənli,
ˌdɪsprəˈpɔːʃ(ə)nəli
AM ˌdɪsprəˈpɔrʃ(ə)nəli

disproportionate
BR ˌdɪsprəˈpɔːʃənət,
ˌdɪsprəˈpɔːʃnət
AM ˌdɪsprəˈpɔrʃ(ə)nət

disproportionately
BR ˌdɪsprəˈpɔːʃənətli,
ˌdɪsprəˈpɔːʃnətli
AM ˌdɪsprəˈpɔrʃ(ə)nətli

disproportionateness
BR ˌdɪsprəˈpɔːʃənətnəs,
ˌdɪsprəˈpɔːʃnətnəs
AM ˌdɪsprəˈpɔrʃ(ə)nətnəs

disproportioned
BR ˌdɪsprəˈpɔːʃnd
AM ˌdɪsprəˈpɔrʃənd

disprovable
BR (ˌ)dɪsˈpruːvəbl
AM dɪsˈpruvəbl

disproval
BR (ˌ)dɪsˈpruːvl, -z
AM dɪsˈpruvəl, -z

disprove
BR (ˌ)dɪsˈpruːv, -z, -ɪŋ,
-d
AM dɪsˈpruv, -z, -ɪŋ, -d

disputable
BR dɪˈspjuːtəbl
AM dəˈspjudəbəl,
ˈdɪspjədəbl

disputably
BR dɪˈspjuːtəbli
AM dəˈspjudəbli,
ˈdɪspjədəbli

disputant
BR ˈdɪspjʊt(ə)nt,
dɪˈspjuːt(ə)nt, -s
AM dəˈspjutnt, -s

disputation
BR ˌdɪspjʊˈteɪʃn, -z
AM ˌdɪspjəˈteɪʃən,
ˌdɪspjuˈteɪʃən, -z

disputatious
BR ˌdɪspjʊˈteɪʃəs
AM ˌdɪspjəˈteɪʃəs,
ˌdɪspjuˈteɪʃəs

disputatiously
BR ˌdɪspjʊˈteɪʃəsli
AM ˌdɪspjəˈteɪʃəsli,
ˌdɪspjuˈteɪʃəsli

disputatiousness
BR ˌdɪspjʊˈteɪʃəsnəs
AM ˌdɪspjəˈteɪʃəsnəs,
ˌdɪspjuˈteɪʃəsnəs

dispute¹
noun
BR dɪˈspjuːt, ˈdɪspjuːt,
-s
AM dəˈspjut, ˈdɪˌspjut,
-s

dispute²
verb
BR dɪˈspjuːt, -s, -ɪŋ, -ɪd
AM dəˈspju|t, -ts, -dɪŋ,
-dəd

disputer
BR dɪˈspjuːtə(r), -z
AM dəˈspjudər, -z

disqualification
BR dɪsˌkwɒlɪfɪˈkeɪʃn,
-z
AM ˌdɪsˌkwɑləfəˈkeɪʃən,
dəˈskwɑləfəˌkeɪʃən,
-z

disqualify
BR dɪsˈkwɒlɪfaɪ, -z, -ɪŋ,
-d
AM dəˈskwɑləˌfaɪ,
dɪsˈkwɑləˌfaɪ, -z, -ɪŋ,
-d

disquiet
BR dɪsˈkwaɪət, -s, -ɪŋ,
-ɪd
AM dɪsˈkwaɪə|t,
dəˈskwaɪə|t, -ts, -dɪŋ,
-dəd

disquieting
BR dɪsˈkwaɪətɪŋ
AM dɪsˈkwaɪədɪŋ,
dəˈskwaɪədɪŋ

disquietingly
BR dɪsˈkwaɪətɪŋli
AM dɪsˈkwaɪədɪŋli,
dəˈskwaɪədɪŋli

disquietude
BR dɪsˈkwaɪɪtjuːd,
dɪsˈkwaɪɪtʃuːd
AM dɪsˈkwaɪəˌt(j)ud,
dəˈskwaɪəˌt(j)ud

disquisition
BR ˌdɪskwɪˈzɪʃn, -z
AM ˌdɪskwəˈzɪʃən, -z

disquisitional
BR ˌdɪskwɪˈzɪʃn(ə)l,
ˌdɪskwɪˈzɪʃən(ə)l
AM ˌdɪskwəˈzɪʃ(ə)nəl

Disraeli
BR dɪzˈreɪli
AM dɪzˈreɪli

disrate
BR (,)dɪs'reɪt, -s, -ɪŋ, -ɪd
AM dɪs'reɪ|t, də'sreɪ|t,
-ts, -dɪŋ, -dɪd

disregard
BR ,dɪsrɪ'gɑːd, -z, -ɪŋ,
-ɪd
AM ,dɪsrə'gɑrd,
'dɪsrɪ'gɑrd, -z, -ɪŋ, -əd

disregardful
BR ,dɪsrɪ'gɑːdf(ʊ)l
AM ,dɪsrə'gɑrdfəl,
'dɪsrɪ'gɑrdfəl

disregardfully
BR ,dɪsrɪ'gɑːdfʊli,
,dɪsrɪ'gɑːdfli
AM ,dɪsrə'gɑrdfəli,
'dɪsrɪ'gɑrdfəli

disrelish
BR (,)dɪs'rɛl|ɪʃ, -ɪʃɪz,
-ɪʃɪŋ, -ɪʃt
AM dɪs'rɛlɪʃ, -ɪz, -ɪŋ, -t

disremember
BR ,dɪsrɪ'mɛmblə(r),
-əz, -(ə)rɪŋ, -əd
AM ,dɪsrə'mɛmbər, -z,
-ɪŋ, -d

disrepair
BR ,dɪsrɪ'pɛː(r)
AM ,dɪsrə'pɛ(ə)r

disreputable
BR dɪs'rɛpjʊtəbl
AM dɪs'rɛpjədəbəl

disreputableness
BR dɪs'rɛpjʊtəblnəs
AM dɪs'rɛpjədəbəlnəs

disreputably
BR dɪs'rɛpjʊtəbli
AM dɪs'rɛpjədəbli

disrepute
BR ,dɪsrɪ'pjuːt
AM ,dɪsrə'pjut

disrespect
BR ,dɪsrɪ'spɛkt
AM ,dɪsrə'spɛk(t)

disrespectful
BR ,dɪsrɪ'spɛk(t)f(ʊ)l
AM ,dɪsrə'spɛk(t)fəl

disrespectfully
BR ,dɪsrɪ'spɛk(t)fʊli,
,dɪsrɪ'spɛk(t)fli
AM ,dɪsrə'spɛk(t)fəli

disrobe
BR (,)dɪs'rəʊb, -z, -ɪŋ, -d
AM dɪs'roʊb, -z, -ɪŋ, -d

disrupt
BR dɪs'rʌpt, -s, -ɪŋ, -ɪd
AM dɪs'rəpt, -s, -ɪŋ, -əd

disrupter
BR dɪs'rʌptə(r), -z
AM dɪs'rəptər, -z

disruption
BR dɪs'rʌpʃn
AM dɪs'rəpʃən

disruptive
BR dɪs'rʌptɪv
AM dɪs'rəptɪv

disruptively
BR dɪs'rʌptɪvli
AM dɪs'rəptəvli

disruptiveness
BR dɪs'rʌptɪvnɪs
AM dɪs'rəptɪvnɪs

Diss
BR dɪs
AM dɪs

dissatisfaction
BR dɪ(s),satɪs'fakʃn,
,dɪsatɪs'fakʃn
AM dɪ(s),sædəs'fækʃən

dissatisfactory
BR dɪ(s),satɪs'fakt(ə)ri,
,dɪsatɪs'fakt(ə)ri
AM dɪ(s),sædəs'fæk,tɔri

dissatisfiedly
BR dɪ(s)'satɪsfʌɪdli
AM dɪ(s)'sædəs,faɪ(ə)dli

dissatisfy
BR dɪ(s)'satɪsfʌɪ, -z,
-ɪŋ, -d
AM dɪ(s)'sædəs,faɪ, -z,
-ɪŋ, -d

dissect
BR dɪ'sɛkt, dʌɪ'sɛkt, -s,
-ɪŋ, -ɪd
AM də'sɛk|(t),
daɪ'sɛk|(t), -(t)s, -tɪŋ,
-təd

dissection
BR dɪ'sɛkʃn,
dʌɪ'sɛkʃn, -z
AM də'sɛkʃən,
daɪ'sɛkʃən, -z

dissector
BR dɪ'sɛktə(r),
dʌɪ'sɛktə(r), -z
AM də'sɛktər,
daɪ'sɛktər, -z

disseise
BR dɪ(s)'siːz, -ɪz, -ɪŋ, -d
AM də(s)'siz, dɪ(s)'siz,
-ɪz, -ɪŋ, -d

disseisin
BR dɪ(s)'siːz(ɪ)n
AM də(s)'sizn,
dɪ(s)'sizn

disseize
BR dɪ(s)'siːz, -ɪz, -ɪŋ, -d
AM də(s)'siz, dɪ(s)'siz,
-ɪz, -ɪŋ, -d

disseizin
BR dɪ(s)'siːz(ɪ)n
AM də(s)'sizn,
dɪ(s)'sizn

dissemblance
BR dɪ'sɛmbləns
AM dɪ(s)'sɛmbləns

dissemble
BR dɪ'sɛmb|l, -lz,
-lɪŋ \-lɪŋ, -ld
AM dɪ'sɛmb|əl, -əlz,
-(ə)lɪŋ, -əld

dissembler
BR dɪ'sɛmblə(r), -z
AM də'sɛmb(ə)lər, -z

dissemblingly
BR dɪ'sɛmblɪŋli,
dɪ'sɛmb|ɪŋli
AM də'sɛmb(ə)lɪŋli

disseminate
BR dɪ'sɛmɪneɪt, -s, -ɪŋ,
-ɪd
AM də'sɛmə,neɪ|t, -ts,
-dɪŋ, -dɪd

dissemination
BR dɪ,sɛmɪ'neɪʃn
AM də,sɛmə'neɪʃən

disseminator
BR dɪ'sɛmɪneɪtə(r), -z
AM də'sɛmə,neɪdər, -z

dissension
BR dɪ'sɛnʃn, -z
AM də'sɛn(t)ʃən, -z

dissent
BR dɪ'sɛnt, -s, -ɪŋ, -ɪd
AM də'sɛn|t, -ts, -(t)ɪŋ,
-(t)əd

dissenter
BR dɪ'sɛntə(r), -z
AM də'sɛn(t)ər, -z

dissentient
BR dɪ'sɛnʃ(ɪ)ənt,
dɪ'sɛnʃnt, -s
AM də'sɛn(t)ʃiənt, -s

dissentingly
BR dɪ'sɛntɪŋli
AM də'sɛn(t)ɪŋli

dissepement
BR dɪ'sɛpɪm(ə)nt, -s
AM də'sɛpəmənt, -s

dissertate
BR 'dɪsəteɪt, -s, -ɪŋ, -ɪd
AM 'dɪsər,teɪ|t, -ts, -dɪŋ,
-dɪd

dissertation
BR ,dɪsə'teɪʃn, -z
AM ,dɪsər'teɪʃən, -z

dissertational
BR ,dɪsə'teɪʃn(ə)l,
,dɪsə'teɪʃən(ə)l
AM ,dɪsər'teɪʃ(ə)nəl

disserve
BR ,dɪs'səːv, dɪ(s)'səːv,
-z, -ɪŋ, -d
AM dɪ(s)'sərv, -z, -ɪŋ, -d

disservice
BR ,dɪs'səːvɪs,
dɪ(s)'səːvɪs
AM dɪ(s)'sərvɪs

dissever
BR dɪ'sɛvə(r), -z, -ɪŋ, -d
AM də'sɛvər, -z, -ɪŋ, -d

disseverance
BR dɪ'sɛv(ə)rəns,
dɪ'sɛv(ə)rns
AM də'sɛv(ə)rəns

disseverment
BR dɪ'sɛvəm(ə)nt
AM də'sɛvərmənt

dissidence
BR 'dɪsɪd(ə)ns
AM 'dɪsədns

dissident
BR 'dɪsɪd(ə)nt, -s
AM 'dɪsədnt, -s

dissimilar
BR ,dɪ(s)'sɪmɪlə(r),
,dɪ(s)'sɪmlə(r),
dɪ(s)'sɪmɪlə(r),
dɪ'sɪmlə(r)
AM dɪ(s)'sɪmɪlər

dissimilarity
BR ,dɪsɪmɪ'larɪti,
dɪ(s),sɪmɪ'larɪt|i, -ɪz
AM dɪ(s),sɪmə'lɛrədi,
-z

dissimilarly
BR ,dɪ(s)'sɪmɪləli,
dɪ(s)'sɪmɪləli
AM dɪ(s)'sɪmɪlərli

dissimilate
BR dɪ'sɪmɪleɪt, -s, -ɪŋ,
-ɪd
AM dɪ'sɪmə,leɪ|t, -ts,
-dɪŋ, -dɪd

dissimilation
BR dɪ,sɪmɪ'leɪʃn, -z
AM də,sɪmə'leɪʃən,
'dɪ,sɪmə'leɪʃən, -z

dissimilatory
BR dɪ'sɪmɪlət(ə)ri
AM dɪ'sɪmələ,tɔri

dissimilitude
BR ,dɪsɪ'mɪlɪtjuːd,
,dɪsɪ'mɪlɪtʃuːd
AM dɪsɪ'mɪlə,t(j)ud

dissimulate
BR dɪ'sɪmjʊleɪt, -s, -ɪŋ,
-ɪd
AM dɪ'sɪmjə,leɪ|t, -ts,
-dɪŋ, -dɪd

dissimulation
BR dɪ,sɪmjʊ'leɪʃn, -z
AM də,sɪmjə'leɪʃən,
'dɪ,sɪmjə'leɪʃən, -z

dissimulator
BR dɪ'sɪmjʊleɪtə(r), -z
AM dɪ'sɪmjə,leɪdər, -z

dissipate
BR 'dɪsɪpeɪt, -s, -ɪŋ, -ɪd
AM 'dɪsə,peɪ|t, -ts, -dɪŋ,
-dɪd

dissipater
BR 'dɪsɪpeɪtə(r), -z
AM 'dɪsə,peɪdər, -z

dissipation
BR ,dɪsɪ'peɪʃn
AM ,dɪsə'peɪʃən

dissipative
BR 'dɪsɪpeɪtɪv
AM 'dɪsə,peɪdɪv

dissipator
BR 'dɪsɪpeɪtə(r), -z
AM 'dɪsə,peɪdər, -z

dissociate
BR dɪ'səʊʃɪeɪt,
dɪ'səʊsɪeɪt, -s, -ɪŋ, -ɪd
AM dɪ'soʊʃi,eɪ|t,
dɪ'soʊsi,eɪ|t, -ts, -dɪŋ,
-dɪd

dissociation
BR dɪˌsəʊʃɪˈeɪʃən,
dɪˌsəʊsɪˈeɪʃn
AM dɪˌsəʊʃiˈeɪʃən,
dɪˌsəʊsiˈeɪʃən

dissociative
BR dɪˈsəʊʃɪətɪv,
dɪˈsəʊsɪətɪv
AM dɪˈsəʊʃiˌeɪdɪv,
dɪˈsəʊsiˌeɪdɪv

dissolubility
BR dɪˌsɒljʊˈbɪlɪti
AM dəˌsɑljəˈbɪlɪdi

dissoluble
BR dɪˈsɒljʊbl
AM dəˈsɑljəbəl

dissolubly
BR dɪˈsɒljʊbli
AM dəˈsɑljəbli

dissolute
BR ˈdɪsəl(j)uːt
AM ˈdɪsəˌlut, ˈdɪsəlˌjut

dissolutely
BR ˈdɪsəl(j)uːtli
AM ˈdɪsəˌlutli,
ˈdɪsəlˌjutli

dissoluteness
BR ˈdɪsəl(j)uːtnəs
AM ˈdɪsəˌlutnəs,
ˈdɪsəlˌjutnəs

dissolution
BR ˌdɪsəˈl(j)uːʃn
AM ˌdɪsəˈluʃən,
ˌdɪsəlˈjuʃən

dissolutionary
BR ˌdɪsəˈl(j)uːʃn(ə)ri
AM ˌdɪsəˈluʃəˌnɛri,
ˌdɪsəlˈjuʃəˌnɛri

dissolvable
BR dɪˈzɒlvəbl
AM dəˈzɑlvəbəl,
dəˈzɑlvəbəl

dissolve
BR dɪˈzɒlv, -z, -ɪŋ, -d
AM dəˈzɑlv, dəˈzɑlv, -z,
-ɪŋ, -d

dissolvent
BR dɪˈzɒlv(ə)nt, -s
AM dəˈzɑlvənt,
dəˈzɑlvənt, -s

dissonance
BR ˈdɪsənəns
AM ˈdɪsənəns

dissonant
BR ˈdɪsənənt
AM ˈdɪsənənt

dissonantly
BR ˈdɪsənəntli
AM ˈdɪsənən(t)li

dissuade
BR dɪˈsweɪd, -z, -ɪŋ, -ɪd
AM dəˈsweɪd, -z, -ɪŋ, -ɪd

dissuader
BR dɪˈsweɪdə(r), -z
AM dəˈsweɪdər, -z

dissuasion
BR dɪˈsweɪʒn
AM dəˈsweɪʒən

dissuasive
BR dɪˈsweɪsɪv
AM dəˈsweɪsɪv

dissyllabic
BR ˌdʌɪsɪˈlabɪk,
ˌdɪsɪˈlabɪk
AM ˈdaɪsəˈlæbɪk,
ˈdɪsəˈlæbɪk

dissyllable
BR ˈdʌɪˌsɪləbl,
ˌdʌɪˈsɪləbl, -z
AM daɪˈsɪləbəl,
dɪˈsɪləbəl, -z

dissymmetrical
BR ˌdɪ(s)sɪˈmɛtrɪkl
AM ˈdɪ(s)sɪˈmɛtrəkəl

dissymmetry
BR dɪ(s)ˈsɪmɪtr|i, -ɪz
AM də(s)ˈsɪmətri,
dɪ(s)ˈsɪmətri, -z

distaff
BR ˈdɪstɑːf, ˈdɪstaf, -s
AM ˈdɪˌstæf, -s

distal
BR ˈdɪstl
AM ˈdɪstl

distally
BR ˈdɪstl̩i, ˈdɪstəli
AM ˈdɪstl̩i

distance
BR ˈdɪst(ə)ns, -ɪz, -ɪŋ, -t
AM ˈdɪstəns, -əz, -ɪŋ, -t

distant
BR ˈdɪst(ə)nt
AM ˈdɪstənt

distantly
BR ˈdɪst(ə)ntli
AM ˈdɪstən(t)li

distantness
BR ˈdɪst(ə)ntnəs
AM ˈdɪstən(t)nəs

distaste
BR (ˌ)dɪsˈteɪst
AM dɪsˈteɪst

distasteful
BR (ˌ)dɪsˈteɪs(t)f(ʊ)l
AM dɪsˈteɪs(t)fəl

distastefully
BR (ˌ)dɪsˈteɪs(t)fʊli,
(ˌ)dɪsˈteɪs(t)fli
AM dɪsˈteɪs(t)fəli

distastefulness
BR (ˌ)dɪsˈteɪs(t)f(ʊ)lnəs
AM dɪsˈteɪs(t)fəlnəs

distemper
BR dɪsˈtɛmp|ə(r), -əz,
-(ə)rɪŋ, -əd
AM dɪsˈtɛmpər, -z, -ɪŋ,
-d

distend
BR dɪsˈtɛnd, -z, -ɪŋ, -ɪd
AM dəsˈtɛnd, -z, -ɪŋ, -əd

distensibility
BR dɪˌstɛnsɪˈbɪlɪti
AM dəˌstɛnsəˈbɪlɪdi

distensible
BR dɪsˈtɛnsɪbl
AM dəsˈtɛnsəbəl

distension
BR dɪsˈtɛnʃn
AM dəsˈtɛnʃən

distich
BR ˈdɪstɪk, -s
AM ˈdɪstɪk, -s

distichous
BR ˈdɪstɪkəs
AM ˈdɪstɪkəs

distil
BR dɪsˈtɪl, -z, -ɪŋ, -d
AM dəsˈtɪl, -z, -ɪŋ, -d

distill
BR dɪsˈtɪl, -z, -ɪŋ, -d
AM dəsˈtɪl, -z, -ɪŋ, -d

distillate
BR ˈdɪstɪlət, ˈdɪstlət,
ˈdɪstɪleɪt, -s
AM ˈdɪstɪlət, ˈdɪstəˌleɪt,
-s

distillation
BR ˌdɪstɪˈleɪʃn
AM ˌdɪstəˈleɪʃən

distillatory
BR dɪˈstɪlət(ə)ri
AM dɪˈstɪləˌtɔri

distiller
BR dɪˈstɪlə(r), -z
AM dəˈstɪlər, -z

distillery
BR dɪˈstɪl(ə)r|i, -ɪz
AM dəˈstɪl(ə)ri, -z

distinct
BR dɪˈstɪŋ(k)t
AM dəˈstɪŋ(k)t,
dəˈstɪŋk(t)

distinction
BR dɪˈstɪŋ(k)ʃn, -z
AM dəˈstɪŋ(k)ʃən, -z

distinctive
BR dɪˈstɪŋ(k)tɪv
AM dəˈstɪŋ(k)tɪv

distinctively
BR dɪˈstɪŋ(k)tɪvli
AM dəˈstɪŋ(k)tɪvli

distinctiveness
BR dɪˈstɪŋ(k)tɪvnɪs
AM dəˈstɪŋ(k)tɪvnɪs

distinctly
BR dɪˈstɪŋ(k)tli
AM dəˈstɪŋ(k)tli,
dəˈstɪŋk(t)li

distinctness
BR dɪˈstɪŋ(k)tnɪs,
AM dəˈstɪŋ(k)tnɪs,
dəˈstɪŋk(t)nɪs

distingué
BR dɪˈstæŋɡeɪ
AM dəˌstɪŋˈɡeɪ

distinguée
BR dɪˈstæŋɡeɪ
AM dəˌstɪŋˈɡeɪ

distinguish
BR dɪˈstɪŋɡw|ɪʃ, -ɪʃɪz,
-ɪʃɪŋ, -ɪʃt
AM dəˈstɪŋɡwɪʃ, -ɪz, -ɪŋ,
-t

distinguishable
BR dɪˈstɪŋɡwɪʃəbl
AM dəˈstɪŋɡwɪʃəbəl

distinguishably
BR dɪˈstɪŋɡwɪʃəbli
AM dəˈstɪŋɡwɪʃəbli

distort
BR dɪˈstɔːt, -s, -ɪŋ, -ɪd
AM dəˈstɔ(ə)rt, -ts,
-ˈstɔrdɪŋ, -ˈstɔrdəd

distortedly
BR dɪˈstɔːtɪdli
AM dəˈstɔrdədli

distortedness
BR dɪˈstɔːtɪdnɪs
AM dəˈstɔrdədnəs

distorter
BR dɪˈstɔːtə(r), -z
AM dəˈstɔrdər, -z

distortion
BR dɪˈstɔːʃn, -z
AM dəˈstɔrʃən, -z

distortional
BR dɪˈstɔːʃn(ə)l,
dɪˈstɔːʃən(ə)l
AM dəˈstɔrʃ(ə)nəl

distortionless
BR dɪˈstɔːʃnləs
AM dəˈstɔrʃənləs

distract
BR dɪˈstrakt, -s, -ɪŋ, -ɪd
AM dəˈstræk|(t), -(t)s,
-tɪŋ, -təd

distracted
BR dɪˈstraktɪd
AM dəˈstræktəd

distractedly
BR dɪˈstraktɪdli
AM dəˈstræktədli

distractedness
BR dɪˈstraktɪdnɪs
AM dəˈstræktədnəs

distraction
BR dɪˈstrakʃn, -z
AM dəˈstrækʃən, -z

distractor
BR dɪˈstraktə(r), -z
AM dəˈstræktər, -z

distrain
BR dɪˈstreɪn, -z, -ɪŋ, -d
AM dəˈstreɪn, -z, -ɪŋ, -d

distrainee
BR dɪˌstreɪˈniː,
ˌdɪstreɪˈniː, -z
AM dəˈstreɪˈni, -z

distrainer
BR dɪˈstreɪnə(r), -z
AM dəˈstreɪnər, -z

distrainment
BR dɪˈstreɪnm(ə)nt
AM dəˈstreɪnmənt

distrainor
BR dɪˈstreɪnə(r), -z
AM dəˈstreɪnər, -z

distraint
BR dɪˈstreɪnt
AM dəˈstreɪnt

distrait
BR dɪ'streɪ, 'dɪstreɪ
AM də'streɪ, di'streɪ

distraite
BR dɪ'streɪt, 'dɪstreɪt
AM də'streɪt, di'streɪt

distraught
BR dɪ'strɔːt
AM də'strɔt, də'strɑt

distress
BR dɪ'strɛs, -ɪz, -ɪŋ, -t
AM də'strɛs, -əz, -ɪŋ, -t

distressful
BR dɪ'strɛsf(ʊ)l
AM də'strɛsfəl

distressfully
BR dɪ'strɛsfʊli, dɪ'strɛsfli
AM də'strɛsfəli

distressing
BR dɪ'strɛsɪŋ
AM də'strɛsɪŋ

distressingly
BR dɪ'strɛsɪŋli
AM də'strɛsɪŋli

distributable
BR dɪ'strɪbjʊtəbl, 'dɪstrɪbjuːtəbl
AM də'strɪbjudəbəl

distributary
BR dɪ'strɪbjʊt(ə)r|i, 'dɪstrɪbjuːt(ə)r|i, -ɪz
AM də'strɪbjuˌtɛri, -z

distribute
BR dɪ'strɪbjuːt, 'dɪstrɪbjuːt, -s, -ɪŋ, -ɪd
AM də'strɪbju|t, -ts, -dɪŋ, -dəd

distribution
BR ˌdɪstrɪ'bjuːʃn, -z
AM ˌdɪstrə'bjuʃən, -z

distributional
BR ˌdɪstrɪ'bjuːʃ|ŋ(ə)l, ˌdɪstrɪ'bjuːʃən(ə)l
AM ˌdɪstrə'bjuʃ(ə)nəl

distributive
BR dɪ'strɪbjʊtɪv
AM də'strɪbjədɪv

distributively
BR dɪ'strɪbjʊtɪvli
AM də'strɪbjədɪvli

distributor
BR dɪ'strɪbjʊtə(r), 'dɪstrɪbjuːtə(r), -z
AM də'strɪbjədər, -z

district
BR 'dɪstrɪkt, -s
AM 'dɪstrɪk(t), -s

distrust
BR (ˌ)dɪs'trʌst, -s, -ɪŋ, -ɪd
AM dɪs'trəst, -s, -ɪŋ, -əd

distruster
BR (ˌ)dɪs'trʌstə(r), -z
AM dɪs'trəstər, -z

distrustful
BR (ˌ)dɪs'trʌs(t)f(ʊ)l
AM dɪs'trəs(t)fəl

distrustfully
BR (ˌ)dɪs'trʌs(t)fʊli, (ˌ)dɪs'trʌs(t)fli
AM dɪs'trəs(t)fəli

distrustfulness
BR (ˌ)dɪs'trʌstf(ʊ)lnəs
AM dɪs'trəs(t)fəlnəs

disturb
BR dɪ'stɜːb, -z, -ɪŋ, -d
AM də'stɜrb, -z, -ɪŋ, -d

disturbance
BR dɪ'stɜːb(ə)ns, -ɪz
AM də'stɜrbəns, -əz

disturber
BR dɪ'stɜːbə(r), -z
AM də'stɜrbər, -z

disturbingly
BR dɪ'stɜːbɪŋli
AM də'stɜrbɪŋli

disulphide
BR dʌɪ'sʌlfʌɪd, -z
AM dɑɪ'səl,faɪd, -z

disunion
BR (ˌ)dɪs'juːnɪən
AM dɪs'junjən

disunite
BR ˌdɪsjʊ'nʌɪt, -s, -ɪŋ, -ɪd
AM ˌdɪsju'naɪt, ˌdɪʃ(j)u'naɪ|t, -ts, -dɪŋ, -dɪd

disunity
BR (ˌ)dɪs'juːnɪti
AM dɪs'junədi, -z

disuse[1]
noun
BR (ˌ)dɪs'juːs
AM dɪs'jus

disuse[2]
verb
BR ˌdɪs'juːz, -ɪz, -ɪŋ, -d
AM dɪs'juz, -əz, -ɪŋ, -d

disutility
BR ˌdɪsjʊ'tɪlɪti
AM ˌdɪsju'tɪlɪdi

disyllabic
BR ˌdʌɪsɪ'labɪk, ˌdɪsɪ'labɪk
AM ˌdaɪsə'læbɪk, ˌdɪsə'læbɪk

disyllable
BR 'dʌɪˌsɪləbl, ˌdʌɪ'sɪləbl, -z
AM daɪ'sɪləbəl, dɪ'sɪləbəl, -z

dit
BR dɪt, -s
AM dɪt, -s

ditch
BR dɪtʃ, -ɪz, -ɪŋ, -t
AM dɪtʃ, -ɪz, -ɪŋ, -t

ditcher
BR 'dɪtʃə(r), -z
AM 'dɪtʃər, -z

ditchwater
BR 'dɪtʃˌwɔːtə(r)
AM 'dɪtʃˌwɔdər, 'dɪtʃˌwɑdər

ditheism
BR 'dʌɪˌθiːɪz(ə)m, ˌdaɪ'θiːɪz(ə)m
AM 'daɪθiˌɪzəm, daɪ'θiˌɪzəm

ditheist
BR 'dʌɪˌθiːɪst, ˌdʌɪ'θiːɪst, -s
AM 'daɪθiɪst, daɪ'θiːɪst, -s

dither
BR 'dɪð|ə(r), -əz, -(ə)rɪŋ, -əd
AM 'dɪð|ər, -ərz, -(ə)rɪŋ, -ərd

ditherer
BR 'dɪð(ə)rə(r), -z
AM 'dɪðərər, -z

dithery
BR 'dɪð(ə)ri
AM 'dɪð(ə)ri

dithionite
BR dʌɪ'θʌɪənʌɪt
AM daɪ'θaɪəˌnaɪt

dithyramb
BR 'dɪθɪram(b)
AM dɪθə,ræm, 'dɪθi,ræm

dithyrambi
BR ˌdɪθɪ'rambʌɪ
AM ˌdɪθə'ræmˌbaɪ

dithyrambic
BR ˌdɪθɪ'rambɪk, -s
AM ˌdɪθə'ræmbɪk, 'dɪθi'ræmbɪk, -s

dithyrambus
BR ˌdɪθɪ'rambəs
AM ˌdɪθə'ræmbəs

ditsy
BR 'dɪts|i, -ɪə(r), -ɪɪst
AM 'dɪtsi, -ər, -ɪst

dittander
BR dɪ'tandə(r)
AM də'tændər

dittany
BR 'dɪtəni, 'dɪtn̩i
AM 'dɪtəni

ditto
BR 'dɪtəʊ, -z
AM 'dɪdoʊ, -z

dittographic
BR ˌdɪtə(ʊ)'grafɪk
AM ˌdɪdoʊ'græfɪk

dittography
BR dɪ'tɒgrəf|i, -ɪz
AM dɪ'tɑgrəfi, -z

Ditton
BR 'dɪtn
AM 'dɪtn

ditty
BR 'dɪt|i, -ɪz
AM 'dɪdi, -z

ditzy
BR 'dɪts|i, -ɪə(r), -ɪɪst
AM 'dɪtsi, -ər, -ɪst

Diu
BR 'diːuː
AM 'diu

diuresis
BR ˌdʌɪjʊ'riːsɪs
AM ˌdaɪjə'risəs

diuretic
BR ˌdʌɪjʊ'rɛtɪk, -s
AM ˌdaɪjə'rɛdɪk, -s

diurnal
BR dʌɪ'ɜːnl
AM daɪ'ɜrnəl

diurnally
BR dʌɪ'ɜːn|li, dʌɪ'ɜːnəli
AM daɪ'ɜrnəli

diva
BR 'diːvə(r), -z
AM 'divə, -z

divagate
BR 'dʌɪvəgeɪt, -s, -ɪŋ, -ɪd
AM 'daɪvəˌgeɪt, 'dɪvəˌgeɪt, -ts, -dɪŋ, -dɪd

divagation
BR ˌdʌɪvə'geɪʃn, -z
AM ˌdaɪvə'geɪʃən, ˌdɪvə'geɪʃən, -z

divalency
BR (ˌ)dʌɪ'veɪlənsi, (ˌ)dʌɪ'veɪlŋsi
AM daɪ'veɪlənsi

divalent
BR (ˌ)dʌɪ'veɪlənt, (ˌ)dʌɪ'veɪlŋt
AM daɪ'veɪlənt

divan
BR dɪ'van, -z
AM 'daɪˌvæn, də'væn, -z

divaricate
BR dʌɪ'varɪkeɪt, dɪ'varɪkeɪt, -s, -ɪŋ, -ɪd
AM daɪ'verəˌkeɪt, də'verəˌkeɪ|t, -ts, -dɪŋ, -dɪd

divarication
BR dʌɪˌvarɪ'keɪʃn, dɪˌvarɪ'keɪʃn
AM daɪˌverə'keɪʃən, dəˌverə'keɪʃən

dive
BR dʌɪv, -z, -ɪŋ, -d
AM daɪv, -z, -ɪŋ, -d

diver
BR 'dʌɪvə(r), -z
AM 'daɪvər, -z

diverge
BR dʌɪ'vɜːdʒ, dɪ'vɜːdʒ, -ɪz, -ɪŋ, -d
AM də'vɜrdʒ, daɪ'vɜrdʒ, -əz, -ɪŋ, -d

divergence
BR dʌɪ'vɜːdʒ(ə)ns, dɪ'vɜːdʒ(ə)ns, -ɪz
AM də'vɜrdʒəns, daɪ'vɜrdʒəns, -əz

divergency
BR dʌɪ'vɜːdʒ(ə)ns|i, dɪ'vɜːdʒ(ə)ns|i, -ɪz

AM dəˈvɜrdʒənsi,
daɪˈvɜrdʒənsi, -z
divergent
BR daɪˈvɜːdʒ(ə)nt,
dɪˈvɜːdʒ(ə)nt
AM dəˈvɜrdʒənt,
daɪˈvɜrdʒənt
divergently
BR daɪˈvɜːdʒ(ə)ntli,
dɪˈvɜːdʒ(ə)ntli
AM dəˈvɜrdʒən(t)li,
daɪˈvɜrdʒən(t)li
divers
BR ˈdaɪvə(ː)z
AM ˈdaɪvɜrz
diverse
BR daɪˈvɜːs
AM dəˈvɜrs, daɪˈvɜrs
diversely
BR daɪˈvɜːsli
AM dəˈvɜrsli,
daɪˈvɜrsli
diversifiable
BR daɪˈvɜːsɪfʌɪəbl
AM dəˈvɜrsəˌfaɪəbəl,
daɪˈvɜrsəˌfaɪəbəl
diversification
BR daɪˌvɜːsɪfɪˈkeɪʃn,
dɪˌvɜːsɪfɪˈkeɪʃn
AM dəˌvɜrsəfəˈkeɪʃən,
daɪˌvɜrsəfəˈkeɪʃən
diversify
BR daɪˈvɜːsɪfʌɪ, -z, -ɪŋ,
-d
AM dəˈvɜrsəˌfaɪ,
daɪˈvɜrsəˌfaɪ, -z, -ɪŋ, -d
diversion
BR daɪˈvɜːʃn, dɪˈvɜːʃn,
-z
AM dəˈvɜrʒən,
daɪˈvɜrʒən, -z
diversional
BR daɪˈvɜːʃn(ə)l,
daɪˈvɜːʃən(ə)l,
dɪˈvɜːʃn(ə)l,
dɪˈvɜːʃən(ə)l
AM dəˈvɜrʒ(ə)nəl,
daɪˈvɜrʒ(ə)nəl
diversionary
BR daɪˈvɜːʃn(ə)ri,
dɪˈvɜːʃn(ə)ri
AM dəˈvɜrʒəˌneri,
daɪˈvɜrʒəˌneri
diversionist
BR daɪˈvɜːʃnɪst,
daɪˈvɜːʃənɪst,
dɪˈvɜːʃnɪst,
dɪˈvɜːʃənɪst, -s
AM dəˈvɜrʒənəst,
daɪˈvɜrʒənəst, -s
diversity
BR daɪˈvɜːsɪt|i,
dɪˈvɜːsɪt|i, -ɪz
AM dəˈvɜrsədi,
daɪˈvɜrsədi, -z
divert
BR daɪˈvɜːt, dɪˈvɜːt, -s,
-ɪŋ, -ɪd

AM dəˈvɜr|t, daɪˈvɜr|t,
-ts, -dɪŋ, -dəd
diverticula
BR ˌdaɪvəˈtɪkjələ(r)
AM ˌdaɪvərˈtɪkjələ
diverticular
BR ˌdaɪvəˈtɪkjələ(r)
AM ˌdaɪvərˈtɪkjələr
diverticulitis
BR ˌdaɪvətɪkjʊˈlʌɪtɪs
AM ˌdaɪvərˌtɪkjəˈlaɪdəs
diverticulosis
BR ˌdaɪvətɪkjʊˈləʊsɪs
AM ˌdaɪvərˌtɪkjəˈlousəs
diverticulum
BR ˌdaɪvəˈtɪkjʊləm
AM ˌdaɪvərˈtɪkjələm
divertimenti
BR dɪˌvɜːtɪˈmenti:
AM dəˌvɜrdəˈmen(t)i
divertimento
BR dɪˌvɜːtɪˈmentəʊ, -z
AM dəˌvɜrdəˈmen(t)ou,
-z
divertingly
BR daɪˈvɜːtɪŋli,
dɪˈvɜːtɪŋli
AM dəˈvɜrdɪŋli,
daɪˈvɜrdɪŋli
divertissement
BR ˌdiːvɛːˈtiːsmɒ̃,
dɪˈvɜːtɪsm(ə)nt, -s
AM dəˈvɜrdəsmənt, -s
Dives
BR ˈdʌɪviːz
AM ˈdaɪˌviz
divest
BR daɪˈvɛst, dɪˈvɛst, -s,
-ɪŋ, -ɪd
AM daɪˈvɛst, dəˈvɛst, -s,
-ɪŋ, -əd
divestiture
BR daɪˈvɛstɪtʃə(r),
dɪˈvɛstɪtʃə(r)
AM daɪˈvɛstəˌtʃ(ʊ)ər,
dəˈvɛstəˌtʃ(ʊ)ər
divestment
BR daɪˈvɛs(t)m(ə)nt,
dɪˈvɛs(t)m(ə)nt, -s
AM daɪˈvɛstmənt,
dəˈvɛstmənt, -s
divesture
BR daɪˈvɛstʃə(r),
dɪˈvɛstʃə(r)
AM daɪˈvɛstʃ(ʊ)ər,
dəˈvɛstʃ(ʊ)ər
divi
BR ˈdɪv|i, -ɪz
AM ˈdɪvi, -z
divide
BR dɪˈvʌɪd, -z, -ɪŋ, -ɪd
AM dəˈvaɪd, -z, -ɪŋ, -ɪd
dividend
BR ˈdɪvɪdɛnd,
ˈdɪvɪd(ə)nd, -z
AM ˈdɪvəˌdɛnd, -z

divider
BR dɪˈvʌɪdə(r), -z
AM dəˈvaɪdər, -z
divi-divi
BR ˌdɪvɪˈdɪv|i, -ɪz
AM ˈdivi'dɪvi, -z
divination
BR ˌdɪvɪˈneɪʃn, -z
AM ˌdɪvəˈneɪʃən, -z
divinatory
BR dɪˈvɪnət(ə)ri
AM dəˈvɪnəˌtori,
ˈdɪvɪnəˌtori,
dəˈvaɪnəˌtori
divine
BR dɪˈvʌɪn, -ə(r), -ɪst
AM dəˈvaɪn, -ər, -ɪst
divinely
BR dɪˈvʌɪnli
AM dəˈvaɪnli
divineness
BR dɪˈvʌɪnnɪs
AM dəˈvaɪ(n)nɪs
diviner
BR dɪˈvʌɪnə(r), -z
AM dəˈvaɪnər, -z
divingboard
BR ˈdaɪvɪŋbɔːd, -z
AM ˈdaɪvɪŋˌbɔ(ə)rd, -z
divinity
BR dɪˈvɪnɪti
AM dəˈvɪnɪdi, -z
divinize
BR ˈdɪvɪnʌɪz, -ɪz, -ɪŋ, -d
AM ˈdɪvɪˌnaɪz, -əz, -ɪŋ,
-d
Divis
BR ˈdɪvɪs
AM ˈdɪvɪs
divisi
BR dɪˈviːsi
AM dəˈvisi
divisibility
BR dɪˌvɪzɪˈbɪlɪti
AM dəˌvɪzəˈbɪlɪdi
divisible
BR dɪˈvɪzɪbl
AM dəˈvɪzəbəl
divisibly
BR dɪˈvɪzɪbli
AM dəˈvɪzəbli
division
BR dɪˈvɪʒn, -z
AM dəˈvɪʒən, -z
divisional
BR dɪˈvɪʒn(ə)l,
dɪˈvɪʒən(ə)l
AM dəˈvɪʒ(ə)nəl
divisionally
BR dɪˈvɪʒnəli, dɪˈvɪʒnli,
dɪˈvɪʒən(ə)li,
dɪˈvɪʒ(ə)nəli
AM dəˈvɪʒəˌneri
divisionary
BR dɪˈvɪʒn(ə)ri
AM dəˈvɪʒəˌneri

divisionism
BR dɪˈvɪʒnɪz(ə)m,
dɪˈvɪʒənɪz(ə)m
AM dəˈvɪʒəˌnɪzəm
divisive
BR dɪˈvʌɪsɪv
AM dəˈvaɪsɪv, dɪˈvɪzɪv
divisively
BR dɪˈvʌɪsɪvli
AM dəˈvaɪsɪvli,
dɪˈvɪzɪvli
divisiveness
BR dɪˈvʌɪsɪvnɪs
AM dəˈvaɪsɪvnɪs,
dɪˈvɪzɪvnɪs
divisor
BR dɪˈvʌɪzə(r), -z
AM dəˈvaɪzər, -z
divorce
BR dɪˈvɔːs, -ɪz, -ɪŋ, -t
AM dəˈvɔ(ə)rs, -əz, -ɪŋ,
-t
divorcé
BR dɪˌvɔːˈsiː, ˌdɪvɔːˈsiː,
-z
AM dəˌvorˈseɪ, -z
divorcée
BR dɪˌvɔːˈsiː, ˌdɪvɔːˈsiː,
-z
AM dəˌvorˈseɪ,
dəˈvɔrˌsi, -z
divorcement
BR dɪˈvɔːsm(ə)nt
AM dəˈvɔrsmənt
divot
BR ˈdɪvət, -s
AM ˈdɪvət, -s
divulgation
BR ˌdaɪvʌlˈgeɪʃn,
ˌdɪvʌlˈgeɪʃn
AM ˌdaɪˌvəlˈgeɪʃən,
dəˌvəlˈgeɪʃən,
ˌdɪvəlˈgeɪʃən
divulge
BR daɪˈvʌldʒ, dɪˈvʌldʒ,
-ɪz, -ɪŋ, -d
AM dəˈvəldʒ, daɪˈvəldʒ,
-əz, -ɪŋ, -d
divulgement
BR daɪˈvʌldʒm(ə)nt,
dɪˈvʌldʒm(ə)nt
AM dəˈvəldʒmənt,
daɪˈvəldʒmənt
divulgence
BR daɪˈvʌldʒ(ə)ns,
dɪˈvʌldʒ(ə)ns
AM dəˈvəldʒəns,
daɪˈvəldʒəns
divvy
BR ˈdɪv|i, -ɪz
AM ˈdɪvi, -z
Diwali
BR dɪˈwɑːli
AM dəˈwɑli
Dixey
BR ˈdɪksi
AM ˈdɪksi

dixie
BR ˈdɪks|i, -ɪz
AM ˈdɪksi, -z
Dixieland
BR ˈdɪksɪland
AM ˈdɪksiˌlænd
Dixon
BR ˈdɪksn
AM ˈdɪksən
dizzily
BR ˈdɪzɪli
AM ˈdɪzɨli
dizziness
BR ˈdɪzɪnɪs
AM ˈdɪzɪnɪs
dizzy
BR ˈdɪz|i, -ɪə(r), -ɪɪst
AM ˈdɪzi, -ər, -ɪst
Djakarta
BR dʒəˈkɑːtə(r)
AM dʒəˈkɑrdə
djellaba
BR ˈdʒɛləbə(r),
dʒəˈlɑːbə(r), -z
AM dʒəˈlɑbə, -z
djellabah
BR ˈdʒɛləbə(r),
dʒəˈlɑːbə(r), -z
AM dʒəˈlɑbə, -z
Djerba
BR ˈdʒɜːbə(r)
AM ˈdʒɜrbə
djibah
BR ˈdʒɪbə(r), -z
AM ˈdʒɪbə, -z
djibba
BR ˈdʒɪbə(r), -z
AM ˈdʒɪbə, -z
Djibouti
BR dʒɪˈbuːti
AM dʒəˈbudi
Djiboutian
BR dʒɪˈbuːtɪən, -z
AM dʒəˈbudiən, -z
djinn
BR dʒɪn, -z
AM dʒɪn, -z
D.Litt.
Doctor of Literature
BR ˌdiːˈlɪt, -s
AM ˌdiˈlɪt, -s
D.Mus.
Doctor of Music
BR ˌdiːˈmʌz, -ɪz
AM ˌdiˈmjuz, -əz
Dnieper
BR ˈ(d)niːpə(r)
AM ˈnipər, dəˈnjɛpər
Dniester
BR ˈ(d)niːstə(r)
AM ˈnistər, dəˈnjɛstər
do
BR duː
AM du, dou
doable
BR ˈduːəbl
AM ˈduəbəl

dob
BR dɒb, -z, -ɪŋ, -d
AM dɑb, -z, -ɪŋ, -d
dobbin
BR ˈdɒbɪn
AM ˈdɑbən
dobe
BR ˈdəʊb|i, -ɪz
AM ˈdoʊbi, -z
Dobell
BR dəʊˈbɛl
AM doʊˈbɛl
Dobermann
BR ˈdəʊbəmən, -z
AM ˈdoʊbərmən, -z
Dobson
BR ˈdɒbsn
AM ˈdɑbsən
doc
BR dɒk, -s
AM dɑk, -s
docent
BR ˈdəʊs(ə)nt, -s
AM ˈdoʊsənt, -s
Docetae
BR dəˈ(ʊ)ˈsiːtiː
AM doʊˈsidi
Docetic
BR dəˈ(ʊ)ˈsiːtɪk
AM doʊˈsidɪk
Docetism
BR dəˈ(ʊ)ˈsiːtɪz(ə)m
AM doʊˈsiˌtɪzəm
Docetist
BR dəˈ(ʊ)ˈsiːtɪst, -s
AM doʊˈsidɪst, -s
doch-an-dorris
BR ˌdɒx(ə)nˈdɒrɪs,
ˌdɒk(ə)nˈdɒrɪs, -ɪz
AM ˌdɑkənˈdɔrəs, -əz
Docherty
BR ˈdɒxəti, ˈdɒkəti
AM ˈdɑkərdi
docile
BR ˈdəʊsʌɪl
AM ˈdɑsəl, ˈdoʊˌsaɪl
docilely
BR ˈdəʊsʌɪlli
AM ˈdɑsə(l)li
docility
BR dəˈ(ʊ)ˈsɪlɨti
AM dɑˈsɪlɨdi
dock
BR dɒk, -s, -ɪŋ, -t
AM dɑk, -s, -ɪŋ, -t
dockage
BR ˈdɒkɪdʒ
AM ˈdɑkɪdʒ
docker
BR ˈdɒkə(r), -z
AM ˈdɑkər, -z
docket
BR ˈdɒk|ɪt, -s, -ɪtɪŋ, -ɪtɪd
AM ˈdɑkət, -s, -ɪŋ, -əd
dockland
BR ˈdɒklənd,
ˈdɒkland, -z

AM ˈdɑkˌlænd, -z
dockominium
BR ˌdɒkəˈmɪnɪəm, -z
AM ˌdɑkəˈmɪniəm, -z
dockside
BR ˈdɒksʌɪd, -z
AM ˈdɑkˌsaɪd, -z
dockyard
BR ˈdɒkjɑːd, -z
AM ˈdɑkˌjɑrd, -z
doctor
BR ˈdɒkt|ə(r), -əz,
-(ə)rɪŋ, -əd
AM ˈdɑkt|ər, -ərz,
-(ə)rɪŋ, -ərd
doctoral
BR ˈdɒkt(ə)rəl,
ˈdɒkt(ə)rl
AM ˈdɑkt(ə)rəl
doctorate
BR ˈdɒkt(ə)rət, -s
AM ˈdɑkt(ə)rət, -s
doctorhood
BR ˈdɒktəhʊd
AM ˈdɑktər(h)ʊd
doctorial
BR dɒkˈtɔːrɪəl
AM dɑkˈtɔriəl
doctorly
BR ˈdɒktəli
AM ˈdɑktərli
doctorship
BR ˈdɒktəʃɪp, -s
AM ˈdɑktərˌʃɪp, -s
doctrinaire
BR ˌdɒktrɪˈnɛː(r)
AM ˌdɑktrəˈnɛ(ə)r
doctrinairism
BR ˌdɒktrɪˈnɛːrɪz(ə)m
AM ˌdɑktrəˈnɛˌrɪzəm
doctrinal
BR dɒkˈtrʌɪnl
AM ˈdɑktrənl,
dɑkˈtraɪnəl
doctrinally
BR dɒkˈtrʌɪnḷi,
dɒkˈtrʌɪnəli
AM ˈdɑktrənəli,
dɑkˈtraɪnəli
doctrinarian
BR ˌdɒktrɪˈnɛːrɪən
AM ˌdɑktrəˈnɛriən
doctrine
BR ˈdɒktr(ɪ)n, -z
AM ˈdɑktrən, -z
doctrinism
BR ˈdɒktrɪnɪz(ə)m
AM ˈdɑktrəˌnɪzəm
doctrinist
BR ˈdɒktrɪnɪst, -s
AM ˈdɑktrənəst, -s
docudrama
BR ˈdɒkjʊˌdrɑːmə(r),
-z
AM ˈdɑkjəˌdrɑmə, -z

AM ˈdɑkˌlænd, -z
document[1]
noun
BR ˈdɒkjʊm(ə)nt, -s
AM ˈdɑkjəmənt, -s
document[2]
verb
BR ˈdɒkjʊmɛnt, -s, -ɪŋ,
-ɪd
AM ˈdɑkjəˌmɛn|t, -ts,
-(t)ɪŋ, -(t)əd
documental
BR ˌdɒkjʊˈmɛntl
AM ˌdɑkjəˈmɛn(t)l
documentalist
BR ˌdɒkjʊˈmɛntəlɪst,
ˌdɒkjʊˈmɛntḷɪst, -s
AM ˌdɑkjəˈmɛn(t)ləst,
-s
documentarily
BR ˌdɒkjʊˈmɛnt(ə)rɪli
AM ˌdɑkjəˈmɛnt(ə)rəli,
ˌdɑkjəˈmɛn(t)ərəli
documentarist
BR ˌdɒkjʊˈmɛnt(ə)rɪst,
-s
AM ˌdɑkjəˈmɛnt(ə)rəst,
ˌdɑkjəˈmɛn(t)ərəst, -s
documentary
BR ˌdɒkjʊˈmɛnt(ə)r|i,
-ɪz
AM ˌdɑkjəˈmɛnt(ə)ri,
ˌdɑkjəˈmɛn(t)əri, -z
documentation
BR ˌdɒkjʊm(ə)nˈteɪʃn,
ˌdɒkjʊmɛnˈteɪʃn
AM ˌdɑkjəmənˈteɪʃən
Dodd
BR dɒd
AM dɑd
dodder
BR ˈdɒd|ə(r), -əz,
-(ə)rɪŋ, -əd
AM ˈdɑdər, -z, -ɪŋ, -d
dodderer
BR ˈdɒd(ə)rə(r), -z
AM ˈdɑdərər, -z
dodderiness
BR ˈdɒd(ə)rɪnɪs
AM ˈdɑdərɪnɪs
doddery
BR ˈdɒd(ə)ri
AM ˈdɑdəri
doddle
BR ˈdɒdl, -z
AM ˈdɑdəl, -z
Dodds
BR dɒdz
AM dɑdz
dodecagon
BR dəʊˈdɛkəɡɒn, -z
AM doʊˈdɛkəˌɡɑn, -z
dodecahedral
BR ˌdəʊdɛkəˈhiːdr(ə)l
AM doʊˌdɛkəˈhidrəl
dodecahedron
BR ˌdəʊdɛkəˈhiːdr(ə)n,
-z
AM doʊˌdɛkəˈhidrən,
-z

Dodecanese
BR ˌdəʊdɪkəˈniːz,
ˌdəʊdɪkəˈniːz
AM doʊˌdekəˈniz

dodecaphonic
BR ˌdəʊdekəˈfɒnɪk,
ˌdəʊdɪkəˈfɒnɪk
AM doʊˌdekəˈfɑnɪk

dodge
BR dɒdʒ, -ɪz, -ɪŋ, -d
AM dɑdʒ, -əz, -ɪŋ, -d

dodgem
BR ˈdɒdʒ(ə)m, -z
AM ˈdɑdʒəm, -z

dodger
BR ˈdɒdʒə(r), -z
AM ˈdɑdʒər, -z

dodgily
BR ˈdɒdʒɪli
AM ˈdɑdʒəli

dodginess
BR ˈdɒdʒɪnɪs
AM ˈdɑdʒɪnɪs

Dodgson
BR ˈdɒdʒsn
AM ˈdɑdʒsən

dodgy
BR ˈdɒdʒ|i, -ɪə(r), -ɪɪst
AM ˈdɑdʒi, -ər, -ɪst

dodo
BR ˈdəʊdəʊ, -z
AM ˈdoʊˌdoʊ, -z

Dodoma
BR ˈdəʊdəmə(r)
AM ˈdoʊdəmə,
doʊˈdamə

Dodson
BR ˈdɒdsn
AM ˈdɑdsən

doe
BR dəʊ, -z
AM doʊ, -z

doek
BR dʊk, -s
AM dʊk, -s

Doenitz
BR ˈdɜːnɪts
AM ˈdənɪts

doer
BR ˈduːə(r), -z
AM ˈduər, -z

does
from do
BR dʌz
AM dəz

doeskin
BR ˈdəʊskɪn, -z
AM ˈdoʊˌskɪn, -z

doesn't
BR ˈdʌznt
AM ˈdəznt

doest
BR ˈduːɪst
AM ˈduəst

doeth
BR ˈduːɪθ
AM ˈduəθ

doff
BR dɒf, -s, -ɪŋ, -t
AM dɔf, daf, -s, -ɪŋ, -t

dog
BR dɒg, -z, -ɪŋ, -d
AM dɔg, dag, -z, -ɪŋ, -d

dogberry
BR ˈdɒgb(ə)r|i, -ɪz
AM ˈdɔgˌbɛri, ˈdagˌbɛri,
-z

dogcart
BR ˈdɒgkɑːt, -s
AM ˈdɔgˌkɑrt,
ˈdagˌkɑrt, -s

dogcatcher
BR ˈdɒgˌkatʃə(r), -z
AM ˈdɔgˌkætʃər,
ˈdagˌkætʃər, -z

doge
BR dəʊ(d)ʒ, -ɪz
AM doʊʒ, -əz

dogface
BR ˈdɒgfeɪs, -ɪz
AM ˈdɔgˌfeɪs, ˈdagˌfeɪs,
-ɪz

dogfight
BR ˈdɒgfʌɪt, -s
AM ˈdɔgˌfaɪt, ˈdagˌfaɪt,
-s

dogfighter
BR ˈdɒgfʌɪtə(r), -z
AM ˈdɔgˌfaɪdər,
ˈdagˌfaɪdər, -z

dogfighting
BR ˈdɒgfʌɪtɪŋ
AM ˈdɔgˌfaɪdɪŋ,
ˈdagˌfaɪdɪŋ

dogfish
BR ˈdɒgfɪʃ, -ɪz
AM ˈdɔgˌfɪʃ, ˈdagˌfɪʃ, -ɪz

dogged
adjective
BR ˈdɒgɪd
AM ˈdɔgəd, ˈdagəd

doggedly
BR ˈdɒgɪdli
AM ˈdɔgədli, ˈdagədli

doggedness
BR ˈdɒgɪdnɪs
AM ˈdɔgədnəs,
ˈdagədnəs

dogger
BR ˈdɒgə(r), -z
AM ˈdɔgər, ˈdagər, -z

doggerel
BR ˈdɒg(ə)rəl,
ˈdɒg(ə)rl̩
AM ˈdɔg(ə)rəl,
ˈdag(ə)rəl

doggie
BR ˈdɒg|i, -ɪz
AM ˈdɔgi, ˈdagi, -z

dogginess
BR ˈdɒgɪnɪs
AM ˈdɔgɪnɪs, ˈdagɪnɪs

doggish
BR ˈdɒgɪʃ
AM ˈdɔgɪʃ, ˈdagɪʃ

doggishly
BR ˈdɒgɪʃli
AM ˈdɔgɪʃli, ˈdagɪʃli

doggishness
BR ˈdɒgɪʃnɪs
AM ˈdɔgɪʃnɪs,
ˈdagɪʃnɪs

doggo
BR ˈdɒgəʊ
AM ˈdɔgoʊ, ˈdagoʊ

doggone
BR ˈdɒgɒn
AM ˈdɔ(g)ˌgɒn,
ˈda(g)ˌgɑn

doggy
BR ˈdɒg|i, -ɪz
AM ˈdɔgi, ˈdagi, -z

doghouse
BR ˈdɒghaʊ|s, -zɪz
AM ˈdɔgˌ(h)aʊ|s,
ˈdagˌ(h)aʊ|s, -zəz

dogie
BR ˈdəʊg|i, -ɪz
AM ˈdoʊgi, -z

dogleg
BR ˈdɒgleg, -z
AM ˈdɔgˌlɛg, ˈdagˌlɛg, -z

doglike
BR ˈdɒglʌɪk
AM ˈdɔgˌlaɪk, ˈdagˌlaɪk

dogma
BR ˈdɒgmə(r), -z
AM ˈdɔgmə, ˈdagmə, -z

dogman
BR ˈdɒgmən, ˈdɒgman
AM ˈdɔgmən,
ˈdɔgˌmæn, ˈdagmən,
ˈdagˌmæn

dogmatic
BR dɒgˈmatɪk, -s
AM dɔgˈmædɪk,
dagˈmædɪk, -s

dogmatically
BR dɒgˈmatɪkli
AM dɔgˈmædək(ə)li,
dagˈmædək(ə)li

dogmatise
BR ˈdɒgmətʌɪz, -ɪz, -ɪŋ,
-d
AM ˈdɔgməˌtaɪz,
ˈdagməˌtaɪz, -ɪz, -ɪŋ, -d

dogmatism
BR ˈdɒgmətɪz(ə)m
AM ˈdɔgməˌtɪzəm,
ˈdagməˌtɪzəm

dogmatist
BR ˈdɒgmətɪst, -s
AM ˈdɔgmədəst,
ˈdagmədəst, -s

dogmatize
BR ˈdɒgmətʌɪz, -ɪz, -ɪŋ,
-d
AM ˈdɔgməˌtaɪz,
ˈdagməˌtaɪz, -ɪz, -ɪŋ, -d

dogmen
BR ˈdɒgmən, ˈdɒgmɛn
AM ˈdɔgmən, ˈdɔgˌmɛn,
ˈdagmən, ˈdagˌmɛn

do-gooder
BR ˌduːˈgʊdə(r), -z
AM ˌduˈgʊdər, -z

do-goodery
BR ˌduːˈgʊd(ə)ri
AM ˌduˈgʊdəri

do-goodism
BR ˌduːˈgʊdɪz(ə)m
AM ˌduˈgʊˌdɪzəm

dogsbody
BR ˈdɒgzbɒd|i, -ɪz
AM ˈdɔgzˌbadi,
ˈdagzˌbadi, -z

dogshore
BR ˈdɒgˌʃɔː(r), -z
AM ˈdɔgzˌʃɔ(ə)r, -z

dogskin
BR ˈdɒgskɪn
AM ˈdɔgzˌskɪn,
ˈdagzˌskɪn

dogtag
BR ˈdɒgtag, -z
AM ˈdɔgˌtæg, ˈdagˌtæg,
-z

dogteeth
BR ˈdɒgtiːθ
AM ˈdɔgˌtiθ, ˈdagˌtiθ

dogtooth
BR ˈdɒgtuːθ
AM ˈdɔgˌtuθ, ˈdagˌtuθ

dogtrot
BR ˈdɒgtrɒt
AM ˈdɔgˌtrɑt, ˈdagˌtrɑt

dogwatch
BR ˈdɒgwɒtʃ, -ɪz
AM ˈdɔgˌwɒtʃ,
ˈdagˌwɒtʃ, -əz

dogwood
BR ˈdɒgwʊd
AM ˈdɔgˌwʊd, ˈdagˌwʊd

doh
BR dəʊ
AM doʊ

Doha
BR ˈdəʊhɑ:(r), ˈdəʊə(r)
AM ˈdoʊˌhɑ

Doherty
BR ˈdɒxəti, ˈdɒhəti,
ˈdəʊəti
AM ˈdɔ(ə)rdi

doily
BR ˈdɔɪl|i, -ɪz
AM ˈdɔɪli, -z

doing
BR ˈduːɪŋ, -z
AM ˈduɪŋ, -z

doit
BR dɔɪt, -s
AM dɔɪt, -s

dojo
BR ˈdəʊdʒəʊ, -z
AM ˈdoʊˌdʒoʊ, -z

Dolan
BR ˈdəʊlən
AM ˈdoʊlən

Dolby®
BR ˈdɒlbi

AM 'doʊlbi, 'dɔlbi

dolce far niente
BR ˌdɒltʃɪ fɑ: nɪ'ɛnti,
ˌdɒltʃeɪ +, + nɪ'ɛnteɪ
AM ˌdoʊltʃə ˌfɑr
ni'ɛnti

Dolcelatte®
BR ˌdɒltʃɪ'lɑti(r)
AM ˌdoʊltʃə'lædi

dolce vita
BR ˌdɒltʃɪ 'vi:tə(r),
ˌdɒltʃeɪ +
AM ˌdoʊltʃə 'vidə

Dolcis®
BR 'dɒlsɪs
AM 'doʊlsəs

doldrums
BR 'dɒldrəmz,
'dəʊldrəmz
AM 'doʊldrəmz,
'dɑldrəmz

dole
BR dəʊl, -z, -ɪŋ, -d
AM doʊl, -z, -ɪŋ, -d

dole-bludger
BR 'dəʊlˌblʌdʒə(r), -z
AM 'doʊlˌblədʒər, -z

doleful
BR 'dəʊlf(ʊ)l
AM 'doʊlfəl

dolefully
BR 'dəʊlfʊli, 'dəʊlfli
AM 'doʊlfəli

dolefulness
BR 'dəʊlf(ʊ)lnəs
AM 'doʊlfəlnəs

dolerite
BR 'dɒlərʌɪt
AM 'dɑləˌraɪt

Dolgellau
BR dɒl'geɬi, dɒl'geθli,
dɒl'geɬʌɪ, dɒl'geθlʌɪ
AM dɔl'geɬi, dɑl'geɬi
WE dɒl'geɬaɪ

dolichocephalic
BR ˌdɒlɪkəʊsɪ'falɪk,
ˌdɒlɪkəʊkɛ'falɪk
AM ˌdɑləkoʊsə'fælɪk

dolichocephalous
BR ˌdɒlɪkəʊ'sɛf(ə)ləs,
ˌdɒlɪkəʊ'sɛfləs,
ˌdɒlɪkəʊ'kɛf(ə)ləs,
ˌdɒlɪkəʊ'kɛfləs
AM ˌdɑləkoʊ'sɛfələs

dolichocephaly
BR ˌdɒlɪkəʊ'sɛfəli,
ˌdɒlɪkəʊ'sɛfli,
ˌdɒlɪkəʊ'kɛfəli,
ˌdɒlɪkəʊ'kɛfli
AM ˌdɑləkoʊ'sɛfəli

dolichosauri
BR ˌdɒlɪkə(ʊ)'sɔːrʌɪ
AM ˌdɑləkə'sɔːˌraɪ

dolichosaurus
BR ˌdɒlɪkə'sɔːrəs, -ɪz
AM ˌdɑləkə'sɔːrəs, -əz

Dolin
BR 'dɒlɪn

AM 'doʊlən

dolina
BR də(ʊ)'li:nə(r), -z
AM də'linə, -z

doline
BR də(ʊ)'li:nə(r), -z
AM də'linə, -z

Dolittle
BR 'du:lɪtl
AM 'duˌlɪdəl

doll
BR dɒl, -z, -ɪŋ, -d
AM dɑl, -z, -ɪŋ, -d

dollar
BR 'dɒlə(r), -z
AM 'dɑlər, -z

Dollfuss
BR 'dɒlfəs
AM 'dɑlfəs

dollhouse
BR 'dɒlhaʊs, -zɪz
AM 'dɑlˌ(h)aʊ|s, -zəz

dollie
BR 'dɒl|i, -ɪz
AM 'dɑli, -z

Dollond
BR 'dɒlənd
AM 'dɒlənd, 'dɑlənd

dollop
BR 'dɒləp, -s
AM 'dɑləp, -s

dolly
BR 'dɒl|i, -ɪz
AM 'dɑli, -z

Dolly Varden
BR ˌdɒlɪ 'vɑːdn, -z
AM ˌdɑli 'vɑrdən, -z

dolma
BR 'dɒlmə(r)
AM 'dɑlmə

dolman
BR 'dɒlmən, -z
AM 'doʊlmən, -z

dolmen
BR 'dɒlmən, -z
AM 'doʊlmən, -z

Dolmetsch
BR 'dɒlmɛtʃ
AM 'dɔlˌmɛtʃ,
ˌdɑlˌmɛtʃ

dolomite
BR 'dɒləmʌɪt
AM 'dɑləˌmaɪt,
'doʊləˌmaɪt, -s

dolomitic
BR ˌdɒlə'mɪtɪk
AM ˌdɑlə'mɪdɪk,
ˌdoʊlə'mɪdɪk

dolor
BR 'dɒlə(r), -z
AM 'doʊlər, -z

Dolores
BR də'lɔːrɪs, də'lɔːrɪz
AM də'lɔrəs

doloroso
BR ˌdɒlə'rəʊsəʊ,
ˌdɒlə'rəʊzəʊ

AM ˌdoʊlə'roʊsoʊ

dolorous
BR 'dɒl(ə)rəs
AM 'doʊlərəs

dolorously
BR 'dɒl(ə)rəsli
AM 'doʊlərəsli

dolorousness
BR 'dɒl(ə)rəsnəs
AM 'doʊlərəsnəs

dolour
BR 'dɒlə(r), -z
AM 'doʊlər, -z

dolphin
BR 'dɒlfɪn, -z
AM 'dɔlfən, 'dɑlfən, -z

dolphinarium
BR ˌdɒlfɪ'nɛːrɪəm, -z
AM ˌdɔlfə'nɛriəm,
ˌdɑlfə'nɛriəm, -z

Dolphus
BR 'dɒlfəs
AM 'dɔlfəs, 'dɑlfəs

dolt
BR dəʊlt, -s
AM doʊlt, -s

doltish
BR 'dəʊltɪʃ
AM 'doʊltɪʃ

doltishly
BR 'dəʊltɪʃli
AM 'doʊltɪʃli

doltishness
BR 'dəʊltɪʃnɪs
AM 'doʊltɪʃnɪs

dom
BR dɒm, -z
AM dɑm, -z

domain
BR də(ʊ)'meɪn, -z
AM doʊ'meɪn,
də'meɪn, -z

domaine
BR də(ʊ)'meɪn, -z
AM doʊ'meɪn,
də'meɪn, -z

domanial
BR də(ʊ)'meɪnɪəl
AM doʊ'meɪnɪəl,
də'meɪnɪəl

Dombey
BR 'dɒmbi
AM 'dɔmbi, 'dɑmbi

dome
BR dəʊm, -z, -d
AM doʊm, -z, -d

domelike
BR 'dəʊmlʌɪk
AM 'doʊmˌlaɪk

Domesday
BR 'du:mzdeɪ
AM 'dumz,deɪ

domestic
BR də'mɛstɪk, -s
AM də'mɛstɪk, -s

domesticable
BR də'mɛstɪkəbl
AM də'mɛstəkəbəl

domestically
BR də'mɛstɪkli
AM də'mɛstək(ə)li

domesticate
BR də'mɛstɪkeɪt, -s, -ɪŋ,
-ɪd
AM də'mɛstəˌkeɪ|t, -ts,
-dɪŋ, -dɪd

domestication
BR dəˌmɛstɪ'keɪʃn
AM dəˌmɛstə'keɪʃən

domesticity
BR ˌdɒmɪ'stɪsɪti,
ˌdɒmɛ'stɪsɪti
AM ˌdoʊˌmɛ'stɪsɪdi

Domestos®
BR də'mɛstɒs
AM də'mɛstəs

domicile
BR 'dɒmɪsʌɪl, -z, -d
AM 'dɑməˌsaɪl,
'doʊməˌsaɪl,
'dæməsəl, -z, -d

domiciliary
BR ˌdɒmɪ'sɪl(ɪ)əri
AM ˌdɑmə'sɪliˌɛri,
ˌdoʊmə'sɪliˌɛri,
ˌdɑmə'sɪljəri,
ˌdoʊmə'sɪljəri

dominance
BR 'dɒmɪnəns
AM 'dɑmənəns

dominant
BR 'dɒmɪnənt
AM 'dɑmənənt

dominantly
BR 'dɒmɪnəntli
AM 'dɑmənən(t)li

dominate
BR 'dɒmɪneɪt, -s, -ɪŋ, -ɪd
AM 'dɑməˌneɪ|t, -ts,
-dɪŋ, -dɪd

domination
BR ˌdɒmɪ'neɪʃn
AM ˌdɑmə'neɪʃən

dominator
BR 'dɒmɪneɪtə(r), -z
AM 'dɑməˌneɪdər, -z

dominatrices
BR ˌdɒmɪ'neɪtrɪsi:z
AM ˌdɑmə'neɪtrəsiz

dominatrix
BR ˌdɒmɪ'neɪtrɪks, -ɪz
AM ˌdɑmə'neɪtrɪks, -ɪz

dominee
BR 'du:mɪni, 'dʊəmɪni
AM 'dumɪni

domineer
BR ˌdɒmɪ'nɪə(r), -z, -ɪŋ,
-d
AM ˌdɑmə'nɪ(ə)r, -z, -ɪŋ,
-d

domineeringly
BR ˌdɒmɪ'nɪərɪŋli
AM ˌdɑmə'nɪrɪŋli

Domingo
BR də'mɪŋgəʊ
AM də'mɪŋgoʊ
Dominic
BR 'dɒmɪnɪk
AM 'dɑmənɪk
Dominica
BR ˌdɒmɪ'niːkə(r),
də'mɪnɪkə(r)
AM ˌdɑmə'nikə
dominical
BR də'mɪnɪkl
AM də'mɪnɪkl
Dominican¹
of Dominica
BR ˌdɒmɪ'niːk(ə)n,
də'mɪnɪk(ə)n, -z
AM ˌdɑmə'nikən, -z
Dominican²
of the Dominican
Republic or religious
order
BR də'mɪnɪk(ə)n, -z
AM də'mɪnəkən, -z
Dominick
BR 'dɒmɪnɪk
AM 'dɒmənɪk,
'dɑmənɪk
dominie
BR 'dɒmɪn|i, -ɪz
AM 'dɑmən|i, -z
dominion
BR də'mɪnɪən, -z
AM də'mɪnjən, -z
Dominique
BR ˌdɒmɪ'niːk
AM ˌdɑmə'nik
domino
BR 'dɒmɪnəʊ, -z
AM 'dɑməˌnoʊ, -z
Domitian
BR də'(ʊ)mɪʃn,
də'(ʊ)mɪʃɪən
AM də'mɪʃən,
doʊ'mɪʃən
don
BR dɒn, -z, -ɪŋ, -d
AM dɑn, -z, -ɪŋ, -d
dona
BR 'dəʊnə(r), -z
AM 'dɑnə, 'doʊnə, -z
doña
BR 'dɒnjə(r)
AM 'dɑnjə, 'doʊnjə
donah
BR 'dəʊnə(r), -z
AM 'dɑnə, 'doʊnə, -z
Donahue
BR 'dɒnəhjuː
AM 'dɑnəˌhju
Donal
BR 'dəʊnl
AM 'dɒnəl, 'dɑnəl
Donald
BR 'dɒnld
AM 'dɒnəl(d),
'dɑnəl(d)

Donaldson
BR 'dɒnlds(ə)n
AM 'dɒnəl(d)sən,
'dɑnəl(d)sən
Donat
BR 'dəʊnat
AM 'doʊˌnɑt
donate
BR də(ʊ)'neɪt, -s, -ɪŋ, -ɪd
AM 'doʊˌneɪ|t,
doʊ'neɪ|t, -ts, -dɪŋ, -dɪd
Donatello
BR ˌdɒnə'tɛləʊ
AM ˌdɑnə'tɛloʊ
donation
BR də(ʊ)'neɪʃn, -z
AM doʊ'neɪʃən, -z
Donatism
BR 'dəʊnətɪz(ə)m
AM 'doʊnəˌtɪzəm,
'dɑnəˌtɪzəm
Donatist
BR 'dəʊnətɪst, -s
AM 'doʊnədəst,
'dɑnədəst, -s
donative
BR 'dəʊnətɪv, -z
AM 'doʊnədɪv,
'dɑnədɪv, -z
donator
BR də(ʊ)'neɪtə(r), -z
AM 'doʊˌneɪdər, -z
Donatus
BR də(ʊ)'neɪtəs
AM doʊ'nɑdəs
Donau
BR 'dəʊnaʊ
AM 'doʊˌnaʊ
Donbas
BR 'dɒnbas
AM 'dɑnˌbæs
Donbass
BR 'dɒnbass
AM 'dɑnˌbæs
Doncaster
BR 'dɒŋkəstə(r),
'dɒŋkɑːstə(r),
'dɒŋkɑːstə(r)
AM 'dɒnˌkæstər,
'dɑnˌkæstər
done
BR dʌn
AM dən
donee
BR dəʊ'niː, -z
AM doʊ'ni, -z
Donegal
BR ˌdɒnɪ'gɔːl
AM ˌdɑnə'gɔl,
ˌdɑnə'gɑl
Donelly
BR 'dɒnəli, 'dɒnˌli
AM 'dɒn(ə)li, 'dɑn(ə)li
Doner
BR 'dɒnə(r)
AM 'dɒnər, 'dɑnər
Donets Basin
BR də'nɛts 'beɪsn

AM də'nɛts 'beɪsn
Donetsk
BR də'nɛtsk
AM də'nɛtsk
dong
BR dɒŋ, -z
AM dɔŋ, dɑŋ, -z
donga
BR 'dɒŋgə(r), -z
AM 'dɑŋgə, 'dɔŋgə, -z
Don Giovanni
BR ˌdɒn dʒə(ʊ)'vaːni,
+ dʒə(ʊ)'vani
AM ˌdɑn dʒ(i)ə'vani,
ˌdɑn dʒ(i)ə'vani
dongle
BR 'dɒŋgl, -z
AM 'dɑŋgəl, -z
Donington
BR 'dɒnɪŋt(ə)n
AM 'dɒnɪŋtən,
'dɑnɪŋtən
Donizetti
BR ˌdɒnɪ'zeti
AM ˌdɑnə'zedi
IT donid'dzetti
donjon
BR 'dɒn(d)ʒ(ə)n,
'dʌn(d)ʒ(ə)n, -z
AM 'dɑndʒən,
'dəndʒən, -z
Don Juan
BR ˌdɒn 'dʒʊən,
+ '(h)waːn, -z
AM ˌdɑn '(h)wɑn, -z
donkey
BR 'dɒŋk|i, -ɪz
AM 'dɔŋki, 'dɑŋki, -z
donkeywork
BR 'dɒŋkɪwəːk
AM 'dɔŋki,wərk,
'dɑŋki,wərk
Donkin
BR 'dɒnkɪn
AM 'dɑnkən
Donleavy
BR dɒn'liːvi
AM 'dɒnˌlivi, 'dɑnˌlivi,
ˌdɒn'livi, ˌdɑn'livi
Donlevy
BR dɒn'liːvi
AM 'dɒnˌlivi, 'dɑnˌlivi,
ˌdɒn'livi, ˌdɑn'livi
donna
BR 'dɒnə(r), -z
AM 'dɑnə, -z
Donne
BR dʌn
AM dən
donné
BR 'dɒneɪ, -z
AM də'neɪ, -z
donnée
BR 'dɒneɪ, -z
AM də'neɪ, -z
Donnegan
BR 'dɒnɪg(ə)n

AM 'dɒnəgən,
'dɑnəgən
Donnell
BR 'dɒnl
AM 'dɒnəl, 'dɑnəl
Donnelly
BR 'dɒnəli, 'dɒnˌli
AM 'dɒn(ə)li, 'dɑn(ə)li
donnish
BR 'dɒnɪʃ
AM 'dɑnɪʃ
donnishly
BR 'dɒnɪʃli
AM 'dɑnɪʃli
donnishness
BR 'dɒnɪʃnɪs
AM 'dɑnɪʃnɪs
donnybrook
BR 'dɒnɪbrʊk, -s
AM 'dɑnɪˌbrʊk, -s
Donoghue
BR 'dɒnəhjuː
AM 'dɒnəˌhju,
'dɑnəˌhju
Donohoe
BR 'dɒnəhəʊ
AM 'dɒnəˌhoʊ,
'dɑnəˌhoʊ
Donohue
BR 'dɒnəhjuː
AM 'dɒnəˌhju,
'dɑnəˌhju
donor
BR 'dəʊnə(r), -z
AM 'doʊnər, -z
Donovan
BR 'dɒnəv(ə)n
AM 'dɑnəvən
Don Pasquale
BR ˌdɒn pa'skaːleɪ,
+ pa'skwaːli
AM ˌdɒn pas'kwɑli,
ˌdɑn pas'kwɑli
Don Quixote
BR ˌdɒn 'kwɪksət,
+ kɪ'(h)əʊti
AM ˌdɑn ki'hoʊdi,
+ 'kwɪksət
don't
BR dəʊnt
AM doʊnt
donut
BR 'dəʊnʌt, -s
AM 'doʊˌnət, -s
doodad
BR 'duːdad, -z
AM 'duˌdæd, -z
doodah
BR 'duːdɑː(r), -z
AM 'duˌdɑ, -z
doodle
BR 'duːd|l, -lz, -lɪŋ \-lɪŋ,
-ld
AM 'dud(ə)l, -əlz, -(ə)lɪŋ,
-əld
doodlebug
BR 'duːdlbʌg, -z
AM 'dudlˌbəg, -z

doodler
BR ˈduːdlə(r),
ˈduːdlə(r), -z
AM ˈdud(ə)lər, -z

doodling
BR ˈduːdlɪŋ, ˈduːdlɪŋ,
-z
AM ˈdudlɪŋ, ˈdudlɪŋ, -z

doohickey
BR ˈduːˌhɪkˌi, -ɪz
AM ˈduˌhɪki, -z

Doolan
BR ˈduːlən
AM ˈdulən

Dooley
BR ˈduːli
AM ˈduli

Doolittle
BR ˈduːlɪtl
AM ˈduˌlɪdəl

doom
BR duːm, -z, -ɪŋ, -d
AM dum, -z, -ɪŋ, -d

doomsday
BR ˈduːmzdeɪ
AM ˈdumzˌdeɪ

doomster
BR ˈduːmstə(r), -z
AM ˈdumstər, -z

doomwatch
BR ˈduːmwɒtʃ, -ɪz
AM ˈdumˌwɑtʃ,
ˈdumˌwɒtʃ, -ə

doomwatcher
BR ˈduːmˌwɒtʃə(r), -z
AM ˈdumˌwɒtʃər,
ˈdumˌwɒtʃər, -z

Doone
BR duːn
AM dun

Doonesbury
BR ˈduːnzb(ə)ri
AM ˈdunzˌberi

door
BR dɔː(r), -z, -d
AM dɔ(ə)r, -z, -d

doorbell
BR ˈdɔːbɛl, -z
AM ˈdɔrˌbɛl, -z

doorcase
BR ˈdɔːkeɪs, -ɪz
AM ˈdɔrˌkeɪs, -ɪz

do-or-die
BR ˌduːɔːˈdaɪ
AM ˈduərˈdaɪ

doorframe
BR ˈdɔːfreɪm, -z
AM ˈdɔrˌfreɪm, -z

doorjamb
BR ˈdɔːdʒam, -z
AM ˈdɔrˌdʒæm, -z

doorkeeper
BR ˈdɔːˌkiːpə(r), -z
AM ˈdɔrˌkipər, -z

doorknob
BR ˈdɔːnɒb, -z
AM ˈdɔrˌnɑb, -z

doorknocker
BR ˈdɔːˌnɒkə(r), -z
AM ˈdɔrˌnɑkər, -z

doorman
BR ˈdɔːmən
AM ˈdɔrmən, ˈdɔrˌmæn

doormat
BR ˈdɔːmat, -s
AM ˈdɔrˌmæt, -s

doormen
BR ˈdɔːmən
AM ˈdɔrmən, ˈdɔrˌmən

doornail
BR ˈdɔːneɪl
AM ˈdɔrˌneɪl

doorplate
BR ˈdɔːpleɪt, -s
AM ˈdɔrˌpleɪt, -s

doorpost
BR ˈdɔːpəʊst, -s
AM ˈdɔrˌpoʊst, -s

doorstep
BR ˈdɔːstɛp, -s, -ɪŋ, -t
AM ˈdɔrˌstɛp, -s, -ɪŋ, -t

doorstop
BR ˈdɔːstɒp, -s
AM ˈdɔrˌstɑp, -s

doorstopper
BR ˈdɔːˌstɒpə(r), -z
AM ˈdɔrˌstɑpər, -z

doorway
BR ˈdɔːweɪ, -z
AM ˈdɔrˌweɪ, -z

dooryard
BR ˈdɔːjɑːd, -z
AM ˈdɔrˌjɑrd, -z

doozy
BR ˈduːzˌi, -ɪz
AM ˈduzi, -z

dop
BR dɒp, -s
AM dɑp, -s

dopa
BR ˈdəʊpə(r)
AM ˈdoʊpə

dopamine
BR ˈdəʊpəmiːn
AM ˈdoʊpəˌmin

dopant
BR ˈdəʊp(ə)nt, -s
AM ˈdoʊpənt, -s

dope
BR dəʊp, -s, -ɪŋ, -t
AM doʊp, -s, -ɪŋ, -t

doper
BR ˈdəʊpə(r), -z
AM ˈdoʊpər, -z

dopesheet
BR ˈdəʊpʃiːt, -s
AM ˈdoʊpˌʃit, -s

dopester
BR ˈdəʊpstə(r), -z
AM ˈdoʊpstər, -z

dopey
BR ˈdəʊpˌi, -ɪə(r), -ɪɪst
AM ˈdoʊpi, -ər, -ɪst

dopiaza
BR ˈdəʊpiɑːzə(r),
ˌdəʊpiˈɑːzə(r)
AM ˌdoʊpiˈɑzə

dopily
BR ˈdəʊpɪli
AM ˈdoʊpəli

dopiness
BR ˈdəʊpɪnɪs
AM ˈdoʊpɪnɪs

doppelgänger
BR ˈdɒplˌgaŋə(r), -z
AM ˈdɑpəlˌgæŋər, -z

Dopper
BR ˈdɒpə(r), -z
AM ˈdɑpər, -z

Doppler
BR ˈdɒplə(r)
AM ˈdɑplər

dopy
BR ˈdəʊpˌi, -ɪə(r), -ɪɪst
AM ˈdoʊpi, -ər, -ɪst

Dora
BR ˈdɔːrə(r)
AM ˈdɔrə

Dorado
BR dəˈrɑːdəʊ
AM dəˈrɑdoʊ

Doran
BR ˈdɔːrən, ˈdɔːrn
AM ˈdɔrən

Dorcas
BR ˈdɔːkəs
AM ˈdɔrkəs

Dorchester
BR ˈdɔːtʃɛstə(r)
AM ˈdɔrˌtʃɛstər

Dordogne
BR dɔːˈdɔɪn
AM dɔrˈdoʊn
FR dɔRdɔɲ

Dordrecht
BR ˈdɔːdrɛkt, ˈdɔːdrɛxt
AM ˈdɔrˌdrɛkt

Doré
BR ˈdɔːreɪ
AM dɔˈreɪ

Doreen
BR ˈdɔːriːn, dəˈriːn
AM ˈdɔrin

Dorian
BR ˈdɔːrɪən
AM ˈdɔrɪən

Doric
BR ˈdɒrɪk
AM ˈdɔrɪk, ˈdɑrɪk

Dorinda
BR dəˈrɪndə(r)
AM dəˈrɪndə

Doris
BR ˈdɒrɪs
AM ˈdɔrəs

dork
BR dɔːk, -s
AM dɔ(ə)rk, -s

Dorking
BR ˈdɔːkɪŋ

AM ˈdɔrkɪŋ

dorm
BR dɔːm, -z
AM dɔ(ə)rm, -z

dormancy
BR ˈdɔːmənsi
AM ˈdɔrmənsi

dormant
BR ˈdɔːm(ə)nt
AM ˈdɔrmənt

dormer
BR ˈdɔːmə(r), -z
AM ˈdɔrmər, -z

dormice
BR ˈdɔːmaɪs
AM ˈdɔrˌmaɪs

dormition
BR dɔːˈmɪʃn
AM dɔrˈmɪʃən

dormitory
BR ˈdɔːmɪt(ə)rˌi, -ɪz
AM ˈdɔrməˌtɔri, -z

Dormobile®
BR ˈdɔːmə(ʊ)biːl, -z
AM ˈdɔrməˌbil, -z

dormouse
BR ˈdɔːmaʊs
AM ˈdɔrˌmaʊs

dormy
BR ˈdɔːmi
AM ˈdɔrmi

Dornoch
BR ˈdɔːnɒk, ˈdɔːnɒx,
ˈdɔːnək, ˈdɔːnəx
AM ˈdɔrnak

doronicum
BR dəˈrɒnɪkəm
AM dəˈrɑnəkəm

Dorothea
BR ˌdɒrəˈθɪə(r),
ˌdɒrəˈθiːə(r)
AM ˌdɔrəˈθiə

Dorothy
BR ˈdɒrəθi
AM ˈdɔrəθi

dorp
BR dɔːp, -s
AM dɔ(ə)rp, -s

Dors
BR dɔːz
AM dɔ(ə)rz

dorsa
BR ˈdɔːsə(r)
AM ˈdɔrsə

dorsal
BR ˈdɔːsl
AM ˈdɔrsəl

dorsally
BR ˈdɔːsˌli, ˈdɔːsəli
AM ˈdɔrsəli

Dorset
BR ˈdɔːsɪt
AM ˈdɔrsət

Dorsey
BR ˈdɔːsi
AM ˈdɔrsi

dorsiflex
BR 'dɔːsɪflɛks
AM 'dɔrsəˌflɛks

dorsum
BR 'dɔːsəm
AM 'dɔrsəm

Dortmund
BR 'dɔːtmənd,
'dɔːtmʊnd
AM 'dɔrtmənd

dory
BR 'dɔːr|i, -ɪz
AM 'dɔri, -z

DOS
BR dɒs
AM dɒs, das

do's
BR duːz
AM duz

dos-à-dos
BR ˌdəʊzɑːˈdəʊ, -z
AM ˌdoʊzəˈdoʊ, -z

dosage
BR 'dəʊs|ɪdʒ, -ɪdʒɪz
AM 'doʊsɪdʒ, -ɪz

dose
BR dəʊs, -ɪz, -ɪŋ, -t
AM doʊs, -əz, -ɪŋ, -t

do-se-do
BR ˌdəʊsɪˈdəʊ, -z
AM ˌdoʊˌsiˈdoʊ, -z

dosh
BR dɒʃ
AM dɑʃ

do-si-do
BR ˌdəʊsɪˈdəʊ, -z
AM ˌdoʊˌsiˈdoʊ, -z

dosimeter
BR dəʊˈsɪmɪtə(r)
AM doʊˈsɪmədər

dosimetric
BR ˌdəʊsɪˈmɛtrɪk
AM ˌdoʊsiˈmɛtrɪk

dosimetry
BR dəʊˈsɪmɪtri
AM doʊˈsɪmətri

Dos Passos
BR dɒs 'pasɒs
AM ˌdas 'pæˌsoʊs

doss
BR dɒs, -ɪz, -ɪŋ, -t
AM das, -əz, -ɪŋ, -t

dossal
BR 'dɒsl
AM 'dasəl

dosser
BR 'dɒsə(r), -z
AM 'dasər, -z

dosshouse
BR 'dɒshaʊ|s, -zɪz
AM 'dɔs,(h)aʊ|s,
'das,(h)aʊs, -zəz

dossier
BR 'dɒsɪə(r), 'dɒsɪeɪ, -z
AM 'dɔsiˌeɪ, 'dasiˌeɪ, -z

dost
BR dʌst

AM dəst

Dostoevsky
BR ˌdɒstɔɪˈɛfski
AM ˌdastəˈjɛfski,
ˌdɔstəˈjɛfski

Dostoyevsky
BR ˌdɒstɔɪˈɛfski
AM ˌdastəˈjɛfski,
ˌdɔstəˈjɛfski

dot
BR dɒt, -s, -ɪŋ, -ɪd
AM dɑ|t, -ts, -dɪŋ, -dəd

dotage
BR 'dəʊtɪdʒ
AM 'doʊdɪdʒ

dotard
BR 'dəʊtəd, -z
AM 'doʊdərd, -z

dote
BR dəʊt, -s, -ɪŋ, -ɪd
AM doʊ|t, -ts, -dɪŋ, -dəd

doter
BR 'dəʊtə(r), -z
AM 'doʊdər, -z

doth
BR dʌθ
AM dəθ, dɒθ, dɑθ

Dotheboys
BR 'duːðəbɔɪz
AM 'duðəˌbɔɪz

dotingly
BR 'dəʊtɪŋli
AM 'doʊdɪŋli

Dotrice
BR də'triːs, dɒ'triːs
AM 'datrəs

Dotson
BR 'dɒtsn
AM 'datsən

dotter
BR 'dɒtə(r), -z
AM 'dadər, -z

dotterel
BR 'dɒtr(ə)l, -z
AM 'datrəl, -z

dottily
BR 'dɒtɪli
AM 'dadəli

dottiness
BR 'dɒtɪnɪs
AM 'dadinɪs

dottle
BR 'dɒtl
AM 'dadəl

dotty
BR 'dɒt|i, -ɪə(r), -ɪɪst
AM 'dadi, -ər, -ɪst

Douai[1]
French town
BR 'duːeɪ
AM du'eɪ
FR dwɛ

Douai[2]
BR 'daʊeɪ, 'daʊi
AM du'eɪ

Douala
BR duːˈɑːlə(r)

AM duː'(w)ɑlə

douane
BR duːˈɑːn, -z
AM dwɑn, -z

Douay
BR 'daʊeɪ, 'daʊi, 'duːeɪ
AM dwaɪ, du'eɪ

double
BR 'dʌb|l, -lz, -|ɪŋ \-lɪŋ,
-ld
AM 'dəb|əl, -əlz, -(ə)lɪŋ,
-əld

Doubleday
BR 'dʌbldeɪ
AM 'dəblˌdeɪ

double entendre
BR ˌduːbl
ɒn'tɒndrə(r),
+ ɒ̃'tɒ̃drə(r)
AM ˌdubəˌlanˈtandrə

double-ganger
BR 'dʌblˌɡaŋə(r)
AM 'dəbəlˌgæŋ(g)ər

doubleheader
BR ˌdʌblˈhɛdə(r), -z
AM ˌdəbəlˈhɛdər, -z

doubleness
BR 'dʌblnəs
AM 'dəbəlnəs

doubler
BR 'dʌblə(r), -z
AM 'dəblər, -z

doublespeak
BR 'dʌblspiːk
AM 'dəbəlˌspik

doublet
BR 'dʌblɪt, -s
AM 'dəblət, -s

doublethink
BR 'dʌblθɪŋk
AM 'dəbəlˌθɪŋk

doubleton
BR 'dʌblt(ə)n, -z
AM 'dəbəltən, -z

doubletree
BR 'dʌbltriː, -z
AM 'dəbəlˌtri, -z

doubloon
BR də'bluːn, -z
AM də'blun, -z

doublure
BR də'blʊə(r),
duː'blʊə(r), -z
AM də'blʊ(ə)r, -z

doubly
BR 'dʌbli
AM 'dəbli

doubt
BR daʊt, -s, -ɪŋ, -ɪd
AM daʊ|t, -ts, -dɪŋ, -dəd

doubtable
BR 'daʊtəbl
AM 'daʊdəbəl

doubter
BR 'daʊtə(r), -z
AM 'daʊdər, -z

doubtful
BR 'daʊtf(ʊ)l
AM 'daʊtfəl

doubtfully
BR 'daʊtfəli, 'daʊtfli
AM 'daʊtfəli

doubtfulness
BR 'daʊtf(ʊ)lnəs
AM 'daʊtfəlnəs

doubtingly
BR 'daʊtɪŋli
AM 'daʊdɪŋli

doubtless
BR 'daʊtləs
AM 'daʊtləs

doubtlessly
BR 'daʊtləsli
AM 'daʊtləsli

douce
BR duːs
AM dus

douceur
BR duːˈsɜː(r), -z
AM du'sər, -z

douche
BR duːʃ, -ɪz
AM duʃ, -əz

Doug
BR dʌg
AM dəg

Dougal
BR 'dʊgl
AM 'dugəl

Dougall
BR 'duːgl
AM 'dugəl

Dougan
BR 'duːg(ə)n
AM 'dugən

dough
BR dəʊ
AM doʊ

doughboy
BR 'dəʊbɔɪ, -z
AM 'doʊˌbɔɪ, -z

Dougherty
BR 'dɒxəti, 'dɒkəti,
'dəʊəti
AM 'dɔrdi

doughiness
BR 'dəʊɪnɪs
AM 'doʊɪnɪs

doughnut
BR 'dəʊnʌt, -s
AM 'doʊˌnət, -s

doughtily
BR 'daʊtɪli
AM 'daʊdəli

doughtiness
BR 'daʊtɪnɪs
AM 'daʊdinɪs

doughty
BR 'daʊt|i, -ɪə(r), -ɪɪst
AM 'daʊdi, -ər, -ɪst

doughy
BR 'dəʊ|i, -ɪə(r), -ɪɪst
AM 'doʊi, -ər, -ɪst

Dougie
BR ˈdʌgi
AM ˈdɒgi
Douglas¹
BR ˈdʌgləs
AM ˈdɒgləs
Douglas²
traditionally
BR ˈduːgləs
AM ˈdɒgləs
Douglass
BR ˈdʌgləs
AM ˈdɒgləs
Doulton®
BR ˈdəʊlt(ə)n
AM ˈdɔːltən, ˈdoʊltən
doum
BR duːm, -z
AM dum, daʊm, -z
Dounreay
BR ˌduːnˈreɪ
AM ˌdunˈreɪ
dour
BR ˈdʊə(r), daʊə(r)
AM ˈdaʊ(ə)r, ˈdʊ(ə)r
dourly
BR ˈdʊəli, ˈdaʊəli
AM ˈdaʊ(ə)rli, ˈdʊrli
dourness
BR ˈdʊənəs, ˈdaʊənəs
AM ˈdaʊ(ə)rnəs, ˈdʊrnəs
Douro
BR ˈdʊərəʊ
AM ˈduˌroʊ
PORT ˈdoru
douroucouli
BR ˌdʊərʊˈkuːlʲi, -ɪz
AM ˌdʊrəˈkuli, -z
douse
BR daʊs, -ɪz, -ɪŋ, -t
AM daʊ|s, daʊ|z, -sɪz\-zɪz, -sɪŋ\-zɪŋ, -st\-zd
dove¹
bird
BR dʌv, -z
AM dəv, -z
dove²
past tense of dive
BR dəʊv
AM doʊv
dovecote
BR ˈdʌvkɒt, ˈdʌvkəʊt, -s
AM ˈdəvˌkoʊt, -s
Dovedale
BR ˈdʌvdeɪl
AM ˈdəvˌdeɪl
dovelike
BR ˈdʌvlaɪk
AM ˈdəvˌlaɪk
Dover
BR ˈdəʊvə(r)
AM ˈdoʊvər
Dovercourt
BR ˈdəʊvəkɔːt
AM ˈdoʊvərˌkɔː(ə)rt

Doveridge
BR ˈdʌv(ə)rɪdʒ
AM ˈdoʊvərɪdʒ, ˈdəvərɪdʒ
dovetail
BR ˈdʌvteɪl, -z, -ɪŋ, -d
AM ˈdəvˌteɪl, -z, -ɪŋ, -d
Dovey
BR ˈdʌvi
AM ˈdəvi
Dow
BR daʊ
AM daʊ
dowager
BR ˈdaʊɪdʒə(r), -z
AM ˈdaʊədʒər, -z
dowdily
BR ˈdaʊdɪli
AM ˈdaʊdəli
dowdiness
BR ˈdaʊdɪnɪs
AM ˈdaʊdinɪs
Dowding
BR ˈdaʊdɪŋ
AM ˈdaʊdɪŋ
dowdy
BR ˈdaʊd|i, -iə(r), -iɪst
AM ˈdaʊdi, -ər, -ɪst
dowel
BR ˈdaʊ(ə)l, -z, -ɪŋ
AM ˈdaʊ(ə)l, -z, -ɪŋ
Dowell
BR ˈdaʊ(ə)l
AM ˈdaʊəl
dower
BR ˈdaʊə(r), -z, -ɪŋ, -d
AM ˈdaʊər, -z, -ɪŋ, -d
dowerless
BR ˈdaʊələs
AM ˈdaʊərləs
Dowlais
BR ˈdaʊlaɪs, ˈdaʊləs
AM ˈdaʊləs
Dowland
BR ˈdaʊlənd
AM ˈdaʊlən(d)
Dowling
BR ˈdaʊlɪŋ
AM ˈdaʊlɪŋ
down
BR daʊn, -z, -ɪŋ, -d
AM daʊn, -z, -ɪŋ, -d
down-and-out¹
adjective
BR ˌdaʊnən(d)ˈaʊt
AM ˌdaʊnənˈaʊt
down-and-out²
noun
BR ˈdaʊnən(d)aʊt, -s
AM ˈdaʊnənˌaʊt, -s
downbeat
BR ˈdaʊnbiːt, -s
AM ˈdaʊnˌbit, -s
downcast
BR ˈdaʊnkɑːst, ˈdaʊnkast
AM ˈdaʊnˌkæst

downcomer
BR ˈdaʊnˌkʌmə(r), -z
AM ˈdaʊnˌkəmər, -z
downdraft
BR ˈdaʊndrɑːft, ˈdaʊndraft, -s
AM ˈdaʊnˌdræft, -s
downer
BR ˈdaʊnə(r), -z
AM ˈdaʊnər, -z
Downes
BR daʊnz
AM daʊnz
Downey
BR ˈdaʊni
AM ˈdaʊni
downfall
BR ˈdaʊnfɔːl, -z
AM ˈdaʊnˌfɔl, ˈdaʊnˌfɑl, -z
downfold
BR ˈdaʊnfəʊld, -z
AM ˈdaʊnˌfoʊld, -z
downgrade
verb
BR ˌdaʊnˈgreɪd
ˈdaʊngreɪd, -z, -ɪŋ, -ɪd
AM ˈdaʊnˌgreɪd, -z, -ɪŋ, -ɪd
down grade
noun
BR ˈdaʊn greɪd, -z
AM ˈdaʊn ˌgreɪd, -z
Downham
BR ˈdaʊnəm
AM ˈdaʊnəm
downhaul
BR ˈdaʊnhɔːl, -z
AM ˈdaʊnˌ(h)ɔl, ˈdaʊnˌ(h)ɑl, -z
downhearted
BR ˌdaʊnˈhɑːtɪd
AM ˈdaʊnˌhɑrdəd
downheartedly
BR ˌdaʊnˈhɑːtɪdli
AM ˈdaʊnˌhɑrdədli
downheartedness
BR ˌdaʊnˈhɑːtɪdnɪs
AM ˈdaʊnˌhɑrdədnəs
downhill
BR ˌdaʊnˈhɪl
AM ˈdaʊnˌhɪl
downhiller
BR ˈdaʊnˌhɪlə(r), -z
AM ˈdaʊnˌ(h)ɪlər, -z
Downie
BR ˈdaʊni
AM ˈdaʊni
downily
BR ˈdaʊnɪli
AM ˈdaʊnəli
downiness
BR ˈdaʊnɪnɪs
AM ˈdaʊninɪs
Downing
BR ˈdaʊnɪŋ
AM ˈdaʊnɪŋ

downland
BR ˈdaʊnland, ˈdaʊnlənd, -z
AM ˈdaʊnˌlænd, -z
downlighter
BR ˈdaʊnˌlaɪtə(r), -z
AM ˈdaʊnˌlaɪdər, -z
download
BR ˈdaʊnˈləʊd, ˈdaʊnləʊd, -z, -ɪŋ, -ɪd
AM ˈdaʊnˈloʊd, -z, -ɪŋ, -əd
downmarket
BR ˌdaʊnˈmɑːkɪt
AM ˈdaʊnˌmɑrkət
downmost
BR ˈdaʊnməʊst
AM ˈdaʊnˌmoʊst
Downpatrick
BR ˌdaʊnˈpatrɪk
AM ˌdaʊnˈpætrək
downpipe
BR ˈdaʊnpʌɪp, -s
AM ˈdaʊnˌpaɪp, -s
downplay
BR ˌdaʊnˈpleɪ, -z, -ɪŋ, -d
AM ˈdaʊnˌpleɪ, -z, -ɪŋ, -d
downpour
BR ˈdaʊnpɔː(r), -z
AM ˈdaʊnˌpɔ(ə)r, -z
downright
BR ˈdaʊnrʌɪt
AM ˈdaʊnˌraɪt
downrightness
BR ˈdaʊnrʌɪtnɪs
AM ˈdaʊnˌraɪtnɪs
downriver
BR ˌdaʊnˈrɪvə(r)
AM ˈdaʊnˈrɪvər
Downs
BR daʊnz
AM daʊnz
downscale
BR ˌdaʊnˈskeɪl, -z, -ɪŋ, -d
AM ˈdaʊnˌskeɪl, -z, -ɪŋ, -d
downshaft
BR ˈdaʊnʃɑːft, ˈdaʊnʃaft, -s, -ɪŋ, -ɪd
AM ˈdaʊnˌʃæft, -s, -ɪŋ, -əd
downshift
BR ˈdaʊnʃɪft, -s, -ɪŋ, -ɪd
AM ˈdaʊnˌʃɪft, -s, -ɪŋ, -ɪd
downside
BR ˈdaʊnsʌɪd, -z
AM ˈdaʊnˌsaɪd, -z
downsize
BR ˈdaʊnˈsʌɪz, -ɪz, -ɪŋ, -d
AM ˈdaʊnˌsaɪz, -əz, -ɪŋ, -d
Downson
BR ˈdaʊns(ə)n
AM ˈdaʊnsən
downspout
BR ˈdaʊnspaʊt, -s

AM 'daʊn,spaʊt, -s

downstage
BR ,daʊn'steɪdʒ
AM ,daʊn'steɪdʒ

downstairs
BR ,daʊn'stɛːz
AM ,daʊn'stɛrz

downstate
BR ,daʊn'steɪt
AM ,daʊn'steɪt

downstream
BR ,daʊn'striːm
AM ,daʊn'strim

downstroke
BR 'daʊnstrəʊk, -s
AM 'daʊn,stroʊk, -s

downswing
BR 'daʊnswɪŋ, -z
AM 'daʊn,swɪŋ, -z

downthrew
BR ,daʊn'θruː
AM 'daʊn,θru

downthrow
BR ,daʊn'θrəʊ, -z, -ɪŋ
AM 'daʊn,θroʊ, -z, -ɪŋ

downthrown
BR ,daʊn'θrəʊn
AM 'daʊn,θroʊn

downtime
BR 'daʊntʌɪm
AM 'daʊn,taɪm

downtown
BR ,daʊn'taʊn
AM ,daʊn'taʊn

downtrodden
BR 'daʊn,trɒdn
AM 'daʊn,trɑdən

downturn
BR 'daʊntəːn, -z
AM 'daʊn,tərn, -z

downward
BR 'daʊnwəd, -z
AM 'daʊnwərd, -z

downwardly
BR 'daʊnwədli
AM 'daʊnwərdli

downwards
BR 'daʊnwədz
AM 'daʊnwərdz

downwarp
BR 'daʊnwɔːp, -s
AM 'daʊnwɔ(ə)rp,-s

downwind
BR ,daʊn'wɪnd
AM ,daʊn'wɪnd

downy
BR 'daʊn|i, -ɪə(r), -ɪɪst
AM 'daʊni, -ər, -ɪst

dowry
BR 'daʊ(ə)r|i, -ɪz
AM 'daʊ(ə)ri, -z

dowse¹
to wet
BR daʊs, -ɪz, -ɪŋ, -t
AM daʊ|s, daʊ|z,
-səz\-zəz, -sɪŋ\-zɪŋ,
-st\-zd

dowse²
to search for water etc
BR daʊz, -ɪz, -ɪŋ, -d
AM daʊ|z, daʊ|s,
-zəz\-səz, -zɪŋ\-sɪŋ,
-zd\-st

dowser¹
water pourer
BR 'daʊsə(r), -z
AM 'daʊsər, 'daʊzər, -z

dowser²
water searcher
BR 'daʊzə(r), -z
AM 'daʊzər, 'daʊsər, -z

Dowsing
BR 'daʊzɪŋ
AM 'daʊzɪŋ

dowsing rod
BR 'daʊzɪŋ rɒd, -z
AM 'daʊzɪŋ ,rɑd,
'daʊsɪŋ +, -z

doxastic
BR dɒk'sastɪk
AM dɑk'sæstɪk

doxological
BR ,dɒksə'lɒdʒɪkl
AM ,dɑksə'lɑdʒəkəl

doxology
BR dɒk'sɒlədʒ|i, -ɪz
AM dɑk'sɑlədʒi, -z

doxy
BR 'dɒks|i, -ɪz
AM 'dɑksi, -z

doyen
BR 'dɔɪən, 'dɔɪɛn, -z
AM 'dɔɪ(j)ɛn, 'dɔjən, -z

doyenne
BR ,dɔɪ'ɛn, -z
AM ,dɔɪ(j)ɛn, dɔ'jɛn, -z

Doyle
BR dɔɪl
AM dɔɪl

doyley
BR 'dɔɪl|i, -ɪz
AM 'dɔɪli, -z

doyly
BR 'dɔɪl|i, -ɪz
AM 'dɔɪli, -z

D'Oyly Carte
BR ,dɔɪlɪ 'kɑːt
AM ,dɔɪli 'kɑrt

doze
BR dəʊz, -ɪz, -ɪŋ, -d
AM doʊz, -əz, -ɪŋ, -d

dozen
BR 'dʌzn, -z
AM 'dəzən, -z

dozenth
BR 'dʌznθ, -s
AM 'dəzənθ, -s

dozer
BR 'dəʊzə(r), -z
AM 'doʊzər, -z

dozily
BR 'dəʊzɪli
AM 'doʊzəli

doziness
BR 'dəʊzɪnɪs
AM 'doʊzɪnɪs

dozy
BR 'dəʊz|i, -ɪə(r), -ɪɪst
AM 'doʊzi, -ər, -ɪst

D.Phil.
Doctor of Philosophy
BR ,diː'fɪl
AM ,di 'fɪl

Dr
BR 'dɒktə(r), -z
AM 'dɑktər, -z

drab
BR drab, -z, -ə(r), -ɪst
AM dræb, -z, -ər, -əst

drabble
BR 'drab|l, -lz,
-lɪŋ\-lɪŋ, -ld
AM 'dræb|əl, -əld,
-(ə)lɪŋ, -əld

drably
BR 'drabli
AM 'dræbli

drabness
BR 'drabnəs
AM 'dræbnəs

drachm
BR dram, -z
AM dræm, -z

drachma
BR 'drakmə(r), -z
AM 'drɑkmə, -z

drachmae
BR 'drakmiː, 'drakmeɪ
AM 'drɑkmi, 'drɑkmeɪ

drack
BR drak
AM dræk

Draco
BR 'dreɪkəʊ
AM 'dreɪkoʊ, 'drɑkoʊ

draconian
BR drə'kəʊnɪən
AM drə'koʊnɪən,
dreɪ'koʊnɪən

draconic
BR drə'kɒnɪk
AM drə'kɑnɪk

draconically
BR drə'kɒnɪkli
AM drə'kɑnək(ə)li

Dracula
BR 'drakjələ(r)
AM 'dræ, kjələ

draff
BR draf
AM dræf

draft
BR drɑːft, draft, -s, -ɪŋ,
-ɪd
AM dræft, -s, -ɪŋ, -əd

draftee
BR ,drɑː'ftiː, ,draf'tiː, -z
AM ,dræf'ti, -z

drafter
BR 'drɑːftə(r),
'draftə(r), -z
AM 'dræftər, -z

drafthorse
BR 'drɑːfthɔːs,
'drafthɔːs, -ɪz
AM 'dræf(t),(h)ɔːrs,
-əz

draftily
BR 'drɑːftɪli, 'draftɪli
AM 'dræftəli

draftiness
BR 'drɑːftɪnɪs,
'draftɪnɪs
AM 'dræftɪnɪs

draftsman
BR 'drɑːf(t)smən,
'draf(t)smən
AM 'dræf(t)smən

draftsmanship
BR 'drɑːf(t)smənʃɪp,
'draf(t)smənʃɪp
AM 'dræf(t)smən,ʃɪp

draftsmen
BR 'drɑːf(t)smən,
'draf(t)smən
AM 'dræf(t)smən

draftswoman
BR 'drɑːf(t)s,wʊmən,
'draf(t)s,wʊmən
AM 'dræf(t)s,wʊmən

draftswomen
BR 'drɑːf(t)s,wɪmɪn,
'draf(t)s,wɪmɪn
AM 'dræf(t)s,wɪmɪn

drafty
BR 'drɑːft|i, 'draft|i,
-ɪə(r), -ɪɪst
AM 'dræfti, -ər, -ɪst

drag
BR drag, -z, -ɪŋ, -d
AM dræg, -z, -ɪŋ, -d

dragée
BR 'draʒeɪ, 'drɑːʒeɪ, -z
AM drɑ'ʒeɪ, -z

draggle
BR 'drag|l, -lz,
-lɪŋ\-lɪŋ, -ld
AM 'dræg|əl, -əld,
-(ə)lɪŋ, -əld

draggletail
BR 'draglteɪl, -z
AM 'drægəl,teɪl, -z

draggle-tailed
BR 'draglteɪld
AM 'drægəl,teɪld

draggy
BR 'drag|i, -ɪə(r), -ɪɪst
AM 'drægi, -ər, -ɪst

dragline
BR 'draglʌɪn, -z
AM 'dræg,laɪn, -z

dragnet
BR 'dragnɛt, -s
AM 'dræg,nɛt, -s

dragoman
BR 'dragə(ʊ)mən, -z
AM 'drægəmən, -z
dragon
BR 'drag(ə)n, -z
AM 'drægən, -z
dragonet
BR 'dragənɪt, 'dragn̩ɪt, -s
AM 'drægənət, -s
dragonfish
BR 'drag(ə)nfɪʃ, -z
AM 'drægən‚fɪʃ, -z
dragonfly
BR 'drag(ə)nflʌɪ, -z
AM 'drægən‚flaɪ, -z
dragonish
BR 'dragənɪʃ, 'dragn̩ɪʃ
AM 'drægənɪʃ
dragonlady
BR 'drag(ə)n‚leɪd|i, -ɪz
AM 'drægən‚leɪdi, -z
dragonnade
BR ‚dragə'neɪd, -z, -ɪŋ, -ɪd
AM ‚drægə'neɪd, -z, -ɪŋ, -ɪd
dragoon
BR drə'gu:n, -z, -ɪŋ, -d
AM drə'gun, dræ'gun, -z, -ɪŋ, -d
dragster
BR 'dragstə(r), -z
AM 'drægztər, 'drægstər, -z
drail
BR dreɪl, -z
AM dreɪl, -z
drain
BR dreɪn, -z, -ɪŋ, -d
AM dreɪn, -z, -ɪŋ, -d
drainage
BR 'dreɪnɪdʒ
AM 'dreɪnɪdʒ
drainboard
BR 'dreɪnbɔːd, -z
AM 'dreɪn‚bɔ(ə)rd, -z
draincock
BR 'dreɪnkɒk, -s
AM 'dreɪn‚kak, -s
drainer
BR 'dreɪnə(r), -z
AM 'dreɪnər, -z
drainpipe
BR 'dreɪnpʌɪp, -s
AM 'dreɪn‚paɪp, -s
drake
BR dreɪk, -s
AM dreɪk, -s
Drakensberg
BR 'drak(ə)nzbəːg
AM 'dreɪkənz‚bərg
Dralon®
BR 'dreɪlɒn
AM 'dreɪ‚lɑn

DRAM
dynamic random access memory
BR 'diːram
AM 'diːˌræm
dram
BR dram, -z
AM dræm, -z
drama
BR 'drɑːmə(r), -z
AM 'drɑmə, -z
dramadoc
BR ‚drɑːmə'dɒk, -s
AM 'drɑmə‚dak, -s
Dramamine®
BR 'dram
əmiːn, -z
AM 'dræmə‚min, -z
dramatic
BR drə'matɪk, -s
AM drə'mædɪk, -s
dramatically
BR drə'matɪkli
AM drə'mædək(ə)li
dramatisation
BR ‚dramətʌɪ'zeɪʃn, -z
AM ‚dramədə'zeɪʃən, ‚drɑmə‚tar'zeɪʃən, ‚dræmədə'zeɪʃən, ‚dræmə‚tar'zeɪʃən, -z
dramatise
BR 'dramətʌɪz, -ɪz, -ɪŋ, -d
AM 'drɑmə‚taɪz, 'dræmə‚taɪz, -ɪz, -ɪŋ, -d
dramatis personae
BR drə‚matɪs pəː'səʊnʌɪ, 'dramətɪs +, + pəː'səʊniː
AM ‚drɑ‚madəs pər'souni, ‚dramədəs +, + pər'sounaɪ
dramatist
BR 'dramətɪst, -s
AM 'drɑmədəst, 'dræmədəst, -s
dramatization
BR ‚dramətʌɪ'zeɪʃn, -z
AM ‚dramədə'zeɪʃən, ‚drɑmə‚tar'zeɪʃən, ‚dræmədə'zeɪʃən, ‚dræmə‚tar'zeɪʃən, -z
dramatize
BR 'dramətʌɪz, -ɪz, -ɪŋ, -d
AM 'drɑmə‚taɪz, 'dræmə‚taɪz, -ɪz, -ɪŋ, -d
dramaturge
BR 'dramətəːdʒ, 'drɑːmətəːdʒ, -ɪz
AM 'drɑmə‚tərdʒ, 'dræmə‚tərdʒ, -əz
dramaturgic
BR ‚dramə'təːdʒɪk, ‚drɑːmə'təːdʒɪk

AM ‚drɑmə'tərdʒɪk, ‚dræmə'tərdʒɪk
dramaturgical
BR ‚dramə'təːdʒɪkl, ‚drɑːmə'təːdʒɪkl
AM ‚drɑmə'tərdʒəkəl, ‚dræmə'tərdʒəkəl
dramaturgy
BR 'dramətəːdʒi, 'drɑːmətəːdʒi
AM 'drɑmə‚tərdʒi, 'dræmə‚tərdʒi
Drambuie®
BR dram'b(j)uː|i, -ɪz
AM dræm'bui, -z
Drammen
BR 'dramən
AM 'dræmən
drank
BR draŋk
AM dræŋk
drape
BR dreɪp, -s, -ɪŋ, -t
AM dreɪp, -s, -ɪŋ, -t
draper
BR 'dreɪpə(r), -z
AM 'dreɪpər, -z
drapery
BR 'dreɪp(ə)r|i, -ɪz
AM 'dreɪp(ə)ri, -z
drastic
BR 'drastɪk, 'drɑːstɪk
AM 'dræstɪk
drastically
BR 'drastɪkli, 'drɑːstɪkli
AM 'dræstək(ə)li
drat
BR drat
AM dræt
dratted
BR 'dratɪd
AM 'drædəd
draught
BR drɑːft, draft, -s
AM dræft, -s
draughtboard
BR 'drɑːf(t)bɔːd, 'draf(t)bɔːd, -z
AM 'dræf(t)‚bɔ(ə)rd, -z
draughthorse
BR 'drɑːftho:s, 'draftho:s, -ɪz
AM 'dræf(t)‚(h)ɔ(ə)rs, -əz
draughtily
BR 'drɑːftɪli, 'draftɪli
AM 'dræftəli
draughtiness
BR 'drɑːftɪnɪs, 'draftɪnɪs
AM 'dræftɪnɪs
draughts
BR drɑːfts, drafts
AM dræf(t)s
draughtsman
BR 'drɑːf(t)smən, 'draf(t)smən

AM 'dræf(t)smən
draughtsmanship
BR 'drɑːf(t)smənʃɪp, 'draf(t)smənʃɪp
AM 'dræf(t)smən‚ʃɪp
draughtsmen
BR 'drɑːf(t)smən, 'draf(t)smən
AM 'dræf(t)smən
draughtswoman
BR 'drɑːf(t)s‚wʊmən, 'draf(t)s‚wʊmən
AM 'dræf(t)s‚wʊmən
draughtswomen
BR 'drɑːft‚wɪmɪn, 'draf(t)s‚wɪmɪn
AM 'dræf(t)s‚wɪmɪn
draughty
BR 'drɑːft|i, 'draft|i, -ɪə(r), -ɪɪst
AM 'dræfti, -ər, -ɪst
Dravidian
BR drə'vɪdɪən, -z
AM drə'vɪdɪən, -z
draw
BR drɔː(r), -z, -ɪŋ
AM drɔ, drɑ, -z, -ɪŋ
drawback
BR 'drɔːbak, -s
AM 'drɔ‚bæk, 'drɑ‚bæk, -s
drawbridge
BR 'drɔːbrɪdʒ, -ɪz
AM 'drɔ‚brɪdʒ, 'drɑ‚brɪdʒ, -ɪz
drawcord
BR 'drɔːkɔːd, -z
AM 'drɔ‚kɔ(ə)rd, 'drɑ‚kɔ(ə)rd, -z
drawee
BR drɔː(r)'iː, -z
AM drɔ'(w)i, drɑ'(w)i, -z
drawer¹
in furniture
BR drɔː(r), -z
AM 'drɔ(ə)r, 'drɑ(ə)r, -z
drawer²
person who draws
BR 'drɔː(r)ə(r), -z
AM 'drɔ(w)ər, 'drɑ(w)ər, -z
drawerful
BR 'drɔːfʊl, -z
AM 'drɔr‚fʊl, -z
drawers
underclothes
BR drɔːz
AM 'drɔ(ə)rz, 'drɑ(ə)rz
drawing
BR 'drɔː(r)ɪŋ, -z
AM 'drɔɪŋ, 'drɑɪŋ, -z
drawl
BR drɔːl, -z, -ɪŋ, -d
AM drɔl, drɑl, -z, -ɪŋ, -d
drawler
BR 'drɔːlə(r), -z
AM 'drɔlər, 'drɑlər, -z

drawn
BR drɔːn
AM drɔn, drɑn

drawstring
BR 'drɔːstrɪŋ, -z
AM 'drɔːstrɪŋ,
'drɑstrɪŋ, -z

Drax
BR draks
AM dræks

dray
BR dreɪ, -z
AM dreɪ, -z

Draycott
BR 'dreɪkət, 'dreɪkɒt
AM 'dreɪˌkɑt

drayman
BR 'dreɪmən
AM 'dreɪmən

draymen
BR 'dreɪmən
AM 'dreɪmən

Drayton
BR 'dreɪtn
AM 'dreɪtn

dread
BR drɛd, -z, -ɪŋ, -ɪd
AM drɛd, -z, -ɪŋ, -əd

dreadful
BR 'drɛdf(ʊ)l
AM 'drɛdfəl

dreadfully
BR 'drɛdfəli, 'drɛdfli
AM 'drɛdfəli

dreadfulness
BR 'drɛdf(ʊ)lnəs
AM 'drɛdfəlnəs

dreadlocked
BR 'drɛdlɒkt
AM 'drɛdˌlɑkt

dreadlocks
BR 'drɛdlɒks
AM 'drɛdˌlɑks

dreadnought
BR 'drɛdnɔːt, -s
AM 'drɛdˌnɔt,
'drɛdˌnɑt, -s

dream
BR driːm, -z, -ɪŋ
AM drim, -z, -ɪŋ

dreamboat
BR 'driːmbəʊt, -s
AM 'drimˌboʊt, -s

dreamed
BR drɛmt, driːmd
AM drimd

dreamer
BR 'driːmə(r), -z
AM 'drimər, -z

dreamful
BR 'driːmf(ʊ)l
AM 'drimfəl

dreamily
BR 'driːmɪli
AM 'drimɪli

dreaminess
BR 'driːmɪnɪs

dreamland
BR 'driːmland, -z
AM 'drimˌlænd, -z

dreamless
BR 'driːmlɪs
AM 'drimlɪs

dreamlessly
BR 'driːmlɪsli
AM 'drimlɪsli

dreamlessness
BR 'driːmlɪsnɪs
AM 'drimlɪsnɪs

dreamlike
BR 'driːmlʌɪk
AM 'drimˌlaɪk

dreamt
BR drɛmt
AM drɛmt

dreamtime
BR 'driːmtʌɪm
AM 'drimˌtaɪm

dreamworld
BR 'driːmwəːld, -z
AM 'drimˌwərld, -z

dreamy
BR 'driːm|i, -ɪə(r), -ɪɪst
AM 'drimi, -ər, -ɪst

drear
BR 'drɪə(r)
AM 'drɪ(ə)r

drearily
BR 'drɪərɪli
AM 'drɪrɪli, 'drɪrɪli

dreariness
BR 'drɪərɪnɪs
AM 'drɪrɪnɪs, 'drɪrɪnɪs

dreary
BR 'drɪər|i, -ɪə(r), -ɪɪst
AM 'drɪri, 'drɪri, -ər,
-ɪst

dreck
BR drɛk
AM drɛk

dredge
BR drɛdʒ, -ɪz, -ɪŋ, -d
AM drɛdʒ, -əz, -ɪŋ, -d

dredger
BR 'drɛdʒə(r), -z
AM 'drɛdʒər, -z

dree
BR driː, -z, -ɪŋ, -d
AM dri, -z, -ɪŋ, -d

Dreft
BR drɛft
AM drɛft

dreg
BR drɛg, -z
AM drɛg, -z

dreggy
BR 'drɛgi
AM 'drɛgi

Dreiser
BR 'drʌɪzə(r)
AM 'draɪzər

drench
BR drɛn(t)ʃ, -ɪz, -ɪŋ, -t

Dresden
BR 'drɛzd(ə)n
AM 'drɛzdən
GER 'dreːzdn

dress
BR drɛs, -ɪz, -ɪŋ, -t
AM drɛs, -əz, -ɪŋ, -t

dressage
BR 'drɛsɑː(d)ʒ
AM drə'sɑʒ

dresser
BR 'drɛsə(r), -z
AM 'drɛsər, -z

dressily
BR 'drɛsɪli
AM 'drɛsəli

dressiness
BR 'drɛsɪnɪs
AM 'drɛsɪnɪs

dressing
BR 'drɛsɪŋ, -z
AM 'drɛsɪŋ, -z

dressmaker
BR 'drɛsˌmeɪkə(r), -z
AM 'drɛsˌmeɪkər, -z

dressmaking
BR 'drɛsˌmeɪkɪŋ
AM 'drɛsˌmeɪkɪŋ

dressy
BR 'drɛs|i, -ɪə(r), -ɪɪst
AM 'drɛsi, -ər, -ɪst

drew
BR druː
AM dru

Drexel
BR 'drɛksl
AM 'drɛksəl

drey
BR dreɪ, -z
AM dreɪ, -z

Dreyfus
BR 'dreɪfəs, 'drʌɪfəs
AM 'dreɪfəs, 'draɪfəs

dribble
BR 'drɪb|l, -lz, -lɪŋ \-lɪŋ,
-ld
AM 'drɪb|əl, -əlz,
-(ə)lɪŋ, -əld

dribbler
BR 'drɪb|ə(r),
'drɪblə(r), -z
AM 'drɪb(ə)lər, -z

dribbly
BR 'drɪb|li, 'drɪbli
AM 'drɪb|li, 'drɪbli

driblet
GER 'drɪblɪt, -s
AM 'drɪblət, -s

dribs and drabs
BR ˌdrɪbz (ə)n 'drabz
AM ˌdrɪbz ən 'dræbz

dried
BR drʌɪd
AM draɪd

drier
BR 'drʌɪə(r), -z

drench
AM drɛn(t)ʃ, -əz, -ɪŋ, -t

Dresden
AM 'draɪ(ə)r, -z

Driffield
BR 'drɪfiːld
AM 'drɪfild

drift
BR drɪft, -s, -ɪŋ, -ɪd
AM drɪft, -s, -ɪŋ, -ɪd

driftage
BR 'drɪftɪdʒ
AM 'drɪftɪdʒ

drifter
BR 'drɪftə(r), -z
AM 'drɪftər, -z

driftnet
BR 'drɪf(t)nɛt, -s
AM 'drɪf(t)ˌnɛt, -s

driftwood
BR 'drɪf(t)wʊd
AM 'drɪf(t)ˌwʊd

Drighlington
BR 'drɪglɪŋt(ə)n
AM 'drɪglɪŋtən

drill
BR drɪl, -z, -ɪŋ, -d
AM drɪl, -z, -ɪŋ, -d

driller
BR 'drɪlə(r), -z
AM 'drɪlər, -z

drillmaster
BR 'drɪlˌmɑːstə(r),
'drɪlˌmɑstə(r), -z
AM 'drɪlˌmæstər, -z

drillstock
BR 'drɪlstɒk, -s
AM 'drɪlˌstɑk, -s

drily
BR 'drʌɪli
AM 'draɪli

drink
BR drɪŋk, -s, -ɪŋ
AM drɪŋk, -s, -ɪŋ

drinkable
BR 'drɪŋkəbl
AM 'drɪŋkəbəl

drinker
BR 'drɪŋkə(r), -z
AM 'drɪŋkər, -z

Drinkwater
BR 'drɪŋkwɔːtə(r)
AM 'drɪŋkˌwɔdər,
'drɪŋkˌwɑdər

drip
BR drɪp, -s, -ɪŋ, -t
AM drɪp, -s, -ɪŋ, -t

dripfed
BR 'drɪpfɛd, ˌdrɪp'fɛd
AM 'drɪpˌfɛd

dripfeed
BR 'drɪpfiːd, ˌdrɪp'fiːd,
-z, -ɪŋ
AM 'drɪpˌfid, -z, -ɪŋ

dripgrind
BR 'drɪpgrʌɪnd,
ˌdrɪp'grʌɪnd, -z, -ɪŋ,
-ɪd
AM 'drɪpˌgraɪnd, -z, -ɪŋ,
-ɪd

drippily
BR ˈdrɪpɪli
AM ˈdrɪpɪli

drippiness
BR ˈdrɪpɪnɪs
AM ˈdrɪpɪnɪs

dripping
BR ˈdrɪpɪŋ
AM ˈdrɪpɪŋ

drippy
BR ˈdrɪp|i, -ɪə(r), -ɪɪst
AM ˈdrɪpi, -ər, -ɪst

Driscoll
BR ˈdrɪskl
AM ˈdrɪskəl

drivable
BR ˈdraɪvəbl
AM ˈdraɪvəbəl

drive
BR draɪv, -z, -ɪŋ
AM draɪv, -z, -ɪŋ

driveable
BR ˈdraɪvəbl
AM ˈdraɪvəbəl

drivel
BR ˈdrɪv|l, -lz, -lɪŋ\-lɪŋ, -ld
AM ˈdrɪvəl, -z, -ɪŋ, -d

driveller
BR ˈdrɪvlə(r), ˈdrɪvlə(r), -z
AM ˈdrɪvələr, -z

driven
BR ˈdrɪvn
AM ˈdrɪvən

driver
BR ˈdraɪvə(r), -z
AM ˈdraɪvər, -z

driverless
BR ˈdraɪvələs
AM ˈdraɪvərləs

driveshaft
BR ˈdraɪvʃɑːft, ˈdraɪvʃaft, -s
AM ˈdraɪvˌʃæft, -s

driveway
BR ˈdraɪvweɪ, -z
AM ˈdraɪvˌweɪ, -z

drizzle
BR ˈdrɪz|l, -lz, -lɪŋ\-lɪŋ, -ld
AM ˈdrɪzəl, -əlz, -(ə)lɪŋ, -əld

drizzly
BR ˈdrɪz|li, -ɪə(r), -ɪɪst
AM ˈdrɪzli, ˈdrɪz|li, -ər, -ɪst

Drogheda
BR ˈdrɔɪɪdə(r)
AM ˈdrɔ(ɪ)ədə, ˈdra(h)ədə

drogue
BR drəʊg, -z
AM droʊg, -z

droit
ᵃʳ drɔɪt, -s
ˈrɔɪt, -s

droit de seigneur
BR ˌdrwaː də seɪnˈjəː(r), + senˈjəː(r)
AM ˌdrwa də seɪnˈjər

droit du seigneur
BR ˌdrwaː də seɪnˈjəː(r), + senˈjəː(r)
AM ˌdrwa də seɪnˈjər

Droitwich
BR ˈdrɔɪtwɪtʃ
AM ˈdrɔɪtwɪtʃ

droll
BR drəʊl, -ə(r), -ɪst
AM droʊl, -ər, -əst

drollery
BR ˈdrəʊl(ə)r|i, -ɪz
AM ˈdroʊl(ə)ri, -z

drollness
BR ˈdrəʊlnəs
AM ˈdroʊlnəs

drolly
BR ˈdrəʊl(l)i
AM ˈdroʊ(l)li

drome
BR drəʊm, -z
AM droʊm, -z

dromedary
BR ˈdrɒmɪd(ə)r|i, -ɪz
AM ˈdraməˌderi, -z

dromoi
BR ˈdrɒmɔɪ
AM ˈdrɒmɔɪ, ˈdraməɪ

dromond
BR ˈdrɒmənd, ˈdrʌmənd, -z
AM ˈdramənd, ˈdrəmənd, -z

Dromore
BR drəˈmɔː(r)
AM drəˈmɔ(ə)r

dromos
BR ˈdrɒmɒs
AM ˈdrɒmɒs, ˈdraməs
GR ˈdrɒmɔs

drone
BR drəʊn, -z, -ɪŋ, -d
AM droʊn, -z, -ɪŋ, -d

Dronfield
BR ˈdrɒnfiːld
AM ˈdranˌfild

drongo
BR ˈdrɒŋgəʊ, -z
AM ˈdraŋgoʊ, -z

droob
BR druːb, -z
AM drub, -z

drool
BR druːl, -z, -ɪŋ, -d
AM drul, -z, -ɪŋ, -d

droop
BR druːp, -s, -ɪŋ, -t
AM drup, -s, -ɪŋ, -t

droopily
BR ˈdruːpɪli
AM ˈdrupəli

droopiness
BR ˈdruːpɪnɪs
AM ˈdrupɪnɪs

droop-snoot
BR ˈdruːpsnuːt, -s
AM ˈdrupˌsnut, -s

droopy
BR ˈdruːp|i, -ɪə(r), -ɪɪst
AM ˈdrupi, -ər, -ɪst

drop
BR drɒp, -s, -ɪŋ, -t
AM drap, -s, -ɪŋ, -t

drophead
BR ˈdrɒphed, -z
AM ˈdrap,(h)ɛd, -z

dropkick
BR ˈdrɒpkɪk, -s, -ɪŋ, -t
AM ˈdrapˌkɪk, -s, -ɪŋ, -t

dropleaf
BR ˈdrɒpliːf
AM ˈdrapˌlif

droplet
BR ˈdrɒplɪt, -s
AM ˈdraplət, -s

dropout
BR ˈdrɒpaʊt, -s
AM ˈdrapˌaʊt, -s

dropper
BR ˈdrɒpə(r), -z
AM ˈdrapər, -z

dropping
BR ˈdrɒpɪŋ, -z
AM ˈdrapɪŋ, -z

dropsical
BR ˈdrɒpsɪkl
AM ˈdrapsəkəl

dropsy
BR ˈdrɒpsi
AM ˈdrapsi

dropwort
BR ˈdrɒpwɜːt
AM ˈdrapˌwɜrt, ˈdrapˌwɔ(ə)rt

droshky
BR ˈdrɒʃk|i, -ɪz
AM ˈdrɒʃki, ˈdraʃki, -z
RUS ˈdrɒʃkʲi

drosophila
BR drəˈsɒfɪlə(r), drɒˈsɒfɪlə(r), -z
AM drəˈsafələ, -z

dross
BR drɒs
AM drɔs, dras

drossy
BR ˈdrɒs|i, -ɪə(r), -ɪɪst
AM ˈdrɔsi, ˈdrasi, -ər, -ɪst

drought
BR draʊt, -s
AM draʊt, -s

droughty
BR ˈdraʊti
AM ˈdraʊdi

drouth
BR draʊθ
AM draʊθ

Drouzhba
BR ˈdruːʒbə(r)
AM ˈdruʒbə

drove
BR drəʊv, -z, -ɪŋ
AM droʊv, -z, -ɪŋ

drover
BR ˈdrəʊvə(r), -z
AM ˈdroʊvər, -z

drown
BR draʊn, -z, -ɪŋ, -d
AM draʊn, -z, -ɪŋ, -d

drowning
BR ˈdraʊnɪŋ, -z
AM ˈdraʊnɪŋ, -z

drowse
BR draʊz, -ɪz, -ɪŋ, -d
AM draʊz, -əz, -ɪŋ, -d

drowsily
BR ˈdraʊzɪli
AM ˈdraʊzəli

drowsiness
BR ˈdraʊzɪnɪs
AM ˈdraʊzɪnɪs

drowsy
BR ˈdraʊz|i, -ɪə(r), -ɪɪst
AM ˈdraʊzi, -ər, -ɪst

drowze
BR draʊz, -ɪz, -ɪŋ, -d
AM draʊz, -əz, -ɪŋ, -d

Droylsden
BR ˈdrɔɪlzd(ə)n
AM ˈdrɔɪlzdən

drub
BR drʌb, -z, -ɪŋ, -d
AM drəb, -z, -ɪŋ, -d

drudge
BR drʌdʒ, -ɪz, -ɪŋ, -d
AM drədʒ, -əz, -ɪŋ, -d

drudgery
BR ˈdrʌdʒ(ə)ri
AM ˈdrədʒ(ə)ri

drug
BR drʌg, -z, -ɪŋ, -d
AM drəg, -z, -ɪŋ, -d

drugget
BR ˈdrʌgɪt, -s
AM ˈdrəgət, -s

druggist
BR ˈdrʌgɪst, -s
AM ˈdrəgəst, -s

druggy
BR ˈdrʌg|i, -ɪə(r), -ɪɪst
AM ˈdrəgi, -ər, -ɪst

drugstore
BR ˈdrʌgstɔː(r), -z
AM ˈdrəgˌstɔ(ə)r, -z

Druid
BR ˈdruːɪd, -z
AM ˈdruəd, -z

Druidess
BR ˈdruːɪdes, -ɪz
AM ˈdruədəs, -əz

Druidic
BR druːˈɪdɪk
AM druˈɪdɪk

Druidical
BR druːˈɪdɪkl
AM druːˈɪdɪkəl

Druidism
BR ˈdruːɪdɪz(ə)m
AM ˈdruəd‿ɪzem

drum
BR drʌm, -z, -ɪŋ, -d
AM drəm, -z, -ɪŋ, -d

Drumalbyn
BR drʌmˈalbɪn
AM drəmˈælbən

drumbeat
BR ˈdrʌmbiːt, -s
AM ˈdrəmˌbit, -s

drumfire
BR ˈdrʌmfʌɪə(r)
AM ˈdrəmˌfaɪ(ə)r

drumhead
BR ˈdrʌmhɛd, -z
AM ˈdrəmˌ(h)ɛd, -z

drumlin
BR ˈdrʌmlɪn, -z
AM ˈdrəmlən, -z

drumlinoid
BR ˈdrʌmlɪnɔɪd
AM ˈdrəmləˌnɔɪd

drummer
BR ˈdrʌmə(r), -z
AM ˈdrəmər, -z

Drummond
BR ˈdrʌm(ə)nd
AM ˈdrəmən(d)

Drumnadrochit
BR ˌdrʌmnəˈdrɒxɪt,
ˌdrʌmnəˈdrɒkɪt
AM ˌdrəmnəˈdrakət

drumstick
BR ˈdrʌmstɪk, -s
AM ˈdrəmˌstɪk, -s

drunk
BR drʌŋk, -s
AM drəŋk, -s

drunkard
BR ˈdrʌŋkəd, -z
AM ˈdrəŋkərd, -z

drunken
BR ˈdrʌŋk(ə)n
AM ˈdrəŋkən

drunkenly
BR ˈdrʌŋk(ə)nli
AM ˈdrəŋkənli

drunkenness
BR ˈdrʌŋk(ə)nnəs
AM ˈdrəŋkə(n)nəs

drupaceous
BR druːˈpeɪʃəs
AM druˈpeɪʃəs

drupe
BR druːp, -s
AM drup, -s

drupel
BR ˈdruːpl, -z
AM ˈdrupəl, -z

drupelet
BR ˈdruːplɪt, -s
AM ˈdruplət, -s

Drury
BR ˈdrʊəri
AM ˈdrʊri

Druse
BR druːz, -ɪz
AM druz, -əz

Drusilla
BR druˈsɪlə(r)
AM druˈsɪlə

druthers
BR ˈdrʌðəz
AM ˈdrəðərz

Druzba
BR ˈdruːzbə(r),
ˈdruːʒbə(r)
AM ˈdruzbə, ˈdruʒbə

Druze
BR druːz, -ɪz
AM druz, -əz

dry
BR drʌɪ, -z, -ɪŋ, -d, -ə(r),
-ɪst
AM draɪ, -z, -ɪŋ, -d, -ər,
-ɪst

dryad
BR ˈdrʌɪad, ˈdrʌɪəd, -z
AM ˈdraɪəd, ˈdraɪæd, -z

dryas
BR ˈdrʌɪəs
AM ˈdraɪəs

Dryden
BR ˈdrʌɪdn
AM ˈdraɪdən

dryer
BR ˈdrʌɪə(r), -z
AM ˈdraɪər, -z

dryish
BR ˈdrʌɪɪʃ
AM ˈdraɪɪʃ

dryland
BR ˈdrʌɪlənd, -z
AM ˈdraɪlənd,
ˈdraɪˌlænd, -z

dryly
BR ˈdrʌɪli
AM ˈdraɪli

dryness
BR ˈdrʌɪnɪs
AM ˈdraɪnɪs

dryopithecine
BR ˌdrʌɪəʊˈpɪθɪsiːn
AM ˌdraɪoʊˈpɪθəˌsin

Dryopithecus
BR ˌdrʌɪəʊˈpɪθɪkəs
AM ˌdraɪoʊˈpɪθəkəs

Drysdale
BR ˈdrʌɪzdeɪl
AM ˈdraɪzˌdeɪl

drystone
BR ˈdrʌɪstəʊn
AM ˈdraɪˌstoʊn

drysuit
BR ˈdrʌɪs(j)uːt, -s
AM ˈdraɪˌsut, -s

drywall
BR ˌdrʌɪˈwɔːl
AM ˈdraɪˌwɔl, ˈdraɪˌwal

dual
BR ˈdjuːəl, dʒuːəl
AM ˈd(j)uəl

dualise
BR ˈdjuːəlʌɪz,
ˈdʒuːəlʌɪz, -ɪz, -ɪŋ, -d
AM ˈd(j)uəˌlaɪz, -ɪz, -ɪŋ,
-d

dualism
BR ˈdjuːəlɪz(ə)m,
ˈdʒuːəlɪz(ə)m
AM ˈd(j)uəˌlɪzəm

dualist
BR ˈdjuːəlɪst,
ˈdʒuːəlɪst, -s
AM ˈd(j)uələst, -s

dualistic
BR ˌdjuːəˈlɪstɪk,
ˌdʒuːəˈlɪstɪk
AM ˌd(j)uəˈlɪstɪk

dualistically
BR ˌdjuːəˈlɪstɪkli,
ˌdʒuːəˈlɪstɪkli
AM ˌd(j)uəˈlɪstɪk(ə)li

duality
BR djuːˈalɪt‿i,
dʒuːˈalɪt‿i, -ɪz
AM d(j)uˈælədi, -z

dualize
BR ˈdjuːəlʌɪz,
ˈdʒuːəlʌɪz, -ɪz, -ɪŋ, -d
AM ˈd(j)uəˌlaɪz, -ɪz, -ɪŋ,
-d

dually
BR ˈdjuːəl(l)i,
ˈdʒuːəl(l)i
AM ˈd(j)uəli

Duane
BR dweɪn, duːˈem
AM dweɪn

dub
BR dʌb, -z, -ɪŋ, -d
AM dəb, -z, -ɪŋ, -d

Dubai
BR ˌduːˈbʌɪ, dʊˈbʌɪ
AM duˈbaɪ

dubbin
BR ˈdʌb|ɪn, -ɪnz, -ɪnɪŋ,
-ɪnd
AM ˈdəbən, -z, -ɪŋ, -d

Dubček
BR ˈdʊbtʃɛk
AM ˈdubˌtʃɛk

dubiety
BR djuːˈbʌɪti,
dʒuːˈbʌɪti
AM d(j)uˈbaɪɪdi

dubious
BR ˈdjuːbɪəs, ˈdʒuːbɪəs
AM ˈd(j)ubiəs

dubiously
BR ˈdjuːbɪəsli,
ˈdʒuːbɪəsli
AM ˈd(j)ubiəsli

dubiousness
BR ˈdjuːbɪəsnəs,
ˈdʒuːbɪəsnəs
AM ˈd(j)ubiəsnəs

dubitation
BR ˌdjuːbɪˈteɪʃn,
ˌdʒuːbɪˈteɪʃn
AM ˌd(j)ubəˈteɪʃən

dubitative
BR ˈdjuːbɪtətɪv,
ˈdʒuːbɪtətɪv
AM ˈd(j)ubəˌteɪdɪv

dubitatively
BR ˈdjuːbɪtətɪvli,
ˈdʒuːbɪtətɪvli
AM ˈd(j)ubəˌteɪdɪvli

Dublin
BR ˈdʌblɪn
AM ˈdəblən

Dubliner
BR ˈdʌblɪnə(r), -z
AM ˈdəblənər, -z

Du Bois
BR dʊ ˈbwɑː(r)
AM du ˈbwɑ

Dubonnet®
BR d(j)ʊˈbɒneɪ
AM ˌdubəˈneɪ

Dubrovnik
BR dʊˈbrɒvnɪk
AM duˈbrɑvnɪk,
duˈbrɑvnɪk

Dubuque
BR dəˈbjuːk
AM dəˈbjuk

ducal
BR ˈdjuːkl, ˈdʒuːkl
AM ˈd(j)ukəl

ducat
BR ˈdʌkət, -s
AM ˈdəkət, -s

Duce
BR ˈduːtʃeɪ
AM ˈdutʃeɪ

Duchamp
BR dʊˈʃɒ̃
AM duˈʃɑm(p)

Duchenne
BR d(j)ʊˈʃɛn
AM d(j)uˈʃɛn

Duchesne
BR d(j)ʊˈʃeɪm
AM duˈʃeɪm, duˈkeɪm

duchess
BR ˈdʌtʃɪs, -ɪz
AM ˈdətʃəs, -əz

duchesse
BR d(j)ʊˈʃɛs, -ɪz
AM ˈd(j)uˈʃɛs, -əz

duchy
BR ˈdʌtʃ|i, -ɪz
AM ˈdətʃi, -z

duck
BR dʌk, -s, -ɪŋ, -t
AM dək, -s, -ɪŋ, -t

duckbill
BR ˈdʌkbɪl, -z
AM ˈdəkˌbɪl, -z

duckboard
BR ˈdʌkbɔːd, -z
AM ˈdəkˌbɔ(ə)rd, -z

duckegg
BR 'dʌkɛg, -z
AM 'dək,ɛg, -z

ducker
BR 'dʌkə(r), -z
AM 'dəkər, -z

Duckett
BR 'dʌkɪt
AM 'dəkət

Duckham
BR 'dʌkəm
AM 'dəkəm

duckie
BR 'dʌk|i, -ɪz
AM 'dəki, -z

duckily
BR 'dʌkɪli
AM 'dəkəli

duckiness
BR 'dʌkɪnɪs
AM 'dəkinɪs

duckling
BR 'dʌklɪŋ, -z
AM 'dəklɪŋ, -z

ducktail
BR 'dʌkteɪl, -z
AM 'dək,teɪl, -z

duckweed
BR 'dʌkwi:d
AM 'dək,wid

Duckworth
BR 'dʌkwəθ, 'dʌkwə:θ
AM 'dək,wərθ

ducky
BR 'dʌk|i, -ɪz, -ɪə(r),
-ɪst
AM 'dəki, -z, -ər, -ɪst

duct
BR 'dʌkt, -s, -ɪŋ, -ɪd-
AM dək|(t), -(t)s, -tɪŋ,
-təd

ductile
BR 'dʌktʌɪl
AM 'dəktl, 'dək,tʌɪl

ductility
BR dʌk'tɪlɪti
AM dək'tɪlɪdi

ductless
BR 'dʌktləs
AM 'dək(t)ləs

dud
BR dʌd, -z
AM dəd, -z

dude
BR dju:d, -z
AM dud, -z

dudgeon
BR 'dʌdʒ(ə)n
AM 'dədʒən

dudish
BR 'dju:dɪʃ
AM 'dudɪʃ

Dudley
BR 'dʌdli
AM 'dədli

due
BR dju:, dʒu:, -z

AM d(j)u, -z

duel
BR 'dju:əl, 'dʒu:əl, -z,
-ɪŋ, -d
AM 'd(j)uəl, -z, -ɪŋ, -d

duelist
BR 'dju:əlɪst,
'dʒu:əlɪst, -s
AM 'd(j)uələst, -s

dueller
BR 'dju:ələ(r),
'dʒu:ələ(r), -z
AM 'd(j)uələr, -z

duellist
BR 'dju:əlɪst,
'dʒu:əlɪst, -s
AM 'd(j)uələst, -s

duende
BR dʊ'ɛndeɪ, -z
AM du'ɛn,deɪ,
'dwɛndeɪ, -z

duenna
BR d(j)ʊ'ɛnə(r),
dʒʊ'ɛnə(r), -z
AM d(j)u'ɛnə, -z

duet
BR dju'ɛt, dʒʊ'ɛt, -s
AM d(j)u'ɛt, -s

duettist
BR dju'ɛtɪst, dʒʊ'ɛtɪst,
-s
AM d(j)u'ɛdəst, -s

Dufay
BR dʊ'feɪ
AM du'feɪ

duff
BR dʌf, -s, -ɪŋ, -t
AM dəf, -s, -ɪŋ, -t

duffel
BR 'dʌfl
AM 'dəfəl

duffer
BR 'dʌfə(r), -z
AM 'dəfər, -z

Duffield
BR 'dʌfi:ld
AM 'dəfild

duffle
BR 'dʌfl
AM 'dəfəl

Duffy
BR 'dʌfi
AM 'dəfi

Dufy
BR 'du:fi
AM du'fi

dug
BR dʌg
AM dəg

Duggan
BR 'dʌg(ə)n
AM 'dəgən

Duggleby
BR 'dʌglbi
AM 'dəgəlbi

dugite
BR 'dju:gʌɪt, -s

AM 'd(j)u,gaɪt, -s

dugong
BR 'd(j)u:gɒŋ, -z
AM 'du,gaŋ, 'du,gɔŋ, -z

dugout
BR 'dʌgaʊt, -s
AM 'dəg,aʊt, -s

duiker
BR 'dʌɪkə(r), -z
AM 'daɪkər, -z
AFK 'dœɪkər

Duisburg
BR 'dju:zbə:g,
'dju:sbə:g
AM 'duz,bərg
GER 'dʏɪsbʊrk

Dukakis
BR d(j)ʊ'ka:kɪs
AM də'kakəs,
d(j)ʊ'kakəs

duke
BR dju:k, dʒu:k, -s
AM d(j)uk, dʒuk, -s

dukedom
BR 'dju:kdəm,
'dʒu:kdəm, -z
AM 'd(j)ukdəm, -z

Dukhobor
BR 'du:kə(ʊ)bɔ:(r), -z
AM 'dukə,bɔ(ə)r, -z

DUKW
BR dʌk, -s
AM dək, -s

Dulais
BR 'dɪlʌɪs, 'dɪləs
AM 'dɪləs

dulcet
BR 'dʌlsɪt
AM 'dəlsət

Dulcie
BR 'dʌlsi
AM 'dəlsi

dulcification
BR ,dʌlsɪfɪ'keɪʃn
AM ,dəlʃəfə'keɪʃən

dulcify
BR 'dʌlsɪfʌɪ, -z, -ɪŋ, -d
AM 'dəlsə,faɪ, -z, -ɪŋ, -d

dulcimer
BR 'dʌlsɪmə(r), -z
AM 'dəlsəmər, -z

dulcitone
BR 'dʌlsɪtəʊn
AM 'dəlsə,toʊn

dulia
BR 'dju:lɪə(r),
'dʒu:lɪə(r),
d(j)ʊ'lʌɪə(r),
dʒʊ'lʌɪə(r)
AM d(j)u'laɪə

dull
BR dʌl, -z, -ɪŋ, -d, -ə(r),
-ɪst
AM dəl, -z, -ɪŋ, -d, -ər,
-əst

dullard
BR 'dʌləd, -z
AM 'dələrd, -z

Dulles
BR 'dʌlɪs
AM 'dələs

dullish
BR 'dʌlɪʃ
AM 'dəlɪʃ

dullness
BR 'dʌlnəs
AM 'dəlnəs

dully
BR 'dʌl(l)i
AM 'dəli

dulse
BR dʌls
AM dəls

Duluth
BR də'lu:θ
AM də'luθ

Dulux®
BR 'dju:lʌks, 'dʒu:lʌks
AM 'd(j)uləks

Dulverton
BR 'dʌlvət(ə)n
AM 'dəlvərtən

Dulwich
BR 'dʌlɪtʃ, 'dʌlɪdʒ
AM 'dəl(w)ɪtʃ

duly
BR 'dju:li, 'dʒu:li
AM 'd(j)uli

Duma
BR 'd(j)u:mə(r), -z
AM 'dumə, -z

Dumas
BR dʊ'ma:(r),
'd(j)u:ma:(r)
AM du'ma(s)

Du Maurier
BR d(j)ʊ'mɒrɪeɪ
AM du 'mɔri,eɪ

dumb
BR dʌm, -ə(r), -ɪst
AM dəm, -ər, -əst

Dumbarton
BR dʌm'ba:tn
AM dəm,bartən

dumbfound
BR (,)dʌm'faʊnd, -z,
-ɪŋ, -ɪd
AM ,dəm'faʊnd, -z, -ɪŋ,
-əd

dumbhead
BR 'dʌmhɛd, -z
AM 'dəm,(h)ɛd, -z

dumbly
BR 'dʌmli
AM 'dəmli

dumbness
BR 'dʌmnəs
AM 'dəmnəs

dumbo
BR 'dʌmbəʊ, -z
AM 'dəmboʊ, -z

dumbshow
BR 'dʌmʃəʊ, -z
AM 'dəm,ʃoʊ, -z

dumbstricken
BR 'dʌm‚strɪk(ə)n
AM 'dəm‚strɪkən

dumbstruck
BR 'dʌmstrʌk
AM 'dəm'strʌk

dumbwaiter
BR ‚dʌm'weɪtə(r), -z
AM 'dəm‚weɪdər, -z

dumdum
BR 'dʌmdʌm, -z
AM 'dəm‚dəm, -z

dumfound
BR (‚)dʌm'faʊnd, -z,
-ɪŋ, -ɪd
AM 'dəm‚faʊnd, -z, -ɪŋ,
-əd

Dumfries
BR dʌm'friːs
AM 'dəmfriz

Dummkopf
BR 'dʌmkʊpf,
'dʊmkʊpf, -s
AM 'dəm‚kɔ(p)f, -s

dummy
BR 'dʌm‖i, -ɪz
AM 'dəmi, -z

dummy run
BR ‚dʌmɪ 'rʌn, -z
AM 'dəmi ‚rən, -z

dump
BR dʌm‖p, -ps, -pɪŋ,
-(p)t
AM dəmp, -s, -ɪŋ, -t

dumper
BR 'dʌmpə(r), -z
AM 'dəmpər, -z

dumpily
BR 'dʌmpɪli
AM 'dəmpəli

dumpiness
BR 'dʌmpɪnɪs
AM 'dəmpinɪs

dumpling
BR 'dʌmplɪŋ, -z
AM 'dəmplɪŋ, -z

dumpster
BR 'dʌm(p)stə(r), -z
AM 'dəm(p)stər, -z

dumpy
BR 'dʌmp‖i, -ɪə(r), -ɪɪst
AM 'dəmpi, -ər, -ɪst

dun
BR dʌn
AM dən

Dunaj
BR 'duːnʌɪ
AM 'du‚naɪ

Dunbar
BR dʌn'bɑː(r)
AM 'dən‚bɑr

Dunblane
BR dʌn'bleɪn
AM dən'bleɪn

Duncan
BR 'dʌŋk(ə)n
AM 'dəŋkən

dunce
BR dʌns, -ɪz
AM dəns, -əz

duncecap
BR 'dʌnskap, -s
AM 'dəns‚kæp, -s

Dunciad
BR 'dʌnsɪad
AM 'dənsi‚æd

Dundalk[1]
place in Ireland
BR dʌn'dɔːk
AM dən'dɔ(l)k

Dundalk[2]
place in US
BR 'dʌndɔːk
AM dən'dɔk, dən'dɑk

Dundas
BR 'dʌndəs
AM 'dəndəs

Dundee
BR dʌn'diː
AM dən'di

dunderhead
BR 'dʌndəhɛd, -z
AM 'dəndər‚(h)ɛd, -z

dunderheaded
BR ‚dʌndə'hɛdɪd
AM 'dəndər‚(h)ɛdəd

Dundonald
BR dʌn'dɒnld
AM dən'dɑnəl(d)

dune
BR djuːn, dʒuːn, -z
AM d(j)un, -z

Dunedin
BR dʌn'iːd(ɪ)n
AM dən'idən

Dunfermline
BR dʌn'fəːmlɪn
AM dən'fərmlən

dung
BR dʌŋ
AM dəŋ

Dungannon
BR dʌn'ganən
AM dən'gænən

dungaree
BR ‚dʌŋgə'riː, -z
AM ‚dəŋgə'ri, -z

Dungarvan
BR dʌn'gɑːv(ə)n
AM dən'gɑrvən

Dungeness
BR ‚dʌn(d)ʒ(ə)'nɛs
AM 'dəndʒənəs

dungeon
BR 'dʌn(d)ʒ(ə)n, -z
AM 'dəndʒən, -z

dunghill
BR 'dʌŋhɪl, -z
AM 'dəŋ‚(h)ɪl, -z

Dunhill
BR 'dʌnhɪl
AM 'dən‚(h)ɪl

dunk
BR dʌŋ‖k, -ks, -kɪŋ,
-(k)t
AM dəŋ‖k, -ks, -kɪŋ,
-(k)t

Dunkeld
BR dʌn'kɛld
AM dən'kɛld

Dunkirk
BR dʌn'kəːk, dʌŋ'kəːk
AM 'dən‚kərk,
dən'kərk

Dunkley
BR 'dʌŋkli
AM 'dəŋkli

Dun Laoghaire
BR dʌn 'lɪəri, duːn +,
+ 'lɛːrə(r)
AM ‚dən 'lɪri, + 'lɛrə
IR duːn 'liːrʲə

Dunlap
BR 'dʌnlap
AM 'dənlɒp, 'dənlæp,
'dənlap

dunlin
BR 'dʌnlɪn, -z
AM 'dənlən, -z

Dunlop[1]
traditional
BR dən'lɒp
AM 'dənlɑp

Dunlop[2]
BR 'dʌnlɒp
AM 'dənlɑp

Dunmow
BR 'dʌnməʊ
AM 'dən‚moʊ

Dunn
BR dʌn
AM dən

dunnage
BR 'dʌnɪdʒ
AM 'dənɪdʒ

Dunne
BR dʌn
AM dən

Dunnet Head
BR ‚dʌnɪt 'hɛd
AM 'dənət 'hɛd

dunno
BR də'nəʊ, dʌ'nəʊ, -z
AM də'noʊ, -z

dunnock
BR 'dʌnək, -s
AM 'dənək, -s

dunny
BR 'dʌn‖i, -ɪz
AM 'dəni, -z

Dunoon
BR də'nuːn, dʌn'uːn
AM də'nun

Dunsinane[1]
in Scotland
BR dʌn'smən
AM 'dənsənən

Dunsinane[2]
in Shakespeare's
'Macbeth'
BR 'dʌnsɪneɪn,
‚dʌnsɪ'neɪn
AM 'dənsə‚neɪn

Duns Scotus
BR ‚dʌnz 'skəʊtəs,
+ 'skʊtəs
AM 'dənz 'skoʊdəs

Dunstable
BR 'dʌnstəbl
AM 'dənstəbəl

Dunstan
BR 'dʌnst(ə)n
AM 'dənstən

Dunwoody
BR dʌn'wʊdi
AM 'dən‚wʊdi

duo
BR 'djuːəʊ, 'dʒuːəʊ, -z
AM 'd(j)uoʊ, -z

duodecimal
BR ‚djuːə(ʊ)'dɛsɪml,
‚dʒuːə(ʊ)'dɛsɪml
AM ‚d(j)uə'dɛsəməl,
'd(j)uoʊ'dɛsəməl

duodecimally
BR ‚djuːə(ʊ)'dɛsɪm‖i,
‚dʒuːə(ʊ)'dɛsɪm‖i,
‚dʒuːə(ʊ)'dɛsɪm‖i,
‚dʒuːə(ʊ)'dɛsɪməli
AM ‚d(j)uə'dɛsəməli,
'd(j)uoʊ'dɛsəməli

duodecimo
BR ‚djuːə(ʊ)'dɛsɪməʊ,
‚dʒuːə(ʊ)'dɛsɪməʊ
AM ‚d(j)uə'dɛsəmoʊ,
'd(j)uoʊ'dɛsəmoʊ

duodena
BR ‚djuːə'diːnə(r),
‚dʒuːə'diːnə(r)
AM ‚d(j)uə'dinə,
d(j)u'ɑdnə

duodenal
BR ‚djuːə'diːnl,
‚dʒuːə'diːnl
AM ‚d(j)uə'dinəl,
d(j)u'ɑdnl

duodenary
BR ‚djuːə'diːn(ə)ri,
‚dʒuːə'diːn(ə)ri
AM ‚d(j)u'ɑdə‚nɛri,
‚d(j)uə'dɛnɛri

duodenitis
BR ‚djuːəd(ɪ)n'ʌɪtɪs,
‚dʒuːəd(ɪ)n'ʌɪtɪs
AM ‚d(j)uədn'aɪdɪs

duodenum
BR ‚djuːə'diːnəm,
‚dʒuːə'diːnəm, -z
AM ‚d(j)uə'dinəm,
d(j)u'ɑdnm, -z

duolog
BR 'djuːəlɒg, 'dʒuːəlɒg,
-z
AM 'd(j)uə‚lɔg,
'd(j)uə‚lɑg, -z

duologue
BR ˈdjuːəlɒg, ˈdʒuːəlɒg,
-z
AM ˈd(j)uəˌlɔg,
ˈd(j)uəˌlɑg, -z

duomo
BR ˈdwəʊməʊ, -z
AM ˈdwoʊmoʊ, -z

duopoly
BR djʊˈɒpəlǀi,
djuˈɒpǀi, dʒʊˈɒpəlǀi,
dʒuˈɒpǀi, -ız
AM d(j)uˈɑpəli, -z

duotone
BR ˈdjuːə(ʊ)təʊn,
ˈdʒuːə(ʊ)təʊn
AM ˈd(j)uəˌtoʊn

dupable
BR ˈdjuːpəbl, ˈdʒuːpəbl
AM ˈd(j)upəbəl

dupe
BR djuːp, dʒuːp, -s, -ıŋ,
-t
AM d(j)up, -s, -ıŋ, -t

duper
BR ˈdjuːpə(r),
ˈdʒuːpə(r), -z
AM ˈd(j)upər, -z

dupery
BR ˈdjuːp(ə)rǀi,
ˈdʒuːp(ə)rǀi, -ız
AM ˈd(j)upəri, -z

dupion
BR ˈdjuːpıɒn,
ˈdʒuːpıɒn, -z
AM ˈdupiˌɑn, -z

duple
BR ˈdjuːpl, ˈdʒuːpl
AM ˈd(j)upəl

duplex
BR ˈdjuːplɛks,
ˈdʒuːplɛks, -ız
AM ˈd(j)uˌplɛks, -əz

duplicable
BR ˈdjuːplıkəbl,
ˈdʒuːplıkəbl
AM ˈd(j)upləkəbəl

duplicate¹
noun, adjective
BR ˈdjuːplıkət,
ˈdʒuːplıkət, -s
AM ˈd(j)upləkət, -s

duplicate²
verb
BR ˈdjuːplıkeıt,
ˈdʒuːplıkeıt, -s, -ıŋ, -ıd
AM ˈd(j)upləˌkeıǀt, -ts,
-dıŋ, -dıd

duplication
BR ˌdjuːplıˈkeıʃn,
ˌdʒuːplıˈkeıʃn, -z
AM ˌd(j)upləˈkeıʃən, -z

duplicator
BR ˈdjuːplıkeıtə(r),
ˈdʒuːplıkeıtə(r), -z
AM ˈd(j)upləˌkeıdər, -z

duplicitous
BR djuˈplısıtəs,
dʒuˈplısıtəs
AM d(j)uˈplısədəs

duplicity
BR djuˈplısıti,
dʒuˈplısıti
AM d(j)uˈplısıdi

Du Pont
BR d(j)ʊ ˈpɒnt
AM d(j)uˈpɑnt

duppy
BR ˈdʌpǀi, -ız
AM ˈdəpi, -z

du Pré
BR d(j)ʊ ˈpreı, + ˈpriː
AM du ˈpreı

Duquesne
BR d(j)ʊˈkeın
AM duˈkeın

dura
BR ˈdjʊərə(r),
ˈdʒʊərə(r), -z
AM ˈd(j)urə, -z

durability
BR ˌdjʊərəˈbılıti,
ˌdʒʊərəˈbılıti,
ˌdjɔːrəˈbılıti,
ˌdʒɔːrəˈbılıti
AM ˌd(j)ʊrəˈbılıdi

durable
BR ˈdjʊərəbl,
ˈdʒʊərəbl, ˈdjɔːrəbl,
ˈdʒɔːrəbl, -z
AM ˈd(j)ʊrəbəl, -z

durableness
BR ˈdjʊərəblnəs,
ˈdʒʊərəblnəs,
ˈdjɔːrəblnəs,
ˈdʒɔːrəblnəs
AM ˈd(j)ʊrəbəlnəs

durably
BR ˈdjʊərəbli,
ˈdʒʊərəbli, ˈdjɔːrəbli,
ˈdʒɔːrəbli
AM ˈd(j)ʊrəbli

Duracell®
BR ˈdjʊərəsɛl,
ˈdʒʊərəsɛl, ˈdjɔːrəsɛl,
ˈdʒɔːrəsɛl
AM ˈdərəˌsɛl

Duraglit®
BR ˈdjʊərəglıt,
ˈdʒʊərəglıt,
ˈdjɔːrəglıt, ˈdʒɔːrəglıt
AM ˈdərəˌglıt

Duralumin®
BR djʊˈraljəmın,
dʒʊˈraljəmın
AM d(j)əˈræljəmən,
d(j)ʊˈræljəmən,
ˌd(j)ʊrəˈlumən

dura mater
BR ˌdjʊərə ˈmeıtə(r),
ˌdʒʊərə +, + ˈmɑːtə(r),
-z
AM ˌd(j)ʊrə ˌmɑdər,
+ ˌmeıdər, -z

duramen
BR djʊˈreımən,
dʒʊˈreımən
AM d(j)ʊˈreımən

durance
BR ˈdjʊərəns, ˈdjʊərn̩s,
ˈdjɔːrəns, ˈdjɔːrn̩s,
ˈdʒʊərəns, ˈdʒʊərn̩s,
ˈdʒɔːrəns, ˈdʒɔːrn̩s
AM ˈd(j)ʊrəns

Durango
BR d(j)ʊˈraŋgəʊ,
dʒʊˈraŋgəʊ
AM dəˈræŋgoʊ

Durante
BR dəˈran(t)i
AM dəˈræn(t)i

duration
BR djʊˈreıʃn,
dʒʊˈreıʃn
AM dəˈreıʃən

durational
BR djʊˈreıʃn(ə)l,
djʊˈreıʃən(ə)l,
dʒʊˈreıʃn(ə)l,
dʒʊˈreıʃən(ə)l
AM dəˈreıʃ(ə)nəl

durative
BR ˈdjʊərətıv,
ˈdʒʊərətıv, ˈdjɔːrətıv,
ˈdʒɔːrətıv
AM ˈd(j)ʊrədıv

Durban
BR ˈdɜːb(ə)n
AM ˈdərbən

durbar
BR dəˈbɑː(r), -z
AM ˈdərˌbɑr, -z

Dürer
BR ˈd(j)ʊərə(r)
AM ˈdʊrər

duress
BR djʊˈrɛs, dʒʊˈrɛs
AM dəˈrɛs

Durex®
BR ˈdjʊərɛks,
ˈdʒʊərɛks, ˈdjɔːrɛks,
ˈdʒɔːrɛks, -ız
AM ˈd(j)ʊˌrɛks, -əz

Durham
BR ˈdʌrəm
AM ˈdərəm

durian
BR ˈd(j)ʊərıən,
ˈdʒʊərıən, -z
AM ˈdʊrıən, -z

during
BR ˈdjʊərıŋ, ˈdʒʊərıŋ
AM ˈd(j)ʊrıŋ

Durkheim
BR ˈdɜːkhʌım
AM ˈdərkˌ(h)aım

Durkheimian
BR ˌdɜːkˈhʌımıən
AM ˌdərkˈ(h)aımıən

durmast
BR dəˈmɑːst, ˈdɜːmast,
-s

duramen (continued)
AM ˈdərˌmæst, -s

durn
BR dɜːn, -d
AM dərn, -d

Durocher
BR dəˈrəʊʃə(r)
AM dəˈroʊʃər

durra
BR ˈdʊ(ə)rə(r), -z
AM ˈdʊrə, -z

Durrant
BR ˈdʌrənt, ˈdʌrn̩t,
dəˈrant
AM dʊˈrænt

Durrell
BR ˈdʌrəl, ˈdʌrl̩
AM dʊˈrɛl

Dürrenmatt
BR ˈd(j)ʊərənmat,
ˈd(j)ʊərn̩mat
AM ˈd(j)ʊrənˌmæt

durrie
BR ˈdʌrǀi, -ız
AM ˈdəri, -z

durry
BR ˈdʌrǀi, -ız
AM ˈdəri, -z

durst
BR dɜːst
AM dərst

durum
BR ˈdʌrəm
AM ˈdərəm

durzi
BR ˈdɜːzǀi, -ız
AM ˈdərzi, dərˈzi, -z

Dushanbe
BR ˌduːˈʃanˈbeı
AM ˌd(j)uˈʃamˈbeı

dusk
BR dʌsk, -s
AM dəsk, -s

duskily
BR ˈdʌskılı
AM ˈdəskəli

duskiness
BR ˈdʌskınɪs
AM ˈdəskinɪs

dusky
BR ˈdʌskǀi, -ıə(r), -ııst
AM ˈdəski, -ər, -ııst

Düsseldorf
BR ˈdʊsldɔːf
AM ˈdʊsəlˌdɔ(ə)rf

dust
BR dʌst, -s, -ıŋ, -ıd
AM dəst, -s, -ıŋ, -əd

dustbin
BR ˈdʌs(t)bın, -z
AM ˈdəs(t)bın, -z

dustbowl
BR ˈdʌs(t)bəʊl, -z
AM ˈdəs(t)ˌboʊl, -z

dustcart
BR ˈdʌs(t)kɑːt, -s
AM ˈdəs(t)ˌkɑrt, -s

duster
BR ˈdʌstə(r), -z
AM ˈdəstər, -z

dustily
BR ˈdʌstɪli
AM ˈdəstəli

Dustin
BR ˈdʌstɪn
AM ˈdəstən

dustiness
BR ˈdʌstɪnɪs
AM ˈdəstɪnɪs

dustless
BR ˈdʌstləs
AM ˈdəs(t)ləs

dustman
BR ˈdʌs(t)mən
AM ˈdəs(t)mən

dustmen
BR ˈdʌs(t)mən
AM ˈdəs(t)mən

dustpan
BR ˈdʌs(t)pan, -z
AM ˈdəs(t)ˌpæn, -z

dustsheet
BR ˈdʌs(t)ʃiːt, -s
AM ˈdəs(t)ˌʃiːt, -s

dusty
BR ˈdʌstli, -ɪə(r), -ɪɪst
AM ˈdəsti, -ər, -ɪst

Dutch
BR dʌtʃ
AM dʌtʃ

Dutchman
BR ˈdʌtʃmən
AM ˈdətʃmən

Dutchmen
BR ˈdʌtʃmən
AM ˈdətʃmən

Dutchwoman
BR ˈdʌtʃˌwʊmən
AM ˈdətʃˌwʊmən

Dutchwomen
BR ˈdʌtʃˌwɪmɪn
AM ˈdətʃˌwɪmɪn

duteous
BR ˈdjuːtɪəs, ˈdʒuːtɪəs
AM ˈd(j)udiəs

duteously
BR ˈdjuːtɪəsli, ˈdʒuːtɪəsli
AM ˈd(j)udiəsli

duteousness
BR ˈdjuːtɪəsnəs, ˈdʒuːtɪəsnəs
AM ˈd(j)udiəsnəs

dutiable
BR ˈdjuːtɪəbl, ˈdʒuːtɪəbl
AM ˈd(j)udiəbəl

dutiful
BR ˈdjuːtɪf(ʊ)l, ˈdʒuːtɪf(ʊ)l
AM ˈd(j)udəfəl, ˈd(j)udifəl

dutifully
BR ˈdjuːtɪfʊli, ˈdjuːtɪfli, ˈdʒuːtɪfʊli, ˈdʒuːtɪfli
AM ˈd(j)udəfəli, ˈd(j)udifəli

dutifulness
BR ˈdjuːtɪf(ʊ)lnəs, ˈdʒuːtɪf(ʊ)lnəs
AM ˈd(j)udəfəlnəs, ˈd(j)udifəlnəs

Du Toit
BR d(j)ʊ ˈtwɑː(r)
AM du ˈtwɑ

Dutton
BR ˈdʌtn
AM ˈdətn

duty
BR ˈdjuːt|i, ˈdʒuːt|i, -ɪz
AM ˈd(j)udi, -z

duumvir
BR djuˈʌmvə(r), dʒʊˈʌmvə(r), -z
AM d(j)uˈəmvər, d(j)uˈəmˌvi(ə)r, -z

duumvirate
BR djuˈʌmv(ɪ)rət, dʒʊˈʌmv(ɪ)rət
AM d(j)uˈəmvərət

Duvalier
BR d(j)ʊˈvaliei
AM duˌvalˈjei

duvet
BR ˈduːveɪ, -z
AM d(j)uˈveɪ, -z

dux
BR dʌks
AM dəks

duyker
BR ˈdaɪkə(r), -z
AM ˈdaɪkər, -z

Dvořák
BR ˈ(d)vɔːʒak
AM ˈdvɔrˌ(ʒ)ɑk

dwale
BR dweɪl
AM dweɪl

Dwane
BR dweɪn
AM dweɪn

dwarf
BR dwɔːf, -s, -ɪŋ, -t
AM d(w)ɔ(ə)rf, -s, -ɪŋ, -t

dwarfish
BR ˈdwɔːfɪʃ
AM ˈd(w)ɔrfɪʃ

dwarfism
BR ˈdwɔːfɪz(ə)m
AM ˈd(w)ɔrˌfɪzəm

dwarves
BR dwɔːvz
AM d(w)ɔ(ə)rvz

dweeb
BR dwiːb, -z
AM dwib, -z

dwell
BR dwɛl, -z, -ɪŋ, -d
AM dwɛl, -z, -ɪŋ, -d

dweller
BR ˈdwɛlə(r), -z
AM ˈdwɛlər, -z

dwelling
BR ˈdwɛlɪŋ, -z
AM ˈdwɛlɪŋ, -z

dwelt
BR dwɛlt
AM dwɛlt

Dwight
BR dwaɪt
AM dwaɪt

dwindle
BR ˈdwɪndl, -lz, -lɪŋ \ -lɪŋ, -ld
AM ˈdwɪn|dəl, -dəlz, -(d)(ə)lɪŋ, -dəld

Dworkin
BR ˈdwɔːkɪn
AM ˈdworkən

Dwyer
BR ˈdwʌɪə(r)
AM ˈdwaɪər

dyad
BR ˈdʌɪad, -z
AM ˈdaɪˌæd, -z

dyadic
BR dʌɪˈadɪk
AM daɪˈædɪk

Dyak
BR ˈdʌɪak, -s
AM ˈdaɪˌæk, -s

dyarchy
BR ˈdʌɪɑːk|i, -ɪz
AM ˈdaɪˌɑrki, -z

dybbuk
BR ˈdɪbʊk, diːˈbuːk, -s
AM ˈdɪbək, -s

dye
BR dʌɪ, -z, -ɪŋ, -d
AM daɪ, -z, -ɪŋ, -d

dyeable
BR ˈdʌɪəbl
AM ˈdaɪəbəl

dyer
BR ˈdʌɪə(r), -z
AM ˈdaɪər, -z

dyestuff
BR ˈdʌɪstʌf, -s
AM ˈdaɪˌstəf, -s

dyeworks
BR ˈdʌɪwɜːks
AM ˈdaɪˌwɜrks

Dyfed
BR ˈdʌvɪd
AM ˈdəvəd
WE ˈdʌved

Dyffryn
BR ˈdʌfr(ɪ)n
AM ˈdaɪfrɪn

dying
BR ˈdʌɪɪŋ
AM ˈdaɪɪŋ

dyke
BR dʌɪk, -s, -ɪŋ, -t
AM daɪk, -s, -ɪŋ, -t

Dylan¹
surname, as in Bob Dylan
BR ˈdɪlən
AM ˈdɪlən

Dylan²
Welsh forename
BR ˈdɪlən, ˈdʌlən
AM ˈdɪlən
WE ˈdʌlan

Dymchurch
BR ˈdɪmtʃəːtʃ
AM ˈdɪmˌtʃərtʃ

Dymo
BR ˈdʌɪməʊ
AM ˈdaɪmoʊ

Dymock
BR ˈdɪmək
AM ˈdɪmək

Dymond
BR ˈdʌɪm(ə)nd
AM ˈdaɪmənd

Dymont
BR ˈdʌɪm(ə)nt
AM ˈdaɪmənt

Dympna
BR ˈdɪmpnə(r)
AM ˈdɪm(p)nə

dynamic
BR dʌɪˈnamɪk, -s
AM daɪˈnæmɪk, -s

dynamical
BR dʌɪˈnamɪkl
AM daɪˈnæməkəl

dynamically
BR dʌɪˈnamɪkli
AM daɪˈnæmək(ə)li

dynamicist
BR dʌɪˈnamɪsɪst, -s
AM daɪˈnæməsəst, -s

dynamisation
BR ˌdʌɪnəmʌɪˈzeɪʃn
AM daɪˌnæməˈzeɪʃən, daɪnəˌmaɪˈzeɪʃən

dynamise
BR ˈdʌɪnəmʌɪz, -ɪz, -ɪŋ, -d
AM ˈdaɪnəˌmaɪz, -ɪz, -ɪŋ, -d

dynamism
BR ˈdʌɪnəmɪz(ə)m
AM ˈdaɪnəˌmɪzəm

dynamist
BR ˈdʌɪnəmɪst, -s
AM ˈdaɪnəməst, -s

dynamite
BR ˈdʌɪnəmʌɪt
AM ˈdaɪnəˌmaɪt

dynamiter
BR ˈdʌɪnəmʌɪtə(r), -z
AM ˈdaɪnəˌmaɪdər, -z

dynamization
BR ˌdʌɪnəmʌɪˈzeɪʃn
AM daɪˌnæməˈzeɪʃən, daɪnəˌmaɪˈzeɪʃən

dynamize
BR ˈdʌɪnəmʌɪz, -ɪz, -ɪŋ, -d

AM 'daɪnə‚maɪz, -ɪz, -ɪŋ, -d

dynamo
BR 'daɪnəməʊ, -z
AM 'daɪnə‚moʊ, -z

dynamometer
BR ‚daɪnə'mɒmɪtə(r), -z
AM ‚daɪnə'mɑmədər, -z

dynast
BR 'dɪnəst, 'dʌɪnəst, 'dɪnast, 'dʌɪnast, -s
AM 'daɪ‚næst, 'daɪnəst, -s

dynastic
BR dɪ'nastɪk, dʌɪ'nastɪk
AM daɪ'næstɪk, də'næstɪk

dynastically
BR dɪ'nastɪkli, dʌɪ'nastɪkli
AM daɪ'næstək(ə)li, də'næstək(ə)li

dynasty
BR 'dɪnəst|i, -ɪz
AM 'daɪnəsti, -z

dynatron
BR 'dʌɪnətrɒn, -z
AM 'daɪnə‚trɑn, -z

dyne
BR dʌɪn, -z
AM daɪn, -z

Dynefor
BR dɪ'nevə(r), 'dɪnɪvə(r)
AM 'dɪnɪvər

Dysart
BR 'dʌɪsət, 'dʌɪsɑːt, 'dʌɪzɑːt
AM 'daɪ‚sɑrt

dyscalculia
BR ‚dɪskal'kjuːlɪə(r)
AM ‚dɪskæl'kjulɪə

dyscrasia
BR dɪs'kreɪzɪə(r)

AM dɪs'kreɪzɪə

dyscrasic
BR dɪs'kreɪzɪk
AM dɪs'kreɪzɪk

dysenteric
BR ‚dɪs(ə)n'tɛrɪk
AM ‚dɪsn'tɛrɪk

dysentery
BR 'dɪs(ə)nt(ə)ri
AM 'dɪsn‚tɛri

dysfunction
BR (‚)dɪs'fʌŋ(k)ʃn
AM dɪs'fəŋkʃən

dysfunctional
BR (‚)dɪs'fʌŋ(k)ʃn(ə)l, (‚)dɪs'fʌŋ(k)ʃən(ə)l
AM dɪs'fəŋkʃ(ə)nəl

dysgenic
BR dɪs'dʒɛnɪk
AM dɪs'dʒɛnɪk

dysgraphia
BR dɪs'grafɪə(r)
AM dɪs'græfɪə

dysgraphic
BR dɪs'grafɪk
AM dɪs'græfɪk

dyslalia
BR dɪs'leɪlɪə(r)
AM dɪs'leɪljə, dɪs'leɪlɪə

dyslectic
BR dɪs'lɛktɪk, -s
AM dəs'lɛktɪk, -s

dyslexia
BR dɪs'lɛksɪə(r)
AM dəs'lɛksɪə

dyslexic
BR dɪs'lɛksɪk, -s
AM dəs'lɛksɪk, -s

dyslogistic
BR ‚dɪslə'dʒɪstɪk
AM ‚dɪslə'dʒɪstɪk

dyslogistically
BR ‚dɪslə'dʒɪstɪkli
AM ‚dɪslə'dʒɪstək(ə)li

dysmenorrhoea
BR ‚dɪsmɛnə'rɪə(r)
AM ‚dɪs‚mɛnə'rɪə

Dyson
BR 'dʌɪsn
AM 'daɪsən

dyspepsia
BR dɪs'pɛpsɪə(r)
AM dɪs'pɛpsɪə, dɪs'pɛpʃə

dyspeptic
BR dɪs'pɛptɪk, -s
AM dɪs'pɛptɪk, -s

dysphagia
BR dɪs'feɪdʒ(ɪ)ə(r)
AM dɪs'feɪdʒ(i)ə

dysphasia
BR dɪs'feɪzɪə(r), dɪs'feɪʒə(r)
AM dɪs'feɪʒ(i)ə, dɪs'feɪzɪə

dysphasic
BR dɪs'feɪzɪk
AM dɪs'feɪzɪk

dysphemism
BR 'dɪsfɪmɪz(ə)m, -z
AM dɪs'fɛmɪzəm, -z

dysphoria
BR dɪs'fɔːrɪə(r)
AM dɪs'fɔrɪə

dysphoric
BR dɪs'fɒrɪk
AM dɪs'fɔrɪk

dysplasia
BR dɪs'pleɪzɪə(r), dɪs'pleɪzə(r)
AM dɪs'pleɪʒ(i)ə, dɪs'pleɪzɪə

dysplastic
BR dɪs'plastɪk
AM dɪs'plæstɪk

dyspnea
BR dɪsp'niːə(r)
AM 'dɪs(p)nɪə

dyspneic
BR dɪsp'niːɪk
AM dɪs(p)'niːɪk

dyspnoea
BR dɪsp'niːə(r)
AM 'dɪs(p)nɪə

dyspnoeic
BR dɪsp'niːɪk
AM dɪs(p)'niːɪk

dyspraxia
BR dɪs'praksɪə(r)
AM dɪs'præksɪə

dysprosium
BR dɪs'prəʊzɪəm
AM də'sprouzɪəm

dysthymia
BR dɪs'θaɪmɪə(r)
AM dɪs'θaɪmɪə

dystocia
BR dɪs'təʊʃ(ɪ)ə(r)
AM də'stouʃ(i)ə

dystopia
BR dɪs'təʊpɪə(r), -z
AM də'stoupɪə, -z

dystopian
BR dɪs'təʊpɪən, -z
AM də'stoupɪən, -z

dystrophic
BR dɪs'trɒfɪk, dɪs'trəʊfɪk
AM dɪs'trɑfɪk

dystrophy
BR 'dɪstrəfi
AM 'dɪstrəfi

dysuria
BR dɪs'jʊərɪə(r), ‚dɪsjə'riːə(r)
AM də'ʃʊrɪə

Dzerzhinsky
BR dʒəː'ʒɪnski
AM dʒər'ʒɪnski

dzho
BR ʒəʊ, zəʊ, -z
AM dʒoʊ, -z

dziggetai
BR '(d)zɪgətʌɪ, 'dʒɪgətʌɪ, -z
AM '(d)zɪgə‚taɪ, -z

dzo
BR ʒəʊ, zəʊ, -z
AM (d)zoʊ, -z

Dzongkha
BR 'zɒŋkə(r)
AM 'zɒŋkə, 'zɑŋkə

Ee

e
BR iː, -z
AM i, -z

ea.
each
BR iːtʃ
AM itʃ

each
BR iːtʃ
AM itʃ

Eadie
BR 'iːdi
AM 'idi

eager
BR 'iːgə(r)
AM 'igər

eagerly
BR 'iːgəli
AM 'igərli

eagerness
BR 'iːgənəs
AM 'igərnəs

eagle
BR 'iːgl, -z
AM 'igəl, -z

eaglet
BR 'iːglɪt, -s
AM 'iglət, -s

eagre
BR 'iːgə(r), -z
AM 'igər, -z

Eakins
BR 'eɪkɪnz
AM 'eɪkɪnz

Ealing
BR 'iːlɪŋ
AM 'ilɪŋ

Eames
BR iːmz
AM imz

Eamon
BR 'eɪmən
AM 'eɪmən

ear
BR ɪə(r), -z, -d
AM ɪ(ə)r, -z, -d

earache
BR 'ɪəreɪk, -s
AM 'ɪrˌeɪk, -s

earbash
BR 'ɪəbaʃ, -ɪz, -ɪŋ, -t
AM 'ɪrˌbæʃ, -əz, -ɪŋ, -t

earbasher
BR 'ɪəˌbaʃə(r), -z
AM 'ɪrˌbæʃər, -z

Eardley
BR 'əːdli
AM 'ərdli

eardrop
BR 'ɪədrɒp, -s
AM 'ɪrˌdrɑp, -s

eardrum
BR 'ɪədrʌm, -z
AM 'ɪrˌdrəm, -z

eared
BR ɪəd
AM ɪ(ə)rd

earflap
BR 'ɪəflap, -s
AM 'ɪrˌflæp, -s

earful
BR 'ɪəfʊl, -z
AM 'ɪrˌfʊl, 'ɪrfəl, -z

Earhart
BR 'ɛːhɑːt
AM 'ɛrˌ(h)ɑrt

earhole
BR 'ɪəhəʊl, -z
AM 'ɪrˌ(h)oʊl, -z

earing
BR 'ɪərɪŋ, -z
AM 'ɪrɪŋ, -z

earl
BR əːl, -z
AM 'ər(ə)l, -z

earldom
BR 'əːldəm, -z
AM 'ərldəm, -z

Earle
BR əːl
AM ərl

earless
BR 'ɪələs
AM 'ɪrləs

Earley
BR 'əːli
AM 'ərli

earliness
BR 'əːlɪnɪs
AM 'ərlinɪs

earlobe
BR 'ɪələʊb, -z
AM 'ɪrˌloʊb, -z

early
BR 'əːl|i, -ɪə(r), -ɪɪst
AM 'ərli, -ər, -ɪst

earmark
BR 'ɪəmɑːk, -s, -ɪŋ, -t
AM 'ɪrˌmɑrk, -s, -ɪŋ, -t

earmuff
BR 'ɪəmʌf, -s
AM 'ɪrˌməf, -s

earn
BR əːn, -z, -ɪŋ, -d\-t
AM ərn, -z, -ɪŋ, -d\-t

earner
BR 'əːnə(r), -z
AM 'ərnər, -z

earnest
BR 'əːnɪst
AM 'ərnəst

earnestly
BR 'əːnɪstli
AM 'ərnəs(t)li

earnestness
BR 'əːnɪs(t)nəs
AM 'ərnəs(t)nəs

earnings
BR 'əːnɪŋz
AM 'ərnɪŋz

Earnshaw
BR 'əːnʃɔː(r)
AM 'ərnˌʃɔ

EAROM
BR 'iːrɒm
AM 'iˌrɑm

Earp
BR əːp
AM ərp

earphone
BR 'ɪəfəʊn, -z
AM 'ɪrˌfoʊn, -z

earpiece
BR 'ɪəpiːs, -ɪz
AM 'ɪrˌpis, -ɪz

earplug
BR 'ɪəplʌg, -z
AM 'ɪrˌpləg, -z

earring
BR 'ɪərɪŋ, -z
AM 'ɪr(r)ɪŋ, -z

earshot
BR 'ɪəʃɒt
AM 'ɪrˌʃɑt

earth
BR əːθ, -s, -ɪŋ, -t
AM ərθ, -s, -ɪŋ, -t

Eartha
BR 'əːθə(r)
AM 'ərθə

earthbound
BR 'əːθbaʊnd
AM 'ərθˌbaʊnd

earthen
BR 'əːθn, 'əːðn
AM 'ərθən

earthenware
BR 'əːθnwɛː(r), 'əːðnwɛː(r)
AM 'ərθən,wɛ(ə)r

earthily
BR 'əːθɪli
AM 'ərθəli

earthiness
BR 'əːθɪnɪs
AM 'ərθinɪs

earthliness
BR 'əːθlɪnɪs
AM 'ərθlinɪs

earthling
BR 'əːθlɪŋ, -z
AM 'ərθlɪŋ, -z

earthly
BR 'əːθl|i, -ɪə(r), -ɪɪst
AM 'ərθli, -ər, -ɪst

earthman
BR 'əːθman
AM 'ərθˌmæn

earthmen
BR 'əːθmen
AM 'ərθˌmɛn

earthnut
BR 'əːθnʌt, -s
AM 'ərθˌnət, -s

earthquake
BR 'əːθkweɪk, -s
AM 'ərθˌkweɪk, -s

earthshaking
BR 'əːθˌʃeɪkɪŋ
AM 'ərθˌʃeɪkɪŋ

earthshattering
BR 'əːθˌʃat(ə)rɪŋ
AM 'ərθˌʃædərɪŋ

earthshatteringly
BR 'əːθˌʃat(ə)rɪŋli
AM 'ərθˌʃædərɪŋli

earthshine
BR 'əːθʃʌɪn
AM 'ərθˌʃaɪn

earthstar
BR 'əːθstɑː(r), -z
AM 'ərθˌstɑr, -z

earthward
BR 'əːθwəd, -z
AM 'ərθwərd, -z

earthwork
BR 'əːθwəːk, -s
AM 'ərθˌwərk, -s

earthworm
BR 'əːθwəm, -z
AM 'ərθˌwərm, -z

earthy
BR 'əːθ|i, -ɪə(r), -ɪɪst
AM 'ərθi, -ər, -ɪst

earwax
BR 'ɪəwaks
AM 'ɪrˌwæks

earwig
BR 'ɪəwɪg, -z
AM 'ɪrˌwɪg, -z

ease
BR iːz, -ɪz, -ɪŋ, -d
AM iz, -ɪz, -ɪŋ, -d

easeful
BR 'iːzf(ʊ)l
AM 'izfəl

easefully
BR 'iːzfʊli, 'iːzfʃi
AM 'izfəli

easefulness
BR 'iːzf(ʊ)lnəs
AM 'izfəlnəs

easel
BR 'iːzl, -z
AM 'izəl, -z

easement
BR 'iːzm(ə)nt, -s
AM 'izmənt, -s

easer
BR 'iːzə(r), -z
AM 'izər, -z

easily
BR 'iːzɪli
AM 'iz(ə)li

easiness
BR 'iːzɪnɪs
AM 'izinɪs

Easington
BR 'iːzɪŋt(ə)n
AM 'izɪŋtən

east
BR iːst, -s
AM ist, -s

eastabout
BR 'iːstəbaʊt
AM 'istə‚baʊt

eastbound
BR 'iːs(t)baʊnd
AM 'is(t)‚baʊnd

Eastbourne
BR 'iːs(t)bɔːn
AM 'is(t)‚bɔː(ə)rn

Eastcheap
BR 'iːs(t)tʃiːp
AM 'is(t)‚tʃip

Easter
BR 'iːstə(r), -z
AM 'istər, -z

easterly
BR 'iːstəl|i, -ɪz
AM 'istərli, -z

eastern
BR 'iːst(ə)n
AM 'istərn

easterner
BR 'iːstənə(r),
'iːstnə(r), -z
AM 'istərnər, -z

easternmost
BR 'iːst(ə)nməʊst
AM 'istərn‚məʊst

Eastertide
BR 'iːstətʌɪd
AM 'istər‚taɪd

easting
BR 'iːstɪŋ, -z
AM 'istɪŋ, -z

Eastleigh
BR ‚iːs(t)'liː, 'iːs(t)liː
AM 'is(t)li

Eastman
BR 'iːs(t)mən
AM 'is(t)mən

Easton
BR 'iːst(ə)n
AM 'istən

eastward
BR 'iːstwəd, -z
AM 'is(t)wərd, -z

eastwardly
BR 'iːstwədli
AM 'is(t)wərdli

East-West
BR ‚iːs(t)'wɛst
AM 'is(t)'wɛst

Eastwood
BR 'iːstwʊd
AM 'is(t)‚wʊd

easy
BR 'iːz|i, -ɪə(r), -ɪɪst
AM 'izi, -ər, -ɪst

easygoing
BR ‚iːzi'gəʊɪŋ
AM 'izi'gəʊɪŋ

easy-peasy
BR ‚iːzɪ'piːzi
AM ‚izi'pizi

eat
BR iːt, -s, -ɪŋ
AM i|t, -ts, -dɪŋ

eatable
BR 'iːtəbl, -z
AM 'idəbəl, -z

eater
BR 'iːtə(r), -z
AM 'idər, -z

eatery
BR 'iːt(ə)r|i, -ɪz
AM 'idəri, -z

Eaton
BR 'iːtn
AM 'itn

eats
BR iːts
AM its

eau de Cologne
BR ‚əʊ də kə'ləʊn
AM ‚oʊ də kə'loʊn

eau-de-Nil
BR ‚əʊ də 'niːl
AM ‚oʊ də 'nil

eau de toilette
BR ‚əʊ də twɑː'lɛt
AM ‚oʊ də twɑ'lɛt

eau-de-vie
BR ‚əʊ də 'viː
AM ‚oʊ də 'vi

eaves
BR iːvz
AM ivz

eavesdrop
BR 'iːvzdrɒp, -s, -ɪŋ, -t
AM 'ivz‚drɑp, -s, -ɪŋ, -t

eavesdropper
BR 'iːvzdrɒpə(r), -z
AM 'ivz‚drɑpər, -z

eavestrough
BR 'iːvztrɒf, -s
AM 'ivz‚trɔf, 'ivz‚trɑf, -s

ebb
BR ɛb, -z, -ɪŋ, -d
AM ɛb, -z, -ɪŋ, -d

ebb-tide
BR ‚ɛb'tʌɪd, 'ɛbtʌɪd, -z
AM 'ɛb‚taɪd, -z

Ebbw Vale
BR ‚ɛbʊ 'veɪl
AM ‚ɛbu 'veɪl

Ebenezer
BR ɛbɪ'niːzə(r)
AM ɛbə'nizər

Ebla
BR 'ɛblə(r)
AM 'ɛblə, 'iblə

Ebola
BR ɪ'bəʊlə(r)
AM i'boʊlə, ə'boʊlə

ebon
BR 'ɛb(ə)n
AM 'ɛbən

Ebonics
BR ɛ'bɒnɪks
AM i'bɑnɪks

ebonise
BR 'ɛbənʌɪz, -ɪz, -ɪŋ, -d
AM 'ɛbə‚naɪz, -ɪz, -ɪŋ, -d

ebonite
BR 'ɛbənʌɪt
AM 'ɛbə‚naɪt

ebonize
BR 'ɛbənʌɪz, -ɪz, -ɪŋ, -d
AM 'ɛbə‚naɪz, -ɪz, -ɪŋ, -d

ebony
BR 'ɛbəni, 'ɛbn̩i
AM 'ɛbəni

Ebor
BR 'iːbɔː(r)
AM 'ibɔ(ə)r

Eboricum
BR ɪ'bɒrəkəm
AM i'bɔrəkəm

Ebro
BR 'iːbrəʊ, 'ɛbrəʊ
AM 'i‚broʊ

ebullience
BR ɪ'bʌlɪəns, ɪ'bʊlɪəns
AM ə'bʊljəns,
i'bʊljəns, ə'bəljəns,
i'bəljəns

ebulliency
BR ɪ'bʌlɪənsi,
ɪ'bʊlɪənsi
AM ə'bʊljənsi,
i'bʊljənsi, ə'bəljənsi,
i'bəljənsi

ebullient
BR ɪ'bʌlɪənt, ɪ'bʊlɪənt
AM ə'bʊliənt,
i'bʊljənt, ə'bəljənt,
i'bəljənt

ebulliently
BR ɪ'bʌlɪəntli,
ɪ'bʊlɪəntli
AM ə'bʊliən(t)li,
i'bʊljən(t)li,
ə'bəljən(t)li,
i'bəljən(t)li

ebullition
BR ‚ɛbə'lɪʃn, -z
AM ‚ɛbə'lɪʃən, -z

Ebury
BR 'iːb(ə)ri
AM 'ibəri

ecad
BR 'iːkad, -z
AM 'i‚kæd, 'ɛ‚kæd, -z

écarté
BR eɪ'kɑːteɪ
AM ‚eɪkɑr'teɪ

Ecce Homo
BR ‚ɛkɪ 'həʊməʊ,
‚ɛtʃeɪ +, ‚ɛksɪ +,
+ 'hɒməʊ
AM ‚ɛtʃeɪ 'hoʊ‚moʊ,
‚ɛtʃə +

eccentric
BR ɪk'sɛntrɪk,
ɛk'sɛntrɪk
AM ɪk'sɛntrɪk

eccentrically
BR ɪk'sɛntrɪkli,
ɛk'sɛntrɪkli
AM ɪk'sɛntrək(ə)li

eccentricity
BR ‚ɛksɛn'trɪsɪt|i,
‚ɛks(ə)n'trɪsɪt|i, -ɪz
AM ‚ɛk‚sɛn'trɪsɪdi, -z

Eccles
BR 'ɛklz
AM 'ɛkəlz

ecclesia
BR ɪ'kliːzɪə(r)
AM ə'kliziə, ə'kliʒiə

ecclesial
BR ɪ'kliːzɪəl
AM ə'kliziəl

Ecclesiastes
BR ɪ‚kliːzɪ'astiːz
AM ə‚klizi'æstiz

ecclesiastic
BR ɪ‚kliːzɪ'astɪk, -s
AM ə‚klizi'æstɪk, -s

ecclesiastical
BR ɪ‚kliːzɪ'astɪkl
AM ə‚klizi'æstəkəl

ecclesiastically
BR ɪ‚kliːzɪ'astɪkli
AM ə‚klizi'æstək(ə)li

ecclesiasticism
BR ɪ‚kliːzɪ'astɪsɪz(ə)m
AM ə‚klizi'æstə‚sɪzəm

Ecclesiasticus
BR ɪ‚kliːzɪ'astɪkəs
AM ə‚klizi'æstəkəs

ecclesiological
BR ɪ‚kliːzɪə'lɒdʒɪkl
AM ə‚kliziə'lɑdʒəkəl

ecclesiologist
BR ɪ‚kliːzɪ'ɒlədʒɪst, -s
AM ə‚klizi'ɑlədʒəst, -s

ecclesiology
BR ɪ‚kliːzɪ'ɒlədʒi
AM ə‚klizi'ɑlədʒi

Ecclestone
BR 'ɛklst(ə)n
AM 'ɛklstən

eccrine
BR 'ɛkrʌɪn, 'ɛkrɪn
AM 'ɛkrən, 'ɛ‚krʌɪn,
'ɛ‚krɪn

ecdysiast
BR ɛk'dɪzɪast, -s
AM ɛk'diziəst, -s

ecdysis
BR 'ɛkdɪsɪs
AM 'ɛkdəsəs

echelon
BR 'ɛʃəlɒn, -z, -ɪŋ, -d
AM 'ɛʃ(ə)ʃɑn, -z, -ɪŋ, -d

echeveria
BR ‚ɛtʃɪ'vɪərɪə(r), -z
AM ‚ɛtʃəvə'riə,
‚ɛtʃəvə'raɪə, -z

echidna
BR ɪ'kɪdnə(r), -z
AM ə'kɪdnə, -z

echinite
BR ˈɛkənʌɪt, ɪˈkʌɪnʌɪt,
-s
AM ˈɛkəˌnaɪt,
əˈkaɪˌnaɪt, iˈkaɪˌnaɪt,
-s

echinoderm
BR ɪˈkʌɪnə(ʊ)dəːm,
ɪˈkɪnə(ʊ)dəːm, -z
AM əˈkaɪnəˌdərm,
əˈkɪnəˌdərm, -z

echinoid
BR ɪˈkʌɪnɔɪd, ˈɛkɪnɔɪd,
ˈɛkɳɔɪd, -z
AM ˈɛkəˌnɔɪd,
əˈkaɪˌnɔɪd, iˈkaɪˌnɔɪd,
-z

echinus
BR ɪˈkʌɪnəs, ˈɛkɪnəs,
ˈɛkɳəs, -ɪz
AM əˈkaɪnəs, iˈkaɪnəs,
-əz

echo
BR ˈɛkəʊ, -z, -ɪŋ, -d
AM ˈɛkoʊ, -z, -ɪŋ, -d

echocardiogram
BR ˌɛkəʊˈkɑːdɪəgram,
-z
AM ˌɛkoʊˈkardiəˌgræm,
-z

echocardiograph
BR ˌɛkəʊˈkɑːdɪəgrɑːf,
ˌɛkəʊˈkɑːdɪəgraf, -s
AM ˌɛkoʊˈkardiəˌgræf,
-s

echocardiographer
BR ˌɛkəʊkɑːdɪˈɒgrəfə(r),
-z
AM ˌɛkoʊˌkardiˈagrəfər,
ˌɛkoʊˈkardiəˌgræfər,
-z

echocardiography
BR ˌɛkəʊkɑːdɪˈɒgrafi,
-ɪz
AM ˌɛkoʊˌkardiˈagrəfi,
-z

echoencephalogram
BR ˌɛkəʊɛnˈsɛf(ə)lə(ʊ)-
gram,
ˌɛkəʊɛnˈsɛflə(ʊ)gram,
ˌɛkəʊɛnˈkɛf(ə)lə(ʊ)-
gram,
ˌɛkəʊɛnˈkɛflə(ʊ)gram,
-z
AM ˌɛkoʊˌɛnˈsɛfələ-
ˌgræm, -z

echoencephalography
BR ˌɛkəʊɛnˌsɛfəˈlɒgrafi,
ˌɛkəʊɛnˌsɛflˈɒgrəfi,
ˌɛkəʊɛnˌkɛfəˈlɒgrafi,
ˌɛkəʊɛnˌkɛflˈɒgrəfi,
AM ˌɛkoʊˌɛnˌsɛfəˈlagrəfi

echoer
BR ˈɛkəʊə(r), -z
AM ˈɛkoʊər, -z

echoey
BR ˈɛkəʊi
AM ˈɛkoʊi

echogram
BR ˈɛkəʊgram, -z
AM ˈɛkoʊˌgræm, -z

echograph
BR ˈɛkəʊgrɑːf,
ˈɛkəʊgraf, -s
AM ˈɛkoʊˌgræf, -s

echoic
BR ɛˈkəʊɪk, ɪˈkəʊɪk
AM əˈkoʊɪk, ɛˈkoʊɪk

echoically
BR ɛˈkəʊɪkli, ɪˈkəʊɪkli
AM əˈkoʊək(ə)li,
ɛˈkoʊək(ə)li

echoism
BR ˈɛkəʊɪzm
AM ˈɛkoʊˌɪzəm

echolalia
BR ˌɛkə(ʊ)ˈleɪliə(r)
AM ˌɛkoʊˈleɪljə,
ˌɛkoʊˈleɪliə

echoless
BR ˈɛkəʊləs
AM ˈɛkoʊləs

echolocate
BR ˈɛkəʊlə(ʊ)ˌkeɪt, -s,
-ɪŋ, -ɪd
AM ˌɛkoʊˈloʊˌkeɪ|t, -ts,
-dɪŋ, -dɪd

echolocation
BR ˌɛkəʊlə(ʊ)ˈkeɪʃn,
ˈɛkəʊlə(ʊ)ˌkeɪʃn
AM ˌɛkoʊˌloʊˈkeɪʃən

echovirus
BR ˈɛkəʊˌvʌɪrəs
AM ˈɛkoʊˌvaɪrəs

echt
BR ɛxt, ɛkt
AM ɛkt

Eckersley
BR ˈɛkəzli
AM ˈɛkərzli

Eckert
BR ˈɛkəːt
AM ˈɛkərt

Eckhart
BR ˈɛkhɑːt
AM ˈɛkərt

éclair
BR ɪˈklɛː(r), eɪˈklɛː(r),
-z
AM eɪˈklɛ(ə)r, ɪˈklɛ(ə)r,
-z

éclaircissement
BR eɪˈklɛːsiːsmɒ̃
AM eɪˌklɛrsiːsˈmant

eclampsia
BR ɪˈklam(p)sɪə(r)
AM ɪˈklæm(p)siə

eclamptic
BR ɪˈklam(p)tɪk
AM ɪˈklæm(p)tɪk

éclat
BR eɪˈklɑː(r), ɛˈklɑː(r),
ˈeɪklɑː(r), ˈɛklɑː(r)

AM eɪˈklɑ

eclectic
BR ɪˈklɛktɪk
AM iˈklɛktɪk, əˈklɛktɪk

eclectically
BR ɪˈklɛktɪkli
AM iˈklɛktək(ə)li,
əˈklɛktək(ə)li

eclecticism
BR ɪˈklɛktɪsɪz(ə)m
AM iˈklɛktəˌsɪzəm,
əˈklɛktəˌsɪzəm

eclipse
BR ɪˈklɪps, -ɪz, -ɪŋ, -t
AM əˈklɪps, iˈklɪps, -ɪz,
-ɪŋ, -t

eclipser
BR ɪˈklɪpsə(r), -z
AM əˈklɪpsər, iˈklɪpsər,
-z

ecliptic
BR ɪˈklɪptɪk, -s
AM əˈklɪptɪk, iˈklɪptɪk,
-s

ecliptically
BR ɪˈklɪptɪkli
AM əˈklɪptək(ə)li,
iˈklɪptək(ə)li

eclogue
BR ˈɛklɒg, -z
AM ˈɛˌklɔg, ˈɛˌklag, -z

eclosion
BR ɪˈkləʊʒn
AM əˈkloʊʒən,
iˈkloʊʒən

Eco
BR ˈɛkəʊ
AM ˈɛkoʊ

ecoclimate
BR ˈiːkəʊˌklʌɪmɪt,
ˈɛkəʊˌklʌɪmɪt, -s
AM ˈɛkoʊˌklaɪmət,
ˈikoʊˌklaɪmət, -s

eco-friendly
BR ˈiːkəʊˈfrɛn(d)li,
ˌɛkəʊˈfrɛn(d)li
AM ˈɛkoʊˌfrɛndli,
ˈikoʊˌfrɛndli

eco-label
BR ˈiːkəʊˌleɪbl,
ˈɛkəʊˌleɪbl, -z
AM ˈɛkoʊˌleɪbəl, -z

eco-labelling
BR ˈiːkəʊˌleɪblɪŋ,
ˈiːkəʊˌleɪblɪŋ,
ˈɛkəʊˌleɪblɪŋ,
ˈɛkəʊˌleɪblɪŋ
AM ˈɛkoʊˌleɪb(ə)lɪŋ,
ˈikoʊˌleɪb(ə)lɪŋ

E. coli
BR ˌiː ˈkəʊlʌɪ
AM ˌi ˈkoʊlaɪ

ecological
BR ˌiːkəˈlɒdʒɪkl,
ˌɛkəˈlɒdʒɪkl
AM ˌɛkəˈladʒəkəl,
ˈikəˈladʒəkəl

ecologically
BR ˌiːkəˈlɒdʒɪkli,
ˌɛkəˈlɒdʒɪkli
AM ˌɛkəˈladʒək(ə)li,
ˈikəˈladʒək(ə)li

ecologist
BR ɪˈkɒlədʒɪst, -s
AM iˈkalədʒəst,
əˈkalədʒəst, -s

ecology
BR ɪˈkɒlədʒi
AM iˈkalədʒi, əˈkalədʒi

econometric
BR ɪˌkɒnəˈmɛtrɪk, -s
AM əˌkanəˈmɛtrɪk,
iˌkanəˈmɛtrɪk, -s

econometrical
BR ɪˌkɒnəˈmɛtrɪkl
AM əˌkanəˈmɛtrəkəl,
iˌkanəˈmɛtrəkəl

econometrically
BR ɪˌkɒnəˈmɛtrɪkli
AM əˌkanəˈmɛtrək(ə)li,
iˌkanəˈmɛtrək(ə)li

econometrician
BR ɪˌkɒnəməˈtrɪʃn, -z
AM əˌkanəməˈtrɪʃən,
-z

econometrist
BR ɪˌkɒnəˈmɛtrɪst, -s
AM əˌkanəˈmɛtrəst,
iˌkanəˈmɛtrəst, -s

economic
BR ˌiːkəˈnɒmɪk,
ˌɛkəˈnɒmɪk, -s
AM ˌɛkəˈnamɪk,
ˈikəˈnamɪk, -s

economical
BR ˌiːkəˈnɒmɪkl,
ˌɛkəˈnɒmɪkl
AM ˌɛkəˈnaməkəl,
ˈikəˈnaməkəl

economically
BR ˌiːkəˈnɒmɪkli,
ˌɛkəˈnɒmɪkli
AM ˌɛkəˈnamək(ə)li,
ˈikəˈnamək(ə)li

economisation
BR ɪˌkɒnəmʌɪˈzeɪʃn
AM əˌkanəməˈzeɪʃən,
iˌkanəˌmaɪˈzeɪʃən,
iˌkanəməˈzeɪʃən,
əˌkanəˈmaɪˈzeɪʃən,
ˌɛkəˌnaməˈzeɪʃən,
ˈikəˌnaməˈzeɪʃən

economise
BR ɪˈkɒnəˌmʌɪz, -ɪz, -ɪŋ,
-d
AM iˈkanəˌmaɪz,
əˈkanəˌmaɪz, -ɪz, -ɪŋ,
-d

economiser
BR ɪˈkɒnəˌmʌɪzə(r), -z
AM iˈkanəˌmaɪzər,
əˈkanəˌmaɪzər, -z

economist
BR ɪˈkɒnəmɪst, -s

economization AM iˈkɑnəməst,
əˈkɑnəməst, -s

economization
BR ɪˌkɒnəmaɪˈzeɪʃn
AM əˌkɑnəməˈzeɪʃən,
iˌkɑnəˌmaɪˈzeɪʃən,
iˌkɑnəməˈzeɪʃən,
əˌkɑnəˌmaɪˈzeɪʃən,
ˈˌɛkəˌnɑməˈzeɪʃən,
ˈˌikəˌnɑməˈzeɪʃən

economize
BR ɪˈkɒnəmaɪz, -ɪz, -ɪŋ,
-d
AM iˈkɑnəˌmaɪz,
əˈkɑnəˌmaɪz, -ɪz, -ɪŋ,
-d

economizer
BR ɪˈkɒnəmaɪzə(r), -z
AM iˈkɑnəˌmaɪzər,
əˈkɑnəˌmaɪzər, -z

economy
BR ɪˈkɒnəmǀi, -ɪz
AM iˈkɑnəmi,
əˈkɑnəmi, -z

écorché
BR ˌeɪkɔːˈʃeɪ
AM ˌeɪkɔrˈʃeɪ

ecosphere
BR ˈiːkəʊsfɪə(r),
ˈɛkəʊsfɪə(r)
AM ˈikoʊˌsfɪ(ə)r,
ˈɛkoʊˌsfɪ(ə)r

écossaise
BR ˌeɪkɒˈseɪz, ˌɛkɒˈseɪz
AM eɪˌkoʊˈseɪz

écossaises
BR ˌeɪkɒˈseɪz,
ˌɛkɒˈseɪz, ˌeɪkɒˈseɪzɪz,
ˌɛkɒˈseɪzɪz
AM eɪˌkoʊˈseɪz(ɪz)

ecosystem
BR ˈiːkəʊˌsɪstɪm,
ˈɛkəʊˌsɪstɪm, -z
AM ˈikoʊˌsɪstəm,
ˈɛkoʊˌsɪstəm, -z

eco-terrorism
BR ˈiːkəʊˌterərɪz(ə)m,
ˈɛkəʊˌterərɪz(ə)m
AM ˈɛkoʊˌterəˌrɪzəm,
ˈikoʊˌterəˌrɪzəm

eco-terrorist
BR ˈiːkəʊˌterərɪst,
ˈɛkəʊˌterərɪst, -s
AM ˈɛkoʊˌterərəst,
ˈikoʊˌterərəst, -s

écru
BR ˈeɪkruː, ɛˈkruː
AM ˈɛkru, ˈeɪkru

ecstasise
BR ˈɛkstəsʌɪz, -ɪz, -ɪŋ,
-d
AM ˈɛkstəˌsaɪz, -ɪz, -ɪŋ,
-d

ecstasize
BR ˈɛkstəsʌɪz, -ɪz, -ɪŋ,
-d
AM ˈɛkstəˌsaɪz, -ɪz, -ɪŋ,
-d

ecstasy
BR ˈɛkstəsǀi, -ɪz
AM ˈɛkstəsi, -z

ecstatic
BR ɪkˈstatɪk, ɛkˈstatɪk
AM ɛkˈstædɪk

ecstatically
BR ɪkˈstatɪkli,
ɛkˈstatɪkli
AM ɛkˈstædək(ə)li

ectoblast
BR ˈɛktə(ʊ)blɑːst,
ˈɛktə(ʊ)blast, -s
AM ˈɛktəˌblæst, -s

ectoblastic
BR ˌɛktə(ʊ)ˈblastɪk
AM ˌɛktəˈblæstɪk

ectoderm
BR ˈɛktə(ʊ)dəːm, -z
AM ˈɛktəˌdərm, -z

ectodermal
BR ˌɛktə(ʊ)ˈdəːml
AM ˌɛktəˈdərməl

ectogenesis
BR ˌɛktə(ʊ)ˈdʒɛnɪsɪs, -s
AM ˌɛktəˈdʒɛnəsəs, -s

ectogenetic
BR ˌɛktə(ʊ)ˈdʒɪˈnɛtɪk
AM ˌɛktədʒəˈnɛdɪk

ectogenetically
BR ˌɛktə(ʊ)ˈdʒɪˈnɛtɪkli
AM ˌɛktədʒəˈnɛdək(ə)li

ectogenic
BR ˌɛktə(ʊ)ˈdʒɛnɪk, -s
AM ˌɛktəˈdʒɛnɪk, -s

ectogenically
BR ˌɛktə(ʊ)ˈdʒɛnɪkli
AM ˌɛktəˈdʒɛnək(ə)li

ectogenous
BR ɛkˈtɒdʒɪnəs
AM ɛkˈtɑdʒənəs

ectomorph
BR ˈɛktə(ʊ)mɔːf, -s
AM ˈɛktəˌmɔ(ə)rf, -s

ectomorphic
BR ˌɛktə(ʊ)ˈmɔːfɪk
AM ˌɛktəˈmorfɪk

ectomorphy
BR ˈɛktə(ʊ)mɔːfi
AM ˈɛktəˌmorfi

ectoparasite
BR ˈɛktə(ʊ)ˌparəsʌɪt,
-s
AM ˌɛktəˈpɛrəˌsaɪt, -s

ectopic
BR ɛkˈtɒpɪk
AM ɛkˈtɑpɪk

ectoplasm
BR ˈɛktə(ʊ)plaz(ə)m
AM ˈɛktəˌplæzəm

ectoplasmic
BR ˌɛktə(ʊ)ˈplazmɪk
AM ˌɛktəˈplæzəmɪk

ectozoon
BR ˌɛktə(ʊ)ˈzuːɒn,
ˌɛktə(ʊ)ˈzəʊɒn, -z

ecstasy AM ˌɛktəˈzoʊən,
ˌɛktəˈzuən, -z

ecu
BR ˈɛkjuː, ˈeɪkjuː, -z
AM eɪˈk(j)u, -z

Ecuador
BR ˈɛkwədɔː(r)
AM ˈɛkwəˌdɔ(ə)r
SP ˌekwaˈðor

Ecuadoran
BR ˌɛkwəˈdɔːrən, -z
AM ˌɛkwəˈdɔrən, -z

Ecuadorean
BR ˌɛkwəˈdɔːrɪən, -z
AM ˌɛkwəˈdɔr(i)ən, -z

Ecuadorian
BR ˌɛkwəˈdɔːrɪən, -z
AM ˌɛkwəˈdɔrɪən, -z

ecumenical
BR ˌiːkjʉˈmɛnɪkl,
ˌɛkjʉˈmɛnɪkl
AM ˌɛkjəˈmɛnəkəl

ecumenicalism
BR ˌiːkjʉˈmɛnɪkəlɪz(ə)m,
ˌiːkjʉˈmɛnɪklɪz(ə)m,
ˌɛkjʉˈmɛnɪkəlɪz(ə)m,
ˌɛkjʉˈmɛnɪklɪzəm
AM ˌɛkjəˈmɛnəkəˌlɪzəm

ecumenically
BR ˌiːkjʉˈmɛnɪkli,
ˌɛkjʉˈmɛnɪkli
AM ˌɛkjəˈmɛnək(ə)li

ecumenicism
BR ˌiːkjʉˈmɛnɪsɪz(ə)m,
ˌɛkjʉˈmɛnɪsɪzəm
AM ˌɛkjəˈmɛnəˌsɪzəm

ecumenicity
BR ˌiːˌkjuːməˈnɪsɪti
AM ˌɛkjəməˈnɪsɪdi

ecumenism
BR ɪˈkjuːmənɪz(ə)m
AM ˈɛkjəməˌnɪzəm,
ɛˈkjuːməˌnɪzəm

eczema
BR ˈɛks(ɪ)mə(r),
ˈɛgzɪmə(r)
AM ˈɛksəmə, ˈɛgzəmə,
ɛɡˈzimə, ɪɡˈzimə

eczematous
BR ɛkˈsɛmətəs,
ɪkˈsɛmətəs,
ɛkˈzɛmətəs,
ɪkˈzɛmətəs
AM ɛɡˈzɛmədəs,
ɛɡˈzimədəs,
ɪɡˈzimədəs,
ɪɡˈzɛmədəs

Ed
BR ɛd
AM ɛd

edacious
BR ɪˈdeɪʃəs
AM əˈdeɪʃəs, iˈdeɪʃəs

edacity
BR ɪˈdasɪti
AM əˈdæsədi, iˈdæsədi

Edale
BR ˈiːdeɪl

Edam
BR ˈiːdam
AM ˈidəm

edaphic
BR ɪˈdafɪk
AM əˈdæfɪk, iˈdæfɪk

Edda
BR ˈɛdə(r), -z
AM ˈɛdə, -z

Eddic
BR ˈɛdɪk
AM ˈɛdɪk

Eddie
BR ˈɛdi
AM ˈɛdi

Eddington
BR ˈɛdɪŋt(ə)n
AM ˈɛdɪŋtən

eddo
BR ˈɛdəʊ, -z
AM ˈɛˌdoʊ, -z

eddy
BR ˈɛdǀi, -ɪz, -ɪŋ, -ɪd
AM ˈɛdi, -z, -ɪŋ, -d

Eddystone
BR ˈɛdɪst(ə)n
AM ˈɛdiˌstoʊn

edelweiss
BR ˈeɪdlvʌɪs
AM ˈeɪdlˌwaɪs,
ˈeɪdlˌvaɪs

edema
BR ɪˈdiːmə(r), -z
AM əˈdimə, -z

edematose
BR ɪˈdiːmətəʊs,
iːˈdiːmətəʊs
AM əˈdiməˌtoʊs,
iˈdiməˌtoʊs,
əˈdiməˌtoʊz,
iˈdiməˌtoʊz

edematous
BR ɪˈdiːmətəs
AM əˈdɛmədəs

Eden
BR ˈiːdn
AM ˈidən

edentate
BR ɪˈdenteɪt
AM əˈdɛnˌteɪt

Edessa
BR ɪˈdɛsə(r)
AM əˈdɛsə

Edgar
BR ˈɛdɡə(r)
AM ˈɛdɡər

Edgbaston
BR ˈɛdʒbəst(ə)n,
ˈɛdʒbast(ə)n
AM ˈɛdʒˌbæstən

edge
BR ɛdʒ, -ɪz, -ɪŋ, -d
AM ɛdʒ, -əz, -ɪŋ, -d

Edgecomb
BR ˈɛdʒkəm
AM ˈɛdʒkəm

Edgecombe
BR ˈɛdʒkəm
AM ˈɛdʒkəm
Edgehill¹
place in UK
BR ˌɛdʒˈhɪl
AM ˌɛdʒˈhɪl
Edgehill²
surname
BR ˈɛdʒhɪl
AM ˈɛdʒˌ(h)ɪl
edgeless
BR ˈɛdʒləs
AM ˈɛdʒləs
edger
BR ˈɛdʒə(r), -z
AM ˈɛdʒər, -z
Edgerton
BR ˈɛdʒət(ə)n
AM ˈɛdʒərtən
edgeways
BR ˈɛdʒweɪz
AM ˈɛdʒˌweɪz
edgewise
BR ˈɛdʒwʌɪz
AM ˈɛdʒˌwaɪz
Edgeworth
BR ˈɛdʒwə(ː)θ
AM ˈɛdʒˌwərθ
edgily
BR ˈɛdʒɪli
AM ˈɛdʒəli
edginess
BR ˈɛdʒɪnɪs
AM ˈɛdʒɪnɪs
edging
BR ˈɛdʒɪŋ, -z
AM ˈɛdʒɪŋ, -z
Edgware
BR ˈɛdʒwɛː(r)
AM ˈɛdʒˌwɛ(ə)r
edgy
BR ˈɛdʒ|i, -ɪə(r), -ɪɪst
AM ˈɛdʒi, -ər, -ɪst
edh
BR ɛð, -z
AM ɛð, -z
edibility
BR ˌɛdɪˈbɪlɪti
AM ˌɛdəˈbɪlɪdi
edible
BR ˈɛdɪbl, -z
AM ˈɛdəbəl, -z
edibleness
BR ˈɛdɪblnəs
AM ˈɛdəbəlnəs
edict
BR ˈiːdɪkt, -s
AM ˈidɪk|(t), -(t)s
edictal
BR ɪˈdɪktl
AM əˈdɪktl, iˈdɪktl
Edie
BR ˈiːdi
AM ˈidi
edification
BR ˌɛdɪfɪˈkeɪʃn

AM ˌɛdəfəˈkeɪʃən
edifice
BR ˈɛdɪfɪs, -ɪz
AM ˈɛdəfəs, -əz
edify
BR ˈɛdɪfʌɪ, -z, -ɪŋ, -d
AM ˈɛdəˌfaɪ, -z, -ɪŋ, -d
edifyingly
BR ˈɛdɪfʌɪŋli
AM ˈɛdəˌfaɪɪŋli
Edinburgh
BR ˈɛd(ɪ)nb(ə)rə(r)
AM ˈɛdənbərə
Edington
BR ˈɛdɪŋt(ə)n
AM ˈɛdɪŋtən
Edison
BR ˈɛdɪs(ə)n
AM ˈɛdəsən
edit
BR ˈɛd|ɪt, -ɪts, -ɪtɪŋ, -ɪtɪd
AM ˈɛdə|t, -ts, -dɪŋ, -dəd
Edith
BR ˈiːdɪθ
AM ˈidɪθ
edition
BR ɪˈdɪʃn, -z
AM əˈdɪʃən, iˈdɪʃən, -z
**editiones
principes**
BR ɪˌdɪʃɪˈəʊniːz
ˈprɪnsɪpiːz
AM eɪˌdidiˈoʊniz
ˈprɪŋkəˌpeɪs,
əˌdɪʃiˈoʊniz
ˈprɪnsəˌpiz
editio princeps
BR ɪˌdɪʃɪəʊ ˈprɪnsɛps
AM eɪˌdidioʊ
ˈprɪnˌkɛps,
+ ˈprɪnˌsɛps
editor
BR ˈɛdɪtə(r), -z
AM ˈɛdədər, -z
editorial
BR ˌɛdɪˈtɔːrɪəl, -z
AM ˌɛdəˈtorial, -z
editorialise
BR ˌɛdɪˈtɔːrɪəlʌɪz, -ɪz,
-ɪŋ, -d
AM ˌɛdəˈtoriəˌlaɪz, -ɪz,
-ɪŋ, -d
editorialist
BR ˌɛdɪˈtɔːrɪəlɪst, -s
AM ˌɛdəˈtoriələst, -s
editorialize
BR ˌɛdɪˈtɔːrɪəlʌɪz, -ɪz,
-ɪŋ, -d
AM ˌɛdəˈtoriəˌlaɪz, -ɪz,
-ɪŋ, -d
editorially
BR ˌɛdɪˈtɔːrɪəli
AM ˌɛdəˈtorɪəli
editorship
BR ˈɛdɪtəʃɪp, -s
AM ˈɛdədərˌʃɪp, -s
Edmond
BR ˈɛdmənd

AM ˈɛdmən(d)
Edmonds
BR ˈɛdmən(d)z
AM ˈɛdmən(d)z
Edmondson
BR ˈɛdmən(d)s(ə)n
AM ˈɛdmən(d)sən
Edmonton
BR ˈɛdmənt(ə)n
AM ˈɛdmənt(ə)n
Edmund
BR ˈɛdmənd
AM ˈɛdmən(d)
Edmunds
BR ˈɛdmən(d)z
AM ˈɛdmən(d)z
Edmundson
BR ˈɛdmən(d)s(ə)n
AM ˈɛdmən(d)sən
Edna
BR ˈɛdnə(r)
AM ˈɛdnə
Edo
BR ˈɛdəʊ
AM ˈidoʊ, ˈɛdoʊ
Edom
BR ˈiːdəm
AM ˈidəm
Edomite
BR ˈiːdəmʌɪt, -s
AM ˈidəˌmaɪt, -s
EDP
BR ˌiːdiːˈpiː
AM ˌidiˈpi
Edrich
BR ˈɛdrɪtʃ
AM ˈɛdrɪtʃ
Edridge
BR ˈɛdrɪdʒ
AM ˈɛdrɪdʒ
Edsel
BR ˈɛdsl
AM ˈɛdzəl, ˈɛdsəl
educability
BR ˌɛdjʉkəˈbɪlɪti,
ˌɛdʒʉkəˈbɪlɪti
AM ˌɛdʒəkəˈbɪlɪdi
educable
BR ˈɛdjʉkəbl,
ˈɛdʒʉkəbl
AM ˈɛdʒəkəbəl
educatable
BR ˈɛdjʉkeɪtəbl,
ˈɛdʒʉkeɪtəbl
AM ˈɛdʒəˌkeɪdəbəl
educate
BR ˈɛdjʉkeɪt,
ˈɛdʒʉkeɪt, -s, -ɪŋ, -ɪd
AM ˈɛdʒəˌkeɪ|t, -ts, -dɪŋ,
-dɪd
education
BR ˌɛdjʉˈkeɪʃn,
ˌɛdʒʉˈkeɪʃn
AM ˌɛdʒəˈkeɪʃən
educational
BR ˌɛdjʉˈkeɪʃn(ə)l,
ˌɛdjʉˈkeɪʃən(ə)l,

AM ˌɛdʒʉˈkeɪʃ(ə)l,
ˌɛdʒʉˈkeɪʃən(ə)l
AM ˌɛdʒəˈkeɪʃ(ə)nəl
educationalist
BR ˌɛdjʉˈkeɪʃnəlɪst,
ˌɛdjʉˈkeɪʃn̩lɪst,
ˌɛdjʉˈkeɪʃənl̩ɪst,
ˌɛdʒʉˈkeɪʃnəlɪst,
ˌɛdʒʉˈkeɪʃn̩lɪst,
ˌɛdʒʉˈkeɪʃənl̩ɪst,
ˌɛdʒʉˈkeɪʃ(ə)nəlɪst, -s
AM ˌɛdʒəˈkeɪʃənl̩əst,
ˌɛdʒəˈkeɪʃnələst, -s
educationally
BR ˌɛdjʉˈkeɪʃn̩əli,
ˌɛdjʉˈkeɪʃn̩li,
ˌɛdjʉˈkeɪʃənl̩i,
ˌɛdjʉˈkeɪʃ(ə)nəli,
ˌɛdʒʉˈkeɪʃn̩əli,
ˌɛdʒʉˈkeɪʃn̩li,
ˌɛdʒʉˈkeɪʃənl̩i,
ˌɛdʒʉˈkeɪʃ(ə)nəli
AM ˌɛdʒəˈkeɪʃ(ə)nəli
educationist
BR ˌɛdjʉˈkeɪʃn̩ɪst,
ˌɛdjʉˈkeɪʃənɪst,
ˌɛdʒʉˈkeɪʃn̩ɪst,
ˌɛdʒʉˈkeɪʃənɪst, -s
AM ˌɛdʒəˈkeɪʃ(ə)nəst,
-s
educative
BR ˈɛdjʉkətɪv,
ˈɛdʒʉkətɪv
AM ˈɛdʒəˌkeɪdɪv
educator
BR ˈɛdjʉkeɪtə(r),
ˈɛdʒʉkeɪtə(r), -z
AM ˈɛdʒəˌkeɪdər, -z
educe
BR ɪˈdjuːs, ɪˈdʒuːs, -ɪz,
-ɪŋ, -t
AM iˈd(j)us, ɪˈd(j)us,
-əz, -ɪŋ, -t
educible
BR ɪˈdjuːsɪbl,
ɪˈdʒuːsɪbl
AM iˈd(j)usəbəl,
ɪˈd(j)usəbəl
eduction
BR ɪˈdʌkʃn
AM iˈdəkʃən, ɪˈdəkʃən
eductive
BR ɪˈdʌktɪv
AM iˈdəktɪv, ɪˈdəktɪv
edulcorate
BR ɪˈdʌlkəreɪt, -s, -ɪŋ,
-ɪd
AM əˈdəlkəˌreɪ|t,
iˈdəlkəˌreɪ|t, -ts, -dɪŋ,
-dɪd
edulcoration
BR ɪˌdʌlkəˈreɪʃn
AM əˌdəlkəˈreɪʃən,
iˌdəlkəˈreɪʃən
edutainment
BR ˌɛdjʉˈteɪmn(ə)nt,
ˌɛdʒʉˈteɪmn(ə)nt

AM ˌɛdʒəˈteɪmmənt

Edward
BR ˈɛdwəd
AM ˈɛdwərd

Edwardes
BR ˈɛdwədz
AM ˈɛdwərdz

Edwardian
BR ɛdˈwɔːdiən, -z
AM ɛdˈwɑrdiən, -z

Edwardiana
BR ɛdˌwɔːdɪˈɑːnə(r)
AM ˌɛdˌwɑrdiˈænə

Edwards
BR ˈɛdwədz
AM ˈɛdwərdz

Edwin
BR ˈɛdwɪn
AM ˈɛdwən

Edwina
BR ɛdˈwiːnə(r)
AM ɛdˈwinə, ɛdˈwinə

Edwinstowe
BR ˈɛdwɪnstəʊ
AM ˈɛdwɪnˌstəʊ

eegit
BR ˈiːdʒɪt, -s
AM ˈidʒɪt, -s

eejit
BR ˈiːdʒɪt, -s
AM ˈidʒɪt, -s

eel
BR iːl, -z
AM il, -z

Eelam
BR ˈiːlam
AM ˈilæm

eelgrass
BR ˈiːlɡrɑːs, ˈiːlɡras
AM ˈilˌɡræs

eelpout
BR ˈiːlpaʊt, -s
AM ˈilˌpaʊt, -s

eelworm
BR ˈiːlwəːm, -z
AM ˈilˌwərm, -z

eely
BR ˈiːli
AM ˈili

e'en
BR iːn
AM in

eeny meeny miny mo
BR ˌiːnɪ ˌmiːnɪ ˌmʌɪni ˈməʊ
AM ˌini ˌmini ˌmaɪni ˈmoʊ

e'er
BR ɛː(r)
AM ɛ(ə)r

eerie
BR ˈɪəri
AM ˈɪri, ˈiri

eerily
BR ˈɪərɪli
AM ˈɪrɪli

eeriness
BR ˈɪərɪnɪs
AM ˈɪrɪnɪs

Eeyore
BR ˈiːɔː(r)
AM ˈiɔ(ə)r

eff
BR ɛf, -s, -ɪŋ, -t
AM ɛf, -s, -ɪŋ, -t

effable
BR ˈɛfəbl
AM ˈɛfəbəl

efface
BR ɪˈfeɪs, -ɪz, -ɪŋ, -t
AM əˈfeɪs, ɛˈfeɪs, iˈfeɪs, -əz, -ɪŋ, -t

effaceable
BR ɪˈfeɪsəbl
AM əˈfeɪsəbəl, ɛˈfeɪsəbəl, iˈfeɪsəbəl

effacement
BR ɪˈfeɪsm(ə)nt
AM əˈfeɪsmənt, ɛˈfeɪsmənt, iˈfeɪsmənt

effect
BR ɪˈfɛkt, -s, -ɪŋ, -ɪd
AM əˈfɛk|(t), iˈfɛk|(t), -(t)s, -tɪŋ, -təd

effective
BR ɪˈfɛktɪv, -z
AM əˈfɛktɪv, iˈfɛktɪv, -z

effectively
BR ɪˈfɛktɪvli
AM əˈfɛktəvli, iˈfɛktəvli

effectiveness
BR ɪˈfɛktɪvnɪs
AM əˈfɛktɪvnɪs, iˈfɛktɪvnɪs

effectivity
BR ˌɛfəkˈtɪvɪti, ˌɪfɛkˈtɪvɪti
AM ˌɛfəkˈtɪvɪdi, ˌɪfəkˈtɪvɪdi

effector
BR ɪˈfɛktə(r), -z
AM əˈfɛktər, iˈfɛktər, -z

effectual
BR ɪˈfɛktʃʊəl, ɪˈfɛktʃ(ʊ)l, ɪˈfɛktjʊəl, ˈfɛktjʊl
AM əˈfɛk(t)ʃ(əw)əl, iˈfɛk(t)ʃ(əw)əl

effectuality
BR ɪˈfɛktʃʊˈalɪti, ˌɪˌfɛktjʊˈalɪti
AM əˌfɛk(t)ʃəˈwælədi, iˌfɛk(t)ʃəˈwælədi

effectually
BR ɪˈfɛktʃʊəli, ɪˈfɛktʃʊli, ɪˈfɛktʃli
AM əˈfɛk(t)ʃ(əw)əli, iˈfɛk(t)ʃ(əw)əli

effectualness
BR ɪˈfɛktʃʊəlnəs, ɪˈfɛktʃ(ʊ)lnəs,

effectuate
BR ɪˈfɛktʃʊeɪt, ɪˈfɛktjʊeɪt, -s, -ɪŋ, -ɪd
AM əˈfɛk(t)ʃəˌweɪt, iˈfɛk(t)ʃəˌweɪt, -ts, -dɪŋ, -dɪd

effectuation
BR ɪˌfɛktʃʊˈeɪʃn, ɪˌfɛktjʊˈeɪʃn
AM əˌfɛk(t)ʃəˈweɪʃən, iˌfɛk(t)ʃəˈweɪʃən

effeminacy
BR ɪˈfɛmɪnəsi
AM əˈfɛmənəsi, iˈfɛmənəsi

effeminate
BR ɪˈfɛmɪnət
AM əˈfɛmənət, iˈfɛmənət

effeminately
BR ɪˈfɛmɪnətli
AM əˈfɛmənətli, iˈfɛmənətli

effendi
BR ɪˈfɛnd|i, ɛˈfɛnd|i, -ɪz
AM əˈfɛndi, ɛˈfɛndi, -z

efference
BR ˈɛf(ə)rəns, ˈɛf(ə)rɲs
AM ˈɛfərəns

efferent
BR ˈɛf(ə)rənt, ˈɛf(ə)rɲt
AM ˈɛfərənt

effervesce
BR ˌɛfəˈvɛs, -ɪz, -ɪŋ, -t
AM ˌɛfərˈvɛs, -əz, -ɪŋ, -t

effervescence
BR ˌɛfəˈvɛsns
AM ˌɛfərˈvɛsəns

effervescency
BR ˌɛfəˈvɛsnsi
AM ˌɛfərˈvɛsənsi

effervescent
BR ˌɛfəˈvɛsnt
AM ˌɛfərˈvɛsənt

effervescently
BR ˌɛfəˈvɛsntli
AM ˌɛfərˈvɛsn(t)li

effete
BR ɪˈfiːt
AM əˈfit, iˈfit

effeteness
BR ɪˈfiːtnɪs
AM əˈfitnɪs, iˈfitnɪs

efficacious
BR ˌɛfɪˈkeɪʃəs
AM ˌɛfəˈkeɪʃəs

efficaciously
BR ˌɛfɪˈkeɪʃəsli
AM ˌɛfəˈkeɪʃəsli

efficaciousness
BR ˌɛfɪˈkeɪʃəsnəs
AM ˌɛfəˈkeɪʃəsnəs

efficacity
BR ˌɛfɪˈkasɪti

ɪˈfɛktjʊəlnəs,
ɪˈfɛktʃ(ɵ)lnəs,

eeriness (cont.)
AM ɪˈfɛktjʊəlnəs,
ɪˈfɛktjɵlnəs
AM əˈfɛk(t)ʃ(əw)əlnəs,
iˈfɛk(t)ʃ(əw)əlnəs

efficacy
BR ˈɛfɪkəsi
AM ˈɛfəkəsi

efficiency
BR ɪˈfɪʃnsi
AM əˈfɪʃənsi, iˈfɪʃənsi

efficient
BR ɪˈfɪʃnt
AM əˈfɪʃənt, iˈfɪʃənt

efficiently
BR ɪˈfɪʃntli
AM əˈfɪʃən(t)li, iˈfɪʃən(t)li

Effie
BR ˈɛfi
AM ˈɛfi

effigy
BR ˈɛfɪdʒ|i, -ɪz
AM ˈɛfɪdʒi, -z

Effingham
BR ˈɛfɪŋəm
AM ˈɛfɪŋəm, ˈɛfɪŋˌhæm

effleurage
BR ˌɛflə'rɑːʒ, -ɪz, -ɪŋ, -d
AM ˌɛflə'rɑʒ, ˌɛfluˈrɑʒ, -əz, -ɪŋ, -d

effloresce
BR ˌɛfləˈrɛs, -ɪz, -ɪŋ, -t
AM ˌɛfləˈrɛs, -əz, -ɪŋ, -t

efflorescence
BR ˌɛfləˈrɛsns
AM ˌɛfləˈrɛsəns

efflorescent
BR ˌɛfləˈrɛsnt
AM ˌɛfləˈrɛsnt

effluence
BR ˈɛfluəns
AM ˈɛˌfluəns

effluent
BR ˈɛfluənt, -s
AM ˈɛˌfluənt, ˈɛfləwənt, -s

effluvia
BR ɪˈfluːvɪə(r)
AM ɛˈfluviə, əˈfluviə

effluvium
BR ɪˈfluːvɪəm
AM ɛˈfluviəm, əˈfluviəm

efflux
BR ˈɛflʌks, -ɪz
AM ˈɛˌflʌks, -əz

effluxion
BR ɪˈflʌkʃn, ɛˈflʌkʃn, -z
AM ɛˈfləkʃən, -z

effort
BR ˈɛfət, -s
AM ˈɛfərt, -s

effortful
BR ˈɛfətf(ɵ)l
AM ˈɛfərtfəl

effortfully
BR ˈɛfətfɵli, ˈɛfətfʃli
AM ˈɛfərtfəli

effortless
BR ˈɛfətləs

effortlessly
AM 'ɛfərtləs
effortlessly
BR 'ɛfətləsli
AM 'ɛfərtləsli
effortlessness
BR 'ɛfətləsnəs
AM 'ɛfərtləsnəs
effrontery
BR ɪ'frʌnt(ə)r|i, -ɪz
AM ə'frəntəri,
i'frəntəri, -z
effulgence
BR ɪ'fʌldʒ(ə)ns
AM ə'fʊldʒəns,
i'fʊldʒəns, ə'fəldʒəns,
i'fəldʒəns
effulgent
BR ɪ'fʌldʒ(ə)nt
AM ə'fʊldʒənt,
ə'fəldʒənt, i'fʊldʒənt,
i'fəldʒənt
effulgently
BR ɪ'fʌldʒ(ə)ntli
AM ə'fʊldʒən(t)li,
ə'fəldʒən(t)li,
i'fʊldʒən(t)li,
i'fəldʒən(t)li
effuse
BR ɪ'fju:z, -ɪz, -ɪŋ, -d
AM ə'fjuz, i'fjuz, -əz,
-ɪŋ, -d
effusion
BR ɪ'fju:ʒn, -z
AM ə'fjuʒən, i'fjuʒən,
-z
effusive
BR ɪ'fju:sɪv
AM ə'fjusɪv, i'fjusɪv,
ə'fjuzɪv, i'fjuzɪv
effusively
BR ɪ'fju:sɪvli
AM ə'fjusəvli, ə'fjuzəvli,
i'fjusəvli, ə'fjuzəvli,
i'fjuzəvli
effusiveness
BR ɪ'fju:sɪvnɪs
AM ə'fjusɪvnɪs,
i'fjusɪvnɪs,
ə'fjuzɪvnɪs,
i'fjuzɪvnɪs
Efik
BR 'ɛfɪk
AM 'ɛfɪk
eft
BR ɛft, -s
AM ɛft, -s
EFTA
BR 'ɛftə(r)
AM 'ɛftə
e.g.
BR ˌi:'dʒi:
AM ˌi'dʒi
egad
BR ɪ'gad
AM i'gæd
egalitarian
BR ɪˌgalɪ'tɛ:rɪən

AM iˌgælə'tɛrɪən,
əˌgælə'tɛrɪən
egalitarianism
BR ɪˌgalɪ'tɛ:rɪənɪz(ə)m
AM iˌgælə'tɛrɪəˌnɪzəm,
əˌgælə'tɛrɪəˌnɪzəm
Egan
BR 'i:g(ə)n
AM 'iɡɪn
Egbert
BR 'ɛgbət
AM 'ɛgbərt
Egerton
BR 'ɛdʒət(ə)n
AM 'ɛdʒərtən
egest
BR ɪ'dʒɛst, -s, -ɪŋ, -ɪd
AM i'dʒɛst, ə'dʒɛst, -s,
-ɪŋ, -əd
egg
BR ɛg, -z, -ɪŋ, -d
AM ɛg, -z, -ɪŋ, -d
eggar
BR 'ɛgə(r), -z
AM 'ɛgər, -z
eggcup
BR 'ɛgkʌp, -s
AM 'ɛgˌkəp, -s
egger
BR 'ɛgə(r), -z
AM 'ɛgər, -z
egghead
BR 'ɛghɛd, -z
AM 'ɛgˌ(h)ɛd, -z
egginess
BR 'ɛgɪnɪs
AM 'ɛgɪnɪs
eggless
BR 'ɛgləs
AM 'ɛgləs
eggnog
BR 'ɛgnɒg, -z
AM 'ɛgˌnɔg, 'ɛgˌnɑg, -z
eggplant
BR 'ɛgplɑːnt, 'ɛgplant,
-s
AM 'ɛgˌplænt, -s
eggshell
BR 'ɛgʃɛl, -z
AM 'ɛgˌʃɛl, -z
eggwhisk
BR 'ɛgwɪsk, -s
AM 'ɛgˌwɪsk, -s
eggy
BR 'ɛg|i, -ɪə(r), -ɪɪst
AM 'ɛgi, -ər, -ɪst
Egham
BR 'ɛgəm
AM 'ɛgəm
egis
BR 'i:dʒɪs
AM 'idʒəs
eglantine
BR 'ɛgləntʌɪn,
'ɛglənti:n
AM 'ɛglənˌtin,
'ɛglənˌtaɪn

Egmont
BR 'ɛgmɒnt
AM 'ɛgˌmɑnt, 'ɛgmənt
ego
BR 'i:gəʊ, -z
AM 'igoʊ, -z
egocentric
BR ˌɛgə(ʊ)'sɛntrɪk,
ˌi:gə(ʊ)'sɛntrɪk
AM ˌigoʊ'sɛntrɪk,
ˌigə'sɛntrɪk
egocentrically
BR ˌɛgə(ʊ)'sɛntrɪkli,
ˌi:gə(ʊ)'sɛntrɪkli
AM ˌigoʊ'sɛntrək(ə)li,
ˌigə'sɛntrək(ə)li
egocentricity
BR ˌɛgə(ʊ)sɛn'trɪsɪti,
ˌɛgə(ʊ)s(ə)n'trɪsɪti,
ˌi:gə(ʊ)sɛn'trɪsɪti,
ˌi:gə(ʊ)s(ə)n'trɪsɪti
AM ˌigoʊsɛn'trɪsɪdi,
ˌigoʊsən'trɪsɪdi
egocentrism
BR ˌɛgə(ʊ)'sɛntrɪz(ə)m,
ˌi:gə(ʊ)'sɛntrɪz(ə)m
AM ˌigoʊ'sɛnˌtrɪzəm,
ˌigə'sɛnˌtrɪzəm
egoism
BR 'ɛgəʊɪz(ə)m,
'i:gəʊɪz(ə)m
AM 'igəˌwɪzəm,
'igoʊˌɪzəm
egoist
BR 'ɛgəʊɪst, 'i:gəʊɪst, -s
AM 'igəwəst, 'igoʊəst,
-s
egoistic
BR ˌɛgəʊ'ɪstɪk,
ˌi:gəʊ'ɪstɪk
AM ˌigə'wɪstɪk,
ˌigoʊ'ɪstɪk
egoistical
BR ˌɛgəʊ'ɪstɪkl,
ˌi:gəʊ'ɪstɪkl
AM ˌigə'wɪstɪkəl,
ˌigoʊ'ɪstɪkəl
egoistically
BR ˌɛgəʊ'ɪstɪkli,
ˌi:gəʊ'ɪstɪkli
AM ˌigə'wɪstɪkəli,
ˌigoʊ'ɪstɪkəli
egomania
BR ˌɛgə(ʊ)'meɪnɪə(r),
ˌi:gə(ʊ)'meɪnɪə(r)
AM ˌigoʊ'meɪnɪə
egomaniac
BR ˌɛgə(ʊ)'meɪnɪak,
ˌi:gə(ʊ)'meɪnɪak, -s
AM ˌigoʊ'meɪniˌæk, -s
egomaniacal
BR ˌɛgə(ʊ)mə'nʌɪəkl,
ˌi:gə(ʊ)mə'nʌɪəkl
AM ˌigoʊmə'naɪəkəl
egotise
BR 'ɛgətʌɪz, 'i:gətʌɪz,
-ɪz, -ɪŋ, -d

Egmont
AM 'igəˌtaɪz, 'igoʊˌtaɪz,
-ɪz, -ɪŋ, -d
egotism
BR 'ɛgətɪz(ə)m,
'i:gətɪz(ə)m
AM 'igəˌtɪzəm,
'igoʊˌtɪzəm
egotist
BR 'ɛgətɪst, 'i:gətɪst, -s
AM 'igədəst, 'igətəst,
'igoʊtəst, -s
egotistic
BR ˌɛgə'tɪstɪk,
ˌi:gə'tɪstɪk
AM ˌigə'tɪstɪk,
ˌigoʊ'tɪstɪk
egotistical
BR ˌɛgə'tɪstɪkl,
ˌi:gə'tɪstɪkl
AM ˌigə'tɪstəkəl,
ˌigoʊ'tɪstəkəl
egotistically
BR ˌɛgə'tɪstɪkli,
ˌi:gə'tɪstɪkli
AM ˌigə'tɪstɪk(ə)li,
ˌigoʊ'tɪstɪk(ə)li
egotize
BR 'ɛgətʌɪz, 'i:gətʌɪz,
-ɪz, -ɪŋ, -d
AM 'igəˌtaɪz, 'igoʊˌtaɪz,
-ɪz, -ɪŋ, -d
egregious
BR ɪ'gri:dʒəs
AM ə'gridʒəs, i'gridʒəs
egregiously
BR ɪ'gri:dʒəsli
AM ə'gridʒəsli,
i'gridʒəsli
egregiousness
BR ɪ'gri:dʒəsnəs
AM ə'gridʒəsnəs,
i'gridʒəsnəs
Egremont
BR 'ɛgrɪmɒnt,
'ɛgrɪm(ə)nt
AM 'ɛgrəˌmɑnt
egress
BR 'i:grɛs, -ɪz
AM 'iˌgrɛs, -əz
egression
BR ɪ'grɛʃn, i:'grɛʃn
AM ə'grɛʃən, i'grɛʃən
egressive
BR ɪ'grɛsɪv, i:'grɛsɪv
AM ə'grɛsɪv, i'grɛsɪv
egret
BR 'i:grɪt, -s
AM 'igrət, 'iˌgrɛt, -s
Egypt
BR 'i:dʒɪpt
AM 'idʒəp(t)
Egyptian
BR ɪ'dʒɪpʃn, -z
AM ə'dʒɪpʃən, -z
Egyptianisation
BR ɪˌdʒɪpʃnʌɪ'zeɪʃn,
ɪˌdʒɪpʃənʌɪ'zeɪʃn

AM ə,dʒɪpʃənə'zeɪʃən,
ə,dʒɪpʃə,naɪ'zeɪʃən
Egyptianise
BR ɪ'dʒɪpʃn̩ʌɪz,
ɪ'dʒɪpʃənʌɪz, -ɪz, -ɪŋ, -d
AM ə'dʒɪpʃə,naɪz, -ɪz,
-ɪŋ, -d
Egyptianization
BR ɪ,dʒɪpʃn̩ʌɪ'zeɪʃn̩,
ɪ,dʒɪpʃənʌɪ'zeɪʃn
AM ə,dʒɪpʃənə'zeɪʃən,
ə,dʒɪpʃə,naɪ'zeɪʃən
Egyptianize
BR ɪ'dʒɪpʃn̩ʌɪz,
ɪ'dʒɪpʃənʌɪz, -ɪz, -ɪŋ, -d
AM ə'dʒɪpʃə,naɪz, -ɪz,
-ɪŋ, -d
Egyptologist
BR ,iːdʒɪp'tɒlədʒɪst, -s
AM ,iˌdʒɪp'tɑlədʒəst, -s
Egyptology
BR ,iːdʒɪp'tɒlədʒi
AM ,iˌdʒɪp'tɑlədʒi
eh
BR eɪ
AM eɪ, ɛ
Ehrlich
BR 'ɛːlɪk, 'ɛːlɪx
AM 'ɛrlɪk
Eichmann
BR 'ʌɪkmən, 'ʌɪxmən
AM 'aɪkmən
Eid
BR iːd
AM id
eider
BR 'ʌɪdə(r), -z
AM 'aɪdər, -z
eiderdown
BR 'ʌɪdədaʊn, -z
AM 'aɪdərˌdaʊn, -z
eidetic
BR ʌɪ'dɛtɪk
AM aɪ'dɛdɪk
eidetically
BR ʌɪ'dɛtɪkli
AM aɪ'dɛdək(ə)li
eidola
BR ʌɪ'dəʊlə(r)
AM aɪ'doʊlə
eidolon
BR ʌɪ'dəʊlɒn, -z
AM aɪ'doʊlən, -z
Eifel
BR 'ʌɪfl
AM 'aɪfəl
Eiffel
BR 'ʌɪfl
AM 'aɪfəl
eigenfrequency
BR 'ʌɪg(ə)n,friːkw(ə)n-
s|i, -ɪz
AM 'aɪgən,frikwənsi,
-z
eigenfunction
BR 'ʌɪg(ə)n,fʌŋ(k)ʃn,
-z
AM 'aɪgən,fəŋkʃən, -z

eigenvalue
BR 'ʌɪg(ə)n,valju:, -z
AM 'aɪgən,vælju, -z
Eiger
BR 'ʌɪgə(r)
AM 'aɪgər
Eigg
BR ɛg
AM ɛg
eight
BR eɪt, -s
AM eɪt, -s
eighteen
BR ,eɪ'ti:n
AM ,eɪ(t)|tin
eighteenmo
BR ,eɪ'ti:nməʊ
AM ,eɪ(t)'tin,moʊ
eighteenth
BR ,eɪ'ti:nθ
AM ,eɪ(t)|tinθ
eightfold
BR 'eɪtfəʊld
AM 'eɪt|foʊld
eighth
BR 'eɪtθ, -s
AM 'eɪ(t)θ, -s
eighthly
BR 'eɪtθli
AM 'eɪ(t)θli
eightieth
BR 'eɪtɪɪθ
AM 'eɪdiəθ
eightsome
BR 'eɪts(ə)m, -z
AM 'eɪtsəm, -z
eighty
BR 'eɪt|i, -ɪz
AM 'eɪdi, -z
eightyfold
BR 'eɪtɪfəʊld
AM 'eɪdi,foʊld
Eilat
BR eɪ'lɑːt, er'lat
AM 'eɪ,lɑt
Eileen
BR 'ʌɪli:n
AM aɪ'lin
Eilidh
BR 'eɪli
AM 'eɪli
Eindhoven
BR 'ʌɪnd,həʊvn
AM 'aɪn(d),(h)oʊvən
einkorn
BR 'ʌɪnkɔ:n
AM 'aɪn,kɔ(ə)rn
Einstein
BR 'ʌɪnstʌɪn
AM 'aɪn,staɪn
einsteinium
BR ʌɪn'stʌɪnɪəm
AM aɪn'staɪniəm
Éire
BR 'ɛːrə(r)
AM 'ɛrə
IR 'e:r'ə

eirenic
BR ʌɪ'ri:nɪk, ʌɪ'rɛnɪk
AM aɪ'rɛnɪk, aɪ'rinɪk
eirenical
BR ʌɪ'ri:nɪkl, ʌɪ'rɛnɪkl
AM aɪ'rinɪkl
eirenicon
BR ʌɪ'ri:nɪkɒn,
ʌɪ'rɛnɪkɒn, -z
AM aɪ'rɛnə,kɑn,
aɪ'rɛnəkən, -z
Eirlys
BR 'ʌɪəlɪs
AM 'aɪrləs
Eisenhower
BR 'ʌɪznhaʊə(r)
AM 'aɪzən,(h)aʊər
Eisenstadt
BR 'ʌɪznstat
AM 'aɪzən,stæt
Eisenstein
BR 'ʌɪznstʌɪn,
'ʌɪznʃtʌɪn
AM 'aɪzən,staɪn,
'aɪzən,ʃtaɪn
eisteddfod
BR ʌɪ'stɛðvɒd,
ʌɪ'stɛdfəd, -z
AM aɪ'stɛð,vɑd,
aɪ'stɛð,vad, -z
WE eɪ'steðvɒd
eisteddfodau
BR ,ʌɪstɛð'vɒdʌɪ
AM ,aɪstɛð'vɑdaɪ
WE eɪ'steðvɒdaɪ
eisteddfodic
BR ,ʌɪstɛð'vɒdɪk,
,ʌɪstɛd'fɒdɪk
AM aɪ'stɛð'vɒdɪk,
aɪ'stɛð,vadɪk
either
BR 'ʌɪðə(r), 'i:ðə(r)
AM 'iðər, 'aɪðər
either/or
BR ,ʌɪðər'ɔ:(r),
,i:ðər'ɔ:(r)
AM 'iðər'ɔ(ə)r,
,aɪðər'ɔ(ə)r
Eithne
BR 'ɛθni
AM 'ɛθni
ejaculate¹
noun
BR ɪ'dʒakjʉlət
AM i'dʒækjələt,
ə'dʒækjələt
ejaculate²
verb
BR ɪ'dʒakjʉleɪt, -s, -ɪŋ,
-ɪd
AM ə'dʒækjəˌleɪt,
i'dʒækjəˌleɪ|t, -ts, -dɪŋ,
-dɪd
ejaculation
BR ɪ,dʒakjʉ'leɪʃn, -z
AM ə,dʒækjə'leɪʃən,
i,dʒækjə'leɪʃən, -z

ejaculator
BR ɪ'dʒakjʉleɪtə(r), -z
AM ə'dʒækjəˌleɪdər,
i'dʒækjəˌleɪdər, -z
ejaculatory
BR ɪ'dʒakjʉlət(ə)ri
AM ə'dʒækjələˌtɔri,
i'dʒækjələˌtɔri
eject
BR ɪ'dʒɛkt, -s, -ɪŋ, -ɪd
AM ə'dʒɛk|(t),
i'dʒɛk|(t), -(t)s, -tɪŋ,
-təd
ejecta
BR ɪ'dʒɛktə(r)
AM ə'dʒɛktə, i'dʒɛktə
ejection
BR ɪ'dʒɛkʃn
AM ə'dʒɛkʃən,
i'dʒɛkʃən
ejective
BR ɪ'dʒɛktɪv
AM ə'dʒɛktɪv, i'dʒɛktɪv
ejectment
BR ɪ'dʒɛk(t)m(ə)nt
AM ə'dʒɛk(t)mənt,
i'dʒɛk(t)mənt
ejector
BR ɪ'dʒɛktə(r), -z
AM ə'dʒɛktər,
i'dʒɛktər, -z
Ekaterinburg
BR ɪ'kat(ə)rɪnbə:g
AM i'kædərən,bərg
RUS jikat'ir'in'burk
Ekco
BR 'ɛkəʊ
AM 'ɛkoʊ
eke
BR i:k, -s, -ɪŋ, -t
AM ik, -s, -ɪŋ, -t
ekistics
BR ɪ'kɪstɪks, i:'kɪstɪks
AM ə'kɪstɪks, i'kɪstɪks
ekka
BR 'ɛkə(r), -z
AM 'ɛ,kɑ, 'ɛkə, -z
Ektachrome®
BR 'ɛktəkrəʊm
AM 'ɛktə,kroʊm
el
BR ɛl, -z
AM ɛl, -z
elaborate¹
adjective
BR ɪ'lab(ə)rət
AM ə'læb(ə)rət,
i'læb(ə)rət
elaborate²
verb
BR ɪ'labəreɪt, -s, -ɪŋ, -ɪd
AM ə'læbəˌreɪt,
i'læbəˌreɪ|t, -ts, -dɪŋ,
-dɪd
elaborately
BR ɪ'lab(ə)rətli
AM ə'læb(ə)rətli,
i'læb(ə)rətli

elaborateness
BR ɪˈlab(ə)rətnəs
AM əˈlæb(ə)rətnəs,
iˈlæb(ə)rətnəs

elaboration
BR ɪˌlabəˈreɪʃn, -z
AM əˌlæbəˈreɪʃən,
iˌlæbəˈreɪʃən, -z

elaborative
BR ɪˈlab(ə)rətɪv
AM əˈlæbəˌreɪdɪv,
əˈlæbəreɪdɪv,
iˈlæbəˌreɪdɪv,
iˈlæbərədɪv

elaborator
BR ɪˈlabəreɪtə(r), -z
AM əˈlæbəˌreɪdər,
iˈlæbəˌreɪdər, -z

Elaine
BR ɪˈleɪn
AM əˈleɪn, iˈleɪn

Elam
BR ˈiːlam
AM ˈiˌlæm, ˈiləm

Elamite
BR ˈiːləmʌɪt, -s
AM ˈiləˌmaɪt, -s

Elan¹
car name
BR ɪˈlan
AM əˈlæn

Elan²
place in Wales
BR ˈiːlən
AM ˈilən
WE ˈelan

élan
BR erˈlan, erˈlɒ̃
AM erˈlɑn, erˈlæn

eland
BR ˈiːlənd, -z
AM ˈilənd, -z

elapid
BR ˈɛləpɪd, -z
AM ˈɛləpəd, -z

elapse
BR ɪˈlaps, -ɪz, -ɪŋ, -t
AM əˈlæps, iˈlæps, -əz,
-ɪŋ, -t

elasmobranch
BR ɪˈlazməbraŋk, -s
AM əˈlæzməˌbræŋk, -s

elasmosaurus
BR ɪˌlazməˈsɔːrəs, -ɪz
AM əˌlæzməˈsɔrəs, -əz

elastane
BR ɪˈlasteɪn
AM iˈlæsˌteɪn,
əˈlæsˌteɪn

elastase
BR ɪˈlasteɪz
AM iˈlæsˌteɪz,
əˈlæsˌteɪz

elastic
BR ɪˈlastɪk
AM əˈlæstɪk, iˈlæstɪk

elastically
BR ɪˈlastɪkli

AM əˈlæstək(ə)li,
iˈlæstək(ə)li

elasticated
BR ɪˈlastɪkeɪtɪd
AM əˈlæstəˌkeɪdɪd,
iˈlæstəˌkeɪdɪd

elasticise
BR ɪˈlastɪsʌɪz, -ɪz, -ɪŋ, -d
AM əˈlæstəˌsaɪz,
iˈlæstəˌsaɪz, -ɪz, -ɪŋ, -d

elasticity
BR ˌiːlaˈstɪsɪti,
ˌɛlaˈstɪsɪti
AM əˌlæˈstɪsɪdi,
iˌlæˈstɪsɪdi

elasticize
BR ɪˈlastɪsʌɪz, -ɪz, -ɪŋ, -d
AM əˈlæstəˌsaɪz,
iˈlæstəˌsaɪz, -ɪz, -ɪŋ, -d

elastomer
BR ɪˈlastəmə(r), -z
AM əˈlæstəmər,
iˈlæstəmər, -z

elastomeric
BR ɪˌlastəˈmɛrɪk
AM əˌlæstəˈmɛrɪk,
iˌlæstəˈmɛrɪk

Elastoplast®
BR ɪˈlastəplɑːst,
ɪˈlastəplast, -s
AM əˈlæstəˌplæst,
iˈlæstəˌplæst, -s

elate
BR ɪˈleɪt, -s, -ɪŋ, -ɪd
AM əˈleɪ|t, iˈleɪ|t, -ts,
-dɪŋ, -dɪd

elated
BR ɪˈleɪtɪd
AM əˈleɪdɪd, iˈleɪdɪd

elatedly
BR ɪˈleɪtɪdli
AM əˈleɪdɪdli, iˈleɪdɪdli

elatedness
BR ɪˈleɪtɪdnɪs
AM əˈleɪdɪdnɪs,
iˈleɪdɪdnɪs

elater
BR ɪˈleɪtə(r), -z
AM əˈleɪdər, iˈleɪdər, -z

elation
BR ɪˈleɪʃn
AM əˈleɪʃən, iˈleɪʃən

Elba
BR ˈɛlbə(r)
AM ˈɛlbə

Elbe
BR ɛlb
AM ɛlb
GER ˈɛlbə

Elbert
BR ˈɛlbət
AM ˈɛlbərt

elbow
BR ˈɛlbəʊ, -z
AM ˈɛlˌboʊ, -z

elbowroom
BR ˈɛlbəʊruːm,
ˈɛlbəʊrʊm

AM ˈɛlbouˌrum,
ˈɛlbouˌrʊm

Elche
BR ˈɛltʃeɪ
AM ˈɛlˌtʃeɪ

eld
BR ɛld
AM ɛld

elder
BR ˈɛldə(r), -z
AM ˈɛldər, -z

elderberry
BR ˈɛldəˌberǀi,
ˈɛldəb(ə)rǀi, -ɪz
AM ˈɛldərˌberi, -z

elderflower
BR ˈɛldəˌflaʊə(r), -z
AM ˈɛldərˌflaʊər, -z

elderliness
BR ˈɛldəlɪnɪs
AM ˈɛldərlinɪs

elderly
BR ˈɛldəli
AM ˈɛldərli

eldership
BR ˈɛldəʃɪp
AM ˈɛldərˌʃɪp

eldest
BR ˈɛldɪst
AM ˈɛldəst

Eldon
BR ˈɛld(ə)n
AM ˈɛldən

eldorado
BR ˌɛldəˈrɑːdəʊ, -z
AM ˌɛldəˈrɑdou,
ˌɛldəˈrædou, -z

eldrich
BR ˈɛldrɪtʃ
AM ˈɛldrɪtʃ

Eldridge
BR ˈɛldrɪdʒ
AM ˈɛldrɪdʒ

eldritch
BR ˈɛldrɪtʃ
AM ˈɛldrɪtʃ

Eleanor
BR ˈɛlənə
AM ˈɛlənər

Eleanora
BR ˌɛləˈnɔːrə(r)
AM ˌɛləˈnɔrə

Eleatic
BR ˌɛlɪˈatɪk, ˌiːlɪˈatɪk, -s
AM ˌɛliˈædɪk, -s

elecampane
BR ˌɛlɪkamˈpeɪn, -z
AM ˌɛləˌkæmˈpeɪn,
ˌɛliˈkæmˌpeɪn,
ˌɛləˈkæmˌpeɪn,
ˌɛliˈkæmˌpeɪn, -z

elect
BR ɪˈlɛkt, -s, -ɪŋ, -ɪd
AM əˈlɛkǀ(t), iˈlɛkǀ(t),
-(t)s, -tɪŋ, -təd

electable
BR ɪˈlɛktəbl

AM əˈlɛktəbəl,
iˈlɛktəbəl

election
BR ɪˈlɛkʃn, -z
AM əˈlɛkʃən, iˈlɛkʃən,
-z

electioneer
BR ɪˌlɛkʃəˈnɪə(r), -z,
-ɪŋ, -d
AM əˌlɛkʃəˈnɪ(ə)r,
iˌlɛkʃəˈnɪ(ə)r, -z, -ɪŋ, -d

electioneering
BR ɪˌlɛkʃəˈnɪərɪŋ
AM əˌlɛkʃəˈnɪrɪŋ,
iˌlɛkʃəˈnɪrɪŋ

elective
BR ɪˈlɛktɪv, -z
AM əˈlɛktɪv, iˈlɛktɪv, -z

electively
BR ɪˈlɛktɪvli
AM əˈlɛktəvli,
iˈlɛktəvli

elector
BR ɪˈlɛktə(r), -z
AM əˈlɛktər, iˈlɛktər,
əˈlɛkˌtɔ(ə)r,
iˈlɛkˌtɔ(ə)r, -z

electoral
BR ɪˈlɛkt(ə)rəl,
ɪˈlɛkt(ə)rǀl
AM əˈlɛkt(ə)rəl,
iˈlɛkt(ə)rəl

electorally
BR ɪˈlɛkt(ə)rəli,
ɪˈlɛkt(ə)rǀli
AM əˈlɛkt(ə)rəli,
iˈlɛkt(ə)rəli

electorate
BR ɪˈlɛkt(ə)rət, -s
AM əˈlɛkt(ə)rət,
iˈlɛkt(ə)rət, -s

electorship
BR ɪˈlɛktəˌʃɪp, -s
AM əˈlɛktərˌʃɪp,
iˈlɛktərˌʃɪp, -s

Electra
BR ɪˈlɛktrə(r)
AM əˈlɛktrə, iˈlɛktrə

Electress
BR ɪˈlɛktrɪs, -ɪz
AM əˈlɛktrəs, iˈlɛktrəs,
-əz

electret
BR ˈlɛktrɪt, -s
AM əˈlɛktrət, iˈlɛktrət,
-s

electric
BR ɪˈlɛktrɪk
AM əˈlɛktrɪk, iˈlɛktrɪk

electrical
BR ɪˈlɛktrɪkl, -z
AM əˈlɛktrəkəl,
iˈlɛktrəkəl, -z

electrically
BR ɪˈlɛktrɪkli
AM əˈlɛktrək(ə)li,
iˈlɛktrək(ə)li

electrician
BR ɪˌlekˈtrɪʃn, -z
AM əˌlekˈtrɪʃən,
iˌlekˈtrɪʃən, -z

electricity
BR ɪˌlekˈtrɪsɪti,
ˌelekˈtrɪsɪti,
ˌelɪkˈtrɪsɪti,
ˌɪlekˈtrɪsɪti,
ˌiːlekˈtrɪsɪti
AM əˌlekˈtrɪsɪdi,
iˌlekˈtrɪsɪdi

electrification
BR ɪˌlektrɪfɪˈkeɪʃn
AM əˌlektrəfəˈkeɪʃən,
iˌlektrəfəˈkeɪʃən

electrifier
BR ɪˈlektrɪfʌɪə(r), -z
AM əˈlektrəˌfaɪər,
iˈlektrəˌfaɪər, -z

electrify
BR ɪˈlektrɪfʌɪ, -z, -ɪŋ, -d
AM əˈlektrəˌfaɪ,
iˈlektrəˌfaɪ, -z, -ɪŋ, -d

electro
BR ɪˈlektrəʊ, -z
AM əˈlektrəʊ,
iˈlektrəʊ, -z

electrobiology
BR ɪˌlektrəʊbʌɪˈɒlədʒi
AM əˌlektrəʊbaɪˈɑlədʒi,
iˌlektrəʊbaɪˈɑlədʒi,
əˌlektrəbaɪˈɑlədʒi,
iˌlektrəbaɪˈɑlədʒi

electrocardiogram
BR ɪˌlektrəʊˈkɑːdɪəˌgram, -z
AM əˌlektrəʊˈkardɪəˌgræm,
əˌlektrəʊˈkardiəʊˌgræm,
əˌlektrəˈkardɪəˌgræm,
iˌlektrəʊˈkardɪəˌgræm,
iˌlektrəʊˈkardiəʊˌgræm,
iˌlektrəˈkardɪəˌgræm, -z

electrocardiograph
BR ɪˌlektrəʊˈkɑːdɪəgrɑːf,
ɪˌlektrəʊˈkɑːdɪəgraf, -s
AM əˌlektrəʊˈkardɪəˌgræf,
əˌlektrəʊˈkardiəʊˌgræf,
əˌlektrəˈkardiəˌgræf,
iˌlektrəʊˈkardiəʊˌgræf,
iˌlektrəʊˈkardiəˌgræf, -s

electrocardiographic
BR ɪˌlektrəʊˌkɑːdɪəˈgrafɪk
AM əˌlektrəʊˌkardɪəˈgræfɪk,
əˌlektrəʊˌkardiəʊˈgræfɪk,
iˌlektrəˌkardiəˈgræfɪk,

iˌlektrəʊˌkardiəˈgræfɪk,
iˌlektrəʊˌkardiəʊˈgræfɪk

electrocardiography
BR ɪˌlektrəʊˈkaːdɪˈɒgrəfi
AM əˌlektrəʊˌkardiˈagrəfi,
əˌlektrəˌkardiˈagrəfi,
iˌlektrəˌkardiˈagrəfi,
iˌlektrəʊˌkardiˈagrəfi

electrochemical
BR ɪˌlektrəʊˈkemɪkl
AM əˌlektrəʊˈkeməkəl,
əˌlektrəˈkeməkəl,
iˌlektrəˈkeməkəl,
iˌlektrəʊˈkeməkəl

electrochemically
BR ɪˌlektrəʊˈkemɪkli
AM əˌlektrəʊˈkemək(ə)li,
əˌlektrəˈkemək(ə)li,
iˌlektrəˈkemək(ə)li,
iˌlektrəʊˈkemək(ə)li

electrochemist
BR ɪˌlektrəʊˈkemɪst, -s
AM əˌlektrəʊˈkeməst,
əˌlektrəˈkeməst,
iˌlektrəˈkeməst,
iˌlektrəʊˈkeməst, -s

electrochemistry
BR ɪˌlektrəʊˈkemɪstri
AM əˌlektrəʊˈkeməstri,
əˌlektrəˈkeməstri,
iˌlektrəˈkeməstri,
iˌlektrəʊˈkeməstri

electroconvulsive
BR ɪˌlektrəʊkənˈvʌlsɪv
AM əˌlektrəʊkənˈvəlsɪv,
əˌlektrəkənˈvəlsɪv,
iˌlektrəkənˈvəlsɪv,
iˌlektrəʊkənˈvəlsɪv

electrocute
BR ɪˈlektrəkjuːt, -s, -ɪŋ, -ɪd
AM əˈlektrəˌkju|t,
iˈlektrəˌkju|t, -ts, -dɪŋ, -dəd

electrocution
BR ɪˌlektrəˈkjuːʃn, -z
AM əˌlektrəˈkjuʃən,
iˈlektrəˈkjuʃən, -z

electrode
BR ɪˈlektrəʊd, -z
AM əˈlektrəʊd,
iˈlektrəʊd, -z

electrodialysis
BR ɪˌletrə(ʊ)dʌɪˈalɪsɪs
AM əˌlektrəʊˌdaɪˈæləsəs,
əˌlektrəˌdaɪˈæləsəs,
iˌlektrəʊˌdaɪˈæləsəs,
iˌlektrəˌdaɪˈæləsəs

electrodynamic
BR ɪˌletrə(ʊ)dʌɪˈnamɪk, -s
AM əˌlektrəʊˌdaɪˈnæmɪk,
əˌlektrəˌdaɪˈnæmɪk,
iˌlektrəʊˌdaɪˈnæmɪk,

iˌlektrəʊˌkardiəˈgræfɪk,
iˌlektrəʊˌkardiəʊˈgræfɪk
electrocardiography
BR ɪˌlektrəʊˈkaːdɪˈɒgrəfi

iˌlektrəˌdaɪˈnæmɪk, -s

electrodynamically
BR ɪˌletrə(ʊ)dʌɪˈnamɪkli
AM əˌlektrəʊˌdaɪˈnæmək(ə)li,
əˌlektrəˌdaɪˈnæmək(ə)li,
iˌlektrəʊˌdaɪˈnæmək(ə)li,
iˌlektrəˌdaɪˈnæmək(ə)li

electroencephalogram
BR ɪˌlektrəʊɪnˈsef(ə)ləgram,
ɪˌlektrəʊɪnˈsefləgram,
ɪˌlektrəʊenˈsef(ə)ləgram,
ɪˌlektrəʊenˈsefləgram,
ɪˌlektrəʊɪnˈkef(ə)ləgram,
ɪˌlektrəʊɪnˈkefləgram,
ɪˌlektrəʊenˈkef(ə)ləgram,
ɪˌlektrəʊenˈkefləgram,
-z
AM əˌlektrəʊənˈsefələgræm,
iˌlektrəʊənˈsefələgræm,
-z

electroencephalograph
BR ɪˌlektrəʊɪnˈsef(ə)ləgraːf,
ɪˌlektrəʊenˈsef(ə)ləgraːf,
ɪˌlektrəʊɪnˈkef(ə)ləgraːf,
ɪˌlektrəʊɪnˈsef(ə)ləgraf,
ɪˌlektrəʊenˈkef(ə)ləgraf,
ɪˌlektrəʊɪnˈkef(ə)ləgraf,
ɪˌlektrəʊenˈkef(ə)ləgraf, -s
AM əˌlektrəʊənˈsefələgræf,
iˌlektrəʊənˈsefələgræf,
-s

electroencephalography
BR ɪˌlektrəʊɪnˌsefəˈlɒgrəfi,
ɪˌlektrəʊenˌsefəˈlɒgrəfi,
ɪˌlektrəʊɪnˌkefəˈlɒgrəfi,
AM əˌlektrəʊˌenˌsefəˈlagrəfi,
iˌlektrəʊˌenˌsefəˈlagrəfi

electroluminescence
BR ɪˌlektrəʊˌluːmɪˈnesns
AM əˌlektrəʊˌlumaˈnesəns,

iˌlektrəʊˌlumaˈnesəns

electroluminescent
BR ɪˌlektrəʊˌluːmɪˈnesnt
AM əˌlektrəʊˌlumaˈnesənt,
iˌlektrəʊˌlumaˈnesənt

Electrolux®
BR ɪˈlektrə(ʊ)lʌks
AM əˈlektrəˌləks

electrolyse
BR ɪˈlektrəlʌɪz, -ɪz, -ɪŋ, -d
AM əˈlektrəˌlaɪz,
iˈlektrəˌlaɪz, -ɪz, -ɪŋ, -d

electrolyser
BR ɪˈlektrəlʌɪzə(r), -z
AM əˈlektrəˌlaɪzər,
iˈlektrəˌlaɪzər, -z

electrolysis
BR ɪˌlekˈtrɒlɪsɪs,
ˌelekˈtrɒlɪsɪs,
ˌelɪkˈtrɒlɪsɪs,
ˌɪlekˈtrɒlɪsɪs,
ˌiːlekˈtrɒlɪsɪs
AM əˌlekˈtrɑləsəs,
iˌlekˈtrɑləsəs

electrolyte
BR ɪˈlektrəlʌɪt, -s
AM əˈlektrəˌlaɪt,
iˈlektrəˌlaɪt, -s

electrolytic
BR ɪˌlektrəˈlɪtɪk
AM əˌlektrəˈlɪdɪk,
iˌlektrəˈlɪdɪk

electrolytical
BR ɪˌlektrəˈlɪtɪkl
AM əˌlektrəˈlɪdɪkəl,
iˌlektrəˈlɪdɪkəl

electrolytically
BR ɪˌlektrəˈlɪtɪkli
AM əˌlektrəˈlɪdɪk(ə)li,
iˌlektrəˈlɪdɪk(ə)li

electrolyze
BR ɪˈlektrəlʌɪz, -ɪz, -ɪŋ, -d
AM əˈlektrəˌlaɪz,
iˈlektrəˌlaɪz, -ɪz, -ɪŋ, -d

electrolyzer
BR ɪˈlektrəlʌɪzə(r), -z
AM əˈlektrəˌlaɪzər,
iˈlektrəˌlaɪzər, -z

electromagnet
BR ɪˌlektrə(ʊ)ˈmagnɪt,
-s
AM əˌlektrəˈmægnət,
iˌlektrəˈmægnət, -s

electromagnetic
BR ɪˌlektrə(ʊ)magˈnetɪk
AM əˌlektrəˌmægˈnedɪk,
iˌlektrəˌmægˈnedɪk

electromagnetically
BR ɪˌlektrə(ʊ)magˈnetɪkli
AM əˌlektrəˌmægˈnedək(ə)li,
iˌlektrəˌmægˈnedək(ə)li

electromagnetism
BR ɪˌlektrə(ʊ)ˈmagnɪtɪz(ə)m

AM əˌlektrəˈmægnə‑
ˌtɪzəm,
iˌlektrəˈmægnəˌtɪzəm
electromechanical
BR ɪˌlektrə(ʊ)mɪˈkanɪkl
AM əˌlektrəməˈkænəkəl,
iˌlektrəməˈkænəkəl
electrometer
BR ɪˌlekˈtrɒmɪtə(r), ‑z
AM əˌlekˈtramədər,
iˌlekˈtramədər, ‑z
electrometric
BR ɪˌlektrə(ʊ)ˈmetrɪk
AM əˌlektrəˈmetrɪk,
iˌlektrəˈmetrɪk
electrometry
BR ɪˌlekˈtrɒmɪtri,
ˌɛlekˈtrɒmɪtri,
ˌɛlɪkˈtrɒmɪtri,
ˌɪlekˈtrɒmɪtri,
ˌiːlekˈtrɒmɪtri
AM əˌlekˈtramətri,
iˌlekˈtramətri
electromotive
BR ɪˌlektrə(ʊ)ˈməʊtɪv
AM əˌlektrəˈmoʊdɪv,
iˌlektrəˈmoʊdɪv
electron
BR ɪˈlektrɒn, ‑z
AM əˈlekˌtran,
iˈlekˌtran, ‑z
electronegative
BR ɪˌlektrə(ʊ)ˈnegətɪv
AM əˌlektrəˈnegədɪv,
iˌlektrəˈnegədɪv
electronic
BR ɪˌlekˈtrɒnɪk,
ˌɛlekˈtrɒnɪk,
ˌɛlɪkˈtrɒnɪk,
ˌɪlekˈtrɒnɪk, ‑s
AM əˌlekˈtranɪk,
iˌlekˈtranɪk, ‑s
electronically
BR ɪˌlekˈtrɒnɪkli,
ˌɛlekˈtrɒnɪkli,
ˌɪlekˈtrɒnɪkli,
ˌiːlekˈtrɒnɪkli
AM əˌlekˈtranək(ə)li,
iˌlekˈtranək(ə)li
electronvolt
BR ɪˈlektrɒnˌvəʊlt, ‑s
AM əˈlektranˌvoʊlt,
iˈlektranˌvoʊlt, ‑s
electrophile
BR ɪˈlektrə(ʊ)fʌɪl, ‑z
AM əˈlektrəˌfaɪl,
iˈlektrəˌfaɪl, ‑z
electrophilic
BR ɪˌlektrə(ʊ)ˈfɪlɪk
AM əˌlektrəˈfɪlɪk,
iˌlektrəˈfɪlɪk
electrophonic
BR ɪˌletrə(ʊ)ˈfɒnɪk
AM əˌlektrəˈfanɪk
electrophoreses
BR ɪˌlektrə(ʊ)fəˈriːsiːz

AM əˌlektrəfəˈrisiz,
iˌlektrəfəˈrisiz
electrophoresic
BR ɪˌlektrə(ʊ)fəˈriːsɪk
AM əˌlektrəfəˈrisɪk,
iˌlektrəfəˈrisɪk
electrophoresis
BR ɪˌlektrə(ʊ)fəˈriːsɪs
AM əˌlektrəfəˈrisɪs,
iˌlektrəfəˈrisɪs
electrophoretic
BR ɪˌlektrə(ʊ)fəˈretɪk
AM əˌlektrəfəˈredɪk,
iˌlektrəfəˈredɪk
electrophorus
BR ɪˌlekˈtrɒf(ə)rəs,
ˌɛlekˈtrɒf(ə)rəs,
ˌɛlɪkˈtrɒf(ə)rəs,
ˌɪlekˈtrɒf(ə)rəs,
ˌiːlekˈtrɒf(ə)rəs
AM əˌlekˈtraf(ə)rəs,
iˌlekˈtraf(ə)rəs
electrophysiolog-
ical
BR ɪˌlektrəʊˌfɪzɪəˈlɒdʒ‑
ɪkl
AM əˌlektrəˌfɪziəˈladʒ‑
əkəl,
iˌlektrəˌfɪziəˈlɒdʒəkəl
electrophysiology
BR ɪˌlektrəʊˌfɪziˈɒlədʒi
AM əˌlektrəˌfɪziˈalədʒi,
iˌlektrəˌfɪziˈalədʒi
electroplate
BR ɪˈlektrə(ʊ)pleɪt,
ɪˌletrə(ʊ)ˈpleɪt, ‑s, ‑ɪŋ,
‑ɪd
AM əˈlektrəˌpleɪ|t,
iˈlektrəˌpleɪ|t, ‑ts,
‑dɪŋ, ‑dɪd
electroplater
BR ɪˈlektrə(ʊ)pleɪtə(r),
ɪˌlektrə(ʊ)ˈpleɪtə(r),
‑z
AM əˈlektrəˌpleɪdər,
iˈlektrəˌpleɪdər, ‑z
electroplexy
BR ɪˈlektrə(ʊ)pleksi
AM əˈlektrəˌpleksi,
iˈlektrəˌpleksi
electropositive
BR ɪˌlektrəʊˈpɒzɪtɪv
AM əˌlektrəˈpazədɪv,
iˌlektrəˈpazədɪv
electroscope
BR ɪˈlektrəskəʊp, ‑s
AM əˈlektrəˌskoʊp,
iˈlektrəˌskoʊp, ‑s
electroscopic
BR ɪˌlektrə(ʊ)ˈskɒpɪk
AM əˌlektrəˈskapɪk,
iˌlektrəˈskapɪk
electrostatic
BR ɪˌlektrə(ʊ)ˈstatɪk,
‑s
AM əˌlektrəˈstædɪk,
iˌlektrəˈstædɪk, ‑s

electrotechnic
BR ɪˌlektrəʊˈteknɪk, ‑s
AM əˌlektrəˈteknɪk,
iˌlektrəˈteknɪk, ‑s
electrotechnical
BR ɪˌlektrəʊˈteknɪkl
AM əˌlektrəˈteknəkəl,
iˌlektrəˈteknəkəl
electrotechnology
BR ɪˌlektrəʊtekˈnɒlədʒi
AM əˌlektrəˌtekˈnalədʒi,
iˌlektrəˌtekˈnalədʒi
electrotherapeutic
BR ɪˌlektrəʊˌθerəˈpjuːtɪk
AM əˌlektrəˌθerəˈpjudɪk,
iˌlektrəˌθerəˈpjudɪk
electrotherapeut-
ical
BR ɪˌlektrəʊˌθerəˈpjuːt‑
ɪkl
AM əˌlektrəˌθerəˈpjud‑
əkəl,
iˌlektrəˌθerəˈpjudəkəl
electrotherapist
BR ɪˌlektrəʊˈθerəpɪst,
‑s
AM əˌlektrəˈθerəpəst,
iˌlektrəˈθerəpəst, ‑s
electrotherapy
BR ɪˌlektrəʊˈθerəpi
AM əˌlektrəˈθerəpi,
iˌlektrəˈθerəpi
electrothermal
BR ɪˌlektrəʊˈθəːml
AM əˌlektrəˈθərməl,
iˌlektrəˈθərməl
electrotype
BR ɪˈlektrə(ʊ)tʌɪp, ‑s
AM əˈlektrəˌtaɪp,
iˈlektrəˌtaɪp, ‑s
electrotyper
BR ɪˈlektrə(ʊ)ˌtʌɪpə(r),
‑z
AM əˈlektrəˌtaɪpər,
iˈlektrəˌtaɪpər, ‑z
electrovalence
BR ɪˌlektrəʊˈveɪləns,
ɪˌlektrəʊˈveɪlŋs
AM əˌlektrəˈveɪləns,
iˌlektrəˈveɪləns
electrovalency
BR ɪˌlektrəʊˈveɪlənsi,
ɪˌlektrəʊˈveɪlŋsi
AM əˌlektrəˈveɪlənsi,
iˌlektrəˈveɪlənsi
electrovalent
BR ɪˌlektrəʊˈveɪlənt,
ɪˌlektrəʊˈveɪlŋt
AM əˌlektrəˈveɪlənt,
iˌlektrəˈveɪlənt
electrum
BR ɪˈlektrəm
AM əˈlektrəm,
iˈlektrəm
electuary
BR ɪˈlektjʊər|i,
ɪˈlektʃʊər|i,
ɪˈlektʃʊr|i, ‑ɪz

electrotechnic
AM əˈlektʃə‚weri,
iˈlektʃə‚weri, ‑z
eleemosynary
BR ˌel(ɪ)iːˈmɒs(ɪ)nəri,
ˌɛl(ɪ)iːˈmɒsŋəri
AM ˌeləˈmasŋəri
elegance
BR ˈelɪg(ə)ns
AM ˈeləgəns
elegant
BR ˈelɪg(ə)nt
AM ˈelǝgənt
elegantly
BR ˈelɪg(ə)ntli
AM ˈelǝgən(t)li
elegiac
BR ˌelɪˈdʒʌɪək, ‑s
AM ˌeləˈdʒaɪək, ‑s
elegiacal
BR ˌelɪˈdʒʌɪəkl
AM ˌeləˈdʒaɪəkəl
elegiacally
BR ˌelɪˈdʒʌɪəkli
AM ˌeləˈdʒaɪəkli
elegise
BR ˈelɪdʒʌɪz, ‑ɪz, ‑ɪŋ, ‑d
AM ˈeləˌdʒaɪz, ‑ɪz, ‑ɪŋ, ‑d
elegist
BR ˈelɪdʒɪst, ‑s
AM ˈelədʒəst, ‑s
elegize
BR ˈelɪdʒʌɪz, ‑ɪz, ‑ɪŋ, ‑d
AM ˈeləˌdʒaɪz, ‑ɪz, ‑ɪŋ, ‑d
elegy
BR ˈelədʒ|i, ‑ɪz
AM ˈelədʒi, ‑z
element
BR ˈelɪm(ə)nt, ‑s
AM ˈeləmənt, ‑s
elemental
BR ˌelɪˈmentl, ‑z
AM ˌeləˈmen(t)l, ‑z
elementalism
BR ˌelɪˈmentəlɪz(ə)m,
ˌɛlɪˈmentlɪz(ə)m
AM ˌeləˈmen(t)lˌɪzəm
elementally
BR ˌelɪˈmentəli,
ˌɛlɪˈmentļi
AM ˌeləˈmen(t)li
elementarily
BR ˌelɪˈment(ə)rɪli
AM ˌeləˈment(ə)rəli
elementariness
BR ˌelɪˈment(ə)rɪnɪs
AM ˌeləˈment(ə)rinɪs
elementary
BR ˌelɪˈment(ə)ri
AM ˌeləˈment(ə)ri
elemi
BR ˈeləm|i, ‑ɪz
AM ˈeləmi, ‑z
elenchus
BR ɪˈleŋkəs
AM əˈleŋkəs, iˈleŋkəs
elenctic
BR ɪˈleŋktɪk

AM əˈleŋktɪk, iˈleŋktɪk

Eleonora
BR ˌɛlɪəˈnɔːrə(r)
AM ˌelɑˈnɔrə

elephant
BR ˈɛlɪf(ə)nt, -s
AM ˈɛləfənt, -s

elephantiasis
BR ˌɛlɪf(ə)nˈtʌɪəsɪs
AM ˌɛləfənˈtaɪəsəs

elephantine
BR ˌɛlɪˈfantʌɪn
AM ˌɛləˈfæn,tin, ˌɛləˈfæn,taɪn, ˈɛləfən,tin, ˈɛləfən,taɪn

elephantoid
BR ˈɛlɪˈfantɔɪd
AM ˌɛləˈfæn,tɔɪd, ˈɛləfən,tɔɪd

Eleusinian
BR ˌɛljəˈsɪnɪən
AM ˌɛl(j)uˈsɪnɪən

Eleusis
BR ɪˈljuːsɪs
AM əˈl(j)usɪs

elevate
BR ˈɛlɪveɪt, -s, -ɪŋ, -ɪd
AM ˈɛlə,veɪ|t, -ts, -dɪŋ, -dɪd

elevation
BR ˌɛlɪˈveɪʃn, -z
AM ˌɛləˈveɪʃən, -z

elevational
BR ˌɛlɪˈveɪʃn̩(ə)l, ˌɛlɪˈveɪʃən(ə)l
AM ˌɛləˈveɪʃ(ə)nəl

elevator
BR ˈɛlɪveɪtə(r), -z
AM ˈɛlə,veɪdər, -z

elevatory
BR ˌɛlɪˈveɪt(ə)ri
AM ˈɛləvə,tɔri

eleven
BR ɪˈlɛvn
AM əˈlɛvən, iˈlɛvən

elevenfold
BR ɪˈlɛvnfəʊld
AM əˈlɛvən,foʊld, iˈlɛvən,foʊld

elevenses
BR ɪˈlɛvnzɪz
AM əˈlɛvənzəz, iˈlɛvənzəz

eleventh
BR ɪˈlɛvnθ
AM əˈlɛvənθ, iˈlɛvənθ

elevon
BR ˈɛlɪvɒn, -z
AM ˈɛlə,vɑn, -z

elf
BR ɛlf
AM ɛlf

Elfed
BR ˈɛlvɛd
AM ˈɛlvɛd

elfin
BR ˈɛlfɪn
AM ˈɛlfən

elfish
BR ˈɛlfɪʃ
AM ˈɛlfɪʃ

elfishly
BR ˈɛlfɪʃli
AM ˈɛlfɪʃli

elfishness
BR ˈɛlfɪʃnɪs
AM ˈɛlfɪʃnɪs

elfland
BR ˈɛlfland
AM ˈɛl,flænd

elflock
BR ˈɛlflɒk, -s
AM ˈɛl,flɑk, -s

Elfreda
BR ɛlˈfriːdə(r)
AM ˌɛlˈfridə

Elfrida
BR ɛlˈfriːdə(r)
AM ˌɛlˈfridə

Elgar
BR ˈɛlgɑː(r), ˈɛlgə(r)
AM ˈɛlgɑr

Elgin
BR ˈɛlgɪn
AM ˈɛlgən

El Giza
BR ˌɛlˈgiːzə(r)
AM ˌɛlˈgizə

Elgon
BR ˈɛlgɒn
AM ˈɛl,gɑn

El Greco
BR ˌɛlˈgrɛkəʊ
AM ˌɛlˈgrɛkoʊ

Eli
BR ˈiːlaɪ
AM ˈi,laɪ

Elia
BR ˈiːlɪə(r)
AM ˈiljə, ˈilɪə

Elias
BR ɪˈlʌɪəs
AM əˈlaɪəs, iˈlaɪəs

elicit
BR ɪˈlɪs|ɪt, -ɪts, -ɪtɪŋ, -ɪtɪd
AM əˈlɪsə|t, iˈlɪsə|t, -ts, -dɪŋ, -dəd

elicitation
BR ɪˌlɪsɪˈteɪʃn, -z
AM əˌlɪsəˈteɪʃən, iˌlɪsəˈteɪʃən, -z

elicitor
BR ɪˈlɪsɪtə(r), -z
AM əˈlɪsədər, iˈlɪsədər, -z

elide
BR ɪˈlʌɪd, -z, -ɪŋ, -ɪd
AM əˈlaɪd, iˈlaɪd, -z, -ɪŋ, -ɪd

eligibility
BR ˌɛlɪdʒɪˈbɪlɪti

AM ˌɛlədʒəˈbɪlɪdi

eligible
BR ˈɛlɪdʒɪbl
AM ˈɛlədʒəbəl

eligibly
BR ˈɛlɪdʒɪbli
AM ˈɛlədʒəbli

Elihu
BR ɪˈlʌɪhjuː, ɛˈlʌɪhjuː
AM ˈɛləh(j)u

Elijah
BR ɪˈlʌɪdʒə(r)
AM əˈlaɪ(d)ʒə, iˈlaɪ(d)ʒə

Elim
BR ˈiːlɪm
AM ˈilɪm

eliminable
BR ɪˈlɪmɪnəbl
AM əˈlɪmənəbəl, iˈlɪmənəbəl

eliminate
BR ɪˈlɪmɪneɪt, -s, -ɪŋ, -ɪd
AM əˈlɪmə,neɪ|t, iˈlɪmə,neɪ|t, -ts, -dɪŋ, -dɪd

elimination
BR ɪˌlɪmɪˈneɪʃn
AM əˌlɪməˈneɪʃən, iˌlɪməˈneɪʃən

eliminator
BR ɪˈlɪmɪneɪtə(r), -z
AM əˈlɪmə,neɪdər, iˈlɪmə,neɪdər, -z

eliminatory
BR ɪˈlɪmɪnət(ə)ri
AM əˈlɪmənə,tɔri, iˈlɪmənə,tɔri

Elinor
BR ˈɛlɪnə(r)
AM ˈɛlənər

ELINT
electronic intelligence
BR ˈɛlɪnt
AM ˈɛ,lɪnt

Eliot
BR ˈɛlɪət
AM ˈɛliət

Elisabeth
BR ɪˈlɪzəbəθ
AM əˈlɪz(ə)bəθ

Elisabethville
BR ɪˈlɪzəbəθvɪl
AM əˈlɪz(ə)bəθ,vɪl

Elisha
BR ɪˈlʌɪʃə(r)
AM əˈlaɪʃə

elision
BR ɪˈlɪʒn, -z
AM əˈlɪʒən, -z

élite
BR ɪˈliːt, eɪˈliːt, -s
AM əˈlit, eɪˈlit, -s

élitism
BR ɪˈliːtɪz(ə)m, eɪˈliːtɪz(ə)m
AM əˈlidɪzəm, eɪˈlidɪzəm

élitist
BR ɪˈliːtɪst, eɪˈliːtɪst, -s
AM əˈlidəst, eɪˈlidəst, -s

elixir
BR ɪˈlɪks(ɪ)ə(r), -z
AM əˈlɪksər, iˈlɪksər, -z

Eliza
BR ɪˈlʌɪzə(r)
AM əˈlaɪzə

Elizabeth
BR ɪˈlɪzəbəθ
AM əˈlɪz(ə)bəθ

Elizabethan
BR ɪˌlɪzəˈbiːθn, -z
AM əˌlɪzəˈbiːθən, iˌlɪzəˈbiːθən, -z

elk
BR ɛlk, -s
AM ɛlk, -s

elkhound
BR ˈɛlkhaʊnd, -z
AM ˈɛlk,(h)aʊnd, -z

Elkie
BR ˈɛlki
AM ˈɛlki

Elkins
BR ˈɛlkɪnz
AM ˈɛlkənz

ell
BR ɛl, -z
AM ɛl, -z

Ella
BR ˈɛlə(r)
AM ˈɛlə

Elland
BR ˈɛlənd
AM ˈɛlənd

Ellen
BR ˈɛlən
AM ˈɛlən

Ellery
BR ˈɛl(ə)ri
AM ˈɛləri

Ellesmere
BR ˈɛlzmɪə(r)
AM ˈɛlz,mɪ(ə)r

Ellice
BR ˈɛlɪs
AM ˈɛləs

Ellie
BR ˈɛli
AM ˈɛli

Ellington
BR ˈɛlɪŋt(ə)n
AM ˈɛlɪŋtən

Elliot
BR ˈɛlɪət
AM ˈɛliət

Elliott
BR ˈɛlɪət
AM ˈɛliət

ellipse
BR ɪˈlɪps, -ɪz
AM əˈlɪps, iˈlɪps, -ɪz

ellipses
plural of ellipsis
BR ɪˈlɪpsiːz

ellipsis
AM əˈlɪpsɪz, iˈlɪpsiz

ellipsis
BR ɪˈlɪpsɪs
AM əˈlɪpsɪs, iˈlɪpsɪs

ellipsoid
BR ɪˈlɪpsɔɪd
AM əˈlɪpsɔɪd, iˈlɪpsɔɪd

ellipsoidal
BR ˌelɪpˈsɔɪdl̩,
ˌɪlɪpˈsɔɪdl̩, ɪˌlɪpˈsɔɪdl̩
AM ˌeləpˈsɔɪdəl,
ˌɪləpˈsɔɪdəl

ellipt
BR ɪˈlɪpt, -s, -ɪŋ, -ɪd
AM əˈlɪpt, iˈlɪpt, -s, -ɪŋ,
-ɪd

elliptic
BR ɪˈlɪptɪk
AM əˈlɪptɪk, iˈlɪptɪk

elliptical
BR ɪˈlɪptɪkli
AM əˈlɪptɪkl, iˈlɪptɪkl

elliptically
BR ɪˈlɪptɪkli
AM əˈlɪptɪk(ə)li,
iˈlɪptɪk(ə)li

ellipticity
BR ˌelɪpˈtɪsɪti,
ˌɪlɪpˈtɪsɪti, ɪˌlɪpˈtɪsɪti
AM əˌlɪpˈtɪsɪdi,
iˌlɪpˈtɪsɪdi

Ellis
BR ˈelɪs
AM ˈeləs

Ellison
BR ˈelɪs(ə)n
AM ˈeləsən

Ellsworth
BR ˈelzwəːθ
AM ˈelzˌwərθ

Ellul
BR ˈiːlʌl, ˈelʌl
AM ˈeləl

elm
BR elm, -z
AM elm, -z

Elmer
BR ˈelmə(r)
AM ˈelmər

Elmet
BR ˈelmɪt
AM ˈelmət

Elmo
BR ˈelməʊ
AM ˈelmoʊ

Elmwood
BR ˈelmwʊd
AM ˈelmˌwʊd

elmy
BR ˈelmi
AM ˈelmi

El Niño
BR el ˈniːnjəʊ
AM ˌel ˈninjoʊ

elocution
BR ˌeləˈkjuːʃn
AM ˌeləˈkjuːʃən

elocutionary
BR ˌeləˈkjuːʃn(ə)ri
AM ˌeləˈkjuːʃəˌneri

elocutionist
BR ˌeləˈkjuːʃnɪst,
ˌeləˈkjuːʃənɪst, -s
AM ˌeləˈkjuːʃənəst, -s

Elohim
BR eˈləʊhɪm, ɪˈləʊhɪm,
ˌeləʊˈhiːm
AM eˈloʊˌhɪm,
əˈloʊˌhɪm, ˌeloʊˈhim

Elohist
BR eˈləʊhɪst, ɪˈləʊhɪst,
-s
AM eˈloʊ(h)əst,
əˈloʊ(h)əst, -s

Eloise
BR ˌeləʊˈiːz, ˈeləʊiːz
AM ˌeləˌwiz

elongate
BR ˈiːlɒŋɡeɪt, -s, -ɪŋ, -ɪd
AM əˈlɒŋˌɡeɪ|t,
iˈlɒŋˌɡeɪ|t, iˈlɑŋˌɡeɪ|t,
əˈlɑŋˌɡeɪ|t, -ts, -dɪŋ,
-dɪd

elongation
BR ˌiːlɒŋˈɡeɪʃn, -z
AM əˌlɒŋˈɡeɪʃən,
iˌlɒŋˈɡeɪʃən,
iˌlɑŋˈɡeɪʃən,
əˌlɑŋˈɡeɪʃən, -z

elope
BR ɪˈləʊp, -s, -ɪŋ, -t
AM əˈloʊp, iˈloʊp, -s, -ɪŋ,
-t

elopement
BR ɪˈləʊpm(ə)nt, -s
AM əˈloʊpmənt,
iˈloʊpmənt, -s

eloper
BR ɪˈləʊpə(r), -z
AM əˈloʊpər, iˈloʊpər,
-z

eloquence
BR ˈeləkw(ə)ns
AM ˈeləkwəns

eloquent
BR ˈeləkw(ə)nt
AM ˈeləkwənt

eloquently
BR ˈeləkw(ə)ntli
AM ˈeləkwən(t)li

El Paso
BR el ˈpasəʊ
AM ˌel ˈpæsoʊ

Elphick
BR ˈelfɪk
AM ˈelfɪk

Elroy
BR ˈelrɔɪ
AM ˈelrɔɪ

Elsa
BR ˈelsə(r)
AM ˈelzə, ˈelsə

Elsan®
BR ˈelsan
AM ˈelzən, ˈelsən

Elsbeth
BR ˈelsbəθ
AM ˈelzbəθ

else
BR els
AM els

elsewhere
BR elsˈweː(r),
ˈelsweː(r)
AM ˈelsˌ(h)weə(ə)r

Elsie
BR ˈelsi
AM ˈelsi

Elsinore
BR ˈelsnɔː(r)
AM ˈelsəˌnɔː(ə)r

Elspeth
BR ˈelspəθ
AM ˈelspəθ

Elstree
BR ˈelstriː
AM ˈelsˌtri

Elsworthy
BR ˈelzwəːði
AM ˈelzˌwərði

Eltham
BR ˈeltəm
AM ˈeltəm

Elton
BR ˈelt(ə)n
AM ˈeltən

eluant
BR ˈeljʊənt, -s
AM ˈel(j)əwənt, -s

eluate
BR ˈeljʊət, -s
AM ˈel(j)əwət,
ˈel(j)əˌweɪt, -s

elucidate
BR ɪˈl(j)uːsɪdeɪt, -s, -ɪŋ,
-ɪd
AM əˈlusəˌdeɪ|t,
iˈlusəˌdeɪ|t, -ts, -dɪŋ,
-dɪd

elucidation
BR ɪˌl(j)uːsɪˈdeɪʃn
AM əˌlusəˈdeɪʃən,
iˌlusəˈdeɪʃən

elucidative
BR ɪˈl(j)uːsɪdeɪtɪv
AM əˈlusəˌdeɪdɪv,
iˈlusəˌdeɪdɪv

elucidator
BR ɪˈl(j)uːsɪdeɪtə(r), -z
AM əˈlusəˌdeɪdər,
iˈlusəˌdeɪdər, -z

elucidatory
BR ɪˈl(j)uːsɪdeɪt(ə)ri,
ɪˌl(j)uːsɪˈdeɪt(ə)ri
AM əˈlusədəˌtɔri,
iˈlusədəˌtɔri

elude
BR ɪˈl(j)uːd, -z, -ɪŋ, -ɪd
AM əˈlud, iˈlud, -z, -ɪŋ,
-əd

eluent
BR ˈeljʊənt, -s
AM ˈel(j)əwənt, -s

Elul
BR ˈiːlʌl, ˈelʌl
AM ˈeləl

Eluned
BR ɛˈlmɛd
AM əˈlməd
WE eˈlmed

elusive
BR ɪˈl(j)uːsɪv
AM əˈlusɪv, iˈlusɪv

elusively
BR ɪˈl(j)uːsɪvli
AM əˈlusɪvli, iˈlusɪvli

elusiveness
BR ɪˈl(j)uːsɪvnɪs
AM əˈlusɪvnɪs,
iˈlusɪvnɪs

elusory
BR ɪˈl(j)uːs(ə)ri
AM iˈluzəri, əˈluzəri,
əˈlusəri, iˈlusəri

elute
BR ɪˈl(j)uːt, -s, -ɪŋ, -ɪd
AM əˈlu|t, iˈlu|t, -ts, -dɪŋ,
-dəd

elution
BR ɪˈl(j)uːʃn
AM əˈluʃən, iˈluʃən

elutriate
BR ɪˈl(j)uːtrɪeɪt, -s, -ɪŋ,
-ɪd
AM əˈlutriˌeɪ|t,
iˈlutriˌeɪ|t, -ts, -dɪŋ,
-dɪd

elutriation
BR ɪˌl(j)uːtrɪˈeɪʃn
AM əˌlutriˈeɪʃən,
iˌlutriˈeɪʃən

elver
BR ˈelvə(r), -z
AM ˈelvər, -z

elves
BR elvz
AM elvz

Elvira
BR elˈvɪərə(r),
elˈvaɪrə(r)
AM elˈvaɪrə

Elvis
BR ˈelvɪs
AM ˈelvəs

elvish
BR ˈelvɪʃ
AM ˈelvɪʃ

elvishly
BR ˈelvɪʃli
AM ˈelvɪʃli

elvishness
BR ˈelvɪʃnɪs
AM ˈelvɪʃnɪs

Elwes
BR ˈelwɪz
AM ˈelwəz

Ely[1]
forename
BR ˈiːlʌɪ
AM ˈiˌlaɪ

Ely²
place in UK
BR 'iːli
AM 'ili

Elyot
BR 'ɛlɪət
AM 'ɛlɪt

Élysée
BR ɪ'liːzeɪ, eɪ'liːzeɪ
AM ˌɛli'zeɪ

Elysian
BR ɪ'lɪziən
AM ə'lɪʒ(i)ən,
ɛ'lɪʒ(i)ən, ɪ'lɪʒ(i)ən

Elysium
BR ɪ'lɪziəm
AM ə'lɪʒiəm, ə'lɪziəm,
ɛ'lɪʒiəm, ɛ'lɪziəm,
ɪ'lɪʒiəm, ɪ'lɪziəm

elytra
BR 'ɛlɪtrə(r)
AM 'ɛlətrə

elytron
BR 'ɛlɪtrɒn, 'ɛlɪtr(ə)n
AM 'ɛləˌtrɑn

Elzevir
BR 'ɛlzɪvɪə(r)
AM 'ɛlzəˌvɪ(ə)r

em
BR ɛm, -z
AM ɛm, -z

'em
BR əm, m
AM əm, m

emaciate
BR ɪ'meɪsieɪt,
ɪ'meɪʃieɪt, -s, -ɪŋ, -ɪd
AM ə'meɪʃiˌeɪ|t,
ɪ'meɪʃiˌeɪ|t, -ts, -dɪŋ,
-dɪd

emaciation
BR ɪˌmeɪsi'eɪʃn
AM əˌmeɪʃi'eɪʃən,
ɪˌmeɪʃi'eɪʃən

email
BR 'iːmeɪl, -z, -ɪŋ, -d
AM 'iˌmeɪl, -z, -ɪŋ, -d

e-mail
BR 'iːmeɪl, -z, -ɪŋ, -d
AM 'iˌmeɪl, -z, -ɪŋ, -d

emanate
BR 'ɛməneɪt, -s, -ɪŋ, -ɪd
AM 'ɛməˌneɪ|t, -ts, -dɪŋ,
-dɪd

emanation
BR ˌɛmə'neɪʃn, -z
AM ˌɛmə'neɪʃən, -z

emanative
BR 'ɛməneɪtɪv,
'ɛmənətɪv
AM 'ɛməˌneɪdɪv

emancipate
BR ɪ'mansɪpeɪt, -s, -ɪŋ,
-ɪd
AM ə'mænsəˌpeɪ|t,
ɪ'mænsəˌpeɪ|t, -ts,
-dɪŋ, -dɪd

emancipation
BR ɪˌmansɪ'peɪʃn
AM əˌmænsə'peɪʃən,
ɪˌmænsə'peɪʃən

emancipationist
BR ɪˌmansɪ'peɪʃn̩ɪst,
ɪˌmansɪ'peɪʃənɪst, -s
AM əˌmænsə'peɪʃənəst,
ɪˌmænsə'peɪʃənəst, -s

emancipator
BR ɪ'mansɪpeɪtə(r), -z
AM ə'mænsəˌpeɪdər,
ɪ'mænsəˌpeɪdər, -z

emancipatory
BR ɪ'mansɪpət(ə)ri,
ɪˌmansɪ'peɪt(ə)ri
AM ə'mænsəpəˌtɔri,
ɪ'mænsəpəˌtɔri

Emanuel
BR ɪ'manjʊ(ə)l
AM ə'mænjəwəl

emasculate
BR ɪ'maskjʊleɪt, -s, -ɪŋ,
-ɪd
AM ə'mæskjəˌleɪ|t,
ɪ'mæskjəˌleɪ|t, -ts,
-dɪŋ, -dɪd

emasculation
BR ɪˌmaskjʊ'leɪʃn
AM əˌmæskjə'leɪʃən,
ɪˌmæskjə'leɪʃən

emasculator
BR ɪ'maskjʊleɪtə(r), -z
AM ə'mæskjəˌleɪdər,
ɪ'mæskjəˌleɪdər, -z

emasculatory
BR ɪ'maskjʊlət(ə)ri
AM ə'mæskjələˌtɔri,
ɪ'mæskjələˌtɔri

embalm
BR ɪm'bɑːm, ɛm'bɑːm,
-z, -ɪŋ, -d
AM əm'bɑ(l)m,
ɛm'bɑ(l)m, -z, -ɪŋ, -d

embalmer
BR ɪm'bɑːmə(r),
ɛm'bɑːmə(r), -z
AM əm'bɑ(l)mər,
ɛm'bɑ(l)mər, -z

embalmment
BR ɪm'bɑːmm(ə)nt,
ɛm'bɑːmm(ə)nt
AM əm'bɑ(m)mənt,
ɛm'bɑ(m)mənt,
əm'bɑ(l)mənt,
ɛm'bɑ(l)mənt

embank
BR ɪm'baŋ|k,
ɛm'baŋ|k, -ks, -kɪŋ,
-(k)t
AM əm'bæŋ|k,
ɛm'bæŋ|k, -ks, -kɪŋ,
-(k)t

embankment
BR ɪm'baŋkm(ə)nt,
ɛm'baŋkm(ə)nt, -s
AM əm'bæŋkmənt,
ɛm'bæŋkmənt, -s

embarcation
BR ˌɛmbɑː'keɪʃn, -z
AM ˌɛmˌbɑr'keɪʃən, -z

embargo
BR ɪm'bɑːgəʊ,
ɛm'bɑːgəʊ, -z, -ɪŋ, -d
AM əm'bɑrgoʊ,
ɛm'bɑrgoʊ, -z, -ɪŋ, -d

embark
BR ɪm'bɑːk, ɛm'bɑːk,
-s, -ɪŋ, -t
AM əm'bɑrk, ɛm'bɑrk,
-s, -ɪŋ, -t

embarkation
BR ˌɛmbɑː'keɪʃn, -z
AM ˌɛmˌbɑr'keɪʃən, -z

embarras de choix
BR ɒmˌbarɑ: də
'ʃwɑː(r)
AM ˌɑmbɑ'rɑ də 'ʃwɑ

embarras de richesse
BR ɒmˌbarɑ: də rɪ'ʃɛs
AM ˌɑmbɑ'rɑ də ri'ʃɛs

embarrass
BR ɪm'barəs,
ɛm'barəs, -ɪz, -ɪŋ, -t
AM əm'bɛrəs,
ɛm'bɛrəs, -əz, -ɪŋ, -t

embarrassedly
BR ɪm'barəstli,
ɛm'barəstli,
ɪm'barəsɪdli,
ɛm'barəsɪdli
AM əm'bɛrəstli,
ɛm'bɛrəstli,
əm'bɛrəsədli,
ɛm'bɛrəsədli

embarrassing
BR ɪm'barəsɪŋ,
ɛm'barəsɪŋ
AM əm'bɛrəsɪŋ,
ɛm'bɛrəsɪŋ

embarrassingly
BR ɪm'barəsɪŋli,
ɛm'barəsɪŋli
AM əm'bɛrəsɪŋli,
ɛm'bɛrəsɪŋli

embarrassment
BR ɪm'barəsm(ə)nt,
ɛm'barəsm(ə)nt, -s
AM əm'bɛrəsmənt,
ɛm'bɛrəsmənt, -s

embassy
BR 'ɛmbəs|i, -ɪz
AM 'ɛmbəsi, -z

embattle
BR ɪm'bat|l, ɛm'bat|l,
-lz, -l̩ɪŋ \ -lɪŋ, -ld
AM əm'bædəl,
ɛm'bædəl, -z, -ɪŋ, -d

embattled
BR ɪm'batld, ɛm'batld
AM əm'bædld,
ɛm'bædld

embay
BR ɪm'beɪ, ɛm'beɪ, -z,
-ɪŋ, -d
AM əm'beɪ, ɛm'beɪ, -z,
-ɪŋ, -d

embayment
BR ɪm'beɪm(ə)nt,
ɛm'beɪm(ə)nt
AM əm'beɪmənt,
ɛm'beɪmənt

embed
BR ɪm'bɛd, ɛm'bɛd, -z,
-ɪŋ, -ɪd
AM əm'bɛd, ɛm'bɛd, -z,
-ɪn, -əd

embedment
BR ɪm'bɛdm(ə)nt,
ɛm'bɛdm(ə)nt
AM əm'bɛdmənt,
ɛm'bɛdmənt

embellish
BR ɪm'bɛl|ɪʃ, ɛm'bɛl|ɪʃ,
-ɪʃɪz, -ɪʃɪŋ, -ɪʃt
AM əm'bɛlɪʃ, ɛm'bɛlɪʃ,
-ɪz, -ɪŋ, -t

embellisher
BR ɪm'bɛlɪʃə(r),
ɛm'bɛlɪʃə(r), -z
AM əm'bɛlɪʃər,
ɛm'bɛlɪʃər, -z

embellishment
BR ɪm'bɛlɪʃm(ə)nt,
ɛm'bɛlɪʃm(ə)nt, -s
AM əm'bɛlɪʃmənt,
ɛm'bɛlɪʃmənt, -s

ember
BR 'ɛmbə(r), -z
AM 'ɛmbər, -z

embezzle
BR ɪm'bɛz|l, ɛm'bɛz|l,
-lz, -l̩ɪŋ \ -lɪŋ, -ld
AM əm'bɛz|əl,
ɛm'bɛz|əl, -əlz, -(ə)lɪŋ,
-əld

embezzlement
BR ɪm'bɛzlm(ə)nt,
ɛm'bɛzlm(ə)nt, -s
AM əm'bɛzəlmənt,
ɛm'bɛzəlmənt, -s

embezzler
BR ɪm'bɛzlə(r),
ɛm'bɛzlə(r), -z
AM əm'bɛzlər,
ɛm'bɛzlər, əm'bɛzlər,
ɛm'bɛzlər, -z

embitter
BR ɪm'bɪt|ə(r),
ɛm'bɪt|ə(r), -əz,
-(ə)rɪŋ, -əd
AM əm'bɪdər,
ɛm'bɪdər, -z, -ɪŋ, -d

embitterment
BR ɪm'bɪtəm(ə)nt,
ɛm'bɪtəm(ə)nt
AM əm'bɪdərmənt,
ɛm'bɪdərmənt

emblazon
BR ɪmˈbleɪz|n,
ɛmˈbleɪz|n, -nz,
-n̩ɪŋ\-ənɪŋ, -nd
AM əmˈbleɪzən,
ɛmˈbleɪzən, -z, -ɪŋ, -d

emblazonment
BR ɪmˈbleɪznm(ə)nt,
ɛmˈbleɪznm(ə)nt
AM əmˈbleɪzənmənt,
ɛmˈbleɪzənmənt

emblazonry
BR ɪmˈbleɪznri,
ɛmˈbleɪznri
AM əmˈbleɪzənri,
ɛmˈbleɪzənri

emblem
BR ˈɛmbləm, -z
AM ˈɛmbləm, -z

emblematic
BR ˌɛmbləˈmatɪk
AM ˌɛmbləˈmædɪk

emblematical
BR ˌɛmbləˈmatɪkl
AM ˌɛmbləˈmædəkəl

emblematically
BR ˌɛmbləˈmatɪkli
AM ˌɛmbləˈmædək(ə)li

emblematise
BR ɛmˈblɛmətʌɪz, -ɪz,
-ɪŋ, -d
AM ɛmˈblɛməˌtaɪz, -ɪz,
-ɪŋ, -d

emblematize
BR ɛmˈblɛmətʌɪz, -ɪz,
-ɪŋ, -d
AM ɛmˈblɛməˌtaɪz, -ɪz,
-ɪŋ, -d

emblements
BR ˈɛmblɪm(ə)nts
AM ɛmˈblɛmən(t)s

embodiment
BR ɪmˈbɒdɪm(ə)nt,
ɛmˈbɒdɪm(ə)nt, -s
AM əmˈbɑdəmənt,
ɛmˈbɑdəmənt,
əmˈbɑdimənt,
ɛmˈbɑdimənt, -s

embody
BR ɪmˈbɒd|i, ɛmˈbɒd|i,
-ɪz, -ɪɪŋ, -ɪd
AM əmˈbɑdi, -z, -ɪŋ, -d

embolden
BR ɪmˈbəʊld|(ə)n,
ɛmˈbəʊld|(ə)n, -(ə)nz,
-ənɪŋ\-n̩ɪŋ, -(ə)nd
AM əmˈboʊld|ən,
ɛmˈboʊld|ən, -ənz,
-(ə)nɪŋ, -ənd

emboli
BR ˈɛmbəlʌɪ, ˈɛmbəliː
AM ˈɛmbəˌlaɪ

embolic
BR ɛmˈbɒlɪk
AM ɛmˈbɑlɪk

embolism
BR ˈɛmbəlɪz(ə)m, -z
AM ˈɛmbəˌlɪzəm, -z

embolismic
BR ˌɛmbəˈlɪzmɪk
AM ˌɛmbəˈlɪzmɪk

embolus
BR ˈɛmbələs
AM ˈɛmbələs

embonpoint
BR ˌɒmbɒnˈpwa(r),
ˌɒbɒ̃ˈpwɒ̃(r)
AM ˌɑmbɔnˈpwɑn

embosom
BR ɪmˈbʊz|(ə)m,
ɛmˈbʊz|(ə)m, -(ə)mz,
-əmɪŋ\-n̩ɪŋ, -(ə)md
AM əmˈbʊzəm,
ɛmˈbʊzəm, -z, -ɪŋ, -d

emboss
BR ɪmˈbɒs, ɛmˈbɒs, -ɪz,
-ɪŋ, -t
AM əmˈbɔs, ɛmˈbɔs,
əmˈbɑs, ɛmˈbɑs, -əz,
-ɪŋ, -t

embosser
BR ɪmˈbɒsə(r),
ɛmˈbɒsə(r), -z
AM əmˈbɔsər,
ɛmˈbɔsər, əmˈbɑsər,
ɛmˈbɑsər, -z

embossment
BR ɪmˈbɒsm(ə)nt,
ɛmˈbɒsm(ə)nt, -s
AM əmˈbɔsmənt,
ɛmˈbɑsmənt,
əmˈbɑsmənt,
ɛmˈbɑsmənt, -s

embouchure
BR ˌɒmbʊˈʃʊə(r), -z
AM ˌɑmbuˈʃʊ(ə)r, -z

embowel
BR ɪmˈbaʊəl,
ɛmˈbaʊəl, -z, -ɪŋ, -d
AM əmˈbaʊəl,
ɛmˈbaʊəl, -z, -ɪŋ, -d

embower
BR ɪmˈbaʊə(r),
ɛmˈbaʊə(r), -z, -ɪŋ, -d
AM əmˈbaʊər,
ɛmˈbaʊər, -z, -ɪŋ, -d

embrace
BR ɪmˈbreɪs, ɛmˈbreɪs,
-ɪz, -ɪŋ, -t
AM əmˈbreɪs, ɛmˈbreɪs,
-ɪz, -ɪŋ, -t

embraceable
BR ɪmˈbreɪsəbl,
ɛmˈbreɪsəbl
AM əmˈbreɪsəbəl,
ɛmˈbreɪsəbəl

embracement
BR ɪmˈbreɪsm(ə)nt,
ɛmˈbreɪsm(ə)nt, -s
AM əmˈbreɪsmənt,
ɛmˈbreɪsmənt, -s

embracer
BR ɪmˈbreɪsə(r),
ɛmˈbreɪsə(r), -z
AM əmˈbreɪsər,
ɛmˈbreɪsər, -z

embranchment
BR ɪmˈbran(t)ʃm(ə)nt,
ɛmˈbran(t)ʃm(ə)nt, -s
AM əmˈbræn(t)ʃmənt,
ɛmˈbræn(t)ʃmənt, -s

embrangle
BR ɪmˈbraŋgl,
ɛmˈbraŋgl, -z, -ɪŋ, -d
AM əmˈbræŋgl|əl,
ɛmˈbræŋgl|əl, -əlz,
-(ə)lɪŋ, -əld

embranglement
BR ɪmˈbraŋglm(ə)nt,
ɛmˈbraŋglm(ə)nt
AM əmˈbræŋglmənt,
ɛmˈbræŋglmənt

embrasure
BR ɪmˈbreɪʒə(r),
ɛmˈbreɪʒə(r), -z, -d
AM əmˈbreɪʒər,
ɛmˈbreɪʒər, -z, -d

embrittle
BR ɪmˈbrɪt|l, ɛmˈbrɪt|l,
-lz, -l̩ɪŋ\-lɪŋ, -ld
AM əmˈbrɪdəl,
ɛmˈbrɪdəl, -z, -ɪŋ, -d

embrittlement
BR ɪmˈbrɪtlm(ə)nt,
ɛmˈbrɪtlm(ə)nt
AM əmˈbrɪdlmənt,
ɛmˈbrɪdlmənt

embrocation
BR ˌɛmbrəˈkeɪʃn, -z
AM ˌɛmbrəˈkeɪʃən, -z

embroider
BR ɪmˈbrɔɪd|ə(r),
ɛmˈbrɔɪd|ə(r), -əz,
-(ə)rɪŋ, -əd
AM əmˈbrɔɪdər,
ɛmˈbrɔɪdər, -z, -ɪŋ, -d

embroiderer
BR ɪmˈbrɔɪd(ə)rə(r),
ɛmˈbrɔɪd(ə)rə(r), -z
AM əmˈbrɔɪdərər,
ɛmˈbrɔɪdərər, -z

embroidery
BR ɪmˈbrɔɪd(ə)ri,
ɛmˈbrɔɪd(ə)ri
AM əmˈbrɔɪd(ə)ri,
ɛmˈbrɔɪd(ə)ri

embroil
BR ɪmˈbrɔɪl, ɛmˈbrɔɪl,
-z, -ɪŋ, -d
AM əmˈbrɔɪl, ɛmˈbrɔɪl,
-z, -ɪŋ, -d

embroilment
BR ɪmˈbrɔɪlm(ə)nt,
ɛmˈbrɔɪlm(ə)nt, -s
AM əmˈbrɔɪlmənt,
ɛmˈbrɔɪlmənt, -s

embrown
BR ɪmˈbraʊn,
ɛmˈbraʊn, -z, -ɪŋ, -d
AM əmˈbraʊn,
ɛmˈbraʊn, -z, -ɪŋ, -d

embryo
BR ˈɛmbrɪəʊ, -z
AM ˈɛmbriˌoʊ, -z

embryogenesis
BR ˌɛmbrɪəʊˈdʒɛnɪsɪs
AM ˌɛmbrioʊˈdʒɛnəsəs

embryoid
BR ˈɛmbrɪɔɪd
AM ˈɛmbriˌɔɪd

embryologic
BR ˌɛmbrɪəˈlɒdʒɪk
AM ˌɛmbriəˈlɑdʒɪk

embryological
BR ˌɛmbrɪəˈlɒdʒɪkl
AM ˌɛmbriəˈlɑdʒəkəl

embryologically
BR ˌɛmbrɪəˈlɒdʒɪkli
AM ˌɛmbriəˈlɑdʒək(ə)li

embryologist
BR ˌɛmbrɪˈɒlədʒɪst, -s
AM ˌɛmbriˈɑlədʒəst, -s

embryology
BR ˌɛmbrɪˈɒlədʒi
AM ˌɛmbriˈɑlədʒi

embryonal
BR ɪmˈbrʌɪənl,
ɛmˈbrʌɪənl
AM ɛmˈbraɪənəl

embryonic
BR ˌɛmbrɪˈɒnɪk
AM ˌɛmbriˈɑnɪk

embryonically
BR ˌɛmbrɪˈɒnɪkli
AM ˌɛmbriˈɑnək(ə)li

Embury
BR ˈɛmb(ə)ri,
ˈɛmbjʊri
AM ˈɛmbəri

embus
BR ɪmˈbʌs, ɛmˈbʌs, -ɪz,
-ɪŋ, -t
AM əmˈbəs, ɛmˈbəs, -əz,
-ɪŋ, -t

emcee
BR ˌɛmˈsiː, -z
AM ˌɛmˈsi, -z

Emeline
BR ˈɛmɪliːn
AM ˈɛməˌlaɪn

emend
BR ɪˈmɛnd, iːˈmɛnd, -z,
-ɪŋ, -ɪd
AM əˈmɛnd, iˈmɛnd, -z,
-ɪŋ, -əd

emendation
BR ˌiːmɛnˈdeɪʃn, -z
AM ˌimɛnˈdeɪʃən,
ˌɛmənˈdeɪʃən, -z

emendator
BR ˈiːmɛndeɪtə(r), -z
AM ˈimɛnˌdeɪdər,
ˈɛmənˌdeɪdər, -z

emendatory
BR ɪˈmɛndət(ə)ri
AM əˈmɛndəˌtɔri

Emeny
BR ˈɛməni
AM ˈɛməni

emerald
BR ˈɛm(ə)rəld,
ˈɛm(ə)r|d, -z

emeraldine
AM 'ɛm(ə)rəld, -z
BR 'ɛm(ə)rəldiːn,
'ɛmr̩ldiːn
AM 'ɛm(ə)rəlˌdin,
'ɛm(ə)rəlˌdaɪn

emerge
BR ɪ'məːdʒ, -ɪz, -ɪŋ, -d
AM ə'mərdʒ, i'mərdʒ,
-əz, -ɪŋ, -d

emergence
BR ɪ'məːdʒ(ə)ns
AM ə'mərdʒəns,
i'mərdʒəns

emergency
BR ɪ'məːdʒ(ə)ns|i, -ɪz
AM ə'mərdʒənsi,
i'mərdʒənsi, -z

emergent
BR ɪ'məːdʒ(ə)nt
AM ə'mərdʒənt,
i'mərdʒənt

emergently
BR ɪ'məːdʒ(ə)ntli
AM ə'mərdʒən(t)li,
i'mərdʒən(t)li

emeritus
BR ɪ'mɛrɪtəs
AM ə'mɛrədəs,
i'mɛrədəs

emerse
BR ɪ'məːs, -t
AM ə'mərs, i'mərs, -t

emersion
BR ɪ'məːʃn
AM ə'mərʒən, i'mərʒn

Emerson
BR 'ɛməs(ə)n
AM 'ɛmərsən

emery
BR 'ɛm(ə)ri
AM 'ɛm(ə)ri

emesis
BR 'ɛməsɪs
AM 'ɛməsəs

emetic
BR ɪ'mɛtɪk, -s
AM ə'mɛdɪk, i'mɛdɪk, -s

émeute
BR eɪ'məːt, -s
AM eɪ'mʊt, -s

emigrant
BR 'ɛmɪgr(ə)nt, -s
AM 'ɛməgrənt, -s

emigrate
BR 'ɛmɪgreɪt, -s, -ɪŋ, -ɪd
AM 'ɛməˌgreɪt, -ts, -dɪŋ, -dɪd

emigration
BR ˌɛmɪ'greɪʃn
AM ˌɛmə'greɪʃən

emigratory
BR 'ɛmɪgreɪt(ə)ri
AM 'ɛməgrəˌtɔri

émigré
BR 'ɛmɪgreɪ, -z
AM 'ɛməˌgreɪ, -z

émigré
BR 'ɛmɪgreɪ, -z
AM 'ɛməˌgreɪ, -z

Emil
BR ɛ'miːl
AM 'eɪmɪl

Emile
BR ɛ'miːl
AM ə'mil

Emily
BR 'ɛmɪli, 'ɛml̩i
AM 'ɛm(ə)li

eminence
BR 'ɛmɪnəns, -ɪz
AM 'ɛmənəns, -əz

éminence grise
BR ˌɛmɪnəns 'griːz
AM ˌɛmənəns 'griz

eminent
BR 'ɛmɪnənt
AM 'ɛmənənt

eminently
BR 'ɛmɪnəntli
AM 'ɛmənən(t)li

emir
BR ɛ'mɪə(r), ɪ'mɪə(r),
eɪ'mɪə(r), -z
AM ə'mɪ(ə)r, eɪ'mɪ(ə)r,
-z

emirate
BR 'ɛmɪrət, 'ɛmɪərət,
ɛ'mɪərət, ɛ'mɪəreɪt, -s
AM ə'mɪˌreɪt, ə'mɪrət,
'ɛməˌreɪt, 'ɛmərət, -s

emissary
BR 'ɛmɪs(ə)r|i, -ɪz
AM 'ɛməˌsɛri, -z

emission
BR ɪ'mɪʃn, -z
AM ə'mɪʃən, i'mɪʃən, -z

emissive
BR ɪ'mɪsɪv
AM ə'mɪsɪv, i'mɪsɪv

emissivity
BR ˌiːmɪˈsɪvɪti,
ˌɪmɪ'sɪvɪti, ˌɛmɪ'sɪvɪti
AM ˌɛmə'sɪvɪdi,
ˌimə'sɪvɪdi

emit
BR ɪ'mɪt, -s, -ɪŋ, -ɪd
AM ə'mɪ|t, i'mɪ|t, -ts,
-dɪŋ, -dɪd

emitter
BR ɪ'mɪtə(r), -z
AM ə'mɪdər, i'mɪdər, -z

Emley
BR 'ɛmli
AM 'ɛmli

Emlyn
BR 'ɛmlɪn
AM 'ɛmlən

Emma
BR 'ɛmə(r)
AM 'ɛmə

Emmanuel
BR ɪ'manjʊəl,
ɪ'manjəl
AM ə'mænjə(wə)l

Emmaus
BR ɪ'meɪəs
AM ə'meɪəs

Emmeline
BR 'ɛməliːn
AM 'ɛmɛˌlaɪn

Emmental
BR 'ɛməntaːl
AM 'ɛmənˌtal

Emmentaler
BR 'ɛməntaːlə(r)
AM 'ɛmənˌtalər

Emmenthal
BR 'ɛməntaːl
AM 'ɛmənˌtal

Emmenthaler
BR 'ɛməntaːlə(r)
AM 'ɛmənˌtalər

emmer
BR 'ɛmə(r)
AM 'ɛmər

Emmerson
BR 'ɛməs(ə)n
AM 'ɛmərsən

emmet
BR 'ɛmɪt, -s
AM 'ɛmət, -s

emmetropia
BR ˌɛmɪ'trəʊpiə(r)
AM ˌɛmə'troʊpiə

emmetropic
BR ˌɛmɪ'trɒpɪk,
ˌɛmɪ'trəʊpɪk
AM ˌɛmə'trapɪk

Emmy
BR 'ɛm|i, -ɪz
AM 'ɛmi, -z

emollience
BR ɪ'mɒliəns
AM ə'maljəns,
i'maljəns

emollient
BR ɪ'mɒliənt, -s
AM ə'maljənt,
i'maljənt, -s

emolument
BR ɪ'mɒljəm(ə)nt
AM ə'maljəmənt,
i'maljəmənt

Emory
BR 'ɛm(ə)ri
AM 'ɛməri

emote
BR ɪ'məʊt, -s, -ɪŋ, -ɪd
AM ə'moʊ|t, i'moʊ|t,
-ts, -dɪŋ, -dəd

emoter
BR ɪ'məʊtə(r), -z
AM ə'moʊdər,
i'moʊdər, -z

emoticon
BR ɪ'mɒtɪkɒn,
ɪ'məʊtɪkɒn, -z
AM ə'moʊdəˌkɑn,
i'moʊdəˌkɑn, -z

emotion
BR ɪ'məʊʃn, -z

emotional
BR ɪ'məʊʃn̩(ə)l,
ɪ'məʊʃən(ə)l
AM ə'moʊʃ(ə)nəl

emotionalise
BR ɪ'məʊʃn̩əlʌɪz,
ɪ'məʊʃn̩lʌɪz,
ɪ'məʊʃən|ʌɪz,
ɪ'məʊʃ(ə)nəlʌɪz, -ɪz,
-ɪŋ, -d
AM ə'moʊʃənlˌɪzəm,
ə'moʊʃnəˌlɪzəm,
i'moʊʃənlˌɪzəm,
i'moʊʃnəˌlɪzəm

emotionalism
BR ɪ'məʊʃn̩əlɪz(ə)m,
ɪ'məʊʃn̩lɪz(ə)m,
ɪ'məʊʃən|ɪz(ə)m,
ɪ'məʊʃ(ə)nəlɪz(ə)m
AM ə'moʊʃənlˌɪzəm,
ə'moʊʃnəˌlɪzəm,
i'moʊʃənlˌɪzəm,
i'moʊʃnəˌlɪzəm

emotionalist
BR ɪ'məʊʃn̩əlɪst,
ɪ'məʊʃn̩lɪst,
ɪ'məʊʃən|ɪst,
ɪ'məʊʃ(ə)nəlɪst, -s
AM ə'moʊʃənələst,
ə'moʊʃnələst, -s

emotionality
BR ɪˌməʊʃə'naliti
AM əˌmoʊʃə'nælədi,
iˌmoʊʃə'nælədi

emotionalize
BR ɪ'məʊʃn̩əlʌɪz,
ɪ'məʊʃn̩lʌɪz,
ɪ'məʊʃən|ʌɪz,
ɪ'məʊʃ(ə)nəlʌɪz, -ɪz,
-ɪŋ, -d
AM ə'moʊʃənəˌlaɪz,
i'moʊʃənəˌlaɪz, -ɪz,
-ɪŋ, -d

emotionally
BR ɪ'məʊʃn̩əli,
ɪ'məʊʃn̩li,
ɪ'məʊʃən|li,
ɪ'məʊʃ(ə)nəli
AM ə'moʊʃ(ə)nəli

emotionless
BR ɪ'məʊʃnləs
AM ə'moʊʃənləs

emotive
BR ɪ'məʊtɪv
AM ə'moʊdɪv,
i'moʊdɪv

emotively
BR ɪ'məʊtɪvli
AM ə'moʊdəvli,
i'moʊdəvli

emotiveness
BR ɪ'məʊtɪvnɪs
AM ə'moʊdɪvnɪs,
i'moʊdɪvnɪs

emotivity
BR ˌiːməʊ'tɪvɪti

AM əˌmoʊˈtɪvɪdi,
iˌmoʊˈtɪvɪdi

empanel
BR ɪmˈpanl, ɛmˈpanl,
-z, -ɪŋ, -d
AM əmˈpænl, -z, -ɪŋ, -d

empanelment
BR ɪmˈpanlm(ə)nt
AM əmˈpænlmənt

empathetic
BR ˌɛmpəˈθɛtɪk
AM ˌɛmpəˈθɛdɪk

empathetically
BR ˌɛmpəˈθɛtɪkli
AM ˌɛmpəˈθɛdək(ə)li

empathic
BR ɪmˈpaθɪk, ɛmˈpaθɪk
AM əmˈpæθɪk,
ɛmˈpæθɪk

empathically
BR ɪmˈpaθɪkli,
ɛmˈpaθɪkli
AM əmˈpæθək(ə)li,
ɛmˈpæθək(ə)li

empathise
BR ˈɛmpəθʌɪz, -ɪz, -ɪŋ,
-d
AM ˈɛmpəˌθaɪz, -ɪz, -ɪŋ,
-d

empathist
BR ˈɛmpəθɪst, -s
AM ˈɛmpəθəst, -s

empathize
BR ˈɛmpəθʌɪz, -ɪz, -ɪŋ,
-d
AM ˈɛmpəˌθaɪz, -ɪz, -ɪŋ,
-d

empathy
BR ˈɛmpəθi
AM ˈɛmpəθi

Empedocles
BR ɛmˈpɛdəkliːz
AM ɛmˈpɛdəˌkliz

empennage
BR ɪmˈpɛnɪdʒ,
ɛmˈpɛnɪdʒ, -ɪz
AM ˌɑmpəˈnɑʒ,
ˌɛmpəˈnɑ(d)ʒ, -əz

emperor
BR ˈɛmp(ə)rə(r), -z
AM ˈɛmp(ə)rər, -z

emperorship
BR ˈɛmp(ə)rəʃɪp, -s
AM ˈɛmp(ə)rərˌʃɪp, -s

emphases
BR ˈɛmfəsiːz
AM ˈɛmfəˌsiz

emphasis
BR ˈɛmfəsɪs
AM ˈɛmfəsəs

emphasise
BR ˈɛmfəsʌɪz, -ɪz, -ɪŋ, -d
AM ˈɛmfəˌsaɪz, -ɪz, -ɪŋ,
-d

emphasize
BR ˈɛmfəsʌɪz, -ɪz, -ɪŋ, -d
AM ˈɛmfəˌsaɪz, -ɪz, -ɪŋ,
-d

emphatic
BR ɪmˈfatɪk, ɛmˈfatɪk
AM əmˈfædɪk,
ɛmˈfædɪk

emphatically
BR ɪmˈfatɪkli
ɛmˈfatɪkli
AM əmˈfædək(ə)li,
ɛmˈfædək(ə)li

emphysema
BR ˌɛmfɪˈsiːmə(r)
AM ˌɛmfəˈsimə,
ˌɛmfəˈzimə

empire
BR ˈɛmpʌɪə(r), -z
AM ˈɛmˌpaɪ(ə)r, -z

**Empire State
Building**
BR ˌɛmpʌɪə ˌsteɪt
ˈbɪldɪŋ
AM ˈɛmˌpaɪ(ə)r ˈsteɪt
ˌbɪldɪŋ

empiric
BR ɪmˈpɪrɪk, ɛmˈpɪrɪk
AM əmˈpɪrɪk, ɛmˈpɪrɪk

empirical
BR ɪmˈpɪrɪkl,
ɛmˈpɪrɪkl
AM əmˈpɪrɪkəl,
ɛmˈpɪrɪkəl

empirically
BR ɪmˈpɪrɪkli,
ɛmˈpɪrɪkli
AM əmˈpɪrɪk(ə)li,
ɛmˈpɪrɪk(ə)li

empiricism
BR ɪmˈpɪrɪsɪz(ə)m,
ɛmˈpɪrɪsɪz(ə)m
AM əmˈpɪrəˌsɪzəm,
ɛmˈpɪrəˌsɪzəm

empiricist
BR ɪmˈpɪrɪsɪst,
ɛmˈpɪrɪsɪst, -s
AM əmˈpɪrəsəst,
ɛmˈpɪrəsəst, -s

emplacement
BR ɪmˈpleɪsm(ə)nt,
ɛmˈpleɪsm(ə)nt, -s
AM əmˈpleɪsmənt,
ɛmˈpleɪsmənt, -s

emplane
BR ɪmˈpleɪn, ɛmˈpleɪn,
-z, -ɪŋ, -d
AM əmˈpleɪn,
ɛmˈpleɪn, -z, -ɪŋ, -d

employ
BR ɪmˈplɔɪ, ɛmˈplɔɪ, -z,
-ɪŋ, -d
AM əmˈplɔɪ, ɛmˈplɔɪ, -z,
-ɪŋ, -d

employability
BR ɪmˌplɔɪəˈbɪlɪti,
ɛmˌplɔɪəˈbɪlɪti
AM əmˌplɔɪəˈbɪlɪdi,
ɛmˌplɔɪəˈbɪlɪdi

employable
BR ɪmˈplɔɪəbl,
ɛmˈplɔɪəbl

AM əmˈplɔɪəbəl,
ɛmˈplɔɪəbəl

employee
BR ˌɛmplɔɪˈiː, ɪmˈplɔɪiː,
ɛmˈplɔɪː, -z
AM əmˌplɔ(ɪ)ˈi,
əmˈplɔˌi, əmˈplɔ(ɪ)ˌi,
ˈɛmˌplɔɪˈi, -z

employer
BR ɪmˈplɔɪə(r),
ɛmˈplɔɪə(r), -z
AM əmˈplɔɪ(j)ər,
ɛmˈplɔɪ(j)ər,
əmˈplɔjər, ɛmˈplɔjər,
-z

employment
BR ɪmˈplɔɪm(ə)nt,
ɛmˈplɔɪm(ə)nt, -s
AM əmˈplɔɪmənt,
ɛmˈplɔɪmənt, -s

empolder
BR ɪmˈpəʊld|ə(r),
ɛmˈpəʊld|ə(r), -əz,
-(ə)rɪŋ, -əd
AM əmˈpoʊldər,
ɛmˈpoʊldər, -d, -ɪŋ, -d

emporia
BR ɪmˈpɔːrɪə(r),
ɛmˈpɔːrɪə(r)
AM əmˈpɔriə, ɛmˈpɔriə

emporium
BR ɪmˈpɔːrɪəm,
ɛmˈpɔːrɪəm, -z
AM əmˈpɔriəm,
ɛmˈpɔriəm, -z

empower
BR ɪmˈpaʊ|ə(r),
ɛmˈpaʊ|ə(r), -əz,
-(ə)rɪŋ, -əd
AM əmˈpaʊ|ər,
ɛmˈpaʊ|ər, -ərd,
-(ə)rɪŋ, -ərd

empowerment
BR ɪmˈpaʊəm(ə)nt,
ɛmˈpaʊəm(ə)nt
AM əmˈpaʊərmənt,
ɛmˈpaʊərmənt

empress
BR ˈɛmprɪs, -ɪz
AM ˈɛmprəs, -əz

Empson
BR ˈɛm(p)sn
AM ˈɛm(p)sən

emptily
BR ˈɛm(p)tɪli
AM ˈɛm(p)təli

emptiness
BR ˈɛm(p)tɪnɪs
AM ˈɛm(p)tinɪs

empty
BR ˈɛm(p)t|i, -ɪz, -ɪɪŋ,
-ɪd, -ɪə(r), -ɪɪst
AM ˈɛm(p)ti, -z, -ɪŋ, -d,
-ər, -ɪst

empurple
BR ɪmˈpəːp|l,
ɛmˈpəːp|l, -lz, -lɪŋ \-lɪŋ,
-ld

AM əmˈplɔɪəbəl,
ɛmˈplɔɪəbəl

empyema
BR ˌɛmpʌɪˈiːmə(r)
AM ˌɛmpaɪˈimə

empyreal
BR ˌɛmpɪˈriːəl,
ˌɛmpʌɪˈriːəl,
ɛmˈpɪrɪəl
AM ɛmˈpɪriəl,
ˌɛmpaɪˈriəl

empyrean
BR ˌɛmpɪˈriːən,
ˌɛmpaɪˈriːən,
ɛmˈpɪriən
AM ɛmˈpɪriən,
ˌɛmpaɪˈriən

Emrys
BR ˈɛmrɪs
AM ˈɛmrəs

Emsworth
BR ˈɛmzwəθ, ˈɛmzwəːθ
AM ˈɛmzˌwərθ

emu
BR ˈiːmjuː, -z
AM ˈim(j)u, -z

emulate
BR ˈɛmjʊlert, -s, -ɪŋ, -ɪd
AM ˈɛmjəˌleɪ|t, -ts, -dɪŋ,
-dɪd

emulation
BR ˌɛmjʊˈleɪʃn
AM ˌɛmjəˈleɪʃən

emulative
BR ˈɛmjʊlətɪv
AM ˈɛmjəˌleɪdɪv

emulator
BR ˈɛmjʊleɪtə(r), -z
AM ˈɛmjəˌleɪdər, -z

emulous
BR ˈɛmjʊləs
AM ˈɛmjələs

emulously
BR ˈɛmjʊləsli
AM ˈɛmjələsli

emulousness
BR ˈɛmjʊləsnəs
AM ˈɛmjələsnəs

emulsifiable
BR ɪˈmʌlsɪfʌɪəbl
AM əˈməlsəˌfaɪəbəl,
iˈməlsəˌfaɪəbəl

emulsification
BR ɪˌmʌlsɪfɪˈkeɪʃn
AM əˌməlsəfəˈkeɪʃən,
iˌməlsəfəˈkeɪʃən

emulsifier
BR ɪˈmʌlsɪfʌɪə(r), -z
AM əˈməlsəˌfaɪər,
iˈməlsəˌfaɪər, -z

emulsify
BR ɪˈmʌlsɪfʌɪ, -z, -ɪŋ, -d
AM əˈməlsəˌfaɪ,
iˈməlsəˌfaɪ, -z, -ɪŋ, -d

emulsion
BR ɪˈmʌlʃn, -z
AM əˈməlʃən,
iˈməlʃən, -z

emulsionise
BR ɪˈmʌlʃṇʌɪz,
ɪˈmʌlʃənʌɪz, -ɪz, -ɪŋ, -d
AM əˈməlʃəˌnʌɪz,
iˈməlʃəˌnaɪz, -ɪz, -ɪŋ, -d

emulsionize
BR ɪˈmʌlʃṇʌɪz,
ɪˈmʌlʃənʌɪz, -ɪz, -ɪŋ, -d
AM əˈməlʃəˌnʌɪz,
iˈməlʃəˌnaɪz, -ɪz, -ɪŋ, -d

emulsive
BR ɪˈmʌlsɪv
AM əˈməlsɪv, iˈməlsɪv

Emyr
BR ˈɛmɪə(r)
AM ˈɛmɪ(ə)r

en
BR ɛn, -z
AM ɛn, -z

Ena
BR ˈiːnə(r)
AM ˈinə

enable
BR ɪnˈeɪb|l̩, ɛnˈeɪb|l̩, -lz,
-|ɪŋ\-|ɪŋ, -ld
AM ɪˈneɪb|əl, ɛˈneɪb|əl,
-əlz, -(ə)lɪŋ, -əld

enablement
BR ɪnˈeɪblm(ə)nt,
ɛnˈeɪblm(ə)nt
AM ɪˈneɪbəlmənt,
ɛˈneɪbəlmənt

enabler
BR ɪnˈeɪblə(r),
ɛnˈeɪblə(r), -z
AM ɪˈneɪblər, ɛˈneɪblər,
-z

enact
BR ɪnˈakt, ɛnˈakt, -s,
-ɪŋ, -ɪd
AM ɪˈnæk|(t),
ɛˈnæk|(t), -(t)s, -tɪŋ,
-təd

enactable
BR ɪnˈaktəbl,
ɛnˈaktəbl
AM ɪˈnæktəbəl,
ɛˈnæktəbəl

enaction
BR ɪnˈakʃn, ɛnˈakʃn
AM ɪˈnækʃən,
ɛˈnækʃən

enactive
BR ɪnˈaktɪv, ɛnˈaktɪv
AM ɪˈnæktɪv, ɛˈnæktɪv

enactment
BR ɪnˈaktm(ə)nt,
ɛˈnaktm(ə)nt, -s
AM ɪˈnæk(t)mənt,
ɛˈnæk(t)mənt, -s

enactor
BR ɪnˈaktə(r),
ɛnˈaktə(r), -z
AM ɪˈnæktər,
ɛˈnæktər, -z

enactory
BR ɪnˈakt(ə)ri,
ɛnˈakt(ə)ri

AM ɪˈnækˌtɔri,
ɛˈnækˌtɔri

enamel
BR ɪˈnam|l̩, -lz,
-|ɪŋ\-əlɪŋ, -ld
AM ɪˈnæm|əl,
ɛˈnæm|əl, -əlz, -(ə)lɪŋ,
-əld

enameller
BR ɪˈnam|ə(r),
ɪˈnaməl|ə(r), -z
AM ɪˈnæm|(ə)lər,
ɛˈnæm|(ə)lər, -z

enamelling
BR ɪˈnam|lɪŋ,
ɪˈnaməlɪŋ
AM ɪˈnæm|(ə)lɪŋ,
ɛˈnæm|(ə)lɪŋ

enamelware
BR ɪˈnamlwɛː(r)
AM ɪˈnæməlˌwɛ(ə)r,
ɛˈnæməlˌwɛ(ə)r

enamelwork
BR ɪˈnamlwəːk
AM ɪˈnæməlˌwərk,
ɛˈnæməlˌwərk

enamor
BR ɪˈnam|ə(r),
ɛˈnam|ə(r), -əz,
-(ə)rɪŋ, -əd
AM ɪˈnæmər, ɛˈnæmər,
-d, -ɪŋ, -d

enamored
BR ɪˈnaməd, ɛˈnaməd
AM ɪˈnæmərd,
ɛˈnæmərd

enamour
BR ɪˈnam|ə(r),
ɛˈnam|ə(r), -əz,
-(ə)rɪŋ, -əd
AM ɪˈnæmər, ɛˈnæmər,
-d, -ɪŋ, -d

enanthema
BR ˌɛnanˈθiːmə(r), -z
AM ɛˌnænˈθimə, -z

enantiomer
BR ɪˈnantɪə(ʊ)mə(r),
ɛˈnantɪə(ʊ)mə(r), -z
AM əˈnæntiouˌmər,
ɛˈnæntiouˌmər, -z

enantiomeric
BR ɪˌnantɪə(ʊ)ˈmɛrɪk,
ɛˌnantɪə(ʊ)ˈmɛrɪk
AM əˌnæntiouˈmɛrɪk,
ɛˌnæntiouˈmɛrɪk

enantiomorph
BR əˈnantɪə(ʊ)mɔːf,
AM əˈnæntiouˌmɔ(ə)rf,
ɛˈnæntiouˌmɔ(ə)rf, -s

enantiomorphic
BR ɪˌnantɪə(ʊ)ˈmɔːfɪk,
ɛˌnantɪə(ʊ)ˈmɔːfɪk
AM əˌnæntiouˈmɔrfɪk,
ɛˌnæntiouˈmɔrfɪk

enantiomorphism
BR ɪˌnantɪə(ʊ)ˈmɔːf-
ɪz(ə)m,

ɛˌnantɪə(ʊ)ˈmɔːf-
ɪz(ə)m
AM əˌnæntiouˈmɔr-
ˌfɪzəm,
ɛˌnæntiouˈmɔrˌfɪzəm

enantiomorphous
BR ɪˌnantɪə(ʊ)ˈmɔːfəs,
ɛˌnantɪə(ʊ)ˈmɔːfəs
AM əˌnæntiouˈmɔrfəs,
ɛˌnæntiouˈmɔrfəs

enarthroses
BR ˌɛnɑːˈθrəʊsiːz
AM ˌɛnɑrˈθroʊsiz

enarthrosis
BR ˌɛnɑːˈθrəʊsɪs
AM ˌɛnɑrˈθroʊsəs

en bloc
BR ˌɒ̃ ˈblɒk, ˌɒn +
AM ɑn ˈblɑk

en brosse
BR ˌɒ̃ ˈbrɒs, ˌɒn +
AM ɑn ˈbrɔs, ɑn ˈbrɑs

encaenia
BR ɪnˈsiːnɪə(r),
ɛnˈsiːnɪə(r), -z
AM ɛnˈsiniə, ɪnˈsiniə,
-z

encage
BR ɪnˈkeɪdʒ, ɛnˈkeɪdʒ,
ɪŋˈkeɪdʒ, ɛŋˈkeɪdʒ, -ɪz,
-ɪŋ, -d
AM ɪnˈkeɪdʒ, ɛnˈkeɪdʒ,
-ɪz, -ɪŋ, -d

encamp
BR ɪnˈkamp, ɛnˈkamp,
ɪŋˈkamp, ɛŋˈkamp, -s,
-ɪŋ, -t
AM ɪnˈkæmp,
ɛnˈkæmp, ɪŋˈkæmp,
ɛŋˈkæmp, -s, -ɪŋ, -t

encampment
BR ɪnˈkampm(ə)nt,
ɛnˈkampm(ə)nt,
ɪŋˈkampm(ə)nt,
ɛŋˈkampm(ə)nt, -s
AM ɪnˈkæmpmənt,
ɛnˈkæmpmənt,
ɪŋˈkæmpmənt,
ɛŋˈkæmpmənt, -s

encapsulate
BR ɪnˈkapsjʉleɪt,
ɛnˈkapsjʉleɪt,
ɪŋˈkapsjʉleɪt,
ɛŋˈkapsjʉleɪt, -s, -ɪŋ,
-ɪd
AM ɪnˈkæps(j)əˌleɪt,
ɛnˈkæps(j)əˌleɪt,
ɪŋˈkæps(j)əˌleɪt,
ɛŋˈkæps(j)əˌleɪt, -ts,
-dɪŋ, -dɪd

encapsulation
BR ɪnˌkapsjʉˈleɪʃn,
ɛnˌkapsjʉˈleɪʃn,
ɪŋˌkapsjʉˈleɪʃn,
ɛŋˌkapsjʉˈleɪʃn,
AM ɪnˌkæps(j)əˈleɪʃən,
ɛnˌkæps(j)əˈleɪʃən,
ɪŋˌkæps(j)əˈleɪʃən,
ɛŋˌkæps(j)ˈleɪʃən

encase
BR ɪnˈkeɪs, ɛnˈkeɪs,
ɪŋˈkeɪs, ɛŋˈkeɪs, -ɪz, -ɪŋ,
-t
AM ɪnˈkeɪs, ɛnˈkeɪs,
ɪŋˈkeɪs, ɛŋˈkeɪs, -ɪz,
-ɪŋ, -t

encasement
BR ɪnˈkeɪsm(ə)nt,
ɛnˈkeɪsmənt,
ɪŋˈkeɪsm(ə)nt,
ɛŋˈkeɪsmənt, -s
AM ɪnˈkeɪsmənt,
ɛnˈkeɪsmənt,
ɪŋˈkeɪsmənt,
ɛŋˈkeɪsmənt, -s

encash
BR ɪnˈkaʃ, ɛnˈkaʃ,
ɪŋˈkaʃ, ɛŋˈkaʃ, -ɪz, -ɪŋ,
-t
AM ɪnˈkæʃ, ɛnˈkæʃ,
ɪŋˈkæʃ, ɛŋˈkæʃ, -əz,
-ɪŋ, -t

encashable
BR ɪnˈkaʃəbl,
ɛnˈkaʃəbl, ɪŋˈkaʃəbl,
ɛŋˈkaʃəbl
AM ɪnˈkæʃəbəl,
ɛnˈkæʃəbəl,
ɪŋˈkæʃəbəl,
ɛŋˈkæʃəbəl

encashment
BR ɪnˈkaʃm(ə)nt,
ɛnˈkaʃm(ə)nt,
ɪŋˈkaʃm(ə)nt,
ɛŋˈkaʃm(ə)nt, -s
AM ɪnˈkæʃmənt,
ɛnˈkæʃmənt,
ɪŋˈkæʃmənt,
ɛŋˈkæʃmənt, -s

encaustic
BR ɪnˈkɔːstɪk,
ɛnˈkɔːstɪk, ɪŋˈkɔːstɪk,
ɛŋˈkɔːstɪk, -s
AM ɪnˈkɔstɪk,
ɛnˈkɔstɪk, ɪnˈkɑstɪk,
ɛŋˈkɔstɪk, ɪŋˈkɔstɪk,
ɛŋˈkɑstɪk, -s

encaustically
BR ɪnˈkɔːstɪkli,
ɛnˈkɔːstɪkli,
ɪŋˈkɔːstɪkli,
ɛŋˈkɔːstɪkli
AM ɪnˈkɔstək(ə)li,
ɛnˈkɔstək(ə)li,
ɪnˈkɑstək(ə)li,
ɛnˈkɑstək(ə)li,
ɪŋˈkɔstɪk(ə)li,
ɛŋˈkɔstɪk(ə)li,
ɪŋˈkɑstɪk(ə)li,
ɛŋˈkɑstɪk(ə)li

enceinte
BR ɒ̃ˈsãt, ɒnˈsant
AM ɑnˈsænt

Enceladus
BR ɪnˈsɛlədəs,
ɛnˈsɛlədəs

encephalic

AM ən'seləðəs,
ɛn'seləðəs

encephalic
BR ,ensɪ'falɪk,
,ɛnkɛ'falɪk,
,ɛŋkɛ'falɪk
AM ,ɛnsə'fælɪk

encephalin
BR ɛn'sɛfəlɪn,
ɛn'sɛf].ɪn, ɛn'kɛfəlɪn,
ɛn'kɛf].ɪn, ɛŋ'kɛfəlɪn,
ɛŋ'kɛf].ɪn
AM ɛn'sɛfələn,
ɛn'sɛfə,lɪn

encephalitic
BR ɛn,sɛfə'lɪtɪk,
ɛn,kɛfə'lɪtɪk,
ɛŋ,kɛfə'lɪtɪk,
,ɛnsɛfə'lɪtɪk,
,ɛnkɛfə'lɪtɪk,
,ɛŋkɛfə'lɪtɪk
AM ɛn,sɛfə'lɪdɪk

encephalitis
BR ɛn,sɛfə'lʌɪtɪs,
ɛn,kɛfə'lʌɪtɪs,
ɛŋ,kɛfə'lʌɪtɪs,
,ɛnsɛfə'lʌɪtɪs,
,ɛnkɛfə'lʌɪtɪs,
,ɛŋkɛfə'lʌɪtɪs
AM ɛn,sɛfə'laɪdəs,
ɛn,sɛfə'laɪdəs

encephalogram
BR ɛn'sɛfələgram,
ɛn'sɛfləgram,
ɛn'kɛfələgram,
ɛn'kɛfləgram,
ɛŋ'kɛfələgram,
ɛŋ'kɛfləgram, -z
AM ɛn'sɛfələ,græm,
ɛn'sɛfələ,græm, -z

encephalograph
BR ɛn'sɛfələgrɑːf,
ɛn'sɛfələgraf,
ɛn'kɛfələgrɑːf,
ɛn'kɛfələgraf,
ɛŋ'kɛfələgrɑːf,
ɛŋ'kɛfələgraf, -s
AM ɛn'sɛfələ,græf,
ɛn'sɛfələ,græf, -s

encephalomyelitis
BR ɛn,sɛfələʊ,mʌɪə-
'lʌɪtɪs,
ɛn,sɛfləʊ,mʌɪə'lʌɪtɪs,
ɛn,kɛfələʊ,mʌɪə'lʌɪtɪs,
ɛn,kɛfləʊ,mʌɪə'lʌɪtɪs,
ɛŋ,kɛfələʊ,mʌɪə'lʌɪtɪs,
ɛŋ,kɛfləʊ,mʌɪə'lʌɪtɪs,
-ɪz
AM ɛn,sɛfələ,maɪə'laɪdɪs,
ɛn,sɛfələ,maɪə'laɪdɪs,
-ɪz

encephalon
BR ɛn'sɛfəlɒn,
ɛn'sɛflɒn, ɛn'kɛfəlɒn,
ɛŋ'kɛflɒn, -z
AM ɪn'sɛfə,lɑn,
ɛn'sɛfə,lɑn,

encephalopathy
BR ɛn,sɛfə'lɒpəθi,
ɛn,kɛfə'lɒpəθi,
ɛŋ,kɛfə'lɒpəθi
AM ɪn,sɛfə'lɑpəθi,
ɛn,sɛfə'lɑpəθi

enchain
BR ɪn'tʃeɪn, ɛn'tʃeɪn,
-z, -ɪŋ, -d
AM ɪn'tʃeɪn, ɛn'tʃeɪn,
-z, -ɪŋ, -d

enchainment
BR ɪn'tʃeɪmm(ə)nt,
ɛn'tʃeɪmm(ə)nt
AM ɪn'tʃeɪmmənt,
ɛn'tʃeɪmmənt

enchant
BR ɪn'tʃɑːnt, ɪn'tʃant,
ɛn'tʃɑːnt, ɛn'tʃant, -s,
-ɪŋ, -ɪd
AM ɪn'tʃænt,
ɛn'tʃæn|t, -ts, -(t)ɪŋ,
-(t)əd

enchantedly
BR ɪn'tʃɑːntɪdli,
ɪn'tʃantɪdli,
ɛn'tʃɑːntɪdli,
ɛn'tʃantɪdli
AM ɪn'tʃæn(t)ədli,
ɛn'tʃæn(t)ədli

enchanter
BR ɪn'tʃɑːntə(r),
ɪn'tʃantə(r),
ɛn'tʃɑːntə(r),
ɛn'tʃantə(r), -z
AM ɪn'tʃæn(t)ər,
ɛn'tʃæn(t)ər, -z

enchanting
BR ɪn'tʃɑːntɪŋ,
ɪn'tʃantɪŋ,
ɛn'tʃɑːntɪŋ,
ɛn'tʃantɪŋ
AM ɪn'tʃæn(t)ɪŋ,
ɛn'tʃæn(t)ɪŋ

enchantingly
BR ɪn'tʃɑːntɪŋli,
ɪn'tʃantɪŋli,
ɛn'tʃɑːntɪŋli,
ɛn'tʃantɪŋli
AM ɪn'tʃæn(t)ɪŋli,
ɛn'tʃæn(t)ɪŋli

enchantment
BR ɪn'tʃɑːntm(ə)nt,
ɪn'tʃantm(ə)nt,
ɛn'tʃɑːntm(ə)nt,
ɛn'tʃantm(ə)nt, -s
AM ɪn'tʃæntmənt,
ɛn'tʃæntmənt, -s

enchantress
BR ɪn'tʃɑːntrɪs,
ɪn'tʃantrɪs,
ɛn'tʃɑːntrɪs,
ɛn'tʃantrɪs, -ɪz
AM ɪn'tʃæntrəs,
ɛn'tʃæntrəs, -əz

enchase
BR ɪn'tʃeɪs, ɛn'tʃeɪs,
-ɪz, -ɪŋ, -t
AM ɪn'tʃeɪs, ɛn'tʃeɪs,
-ɪz, -ɪŋ, -t

enchilada
BR ,entʃɪ'lɑːdə(r), -z
AM ,entʃə'lɑdə, -z

enchiridia
BR ,ɛnkʌɪ'rɪdɪə(r),
,ɛŋkʌɪ'rɪdɪə(r)
AM ,ɛŋkə'rɪdɪə,
,ɛn,kaɪ'rɪdɪə

enchiridion
BR ,ɛnkʌɪ'rɪdɪən,
,ɛŋkʌɪ'rɪdɪən, -z
AM ,ɛŋkə'rɪdɪən,
,ɛn,kaɪ'rɪdɪən, -z

encipher
BR ɪn'sʌɪfə(r),
ɛn'sʌɪf]ə(r), -əz,
-(ə)rɪŋ, -əd
AM ɪn'saɪf]ər,
ɛn'saɪf]ər, -ərz,
-(ə)rɪŋ, -ərd

encipherment
BR ɪn'sʌɪfəm(ə)nt,
ɛn'sʌɪfəm(ə)nt
AM ɪn'saɪfərmənt,
ɛn'saɪfərmənt

encircle
BR ɪn'sə:k|l, ɛn'sə:k|l,
-lz, -]ɪŋ \-lɪŋ, -ld
AM ɪn'sərk|əl,
ɛn'sərk|əl, -əlz,
-(ə)lɪŋ, -əld

encirclement
BR ɪn'sə:klm(ə)nt,
ɛn'sə:klm(ə)nt
AM ɪn'sərkəlmənt,
ɛn'sərkəlmənt

en clair
BR ,ɒ̃ 'klɛː(r), ,ɒn +
AM ɑn 'klɛ(ə)r

enclasp
BR ɪn'klɑːsp, ɪn'klasp,
ɛn'klɑːsp, ɛn'klasp,
ɪŋ'klɑːsp, ɪŋ'klasp,
ɛŋ'klɑːsp, ɛŋ'klasp, -s,
-ɪŋ, -t
AM ɪn'klæsp,
ɛn'klæsp, ɪŋ'klæsp,
ɛŋ'klæsp, -s, -ɪŋ, -t

enclave
BR 'ɛnkleɪv, 'ɛŋkleɪv,
'ɒŋkleɪv, -z
AM 'ɛn,kleɪv, 'ɑŋ,kleɪv,
-z

enclitic
BR ɪn'klɪtɪk, ɛn'klɪtɪk,
ɪŋ'klɪtɪk, ɛŋ'klɪtɪk, -s
AM ɛn'klɪdɪk,
ɪn'klɪdɪk, ɛŋ'klɪdɪk,
ɪŋ'klɪdɪk, -s

enclitically
BR ɪn'klɪtɪkli,
ɛn'klɪtɪkli, ɪŋ'klɪtɪkli,
ɛŋ'klɪtɪkli

enclose
BR ɪn'kləʊz, ɛn'kləʊz,
ɪŋ'kləʊz, ɛŋ'kləʊz, -ɪz,
-ɪŋ, -d
AM ɪn'kloʊz, ɛn'kloʊz,
ɪŋ'kloʊz, ɛŋ'kloʊz,
-əz, -ɪŋ, -d

enclosure
BR ɪn'kləʊʒə(r),
ɛn'kləʊʒə(r),
ɪŋ'kləʊʒə(r),
ɛŋ'kləʊʒə(r), -z
AM ɪn'kloʊʒər,
ɛn'kloʊʒər,
ɪŋ'kloʊʒər,
ɛŋ'kloʊʒər, -z

encode
BR ɪn'kəʊd, ɛn'kəʊd,
ɪŋ'kəʊd, ɛŋ'kəʊd, -z,
-ɪŋ, -ɪd
AM ɪn'koʊd, ɛn'koʊd,
ɪŋ'koʊd, ɛŋ'koʊd, -z,
-ɪŋ, -əd

encoder
BR ɪn'kəʊdə(r),
ɛn'kəʊdə(r),
ɪŋ'kəʊdə(r),
ɛŋ'kəʊdə(r), -z
AM ɪn'koʊdər,
ɛn'koʊdər, ɪŋ'koʊdər,
ɛŋ'koʊdər, -z

encomia
BR ɪn'kəʊmɪə(r),
ɛn'kəʊmɪə(r),
ɪŋ'kəʊmɪə(r),
ɛŋ'kəʊmɪə(r)
AM ɪn'koʊmiə,
ɛn'koʊmiə,
ɪŋ'koʊmiə,
ɛŋ'koʊmiə

encomiast
BR ɪn'kəʊmɪast,
ɛn'kəʊmɪast,
ɪŋ'kəʊmɪast,
ɛŋ'kəʊmɪast, -s
AM ɪn'koʊmi,æst,
ɛn'koʊmi,æst,
ɪŋ'koʊmi,æst,
ɛŋ'koʊmi,æst, -s

encomiastic
BR ɪn,kəʊmɪ'astɪk,
ɛn,kəʊmɪ'astɪk,
ɪŋ,kəʊmɪ'astɪk,
ɛŋ,kəʊmɪ'astɪk
AM ɪn,koʊmi'æstɪk,
ɛn,koʊmi'æstɪk,
ɪŋ,koʊmi'æstɪk,
ɛŋ,koʊmi'æstɪk

encomium
BR ɪn'kəʊmɪəm,
ɛn'kəʊmɪəm,
ɪŋ'kəʊmɪəm,
ɛŋ'kəʊmɪəm, -z
AM ɪn'koʊmiəm,
ɛn'koʊmiəm,

encompass
ɪŋ'koʊmiəm,
eŋ'koʊmiəm, -z
encompass
BR ɪn'kʌmpəs,
ɛn'kʌmpəs,
ɪŋ'kʌmpəs,
eŋ'kʌmpəs, -ɪz, -ɪŋ, -t
AM ɪn'kəmpəs,
ɛn'kəmpəs,
ɪŋ'kəmpəs,
eŋ'kəmpəs, -əz, -ɪŋ, -t
encompassment
BR ɪn'kʌmpəsm(ə)nt,
ɛn'kʌmpəsm(ə)nt,
ɪŋ'kʌmpəsm(ə)nt,
eŋ'kʌmpəsm(ə)nt
AM ɪn'kəmpəsmənt,
ɛn'kəmpəsmənt,
ɪŋ'kəmpəsmənt,
eŋ'kəmpəsmənt
encore
BR 'ɒŋkɔː(r), -z, -ɪŋ, -d
AM 'ɑn,kɔ(ə)r,
'ɑŋ,kɔ(ə)r, -z, -ɪŋ, -d
encounter
BR ɪn'kaʊnt|ə(r),
ɛn'kaʊnt|ə(r),
ɪŋ'kaʊnt|ə(r),
eŋ'kaʊnt|ə(r), -əz,
-(ə)rɪŋ, -əd
AM ɪn'kaʊn(t)ər,
ɛn'kaʊn(t)ər,
ɪŋ'kaʊn(t)ər,
eŋ'kaʊn(t)ər, -z, -ɪŋ, -d
encourage
BR ɪn'kʌr|ɪdʒ,
ɛn'kʌr|ɪdʒ, ɪŋ'kʌr|ɪdʒ,
eŋ'kʌr|ɪdʒ, -ɪdʒɪz,
-ɪdʒɪŋ, -ɪdʒd
AM ɪn'kərɪdʒ,
ɛn'kərɪdʒ, ɪŋ'kərɪdʒ,
eŋ'kərɪdʒ, -əz, -ɪŋ, -d
encouragement
BR ɪn'kʌrɪdʒm(ə)nt,
ɛn'kʌrɪdʒm(ə)nt,
ɪŋ'kʌrɪdʒm(ə)nt,
eŋ'kʌrɪdʒm(ə)nt, -s
AM ɪn'kərɪdʒmənt,
ɛn'kərɪdʒmənt,
ɪŋ'kərɪdʒmənt,
eŋ'kərɪdʒmənt, -s
encourager
BR ɪn'kʌrɪdʒə(r),
ɛn'kʌrɪdʒə(r),
ɪŋ'kʌrɪdʒə(r),
eŋ'kʌrɪdʒə(r), -z
AM ɪn'kərɪdʒər,
ɛn'kərɪdʒər,
ɪŋ'kərɪdʒər,
eŋ'kərɪdʒər, -z
encouragingly
BR ɪn'kʌrɪdʒɪŋli,
ɛn'kʌrɪdʒɪŋli,
ɪŋ'kʌrɪdʒɪŋli,
eŋ'kʌrɪdʒɪŋli
AM ɪn'kərɪdʒɪŋli,
ɛn'kərɪdʒɪŋli,
ɪŋ'kərɪdʒɪŋli,
eŋ'kərɪdʒɪŋli

encrinite
BR 'ɛŋkrɪnʌɪt, -s
AM 'ɛŋkrə,naɪt, -s
encroach
BR ɪn'krəʊtʃ,
ɛn'krəʊtʃ, ɪŋ'krəʊtʃ,
eŋ'krəʊtʃ, -ɪz, -ɪŋ, -t
AM ɪn'kroʊtʃ,
ɛn'kroʊtʃ, ɪŋ'kroʊtʃ,
eŋ'kroʊtʃ, -əz, -ɪŋ, -t
encroacher
BR ɪn'krəʊtʃə(r),
ɛn'krəʊtʃə(r),
ɪŋ'krəʊtʃə(r),
eŋ'krəʊtʃə(r), -z
AM ɪn'kroʊtʃər,
ɛn'kroʊtʃər,
ɪŋ'kroʊtʃər,
eŋ'kroʊtʃər, -z
encroachment
BR ɪn'krəʊtʃm(ə)nt,
ɛn'krəʊtʃm(ə)nt,
ɪŋ'krəʊtʃm(ə)nt,
eŋ'krəʊtʃm(ə)nt, -s
AM ɪn'kroʊtʃmənt,
ɛn'kroʊtʃmənt,
ɪŋ'kroʊtʃmənt,
eŋ'kroʊtʃmənt, -s
encrust
BR ɪn'krʌst, ɛn'krʌst,
ɪŋ'krʌst, eŋ'krʌst, -s,
-ɪŋ, -ɪd
AM ɪn'krəst, ɛn'krəst,
ɪŋ'krəst, eŋ'krəst, -s,
-ɪŋ, -əd
encrustation
BR ˌɪnkrʌ'steɪʃn,
ˌɛnkrʌ'steɪʃn,
ˌɪŋkrʌ'steɪʃn,
ˌeŋkrʌ'steɪʃn
AM ɪn,krəs'teɪʃən,
ɛn,krəs'teɪʃən,
ɪŋ,krəs'teɪʃən,
eŋ,krəs'teɪʃən
encrustment
BR ɪn'krʌs(t)m(ə)nt,
ɛn'krʌs(t)m(ə)nt,
ɪŋ'krʌs(t)m(ə)nt,
eŋ'krʌs(t)m(ə)nt
AM ɪn'krəs(t)mənt,
ɛn'krəs(t)mənt,
ɪŋ'krəs(t)mənt,
eŋ'krəs(t)mənt
encrypt
BR ɪn'krɪpt, ɛn'krɪpt,
ɪŋ'krɪpt, eŋ'krɪpt, -s,
-ɪŋ, -ɪd
AM ɪn'krɪpt, ɛn'krɪpt,
ɪŋ'krɪpt, eŋ'krɪpt, -s,
-ɪŋ, -ɪd
encryption
BR ɪn'krɪpʃn,
ɛn'krɪpʃn, ɪŋ'krɪpʃn,
eŋ'krɪpʃn, -z
AM ɪn'krɪpʃən,
ɛn'krɪpʃən,
ɪŋ'krɪpʃən,
eŋ'krɪpʃən, -z

encumber
BR ɪn'kʌmb|ə(r),
ɛn'kʌmb|ə(r),
ɪŋ'kʌmb|ə(r),
eŋ'kʌmb|ə(r), -əz,
-(ə)rɪŋ, -əd
AM ɪn'kəmb|ər,
ɛn'kəmb|ər,
ɪŋ'kəmb|ər,
eŋ'kəmb|ər, -ərz,
-(ə)rɪŋ, -ərd
encumberment
BR ɪn'kʌmbəm(ə)nt,
ɛn'kʌmbəm(ə)nt,
ɪŋ'kʌmbəm(ə)nt,
eŋ'kʌmbəm(ə)nt
AM ɪn'kəmbərmənt,
ɛn'kəmbərmənt,
ɪŋ'kəmbərmənt,
eŋ'kəmbərmənt
encumbrance
BR ɪn'kʌmbr(ə)ns,
ɛn'kʌmbr(ə)ns,
ɪŋ'kʌmbr(ə)ns,
eŋ'kʌmbr(ə)ns, -ɪz
AM ɪn'kəmb(ə)rəns,
ɛn'kʌmb(ə)rəns,
ɪŋ'kəmb(ə)rəns,
eŋ'kʌmb(ə)rəns, -əz
encyclic
BR ɪn'sʌɪklɪk,
ɛn'sʌɪklɪk, ɪn'sɪklɪk,
ɛn'sɪklɪk
AM ɪn'sɪklɪk, ɛn'sɪklɪk
encyclical
BR ɪn'sɪklɪkl,
ɛn'sɪklɪkl, -z
AM ɪn'sɪkləkəl,
ɛn'sɪkləkəl, -z
encyclopaedia
BR ɪn,sʌɪklə(ʊ)'piːdɪə(r),
ɛn,sʌɪklə(ʊ)'piːdɪə(r),
-z
AM ɪn,saɪklə'pidɪə,
ɛn,saɪklə'pidɪə, -z
encyclopaedic
BR ɪn,sʌɪklə'piːdɪk,
ɛn,sʌɪklə'piːdɪk
AM ɪn,saɪklə'pidɪk,
ɛn,saɪklə'pidɪk
encyclopaedically
BR ɪn,sʌɪklə'piːdɪkli,
ɛn,sʌɪklə'piːdɪkli
AM ɪn,saɪklə'pidɪk(ə)li,
ɛn,saɪklə'pidɪk(ə)li
encyclopaedism
BR ɪn,sʌɪklə'piːdɪz(ə)m,
ɛn,sʌɪklə'piːdɪz(ə)m
AM ɪn,saɪklə'pi,dɪzəm,
ɛn,saɪklə'pi,dɪzəm
encyclopaedist
BR ɪn,sʌɪklə'piːdɪst,
ɛn,sʌɪklə'piːdɪst, -s
AM ɪn,saɪklə'pidɪst,
ɛn,saɪklə'pidɪst, -s
encyclopedia
BR ɪn,sʌɪklə(ʊ)'piːdɪə(r),
ɛn,sʌɪklə(ʊ)'piːdɪə(r),
-z

encyclopedic
AM ɪn,saɪklə'pidɪə,
ɛn,saɪklə'pidɪə, -z
encyclopedic
BR ɪn,sʌɪklə'piːdɪk,
ɛn,sʌɪklə'piːdɪk
AM ɪn,saɪklə'pidɪk,
ɛn,saɪklə'pidɪk
encyclopedically
BR ɪn,sʌɪklə'piːdɪkli,
ɛn,sʌɪklə'piːdɪkli
AM ɪn,saɪklə'pidɪk(ə)li,
ɛn,saɪklə'pidɪk(ə)li
encyclopedism
BR ɪn,sʌɪklə'piːdɪz(ə)m,
ɛn,sʌɪklə'piːdɪz(ə)m
AM ɪn,saɪklə'pi,dɪzəm,
ɛn,saɪklə'pi,dɪzəm
encyclopedist
BR ɪn,sʌɪklə'piːdɪst,
ɛn,sʌɪklə'piːdɪst, -s
AM ɪn,saɪklə'pidɪst,
ɛn,saɪklə'pidɪst, -s
encyst
BR ɛn'sɪst, -s, -ɪŋ, -ɪd
AM ɛn'sɪst, -s, -ɪŋ, -ɪd
encystation
BR ,ɛnsɪ'steɪʃn
AM ,ɛnsə'steɪʃən
encystment
BR ɛn'sɪs(t)m(ə)nt
AM ɛn'sɪs(t)mənt
end
BR ɛnd, -z, -ɪŋ, -ɪd
AM ɛnd, -z, -ɪŋ, -əd
endanger
BR ɪn'deɪn(d)ʒ|ə(r),
ɛn'deɪn(d)ʒ|ə(r), -əz,
-(ə)rɪŋ, -əd
AM ɪn'deɪnd|ʒ|ər,
ɛn'deɪnd|ʒ|ər, -ərz,
-(ə)rɪŋ, -ərd
endangerment
BR ɪn'deɪn(d)ʒəm(ə)nt,
ɛn'deɪn(d)ʒəm(ə)nt
AM ɪn'deɪndʒərmənt,
ɛn'deɪndʒərmənt
endear
BR ɪn'dɪə(r), ɛn'dɪə(r),
-z, -ɪŋ, -d
AM ɪn'dɪ(ə)r, ɛn'dɪ(ə)r,
-z, -ɪŋ, -d
endearingly
BR ɪn'dɪərɪŋli,
ɛn'dɪərɪŋli
AM ɪn'dɪrɪŋli,
ɛn'dɪrɪŋli
endearment
BR ɪn'dɪəm(ə)nt,
ɛn'dɪəm(ə)nt, -s
AM ɪn'dɪrmənt,
ɛn'dɪrmənt, -s
endeavor
BR ɪn'dɛv|ə(r),
ɛn'dɛv|ə(r), -əz,
-(ə)rɪŋ, -əd
AM ən'dɛv|ər,
ɛn'dɛv|ər, -ərz,
-(ə)rɪŋ, -ərd

endeavour
BR ɪnˈdɛv|ə(r),
ɛnˈdɛv|ə(r), -əz,
-(ə)rɪŋ, -əd
AM ənˈdɛv|ər,
ɛnˈdɛv|ər, -ərz,
-(ə)rɪŋ, -ərd

endemic
BR ɛnˈdɛmɪk,
ɪnˈdɛmɪk
AM ɛnˈdɛmɪk

endemically
BR ɛnˈdɛmɪkli,
ɪnˈdɛmɪkli
AM ɛnˈdɛmək(ə)li

endemicity
BR ˌɛndɪˈmɪsɪti
AM ˌɛndəˈmɪsɪdi

endemism
BR ˈɛndɪmɪz(ə)m
AM ˈɛndəˌmɪzəm

ender
BR ˈɛndə(r), -z
AM ˈɛndər, -z

Enderby
BR ˈɛndəbi
AM ˈɛndərbi

endermic
BR ɛnˈdəːmɪk
AM ɛnˈdərmɪk

endermically
BR ɛnˈdəːmɪkli
AM ɛnˈdərmək(ə)li

Enders
BR ˈɛndəz
AM ˈɛndərz

endgame
BR ˈɛn(d)geɪm, -z
AM ˈɛn(d)ˌgeɪm, -z

ending
BR ˈɛndɪŋ, -z
AM ˈɛndɪŋ, -z

endite
BR ˈɛndʌɪt, -s
AM ˈɛndaɪt, -s

endive
BR ˈɛndɪv, ˈɛndʌɪv, -z
AM ˈɛnˌdaɪv, -z

endless
BR ˈɛndləs
AM ˈɛn(d)ləs

endlessly
BR ˈɛndləsli
AM ˈɛn(d)ləsli

endlessness
BR ˈɛndləsnəs
AM ˈɛn(d)ləsnəs

endlong
BR ˈɛndlɒŋ
AM ˈɛn(d)ˈlɔŋ,
ˈɛn(d)ˌlaŋ

endmost
BR ˈɛn(d)məʊst
AM ˈɛn(d)ˌmoʊst

endnote
BR ˈɛn(d)nəʊt, -s
AM ˈɛn(d)ˌnoʊt, -s

endocardia
BR ˌɛndə(ʊ)ˈkɑːdɪə(r)
AM ˌɛndoʊˈkɑrdiə

endocarditic
BR ˌɛndə(ʊ)kɑːˈdɪtɪk
AM ˌɛndoʊˌkɑrˈdɪdɪk

endocarditis
BR ˌɛndəʊkɑːˈdʌɪtɪs
AM ˌɛndoʊˌkɑrˈdaɪdɪs

endocardium
BR ˌɛndə(ʊ)ˈkɑːdɪəm
AM ˌɛndoʊˈkɑrdiəm

endocarp
BR ˈɛndə(ʊ)kɑːp, -s
AM ˈɛndoʊˈkɑrp, -s

endocarpic
BR ˌɛndə(ʊ)ˈkɑːpɪk
AM ˌɛndoʊˈkɑrpɪk

endocentric
BR ˌɛndə(ʊ)ˈsɛntrɪk
AM ˌɛndoʊˈsɛntrɪk

endocentrically
BR ˌɛndə(ʊ)ˈsɛntrɪkli
AM ˌɛndəˈsɛntrək(ə)li,
ˌɛndoʊˈsɛntrək(ə)li

endocrine
BR ˈɛndə(ʊ)krʌɪn,
ˈɛndə(ʊ)krɪn
AM ˈɛndəkrən,
ˈɛndəˌkrɪn,
ˈɛndəˌkraɪn

endocrinological
BR ˌɛndə(ʊ)krɪnəˈlɒdʒ-
ɪkl
AM ˌɛndəkrənəˈlɑdʒəkəl

endocrinologist
BR ˌɛndə(ʊ)krɪˈnɒlə-
dʒɪst, -s
AM ˌɛndəkrəˈnɑlədʒəst,
ˌɛndoʊkrəˈnɑlədʒəst,
-s

endocrinology
BR ˌɛndə(ʊ)krɪˈnɒlədʒi
AM ˌɛndəkrəˈnɑlədʒi,
ˌɛndoʊkrəˈnɑlədʒi

endoderm
BR ˈɛndə(ʊ)dəːm, -z
AM ˈɛndəˌdərm, -z

endodermal
BR ˌɛndə(ʊ)ˈdəːml
AM ˌɛndəˈdərməl,
ˌɛndoʊˈdərməl

endodermic
BR ˌɛndə(ʊ)ˈdəːmɪk
AM ˌɛndəˈdərmɪk,
ˌɛndoʊˈdərmɪk

endogamous
BR ɛnˈdɒgəməs
AM ɛnˈdɑgəməs

endogamy
BR ɛnˈdɒgəmi
AM ɛnˈdɑgəmi

endogen
BR ˈɛndədʒ(ə)n, -z
AM ˈɛndədʒən, -z

endogenesis
BR ˌɛndə(ʊ)ˈdʒɛnɪsɪs

AM ˌɛndəˈdʒɛnəsəs,
ˌɛndoʊˈdʒɛnəsəs

endogenous
BR ɛnˈdɒdʒɪnəs,
ɛnˈdɒdʒnəs
AM ɛnˈdɑdʒənəs

endogeny
BR ɛnˈdɒdʒəni,
ɛnˈdɒdʒni
AM ɛnˈdɑdʒəni

endolymph
BR ˈɛndə(ʊ)lɪmf
AM ˈɛndəˌlɪmf,
ˈɛndoʊˌlɪmf

endometria
BR ˌɛndə(ʊ)ˈmiːtrɪə(r)
AM ˌɛndəˈmitriə,
ˌɛndoʊˈmitriə

endometrial
BR ˌɛndə(ʊ)ˈmiːtrɪəl
AM ˌɛndəˈmitriəl,
ˌɛndoʊˈmitriəl

endometriosis
BR ˌɛndə(ʊ)miːtrɪˈəʊsɪs
AM ˌɛndoʊˌmitriˈoʊsəs

endometritis
BR ˌɛndəʊmɪˈtrʌɪtɪs
AM ˌɛndəməˈtraɪdɪs,
ˌɛndoʊməˈtraɪdɪs

endometrium
BR ˌɛndə(ʊ)ˈmiːtrɪəm
AM ˌɛndəˈmitriəm,
ˌɛndoʊˈmitriəm

endomorph
BR ˈɛndə(ʊ)mɔːf, -s
AM ˈɛndəˌmɔ(ə)rf, -s

endomorphic
BR ˌɛndə(ʊ)ˈmɔːfɪk
AM ˌɛndəˈmɔrfɪk,
ˌɛndoʊˈmɔrfɪk

endomorphy
BR ˈɛndə(ʊ)mɔːfi
AM ˈɛndəˌmɔrfi,
ˈɛndoʊˌmɔrfi

endoparasite
BR ˌɛndəʊˈparəsʌɪt, -s
AM ˌɛndəˈpɛrəˌsaɪt,
ˌɛndoʊˈpɛrəˌsaɪt, -s

endoplasm
BR ˈɛndə(ʊ)plaz(ə)m
AM ˈɛndəˌplæz(ə)m,
ˈɛndoʊˌplæzəm

endorphin
BR ɛnˈdɔːfɪn, -z
AM ˌɛnˈdɔrfɪn, -z

endorsable
BR ɪnˈdɔːsəbl,
ɛnˈdɔːsəbl
AM ɪnˈdɔrsəbəl,
ɛnˈdɔrsəbəl

endorse
BR ɪnˈdɔːs, ɛnˈdɔːs, -ɪz,
-ɪŋ, -t
AM ɪnˈdɔ(ə)rs,
ɛnˈdɔ(ə)rs, -əz, -ɪŋ, -t

endorsee
BR ɪnˌdɔːˈsiː, ɛnˌdɔːˈsiː,
-z

AM ɪnˌdɔrˈsi, ɛnˌdɔrˈsi,
-z

endorsement
BR ɪnˈdɔːsm(ə)nt,
ɛnˈdɔːsm(ə)nt, -s
AM ɪnˈdɔrsmənt,
ɛnˈdɔrsmənt, -s

endorser
BR ɪnˈdɔːsə(r),
ɛnˈdɔːsə(r), -z
AM ɪnˈdɔrsər,
ɛnˈdɔrsər, -z

endoscope
BR ˈɛndəskəʊp, -s
AM ˈɛndəˌskoʊp, -s

endoscopic
BR ˌɛndəˈskɒpɪk
AM ˌɛndəˈskɑpɪk

endoscopically
BR ˌɛndəˈskɒpɪkli
AM ˌɛndəˈskɑpək(ə)li

endoscopist
BR ɛnˈdɒskəpɪst, -s
AM ɛnˈdɑskəpəst, -s

endoscopy
BR ɛnˈdɒskəp|i, -ɪz
AM ɛnˈdɑskəpi, -z

endoskeleton
BR ˈɛndəʊˌskɛlɪt(ə)n,
-z
AM ˈɛndəˌskɛlətn,
ˈɛndoʊˌskɛlətn, -z

endosperm
BR ˈɛndə(ʊ)spəːm, -z
AM ˈɛndəˌspərm,
ˈɛndoʊˌspərm, -z

endospore
BR ˈɛndə(ʊ)spɔː(r), -z
AM ˈɛndəˌspɔ(ə)r,
ˈɛndoʊˌspɔ(ə)r, -z

endothelia
BR ˌɛndə(ʊ)ˈθiːlɪə(r)
AM ˌɛndəˈθiliə,
ˌɛndoʊˈθiliə

endothelial
BR ˌɛndə(ʊ)ˈθiːlɪəl
AM ˌɛndəˈθiliəl,
ˌɛndoʊˈθiliəl

endothelium
BR ˌɛndə(ʊ)ˈθiːlɪəm
AM ˌɛndəˈθiliəm,
ˌɛndoʊˈθiliəm

endothermic
BR ˌɛndə(ʊ)ˈθəːmɪk
AM ˌɛndəˈθərmɪk,
ˌɛndoʊˈθərmɪk

endothermically
BR ˌɛndə(ʊ)ˈθəːmɪkli
AM ˌɛndəˈθərmək(ə)li,
ˌɛndoʊˈθərmək(ə)li

endothermy
BR ˈɛndə(ʊ)θəːmi
AM ˈɛndəˌθərmi,
ˈɛndoʊˌθərmi

endow
BR ɪnˈdaʊ, ɛnˈdaʊ, -z,
-ɪŋ, -d

endower
AM ɪn'daʊ, ɛn'daʊ, -z, -ɪŋ, -d

endower
BR ɪn'daʊə(r), ɛn'daʊə(r), -z
AM ɪn'daʊər, ɛn'daʊər, -z

endowment
BR ɪn'daʊm(ə)nt, ɛn'daʊm(ə)nt, -s
AM ɪn'daʊmənt, ɛn'daʊmənt, -s

endpaper
BR 'ɛn(d)ˌpeɪpə(r), -z
AM 'ɛn(d)ˌpeɪpər, -z

endplay
BR 'ɛn(d)pleɪ, -z, -ɪŋ, -d
AM 'ɛn(d)ˌpleɪ, -z, -ɪŋ, -d

endpoint
BR 'ɛn(d)pɔɪnt, -s
AM 'ɛn(d)ˌpɔɪnt, -s

endrun
BR 'ɛndrʌn, -z
AM ˌɛn(d)'rən, -z

endue
BR ɪn'djuː, ɛn'djuː, ɪn'dʒuː, ɛn'dʒuː, -z, -ɪŋ, -d
AM ɪn'd(j)u, ɛn'd(j)u, -z, -ɪŋ, -d

endurability
BR ɪnˌdjʊərə'bɪlɪti, ɛnˌdjʊərə'bɪlɪti, ɪnˌdʒʊərə'bɪlɪti, ɛnˌdʒʊərə'bɪlɪti, ɪnˌdjɔːrə'bɪlɪti, ɛnˌdjɔːrə'bɪlɪti, ɪnˌdʒɔːrə'bɪlɪti, ɛnˌdʒɔːrə'bɪlɪti
AM ɪnˌd(j)ʊrə'bɪlɪdi, ɛnˌd(j)ʊrə'bɪlɪdi

endurable
BR ɪn'djʊərəbl, ɛn'djʊərəbl, ɪn'dʒʊərəbl, ɛn'dʒʊərəbl, ɪn'djɔːrəbl, ɛn'djɔːrəbl, ɪn'dʒɔːrəbl, ɛn'dʒɔːrəbl
AM ɪn'd(j)ʊrəbəl, ɛn'd(j)ʊrəbəl

endurance
BR ɪn'djʊərn̩s, ɛn'djʊərn̩s, ɪn'dʒʊərn̩s, ɛn'dʒʊərn̩s, ɪn'dʒɔːrn̩s, ɛn'djɔːrn̩s, ɪn'dʒɔːrn̩s, ɛn'dʒɔːrn̩s
AM ɪn'd(j)ʊrəns, ɛn'd(j)ʊrəns

endure
BR ɪn'djʊə(r), ɛn'djʊə(r), ɪn'dʒʊə(r), ɛn'dʒʊə(r), ɪn'djɔː(r), ɛn'djɔː(r), ɪn'dʒɔː(r), ɛn'dʒɔː(r), -z, -ɪŋ, -d
AM ɪn'd(j)ʊ(ə)r,

en'd(j)ʊ(ə)r, -z, -ɪŋ, -d

enduringly
BR ɪn'djʊərɪŋli, ɛn'djʊərɪŋli, ɪn'dʒʊərɪŋli, ɛn'dʒʊərɪŋli, ɪn'djɔːrɪŋli, ɛn'djɔːrɪŋli, ɪn'dʒɔːrɪŋli, ɛn'dʒɔːrɪŋli AM ɪn'd(j)ʊrɪŋli, ɛn'd(j)ʊrɪŋli

enduro
BR ɪn'djʊərəʊ, ɛn'djʊərəʊ, ɪn'dʒʊərəʊ, ɛn'dʒʊərəʊ, ɪn'djɔːrəʊ, ɛn'djɔːrəʊ, ɪn'dʒɔːrəʊ, ɛn'dʒɔːrəʊ, -z AM ɪn'd(j)ʊrəʊ, ɛn'd(j)ʊrəʊ, -z

endways
BR 'ɛndweɪz
AM 'ɛn(d)ˌweɪz

endwise
BR 'ɛndwaɪz
AM 'ɛn(d)ˌwaɪz

Endymion
BR ɛn'dɪmiən
AM ɛn'dɪmiən

endzone
BR 'ɛn(d)zəʊn, -z
AM 'ɛn(d)ˌzoʊn, -z

Eneas
BR iː'niːəs, ɪ'niːəs
AM ə'niəs, eɪ'niəs

Eneid
BR 'iːnɪɪd, iː'niːɪd, ɪ'niːɪd
AM ə'niəd, eɪ'niəd

enema
BR 'ɛnɪmə(r), -z
AM 'ɛnəmə, -z

enemy
BR 'ɛnɪm|i, -ɪz
AM 'ɛnəmi, -z

Energen
BR 'ɛnədʒ(ə)n
AM 'ɛnərdʒən

energetic
BR ˌɛnə'dʒɛtɪk, -s
AM ˌɛnər'dʒɛdɪk, -s

energetically
BR ˌɛnə'dʒɛtɪkli
AM ˌɛnər'dʒɛdək(ə)li

energise
BR 'ɛnədʒaɪz, -ɪz, -ɪŋ, -d
AM 'ɛnərˌdʒaɪz, -ɪz, -ɪŋ, -d

energiser
BR 'ɛnədʒaɪzə(r), -z
AM 'ɛnərˌdʒaɪzər, -z

energize
BR 'ɛnədʒaɪz, -ɪz, -ɪŋ, -d
AM 'ɛnərˌdʒaɪz, -ɪz, -ɪŋ, -d

energizer
BR 'ɛnədʒaɪzə(r), -z
AM 'ɛnərˌdʒaɪzər, -z

energumen
BR ˌɛnə'gjuːmən, -z
AM ˌɛnər'gjumən, -z

energy
BR 'ɛnədʒ|i, -ɪz
AM 'ɛnərdʒi, -z

enervate
BR 'ɛnəveɪt, -s, -ɪŋ, -ɪd
AM 'ɛnərˌveɪ|t, -ts, -dɪŋ, -dɪd

enervation
BR ˌɛnə'veɪʃn
AM ˌɛnər'veɪʃən

Enesco
BR ɪ'nɛskəʊ
AM ə'nɛskoʊ

Enewetak
BR ˌɛnɪ'wiːtak
AM ˌɛnə'wiˌtak

en famille
BR ˌɒ̃ faˈmiː, ˌɒn +
AM ˌɑn fɑ'mi

enfant gâté
BR ˌɒ̃fɒ̃ ga'teɪ, ˌɒnfɒn gaˈteɪ, ˌɑːnfɑːn ga'teɪ
AM ˌɑnfɑn ga'teɪ

enfants gâtés
BR ˌɒ̃fɒ̃ ga'teɪ, ˌɒnfɒn +, ˌɑːnfɑːn +
AM ˌɑnfɑn ga'teɪ

enfants terribles
BR ˌɒ̃fɒ̃ tɛ'ri:blə(r), ˌɒnfɒn +, ˌɑːnfɑːn +
AM ˌɑnfɑn tɛ'ribl(ə)

enfant terrible
BR ˌɒ̃fɒ̃ tə'ri:blə(r), ˌɒnfɒn +, ˌɑːnfɑːn +
AM ˌɑnfɑn tɛ'ribl(ə)

enfeeble
BR ɪn'fiːb|l, ɛn'fiːb|l, -lz, -lɪŋ \-lɪŋ, -ld
AM ɪn'fibləl, ɛn'fibləl, -əlz, -(ə)lɪŋ, -əld

enfeeblement
BR ɪn'fiːblm(ə)nt, ɛn'fiːblm(ə)nt
AM ɪn'fibləmənt, ɛn'fibləmənt

enfeoff
BR ɪn'fiːf, ɛn'fiːf, ɪn'fɛf, ɛn'fɛf, -s, -ɪŋ, -t
AM ɪn'fif, ɛn'fif, -s, -ɪŋ, -t

enfeoffment
BR ɪn'fiːfm(ə)nt, ɛn'fiːfm(ə)nt, ɪn'fɛfm(ə)nt, ɛn'fɛfm(ə)nt
AM ɪn'fifmənt, ɛn'fifmənt

en fête
BR ˌɒ̃ 'fɛt, ˌɒn +, + 'feɪt
AM ˌɑn 'feɪt, + 'fɛt

enfetter
BR ɪn'fɛt|ə(r), ɛn'fɛt|ə(r), -əz, -(ə)rɪŋ, -əd
AM ɪn'fɛdər, ɛn'fɛdər, -z, -ɪŋ, -t

Enfield
BR 'ɛnfiːld
AM 'ɛnˌfild

enfilade¹
noun
BR 'ɛnfɪleɪd, -z
AM 'ɛnfəˈlad, ˈɛnfəˌleɪd, -z

enfilade²
verb
BR ˌɛnfɪ'leɪd, 'ɛnfɪleɪd, -z, -ɪŋ, -ɪd
AM 'ɛnfəˈlad, ˈɛnfəˌleɪd, -z, -ɪŋ, -ɪd \-əd

enfold
BR ɪn'fəʊld, ɛn'fəʊld, -z, -ɪŋ, -ɪd
AM ɪn'foʊld, ɛn'foʊld, -z, -ɪŋ, -əd

enforce
BR ɪn'fɔːs, ɛn'fɔːs, -ɪz, -ɪŋ, -t
AM ɪn'fɔ(ə)rs, ɛn'fɔ(ə)rs, -əz, -ɪŋ, -t

enforceability
BR ɪnˌfɔːsə'bɪlɪti, ɛn'fɔːsə'bɪlɪti
AM ɪnˌfɔrsə'bɪlɪdi, ɛnˌfɔrsə'bɪlɪdi

enforceable
BR ɪn'fɔːsəbl, ɛn'fɔːsəbl
AM ɪn'fɔrsəbəl, ɛn'fɔrsəbəl

enforceably
BR ɪn'fɔːsəbli, ɛn'fɔːsəbli
AM ɪn'fɔrsəbli, ɛn'fɔrsəbli

enforcedly
BR ɪn'fɔːsɪdli, ɛn'fɔːsɪdli
AM ɪn'fɔrsədli, ɛn'fɔrsədli

enforcement
BR ɪn'fɔːsm(ə)nt, ɛn'fɔːsm(ə)nt
AM ɪn'fɔrsmənt, ɛn'fɔrsmənt

enforcer
BR ɪn'fɔːsə(r), ɛn'fɔːsə(r), -z
AM ɪn'fɔrsər, ɛn'fɔrsər, -z

enfranchise
BR ɪn'fran(t)ʃaɪz, ɛn'fran(t)ʃaɪz, -ɪz, -ɪŋ, -d
AM ɪn'fræn,tʃaɪz, ɛn'fræn,tʃaɪz, -ɪz, -ɪŋ, -d

enfranchisement
BR ɪnˈfran(t)ʃɪzm(ə)nt,
ɛnˈfran(t)ʃɪzm(ə)nt
AM ənˈfræn͵tʃaɪzmənt

Engadine
BR ˈɛŋɡədiːn,
͵ɛŋɡəˈdiːn
AM ˈɛŋɡə͵din

engage
BR ɪnˈɡeɪdʒ, ɛnˈɡeɪdʒ,
ɪŋˈɡeɪdʒ, ɛŋˈɡeɪdʒ, -ɪz,
-ɪŋ, -d
AM ɪnˈɡeɪdʒ, ɛnˈɡeɪdʒ,
ɪŋˈɡeɪdʒ, ɛŋˈɡeɪdʒ, -ɪz,
-ɪŋ, -d

engagé
BR ͵ɒ̃ɡaˈʒeɪ
AM ͵ɑŋɡɑˈʒeɪ, ͵ɑŋɡɑˈʒeɪ

engagement
BR ɪnˈɡeɪdʒm(ə)nt,
ɛnˈɡeɪdʒm(ə)nt,
ɪŋˈɡeɪdʒm(ə)nt,
ɛŋˈɡeɪdʒm(ə)nt, -s
AM ɪnˈɡeɪdʒmənt,
ɛnˈɡeɪdʒmənt,
ɪŋˈɡeɪdʒmənt,
ɛŋˈɡeɪdʒmənt, -s

engager
BR ɪnˈɡeɪdʒə(r),
ɛnˈɡeɪdʒə(r),
ɪŋˈɡeɪdʒə(r),
ɛŋˈɡeɪdʒə(r), -z
AM ɪnˈɡeɪdʒər,
ɛnˈɡeɪdʒər,
ɪŋˈɡeɪdʒər,
ɛnˈɡeɪdʒər, -z

engaging
BR ɪnˈɡeɪdʒɪŋ,
ɛnˈɡeɪdʒɪŋ,
ɪŋˈɡeɪdʒɪŋ, ɛŋˈɡeɪdʒɪŋ
AM ɪnˈɡeɪdʒɪŋ,
ɛnˈɡeɪdʒɪŋ,
ɪŋˈɡeɪdʒɪŋ, ɛŋˈɡeɪdʒɪŋ

engagingly
BR ɪnˈɡeɪdʒɪŋli,
ɛnˈɡeɪdʒɪŋli,
ɪŋˈɡeɪdʒɪŋli,
ɛŋˈɡeɪdʒɪŋli
AM ɪnˈɡeɪdʒɪŋli,
ɛnˈɡeɪdʒɪŋli,
ɪŋˈɡeɪdʒɪŋli,
ɛŋˈɡeɪdʒɪŋli

engagingness
BR ɪnˈɡeɪdʒɪŋnɪs,
ɛnˈɡeɪdʒɪŋnɪs,
ɪŋˈɡeɪdʒɪŋnɪs,
ɛŋˈɡeɪdʒɪŋnɪs
AM ɪnˈɡeɪdʒɪŋnɪs,
ɛnˈɡeɪdʒɪŋnɪs,
ɪŋˈɡeɪdʒɪŋnɪs,
ɛŋˈɡeɪdʒɪŋnɪs

en garde
BR ͵ɒ̃ ˈɡɑːd, ͵ɒn +
AM ͵ɑn ˈɡɑrd

engarland
BR ɪnˈɡɑːlənd,
ɛnˈɡɑːlənd,
ɪŋˈɡɑːlənd,
ɛŋˈɡɑːlənd, -z, -ɪŋ, -ɪd

AM ɪnˈɡɑrlənd,
ɛnˈɡɑrlənd,
ɪŋˈɡɑrlənd,
ɛŋˈɡɑrlənd, -z, -ɪŋ, -əd

Engelbert
BR ˈɛŋɡlbəːt
AM ˈɛŋɡəl͵bərt

Engels
BR ˈɛŋɡlz
AM ˈɛŋɡəlz

engender
BR ɪnˈdʒɛnd|ə(r),
ɛnˈdʒɛnd|ə(r), -əz,
-(ə)rɪŋ, -əd
AM ənˈdʒɛnd|ər, -ərz,
-(ə)rɪŋ, -ərd

engine
BR ˈɛn(d)ʒ(ɪ)n, -z
AM ˈɛndʒən, -z

engineer
BR ͵ɛn(d)ʒɪˈnɪə(r), -z,
-ɪŋ, -d
AM ͵ɛndʒəˈnɪ(ə)r, -z,
-ɪŋ, -d

engineering
BR ͵ɛn(d)ʒɪˈnɪərɪŋ
AM ͵ɛndʒəˈnɪrɪŋ

engineership
BR ͵ɛn(d)ʒɪˈnɪəʃɪp
AM ͵ɛndʒəˈnɪr͵ʃɪp

engineless
BR ˈɛn(d)ʒ(ɪ)nlɪs
AM ˈɛndʒənləs

enginery
BR ˈɛn(d)ʒɪn(ə)ri,
ˈɛn(d)ʒn(ə)ri
AM ˈɛndʒənri

engird
BR ɪnˈɡəːd, ɛnˈɡəːd,
ɪŋˈɡəːd, ɛŋˈɡəːd, -z, -ɪŋ,
-ɪd
AM ɪnˈɡərd, ɛnˈɡərd,
ɪŋˈɡərd, ɛŋˈɡərd, -z,
-ɪŋ, -əd

engirdle
BR ɪnˈɡəːd|l̩, ɛnˈɡəːd|l̩,
ɪŋˈɡəːd|l̩, ɛŋˈɡəːd|l̩, -lz,
-l̩ɪŋ \-l̩ɪŋ, -ld
AM ɪnˈɡərdəl,
ɛnˈɡərd|əl, ɪŋˈɡərdəl,
ɛŋˈɡərd|əl, -əlz, -(ə)lɪŋ,
-əld

England
BR ˈɪŋɡlənd
AM ˈɪŋ(ɡ)lənd

Englefield
BR ˈɛŋɡlfiːld
AM ˈɛŋɡəl͵fild

Englewood
BR ˈɛŋɡlwʊd
AM ˈɛŋɡəl͵wʊd

English
BR ˈɪŋɡlɪʃ
AM ˈɪŋ(ɡ)lɪʃ

Englishman
BR ˈɪŋɡlɪʃmən
AM ˈɪŋ(ɡ)lɪʃmən

Englishmen
BR ˈɪŋɡlɪʃmən
AM ˈɪŋ(ɡ)lɪʃmən

Englishness
BR ˈɪŋɡlɪʃnɪs
AM ˈɪŋ(ɡ)lɪʃnɪs

Englishwoman
BR ˈɪŋɡlɪʃ͵wʊmən
AM ˈɪŋ(ɡ)lɪʃ͵wʊmən

Englishwomen
BR ˈɪŋɡlɪʃ͵wɪmɪn
AM ˈɪŋ(ɡ)lɪʃ͵wɪmɪn

engorge
BR ɪnˈɡɔːdʒ, ɛnˈɡɔːdʒ,
ɪŋˈɡɔːdʒ, ɛŋˈɡɔːdʒ, -ɪz,
-ɪŋ, -d
AM ɪnˈɡɔrdʒ, ɛnˈɡɔrdʒ,
ɪŋˈɡɔrdʒ, ɛŋˈɡɔrdʒ,
-əz, -ɪŋ, -t

engorgement
BR ɪnˈɡɔːdʒm(ə)nt,
ɛnˈɡɔːdʒm(ə)nt,
ɪŋˈɡɔːdʒm(ə)nt,
ɛŋˈɡɔːdʒm(ə)nt
AM ɪnˈɡɔrdʒmənt,
ɛnˈɡɔrdʒmənt,
ɪŋˈɡɔrdʒmənt,
ɛŋˈɡɔrdʒmənt

engraft
BR ɪnˈɡrɑːft, ɛnˈɡrɑːft,
ɪnˈɡraft, ɛnˈɡraft,
ɪŋˈɡrɑːft, ɛŋˈɡrɑːft,
ɪŋˈɡraft, ɛŋˈɡraft, -s,
-ɪŋ, -ɪd
AM ɪnˈɡræft, ɛnˈɡræft,
ɪŋˈɡræft, ɛŋˈɡræft, -s,
-ɪŋ, -əd

engraftment
BR ɪnˈɡrɑːf(t)m(ə)nt,
ɛnˈɡrɑːf(t)m(ə)nt,
ɪnˈɡraf(t)m(ə)nt,
ɛnˈɡraf(t)m(ə)nt,
ɪŋˈɡrɑːf(t)m(ə)nt,
ɛŋˈɡrɑːf(t)m(ə)nt,
ɪŋˈɡraf(t)m(ə)nt,
ɛŋˈɡraf(t)m(ə)nt
AM ɪnˈɡræf(t)mənt,
ɛnˈɡræf(t)mənt,
ɪŋˈɡræf(t)mənt,
ɛŋˈɡræf(t)mənt

engrail
BR ɪnˈɡreɪl, ɛnˈɡreɪl,
ɪŋˈɡreɪl, ɛŋˈɡreɪl, -z,
-ɪŋ, -d
AM ɪnˈɡreɪl, ɛnˈɡreɪl,
ɪŋˈɡreɪl, ɛŋˈɡreɪl, -z,
-ɪŋ, -d

engrain
BR ɪnˈɡreɪn, ɛnˈɡreɪn,
ɪŋˈɡreɪn, ɛŋˈɡreɪn, -z,
-ɪŋ, -d
AM ɪnˈɡreɪn, ɛnˈɡreɪn,
ɪŋˈɡreɪn, ɛŋˈɡreɪn, -z,
-ɪŋ, -d

engram
BR ˈɛnɡram, ˈɛŋɡram,
-z
AM ˈɛnɡræm,
ˈɛŋɡræm, -z

---

engrammatic
BR ͵ɛnɡrəˈmatɪk,
͵ɛŋɡrəˈmatɪk
AM ͵ɪnɡrəˈmædɪk,
͵ɛnɡrəˈmædɪk,
͵ɪŋɡrəˈmædɪk,
͵ɛŋɡrəˈmædɪk

engrave
BR ɪnˈɡreɪv, ɛnˈɡreɪv,
ɪŋˈɡreɪv, ɛŋˈɡreɪv, -z,
-ɪŋ, -d
AM ɪnˈɡreɪv, ɛnˈɡreɪv,
ɪŋˈɡreɪv, ɛŋˈɡreɪv, -z,
-ɪŋ, -d

engraver
BR ɪnˈɡreɪvə(r),
ɛnˈɡreɪvə(r),
ɪŋˈɡreɪvə(r),
ɛŋˈɡreɪvə(r), -z
AM ɪnˈɡreɪvər,
ɛnˈɡreɪvər,
ɪŋˈɡreɪvər,
ɛŋˈɡreɪvər, -z

engraving
BR ɪnˈɡreɪvɪŋ,
ɛnˈɡreɪvɪŋ,
ɪŋˈɡreɪvɪŋ,
ɛŋˈɡreɪvɪŋ, -z

engross
BR ɪnˈɡrəʊs, ɛnˈɡrəʊs,
ɪŋˈɡrəʊs, ɛŋˈɡrəʊs, -ɪz,
-ɪŋ, -t
AM ɪnˈɡroʊs, ɛnˈɡroʊs,
ɪŋˈɡroʊs, ɛŋˈɡroʊs,
-əz, -ɪŋ, -t

engrossment
BR ɪnˈɡrəʊsm(ə)nt,
ɛnˈɡrəʊsm(ə)nt,
ɪŋˈɡrəʊsm(ə)nt,
ɛŋˈɡrəʊsm(ə)nt
AM ɪnˈɡroʊsmənt,
ɛnˈɡroʊsmənt,
ɪŋˈɡroʊsmənt,
ɛŋˈɡroʊsmənt

engulf
BR ɪnˈɡʌlf, ɛnˈɡʌlf,
ɪŋˈɡʌlf, ɛŋˈɡʌlf, -s, -ɪŋ,
-t
AM ɪnˈɡəlf, ɛnˈɡəlf,
ɪŋˈɡəlf, ɛŋˈɡəlf, -s, -ɪŋ,
-t

engulfment
BR ɪnˈɡʌlfm(ə)nt,
ɛnˈɡʌlfm(ə)nt,
ɪŋˈɡʌlfm(ə)nt,
ɛŋˈɡʌlfm(ə)nt
AM ɪnˈɡəlfmənt,
ɛnˈɡəlfmənt,
ɪŋˈɡəlfmənt,
ɛŋˈɡəlfmənt

enhance
BR ɪnˈhɑːns, ɛnˈhɑːns,
ɪnˈhans, ɛnˈhans, -ɪz,
-ɪŋ, -t

AM ɪnˈhæns, ɛnˈhæns,
-əz, -ɪŋ, -t

enhancement
BR ɪnˈhɑːnsm(ə)nt,
ɛnˈhɑːnsm(ə)nt,
ɪnˈhansm(ə)nt,
ɛnˈhansm(ə)nt, -s
AM ɪnˈhænsmənt,
ɛnˈhænsmənt, -s

enhancer
BR ɪnˈhɑːnsə(r),
ɛnˈhɑːnsə(r),
ɪnˈhansə(r),
ɛnˈhansə(r), -z
AM ɪnˈhænsər,
ɛnˈhænsər, -z

enharmonic
BR ˌɛnhɑːˈmɒnɪk
AM ɪnˌ(h)ɑrˈmɑnɪk,
ɛnˌ(h)ɑrˈmɑnɪk

enharmonically
BR ˌɛnhɑːˈmɒnɪkli
AM ɪnˌ(h)ɑrˈmɑnək(ə)li,
ɛnˌ(h)ɑrˈmɑnɪək(ə)li

Enid
BR ˈiːnɪd
AM ˈinɪd, ˈeɪnɪd

enigma
BR ɪˈnɪgmə(r),
ɛˈnɪgmə(r), -z
AM ɪˈnɪgmə, ɛˈnɪgmə, -z

enigmatic
BR ˌɛnɪgˈmatɪk
AM ˌɛnɪgˈmædɪk

enigmatical
BR ˌɛnɪgˈmatɪkl
AM ˌɛnɪgˈmædəkəl

enigmatically
BR ˌɛnɪgˈmatɪkli
AM ˌɛnɪgˈmædək(ə)li

enigmatise
BR ɪˈnɪgmətʌɪz,
ɛˈnɪgmətʌɪz, -ɪz, -ɪŋ, -d
AM ɪˈnɪgməˌtaɪz,
ɛˈnɪgməˌtaɪz, -ɪz, -ɪŋ,
-d

enigmatize
BR ɪˈnɪgmətʌɪz,
ɛˈnɪgmətʌɪz, -ɪz, -ɪŋ, -d
AM ɪˈnɪgməˌtaɪz,
ɛˈnɪgməˌtaɪz, -ɪz, -ɪŋ,
-d

Eniwetok
BR ˌɛnɪˈwiːtɒk
AM ˌɛnəˈwiˌtɑk

enjambment
BR ɪnˈdʒam(b)m(ə)nt,
ɛnˈdʒam(b)m(ə)nt, -s
AM ɪnˈdʒæm(b)mənt,
ɛnˈdʒæm(b)mənt, -s

enjoin
BR ɪnˈdʒɔɪn, ɛnˈdʒɔɪn,
-z, -ɪŋ, -d
AM ɪnˈdʒɔɪn, ɛnˈdʒɔɪn,
-z, -ɪŋ, -d

enjoinment
BR ɪnˈdʒɔɪnm(ə)nt,
ɛnˈdʒɔɪnm(ə)nt

AM ɪnˈdʒɔɪnmənt,
ɛnˈdʒɔɪnmənt

enjoy
BR ɪnˈdʒɔɪ, ɛnˈdʒɔɪ, -z,
-ɪŋ, -d
AM ɪnˈdʒɔɪ, ɛnˈdʒɔɪ, -z,
-ɪŋ, -d

enjoyability
BR ɪnˌdʒɔɪəˈbɪlɪti,
ɛnˌdʒɔɪəˈbɪlɪti
AM ɪnˌdʒɔɪəˈbɪlɪdi,
ɛnˌdʒɔɪəˈbɪlɪdi

enjoyable
BR ɪnˈdʒɔɪəbl,
ɛnˈdʒɔɪəbl
AM ɪnˈdʒɔɪəbəl,
ɛnˈdʒɔɪəbəl

enjoyableness
BR ɪnˈdʒɔɪəblnəs,
ɛnˈdʒɔɪəblnəs
AM ɪnˈdʒɔɪəbəlnəs,
ɛnˈdʒɔɪəbəlnəs

enjoyably
BR ɪnˈdʒɔɪəbli,
ɛnˈdʒɔɪəbli
AM ɪnˈdʒɔɪəbli,
ɛnˈdʒɔɪəbli

enjoyer
BR ɪnˈdʒɔɪə(r),
ɛnˈdʒɔɪə(r), -z
AM ɪnˈdʒɔɪər,
ɛnˈdʒɔɪər, -z

enjoyment
BR ɪnˈdʒɔɪm(ə)nt,
ɛnˈdʒɔɪm(ə)nt, -s
AM ɪnˈdʒɔɪmənt,
ɛnˈdʒɔɪmənt, -s

enkephalin
BR ɪnˈkɛfəlɪn,
ɛnˈkɛflɪn, ɛŋˈkɛfəlɪn,
ɛŋˈkɛflɪn, -z
AM ɛnˈkɛfələn,
ɛnˈkɛfəˌlin, -z

enkindle
BR ɪnˈkɪndl̩, ɛnˈkɪndl̩,
ŋˈkɪndl̩, ɛŋˈkɪndl̩,
-lz, -lɪŋ \-lɪŋ, -ld
AM ɪnˈkɪndəl,
ɛnˈkɪndəl, ŋˈkɪndəl,
ɛŋˈkɪndəl, -lz, -lɪŋ, -ld

enlace
BR ɪnˈleɪs, ɛnˈleɪs, -ɪz,
-ɪŋ, -t
AM ɪnˈleɪs, ɛnˈleɪs, -ɪz,
-ɪŋ, -t

enlacement
BR ɪnˈleɪsm(ə)nt,
ɛnˈleɪsm(ə)nt
AM ɪnˈleɪsmənt,
ɛnˈleɪsmənt

enlarge
BR ɪnˈlɑːdʒ, ɛnˈlɑːdʒ,
-ɪz, -ɪŋ, -d
AM ɪnˈlɑrdʒ, ɛnˈlɑrdʒ,
-əz, -ɪŋ, -t

enlargeable
BR ɪnˈlɑːdʒəbl,
ɛnˈlɑːdʒəbl

AM ɪnˈlɑːdʒəbəl,
ɛnˈlɑːdʒəbəl

enlargement
BR ɪnˈlɑːdʒm(ə)nt,
ɛnˈlɑːdʒm(ə)nt, -s
AM ɪnˈlɑrdʒmənt,
ɛnˈlɑrdʒmənt, -s

enlarger
BR ɪnˈlɑːdʒə(r),
ɛnˈlɑːdʒə(r), -z
AM ɪnˈlɑrdʒər,
ɛnˈlɑrdʒər, -z

enlighten
BR ɪnˈlʌɪt|n, ɛnˈlʌɪt|n,
-nz, -ŋɪŋ \-nɪŋ, -nd
AM ɪnˈlaɪtn, ɛnˈlaɪtn,
-z, -ɪŋ, -d

enlightener
BR ɪnˈlʌɪtnə(r),
ɛnˈlʌɪtnə(r), -z
AM ɪnˈlaɪtn̩ər,
ɛnˈlaɪtn̩ər, -z

enlightenment
BR ɪnˈlʌɪtn̩m(ə)nt,
ɛnˈlʌɪtn̩m(ə)nt, -s
AM ɪnˈlaɪtnmənt,
ɛnˈlaɪtnmənt, -s

enlist
BR ɪnˈlɪst, ɛnˈlɪst, -s,
-ɪŋ, -ɪd
AM ɪnˈlɪst, ɛnˈlɪst, -s,
-ɪŋ, -ɪd

enlister
BR ɪnˈlɪstə(r),
ɛnˈlɪstə(r), -z
AM ɪnˈlɪstər, ɛnˈlɪstər,
-z

enlistment
BR ɪnˈlɪs(t)m(ə)nt,
ɛnˈlɪs(t)m(ə)nt
AM ɪnˈlɪs(t)mənt,
ɛnˈlɪs(t)mənt

enliven
BR ɪnˈlʌɪv|n, ɛnˈlʌɪv|n,
-nz, -ŋɪŋ \-nɪŋ, -nd
AM ɪnˈlaɪv|ən,
ɛnˈlaɪv|ən, -ənz,
-(ə)nɪŋ, -ənd

enlivener
BR ɪnˈlʌɪvnə(r),
ɛnˈlʌɪvnə(r), -z
AM ɪnˈlaɪv(ə)nər,
ɛnˈlaɪv(ə)nər, -z

enlivenment
BR ɪnˈlʌɪvnm(ə)nt,
ɛnˈlʌɪvnm(ə)nt
AM ɪnˈlaɪvənmənt,
ɛnˈlaɪvənmənt

en masse
BR ˌɒ̃ ˈmas, ˌɒn +,
ˌɒm +
AM ˌɑn ˈmæs, ˌɛn ˈmæs

enmesh
BR ɪnˈmɛʃ, ɛnˈmɛʃ, -ɪz,
-ɪŋ, -t
AM ɪnˈmɛʃ, ɛnˈmɛʃ, -əz,
-ɪŋ, -t

enmeshment
BR ɪnˈmɛʃm(ə)nt,
ɛnˈmɛʃm(ə)nt
AM ɪnˈmɛʃmənt,
ɛnˈmɛʃmənt

enmity
BR ˈɛnmɪt|i, -ɪz
AM ˈɛnmədi, -z

Ennals
BR ˈɛnlz
AM ˈɛnəlz

ennead
BR ˈɛnɪad, -z
AM ˈɛni̯æd, ˈɛniəd, -z

Ennis
BR ˈɛnɪs
AM ˈɛnəs

Enniskillen
BR ˌɛnɪˈskɪlɪn
AM ˌɛnəˈskɪlən

Ennius
BR ˈɛnɪəs
AM ˈɛniəs

ennoble
BR ɪˈnəʊb|l, ɛˈnəʊb|l,
-lz, -lɪŋ \-lɪŋ, -ld
AM əˈnoʊb|əl,
ɛˈnoʊb|əl, -əlz, -(ə)lɪŋ,
-əld

ennoblement
BR ɪˈnəʊblm(ə)nt,
ɛˈnəʊblm(ə)nt
AM əˈnoʊbəlmənt,
ɛˈnoʊbəlmənt

ennui
BR ɒnˈwiː, ˈɒnwiː
AM ɑnˈwi

Eno®
BR ˈiːnəʊ
AM ˈinoʊ

Enoch
BR ˈiːnɒk
AM ˈinək, ˈiˌnɑk

enologist
BR iːˈnɒlədʒɪst, -s
AM iˈnɑlədʒəst, -s

enology
BR iːˈnɒlədʒi
AM iˈnɑlədʒi

enormity
BR ɪˈnɔːmɪt|i, -ɪz
AM ɪˈnɔrmədi, -z

enormous
BR ɪˈnɔːməs
AM ɪˈnɔrməs

enormously
BR ɪˈnɔːməsli
AM ɪˈnɔrməsli

enormousness
BR ɪˈnɔːməsnəs
AM ɪˈnɔrməsnəs

enosis
BR ˈɛnə(ʊ)sɪs, ɪˈnəʊsɪs
AM əˈnoʊsəs, iˈnoʊsəs,
ɛˈnoʊsəs

enough
BR ɪˈnʌf
AM ɪˈnəf, iˈnəf

enounce
BR ɪ'naʊns, -ɪz, -ɪŋ, -t
AM ɪ'naʊns, i'naʊns,
-əz, -ɪŋ, -t

enouncement
BR ɪ'naʊnsm(ə)nt
AM ɪ'naʊnsmənt,
i'naʊnsmənt

en passant
BR ˌɒ̃ pa'sɒ̃, ˌɒn +,
+ pa'sɑːnt, ˌɒn
pa'sɑːnt
AM ˌɑn pa'sɑn(t)

en pension
BR ˌɒ̃ pɒ̃'sjɒ̃
AM ˌɑn pɑn'sjɔn, ˌɑn
pɑn'sjɑn

enplane
BR ɪn'pleɪn, ɛn'pleɪn,
-z, -ɪŋ, -d
AM ɪn'pleɪn, ɛn'pleɪn,
-z, -ɪŋ, -d

enprint
BR 'ɛnprɪnt, -s
AM ɪn'prɪnt, ɛn'prɪnt,
-s

enquire
BR ɪn'kwʌɪə(r),
ɛn'kwʌɪə(r),
ɪŋ'kwʌɪə(r),
ɛŋ'kwʌɪə(r), -z, -ɪŋ, -d
AM ɪn'kwaɪ(ə)r,
ɛn'kwaɪ(ə)r, -z, -ɪŋ, -d

enquirer
BR ɪn'kwʌɪərə(r),
ɛn'kwʌɪərə(r),
ɪŋ'kwʌɪərə(r),
ɛŋ'kwʌɪərə(r), -z
AM ɪn'kwaɪ(ə)rər,
ɛn'kwaɪ(ə)rər, -z

enquiringly
BR ɪn'kwʌɪərɪŋli,
ɛn'kwʌɪərɪŋli,
ɪŋ'kwʌɪərɪŋli,
ɛŋ'kwʌɪərɪŋli
AM ɪn'kwaɪ(ə)rɪŋli,
ɛn'kwaɪ(ə)rɪŋli

enquiry
BR ɪn'kwʌɪər|i,
ɛn'kwʌɪər|i,
ɪŋ'kwʌɪər|i,
ɛŋ'kwʌɪər|i, -ɪz
AM ən'kwaɪ(ə)ri,
'ɪn,kwaɪ(ə)ri,
'ɛn,kwaɪ(ə)ri, -z

enrage
BR ɪn'reɪdʒ, ɛn'reɪdʒ,
-ɪz, -ɪŋ, -d
AM ɪn'reɪdʒ, ɛn'reɪdʒ,
-ɪz, -ɪŋ, -d

enragement
BR ɪn'reɪdʒm(ə)nt,
ɛn'reɪdʒm(ə)nt
AM ɪn'reɪdʒmənt,
ɛn'reɪdʒmənt

en rapport
BR ˌɒ̃ ra'pɔː(r), ˌɒn +
AM ˌɑn ra'pɔ(ə)r(t)

enrapt
BR ɪn'rapt, ɛn'rapt
AM ɪn'ræpt, ɛn'ræpt

enrapture
BR ɪn'raptʃə(r),
ɛn'raptʃə(r), -z, -ɪŋ, -d
AM ɪn'ræptʃər,
ɛn'ræptʃər, -z, -ɪŋ, -d

enrich
BR ɪn'rɪtʃ, ɛn'rɪtʃ, -ɪz,
-ɪŋ, -t
AM ɪn'rɪtʃ, ɛn'rɪtʃ, -ɪz,
-ɪŋ, -t

enrichment
BR ɪn'rɪtʃm(ə)nt,
ɛn'rɪtʃm(ə)nt, -s
AM ɪn'rɪtʃmənt,
ɛn'rɪtʃmənt, -s

Enright
BR 'ɛnrʌɪt
AM 'ɛn,raɪt

enrobe
BR ɪn'rəʊb, ɛn'rəʊb, -z,
-ɪŋ, -d
AM ɪn'roʊb, ɛn'roʊb, -z,
-ɪŋ, -d

enrol
BR ɪn'rəʊl, ɛnrəʊl, -z,
-ɪŋ, -d
AM ɪn'roʊl, ɛn'roʊl, -z,
-ɪŋ, -d

enroll
BR ɪn'rəʊl, ɛnrəʊl, -z,
-ɪŋ, -d
AM ɪn'roʊl, ɛn'roʊl, -z,
-ɪŋ, -d

enrollee
BR ˌɪnrəʊ'liː, ˌɛnrəʊ'liː,
-z
AM ɪn,roʊ'li, ɛn,roʊ'li,
-z

enroller
BR ɪn'rəʊlə(r),
ɛnrəʊlə(r), -z
AM ɪn'roʊlər,
ɛn'roʊlər, -z

enrollment
BR ɪn'rəʊlm(ə)nt,
ɛn'rəʊlm(ə)nt, -s
AM ɪn'roʊlmənt,
ɛn'roʊlmənt, -s

enrolment
BR ɪn'rəʊlm(ə)nt,
ɛn'rəʊlm(ə)nt, -s
AM ɪn'roʊlmənt,
ɛn'roʊlmənt, -s

en route
BR ˌɒ̃ 'ruːt, ˌɒn +
AM ˌɑn 'rut, ˌɑn 'rʊt

ENSA
BR 'ɛnsə(r)
AM 'ɛnsə

ensanguined
BR ɪn'saŋgwɪnd,
ɛn'saŋgwɪnd
AM ən'sæŋgwənd,
ɛn'sæŋgwənd

ensconce
BR ɪn'skɒns, ɛn'skɒns,
-ɪz, -ɪŋ, -t
AM ənz'kɑns,
ən'skɑns, ɛnz'kɑns,
ɛn'skɑns, -əz, -ɪŋ, -t

ensemble
BR ɒ̃'sɒ̃bl, ɑ̃ː'sɑːbl,
ɒn'sɒmbl, -z
AM ɑn'sɑmbəl, -z

enshrine
BR ɪn'ʃrʌɪn, ɛn'ʃrʌɪn,
-z, -ɪŋ, -d
AM ɪn'ʃraɪn, ɛn'ʃraɪn,
-z, -ɪŋ, -d

enshrinement
BR ɪn'ʃrʌɪnm(ə)nt,
ɛn'ʃrʌɪnm(ə)nt
AM ɪn'ʃraɪnmənt,
ɛn'ʃraɪnmənt

enshroud
BR ɪn'ʃraʊd, ɛn'ʃraʊd,
-z, -ɪŋ, -ɪd
AM ɪn'ʃraʊd, ɛn'ʃraʊd,
-z, -ɪŋ, -əd

ensiform
BR 'ɛnsɪfɔːm
AM 'ɛnsə,fɔ(ə)rm

ensign[1]
flag
BR 'ɛnsn, -z
AM 'ɛnsən, -z

ensign[2]
officer
BR 'ɛnsʌɪn, 'ɛnsn, -z
AM 'ɛnsən, -z

ensigncy
BR 'ɛnsʌɪns|i, -ɪz
AM 'ɛnsənsi, -z

ensilage
BR 'ɛnsɪl|ɪdʒ, 'ɛns||ɪdʒ,
ɪn'sʌɪl|ɪdʒ,
ɛn'sʌɪl|ɪdʒ, -ɪdʒɪz,
-ɪdʒɪŋ, -ɪdʒd
AM 'ɛnsəlɪdʒ, -ɪz, -ɪŋ, -d

ensile
BR ɪn'sʌɪl, ɛn'sʌɪl, -z,
-ɪŋ, -d
AM ɪn'saɪl, ɛn'saɪl, -z,
-ɪŋ, -d

enslave
BR ɪn'sleɪv, ɛn'sleɪv, -z,
-ɪŋ, -d
AM ɪn'sleɪv, ɛn'sleɪv, -z,
-ɪŋ, -d

enslavement
BR ɪn'sleɪvm(ə)nt,
ɛn'sleɪvm(ə)nt
AM ɪn'sleɪvmənt,
ɛn'sleɪvmənt

enslaver
BR ɪn'sleɪvə(r),
ɛn'sleɪvə(r), -z
AM ɪn'sleɪvər,
ɛn'sleɪvər, -z

ensnare
BR ɪn'snɛː(r),
ɛn'snɛː(r), -z, -ɪŋ, -d

ensconce
AM ən'snɛ(ə)r,
ɛn'snɛ(ə)r, -z, -ɪŋ, -d

ensnarement
BR ɪn'snɛːm(ə)nt,
ɛn'snɛːm(ə)nt
AM ən'snɛrmənt,
ɛn'snɛrmənt

ensnarl
BR ɪn'snɑːl, ɛn'snɑːl,
-z, -ɪŋ, -d
AM ən'snɑrl, ɛn'snɑrl,
-z, -ɪŋ, -d

Ensor
BR 'ɛnsɔː(r)
AM 'ɛn,sɔ(ə)r

enstatite
BR 'ɛnstətʌɪt
AM 'ɛnstə,taɪt

ensue
BR ɪn'sjuː, ɛn'sjuː, -z,
-ɪŋ, -d
AM ɪn'su, ɛn'su, -z, -ɪŋ,
-d

en suite
BR ˌɒ̃ 'swiːt, ˌɒn +
AM ˌɑn 'swit

ensure
BR ɪn'ʃʊə(r),
ɛn'ʃʊə(r), ɪn'ʃɔː(r),
ɛn'ʃɔː(r), -z, -ɪŋ, -d
AM ɪn'ʃʊ(ə)r,
ɛn'ʃʊ(ə)r, -z, -ɪŋ, -d

ensurer
BR ɪn'ʃʊərə(r),
ɛn'ʃʊərə(r),
ɪn'ʃɔːrə(r),
ɛn'ʃɔːrə(r), -z
AM ɪn'ʃʊrər, ɛn'ʃʊrər,
-z

enswathe
BR ɪn'sweɪð, ɛn'sweɪð,
-z, -ɪŋ, -d
AM ən'swɑð, ɛn'swɑð,
-z, -ɪŋ, -d

enswathement
BR ɪn'sweɪðm(ə)nt,
ɛn'sweɪðm(ə)nt
AM ən'swɑðmənt,
ɛn'swɑðmənt

entablature
BR ɪn'tablətʃə(r),
ɛn'tablətʃə(r), -z
AM ən'tæblət,ʃʊ(ə)r,
ən'tæblətʃər,
ən'tæblə,tjʊ(ə)r, -z

entablement
BR ɪn'teɪblm(ə)nt,
ɛn'teɪblm(ə)nt
AM ən'teɪbəlmənt,
ɛn'teɪbəlmənt

entail[1]
noun
BR ɪn'teɪl, ɛn'teɪl, -z
AM ɪn'teɪl, ɛn'teɪl, -z

entail[2]
verb
BR ɪn'teɪl, ɛn'teɪl, -z,
-ɪŋ, -d

AM ɪnˈteɪl, ɛnˈteɪl, -z,
-ɪŋ, -d

entailment
BR ɪnˈteɪlm(ə)nt,
ɛnˈteɪlm(ə)nt, -s
AM ɪnˈteɪlmənt,
ɛnˈteɪlmənt, -s

entangle
BR ɪnˈtaŋgl̩, ɛnˈtaŋgl̩,
-lz, -lɪŋ\-lɪŋ, -ld
AM ɪnˈtæŋgl̩əl,
ɛnˈtæŋgl̩əl, -əlz,
-(ə)lɪŋ, -əld

entanglement
BR ɪnˈtaŋglm(ə)nt,
ɛnˈtaŋglm(ə)nt, -s
AM ɪnˈtæŋgəlmənt,
ɛnˈtæŋgəlmənt, -s

entases
BR ˈɛntəsiːz
AM ˈɛn(t)əsiz

entasis
BR ˈɛntəsɪs
AM ˈɛn(t)əsəs

Entebbe
BR ɛnˈtɛbi, ɪnˈtɛbi
AM ɛnˈtɛbi

entelechy
BR ɛnˈtɛləki, ɪnˈtɛləki
AM ənˈtɛləki, ɛnˈtɛləki

entellus
BR ɪnˈtɛləs, ɛnˈtɛləs, -ɪz
AM ənˈtɛləs, ɛnˈtɛləs,
-əz

entendre
BR ɒnˈtɒndrə(r),
ɒ̃ˈtɒ̃drə(r), -z
AM ɑnˈtɑndrə -z

entente
BR ɑːnˈtɑːnt, ɒnˈtɒnt,
ɒ̃ˈtɒ̃t, -s
AM ɑnˈtɑnt, -s

entente cordiale
BR ɑːnˌtɑːnt ˌkɔːdɪˈɑːl,
ɒnˈtɒnt +, ɒ̃ˌtɒ̃t +
AM ɑnˈtɑnt
ˌkɔrd(ʒ)iˈɑl

enter
BR ˈɛntə(r), -əz,
-(ə)rɪŋ, -əd
AM ˈɛn|t(ər, -(t)ərz,
-t(ə)rɪŋ\-ərɪŋ, -(t)ərd

enterable
BR ˈɛnt(ə)rəbl̩
AM ˈɛn(t)ərəbəl

enterer
BR ˈɛnt(ə)rə(r), -z
AM ˈɛn(t)ərər, -z

enteric
BR ɛnˈtɛrɪk
AM ɛnˈtɛrɪk

enteritis
BR ˌɛntəˈrʌɪtɪs
AM ˌɛn(t)əˈraɪdɪs

enterostomy
BR ˌɛntəˈrɒstəm|i, -ɪz
AM ˌɛn(t)əˈrɑstəmi, -z

enterotomy
BR ˌɛntəˈrɒtəm|i, -ɪz
AM ˌɛn(t)əˈradəmi, -z

enterovirus
BR ˈɛnt(ə)rəʊˌvʌɪrəs,
-ɪz
AM ˈɛn(t)əroʊˌvaɪrəs,
-əz

enterprise
BR ˈɛntəprʌɪz, -ɪz
AM ˈɛn(t)ərˌpraɪz, -ɪz

enterpriser
BR ˈɛntəprʌɪzə(r), -z
AM ˈɛn(t)ərˌpraɪzər, -z

enterprising
BR ˈɛntəprʌɪzɪŋ
AM ˈɛn(t)ərˌpraɪzɪŋ

enterprisingly
BR ˈɛntəprʌɪzɪŋli
AM ˈɛn(t)ərˌpraɪzɪŋli

entertain
BR ˌɛntəˈteɪn, -z, -ɪŋ, -d
AM ˌɛn(t)ərˈteɪn, -z, -ɪŋ,
-d

entertainer
BR ˌɛntəˈteɪnə(r), -z
AM ˌɛn(t)ərˈteɪnər, -z

entertaining
BR ˌɛntəˈteɪnɪŋ
AM ˌɛn(t)ərˈteɪnɪŋ

entertainingly
BR ˌɛntəˈteɪnɪŋli
AM ˌɛn(t)ərˈteɪnɪŋli

entertainment
BR ˌɛntəˈteɪnm(ə)nt, -s
AM ˌɛn(t)ərˈteɪ(n)mənt,
-s

enthalpy
BR ˈɛnθalpi, ˈɛnθ(ə)lpi,
ɛnˈθalpi, ɪnˈθalpi
AM ˈɛn,θælpi,
ənˈθælpi, ɛnˈθælpi

enthral
BR ɪnˈθrɔːl, ɛnˈθrɔːl, -z,
-ɪŋ, -d
AM ɪnˈθrɔl, ɛnˈθrɔl,
ɪnˈθral, ɛnˈθral, -z, -ɪŋ,
-d

enthrall
BR ɪnˈθrɔːl, ɛnˈθrɔːl, -z,
-ɪŋ, -d
AM ɪnˈθrɔl, ɛnˈθrɔl,
ɪnˈθral, ɛnˈθral, -z, -ɪŋ,
-d

enthrallment
BR ɪnˈθrɔːlm(ə)nt,
ɛnˈθrɔːlm(ə)nt
AM ɪnˈθrɔlmənt,
ɛnˈθrɔlmənt,
ɪnˈθralmənt,
ɛnˈθralmənt

enthralment
BR ɪnˈθrɔːlm(ə)nt,
ɛnˈθrɔːlm(ə)nt
AM ɪnˈθrɔlmənt,
ɛnˈθrɔlmənt,
ɪnˈθralmənt,
ɛnˈθralmənt

enthrone
BR ɪnˈθrəʊn, ɛnˈθrəʊn,
-z, -ɪŋ, -d
AM ənˈθroʊn,
ɛnˈθroʊn, -z, -ɪŋ, -d

enthronement
BR ɪnˈθrəʊnm(ə)nt,
ɛnˈθrəʊnm(ə)nt, -s
AM ənˈθroʊnmənt,
ɛnˈθroʊnmənt, -s

enthronisation
BR ɪnˌθrəʊnʌɪˈzeɪʃn,
ɛnˌθrəʊnʌɪˈzeɪʃn
AM ənˌθroʊnəˈzeɪʃən,
ɛnˌθroʊnəˈzeɪʃən,
ənˌθroʊˌnaɪˈzeɪʃən,
ɛnˌθroʊˌnaɪˈzeɪʃən

enthronization
BR ɪnˌθrəʊnʌɪˈzeɪʃn,
ɛnˌθrəʊnʌɪˈzeɪʃn
AM ənˌθroʊnəˈzeɪʃən,
ɛnˌθroʊnəˈzeɪʃən,
ənˌθroʊˌnaɪˈzeɪʃən,
ɛnˌθroʊˌnaɪˈzeɪʃən

enthuse
BR ɪnˈθjuːz, ɛnˈθjuːz,
-ɪz, -ɪŋ, -d
AM ɪnˈθ(j)uz, ɛnˈθ(j)uz,
-əz, -ɪŋ, -t

enthusiasm
BR ɪnˈθjuːzɪaz(ə)m,
ɛnˈθjuːzɪaz(ə)m, -z
AM ɪnˈθ(j)uziˌæzəm,
ɛnˈθ(j)uziˌæzəm, -z

enthusiast
BR ɪnˈθjuːzɪast,
ɛnˈθjuːzɪast, -s
AM ɪnˈθ(j)uziˌæst,
ɛnˈθ(j)uziˌæst, -s

enthusiastic
BR ɪnˌθjuːzɪˈastɪk,
ɛnˌθjuːzɪˈastɪk
AM ənˌθ(j)uziˈæstɪk,
ɛnˌθ(j)uziˈæstɪk

enthusiastically
BR ɪnˌθjuːzɪˈastɪkli,
ɛnˌθjuːzɪˈastɪkli
AM ənˌθ(j)uziˈæstək(ə)li,
ɛnˌθ(j)uziˈæstək(ə)li

enthymeme
BR ˈɛnθɪmiːm
AM ˈɛnθəˌmim

entice
BR ɪnˈtʌɪs, ɛnˈtʌɪs, -ɪz,
-ɪŋ, -t
AM ɪnˈtaɪs, ɛnˈtaɪs, -ɪz,
-ɪŋ, -t

enticement
BR ɪnˈtʌɪsm(ə)nt,
ɛnˈtʌɪsm(ə)nt, -s
AM ɪnˈtaɪsmənt,
ɛnˈtaɪsmənt, -s

enticer
BR ɪnˈtʌɪsə(r),
ɛnˈtʌɪsə(r), -z
AM ɪnˈtaɪsər, ɛnˈtaɪsər,
-z

enticing
BR ɪnˈtʌɪsɪŋ, ɛnˈtʌɪsɪŋ
AM ɪnˈtaɪsɪŋ, ɛnˈtaɪsɪŋ

enticingly
BR ɪnˈtʌɪsɪŋli
AM ɪnˈtaɪsɪŋli,
ɛnˈtaɪsɪŋli

entire
BR ɪnˈtʌɪə(r),
ɛnˈtʌɪə(r)
AM ənˈtaɪ(ə)r,
ɛnˈtaɪ(ə)r

entirely
BR ɪnˈtʌɪəli, ɛnˈtʌɪəli
AM ənˈtaɪ(ə)rli,
ɛnˈtaɪ(ə)rli

entirety
BR ɪnˈtʌɪərɪti,
ɛnˈtʌɪərɪti
AM ɪnˈtaɪrədi,
ɪnˈtaɪ(ə)rdi,
ɛnˈtaɪrədi,
ɛnˈtaɪ(ə)rdi

entitative
BR ˈɛntɪtətɪv
AM ˈɛn(t)əˌteɪdɪv,
ˈɛn(t)ədədɪv

entitle
BR ɪnˈtʌɪtl̩, ɛnˈtʌɪtl̩,
-lz, -lɪŋ\-lɪŋ, -ld
AM ɪnˈtaɪdəl, ɛnˈtaɪdəl,
-z, -ɪŋ, -d

entitlement
BR ɪnˈtʌɪtlm(ə)nt,
ɛnˈtʌɪtlm(ə)nt, -s
AM ɪnˈtaɪdlmənt,
ɛnˈtaɪdlmənt, -s

entity
BR ˈɛntɪt|i, -ɪz
AM ˈɛn(t)ədi, -z

entomb
BR ɪnˈtuːm, ɛnˈtuːm, -z,
-ɪŋ, -d
AM ɪnˈtum, ɛnˈtum, -z,
-ɪŋ, -d

entombment
BR ɪnˈtuːmm(ə)nt,
ɛnˈtuːmm(ə)nt, -s
AM ɪnˈtu(m)mənt,
ɛnˈtu(m)mənt, -s

entomic
BR ɛnˈtɒmɪk
AM ɛnˈtɑmɪk

entomological
BR ˌɛntəməˈlɒdʒɪkl̩
AM ˌɛn(t)əməˈlɑdʒəkəl

entomologically
BR ˌɛntəməˈlɒdʒɪkli
AM ˌɛn(t)əməˈlɑdʒək(ə)li

entomologist
BR ˌɛntəˈmɒlədʒɪst, -s
AM ˌɛn(t)əˈmɑlədʒəst,
-s

entomology
BR ˌɛntəˈmɒlədʒi
AM ˌɛn(t)əˈmɑlədʒi

entomophagous
BR ˌentəˈmɒfəgəs
AM ˌen(t)əˈmɑfəgəs

entomophilous
BR ˌentəˈmɒfɪləs
AM ˌen(t)əˈmɑfələs

entoparasite
BR ˌentəʊˈparəsʌɪt, -s
AM ˌen(t)oʊˈpɛrəˌsaɪt, -s

entophyte
BR ˈentəfʌɪt, -s
AM ˈen(t)əˌfaɪt, -s

entourage
BR ˈɒntʊrɑːʒ, ˈɒtʊrɑːʒ, -ɪz
AM ˌantəˈrɑʒ, ˈantʊˌrɑʒ, -əz

entr'acte
BR ˈɒntrakt, ɒnˈtrakt, ˈɒtrakt, ɒˈtrakt, -s
AM ˈɑnˌtrækt, ˈɑnˌtrakt, -s

entrails
BR ˈentreɪlz
AM ˈentrəlz, ˈentreɪlz

entrain
BR ɪnˈtreɪn, ɛnˈtreɪn, -z, -ɪŋ, -d
AM ɪnˈtreɪn, ɛnˈtreɪn, -z, -ɪŋ, -d

entrainment
BR ɪnˈtreɪnm(ə)nt, ɛnˈtreɪnm(ə)nt
AM ɪnˈtreɪnmənt, ɛnˈtreɪnmənt

entrammel
BR ɪnˈtram|l, ɛnˈtram|l, -lz, -|ɪŋ\-əlɪŋ, -ld
AM ɪnˈtræməl, ɛnˈtræməl, -z, -ɪŋ, -d

entrance¹
noun
BR ˈɛntr(ə)ns, -ɪz
AM ˈɛntrəns, -əz

entrance²
verb
BR ɪnˈtrɑːns, ɛnˈtrɑːns, ɪnˈtrans, ɛnˈtrans, -ɪz, -ɪŋ, -t
AM ɪnˈtræns, ɛnˈtræns, -əz, -ɪŋ, -t

entrancement
BR ɪnˈtrɑːnsm(ə)nt, ɛnˈtrɑːnsm(ə)nt, ɪnˈtransm(ə)nt, ɛnˈtransm(ə)nt
AM ɪnˈtrænsmənt, ɛnˈtrænsmənt

entrancingly
BR ɪnˈtrɑːnsɪŋli, ɛnˈtrɑːnsɪŋli, ɪnˈtransɪŋli, ɛnˈtransɪŋli
AM ɪnˈtrænsɪŋli, ɛnˈtrænsɪŋli

entrant
BR ˈɛntr(ə)nt, -s
AM ˈɛntrənt, -s

entrap
BR ɪnˈtrap, ɛnˈtrap, -s, -ɪŋ, -t
AM ɪnˈtræp, ɛnˈtræp, -s, -ɪŋ, -t

entrapment
BR ɪnˈtrapm(ə)nt, ɛnˈtrapm(ə)nt, -s
AM ɪnˈtræpmənt, ɛnˈtræpmənt, -s

entrapper
BR ɪnˈtrapə(r), ɛnˈtrapə(r), -z
AM ɪnˈtræpər, ɛnˈtræpər, -z

entreat
BR ɪnˈtriːt, ɛnˈtriːt, -s, -ɪŋ, -ɪd
AM ɪnˈtri|t, ɛnˈtri|t, -ts, -dɪŋ, -dɪd

entreatingly
BR ɪnˈtriːtɪŋli, ɛnˈtriːtɪŋli
AM ɪnˈtridɪŋli, ɛnˈtridɪŋli

entreaty
BR ɪnˈtriːt|i, ɛnˈtriːt|i, -ɪz
AM ɪnˈtridi, ɛnˈtridi, -z

entrechat
BR ˈɒtrəʃɑ:(r), ˈɒntrəʃɑ:(r), ˈɑ:ntrəʃɑ:(r), -z
AM ˌantrəˈʃa, -z

entrecôte
BR ˈɒntrəkəʊt, ˈɒtrəkəʊt, -s
AM ˌantrəˌkoʊt, -s

entrée¹
dinner
BR ˈɒntreɪ, ˈɒtreɪ, -z
AM ˈɑnˌtreɪ, -z

entrée²
introduction
BR ˈɒntreɪ, ˈɒtreɪ, -z
AM ˌɑnˈtreɪ, ˈɑnˌtreɪ, -z

entremets
BR ˈɒntrəmeɪ, ˈɒtrəmeɪ, -z
AM ˈantrəˌmeɪ, -z

entrench
BR ɪnˈtrɛn(t)ʃ, ɛnˈtrɛn(t)ʃ, -ɪz, -ɪŋ, -t
AM ɪnˈtrɛn(t)ʃ, ɛnˈtrɛn(t)ʃ, -əz, -ɪŋ, -t

entrenchment
BR ɪnˈtrɛn(t)ʃm(ə)nt, ɛnˈtrɛn(t)ʃm(ə)nt, -s
AM ɪnˈtrɛn(t)ʃmənt, ɛnˈtrɛn(t)ʃmənt, -s

entre nous
BR ˌɒntrə ˈnuː, ˌɒtrə +, ˈɑːntrə +
AM ˌantrə ˈnu

entrepôt
BR ˈɒntrəpəʊ, ˈɒtrəpəʊ, -z
AM ˈantrəˌpoʊ, -z

entrepreneur
BR ˌɒntrəprəˈnə:(r), ˌɒtrəprəˈnə:(r), ˌɑːntrəprəˈnə:(r), -z
AM ˌantrəprəˈnʊ(ə)r, ˌantrəprəˈnər, -z

entrepreneurial
BR ˌɒntrəprəˈnə:rɪəl, ˌɒtrəprəˈnə:rɪəl, ˌɑːntrəprəˈnə:rɪəl
AM ˌantrəprəˈnərɪəl, ˌantrəprəˈnʊrɪəl

entrepreneurialism
BR ˌɒntrəprəˈnə:rɪəlɪz(ə)m, ˌɒtrəprəˈnə:rɪəlɪz(ə)m, ˌɑːntrəprəˈnə:rɪəlɪz(ə)m
AM ˌantrəprəˈnərɪəˌlɪzəm, ˌantrəprəˈnʊrɪəˌlɪzəm

entrepreneurially
BR ˌɒntrəprəˈnə:rɪəli, ˌɒtrəprəˈnə:rɪəli, ˌɑːntrəprəˈnə:rɪəli
AM ˌantrəprəˈnərɪəli, ˌantrəprəˈnʊrɪəli

entrepreneurship
BR ˌɒntrəprəˈnə:ʃɪp, ˌɒtrəprəˈnə:ʃɪp, ˌɑːntrəprəˈnə:ʃɪp
AM ˌantrəprəˈnərˌʃɪp, ˌantrəprəˈnʊrˌʃɪp

entresol
BR ˈɒntrəsɒl, ˈɒtrəsɒl, -z
AM ˈɛn(t)ərˌsal, ˈantrəˌsal, -z

entrism
BR ˈɛntrɪz(ə)m
AM ˈɛnˌtrɪzəm

entrist
BR ˈɛntrɪst, -s
AM ˈɛntrəst, -s

entropic
BR ɛnˈtrɒpɪk, ɛnˈtrəʊpɪk
AM ɛnˈtrapɪk

entropically
BR ɛnˈtrɒpɪkli
AM ɛnˈtrapək(ə)li

entropy
BR ˈɛntrəpi
AM ˈɛntrəpi

entrust
BR ɪnˈtrʌst, ɛnˈtrʌst, -s, -ɪŋ, -ɪd
AM ənˈtrəst, ɛnˈtrəst, -s, -ɪŋ, -əd

entrustment
BR ɪnˈtrʌs(t)m(ə)nt, ɛnˈtrʌs(t)m(ə)nt
AM ənˈtrəs(t)mənt, ɛnˈtrəs(t)mənt

entry
BR ˈɛntr|i, -ɪz
AM ˈɛntri, -z

entryism
BR ˈɛntrɪɪz(ə)m
AM ˈɛntriˌɪzəm

entryist
BR ˈɛntrɪɪst, -s
AM ˈɛntriɪst, -s

entryphone®
BR ˈɛntrɪfəʊn, -z
AM ˈɛntriˌfoʊn, -z

entryway
BR ˈɛntrɪweɪ, -z
AM ˈɛntriˌweɪ, -z

entwine
BR ɪnˈtwʌɪn, ɛnˈtwʌɪn, -z, -ɪŋ, -d
AM ənˈtwaɪn, ɛnˈtwaɪn, -z, -ɪŋ, -d

entwinement
BR ɪnˈtwʌɪnm(ə)nt, ɛnˈtwʌɪnm(ə)nt
AM ənˈtwaɪnmənt, ɛnˈtwaɪnmənt

enucleate
BR ɪˈnjuːklɪeɪt, -s, -ɪŋ, -ɪd
AM əˈn(j)ukliˌeɪt, iˈn(j)ukliˌeɪt, -ts, -dɪŋ, -dɪd

enucleation
BR ɪˌnjuːklɪˈeɪʃn
AM əˌn(j)ukliˈeɪʃən, iˌn(j)ukliˈeɪʃən

Enugu
BR ɪˈnuːguː, ɛˈnuːguː
AM əˈnugu

enumerable
BR ɪˈnjuːm(ə)rəbl
AM əˈn(j)umərəbəl, iˈn(j)umərəbəl

enumerate
BR ɪˈnjuːməreɪt, -s, -ɪŋ, -ɪd
AM əˈn(j)uməˌreɪt, iˈn(j)uməˌreɪt, -ts, -dɪŋ, -dɪd

enumeration
BR ɪˌnjuːməˈreɪʃn, -z
AM əˌn(j)uməˈreɪʃən, iˌn(j)uməˈreɪʃən, -z

enumerative
BR ɪˈnjuːm(ə)rətɪv
AM əˈn(j)umərədɪv, iˈn(j)umərədɪv, əˈn(j)uməˌreɪdɪv, iˈn(j)uməˌreɪdɪv

enumerator
BR ɪˈnjuːməreɪtə(r), -z
AM əˈn(j)uməˌreɪdər, iˈn(j)uməˌreɪdər, -z

enunciate
BR ɪˈnʌnsɪeɪt, ɪˈnʌnʃɪeɪt, -s, -ɪŋ, -ɪd
AM iˈnənsiˌeɪt, əˈnənsiˌeɪt, -ts, -dɪŋ, -dɪd

enunciation
BR ɪˌnʌnsɪˈeɪʃn,
ɪˌnʌnʃɪˈeɪʃn, -z
AM iˌnənsiˈeɪʃən,
əˌnənsiˈeɪʃən, -z

enunciative
BR ɪˈnʌnsɪətɪv,
ɪˈnʌnʃɪətɪv,
ɪˈnʌnsɪeɪtɪv,
ɪˈnʌnʃɪeɪtɪv
AM iˈnənsiədɪv,
əˈnənsiədɪv,
iˈnənsiˌeɪdɪv,
əˈnənsiˌeɪdɪv

enunciatively
BR ɪˈnʌnsɪətɪvli,
ɪˈnʌnʃɪətɪvli
AM iˈnənsiəˌtɪvli,
əˈnənsiəˌtɪvli,
iˈnənsiˌeɪdɪvli,
əˈnənsiˌeɪdɪvli

enunciator
BR ɪˈnʌnsɪeɪtə(r), -z
AM iˈnənsiˌeɪdər,
əˈnənsiˌeɪdər, -z

enure
BR ɪˈnjʊə(r), ɪˈnjɔː(r),
-z, -ɪŋ, -d
AM əˈn(j)ʊər, -z, -ɪŋ, -d

enuresis
BR ˌenjʊˈriːsɪs
AM ˌenjəˈrisəs

enuretic
BR ˌenjʊˈrɛtɪk, -s
AM ˌenjəˈrɛdɪk, -s

envelop
BR ɪnˈvɛləp, ɛnˈvɛləp,
-s, -ɪŋ, -t
AM ənˈvɛləp, ɛnˈvɛləp,
-s, -ɪŋ, -t

envelope
BR ˈɛnvələʊp,
ˈɒnvələʊp, -s
AM ˈɛnvəˌloʊp,
ˈɑnvəˌloʊp, -s

envelopment
BR ɪnˈvɛləpm(ə)nt,
ɛnˈvɛləpm(ə)nt, -s
AM ənˈvɛləpmənt,
ɛnˈvɛləpmənt, -s

envenom
BR ɪnˈvɛnəm,
ɛnˈvɛnəm, -z, -ɪŋ, -d
AM ənˈvɛnəm,
ɛnˈvɛnəm, -z, -ɪŋ, -d

enviable
BR ˈɛnvɪəbl
AM ˈɛnviəbəl

enviably
BR ˈɛnvɪəbli
AM ˈɛnviəbli

envier
BR ˈɛnvɪə(r), -z
AM ˈɛnviər, -z

envious
BR ˈɛnvɪəs

AM ˈɛnviəs

enviously
BR ˈɛnvɪəsli
AM ˈɛnviəsli

environ
BR ɪnˈvaɪrən, ɪnˈvaɪrŋ,
ɛnˈvaɪrən, ɛnˈvaɪrŋ,
-z, -ɪŋ, -d
AM ənˈvaɪrən,
ənˈvaɪ(ə)rn,
ɛnˈvaɪrən,
ɛnˈvaɪ(ə)rn, -z, -ɪŋ, -d

environment
BR ɪnˈvaɪrənm(ə)nt,
ɪnˈvaɪrŋm(ə)nt,
ɛnˈvaɪrənm(ə)nt,
ɛnˈvaɪrŋm(ə)nt, -s
AM ənˈvaɪrənmənt,
ənˈvaɪ(ə)rnmənt,
ɛnˈvaɪrənmənt,
ɛnˈvaɪ(ə)rnmənt, -s

environmental
BR ɪnˌvaɪrənˈmɛntl,
ɪnˌvaɪrŋˈmɛntl,
ɛnˌvaɪrənˈmɛntl,
ɛnˌvaɪrŋˈmɛntl
AM ənˌvaɪrənˈmɛn(t)l,
ənˌvaɪ(ə)rnˈmɛn(t)l,
ɛnˌvaɪrənˈmɛn(t)l,
ɛnˌvaɪ(ə)rnˈmɛn(t)l

environmentalism
BR ɪnˌvaɪrənˈmɛntl̩-
ɪz(ə)m,
ɪnˌvaɪrŋˈmɛntl̩ɪz(ə)m,
ɛnˌvaɪrənˈmɛntl̩ɪz(ə)m,
ɛnˌvaɪrŋˈmɛntl̩ɪz(ə)m
AM ənˌvaɪrənˈmɛn(t)l̩-
ˌɪzəm,
ənˌvaɪ(ə)rnˈmɛn(t)l̩-
ˌɪzəm,
ɛnˌvaɪrənˈmɛn(t)l̩-
ˌɪzəm,
ɛnˌvaɪ(ə)rnˈmɛn(t)l̩-
ˌɪzəm

environmentalist
BR ɪnˌvaɪrənˈmɛntl̩ɪst,
ɪnˌvaɪrŋˈmɛntl̩ɪst,
ɛnˌvaɪrənˈmɛntl̩ɪst,
ɛnˌvaɪrŋˈmɛntl̩ɪst, -s
AM ənˌvaɪrənˈmɛn(t)l̩-
əst,
ənˌvaɪ(ə)rnˈmɛn(t)l̩əst,
ɛnˌvaɪrənˈmɛn(t)l̩əst,
ɛnˌvaɪ(ə)rnˈmɛn(t)l̩əst,
-s

environmentally
BR ɪnˌvaɪrənˈmɛntl̩i,
ɪnˌvaɪrŋˈmɛntl̩i,
ɛnˌvaɪrənˈmɛntl̩i,
ɛnˌvaɪrŋˈmɛntl̩i,
ɪnˌvaɪrənˈmɛntəli,
ɪnˌvaɪrŋˈmɛntəli,
ɛnˌvaɪrənˈmɛntəli,
ɛnˌvaɪrŋˈmɛntəli
AM ənˌvaɪrənˈmɛn(t)l̩i,
ənˌvaɪ(ə)rnˈmɛn(t)l̩i,
ɛnˌvaɪrənˈmɛn(t)l̩i,
ɛnˌvaɪ(ə)rnˈmɛn(t)l̩i

environs
plural noun
BR ɪnˈvaɪrənz,
ɪnˈvaɪrŋz, ɛnˈvaɪrənz,
ɛnˈvaɪrŋz
AM ənˈvaɪrənz,
ənˈvaɪ(ə)rnz,
ɛnˈvaɪrənz,
ɛnˈvaɪ(ə)rnz

envisage
BR ɪnˈvɪz|ɪdʒ,
ɛnˈvɪz|ɪdʒ, -ɪdʒɪz,
-ɪdʒɪŋ, -ɪdʒd
AM ənˈvɪzɪdʒ,
ɛnˈvɪzɪdʒ, -ɪz, -ɪŋ, -d

envisagement
BR ɪnˈvɪzɪdʒm(ə)nt,
ɛnˈvɪzɪdʒm(ə)nt
AM ənˈvɪzɪdʒmənt,
ɛnˈvɪzɪdʒmənt

envision
BR ɪnˈvɪʒ|n, ɛnˈvɪʒ|n,
-ənz, -ŋɪŋ \-nɪŋ, -ənd
AM ənˈvɪʒən, ɛnˈvɪʒən,
-d, -ɪŋ, -d

envoi
BR ˈɛnvɔɪ, -z
AM ˈɛnˌvɔɪ, ˈɑnˌvɔɪ, -z

envoy
BR ˈɛnvɔɪ, -z
AM ˈɛnˌvɔɪ, ˈɑnˌvɔɪ, -z

envoyship
BR ˈɛnvɔɪʃɪp, -s
ɛnˌvɔɪˌʃɪp,
ˈɑnˌvɔɪˌʃɪp, -s

envy
BR ˈɛnv|i, -ɪz, -ɪɪŋ, -ɪd
AM ˈɛnvi, -z, -ɪŋ, -d

enweave
BR ɪnˈwiːv, ɛnˈwiːv, -z,
-ɪŋ
AM ənˈwiv, ɛnˈwiv, -z,
-ɪŋ

enwind
BR ɪnˈwʌɪnd,
ɛnˈwʌɪnd, -z, -ɪŋ, -ɪd
AM ənˈwaɪn|d,
ɛnˈwaɪnd, -z, -ɪŋ, -ɪd

enwove
BR ɪnˈwəʊv, ɛnˈwəʊv
AM ənˈwoʊv, ɛnˈwoʊv

enwoven
BR ɪnˈwəʊvn,
ɛnˈwəʊvn
AM ənˈwoʊvən,
ɛnˈwoʊvən

enwrap
BR ɪnˈrap, ɛnˈrap, -s,
-ɪŋ, -t
AM ənˈræp, ɛnˈræp, -s,
-ɪŋ, -t

enwreathe
BR ɪnˈriːð, ɛnˈriːð, -z,
-ɪŋ, -d
AM ənˈrið, ɛnˈrið, -z, -ɪŋ,
-d

Enzed
BR ɛnˈzɛd

AM ɛnˈzɛd

Enzedder
BR ɛnˈzɛdə(r), -z
AM ɛnˈzɛdər, -z

enzootic
BR ˌenzuːˈɒtɪk,
ˌenzəʊˈɒtɪk,
AM ˌenzəˈwɑdɪk,
ˌenzoʊˈɑdɪk

enzymatic
BR ˌenzʌɪˈmatɪk
AM ˌenzəˈmædɪk,
ˌenˌzaɪˈmædɪk

enzyme
BR ˈɛnzʌɪm, -z
AM ˈɛnˌzaɪm, -z

enzymic
BR ɛnˈzʌɪmɪk
AM ɛnˈzaɪmɪk,
ɛnˈzɪmɪk

enzymology
BR ˌenzʌɪˈmɒlədʒi
AM ˌenzəˈmɑlədʒi,
ˌenzaɪˈmɑlədʒi

Eocene
BR ˈiːə(ʊ)siːn
AM ˈiəˌsin

eohippus
BR ˌiːəʊˈhɪpəs
AM ˌioʊˈhɪpəs

EOKA
BR eɪˈəʊkə(r)
AM ˌiˌoʊˌkeɪˈeɪ

Eolian
BR ɪˈəʊlɪən, eɪˈəʊlɪən
AM iˈoʊljən, iˈoʊliən

eolith
BR ˈiːəlɪθ, -s
AM ˈiəˌlɪθ, -s

Eolithic
BR ˌiːə(ʊ)ˈlɪθɪk
AM ˌiəˈlɪθɪk

eon
BR ˈiːən, ˈiːɒn, -z
AM ˈiən, ˈiˌɑn, -z

Eos
BR ˈiːɒs
AM ˈiəs, ˈiˌɑs

eosin
BR ˈiːə(ʊ)sɪn
AM ˈiəsən

eosinophil
BR ˌiːə(ʊ)ˈsɪnə(ʊ)fɪl, -z
AM ˌiəˈsɪnəˌfɪl, -z

eosinophile
BR ˌiːə(ʊ)ˈsɪnə(ʊ)fʌɪl,
-z
AM ˌiəˈsɪnəˌfaɪl, -z

epact
BR ˈiːpakt, ˈɛpakt, -s
AM ˈiˌpæk|(t),
ˈɛˌpæk|(t), -(t)s

Epaminondas
BR ɪˌpamɪˈnɒndas,
ɛˌpamɪˈnɒndas
AM əˌpaməˈnɑndəs

eparch
BR ˈepɑːk, -s
AM ˈɛˌpɑrk, -s

eparchy
BR ˈepɑːk|i, -ɪz
AM ˈɛˌpɑrki, -z

epaulet
BR ˌepəˈlɛt, -s
AM ˈepəˌlɛt, -s

epaulette
BR ˌepəˈlɛt, -s
AM ˈepəˌlɛt, -s

Epcot®
BR ˈepkɒt
AM ˈɛpˌkɑt

épée
BR ˈepeɪ, -z
AM ˌɛˈpeɪ, -z

epeirogeneses
BR ɪˌpaɪrə(ʊ)ˈdʒenɪsiːz
AM əˌpaɪroʊˈdʒenəsiz

epeirogenesis
BR ɪˌpaɪrə(ʊ)ˈdʒenɪsɪs
AM əˌpaɪroʊˈdʒenəsəs

epeirogenic
BR ɪˌpaɪrə(ʊ)ˈdʒenɪk
AM əˌpaɪroʊˈdʒenɪk

epeirogeny
BR ˌepaɪˈrɒdʒɪni,
ˌepʌɪˈrɒdʒṇi
AM ɛˌpaɪˈrɑdʒəni

epentheses
BR ɪˈpenθɪsiːz,
ɛˈpenθɪsiːz
AM əˈpenθəˌsiz,
ɛˈpenθəˌsiz

epenthesis
BR ɪˈpenθɪsɪs,
ɛˈpenθɪsɪs
AM əˈpenθəsəs,
ɛˈpenθəsəs

epenthetic
BR ˌepenˈθetɪk
AM ˌepenˈθedɪk

epergne
BR ɪˈpɜːn, ɛˈpɜːn, -z
AM əˈpɜrn, ɪˈpɜrn,
eɪˈpɜrn, -z

epexegeses
BR ɛˌpeksɪˈdʒiːsiːz,
ɪˌpeksɪˈdʒiːsiːz
AM ɛˌpeksəˈdʒisiz

epexegesis
BR ɛˌpeksɪˈdʒiːsɪs,
ɪˌpeksɪˈdʒiːsɪs
AM ɛˌpeksəˈdʒisɪs

epexegetic
BR ɛˌpeksɪˈdʒetɪk,
ɪˌpeksɪˈdʒetɪk
AM ɛˌpeksəˈdʒedɪk

epexegetical
BR ɛˌpeksɪˈdʒetɪkl̩,
ɪˌpeksɪˈdʒetɪkl̩
AM ɛˌpeksəˈdʒedəkəl

epexegetically
BR ɛˌpeksɪˈdʒetɪkl̩i,
ɪˌpeksɪˈdʒetɪkli
AM ɛˌpeksəˈdʒedək(ə)li

ephebe
BR ˈefiːb, ɛˈfiːb, ɪˈfiːb, -z
AM ˈɛˌfib, əˈfib, ɛˈfib, -z

ephebic
BR ɛˈfiːbɪk, ɪˈfiːbɪk
AM əˈfibɪk, ɛˈfibɪk

ephedra
BR ɛˈfedrə(r),
ɪˈfedrə(r), ˈefɪdrə(r), -z
AM əˈfedrə, ˈɛfədrə, -z

ephedrine
BR ˈefɪdriːn, ˈefɪdrɪn,
ɪˈfedrɪn
AM əˈfedrən, ɛˈfedrən,
ˈefədrən, ˈefəˌdrin

ephemera
BR ɪˈfem(ə)rə(r),
ɛˈfem(ə)rə(r)
AM əˈfem(ə)rə

ephemeral
BR ɪˈfem(ə)rəl,
ɪˈfem(ə)rl̩,
ɛˈfem(ə)rəl,
ɛˈfem(ə)rl̩
AM əˈfem(ə)rəl,
iˈfem(ə)rəl

ephemerality
BR ɪˌfeməˈralɪti,
ɛˌfeməˈralɪti
AM əˌfem(ə)ˈrælədi,
iˌfem(ə)ˈrælədi

ephemerally
BR ɪˈfem(ə)rl̩i,
ɪˈfem(ə)rəli,
ɛˈfem(ə)rl̩i,
ɛˈfem(ə)rəli
AM əˈfem(ə)rəli,
iˈfem(ə)rəli

ephemeralness
BR ɪˈfem(ə)rl̩nəs,
ɪˈfem(ə)rəlnəs,
ɛˈfem(ə)rl̩nəs,
ɛˈfem(ə)rəlnəs
AM əˈfem(ə)rəlnəs,
iˈfem(ə)rəlnəs

ephemeris
BR ɪˈfem(ə)rɪs,
ɛˈfem(ə)rɪs, -ɪz
AM əˈfem(ə)rəs,
iˈfem(ə)rəs, -ɪz

ephemerist
BR ɪˈfem(ə)rɪst,
ɛˈfem(ə)rɪst, -s
AM əˈfem(ə)rəst,
iˈfem(ə)rəst, -s

ephemeron
BR ɪˈfem(ə)rɒn,
ɛˈfem(ə)rɒn
AM əˈfeməˌrɑn

Ephemeroptera
BR ɪˌfeməˈrɒpt(ə)rə(r),
ɛˌfeməˈrɒpt(ə)rə(r)
AM əˌfeməˈrɑptərə

ephemeropteran
BR ɪˌfeməˈrɒpt(ə)rən,
ɪˌfeməˈrɒpt(ə)rṇ,
ɛˌfeməˈrɒpt(ə)rən,
ɛˌfeməˈrɒpt(ə)rṇ, -z

AM əˌfeməˈrɑptərən, -z

ephemeropterous
BR ɪˌfeməˈrɒpt(ə)rəs,
ɛˌfeməˈrɒpt(ə)rəs
AM əˌfeməˈrɑptərəs

Ephesian
BR ɪˈfiːʒn, -z
AM əˈfiʒən, -z

Ephesus
BR ˈefɪsəs
AM ˈefəsəs

ephod
BR ˈiːfɒd, ˈefɒd, -z
AM ˈɛˌfɑd, ˈiˌfɑd, ˈefəd,
-z

ephor
BR ˈiːfɔː(r), ˈefɔː(r), -z
AM ɛˌfɔ(ə)r, ˈefər,
ˈiˌfɔ(ə)r, -z

ephorate
BR ˈiːf(ə)rət, ˈef(ə)rət,
-s
AM ˈefəˌreɪt, ˈefərət, -s

ephori
BR ˈiːfərʌɪ, ˈefərʌɪ
AM ˈefəˌraɪ

ephorship
BR ˈiːfəʃɪp, ˈefəʃɪp
AM ˈefərˌʃɪp, ˈɛˌfərˌʃɪp,
ˈiˌfərˌʃɪp

Ephraim
BR ˈiːfreɪm
AM ˈifrəm

epiblast
BR ˈepɪblɑːst,
ˈepɪblast, -s
AM ˈepəˌblæst, -s

epic
BR ˈepɪk, -s
AM ˈepɪk, -s

epical
BR ˈepɪkl
AM ˈepəkəl

epically
BR ˈepɪkli
AM ˈepək(ə)li

epicanthic
BR ˌepɪˈkanθɪk
AM ˌepəˈkænθɪk,
ˌepiˈkænθɪk

epicarp
BR ˈepɪkɑːp, -s
AM ˈepəˌkɑrp, -s

epicedia
BR ˌepɪˈsiːdɪə(r)
AM ˌepəˈsidiə

epicedian
BR ˌepɪˈsiːdɪən
AM ˌepəˈsidiən

epicedium
BR ˌepɪˈsiːdɪəm
AM ˌepəˈsidiəm

epicene
BR ˈepɪsiːn, -z
AM ˈepəˌsin, -z

epicenter
BR ˈepɪˌsentə(r), -z

epicentral
BR ˌepɪˈsentr(ə)l
AM ˌepəˈsentrəl,
ˈepiˈsentrəl

epicentre
BR ˈepɪˌsentə(r), -z
AM ˈepəˌsen(t)ər,
ˈepiˌsen(t)ər, -z

epicleses
BR ˌepɪˈkliːsiːz
AM ˌepəˈklisiz

epiclesis
BR ˌepɪˈkliːsɪs
AM ˌepəˈklisɪs

epicondilitis
BR ˌepɪkɒndɪˈlaɪtɪs
AM ˌepəkɑndəˈlaɪdɪs

epicontinental
BR ˌepɪkɒntɪˈnentl
AM ˌepəˌkɑn(t)əˈnen(t)l,
ˌepiˌkɑn(t)əˈnen(t)l

epicotyl
BR ˈepɪkɒtl, -z
AM ˈepəˈkɑdl, -z

Epictetus
BR ˌepɪkˈtiːtəs
AM ˌepəkˈtidəs

epicure
BR ˈepɪkjʊə(r),
ˈepɪkjɔː(r), -z
AM ˈepəˌkjʊ(ə)r,
ˈepiˌkjʊ(ə)r, -z

epicurean
BR ˌepɪkjəˈriːən, -z
AM ˌepəkjəˈriən,
ˌepəˈkjʊriən, -z

Epicureanism
BR ˌepɪkjəˈriːənɪz(ə)m
AM ˌepəkjəˈriəˌnɪzəm,
ˌepəˈkjʊriəˌnɪzəm

epicurism
BR ˈepɪkjərɪz(ə)m
AM ˈepəˌkjʊˌrɪzəm,
ˌepəˈkjʊˌrɪzəm

Epicurus
BR ˌepɪˈkjʊərəs,
ˌepɪˈkjɔːrəs
AM ˌepəˈkjʊrəs,
ˌepəˈkjʊrəs

epicycle
BR ˈepɪˌsʌɪkl, -z
AM ˈepəˌsaɪkəl, -z

epicyclic
BR ˌepɪˈsʌɪklɪk
AM ˌepəˈsaɪklɪk,
ˌepəˈsɪklɪk

epicycloid
BR ˌepɪˈsʌɪklɔɪd, -z
AM ˌepəˈsaɪˌklɔɪd, -z

epicycloidal
BR ˌepɪsʌɪˈklɔɪdl
AM ˌepəˌsaɪˈklɔɪdəl

Epidaurus
BR ˌepɪˈdɔːrəs
AM ˌepəˈdɔrəs

epideictic
BR ˌepɪˈdʌɪktɪk
AM ˌepəˈdaɪktɪk

epidemic
BR ˌepɪˈdemɪk, -s
AM ˌepəˈdemɪk, -s

epidemical
BR ˌepɪˈdemɪkl
AM ˌepəˈdeməkəl

epidemically
BR ˌepɪˈdemɪkli
AM ˌepəˈdemək(ə)li

epidemiological
BR ˌepɪdiːmɪəˈlɒdʒɪkl
AM ˌepəˌdimiəˈladʒəkəl

epidemiologist
BR ˌepɪdiːmɪˈɒlədʒɪst, -s
AM ˌepəˌdimiˈalədʒəst, -s

epidemiology
BR ˌepɪdiːmɪˈɒlədʒi
AM ˌepəˌdimiˈalədʒi

epidermal
BR ˌepɪˈdɜːml
AM ˌepəˈdɜrməl

epidermic
BR ˌepɪˈdɜːmɪk
AM ˌepəˈdɜrmɪk

epidermis
BR ˌepɪˈdɜːmɪs
AM ˌepəˈdɜrmɪs

epidermoid
BR ˌepɪˈdɜːmɔɪd
AM ˌepəˈdɜrˌmɔɪd

epidiascope
BR ˌepɪˈdaɪəskəʊp, -s
AM ˌepəˈdaɪəˌskoʊp, -s

epididymides
BR ˌepɪˈdɪdɪmɪdiːz, ˌepɪdɪˈdɪmɪdiːz
AM ˌepəˈdɪdəməˌdiz, ˌepədəˈdɪməˌdiz, ˌepəˌdaɪˈdɪməˌdiz

epididymis
BR ˌepɪˈdɪdɪmɪs, -ɪz
AM ˌepəˈdɪdəməs, -əz

epidural
BR ˌepɪˈdjʊərəl, ˌepɪˈdjʊər], ˌepɪˈdʒʊərəl, ˌepɪˈdʒʊər], ˌepɪˈdjɔːrəl, ˌepɪˈdjɔːr], ˌepɪˈdʒɔːrəl, ˌepɪˈdʒɔːr], -z
AM ˌepəˈd(j)ʊrəl, ˌepɪˈd(j)ʊrəl, -z

epifauna
BR ˌepɪˈfɔːnə(r)
AM ˌepəˈfɔnə, ˌepəˈfɑnə

epigastria
BR ˌepɪˈgastrɪə(r)
AM ˌepəˈgæstrɪə

epigastric
BR ˌepɪˈgastrɪk
AM ˌepəˈgæstrɪk

epigastrium
BR ˌepɪˈgastrɪəm
AM ˌepəˈgæstriəm

epigeal
BR ˌepɪˈdʒiːəl
AM ˌepəˈdʒiəl

epigene
BR ˈepɪdʒiːn
AM ˈepəˌdʒin

epigenesis
BR ˌepɪˈdʒenɪsɪs
AM ˌepəˈdʒenəsəs

epigenetic
BR ˌepɪdʒɪˈnetɪk
AM ˌepədʒəˈnedɪk

epiglottal
BR ˌepɪˈglɒtl
AM ˌepəˈgladl

epiglottic
BR ˌepɪˈglɒtɪk
AM ˌepəˈgladɪk

epiglottis
BR ˌepɪˈglɒtɪs, -ɪz
AM ˌepəˈgladəs, -əz

epigone
BR ˈepɪgəʊn, -z
AM ˈepəˌgoʊn, -z

epigram
BR ˈepɪgram, -z
AM ˈepəˌgræm, -z

epigrammatic
BR ˌepɪgrəˈmatɪk
AM ˌepəgrəˈmædɪk

epigrammatically
BR ˌepɪgrəˈmatɪkli
AM ˌepəgrəˈmædək(ə)li

epigrammatise
BR ˌepɪˈgramətʌɪz, -ɪz, -ɪŋ, -d
AM ˌepəˈgræməˌtaɪz, -ɪz, -ɪŋ, -d

epigrammatist
BR ˌepɪˈgramətɪst, -s
AM ˌepəˈgræmədəst, -s

epigrammatize
BR ˌepɪˈgramətʌɪz, -ɪz, -ɪŋ, -d
AM ˌepəˈgræməˌtaɪz, -ɪz, -ɪŋ, -d

epigraph
BR ˈepɪgrɑːf, ˈepɪgraf, -s
AM ˈepəˌgræf, -s

epigraphic
BR ˌepɪˈgrafɪk
AM ˌepəˈgræfɪk

epigraphical
BR ˌepɪˈgrafɪkl
AM ˌepəˈgræfəkəl

epigraphically
BR ˌepɪˈgrafɪkli
AM ˌepəˈgræfək(ə)li

epigraphist
BR ɪˈpɪgrəfɪst, eˈpɪgrəfɪst, -s
AM əˈpɪgrəfəst, eˈpɪgrəfəst, -s

epigraphy
BR ɪˈpɪgrəfi, eˈpɪgrəfi
AM əˈpɪgrəfi, eˈpɪgrəfi

epilate
BR ˈepɪleɪt, -s, -ɪŋ, -ɪd
AM ˈepəˌleɪ|t, -ts, -dɪŋ, -dɪd

epilation
BR ˌepɪˈleɪʃn
AM ˌepəˈleɪʃən

epilepsy
BR ˈepɪlepsi
AM ˈepəˌlepsi

epileptic
BR ˌepɪˈleptɪk, -s
AM ˌepəˈleptɪk, -s

epilimnia
BR ˌepɪˈlɪmnɪə(r)
AM ˌepəˈlɪmniə

epilimnion
BR ˌepɪˈlɪmnɪən, ˌepɪˈlɪmnɪɒn
AM ˌepəˈlɪmniˌɑn, ˌepəˈlɪmniən

epilog
BR ˈepɪlɒg, -z
AM ˈepəˌlɔg, ˈepəˌlɑg, ˈepiˌlɑg, -z

epilogist
BR ɪˈpɪlədʒɪst, eˈpɪlədʒɪst, ˈepɪlɑgɪst, -s
AM əˈpɪlədʒəst, eˈpɪlədʒəst, ˈepəˌlɔgəst, ˈepəˌlɑgəst, -s

epilogue
BR ˈepɪlɒg, -z
AM ˈepəˌlɔg, ˈepəˌlɑg, ˈepiˌlɑg, -z

epimer
BR ˈepɪmə(r), -z
AM ˈepəmər, -z

epimeric
BR ˌepɪˈmerɪk
AM ˌepəˈmerɪk

epimerise
BR ɪˈpɪmərʌɪz, eˈpɪmərʌɪz, ˈepɪmərʌɪz, -ɪz, -ɪŋ, -d
AM ˈepəməˌraɪz, -ɪz, -ɪŋ, -d

epimerism
BR ɪˈpɪmərɪz(ə)m, eˈpɪmərɪz(ə)m, ˈepɪmərɪz(ə)m
AM ˈepəm+ˌrɪzəm

epimerize
BR ɪˈpɪmərʌɪz, eˈpɪmərʌɪz, ˈepɪmərʌɪz, -ɪz, -ɪŋ, -d
AM ˈepəməˌraɪz, -ɪz, -ɪŋ, -d

epinasty
BR ˈepɪnasti
AM ˈepəˌnæsti

epinephrine
BR ˌepɪˈnefrɪn, ˌepɪˈnefriːn
AM ˌepəˈnefrən

epiphanic
BR ˌepɪˈfanɪk
AM ˌepəˈfænɪk

epiphany
BR ɪˈpɪfəni, ɪˈpɪfn̩i
AM əˈpɪfəni, ɪˈpɪfəni

epiphenomena
BR ˌepɪfɪˈnɒmɪnə(r)
AM ˌepəfəˈnamənə, ˌepɪfəˈnamənə

epiphenomenal
BR ˌepɪfɪˈnɒmɪnl
AM ˌepəfəˈnamənəl, ˌepɪfəˈnamənəl

epiphenomenon
BR ˌepɪfɪˈnɒmɪnən
AM ˌepəfəˈnamənən, ˌepɪfəˈnamənən

epiphyses
BR ɪˈpɪfɪsiːz, eˈpɪfɪsiːz
AM əˈpɪfəsiz

epiphysis
BR ɪˈpɪfɪsɪs, eˈpɪfɪsɪs
AM əˈpɪfəsəs

epiphytal
BR ˌepɪˈfʌɪtl
AM ˌepəˈfaɪdl

epiphyte
BR ˈepɪfʌɪt, -s
AM ˈepəˌfaɪt, -s

epiphytic
BR ˌepɪˈfɪtɪk
AM ˌepəˈfɪdɪk

epirogenic
BR ɪˌpʌɪrə(ʊ)ˈdʒenɪk
AM əˌpaɪroʊˈdʒenɪk

epirogeny
BR ˌepʌɪˈrɒdʒɪni
AM ˌeˌpaɪˈrɑdʒəni

Epirot
BR eˈpʌɪrət, ɪˈpʌɪrət, -s
AM ˈepəˌrat, əˈpaɪrət, iˈpaɪrət, -s

Epirote
BR eˈpʌɪrəʊt, ɪˈpʌɪrəʊt, -s
AM ˈepəˌrat, eˈpaɪroʊt, iˈpaɪroʊt, -s

Epirus
BR eˈpʌɪrəs, ɪˈpʌɪrəs
AM ˈepərəs, əˈpaɪrəs, iˈpaɪrəs

episcopacy
BR ɪˈpɪskəpəsɪi, -ɪz
AM əˈpɪskəpəsi, iˈpɪskəpəsi, -z

episcopal
BR ɪˈpɪskəpl
AM əˈpɪskəpəl, iˈpɪskəpəl

episcopalian
BR ɪˌpɪskəˈpeɪlɪən, -z
AM əˌpɪskəˈpeɪljən, iˌpɪskəˈpeɪljən,

ə,pɪskə'peɪliən,
i,pɪskə'peɪliən, -z

episcopalianism
BR ɪ,pɪskə'peɪliənɪz(ə)m
AM ə,pɪskə'peɪljə,nɪzəm,
i,pɪskə'peɪljə,nɪzəm,
ə,pɪskə'peɪliə,nɪzəm,
i,pɪskə'peɪliə,nɪzəm

episcopalism
BR ɪ'pɪskəpɪlɪz(ə)m,
ɪ'pɪskəpəlɪz(ə)m
AM ə'pɪskəpə,lɪzəm,
i'pɪskəpə,lɪzəm

episcopally
BR ɪ'pɪskəpḷi,
ɪ'pɪskəpəli
AM ə'pɪskəp(ə)li,
i'pɪskəp(ə)li

episcopate
BR ɪ'pɪskəpət, -s
AM ə'pɪskəpət,
ə'pɪskə,peɪt,
i'pɪskəpət,
i'pɪskə,peɪt, -s

episcope¹
projector
BR 'epɪskəʊp, -s
AM 'epə,skoʊp, -s

episcope²
*supervision by a
bishop*
BR ɪ'pɪskəpi
AM ə'pɪskəpi,
i'pɪskəpi

episematic
BR ,epɪsɪ'mætɪk
AM ,epəsə'mædɪk,
,epɪsə'mædɪk

episiotomy
BR ɪ,pi:zi'ɒtəm|i, -ɪz
AM ə'pizi,ɑdəmi, -z

episode
BR 'epɪsəʊd, -z
AM 'epə,soʊd, -z

episodic
BR ,epɪ'sɒdɪk
AM ,epə'sɑdɪk

episodically
BR ,epɪ'sɒdɪkli
AM ,epə'sɑdək(ə)li

epistaxes
BR ,epɪ'stæksi:z
AM ,epə'stæksiz

epistaxis
BR ,epɪ'stæksɪs
AM ,epə'stæksəs

epistemic
BR ,epɪ'sti:mɪk
AM ,epə'stemɪk,
,epə'stimɪk

epistemically
BR ,epɪ'sti:mɪkli
AM ,epə'stemək(ə)li,
,epə'stimɪk(ə)li

epistemological
BR ɪ,pɪstəmə'lɒdʒɪkl
AM ə,pɪstəmə'lɑdʒəkəl

epistemologically
BR ɪ,pɪstəmə'lɒdʒɪkli
AM ə,pɪstəmə'lɑdʒək-
(ə)li

epistemologist
BR ɪ,pɪstə'mɒlədʒɪst,
-s
AM ə,pɪstə'mɑlədʒɪst,
ɛ,pɪstə'mɑlədʒəst,
i,pɪstə'mɑlədʒəst, -s

epistemology
BR ɪ,pɪstə'mɒlədʒi
AM ə,pɪstə'mɑlədʒi,
ɛ,pɪstə'mɑlədʒi,
i'pɪstə'mɑlədʒi

epistle
BR ɪ'pɪsl, -z
AM ə'pɪsəl, i'pɪsəl, -z

epistolary
BR ɪ'pɪstəl(ə)ri,
ɪ'pɪstḷ(ə)ri
AM ə'pɪstə,leri,
i'pɪstə,leri

epistoler
BR ɪ'pɪstələ(r),
ɪ'pɪstḷ(ə)r, -z
AM ə'pɪstələr,
i'pɪstələr, -z

epistrophe
BR ɪ'pɪstrəf|i, -ɪz
AM ə'pɪstrəfi, -z

epistyle
BR 'epɪstʌɪl, -z
AM 'epə,staɪl, -z

epitaph
BR 'epɪtɑːf, 'epɪtaf, -s
AM 'epə,tæf, -s

epitaxial
BR ,epɪ'taksɪəl
AM ,epə'tæksɪəl

epitaxy
BR 'epɪtaksi
AM 'epə,tæksi,
,epə'tæksi

epithalamia
BR ,epɪθə'leɪmɪə(r)
AM ,epəθə'leɪmɪə

epithalamial
BR ,epɪθə'leɪmɪəl
AM ,epəθə'leɪmɪəl

epithalamic
BR ,epɪθə'læmɪk
AM ,epəθə'læmɪk

epithalamium
BR ,epɪθə'leɪmɪəm, -z
AM ,epə'θælmiəm, -z

epithelia
BR ,epɪ'θi:lɪə(r)
AM ,epə'θiliə

epithelial
BR ,epɪ'θi:lɪəl
AM ,epə'θiliəl

epithelium
BR ,epɪ'θi:lɪəm
AM ,epə'θiliəm

epithet
BR 'epɪθɛt, -s
AM 'epə,θɛt, -s

epithetic
BR ,epɪ'θɛtɪk
AM ,epə'θɛdɪk

epithetical
BR ,epɪ'θɛtɪkl
AM ,epə'θɛdəkəl

epithetically
BR ,epɪ'θɛtɪkli
AM ,epə'θɛdək(ə)li

epitome
BR ɪ'pɪtəmi
AM ə'pɪdəmi, i'pɪdəmi

epitomisation
BR ɪ,pɪtəmʌɪ'zeɪʃn
AM ə,pɪdəmə'zeɪʃən,
i,pɪdəmə'zeɪʃən,
ə,pɪdə,maɪ'zeɪʃən,
'i,pɪdə,maɪ'zeɪʃən

epitomise
BR ɪ'pɪtəmʌɪz, -ɪz, -ɪŋ,
-d
AM ə'pɪdə,maɪz,
i'pɪdə,maɪz, -ɪz, -ɪŋ, -d

epitomist
BR ɪ'pɪtəmɪst, -s
AM ə'pɪdəməst,
i'pɪdəməst, -s

epitomization
BR ɪ,pɪtəmʌɪ'zeɪʃn
AM ə,pɪdəmə'zeɪʃən,
i,pɪdəmə'zeɪʃən,
ə,pɪdə,maɪ'zeɪʃən,
'i,pɪdə,maɪ'zeɪʃən

epitomize
BR ɪ'pɪtəmʌɪz, -ɪz, -ɪŋ,
-d
AM ə'pɪdə,maɪz,
i'pɪdə,maɪz, -ɪz, -ɪŋ, -d

epizoa
BR ,epɪ'zəʊə(r)
AM ,epə'zoʊə

epizoon
BR ,epɪ'zu:ɒn,
,epɪ'zəʊɒn
AM ,epə'zoʊ,ɑn

epizootic
BR ,epɪzu:'ɒtɪk,
,epɪzəʊ'ɒtɪk
AM ,epəzə'wɑdɪk

epoch
BR 'i:pɒk, -s
AM 'epək, 'i,pɑk, -s

epochal
BR 'epəkl, 'epɒkl,
'i:pɒkl, i:'pɒkl
AM 'epəkəl

epode
BR 'epəʊd, -z
AM 'ɛ,poʊd, -z

eponym
BR 'epənɪm, -z
AM 'epə,nɪm, -z

eponymous
BR ɪ'pɒnɪməs
AM ə'pɑnəməs,
ɛ'pɑnəməs

EPOS
BR 'i:pɒs, 'i:pɒz

AM 'i,pɑs, ,i,pi,oʊ'ɛs

epoxide
BR ɪ'pɒksʌɪd, -z
AM ə'pak,saɪd, -z

epoxy
BR ɪ'pɒksi
AM ə'paksi

Epping
BR 'epɪŋ
AM 'epɪŋ

EPROM
BR 'eprɒm, 'i:prɒm, -z
AM 'i,prɑm, -z

epsilon
BR 'epsɪlɒn, 'epsɪlən,
ɛp'sʌɪlən, -z
AM 'epsɪ,lɑn, -z

Epsom
BR 'eps(ə)m
AM 'epsəm

Epson
BR 'epsɒn, 'eps(ə)n
AM 'epsən

Epstein
BR 'epstʌɪn
AM 'ep,staɪn

epyllia
BR ɪ'pɪlɪə(r), ɛ'pɪlɪə(r)
AM ə'pɪljə, ə'pɪliə

epyllion
BR ɪ'pɪliən, ɛ'pɪliən
AM ə'pɪljən, ə'pɪli,ɑn

equability
BR ,ekwə'bɪlɪti
AM ,ekwə'bɪlɪdi,
,ikwə'bɪlɪdi

equable
BR 'ekwəbl
AM 'ekwəbəl, 'ikwəbəl

equableness
BR 'ekwəblnəs
AM 'ekwəbəlnəs,
'ikwəbəlnəs

equably
BR 'ekwəbli
AM 'ekwəbli, 'ikwəbli

equal
BR 'i:kw|(ə)l, -(ə)lz,
-əlɪŋ \-,lɪŋ, -(ə)ld
AM 'ikwəl, -z, -ɪŋ, -d

equalisation
BR ,i:kwəlʌɪ'zeɪʃn,
,i:kwḷʌɪ'zeɪʃn
AM ,ikwələ'zeɪʃən,
,ikwə,laɪ'zeɪʃən

equalise
BR 'i:kwəlʌɪz,
'i:kwḷʌɪz, -ɪz, -ɪŋ, -d
AM 'ikwə,laɪz, -ɪz, -ɪŋ,
-d

equaliser
BR 'i:kwəlʌɪzə(r),
'i:kwḷʌɪzə(r), -z
AM 'ikwə,laɪzər, -z

equalitarian
BR ɪ,kwɒlɪ'tɛːrɪən
AM i,kwɑlə'tɛrɪən,
ə,kwɑlə'tɛrɪən

equalitarianism
BR ɪˌkwɒlɪˈtɛːrɪənɪz(ə)m
AM iˌkwɑlǝˈtɛriǝˌnɪzǝm,
ǝˌkwɑlǝˈtɛriǝˌnɪzǝm

equality
BR ɪˈkwɒlɪti
AM iˈkwɑlǝdi,
ǝˈkwɑlǝdi, iˈkwɔlǝdi,
ǝˈkwɔlǝdi

equalization
BR ˌiːkwǝlʌɪˈzeɪʃn,
ˌiːkwˌlʌɪˈzeɪʃn
AM ˌikwǝlǝˈzeɪʃǝn,
ˌikwǝˌlaɪˈzeɪʃǝn

equalize
BR ˈiːkwǝlʌɪz,
ˈiːkwˌlʌɪz, -ɪz, -ɪŋ, -d
AM ˈikwǝˌlaɪz, -ɪz, -ɪŋ,
-d

equalizer
BR ˈiːkwǝlʌɪzǝ(r),
ˈiːkwˌlʌɪzǝ(r), -z
AM ˈikwǝˌlaɪzǝr, -z

equally
BR ˈiːkwˌli, ˈiːkwǝli
AM ˈikwǝli

equanimity
BR ˌiːkwǝˈnɪmɪti,
ˌɛkwǝˈnɪmɪti
AM ˌɛkwǝˈnɪmɪdi,
ˌikwǝˈnɪmɪdi

equanimous
BR iːˈkwanɪmǝs,
ɪˈkwanɪmǝs,
ɛˈkwanɪmǝs
AM iˈkwanǝmǝs,
ǝˈkwanǝmǝs

equatable
BR ɪˈkweɪtǝbl
AM ǝˈkweɪdɪbǝl

equatably
BR ɪˈkweɪtǝbli
AM ǝˈkweɪdɪbli

equate
BR ɪˈkweɪt, -s, -ɪŋ, -ɪd
AM ǝˈkweɪ|t, iˈkweɪ|t,
-ts, -dɪŋ, -dɪd

equation
BR ɪˈkweɪʒn, -z
AM ǝˈkweɪʒǝn,
iˈkweɪʒǝn, -z

equational
BR ɪˈkweɪʒn̩(ǝ)l,
ɪˈkweɪʒǝn(ǝ)l
AM ǝˈkweɪʒ(ǝ)nǝl,
iˈkweɪʒ(ǝ)nǝl

equator
BR ɪˈkweɪtǝ(r), -z
AM ǝˈkweɪdǝr,
iˈkweɪdǝr, -z

equatorial
BR ˌɛkwǝˈtɔːrɪǝl
AM ˌɛkwǝˈtɔriǝl

equatorially
BR ˌɛkwǝˈtɔːrɪǝli
AM ˌɛkwǝˈtɔriǝli

equerry
BR ˈɛkwǝr|i, ɪˈkwɛr|i,
-ɪz
AM ˈɛkwǝri, ǝˈkwɛri,
iˈkwɛri, ɛˈkwɛri, -z

eques
BR ˈɛkweɪz
AM ˈɛkweɪz, ˈɛkwiz

equestrian
BR ɪˈkwɛstrɪǝn, -z
AM ǝˈkwɛstriǝn,
iˈkwɛstriǝn, -z

equestrianism
BR ɪˈkwɛstrɪǝnɪz(ǝ)m
AM ǝˈkwɛstriǝˌnɪzǝm,
iˈkwɛstriǝˌnɪzǝm

equestrienne
BR ɪˌkwɛstrɪˈɛn, -z
AM ǝˌkwɛstriˈɛn,
iˌkwɛstriˈɛn, -z

equiangular
BR ˌiːkwɪˈaŋɡjʉlǝ(r),
ˌɛkwɪˈaŋɡjʉlǝ(r)
AM ˌɛkwǝˈæŋɡjǝlǝr,
ˌɛkwiˈæŋɡjǝlǝr,
ˌikwǝˈæŋɡjǝlǝr,
ˌikwiˈæŋɡjǝlǝr

equid
BR ˈɛkwɪd, -z
AM ˈɛkwɪd, -z

equidistant
BR ˌiːkwɪˈdɪst(ǝ)nt,
ˌɛkwɪˈdɪst(ǝ)nt
AM ˌɛkwǝˈdɪstnt,
ˌɛkwiˈdɪstnt,
ˌikwǝˈdɪstnt,
ˌikwiˈdɪstnt

equidistantly
BR ˌiːkwɪˈdɪst(ǝ)ntli,
ˌɛkwɪˈdɪst(ǝ)ntli
AM ˌɛkwǝˈdɪstǝn(t)li,
ˌɛkwiˈdɪstǝn(t)li,
ˌikwǝˈdɪstǝn(t)li,
ˌikwiˈdɪstǝn(t)li

equilateral
BR ˌiːkwɪˈlat(ǝ)rǝl,
ˌiːkwɪˈlat(ǝ)r̩,
ˌɛkwɪˈlat(ǝ)rǝl,
ˌɛkwɪˈlat(ǝ)r̩
AM ˌɛkwǝˈlædǝrǝl,
ˌɛkwiˈlædǝrǝl,
ˌikwǝˈlædǝrǝl,
ˌikwiˈlædǝrǝl,
ˌikwǝˈlætrǝl,
ˌikwiˈlætrǝl,
ˌɛkwǝˈlætrǝl,
ˌɛkwiˈlætrǝl

equilibrate
BR ˌiːkwɪˈlʌɪbreɪt,
ˌɛkwɪˈlʌɪbreɪt,
ˌiːkwɪˈlɪbreɪt,
ˌɛkwɪˈlɪbreɪt,
iːˈkwɪlɪbreɪt,
ɪˈkwɪlɪbreɪt, -s, -ɪŋ, -ɪd
AM ǝˈkwɪlǝˌbreɪ|t,
ɛˈkwɪlǝˌbreɪt,
iˈkwɪlǝˌbreɪ|t, -ts, -dɪŋ,
-dɪd

equilibration
BR ˌiːkwɪlʌɪˈbreɪʃn,
ˌɛkwɪlʌɪˈbreɪʃn,
ˌiːkwɪlˈbreɪʃn,
ˌɛkwɪlˈbreɪʃn,
iːˌkwɪlɪˈbreɪʃn,
ɪˌkwɪlɪˈbreɪʃn
AM ǝˌkwɪlǝˈbreɪʃǝn,
ɛˌkwɪlǝˈbreɪʃǝn,
iˌkwɪlǝˈbreɪʃǝn

equilibrator
BR ˌiːkwɪˈlʌɪbreɪtǝ(r),
ˌɛkwɪˈlʌɪbreɪtǝ(r),
ˌiːkwɪˈlɪbreɪtǝ(r),
ˌɛkwɪˈlɪbreɪtǝ(r),
iːˈkwɪlɪbreɪtǝ(r),
ɪˈkwɪlɪbreɪtǝ(r), -z
AM ǝˈkwɪlǝˌbreɪdǝr,
ɛˈkwɪlǝˌbreɪdǝr,
iˈkwɪlǝˌbreɪdǝr, -z

equilibrist
BR ˌiːkwɪˈlɪbrɪst,
ˌɛkwɪˈlɪbrɪst,
ɪˈkwɪlɪbrɪst,
ɛˈkwɪlɪbrɪst, -s
AM ˌikwǝˈlɪbrɪst,
ˌɛkwǝˈlɪbrɪst,
ǝˈkwɪlǝbrǝst, -s

equilibrium
BR ˌiːkwɪˈlɪbrɪǝm,
ˌɛkwɪˈlɪbrɪǝm
AM ˌɛkwǝˈlɪbriǝm,
ˌikwǝˈlɪbriǝm

equine
BR ˈɛkwʌɪn, ˈiːkwʌɪn
AM ˈɛkwaɪn, ˈikwaɪn

equinoctial
BR ˌiːkwɪˈnɒkʃl,
ˌɛkwɪˈnɒkʃl
AM ˌɛkwǝˈnakʃǝl,
ˌikwǝˈnakʃǝl

equinox
BR ˈiːkwɪnɒks,
ˈɛkwɪnɒks, -ɪz
AM ˈɛkwǝˌnaks,
ˈikwǝˌnaks, -ǝz

equip
BR ɪˈkwɪp, -s, -ɪŋ, -t
AM ǝˈkwɪp, iˈkwɪp, -s,
-ɪŋ, -t

equipage
BR ˈɛkwɪpɪdʒ
AM ˈɛkwǝpɪdʒ

equipartition
BR ˌiːkwɪpɑːˈtɪʃn,
ˌɛkwɪpɑːˈtɪʃn
AM ˌɛkwǝˌpɑrˈtɪʃǝn,
ˌikwǝˌpɑrˈtɪʃǝn

equipment
BR ɪˈkwɪpm(ǝ)nt
AM ǝˈkwɪpmǝnt,
iˈkwɪpmǝnt

equipoise
BR ˈɛkwɪpɔɪz
AM ˈɛkwǝˌpɔɪz

equipollence
BR ˌiːkwɪˈpɒlǝns,
ˌiːkwɪˈpɒlns,

equipollens
ˌɛkwɪˈpɒlǝns,
ˌɛkwɪˈpɒlns
AM ˌɛkwǝˈpɑlǝns,
ˌikwǝˈpɑlǝns

equipollency
BR ˌiːkwɪˈpɒlǝnsi,
ˌiːkwɪˈpɒln̩si,
ˌɛkwɪˈpɒlǝnsi,
ˌɛkwɪˈpɒln̩si
AM ˌɛkwǝˈpɑlǝnsi,
ˌikwǝˈpɑlǝnsi

equipollent
BR ˌiːkwɪˈpɒlǝnt,
ˌiːkwɪˈpɒlnt,
ˌɛkwɪˈpɒlǝnt,
ˌɛkwɪˈpɒlnt, -s
AM ˌɛkwǝˈpɑlǝnt,
ˌikwǝˈpɑlǝnt, -s

equiponderant
BR ˌiːkwɪˈpɒnd(ǝ)rǝnt,
ˌiːkwɪˈpɒnd(ǝ)rn̩t,
ˌɛkwɪˈpɒnd(ǝ)rǝnt,
ˌɛkwɪˈpɒnd(ǝ)rn̩t
AM ˌɛkwǝˈpɑndǝrǝnt,
ˌikwǝˈpɑndǝrǝnt

equiponderate
BR ˌiːkwɪˈpɒndǝreɪt,
ˌɛkwɪˈpɒndǝreɪt, -s,
-ɪŋ, -ɪd
AM ˌɛkwǝˈpɑndǝˌreɪ|t,
ˌikwǝˈpɑndǝˌreɪ|t, -ts,
-dɪŋ, -dɪd

equipotential
BR ˌiːkwɪpǝˈtɛnʃl,
ˌɛkwɪpǝˈtɛnʃl
AM ˌɛkwǝpǝˈtɛn(t)ʃǝl,
ˌikwǝpǝˈtɛn(t)ʃǝl

equipper
BR ɪˈkwɪpǝ(r), -z
AM ǝˈkwɪpǝr, iˈkwɪpǝr,
-z

equiprobability
BR ˌiːkwɪˌprɒbǝˈbɪlɪti,
ˌɛkwɪˌprɒbǝˈbɪlɪti
AM ˌɛkwǝˌprɑbǝˈbɪlɪdi,
ˌikwǝˌprɑbǝˈbɪlɪdi

equiprobable
BR ˌiːkwɪˈprɒbǝbl,
ˌɛkwɪˈprɒbǝbl
AM ˌɛkwǝˈprɑbǝbǝl,
ˌikwǝˈprɑbǝbǝl

equitable
BR ˈɛkwɪtǝbl
AM ˈɛkwǝdǝbǝl

equitableness
BR ˈɛkwɪtǝblnǝs
AM ˈɛkwǝdǝbǝlnǝs

equitably
BR ˈɛkwɪtǝbli
AM ˈɛkwǝdǝbli

equitant
BR ˈɛkwɪt(ǝ)nt
AM ˈɛkwǝdǝnt

equitation
BR ˌɛkwɪˈteɪʃn
AM ˌɛkwǝˈteɪʃǝn

equites
BR ˈɛkwɪteɪz

AM 'ɛkwə,teɪz,
'ɛkwə,tiz
equity
BR 'ɛkwɪt|i, -ɪz
AM 'ɛkwədi, -z
equivalence
BR ɪ'kwɪvələns,
ɪ'kwɪvəlns̩,
ɪ'kwɪvl̩(ə)ns
AM ə'kwɪv(ə)ləns,
i'kwɪv(ə)ləns
equivalency
BR ɪ'kwɪvələns|i,
ɪ'kwɪvəlnsi,
ɪ'kwɪvl̩(ə)nsi, -ɪz
AM ə'kwɪv(ə)lənsi,
i'kwɪv(ə)lənsi, -z
equivalent
BR ɪ'kwɪvələnt,
ɪ'kwɪvəlnt,
ɪ'kwɪvl̩(ə)nt, -s
AM ə'kwɪv(ə)lənt,
i'kwɪv(ə)lənt, -s
equivalently
BR ɪ'kwɪvələntli,
ɪ'kwɪv(ə)lntli,
ɪ'kwɪvl̩(ə)ntli
AM ə'kwɪvələn(t)li,
i'kwɪvələn(t)li
equivocacy
BR ɪ'kwɪvəkəsi,
AM ə'kwɪvəkəsi,
i'kwɪvəkəsi
equivocal
BR ɪ'kwɪvəkl
AM ə'kwɪvəkəl,
i'kwɪvəkəl
equivocality
BR ɪ,kwɪvə'kalɪti
AM ə,kwɪvə'kælədi,
i,kwɪvə'kælədi
equivocally
BR ɪ'kwɪvəkl̩i,
ɪ'kwɪvəkəli
AM ə'kwɪvək(ə)li,
i'kwɪvək(ə)li
equivocalness
BR ɪ'kwɪvəklnəs
AM ə'kwɪvəkəlnəs,
i'kwɪvəkəlnəs
equivocate
BR ɪ'kwɪvəkeɪt, -s, -ɪŋ,
-ɪd
AM ə'kwɪvə,keɪ|t,
i'kwɪvə,keɪ|t, -ts, -ɪŋ,
-dɪd
equivocation
BR ɪ,kwɪvə'keɪʃn, -z
AM ə,kwɪvə'keɪʃən,
i'kwɪvə'keɪʃən, -z
equivocator
BR ɪ'kwɪvəkeɪtə(r), -z
AM ə'kwɪvə,keɪdər,
i'kwɪvə,keɪdər, -z
equivocatory
BR ɪ'kwɪvəkeɪt(ə)ri
AM ə'kwɪvəkə,tɔri,
i'kwɪvəkə,tɔri

equivoke
BR 'ɛkwɪvəʊk, -s
AM 'ɛkwə,voʊk,
'ikwə,voʊk, -s
equivoque
BR 'ɛkwɪvəʊk, -s
AM 'ɛkwə,voʊk,
'ikwə,voʊk, -s
Equuleus
BR ɪ'kwʊliəs
AM i'kwʊliəs
equus
BR 'ɛkwəs
AM 'ɛkwəs
er
BR ə:(r)
AM ər
era
BR 'ɪərə(r), -z
AM 'ɛrə, 'ɪrə, -z
eradicable
BR ɪ'radɪkəbl
AM ə'rædəkəbəl,
i'rædəkəbəl
eradicate
BR ɪ'radɪkeɪt, -s, -ɪŋ, -ɪd
AM ə'rædə,keɪ|t,
i'rædə,keɪ|t, -ts, -dɪŋ,
-dɪd
eradication
BR ɪ,radɪ'keɪʃn
AM ə,rædə'keɪʃən,
i,rædə'keɪʃən
eradicator
BR ɪ'radɪkeɪtə(r), -z
AM ə'rædə,keɪdər,
i'rædə,keɪdər, -z
erasable
BR ɪ'reɪzəbl
AM ə'reɪsəbəl,
i'reɪsəbəl
erase
BR ɪ'reɪz, -ɪz, -ɪŋ, -d
AM ə'reɪs, i'reɪs, -ɪz, -ɪŋ,
-t
eraser
BR ɪ'reɪzə(r), -z
AM ə'reɪsər, i'reɪsər, -z
Erasmus
BR ɪ'razməs
AM ə'ræzməs
Erastian
BR ɪ'rastɪən, ɛ'rastɪən,
-z
AM ə'ræstɪən,
i'ræstɪən, ə'ræstʃən,
i'ræstʃən, -z
Erastianism
BR ɪ'rastɪənɪz(ə)m,
ɛ'rastɪənɪz(ə)m
AM ə'ræstɪə,nɪzəm,
i'ræstɪə,nɪzəm,
ə'ræstʃə,nɪzəm,
i'ræstʃə,nɪzəm
erasure
BR ɪ'reɪʒə(r), -z
AM ə'reɪʃər, i'reɪʃər, -z

Erato
BR 'ɛrətəʊ
AM 'ɛrədoʊ
Eratosthenes
BR ,ɛrə'tɒsθθəni:z
AM ,ɛrə'tɑsθə,niz
erbium
BR 'ə:bɪəm
AM 'ərbiəm
ere
before
BR ɛ:(r)
AM ɛ(ə)r
'ere
here
BR ɪə(r)
AM ɪ(ə)r
Erebus
BR 'ɛrɪbəs
AM 'ɛrəbəs
Erechtheum
BR ,ɛrɛk'θi:əm,
,ɛrɪk'θi:əm
AM ,ɛrɛk'θiəm
Erechtheus
BR ɪ'rɛkθɪəs, ɛ'rɛkθɪəs
AM ə'rɛkθiəs
erect
BR ɪ'rɛkt, -s, -ɪŋ, -ɪd
AM ə'rɛk|(t), i'rɛk|(t),
-(t)s, -tɪŋ, -təd
erectable
BR ɪ'rɛktəbl
AM ə'rɛktəbəl,
i'rɛktəbəl
erectile
BR ɪ'rɛktʌɪl
AM ə'rɛktl, ə'rɛk,taɪl,
i'rɛktl, i'rɛk,taɪl
erection
BR ɪ'rɛkʃn, -z
AM ə'rɛkʃən, i'rɛkʃən,
-z
erectly
BR ɪ'rɛktli
AM ə'rɛk(t)li, i'rɛk(t)li
erectness
BR ɪ'rɛk(t)nəs
AM ə'rɛk(t)nəs,
i'rɛk(t)nəs
erector
BR ɪ'rɛktə(r), -z
AM ə'rɛktər, i'rɛktər, -z
eremite
BR 'ɛrɪmʌɪt, -s
AM 'ɛrə,maɪt, -s
eremitic
BR ,ɛrɪ'mɪtɪk
AM ,ɛrə'mɪdɪk
eremitical
BR ,ɛrɪ'mɪtɪkl
AM ,ɛrə'mɪdɪkəl
eremitism
BR ,ɛrɪmɪtɪz(ə)m
AM ,ɛrə'mɪ,dɪzəm
erethism
BR 'ɛrɪθɪz(ə)m
AM 'ɛrə,θɪzəm

Erewhon
BR 'ɛrɪwɒn
AM 'ɛrə(h)wɑn
erg
BR ə:g, -z
AM ərg, -z
ergative
BR 'ə:gətɪv, -z
AM 'ərgədɪv, -z
ergatively
BR 'ə:gətɪvli
AM 'ərgədəvli
ergativity
BR ,ə:gə'tɪvɪti
AM ,ərgə'tɪvɪdi
ergo
BR 'ə:gəʊ
AM 'ərgoʊ, 'ɛrgoʊ
ergocalciferol
BR ,ə:gə(ʊ)kal'sɪfərɒl,
-z
AM ,ərgə,kæl'sɪfərɑl,
-z
ergonomic
BR ,ə:gə'nɒmɪk, -s
AM ,ərgə'nɑmɪk, -s
ergonomically
BR ,ə:gə'nɒmɪkli
AM ,ərgə'nɑmək(ə)li
ergonomist
BR ə:'gɒnəmɪst, -s
AM ər'gɑnəməst, -s
ergosterol
BR ə:'gɒstərɒl
AM ər'gɑstə,roʊl,
ər'gɑstə,rɑl
ergot
BR 'ə:gət, 'ə:gɒt, -s
AM 'ərgət, 'ər,gɑt, -s
ergotism
BR 'ə:gətɪz(ə)m
AM 'ərgə,tɪzəm
erhu
BR ə:'hu:, -z
AM ər'hu, -z
Eric
BR 'ɛrɪk
AM 'ɛrɪk
erica
BR 'ɛrɪkə(r), -z
AM 'ɛrəkə, -z
ericaceous
BR ,ɛrɪ'keɪʃəs
AM ,ɛrə'keɪʃəs
Erickson
BR 'ɛrɪksn
AM 'ɛrɪksən
Ericsson
BR 'ɛrɪksn
AM 'ɛrɪksən
Eridanus
BR ɪ'rɪdənəs, ɪ'rɪdn̩əs
AM ə'rɪdənəs
Erie
BR 'ɪəri
AM 'ɪri

erigeron
BR ɪˈrɪdʒərɒn,
ɛˈrɪdʒərɒn
AM əˈrɪdʒərən,
əˈrɪdʒəˌrɑn

Erin
BR ˈɛrɪn
AM ˈɛrən

Erinys
BR ˈɛrɪnɪs, -ɪz
AM ˈɛrənəs, -əz

Eris
BR ˈɛrɪs
AM ˈɛrəs

eristic
BR ɛˈrɪstɪk, ɪˈrɪstɪk, -s
AM əˈrɪstɪk, ɛˈrɪstɪk, -s

eristically
BR ɛˈrɪstɪkli, ɪˈrɪstɪkli
AM əˈrɪstək(ə)li,
ɛˈrɪstək(ə)li

Eritrea
BR ˌɛrɪˈtreɪə(r),
ˌɛrɪˈtriːə(r)
AM ˌɛrəˈtriːə, ˌɛrəˈtreɪə

Eritrean
BR ˌɛrɪˈtreɪən,
ˌɛrɪˈtriːən, -z
AM ˌɛrəˈtriːən,
ˌɛrəˈtreɪən, -z

erk
BR əːk, -s
AM ɜrk, -s

Erlang
BR ˈəːlaŋ
AM ˈərˌlæŋ

Erlanger
BR ˈəːlaŋə(r)
AM ˈərˌlæŋgər

Erle
BR əːl
AM ɜrl

erl-king
BR ˈəːlkɪŋ, -z
AM ˈər(ə)lˌkɪŋ, -z

ermine
BR ˈəːmɪn, -z, -d
AM ˈɜrmən, -z, -d

Ermintrude
BR ˈəːmɪntruːd
AM ˈɜrmənˌtrud

ern
BR əːn, -z
AM ɜrn, -z

erne
BR əːn, -z
AM ɜrn, -z

Ernest
BR ˈəːnɪst
AM ˈɜrnəst

Ernestine
BR ˈəːnɪstiːn
AM ˈɜrnəsˌtin

Ernie
BR ˈəːni
AM ˈɜrni

Ernle
BR ˈəːnli
AM ˈɜrnli

Ernst
BR ɛːnst, əːnst
AM ɜrnst

erode
BR ɪˈrəʊd, -z, -ɪŋ, -ɪd
AM əˈroʊd, iˈroʊd, -z,
-ɪŋ, -əd

erogenous
BR ɪˈrɒdʒɪnəs,
ɪˈrɒdʒnəs, ɛˈrɒdʒɪnəs,
ɛˈrɒdʒnəs
AM əˈradʒənəs,
iˈradʒənəs,
ɛˈradʒənəs

Eroica
BR ɪˈrəʊɪkə(r),
ɛˈrəʊɪkə(r)
AM ɛˈroʊɪkə

Eros
BR ˈɪərɒs
AM ˈɛˌrɑs, ˈiˌrɑs

erosion
BR ɪˈrəʊʒn
AM əˈroʊʒən, iˈroʊʒən

erosional
BR ɪˈrəʊʒn(ə)l,
ɪˈrəʊʒən(ə)l
AM əˈroʊʒ(ə)nəl,
iˈroʊʒ(ə)nəl

erosive
BR ɪˈrəʊsɪv
AM əˈroʊsɪv

erosively
BR ɪˈrəʊsɪvli
AM əˈroʊsəvli

erotic
BR ɪˈrɒtɪk
AM əˈradɪk, iˈradɪk

erotica
BR ɪˈrɒtɪkə(r)
AM əˈradəkə, iˈradəkə

erotically
BR ɪˈrɒtɪkli
AM əˈradək(ə)li,
iˈradək(ə)li

eroticise
BR ɪˈrɒtɪsaɪz, -ɪz, -ɪŋ, -d
AM əˈradəˌsaɪz,
iˈradəˌsaɪz, -ɪz, -ɪŋ, -d

eroticism
BR ɪˈrɒtɪsɪz(ə)m
AM əˈradəˌsɪzəm,
iˈradəˌsɪzəm

eroticize
BR ɪˈrɒtɪsaɪz, -ɪz, -ɪŋ, -d
AM əˈradəˌsaɪz,
iˈradəˌsaɪz, -ɪz, -ɪŋ, -d

erotism
BR ˈɛrətɪz(ə)m
AM əˈradɪzəm,
iˈradɪzəm

erotogenic
BR ɪˌrɒtə(ʊ)ˈdʒɛnɪk
AM əˌradəˈdʒɛnɪk,
iˌradəˈdʒɛnɪk

erotogenous
BR ɪˌrɒtˈɒdʒɪnəs
AM ˌɛrəˈtadʒənəs

erotology
BR ˌɛrəˈtɒlədʒi
AM ˌɛrəˈtalədʒi

erotomania
BR ɪˌrɒtə(ʊ)ˈmeɪnɪə(r)
AM əˌradəˈmeɪnɪə,
iˌradəˈmeɪniə

erotomaniac
BR ɪˌrɒtə(ʊ)ˈmeɪnɪak,
-s
AM əˌradəˈmeɪniæk,
iˌradəˈmeɪniˌæk, -s

err
BR əː(r), -z, -ɪŋ, -d
AM ɜr, ɛ(ə)r, -z, -ɪŋ, -d

errancy
BR ˈɛrənsi, ˈɛrn̩si
AM ˈɛrənsi

errand
BR ˈɛrənd, ˈɛrn̩d, -z
AM ˈɛrənd, -z

errant
BR ˈɛrənt, ˈɛrn̩t
AM ˈɛrənt

errantly
BR ˈɛrəntli, ˈɛrn̩tli
AM ˈɛrən(t)li

errantry
BR ˈɛrəntri, ˈɛrn̩tri
AM ˈɛrəntri

errata
BR ɛˈrɑːtə(r), ɪˈrɑːtə(r)
AM ɛˈradə

erratic
BR ɪˈratɪk
AM əˈrædɪk, ɛˈrædɪk,
iˈrædɪk

erratically
BR ɪˈratɪkli
AM əˈrædək(ə)li,
ɛˈrædək(ə)li,
iˈrædək(ə)li

erraticism
BR ɪˈratɪsɪz(ə)m
AM əˈrædəˌsɪzəm,
ɛˈrædəˌsɪzəm,
iˈrædəˌsɪzəm

erratum
BR ɛˈrɑːtəm, ɪˈrɑːtəm
AM ɛˈradəm

Errol
BR ˈɛrəl, ˈɛrl̩
AM ˈɛrəl

Erroll
BR ˈɛrəl, ˈɛrl̩
AM ˈɛrəl

erroneous
BR ɪˈrəʊnɪəs
AM ɛˈroʊnɪəs,
iˈroʊnɪəs, iˈroʊnjəs,
ɛˈroʊnjəs

erroneously
BR ɪˈrəʊnɪəsli
AM ɛˈroʊnɪəsli,
iˈroʊnɪəsli,
iˈroʊnjəsli,
ɛˈroʊnjəsli

erroneousness
BR ɪˈrəʊnɪəsnəs
AM ɛˈroʊnɪəsnəs,
iˈroʊnɪəsnəs,
iˈroʊnjəsnəs,
ɛˈroʊnjəsnəs

error
BR ˈɛrə(r), -z
AM ˈɛrər, -z

errorless
BR ˈɛrələs
AM ˈɛrərləs

ersatz
BR ˈəːsats, ˈɛːsats,
ˈəːzats, ˈɛːzats
AM ˈɛrˌsats, ˈɛrˌzæts,
ˈɛrˌzats

Erse
BR əːs
AM ərs

erst
BR əːst
AM ɜrst

erstwhile
BR ˈəːstwaɪl
AM ˈɜrst,(h)waɪl

Ertebølle
BR ˌəːtəˈbəːlə(r)
AM ˌɜrdəˈbalə
DAN ˈaʌdəˌbœlə

erubescence
BR ˌɛrʊˈbɛsns
AM ˌɛruˈbɛsəns

erubescent
BR ˌɛrʊˈbɛsnt
AM ˌɛruˈbɛsənt

eructation
BR ˌiːrʌkˈteɪʃn,
ɪˌrʌkˈteɪʃn,
ˌɛrʌkˈteɪʃn, -z
AM əˌrəkˈteɪʃən,
iˌrəkˈteɪʃən, -z

erudite
BR ˈɛr(j)ʊdʌɪt
AM ˈɛr(j)əˌdaɪt

eruditely
BR ˈɛr(j)ʊdʌɪtli
AM ˈɛr(j)əˌdaɪtli

erudition
BR ˌɛr(j)ʊˈdɪʃn
AM ˌɛrəˈdɪʃən,
ˈɛr(j)ʊˌdɪʃən

erupt
BR ɪˈrʌpt, -s, -ɪŋ, -ɪd
AM əˈrəpt, iˈrəpt, -s, -ɪŋ,
-əd

eruption
BR ɪˈrʌpʃn, -z
AM əˈrəpʃən, iˈrəpʃən,
-z

eruptive
BR ɪˈrʌptɪv
AM əˈrəptɪv, iˈrəptɪv

eruptively
BR ɪˈrʌptɪvli

eruptivity
AM ə'rəptəvli,
i'rəptəvli

eruptivity
BR ɪˌrʌp'tɪvɪti
AM əˌrəp'tɪvɪdi,
iˌrəp'tɪvɪdi

Erving
BR 'ə:vɪŋ
AM 'ərvɪŋ

eryngo
BR ɪ'rɪŋgəʊ
AM ə'rɪŋgoʊ

erysipelas
BR ˌɛrɪ'sɪpɪləs,
ˌɛrɪ'sɪpləs
AM ˌɛrə'sɪp(ə)ləs

erythema
BR ˌɛrɪ'θiːmə(r)
AM ˌɛrə'θiːmə

erythemal
BR ˌɛrɪ'θiːml
AM ˌɛrə'θiːməl

erythematic
BR ˌɛrɪθɪ'mætɪk
AM ˌɛrəθə'mædɪk

erythroblast
BR ɪ'rɪθrə(ʊ)blɑːst,
ɪ'rɪθrə(ʊ)blast, -s
AM ə'rɪθroʊˌblæst,
ɪ'rɪθroʊˌblæst, -s

erythrocyte
BR ɪ'rɪθrəsʌɪt, -s
AM ə'rɪθroʊˌsaɪt,
ɪ'rɪθroʊˌsaɪt, -s

erythrocytic
BR ɪˌrɪθrə'sʌɪtɪk
AM əˌrɪθrə'sɪdɪk,
iˌrɪθrə'sɪdɪk

erythroid
BR ɪ'rɪθrɔɪd
AM ə'rɪθˌrɔɪd, i'rɪθˌrɔɪd

erythromycin
BR ɪˌrɪθrə(ʊ)'mʌɪsɪn
AM əˌrɪθroʊ'maɪsɪn,
iˌrɪθroʊ'maɪsɪn

erythropoietic
BR ɪˌrɪθrə(ʊ)pɔɪ'ɛtɪk
AM əˌrɪθrəˌpɔɪ'ɛdɪk,
iˌrɪθrəˌpɔɪ'ɛdɪk

Erzgebirge
BR 'ə:tsgəˌbə:gə(r)
AM 'ɛrtsgəˌbɪrgə
GER 'eːɐtsgəbɪrgə

Esau
BR 'i:sɔː(r)
AM 'isɔ, 'isɑ

Esbjerg
BR 'ɛsbjə:g
AM 'ɛsˌb(j)ər(g)
DAN 'ɛsˌbjaʌ'

escadrille
BR ˌɛskədrɪl,
ˌɛskə'drɪl, -z
AM ˌɛskəˌdrɪl,
ˌɛskə'drɪl, -z

escalade
BR ˌɛskə'leɪd, -z, -ɪŋ, -ɪd
AM ˌɛskə'leɪd, -z, -ɪŋ, -ɪd

escalate
BR 'ɛskəleɪt, -s, -ɪŋ, -ɪd
AM 'ɛskəˌleɪ|t, -ts, -dɪŋ,
-dɪd

escalation
BR ˌɛskə'leɪʃn, -z
AM ˌɛskə'leɪʃən, -z

escalator
BR 'ɛskəleɪtə(r), -z
AM 'ɛskəˌleɪdər, -z

escallonia
BR ˌɛskə'ləʊnɪə(r), -z
AM ˌɛkə'loʊniə, -z

escallop
BR ɪ'skaləp, ɛ'skaləp,
'ɛskəlɒp, ˌɛskə'lɒp, -s
AM ə'skaləp, ɛ'skaləp,
ə'skæləp, ɛ'skæləp, -s

escalope
BR ɪ'skaləp, ɛ'skaləp,
'ɛskəlɒp, ˌɛskə'lɒp,
'ɛskələʊp, -s
AM ə'skaləp, ɛ'skaləp,
ə'skæləp, ɛ'skæləp, -s

escapable
BR ɪ'skeɪpəbl
AM ə'skeɪpəbəl,
ɛ'skeɪpəbəl

escapade
BR 'ɛskəpeɪd, -z
AM 'ɛskəˌpeɪd, -z

escape
BR ɪ'skeɪp, -s, -ɪŋ, -t
AM ə'skeɪp, ɛ'skeɪp, -s,
-ɪŋ, -t

escapee
BR ɛskeɪ'pi:, -z
AM ɛsˌkeɪ'pi, ə'skeɪˌpi,
-z

escapement
BR ɪ'skeɪpm(ə)nt, -s
AM ə'skeɪpmənt,
ɛ'skeɪpmənt, -s

escaper
BR ɪ'skeɪpə(r), -z
AM ə'skeɪpər,
ɛ'skeɪpər, -z

escapism
BR ɪ'skeɪpɪz(ə)m
AM ə'skeɪpˌɪzəm,
ɛ'skeɪpˌɪzəm

escapist
BR ɪ'skeɪpɪst, -s
AM ə'skeɪpɪst,
ɛ'skeɪpɪst, -s

escapologist
BR ˌɛskə'pɒlədʒɪst, -s
AM əˌsker'palədʒəst,
ɛˌsker'palədʒəst, -s

escapology
BR ˌɛskə'pɒlədʒi
AM əˌsker'palədʒi,
ɛˌsker'palədʒi

escargot
BR ɪ'skɑːgəʊ,
ɛ'skɑːgəʊ, -z
AM ˌɛskɑr'goʊ, -z

escarp
BR ɪ'skɑːp, ɛ'skɑːp, -s
AM ə'skɑrp, ɛ'skɑrp, -s

escarpment
BR ɪ'skɑːpm(ə)nt,
ɛ'skɑːpm(ə)nt, -s
AM ə'skɑrpmənt,
ɛ'skɑrpmənt, -s

eschar
BR 'ɛskɑː(r), -z
AM 'ɛskɑr, 'ɛskər, -z

eschatological
BR ˌɛskətə'lɒdʒɪkl,
ˌɛskatə'lɒdʒɪkl
AM ˌɛsˌkædl'adʒəkəl,
ˌɛskədl'adʒəkəl

eschatologist
BR ˌɛskə'tɒlədʒɪst, -s
AM ˌɛskə'talədʒəst, -s

eschatology
BR ˌɛskə'tɒlədʒi
AM ˌɛskə'talədʒi

eschaton
BR 'ɛskətɒn
AM 'ɛskəˌtan

escheat
BR ɪs'tʃiːt, ɛs'tʃiːt, -s,
-ɪŋ, -ɪd
AM əs'tʃi|t, əʃ'tʃi|t,
ɛs'tʃi|t, ɛʃ'tʃi|t, -ts,
-dɪŋ, -dɪd

eschew
BR ɪs'tʃuː, ɛs'tʃuː, -z,
-ɪŋ, -d
AM əs'tʃu, ɛs'tʃu, -z, -ɪŋ,
-d

eschewal
BR ɪs'tʃʊəl, ɛs'tʃʊəl
AM əs'tʃʊəl, ɛs'tʃʊəl

eschscholtzia
BR ɪ'ʃɒltsɪə(r),
ɛ'ʃɒltsɪə(r),
ɪ'skɒltsɪə(r),
ɛ'skɒltsɪə(r),
ɪ'skɒlʃə(r),
ɛ'skɒlʃə(r)
AM ə'ʃaltsɪə

Escoffier
BR ɪ'skɒfɪeɪ, ɛ'skɒfɪeɪ
AM ˌɛskɒf'jeɪ, ˌɛskaf'jeɪ

Escondido
BR ˌɛskɒn'diːdəʊ,
ˌɛsk(ə)n'diːdəʊ
AM ˌɛskən'didoʊ

Escorial
BR ˌɛskɒrɪ'ɑːl,
ɛ'skɔːrɪəl, ɛ'skɔːrɪal
AM ˌɛskɔr'jal

escort¹
noun
BR 'ɛskɔːt, -s
AM 'ɛsˌkɔ(ə)rt, -s

escort²
verb
BR ɪ'skɔːt, ɛ'skɔːt, -s,
-ɪŋ, -ɪd

escribe
BR ɪ'skrʌɪb, ɛ'skrʌɪb,
-z, -ɪŋ, -d
AM ə'skraɪb, -z, -ɪŋ, -d

escritoire
BR ˌɛskrɪ'twɑː(r), -z
AM ˌɛskrəˌtwɑr,
ˌɛskrə'twɑr, -z

escrow
BR 'ɛskrəʊ, ɛ'skrəʊ
AM 'ɛskˌroʊ, ɛ'skroʊ

escudo
BR ɛ'sk(j)uːdəʊ,
ɪ'sk(j)uːdəʊ,
ɛ'ʃkuːdəʊ, ɪ'ʃkuːdəʊ,
-z
AM ə'sk(j)udoʊ,
ɛ'sk(j)udoʊ, -z

esculent
BR 'ɛskjʊlənt,
'ɛskjʊlnt
AM 'ɛskjələnt

escutcheon
BR ɪ'skʌtʃ(ə)n, -z
AM ə'skətʃən,
ɛ'skətʃən, -z

escutcheoned
BR ɪ'skʌtʃ(ə)nd
AM ə'skətʃənd,
ɛ'skətʃənd

Esdras
BR 'ɛzdras, 'ɛzdrəs
AM 'ɛzdrəs

Esfahan
BR ˌɛsfə'hɑːn
AM ˌɛsfə'hɑn

Esher
BR 'i:ʃə(r)
AM 'iʃər

Esk
BR ɛsk
AM ɛsk

eskar
BR 'ɛskə(r), -z
AM 'ɛskər, -z

Eskdale
BR 'ɛskdeɪl
AM 'ɛskˌdeɪl

esker
BR 'ɛskə(r), -z
AM 'ɛskər, -z

Eskimo
BR 'ɛskɪməʊ, -z
AM 'ɛskəˌmoʊ, -z

Esky®
BR 'ɛsk|i, -iz
AM 'ɛski, -z

Esme
BR 'ɛzmi
AM 'ɛzmi

Esmeralda
BR ˌɛzmə'raldə(r)
AM ˌɛzmə'raldə

Esmond
BR 'ɛzmənd

AM ˈɛzmənd

ESOL
BR ˈiːsɒl
AM ˈiˌsɑl

esophageal
BR ɪˌsɒfəˈdʒiːəl,
iːˌsɒfəˈdʒiːəl
AM əˌsɑfəˈdʒiəl,
iˌsɑfəˈdʒiəl

esophagi
BR ɪˈsɒfəɡʌɪ,
iːˈsɒfəɡʌɪ, ɪˈsɒfədʒʌɪ,
iːˈsɒfədʒʌɪ
AM əˈsɑfəˌɡɑɪ,
iˈsɑfəˌɡɑɪ, əˈsɑfəˌdʒɑɪ,
iˈsɑfəˌdʒɑɪ

esophagus
BR ɪˈsɒfəɡəs, iːˈsɒfəɡəs
AM əˈsɑfəɡəs, iˈsɑfəɡəs

esoteric
BR ˌɛsə(ʊ)ˈtɛrɪk,
ˌiːsə(ʊ)ˈtɛrɪk
AM ˌɛsəˈtɛrɪk

esoterical
BR ˌɛsə(ʊ)ˈtɛrɪkl,
ˌiːsə(ʊ)ˈtɛrɪkl
AM ˌɛsəˈtɛrəkəl

esoterically
BR ˌɛsə(ʊ)ˈtɛrɪkli,
ˌiːsə(ʊ)ˈtɛrɪkli
AM ˌɛsəˈtɛrək(ə)li

esotericism
BR ˌɛsə(ʊ)ˈtɛrɪsɪz(ə)m,
ˌiːsə(ʊ)ˈtɛrɪsɪz(ə)m
AM ˌɛsəˈtɛrəˌsɪzəm

esotericist
BR ˌɛsə(ʊ)ˈtɛrɪsɪst,
ˌiːsə(ʊ)ˈtɛrɪsɪst, -s
AM ˌɛsəˈtɛrəsəst, -s

espadrille
BR ˈɛspədrɪl,
ˌɛspəˈdrɪl, -z
AM ˌɛspəˈdrɪl, -z

espalier
BR ɪˈspalɪə(r),
ɛˈspalɪə(r), ɪˈspalɪeɪ,
ɛˈspalɪeɪ, -z
AM əsˈpæljər,
ɛsˈpæljər, əsˈpaljər,
ɛsˈpaljər, əsˈpeɪljər,
ɛsˈpeɪljər, -z

esparto
BR ɪˈspɑːtəʊ, ɛˈspɑːtəʊ,
-z
AM əˈspɑrdoʊ,
ɛˈspɑrdoʊ, -z

especial
BR ɪˈspɛʃl, ɛˈspɛʃl
AM əsˈpɛʃəl, ɛsˈpɛʃəl

especially
BR ɪˈspɛʃli, ɪˈspɛʃəli,
ɛˈspɛʃli, ɛˈspɛʃəli
AM əsˈpɛʃəli, ɛsˈpɛʃəli

Esperantist
BR ˌɛspəˈrantɪst, -s
AM ˌɛspəˈrɑn(t)əst, -s

Esperanto
BR ˌɛspəˈrantəʊ

AM ˌɛspəˈrɑn(t)oʊ

espial
BR ɪˈspʌɪəl, ɛˈspʌɪəl
AM əsˈpaɪ(ə)l,
ɛsˈpaɪ(ə)l

espionage
BR ˈɛspɪənɑː(d)ʒ
AM ˈɛspiəˌnɑʒ

esplanade
BR ˌɛspləˈneɪd,
ˈɛspləneɪd, -z
AM ˌɛspləˈnɑd,
ˌɛspləˈneɪd, -z

Esposito
BR ˌɛspəˈziːtəʊ
AM ˌɛspəˈzidoʊ

espousal
BR ɪˈspaʊzl, ɛˈspaʊzl, -z
AM əsˈpaʊzəl,
ɛsˈpaʊzəl, -z

espouse
BR ɪˈspaʊz, ɛˈspaʊz, -ɪz,
-ɪŋ, -d
AM əsˈpaʊz, ɛsˈpaʊz,
-əz, -ɪŋ, -t

espouser
BR ɪˈspaʊzə(r),
ɛˈspaʊzə(r), -z
AM əsˈpaʊzər,
ɛsˈpaʊzər, -z

espresso
BR ɛˈsprɛsəʊ, -z
AM ɛsˈprɛsoʊ, -z

esprit
BR ɛˈspriː, ˈɛspriː
AM əsˈpri, ɛsˈpri

esprit de corps
BR ɛˌspri: də ˈkɔː(r),
ˌɛspri: +
AM ɛsˌpri də ˈkɔ(ə)r

**esprit de
l'escalier**
BR ɛˌspri: də lɛˈskalɪeɪ,
ˌɛspri: +
AM ɛsˌpri də ˌlɛskəlˈjeɪ

espy
BR ɪˈspʌɪ, ɛˈspʌɪ, -z, -ɪŋ,
-d
AM əsˈpaɪ, ɛsˈpaɪ, -z, -ɪŋ,
-d

Esq.
BR ɪˈskwʌɪə(r),
ɛˈskwʌɪə(r), -z
AM ˈɛsˌkwaɪ(ə)r ,
əsˈkwaɪ(ə)r, -z

Esquimau
BR ˈɛskɪməʊ, -z
AM ˈɛskəˌmoʊ, -z

Esquimaux
BR ˈɛskəməʊz
AM ˈɛskəˌmoʊz

esquire
BR ɪˈskwʌɪə(r),
ɛˈskwʌɪə(r), -z
AM ˈɛsˌkwaɪ(ə)r,
əsˈkwaɪ(ə)r, -z

essay¹
noun
BR ˈɛseɪ, -z
AM ˈɛseɪ, -z

essay²
verb
BR ɛˈseɪ, -z, -ɪŋ, -d
AM ɛˈseɪ, -z, -ɪŋ, -d

essayist
BR ˈɛseɪɪst, -s
AM ˈɛseɪəst, -s

Essen
BR ˈɛsn
AM ˈɛsən

essence
BR ˈɛsns, -ɪz
AM ˈɛsəns, -əz

Essendon
BR ˈɛsnd(ə)n
AM ˈɛsənd(ə)n

Essene
BR ˈɛsiːn, ɛˈsiːn, -z
AM əˈsin, ɛˈsin, ˈɛˌsin, -z

essential
BR ɪˈsɛnʃl
AM əˈsɛn(t)ʃəl

essentialism
BR ɪˈsɛnʃlɪz(ə)m,
ɪˈsɛnʃəlɪz(ə)m
AM əˈsɛn(t)ʃəˌlɪzəm

essentialist
BR ɪˈsɛnʃlɪst,
ɪˈsɛnʃəlɪst, -s
AM əˈsɛn(t)ʃ(ə)ləst, -s

essentiality
BR ɪˌsɛnʃɪˈalɪti
AM əˌsɛn(t)ʃiˈælədi

essentially
BR ɪˈsɛnʃli, ɪˈsɛnʃəli
AM əˈsɛn(t)ʃəli

essentialness
BR ɪˈsɛnʃ(ə)lnəs
AM əˈsɛn(t)ʃəlnəs

Essequibo
BR ˌɛsɪˈkwiːbəʊ
AM ˌɛsəˈkwiboʊ

Essex
BR ˈɛsɪks
AM ˈɛsəks

essive
BR ˈɛsɪv, -z
AM ˈɛsɪv, -z

Esso®
BR ˈɛsəʊ
AM ˈɛsoʊ

Essoldo
BR ɛˈsɒldəʊ, ɪˈsɒldəʊ
AM ɛˈsɑldoʊ, ɛˈsɑldoʊ

establish
BR ɪˈstablɪʃ, ɛˈstablɪʃ,
-ɪʃɪz, -ɪʃɪŋ, -ɪʃt
AM əsˈtæblɪʃ,
ɛsˈtæblɪʃ, -ɪz, -ɪŋ, -t

establisher
BR ɪˈstablɪʃə(r),
ɛˈstablɪʃə(r), -z
AM əsˈtæblɪʃər,
ɛsˈtæblɪʃər, -z

establishment
BR ɪˈstablɪʃm(ə)nt,
ɛˈstablɪʃm(ə)nt, -s
AM əsˈtæblɪʃmənt,
ɛsˈtæblɪʃmənt, -s

establishmentarian
BR ɪˌstablɪʃm(ə)nˈtɛːrɪən,
ɛˌstablɪʃm(ə)nˈtɛːrɪən,
-z
AM əsˌtæblɪʃmənˈtɛriən,
ɛsˌtæblɪʃmənˈtɛriən,
-z

establishmentarianism
BR ɪˌstablɪʃm(ə)nˈtɛːrɪənɪz(ə,
ɛstablɪʃm(ə)nˈtɛːrɪənɪz(ə)m
AM əsˌtæblɪʃmənˈtɛriəˌnɪzəm
ɛsˌtæblɪʃmənˈtɛriəˌnɪzəm

estaminet
BR ɛˈstamɪneɪ, -z
AM ɛsˌtæmiˈneɪ, -z

estancia
BR ɪˈstansɪə(r),
ɛˈstansɪə(r), -z
AM ɛˈstænsiə, -z

estate
BR ɪˈsteɪt, ɛˈsteɪt, -s
AM əsˈteɪt, ɛsˈteɪt, -s

esteem
BR ɪˈstiːm, ɛˈstiːm, -z,
-ɪŋ, -d
AM əsˈtim, ɛsˈtim, -z,
-ɪŋ, -d

Estella
BR ɪˈstɛlə(r), ɛˈstɛlə(r)
AM ɛsˈtɛlə

Estelle
BR ɛˈstɛl
AM əˈstɛl

ester
BR ˈɛstə(r), -z
AM ˈɛstər, -z

Esterhazy
BR ˈɛstəhɑːzi
AM ˈɛstərˌ(h)ɑzi

esterify
BR ɪˈstɛrɪfʌɪ, ɛˈstɛrɪfʌɪ,
-z, -ɪŋ, -d
AM əˈstɛrəˌfaɪ, -z, -ɪŋ, -d

Estes
BR ˈɛstɪz, ˈɛsteɪz
AM ˈɛstiz

Esther
BR ˈɛstə(r), ˈɛsθə(r)
AM ˈɛstər

esthete
BR ˈiːsθiːt, -s
AM ˈɛsˌθit, -s

esthetic
BR iːsˈθɛtɪk, ɪsˈθɛtɪk, -s
AM ɛsˈθɛdɪk, -s

esthetical
BR iːsˈθɛtɪkl, ɪsˈθɛtɪkl
AM ɛsˈθɛdəkəl

esthetically
BR iːsˈθɛtɪkli,
ɪsˈθɛtɪkli
AM ɛsˈθɛdək(ə)li

esthetician
BR ˌiːsθəˈtɪʃn
AM ˌɛsθəˈtɪʃən

estheticism
BR iːsˈθetɪsɪz(ə)m,
ɪsˈθetɪsɪz(ə)m
AM ɛsˈθedəˌsɪzəm

estimable
BR ˈestɪməbl
AM ˈestəməbəl

estimableness
BR ˈestɪməblnəs
AM ˈestəməbəlnəs

estimably
BR ˈestɪməbli
AM ˈestəməbli

estimate¹
noun
BR ˈestɪmət, -s
AM ˈestɪmət, -s

estimate²
verb
BR ˈestɪmeɪt, -s, -ɪŋ, -ɪd
AM ˈestəˌmeɪ|t, -ts, -dɪŋ, -dɪd

estimation
BR ˌestɪˈmeɪʃn
AM ˌestəˈmeɪʃən

estimative
BR ˈestɪmətɪv
AM ˈestəˌmeɪdɪv, ˈestəmədɪv

estimator
BR ˈestɪmeɪtə(r), -z
AM ˈestəˌmeɪdər, -z

estival
BR iːˈstɪvl, ˈestɪvl, iːˈstʌɪvl, ɛˈstʌɪvl
AM ˈestəvəl

estivate
BR iːˈstɪveɪt, ˈestɪveɪt, -s, -ɪŋ, -ɪd
AM ˈestəˌveɪ|t, -ts, -dɪŋ, -dɪd

estivation
BR ˌiːstɪˈveɪʃn, ˌestɪˈveɪʃn, -z
AM ˌestəˈveɪʃən, -z

estoile
BR ɪˈstɔɪl, ɛˈstɔɪl, -z
AM əˈstɔɪl, ɛˈstɔɪl, -z

Estonia
BR ɛˈstəʊnɪə(r), ɪˈstəʊnɪə(r)
AM ɛˈstoʊnɪə

Estonian
BR ɛˈstəʊnɪən, ɪˈstəʊnɪən, -z
AM ɛˈstoʊnɪən, -z

estop
BR ɪˈstɒp, ɛˈstɒp, -s, -ɪŋ, -t
AM əˈstɑp, ɛˈstɑp, -s, -ɪŋ, -t

estoppage
BR ɪˈstɒpɪdʒ, ɛˈstɒpɪdʒ
AM əˈstɑpɪdʒ, ɛˈstɑpɪdʒ

estoppel
BR ɪˈstɒpl, ɛˈstɒpl
AM əˈstɑpəl, ɛˈstɑpəl

Estoril
BR ˌestəˈrɪl
AM ˌestəˈrɪl
B PORT isˈtoriw
L PORT əʃtuˈril

estovers
BR ɪˈstəʊvəz, ɛˈstəʊvəz
AM əˈstoʊvərz, ɛˈstoʊvərz

estrade
BR ɛˈstrɑːd, ɪˈstrɑːd, -z
AM ɛˈstrɑd, -z

estragon
BR ˈestrəgɒn, ˈestrəg(ə)n
AM ˈestrəˌgɑn

estrange
BR ɪˈstreɪn(d)ʒ, ɛˈstreɪn(d)ʒ, -ɪz, -ɪŋ, -d
AM əˈstreɪndʒ, ɛˈstreɪndʒ, -ɪz, -ɪŋ, -d

estrangement
BR ɪˈstreɪn(d)ʒm(ə)nt, ɪˈstreɪn(d)ʒm(ə)nt, -s
AM əˈstreɪndʒmənt, ɛˈstreɪndʒmənt, -s

estreat
BR ɪˈstriːt, ɛˈstriːt
AM əˈstrit, ɛˈstrit

Estremadura
BR ˌestrəməˈd(j)ʊərə(r), ˌestrəməˈdʒʊərə(r)
AM ˌestrəməˈd(j)ʊrə

estrogen
BR ˈiːstrədʒ(ə)n, ˈestrədʒ(ə)n
AM ˈestrədʒən

estrous
BR ˈiːstrəs, ˈestrəs
AM ˈestrəs

estrus
BR ˈiːstrəs, ˈestrəs
AM ˈestrəs

estuarine
BR ˈestjʊərʌɪn, ˈestjʊərʌɪn, ˈestʃʊərʌɪn
AM ˈestʃəwəˌraɪn, ˈestʃəwərən, ˈestʃəwəˌrin

estuary
BR ˈestjʊr|i, ˈestjʊər|i, ˈestʃʊr|i, -ɪz
AM ˈestʃəˌweri, -z

esurience
BR ɪˈsjʊərɪəns, ɛˈsjʊərɪəns, ɪˈsjɔːrɪəns, ɛˈsjɔːrɪəns, ɪˈsʊərɪəns, ɛˈsʊərɪəns
AM əˈsʊrɪəns, iˈsʊrɪəns

esuriency
BR ɪˈsjʊərɪənsi, ɛˈsjʊərɪənsi, ɪˈsjɔːrɪənsi,

ɛˈsjɔːrɪənsi, ɪˈsʊərɪənsi, ɛˈsʊərɪənsi
AM əˈsʊrɪənsi, iˈsʊrɪənsi

esurient
BR ɪˈsjʊərɪənt, ɛˈsjʊərɪənt, ɪˈsjɔːrɪənt, ɛˈsjɔːrɪənt, ɪˈsʊərɪənt, ɛˈsʊərɪənt
AM əˈsʊrɪənt, iˈsʊrɪənt

esuriently
BR ɪˈsjʊərɪəntli, ɛˈsjʊərɪəntli, ɪˈsjɔːrɪəntli, ɛˈsjɔːrɪəntli, ɪˈsʊərɪəntli, ɛˈsʊərɪəntli
AM əˈsʊrɪən(t)li, iˈsʊrɪən(t)li

ETA
Basque organization
BR ˈetə(r)
AM ˈedə

eta
Greek letter
BR ˈiːtə(r)
AM ˈeɪdə, ˈidə

etaerio
BR ɛˈtɪərɪəʊ, -z
AM ɛˈtɪrioʊ, -z

et al.
BR ˌet ˈal
AM ˌetˈæl, ˌetˈɑl

etalon
BR ˈetəlɒn, -z
AM ˈeɪdlˌɑn, -z

Etam®
BR ˈiːtam
AM ˈidəm

etc
UNIX directory
BR ˈetsi
AM ˈetsi

etc.
BR ˌet ˈset(ə)rə(r)
AM ɛt ˈsedərə

et cetera
BR ˌet ˈset(ə)rə(r)
AM ɛt ˈsedərə

etch
BR etʃ, -ɪz, -ɪŋ, -t
AM etʃ, -əz, -ɪŋ, -t

etchant
BR ˈetʃ(ə)nt, -s
AM ˈetʃənt, -s

etcher
BR ˈetʃə(r), -z
AM ˈetʃər, -z

etching
BR ˈetʃɪŋ, -z
AM ˈetʃɪŋ, -z

eternal
BR ɪˈtəːnl
AM əˈtərnəl, iˈtərnəl

eternalise
BR ɪˈtəːnəlʌɪz, ɪˈtəːnlˌʌɪz, -ɪz, -ɪŋ, -d
AM əˈtərnlˌaɪz, iˈtərnlˌaɪz, -ɪz, -ɪŋ, -d

eternality
BR ɪˌtəːˈnalɪti
AM ˌidərˈnælədi

eternalize
BR ɪˈtəːnəlʌɪz|
ɪˈtəːnlˌʌɪz, -ɪz, -ɪŋ, -d
AM əˈtərnlˌaɪz, iˈtərnlˌaɪz, -ɪz, -ɪŋ, -d

eternally
BR ɪˈtəːnli, ɪˈtəːnəli
AM əˈtərnəli, iˈtərnəli

eternalness
BR ɪˈtəːnlnəs
AM əˈtərnlnəs, iˈtərnlnəs

eternise
BR ɪˈtəːnʌɪz, -ɪz, -ɪŋ, -d
AM əˈtərˌnaɪz, iˈtərˌnaɪz, -ɪz, -ɪŋ, -d

eternity
BR ɪˈtəːnɪt|i, -ɪz
AM əˈtərnədi, iˈtərnədi, -z

eternize
BR ɪˈtəːnʌɪz, -ɪz, -ɪŋ, -d
AM iˈtərˌnaɪz, əˈtərˌnaɪz, -ɪz, -ɪŋ, -d

Etesian
BR ɪˈtiːzɪən, ɪˈtiːʒən, ɪˈtiːʒn
AM əˈtiʒən, iˈtiʒən

eth
BR ɛð, -z
AM ɛð, -z

Ethan
BR ˈiːθn
AM ˈiθən

ethanal
BR ˈeθənal
AM ˈeθəˌnɑl

ethane
BR ˈiːθeɪn, ˈeθeɪn
AM ˈeθˌeɪn

ethanoate
BR ˈiːθeɪnəʊət, ˈeθeɪnəʊət, -s
AM ˈeθənəwət, ɛˈθeɪnəwət, -s

ethanoic
BR ˌeθəˈnəʊɪk
AM ˌeθəˈnoʊɪk

ethanol
BR ˈeθənɒl
AM ˈeθəˌnɔl, ˈeθəˌnɑl

Ethel
BR ˈeθl
AM ˈeθəl

Ethelbert
BR ˈeθlbəːt
AM ˈeθəlˌbərt

Ethelberta
BR ˌeθlˈbəːtə(r), ˈeθlbəːtə(r)
AM ˌeθəlˈbərdə

Ethelburga
BR ˌeθlˈbəːgə(r), ˈeθlbəːgə(r)
AM ˌeθəlˈbərgə

Etheldreda
BR ˌεθl'dri:də(r),
'εθldri:də(r)
AM ˌεθəl'drεdə

Ethelred
BR 'εθlrεd
AM 'εθəlˌrεd

ethene
BR 'i:θi:n, 'εθi:n
AM 'εθin

ether
BR 'i:θə(r)
AM 'iθər

ethereal
BR ɪ'θɪərɪəl
AM ə'θɪriəl, i'θɪriəl,
ε'θɪriəl

etherealise
BR ɪ'θɪərɪəlʌɪz, -ɪz, -ɪŋ,
-d
AM ə'θɪriəˌlaɪz,
i'θɪriəˌlaɪz,
ε'θɪriəˌlaɪz, -ɪz, -ɪŋ, -d

ethereality
BR ɪˌθɪərɪ'alɪti
AM əˌθɪriə'ælədi,
iˌθɪriə'ælədi,
εˌθɪriə'ælədi

etherealize
BR ɪ'θɪərɪəlʌɪz, -ɪz, -ɪŋ,
-d
AM ə'θɪriəˌlaɪz,
i'θɪriəˌlaɪz,
ε'θɪriəˌlaɪz, -ɪz, -ɪŋ, -d

ethereally
BR ɪ'θɪərɪəli
AM ə'θɪriəli, i'θɪriəli,
ε'θɪriəli

Etheredge
BR 'εθ(ə)rɪdʒ
AM 'εθ(ə)rədʒ

etherial
BR ɪ'θɪərɪəl
AM ə'θɪriəl, i'θɪriəl,
ε'θɪriəl

etheric
BR i:'θεrɪk, ɪ'θεrɪk
AM ə'θεrɪk, i'θεrɪk,
ε'θεrɪk

Etheridge
BR 'εθ(ə)rɪdʒ
AM 'εθ(ə)rədʒ

etherisation
BR ˌi:θ(ə)rʌɪ'zeɪʃn
AM ˌiθərə'zeɪʃən,
ˌiθəˌraɪ'zeɪʃən

etherise
BR 'i:θərʌɪz, -ɪz, -ɪŋ, -d
AM 'iθəˌraɪz, -ɪz, -ɪŋ, -d

etherization
BR ˌi:θ(ə)rʌɪ'zeɪʃn
AM ˌiθərə'zeɪʃən,
ˌiθəˌraɪ'zeɪʃən

etherize
BR 'i:θ(ə)rʌɪz, -ɪz, -ɪŋ, -d
AM 'iθəˌraɪz, -ɪz, -ɪŋ, -d

Ethernet
BR 'i:θənεt, -s

ethic
BR 'εθɪk, -s
AM 'εθɪk, -s

ethical
BR 'εθɪkl
AM 'εθəkəl

ethicality
BR ˌεθɪ'kalɪti
AM ˌεθə'kælədi

ethically
BR 'εθɪkli
AM 'εθək(ə)li

ethicise
BR 'εθɪsʌɪz, -ɪz, -ɪŋ, -d
AM 'εθəˌsaɪz, -ɪz, -ɪŋ, -d

ethicist
BR 'εθɪsɪst, -s
AM 'εθəsəst, -s

ethicize
BR 'εθɪsʌɪz, -ɪz, -ɪŋ, -d
AM 'εθəˌsaɪz, -ɪz, -ɪŋ, -d

Ethiopia
BR ˌi:θɪ'əʊpɪə(r)
AM ˌiθi'oʊpiə

Ethiopian
BR ˌi:θɪ'əʊpɪən, -z
AM ˌiθi'oʊpiən, -z

Ethiopic
BR ˌi:θɪ'əʊpɪk,
ˌi:θɪ'ɒpɪk
AM ˌiθi'apɪk, ˌiθi'oʊpɪk

ethmoid
BR 'εθmɔɪd, -z
AM 'εˌθmɔɪd, -z

ethmoidal
BR εθ'mɔɪdl
AM ˌεθ'mɔɪdəl

ethnarch
BR 'εθnɑ:k, -s
AM 'εˌθnɑrk, -s

ethnarchy
BR 'εθnɑ:kʃi, -ɪz
AM 'εˌθnɑrki, -z

Ethne
BR 'εθni
AM 'εθni

ethnic
BR 'εθnɪk
AM 'εθnɪk

ethnical
BR 'εθnɪkl
AM 'εθnəkəl

ethnically
BR 'εθnɪkli
AM 'εθnək(ə)li

ethnicity
BR εθ'nɪsɪti
AM εθ'nɪsɪdi

**ethnoarchaeo-
logical**
BR ˌεθnəʊˌɑ:kɪə'lɒdʒɪkl
AM ˌεθnoʊˌɑrkiə'lɑdʒ-
əkəl

**ethnoarchaeolo-
gist**
BR ˌεθnəʊˌɑ:kɪ'ɒlədʒɪst,
-s
AM ˌεθnoʊˌɑrki'ɑlədʒəst,
-s

ethnoarchaeology
BR ˌεθnəʊˌɑ:kɪ'ɒlədʒi
AM ˌεθnoʊˌɑrki'ɑlədʒi

ethnocentric
BR ˌεθnə(ʊ)'sεntrɪk
AM ˌεθnoʊ'sεntrɪk

ethnocentrically
BR ˌεθnə(ʊ)'sεntrɪkli
AM ˌεθnoʊ'sεntrək(ə)li

ethnocentricity
BR ˌεθnə(ʊ)sεn'trɪsɪti
AM ˌεθnoʊˌsεn'trɪsɪdi

ethnocentrism
BR ˌεθnə(ʊ)'sεntrɪz(ə)m
AM ˌεθnoʊ'sεnˌtrɪzəm

ethnographer
BR εθ'nɒgrəfə(r), -z
AM εθ'nɑgrəfər, -z

ethnographic
BR ˌεθnə'grafɪk
AM ˌεθnə'græfɪk

ethnographical
BR ˌεθnə'grafɪkl
AM ˌεθnə'græfɪkl

ethnographically
BR ˌεθnə'grafɪkli
AM ˌεθnə'græfək(ə)li

ethnography
BR εθ'nɒgrəfi
AM εθ'nɑgrəfi

ethnohistory
BR ˌεθnəʊ'hɪst(ə)ri
AM ˌεθnoʊ'hɪst(ə)ri

ethnologic
BR ˌεθnə'lɒdʒɪk
AM ˌεθnə'lɑdʒɪk

ethnological
BR ˌεθnə'lɒdʒɪkl
AM ˌεθnə'lɑdʒəkəl

ethnologically
BR ˌεθnə'lɒdʒɪkli
AM ˌεθnə'lɑdʒək(ə)li

ethnologist
BR εθ'nɒlədʒɪst, -s
AM εθ'nɑlədʒəst, -s

ethnology
BR εθ'nɒlədʒi
AM εθ'nɑlədʒi

**ethnomethodo-
logical**
BR ˌεθnəʊˌmεθədə'lɒdʒ-
ɪkl
AM ˌεθnoʊˌmεθədə'lɑdʒ-
əkəl

**ethnomethodolo-
gist**
BR ˌεθnəʊˌmεθə'dɒlə-
dʒɪst, -s
AM ˌεθnoʊˌmεθə'dɑlə-
dʒəst, -s

ethnomethodology
BR ˌεθnəʊˌmεθə'dɒlədʒi

ethnomusicologi
AM ˌεθnoʊˌmεθə'dɑlədʒi

ethnomusicologist
BR ˌεθnəʊˌmju:zɪ'kɒlə-
dʒɪst, -s
AM ˌεθnoʊˌmjuzə'kɑlə-
dʒəst, -s

ethnomusicology
BR ˌεθnəʊˌmju:zɪ'kɒl-
ədʒi
AM ˌεθnoʊˌmjuzə'kɑl-
ədʒi

ethogram
BR 'i:θəgram, -z
AM 'iθəˌgræm,
'εθəˌgræm, -z

ethological
BR ˌi:θə'lɒdʒɪkl
AM ˌiθə'lɑdʒəkəl,
ˌεθə'lɑdʒəkəl

ethologically
BR ˌi:θə'lɒdʒɪkli
AM ˌiθə'lɑdʒək(ə)li,
ˌεθə'lɑdʒək(ə)li

ethologist
BR i:'θɒlədʒɪst, -s
AM i'θɑlədʒəst,
ε'θɑlədʒəst, -s

ethology
BR i:'θɒlədʒi
AM i'θɑlədʒi, ε'θɑlədʒi

ethos
BR 'i:θɒs
AM 'iθas

ethoxyethane
BR ɪˌθɒksɪ'i:θeɪn,
ɪˌθɒksɪ'εθeɪn
AM əˌθaksi'εθˌem

ethyl
BR 'εθ(ɪ)l, 'εθʌɪl, 'i:θʌɪl
AM 'εθəl

ethylene
BR 'εθɪli:n, 'εθβli:n
AM 'εθəˌlin

ethylenic
BR ˌεθɪ'lεnɪk
AM ˌεθə'lεnɪk

Etienne
BR ˌεti'εn
AM ˌeɪdi'εn, ˌer'tiεn

etiolate
BR 'i:tɪə(ʊ)leɪt
AM 'idiəˌleɪt, i'tiəˌleɪt

etiolation
BR ˌi:tɪə(ʊ)'leɪʃn
AM ˌidiə'leɪʃən

etiologic
BR ˌi:tɪə'lɒdʒɪk,
ˌεtɪə'lɒdʒɪk
AM ˌidiə'lɑdʒɪk,
ˌεdiə'lɑdʒɪk

etiological
BR ˌi:tɪə'lɒdʒɪkl,
ˌεtɪə'lɒdʒɪkl
AM ˌidiə'lɑdʒəkəl,
ˌεdiə'lɑdʒəkəl

etiologically
BR ˌi:tɪə'lɒdʒɪkli,
ˌεtɪə'lɒdʒɪkli

AM ˌidiəˈlɑdʒək(ə)li, ˌɛdiəˈlɑdʒək(ə)li

etiology
BR ˌiːtɪˈɒlədʒi, ˌɛtɪˈɒlədʒi
AM ˌidiˈɑlədʒi, ˌɛdiˈɑlədʒi

etiquette
BR ˈɛtɪkɛt, ˈɛtɪkət
AM ˈɛdəkət

Etive
BR ˈɛtɪv
AM ˈɛdɪv

Etna
BR ˈɛtnə(r)
AM ˈɛtnə

Eton
BR ˈiːtn
AM ˈitn

Etonian
BR iːˈtəʊnɪən, -z
AM iˈtoʊniən, -z

étouffée
BR ˌeɪtuːˈfeɪ, -z
AM ˌeɪtuˈfeɪ, -z

Etruria
BR ɪˈtrʊərɪə(r)
AM əˈtrʊriə

Etruscan
BR ɪˈtrʌsk(ə)n, -z
AM əˈtrəskən, -z

Etruscology
BR ɪˌtrʌsˈkɒlədʒi
AM əˌtrəsˈkɑlədʒi

Ettrick
BR ˈɛtrɪk
AM ˈɛtrək

étude
BR eɪˈt(j)uːd, eɪˈtʃuːd, ˈeɪt(j)uːd, ˈeɪtʃuːd, -z
AM eɪˈt(j)ud, -z

etyma
BR ˈɛtɪmə(r)
AM ˈɛdəmə

etymologic
BR ˌɛtɪməˈlɒdʒɪk
AM ˌɛdəməˈlɑdʒɪk

etymological
BR ˌɛtɪməˈlɒdʒɪkl
AM ˌɛdəməˈlɑdʒəkəl

etymologically
BR ˌɛtɪməˈlɒdʒɪkli
AM ˌɛdəməˈlɑdʒək(ə)li

etymologise
BR ˌɛtɪˈmɒlədʒʌɪz, -ɪz, -ɪŋ, -d
AM ˌɛdəˈmɑləˌdʒaɪz, -ɪz, -ɪŋ, -d

etymologist
BR ˌɛtɪˈmɒlədʒɪst, -s
AM ˌɛdəˈmɑlədʒəst, -s

etymologize
BR ˌɛtɪˈmɒlədʒʌɪz, -ɪz, -ɪŋ, -d
AM ˌɛdəˈmɑləˌdʒaɪz, -ɪz, -ɪŋ, -d

etymology
BR ˌɛtɪˈmɒlədʒ|i, -ɪz
AM ˌɛdəˈmɑlədʒi, -z

etymon
BR ˈɛtɪmɒn, ˈɛtɪmən, -z
AM ˈɛdəˌmɑn, -z

Euan
BR ˈjuːən
AM ˈjʊən

eubacteria
BR ˌjuːbakˈtɪərɪə(r)
AM ˌjubækˈtɪriə

eubacterium
BR ˌjuːbakˈtɪərɪəm
AM ˌjubækˈtɪriəm

Euboea
BR juːˈbiːə(r), jʊˈbiːə(r)
AM juˈbiə

eucalypt
BR ˈjuːkəlɪpt, -s
AM ˈjukəˌlɪpt, -s

eucalyptus
BR ˌjuːkəˈlɪptəs, -ɪz
AM ˌjukəˈlɪptəs, -əz

eucaryote
BR juːˈkarɪət, juːˈkarɪɒt
AM juˈkɛriˌoʊt

eucaryotic
BR ˌjuːkarɪˈɒtɪk
AM ˌjukɛriˈɑdɪk

eucharis
BR ˈjuːkərɪs, -ɪz
AM ˈjuk(ə)rəs, -əz

Eucharist
BR ˈjuːkərɪst
AM ˈjuk(ə)rəst

eucharist
BR ˈjuːkərɪst, -s
AM ˈjuk(ə)rəst, -s

eucharistic
BR ˌjuːkəˈrɪstɪk
AM ˌjukəˈrɪstɪk

Eucharistical
BR ˌjuːkəˈrɪstɪkl
AM ˌjukəˈrɪstəkəl

euchre
BR ˈjuːkə(r)
AM ˈjukər

Euclid
BR ˈjuːklɪd
AM ˈjuˌklɪd

Euclidean
BR juːˈklɪdɪən
AM juˈklɪdiən

euclidean
BR juːˈklɪdɪən
AM juˈklɪdiən

euclidian
BR juːˈklɪdɪən
AM juˈklɪdiən

eudaemonic
BR ˌjuːdiːˈmɒnɪk, ˌjuːdɪˈmɒnɪk
AM ˌjudəˈmɑnɪk

eudaemonism
BR juːˈdiːmənɪz(ə)m
AM juˈdiməˌnɪzəm

eudaemonist
BR juːˈdiːmənɪst, -s
AM juˈdimənəst, -s

eudaemonistic
BR juːˌdiːməˈnɪstɪk
AM juˌdiməˈnɪstɪk

eudemonic
BR ˌjuːdiːˈmɒnɪk, ˌjuːdɪˈmɒnɪk
AM ˌjudəˈmɑnɪk

eudemonism
BR juːˈdiːmənɪz(ə)m
AM juˈdiməˌnɪzəm

eudemonist
BR juːˈdiːmənɪst, -s
AM juˈdimənəst, -s

eudemonistic
BR juːˌdiːməˈnɪstɪk
AM juˌdiməˈnɪstɪk

eudiometer
BR ˌjuːdɪˈɒmɪtə(r), -z
AM ˌjudiˈɑmədər, -z

eudiometric
BR ˌjuːdɪə(ʊ)ˈmɛtrɪk
AM ˌjudioʊˈmɛtrɪk

eudiometrical
BR ˌjuːdɪə(ʊ)ˈmɛtrɪkl
AM ˌjudioʊˈmɛtrəkəl

eudiometry
BR ˌjuːdɪˈɒmɪtri
AM ˌjudiˈɑmətri

Eudora
BR jʊˈdɔːrə(r)
AM juˈdɔrə

Euen
BR ˈjuːən
AM ˈjuən

Eugene
BR ˈjuːdʒiːn, juːˈdʒiːn
AM ˈjuˌdʒin

Eugene Onegin
BR ˌjuːdʒiːn ɒˈneɪɡɪn, juːˈdʒiːn
AM ˈjuˌdʒin oʊˈnɛɡɪn

Eugenia
BR juːˈdʒiːnɪə(r)
AM ˌjuˈdʒiniə

eugenic
BR juːˈdʒɛnɪk, -s
AM juˈdʒɛnɪk, -s

eugenically
BR juːˈdʒɛnɪkli
AM juˈdʒɛnək(ə)li

eugenicist
BR juːˈdʒɛnɪsɪst, -s
AM juˈdʒɛnəsəst, -s

Eugénie
BR juːˈʒeɪni
AM juˌʒeɪˈni

eugenist
BR juːˈdʒɛnɪst, -s
AM juˈdʒɛnəst, -s

euglena
BR juːˈɡliːnə(r), -z
AM juˈɡlinə, -z

euhemerism
BR juːˈhiːmərɪz(ə)m
AM juˈhiməˌrɪzəm

eukaryote
BR juːˈkarɪət, juːˈkarɪɒt
AM juˈkɛriˌoʊt

eukaryotic
BR ˌjuːkarɪˈɒtɪk
AM ˌjukɛriˈɑdɪk

Eulalia
BR juːˈleɪlɪə(r)
AM uˈleɪljə, uˈleɪliə

Euler
BR ˈɔɪlə(r), ˈjuːlə(r)
AM ˈɔɪlər

eulogia
BR juːˈləʊdʒɪə(r)
AM juˈloʊdʒiə

eulogise
BR ˈjuːlədʒʌɪz, -ɪz, -ɪŋ, -d
AM ˈjuləˌdʒaɪz, -ɪz, -ɪŋ, -d

eulogist
BR ˈjuːlədʒɪst, -s
AM ˈjulədʒəst, -s

eulogistic
BR ˌjuːləˈdʒɪstɪk
AM ˌjuləˈdʒɪstɪk

eulogistically
BR ˌjuːləˈdʒɪstɪkli
AM ˈjuləˈdʒɪstək(ə)li

eulogium
BR juːˈləʊdʒɪəm, -z
AM juˈloʊdʒiəm, -z

eulogize
BR ˈjuːlədʒʌɪz, -ɪz, -ɪŋ, -d
AM ˈjuləˌdʒaɪz, -ɪz, -ɪŋ, -d

eulogy
BR ˈjuːlədʒ|i, -ɪz
AM ˈjulədʒi, -z

Eumenides
BR juːˈmɛnɪdiːz
AM juˈmɛnəˌdiz

Eunice
BR ˈjuːnɪs
AM ˈjunəs

eunuch
BR ˈjuːnək, -s
AM ˈjunək, -s

eunuchoid
BR ˈjuːnəkɔɪd
AM ˈjunəˌkɔɪd

euonymus
BR juːˈɒnɪməs
AM juˈɑnəməs

eupeptic
BR juːˈpɛptɪk
AM juˈpɛptɪk

Euphemia
BR juːˈfiːmɪə(r)
AM juˈfimiə

euphemise
BR ˈjuːfɪmʌɪz, -ɪz, -ɪŋ, -d
AM ˈjufəˌmaɪz, -ɪz, -ɪŋ,
-d

euphemism
BR ˈjuːfɪmɪz(ə)m, -z
AM ˈjufəˌmɪzəm,
ˈjufɱɪzəm, -z

euphemist
BR ˈjuːfɪmɪst, -s
AM ˈjufəməst, -s

euphemistic
BR ˌjuːfɪˈmɪstɪk
AM ˌjufəˈmɪstɪk,
ˌjufɱɪstɪk

euphemistically
BR ˌjuːfɪˈmɪstɪkli
AM ˌjufəˈmɪstək(ə)li,
ˌjufɱˈɪstək(ə)li

euphemize
BR ˈjuːfɪmʌɪz, -ɪz, -ɪŋ, -d
AM ˈjufəˌmaɪz, -ɪz, -ɪŋ,
-d

euphonic
BR juːˈfɒnɪk
AM juˈfɑnɪk

euphonious
BR juːˈfəʊnɪəs
AM juˈfoʊnɪəs,
juˈfoʊnjəs

euphoniously
BR juːˈfəʊnɪəsli
AM juˈfoʊnɪəsli,
juˈfoʊnjəsli

euphonise
BR ˈjuːfənʌɪz, ˈjuːfɱʌɪz,
-ɪz, -ɪŋ, -d
AM ˈjufəˌnaɪz, -ɪz, -ɪŋ, -d

euphonium
BR juːˈfəʊnɪəm, -z
AM juˈfoʊnɪəm, -z

euphonize
BR ˈjuːfənʌɪz, ˈjuːfɱʌɪz,
-ɪz, -ɪŋ, -d
AM ˈjufəˌnaɪz, -ɪz, -ɪŋ, -d

euphony
BR ˈjuːfəni, ˈjuːfɱi
AM ˈjufəni

euphorbia
BR juːˈfɔːbɪə(r), -z
AM juˈfɔrbɪə, -z

euphoria
BR juːˈfɔːrɪə(r)
AM juˈfɔrɪə

euphoriant
BR juːˈfɔːrɪənt, -s
AM juˈfɔrɪənt, -s

euphoric
BR juːˈfɒrɪk
AM juˈfɔrɪk

euphorically
BR juːˈfɒrɪkli
AM juˈfɔrək(ə)li

euphrasy
BR ˈjuːfrəʒli, -ɪz
AM ˈjufrəsi, -z

Euphrates
BR juːˈfreɪtiːz

Euphues
AM juːˈfreɪdiz
BR ˈjuːfjuːz
AM ˈjuˌfjuiz

euphuism
BR ˈjuːfjʊɪz(ə)m
AM ˈjufjəˌwɪzəm

euphuist
BR ˈjuːfjʊɪst, -s
AM ˈjufjəˌwəst, -s

euphuistic
BR ˌjuːfjʊˈɪstɪk
AM ˌjufjəˈwɪstɪk

euphuistically
BR ˌjuːfjʊˈɪstɪkli
AM ˌjufjəˈwɪstək(ə)li

euploid
BR ˈjuːplɔɪd, -z
AM ˈjuˌplɔɪd, -z

Eurasian
BR jʊˈreɪʒn, jʊˈreɪʃn,
-z
AM jərˈeɪʒən,
jʊrˈeɪʒən, jərˈeɪʃən,
jʊrˈeɪʃən, -z

Euratom
BR jʊrˈatəm
AM jərˈædəm,
jʊrˈædəm

eureka
BR jʊˈriːkə(r)
AM jəˈrikə, juˈrikə

eurhythmic
BR jʊˈrɪðmɪk, -s
AM juˈrɪðmɪk, -s

Euripides
BR jʊˈrɪpɪdiːz
AM jəˈrɪpəˌdiz,
juˈrɪpəˌdiz

Euro-
BR ˈjʊərə(ʊ), ˈjɔːrə(ʊ)
AM ˈjərou, ˈjərə, ˈjurou,
ˈjurə

euro
BR ˈjʊərə(ʊ), ˈjɔːrəʊ, -z
AM ˈjərou, ˈjurou, -z

Eurobond
BR ˈjʊərə(ʊ)bɒnd,
ˈjɔːrə(ʊ)bɒnd, -z
AM ˈjərouˌband,
ˈjərəˌband,
ˈjurouˌband, -z

Eurocentric
BR ˌjʊərəʊˈsɛntrɪk,
ˌjɔːrəʊˈsɛntrɪk
AM ˌjərouˈsɛntrɪk,
ˌjurouˈsɛntrɪk

Eurocentrism
BR ˌjʊərəʊˈsɛntrɪz(ə)m,
ˌjɔːrəʊˈsɛntrɪz(ə)m
AM ˌjərouˈsɛnˌtrɪzəm,
ˌjurouˈsɛnˌtrɪzəm

Eurocheque
BR ˈjʊərəʊtʃɛk,
ˈjɔːrəʊtʃɛk, -s
AM ˈjərouˌtʃɛk,
ˈjərəˌtʃɛk,

ˈjʊrəʊˌtʃɛk,
ˈjʊrəˌtʃɛk, -s

Eurocommunism
BR ˌjʊərəʊˈkɒmjʊn-
ɪz(ə)m,
ˌjɔːrəʊˈkɒmjʊnɪz(ə)m
AM ˌjərouˈkamjəˌnɪzəm,
ˌjurouˈkamjəˌnɪzəm

Eurocommunist
BR ˌjʊərəʊˈkɒmjʊnɪst,
ˌjɔːrəʊˈkɒmjʊnɪst, -s
AM ˌjərouˈkamjənəst,
ˌjurouˈkamjənəst, -s

Eurocrat
BR ˈjʊərə(ʊ)krat,
ˈjɔːrə(ʊ)krat, -s
AM ˈjərəˌkræt,
ˈjurəˌkræt, -s

Euro-currency
BR ˈjʊərəʊˌkʌrənsi,
ˈjʊərəʊˌkʌrnsi,
ˈjɔːrəʊˌkʌrənsi,
ˈjɔːrəʊˌkʌrnsi
AM ˈjərouˌkərənsi,
ˈjurouˌkərənsi

Eurodollar
BR ˈjʊərə(ʊ)ˌdɒlə(r),
ˈjɔːrə(ʊ)ˌdɒlə(r), -z
AM ˈjərouˌdalər,
ˈjurouˌdalər, -z

Euro-election
BR ˈjʊərəʊɪˌlɛkʃn,
ˈjɔːrəʊɪˌlɛkʃn, -z
AM ˈjərouəˈlɛkʃən,
ˈjurouəˈlɛkʃən, -z

Euromarket
BR ˈjʊərəʊˌmaːkɪt,
ˈjɔːrəʊˌmaːkɪt, -s
AM ˈjərouˌmarkət,
ˈjurouˌmarkət, -s

Europa
BR jʊˈrəʊpə(r)
AM juˈroupə

Europarliament
BR ˈjʊərəʊˌpaːləm(ə)nt,
ˈjɔːrəʊˌpaːləm(ə)nt
AM ˈjərouˌparləmənt,
ˈjurouˌparləmənt

**Europarliamen-
tarian**
BR ˌjʊərəʊˌpaːləm(ə)n-
ˈtɛːrɪən,
ˌjɔːrəʊˌpaːləm(ə)n-
ˈtɛːrɪən, -z
AM ˌjərouˌparləmən-
ˈtɛrɪən,
ˌjurouˌparləmən-
ˈtɛrɪən, -z

**Europarliamen-
tary**
BR ˌjʊərəʊˌpaːləˈmɛnt-
(ə)ri,
ˌjɔːrəʊˌpaːləˈmɛnt(ə)ri
AM ˌjərouˌparləˈmɛn-
(t)əri,
ˌjurouˌparləˈmɛn(t)əri

Europe
BR ˈjʊərəp, ˈjɔːrəp

AM ˈjərəp, ˈjurəp

European
BR ˌjʊərəˈpiːən,
ˌjɔːrəˈpiːən, -z
AM ˌjərəˈpiən,
ˌjurəˈpiən, -z

Europeanisation
BR ˌjʊərəpiːənʌɪˈzeɪʃn,
ˌjɔːrəpiːənʌɪˈzeɪʃn
AM ˌjərəˌpiənəˈzeɪʃən,
ˌjurəˌpiənəˈzeɪʃən,
ˌjərəˌpiəˌnaɪˈzeɪʃən,
ˌjurəˌpiəˌnaɪˈzeɪʃən

Europeanise
BR ˌjʊərəˈpiːənʌɪz,
ˌjɔːrəˈpiːənʌɪz, -ɪz, -ɪŋ,
-d
AM ˌjərəˈpiəˌnaɪz,
ˌjurəˈpiəˌnaɪz, -ɪz, -ɪŋ,
-d

Europeanism
BR ˌjʊərəˈpiːənɪz(ə)m,
ˌjɔːrəˈpiːənɪz(ə)m
AM ˌjərəˈpiəˌnɪzəm,
ˌjurəˈpiəˌnɪzəm

Europeanization
BR ˌjʊərəpiːənʌɪˈzeɪʃn,
ˌjɔːrəpiːənʌɪˈzeɪʃn
AM ˌjərəˌpiənəˈzeɪʃən,
ˌjurəˌpiənəˈzeɪʃən,
ˌjərəˌpiəˌnaɪˈzeɪʃən,
ˌjurəˌpiəˌnaɪˈzeɪʃən

Europeanize
BR ˌjʊərəˈpiːənʌɪz,
ˌjɔːrəˈpiːənʌɪz, -ɪz, -ɪŋ,
-d
AM ˌjərəˈpiəˌnaɪz,
ˌjurəˈpiəˌnaɪz, -ɪz, -ɪŋ,
-d

Europhile
BR ˈjʊərə(ʊ)fʌɪl,
ˈjɔːrə(ʊ)fʌɪl, -z
AM ˈjərəˌfaɪl, ˈjurəˌfaɪl,
-z

europium
BR jʊˈrəʊpɪəm
AM jəˈroupɪəm,
juˈroupɪəm

Europort
BR ˈjʊərəʊpɔːt,
ˈjɔːrəʊpɔːt
AM ˈjərouˌpɔ(ə)rt,
ˈjurouˌpɔ(ə)rt

Eurotunnel
BR ˈjʊərəʊˌtʌnl,
ˈjɔːrəʊˌtʌnl
AM ˈjərouˌtənəl,
ˈjurouˌtənəl

Eurovision
BR ˈjʊərəvɪʒn,
ˈjɔːrəvɪʒn
AM ˈjərouˌvɪʒən,
ˈjurouˌvɪʒən

Eurydice
BR jʊˈrɪdɪsi, jʊˈrɪdɪsiː,
jʊərˈdiːtʃi,
jʊərɪˈdiːtʃeɪ
AM jəˈrɪdəsi, jəˈrɪdətʃi

eurythmic
BR jəˈrɪðmɪk, -s
AM juˈrɪðmɪk, -s

Eusebius
BR juːˈsiːbɪəs
AM juˈseɪbɪəs

Eustace
BR ˈjuːstəs
AM ˈjustəs

eustachian
BR juːˈsteɪʃn
AM juˈsteɪʃ(i)ən

eustacy
BR ˈjuːstəsi
AM ˈjustəsi

eustasy
BR ˈjuːstəsi
AM ˈjustəsi

eustatic
BR juːˈstatɪk
AM juˈstædɪk

Euston
BR ˈjuːst(ə)n
AM ˈjustən

eutectic
BR juːˈtɛktɪk, -s
AM juˈtɛktɪk, -s

Euterpe
BR juːˈtəːpi
AM juˈtərpi

euthanasia
BR ˌjuːθəˈneɪzɪə(r),
ˌjuːθəˈneɪʒə(r)
AM ˌjuθəˈneɪʒ(i)ə,
ˌjuθəˈneɪziə

eutherian
BR juːˈθɪərɪən, -z
AM juˈθɪrɪən, -z

eutrophic
BR juːˈtrɒfɪk,
juːˈtrəʊfɪk
AM juˈtrɑfɪk

eutrophicate
BR juːˈtrəʊfɪkeɪt,
juːˈtrɒfɪkeɪt, -s, -ɪŋ, -ɪd
AM juˈtrɑfəˌkeɪt, -ts,
-dɪŋ, -dɪd

eutrophication
BR ˌjuːtrə(ʊ)fɪˈkeɪʃn
AM juˌtrɑfəˈkeɪʃən

eutrophy
BR ˈjuːtrəfi
AM ˈjutrəfi

Euxine
BR ˈjuːksʌɪn
AM ˈjʊksən, ˈjʊkˌsaɪn

Eva
BR ˈiːvə(r)
AM ˈivə

evacuant
BR ɪˈvakjʊənt, -s
AM əˈvækjəwənt,
iˈvækjəwənt, -s

evacuate
BR ɪˈvakjʊeɪt, -s, -ɪŋ, -ɪd
AM əˈvækjəˌweɪ|t,
iˈvækjəˌweɪ|t, -ts, -dɪŋ,
-dɪd

evacuation
BR ɪˌvakjʊˈeɪ|ʃn, -z
AM əˌvækjəˈweɪʃən,
iˌvækjəˈweɪʃən, -z

evacuative
BR ɪˈvakjʊətɪv
AM əˈvækjəˌweɪdɪv,
iˈvækjəˌweɪdɪv

evacuator
BR ɪˈvakjʊeɪtə(r), -z
AM əˈvækjəˌweɪdər,
iˈvækjəˌweɪdər, -z

evacuee
BR ɪˌvakjʊˈiː, -z
AM əˌvækjəˈwi,
iˌvækjəˈwi, -z

evadable
BR ɪˈveɪdəbl
AM əˈveɪdəbəl,
iˈveɪdəbəl

evade
BR ɪˈveɪd, -z, -ɪŋ, -ɪd
AM əˈveɪd, iˈveɪd, -z, -ɪŋ,
-ɪd

evader
BR ɪˈveɪdə(r), -z
AM əˈveɪdər, iˈveɪdər,
-z

Evadne
BR ɪˈvadni
AM əˈvædni, iˈvædni

evaginate
BR ɪˈvadʒɪneɪt, -s, -ɪŋ,
-ɪd
AM əˈvædʒəˌneɪ|t,
iˈvædʒəˌneɪ|t, -ts, -dɪŋ,
-dɪd

evagination
BR ɪˌvadʒɪˈneɪʃn
AM əˌvædʒəˈneɪʃən,
iˌvædʒəˈneɪʃən

evaluate
BR ɪˈvaljʊeɪt, -s, -ɪŋ, -ɪd
AM əˈvæljəˌweɪ|t,
iˈvæljəˌweɪ|t, -ts, -dɪŋ,
-dɪd

evaluation
BR ɪˌvaljʊˈeɪʃn, -z
AM əˌvæljəˈweɪʃən,
iˌvæljəˈweɪʃən, -z

evaluative
BR ɪˈvaljʊətɪv
AM əˈvæljəˌweɪdɪv,
iˈvæljəˌweɪdɪv

evaluator
BR ɪˈvaljʊeɪtə(r), -z
AM əˈvæljəˌweɪdər,
iˈvæljəˌweɪdər, -z

Evan
BR ˈɛvn
AM ˈɛvən

evanesce
BR ˌɛvəˈnɛs, -ɪz, -ɪŋ, -t
AM ˌɛvəˈnɛs, -əz, -ɪŋ, -t

evanescence
BR ˌɛvəˈnɛsns
AM ˌɛvəˈnɛsəns

evanescent
BR ˌɛvəˈnɛsnt
AM ˌɛvəˈnɛsənt

evanescently
BR ˌɛvəˈnɛsntli
AM ˌɛvəˈnɛsn(t)li

evangel
BR iːˈvan(d)ʒ(ə)l, -z
AM iˈvændʒəl,
ɛˈvændʒəl, -z

evangelic
BR ˌiːvanˈdʒɛlɪk
AM ˌiːvænˈdʒɛlɪk,
ˌɛvənˈdʒɛlɪk

evangelical
BR ˌiːvanˈdʒɛlɪkl, -z
AM ˌiːvænˈdʒɛləkəl,
ˌɛvənˈdʒɛləkəl, -z

evangelicalism
BR ˌiːvanˈdʒɛlɪkəl-
ɪz(ə)m,
ˌiːvanˈdʒɛlɪkˌlɪz(ə)m
AM ˌiːvænˈdʒɛləkə-
ˌlɪzəm,
ˌɛvənˈdʒɛləkəˌlɪzəm

evangelically
BR ˌiːvanˈdʒɛlɪkli
AM ˌiːvænˈdʒɛlək(ə)li,
ˌɛvənˈdʒɛlək(ə)li

Evangeline
BR ɪˈvan(d)ʒəliːn
AM əˈvændʒəˌlaɪn

evangelisation
BR ɪˌvan(d)ʒəlʌɪˈzeɪʃn,
ɪˌvan(d)ʒlʌɪˈzeɪʃn
AM əˌvændʒələˈzeɪʃən,
iˌvændʒələˈzeɪʃən,
əˌvændʒəˌlaɪˈzeɪʃən,
iˌvændʒəˌlaɪˈzeɪʃən

evangelise
BR ɪˈvan(d)ʒəlʌɪz,
ɪˈvan(d)ʒlʌɪz, -ɪz, -ɪŋ,
-d
AM əˈvændʒəˌlaɪz,
iˈvændʒəˌlaɪz, -ɪz, -ɪŋ,
-d

evangeliser
BR ɪˈvan(d)ʒəlʌɪzə(r),
ɪˈvan(d)ʒlʌɪzə(r), -z
AM əˈvændʒəˌlaɪzər,
iˈvændʒəˌlaɪzər, -z

evangelism
BR ɪˈvan(d)ʒəlɪz(ə)m,
ɪˈvan(d)ʒlɪz(ə)m
AM əˈvændʒəˌlɪzəm,
iˈvændʒəˌlɪzəm

evangelist
BR ɪˈvan(d)ʒəlɪst,
ɪˈvan(d)ʒlɪst, -s
AM əˈvændʒələst,
iˈvændʒələst, -s

evangelistic
BR ɪˌvan(d)ʒəˈlɪstɪk,
ɪˌvan(d)ʒlˈɪstɪk
AM əˌvændʒəˈlɪstɪk,
iˌvændʒəˈlɪstɪk

evangelistically
BR ɪˌvan(d)ʒəˈlɪstɪkli,
ɪˌvan(d)ʒlˈɪstɪkli
AM əˌvændʒəˈlɪstək(ə)li,
iˈvændʒəˈlɪstək(ə)li

evangelization
BR ɪˌvan(d)ʒəlʌɪˈzeɪʃn,
ɪˌvan(d)ʒlʌɪˈzeɪʃn
AM əˌvændʒələˈzeɪʃən,
iˌvændʒələˈzeɪʃən,
əˌvændʒəˌlaɪˈzeɪʃən,
iˌvændʒəˌlaɪˈzeɪʃən

evangelize
BR ɪˈvan(d)ʒəlʌɪz,
ɪˈvan(d)ʒlʌɪz, -ɪz, -ɪŋ,
-d
AM əˈvændʒəˌlaɪz,
iˈvændʒəˌlaɪz, -ɪz, -ɪŋ,
-d

evangelizer
BR ɪˈvan(d)ʒəlʌɪzə(r),
ɪˈvan(d)ʒlʌɪzə(r), -z
AM əˈvændʒəˌlaɪzər,
iˈvændʒəˌlaɪzər, -z

Evans
BR ˈɛvnz
AM ˈɛvənz

evaporable
BR ɪˈvap(ə)rəbl
AM əˈvæpərəbəl,
iˈvæpərəbəl

evaporate
BR ɪˈvapəreɪt, -s, -ɪŋ, -ɪd
AM əˈvæpəˌreɪ|t,
iˈvæpəˌreɪ|t, -ts, -dɪŋ,
-dɪd

evaporation
BR ɪˌvapəˈreɪʃn
AM əˌvæpəˈreɪʃən,
iˌvæpəˈreɪʃən

evaporative
BR ɪˈvap(ə)rətɪv
AM əˈvæpəˌreɪdɪv,
iˈvæpəˌreɪdɪv

evaporator
BR ɪˈvapəreɪtə(r), -z
AM əˈvæpəˌreɪdər,
iˈvæpəˌreɪdər, -z

evasion
BR ɪˈveɪʒn, -z
AM əˈveɪʒən, iˈveɪʒən,
-z

evasive
BR ɪˈveɪsɪv
AM əˈveɪsɪv, iˈveɪsɪv

evasively
BR ɪˈveɪsɪvli
AM əˈveɪsɪvli,
iˈveɪsɪvli

evasiveness
BR ɪˈveɪsɪvnɪs
AM əˈveɪsɪvnɪs,
iˈveɪsɪvnɪs

eve
BR iːv, -z
AM iv, -z

evection
BR ɪˈvɛkʃn

AM ə'vɛkʃən, ɪ'vɛkʃən
Evelyn
BR 'i:vlɪn, 'ɛvlɪn
AM 'ɛv(ə)lən
even
BR 'i:vn, -z
AM 'ivən, -z
evening
BR 'i:vnɪŋ, -z
AM 'iv(ə)nɪŋ, -z
Evenlode
BR 'i:vnləʊd
AM 'ivən,loʊd
evenly
BR 'i:vnli
AM 'ivənli
evenness
BR 'i:vnnəs
AM 'ivə(n)nəs
evensong
BR 'i:vnsɒŋ
AM 'ivən,sɔŋ, 'ivən,sɑŋ
event
BR ɪ'vɛnt, -s, -ɪŋ, -ɪd
AM ə'vɛn|t, ɪ'vɛn|t, -ts, -(t)ɪŋ, -(t)əd
eventer
BR ɪ'vɛntə(r), -z
AM ə'vɛn(t)ər, ɪ'vɛn(t)ər, -z
eventful
BR ɪ'vɛntf(ʊ)l
AM ə'vɛntfəl, ɪ'vɛntfəl
eventfully
BR ɪ'vɛntfʊli, ɪ'vɛntfʃi
AM ə'vɛntfəli, ɪ'vɛntfəli
eventfulness
BR ɪ'vɛntf(ʊ)lnəs
AM ə'vɛntfəlnəs, ɪ'vɛntfəlnəs
eventide
BR i:vntʌɪd, -z
AM 'ivən,taɪd, -z
eventless
BR ɪ'vɛntləs
AM ə'vɛn(t)ləs, ɪ'vɛn(t)ləs
eventlessly
BR ɪ'vɛntləsli
AM ə'vɛn(t)ləsli, ɪ'vɛn(t)ləsli
eventual
BR ɪ'vɛn(t)ʃʊəl, ɪ'vɛn(t)ʃ(ʊ)l
AM ə'vɛn(t)ʃ(əw)əl, ɪ'vɛn(t)ʃ(əw)əl
eventuality
BR ɪ,vɛn(t)ʃʊ'alɪt|i, -ɪz
AM ə,vɛn(t)ʃə'wælədi, ɪ,vɛn(t)ʃə'wælədi, -z
eventually
BR ɪ'vɛn(t)ʃʊəli, ɪ'vɛn(t)ʃʊli, ɪ'vɛn(t)ʃʃi
AM ə'vɛn(t)ʃəli, ə'vɛn(t)ʃ(ə)wəli,

i'vɛn(t)ʃəli, i'vɛn(t)ʃ(ə)wəli
eventuate
BR ɪ'vɛn(t)ʃʊeɪt, -s, -ɪŋ, -ɪd
AM ə'vɛn(t)ʃə,weɪt, ɪ'vɛn(t)ʃə,weɪt, -ts, -dɪŋ, -dɪd
eventuation
BR ɪ,vɛn(t)ʃʊ'eɪʃn
AM ə,vɛn(t)ʃə'weɪʃən, ɪ,vɛn(t)ʃə'weɪʃən
ever
BR 'ɛvə(r)
AM 'ɛvər
Everard
BR 'ɛv(ə)rɑ:d
AM 'ɛvə,rɑrd
Everest
BR 'ɛv(ə)rɪst
AM 'ɛv(ə)rəst
Everett
BR 'ɛv(ə)rɪt, 'ɛv(ə)rɛt
AM 'ɛvərət
Everglades
BR 'ɛvəgleɪdz
AM 'ɛvər,gleɪdz
evergreen
BR 'ɛvəgri:n, -z
AM 'ɛvər,grin, -z
everlasting
BR ,ɛvə'lɑ:stɪŋ, ,ɛvə'lastɪŋ
AM 'ɛvər'læstɪŋ
everlastingly
BR ,ɛvə'lɑ:stɪŋli, ,ɛvə'lastɪŋli
AM 'ɛvər'læstɪŋli
everlastingness
BR ,ɛvə'lɑ:stɪŋnɪs, ,ɛvə'lastɪŋnɪs
AM 'ɛvər'læstɪŋnɪs
Everley
BR 'ɛvəli
AM 'ɛvərli
Everly
BR 'ɛvəli
AM 'ɛvərli
evermore
BR ,ɛvə'mɔ:(r)
AM 'ɛvər'mɔ(ə)r
everpresent
BR ,ɛvə'prɛznt
AM 'ɛvər'prɛzənt
Evers
BR 'ɛvəz
AM 'ɛvərz
Evershed
BR 'ɛvəʃɛd
AM 'ɛvər,ʃɛd
Eversholt
BR 'ɛvəʃɒlt, 'ɛvəʃəʊlt
AM 'ɛvər,ʃoʊlt
eversion
BR ɪ'və:ʃn
AM ə'vərʒən, ɪ'vərʒən

Evert
BR 'ɛvət
AM 'ɛvərt
evert
BR ɪ'və:t, -s, -ɪŋ, -ɪd
AM ə'vər|t, ɪ'vər|t, -ts, -dɪŋ, -dəd
Everton
BR 'ɛvət(ə)n
AM 'ɛvərt(ə)n
every
BR 'ɛvri
AM 'ɛv(ə)ri
everybody
BR 'ɛvrɪbɒdi, 'ɛvrɪbədi
AM 'ɛv(ə)ri,bədi, 'ɛv(ə)ri,bɑdi
everyday
BR ,ɛvrɪ'deɪ
AM 'ɛv(ə)ri'deɪ
everyman
BR 'ɛvrɪman
AM 'ɛv(ə)ri,mæn
everyone
BR 'ɛvrɪwʌn
AM 'ɛv(ə)ri,wən
everyplace
BR 'ɛvrɪpleɪs
AM 'ɛv(ə)ri,pleɪs
everything
BR 'ɛvrɪθɪŋ
AM 'ɛv(ə)ri,θɪŋ
everyway
BR 'ɛvrɪ'weɪ
AM 'ɛv(ə)ri,weɪ
everywhere
BR 'ɛvrɪwɛ:(r)
AM 'ɛv(ə)ri,(h)wɛ(ə)r
everywoman
BR 'ɛvrɪ,wʊmən
AM 'ɛv(ə)ri,wʊmən
Evesham
BR 'i:v(ɪ)ʃ(ə)m
AM 'ivʃəm
Évian®
BR 'eɪviən, 'eɪvjɒ̃
AM 'ɛviən, 'ɛvi,jɑn
evict
BR ɪ'vɪkt, -s, -ɪŋ, -ɪd
AM ə'vɪk|(t), ɪ'vɪk|(t), -(t)s, -tɪŋ, -tɪd
eviction
BR ɪ'vɪkʃn, -z
AM ə'vɪkʃən, ɪ'vɪkʃən, -z
evictor
BR ɪ'vɪktə(r), -z
AM ə'vɪktər, ɪ'vɪktər, -z
evidence
BR 'ɛvɪd(ə)ns, -ɪz, -ɪŋ, -t
AM 'ɛvədns, 'ɛvə,dɛns, -əz, -ɪŋ, -t
evident
BR 'ɛvɪd(ə)nt
AM 'ɛvəd(ə)nt, 'ɛvə,dɛnt

evidential
BR ,ɛvɪ'dɛnʃl
AM ,ɛvə'dɛn(t)ʃəl
evidentially
BR ,ɛvɪ'dɛnʃʃi, ,ɛvɪ'dɛnʃəli
AM ,ɛvə'dɛntʃəli
evidentiary
BR ,ɛvɪ'dɛnʃ(ə)ri
AM ,ɛvə'dɛn(t)ʃəri
evidently
BR 'ɛvɪd(ə)ntli
AM 'ɛvə,dɛntli, 'ɛvəd(ə)n(t)li, ,ɛvə'dɛn(t)li
evil
BR 'i:vl, -z
AM 'ivəl, -z
evildoer
BR 'i:vl,du:ə(r), ,i:vl'du:ə(r), -z
AM 'ivəl'duər, -z
evildoing
BR 'i:vl,du:ɪŋ, ,i:vl'du:ɪŋ
AM 'ivəl'duɪŋ
evilly
BR 'i:vl(l)i
AM 'ivə(l)li
evilness
BR 'i:vlnəs
AM 'ivəlnəs
evince
BR ɪ'vɪns, -ɪz, -ɪŋ, -t
AM ə'vɪns, ɪ'vɪns, -ɪz, -ɪŋ, -t
evincible
BR ɪ'vɪnsɪbl
AM ə'vɪnsəbəl, ɪ'vɪnsəbəl
evincive
BR ɪ'vɪnsɪv
AM ə'vɪnsɪv, ɪ'vɪnsɪv
eviscerate
BR ɪ'vɪsəreɪt, -s, -ɪŋ, -ɪd
AM ə'vɪsə,reɪ|t, ɪ'vɪsə,reɪ|t, -ts, -dɪŋ, -dɪd
evisceration
BR ɪ,vɪsə'reɪʃn
AM ə,vɪsə'reɪʃən, ɪ,vɪsə'reɪʃən
Evita
BR ɪ'vi:tə(r), ɛ'vi:tə(r)
AM ə'vidə
evocation
BR ,i:və(ʊ)'keɪʃn, ,ɛvə(ʊ)'keɪʃn, -z
AM ,ivoʊ'keɪʃən, ,ɛvə'keɪʃən, ,ɛvoʊ'keɪʃən, -z
evocative
BR ɪ'vɒkətɪv
AM ə'vɑkədɪv, ɪ'vɑkədɪv
evocatively
BR ɪ'vɒkətɪvli

AM əˈvɑkədəvli,
iˈvɑkədəvli

evocativeness
BR ɪˈvɒkətɪvnɪs
AM əˈvɑkədɪvnɪs,
iˈvɑkədɪvnɪs

evocatory
BR ɪˈvɒkət(ə)ri
AM əˈvɑkəˌtɔri

evoke
BR ɪˈvəʊk, -s, -ɪŋ, -t
AM əˈvoʊk, iˈvoʊk, -s,
-ɪŋ, -t

evoker
BR ɪˈvəʊkə(r), -z
AM əˈvoʊkər, iˈvoʊkər,
-z

evolute
BR ˈiːvəl(j)uːt,
ˈɛvəl(j)uːt, -s, -ɪŋ, -ɪd
AM ˈɛvəˌl(j)uǀt, -ts, -dɪŋ,
-dəd

evolution
BR ˌiːvəˈl(j)uːʃn,
ˌɛvəˈl(j)uːʃn, -z
AM ˌɛvəˈluʃən, -z

evolutional
BR ˌiːvəˈl(j)uːʃn(ə)l,
ˌiːvəˈl(j)uːʃən(ə)l,
ˌɛvəˈl(j)uːʃn(ə)l,
ˌɛvəˈl(j)uːʃən(ə)l
AM ˌɛvəˈluʃ(ə)nəl

evolutionally
BR ˌiːvəˈl(j)uːʃnəli,
ˌiːvəˈl(j)uːʃnˌli,
ˌiːvəˈl(j)uːʃənˌli,
ˌiːvəˈl(j)uːʃ(ə)nəli,
ˌɛvəˈl(j)uːʃnəli,
ˌɛvəˈl(j)uːʃnˌli,
ˌɛvəˈl(j)uːʃənˌli,
ˌɛvəˈl(j)uːʃ(ə)nəli
AM ˌɛvəˈluʃ(ə)nəli

evolutionarily
BR ˌiːvəˈl(j)uːʃnərɪli,
ˌɛvəˈl(j)uːʃnərɪli
AM ˌɛvəˌluʃəˈnɛrəli

evolutionary
BR ˌiːvəˈl(j)uːʃn(ə)ri,
ˌɛvəˈl(j)uːʃn(ə)ri
AM ˌɛvəˈluʃəˌnɛri

evolutionism
BR ˌiːvəˈl(j)uːʃnɪz(ə)m,
ˌɛvəˈl(j)uːʃnɪz(ə)m
AM ˌɛvəˈluʃəˌnɪzəm

evolutionist
BR ˌiːvəˈl(j)uːʃnɪst,
ˌɛvəˈl(j)uːʃnɪst, -s
AM ˌɛvəˈluʃənəst, -s

evolutionistic
BR ˌiːvəˌl(j)uːʃəˈnɪstɪk,
ˌiːvəˌl(j)uːʃnˈɪstɪk,
ˌɛvəˌl(j)uːʃəˈnɪstɪk,
ˌɛvəˌl(j)uːʃnˈɪstɪk
AM ˌɛvəˌluʃəˈnɪstɪk

evolutive
BR ˌiːvəˈl(j)uːtɪv,
ˌɛvəˈl(j)uːtɪv
AM ˌɛvəˈludɪv

evolvable
BR ɪˈvɒlvəbl
AM əˈvɒlvəbəl,
iˈvɒlvəbəl,
əˈvɑlvəbəl, iˈvɑlvəbəl

evolve
BR ɪˈvɒlv, -z, -ɪŋ, -d
AM əˈvɒlv, iˈvɒlv,
əˈvɑlv, iˈvɑlv, -z, -ɪŋ, -d

evolvement
BR ɪˈvɒlvm(ə)nt
AM əˈvɒlvmənt,
iˈvɒlvmənt,
əˈvɑlvmənt,
iˈvɑlvmənt

Evonne
BR ɪˈvɒn, ˌiːˈvɒn
AM ɪˈvɑn, iˈvɑn

Evo-stik®
BR ˈiːvəʊstɪk
AM ˈivoʊˌstɪk

evulsion
BR ɪˈvʌlʃn
AM əˈvəlʒən, iˈvəlʒən

evzone
BR ˈɛvzəʊn, -z
AM ˈɛvˌzoʊn, -z

Ewan
BR ˈjuːən
AM ˈjuən

Ewart
BR ˈjuːət
AM ˈjuərt

Ewbank
BR ˈjuːbaŋk
AM ˈjuˌbæŋk

Ewe¹
*African language
and people*
BR ˈeɪweɪ, ˈɛweɪ
AM ˈeɪweɪ

Ewe²
Scottish loch
BR juː
AM ju

ewe
BR juː, -z
AM ju, -z

Ewen
BR ˈjuːən
AM ˈjuən

ewer
BR ˈjuːə(r), -z
AM ˈjuər, -z

Ewhurst
BR ˈjuːhəːst
AM ˈjuˌhərst

Ewing
BR ˈjuːɪŋ
AM ˈjuɪŋ

Ewyas
BR ˈjuːəs
AM ˈjuəs

ex
BR ɛks, -ɪz
AM ɛks, -əz

exacerbate
BR ɪgˈzasəbeɪt,
ɛgˈzasəbeɪt, -s, -ɪŋ, -ɪd
AM ɪgˈzæsərˌbeɪǀt,
ɛgˈzæsərˌbeɪǀt, -ts,
-dɪŋ, -dɪd

exacerbation
BR ɪgˌzasəˈbeɪʃn,
ɛgˌzasəˈbeɪʃn, -z
AM ɪgˌzæsərˈbeɪʃən,
ɛgˌzæsərˈbeɪʃən, -z

exact
BR ɪgˈzakt, ɛgˈzakt, -s,
-ɪŋ, -ɪd
AM ɪgˈzækǀ(t),
ɛgˈzækǀ(t), -(t)s, -tɪŋ,
-təd

exacta
BR ɪgˈzaktə(r),
ɛgˈzaktə(r)
AM ɪgˈzæktə, ɛgˈzæktə

exactable
BR ɪgˈzaktəbl,
ɛgˈzaktəbl
AM ɪgˈzæktəbəl,
ɛgˈzæktəbəl

exacting
BR ɪgˈzaktɪŋ, ɛgˈzaktɪŋ
AM ɪgˈzæktɪŋ,
ɛgˈzæktɪŋ

exactingly
BR ɪgˈzaktɪŋli,
ɛgˈzaktɪŋli
AM ɪgˈzæktɪŋli,
ɛgˈzæktɪŋli

exactingness
BR ɪgˈzaktɪŋnɪs,
ɛgˈzaktɪŋnɪs
AM ɪgˈzæktɪŋnəs,
ɛgˈzæktɪŋnəs

exaction
BR ɪgˈzakʃn, ɛgˈzakʃn,
-z
AM ɪgˈzækʃən,
ɛgˈzækʃən, -z

exactitude
BR ɪgˈzaktɪtjuːd,
ɪgˈzaktɪtʃuːd,
ɛgˈzaktɪtjuːd,
ɛgˈzaktɪtʃuːd
AM ɪgˈzæktəˌt(j)ud,
ɛgˈzæktəˌt(j)ud

exactly
BR ɪgˈzak(t)li,
ɛgˈzak(t)li
AM ɪgˈzæk(t)li,
ɛgˈzæk(t)li

exactness
BR ɪgˈzak(t)nəs,
ɛgˈzak(t)nəs
AM ɪgˈzæk(t)nəs,
ɛgˈzæk(t)nəs

exactor
BR ɪgˈzaktə(r),
ɛgˈzaktə(r), -z
AM ɪgˈzæktər,
ɛgˈzæktər, -z

exaggerate
BR ɪgˈzadʒəreɪt,
ɛgˈzadʒəreɪt, -s, -ɪŋ, -ɪd
AM ɪgˈzædʒəˌreɪǀt,
ɛgˈzædʒəˌreɪǀt, -ts,
-dɪŋ, -dɪd

exaggeratedly
BR ɪgˈzadʒəreɪtɪdli,
ɛgˈzadʒəreɪtɪdli
AM ɪgˈzædʒəˌreɪdɪdli,
ɛgˈzædʒəˌreɪdɪdli

exaggeratingly
BR ɪgˈzadʒəreɪtɪŋli,
ɛgˈzadʒəreɪtɪŋli
AM ɪgˈzædʒəˌreɪdɪŋli,
ɛgˈzædʒəˌreɪdɪŋli

exaggeration
BR ɪgˌzadʒəˈreɪʃn,
ɛgˌzadʒəˈreɪʃn, -z
AM ɪgˌzædʒəˈreɪʃən,
ɛgˌzædʒəˈreɪʃən, -z

exaggerative
BR ɪgˈzadʒ(ə)rətɪv,
ɛgˈzadʒ(ə)rətɪv
AM ɪgˈzædʒəˌreɪdɪv,
ɛgˈzædʒəˌreɪdɪv

exaggerator
BR ɪgˈzadʒəreɪtə(r),
ɛgˈzadʒəreɪtə(r), -z
AM ɪgˈzædʒəˌreɪdər,
ɛgˈzædʒəˌreɪdər, -z

exalt
BR ɪgˈzɔːlt, ɛgˈzɔːlt,
ɪgˈzɒlt, ɛgˈzɒlt, -s, -ɪŋ,
-ɪd
AM ɪgˈzɔlt, ɛgˈzɔlt,
ɪgˈzɑlt, ɛgˈzɑlt, -s, -ɪŋ,
-əd

exaltation
BR ˌɛgzɔːˈleɪʃn,
ˌɛgzɒlˈteɪʃn
AM ˌɛgˌzɔlˈteɪʃən,
ˌɛgˌzɑlˈteɪʃən

exaltedly
BR ɪgˈzɔːltɪdli,
ɛgˈzɔːltɪdli,
ɪgˈzɒltɪdli, ɛgˈzɒltɪdli
AM ɪgˈzɔltədli,
ɛgˈzɔltədli,
ɪgˈzɑltədli, ɛgˈzɑltədli

exaltedness
BR ɪgˈzɔːltɪdnɪs,
ɛgˈzɔːltɪdnɪs,
ɪgˈzɒltɪdnɪs,
ɛgˈzɒltɪdnɪs
AM ɪgˈzɔltədnəs,
ɛgˈzɔltədnəs,
ɪgˈzɑltədnəs,
ɛgˈzɑltədnəs

exalter
BR ɪgˈzɔːltə(r),
ɛgˈzɔːltə(r),
ɪgˈzɒltə(r),
ɛgˈzɒltə(r), -z
AM ɪgˈzɔltər, ɛgˈzɔltər,
ɪgˈzɑltər, ɛgˈzɑltər, -z

exam
BR ɪgˈzam, ɛgˈzam, -z
AM ɪgˈzæm, ɛgˈzæm, -z

examen
BR ɛg'zeɪmɛn, -z
AM ɪg'zeɪmən,
ɛg'zeɪmən, -z

examinable
BR ɪg'zamɪnəbl,
ɛg'zamɪnəbl
AM ɪg'zæmənəbəl,
ɛg'zæmənəbəl

examination
BR ɪg,zamɪ'neɪʃn,
ɛg,zamɪ'neɪʃn, -z
AM ɪg,zæmə'neɪʃən,
ɛg,zæmə'neɪʃən, -z

examinational
BR ɪg,zamɪ'neɪʃŋ(ə)l,
ɪg,zamɪ'neɪʃən(ə)l,
ɛg,zamɪ'neɪʃŋ(ə)l,
ɛg,zamɪ'neɪʃən(ə)l
AM ɪg,zæmə'neɪʃ(ə)nəl,
ɛg,zæmə'neɪʃ(ə)nəl

examine
BR ɪg'zam|ɪn,
ɛg'zam|ɪn, -ɪnz, -ɪnɪŋ,
-ɪnd
AM ɪg'zæmən,
ɛg'zæmən, -z, -ɪŋ, -d

examinee
BR ɪg,zamɪ'niː,
ɛg,zamɪ'niː, -z
AM ɪg,zæmə'ni,
ɛg,zæmə'ni, -z

examiner
BR ɪg'zamɪnə(r),
ɛg'zamɪnə(r), -z
AM ɪg'zæmənər,
ɛg'zæmənər, -z

example
BR ɪg'zɑːmpl,
ɪg'zampl, ɛg'zɑːmpl,
ɛg'zampl, -z
AM ɪg'zæmpəl,
ɛg'zæmpəl, -z

exanthema
BR ,ɛksan'θiːmə(r),
ɪk'sanθɪmə(r)
AM ,ɛgzæn'θimə,
,ɪgzæn'θimə

exarch
BR 'ɛksɑːk, -s
AM 'ɛk,sɑrk, -s

exarchate
BR 'ɛksɑːkeɪt, -s
AM 'ɛksɑr,keɪt, -s

ex-army
BR ,ɛks'ɑːmi
AM ,ɛks'ɑrmi

exasperate
BR ɪg'zasp(ə)reɪt,
ɪg'zɑːsp(ə)reɪt,
ɛg'zasp(ə)reɪt,
ɛg'zɑːsp(ə)reɪt, -s, -ɪŋ,
-ɪd
AM ɪg'zæspə,reɪt,
ɛg'zæspə,reɪt, -ts,
-dɪŋ, -dɪd

exasperatedly
BR ɪg'zasp(ə)reɪtɪdli,
ɪg'zɑːsp(ə)reɪtɪdli,
ɛg'zasp(ə)reɪtɪdli,
ɛg'zɑːsp(ə)reɪtɪdli
AM ɪg'zæspə,reɪdɪdli,
ɛg'zæspə,reɪdɪdli

exasperatingly
BR ɪg'zasp(ə)reɪtɪŋli,
ɪg'zɑːsp(ə)reɪtɪŋli,
ɛg'zasp(ə)reɪtɪŋli,
ɛg'zɑːsp(ə)reɪtɪŋli
AM ɪg'zæspə,reɪdɪŋli,
ɛg'zæspə,reɪdɪŋli

exasperation
BR ɪg'zaspə'reɪʃn,
ɪg,zɑːspə'reɪʃn,
ɛg,zaspə'reɪʃn,
ɛg,zɑːspə'reɪʃn
AM ɪg,zæspə'reɪʃən,
ɛg,zæspə'reɪʃən

Excalibur
BR ɛk'skalɪbə(r)
AM ɛk'skæləbər

ex cathedra
BR ,ɛks kə'θiːdrə(r)
AM ,ɛks kə'θidrə

excavate
BR 'ɛkskəveɪt, -s, -ɪŋ,
-ɪd
AM 'ɛkskə,veɪ|t, -ts,
-dɪŋ, -dɪd

excavation
BR ,ɛkskə'veɪʃn, -z
AM ,ɛkskə'veɪʃən, -z

excavator
BR 'ɛkskəveɪtə(r), -z
AM 'ɛkskə,veɪdər, -z

exceed
BR ɪk'siːd, ɛk'siːd, -z,
-ɪŋ, -ɪd
AM ɪk'sid, ɛk'sid, -z, -ɪŋ,
-ɪd

exceeding
BR ɪk'siːdɪŋ, ɛk'siːdɪŋ
AM ɪk'sidɪŋ, ɛk'sidɪŋ

exceedingly
BR ɪk'siːdɪŋli,
ɛk'siːdɪŋli
AM ɪk'sidɪŋli,
ɛk'sidɪŋli

excel
BR ɪk'sɛl, ɛk'sɛl, -z, -ɪŋ,
-d
AM ɪk'sɛl, ɛk'sɛl, -z, -ɪŋ,
-d

excellence
BR 'ɛksələns, 'ɛksəlŋs,
'ɛksl(ə)ns
AM 'ɛks(ə)ləns

excellency
BR 'ɛksələns|i,
'ɛksəlŋs|i,
'ɛksl(ə)ns|i, -ɪz
AM 'ɛks(ə)lənsi, -z

excellent
BR 'ɛksələnt, 'ɛksəlŋt,
'ɛksl(ə)nt

AM 'ɛks(ə)lənt

excellently
BR 'ɛksələntli,
'ɛksəlŋtli, 'ɛksl(ə)ntli
AM 'ɛks(ə)lən(t)li

excelsior
BR ɪk'sɛlsɪɔː(r),
ɛk'sɛlsɪɔː(r),
ɪk'sɛlsɪə(r),
ɛk'sɛlsɪə(r)
AM ɪk'sɛlsiər,
ɛk'sɛlsiər

excentric
BR ɪk'sɛntrɪk,
ɛk'sɛntrɪk, -s
AM ɪk'sɛntrɪk,
ɛk'sɛntrɪk, -s

except
BR ɪk'sɛpt, ɛk'sɛpt, -s,
-ɪŋ, -ɪd
AM ɪk'sɛpt, ɛk'sɛpt, -s,
-ɪŋ, -əd

excepting
BR ɪk'sɛptɪŋ, ɛk'sɛptɪŋ
AM ɪk'sɛptɪŋ, ɛk'sɛptɪŋ

exception
BR ɪk'sɛpʃn, ɛk'sɛpʃn,
-z
AM ɪk'sɛpʃən,
ɛk'sɛpʃən, -z

exceptionable
BR ɪk'sɛpʃŋəbl,
ɪk'sɛpʃ(ə)nəbl,
ɛk'sɛpʃŋəbl,
ɛk'sɛpʃ(ə)nəbl
AM ɪk'sɛpʃ(ə)nəbəl,
ɛk'sɛpʃ(ə)nəbəl

exceptionableness
BR ɪk'sɛpʃŋəblnəs,
ɪk'sɛpʃ(ə)nəblnəs,
ɛk'sɛpʃŋəblnəs,
ɛk'sɛpʃ(ə)nəblnəs
AM ɪk'sɛpʃ(ə)nəbəlnəs,
ɛk'sɛpʃ(ə)nəblnəs

exceptionably
BR ɪk'sɛpʃŋəbli,
ɪk'sɛpʃ(ə)nəbli,
ɛk'sɛpʃŋəbli,
ɛk'sɛpʃ(ə)nəbli
AM ɪk'sɛpʃ(ə)nəbli,
ɛk'sɛpʃ(ə)nəbli

exceptional
BR ɪk'sɛpʃŋ(ə)l,
ɪk'sɛpʃən(ə)l,
ɛk'sɛpʃŋ(ə)l,
ɛk'sɛpʃən(ə)l
AM ɪk'sɛpʃ(ə)nəl,
ɛk'sɛpʃ(ə)nəl

exceptionality
BR ɪk,sɛpʃə'nalɪti,
ɛk,sɛpʃə'nalɪti
AM ɪk,sɛpʃə'næləedi,
ɛk,sɛpʃə'nælədi

exceptionally
BR ɪk'sɛpʃŋəli,
ɪk'sɛpʃŋli,
ɪk'sɛpʃən|i,
ɪk'sɛpʃ(ə)nəli,

AM 'ɛks(ə)lənt

excellently
BR 'ɛksələntli,
'ɛksəlŋtli, 'ɛksl(ə)ntli
AM 'ɛks(ə)lən(t)li

ɛk'sɛpʃŋəli,
ɛk'sɛpʃŋli,
ɛk'sɛpʃənli,
ɛk'sɛpʃ(ə)nəli
AM ɪk'sɛpʃ(ə)nəli,
ɛk'sɛpʃ(ə)nəli

excerpt¹
noun
BR 'ɛksəːpt, 'ɛgzəːpt, -s
AM 'ɛk,sərpt, ɛg'zərpt,
-s

excerpt²
verb
BR ɪk'səːpt, ɛk'səːpt,
ɪg'zəːpt, ɛg'zəːpt, -s,
-ɪŋ, -ɪd
AM ɪk'sərpt, ɪk'sərpt,
ɛg'zərpt, ɪg'zərpt, -s,
-ɪŋ, -əd

excerptible
BR ɪk'səːptəbl,
ɛk'səːptəbl,
ɪg'zəːptəbl,
ɛg'zəːptəbl
AM ɛk'sərptəbəl,
ɪk'sərptəbəl,
ɛg'zərptəbəl,
ɪg'zərptəbəl

excerption
BR ɪk'səːpʃn,
ɛk'səːpʃn, ɪg'zəːpʃn,
ɛg'zəːpʃn
AM ɛk'sərpʃən,
ɪk'sərpʃən,
ɛg'zərpʃən,
ɪg'zərpʃən

excess¹
adjective
BR 'ɛksɛs, ɛk'sɛs,
ɪk'sɛs
AM 'ɛk,sɛs, ɪk'sɛs,
ɛk'sɛs

excess²
noun
BR ɪk'sɛs, ɛk'sɛs,
'ɛksɛs, -ɪz
AM ɪk'sɛs, ɛk'sɛs, -əz

excessive
BR ɪk'sɛsɪv, ɛk'sɛsɪv
AM ɪk'sɛsɪv, ɛk'sɛsɪv

excessively
BR ɪk'sɛsɪvli
AM ɪk'sɛsəvli,
ɛk'sɛsəvli

excessiveness
BR ɪk'sɛsɪvnɪs,
ɛk'sɛsɪvnɪs
AM ɪk'sɛsɪvnɪs,
ɛk'sɛsɪvnɪs

exchange
BR ɪks'tʃeɪn(d)ʒ,
ɛks'tʃeɪn(d)ʒ, -ɪz, -ɪŋ,
-d
AM ɪks'tʃeɪndʒ,
ɛks'tʃeɪndʒ, -ɪz, -ɪŋ, -d

exchangeability
BR ɪks,tʃeɪn(d)ʒə'bɪlɪti,
ɛks,tʃeɪn(d)ʒə'bɪlɪti

AM ɪks,tʃeɪndʒə'bɪlɪdi,
ɛks,tʃeɪndʒə'bɪlɪdi

exchangeable
BR ɪks'tʃeɪn(d)ʒəbl,
ɛks'tʃeɪn(d)ʒəbl
AM ɪks'tʃeɪndʒəbəl,
ɛks'tʃeɪndʒəbəl

exchanger
BR ɪks'tʃeɪn(d)ʒə(r),
ɛks'tʃeɪn(d)ʒə(r), -z
AM ɪks'tʃeɪndʒər,
ɛks'tʃeɪndʒər, -z

exchequer
BR ɪks'tʃɛkə(r),
ɛks'tʃɛkə(r), -z
AM ɛks'tʃɛkər,
ɪks'tʃɛkər, -z

excipient
BR ɪk'sɪpɪənt,
ɛk'sɪpɪənt, -s
AM ɪk'sɪpiənt,
ɛk'sɪpiənt, -s

excisable
BR ɪk'sʌɪzəbl,
ɛk'sʌɪzəbl
AM ɪk'saɪzəbəl,
ɛk'saɪzəbəl

excise[1]
noun
BR 'ɛksʌɪz
AM 'ɛk,saɪz

excise[2]
verb
BR ɪk'sʌɪz, ɛk'sʌɪz, -ɪz,
-ɪŋ, -d
AM ɪk'saɪz, ɛk'saɪz, -ɪz,
-ɪŋ, -d

exciseman
BR 'ɛksʌɪzmən
AM 'ɛk,saɪzmən

excisemen
BR 'ɛksʌɪzmən
AM 'ɛk,saɪzmən

excision
BR ɪk'sɪʒn, ɛk'sɪʒn, -z
AM ɪk'sɪʒən, ɛk'sɪʒən,
-z

excitability
BR ɪk,sʌɪtə'bɪlɪti,
ɛk,sʌɪtə'bɪlɪti
AM ɪk,saɪdə'bɪlɪdi,
ɛk,saɪdə'bɪlɪdi

excitable
BR ɪk'sʌɪtəbl,
ɛk'sʌɪtəbl
AM ɪk'saɪdəbəl,
ɛk'saɪdəbəl

excitableness
BR ɪk'sʌɪtəblnəs,
ɛk'sʌɪtəblnəs
AM ɪk'saɪdəbəlnəs,
ɛk'saɪdəbəlnəs

excitably
BR ɪk'sʌɪtəbli,
ɛk'sʌɪtəbli
AM ɪk'saɪdəbli,
ɛk'saɪdəbli

excitant
BR ɪk'sʌɪtnt, ɛk'sʌɪtnt,
-s
AM ɪk'saɪtnt, ɛk'saɪtnt,
-s

excitation
BR ,ɛksʌɪ'teɪʃn
AM ,ɛksə'teɪʃən,
ɛk,saɪ'teɪʃən

excitative
BR ɪk'sʌɪtətɪv,
ɛk'sʌɪtətɪv
AM ɪk'saɪdədɪv,
ɛk'saɪdədɪv

excitatory
BR ɪk'sʌɪtət(ə)ri,
ɛk'sʌɪtət(ə)ri
AM ɪk'saɪdə,tɔri,
ɛk'saɪdə,tɔri

excite
BR ɪk'sʌɪt, ɛk'sʌɪt, -s,
-ɪŋ, -ɪd
AM ɪk'saɪ|t, ɛk'saɪ|t, -ts,
-dɪŋ, -dɪd

excitedly
BR ɪk'sʌɪtɪdli,
ɛk'sʌɪtɪdli
AM ɪk'saɪdɪdli,
ɛk'saɪdɪdli

excitedness
BR ɪk'sʌɪtɪdnɪs,
ɛk'sʌɪtɪdnɪs
AM ɪk'saɪdɪdnɪs,
ɛk'saɪdɪdnɪs

excitement
BR ɪk'sʌɪtm(ə)nt,
ɛk'sʌɪtm(ə)nt, -s
AM ɪk'saɪtmənt,
ɛk'saɪtmənt, -s

exciter
BR ɪk'sʌɪtə(r),
ɛk'sʌɪtə(r), -z
AM ɪk'saɪdər,
ɛk'saɪdər, -z

excitingly
BR ɪk'sʌɪtɪŋli,
ɛk'sʌɪtɪŋli
AM ɪk'saɪdɪŋli,
ɛk'saɪdɪŋli

excitingness
BR ɪk'sʌɪtɪŋnɪs,
ɛk'sʌɪtɪŋnɪs
AM ɪk'saɪdɪŋnɪs,
ɛk'saɪdɪŋnɪs

exciton
BR 'ɛksɪtɒn, -z
AM 'ɛksə,tɑn, -z

exclaim
BR ɪk'skleɪm,
ɛk'skleɪm, -z, -ɪŋ, -d
AM ɪk'skleɪm,
ɛk'skleɪm, -z, -ɪŋ, -d

exclamation
BR ,ɛksklə'meɪʃn, -z
AM ,ɛksklə'meɪʃən, -z

exclamatory
BR ɪk'sklamət(ə)ri,
ɛk'sklamət(ə)ri

AM ɪk'sklæmə,tɔri,
ɛk'sklæmə,tɔri

exclave
BR 'ɛkskleɪv, -z
AM 'ɛk,skleɪv, -z

exclosure
BR ɪk'skləʊʒə(r),
ɛk'skləʊʒə(r), -z
AM ɪk'skloʊʒər,
ɛk'skloʊʒər, -z

excludable
BR ɪk'sklu:dəbl,
ɛk'sklu:dəbl
AM ɪk'skludəbəl,
ɛk'skludəbəl

exclude
BR ɪk'sklu:d,
ɛk'sklu:d, -z, -ɪŋ, -ɪd
AM ɪk'sklud, ɛk'sklud,
-z, -ɪŋ, -əd

excluder
BR ɪk'sklu:də(r),
ɛk'sklu:də(r), -z
AM ɪk'skludər,
ɛk'skludər, -z

exclusion
BR ɪk'sklu:ʒn,
ɛk'sklu:ʒn
AM ɪk'skluʒən,
ɛk'skluʒən

exclusionary
BR ɪk'sklu:ʒən(ə)ri,
ɪk'sklu:ʒn(ə)ri,
ɛk'sklu:ʒən(ə)ri,
ɛk'sklu:ʒn(ə)ri
AM ɪk'skluʒə,nɛri,
ɛk'skluʒə,nɛri

exclusionist
BR ɪk'sklu:ʒənɪst,
ɪk'sklu:ʒnɪst,
ɛk'sklu:ʒənɪst,
ɛk'sklu:ʒnɪst, -s
AM ɪk'skluʒənəst,
ɛk'skluʒənəst, -s

exclusive
BR ɪk'sklu:sɪv,
ɛk'sklu:sɪv
AM ɪk'sklusɪv,
ɪk'skluzɪv,
ɛk'sklusɪv, ɛk'skluzɪv

exclusively
BR ɪk'sklu:sɪvli,
ɛk'sklu:sɪvli
AM ɪk'sklusəvli,
ɪk'skluzəvli,
ɛk'sklusəvli,
ɛk'skluzəvli

exclusiveness
BR ɪk'sklu:sɪvnɪs,
ɛk'sklu:sɪvnɪs
AM ɪk'sklusɪvnɪs,
ɪk'skluzɪvnɪs,
ɛk'sklusɪvnɪs,
ɛk'skluzɪvnɪs

exclusivity
BR ,ɛksklu:'sɪvɪti
AM ,ɛksklu'sɪvɪdi

excogitable
BR ɛks'kɒdʒɪtəbl,
ɪks'kɒdʒɪtəbl
AM ɛk'skɑdʒədəbəl

excogitate
BR ɛks'kɒdʒɪteɪt,
ɪks'kɒdʒɪteɪt, -s, -ɪŋ,
-ɪd
AM ɛk'skɑdʒə,teɪ|t, -ts,
-dɪŋ, -dɪd

excogitation
BR ,ɛkskɒdʒɪ'teɪʃn,
ɛks,kɒdʒɪ'teɪʃn,
,ɪkskɒdʒɪ'teɪʃn,
ɪks,kɒdʒɪ'teɪʃn, -z
AM ɛk,skɑdʒə'teɪʃən,
-z

excogitative
BR ɛks'kɒdʒɪtətɪv,
ɪks'kɒdʒɪtətɪv
AM ɛk'skɑdʒə,teɪdɪv

excommunicate
BR ,ɛkskə'mju:nɪkeɪt,
-s, -ɪŋ, -ɪd
AM ,ɛkskə'mjunə,keɪ|t,
-ts, -dɪŋ, -dɪd

excommunication
BR ,ɛkskə,mju:nɪ'keɪʃn,
-z
AM ,ɛkskə,mjunə'keɪʃən,
-z

excommunicative
BR ,ɛkskə'mju:nɪkətɪv
AM ,ɛkskə'mjunə,keɪdɪv

excommunicator
BR ,ɛkskə'mju:nɪkeɪtə(r),
-z
AM ,ɛkskə'mjunə,keɪdər,
-z

excommunicatory
BR ,ɛkskə'mju:nɪkət(ə)ri
AM ,ɛkskə'mjunəkə,tɔri

excoriate
BR ɛk'skɔ:rɪeɪt,
ɪk'skɔ:rɪeɪt,
ɛk'skɒrɪeɪt,
ɪk'skɒrɪeɪt, -s, -ɪŋ, -ɪd
AM ɪk'skɔri,eɪ|t,
ɛk'skɔri,eɪ|t, -ts, -dɪŋ,
-dɪd

excoriation
BR ɛk,skɔ:rɪ'eɪʃn,
ɪk,skɔ:rɪ'eɪʃn,
ɛk,skɒrɪ'eɪʃn,
ɪk,skɒrɪ'eɪʃn, -z
AM ɪk,skɔri'eɪʃən,
ɛk,skɔri'eɪʃən, -z

excrement
BR 'ɛkskrɪm(ə)nt
AM 'ɛkskrəmənt

excremental
BR ,ɛkskrɪ'mentl
AM ,ɛkskrə'mɛn(t)l

excrescence
BR ɪk'skrɛsns,
ɛk'skrɛsns, -ɪz
AM ɪk'skrɛsəns,
ɛk'skrɛsəns, -əz

excrescent BR ɪkˈskresnt, ekˈskresnt AM ɪkˈskresnt, ekˈskresnt	**exculpatory** BR ɪksˈkʌlpət(ə)ri, eksˈkʌlpət(ə)ri AM ˌeksˈkəlpəˌtɔri	**excuse²** *verb* BR ɪkˈsjuːz, ekˈskjuːz, -ɪz, -ɪŋ, -d AM ɪkˈskjuz, ekˈskjuz, -əz, -ɪŋ, -d	AM ɪgˈzekjədɪv, egˈzekjədɪv, -z **executively** BR ɪgˈzekjətɪvli, egˈzekjətɪvli
excrescential BR ˌekskrɪˈsenʃl AM ˌekskrəˈsentʃəl	**excursion** BR ɪkˈskəːʃn, ekˈskəːʃn, -z AM ɪkˈskəːʒən, ekˈskəːʒən, -z	**excuse-me** BR ɪkˈsjuːzmiː, ekˈskjuːzmiː, -z AM ɪkˈskjuzˌmi,	AM ɪgˈzekjədəvli, egˈzekjədəvli **executor** BR ɪgˈzekjətə(r), egˈzekjətə(r), -z
excreta BR ɪkˈskriːtə(r), ekˈskriːtə(r) AM ekˈskridə, ɪkˈskridə	**excursional** BR ɪkˈskəːʃn(ə)l, ɪkˈskəːʃən(ə)l, ekˈskəːʃn(ə)l, ekˈskəːʃən(ə)l	ekˈskjuzˌmi, -z **ex-directory** BR ˌeksdɪˈrekt(ə)ri, ˌeksdaɪˈrekt(ə)ri AM ˌeksdəˈrekt(ə)ri	AM ɪgˈzekjədər, egˈzekjədər, ˈeksəˌkjudər, -z **executorial** BR ɪgˌzekjəˈtɔːriəl,
excrete BR ɪkˈskriːt, ekˈskriːt, -s, -ɪŋ, -ɪd AM ɪkˈskri|t, ekˈskri|t, -ts, -dɪŋ, -dɪd	AM ɪkˈskəːʒ(ə)nəl, ekˈskəːʒ(ə)nəl **excursionary** BR ɪkˈskəːʃ(ə)ri, ekˈskəːʃ(ə)ri	**Exe** BR eks AM eks **exeat** BR ˈeksɪət, -s	egˌzekjəˈtɔːriəl AM ɪgˌzekjəˈtɔriəl, egˌzekjəˈtɔriəl **executorship** BR ɪgˈzekjətəʃɪp,
excreter BR ɪkˈskriːtə(r), ekˈskriːtə(r), -z AM ɪkˈskridər, ekˈskridər, -z	AM ɪkˈskəːʒəˌneri, ekˈskəːʒəˌneri **excursionist** BR ɪkˈskəːʃnɪst, ɪkˈskəːʃənɪst,	AM ˈeksiˌæt, -s **exec** BR ɪgˈzek, egˈzek, -s AM egˈzek, -s	egˈzekjətəʃɪp, -s AM ɪgˈzekjədərˌʃɪp, egˈzekjədərˌʃɪp, -s **executory**
excretion BR ɪkˈskriːʃn, ekˈskriːʃn, -z AM ɪkˈskriʃən, ekˈskriʃən, -z	ekˈskəːʃnɪst, ekˈskəːʃənɪst, -s AM ɪkˈskəːʒ(ə)nəst, ekˈskəːʒ(ə)nəst, -s	**execrable** BR ˈeksɪkrəbl AM ˈeksəkrəbəl **execrably**	BR ɪgˈzekjət(ə)ri, egˈzekjət(ə)ri AM ɪgˈzekjəˌtɔri, egˈzekjəˌtɔri
excretive BR ɪkˈskriːtɪv, ekˈskriːtɪv AM ˈekskrədɪv, ɪkˈskridɪv, ekˈskridɪv	**excursive** BR ɪkˈskəːsɪv, ekˈskəːsɪv AM ɪkˈskəːsɪv, ekˈskəːsɪv	BR ˈeksɪkrəbli AM ˈeksəkrəbli **execrate** BR ˈeksɪkreɪt, -s, -ɪŋ, -ɪd AM ˈeksəˌkreɪ|t, -ts,	**executrices** BR ɪgˈzekjətrɪsiːz AM ɪgˈzekjəˌtrɪsiz, egˈzekjəˌtrɪsiz **executrix**
excretory BR ɪkˈskriːt(ə)ri, ekˈskriːt(ə)ri AM ˈekskrəˌtɔri	**excursively** BR ɪkˈskəːsɪvli, ekˈskəːsɪvli AM ɪkˈskəːsəvli, ekˈskəːsəvli	-dɪŋ, -dɪd **execration** BR ˌeksɪˈkreɪʃn, -z AM ˌeksəˈkreɪʃən, -z	BR ɪgˈzekjətrɪks, egˈzekjətrɪks, -ɪz AM ɪgˈzekjəˌtrɪks, egˈzekjəˌtrɪks, -ɪz
excretum BR ɪkˈskriːtəm, ekˈskriːtəm AM ekˈskridəm, ɪkˈskridəm	**excursiveness** BR ɪkˈskəːsɪvnɪs, ekˈskəːsɪvnɪs AM ɪkˈskəːsɪvnɪs, ekˈskəːsɪvnɪs	**execrative** BR ˈeksɪkreɪtɪv AM ˈeksəˌkreɪdɪv **execratory** BR ˈeksɪkreɪt(ə)ri	**exegeses** BR ˌeksɪˈdʒiːsiːz AM ˌeksəˈdʒisiz **exegesis** BR ˌeksɪˈdʒiːsɪs
excruciate BR ɪkˈskruːʃieɪt, ekˈskruːʃieɪt, -s, -ɪŋ, -ɪd AM ɪkˈskruʃiˌeɪ|t, ekˈskruʃiˌeɪ|t, -ts, -dɪŋ, -dɪd	**excursus** BR ɪkˈskəːsəs, ekˈskəːsəs AM ekˈskəːsəs	AM ˈeksəkrəˌtɔri **executable** BR ˈeksɪkjuːtəbl AM ˌeksəˈkjudəbəl	AM ˌeksəˈdʒisɪs **exegete** BR ˈeksɪdʒiːt, -s AM ˈeksəˌdʒit, -s
	excusable BR ɪkˈskjuːzəbl, ekˈsjuːzəbl AM ɪkˈskjuzəbəl, ekˈskjuzəbəl	**executant** BR ɪgˈzekjət(ə)nt, egˈzekjət(ə)nt, -s AM ɪgˈzekjədnt, egˈzekjədnt, -s	**exegetic** BR ˌeksɪˈdʒetɪk AM ˌeksəˈdʒedɪk **exegetical** BR ˌeksɪˈdʒetɪkl
excruciatingly BR ɪkˈskruːʃieɪtɪŋli, ekˈskruːʃieɪtɪŋli AM ɪkˈskruʃiˌeɪdɪŋli, ekˈskruʃiˌeɪdɪŋli	**excusably** BR ɪkˈskjuːzəbli, ekˈsjuːzəbli AM ɪkˈskjuzəbli, ekˈskjuzəbli	**execute** BR ˈeksɪkjuːt, -s, -ɪŋ, -ɪd AM ˈeksəˌkju|t, -ts, -dɪŋ, -dəd	AM ˌeksɪˈdʒedəkəl **exegetist** BR ˈeksɪdʒiːtɪst, -s AM ˈeksəˌdʒedəst, -s
excruciation BR ɪkˌskruːʃɪˈeɪʃn, ekˌskruːʃɪˈeɪʃn AM ɪkˌskruʃiˌeɪʃən, ekˌskruʃiˈeɪʃən	**excusatory** BR ɪkˈskjuːzət(ə)ri, ekˈskjuːzət(ə)ri AM ɪkˈskjuzəˌtɔri, ekˈskjuzəˌtɔri	**execution** BR ˌeksɪˈkjuːʃn, -z AM ˌeksəˈkjuʃən, -z **executionary** BR ˌeksɪˈkjuːʃ(ə)ri	**exempla** BR ɪgˈzemplə(r), egˈzemplə(r) AM ɪgˈzemplə, egˈzemplə
exculpate BR ˈekskʌlpeɪt, -s, -ɪŋ, -ɪd AM ˈekskəlˌpeɪl|t, -ts, -dɪŋ, -dɪd	**excuse¹** *noun* BR ɪkˈskjuːs, ekˈskjuːs, -ɪz	AM ˌeksəˈkjuʃənˌeri **executioner** BR ˌeksɪˈkjuːʃnə(r), ˌeksɪˈkjuːʃənə(r), -z	**exemplar** BR ɪgˈzemplə(r), egˈzemplə(r), -z AM ɪgˈzemplər,
exculpation BR ˌekskʌlˈpeɪʃn AM ˌekskəlˈpeɪʃən	AM ɪkˈskjus, ekˈskjus, -əz	AM ˌeksəˈkjuʃ(ə)nər, -z **executive** BR ɪgˈzekjətɪv, egˈzekjətɪv, -z	egˈzemplər, -z **exemplarily** BR ɪgˈzemplərɪli, egˈzemplərɪli

exemplariness
AM ɪgˈzemplərəli,
egˈzemplərəli,
ɪgzemˈplərəli,
egzəmˈplərəli

exemplariness
BR ɪgˈzemplərɪnɪs,
egˈzemplərɪnɪs
AM ɪgˈzemplərɪnɪs,
egˈzemplərɪnɪs

exemplary
BR ɪgˈzempləri,
egˈzempləri
AM ɪgˈzempləri,
egˈzempləri

exemplification
BR ɪgˌzemplɪfɪˈkeɪʃn,
egˌzemplɪfɪˈkeɪʃn, -z
AM ɪgˌzempləfəˈkeɪʃən,
egˌzempləfəˈkeɪʃən,
-z

exemplify
BR ɪgˈzemplɪfʌɪ,
egˈzemplɪfʌɪ, -z, -ɪŋ, -d
AM ɪgˈzempləˌfaɪ,
egˈzempləˌfaɪ, -z, -ɪŋ,
-d

exemplum
BR ɪgˈzempləm,
egˈzempləm
AM ɪgˈzempləm,
egˈzempləm

exempt
BR ɪgˈzem(p)t,
egˈzem(p)t, -s, -ɪŋ, -ɪd
AM ɪgˈzem(p)t,
egˈzem(p)t, -s, -ɪŋ, -əd

exemption
BR ɪgˈzem(p)ʃn,
egˈzem(p)ʃn, -z
AM ɪgˈzem(p)ʃən,
egˈzem(p)ʃən, -z

exequatur
BR ˌeksɪˈkweɪtə(r), -z
AM ˌeksəˈkweɪdər, -z

exequies
BR ˈeksɪkwɪz
AM ˈeksəkwɪz

exercisable
BR ˈeksəsʌɪzəbl
AM ˈeksərˌsaɪzəbəl

exercise
BR ˈeksəsʌɪz, -ɪz, -ɪŋ, -d
AM ˈeksərˌsaɪz, -ɪz, -ɪŋ,
-d

exerciser
BR ˈeksəsʌɪzə(r), -z
AM ˈeksərˌsaɪzər, -z

exergual
BR ek'sə:gl, ˈeksə:gl
AM ek'sərgəl,
egˈzərgəl

exergue
BR ek'sə:g, ˈeksə:g, -z
AM ek'sərg, eg'zərg,
ˈeksərg, ˈegzərg, -z

exert
BR ɪgˈzəːt, egˈzəːt, -s,
-ɪŋ, -ɪd

AM ɪgˈzərt, egˈzert, -s,
-dɪŋ, -dəd

exertion
BR ɪgˈzəːʃn, egˈzəːʃn, -z
AM ɪgˈzərʃən,
egˈzerʃən, -z

Exeter
BR ˈeksɪtə(r)
AM ˈeksətər, ˈegzətər

exeunt
BR ˈeksɪʌnt, ˈeksɪʊnt
AM ˈeksiˌənt, ˈeksiˌʊnt

exfiltrate
BR ˈeksfɪltreɪt, -s, -ɪŋ,
-ɪd
AM ekˈsfɪlˌtreɪt,
ɪkˈsfɪlˌtreɪt, -ts, -dɪŋ,
-dɪd

exfiltration
BR ˌeksfɪlˈtreɪʃn
AM ekˌsfɪlˈtreɪʃən,
ɪkˌsfɪlˈtreɪʃən

exfoliate
BR (ˌ)eksˈfəʊlɪeɪt,
ɪksˈfəʊlɪeɪt, -s, -ɪŋ, -ɪd
AM ekˈsfoʊliˌeɪt,
ɪkˈsfoʊliˌeɪt, -ts, -dɪŋ,
-dɪd

exfoliation
BR eksˌfəʊlɪˈeɪʃn,
ɪksˌfəʊlɪˈeɪʃn, -z
AM ekˌsfoʊliˈeɪʃən,
ɪkˌsfoʊliˈeɪʃən, -z

exfoliative
BR eksˈfəʊlɪətɪv,
ɪksˈfəʊlɪətɪv
AM ekˈsfoʊliˌeɪdɪv,
ɪkˈsfoʊliˌeɪdɪv

ex gratia
BR ˌeks ˈgreɪʃə(r)
AM eks ˈgreɪdiə,
+ ˈgreɪʃ(i)ə

exhalable
BR eksˈheɪləbl,
ɪksˈheɪləbl
AM eksˈheɪləbəl,
ɪksˈheɪləbəl,
ˈeksˌheɪləbəl

exhalation
BR ˌeks(h)əˈleɪʃn, -z
AM ˌeks(h)əˈleɪʃən, -z

exhale
BR eksˈheɪl, ɪksˈheɪl,
-z, -ɪŋ, -d
AM eksˈheɪl, ɪksˈheɪl,
ˈeks,(h)eɪl, -z, -ɪŋ, -d

exhaust
BR ɪgˈzɔːst, egˈzɔːst, -s,
-ɪŋ, -ɪd
AM ɪgˈzɔst, egˈzɔst,
ɪgˈzast, egˈzast, -s, -ɪŋ,
-əd

exhauster
BR ɪgˈzɔːstə(r),
egˈzɔːstə(r), -z
AM ɪgˈzɔstər, egˈzɔstər,
ɪgˈzastər, egˈzastər, -z

---

exhaustibility
BR ɪgˌzɔːstɪˈbɪlɪti,
egˌzɔːstɪˈbɪlɪti
AM ɪgˌzɔstəˈbɪlɪdi,
egˌzɔstəˈbɪlɪdi,
ɪgˌzastəˈbɪlɪdi,
egˌzastəˈbɪlɪdi

exhaustible
BR ɪgˈzɔːstɪbl,
egˈzɔːstɪbl
AM ɪgˈzɔstəbəl,
egˈzɔstəbəl,
ɪgˈzastəbəl,
egˈzastəbəl

exhaustibly
BR ɪgˈzɔːstɪbli,
egˈzɔːstɪbli
AM ɪgˈzɔstəbli,
egˈzɔstəbli,
ɪgˈzastəbli,
egˈzastəbli

exhaustion
BR ɪgˈzɔːstʃ(ə)n,
egˈzɔːstʃ(ə)n
AM ɪgˈzɔstʃən,
egˈzɔstʃən,
ɪgˈzastʃən, egˈzastʃən

exhaustive
BR ɪgˈzɔːstɪv, egˈzɔːstɪv
AM ɪgˈzɔstɪv, egˈzɔstɪv,
ɪgˈzastɪv, egˈzastɪv

exhaustively
BR ɪgˈzɔːstɪvli,
egˈzɔːstɪvli
AM ɪgˈzɔstɪvli,
egˈzɔstəvli,
ɪgˈzastəvli,
egˈzastəvli

exhaustiveness
BR ɪgˈzɔːstɪvnɪs,
egˈzɔːstɪvnɪs
AM ɪgˈzɔstɪvnɪs,
egˈzɔstɪvnɪs,
ɪgˈzastɪvnɪs,
egˈzastɪvnɪs

exhibit
BR ɪgˈzɪbˌɪt, egˈzɪbˌɪt, -s,
-ɪtɪŋ, -ɪtɪd
AM ɪgˈzɪbəˌt, egˈzɪbəˌt,
-ts, -ɪŋ, -dəd

exhibition
BR ˌeksɪˈbɪʃn, -z
AM ˌeksəˈbɪʃən, -z

exhibitioner
BR ˌeksɪˈbɪʃnə(r),
ˌeksɪˈbɪʃənə(r), -z
AM ˌeksəˈbɪʃənər, -z

exhibitionism
BR ˌeksɪˈbɪʃnɪz(ə)m,
ˌeksɪˈbɪʃənɪz(ə)m
AM ˌeksəˈbɪʃəˌnɪzəm

exhibitionist
BR ˌeksɪˈbɪʃnɪst,
ˌeksɪˈbɪʃənɪst, -s
AM ˌeksəˈbɪʃ(ə)nəst, -s

exhibitionistic
BR ˌeksɪˌbɪʃəˈnɪstɪk,
ˌeksɪˌbɪʃnˈɪstɪk

AM ˌeksəˌbɪʃəˈnɪstɪk

exhibitionistically
BR ˌeksɪˌbɪʃəˈnɪstɪkli
AM ˌeksəˌbɪʃəˈnɪstɪk(ə)li

exhibitor
BR ɪgˈzɪbɪtə(r),
egˈzɪbɪtə(r), -z
AM ɪgˈzɪbədər,
egˈzɪbədər, -z

exhibitory
BR ɪgˈzɪbɪt(ə)ri,
egˈzɪbɪt(ə)ri
AM ɪgˈzɪbəˌtɔri,
egˈzɪbəˌtɔri

exhilarant
BR ɪgˈzɪlərənt,
ɪgˈzɪlərnt, egˈzɪlərənt,
egˈzɪlərnt, -s
AM ɪgˈzɪlərənt,
egˈzɪlərənt, -s

exhilarate
BR ɪgˈzɪləreɪt,
egˈzɪlərert, -s, -ɪŋ, -ɪd
AM ɪgˈzɪləˌreɪt,
egˈzɪləˌreɪt, -ts, -dɪŋ,
-dɪd

exhilaratingly
BR ɪgˈzɪləreɪtɪŋli,
egˈzɪlərertɪŋli
AM ɪgˈzɪləˌreɪdɪŋli,
egˈzɪləˌreɪdɪŋli

exhilaration
BR ɪgˌzɪləˈreɪʃn,
egˌzɪləˈreɪʃn
AM ɪgˌzɪləˈreɪʃən,
egˌzɪləˈreɪʃən

exhilarative
BR ɪgˈzɪl(ə)rətɪv,
egˈzɪl(ə)rətɪv
AM ɪgˈzɪləˌreɪdɪv,
egˈzɪləˌreɪdɪv

exhort
BR ɪgˈzɔːt, egˈzɔːt, -s,
-ɪŋ, -ɪd
AM ɪgˈzɔ(ə)rt,
egˈzɔ(ə)rt, -ts,
-ˈzɔrdɪŋ, -ˈzɔrdəd

exhortation
BR ˌegzɔːˈteɪʃn,
ˌeksɔːˈteɪʃn, -z
AM ˌeg,zɔrˈteɪʃən,
ˌek,sɔrˈteɪʃən,
ˌeksərˈteɪʃən,
ˌeks,(h)ɔrˈteɪʃən, -s

exhortative
BR ɪgˈzɔːtətɪv,
egˈzɔːtətɪv
AM ɪgˈzɔrdədɪv,
egˈzɔrdədɪv

exhortatory
BR ɪgˈzɔːtət(ə)ri,
egˈzɔːtət(ə)ri
AM ɪgˈzɔrdəˌtɔri,
egˈzɔrdəˌtɔri

exhorter
BR ɪgˈzɔːtə(r),
egˈzɔːtə(r), -z

AM ɪɡˈzɔːrdər,
ɛɡˈzɔːrdər, -z
exhumation
BR ˌɛks(h)juˈmeɪʃn,
ˌɛɡzjʉˈmeɪʃn, -z
AM ˌɛks(h)juˈmeɪʃən,
ˌɛɡz(j)uˈmeɪʃən, -z
exhume
BR ɛksˈhjuːm,
ɪɡˈzjuːm, ɛɡˈzjuːm, -z,
-ɪŋ, -d
AM ɪɡˈz(j)um,
ɛɡˈz(j)um, -z, -ɪŋ, -d
ex hypothesi
BR ˌɛks hʌɪˈpɒθɪsʌɪ
AM ˌɛks haɪˈpɑθəˌsaɪ
Exide®
BR ˈɛksaɪd
AM ˈɛksaɪd, ˈɛɡzaɪd
exigence
BR ˈɛksɪdʒ(ə)ns,
ˈɛɡzɪdʒ(ə)ns, -ɪz
AM ˈɛksədʒəns,
ˈɛɡzədʒəns, -əz
exigency
BR ˈɛksɪdʒ(ə)ns|i,
ˈɛɡzɪdʒ(ə)ns|i,
ɪɡˈzɪdʒ(ə)ns|i, -ɪz
AM ˈɛɡzədʒənsi,
ˈɛksədʒənsi, -z
exigent
BR ˈɛksɪdʒ(ə)nt,
ˈɛɡzɪdʒ(ə)nt
AM ˈɛɡzədʒənt,
ˈɛksədʒənt
exigently
BR ˈɛksɪdʒ(ə)ntli,
ˈɛɡzɪdʒ(ə)ntli
AM ˈɛɡzədʒən(t)li,
ˈɛksədʒən(t)li
exigible
BR ˈɛksɪdʒəbl,
ˈɛɡzɪdʒəbl
AM ˈɛɡzədʒəbəl,
ˈɛksədʒəbəl
exiguity
BR ˌɛksɪˈgjuːɪti,
ˌɛɡzɪˈgjuːɪti
AM ˌɛɡzəˈgjuədi,
ˌɛksəˈgjuədi
exiguous
BR ɪɡˈzɪɡjʊəs,
ɛɡˈzɪɡjʊəs, ɪkˈsɪɡjʊəs,
ɛkˈsɪɡjʊəs
AM ɛɡˈzɪɡjəwəs,
ɛkˈsɪɡjəwəs
exiguously
BR ɛɡˈzɪɡjʊəsli,
ɪɡˈzɪɡjʊəsli,
ɪkˈsɪɡjʊəsli,
ɛkˈsɪɡjʊəsli
AM ɛɡˈzɪɡjəwəsli,
ɛkˈsɪɡjəwəsli
exiguousness
BR ɛɡˈzɪɡjʊəsnəs,
ɪɡˈzɪɡjʊəsnəs,
ɪkˈsɪɡjʊəsnəs,
ɛkˈsɪɡjʊəsnəs

AM ɛɡˈzɪɡjəwəsnəs,
ɛkˈsɪɡjəwəsnəs
exile
BR ˈɛkzʌɪl, ˈɛɡzʌɪl, -z,
-ɪŋ, -d
AM ˈɛɡˌzaɪl, ˈɛkˌsaɪl, -z,
-ɪŋ, -d
exilic
BR ɛkˈsɪlɪk, ɛɡˈzɪlɪk
AM ɛɡˈzɪlɪk, ɛkˈsɪlɪk
eximious
BR ɪɡˈzɪmɪəs,
ɛɡˈzɪmɪəs, ɛkˈsɪmɪəs
AM ɪɡˈzɪmɪəs,
ɛkˈsɪmɪəs
exist
BR ɪɡˈzɪst, ɛɡˈzɪst, -s,
-ɪŋ, -ɪd
AM ɪɡˈzɪst, ɛɡˈzɪst, -s,
-ɪŋ, -ɪd
existence
BR ɪɡˈzɪst(ə)ns,
ɛɡˈzɪst(ə)ns
AM ɪɡˈzɪstns, ɛɡˈzɪstns
existent
BR ɪɡˈzɪst(ə)nt,
ɛɡˈzɪst(ə)nt
AM ɪɡˈzɪstənt,
ɛɡˈzɪstənt
existential
BR ˌɛɡzɪˈstɛnʃl
AM ˌɛɡzəˈstɛn(t)ʃəl,
ˌɛksəˈstɛn(t)ʃəl
existentialism
BR ˌɛɡzɪˈstɛnʃəlɪz(ə)m,
ˌɛɡzɪˈstɛnʃlɪz(ə)m
AM ˌɛɡzəˈstɛn(t)ʃəˌlɪzəm,
ˌɛksəˈstɛn(t)ʃəˌlɪzəm
existentialist
BR ˌɛɡzɪˈstɛnʃəlɪst,
ˌɛɡzɪˈstɛnʃlɪst, -s
AM ˌɛɡzəˈstɛn(t)ʃələst,
ˌɛksəˈstɛn(t)ʃələst, -s
existentially
BR ˌɛɡzɪˈstɛnʃli,
ˌɛɡzɪˈstɛnʃəli
AM ˌɛɡzəˈstɛn(t)ʃəli,
ˌɛksəˈstɛn(t)ʃəli
exit
BR ˈɛks|ɪt, ˈɛɡz|ɪt, -ɪts,
-ɪtɪŋ, -ɪtɪd
AM ˈɛɡzə|t, ˈɛksə|t, -ts,
-dɪŋ, -dəd
Ex-lax®
BR ˈɛkslaks
AM ˈɛksˌlæks
ex libris
BR ˌɛks ˈlɪbrɪs
AM ˌɛks ˈlibrɪs
Exmoor
BR ˈɛksmʊə(r),
ˈɛksmɔː(r)
AM ˈɛksˌmɔ(ə)r
Exmouth
BR ˈɛksməθ, ˈɛksmaʊθ
AM ˈɛksməθ
ex nihilo
BR ˌɛks ˈnʌɪɪləʊ

AM ˌɛks ˈni(h)əloʊ
exobiologist
BR ˌɛksəʊbʌɪˈɒlədʒɪst,
-s
AM ˌɛksəˌbaɪˈɑlədʒəst,
-s
exobiology
BR ˌɛksəʊbʌɪˈɒlədʒi
AM ˌɛksəˌbaɪˈɑlədʒi
exocentric
BR ˌɛksə(ʊ)ˈsɛntrɪk
AM ˌɛksoʊˈsɛntrɪk
Exocet®
BR ˈɛksəsɛt, -s
AM ˈɛksəˌsɛt, -s
exocrine
BR ˈɛksə(ʊ)krʌɪn,
ˈɛksə(ʊ)krɪn
AM ˈɛksəkrən,
ˈɛksəˌkraɪn,
ˈɛksəˌkrɪn
exoderm
BR ˈɛksə(ʊ)dəːm, -z
AM ˈɛksəˌdərm, -z
exodus
BR ˈɛksədəs, -ɪz
AM ˈɛksədəs, ˈɛɡzədəs,
-əz
ex officio
BR ˌɛks əˈfɪʃɪəʊ
AM ˌɛks əˈfɪʃioʊ
exogamous
BR ɛkˈsɒɡəməs
AM ɛkˈsɑɡəməs
exogamy
BR ɛkˈsɒɡəmi
AM ɛkˈsɑɡəmi
exogen
BR ˈɛksədʒ(ə)n, -z
AM ˈɛksədʒən,
ˈɛɡzədʒən, -z
exogenous
BR ɛkˈsɒdʒɪnəs,
ɛkˈsɒdʒnəs,
ɪkˈsɒdʒɪnəs,
ɪkˈsɒdʒnəs
AM ɪɡˈzɑdʒənəs,
ɛɡˈzɑdʒənəs
exogenously
BR ɛkˈsɒdʒɪnəsli,
ɛkˈsɒdʒɪnəsli,
ɪkˈsɒdʒɪnəsli,
ɪkˈsɒdʒnəsli
AM ɪɡˈzɑdʒənəsli,
ɛɡˈzɑdʒənəsli
exon
BR ˈɛksɒn, -z
AM ˈɛkˌsɑn, -z
exonerate
BR ɪɡˈzɒnəreɪt,
ɛɡˈzɒnəreɪt, -s, -ɪŋ, -ɪd
AM ɪɡˈzɑnəˌreɪ|t,
ɛɡˈzɑnəˌreɪ|t, -ts, -dɪŋ,
-dɪd
exoneration
BR ɪɡˌzɒnəˈreɪʃn,
ɛɡˌzɒnəˈreɪʃn

AM ɪɡˌzɑnəˈreɪʃən,
ɛɡˌzɑnəˈreɪʃən
exonerative
BR ɪɡˈzɒn(ə)rətɪv,
ɛɡˈzɒn(ə)rətɪv
AM ɪɡˈzɑnəˌreɪdɪv,
ɛɡˈzɑnəˌreɪdɪv
exophera
BR ɛkˈsɒf(ə)rə(r),
ɪkˈsɒf(ə)rə(r)
AM ɛkˈsɑf(ə)rə
exophoric
BR ˌɛksə(ʊ)ˈfɒrɪk
AM ˌɛksoʊˈfɔrɪk
exophthalmia
BR ˌɛksɒfˈθalmɪə(r)
AM ˌɛksɑfˈθælmɪə,
ˌɛksɑpˈθælmɪə
exophthalmic
BR ˌɛksɒfˈθalmɪk
AM ˌɛksɑfˈθælmɪk,
ˌɛksɑpˈθælmɪk
exophthalmos
BR ˌɛksɒfˈθalmɒs
AM ˌɛksɑfˈθælməs,
ˌɛksɑpˈθælməs
exophthalmus
BR ˌɛksɒfˈθalməs
AM ˌɛksɑfˈθælməs,
ˌɛksɑpˈθælməs
exoplasm
BR ˈɛksə(ʊ)plaz(ə)m
AM ˈɛksoʊˌplæz(ə)m
exorbitance
BR ɪɡˈzɔːbɪt(ə)ns,
ɛɡˈzɔːbɪt(ə)ns
AM ɪɡˈzɔrbədəns,
ɛɡˈzɔrbədəns
exorbitant
BR ɪɡˈzɔːbɪt(ə)nt,
ɛɡˈzɔːbɪt(ə)nt
AM ɪɡˈzɔrbədnt,
ɛɡˈzɔrbədnt
exorbitantly
BR ɪɡˈzɔːbɪt(ə)ntli,
ɛɡˈzɔːbɪt(ə)ntli
AM ɪɡˈzɔrbədən(t)li,
ɛɡˈzɔrbədən(t)li,
ɪɡˈzɔrbətn(t)li,
ɛɡˈzɔrbətn(t)li
exorcisation
BR ˌɛksəsʌɪˈzeɪʃn,
ˌɛksɔːsʌɪˈzeɪʃn
AM ˌɛkˌsɔrsəˈzeɪʃən,
ˌɛksərsəˈzeɪʃən,
ˌɛkˌsɔrˌsaɪˈzeɪʃən,
ˌɛksərˌsaɪˈzeɪʃən
exorcise
BR ˈɛksɔːsʌɪz,
ˈɛksəsʌɪz, -ɪz, -ɪŋ, -d
AM ˈɛkˌsɔrˌsaɪz,
ˈɛksərˌsaɪz, -ɪz, -ɪŋ, -d
exorcism
BR ˈɛksɔːsɪz(ə)m,
ˈɛksəsɪz(ə)m, -z
AM ˈɛkˌsɔrˌsɪzəm,
ˈɛksərˌsɪzəm, -z

exorcist
BR ˈɛksɔːsɪst, ˈɛksəsɪst
AM ˈɛkˌsɔrˌsəst,
ˈɛksərˌsəst

exorcization
BR ˌɛksɔːsaɪˈzeɪʃn,
ˌɛksəsaɪˈzeɪʃn
AM ˌɛkˌsɔrsəˈzeɪʃən,
ˌɛksərsəˈzeɪʃən,
ˌɛkˌsɔrˌsaɪˈzeɪʃən,
ˌɛksərˌsaɪˈzeɪʃən

exorcize
BR ˈɛksɔːsaɪz,
ˈɛksəsaɪz, -ɪz, -ɪŋ, -d
AM ˈɛkˌsɔrˌsaɪz,
ˈɛksərˌsaɪz, -ɪz, -ɪŋ, -d

exordia
BR ɪgˈzɔːdɪə(r),
ɛgˈzɔːdɪə(r)
AM ɪgˈzɔrdiə, ɛgˈzɔrdiə

exordial
BR ɪgˈzɔːdɪəl,
ɛgˈzɔːdɪəl
AM ɪgˈzɔrdiəl,
ɛgˈzɔrdiəl

exordially
BR ɪgˈzɔːdɪəli,
ɛgˈzɔːdɪəli
AM ɪgˈzɔrdiəli,
ɛgˈzɔrdiəli

exordium
BR ɪgˈzɔːdɪəm,
ɛgˈzɔːdɪəm
AM ɪgˈzɔrdiəm,
ɛgˈzɔrdiəm

exoskeletal
BR ˌɛksə(ʊ)ˈskɛlɪtl
AM ˌɛksəˈskɛlədl

exoskeleton
BR ˈɛksə(ʊ)ˌskɛlɪt(ə)n,
-z
AM ˌɛksəˈskɛlətn, -z

exosphere
BR ˌɛksə(ʊ)sfɪə(r), -z
AM ˌɛksoʊˈsfɪ(ə)r, -z

exoteric
BR ˌɛksə(ʊ)ˈtɛrɪk, -s
AM ˌɛksəˈtɛrɪk, -s

exoterical
BR ˌɛksə(ʊ)ˈtɛrɪkl
AM ˌɛksəˈtɛrəkəl

exoterically
BR ˌɛksə(ʊ)ˈtɛrɪkli
AM ˌɛksəˈtɛrək(ə)li

exotericism
BR ˌɛksə(ʊ)ˈtɛrɪsɪz(ə)m
AM ˌɛksəˈtɛrəˌsɪzəm

exothermal
BR ˌɛksə(ʊ)ˈθəːml
AM ˌɛksəˈθərməl

exothermally
BR ˌɛksə(ʊ)ˈθəːml̩i,
ˌɛksə(ʊ)ˈθəːməli
AM ˌɛksəˈθərməli

exothermic
BR ˌɛksə(ʊ)ˈθəːmɪk
AM ˌɛksəˈθərmɪk

exothermically
BR ˌɛksə(ʊ)ˈθəːmɪkli
AM ˌɛksəˈθərmək(ə)li

exotic
BR ɪgˈzɒtɪk, ɛgˈzɒtɪk
AM ɪgˌzɑdɪk, ɛgˈzɑdɪk

exotica
BR ɪgˈzɒtɪkə(r),
ɛgˈzɒtɪkə(r)
AM ɪgˌzɑdɪkə,
ɛgˈzɑdɪkə

exotically
BR ɪgˈzɒtɪkli,
ɛgˈzɒtɪkli
AM ɪgˌzɑdək(ə)li,
ɛgˈzɑdək(ə)li

exoticism
BR ɪgˈzɒtɪsɪz(ə)m,
ɛgˈzɒtɪsɪz(ə)m
AM ɪgˌzɑdəˌsɪzəm,
ɛgˈzɑdəˌsɪzəm

expand
BR ɪkˈspand, ɛkˈspand,
-z, -ɪŋ, -ɪd
AM ɪkˈspænd,
ɛkˈspænd, -z, -ɪŋ, -əd

expandable
BR ɪkˈspandəbl,
ɛkˈspandəbl
AM ɪkˈspændəbəl,
ɛkˈspændəbəl

expander
BR ɪkˈspandə(r),
ɛkˈspandə(r), -z
AM ɪkˈspændər,
ɛkˈspændər, -z

expanse
BR ɪkˈspans, ɛkˈspans,
-ɪz
AM ɪkˈspæns,
ɛkˈspæns, -əz

expansibility
BR ɪkˌspansɪˈbɪlɪti,
ɛkˌspansɪˈbɪlɪti
AM ɪkˌspænsəˈbɪlɪdi,
ɛkˌspænsəˈbɪlɪdi

expansible
BR ɪkˈspansɪbl,
ɛkˈspansɪbl
AM ɪkˈspænsəbəl,
ɛkˈspænsəbəl

expansile
BR ɪkˈspansʌɪl,
ɛkˈspansʌɪl
AM ɪkˈspænsl,
ɛkˈspænsl,
ɪkˈspænˌsaɪl,
ɛkˈspænˌsaɪl

expansion
BR ɪkˈspanʃn,
ɛkˈspanʃn, -z
AM ɪkˈspænʃən,
ɛkˈspænʃən, -z

expansionary
BR ɪkˈspanʃn̩(ə)ri,
ɛkˈspanʃn̩(ə)ri,
ɪkˈspanʃən(ə)ri,
ɛkˈspanʃən(ə)ri

expansionism
BR ɪkˈspanʃnɪz(ə)m,
ɛkˈspanʃnɪz(ə)m,
ɪkˈspanʃənɪz(ə)m,
ɛkˈspanʃənɪz(ə)m
AM ɪkˈspænʃəˌnɪzəm,
ɛkˈspænʃəˌnɪzəm

expansionist
BR ɪkˈspanʃnɪst,
ɛkˈspanʃnɪst,
ɪkˈspanʃənɪst,
ɛkˈspanʃənɪst, -s
AM ɪkˈspæn(t)ʃ(ə)nəst,
ɛkˈspæn(t)ʃ(ə)nəst,
-s

expansionistic
BR ɪkˈspanʃəˈnɪstɪk,
ɛkˌspanʃəˈnɪstɪk,
ɪkˌspanʃn̩ˈɪstɪk,
ɛkˌspanʃn̩ˈɪstɪk
AM ɪkˌspæn(t)ʃəˈnɪstɪk,
ɛkˌspæn(t)ʃəˈnɪstɪk

expansive
BR ɪkˈspansɪv,
ɛkˈspansɪv
AM ɪkˈspænsɪv,
ɛkˈspænsɪv

expansively
BR ɪkˈspansɪvli,
ɛkˈspansɪvli
AM ɪkˈspænsəvli,
ɛkˈspænsəvli

expansiveness
BR ɪkˈspansɪvnɪs,
ɛkˈspansɪvnɪs
AM ɪkˈspænsɪvnɪs,
ɛkˈspænsɪvnɪs

expansivity
BR ɪkˌspanˈsɪvɪti,
ɛkˌspanˈsɪvɪti
AM ɪkˌspænˈsɪvɪdi,
ɛkˌspænˈsɪvɪdi

ex parte
BR ˌɛks ˈpɑːti
AM ˌɛks ˈpɑrdi

expat
BR ˌɛksˈpat, -s
AM ˌɛksˈpæt, -s

expatiate
BR ɪkˈspeɪʃɪeɪt,
ɛkˈspeɪʃɪeɪt, -s, -ɪŋ, -ɪd
AM ɪkˈspeɪʃiˌeɪt,
ɛkˈspeɪʃiˌeɪt, -ts, -ɪŋ,
-dɪd

expatiation
BR ɪkˌspeɪʃɪˈeɪʃn,
ɛkˌspeɪʃɪˈeɪʃn
AM ɪkˌspeɪʃiˈeɪʃən,
ɛkˌspeɪʃiˈeɪʃən

expatiatory
BR ɪkˈspeɪʃɪətri,
ɛkˈspeɪʃɪətri
AM ɪkˈspeɪʃiəˌtɔri,
ɛkˈspeɪʃiəˌtɔri

AM ɪkˈspænʃəˌnɛri,
ɛkˈspænʃəˌnɛri

expatriate[1]
noun, adjective
BR ɛksˈpatrɪət,
ɪksˈpatrɪət,
ɛksˈpeɪtrɪət,
ɪksˈpeɪtrɪət, -s
AM ɛkˈspeɪtrɪət, -s

expatriate[2]
verb
BR ɛksˈpatrɪeɪt,
ɪksˈpatrɪeɪt,
ɪksˈpeɪtrɪeɪt, -s, -ɪŋ, -ɪd
AM ɛkˈspeɪtriˌeɪ|t, -ts,
-dɪŋ, -dɪd

expatriation
BR ɛksˌpatrɪˈeɪʃn,
ɪksˌpatrɪˈeɪʃn,
ɛksˌpeɪtrɪˈeɪʃn,
ɪksˌpeɪtrɪˈeɪʃn
AM ɛkˌspeɪtriˈeɪʃən

expect
BR ɪkˈspɛkt, ɛkˈspɛkt,
-s, -ɪŋ, -ɪd
AM ɪkˈspɛk|(t),
ɛkˈspɛk|(t), -(t)s, -tɪŋ,
-təd

expectable
BR ɪkˈspɛktəbl,
ɛkˈspɛktəbl
AM ɪkˈspɛktəbəl,
ɛkˈspɛktəbəl

expectance
BR ɪkˈspɛkt(ə)ns,
ɛkˈspɛkt(ə)ns
AM ɪkˈspɛktns,
ɛkˈspɛktns

expectancy
BR ɪkˈspɛkt(ə)nsi,
ɛkˈspɛkt(ə)nsi
AM ɪkˈspɛktənsi,
ɛkˈspɛktnsi

expectant
BR ɪkˈspɛkt(ə)nt,
ɛkˈspɛkt(ə)nt
AM ɪkˈspɛktnt,
ɛkˈspɛktnt

expectantly
BR ɪkˈspɛkt(ə)ntli,
ɛkˈspɛkt(ə)ntli
AM ɪkˈspɛktən(t)li,
ɛkˈspɛktən(t)li

expectation
BR ˌɛkspɛkˈteɪʃn, -z
AM ˌɛkˌspɛkˈteɪʃən,
ɪkˌspɛkˈteɪʃən, -z

expectorant
BR ɪkˈspɛkt(ə)rənt,
ɛkˈspɛkt(ə)rənt,
ɪkˈspɛkt(ə)rn̩t,
ɛkˈspɛkt(ə)rn̩t, -s
AM ɪkˈspɛktərənt,
ɛkˈspɛktərənt, -s

expectorate
BR ɪkˈspɛktəreɪt,
ɛkˈspɛktəreɪt, -s, -ɪŋ,
-ɪd

AM ɪkˈspɛktəˌreɪ|t,
ɛkˈspɛktəˌreɪ|t, -ts,
-dɪŋ, -dɪd
expectoration
BR ɪkˌspɛktəˈreɪʃn,
ɛkˌspɛktəˈreɪʃn
AM ˌɛkˌspɛktəˈreɪʃən,
ɪkˌspɛktəˈreɪʃən
expectorator
BR ɪkˈspɛktəreɪtə(r),
ɛkˈspɛktəreɪtə(r), -z
AM ɪkˈspɛktəˌreɪdər,
ɛkˈspɛktəˌreɪdər, -z
expedience
BR ɪkˈspiːdɪəns,
ɛkˈspiːdɪəns
AM ɪkˈspidiəns,
ɛkˈspidiəns
expediency
BR ɪkˈspiːdɪənsi,
ɛkˈspiːdɪənsi
AM ɪkˈspidiənsi,
ɛkˈspidiənsi
expedient
BR ɪkˈspiːdɪənt,
ɛkˈspiːdɪənt
AM ɪkˈspidiənt,
ɛkˈspidiənt
expediently
BR ɪkˈspiːdɪəntli,
ɛkˈspiːdɪəntli
AM ɪkˈspidiən(t)li,
ɛkˈspidiən(t)li
expedite
BR ˈɛkspɪdʌɪt, -s, -ɪŋ,
-ɪd
AM ˈɛkspəˌdaɪ|t, -ts,
-dɪŋ, -dɪd
expediter
BR ˈɛkspɪdʌɪtə(r), -z
AM ˈɛkspəˌdaɪdər, -z
expedition
BR ˌɛkspɪˈdɪʃn, -z
AM ˌɛkspəˈdɪʃən, -z
expeditionary
BR ˌɛkspɪˈdɪʃn(ə)ri
AM ˌɛkspəˈdɪʃəˌnɛri
expeditionist
BR ˌɛkspɪˈdɪʃnɪst,
ˌɛkspɪˈdɪʃənɪst, -s
AM ˌɛkspəˈdɪʃənəst, -s
expeditious
BR ˌɛkspɪˈdɪʃəs
AM ˌɛkspəˈdɪʃəs
expeditiously
BR ˌɛkspɪˈdɪʃəsli
AM ˌɛkspəˈdɪʃəsli
expeditiousness
BR ˌɛkspɪˈdɪʃəsnəs
AM ˌɛkspəˈdɪʃəsnəs
expel
BR ɪkˈspɛl, ɛkˈspɛl, -z,
-ɪŋ, -d
AM ɪkˈspɛl, ɛkˈspɛl, -z,
-ɪŋ, -d
expellable
BR ɪkˈspɛləbl,
ɛkˈspɛləbl

AM ɪkˈspɛləbəl,
ɛkˈspɛləbəl
expellee
BR ɪkˌspɛˈliː, ɛkˌspɛˈliː,
ˌɛkspɛˈliː, -z
AM ɪkˌspɛˈli, ɛkˌspɛˈli,
-z
expellent
BR ɪkˈspɛlənt,
ɛkˈspɛlənt, ɪkˈspɛlnt̩,
ɛkˈspɛlnt̩, -s
AM ɪkˈspɛlənt,
ɛkˈspɛlənt, -s
expeller
BR ɪkˈspɛlə(r),
ɛkˈspɛlə(r), -z
AM ɪkˈspɛlər,
ɛkˈspɛlər, -z
expend
BR ɪkˈspɛnd, ɛkˈspɛnd,
-z, -ɪŋ, -ɪd
AM ɪkˈspɛnd, ɛkˈspɛnd,
-z, -ɪŋ, -əd
expendability
BR ɪkˌspɛndəˈbɪlɪti,
ɛkˌspɛndəˈbɪlɪti
AM ɪkˌspɛndəˈbɪlɪdi,
ɛkˌspɛndəˈbɪlɪdi
expendable
BR ɪkˈspɛndəbl,
ɛkˈspɛndəbl, -z
AM ɪkˈspɛndəbəl,
ɛkˈspɛndəbəl, -z
expendably
BR ɪkˈspɛndəbli,
ɛkˈspɛndəbli
AM ɪkˈspɛndəbli,
ɛkˈspɛndəbli
expenditure
BR ɪkˈspɛndɪtʃə(r),
ɛkˈspɛndɪtʃə(r), -z
AM ɪkˈspɛndətʃər,
ɛkˈspɛndətʃər,
ɪkˈspɛndəˌtʃʊ(ə)r,
ɛkˈspɛndəˌtʃʊ(ə)r, -z
expense
BR ɪkˈspɛns, ɛkˈspɛns,
-ɪz
AM ɪkˈspɛns, ɛkˈspɛns,
-əz
expensive
BR ɪkˈspɛnsɪv,
ɛkˈspɛnsɪv
AM ɪkˈspɛnsɪv,
ɛkˈspɛnsɪv
expensively
BR ɪkˈspɛnsɪvli,
ɛkˈspɛnsɪvli
AM ɪkˈspɛnsəvli,
ɛkˈspɛnsəvli
expensiveness
BR ɪkˈspɛnsɪvnɪs,
ɛkˈspɛnsɪvnɪs
AM ɪkˈspɛnsɪvnɪs,
ɛkˈspɛnsɪvnɪs
experience
BR ɪkˈspɪərɪəns,
ɛkˈspɪərɪəns, -ɪz, -ɪŋ, -t

AM ɪkˈspɪriəns,
ɛkˈspɪriəns,
ɪkˈspɪriəns,
ɛkˈspɪriəns, -əz, -ɪŋ, -t
experienceable
BR ɪkˈspɪərɪənsəbl,
ɛkˈspɪərɪənsəbl
AM ɪkˈspɪriənsəbəl,
ɛkˈspɪriənsəbəl,
ɪkˈspɪriənsəbəl,
ɛkˈspɪriənsəbəl
experiential
BR ɪkˌspɪərɪˈɛnʃl,
ɛkˌspɪərɪˈɛnʃl
AM ɛkˌspɪriˈɛn(t)ʃəl,
ɪkˌspɪriˈɛn(t)ʃəl
experientialism
BR ɪkˌspɪərɪˈɛnʃlɪz(ə)m,
ɛkˌspɪərɪˈɛnʃlɪz(ə)m,
ɪkˌspɪərɪˈɛnʃəlɪz(ə)m,
ɛkˌspɪərɪˈɛnʃəlɪz(ə)m
AM ɛkˌspɪriˈɛn(t)ʃəˌlɪ-
zəm,
ɪkˌspɪriˈɛn(t)ʃəˌlɪzəm
experientialist
BR ɪkˌspɪərɪˈɛnʃlɪst,
ɛkˌspɪərɪˈɛnʃlɪst,
ɪkˌspɪərɪˈɛnʃəlɪst,
ɛkˌspɪərɪˈɛnʃəlɪst, -s
AM ɛkˌspɪriˈɛn(t)ʃ(ə)l-
əst,
ɪkˌspɪriˈɛn(t)ʃ(ə)ləst,
-s
experientially
BR ɪkˌspɪərɪˈɛnʃli,
ɛkˌspɪərɪˈɛnʃli,
ɪkˌspɪərɪˈɛnʃəli,
ɛkˌspɪərɪˈɛnʃəli
AM ɛkˌspɪriˈɛn(t)ʃəli,
ɪkˌspɪriˈɛn(t)ʃəli
experiment¹
noun
BR ɪkˈspɛrɪm(ə)nt,
ɛkˈspɛrɪm(ə)nt, -s
AM ɪkˈspɛrəmənt,
ɛkˈspɛrəmənt, -s
experiment²
verb
BR ɪkˈspɛrɪm(ə)nt,
ɛkˈspɛrɪm(ə)nt,
ɪkˈspɛrɪment,
ɛkˈspɛrɪment, -s, -ɪŋ,
-ɪd
AM ɪkˈspɛrəmən|t,
ɛkˈspɛrəmən|t, -ts,
-(t)ɪŋ, -(t)əd
experimental
BR ɪkˌspɛrɪˈmɛntl,
ɛkˌspɛrɪˈmɛntl
AM ɪkˌspɛrəˈmɛn(t)l,
ɛkˌspɛrəˈmɛn(t)l
experimentalise
BR ɪkˌspɛrɪˈmɛntl̩ʌɪz,
ɛkˌspɛrɪˈmɛntl̩ʌɪz,
ɪkˌspɛrɪˈmɛntəlʌɪz,
ɛkˌspɛrɪˈmɛntəlʌɪz,
-ɪz, -ɪŋ, -d

AM ɪkˌspɛrəˈmɛntəˌlaɪz,
ɛkˌspɛrəˈmɛntəˌlaɪz,
-ɪz, -ɪŋ, -d
experimentalism
BR ɪkˌspɛrɪˈmɛntlɪz(ə)m,
ɛkˌspɛrɪˈmɛntlɪz(ə)m,
ɪkˌspɛrɪˈmɛntəlɪz(ə)m,
ɛkˌspɛrɪˈmɛntəlɪz(ə)m
AM ɪkˌspɛrəˈmɛn(t)ə-
ˌlɪzəm,
ɛkˌspɛrəˈmɛn(t)əˌlɪzəm
experimentalist
BR ɪkˌspɛrɪˈmɛntlɪst,
ɛkˌspɛrɪˈmɛntlɪst,
ɪkˌspɛrɪˈmɛntəlɪst,
ɛkˌspɛrɪˈmɛntəlɪst, -s
AM ɪkˌspɛrəˈmɛn(t)ləst,
ɛkˌspɛrəˈmɛn(t)ləst,
-s
experimentalize
BR ɪkˌspɛrɪˈmɛntl̩ʌɪz,
ɛkˌspɛrɪˈmɛntl̩ʌɪz,
ɪkˌspɛrɪˈmɛntəlʌɪz,
ɛkˌspɛrɪˈmɛntəlʌɪz,
-ɪz, -ɪŋ, -d
AM ɪkˌspɛrəˈmɛn(t)əˌlaɪz,
ɛkˌspɛrəˈmɛn(t)əˌlaɪz,
-ɪz, -ɪŋ, -d
experimentally
BR ɪkˌspɛrɪˈmɛntli,
ɛkˌspɛrɪˈmɛntli,
ɪkˌspɛrɪˈmɛntəli,
ɛkˌspɛrɪˈmɛntəli
AM ɪkˌspɛrəˈmɛn(t)li,
ɛkˌspɛrəˈmɛn(t)li
experimentation
BR ɪkˌspɛrɪmɛnˈteɪʃn,
ɛkˌspɛrɪmɛnˈteɪʃn,
ɪkˌspɛrɪm(ə)nˈteɪʃn,
ɛkˌspɛrɪm(ə)nˈteɪʃn
AM ɪkˌspɛrəmənˈteɪʃən,
ɛkˌspɛrəmənˈteɪʃən
experimenter
BR ɪkˈspɛrɪmɛntə(r),
ɛkˈspɛrɪmɛntə(r),
ɪkˈspɛrɪm(ə)ntə(r),
ɛkˈspɛrɪm(ə)ntə(r), -z
AM ɪkˈspɛrəˌmɛn(t)ər,
ɛkˈspɛrəˌmɛn(t)ər, -z
expert
BR ˈɛkspəːt, -s
AM ˈɛkˌspərt, -s
expertise
noun
BR ˌɛkspəːˈtiːz,
ˌɛkspəˈtiːz
AM ˌɛkˌspərˈtiːz,
ˌɛkˌspərˈtis
expertize
verb
BR ˈɛkspətʌɪz,
ˈɛkspəːtʌɪz, -ɪz, -ɪŋ, -d
AM ˈɛkspərˌtaɪz, -ɪz, -ɪŋ,
-d
expertly
BR ˈɛkspəːtli
AM ˈɛkˌspərtli
expertness
BR ˈɛkspəːtnəs

AM ˌekˈspɜːtnəs

expiable
BR ˈekspɪəbl
AM ˈekspɪəbəl

expiate
BR ˈekspɪeɪt, -s, -ɪŋ, -ɪd
AM ˈekspiˌeɪ|t, -ts, -dɪŋ, -dɪd

expiation
BR ˌekspɪˈeɪʃn
AM ˌekspiˈeɪʃən

expiator
BR ˈekspɪeɪtə(r), -z
AM ˈekspiˌeɪdər, -z

expiatory
BR ˈekspɪət(ə)ri
AM ˈekspiəˌtɔri

expiration
BR ˌekspɪˈreɪʃn
AM ˌekspəˈreɪʃən

expiratory
BR ɪkˈspʌɪərət(ə)ri, ɛkˈspʌɪərət(ə)ri
AM ɪkˈspʌɪ(ə)rəˌtɔri, ɛkˈspʌɪ(ə)rəˌtɔri

expire
BR ɪkˈspʌɪə(r), ɛkˈspʌɪə(r), -z, -ɪŋ, -d
AM ɪkˈspʌɪ(ə)r, ɛkˈspʌɪ(ə)r, -z, -ɪŋ, -d

expiry
BR ɪkˈspʌɪəri, ɛkˈspʌɪəri
AM ɪkˈspʌɪri, ɛkˈspʌɪri

explain
BR ɪkˈspleɪn, ɛkˈspleɪn, -z, -ɪŋ, -d
AM ɪkˈspleɪn, ɛkˈspleɪn, -z, -ɪŋ, -d

explainable
BR ɪkˈspleɪnəbl, ɛkˈspleɪnəbl
AM ɪkˈspleɪnəbəl, ɛkˈspleɪnəbəl

explainer
BR ɪkˈspleɪnə(r), ɛkˈspleɪnə(r), -z
AM ɪkˈspleɪnər, ɛkˈspleɪnər, -z

explananda
BR ˌekspləˈnandə(r)
AM ˌekspləˈnɑndə

explanandum
BR ˌekspləˈnandəm
AM ˌekspləˈnɑndəm

explanans
BR ˌekspləˈnanz
AM ˌekspləˈnænz, ˌeksˈplænənz

explanantia
BR ˌekspləˈnantɪə(r)
AM ˌekspləˈnæn(t)iə

explanation
BR ˌekspləˈneɪʃn, -z
AM ˌekspləˈneɪʃən, -z

explanatorily
BR ɪkˈsplanət(ə)rɪli, ɛkˈsplanət(ə)rɪli

AM ɪkˈsplænəˌtɔrəli, ɛkˈsplænəˌtɔrəli

explanatory
BR ɪkˈsplanət(ə)ri, ɛkˈsplanət(ə)ri
AM ɪkˈsplænəˌtɔri, ɛkˈsplænəˌtɔri

explant
BR ɪksˈplɑːnt, ɛksˈplɑːnt, ɪksˈplant, ɛksˈplant, -s, -ɪŋ, -ɪd
AM ɪkˈsplæn|t, ɛkˈsplæn|t, -ts, -(t)ɪŋ, -(t)əd

explantation
BR ɪksˌplɑːnˈteɪʃn, ɛksˌplɑːnˈteɪʃn, ɪksˌplanˈteɪʃn, ɛksˌplanˈteɪʃn
AM ɪkˌsplænˈteɪʃən, ɛkˌsplænˈteɪʃən

expletive
BR ɪkˈspliːtɪv, ɛkˈspliːtɪv, -z
AM ˈeksplədɪv, -z

explicable
BR ɪkˈsplɪkəbl, ɛkˈsplɪkəbl, ˈeksplɪkəbl
AM ɛkˈsplɪkəbəl, ɪkˈsplɪkəbəl, ˈeksplərkəbəl

explicably
BR ɪkˈsplɪkəbli, ɛkˈsplɪkəbli, ˈeksplɪkəbli
AM ɛkˈsplɪkɪbli, ɪkˈsplɪkɪbli, ˈeksplərkɪbli

explicate
BR ˈeksplɪkeɪt, -s, -ɪŋ, -ɪd
AM ˈeksplɪˌkeɪ|t, -ts, -dɪŋ, -dɪd

explication
BR ˌeksplɪˈkeɪʃn, -z
AM ˌekspləˈkeɪʃən, -z

explicative
BR ɪkˈsplɪkətɪv, ɛkˈsplɪkətɪv, ˈeksplɪkətɪv
AM ˈekspləˌkeɪdɪv

explicator
BR ˈeksplɪkeɪtə(r), -z
AM ˈekspləˌkeɪdər, -z

explicatory
BR ɪkˈsplɪkət(ə)ri, ɛkˈsplɪkət(ə)ri, ˈeksplɪkət(ə)ri
AM ɪkˈsplɪkəˌtɔri, ɛkˈsplɪkəˌtɔri

explicature
BR ɪkˈsplɪkətʃə(r), ɛkˈsplɪkətʃə(r), ˈeksplɪkətʃə(r), -z
AM ɪkˈsplɪkətʃər, ɛkˈsplɪkətʃər, -z

explicit
BR ɪkˈsplɪsɪt, ɛkˈsplɪsɪt
AM ɪkˈsplɪsɪt, ɛkˈsplɪsɪt

explicitly
BR ɪkˈsplɪsɪtli, ɛkˈsplɪsɪtli
AM ɪkˈsplɪsɪtli, ɛkˈsplɪsɪtli

explicitness
BR ɪkˈsplɪsɪtnɪs, ɛkˈsplɪsɪtnɪs
AM ɪkˈsplɪsɪtnɪs, ɛkˈsplɪsɪtnɪs

explode
BR ɪkˈspləʊd, ɛkˈspləʊd, -z, -ɪŋ, -ɪd
AM ɪkˈsploʊd, ɛkˈsploʊd, -z, -ɪŋ, -əd

exploder
BR ɪkˈspləʊdə(r), ɛkˈspləʊdə(r), -z
AM ɪkˈsploʊdər, ɛkˈsploʊdər, -z

exploit¹
noun
BR ˈeksplɔɪt, -s
AM ˈekˌsplɔɪt, -s

exploit²
verb
BR ɪkˈsplɔɪt, ɛkˈsplɔɪt, -s, -ɪŋ, -ɪd
AM ɪkˈsplɔɪ|t, ɛkˈsplɔɪ|t, -ts, -dɪŋ, -dɪd

exploitable
BR ɪkˈsplɔɪtəbl, ɛkˈsplɔɪtəbl
AM ɪkˈsplɔɪdəbəl, ɛkˈsplɔɪdəbəl

exploitation
BR ˌeksplɔɪˈteɪʃn
AM ˌekˌsplɔɪˈteɪʃən

exploitative
BR ɪkˈsplɔɪtətɪv, ɛkˈsplɔɪtətɪv
AM ɪkˈsplɔɪdədɪv, ɛkˈsplɔɪdədɪv

exploitatively
BR ɪkˈsplɔɪtətɪvli, ɛkˈsplɔɪtətɪvli
AM ɪkˈsplɔɪdədəvli, ɛkˈsplɔɪdədəvli

exploiter
BR ɪkˈsplɔɪtə(r), ɛkˈsplɔɪtə(r), -z
AM ɪkˈsplɔɪdər, ɛkˈsplɔɪdər, -z

exploitive
BR ɪkˈsplɔɪtɪv, ɛkˈsplɔɪtɪv
AM ɪkˈsplɔɪdɪv, ɛkˈsplɔɪdɪv

exploration
BR ˌekspləˈreɪʃn, -z
AM ˌekspləˈreɪʃən, -z

explorational
BR ˌekspləˈreɪʃ(ə)l, ˌekspləˈreɪʃən(ə)l
AM ˌekspləˈreɪʃ(ə)nəl

explorative
BR ɪkˈsplɒrətɪv, ɛkˈsplɒrətɪv
AM ɪkˈsplɔrədɪv, ɛkˈsplɔrədɪv

exploratory
BR ɪkˈsplɒrət(ə)ri, ɛkˈsplɒrət(ə)ri
AM ɪkˈsplɔrəˌtɔri, ɛkˈsplɔrəˌtɔri

explore
BR ɪkˈsplɔː(r), ɛkˈsplɔː(r), -z, -ɪŋ, -d
AM ɪkˈsplɔ(ə)r, ɛkˈsplɔ(ə)r, -z, -ɪŋ, -d

explorer
BR ɪkˈsplɔːrə(r), ɛkˈsplɔːrə(r), -z
AM ɪkˈsplɔrər, ɛkˈsplɔrər, -z

explosion
BR ɪkˈspləʊʒn, ɛkˈspləʊʒn, -z
AM ɪkˈsploʊʒən, ɛkˈsploʊʒən, -z

explosive
BR ɪkˈspləʊsɪv, ɪkˈspləʊzɪv, ɛkˈspləʊsɪv, ɛkˈspləʊzɪv, -z
AM ɪkˈsploʊsɪv, ɛkˈsploʊsɪv, ɪkˈsploʊzɪv, ɛkˈsploʊzɪv, -z

explosively
BR ɪkˈspləʊsɪvli, ɪkˈspləʊzɪvli, ɛkˈspləʊsɪvli, ɛkˈspləʊzɪvli
AM ɪkˈsploʊsəvli, ɛkˈsploʊsəvli, ɪkˈsploʊzəvli, ɛkˈsploʊzəvli

explosiveness
BR ɪkˈspləʊsɪvnɪs, ɪkˈspləʊzɪvnɪs, ɛkˈspləʊsɪvnɪs, ɛkˈspləʊzɪvnɪs
AM ɪkˈsploʊsɪvnɪs, ɛkˈsploʊsɪvnɪs, ɪkˈsploʊzɪvnɪs, ɛkˈsploʊzɪvnɪs

Expo
BR ˈekspəʊ, -z
AM ˈekˌspoʊ, -z

exponent
BR ɪkˈspəʊnənt, ɛkˈspəʊnənt, -s
AM ɪkˈspoʊnənt, ɛkˈspoʊnənt, ˈekspoʊnənt, -s

exponential
BR ˌekspə(ʊ)ˈnenʃl
AM ˌekspəˈnen(t)ʃəl, ˌekspoʊˈnen(t)ʃəl

exponentially
BR ˌekspəˈnenʃli,
ˌekspəˈnenʃəli
AM ˌekspəˈnen(t)ʃəli,
ˌekspoʊˈnen(t)ʃəli

export¹
noun
BR ˈekspɔːt, -s
AM ˈekˌspɔ(ə)rt, -s

export²
verb
BR ɪkˈspɔːt, ekˈspɔːt, -s,
-ɪŋ, -ɪd
AM ɪkˈspɔ(ə)r|t,
ekˈspɔ(ə)r|t, -ts, -dɪŋ,
-dəd

exportability
BR ɪkˌspɔːtəˈbɪlɪti,
ekˌspɔːtəˈbɪlɪti
AM ɪkˌspɔrdəˈbɪlɪdi,
ekˌspɔrdəˈbɪlɪdi

exportable
BR ɪkˈspɔːtəbl,
ekˈspɔːtəbl
AM ɪkˈspɔrdəbəl,
ekˈspɔrdəbəl

exportation
BR ˌekspɔːˈteɪʃn
AM ˌekˌspɔrˈteɪʃən,
ˌekspərˈteɪʃən

exporter
BR ɪkˈspɔːtə(r),
ekˈspɔːtə(r), -z
AM ˈekspɔrdər,
ɪkˈspɔrdər, -z

expose
BR ɪkˈspəʊz, ekˈspəʊz,
-ɪz, -ɪŋ, -d
AM ɪkˈspoʊz, ekˈspoʊz,
-əz, -ɪŋ, -d

exposé
BR ɪkˈspəʊzeɪ,
ekˈspəʊzeɪ, -z
AM ˌekspoʊˈzeɪ,
ˈekspəˈzeɪ, -z

exposer
BR ɪkˈspəʊzə(r),
ekˈspəʊzə(r), -z
AM ɪkˈspoʊzər,
ekˈspoʊzər, -z

exposition
BR ˌekspəˈzɪʃn, -z
AM ˌekspəˈzɪʃən,
ˌekspoʊˈzɪʃən, -z

expositional
BR ˌekspəˈzɪʃn(ə)l,
ˌekspəˈzɪʃən(ə)l
AM ˌekspəˈzɪʃ(ə)nəl,
ˌekspoʊˈzɪʃ(ə)nəl

expositive
BR ɪkˈspɒzɪtɪv,
ekˈspɒzɪtɪv
AM ɪkˈspɑzədɪv,
ekˈspɑzədɪv

expositor
BR ɪkˈspɒzɪtə(r),
ekˈspɒzɪtə(r), -z

AM ɪkˈspɑzədər,
ekˈspɑzədər, -z

expository
BR ɪkˈspɒzɪt(ə)ri,
ekˈspɒzɪt(ə)ri
AM ɪkˈspɑzəˌtɔri,
ekˈspɑzəˌtɔri

ex post facto
BR ˌeks pəʊs(t) ˈfaktəʊ
AM ˌekˌspoʊs(t)
ˌfæktoʊ

expostulate
BR ɪkˈspɒstjʊleɪt,
ekˈspɒstjʊleɪt,
ɪkˈspɒstʃʊleɪt,
ekˈspɒstʃʊleɪt, -s, -ɪŋ,
-ɪd
AM ɪkˈspɑstʃəˌleɪ|t,
ekˈspɑstʃəˌleɪ|t, -ts,
-dɪŋ, -dɪd

expostulation
BR ɪkˌspɒstjʊˈleɪʃn,
ekˌspɒstjʊˈleɪʃn,
ɪkˌspɒstʃʊˈleɪʃn,
ekˌspɒstʃʊˈleɪʃn, -z
AM ɪkˌspɑstʃəˈleɪʃən,
ekˌspɑstʃəˈleɪʃən, -z

expostulatory
BR ɪkˈspɒstjʊlət(ə)ri,
ekˈspɒstjʊlət(ə)ri,
ɪkˈspɒstʃʊlət(ə)ri,
ekˈspɒstʃʊlət(ə)ri
AM ɪkˈspɑstʃələˌtɔri,
ekˈspɑstʃələˌtɔri

exposure
BR ɪkˈspəʊʒə(r),
ekˈspəʊʒə(r), -z
AM ɪkˈspoʊʒər,
ekˈspoʊʒər, -z

expound
BR ɪkˈspaʊnd,
ekˈspaʊnd, -z, -ɪŋ, -ɪd
AM ɪkˈspaʊnd,
ekˈspaʊnd, -z, -ɪŋ, -əd

expounder
BR ɪkˈspaʊndə(r),
ekˈspaʊndə(r), -z
AM ɪkˈspaʊndər,
ekˈspaʊndər, -z

ex-president
BR eksˈprezɪd(ə)nt, -s
AM eksˈprezədnt, -s

express
BR ɪkˈspres, ekˈspres,
-ɪz, -ɪŋ, -t
AM ɪkˈspres, ekˈspres,
-əz, -ɪŋ, -t

expresser
BR ɪkˈspresə(r),
ekˈspresə(r), -z
AM ɪkˈspresər,
ekˈspresər, -z

expressible
BR ɪkˈspresɪbl,
ekˈspresɪbl
AM ɪkˈspresəbəl,
ekˈspresəbəl

expression
BR ɪkˈspreʃn,
ekˈspreʃn, -z
AM ɪkˈspreʃən,
ekˈspreʃən, -z

expressional
BR ɪkˈspreʃṇ(ə)l,
ekˈspreʃṇ(ə)l,
ɪkˈspreʃən(ə)l,
ekˈspreʃən(ə)l
AM ɪkˈspreʃ(ə)nəl,
ekˈspreʃ(ə)nəl

expressionism
BR ɪkˈspreʃnɪz(ə)m,
ekˈspreʃnɪz(ə)m,
ɪkˈspreʃənɪz(ə)m,
ekˈspreʃənɪz(ə)m
AM ɪkˈspreʃəˌnɪzəm,
ekˈspreʃəˌnɪzəm

expressionist
BR ɪkˈspreʃnɪst,
ekˈspreʃnɪst,
ɪkˈspreʃənɪst,
ekˈspreʃənɪst, -s
AM ɪkˈspreʃ(ə)nəst,
ekˈspreʃ(ə)nəst, -s

expressionistic
BR ɪkˌspreʃəˈnɪstɪk,
ekˌspreʃəˈnɪstɪk,
ɪkˌspreʃṇˈɪstɪk,
ekˌspreʃṇˈɪstɪk
AM ɪkˌspreʃəˈnɪstɪk,
ekˌspreʃəˈnɪstɪk

**expressionistic-
ally**
BR ɪkˌspreʃəˈnɪstɪkli,
ekˌspreʃəˈnɪstɪkli,
ɪkˌspreʃṇˈɪstɪkli,
ekˌspreʃṇˈɪstɪkli
AM ɪkˌspreʃəˈnɪstək-
(ə)li,
ekˌspreʃəˈnɪstək(ə)li

expressionless
BR ɪkˈspreʃnləs,
ekˈspreʃnləs
AM ɪkˈspreʃənləs,
ekˈspreʃənləs

expressionlessly
BR ɪkˈspreʃnləsli,
ekˈspreʃnləsli
AM ɪkˈspreʃənləsli,
ekˈspreʃənləsli

**expressionless-
ness**
BR ɪkˈspreʃnləsnəs,
ekˈspreʃnləsnəs
AM ɪkˈspreʃənləsnəs,
ekˈspreʃənləsnəs

expressive
BR ɪkˈspresɪv,
ekˈspresɪv
AM ɪkˈspresɪv,
ekˈspresɪv

expressively
BR ɪkˈspresɪvli,
ekˈspresɪvli
AM ɪkˈspresəvli,
ekˈspresəvli

expressiveness
BR ɪkˈspresɪvnɪs,
ekˈspresɪvnɪs
AM ɪkˈspresɪvnɪs,
ekˈspresɪvnɪs

expressivity
BR ˌekspreˈsɪvɪti
AM ˌekspreˈsɪvɪdi

expressly
BR ɪkˈspresli,
ekˈspresli
AM ɪkˈspresli,
ekˈspresli

expresso
BR ɪkˈspresəʊ,
ekˈspresəʊ, -z
AM ɪkˈspresoʊ,
ekˈspresoʊ, -z

expressway
BR ɪkˈspreswei,
ekˈspreswei, -z
AM ɪkˈspresˌwei,
ekˈspresˌwei, -z

expropriate
BR ɪkˈsprəʊprieɪt,
ekˈsprəʊprieɪt, -s, -ɪŋ,
-ɪd
AM ˌeksˈproʊpriˌeɪ|t,
ɪkˈsproʊpriˌeɪ|t, -ts,
-dɪŋ, -dɪd

expropriation
BR ɪkˌsprəʊprɪˈeɪʃn,
ekˌsprəʊprɪˈeɪʃn, -z
AM ˌeksˌproʊpriˈeɪʃən,
ɪkˌsproʊpriˈeɪʃən, -z

expropriator
BR ɪkˈsprəʊprieɪtə(r),
ekˈsprəʊprieɪtə(r), -z
AM ˌeksˈproʊpriˌeɪdər,
ɪkˈsproʊpriˌeɪdər, -z

expulsion
BR ɪkˈspʌlʃn,
ekˈspʌlʃn, -z
AM ɪkˈspəlʃən,
ekˈspəlʃən, -z

expulsive
BR ɪkˈspʌlsɪv,
ekˈspʌlsɪv
AM ɪkˈspəlsɪv,
ekˈspəlsɪv

expunction
BR ɪkˈspʌŋ(k)ʃn,
ekˈspʌŋ(k)ʃn
AM ɪkˈspəŋkʃən,
ekˈspəŋkʃən

expunge
BR ɪkˈspʌn(d)ʒ,
ekˈspʌn(d)ʒ, -ɪz, -ɪŋ, -d
AM ɪkˈspəndʒ,
ekˈspəndʒ, -əz, -ɪŋ, -t

expunger
BR ɪkˈspʌn(d)ʒə(r),
ekˈspʌn(d)ʒə(r), -z
AM ɪkˈspəndʒər,
ekˈspəndʒər, -z

expurgate
BR ˈekspəgeɪt, -s, -ɪŋ,
-ɪd

AM 'ɛkspər,geɪ|t, -ts,
-dɪŋ, -dɪd

expurgation
BR ,ɛkspə'geɪʃn, -z
AM ,ɛkspər'geɪʃən, -z

expurgator
BR 'ɛkspəgeɪtə(r), -z
AM 'ɛkspər,geɪdər, -z

expurgatorial
BR ɪk,spə:gə'tɔ:rɪəl,
ɛk,spə:gə'tɔ:rɪəl
AM ɪk,spərgə'tɔrɪəl,
ɛk,spərgə'tɔrɪəl

expurgatory
BR ɪk'spə:gət(ə)ri,
ɛk'spə:gət(ə)ri
AM ɪk'spərgə,tɔri,
ɛk'spərgə,tɔri

exquisite
BR ɪk'skwɪzɪt,
ɛk'skwɪzɪt,
'ɛkskwɪzɪt
AM ɪk'skwɪzət,
'ɛk,skwɪzət,
'ɛkskwəzət

exquisitely
BR ɪk'skwɪzɪtli,
ɛk'skwɪzɪtli,
'ɛkskwɪzɪtli
AM ɛk'skwɪzətli,
'ɛk,skwɪzətli,
'ɛkskwəzətli

exquisiteness
BR ɪk'skwɪzɪtnɪs,
ɛk'skwɪzɪtnɪs,
'ɛkskwɪzɪtnɪs
AM ɛk'skwɪzətnəs,
'ɛk,skwɪzətnəs,
'ɛkskwəzətnəs

exsanguinate
BR ɛk'saŋgwɪneɪt, -s,
-ɪŋ, -ɪd
AM ɛk'sæŋgwə,neɪ|t,
ɪk'sæŋgwə,neɪ|t, -ts,
-dɪŋ, -dɪd

exsanguination
BR ɛk,saŋgwɪ'neɪʃn
AM ɛk,sæŋwə'neɪʃən,
ɪk,sæŋwə'neɪʃən

exsanguinity
BR ,ɛksaŋ'gwɪnɪti
AM ɛk,sæŋ'gwɪnɪdi,
ɪk,sæŋ'gwɪnɪdi

exscind
BR ɪk'sɪnd, ɛk'sɪnd, -z,
-ɪŋ, -ɪd
AM ɛk'sɪnd, ɪk'sɪnd, -z,
-ɪŋ, -ɪd

exsert
BR ɪk'sə:t, ɛk'sə:t, -s,
-ɪŋ, -ɪd
AM ɛk'sər|t, ɪk'sər|t,
-ts, -dɪŋ, -dəd

exsiccate
BR 'ɛksɪkeɪt, -s, -ɪŋ, -ɪd
AM 'ɛksə,keɪ|t, -ts, -dɪŋ,
-dɪd

ex silentio
BR ,ɛks sɪ'lɛn(t)ʃɪəʊ
AM ,ɛk(s) sə'lɛn(t)ʃɪoʊ

exsolve
BR ɪk'sɒlv, ɛk'sɒlv, -z,
-ɪŋ, -d
AM ɪk'sɑlv, ɛk'sɑlv, -z,
-ɪŋ, -d

extant
BR ɛk'stant, ɪk'stant,
'ɛkst(ə)nt
AM 'ɛkstənt, ɛk'stænt,
'ɛk,stænt

Extel
BR 'ɛkstɛl
AM 'ɛks,tɛl

extemporaneous
BR ɪk,stɛmpə'reɪnɪəs,
ɛk,stɛmpə'reɪnɪəs
AM ɪk,stɛmpə'reɪnɪəs,
ɛk,stɛmpə'reɪnɪəs

extemporaneously
BR ɪk,stɛmpə'reɪnɪəsli,
ɛk,stɛmpə'reɪnɪəsli
AM ɪk,stɛmpə'reɪnɪəsli,
ɛk,stɛmpə'reɪnɪəsli

**extemporaneous-
ness**
BR ɪk,stɛmpə'reɪnɪəs-
nəs,
ɛk,stɛmpə'reɪnɪəsnəs
AM ɪk,stɛmpə'reɪnɪəs-
nəs,
ɛk,stɛmpə'reɪnɪəsnəs

extemporarily
BR ɪk'stɛmp(ə)rərɪli,
ɛk'stɛmp(ə)rərɪli
AM ɪk,stɛmpə'rɛrəli,
ɛk,stɛmpə'rɛrəli

extemporariness
BR ɪk'stɛmp(ə)rərɪnɪs,
ɛk'stɛmp(ə)rərɪnɪs
AM ɪk'stɛmpə'rɛrɪnɪs,
ɛk'stɛmpə,rɛrɪnɪs

extemporary
BR ɪk'stɛmp(ə)r(ər)i,
ɛk'stɛmp(ə)r(ər)i
AM ɪk'stɛmpə,rɛri,
ɛk'stɛmpə,rɛri

extempore
BR ɪk'stɛmp(ə)ri,
ɛk'stɛmp(ə)ri
AM ɪk'stɛmpəri,
ɛk'stɛmpəri

extemporisation
BR ɪk,stɛmpərʌɪ'zeɪʃn,
ɛk,stɛmpərʌɪ'zeɪʃn,
ɪk,stɛmpərə'zeɪʃn,
ɛk,stɛmpərə'zeɪʃn, -z
AM ɪk,stɛmpərə'zeɪʃən,
ɛk,stɛmpərə'zeɪʃən,
ɪk,stɛmpə,raɪ'zeɪʃən,
ɛk,stɛmpə,raɪ'zeɪʃən,
-z

extemporise
BR ɪk'stɛmpərʌɪz,
ɛk'stɛmpərʌɪz, -ɪz, -ɪŋ,
-d

AM ɪk'stɛmpə,raɪz,
ɛk'stɛmpə,raɪz, -ɪz,
-ɪŋ, -d

extemporization
BR ɪk,stɛmpərʌɪ'zeɪʃn,
ɛk,stɛmpərʌɪ'zeɪʃn,
ɪk,stɛmpərə'zeɪʃn,
ɛk,stɛmpərə'zeɪʃn, -z
AM ɪk,stɛmpərə'zeɪʃən,
ɛk,stɛmpərə'zeɪʃən,
ɪk,stɛmpə,raɪ'zeɪʃən,
ɛk,stɛmpə,raɪ'zeɪʃən,
-z

extemporize
BR ɪk'stɛmpərʌɪz,
ɛk'stɛmpərʌɪz, -ɪz, -ɪŋ,
-d
AM ɪk'stɛmpə,raɪz,
ɛk'stɛmpə,raɪz, -ɪz,
-ɪŋ, -d

extend
BR ɪk'stɛnd, ɛk'stɛnd,
-z, -ɪŋ, -ɪd
AM ɪk'stɛnd, ɛk'stɛnd,
-z, -ɪŋ, -əd

extendability
BR ɪk,stɛndə'bɪlɪti,
ɛk,stɛndə'bɪlɪti
AM ɪk,stɛndə'bɪlɪdi,
ɛk,stɛndə'bɪlɪdi

extendable
BR ɪk'stɛndəbl,
ɛk'stɛndəbl
AM ɪk'stɛndəbəl,
ɛk'stɛndəbəl

extender
BR ɪk'stɛndə(r),
ɛk'stɛndə(r), -z
AM ɪk'stɛndər,
ɛk'stɛndər, -z

extendibility
BR ɪk,stɛndɪ'bɪlɪti,
ɛk,stɛndɪ'bɪlɪti
AM ɪk,stɛndə'bɪlɪdi,
ɛk,stɛndə'bɪlɪdi

extendible
BR ɪk'stɛndɪbl,
ɛk'stɛndɪbl
AM ɪk'stɛndəbəl,
ɛk'stɛndəbəl

extensibility
BR ɪk,stɛnsɪ'bɪlɪti,
ɛk,stɛnsɪ'bɪlɪti
AM ɪk,stɛnsə'bɪlɪdi,
ɛk,stɛnsə'bɪlɪdi

extensible
BR ɪk'stɛnsɪbl,
ɛk'stɛnsɪbl
AM ɪk'stɛnsəbəl,
ɛk'stɛnsəbəl

extensile
BR ɪk'stɛnsʌɪl,
ɛk'stɛnsʌɪl
AM ɪk'stɛnsəl,
ɛk'stɛnsəl,
ɪk'stɛn,saɪl,
ɛk'stɛn,saɪl

ex silentio (col.2 top)
AM ɪk'stɛmpə,raɪz,
ɛk'stɛmpə,raɪz, -ɪz,
-ɪŋ, -d

extension
BR ɪk'stɛnʃn,
ɛk'stɛnʃn, -z
AM ɪk'stɛn(t)ʃən,
ɛk'stɛn(t)ʃən, -z

extensional
BR ɪk'stɛnʃn(ə)l,
ɛk'stɛnʃ(ə)l,
ɪk'stɛnʃən(ə)l,
ɛk'stɛnʃən(ə)l
AM ɪk'stɛn(t)ʃ(ə)nəl,
ɛk'stɛn(t)ʃ(ə)nəl

extensionality
BR ɪk,stɛnʃə'nalɪti,
ɛk,stɛnʃə'nalɪti
AM ɪk,stɛn(t)ʃə'nælədi,
ɛk,stɛn(t)ʃə'nælədi

extensive
BR ɪk'stɛnsɪv,
ɛk'stɛnsɪv
AM ɪk'stɛnsɪv,
ɛk'stɛnsɪv

extensively
BR ɪk'stɛnsɪvli,
ɛk'stɛnsɪvli
AM ɪk'stɛnsəvli,
ɛk'stɛnsəvli

extensiveness
BR ɪk'stɛnsɪvnɪs,
ɛk'stɛnsɪvnɪs
AM ɪk'stɛnsɪvnɪs,
ɛk'stɛnsɪvnɪs

extensometer
BR ,ɛkstɛn'sɒmɪtə(r),
-z
AM ɪk,stɛn'sɑmədər,
ɛk,stɛn'sɑmədər, -z

extensor
BR ɪk'stɛnsə(r),
ɛk'stɛnsə(r), -z
AM ɪk'stɛnsər,
ɛk'stɛnsər, -z

extent
BR ɪk'stɛnt, ɛk'stɛnt, -s
AM ɪk'stɛnt, ɛk'stɛnt, -s

extenuate
BR ɪk'stɛnjʊeɪt,
ɛk'stɛnjʊeɪt, -s, -ɪŋ, -ɪd
AM ɪk'stɛnjə,weɪ|t,
ɛk'stɛnjə,weɪ|t, -ts,
-dɪŋ, -dɪd

extenuatingly
BR ɪk'stɛnjʊeɪtɪŋli,
ɛk'stɛnjʊeɪtɪŋli
AM ɪk'stɛnjə,weɪdɪŋli,
ɛk'stɛnjə,weɪdɪŋli

extenuation
BR ɪk,stɛnjʊ'eɪʃn,
ɛk,stɛnjʊ'eɪʃn, -z
AM ɪk,stɛnjə'weɪʃən,
ɛk,stɛnjə'weɪʃən, -z

extenuatory
BR ɪk'stɛnjʊət(ə)ri,
ɛk'stɛnjʊət(ə)ri
AM ɪk'stɛnjəwə,tɔri,
ɛk'stɛnjəwə,tɔri

exterior
BR ɪkˈstɪərɪə(r),
ɛkˈstɪərɪə(r), -z
AM ɪkˈstɪrɪər,
ɛkˈstɪrɪər, ɛkˈstɪrɪər,
ɪkˈstɪrɪər, -z

exteriorise
BR ɪkˈstɪərɪərʌɪz,
ɛkˈstɪərɪərʌɪz, -ɪz, -ɪŋ,
-d
AM ɪkˈstɪrɪəˌraɪz,
ɛkˈstɪrɪəˌraɪz,
ɛkˈstɪrɪəˌraɪz,
ɪkˈstɪrɪəˌraɪz, -ɪz, -ɪŋ,
-d

exteriority
BR ɪkˌstɪərɪˈɒrɪti,
ɛkˌstɪərɪˈɒrɪti
AM ɪkˌstɪrɪˈɔrədi,
ɛkˌstɪrɪˈɔrədi,
ɛkˌstɪrɪˈɔrədi,
ɪkˌstɪrɪˈɔrədi

exteriorize
BR ɪkˈstɪərɪərʌɪz,
ɛkˈstɪərɪərʌɪz, -ɪz, -ɪŋ,
-d
AM ɪkˈstɪrɪəˌraɪz,
ɛkˈstɪrɪəˌraɪz,
ɛkˈstɪrɪəˌraɪz,
ɪkˈstɪrɪəˌraɪz, -ɪz, -ɪŋ,
-d

exteriorly
BR ɪkˈstɪərɪəli,
ɛkˈstɪərɪəli
AM ɪkˈstɪrɪərli,
ɛkˈstɪrɪərli,
ɛkˈstɪrɪərli,
ɪkˈstɪrɪərli

exterminate
BR ɪkˈstəːmɪneɪt,
ɛkˈstəːmɪneɪt, -s, -ɪŋ,
-ɪd
AM ɪkˈstɜːrməˌneɪt,
ɛkˈstɜːrməˌneɪt, -ts,
-dɪŋ, -dɪd

extermination
BR ɪkˌstəːmɪˈneɪʃn,
ɛkˌstəːmɪˈneɪʃn, -z
AM ɪkˌstɜːrməˈneɪʃən,
ɛkˌstɜːrməˈneɪʃən, -z

exterminator
BR ɪkˈstəːmɪneɪtə(r),
ɛkˈstəːmɪneɪtə(r), -z
AM ɪkˈstɜːrməˌneɪdər,
ɛkˈstɜːrməˌneɪdər, -z

exterminatory
BR ɪkˈstəːmɪnət(ə)ri,
ɛkˈstəːmɪnət(ə)ri
AM ɪkˈstɜːrmənəˌtɔri,
ɛkˈstɜːrmənəˌtɔri

extern
BR ˈɛkstəːn, -z
AM ˈɛksˌtɜrn, -z

external
BR ɪkˈstəːnl, ɛkˈstəːnl,
-z
AM ɪkˈstɜrnəl,
ɛkˈstɜrnəl-z

externalisation
BR ɪkˌstəːnəlʌɪˈzeɪʃn,
ɛkˌstəːnəlʌɪˈzeɪʃn,
ɪkˌstəːnlʌɪˈzeɪʃn,
ɛkˌstəːnlʌɪˈzeɪʃn
AM ɪkˌstɜrnləˈzeɪʃən,
ɛkˌstɜrnləˈzeɪʃən,
ɪkˌstɜrnəˌlaɪˈzeɪʃən,
ɛkˌstɜrnəˌlaɪˈzeɪʃən

externalise
BR ɪkˈstəːnəlʌɪz,
ɛkˈstəːnəlʌɪz,
ɪkˈstəːnlʌɪz,
ɛkˈstəːnlʌɪz, -ɪz, -ɪŋ, -d
AM ɪkˈstɜrnəˌlaɪz,
ɛkˈstɜrnəˌlaɪz, -ɪz, -ɪŋ,
-d

externality
BR ˌɛkstəːˈnalɪt|i, -ɪz
AM ˌɛkˌstərˈnælədi,
ɪkˌstərˈnælədi, -z

externalization
BR ɪkˌstəːnlʌɪˈzeɪʃn,
ɛkˌstəːnlʌɪˈzeɪʃn
AM ɪkˌstɜrnləˈzeɪʃən,
ɛkˌstɜrnləˈzeɪʃən,
ɪkˌstɜrnəˌlaɪˈzeɪʃən,
ɛkˌstɜrnəˌlaɪˈzeɪʃən

externalize
BR ɪkˈstəːnəlʌɪz,
ɛkˈstəːnəlʌɪz,
ɪkˈstəːnlʌɪz,
ɛkˈstəːnlʌɪz, -ɪz, -ɪŋ, -d
AM ɪkˈstɜrnəˌlaɪz,
ɛkˈstɜrnəˌlaɪz, -ɪz, -ɪŋ,
-d

externally
BR ɪkˈstəːnli,
ɛkˈstəːnli, ɪkˈstəːnəli,
ɛkˈstəːnəli
AM ˌɛkˈstɜrnəli,
ɪkˈstɜrnəli

exteroceptive
BR ˌɛkstərə(ʊ)ˈsɛptɪv
AM ˌɛkstəroʊˈsɛptɪv

exterritorial
BR ˌɛkstɛrɪˈtɔːrɪəl
AM ˌɛksˌtɛrəˈtoriəl

exterritoriality
BR ˌɛkstɛrɪˌtɔːrɪˈalɪti
AM ˌɛksˌtɛrəˌtoriˈælədi

extinct
BR ɪkˈstɪŋ(k)t,
ɛkˈstɪŋ(k)t
AM ɪkˈstɪŋ(k)t,
ɛkˈstɪŋ(k)t,
ɪkˈstɪŋk(t),
ɛkˈstɪŋk(t)

extinction
BR ɪkˈstɪŋ(k)ʃn,
ɛkˈstɪŋ(k)ʃn
AM ɪkˈstɪŋ(k)ʃən,
ɛkˈstɪŋ(k)ʃən

extinctive
BR ɪkˈstɪŋ(k)tɪv,
ɛkˈstɪŋ(k)tɪv
AM ɪkˈstɪŋ(k)tɪv,
ɛkˈstɪŋ(k)tɪv

extinguish
BR ɪkˈstɪŋgwɪʃ,
ɛkˈstɪŋgwɪʃ, -ɪʃɪz,
-ɪʃɪŋ, -ɪʃt
AM ɪkˈstɪŋgwɪʃ,
ɛkˈstɪŋgwɪʃ, -ɪz, -ɪŋ, -t

extinguishable
BR ɪkˈstɪŋgwɪʃəbl,
ɛkˈstɪŋgwɪʃəbl
AM ɪkˈstɪŋgwɪʃəbəl,
ɛkˈstɪŋgwɪʃəbəl

extinguisher
BR ɪkˈstɪŋgwɪʃə(r),
ɛkˈstɪŋgwɪʃə(r), -z
AM ɪkˈstɪŋgwɪʃər,
ɛkˈstɪŋgwɪʃər, -z

extinguishment
BR ɪkˈstɪŋgwɪʃm(ə)nt,
ɛkˈstɪŋgwɪʃm(ə)nt
AM ɪkˈstɪŋgwɪʃmənt,
ɛkˈstɪŋgwɪʃmənt

extirpate
BR ˈɛkstəpeɪt, -s, -ɪŋ, -ɪd
AM ˈɛkstərˌpeɪ|t, -ts,
-dɪŋ, -dɪd

extirpation
BR ˌɛkstəˈpeɪʃn, -z
AM ˌɛkstərˈpeɪʃən, -z

extirpator
BR ˈɛkstəpeɪtə(r), -z
AM ˈɛkstərˌpeɪdər, -z

extol
BR ɪkˈstəʊl, ɪkˈstɒl,
ɛkˈstəʊl, ɛkˈstɒl, -z,
-ɪŋ, -d
AM ɪkˈstoʊl, ɛkˈstoʊl,
-z, -ɪŋ, -d

extoller
BR ɪkˈstəʊlə(r),
ɪkˈstɒlə(r),
ɛkˈstəʊlə(r),
ɛkˈstɒlə(r), -z
AM ɪkˈstoʊlər,
ɛkˈstoʊlər, -z

extolment
BR ɪkˈstəʊlm(ə)nt,
ɪkˈstɒlm(ə)nt,
ɛkˈstəʊlm(ə)nt,
ɛkˈstɒlm(ə)nt
AM ɪkˈstoʊlmənt,
ɛkˈstoʊlmənt

Exton
BR ˈɛkst(ə)n
AM ˈɛkstən

extort
BR ɪkˈstɔːt, ɛkˈstɔːt, -s,
-ɪŋ, -ɪd
AM ɪkˈstɔ(ə)r|t,
ɛkˈstɔ(ə)r t, -ts, -dɪŋ,
-dəd

extorter
BR ɪkˈstɔːtə(r),
ɛkˈstɔːtə(r), -z
AM ɪkˈstɔrdər,
ɛkˈstɔrdər, -z

extortion
BR ɪkˈstɔːʃn, ɛkˈstɔːʃn,
-z

extortionate
BR ɪkˈstɔːʃnət,
ɪkˈstɔːʃ(ə)nət,
ɛkˈstɔːʃnət,
ɛkˈstɔːʃ(ə)nət
AM ɪkˈstɔrʃ(ə)nət,
ɛkˈstɔrʃ(ə)nət

extortionately
BR ɪkˈstɔːʃnətli,
ɪkˈstɔːʃ(ə)nətli,
ɛkˈstɔːʃnətli,
ɛkˈstɔːʃ(ə)nətli
AM ɪkˈstɔrʃ(ə)nətli,
ɛkˈstɔrʃ(ə)nətli

extortioner
BR ɪkˈstɔːʃnə(r),
ɛkˈstɔːʃnə(r), -z
AM ɪkˈstɔrʃənər,
ɛkˈstɔrʃənər, -z

extortionist
BR ɪkˈstɔːʃnɪst,
ɛkˈstɔːʃnɪst, -s
AM ɪkˈstɔrʃənəst,
ɛkˈstɔrʃənəst, -s

extortive
BR ɪkˈstɔːtɪv, ɛkˈstɔːtɪv
AM ɪkˈstɔrdɪv,
ɛkˈstɔrdɪv

extra
BR ˈɛkstrə(r), -z
AM ˈɛkstrə, -z

extracellular
BR ˌɛkstrəˈsɛljʉlə(r)
AM ˌɛkstrəˈsɛljələr

extracranial
BR ˌɛkstrəˈkreɪnɪəl
AM ˌɛkstrəˈkreɪniəl

extract¹
noun
BR ˈɛkstrakt, -s
AM ˈɛkˌstræk(t), -s

extract²
verb
BR ɪkˈstrakt,
ɛkˈstrakt, -s, -ɪŋ, -ɪd
AM ɪkˈstræk|(t),
ɛkˈstræk|(t), -(t)s,
-tɪŋ, -təd

extractability
BR ɪkˌstraktəˈbɪlɪti,
ɛkˌstraktəˈbɪlɪti
AM ɪkˌstræktəˈbɪlɪdi,
ɛkˌstræktəˈbɪlɪdi

extractable
BR ɪkˈstraktəbl,
ɛkˈstraktəbl
AM ɪkˈstræktəbəl,
ɛkˈstræktəbəl

extraction
BR ɪkˈstrakʃn,
ɛkˈstrakʃn
AM ɪkˈstrækʃən,
ɛkˈstrækʃən

extractive
BR ɪkˈstraktɪv,
ɛkˈstraktɪv

AM ɪk'stræktɪv,
ɛk'stræktɪv
extractor
BR ɪk'straktə(r),
ɛk'straktə(r), -z
AM ɪk'stræktər,
ɛk'stræktər, -z
extracurricular
BR ,ɛkstrəkə'rɪkjʊlə(r)
AM 'ɛkstrəkə'rɪkjələr
extraditable
BR 'ɛkstrədʌɪtəbl,
,ɛkstrə'dʌɪtəbl
AM ,ɛkstrə,daɪdəbəl,
,ɛkstrə'daɪdəbəl
extradite
BR 'ɛkstrədʌɪt, -s, -ɪŋ,
-ɪd
AM 'ɛkstrə,daɪt, -ts,
-dɪŋ, -dɪd
extradition
BR ,ɛkstrə'dɪʃn, -z
AM ,ɛkstrə'dɪʃən, -z
extrados
BR ɛk'streɪdɒs,
ɪk'streɪdɒs, -ɪz
AM 'ɛkstrə,dɑs,
ɛk'stra,das, -əz
extragalactic
BR ,ɛkstrəgə'laktɪk
AM 'ɛkstrəgə'læktɪk
extrajudicial
BR ,ɛkstrədʒuː'dɪʃl
AM 'ɛkstrədʒu'dɪʃəl
extrajudicially
BR ,ɛkstrədʒuː'dɪʃli,
AM ,ɛkstrədʒu:'dɪʃ(ə)li
extralinguistic
BR ,ɛkstrəlɪŋ'gwɪstɪk
AM ,ɛkstrə,lɪŋ'gwɪstɪk
extramarital
BR ,ɛkstrə'marɪtl
AM ,ɛkstrə'mɛrədl
extramaritally
BR ,ɛkstrə'marɪtļi
AM ,ɛkstrə'mɛrədəli
extramundane
BR ,ɛkstrəmʌn'deɪn
AM ,ɛkstrəmən'deɪn
extramural
BR ,ɛkstrə'mjʊərəl,
,ɛkstrə'mjʊərļ,
,ɛkstrə'mjɔːrəl,
,ɛkstrə'mjɔːrļ
AM ,ɛkstrə'mjurəl,
,ɛkstrə'mjurəl
extramurally
BR ,ɛkstrə'mjʊərəli,
,ɛkstrə'mjʊərļi,
,ɛkstrə'mjɔːrəli,
,ɛkstrə'mjɔːrļi
AM ,ɛkstrə'mjurəli,
,ɛkstrə'mjurəli
extraneous
BR ɪk'streɪnɪəs,
ɛk'streɪnɪəs

AM ɪk'streɪnɪəs,
ɛk'streɪnɪəs
extraneously
BR ɪk'streɪnɪəsli,
ɛk'streɪnɪəsli
AM ɪk'streɪnɪəsli,
ɛk'streɪnɪəsli
extraneousness
BR ɪk'streɪnɪəsnəs,
ɛk'streɪnɪəsnəs
AM ɪk'streɪnɪəsnəs,
ɛk'streɪnɪəsnəs
extraordinarily
BR ɪk'strɔːdn(ə)rəli,
ɛk'strɔːdn(ə)rəli,
,ɛkstrə'ɔːdn(ə)rəli
AM ɪk'strɔrdn,ɛrəli,
ɛk'strɔrdn,ɛrəli
extraordinariness
BR ɪk'strɔːdn(ə)rmɪs,
ɛk'strɔːdn(ə)rmɪs,
,ɛkstrə'ɔːdn(ə)rmɪs
AM ɪk'strɔrdn,ɛrmɪs,
ɛk'strɔrdn,ɛrmɪs
extraordinary
BR ɪk'strɔːdn(ə)ri,
ɛk'strɔːdn(ə)ri,
,ɛkstrə'ɔːdn(ə)ri
AM ɪk'strɔrdn,ɛri,
ɛk'strɔrdn,ɛri
extraphysical
BR ,ɛkstrə'fɪzɪkl
AM ,ɛkstrə'fɪzɪkəl
extrapolate
BR ɪk'strapəleɪt,
ɛk'strapəleɪt, -s, -ɪŋ,
-ɪd
AM ɪk'stræpə,leɪt,
ɛk'stræpə,leɪt, -ts,
-dɪŋ, -dɪd
extrapolation
BR ɪk,strapə'leɪʃn,
ɛk,strapə'leɪʃn
AM ɪk,stræpə'leɪʃən,
ɛk,stræpə'leɪʃən
extrapolative
BR ɪk'strapələtɪv,
ɛk'strapələtɪv
AM ɪk'stræpə,leɪdɪv,
ɛk'stræpə,leɪdɪv
extrapolator
BR ɪk'strapələtə(r),
ɛk'strapələtə(r), -z
AM ɪk'stræpə,leɪdər,
ɛk'stræpə,leɪdər, -z
extrasensory
BR ,ɛkstrə'sɛns(ə)ri
AM ,ɛkstrə'sɛnsəri
extraterrestrial
BR ,ɛkstrətɪ'rɛstrɪəl
AM ,ɛkstrətə'rɛstrɪəl
extraterritorial
BR ,ɛkstrə,tɛrɪ'tɔːrɪəl
AM ,ɛkstrə,tɛrə'tɔːrɪəl
extraterritoriality
BR ,ɛkstrə,tɛrɪtɔːrɪ'alɪti
AM ,ɛkstrə,tɛrə,tɔːri'æl-
ədi

extravagance
BR ɪk'stravəg(ə)ns,
ɛk'stravəg(ə)ns, -ɪz
AM ɪk'strævəgəns,
ɛk'strævəgəns, -əz
extravagancy
BR ɪk'stravəg(ə)ns|i,
ɛk'stravəg(ə)ns|i, -ɪz
AM ɪk'strævəgənsi,
ɛk'strævəgənsi, -z
extravagant
BR ɪk'stravəg(ə)nt,
ɛk'stravəg(ə)nt
AM ɪk'strævəgənt,
ɛk'strævəgənt
extravagantly
BR ɪk'stravəg(ə)ntli,
ɛk'stravəg(ə)ntli
AM ɪk'strævəgən(t)li,
ɛk'strævəgən(t)li
extravaganza
BR ɪk,stravə'ganzə(r),
ɛk,stravə'ganzə(r), -z
AM ɪk,strævə'gænzə,
ɛk,strævə'gænzə, -z
extravasate
BR ɪk'stravəseɪt,
ɛk'stravəseɪt, -s, -ɪŋ,
-ɪd
AM ɪk'strævə,seɪt,
ɛk'strævə,seɪt, -ts,
-dɪŋ, -dɪd
extravasation
BR ɪk,stravə'seɪʃn,
ɛk,stravə'seɪʃn
AM ɪk,strævə'seɪʃən,
ɛk,strævə'seɪʃən
extravehicular
BR ,ɛkstrəvɪ'(h)ɪkjʊ-
lə(r)
AM ,ɛkstrəvə'hɪkjələr,
,ɛkstrəvi'hɪkjələr
extraversion
BR ,ɛkstrə'vəːʃn
AM 'ɛkstrə'vərʒən
extravert
BR 'ɛkstrəvəːt, -s
AM 'ɛkstrə,vərt, -s
extrema
BR ɪk'striːmə(r),
ɛk'striːmə(r)
AM ɪk'strimə,
ɛk'strimə
extremal
BR ɪk'striːml,
ɛk'striːml
AM ɪk'striməl,
ɛk'striməl
extreme
BR ɪk'striːm,
ɛk'striːm, -z
AM ɪk'strim, ɛk'strim,
-z
extremely
BR ɪk'striːmli,
ɛk'striːmli
AM ɪk'strimli,
ɛk'strimli

extremeness
BR ɪk'striːmnɪs,
ɛk'striːmnɪs
AM ɪk'strimnɪs,
ɛk'strimnɪs
extremis
BR ɪk'striːmɪs,
ɛk'striːmɪs
AM ɪk'strimɪs,
ɛk'strimɪs
extremism
BR ɪk'striːmɪz(ə)m,
ɛk'striːmɪz(ə)m
AM ɪk'stri,mɪzəm,
ɛk'stri,mɪzəm
extremist
BR ɪk'striːmɪst,
ɛk'striːmɪst, -s
AM ɪk'strimɪst,
ɛk'strimɪst, -s
extremity
BR ɪk'strɛmɪt|i,
ɛk'strɛmɪt|i, -ɪz
AM ɪk'strɛmədi,
ɛk'strɛmədi, -z
extremum
BR ɪk'striːməm,
ɛk'striːməm, -z
AM ɪk'striməm,
ɛk'striməm, -z
extricable
BR ɪk'strɪkəbl,
ɛk,strɪkəbl,
'ɛkstrɪkəbl
AM ɪk'strɪkəbəl,
ɛk'strɪkəbəl,
'ɛkstrɪkəbəl
extricate
BR 'ɛkstrɪkeɪt, -s, -ɪŋ,
-ɪd
AM 'ɛkstrə,keɪ|t, -ts,
-dɪŋ, -dɪd
extrication
BR ,ɛkstrɪ'keɪʃn
AM ,ɛkstrə'keɪʃən
extrinsic
BR ɛk'strɪnsɪk,
ɪk'strɪnsɪk,
ɛk'strɪnzɪk,
ɪk'strɪnzɪk
AM ɪk'strɪnzɪk,
ɛk'strɪnzɪk,
ɛk'strɪnsɪk,
ɪk'strɪnsɪk
extrinsically
BR ɛk'strɪnsɪkli,
ɪk'strɪnsɪkli,
ɛk'strɪnzɪkli,
ɪk'strɪnzɪkli
AM ɪk'strɪnzək(ə)li,
ɛk'strɪnzək(ə)li,
ɛk'strɪnsək(ə)li,
ɪk'strɪnsək(ə)li
extroversion
BR ,ɛkstrə'vəːʃn
AM 'ɛkstrə'vərʒən,
'ɛkstroʊ'vərʒən

extrovert
BR 'ɛkstrəvɜ:t, -s
AM 'ɛkstrə,vɜrt, -s

extroverted
BR ,ɛkstrəvɜ:tɪd
AM 'ɛkstrə,vɜrdəd

extrude
BR ɪk'stru:d, ɛk'stru:d,
-z, -ɪŋ, -ɪd
AM ɪk'strud, ɛk'strud,
-z, -ɪŋ, -əd

extrusile
BR ɪk'stru:sʌɪl,
ɛk'stru:sʌɪl
AM ɪk'strusəl,
ɛk'strusəl,
ɪk'stru,saɪl,
ɛk'stru,saɪl

extrusion
BR ɪk'stru:ʒn,
ɛk'stru:ʒn
AM ɪk'stru:ʒn,
ɛk'struʒən

extrusive
BR ɪk'stru:sɪv,
ɛk'stru:sɪv
AM ɪk'strusɪv,
ɛk'strusɪv

exuberance
BR ɪg'z(j)u:b(ə)rəns,
ɛg'z(j)u:b(ə)rəns,
ɪg'z(j)u:b(ə)rns,
ɛg'z(j)u:b(ə)rns
AM ɪg'zub(ə)rəns,
ɛg'zub(ə)rəns

exuberant
BR ɪg'z(j)u:b(ə)rənt,
ɛg'z(j)u:b(ə)rənt,
ɪg'z(j)u:b(ə)rnt,
ɛg'z(j)u:b(ə)rnt
AM ɪg'zub(ə)rənt,
ɛg'zub(ə)rənt

exuberantly
BR ɪg'z(j)u:b(ə)rəntli,
ɛg'z(j)u:b(ə)rəntli,
ɪg'z(j)u:b(ə)rntli,
ɛg'z(j)u:b(ə)rntli
AM ɪg'zub(ə)rən(t)li,
ɛg'zub(ə)rən(t)li

exuberate
BR ɪg'z(j)u:bəreɪt,
ɛg'z(j)u:bəreɪt, -s, -ɪŋ,
-ɪd
AM ɪg'zubə,reɪt,
ɛg'zubə,reɪt, -ts, -dɪŋ,
-dɪd

exudate
BR 'ɛksjʊdeɪt,
'ɛgzjʊdeɪt, -s, -ɪŋ, -ɪd
AM 'ɛksə,deɪt,
'ɛksju,deɪt, -ts, -dɪŋ,
-dɪd

exudation
BR ,ɛksjʊ'deɪʃn,
,ɛgzjʊ'deɪʃn
AM ,ɛksə'deɪʃən,
,ɛksju'deɪʃən

exudative
BR 'ɛksjʊdeɪtɪv,
'ɛgzjʊdeɪtɪv
AM 'ɛksə,deɪdɪv,
'ɛksju,deɪdɪv

exude
BR ɪg'zju:d, ɛg'zju:d, -z,
-ɪŋ, -ɪd
AM ɪg'zud, ɛg'zud, -z,
-ɪŋ, -əd

exult
BR ɪg'zʌlt, ɛg'zʌlt, -s,
-ɪŋ, -ɪd
AM ɪg'zəlt, ɛg'zəlt, -s,
-ɪŋ, -əd

exultancy
BR ɪg'zʌlt(ə)nsi,
ɛg'zʌlt(ə)nsi
AM ɪg'zəltnsi,
ɛg'zəltnsi

exultant
BR ɪg'zʌlt(ə)nt,
ɛg'zʌlt(ə)nt
AM ɪg'zəltnt, ɛg'zəltnt

exultantly
BR ɪg'zʌlt(ə)ntli,
ɛg'zʌlt(ə)ntli
AM ɪg'zəltn(t)li,
ɛg'zəltn(t)li

exultation
BR ,ɛgz(ʌ)l'teɪʃn,
,ɛks(ʌ)l'teɪʃn
AM ,ɛksəl'teɪʃən,
,ɛgzəl'teɪʃən

exultingly
BR ɪg'zʌltɪŋli,
ɛg'zʌltɪŋli
AM ɪg'zəltɪŋli,
ɛg'zəltɪŋli

exurb
BR 'ɛksə:b, -z
AM 'ɛksɜrb, 'ɛgzɜrb, -z

exurban
BR (,)ɛks'ə:b(ə)n
AM ɛk'sɜrbən,
ɛg'zɜrbən

exurbanite
BR (,)ɛks'ə:bənʌɪt, -s
AM ɛk'sɜrbə,naɪt,
ɛg'zɜrbə,naɪt, -s

exurbia
BR (,)ɛks'ə:bɪə(r)
AM ɛk'sɜrbiə,
ɛg'zɜrbiə

exuviae
BR ɪg'zju:vii:,
ɛg'zju:vii:,
ɪg'zju:vɪʌɪ, ɛg'zju:vɪʌɪ
AM ɪg'zuvi,i, ɛg'zuvi,i,
ɪg'zuvi,aɪ, ɛg'zuvi,aɪ

exuvial
BR ɪg'zju:vɪəl,
ɛg'zju:vɪəl
AM ɪg'zuvɪəl, ɛg'zuvɪəl

exuviate
BR ɪg'zju:vɪeɪt,
ɛg'zju:vɪeɪt, -s, -ɪŋ, -ɪd

exuviation
BR ɪg,zju:vi'eɪʃn,
ɛg,zju:vi'eɪʃən
AM ɪg,zuvi'eɪʃən,
ɛg,zuvi'eɪʃən

ex voto
BR ,ɛks 'vəʊtəʊ, -z
AM ,ɛks 'voʊdoʊ, -z

Exxon®
BR 'ɛksɒn
AM 'ɛk,sɑn

Eyam
BR i:m
AM im

eyas
BR 'ʌɪəs, -ɪz
AM 'aɪəs, -əz

eye
BR ʌɪ, -z, -ɪŋ, -d
AM aɪ, -z, -ɪŋ, -d

eyeball
BR 'ʌɪbɔ:l, -z, -ɪŋ, -d
AM 'aɪ,bɔl, 'aɪ,bɑl, -z,
-ɪŋ, -d

eyebath
BR 'ʌɪ|bɑ:θ, 'ʌɪ|baθ,
-bɑ:ðz\-bɑ:θs\-baθs
AM 'aɪ,bæθ, -s, -ðz

eyeblack
BR 'ʌɪblak
AM 'aɪ,blæk

eyebright
BR 'ʌɪbrʌɪt
AM 'aɪ,braɪt

eyebrow
BR 'ʌɪbraʊ, -z
AM 'aɪ,braʊ, -z

eyedropper
BR 'ʌɪ,drɒpə(r), -z
AM 'aɪ,drɑpər, -z

eyeful
BR 'ʌɪfʊl, -z
AM 'aɪ,fʊl, -z

eyeglass
BR 'ʌɪglɑ:s, 'ʌɪglas, -ɪz
AM 'aɪ,glæs, -əz

eyehole
BR 'ʌɪhəʊl, -z
AM 'aɪ,(h)oʊl, -z

eyelash
BR 'ʌɪlaʃ, -ɪz
AM 'aɪ,læʃ, -əz

eyeless
BR 'ʌɪlɪs
AM 'aɪlɪs

eyelet
BR 'ʌɪlɪt, -s
AM 'aɪlət, -s

eyelevel
BR 'ʌɪ,lɛvl
AM 'aɪ,lɛvəl

eyelid
BR 'ʌɪlɪd, -z
AM 'aɪ,lɪd, -z

eyeliner
BR 'ʌɪ,lʌɪnə(r), -z
AM 'aɪ,laɪnər, -z

eyepatch
BR 'ʌɪpatʃ, -ɪz
AM 'aɪ,pætʃ, -əz

eyepiece
BR 'ʌɪpi:s, -ɪz
AM 'aɪ,pis, -ɪz

eyeshade
BR 'ʌɪʃeɪd, -z
AM 'aɪ,ʃeɪd, -z

eyeshadow
BR 'ʌɪ,ʃadəʊ, -z
AM 'aɪ,ʃædoʊ, -z

eyeshot
BR 'ʌɪʃɒt
AM 'aɪ,ʃɑt

eyesight
BR 'ʌɪsʌɪt
AM 'aɪ,saɪt

eyesore
BR 'ʌɪsɔ:(r), -z
AM 'aɪ,sɔ(ə)r, -z

eyess
BR 'ʌɪəs, -ɪz
AM 'aɪəs, -əz

eyestrain
BR 'ʌɪstreɪn
AM 'aɪ,streɪn

eyeteeth
BR 'ʌɪti:θ, ,ʌɪ'ti:θ
AM 'aɪ,tiθ

Eyetie
BR 'ʌɪtʌɪ, -z
AM 'aɪ,taɪ, -z

eyetooth
BR 'ʌɪtu:θ, ,ʌɪ'tu:θ
AM 'aɪ,tuθ

eyewash
BR 'ʌɪwɒʃ
AM 'aɪ,wɒʃ, 'aɪ,wɑʃ

eyewitness
BR 'ʌɪ,wɪtnɪs, -ɪz
AM 'aɪ,wɪtnəs, -əz

Eynon
BR 'ʌɪnən
AM 'aɪnən
WE 'eɪnɒn

Eynsford
BR 'eɪnzfəd
AM 'eɪnzfərd

Eynsham
BR 'eɪnʃ(ə)m
AM 'eɪnʃəm

eyot
BR eɪt, 'eɪət, -s
AM eɪt, 'eɪət, -s

eyra
BR 'eɪrə(r), -z
AM 'eɪrə, -z

Eyre
BR ɛ:(r)
AM ɛ(ə)r

eyrie
BR 'ɪər|i, 'ʌɪr|i, 'ɛ:r|i, -ɪz
AM 'aɪri, 'ɛri, 'iri, 'ɪri, -z

eyry
BR ˈɪərˌi, ˈʌɪrˌi, ˈɛːrˌi, -ɪz-
AM ˈaɪri, ˈɛri, ˈiri, ˈɪri, -z

Eysenck
BR ˈʌɪzɛŋk
AM ˈaɪzəŋk

Ezekiel
BR ɪˈziːkɪəl
AM əˈzikiəl, iˈzikiəl

Ezra
BR ˈɛzrə(r)
AM ˈɛzrə

Ff

f
BR ɛf, -s
AM ɛf, -s

FA
BR ˌɛf 'eɪ
AM ˌɛf 'eɪ

fa
BR fɑː(r)
AM fɑ

fab
BR fab
AM fæb

Fabergé
BR 'fabəʒeɪ
AM ˌfæbər'ʒeɪ

Fabia
BR 'feɪbɪə(r)
AM 'feɪbiə

Fabian
BR 'feɪbɪən, -z
AM 'feɪbiən, -z

Fabianism
BR 'feɪbɪənɪz(ə)m
AM 'feɪbiəˌnɪzəm

Fabianist
BR 'feɪbɪənɪst, -s
AM 'feɪbiənəst, -s

Fabius
BR 'feɪbɪəs
AM 'feɪbiəs

fable
BR 'feɪbl, -z, -d
AM 'feɪbəl, -z, -d

fabler
BR 'feɪblə(r), -z
AM 'feɪb(ə)lər, -z

fabliau
BR 'fablɪəʊ, -z
AM 'fæblioʊ, -z

Fablon®
BR 'fablɒn
AM 'fæblən

fabric
BR 'fabrɪk, -s
AM 'fæbrɪk, -s

fabricate
BR 'fabrɪkeɪt, -s, -ɪŋ, -ɪd
AM 'fæbrəˌkeɪt, -ts, -dɪŋ, -dɪd

fabrication
BR ˌfabrɪ'keɪʃn, -z
AM ˌfæbrə'keɪʃən, -z

fabricator
BR 'fabrɪkeɪtə(r), -z
AM 'fæbrəˌkeɪdər, -z

fabulist
BR 'fabjʊlɪst, -s
AM 'fæbjələst, -s

fabulosity
BR ˌfabjʊ'lɒsɪti
AM ˌfæbjʊ'lɑsədi

fabulous
BR 'fabjʊləs
AM 'fæbjələs

fabulously
BR 'fabjʊləsli
AM 'fæbjələsli

fabulousness
BR 'fabjʊləsnəs
AM 'fæbjələsnəs

facade
BR fə'sɑːd, -z
AM fə'sɑd, -z

façade
BR fə'sɑːd, -z
AM fə'sɑd, -z

face
BR feɪs, -ɪz, -ɪŋ, -t
AM feɪs, -ɪz, -ɪŋ, -t

facecloth
BR 'feɪsklɒ|θ, -θs\-ðz
AM 'feɪsˌklɔ|θ, 'feɪsˌklɑ|θ, -θs\-ðz

faceless
BR 'feɪslɪs
AM 'feɪslɪs

facelessly
BR 'feɪslɪsli
AM 'feɪslɪsli

facelessness
BR 'feɪslɪsnɪs
AM 'feɪslɪsnɪs

facelift
BR 'feɪslɪf|t, -(t)s
AM 'feɪsˌlɪft, -s

facemask
BR 'feɪsmɑːsk, 'feɪsmask, -s
AM 'feɪsˌmæsk, -s

faceplate
BR 'feɪspleɪt, -s
AM 'feɪsˌpleɪt, -s

facer
BR 'feɪsə(r), -z
AM 'feɪsər, -z

facet
BR 'fasɪt, 'fasɛt, -s
AM 'fæsət, -s

faceted
BR 'fasɪtɪd
AM 'fæsədəd

facetiae
BR fə'siːʃiː
AM fə'siːʃi,i, fə'siːʃi,aɪ

facetious
BR fə'siːʃəs
AM fə'siːʃəs

facetiously
BR fə'siːʃəsli
AM fə'siːʃəsli

facetiousness
BR fə'siːʃəsnəs
AM fə'siːʃəsnəs

facetted
BR 'fasɪtɪd
AM 'fæsədəd

faceworker
BR 'feɪsˌwəːkə(r), -z

facia
BR 'feɪʃə(r), -z
AM 'fæʃ(i)ə, 'feɪʃ(i)ə, -z

facial
BR 'feɪʃl
AM 'feɪʃəl

facially
BR 'feɪʃli, 'feɪʃəli
AM 'feɪʃəli

facies
BR 'feɪʃriːz
AM 'feɪʃiz, 'feɪʃi,iz

facile
BR 'fasʌɪl
AM 'fæsəl

facilely
BR 'fasʌɪl(l)i
AM 'fæsə(l)li

facileness
BR 'fasʌɪlnɪs
AM 'fæsəlnəs

facilitate
BR fə'sɪlɪteɪt, -s, -ɪŋ, -ɪd
AM fə'sɪləˌteɪ|t, -ts, -dɪŋ, -dɪd

facilitation
BR fəˌsɪlɪ'teɪʃn
AM fəˌsɪlə'teɪʃən

facilitative
BR fəˌsɪlɪtətɪv
AM fə'sɪləˌteɪdɪv

facilitator
BR fə'sɪlɪteɪtə(r), -z
AM fə'sɪləˌteɪdər, -z

facility
BR fə'sɪlɪt|i, -ɪz
AM fə'sɪlədi, -z

facing
BR 'feɪsɪŋ, -z
AM 'feɪsɪŋ, -z

facsimile
BR fak'sɪmɪl|i, fak'sɪml|i, -ɪz
AM fæk'sɪməli, -z

fact
BR fakt, -s
AM fæk|(t), -(t)s

facta
BR 'faktə(r)
AM 'fæktə

fact-finding
BR 'fak(t)ˌfʌɪndɪŋ
AM 'fæk(t)ˌfaɪndɪŋ

factice
BR 'faktɪs
AM 'fæktəs

faction
BR 'fakʃn, -z
AM 'fækʃən, -z

factional
BR 'fakʃn(ə)l, 'fakʃən(ə)l
AM 'fækʃ(ə)nəl

factionalise
BR 'fakʃnəlʌɪz, 'fakʃnlʌɪz,

'fakʃənlʌɪz,
'fakʃ(ə)nəlʌɪz, -ɪz, -ɪŋ, -d
AM 'fækʃ(ə)nəˌlaɪz, -ɪz, -ɪŋ, -d

factionalism
BR 'fakʃnəlɪz(ə)m, 'fakʃnlɪz(ə)m, 'fakʃənlɪz(ə)m, 'fakʃ(ə)nəlɪz(ə)m
AM 'fækʃənlˌɪzəm, 'fækʃnəˌlɪzəm

factionalize
BR 'fakʃnəlʌɪz, 'fakʃnlʌɪz, 'fakʃənlʌɪz, 'fakʃ(ə)nəlʌɪz, -ɪz, -ɪŋ, -d
AM 'fækʃ(ə)nəˌlaɪz, -ɪz, -ɪŋ, -d

factionally
BR 'fakʃnəli, 'fakʃnli, 'fakʃənli, 'fakʃ(ə)nəli
AM 'fækʃ(ə)nəli

factious
BR 'fakʃəs
AM 'fækʃəs

factiously
BR 'fakʃəsli
AM 'fækʃəsli

factiousness
BR 'fakʃəsnəs
AM 'fækʃəsnəs

factitious
BR fak'tɪʃəs
AM fæk'tɪʃəs

factitiously
BR fak'tɪʃəsli
AM fæk'tɪʃəsli

factitiousness
BR fak'tɪʃəsnəs
AM fæk'tɪʃəsnəs

factitive
BR 'faktɪtɪv
AM 'fæktəˌtɪv

facto
BR 'faktəʊ
AM 'fæktoʊ

factoid
BR 'faktɔɪd, -z
AM 'fækˌtɔɪd, -z

factor
BR 'faktə(r), -z
AM 'fæktər, 'fæktɔ(ə)r, -z

factorable
BR 'fakt(ə)rəbl
AM 'fæktərəbəl

factorage
BR 'fakt(ə)r|ɪdʒ, -ɪdʒɪz
AM 'fæktərɪdʒ, -ɪz

factorial
BR fak'tɔːrɪəl, -z
AM fæk'tɔriəl, -z

factorially
BR fak'tɔːrɪəli
AM fæk'tɔriəli

factorisation
BR ˌfakt(ə)rʌɪˈzeɪʃn
AM ˌfæktərəˈzeɪʃən,
ˌfæktəˌraɪˈzeɪʃən

factorise
BR ˈfaktərʌɪz, -ɪz, -ɪŋ, -d
AM ˈfæktəˌraɪz, -ɪz, -ɪŋ, -d

factorization
BR ˌfakt(ə)rʌɪˈzeɪʃn
AM ˌfæktərəˈzeɪʃən,
ˌfæktəˌraɪˈzeɪʃən

factorize
BR ˈfaktərʌɪz, -ɪz, -ɪŋ, -d
AM ˈfæktəˌraɪz, -ɪz, -ɪŋ, -d

factory
BR ˈfakt(ə)r|i, -ɪz
AM ˈfækt(ə)ri, -z

factotum
BR fakˈtəʊtəm, -z
AM fækˈtoʊdəm, -z

factual
BR ˈfaktʃʊəl,
ˈfaktʃ(ʉ)l, ˈfaktjʊəl,
ˈfaktjʉl
AM ˈfæk(t)ʃ(əw)əl

factualism
BR ˈfaktʃʊəlɪz(ə)m,
ˈfaktʃʉlɪz(ə)m,
ˈfaktʃlɪz(ə)m
AM ˈfæk(t)ʃ(əw)əˌlɪzəm

factualist
BR ˈfaktʃʊəlɪst,
ˈfaktʃʉlɪst, ˈfaktʃlɪst,
-s
AM ˈfæk(t)ʃ(əw)ələst,
-s

factuality
BR ˌfaktʃʊˈalɪti,
ˌfaktjʊˈalɪti
AM ˌfæk(t)ʃəˈwælədi

factually
BR ˈfaktʃʊəli,
ˈfaktʃʉli, ˈfaktʃli
AM ˈfæk(t)ʃ(əw)əli

factualness
BR ˈfaktʃʊəlnəs,
ˈfaktʃ(ʉ)lnəs
AM ˈfæk(t)ʃ(əw)əlnəs

factum
BR ˈfaktəm, -z
AM ˈfæktəm, -z

facture
BR ˈfaktʃə(r), -z
AM ˈfæk(t)ʃər, -z

facula
BR ˈfakjʉlə(r)
AM ˈfækjələ

facular
BR ˈfakjʉlə(r)
AM ˈfækjələr

faculous
BR ˈfakjʉləs
AM ˈfækjələs

facultative
BR ˈfakltətɪv
AM ˈfækəlˌteɪdɪv

facultatively
BR ˈfakltətɪvli
AM ˈfækəlˌteɪdɪvli

faculty
BR ˈfaklt|i, -ɪz
AM ˈfækəlti, ˈfækəldi,
-z

fad
BR fad, -z
AM fæd, -z

faddily
BR ˈfadɪli
AM ˈfædəli

faddiness
BR ˈfadɪnɪs
AM ˈfædinɪs

faddish
BR ˈfadɪʃ
AM ˈfædɪʃ

faddishly
BR ˈfadɪʃli
AM ˈfædɪʃli

faddishness
BR ˈfadɪʃnɪs
AM ˈfædɪʃnɪs

faddism
BR ˈfadɪz(ə)m
AM ˈfæˌdɪzəm

faddist
BR ˈfadɪst, -s
AM ˈfædəst, -s

faddy
BR ˈfadi
AM ˈfædi

fade
BR feɪd, -z, -ɪŋ, -ɪd
AM feɪd, -z, -ɪŋ, -ɪd

fadeaway
BR ˈfeɪdəweɪ
AM ˈfeɪdəˌweɪ

fadeless
BR ˈfeɪdlɪs
AM ˈfeɪdlɪs

fader
BR ˈfeɪdə(r), -z
AM ˈfeɪdər, -z

fadge
BR fadʒ, -ɪz
AM fædʒ, -əz

faecal
BR ˈfiːkl
AM ˈfikəl

faeces
BR ˈfiːsiːz
AM ˈfisiz

Faenza
BR fɑːˈɛntsə(r)
AM fɑˈɛn(t)zə

faerie
BR ˈfɛːri
AM ˈfɛri

Faeroe Islands
BR ˈfɛːrəʊ ˌʌɪlən(d)z
AM ˈfɛroʊ ˈaɪlən(d)z

Faeroes
BR ˈfɛːrəʊz
AM ˈfɛroʊz

Faeroese
BR ˌfɛːrəʊˈiːz
AM ˈfɛrəˈwiz

faery
BR ˈfɛːri
AM ˈfɛri

faff
BR faf, -s, -ɪŋ, -t
AM fæf, -s, -ɪŋ, -t

fag
BR fag, -z, -ɪŋ, -d
AM fæg, -z, -ɪŋ, -d

Fagan
BR ˈfeɪg(ə)n
AM ˈfeɪgən

faggot
BR ˈfagət, -s, -ɪŋ, -ɪd
AM ˈfægə|t, -ts, -dɪŋ,
-dəd

faggotry
BR ˈfagətri
AM ˈfægətri

faggoty
BR ˈfagəti
AM ˈfægədi

Fagin
BR ˈfeɪgɪn
AM ˈfeɪgɪn

fagot
BR ˈfagət, -s, -ɪŋ, -ɪd
AM ˈfægə|t, -ts, -dɪŋ,
-dəd

fah
BR fɑː(r)
AM fɑ

Fahd
BR fɑːd
AM fɑd

Fahrenheit
BR ˈfarənhʌɪt,
ˈfarnhʌɪt
AM ˈfɛrənˌ(h)aɪt

Fahy
BR ˈfɑːhi
AM ˈfeɪˌhi

faience
BR fʌɪˈɑːns, fʌɪˈɒs
AM faɪˈans, feɪˈans

fail
BR feɪl, -z, -ɪŋ, -d
AM feɪl, -z, -ɪŋ, -d

failing
BR ˈfeɪlɪŋ, -z
AM ˈfeɪlɪŋ, -z

faille
BR feɪl
AM faɪl

failure
BR ˈfeɪljə(r), -z
AM ˈfeɪljər, -z

fain
BR feɪn
AM feɪn

fainéancy
BR ˈfeɪnɪəns|i,
ˈfeɪnɛ̃s|i, -ɪz
AM ˈfeɪniənsi, -z

fainéant
BR ˈfeɪnɪənt, ˈfeɪnɛɪ̃,
-s
AM ˈfeɪniənt, -s

faint
BR feɪnt, -s, -ɪŋ, -ɪd,
-ə(r), -ɪst
AM feɪn|t, -ts, -(t)ɪŋ,
-(t)ɪd, -(t)ər, -(t)ɪst

faintly
BR ˈfeɪntli
AM ˈfeɪn(t)li

faintness
BR ˈfeɪntnɪs
AM ˈfeɪn(t)nɪs

fair
BR fɛː(r)
AM fɛ(ə)r

Fairbairn
BR ˈfɛːbɛːn
AM ˈfɛrˌbɛrn

Fairbanks
BR ˈfɛːbaŋks
AM ˈfɛrˌbæŋks

Fairbourn
BR ˈfɛːbɔːn
AM ˈfɛrˌbɔ(ə)rn

Fairbourne
BR ˈfɛːbɔːn
AM ˈfɛrˌbɔ(ə)rn

Fairbrother
BR ˈfɛːˌbrʌðə(r)
AM ˈfɛrˌbrəðər

Fairchild
BR ˈfɛːtʃʌɪld
AM ˈfɛrˌtʃaɪld

Fairclough
BR ˈfɛːklʌf
AM ˈfɛrˌkləf

Fairfax
BR ˈfɛːfaks
AM ˈfɛrˌfæks

Fairford
BR ˈfɛːfəd
AM ˈfɛrfərd

fairground
BR ˈfɛːgraʊnd, -z
AM ˈfɛrˌgraʊnd, -z

Fairhaven
BR ˈfɛːˌheɪvn
AM ˈfɛrˌ(h)eɪvən

Fairhurst
BR ˈfɛːhəːst
AM ˈfɛrˌ(h)ərst

fairing
BR ˈfɛːrɪŋ, -z
AM ˈfɛrɪŋ, -z

fairish
BR ˈfɛːrɪʃ
AM ˈfɛrɪʃ

fairlead
BR ˈfɛːliːd, -z
AM ˈfɛrˌlid, -z

Fairley
BR ˈfɛːli
AM ˈfɛrli

Fairlie
BR 'fɛːli
AM 'fɛrli

fairly
BR 'fɛːli
AM 'fɛrli

fairness
BR 'fɛːnəs
AM 'fɛrnəs

Fairport
BR 'fɛːpɔːt
AM 'fɛr,pɔ(ə)rt

fairway
BR 'fɛːweɪ, -z
AM 'fɛr,weɪ, -z

fairy
BR 'fɛːr|i, -ɪz
AM 'fɛri, -z

fairyland
BR 'fɛːrɪland, -z
AM 'fɛri,lænd, -z

Faisal
BR 'fʌɪsl
AM 'faɪ'zɑl

Faisalabad
BR 'fʌɪs(ə)ləbad,
,fʌɪs|əbad,
'fʌɪs(ə)ləbɑːd,
,fʌɪs|əbɑːd
AM ,faɪ'zɑlə,bɑd,
,faɪ'zɑlə,bæd

fait accompli
BR ,feɪt ə'kɒmpli, ,fɛt +
AM ,fɛt əkɑm'pli,
,feɪt +

faith
BR feɪθ, -s
AM feɪθ, -s

faithful
BR 'feɪθf(ʊ)l
AM 'feɪθfəl

Faithfull
BR 'feɪθf(ʊ)l
AM 'feɪθfəl

faithfully
BR 'feɪθfʊli, 'feɪθf|i
AM 'feɪθfəli

faithfulness
BR 'feɪθf(ʊ)lnəs
AM 'feɪθfəlnəs

faithless
BR 'feɪθlɪs
AM 'feɪθlɪs

faithlessly
BR 'feɪθlɪsli
AM 'feɪθlɪsli

faithlessness
BR 'feɪθlɪsnɪs
AM 'feɪθlɪsnɪs

fake
BR feɪk, -s, -ɪŋ, -t
AM feɪk, -s, -ɪŋ, -t

Fakenham
BR 'feɪkənəm,
'feɪkn̩əm
AM 'feɪkənəm

faker
BR 'feɪkə(r), -z
AM 'feɪkər, -z

fakery
BR 'feɪk(ə)ri
AM 'feɪkəri

fakir
BR 'feɪkɪə(r), 'fakɪə(r),
fə'kɪə(r), -z
AM fə'kɪ(ə)r, -z

falafel
BR fə'lɑːfl
AM fə'lɑfəl

Falange
BR fə'lan(d)ʒ
AM fə'lændʒ
SP fa'laŋxe

Falangism
BR fə'lan(d)ʒɪz(ə)m
AM fə'læn,dʒɪzəm,
feɪ'læn,dʒɪzəm

Falangist
BR fə'lan(d)ʒɪst, -s
AM fə'lændʒəst,
feɪ'lændʒəst, -s

Falasha
BR fə'laʃə(r)
AM fə'lɑʃə

falbala
BR 'falbələ(r)
AM 'fælbələ

falcate
BR 'falkeɪt
AM 'fæl,keɪt, 'fɒl,keɪt,
'fæl,keɪt, 'fal,keɪt

falchion
BR 'fɔːl(t)ʃ(ə)n, -z
AM 'fɒl(t)ʃən,
'fal(t)ʃən, -z

falciform
BR 'falsɪfɔːm
AM 'fælsə,fɔ(ə)rm

falcon
BR 'fɔː(l)k(ə)n,
'fɒlk(ə), 'falk(ə)n, -z
AM 'fælkən, -z

falconer
BR 'fɔː(l)kənə(r),
'fɔː(l)kn̩ə(r),
'fɒlkənə(r), 'fɒlkn̩ə(r),
'falkənə(r),
'falkn̩ə(r), -z
AM 'fælkənər, -z

falconet
BR 'fɔː(l)kənɪt,
'fɔː(l)kn̩ɪt, 'fɔː(l)kənɪt,
'fɔː(l)kn̩ɪt, 'fɒlkənɪt,
'fɒlkn̩ɪt, 'falkənɪt,
'falkn̩ɪt, -s
AM 'fælkənət, -s

falconry
BR 'fɔː(l)k(ə)nri,
'fɒlk(ə)nri,
'falk(ə)nri
AM 'fælkənri

falderal
BR 'faldəral, -z

AM 'fɒldə,rɒl,
'fældə,ræl, 'fɑldə,rɑl,
-z

Faldo
BR 'faldəʊ
AM 'fɔldoʊ, 'faldoʊ

faldstool
BR 'fɔːl(d)stuːl, -z
AM 'fɒl(d),stul,
'fal(d),stul, -z

Falernian
BR fə'lə:nɪən
AM fə'lɜrnɪən

Falk
BR 'fɔː(l)k
AM fɒk, fak

Falkender
BR 'fɔːlk(ə)ndə(r)
AM 'fɒlkəndər,
'fɑlkəndər

Falkirk
BR 'fɔːlkə:k, 'fɒlkə:k
AM 'fɒl,kɜrk, 'fɑl,kɜrk

Falkland Islands
BR 'fɔː(l)klənd
,aɪlən(d)z, 'fɒlklənd +
AM 'fɒklən(d)
'aɪlən(d)z, 'faklən(d)
'aɪlən(d)z

Falklands
BR 'fɔː(l)kləndz,
'fɒlkləndz
AM 'fɒklən(d)z,
'faklən(d)z

fall
BR fɔːl, -z, -ɪŋ
AM fɒl, fal, -z, -ɪŋ

fallacious
BR fə'leɪʃəs
AM fə'leɪʃəs

fallaciously
BR fə'leɪʃəsli
AM fə'leɪʃəsli

fallaciousness
BR fə'leɪʃəsnəs
AM fə'leɪʃəsnəs

fallacy
BR 'faləs|i, -ɪz
AM 'fæləsi, -z

fallback
BR 'fɔːlbak, -s
AM 'fɒl,bæk, 'fal,bæk,
-s

fallen
BR 'fɔːlən
AM 'fɒlən, 'falən

fallenness
BR 'fɔːlənnəs
AM 'fɒlə(n)nəs,
'falə(n)nəs

faller
BR 'fɔːlə(r), -z
AM 'fɒlər, 'falər, -z

fallibility
BR ,falɪ'bɪlɪti
AM ,fælə'bɪlɪdi

fallible
BR 'falɪbl

fallibleness
BR 'falɪblnəs
AM 'fæləbəlnəs

fallibly
BR 'falɪbli
AM 'fæləbli

Fallon
BR 'falən
AM 'fælən

fallopian
BR fə'ləʊpɪən
AM fə'loʊpɪən

fallout
BR 'fɔːlaʊt
AM 'fɒl,aʊt, 'fal,aʊt

fallow
BR 'faləʊ
AM 'fæloʊ

Fallowfield
BR 'falə(ʊ)fiːld
AM 'fæloʊ,fild

fallowness
BR 'faləʊnəs
AM 'fæloʊnəs

Falmouth
BR 'falməθ
AM 'fælməθ

false
BR fɔːls, fɒls, -ə(r), -ɪst
AM fɒls, fals, -ər, -əst

falsehood
BR 'fɔːlshʊd, 'fɒlshʊd,
-z
AM 'fɒls,(h)ʊd,
'fals,(h)ʊd, -z

falsely
BR 'fɔːlsli, 'fɒlsli
AM 'fɒlsli, 'falsli

falseness
BR 'fɔːlsnəs, 'fɒlsnəs
AM 'fɒlsnəs, 'falsnəs

falsetto
BR ,fɔːl'sɛtəʊ,
,fɒl'sɛtəʊ, -z
AM fɒl'sɛdoʊ,
fal'sɛdoʊ, -z

falsework
BR 'fɔːlswə:k,
'fɒlswə:k
AM 'fɒls,wɜrk,
'fals,wɜrk

falsies
BR 'fɔːlsɪz, 'fɒlsɪz
AM 'fɒlsiz, 'falsiz

falsifiability
BR ,fɔːlsɪfʌɪə'bɪlɪti,
,fɒlsɪfʌɪə'bɪlɪti
AM ,fɒlsə,faɪə'bɪlɪdi

falsifiable
BR 'fɔːlsɪfʌɪəbl,
'fɒlsɪfʌɪəbl
AM 'fɒlsə,faɪəbəl,
'falsə,faɪəbəl

falsification
BR ,fɔːlsɪfɪ'keɪʃn,
,fɒlsɪfɪ'keɪʃn, -z

falsify
AM ˌfɒlsəfəˈkeɪʃən,
ˌfɑlsəfəˈkeɪʃən, -z

falsify
BR ˈfɔːlsɪfʌɪ, ˈfɒlsɪfʌɪ,
-z, -ɪŋ, -d
AM ˈfɔlsəˌfaɪ, ˈfɑlsəˌfaɪ,
-z, -ɪŋ, -d

falsity
BR ˈfɔːlsɪti, ˈfɒlsɪti
AM ˈfɔlsədi, ˈfɑlsədi

Falstaff
BR ˈfɔːlstɑːf, ˈfɔːlstaf,
ˈfɒlstɑːf, ˈfɒlstaf
AM ˈfɔlˌstæf, ˈfɑlˌstæf

Falstaffian
BR fɔːlˈstɑːfɪən,
fɔːlˈstafɪən,
fɒlˈstɑːfɪən,
fɒlˈstafɪən
AM fɔlˈstæfɪən,
fɑlˈstæfɪən

Falster
BR ˈfɔːlstə(r), ˈfɒlstə(r)
AM ˈfɒlstər, ˈfɑlstər

falter
BR ˈfɔːl|tə(r), ˈfɒlt|ə(r),
-əz, -(ə)rɪŋ, -əd
AM ˈfɒlt|ər, ˈfɑlt|ər,
-ərz, -(ə)rɪŋ, -ərd

falterer
BR ˈfɔːlt(ə)rə(r),
ˈfɒlt(ə)rə(r), -z
AM ˈfɒltərər, ˈfɑltərər,
-z

faltering
BR ˈfɔːlt(ə)rɪŋ,
ˈfɒlt(ə)rɪŋ
AM ˈfɒlt(ə)rɪŋ,
ˈfɑlt(ə)rɪŋ

falteringly
BR ˈfɔːlt(ə)rɪŋli,
ˈfɒlt(ə)rɪŋli
AM ˈfɒlt(ə)rɪŋli,
ˈfɑlt(ə)rɪŋli

Falwell
BR ˈfɔːlwɛl, ˈfɒlwɛl
AM ˈfɒlˌwɛl, ˈfɑlˌwɛl

Famagusta
BR ˌfaməˈgustə(r)
AM ˌfaməˈgustə

fame
BR feɪm, -d
AM feɪm, -d

familial
BR fəˈmɪlɪəl
AM fəˈmɪljəl, fəˈmɪlɪəl

familiar
BR fəˈmɪlɪə(r)
AM fəˈmɪljər, fəˈmɪlɪər

familiarisation
BR fəˌmɪlɪərʌɪˈzeɪʃn
AM fəˌmɪljərəˈzeɪʃən,
fəˌmɪljəˌraɪˈzeɪʃən

familiarise
BR fəˈmɪlɪərʌɪz, -ɪz, -ɪŋ,
-d
AM fəˈmɪljəˌraɪz, -ɪz,
-ɪŋ, -d

familiarity
BR fəˌmɪlɪˈarɪt|i, -ɪz
AM fəˌmɪliˈɛrədi,
fəˌmɪlˈjərədi, -z

familiarization
BR fəˌmɪlɪərʌɪˈzeɪʃn
AM fəˌmɪljərəˈzeɪʃən,
fəˌmɪljəˌraɪˈzeɪʃən

familiarize
BR fəˈmɪlɪərʌɪz, -ɪz, -ɪŋ,
-d
AM fəˈmɪljəˌraɪz, -ɪz,
-ɪŋ, -d

familiarly
BR fəˈmɪlɪəli
AM fəˈmɪljərli

famille jaune
BR fəˌmi: ˈʒɔːn
AM fəˌmi ˈʒoʊn

famille noire
BR fəˌmi: ˈnwɑː(r)
AM fəˌmi ˈnwɑr

famille rose
BR fəˌmi: ˈrəʊz
AM fəˌmi ˈroʊz

famille verte
BR fəˌmi: ˈvɛːt
AM fəˌmi ˈvɛr(t)

family
BR ˈfam(ɪ)l|i, ˈfam|l|i,
-ɪz
AM ˈfæm(ə)li, -z

famine
BR ˈfamɪn, -z
AM ˈfæmən, -z

famish
BR ˈfam|ɪʃ, -ɪʃɪz, -ɪʃɪŋ,
-ɪʃt
AM ˈfæmɪʃ, -ɪz, -ɪŋ, -t

famous
BR ˈfeɪməs
AM ˈfeɪməs

famously
BR ˈfeɪməsli
AM ˈfeɪməsli

famousness
BR ˈfeɪməsnəs
AM ˈfeɪməsnəs

famuli
BR ˈfamjʊlʌɪ, ˈfamjʊli:
AM ˈfæmjəˌlaɪ

famulus
BR ˈfamjʊləs
AM ˈfæmjələs

fan
BR fan, -z, -ɪŋ, -d
AM fæn, -z, -ɪŋ, -d

Fanagalo
BR ˌfanəgəˈləʊ,
ˈfanəgələʊ, ˈfanəg|əʊ
AM ˌfænəgəˈloʊ

fanatic
BR fəˈnatɪk, -s
AM fəˈnædɪk, -s

fanatical
BR fəˈnatɪkl
AM fəˈnædəkəl

fanatically
BR fəˈnatɪkli
AM fəˈnædək(ə)li

fanaticise
BR fəˈnatɪsʌɪz, -ɪz, -ɪŋ,
-d
AM fəˈnædəˌsaɪz, -ɪz,
-ɪŋ, -d

fanaticism
BR fəˈnatɪsɪz(ə)m, -z
AM fəˈnædəˌsɪzəm, -z

fanaticize
BR fəˈnatɪsʌɪz, -ɪz, -ɪŋ,
-d
AM fəˈnædəˌsaɪz, -ɪz,
-ɪŋ, -d

fanbelt
BR ˈfanbɛlt, -s
AM ˈfænˌbɛlt, -s

fanciable
BR ˈfansɪəbl
AM ˈfænsɪəbl

fancier
BR ˈfansɪə(r), -z
AM ˈfænsɪər, -z

fanciful
BR ˈfansɪf(ʊ)l
AM ˈfænsɪfəl

fancifully
BR ˈfansɪfʊli, ˈfansɪfˌli
AM ˈfænsɪf(ə)li

fancifulness
BR ˈfansɪf(ʊ)lnəs
AM ˈfænsɪfəlnəs

fancily
BR ˈfansɪli
AM ˈfænsəli

fanciness
BR ˈfansɪnɪs
AM ˈfænsɪnɪs

fancy
BR ˈfans|i, -ɪz, -ɪɪŋ, -ɪd
AM ˈfænsi, -z, -ɪŋ, -d

fancywork
BR ˈfansɪwəːk
AM ˈfænsiˌwərk

fandangle
BR fanˈdaŋgl, -z
AM fænˈdæŋgəl, -z

fandango
BR fanˈdaŋgəʊ, -z
AM fænˈdæŋgoʊ, -z

fandom
BR ˈfandəm
AM ˈfændəm

fane
BR feɪn, -z
AM feɪn, -z

fanfare
BR ˈfanfɛː(r), -z
AM ˈfænˌfɛ(ə)r, -z

fanfaronade
BR ˌfanfarəˈneɪd, -z
AM ˌfænˌfɛrəˈneɪd, -z

fanfold
BR ˈfanfəʊld
AM ˈfænˌfoʊld

fang
BR faŋ, -z, -d
AM fæŋ, -z, -d

Fangio
BR ˈfan(d)ʒɪəʊ
AM ˈfɑndʒ(i)oʊ

fangless
BR ˈfaŋləs
AM ˈfæŋləs

fanlight
BR ˈfanlʌɪt, -s
AM ˈfænˌlaɪt, -s

fanlike
BR ˈfanlʌɪk
AM ˈfænˌlaɪk

fanner
BR ˈfanə(r), -z
AM ˈfænər, -z

Fannie
BR ˈfani
AM ˈfæni

fanny
BR ˈfan|i, -ɪz
AM ˈfæni, -z

Fanshawe
BR ˈfanʃɔː(r)
AM ˈfænˌsɔ

Fanta®
BR ˈfantə(r), -z
AM ˈfæn(t)ə, -z

fantail
BR ˈfanteɪl, -z, -d
AM ˈfænˌteɪl, -z, -d

fan-tan
BR ˈfantan
AM ˈfænˌtæn

fantasia
BR fanˈteɪzɪə(r),
ˌfantəˈziːə(r), -z
AM fænˈteɪʒ(i)ə,
fænˈteɪzɪə, -z

fantasise
BR ˈfantəsʌɪz, -ɪz, -ɪŋ, -d
AM ˈfæn(t)əˌsaɪz, -ɪz,
-ɪŋ, -d

fantasist
BR ˈfantəsɪst, -s
AM ˈfæn(t)əsəst, -s

fantasize
BR ˈfantəsʌɪz, -ɪz, -ɪŋ, -d
AM ˈfæn(t)əˌsaɪz, -ɪz,
-ɪŋ, -d

fantasmatic
BR ˌfantəzˈmatɪk
AM ˌfæn(t)əzˈmædɪk,
ˌfænˌtæzˈmædɪk

fantast
BR ˈfantast, -s
AM ˈfænˌtæst, -s

fantastic
BR fanˈtastɪk
AM fænˈtæstɪk

fantastical
BR fanˈtastɪkl
AM fænˈtæstəkəl

fantasticality
BR fanˌtastɪˈkalɪti

AM fæn‚tæstə'kælədi

fantastically
BR fan'tastıkli
AM fæn'tæstək(ə)li

fantasticate
BR fan'tastıkeıt, -s, -ıŋ,
-ıd
AM fæn'tæstə‚keıʃt, -ts,
-dıŋ, -dıd

fantastication
BR fan‚tastı'keıʃn
AM fæn‚tæstə'keıʃən

fantasticism
BR fan'tastısız(ə)m
AM fæn'tæstə‚sızəm

fantasy
BR 'fantəs|i, -ız
AM 'fæn(t)əsi, -z

Fante
BR 'fanti, -ız
AM 'fɑnti, -z

Fanti
BR 'fanti, -ız
AM 'fɑnti, -z

fantod
BR 'fantɒd, -z
AM 'fæn‚tad, -z

Fanum
BR 'feınəm
AM 'feınəm

fanzine
BR 'fanziːn, -z
AM 'fæn‚zin, -z

faquir
BR 'feıkıə(r), 'fakıə(r),
fə'kıə(r), -z
AM fə'kı(ə)r, -z

far
BR fɑː(r)
AM fɑr

Fara
BR 'farə(r)
AM 'fɛrə

farad
BR 'farad, 'farəd, -z
AM 'fɛr‚æd, -z

faradaic
BR ‚farə'deıık
AM ‚fɛrə'deıık

faraday
BR 'farədeı, -z
AM 'fɛrə‚deı, -z

faradic
BR fə'radık
AM fə'rædık

Farah
BR 'farə(r)
AM 'fɛrə

farandole
BR 'farəndəʊl,
'farṇdəʊl, -z
AM 'fɛrəndoʊl, -z

faraway
BR ‚fɑːrə'weı
AM ‚farə‚weı

farce
BR fɑːs, -ız

AM fɑrs, -əz

farceur
BR ‚fɑː'sɔː(r), -z
AM fɑr'sər, -z

farcical
BR 'fɑːsıkl
AM 'fɑrsəkəl

farcicality
BR ‚fɑː'sı'kalıti
AM ‚fɑrsə'kælədi

farcically
BR 'fɑːsıkḷi
AM 'fɑrsək(ə)li

farcy
BR 'fɑːsi
AM 'fɑrsi

farded
BR 'fɑːdıd
AM 'fɑrdəd

fare
BR fɛː(r), -z, -ıŋ, -d
AM fɛ(ə)r, -z, -ıŋ, -d

Fareham
BR 'fɛːrəm
AM 'fɛrəm

farewell
BR ‚fɛː'wɛl, -z
AM ‚fɛr'wɛl, -z

farfalle
BR fɑː'faleı, fɑː'fali
AM ‚fɑr'falə, 'fɑrfələ

farfetched
BR ‚fɑː'fɛtʃt
AM 'fɑr'fɛtʃt

farfetchedness
BR ‚fɑː'fɛtʃtnəs,
‚fɑː'fɛtʃıdnıs
AM 'fɑr'fɛtʃ(t)nəs,
'fɑr'fɛtʃədnəs

Fargo
BR 'fɑːgəʊ
AM 'fɑrgoʊ

Faridabad
BR fə'riːdəbad,
fə'riːdəbaːd
AM fə'ridə‚bad,
fə'ridə‚bæd

farina
BR fə'riːnə(r),
fə'rʌmə(r)
AM fə'rinə

farinaceous
BR ‚farı'neıʃəs
AM ‚fɛrə'neıʃəs

Faringdon
BR 'farıŋd(ə)n
AM 'fɛrıŋdən

Farjeon
BR 'fɑːdʒ(ə)n
AM 'fɑrdʒən

farl
BR fɑːl, -z
AM fɑr(ə)l, -z

Farleigh
BR 'fɑːli
AM 'fɑrli

Farley
BR 'fɑːli
AM 'fɑrli

farm
BR fɑːm, -z, -ıŋ, -d
AM fɑrm, -z, -ıŋ, -d

farmable
BR 'fɑːməbl
AM 'fɑrməbəl

farmer
BR 'fɑːmə(r), -z
AM 'fɑrmər, -z

farmhand
BR 'fɑːmhand, -z
AM 'fɑrm‚(h)ænd, -z

farmhouse
BR 'fɑːmhaʊ|s, -zız
AM 'fɑrm‚(h)aʊ|s, -zəz

farmland
BR 'fɑːmland, -z
AM 'fɑrm‚lænd, -z

farmstead
BR 'fɑːmstɛd, -z
AM 'fɑrm‚stɛd, -z

farmwork
BR 'fɑːmwəːk
AM 'fɑrm‚wərk

farmworker
BR 'fɑːm‚wəːkə(r), -z
AM 'fɑrm‚wərkər, -z

farmyard
BR 'fɑːmjɑːd, -z
AM 'fɑrm‚jɑrd, -z

Farnborough
BR 'fɑːnb(ə)rə(r)
AM 'fɑrnb(ə)rə

Farne Islands
BR 'fɑːn ‚ʌılən(d)z
AM 'fɑrn 'ʌılən(d)z

Farnese
BR fɑː'neızi
AM fɑr‚neızi

farness
BR 'fɑːnəs
AM 'fɑrnəs

Farnham
BR 'fɑːnəm
AM 'fɑrnəm

Farnley
BR 'fɑːnli
AM 'fɑrnli

Farnworth
BR 'fɑːnwəːθ
AM 'fɑrn‚wərθ

Faro
place in Portugal
BR 'fɑːrəʊ, 'fɛːrəʊ
AM 'fɛroʊ
PORT 'faru

faro
card-game
BR 'fɛːrəʊ
AM 'fɛroʊ

Faroe
BR 'fɛːrəʊ, -z
AM 'fɛroʊ, -z

Faroese
BR ‚fɛːrəʊ'iːz
AM ‚fɛrə'wiz

far-off
BR ‚fɑː'ɒf
AM ‚fɑː'rɒf, 'fɑ‚rɒf

farouche
BR fə'ruːʃ
AM fə'ruʃ

Farouk
BR fə'ruːk
AM fə'ruk

Farquhar
BR 'fɑːk(w)ɑ(r)
AM 'fɑr‚kwɑr

Farquharson
BR 'fɑːk(w)əs(ə)n
AM 'fɑrk(w)əsən,
'fɑrk‚wɑrsən

Farr
BR fɑː(r)
AM fɑr

farraginous
BR fə'radʒınəs
AM fə'rædʒənəs

farrago
BR fə'rɑːgəʊ, -z
AM fə'ragoʊ, fə'reıgoʊ,
-z

Farrah
BR 'farə(r)
AM 'fɛrə

Farrar
BR 'farə(r)
AM fə'rɑr, 'fɛrər

Farrell
BR 'farəl, 'farḷ
AM 'fɛrəl

Farrelly
BR 'farəli, 'farḷi
AM 'far(ə)li

farrier
BR 'farıə(r), -z
AM 'fɛrıər, -z

farriery
BR 'farıəri
AM 'fɛrıəri, 'fɛrjəri

Farringdon
BR 'farıŋd(ə)n
AM 'fɛrıŋdən

Farris
BR 'farıs
AM 'fɛrəs

farrow
BR 'farəʊ, -z, -ıŋ, -d
AM 'fɛroʊ, -z, -ıŋ, -d

farruca
BR fə'ruːkə(r), -z
AM fə'rukə, -z

far-seeing
BR ‚fɑː'siːıŋ
AM 'fɑr'siıŋ

Farsi
BR 'fɑːsiː, ‚fɑː'si
AM 'fɑrsi

fart
BR fɑːt, -s, -ıŋ, -ıd

AM 'fɑːr|t, -ts, -dɪŋ, -dəd

farther
BR 'fɑːðə(r)
AM 'fɑrðər

farthest
BR 'fɑːðɪst
AM 'fɑrðəst

farthing
BR 'fɑːðɪŋ
AM 'fɑrðɪŋ

farthingale
BR 'fɑːðɪŋgeɪl, -z
AM 'fɑrðɪŋ,geɪl, -z

fartlek
BR 'fɑːtlɛk
AM 'fɑrtlək

fasces
BR 'fasiːz
AM 'fæsiz

fascia¹
BR 'feɪʃɪə(r), -z
AM 'fæʃ(i)ə, 'feɪʃ(i)ə, -z

fascia²
architectural
BR 'feɪsɪə(r), -z
AM 'fæʃ(i)ə, 'feɪʃ(i)ə, -z

fascia³
medical
BR 'faʃɪə(r), -z
AM 'fæʃ(i)ə, -z

fascial
BR 'feɪʃl
AM 'fæʃ(i)əl

fasciate
BR 'faʃɪeɪt, -s, -ɪŋ, -ɪd
AM 'fæʃi,eɪ|t, -ts, -dɪŋ, -dɪd

fasciation
BR ,faʃɪ'eɪʃn
AM ,fæʃi'eɪʃən

fascicle
BR 'fasɪkl, -z, -d
AM 'fæsəkəl, -z, -d

fascicular
BR fə'sɪkjələ(r)
AM fə'sɪkjələr

fasciculate
BR fə'sɪkjələɪt, fə'sɪkjələt
AM fə'sɪkjə,leɪt, fə'sɪkjələt

fasciculation
BR fə,sɪkjə'leɪʃn
AM fə,sɪkjə'leɪʃən

fascicule
BR 'fasɪkjuːl, -z
AM 'fæsə,kjul, -z

fasciculi
BR fə'sɪkjələʌɪ, fə'sɪkjəliː
AM fə'sɪkjə,lʌɪ

fasciculus
BR fə'sɪkjələs
AM fə'sɪkjələs

fasciitis
BR ,fasɪ'ʌɪtɪs, ,faʃɪ'ʌɪtɪs

AM ,fæʃi'aɪdɪs

fascinate
BR 'fasɪneɪt, -s, -ɪŋ, -ɪd
AM 'fæsə,neɪ|t, -ts, -dɪŋ, -dɪd

fascinatingly
BR 'fasɪneɪtɪŋli
AM 'fæsə,neɪdɪŋli

fascination
BR ,fasɪ'neɪʃn, -z
AM ,fæsə'neɪʃən, -z

fascinator
BR 'fasɪneɪtə(r), -z
AM 'fæsə,neɪdər, -z

fascine
BR fa'siːn, -z
AM fə'sin, -z

fascism
BR 'faʃɪz(ə)m
AM 'fæ,ʃɪzəm

fascist
BR 'faʃɪst, -s
AM 'fæʃəst, -s

fascistic
BR fə'ʃɪstɪk
AM fæ'ʃɪstɪk, fə'ʃɪstɪk

Fashanu
BR 'faʃənuː
AM 'fæʃənu

fashion
BR 'faʃ|n, -nz, -ŋɪŋ\-ənɪŋ, -nd
AM 'fæʃ|ən, -ənz, -(ə)nɪŋ, -ənd

fashionability
BR ,faʃ(ə)nə'bɪlɪti, ,faʃnə'bɪlɪti
AM ,fæʃ(ə)nə'bɪlɪdi

fashionable
BR 'faʃ(ə)nəbl, 'faʃnəbl
AM 'fæʃ(ə)nəbəl

fashionableness
BR 'faʃ(ə)nəblnəs, 'faʃnəblnəs
AM 'fæʃ(ə)nəbəlnəs

fashionably
BR 'faʃ(ə)nəbli, 'faʃnəbli
AM 'fæʃ(ə)nəbli

fashioner
BR 'faʃənə(r), 'faʃnə(r), -z
AM 'fæʃ ənər, -z

Fashoda
BR fə'ʃəʊdə(r)
AM fə'ʃoʊdə

Faslane
BR faz'leɪn
AM fæz'leɪn

Fassbinder
BR 'fasbʌɪndə(r)
AM 'fæs,baɪndər
GER 'fasbɪndɐ

fast
BR fɑːst, fast, -s, -ɪŋ, -ɪd, -ə(r), -ɪst

AM fæst, -s, -ɪŋ, -əd, -ər, -əst

fastback
BR 'fɑːs(t)bak, 'fas(t)bak, -s
AM 'fæs(t),bæk, -s

fastball
BR 'fɑːs(t)bɔːl, 'fas(t)bɔːl
AM 'fæs(t),bɔl, 'fæs(t),bɑl

fasten
BR 'fɑːs|n, 'fas|n, -nz, -nɪŋ\-nɪŋ, -nd
AM 'fæsn, -z, -ɪŋ, -d

fastener
BR 'fɑːsnə(r), 'fɑːsnə(r), 'fasnə(r), 'fasnə(r), -z
AM 'fæs(ə)nər, -z

fastening
BR 'fɑːsnɪŋ, 'fɑːsnɪŋ, 'fasnɪŋ, 'fasnɪŋ, -z
AM 'fæs(ə)nɪŋ, -z

faster
BR 'fɑːstə(r), 'fastə(r), -z
AM 'fæstər, -z

fastidious
BR fa'stɪdɪəs
AM fæ'stɪdiəs

fastidiously
BR fa'stɪdɪəsli
AM fæ'stɪdiəsli

fastidiousness
BR fa'stɪdɪəsnəs
AM fæ'stɪdiəsnəs

fastigiate
BR fa'stɪdʒɪət, fa'stɪdʒɪeɪt
AM fə'stɪdʒiət

fasting
BR 'fɑːstɪŋ, 'fastɪŋ, -z
AM 'fæstɪŋ, -z

fastness
BR 'fɑːs(t)nəs, 'fas(t)nəs, -ɪz
AM 'fæs(t)nəs, -əz

Fastnet
BR 'fɑːs(t)nɛt, 'fɑːs(t)nɪt, 'fas(t)nɛt, 'fas(t)nɪt
AM 'fæs(t),nɛt

fat
BR fat, -ə(r), -ɪst
AM fæ|t, -ər, -dəst

Fatah, Al
BR ,al fə'tɑː(r), 'fatə(r)
AM ,ɑl fə'tɑ

fatal
BR 'feɪtl
AM 'feɪdl

fatalism
BR 'feɪtl|ɪz(ə)m, 'feɪtlɪz(ə)m
AM 'feɪdl,ɪzəm

fatalist
BR 'feɪt|ɪst, 'feɪtəlɪst, -s
AM 'feɪdlɪst, -s

fatalistic
BR ,feɪtl'ɪstɪk, ,feɪtə'lɪstɪk
AM ,feɪdl'ɪstɪk

fatalistically
BR ,feɪtl'ɪstɪkli, ,feɪtə'lɪstɪkli
AM ,feɪdl'ɪstək(ə)li

fatality
BR fə'talɪt|i, -ɪz
AM feɪ'tælədi, fə'tælədi, -z

fatally
BR 'feɪtli, 'feɪtəli
AM 'feɪdli

fatalness
BR 'feɪtlnəs
AM 'feɪdlnəs

Fata Morgana
BR ,fɑːtə ,mɔː'gɑːnə(r), ,fatə mɔː'ganə(r)
AM ,fɑdə ,mɔr'gɑnə

fatback
BR 'fatbak, -s
AM 'fæt,bæk, -s

fatcat
BR 'fatkat, -s
AM 'fæt,kæt, -s

fate
BR feɪt, -s, -ɪd
AM feɪ|t, -ts, -dɪd

fateful
BR 'feɪtf(ʊ)l
AM 'feɪtfəl

fatefully
BR 'feɪtfʊli, 'feɪtfʃli
AM 'feɪtfəli

fatefulness
BR 'feɪtf(ʊ)lnəs
AM 'feɪtfəlnəs

Fates
BR feɪts
AM feɪts

fathead
BR 'fathɛd, -z
AM 'fæt,(h)ɛd, -z

fatheaded
BR 'fat'hɛdɪd
AM 'fæt'hɛdəd

father
BR 'fɑːð|ə(r), -əz, -(ə)rɪŋ, -əd
AM 'fɑð|ər, -ərz, -(ə)rɪŋ, -ərd

fatherhood
BR 'fɑːðəhʊd
AM 'fɑðər,(h)ʊd

fatherland
BR 'fɑːðəland, -z
AM 'fæðər,lænd, -z

fatherless
BR 'fɑːðələs
AM 'fɑðərləs

fatherlessness
BR 'fɑːðələsnəs
AM 'fɑðərləsnəs
fatherlike
BR 'fɑːðəlaɪk
AM 'fɑðər‚laɪk
fatherliness
BR 'fɑːðəlɪnɪs
AM 'fɑðərlɪnɪs
fatherly
BR 'fɑːðəli
AM 'fɑðərli
fathership
BR 'fɑːðəʃɪp
AM 'fɑðər‚ʃɪp
fathom
BR 'fæðǀ(ə)m, -(ə)mz,
-əmɪŋ \-mɪŋ, -(ə)md
AM 'fæðəm, -z, -ɪŋ, -d
fathomable
BR 'faðəməbl, 'faðməbl
AM 'fæðəməbəl
Fathometer®
BR fa'ðɒmɪtə(r), -z
AM fæ'ðɑmədər,
'fæðə(m)‚mɪdər, -z
fathomless
BR 'fað(ə)mləs
AM 'fæðəmləs
fatidical
BR feɪ'tɪdɪkl, fə'tɪdɪkl
AM feɪ'tɪdɪkəl,
fə'tɪdɪkəl
fatiguability
BR fə‚tiːgə'bɪlɪti
AM fə‚tigə'bɪlɪdi
fatiguable
BR fə'tiːgəbl
AM fə'tigəbəl
fatigue
BR fə'tiːg, -z, -ɪŋ, -d
AM fə'tig, -z, -ɪŋ, -d
fatigueless
BR fə'tiːglɪs
AM fə'tiglɪs
Fatiha
BR 'fɑːtɪhə(r),
'fatɪhə(r)
AM 'fɑdi‚hɑ
Fatihah
BR 'fɑːtɪhə(r),
'fatɪhə(r)
AM 'fɑdi‚hɑ
Fatima
BR 'fatɪmə(r)
AM 'fatɪmə, 'fædəmə
Fatimid
BR 'fatɪmɪd, -z
AM 'fædəməd,
'fædə‚mɪd, -z
Fatimite
BR 'fatɪmʌɪt, -s
AM 'fædə‚maɪt, -s
fatism
BR 'feɪtɪz(ə)m
AM 'feɪdɪzəm

fatist
BR 'feɪtɪst, -s
AM 'feɪdɪst, -s
fatless
BR 'fatləs
AM 'fætləs
fatling
BR 'fatlɪŋ, -z
AM 'fætlɪŋ, -z
fatly
BR 'fatli
AM 'fætli
fatness
BR 'fatnəs
AM 'fætnəs
fatsia
BR 'fatsɪə(r)
AM 'fætsɪə
fatso
BR 'fatsəʊ, -z
AM 'fætsoʊ, -z
fatstock
BR 'fatstɒk
AM 'fæt‚stɑk
fatted
BR 'fatɪd
AM 'fædəd
fatten
BR 'fatǀn, -nz,
-nɪŋ \-nɪŋ, -nd
AM 'fætn, -z, -ɪŋ, -d
fattily
BR 'fatɪli
AM 'fædəli
fattiness
BR 'fatɪnɪs
AM 'fædɪnɪs
fattish
BR 'fatɪʃ
AM 'fædɪʃ
fattism
BR 'fatɪz(ə)m
AM 'fædɪzəm
fattist
BR 'fatɪst, -s
AM 'fædəst, -s
fatty
BR 'fati
AM 'fædi
fatuity
BR fə'tjuːɪti, fə'tʃuːɪti
AM fə'tuədi
fatuous
BR 'fatjʊəs, 'fatʃʊəs
AM 'fætʃ(əw)əs
fatuously
BR 'fatjʊəsli, 'fatʃʊəsli
AM 'fætʃ(əw)əsli
fatuousness
BR 'fatjʊəsnəs,
'fatʃʊəsnəs
AM 'fætʃ(əw)əsnəs
fatwa
BR 'fatwɑː(r),
'fatwə(r), -z
AM 'fætwə, -z

faubourg
BR 'fəʊbʊəg, -z
AM 'foʊbərg,
foʊ'bʊ(ə)r, -z
fauces
BR 'fɔːsiːz
AM 'foʊ‚siz
faucet
BR 'fɔːsɪt, -s
AM 'fɔsət, 'fasət, -s
Faucett
BR 'fɔːsɪt
AM 'fɔsət, 'fasət
faucial
BR 'fɔːʃl
AM 'fɔʃəl, 'faʃəl
Faucitt
BR 'fɔːsɪt
AM 'fɔsət, 'fasət
Faulds
BR fəʊldz, fɔːldz
AM fɔldz, foʊldz
Faulkner
BR 'fɔː(l)knə(r)
AM 'foknər, 'faknər
fault
BR fɔːlt, fɒlt, -s, -ɪŋ, -ɪd
AM fɔlt, falt, -s, -ɪŋ, -əd
faultfinder
BR 'fɔːlt‚fʌɪndə(r),
'fɒlt‚fʌɪndə(r), -z
AM 'fɔlt‚faɪndər,
'falt‚faɪndər, -z
faultfinding
BR 'fɔːlt‚fʌɪndɪŋ,
'fɒlt‚fʌɪndɪŋ
AM 'fɔlt‚faɪndɪŋ,
'falt‚faɪndɪŋ
faultily
BR 'fɔːltɪli, 'fɒltɪli
AM 'fɔltəli, 'faltəli
faultiness
BR 'fɔːltɪnɪs, 'fɒltɪnɪs
AM 'fɔltɪnɪs, 'faltɪnɪs
faultless
BR 'fɔːltləs, 'fɒltləs
AM 'fɔltləs, 'faltləs
faultlessly
BR 'fɔːltləsli, 'fɒltləsli
AM 'fɔltləsli, 'faltləsli
faultlessness
BR 'fɔːltləsnəs,
'fɒltləsnəs
AM 'fɔltləsnəs,
'faltləsnəs
faulty
BR 'fɔːlti, 'fɒlti
AM 'fɔlti, 'falti
faun
BR fɔːn, -z
AM fɔn, fan, -z
fauna
BR 'fɔːnə(r)
AM 'fɔnə, 'fanə
faunal
BR 'fɔːnl
AM 'fɔnəl, 'fanəl

faunist
BR 'fɔːnɪst, -s
AM 'fɔnəst, 'fanəst, -s
faunistic
BR 'fɔːnɪstɪk
AM fə'nɪstɪk, fɑ'nɪstɪk
faunistical
BR 'fɔːnɪstɪkl
AM fə'nɪstəkəl,
fɑ'nɪstəkəl
Fauntleroy
BR 'fɒntlərɔɪ,
'fɔːntlərɔɪ
AM 'fɑntlə‚rɔɪ,
'fantlə‚rɔɪ
Faunus
BR 'fɔːnəs
AM 'fɔnəs, 'fanəs
Fauré
BR 'fɔːreɪ
AM fɔ'reɪ
Faust
BR faʊst
AM faʊst
Faustian
BR 'faʊstɪən
AM 'faʊstɪən
Faustus
BR 'faʊstəs
AM 'faʊstəs
faute de mieux
BR ‚fəʊt də 'mjəː(r)
AM ‚foʊt də 'mjə
fauteuil
BR fəʊ'təːɪ, -z
AM foʊ'təɪ, -z
fauve
BR fəʊv, -z
AM foʊv, -z
fauvism
BR 'fəʊvɪz(ə)m
AM 'foʊ‚vɪzəm
fauvist
BR 'fəʊvɪst, -s
AM 'foʊvəst, -s
Faux
BR fɔːks, fəʊ
AM foʊ
faux pas
BR ‚fəʊ 'pɑː(r), -z
AM ‚foʊ 'pɑ, -z
fave
BR feɪv
AM feɪv
favela
BR fə'vɛlə(r), -z
AM fə'vɛlə, -z
Favell
BR 'feɪvl
AM fɑ'vɛl, 'feɪvəl
Faversham
BR 'favəʃ(ə)m
AM 'fævərʃəm
favor
BR 'feɪvǀə(r), -əz,
-(ə)rɪŋ, -əd

favorable
AM 'feɪv|ər, -ərz,
-(ə)rɪŋ, -ərd
favorable
BR 'feɪv(ə)rəbl
AM 'feɪvər(ə)bəl,
'feɪvrəbəl
favorableness
BR 'feɪv(ə)rəblnəs
AM 'feɪvər(ə)bəlnəs,
'feɪvrəbəlnəs
favorably
BR 'feɪv(ə)rəbli
AM 'feɪvər(ə)bli,
'feɪvrəbli
favorer
BR 'feɪv(ə)rə(r), -z
AM 'feɪv(ə)rər, -z
favorite
BR 'feɪv(ə)rɪt, -s
AM 'feɪv(ə)rɪt, -s
favoritism
BR 'feɪv(ə)rɪtɪz(ə)m
AM 'feɪv(ə)rɪ̩tɪzəm
favour
BR 'feɪv|ə(r), -əz,
-(ə)rɪŋ, -əd
AM 'feɪv|ər, -ərz,
-(ə)rɪŋ, -ərd
favourable
BR 'feɪv(ə)rəbl
AM 'feɪv(ə)r(ə)bəl
favourableness
BR 'feɪv(ə)rəblnəs
AM 'feɪvər(ə)bəlnəs,
'feɪvrəbəlnəs
favourably
BR 'feɪv(ə)rəbli
AM 'feɪvər(ə)bli,
'feɪvrəbli
favourer
BR 'feɪv(ə)rə(r), -z
AM 'feɪv(ə)rər, -z
favourite
BR 'feɪv(ə)rɪt, -s
AM 'feɪv(ə)rɪt, -s
favouritism
BR 'feɪv(ə)rɪtɪz(ə)m
AM 'feɪv(ə)rɪ̩tɪzəm
Fawcett
BR 'fɔːsɪt
AM 'fɔsət, 'fasət
Fawkes
BR fɔːks
AM fɔks, faks
Fawley
BR 'fɔːli
AM 'fɔli, 'fali
fawn
BR fɔːn, -z, -ɪŋ, -d
AM fɔn, fan, -z, -ɪŋ, -d
fawner
BR 'fɔːnə(r), -z
AM 'fɔnər, 'fanər, -z
fawningly
BR 'fɔːnɪŋli
AM 'fɔnɪŋli, 'fanɪŋli

fawr
BR 'vaʊə(r)
AM 'vaʊər
WE vaʊr
fax
BR faks, -ɪz, -ɪŋ, -t
AM fæks, -əz, -ɪŋ, -t
fay
BR feɪ
AM feɪ
Faye
BR feɪ
AM feɪ
Fayette
BR feɪ'ɛt
AM ̩feɪ'ɛt
Fayetteville
BR 'feɪtvɪl
AM 'feɪt̩vɪl
fayre
BR fɛː(r), -z
AM fɛ(ə)r, -z
Fazackerley
BR fə'zakəli
AM fə'zækərli
Fazakerley
BR fə'zakəli
AM fə'zækərli
faze
BR feɪz, -ɪz, -ɪŋ, -d
AM feɪz, -ɪz, -ɪŋ, -d
fazenda
BR fə'zɛndə(r), -z
AM fə'zɛndə, -z
fealty
BR 'fiː|əlt|i, -ɪz
AM 'fi(ə)lti, -z
fear
BR fɪə(r), -z, -ɪŋ, -d
AM fɪ(ə)r, -z, -ɪŋ, -d
fearful
BR 'fɪəf(ʊ)l
AM 'fɪrfəl
fearfully
BR 'fɪəfʊli, 'fɪəf̩li
AM 'fɪrfəli
fearfulness
BR 'fɪəf(ʊ)lnəs
AM 'fɪrfəlnəs
Feargal
BR 'fəːgl
AM 'fərgəl
Feargus
BR 'fəːgəs
AM 'fərgəs
fearless
BR 'fɪələs
AM 'fɪrləs
fearlessly
BR 'fɪələsli
AM 'fɪrləsli
fearlessness
BR 'fɪələsnəs
AM 'fɪrləsnəs
fearsome
BR 'fɪəs(ə)m
AM 'fɪrsəm

fearsomely
BR 'fɪəs(ə)mli
AM 'fɪrsəmli
fearsomeness
BR 'fɪəs(ə)mnəs
AM 'fɪrsəmnəs
feasibility
BR ̩fiːzɪ'bɪlɪti
AM ̩fizə'bɪlɪdi
feasible
BR 'fiːzɪbl
AM 'fizəbəl
feasibly
BR 'fiːzɪbli
AM 'fizəbli
feast
BR fiːst, -s, -ɪŋ, -ɪd
AM fis|t, -s, -ɪŋ, -ɪd
feaster
BR 'fiːstə(r), -z
AM 'fistər, -z
feat
BR fiːt, -s
AM fit, -s
feather
BR 'fɛð|ə(r), -əz,
-(ə)rɪŋ, -əd
AM 'fɛð|ər, -ərz, -(ə)rɪŋ,
-ərd
featherbed
verb
BR 'fɛðəbɛd, ̩fɛðə'bɛd,
-z, -ɪŋ, -ɪd
AM 'fɛðər̩bɛd, -z, -ɪŋ,
-əd
featherbrained
BR 'fɛðəbreɪnd
AM 'fɛðər̩breɪnd
featherhead
BR 'fɛðəhɛd, -z
AM 'fɛðər̩(h)ɛd, -z
featheriness
BR 'fɛð(ə)rɪnɪs
AM 'fɛð(ə)rɪnɪs
featherless
BR 'fɛðələs
AM 'fɛðərləs
featherlight
BR 'fɛðəlaɪt
AM 'fɛðər̩laɪt
Featherstone
BR 'fɛðəst(ə)n,
'fəːst(ə)n
AM 'fɛðərstən
**Featherstone-
haugh**
BR 'fɛðəst(ə)nhɔː(r),
'fanʃɔː(r),
'fɛst(ə)nhɔː(r),
'fɪəst(ə)nhɔː(r)
AM 'fɛðərstən̩(h)ɔ
featherweight
BR 'fɛðəweɪt, -s
AM 'fɛðər̩weɪt, -s
feathery
BR 'fɛð(ə)ri
AM 'fɛð(ə)ri

feature
BR 'fiːtʃ|ə(r), -əz,
-(ə)rɪŋ, -əd
AM 'fitʃər, -z, -ɪŋ, -d
featureless
BR 'fiːtʃələs
AM 'fitʃərləs
febrifugal
BR fɪ'brɪfjʊgl,
'fɛbrɪ̩fjuːgl
AM fə'brɪf(j)ugəl,
'fɛbrɪ̩f(j)ugəl
febrifuge
BR 'fɛbrɪfjuːdʒ, -ɪz
AM 'fɛbrə̩fjudʒ, -əz
febrile
BR 'fiːbrʌɪl, 'fɛbrʌɪl
AM 'fɛ̩braɪl, 'fi̩braɪl
febrility
BR fɪ'brɪlɪti
AM fɛ'brɪlɪdi, fi'brɪlɪdi
February
BR 'fɛbr(ər)|i,
'fɛbjʊər|i, 'fɛbjʊər|i, -ɪz
AM 'fɛb(j)ə̩wɛri,
'fɛbrə̩wɛri, -z
fecal
BR 'fiːkl
AM 'fikəl
feces
BR 'fiːsiːz
AM 'fisiz
feckless
BR 'fɛkləs
AM 'fɛkləs
fecklessly
BR 'fɛkləsli
AM 'fɛkləsli
fecklessness
BR 'fɛkləsnəs
AM 'fɛkləsnəs
feculence
BR 'fɛkjʊləns,
'fɛkjʊlns
AM 'fɛkjələns
feculent
BR 'fɛkjʊlənt,
'fɛkjʊlnt
AM 'fɛkjələnt
fecund
BR 'fɛk(ə)nd, 'fɛkʌnd,
'fiːk(ə)nd, 'fiːkʌnd
AM 'fɛkənd, 'fikənd
fecundability
BR fɪ̩kʌndə'bɪlɪti,
fɛ̩kʌndə'bɪlɪti
AM fɛ̩kəndə'bɪlɪdi,
fi̩kəndə'bɪlɪdi
fecundate
BR 'fɛk(ə)ndeɪt,
'fɛkʌndeɪt,
'fiːk(ə)ndeɪt,
'fiːkʌndeɪt, -s, -ɪŋ, -ɪd
AM 'fɛkən̩deɪ|t, -ts,
-dɪŋ, -dɪd
fecundation
BR ̩fɛk(ə)n'deɪʃn,
̩fɛkʌn'deɪʃn,

ˌfiːk(ə)nˈdeɪʃn,
ˌfiːkʌnˈdeɪʃn
AM ˌfɪk(ə)nˈdeɪʃ(ə)n
fecundity
BR frˈkʌndɪti,
fɛˈkʌndɪti
AM fɛˈkəndədi,
frˈkəndədi
fed
BR fɛd, -z
AM fɛd, -z
fedayeen
BR ˌfɛdaɪˈiːn, frˈdɑːjiːn
AM ˌfɛdeɪˈin
federal
BR ˈfɛd(ə)rəl, ˈfɛd(ə)rl̩
AM ˈfɛd(ə)rəl
federalisation
BR ˌfɛd(ə)rəlaɪˈzeɪʃn,
ˌfɛd(ə)rl̩aɪˈzeɪʃn
AM ˌfɛd(ə)rələˈzeɪʃən,
ˌfɛd(ə)rəˌlaɪˈzeɪʃən
federalise
BR ˈfɛd(ə)rəlaɪz,
ˈfɛd(ə)rl̩aɪz, -ɪz, -ɪŋ, -d
AM ˈfɛd(ə)rəˌlaɪz, -ɪz,
-ɪŋ, -d
federalism
BR ˈfɛd(ə)rəlɪz(ə)m,
ˈfɛd(ə)rl̩ɪz(ə)m
AM ˈfɛd(ə)rəˌlɪzəm
federalist
BR ˈfɛd(ə)rəlɪst,
ˈfɛd(ə)rl̩ɪst, -s
AM ˈfɛd(ə)rələst, -s
federalization
BR ˌfɛd(ə)rəlaɪˈzeɪʃn,
ˌfɛd(ə)rl̩aɪˈzeɪʃn
AM ˌfɛd(ə)rələˈzeɪʃən,
ˌfɛd(ə)rəˌlaɪˈzeɪʃən
federalize
BR ˈfɛd(ə)rəlaɪz,
ˈfɛd(ə)rl̩aɪz, -ɪz, -ɪŋ, -d
AM ˈfɛd(ə)rəˌlaɪz, -ɪz,
-ɪŋ, -d
federally
BR ˈfɛd(ə)rəli,
ˈfɛd(ə)rl̩i
AM ˈfɛd(ə)rəli
federate
BR ˈfɛdəreɪt, -s, -ɪŋ, -ɪd
AM ˈfɛdəˌreɪ|t, -ts, -dɪŋ, -dɪd
federation
BR ˌfɛdəˈreɪʃn, -z
AM ˌfɛdəˈreɪʃən, -z
federationist
BR ˌfɛdəˈreɪʃnɪst, -s
AM ˌfɛdəˈreɪʃənəst, -s
federative
BR ˈfɛd(ə)rətɪv
AM ˈfɛdərəˌtɪv, ˈfɛdəˌreɪdɪv
fedora
BR frˈdɔːrə(r), -z
AM fəˈdɔrə, -z
fed up
BR ˌfɛd ˈʌp

AM ˌfɛd ˈəp
fee
BR fiː, -z, -ɪŋ, -d
AM fi, -z, -ɪŋ, -d
feeble
BR ˈfiːbl
AM ˈfibəl
feebleness
BR ˈfiːblnəs
AM ˈfibəlnəs
feeblish
BR ˈfiːblɪʃ
AM ˈfiblɪʃ
feebly
BR ˈfiːbli
AM ˈfibli
feed
BR fiːd, -z, -ɪŋ
AM fid, -z, -ɪŋ
feedable
BR ˈfiːdəbl
AM ˈfidəbəl
feedback
BR ˈfiːdbak
AM ˈfidˌbæk
feedbag
BR ˈfiːdbag, -z
AM ˈfidˌbæg, -z
feeder
BR ˈfiːdə(r), -z
AM ˈfidər, -z
feedlot
BR ˈfiːdlɒt, -s
AM ˈfidˌlɑt, -s
feedstock
BR ˈfiːdstɒk
AM ˈfidˌstɑk
feedstuff
BR ˈfiːdstʌf, -s
AM ˈfidˌstəf, -s
feel
BR fiːl, -z, -ɪŋ
AM fil, -z, -ɪŋ
feeler
BR ˈfiːlə(r), -z
AM ˈfilər, -z
feeling
BR ˈfiːlɪŋ, -z
AM ˈfilɪŋ, -z
feelingless
BR ˈfiːlɪŋlɪs
AM ˈfilɪŋlɪs
feelingly
BR ˈfiːlɪŋli
AM ˈfilɪŋli
feelings
BR ˈfiːlɪŋz
AM ˈfilɪŋz
Feeney
BR ˈfiːni
AM ˈfini
feet
BR fiːt
AM fit
feign
BR feɪn, -z, -ɪŋ, -d
AM feɪn, -z, -ɪŋ, -d

feignedly
BR ˈfeɪnɪdli
AM ˈfeɪnɪdli
feijoa
BR feɪˈ(d)ʒəʊə(r),
fɛˈ(d)ʒəʊə(r),
fiːˈ(d)ʒəʊə(r),
feɪˈjəʊə(r), fɛˈjəʊə(r),
fiːˈjəʊə(r), -z
AM feɪˈdʒəʊə, feɪˈhoʊə, -z
feint
BR feɪnt, -s, -ɪŋ, -ɪd
AM feɪn|t, -ts, -(t)ɪŋ, -(t)ɪd
feis
BR fɛʃ, feɪʃ
AM fɛʃ
IR ˈfesʲ
Feisal
BR ˈfaɪsl
AM ˈfaɪˈzal
feiseanna
BR ˈfɛʃənə(r), ˈfeɪʃənə(r)
AM ˈfeɪʃənə
IR ˈfesʲenə
feistiness
BR ˈfaɪstɪnɪs
AM ˈfaɪstɪnɪs
feisty
BR ˈfaɪsti
AM ˈfaɪsti
felafel
BR frˈlafl, frˈlɑːfl
AM fəˈlafəl
felching
BR ˈfɛltʃɪŋ
AM ˈfɛltʃɪŋ
Feldman
BR ˈfɛldmən
AM ˈfɛl(d)mən
feldspar
BR ˈfɛl(d)spɑː(r)
AM ˈfɛldˌspar
feldspathic
BR ˈfɛl(d)ˈspaθɪk
AM ˈfɛlzˈpæθɪk, ˌfɛl(d)ˈspæθɪk
feldspathoid
BR ˈfɛl(d)spəθɔɪd, -z
AM ˈfɛlzˈpæˌθɔɪd, ˌfɛl(d)ˈspæˌθɔɪd, -z
Felicia
BR frˈlɪsɪə(r)
AM fəˈliʃ(i)ə
felicific
BR ˌfiːlɪˈsɪfɪk, ˌfɛlɪˈsɪfɪk
AM ˌfɛləˈsɪfɪk
felicitate
BR frˈlɪsɪteɪt, -s, -ɪŋ, -ɪd
AM fəˈlɪsɪˌteɪ|t, -ts, -dɪŋ, -dɪd
felicitation
BR fɪˌlɪsɪˈteɪʃn, -z
AM fəˌlɪsɪˈteɪʃən, -z
felicitous
BR frˈlɪsɪtəs

AM fəˈlɪsɪtəs
felicitously
BR frˈlɪsɪtəsli
AM fəˈlɪsɪdɪsli
felicitousness
BR frˈlɪsɪtəsnəs
AM fəˈlɪsɪdɪsnɪs
felicity
BR frˈlɪsɪt|i, -ɪz
AM fəˈlɪsɪdi, -z
Felindre
BR vɪˈlɪndrə(r)
AM fəˈlɪndər
WE veˈlɪndre
feline
BR ˈfiːlaɪn
AM ˈfiˌlaɪn
felinity
BR frˈlɪnɪti
AM fiˈlɪnɪdi
Felix
BR ˈfiːlɪks
AM ˈfiˌlɪks
Felixstowe
BR ˈfiːlɪkstəʊ
AM ˈfilɪkˌstoʊ
fell
BR fɛl, -z
AM fɛl, -z
fellah
BR ˈfɛlə(r), -z
AM ˈfɛlə, -z
fellate
BR fɛˈleɪt, frˈleɪt, -s, -ɪŋ, -ɪd
AM ˈfɛlˌeɪ|t, -ts, -dɪŋ, -dɪd
fellatio
BR fɛˈleɪʃɪəʊ, frˈleɪʃɪəʊ
AM fəˈleɪʃioʊ
fellation
BR fɛˈleɪʃn, frˈleɪʃn, -z
AM fəˈleɪʃən, -z
fellator
BR fɛˈleɪtə(r), frˈleɪtə(r), -z
AM ˈfɛlˌeɪdər, -z
feller
BR ˈfɛlə(r), -z
AM ˈfɛlər, -z
Fellini
BR fɛˈliːni, frˈliːni
AM fəˈlini
fellmonger
BR ˈfɛlˌmʌŋgə(r)
AM ˈfɛlˌmʌŋgər, ˈfɛlˌməŋgər
felloe
BR ˈfɛləʊ, -z
AM ˈfɛloʊ, -z
fellow
BR ˈfɛləʊ, ˈfɛlə(r), -z
AM ˈfɛloʊ, ˈfɛlə, -z
Fellowes
BR ˈfɛləʊz
AM ˈfɛloʊz

Fellows
BR ˈfɛləʊz
AM ˈfɛloʊz

fellowship
BR ˈfɛlə(ʊ)ʃɪp, -s
AM ˈfɛloʊˌʃɪp, ˈfɛləˌʃɪp, -s

fellwort
BR ˈfɛlwəːt
AM ˈfɛlwərt, ˈfɛlwə(ə)rt

felly
BR ˈfɛl|i, -ɪz
AM ˈfɛli, -z

felon
BR ˈfɛlən, -z
AM ˈfɛlən, -z

felonious
BR frˈləʊnɪəs
AM fəˈloʊnɪəs, fɛˈloʊnɪəs

feloniously
BR frˈləʊnɪəsli
AM fəˈloʊnɪəsli, fɛˈloʊnɪəsli

feloniousness
BR frˈləʊnɪəsnəs
AM fəˈloʊnɪəsnəs, fɛˈloʊnɪəsnəs

felonry
BR ˈfɛlənri
AM ˈfɛlənri

felony
BR ˈfɛlən|i, -ɪz
AM ˈfɛləni, -z

felspar
BR ˈfɛlspɑː(r)
AM ˈfɛlˌspɑr

Felstead
BR ˈfɛlstɛd
AM ˈfɛlˌstɛd

felt
BR fɛlt, -s, -ɪŋ, -ɪd
AM fɛlt, -s, -ɪŋ, -əd

Feltham[1]
place in UK
BR ˈfɛltəm
AM ˈfɛltəm

Feltham[2]
surname
BR ˈfɛltəm, ˈfɛlθ(ə)m
AM ˈfɛltəm, ˈfɛlθəm

Felton
BR ˈfɛlt(ə)n
AM ˈfɛltən

felty
BR ˈfɛlti
AM ˈfɛlti

felucca
BR fɛˈlʌkə(r), fɪˈlʌkə(r), -z
AM fəˈlukə, -z

felwort
BR ˈfɛlwəːt
AM ˈfɛlwərt, ˈfɛlwə(ə)rt

female
BR ˈfiːmeɪl, -z

AM ˈfiˌmeɪl, -z

femaleness
BR ˈfiːmeɪlnɪs
AM ˈfiˌmeɪlnɪs

feme
BR fiːm, fɛm, -z
AM fɛm, -z

feme covert
BR ˌfiːm ˈkʌvət, ˌfɛm +
AM ˈfɛm ˈkəvərt

femes covert
BR ˌfiːmz ˈkʌvət, ˌfɛmz +
AM ˈfɛmz ˈkəvərt

feme sole
BR ˌfiːm ˈsəʊl, ˌfɛm +
AM ˈfɛm ˈsoʊl

femes sole
BR ˌfiːmz ˈsəʊl, ˌfɛmz +
AM ˈfɛmz ˈsoʊl

feminal
BR ˈfɛmɪnl
AM ˈfɛmənəl

feminality
BR ˌfɛmɪˈnalɪti
AM ˌfɛməˈnælədi

femineity
BR ˌfɛmɪˈniːɪti
AM ˌfɛməˈniɪdi

feminine
BR ˈfɛmɪnɪn
AM ˈfɛmənən

femininely
BR ˈfɛmɪnɪnli
AM ˈfɛmənənli

feminineness
BR ˈfɛmɪnɪnnɪs
AM ˈfɛmənə(n)nəs

femininity
BR ˌfɛmɪˈnɪnɪti
AM ˌfɛməˈnɪnɪdi

feminisation
BR ˌfɛmɪnʌɪˈzeɪʃn
AM ˌfɛmənəˈzeɪʃən, ˌfɛmɛˌnaɪˈzeɪʃən

feminise
BR ˈfɛmɪnʌɪz, -ɪz, -ɪŋ, -d
AM ˈfɛməˌnaɪz, -ɪz, -ɪŋ, -d

feminism
BR ˈfɛmɪnɪz(ə)m
AM ˈfɛməˌnɪzəm

feminist
BR ˈfɛmɪnɪst, -s
AM ˈfɛmənəst, -s

feminity
BR frˈmɪnɪti
AM fəˈmɪnɪdi

feminization
BR ˌfɛmɪnʌɪˈzeɪʃn
AM ˌfɛmənəˈzeɪʃən, ˌfɛmɛˌnaɪˈzeɪʃən

feminize
BR ˈfɛmɪnʌɪz, -ɪz, -ɪŋ, -d
AM ˈfɛməˌnaɪz, -ɪz, -ɪŋ, -d

femme
BR fam, fɛm, -z
AM fɛm, -z

femme fatale
BR ˌfam fəˈtɑːl, -z
AM ˌfɛm fəˈtæl, + fəˈtɑl, -z

femora
BR ˈfɛm(ə)rə(r)
AM ˈfɛmərə

femoral
BR ˈfɛm(ə)rəl, ˈfɛm(ə)rl̩
AM ˈfɛmərəl

femtometer
BR ˈfɛmtəˌmiːtə(r), -z
AM ˈfɛmtəˌmidər, -z

femtometre
BR ˈfɛmtəˌmiːtə(r), -z
AM ˈfɛmtəˌmidər, -z

femur
BR ˈfiːmə(r), -z
AM ˈfimər, -z

fen
BR fɛn, -z
AM fɛn, -z

fen-berry
BR ˈfɛnb(ə)r|i, -ɪz
AM ˈfɛnˌbɛri, -z

fence
BR fɛns, -ɪz, -ɪŋ, -t
AM fɛns, -əz, -ɪŋ, -t

fenceless
BR ˈfɛnsləs
AM ˈfɛnsləs

fencer
BR ˈfɛnsə(r), -z
AM ˈfɛnsər, -z

Fenchurch
BR ˈfɛntʃəːtʃ
AM ˈfɛnˌtʃərtʃ

fencible
BR ˈfɛnsɪbl̩, -z
AM ˈfɛnsəbəl, -z

fend
BR fɛnd, -z, -ɪŋ, -ɪd
AM fɛnd, -z, -ɪŋ, -əd

fender
BR ˈfɛndə(r), -z
AM ˈfɛndər, -z

Fenella
BR frˈnɛlə(r)
AM fəˈnɛlə

fenestella
BR ˌfɛnɪˈstɛlə(r), -z
AM ˌfɛnəˈstɛlə, -z

fenestra
BR frˈnɛstrə(r)
AM fəˈnɛstrə

fenestrae
BR frˈnɛstriː
AM fəˈnɛstri, fəˈnɛˌstraɪ

fenestrate
BR ˈfɛnɪstreɪt, -s, -ɪŋ, -ɪd
AM ˈfɛnəˌstreɪ|t, -ts, -dɪŋ, -dɪd

fenestration
BR ˌfɛnɪˈstreɪʃn
AM ˌfɛnəˈstreɪʃən

feng shui
BR ˌfɛŋ ˈʃuːi, ˌfʌŋ ˈʃweɪ
AM ˌfɛŋ ˈʃui

Fenian
BR ˈfiːnɪən, -z
AM ˈfiniən, -z

Fenianism
BR ˈfiːnɪənɪz(ə)m
AM ˈfiniəˌnɪzəm

Fenimore
BR ˈfɛnɪmɔː(r)
AM ˈfɛnəˌmɔ(ə)r

fenland
BR ˈfɛnland, ˈfɛnlənd, -z
AM ˈfɛnˌlænd, -z

fenman
BR ˈfɛnman, ˈfɛnmən
AM ˈfɛnˌmæn

fenmen
BR ˈfɛnmɛn, ˈfɛnmən
AM ˈfɛnˌmɛn

fennec
BR ˈfɛnɪk, -s
AM ˈfɛnɪk, -s

fennel
BR ˈfɛnl̩
AM ˈfɛnəl

Fennimore
BR ˈfɛnɪmɔː(r)
AM ˈfɛnəˌmɔ(ə)r

Fennoscandia
BR ˌfɛnə(ʊ)ˈskandɪə(r)
AM ˌfɛnəˈskændiə

fenny
BR ˈfɛni
AM ˈfɛni

Fens
BR fɛnz
AM fɛnz

Fenton
BR ˈfɛnt(ə)n
AM ˈfɛn(t)ən

fenugreek
BR ˈfɛnjʊgriːk
AM ˈfɛn(j)əˌgrik

Fenwick
BR ˈfɛn(w)ɪk
AM ˈfɛnˌwɪk

feoff
BR fiːf, fɛf, -s, -ɪŋ, -t
AM fif, -s, -ɪŋ, -t

feoffee
BR fɛˈfiː, fiːˈfiː, -z
AM fɛˈfi, fiˈfi, -z

feoffment
BR ˈfiːfm(ə)nt, ˈfɛfm(ə)nt, -s
AM ˈfifmənt, -s

feoffor
BR 'fi:fə(r), 'fefə(r), -z
AM 'fifər, -z

feral
BR 'fɛrəl, 'fɛr|
AM 'fɛrəl, 'fɪrəl

fer de lance
BR ,fɛː də 'lɑːns,
+ 'lans, -ɪz
AM ,fɛr də ,læns, -əz

Ferdinand
BR 'fəːdɪnand,
'fəːdɪnənd
AM 'fərd(ə),nænd

feretory
BR 'fɛrət(ə)r|i, -ɪz
AM 'fɛrə,tɔri, -z

Fergal
BR 'fəːgl
AM 'fərgəl

Fergie
BR 'fəːgi
AM 'fərgi

Fergus
BR 'fəːgəs
AM 'fərgəs

Ferguson
BR 'fəːgəs(ə)n
AM 'fərgəsən

ferial
BR 'fɪərɪəl, 'fɛrɪəl
AM 'fɛrɪəl, 'fɪrɪəl

Fermanagh
BR fə'manə(r)
AM fər'mænə

Fermat
BR 'fəːmɑː(r), fə'mat,
'fəːmat
AM fər'mɑt

fermata
BR fəː'mɑːtə(r), -z
AM fər'mɑdə, -z

ferment¹
noun
BR 'fəːmɛnt, -s
AM 'fər,mɛnt, -s

ferment²
verb
BR fə(ː)'mɛnt, -s, -ɪŋ, -ɪd
AM fər'mɛn|t, -ts, -(t)ɪŋ,
-(t)əd

fermentable
BR fə'mɛntəbl
AM fər'mɛn(t)əbəl

fermentation
BR ,fəːmɛn'teɪʃn,
,fəːm(ə)n'teɪʃn, -z
AM ,fərmən'teɪʃən, -z

fermentative
BR fə'mɛntətɪv
AM fər'mɛn(t)ədɪv

fermenter
BR fə'mɛntə(r), -z
AM fər'mɛn(t)ər, -z

fermi
BR 'fəːm|i, 'fɛːm|i, -ɪz
AM 'fɛr,mi, -z

fermion
BR 'fəːmɪɒn, 'fəːmɪən
AM 'fɛrmɪɑn, 'fərmɪɑn

fermium
BR 'fəːmɪəm
AM 'fɛrmɪəm,
'fərmɪəm

Fermor
BR 'fəːmɔː(r)
AM 'fər,mɔː(ə)r

Fermoy
BR fə'mɔɪ
AM 'fər,mɔɪ

fern
BR fəːn, -z
AM fərn, -z

Fernández
BR fə'nandez
AM fər'nændɛz

Fernando Póo
BR fə,nandəʊ 'pəʊ
AM fər',nændoʊ 'poʊ

fernery
BR 'fəːn(ə)r|i, -ɪz
AM 'fərnəri, -z

Ferneyhough
BR 'fəːnɪhʌf, 'fəːnɪhəʊ
AM 'fərnɪhəf

Fernihough
BR 'fəːnɪhʌf, 'fəːnɪhəʊ
AM 'fərnɪhəf

fernless
BR 'fəːnləs
AM 'fərnləs

ferny
BR 'fəːn|i, -ɪə(r), -ɪɪst
AM 'fərni, -ər, -ɪst

Fernyhough
BR 'fəːnɪhʌf, 'fəːnɪhəʊ
AM 'fərnɪhəf

ferocious
BR fɪ'rəʊʃəs
AM fə'roʊʃəs

ferociously
BR fɪ'rəʊʃəsli
AM fə'roʊʃəsli

ferociousness
BR fɪ'rəʊʃəsnəs
AM fə'roʊʃəsnəs

ferocity
BR fɪ'rɒsɪti
AM fə'rɑsədi

Ferodo
BR fə'rəʊdəʊ
AM fə'roʊdoʊ

Ferranti
BR fɪ'ranti
AM fə'rɑn(t)i

Ferrara
BR fə'rɑːrə(r)
AM fə'rɑrə

Ferrari®
BR fə'rɑːr|i, -ɪz
AM fə'rɑri, -z

ferrate
BR 'fɛreɪt, -s
AM 'fɛ,reɪt, -s

ferrel
BR 'fɛrəl, 'fɛr|, -z
AM 'fɛrəl, -z

Ferrell
BR 'fɛrəl, 'fɛr|
AM 'fɛrəl

Ferrer
BR 'fɛrə(r)
AM fə'rɑr, 'fɛrər

ferret
BR 'fɛrɪt, -s, -ɪŋ, -ɪd
AM 'fɛrə|t, -ts, -dɪŋ, -dəd

ferreter
BR 'fɛrɪtə(r), -z
AM 'fɛrədər, -z

ferrety
BR 'fɛrɪti
AM 'fɛrədi

ferriage
BR 'fɛrɪ|ɪdʒ, -ɪdʒɪz
AM 'fɛrɪɪdʒ, -ɪz

ferric
BR 'fɛrɪk
AM 'fɛrɪk

Ferrier
BR 'fɛrɪə(r)
AM 'fɛrɪər

ferrimagnetic
BR ,fɛrɪmag'nɛtɪk
AM ,fɛri,mæg'nɛdɪk

ferrimagnetism
BR ,fɛrɪ'magnɪtɪz(ə)m
AM ,fɛri'mægnə,tɪzəm

Ferris
BR 'fɛrɪs
AM 'fɛrəs

ferrite
BR 'fɛrʌɪt
AM 'fɛraɪt

ferritic
BR fɪ'rɪtɪk
AM fə'rɪdɪk

ferroconcrete
BR ,fɛrə(ʊ)'kɒŋkriːt
AM 'fɛroʊ'kɑn,krit

ferroelectric
BR ,fɛrəʊɪ'lɛktrɪk
AM ,fɛroʊə'lɛktrɪk,
'fɛroʊɪ'lɛktrɪk

ferroelectricity
BR ,fɛrəʊɪlɛk'trɪsɪti
AM ,fɛroʊə,lɛk'trɪsɪdi,
'fɛroʊɪ,lɛk'trɪsɪdi

Ferrograph®
BR 'fɛrə(ʊ)grɑːf,
'fɛrə(ʊ)graf
AM 'fɛrə,græf

ferromagnetic
BR ,fɛrə(ʊ)mag'nɛtɪk
AM ,fɛroʊ,mæg'nɛdɪk

ferromagnetism
BR ,fɛrə(ʊ)'magnɪtɪz(ə)m
AM ,fɛroʊ'mægnə,tɪzəm

ferrous
BR 'fɛrəs
AM 'fɛrəs

ferruginous
BR fɪ'ruːdʒɪnəs,
fɪ'ruːdʒnəs,
fɛ'ruːdʒɪnəs
fɛ'ruːdʒnəs
AM fə'rudʒənəs

ferrule
BR 'fɛr(j)uːl, 'fɛrəl,
'fɛr|, -z
AM 'fɛrəl, 'fɛ,rul, -z

ferry
BR 'fɛr|i, -ɪz, -ɪɪŋ, -ɪd
AM 'fɛri, -z, -ɪŋ, -d

ferryage
BR 'fɛrɪ|ɪdʒ, -ɪdʒɪz
AM 'fɛriɪdʒ, -ɪz

ferryboat
BR 'fɛrɪbəʊt, -s
AM 'fɛri,bout, -s

Ferrybridge
BR 'fɛrɪbrɪdʒ
AM 'fɛri,brɪdʒ

ferryman
BR 'fɛrɪmən
AM 'fɛri,mæn, fɛrɪmən

ferrymen
BR 'fɛrɪmən
AM 'fɛri,mɛn

fers de lance
BR ,fɛː də 'lɑːns, + 'lans
AM ,fɛ(ə)r(z) də 'læns

fertile
BR 'fəːtʌɪl
AM 'fərdl

fertilisable
BR 'fəːtɪlʌɪzəbl,
'fəːtlʌɪzəbl
AM 'fərdl,aɪzəbəl

fertilisation
BR ,fəːtɪlʌɪ'zeɪʃn,
,fəːtlʌɪ'zeɪʃn
AM ,fərdlə'zeɪʃən,
,fərdl,aɪ'zeɪʃən

fertilise
BR 'fəːtɪlʌɪz, 'fəːtlʌɪz,
-ɪz, -ɪŋ, -d
AM 'fərdl,aɪz, -ɪz, -ɪŋ, -d

fertiliser
BR 'fəːtɪlʌɪzə(r),
'fəːtlʌɪzə(r), -z
AM 'fərdl,aɪzər, -z

fertility
BR fə(ː)'tɪlɪti
AM fər'tɪlɪdi

fertilizable
BR 'fəːtɪlʌɪzəbl,
'fəːtlʌɪzəbl
AM 'fərdl,aɪzəbəl

fertilization
BR ,fəːtɪlʌɪ'zeɪʃn,
,fəːtlʌɪ'zeɪʃn
AM ,fərdlə'zeɪʃən,
,fərdl,aɪ'zeɪʃən

fertilize
BR 'fəːtɪlʌɪz, 'fəːtlʌɪz,
-ɪz, -ɪŋ, -d
AM 'fərdl,aɪz, -ɪz, -ɪŋ, -d

fertilizer
BR ˈfəːtɪlʌɪzə(r),
ˈfəːtlʌɪzə(r), -z
AM ˈfərdl͟ʌɪzər, -z
Fertö Tó
BR ˌfɛːtəʊ ˈtəʊ
AM ˈfɛrdoʊ ˈtoʊ
HU ˈfɛrtœ ˈtɔː
ferula
BR ˈfɛr(j)ʉlə(r), -z
AM ˈfɛrələ, -z
ferule
BR ˈfɛr(j)uːl, ˈfɛrəl,
ˈfɛrl̩, -z
AM ˈfɛrəl, -z
fervency
BR ˈfəːvns|i, -ɪz
AM ˈfərvənsi, -z
fervent
BR ˈfəːv(ə)nt
AM ˈfərvənt
fervently
BR ˈfəːv(ə)ntli
AM ˈfərvən(t)li
ferventness
BR ˈfəːv(ə)ntnəs
AM ˈfərvən(t)nəs
fervid
BR ˈfəːvɪd
AM ˈfərvəd
fervidly
BR ˈfəːvɪdli
AM ˈfərvədli
fervidness
BR ˈfəːvɪdnɪs
AM ˈfərvədnəs
fervor
BR ˈfəːvə(r)
AM ˈfərvər
fervour
BR ˈfəːvə(r)
AM ˈfərvər
Fès
BR fɛz, -ɪz
AM fɛz, -əz
Fescennine
BR ˈfɛsɪnʌɪn, ˈfɛsn̩ʌɪn
AM ˈfɛsn̩ˌin, ˈfɛsn̩ˌʌɪn
fescue
BR ˈfɛskjuː
AM ˈfɛskju
fess
BR fɛs, -ɪz
AM fɛs, -əz
fesse
BR fɛs, -ɪz
AM fɛs, -əz
festal
BR ˈfɛstl̩
AM ˈfɛstl
festally
BR ˈfɛstl̩i, ˈfɛstəli
AM ˈfɛstəli
fester
BR ˈfɛst|ə(r), -əz,
-(ə)rɪŋ, -əd

AM ˈfɛst|ər, -ərz,
-(ə)rɪŋ, -ərd
festination
BR ˌfɛstɪˈneɪʃn
AM ˌfɛstəˈneɪʃən
festival
BR ˈfɛstɪvl, -z
AM ˈfɛstəvəl, -z
festive
BR ˈfɛstɪv
AM ˈfɛstɪv
festively
BR ˈfɛstɪvli
AM ˈfɛstɪvli
festiveness
BR ˈfɛstɪvnɪs
AM ˈfɛstɪvnɪs
festivity
BR fɛˈstɪvɪt|i, -ɪz
AM fɛˈstɪvɪdi, -z
festoon
BR fɛˈstuːn, -z, -ɪŋ, -d
AM fɛˈstun, -z, -ɪŋ, -d
festoonery
BR fɛˈstuːn(ə)ri
AM fɛˈstunəri
Festschrift
BR ˈfɛs(t)ʃrɪft, -s
AM ˈfɛs(t)ˌʃrɪft, -s
Festschriften
BR ˈfɛs(t)ʃrɪftən
AM ˈfɛs(t)ˌʃrɪftən
Festus
BR ˈfɛstəs
AM ˈfɛstəs
feta
BR ˈfɛtə(r)
AM ˈfɛdə
fetal
BR ˈfiːtl
AM ˈfidl
fetch
BR fɛtʃ, -ɪz, -ɪŋ, -t
AM fɛtʃ, -əz, -ɪŋ, -t
fetcher
BR ˈfɛtʃə(r), -z
AM ˈfɛtʃər, -z
fetchingly
BR ˈfɛtʃɪŋli
AM ˈfɛtʃɪŋli
fête
BR feɪt, -s, -ɪŋ, -ɪd
AM feɪt, -ts, -dɪŋ, -dɪd
fête champêtre
BR feɪt ʃɒˈpeɪtr(ə), -z
AM ˈfeɪt ʃamˈpɛtr(ə), -z
fête galante
BR feɪt gəˈlɑːnt
AM ˈfeɪt gəˈlant
fêtes champêtres
BR feɪt ʃɒˈpeɪtr(ə)z
AM ˈfeɪt ʃamˈpɛtr(ə)z
fêtes galantes
BR feɪt gəˈlɑːnt
AM ˈfeɪt(s) gəˈlant

feticide
BR ˈfɛtɪsʌɪd
AM ˈfɛdəˌsaɪd
fetid
BR ˈfɛtɪd
AM ˈfɛdɪd
fetidly
BR ˈfɛtɪdli
AM ˈfɛdɪdli
fetidness
BR ˈfɛtɪdnɪs
AM ˈfɛdɪdnɪs
fetish
BR ˈfɛt|ɪʃ, -ɪʃɪz
AM ˈfɛdɪʃ, -ɪz
fetishise
BR ˈfɛtɪʃʌɪz, -ɪz, -ɪŋ, -d
AM ˈfɛdəˌʃaɪz, -ɪz, -ɪŋ, -d
fetishism
BR ˈfɛtɪʃɪz(ə)m
AM ˈfɛdɪʃˌɪzəm
fetishist
BR ˈfɛtɪʃɪst, -s
AM ˈfɛdɪʃɪst, -s
fetishistic
BR ˌfɛtɪˈʃɪstɪk
AM ˌfɛdəˈʃɪstɪk
fetishize
BR ˈfɛtɪʃʌɪz, -ɪz, -ɪŋ, -d
AM ˈfɛdəˌʃaɪz, -ɪz, -ɪŋ, -d
Fetlar
BR ˈfɛtlə(r)
AM ˈfɛtlər
fetlock
BR ˈfɛtlɒk, -s
AM ˈfɛtˌlak, -s
fetor
BR ˈfiːtə(r)
AM ˈfidər
fetta
BR ˈfɛtə(r)
AM ˈfɛdə
fetter
BR ˈfɛt|ə(r), -əz, -(ə)rɪŋ,
-əd
AM ˈfɛdər, -z, -ɪŋ, -d
fetterlock
BR ˈfɛtəlɒk, -s
AM ˈfɛdərˌlak, -s
fettle
BR ˈfɛt|l, -lz, -lɪŋ\-lɪŋ,
-ld
AM ˈfɛdəl, -z, -ɪŋ, -d
fettler
BR ˈfɛtlə(r), ˈfɛtlə(r), -z
AM ˈfɛdlər, -z
fettuccine
BR ˌfɛtʊˈtʃiːni
AM ˌfɛdəˈtʃini
fettucine
BR ˌfɛtʊˈtʃiːni
AM ˌfɛdəˈtʃini
fettucini
BR ˌfɛtʊˈtʃiːni
AM ˌfɛdəˈtʃini
fetus
BR ˈfiːtəs, -ɪz

AM ˈfidəs, -əz
feu
BR fjuː, -z, -ɪŋ, -d
AM fju, -z, -ɪŋ, -d
feud
BR fjuːd, -z, -ɪŋ, -ɪd
AM fjud, -z, -ɪŋ, -əd
feudal
BR ˈfjuːdl
AM ˈfjudəl
feudalisation
BR ˌfjuːdlʌɪˈzeɪʃn
AM ˌfjudləˈzeɪʃən,
fjudlˌaɪˈzeɪʃən
feudalise
BR ˈfjuːdlʌɪz, -ɪz, -ɪŋ, -d
AM ˈfjudlˌaɪz, -ɪz, -ɪŋ, -d
feudalism
BR ˈfjuːdlɪz(ə)m
AM ˈfjudlˌɪzəm
feudalist
BR ˈfjuːdlɪst, -s
AM ˈfjudləst, -s
feudalistic
BR ˌfjuːdlˈɪstɪk
AM ˌfjudlˈɪstɪk
feudalistically
BR ˌfjuːdlˈɪstɪkli
AM ˈfjudlˈɪstək(ə)li
feudality
BR fjuːˈdalɪti
AM fjuˈdælədi
feudalization
BR ˌfjuːdlʌɪˈzeɪʃn
AM ˌfjudləˈzeɪʃən,
fjudlˌaɪˈzeɪʃən
feudalize
BR ˈfjuːdlʌɪz, -ɪz, -ɪŋ, -d
AM ˈfjudlˌaɪz, -ɪz, -ɪŋ, -d
feudally
BR ˈfjuːdli
AM ˈfjudli
feudatory
BR ˈfjuːdət(ə)ri
AM ˈfjudəˌtɔri
feu de joie
BR ˌfəː də ˈʒwɑː(r)
AM ˌfə də ˈʒwɑ
feudist
BR ˈfjuːdɪst, -s
AM ˈfjudəst, -s
feuilleton
BR ˈfəːɪtɒ̃, -z
AM ˈfəɪˌtɒn, -z
feux de joie
BR ˌfəː də ˈʒwɑː(r)
AM ˌfə(z) də ˈʒwɑ
fever
BR ˈfiːvə(r), -z, -d
AM ˈfivər, -z, -d
feverfew
BR ˈfiːvəfjuː
AM ˈfivərˌfju
feverish
BR ˈfiːv(ə)rɪʃ
AM ˈfiv(ə)rɪʃ

feverishly
BR ˈfiːv(ə)rɪʃli
AM ˈfiv(ə)rɪʃli

feverishness
BR ˈfiːv(ə)rɪʃnɪs
AM ˈfiv(ə)rɪʃnɪs

feverous
BR ˈfiːv(ə)rəs
AM ˈfiv(ə)rəs

few
BR fjuː, -ə(r), -ɪst
AM fju, -ər, -əst

fewness
BR ˈfjuːnəs
AM ˈfjunəs

fey
BR feɪ
AM feɪ

Feydeau
BR ˈfeɪdəʊ
AM feɪˈdou, ˈfeɪdou

feyly
BR ˈfeɪli
AM ˈfeɪli

feyness
BR ˈfeɪnɪs
AM ˈfeɪnɪs

Feynman
BR ˈfaɪnmən
AM ˈfaɪnmən

fez
BR fɛz, -ɪz, -d
AM fɛz, -əz, -d

Ffestiniog
BR fɛˈstɪnɪɒg
AM fəˈstɪniˌɒg, fɛsˈtiniˌɑg

Ffolkes
BR fəʊks
AM foʊks

Ffoulkes
BR fuːks, fəʊks
AM foʊks, fuks

fiacre
BR fɪˈɑːkrə(r), fɪˈakrə(r), -z
AM fiˈækrə, -z

fiancé
BR fɪˈɑːnseɪ
AM ˌfiˌɑnˈseɪ, fiˈɑnˌseɪ, -z

fiancée
BR fɪˈɑːnseɪ, -z
AM ˌfiˌɑnˈseɪ, fiˈɑnˌseɪ, -z

fianchetto
BR ˌfɪənˈtʃɛtəʊ, ˌfɪənˈkɛtəʊ, -z
AM ˌfɪənˈtʃɛdou, ˌfɪənˈkɛdou, -z

Fianna Fáil
BR fɪˌanə ˈfɔɪl
AM fiˌɑnə ˈfɔɪl
IR ˌfiənə ˈfaːlʲ

fiasco
BR fɪˈaskəʊ, -z
AM fiˈæskoʊ, -z

fiat
BR ˈfiːat, ˈfaɪat, -s
AM ˈfiət, ˈfiˌɑt, -s

fib
BR fɪb, -z, -ɪŋ, -d
AM fɪb, -z, -ɪŋ, -d

fibber
BR ˈfɪbə(r), -z
AM ˈfɪbər, -z

fiber
BR ˈfaɪbə(r), -z, -d
AM ˈfaɪbər, -z, -d

fiberboard
BR ˈfaɪbəbɔːd
AM ˈfaɪbərˌbɔ(ə)rd

fiberfill
BR ˈfaɪbəfɪl
AM ˈfaɪbərˌfɪl

fiberglass
BR ˈfaɪbəglɑːs, ˈfaɪbəglas
AM ˈfaɪbərˌglæs

fiberless
BR ˈfaɪbələs
AM ˈfaɪbərləs

Fibonacci
BR fɪbəˈnɑːtʃi
AM fɪbəˈnatʃi

fibre
BR ˈfaɪbə(r), -z, -d
AM ˈfaɪbər, -z, -d

fibreboard
BR ˈfaɪbəbɔːd
AM ˈfaɪbərˌbɔ(ə)rd

fibrefill
BR ˈfaɪbəfɪl
AM ˈfaɪbərˌfɪl

fibreglass
BR ˈfaɪbəglɑːs, ˈfaɪbəglas
AM ˈfaɪbərˌglæs

fibreless
BR ˈfaɪbələs
AM ˈfaɪbərləs

fibriform
BR ˈfɪbrɪfɔːm, ˈfaɪbrɪfɔːm
AM ˈfɪbrəˌfɔ(ə)rm

fibril
BR ˈfaɪbr(ɪ)l, -z
AM ˈfaɪbrəl, -z

fibrillar
BR fɪˈbrɪlə(r), faɪˈbrɪlə(r)
AM ˈfɪbrələr

fibrillary
BR fɪˈbrɪl(ə)ri, faɪˈbrɪl(ə)ri
AM ˈfɪbrəˌlɛri

fibrillate
BR ˈfɪbrɪleɪt, ˈfaɪbrɪleɪt, -s, -ɪŋ, -ɪd
AM ˈfɪbrəˌleɪt, -ts, -dɪŋ, -dɪd

fibrillation
BR ˌfɪbrɪˈleɪʃn, ˌfaɪbrɪˈleɪʃn
AM ˌfɪbrəˈleɪʃən

fibrin
BR ˈfaɪbrɪn, ˈfɪbrɪn
AM ˈfaɪbrɪn

fibrinogen
BR fʌɪˈbrɪnədʒ(ə)n, fɪˈbrɪnədʒ(ə)n
AM faɪˈbrɪnədʒən

fibrinoid
BR ˈfaɪbrɪnɔɪd, ˈfɪbrɪnɔɪd
AM ˈfaɪbrəˌnɔɪd

fibro
BR ˈfaɪbrəʊ, -z
AM ˈfaɪbroʊ, -z

fibroid
BR ˈfaɪbrɔɪd, -z
AM ˈfaɪˌbrɔɪd, -z

fibroin
BR ˈfaɪbrəʊɪn
AM ˈfaɪbrəwən

fibroma
BR fʌɪˈbrəʊmə(r), -z
AM faɪˈbroʊmə, -z

fibromata
BR fʌɪˈbrəʊmətə(r)
AM faɪˈbroʊmədə

fibrosis
BR fʌɪˈbrəʊsɪs
AM faɪˈbroʊsəs

fibrositic
BR ˌfaɪbrəˈsɪtɪk
AM ˌfaɪbrəˈsɪdɪk

fibrositis
BR ˌfaɪbrəˈsʌɪtɪs
AM ˌfaɪbrəˈsaɪdɪs

fibrotic
BR fʌɪˈbrɒtɪk
AM faɪˈbrɑdɪk

fibrous
BR ˈfaɪbrəs
AM ˈfaɪbrəs

fibrously
BR ˈfaɪbrəsli
AM ˈfaɪbrəsli

fibrousness
BR ˈfaɪbrəsnəs
AM ˈfaɪbrəsnəs

fibula
BR ˈfɪbjʊlə(r), -z
AM ˈfɪbjələ, -z

fibular
BR ˈfɪbjʊlə(r)
AM ˈfɪbjələr

fiche
BR fiːʃ, -ɪz
AM fiʃ, -ɪz

Fichte
BR fɪxt
AM ˈfɪktə
GER ˈfɪçtə

Fichtean
BR ˈfɪxtɪən
AM ˈfɪktiən

fichu
BR ˈfiːʃuː, ˈfɪʃuː, -z
AM ˈfɪˌʃu, -z

fickle
BR ˈfɪkl̩, -ə(r), -ɪst
AM ˈfɪkl̩əl, -(ə)lər, -(ə)ləst

fickleness
BR ˈfɪklnəs
AM ˈfɪkəlnəs

fickly
BR ˈfɪkl̩(l)i
AM ˈfɪk(ə)li

fictile
BR ˈfɪktaɪl, ˈfɪkt(ɪ)l
AM ˈfɪktl, ˈfɪkˌtaɪl

fiction
BR ˈfɪkʃn, -z
AM ˈfɪkʃən, -z

fictional
BR ˈfɪkʃn̩(ə)l, ˈfɪkʃən(ə)l
AM ˈfɪkʃ(ə)nəl

fictionalisation
BR ˌfɪkʃnəlʌɪˈzeɪʃn, ˌfɪkʃn̩lʌɪˈzeɪʃn, ˌfɪkʃənlʌɪˈzeɪʃn, ˌfɪkʃ(ə)nəlʌɪˈzeɪʃn, -z
AM ˌfɪkʃənləˈzeɪʃən, ˌfɪkʃnələˈzeɪʃən, ˌfɪkʃnəˌlaɪˈzeɪʃən, -z

fictionalise
BR ˈfɪkʃnəlʌɪz, ˈfɪkʃn̩lʌɪz, ˈfɪkʃənlʌɪz, ˈfɪkʃ(ə)nəlʌɪz, -ɪz, -ɪŋ, -d
AM ˈfɪkʃ(ə)nəˌlaɪz, -ɪz, -ɪŋ, -d

fictionality
BR ˌfɪkʃəˈnalɪti
AM ˌfɪkʃəˈnælədi

fictionalization
BR ˌfɪkʃnəlʌɪˈzeɪʃn, ˌfɪkʃn̩lʌɪˈzeɪʃn, ˌfɪkʃənlʌɪˈzeɪʃn, ˌfɪkʃ(ə)nəlʌɪˈzeɪʃn, -z
AM ˌfɪkʃənləˈzeɪʃən, ˌfɪkʃnələˈzeɪʃən, ˌfɪkʃnəˌlaɪˈzeɪʃən, -z

fictionalize
BR ˈfɪkʃnəlʌɪz, ˈfɪkʃn̩lʌɪz, ˈfɪkʃənlʌɪz, ˈfɪkʃ(ə)nəlʌɪz, -ɪz, -ɪŋ, -d
AM ˈfɪkʃ(ə)nəˌlaɪz, -ɪz, -ɪŋ, -d

fictionally
BR ˈfɪkʃnəli, ˈfɪkʃn̩li, ˈfɪkʃənl̩i, ˈfɪkʃ(ə)nəli
AM ˈfɪkʃ(ə)nəli

fictionist
BR ˈfɪkʃn̩ɪst, ˈfɪkʃənɪst, -s
AM ˈfɪkʃ(ə)nəst, -s

fictitious
BR fɪkˈtɪʃəs
AM fɪkˈtɪʃəs

fictitiously
BR fɪkˈtɪʃəsli

AM fɪk'tɪʃəsli
fictitiousness
BR fɪk'tɪʃəsnəs
AM fɪk'tɪʃəsnəs
fictive
BR 'fɪktɪv
AM 'fɪktɪv
fictively
BR 'fɪktɪvli
AM 'fɪktɪvli
fictiveness
BR 'fɪktɪvnɪs
AM 'fɪktɪvnɪs
fid
BR fɪd, -z
AM fɪd, -z
fiddle
BR 'fɪd|l, -lz, -lɪŋ \-lɪŋ,
-ld
AM 'fɪd|əl, -əlz, -(ə)lɪŋ,
-əld
fiddle-de-dee
BR ,fɪdldɪ'di:
AM 'fɪdəldi'di
fiddler
BR 'fɪdlə(r), -z
AM 'fɪd(ə)lər, -z
fiddlestick
BR 'fɪdlstɪk, -s
AM 'fɪdl,stɪk, -s
fiddly
BR 'fɪdli, 'fɪdli
AM 'fɪdl̩i
Fidei Defensor
BR ,fɪdeɪi: dɪ'fɛnsɔ:(r),
,fʌɪdɪʌɪ +
AM 'fɪdeɪ,i
də'fɛn,sɔ(ə)r
fideism
BR 'fi:deɪɪz(ə)m,
'fʌɪdɪɪz(ə)m
AM 'fɪdeɪ,ɪzəm
fideist
BR 'fi:deɪɪst, 'fʌɪdɪɪst,
-s
AM 'fɪdeɪɪst, -s
fideistic
BR ,fi:deɪ'ɪstɪk,
,fʌɪdɪ'ɪstɪk
AM ,fɪdeɪ'ɪstɪk
Fidel
BR fɪ'dɛl
AM fə'dɛl
Fidelio
BR fɪ'deɪlɪəʊ
AM fɪ'deɪlioʊ
Fidelis
BR fɪ'deɪlɪs
AM fɪ'deɪlɪs
fidelity
BR fɪ'dɛlɪti
AM fɪ'dɛlədi
fidget
BR 'fɪdʒɪt, -s, -ɪŋ, -ɪd
AM 'fɪdʒɪ|t, -ts, -dɪŋ,
-dɪd

fidgetiness
BR 'fɪdʒɪtɪnɪs
AM 'fɪdʒɪdinɪs
fidgety
BR 'fɪdʒɪti
AM 'fɪdʒɪdi
Fidler
BR 'fɪdlə(r), 'fi:dlə(r)
AM 'frdlər, 'fidlər
Fido
BR 'fʌɪdəʊ
AM 'faɪdoʊ
fiducial
BR fɪ'dju:ʃ(ə)l,
fɪ'dʒu:ʃ(ə)l,
fɪ'dju:ʃɪəl, fɪ'dʒu:ʃɪəl,
fɪ'dju:sɪəl, fɪ'dʒu:sɪəl
AM fə'duʃɪəl
fiducially
BR fɪ'dju:ʃli,
fɪ'dju:ʃəli, fɪ'dʒu:ʃʃi,
fɪ'dʒu:ʃəli,
fɪ'dju:ʃɪəli,
fɪ'dʒu:ʃɪəli,
fɪ'dju:sɪəli,
fɪ'dʒu:sɪəli
AM fə'duʃ(i)əli
fiduciary
BR fɪ'dju:ʃ(ə)r|i,
fɪ'dʒu:ʃ(ə)r|i
fɪ'dju:s(ə)r|i,
fɪ'dʒu:s(ə)ri,
fɪ'dju:ʃɪər|i,
fɪ'dʒu:ʃɪəri,
fɪ'dju:sɪəri, -ɪz
AM fə'duʃi,ɛri,
fə'dusi,ɛri, -z
fidus Achates
BR ,fʌɪdəs ə'keɪti:z
AM 'faɪdəs ə'kɑdiz
fie
BR fʌɪ
AM faɪ
Fiedler
BR 'fi:dlə(r)
AM 'fidlər
fief
BR fi:f, -s
AM fif, -s
fiefdom
BR 'fi:fdəm, -z
AM 'fifdəm, -z
field
BR fi:ld, -z, -ɪŋ, -ɪd
AM fild, -z, -ɪŋ, -ɪd
Fielden
BR 'fi:ld(ə)n
AM 'fildən
fielder
BR 'fi:ldə(r), -z
AM 'fildər, -z
fieldfare
BR 'fi:ldfɛ:(r), -z
AM 'fild(d),fɛ(ə)r, -z
Fielding
BR 'fi:ldɪŋ
AM 'fildɪŋ

fieldmice
BR 'fi:ldmʌɪs
AM 'fil(d),maɪs
fieldmouse
BR 'fi:ldmaʊs
AM 'fil(d),maʊs
Fields
BR fi:ldz
AM fil(d)z
fieldsman
BR 'fi:ldzmən
AM 'fil(d)zmən
fieldsmen
BR 'fi:ldzmən
AM 'fil(d)zmən
fieldstone
BR 'fi:ldstəʊn, -z
AM 'fil(d),stoʊn, -z
fieldwork
BR 'fi:ldwə:k
AM 'fil(d),wərk
fieldworker
BR 'fi:ldwə:kə(r), -z
AM 'fil(d),wərkər, -z
fiend
BR fi:nd, -z
AM find, -z
fiendish
BR 'fi:ndɪʃ
AM 'findɪʃ
fiendishly
BR 'fi:ndɪʃli
AM 'findɪʃli
fiendishness
BR 'fi:ndɪʃnɪs
AM 'findɪʃnɪs
fiendlike
BR 'fi:ndlʌɪk
AM 'fin(d),laɪk
Fiennes
BR fʌɪnz
AM faɪnz
fierce
BR fɪəs, -ə(r), -ɪst
AM fɪ(ə)rs, -ər, -ɪst
fiercely
BR 'fɪəsli
AM 'fɪrsli
fierceness
BR 'fɪəsnəs
AM 'fɪrsnəs
fieri facias
BR ,fʌɪərʌɪ 'feɪʃɪas
AM ,faɪri 'feɪʃ(i)əs
fierily
BR 'fʌɪərɪli
AM 'faɪrəli
fieriness
BR 'fʌɪərɪnɪs
AM 'faɪrinɪs
fiery
BR 'fʌɪər|i, -ɪə(r), -ɪɪst
AM 'faɪri, -ər, -ɪst
fiesta
BR fɪ'ɛstə(r)
AM fi'ɛstə

FIFA
BR 'fi:fə(r)
AM 'fifə
fife
BR fʌɪf, -s, -ɪŋ, -t
AM faɪf, -s, -ɪŋ, -t
fifer
BR 'fʌɪfə(r), -z
AM 'faɪfər, -z
Fifi
BR 'fi:fi:
AM 'fifi
Fifield
BR 'fʌɪfi:ld
AM 'faɪ,fild
FIFO
BR 'fi:fəʊ
AM 'fi,foʊ
fifteen
BR fɪf'ti:n
AM ,fɪf,tin
fifteenth
BR ,fɪf'ti:nθ
AM ,fɪf'tinθ
fifth
BR fɪfθ
AM fɪ(f)θ
fifthly
BR 'fɪfθli
AM 'fɪ(f)θli
Fifth Monarchy
BR ,fɪfθ 'mɒnəki
AM 'fɪ(f)θ 'mɑnərki
fiftieth
BR 'fɪftɪɪθ
AM 'fɪftiɪθ
fifty
BR 'fɪfti
AM 'fɪfti
fifty-fifty
BR ,fɪftɪ'fɪfti
AM ,fɪfti'fɪfti
fiftyfold
BR 'fɪftɪfəʊld
AM 'fɪfti,foʊld
fig
BR fɪg, -z
AM fɪg, -z
Figaro
BR 'fɪgərəʊ
AM 'fɪgəroʊ
Figg
BR fɪg
AM fɪg
Figgis
BR 'fɪgɪs
AM 'fɪgɪs
fight
BR fʌɪt, -s, -ɪŋ
AM faɪ|t, -ts, -dɪŋ
fightback
BR 'fʌɪtbak, -s
AM 'faɪt,bæk, -s
fighter
BR 'fʌɪtə(r), -z
AM 'faɪdər, -z

figleaf
BR ˈfɪgliːf
AM ˈfɪgˌlif

figleaves
BR ˈfɪgliːvz
AM ˈfɪgˌlivz

figment
BR ˈfɪgm(ə)nt, -s
AM ˈfɪgmənt, -s

figtree
BR ˈfɪgtriː, -z
AM ˈfɪgˌtri, -z

Figueroa
BR ˌfɪgəˈrəʊə(r)
AM ˌfɪgəˈroʊə

figura
BR fɪˈgjʊərə(r), fɪˈgjɔːrə(r), -z
AM fɪˈgjərə, -z

figural
BR ˈfɪgjʊrəl, ˈfɪgjʊrl̩
AM fɪˈgjərəl

figurant
BR ˈfɪgjʊrənt, ˈfɪgjʊrn̩t, -s
AM ˈfɪg(j)ərənt, ˌfɪg(j)əˈrɑnt, -s

figurante
BR ˌfɪgjʊˈrɑntǀi, -ɪz
AM ˌfɪgjəˈrɑn(t)i, -z

figuranti
BR ˌfɪgjʊˈrɑntǀi, -ɪz
AM ˌfɪgjəˈrɑn(t)i, -z

figuration
BR ˌfɪgjʊˈreɪʃn, -z
AM ˌfɪgjəˈreɪʃən, -z

figurative
BR ˈfɪg(ə)rətɪv, ˈfɪgjʊrətɪv
AM ˈfɪgjərədɪv

figuratively
BR ˈfɪg(ə)rətɪvli, ˈfɪgjʊrətɪvli
AM ˈfɪgjərədəvli

figurativeness
BR ˈfɪg(ə)rətɪvnɪs, ˈfɪgjʊrətɪvnɪs
AM ˈfɪgjərədɪvnɪs

figure
BR ˈfɪgə(r), -z, -ɪŋ, -d
AM ˈfɪgjər, -z, -ɪŋ, -d

figurehead
BR ˈfɪgəhɛd, -z
AM ˈfɪgjərˌ(h)ɛd, -z

figureless
BR ˈfɪgələs
AM ˈfɪgjərləs

figurine
BR ˌfɪgəˈriːn, -z
AM ˌfɪgjəˈrin, -z

figwort
BR ˈfɪgwəːt
AM ˈfɪgˌwərt, ˈfɪgˌwɔ(ə)rt

Fiji
BR ˈfiːdʒiː, ˌfiːˈdʒiː
AM ˈfiˌdʒi

Fijian
BR fɪˈdʒiːən, fiːˈdʒiːən, -z
AM fiˈdʒiən, fəˈdʒiən, -z

filagree
BR ˈfɪləgriː, -z
AM ˈfɪləˌgri, -z

filament
BR ˈfɪləm(ə)nt, -s
AM ˈfɪləmənt, -s

filamentary
BR ˌfɪləˈmɛnt(ə)ri
AM ˌfɪləˈmɛn(t)əri

filamented
BR ˈfɪləmɛntɪd
AM ˈfɪləˌmɛn(t)əd

filamentous
BR ˌfɪləˈmɛntəs
AM ˌfɪləˈmɛn(t)əs

filaria
BR fɪˈlɛːrɪə(r), -z
AM fəˈlɛriə, -z

filariae
BR fɪˈlɛːriː
AM fəˈlɛriˌi, fəˈlɛriˌaɪ

filarial
BR fɪˈlɛːrɪəl
AM fəˈlɛriəl

filariasis
BR ˌfɪləˈraɪəsɪs, fɪˌlɛːrɪˈeɪsɪs
AM ˌfɪləˈraɪəsəs

filature
BR ˈfɪlətʃə(r), ˈfɪlətʃʊə(r), -z
AM ˈfɪlətʃər, ˈfɪləˌtʃʊ(ə)r, -z

filbert
BR ˈfɪlbət, -s
AM ˈfɪlbərt, -s

filch
BR fɪltʃ, -ɪz, -ɪŋ, -t
AM fɪltʃ, -ɪz, -ɪŋ, -t

filcher
BR ˈfɪltʃə(r), -z
AM ˈfɪltʃər, -z

file
BR faɪl, -z, -ɪŋ, -d
AM faɪl, -z, -ɪŋ, -d

filefish
BR ˈfaɪlfɪʃ
AM ˈfaɪlˌfɪʃ

filename
BR ˈfaɪlneɪm, -z
AM ˈfaɪlˌneɪm, -z

filer
BR ˈfaɪlə(r), -z
AM ˈfaɪlər, -z

filet
BR ˈfɪlɪt, ˈfɪleɪ, -s \-z
AM frˈleɪ, ˈfɪleɪ, -z

filet mignon
BR ˈfɪleɪ ˈmiːnjɔ̃, + ˈmɪnjɔ̃, -z
AM frˈleɪ mɪnˈjɑn, -z

Filey
BR ˈfaɪli

filial
BR ˈfɪlɪəl
AM ˈfɪljəl, ˈfɪliəl

filially
BR ˈfɪlɪəli
AM ˈfɪljəli, ˈfɪliəli

filialness
BR ˈfɪlɪəlnəs
AM ˈfɪljəlnəs, ˈfɪliəlnəs

filiation
BR ˌfɪlɪˈeɪʃn
AM ˌfɪliˈeɪʃən

filibeg
BR ˈfɪlɪbɛg, -z
AM ˈfɪləˌbɛg, -z

filibuster
BR ˈfɪlɪbʌstǀə(r), -əz, -(ə)rɪŋ, -əd
AM ˈfɪləˌbəstǀər, -ərz, -(ə)rɪŋ, -ərd

filibusterer
BR ˈfɪlɪbʌst(ə)rə(r), -z
AM ˈfɪləˌbəstərər, -z

filicide
BR ˈfɪlɪsʌɪd, -z
AM ˈfɪləˌsaɪd, -z

filiform
BR ˈfʌɪlɪfɔːm
AM ˈfɪləˌfɔ(ə)rm, ˈfaɪləˌfɔ(ə)rm

filigree
BR ˈfɪlɪgriː
AM ˈfɪləˌgri

filigreed
BR ˈfɪlɪgriːd
AM ˈfɪləˌgrid

filing
BR ˈfʌɪlɪŋ, -z
AM ˈfaɪlɪŋ, -z

filings
BR ˈfʌɪlɪŋz
AM ˈfaɪlɪŋz

Filioque
BR ˌfiːlɪˈəʊkwi, ˌfɪlɪˈəʊkwi
AM ˌfɪliˈoʊkwə

Filipina
BR ˌfɪlɪˈpiːnə(r), -z
AM ˈfɪləˈpinə, -z

Filipino
BR ˌfɪlɪˈpiːnəʊ, -z
AM ˈfɪləˈpinoʊ, -z

fill
BR fɪl, -z, -ɪŋ, -d
AM fɪl, -z, -ɪŋ, -d

fille de joie
BR ˌfiː də ˈʒwɑː(r)
AM ˌfɪ də ˈʒwɑ

filler
BR ˈfɪlə(r), -z
AM ˈfɪlər, -z

filles de joie
BR ˌfiː də ˈʒwɑː(r)
AM ˌfɪ(z) də ˈʒwɑ

fillet
BR ˈfɪlɪt, -s, -ɪŋ, -ɪd

faɪli

filleter
BR ˈfɪlɪtə(r), -z
AM ˈfɪlɪdər, -z

fill-in
BR ˈfɪlɪn, -z
AM ˈfɪlˌɪn, -z

filling
BR ˈfɪlɪŋ, -z
AM ˈfɪlɪŋ, -z

fillip
BR ˈfɪlɪp, -s, -ɪŋ, -t
AM ˈfɪlɪp, -s, -ɪŋ, -t

fillis
BR ˈfɪlɪs
AM ˈfɪlɪs

fillister
BR ˈfɪlɪstə(r), -z
AM ˈfɪlɪstər, -z

Fillmore
BR ˈfɪlmɔː(r)
AM ˈfɪlˌmɔ(ə)r

fill-up
BR ˈfɪlʌp, -s
AM ˈfɪləp, -s

filly
BR ˈfɪlǀi, -ɪz
AM ˈfɪli, -z

film
BR fɪlm, -z, -ɪŋ, -d
AM fɪlm, -z, -ɪŋ, -d

filmable
BR ˈfɪlməbl
AM ˈfɪlməbəl

filmgoer
BR ˈfɪlmˌgəʊə(r), -z
AM ˈfɪlmˌgoʊər, -z

filmic
BR ˈfɪlmɪk
AM ˈfɪlmɪk

filmily
BR ˈfɪlmɪli
AM ˈfɪlmɪli

filminess
BR ˈfɪlmɪnɪs
AM ˈfɪlmɪnɪs

filmmaker
BR ˈfɪlmˌmeɪkə(r), -z
AM ˈfɪlmˌmeɪkər, -z

filmmaking
BR ˈfɪlmˌmeɪkɪŋ
AM ˈfɪlmˌmeɪkɪŋ

film noir
BR ˌfɪlm ˈnwɑː(r)
AM ˌfɪlm ˈnwɑr

filmography
BR fɪlˈmɒgrəfi
AM fɪlˈmɑgrəfi

filmset
BR ˈfɪlmsɛt, -s, -ɪŋ
AM ˈfɪlmˌsɛǀt, -ts, -dɪŋ

filmsetter
BR ˈfɪlmˌsɛtə(r), -z
AM ˈfɪlmˌsɛdər, -z

filmstrip
BR ˈfɪlmstrɪp, -s
AM ˈfɪlmˌstrɪp, -s

filmy
BR ˈfɪlm|i, -ɪə(r), -ɪɪst
AM ˈfɪlmi, -ər, -ɪst

filo
BR ˈfiːləʊ
AM ˈfiːloʊ

Filofax®
BR ˈfaɪlə(ʊ)faks, -ɪz
AM ˈfaɪloʊˌfæks

filoplume
BR ˈfaɪlə(ʊ)pluːm, -z
AM ˈfiːləˌplum, ˈfaɪləˌplum, -z

filoselle
BR ˈfɪləsɛl
AM ˌfɪləˈsɛl

filovirus
BR ˈfiːləʊˌvʌɪrəs
AM ˈfiːloʊˌvaɪrəs, ˈfɪləˌvaɪrəs

fils
BR fiːs
AM fis

filter
BR ˈfɪlt|ə(r), -əz, -(ə)rɪŋ, -əd
AM ˈfɪlt|ər, -ərz, -(ə)rɪŋ, -ərd

filterable
BR ˈfɪlt(ə)rəbl
AM ˈfɪlt(ə)rəbəl

filth
BR fɪlθ
AM fɪlθ

filthily
BR ˈfɪlθɪli
AM ˈfɪlθɪli

filthiness
BR ˈfɪlθɪnɪs
AM ˈfɪlθɪnɪs

filthy
BR ˈfɪlθ|i, -ɪə(r), -ɪɪst
AM ˈfɪlθi, -ər, -ɪst

Filton
BR ˈfɪlt(ə)n
AM ˈfɪltən

filtrable
BR ˈfɪltrəbl
AM ˈfɪltrəbəl

filtrate
BR ˈfɪltreɪt, -s, -ɪŋ, -ɪd
AM ˈfɪltˌreɪ|t, -ts, -dɪŋ, -dɪd

filtration
BR fɪlˈtreɪʃn
AM fɪlˈtreɪʃən

fimbria
BR ˈfɪmbrɪə(r)
AM ˈfɪmbrɪə

fimbriae
BR ˈfɪmbriː
AM ˈfɪmbriː, ˈfɪmbriaɪ

fimbriate
BR ˈfɪmbrɪeɪt, ˈfɪmbrɪət
AM ˈfɪmbrɪət

fimbriated
BR ˈfɪmbrɪeɪtɪd
AM ˈfɪmbriˌeɪdɪd

fin
BR fɪn, -z, -d
AM fɪn, -z, -d

finable
BR ˈfʌɪnəbl
AM ˈfaɪnəbəl

finagle
BR fɪˈneɪg|l, -lz, -lɪŋ \-lɪŋ, -ld
AM fɪˈneɪg|əl, -əlz, -(ə)lɪŋ, -əld

finagler
BR fɪˈneɪglə(r), fɪˈneɪglə(r), -z
AM fɪˈneɪg(ə)lər, -z

final
BR ˈfʌɪnl, -z
AM ˈfaɪnl, -z

finale
BR fɪˈnɑːl|i, -ɪz
AM fɪˈnæli, fɪˈnɑli, -z

finalisation
BR ˌfʌɪnəlʌɪˈzeɪʃn, ˌfʌɪnl̩ʌɪˈzeɪʃn
AM ˌfaɪnələˈzeɪʃən, ˌfaɪnəˌlaɪˈzeɪʃən

finalise
BR ˈfʌɪnəlʌɪz, ˈfʌɪnl̩ʌɪz, -ɪz, -ɪŋ, -d
AM ˈfaɪnlˌaɪz, -ɪz, -ɪŋ, -d

finalism
BR ˈfʌɪnəlɪz(ə)m, ˈfʌɪnl̩ɪz(ə)m
AM ˈfaɪnlˌɪzəm

finalist
BR ˈfʌɪnəlɪst, ˈfʌɪnl̩ɪst, -s
AM ˈfaɪnl̩ɪst, -s

finalistic
BR ˌfʌɪnəˈlɪstɪk, ˌfʌɪnl̩ˈɪstɪk
AM ˌfaɪnl̩ˈɪstɪk

finality
BR fʌɪˈnalɪti
AM faɪˈnælədi, fɪˈnælədi

finalization
BR ˌfʌɪnəlʌɪˈzeɪʃn, ˌfʌɪnl̩ʌɪˈzeɪʃn
AM ˌfaɪnələˈzeɪʃən, ˌfaɪnəˌlaɪˈzeɪʃən

finalize
BR ˈfʌɪnəlʌɪz, ˈfʌɪnl̩ʌɪz, -ɪz, -ɪŋ, -d
AM ˈfaɪnlˌaɪz, -ɪz, -ɪŋ, -d

finally
BR ˈfʌɪnəli, ˈfʌɪnl̩i
AM ˈfaɪn(ə)li

finance
BR fʌɪˈnans, fɪˈnans, ˈfʌɪnans, -ɪz, -ɪŋ, -t
AM ˈfaɪˌnæns, fɪˈnæns, -əz, -ɪŋ, -t

financial
BR fɪˈnanʃl, fʌɪˈnanʃl

financially
BR fɪˈnanʃl̩i, fɪˈnanʃəli, fʌɪˈnanʃl̩i, fʌɪˈnanʃəli
AM fɪˈnæn(t)ʃ(ə)li, faɪˈnæn(t)ʃ(ə)li

financier
BR fɪˈnansɪə(r), -z
AM ˌfɪnənˈsɪ(ə)r, -z

Finbar
BR ˈfɪnbɑː(r)
AM ˈfɪnˌbɑr

finca
BR ˈfɪŋkə(r), -z
AM ˈfɪŋkə, -z

finch
BR fɪn(t)ʃ, -ɪz
AM fɪn(t)ʃ, -ɪz

Finchale
BR ˈfɪŋkl
AM ˈfɪŋkəl

Finchampstead
BR ˈfɪn(t)ʃəm(p)stɛd, ˈfɪn(t)ʃəm(p)stɪd
AM ˈfɪn(t)ʃəm(p)ˌstɛd

Finchley
BR ˈfɪn(t)ʃli
AM ˈfɪn(t)ʃli

find
BR fʌɪnd, -z, -ɪŋ
AM faɪnd, -z, -ɪŋ

findable
BR ˈfʌɪndəbl
AM ˈfaɪndəbəl

finder
BR ˈfʌɪndə(r), -z
AM ˈfaɪndər, -z

fin de siècle
BR ˌfã də ˈsjɛklə(r)
AM ˌfan də sˈjɛkl

Findhorn
BR ˈfɪndhɔːn
AM ˈfaɪndˌ(h)ɔ(ə)rn

finding
BR ˈfʌɪndɪŋ, -z
AM ˈfaɪndɪŋ, -z

Findlater
BR ˈfɪn(d)lətə(r)
AM ˈfɪn(d)lədər

Findlay
BR ˈfɪn(d)li
AM ˈfɪnli

Findon
BR ˈfɪnd(ə)n
AM ˈfɪndən

findspot
BR ˈfʌɪn(d)spɒt, -s
AM ˈfaɪn(d)ˌspat, -s

Findus
BR ˈfɪndəs
AM ˈfɪndəs

fine
BR fʌɪn, -z, -ɪŋ, -d, -ə(r), -ɪst

AM faɪn, -z, -ɪŋ, -d, -ər, -ɪst

fineable
BR ˈfʌɪnəbl
AM ˈfaɪnəbəl

Fine Gael
BR ˌfɪnə ˈgeɪl
AM ˌfɪnə ˈgeɪl
IR ˌfʲɪnʲə ˈgeːl

finely
BR ˈfʌɪnli
AM ˈfaɪnli

fineness
BR ˈfʌɪnnɪs
AM ˈfaɪ(n)nɪs

finery
BR ˈfʌɪnəri
AM ˈfaɪnəri

fines herbes
BR ˌfiːn(z) ˈɛːb
AM ˌfin ˈ(z)ɛrb

fine-spun
BR ˌfʌɪnˈspʌn
AM ˈfaɪnˌspən

finesse
BR fɪˈnɛs
AM fɪˈnɛs

Fingal
BR ˈfɪŋgl
AM ˈfɪŋgəl

finger
BR ˈfɪŋg|ə(r), -əz, -(ə)rɪŋ, -əd
AM ˈfɪŋg|ər, -ərz, -(ə)rɪŋ, -ərd

fingerboard
BR ˈfɪŋgəbɔːd, -z
AM ˈfɪŋgərˌbɔ(ə)rd, -z

fingering
BR ˈfɪŋg(ə)rɪŋ, -z
AM ˈfɪŋgərɪŋ, -z

fingerless
BR ˈfɪŋgələs
AM ˈfɪŋgərləs

fingerling
BR ˈfɪŋgəlɪŋ, -z
AM ˈfɪŋgərlɪŋ, -z

fingernail
BR ˈfɪŋgəneɪl, -z
AM ˈfɪŋgərˌneɪl, -z

fingerplate
BR ˈfɪŋgəpleɪt, -s
AM ˈfɪŋgərˌpleɪt, -s

fingerpost
BR ˈfɪŋgəpəʊst, -s
AM ˈfɪŋgərˌpoʊst, -s

fingerprint
BR ˈfɪŋgəprɪnt, -s, -ɪŋ, -ɪd
AM ˈfɪŋgərˌprɪn|t, -ts, -dɪŋ, -dɪd

fingerstall
BR ˈfɪŋgəstɔːl, -z
AM ˈfɪŋgərˌstɔl, ˈfɪŋgərˌstal, -z

fingertip
BR ˈfɪŋgətɪp, -s

AM ˈfɪŋɡərˌtɪp, -s

finial
BR ˈfɪniəl, ˈfʌɪniəl, -z
AM ˈfɪniəl, -z

finical
BR ˈfɪnɪkl
AM ˈfɪnɪkəl

finicality
BR ˌfɪnɪˈkalɪti
AM ˌfɪnɪˈkælədi

finically
BR ˈfɪnɪkli, ˈfɪnɪkəli
AM ˈfɪnɪk(ə)li

finicalness
BR ˈfɪnɪklnəs
AM ˈfɪnɪkəlnəs

finickily
BR ˈfɪnɪkɪli, ˈfɪnɪkļi
AM ˈfɪnɪk(ə)li

finickiness
BR ˈfɪnɪkɪnɪs
AM ˈfɪnɪkinɪs

finicking
BR ˈfɪnɪkɪŋ
AM ˈfɪnɪkɪŋ

finickity
BR frˈnɪkɪti
AM fəˈnɪkɪdi

finicky
BR ˈfɪnɪk|i, -ɪə(r), -ɪɪst
AM ˈfɪnɪki, -ər, -ɪst

finis
BR ˈfiːnɪs, ˈfɪnɪs, ˈfʌɪnɪs
AM ˈfɪnɪs, ˈfɪni, frˈni

finish
BR ˈfɪn|ɪʃ, -ɪʃɪz, -ɪʃɪŋ, -ɪʃt
AM ˈfɪnɪʃ, -ɪz, -ɪŋ, -t

finisher
BR ˈfɪnɪʃə(r), -z
AM ˈfɪnɪʃər, -z

Finisterre
BR ˌfɪnɪˈstɜː(r)
AM ˌfɪnɪsˈtɛ(ə)r

finite
BR ˈfʌɪnʌɪt
AM ˈfaɪˌnaɪt

finitely
BR ˈfʌɪnʌɪtli
AM ˈfaɪˌnaɪtli

finiteness
BR ˈfʌɪnʌɪtnɪs
AM ˈfaɪˌnaɪtnɪs

finitism
BR ˈfʌɪnʌɪtɪz(ə)m
AM ˈfaɪnəˌtɪzəm

finitist
BR ˈfʌɪnʌɪtɪst, -s
AM ˈfaɪˌnaɪdɪst, -s

finitude
BR ˈfɪnɪtjuːd,
ˈfʌɪnɪtjuːd, ˈfɪnɪtʃuːd,
ˈfʌɪnɪtʃuːd
AM ˈfɪnəˌt(j)ud,
ˈfaɪnəˌt(j)ud

fink
BR fɪŋk, -s

AM fɪŋk, -s

Finkelstein
BR ˈfɪŋklstʌɪn
AM ˈfɪŋkəlˌstin,
ˈfɪŋkəlˌstaɪn

Finland
BR ˈfɪnlənd
AM ˈfɪnlənd

Finlandia
BR fɪnˈlandiə(r)
AM fɪnˈlændiə

Finlay
BR ˈfɪnli, ˈfɪnleɪ
AM ˈfɪnli

Finlayson
BR ˈfɪnlɪs(ə)n
AM ˈfɪnlisən

finless
BR ˈfɪnlɪs
AM ˈfɪnlɪs

Finley
BR ˈfɪnli
AM ˈfɪnli

Finn
BR fɪn, -z
AM fɪn, -z

Finnair
BR ˌfɪnˈɛː(r), ˈfɪnɛː(r)
AM ˌfɪnˈɛ(ə)r

finnan
BR ˈfɪnən, -z
AM ˈfɪnən, -z

finnanhaddie
BR ˌfɪnənˈhadi
AM ˌfɪnənˈhædi

Finnegan
BR ˈfɪnɪɡ(ə)n
AM ˈfɪnəɡən

finner
BR ˈfɪnə(r), -z
AM ˈfɪnər, -z

finnesko
BR ˈfɪn(ɪ)skəʊ, -z
AM ˈfɪnəˌskoʊ, -z

finneskoe
BR ˈfɪn(ɪ)skəʊ, -z
AM ˈfɪnzkoʊ,
ˈfɪnəˌskoʊ, -z

Finney
BR ˈfɪni
AM ˈfɪni

Finnic
BR ˈfɪnɪk
AM ˈfɪnɪk

Finningley
BR ˈfɪnɪŋli
AM ˈfɪnɪŋli

Finnish
BR ˈfɪnɪʃ
AM ˈfɪnɪʃ

Finno-Ugrian
BR ˌfɪnəʊˈjuːɡriən
AM ˌfɪnoʊˈugriən

Finno-Ugric
BR ˌfɪnəʊˈjuːɡrɪk
AM ˌfɪnoʊˈugrɪk

finny
BR ˈfɪni
AM ˈfɪni

fino
BR ˈfiːnəʊ, -z
AM ˈfinoʊ, -z

Finola
BR frˈnəʊlə(r)
AM fəˈnoʊlə

Finsberg
BR ˈfɪnzbəːɡ
AM ˈfɪnzˌbərɡ

Finsbury
BR ˈfɪnzb(ə)ri
AM ˈfɪnzˌbɛri

Finucane
BR frˈnuːk(ə)n
AM ˈfɪnəˌkeɪn

Fiona
BR frˈəʊnə(r)
AM fiˈoʊnə

fiord
BR ˈfiːɔːd, frˈɔːd, fjɔːd, -z
AM fiˈɔ(ə)rd, fjɔ(ə)rd,
-z

fioritura
BR fɪˌɔːriˈtʊərə(r)
AM fiˌɔrəˈtʊrə

fioriture
BR fɪˌɔːriˈtʊəri,
fɪˌɔːriˈtʊəreɪ
AM fiˌɔrəˈtʊˌreɪ

fipple
BR ˈfɪpl, -z
AM ˈfɪpəl, -z

fir
BR fəː(r), -z
AM fər, -z

fire
BR ˈfʌɪə(r), -z, -ɪŋ, -d
AM ˈfaɪ(ə)r, -z, -ɪŋ, -d

firearm
BR ˈfʌɪərɑːm, -z
AM ˈfaɪ(ə)rˌɑrm, -z

fireback
BR ˈfʌɪəbak, -s
AM ˈfaɪ(ə)rˌbæk, -s

fireball
BR ˈfʌɪəbɔːl, -z
AM ˈfaɪ(ə)rˌbɔl,
ˈfaɪ(ə)rˌbɑl, -z

firebird
BR ˈfʌɪəbəːd, -z
AM ˈfaɪ(ə)rˌbərd, -z

firebomb
BR ˈfʌɪəbɒm, -z, -ɪŋ, -d
AM ˈfaɪ(ə)rˌbɑm, -z, -ɪŋ,
-d

firebox
BR ˈfʌɪəbɒks, -ɪz
AM ˈfaɪ(ə)rˌbɑks, -əz

firebrand
BR ˈfʌɪəbrand, -z
AM ˈfaɪ(ə)rˌbrænd, -z

firebrat
BR ˈfʌɪəbrat, -s
AM ˈfaɪ(ə)rˌbræt, -s

firebreak
BR ˈfʌɪəbreɪk, -s
AM ˈfaɪ(ə)rˌbreɪk, -s

firebrick
BR ˈfʌɪəbrɪk, -s
AM ˈfaɪ(ə)rˌbrɪk, -s

firebug
BR ˈfʌɪəbʌɡ, -z
AM ˈfaɪ(ə)rˌbəɡ, -z

firecat
BR ˈfʌɪəkat, -s
AM ˈfaɪ(ə)rˌkæt, -s

fireclay
BR ˈfʌɪəkleɪ
AM ˈfaɪ(ə)rˌkleɪ

firecracker
BR ˈfʌɪəˌkrakə(r), -z
AM ˈfaɪ(ə)rˌkrækər, -z

firecrest
BR ˈfʌɪəkrɛst, -s
AM ˈfaɪ(ə)rˌkrɛst, -s

firedamp
BR ˈfʌɪədamp
AM ˈfaɪ(ə)rˌdæmp

firedog
BR ˈfʌɪədɒɡ, -z
AM ˈfaɪ(ə)rˌdɔɡ,
ˈfaɪ(ə)rˌdɑɡ, -z

firefly
BR ˈfʌɪəflʌɪ, -z
AM ˈfaɪ(ə)rˌflaɪ, -z

fireguard
BR ˈfʌɪəɡɑːd, -z
AM ˈfaɪ(ə)rˌɡɑrd, -z

firehouse
BR ˈfʌɪəhaʊ|s, -zɪz
AM ˈfaɪ(ə)r,(h)aʊ|s,
-zəz

fireless
BR ˈfʌɪələs
AM ˈfaɪ(ə)rləs

firelight
BR ˈfʌɪəlʌɪt
AM ˈfaɪ(ə)rˌlaɪt

firelighter
BR ˈfʌɪəlʌɪtə(r), -z
AM ˈfaɪ(ə)rˌlaɪdər, -z

firelock
BR ˈfʌɪəlɒk, -s
AM ˈfaɪ(ə)rˌlɑk, -s

fireman
BR ˈfʌɪəmən
AM ˈfaɪ(ə)rmən

firemen
BR ˈfʌɪəˌmɛn, ˈfʌɪəmən
AM ˈfaɪ(ə)rˌmɛn,
ˈfaɪ(ə)rmən

Firenze
BR frˈrɛnzi
AM frˈrɛn(t)zə
IT fiˈrɛntse

fireplace
BR ˈfʌɪəpleɪs, -ɪz
AM ˈfaɪ(ə)rˌpleɪs, -ɪz

fireplug
BR ˈfʌɪəplʌɡ, -z
AM ˈfaɪ(ə)rˌpləɡ, -z

firepower
BR ˈfaɪəˌpaʊə(r)
AM ˈfaɪ(ə)rˌpaʊər
fireproof
BR ˈfaɪəpruːf
AM ˈfaɪ(ə)rˌpruf
firer
BR ˈfaɪərə(r), -z
AM ˈfaɪ(ə)rər, -z
fire sale
BR ˈfaɪə seɪl, -z
AM ˈfaɪ(ə)r ˌseɪl, -z
fire screen
BR ˈfaɪə skriːn, -z
AM ˈfaɪ(ə)r ˌskrin, -z
fireship
BR ˈfaɪəʃɪp, -s
AM ˈfaɪ(ə)rˌʃɪp, -s
fireside
BR ˈfaɪəsʌɪd, -z
AM ˈfaɪ(ə)rˌsaɪd, -z
firestorm
BR ˈfaɪəstɔːm, -z
AM ˈfaɪ(ə)rˌstɔ(ə)rm, -z
firetrap
BR ˈfaɪətrap, -s
AM ˈfaɪ(ə)rˌtræp, -s
firewalker
BR ˈfaɪəˌwɔːkə(r), -z
AM ˈfaɪ(ə)rˌwɔkər,
ˈfaɪ(ə)rˌwakər, -z
firewalking
BR ˈfaɪəˌwɔːkɪŋ
AM ˈfaɪ(ə)rˌwɔkɪŋ,
ˈfaɪ(ə)rˌwakɪŋ
firewatcher
BR ˈfaɪəˌwɒtʃə(r), -z
AM ˈfaɪ(ə)rˌwatʃər,
ˈfaɪ(ə)rˌwɒtʃər, -z
firewatching
BR ˈfaɪəˌwɒtʃɪŋ
AM ˈfaɪ(ə)rˌwatʃɪŋ,
ˈfaɪ(ə)rˌwɒtʃɪŋ
firewater
BR ˈfaɪəˌwɔːtə(r)
AM ˈfaɪ(ə)rˌwɔdər,
ˈfaɪ(ə)rˌwadər
fireweed
BR ˈfaɪəwiːd
AM ˈfaɪ(ə)rˌwid
firewoman
BR ˈfaɪəˌwʊmən
AM ˈfaɪ(ə)rˌwʊmən
firewomen
BR ˈfaɪəˌwɪmɪn
AM ˈfaɪ(ə)rˌwɪmɪn
firewood
BR ˈfaɪəwʊd
AM ˈfaɪ(ə)rˌwʊd
firework
BR ˈfaɪəwəːk, -s
AM ˈfaɪ(ə)rˌwərk, -s
firing
BR ˈfaɪərɪŋ, -z
AM ˈfaɪ(ə)rɪŋ, -z
firkin
BR ˈfəːkɪn, -z

firm
BR fəːm, -z, -ɪŋ, -d, -ə(r),
-ɪst
AM fərm, -z, -ɪŋ, -d, -ər,
-əst
firmament
BR ˈfəːməm(ə)nt
AM ˈfərməmənt
firmamental
BR ˌfəːməˈmɛntl
AM ˌfərməˈmɛn(t)l
firman
BR ˈfəːmən, -z
AM ˈfərmən, -z
firmly
BR ˈfəːmli
AM ˈfərmli
firmness
BR ˈfəːmnəs
AM ˈfərmnəs
firmware
BR ˈfəːmwɛː(r)
AM ˈfərmˌwɛ(ə)r
firry
BR ˈfəːri
AM ˈfəri
first
BR fəːst, -s
AM fərst, -s
firstborn
BR ˈfəːs(t)bɔːn, -z
AM ˈfərs(t)ˌbɔ(ə)rn, -z
firstfruits
BR ˈfəːs(t)fruːts
AM ˈfərs(t)ˌfruts
firsthand
BR ˌfəːstˈhand
AM ˌfərstˈhænd
firstling
BR ˈfəːs(t)lɪŋ, -z
AM ˈfərs(t)lɪŋ, -z
firstly
BR ˈfəːstli
AM ˈfərs(t)li
first-nighter
BR ˌfəːs(t)ˈnʌɪtə(r), -z
AM ˌfərs(t)ˈnaɪdər, -z
firth
BR fəːθ, -s
AM fərθ, -s
firtree
BR ˈfəːtriː, -z
AM ˈfərˌtri, -z
fisc
BR fɪsk, -s
AM fɪsk, -s
fiscal
BR ˈfɪskl, -z
AM ˈfɪskəl, -z
fiscality
BR fɪˈskalɪti
AM fɪˈskælədi
fiscally
BR ˈfɪskl̩i, ˈfɪskəli
AM ˈfɪskəli

Fischer
BR ˈfɪʃə(r)
AM ˈfɪʃər
Fischer-Dieskau
BR ˌfɪʃəˈdɪskaʊ
AM ˈfɪʃərˈdiskaʊ
fish
BR fɪʃ, -ɪz, -ɪŋ, -t
AM fɪʃ, -ɪz, -ɪŋ, -t
fishable
BR ˈfɪʃəbl
AM ˈfɪʃəbəl
fishbowl
BR ˈfɪʃbəʊl, -z
AM ˈfɪʃˌboʊl, -z
fishcake
BR ˈfɪʃkeɪk, -s
AM ˈfɪʃˌkeɪk, -s
fisher
BR ˈfɪʃə(r), -z
AM ˈfɪʃər, -z
fisherfolk
BR ˈfɪʃəfəʊk
AM ˈfɪʃərˌfoʊk
fisherman
BR ˈfɪʃəmən
AM ˈfɪʃərmən
fishermen
BR ˈfɪʃəmən
AM ˈfɪʃərˌmɛn,
ˈfɪʃərmən
fisherwoman
BR ˈfɪʃəˌwʊmən
AM ˈfɪʃərˌwʊmən
fisherwomen
BR ˈfɪʃəˌwɪmɪn
AM ˈfɪʃərˌwɪmɪn
fishery
BR ˈfɪʃ(ə)r|i, -ɪz
AM ˈfɪʃəri, -z
Fishguard
BR ˈfɪʃɡɑːd
AM ˈfɪʃˌɡɑrd
fishhook
BR ˈfɪʃhʊk, -s
AM ˈfɪʃˌ(h)ʊk, -s
fishily
BR ˈfɪʃɪli
AM ˈfɪʃɪli
fishiness
BR ˈfɪʃɪnɪs
AM ˈfɪʃɪnɪs
fishlike
BR ˈfɪʃlʌɪk
AM ˈfɪʃˌlaɪk
Fishlock
BR ˈfɪʃlɒk
AM ˈfɪʃˌlak
fishmeal
BR ˈfɪʃmiːl
AM ˈfɪʃˌmil
fishmonger
BR ˈfɪʃˌmʌŋɡə(r), -z
AM ˈfɪʃˌmaŋɡər,
ˈfɪʃˌməŋɡər, -z
fishnet
BR ˈfɪʃnɛt, -s

Fischer AM ˈfɪʃˌnɛt, -s
fishplate
BR ˈfɪʃpleɪt, -s
AM ˈfɪʃˌpleɪt, -s
fishpot
BR ˈfɪʃpɒt, -s
AM ˈfɪʃˌpat, -s
fishstick
BR ˈfɪʃstɪk, -s
AM ˈfɪʃˌstɪk, -s
fishtail
BR ˈfɪʃteɪl
AM ˈfɪʃˌteɪl
Fishwick
BR ˈfɪʃwɪk
AM ˈfɪʃˌwɪk
fishwife
BR ˈfɪʃwʌɪf
AM ˈfɪʃˌwaɪf
fishwives
BR ˈfɪʃwʌɪvz
AM ˈfɪʃˌwaɪvz
fishy
BR ˈfɪʃ|i, -ɪə(r), -ɪɪst
AM ˈfɪʃi, -ər, -ɪɪst
fisk
BR fɪsk, -s
AM fɪsk, -s
Fiske
BR fɪsk
AM fɪsk
Fison
BR ˈfʌɪsn
AM ˈfaɪsən
fissile
BR ˈfɪsʌɪl
AM ˈfɪsəl, ˈfɪˌsaɪl
fissility
BR fɪˈsɪlɪti
AM fɪˈsɪlɪdi
fission
BR ˈfɪʃn
AM ˈfɪʃən
fissionable
BR ˈfɪʃnəbl, ˈfɪʃənəbl
AM ˈfɪʃ(ə)nəbəl
fissiparity
BR ˌfɪsɪˈparɪti
AM ˌfɪsəˈpɛrədi
fissiparous
BR fɪˈsɪp(ə)rəs
AM fɪˈsɪp(ə)rəs
fissiparously
BR fɪˈsɪp(ə)rəsli
AM fɪˈsɪp(ə)rəsli
fissiparousness
BR fɪˈsɪp(ə)rəsnəs
AM fɪˈsɪp(ə)rəsnəs
fissure
BR ˈfɪʃə(r), -z
AM ˈfɪʃər, -z
fist
BR fɪst, -s
AM fɪst, -s
fistful
BR ˈfɪs(t)fʊl
AM ˈfɪs(t)ˌfʊl

fistic
BR ˈfɪstɪk
AM ˈfɪstɪk

fistical
BR ˈfɪstɪkl
AM ˈfɪstɪkəl

fisticuffs
BR ˈfɪstɪkʌfs
AM ˈfɪstɪˌkəfs

fistula
BR ˈfɪstjʊlə(r),
ˈfɪstʃʊlə(r), -z
AM ˈfɪstʃələ, ˈfɪʃtʃələ,
-z

fistular
BR ˈfɪstjʊlə(r),
ˈfɪstʃʊlə(r)
AM ˈfɪstʃələr, ˈfɪʃtʃələr

fistulous
BR ˈfɪstjʊləs, ˈfɪstʃʊləs
AM ˈfɪstʃələs, ˈfɪʃtʃələs

fit
BR fɪt, -s, -ɪŋ, -ɪd, -ə(r),
-ɪst
AM fɪ|t, -ts, -dɪŋ, -dɪd,
-dər, -dəst

fitch
BR fɪtʃ, -ɪz
AM fɪtʃ, -ɪz

fitchew
BR ˈfɪtʃuː, -z
AM ˈfɪtʃu, -z

fitful
BR ˈfɪtf(ʊ)l
AM ˈfɪtfəl

fitfully
BR ˈfɪtfʊli, ˈfɪtfli
AM ˈfɪtfəli

fitfulness
BR ˈfɪtf(ʊ)lnəs
AM ˈfɪtfəlnəs

fitly
BR ˈfɪtli
AM ˈfɪtli

fitment
BR ˈfɪtm(ə)nt, -s
AM ˈfɪtmənt, -s

fitness
BR ˈfɪtnɪs
AM ˈfɪtnɪs

fitter
BR ˈfɪtə(r), -z
AM ˈfɪdər, -z

fitting
BR ˈfɪtɪŋ, -z
AM ˈfɪdɪŋ, -z

fittingly
BR ˈfɪtɪŋli
AM ˈfɪdɪŋli

fittingness
BR ˈfɪtɪŋnɪs
AM ˈfɪdɪŋnɪs

Fittipaldi
BR ˌfɪtɪˈpaldi
AM ˌfɪdəˈpɑldi

Fitz
BR fɪts

AM fɪts

Fitzgerald
BR ˌfɪtsˈdʒɛrəld,
ˌfɪtsˈdʒɛrld
AM ˌfɪtsˈdʒɛrəld

Fitzgibbon
BR fɪtsˈgɪb(ə)n
AM fɪtsˈgɪbən

Fitzjames
BR fɪtsˈdʒeɪmz
AM fɪtsˈdʒeɪmz

Fitzjohn
BR fɪtsˈdʒɒn
AM fɪtsˈdʒɑn

Fitzpatrick
BR fɪtsˈpatrɪk
AM fɪtsˈpætrək

Fitzrovia
BR fɪtsˈrəʊviə(r)
AM fɪtsˈrouviə

Fitzroy
BR ˈfɪtsrɔɪ, fɪtsˈrɔɪ
AM ˈfɪtsˌrɔɪ, ˌfɪtsˈrɔɪ

Fitzsimmons
BR fɪt(s)ˈsɪmənz
AM fɪtsˈsɪmənz

Fitzwalter
BR fɪtsˈwɔːltə(r)
AM fɪtsˈwɔltər,
fɪtsˈwɑltər

Fitzwilliam
BR ˌfɪtsˈwɪliəm
AM ˌfɪtsˈwɪljəm,
ˌfɪtsˈwɪliəm

Fiume
BR ˈfjuːmeɪ
AM ˈfjuˌmeɪ

five
BR fʌɪv, -z
AM faɪv, -z

five-a-side
BR ˌfʌɪvəˈsʌɪd, -z
AM ˌfaɪvəˈsaɪd, -z

fivefold
BR ˈfʌɪvfəʊld
AM ˈfaɪvˌfould

fivepence
BR ˈfʌɪvp(ə)ns,
ˈfʌɪfp(ə)ns, -ɪz
AM ˈfaɪvˌpɛns, -əz

fivepenny
BR ˈfʌɪvpən|i,
ˈfʌɪvpŋ|i, -ɪz
AM ˈfaɪvˌpɛni, -z

fiver
BR ˈfʌɪvə(r), -z
AM ˈfaɪvər, -z

fivestones
BR ˈfʌɪvstəʊnz
AM ˈfaɪvˌstoʊnz

fix
BR fɪks, -ɪz, -ɪŋ, -t
AM fɪks, -ɪz, -ɪŋ, -t

fixable
BR ˈfɪksəbl
AM ˈfɪksəbəl

fixate
BR fɪkˈseɪt, -s, -ɪŋ, -ɪd
AM ˈfɪkˌseɪ|t, -ts, -dɪŋ,
-dɪd

fixatedly
BR fɪkˈseɪtɪdli
AM ˈfɪkˌseɪdɪdli

fixation
BR fɪkˈseɪʃn, -z
AM fɪkˈseɪʃən, -z

fixative
BR ˈfɪksətɪv, -z
AM ˈfɪksədɪv, -z

fixedly
BR ˈfɪksɪdli
AM ˈfɪksɪdli

fixedness
BR ˈfɪksɪdnɪs
AM ˈfɪksɪdnɪs

fixer
BR ˈfɪksə(r), -z
AM ˈfɪksər, -z

fixings
BR ˈfɪksɪŋz
AM ˈfɪksɪŋz, ˈfɪksɪnz

fixity
BR ˈfɪksɪti
AM ˈfɪksɪdi

fixture
BR ˈfɪkstʃə(r), -z
AM ˈfɪkstʃər, -z

fizgig
BR ˈfɪzgɪg, -z
AM ˈfɪzˌgɪg, -z

fizz
BR fɪz, -ɪz, -ɪŋ, -d
AM fɪz, -ɪz, -ɪŋ, -d

fizzer
BR ˈfɪzə(r), -z
AM ˈfɪzər, -z

fizzily
BR ˈfɪzɪli
AM ˈfɪzɪli

fizziness
BR ˈfɪzɪnɪs
AM ˈfɪzɪnɪs

fizzle
BR ˈfɪz|l, -lz, -lɪŋ \ -lɪŋ,
-ld
AM ˈfɪz|əl, -əlz, -(ə)lɪŋ,
-əld

fizzy
BR ˈfɪz|i, -ɪə(r), -ɪɪst
AM ˈfɪzi, -ər, -ɪst

fjord
BR fiːɔːd, fɪˈɔːd, fjɔːd
AM fiˈɔ(ə)rd, fjɔ(ə)rd

flab
BR flab
AM flæb

flabbergast
BR ˈflabəgɑːst,
ˈflabəgast, -s, -ɪŋ, -ɪd
AM ˈflæbərˌgæst, -s, -ɪŋ,
-əd

flabbily
BR ˈflabɪli

AM ˈflæbəli

flabbiness
BR ˈflabɪnɪs
AM ˈflæbɪnɪs

flabby
BR ˈflab|i, -ɪə(r), -ɪɪst
AM ˈflæbi, -ər, -ɪst

flaccid
BR ˈfla(k)sɪd
AM ˈflæ(k)səd

flaccidity
BR flaˈsɪdɪti,
fla(k)ˈsɪdɪti
AM flæ(k)ˈsɪdɪdi

flaccidly
BR ˈfla(k)sɪdli
AM ˈflæ(k)sədli

flaccidness
BR ˈfla(k)sɪdnɪs
AM ˈflæ(k)sədnəs

flack
BR flak
AM flæk

flag
BR flag, -z, -ɪŋ, -d
AM flæg, -z, -ɪŋ, -d

flagella
BR fləˈdʒɛlə(r)
AM ˌfləˈdʒɛlə

flagellant
BR ˈfladʒɪlənt,
ˈfladʒɪlŋt,
ˈfladʒl̩(ə)nt,
fləˈdʒɛlənt, fləˈdʒɛlŋt,
-s
AM ˈflædʒələnt,
fləˈdʒɛlənt, -s

flagellar
BR ˈfladʒɪlə(r),
ˈfladʒl̩ə(r),
fləˈdʒɛlə(r)
AM ˈflædʒələr

flagellate¹
noun, adjective
BR ˈfladʒɪlət, ˈfladʒl̩ət,
ˈfladʒɪleɪt, ˈfladʒl̩eɪt,
-s
AM ˈflædʒələt,
ˈflædʒəˌleɪt, -s

flagellate²
verb
BR ˈfladʒɪleɪ|t, -s, -ɪŋ, -ɪd
AM ˈflædʒəˌleɪ|t, -ts,
-dɪŋ, -dɪd

flagellation
BR ˌfladʒɪˈleɪʃn, -z
AM ˌflædʒəˈleɪʃən, -z

flagellator
BR ˈfladʒɪleɪtə(r), -z
AM ˈflædʒəˌleɪdər, -z

flagellatory
BR ˈfladʒɪleɪt(ə)ri
AM ˌflæˈdʒɛləˌtɔri

flagelliform
BR fləˈdʒɛlɪfɔːm
AM ˌfləˈdʒɛləˌfɔ(ə)rm

flagellum
BR fləˈdʒɛləm

AM ˌflæˈdʒɛləm
flageolet
BR ˌfladʒəˈlɛt,
ˈfladʒəlɪt, -s
AM ˌflædʒəˈlɛt, -s
Flagg
BR flag
AM flæg
flagger
BR ˈflagə(r), -z
AM ˈflægər, -z
flagitious
BR fləˈdʒɪʃəs
AM fləˈdʒɪʃəs
flagitiously
BR fləˈdʒɪʃəsli
AM fləˈdʒɪʃəsli
flagitiousness
BR fləˈdʒɪʃəsnəs
AM fləˈdʒɪʃəsnəs
flagman
BR ˈflagmən
AM ˈflægmæn
flagmen
BR ˈflagmən
AM ˈflægmən
flagon
BR ˈflag(ə)n, -z
AM ˈflægən, -z
flagpole
BR ˈflagpəʊl, -z
AM ˈflægˌpoʊl, -z
flagrancy
BR ˈfleɪgr(ə)nsi
AM ˈfleɪgrənsi
flag-rank
BR ˈflagraŋk, -s
AM ˈflægˌræŋk, -s
flagrant
BR ˈfleɪgr(ə)nt
AM ˈfleɪgrənt
flagrante
BR fləˈgranti
AM fləˈgran(t)i
flagrantly
BR ˈfleɪgr(ə)ntli
AM ˈfleɪgrən(t)li
flagship
BR ˈflagˌʃɪp, -s
AM ˈflægˌʃɪp, -s
flagstaff
BR ˈflagstɑːf, ˈflagstaf, -s
AM ˈflægˌstæf, -s
flagstick
BR ˈflagstɪk, -s
AM ˈflægˌstɪk, -s
flagstone
BR ˈflagstəʊn, -z, -d
AM ˈflægˌstoʊn, -z, -d
Flaherty
BR ˈflɑː(h)əti
AM ˈflɛrdi
flail
BR fleɪl, -z, -ɪŋ, -d
AM fleɪl, -z, -ɪŋ, -d

flair
BR flɛː(r)
AM flɛ(ə)r
flak
BR flak
AM flæk
flake
BR fleɪk, -s, -ɪŋ, -t
AM fleɪk, -s, -ɪŋ, -t
flakily
BR ˈfleɪkɪli
AM ˈfleɪkɪli
flakiness
BR ˈfleɪkɪnɪs
AM ˈfleɪkɪnɪs
flaky
BR ˈfleɪk|i, -ɪə(r), -ɪɪst
AM ˈfleɪki, -ər, -ɪst
flam
BR flam, -z
AM flæm, -z
flambé
BR ˈflɒmbeɪ, ˈflambeɪ, ˈflɑːmbeɪ
AM flɑmˈbeɪ
flambeau
BR ˈflambəʊ, -z
AM ˈflæmboʊ, -z
flambeaux
BR ˈflambəʊz
AM ˈflæmboʊ
flambée
BR ˈflɒmbeɪ, ˈflambeɪ, ˈflɑːmbeɪ, -d
AM flɑmˈbeɪ, -d
Flamborough
BR ˈflamb(ə)rə(r)
AM ˈflæmˌbəroʊ, ˈflæmˌbərə
flamboyance
BR flamˈbɔɪəns
AM flæmˈbɔɪ(j)əns
flamboyancy
BR flamˈbɔɪənsi
AM flæmˈbɔɪ(j)ənsi
flamboyant
BR flamˈbɔɪənt
AM flæmˈbɔɪ(j)ənt
flamboyantly
BR flamˈbɔɪəntli
AM flæmˈbɔɪ(j)ən(t)li
flame
BR fleɪm, -z, -ɪŋ, -d
AM fleɪm, -z, -ɪŋ, -d
flameless
BR ˈfleɪmlɪs
AM ˈfleɪmlɪs
flamelike
BR ˈfleɪmlʌɪk
AM ˈfleɪmˌlaɪk
flamen
BR ˈfleɪmɛn, ˈflɑːmɛn, -z
AM ˈfleɪmən, -z
flamenco
BR fləˈmɛŋkəʊ, -z
AM fləˈmɛŋkoʊ, -z

flameproof
BR ˈfleɪmpruːf
AM ˈfleɪmˌpruf
flamingo
BR fləˈmɪŋgəʊ, -z
AM fləˈmɪŋgoʊ, -z
flammability
BR ˌflaməˈbɪlɪti
AM ˌflæməˈbɪlɪdi
flammable
BR ˈflaməbl
AM ˈflæməbəl
Flamsteed
BR ˈflamstiːd
AM ˈflæmˌstid
flamy
BR ˈfleɪm|i, -ɪə(r), -ɪɪst
AM ˈfleɪmi, -ər, -ɪst
flan
BR flan, -z
AM flæn, -z
Flanagan
BR ˈflanəg(ə)n
AM ˈflænəgən
flanch
BR flɑːn(t)ʃ, flan(t)ʃ, -ɪz, -ɪŋ, -t
AM flæn(t)ʃ, -əz, -ɪŋ, -t
Flanders
BR ˈflɑːndəz, ˈflandəz
AM ˈflændərz
flânerie
BR ˌflɑːnˈriː
AM ˌflɑn(ə)ˈri
flâneur
BR flɑːˈnəː(r), -z
AM flɑˈnər, -z
flange
BR flan(d)ʒ, -ɪz
AM flænd ʒ, -əz
flangeless
BR ˈflan(d)ʒləs
AM ˈflænd ʒləs
flank
BR flaŋ|k, -ks, -kɪŋ, -(k)t
AM flæŋ|k, -ks, -kɪŋ, -(k)t
flanker
BR ˈflaŋkə(r), -z
AM ˈflæŋkər, -z
flannel
BR ˈflan|l, -lz, -l̩ɪŋ \ -əlɪŋ, -ld
AM ˈflænəl, -z, -ɪŋ, -d
flannelboard
BR ˈflanlbɔːd, -z
AM ˈflænlˌbɔ(ə)rd, -z
flannelette
BR ˌflanəˈlɛt, ˌflanlˈɛt
AM ˌflænlˈɛt
flannelgraph
BR ˈflanlgrɑːf, ˈflanlgraf, -s
AM ˈflænlˌgræf, -s
flannelly
BR ˈflanli

AM ˈflænl̩i
flannely
BR ˈflanl̩i
AM ˈflænl̩i
flap
BR flap, -s, -ɪŋ, -t
AM flæp, -s, -ɪŋ, -t
flapdoodle
BR ˈflap,duːdl
AM ˈflæp,dudəl
flapjack
BR ˈflapdʒak, -s
AM ˈflæp,dʒæk, -s
flapper
BR ˈflapə(r), -z
AM ˈflæpər, -z
flappy
BR ˈflap|i, -ɪə(r), -ɪɪst
AM ˈflæpi, -ər, -ɪst
flare
BR flɛː(r), -z, -ɪŋ, -d
AM flɛ(ə)r, -z, -ɪŋ, -d
flash
BR flaʃ, -ɪz, -ɪŋ, -t
AM flæʃ, -əz, -ɪŋ, -t
flashback
BR ˈflaʃbak, -s
AM ˈflæʃˌbæk, -s
flashbulb
BR ˈflaʃbʌlb, -z
AM ˈflæʃˌbəlb, -z
flashcard
BR ˈflaʃkɑːd, -z
AM ˈflæʃˌkɑrd, -z
flashcube
BR ˈflaʃkjuːb, -z
AM ˈflæʃˌkjub, -z
flasher
BR ˈflaʃə(r), -z
AM ˈflæʃər, -z
flashgun
BR ˈflaʃgʌn, -z
AM ˈflæʃˌgən, -z
flashily
BR ˈflaʃɪli
AM ˈflæʃəli
flashiness
BR ˈflaʃɪnɪs
AM ˈflæʃɪnɪs
flashing
BR ˈflaʃɪŋ, -z
AM ˈflæʃɪŋ, -z
flash lamp
BR ˈflaʃ lamp, -s
AM ˈflæʃ ˌlæmp, -s
flashlight
BR ˈflaʃlʌɪt, -s
AM ˈflæʃˌlaɪt, -s
Flashman
BR ˈflaʃmən
AM ˈflæʃmən
flashover
BR ˈflaʃˌəʊvə(r), -z
AM ˈflæʃˌoʊvər, -z
flashpoint
BR ˈflaʃpɔɪnt, -s
AM ˈflæʃˌpɔɪnt, -s

flashy
BR 'flaʃ|i, -ɪə(r), -ɪɪst
AM 'flæʃi, -ər, -ɪst

flask
BR flɑːsk, flask, -s
AM flæsk, -s

flat
BR flat, -s, -ə(r), -ɪst
AM flæ|t, -ts, -dər, -dəst

flatbed
BR 'flatbɛd, -z
AM 'flæt,bɛd, -z

flatboat
BR 'flatbəʊt, -s
AM 'flæt,bəʊt, -s

flatbread
BR 'flatbrɛd, -z
AM 'flæt,brɛd, -z

flatcar
BR 'flatkɑː(r), -z
AM 'flæt,kɑr, -z

flatfeet
BR 'flatfiːt
AM 'flæt,fit

flatfish
BR 'flatfɪʃ, -ɪz
AM 'flæt,fɪʃ, -ɪz

flatfoot
BR 'flatfʊt
AM 'flæt,fʊt

Flathead
BR 'flathɛd
AM 'flæt,(h)ɛd

flatiron
BR 'flatʌɪən, -z
AM 'flæt,aɪərn, -z

flatland
BR 'flatland, -z
AM 'flæt,lænd, -z

flatlander
BR 'flat,landə(r), -z
AM 'flæt,lændər, -z

flatlet
BR 'flatlɪt, -s
AM 'flætlət, -s

flatly
BR 'flatli
AM 'flætli

flatmate
BR 'flatmeɪt, -s
AM 'flæt,meɪt, -s

flatness
BR 'flatnəs
AM 'flætnəs

flatshare
BR 'flatʃɛː(r), -z
AM 'flæt,ʃɛ(ə)r, -z

flatsie
BR 'flats|i, -ɪz
AM 'flætsi, -z

flatten
BR 'flat|n, -nz,
-nɪŋ \-nɪŋ, -nd
AM 'flætn, -z, -ɪŋ, -d

flattener
BR 'flatnə(r),
'flatnə(r), -z

flatter
BR 'flat|ə(r), -əz,
-(ə)rɪŋ, -əd
AM 'flædər, -z, -ɪŋ, -d

flatterer
BR 'flat(ə)rə(r), -z
AM 'flædərər, -z

flatteringly
BR 'flat(ə)rɪŋli
AM 'flædərɪŋli

flattery
BR 'flat(ə)r|i, -ɪz
AM 'flædəri, -z

flattie
BR 'flat|i, -ɪz
AM 'flædi, -z

flattish
BR 'flatɪʃ
AM 'flædɪʃ

flattop
BR 'flattɒp, -s
AM 'flæt,tɑp, -s

flatulence
BR 'flatjʊləns,
'flatjʊlns, 'flatʃʊləns,
'flatʃʊlns
AM 'flætʃələns

flatulency
BR 'flatjʊlənsi,
'flatjʊlnsi,
'flatʃʊlənsi,
'flatʃʊlnsi
AM 'flætʃələnsi

flatulent
BR 'flatjʊlənt,
'flatjʊlnt, 'flatʃʊlənt,
'flatʃʊlnt
AM 'flætʃələnt

flatulently
BR 'flatjʊləntli,
'flatjʊlntli,
'flatʃʊləntli,
'flatʃʊlntli
AM 'flætʃələn(t)li

flatus
BR 'fleɪtəs, -ɪz
AM 'fleɪdəs, -əz

flatware
BR 'flatwɛː(r)
AM 'flæt,wɛ(ə)r

flatworm
BR 'flatwəːm, -z
AM 'flæt,wərm, -z

Flaubert
BR 'fləʊbɛː(r)
AM floʊ'bɛ(ə)r

flaunch
BR flɔːn(t)ʃ, -ɪz, -ɪŋ, -t
AM flɑntʃ, flantʃ, -əz,
-ɪŋ, -t

flaunt
BR flɔːnt, -s, -ɪŋ, -ɪd
AM flɑn|t, flan|t, -ts,
-(t)ɪŋ, -(t)əd

flaunter
BR 'flɔːntə(r), -z

flaunty
BR 'flɔːnti
AM 'flɔn(t)i, 'flan(t)i

flautist
BR 'flɔːtɪst, -s
AM 'flɑdəst, 'flaʊdəst, -s

flavescent
BR flə'vɛsnt
AM flə'vɛsənt

Flavia
BR 'fleɪvɪə(r)
AM 'fleɪvɪə

Flavian
BR 'fleɪvɪən, -z
AM 'fleɪvɪən, -z

flavin
BR 'fleɪvɪn, -z
AM 'fleɪvɪn, -z

flavine
BR 'fleɪviːn
AM 'fleɪvin

Flavius
BR 'fleɪvɪəs
AM 'fleɪvɪəs

flavone
BR 'fleɪvəʊn
AM 'fleɪ,voʊn

flavoprotein
BR ,fleɪvə(ʊ)'prəʊtiːn, -z
AM ,fleɪvə'proʊ,tin, -z

flavor
BR 'fleɪv|ə(r), -əz,
-(ə)rɪŋ, -əd
AM 'fleɪv|ər, -ərz,
-(ə)rɪŋ, -ərd

flavorful
BR 'fleɪvəf(ʊ)l
AM 'fleɪvərfəl

flavorfully
BR 'fleɪvəfʊli,
'fleɪvəfḷi
AM 'fleɪvərf(ə)li

flavoring
BR 'fleɪv(ə)rɪŋ, -z
AM 'fleɪvərɪŋ, -z

flavorless
BR 'fleɪvələs
AM 'fleɪvərləs

flavorous
BR 'fleɪv(ə)rəs
AM 'fleɪvərəs

flavorously
BR 'fleɪv(ə)rəsli
AM 'fleɪvərəsli

flavorsome
BR 'fleɪvəs(ə)m
AM 'fleɪvərsəm

flavour
BR 'fleɪv|ə(r), -əz,
-(ə)rɪŋ, -əd
AM 'fleɪv|ər, -ərz,
-(ə)rɪŋ, -ərd

flavourful
BR 'fleɪvəf(ʊ)l
AM 'fleɪvərfəl

flavourfully
BR 'fleɪvəfʊli,
'fleɪvəfḷi
AM 'fleɪvərf(ə)li

flavouring
BR 'fleɪv(ə)rɪŋ, -z
AM 'fleɪvərɪŋ, -z

flavourless
BR 'fleɪvələs
AM 'fleɪvərləs

flavourous
BR 'fleɪv(ə)rəs
AM 'fleɪvərəs

flavourously
BR 'fleɪv(ə)rəsli
AM 'fleɪvərəsli

flavoursome
BR 'fleɪvəs(ə)m
AM 'fleɪvərsəm

flaw
BR flɔː(r), -z, -ɪŋ, -d
AM flɔ, flɑ, -z, -ɪŋ, -d

flawless
BR 'flɔːləs
AM 'flɔləs, 'flɑləs

flawlessly
BR 'flɔːləsli
AM 'flɔləsli, 'flɑləsli

flawlessness
BR 'flɔːləsnəs
AM 'flɔləsnəs, 'flɑləsnəs

flax
BR flaks
AM flæks

flaxen
BR 'flaksn
AM 'flæksən

Flaxman
BR 'flaksmən
AM 'flæksmən

flaxseed
BR 'flak(s)siːd
AM 'flæk(s),sid

flay
BR fleɪ, -z, -ɪŋ, -d
AM fleɪ, -z, -ɪŋ, -d

flayer
BR 'fleɪə(r), -z
AM 'fleɪər, -z

flea
BR fliː, -z
AM fli, -z

fleabag
BR 'fliːbag, -z
AM 'fli,bag, -z

fleabane
BR 'fliːbeɪn
AM 'fli,beɪn

fleabite
BR 'fliːbʌɪt, -s
AM 'fli,baɪt, -s

fleapit
BR 'fliːpɪt, -s

AM 'fli,pɪt, -s

flèche
BR fleɪʃ, flɛʃ, -ɪz
AM fleɪʃ, flɛʃ, -ɪz

fleck
BR flɛk, -s, -ɪŋ, -t
AM flɛk, -s, -ɪŋ, -t

Flecker
BR 'flɛkə(r)
AM 'flɛkər

flection
BR 'flɛkʃn, -z
AM 'flɛkʃən, -z

flectional
BR 'flɛkʃn(ə)l, 'flɛkʃən(ə)l
AM 'flɛkʃ(ə)nəl

flectionless
BR 'flɛkʃnləs
AM 'flɛkʃənləs

fled
BR flɛd
AM flɛd

Fledermaus, Die
BR ,di: 'fleɪdəmaʊs
AM ,di 'fleɪdər,maʊs

fledge
BR flɛdʒ, -ɪz, -ɪŋ, -d
AM flɛdʒ, -əz, -ɪŋ, -d

fledgeling
BR 'flɛdʒlɪŋ, -z
AM 'flɛdʒlɪŋ, -z

fledgling
BR 'flɛdʒlɪŋ, -z
AM 'flɛdʒlɪŋ, -z

flee
BR fli:, -z, -ɪŋ
AM fli, -z, -ɪŋ

fleece
BR fli:s, -ɪz, -ɪŋ, -t
AM flis, -ɪz, -ɪŋ, -t

fleeceable
BR 'fli:səbl
AM 'flisəbəl

fleecily
BR 'fli:sɪli
AM 'flisɪli

fleeciness
BR 'fli:sɪnɪs
AM 'flisɪnɪs

fleecy
BR 'fli:s|i, -ɪə(r), -ɪɪst
AM 'flisi, -ər, -ɪst

fleer
BR 'flɪə(r), -z, -rɪŋ, -d
AM 'flɪ|(ə)r, -ərd, -(ə)rɪŋ, -ərd

fleet
BR fli:t, -s, -ɪŋ
AM fli|t, -ts, -dɪŋ

Fleet Air Arm
BR ,fli:t 'ɛːr ɑːm
AM ,flid 'ɛr ,ɑrm

fleeting
BR 'fli:tɪŋ
AM 'flidɪŋ

fleetingly
BR 'fli:tɪŋli
AM 'flidɪŋli

fleetly
BR 'fli:tli
AM 'flitli

fleetness
BR 'fli:tnɪs
AM 'flitnɪs

Fleetwood
BR 'fli:twʊd
AM 'flit,wʊd

Fleming
BR 'flɛmɪŋ, -z
AM 'flɛmɪŋ, -z

Flemish
BR 'flɛmɪʃ
AM 'flɛmɪʃ

flense
BR flɛns, -ɪz, -ɪŋ, -t
AM flɛns, -əz, -ɪŋ, -t

flesh
BR flɛʃ, -ɪz, -ɪŋ, -t
AM flɛʃ, -əz, -ɪŋ, -t

flesher
BR 'flɛʃə(r), -z
AM 'flɛʃər, -z

fleshiness
BR 'flɛʃɪnɪs
AM 'flɛʃɪnɪs

fleshings
BR 'flɛʃɪŋz
AM 'flɛʃɪŋz

fleshless
BR 'flɛʃləs
AM 'flɛʃləs

fleshliness
BR 'flɛʃlɪnɪs
AM 'flɛʃlɪnɪs

fleshly
BR 'flɛʃli
AM 'flɛʃli

fleshpot
BR 'flɛʃpɒt, -s
AM 'flɛʃ,pɑt, -s

fleshy
BR 'flɛʃ|i, -ɪə(r), -ɪɪst
AM 'flɛʃi, -ər, -ɪst

fletcher
BR 'flɛtʃə(r), -z
AM 'flɛtʃər, -z

Fleur
BR flə:(r), -z
AM flər, -z

fleur-de-lis
BR ,flə: də 'li:, -z
AM ,flər də 'li, -z

fleur-de-lys
BR ,flə:də'li:, -z
AM ,flərdə'li, -z

fleurette
BR ,fluə'rɛt, ,flə:'rɛt, -s
AM ,flə'rɛt, flʊ'rɛt, -s

fleuron
BR 'fluərɒn, 'flə:rɒn, -z
AM 'flə,rɑn, 'flʊ,rɑn, -z

fleury
BR 'fluəri
AM 'fləri

flew
BR flu:, -z
AM flu, -z

flex
BR flɛks, -ɪz, -ɪŋ, -t
AM flɛks, -əz, -ɪŋ, -t

flexibility
BR ,flɛksɪ'bɪlɪti
AM ,flɛksə'bɪlɪdi

flexible
BR 'flɛksɪbl
AM 'flɛksəbəl

flexibleness
BR 'flɛksɪblnəs
AM 'flɛksəbəlnəs

flexibly
BR 'flɛksɪbli
AM 'flɛksəbli

flexile
BR 'flɛksʌɪl
AM 'flɛksəl

flexility
BR flɛk'sɪlɪt|i, -ɪz
AM flɛk'sɪlɪdi, -z

flexion
BR 'flɛkʃn
AM 'flɛkʃən

flexional
BR 'flɛkʃn(ə)l, 'flɛkʃən(ə)l
AM 'flɛkʃ(ə)nəl

flexionless
BR 'flɛkʃnləs
AM 'flɛkʃənləs

flexitime
BR 'flɛksɪtʌɪm
AM 'flɛksi,taɪm

Flexner
BR 'flɛksnə(r)
AM 'flɛksnər

flexographic
BR ,flɛksə'grafɪk
AM ,flɛksə'græfɪk

flexography
BR flɛk'sɒgrəfi
AM flɛk'sɑgrəfi

flexor
BR 'flɛksə(r), -z
AM 'flɛksər, 'flɛk,sɔ(ə)r, -z

flextime
BR 'flɛkstʌɪm
AM 'flɛks,taɪm

flexuosity
BR ,flɛksjʊ'ɒsɪti, ,flɛkʃʊ'ɒsɪti
AM ,flɛkʃə'wɑsədi

flexuous
BR 'flɛksjʊəs, 'flɛkʃʊəs
AM 'flɛkʃəwəs

flexuously
BR 'flɛksjʊəsli, 'flɛkʃʊəsli

AM 'flɛkʃəwəsli

flexural
BR 'flɛksjʊrəl, 'flɛksjʊrl, 'flɛkʃ(ə)rəl, 'flɛkʃ(ə)r|
AM 'flɛkʃ(ə)rəl

flexure
BR 'flɛkʃə(r), -z
AM 'flɛkʃər, -z

flibbertigibbet
BR 'flɪbəti,dʒɪbɪt, -s
AM ,flɪbərdi'dʒɪbɪt, -s

flick
BR flɪk, -s, -ɪŋ, -t
AM flɪk, -s, -ɪŋ, -t

flicker
BR 'flɪk|ə(r), -əz, -(ə)rɪŋ, -əd
AM 'flɪk|ər, -ərz, -(ə)rɪŋ, -ərd

flickering
BR 'flɪk(ə)rɪŋ, -z
AM 'flɪk(ə)rɪŋ, -z

flier
BR 'flʌɪə(r), -z
AM 'flaɪər, -z

flies
BR flʌɪz
AM flaɪz

flight
BR flʌɪt, -s
AM flaɪt, -s

flightily
BR 'flʌɪtɪli
AM 'flaɪdɪli

flightiness
BR 'flʌɪtɪnɪs
AM 'flaɪdɪnɪs

flightless
BR 'flʌɪtlɪs
AM 'flaɪtlɪs

flighty
BR 'flʌɪt|i, -ɪə(r), -ɪɪst
AM 'flaɪdi, -ər, -ɪst

flimflam
BR 'flɪmflam, -z, -ɪŋ, -d
AM 'flɪm,flæm, -z, -ɪŋ, -d

flimflammer
BR 'flɪm,flamə(r), -z
AM 'flɪm,flæmər, -z

flimflammery
BR 'flɪm,flam(ə)ri
AM 'flɪm,flæməri

flimsily
BR 'flɪmzɪli
AM 'flɪmzɪli

flimsiness
BR 'flɪmzɪnɪs
AM 'flɪmzɪnɪs

flimsy
BR 'flɪmz|i, -ɪə(r), -ɪɪst
AM 'flɪmzi, -ər, -ɪst

flinch
BR flɪn(t)ʃ, -ɪz, -ɪŋ, -t
AM flɪn(t)ʃ, -ɪz, -ɪŋ, -t

flincher
BR ˈflɪn(t)ʃə(r), -z
AM ˈflɪn(t)ʃər, -z
flinchingly
BR ˈflɪn(t)ʃɪŋli
AM ˈflɪn(t)ʃɪŋli
flinders
BR ˈflɪndəz
AM ˈflɪndərz
fling
BR flɪŋ, -z, -ɪŋ
AM flɪŋ, -z, -ɪŋ
flinger
BR ˈflɪŋə(r), -z
AM ˈflɪŋər, -z
Flinn
BR flɪn
AM flɪn
flint
BR flɪnt, -s
AM flɪnt, -s
flintily
BR ˈflɪntɪli
AM ˈflɪn(t)ɪli
flintiness
BR ˈflɪntɪnɪs
AM ˈflɪn(t)inɪs
flintlock
BR ˈflɪntlɒk, -s
AM ˈflɪntˌlɑk, -s
Flintshire
BR ˈflɪntʃ(ɪ)ə(r)
AM ˈflɪn(t)ʃɪ(ə)r
Flintstones
BR ˈflɪntstəʊnz
AM ˈflɪn(t)ˌstoʊnz
flinty
BR ˈflɪnt|i, -ɪə(r), -ɪɪst
AM ˈflɪn(t)i, -ər, -ɪst
flip
BR flɪp, -s, -ɪŋ, -t
AM flɪp, -s, -ɪŋ, -t
flipflop
BR ˈflɪpflɒp, -s, -ɪŋ, -t
AM ˈflɪpˌflɑp, -s, -ɪŋ, -t
flippancy
BR ˈflɪp(ə)nsi
AM ˈflɪpənsi
flippant
BR ˈflɪp(ə)nt
AM ˈflɪpənt
flippantly
BR ˈflɪp(ə)ntli
AM ˈflɪpən(t)li
flippantness
BR ˈflɪp(ə)ntnəs
AM ˈflɪpən(t)nəs
flipper
BR ˈflɪpə(r), -z
AM ˈflɪpər, -z
FLIR
BR flɪə(r)
AM flɪ(ə)r
flirt
BR flɜːt, -s, -ɪŋ, -ɪd
AM flɜr|t, -ts, -dɪŋ, -dəd

flirtation
BR fləˈteɪʃn, -z
AM flərˈteɪʃən, -z
flirtatious
BR fləˈteɪʃəs
AM flərˈteɪʃəs
flirtatiously
BR fləˈteɪʃəsli
AM flərˈteɪʃəsli
flirtatiousness
BR fləˈteɪʃəsnəs
AM flərˈteɪʃəsnəs
flirty
BR ˈflɜːt|i, -ɪə(r), -ɪɪst
AM ˈflɜrdi, -ər, -ɪst
flit
BR flɪt, -s, -ɪŋ, -ɪd
AM flɪ|t, -ts, -dɪŋ, -dɪd
flitch
BR flɪtʃ, -ɪz
AM flɪtʃ, -ɪz
flitter
BR ˈflɪt|ə(r), -əz, -(ə)rɪŋ, -əd
AM ˈflɪd|ər, -ərd, -(ə)rɪŋ, -ərd
Flitton
BR ˈflɪtn
AM ˈflɪtn
flivver
BR ˈflɪvə(r), -z
AM ˈflɪvər, -z
Flixton
BR ˈflɪkst(ə)n
AM ˈflɪkstən
flixweed
BR ˈflɪkswiːd
AM ˈflɪksˌwid
Flo
BR fləʊ
AM floʊ
float
BR fləʊt, -s, -ɪŋ, -ɪd
AM floʊ|t, -ts, -dɪŋ, -dəd
floatability
BR ˌfləʊtəˈbɪlɪti
AM ˌfloʊdəˈbɪlɪdi
floatable
BR ˈfləʊtəbl
AM ˈfloʊdəbəl
floatage
BR ˈfləʊtɪdʒ
AM ˈfloʊdɪdʒ
floatation
BR fləʊˈteɪʃn, -z
AM floʊˈteɪʃən, -z
floater
BR ˈfləʊtə(r), -z
AM ˈfloʊdər, -z
floatingly
BR ˈfləʊtɪŋli
AM ˈfloʊdɪŋli
floatplane
BR ˈfləʊtpleɪn, -z
AM ˈfloʊtˌpleɪn, -z
floaty
BR ˈfləʊt|i, -ɪz

floc
AM ˈfloʊdi, -z
floc
BR flɒk, -s
AM flɑk, -s
flocci
BR ˈflɒksʌɪ
AM ˈflɑˌkaɪ, ˈflɑkˌsaɪ
flocculate
BR ˈflɒkjʊleɪt, -s, -ɪŋ, -ɪd
AM ˈflɑkjəˌleɪ|t, -ts, -dɪŋ, -dɪd
flocculation
BR ˌflɒkjʊˈleɪʃn
AM ˌflɑkjəˈleɪʃən
floccule
BR ˈflɒkjuːl, -z
AM ˈflɑˌkjul, -z
flocculence
BR ˈflɒkjələns, ˈflɒkjʊlns
AM ˈflɑkjələns
flocculent
BR ˈflɒkjʊlənt, ˈflɒkjəlnt
AM ˈflɑkjələnt
flocculently
BR ˈflɒkjʊləntli, ˈflɒkjəlntli
AM ˈflɑkjələn(t)li
flocculi
BR ˈflɒkjʊlʌɪ
AM ˈflɑkjəˌlaɪ
flocculus
BR ˈflɒkjʊləs
AM ˈflɑkjələs
floccus
BR ˈflɒkəs
AM ˈflɑkəs
flock
BR flɒk, -s, -ɪŋ, -t
AM flɑk, -s, -ɪŋ, -t
flocky
BR ˈflɒk|i, -ɪə(r), -ɪɪst
AM ˈflɑki, -ər, -ɪst
Flodden Field
BR ˌflɒdn ˈfiːld
AM ˌflɑdən ˈfild
floe
BR fləʊ, -z
AM floʊ, -z
Floella
BR fləʊˈɛlə(r)
AM fləˈwɛlə
flog
BR flɒg, -z, -ɪŋ, -d
AM flɑg, -z, -ɪŋ, -d
flogger
BR ˈflɒgə(r), -z
AM ˈflɑgər, -z
flong
BR flɒŋ
AM flɒŋ, flɑŋ
flood
BR flʌd, -z, -ɪŋ, -ɪd
AM fləd, -z, -ɪŋ, -əd

floodgate
BR ˈflʌdgeɪt, -s
AM ˈflədˌgeɪt, -s
floodlight
BR ˈflʌdlʌɪt, -s, -ɪŋ, -ɪd
AM ˈflədˌlaɪ|t, -ts, -dɪŋ, -dɪd
floodlit
BR ˈflʌdlɪt
AM ˈflədˌlɪt
Flook
BR flʊk, fluːk
AM flʊk, fluk
floor
BR flɔː(r), -z, -ɪŋ, -d
AM flɔ(ə)r, -z, -ɪŋ, -d
floorboard
BR ˈflɔːbɔːd, -z
AM ˈflɔrˌbɔ(ə)rd, -z
floorcloth
BR ˈflɔː klɒ|θ, -θs\-ðz
AM ˈflɔr ˌklɔ|θ, ˈflɔr ˌklɑ|θ, -θs\-ðz
flooring
BR ˈflɔːrɪŋ, -z
AM ˈflɔrɪŋ, -z
floorless
BR ˈflɔːləs
AM ˈflɔrləs
floosie
BR ˈfluːz|i, -ɪz
AM ˈfluzi, -z
floosy
BR ˈfluːz|i, -ɪz
AM ˈfluzi, -z
floozie
BR ˈfluːz|i, -ɪz
AM ˈfluzi, -z
floozy
BR ˈfluːz|i, -ɪz
AM ˈfluzi, -z
flop
BR flɒp, -s, -ɪŋ, -t
AM flɑp, -s, -ɪŋ, -t
flophouse
BR ˈflɒphaʊ|s, -zɪz
AM ˈflɑp,(h)aʊ|s, -zəz
floppily
BR ˈflɒpɪli
AM ˈflɑpəli
floppiness
BR ˈflɒpɪnɪs
AM ˈflɑpɪnɪs
floppy
BR ˈflɒp|i, -ɪə(r), -ɪɪst
AM ˈflɑpi, -ər, -ɪst
flora
BR ˈflɔːrə(r)
AM ˈflɔrə
floral
BR ˈflɔːrəl, ˈflɔːr|
AM ˈflɔrəl
florally
BR ˈflɔːr|i, ˈflɔːrəli
AM ˈflɔrəli
floreat
BR ˈflɒrɪat, ˈflɔːrɪat

AM ˈflɒriˌæt
Florence
BR ˈflɒrəns, ˈflɒrns
AM ˈflɔːrəns
Florentine
BR ˈflɒrəntʌɪn, ˈflɒrntʌɪn, ˈflɒrəntiːn, ˈflɒrntiːn, -z
AM ˈflɔːrənˌtin, -z
Flores
BR ˈflɔːrɪz, ˈflɔːriːz, ˈflɔːrɪs
AM ˈflɔːrəs
florescence
BR fləˈrɛsns, flɔːˈrɛsns, flʊˈrɛsns
AM flʊˈrɛsəns, flɔːˈrɛsəns, fləˈrɛsəns
floret
BR ˈflɒrɪt, ˈflɔːrɪt, -s
AM ˈflɔːrət, -s
Florey
BR ˈflɔːri
AM ˈflɒri
floriate
BR ˈflɒrɪeɪt, ˈflɔːrɪeɪt, -s, -ɪŋ, -ɪd
AM ˈflɒriˌeɪ|t, -ts, -dɪŋ, -dɪd
floribunda
BR ˌflɒrɪˈbʌndə(r), ˌflɔːrɪˈbʌndə(r)
AM ˌflɔːrəˈbəndə
floricultural
BR ˌflɔːrɪˈkʌltʃ(ə)rəl, ˌflɔːrɪˈkʌltʃ(ə)rl̩, ˌflɒrɪˈkʌltʃ(ə)rəl, ˌflɒrɪˈkʌltʃ(ə)rl̩
AM ˈflɔːrəˌkəltʃ(ə)rəl
floriculture
BR ˈflɔːrɪˌkʌltʃə(r), ˈflɒrɪˌkʌltʃə(r)
AM ˈflɔːrəˌkəltʃər
floriculturist
BR ˌflɔːrɪˈkʌltʃ(ə)rɪst, ˌflɒrɪˈkʌltʃ(ə)rɪst, -s
AM ˈflɔːrəˌkəltʃ(ə)rəst, -s
florid
BR ˈflɒr|ɪd, -ɪdɪst
AM ˈflɔːrɪd, ˈflɑːrɪd, -ɪst
Florida
BR ˈflɒrɪdə(r)
AM ˈflɔːrɪdə
Floridian
BR flɒˈrɪdɪən, fləˈrɪdɪən, -z
AM ˈflɔːrɪdiən, -z
floridity
BR flɒˈrɪdɪti, fləˈrɪdɪti
AM fləˈrɪdɪdi
floridly
BR ˈflɒrɪdli
AM ˈflɒrɪdli, ˈflɑːrɪdli
floridness
BR ˈflɒrɪdnɪs
AM ˈflɔːrɪdnɪs, ˈflɑːrɪdnɪs

floriferous
BR flɒˈrɪf(ə)rəs, fləˈrɪf(ə)rəs
AM flɔːˈrɪfərəs
florilegia
BR ˌflɒrɪˈliːdʒɪə(r), ˌflɔːrɪˈliːdʒɪə(r)
AM ˌflɒriˈlidʒiə
florilegium
BR ˌflɒrɪˈliːdʒɪəm, ˌflɔːrɪˈliːdʒɪəm
AM ˌflɒriˈlidʒiəm
florin
BR ˈflɒrɪn, -z
AM ˈflɔːrən, ˈflɑːrən, -z
Florio
BR ˈflɒrɪəʊ
AM ˈflɔːrioʊ
florist
BR ˈflɒrɪst, -s
AM ˈflɔːrəst, -s
floristic
BR flɒˈrɪstɪk, fləˈrɪstɪk, -s
AM fləˈrɪstɪk, -s
floristically
BR flɒˈrɪstɪkli, fləˈrɪstɪkli
AM fləˈrɪstɪk(ə)li
floristry
BR ˈflɒrɪstri
AM ˈflɔːrəstri
Florrie
BR ˈflɒri
AM ˈflɔːri
floruit
BR ˈflɒrʊɪt, ˈflɔːrʊɪt
AM ˈflɔːrəwət
flory
BR ˈflɔːri
AM ˈflɒri
floscular
BR ˈflɒskjələ(r)
AM ˈflɑːskjələr
flosculous
BR ˈflɒskjələs
AM ˈflɑːskjələs
floss
BR flɒs, -ɪz, -ɪŋ, -t
AM flɔːs, flɑːs, -əz, -ɪŋ, -t
Flossie
BR ˈflɒsi
AM ˈflɔːsi, ˈflɑːsi
flossy
BR ˈflɒs|i, -ɪə(r), -ɪɪst
AM ˈflɔːsi, ˈflɑːsi, -ər, -ɪɪst
flotation
BR fləˈ(ʊ)teɪʃn, -z
AM floʊˈteɪʃən, -z
flote
BR fləʊt
AM floʊt
flotilla
BR fləˈtɪlə(r), -z
AM floʊˈtɪlə, fləˈtɪlə, -z
flotsam
BR ˈflɒts(ə)m

AM ˈflɑːtsəm
Flotta
BR ˈflɒtə(r)
AM ˈflɑːdə, ˈfladə
flounce
BR flaʊns, -ɪz, -ɪŋ, -t
AM flaʊns, -əz, -ɪŋ, -t
flounder
BR ˈflaʊnd|ə(r), -əz, -(ə)rɪŋ, -əd
AM ˈflaʊnd|ər, -ərz, -(ə)rɪŋ, -ərd
flounderer
BR ˈflaʊnd(ə)rə(r), -z
AM ˈflaʊndərər, -z
flour
BR ˈflaʊə(r), -z, -ɪŋ, -d
AM ˈflaʊ(ə)r, -z, -ɪŋ, -d
flouresce
BR flʊəˈrɛs, flʊˈrɛs, -ɪz, -ɪŋ, -t
AM fləˈrɛs, flɔːˈrɛs, -əz, -ɪŋ, -t
flouriness
BR ˈflaʊ(ə)rɪnɪs
AM ˈflaʊ(ə)rinɪs
flourish
BR ˈflʌr|ɪʃ, -ɪʃɪz, -ɪʃɪŋ, -ɪʃt
AM ˈfləːrɪʃ, -ɪz, -ɪŋ, -t
flourisher
BR ˈflʌrɪʃə(r)
AM ˈfləːrɪʃər
flourishy
BR ˈflʌrɪʃi
AM ˈfləːrɪʃi
flourmill
BR ˈflaʊəmɪl, -z
AM ˈflaʊ(ə)rˌmɪl, -z
floury
BR ˈflaʊ(ə)r|i, -ɪə(r), -ɪɪst
AM ˈflaʊ(ə)ri, -ər, -ɪɪst
flout
BR flaʊt, -s, -ɪŋ, -ɪd
AM flaʊ|t, -ts, -dɪŋ, -dəd
flow
BR fləʊ, -z, -ɪŋ, -d
AM floʊ, -z, -ɪŋ, -d
flowage
BR ˈfləʊ|ɪdʒ, -ɪdʒɪz
AM ˈfloʊɪdʒ, -ɪz
flowchart
BR ˈfləʊtʃɑː|t, -s
AM ˈfloʊˌtʃɑrt, -s
flower
BR ˈflaʊə(r), -z, -ɪŋ, -d
AM ˈfla|ʊər, -ʊərz, -ʊ(ə)rɪŋ, -ʊərd
flowerbed
BR ˈflaʊəbɛd, -z
AM ˈflaʊərˌbɛd, -z
flowerer
BR ˈflaʊərə(r), -z
AM ˈflaʊərər, -z
floweret
BR ˈflaʊərɪt, -s

AM ˈflaʊəˌrɛt, -s
flowerily
BR ˈflaʊərɪli
AM ˈflaʊ(ə)rɪli
floweriness
BR ˈflaʊ(ə)rɪnɪs
AM ˈflaʊ(ə)rinɪs
flowerless
BR ˈflaʊələs
AM ˈflaʊərləs
flowerlike
BR ˈflaʊəlʌɪk
AM ˈflaʊərˌlaɪk
flowerpot
BR ˈflaʊəpɒt, -s
AM ˈflaʊərˌpɑt, -s
Flowers
BR ˈflaʊəz
AM ˈflaʊərz
flowery
BR ˈflaʊər|i, -ɪə(r), -ɪɪst
AM ˈfla|ʊ(ə)ri, -ʊ(ə)riər, -ʊ(ə)riɪst
flowing
BR ˈfləʊɪŋ
AM ˈfloʊɪŋ
flowingly
BR ˈfləʊɪŋli
AM ˈfloʊɪŋli
flown
BR fləʊn
AM floʊn
flowsheet
BR ˈfləʊʃiːt, -s
AM ˈfloʊˌʃit, -s
flowstone
BR ˈfləʊstəʊn
AM ˈfloʊˌstoʊn
Floyd
BR flɔɪd
AM flɔɪd
flu
BR fluː, -z
AM flu, -z
flub
BR flʌb, -z
AM fləb, -z
Fluck
BR flʌk
AM flək
fluctuate
BR ˈflʌktʃʊeɪt, ˈflʌktjʊeɪt, -s, -ɪŋ, -ɪd
AM ˈfləktʃəˌweɪ|t, -ts, -dɪŋ, -dɪd
fluctuation
BR ˌflʌktʃʊˈeɪʃn, ˌflʌktjʊˈeɪʃn, -z
AM ˌfləktʃəˈweɪʃən, -z
flue
BR fluː, -z
AM flu, -z
fluence
BR ˈfluːəns
AM ˈfluəns
fluency
BR ˈfluːənsi

AM 'fluənsi

fluent
BR 'fluːənt
AM 'fluənt

fluently
BR 'fluːəntli
AM 'fluən(t)li

fluff
BR flʌf, -s, -ɪŋ, -t
AM fləf, -s, -ɪŋ, -t

fluffily
BR 'flʌfɪli
AM 'fləfəli

fluffiness
BR 'flʌfɪnɪs
AM 'fləfɪnɪs

fluffy
BR 'flʌf|i, -ɪə(r), -ɪɪst
AM 'fləfi, -ər, -ɪst

Flügelhorn
BR 'fluːglhɔːn, -z
AM 'flugəl,(h)ɔː(ə)rn, -z

fluid
BR 'fluːɪd, -z
AM 'fluɪd, -z

fluidic
BR fluː'ɪdɪk, -s
AM 'fluɪdɪk, -s

fluidify
BR fluː'ɪdɪfʌɪ, -z, -ɪŋ, -d
AM fluː'ɪdə,faɪ, -z, -ɪŋ, -d

fluidisation
BR ,fluːɪdʌɪ'zeɪʃn
AM ,fluədə'zeɪʃən,
,fluə,daɪ'zeɪʃən

fluidise
BR 'fluːɪdʌɪz, -ɪz, -ɪŋ, -d
AM 'fluə,daɪz, -ɪz, -ɪŋ, -d

fluidity
BR fluː'ɪdɪti
AM flu'ɪdɪdi

fluidization
BR ,fluːɪdʌɪ'zeɪʃn
AM ,fluədə'zeɪʃən,
,fluə,daɪ'zeɪʃən

fluidize
BR 'fluːɪdʌɪz, -ɪz, -ɪŋ, -d
AM 'fluə,daɪz, -ɪz, -ɪŋ, -d

fluidly
BR 'fluːɪdli
AM 'fluɪdli

fluidness
BR 'fluːɪdnɪs
AM 'fluɪdnɪs

fluidounce
BR ,fluːɪd'aʊns, -ɪz
AM 'fluɪd'aʊns, -əz

fluke
BR fluːk, -s
AM fluk, -s

flukey
BR 'fluːk|i, -ɪə(r), -ɪɪst
AM 'fluki, -ər, -ɪst

flukily
BR 'fluːkɪli
AM 'flukɪli

flukiness
BR 'fluːkɪnɪs
AM 'flukɪnɪs

fluky
BR 'fluːk|i, -ɪə(r), -ɪɪst
AM 'fluki, -ər, -ɪst

flume
BR fluːm, -z
AM flum, -z

flummery
BR 'flʌm(ə)ri
AM 'fləməri

flummox
BR 'flʌməks, -ɪz, -ɪŋ, -t
AM 'fləməks, -əz, -ɪŋ, -t

flump
BR flʌm|p, -ps, -pɪŋ,
-(p)t
AM fləmp, -s, -ɪŋ, -t

flung
BR flʌŋ
AM fləŋ

flunk
BR flʌŋ|k, -ks, -kɪŋ,
-(k)t
AM fləŋ|k, -ks, -kɪŋ,
-(k)t

flunkey
BR 'flʌŋk|i, -ɪz
AM 'fləŋki, -z

flunkeyism
BR 'flʌŋkɪɪz(ə)m
AM 'fləŋki,ɪzəm

flunky
BR 'flʌŋk|i, -ɪz
AM 'fləŋki, -z

Fluon®
BR 'fluːɒn
AM 'flu,ɑn

fluoresce
BR fluə'rɛs, flɔː'rɛs,
flʊ'rɛs, -ɪz, -ɪŋ, -t
AM flʊ'rɛs, flɔː'rɛs, -əz,
-ɪŋ, -t

fluorescence
BR fluə'rɛsns,
flɔː'rɛsns, flʊ'rɛsns
AM flʊ'rɛsəns,
flɔ'rɛsəns, flə'rɛsəns

fluorescent
BR fluə'rɛsnt,
flɔː'rɛsnt, flʊ'rɛsnt
AM flʊ'rɛsənt,
flɔ'rɛsənt

fluoridate
BR 'fluərɪdeɪt,
'flɔːrɪdeɪt
AM 'flʊrə,deɪt,
'flɔrə,deɪt

fluoridation
BR ,fluərɪ'deɪʃn,
,flɔːrɪ'deɪʃn
AM ,flʊrə'deɪʃən,
,flɔrə'deɪʃən

fluoride
BR 'fluərʌɪd, 'flɔːrʌɪd
AM 'flʊ,raɪd, 'flɔ,raɪd

fluoridisation
BR ,fluərɪdʌɪ'zeɪʃn,
,flɔːrɪdʌɪ'zeɪʃn
AM ,flʊrɪdə'zeɪʃən,
,flʊrɪ,daɪ'zeɪʃən

fluoridization
BR ,fluərɪdʌɪ'zeɪʃn,
,flɔːrɪdʌɪ'zeɪʃn
AM ,flʊrɪdə'zeɪʃən,
,flʊrɪ,daɪ'zeɪʃən

fluorinate
BR 'fluərɪneɪt,
'flɔːrɪneɪt, -s, -ɪŋ, -ɪd
AM 'flʊrə,neɪ|t,
'flɔrə,neɪ|t, -ts, -dɪŋ,
-dɪd

fluorination
BR ,fluərɪ'neɪʃn,
,flɔːrɪ'neɪʃn
AM ,flʊrə'neɪʃən,
,flɔrə'neɪʃən

fluorine
BR 'fluəriːn, 'flɔːriːn
AM 'flʊ,rin, 'flɔ,rin

fluorite
BR 'fluərʌɪt, 'flɔːrʌɪt
AM 'flʊ,raɪt, 'flɔ,raɪt

fluorocarbon
BR 'fluərə(ʊ),kɑːb(ə)n,
'flɔːrə(ʊ),kɑː(b(ə)n, -z
AM 'flʊroʊ,kɑrbən,
'flɔroʊ,kɑrbən, -z

fluoroscope
BR 'fluərəskəʊp,
'flɔːrəskəʊp, -s
AM 'flʊrə,skoʊp,
'flɔrə,skoʊp, -s

fluoroscopy
BR fluə'rɒskəpi,
flɔː'rɒskəpi,
flə'rɒskəpi
AM flʊ'rɑskəpi,
flɔ'raskəpi

fluorosis
BR fluə'rəʊsɪs,
flɔː'rəʊsɪs, flə'rəʊsɪs
AM flʊ'roʊsəs,
flɔ'roʊsəs

fluorspar
BR 'fluəspɑː(r),
'flɔːspɑː(r)
AM 'flʊr,spɑr,
'flɔr,spɑr

flurry
BR 'flʌr|i, -ɪz, -ɪɪŋ, -ɪd
AM 'fləri, -z, -ɪŋ, -d

flush
BR flʌʃ, -ɪz, -ɪŋ, -t
AM fləʃ, -əz, -ɪŋ, -t

flusher
BR 'flʌʃə(r), -z
AM 'fləʃər, -z

Flushing
BR 'flʌʃɪŋ
AM 'fləʃɪŋ

flushness
BR 'flʌʃnəs
AM 'fləʃnəs

fluster
BR 'flʌst|ə(r), -əz,
-(ə)rɪŋ, -əd
AM 'fləst|ər, -ərz,
-(ə)rɪŋ, -ərd

flute
BR fluːt, -s, -ɪŋ, -ɪd
AM flu|t, -ts, -dɪŋ, -dəd

flutelike
BR 'fluːtlʌɪk
AM 'flut,laɪk

flutey
BR 'fluːt|i, -ɪə(r), -ɪɪst
AM 'fludi, -ər, -ɪst

flutist
BR 'fluːtɪst, -s
AM 'fludəst, -s

flutter
BR 'flʌt|ə(r), -əz,
-(ə)rɪŋ, -əd
AM 'flədər, -z, -ɪŋ, -d

flutterer
BR 'flʌt(ə)rə(r), -z
AM 'flədərər, -z

fluttery
BR 'flʌt(ə)ri
AM 'flədəri

fluty
BR 'fluːt|i, -ɪə(r), -ɪɪst
AM 'fludi, -ər, -ɪst

fluvial
BR 'fluːvɪəl
AM 'fluviəl

fluviatile
BR 'fluːvɪətʌɪl
AM 'fluviə,taɪl

fluvioglacial
BR ,fluːvɪəʊ'gleɪʃl
AM ,fluvioʊ'gleɪʃəl

fluviometer
BR ,fluːvɪ'ɒmɪtə(r), -z
AM ,fluvi'ɑmədər, -z

flux
BR flʌks, -ɪz
AM fləks, -əz

fluxion
BR 'flʌkʃn, -z
AM 'fləkʃən, -z

fluxional
BR 'flʌkʃn(ə)l,
'flʌkʃən(ə)l
AM 'fləkʃ(ə)nəl

fluxionary
BR 'flʌkʃn̩ri
AM 'fləkʃə,nɛri

fly
BR flʌɪ, -z, -ɪŋ
AM flaɪ, -z, -ɪŋ

flyable
BR 'flʌɪəbl
AM 'flaɪəbəl

flyaway
BR 'flʌɪəweɪ
AM 'flaɪə,weɪ

flyback
BR 'flʌɪbak
AM 'flaɪ,bæk

flyblown
BR ˈflaɪbləʊn
AM ˈflaɪˌbloʊn

flyby
BR ˈflaɪbʌɪ, -z
AM ˈflaɪˌbaɪ, -z

flycatcher
BR ˈflʌɪˌkatʃə(r), -z
AM ˈflaɪˌkætʃər, -z

flyer
BR ˈflʌɪə(r), -z
AM ˈflaɪər, -z

flyleaf
BR ˈflʌɪliːf
AM ˈflaɪˌlif

flyleaves
BR ˈflʌɪliːvz
AM ˈflaɪˌlivz

Flymo®
BR ˈflʌɪməʊ, -z
AM ˈflaɪmoʊ, -z

flyness
BR ˈflaɪnɪs
AM ˈflaɪnɪs

Flynn
BR flɪn
AM flɪn

flyover
BR ˈflʌɪˌ(ˌ)əʊvə(r), -z
AM ˈflaɪˌoʊvər, -z

flypaper
BR ˈflʌɪˌpeɪpə(r), -z
AM ˈflaɪˌpeɪpər, -z

flypast
BR ˈflʌɪpɑːst, ˈflʌɪpast, -s
AM ˈflaɪˌpæst, -s

flysheet
BR ˈflʌɪʃiːt, -s
AM ˈflaɪˌʃit, -s

flyswatter
BR ˈflʌɪˌswɒtə(r), -z
AM ˈflaɪˌswɑdər, -z

flyting
BR ˈflʌɪtɪŋ, -z
AM ˈflaɪdɪŋ, -z

flytrap
BR ˈflʌɪtrap, -s
AM ˈflaɪˌtræp, -s

flyway
BR ˈflʌɪweɪ, -z
AM ˈflaɪˌweɪ, -z

flyweight
BR ˈflʌɪweɪt, -s
AM ˈflaɪˌweɪt, -s

flywheel
BR ˈflʌɪwiːl, -z
AM ˈflaɪˌ(h)wil, -z

flywhisk
BR ˈflʌɪwɪsk, -s
AM ˈflaɪˌ(h)wɪsk, -s

FNMA
BR ˌfanɪˈmeɪ
AM ˌfæniˈmeɪ

foal
BR fəʊl, -z, -ɪŋ, -d
AM foʊl, -z, -ɪŋ, -d

foam
BR fəʊm, -z, -ɪŋ, -d
AM foʊm, -z, -ɪŋ, -d

foaminess
BR ˈfəʊmɪnɪs
AM ˈfoʊmɪnɪs

foamless
BR ˈfəʊmləs
AM ˈfoʊmləs

foamy
BR ˈfəʊmi
AM ˈfoʊmi

fob
BR fɒb, -z, -ɪŋ, -d
AM fab, -z, -ɪŋ, -d

fobwatch
BR ˈfɒbwɒtʃ, -ɪz
AM ˈfab,watʃ, ˈfab,wɔtʃ, -əz

focaccia
BR fəˈkatʃə(r)
AM foʊˈkatʃiə

focal
BR ˈfəʊkl
AM ˈfoʊkəl

focalisation
BR ˌfəʊkəlʌɪˈzeɪʃn, ˌfəʊklʌɪˈzeɪʃn
AM ˌfoʊkələˈzeɪʃən, ˌfoʊkəˌlaɪˈzeɪʃən

focalise
BR ˈfəʊkəlʌɪz, ˈfəʊkḷʌɪz, -ɪz, -ɪŋ, -d
AM ˈfoʊkəˌlaɪz, -ɪz, -ɪŋ, -d

focalization
BR ˌfəʊkəlʌɪˈzeɪʃn, ˌfəʊklʌɪˈzeɪʃn
AM ˌfoʊkələˈzeɪʃən, ˌfoʊkəˌlaɪˈzeɪʃən

focalize
BR ˈfəʊkəlʌɪz, ˈfəʊkḷʌɪz, -ɪz, -ɪŋ, -d
AM ˈfoʊkəˌlaɪz, -ɪz, -ɪŋ, -d

Foch
BR fɒʃ
AM fɔʃ, faʃ

Fochabers
BR ˈfɒxəbəz, ˈfɒkəbəz
AM ˈfakəbərs

foci
BR ˈfəʊkʌɪ, ˈfəʊsʌɪ
AM ˈfoʊˌsaɪ

foc's'le
BR ˈfəʊksl, -z
AM ˈfoʊksəl, -z

fo'c'sle
BR ˈfəʊksl, -z
AM ˈfoʊksəl, -z

fo'c's'le
BR ˈfəʊksl, -z
AM ˈfoʊksəl, -z

focus
BR ˈfəʊkəs, -ɪz, -ɪŋ, -t
AM ˈfoʊkəs, -əz, -ɪŋ, -t

focuser
BR ˈfəʊkəsə(r), -z

AM ˈfoʊkəsər, -z

fodder
BR ˈfɒd|ə(r), -əz, -(ə)rɪŋ, -əd
AM ˈfadər, -z, -ɪŋ, -d

Foden
BR ˈfəʊdn
AM ˈfoʊdən

foe
BR fəʊ, -z
AM foʊ, -z

foehn
BR fəːn
AM fən

foeman
BR ˈfəʊmən
AM ˈfoʊmən

foemen
BR ˈfəʊmən, ˈfəʊmɛn
AM ˈfoʊˌmɛn, ˈfoʊmən

foetal
BR ˈfiːtl
AM ˈfidl

foeticide
BR ˈfiːtɪsʌɪd
AM ˈfidəˌsaɪd

foetid
BR ˈfɛtɪd, ˈfiːtɪd
AM ˈfɛdəd

foetus
BR ˈfiːtəs, -ɪz
AM ˈfidəs, -əz

fog
BR fɒg, -z, -ɪŋ, -d
AM fɔg, fag, -z, -ɪŋ, -d

Fogarty
BR ˈfɒgəti
AM ˈfoʊgərdi

fogau
BR ˈfəʊguː, ˈfəʊgəʊ, -z
AM ˈfoʊgu, ˈfoʊgoʊ, -z

fogbank
BR ˈfɒgbaŋk, -s
AM ˈfɔg,bæŋk, ˈfag,bæŋk, -s

fogbound
BR ˈfɒgbaʊnd
AM ˈfɔg,baʊnd, ˈfag,baʊnd

fog-bow
BR ˈfɒgbəʊ, -z
AM ˈfɔg,boʊ, ˈfag,boʊ, -z

Fogerty
BR ˈfɒgəti
AM ˈfoʊgərdi

fogey
BR ˈfəʊg|i, -ɪz
AM ˈfoʊgi, -z

fogeydom
BR ˈfəʊgɪdəm
AM ˈfoʊgɪdəm

fogeyish
BR ˈfəʊgɪɪʃ
AM ˈfoʊgiɪʃ

Fogg
BR fɒg
AM fɔg, fag

foggily
BR ˈfɒgɪli
AM ˈfɔgəli, ˈfagəli

fogginess
BR ˈfɒgɪnɪs
AM ˈfɔgɪnɪs, ˈfagɪnɪs

foggy
BR ˈfɒg|i, -ɪə(r), -ɪɪst
AM ˈfɔgi, ˈfagi, -ər, -ɪst

foghorn
BR ˈfɒghɔːn, -z
AM ˈfɔg,(h)ɔ(ə)rn, ˈfag,(h)ɔ(ə)rn, -z

fogy
BR ˈfəʊg|i, -ɪz
AM ˈfoʊgi, -z

fogydom
BR ˈfəʊgɪdəm
AM ˈfoʊgɪdəm

fogyish
BR ˈfəʊgɪɪʃ
AM ˈfoʊgiɪʃ

fohn
BR fəːn
AM fən

föhn
BR fəːn
AM fən

foible
BR ˈfɔɪbl, -z
AM ˈfɔɪbəl, -z

foie gras
BR ˌfwɑː ˈgrɑː(r)
AM ˌfwɑ ˈgrɑ

foil
BR fɔɪl, -z, -ɪŋ, -d
AM fɔɪl, -z, -ɪŋ, -d

foilist
BR ˈfɔɪlɪst, -s
AM ˈfɔɪlɪst, -s

foist
BR fɔɪst, -s, -ɪŋ, -ɪd
AM fɔɪst, -s, -ɪŋ, -ɪd

Fokker®
BR ˈfɒkə(r), -z
AM ˈfakər, -z

folacin
BR ˈfəʊləsɪn
AM ˈfɔləsən, ˈfaləsən

fold
BR fəʊld, -z, -ɪŋ, -ɪd
AM foʊld, -z, -ɪŋ, -əd

foldable
BR ˈfəʊldəbl
AM ˈfoʊldəbəl

foldaway
BR ˈfəʊldəweɪ
AM ˈfoʊldə,weɪ

foldback
BR ˈfəʊl(d)bak, -s
AM ˈfoʊl(d),bæk, -s

foldboat
BR ˈfəʊl(d)bəʊt, -s
AM ˈfoʊl(d),boʊt, -s

folder
BR ˈfəʊldə(r), -z
AM ˈfoʊldər, -z

folderol
BR ˈfɒldərɒl, -z
AM ˈfɔldəˌrɔl, ˈfɑldəˌrɑl, -z

foldout
BR ˈfəʊldaʊt, -s
AM ˈfoʊlˌdaʊt, -s

fold-up
BR ˈfəʊldʌp
AM ˈfoʊldəp

Foley
BR ˈfəʊli
AM ˈfoʊli

Folger
BR ˈfəʊldʒə(r), ˈfɒldʒə(r)
AM ˈfoʊldʒər

folia
BR ˈfəʊlɪə(r)
AM ˈfoʊljə, ˈfoʊliə

foliaceous
BR ˌfəʊlɪˈeɪʃəs
AM ˌfoʊliˈeɪʃəs

foliage
BR ˈfəʊlɪɪdʒ
AM ˈfoʊl(i)ɪdʒ

foliar
BR ˈfəʊlɪə(r)
AM ˈfoʊljər, ˈfoʊliər

foliate[1]
adjective
BR ˈfəʊlɪət, ˈfəʊlɪeɪt
AM ˈfoʊliət, ˈfoʊliˌeɪt

foliate[2]
verb
BR ˈfəʊlɪeɪt, -s, -ɪŋ, -ɪd
AM ˈfoʊliˌeɪ|t, -ts, -dɪŋ, -dɪd

foliation
BR ˌfəʊlɪˈeɪʃn, -z
AM ˌfoʊliˈeɪʃən, -z

folic
BR ˈfəʊlɪk, ˈfɒlɪk
AM ˈfoʊlɪk, ˈfɑlɪk

Folies-Bergère
BR ˌfɒlɪbəˈʒɛː(r), ˌfɒlɪbɛːˈʒɛː(r)
AM fɔˌlibərˈʒɛ(ə)r

folio
BR ˈfəʊlɪəʊ, -z
AM ˈfoʊlioʊ, -z

foliole
BR ˈfəʊlɪəʊl, -z
AM ˈfoʊliˌoʊl, -z

foliot
BR ˈfɒlɪət, -s
AM ˈfoʊliət, -s

folium
BR ˈfəʊlɪəm
AM ˈfoʊliəm

folk
BR fəʊk, -s
AM foʊk, -s

Folkestone
BR ˈfəʊkst(ə)n
AM ˈfoʊkˌstoʊn

folkie
BR ˈfəʊk|i, -ɪz
AM ˈfoʊki, -z

folkiness
BR ˈfəʊkɪnɪs
AM ˈfoʊkinɪs

folkish
BR ˈfəʊkɪʃ
AM ˈfoʊkɪʃ

folklore
BR ˈfəʊklɔː(r)
AM ˈfoʊkˌlɔ(ə)r

folkloric
BR fəʊkˈlɔːrɪk
AM foʊkˈlɔrɪk

folklorist
BR ˈfəʊklɔːrɪst, -s
AM ˈfoʊkˌlɔrəst, -s

folkloristic
BR ˌfəʊkləˈrɪstɪk
AM ˌfoʊkləˈrɪstɪk

folksily
BR ˈfəʊksɪli
AM ˈfoʊksəli

folksiness
BR ˈfəʊksɪnɪs
AM ˈfoʊksinɪs

folksong
BR ˈfəʊksɒŋ, -z
AM ˈfoʊkˌsɔŋ, ˈfoʊkˌsɑŋ, -z

folksy
BR ˈfəʊks|i, -ɪə(r), -ɪɪst
AM ˈfoʊksi, -ər, -ɪst

folktale
BR ˈfəʊkteɪl, -z
AM ˈfoʊkˌteɪl, -z

folkway
BR ˈfəʊkweɪ, -z
AM ˈfoʊkˌweɪ, -z

folkweave
BR ˈfəʊkwiːv
AM ˈfoʊkˌwiv

folky
BR ˈfəʊki
AM ˈfoʊki

Follick
BR ˈfɒlɪk
AM ˈfɑlək

follicle
BR ˈfɒlɪkl, -z
AM ˈfɑləkəl, -z

follicular
BR fɒˈlɪkjʉlə(r), fəˈlɪkjʉlə(r)
AM fəˈlɪkjələr

folliculate
BR fɒˈlɪkjʉlət, fəˈlɪkjʉlət
AM fəˈlɪkjələt, fəˈlɪkjəˌleɪt

folliculated
BR fɒˈlɪkjʉleɪtɪd, fəˈlɪkjʉleɪtɪd
AM fəˈlɪkjəˌleɪdɪd

follow
BR ˈfɒləʊ, -z, -ɪŋ, -d
AM ˈfɑloʊ, -z, -ɪŋ, -d

follower
BR ˈfɒləʊə(r), -z
AM ˈfɑloʊər, -z

following
BR ˈfɒləʊɪŋ, -z
AM ˈfɑloʊɪŋ, -z

follow-my-leader
BR ˌfɒlə(ʊ)məˈliːdə(r)
AM ˌfɑloʊmaɪˈlidər

folly
BR ˈfɒl|i, -ɪz
AM ˈfɑli, -z

Folsom[1]
places in US
BR ˈfəʊls(ə)m
AM ˈfoʊlsəm

Folsom[2]
surname
BR ˈfəʊls(ə)m, ˈfɒls(ə)m
AM ˈfoʊlsəm

Fomalhaut
BR ˈfɒml̩əʊt, ˈfɒmələʊt
AM ˈfoʊməlˌ(h)ɔt, ˈfoʊməlˌ(h)ɑt

foment[1]
noun
BR ˈfəʊmɛnt
AM ˈfoʊˌmɛnt

foment[2]
verb
BR fəˈmɛnt, -s, -ɪŋ, -ɪd
AM ˌfoʊˈmɛn|t, -ts, -(t)ɪŋ, -(t)əd

fomentation
BR ˌfəʊmɛnˈteɪʃn, ˌfəʊm(ə)nˈteɪʃn
AM ˌfoʊmɛnˈteɪʃən, ˌfoʊmənˈteɪʃən

fomenter
BR fəˈmɛntə(r), -z
AM ˌfoʊˈmɛn(t)ər, -z

fomites
BR ˈfəʊmɪtiːz
AM ˈfoʊməˌtiz

fond
BR fɒnd, -ə(r), -ɪst
AM fɑnd, -ər, -əst

Fonda
BR ˈfɒndə(r)
AM ˈfɑndə

fondant
BR ˈfɒnd(ə)nt, -s
AM ˈfɑndnt, -s

fondle
BR ˈfɒnd|l, -lz, -l̩ɪŋ\-lɪŋ, -ld
AM ˈfɑn|dəl, -dəlz, -(d)(ə)lɪŋ, -dəld

fondler
BR ˈfɒndl̩ə(r), ˈfɒndlə(r), -z
AM ˈfɑn(də)lər, -z

fondly
BR ˈfɒndli
AM ˈfɑn(d)li

fondness
BR ˈfɒn(d)nəs
AM ˈfɑn(d)nəs

fondu
BR ˈfɒnd(j)uː, -z
AM ˌfɑnˈd(j)u, -z

fondue
BR ˈfɒnd(j)uː, -z
AM ˌfɑnˈd(j)u, -z

font
BR fɒnt, -s
AM fɑnt, -s

Fontainebleau
BR ˈfɒntɪnbləʊ
AM ˈfɑntnˌbloʊ

fontal
BR ˈfɒntl
AM ˈfɑntl

Fontana
BR fɒnˈtɑːnə(r)
AM ˌfɑnˈtænə

fontanel
BR ˌfɒntəˈnɛl, -z
AM ˌfɑntnˈɛl, -z

fontanelle
BR ˌfɒntəˈnɛl, -z
AM ˌfɑntnˈɛl, -z

Fonteyn
BR ˈfɒnteɪn
AM ˌfɑnˈteɪn

Fontwell
BR ˈfɒntw(ɛ)l
AM ˈfɑntˌwɛl

Foochow
BR ˈfuːˈtʃaʊ
AM ˈfuˈtʃaʊ

food
BR fuːd, -z
AM fud, -z

foodie
BR ˈfuːd|i, -ɪz
AM ˈfudi, -z

foodism
BR ˈfuːdɪz(ə)m
AM ˈfudɪzəm

foodstuff
BR ˈfuːdstʌf, -s
AM ˈfudˌstəf, -s

Fookes
BR fuːks
AM fuks

fool
BR fuːl, -z, -ɪŋ, -d
AM ful, -z, -ɪŋ, -d

foolery
BR ˈfuːlər|i, -ɪz
AM ˈfuləri, -z

foolhardily
BR ˈfuːlˌhɑːdɪli
AM ˈfulˌ(h)ɑrdəli

foolhardiness
BR ˈfuːlˌhɑːdɪnɪs
AM ˈfulˌ(h)ɑrdinɪs

foolhardy
BR ˈfuːlˌhɑːdi
AM ˈfulˌ(h)ɑrdi

foolish
BR ˈfuːlɪʃ
AM ˈfulɪʃ
foolishly
BR ˈfuːlɪʃli
AM ˈfulɪʃli
foolishness
BR ˈfuːlɪʃnɪs
AM ˈfulɪʃnɪs
foolproof
BR ˈfuːlpruːf
AM ˈfulˌpruf
foolscap
BR ˈfuːlskap, ˈfuːlzkap
AM ˈfʊlzˌkæp
Foord
BR fɔːd
AM fɔ(ə)rd
foot
BR fʊt, -s, -ɪŋ, -ɪd
AM fʊ|t, -ts, -ɪŋ, -dəd
footage
BR ˈfʊtɪdʒ
AM ˈfʊdɪdʒ
football
BR ˈfʊtbɔːl, -z
AM ˈfʊtˌbɔl, ˈfʊtˌbal, -z
footballer
BR ˈfʊtbɔːlə(r), -z
AM ˈfʊtˌbɔlər,
ˈfʊtˌbalər, -z
footbath
BR ˈfʊt|bɑːθ, ˈfʊt|baθ,
-bɑːðz\-baˈθs\-baθs
AM ˈfʊtˌbæθ, -s, -ðz
footbed
BR ˈfʊtbɛd, -z
AM ˈfʊtˌbɛd, -z
footboard
BR ˈfʊtbɔːd, -z
AM ˈfʊtˌbɔ(ə)rd, -z
footbrake
BR ˈfʊtbreɪk, -s
AM ˈfʊtˌbreɪk, -s
footbridge
BR ˈfʊtbrɪdʒ, -ɪz
AM ˈfʊtˌbrɪdʒ, -ɪz
footcandle
BR ˈfʊtˌkandl, -z
AM ˈfʊtˌkændəl, -z
Foote
BR fʊt
AM fʊt
footer
BR ˈfʊtə(r)
AM ˈfʊdər
footfall
BR ˈfʊtfɔːl, -z
AM ˈfʊtˌfɔl, ˈfʊtˌfal, -z
footgear
BR ˈfʊtgɪə(r)
AM ˈfʊtˌgɪ(ə)r
foothill
BR ˈfʊthɪl, -z
AM ˈfʊtˌ(h)ɪl, -z
foothold
BR ˈfʊthəʊld, -z

foothold (cont.)
AM ˈfʊtˌ(h)oʊld, -z
footing
BR ˈfʊtɪŋ, -z
AM ˈfʊdɪŋ, -z
footle
BR ˈfuːt|l, -lz, -lɪŋ \-lɪŋ,
-ld
AM ˈfudəl, -z, -ɪŋ, -d
footless
BR ˈfʊtləs
AM ˈfʊtləs
footlights
BR ˈfʊtlʌɪts
AM ˈfʊtˌlaɪts
footlocker
BR ˈfʊtˌlɒkə(r), -z
AM ˈfʊtˌlakər, -z
footloose
BR ˈfʊtluːs
AM ˈfʊtˌlus
footman
BR ˈfʊtmən
AM ˈfʊtmən
footmark
BR ˈfʊtmɑːk, -s
AM ˈfʊtˌmark, -s
footmen
BR ˈfʊtmən
AM ˈfʊtˌmɛn, fʊtmən
footnote
BR ˈfʊtnəʊt, -s, -ɪŋ, -ɪd
AM ˈfʊtˌnoʊ|t, -ts, -dɪŋ,
-dəd
footpad
BR ˈfʊtpad, -z
AM ˈfʊtˌpæd, -z
footpath
BR ˈfʊtpɑː|θ, ˈfʊtpa|θ,
-ðz
AM ˈfʊtˌpæ|θ, -ðz
footplate
BR ˈfʊtpleɪt, -s
AM ˈfʊtˌpleɪt, -s
footprint
BR ˈfʊtprɪnt, -s
AM ˈfʊtˌprɪnt, -s
footrest
BR ˈfʊtrɛst, -s
AM ˈfʊtˌrɛst, -s
footsie
BR ˈfʊtsi
AM ˈfʊtsi
footslog
BR ˈfʊtslɒg, -z, -ɪŋ, -d
AM ˈfʊtˌslag, -z, -ɪŋ, -d
footslogger
BR ˈfʊtˌslɒgə(r), -z
AM ˈfʊtˌslagər, -z
footsore
BR ˈfʊtsɔː(r)
AM ˈfʊtˌsɔ(ə)r
footstalk
BR ˈfʊtstɔːk, -s
AM ˈfʊtˌstɔk, ˈfʊtˌstak,
-s
footstep
BR ˈfʊtstɛp, -s

footstep (cont.)
AM ˈfʊtˌstɛp, -s
footstool
BR ˈfʊtstuːl, -z
AM ˈfʊtˌstul, -z
footstrap
BR ˈfʊtstrap, -s
AM ˈfʊtˌstræp, -s
footsure
BR ˈfʊtʃʊə(r), ˈfʊtʃɔː(r)
AM ˈfʊtˌʃʊr
footway
BR ˈfʊtweɪ, -z
AM ˈfʊtˌweɪ, -z
footwear
BR ˈfʊtwɛː(r)
AM ˈfʊtˌwɛ(ə)r
footwork
BR ˈfʊtwəːk
AM ˈfʊtˌwərk
foozle
BR ˈfuːz|l, -lz, -lɪŋ \-lɪŋ,
-ld
AM ˈfuzəl, -z, -ɪŋ, -d
foozler
BR ˈfuːz|ə(r), -z
AM ˈfuz(ə)lər, -z
fop
BR fɒp
AM fɑp
foppery
BR ˈfɒp(ə)ri
AM ˈfɑpəri
foppish
BR ˈfɒpɪʃ
AM ˈfɑpɪʃ
foppishly
BR ˈfɒpɪʃli
AM ˈfɑpɪʃli
foppishness
BR ˈfɒpɪʃnɪs
AM ˈfɑpɪʃnɪs
for¹
strong form
BR fɔː(r)
AM fɔ(ə)r
for²
weak form
BR fə(r)
AM fər
fora
BR ˈfɔːrə(r)
AM ˈfɔrə
forage
BR ˈfɒr|ɪdʒ, -ɪdʒɪz,
-ɪdʒɪŋ, -ɪdʒd
AM ˈfɔrɪdʒ, ˈfɑrɪdʒ, -ɪz,
-ɪŋ, -d
forager
BR ˈfɒrɪdʒə(r), -z
AM ˈfɔrɪdʒər, ˈfɑrɪdʒər,
-z
foramen
BR fəˈreɪmɛn
AM fəˈreɪmən
foramina
BR fəˈramɪnə(r)
AM fəˈræmənə

foraminate
BR fəˈramɪneɪt
AM fəˈræməˌneɪt
foraminated
BR fəˈramɪneɪtɪd
AM fəˈræməˌneɪdɪd
foraminifer
BR ˌfɒrəˈmɪnɪfə(r), -z
AM ˌfɔrəˈmɪnəfər, -z
foraminiferan
BR fəˌramɪˈnɪf(ə)rən,
fəˌramɪˈnɪf(ə)rn,
ˌfɒrəmɪˈnɪf(ə)rən,
ˌfɒrəmɪˈnɪf(ə)rn, -z
AM fəˈræməˌnɪf(ə)rən,
-z
foraminiferous
BR fəˌramɪˈnɪf(ə)rəs,
ˌfɒrəmɪˈnɪf(ə)rəs
AM fəˈræməˌnɪf(ə)rəs
forasmuch
BR ˌf(ə)rəzˈmʌtʃ
AM ˌfɔrəzˈmətʃ,
ˌfərəzˈmətʃ
forastero
BR ˌfɒrəˈstɛːrəʊ, -z
AM ˌfɔrəˈstɛroʊ, -z
foray
BR ˈfɒreɪ, -z, -ɪŋ, -d
AM ˈfɔˌreɪ, ˈfɑˌreɪ, -z, -ɪŋ,
-d
forb
BR fɔːb, -z
AM fɔ(ə)rb, -z
forbad
BR fəˈbad
AM fərˈbæd, fɔrˈbæd
forbade
BR fəˈbad, fəˈbeɪd
AM fərˈbæd, fɔrˈbæd,
fərˈbeɪd, fɔrˈbeɪd
forbear¹
noun, ancestor
BR ˈfɔːbɛː(r), -z
AM ˈfɔrˌbɛ(ə)r, -z
forbear²
verb
BR fəˈbɛː(r), fɔːˈbɛː(r),
-z, -ɪŋ
AM fərˈbɛ(ə)r,
fɔrˈbɛ(ə)r, -z, -ɪŋ
forbearance
BR fəˈbɛːrəns,
fəˈbɛːrns, fɔːˈbɛːrəns,
fɔːˈbɛːrns
AM fərˈbɛrəns,
fɔrˈbɛrəns
forbearingly
BR fəˈbɛːrɪŋli,
fɔːˈbɛːrɪŋli
AM fərˈbɛrɪŋli,
fɔrˈbɛrɪŋli
Forbes
BR fɔːbz, ˈfɔːbɪs, fɔːˈbɪs
AM fɔrbz
forbid
BR fəˈbɪd, -z, -ɪŋ

AM fərˈbɪd, fɔrˈbɪd, -z, -ɪŋ

forbiddance
BR fəˈbɪdns
AM fərˈbɪdns, fɔrˈbɪdns

forbidden
BR fəˈbɪdn
AM fərˈbɪdən, fɔrˈbɪdən

forbidding
BR fəˈbɪdɪŋ
AM fərˈbɪdɪŋ, fɔrˈbɪdɪŋ

forbiddingly
BR fəˈbɪdɪŋli
AM fərˈbɪdɪŋli, fɔrˈbɪdɪŋli

forbore
BR fəˈbɔː(r), fɔːˈbɔː(r)
AM fərˈbɔ(ə)r, fɔrˈbɔ(ə)r

forborne
BR fəˈbɔːn, fɔːˈbɔːn
AM fərˈbɔ(ə)rn, fɔrˈbɔ(ə)rn

forbye
BR fəˈbʌɪ, fɔːˈbʌɪ
AM fərˈbaɪ, fɔrˈbaɪ

force
BR fɔːs, -ɪz, -ɪŋ, -t
AM fɔ(ə)rs, -əz, -ɪŋ, -t

forceable
BR ˈfɔːsəbl
AM ˈfɔrsəbəl

forceful
BR ˈfɔːsf(ʊ)l
AM ˈfɔrsfəl

forcefully
BR ˈfɔːsfʊli, ˈfɔːsfli
AM ˈfɔrsfəli

forcefulness
BR ˈfɔːsf(ʊ)lnəs
AM ˈfɔrsfəlnəs

force majeure
BR ˌfɔːs maˈʒɜː(r)
AM ˌfɔ(ə)rs maˈʒər

forcemeat
BR ˈfɔːsmiːt
AM ˈfɔrsˌmit

forceps
BR ˈfɔːsɛps, ˈfɔːsɪps
AM ˈfɔrsəps, ˈfɔrˌsɛps

forcer
BR ˈfɔːsə(r), -z
AM ˈfɔrsər, -z

forcible
BR ˈfɔːsɪbl
AM ˈfɔrsəbəl

forcibleness
BR ˈfɔːsɪblnəs
AM ˈfɔrsəbəlnəs

forcibly
BR ˈfɔːsɪbli
AM ˈfɔrsəbli

ford
BR fɔːd, -z, -ɪŋ, -ɪd
AM fɔ(ə)rd, -z, -ɪŋ, -əd

fordable
BR ˈfɔːdəbl
AM ˈfɔrdəbəl

Forde
BR fɔːd
AM fɔ(ə)rd

Fordham
BR ˈfɔːdəm
AM ˈfɔrdəm

Fordingbridge
BR ˈfɔːdɪŋbrɪdʒ
AM ˈfɔrdɪŋˌbrɪdʒ

fordless
BR ˈfɔːdləs
AM ˈfɔrdləs

Fordyce
BR ˈfɔːdʌɪs, fɔːˈdʌɪs
AM ˈfɔrˌdaɪs

fore
BR fɔː(r)
AM fɔ(ə)r

forearm¹
noun
BR ˈfɔːrɑːm, -z
AM ˈfɔrˌɑrm, -z

forearm²
verb
BR (ˌ)fɔːrˈɑːm, -z, -ɪŋ, -d
AM ˌfɔrˈɑrm, -z, -ɪŋ, -d

forebad
BR fəˈbad, fəˈbeɪd
AM fərˈbæd, fɔrˈbeɪd

forebade
BR fəˈbad, fəˈbeɪd
AM fərˈbæd, fɔrˈbeɪd

forebear
BR ˈfɔːbɛː(r), -z
AM ˈfɔrˌbɛ(ə)r, -z

forebode
BR fəˈbəʊd, fɔːˈbəʊd, -z, -ɪŋ, -ɪd
AM fərˈboʊd, -z, -ɪŋ, -əd

foreboding
BR fəˈbəʊdɪŋ, fɔːˈbəʊdɪŋ, -z
AM fərˈboʊdɪŋ, -z

forebodingly
BR fəˈbəʊdɪŋli, fɔːˈbəʊdɪŋli
AM fərˈboʊdɪŋli

forebrain
BR ˈfɔːbreɪn, -z
AM ˈfɔrˌbreɪn, -z

forecast
BR ˈfɔːkɑːst, ˈfɔːkast, -s, -ɪŋ, -ɪd
AM ˈfɔrˌkæst, -s, -ɪŋ, -əd

forecaster
BR ˈfɔːkɑːstə(r), ˈfɔːkastə(r), -z
AM ˈfɔrˌkæstər, -z

forecastle
BR ˈfəʊksl, -z
AM ˈfoʊksəl, ˈfɔrˌkæsəl, -z

foreclose
BR (ˌ)fɔːˈkləʊz, -ɪz, -ɪŋ, -d

AM ˌfɔrˈkloʊz, -ɪz, -ɪŋ, -d

foreclosure
BR (ˌ)fɔːˈkləʊʒə(r), -z
AM ˌfɔrˈkloʊʒər, -z

foreconscious
BR ˈfɔːˌkɒnʃəs
AM ˈfɔrˌkɑnʃəs

forecourt
BR ˈfɔːkɔːt, -s
AM ˈfɔrˌkɔ(ə)rt, -s

foredeck
BR ˈfɔːdɛk, -s
AM ˈfɔrˌdɛk, -s

foredge
BR ˈfɔːrɛdʒ, -ɪz
AM ˈfɔrˌɛdʒ, -əz

foredoom
BR (ˌ)fɔːˈduːm, -z, -ɪŋ, -d
AM ˌfɔrˈdum, -z, -ɪŋ, -d

forefather
BR ˈfɔːˌfɑːðə(r), -z
AM ˈfɔrˌfɑðər, -z

forefeel
BR (ˌ)fɔːˈfiːl, -z, -ɪŋ
AM ˌfɔrˈfil, -z, -ɪŋ

forefeet
BR ˈfɔːfiːt
AM ˈfɔrˌfit

forefelt
BR (ˌ)fɔːˈfɛlt
AM ˌfɔrˈfelt

forefinger
BR ˈfɔːˌfɪŋɡə(r), -z
AM ˈfɔrˌfɪŋɡər, -z

forefoot
BR ˈfɔːfʊt
AM ˈfɔrˌfʊt

forefront
BR ˈfɔːfrʌnt
AM ˈfɔrˌfrʌnt

foregather
BR fəˈɡaðə(r), (ˌ)fɔːˈɡaðə(r), -əz, -(ə)rɪŋ, -əd
AM fərˈɡæðər, fɔrˈɡæðər, -z, -ɪŋ, -d

forego
verb, give up, renounce
BR fəˈɡəʊ, (ˌ)fɔːˈɡəʊ, -z, -ɪŋ
AM fərˈɡoʊ, fɔrˈɡoʊ, -z, -ɪŋ

foregoer
BR fəˈɡəʊə(r), (ˌ)fɔːˈɡəʊə(r), -z
AM fərˈɡoʊər, fɔrˈɡoʊər, -z

foregoing
adjective, preceding
BR ˈfɔːˌɡəʊɪŋ
AM ˈfɔrˌɡoʊɪŋ

foregone
BR (ˌ)fɔːˈɡɒn
AM ˈfɔrˌɡɔn

foreground
BR ˈfɔːɡraʊnd, -z
AM ˈfɔrˌɡraʊnd, -z

forehand
BR ˈfɔːhand, -z
AM ˈfɔrˌ(h)ænd, -z

forehead
BR ˈfɒrɪd, ˈfɔːhɛd, -z
AM ˈfɔrˌ(h)ɛd, -z

forehock
BR ˈfɔːhɒk, -s
AM ˈfɔrˌ(h)ɑk, -s

forehold
BR ˈfɔːhəʊld, -z
AM ˈfɔrˌ(h)oʊld, -z

foreign
BR ˈfɒrɪn, ˈfɒrn
AM ˈfɔrən

foreigner
BR ˈfɒrɪnə(r), ˈfɒrnə(r), -z
AM ˈfɔrənər, -z

foreignness
BR ˈfɒrɪnnɪs, ˈfɒrnnəs
AM ˈfɔrə(n)nəs

forejudge
BR fəˈdʒʌdʒ, (ˌ)fɔːˈdʒʌdʒ, -ɪz, -ɪŋ, -d
AM fərˈdʒʌdʒ, fɔrˈdʒʌdʒ, -əz, -ɪŋ, -d

foreknew
BR (ˌ)fɔːˈnjuː
AM fɔrˈn(j)u

foreknow
BR (ˌ)fɔːˈnəʊ, -z, -ɪŋ
AM fɔrˈnoʊ, -z, -ɪŋ

foreknowledge
BR (ˌ)fɔːˈnɒlɪdʒ
AM ˈfɔrˌnɑlədʒ

foreknown
BR (ˌ)fɔːˈnəʊn
AM fɔrˈnoʊn

forelady
BR ˈfɔːˌleɪdli, -ɪz
AM ˈfɔrˌleɪdi, -z

foreland
BR ˈfɔːlənd, -z
AM ˈfɔrlənd, -z

foreleg
BR ˈfɔːlɛɡ, -z
AM ˈfɔrˌlɛɡ, -z

forelimb
BR ˈfɔːlɪm, -z
AM ˈfɔrˌlɪm, -z

forelock
BR ˈfɔːlɒk, -s
AM ˈfɔrˌlɑk, -s

foreman
BR ˈfɔːmən
AM ˈfɔrmən

foremast
BR ˈfɔːmɑːst, ˈfɔːmast, ˈfɔːməst, -s
AM ˈfɔrˌmæst, ˈfɔrməst, -s

foremen
BR ˈfɔːmən
AM ˈfɔrˌmɛn, fɔrmən

foremost
BR ˈfɔːməʊst

AM ˈfɔːˌmoʊst

forename
BR ˈfɔːneɪm, -z
AM ˈfɔrˌneɪm, -z

forenoon
BR ˈfɔːnuːn
AM ˈfɔrˌnun

forensic
BR fəˈrɛnzɪk, fəˈrɛnsɪk
AM fəˈrɛnzɪk, fəˈrɛnsɪk

forensically
BR fəˈrɛnzɪkli,
fəˈrɛnsɪkli
AM fəˈrɛnzɪkli,
fəˈrɛnsək(ə)li

foreordain
BR ˌfɔːrɔːˈdeɪn, -z, -ɪŋ,
-d
AM ˌfɔrɔrˈdeɪn, -z, -ɪŋ,
-d

foreordination
BR ˌfɔːrɔːdɪˈneɪʃn
AM fɔrˌɔrdəˈneɪʃən

forepart
BR ˈfɔːpɑːt, -s
AM ˈfɔrˌpɑrt, -s

forepaw
BR ˈfɔːpɔː(r), -z
AM ˈfɔrˌpɔ, ˈfɔrˌpɑ, -z

forepeak
BR ˈfɔːpiːk, -s
AM ˈfɔrˌpik, -s

foreplay
BR ˈfɔːpleɪ
AM ˈfɔrˌpleɪ

forequarter
BR ˈfɔːˌkwɔːtə(r), -z
AM ˈfɔrˌkwɔrdər, -z

foreran
BR (ˌ)fɔːˈran
AM fɔ(r)ˈræn

forerun
BR (ˌ)fɔːˈrʌn, -z, -ɪŋ
AM fɔ(r)ˈrən, -z, -ɪŋ

forerunner
BR ˈfɔːˌrʌnə(r), -z
AM ˈfɔrˌrənər, -z

foresail
BR ˈfɔːseɪl, ˈfɔːsl, -z
AM ˈfɔrˌseɪl, ˈfɔrsəl, -z

foresaw
BR fəˈsɔː(r), (ˌ)fɔːˈsɔː(r)
AM fərˈsɔ, fɔrˈsɔ, fərˈsɑ,
fɔrˈsɑ

foresee
BR fəˈsiː, (ˌ)fɔːˈsiː, -z, -ɪŋ
AM fərˈsi, fɔrˈsi, -z, -ɪŋ

foreseeability
BR fəˌsiːəˈbɪlɪti,
fɔːˌsiːəˈbɪlɪti
AM fərˌsiəˈbɪlɪdi,
fɔrˌsiəˈbɪlɪdi

foreseeable
BR fəˈsiːəbl,
(ˌ)fɔːˈsiːəbl
AM fərˈsiəbəl,
fɔrˈsiəbəl

foreseeably
BR fəˈsiːəbli,
(ˌ)fɔːˈsiːəbli
AM fərˈsiəbli,
fɔrˈsiəbli

foreseen
BR fəˈsiːn, (ˌ)fɔːˈsiːn
AM fərˈsin, fɔrˈsin

foreseer
BR fəˈsiːə(r),
(ˌ)fɔːˈsiːə(r), -z
AM fərˈsiər, fɔrˈsiər, -z

foreshadow
BR fəˈʃadəʊ,
(ˌ)fɔːˈʃadəʊ, -z, -ɪŋ, -d
AM fərˈʃædoʊ,
fɔrˈʃædoʊ, -z, -ɪŋ, -d

foresheets
BR ˈfɔːʃiːts
AM ˈfɔrˌʃits

foreshore
BR ˈfɔːʃɔː(r), -z
AM ˈfɔrˌʃɔ(ə)r, -z

foreshorten
BR fəˈʃɔːt|n,
(ˌ)fɔːˈʃɔːt|n, -nz,
-nɪŋ \- n̩ɪŋ, -nd
AM fərˈʃɔrtən,
fɔrˈʃɔrtən, -z, -ɪŋ, -d

foreshow
BR fəˈʃəʊ, (ˌ)fɔːˈʃəʊ, -z,
-ɪŋ, -d
AM fərˈʃoʊ, -z, -ɪŋ, -d

foreshown
BR fəˈʃəʊn, (ˌ)fɔːˈʃəʊn
AM fərˈʃoʊn

foresight
BR ˈfɔːsaɪt, -s
AM ˈfɔrˌsaɪt, -s

foresighted
BR ˈfɔːsaɪtɪd
AM ˈfɔrˌsaɪdɪd

foresightedly
BR ˈfɔːsaɪtɪdli
AM ˈfɔrˌsaɪdɪdli

foresightedness
BR ˈfɔːsaɪtɪdnɪs
AM ˈfɔrˌsaɪdɪdnɪs

foreskin
BR ˈfɔːskɪn, -z
AM ˈfɔrˌskɪn, -z

forest
BR ˈfɒrɪst, -s
AM ˈfɔrəst, -s

forestall
BR (ˌ)fɔːˈstɔːl, -z, -ɪŋ, -d
AM fərˈstɔl, fɔrˈstɔl,
fərˈstɑl, fɔrˈstɑl, -z,
-ɪŋ, -d

forestaller
BR (ˌ)fɔːˈstɔːlə(r), -z
AM fərˈstɔlər,
fərˈstɑlər, fɔrˈstɑlər,
fɔrˈstɑlər, -z

forestalment
BR (ˌ)fɔːˈstɔːlm(ə)nt
AM fərˈstɔlmənt,
fɔrˈstɔlmənt,

fərˈstɑlmənt,
fɔrˈstɑlmənt

forestation
BR ˌfɒrɪˈsteɪʃn
AM ˌfɔrəˈsteɪʃən

forestay
BR ˈfɔːsteɪ, -z
AM ˈfɔrˌsteɪ, -z

forester
BR ˈfɒrɪstə(r), -z
AM ˈfɔrəstər, -z

forestry
BR ˈfɒrɪstri
AM ˈfɔrəstri

foreswear
BR fəˈswɛː(r),
(ˌ)fɔːˈswɛː(r), -z, -ɪŋ
AM fərˈswɛ(ə)r,
fərˈswɛə)r, -z, -ɪŋ

foreswore
BR fəˈswɔː(r),
(ˌ)fɔːˈswɔː(r)
AM fərˈswɔ(ə)r,
fɔrˈswɔ(ə)r

foresworn
BR fəˈswɔːn,
(ˌ)fɔːˈswɔːn
AM fərˈswɔ(ə)rn,
fɔrˈswɔ(ə)rn

foretaste
BR ˈfɔːteɪst, -s
AM ˈfɔrˌteɪst, -s

foretell
BR fəˈtɛl, (ˌ)fɔːˈtɛl, -z,
-ɪŋ
AM fərˈtɛl, fɔrˈtɛl, -z, -ɪŋ

foreteller
BR fəˈtɛlə(r),
(ˌ)fɔːˈtɛlə(r), -z
AM fərˈtɛlər, fɔrˈtɛlər,
-z

forethought
BR ˈfɔːθɔːt
AM ˈfɔrˌθɔt, ˈfɔrˌθɑt

foretoken
BR (ˌ)fɔːˈtəʊk|(ə)n,
-(ə)nz, -ənɪŋ \-n̩ɪŋ,
-(ə)nd
AM fərˈtoʊkən, -z, -ɪŋ,
-d

foretold
BR fəˈtəʊld, (ˌ)fɔːˈtəʊld
AM fərˈtoʊld, fɔrˈtoʊld

foretop
BR ˈfɔːtɒp, -s
AM ˈfɔrˌtɑp, -s

forever
BR fəˈrɛvə(r)
AM fəˈrɛvər

forevermore
BR fəˌrɛvəˈmɔː(r)
AM fəˌrɛvərˈmɔ(ə)r

forewarn
BR fəˈwɔːn, (ˌ)fɔːˈwɔːn,
-z, -ɪŋ, -d
AM fərˈwɔ(ə)rn,
fɔrˈwɔ(ə)rn, -z, -ɪŋ, -d

forewarner
BR fəˈwɔːnə(r),
(ˌ)fɔːˈwɔːnə(r), -z
AM fərˈwɔrnər,
fɔrˈwɔrnər, -z

forewent
BR fəˈwɛnt, (ˌ)fɔːˈwɛnt
AM fɔrˈwɛnt

forewing
BR ˈfɔːwɪŋ, -z
AM ˈfɔrˌwɪŋ, -z

forewoman
BR ˈfɔːˌwʊmən
AM ˈfɔrˌwʊmən

forewomen
BR ˈfɔːˌwɪmɪn
AM ˈfɔrˌwɪmɪn

foreword
BR ˈfɔːwəːd, -z
AM ˈfɔrˌwərd, -z

foreyard
BR ˈfɔːjɑːd, -z
AM ˈfɔrˌjɑrd, -z

Forfar
BR ˈfɔːfə(r)
AM ˈfɔrfər

Forfarshire
BR ˈfɔːfəʃ(ɪ)ə(r)
AM ˈfɔrfɑrˌʃɪ(ə)r

forfeit
BR ˈfɔːfɪt, -s, -ɪŋ, -ɪd
AM ˈfɔrfeɪt, -ts, -dɪŋ,
-dəd

forfeitable
BR ˈfɔːfɪtəbl
AM ˈfɔrfədəbəl

forfeiter
BR ˈfɔːfɪtə(r), -z
AM ˈfɔrfədər, -z

forfeiture
BR ˈfɔːfɪtʃə(r)
AM ˈfɔrfətju(ə)r,
ˈfɔrfətʃər

forfend
BR fɔːˈfɛnd, -z, -ɪŋ, -ɪd
AM fɔrˈfɛnd, -z, -ɪŋ, -əd

forgather
BR fəˈgað|ə(r),
(ˌ)fɔːˈgað|ə(r), -ə(r)z,
-(ə)rɪŋ, -ə(r)d
AM fərˈgæðər,
fɔrˈgæðər, -z, -ɪŋ, -d

forgave
BR fəˈgeɪv
AM fərˈgeɪv

forge
BR fɔːdʒ, -ɪz, -ɪŋ, -d
AM fɔrdʒ, -əz, -ɪŋ, -t

forgeable
BR ˈfɔːdʒəbl
AM ˈfɔrdʒəbəl

forger
BR ˈfɔːdʒə(r), -z
AM ˈfɔrdʒər, -z

forgery
BR ˈfɔːdʒ(ə)r|i, -ɪz
AM ˈfɔrdʒəri, -z

forget
BR fə'gɛt, -s, -ɪŋ
AM fər'gɛ|t, -ts, -dɪŋ
forgetful
BR fə'gɛtf(ə)l
AM fər'gɛtfəl
forgetfully
BR fə'gɛtfəli, fə'gɛtfʃi
AM fər'gɛtfəli
forgetfulness
BR fə'gɛtf(ə)lnəs
AM fər'gɛtfəlnəs
forget-me-not
BR fə'gɛtmɪnʊt, -s
AM fər'gɛdmɪˌnɑt, -s
forgettable
BR fə'gɛtəbl
AM fər'gɛdəbəl
forgetter
BR fə'gɛtə(r), -z
AM fər'gɛdər, -z
forgivable
BR fə'gɪvəbl
AM fər'gɪvəbəl
forgivably
BR fə'gɪvəbli
AM fər'gɪvəbli
forgive
BR fə'gɪv, -z, -ɪŋ
AM fər'gɪv, -z, -ɪŋ
forgiven
BR fə'gɪvn
AM fər'gɪvən
forgiveness
BR fə'gɪvnɪs
AM fər'gɪvnɪs
forgiver
BR fə'gɪvə(r), -z
AM fər'gɪvər, -z
forgivingly
BR fə'gɪvɪŋli
AM fər'gɪvɪŋli
forgo
BR fə'gəʊ, fɔː'gəʊ, -z, -ɪŋ
AM fər'goʊ, fɔr'goʊ, -z, -ɪŋ
forgot
BR fə'gɒt
AM fər'gɑt
forgotten
BR fə'gɒtn
AM fər'gɑtn
forint
BR 'fɒrɪnt, -s
AM 'fɔrɪnt, -s
fork
BR fɔːk, -s, -ɪŋ, -t
AM fɔ(ə)rk, -s, -ɪŋ, -t
forkful
BR 'fɔːkfʊl, -z
AM 'fɔrkˌfʊl, -z
forklift
BR 'fɔːklɪft, -s
AM 'fɔrkˌlɪft, -s
forlorn
BR fə'lɔːn
AM fər'lɔ(ə)rn

forlornly
BR fə'lɔːnli
AM fər'lɔrnli
forlornness
BR fə'lɔːnnəs
AM fər'lɔr(n)nəs
form
BR fɔːm, -z, -ɪŋ, -d
AM fɔ(ə)rm, -z, -ɪŋ, -d
formal
BR 'fɔːml
AM 'fɔrməl
formaldehyde
BR fɔː'maldɪhaɪd,
fə'maldɪhaɪd
AM fɔr'mældəˌhaɪd,
fər'mældəˌhaɪd
formalin
BR 'fɔːməlɪn
AM 'fɔrməlɪn
formalisation
BR ˌfɔːmlʌɪ'zeɪʃn
AM ˌfɔrmələ'zeɪʃən,
ˌfɔrməˌlaɪ'zeɪʃən
formalise
BR 'fɔːməlʌɪz,
'fɔːmlʌɪz, -ɪz, -ɪŋ, -d
AM 'fɔrməˌlaɪz, -ɪz, -ɪŋ, -d
formalism
BR 'fɔːməlɪz(ə)m,
'fɔːmlɪz(ə)m
AM 'fɔrməˌlɪzəm
formalist
BR 'fɔːməlɪst,
'fɔːmlɪst, -s
AM 'fɔrmələst, -s
formalistic
BR ˌfɔːmə'lɪstɪk,
ˌfɔːml'ɪstɪk
AM ˌfɔrmə'lɪstɪk
formality
BR fə'malɪt|i,
fɔː'malɪt|i, -ɪz
AM fər'mælədi, -z
formalization
BR ˌfɔːmlʌɪ'zeɪʃn
AM ˌfɔrmələ'zeɪʃən,
ˌfɔrməˌlaɪ'zeɪʃən
formalize
BR 'fɔːməlʌɪz,
'fɔːmlʌɪz, -ɪz, -ɪŋ, -d
AM 'fɔrməˌlaɪz, -ɪz, -ɪŋ,
-d
formally
BR 'fɔːmli
AM 'fɔrməli
formalness
BR 'fɔːmlnəs
AM 'fɔrməlnəs
formant
BR 'fɔːm(ə)nt, -s
AM 'fɔrmənt, -s
format
BR 'fɔːmat, -s, -ɪŋ, -ɪd
AM 'fɔrˌmæ|t, -ts, -dɪŋ,
-dəd

formate
BR 'fɔːmeɪt
AM 'fɔrˌmeɪt
formation
BR fə'meɪʃn,
fɔː'meɪʃn, -z
AM fɔr'meɪʃən,
fər'meɪʃən, -z
formational
BR fə'meɪʃn(ə)l,
fə'meɪʃən(ə)l,
fɔː'meɪʃn(ə)l,
fɔː'meɪʃən(ə)l
AM fɔr'meɪʃ(ə)nəl,
fər'meɪʃ(ə)nəl
formative
BR 'fɔːmətɪv
AM 'fɔrmədɪv
formatively
BR 'fɔːmətɪvli
AM 'fɔrmədəvli
formbook
BR 'fɔːmbʊk
AM 'fɔrmˌbʊk
Formby
BR 'fɔːmbi
AM 'fɔrmbi
forme
BR fɔːm, -z
AM fɔ(ə)rm, -z
former
BR 'fɔːmə(r)
AM 'fɔrmər
formerly
BR 'fɔːməli
AM 'fɔrmərli
formic
BR 'fɔːmɪk
AM 'fɔrmɪk
Formica®
BR fɔː'mʌɪkə(r),
fə'mʌɪkə(r)
AM fər'maɪkə,
fɔr'maɪkə
formication
BR ˌfɔːmɪ'keɪʃn
AM ˌfɔrmə'keɪʃən
formidable
BR 'fɔːmɪdəbl,
fə'mɪdəbl
AM 'fɔrmədəbəl,
fər'mɪdəbəl
fɔr'mɪdəbəl
formidableness
BR 'fɔːmɪdəblnəs,
fə'mɪdəblnəs
AM 'fɔrmədəbəlnəs,
fər'mɪdəbəlnəs,
fɔr'mɪdəbəlnəs
formidably
BR 'fɔːmɪdəbli,
fə'mɪdəbli
AM 'fɔrmədəbli,
fər'mɪdəbli,
fɔr'mɪdəbli
formless
BR 'fɔːmləs
AM 'fɔrmləs

formlessly
BR 'fɔːmləsli
AM 'fɔrmləsli
formlessness
BR 'fɔːmləsnəs
AM 'fɔrmləsnəs
Formosa
BR fɔː'məʊsə(r),
fɔː'məʊzə(r)
AM fɔr'moʊsə
Formosan
BR fɔː'məʊsn,
fɔː'məʊzn, -z
AM fɔr'moʊsən, -z
formula
BR 'fɔːmjʊlə(r), -z
AM 'fɔrmjələ, -z
formulae
BR 'fɔːmjʊliː
AM 'fɔrmjəˌli,
'fɔrmjəˌlaɪ
formulaic
BR ˌfɔːmjʊ'leɪɪk
AM ˌfɔrmjə'leɪɪk
formularise
BR 'fɔːmjʊlərʌɪz, -ɪz,
-ɪŋ, -d
AM 'fɔrmjələˌraɪz, -ɪz,
-ɪŋ, -d
formularize
BR 'fɔːmjʊlərʌɪz, -ɪz,
-ɪŋ, -d
AM 'fɔrmjələˌraɪz, -ɪz,
-ɪŋ, -d
formulary
BR 'fɔːmjʊlər|i, -ɪz
AM 'fɔrmjəˌlɛri, -z
formulate
BR 'fɔːmjʊleɪt, -s, -ɪŋ,
-ɪd
AM 'fɔrmjəˌleɪ|t, -ts,
-dɪŋ, -dɪd
formulation
BR ˌfɔːmjʊ'leɪʃn, -z
AM ˌfɔrmjə'leɪʃən, -z
formulator
BR 'fɔːmjʊleɪtə(r), -z
AM 'fɔrmjəˌleɪdər, -z
formulise
BR 'fɔːmjʊlʌɪz, -ɪz, -ɪŋ,
-d
AM 'fɔrmjəˌlaɪz, -ɪz, -ɪŋ,
-d
formulism
BR 'fɔːmjʊlɪz(ə)m
AM 'fɔrmjəˌlɪzəm
formulist
BR 'fɔːmjʊlɪst, -s
AM 'fɔrmjələst, -s
formulistic
BR ˌfɔːmjʊ'lɪstɪk
AM ˌfɔrmjə'lɪstɪk
formulize
BR 'fɔːmjʊlʌɪz, -ɪz, -ɪŋ,
-d
AM 'fɔrmjəˌlaɪz, -ɪz, -ɪŋ,
-d

formwork
BR ˈfɔːmwəːk
AM ˈfɔrmˌwɚrk
fornicate
BR ˈfɔːnɪkeɪt, -s, -ɪŋ, -ɪd
AM ˈfɔrnəˌkeɪ|t, -ts, -dɪŋ, -dɪd
fornication
BR ˌfɔːnɪˈkeɪʃn
AM ˌfɔrnəˈkeɪʃən
fornicator
BR ˈfɔːnɪkeɪtə(r), -z
AM ˈfɔrnəˌkeɪdər, -z
fornices
BR ˈfɔːnɪsiːz
AM ˈfɔrnəˌsiz
fornix
BR ˈfɔːnɪks
AM ˈfɔrnɪks
forrader
BR ˈfɒrədə(r)
AM ˈfɔrədər
Forres
BR ˈfɒrɪs
AM ˈfɔrəs, ˈfɑrəs
Forrest
BR ˈfɒrɪst
AM ˈfɔrəst
Forrester
BR ˈfɒrɪstə(r)
AM ˈfɔrəstər, ˈfɑrəstər
forsake
BR fəˈseɪk, fɔːˈseɪk, -s, -ɪŋ
AM fərˈseɪk, -s, -ɪŋ
forsaken
BR fəˈseɪk(ə)n, fɔːˈseɪk(ə)n
AM fərˈseɪkən
forsakenness
BR fəˈseɪknnəs, fɔːˈseɪknnəs
AM fərˈseɪkə(n)nəs
forsaker
BR fəˈseɪkə(r), fɔːˈseɪkə(r), -z
AM fərˈseɪkər, -z
Forshaw
BR ˈfɔːʃɔː(r)
AM ˈfɔrˌʃɔ
forsook
BR fəˈsʊk, fɔːˈsʊk
AM fərˈsʊk
forsooth
BR fəˈsuːθ, fɔːˈsuːθ
AM fərˈsuːθ
Forster
BR ˈfɔːstə(r)
AM ˈfɔrstər
forswear
BR fəˈswɛː(r), fɔːˈswɛː(r), -z, -ɪŋ
AM fərˈswɛ(ə)r, fɔ(ə)rˈswɛ(ə)r, -z, -ɪŋ
forswore
BR fəˈswɔː(r), fɔːˈswɔː(r)

AM fərˈswɔ(ə)r, fɔrˈswɔ(ə)r
Forsyte
BR ˈfɔːsʌɪt
AM ˈfɔrsaɪt
Forsyth
BR ˈfɔːsʌɪθ, fɔːˈsʌɪθ
AM ˈfɔrˌsaɪθ
forsythia
BR fɔːˈsʌɪθɪə(r), fəˈsʌɪθɪə(r)
AM fərˈsɪθiə, fɔrˈsɪθiə
fort
BR fɔːt, -s
AM fɔ(ə)rt, -s
fortalice
BR ˈfɔːtəlɪs, -ɪz
AM ˈfɔrdələs, -əz
Fort-de-France
BR ˌfɔː(t)dəˈfrɑːns, ˌfɔː(t)dəˈfrans
AM ˌfɔrdəˈfræns
forte
BR ˈfɔːteɪ, -z
AM ˈfɔrˌteɪ, fɔ(ə)rt, -z
Fortean
BR ˈfɔːtɪən
AM ˈfɔrdiən
forte-piano
BR ˌfɔːteɪˈpɪˈanəʊ, ˌfɔːtɪˈpjɑːnəʊ
AM ˈfɔrˌteɪˈpjɑnoʊ
Fortescue
BR ˈfɔːtɪskjuː
AM ˈfɔrdəsˌkju
forth
BR fɔːθ
AM fɔ(ə)rθ
forthcoming
BR ˌfɔːθˈkʌmɪŋ
AM ˈfɔrθˈkəmɪŋ
forthcomingness
BR ˌfɔːθˈkʌmɪŋnɪs
AM ˈfɔrθˈkəmɪŋnɪs
forthright
BR ˈfɔːθrʌɪt
AM ˈfɔrθˌraɪt
forthrightly
BR ˈfɔːθrʌɪtli
AM ˈfɔrθˈraɪtli
forthrightness
BR ˈfɔːθrʌɪtnɪs
AM ˈfɔrθˌraɪtnɪs
forthwith
BR ˌfɔːθˈwɪð, fɔːˈθwɪθ
AM ˈfɔrθˈwɪθ
fortieth
BR ˈfɔːtɪθ
AM ˈfɔrdiɪθ
fortifiable
BR ˈfɔːtɪfʌɪəbl
AM ˈfɔrdəˌfaɪəbəl
fortification
BR ˌfɔːtɪfɪˈkeɪʃn, -z
AM ˌfɔrdəfəˈkeɪʃən, -z
fortifier
BR ˈfɔːtɪfʌɪə(r), -z

AM ˈfɔrdəˌfaɪər, -z
fortify
BR ˈfɔːtɪfʌɪ, -z, -ɪŋ, -d
AM ˈfɔrdəˌfaɪ, -z, -ɪŋ, -d
Fortinbras
BR ˈfɔːt(ɪ)nbras
AM ˈfɔrtnˌbræs
fortis
BR ˈfɔːtɪs
AM ˈfɔrdəs
fortissimo
BR fɔːˈtɪsɪməʊ
AM fɔrˈtɪsəmoʊ
fortitude
BR ˈfɔːtɪtjuːd, fɔːtɪtʃuːd
AM ˈfɔrdəˌtud
Fort Knox
BR ˌfɔːt ˈnɒks
AM ˌfɔ(ə)rt ˈnaks
fortnight
BR ˈfɔːtnʌɪt, -s
AM ˈfɔrtˌnaɪt, -s
fortnightly
BR ˈfɔːtnʌɪtl|i, -ɪz
AM ˈfɔrtˌnaɪtli, -z
Fortnum and Mason
BR ˌfɔːtnəm (ə)n(d) ˈmeɪsn
AM ˈfɔrtnəm ən ˈmeɪsən
FORTRAN
BR ˈfɔːtran
AM ˈfɔrˌtræn
fortress
BR ˈfɔːtrɪs, -ɪz
AM ˈfɔrtrəs, -əz
fortuitism
BR fɔːˈtjuːɪtɪz(ə)m, fɔːˈtʃuːɪtɪz(ə)m
AM fɔrˈtuəˌtɪzəm
fortuitist
BR fɔːˈtjuːɪtɪst, fɔːˈtʃuːɪtɪst, -s
AM fɔrˈtuədəst, -s
fortuitous
BR fɔːˈtjuːɪtəs, fɔːˈtʃuːɪtəs
AM fɔrˈtuədəs
fortuitously
BR fɔːˈtjuːɪtəsli, fɔːˈtʃuːɪtəsli
AM fɔrˈtuədəsli
fortuitousness
BR fɔːˈtjuːɪtəsnəs, fɔːˈtʃuːɪtəsnəs
AM fɔrˈtuədəsnəs
fortuity
BR fɔːˈtjuːɪt|i, fɔːˈtʃuːɪt|i, -ɪz
AM fɔrˈtuədi, -z
fortunate
BR ˈfɔːtʃnət, ˈfɔːtʃ(ə)nət, ˈfɔːtjʉnət
AM ˈfɔrtʃ(ə)nət

fortunately
BR ˈfɔːtʃnətli, ˈfɔːtʃ(ə)nətli, ˈfɔːtjʉnətli
AM ˈfɔrtʃ(ə)nətli
fortune
BR ˈfɔːtʃuːn, ˈfɔːtʃ(ə)n, ˈfɔːtjuːn, -z
AM ˈfɔrtʃən, -z
forty
BR ˈfɔːti
AM ˈfɔrdi
fortyfold
BR ˈfɔːtɪfəʊld
AM ˈfɔrdiˌfoʊld
forty-niner
BR ˌfɔːtɪˈnʌɪmə(r), -z
AM ˌfɔrdiˈnaɪnər, -z
forum
BR ˈfɔːrəm, -z
AM ˈfɔrəm, -z
forward
BR ˈfɔːwəd, -z, -ɪŋ, -ɪd
AM ˈfɔrwərd, -z, -ɪŋ, -əd
forwarder
BR ˈfɔːwədə(r), -z
AM ˈfɔrwərdər, -z
forwardly
BR ˈfɔːwədli
AM ˈfɔrwərdli
forwardness
BR ˈfɔːwədnəs
AM ˈfɔrwərdnəs
forwards
BR ˈfɔːwədz
AM ˈfɔrwərdz
forwent
BR (ˌ)fɔːˈwɛnt
AM fɔrˈwɛnt
Fosbury
BR ˈfɒzb(ə)ri
AM ˈfas ˌbɛri
Fosdick
BR ˈfɒzdɪk
AM ˈfazdɪk
Fosdyke
BR ˈfɒzdʌɪk
AM ˈfazˌdaɪk
foss
BR fɒs, -ɪz
AM fɔs, fas, -əz
fossa
BR ˈfɒsə(r), -z
AM ˈfɔsə, ˈfasə, -z
fossae
BR ˈfɒsiː
AM ˈfɔsi, ˈfɔˌsaɪ, ˈfasi, ˈfaˌsaɪ
fosse
BR fɒs, -ɪz
AM fas, -əz
fossick
BR ˈfɒs|ɪk, -ɪks, -ɪkɪŋ, -ɪkt
AM ˈfasɪk, -s, -ɪŋ, -t
fossicker
BR ˈfɒsɪkə(r), -z

AM 'fasɪkər, -z

fossil
BR 'fɒsl, -z
AM 'fɑsəl, -z

fossil fuel
BR ˌfɒsl 'fjuːəl
AM 'fɑsəl ˌfjuˈ(ə)l

fossiliferous
BR ˌfɒsɪ'lɪf(ə)rəs
AM ˌfɑsə'lɪfərəs

fossilisation
BR ˌfɒslˌʌɪ'zeɪʃn,
ˌfɒsɪlʌɪ'zeɪʃn
AM ˌfɑsələ'zeɪʃən,
ˌfɑsəˌlaɪˈzeɪʃən

fossilise
BR 'fɒslˌʌɪz, 'fɒsɪlʌɪz,
-ɪz, -ɪŋ, -d
AM 'fɑsəˌlaɪz, -ɪz, -ɪŋ, -d

fossilization
BR ˌfɒslˌʌɪ'zeɪʃn,
ˌfɒsɪlʌɪ'zeɪʃn
AM ˌfɑsələ'zeɪʃən,
ˌfɑsəˌlaɪˈzeɪʃən

fossilize
BR 'fɒslˌʌɪz, 'fɒsɪlʌɪz,
-ɪz, -ɪŋ, -d
AM 'fɑsəˌlaɪz, -ɪz, -ɪŋ, -d

fossorial
BR fɒ'sɔːrɪəl
AM fɑ'sɔrɪəl

foster
BR 'fɒst|ə(r), -əz,
-(ə)rɪŋ, -əd
AM 'fɑst|ər, 'fɑst|ər,
-ərz, -(ə)rɪŋ, -ərd

fosterage
BR 'fɒst(ə)rɪdʒ
AM 'fɑstərɪdʒ,
'fɑstərɪdʒ

fosterer
BR 'fɒst(ə)rə(r), -z
AM 'fɑstərər, 'fɑstərər,
-z

fosterling
BR 'fɒstəlɪŋ, -z
AM 'fɑstərlɪŋ,
'fɑstərlɪŋ, -z

Fothergill
BR 'fɒðəgɪl
AM 'fɑðərˌgɪl

Fotheringay
BR 'fɒð(ə)rɪŋgeɪ
AM 'fɑðərən‚geɪ

Fotheringham
BR 'fɒð(ə)rɪŋg(ə)m
AM 'fɑðərɪŋəm

Foucault
BR fuː'kəʊ
AM fu'koʊ

fouetté
BR 'fwɛteɪ, 'fuːəteɪ, -z
AM ‚fuə'teɪ, -z

fought
BR fɔːt
AM fɔt, fɑt

foul
BR faʊl, -z, -ɪŋ, -d, -ə(r),
-ɪst
AM faʊl, -z, -ɪŋ, -d, -ər,
-əst

Foula
BR 'fuːlə(r)
AM 'fulə

foulard
BR 'fuːlɑː(r), 'fuːlɑːd,
fuː'lɑː(r), fuː'lɑːd, -z
AM fu'lɑrd, fə'lɑrd, -z

Foulds
BR fəʊldz
AM foʊl(d)z

Foulkes
BR fəʊks, faʊks
AM foʊlks

foully
BR 'faʊlli
AM 'faʊ(l)li

foulmart
BR 'fuːmət, 'fuːmɑːt, -s
AM 'fumərt, 'fuˌmɑrt,
-s

foulness
BR 'faʊlnəs
AM 'faʊlnəs

foumart
BR 'fuːmət, 'fuːmɑːt, -s
AM 'fumərt, 'fuˌmɑrt,
-s

found
BR faʊnd
AM faʊnd

foundation
BR faʊn'deɪʃn, -z
AM faʊn'deɪʃən, -z

foundational
BR faʊn'deɪʃn(ə)l,
faʊn'deɪʃən(ə)l
AM faʊn'deɪʃ(ə)nəl

foundationer
BR faʊn'deɪʃnə(r),
faʊn'deɪʃ(ə)nə(r), -z
AM faʊn'deɪʃ(ə)nər, -z

founder
BR 'faʊnd|ə(r), -əz,
-(ə)rɪŋ, -əd
AM 'faʊnd|ər, -ərz,
-(ə)rɪŋ, -ərd

foundership
BR 'faʊndəʃɪp
AM 'faʊndər‚ʃɪp

foundling
BR 'faʊndlɪŋ, -z
AM 'faʊndlɪŋ, -z

foundress
BR 'faʊndrɪs, -ɪz
AM 'faʊndrəs, -əz

foundry
BR 'faʊndr|i, -ɪz
AM 'faʊndri, -z

fount¹
in printing
BR fɒnt, faʊnt, -s
AM fɑnt, faʊnt, -s

fount²
spring of water,
beginning
BR faʊnt, -s
AM faʊnt, -s

fountain
BR 'faʊnt(ɪ)n, -z, -d
AM 'faʊnt(ə)n, -z, -d

fountainhead
BR 'faʊnt(ɪ)nhɛd, -z
AM 'faʊnt(ə)nˌ(h)ɛd, -z

fountainpen
BR 'faʊnt(ɪ)npɛn, -z
AM 'faʊnt(ə)nˌpɛn, -z

four
BR fɔː(r), -z
AM fɔ(ə)r, -z

four-bagger
BR 'fɔːˌbagə(r), -z
AM ˌfɔr'bægər, -z

fourchette
BR 'fʊə'ʃɛt, ˌfɔː'ʃɛt, -s
AM ˌfur'ʃɛt, -s

fourdrinier
BR ˌfʊə'drɪnɪə(r),
ˌfʊə'drɪnɪeɪ,
ˌfɔː'drɪnɪə(r),
ˌfɔː'drɪnɪeɪ, -z
AM ˌfɔrdrə'nɪ(ə)r, -z

fourfold
BR 'fɔːfəʊld
AM 'fɔrˌfoʊld

Fourier
BR 'fʊrɪə(r), 'fʊrɪeɪ
AM ˌfuri'eɪ

Fourierism
BR 'fʊrɪərɪz(ə)m
AM 'furiəˌrɪzəm

fourpence
BR 'fɔːp(ə)ns, -ɪz
AM 'fɔr‚pens, -əz

fourpenny
BR 'fɔːpn|i, 'fɔːpn|i, -ɪz
AM 'fɔrˌpɛni, -z

fourscore
BR ˌfɔː'skɔː(r)
AM 'fɔr'skɔ(ə)r

foursome
BR 'fɔːs(ə)m, -z
AM 'fɔrsəm, -z

foursquare
BR ˌfɔː'skwɛː(r)
AM ˌfɔr'skwɛ(ə)r

fourteen
BR ˌfɔː'tiːn, -z
AM ˌfɔr'tin, -z

fourteenth
BR ˌfɔː'tiːnθ
AM ˌfɔr'tinθ

fourth
BR fɔːθ, -s
AM fɔ(ə)rθ, -s

fourthly
BR 'fɔːθli
AM 'fɔrθli

fovea
BR 'fəʊvɪə(r)

AM 'foʊvɪə

foveae
BR 'fəʊviː
AM 'foʊviˌi, 'foʊviˌaɪ

foveal
BR 'fəʊvɪəl
AM 'foʊvɪəl

foveate
BR 'fəʊvɪət
AM 'foʊviˌeɪt, 'foʊvɪət

foveola
BR fə(ʊ)'viːələ(r)
AM foʊ'vɪələ

foveolae
BR fə(ʊ)'viːəliː
AM foʊ'vɪəli:
foʊ'vɪəˌlaɪ

foveolate
BR fə(ʊ)'viːələt
AM foʊ'vɪəˌleɪt,
foʊ'vɪələt

Fowey
BR fɔɪ
AM fɔɪ

Fowkes
BR fəʊks, faʊks
AM foʊks, faʊks

fowl
BR faʊl, -z
AM faʊl, -z

fowler
BR 'faʊlə(r), -z
AM 'faʊlər, -z

Fowles
BR faʊlz
AM faʊls, foʊls

fowling
BR 'faʊlɪŋ
AM 'faʊlɪŋ

Fowlmere
BR 'faʊlmɪə(r)
AM 'faʊlˌmaɪər

fox
BR fɒks, -ɪz
AM fɑks, -əz

Foxcroft
BR 'fɒkskrɒft
AM 'fɑksˌkrɔft,
'fɑksˌkrɑft

Foxe
BR fɒks
AM fɑks

foxfire
BR 'fɒksfʌɪə(r)
AM 'fɑksˌfaɪ(ə)r

foxglove
BR 'fɒksglʌv, -z
AM 'fɑksˌglʌv, -z

foxhole
BR 'fɒkshəʊl, -z
AM 'fɑksˌ(h)oʊl, -z

foxhound
BR 'fɒkshaʊnd, -z
AM 'fɑksˌ(h)aʊnd, -z

foxhunt
BR 'fɒkshʌnt, -s, -ɪŋ, -ɪd

foxily
AM 'fɑks,(h)ən|t, -ts, -(t)ɪŋ, -(t)əd

foxily
BR 'fɒksɪli
AM 'fɑksəli

foxiness
BR 'fɒksɪnɪs
AM 'fɑksɪnɪs

foxlike
BR 'fɒkslʌɪk
AM 'fɑks,laɪk

foxtail
BR 'fɒksteɪl, -z
AM 'fɑks,teɪl, -z

Foxton
BR 'fɒkst(ə)n
AM 'fɑkstən

foxtrot
BR 'fɒkstrɒt, -s
AM 'fɑks,trɑt, -s

foxy
BR 'fɒks|i, -ɪə(r), -ɪɪst
AM 'fɑksi, -ər, -ɪst

foyer
BR 'fɔɪeɪ, 'fɔɪə(r), -z
AM 'fɔɪər, -z

Foyle
BR fɔɪl
AM fɔɪl

Fra
BR frɑː(r)
AM frɑ

frabjous
BR 'frabdʒəs
AM 'fræbdʒəs

frabjously
BR 'frabdʒəsli
AM 'fræbdʒəsli

fracas¹
singular
BR 'frakɑː(r)
AM 'freɪkəs, 'frækəs

fracas²
plural
BR 'frakɑːz
AM 'freɪkəs, 'frækəs

fracases
BR 'frakəsɪz
AM 'freɪkəsəz, 'frækəsəz

fractal
BR 'fraktl, -z
AM 'fræktəl, -z

fraction
BR 'frakʃn, -z
AM 'frækʃən, -z

fractional
BR 'frakʃn(ə)l, 'frakʃən(ə)l
AM 'frækʃ(ə)nəl

fractionalise
BR 'frakʃnəlʌɪz, 'frakʃn̩lʌɪz, 'frakʃənlʌɪz, 'frakʃ(ə)nəlʌɪz, -ɪz, -ɪŋ, -d

fractionalize
BR 'frakʃn̩əlʌɪz, 'frakʃn̩lʌɪz, 'frakʃənlʌɪz, 'frakʃ(ə)nəlʌɪz, -ɪz, -ɪŋ, -d

fractionally
BR 'frakʃn̩əli, 'frakʃn̩li, 'frakʃənli, 'frakʃ(ə)nəli
AM 'frækʃ(ə)nəli

fractionary
BR 'frakʃn̩(ə)ri
AM 'frækʃə,neri

fractionate
BR 'frakʃəneɪt, 'frakʃn̩eɪt, -s, -ɪŋ, -ɪd
AM 'frækʃə,neɪ|t, -ts, -dɪŋ, -dɪd

fractionation
BR ,frakʃə'neɪʃn
AM ,frækʃə'neɪʃən

fractionator
BR 'frakʃəneɪtə(r), 'frakʃn̩eɪtə(r), -z
AM 'frækʃə,neɪdər, -z

fractionise
BR 'frakʃənʌɪz, 'frakʃn̩ʌɪz, -ɪz, -ɪŋ, -d
AM 'frækʃə,naɪz, -ɪz, -ɪŋ, -d

fractionize
BR 'frakʃənʌɪz, 'frakʃn̩ʌɪz, -ɪz, -ɪŋ, -d
AM 'frækʃə,naɪz, -ɪz, -ɪŋ, -d

fractious
BR 'frakʃəs
AM 'frækʃəs

fractiously
BR 'frakʃəsli
AM 'frækʃəsli

fractiousness
BR 'frakʃəsnəs
AM 'frækʃəsnəs

fracture
BR 'fraktʃ|ə(r), -əz, -(ə)rɪŋ, -əd
AM 'fræktʃər, -ərz, -ərɪŋ, -ərd

fraena
BR 'friːnə(r)
AM 'frinə

fraenula
BR 'friːnjʉlə(r), 'frɛnjʉlə(r)
AM 'frɛnjələ

fraenulum
BR 'friːnjʉləm, 'frɛnjʉləm
AM 'frɛnjələm

fraenum
BR 'friːnəm
AM 'frɛnəm

fragile
BR 'fradʒʌɪl
AM 'frædʒəl

fragilely
BR 'fradʒʌɪl(l)i
AM 'frædʒə(l)li

fragility
BR frə'dʒɪlɪti
AM frə'dʒɪlɪdi

fragment¹
noun
BR 'fragm(ə)nt, -s
AM 'frægmənt, -s

fragment²
verb
BR frag'mɛnt, -s, -ɪŋ, -ɪd
AM ˌfræg'mɛn|t, -ts, -(t)ɪŋ, -(t)əd

fragmental
BR frag'mɛntl
AM fræg'mɛn(t)l

fragmentarily
BR 'fragm(ə)nt(ə)rɪli
AM 'frægmənˌtɛrəli

fragmentary
BR 'fragm(ə)ntri
AM 'frægmənˌtɛri

fragmentation
BR ˌfragm(ə)n'teɪʃn, ˌfragmɛn'teɪʃn
AM ˌfrægmən'teɪʃən

fragmentise
BR 'fragm(ə)ntʌɪz, -ɪz, -ɪŋ, -d
AM 'frægmənˌtaɪz, -ɪz, -ɪŋ, -d

fragmentize
BR 'fragm(ə)ntʌɪz, -ɪz, -ɪŋ, -d
AM 'frægmənˌtaɪz, -ɪz, -ɪŋ, -d

Fragonard
BR 'fragənɑː(r)
AM ˌfrægə'nɑr

fragrance
BR 'freɪgr(ə)ns, -ɪz
AM 'freɪgrəns, -əz

fragranced
BR 'freɪgr(ə)nst
AM 'freɪgrənst

fragrancy
BR 'freɪgr(ə)nsi
AM 'freɪgrənsi

fragrant
BR 'freɪgr(ə)nt
AM 'freɪgrənt

fragrantly
BR 'freɪgr(ə)ntli
AM 'freɪgrən(t)li

fragrantness
BR 'freɪgr(ə)ntnəs
AM 'freɪgrən(t)nəs

frail
BR freɪl, -ə(r), -ɪst

frailer
AM freɪ(ə)l, -ər, -ɪst

frailly
BR 'freɪlli
AM 'freɪ(əl)li

frailness
BR 'freɪlnɪs
AM 'freɪ(ə)lnɪs

frailty
BR 'freɪlt|i, -ɪz
AM 'freɪ(ə)lti, -z

fraise
BR frɛz, freɪz
AM frɛz

fraises
BR frɛz, freɪz
AM frɛz

Fraktur
BR 'fraktʊə(r), frak'tʊə(r)
AM fræk'tʊ(ə)r

framable
BR 'freɪməbl
AM 'freɪməbəl

frambesia
BR fram'biːzɪə(r), fram'biːʒə(r)
AM fræm'biʒə

framboesia
BR fram'biːzɪə(r), fram'biːʒə(r)
AM fræm'biʒə

frame
BR freɪm, -z, -ɪŋ, -d
AM freɪm, -z, -ɪŋ, -d

frameless
BR 'freɪmlɪs
AM 'freɪmlɪs

framer
BR 'freɪmə(r), -z
AM 'freɪmər, -z

framework
BR 'freɪmwəːk, -s
AM 'freɪm,wərk, -s

Framlingham
BR 'framlɪŋ(ə)m
AM 'fræmlɪŋəm

Framlington
BR 'framlɪŋt(ə)n
AM 'fræmlɪŋtən

Frampton
BR 'fram(p)t(ə)n
AM 'fræmtən

Fran
BR fran
AM fræn

franc
BR fraŋk, -s
AM fræŋk, -s

France
BR frɑːns, frans
AM fræns

Frances
BR 'frɑːnsɪs, 'fransɪs
AM 'frænsəs

Francesca
BR fran'tʃɛskə(r)
AM fræn'(t)ʃɛskə

Franche-Comté
BR ˌfrɒʃˈkɒ̃teɪ
AM ˌfrɑːnʃˌkɒnˈteɪ

franchise
BR ˈfran(t)ʃaɪz, -ɪz, -ɪŋ, -d
AM ˈfræn,(t)ʃaɪz, -ɪz, -ɪŋ, -d

franchisee
BR ˌfran(t)ʃaɪˈziː, -z
AM ˌfræn,(t)ʃaɪˈzi, -z

franchiser
BR ˈfran(t)ʃaɪzə(r), -z
AM ˈfræn,(t)ʃaɪzər, -z

Francine
BR frɑːnˈsiːn, franˈsiːn
AM ˌfrænˈsin

Francis
BR ˈfrɑːnsɪs, ˈfransɪs
AM ˈfrænsəs

Franciscan
BR franˈsɪsk(ə)n, -z
AM frænˈsɪskən, -z

francium
BR ˈfransɪəm, ˈfrɑːnsɪəm
AM ˈfræn(t)sɪəm

Franck
BR frɑːŋk
AM fraŋk

Franco
BR ˈfraŋkəʊ
AM ˈfræŋkoʊ

Franco-
BR ˈfraŋkəʊ
AM ˈfræŋkoʊ

Franco-German
BR ˈfraŋkəʊˈdʒəːmən
AM ˌfræŋkoʊˈdʒərmən

François
BR ˈfrɒnswɑː(r), ˈfrɑːnswɑː(r), ˈfranswɑː(r)
AM ˌfrænˈswɑ

Françoise
BR ˈfrɒnswɑː(r), ˈfrɑːnswɑː(r), ˈfranswɑː(r)
AM ˌfrænˈswɑz

francolin
BR ˈfraŋkəlɪn, -z
AM ˈfræŋkələn, -z

Francomania
BR ˌfraŋkəʊˈmeɪnɪə(r)
AM ˌfræŋkoʊˈmeɪnɪə

Franconia
BR fraŋˈkəʊnɪə(r)
AM fræŋˈkoʊnɪə

Francophile
BR ˈfraŋkə(ʊ)fʌɪl, -z
AM ˈfræŋkəˌfaɪl, -z

Francophobe
BR ˈfraŋkə(ʊ)fəʊb, -z
AM ˈfræŋkəˌfoʊb, -z

Francophobia
BR ˌfraŋkə(ʊ)ˈfəʊbɪə(r)
AM ˌfræŋkəˈfoʊbɪə

francophone
BR ˈfraŋkə(ʊ)fəʊn
AM ˈfræŋkəˌfoʊn

frangibility
BR ˌfran(d)ʒɪˈbɪlɪti
AM ˌfrændʒəˈbɪlɪdi

frangible
BR ˈfran(d)ʒɪbl
AM ˈfrændʒəbəl

frangibleness
BR ˈfran(d)ʒɪblnəs
AM ˈfrændʒəbəlnəs

frangipane
BR ˈfran(d)ʒɪpeɪn, -z
AM ˈfrændʒəˌpeɪn, -z

frangipani
BR ˌfran(d)ʒɪˈpɑːnʲi, -ɪz
AM ˌfrændʒəˈpɑni, ˌfræn(d)ʒəˈpæni, -z

franglais
BR ˈfrɑːŋgleɪ, ˈfrɒŋgleɪ
AM ˈfrɑŋˈgleɪ

frank
BR fraŋ|k, -ks, -kɪŋ, -(k)t, -kə(r), -kɪst
AM fræŋ|k, -ks, -kɪŋ, -(k)t, -kər, -kəst

frankable
BR ˈfraŋkəbl
AM ˈfræŋkəbəl

Frankenstein
BR ˈfraŋk(ɪ)nstʌɪn
AM ˈfræŋkənˌstaɪn

franker
BR ˈfraŋkə(r), -z
AM ˈfræŋkər, -z

Frankfort
BR ˈfraŋkfət
AM ˈfræŋkfərt

Frankfurt
BR ˈfraŋkfə(ː)t
AM ˈfræŋkfərt

frankfurter
BR ˈfraŋkfəːtə(r), -z
AM ˈfræŋkfərdər, -z

Frankie
BR ˈfraŋki
AM ˈfræŋki

frankincense
BR ˈfraŋk(ɪ)nsɛns
AM ˈfræŋkənˌsɛns

Frankish
BR ˈfraŋkɪʃ
AM ˈfræŋkɪʃ

Frankland
BR ˈfraŋklənd
AM ˈfræŋklənd

franklin
BR ˈfraŋklɪn, -z
AM ˈfræŋklən, -z

frankly
BR ˈfraŋkli
AM ˈfræŋkli

Franklyn
BR ˈfraŋklɪn
AM ˈfræŋklən

frankness
BR ˈfraŋknəs
AM ˈfræŋknəs

Franks
BR fraŋks
AM fræŋks

frantic
BR ˈfrantɪk
AM ˈfræn(t)ɪk

frantically
BR ˈfrantɪkli
AM ˈfræn(t)ək(ə)li

franticly
BR ˈfrantɪkli
AM ˈfræn(t)ək(ə)li

franticness
BR ˈfrantɪknɪs
AM ˈfræn(t)ɪknɪs

Franz Joseph Land
BR ˌfran(t)s ˈdʒəʊsɪf ˌland
AM ˌfran(t)s ˈdʒoʊsəf ˌlænd

frap
BR frap, -s, -ɪŋ, -t
AM fræp, -s, -ɪŋ, -t

frappé
BR ˈfrapeɪ
AM fræˈpeɪ, fræp

Frascati
BR fraˈskɑːti
AM fræsˈkɑdi

Fraser
BR ˈfreɪzə(r)
AM ˈfreɪzər, ˈfreɪʒər

Fraserburgh
BR ˈfreɪzəb(ə)rə(r), ˈfreɪzəˌbʌrə(r)
AM ˈfreɪzərˌbərə

frass
BR fras
AM fræs

frat
BR frat
AM fræt

fratchiness
BR ˈfratʃɪnɪs
AM ˈfrætʃɪnɪs

fratchy
BR ˈfratʃi
AM ˈfrætʃi

fraternal
BR frəˈtəːnl
AM frəˈtərnəl

fraternalism
BR frəˈtəːnlɪz(ə)m, frəˈtəːnəlɪz(ə)m
AM frəˈtərnlˌɪzəm

fraternally
BR frəˈtəːnli, frəˈtəːnəli
AM frəˈtərnəli

fraternisation
BR ˌfratənʌɪˈzeɪʃn
AM ˌfrædərnəˈzeɪʃən, ˈfrædərˌnaɪˈzeɪʃən

fraternise
BR ˈfratənʌɪz, -ɪz, -ɪŋ, -d
AM ˈfrædərˌnaɪz, -ɪz, -ɪŋ, -d

fraternity
BR frəˈtəːnɪtʲi, -ɪz
AM frəˈtərnədi, -z

fraternization
BR ˌfratənʌɪˈzeɪʃn
AM ˌfrædərnəˈzeɪʃən, ˈfrædərˌnaɪˈzeɪʃən

fraternize
BR ˈfratənʌɪz, -ɪz, -ɪŋ, -d
AM ˈfrædərˌnaɪz, -ɪz, -ɪŋ, -d

fratricidal
BR ˌfratrɪˈsʌɪdl
AM ˈfrætrəˌsaɪdəl

fratricide
BR ˈfratrɪsʌɪd, -z
AM ˈfrætrəˌsaɪd, -z

Frau
BR frau, -z
AM frau, -z

fraud
BR frɔːd, -z
AM frɔd, frɑd, -z

fraudster
BR ˈfrɔːdstə(r), -z
AM ˈfrɔdˌstər, -z

fraudulence
BR ˈfrɔːdjʊləns, ˈfrɔːdjʊlns, ˈfrɔːdʒʊləns, ˈfrɔːdʒʊlns, ˈfrɔːdʒ(ə)ns
AM ˈfrɔdʒələns, ˈfradʒələns

fraudulent
BR ˈfrɔːdjʊlənt, ˈfrɔːdjʊlnt, ˈfrɔːdʒʊlənt, ˈfrɔːdʒʊlnt, ˈfrɔːdʒ(ə)nt
AM ˈfrɔdʒələnt, ˈfradʒələnt

fraudulently
BR ˈfrɔːdjʊləntli, ˈfrɔːdjʊlntli, ˈfrɔːdʒʊləntli, ˈfrɔːdʒʊlntli, ˈfrɔːdʒlntli
AM ˈfrɔdʒələn(t)li, ˈfradʒələn(t)li

fraught
BR frɔːt
AM frɔt, frɑt

Fräulein
BR ˈfrɔɪlʌɪn, -z
AM ˈfrɔɪˌlaɪn, -z

fraulein
BR ˈfrɔɪlʌɪn, -z
AM ˈfrɔɪˌlaɪn, -z

Fraunhofer
BR ˈfraʊnhəʊfə(r)
AM ˈfraʊnˌ(h)oʊfər

fraxinella
BR ˌfraksɪˈnɛlə(r)
AM ˌfræksəˈnɛlə

fray
BR freɪ, -z, -ɪŋ, -d
AM freɪ, -z, -ɪŋ, -d

Fray Bentos
BR ˌfreɪ ˈbɛntɒs
AM ˌfreɪ ˈbɛn(t)əs

Frayn
BR freɪn
AM freɪn

Frayne
BR freɪn
AM freɪn

Frazer
BR ˈfreɪzə(r)
AM ˈfreɪzər, ˈfreɪʒər

Frazier
BR ˈfreɪzɪə(r)
AM ˈfreɪzər, ˈfreɪʒər

frazil
BR ˈfreɪz(ɪ)l, frəˈzɪl
AM ˈfreɪzl, ˈfræzəl

frazzle
BR ˈfraz|l, -lz, -lɪŋ \-l-lɪŋ, -ld
AM ˈfræz|əl, -əlz, -(ə)lɪŋ, -əld

freak
BR friːk, -s, -ɪŋ, -t
AM frik, -s, -ɪŋ, -t

freakily
BR ˈfriːkɪli
AM ˈfrikɪli

freakiness
BR ˈfriːkɪnɪs
AM ˈfrikɪnɪs

freakish
BR ˈfriːkɪʃ
AM ˈfrikɪʃ

freakishly
BR ˈfriːkɪʃli
AM ˈfrikɪʃli

freakishness
BR ˈfriːkɪʃnɪs
AM ˈfrikɪʃnɪs

freaky
BR ˈfriːk|i, -iə(r), -iɪst
AM ˈfriki, -ər, -iɪst

freckle
BR ˈfrɛkl, -z, -d
AM ˈfrɛkəl, -z, -d

freckly
BR ˈfrɛkli
AM ˈfrɛkli, ˈfrɛkli

Fred
BR frɛd
AM frɛd

Freddie
BR ˈfrɛdi
AM ˈfrɛdi

Freddy
BR ˈfrɛdi
AM ˈfrɛdi

Frederic
BR ˈfrɛd(ə)rɪk

Frederica
BR ˌfrɛdəˈriːkə(r),
frɛˈdriːkə(r)
AM ˌfrɛd(ə)ˈrikə

Frederick
BR ˈfrɛd(ə)rɪk
AM ˈfrɛdrɪk

Fredericton
BR ˈfrɛd(ə)rɪkt(ə)n
AM ˈfrɛdrɪktən

free
BR friː, -z, -ɪŋ, -d, -ə(r),
-ɪst
AM fri, -s, -ɪŋ, -d, -ər, -ɪst

freebase
BR ˈfriːbeɪs, -ɪz, -ɪŋ, -d
AM ˈfriˌbeɪs, -ɪz, -ɪŋ, -d

freebee
BR ˈfriːb|i, -ɪz
AM ˈfribi, -z

freebie
BR ˈfriːb|i, -ɪz
AM ˈfribi, -z

freeboard
BR ˈfriːbɔːd, -z
AM ˈfriˌbɔ(ə)rd, -z

freeboot
BR ˈfriːbuːt, -s, -ɪŋ, -ɪd
AM ˈfriˌbu|t, -ts, -dɪŋ, -dəd

freebooter
BR ˈfriːˌbuːtə(r), -z
AM ˈfriˌbudər, -z

freeborn
BR ˌfriːˈbɔːn
AM ˈfriˈbɔ(ə)rn

freedman
BR ˈfriːdman,
ˈfriːdmən
AM ˈfridˌmæn,
ˈfridmən

freedmen
BR ˈfriːdmɛn,
ˈfriːdmən
AM ˈfridˌmɛn,
ˈfridmən

freedom
BR ˈfriːdəm, -z
AM ˈfridəm, -z

freedwoman
BR ˈfriːdˌwʊmən
AM ˈfridˌwʊmən

freedwomen
BR ˈfriːdˌwɪmɪn
AM ˈfridˌwɪmɪn

Freefone®
BR ˈfriːfəʊn
AM ˈfriˌfoʊn

freehand
BR ˈfriːhand
AM ˈfriˌ(h)ænd

freehold
BR ˈfriːhəʊld, -z
AM ˈfriˌ(h)oʊld, -z

freeholder
BR ˈfriːhəʊldə(r), -z

freelance
BR ˈfriːlɑːns, ˈfriːlans,
-ɪz, -ɪŋ, -t
AM ˈfriˌlæns, -əz, -ɪŋ, -t

freeload
BR ˈfriːləʊd, -z, -ɪŋ, -ɪd
AM ˈfriˌloʊd, -z, -ɪŋ, -əd

freeloader
BR ˈfriːləʊdə(r), -z
AM ˈfriˌloʊdər, -z

freely
BR ˈfriːli
AM ˈfrili

Freeman
BR ˈfriːmən
AM ˈfrimən

freeman
BR ˈfriːmən
AM ˈfrimən, friˌmæn

freemartin
BR ˈfriːˌmɑːtɪn, -z
AM ˈfriˌmartn, -z

Freemason
BR ˈfriːˌmeɪsn, -z
AM ˈfriˌmeɪsən, -z

freemasonry
BR ˈfriːˌmeɪsnri
AM ˈfriˌmeɪsnri

freemen
BR ˈfriːmən
AM ˈfrimən, friˌmɛn

freeness
BR ˈfriːnɪs
AM ˈfrinɪs

freephone
BR ˈfriːfəʊn
AM ˈfriˌfoʊn

Freeport
BR ˈfriːpɔːt
AM ˈfriˌpɔ(ə)rt

Freepost
BR ˈfriːpəʊst
AM ˈfriˌpoʊst

Freer
BR frɪə(r)
AM ˈfri(ə)r

freer
BR ˈfriːə(r)
AM ˈfriər

freesheet
BR ˈfriːʃiːt, -s
AM ˈfriˌʃit, -s

freesia
BR ˈfriːzɪə(r), ˈfriːʒə(r),
-z
AM ˈfriʒ(i)ə, ˈfriziə, -z

freest
BR ˈfriːɪst
AM ˈfriɪst

freestanding
BR ˌfriːˈstandɪŋ
AM ˈfriˈstændɪŋ

freestone
BR ˈfriːstəʊn
AM ˈfriˌstoʊn

freestyle
BR ˈfriːstaɪl
AM ˈfriˌstaɪl

freestyler
BR ˈfriːstaɪlə(r), -z
AM ˈfriˌstaɪlər, -z

freethinker
BR ˌfriːˈθɪŋkə(r), -z
AM ˈfriˈθɪŋkər, -z

freethinking
BR ˌfriːˈθɪŋkɪŋ
AM ˈfriˈθɪŋkɪŋ

Freetown
BR ˈfriːtaʊn
AM ˈfriˌtaʊn

freeware
BR ˈfriːwɛː(r)
AM ˈfriˌwɛ(ə)r

freeway
BR ˈfriːweɪ, -z
AM ˈfriˌweɪ, -z

freewheel
BR ˌfriːˈwiːl, -z, -ɪŋ, -d
AM ˈfriˈ(h)wil, -z, -ɪŋ, -d

freewheeler
BR ˌfriːˈwiːlə(r), -z
AM ˈfriˈ(h)wilər, -z

freewill
BR ˌfriːˈwɪl
AM ˈfriˈwɪl

freezable
BR ˈfriːzəbl
AM ˈfrizəbəl

freeze
BR friːz, -ɪz, -ɪŋ
AM friz, -ɪz, -ɪŋ

freezer
BR ˈfriːzə(r), -z
AM ˈfrizər, -z

Freiburg
BR ˈfraɪbəːg
AM ˈfraɪˌbɜrg

freight
BR freɪt, -s, -ɪŋ, -ɪd
AM freɪ|t, -ts, -dɪŋ, -dɪd

freightage
BR ˈfreɪtɪdʒ
AM ˈfreɪdɪdʒ

freighter
BR ˈfreɪtə(r), -z
AM ˈfreɪdər, -z

freightliner
BR ˈfreɪtˌlaɪnə(r), -z
AM ˈfreɪtˌlaɪnər, -z

Freischütz, Der
BR ˌdə: ˈfraɪʃuːts
AM ˌdər ˈfraɪˌʃuts

Frelimo
BR frɛˈliːməʊ,
frɪˈliːməʊ
AM frɛˈlimoʊ

Fremantle
BR ˈfriːmantl
AM ˈfriˌmæn(t)əl

fremitus
BR ˈfrɛmɪtəs
AM ˈfrɛmədəs

Frémont
BR ˈfriːmɒnt
AM ˈfriˌmɑnt

frena
BR ˈfriːnə(r)
AM ˈfrinə

French
BR frɛn(t)ʃ
AM frɛn(t)ʃ

Frenchification
BR ˌfrɛn(t)ʃɪfɪˈkeɪʃn
AM ˌfrɛn(t)ʃəfəˈkeɪʃən

Frenchify¹
BR ˈfrɛn(t)ʃɪfʌɪ, -z, -ɪŋ, -d
AM ˈfrɛn(t)ʃəˌfaɪ, -z, -ɪŋ, -d

Frenchify²
BR ˈfrɛn(t)ʃɪfʌɪ, -z, -ɪŋ, -d
AM ˈfrɛntʃəˌfaɪ, -z, -ɪŋ, -d

Frenchman
BR ˈfrɛn(t)ʃmən
AM ˈfrɛn(t)ʃmən

Frenchmen
BR ˈfrɛn(t)ʃmən
AM ˈfrɛn(t)ʃmən

Frenchness
BR ˈfrɛn(t)ʃnəs
AM ˈfrɛn(t)ʃnəs

Frenchwoman
BR ˈfrɛn(t)ʃˌwʊmən
AM ˈfrɛn(t)ʃˌwʊmən

Frenchwomen
BR ˈfrɛn(t)ʃˌwɪmɪn
AM ˈfrɛn(t)ʃˌwɪmɪn

Frenchy
BR ˈfrɛn(t)ʃli, -ɪz
AM ˈfrɛn(t)ʃi, -z

frenetic
BR frɪˈnɛtɪk
AM frəˈnɛdɪk

frenetically
BR frɪˈnɛtɪkli
AM frəˈnɛdək(ə)li

frenula
BR ˈfrɛnjələ(r)
AM ˈfrɛnjələ

frenulum
BR ˈfrɛnjələm
AM ˈfrɛnjələm

frenum
BR ˈfriːnəm
AM ˈfrinəm

frenzied
BR ˈfrɛnzid
AM ˈfrɛnzid

frenziedly
BR ˈfrɛnzidli
AM ˈfrɛnzidli

frenzy
BR ˈfrɛnz|i, -ɪz
AM ˈfrɛnzi, -z

Freon®
BR ˈfriːɒn, -z
AM ˈfriˌɑn, -z

frequency
BR ˈfriːkw(ə)ns|i, -ɪz
AM ˈfrikwənsi, -z

frequent¹
adjective
BR ˈfriːkw(ə)nt
AM ˈfrikwənt

frequent²
verb
BR frɪˈkwɛnt, -s, -ɪŋ, -ɪd
AM friˈkwɛn|t, -ts, -(t)ɪŋ, -(t)əd

frequentation
BR ˌfriːkw(ə)nˈteɪʃn
AM ˌfrikwənˈteɪʃən

frequentative
BR frɪˈkwɛntətɪv
AM frɪˈkwən(t)ədɪv

frequenter
BR frɪˈkwɛntə(r), -z
AM friˈkwɛn(t)ər, -z

frequently
BR ˈfriːkw(ə)ntli
AM ˈfrikwən(t)li

Frere
BR frɪə(r), frɛː(r)
AM ˈfrɛr(i)

fresco
BR ˈfrɛskəʊ, -z, -d
AM ˈfrɛskoʊ, -z, -d

fresco secco
BR ˌfrɛskəʊ ˈsɛkəʊ
AM ˌfrɛskoʊ ˈsɛkoʊ

fresh
BR frɛʃ, -ə(r), -ɪst
AM frɛʃ, -ər, -əst

freshen
BR ˈfrɛʃ|n, -nz, -nɪŋ \ -(ə)nɪŋ, -nd
AM ˈfrɛʃ|ən, -ənz, -(ə)nɪŋ, -ənd

fresher
BR ˈfrɛʃə(r), -z
AM ˈfrɛʃər, -z

freshet
BR ˈfrɛʃɪt, -s
AM ˈfrɛʃət, -s

freshly
BR ˈfrɛʃli
AM ˈfrɛʃli

freshness
BR ˈfrɛʃnəs
AM ˈfrɛʃnəs

freshwater
BR ˈfrɛʃˌwɔːtə(r)
AM ˈfrɛʃˌwɔdər, ˈfrɛʃˌwɑdər

freshwoman
BR ˈfrɛʃˌwʊmən
AM ˈfrɛʃˌwʊmən

freshwomen
BR ˈfrɛʃˌwɪmɪn
AM ˈfrɛʃˌwɪmɪn

Fresnel
BR ˈfreɪnɛl, frəˈnɛl
AM frəˈnɛl

Fresno
BR ˈfrɛznəʊ
AM ˈfrɛznoʊ

fret
BR frɛt, -s, -ɪŋ, -ɪd
AM frɛ|t, -ts, -dɪŋ, -dəd

fretboard
BR ˈfrɛtbɔːd, -z
AM ˈfrɛtˌbɔ(ə)rd, -z

fretful
BR ˈfrɛtf(ʊ)l
AM ˈfrɛtfəl

fretfully
BR ˈfrɛtfʊli, ˈfrɛtfli
AM ˈfrɛtfəli

fretfulness
BR ˈfrɛtf(ʊ)lnəs
AM ˈfrɛtfəlnəs

fretless
BR ˈfrɛtləs
AM ˈfrɛtləs

fretsaw
BR ˈfrɛtsɔː(r), -z
AM ˈfrɛtˌsɔ, ˈfrɛtˌsɑ, -z

fretwork
BR ˈfrɛtwəːk
AM ˈfrɛtˌwərk

Freud
BR frɔɪd
AM frɔɪd

Freudian
BR ˈfrɔɪdiən
AM ˈfrɔɪdiən

Freudianism
BR ˈfrɔɪdiənɪz(ə)m
AM ˈfrɔɪdiəˌnɪzəm

Frey
BR freɪ
AM freɪ

Freya
BR ˈfreɪə(r)
AM ˈfreɪə

Freyr
BR ˈfreɪə(r)
AM ˈfreɪər

friability
BR ˌfrʌɪəˈbɪlɪti
AM ˌfraɪəˈbɪlɪdi

friable
BR ˈfrʌɪəbl
AM ˈfraɪəbəl

friableness
BR ˈfrʌɪəblnəs
AM ˈfraɪəbəlnəs

friar
BR ˈfrʌɪə(r), -z
AM ˈfraɪər, -z

friarly
BR ˈfrʌɪəli
AM ˈfraɪərli

friary
BR ˈfrʌɪər|i, -ɪz
AM ˈfraɪəri, -z

fribble
BR ˈfrɪbl, -z, -ɪŋ, -d
AM ˈfrɪb|əl, -əld, -(ə)lɪŋ, -əld

fricandeau
BR ˈfrɪk(ə)ndəʊ, -z
AM ˈfrɪkənˌdoʊ, ˌfrɪkənˈdoʊ, -z

fricandeaux
BR ˈfrɪk(ə)ndəʊz
AM ˈfrɪkənˌdoʊz, ˌfrɪkənˈdoʊ

fricassee
BR ˈfrɪkəsiː, ˌfrɪkəˈsiː, -z, -ɪŋ, -d
AM ˈfrɪkəˌsi, ˌfrɪkəˈsi, -z, -ɪŋ, -d

fricative
BR ˈfrɪkətɪv, -z
AM ˈfrɪkədɪv, -z

friction
BR ˈfrɪkʃn
AM ˈfrɪkʃən

frictional
BR ˈfrɪkʃn(ə)l, ˈfrɪkʃən(ə)l, -z
AM ˈfrɪkʃ(ə)nəl, -z

frictionally
BR ˈfrɪkʃnəli, ˈfrɪkʃn̩li, ˈfrɪkʃənli, ˈfrɪkʃ(ə)nəli
AM ˈfrɪkʃ(ə)nəli

frictionless
BR ˈfrɪkʃnləs
AM ˈfrɪkʃənləs

Friday
BR ˈfrʌɪdeɪ, ˈfrʌɪd|i, -eɪz \ -ɪz
AM ˈfraɪˌdeɪ, ˈfraɪdi, -z

fridge
BR frɪdʒ, -ɪz
AM frɪdʒ, -ɪz

Friedan
BR friˈdan
AM friˈdæn

Friedman
BR ˈfriːdmən
AM ˈfridmən

Friedrich
BR ˈfriːdrɪk
AM ˈfridrɪk

friend
BR frɛnd, -z
AM frɛnd, -z

friendless
BR ˈfrɛndləs
AM ˈfrɛn(d)ləs

friendlessness
BR ˈfrɛndləsnəs
AM ˈfrɛn(d)ləsnəs

friendlily
BR ˈfrɛndlɪli
AM ˈfrɛn(d)ləli

friendliness
BR ˈfrɛndlɪnɪs

friendly
AM ˈfren(d)linɪs

friendly
BR ˈfrendli
AM ˈfren(d)li

friendship
BR ˈfren(d)ʃɪp, -s
AM ˈfren(d)ˌʃɪp, -s

frier
BR ˈfrʌɪə(r), -z
AM ˈfraɪər, -z

Friern Barnet
BR ˌfrʌɪən ˈbɑːnɪt
AM ˌfraɪərn ˈbɑrnət

Fries
BR friːz
AM friz

Friesian
BR ˈfriːʒn, -z
AM ˈfriʒən, ˈfriʒən, -z

Friesland
BR ˈfriːzlənd
AM ˈfrizlənd

frieze
BR friːz, -ɪz
AM friz, -ɪz

frig¹
noun, refrigerator
BR frɪdʒ, -ɪz
AM frɪdʒ, -ɪz

frig²
verb, copulate,
masturbate
BR frɪg, -z, -ɪŋ, -d
AM frɪg, -z, -ɪŋ, -d

frigate
BR ˈfrɪgɪt, -s
AM ˈfrɪgɪt, -s

Frigg
BR frɪg
AM frɪg

Frigga
BR ˈfrɪgə(r)
AM ˈfrɪgə

fright
BR frʌɪt, -s
AM fraɪt, -s

frighten
BR ˈfrʌɪt|n, -nz,
-nɪŋ\-nɪŋ, -nd
AM ˈfraɪtn, -z, -ɪŋ, -d

frightener
BR ˈfrʌɪtnə(r),
ˈfrʌɪtnə(r), -z
AM ˈfraɪtnər, ˈfraɪtnər,
-z

frighteningly
BR ˈfrʌɪtnɪŋli,
ˈfrʌɪtnɪŋli
AM ˈfraɪtnɪŋli,
ˈfraɪtnɪŋli

frightful
BR ˈfrʌɪtf(ʊ)l
AM ˈfraɪtfəl

frightfully
BR ˈfrʌɪtfʊli, ˈfrʌɪtfli
AM ˈfraɪtfəli

frightfulness
BR ˈfrʌɪtf(ʊ)lnəs
AM ˈfraɪtfəlnəs

frigid
BR ˈfrɪdʒɪd
AM ˈfrɪdʒɪd

Frigidaire®
BR ˌfrɪdʒɪˈdɛː(r), -z
AM ˌfrɪdʒɪˈdɛ(ə)r, -z

frigidaria
BR ˌfrɪdʒɪˈdɛːrɪə(r)
AM ˌfrɪdʒəˈdɛrɪə

frigidarium
BR ˌfrɪdʒɪˈdɛːrɪəm, -z
AM ˌfrɪdʒəˈdɛriəm, -z

frigidity
BR frɪˈdʒɪdɪti
AM frəˈdʒɪdɪdi

frigidly
BR ˈfrɪdʒɪdli
AM ˈfrɪdʒɪdli

frigidness
BR ˈfrɪdʒɪdnɪs
AM ˈfrɪdʒɪdnɪs

frijoles
BR frɪˈhəʊles
AM friˈhouˌleis

frill
BR frɪl, -z, -d
AM frɪl, -z, -d

frillery
BR ˈfrɪlər|i, -ɪz
AM ˈfrɪləri, -z

frilliness
BR ˈfrɪlɪnɪs
AM ˈfrɪlɪnɪs

frilling
BR ˈfrɪlɪŋ, -z
AM ˈfrɪlɪŋ, -z

frilly
BR ˈfrɪli
AM ˈfrɪli

fringe
BR frɪn(d)ʒ, -ɪz
AM frɪndʒ, -ɪz

fringeless
BR ˈfrɪn(d)ʒlɪs
AM ˈfrɪndʒləs

fringy
BR ˈfrɪn(d)ʒi
AM ˈfrɪndʒi

Frink
BR frɪŋk
AM frɪŋk

Frinton
BR ˈfrɪnt(ə)n
AM ˈfrɪn(t)ən

frippery
BR ˈfrɪp(ə)r|i, -ɪz
AM ˈfrɪp(ə)ri, -z

frippet
BR ˈfrɪpɪt, -s
AM ˈfrɪpɪt, -s

frisbee®
BR ˈfrɪzb|iː, -ɪz
AM ˈfrɪzˌbi, -z

Frisch
BR frɪʃ
AM frɪʃ

frisé
BR ˈfriːzeɪ, ˈfrizeɪ
AM friˈzei

frisée
BR ˈfriːzeɪ, ˈfrizeɪ
AM friˈzei

Frisia
BR ˈfrɪzɪə(r), ˈfrɪʒə(r),
ˈfriːzɪə(r), ˈfriːʒə(r)
AM ˈfrɪʒə, ˈfriʒə

Frisian
BR ˈfrɪzɪən, ˈfrɪʒn,
ˈfriːzɪən, ˈfriːʒn, -z
AM ˈfrɪʒən, ˈfrɪʒən, -z

frisk
BR frɪsk, -s, -ɪŋ, -t
AM frɪsk, -s, -ɪŋ, -t

frisker
BR ˈfrɪskə(r), -z
AM ˈfrɪskər, -z

frisket
BR ˈfrɪskɪt, -s
AM ˈfrɪskɪt, -s

friskily
BR ˈfrɪskɪli
AM ˈfrɪskɪli

friskiness
BR ˈfrɪskɪnɪs
AM ˈfrɪskɪnɪs

frisky
BR ˈfrɪski
AM ˈfrɪski

frisson
BR ˈfriːsɒn, ˈfrɪsɒn, -z
AM friˈsɔn, -z

frit
BR frɪt, -s, -ɪŋ, -ɪd
AM frɪ|t, -ts, -dɪŋ, -dɪd

frites
plural noun
BR friːt
AM frit

frith
BR frɪθ, -s
AM frɪθ, -s

fritillary
BR frɪˈtɪl(ə)r|i, -ɪz
AM ˈfrɪdlˌɛri, -z

fritter
BR ˈfrɪt|ə(r), -əz,
-(ə)rɪŋ, -əd
AM ˈfrɪdər, -z, -ɪŋ, -d

fritto misto
BR ˌfrɪtəʊ ˈmɪstəʊ
AM ˌfrɪtou ˈmɪstou

Fritz
BR frɪts
AM frɪts

Friuli
BR frɪˈuːli
AM friˈuli

Friulian
BR frɪˈuːlɪən
AM friˈuljən, friˈulian

frivol
BR ˈfrɪv|l, -lz, -lɪŋ\-lɪŋ,
-ld
AM ˈfrɪv|əl, -əlz, -(ə)lɪŋ,
-əld

frivolity
BR frɪˈvɒlɪt|i, -ɪz
AM frɪˈvalədi, -z

frivolous
BR ˈfrɪvələs, ˈfrɪvjələs
AM ˈfrɪvələs

frivolously
BR ˈfrɪvələsli,
ˈfrɪvjələsli
AM ˈfrɪvələsli

frivolousness
BR ˈfrɪvələsnəs,
ˈfrɪvjələsnəs
AM ˈfrɪvələsnəs

friz
BR frɪz, -ɪz, -ɪŋ, -d
AM frɪz, -ɪz, -ɪŋ, -d

frizz
BR frɪz, -ɪz, -ɪŋ, -d
AM frɪz, -ɪz, -ɪŋ, -d

frizzily
BR ˈfrɪzɪli
AM ˈfrɪzɪli

frizziness
BR ˈfrɪzɪnɪs
AM ˈfrɪzɪnɪs

frizzle
BR ˈfrɪz|l, -lz, -lɪŋ\-lɪŋ,
-ld
AM ˈfrɪz|əl, -əlz, -(ə)lɪŋ,
-əld

frizzly
BR ˈfrɪz|i, ˈfrɪzli
AM ˈfrɪz|i, ˈfrɪzli

frizzy
BR ˈfrɪz|i, -ɪə(r), -ɪɪst
AM ˈfrɪzi, -ər, -ɪst

fro
BR frəʊ
AM frou

Frobisher
BR ˈfrəʊbɪʃə(r)
AM ˈfroubɪʃər

frock
BR frɒk, -s
AM frak, -s

Frodsham
BR ˈfrɒdʃ(ə)m
AM ˈfrɑdʃəm, ˈfrɑdʃəm

froe
BR frəʊ, -z
AM frou, -z

Froebel
BR ˈfrəʊbl, ˈfrəːbl
AM ˈfreɪbəl

Froebelian
BR frə(ʊ)ˈbiːlɪən,
frəːˈbiːlɪən, -z
AM frəˈbiliən, -z

Froebelism
BR ˈfrəʊbɪlɪz(ə)m,
ˈfrəʊblɪz(ə)m,

'frəːbɪlɪz(ə)m,
'frəːblɪz(ə)m
AM 'freɪbə͵lɪzəm

frog
BR frɒg, -z, -d
AM frɔg, frag, -z, -d

frogbit
BR 'frɒgbɪt, -s
AM 'frɔg͵bɪt, 'frag͵bɪt,
-s

frogfish
BR 'frɒgfɪʃ, -ɪz
AM 'frɔg͵fɪʃ, 'frag͵fɪʃ,
-ɪz

Froggie
BR 'frɒg|i, -iz
AM 'frɔgi, 'fragi, -z

frogging
BR 'frɒgɪŋ, -z
AM 'frɔgɪŋ, 'fragɪŋ, -z

froggy
BR 'frɒgi
AM 'frɔgi, 'fragi

froghopper
BR 'frɒg͵hɒpə(r), -z
AM 'frɔg͵(h)ɑpər,
'frag͵(h)ɑpər, -z

frogman
BR 'frɒgmən
AM 'frɔgmən,
'frɒg͵mæn, 'fragmən,
'frag͵mæn

frogmarch
BR 'frɒgmɑːtʃ, -ɪz, -ɪŋ,
-t
AM 'frɔg͵mɑrtʃ,
'frag͵mɑrtʃ, -əz, -ɪŋ, -t

frogmen
BR 'frɒgmən
AM 'frɔgmən,
'frɒg͵mɛn, 'fragmən,
'frag͵mɛn

Frogmore
BR 'frɒgmɔː(r)
AM 'frɔg͵mɔ(ə)r,
'frag͵mɔ(ə)r

frogmouth
BR 'frɒgmaʊθ, -ðz
AM 'frɔg͵maʊθ,
'frag͵maʊθ, -θz \ -ðz

frogspawn
BR 'frɒgspɔːn
AM 'frɔg͵spɔn,
'frag͵spɑn

froing
BR 'frəʊɪŋ, -z
AM 'froʊɪŋ, -z

frolic
BR 'frɒl|ɪk, -ɪks, -ɪkɪŋ,
-ɪkt
AM 'frɑlɪk, -s, -ɪŋ, -t

frolicker
BR 'frɒlɪkə(r), -z
AM 'frɑlɪkər, -z

frolicsome
BR 'frɒlɪks(ə)m
AM 'frɑlɪksəm

frolicsomely
BR 'frɒlɪks(ə)mli
AM 'frɑlɪksəmli

frolicsomeness
BR 'frɒlɪks(ə)mnəs
AM 'frɑlɪksəmnəs

from[1]
strong form
BR frɒm
AM frɑm

from[2]
weak form
BR frəm
AM frəm

fromage blanc
BR ͵frɒmɑːʒ 'blɒ̃
AM froʊˈmɑʒ 'blɑŋk

fromage frais
BR ͵frɒmɑːʒ 'freɪ
AM froʊˈmɑʒ 'freɪ

Frome[1]
Australia
BR frəʊm
AM froʊm

Frome[2]
England, West Indies
BR fruːm
AM frum

Fron
in Welsh placenames
BR vrɒn
AM vrɑn

frond
BR frɒnd, -z
AM frɑnd, -z

frondage
BR 'frɒndɪdʒ
AM 'frandɪdʒ

Fronde
BR frɒnd
AM frɑnd

Frondes
BR frɒnd
AM frɑnd

frondeur
BR ͵frɒn'dɜː(r)
AM frɔn'dɜr

frondeurs
BR ͵frɒn'dɜː(r),
͵frɒn'dɜːz
AM frɔn'dɜrz,
͵fran'dɜrz

frondose
BR frɒn'dəʊs
AM frɑn͵doʊs,
'fran͵doʊs

front
BR frʌnt, -s, -ɪŋ, -ɪd
AM frən|t, -ts, -(t)ɪŋ,
-(t)əd

frontage
BR 'frʌnt|ɪdʒ, -ɪdʒɪz
AM 'frən(t)ɪdʒ, -ɪz

frontager
BR 'frʌntɪdʒə(r), -z
AM 'frən(t)ɪdʒər, -z

frontal
BR 'frʌntl, -z

AM 'frən(t)l, -z

frontally
BR 'frʌntli
AM 'frən(t)li

frontbench
adjective
BR ͵frʌn'tbɛn(t)ʃ
AM ͵'frən(t)'bɛn(t)ʃ

front bench
noun
BR ͵frʌnt 'bɛn(t)ʃ, -ɪz
AM ͵'frən(t) 'bɛn(t)ʃ, -əz

front-bencher
BR ͵frʌn'tbɛn(t)ʃə(r),
-z
AM ͵'frən(t)'bɛn(t)ʃər, -z

frontier
BR 'frʌntɪə(r),
frʌn'tɪə(r), -z
AM frən'tɪ(ə)r, -z

frontierless
BR 'frʌntɪələs,
frʌn'tɪələs
AM frən'tɪrləs

frontiersman
BR 'frʌntɪəzmən,
frʌn'tɪəzmən
AM frən'tɪrzmən

frontiersmen
BR 'frʌntɪəzmən,
frʌn'tɪəzmən
AM frən'tɪrzmən

frontierswoman
BR 'frʌntɪəz͵wʊmən,
frʌn'tɪəz͵wʊmən
AM frən'tɪrz͵wʊmən

frontierswomen
BR 'frʌntɪəz͵wɪmɪn,
frʌn'tɪəz͵wɪmɪn
AM frən'tɪrz͵wɪmɪn

frontispiece
BR 'frʌntɪspiːs, -ɪz
AM 'frən(t)ɪs͵pis, -ɪz

frontless
BR 'frʌntləs
AM 'frən(t)ləs

frontlet
BR 'frʌntlɪt, -s
AM 'frən(t)lət, -s

frontline
BR ͵frʌnt'lʌɪn
AM ͵'frən(t)'laɪn

frontman
BR 'frʌntman
AM 'frən(t)͵mæn

frontmen
BR 'frʌntmɛn
AM 'frən(t)mɛn

frontogenesis
BR ͵frʌntə(ʊ)'dʒɛnɪsɪs
AM ͵'frən(t)oʊ'dʒɛnəsəs,
͵'fran(t)oʊ'dʒɛnəsəs

frontogenetic
BR ͵frʌntə(ʊ)dʒɪ'nɛtɪk
AM ͵'frən(t)oʊdʒə'nɛdɪk,
͵'fran(t)oʊdʒə'nɛdɪk

fronton
BR 'frʌnt(ə)n, -z

AM 'frʌn͵tɑn, -z

frontpage
BR ͵frʌnt'peɪdʒ
AM 'frən(t)'peɪdʒ

front-runner
BR ͵frʌnt'rʌnə(r),
'frʌnt͵rʌnə(r), -z
AM 'frən(t)͵rənər, -z

frontward
BR 'frʌntwəd, -z
AM 'frəntwərd, -z

frore
BR frɔː(r)
AM frɔ(ə)r

frosh
BR frɒʃ, -ɪz
AM frɔʃ, fraʃ, -əz

frost
BR frɒst, -s, -ɪŋ, -ɪd
AM frɔst, frast, -s, -ɪŋ,
-əd

frostbite
BR 'frɒs(t)bʌɪt
AM 'frɔs(t)͵baɪt,
'fras(t)͵baɪt

frostbitten
BR 'frɒs(t)͵bɪtn
AM 'frɔs(t)͵bɪtn,
'fras(t)͵bɪtn

frostbound
BR 'frɒs(t)baʊnd
AM 'frɔs(t)͵baʊnd,
'fras(t)͵baʊnd

frost-free
BR ͵frɒs(t)'friː
AM ͵'frɔs(t)'fri,
'fras(t)'fri

frostily
BR 'frɒstɪli
AM 'frɔstəli, 'frastəli

frostiness
BR 'frɒstɪnɪs
AM 'frɔstɪnɪs,
'frastɪnɪs

frosting
BR 'frɒstɪŋ, -z
AM 'frɔstɪŋ, 'frastɪŋ, -z

frostless
BR 'frɒs(t)ləs
AM 'frɔs(t)ləs,
'fras(t)ləs

frost-work
BR 'frɒstwɜːk
AM 'frɔs(t)͵wərk,
'fras(t)͵wərk

frosty
BR 'frɒst|i, -ɪə(r), -ɪɪst
AM 'frɔsti, 'frasti, -ər,
-ɪst

froth
BR frɒθ, -s, -ɪŋ, -t
AM frɔθ, fraθ, -s, -ɪŋ, -t

frothily
BR 'frɒθɪli
AM 'frɔθəli, 'fraθəli

frothiness
BR 'frɒθɪnɪs
AM 'frɔθɪnɪs, 'fraθɪnɪs

frothy
BR 'frɒθ|i, -ɪə(r), -ɪɪst
AM 'frɔːθi, 'fraθi, -ər, -ɪst

frottage
BR 'frɒtɑːʒ, 'frɒtɪdʒ,
frɒ'tɑːʒ
AM frɔ'tɑʒ

froufrou
BR 'fruːfruː, -z
AM 'fru,fru, -z

frow
BR frəʊ, -z
AM froʊ, -z

froward
BR 'frəʊəd
AM 'froʊ(w)ərd

frowardly
BR 'frəʊədli
AM 'froʊ(w)ərdli

frowardness
BR 'frəʊədnəs
AM 'froʊ(w)ərdnəs

frown
BR fraʊn, -z, -ɪŋ, -d
AM fraʊn, -z, -ɪŋ, -d

frowner
BR 'fraʊnə(r)
AM 'fraʊnər

frowningly
BR 'fraʊnɪŋli
AM 'fraʊnɪŋli

frowsily
BR 'fraʊzɪli
AM 'fraʊzəli

frowst
BR fraʊst, -s, -ɪŋ, -ɪd
AM fraʊst, -s, -ɪŋ, -əd

frowster
BR 'fraʊstə(r), -z
AM 'fraʊstər, -z

frowstily
BR 'fraʊstɪli
AM 'fraʊstəli

frowstiness
BR 'fraʊstɪnɪs
AM 'fraʊstɪnɪs

frowsty
BR 'fraʊst|i, -ɪə(r), -ɪɪst
AM 'fraʊsti, -ər, -ɪst

frowsy
BR 'fraʊz|i, -ɪə(r), -ɪɪst
AM 'fraʊzi, -ər, -ɪst

frowzily
BR 'fraʊzɪli
AM 'fraʊzəli

frowziness
BR 'fraʊzɪnɪs
AM 'fraʊzɪnɪs

frowzy
BR 'fraʊz|i, -ɪə(r), -ɪɪst
AM 'fraʊzi, -ər, -ɪst

froze
BR frəʊz
AM froʊz

frozen
BR 'frəʊzn
AM 'froʊzən

frozenly
BR 'frəʊznli
AM 'froʊzənli

fructiferous
BR ,frʌk'tɪf(ə)rəs
AM ,frək'tɪfərəs

fructification
BR ,frʌktɪfɪ'keɪʃn
AM ,frəktəfə'keɪʃən

fructify
BR 'frʌktɪfʌɪ, -z, -ɪŋ, -d
AM 'frəktə,faɪ, -z, -ɪŋ, -d

fructose
BR 'frʌktəʊz,
'frʌktəʊs, 'frʊktəʊz,
'frʊktəʊs
AM 'frʊk,toʊs,
'frək,toʊs, 'frʊk,toʊz,
'frək,toʊz

fructuous
BR 'frʌktjʊəs,
'frʌktʃʊəs
AM 'frək(t)ʃ(əw)əs

frugal
BR 'fruːgl
AM 'fruːgəl

frugality
BR fruː'galɪti
AM fru'gæləti

frugally
BR 'fruːgli, 'fruːgəli
AM 'fruːgəli

frugalness
BR 'fruːglnəs
AM 'fruːgəlnəs

frugivorous
BR fruː'dʒɪv(ə)rəs
AM fru'dʒɪvərəs

fruit
BR fruːt, -s, -ɪŋ, -ɪd
AM fruɪt, -ts, -dɪŋ, -dəd

fruitage
BR 'fruːtɪdʒ
AM 'frudɪdʒ

fruitarian
BR fruː'teːrɪən, -z
AM fru'terɪən, -z

fruitbat
BR 'fruːtbat, -s
AM 'frut,bæt, -s

fruitcake
BR 'fruːtkeɪk, -s
AM 'frut,keɪk, -s

fruiter
BR 'fruːtə(r), -z
AM 'frudər, -z

fruiterer
BR 'fruːt(ə)rə(r), -z
AM 'frudərər, -z

fruitful
BR 'fruːtf(ʊ)l
AM 'frutfəl

fruitfully
BR 'fruːtfʊli, 'fruːtfļi
AM 'frutfəli

fruitfulness
BR 'fruːtf(ʊ)lnəs

fruitfulness
AM 'frutfəlnəs

fruitily
BR 'fruːtɪli
AM 'frudəli

fruitiness
BR 'fruːtɪnɪs
AM 'frudɪnɪs

fruition
BR fruː'ɪʃn
AM fru'ɪʃən

fruitless
BR 'fruːtləs
AM 'frutləs

fruitlessly
BR 'fruːtləsli
AM 'frutləsli

fruitlessness
BR 'fruːtləsnəs
AM 'frutləsnəs

fruitlet
BR 'fruːtlɪt, -s
AM 'frutlət, -s

fruitwood
BR 'fruːtwʊd, -z
AM 'frut,wʊd, -z

fruity
BR 'fruːt|i, -ɪə(r), -ɪɪst
AM 'frudi, -ər, -ɪst

frumenty
BR 'fruːm(ə)nti
AM 'frumən(t)i

frump
BR frʌmp, -s
AM frəmp, -s

frumpily
BR 'frʌmpɪli
AM 'frəmpəli

frumpiness
BR 'frʌmpɪnɪs
AM 'frəmpɪnɪs

frumpish
BR 'frʌmpɪʃ
AM 'frəmpɪʃ

frumpishly
BR 'frʌmpɪʃli
AM 'frəmpɪʃli

frumpy
BR 'frʌmp|i, -ɪə(r), -ɪɪst
AM 'frəmpi, -ər, -ɪst

frusemide
BR 'fruːsəmʌɪd
AM 'frusə,maɪd

frusta
BR 'frʌstə(r)
AM 'frəstə

frustrate
BR frʌ'streɪt, -s, -ɪŋ, -ɪd
AM 'frə,streɪ|t, -ts, -dɪŋ, -dɪd

frustratedly
BR frʌ'streɪtɪdli
AM 'frə,streɪdɪdli

frustrater
BR frʌ'streɪtə(r), -z
AM 'frə,streɪdər, -z

frustratingly
BR frʌ'streɪtɪŋli

frustalness AM 'frutfəlnəs
AM 'frutfəlnəs

frustration
BR frʌ'streɪʃn, -z
AM frə'streɪʃən, -z

frustule
BR 'frʌstjuːl,
'frʌstʃuːl, -z
AM 'frəs,tʃul, -z

frustum
BR 'frʌstəm, -z
AM 'frəstəm, -z

frutescent
BR fruː'tɛsnt
AM fru'tɛsənt

frutex
BR 'fruːtɛks, -ɪz
AM 'fru,dɛks, -əz

frutices
BR 'fruːtɪsiːz
AM 'frudə,siz

fruticose
BR 'fruːtɪkəʊz,
'fruːtɪkəʊs
AM 'frudə,koʊs

fry
BR frʌɪ, -z, -ɪŋ, -d
AM fraɪ, -z, -ɪŋ, -d

Frye
BR frʌɪ
AM fraɪ

fryer
BR 'frʌɪə(r), -z
AM 'fraɪər, -z

frypan
BR 'frʌɪpan, -z
AM 'fraɪ,pæn, -z

Fryston
BR 'frʌɪst(ə)n
AM 'fraɪstən

fry-up
BR 'frʌɪʌp, -s
AM 'fraɪ,əp, -s

FT-SE
BR 'fʊtsi
AM 'fʊtsi

fubsy
BR 'fʌbs|i, -ɪə(r), -ɪɪst
AM 'fəbsi, -ər, -ɪst

Fuchs
BR fuːks, fʊks
AM f(j)uks

fuchsia
BR 'fjuːʃə(r), -z
AM 'fjuʃə, -z

fuchsine
BR 'fuːksiːn
AM 'fjuksən, 'fjuk,sin

fuci
BR 'fjuːsʌɪ
AM 'fju,saɪ

fuck
BR fʌk, -s, -ɪŋ, -t
AM fək, -s, -ɪŋ, -t

fucker
BR 'fʌkə(r), -z
AM 'fəkər, -z

fucoid
BR ˈfjuːkɔɪd
AM ˈfjuˌkɔɪd

fucous
BR ˈfjuːkəs
AM ˈfjukəs

fucus
BR ˈfjuːkəs
AM ˈfjukəs

fuddle
BR ˈfʌd|l̩, -lz, -l̩ɪŋ \ -lɪŋ, -ld
AM ˈfəd|əl, -əlz, -(ə)lɪŋ, -əld

fuddy-duddy
BR ˈfʌdɪˌdʌdi, -iz
AM ˈfədiˌdədi, -z

fudge
BR fʌdʒ, -ɪz, -ɪŋ, -d
AM fədʒ, -əz, -ɪŋ, -d

fudgeable
BR ˈfʌdʒəbl
AM ˈfədʒəbəl

fudgicle
BR ˈfʌdʒɪkl, -z
AM ˈfədʒəkəl, -z

fuehrer
BR ˈfjʊərə(r), -z
AM ˈfjʊrər, -z

fuel
BR ˈfjuːəl, -z, -ɪŋ, -d
AM ˈfju(ə)l, -z, -ɪŋ, -d

Fuentes
BR fʊˈɛnteɪs
AM fʊˈɛnteɪs, ˈfwɛnteɪs

fug
BR fʌg, -z
AM fəg, -z

fugacious
BR fjuːˈɡeɪʃəs
AM fjuˈɡeɪʃəs

fugaciously
BR fjuːˈɡeɪʃəsli
AM fjuˈɡeɪʃəsli

fugaciousness
BR fjuːˈɡeɪʃəsnəs
AM fjuˈɡeɪʃəsnəs

fugacity
BR fjuːˈɡasɪti
AM fjuˈɡæsədi

fugal
BR ˈfjuːɡl
AM ˈfjuɡəl

fugally
BR ˈfjuːɡli, ˈfjuːɡəli
AM ˈfjuɡəli

fugginess
BR ˈfʌɡɪnɪs
AM ˈfəɡɪnɪs

fuggy
BR ˈfʌɡi, -ɪə(r), -ɪɪst
AM ˈfəɡi, -ər, -ɪst

fugitive
BR ˈfjuːdʒɪtɪv, -z
AM ˈfjudʒədɪv, ˈfjudʒəˌtɪv, -z

fugitively
BR ˈfjuːdʒɪtɪvli
AM ˈfjudʒədəvli, ˈfjudʒəˌtɪvli

fugle
BR ˈfjuːɡ|l, -lz, -l̩ɪŋ \ -lɪŋ, -ld
AM ˈfjuɡ|əl, -əlz, -(ə)lɪŋ, -əld

fugleman
BR ˈfjuːɡlmən
AM ˈfjuɡəlmən

fuglemen
BR ˈfjuːɡlmən
AM ˈfjuɡəlmən

fugu
BR ˈfuːɡuː, -z
AM ˈf(j)uɡu, -z

fugue
BR ˈfjuːɡ, -z
AM fjuɡ, -z

fuguist
BR ˈfjuːɡɪst, -s
AM ˈfjuɡəst, -s

Führer
BR ˈfjʊərə(r)
AM ˈfjʊrər

Fujairah
BR fəˈdʒaɪrə(r)
AM fuˈdʒaɪrə

Fuji
BR ˈfuːdʒi
AM ˈfudʒi

Fujian
BR ˈfuːdʒɪən
AM ˈfudʒiən

Fujica
BR ˈfuːdʒɪkə(r)
AM ˈfudʒəkə

Fujitsu
BR fuːˈdʒɪtsuː
AM fuˈdʒɪtsu

Fujiyama
BR ˌfuːdʒɪˈjɑːmə(r)
AM ˌfudʒiˈjɑmə

Fulani
BR fəˈlɑːni
AM fəˈlɑni

Fulbright
BR ˈfʊlbraɪt
AM ˈfʊlˌbraɪt

fulcra
BR ˈfʊlkrə(r)
AM ˈfʊlkrə, ˈfəlkrə

fulcrum
BR ˈfʊlkrəm, -z
AM ˈfʊlkrəm, ˈfəlkrəm, -z

fulfil
BR fʊlˈfɪl, -z, -ɪŋ, -d
AM fʊlˈfɪl, -z, -ɪŋ, -d

fulfill
BR fʊlˈfɪl, -z, -ɪŋ, -d
AM fʊlˈfɪl, -z, -ɪŋ, -d

fulfillable
BR fʊlˈfɪləbl
AM fʊlˈfɪləbəl

fulfiller
BR fʊlˈfɪlə(r), -z
AM fʊlˈfɪlər, -z

fulfillment
BR fʊlˈfɪlm(ə)nt, -s
AM fʊlˈfɪlmənt, -s

fulfilment
BR fʊlˈfɪlm(ə)nt, -s
AM fʊlˈfɪlmənt, -s

Fulford
BR ˈfʊlfəd
AM ˈfʊlfərd

fulgent
BR ˈfʌldʒ(ə)nt
AM ˈfəldʒənt

fulgid
BR ˈfʌldʒɪd
AM ˈfəldʒəd

fulguration
BR ˌfʌlɡjʊˈreɪʃn
AM ˌfʊlɡ(j)əˈreɪʃən

fulgurite
BR ˈfʌlɡjʊrʌɪt
AM ˈfʊlɡ(j)əˌraɪt

Fulham
BR ˈfʊləm
AM ˈfʊləm

fuliginous
BR fjuːˈlɪdʒɪnəs
AM fjuˈlɪdʒənəs

fuliginously
BR fjuːˈlɪdʒɪnəsli
AM fjuˈlɪdʒənəsli

full
BR fʊl, -z, -ɪŋ, -d, -ə(r), -ɪst
AM fʊl, -z, -ɪŋ, -d, -ər, -əst

fullback
BR ˈfʊlbak, -s
AM ˈfʊlˌbæk, ˈfə(l)ˌbæk, -s

fuller
BR ˈfʊlə(r), -z
AM ˈfʊlər, -z

fullness
BR ˈfʊlnəs
AM ˈfʊlnəs

fully
BR ˈfʊli
AM ˈfʊli

fulmar
BR ˈfʊlmə(r), ˈfʊlmɑː(r), -z
AM ˈfʊlmər, ˈfʊlˌmɑr, -z

fulminant
BR ˈfʊlmɪnənt, ˈfʌlmɪnənt
AM ˈfʊlmənənt

fulminate
BR ˈfʊlmɪneɪt, ˈfʌlmɪneɪt, -s, -ɪŋ, -ɪd
AM ˈfʊlməˌneɪt, -ts, -dɪŋ, -dɪd

fulmination
BR ˌfʊlmɪˈneɪʃn, ˌfʌlmɪˈneɪʃn, -z
AM ˌfəlməˈneɪʃən, -z

fulminatory
BR ˈfʊlmɪnət(ə)ri, ˈfʌlmɪnət(ə)ri
AM ˈfəlmɪnəˌtɔri

fulminic acid
BR fʊlˌmɪnɪk ˈasɪd, fʌlˌmɪnɪk +
AM fəlˈmɪnɪk ˈæsəd

fulness
BR ˈfʊlnəs
AM ˈfʊlnəs

fulsome
BR ˈfʊls(ə)m
AM ˈfʊlsəm

fulsomely
BR ˈfʊls(ə)mli
AM ˈfʊlsəmli

fulsomeness
BR ˈfʊls(ə)mnəs
AM ˈfʊlsəmnəs

Fulton
BR ˈfʊlt(ə)n
AM ˈfʊlt(ə)n

fulvescent
BR fʌlˈvɛsnt, fʊlˈvɛsnt
AM fəlˈvɛsənt

fulvous
BR ˈfʌlvəs, ˈfʊlvəs
AM ˈfʊlvəs, ˈfəlvəs

Fulwell
BR ˈfʊlwɛl
AM ˈfʊlˌwɛl

Fulwood
BR ˈfʊlwʊd
AM ˈfʊlˌwʊd

Fu Manchu
BR ˌfuː manˈtʃuː
AM ˌfu ˌmænˈtʃu

fumaric
BR fjʊˈmarɪk, fjuːˈmarɪk
AM fjuˈmɛrɪk

fumarole
BR ˈfjuːmərəʊl, -z
AM ˈfjuməˌroʊl, -z

fumarolic
BR ˌfjuːməˈrɒlɪk
AM ˌfjuməˈroʊlɪk, ˌfjuməˈrɑlɪk

fumble
BR ˈfʌmb|l, -lz, -l̩ɪŋ \ -lɪŋ, -ld
AM ˈfəmb|əl, -əlz, -(ə)lɪŋ, -əld

fumbler
BR ˈfʌmblə(r), ˈfʌmblə(r), -z
AM ˈfəmb(ə)lər, -z

fumblingly
BR ˈfʌmblɪŋli
AM ˈfəmb(ə)lɪŋli

fume
BR fjuːm, -z, -ɪŋ, -d
AM fjum, -z, -ɪŋ, -d

fumeless
BR ˈfjuːmləs
AM ˈfjumləs

fumigant
BR ˈfjuːmɪg(ə)nt, -s
AM ˈfjuməgənt, -s

fumigate
BR ˈfjuːmɪgeɪt, -s, -ɪŋ,
-ɪd
AM ˈfjuməˌgeɪt, -ts,
-dɪŋ, -dɪd

fumigation
BR ˌfjuːmɪˈgeɪʃn
AM ˌfjuməˈgeɪʃən

fumigator
BR ˈfjuːmɪgeɪtə(r), -z
AM ˈfjuməˌgeɪdər, -z

fumingly
BR ˈfjuːmɪŋli
AM ˈfjuːmɪŋli

fumitory
BR ˈfjuːmɪt(ə)r|i, -ɪz
AM ˈfjuːməˌtɔːri, -z

fumy
BR ˈfjuːm|i, -ɪə(r), -ɪɪst
AM ˈfjuːmi, -ər, -ɪst

fun
BR fʌn
AM fən

Funafuti
BR ˌfuːnəˈfuːti
AM ˌf(j)unəˈf(j)udi

funambulist
BR fjuːˈnæmbjəlɪst, -s
AM fjuˈnæmbjələst, -s

funboard
BR ˈfʌnbɔːd, -z
AM ˈfənˌbɔ(ə)rd, -z

Funchal
BR fʊnˈtʃɑːl
AM fʊnˈʃɑl, fənˈʃɑl

function
BR ˈfʌŋ(k)ʃ|n, -nz,
-ŋɪŋ \ -ənɪŋ, -nd
AM ˈfəŋ(k)ʃ|ən, -ənz,
-(ə)nɪŋ, -ənd

functional
BR ˈfʌŋ(k)ʃŋ(ə)l,
ˈfʌŋ(k)ʃən(ə)l
AM ˈfəŋ(k)ʃ(ə)nəl

functionalism
BR ˈfʌŋ(k)ʃŋəlɪz(ə)m,
ˈfʌŋ(k)ʃŋlɪz(ə)m,
ˈfʌŋ(k)ʃənlɪz(ə)m,
ˈfʌŋ(k)ʃ(ə)nəlɪz(ə)m
AM ˈfəŋ(k)ʃənlˌɪzəm,
ˈfəŋ(k)ʃnəˌlɪzəm

functionalist
BR ˈfʌŋ(k)ʃŋəlɪst,
ˈfʌŋ(k)ʃŋlɪst,
ˈfʌŋ(k)ʃənlɪst,
ˈfʌŋ(k)ʃ(ə)nəlɪst, -s
AM ˈfʌŋ(k)ʃənləst,
ˈfəŋ(k)ʃnələst, -s

functionality
BR ˌfʌŋ(k)ʃəˈnalɪt|i, -ɪz
AM ˌfəŋ(k)ʃəˈnælədi,
-z

functionally
BR ˈfʌŋ(k)ʃŋəli,
ˈfʌŋ(k)ʃŋli,

ˈfʌŋ(k)ʃənˌli,
ˈfʌŋ(k)ʃ(ə)nəli
AM ˈfəŋ(k)ʃ(ə)nəli

functionary
BR ˈfʌŋ(k)ʃŋ(ə)r|i, -ɪz
AM ˈfəŋ(k)ʃəˌnɛri, -z

functionate
BR ˈfʌŋ(k)ʃəneɪt,
ˈfʌŋ(k)ʃneɪt, -s, -ɪŋ, -ɪd
AM ˈfəŋ(k)ʃəˌneɪ|t, -ts,
-dɪŋ, -dɪd

functionless
BR ˈfʌŋ(k)ʃnləs
AM ˈfəŋ(k)ʃənləs

functor
BR ˈfʌŋ(k)tə(r), -z
AM ˈfəŋ(k)tər, -z

fund
BR fʌnd, -z, -ɪŋ, -ɪd
AM fənd, -z, -ɪŋ, -əd

fundament
BR ˈfʌndəm(ə)nt, -s
AM ˈfəndəmənt, -s

fundamental
BR ˌfʌndəˈmentl
AM ˌfəndəˈmen(t)l

fundamentalism
BR ˌfʌndəˈmentlɪz(ə)m
AM ˌfəndəˈmen(t)lˌɪzəm

fundamentalist
BR ˌfʌndəˈmentlɪst, -s
AM ˌfəndəˈmen(t)ləst,
-s

fundamentality
BR ˌfʌndəmɛnˈtalɪti
AM ˌfəndəmənˈtælədi

fundamentally
BR ˌfʌndəˈmentli
AM ˌfəndəˈmen(t)li

fundholder
BR ˈfʌndˌhəʊldə(r), -z
AM ˈfən(d)ˌ(h)oʊldər,
-z

fundholding
BR ˈfʌndˌhəʊldɪŋ
AM ˈfən(d)ˌ(h)oʊldɪŋ

fundi
BR ˈfʌndʌɪ
AM ˈfənˌdaɪ

fundus
BR ˈfʌndəs
AM ˈfəndəs

Fundy
BR ˈfʌndi
AM ˈfəndi

funebrial
BR fjuːˈniːbrɪəl,
fjuːˈnɛbrɪəl
AM fjuˈnibrɪəl,
fjuˈnɛbrɪəl

funeral
BR ˈfjuːn(ə)rəl,
ˈfjuːn(ə)r|l, -z
AM ˈfjun(ə)rəl, -z

funerary
BR ˈfjuːn(ə)rəri
AM ˈfjunəˌrɛri

funereal
BR fjəˈnɪərɪəl,
fjuːˈnɪərɪəl
AM fjəˈnɪriəl

funereally
BR fjəˈnɪərɪəli,
fjuːˈnɪərɪəli
AM fjəˈnɪriəli

funfair
BR ˈfʌnfɛː(r), -z
AM ˈfənˌfɛ(ə)r, -z

fungal
BR ˈfʌŋgl
AM ˈfəŋgəl

fungi
BR ˈfʌŋgʌɪ, ˈfʌn(d)ʒʌɪ
AM ˈfənˌdʒaɪ, ˈfəŋˌgaɪ

fungibility
BR ˌfʌn(d)ʒɪˈbɪlɪti
AM ˌfəndʒəˈbɪlɪdi

fungible
BR ˈfʌn(d)ʒɪbl
AM ˈfəndʒəbəl

fungicidal
BR ˌfʌn(d)ʒɪˈsʌɪdl,
ˌfʌŋgɪˈsʌɪdl
AM ˌfəndʒəˌsaɪdəl,
ˈfəŋgəˌsaɪdəl

fungicide
BR ˈfʌn(d)ʒɪsʌɪd,
ˈfʌŋgɪsʌɪd, -z
AM ˈfəndʒəˌsaɪd,
ˈfəŋgəˌsaɪd, -z

fungiform
BR ˈfʌn(d)ʒɪfɔːm,
ˈfʌŋgɪfɔːm
AM ˈfəndʒəˌfɔ(ə)rm,
ˈfəŋgəˌfɔ(ə)rm

fungistatic
BR ˌfʌn(d)ʒɪˈstatɪk,
ˌfʌŋgɪˈstatɪk
AM ˌfəndʒəˈstædɪk,
ˌfəŋgəˈstædɪk

fungistatically
BR ˌfʌn(d)ʒɪˈstatɪkli,
ˌfʌŋgɪˈstatɪkli
AM ˌfəndʒəˈstædək(ə)li,
ˌfəŋgəˈstædək(ə)li

fungivorous
BR ˌfʌn(d)ʒɪv(ə)rəs
AM fənˈdʒɪvərəs,
ˌfənˈgɪvərəs

fungo
BR ˈfʌŋgəʊ, -z
AM ˈfəŋgoʊ, -z

fungoid
BR ˈfʌŋgɔɪd
AM ˈfəŋˌgɔɪd

fungous
BR ˈfʌŋgəs
AM ˈfəŋgəs

fungus
BR ˈfʌŋgəs, -ɪz
AM ˈfəŋgəs, -əz

funhouse
BR ˈfʌnhaʊ|s, -zɪz
AM ˈfənˌ(h)aʊ|s, -zəz

funicle
BR ˈfjuːnɪkl, -z
AM ˈfjunəkl, -z

funicular
BR f(j)ʉˈnɪkjələ(r), -z
AM fjuˈnɪkjələr, -z

funiculi
BR fjʉˈnɪkjʉlʌɪ
AM ˌfjuˈnɪkjəˌlaɪ

funiculus
BR fjʉˈnɪkjʉləs
AM fjuˈnɪkjələs

funk
BR fʌŋ|k, -ks, -kɪŋ, -(k)t
AM fəŋ|k, -ks, -kɪŋ, -(k)t

funkia
BR ˈfʌŋkɪə(r), -z
AM ˈfəŋkiə, ˈfʊŋkiə, -z

funkily
BR ˈfʌŋkɪli
AM ˈfəŋkəli

funkiness
BR ˈfʌŋkɪnɪs
AM ˈfəŋkɪnɪs

funkster
BR ˈfʌŋ(k)stə(r), -z
AM ˈfəŋ(k)stər, -z

funky
BR ˈfʌŋk|i, -ɪə(r), -ɪɪst
AM ˈfəŋki, -ər, -ɪst

fun-lover
BR ˈfʌnˌlʌvə(r), -z
AM ˈfənˌləvər, -z

fun-loving
BR ˈfʌnˌlʌvɪŋ
AM ˈfənˌləvɪŋ

funnel
BR ˈfʌn|l, -lz, -lɪŋ \ -əlɪŋ,
-ld
AM ˈfənəl, -z, -ɪŋ, -d

funnily
BR ˈfʌnɪli
AM ˈfənəli

funniness
BR ˈfʌnɪnɪs
AM ˈfənɪnɪs

funniosity
BR ˌfʌnɪˈɒsɪti, -ɪz
AM ˌfəniˈɑsədi, -z

funny
BR ˈfʌn|i, -ɪz, -ɪə(r), -ɪɪst
AM ˈfəni, -z, -ər, -ɪst

funster
BR ˈfʌnstə(r), -z
AM ˈfənstər, -z

fur
BR fəː(r), -z
AM fər, -z

furbelow
BR ˈfəːbɪləʊ, -z
AM ˈfərbəˌloʊ, -z

furbish
BR ˈfəːb|ɪʃ, -ɪʃɪz, -ɪʃɪŋ,
-ɪʃt
AM ˈfərbɪʃ, -ɪz, -ɪŋ, -t

furbisher
BR ˈfəːbɪʃə(r), -z

AM ˈfɜːbɪʃər, -z

Furby
BR ˈfɜːbi
AM ˈfɜːbi

furcate
BR ˈfɜːkeɪt, fəˈkeɪt, -s, -ɪŋ, -ɪd
AM ˈfɜːrˌkeɪ|t, -ts, -dɪŋ, -dɪd

furcation
BR fəˈkeɪʃn
AM fərˈkeɪʃən

furfuraceous
BR ˌfɜːfəˈreɪʃəs
AM ˈfɜːf(j)əˈreɪʃəs

Furies
BR ˈfjʊərɪz, ˈfjɔːrɪz
AM ˈfjʊriz

furious
BR ˈfjʊərɪəs, ˈfjɔːrɪəs
AM ˈfjʊriəs

furiously
BR ˈfjʊərɪəsli, ˈfjɔːrɪəsli
AM ˈfjʊriəsli

furiousness
BR ˈfjʊərɪəsnəs, ˈfjɔːrɪəsnəs
AM ˈfjʊriəsnəs

furl
BR fɜːl, -z, -ɪŋ, -d
AM fɜːrl, -z, -ɪŋ, -d

furlable
BR ˈfɜːləbl
AM ˈfɜːrləbəl

furless
BR ˈfɜːləs
AM ˈfɜːrləs

furlong
BR ˈfɜːlɒŋ, -z
AM ˈfɜːrˌlɔŋ, ˈfɜːrˌlɑŋ, -z

furlough
BR ˈfɜːləʊ, -z
AM ˈfɜːrˌloʊ, -z

furmety
BR ˈfɜːməti
AM ˈfɜːrmədi

furnace
BR ˈfɜːnɪs, -ɪz
AM ˈfɜːrnəs, -əz

Furneaux
BR ˈfɜːnəʊ
AM ˈfɜːrnoʊ

Furness
BR ˈfɜːnɪs, fəˈnɛs
AM fərˈnɛs

furnish
BR ˈfɜːn|ɪʃ, -ɪʃɪz, -ɪʃɪŋ, -ɪʃt
AM ˈfɜːrnɪʃ, -ɪz, -ɪŋ, -t

furnisher
BR ˈfɜːnɪʃə(r), -z
AM ˈfɜːrnɪʃər, -z

furnishing
BR ˈfɜːnɪʃɪŋ, -z
AM ˈfɜːrnɪʃɪŋ, -z

furnishings
BR fəˈnɪʃɪŋz
AM ˈfɜːrnɪʃɪŋz

furniture
BR ˈfɜːnɪtʃə(r)
AM ˈfɜːrnɪtʃər, ˈfɜːrnɪtʃʊ(ə)r

Furnivall
BR ˈfɜːnɪvl
AM ˈfɜːrnəvəl

furor
BR ˈfjʊərɔː(r), ˈfjɔːrɔː(r), -z
AM ˈfjʊˌrɔ(ə)r, ˈfjuˌrɔ(ə)r, -z

furore
BR fjʊˈrɔːri, ˈfjʊərɔː(r), ˈfjɔːrɔː(r)
AM ˈfjʊˌrɔ(ə)r, ˈfjuˌrɔ(ə)r

furores
BR fjʊˈrɔːrɪz, ˈfjʊərɔːz, ˈfjɔːrɔːz
AM ˈfjʊˌrɔ(ə)rz, ˈfjuˌrɔ(ə)rz

furphy
BR ˈfɜːf|i, -ɪz
AM ˈfɜːrfi, -z

furrier
BR ˈfʌrɪə(r), -z
AM ˈfɜːriər, -z

furriery
BR ˈfʌrɪəri
AM ˈfɜːriəri

furriness
BR ˈfɜːrɪnɪs
AM ˈfɜːrɪnɪs

furring
BR ˈfɜːrɪŋ
AM ˈfɜːrɪŋ

furrow
BR ˈfʌrəʊ, -z, -ɪŋ, -d
AM ˈfɜːroʊ, -z, -ɪŋ, -d

furrowless
BR ˈfʌrəʊləs
AM ˈfɜːroʊləs

furrowy
BR ˈfʌrəʊi
AM ˈfɜːrəwi

furry
BR ˈfɜː|r|i, -ɪə(r), -ɪɪst
AM ˈfɜːri, -ər, -ɪst

further
BR ˈfɜːð|ə(r), -əz, -(ə)rɪŋ, -əd
AM ˈfɜːrðər, -z, -ɪŋ, -d

furtherance
BR ˈfɜːð(ə)rəns, ˈfɜːð(ə)rns
AM ˈfɜːrð(ə)rəns

furtherer
BR ˈfɜːð(ə)rə(r), -z
AM ˈfɜːrðərər, -z

furthermore
BR ˌfɜːðəˈmɔː(r), ˈfɜːðəmɔː(r)
AM ˈfɜːrðərˌmɔ(ə)r, ˌfɜːrðərˈmɔ(ə)r

furthermost
BR ˈfɜːðəməʊst
AM ˈfɜːrðərˌmoʊst

furthest
BR ˈfɜːðɪst
AM ˈfɜːrðəst

furtive
BR ˈfɜːtɪv
AM ˈfɜːrdɪv

furtively
BR ˈfɜːtɪvli
AM ˈfɜːrdɪvli

furtiveness
BR ˈfɜːtɪvnɪs
AM ˈfɜːrdɪvnɪs

furuncle
BR ˈfjʊərʌŋkl, ˈfjɔːrʌŋkl, -z
AM ˈfjuˌrəŋkəl, -z

furuncular
BR fjʊˈrʌŋkjʊlə(r)
AM fjuˈrəŋkjələr

furunculosis
BR fjʊˌrʌŋkjʊˈləʊsɪs
AM fjuˌrəŋkjəˈloʊsəs

furunculous
BR fjʊˈrʌŋkjʊləs
AM fjuˈrəŋkjələs

fury
BR ˈfjʊəri, ˈfjɔːri
AM ˈfjʊri

furze
BR fɜːz
AM fɜːrz

furzy
BR ˈfɜːzi
AM ˈfɜːrzi

fusaria
BR fjuːˈzeːrɪə(r)
AM fjəˈzɛrɪə

fusarium
BR fjuːˈzeːrɪəm
AM fjəˈzɛriəm

fuscous
BR ˈfʌskəs
AM ˈfəskəs

fuse
BR fjuːz, -ɪz, -ɪŋ, -d
AM fjuz, -əz, -ɪŋ, -d

fusee
BR fjuːˈziː, -z
AM fjuˈzi, -z

fusel
BR ˈfjuːzl
AM ˈfjuzəl

fuselage
BR ˈfjuːzɪlɑːʒ, ˈfjuːzɪlˌɪdʒ, -ɑːʒɪz\-ɪdʒɪz
AM ˈfjusəˌlɑʒ, ˈfjuzəˌlɑʒ, -ɪz

fuseless
BR ˈfjuːzləs
AM ˈfjuzləs

fusibility
BR ˌfjuːzɪˈbɪlɪti

AM ˌfjuzəˈbɪlɪdi

fusible
BR ˈfjuːzɪbl
AM ˈfjuzəbəl

fusiform
BR ˈfjuːzɪfɔːm
AM ˈfjuzəˌfɔ(ə)rm

fusil
BR ˈfjuːz(ɪ)l, -z
AM ˈfjuzəl, -z

fusilier
BR ˌfjuːzɪˈlɪə(r), -z
AM ˌfjuzəˈlɪ(ə)r, -z

fusillade
BR ˌfjuːzɪˈleɪd, ˌfjuːzɪˈleɪd
AM ˌfjuzəˈleɪd, ˌfjuzəˈlad, -z

fusilli
BR f(j)ʊˈziːli
AM ˌfjuˈsɪli

fusion
BR ˈfjuːʒn
AM ˈfjuʒən

fusional
BR ˈfjuːʒn(ə)l, ˈfjuːʒən(ə)l
AM ˈfjuʒ(ə)nəl

fusionist
BR ˈfjuːʒnɪst, ˈfjuːʒənɪst, -s
AM ˈfjuʒənəst, -s

fuss
BR fʌs, -ɪz, -ɪŋ, -t
AM fəs, -əz, -ɪŋ, -t

fusser
BR ˈfʌsə(r), -z
AM ˈfəsər, -z

fussily
BR ˈfʌsɪli
AM ˈfəsəli

fussiness
BR ˈfʌsɪnɪs
AM ˈfəsɪnɪs

fusspot
BR ˈfʌspɒt, -s
AM ˈfəsˌpɑt, -s

fussy
BR ˈfʌs|i, -ɪə(r), -ɪɪst
AM ˈfəsi, -ər, -ɪst

fustanella
BR ˌfʌstəˈnɛlə(r), -z
AM ˌfʌstəˈnɛlə, -z

fustian
BR ˈfʌstɪən
AM ˈfəstʃən

fustic
BR ˈfʌstɪk
AM ˈfəstɪk

fustigate
BR ˈfʌstɪgeɪt, -s, -ɪŋ, -ɪd
AM ˈfəstəˌgeɪ|t, -ts, -dɪŋ, -dɪd

fustigation
BR ˌfʌstɪˈgeɪʃn, -z
AM ˌfəstəˈgeɪʃən, -z

fustily
BR ˈfʌstɪli
AM ˈfəstəli
fustiness
BR ˈfʌstɪnɪs
AM ˈfəstɪnɪs
fusty
BR ˈfʌst|i, -ɪə(r), -ɪɪst
AM ˈfəsti, -ər, -ɪɪst
futharc
BR ˈfuːθɑːk
AM ˈfuˌθɑrk
futhorc
BR ˈfuːθɔːk
AM ˈfuˌθɔ(ə)rk
futile
BR ˈfjuːtʌɪl
AM ˈfjudl
futilely
BR ˈfjuːtʌɪlli
AM ˈfjud(l)li
futileness
BR ˈfjuːtʌɪlnɪs
AM ˈfjudlnəs
futilitarian
BR ˌfjuːtɪlɪˈtɛːrɪən
AM fjuˌtɪləˈtɛrɪən
futility
BR fjuːˈtɪlɪti, fjəˈtɪlɪti

AM ˈfjuːˈtɪlɪdi
futon
BR ˈf(j)uːtɒn, ˌfuːˈtɒn, -z
AM ˈf(j)uˌtɑn, -z
futtock
BR ˈfʌtək, -s
AM ˈfədək, -s
future
BR ˈfjuːtʃə(r), -z
AM ˈfjutʃər, -z
futureless
BR ˈfjuːtʃələs
AM ˈfjutʃərləs
futurism
BR ˈfjuːtʃ(ə)rɪz(ə)m
AM ˈfjutʃəˌrɪzəm
futurist
BR ˈfjuːtʃ(ə)rɪst, -s
AM ˈfjutʃəˌrəst, -s
futuristic
BR ˌfjuːtʃəˈrɪstɪk
AM ˌfjutʃəˈrɪstɪk
futuristically
BR ˌfjuːtʃəˈrɪstɪkli
AM ˌfjutʃəˈrɪstək(ə)li
futurity
BR fjəˈtjʊərɪt|i, fjəˈtʃʊərɪt|i,

fjəˈtjɔːrɪt|i,
fjəˈtʃɔːrɪt|i-ɪz
AM fjəˈtʊrədi,
fjəˈturədi, fjəˈtʃurədi, -z
futurologist
BR ˌfjuːtʃəˈrɒlədʒɪst, -s
AM ˌfjutʃəˈrɑlədʒəst, -s
futurology
BR ˌfjuːtʃəˈrɒlədʒi
AM ˌfjutʃəˈrɑlədʒi
futz
BR fʌts, -ɪz, -ɪŋ, -t
AM fəts, -əz, -ɪŋ, -t
fuze
BR fjuːz, -ɪz, -ɪŋ, -d
AM fjuz, -əz, -ɪŋ, -d
fuzee
BR fjuːˈziː, -z
AM fjuˈzi, -z
fuzz
BR fʌz
AM fəz
fuzzily
BR ˈfʌzɪli
AM ˈfəzəli
fuzziness
BR ˈfʌzɪnɪs
AM ˈfəzɪnɪs

fuzzy
BR ˈfʌz|i, -ɪə(r), -ɪɪst
AM ˈfəzi, -ər, -ɪɪst
fuzzy-wuzzy
BR ˈfʌzɪˌwʌz|i, -ɪz
AM ˈfəziˈwəzi, -z
Fyfe
BR fʌɪf
AM faɪf
Fyffe
BR fʌɪf
AM faɪf
Fylde
BR fʌɪld
AM faɪld
fylfot
BR ˈfɪlfɒt, -s
AM ˈfɪlˌfɑt, -s
Fylingdales
BR ˈfʌlɪŋdeɪlz
AM ˈfaɪlɪŋˌdeɪlz
Fyne
BR fʌɪn
AM faɪn
fyrd
BR fəːd, fɪəd, -z
AM fərd, fɪ(ə)rd, -z
fytte
BR fɪt
AM fɪt

Gg

g
BR dʒiː, -z
AM dʒi, -z

gab
BR gab, -z, -ɪŋ, -d
AM gæb, -z, -ɪŋ, -d

Gabalfa
BR gə'balvə(r),
gə'balfə(r)
AM gə'bælfə

gabardine
BR 'gabədiːn,
ˌgabə'diːn, -z
AM 'gæbər,din, -z

gabber
BR 'gabə(r), -z
AM 'gæbər, -z

Gabbitas
BR 'gabɪtas
AM 'gæbədəs

gabble
BR 'gab|l, -lz, -|ɪŋ\-l|ɪŋ,
-ld
AM 'gæb|əl, -əlz, -(ə)lɪŋ,
-əld

gabbler
BR 'gablə(r), -z
AM 'gæblər, -z

gabbro
BR 'gabrəʊ, -z
AM 'gæbroʊ, -z

gabbroic
BR ga'brəʊɪk
AM gə'broʊɪk

gabbroid
BR 'gabrɔɪd
AM 'gæ,brɔɪd

gabby
BR 'gab|i, -iə(r), -ɪɪst
AM 'gæbi, -ər, -ɪst

gabelle
BR ga'bɛl, gə'bɛl, -z
AM gə'bɛl, -z

gaberdine
BR 'gabədiːn,
ˌgabə'diːn, -z
AM 'gæbər,din, -z

gabfest
BR 'gabfɛst, -s
AM 'gæb,fɛst, -s

gabion
BR 'geɪbɪən, -z
AM 'geɪbɪən, -z

gabionade
BR ˌgeɪbɪə'neɪd, -z
AM ˌgeɪbɪə'neɪd, -z

gabionage
BR 'geɪbɪənɪdʒ
AM 'geɪbɪəˌnɑ(d)ʒ

gable
BR 'geɪbl, -z, -d

gablet
AM 'geɪbəl, -z, -d

Gabo
BR 'gɑːbəʊ
AM 'gaboʊ

Gabon
BR gə'bɒn
AM gə'bɑn, gə'boʊn

Gabonese
BR ˌgabə'niːz
AM ˌgæbə'niz

Gábor
BR gə'bɔː(r)
AM gə'bɔ(ə)r
HU 'gɑːbɔr

Gaborone
BR ˌgabə'rəʊni
AM ˌgabə'roʊn

Gabriel
BR 'geɪbrɪəl
AM 'geɪbriəl

Gabrielle
BR ˌgeɪbrɪ'ɛl
AM ˌgæbri'ɛl

gad
BR gad, -z, -ɪŋ, -ɪd
AM gæd, -z, -ɪŋ, -ɪd

gadabout
BR 'gadəbaʊt, -s
AM 'gædə,baʊt, -s

Gadarene
BR 'gadəriːn,
ˌgadə'riːn
AM 'gædə,rin,
ˌgædə'rin

Gaddafi
BR gə'dɑːfi, gə'dafi
AM gə'dɑfi

gadfly
BR 'gadflʌɪ, -z
AM 'gæd,flaɪ, -z

gadget
BR 'gadʒɪt, -s
AM 'gædʒət, -s

gadgeteer
BR ˌgadʒɪ'tɪə(r), -z
AM ˌgædʒə'tɪ(ə)r, -z

gadgetry
BR 'gadʒɪtri
AM 'gædʒətri

gadgety
BR 'gadʒɪti
AM 'gædʒədi

Gadhelic
BR gə'dɛlɪk, ga'dɛlɪk
AM gə'dɛlɪk, gæ'dɛlɪk

gadid
BR 'geɪdɪd, -z
AM 'geɪdɪd, -z

gadoid
BR 'gadɔɪd, -z
AM 'geɪ,dɔɪd, 'gæ,dɔɪd,
-z

gadolinite
BR 'gadəlɪnʌɪt,
'gad],ɪnʌɪt,
gə'dəʊlɪnʌɪt
AM 'gædlə,naɪt

gadolinium
BR ˌgadə'lɪnɪəm,
ˌgad]'ɪnɪəm
AM ˌgædl'ɪnɪəm

gadroon
BR gə'druːn, -z
AM gə'drun, -z, -d

gadwall
BR 'gadwɔːl, -z
AM 'gæ,dwɔl,
'gæ,dwɑl, -z

gadzooks
BR (ˌ)gad'zuːks
AM gæd'zuks

Gaea
BR 'dʒiːə(r)
AM 'dʒiə

Gael
BR geɪl, -z
AM geɪl, -z

Gaeldom
BR 'geɪldəm
AM 'geɪldəm

Gaelic
BR 'geɪlɪk, 'galɪk
AM 'geɪlɪk

Gaeltacht
BR 'geɪltaxt
AM 'geɪl,tækt
IR 'geːltəxt

Gaenor
BR 'geɪnə(r)
AM 'geɪnər

gaff
BR gaf, -s, -ɪŋ, -t
AM gæf, -s, -ɪŋ, -t

gaffe
BR gaf, -s
AM gæf, -s

gaffer
BR 'gafə(r), -z
AM 'gæfər, -z

Gaffney
BR 'gafni
AM 'gæfni

Gafsa
BR 'gafsə(r)
AM 'gæfsə

gag
BR gag, -z, -ɪŋ, -d
AM gæg, -z, -ɪŋ, -d

gaga
BR 'gɑːgɑː(r)
AM 'ga,ga

Gagarin
BR gə'gɑːrɪn
AM gə'gɑrən

gage
BR geɪdʒ, -ɪz, -ɪŋ, -d
AM geɪdʒ, -ɪz, -ɪŋ, -d

gaggle
BR 'gagl, -z

gadolinite
AM 'gægəl, -z

gagman
BR 'gagman
AM 'gæg,mæn

gagmen
BR 'gagmɛn
AM 'gæg,mɛn

gagster
BR 'gagstə(r), -z
AM 'gægstər, -z

Gaia
BR 'gʌɪə(r)
AM 'gaɪə

Gaian
BR 'gʌɪən, -z
AM 'gaɪən, -z

gaiety
BR 'geɪti
AM 'gaɪɪdi

gaijin
BR (ˌ)gʌɪ'dʒɪn
AM gaɪ'dʒɪn

Gail
BR geɪl
AM geɪl

gaillardia
BR geɪ'lɑːdɪə(r),
gə'lɑːdɪə(r), -z
AM gə'lard(i)ə, -z

gaily
BR 'geɪli
AM 'geɪli

gain
BR geɪn, -z, -ɪŋ, -d
AM geɪn, -z, -ɪŋ, -d

gainable
BR 'geɪnəbl
AM 'geɪnəbəl

gainer
BR 'geɪnə(r), -z
AM 'geɪnər, -z

Gaines
BR geɪnz
AM geɪnz

gainful
BR 'geɪnf(ʊ)l
AM 'geɪnfəl

gainfully
BR 'geɪnfəli, 'geɪnf]i
AM 'geɪnfəli

gainfulness
BR 'geɪnf(ʊ)lnəs
AM 'geɪnfəlnəs

gainings
BR 'geɪnɪŋz
AM 'geɪnɪŋz

gainsaid
BR ˌgeɪn'sɛd
AM 'geɪn,seɪd

gainsay
BR ˌgeɪn'seɪ, -z, -ɪŋ
AM ˌgeɪn,seɪ, -z, -ɪŋ

gainsayer
BR ˌgeɪn'seɪə(r), -z
AM 'geɪn,seɪər, -z

Gainsborough
BR 'geɪnzb(ə)rə(r)

AM ˈɡeɪnzbərə

'gainst
BR ɡɛnst, ɡeɪnst
AM ɡɛnst, ɡeɪnst

Gairloch
BR ˈɡɛːlɒx, ˈɡɛːlɒk
AM ˈɡɛrlɑk

gait
BR ɡeɪt, -s
AM ɡeɪt, -s

gaiter
BR ˈɡeɪtə(r), -z, -d
AM ˈɡeɪdər, -z, -d

Gaitskell
BR ˈɡeɪtsk(ɪ)l
AM ˈɡeɪtskəl

Gaius
BR ˈɡʌɪəs
AM ˈɡaɪəs

gal
BR ɡal, -z
AM ɡæl, -z

gala
BR ˈɡɑːlə(r), ˈɡeɪlə(r), -z
AM ˈɡeɪlə, ˈɡælə, -z

galactagogue
BR ɡəˈlaktəɡɒɡ, -z
AM ɡəˈlæktəˌɡɑɡ, -z

galactic
BR ɡəˈlaktɪk
AM ɡəˈlæktɪk

galactogogue
BR ɡəˈlaktəɡɒɡ, -z
AM ɡəˈlæktəˌɡɑɡ, -z

galactose
BR ɡəˈlaktəʊz, ɡəˈlaktəʊs
AM ɡəˈlækˌtoʊs, ɡəˈlækˌtoʊz

galago
BR ɡəˈleɪɡəʊ, -z
AM ɡəˈleɪɡoʊ, ɡəˈlɑɡoʊ, ˈɡæləˌɡoʊ, -z

galah
BR ɡəˈlɑː(r), -z
AM ɡəˈlɑ, -z

Galahad
BR ˈɡaləhad
AM ˈɡæləˌhæd

galantine
BR ˈɡaləntiːn, ˈɡalɲtiːn, ˌɡalənˈtiːn, ˌɡalɲˈtiːn, -z
AM ˈɡælənˌtin, -z

galanty show
BR ɡəˈlantɪ ʃəʊ, -z
AM ɡəˈlæn(t)i ˌʃoʊ, -z

Galapagos
BR ɡəˈlapəɡəs
AM ɡəˈlɑpəˌɡoʊs, ɡəˈlapəɡəs

Galashiels
BR ˌɡaləˈʃiːlz
AM ˌɡæləˈʃilz

Galatea
BR ˌɡaləˈtɪə(r)

Galatia
BR ɡəˈleɪʃ(ɪ)ə(r)
AM ɡəˈleɪʃ(i)ə

Galatian
BR ɡəˈleɪʃ(ə)n, -z
AM ɡəˈleɪʃ(i)ən, -z

galaxy
BR ˈɡaləksˌi, -ɪz
AM ˈɡæləksi, -z

Galba
BR ˈɡalbə(r)
AM ˈɡælbə

galbanum
BR ˈɡalbənəm
AM ˈɡælbənəm

Galbraith
BR ɡalˈbreɪθ
AM ˈɡælˌbreɪθ

gale
BR ɡeɪl, -z
AM ɡeɪl, -z

galea
BR ˈɡeɪlɪə(r), -z
AM ˈɡeɪliə, -z

galeae
BR ˈɡeɪlɪʌɪ
AM ˈɡeɪliˌi, ˈɡeɪliˌaɪ

galeate
BR ˈɡeɪlɪət
AM ˈɡeɪliət

galeated
BR ˈɡeɪlɪeɪtɪd
AM ˈɡeɪliˌeɪdɪd

Galen
BR ˈɡeɪlɪn
AM ˈɡeɪlən

galena
BR ɡəˈliːnə(r)
AM ɡəˈlinə

galenic
BR ɡəˈlɛnɪk
AM ɡeɪˈlɛnɪk, ɡəˈlɛnɪk

galenical
BR ɡəˈlɛnɪkl
AM ɡeɪˈlɛnəkəl, ɡəˈlɛnəkəl

galette
BR ɡəˈlɛt, -s
AM ɡəˈlɛt, -s

Galicia
BR ɡəˈlɪsɪə(r), ɡəˈlɪʃ(ɪ)ə(r)
AM ɡəˈlɪʃə
SP ɡaˈliθja, ɡaˈlisja

Galician
BR ɡəˈlɪsɪən, ɡəˈlɪʃ(ɪ)ən, ɡəˈlɪʃ(i)n, -z
AM ɡəˈlɪʃən, -z

Galilean
BR ˌɡalɪˈliːən
AM ˌɡæləˈliən

Galilee
BR ˈɡalɪliː, -z
AM ˈɡæləˌli, -z

Galileo
BR ˌɡalɪˈleɪəʊ

AM ˌɡæləˈleɪoʊ

galimatias
BR ˌɡalɪˈmatɪəs, ˌɡalɪˈmeɪʃəs
AM ˌɡæləˈmeɪʃəs, ˌɡæləˈmædiəs

galingale
BR ˈɡalɪŋɡeɪl, -z
AM ˈɡælənˌɡeɪl, -z

galiot
BR ˈɡalɪət, -s
AM ˈɡæliət, ˈɡæliˌɑt, -s

galipot
BR ˈɡalɪpɒt
AM ˈɡæliˌpɑt

gall
BR ɡɔːl, -z, -ɪŋ, -d
AM ɡɔl, ɡɑl, -z, -ɪŋ, -d

Galla
BR ˈɡalə(r), -z
AM ˈɡælə, ˈɡɑlə, -z

Gallacher
BR ˈɡaləhə(r), ˈɡaləxə(r)
AM ˈɡæləkər

Gallagher
BR ˈɡaləhə(r), ˈɡaləxə(r), ˈɡaləɡə(r)
AM ˈɡæləɡər

Gallaher
BR ˈɡaləhə(r), ˈɡaləxə(r)
AM ˈɡæləˌhər

gallant¹
adjective, brave, splendid
BR ˈɡalənt, ˈɡalɲt
AM ˈɡælənt

gallant²
noun, adjective, courteous
BR ˈɡalənt, ˈɡalɲt, ɡəˈlant, -s
AM ɡəˈlænt, ɡəˈlant, ˈɡælənt, -s

gallant³
verb
BR ɡəˈlant, -s, -ɪŋ, -ɪd
AM ɡəˈlæn|t, ɡəˈlan|t, -ts, -(t)ɪŋ, -(t)əd

gallantly
BR ˈɡaləntli, ˈɡalɲtli
AM ˈɡælən(t)li

gallantry
BR ˈɡaləntri, ˈɡalɲtri
AM ˈɡæləntri

Galle
BR ɡɔːl
AM ɡɔl, ɡɑl

galleon
BR ˈɡalɪən, -z
AM ˈɡæliən, ˈɡæljən, -z

galleria
BR ˌɡaləˈriːə(r), -z
AM ˌɡæləˈriə, -z

gallery
BR ˈɡal(ə)r|i, -ɪz, -d
AM ˈɡæl(ə)ri, -z, -d

galleryite
BR ˈɡalərɪʌɪt, -s
AM ˈɡæl(ə)riˌaɪt, -s

galley
BR ˈɡal|i, -ɪz
AM ˈɡæli, -z

galliambic
BR ˌɡalɪˈambɪk, -s
AM ˌɡæliˈæmbɪk, -s

galliard
BR ˈɡalɪɑːd, -z
AM ˈɡæljərd, -z

Gallic
BR ˈɡalɪk
AM ˈɡælɪk

Gallican
BR ˈɡalɪk(ə)n, -z
AM ˈɡæləkən, -z

Gallicanism
BR ˈɡalɪkənɪz(ə)m, ˈɡalɪˌknɪz(ə)m
AM ˈɡæləkəˌnɪzəm

gallice
BR ˈɡalɪsiː
AM ˈɡæləs

Gallicise
BR ˈɡalɪsaɪz, -ɪz, -ɪŋ, -d
AM ˈɡæləˌsaɪz, -ɪz, -ɪŋ, -d

Gallicism
BR ˈɡalɪsɪz(ə)m, -z
AM ˈɡæləˌsɪzəm, -z

Gallicize
BR ˈɡalɪsaɪz, -ɪz, -ɪŋ, -d
AM ˈɡæləˌsaɪz, -ɪz, -ɪŋ, -d

galligaskins
BR ˌɡalɪˌɡaskɪnz
AM ˌɡæləˈɡæskənz, ˌɡæliˈɡæskənz

gallimaufry
BR ˌɡalɪˈmɔːfr|i, -ɪz
AM ˌɡæləˈmɔfri, ˌɡæləˈmɑfri, -z

gallinaceous
BR ˌɡalɪˈneɪʃəs
AM ˌɡæləˈneɪʃəs

gallingly
BR ˈɡɔːlɪŋli
AM ˈɡɔlɪŋli, ˈɡɑlɪŋli

gallinule
BR ˈɡalɪnjuːl, -z
AM ˈɡæləˌn(j)ul, -z

galliot
BR ˈɡalɪət, -s
AM ˈɡæliət, ˈɡæliˌɑt, -s

Gallipoli
BR ɡəˈlɪpəli, ɡəˈlɪpˌli
AM ɡəˈlɪp(ə)li

gallipot
BR ˈɡalɪpɒt, -s
AM ˈɡæliˌpɑt, -s

gallium
BR ˈɡalɪəm
AM ˈɡæliəm

gallivant
BR ˈɡalɪvant, -s, -ɪŋ, -ɪd

AM ˈgæləˌvænǀt, -ts, -(t)ɪŋ, -(t)əd
galliwasp
BR ˈgalɪwɒsp, -s
AM ˈgælə,wɑsp, -s
gallnut
BR ˈgalnʌt, -s
AM ˈgælˌnət, -s
Gallo
BR ˈgaləʊ
AM ˈgæləʊ
Gallo-
BR ˈgaləʊ
AM ˈgæləʊ
Gallois
BR ˈgalwɑ:(r)
AM gal'wɑ
Gallomania
BR ˌgalə(ʊ)ˈmeɪnɪə(r)
AM ˌgæləʊˈmeɪnɪə
Gallomaniac
BR ˌgalə(ʊ)ˈmeɪnɪak, -s
AM ˌgæləʊˈmeɪniˌæk, -s
gallon
BR ˈgalən, -z
AM ˈgælən, -z
gallonage
BR ˈgalənǀɪdʒ, -ɪdʒɪz
AM ˈgælənɪdʒ, -ɪz
galloon
BR gəˈlu:n
AM gəˈlun
gallop
BR ˈgaləp, -s, -ɪŋ, -t
AM ˈgæləp, -s, -ɪŋ, -t
galloper
BR ˈgaləpə(r), -z
AM ˈgæləpər, -z
Gallophile
BR ˈgalə(ʊ)fʌɪl, -z
AM ˈgæləˌfaɪl, -z
Gallophobe
BR ˈgalə(ʊ)fəʊb, -z
AM ˈgæləˌfəʊb, -z
Gallophobia
BR ˌgalə(ʊ)ˈfəʊbɪə(r)
AM ˌgæləˈfəʊbɪə
Gallo-Roman
BR ˌgaləʊˈrəʊmən, -z
AM ˌgæləʊˈrəʊmən, -z
galloway
BR ˈgaləweɪ, -z
AM ˈgæləˌweɪ, -z
gallowglass
BR ˈgaləʊglɑ:s, ˈgaləʊglas, -ɪz
AM ˈgæləʊˌglæs, -əz
gallows
BR ˈgaləʊz
AM ˈgæləʊz
gallstone
BR ˈgɔ:lstəʊn, -z
AM ˈgɔlˌstoʊn, ˈgɑlˌstoʊn, -z

Gallup
BR ˈgaləp
AM ˈgæləp
galluses
BR ˈgaləsɪz
AM ˈgæləsəz
gall-wasp
BR ˈgɔ:lwɒsp, -s
AM ˈgɔlˌwasp, ˈgalˌwasp, -s
galoot
BR gəˈlu:t, -s
AM gəˈlut, -s
galop
BR ˈgaləp, -s, -ɪŋ, -t
AM ˈgæləp, -s, -ɪŋ, -t
galore
BR gəˈlɔ:(r)
AM gəˈlɔ(ə)r
galosh
BR gəˈlɒʃ, -ɪz
AM gəˈlɑʃ, -əz
Galsworthy
BR ˈgɔ:lz,wə:ði
AM ˈgɔlz,wərði, ˈgalz,wərði
Galt
BR gɔ:lt, gɒlt
AM gɔlt, galt
Galton
BR ˈgɔ:lt(ə)n, ˈgɒlt(ə)n
AM ˈgɔltən, ˈgaltən
galumph
BR gəˈlʌmf, -s, -ɪŋ, -t
AM gəˈləm(p)f, -s, -ɪŋ, -t
Galvani
BR galˈvɑ:ni
AM gælˈvɑni
galvanic
BR galˈvanɪk
AM gælˈvænɪk
galvanically
BR galˈvanɪkli
AM gælˈvænək(ə)li
galvanise
BR ˈgalvənʌɪz, -ɪz, -ɪŋ, -d
AM ˈgælvəˌnaɪz, -ɪz, -ɪŋ, -d
galvaniser
BR ˈgalvənʌɪzə(r), -z
AM ˈgælvəˌnaɪzər, -z
galvanism
BR ˈgalvənɪz(ə)m
AM ˈgælvəˌnɪzəm
galvanist
BR ˈgalvənɪst, -s
AM ˈgælvənəst, -s
galvanization
BR ˌgalvənʌɪˈzeɪʃn
AM ˌgælvənəˈzeɪʃən, ˌgælvəˌnaɪˈzeɪʃən
galvanize
BR ˈgalvənʌɪz, -ɪz, -ɪŋ, -d
AM ˈgælvəˌnaɪz, -ɪz, -ɪŋ, -d

galvanizer
BR ˈgalvənʌɪzə(r), -z
AM ˈgælvəˌnaɪzər, -z
galvanometer
BR ˌgalvəˈnɒmɪtə(r), -z
AM ˌgælvəˈnɑmədər, -z
galvanometric
BR ˌgalvənəˈmɛtrɪk, ˌgalvnəˈmɛtrɪk
AM ˌgælvənəˈmɛtrɪk
Galveston
BR ˈgalvɪst(ə)n
AM ˈgælvəstən
galvo
BR ˈgalvəʊ, -z
AM ˈgælˌvoʊ, -z
Galway
BR ˈgɔ:lweɪ
AM ˈgɔlˌweɪ, ˈgalˌweɪ
gam
BR gam, -z
AM gæm, -z
Gama, da
BR də ˈgɑ:mə(r)
AM də ˈgæmə
Gamage
BR ˈgamɪdʒ
AM ˈgæmɪdʒ
Gamaliel
BR gəˈmeɪlɪəl
AM gəˈmeɪlɪəl
gamay
BR ˈgameɪ, -z
AM gæˈmeɪ, -z
gamba
BR ˈgambə(r), -z
AM ˈgæmbə, ˈgambə, -z
Gambaccini
BR ˌgambəˈtʃi:ni
AM ˌgæmbəˈtʃini
gambade
BR gamˈbeɪd, gamˈbɑ:d, -z
AM gæmˈbeɪd, gæmˈbad, -z
gambado
BR gamˈbeɪdəʊ, gamˈbɑ:dəʊ, -z
AM gæmˈbeɪˌdoʊ, gæmˈbɑˌdoʊ, -z
Gambia
BR ˈgambɪə(r)
AM ˈgæmbɪə
Gambian
BR ˈgambɪən, -z
AM ˈgæmbɪən, -z
gambier
BR ˈgambɪə(r), -z
AM ˈgæmˌbɪ(ə)r, -z
gambit
BR ˈgambɪt, -s
AM ˈgæmbət, -s
gamble
BR ˈgambǀl, -lz, -lɪŋ\-lɪŋ, -ld
AM ˈgæmbǀəl, -əlz, -(ə)lɪŋ, -əld

gambler
BR ˈgamblə(r), -z
AM ˈgæmblər, -z
gamboge
BR gamˈbəʊ(d)ʒ, gamˈbu:ʒ
AM gæmˈboʊdʒ, gæmˈbuʒ
gambol
BR ˈgambǀl, -lz, -lɪŋ\-lɪŋ, -ld
AM ˈgæmbǀəl, -əlz, -(ə)lɪŋ, -əld
gambrel
BR ˈgambr(ə)l, -z
AM ˈgæmbrəl, -z
game
BR geɪm, -z, -ɪŋ, -d, -ə(r), -ɪst
AM geɪm, -z, -ɪŋ, -d, -ər, -ɪst
gamebook
BR ˈgeɪmbʊk, -s
AM ˈgeɪmˌbʊk, -s
gamecock
BR ˈgeɪmkɒk, -s
AM ˈgeɪmˌkak, -s
gamefowl
BR ˈgeɪmfaʊl, -z
AM ˈgeɪmˌfaʊl, -z
gamekeeper
BR ˈgeɪmˌki:pə(r), -z
AM ˈgeɪmˌkipər, -z
gamekeeping
BR ˈgeɪmˌki:pɪŋ
AM ˈgeɪmˌkipɪŋ
gamelan
BR ˈgamɪlan
AM ˈgæməˌlæn
gamely
BR ˈgeɪmli
AM ˈgeɪmli
gameness
BR ˈgeɪmnɪs
AM ˈgeɪmnɪs
gamesman
BR ˈgeɪmzmən
AM ˈgeɪmzmən
gamesmanship
BR ˈgeɪmzmənˌʃɪp
AM ˈgeɪmzmənˌʃɪp
gamesmen
BR ˈgeɪmzmən
AM ˈgeɪmzmən
gamesome
BR ˈgeɪms(ə)m
AM ˈgeɪmsəm
gamesomely
BR ˈgeɪms(ə)mli
AM ˈgeɪmsəmli
gamesomeness
BR ˈgeɪms(ə)mnəs
AM ˈgeɪmsəmnəs
gamesplayer
BR ˈgeɪmzˌpleɪə(r), -z
AM ˈgeɪmzˌpleɪər, -z

gamester
BR ˈgeɪmstə(r), -z
AM ˈgeɪmstər, -z

gametangia
BR ˌgæmɪˈtan(d)ʒ(ɪ)ə(r)
AM ˌgæməˈtændʒ(i)ə

gametangium
BR ˌgæmɪˈtan(d)ʒɪəm
AM ˌgæməˈtændʒiəm

gamete
BR ˈgamiːt, gaˈmiːt
AM ˈgæmˌit, gəˈmit

gametic
BR gəˈmɛtɪk, gaˈmɛtɪk
AM gəˈmɛdɪk

gametocyte
BR gəˈmiːtə(ʊ)sʌɪt, ˈgamɪtəsʌɪt, -s
AM gəˈmidəˌsaɪt, -s

gametogenesis
BR gəˌmiːtə(ʊ)ˈdʒɛnɪsɪs, ˌgamɪtə(ʊ)ˈdʒɛnɪsɪs
AM gəˌmidəˈdʒɛnəsəs, ˌgæmɛdoʊˈdʒɛnəsəs

gametophyte
BR gəˈmiːtə(ʊ)fʌɪt, ˈgamɪtəfʌɪt, -s
AM gəˈmidəˌfaɪt, -s

gametophytic
BR gəˌmiːtə(ʊ)ˈfɪtɪk, ˌgamɪtə(ʊ)ˈfɪtɪk
AM gəˌmidəˈfɪdɪk

gamey
BR ˈgeɪm|i, -ɪə(r), -ɪɪst
AM ˈgeɪmi, -ər, -ɪst

gamily
BR ˈgeɪmɪli
AM ˈgeɪmɪli

gamin
BR ˈgamɪn, -z
AM ˈgæmən, -z

gamine
BR ˈgamiːn, -z
AM ˈgæmin, -z

gaminess
BR ˈgeɪmɪnɪs
AM ˈgeɪmɪnɪs

gamma
BR ˈgamə(r), -z
AM ˈgæmə, -z

gammadion
BR gəˈmeɪdɪən, gaˈmeɪdɪən, gəˈmadɪən, gaˈmadɪən, -z
AM gəˈmeɪdiˌɑn, gəˈmeɪdɪən, gəˈmædɪən, gæˈmeɪdiˌɑn, gæˈmædiˌɑn, gæˈmeɪdɪən, gæˈmædɪən, -z

gammer
BR ˈgamə(r), -z
AM ˈgæmər, -z

gamminess
BR ˈgamɪnɪs

AM ˈgæmɪnɪs

gammon
BR ˈgamən, -z
AM ˈgæmən, -z

gammy
BR ˈgam|i, -ɪə(r), -ɪɪst
AM ˈgæmi, -ər, -ɪst

Gamow
BR ˈgaməʊ
AM ˈgæˌmoʊ
RUS ˈgaməf

gamp
BR gamp, -s
AM gæmp, -s

gamut
BR ˈgamət, -s
AM ˈgæmət, -s

gamy
BR ˈgeɪm|i, -ɪə(r), -ɪɪst
AM ˈgeɪmi, -ər, -ɪst

gander
BR ˈgandə(r), -z
AM ˈgændər, -z

Gandhi
BR ˈgandi, ˈgɑːndi
AM ˈgɑndi

Ganesha
BR gəˈneɪʃə(r)
AM gəˈneɪʃə

gang
BR gaŋ, -z, -ɪŋ, -d
AM gæŋ, -z, -ɪŋ, -d

gangboard
BR ˈgaŋbɔːd, -z
AM ˈgæŋˌbɔ(ə)rd, -z

gangbuster
BR ˈgaŋˌbʌstə(r), -z
AM ˈgæŋˌbəstər, -z

ganger
BR ˈgaŋə(r), -z
AM ˈgæŋər, -z

Ganges
BR ˈgandʒiːz
AM ˈgænˌdʒiz

Gangetic
BR ganˈdʒetɪk
AM gænˈdʒɛdɪk

gangland
BR ˈgaŋland
AM ˈgæŋˌlænd

gangle
BR ˈgaŋg|l, -lz, -lɪŋ \ -lɪŋ, -ld
AM ˈgæŋg|əl, -əlz, -(ə)lɪŋ, -əld

ganglia
BR ˈgaŋglɪə(r)
AM ˈgæŋglɪə

gangliar
BR ˈgaŋglɪə(r)
AM ˈgæŋglɪər

gangliform
BR ˈgaŋglɪfɔːm
AM ˈgæŋgləˌfɔː(ə)rm

gangling
BR ˈgaŋglɪŋ
AM ˈgæŋglɪŋ

ganglion
BR ˈgaŋglɪən, -z
AM ˈgæŋglɪən, -z

ganglionated
BR ˈgaŋglɪəneɪtɪd
AM ˈgæŋgliəˌneɪdɪd

ganglionic
BR ˌgaŋglɪˈɒnɪk
AM ˌgæŋgliˈɑnɪk

gangly
BR ˈgaŋgl|i, -ɪə(r), -ɪɪst
AM ˈgæŋgli, -ər, -ɪst

gangplank
BR ˈgaŋplaŋk, -s
AM ˈgæŋˌplæŋk, -s

gangrene
BR ˈgaŋgriːn
AM ˈgæŋgrin

gangrenous
BR ˈgaŋgrɪnəs
AM ˈgæŋgrənəs

gangster
BR ˈgaŋstə(r), -z
AM ˈgæŋgstər, -z

gangsterism
BR ˈgaŋst(ə)rɪz(ə)m
AM ˈgæŋgstəˌrɪzəm

gangue
BR gaŋ
AM gæŋ

gangway
BR ˈgaŋweɪ, -z
AM ˈgæŋˌweɪ, -z

ganister
BR ˈganɪstə(r)
AM ˈgænəstər

ganja
BR ˈgandʒə(r)
AM ˈgɑndʒə, ˈgændʒə

gannet
BR ˈganɪt, -s
AM ˈgænət, -s

gannetry
BR ˈganɪtr|i, -ɪz
AM ˈgænətri, -z

Gannex
BR ˈganɛks
AM ˈgænəks

gannister
BR ˈganɪstə(r)
AM ˈgænəstər

Gannon
BR ˈganən
AM ˈgænən

ganoid
BR ˈganɔɪd, -z
AM ˈgæˌnɔɪd, -z

gantlet
BR ˈgantlɪt, ˈgɔːntlɪt, -s
AM ˈgɒntlət, ˈgæntlət, -s

gantry
BR ˈgantr|i, -ɪz
AM ˈgæntri, -z

Ganymede
BR ˈganɪmiːd
AM ˈgænəˌmid

gaol
BR dʒeɪl, -z, -ɪŋ, -d
AM dʒeɪl, -z, -ɪŋ, -d

gaolbird
BR ˈdʒeɪlbəːd, -z
AM ˈdʒeɪlˌbərd, -z

gaoler
BR ˈdʒeɪlə(r), -z
AM ˈdʒeɪlər, -z

gap
BR gap, -s, -ɪŋ, -t
AM gæp, -s, -ɪŋ, -t

gape
BR geɪp, -s, -ɪŋ, -t
AM geɪp, -s, -ɪŋ, -t

gaper
BR ˈgeɪpə(r), -z
AM ˈgeɪpər, -z

gapeworm
BR ˈgeɪpwəːm, -z
AM ˈgeɪpˌwərm, -z

gapingly
BR ˈgeɪpɪŋli
AM ˈgeɪpɪŋli

gappy
BR ˈgap|i, -ɪə(r), -ɪɪst
AM ˈgæpi, -ər, -ɪst

gar
BR gɑː(r)
AM gɑr

garage
BR ˈgarɑː(d)ʒ, ˈgarɪdʒ, gəˈrɑː(d)ʒ, ˈgarɑː(d)ʒɪˈgarɪdʒɪz\, gəˈrɑː(d)ʒɪz, ˈgarɑː(d)ʒɪŋ\ˈgarɪdʒɪŋ\, gəˈrɑː(d)ʒɪŋ, ˈgarɑː(d)ʒdˈgarɪdʒd\, gəˈrɑː(d)ʒd
AM gəˈrɑʒ, -əz, -ɪŋ, -t

garam masala
BR ˌgɑːrəm məˈsɑːlə(r)
AM ˌgɑrəm məˈsɑlə

Garard
BR ˈgarɑːd
AM ˈgɛrɑrd

garb
BR gɑːb, -z, -d
AM gɑrb, -z, -d

garbage
BR ˈgɑːbɪdʒ
AM ˈgɑrbɪdʒ

garbanzo
BR gɑːˈbanzəʊ, -z
AM gɑrˈbanzoʊ, -z

Garbett
BR ˈgɑːbɪt
AM ˈgɑːrbət

garble
BR ˈgɑːb|l, -lz, -lɪŋ \ -lɪŋ, -ld
AM ˈgɑrb|əl, -əlz, -(ə)lɪŋ, -əld

garbler
BR ˈgɑːblə(r), -z
AM ˈgɑrb(ə)lər, -z

Garbo
BR ˈgɑːbəʊ
AM ˈgɑrˌboʊ

garboard
BR ˈgɑːbɔːd, -z
AM ˈgɑr,bɔ(ə)rd, -z

García
BR gɑːˈsiːə(r)
AM gɑrˈsiə
SP garˈθia, garˈsia

garçon
BR ˈgɑːsɒn, ˌgɑːsɒ̃, -z
AM gɑrˈsɔn, -z

Garda
BR ˈgɑːdə(r)
AM ˈgɑrdə

Gardaí
BR (ˌ)gɑːˈdiː
AM gɑrˈdi

garden
BR ˈgɑːdn̩, -nz,
-n̩ɪŋ \-nɪŋ, -nd
AM ˈgɑrdən, -z, -ɪŋ, -d

gardener
BR ˈgɑːdnə(r),
ˈgɑːdnə(r), -z
AM ˈgɑrdnər, -z

gardenesque
BR ˌgɑːdnˈɛsk
AM ˌgɑrdnˈɛsk

gardenia
BR gɑːˈdiːniə(r), -z
AM gɑrˈdinjə, -z

Gardiner
BR ˈgɑːdnə(r)
AM ˈgɑrd(ə)nər

Gardner
BR ˈgɑːdnə(r)
AM ˈgɑrdnər

Gardyne
BR gɑːˈdʌɪn, ˈgɑːdʌɪn
AM ˈgɑrdaɪn

Gareloch
BR ˈgɛːlɒx, ˈgɛːlɒk
AM ˈgɛrlɑk

Gareth
BR ˈgarəθ
AM ˈgɛrəθ

Garfield
BR ˈgɑːfiːld
AM ˈgɑrˌfild

garfish
BR ˈgɑːfɪʃ
AM ˈgɑrˌfɪʃ

Garforth
BR ˈgɑːfɔːθ, ˈgɑːfəθ
AM ˈgɑrˌfɔ(ə)rθ

Garfunkel
BR gɑːˈfʌŋkl̩, ˈgɑːˌfʌŋkl̩
AM ˈgɑrˌfəŋkəl

garganey
BR ˈgɑːgənli, ˈgɑːgn̩li, -ɪz
AM ˈgɑrgəni, -z

Gargantua
BR gɑːˈgantjʊə(r), gɑːˈgantʃʊə(r)
AM ˌgɑrˈgæn(t)ʃuə

gargantuan
BR gɑːˈgantjʊən, gɑːˈgantʃʊən
AM gɑrˈgæn(t)ʃ(ə(w)ə)n

garget
BR ˈgɑːgɪt
AM ˈgɑrgət

gargle
BR ˈgɑːgl̩, -lz, -l̩ɪŋ \-lɪŋ, -ld
AM ˈgɑrgl̩əl, -əlz, -(ə)lɪŋ, -əld

gargoyle
BR ˈgɑːgɔɪl, -z
AM ˈgɑrˌgɔɪl, -z

gargoylism
BR ˈgɑːgɔɪlɪz(ə)m
AM ˈgɑrˌgɔɪˌlɪzəm

Garibaldi
BR ˌgarɪˈbɔːldi, ˌgarɪˈbɒldi, ˌgarɪˈbaldi
AM ˌgɛrəˈbɔldi, ˌgɛrəˈbaldi

garish
BR ˈgɛːrɪʃ, ˈgarɪʃ
AM ˈgɛrɪʃ

garishly
BR ˈgɛːrɪʃli, ˈgarɪʃli
AM ˈgɛrəʃli

garishness
BR ˈgɛːrɪʃnɪs, ˈgarɪʃnɪs
AM ˈgɛrɪʃnɪs

garland
BR ˈgɑːlənd, -z, -ɪŋ, -ɪd
AM ˈgɑrlən(d), -z, -ɪŋ, -əd

garlic
BR ˈgɑːlɪk
AM ˈgɑrlɪk

garlicky
BR ˈgɑːlɪki
AM ˈgɑrlɪki

Garman
BR ˈgɑːmən
AM ˈgɑrmən

garment
BR ˈgɑːm(ə)nt, -s, -ɪd
AM ˈgɑrmən|t, -ts, -(t)əd

Garmondsway
BR ˈgɑːmən(d)zweɪ
AM ˈgɑrmənz,weɪ

Garmonsway
BR ˈgɑːmənzweɪ
AM ˈgɑrmənz,weɪ

garner
BR ˈgɑːn|ə(r), -əz, -(ə)rɪŋ, -əd
AM ˈgɑrnər, -z, -ɪŋ, -d

garnet
BR ˈgɑːnɪt, -s
AM ˈgɑrnət, -s

Garnett
BR ˈgɑːnɪt
AM ˈgɑrnət

garnish
BR ˈgɑːn|ɪʃ, -ɪʃɪz, -ɪʃɪŋ, -ɪʃt
AM ˈgɑrnɪʃ, -ɪz, -ɪŋ, -t

garnishee
BR ˌgɑːnɪˈʃiː, -z
AM ˌgɑrnɪˈʃi, -z

garnishing
BR ˈgɑːnɪʃɪŋ, -z
AM ˈgɑrnɪʃɪŋ, -z

garnishment
BR ˈgɑːnɪʃm(ə)nt
AM ˈgɑrnɪʃmənt

garniture
BR ˈgɑːnɪtʃə(r)
AM ˈgɑrnətʃʊ(ə)r, ˈgɑrnətʃər

Garonne
BR gəˈrɒn
AM gəˈrɑn, gəˈrɔn

garotte
BR gəˈrɒt, -s, -ɪŋ, -ɪd
AM gəˈrɑ|t, -ts, -dɪŋ, -dəd

garpike
BR ˈgɑːpʌɪk
AM ˈgærˌpaɪk

Garrard
BR ˈgarɑːd, ˈgarəd
AM gəˈrɑrd

Garratt
BR ˈgarət
AM ˈgɛrət

garret
BR ˈgarət, -s
AM ˈgɛrət, -s

garreteer
BR ˌgarɪˈtiːə(r), -z
AM ˌgɛrəˈti(ə)r, -z

Garrick
BR ˈgarɪk
AM ˈgɛrɪk

garrison
BR ˈgarɪs(ə)n, -z, -ɪŋ, -d
AM ˈgɛrəsən, -z, -ɪŋ, -d

garrote
BR gəˈrɒt, -s, -ɪŋ, -ɪd
AM gəˈrɑ|t, -ts, -dɪŋ, -dəd

garrotte
BR gəˈrɒt, -s, -ɪŋ, -ɪd
AM gəˈrɑ|t, -ts, -dɪŋ, -dəd

garrotter
BR gəˈrɒtə(r), -z
AM gəˈrɑdər, -z

garrulity
BR gəˈr(j)uːlɪti, gaˈr(j)uːlɪti
AM gəˈrulədi

garrulous
BR ˈgar(j)ʊləs
AM ˈgɛrələs

garrulously
BR ˈgar(j)ʊləsli
AM ˈgɛrələsli

garrulousness
BR ˈgar(j)ʊləsnəs
AM ˈgɛrələsnəs

Garry
BR ˈgari
AM ˈgɛri

garrya
BR ˈgarɪə(r), -z
AM ˈgɛriə, -z

garter
BR ˈgɑːt|ə(r), -əz, -(ə)rɪŋ, -əd
AM ˈgɑrdər, -z, -ɪŋ, -d

garth
BR gɑːθ, -s
AM gɑrθ, -s

garuda
BR ˈgarʊdə(r), -z
AM gəˈrudə, -z

Garvey
BR ˈgɑːvi
AM ˈgɑrvi

Gary
BR ˈgari
AM ˈgɛri

Garza
BR ˈgɑːzə(r)
AM ˈgɑrzə

gas
BR gas, -ɪz, -ɪŋ, -t
AM gæs, -əz, -ɪŋ, -t

gasbag
BR ˈgasbag, -z
AM ˈgæs,bæg, -z

gas chamber
BR ˈgas ˌtʃeɪmbə(r), -z
AM ˈgæs ˌtʃeɪmbər, -z

Gascogne
BR ˈgaskɔɪn
AM gæsˈkɔɪn
FR gaskɔɲ

Gascoigne
BR ˈgaskɔɪn
AM gæsˈkɔɪn

Gascoin
BR ˈgaskɔɪn
AM gæsˈkɔɪn

Gascoine
BR ˈgaskɔɪn
AM gæsˈkɔɪn

Gascon
BR ˈgaskən, -z
AM ˈgæskən, -z

gasconade
BR ˌgaskəˈneɪd, -z, -ɪŋ, -ɪd
AM ˌgæskəˈneɪd, -z, -ɪŋ, -ɪd

Gascony
BR ˈgaskəni
AM ˈgæskəni

gaseous
BR ˈgasɪəs, ˈgeɪsɪəs
AM ˈgæʃ(j)əs, ˈgæsɪəs

gaseousness
BR ˈɡasɪəsnəs,
ˈɡeɪsɪəsnəs
AM ˈɡæʃ(j)əsnəs,
ˈɡæsɪəsnəs
gasfield
BR ˈɡasfiːld, -z
AM ˈɡæsˌfild, -z
gash
BR ɡaʃ, -ɪz, -ɪŋ, -t
AM ɡæʃ, -əz, -ɪŋ, -t
gasholder
BR ˈɡasˌhəʊldə(r), -z
AM ˈɡæsˌ(h)oʊldər, -z
gashouse
BR ˈɡashaʊ|s, -zɪz
AM ˈɡæsˌ(h)aʊ|s, -zəz
gasification
BR ˌɡasɪfɪˈkeɪʃn
AM ˌɡæsəfəˈkeɪʃən
gasify
BR ˈɡasɪfʌɪ, -z, -ɪŋ, -d
AM ˈɡæsəˌfaɪ, -z, -ɪŋ, -d
Gaskell
BR ˈɡaskl
AM ˈɡæskəl
gasket
BR ˈɡaskɪt, -s
AM ˈɡæskət, -s
gaskin
BR ˈɡaskɪn, -z
AM ˈɡæskən, -z
gaslamp
BR ˈɡaslamp, -s
AM ˈɡæsˌlæmp, -s
gaslight
BR ˈɡaslʌɪt
AM ˈɡæsˌlaɪt
gasman
BR ˈɡasman
AM ˈɡæsmən
gasmen
BR ˈɡasmɛn
AM ˈɡæsmən
gasohol
BR ˈɡasəhɒl
AM ˈɡæsəˌhɔl,
ˈɡæsəˌhɑl
gasolene
BR ˈɡasəliːn, ˌɡasəˈliːn
AM ˈɡæsəlin, ˌɡæsəˈlin
gasoline
BR ˈɡasəliːn, ˌɡasəˈliːn
AM ˈɡæsəlin, ˌɡæsəˈlin
gasometer
BR ɡaˈsɒmɪtə(r),
ɡəˈsɒmɪtə(r), -z
AM ɡæˈsɑmədər, -z
gasp
BR ɡɑːsp, ɡasp, -s, -ɪŋ, -t
AM ɡæsp, -s, -ɪŋ, -t
gasper
BR ˈɡɑːspə(r),
ˈɡaspə(r), -z
AM ˈɡæspər, -z
gaspereau
BR ˈɡaspərəʊ, -z

AM ˈɡæspərəʊ, -z
gaspereaux
BR ˈɡaspərəʊz
AM ˈɡæspərəʊ
gasproof
BR ˈɡaspruːf
AM ˈɡæsˌpruf
Gassendi
BR ɡəˈsɛndi
AM ɡəˈsɛndi
gasser
BR ˈɡasə(r), -z
AM ˈɡæsər, -z
gassiness
BR ˈɡasɪnɪs
AM ˈɡæsɪnɪs
gassy
BR ˈɡas|i, -ɪə(r), -ɪɪst
AM ˈɡæsi, -ər, -ɪɪst
gasteropod
BR ˈɡast(ə)rəpɒd, -z
AM ˈɡæst(ə)rəˌpad, -z
Gasthaus
BR ˈɡasthaʊ|s, -zɪz
AM ˈɡast,(h)aʊ|s, -zəz
Gasthäuser
BR ˈɡasthɔɪzə(r)
AM ˈɡast,(h)ɔɪzər
Gasthof
BR ˈɡasthɒf, -s
AM ˈɡast,(h)ɔf,
ˈɡast,(h)af, -s
Gasthöfe
BR ˈɡast,hɒfə(r)
AM ˈɡas(t),(h)ɔfə,
ˈɡas(t),(h)afə
gastrectomy
BR ɡaˈstrɛktəm|i, -ɪz
AM ɡæˈstrɛktəmi, -ɪz
gastric
BR ˈɡastrɪk
AM ˈɡæstrɪk
gastritis
BR ɡaˈstrʌɪtɪs
AM ɡæˈstraɪdɪs
gastroenteric
BR ˌɡastrəʊɛnˈtɛrɪk
AM ˌɡæstroʊˌɛnˈtɛrɪk
gastroenteritis
BR ˌɡastrəʊˌɛntəˈrʌɪtɪs
AM ˌɡæstroʊˌɛn(t)əˈraɪ-
dɪs
gastroenterology
BR ˌɡastrəʊˌɛntəˈrɒl-
ədʒi
AM ˌɡæstroʊˌɛn(t)əˈral-
ədʒi
gastrointestinal
BR ˌɡastrəʊɪnˈtɛstɪnl,
ˌɡastrəʊˌɪntɛˈstʌɪnl
AM ˌɡæstroʊɪnˈtɛstənəl
gastronome
BR ˈɡastrənəʊm, -z
AM ˈɡæstrəˌnoʊm, -z
gastronomic
BR ˌɡastrəˈnɒmɪk
AM ˌɡæstrəˈnamɪk

gastronomical
BR ˌɡastrəˈnɒmɪkl
AM ˌɡæstrəˈnaməkəl
gastronomically
BR ˌɡastrəˈnɒmɪkli
AM ˌɡæstrəˈnamək(ə)li
gastronomy
BR ɡaˈstrɒnəmi
AM ɡæˈstrɑnəmi
gastropod
BR ˈɡastrəpɒd, -z
AM ˈɡæstrəˌpad, -z
gastropodous
BR ɡaˈstrɒpədəs
AM ɡæˈstrɑpədəs
gastroscope
BR ˈɡastrəskəʊp, -s
AM ˈɡæstrəˌskoʊp, -s
gastrula
BR ˈɡastrʊlə(r), -z
AM ˈɡæstrələ, -z
gastrulae
BR ˈɡastrʊliː
AM ˈɡæstrəˌli,
ˈɡæstrəˌlaɪ
gasworks
BR ˈɡaswəːks
AM ˈɡæsˌwərks
gat
BR ɡat, -s
AM ɡæt, -s
gate
BR ɡeɪt, -s, -ɪŋ, -ɪd
AM ɡeɪ|t, -ts, -dɪŋ, -dɪd
gateau
BR ˈɡatəʊ, -z
AM ɡɑˈtoʊ, ɡæˈtoʊ, -z
gateaux
BR ˈɡatəʊz
AM ɡɑˈtoʊ, ɡæˈtoʊ
gatecrash
BR ˈɡeɪtkraʃ, -ɪz, -ɪŋ, -t
AM ˈɡeɪtˌkræʃ, -əz, -ɪŋ,
-t
gatecrasher
BR ˈɡeɪtkraʃə(r), -z
AM ˈɡeɪtˌkræʃər, -z
gatefold
BR ˈɡeɪtfəʊld, -z
AM ˈɡeɪtˌfoʊld, -z
gatehouse
BR ˈɡeɪthaʊ|s, -zɪz
AM ˈɡeɪtˌ(h)aʊ|s, -zɪz
gatekeeper
BR ˈɡeɪtˌkiːpə(r), -z
AM ˈɡeɪtˌkipər, -z
gateleg
BR ˈɡeɪtlɛɡ, -z
AM ˈɡeɪtˌlɛɡ, -z
gatelegged
BR ˌɡeɪtˈlɛɡd
AM ˈɡeɪtˌlɛɡəd
gateman
BR ˈɡeɪtman
AM ˈɡeɪtmən
gatemen
BR ˈɡeɪtmɛn

AM ˈɡeɪtmən
gatepost
BR ˈɡeɪtpəʊst, -s
AM ˈɡeɪtˌpoʊst, -s
Gates
BR ɡeɪts
AM ɡeɪts
Gateshead
BR ˈɡeɪtshɛd,
ˌɡeɪtsˈhɛd
AM ˈɡeɪts,(h)ɛd
gateway
BR ˈɡeɪtweɪ, -z
AM ˈɡeɪtˌweɪ, -z
gather
BR ˈɡað|ə(r), -əz,
-(ə)rɪŋ, -əd
AM ˈɡæð|ər, -ərz,
-(ə)rɪŋ, -ərd
gatherer
BR ˈɡað(ə)rə(r), -z
AM ˈɡæðərər, -z
gathering
BR ˈɡað(ə)rɪŋ, -z
AM ˈɡæð(ə)rɪŋ, -z
Gatling
BR ˈɡatlɪŋ, -z
AM ˈɡætˌlɪŋ, -z
'gator
BR ˈɡeɪtə(r), -z
AM ˈɡeɪdər, -z
GATT
BR ɡat
AM ɡæt
Gatting
BR ˈɡatɪŋ
AM ˈɡædɪŋ
Gatwick
BR ˈɡatwɪk
AM ˈɡætˌwɪk
gauche
BR ɡəʊʃ
AM ɡoʊʃ
gauchely
BR ˈɡəʊʃli
AM ˈɡoʊʃli
gaucheness
BR ˈɡəʊʃnəs
AM ˈɡoʊʃnəs
gaucherie
BR ˈɡəʊʃ(ə)r|i, -ɪz
AM ˈɡoʊʃəri, -z
gaucho
BR ˈɡaʊtʃəʊ, -z
AM ˈɡaʊtʃoʊ, -z
gaud
BR ɡɔːd, -z
AM ɡɔd, ɡad, -z
gaudeamus
BR ˌɡaʊdɪˈɑːməs
AM ˌɡaʊdiˈaməs
Gaudí
BR ˈɡaʊdi
AM ˈɡaʊdi
gaudily
BR ˈɡɔːdɪli
AM ˈɡɔdəli, ˈɡadəli

gaudiness
BR 'gɔːdɪnɪs
AM 'gɔdinɪs, 'gɑdinɪs
gaudy
BR 'gɔːd|i, -ɪə(r), -ɪɪst
AM 'gɔdi, 'gɑdi, -ər, -ɪst
gauge
BR geɪdʒ, -ɪz, -ɪŋ, -d
AM geɪdʒ, -ɪz, -ɪŋ, -d
gaugeable
BR 'geɪdʒəbl
AM 'geɪdʒəbəl
gauger
BR 'geɪdʒə(r), -z
AM 'geɪdʒər, -z
Gauguin
BR 'gəʊgã, 'gəʊgan
AM gɔ'gɛn, gɑ'gɛn
Gaul
BR gɔːl, -z
AM gɔl, gɑl, -z
gauleiter
BR 'gaʊlʌɪtə(r), -z
AM 'gaʊˌlaɪdər, -z
Gaulish
BR 'gɔːlɪʃ
AM 'gɔlɪʃ, 'gɑlɪʃ
Gaullism
BR 'gəʊlɪz(ə)m
AM 'gɔˌlɪzəm, 'gɑˌlɪzəm
Gaullist
BR 'gəʊlɪst, -s
AM 'gɔləst, 'gɑləst, -s
Gauloise
BR 'gəʊlwɑːz,
'gɔːlwɑːz, -ɪz
AM 'gɔlˌwɑz, 'gɑlˌwɑz,
-əz
gault
BR gɔːlt, gɒlt
AM gɔlt, gɑlt
gaultheria
BR gɔːl'tɪrɪə(r), -z
AM gɔl'θɪriə, gɑl'θɪriə,
-z
gaunt
BR gɔːnt, -ə(r), -ɪst
AM gɔnt, gɑnt, -ər, -əst
gauntlet
BR 'gɔːntlɪt, -s
AM 'gɒn(t)lət,
'gɑn(t)lət, -s
gauntly
BR 'gɔːntli
AM 'gɒn(t)li, 'gɑn(t)li
gauntness
BR 'gɔːntnəs
AM 'gɒn(t)nəs,
'gɑn(t)nəs
gauntry
BR 'gɔːntr|i, -ɪz
AM 'gɒntri, 'gɑntri, -z
gaur
BR 'gaʊə(r), -z
AM 'gaʊ(ə)r, -z
Gauss
BR gaʊs, -ɪz, -ɪŋ, -t

AM gaʊs, -əz, -ɪŋ, -t
Gaussian
BR 'gaʊsɪən
AM 'gaʊsɪən
Gautama
BR 'gaʊtəmə(r),
'gəʊtəmə(r)
AM 'gɔdəmə, 'gaʊdəmə
gauze
BR gɔːz
AM gɔz, gɑz
gauzily
BR 'gɔːzɪli
AM 'gɔzəli, 'gazəli
gauziness
BR 'gɔːzɪnɪs
AM 'gɔzɪnɪs, 'gazɪnɪs
gauzy
BR 'gɔːz|i, -ɪə(r), -ɪɪst
AM 'gɔzi, 'gazi, -ər, -ɪst
gave
BR geɪv
AM geɪv
gavel
BR 'gavl, -z
AM 'gævəl, -z
gavial
BR 'geɪvɪəl, 'gavɪəl, -z
AM 'geɪvɪəl, -z
Gavin
BR 'gavɪn
AM 'gævən
gavotte
BR gə'vɒt, -s
AM gə'vɑt, -s
Gawain
BR 'gɑːweɪn, 'gaweɪn,
gə'weɪn
AM gə'weɪn, 'gaweɪn
Gawd
God in exclamations
BR gɔːd
AM gɔd, gad
gawk
BR gɔːk, -s, -ɪŋ, -t
AM gɔk, gak, -s, -ɪŋ, -t
gawkily
BR 'gɔːkɪli
AM 'gɔkəli, 'gakəli
gawkiness
BR 'gɔːkɪnɪs
AM 'gɔkɪnɪs, 'gakɪnɪs
gawkish
BR 'gɔːkɪʃ
AM 'gɔkɪʃ, 'gakɪʃ
gawky
BR 'gɔːk|i, -ɪə(r), -ɪɪst
AM 'gɔki, 'gaki, -ər, -ɪst
gawp
BR gɔːp, -s, -ɪŋ, -t
AM gɔp, gap, -s, -ɪŋ, -t
gawper
BR 'gɔːpə(r), -z
AM 'gɔpər, 'gapər, -z
gay
BR geɪ, -ə(r), -ɪst
AM geɪ, -ər, -ɪst

gayal
BR gʌɪ'jɑːl, gʌɪ'jal, -z
AM gə'jal, -z
Gaydon
BR 'geɪdn
AM 'geɪdən
Gaye
BR geɪ
AM geɪ
gayety
BR 'geɪɪti
AM 'geɪɪdi
Gayle
BR geɪl
AM geɪl
Gay-Lussac
BR ˌgeɪ'luːsak
AM 'geɪlə'sæk
gayness
BR 'geɪnɪs
AM 'geɪnɪs
Gaynor
BR 'geɪnə(r)
AM 'geɪnər
Gaza
BR 'gɑːzə(r)
AM 'gazə
gazania
BR gə'zeɪnɪə(r), -z
AM gə'zeɪnɪə, -z
gaze
BR geɪz, -ɪz, -ɪŋ, -d
AM geɪz, -ɪz, -ɪŋ, -d
gazebo
BR gə'ziːbəʊ, -z
AM gə'ziboʊ, -z
gazelle
BR gə'zɛl, -z
AM gə'zɛl, -z
gazer
BR 'geɪzə(r), -z
AM 'geɪzər, -z
gazette
BR gə'zɛt, -s, -ɪŋ, -ɪd
AM gə'zɛ|t, -ts, -dɪŋ,
-dəd
gazetteer
BR ˌgazɪ'tɪə(r), -z
AM ˌgazəə'tɪ(ə)r, -z
gazpacho
BR gaz'patʃəʊ,
gə'spatʃəʊ,
gə'spatʃəʊ,
gə'spɑːtʃəʊ,
gə'spɑːtʃəʊ, -z
AM gəz'patʃoʊ, -z
gazump
BR gə'zʌm|p, -ps, -pɪŋ,
-(p)t
AM gə'zəmp, -s, -ɪŋ, -t
gazumper
BR gə'zʌmpə(r), -z
AM gə'zəmpər, -z
gazunder
BR gə'zʌnd|ə(r), -əz,
-(ə)rɪŋ, -əd
AM gə'zənd|ər, -ərz,
-(ə)rɪŋ, -ərd

Gdansk
BR gə'dansk
AM gə'dɑnsk
Gdańsk
BR gə'dansk
AM gə'dɑnsk
GDP
BR ˌdʒiː'diː'piː
AM ˌdʒi'di'pi
Gdynia
BR gə'dɪnɪə(r)
AM gə'dɪnɪə
gean
BR giːn, -z
AM gin, -z
gear
BR gɪə(r), -z, -ɪŋ, -d
AM gɪ(ə)r, -z, -ɪŋ, -d
gearbox
BR 'gɪəbɒks, -ɪz
AM 'gɪrˌbaks, -əz
gearing
BR 'gɪərɪŋ
AM 'gɪrɪŋ
gearstick
BR 'gɪəstɪk, -s
AM 'gɪrˌstɪk, -s
gearwheel
BR 'gɪəwiːl, -z
AM 'gɪrˌ(h)wil, -z
Geary
BR 'gɪəri
AM 'gɪri
Geber
BR 'dʒiːbə(r)
AM 'dʒibər
gecko
BR 'gɛkəʊ, -z
AM 'gɛkoʊ, -z
Geddes
BR 'gɛdɪs
AM 'gɛdiz
gee
BR dʒiː, -z, -ɪŋ, -d
AM dʒi, -z, -ɪŋ, -d
Geechee
BR 'giːtʃi
AM 'giˌtʃi
gee-gee
BR 'dʒiːdʒiː, -z
AM 'dʒiˌdʒi, -z
geek
BR giːk, -s
AM gik, -s
Geelong
BR dʒi:'lɒŋ, dʒɪ'lɒŋ
AM dʒi'lɒŋ, dʒi'lɑŋ
geese
BR giːs
AM gis
gee-string
BR 'dʒiːstrɪŋ, -z
AM 'dʒiˌstrɪŋ, -z
gee-whiz
BR ˌdʒiː'wɪz
AM 'dʒi'(h)wɪz

gee-whizz
BR ˌdʒiːˈwɪz
AM ˈdʒiːˈ(h)wɪz

Ge'ez
BR ˈgiːɛz
AM giˈɛz, geɪˈɛz

geezer
BR ˈgiːzə(r), -z
AM ˈgizər, -z

gefilte fish
BR gɪˈfɪltə fɪʃ
AM gəˈfɪltə ˌfɪʃ

Gehenna
BR gɪˈhɛnə(r)
AM gəˈhɛnə

Gehrig
BR ˈgɛrɪg
AM ˈgɛrɪg

Geiger counter
BR ˈgaɪgə ˌkaʊntə(r),
-z
AM ˈgaɪgər ˌkaʊn(t)ər,
-z

Geikie
BR ˈgiːki
AM ˈgiki

Geisel
BR ˈgaɪsl
AM ˈgaɪsəl

geisha
BR ˈgeɪʃə(r), -z
AM ˈgeɪʃə, ˈgiʃə, -z

Geissler
BR ˈgaɪslə(r)
AM ˈgeɪslər

gel
BR dʒɛl, -z, -ɪŋ, -d
AM dʒɛl, -z, -ɪŋ, -d

gelada
BR dʒɪˈlɑːdə(r), -z
AM ˈdʒɛlədə, ˈgɛlədə,
dʒəˈlɑdə, gəˈlɑdə, -z

gelatin
BR ˈdʒɛlətɪn
AM ˈdʒɛlətn, ˈdʒɛlədən

gelatine
BR ˈdʒɛlətiːn
AM ˈdʒɛlətn, ˈdʒɛlədən

gelatinisation
BR dʒɪˌlatɪnʌɪˈzeɪʃn
AM dʒɛˌlætn̩ˌaɪˈzeɪʃən,
ˌdʒɛlədəˌnaɪˈzeɪʃən,
dʒɛˌlætn̩əˈzeɪʃən,
ˌdʒɛlədənəˈzeɪʃən

gelatinise
BR dʒɪˈlatɪnʌɪz, -ɪz, -ɪŋ,
-d
AM dʒəˈlætn̩ˌaɪz,
ˈdʒɛlədəˌnaɪz, -ɪz, -ɪŋ,
-d

gelatinization
BR dʒɪˌlatɪnʌɪˈzeɪʃn
AM dʒɛˌlætn̩ˌaɪˈzeɪʃən,
ˌdʒɛlədəˌnaɪˈzeɪʃən,
dʒɛˌlætn̩əˈzeɪʃən,
ˌdʒɛlədənəˈzeɪʃən

gelatinize
BR dʒɪˈlatɪnʌɪz, -ɪz, -ɪŋ,
-d
AM dʒəˈlætn̩ˌaɪz,
ˈdʒɛlədəˌnaɪz, -ɪz, -ɪŋ,
-d

gelatinous
BR dʒɪˈlatɪnəs
AM dʒəˈlætn̩əs

gelatinously
BR dʒɪˈlatɪnəsli
AM dʒəˈlætn̩əsli

gelation
BR dʒɪˈleɪʃn, dʒɛˈleɪʃn
AM dʒəˈleɪʃən,
dʒɛˈleɪʃən

gelato
BR dʒɪˈlatəʊ
AM dʒəˈlædoʊ

gelcoat
BR ˈdʒɛlkəʊt, -s
AM ˈdʒɛlˌkoʊt, -s

geld
BR gɛld, -z, -ɪŋ, -ɪd
AM gɛld, -z, -ɪŋ, -əd

Geldart
BR ˈgɛldɑːt
AM ˈgɛldɑrt

Gelderland
BR ˈgɛldəland
AM ˈgɛldərˌlænd
DU ˈxɛldərˌlɑnt

gelding
BR ˈgɛldɪŋ, -z
AM ˈgɛldɪŋ, -z

Geldof
BR ˈgɛldɒf
AM ˈgɛldɒf, ˈgɛldɑf

gelid
BR ˈdʒɛlɪd
AM ˈdʒɛlid

gelignite
BR ˈdʒɛlɪgnʌɪt
AM ˈdʒɛləgˌnaɪt

Gell
BR dʒɛl, gɛl
AM gel

Gelligaer
BR ˌgɛɬɪˈgʌɪə(r),
ˌgɛɬɪgˈʌɪə(r),
ˌgɛɬɪˈgɛː(r),
ˌgɛɬɪˈgɛː(r)
AM ˌgɛləˈgɛ(ə)r

Gell-Mann
BR ˌgɛlˈman
AM ˌgɛlˈmæn

gelly
BR ˈdʒɛli
AM ˈdʒɛli

gelsemium
BR dʒɛlˈsiːmɪəm
AM dʒɛlˈsimiəm

gelt
BR gɛlt
AM gɛlt

gem
BR dʒɛm, -z
AM dʒɛm, -z

Gemara
BR gəˈmɑːrə(r),
gɛˈmɑːrə(r)
AM gəˈmɑrə

gematria
BR gɪˈmeɪtrɪə(r)
AM gəˈmeɪtriə

geminal
BR ˈdʒɛmɪnl
AM ˈdʒɛmənəl

geminally
BR ˈdʒɛmɪnəli,
ˈdʒɛmɪn̩li
AM ˈdʒɛmənəli

geminate[1]
adjective
BR ˈdʒɛmɪnət
AM ˈdʒɛmənət

geminate[2]
verb
BR ˈdʒɛmɪneɪt, -s, -ɪŋ,
-ɪd
AM ˈdʒɛməˌneɪ|t, -ts,
-dɪŋ, -dɪd

gemination
BR ˌdʒɛmɪˈneɪʃn
AM ˌdʒɛməˈneɪʃən

Gemini[1]
constellation
BR ˈdʒɛmɪnʌɪ,
ˈdʒɛmɪniː
AM ˈdʒɛməˌnaɪ,
ˈdʒɛməˌni

Gemini[2]
spacecraft
BR ˈdʒɛmɪniː
AM ˈdʒɛməˌnaɪ

Geminian
BR ˌdʒɛmɪˈnʌɪən,
ˌdʒɛmɪˈniːən, -z
AM ˌdʒɛməˈnaɪən,
ˌdʒɛməˈniən, -z

Geminids
BR ˈdʒɛmɪnɪdz
AM ˈdʒɛmənɪdz

gemlike
BR ˈdʒɛmlʌɪk
AM ˈdʒɛmˌlaɪk

gemma
BR ˈdʒɛmə(r), -z
AM ˈdʒɛmə, -z

gemmae
BR ˈdʒɛmiː
AM ˈdʒɛmi, ˈdʒɛmaɪ

gemmation
BR dʒɛˈmeɪʃn
AM dʒɛˈmeɪʃən

Gemmell
BR ˈgɛml
AM ˈgɛml

gemmiferous
BR dʒɛˈmɪf(ə)rəs
AM dʒɛˈmɪf(ə)rəs

Gemmill
BR ˈgɛml
AM ˈgɛml

gemmiparous
BR dʒɛˈmɪp(ə)rəs

Gemara
AM dʒɛˈmɪpərəs

gemmologist
BR dʒɛˈmɒlədʒɪst, -s
AM dʒɛˈmɑlədʒəst, -s

gemmology
BR dʒɛˈmɒlədʒi
AM dʒɛˈmɑlədʒi

gemmule
BR ˈdʒɛmjuːl, -z
AM ˈdʒɛˌm(j)ul, -z

gemmy
BR ˈdʒɛmi
AM ˈdʒɛmi

gemologist
BR dʒɛˈmɒlədʒɪst, -s
AM dʒɛˈmɑlədʒəst, -s

gemology
BR dʒɛˈmɒlədʒi
AM dʒɛˈmɑlədʒi

gemsbok
BR ˈgɛmzbɒk, -s
AM ˈgɛmzˌbak, -s

gemstone
BR ˈdʒɛmstəʊn, -z
AM ˈdʒɛmˌstoʊn, -z

gemütlich
BR gəˈmuːtlɪk,
gəˈmuːtlɪʃ, gəˈmuːtlɪx
AM gəˈmʊtlɪk

gen
BR dʒɛn, -z, -ɪŋ, -d
AM dʒɛn, -z, -ɪŋ, -d

gendarme
BR ˈʒɒndɑːm, ˈʒɒ̃dɑːm,
-z
AM ˌʒɑnˈdɑrm, -z

gendarmerie
BR ʒɒnˈdɑːm(ə)r|i,
ʒɒ̃ˈdɑːm(ə)r|i, -ɪz
AM ˌʒɑnˈdɑrməri, -z

gender
BR ˈdʒɛndə(r), -z
AM ˈdʒɛndər, -z

gene
BR dʒiːn, -z
AM dʒin, -z

genealogical
BR ˌdʒiːnɪəˈlɒdʒɪkl
AM ˌdʒiniəˈlɑdʒəkəl

genealogically
BR ˌdʒiːnɪəˈlɒdʒɪkli
AM ˌdʒiniəˈlɑdʒək(ə)li

genealogise
BR ˌdʒiːnɪˈalədʒʌɪz, -ɪz,
-ɪŋ, -d
AM ˌdʒiniˈalәˌdʒaɪz, -ɪz,
-ɪŋ, -d

genealogist
BR ˌdʒiːnɪˈalədʒɪst, -s
AM ˌdʒiniˈalədʒəst,
ˌdʒiniˈælədʒəst, -s

genealogize
BR ˌdʒiːnɪˈalədʒʌɪz, -ɪz,
-ɪŋ, -d
AM ˌdʒiniˈalәˌdʒaɪz, -ɪz,
-ɪŋ, -d

genealogy
BR ˌdʒiːnɪˈaladʒ|i, -ɪz
AM ˌdʒini'alədʒi,
ˌdʒini'æledʒi, -z

genera
BR 'dʒɛn(ə)rə(r)
AM 'dʒɛnərə

generable
BR 'dʒɛn(ə)rəbl
AM 'dʒɛnərəbəl

general
BR 'dʒɛn(ə)rəl,
'dʒɛn(ə)r|, -z
AM 'dʒɛn(ə)rəl, -z

generalisability
BR ˌdʒɛn(ə)rəlʌɪzə'bɪl-
ɪti,
ˌdʒɛn(ə)r|ʌɪzə'bɪlɪti
AM ˌdʒɛn(ə)rə,laɪzə-
'bɪlɪdi

generalisable
BR 'dʒɛn(ə)rəlʌɪzəbl,
'dʒɛn(ə)r|ʌɪzəbl
AM 'dʒɛn(ə)rə,laɪzəbəl

generalisation
BR ˌdʒɛn(ə)rəlʌɪ'zeɪʃn,
ˌdʒɛn(ə)r|ʌɪ'zeɪʃn, -z
AM ˌdʒɛn(ə)rələ'zeɪʃən,
ˌdʒɛn(ə)rə,laɪ'zeɪʃən,
-z

generalise
BR 'dʒɛn(ə)rəlʌɪz,
'dʒɛn(ə)r|ʌɪz, -ɪz, -ɪŋ,
-d
AM 'dʒɛn(ə)rə,laɪz, -ɪz,
-ɪŋ, -d

generaliser
BR 'dʒɛn(ə)rəlʌɪzə(r),
'dʒɛn(ə)r|ʌɪzə(r), -z
AM 'dʒɛn(ə)rə,laɪzər,
-z

generalissimo
BR ˌdʒɛn(ə)rə'lɪsɪməʊ,
-z
AM ˌdʒɛn(ə)rə'lɪsə,moʊ,
-z

generalist
BR 'dʒɛn(ə)rəlɪst,
'dʒɛn(ə)r|ɪst, -s
AM 'dʒɛn(ə)rələst, -s

generality
BR ˌdʒɛnə'ralɪt|i, -ɪz
AM ˌdʒɛnə'rælədi, -z

generalizability
BR ˌdʒɛn(ə)rəlʌɪzə'bɪl-
ɪti,
ˌdʒɛn(ə)r|ʌɪzə'bɪlɪti
AM ˌdʒɛn(ə)rə,laɪzə-
'bɪlɪdi

generalizable
BR 'dʒɛn(ə)rəlʌɪzəbl,
'dʒɛn(ə)r|ʌɪzəbl
AM 'dʒɛn(ə)rə,laɪzəbəl

generalization
BR ˌdʒɛn(ə)rəlʌɪ'zeɪʃn,
ˌdʒɛn(ə)r|ʌɪ'zeɪʃn, -z

AM ˌdʒɛn(ə)rələ'zeɪʃən,
ˌdʒɛn(ə)rə,laɪ'zeɪʃən,
-z

generalize
BR 'dʒɛn(ə)rəlʌɪz,
'dʒɛn(ə)r|ʌɪz, -ɪz, -ɪŋ,
-d
AM 'dʒɛn(ə)rə,laɪz, -ɪz,
-ɪŋ, -d

generalizer
BR 'dʒɛn(ə)rəlʌɪzə(r),
'dʒɛn(ə)r|ʌɪzə(r), -z
AM 'dʒɛn(ə)rə,laɪzər,
-z

generally
BR 'dʒɛn(ə)rəli,
'dʒɛn(ə)r|i
AM 'dʒɛn(ə)rəli

generalness
BR 'dʒɛn(ə)rəlnəs,
'dʒɛn(ə)r|nəs
AM 'dʒɛn(ə)rəlnəs

generalship
BR 'dʒɛn(ə)rəlʃɪp,
'dʒɛn(ə)r|ʃɪp, -s
AM 'dʒɛn(ə)rəlʃɪp, -s

generate
BR 'dʒɛnəreɪt, -s, -ɪŋ,
-ɪd
AM 'dʒɛnə,reɪ|t, -ts,
-dɪŋ, -dɪd

generation
BR ˌdʒɛnə'reɪʃn, -z
AM ˌdʒɛnə'reɪʃən, -z

generational
BR ˌdʒɛnə'reɪʃn(ə)l,
ˌdʒɛnə'reɪʃən(ə)l
AM ˌdʒɛnə'reɪʃ(ə)nəl

generative
BR 'dʒɛn(ə)rətɪv
AM 'dʒɛn(ə)rədɪv,
'dʒɛnə,reɪdɪv

generatively
BR 'dʒɛn(ə)rətɪvli
AM 'dʒɛn(ə)rədɪvli,
'dʒɛnə,reɪdɪvli

generativeness
BR 'dʒɛn(ə)rətɪvnɪs
AM 'dʒɛn(ə)rədɪvnɪs,
'dʒɛnə,reɪdɪvnɪs

generator
BR 'dʒɛnəreɪtə(r), -z
AM 'dʒɛnə,reɪdər, -z

generic
BR dʒɪ'nɛrɪk
AM dʒə'nɛrɪk

generically
BR dʒɪ'nɛrɪkli
AM dʒə'nɛrək(ə)li

generosity
BR ˌdʒɛnə'rɒsɪti
AM ˌdʒɛnə'rɑsədi

generous
BR 'dʒɛn(ə)rəs
AM 'dʒɛn(ə)rəs

generously
BR 'dʒɛn(ə)rəsli
AM 'dʒɛn(ə)rəsli

generousness
BR 'dʒɛn(ə)rəsnəs
AM 'dʒɛn(ə)rəsnəs

genesis
BR 'dʒɛnɪsɪs, -ɪz
AM 'dʒɛnəsəs, -əz

Genet
BR ʒə'neɪ
AM dʒə'neɪ

genet
BR 'dʒɛnɪt, -s
AM 'dʒɛnət, -s

genetic
BR dʒɪ'nɛtɪk, -s
AM dʒə'nɛdɪk, -s

genetically
BR dʒɪ'nɛtɪkli
AM dʒə'nɛdək(ə)li

geneticist
BR dʒɪ'nɛtɪsɪst, -s
AM dʒə'nɛdəsəst, -s

genette
BR dʒɪ'nɛt, -s
AM 'dʒɛnət, -s

Geneva
BR dʒɪ'niːvə(r)
AM dʒə'nivə

Genevan
BR dʒɪ'niːvn, -z
AM dʒə'nivən, -z

genever
BR dʒɪ'niːvə(r)
AM dʒə'nivər

Genevieve
BR 'dʒɛnɪviːv
AM 'dʒɛnəviv

Genghis Khan
BR ˌgɛŋgɪs 'kɑːn
AM ˌgɛŋgɪs 'kan

genial¹
jovial, kindly
BR 'dʒiːnɪəl
AM 'dʒinjəl, 'dʒiniəl

genial²
of the chin
BR dʒɪ'niːəl, dʒɪ'nʌɪəl
AM dʒə'niəl

geniality
BR ˌdʒiːnɪ'alɪt|i, -ɪz
AM ˌdʒini'ælədi,
ˌdʒin'jælədi, -z

genially
BR 'dʒiːnɪəli
AM 'dʒinjəli, 'dʒiniəli

genic
BR 'dʒɛnɪk
AM 'dʒɛnɪk

genie
BR 'dʒiːn|i, -ɪz
AM 'dʒini, -z

genii
BR 'dʒiːnɪʌɪ
AM 'dʒini,aɪ

genipapo
BR ˌdʒɛnɪ'papəʊ, -z
AM ˌdʒɛnə'papoʊ, -z

genital
BR 'dʒɛnɪtl, -z
AM 'dʒɛnədl, -z

genitalia
BR ˌdʒɛnɪ'teɪlɪə(r)
AM dʒɛnə'teɪljə,
ˌdʒɛnə'teɪliə

genitally
BR 'dʒɛnɪtļi
AM 'dʒɛnədļi

genitival
BR ˌdʒɛnɪ'tʌɪvl
AM ˌdʒɛnə'taɪvəl

genitivally
BR ˌdʒɛnɪ'tʌɪvļi
AM ˌdʒɛnə'taɪvəli

genitive
BR 'dʒɛnɪtɪv, -z
AM 'dʒɛnədɪv, -z

genito-urinary
BR ˌdʒɛnɪtəʊ'jʊərɪn(ə)ri,
ˌdʒɛnɪtəʊ'jɔːrɪn(ə)ri
AM ˌdʒɛnətoʊ'jʊrə,nɛri

genius
BR 'dʒiːnɪəs, -ɪz
AM 'dʒinjəs, -ɪz

genizah
BR dʒɛ'niːzə(r),
gɛ'niːzə(r), -z
AM dʒə'ni,zɑ, -z

genlock
BR 'dʒɛnlɒk, -s
AM 'dʒɛn,lak, -s

Gennesaret
BR gɪ'nɛz(ə)rɪt
AM gɛ'nɛzərət

Gennesareth
BR gɪ'nɛz(ə)rɪt
AM gɛ'nɛzərət

genoa
BR 'dʒɛnəʊə(r),
dʒɪ'nəʊə(r), -z
AM dʒə'noʊə, -z

genocidal
BR ˌdʒɛnə'sʌɪdl
AM ˌdʒɛnə'saɪdəl

genocide
BR 'dʒɛnəsʌɪd
AM 'dʒɛnə,saɪd

Genoese
BR ˌdʒɛnəʊ'iːz
AM 'dʒɛnoʊ'iz

genome
BR 'dʒiːnəʊm, -z
AM 'dʒi,noʊm, -z

genotype
BR 'dʒɛnətʌɪp, -s
AM 'dʒinə,taɪp,
'dʒɛnə,taɪp

genotypic
BR ˌdʒɛnə'tɪpɪk
AM ˌdʒɛnə'tɪpɪk

Genova
BR 'dʒɛnəvə(r)
AM 'dʒɛnəvə

genre BR ˈʒɒrə(r), ˈʒɒnrə(r), ˈʒɑːnrə(r), -z AM ˈʒɑnrə, -z

gens BR dʒɛnz, -ɪz AM dʒɛnz, -əz

gent BR dʒɛnt, -s AM dʒɛnt, -s

genteel BR dʒɛnˈtiːl AM dʒɛnˈtil

genteelism BR dʒɛnˈtiːlɪz(ə)m AM dʒɛnˈtiˌlɪzəm

genteelly BR dʒɛnˈtiːlli AM dʒɛnˈti(l)li

genteelness BR dʒɛnˈtiːlnɪs AM dʒɛnˈtilnɪs

gentes BR ˈdʒɛntiːz AM ˈdʒɛnˌtiz

gentian BR ˈdʒɛnʃn, ˈdʒɛnʃɪən, -z AM ˈdʒɛn(t)ʃən, -z

gentile BR ˈdʒɛntʌɪl, -z AM ˈdʒɛnˌtaɪl, -z

gentility BR dʒɛnˈtɪlɪti AM dʒɛnˈtɪlɪdi

gentle BR ˈdʒɛntl, -ə(r), -ɪst AM ˈdʒɛn(t)əl, -ər, -əst

gentlefolk BR ˈdʒɛntlfəʊk, -s AM ˈdʒɛn(t)lˌfoʊk, -s

gentleman BR ˈdʒɛntlmən AM ˈdʒɛn(t)lmən

gentlemanliness BR ˈdʒɛntlmənlɪnɪs AM ˈdʒɛn(t)lmənlinɪs

gentlemanly BR ˈdʒɛntlmənli AM ˈdʒɛn(t)lmənli

gentlemen BR ˈdʒɛntlmən AM ˈdʒɛn(t)lmən

gentleness BR ˈdʒɛntlnəs AM ˈdʒɛn(t)lnəs

gentlewoman BR ˈdʒɛntlˌwʊmən AM ˈdʒɛn(t)lˌwʊmən

gentlewomen BR ˈdʒɛntlˌwɪmɪn AM ˈdʒɛn(t)lˌwɪmɪn

gently BR ˈdʒɛntli AM ˈdʒɛn(t)li

gentoo BR ˈdʒɛntuː, -z

gentoo AM ˈdʒɛnˌtu, -z

gentrification BR ˌdʒɛntrɪfɪˈkeɪʃn AM ˌdʒɛntrəfəˈkeɪʃən

gentrifier BR ˈdʒɛntrɪfʌɪə(r), -z AM ˈdʒɛntrəˌfaɪər, -z

gentrify BR ˈdʒɛntrɪfʌɪ, -z, -ɪŋ, -d AM ˈdʒɛntrəˌfaɪ, -z, -ɪŋ, -d

gentry BR ˈdʒɛntri AM ˈdʒɛntri

genuflect BR ˈdʒɛnjʊflɛkt, -s, -ɪŋ, -ɪd AM ˈdʒɛnjəˌflɛk|(t), -(t)s, -tɪŋ, -təd

genuflection BR ˌdʒɛnjʊˈflɛkʃn, -z AM ˌdʒɛnjəˈflɛkʃən, -z

genuflector BR ˌdʒɛnjʊˈflɛktə(r), -z AM ˈdʒɛnjəˌflɛktər, -z

genuflectory BR ˌdʒɛnjʊˈflɛkt(ə)ri AM ˌdʒɛnjəˈflɛkˌtɔri

genuflexion BR ˌdʒɛnjʊˈflɛkʃn, -z AM ˌdʒɛnjəˈflɛkʃən, -z

genuine BR ˈdʒɛnjʊɪn AM ˈdʒɛnjəwən

genuinely BR ˈdʒɛnjʊɪnli AM ˈdʒɛnjəwənli

genuineness BR ˈdʒɛnjʊɪnnəs AM ˈdʒɛnjəwə(n)nəs

genus BR ˈdʒiːnəs AM ˈdʒinəs

geobotanist BR ˌdʒiːəʊˈbɒtənɪst, ˌdʒiːəʊˈbɒtnɪst, -s AM ˈdʒioʊˈbɑtnəst, -s

geobotany BR ˌdʒiːəʊˈbɒtəni, ˌdʒiːəˈbɒtn̩i AM ˈdʒioʊˈbɑtn̩i

geocentric BR ˌdʒiːəˈ(ʊ)sɛntrɪk, dʒɪəˈsɛntrɪk AM ˈdʒioʊˈsɛntrɪk

geocentrically BR ˌdʒiːəˈ(ʊ)sɛntrɪkli, dʒɪəˈsɛntrɪkli AM ˈdʒioʊˈsɛntrək(ə)li

geochemical BR ˌdʒiːəʊˈkɛmɪkl AM ˈdʒioʊˈkɛməkəl

geochemist BR ˌdʒiːəʊˈkɛmɪst, -s AM ˈdʒioʊˈkɛməst, -s

geochemistry BR ˌdʒiːəʊˈkɛmɪstri AM ˈdʒioʊˈkɛməstri

geochronological BR ˌdʒiːəʊˌkrɒnəˈlɒdʒ-ɪkl AM ˈdʒioʊˌkrɑnəˈlɑdʒ-əkəl

geochronologist BR ˌdʒiːəʊkrəˈnɒlədʒɪst, -s AM ˈdʒioʊkrəˈnɑlədʒəst, -s

geochronology BR ˌdʒiːəʊkrəˈnɒlədʒi AM ˈdʒioʊkrəˈnɑlədʒi

geode BR ˈdʒiːəʊd, -z AM ˈdʒiˌoʊd, -z

geodesic BR ˌdʒiːəˈ(ʊ)dɛsɪk, ˌdʒiːəˈ(ʊ)diːsɪk, ˌdʒiːəˈ(ʊ)diːzɪk, dʒɪəˈdɛsɪk, dʒɪəˈdiːsɪk, dʒɪəˈdiːzɪk AM ˈdʒioʊˈdɛsɪk

geodesist BR dʒɪˈɒdɪsɪst, -s AM dʒiˈɑdəsəst, -s

geodesy BR dʒɪˈɒdɪsi AM dʒiˈɑdəsi

geodetic BR ˌdʒiːəˈ(ʊ)dɛtɪk, dʒɪəˈdɛtɪk AM ˈdʒiəˈdɛdɪk

geodic BR ˈdʒiːɒdɪk AM dʒiˈɑdɪk

Geoff BR dʒɛf AM dʒɛf

Geoffrey BR ˈdʒɛfri AM ˈdʒɛfri

geographer BR dʒɪˈɒɡrəfə(r), ˈdʒɒɡrəfə(r), -z AM dʒɪˈɑɡrəfər, -z

geographic BR ˌdʒiːəˈɡrafɪk, dʒɪəˈɡrafɪk AM ˌdʒiəˈɡræfɪk

geographical BR ˌdʒiːəˈɡrafɪkl, dʒɪəˈɡrafɪkl AM ˌdʒiəˈɡræfəkəl

geographically BR ˌdʒiːəˈɡrafɪkli, dʒɪəˈɡrafɪkli AM ˌdʒiəˈɡræfək(ə)li

geography BR dʒɪˈɒɡrəfi, ˈdʒɒɡrəfi AM dʒɪˈɑɡrəfi

geoid BR ˈdʒiːɔɪd, -z

geologic BR ˌdʒiːəˈlɒdʒɪk, dʒɪəˈlɒdʒɪk AM ˌdʒiəˈlɑdʒɪk

geological BR ˌdʒiːəˈlɒdʒɪkl, dʒɪəˈlɒdʒɪkl AM ˌdʒiəˈlɑdʒəkəl

geologically BR ˌdʒiːəˈlɒdʒɪkli, dʒɪəˈlɒdʒɪkli AM ˌdʒiəˈlɑdʒək(ə)li

geologise BR dʒɪˈɒlədʒʌɪz, -ɪz, -ɪŋ, -d AM dʒiˈɑləˌdʒaɪz, -ɪz, -ɪŋ, -d

geologist BR dʒɪˈɒlədʒɪst, -s AM dʒiˈɑlədʒəst, -s

geologize BR dʒɪˈɒlədʒʌɪz, -ɪz, -ɪŋ, -d AM dʒiˈɑləˌdʒaɪz, -ɪz, -ɪŋ, -d

geology BR dʒɪˈɒlədʒi AM dʒiˈɑlədʒi

geomagnetic BR ˌdʒiːəˈ(ʊ)maɡˈnɛtɪk AM ˈdʒiəˌmæɡˈnɛdɪk

geomagnetically BR ˌdʒiːəˈ(ʊ)maɡˈnɛtɪkli AM ˈdʒiəˌmæɡˈnɛdək(ə)li

geomagnetism BR ˌdʒiːəʊˈmaɡnɪtɪz(ə)m AM ˈdʒiəˈmæɡnəˌtɪzəm

geomancy BR ˈdʒiːəmansi AM ˈdʒiəˌmænsi

geomantic BR ˌdʒiːəˈ(ʊ)mantɪk AM ˈdʒiəˈmæn(t)ɪk

geometer BR dʒɪˈɒmɪtə(r), -z AM dʒiˈɑmədər, -z

geometric BR ˌdʒiːəˈmɛtrɪk, dʒɪəˈmɛtrɪk AM ˌdʒiəˈmɛtrɪk

geometrical BR ˌdʒiːəˈmɛtrɪkl, dʒɪəˈmɛtrɪkl AM ˌdʒiəˈmɛtrəkəl

geometrically BR ˌdʒiːəˈmɛtrɪkli, dʒɪəˈmɛtrɪkli AM ˌdʒiəˈmɛtrək(ə)li

geometrician BR ˌdʒiːəˈ(ʊ)mɪˈtrɪʃn, -z AM dʒiˌɑməˈtrɪʃən, -z

geometrise BR dʒɪˈɒmɪtrʌɪz, ˈdʒɒmɪtrʌɪz, -ɪz, -ɪŋ, -d AM dʒiˈɑməˌtraɪz, -ɪz, -ɪŋ, -d

geometrize
BR 'dʒɪ'ɒmɪtrʌɪz,
'dʒɒmɪtrʌɪz, -ɪz, -ɪŋ, -d
AM dʒɪ'ɑmə,traɪz, -ɪz,
-ɪŋ, -d
geometry
BR dʒɪ'ɒmɪtri,
'dʒɒmɪtri
AM dʒɪ'ɑmətri
geomorphological
BR ,dʒɪəʊ,mɔ:fə'lɒdʒɪkl
AM 'dʒiəʊ,mɔrfə'ladʒ-
əkəl
geomorphologist
BR ,dʒɪə(ʊ)mɔ:'fɒlə-
dʒɪst, -s
AM 'dʒiəʊ,mɔr'fɑlə-
dʒəst, -s
geomorphology
BR ,dʒɪə(ʊ)mɔ:'fɒlədʒi
AM 'dʒiəʊ,mɔr'fɑlədʒi
geophagy
BR dʒɪ'ɒfədʒi
AM dʒɪ'ɑfədʒi
geophone
BR 'dʒi:ə(ʊ)fəʊn, -z
AM 'dʒiə,fəʊn, -z
geophysical
BR ,dʒi:ə(ʊ)'fɪzɪkl
AM ,dʒiə'fɪzɪkəl
geophysically
BR ,dʒi:ə(ʊ)'fɪzɪkli
AM ,dʒiə'fɪzɪk(ə)li
geophysicist
BR ,dʒi:ə(ʊ)'fɪzɪsɪst, -s
AM ,dʒiə'fɪzɪsɪst, -s
geophysics
BR ,dʒi:ə(ʊ)'fɪzɪks
AM ,dʒiə'fɪzɪks
geopolitical
BR ,dʒi:əʊpə'lɪtɪkl
AM ,dʒiəʊpə'lɪdɪkəl
geopolitically
BR ,dʒi:əʊpə'lɪtɪkli
AM ,dʒiəʊpə'lɪdɪk(ə)li
geopolitician
BR ,dʒi:əʊ,pɒlɪ'tɪʃn, -z
AM 'dʒiəʊ,pɑlə'tɪʃən,
-z
geopolitics
BR ,dʒi:ə(ʊ)'pɒlɪtɪks
AM ,dʒiəʊ'pɑlədɪks
Geordie
BR 'dʒɔːd|i, -ɪz
AM 'dʒɔrdi, -z
George
BR dʒɔːdʒ
AM dʒɔrdʒ
Georgetown
BR 'dʒɔːdʒtaʊn
AM 'dʒɔrdʒ,taʊn
Georgette
BR dʒɔː'dʒɛt
AM dʒɔr'dʒɛt
Georgia
BR 'dʒɔːdʒə(r)
AM 'dʒɔrdʒə

Georgian
BR 'dʒɔːdʒ(ə)n, -z
AM 'dʒɔrdʒən, -z
Georgiana
BR ,dʒɔːdʒi'ɑ:nə(r)
AM ,dʒɔrdʒi'ænə
georgic
BR 'dʒɔːdʒɪk, -s
AM 'dʒɔrdʒɪk, -s
Georgie
BR 'dʒɔːdʒi
AM 'dʒɔrdʒi
Georgina
BR dʒɔː'dʒiːnə(r)
AM dʒɔr'dʒinə
geoscience
BR ,dʒi:əʊ'sʌɪəns, -ɪz
AM 'dʒiəʊ'saɪəns, -əz
geoscientist
BR ,dʒi:əʊ'sʌɪəntɪst, -s
AM ,dʒiəʊ'saɪən(t)əst,
-s
geosphere
BR 'dʒi:ə(ʊ)sfɪə(r), -z
AM 'dʒiəʊ,sfɪ(ə)r, -z
geostationary
BR ,dʒi:ə(ʊ)'steɪʃn(ə)ri
AM ,dʒiəʊ'steɪʃənɛri
geostrophic
BR ,dʒi:ə'strɒfɪk,
,dʒi:ə'strəʊfɪk
AM ,dʒiə'strɑfɪk
geosynchronous
BR ,dʒi:ə(ʊ)'sɪŋkrənəs
AM ,dʒiəʊ'sɪŋkrənəs
geotechnical
BR ,dʒi:ə(ʊ)'tɛknɪkl
AM ,dʒiə'tɛknəkəl
geothermal
BR ,dʒi:ə(ʊ)'θɜːml
AM ,dʒiəʊ'θɜrməl
geothermally
BR ,dʒi:ə(ʊ)'θɜːmli
AM ,dʒiəʊ'θɜrməli
geotropic
BR ,dʒi:ə'trɒpɪk,
,dʒi:ə'trəʊpɪk
AM ,dʒiə'trɑpɪk
geotropism
BR ,dʒi:əʊ'trəʊpɪz(ə)m
AM ,dʒiə'trɑ,pɪzəm
Geraint
BR 'gɛrʌɪnt
AM 'dʒɛraɪnt
Gerald
BR 'dʒɛrəld, 'dʒɛrld
AM 'dʒɛrəl(d)
Geraldine
BR 'dʒɛrəldi:n,
'dʒɛrldi:n
AM 'dʒɛrəl,din
Geraldton
BR 'dʒɛrəld(ə)t(ə)n,
'dʒɛrl(d)t(ə)n
AM 'dʒɛrəld(ə)tən
geranium
BR dʒɪ'reɪnɪəm, -z

AM dʒə'reɪniəm,
dʒə'reɪnjəm, -z
Gerard
BR 'dʒɛrɑːd, dʒə'rɑːd
AM dʒə'rɑrd
gerbera
BR 'dʒəː(b)ə)rə(r),
'gəːb(ə)rə(r), -z
AM 'gɜrbərə,
'dʒɜrbərə, dʒɜr'bɛrə,
-z
gerbil
BR 'dʒəː(b)(ɪ)l, -z
AM 'dʒɜrbəl, -z
Gerda
BR 'gəːdə(r)
AM 'gɜrdə
gerenuk
BR 'gɛrənʊk,
'dʒɛrənʊk, -s
AM 'gɛrə,nʊk,
gə'rɛnək, -s
gerfalcon
BR 'dʒəː,fɔːlk(ə)n,
'dʒəː,falk(ə)n, -z
AM 'dʒɜr,fælkən, -z
geriatric
BR ,dʒɛrɪ'atrɪk, -s
AM ,dʒɛri'ætrɪk, -s
geriatrician
BR ,dʒɛrɪə'trɪʃn, -z
AM ,dʒɛriə'trɪʃən, -z
geriatrist
BR ,dʒɛrɪ'atrɪst, -s
AM ,dʒɛri'ætrəst, -s
gerkin
BR 'gəːkɪn, -z
AM 'gɜrkən, -z
germ
BR dʒəːm, -z
AM dʒɜrm, -z
Germaine
BR ʒəː'meɪn
AM ʒɜr'meɪn
German
BR 'dʒəːmən, -z
AM 'dʒɜrmən, -z
germander
BR dʒə'mandə(r),
dʒə'mɑndə(r), -z
AM dʒɜr'mændər, -z
germane
BR dʒə'meɪn,
dʒə'meɪn
AM dʒɜr'meɪn
germanely
BR dʒə'meɪnli,
dʒə'meɪnli
AM dʒɜr'meɪnli
germaneness
BR dʒə'meɪnnɪs,
dʒə'meɪnnɪs
AM dʒɜr'meɪ(n)nɪs
Germanic
BR dʒə'manɪk
AM dʒɜr'mænɪk

Germanicism
BR dʒə'manɪsɪz(ə)m,
-z
AM dʒɜr'mænə,sɪzəm,
-z
Germanicus
BR dʒə'manɪkəs
AM ,dʒɜr'mænəkəs
Germanisation
BR ,dʒə'mənʌɪ'zeɪʃn
AM ,dʒɜrmənə'zeɪʃən,
,dʒɜrmə,naɪ'zeɪʃən
Germanise
BR 'dʒə'mənʌɪz, -ɪz,
-ɪŋ, -d
AM 'dʒɜrmə,naɪz, -ɪz,
-ɪŋ, -d
Germaniser
BR 'dʒə'mənʌɪzə(r), -z
AM 'dʒɜrmə,naɪzər, -z
Germanism
BR 'dʒə'mənɪz(ə)m, -z
AM 'dʒɜrmə,nɪzəm, -z
Germanist
BR 'dʒə'mənɪst, -s
AM 'dʒɜrmənəst, -s
germanium
BR dʒəː'meɪnɪəm,
dʒə'meɪnɪəm
AM dʒɜr'meɪniəm
Germanization
BR ,dʒə'mənʌɪ'zeɪʃən
AM ,dʒɜrmənə'zeɪʃən,
,dʒɜrmə,naɪ'zeɪʃən
Germanize
BR 'dʒə'mənʌɪz, -ɪz,
-ɪŋ, -d
AM 'dʒɜrmə,naɪz, -ɪz,
-ɪŋ, -d
Germanizer
BR 'dʒə'mənʌɪzə(r), -z
AM 'dʒɜrmə,naɪzər, -z
germanous
BR 'dʒə'mənəs
AM 'dʒɜrmənəs
Germany
BR 'dʒə'mən|i, -ɪz
AM 'dʒɜrməni, -z
germen
BR 'dʒə'mən, -z
AM 'dʒɜrmən, -z
germicidal
BR ,dʒəː'mɪ'sʌɪdl
AM 'dʒɜrmə'saɪdəl
germicide
BR 'dʒə'mɪsʌɪd, -z, -əl
AM 'dʒɜrmə,saɪd, -z, -əl
germinal
BR 'dʒə'mɪnl
AM 'dʒɜrmənəl
germinally
BR 'dʒə'mɪnl̩i
AM 'dʒɜrmənəli
germinant
BR 'dʒə'mɪnənt
AM 'dʒɜrmənənt

germinate
BR 'dʒɜːmɪneɪt, -s, -ɪŋ, -ɪd
AM 'dʒɜrməˌneɪ|t, -ts, -dɪŋ, -dɪd

germination
BR ˌdʒɜːmɪ'neɪʃn
AM ˌdʒɜrmə'neɪʃən

germinative
BR 'dʒɜːmɪnətɪv
AM 'dʒɜrməˌneɪdɪv

germinator
BR 'dʒɜːmɪneɪtə(r), -z
AM 'dʒɜrməˌneɪdər, -z

Germiston
BR 'dʒɜː'mɪst(ə)n
AM 'dʒɜrməstən

Germolene
BR 'dʒɜː'məliːn
AM 'dʒɜrməˌliːn

germon
BR 'dʒɜːmən, -z
AM ʒɜr'mɔn, ʒɜr'mɑn, -z

germy
BR 'dʒɜːm|i, -ɪə(r), -ɪɪst
AM 'dʒɜrmi, -ər, -ɪst

Geronimo
BR dʒɪ'rɒnɪməʊ
AM dʒə'rɑnəˌmoʊ

gerontocracy
BR ˌdʒɛrən'tɒkrəs|i, ˌdʒɛrn'tɒkrəsi, -ɪz
AM ˌdʒɛrən'takrəsi, -z

gerontological
BR dʒəˌrɒntə'lɒdʒɪkl, ˌdʒɜːntə'lɒdʒɪkl
AM dʒəˌran(t)ə'ladʒəkəl

gerontologist
BR ˌdʒɛrən'tɒlədʒɪst, ˌdʒɜːn'tɒlədʒɪst, -s
AM ˌdʒɛrən'talədʒəst, -s

gerontology
BR ˌdʒɛrən'tɒlədʒi, ˌdʒɜːn'tɒlədʒi
AM ˌdʒɛrən'talədʒi

Gerrard
BR 'dʒɛrɑːd, dʒə'rɑːd
AM dʒə'rɑrd

Gerry
BR 'dʒɛri
AM 'dʒɛri

gerrymander
BR 'dʒɛrɪmand|ə(r), -əz, -(ə)rɪŋ, -əd
AM 'dʒɛriˌmændər, -ərz, -(ə)rɪŋ, -ərd

gerrymanderer
BR 'dʒɜrɪmand(ə)rə(r), -z
AM 'dʒɛriˌmænd(ə)rər, -z

Gershwin
BR 'gɜː'ʃwɪn
AM 'gɜrˌʃwɪn

Gertie
BR 'gɜːti

AM 'gɜːdi

Gertrude
BR 'gɜː'truːd
AM 'gɜrˌtrud

gerund
BR 'dʒɛrənd, 'dʒɜːnd, 'dʒɛrʌnd, -z
AM 'dʒɛrənd, -z

gerundial
BR dʒɪ'rʌndɪəl, dʒɛ'rʌndɪəl
AM dʒə'rəndiəl

gerundival
BR ˌdʒɛrən'dʌɪvl, ˌdʒɛrɪn'dʌɪvl, ˌdʒɛrʌn'dʌɪvl
AM ˌdʒɛrən'daɪvəl

gerundive
BR dʒɪ'rʌndɪv, dʒɛ'rʌndɪv, -z
AM dʒə'rəndɪv, -z

Gervaise
BR 'dʒɜːˌveɪz, dʒɜː'veɪz, 'dʒɜːˌveɪs, dʒɜː'veɪs
AM ʒɜr'veɪ(z)

Gervase
BR 'dʒɜːˌveɪz, dʒɜː'veɪz, 'dʒɜːˌveɪs, dʒɜː'veɪs
AM ʒɜr'veɪ(z)

gesnieriad
BR gɛs'nɪərɪəd, dʒɛs'nɪərɪəd, -z
AM gɛs'nɪriæd, dʒɛs'nɪriæd, -z

gesso
BR 'dʒɛsəʊ
AM 'dʒɛsoʊ

gest
BR dʒɛst, -s
AM dʒɛst, -s

gestagen
BR 'dʒɛstədʒ(ə)n, -z
AM 'dʒɛstədʒən, 'dʒɛstəˌdʒɛn, -z

gestagenic
BR ˌdʒɛstə'dʒɛnɪk
AM ˌdʒɛstə'dʒɛnɪk

gestalt
BR gə'ʃtalt, gə'ʃtɑːlt
AM gə'ʃtalt, gə'ʃtɑlt

gestaltism
BR gə'ʃtaltɪz(ə)m, gə'ʃtɑːltɪz(ə)m, gə'stal,tɪzəm, gə'stal,tɪzəm

gestaltist
BR gə'ʃtaltɪst, gə'ʃtɑːltɪst, -s
AM gə'ʃtaltəst, gə'staltəst, -s

Gestapo
BR gɛ'stɑːpəʊ, gə'stɑːpəʊ
AM gə'stɑpoʊ

gestate
BR dʒɛ'steɪt, 'dʒɛsteɪt, -s, -ɪŋ, -ɪd

AM 'dʒɛˌsteɪ|t, -ts, -dɪŋ, -dɪd

gestation
BR dʒɛ'steɪʃn
AM dʒɛ'steɪʃən

gestatorial
BR ˌdʒɛstə'tɔːrɪəl
AM ˌdʒɛstə'tɔriəl

gestatory
BR dʒɛ'steɪt(ə)ri, 'dʒɛstət(ə)ri
AM 'dʒɛstəˌtɔri

Gestetner
BR gɛ'stɛtnə(r), gɪ'stɛtnə(r)
AM gə'stɛtnər

gesticulate
BR dʒɛ'stɪkjʉleɪt, dʒə'stɪkjʉleɪt, -s, -ɪŋ, -ɪd
AM dʒɛ'stɪkjəˌleɪ|t, -ts, -dɪŋ, -dɪd

gesticulation
BR dʒɛˌstɪkjʉ'leɪʃn, dʒəˌstɪkjʉ'leɪʃn, -z
AM dʒɛˌstɪkjə'leɪʃən, -z

gesticulative
BR dʒɛ'stɪkjʉlətɪv, dʒə'stɪkjʉlətɪv
AM dʒɛ'stɪkjəˌleɪdɪv, dʒɛ'stɪkjələdɪv

gesticulator
BR dʒɛ'stɪkjʉleɪtə(r), dʒə'stɪkjʉleɪtə(r), -z
AM dʒɛ'stɪkjəˌleɪdər, -z

gesticulatory
BR dʒɛ'stɪkjʉlət(ə)ri, dʒə'stɪkjʉlət(ə)ri
AM ˌdʒɛstə'kjʉləˌtɔri

gestural
BR 'dʒɛstʃ(ə)rəl, 'dʒɛstʃ(ə)rl
AM 'dʒɛstʃ(ə)rəl, 'dʒɛtʃ(ə)rəl

gesture
BR 'dʒɛstʃ|ə(r), -əz, -(ə)rɪŋ, -əd
AM 'dʒɛstʃər, 'dʒɛʃtʃər, -z, -ɪŋ, -d

gesturer
BR 'dʒɛstʃ(ə)rə(r), -z
AM 'dʒɛstʃərər, 'dʒɛʃtʃərər, -z

gesundheit
BR gə'zʊndhʌɪt, gə'zʊnthʌɪt
AM gə'zʊn(d)ˌ(h)aɪt

get
BR gɛt, -s, -ɪŋ
AM gɛ|t, -ts, -dɪŋ

geta
BR 'geɪtə(r)
AM 'gɛˌta

get-at-able
BR ˌgɛt'atəbl
AM gɛd'ædəbəl

getaway
BR 'gɛtəweɪ, -z

AM 'dʒɛˌsteɪ|t, -ts, -dɪŋ, -dɪd

Gethin
BR 'gɛθɪn
AM 'gɛθən

Gethsemane
BR gɛθ'sɛmənɪ
AM ˌgɛθ'sɛmənɪ

gettable
BR 'gɛtəbl
AM 'gɛdəbəl

getter
BR 'gɛtə(r), -z
AM 'gɛdər, -z

Getty
BR 'gɛti
AM 'gɛdi

Gettysburg
BR 'gɛtɪzbəːg
AM 'gɛdiz,bɜrg

geum
BR 'dʒiːəm, -z
AM 'dʒiəm, -z

gewgaw
BR 'gjuːgɔː(r), -z
AM 'gju,gɔ, 'gju,gɑ, -z

Gewürztraminer
BR gə'vʊətstrəˌmiːnə(r), -z
AM gə'wɜrts,trɑmənər, -z

geyser
BR 'giːzə(r), 'gaɪzə(r), -z
AM 'gaɪzər, -z

Ghana
BR 'gɑːnə(r)
AM 'gɑnə

Ghanaian
BR gɑː'neɪən, -z
AM gɑniən, -z

gharial
BR 'garɪəl, 'garɪɑːl, 'gɛːrɪəl, ˌgʌrɪ'ɑːl, -z
AM 'gɛriəl, -z

gharry
BR 'gar|i, -ɪz
AM 'gɛri, -z

ghastlily
BR 'gɑːs(t)lɪli, 'gas(t)lɪli
AM 'gæs(t)ləli

ghastliness
BR 'gɑːs(t)lɪnɪs, 'gas(t)lɪnɪs
AM 'gæs(t)linɪs

ghastly
BR 'gɑːs(t)l|i, 'gas(t)l|i, -ɪə(r), -ɪɪst
AM 'gæs(t)li, -ər, -ɪst

ghat
BR gɑːt, gɔːt, gʌt, -s
AM gɑt, gɔt, gɑt, -s

ghaut
BR gɑːt, gɔːt, gʌt, -s
AM gɑt, gɔt, gɑt, -s

Ghazi
BR 'gɑːz|i, -ɪz

AM ˈgɑ,zi, -z

ghee
BR giː
AM gi

Gheg
BR gɛg, -z
AM gɛg, -z

Ghent
BR gɛnt
AM gɛnt

gherao
BR gɛˈrau, -z, -ɪŋ, -d
AM gəˈrau, -z, -ɪŋ, -d

gherkin
BR ˈgɜːkɪn, -z
AM ˈgɜrkən, -z

ghetto
BR ˈgɛtəʊ, -z
AM ˈgɛdoʊ, -z

ghettoise
BR ˈgɛtəʊaɪz, -ɪz, -ɪŋ, -d
AM ˈgɛdoʊ,aɪz, -ɪz, -ɪŋ, -d

ghettoize
BR ˈgɛtəʊaɪz, -ɪz, -ɪŋ, -d
AM ˈgɛdoʊ,aɪz, -ɪz, -ɪŋ, -d

ghi
BR giː
AM gi

Ghibelline
BR ˈgɪbɪliːn, ˈgɪbɪlʌɪn, -z
AM ˈgɪbə,lin, ˈgɪbə,laɪn, ˈgɪbələn, -z

Ghibellinism
BR ˈgɪbɪlɪnɪz(ə)m
AM ˈgɪbələ,nɪzəm, ˈgɪbə,laɪ,nɪzəm

Ghiberti
BR gɪˈbɛːti
AM giˈbɛrdi

ghillie
BR ˈgɪlʲi, -ɪz
AM ˈgɪlʲi, -z

ghost
BR gəʊst, -s, -ɪŋ, -ɪd
AM goʊst, -s, -ɪŋ, -əd

ghostbuster
BR ˈgəʊs(t),bʌstə(r), -z
AM ˈgoʊs(t),bəstər, -z

ghostbusting
BR ˈgəʊs(t),bʌstɪŋ
AM ˈgoʊs(t),bəstɪŋ

ghostlike
BR ˈgəʊs(t)lʌɪk
AM ˈgoʊs(t),laɪk

ghostliness
BR ˈgəʊs(t)lɪnɪs
AM ˈgoʊs(t)linɪs

ghostly
BR ˈgəʊs(t)lʲi, -ɪə(r), -ɪst
AM ˈgoʊs(t)li, -ər, -ɪst

ghostwriter
BR ˈgəʊs(t),rʌɪtə(r), -z
AM ˈgoʊs(t),raɪdər, -z

ghoul
BR guːl, -z
AM gul, -z

ghoulish
BR ˈguːlɪʃ
AM ˈgulɪʃ

ghoulishly
BR ˈguːlɪʃli
AM ˈgulɪʃli

ghoulishness
BR ˈguːlɪʃnɪs
AM ˈgulɪʃnɪs

ghyll
BR gɪl, -z
AM gɪl, -z

Giacometti
BR ,dʒakəˈmɛti
AM ,dʒækəˈmɛdi

giant
BR ˈdʒʌɪənt, -s
AM ˈdʒaɪənt, -s

giantess
BR ˈdʒʌɪəntɪs, ˈdʒʌɪəntɛs, ,dʒʌɪənˈtɛs, -ɪz
AM ˈdʒaɪən(t)əs, -əz

giantism
BR ˈdʒʌɪəntɪz(ə)m
AM ˈdʒaɪən(t),ɪzəm

giaour
BR ˈdʒaʊə(r), -z
AM ˈdʒaʊ(ə)r, -z

giardiasis
BR ,dʒɪɑːˈdaɪəsɪs
AM ,dʒ(i)ɑrˈdaɪəsɪs

gib
BR dʒɪb, -z, -ɪŋ, -d
AM dʒɪb, -z, -ɪŋ, -d

Gibb
BR gɪb
AM gɪb

gibber
BR ˈdʒɪbʲə(r), -əz, -(ə)rɪŋ, -əd
AM ˈdʒɪbʲər, -ərz, -(ə)rɪŋ, -ərd

gibberellin
BR ,dʒɪbəˈrɛlɪn
AM ,dʒɪbəˈrɛlən

gibberish
BR ˈdʒɪb(ə)rɪʃ
AM ˈdʒɪb(ə)rɪʃ

gibbet
BR ˈdʒɪbɪt, -s
AM ˈdʒɪbɪt, -s

gibbon
BR ˈgɪbən, -z
AM ˈgɪbən, -z

Gibbons
BR ˈgɪbənz
AM ˈgɪbənz

gibbosity
BR gɪˈbɒsɪti
AM gɪˈbɑsədi

gibbous
BR ˈgɪbəs
AM ˈgɪbəs

gibbously
BR ˈgɪbəsli
AM ˈgɪbəsli

gibbousness
BR ˈgɪbəsnəs
AM ˈgɪbəsnəs

Gibbs
BR gɪbz
AM gɪbz

gibe
BR dʒʌɪb, -z, -ɪŋ, -d
AM dʒaɪb, -z, -ɪŋ, -d

Gibeon
BR ˈgɪbɪən
AM ˈgɪbiən

Gibeonite
BR ˈgɪbɪənʌɪt
AM ˈgɪbiə,naɪt

giber
BR ˈdʒʌɪbə(r), -z
AM ˈdʒaɪbər, -z

giblets
BR ˈdʒɪblɪts
AM ˈdʒɪbləts

Gibraltar
BR dʒɪˈbrɔːltə(r), dʒɪˈbrʊltə(r)
AM dʒəˈbrɔltər, dʒəˈbrɑltər

Gibraltarian
BR ,dʒɪbrɔːˈltɛːrɪən, ,dʒɪbrɒlˈtɛːrɪən, -z
AM ,dʒɪbrɔlˈtɛrɪən, ,dʒɪbrɑlˈtɛrɪən, -z

Gibson
BR ˈgɪbsn
AM ˈgɪbsən

gid
BR gɪd
AM gɪd

giddily
BR ˈgɪdɪli
AM ˈgɪdɪli

giddiness
BR ˈgɪdɪnɪs
AM ˈgɪdɪnɪs

giddy
BR ˈgɪdʲi, -ɪə(r), -ɪɪst
AM ˈgɪdi, -ər, -ɪst

Gide
BR ʒiːd
AM ʒid

Gideon
BR ˈgɪdɪən
AM ˈgɪdiən

gie
BR giː, -z, -ɪŋ, -d
AM gi, -z, -ɪŋ, -d

Gielgud
BR ˈgiːlgʊd
AM ˈgil,gʊd

gift
BR gɪft, -s, -ɪd
AM gɪft, -s, -ɪd

giftedly
BR ˈgɪftɪdli
AM ˈgɪftɪdli

giftedness
BR ˈgɪftɪdnɪs
AM ˈgɪftɪdnɪs

giftware
BR ˈgɪftwɛː(r)
AM ˈgɪf(t),wɛ(ə)r

giftwrap
BR ,gɪftˈrap, ˈgɪftrap, -s, -ɪŋ, -t
AM ˈgɪf(t),ræp, -s, -ɪŋ, -t

gig
BR gɪg, -z
AM gɪg, -z

gigabit
BR ˈgɪgəbɪt, -s
AM ˈgɪgə,bɪt, -s

gigabyte
BR ˈgɪgəbʌɪt, -s
AM ˈgɪgə,baɪt, -s

gigaflop
BR ˈgɪgəflɒp, -s
AM ˈgɪgə,flɑp, -s

gigametre
BR ˈgɪgə,miːtə(r), -z
AM ˈgɪgə,midər, -z

gigantesque
BR ,dʒʌɪgənˈtɛsk
AM ,dʒaɪgənˈtɛsk

gigantic
BR dʒʌɪˈgantɪk
AM dʒaɪˈgæn(t)ɪk

gigantically
BR dʒʌɪˈgantɪkli
AM dʒaɪˈgæn(t)ək(ə)li

gigantism
BR dʒʌɪˈgantɪz(ə)m
AM dʒaɪˈgæn,tɪzəm

Gigantopithecus
BR dʒʌɪ,gantəʊˈpɪθɪkəs, ,dʒʌɪgantəʊˈpɪθɪkəs
AM dʒaɪ,gæn(t)oʊˈpɪθɪkəs

gigawatt
BR ˈgɪgəwɒt, -s
AM ˈgɪgə,wɑt, -s

giggle
BR ˈgɪg|l, -lz, -lɪŋ \-lɪŋ, -ld
AM ˈgɪg|əl, -əlz, -(ə)lɪŋ, -əld

giggler
BR ˈgɪglə(r), ˈgɪglə(r), -z
AM ˈgɪg(ə)lər, -z

Giggleswick
BR ˈgɪglzwɪk
AM ˈgɪgəlzwɪk

giggliness
BR ˈgɪg|lɪnɪs, ˈgɪglɪnɪs
AM ˈgɪg(ə)linɪs

giggly
BR ˈgɪgl|i, -ɪə(r), -ɪɪst
AM ˈgɪgli, ˈgɪgl|i, -ər, -ɪst

Gigli
BR ˈdʒiːli
AM ˈdʒili
IT ˈdʒiʎʎi

GIGO
BR ˈgɪgəʊ
AM ˈgɪˌgoʊ

gigolo
BR (ˈd)ʒɪgələʊ, -z
AM ˈdʒɪgəˌloʊ, -z

gigot
BR ˈdʒɪgət, -s
AM ˈdʒɪgət, -s

gigue
BR ʒiːg, -z
AM ʒig, -z

Gila monster
BR ˈhiːlə ˌmʊnstə(r), -z
AM ˈhilə ˌmɑnstər, -z

Gilbert
BR ˈgɪlbət
AM ˈgɪlbərt

Gilbertian
BR gɪlˈbəːtɪən
AM gɪlˈbərdiən

gild
BR gɪld, -z, -ɪŋ, -ɪd
AM gɪld, -z, -ɪŋ, -ɪd

gilder
BR ˈgɪldə(r), -z
AM ˈgɪldər, -z

Gilead
BR ˈgɪlɪəd
AM ˈgɪliˌæd

Giles
BR dʒʌɪlz
AM dʒaɪlz

gilet
BR (d)ʒɪˈleɪ, -z
AM ʒəˈleɪ, -z

gilgai
BR ˈgɪlgʌɪ, -z
AM ˈgɪlˌgaɪ, -z

Gilgamesh
BR ˈgɪlgəmeʃ
AM ˈgɪlgəˌmeʃ

Gilgit
BR ˈgɪlgɪt
AM ˈgɪlgɪt

Gill¹
surname
BR gɪl
AM gɪl

Gill²
woman's forename
BR dʒɪl
AM dʒɪl

gill¹
liquid measure
BR dʒɪl, -z
AM dʒɪl, -z

gill²
of fish
BR gɪl, -z
AM gɪl, -z

gill³
verb
BR gɪl, -z, -ɪŋ, -d
AM gɪl, -z, -ɪŋ, -d

Gillard
BR ˈgɪlɑːd

AM ˈgɪlərd

gillaroo
BR ˌgɪləˈruː, -z
AM ˌgɪləˈru, -z

gill cover
BR ˈgɪl ˌkʌvə(r), -z
AM ˈgɪl ˌkəvər, -z

Gillespie
BR gɪˈlɛspi
AM gəˈlɛspi

Gillette
BR dʒɪˈlet
AM dʒəˈlɛt

Gillian
BR ˈdʒɪlɪən
AM ˈdʒɪljən, ˈdʒɪliən

gillie
BR ˈgɪlˌji, -ɪz
AM ˈgɪli, -z

Gillies
BR ˈgɪlɪz
AM ˈgɪliz

Gilligan
BR ˈgɪlɪg(ə)n
AM ˈgɪlɪgən

Gillingham¹
place in Kent, UK
BR ˈdʒɪlɪŋəm
AM ˈdʒɪlɪŋəm

Gillingham²
places in Dorset and Norfolk, UK
BR ˈgɪlɪŋəm
AM ˈgɪlɪŋəm

gillion
BR ˈgɪljən, -z
AM ˈgɪljən, -z

gill-net
BR ˈgɪlnɛt, -s
AM ˈgɪlˌnɛt, -s

Gillow
BR ˈgɪləʊ
AM ˈgɪloʊ

Gilly
BR ˈdʒɪli
AM ˈdʒɪli

gilly
BR ˈgɪlˌji, -ɪz
AM ˈgɪli, -z

gillyflower
BR ˈdʒɪliˌflaʊə(r), -z
AM ˈdʒɪliˌflaʊər, -z

Gilman
BR ˈgɪlmən
AM ˈgɪlmən

Gilmore
BR ˈgɪlmɔː(r)
AM ˈgɪlˌmɔ(ə)r

Gilmour
BR ˈgɪlmɔː(r)
AM ˈgɪlˌmɔ(ə)r

Gilpin
BR ˈgɪlpɪn
AM ˈgɪlpɪn

Gilroy
BR ˈgɪlrɔɪ
AM ˈgɪlˌrɔɪ

gilt
BR gɪlt, -s
AM gɪlt, -s

gilt-edged
BR ˌgɪltˈɛdʒd
AM ˈgɪltˌɛdʒd

giltwood
BR ˈgɪltwʊd
AM ˈgɪltˌwʊd

gimbal
BR ˈdʒɪmbl, ˈgɪmbl, -z
AM ˈgɪmbəl, ˈdʒɪmbəl, -z

gimcrack
BR ˈdʒɪmkrak
AM ˈdʒɪmˌkræk

gimcrackery
BR ˈdʒɪmkrak(ə)ri
AM ˈdʒɪmˌkrækəri

gimcracky
BR ˈdʒɪmkraki
AM ˈdʒɪmˌkræki

gimlet
BR ˈgɪmlɪt, -s
AM ˈgɪmlət, -s

gimme
BR ˈgɪmi
AM ˈgɪmi

gimmick
BR ˈgɪmɪk, -s
AM ˈgɪmɪk, -s

gimmickry
BR ˈgɪmɪkri
AM ˈgɪmɪkri

gimmicky
BR ˈgɪmɪki
AM ˈgɪmɪki

gimp
BR gɪm|p, -ps, -pɪŋ, -(p)t
AM gɪm|p, -(p)s, -pɪŋ, -(p)t

gimpy
BR ˈgɪmpi
AM ˈgɪmpi

Gimson
BR ˈgɪmsn, ˈdʒɪmsn
AM ˈgɪmsən, ˈdʒɪmsən

gin
BR dʒɪn, -z
AM dʒɪn, -z

Gina
BR ˈdʒiːnə(r)
AM ˈdʒinə

ging
BR gɪŋ, -z, -ɪŋ, -d
AM gɪŋ, -z, -ɪŋ, -d

ginger
BR ˈdʒɪn(d)ʒ|ə(r), -əz, -(ə)rɪŋ, -əd
AM ˈdʒɪn(d)ʒ|ər, -ərz, -(ə)rɪŋ, -ərd

ginger ale
BR ˌdʒɪn(d)ʒər ˈeɪl
AM ˈdʒɪn(d)ʒər ˌeɪl, ˌdʒɪn(d)ʒər ˈeɪl

gingerbread
BR ˈdʒɪn(d)ʒəbrɛd

AM ˈdʒɪn(d)ʒərˌbrɛd

gingerliness
BR ˈdʒɪn(d)ʒəlɪnɪs
AM ˈdʒɪn(d)ʒərlɪnɪs

gingerly
BR ˈdʒɪn(d)ʒəli
AM ˈdʒɪn(d)ʒərli

gingery
BR ˈdʒɪn(d)ʒ(ə)ri
AM ˈdʒɪn(d)ʒəri

gingham
BR ˈgɪŋəm
AM ˈgɪŋəm

gingili
BR ˈdʒɪn(d)ʒɪli
AM ˈdʒɪn(d)ʒəli

gingiva
BR dʒɪnˈdʒʌɪvə(r), ˈdʒɪn(d)ʒɪvə(r)
AM dʒənˈdʒaɪvə

gingivae
BR dʒɪnˈdʒʌɪviː, ˈdʒɪn(d)ʒɪviː
AM dʒənˈdʒaɪvi, ˈdʒɪn(d)ʒəˌvaɪ

gingival
BR dʒɪnˈdʒʌɪvl, ˈdʒɪn(d)ʒɪvl
AM dʒənˈdʒaɪvəl, ˈdʒɪn(d)ʒəvəl

gingivitis
BR ˌdʒɪn(d)ʒɪˈvʌɪtɪs
AM ˌdʒɪn(d)ʒəˈvaɪdɪs

gingko
BR ˈgɪŋkəʊ, -z
AM ˈgɪŋkoʊ, -z

ginglymi
BR ˈgɪŋglɪmʌɪ, ˈgɪŋglɪmiː, ˈdʒɪŋglɪmʌɪ, ˈdʒɪŋglɪmiː
AM ˈdʒɪŋgləˌmaɪ, ˈgɪŋgləˌmaɪ, ˈdʒɪŋgləmi, ˈgɪŋgləmi

ginglymus
BR ˈgɪŋglɪməs, ˈdʒɪŋglɪməs
AM ˈdʒɪŋgləməs, ˈgɪŋgləməs

Gingold
BR ˈgɪŋgəʊld
AM ˈgɪŋˌgoʊld

gink
BR gɪŋk, -s
AM gɪŋk, -s

ginkgo
BR ˈgɪŋkəʊ, -z
AM ˈgɪŋkoʊ, -z

Ginn
BR gɪn
AM gɪn, dʒɪn

ginner
BR ˈdʒɪnə(r), -z
AM ˈdʒɪnər, -z

Ginny
BR ˈdʒɪni
AM ˈdʒɪni

Gino
BR 'dʒiːnəʊ
AM 'dʒinoʊ

ginormous
BR dʒʌɪ'nɔːməs
AM dʒaɪ'nɔrməs

Ginsberg
BR 'gɪnzbəːg
AM 'gɪnz,bərg

ginseng
BR 'dʒɪnsɛŋ
AM 'dʒɪn,ˈsɛŋ

Ginsu
BR 'gɪnsuː
AM 'gɪnsu

Gioconda, La
BR la ,dʒiə'kɒndə(r)
AM ,la dʒɔ'kɒndə,
,la dʒɑ'kandə

Giorgione
BR ,dʒɔː'dʒɪ'əʊni
AM 'dʒɔr'dʒ(i)oʊni

Giotto
BR 'dʒɒtəʊ, dʒɪ'ɒtəʊ
AM 'dʒoɔdoʊ, 'dʒadoʊ

Giovanni
BR dʒə(ʊ)'vɑːni,
,dʒiːə'vɑːni,
dʒə(ʊ)'vani,
,dʒiːə'vani
AM dʒə'vɑni,
,dʒiə'vani

gip
BR dʒɪp, -s, -ɪŋ, -t
AM dʒɪp, -s, -ɪŋ, -t

gippo
BR 'dʒɪpəʊ, -z
AM 'dʒɪpoʊ, -z

gippy
BR 'dʒɪpi
AM 'dʒɪpi

Gipsy
BR 'dʒɪps|i, -ɪz
AM 'dʒɪpsi, -z

giraffe
BR dʒɪ'rɑːf, dʒɪ'raf, -s
AM dʒə'ræf, -s

**Giraldus
Cambrensis**
BR dʒɪ,raldəs
kam'brɛnsɪs
AM dʒə,rɔldəs
kæm'brɛnsəs,
dʒə,raldəs
kæm'brɛnsəs

girandole
BR 'dʒɪrəndəʊl,
'dʒɪrn̩dəʊl, -z
AM 'dʒɪrən,doʊl, -z

Girard
BR 'dʒɛrɑːd, dʒə'rɑːd
AM dʒə'rard

girasol
BR 'dʒɪrəsɒl, -z
AM 'dʒɪrə,sal, -z

girasole
BR 'dʒɪrəsəʊl, -z
AM 'dʒɪrə,soʊl, -z

gird
BR gəːd, -z, -ɪŋ, -ɪd
AM gərd, -z, -ɪŋ, -əd

girder
BR 'gəːdə(r), -z
AM 'gərdər, -z

girdle
BR 'gəːd|l, -lz, -l̩ɪŋ\-lɪŋ,
-ld
AM 'gərd|əl, -əlz,
-(ə)lɪŋ, -əld

girl
BR gəːl, -z
AM gərl, -z

girlfriend
BR 'gəːlfrɛnd, -z
AM 'gərl,frɛnd, -z

girlhood
BR 'gəːlhʊd
AM 'gərl,(h)ʊd

girlie
BR 'gəːli
AM 'gərli

girlish
BR 'gəːlɪʃ
AM 'gərlɪʃ

girlishly
BR 'gəːlɪʃli
AM 'gərlɪʃli

girlishness
BR 'gəːlɪʃnɪs
AM 'gərlɪʃnɪs

girly
BR 'gəːli
AM 'gərli

giro[1]
banking
BR 'dʒʌɪrəʊ, -z
AM 'dʒɪroʊ, -z

giro[2]
gyroscope
BR 'dʒʌɪrəʊ, -z
AM 'dʒaɪroʊ, -z

giro[3]
verb
BR 'dʒʌɪrəʊ, -z, -ɪŋ, -d
AM 'dʒɪroʊ, -z, -ɪŋ, -d

Gironde
BR (d)ʒɪ'rɒnd
AM dʒə'rand

Girondin
BR (d)ʒɪ'rɒndɪn, -z
AM dʒə'randən, -z
FR ʒirɔ̃dɛ̃

Girondist
BR (d)ʒɪ'rɒndɪst, -s
AM dʒə'randəst, -s

girt
BR gəːt
AM gərt

girth
BR gəːθ, -s
AM gərθ, -s

Girton
BR 'gəːtn
AM 'gərtən

Gisborne
BR 'gɪzbəːn
AM 'gɪzbərn

Giselle
BR (d)ʒɪ'zɛl
AM ʒə'zɛl

Gish
BR gɪʃ
AM gɪʃ

gismo
BR 'gɪzməʊ, -z
AM 'gɪzmoʊ, -z

Gissing
BR 'gɪsɪŋ
AM 'gɪsɪŋ

gist
BR dʒɪst
AM dʒɪst

git
BR gɪt, -s
AM gɪt, -s

gîte
BR ʒiːt, -s
AM ʒit, -s

gittern
BR 'gɪtəːn, -z
AM 'gɪdərn, -z

Gittins
BR 'gɪtɪnz
AM 'gɪtnz

Giuseppe
BR dʒʊ'zɛpi, dʒʊ'sɛpi
AM dʒə'sɛpi

givable
BR 'gɪvəbl
AM 'gɪvəbəl

give
BR gɪv, -z, -ɪŋ
AM gɪv, -z, -ɪŋ

giveable
BR 'gɪvəbl
AM 'gɪvəbəl

giveaway
BR 'gɪvəweɪ, -z
AM 'gɪvə,weɪ, -z

given
BR 'gɪvn
AM 'gɪvən

Givenchy
BR ʒɪ'vɒʃi, ʒiː'vɒʃi,
ʒɪ'vɒnʃi, ʒiː'vɒnʃi
AM ʒə'vɑnʃi

giver
BR 'gɪvə(r), -z
AM 'gɪvər, -z

gizmo
BR 'gɪzməʊ, -z
AM 'gɪzmoʊ, -z

gizzard
BR 'gɪzəd, -z
AM 'gɪzərd, -z

glabella
BR glə'bɛlə(r)
AM glə'bɛlə

glabellae
BR glə'bɛliː
AM glə'bɛli, glə'bɛ,laɪ

glabellar
BR glə'bɛlə(r)
AM glə'bɛlər

glabrous
BR 'gleɪbrəs
AM 'gleɪbrəs

glacé
BR 'glaseɪ
AM glæ'seɪ, glɑ'seɪ

glacial
BR 'gleɪʃl, 'gleɪsɪəl
AM 'gleɪʃəl

glacially
BR 'gleɪʃli, 'gleɪʃəli,
'gleɪsɪəli
AM 'gleɪʃəli

glaciate
BR 'gleɪsɪeɪt, 'gleɪʃɪeɪt,
-s, -ɪŋ, -ɪd
AM 'gleɪʃi,eɪ|t, -ts, -dɪŋ,
-dɪd

glaciated
BR 'gleɪsɪeɪtɪd,
'gleɪʃɪeɪtɪd
AM 'gleɪʃi,eɪdɪd

glaciation
BR ,gleɪsɪ'eɪʃn,
,gleɪʃɪ'eɪʃn, -z
AM ,gleɪʃi'eɪʃən, -z

glacier
BR 'glasɪə(r),
'gleɪsɪə(r), -z
AM 'gleɪʃər, -z

glaciological
BR ,gleɪsɪə'lɒdʒɪkl,
,gleɪʃɪə'lɒdʒɪkl
AM ,gleɪʃiə'lɑdʒəkəl

glaciologist
BR ,gleɪsɪ'ɒlədʒɪst,
,gleɪʃɪ'ɒlədʒɪst, -s
AM ,gleɪʃi'ɑlədʒəst, -s

glaciology
BR ,gleɪsɪ'ɒlədʒi,
,gleɪʃɪ'ɒlədʒi
AM ,gleɪʃi'ɑlədʒi

glacis[1]
singular
BR 'glas|ɪs, 'glas|i, -ɪsɪz
AM 'glæsiz, 'glæsəs,
'gleɪsɪz, -ɪsɪz

glacis[2]
plural
BR 'glasɪz
AM 'gleɪsɪz

glad
BR glad, -ə(r), -ɪst
AM glæd, -ər, -əst

gladden
BR 'gladn, -z, -ɪŋ, -d
AM 'glæd(ə)n, -z, -ɪŋ, -d

gladdener
BR 'gladnə(r), -z
AM 'glædnər, -z

gladdie
BR 'glad|i, -ɪz
AM 'glædi, -z

gladdon
BR 'gladn, -z

AM 'glæd(ə)n, -z

glade
BR gleɪd, -z
AM gleɪd, -z

gladiator
BR 'glædɪeɪtə(r), -z
AM 'glædiˌeɪdər, -z

gladiatorial
BR ˌglædɪə'tɔːriəl
AM ˌglædiə'tɔːriəl

gladioli
BR ˌglædɪ'əʊlʌɪ
AM ˌglædi'oʊˌlaɪ

gladiolus
BR ˌglædɪ'əʊləs, -ɪz
AM ˌglædi'oʊləs, -ɪz

gladly
BR 'glædli
AM 'glædli

gladness
BR 'glædnəs
AM 'glædnəs

gladsome
BR 'glæds(ə)m
AM 'glædsəm

gladsomely
BR 'glæds(ə)mli
AM 'glædsəmli

gladsomeness
BR 'glæds(ə)mnəs
AM 'glædsəmnəs

Gladstone
BR 'glædst(ə)n
AM 'glædzˌtoʊn

Gladwin
BR 'glædwɪn
AM 'glædwɪn

Gladys
BR 'glædɪs
AM 'glædəs

Glagolitic
BR ˌglagə'lɪtɪk
AM ˌglægə'lɪdɪk

glair
BR glɛː(r)
AM glɛ(ə)r

glaire
BR glɛː(r)
AM glɛ(ə)r

glaireous
BR 'glɛːrəs
AM 'glɛrəs

glairiness
BR 'glɛːrɪnɪs
AM 'glɛrɪnɪs

glairy
BR 'glɛːri
AM 'glɛri

glaive
BR gleɪv, -z
AM gleɪv, -z

glam
BR glam, -z, -ɪŋ, -d
AM glæm, -z, -ɪŋ, -d

Glamis
BR glɑːmz
AM glɑmz

glamor
BR 'glamə(r)
AM 'glæmər

Glamorgan
BR glə'mɔːg(ə)n
AM glə'mɔrgən

glamorisation
BR ˌglam(ə)rʌɪ'zeɪʃn
AM ˌglæm(ə)rə'zeɪʃən,
ˌglæməˌraɪ'zeɪʃən

glamorise
BR 'glamərʌɪz, -ɪz, -ɪŋ, -d
AM 'glæməˌraɪz, -ɪz, -ɪŋ, -d

glamorization
BR ˌglam(ə)rʌɪ'zeɪʃn
AM ˌglæm(ə)rə'zeɪʃən,
ˌglæməˌraɪ'zeɪʃən

glamorize
BR 'glamərʌɪz, -ɪz, -ɪŋ, -d
AM 'glæməˌraɪz, -ɪz, -ɪŋ, -d

glamorous
BR 'glam(ə)rəs
AM 'glæm(ə)rəs

glamorously
BR 'glam(ə)rəsli
AM 'glæm(ə)rəsli

glamour
BR 'glamə(r)
AM 'glæmər

glamourisation
BR ˌglam(ə)rʌɪ'zeɪʃn
AM ˌglæm(ə)rə'zeɪʃən,
ˌglæməˌraɪ'zeɪʃən

glamourise
BR 'glamərʌɪz, -ɪz, -ɪŋ, -d
AM 'glæməˌraɪz, -ɪz, -ɪŋ, -d

glamourization
BR ˌglam(ə)rʌɪ'zeɪʃn
AM ˌglæm(ə)rə'zeɪʃən,
ˌglæməˌraɪ'zeɪʃən

glamourize
BR 'glamərʌɪz, -ɪz, -ɪŋ, -d
AM 'glæməˌraɪz, -ɪz, -ɪŋ, -d

glamourous
BR 'glam(ə)rəs
AM 'glæm(ə)rəs

glamourously
BR 'glam(ə)rəsli
AM 'glæm(ə)rəsli

glance
BR glɑːns, glans, -ɪz, -ɪŋ, -t
AM glæns, -əz, -ɪŋ, -t

glancingly
BR 'glɑːnsɪŋli, 'glansɪŋli
AM 'glænsɪŋli

gland
BR gland, -z
AM glænd, -z

glandered
BR 'glandəd
AM 'glændərd

glanderous
BR 'gland(ə)rəs
AM 'glændərəs

glanders
BR 'glandəz
AM 'glændərz

glandes
BR 'glandiːz
AM 'glændiz

glandular
BR 'glandjʉlə(r),
'glandʒʉlə(r)
AM 'glændʒələr,
'glændjələr

glandule
BR 'glandjuːl,
'glandʒuːl, -z
AM 'glændʒul,
'glændjul, -z

glans
BR glanz
AM glænz

Glanville
BR 'glanvɪl
AM 'glæn.vɪl

Glanyrafon
BR ˌglanər'avn
AM ˌglænər'ævən

Glaramara
BR ˌglarə'mɑːrə(r)
AM ˌglɛrə'mɑrə

glare
BR glɛː(r), -z, -ɪŋ, -d
AM glɛ(ə)r, -z, -ɪŋ, -d

glaringly
BR 'glɛːrɪŋli
AM 'glɛrɪŋli

glaringness
BR 'glɛːrɪŋnɪs
AM 'glɛrɪŋnɪs

glary
BR 'glɛːri
AM 'glɛri

Glaser
BR 'gleɪzə(r)
AM 'gleɪzər

Glasgow
BR 'glazgəʊ, 'glɑːzgəʊ
AM 'glæz.goʊ,
'glæs.goʊ

Glaslyn
BR 'glaslɪn
AM 'glæslən

glasnost
BR 'glaznɒst
AM 'glazˌnoʊst,
'glazˌnɒst, 'glazˌnɑst

glass
BR glɑːs, glas, -ɪz
AM glæs, -əz

glassful
BR 'glɑːsfʊl, 'glasfʊl, -z
AM 'glæsˌfʊl, -z

glassfull
BR 'glɑːsfʊl, 'glasfʊl, -z
AM 'glæsˌfʊl, -z

glasshouse
BR 'glɑːshaʊ|s,
'glashaʊ|s, -zɪz
AM 'glæs,(h)aʊ|s, -zəz

glassie
BR 'glɑːs|i, 'glas|i, -ɪz
AM 'glæs|i, -z

glassily
BR 'glɑːsɪli, 'glasɪli
AM 'glæsəli

glassine
BR 'glɑːsiːn, 'glasiːn
AM 'glæˌsin

glassiness
BR 'glɑːsɪnɪs, 'glasɪnɪs
AM 'glæsɪnɪs

glassless
BR 'glɑːsləs, 'glasləs
AM 'glæsləs

glasslike
BR 'glɑːslʌɪk, 'glaslʌɪk
AM 'glæsˌlaɪk

glassmaker
BR 'glɑːsˌmeɪkə(r),
'glasˌmeɪkə(r), -z
AM 'glæsˌmeɪkər, -z

glasspaper
BR 'glɑːsˌpeɪpə(r),
'glasˌpeɪpə(r)
AM 'glæsˌpeɪpər

glassware
BR 'glɑːsˌwɛː(r),
'glasˌwɛː(r)
AM 'glæsˌwɛ(ə)r

glasswork
BR 'glɑːsˌwɜːk,
'glasˌwɜːk, -s
AM 'glæsˌwɜrk, -s

glasswort
BR 'glɑːsˌwɜːt,
'glasˌwɜːt, -s
AM 'glæsˌwɜrt,
'glæsˌwɔ(ə)rt, -s

glassy
BR 'glɑːs|i, 'glas|i,
-ɪ-(r), -ɪst
AM 'glæsi, -ər, -ɪst

Glastonbury
BR 'glast(ə)nb(ə)ri,
'glɑːst(ə)nb(ə)ri
AM 'glæstən,bɛri

Glaswegian
BR glaz'wiːdʒ(ə)n,
glɑːz'wiːdʒ(ə)n, -z
AM glæz'widʒiən,
glæs'widʒiən, -z

glaucoma
BR glɔː'kəʊmə(r),
glaʊ'kəʊmə(r)
AM glɔ'koʊmə,
glaʊ'koʊmə

glaucomatous
BR glɔː'kəʊmətəs,
glaʊ'kəʊmətəs

glaucous
AM glɔ'koʊmədəs,
glɔ'kɑmədəs,
glɑ'koʊmədəs,
glɑ'kɑmədəs

glaucous
BR 'glɔːkəs
AM 'glɔkəs, 'glɑkəs

Glaxo
BR 'glaksəʊ
AM 'glæksoʊ

glaze
BR gleɪz, -ɪz, -ɪŋ, -d
AM gleɪz, -ɪz, -ɪŋ, -d

glazer
BR 'gleɪzə(r), -z
AM 'gleɪzər, -z

glazier
BR 'gleɪzɪə(r), -z
AM 'gleɪʒər, 'gleɪzɪər, -z

glaziery
BR 'gleɪzɪəri
AM 'gleɪʒəri, 'gleɪzɪˌɛri

glazy
BR 'gleɪzi
AM 'gleɪzi

gleam
BR gliːm, -z, -ɪŋ, -d
AM glim, -z, -ɪŋ, -d

gleamingly
BR 'gliːmɪŋli
AM 'glimɪŋli

gleamy
BR 'gliːmi
AM 'glimi

glean
BR gliːn, -z, -ɪŋ, -d
AM glin, -z, -ɪŋ, -d

gleaner
BR 'gliːnə(r), -z
AM 'glinər, -z

gleanings
BR 'gliːnɪŋz
AM 'glinɪŋz

Gleason
BR 'gliːs(ə)n
AM 'glisən

Gleave
BR gliːv
AM gliv

glebe
BR gliːb, -z
AM glib, -z

glee
BR gliː
AM gli

gleeful
BR 'gliːf(ʊ)l
AM 'glifəl

gleefully
BR 'gliːfʊli, 'gliːfʃi
AM 'glifəli

gleefulness
BR 'gliːf(ʊ)lnəs
AM 'glifəlnəs

gleesome
BR 'gliːs(ə)m
AM 'glisəm

Gleeson
BR 'gliːs(ə)n
AM 'glisən

Gleichschaltung
BR 'glaɪk.ʃaltʊŋ
AM 'glaɪk.ʃæltʊŋ

glen
BR glɛn, -z
AM glɛn, -z

Glencoe
BR glɛn'kəʊ
AM glɛn.koʊ

Glenda
BR 'glɛndə(r)
AM 'glɛndə

Glendale
BR 'glɛndeɪl
AM 'glɛn.deɪl

Glendenning
BR glɛn'dɛnɪŋ
AM glɛn'dɛnɪŋ

Glendinning
BR glɛn'dɪnɪŋ
AM glɛn'dɪnɪŋ

Glendower
BR glɛn'daʊə(r)
AM 'glɛndaʊər

Gleneagles
BR glɛn'iːglz
AM glɛn'igəlz

Glenfiddich
BR glɛn'fɪdɪk,
glɛn'fɪdɪx
AM glɛn'fɪdɪk,
glɛn'fɪdɪtʃ

glengarry
BR glɛn'garˌi, -ɪz
AM glɛn'gɛri, -z

Glenlivet
BR glɛn'lɪvɪt
AM glɛn'lɪvɪt

Glenn
BR glɛn
AM glɛn

glenoid cavity
BR ˌgliːnɔɪd 'kavɪtˌi, -ɪz
AM ˌglɛˌnɔɪd 'kævədi,
-z

Glenrothes
BR glɛn'rʊθɪs
AM glɛn'rɑθəs

Glenys
BR 'glɛnɪs
AM 'glɛnəs

gley
BR gleɪ, -z
AM gleɪ, -z

glia
BR 'glaɪə(r), 'gliːə(r), -z
AM 'gliə, 'glaɪə, -z

glial
BR 'glaɪəl, 'gliːəl
AM 'gliəl, 'glaɪəl

glib
BR glɪb, -ə(r), -ɪst
AM glɪb, -ər, -ɪst

glibly
BR 'glɪbli
AM 'glɪbli

glibness
BR 'glɪbnɪs
AM 'glɪbnɪs

glide
BR glʌɪd, -z, -ɪŋ, -d
AM glaɪd, -z, -ɪŋ, -d

glider
BR 'glʌɪdə(r), -z
AM 'glaɪdər, -z

glidingly
BR 'glʌɪdɪŋli
AM 'glaɪdɪŋli

glim
BR glɪm, -z
AM glɪm, -z

glimmer
BR 'glɪm|ə(r), -əz,
-(ə)rɪŋ, -əd
AM 'glɪmər, -z, -ɪŋ, -d

glimmering
BR 'glɪm(ə)rɪŋ, -z
AM 'glɪmərɪŋ, -z

glimmeringly
BR 'glɪm(ə)rɪŋli
AM 'glɪmərɪŋli

glimpse
BR glɪm(p)s, -ɪz, -ɪŋ, -t
AM glɪm(p)s, -ɪz, -ɪŋ, -t

Glinka
BR 'glɪŋkə(r)
AM 'glɪŋkə

glint
BR glɪnt, -s, -ɪŋ, -d
AM glɪn|t, -ts, -(t)ɪŋ,
-(t)d

glioma
BR glʌɪ'əʊmə(r), -z
AM glaɪ'oʊmə, -z

glissade
BR glɪ'sɑːd, glɪ'seɪd, -z,
-ɪŋ, -ɪd
AM glə'sɑd, -z, -ɪŋ, -əd

glissandi
BR glɪ'sandi:
AM glə'sɑnˌdaɪ

glissando
BR glɪ'sandəʊ, -z
AM glə'sɑndoʊ, -z

glissé
BR glɪ'seɪ, -z
AM glə'seɪ, gli'seɪ, -z

glisten
BR 'glɪs|n, -nz
-nɪŋ \-nˌɪŋ, -nd
AM 'glɪsn, -z, -ɪŋ, -d

glister
BR 'glɪst|ə(r), -əz,
-(ə)rɪŋ, -əd
AM 'glɪst|ər, -ərz,
-(ə)rɪŋ, -ərd

glitch
BR glɪtʃ, -ɪz
AM glɪtʃ, -ɪz

glitter
BR 'glɪt|ə(r), -əz,
-(ə)rɪŋ, -əd
AM 'glɪdər, -z, -ɪŋ, -d

glitterati
BR ˌglɪtə'rɑːti
AM ˌglɪdə'radi

glitteringly
BR 'glɪt(ə)rɪŋli
AM 'glɪdərɪŋli

glittery
BR 'glɪt(ə)ri
AM 'glɪdəri

glitz
BR glɪts
AM glɪts

glitzily
BR 'glɪtsɪli
AM 'glɪtsɪli

glitziness
BR 'glɪtsɪnɪs
AM 'glɪtsɪnɪs

glitzy
BR 'glɪts|i, -ɪə(r), -ɪɪst
AM 'glɪtsi, -ər, -ɪst

gloaming
BR 'gləʊmɪŋ
AM 'gloʊmɪŋ

gloat
BR gləʊt, -s, -ɪŋ, -d
AM gloʊ|t, -ts, -dɪŋ, -dəd

gloater
BR 'gləʊtə(r), -z
AM 'gloʊdər, -z

gloatingly
BR 'gləʊtɪŋli
AM 'gloʊdɪŋli

glob
BR glɒb, -z
AM glɑb, -z

global
BR 'gləʊbl
AM 'gloʊbəl

globalisation
BR ˌgləʊbl̩ʌɪ'zeɪʃn,
ˌgləʊbəlʌɪ'zeɪʃn
AM ˌgloʊbələ'zeɪʃən,
ˌgloʊbəˌlaɪ'zeɪʃən

globalise
BR 'gləʊbl̩ʌɪz,
ˌgləʊbəlʌɪz, -ɪz, -ɪŋ, -d
AM 'gloʊbəˌlaɪz, -ɪz, -ɪŋ,
-d

globalization
BR ˌgləʊbl̩ʌɪ'zeɪʃn,
ˌgləʊbəlʌɪ'zeɪʃn
AM ˌgloʊbələ'zeɪʃən,
ˌgloʊbəˌlaɪ'zeɪʃən

globalize
BR 'gləʊbl̩ʌɪz,
ˌgləʊbəlʌɪz, -ɪz, -ɪŋ, -d
AM 'gloʊbəˌlaɪz, -ɪz, -ɪŋ,
-d

globally
BR 'gləʊbl̩i, 'gləʊbəli
AM 'gloʊbəli

globe
BR gləʊb, -z

AM gloʊb, -z
globefish
BR ˈgləʊbfɪʃ, -ɪz
AM ˈgloʊb,fɪʃ, -ɪz
globelike
BR ˈgləʊblʌɪk
AM ˈgloʊb,laɪk
globetrotter
BR ˈgləʊb,trɒtə(r), -z
AM ˈgloʊb,trɑdər, -z
globigerina
BR ˌgləʊbɪdʒəˈrʌmə(r),
-z
AM gloʊˌbɪdʒəˈraɪnə,
gloʊˌbɪdʒəˈrinə, -z
globigerinae
BR ˌgləʊbɪdʒəˈrʌmiː
AM gloʊˌbɪdʒəˈraɪni,
gloʊˌbɪdʒəˈriˌnaɪ
globoid
BR ˈgləʊbɔɪd, -z
AM ˈgloʊˌbɔɪd, -z
globose
BR ˈgləʊbəʊs,
gləʊˈbəʊs
AM ˈgloʊˌboʊs
globosely
BR ˈgləʊbəʊsli,
gləʊˈbəʊsli
AM ˈgloʊˌboʊsli
globoseness
BR ˈgləʊbəʊsnəs,
gləʊˈbəʊsnəs
AM ˈgloʊˌboʊsnəs
globular
BR ˈglɒbjʉlə(r)
AM ˈglɑbjələr
globularity
BR ˌglɒbjʉˈlarɪti
AM ˌglɑbjəˈlɛrədi
globularly
BR ˈglɒbjʉləli
AM ˈglɑbjələrli
globule
BR ˈglɒbjuːl, -z
AM ˈglɑbˌjul, -z
globulin
BR ˈglɒbjʉlɪn
AM ˈglɑbjələn
globulous
BR ˈglɒbjʉləs
AM ˈglɑbjələs
Glockenspiel
BR ˈglɒk(ə)nspiːl,
ˈglɒk(ə)nˌʃpiːl, -z
AM ˈglɑkənˌspil,
ˈglɑkənˌʃpil, -z
glom
BR glɒm, -z, -ɪŋ, -d
AM glɑm, -z, -ɪŋ, -d
glomata
BR glʌɪˈəʊmətə(r)
AM glaɪˈoʊmədə
glomerate[1]
adjective
BR ˈglɒm(ə)rət
AM ˈglɑməˌreɪt,
ˈglɑmərət

glomerate[2]
verb
BR ˈglɒməreɪt, -s, -ɪŋ,
-ɪd
AM ˈglɑməˌreɪ|t, -ts,
-dɪŋ, -dɪd
glomerular
BR glɒˈmɛr(j)ʉlə(r)
AM gləˈmɛr(j)ələr
glomerule
BR ˈglɒməruːl, -z
AM ˈglɑməˌrul, -z
glomeruli
BR glɒˈmɛr(j)ʉlʌɪ,
glɒˈmɛr(j)ʉliː
AM gləˈmɛrjəˌlaɪ
glomerulus
BR glɒˈmɛr(j)ʉləs
AM gləˈmɛrjələs
gloom
BR gluːm
AM glum
gloomily
BR ˈgluːmɪli
AM ˈgluməli
gloominess
BR ˈgluːmɪnɪs
AM ˈglumɪnɪs
gloomy
BR ˈgluːm|i, -ɪə(r), -ɪɪst
AM ˈglumi, -ər, -ɪst
glop
BR glɒp, -s
AM glɑp, -s
Gloria
BR ˈglɔːrɪə(r)
AM ˈglɔrɪə
Gloriana
BR ˌglɔːrɪˈɑːnə(r)
AM ˌglɔriˈænə
glorification
BR ˌglɔːrɪfɪˈkeɪʃn
AM ˌglɔrəfəˈkeɪʃən
glorifier
BR ˈglɔːrɪfʌɪə(r), -z
AM ˈglɔrəˌfaɪ(ə)r, -z
glorify
BR ˈglɔːrɪfʌɪ, -z, -ɪŋ, -d
AM ˈglɔrəˌfaɪ, -z, -ɪŋ, -d
gloriole
BR ˈglɔːrɪəʊl, -z
AM ˈglɔrɪoʊl, -z
glorious
BR ˈglɔːrɪəs
AM ˈglɔrɪəs
gloriously
BR ˈglɔːrɪəsli
AM ˈglɔrɪəsli
gloriousness
BR ˈglɔːrɪəsnəs
AM ˈglɔrɪəsnəs
glory
BR ˈglɔːr|i, -ɪz
AM ˈglɔri, -z
gloss
BR glɒs, -ɪz, -ɪŋ, -t
AM glɑs, glas, -əz, -ɪŋ, -t

glossal
BR ˈglɒsl
AM ˈglasəl
glossarial
BR glɒˈsɛːrɪəl
AM glɒˈsɛrɪəl,
glaˈsɛrɪəl
glossarist
BR ˈglɒsərɪst, -s
AM ˈglɑsərəst,
ˈglasərəst, -s
glossary
BR ˈglɒs(ə)r|i, -ɪz
AM ˈglɑsəri, ˈglasəri, -z
glossator
BR ˈglɒseɪtə(r),
glɒˈseɪtə(r), -z
AM ˈglɑˌseɪdər,
ˈglaˌseɪdər, -z
glosseme
BR ˈglɒsiːm, -z
AM ˈglɔˌsim, ˈglɑˌsim,
-z
glosser
BR ˈglɒsə(r), -z
AM ˈglɔsər, ˈglasər, -z
glossily
BR ˈglɒsɪli
AM ˈglɔsəli, ˈglasəli
glossiness
BR ˈglɒsɪnɪs
AM ˈglɔsɪnɪs, ˈglasɪnɪs
glossitis
BR glɒˈsʌɪtɪs
AM glɔˈsaɪdɪs
glaˈsaɪdɪs
glossographer
BR glɒˈsɒgrəfə(r), -z
AM glɔˈsɑgrəfər,
glaˈsɑgrəfər, -z
glossolalia
BR ˌglɒsəˈleɪlɪə(r)
AM ˌglɑsəˈleɪljə,
ˌglɔsəˈleɪlɪə,
ˌglɔsəˈleɪlɪə
glosso-laryngeal
BR ˌglɒsəʊləˈrɪndʒɪəl,
ˌglɒsəʊˌlarɪnˈdʒiːəl,
ˌglɒsəʊˌlarŋˈdʒiːəl
AM ˌglɑsoʊləˈrɪndʒəl,
ˌglasoʊləˈrɪndʒəl
glossology
BR glɒˈsɒlədʒi
AM glɔˈsalədʒi,
glaˈsalədʒi
Glossop
BR ˈglɒsəp
AM ˈglɔsəp, ˈglasəp
glossy
BR ˈglɒs|i, -ɪz, -ɪə(r),
-ɪɪst
AM ˈglɔsi, ˈglasi, -z, -ər,
-ɪst
Gloster
BR ˈglɒstə(r)
AM ˈglɔstər, ˈglastər

glottal
BR ˈglɒtl, -z
AM ˈglɑdl, -z
glottalisation
BR ˌglɒtlʌɪˈzeɪʃn
AM ˌglɑdləˈzeɪʃən,
ˌglɑdlˌaɪˈzeɪʃən
glottalise
BR ˈglɒtlˌʌɪz, -ɪz, -ɪŋ, -d
AM ˈglɑdlˌaɪz, -ɪz, -ɪŋ, -d
glottalization
BR ˌglɒtlʌɪˈzeɪʃn
AM ˌglɑdləˈzeɪʃən,
ˌglɑdlˌaɪˈzeɪʃən
glottalize
BR ˈglɒtlˌʌɪz, -ɪz, -ɪŋ, -d
AM ˈglɑdlˌaɪz, -ɪz, -ɪŋ, -d
glottis
BR ˈglɒtɪs, -ɪz
AM ˈgladəs, -ɪz
glottochronology
BR ˌglɒtəʊkrəˈnɒlədʒi
AM ˌgladoʊkrəˈnalədʒi
Gloucester
BR ˈglɒstə(r)
AM ˈglɔstər, ˈglastər
glove
BR glʌv, -z
AM gləv, -z
Glover
BR ˈglʌvə(r)
AM ˈgləvər
glow
BR gləʊ, -z, -ɪŋ, -d
AM gloʊ, -z, -ɪŋ, -d
glower
BR ˈglaʊə(r), -z, -ɪŋ, -d
AM ˈglaʊər, ˈgloʊər, -z,
-(ə)rɪŋ, -d
gloxinia
BR glɒkˈsɪnɪə(r)
AM glakˈsɪnɪə
Gloy
BR glɔɪ
AM glɔɪ
Gluck
BR glʊk
AM glʊk
glucose
BR ˈgluːkəʊz, ˈgluːkəʊs
AM ˈgluˌkoʊs
glucoside
BR ˈgluːkəsʌɪd
AM ˈglukəˌsaɪd
glucosidic
BR ˌgluːkəˈsɪdɪk
AM ˌglukəˈsɪdɪk
glue
BR gluː, -z, -ɪŋ, -d
AM glu, -z, -ɪŋ, -d
gluer
BR ˈgluːə(r), -z
AM ˈgluər, -z
gluey
BR ˈgluː|i, -ɪə(r), -ɪɪst
AM ˈglui, -ər, -ɪst

glueyly
BR 'glu:ɪli
AM 'gluəli

glueyness
BR 'glu:ɪnɪs
AM 'gluinɨs

glug
BR glʌg, -z, -ɪŋ, -d
AM gləg, -z, -ɪŋ, -d

Glühwein
BR 'glu:vʌɪn, -z
AM 'glu,vaɪn,
'glu,waɪn, -z

glum
BR glʌm, -ə(r), -ɨst
AM gləm, -ər, -əst

glumaceous
BR glu:'meɪʃəs
AM glu'meɪʃəs

glume
BR glu:m, -z
AM glum, -z

glumly
BR 'glʌmli
AM 'gləmli

glumness
BR 'glʌmnəs
AM 'gləmnəs

glumose
BR 'glʌməʊs
AM 'gləmoʊs, 'gləmoʊz

gluon
BR 'glu:ɒn
AM 'glu,ɑn

glut
BR glʌt, -s, -ɪŋ, -ɨd
AM glə|t, -ts, -dɪŋ, -dəd

glutamate
BR 'glu:təmeɪt
AM 'gludə,meɪt

glutamic
BR glu:'tamɪk
AM glu'tæmɪk

gluteal
BR 'glu:tɪəl
AM 'gludiəl

gluten
BR 'glu:t(ɪ)n
AM 'glutn

gluteus
BR 'glu:tɪəs
AM 'gludiəs

glutinous
BR 'glu:tɨnəs, 'glu:tn̩əs
AM 'glutn̩əs, 'gludənəs

glutinously
BR 'glu:tɨnəsli,
'glu:tn̩əsli
AM 'glutn̩əsli,
'gludənəsli

glutinousness
BR 'glu:tɨnəsnəs,
'glu:tn̩əsnəs
AM 'glutn̩əsnəs,
'gludənəsnəs

glutton
BR 'glʌtn, -z
AM 'glətn, -z

gluttonise
BR 'glʌtənʌɪz,
'glʌtn̩ʌɪz, -ɨz, -ɪŋ, -d
AM 'glətn,aɪz,
'glədə,naɪz, -ɨz, -ɪŋ, -d

gluttonize
BR 'glʌtənʌɪz,
'glʌtn̩ʌɪz, -ɨz, -ɪŋ, -d
AM 'glətn,aɪz,
'glədə,naɪz, -ɨz, -ɪŋ, -d

gluttonous
BR 'glʌtənəs, 'glʌtn̩əs
AM 'glətnəs, 'glədənəs

gluttonously
BR 'glʌtənəsli,
'glʌtn̩əsli
AM 'glətnəsli,
'glədənəs

gluttony
BR 'glʌtəni, 'glʌtn̩i
AM 'glətni, 'glədəni

glyceride
BR 'glɪsərʌɪd, -z
AM 'glɪsə,raɪd, -z

glycerin
BR 'glɪs(ə)rɪn
AM 'glɪsərən, 'glɪsrɨn

glycerine
BR 'glɪs(ə)ri:n,
'glɪs(ə)rɪn
AM 'glɪsərən, 'glɪsrɨn

glycerol
BR 'glɪsərɒl
AM 'glɪsərɔl, 'glɪsə,rɑl

glycin
BR 'glʌɪsɪn
AM 'glaɪsən

glycine
BR 'glʌɪsi:n
AM 'glaɪ,sin

glycogen
BR 'glʌɪkədʒ(ə)n
AM 'glaɪkədʒən,
'glaɪkə,dʒɛn

glycogenesis
BR ,glʌɪkə'dʒɛnɨsɪs
AM ,glaɪkə'dʒɛnəsəs

glycogenic
BR ,glʌɪkə'dʒɛnɪk
AM ,glaɪkə'dʒɛnɪk

glycol
BR 'glʌɪkɒl
AM 'glaɪkɔl, 'glaɪ,kɑl

glycolic
BR glʌɪ'kɒlɪk
AM glaɪ'kɔlɪk,
glaɪ'kɑlɪk

glycollic
BR glʌɪ'kɒlɪk
AM glaɪ'kɔlɪk,
,glaɪ'kɑlɪk

glycolyses
BR glʌɪ'kɒlɨsi:z
AM glaɪ'kɔlə,siz,
,glaɪ'kɑlə,siz

glycolysis
BR glʌɪ'kɒlɨsɪs
AM ,glaɪ'kɔləsəs,
,glaɪ'kɑləsəs

glycoprotein
BR ,glʌɪkəʊ'prəʊti:n,
-z
AM ¦glaɪkoʊ'proʊ,tin,
-z

glycoside
BR 'glʌɪkəsʌɪd, -z
AM 'glaɪkə,saɪd, -z

glycosidic
BR ,glʌɪkə(ʊ)'sɪdɪk
AM ¦glaɪkoʊ'sɪdɪk

glycosuria
BR ,glʌɪkə'sjʊərɪə(r),
,glʌɪkə'ʃʊərɪə(r),
,glʌɪkə'sjɔ:rɪə(r),
,glʌɪkə'ʃɔ:rɪə(r)
AM ¦glaɪkoʊ'sʊriə,
¦glaɪkoʊ'ʃʊriə

glycosuric
BR ,glʌɪkə'sjʊərɪk,
,glʌɪkə'ʃʊərɪk,
,glʌɪkə'sjɔ:rɪk,
,glʌɪkə'ʃɔ:rɪk
AM ¦glaɪkoʊ'sʊrɪk,
¦glaɪkoʊ'ʃʊrɪk

Glyn
BR glɪn
AM glɪn

Glyndebourne
BR 'glʌɪn(d)bɔ:n
AM 'glaɪn(d),bɔ(ə)rn

Glynis
BR 'glɪnɪs
AM 'glɪnɨs

Glynn
BR glɪn
AM glɪn

glyph
BR glɪf, -s
AM glɪf, -s

glyphic
BR 'glɪfɪk
AM 'glɪfɪk

glyptal
BR 'glɪptl, -z
AM 'glɪptl, -z

glyptic
BR 'glɪptɪk
AM 'glɪptɪk

glyptodon
BR 'glɪptədɒn, -z
AM 'glɪptə,dɑn, -z

glyptodont
BR 'glɪptədɒnt, -s
AM 'glɪptə,dɑnt, -s

glyptography
BR glɪp'tɒgrəfi
AM glɪp'tɑgrəfi

gnamma
BR 'namə(r), -z
AM (gə)'næmə, -z

gnarl
BR nɑ:l, -z
AM nɑrl, -z, -d

gnarly
BR 'nɑ:l|i, -ɪə(r), -ɪɨst
AM 'nɑrli, -ər, -ɨst

gnash
BR naʃ, -ɨz, -ɪŋ, -t
AM næʃ, -əz, -ɪŋ, -t

gnasher
BR 'naʃə(r), -z
AM 'næʃər, -z

gnat
BR nat, -s
AM næt, -s

gnathic
BR 'naθɪk
AM 'næθɪk

gnaw
BR nɔ:(r), -z, -ɪŋ, -d
AM nɔ, nɑ, -z, -ɪŋ, -d

gnawingly
BR 'nɔ:(r)ɪŋli
AM 'nɔɪŋli

gneiss
BR nʌɪs
AM naɪs

gneissic
BR 'nʌɪsɪk
AM 'naɪsɪk

gneissoid
BR 'nʌɪsɔɪd
AM 'naɪ,sɔɪd

gneissose
BR 'nʌɪsəʊs
AM 'naɪ,soʊs

gnocchi
BR 'nɒki
AM 'nɑki

gnome
BR nəʊm, -z
AM noʊm, -z

gnomic
BR 'nəʊmɪk
AM 'noʊmɪk

gnomically
BR 'nəʊmɪkli
AM 'noʊmək(ə)li

gnomish
BR 'nəʊmɪʃ
AM 'noʊmɪʃ

gnomon
BR 'nəʊmɒn, -z
AM 'noʊ,mɑn,
'noʊmən, -z

gnomonic
BR nəʊ'mɒnɪk
AM noʊ'mɑnɪk

gnoses
BR 'nəʊsi:z
AM 'noʊsiz

gnosis
BR 'nəʊsɪs
AM 'noʊsəs

gnostic
BR 'nɒstɪk, -s
AM 'nɑstɪk, -s

gnosticism
BR 'nɒstɪsɪz(ə)m
AM 'nɑstə,sɪzəm

gnosticize
BR 'nɒstɪsʌɪz, -ɨz, -ɪŋ, -d

AM 'nɑstə͵saɪz, -ɪz, -ɪŋ, -d

gnotobiotic
BR ͵nəʊtə(ʊ)baɪ'ɒtɪk
AM ͵noʊdə͵baɪ'ɑdɪk

gnu
BR n(j)uː, -z
AM n(j)u, -z

go
BR gəʊ, -z, -ɪŋ
AM goʊ, -z, -ɪŋ

goa
BR 'gəʊə(r), -z
AM 'goʊə, -z

goad
BR gəʊd, -z, -ɪŋ, -ɪd
AM goʊd, -z, -ɪŋ, -əd

go-ahead
BR 'gəʊəhɛd
AM 'goʊə͵hɛd

goal
BR gəʊl, -z
AM goʊl, -z

goalball
BR 'gəʊl͵bɔːl
AM 'goʊl͵bɔl, 'goʊl͵bɑl

goalie
BR 'gəʊl|i, -ɪz
AM 'goʊli, -z

goalkeeper
BR 'gəʊl͵kiːpə(r), -z
AM 'goʊl͵kipər, -z

goalkeeping
BR 'gəʊl͵kiːpɪŋ
AM 'goʊl͵kipɪŋ

goalless
BR 'gəʊlləs
AM 'goʊ(l)ləs

goalminder
BR 'gəʊl͵maɪndə(r), -z
AM 'goʊl͵maɪndər, -z

goalmouth
BR 'gəʊlmaʊ|θ, -ðs
AM 'goʊl͵maʊθ, -s

goalpost
BR 'gəʊlpəʊst, -s
AM 'goʊl͵poʊst, -s

goalscorer
BR 'gəʊl͵skɔːrə(r), -z
AM 'goʊl͵skɔrər, -z

goalscoring
BR 'gəʊl͵skɔːrɪŋ
AM 'goʊl͵skɔrɪŋ

goaltender
BR 'gəʊl͵tɛndə(r), -z
AM 'goʊl͵tɛndər, -z

goaltending
BR 'gəʊl͵tɛndɪŋ
AM 'goʊl͵tɛndɪŋ

Goan
BR 'gəʊən
AM 'goʊən

Goanese
BR ͵gəʊə'niːz
AM goʊə'niz

goanna
BR gəʊ'anə(r), -z

AM goʊ'ænə, -z

goat
BR gəʊt, -s
AM goʊt, -s

goatee
BR ͵gəʊ'tiː, -z
AM goʊ'ti, -z

goatherd
BR 'gəʊthəːd, -z
AM 'goʊt͵(h)ərd, -z

Goathland
BR 'gəʊθlənd
AM 'goʊθ͵lænd

goatish
BR 'gəʊtɪʃ
AM 'goʊdɪʃ

goatling
BR 'gəʊtlɪŋ, -z
AM 'goʊtlɪŋ, -z

goatsbeard
BR 'gəʊtsbɪəd, -z
AM 'goʊts͵bɪ(ə)rd, -z

goatskin
BR 'gəʊtskɪn, -z
AM 'goʊt͵skɪn, -z

goatsucker
BR 'gəʊt͵sʌkə(r), -z
AM 'goʊt͵səkər, -z

goaty
BR 'gəʊt|i, -ɪə(r), -ɪɪst
AM 'goʊdi, -ər, -ɪst

gob
BR gɒb, -z
AM gɑb, -z

gobang
BR ͵gəʊ'baŋ
AM goʊ'baŋ

gobbet
BR 'gɒbɪt, -s
AM 'gɑbət, -s

Gobbi
BR 'gɒbi
AM 'gɑbi

gobble
BR 'gɒb|l, -lz, -lɪŋ \-lɪŋ, -ld
AM 'gɑbəl, -əlz, -(ə)lɪŋ, -əld

gobbledegook
BR 'gɒbldɪguːk
AM 'gɑbəldɪ͵gʊk

gobbledygook
BR 'gɒbldɪguːk
AM 'gɑbəldɪ͵gʊk

gobbler
BR 'gɒblə(r), -z
AM 'gɑb(ə)lər, -z

gobby
BR 'gɒb|i, -ɪz
AM 'gɑbi, -z

Gobelins
BR 'gəʊbəlɪnz, 'gəʊb|ɪnz
AM 'goʊbələnz
FR gɔblɛ̃

gobemouche
BR 'gɒbmuːʃ, -ɪz

AM goʊb'muʃ, -əz

go-between
BR 'gəʊbɪtwiːn, -z
AM 'goʊbə͵twin, -z

Gobi Desert
BR ͵gəʊbɪ 'dɛzət
AM ͵goʊbi 'dɛzərt

Gobineau
BR 'gɒbɪnəʊ
AM 'gabə͵noʊ

goblet
BR 'gɒblɪt, -s
AM 'gablət, -s

goblin
BR 'gɒblɪn, -z
AM 'gablən, -z

gobsmack
BR 'gɒbsmak, -s, -ɪŋ, -t
AM 'gab͵smæk, -s, -ɪŋ, -t

goby
fish
BR 'gəʊb|i, -ɪz
AM 'goʊbi, -z

go-by
BR 'gəʊbʌɪ
AM 'goʊ͵baɪ

go-cart
BR 'gəʊkɑːt, -s
AM 'goʊ͵kɑrt, -s

god
BR gɒd, -z
AM gɑd, -z

Godalming
BR 'gɒdlmɪŋ
AM 'gadəlmɪŋ

Godard
BR 'gɒdɑː(d)
AM 'goʊ͵dard, 'gadərd

godchild
BR 'gɒdtʃʌɪld
AM 'gad͵tʃaɪld

godchildren
BR 'gɒd͵tʃɪldr(ə)n
AM 'gad͵tʃɪldrən

Godd
BR gɒd
AM gɑd

goddam
BR 'gɒdam, -d
AM 'gad|'dæm, -d

goddamn
BR 'gɒdam, -d
AM 'gad|'dæm, -d

Goddard
BR 'gɒdɑːd, 'gɒdəd
AM 'gadərd

goddess
BR 'gɒdɪs, 'gɒdɛs, -ɪz
AM 'gadəs, -əz

Gödel
BR 'gəʊdl
AM 'goʊdəl

godet
BR ͵gəʊ'dɛt, 'gəʊdeɪ
AM goʊ'dɛt

godetia
BR gə(ʊ)'diː͵ʃ(ɪ)ə(r), -z

AM gə'diʃə, -z

godets
BR ͵gəʊ'dɛts, 'gəʊdeɪz
AM goʊ'dɛts

go-devil
BR 'gəʊ͵dɛvl, -z
AM 'goʊ͵dɛvəl, -z

godfather
BR 'gɒd͵fɑː͵ðə(r), -z
AM 'gad͵fɑðər, -z

godfearing
BR 'gɒd͵fɪərɪŋ
AM 'gad͵fɪrɪŋ

godforsaken
BR 'gɒdfə͵seɪk(ə)n
AM 'gadfər͵seɪkən

Godfrey
BR 'gɒdfri
AM 'gadfri

Godgiven
BR 'gɒd͵gɪvn
AM 'gad͵gɪvən

godhead
BR 'gɒdhɛd, -z
AM 'gad͵(h)ɛd, -z

godhood
BR 'gɒdhʊd, -z
AM 'gad͵(h)ʊd, -z

Godiva
BR gə'dʌɪvə(r)
AM gə'daɪvə

godless
BR 'gɒdləs
AM 'gadləs

godlessly
BR 'gɒdləsli
AM 'gadləsli

godlessness
BR 'gɒdləsnəs
AM 'gadləsnəs

godlike
BR 'gɒdlʌɪk
AM 'gad͵laɪk

godliness
BR 'gɒdlɪnɪs
AM 'gadlinɪs

godly
BR 'gɒdl|i, -ɪə(r), -ɪɪst
AM 'gadli, -ər, -ɪst

Godman
BR 'gɒdmən
AM 'gadmən

godmother
BR 'gɒd͵mʌðə(r), -z
AM 'gad͵məðər, -z

Godolphin
BR gə'dɒlfɪn
gə'dɑlfən

godown
BR 'gəʊdaʊn, -z
AM 'goʊ͵daʊn, -z

godparent
BR 'gɒd͵pɛːrənt, 'gɒd͵pɛːrnt, -s
AM 'gad͵pɛrənt, -s

godsend
BR 'gɒdsɛnd, -z
AM 'gɑd,sɛnd,-z

godship
BR 'gɒdʃɪp, -s
AM 'gɑd,ʃɪp, -s

godson
BR 'gɒdsʌn, -z
AM 'gɑd,sən, -z

god-speed
BR ,gɒd'spiːd
AM ,gɑdz'pid,
,gɑd'spid

Godunov
BR 'gɒdənɒf
AM 'gɒdə,nɒv,
'gɒdə,nɔf, 'gɑdə,nɑv,
'gɑdə,nɑf
RUS gədu'nof

godward
BR 'gɒdwəd, -z
AM 'gɑdwərd, -z

Godwin
BR 'gɒdwɪn
AM 'gɑdwən

godwit
BR 'gɒdwɪt, -s
AM 'gɑd,wɪt, -s

Godwottery
BR ,gɒd'wɒt(ə)ri
AM 'gɑd,wɑdəri

Godzilla
BR gɒd'zɪlə(r)
AM gɑd'zɪlə

Goebbels
BR 'gəːblz
AM 'gʊbəlz

goer
BR 'gəʊə(r), -z
AM 'goʊ(ə)r,-z

Goering
BR 'gəːrɪŋ
AM 'gʊrɪŋ

goest
BR 'gəʊɪst
AM 'goʊ(ə)st

goeth
BR 'gəʊɪθ
AM 'goʊ(ə)θ

Goethe
BR 'gəːtə(r)
AM 'gʊdə

Goethean
BR 'gəːtɪən, -z
AM 'gʊdiən, -z

Goethian
BR 'gəːtɪən, -z
AM 'gʊdiən, -z

gofer
BR 'gəʊfə(r), -z
AM 'goʊfər, -z

Goff
BR gɒf
AM gɒf, gɑf

goffer
BR 'gəʊf]ə(r), 'gɒf]ə(r),
-əz, -(ə)rɪŋ, -əd

Gog
AM 'gɒfər, 'gɑfər, -z, -ɪŋ,
-d

Gog
BR gɒg
AM gɒg, gag

go-getter
BR ,gəʊ'gɛtə(r),
'gəʊ,gɛtə(r),-z
AM ,goʊ'gɛdər, -z

goggle
BR 'gɒg|l, -lz, -lɪŋ \-lɪŋ,
-ld
AM 'gag|əl, -əlz, -(ə)lɪŋ,
-əld

goglet
BR 'gɒglɪt, -s
AM 'gaglət, -s

Gogmagog
BR ,gɒgmə'gɒg
AM ,gɒgmə'gɒg,
,gagmə'gag

go-go
BR 'gəʊgəʊ
AM 'goʊ,goʊ

Gogol
BR 'gəʊgɒl
AM 'goʊ,gɒl, 'goʊgəl
RUS 'gogəlʲ

Goiânia
BR gɔɪ'anɪə(r)
AM gɔɪ'ænɪə

Goidel
BR 'gɔɪdl, -z
AM 'gɔɪdəl, -z

Goidelic
BR gɔɪ'dɛlɪk
AM gɔɪ'dɛlɪk

going
BR 'gəʊɪŋ, -z
AM 'goʊɪŋ, -z

goiter
BR 'gɔɪtə(r), -z, -d
AM 'gɔɪdər, -z, -d

goitre
BR 'gɔɪtə(r), -z, -d
AM 'gɔɪdər, -z, -d

goitrous
BR 'gɔɪtrəs
AM 'gɔɪtrəs

go-kart
BR 'gəʊkaːt, -s
AM 'goʊ,kart, -s

Golan Heights
BR ,gəʊlan 'hʌɪts,
,gəʊlaːn +, gəʊ'laːn +
AM 'goʊlan 'haɪts

Golborne
BR 'gəʊlbɔːn
AM 'goʊl,bɔ(ə)rn

Golconda
BR gɒl'kɒndə(r), -z
AM gal'kɑndə, -z

gold
BR gəʊld
AM goʊld

Golda
BR 'gəʊldə(r)

Gould
AM 'goʊldə

Goldberg
BR 'gəʊl(d)bəːg
AM 'goʊl(d),bərg

golden
BR 'gəʊld(ə)n
AM 'goʊldən

golden-ager
BR ,gəʊld(ə)n'eɪdʒə(r),
-z
AM 'goʊldən'eɪdʒər, -z

goldeneye
BR 'gəʊldənʌɪ,
'gəʊldnʌɪ, -z
AM 'goʊldən,aɪ, -z

goldenly
BR 'gəʊld(ə)nli
AM 'goʊldənli

goldenness
BR 'gəʊld(ə)nnəs
AM 'goʊldə(n)nəs

goldenrod
BR 'gəʊld(ə)nrɒd,
,gəʊld(ə)n'rɒd
AM 'goʊldən,rad

goldfield
BR 'gəʊl(d)fiːld, -z
AM 'goʊl(d),fild, -z

goldfinch
BR 'gəʊl(d)fɪn(t)ʃ, -ɪz
AM 'goʊl(d),fɪn(t)ʃ, -ɪz

goldfish
BR 'gəʊl(d)fɪʃ
AM 'goʊl(d),fɪʃ

Goldie
BR 'gəʊldi
AM 'goʊldi

Goldilocks
BR 'gəʊldɪlɒks
AM 'goʊldi,laks

Golding
BR 'gəʊldɪŋ
AM 'goʊldɪŋ

Goldman
BR 'gəʊl(d)mən
AM 'goʊl(d)mən

Goldmark
BR 'gəʊl(d)maːk
AM 'goʊl(d),mark

goldmine
BR 'gəʊl(d)mʌɪn, -z
AM 'goʊl(d),maɪn, -z

Goldschmidt
BR 'gəʊl(d)ʃmɪt
AM 'goʊl(d),ʃmɪt

goldsmith
BR 'gəʊl(d)smɪθ, -s
AM 'goʊl(d),smɪθ, -s

Goldstein
BR 'gəʊl(d)stiːn,
'gəʊl(d)staɪn
AM 'goʊl(d),staɪn,
'goʊl(d),stin

Goldwater
BR 'gəʊld,wɔːtə(r)
AM 'goʊl(d),wɔdər,
'goʊl(d),wadər

Goldwyn
BR 'gəʊldwɪn
AM 'goʊl(d)wən

golem
BR 'gəʊləm, 'gɔɪləm, -z
AM 'goʊləm, -z

golf
BR gɒlf, -ɪŋ
AM gɔlf, galf, -ɪŋ

golfer
BR 'gɒlfə(r), -z
AM 'gɔlfər, 'galfər, -z

Golgi
BR 'gɒldʒi
AM 'gɒldʒi, 'goʊldʒi

Golgotha
BR 'gɒlgəθə(r),
gɒl'gɒðə(r)
AM 'galgəθə, 'gɔlgəθə,
,gal'gaθə, ,gɒl'gɒθə

Goliath
BR gə'lʌɪəθ, -s
AM gə'laɪəθ, -s

Golightly
BR gə(ʊ)'lʌɪtli
AM goʊ'laɪtli

Gollancz
BR 'gɒlaŋks, gə'laŋks
AM 'galæŋks,
gə'læŋkʃ

golliwog
BR 'gɒlɪwɒg, -z
AM 'gali,wag, -z

gollop
BR 'gɒləp, -s, -ɪŋ, -t
AM 'galəp, -s, -ɪŋ, -t

golly
BR 'gɒli
AM 'gali

gollywog
BR 'gɒlɪwɒg, -z
AM 'gali,wag, -z

golosh
BR gə'lɒʃ, -ɪz
AM gə'laʃ, -əz

gombeen
BR gɒm'biːn, -z
AM gam'bin, -z

Gomer
BR 'gəʊmə(r)
AM 'goʊmər

Gomes
BR 'gəʊmɛz
AM 'goʊmɛz

Gómez
BR 'gəʊmɛz
AM 'goʊmɛz

Gomorrah
BR gə'mɒrə(r)
AM gə'mɔrə

Gompers
BR 'gɒmpəz
AM 'gampərz

gonad
BR 'gəʊnad, 'gɒnad, -z
AM 'goʊ,næd, -z

gonadal
BR gə(ʊ)'neɪdl
AM goʊ'nædəl

gonadotrophic
BR ˌgəʊnədə'trɒfɪk,
ˌgəʊnədə'trəʊfɪk,
ˌgɒnədə'trɒfɪk,
ˌgɒnədə'trəʊfɪk
AM ˌgoʊˌnædə'trafɪk,
ˌgoʊˌnædə'troʊfɪk

gonadotrophin
BR ˌgəʊnədə'trəʊfɪn,
ˌgəʊnədə'trɒfɪn,
ˌgɒnədə'trəʊfɪn,
ˌgɒnədə'trɒfɪn
AM ˌgoʊˌnædə'troʊfən

gonadotropic
BR ˌgəʊnədə'trɒpɪk,
ˌgəʊnədə'trəʊpɪk,
ˌgɒnədə'trɒpɪk,
ˌgɒnədə'trəʊpɪk
AM ˌgoʊˌnædə'trapɪk

Goncourt
BR 'gɒŋkʊə(r),
'gɒŋkɔ:(r)
AM 'gɑn,kʊ(ə)r,
'gɑn,kʊ(ə)r

gondola
BR 'gɒndələ(r),
'gɒndlə(r), -z
AM 'gɑndələ, -z

gondolier
BR ˌgɒndə'lɪə(r), -z
AM ˌgɑndə'lɪ(ə)r, -z

Gondwana
BR gɒn'dwɑ:nə(r)
AM gɑn'dwɑnə

Gondwanaland
BR gɒn'dwɑ:nəland
AM gɑn'dwɑnəˌlænd

gone
BR gɒn
AM gɔn, gɑn

goner
BR 'gɒnə(r), -z
AM 'gɔnər, 'gɑnər, -z

Goneril
BR 'gɒn(ə)rɪl,
'gɒn(ə)rl̩
AM 'gɑnərəl

gonfalon
BR 'gɒnfələn,
'gɒnflən, -z
AM 'gɑnfələn, -z

gonfalonier
BR ˌgɒnfələ'nɪə(r),
ˌgɒnflə'nɪə(r), -z
AM ˌgɑnfələ'nɪ(ə)r, -z

gong
BR gɒŋ, -z
AM gɔŋ, gɑŋ, -z

goniometer
BR ˌgəʊnɪ'ɒmɪtə(r), -z
AM ˌgoʊni'amədər, -z

goniometric
BR ˌgəʊnɪə'metrɪk
AM ˌgoʊniə'metrɪk

goniometrical
BR ˌgəʊnɪə'metrɪkl
AM ˌgoʊniə'metrəkəl

goniometrically
BR ˌgəʊnɪə'metrɪkli
AM ˌgoʊniə'metrək(ə)li

goniometry
BR ˌgəʊnɪ'ɒmɪtri
AM ˌgoʊni'amɛtri

gonk
BR gɒŋk, -s
AM gɔŋk, gɑŋk, -s

gonna¹
strong form
BR 'gɒnə(r)
AM 'gənə, 'gɔnə, 'gɑnə

gonna²
weak form
BR 'gənə(r), 'gn̩ə(r)
AM 'gənə

gonococcal
BR ˌgɒnə'kɒkl
AM ˌgɑnə'kakəl

gonococci
BR ˌgɒnə'kɒk(s)ʌɪ,
ˌgɒnə'kɒk(s)i:
AM ˌgɑnə'ka(k)ˌsaɪ

gonococcus
BR ˌgɒnə'kɒkəs
AM ˌgɑnə'kakəs

gonorrhea
BR ˌgɒnə'rɪə(r)
AM ˌgɑnə'riə

gonorrheal
BR ˌgɒnə'rɪəl
AM ˌgɑnə'riəl

gonorrhoea
BR ˌgɒnə'rɪə(r)
AM ˌgɑnə'riə

gonorrhoeal
BR ˌgɒnə'rɪəl
AM ˌgɑnə'riəl

Gonville
BR 'gɒnvɪl
AM 'gɑnˌvɪl

Gonzales
BR gɒn'zɑ:lɪz,
gɒn'zɑ:lez, gən'zɑ:lɪz,
gən'zɑ:lez
AM gɑn'zɑləs,
gɑn'zɑlez

González
BR gɒn'zɑ:lɪz,
gɒn'zɑ:lez, gən'zɑ:lɪz,
gən'zɑ:lez
AM gɑn'zɑləs,
gɑn'zɑlez
SP gon'θɑleθ,
gon'sɑles

gonzo
BR 'gɒnzəʊ, -z
AM 'gɑnzoʊ, -z

goo
BR gu:, -z
AM gu, -z

goober
BR 'gu:bə(r), -z
AM 'gubər, -z

Gooch
BR gu:tʃ
AM gutʃ

good
BR gʊd, -z
AM gʊd, -z

Goodall
BR 'gʊdɔ:l
AM 'gʊd,ɔl, 'gʊd,ɑl

Goodbody
BR 'gʊd,bɒdi
AM 'gʊd,bɑdi

goodby
BR (ˌ)gʊd'bʌɪ, -z
AM gʊd'baɪ, -z

goodbye
BR (ˌ)gʊd'bʌɪ, -z
AM gʊd'baɪ, -z

Goodchild
BR 'gʊdtʃʌɪld
AM 'gʊdˌtʃaɪld

Goode
BR gʊd
AM gʊd

Goodenough
BR 'gʊdɪnʌf, 'gʊdn̩ʌf
AM 'gʊdənəf

Goodfellow
BR 'gʊdˌfɛləʊ
AM 'gʊdˌfɛloʊ

Goodge
BR gu:dʒ
AM gʊdʒ

Goodhart
BR 'gʊdhɑ:t
AM 'gʊd,(h)ɑrt

good-hearted
BR 'gʊd'hɑ:tɪd
AM 'gʊdˌ(h)ɑrdəd

good-heartedness
BR 'gʊd'hɑ:tɪdnɪs
AM 'gʊdˌ(h)ɑrdədnəs

goodie
BR 'gʊdˌi, -ɪz
AM 'gʊdi, -z

goodish
BR 'gʊdɪʃ
AM 'gʊdɪʃ

Goodison
BR 'gʊdɪs(ə)n
AM 'gʊdəsən

goodliness
BR 'gʊdlɪnɪs
AM 'gʊdlɪnɪs

goodly
BR 'gʊdlˌi, -ɪə(r), -ɪɪst
AM 'gʊdli, -ər, -ɪst

goodman
BR 'gʊdmən
AM 'gʊdmən

goodmen
BR 'gʊdmən
AM 'gʊdmən

good-natured
BR ˌgʊd'neɪtʃəd
AM ˌgʊdˌ'neɪtʃərd

good-naturedly
BR ˌgʊd'neɪtʃədli
AM ˌgʊdˌ'neɪtʃərdli

goodness
BR 'gʊdnəs
AM 'gʊdnəs

goodnight
BR (ˌ)gʊd'nʌɪt, -s
AM gʊd'naɪt, -s

goodo
BR ˌgʊd'əʊ
AM ˌgʊd'oʊ

good-oh
BR ˌgʊd'əʊ
AM ˌgʊd'oʊ

Goodrich
BR 'gʊdrɪtʃ
AM 'gʊdrɪtʃ

goods
BR gʊdz
AM gʊdz

goodwife
BR 'gʊdwʌɪf
AM 'gʊdˌwaɪf

goodwill
BR ˌgʊd'wɪl
AM ˌgʊd'wɪl

Goodwin
BR 'gʊdwɪn
AM 'gʊdwɪn

goodwives
BR 'gʊdwʌɪvz
AM 'gʊdˌwaɪvz

Goodwood
BR 'gʊdwʊd
AM 'gʊd,wʊd

Goodwright
BR 'gʊdrʌɪt
AM 'gʊd,raɪt

goody
BR 'gʊdˌi, -ɪz
AM 'gʊdi, -z

Goodyear
BR 'gʊdjɪə(r),
'gʊdjə:(r)
AM 'gʊd,jɪ(ə)r

gooey
BR 'gu:ˌi, -ɪə(r), -ɪɪst
AM 'gui, -ər, -ɪst

gooeyly
BR 'gu:ɪli
AM 'gʊəli

gooeyness
BR 'gu:ɪnɪs
AM 'guinɪs

goof
BR gu:f, -s, -ɪŋ, -t
AM gʊf, -s, -ɪŋ, -t

goofball
BR 'gu:fbɔ:l, -z
AM 'gʊf,bɔl, 'gʊf,bɑl, -z

goofily
BR 'gu:fɪli
AM 'gʊfəli

goofiness
BR 'gu:fɪnɪs
AM 'gʊfɪnɪs

goofy
BR ˈɡuːfǀi, -ɪə(r), -ɪɪst
AM ˈɡufi, -ər, -ɪst

goog
BR ɡuːɡ, -z
AM ɡuɡ, -z

Googie
BR ˈɡuːɡi
AM ˈɡuɡi

googly
BR ˈɡuːɡlǀi, -ɪz
AM ˈɡuɡli, -z

googol
BR ˈɡuːɡɒl
AM ˈɡuɡəl, ˈɡuˌɡɒl,
ˈɡuˌɡɑl

gook
BR ɡuːk, -s
AM ɡʊk, -s

Goole
BR ɡuːl
AM ɡul

goolie
BR ˈɡuːlǀi, -ɪz
AM ˈɡuli, -z

goon
BR ɡuːn, -z
AM ɡun, -z

goonery
BR ˈɡuːn(ə)ri
AM ˈɡunəri

gooney
BR ˈɡuːni
AM ˈɡuni

Goonhilly
BR ɡʊnˈhɪli, ˌɡuːnˈhɪli
AM ɡʊnˈhɪli

goop
BR ɡuːp, -s
AM ɡup, -s

goopiness
BR ˈɡuːpɪnɪs
AM ˈɡupɪnɪs

goopy
BR ˈɡuːpǀi, -ɪə(r), -ɪɪst
AM ˈɡupi, -ər, -ɪst

goosander
BR ɡuːˈsandə(r), -z
AM ɡuˈsændər, -z

goose
BR ɡuːs, -ɪz, -ɪŋ, -t
AM ɡus, -əz, -ɪŋ, -t

gooseberry
BR ˈɡʊzb(ə)rǀi, -ɪz
AM ˈɡus,bɛri, -z

goosebumps
BR ˈɡuːsbʌmps
AM ˈɡus,bəm(p)s

gooseflesh
BR ˈɡuːsflɛʃ
AM ˈɡusˌflɛʃ

goosefoot
BR ˈɡuːsfʊt, -s
AM ˈɡusˌfʊt, -s

goosegog
BR ˈɡʊzɡɒɡ, -z
AM ˈɡʊzˌɡɑɡ, -z

goosegrass
BR ˈɡuːsɡrɑːs,
ˈɡuːsɡras, -ɪz
AM ˈɡusˌɡræs, -əz

gooseherd
BR ˈɡuːshəːd, -z
AM ˈɡus,(h)ərd, -z

goosestep
BR ˈɡuːsstɛp, -s, -ɪŋ, -t
AM ˈɡu(s)ˌstɛp, -s, -ɪŋ, -t

goosey
BR ˈɡuːsi
AM ˈɡusi

Goossens
BR ˈɡuːsnz
AM ˈɡusəns

gopher
BR ˈɡəʊfə(r), -z
AM ˈɡoʊfər, -z

goral
BR ˈɡɔːrəl, ˈɡɔːrl̩, -z
AM ˈɡoʊrəl, -z

Gorbachev
BR ˈɡɔːbətʃɒf
AM ˈɡɔrbəˌtʃɔv,
ˈɡɔrbəˌtʃɔf,
ˈɡɔrbəˌtʃav,
ˈɡɔrbəˌtʃaf

Gorbals
BR ˈɡɔːblz
AM ˈɡɔrbəlz

gorblimey
BR (ˌ)ɡɔːˈblʌɪmǀi, -ɪz
AM ɡɔrˈblaɪmi, -z

gorcock
BR ˈɡɔːkɒk, -s
AM ˈɡɔrˌkak, -s

Gordian
BR ˈɡɔːdɪən
AM ˈɡɔrdiən

Gordimer
BR ˈɡɔːdɪmə(r)
AM ˈɡɔrdəmər

Gordium
BR ˈɡɔːdɪəm
AM ˈɡɔrdiəm

gordo
BR ˈɡɔːdəʊ, -z
AM ˈɡɔrˌdoʊ, -z

Gordon
BR ˈɡɔːdn
AM ˈɡɔrdən

Gordonstoun
BR ˈɡɔːdnst(ə)n,
ˈɡɔːdnzt(ə)n
AM ˈɡɔrdənˌstoʊn

gore
BR ɡɔː(r), -z, -ɪŋ, -d
AM ɡɔ(ə)r, -z, -ɪŋ, -d

Górecki
BR ɡəˈrɛtski
AM ɡʊˈrɛtski

Gore-tex®
BR ˈɡɔːtɛks
AM ˈɡɔrˌtɛks

gorge
BR ɡɔːdʒ, -ɪz, -ɪŋ, -d
AM ɡɔrdʒ, -əz, -ɪŋ, -t

gorgeous
BR ˈɡɔːdʒəs
AM ˈɡɔrdʒəs

gorgeously
BR ˈɡɔːdʒəsli
AM ˈɡɔrdʒəsli

gorgeousness
BR ˈɡɔːdʒəsnəs
AM ˈɡɔrdʒəsnəs

gorger
BR ˈɡɔːdʒə(r), -z
AM ˈɡɔrdʒər, -z

gorget
BR ˈɡɔːdʒɪt, -s
AM ˈɡɔrdʒət, -s

Gorgio
BR ˈɡɔːdʒəʊ, -z
AM ˈɡɔrˌdʒoʊ, -z

gorgon
BR ˈɡɔːɡ(ə)n, -z
AM ˈɡɔrɡən, -z

gorgonia
BR ɡɔːˈɡəʊnɪə(r), -z
AM ɡɔrˈɡoʊniə, -z

gorgoniae
BR ɡɔːˈɡəʊniː
AM ɡɔrˈɡoʊniˌi,
ɡɔrˈɡoʊniˌaɪ

gorgonian
BR ɡɔːˈɡəʊnɪən, -z
AM ɡɔrˈɡoʊniən, -z

gorgonise
BR ˈɡɔːɡənʌɪz,
ˈɡɔːɡnʌɪz, -ɪz, -ɪŋ, -d
AM ˈɡɔrɡəˌnaɪz, -ɪz, -ɪŋ,
-d

gorgonize
BR ˈɡɔːɡənʌɪz,
ˈɡɔːɡnʌɪz, -ɪz, -ɪŋ, -d
AM ˈɡɔrɡəˌnaɪz, -ɪz, -ɪŋ,
-d

Gorgonzola
BR ˌɡɔːɡ(ə)nˈzəʊlə(r)
AM ˌɡɔrɡənˈzoʊlə

gorilla
BR ɡəˈrɪlə(r), -z
AM ɡəˈrɪlə, -z

gorily
BR ˈɡɔːrɪli
AM ˈɡɔrəli

goriness
BR ˈɡɔːrɪnɪs
AM ˈɡɔrɪnɪs

Goring
BR ˈɡɔːrɪŋ
AM ˈɡɔrɪŋ

Gorki
BR ˈɡɔːki
AM ˈɡɔrki

Gorky
BR ˈɡɔːki
AM ˈɡɔrki

Gorman
BR ˈɡɔːmən
AM ˈɡɔrmən

gormandise
BR ˈɡɔːm(ə)ndʌɪz, -ɪz,
-ɪŋ, -d
AM ˈɡɔrmənˌdaɪz, -ɪz,
-ɪŋ, -d

gormandiser
BR ˈɡɔːm(ə)ndʌɪzə(r),
-z
AM ˈɡɔrmənˌdaɪzər, -z

gormandize
BR ˈɡɔːm(ə)ndʌɪz, -ɪz,
-ɪŋ, -d
AM ˈɡɔrmənˌdaɪz, -ɪz,
-ɪŋ, -d

gormandizer
BR ˈɡɔːm(ə)ndʌɪzə(r),
-z
AM ˈɡɔrmənˌdaɪzər, -z

gormless
BR ˈɡɔːmləs
AM ˈɡɔrmləs

gormlessly
BR ˈɡɔːmləsli
AM ˈɡɔrmləsli

gormlessness
BR ˈɡɔːmləsnəs
AM ˈɡɔrmləsnəs

Gormley
BR ˈɡɔːmli
AM ˈɡɔrmli

Goronwy
BR ɡəˈrɒnwi
AM ɡəˈrɑnwi

go-round
BR ˈɡəʊraʊnd
AM ˈɡoʊˌraʊnd

Gor-Ray
BR ˈɡɔːreɪ
AM ˈɡɔ(r)ˌreɪ

gorse
BR ɡɔːs
AM ɡɔ(ə)rs

Gorsedd
BR ˈɡɔːsɛð
AM ˈɡɔrsɛð

Gorseinon
BR ɡɔːˈsʌɪnən
AM ɡɔrˈsaɪnən

gorsy
BR ˈɡɔːsǀi, -ɪə(r), -ɪɪst
AM ˈɡɔrsi, -ər, -ɪst

Gorton
BR ˈɡɔːtn
AM ˈɡɔrt(ə)n

gory
BR ˈɡɔːrǀi, -ɪə(r), -ɪɪst
AM ˈɡɔri, -ər, -ɪst

Gosforth
BR ˈɡɒsfəθ, ˈɡɒsfɔːθ
AM ˈɡasfərθ

gosh
BR ɡɒʃ
AM ɡaʃ

goshawk
BR ˈɡɒshɔːk, -s
AM ˈɡas,(h)ɔk,
ˈɡas,(h)ak, -s

Goshen
BR ˈgəʊʃn
AM ˈgoʊʃən
gosling
BR ˈgɒzlɪŋ, -z
AM ˈgɑːzlɪŋ, -z
go-slow
BR ˌgəʊˈsləʊ, -z
AM ˌgoʊˈsloʊ, -z
gospel
BR ˈgɒspl, -z
AM ˈgɑspəl, -z
gospeler
BR ˈgɒspələ(r),
ˈgɒsplə(r), -z
AM ˈgɑspələr, -z
gospeller
BR ˈgɒspələ(r),
ˈgɒsplə(r), -z
AM ˈgɑspələr, -z
Gosport
BR ˈgɒspɔːt
AM ˈgɑsˌpɔ(ə)rt
Goss
BR gɒs
AM gɔs, gɑs
gossamer
BR ˈgɒsəmə(r), -d
AM ˈgɑsəmər, -d
gossamery
BR ˈgɒsəm(ə)ri
AM ˈgɑsəˌmɛri
gossan
BR ˈgɒzn
AM ˈgɑsən
Gosse
BR gɒs
AM gɔs, gɑs
gossip
BR ˈgɒsɪp, -ɪps, -ɪpɪŋ, -ɪpt
AM ˈgɑsəp, -s, -ɪŋ, -t
gossiper
BR ˈgɒsɪpə(r), -z
AM ˈgɑsəpər, -z
gossipmonger
BR ˈgɒsɪpˌmʌŋgə(r), -z
AM ˈgɑsəpˌmɑŋgər,
ˈgɑsəpˌməŋgər, -z
gossipy
BR ˈgɒsɪpi
AM ˈgɑsəpi
gossoon
BR gɒˈsuːn, -z
AM gɑˈsun, -z
got
BR gɒt
AM gɑt
gotcha
BR ˈgɒtʃə(r), -z
AM ˈgɑtʃə, -z
Goth
BR gɒθ, -s
AM gɔθ, gɑθ, -s
Gotha
BR ˈgəʊθə(r), ˈgəʊtə(r)
AM ˈgoʊθə

Gotham¹
New York
BR gɒθ(ə)m
AM ˈgɑθəm
Gotham²
place in UK
BR ˈgəʊtəm, ˈgɒtəm
AM ˈgoʊdəm
Gothamite
BR ˈgɒθəmʌɪt,
ˈgɒθmʌɪt, -s
AM ˈgɑθəˌmaɪt, -s
Gothard
BR ˈgɒθɑːd
AM ˈgɑθərd
Gothenburg
BR ˈgɒθnbəːg
AM ˈgɑθənˌbərg
Gothic
BR ˈgɒθɪk
AM ˈgɑθɪk
Gothically
BR ˈgɒθɪkli
AM ˈgɑθək(ə)li
Gothicise
BR ˈgɒθɪsʌɪz, -ɪz, -ɪŋ, -d
AM ˈgɑθəˌsaɪz, -ɪz, -ɪŋ, -d
Gothicism
BR ˈgɒθɪsɪz(ə)m
AM ˈgɑθəˌsɪzəm
Gothicize
BR ˈgɒθɪsʌɪz, -ɪz, -ɪŋ, -d
AM ˈgɑθəˌsaɪz, -ɪz, -ɪŋ, -d
Gotland
BR ˈgɒtland
AM ˈgɑtˌlænd
gotta
BR ˈgɒtə(r)
AM ˈgɑdə
gotten
BR ˈgɒtn
AM ˈgɑtn
Götterdämmerung
BR ˌgɒtəˈdamərʊŋ,
ˌgəːtəˈdamərʊŋ,
ˌgɒtəˈdamərʌŋ,
ˌgəːtəˈdamərʌŋ
AM ˌgədərˈdæmərʊŋ
GER ˈgœtɐdɛmərʊŋ
gouache
BR gʊˈɑːʃ, gwɑːʃ, -ɪz
AM gwaʃ, guˈaʃ, -əz
Gouda
BR ˈgaʊdə(r), ˈguːdə(r)
AM ˈgudə
DU ˈxɔʊda
Goudge
BR guːdʒ
AM gudʒ
Goudy
BR ˈgaʊdi
AM ˈgaʊdi
gouge
BR gaʊdʒ, -ɪz, -ɪŋ, -d
AM gaʊdʒ, -əz, -ɪŋ, -t

gouger
BR ˈgaʊdʒə(r), -z
AM ˈgaʊdʒər, -z
Gough
BR gɒf
AM gɔf, gɑf
goujons
BR ˈguː(d)ʒ(ə)nz,
ˈguː(d)ʒɒnz, ˈguːʒɒ̃
AM ˈgudʒɒnz
goulash
BR ˈguːlaʃ, -ɪz
AM ˈguˌlɑʃ, -əz
Gould
BR guːld
AM guld
Gounod
BR ˈguːnəʊ
AM guˈnoʊ
gourami
BR gʊˈrɑːmˌi,
ˈgʊərəmˌi, -ɪz
AM gəˈrami, -z
gouramy
BR gʊˈrɑːmˌi,
ˈgʊərəmˌi, -ɪz
AM gəˈrami, -z
gourd
BR gʊəd, gɔːd, -z
AM gɔ(ə)rd, -z
gourdful
BR ˈgʊədfʊl, ˈgɔːdfʊl, -z
AM ˈgɔrdˌfʊl, -z
Gourlay
BR ˈgʊəli
AM ˈgərli
Gourley
BR ˈgʊəli
AM ˈgərli
gourmand
BR ˈgʊəmənd,
ˈgɔːmənd, -z
AM gʊrˈmɑnd, -z
gourmandise
BR ˈgʊəm(ə)ndʌɪz,
ˈgɔːm(ə)ndʌɪz, -ɪz, -ɪŋ, -d
AM ˈgʊrmənˌdaɪz, -ɪz, -ɪŋ, -d
gourmandism
BR ˈgʊəm(ə)ndɪz(ə)m,
ˈgɔːm(ə)ndɪz(ə)m
AM ˈgʊrmənˌdɪzəm
gourmandize
BR ˈgʊəm(ə)ndʌɪz,
ˈgɔːm(ə)ndʌɪz, -ɪz, -ɪŋ, -d
AM ˈgʊrmənˌdaɪz, -ɪz, -ɪŋ, -d
gourmet
BR ˈgʊəmeɪ, ˈgɔːmeɪ, -z
AM ˌgʊrˈmeɪ, ˌgɔrˈmeɪ, -z
gout
BR gaʊt
AM gaʊt
goutily
BR ˈgaʊtɪli

AM ˈgaʊdəli
goutiness
BR ˈgaʊtɪnɪs
AM ˈgaʊdɪnɪs
goutweed
BR ˈgaʊtwiːd
AM ˈgaʊtˌwid
gouty
BR ˈgaʊtˌli, -ɪə(r), -ɪɪst
AM ˈgaʊdi, -ər, -ɪst
Govan
BR ˈgʌvn
AM ˈgəvən
govern
BR ˈgʌv|n, -nz,
-nɪŋ \-ənɪŋ, -nd
AM ˈgəvərn, -z, -ɪŋ, -d
governability
BR ˌgʌvnəˈbɪlɪti,
ˌgʌvənəˈbɪlɪti
AM ˌgəvərnəˈbɪlɪdi
governable
BR ˈgʌvnəbl, ˈgʌvənəbl
AM ˈgəvərnəbəl
governableness
BR ˈgʌvnəblnəs,
ˈgʌv(ə)nəblnəs
AM ˈgəvərnəbəlnəs
governance
BR ˈgʌvnəns,
ˈgʌvənəns
AM ˈgəvərnəns
governess
BR ˈgʌvnɪs, ˈgʌvnɛs, -ɪz
AM ˈgəvərnəs, -əz
governessy
BR ˈgʌvnɪsi
AM ˈgəvərnəsi
government
BR ˈgʌvnm(ə)nt,
ˈgʌvəm(ə)nt, -s
AM ˈgəvər(n)mənt,
ˈgəvə(r)mənt, -s
governmental
BR ˌgʌvnˈmɛntl,
ˌgʌvəˈmɛntl
AM ˌgəvər(n)ˈmɛn(t)l
governmentally
BR ˌgʌvnˈmɛntˌli,
ˌgʌvəˈmɛntˌli,
ˌgʌvnˈmɛntəli,
ˌgʌvəˈmɛntəli
AM ˌgəvər(n)ˈmɛn(t)li
governor
BR ˈgʌvnə(r),
ˈgʌvənə(r), -z
AM ˈgəv(ə)nər, -z
governorate
BR ˈgʌvnərət,
ˈgʌvənərət, -s
AM ˈgəv(ə)nərət,
ˈgəv(ə)nəˌreɪt, -s
governorship
BR ˈgʌvnəˌʃɪp,
ˈgʌvənəˌʃɪp, -s
AM ˈgəv(ə)nərˌʃɪp, -s
Gow
BR gaʊ

gowan
AM gaʊ

gowan
BR ˈgaʊən, -z
AM ˈgoʊən, -z

Gower
BR ˈgaʊə(r)
AM ˈgaʊər

Gowing
BR ˈgaʊɪŋ
AM ˈgaʊɪŋ

gowk
BR gaʊk, -s
AM gaʊk, -s

gown
BR gaʊn, -z
AM gaʊn, -z

gownsman
BR ˈgaʊnzmən
AM ˈgaʊnzmən

gownsmen
BR ˈgaʊnzmən
AM ˈgaʊnzmən

Gowrie
BR ˈgaʊri
AM ˈgaʊri

goy
BR gɔɪ, -z
AM gɔɪ, -z

Goya
BR ˈgɔɪə(r)
AM ˈgɔɪə

goyim
BR ˈgɔɪ(j)ɪm
AM ˈgɔɪ(j)ɪm

goyisch
BR gɔɪˈ(j)ɪʃ
AM ˈgɔɪɪʃ

goyish
BR gɔɪˈ(j)ɪʃ
AM ˈgɔɪɪʃ

Gozo
BR ˈgəʊzəʊ
AM ˈgoʊˌzoʊ

Graafian
BR ˈgrɑːfiən, ˈgrɑfiən
AM ˈgrɑfiən, ˈgræfiən

grab
BR grab, -z, -ɪŋ, -d
AM græb, -z, -ɪŋ, -d

grabber
BR ˈgrabə(r), -z
AM ˈgræbər, -z

grabble
BR ˈgrab|l, -lz,
-lɪŋ \-lɪŋ, -ld
AM ˈgræb|əl, -əlz,
-(ə)lɪŋ, -əld

grabby
BR ˈgrab|i, -ɪə(r), -ɪɪst
AM ˈgræbi, -ər, -ɪst

graben
BR ˈgrɑːb(ə)n, -z
AM ˈgrɑbən, -z

Gracchus
BR ˈgrakəs
AM ˈgrækəs

grace
BR greɪs, -ɪz, -ɪŋ, -t
AM greɪs, -ɪz, -ɪŋ, -t

graceful
BR ˈgreɪsf(ʊ)l
AM ˈgreɪsfəl

gracefully
BR ˈgreɪsfʊli, ˈgreɪsfʃi
AM ˈgreɪsfəli

gracefulness
BR ˈgreɪsf(ʊ)lnəs
AM ˈgreɪsfəlnəs

graceless
BR ˈgreɪslɪs
AM ˈgreɪslɪs

gracelessly
BR ˈgreɪslɪsli
AM ˈgreɪslɪsli

gracelessness
BR ˈgreɪslɪsnɪs
AM ˈgreɪslɪsnɪs

Gracie
BR ˈgreɪsi
AM ˈgreɪsi

gracile
BR ˈgrasɪl, ˈgrasʌɪl
AM ˈgræsəl, ˈgræˌsaɪl

gracility
BR graˈsɪlɪti, grəˈsɪlɪti
AM græˈsɪlɪdi,
grəˈsɪlɪdi

graciosity
BR ˌgreɪʃɪˈɒsɪti,
ˌgreɪsɪˈɒsɪti
AM ˌgreɪʃiˈɑsədi,
ˌgreɪsɪˈɑsədi

gracious
BR ˈgreɪʃəs
AM ˈgreɪʃəs

graciously
BR ˈgreɪʃəsli
AM ˈgreɪʃəsli

graciousness
BR ˈgreɪʃəsnəs
AM ˈgreɪʃəsnəs

grackle
BR ˈgrakl, -z
AM ˈgrækəl, -z

grad
BR grad, -z
AM græd, -z

gradability
BR ˌgreɪdəˈbɪlɪti
AM ˌgreɪdəˈbɪlɪdi

gradable
BR ˈgreɪdəbl
AM ˈgreɪdəbəl

gradate
BR grəˈdeɪt, -s, -ɪŋ, -ɪd
AM ˈgreɪˌdeɪ|t, -ts, -dɪŋ,
-dɪd

gradation
BR grəˈdeɪʃn, -z
AM greɪˈdeɪʃən, -z

gradational
BR grəˈdeɪʃ(n(ə)l,
grəˈdeɪʃən(ə)l

grader
BR ˈgreɪdə(r), -z
AM ˈgreɪdər, -z

Gradgrind
BR ˈgradgrʌɪnd
AM ˈgræd.graɪnd

gradience
BR ˈgreɪdɪəns
AM ˈgreɪdiəns

gradient
BR ˈgreɪdɪənt, -s
AM ˈgreɪdiənt, -s

gradin
BR ˈgreɪdɪn, -z
AM ˈgreɪdn, -z

gradine
BR ˈgreɪdiːn, -z
AM greɪˌdin, grəˈdin,
-z

grading
BR ˈgreɪdɪŋ, -z
AM ˈgreɪdɪŋ, -z

gradual
BR ˈgradʒʊəl,
ˈgradjʊəl, ˈgradʒ(ʊ)l
AM ˈgrædʒ(ə)wəl,
ˈgrædʒəl

gradualism
BR ˈgradʒʊəlɪz(ə)m,
ˈgradjʊəlɪz(ə)m,
ˈgradʒʊlɪz(ə)m,
ˈgradʒlɪz(ə)m
AM ˈgrædʒ(ə)wəˌlɪzəm,
ˈgrædʒəˌlɪzəm

gradualist
BR ˈgradʒʊəlɪst,
ˈgradjʊəlɪst,
ˈgradʒlɪst,
ˈgradʒlɪst, -s
AM ˈgrædʒ(ə)wələst,
ˈgrædʒələst, -s

gradualistic
BR ˌgradʒʊəˈlɪstɪk,
ˌgradjʊəˈlɪstɪk,
ˌgradʒ(ʊ)lˈɪstɪk
AM ˌgrædʒ(ə)wəˈlɪstɪk,
ˌgrædʒəˈlɪstɪk

gradually
BR ˈgradʒʊli,
ˈgradjʊəli
AM ˈgrædʒ(ə)wəli,
ˈgrædʒəli

gradualness
BR ˈgradʒʊəlnəs,
ˈgradʒəlnəs,
ˈgradjʊəlnəs
AM ˈgrædʒ(ə)wəlnəs,
ˈgrædʒəlnəs

graduand
BR ˈgradʒʊand,
ˈgradjʊand, -z
AM ˈgrædʒ(ə)wənd, -z

graduate¹
noun
BR ˈgradʒʊət,
ˈgradjʊət, -s
AM ˈgrædʒ(ə)wət, -s

graduate²
verb
BR ˈgradʒʊeɪt,
ˈgradjʊeɪt, -s, -ɪŋ, -ɪd
AM ˈgrædʒəˌweɪ|t, -ts,
-dɪŋ, -dɪd

graduation
BR ˌgradʒʊˈeɪʃn,
ˌgradjʊˈeɪʃn, -z
AM ˌgrædʒəˈweɪʃən, -z

graduator
BR ˈgradʒʊeɪtə(r),
ˈgradjʊeɪtə(r), -z
AM ˈgrædʒəˌweɪdər, -z

Grady
BR ˈgreɪdi
AM ˈgreɪdi

Graecise
BR ˈgriːsʌɪz, ˈgrʌɪsʌɪz,
-ɪz, -ɪŋ, -d
AM ˈgriˌsaɪz, -ɪz, -ɪŋ, -d

Graecism
BR ˈgriːsɪz(ə)m,
ˈgrʌɪsɪz(ə)m, -z
AM ˈgriˌsɪzəm, -z

Graecize
BR ˈgriːsʌɪz, ˈgrʌɪsʌɪz,
-ɪz, -ɪŋ, -d
AM ˈgriˌsaɪz, -ɪz, -ɪŋ, -d

Graeco-
BR ˈgriːkəʊ, ˈgrʌɪkəʊ,
ˈgrɛkəʊ
AM ˈgrɛkoʊ

Graecomania
BR ˌgriːkəʊˈmeɪnɪə(r),
ˌgrʌɪkəʊˈmeɪnɪə(r),
ˌgrɛkəʊˈmeɪnɪə(r)
AM ˌgrɛkoʊˈmeɪnɪə

Graecomaniac
BR ˌgriːkəʊˈmeɪnɪak,
ˌgrʌɪkəʊˈmeɪnɪak,
ˌgrɛkəʊˈmeɪnɪak, -s
AM ˌgrɛkoʊˈmeɪniˌæk,
-s

Graecophile
BR ˈgriːkəʊfʌɪl,
ˈgrʌɪkəʊfʌɪl,
ˈgrɛkəʊfʌɪl, -z
AM ˈgrɛkoʊˌfaɪl, -z

Graeco-Roman
BR ˌgriːkəʊˈrəʊmən,
ˌgrʌɪkəʊˈrəʊmən,
ˌgrɛkəʊˈrəʊmən
AM ˌgrɛkoʊˈroʊmən

Graeme
BR ˈgreɪəm
AM ˈgreɪəm

Graf
BR grɑːf, graf

AM grɑːf, græf

graffiti
BR grəˈfiːt|i, -ɪd
AM grəˈfidi, -d

graffitist
BR grəˈfiːtɪst, -s
AM grəˈfidɪst, -s

graffito
BR grəˈfiːtəʊ
AM grəˈfidoʊ

graft
BR grɑːft, graft, -s, -ɪŋ, -ɪd
AM græft, -s, -ɪŋ, -əd

grafter
BR ˈgrɑːftə(r), ˈgraftə(r), -z
AM ˈgræftər, -z

Grafton
BR ˈgrɑːft(ə)n, ˈgraft(ə)n
AM ˈgræftən

graham
BR ˈgreɪəm, -z
AM græm, ˈgreɪəm, -z

Grahame
BR ˈgreɪəm
AM ˈgreɪəm

Grahamstown
BR ˈgreɪəmztaʊn
AM ˈgreɪəmzˌtaʊn

Graig
BR grʌɪg
AM graɪg, greɪg

Grail
BR greɪl
AM greɪl

grail
BR greɪl, -z
AM greɪl, -z

grain
BR greɪn, -z
AM greɪn, -z

grainer
BR ˈgreɪnə(r), -z
AM ˈgreɪnər, -z

grainfield
BR ˈgreɪnfiːld, -z
AM ˈgreɪnˌfild, -z

Grainger
BR ˈgreɪn(d)ʒə(r)
AM ˈgreɪndʒər

grainily
BR ˈgreɪnɪli
AM ˈgreɪnɪli

graininess
BR ˈgreɪnɪnɪs
AM ˈgreɪnɪnɪs

grainless
BR ˈgreɪnlɪs
AM ˈgreɪnlɪs

grainy
BR ˈgreɪn|i, -iə(r), -ɪɪst
AM ˈgreɪni, -ər, -ɪst

grallatorial
BR ˌgraləˈtɔːrɪəl
AM ˈgræləˈtɔrɪəl

gram
BR gram, -z
AM græm, -z

graminaceous
BR ˌgramɪˈneɪʃəs
AM ˌgræməˈneɪʃəs

gramineous
BR grəˈmɪnɪəs
AM grəˈmɪnɪəs

graminivorous
BR ˌgramɪˈnɪv(ə)rəs
AM ˌgræməˈnɪvərəs

grammalogue
BR ˈgramalɒg, -z
AM ˈgræməˌlag, ˈgræməˌlɔg, -z

grammar
BR ˈgramə(r), -z
AM ˈgræmər, -z

grammarian
BR grəˈmɛːrɪən, -z
AM grəˈmɛrɪən, -z

grammarless
BR ˈgramələs
AM ˈgræmərləs

grammatical
BR grəˈmatɪkl
AM grəˈmædəkəl

grammaticality
BR grəˌmatrˈkalɪti
AM grəˌmædəˈkælədi

grammatically
BR grəˈmatɪkli
AM grəˈmædək(ə)li

grammaticalness
BR grəˈmatɪklnəs
AM grəˈmædəkəlnəs

grammaticise
BR grəˈmatɪsʌɪz, -ɪz, -ɪŋ, -d
AM grəˈmædəˌsaɪz, -ɪz, -ɪŋ, -d

grammaticize
BR grəˈmatɪsʌɪz, -ɪz, -ɪŋ, -d
AM grəˈmædəˌsaɪz, -ɪz, -ɪŋ, -d

gramme
BR gram, -z
AM græm, -z

Grammy
BR ˈgram|i, -ɪz
AM ˈgræmi, -z

gramophone
BR ˈgraməfəʊn, -z
AM ˈgræməˌfoʊn, -z

gramophonic
BR ˌgraməˈfɒnɪk
AM ˌgræməˈfɑnɪk

Grampian
BR ˈgrampɪən, -z
AM ˈgræmpɪən, -z

grampus
BR ˈgrampəs, -ɪz
AM ˈgræmpəs, -əz

Gramsci
BR ˈgramʃi

AM ˈgræmʃi

gran
BR gran, -z
AM græn, -z

Granada
BR grəˈnɑːdə(r)
AM grəˈnadə

granadilla
BR ˌgranəˈdɪlə(r), -z
AM ˌgrænəˈdɪlə, -z

Granados
BR grəˈnɑːdɒs
AM grəˈnadəs

granary
BR ˈgran(ə)r|i, -ɪz
AM ˈgreɪn(ə)ri, ˈgræn(ə)ri, -z

Gran Canaria
BR ˌgran kəˈnɛːrɪə(r)
AM ˌgræn kəˈnɛrɪə

Gran Chaco
BR ˌgran ˈtʃɑːkəʊ, + ˈtʃakəʊ
AM ˌgran ˈtʃakoʊ

grand
BR grand, -ə(r), -ɪst
AM grænd, -ər, -əst

grandad
BR ˈgrandad, -z
AM ˈgrænˌdæd, -z

grandam
BR ˈgrandam, -z
AM ˈgrænˌdæm, ˈgrændəm, -z

grandame
BR ˈgrandeɪm, -z
AM ˈgrænˌdeɪm, ˈgrændəm, -z

grandchild
BR ˈgran(d)tʃʌɪld
AM ˈgræn(d)tʃaɪld

grandchildren
BR ˈgran(d)ˌtʃɪldr(ə)n
AM ˈgræn(d)ˌtʃɪldrən

Grand Coulee
BR ˌgran(d) ˈkuːli
AM ˌgræn(d) ˈkuli

granddad
BR ˈgrandad, -z
AM ˈgrænˌdæd, -z

granddaddy
BR ˈgranˌdad|i, -ɪz
AM ˈgrænˌdædi, -z

granddaughter
BR ˈgranˌdɔːtə(r), -z
AM ˈgrænˌdɔdər, ˈgrænˌdɑdər, -z

grandee
BR granˈdiː, -z
AM grænˈdi, -z

grandeur
BR ˈgran(d)ʒə(r), ˈgrandjʊə(r)
AM ˈgrændʒər, ˈgrænd(j)ʊr

grandfather
BR ˈgran(d)ˌfɑːðə(r), -z

grandmaster
AM ˈgræm ʃi

grandfatherly
BR ˈgran(d)ˌfɑːðəli
AM ˈgræn(d)ˌfɑðərli

Grand Guignol
BR ˌgrɒn ˈgiːnjɒl, ˌgrɒ̃ +
AM ˈgræn(d) ˈginjɔl

grandiflora
BR ˌgrandɪˈflɔːrə(r)
AM ˈgrændəˌflɔrə

grandiloquence
BR granˈdɪləkw(ə)ns
AM grænˈdɪləkwəns

grandiloquent
BR granˈdɪləkw(ə)nt
AM grænˈdɪləkwənt

grandiloquently
BR granˈdɪləkw(ə)ntli
AM grænˈdɪləkwən(t)li

grandiose
BR ˈgrandɪəʊs, ˈgrandɪəʊz
AM ˈgrændiˌoʊs, ˌgrændiˈoʊs, ˈgrændiˌoʊz, ˌgrændiˈoʊz

grandiosely
BR ˈgrandɪəʊsli, ˈgrandɪəʊzli
AM ˈgrændiˌoʊsli, ˌgrændiˈoʊsli, ˈgrændiˌoʊzli, ˌgrændiˈoʊzli

grandiosity
BR ˌgrandɪˈɒsɪti
AM ˌgrændiˈɑsədi

Grandison
BR ˈgrandɪs(ə)n
AM ˈgrændəsən

Grandisonian
BR ˌgrandɪˈsəʊnɪən
AM ˌgrændəˈsoʊnɪən

grandly
BR ˈgrandli
AM ˈgræn(d)li

grandma
BR ˈgran(d)mɑː(r), -z
AM ˈgræn(d)ˌmɑ, ˈgræ(m)ˌmɑ, -z

grand mal
BR ˌgrɒn ˈmal, ˌgrɒ̃ +
AM ˈgræn(d) ˈmal

grandmama
BR ˈgran(d)məˌmɑː(r), -z
AM ˈgræn(d)ˌmɑmə, ˈgræn(d)məˌmɑ, -z

grandmamma
BR ˈgran(d)məˌmɑː(r), -z
AM ˈgræn(d)ˌmɑmə, ˈgræn(d)məˌmɑ, -z

grandmaster
BR ˈgran(d)ˌmɑːstə(r), ˌgran(d)ˈmɑstə(r), AM -z
ˌgræn(d)ˈmæstər, -z

grandmother
BR 'gran(d)ˌmʌðə(r),
-z
AM 'græn(d)ˌməðər, -z
grandmotherly
BR 'gran(d)ˌmʌðəli
AM 'græn(d)ˌməðərli
grandness
BR 'gran(d)nəs
AM 'græn(d)nəs
grandpa
BR 'gran(d)pɑː(r),
'grampɑː(r), -z
AM 'græn(d)ˌpɑ,
'græm,pɑ, -z
grandpapa
BR 'gran(d)pəˌpɑː(r),
-z
AM 'græn(d)ˌpɑpə,
'græn(d)pəˌpɑ, -z
grandparent
BR 'gran(d)ˌpɛːrənt,
'gran(d)ˌpɛːrn̩t, -s
AM 'græn(d)ˌpɛrənt, -s
Grand Prix
BR ˌgrɒ̃ 'priː
AM ˌgrɑn 'pri,
ˌgræn(d) +
grandsire
BR 'gran(d)saɪə(r), -z
AM 'græn(d)ˌsaɪ(ə)r, -z
grandson
BR 'gran(d)sʌn, -z
AM 'græn(d)ˌsən, -z
Grands Prix
BR ˌgrɒ̃ 'priː(z)
AM ˌgrɑn 'pri,
ˌgræn(d) +
grandstand
BR 'gran(d)stand, -z
AM 'græn(d)ˌstænd, -z
granduncle
BR 'grandˌʌŋkl
AM 'grænd,əŋkəl
grange
BR greɪn(d)ʒ, -ɪz
AM greɪndʒ, -ɪz
Grangemouth
BR 'greɪn(d)ʒmaʊθ
AM 'greɪndʒmaʊθ
graniferous
BR grə'nɪf(ə)rəs,
gra'nɪf(ə)rəs
AM grə'nɪf(ə)rəs
graniform
BR 'granɪfɔːm
AM 'grænəˌfɔ(ə)rm
granita
BR grə'niːtə(r),
gra'niːtə(r)
AM grə'nidə
granite[1]
BR 'granɪt
AM 'grænət
granite[2]
plural of granita
BR grə'niːti, gra'niːti
AM grə'nidi

graniteware
BR 'granɪtwɛː(r)
AM 'grænət,wɛ(ə)r
granitic
BR grə'nɪtɪk, gra'nɪtɪk
AM grə'nɪdɪk
granitoid
BR 'granɪtɔɪd
AM 'grænəˌtɔɪd
granivore
BR 'granɪvɔː(r), -z
AM 'grænəˌvɔ(ə)r, -z
granivorous
BR grə'nɪv(ə)rəs,
gra'nɪv(ə)rəs
AM grə'nɪv(ə)rəs
granma
BR 'granmɑː(r), -z
AM 'græn,mɑ,
'græ(m),mɑ, -z
grannie
BR 'gran|i, -ɪz
AM 'græni, -z
granny
BR 'gran|i, -ɪz
AM 'græni, -z
granola
BR grə'nəʊlə(r),
gra'nəʊlə(r)
AM grə'noʊlə
granolithic
BR ˌgranə'lɪθɪk
AM ˌgrænə'lɪθɪk
granophyre
BR 'granə(ʊ)faɪə(r)
AM 'grænəˌfaɪ(ə)r
granpa
BR 'granpɑː(r),
'grampɑː(r), -z
AM 'græn,pɑ,
'græm,pɑ, -z
grant
BR grɑːnt, grant, -s, -ɪŋ,
-ɪd
AM grænt, -ts, -(t)ɪŋ,
-(t)əd
Granta
BR 'grɑːntə(r),
'grantə(r)
AM 'græn(t)ə
grantable
BR 'grɑːntəbl,
'grantəbl
AM 'græn(t)əbəl
Grantchester
BR 'grɑːntʃɪstə(r),
'grantʃɪstə(r)
AM 'græn,(t)ʃestər
grantee
BR (ˌ)grɑː'niː,
(ˌ)gran'tiː, -z
AM græn'ti, -z
granter
BR 'grɑːntə(r),
'grantə(r), -z
AM 'græn(t)ər, -z
Granth
BR grʌnt

AM grɒnt
Grantha
BR 'grʌntə(r)
AM 'grən(t)ə
Grantham
BR 'granθəm
AM 'grænθəm
Grantley
BR 'grɑːntli, 'grantli
AM 'græn(t)li
grantor
BR (ˌ)grɑː'ntɔː(r),
(ˌ)gran'tɔː(r),
'grɑːntə(r),
'grantə(r), -z
AM græn'tɔ(ə)r, -z
grantsmanship
BR 'grɑːntsmənˌʃɪp,
'grantsmənʃɪp
AM 'græn(t)smənˌʃɪp
gran turismo
BR ˌgran tʊə'rɪzməʊ,
+ tʊ'rɪzməʊ,
+ tɔː'rɪzməʊ, -z
AM ˌgræn tʊ'rɪzmoʊ, -z
granular
BR 'granjʊlə(r)
AM 'grænjələr
granularity
BR ˌgranjʊ'larɪti
AM ˌgrænjə'lɛrədi
granularly
BR 'granjʊləli
AM 'grænjələrli
granulate
BR 'granjʊleɪt, -s, -ɪŋ,
-ɪd
AM 'grænjəˌleɪ|t, -ts,
-dɪŋ, -dɪd
granulation
BR ˌgranjʊ'leɪʃn
AM ˌgrænjə'leɪʃən
granulator
BR 'granjʊleɪtə(r), -z
AM 'grænjəˌleɪdər, -z
granule
BR 'granjuːl, -z
AM 'grænˌjul, -z
granulocyte
BR 'granjʊləsaɪt, -s
AM 'grænjələˌsaɪt, -s
granulocytic
BR ˌgranjʊlə'sɪtɪk
AM ˌgrænjələ'sɪdɪk
granulometric
BR ˌgranjʊlə'mɛtrɪk
AM ˌgrænjələ'mɛtrɪk
Granville
BR 'granv(ɪ)l
AM 'græn,vɪl
grape
BR greɪp, -s
AM greɪp, -s
grapefruit
BR 'greɪpfruːt, -s
AM 'greɪp,frut, -s

grapery
BR 'greɪp(ə)r|i, -ɪz
AM 'greɪpəri, -z
grapeseed
BR 'greɪpsiːd
AM 'greɪp,sid
grapeshot
BR 'greɪpʃɒt
AM 'greɪp,ʃat
grapevine
BR 'greɪpvʌɪn, -z
AM 'greɪp,vaɪn, -z
grapey
BR 'greɪp|i, -ɪə(r), -ɪɪst
AM 'greɪpi, -ər, -ɪst
graph
BR grɑːf, graf, -s
AM græf, -s
graphematic
BR ˌgrafə'matɪk
AM ˌgræfə'mædɪk
grapheme
BR 'grafiːm, -z
AM 'græfim, -z
graphemic
BR gra'fiːmɪk,
grə'fiːmɪk, -s
AM grə'fimɪk, -s
graphemically
BR gra'fiːmɪkli,
grə'fiːmɪkli
AM grə'fimək(ə)li
graphic
BR 'grafɪk, -s
AM 'græfɪk, -s
graphicacy
BR 'grafɪkəsi
AM 'græfəkəsi
graphical
BR 'grafɪkl
AM 'græfəkəl
graphically
BR 'grafɪkli
AM 'græfək(ə)li
graphicness
BR 'grafɪknɪs
AM 'græfɪknɪs
graphite
BR 'grafʌɪt
AM 'græ,faɪt
graphitic
BR grə'fɪtɪk, gra'fɪtɪk
AM grə'fɪdɪk
graphitise
BR 'grafɪtʌɪz, -ɪz, -ɪŋ, -d
AM 'græfəˌtaɪz, -ɪz, -ɪŋ,
-d
graphitize
BR 'grafɪtʌɪz, -ɪz, -ɪŋ, -d
AM 'græfəˌtaɪz, -ɪz, -ɪŋ,
-d
graphological
BR ˌgrafə'lɒdʒɪkl
AM ˌgræfə'lɑdʒəkəl
graphologist
BR grə'fɒlədʒɪst,
gra'fɒlədʒɪst, -s

AM grə'fɑlədʒəst, -s
graphology
BR grə'fɒlədʒi,
gra'fɒlədʒi
AM grə'fɑlədʒi
grapnel
BR 'græpnl, -z
AM 'græpnəl, -z
grappa
BR 'græpə(r)
AM 'grɑpə
Grappelli
BR grə'pɛli
AM grə'pɛli
grapple
BR 'græp|l, -lz,
-|ɪŋ\-lɪŋ, -ld
AM 'græp|əl, -əlz,
-(ə)lɪŋ, -əld
grappler
BR 'græp|ə(r),
'græplə(r), -z
AM 'græp(ə)lər, -z
graptolite
BR 'græptəlʌɪt, -s
AM 'græptəˌlaɪt, -s
grapy
BR 'greɪp|i, -ɪə(r), -ɪɪst
AM 'greɪpi, -ər, -ɪst
Grasmere
BR 'grasmɪə(r),
'grɑːsmɪə(r)
AM 'græsˌmɪ(ə)r
grasp
BR grɑːsp, grasp, -s, -ɪŋ,
-t
AM græsp, -s, -ɪŋ, -t
graspable
BR 'grɑːspəbl,
'graspəbl
AM 'græspəbəl
grasper
BR 'grɑːspə(r),
'graspə(r), -z
AM 'græspər, -z
graspingly
BR 'grɑːspɪŋli,
'graspɪŋli
AM 'græspɪŋli
graspingness
BR 'grɑːspɪŋnɪs,
'graspɪŋnɪs
AM 'græspɪŋnɪs
grass
BR grɑːs, gras, -ɪz
AM græs, -əz
grasscloth
BR 'grɑːsklɒ|θ,
'grasklɒ|θ, -θs\-ðz
AM 'græsˌklɔ|θ,
'græsˌklɑ|θ, -θs\-ðz
Grasse
BR grɑːs
AM grɑs
grasshopper
BR 'grɑːsˌhɒpə(r),
'grasˌhɒpə(r), -z
AM 'græsˌ(h)ɑpər, -z

grassiness
BR 'grɑːsɪnɪs,
'grasɪnɪs
AM 'græsɪnɪs
Grassington
BR 'grasɪŋt(ə)n,
'grɑːsɪŋt(ə)n
AM 'græsɪŋt(ə)n
grassland
BR 'grɑːsland,
'grasland, -z
AM 'græsˌlænd, -z
grassless
BR 'grɑːsləs, 'grasləs
AM 'græsləs
grasslike
BR 'grɑːslʌɪk,
'graslʌɪk
AM 'græsˌlaɪk
grassy
BR 'grɑːs|i, 'gras|i,
-ɪə(r), -ɪɪst
AM 'græsi, -ər, -ɪst
grate
BR greɪt, -s, -ɪŋ, -ɪd
AM greɪ|t, -ts, -dɪŋ, -dɪd
grateful
BR 'greɪtf(ʊ)l
AM 'greɪtfəl
gratefully
BR 'greɪtfəli, 'greɪtfli
AM 'greɪtfəli
gratefulness
BR 'greɪtf(ʊ)lnəs
AM 'greɪtfəlnəs
grater
BR 'greɪtə(r), -z
AM 'greɪdər, -z
graticule
BR 'gratɪkjuːl, -z
AM 'grædəˌkjul, -z
gratification
BR ˌgratɪfɪ'keɪ|n
AM ˌgrædəfə'keɪʃən
gratifier
BR 'gratɪfʌɪə(r), -z
AM 'grædəˌfaɪ(ə)r, -z
gratify
BR 'gratɪfʌɪ, -z, -ɪŋ, -d
AM 'grædəˌfaɪ, -z, -ɪŋ, -d
gratifyingly
BR 'gratɪfʌɪɪŋli
AM 'grædəˌfaɪɪŋli
gratin
BR 'gratã, 'grataŋ, -z
AM 'gratn, 'grætn,
grə'tan, -z
gratiné
BR 'gratɪneɪ, -z
AM ˌgrætn'eɪ, -z
gratinée
BR 'gratɪneɪ, -z
AM ˌgrætn'eɪ, -z
grating
BR 'greɪtɪŋ, -z
AM 'greɪdɪŋ, -z

gratingly
BR 'greɪtɪŋli
AM 'greɪdɪŋli
gratis
BR 'gratɪs, 'grɑːtɪs,
'greɪtɪs
AM 'grædəs
gratitude
BR 'gratɪtjuːd,
'gratɪtʃuːd
AM 'grædəˌt(j)ud
Grattan
BR 'gratn
AM 'grætn
Gratton
BR 'gratn
AM 'grætn
gratuitous
BR grə'tjuːɪtəs,
grə'tʃuːɪtəs
AM grə't(j)uədəs
gratuitously
BR grə'tjuːɪtəsli,
grə'tʃuːɪtəsli
AM grə't(j)uədəsli
gratuitousness
BR grə'tjuːɪtəsnəs,
grə'tʃuːɪtəsnəs
AM grə't(j)uədəsnəs
gratuity
BR grə'tjuːɪt|i,
grə'tʃuːɪt|i, -ɪz
AM grə't(j)uədi, -z
gratulatory
BR 'gratjʊlət(ə)ri,
'gratʃʊlət(ə)ri
AM 'grætʃələˌtɔri
graunch
BR grɔːn(t)ʃ, -ɪz, -ɪŋ, -t
AM grɑntʃ, grantʃ, -əz,
-ɪŋ, -t
gravadlax
BR 'gravɛdlaks
AM 'gravədˌlaks
gravamen
BR grə'veɪmɛn,
grə'veɪmən,
grə'vɑːmən,
'gravəmɛn,
'gravəmən, -z
AM grə'veɪmən,
grə'vaman,
'gravəmən,
'grævəmən, -z
gravamina
BR grə'veɪmɪnə(r),
grə'vɑːmɪnə(r)
AM grə'vamənə,
grə'vɑmənə
grave¹
accent
BR grɑːv, -z
AM grɑv, greɪv, -z
grave²
burial place
BR greɪv, -z
AM greɪv, -z

grave³
adjective
BR greɪv, -ə(r), -ɪst
AM greɪv, -ər, -əst
gravedigger
BR 'greɪvˌdɪɡə(r), -z
AM 'greɪvˌdɪɡər, -z
gravel
BR 'gravl, -d
AM 'grævəl, -d
graveless
BR 'greɪvlɪs
AM 'greɪvlɪs
gravelly
BR 'gravlɪ
AM 'grævəli
gravely
BR 'greɪvli
AM 'greɪvli
graven
BR 'greɪvn
AM 'greɪvən
graveness
BR 'greɪvnɪs
AM 'greɪvnɪs
Graveney
BR 'greɪvni
AM 'greɪvni
graver
BR 'greɪvə(r), -z
AM 'greɪvər, -z
Graves¹
surname
BR greɪvz
AM greɪvz
Graves²
wine
BR grɑːv
AM grɑv
Gravesend
BR ˌgreɪvz'ɛnd
AM ˌgreɪvz'ɛnd
graveside
BR 'greɪvsʌɪd
AM 'greɪvˌsaɪd
gravestone
BR 'greɪvstəʊn, -z
AM 'greɪvˌstoʊn, -z
Gravettian
BR grə'vɛtiən
AM grə'vɛdiən
graveward
BR 'greɪvwəd
AM 'greɪvwərd
graveyard
BR 'greɪvjɑːd, -z
AM 'greɪvˌjard, -z
gravid
BR 'gravɪd
AM 'grævəd
gravimeter
BR grə'vɪmɪtə(r), -z
AM grə'vɪmədər,
græ'vɪmədər, -z
gravimetric
BR ˌgravɪ'mɛtrɪk
AM ˌgrævə'mɛtrɪk

gravimetry
BR grəˈvɪmɪtri
AM grəˈvɪmətri,
græˈvɪmətri

gravitas
BR ˈɡravɪtas,
ˈɡravɪtɑːs
AM ˈɡrævəˌtɑs

gravitate
BR ˈɡravɪteɪt, -s, -ɪŋ, -ɪd
AM ˈɡrævəˌteɪt, -ts,
-dɪŋ, -dɪd

gravitation
BR ˌɡravɪˈteɪʃn
AM ˌɡrævəˈteɪʃən

gravitational
BR ˌɡravɪˈteɪʃn(ə)l,
ˌɡravɪˈteɪʃən(ə)l
AM ˌɡrævəˈteɪʃ(ə)nəl

gravitationally
BR ˌɡravɪˈteɪʃnəli,
ˌɡravɪˈteɪʃn̩li,
ˌɡravɪˈteɪʃənli,
ˌɡravɪˈteɪʃ(ə)nəli
AM ˌɡrævəˈteɪʃ(ə)nəli

graviton
BR ˈɡravɪtɒn, -z
AM ˈɡrævəˌtɑn, -z

gravity
BR ˈɡravɪti
AM ˈɡrævədi

gravlax
BR ˈɡravlaks
AM ˈɡrɑvˌlaks

gravure
BR ɡrəˈvjʊə(r),
ɡrəˈvjɔː(r)
AM ɡrəˈvjʊ(ə)r

gravy
BR ˈɡreɪvi
AM ˈɡreɪvi

gray
BR ɡreɪ, -z, -ɪŋ, -d, -ə(r),
-ɪst
AM ɡreɪ, -z, -ɪŋ, -d, -ər,
-ɪst

graybeard
BR ˈɡreɪbɪəd, -z
AM ˈɡreɪˌbɪ(ə)rd, -z

grayish
BR ˈɡreɪɪʃ
AM ˈɡreɪɪʃ

grayling
BR ˈɡreɪlɪŋ, -z
AM ˈɡreɪlɪŋ, -z

Grayson
BR ˈɡreɪsn
AM ˈɡreɪsən

graywacke
BR ˈɡreɪˌwakə(r)
AM ˈɡreɪˌwækə

Graz
BR ɡrɑːts
AM ɡrɑts

graze
BR ɡreɪz, -ɪz, -ɪŋ, -d
AM ɡreɪz, -ɪz, -ɪŋ, -d

grazer
BR ˈɡreɪzə(r), -z
AM ˈɡreɪzər, -z

grazier
BR ˈɡreɪzɪə(r), -z
AM ˈɡreɪzɪər, ˈɡreɪʒər,
-z

graziery
BR ˈɡreɪzɪər|i, -ɪz
AM ˈɡreɪzɪəri,
ˈɡreɪʒəri, -z

grease¹
noun
BR ɡriːs, -ɪz
AM ɡris, -ɪz

grease²
verb
BR ɡriː|s, ɡriː|z,
-sɪz\-zɪz, -sɪŋ\-zɪŋ,
-st\-zd
AM ɡri|s, ɡri|z,
-sɪz\-zɪz, -sɪŋ\-zɪŋ,
-st\-zd

greaseless
BR ˈɡriːslɪs
AM ˈɡrislɪs

greasepaint
BR ˈɡriːspeɪnt
AM ˈɡrisˌpeɪnt

greaseproof
BR ˈɡriːspruːf
AM ˈɡrisˌpruf

greaser
BR ˈɡriːsə(r),
ˈɡriːzə(r), -z
AM ˈɡrisər, ˈɡrizər, -z

greasily
BR ˈɡriːsɪli, ˈɡriːzɪli
AM ˈɡrisɪli, ˈɡrizɪli

greasiness
BR ˈɡriːsɪnɪs, ˈɡriːzɪnɪs
AM ˈɡrisɪnɪs, ˈɡrizɪnɪs

greasy
BR ˈɡriːs|i, ˈɡriːz|i,
-ɪə(r), -ɪɪst
AM ˈɡrisi, ˈɡrizi, -ər, -ɪst

great
BR ɡreɪt, -ə(r), -ɪst
AM ɡreɪ|t, -dər, -dɪst

greatcoat
BR ˈɡreɪtkəʊt, -s
AM ˈɡreɪtˌkoʊt, -s

greatness
BR ˈɡreɪtnɪs
AM ˈɡreɪtnɪs

greave
BR ɡriːv, -z, -ɪŋ, -d
AM ɡriv, -z, -ɪŋ, -d

Greaves
BR ɡriːvz
AM ɡrivz

grebe
BR ɡriːb, -z
AM ɡrib, -z

grebo
BR ˈɡriːbəʊ, -z
AM ˈɡreɪˌboʊ, -z

Grecian
BR ˈɡriːʃn
AM ˈɡriʃən

Grecise
BR ˈɡriːsʌɪz, -ɪz, -ɪŋ, -d
AM ˈɡriˌsaɪz, -ɪz, -ɪŋ, -d

Grecism
BR ˈɡriːsɪz(ə)m, -z
AM ˈɡriˌsɪzəm, -z

Grecize
BR ˈɡriːsʌɪz, -ɪz, -ɪŋ, -d
AM ˈɡriˌsaɪz, -ɪz, -ɪŋ, -d

Greco-
BR ˈɡriːkəʊ, ˈɡrɛkəʊ
AM ˈɡrɛkoʊ

Grecomania
BR ˈɡriːkəʊˌmeɪnɪə(r),
ˈɡrɛkəʊˌmeɪnɪə(r)
AM ˌɡrɛkoʊˈmeɪnɪə

Grecomaniac
BR ˌɡriːkəʊˈmeɪnɪak,
ˌɡrɛkəʊˈmeɪnɪak, -s
AM ˌɡrɛkoʊˈmeɪnɪˌæk,
-s

Grecophile
BR ˈɡriːkəʊfʌɪl,
ˈɡrɛkəʊfʌɪl, -z
AM ˈɡriːkəʊˌfaɪl, -z

Greece
BR ɡriːs
AM ɡris

greed
BR ɡriːd
AM ɡrid

greedily
BR ˈɡriːdɪli
AM ˈɡridɪli

greediness
BR ˈɡriːdɪnɪs
AM ˈɡridɪnɪs

greedy
BR ˈɡriːd|i, -ɪə(r), -ɪɪst
AM ˈɡridi, -ər, -ɪst

greegree
BR ˈɡriːɡriː, -z
AM ˈɡriˌɡri, -z

Greek
BR ɡriːk, -s
AM ɡrik, -s

Greekness
BR ˈɡriːknɪs
AM ˈɡriknɪs

Greeley
BR ˈɡriːli
AM ˈɡrili

Greely
BR ˈɡriːli
AM ˈɡrili

green
BR ɡriːn, -z, -ɪŋ, -ə(r),
-ɪst
AM ɡrin, -z, -ɪŋ, -ər, -ɪst

Greenaway
BR ˈɡriːnəweɪ
AM ˈɡrinəˌweɪ

greenback
BR ˈɡriːnbak, -s

Grecian
AM ˈɡrinˌbæk, -s

Greenbaum
BR ˈɡriːnbaʊm
AM ˈɡrinˌbɑm

Green Beret
BR ˌɡriːn ˈbɛreɪ, -z
AM ˌɡrin bəˈreɪ, -z

greenbottle
BR ˈɡriːnˌbɒtl, -z
AM ˈɡrinˌbɑdəl, -z

greenbrier
BR ˈɡriːnˌbrʌɪə(r)
AM ˈɡrinˌbraɪ(ə)r

Greene
BR ɡriːn
AM ɡrin

greenery
BR ˈɡriːn(ə)ri
AM ˈɡrinəri

greenfeed
BR ˈɡriːnfiːd
AM ˈɡrinˌfid

Greenfield
BR ˈɡriːnfiːld
AM ˈɡrinˌfild

greenfinch
BR ˈɡriːnfɪn(t)ʃ, -ɪz
AM ˈɡrinˌfɪn(t)ʃ, -ɪz

greenfly
BR ˈɡriːnflʌɪ, -z
AM ˈɡrinˌflaɪ, -z

greengage
BR ˈɡriːnɡeɪdʒ, -ɪz
AM ˈɡrinˌɡeɪdʒ, -ɪz

greengrocer
BR ˈɡriːnˌɡrəʊsə(r), -z
AM ˈɡrinˌɡroʊsər, -z

greengrocery
BR ˈɡriːnˌɡrəʊs(ə)r|i,
-ɪz
AM ˈɡrinˌɡroʊs(ə)ri, -z

Greengross
BR ˈɡriːnɡrɒs
AM ˈɡrinˌɡrɒs,
ˈɡrinˌɡrɑs

Greenhalgh
BR ˈɡriːnhalʃ,
ˈɡriːnhɔːlʃ,
ˈɡriːnhɒlʃ,
ˈɡriːnhaldʒ
AM ˈɡrin(h)ælʃ

Greenham
BR ˈɡriːnəm
AM ˈɡrinəm

greenhead
BR ˈɡriːnhɛd, -z
AM ˈɡrin(h)ɛd, -z

greenheart
BR ˈɡriːnhɑːt, -s
AM ˈɡrin(h)ɑrt, -s

greenhide
BR ˈɡriːnhʌɪd, -z
AM ˈɡrin(h)aɪd, -z

greenhorn
BR ˈɡriːnhɔːn, -z
AM ˈɡrin(h)ɔ(ə)rn, -z

Greenhough
BR ˈgriːn(h)ɒf,
ˈgriːn(h)ʌf, ˈgriːnhəʊ,
ˈgriːnhaʊ
AM ˈgriːn(h)əf
greenhouse
BR ˈgriːnhaʊs, -zɪz
AM ˈgriːn(h)aʊs, -zəz
greening
BR ˈgriːnɪŋ, -z
AM ˈgriːnɪŋ, -z
greenish
BR ˈgriːnɪʃ
AM ˈgriːnɪʃ
greenishness
BR ˈgriːnɪʃnɪs
AM ˈgriːnɪʃnɪs
greenkeeper
BR ˈgriːnˌkiːpə(r), -z
AM ˈgriːnˌkiːpər, -z
greenkeeping
BR ˈgriːnˌkiːpɪŋ
AM ˈgriːnˌkiːpɪŋ
Greenland
BR ˈgriːnlənd
AM ˈgriːnlənd
Greenlander
BR ˈgriːnləndə(r), -z
AM ˈgriːnləndər, -z
greenlet
BR ˈgriːnlɪt, -s
AM ˈgriːnlət, -s
greenly
BR ˈgriːnli
AM ˈgriːnli
greenmail
BR ˈgriːnmeɪl
AM ˈgriːnˌmeɪl
greenmailer
BR ˈgriːnˌmeɪlə(r), -z
AM ˈgriːnˌmeɪlər, -z
greenness
BR ˈgriːnnɪs
AM ˈgri(n)nɪs
Greenock
BR ˈgriːnək
AM ˈgriːnək
Greenough
BR ˈgriːnəʊ
AM ˈgriːnoʊ
Greenpeace
BR ˈgriːnpiːs
AM ˈgriːnˌpis
greenroom
BR ˈgriːnruːm,
ˈgriːnrʊm, -z
AM ˈgriːnˌrum,
ˈgriːnˌrʊm, -z
greensand
BR ˈgriːnsand, -z
AM ˈgriːnˌsænd, -z
greenshank
BR ˈgriːnʃaŋk, -s
AM ˈgriːnˌʃæŋk, -s
greensick
BR ˈgriːnsɪk
AM ˈgriːnˌsɪk

greensickness
BR ˈgriːnˌsɪknɪs
AM ˈgriːnˌsɪknɪs
greenskeeper
BR ˈgriːnzˌkiːpə(r), -z
AM ˈgriːnzˌkipər, -z
Greenslade
BR ˈgriːnsleɪd
AM ˈgriːnˌsleɪd
Greensleeves
BR ˈgriːnsliːvz
AM ˈgriːnˌslivz
greenstick
BR ˈgriːnstɪk
AM ˈgriːnˌstɪk
greenstone
BR ˈgriːnstəʊn
AM ˈgriːnˌstoʊn
Greenstreet
BR ˈgriːnstriːt
AM ˈgriːnˌstrit
greenstuff
BR ˈgriːnstʌf
AM ˈgriːnˌstəf
greensward
BR ˈgriːnswɔːd
AM ˈgriːnˌswɔː(ə)rd,
ˈgriːnˌswɑrd
greenweed
BR ˈgriːnwiːd, -z
AM ˈgriːnˌwid, -z
Greenwell
BR ˈgriːnw(ɛ)l
AM ˈgriːnˌwɛl
Greenwich
BR ˈgrɛnɪtʃ, ˈgrɪnɪtʃ,
ˈgrɛnɪdʒ, ˈgrɪnɪdʒ
AM ˈgrɛnɪtʃ
greenwood
BR ˈgriːnwʊd, -z
AM ˈgriːnˌwʊd, -z
greeny
BR ˈgriːni
AM ˈgrini
greenyard
BR ˈgriːnjɑːd, -z
AM ˈgriːnˌjɑrd, -z
Greer
BR grɪə(r)
AM grɪ(ə)r
greet
BR griːt, -s, -ɪŋ, -ɪd
AM grit, -ts, -dɪŋ, -dɪd
greeter
BR ˈgriːtə(r), -z
AM ˈgridər, -z
greeting
BR ˈgriːtɪŋ, -z
AM ˈgridɪŋ, -z
greffier
BR ˈgrɛfɪə(r), -z
AM ˈgrɛfiˌeɪ, -z
Greg
BR grɛg
AM grɛg
gregarious
BR grɪˈgɛːrɪəs

AM grəˈgɛːrɪəs
gregariously
BR grɪˈgɛːrɪəsli
AM grəˈgɛːrɪəsli
gregariousness
BR grɪˈgɛːrɪəsnəs
AM grəˈgɛːrɪəsnəs
Gregg
BR grɛg
AM grɛg
Gregor
BR ˈgrɛgə(r)
AM ˈgrɛgər
Gregorian
BR grɪˈgɔːrɪən
AM grəˈgɔːrɪən
Gregory
BR ˈgrɛg(ə)ri
AM ˈgrɛg(ə)ri
Gregson
BR ˈgrɛgsn
AM ˈgrɛgsən
Greig
BR grɛg
AM grɛg
greisen
BR ˈgrʌɪzn
AM ˈgraɪzn
gremial
BR ˈgriːmɪəl, -z
AM ˈgrimɪəl, -z
gremlin
BR ˈgrɛmlɪn, -z
AM ˈgrɛmlən, -z
Grenada
BR grɪˈneɪdə(r)
AM grəˈneɪdə
grenade
BR grɪˈneɪd, -z
AM grəˈneɪd, -z
Grenadian
BR grɪˈneɪdɪən, -z
AM grəˈneɪdɪən, -z
grenadier
BR ˌgrɛnəˈdɪə(r), -z
AM ˌgrɛnəˈdɪ(ə)r, -z
grenadilla
BR ˌgrɛnəˈdɪlə(r), -z
AM ˌgrɛnəˈdɪlə, -z
grenadine
BR ˈgrɛnədiːn,
ˌgrɛnəˈdiːn, -z
AM ˈgrɛnəˌdin, -z
Grendel
BR ˈgrɛndl
AM ˈgrɛndəl
Grendon
BR ˈgrɛnd(ə)n
AM ˈgrɛnd(ə)n
Grenfell
BR ˈgrɛnf(ɛ)l
AM ˈgrɛnˌfɛl
Grenoble
BR grɪˈnəʊbl
AM grəˈnoʊbəl
FR grənɔbl

Grenville
BR ˈgrɛnv(ɪ)l
AM ˈgrɛnvəl
Grepo
BR ˈgrɛpəʊ, -z
AM ˈgrɛˌpoʊ, -z
Gresham
BR ˈgrɛʃəm
AM ˈgrɛʃəm
gressorial
BR grɛˈsɔːrɪəl
AM grɛˈsɔːrɪəl
Greta
BR ˈgrɛtə(r), ˈgriːtə(r)
AM ˈgrɛdə
Gretel
BR ˈgrɛtl
AM ˈgrɛdəl
Gretna Green
BR ˌgrɛtnə ˈgriːn
AM ˌgrɛtnə ˈgrin
Gretzky
BR ˈgrɛtski
AM ˈgrɛtski
Greville
BR ˈgrɛv(ɪ)l
AM ˈgrɛvɨl
grew
BR gruː
AM gru
grey
BR greɪ, -z, -ɪŋ, -d, -ə(r),
-ɪst
AM greɪ, -z, -ɪŋ, -d, -ər,
-ɪst
greybeard
BR ˈgreɪbɪəd, -z
AM ˈgreɪˌbɪ(ə)rd, -z
Greyfriars
BR ˈgreɪfrʌɪəz
AM ˈgreɪˌfraɪ(ə)rz
greyhen
BR ˈgreɪhɛn, -z
AM ˈgreɪˌ(h)ɛn, -z
greyhound
BR ˈgreɪhaʊnd, -z
AM ˈgreɪˌ(h)aʊnd, -z
greyish
BR ˈgreɪɪʃ
AM ˈgreɪɪʃ
greylag
BR ˈgreɪlag, -z
AM ˈgreɪˌlæg, -z
greyly
BR ˈgreɪli
AM ˈgreɪli
greyness
BR ˈgreɪnɪs
AM ˈgreɪnɪs
Greystoke
BR ˈgreɪstəʊk
AM ˈgreɪˌstoʊk
greywacke
BR ˈgreɪˌwakə(r)
AM ˈgreɪˌwækə
Gribble
BR ˈgrɪbl

AM ˈɡrɪbəl
gricer
BR ˈɡrʌɪsə(r), -z
AM ˈɡraɪsər, -z
grid
BR ɡrɪd, -z, -ɪd
AM ɡrɪd, -z, -ɪd
griddle
BR ˈɡrɪdl, -z
AM ˈɡrɪdəl, -z
griddlecake
BR ˈɡrɪdlkeɪk, -s
AM ˈɡrɪdl̩keɪk, -s
gridiron
BR ˈɡrɪdˌʌɪən, -z
AM ˈɡrɪdˌaɪ(ə)rn, -z
gridlock
BR ˈɡrɪdlɒk, -s, -t
AM ˈɡrɪdˌlɑk, -s, -t
grief
BR ɡriːf, -s
AM ɡriːf, -s
Grieg
BR ɡriːɡ
AM ɡriːɡ
Grier
BR ɡrɪə(r)
AM ɡrɪ(ə)r
Grierson
BR ˈɡrɪəsn
AM ˈɡrɪrsən
grievance
BR ˈɡriːvns, -ɪz
AM ˈɡriːvəns, -əz
grieve
BR ɡriːv, -z, -ɪŋ, -d
AM ɡriːv, -z, -ɪŋ, -d
griever
BR ˈɡriːvə(r), -z
AM ˈɡriːvər, -z
grievous
BR ˈɡriːvəs
AM ˈɡriːvəs
grievously
BR ˈɡriːvəsli
AM ˈɡriːvəsli
grievousness
BR ˈɡriːvəsnəs
AM ˈɡriːvəsnəs
griff
BR ɡrɪf, -s
AM ɡrɪf, -s
griffe
BR ɡrɪf, -s
AM ɡrɪf, -s
griffin
BR ˈɡrɪf(ɪ)n, -z
AM ˈɡrɪfən, -z
Griffith
BR ˈɡrɪfɪθ
AM ˈɡrɪfɪθ
Griffiths
BR ˈɡrɪfɪθs
AM ˈɡrɪfɪθs
griffon
BR ˈɡrɪfn, -z
AM ˈɡrɪfən, -z

grift
BR ɡrɪft
AM ɡrɪft
grifter
BR ˈɡrɪftə(r), -z
AM ˈɡrɪftər, -z
grig
BR ɡrɪɡ, -z
AM ɡrɪɡ, -z
Griggs
BR ɡrɪɡz
AM ɡrɪɡz
Grignard
BR ˈɡriːnjɑː(r)
AM ˈɡrinˌjɑrd
Grigson
BR ˈɡrɪɡsn
AM ˈɡrɪɡsən
grike
BR ɡrʌɪk, -s
AM ɡraɪk, -s
grill
BR ɡrɪl, -z, -ɪŋ, -d
AM ɡrɪl, -z, -ɪŋ, -d
grillade
BR ɡrɪˈleɪd, ɡrɪˈjɑːd,
ˈɡriːɑːd, -z
AM ɡrəˈlad, ɡriˈjɑd, -z
grillage
BR ˈɡrɪl|ɪdʒ, -ɪdʒɪz
AM ˈɡrɪlɪdʒ, ɡrəˈlɑʒ, -əz
grille
BR ɡrɪl, -z
AM ɡrɪl, -z
griller
BR ˈɡrɪlə(r), -z
AM ˈɡrɪlər, -z
grilling
BR ˈɡrɪlɪŋ, -z
AM ˈɡrɪlɪŋ, -z
grillroom
BR ˈɡrɪlruːm, ˈɡrɪlrʊm,
-z
AM ˈɡrɪlˌrum,
ˈɡrɪlˌrʊm, -z
grillwork
BR ˈɡrɪlwəːk
AM ˈɡrɪlˌwərk
grilse
BR ɡrɪls
AM ɡrɪls
grim
BR ɡrɪm, -ə(r), -ɪst
AM ɡrɪm, -ər, -ɪst
grimace
BR ˈɡrɪməs, ɡrɪˈmeɪs,
-ɪz, -ɪŋ, -t
AM ˈɡrɪməs, ɡrəˈmeɪs,
-ɪz, -ɪŋ, -t
grimacer
BR ˈɡrɪməsə(r),
ɡrɪˈmeɪsə(r), -z
AM ˈɡrɪməsər,
ɡrəˈmeɪsər, -z
Grimaldi
BR ɡrɪˈmɔːldi,
ɡrɪˈmɒldi

AM ɡrəˈmɔːldi,
ɡrəˈmɒldi
grimalkin
BR ɡrɪˈmalkɪn,
ɡrɪˈmɔːlkɪn, -z
AM ɡrəˈmalkən, -z
grime
BR ɡrʌɪm, -z, -ɪŋ, -d
AM ɡraɪm, -z, -ɪŋ, -d
Grimes
BR ɡrʌɪmz
AM ɡraɪmz
Grimethorpe
BR ˈɡrʌɪmθɔːp
AM ˈɡraɪmˌθɔ(ə)rp
grimily
BR ˈɡrʌɪmɪli
AM ˈɡraɪmɪli
griminess
BR ˈɡrʌɪmɪnɪs
AM ˈɡraɪmɪnɪs
grimly
BR ˈɡrɪmli
AM ˈɡrɪmli
Grimm
BR ɡrɪm
AM ɡrɪm
grimness
BR ˈɡrɪmnɪs
AM ˈɡrɪmnɪs
Grimond
BR ˈɡrɪmənd
AM ˈɡrɪmənd
Grimsby
BR ˈɡrɪmzbi
AM ˈɡrɪmzbi
Grimshaw
BR ˈɡrɪmʃɔː(r)
AM ˈɡrɪmˌʃɔ
grimy
BR ˈɡrʌɪm|i, -ɪə(r), -ɪst
AM ˈɡraɪmi, -ər, -ɪst
grin
BR ɡrɪn, -z, -ɪŋ, -d
AM ɡrɪn, -z, -ɪŋ, -d
grind
BR ɡrʌɪnd, -z, -ɪŋ
AM ɡraɪnd, -z, -ɪŋ
grinder
BR ˈɡrʌɪndə(r), -z
AM ˈɡraɪndər, -z
grindingly
BR ˈɡrʌɪndɪŋli
AM ˈɡraɪndɪŋli
grindstone
BR ˈɡrʌɪn(d)stəʊn, -z
AM ˈɡraɪn(d)ˌstoʊn, -z
gringo
BR ˈɡrɪŋɡəʊ, -z
AM ˈɡrɪŋɡoʊ, -z
grinner
BR ˈɡrɪnə(r), -z
AM ˈɡrɪnər, -z
grinningly
BR ˈɡrɪnɪŋli
AM ˈɡrɪnɪŋli

Grinstead
BR ˈɡrɪnstɛd, ˈɡrɪnstrɪd
AM ˈɡrɪnˌstɛd
grip
BR ɡrɪp, -s, -ɪŋ, -t
AM ɡrɪp, -s, -ɪŋ, -t
gripe
BR ɡrʌɪp, -s, -ɪŋ, -t
AM ɡraɪp, -s, -ɪŋ, -t
griper
BR ˈɡrʌɪpə(r), -z
AM ˈɡraɪpər, -z
gripingly
BR ˈɡrʌɪpɪŋli
AM ˈɡraɪpɪŋli
grippe
BR ɡrɪp, ɡriːp
AM ɡrɪp
gripper
BR ˈɡrɪpə(r), -z
AM ˈɡrɪpər, -z
grippingly
BR ˈɡrɪpɪŋli
AM ˈɡrɪpɪŋli
grippy
BR ˈɡrɪp|i, -ɪə(r), -ɪst
AM ˈɡrɪpi, -ər, -ɪst
Griqua
BR ˈɡriːk(w)ə(r)
AM ˈɡrikwə
Griqualand
BR ˈɡriːk(w)əland
AM ˈɡrikwəˌlænd
grisaille
BR ɡrɪˈzeɪl, ɡrɪˈzʌɪ(l)
AM ɡrəˈzaɪ, ɡrəˈzeɪl
Griselda
BR ɡrɪˈzɛldə(r)
AM ɡrəˈzɛldə
griseofulvin
BR ˌɡrɪzɪə(ʊ)ˈfʊlvɪn
AM ˌɡrɪzioʊˈfʊlvən
grisette
BR ɡrɪˈzɛt, -s
AM ɡrəˈzɛt, -s
Grisewood
BR ˈɡrʌɪzwʊd
AM ˈɡraɪzˌwʊd
griskin
BR ˈɡrɪskɪn, -z
AM ˈɡrɪskɪn, -z
grisliness
BR ˈɡrɪzlɪnɪs
AM ˈɡrɪzlɪnɪs
grisly
BR ˈɡrɪzl|i, -ɪə(r), -ɪst
AM ˈɡrɪzli, -ər, -ɪst
grison
BR ˈɡrɪzn, ˈɡrʌɪsn
AM ˈɡrɪzn
grissini
BR ɡrɪˈsiːni
AM ɡrəˈsini
grist
BR ɡrɪst
AM ɡrɪst

gristle
BR ˈɡrɪsl
AM ˈɡrɪsəl

gristly
BR ˈɡrɪsl̩i, ˈɡrɪsl̩i,
-ɪə(r), -ɪst
AM ˈɡrɪs(ə)li, -ər, -ɪst

gristmill
BR ˈɡrɪs(t)mɪl, -z
AM ˈɡrɪs(t)ˌmɪl, -z

Griswold
BR ˈɡrɪzwld,
ˈɡrɪzwəʊld
AM ˈɡrɪzˌwɒld,
ˈɡrɪzˌwɑld

grit
BR ɡrɪt, -s
AM ɡrɪt, -s

gritstone
BR ˈɡrɪtstəʊn, -z
AM ˈɡrɪtˌstoʊn, -z

gritter
BR ˈɡrɪtə(r), -z
AM ˈɡrɪdər, -z

grittily
BR ˈɡrɪtɪli
AM ˈɡrɪdɪli

grittiness
BR ˈɡrɪtɪnɪs
AM ˈɡrɪdɪnɪs

gritty
BR ˈɡrɪtl̩i, -ɪə(r), -ɪst
AM ˈɡrɪdi, -ər, -ɪst

Grizedale
BR ɡrʌɪzdeɪl
AM ˈɡraɪzˌdeɪl

grizzle
BR ˈɡrɪzl̩l, -lz, -l̩ɪŋ\-lɪŋ,
-ld
AM ˈɡrɪzǝl, -ǝlz, -(ǝ)lɪŋ,
-ǝld

grizzler
BR ˈɡrɪzlǝ(r), -z
AM ˈɡrɪz(ǝ)lǝr, -z

grizzly
BR ˈɡrɪzl̩i, -ɪz, -ɪǝ(r),
-ɪst
AM ˈɡrɪzli, -z, -ǝr, -ɪst

groan
BR ɡrǝʊn, -z, -ɪŋ, -d
AM ɡroʊn, -z, -ɪŋ, -d

groaner
BR ˈɡrǝʊnǝ(r), -z
AM ˈɡroʊnǝr, -z

groaningly
BR ˈɡrǝʊnɪŋli
AM ˈɡroʊnɪŋli

groat
BR ɡrǝʊt, -s
AM ɡroʊt, -s

Gro-bag®
BR ˈɡrǝʊbaɡ, -z
AM ˈɡroʊˌbæɡ, -z

Grobian
BR ˈɡrǝʊbɪǝn
AM ˈɡroʊbɪǝn

grocer
BR ˈɡrǝʊsǝ(r), -z
AM ˈɡroʊsǝr, -z

grocery
BR ˈɡrǝʊs(ǝ)r|i, -ɪz
AM ˈɡroʊs(ǝ)ri, -z

grockle
BR ˈɡrɒkl, -z
AM ˈɡrɑkǝl, -z

Grocott
BR ˈɡrǝʊkɒt
AM ˈɡroʊˌkɑt

Grodno
BR ˈɡrɒdnǝʊ
AM ˈɡrɑdˌnoʊ

grog
BR ɡrɒɡ
AM ɡrɑɡ

Grogan
BR ˈɡrǝʊɡ(ǝ)n
AM ˈɡroʊɡǝn

groggily
BR ˈɡrɒɡɪli
AM ˈɡraɡǝli

grogginess
BR ˈɡrɒɡɪnɪs
AM ˈɡraɡɪnɪs

groggy
BR ˈɡrɒɡ|i, -ɪǝ(r), -ɪst
AM ˈɡraɡi, -ǝr, -ɪst

grogram
BR ˈɡrɒɡrǝm
AM ˈɡraɡrǝm

groin
BR ɡrɔɪn, -z
AM ɡrɔɪn, -z

Grolier
BR ˈɡrǝʊlɪǝ(r)
AM ˈɡroʊliǝr

grommet
BR ˈɡrɒmɪt, ˈɡrʌmɪt, -s
AM ˈɡramǝt, -s

gromwell
BR ˈɡrɒmw(ɛ)l, -z
AM ˈɡramwǝl, -z

Gromyko
BR ɡrǝˈmiːkǝʊ
AM ɡrǝˈmikoʊ
RUS ɡraˈmɨkǝ

Groningen
BR ˈɡrǝʊnɪŋǝn,
ˈɡrɒnɪŋǝn
AM ˈɡroʊnɪŋǝn
DU ˈxronɪŋǝ(n)

groom
BR ɡruːm, -z, -ɪŋ, -d
AM ɡrum, -z, -ɪŋ, -d

groomsman
BR ˈɡruːmzmǝn
AM ˈɡrumzmǝn

groomsmen
BR ˈɡruːmzmǝn
AM ˈɡrumzmǝn

groove
BR ɡruːv, -z, -ɪŋ, -d
AM ɡruv, -z, -ɪŋ, -d

groover
BR ˈɡruːvǝ(r), -z
AM ˈɡruvǝr, -z

groovily
BR ˈɡruːvɪli
AM ˈɡruvǝli

grooviness
BR ˈɡruːvɪnɪs
AM ˈɡruvɪnɪs

groovy
BR ˈɡruːv|i, -ɪǝ(r), -ɪst
AM ˈɡruvi, -ǝr, -ɪst

grope
BR ɡrǝʊp, -s, -ɪŋ, -t
AM ɡroʊp, -s, -ɪŋ, -t

groper
BR ˈɡrǝʊpǝ(r), -z
AM ˈɡroʊpǝr, -z

gropingly
BR ˈɡrǝʊpɪŋli
AM ˈɡroʊpɪŋli

Gropius
BR ˈɡrǝʊpɪǝs
AM ˈɡroʊpɪǝs

grosbeak
BR ˈɡrǝʊsbiːk,
ˈɡrɒsbiːk, -s
AM ˈɡroʊsˌbik, -s

groschen
BR ˈɡrǝʊʃn, ˈɡrɒʃn
AM ˈɡroʊʃǝn

grosgrain
BR ˈɡrǝʊɡreɪn
AM ˈɡroʊˌɡreɪn

Grosmont¹
in Monmouthshire,
UK
BR ˈɡrɒsm(ǝ)nt,
ˈɡrǝʊsm(ǝ)nt,
ˈɡrɒsmɒnt,
ˈɡrǝʊsmɒnt
AM ˈɡroʊsˌmant

Grosmont²
in Yorkshire, UK
BR ˈɡrǝʊ(s)m(ǝ)nt,
ˈɡrǝʊ(s)mɒnt
AM ˈɡroʊsˌmant

gros point
BR ˌɡrǝʊ ˈpɔɪnt
AM ˌɡroʊ ˌpɔɪnt

gross
BR ɡrǝʊs, -ɪz, -ɪŋ, -t,
-ǝ(r), -ɪst
AM ɡroʊs, -ǝz, -ɪŋ, -t, -ǝr,
-ǝst

Grosseteste
BR ˈɡrǝʊstɛst,
ˈɡrǝʊsteɪt
AM ˈɡroʊsˌtɛst

grossly
BR ˈɡrǝʊsli
AM ˈɡroʊsli

Grossmith
BR ˈɡrǝʊsmɪθ
AM ˈɡroʊˌsmɪθ

grossness
BR ˈɡrǝʊsnǝs
AM ˈɡroʊsnǝs

Grosvenor
BR ˈɡrǝʊvnǝ(r),
ˈɡrǝʊvnǝ(r)
AM ˈɡroʊvnǝr

Grosz
BR ɡrǝʊs
AM ɡroʊs

grot
BR ɡrɒt, -s
AM ɡrɑt, -s

grotesque
BR ɡrǝ(ʊ)ˈtɛsk
AM ɡroʊˈtɛsk, ɡrǝˈtɛsk

grotesquely
BR ɡrǝ(ʊ)ˈtɛskli
AM ɡroʊˈtɛskli,
ɡrǝˈtɛskli

grotesqueness
BR ɡrǝ(ʊ)ˈtɛsknǝs
AM ɡroʊˈtɛsknǝs,
ɡrǝˈtɛsknǝs

grotesquerie
BR ɡrǝ(ʊ)ˈtɛsk(ǝ)r|i,
-ɪz
AM ɡroʊˈtɛskǝri, -z

grotesquery
BR ɡrǝ(ʊ)ˈtɛsk(ǝ)r|i,
-ɪz
AM ɡroʊˈtɛskǝri, -z

Grotius
BR ˈɡrǝʊtɪǝs
AM ˈɡroʊʃ(i)ǝs

grottily
BR ˈɡrɒtɪli
AM ˈɡradǝli

grottiness
BR ˈɡrɒtɪnɪs
AM ˈɡradɪnɪs

grotto
BR ˈɡrɒtǝʊ, -z
AM ˈɡradoʊ, -z

grotty
BR ˈɡrɒt|i, -ɪǝ(r), -ɪst
AM ˈɡradi, -ǝr, -ɪst

grouch
BR ɡraʊtʃ, -ɪz, -ɪŋ, -t
AM ɡraʊtʃ, -ǝz, -ɪŋ, -t

grouchily
BR ˈɡraʊtʃɪli
AM ˈɡraʊtʃǝli

grouchiness
BR ˈɡraʊtʃɪnɪs
AM ˈɡraʊtʃɪnɪs

Groucho
BR ˈɡraʊtʃǝʊ
AM ˈɡraʊtʃoʊ

grouchy
BR ˈɡraʊtʃ|i, -ɪǝ(r),
-ɪst
AM ˈɡraʊtʃi, -ǝr, -ɪst

ground
BR ɡraʊnd, -z, -ɪŋ, -ɪd
AM ɡraʊnd, -z, -ɪŋ, -ǝd

groundage
BR ˈɡraʊndɪdʒ
AM ˈɡraʊndɪdʒ

groundbait
BR 'graʊn(d)beɪt, -s
AM 'graʊn(d)ˌbeɪt, -s

grounder
BR 'graʊndə(r), -z
AM 'graʊndər, -z

groundhog
BR 'graʊndhɒg, -z
AM 'graʊn(d)ˌ(h)ɔg,
'graʊn(d)ˌ(h)ɑg, -z

grounding
BR 'graʊndɪŋ, -z
AM 'graʊndɪŋ, -z

groundless
BR 'graʊndləs
AM 'graʊn(d)ləs

groundlessly
BR 'graʊndləsli
AM 'graʊn(d)ləsli

groundlessness
BR 'graʊndləsnəs
AM 'graʊn(d)ləsnəs

groundling
BR 'graʊndlɪŋ, -z
AM 'graʊn(d)lɪŋ, -z

groundnut
BR 'graʊn(d)nʌt, -s
AM 'graʊn(d)ˌnət, -s

groundout
BR 'graʊndaʊt, -s
AM 'graʊnˌdaʊt, -s

grounds
BR graʊn(d)z
AM graʊn(d)z

groundsel
BR 'graʊn(d)sl
AM 'graʊn(d)səl

groundsheet
BR 'graʊn(d)ʃiːt, -s
AM 'graʊn(d)ˌʃit, -s

groundsman
BR 'graʊn(d)zmən
AM 'graʊn(d)zmən

groundsmen
BR 'graʊn(d)zmən
AM 'graʊn(d)zmən,
'graʊn(d)zˌmɛn

groundswell
BR 'graʊn(d)swɛl
AM 'graʊn(d)ˌswɛl

groundwater
BR 'graʊndˌwɔːtə(r), -z
AM 'graʊn(d)ˌwɔdər,
'graʊn(d)ˌwɑdər, -z

groundwork
BR 'graʊndwɜːk
AM 'graʊn(d)ˌwɜrk

group
BR gruːp, -s, -ɪŋ, -t
AM grup, -s, -ɪŋ, -t

groupage
BR 'gruːpɪdʒ
AM 'grupɪdʒ

grouper
BR 'gruːpə(r), -z
AM 'grupər, -z

groupie
BR 'gruːpˌi, -ɪz
AM 'grupi, -z

grouping
BR 'gruːpɪŋ, -z
AM 'grupɪŋ, -z

groupware
BR 'gruːpwɛː(r)
AM 'grupˌwɛ(ə)r

grouse
BR graʊs, -ɪz, -ɪŋ, -t
AM graʊs, -əz, -ɪŋ, -t

grouser
BR 'graʊsə(r), -z
AM 'graʊsər, -z

grout
BR graʊt, -s, -ɪŋ, -ɪd
AM graʊ|t, -ts, -dɪŋ,
-dəd

grouter
BR 'graʊtə(r), -z
AM 'graʊdər, -z

grove
BR grəʊv, -z
AM groʊv, -z

grovel
BR 'grɒv|l, -lz,
-lɪŋ \-lɪŋ, -ld
AM 'grav|əl, 'grəv|əl,
-əlz, -(ə)lɪŋ, -əld

groveler
BR 'grɒvlə(r),
'grɒvlə(r), -z
AM 'grav(ə)lər,
'grəv(ə)lər, -z

grovelingly
BR 'grɒvlɪŋli,
'grɒvlɪŋli
AM 'grav(ə)lɪŋli

groveller
BR 'grɒvlə(r),
'grɒvlə(r), -z
AM 'grav(ə)lər,
'grəv(ə)lər, -z

grovellingly
BR 'grɒvlɪŋli,
'grɒvlɪŋli
AM 'grav(ə)lɪŋli

Grover
BR 'grəʊvə(r)
AM 'groʊvər

Groves
BR grəʊvz
AM groʊvz

grovy
BR 'grəʊvi
AM 'groʊvi

grow
BR grəʊ, -z, -ɪŋ
AM groʊ, -z, -ɪŋ

growable
BR 'grəʊəbl
AM 'groʊəbəl

growbag
BR 'grəʊbag, -z
AM 'groʊˌbæg, -z

grower
BR 'grəʊə(r), -z

AM 'groʊər, -z

growl
BR graʊl, -z, -ɪŋ, -d
AM graʊl, -z, -ɪŋ, -d

growler
BR 'graʊlə(r), -z
AM 'graʊlər, -z

growlingly
BR 'graʊlɪŋli
AM 'graʊlɪŋli

Growmore
BR 'grəʊmɔː(r)
AM 'groʊˌmɔ(ə)r

grown
BR grəʊn
AM groʊn

grownup
noun
BR 'grəʊnʌp, -s
AM 'groʊˌnəp, -s

grown-up
adjective
BR ˌgrəʊnˈʌp
AM 'groʊˌnəp

growth
BR grəʊθ, -s
AM groʊθ, -s

groyne
BR grɔɪn, -z
AM grɔɪn, -z

Grozny
BR 'grɒzni
AM 'grɔzni, 'grɑzni

grub
BR grʌb, -z, -ɪŋ, -d
AM grəb, -z, -ɪŋ, -d

grubber
BR 'grʌbə(r), -z
AM 'grəbər, -z

grubbily
BR 'grʌbɪli
AM 'grəbəli

grubbiness
BR 'grʌbɪnɪs
AM 'grəbɪnɪs

grubby
BR 'grʌb|i, -ɪə(r), -ɪɪst
AM 'grəbi, -ər, -ɪst

grubstake
BR 'grʌbsteɪk, -s
AM 'grəbˌsteɪk, -s

grubstaker
BR 'grʌbsteɪkə(r), -z
AM 'grəbˌsteɪkər, -z

grudge
BR grʌdʒ, -ɪz, -ɪŋ, -d
AM grədʒ, -əz, -ɪŋ, -d

grudger
BR 'grʌdʒə(r), -z
AM 'grədʒər, -z

grudgingly
BR 'grʌdʒɪŋli
AM 'grədʒɪŋli

grudgingness
BR 'grʌdʒɪŋnɪs
AM 'grədʒɪŋnɪs

AM 'groʊər, -z

gruel
BR 'gruːəl
AM 'gru(ə)l

grueling
BR 'gruːəlɪŋ
AM 'gru(ə)lɪŋ

gruelingly
BR 'gruːəlɪŋli
AM 'gru(ə)lɪŋli

gruelling
BR 'gruːəlɪŋ
AM 'gru(ə)lɪŋ

gruellingly
BR 'gruːəlɪŋli
AM 'gru(ə)lɪŋli

gruesome
BR 'gruːs(ə)m
AM 'grusəm

gruesomely
BR 'gruːs(ə)mli
AM 'grusəmli

gruesomeness
BR 'gruːs(ə)mnəs
AM 'grusəmnəs

gruff
BR grʌf, -ə(r), -ɪst
AM grəf, -ər, -əst

gruffly
BR 'grʌfli
AM 'grəfli

gruffness
BR 'grʌfnəs
AM 'grəfnəs

Gruffydd
BR 'grɪfɪð
AM 'grɪfɪθ

grumble
BR 'grʌmbl, -z, -ɪŋ, -d
AM 'grəmb|əl, -əlz,
-(ə)lɪŋ, -əld

grumbler
BR 'grʌmblə(r), -z
AM 'grəmb(ə)lər, -z

grumbling
BR 'grʌmblɪŋ, -z
AM 'grəmb(ə)lɪŋ, -z

grumblingly
BR 'grʌmblɪŋli
AM 'grəmb(ə)lɪŋli

grumbly
BR 'grʌmbli
AM 'grəmb(ə)li

grummet
BR 'grʌmɪt, -s
AM 'grəmət, -s

grumous
BR 'gruːməs
AM 'grəməs

grump
BR grʌm|p, -(p)s
AM grəm|p, -(p)s

grumpily
BR 'grʌmpɪli
AM 'grəmpəli

grumpiness
BR 'grʌmpɪnɪs
AM 'grəmpɪnɪs

grumpish
BR 'grʌmpɪʃ
AM 'grəmpɪʃ

grumpishly
BR 'grʌmpɪʃli
AM 'grəmpɪʃli

grumpy
BR 'grʌmp|i, -ɪə(r),
-ɪɪst
AM 'grəmpi, -ər, -ɪst

Grundig
BR 'grʌndɪg, 'grʊndɪg
AM 'grəndɪg

Grundy
BR 'grʌnd|i, -ɪz
AM 'grəndi, -z

Grundyism
BR 'grʌndɪɪz(ə)m
AM 'grəndi,ɪzəm

grunge
BR grʌn(d)ʒ
AM grəndʒ

grungy
BR 'grʌn(d)ʒi
AM 'grəndʒi

grunion
BR 'grʌnjən
AM 'grənjən

grunt
BR grʌnt, -s, -ɪŋ, -ɪd
AM grən|t, -ts, -(t)ɪŋ,
-(t)əd

grunter
BR 'grʌntə(r), -z
AM 'grən(t)ər, -z

Grunth
BR grʌnt
AM grənθ

Gruyère
BR 'gru:jɛ:(r),
grʊ'jɛ:(r)
AM gru'jɛ(ə)r

Gruyères
BR 'gru:jɛ:(r),
grʊ'jɛ:(r)
AM gru'jɛ(ə)r(z)

gryphon
BR 'grɪfn, -z
AM 'grɪfən, -z

grysbok
BR 'grʌɪsbɒk,
'xreɪsbɒk, -s
AM 'greɪs,bak,
'graɪs,bak, -s

guacamole
BR ,gwɑ:kə'məʊli
AM ,gwɑkə'moʊli

guacharo
BR 'gwɑ:tʃərəʊ, -z
AM 'gwɑtʃə,roʊ, -z

Guadalajara
BR ,gwɑ:dələ'hɑ:rə(r)
AM ,gwɑdələ'hɑrə

Guadalcanál
BR ,gwɑ:dlkə'nal
AM ,gwɑdəlkə'næl

Guadaloupe
BR ,gwɑ:də'lu:p
AM ,gwɑdə'lup

Guadaloupian
BR ,gwɑ:də'lu:piən, -z
AM ,gwɑdə'lupiən, -z

Guadalquivír
BR ,gwɑ:dlkwɪ'vɪə(r),
,gwɑ:dl'kwɪvə(r)
AM ,gwɑdl'k(w)ɪvər

Guadeloupe
BR ,gwɑ:də'lu:p
AM ,gwɑdə'lup

Guadeloupian
BR ,gwɑ:də'lu:pɪən, -z
AM ,gwɑdə'lupiən, -z

guaiac
BR 'g(w)ʌɪak,
'g(w)ʌɪək, -s
AM 'g(w)aɪ,æk,
'g(w)aɪək, -s

guaiacum
BR 'g(w)ʌɪəkəm, -z
AM 'g(w)aɪəkəm, -z

Guam
BR gwɑ:m
AM gwɑm

guan
BR gwɑ:n, -z
AM gwɑn, -z

guanaco
BR 'gwɑ:nəkəʊ, -z
AM gwə'nakoʊ, -z

Guangdong
BR 'gwaŋ'dɒŋ
AM 'gwaŋ'dɒŋ,
'gwaŋ'daŋ

guanine
BR 'gwɑ:ni:n,
'gu:əni:n
AM 'gwɑ,nin, 'gwanən

guano
BR 'gwɑ:nəʊ
AM 'gwanoʊ

Guantánamo
BR gwan'tanəməʊ,
gwɑ:n'tanəməʊ
AM gwan'tanəmoʊ

guar
BR gwɑ:(r), 'gu:ɑ:(r)
AM gwɑr

Guarani
BR ,gwɑ:rə'ni:,
'gwɑ:rəni, 'gwɑ:rɲi, -z
AM 'gwɑrə'ni, -z

guarantee
BR ,garən'ti:, ,garɲ'ti:,
-z, -ɪŋ, -d
AM ,gɛrən'ti, -z, -ɪŋ, -d

guarantor
BR ,garən'tɔ:(r),
,garɲ'tɔ:(r), -z
AM ,gɛ(ə)rən'tɔ(ə)r, -z

guaranty
BR 'garənt|i, 'garɲt|i,
-ɪz
AM 'gɛrənti, -z

guard
BR gɑ:d, -z, -ɪŋ, -ɪd
AM gɑrd, -z, -ɪŋ, -əd

guardant
BR 'gɑ:dnt
AM 'gɑrdənt

guardedly
BR 'gɑ:dɪdli
AM 'gɑrdədli

guardedness
BR 'gɑ:dɪdnɪs
AM 'gɑrdədnəs

guardee
BR ,gɑ:'di:, -z
AM ,gɑr'di, -z

guarder
BR 'gɑ:də(r), -z
AM 'gɑrdər, -z

guardhouse
BR 'gɑ:dhaʊ|s, -zɪz
AM 'gɑrd,(h)aʊ|s, -zəz

Guardi
BR 'gwɑ:di
AM 'gɑrdi

guardian
BR 'gɑ:dɪən, -z
AM 'gɑrdiən, -z

guardianship
BR 'gɑ:dɪənʃɪp, -s
AM 'gɑrdiənʃɪp, -s

guardless
BR 'gɑ:dləs
AM 'gɑrdləs

guardrail
BR 'gɑ:dreɪl, -z
AM 'gɑrd,reɪl, -z

guardroom
BR 'gɑ:dru:m,
'gɑ:drɒm, -z
AM 'gɑrd,rum,
'gɑrd,rʊm, -z

guardsman
BR 'gɑ:dzmən
AM 'gɑrdzmən

guardsmen
BR 'gɑ:dzmən
AM 'gɑrdzmən,
'gɑrdz,mɛn

Guarneri
BR gwɑ:'nɛ:ri
AM ,gwɑr'nɛri

Guarnerius
BR gwɑ:'nɪərɪəs,
gwɑ:'nɛ:rɪəs
AM gwɑr'nɛriəs

Guatemala
BR ,gwɑ:tə'mɑ:lə(r),
,gwatə'mɑ:lə(r)
AM ,gwɑdə'mɑlə

Guatemalan
BR ,gwɑ:tə'mɑ:lən,
,gwatə'mɑ:lən, -z
AM ,gwɑdə'mɑlən, -z

guava
BR 'gwɑ:və(r), -z
AM 'gwɑvə, -z

Guayaquil
BR ,gwʌɪə'ki:l
AM ,gaɪə'ki(ə)l

guayule
BR (g)wɑ:'(j)u:l|i, -ɪz
AM (g)wɑ'juli, -z

gubbins
BR 'gʌbɪnz
AM 'gəbənz

gubernatorial
BR ,gu:bənə'tɔ:rɪəl
AM ,gubə(r)nə'tɔriəl

Gucci
BR 'gu:tʃi
AM 'gutʃi

gudgeon
BR 'gʌdʒ(ə)n, -z
AM 'gədʒən, -z

Gudrun
BR 'gʊdrən, 'gʊdru:n
AM 'gʊdrən, 'gudrən

guelder-rose
BR 'gɛldərəʊz,
,gɛldə'rəʊz, -ɪz
AM 'gɛldər,roʊz, -ɪz

Guelph
BR gwɛlf, -s
AM gwɛlf, -s

Guelphic
BR 'gwɛlfɪk
AM 'gwɛlfɪk

Guelphism
BR 'gwɛlfɪz(ə)m
AM 'gwɛl,fɪzəm

guenon
BR gə'nɒn, 'gweɪnɒn,
-z
AM gə'nan, -z

guerdon
BR 'gə:dn, -z
AM 'gərdən, -z

guerilla
BR gə'rɪlə(r),
gɛ'rɪlə(r), -z
AM gə'rɪlə, -z

Guernica
BR 'gə:nɪkə(r),
gə:'ni:kə(r)
AM gɛr,nikə, gɛr'nikə

Guernsey
BR 'gə:nz|i, -ɪz
AM 'gərnzi, -z

Guerrero
BR gɛ'rɛ:rəʊ, gə'rɛ:rəʊ
AM gə'rɛroʊ

guerrilla
BR gə'rɪlə(r),
gɛ'rɪlə(r), -z
AM gə'rɪlə, -z

guess
BR gɛs, -ɪz, -ɪŋ, -t
AM gɛs, -əz, -ɪŋ, -t

guessable
BR 'gɛsəbl
AM 'gɛsəbəl

guesser
BR 'gɛsə(r), -z

AM ˈgɛsər, -z

guesstimate¹
noun
BR ˈgɛstɪmət, -s
AM ˈgɛstəmət, -s

guesstimate²
verb
BR ˈgɛstɪmeɪt, -s, -ɪŋ, -ɪd
AM ˈgɛstəˌmeɪlt, -ts, -dɪŋ, -dɪd

guesswork
BR ˈgɛswɜːk
AM ˈgɛsˌwɜrk

guest
BR gɛst, -s, -ɪŋ, -ɪd
AM gɛst, -s, -ɪŋ, -əd

guesthouse
BR ˈgɛsthaʊ|s, -zɪz
AM ˈgɛst,(h)aʊ|s, -zəz

guestimate¹
noun
BR ˈgɛstɪmət, -s
AM ˈgɛstəmət, -s

guestimate²
verb
BR ˈgɛstɪmeɪt, -s, -ɪŋ, -ɪd
AM ˈgɛstəˌmeɪlt, -ts, -dɪŋ, -dɪd

guestroom
BR ˈgɛstruːm, ˈgɛstrʊm, -z
AM ˈgɛstˌrum, ˈgɛstˌrʊm, -z

guestship
BR ˈgɛstʃɪp
AM ˈgɛs(t)ˌʃɪp

Guevara
BR gɪˈvɑːrə(r), gɛˈvɑːrə(r)
AM gəˈvɑrə

guff
BR gʌf
AM gəf

guffaw
BR gəˈfɔː(r), -z, -ɪŋ, -d
AM gəˈfɔ, gəˈfɑ, -z, -ɪŋ, -d

Guggenheim
BR ˈgʊg(ə)nhʌɪm
AM ˈgʊgənˌ(h)aɪm

guggle
BR ˈgʌg|l, -lz, -lɪŋ \-lɪŋ, -ld
AM ˈgəg|əl, -əlz, -(ə)lɪŋ, -əld

Guiana
BR gʌɪˈɑːnə(r), gɪˈɑːnə(r), gʌɪˈɑnə(r)
AM gɪˈɑnə

Guianese
BR ˌgʌɪəˈniːz
AM ˌgiəˈniz

guidable
BR ˈgʌɪdəbl
AM ˈgaɪdəbəl

guidance
BR ˈgʌɪdns

AM ˈgaɪdns

guide
BR gʌɪd, -z, -ɪŋ, -ɪd
AM gaɪd, -z, -ɪŋ, -ɪd

guidebook
BR ˈgʌɪdbʊk, -s
AM ˈgaɪdˌbʊk, -s

guideline
BR ˈgʌɪdlʌɪn, -z
AM ˈgaɪdˌlaɪn, -z

guidepost
BR ˈgʌɪdpəʊst, -s
AM ˈgaɪdˌpoʊst, -s

Guider
BR ˈgʌɪdə(r), -z
AM ˈgaɪdər, -z

guideway
BR ˈgʌɪdweɪ, -z
AM ˈgaɪdˌweɪ, -z

Guido
BR ˈg(w)iːdəʊ
AM ˈg(w)idoʊ

guidon
BR ˈgʌɪdn, -z
AM ˈgaɪˌdan, ˈgaɪdən, -z

Guignol
BR giːnˈjɒl
AM ginˈjɔl, ginˈjɑl

Guignolesque
BR ˌgiːnjəˈlɛsk
AM ˌginjəˈlɛsk

guild
BR gɪld, -z
AM gɪld, -z

guilder
BR ˈgɪldə(r), -z
AM ˈgɪldər, -z

Guildford
BR ˈgɪl(d)fəd
AM ˈgɪl(d)fərd

guildhall
BR ˈgɪldhɔːl, -z
AM ˈgɪl(d),(h)ɔl, ˈgɪl(d),(h)ɑl, -z

guildsman
BR ˈgɪldzmən
AM ˈgɪl(d)zmən

guildsmen
BR ˈgɪldzmən
AM ˈgɪl(d)zmən

guildswoman
BR ˈgɪldzˌwʊmən
AM ˈgɪl(d)zˌwʊmən

guildswomen
BR ˈgɪldzˌwɪmɪn
AM ˈgɪl(d)zˌwɪmɪn

guile
BR gʌɪl
AM gaɪl

guileful
BR ˈgʌɪlf(ʊ)l
AM ˈgaɪlfəl

guilefully
BR ˈgʌɪlfʊli, ˈgʌɪlflˌi
AM ˈgaɪlfəli

guilefulness
BR ˈgʌɪlf(ʊ)lnəs

AM ˈgaɪlfəlnəs

guileless
BR ˈgʌɪllɪs
AM ˈgaɪ(l)lɪs

guilelessly
BR ˈgʌɪllɪsli
AM ˈgaɪ(l)lɪsli

guilelessness
BR ˈgʌɪllɪsnɪs
AM ˈgaɪ(l)lɪsnɪs

Guillaume
BR ˈgiːəʊm
AM giˈoʊm

guillemot
BR ˈgɪlɪmɒt, -s
AM ˈgɪləˌmɑt, -s

guilloche
BR gɪˈləʊʃ, gɪˈlɒʃ, -ɪz
AM gəˈloʊʃ, gɪˈjoʊʃ, -əz

guillotine
BR ˈgɪləti:n, ˌgɪləˈti:n, ˌgi:jəˈti:n, -z, -ɪŋ, -d
AM ˈgɪləˌtin, ˈgi(j)əˌtin, -z, -ɪŋ, -d

guillotiner
BR ˈgɪlətiˌnə(r), ˌgɪləˈti:nə(r), ˌgi:jəˈti:nə(r), -z
AM ˈgɪləˌtinər, ˈgi(j)əˌtinər, -z

guilt
BR gɪlt
AM gɪlt

guiltily
BR ˈgɪltɪli
AM ˈgɪltɪli

guiltiness
BR ˈgɪltɪnɪs
AM ˈgɪltɪnɪs

guiltless
BR ˈgɪltlɪs
AM ˈgɪltlɪs

guiltlessly
BR ˈgɪltlɪsli
AM ˈgɪltlɪsli

guiltlessness
BR ˈgɪltlɪsnɪs
AM ˈgɪltlɪsnɪs

guilty
BR ˈgɪlt|i, -ɪə(r), -ɪɪst
AM ˈgɪlti, -ər, -ɪst

guimp
BR gɪmp, -s
AM gɪmp, -s

guimpe
BR gɪmp, -s
AM gɪmp, -s

guinea
BR ˈgɪn|i, -ɪz
AM ˈgɪni, -z

Guinea-Bissau
BR ˌgɪnɪbɪˈsaʊ
AM ˌgɪnɪbɪˈsaʊ

Guinean
BR ˈgɪnɪən, -z
AM ˈgɪnɪən, -z

Guinevere
BR ˈgwɪnɪvɪə(r)
AM ˈgwɪnɪˌvɪ(ə)r

Guinness
BR ˈgɪnɪs, -ɪz
AM ˈgɪnɪs, -ɪz

guipure
BR gɪˈpjʊə(r)
AM gɪˈp(j)u(ə)r

guise
BR gʌɪz, -ɪz
AM gaɪz, -ɪz

Guiseley
BR ˈgʌɪzli
AM ˈgaɪzli

guitar
BR gɪˈtɑː(r), -z
AM gəˈtɑr, -z

guitarist
BR gɪˈtɑːrɪst, -s
AM gəˈtɑrəst, -s

guiver
BR ˈgʌɪvə(r)
AM ˈgaɪvər

Gujarat
BR ˌgʊdʒəˈrɑːt, ˌgu:dʒəˈrɑːt
AM ˌgʊdʒəˈrɑt

Gujarati
BR ˌgʊdʒəˈrɑːt|i, ˌgu:dʒəˈrɑːti, -ɪz
AM ˌgʊdʒəˈrɑd|i, -z

Gujerat
BR ˌgʊdʒəˈrɑːt, ˌgu:dʒəˈrɑːt
AM ˌgʊdʒəˈrɑt

Gujerati
BR ˌgʊdʒəˈrɑːt|i, ˌgu:dʒəˈrɑːt|i, -ɪz
AM ˌgʊdʒəˈrɑdi, -z

Gujranwala
BR ˌgʊdʒrənˈwɑːlə(r)
AM ˈgʊdʒrənˈwɑlə

Gujrat
BR ˌgʊdʒ(ə)ˈrɑːt, ˌgu:dʒəˈrɑːt
AM ˌgʊdʒ(ə)ˈrɑt

gulag
BR ˈguːlag, -z
AM ˈguˌlag, -z

gular
BR ˈgjuːlə(r)
AM ˈg(j)ulər

Gulbenkian
BR gʊlˈbɛŋkɪən
AM gʊlˈbɛŋkiən

gulch
BR gʌltʃ, -ɪz
AM gəltʃ, -əz

gulden
BR ˈgʊld(ə)n, -z
AM ˈguldən, ˈgʊldən, -z
DU ˈxəldə(n)

gules
BR gjuːlz
AM gjulz

gulf
BR gʌlf, -s
AM gəlf, -s

gulfweed
BR 'gʌlfwiːd
AM 'gəlf͵wid

gull
BR gʌl, -z, -ɪŋ, -d
AM gəl, -z, -ɪŋ, -d

Gullah
BR 'gʌlə(r)
AM 'gələ

gullery
BR 'gʌl(ə)r|i, -ɪz
AM 'gæləri, -z

gullet
BR 'gʌlɪt, -s
AM 'gələt, -s

gulley
BR 'gʌl|i, -ɪz, -ɪd
AM 'gəli, -z, -d

gullibility
BR ͵gʌlə'bɪlɪti
AM ͵gələ'bɪlɪdi

gullible
BR 'gʌlɪbl
AM 'gələbəl

gullibly
BR 'gʌlɪbli
AM 'gələbli

Gulliver
BR 'gʌlɪvə(r)
AM 'gələvər

gully
BR 'gʌl|i, -ɪz, -ɪd
AM 'gəli, -z, -d

gulp
BR gʌlp, -s, -ɪŋ, -t
AM gəlp, -s, -ɪŋ, -t

gulper
BR 'gʌlpə(r), -z
AM 'gəlpər, -z

gulpingly
BR 'gʌlpɪŋli
AM 'gəlpɪŋli

gulpy
BR 'gʌlpi
AM 'gəlpi

gum
BR gʌm, -z, -ɪŋ, -d
AM gəm, -z, -ɪŋ, -d

gumbo
BR 'gʌmbəʊ, -z
AM 'gəm͵boʊ, -z

gumboil
BR 'gʌmbɔɪl, -z
AM 'gəm͵bɔɪl, -z

gumboot
BR 'gʌmbuːt, -s
AM 'gəm͵but, -s

gumdrop
BR 'gʌmdrɒp, -s
AM 'gəm͵drɑp, -s

gumma
BR 'gʌmə(r), -z
AM 'gəmə, -z

gummatous
BR 'gʌmətəs
AM 'gəmə͵toʊs

Gummer
BR 'gʌmə(r)
AM 'gəmər

Gummidge
BR 'gʌmɪdʒ
AM 'gəmɪdʒ

gummily
BR 'gʌmɪli
AM 'gəməli

gumminess
BR 'gʌmɪnɪs
AM 'gəmɪnɪs

gummy
BR 'gʌmi
AM 'gəmi

gumption
BR 'gʌm(p)ʃn
AM 'gəm(p)ʃən

gumshield
BR 'gʌmʃiːld, -z
AM 'gəm͵ʃild, -z

gumshoe
BR 'gʌmʃuː, -z
AM 'gəm͵ʃu, -z

gun
BR gʌn, -z, -ɪŋ, -d
AM gən, -z, -ɪŋ, -d

gunboat
BR 'gʌnbəʊt, -s
AM 'gən͵boʊt, -s

gundi
BR 'gʌnd|i, -ɪz
AM 'gʊndi, 'gəndi, -z

gundog
BR 'gʌndɒg, -z
AM 'gən͵dɔg, 'gən͵dɑg, -z

gundy
BR 'gʌndi
AM 'gəndi

gunfight
BR 'gʌnfʌɪt, -s
AM 'gən͵faɪt, -s

gunfighter
BR 'gʌn͵fʌɪtə(r), -z
AM 'gən͵faɪdər, -z

gunfire
BR 'gʌn͵fʌɪə(r)
AM 'gən͵faɪ(ə)r

Gunga Din
BR ͵gʌŋgə 'dɪn
AM ͵gəŋgə 'dɪn

gunge
BR gʌn(d)ʒ
AM gəndʒ

gung-ho
BR ͵gʌn'həʊ
AM ͵gən͵'hoʊ

gungy
BR 'gʌn(d)ʒi
AM 'gəndʒi

gunk
BR gʌŋk
AM gəŋk

gunless
BR 'gʌnləs
AM 'gənləs

gunlock
BR 'gʌnlɒk, -s
AM 'gən͵lɑk, -s

gunmaker
BR 'gʌn͵meɪkə(r), -z
AM 'gən͵meɪkər, -z

gunman
BR 'gʌnmən, 'gʌnman
AM 'gənmən

gunmen
BR 'gʌnmən, 'gʌnmɛn
AM 'gənmən, 'gən͵mɛn

gunmetal
BR 'gʌn͵mɛtl
AM 'gən͵mɛdl

Gunn
BR gʌn
AM gən

gunnel
BR 'gʌnl, -z
AM 'gənəl, -z

gunner
BR 'gʌnə(r), -z
AM 'gənər, -z

gunnera
BR 'gʌn(ə)rə(r), -z
AM 'gən(ə)rə, -z

gunnery
BR 'gʌn(ə)ri
AM 'gən(ə)ri

gunny
BR 'gʌn|i, -ɪz
AM 'gəni, -z

gunnysack
BR 'gʌnɪsak, -s
AM 'gəni͵sæk, -s

gunplay
BR 'gʌnpleɪ, -z
AM 'gən͵pleɪ, -z

gunpoint
BR 'gʌnpɔɪnt
AM 'gən͵pɔɪnt

gunpowder
BR 'gʌn͵paʊdə(r)
AM 'gən͵paʊdər

gunpower
BR 'gʌnpaʊə(r)
AM 'gən͵paʊər

gunroom
BR 'gʌnruːm, 'gʌnrʊm, -z
AM 'gən͵rum, 'gən͵rʊm, -z

gunrunner
BR 'gʌn͵rʌnə(r), -z
AM 'gən͵rənər, -z

gunrunning
BR 'gʌn͵rʌnɪŋ
AM 'gən͵rənɪŋ

gunsel
BR 'gʌnsl, -z
AM 'gən(t)səl, -z

gunship
BR 'gʌnʃɪp, -s

AM 'gən͵ʃɪp, -s

gunshot
BR 'gʌnʃɒt, -s
AM 'gən͵ʃɑt, -s

gunshy
BR 'gʌnʃʌɪ
AM 'gən͵ʃaɪ

gunsight
BR 'gʌnsʌɪt, -s
AM 'gən͵saɪt, -s

gunslinger
BR 'gʌn͵slɪŋə(r), -z
AM 'gən͵slɪŋər, -z

gunslinging
BR 'gʌn͵slɪŋɪŋ
AM 'gən͵slɪŋɪŋ

gunsmith
BR 'gʌnsmɪθ, -s
AM 'gən͵smɪθ, -s

gunstock
BR 'gʌnstɒk, -s
AM 'gən͵stɑk, -s

Gunter
BR 'gʌntə(r), 'gʊntə(r)
AM 'gən(t)ər

Gunther
BR 'gʌnθə(r), 'gʊntə(r)
AM 'gənθər, 'gʊn(t)ər

gunwale
BR 'gʌnl, -z
AM 'gənl, -z

gunyah
BR 'gʌnjə(r), -z
AM 'gənjə, -z

Guomindang
BR ͵gwəʊmɪm'daŋ
AM 'gwɔ͵mɪn'dæŋ

guppy
BR 'gʌp|i, -ɪz
AM 'gəpi, -z

Gupta
BR 'gʊptə(r)
AM 'gʊptə

gurdwara
BR 'gəːdwɑːrə(r), gəd'wɑːrə(r), -z
AM 'gərd͵'warə, -z

gurgitation
BR ͵gəːdʒɪ'teɪʃn
AM ͵gərdʒə'teɪʃən

gurgle
BR 'gəːg|l, -lz, -l̩ɪŋ \-lɪŋ, -ld
AM 'gərg|əl, -əlz, -(ə)lɪŋ, -əld

gurgler
BR 'gəːglə(r), 'gəːglə(r), -z
AM 'gərg(ə)lər, -z

gurjun
BR 'gəːdʒ(ə)n, -z
AM 'gərjən, -z

Gurkha
BR 'gəːkə(r), 'gʊəkə(r), -z
AM 'gʊrkə, 'gərkə, -z

Gurkhali
BR ˌgəˈkɑːli
AM ˌgərˈkɑli

gurnard
BR ˈgɜːnəd, -z
AM ˈgɜrnərd, -z

gurnet
BR ˈgɜːnɪt, -s
AM ˈgɜrnət, -s

gurney
BR ˈgɜːn|i, -ɪz
AM ˈgɜrni, -z

guru
BR ˈgʊruː, -z
AM ˈgʊˌru, gəˈru, -z

Gus
BR gʌs
AM gəs

gush
BR gʌʃ, -ɪz, -ɪŋ, -t
AM gəʃ, -əz, -ɪŋ, -t

gusher
BR ˈgʌʃə(r), -z
AM ˈgəʃər, -z

gushily
BR ˈgʌʃɪli
AM ˈgəʃəli

gushiness
BR ˈgʌʃɪnɪs
AM ˈgəʃinɪs

gushing
BR ˈgʌʃɪŋ
AM ˈgəʃɪŋ

gushingly
BR ˈgʌʃɪŋli
AM ˈgəʃɪŋli

gushy
BR ˈgʌʃ|i, -ɪə(r), -ɪɪst
AM ˈgəʃi, -ər, -ɪst

gusset
BR ˈgʌs|ɪt, -ɪts, -ɪtɪd
AM ˈgəsə|t, -ts, -dəd

gust
BR gʌst, -s, -ɪŋ, -ɪd
AM gəst, -s, -ɪŋ, -əd

Gustafson
BR ˈgʊstɑːfs(ə)n,
ˈgʌstɑːfs(ə)n,
ˈgʊstafs(ə)n,
ˈgʌstafs(ə)n
AM ˈgəstəfsən

gustation
BR gʌˈsteɪʃn
AM gəˈsteɪʃən

gustative
BR ˈgʌstətɪv, gʌˈsteɪtɪv
AM ˈgəstədɪv

gustatory
BR ˈgʌstət(ə)ri,
gʌˈsteɪt(ə)ri
AM ˈgəstəˌtɔri

Gustave
BR ˈgʊstɑːv, ˈgʌstɑːv
AM ˈgʊsˌtɑv

Gustavus
BR gʊˈstɑːvəs,
gʌˈstɑːvəs

gustily
BR ˈgʌstɪli
AM ˈgəstəli

gustiness
BR ˈgʌstɪnɪs
AM ˈgəstinɪs

gusto
BR ˈgʌstəʊ
AM ˈgəstoʊ

gusty
BR ˈgʌst|i, -ɪə(r), -ɪɪst
AM ˈgəsti, -ər, -ɪst

gut
BR gʌt, -s, -ɪŋ, -ɪd
AM gə|t, -ts, -dɪŋ, -dəd

Gutenberg
BR ˈguːtnbəːg,
ˈgʊtnbəːg
AM ˈgʊtnˌbərg

Guthrie
BR ˈgʌθri
AM ˈgəθri

Gutiérrez
BR ˌgʊtiˈɛːrez
AM ˌgudiˈɛrəs,
ˌgudiˈɛrəz
SP guˈtjerreθ
gu'tjerres

gutless
BR ˈgʌtləs
AM ˈgətləs

gutlessly
BR ˈgʌtləsli
AM ˈgətləsli

gutlessness
BR ˈgʌtləsnəs
AM ˈgətləsnəs

gutrot
BR ˈgʌtrɒt
AM ˈgətˌrɑt

gutser
BR ˈgʌtsə(r), -z
AM ˈgətsər, -z

gutsily
BR ˈgʌtsɪli
AM ˈgətsəli

gutsiness
BR ˈgʌtsɪnɪs
AM ˈgətsinɪs

gutsy
BR ˈgʌts|i, -ɪə(r), -ɪɪst
AM ˈgətsi, -ər, -ɪst

guttapercha
BR ˌgʌtəˈpəːtʃə(r)
AM ˌgədəˈpərtʃə

guttate
BR ˈgʌteɪt
AM ˈgədˌeɪt

gutter
BR ˈgʌt|ə(r), -əz,
-(ə)rɪŋ, -əd
AM ˈgədər, -z, -ɪŋ, -d

guttersnipe
BR ˈgʌtəsnʌɪp, -s
AM ˈgədərˌsnaɪp, -s

guttle
BR ˈgʌt|l, -lz, -l̩ɪŋ \-lɪŋ,
-ld
AM ˈgədəl, -z, -ɪŋ, -d

guttural
BR ˈgʌt(ə)rəl,
ˈgʌt(ə)r̩l, -z
AM ˈgədərəl, -z

gutturalise
BR ˈgʌt(ə)rəlʌɪz,
ˈgʌt(ə)r̩lʌɪz, -ɪz, -ɪŋ, -d
AM ˈgədərəˌlaɪz, -ɪz, -ɪŋ,
-d

gutturalism
BR ˈgʌt(ə)rəlɪz(ə)m,
ˈgʌt(ə)r̩lɪz(ə)m
AM ˈgədərəˌlɪzəm

gutturality
BR ˌgʌtəˈralɪti
AM ˌgədəˈrælədi

gutturalize
BR ˈgʌt(ə)rəlʌɪz,
ˈgʌt(ə)r̩lʌɪz, -ɪz, -ɪŋ, -d
AM ˈgədərəˌlaɪz, -ɪz, -ɪŋ,
-d

gutturally
BR ˈgʌt(ə)rəli,
ˈgʌt(ə)r̩li
AM ˈgədərəli

gutty
BR ˈgʌti
AM ˈgədi

gutzer
BR ˈgʌtsə(r), -z
AM ˈgətsər, -z

guv
BR gʌv
AM gəv

guvnor
BR ˈgʌvnə(r), -z
AM ˈgəvnər, -z

guv'nor
BR ˈgʌvnə(r), -z
AM ˈgəvnər, -z

guy
BR gʌɪ, -z, -ɪŋ, -d
AM gaɪ, -z, -ɪŋ, -d

Guyana
BR gʌɪˈɑnə(r)
AM gaɪˈɑnə

Guyanese
BR ˌgʌɪəˈniːz
AM ˌgiəˈniz

Guyenne
BR g(w)ɪˈjɛn
AM g(w)iˈ(j)ɛn
FR gɥijɛn

Guy Fawkes
BR ˌgʌɪ ˈfɔːks
AM ˌgaɪ ˈfɔks, ˌgɑ̃ks ˈfɑks

Guzmán
BR ˈgʊθmən
AM ˈgusmən
SP guθˈman, gusˈman

guzzle
BR ˈgʌz|l, -lz, -l̩ɪŋ \-lɪŋ,
-ld

guttle AM ˈgəz|əl, -əlz, -(ə)lɪŋ,
-əld

guzzler
BR ˈgʌz|lə(r), ˈgʌzlə(r),
-z
AM ˈgəz(ə)lər, -z

Gwalia
BR ˈgwɑːlɪə(r)
AM ˈgwɑljə, ˈgwɑliə

Gwalior
BR ˈgwɑːlɪɔː(r)
AM ˈgwɑliˌɔ(ə)r

Gwen
BR gwɛn
AM gwɛn

Gwenda
BR ˈgwɛndə(r)
AM ˈgwɛndə

Gwendolen
BR ˈgwɛndəlɪn,
ˈgwɛndl̩ɪn
AM ˈgwɛndələn

Gwendoline
BR ˈgwɛndəlɪn,
ˈgwɛndl̩ɪn
AM ˈgwɛndələn

Gwendraeth
BR ˈgwɛndrʌɪθ
AM ˈgwɛnˌdraɪθ

Gwenllian
BR ˈgwɛnɬɪən
AM ˈgwɛnljən

Gwent
BR gwɛnt
AM gwɛnt

Gwenyth
BR ˈgwɛnɪθ
AM ˈgwɛnɪθ

Gwyn
BR gwɪn
AM gwɪn

Gwynedd
BR ˈgwɪnəð
AM ˈgwɪnəð

Gwyneth
BR ˈgwɪnɪθ
AM ˈgwɪnɪθ

Gwynfor
BR ˈgwɪnvɔː(r),
ˈgwɪnvə(r)
AM ˈgwɪnvɔ(ə)r

Gwynn
BR gwɪn
AM gwɪn

gybe
BR dʒʌɪb, -z, -ɪŋ, -d
AM dʒaɪb, -z, -ɪŋ, -d

Gyles
BR dʒʌɪlz
AM dʒaɪlz

gym
BR dʒɪm, -z
AM dʒɪm, -z

gymkhana
BR dʒɪmˈkɑːnə(r), -z
AM dʒɪmˈkɑnə,
dʒɪmˈkænə, -z

gymnasia
BR dʒɪmˈneɪzɪə(r)
AM dʒɪmˈneɪzɪə,
dʒɪmˈneɪʒə

gymnasial
BR dʒɪmˈneɪzɪəl
AM dʒɪmˈneɪzɪəl

gymnasium
BR dʒɪmˈneɪzɪəm, -z
AM dʒɪmˈneɪzɪəm, -z

gymnast
BR ˈdʒɪmnast, -s
AM ˈdʒɪmnəst,
ˈdʒɪmˌnæst, -s

gymnastic
BR dʒɪmˈnastɪk, -s
AM dʒɪmˈnæstɪk, -s

gymnastically
BR dʒɪmˈnastɪkli
AM dʒɪmˈnæstək(ə)li

gymnosophist
BR dʒɪmˈnɒsəfɪst, -s
AM dʒɪmˈnɑsəfəst, -s

gymnosophy
BR dʒɪmˈnɒsəfi
AM dʒɪmˈnɑsəfi

gymnosperm
BR ˈdʒɪmnə(ʊ)spəːm,
-z
AM ˈdʒɪmnəˌspɜrm, -z

gymnospermous
BR ˌdʒɪmnə(ʊ)ˈspəːməs
AM ˌdʒɪmnəˈspɜrməs

gymp
BR gɪm|p, -ps, -pɪŋ, -(p)t
AM gɪm|p, -ps, -pɪŋ,
-(p)t

gymslip
BR ˈdʒɪmslɪp, -s
AM ˈdʒɪmˌslɪp, -s

gynaecea
BR ˌdʒaɪnɪˈsiːə(r),
ˌgaɪnɪˈsiːə(r)
AM ˌdʒɪnəˈsiə

gynaeceum
BR ˌdʒaɪnɪˈsiːəm,
ˌgaɪnɪˈsiːəm, -z
AM ˌdʒɪnəˈsiəm, -z

gynaecocracy
BR ˌgaɪnəˈkɒkrəs|i,
ˌdʒaɪnəˈkɒkrəs|i, -ɪz
AM ˌgaɪnəˈkɑkrəsi, -z

gynaecologic
BR ˌgaɪnəkəˈlɒdʒɪk
AM ˌgaɪnəkəˈlɑdʒɪk

gynaecological
BR ˌgaɪnəkəˈlɒdʒɪkl
AM ˌgaɪnəkəˈlɑdʒəkəl

gynaecologically
BR ˌgaɪnəkəˈlɒdʒɪkli
AM ˌgaɪnəkəˈlɑdʒək(ə)li

gynaecologist
BR ˌgaɪnəˈkɒlədʒɪst, -s
AM ˌgaɪnəˈkɑlədʒəst, -s

gynaecology
BR ˌgaɪnəˈkɒlədʒi
AM ˌgaɪnəˈkɑlədʒi

gynaecomastia
BR ˌgaɪnəkə(ʊ)ˈmast-
ɪə(r)
AM ˌgaɪnəkoʊˈmæstiə

gynandromorph
BR dʒɪˈnandrəmɔːf, -s
AM dʒɪˈnændrəˌmɔ(ə)rf,
-s

gynandromorphic
BR dʒɪˌnandrəˈmɔːfɪk
AM dʒɪˌnændrəˈmɔrfɪk

**gynandromorph-
ism**
BR dʒɪˌnandrəˈmɔːf-
ɪz(ə)m
AM dʒɪˌnændrəˈmɔr-
ˌfɪzəm

gynandrous
BR dʒɪˈnandrəs
AM dʒɪˈnændrəs

gynecia
BR gaɪˈniːsɪə(r),
dʒaɪˈniːsɪə(r)
AM gaɪˈniʃiə

gynecium
BR gaɪˈniːsɪəm,
dʒaɪˈniːsɪəm, -z
AM gaɪˈniʃiəm, -z

gynecocracy
BR ˌgaɪnəˈkɒkrəs|i,
ˌdʒaɪnəˈkɒkrəsi, -ɪz
AM ˌgaɪnəˈkakrəsi, -z

gynecologic
BR ˌgaɪnəkəˈlɒdʒɪk
AM ˌgaɪnəkəˈladʒɪk

gynecological
BR ˌgaɪnəkəˈlɒdʒɪkl
AM ˌgaɪnəkəˈladʒəkəl

gynecologically
BR ˌgaɪnəkəˈlɒdʒɪkli
AM ˌgaɪnəkəˈladʒək(ə)li

gynecologist
BR ˌgaɪnəˈkɒlədʒɪst, -s
AM ˌgaɪnəˈkɑlədʒəst, -s

gynecology
BR ˌgaɪnəˈkɒlədʒi
AM ˌgaɪnəˈkɑlədʒi

gynecomastia
BR ˌgaɪnəkəˈmastɪə(r)
AM ˌgaɪnəkoʊˈmæstiə

gynobase
BR ˈgaɪnə(ʊ)beɪs, -ɪz
AM ˈgaɪnoʊˌbeɪs, -ɪz

gynocracy
BR gaɪˈnɒkrəs|i,
dʒaɪˈnɒkrəsi, -ɪz
AM gaɪˈnakrəsi, -z

gynoecia
BR gaɪˈniːsɪə(r),
dʒaɪˈniːsɪə(r)
AM gaɪˈniʃiə

gynoecium
BR gaɪˈniːsɪəm
AM gaɪˈniʃiəm

gynophobia
BR ˌgaɪnəˈfəʊbɪə(r),
ˌdʒaɪnəˈfəʊbɪə(r)
AM ˌgaɪnəˈfoʊbiə

gyp
BR dʒɪp, -s
AM dʒɪp, -s

gyppy tummy
BR ˌdʒɪpi ˈtʌmi
AM ˈdʒɪpi ˈtəmi

gypseous
BR ˈdʒɪpsɪəs
AM ˈdʒɪpsiəs

gypsiferous
BR dʒɪpˈsɪf(ə)rəs
AM dʒɪpˈsɪf(ə)rəs

gypsophila
BR dʒɪpˈsɒfɪlə(r), -z
AM dʒɪpˈsafələ, -z

gypsum
BR ˈdʒɪps(ə)m
AM ˈdʒɪpsəm

Gypsy
BR ˈdʒɪps|i, -ɪz
AM ˈdʒɪpsi, -z

Gypsydom
BR ˈdʒɪpsɪdəm
AM ˈdʒɪpsɪdəm

Gypsyfied
BR ˈdʒɪpsɪfaɪd
AM ˈdʒɪpsəˌfaɪd

Gypsyhood
BR ˈdʒɪpsɪhʊd
AM ˈdʒɪpsiˌhʊd

Gypsyish
BR ˈdʒɪpsɪɪʃ
AM ˈdʒɪpsiɪʃ

gyrate
BR dʒʌɪˈreɪt, -s, -ɪŋ, -ɪd
AM ˈdʒaɪˌreɪ|t, -ts, -dɪŋ,
-dɪd

gyration
BR dʒʌɪˈreɪʃn, -z
AM dʒaɪˈreɪʃən, -z

gyrator
BR dʒʌɪˈreɪtə(r), -z
AM ˈdʒaɪˌreɪdər, -z

gyratory
BR dʒʌɪˈreɪt(ə)ri,
ˈdʒʌɪrət(ə)ri
AM ˈdʒaɪrəˌtɔri

gyre
BR ˈdʒʌɪə(r), -z
AM ˈdʒaɪ(ə)r, -z

gyrfalcon
BR ˈdʒəːˌfɔːlk(ə)n,
ˈdʒəːˌfalk(ə)n, -z
AM ˈdʒɜrˌfælkən, -z

gyri
BR ˈdʒʌɪrʌɪ
AM ˈdʒaɪˌraɪ

gyro¹
gyroscope
BR ˈdʒʌɪrəʊ
AM ˈdʒaɪroʊ

gyro²
sandwich
BR ˈjɪərəʊ, ˈdʒɪərəʊ,
ˈdʒʌɪrəʊ, -z
AM ˈdʒirou, ˈjɪroʊ, -z

gyrocompass
BR ˈdʒʌɪrə(ʊ)ˌkʌmpəs,
-ɪz
AM ˈdʒaɪroʊˌkəmpəs,
-əz

gyrograph
BR ˈdʒʌɪrəʊgrɑːf,
ˈdʒʌɪrəgraf, -s
AM ˈdʒaɪrəˌgræf, -s

gyromagnetic
BR ˌdʒʌɪrə(ʊ)magˈnɛtɪk
AM ˌdʒaɪroʊˌmægˈnɛdɪk

gyronny
BR dʒʌɪˈrɒni
AM dʒaɪˈrani

gyropilot
BR ˈdʒʌɪrə(ʊ)ˌpʌɪlət, -s
AM ˈdʒaɪrəˌpaɪlət, -s

gyroplane
BR ˈdʒʌɪrəpleɪn, -z
AM ˈdʒaɪrəˌpleɪn, -z

gyroscope
BR ˈdʒʌɪrəskəʊp, -s
AM ˈdʒaɪrəˌskoʊp, -s

gyroscopic
BR ˌdʒʌɪrəˈskɒpɪk
AM ˌdʒaɪrəˈskɑpɪk

gyrostabiliser
BR ˈdʒʌɪrəʊˌsteɪbɪlʌɪzə(r),
ˈdʒʌɪrəʊˌsteɪbl̩ʌɪzə(r),
-z
AM ˈdʒaɪroʊˌsteɪbəˌlaɪzər,
-z

gyrostabilizer
BR ˈdʒʌɪrəʊˌsteɪbɪlʌɪzə(r),
ˈdʒʌɪrəʊˌstabl̩ʌɪzə(r),
ˈdʒʌɪrəʊˌsteɪbl̩ʌɪzə(r),
-z
AM ˈdʒaɪroʊˈsteɪbəˌlaɪzər,
-z

gyrostatic
BR ˌdʒʌɪrəˈstatɪk
AM ˌdʒaɪrəˈstædɪk

gyrus
BR ˈdʒʌɪrəs
AM ˈdʒaɪrəs

gyttja
BR ˈjɪtʃə(r)
AM ˈjɪˌtʃɑ

gyve
BR dʒʌɪv, -z, -ɪŋ, -d
AM dʒaɪv, -z, -ɪŋ, -d

gyver
BR ˈgʌɪvə(r)
AM ˈgaɪvər

Hh

h
BR eɪtʃ, -ɪz
AM eɪtʃ, -ɪz

ha
BR hɑː(r)
AM hɑ

haar
BR hɑː(r), -z
AM (h)ɑr, -z

Haarlem
BR 'hɑːləm
AM 'hɑrləm

Haas
BR hɑːs, has
AM hɑs

Habakkuk
BR 'habəkʌk
AM 'hæbə,kʊk,
hə'bækək

habanera
BR ,habə'nɛːrə(r),
,(h)ɑːbə'nɛːrə(r), -z
AM (h)ɑbə'nɛrə, -z

habeas corpus
BR ,heɪbɪəs 'kɔːpəs
AM 'heɪbiə 'skɔrpəs

Haber-Bosch
BR ,heɪbə'bɒʃ
AM 'heɪbər'bɔʃ,
'heɪbər'bɑʃ

haberdasher
BR 'habədaʃə(r), -z
AM 'habər,dæʃər, -z

haberdashery
BR 'habədaʃ(ə)r|i, -ɪz
AM 'habər,dæʃəri, -z

habergeon
BR 'habədʒ(ə)n, -z
AM 'hæbərdʒən,
hə'bərdʒ(i)ən, -z

Habgood
BR 'habgʊd
AM 'hæb,gʊd

habile
BR 'habɪl
AM 'hæbəl

habiliment
BR hə'bɪlɪm(ə)nt, -s
AM hə'bɪləmənt, -s

habilitate
BR hə'bɪlɪteɪt, -s, -ɪŋ,
-ɪd
AM hə'bɪlə,teɪ|t, -ts,
-dɪŋ, -dɪd

habilitation
BR hə,bɪlɪ'teɪʃn
AM hə,bɪlə'teɪʃən

habit
BR 'habɪt, -s
AM 'hæbət, -s

habitability
BR ,habɪtə'bɪlɪti
AM ,hæbədə'bɪlɪdi

habitable
BR 'habɪtəbl
AM 'hæbədəbəl

habitableness
BR 'habɪtəblnəs
AM 'hæbədəbəlnəs

habitably
BR 'habɪtəbli
AM 'hæbədəbli

habitant
BR 'habɪt(ə)nt, -s
AM 'hæbədənt,
'hæbətnt, -s

habitat
BR 'habɪtat, -s
AM 'hæbə,tæt, -s

habitation
BR ,habɪ'teɪʃn, -z
AM ,hæbə'teɪʃən, -z

habited
BR 'habɪtɪd
AM 'hæbədəd

habitual
BR hə'bɪtʃʊəl,
hə'bɪtʃ(ʊ)l,
hə'bɪtjʊəl, hə'bɪtjʊl
AM hə'bɪtʃ(əw)əl

habitually
BR hə'bɪtʃʊəli,
hə'bɪtʃʊli, hə'bɪtʃli,
hə'bɪtjʊəli, hə'bɪtjʊli
AM hə'bɪtʃ(əw)əli

habitualness
BR hə'bɪtʃʊəlnəs,
hə'bɪtʃ(ʊ)lnəs,
hə'bɪtjʊəlnəs,
hə'bɪtjʊlnəs
AM hə'bɪtʃ(əw)əlnəs

habituate
BR hə'bɪtʃʊeɪt,
hə'bɪtjʊeɪt, -s, -ɪŋ, -ɪd
AM hə'bɪtʃə,weɪ|t, -ts,
-dɪŋ, -dɪd

habituation
BR hə,bɪtʃʊ'eɪʃn,
hə,bɪtjʊ'eɪʃn
AM hə,bɪtʃə'weɪʃən

habitude
BR 'habɪtʃuːd,
'habɪtjuːd, -z
AM 'hæbə,t(j)ud, -z

habitué
BR hə'bɪtʃʊeɪ,
hə'bɪtjʊeɪ, -z
AM hə'bɪtʃə,weɪ,
hə,bɪtʃə'weɪ, -z

Habsburg
BR 'hapsbəːg,
'habzbəːg, -z
AM 'hæps,bərg,
'habs,bərg, -z

habutai
BR 'hɑːbʊtʌɪ
AM 'hɑbə,taɪ

haček
BR 'hatʃɛk, 'hɑːtʃɛk, -s
AM 'hæ,tʃɛk, 'hɑ,tʃɛk,
-s

hachure
BR 'haʃə(r), ha'ʃʊə(r),
'haʃəz\ha'ʃʊəz,
'haʃ(ə)rɪŋ\ha'ʃʊərɪŋ,
'haʃəd\ha'ʃʊəd
AM hæ'ʃʊ(ə)r, 'hæʃər,
-z, -ɪŋ, -d

hacienda
BR ,hasɪ'ɛndə(r), -z
AM ,hɑsi'ɛndə, -z

hack
BR hak, -s, -ɪŋ, -t
AM hæk, -s, -ɪŋ, -t

hackamore
BR 'hakəmɔː(r), -z
AM 'hækə,mɔ(ə)r, -z

hackberry
BR 'hakb(ə)r|i, -ɪz
AM 'hæk,bɛri, -z

hacker
BR 'hakə(r), -z
AM 'hækər, -z

hackery
BR 'hak(ə)r|i, -ɪz
AM 'hækəri, -z

Hackett
BR 'hakɪt
AM 'hækət

hackette
BR ha'kɛt, -s
AM hæ'kɛt, -s

hackle
BR 'hakl, -lz, -lɪŋ\-lɪŋ,
-ld
AM 'hæk|əl, -əlz,
-(ə)lɪŋ, -əld

hackly
BR 'hakli
AM 'hækli

hackmatack
BR 'hakmətak, -s
AM 'hækmə,tæk, -s

hackney
BR 'hakn|i, -ɪz, -ɪd
AM 'hækni, -z, -d

hacksaw
BR 'haksɔː(r), -z
AM 'hæk,sɔ, 'hæk,sɑ, -z

hackwork
BR 'hakwəːk
AM 'hæk,wərk

had¹
strong form
BR had
AM hæd

had²
weak form
BR həd, əd, d
AM həd, əd, d

haddie
BR 'had|i, -ɪz
AM 'hædi, -z

Haddington
BR 'hadɪŋt(ə)n

Haddon
BR 'hadn
AM 'hædən

hade
BR heɪd, -z, -ɪŋ, -ɪd
AM heɪd, -z, -ɪŋ, -ɪd

Hadean
BR 'heɪdɪən
AM 'heɪdiən

Hades
BR 'heɪdiːz
AM 'heɪdiz

Hadfield
BR 'hadfiːld
AM 'hæd,fild

Hadith
BR hə'diːθ
AM hə'diθ

hadj
BR hadʒ, hɑːdʒ, -ɪz
AM hadʒ, hædʒ, -əz

hadji
BR 'hadʒiː, 'hɑːdʒiː,
-ɪz\-iːz
AM 'hadʒi, 'hædʒi, -z

Hadlee
BR 'hadli
AM 'hædli

Hadley
BR 'hadli
AM 'hædli

hadn't
BR 'hadnt
AM 'hædnt

Hadrian
BR 'heɪdrɪən
AM 'heɪdriən

hadron
BR 'hadrɒn, 'hadrən,
-z
AM 'hædrən,
'hæd,rɑn, -z

hadronic
BR ha'drɒnɪk
AM hæd'rɑnɪk

hadrosaur
BR 'hadrəsɔː(r), -z
AM 'hædrə,sɔ(ə)r, -z

hadst¹
strong form
BR hadst
AM hædst

hadst²
weak form
BR hədst
AM hədst

haecceity
BR hɛk'siːɪt|i,
hiːk'siːɪti, -ɪz
AM hæk'siɪdi, -z

haem
BR hiːm
AM him

haemal
BR ˈhiːml
AM ˈhiməl
haematic
BR hiːˈmatɪk
AM hiˈmædɪk
haematin
BR ˈhiːmətɪn
AM ˈhimə,tin
haematite
BR ˈhiːmətʌɪt
AM ˈhimə,taɪt
haematocele
BR hiˈmatəsiːl
AM hiˈmædoʊ,sil
haematocrit
BR hɪˈmatəkrɪt
AM hiˈmædə,krɪt
haematologic
BR ˌhiːmətəˈlɒdʒɪk
AM ˈhimədoʊˈladʒɪk
haematological
BR ˌhiːmətəˈlɒdʒɪkl
AM ˈhimədoʊˈladʒəkəl
haematologist
BR ˌhiːməˈtɒlədʒɪst, -s
AM ˌhiməˈtalədʒəst, -s
haematology
BR ˌhiːməˈtɒlədʒi
AM ˌhiməˈtalədʒi
haematoma
BR ˌhiːməˈtəʊmə(r), -z
AM ˌhiməˈtoʊmə, -z
haematuria
BR ˌhiːməˈtjʊərɪə(r)
AM ˌhiməˈtʊriə
haemocyanin
BR ˌhiːməˈ(ʊ)sʌɪənɪn
AM ˌhiməˈsaɪənən
haemodialysis
BR ˌhiːməˈ(ʊ)dʌɪˈalɪsɪs
AM ˌhimoʊdaɪˈæləsəs
haemodynamic
BR ˌhiːməˈ(ʊ)dʌɪˈnamɪk
AM ˌhimoʊdaɪˈnæmɪk
haemoglobin
BR ˌhiːməˈɡləʊbɪn
AM ˈhimə,gloʊbən
haemolysis
BR hiːˈmɒlɪsɪs
AM hiˈmaləsəs
haemolytic
BR ˌhiːməˈlɪtɪk
AM ˌhiməˈlɪdɪk
haemophilia
BR ˌhiːməˈfɪlɪə(r)
AM ˌhiməˈfɪljə,
ˌhiməˈfɪliə
haemophiliac
BR ˌhiːməˈfɪlɪak, -s
AM ˌhiməˈfɪli,æk, -s
haemophilic
BR ˌhiːməˈfɪlɪk
AM ˌhiməˈfɪlɪk
haemorrhage
BR ˈhɛm(ə)r|ɪdʒ, -ɪdʒɪz,
-ɪdʒɪŋ, -ɪdʒd

AM ˈhɛm(ə)rɪdʒ, -ɪz,
-ɪŋ, -d
haemorrhagic
BR ˌhɛməˈradʒɪk
AM ˌhɛməˈrædʒɪk
haemorrhoid
BR ˈhɛmərɔɪd, -z
AM ˈhɛm(ə)ˌrɔɪd, -z
haemorrhoidal
BR ˌhɛməˈrɔɪdl
AM ˌhɛm(ə)ˈrɔɪdəl
haemostasis
BR ˌhiːməˈ(ʊ)ˈsteɪsɪs
AM ˌhiməˈsteɪsəs
haemostatic
BR ˌhiːməˈstatɪk
AM ˌhiməˈstædɪk
haere mai
BR ˈhʌɪrə ˈmʌɪ
AM ˈhirə ˈmaɪ
hafiz
BR ˈhaːfɪz, -ɪz
AM ˈhafəz, -əz
hafnium
BR ˈhafnɪəm
AM ˈhæfniəm
Hafod
BR ˈhavɒd
AM ˈhævəd
haft
BR haːft, haft, -s, -ɪŋ, -ɪd
AM hæft, -s, -ɪŋ, -əd
haftara
BR ˌhaːftəˈraː(r),
ˌhaftəˈraː(r)
AM ˌhaftəˈra
haftarah
BR ˌhaːftəˈraː(r),
ˌhaftəˈraː(r)
AM ˌhaftəˈra
hag
BR hag, -z
AM hæg, -z
Hagan
BR ˈheɪg(ə)n
AM ˈheɪgən
Hagar
BR ˈheɪgaː(r), ˈheɪgə(r)
AM ˈheɪgər
hagfish
BR ˈhagfɪʃ, -ɪz
AM ˈhæg,fɪʃ, -ɪz
Haggada
BR hə'ga:də(r),
ˌhagəˈdaː(r)
AM həˈgadə
Haggadah
BR hə'ga:də(r),
ˌhagəˈdaː(r)
AM həˈgadə
Haggadic
BR hə'ga:dɪk, hə'gadɪk
AM həˈgadɪk
Haggadoth
BR hə'ga:dəʊt,
ˌhagəˈdəʊt
AM hə'ga,doʊθ

Haggai
BR ˈhagʌɪ, ˈhagɪʌɪ,
ˈhageɪʌɪ
AM ˈhægaɪ
haggard
BR ˈhagəd
AM ˈhægərd
haggardly
BR ˈhagədli
AM ˈhægərdli
haggardness
BR ˈhagədnəs
AM ˈhægərdnəs
haggis
BR ˈhag|ɪs, -ɪsɪz
AM ˈhagəs, -əz
haggish
BR ˈhagɪʃ
AM ˈhægɪʃ
haggle
BR ˈhag|l, -lz, -ḷɪŋ \-lɪŋ,
-ld
AM ˈhæg|əl, -əlz,
-(ə)lɪŋ, -əld
haggler
BR ˈhaglə(r),
ˈhaglə(r), -z
AM ˈhæg(ə)lər, -z
hagiocracy
BR ˌhagɪˈɒkrəs‖i, -ɪz
AM ˌhægɪˈakrəsi,
ˌheɪgiˈakrəsi,
ˌhagiˈakrəsi, -z
Hagiographa
BR ˌhagɪˈɒɡrəfə(r)
AM ˌhægɪˈagrəfə,
ˌheɪgiˈagrəfə,
ˌhagiˈagrəfə
hagiographer
BR ˌhagɪˈɒɡrəfə(r), -z
AM ˌhægɪˈagrəfər,
ˌheɪgiˈagrəfər,
ˌhagiˈagrəfər, -z
hagiographic
BR ˌhagɪəˈgrafɪk
AM ˌhægɪəˈgræfɪk,
ˌheɪgiəˈgræfɪk,
ˌhagiəˈgræfɪk
hagiographical
BR ˌhagɪəˈgrafɪkl
AM ˌhægɪəˈgræfəkəl,
ˌheɪgiəˈgræfəkəl,
ˌhagiəˈgræfɪkəl
hagiography
BR ˌhagɪˈɒɡrəfi
AM ˌhægɪˈagrəfi,
ˌheɪgiˈagrəfi,
ˌhagiˈagrəfi
hagiolater
BR ˌhagɪˈɒlətə(r), -z
AM ˌhagiˈalədər,
ˌheɪgiˈalədər,
ˌhagiˈalədər, -z
hagiolatry
BR ˌhagɪˈɒlətri
AM ˌhagiˈalətri,
ˌheɪgiˈalətri,
ˌhagiˈalətri

hagiological
BR ˌhagɪəˈlɒdʒɪkl
AM ˌhagiəˈladʒəkəl,
ˌheɪgiəˈladʒəkəl,
ˌhagiəˈladʒəkəl
hagiologist
BR ˌhagɪˈɒlədʒɪst, -s
AM ˌhægiˈalədʒəst,
ˌheɪgiˈalədʒəst,
ˌhagiˈalədʒəst, -s
hagiology
BR ˌhagɪˈɒlədʒi
AM ˌhægiˈalədʒi,
ˌheɪgiˈalədʒi,
ˌhagiˈalədʒi
hagioscope
BR ˈhagɪəskəʊp, -s
AM ˈhægiə,skoʊp,
ˈheɪgiə,skoʊp,
ˈhagiə,skoʊp, -s
hagioscopic
BR ˌhagɪəˈskɒpɪk
AM ˌhægiəˈskapɪk,
ˌheɪgiəˈskapɪk,
ˌhagiəˈskapɪk
hagridden
BR ˈhag,rɪdn
AM ˈhæg,rɪdən
Hague
BR heɪg
AM heɪg
hah
interjection
BR haː(r)
AM ha
ha-ha¹
ditch
BR ˈhaːhaː(r), -z
AM ˈha,ha, -z
ha-ha²
interjection, laughter
BR (,)haːˈhaː(r), -z
AM ˈha,ha, -z
Hahn
BR haːn
AM han
hahnium
BR ˈhaːnɪəm
AM ˈhaniəm
haick
BR hʌɪk, ˈhaːɪk, heɪk, -s
AM haɪk, -s
Haida
BR ˈhʌɪdə(r), -z
AM ˈhaɪdə, -z
Haifa
BR ˈhʌɪfə(r)
AM ˈhaɪfə
Haig
BR heɪg
AM heɪg
Haigh¹
placename
BR heɪ
AM heɪ
Haigh²
surname
BR heɪg

AM heɪɡ
Haight
BR hʌɪt, heɪt
AM heɪt
Haight-Ashbury
BR ˌhʌɪt'aʃb(ə)ri
AM ˌheɪt'aʃbɛri
haik
BR hʌɪk, 'hɑːɪk, heɪk, -s
AM haɪk, -s
haiku
BR 'hʌɪkuː, -z
AM 'haɪˌku, -z
hail
BR heɪl, -z, -ɪŋ, -d
AM heɪl, -z, -ɪŋ, -d
hailer
BR 'heɪlə(r), -z
AM 'heɪlər, -z
Haile Selassie
BR ˌhʌɪli sɪ'lasi
AM ˌhaɪli sə'læsi
Hailey
BR 'heɪli
AM 'heɪli
Haileybury
BR 'heɪlɪb(ə)ri
AM 'heɪliˌbɛri
Hailsham
BR 'heɪlʃ(ə)m
AM 'heɪlʃəm
hailstone
BR 'heɪlstəʊn, -z
AM 'heɪlˌstoʊn, -z
hailstorm
BR 'heɪlstɔːm, -z
AM 'heɪlˌstɔ(ə)rm, -z
Hailwood
BR 'heɪlwʊd
AM 'heɪlˌwʊd
haily
BR 'heɪli
AM 'heɪli
Hain
BR heɪn
AM heɪn
Hainault
BR 'heɪnɔː(l)t, 'heɪnlt
AM (h)eɪ'noʊ
Haines
BR heɪnz
AM heɪnz
Hainsworth
BR 'heɪnzwəːθ, 'heɪnzwəθ
AM 'heɪnzˌwərθ
Haiphong
BR ˌhʌɪ'fɒŋ
AM 'haɪ'fɒŋ, 'haɪ'fɑŋ
hair
BR hɛː(r), -z, -d
AM hɛ(ə)r, -z, -d
hairbreadth
BR 'hɛːbrɛdθ, 'hɛːbrɛtθ
AM 'hɛːr,brɛ(d)θ

hairbrush
BR 'hɛːbrʌʃ, -ɪz
AM 'hɛr,brʌʃ, -əz
haircare
BR 'hɛːkɛː(r)
AM 'hɛr,kɛ(ə)r
haircloth
BR 'hɛːklɒθ,-θs\-ðz
AM 'hɛr,klɒθ, 'hɛr,klɑθ, -θs\-ðz
haircut
BR 'hɛːkʌt, -s, -ɪŋ
AM 'hɛr,kət, -s, -ɪŋ
hairdo
BR 'hɛːduː, -z
AM 'hɛr,du, -z
hairdresser
BR 'hɛːˌdrɛsə(r), -z
AM 'hɛr,drɛsər, -z
hairdressing
BR 'hɛːˌdrɛsɪŋ
AM 'hɛr,drɛsɪŋ
hairdrier
BR 'hɛːˌdrʌɪə(r), -z
AM 'hɛr,draɪər, -z
hairdryer
BR 'hɛːˌdrʌɪə(r), -z
AM 'hɛr,draɪər, -z
hairgrip
BR 'hɛːɡrɪp, -s
AM 'hɛr,ɡrɪp, -s
hairily
BR 'hɛːrɪli
AM 'hɛrəli
hairiness
BR 'hɛːrɪnɪs
AM 'hɛrɪnɪs
hairless
BR 'hɛːləs
AM 'hɛrləs
hairlessness
BR 'hɛːləsnəs
AM 'hɛrləsnəs
hairlike
BR 'hɛːlʌɪk
AM 'hɛr,lʌɪk
hairline
BR 'hɛːlʌɪn, -z
AM 'hɛr,laɪn, -z
hairnet
BR 'hɛːnɛt, -s
AM 'hɛr,nɛt, -s
hairpiece
BR 'hɛːpiːs, -ɪz
AM 'hɛr,pis, -ɪz
hairpin
BR 'hɛːpɪn, -z
AM 'hɛr,pɪn, -z
hairsbreadth
BR 'hɛːzbrɛdθ, 'hɛːzbrɛtθ
AM 'hɛrz,brɛ(d)θ
hairspray
BR 'hɛːspreɪ, -z
AM 'hɛr,spreɪ, -z
hairspring
BR 'hɛːsprɪŋ, -z

hairstreak
AM 'hɛr,sprɪŋ, -z
hairstreak
BR 'hɛːstriːk, -s
AM 'hɛr,strik, -s
hairstyle
BR 'hɛːstʌɪl, -z
AM 'hɛr,staɪl, -z
hairstyling
BR 'hɛːˌstʌɪlɪŋ
AM 'hɛr,staɪlɪŋ
hairstylist
BR 'hɛːˌstʌɪlɪst, -s
AM 'hɛr,staɪlɪst, -s
hairy
BR 'hɛːr|i, -ɪə(r), -ɪɪst
AM 'hɛri, -ər, -ɪst
Haiti
BR 'heɪti, 'hʌɪti, her'iːti, hʌɪ'iːti, hɑː'iːti
AM 'heɪdi
Haitian
BR 'heɪʃn, 'heɪʃiən, 'heɪtiən, 'hʌɪʃn, her'iːʃn, hʌɪ'iːʃn, hɑː'iːʃn, -z
AM 'heɪʃən, -z
haj
BR hadʒ, hɑːdʒ, -ɪz
AM hadʒ, hædʒ, -ɪz
haji
BR 'hadʒ|i, 'hadʒ|iː, 'hɑːdʒ|i, 'hɑːdʒ|iː, -ɪz\-iːz
AM 'hɑdʒi, 'hædʒi, -z
hajj
BR hadʒ, hɑːdʒ, -ɪz
AM hadʒ, hædʒ, -ɪz
hajji
BR 'hadʒ|i, 'hadʒ|iː, 'hɑːdʒ|i, 'hɑːdʒ|iː, -ɪz\-iːz
AM 'hɑdʒi, 'hædʒi, -z
haka
BR 'hɑːkə(r), -z
AM 'hɑkə, -z
hake
BR heɪk, -s
AM heɪk, -s
Hakenkreuz
BR 'hɑːk(ə)nkrɔɪts
AM 'hɑkən,krɔɪts
Hakenkreuze
BR 'hɑːk(ə)n,krɔɪtsə(r)
AM 'hɑkən,krɔɪtsə
hakim
BR ha'kiːm, -z
AM ha'kim, -z
Hakka
BR 'hakə(r), -z
AM 'hɑkə, 'hækə, -z
Hakluyt
BR 'hakluːt
AM 'hæˌklut
Hal
BR hal
AM hæl

Halacha
BR ˌhalɑː'xɑː(r), hə'lɑːxə(r), hə'lɑːkɑː(r)
AM hɑ'lɑkɑ
Halachic
BR hə'lɑːkɪk
AM hə'lɑkɪk
Halafian
BR hə'lɑːfiən
AM hə'lɑfiən
Halakah
BR ˌhalɑː'xɑː(r), hə'lɑːxə(r), hə'lɑːkɑː(r)
AM hɑ'lɑkɑ
halal
BR hə'lɑːl, hə'lal, 'halal
AM hə'lɑl, hə'læl
halation
BR hə'leɪʃn
AM hə'leɪʃən
halberd
BR 'halbəd, -z
AM 'hælbərd, 'hɒlbərd, 'halbərd, -z
halberdier
BR ˌhalbə'dɪə(r), -z
AM ˌhælbər'dɪ(ə)r, ˌhɒlbər'dɪ(ə)r, ˌhalbər'dɪ(ə)r, -z
halcyon
BR 'halsɪən
AM 'hælsiən, 'hælsiˌɑn
Haldane
BR 'hɔːldeɪn, 'hɒldeɪn, 'haldeɪn
AM 'hælˌdeɪn, 'hɒlˌdeɪn, 'halˌdeɪn
hale
BR heɪl, -z, -ɪŋ, -d
AM heɪl, -z, -ɪŋ, -d
haleness
BR 'heɪlnəs
AM 'heɪlnɪs
háleř
currency
BR 'hɑːlə(r)
AM 'hɑlər
cz 'hʌle:(r)ʒ
haleru
BR 'hɑːləruː
AM 'hɑləru
Hales
BR heɪlz
AM heɪlz
Halesowen
BR (ˌ)heɪlz'əʊən
AM 'heɪlz'oʊən
Halesworth
BR 'heɪlzwəːθ, 'heɪlzwəθ
AM 'heɪlz,wərθ
Halewood
BR 'heɪlwʊd
AM 'heɪlˌwʊd

Halex®
BR ˈheɪlɛks
AM ˈheɪlɛks

Haley
BR ˈheɪli
AM ˈheɪli

half
BR hɑːf
AM hæf

halfback
BR ˈhɑːfbak, -s
AM ˈhæfˌbæk, -s

halfpence
BR ˈheɪp(ə)ns
AM ˈhæfˌpɛns,
ˈheɪpəns

halfpenny
BR ˈheɪpn‖i, -ɪz
AM ˈhæfˌpɛni,
ˈheɪp(ə)ni, -z

halfpennyworth
BR ˈheɪpnɪwəːθ,
ˌhɑːfˈpɛnəθ, -s
AM ˈhæfˌpɛniˌwərθ,
ˈheɪpnɪˌwərθ, -s

halftime
BR ˌhɑːfˈtaɪm
AM ˈhæfˌtaɪm

halftone
BR ˈhɑːfˌtəʊn,
ˌhɑːfˈtəʊn, -z
AM ˈhæfˌtoʊn, -z

halftrack
noun
BR ˈhɑːftrak, -s
AM ˈhæfˌtræk, -s

half-track
adjective
BR ˌhɑːfˈtrak, -t
AM ˌhæfˈtræk, -t

halfway
BR ˌhɑːfˈweɪ
AM ˌhæfˈweɪ

halfwit
BR ˈhɑːfwɪt, -s
AM ˈhæfˌwɪt, -s

half-witted
BR ˌhɑːfˈwɪtɪd
AM ˌhæfˈwɪdɪd

half-wittedly
BR ˌhɑːfˈwɪtɪdli
AM ˌhæfˈwɪdɪdli

half-wittedness
BR ˌhɑːfˈwɪtɪdnɪs
AM ˌhæfˈwɪdɪdnɪs

halibut
BR ˈhalɪbət, -s
AM ˈhæləbət, -s

Halicarnassus
BR ˌhalɪkɑːˈnasəs
AM ˌhæləˌkɑrˈnæsəs

halide
BR ˈheɪlʌɪd, ˈhalʌɪd, -z
AM ˈheɪˌlaɪd, ˈhæˌlaɪd,
-z

halieutic
BR ˌhalɪˈjuːtɪk, -s
AM ˌhæliˈ(j)udɪk, -s

Halifax
BR ˈhalɪfaks
AM ˈhæləˌfæks

haliotis
BR ˌhalɪˈəʊtɪs
AM ˌhæliˈoʊdəs

halite
BR ˈhalʌɪt, -s
AM ˈhæˌlaɪt, ˈheɪˌlaɪt, -s

halitosis
BR ˌhalɪˈtəʊsɪs
AM ˌhæləˈtoʊsəs

hall
BR hɔːl, -z
AM hɔl, hɑl, -z

hallal
BR həˈlɑːl, həˈlal,
ˈhalal
AM həˈlal, həˈlæl

Hallam
BR ˈhaləm
AM ˈhæləm

Halle
BR ˈhalə(r)
AM ˈhalə

Hallé
BR ˈhaleɪ, ˈhali
AM ˈhaleɪ

halleluja
BR ˌhalɪˈluːjə(r), -z
AM ˌhæləˈlujə, -z

hallelujah
BR ˌhalɪˈluːjə(r), -z
AM ˌhæləˈlujə, -z

Haller
BR ˈhalə(r)
AM ˈhælər

Halley
BR ˈhali
AM ˈhæli

halliard
BR ˈhaljəd, -z
AM ˈhæljərd, -z

Halliday
BR ˈhalɪdeɪ
AM ˈhæləˌdeɪ

Halliwell
BR ˈhalɪwɛl
AM ˈhæləˌwɛl

hallmark
BR ˈhɔːlmɑːk, -s, -ɪŋ, -t
AM ˈhɔlˌmɑrk,
ˈhalˌmɑrk, -s, -ɪŋ, -t

hallo
BR həˈləʊ, -z
AM həˈloʊ, -z

halloo
BR həˈluː, -z, -ɪŋ, -d
AM həˈlu, -z, -ɪŋ, -d

hallow
BR ˈhaləʊ, -z, -ɪŋ, -d
AM ˈhæloʊ, -z, -ɪŋ, -d

Halloween
BR ˌhaləʊˈiːn
AM ˌhæləˈwin,
ˌhaləˈwin

Hallowe'en
BR ˌhaləʊˈiːn
AM ˌhæləˈwin,
ˌhaləˈwin

Hallowes
BR ˈhaləʊz
AM ˈhæloʊz

hallstand
BR ˈhɔːlstand, -z
AM ˈhɔlˌstænd,
ˈhalˌstænd, -z

Hallstatt
BR ˈhɑːlʃtɑːt, ˈhɑːlʃtat
AM ˈhalˌʃtat, ˈhalˌstat

halluces
BR ˈhaljʊsiːz
AM ˈhæləˌsiz

hallucinant
BR həˈl(j)uːsɪnənt, -s
AM həˈlusənənt, -s

hallucinate
BR həˈl(j)uːsɪneɪt, -s,
-ɪŋ, -ɪd
AM həˈlusnˌeɪt, -ts,
-dɪŋ, -dɪd

hallucination
BR həˌl(j)uːsɪˈneɪʃn, -z
AM həˌlusnˈeɪʃn, -z

hallucinator
BR həˈl(j)uːsɪneɪtə(r),
-z
AM həˈlusnˌeɪdər, -z

hallucinatory
BR həˈl(j)uːsɪnət(ə)ri,
həˈl(j)uːsɪˈsnət(ə)ri,
həˌl(j)uːsɪˈneɪt(ə)ri
AM həˈlusnəˌtɔri

hallucinogen
BR həˈl(j)uːsɪ(ɪ)nədʒ(ə)n,
həˈl(j)uːsɪˈsnədʒ(ə)n, -z
AM həˈlusnəˌdʒɛn, -z

hallucinogenic
BR həˌl(j)uːsɪ(ɪ)nə-
ˈdʒɛnɪk,
həˈl(j)uːsɪˈsnəˈdʒɛnɪk
AM həˌlusnəˈdʒɛnɪk

hallux
BR ˈhaləks, -ɪz
AM ˈhæləks, -əz

hallway
BR ˈhɔːlweɪ, -z
AM ˈhɔlˌweɪ, ˈhalˌweɪ,
-z

halm
BR hɔːm, -z
AM hɔm, hɑ(l)m, -z

halma
BR ˈhalmə(r)
AM ˈhælmə

Halmahera
BR ˌhalməˈhɛːrə(r)
AM ˌhælməˈhɛrə

halo
BR ˈheɪləʊ, -z, -d
AM ˈheɪloʊ, -z, -d

halocarbon
BR ˈhalə(ʊ)ˌkɑːbn, -z
AM ˈhæləˌkɑrbən, -z

halogen
BR ˈhaləd͡ʒ(ə)n, -z
AM ˈhælədʒən, -z

halogenation
BR ˌhalədʒəˈneɪʃn
AM ˌhælədʒəˈneɪʃən,
həˌladʒəˈneɪʃən

halogenic
BR ˌhaləˈdʒɛnɪk
AM ˌhæləˈdʒɛnɪk

halon
BR ˈheɪlɒn
AM ˈheɪlɑn

halophyte
BR ˈhaləfʌɪt, -s
AM ˈhæləˌfaɪt, -s

Halpern
BR ˈhalp(ə)n
AM ˈhælpərn

Halpin
BR ˈhalpɪn
AM ˈhælpən

Hals
BR hals, halz
AM hɑls

Halstead
BR ˈhalstɛd, ˈhalstɪd,
ˈhɔːlstɛd, ˈhɔːlstɪd,
ˈhɒlstɛd, ˈhɒlstɪd
AM ˈhɔlˌstɛd, ˈhalˌstɛd

halt
BR hɔːlt, hɒlt, -s, -ɪŋ, -ɪd
AM hɔlt, hɑlt, -s, -ɪŋ, -əd

Haltemprice
BR ˈhɔːltəmprʌɪs,
ˈhɒltəmprʌɪs
AM ˈhɔltəmˌpraɪs,
ˈhaltəmˌpraɪs

halter
BR ˈhɔːltə(r), ˈhɒltə(r),
-z
AM ˈhɔltər, ˈhaltər, -z

halteres
BR ˈhaltɪəz, ˈhɔːltɪəz,
ˈhɒltɪəz, halˈtɪəz
AM ˈhælˌtɪ(ə)rz,
ˈhɔlˌtɪ(ə)rz,
ˈhalˌtɪ(ə)rz

halterneck
BR ˈhɔːltənɛk,
ˈhɒltənɛk, -s
AM ˈhɔltərˌnɛk,
ˈhaltərˌnɛk, -s

haltingly
BR ˈhɔːltɪŋli, ˈhɒltɪŋli
AM ˈhɔltɪŋli, ˈhaltɪŋli

Halton
BR ˈhɔːlt(ə)n, ˈhɒlt(ə)n
AM ˈhɔltən, ˈhaltən

halva
BR ˈhalvə(r),
ˈhalvɑː(r), -z
AM ˈhalˈvɑ, -z

halvah
BR ˈhalvə(r),
ˈhalvɑː(r), -z
AM ˈhalˈvɑ, -z

halve
BR hɑːv, -z, -ɪŋ, -d
AM hæv, -z, -ɪŋ, -d
halyard
BR ˈhaljəd, -z
AM ˈhæljərd, -z
ham
BR ham, -z, -ɪŋ, -d
AM hæm, -z, -ɪŋ, -d
Hamada
BR həˈmɑːdə(r)
AM həˈmɑdə
hamadryad
BR ˌhaməˈdraɪəd,
ˌhaməˈdrʌɪad, -z
AM ˌhæməˈdraɪɛd,
ˌhæməˈdraɪˌæd, -z
hamadryas
BR ˌhaməˈdrʌɪəs,
ˌhaməˈdrʌɪas, -ɪz
AM ˌhæməˈdraɪəs, -ɪz
hamamelis
BR ˌhaməˈmiːlɪs, -ɪsɪz
AM ˌhæməˈmiːlɪs, -ɪz
hamartia
BR həˈmɑːtɪə(r)
AM həˈmɑrdiə
Hamas
BR haˈmas
AM hɑˈmas
Hambly
BR ˈhambli
AM ˈhæmbli
hambone
BR ˈhambəʊn, -z
AM ˈhæmˌboʊn, -z
Hambro
BR ˈhambrəʊ
AM ˈhæmbroʊ
Hamburg
BR ˈhambəːg
AM ˈhæmˌbərg
hamburger
BR ˈhamˌbəːgə(r), -z
AM ˈhæmˌbərgər, -z
Hamelin
BR ˈham(ɪ)lɪn
AM ˈhæm(ə)lən
Hamer
BR ˈheɪmə(r)
AM ˈheɪmər
hames
BR heɪmz
AM heɪmz
Hamilcar
BR ˈham(ɪ)lkɑː(r),
həˈmɪlkɑː(r)
AM həˈmɪlˌkɑr,
ˈhæməlˌkɑr
Hamill
BR ˈham(ɪ)l
AM ˈhæməl
Hamilton
BR ˈham(ɪ)lt(ə)n
AM ˈhæməltən
Hamish
BR ˈheɪmɪʃ

AM ˈheɪmɪʃ
Hamite
BR ˈhamʌɪt, -s
AM ˈhæˌmaɪt, -s
Hamitic
BR haˈmɪtɪk, həˈmɪtɪk
AM həˈmɪdɪk
Hamito-Semitic
BR ˌhamɪtəʊsɪˈmɪtɪk
AM ˌhæməˌtoʊsəˈmɪdɪk
hamlet
BR ˈhamlɪt, -s
AM ˈhæmlət, -s
Hamley
BR ˈhamli
AM ˈhæmli
Hamlin
BR ˈhamlɪn
AM ˈhæmlən
Hamlyn
BR ˈhamlɪn
AM ˈhæmlən
hammam
BR ˈhamam, həˈmɑːm,
ˈhʌmʌm, -z
AM həˈmɑm, -z
hammer
BR ˈham|ə(r), -əz,
-(ə)rɪŋ, -əd
AM ˈhæmər, -z, -ɪŋ, -d
hammerbeam
BR ˈhaməbiːm, -z
AM ˈhæmərˌbim, -z
hammerer
BR ˈham(ə)rə(r), -z
AM ˈhæmərər, -z
Hammerfest
BR ˈhaməfɛst
AM ˈhæmərˌfɛst
hammerhead
BR ˈhaməhɛd, -z
AM ˈhæmər(ˌh)ɛd, -z
hammering
BR ˈham(ə)rɪŋ, -z
AM ˈhæmərɪŋ, -z
hammerless
BR ˈhamələs
AM ˈhæmərləs
hammerlock
BR ˈhamələk, -s
AM ˈhæmərˌlak, -s
hammerman
BR ˈhaməman
AM ˈhæmərˌmæn
hammermen
BR ˈhaməmɛn
AM ˈhæmərˌmɛn
Hammersmith
BR ˈhaməsmɪθ
AM ˈhæmərˌsmɪθ
Hammerstein
BR ˈhaməstʌɪn
AM ˈhæmərˌstin,
ˈhæmərˌstaɪn
Hammett
BR ˈhamɪt
AM ˈhæmət

hammock
BR ˈhamək, -s
AM ˈhæmək, -s
Hammond
BR ˈhamənd
AM ˈhæmənd
Hammurabi
BR ˌhaməˈrɑːbi
AM ˌhæməˈrɑbi
hammy
BR ˈham|i, -ɪə(r), -ɪɪst
AM ˈhæmi, -ər, -ɪst
Hamnett
BR ˈhamnɪt
AM ˈhæmnət
hamper
BR ˈhamp|ə(r), -əz,
-(ə)rɪŋ, -əd
AM ˈhæmp|ər, -ərz,
-(ə)rɪŋ, -ərd
Hampshire
BR ˈham(p)ʃ(ɪ)ə(r)
AM ˈhæm(p)ʃɪ(ə)r
Hampson
BR ˈham(p)s(ə)n
AM ˈhæm(p)sən
Hampstead
BR ˈham(p)stɪd,
ˈham(p)stɛd
AM ˈhæm(p)stɛd
Hampton
BR ˈham(p)t(ə)n
AM ˈhæm(p)tən
Hampton Court
BR ˌham(p)t(ə)n ˈkɔːt
AM ˈhæm(p)tən
ˈkɔ(ə)rt
Hampton Roads
BR ˌham(p)t(ə)n
ˈrəʊdz
AM ˈhæm(p)tən ˈroʊdz
hamsin
BR ˈhamsɪn
AM ˈhæmsɪn
hamster
BR ˈhamstə(r), -z
AM ˈhæmstər, -z
hamstring
BR ˈhamstrɪŋ, -z, -ɪŋ
AM ˈhæmˌstrɪŋ, -z, -ɪŋ
hamstrung
BR ˈhamstrʌŋ
AM ˈhæmˌstrəŋ
hamuli
BR ˈhamjəlʌɪ,
ˈhamjəli:
AM ˈhæmjəˌlaɪ
hamulus
BR ˈhamjələs
AM ˈhæmjələs
hamza
BR ˈhamzə(r), -z
AM ˈhæmzə, -z
hamzah
BR ˈhamzə(r), -z
AM ˈhæmzə, -z

Han
BR han
AM hæn
Hancock
BR ˈhankɒk, ˈhaŋkɒk
AM ˈhænˌkak,
ˈhæŋˌkak
Hancox
BR ˈhankɒks,
ˈhaŋkɒks
AM ˈhænkaks,
ˈhæŋkaks
hand
BR hand, -z, -ɪŋ, -ɪd
AM hænd, -z, -ɪŋ, -əd
hand-axe
BR ˈhandaks, -ɪz
AM ˈhændˌæks, -əz
handbag
BR ˈhan(d)bag, -z
AM ˈhæn(d)ˌbæg, -z
handball
BR ˈhan(d)bɔːl, -z
AM ˈhæn(d)ˌbɔl,
ˈhæn(d)ˌbal, -z
handbasin
BR ˈhan(d)ˌbeɪsn, -z
AM ˈhæn(d)ˌbeɪsn, -z
handbell
BR ˈhan(d)bɛl, -z
AM ˈhæn(d)ˌbɛl, -z
handbill
BR ˈhan(d)bɪl, -z
AM ˈhæn(d)ˌbɪl, -z
handbook
BR ˈhan(d)bʊk, -s
AM ˈhæn(d)ˌbʊk, -s
handbrake
BR ˈhan(d)breɪk, -s
AM ˈhæn(d)ˌbreɪk, -s
handbreadth
BR ˈhan(d)brɛdθ,
ˈhan(d)brɛtθ, -s
AM ˈhæn(d)ˌbrɛ(d)θ, -s
handcar
BR ˈhan(d)kɑː(r), -z
AM ˈhæn(d)ˌkar, -z
handcart
BR ˈhan(d)kɑːt, -s
AM ˈhæn(d)ˌkart, -s
handclap
BR ˈhan(d)klap, -s
AM ˈhæn(d)ˌklæp, -s
handclapping
BR ˈhan(d)ˌklapɪŋ
AM ˈhæn(d)ˌklæpɪŋ
handcraft
BR ˈhan(d)krɑːft,
ˈhan(d)kraft, -s, -ɪŋ,
-ɪd
AM ˈhæn(d)ˌkræft, -s,
-ɪŋ, -d
handcuff
BR ˈhan(d)kʌf, -s, -ɪŋ, -t
AM ˈhæn(d)ˌkəf, -s, -ɪŋ,
-t
handedness
BR ˈhandɪdnɪs

AM ˈhændədnəs
Handel
BR ˈhændl
AM ˈhɑndəl
Handelian
BR hanˈdiːlɪən
AM hænˈdɛlɪən
handful
BR ˈhan(d)fʊl, -z
AM ˈhæn(d)fʊl, -z
handglass
BR ˈhan(d)glɑːs,
ˈhan(d)glas, -ɪz
AM ˈhæn(d)ˌglæs, -əz
handgrip
BR ˈhan(d)grɪp, -s
AM ˈhæn(d)ˌgrɪp, -s
handgun
BR ˈhan(d)gʌn, -z
AM hæn(d)ˌgən, -z
handhold
BR ˈhandhəʊld, -z
AM ˈhæn(d)ˌ(h)oʊld, -z
hand-holding
BR ˈhandˌhəʊldɪŋ
AM ˈhæn(d)ˌ(h)oʊldɪŋ
handicap
BR ˈhandɪkap, -s, -ɪŋ, -t
AM ˈhandiˌkæp, -s, -ɪŋ, -t
handicapper
BR ˈhandɪˌkapə(r), -z
AM ˈhandiˌkæpər, -z
handicraft
BR ˈhandɪkrɑːft,
ˈhandɪkraft, -s
AM ˈhandiˌkræft, -s
handily
BR ˈhandɪli
AM ˈhændəli
handiness
BR ˈhandɪnɪs
AM ˈhændɪnɪs
handiwork
BR ˈhandɪwəːk
AM ˈhændiˌwərk
handkerchief
BR ˈhaŋkətʃɪf,
ˈhaŋkətʃiːf
AM ˈhæŋkərtʃəf,
ˈhæŋkərˌtʃif
handkerchiefs
BR ˈhaŋkətʃɪfs,
ˈhaŋkətʃiːfs,
ˈhaŋkətʃiːvz
AM ˈhæŋkərtʃəfs,
ˈhæŋkərˌtʃivz,
ˈhæŋkərˌtʃifs
handle
BR ˈhandl̩, -lz,
-lɪŋ\-lɪŋ, -ld
AM ˈhændl̩dəl, -dəlz,
-(d)(ə)lɪŋ, -dəld
handleability
BR ˌhandləˈbɪlɪti,
ˌhandləˈbɪlɪti
AM ˌhændl̩əˈbɪlɪdi

handleable
BR ˈhandləbl̩,
ˈhandl̩əbl̩
AM ˈhændl̩əbəl
handlebar
BR ˈhandlbɑː(r), -z
AM ˈhændl̩ˌbɑr, -z
handler
BR ˈhandlə(r),
ˈhandl̩ə(r), -z
AM ˈhæn(d)ələr, -z
handless
BR ˈhandləs
AM ˈhæn(d)ləs
Handley
BR ˈhandli
AM ˈhæn(d)li
handline
BR ˈhan(d)lʌɪn, -z, -ɪŋ, -d
AM ˈhæn(d)ˌlaɪn, -z, -ɪŋ, -d
handlist
BR ˈhan(d)lɪst, -s
AM ˈhæn(d)ˌlɪst, -s
handloom
BR ˈhan(d)luːm, -z
AM ˈhæn(d)ˌlum, -z
handmade
BR ˌhan(d)ˈmeɪd
AM ˈhæn(d)ˌmeɪd
handmaid
BR ˈhan(d)meɪd, -z
AM ˈhæn(d)ˌmeɪd, -z
handmaiden
BR ˈhan(d)ˌmeɪdn, -z
AM ˈhæn(d)ˌmeɪdən, -z
handout
BR ˈhandaʊt, -s
AM ˈhændˌaʊt, -s
handover
BR ˈhandˌəʊvə(r), -z
AM ˈhændˌoʊvər, -z
hand-painted
BR ˌhan(d)ˈpaɪntɪd
AM ˈhæn(d)ˌpeɪm(t)ɪd
hand-pick
BR ˌhan(d)ˈpɪk, -s, -ɪŋ, -t
AM ˈhæn(d)ˌpɪk, -s, -ɪŋ, -t
handpicked
BR ˌhan(d)ˈpɪkt
AM ˈhæn(d)ˌpɪkt
handpump
BR ˈhan(d)pʌmp, -s
AM ˈhæn(d)ˌpəmp, -s
handrail
BR ˈhandreɪl, -z
AM ˈhæn(d)ˌreɪl, -z
handsaw
BR ˈhan(d)sɔː(r), -z
AM ˈhæn(d)ˌsɔ,
ˈhæn(d)ˌsɑ, -z
handsbreadth
BR ˈhan(d)zbrɛdθ,
ˈhan(d)zbrɛtθ, -s

AM ˈhæn(d)zˌbrɛ(d)θ, -s
handsel
BR ˈhan(d)s|l, -lz,
-əlɪŋ\-lɪŋ, -ld
AM ˈhæn(t)s|əl, -əlz,
-(ə)lɪŋ, -əld
handset
BR ˈhan(d)sɛt, -s
AM ˈhæn(d)ˌsɛt, -s
handshake
BR ˈhan(d)ʃeɪk, -s
AM ˈhæn(d)ˌʃeɪk, -s
handsome
BR ˈhans(ə)m,
-əmə(r)\-mə(r),
-əmɪst\-mɪst
AM ˈhæn(t)səm, -ər,
-əst
handsomely
BR ˈhans(ə)mli
AM ˈhæn(t)səmli
handsomeness
BR ˈhans(ə)mnəs
AM ˈhæn(t)səmnəs
handspike
BR ˈhan(d)spʌɪk, -s
AM ˈhæn(d)ˌspaɪk, -s
handspring
BR ˈhan(d)sprɪŋ, -z
AM ˈhæn(d)ˌsprɪŋ, -z
handstand
BR ˈhan(d)stand, -z
AM ˈhæn(d)ˌstænd, -z
handwork
BR ˈhandwəːk
AM ˈhæn(d)ˌwərk
handworked
BR ˌhandˈwəːkt
AM ˈhæn(d)ˈwərkt
handwriting
BR ˈhandˌrʌɪtɪŋ
AM ˈhæn(d)ˌraɪdɪŋ
handwritten
BR ˌhandˈrɪtn
AM ˌhæn(d)ˈrɪtn
handy
BR ˈhand|i, -ɪə(r), -ɪɪst
AM ˈhændi, -ər, -ɪst
handyman
BR ˈhandɪman
AM ˈhændiˌmæn
handymen
BR ˈhandɪmɛn
AM ˈhændiˌmɛn
Haney
BR ˈheɪni
AM ˈheɪni
hang
BR haŋ, -z, -ɪŋ, -d
AM hæŋ, -z, -ɪŋ, -d
hangar
BR ˈhaŋ(g)ə(r), -z
AM ˈhæŋər, -z
hangarage
BR ˈhaŋ(g)(ə)rɪdʒ
AM ˈhæŋərɪdʒ

Hangchow
BR ˌhaŋˈtʃaʊ
AM ˈhæŋˈtʃaʊ
hangdog
BR ˈhaŋdog
AM ˈhæŋˌdɔg,
ˈhæŋˌdɑg
hanger
BR ˈhaŋə(r), -z
AM ˈhæŋər, -z
hangi
BR ˈhaŋi, ˈhɑːŋi, -ɪz
AM ˈhæŋi, -z
hanging
BR ˈhaŋɪŋ, -z
AM ˈhæŋɪŋ, -z
hangman
BR ˈhaŋmən, ˈhaŋman
AM ˈhæŋmən,
ˈhæŋˌmæn
hangmen
BR ˈhaŋmən, ˈhaŋmɛn
AM ˈhæŋmən,
ˈhæŋˌmɛn
hangnail
BR ˈhaŋneɪl, -z
AM ˈhæŋˌneɪl, -z
hangout
BR ˈhaŋaʊt, -s
AM ˈhæŋˌaʊt, -s
hangover
BR ˈhaŋˌəʊvə(r), -z
AM ˈhæŋˌoʊvər, -z
Hang Seng
BR ˌhaŋ ˈsɛŋ
AM ˈhæŋ ˈsɛŋ
hangup
BR ˈhaŋʌp, -s
AM ˈhæŋˌəp, -s
Hangzhou
BR ˌhaŋˈ(d)ʒaʊ
AM ˈhæŋˈ(d)ʒaʊ
Hanif
BR haˈniːf
AM həˈnif
hank
BR haŋk, -s
AM hæŋk, -s
hanker
BR ˈhaŋk|ə(r), -əz,
-(ə)rɪŋ, -əd
AM ˈhæŋk|ər, -ərz,
-(ə)rɪŋ, -ərd
hankerer
BR ˈhaŋk(ə)rə(r), -z
AM ˈhæŋk(ə)rər, -z
hankering
BR ˈhaŋk(ə)rɪŋ, -z
AM ˈhæŋk(ə)rɪŋ, -z
hankie
BR ˈhaŋk|i, -ɪz
AM ˈhæŋki, -z
Hanks
BR haŋks
AM hæŋks
hanky
BR ˈhaŋk|i, -ɪz

AM 'hæŋki, -z

hanky-panky
BR ˌhæŋkɪ'pæŋki
AM ˌhæŋki'pæŋki

Hanley
BR 'hanli
AM 'hænli

Hanna
BR 'hanə(r)
AM 'hænə

Hannah
BR 'hanə(r)
AM 'hænə

Hannibal
BR 'hanɪbl
AM 'hænəbəl

Hannon
BR 'hanən
AM 'hænən

Hannover
BR 'hanə(ʊ)və(r)
AM 'hæn,ouvər
GER ha'no:fɐ

Hanoi
BR ha'nɔɪ
AM hæ'nɔɪ

Hanover
BR 'hanə(ʊ)və(r)
AM 'hæn,ouvər

Hanoverian
BR ˌhanə(ʊ)'vɛːrɪən, ˌhanə(ʊ)'vɪərɪən, -z
AM ˌhænə'vɛrɪən, -z

Hanrahan
BR 'hanrəhən, 'hanrəhan
AM 'hænrə,hæn

Hanratty
BR han'rati
AM 'hæn,rædi

Hans
BR hans, hanz
AM hɑns

Hansa
BR 'hansə(r)
AM 'hænsə

Hansard
BR 'hansɑːd
AM 'hænsɑrd

Hanse
BR hans, -ɪz
AM hænz, hɑns, -əz

Hanseatic
BR ˌhansɪ'atɪk
AM ˌhænsi'ædɪk

Hänsel
BR 'hansl
AM 'han(t)səl, 'hæn(t)səl
GER 'hɛnzl

hansel
BR 'hans|l, -lz, -lɪŋ\-əlɪŋ, -ld
AM 'hæn(t)s|əl, -əlz, -(ə)lɪŋ, -əld

Hansen
BR 'hansn

AM 'hænsən

hansom
BR 'hans(ə)m, -z
AM 'hænsəm, -z

Hanson
BR 'hansn
AM 'hænsən

Hants
Hampshire
BR hants
AM hænts

Hanukkah
BR 'hanʊkə(r), 'xanʊkə(r), 'hɑːnʊkə(r), 'xɑːnʊkə(r), -z
AM 'hanəkə, -z

Hanuman
BR ˌhʌnʊ'mɑːn
AM 'hanə'man

hanuman
BR ˌhʌnʊ'mɑːn, -z
AM ˌhænə,man, hə'nʊmən, -z

hap
BR hap, -s, -ɪŋ, -t
AM hæp, -s, -ɪŋ, -t

hapax
BR 'hapaks
AM 'hæ,pæks

hapax legomena
BR ˌhapaks lɪ'gʊmɪnə(r)
AM ˌhæpæks lə'gamənə

hapax legomenon
BR ˌhapaks lɪ'gʊmɪnən, + lɪ'gʊmɪnɒn
AM ˌhæpæks lə'gamə,nan

ha'penny
BR 'heɪpn|i, -ɪz
AM 'heɪp(ə)ni, -z

haphazard
BR ˌhap'hazəd
AM ˌhæp'hæzərd

haphazardly
BR ˌhap'hazədli
AM ˌhæp'hæzərdli

haphazardness
BR ˌhap'hazədnəs
AM ˌhæp'hæzərdnəs

haphtarah
BR ˌhaː'ftaː'raː(r)
AM ˌhaftə'ra

haphtaroth
BR ˌhaː'ftaː'rəʊt
AM ˌhaftə'raθ

haphtorah
BR ˌhaː'ftəʊraː(r), ˌhaː'ftəʊrə(r)
AM ˌhaftə'ra

hapless
BR 'hapləs
AM 'hæpləs

haplessly
BR 'haplǝsli
AM 'hæpləsli

haplessness
BR 'haplǝsnǝs
AM 'hæpləsnǝs

haplography
BR hap'lɒgrəfi
AM hæp'lagrəfi

haploid
BR 'haplɔɪd
AM 'hæp,lɔɪd

haplology
BR hap'lɒlədʒ|i, -ɪz
AM hæp'lalədʒi, -z

haply
BR 'hapli
AM 'hæpli

hap'orth
BR 'heɪpəθ, -s
AM 'heɪpərθ, -s

ha'p'orth
BR 'heɪpəθ
AM 'heɪpərθ

happen
BR 'hap|(ə)n, -(ə)nz, -(ə)nɪŋ\-ˌnɪŋ, -(ə)nd
AM 'hæp|ən, -ənz\ˌmz, -(ə)nɪŋ, -ənd\ˌnd

happening
BR 'hap(ə)nɪŋ, 'hapnɪŋ, -z
AM 'hæp(ə)nɪŋ, -z

happenstance
BR 'hap(ə)nstans, 'hap(ə)nsta:ns
AM 'hæpən,stæns

happi
BR 'hap|i, -ɪz
AM 'hæpi, -z

happi-coat
BR 'hapɪkəʊt, -s
AM 'hæpi,koʊt, -s

happily
BR 'hapɪli
AM 'hæp(ə)li

happiness
BR 'hapɪnɪs, -ɪz
AM 'hæpɪnɪs, -ɪz

Happisburgh
BR 'heɪzb(ə)rə(r)
AM 'heɪzbərə

happy
BR 'hap|i, -ɪə(r), -ɪɪst
AM 'hæpi, -ər, -ɪst

happy-go-lucky
BR ˌhapɪgə(ʊ)'lʌki
AM ˌhæpi,goʊ'ləki

Hapsburg
BR 'hapsbəːg, 'habzbəːg, -z
AM 'hæps,bərg, 'habs,bərg, -z

haptic
BR 'haptɪk
AM 'hæptɪk

hara-kiri
BR ˌharə'kɪri
AM ˌhɛrə'kɪri, ˌhɛrə'kɛri

harangue
BR hə'raŋ, -z, -ɪŋ, -d
AM hə'ræŋ, -z, -ɪŋ, -d

haranguer
BR hə'raŋə(r), -z
AM hə'ræŋər, -z

Harappa
BR hə'rapə(r)
AM hə'ræpə

Harare
BR hə'raːri
AM hə'rari

harass
BR 'harəs, hə'ras, -ɪz, -ɪŋ, -t
AM 'hæras, 'hɛrəs, -əz, -ɪŋ, -t

harasser
BR 'harəsə(r), hə'rasə(r), -z
AM hə'ræsər, 'hɛrəsər, -z

harassingly
BR 'harəsɪŋli, hə'rasɪŋli
AM hə'ræsɪŋli, 'hɛrəsɪŋli

harassment
BR 'harəsm(ə)nt, hə'rasm(ə)nt
AM hə'ræsmənt, 'hɛrəsmənt

Harben
BR 'haːb(ə)n
AM 'harbən

harbinger
BR 'haːbɪn(d)ʒə(r), -z
AM 'harbəndʒər, -z

harbor
BR 'haːb|ə(r), -əz, -(ə)rɪŋ, -əd
AM 'harbər, -z, -ɪŋ, -d

harborage
BR 'haːb(ə)rɪdʒ
AM 'harbərɪdʒ

harborless
BR 'haːbələs
AM 'harbərləs

harbormaster
BR 'haːbə,maːstə(r), 'haːbə,mastə(r), -z
AM 'harbər,mæstər, -z

harbour
BR 'haːb|ə(r), -əz, -(ə)rɪŋ, -əd
AM 'harbər, -z, -ɪŋ, -d

harbourage
BR 'haːb(ə)rɪdʒ
AM 'harbərɪdʒ

harbourless
BR 'haːbələs
AM 'harbərləs

harbourmaster
BR 'hɑːbəˌmɑːstə(r),
'hɑːbəˌmɑstə(r), -z
AM 'hɑrbərˌmæstər, -z

Harcourt
BR 'hɑːkɔːt
AM 'hɑrˌkɔ(ə)rt

hard
BR hɑːd, -ə(r), -ɪst
AM hɑrd, -ər, -əst

hardback
BR 'hɑːdbak, -s
AM 'hɑrdˌbæk, -s

hardbake
BR 'hɑːdbeɪk
AM 'hɑrdˌbeɪk

hardball
BR 'hɑːdbɔːl
AM 'hɑrdˌbɔl,
'hɑrdˌbal

hardbitten
BR ˌhɑːd'bɪtn
AM ˌhɑrd'bɪtn

hardboard
BR 'hɑːdbɔːd
AM 'hɑrdˌbɔ(ə)rd

hardbound
BR 'hɑːdbaʊnd
AM 'hɑrdˌbaʊnd

Hardcastle
BR 'hɑːdˌkɑːsl,
'hɑːdˌkɑsln
AM 'hɑrdˌkæsəl

hardcore
noun
BR 'hɑːdkɔː(r)
AM 'hærdˌkɔ(ə)r

hard-core
adjective
BR ˌhɑːd'kɔː(r)
AM 'hɑrdˌkɔ(ə)r

hardcover
BR ˌhɑːd'kʌvə(r)
AM 'hɑrdˌkʌvər

harden
BR 'hɑːd|n, -nz,
-nɪŋ \ -nɪŋ, -nd
AM 'hɑrdən, -z, -ɪŋ, -d

hardener
BR 'hɑːdnə(r),
'hɑːdnə(r), -z
AM 'hɑrdnər, -z

hardhat
BR 'hɑːdhat, -s
AM 'hɑrdˌ(h)æt, -s

hardheaded
BR ˌhɑːd'hɛdɪd
AM 'hɑrdˌhɛdəd

hard-headedly
BR ˌhɑːd'hɛdɪdli
AM 'hɑrdˌhɛdədli

hard-
headedness
BR ˌhɑːd'hɛdɪdnɪs
AM 'hɑrdˌhɛdədnəs

hard-hearted
BR ˌhɑːd'hɑːtɪd
AM 'hɑrd'hɑrdəd

hard-heartedly
BR ˌhɑːd'hɑːtɪdli
AM 'hɑrd'hɑrdədli

hard-
heartedness
BR ˌhɑːd'hɑːtɪdnɪs
AM 'hɑrd'hɑrdədnəs

Hardicanute
BR 'hɑːdɪkəˌnjuːt
AM 'hɑrdəkəˌnut

Hardie
BR 'hɑːdi
AM 'hɑrdi

hardihood
BR 'hɑːdɪhʊd
AM 'hɑrdiˌ(h)ʊd

hardily
BR 'hɑːdɪli
AM 'hɑrdəli

Hardin
BR 'hɑːdɪn
AM 'hɑrdən

hardiness
BR 'hɑːdɪnɪs
AM 'hɑrdinɪs

Harding
BR 'hɑːdɪŋ
AM 'hɑrdɪŋ

hardish
BR 'hɑːdɪʃ
AM 'hɑrdɪʃ

hardline
adjective
BR ˌhɑːd'lʌɪn
AM 'hɑrdˌlaɪn

hardliner
BR ˌhɑːd'lʌɪnə(r), -z
AM 'hɑrdˌlaɪnər, -z

hardly
BR 'hɑːdli
AM 'hɑrdli

Hardman
BR 'hɑːdmən
AM 'hɑrdmən

hardness
BR 'hɑːdnəs
AM 'hɑrdnəs

hardpan
BR 'hɑːdpan, -z
AM 'hɑrdˌpæn, -z

hardshell
BR 'hɑːdʃɛl, -z
AM 'hɑrdˌʃɛl, -z

hardship
BR 'hɑːdʃɪp, -s
AM 'hɑrdˌʃɪp, -s

hardstanding
BR ˌhɑːd'standɪŋ
AM 'hɑrd'stændɪŋ

hardtack
BR 'hɑːdtak
AM 'hɑrdˌtæk

hardtop
BR 'hɑːdtɒp, -s
AM 'hɑrdˌtɑp, -s

Hardwar
BR 'hɑːdwɑː(r)

hardware
BR 'hɑːdweː(r)
AM 'hɑrdˌwɛ(ə)r

hardwearing
BR ˌhɑːd'wɛːrɪŋ
AM 'hɑrd'werɪŋ

Hardwick
BR 'hɑːdwɪk
AM 'hɑrdˌwɪk

Hardwicke
BR 'hɑːdwɪk
AM 'hɑrdˌwɪk

hardwood
BR 'hɑːdwʊd, -z
AM 'hɑrdˌwʊd, -z

hardworking
BR ˌhɑːd'wəːkɪŋ
AM 'hɑrd'wərkɪŋ

hardy
BR 'hɑːd|i, -ɪə(r), -ɪɪst
AM 'hɑrdi, -ər, -ɪst

hare
BR hɛː(r), -z, -ɪŋ, -d
AM hɛ(ə)r, -z, -ɪŋ, -d

harebell
BR 'hɛːbɛl, -z
AM 'hɛrˌbɛl, -z

harebrained
BR 'hɛːbreɪnd
AM 'hɛrˌbreɪn(d)

Hare Krishna
BR ˌhari 'krɪʃnə(r)
AM ˌhari 'krɪʃnə,
ˌhɛri +

harelip
BR ˌhɛː'lɪp, -s
AM 'hɛrˌlɪp, -s

harelipped
BR ˌhɛː'lɪpt
AM 'hɛr'lɪpt

harem
BR 'hɛːrəm, 'hɑːriːm,
(ˌ)hɑː'riːm, -z
AM 'hɛrəm, -z

Harewood[1]
name of Earl and
House in UK
BR 'hɑːwʊd
AM 'hɑrˌwʊd

Harewood[2]
place in UK
BR 'hɛːwʊd
AM 'hɛrˌwʊd

harewood
BR 'hɛːwʊd
AM 'hɛrˌwʊd

Hargraves
BR 'hɑːgreɪvz
AM 'hɑrˌgreɪvz

Hargreaves
BR 'hɑːgriːvz,
'hɑːgreɪvz
AM 'hɑrˌgreɪvz

haricot
BR 'harɪkəʊ, -z
AM 'hɛrəˌkoʊ, -z

Harijan
BR 'hʌrɪdʒ(ə)n,
'harɪdʒ(ə)n,
'harɪdʒan, -z
AM 'hɛrəˌdʒæn, -z

hark
BR hɑːk, -s, -ɪŋ, -t
AM hɑrk, -s, -ɪŋ, -t

harken
BR 'hɑːk|n, -nz,
-nɪŋ \ -(ə)nɪŋ, -nd
AM 'hɑrk|ən, -ənz,
-(ə)nɪŋ, -ənd

Harkness
BR 'hɑːknɪs
AM 'hɑrknəs

harl
BR hɑːl, -z
AM hɑrl, -z

Harland
BR 'hɑːlənd
AM 'hɑrlən(d)

harle
BR hɑːl
AM hɑrl

Harlech
BR 'hɑːləx, 'hɑːlək
AM 'hɑrlɛk

Harlem
BR 'hɑːləm
AM 'hɑrləm

harlequin
BR 'hɑːlɪkwɪn, -z
AM 'hɑrlək(w)ən, -z

harlequinade
BR ˌhɑːlɪkwɪ'neɪd, -z
AM ˌhɑrlək(w)ə'neɪd,
-z

Harlesden
BR 'hɑːlzd(ə)n
AM 'hɑrlzdən

Harley Street
BR 'hɑːlɪ striːt
AM 'hɑrli ˌstrit

harlot
BR 'hɑːlət, -s
AM 'hɑrlət, -s

harlotry
BR 'hɑːlətri
AM 'hɑrlətri

Harlow
BR 'hɑːləʊ
AM 'hɑrloʊ

Harlowe
BR 'hɑːləʊ
AM 'hɑrloʊ

harm
BR hɑːm, -z, -ɪŋ, -d
AM hɑrm, -z, -ɪŋ, -d

Harman
BR 'hɑːmən
AM 'hɑrmən

harmattan
BR hɑː'matn, -z
AM ˌhɑrmə'tan, -z

Harmer
BR 'hɑːmə(r)

AM ˈhɑːrmər
harmful
BR ˈhɑːmf(ʊ)l
AM ˈhɑːrmfəl
harmfully
BR ˈhɑːmfəli, ˈhɑːmfˌli
AM ˈhɑːrmfəli
harmfulness
BR ˈhɑːmf(ʊ)lnəs
AM ˈhɑːrmfəlnəs
harmless
BR ˈhɑːmləs
AM ˈhɑːrmləs
harmlessly
BR ˈhɑːmləsli
AM ˈhɑːrmləsli
harmlessness
BR ˈhɑːmləsnəs
AM ˈhɑːrmləsnəs
Harmon
BR ˈhɑːmən
AM ˈhɑːrmən
Harmondsworth
BR ˈhɑːmən(d)zwəːθ
AM ˈhɑːrmən(d)zˌwərθ
harmonic
BR hɑːˈmɒnɪk
AM hɑrˈmɑnɪk
harmonica
BR hɑːˈmɒnɪkə(r), -z
AM hɑrˈmɑnəkə, -z
harmonically
BR hɑːˈmɒnɪkli
AM hɑrˈmɑnək(ə)li
harmonious
BR hɑːˈməʊnɪəs
AM hɑrˈmoʊnɪəs
harmoniously
BR hɑːˈməʊnɪəsli
AM hɑrˈmoʊnɪəsli
harmoniousness
BR hɑːˈməʊnɪəsnəs
AM hɑrˈmoʊnɪəsnəs
harmonisation
BR ˌhɑːmənʌɪˈzeɪʃn, -z
AM ˌhɑrmənəˈzeɪʃən, ˌhɑrməˌnaɪˈzeɪʃən, -z
harmonise
BR ˈhɑːmənʌɪz, -ɪz, -ɪŋ, -d
AM ˈhɑrməˌnaɪz, -ɪz, -ɪŋ, -d
harmonist
BR ˈhɑːmənɪst, -s
AM ˈhɑrmənəst, -s
harmonistic
BR ˌhɑːməˈnɪstɪk
AM ˌhɑrməˈnɪstɪk
harmonium
BR hɑːˈməʊnɪəm, -z
AM hɑrˈmoʊnɪəm, -z
harmonization
BR ˌhɑːmənʌɪˈzeɪʃn, -z
AM ˌhɑrmənəˈzeɪʃən, ˌhɑrməˌnaɪˈzeɪʃən, -z

harmonize
BR ˈhɑːmənʌɪz, -ɪz, -ɪŋ, -d
AM ˈhɑrməˌnaɪz, -ɪz, -ɪŋ, -d
harmony
BR ˈhɑːmənˌi, -ɪz
AM ˈhɑrməni, -z
Harmsworth
BR ˈhɑːmzwəːθ
AM ˈhɑrmzˌwərθ
harness
BR ˈhɑːnɪs, -ɪz, -ɪŋ, -t
AM ˈhɑrnəs, -əz, -ɪŋ, -t
harnesser
BR ˈhɑːnɪsə(r), -z
AM ˈhɑrnəsər, -z
Harold
BR ˈhærˌld
AM ˈhɛrəld
harp
BR hɑːp, -s, -ɪŋ, -t
AM hɑrp, -s, -ɪŋ, -t
Harpenden
BR ˈhɑːp(ə)ndən
AM ˈhɑrpəndən
harper
BR ˈhɑːpə(r), -z
AM ˈhɑrpər, -z
Harpic®
BR ˈhɑːpɪk
AM ˈhɑrpək
harpie
BR ˈhɑːpˌi, -ɪz
AM ˈhɑrpi, -z
harpist
BR ˈhɑːpɪst, -s
AM ˈhɑrpəst, -s
Harpocrates
BR hɑːˈpɒkrəti:z
AM hɑrˈpɑkrəˌtiz
harpoon
BR hɑːˈpuːn, -z, -ɪŋ, -d
AM ˌhɑrˈpun, -z, -ɪŋ, -d
harpooner
BR hɑːˈpuːnə(r), -z
AM ˌhɑrˈpunər, -z
harpsichord
BR ˈhɑːpsɪkɔːd, -z
AM ˈhɑrpsəˌkɔ(ə)rd, -z
harpsichordist
BR ˈhɑːpsɪkɔːdɪst, -s
AM ˈhɑrpsəˌkordəst, -s
harpy
BR ˈhɑːpˌi, -ɪz
AM ˈhɑrpi, -z
harquebus
BR ˈ(h)ɑːkwɪbəs, -ɪz
AM ˈ(h)ɑrk(w)əbəs, -əz
harquebusier
BR ˌ(h)ɑːkwɪbəˈsɪə(r), -z
AM ˌ(h)ɑrk(w)əbəˈsɪ(ə)r, -z
Harrap
BR ˈhærəp
AM ˈhɛrəp

Harrell
BR ˈhærəl, ˈharl̩
AM ˈhɛrəl
harridan
BR ˈhærɪd(ə)n, -z
AM ˈhɛrədən, -z
harrier
BR ˈhærɪə(r), -z
AM ˈhɛrɪər, -z
Harries
BR ˈhærɪs, ˈharɪz
AM ˈhɛriz
Harriet
BR ˈhærɪət
AM ˈhɛriət
Harriman
BR ˈharɪmən
AM ˈhɛrəmən
Harrington
BR ˈharɪŋt(ə)n
AM ˈhɛrɪŋtən
Harris
BR ˈharɪs
AM ˈhɛrəs
Harrisburg
BR ˈharɪsbəːg
AM ˈhɛrəsˌbərg
Harrison
BR ˈharɪs(ə)n
AM ˈhɛrəsən
Harrod
BR ˈharəd, -z
AM ˈhɛrəd, -z
Harrogate
BR ˈharəgət, ˈharəgeɪt
AM ˈhɛrəˌgeɪt
Harrovian
BR həˈrəʊvɪən, hɑˈrəʊvɪən, -z
AM həˈroʊvɪən, -z
harrow
BR ˈharəʊ, -z, -ɪŋ, -d
AM ˈhɛr|oʊ, -oʊz, -əwɪŋ, -oʊd
harrower
BR ˈharəʊə(r), -z
AM ˈhɛrəwər, -z
harrowingly
BR ˈharəʊɪŋli
AM ˈhɛrəwɪŋli
harrumph
BR həˈrʌmf, -s, -ɪŋ, -t
AM həˈrəm(p)f, -s, -ɪŋ, -t
harry
BR ˈhar|i, -ɪz, -ɪɪŋ, -ɪd
AM ˈhɛri, -z, -ɪŋ, -d
harsh
BR hɑːʃ, -ə(r), -ɪst
AM hɑrʃ, -ər, -əst
harshen
BR ˈhɑːʃ|n, -nz, -nɪŋ \ -ənɪŋ, -nd
AM ˈhɑrʃ|ən, -ənz, -(ə)nɪŋ, -ənd
harshly
BR ˈhɑːʃli
AM ˈhɑrʃli

harshness
BR ˈhɑːʃnəs
AM ˈhɑrʃnəs
harslet
BR ˈhɑːslɪt
AM ˈhɑrslət
hart
BR hɑːt, -s
AM hɑrt, -s
hartal
BR ˈhɑːtɑːl, ˈhəːtɑːl, hɑːˈtɑːl, həːˈtɑːl
AM hɑrˈtɑl
Harte
BR hɑːt
AM hɑrt
hartebeest
BR ˈhɑːtɪbiːst, -s
AM ˈhɑrdəˌbist, -s
Hartford
BR ˈhɑːtfəd
AM ˈhɑrtfərd
Hartland
BR ˈhɑːtlənd
AM ˈhɑrtlənd
Hartlepool
BR ˈhɑːtlɪpuːl
AM ˈhɑrtliˌpul
Hartley
BR ˈhɑːtli
AM ˈhɑrtli
Hartman
BR ˈhɑːtmən
AM ˈhɑrtmən
Hartnell
BR ˈhɑːtnl
AM ˈhɑrtnəl
hartshorn
BR ˈhɑːtshɔːn
AM ˈhɑrts,(h)ɔ(ə)rn
Hartshorne
BR ˈhɑːtshɔːn
AM ˈhɑrt,ʃɔ(ə)rn
harum-scarum
BR ˌhɛːrəmˈskɛːrəm
AM ˌhɛrəmˈskɛrəm
haruspex
BR həˈrʌspɛks, haˈrʌspɛks, ˈharəspɛks
AM həˈrəˌspɛks, ˈhɛrəspɛks
haruspices
BR həˈrʌspɪsiːz, haˈrʌspɪsiːz
AM həˈrəspəˌsiz
haruspicy
BR həˈrʌspɪsi, haˈrʌspɪsi
AM həˈrəspəsi
Harvard
BR ˈhɑːvəd
AM ˈhɑrvərd
harvest
BR ˈhɑːvɪst, -s, -ɪŋ, -ɪd
AM ˈhɑrvəst, -s, -ɪŋ, -əd

harvestable
BR ˈhɑːvɪstəbl
AM ˈhɑrvəstəbəl
harvester
BR ˈhɑːvɪstə(r), -z
AM ˈhɑrvəstər, -z
harvestman
BR ˈhɑːvɪs(t)mən
AM ˈhɑrvəs(t)mən
harvestmen
BR ˈhɑːvɪs(t)mən
AM ˈhɑrvəs(t)mən
Harvey
BR ˈhɑːvi
AM ˈhɑrvi
Harwich
BR ˈharɪdʒ, ˈharɪtʃ
AM ˈhɛrɪdʒ
Harwood
BR ˈhɑːwʊd
AM ˈhɑrˌwʊd
Haryana
BR ˌhariˈɑːnə(r)
AM ˌhariˈɑnə
Harz
BR ˈhɑːts
AM ˈhɑrts
has¹
strong
BR haz
AM hæz
has²
weak
BR (h)əz, z, s
AM (h)əz, z, s
Hasdrubal
BR ˈhazdrʊbl,
ˈhazdruːbl,
ˈhazdrʊbal
AM ˈhæzdrubəl
Hašek
BR ˈhaʃɛk
AM ˈhæʃɛk
CZ ˈhʌʃɛk
Haseldine
BR ˈheɪzldʌɪn
AM ˈheɪzəlˌdaɪn
hash
BR haʃ, -ɪz, -ɪŋ, -t
AM hæʃ, -əz, -ɪŋ, -t
hash-browns
BR ˌhaʃˈbraʊnz
AM ˈhæʃˌbraʊnz
hasheesh
BR ˈhaʃiːʃ, ˈhaʃɪʃ,
haˈʃiːʃ
AM ˌhæˈʃiʃ, haˈʃiʃ
Hashemite
BR ˈhaʃɪmʌɪt, -s
AM ˈhæʃəˌmaɪt, -s
hashish
BR ˈhaʃiːʃ, ˈhaʃɪʃ,
haˈʃiːʃ
AM hæˈʃiʃ, haˈʃiʃ
Hasid
BR ˈhasɪd
AM ˈhæsɪd

hasidic
BR haˈsɪdɪk
AM həˈsɪdɪk
Hasidim
BR ˈhasɪdɪm
AM həˈsidɪm
Hasidism
BR ˈhasɪdɪz(ə)m
AM ˈhæsəˌdɪzəm
Haslam
BR ˈhazləm
AM ˈhæzləm
Haslemere
BR ˈheɪzlmɪə(r)
AM ˈheɪzəlˌmɪ(ə)r
haslet
BR ˈhazlɪt, ˈheɪzlɪt
AM ˈhæslət, ˈheɪzlət
Haslett
BR ˈheɪzlɪt, ˈhazlɪt
AM ˈhæzlət
Hasmonean
BR ˌhazməˈniːən
AM ˌhæzməˈniən
hasn't
BR ˈhaznt
AM ˈhæznt
hasp
BR hɑːsp, hasp, -s
AM hæsp, -s
Hassall
BR ˈhasl
AM ˈhæsəl
Hassan
BR həˈsɑːn, haˈsɑːn,
ˈhasn
AM hɑˈsan
Hasselt
BR ˈhaslt
AM ˈhæsəlt
hassle
BR ˈhas|l, -lz, -l̩ŋ\-lɪŋ,
-ld
AM ˈhæs|əl, -əlz, -(ə)lɪŋ,
-əld
hassock
BR ˈhasək, -s
AM ˈhæsək, -s
hast
BR hast
AM hæst
hastate
BR ˈhasteɪt
AM ˈhæˌsteɪt
haste
BR heɪst
AM heɪst
hasten
BR ˈheɪs|n, -nz,
-n̩ɪŋ\-nɪŋ, -nd
AM ˈheɪs|n, -nz, -n̩ɪŋ,
-nd
Hastie
BR ˈheɪsti
AM ˈheɪsti
hastily
BR ˈheɪstɪli

AM ˈheɪstɪli
hastiness
BR ˈheɪstɪnɪs
AM ˈheɪstinɪs
Hastings
BR ˈheɪstɪŋz
AM ˈheɪstɪŋz
hasty
BR ˈheɪst|i, -ɪə(r), -ɪɪst
AM ˈheɪsti, -ər, -ɪst
hat
BR hat, -s
AM hæt, -s
hatable
BR ˈheɪtəbl
AM ˈheɪdəbəl
hatband
BR ˈhatband, -z
AM ˈhætˌbænd, -z
hatbox
BR ˈhatbɒks, -ɪz
AM ˈhætˌbɑks, -əz
hatch
BR hatʃ, -ɪz, -ɪŋ, -t
AM hætʃ, -ɪz, -ɪŋ, -t
hatchback
BR ˈhatʃbak, -s
AM ˈhætʃˌbæk, -s
Hatcher
BR ˈhatʃə(r)
AM ˈhætʃər
hatchery
BR ˈhatʃ(ə)r|i, -ɪz
AM ˈhætʃəri, -z
hatchet
BR ˈhatʃɪt, -s
AM ˈhætʃət, -s
hatching
BR ˈhatʃɪŋ, -z
AM ˈhætʃɪŋ, -z
hatchling
BR ˈhatʃlɪŋ, -z
AM ˈhætʃlɪŋ, -z
hatchment
BR ˈhatʃm(ə)nt, -s
AM ˈhætʃmənt, -s
hatchway
BR ˈhatʃweɪ, -z
AM ˈhætʃˌweɪ, -z
hate
BR heɪt, -s, -ɪŋ, -ɪd
AM heɪt, -ts, -dɪŋ, -dɪd
hateful
BR ˈheɪtf(ʊ)l
AM ˈheɪtfəl
hatefully
BR ˈheɪtfʊli, ˈheɪtfḷi
AM ˈheɪtfəli
hatefulness
BR ˈheɪtf(ʊ)lnəs
AM ˈheɪtfəlnəs
hater
BR ˈheɪtə(r), -z
AM ˈheɪdər, -z
Hatfield
BR ˈhatfiːld
AM ˈhætˌfild

hatful
BR ˈhatfʊl, -z
AM ˈhætˌfʊl, -z
hath
BR haθ
AM hæθ
Hathaway
BR ˈhaθəweɪ
AM ˈhæθəˌweɪ
hatha-yoga
BR ˌhʌtəˈjəʊgə(r),
ˌhaθəˈjəʊgə(r)
AM ˈhɑθəˈjəʊgə,
ˈhɑdəˈjəʊgə
Hatherley
BR ˈhaðəli
AM ˈhæðərli
Hathern
BR ˈhaðn
AM ˈhæðərn
Hathersage
BR ˈhaðəseɪdʒ,
ˈhaðəsɪdʒ
AM ˈhæðərˌseɪdʒ,
ˈhæðərsɪdʒ
Hathor
BR ˈhaθɔː(r)
AM ˈhæθər
hatless
BR ˈhatləs
AM ˈhætləs
hatpeg
BR ˈhatpɛg, -z
AM ˈhætˌpɛg, -z
hatpin
BR ˈhatpɪn, -z
AM ˈhætˌpɪn, -z
hatred
BR ˈheɪtrɪd
AM ˈheɪtrəd
Hatshepsut
BR hatˈʃɛpsuːt
AM hætˈʃɛpˌsut
hatstand
BR ˈhatstand, -z
AM ˈhætˌstænd, -z
hatter
BR ˈhatə(r), -z
AM ˈhædər, -z
Hatteras
BR ˈhat(ə)rəs
AM ˈhædərəs
Hattersley
BR ˈhatəzli
AM ˈhædərzli
Hattie
BR ˈhati
AM ˈhædi
Hatton
BR ˈhatn
AM ˈhætn
Hattusas
BR hatˈtuːsəs
AM hæ(t)ˈtusəs
hauberk
BR ˈhɔːbəːk, -s
AM ˈhɔbərk, ˈhabərk, -s

Haugh
BR hɔ:(r), hɔ:f
AM hɑʊ, hɔf, hɑf

Haughey
BR 'hɒxi, 'hɔ:hi
AM 'hɑʊi, 'hɔi

haughtily
BR 'hɔ:tɪli
AM 'hɑdəli, 'hɑdəli

haughtiness
BR 'hɔ:tɪnɪs
AM 'hɑdɪnɪs, 'hɑdɪnɪs

Haughton
BR 'hɔ:tn
AM 'hɔtn, 'hɑtn

haughty
BR 'hɔ:t|i, -ɪə(r), -ɪɪst
AM 'hɑdi, 'hɑdi, -ər, -ɪɪst

haul
BR hɔ:l, -z, -ɪŋ, -d
AM hɔl, hɑl, -z, -ɪŋ, -d

haulage
BR 'hɔ:lɪdʒ
AM 'hɔlɪdʒ, 'hɑlɪdʒ

hauler
BR 'hɔ:lə(r), -z
AM 'hɔlər, 'hɑlər, -z

haulier
BR 'hɔ:lɪə(r), -z
AM 'hɔljər, 'hɑljər, -z

haulm
BR hɔ:m, -z
AM hɔm, hɑ(l)m, -z

haulyard
BR 'hɔ:ljəd, -z
AM 'hɔljərd, 'hɑljərd, -z

haunch
BR hɔ:n(t)ʃ, -ɪz
AM hɒn(t)ʃ, hɑn(t)ʃ, -əz

haunt
BR hɔ:nt, -s, -ɪŋ, -ɪd
AM hɒn|t, hɑn|t, -ts, -(t)ɪŋ, -(t)əd

haunter
BR 'hɔ:ntə(r), -z
AM 'hɒn(t)ər, 'hɑn(t)ər, -z

hauntingly
BR 'hɔ:ntɪŋli
AM 'hɒn(t)ɪŋli, 'hɑn(t)ɪŋli

Hauptmann
BR 'haʊp(t)mən
AM 'haʊp(t)mɑn

Hausa
BR 'haʊsə(r), 'haʊzə(r), -z
AM 'haʊsə, 'haʊzə, -z

Hausfrau
BR 'haʊsfraʊ, -z
AM 'haʊs,fraʊ, -z

hautbois
BR '(h)əʊbɔɪ, -z
AM '(h)oʊ(t),bɔɪ, -z

hautboy
BR '(h)əʊbɔɪ, -z
AM '(h)oʊ(t),bɔɪ, -z

haute couture
BR ,əʊt kə'tjʊə(r), + kə'tʃʊə(r)
AM ,(h)oʊt ,ku'tʊ(ə)r

haute cuisine
BR ,əʊt kwɪ'zi:n
AM ,(h)oʊt ,kwə'zin

haute école
BR ,əʊt eɪ'kɒl
AM ,(h)oʊ 'tɛkɔl
FR 'ot ekɔl

hauteur
BR əʊ'tə:(r), hɔ:'tə:(r)
AM ,(h)oʊ'tər

haut monde
BR ,əʊ 'mɒnd
AM ,(h)oʊ 'mɔnd, + 'mɑnd

Havana
BR hə'vanə(r), -z
AM hə'vænə, hə'vɑnə, -z

Havant
BR 'havnt
AM 'hævənt

have¹
strong
BR hav, -z, -ɪŋ
AM hæv, -z, -ɪŋ

have²
weak
BR həv, (ə)v
AM həv, (ə)v

have-a-go
BR ,havə'gəʊ
AM ,hævə'goʊ

Havel
BR 'hɑ:v(ə)l
AM 'hɑvəl

Havelock
BR 'havlɒk
AM 'hævə,lɑk, 'hæv(ə),lɑk, 'hæv,lɑk

havelock
BR 'havlɒk, 'havlək, -s
AM 'hævə,lɑk, 'hæv(ə),lɑk, 'hæv,lɑk, -s

haven
BR 'heɪvn, -z
AM 'heɪvən, -z

have-not
BR ,hav'nɒt, 'havnɒt, -s
AM 'hæv,nɑt, -s

haven't
BR 'havnt
AM 'hævənt

haver
BR 'heɪv|ə(r), -əz, -(ə)rɪŋ, -əd
AM 'heɪvər, -z, -ɪŋ, -d

Haverfordwest
BR ,havəfəd'west
AM ,hævərfərd'west

Haverhill
BR 'heɪv(ə)rɪl, 'heɪv(ə)rl, 'heɪvəhɪl
AM 'hævər,hɪl

Havering
BR 'heɪv(ə)rɪŋ
AM 'hævərɪŋ

Havers
BR 'heɪvəz
AM 'heɪvərs

haversack
BR 'havəsak, -s
AM 'hævər,sæk, -s

haversine
BR 'havəsaɪn, -z
AM 'hævər,saɪn, -z

haves
BR havz
AM hævz

Haviland
BR 'havɪlənd
AM 'hævələnd

havildar
BR 'hav(ɪ)ldɑ:(r), -z
AM 'hævəl,dɑr, -z

havoc
BR 'havək
AM 'hævək

haw
BR hɔ:(r), -z, -ɪŋ, -d
AM hɔ, hɑ, -z, -ɪŋ, -d

Hawaii
BR hə'wʌɪi:
AM hə'waɪ(j)i

Hawaiian
BR hə'wʌɪən, -z
AM hə'waɪ(j)ən, -z

Hawes
BR hɔ:z
AM hɔz, haz

hawfinch
BR 'hɔ:fɪn(t)ʃ, -ɪz
AM 'hɔ,fɪntʃ, 'hɑ,fɪntʃ, -ɪz

haw-haw¹
interjection
BR ,hɔ:'hɔ:(r)
AM ,hɔ'hɔ, 'hɑ'ha

haw-haw²
noun
BR 'hɔ:hɔ:(r)
AM 'hɔ'hɔ, 'hɑ'ha

Hawick
BR 'hɔ:ɪk, hɔɪk
AM 'hɔwɪk, 'hɑwɪk

hawk
BR hɔ:k, -s, -ɪŋ, -t
AM hɔk, hɑk, -s, -ɪŋ, -t

hawkbit
BR 'hɔ:kbɪt, -s
AM 'hɔk,bɪt, 'hɑk,bɪt, -s

Hawke
BR hɔ:k
AM hɔk, hɑk

Hawke Bay
BR ,hɔ:k 'beɪ
AM 'hɔk 'beɪ, 'hɑk 'beɪ

hawker
BR 'hɔ:kə(r), -z
AM 'hɔkər, 'hɑkər, -z

Hawkes
BR hɔ:ks
AM hɔks, haks

Hawke's Bay
BR ,hɔ:ks 'beɪ
AM 'hɔks 'beɪ, 'haks 'beɪ

Hawking
BR 'hɔ:kɪŋ
AM 'hɔkɪŋ, 'hɑkɪŋ

Hawkins
BR 'hɔ:kɪnz
AM 'hɔkɪnz, 'hɑkɪnz

hawkish
BR 'hɔ:kɪʃ
AM 'hɔkɪʃ, 'hɑkɪʃ

hawkishness
BR 'hɔ:kɪʃnɪs
AM 'hɔkɪʃnɪs, 'hɑkɪʃnɪs

hawklike
BR 'hɔ:klʌɪk
AM 'hɔk,laɪk, 'hɑk,laɪk

hawkmoth
BR 'hɔ:kmɒθ, -s
AM 'hɔk,mɔθ, 'hɑk,mɑθ, -s

hawksbill
BR 'hɔ:ksbɪl, -z
AM 'hɔks,bɪl, 'haks,bɪl, -z

Hawksmoor
BR 'hɔ:ksmʊə(r), 'hɔ:ksmɔ:(r)
AM 'hɔks,mʊ(ə)r, 'haks,mɔ(ə)r

hawkweed
BR 'hɔ:kwi:d, -z
AM 'hɔk,wid, 'hak,wid, -z

Hawley
BR 'hɔ:li
AM 'hɔli, 'hali

Haworth
BR 'haʊəθ, 'hɔ:wəθ
AM 'hɔ,wərθ, 'ha,wərθ

hawse
BR hɔ:z, -ɪz
AM hɔz, haz, -əz

hawser
BR 'hɔ:zə(r), -z
AM 'hɔzər, 'hazər, -z

hawthorn
BR 'hɔ:θɔ:n, -z
AM 'hɔ,θɔ(ə)rn, 'ha,θɔ(ə)rn, -z

Hawtrey
BR 'hɔ:tri
AM 'hɔtri, 'hɑtri

Haxey
BR 'haksi
AM 'hæksi

hay
BR heɪ
AM heɪ

Hayakawa AM ˈheɪˌræk, -s
BR ˌhʌɪəˈkɑːwə(r)
AM ˌhaɪəˈkawə
haybox
BR ˈheɪbɒks, -ɪz
AM ˈheɪˌbɑks, -əz
haycock
BR ˈheɪkɒk, -s
AM ˈheɪˌkɑk, -s
Hayden
BR ˈheɪdn
AM ˈheɪd(ə)n
Haydn[1]
composer
BR ˈhʌɪdn
AM ˈhaɪdn
Haydn[2]
forename
BR ˈheɪdn
AM ˈheɪd(ə)n
Hayek
BR ˈhʌɪɛk, ˈhɑːjɛk
AM ˈhaɪɛk
Hayes
BR heɪz
AM heɪz
hayfield
BR ˈheɪfiːld, -z
AM ˈheɪˌfild, -z
hayfork
BR ˈheɪfɔːk, -s
AM ˈheɪˌfɔ(ə)rk, -s
haylage
BR ˈheɪlɪdʒ
AM ˈheɪlɪdʒ
Hayle
BR heɪl
AM heɪl
Hayley
BR ˈheɪli
AM ˈheɪli
Hayling
BR ˈheɪlɪŋ
AM ˈheɪlɪŋ
hayloft
BR ˈheɪlɒft, -s
AM ˈheɪˌlɔft, ˈheɪˌlɑft, -s
haymaker
BR ˈheɪˌmeɪkə(r), -z
AM ˈheɪˌmeɪkər, -z
haymaking
BR ˈheɪˌmeɪkɪŋ
AM ˈheɪˌmeɪkɪŋ
Hayman
BR ˈheɪmən
AM ˈheɪmən
Haymarket
BR ˈheɪˌmɑːkɪt
AM ˈheɪˌmɑrkət
haymow
BR ˈheɪməʊ
AM ˈheɪˌmoʊ
Haynes
BR heɪnz
AM heɪnz
hayrack
BR ˈheɪrak, -s

hayrick
BR ˈheɪrɪk, -s
hayride
BR ˈheɪrʌɪd, -z
AM ˈheɪˌraɪd, -z
Hays
BR heɪz
AM heɪz
hayseed
BR ˈheɪsiːd, -z
AM ˈheɪˌsid, -z
haystack
BR ˈheɪstak, -s
AM ˈheɪˌstæk, -s
Hayter
BR ˈheɪtə(r)
AM ˈheɪdər
haywain
BR ˈheɪweɪn, -z
AM ˈheɪˌweɪn, -z
Hayward
BR ˈheɪwəd
AM ˈheɪwərd
haywire
BR ˈheɪˌwʌɪə(r)
AM ˈheɪˌwaɪ(ə)r
Haywood
BR ˈheɪwʊd, ˈheɪwəd
AM ˈheɪˌwʊd
Hayworth
BR ˈheɪwəθ, ˈheɪwəːθ
AM ˈheɪˌwərθ
Hazan
BR həˈzan
AM həˈzɑn
hazard
BR ˈhazəd, -z, -ɪŋ, -ɪd
AM ˈhæzərd, -z, -ɪŋ, -əd
hazardous
BR ˈhazədəs
AM ˈhæzərdəs
hazardously
BR ˈhazədəsli
AM ˈhæzərdəsli
hazardousness
BR ˈhazədəsnəs
AM ˈhæzərdəsnəs
haze
BR heɪz, -ɪz
AM heɪz, -ɪz
hazel
BR ˈheɪzl, -z
AM ˈheɪzəl, -z
hazelnut
BR ˈheɪzlnʌt, -s
AM ˈheɪzəlˌnət, -s
hazily
BR ˈheɪzɪli
AM ˈheɪzɪli
haziness
BR ˈheɪzɪnɪs
AM ˈheɪzɪnɪs
Hazlitt
BR ˈhazlɪt, ˈheɪzlɪt
AM ˈhæzlət

hazy
BR ˈheɪz|i, -ɪə(r), -ɪɪst
AM ˈheɪzi, -ər, -ɪst
Hazzard
BR ˈhazəd
AM ˈhæzərd
he[1]
noun
BR hiː, -z
AM hi, -z
he[2]
strong form pronoun
BR hiː
AM hi
he[3]
weak form pronoun
BR (h)i:
AM (h)i
head
BR hɛd, -z, -ɪŋ, -ɪd
AM hɛd, -z, -ɪŋ, -əd
headache
BR ˈhɛdeɪk, -s
AM ˈhɛdˌeɪk, -s
headachy
BR ˈhɛdeɪki
AM ˈhɛdˌeɪki
headage
BR ˈhɛdɪdʒ
AM ˈhɛdɪdʒ
headband
BR ˈhɛdband, -z
AM ˈhɛdˌbænd, -z
headbanger
BR ˈhɛdˌbaŋə(r), -z
AM ˈhɛdˌbæŋər, -z
headbanging
BR ˈhɛdˌbaŋɪŋ
AM ˈhɛdˌbæŋɪŋ
headboard
BR ˈhɛdbɔːd, -z
AM ˈhɛdˌbɔ(ə)rd, -z
headcheese
BR ˈhɛdtʃiːz
AM ˈhɛdˌtʃiz
headcount
BR ˈhɛdkaʊnt, -s
AM ˈhɛdˌkaʊnt, -s
headdress
BR ˈhɛddrɛs, -ɪz
AM ˈhɛ(d)ˌdrɛs, -əz
header
BR ˈhɛdə(r), -z
AM ˈhɛdər, -z
headfast
BR ˈhɛdfɑːst, ˈhɛdfast, -s
AM ˈhɛdˌfæst, -s
headfirst
BR ˌhɛdˈfəːst
AM ˌhɛdˈfərst
headgear
BR ˈhɛdɡɪə(r)
AM ˈhɛdˌɡɪ(ə)r
headhunt
BR ˈhɛdhʌnt, -s, -ɪŋ, -ɪd

hazy AM ˈhɛd(h)ən|t, -ts,
-(t)ɪŋ, -(t)əd
headhunter
BR ˈhɛdˌhʌntə(r), -z
AM ˈhɛd(h)ən(t)ər, -z
headily
BR ˈhɛdɪli
AM ˈhɛdəli
headiness
BR ˈhɛdɪnɪs
AM ˈhɛdɪnɪs
heading
BR ˈhɛdɪŋ, -z
AM ˈhɛdɪŋ, -z
headlamp
BR ˈhɛdlamp, -s
AM ˈhɛdˌlæmp, -s
headland
BR ˈhɛdlənd, -z
AM ˈhɛdlənd,
ˈhɛdˌlænd, -z
headless
BR ˈhɛdləs
AM ˈhɛdləs
headlight
BR ˈhɛdlʌɪt, -s
AM ˈhɛdˌlaɪt, -s
headline
BR ˈhɛdlʌɪn, -z, -ɪŋ, -d
AM ˈhɛdˌlaɪn, -z, -ɪŋ, -d
headliner
BR ˈhɛdˌlʌɪnə(r), -z
AM ˈhɛdˌlaɪnər, -z
headlock
BR ˈhɛdlɒk, -s
AM ˈhɛdˌlɑk, -s
headlong
BR ˈhɛdlɒŋ
AM ˈhɛdˌlɔŋ, ˈhɛdˌlɑŋ
headman[1]
chief
BR ˈhɛdmən, ˈhɛdman
AM ˈhɛdˈmæn
headman[2]
executioner
BR ˈhɛdmən, ˈhɛdman
AM ˈhɛdmən
headmaster
BR ˌhɛdˈmɑːstə(r),
ˌhɛdˈmɑstə(r), -z
AM ˈhɛdˈmæstər, -z
headmasterly
BR ˌhɛdˈmɑːstəli,
ˌhɛdˈmɑstəli
AM ˈhɛdˈmæstərli
headmen[1]
chiefs
BR ˈhɛdmən, ˈhɛdmɛn
AM ˈhɛdˈmɛn
headmen[2]
executioners
BR ˈhɛdmən, ˈhɛdmɛn
AM ˈhɛdmən
headmistress
BR ˌhɛdˈmɪstrɪs, -ɪz
AM ˈhɛdˈmɪstrɪs, -ɪz

headmost
BR ˈhɛdməʊst
AM ˈhɛdˌmoʊst
headnote
BR ˈhɛdnəʊt, -s
AM ˈhɛdˌnoʊt, -s
headphone
BR ˈhɛdfəʊn, -z
AM ˈhɛdˌfoʊn, -z
headpiece
BR ˈhɛdpiːs, -ɪz
AM ˈhɛdˌpis, -ɪz
headpin
BR ˈhɛdpɪn, -z
AM ˈhɛdˌpɪn, -z
headquarter
verb
BR ˈhɛdˌkwɔːt|ə(r), -əz,
-(ə)rɪŋ, -əd
AM ˈhɛdˌkwɔrdər, -ərz,
-(ə)rɪŋ, -ərd
headquarters
noun
BR ˌhɛdˈkwɔːtəz,
ˈhɛdˌkwɔːtəz
AM ˈhɛdˌkwɔrdərz
headrest
BR ˈhɛdrɛst, -s
AM ˈhɛdˌrɛst, -s
headroom
BR ˈhɛdruːm, ˈhɛdrʊm
AM ˈhɛdˌrum,
ˈhɛdˌrʊm
headsail
BR ˈhɛdseɪl, -z
AM ˈhɛdˌseɪl, -z
headscarf
BR ˈhɛdskɑːf
AM ˈhɛdˌskɑrf
headscarves
BR ˈhɛdskɑːvz
AM ˈhɛdˌskɑrvz
headset
BR ˈhɛdsɛt, -s
AM ˈhɛdˌsɛt, -s
headship
BR ˈhɛdʃɪp, -s
AM ˈhɛdˌʃɪp, -s
headshrinker
BR ˈhɛdˌʃrɪŋkə(r), -z
AM ˈhɛdˌʃrɪŋkər, -z
headsman
BR ˈhɛdzmən
AM ˈhɛdzmən
headsmen
BR ˈhɛdzmən
AM ˈhɛdzmən
headspace
BR ˈhɛdspeɪs
AM ˈhɛdˌspeɪs
headspring
BR ˈhɛdsprɪŋ, -z
AM ˈhɛdˌsprɪŋ, -z
headsquare
BR ˈhɛdskwɛː(r), -z
AM ˈhɛdˌskwɛ(ə)r, -z

headstall
BR ˈhɛdstɔːl, -z
AM ˈhɛdˌstɔl, ˈhɛdˌstal,
-z
headstock
BR ˈhɛdstɒk, -s
AM ˈhɛdˌstak, -s
headstone
BR ˈhɛdstəʊn, -z
AM ˈhɛdˌstoʊn, -z
headstrong
BR ˈhɛdstrɒŋ
AM ˈhɛdˌstrɔŋ,
ˈhɛdˌstrɑŋ
headstrongly
BR ˈhɛdstrɒŋli
AM ˈhɛdˌstrɔŋli,
ˈhɛdˌstrɑŋli
headstrongness
BR ˈhɛdstrɒŋnəs
AM ˈhɛdˌstrɔŋnəs,
ˈhɛdˌstrɑŋnəs
headteacher
BR ˌhɛdˈtiːtʃə(r), -z
AM ˌhɛdˈtitʃər, -z
headward
BR ˈhɛdwəd
AM ˈhɛdwərd
headwater
BR ˈhɛdˌwɔːtə(r), -z
AM ˈhɛdˌwɔdər,
ˈhɛdˌwɑdər, -z
headway
BR ˈhɛdweɪ
AM ˈhɛdˌweɪ
headwind
BR ˈhɛdwɪnd, -z
AM ˈhɛdˌwɪnd, -z
headword
BR ˈhɛdwɜːd, -z
AM ˈhɛdˌwɜrd, -z
headwork
BR ˈhɛdwɜːk
AM ˈhɛdˌwɜrk
heady
BR ˈhɛd|i, -ɪə(r), -ɪɪst
AM ˈhɛdi, -ər, -ɪst
heal
BR hiːl, -z, -ɪŋ, -d
AM hil, -z, -ɪŋ, -d
healable
BR ˈhiːləbl
AM ˈhiləbəl
heald
BR hiːld, -z
AM hild, -z
healer
BR ˈhiːlə(r), -z
AM ˈhilər, -z
Healey
BR ˈhiːli
AM ˈhili
health
BR hɛlθ
AM hɛlθ
healthful
BR ˈhɛlθf(ʊ)l

AM ˈhɛlθfəl
healthfully
BR ˈhɛlθfəli, ˈhɛlθfʃi
AM ˈhɛlθfəli
healthfulness
BR ˈhɛlθf(ʊ)lnəs
AM ˈhɛlθfəlnəs
healthily
BR ˈhɛlθɪli
AM ˈhɛlθəli
healthiness
BR ˈhɛlθɪnɪs
AM ˈhɛlθinɪs
healthy
BR ˈhɛlθ|i, -ɪə(r), -ɪɪst
AM ˈhɛlθi, -ər, -ɪst
Healy
BR ˈhiːli
AM ˈhili
Heaney
BR ˈhiːni
AM ˈhini
Heanor
BR ˈhiːnə(r)
AM ˈhinər
heap
BR hiːp, -s, -ɪŋ, -t
AM hip, -s, -ɪŋ, -t
hear
BR hɪə(r), -z, -ɪŋ
AM hɪ|(ə)r, -(ə)rz, -rɪŋ
hearable
BR ˈhɪərəbl
AM ˈhɪrəbəl
Heard
BR hɜːd
AM hɜrd
hearer
BR ˈhɪərə(r), -z
AM ˈhɪrər, -z
hearken
BR ˈhɑːk|(ə)n, -(ə)nz,
-ɳɪŋ \-(ə)nɪŋ, -(ə)nd
AM ˈhɑrkən, -z, -ɪŋ, -d
Hearn
BR hɜːn
AM hɜrn
Hearne
BR hɜːn
AM hɜrn
hearsay
BR ˈhɪəseɪ
AM ˈhɪrˌseɪ
hearse
BR hɜːs, -ɪz
AM hɜrs, -əz
Hearst
BR hɜːst
AM hɜrst
heart
BR hɑːt, -s
AM hɑrt, -s
heartache
BR ˈhɑːteɪk, -s
AM ˈhɑrˌdeɪk, -s
heartbeat
BR ˈhɑːtbiːt, -s

AM ˈhɑrtˌbit, -s
heartbreak
BR ˈhɑːtbreɪk, -s, -ɪŋ
AM ˈhɑrtˌbreɪk, -s, -ɪŋ
heartbreaker
BR ˈhɑːtˌbreɪkə(r), -z
AM ˈhɑrtˌbreɪkər, -z
heartbreaking
BR ˈhɑːtˌbreɪkɪŋ
AM ˈhɑrtˌbreɪkɪŋ
heartbroken
BR ˈhɑːtˌbrəʊk(ə)n
AM ˈhɑrtˌbroʊkən
heartburn
BR ˈhɑːtbɜːn
AM ˈhɑrtˌbɜrn
hearten
BR ˈhɑːt|n, -nz,
-ɳɪŋ \-nɪŋ, -nd
AM ˈhɑrtən, -z, -ɪŋ, -d
hearteningly
BR ˈhɑːtnɪŋli,
ˈhɑːtnɪŋli
AM ˈhɑrtnɪŋli
heartfelt
BR ˈhɑːtfɛlt
AM ˈhɑrtˌfɛlt
hearth
BR hɑːθ, -s
AM hɑrθ, -s
hearthrug
BR ˈhɑːθrʌɡ, -z
AM ˈhɑrθˌrəɡ, -z
hearthstone
BR ˈhɑːθstəʊn, -z
AM ˈhɑrθˌstoʊn, -z
heartily
BR ˈhɑːtɪli
AM ˈhɑrdəli
heartiness
BR ˈhɑːtɪnɪs
AM ˈhɑrdinɪs
heartland
BR ˈhɑːtlənd,
ˈhɑːtland, -z
AM ˈhɑrtˌlænd, -z
heartless
BR ˈhɑːtləs
AM ˈhɑrtləs
heartlessly
BR ˈhɑːtləsli
AM ˈhɑrtləsli
heartlessness
BR ˈhɑːtləsnəs
AM ˈhɑrtləsnəs
heartrending
BR ˈhɑːtˌrɛndɪŋ
AM ˈhɑrtˌrɛndɪŋ
heartsearching
BR ˈhɑːtˌsəːtʃɪŋ
AM ˈhɑrtˌsərtʃɪŋ
heartsease
BR ˈhɑːtsiːz
AM ˈhɑrtˌsiz
heartsick
BR ˈhɑːtsɪk
AM ˈhɑrtˌsɪk

heartsickness
BR ˈhɑːtˌsɪknɪs
AM ˈhɑrtˌsɪknɪs
heartsore
BR ˈhɑːtsɔː(r)
AM ˈhɑrtˌsɔ(ə)r
heartstrings
BR ˈhɑːtstrɪŋz
AM ˈhɑrtˌstrɪŋz
heartthrob
BR ˈhɑːtθrɒb, -z
AM ˈhɑrtˌθrɑb, -z
heart-to-heart
BR ˌhɑːttəˈhɑːt, -s
AM ˌhɑr(t)təˈhɑrt, -s
heartwarming
BR ˈhɑːtˌwɔːmɪŋ
AM ˈhɑrtˌwɔrmɪŋ
heartwarmingly
BR ˈhɑːtˌwɔːmɪŋli
AM ˈhɑrtˌwɔrmɪŋli
heartwood
BR ˈhɑːtwʊd
AM ˈhɑrtˌwʊd
hearty
BR ˈhɑːt|i, -ɪə(r), -ɪɪst
AM ˈhɑrdi, -ər, -ɪst
heat
BR hiːt, -s, -ɪŋ, -ɪd
AM hi|t, -ts, -dɪŋ, -dɪd
heatedly
BR ˈhiːtɪdli
AM ˈhidɪdli
heater
BR ˈhiːtə(r), -z
AM ˈhidər, -z
heath
BR hiːθ, -s
AM hiθ, -s
Heathcliff
BR ˈhiːθklɪf
AM ˈhiθˌklɪf
Heathcliffe
BR ˈhiːθklɪf
AM ˈhiθˌklɪf
Heathcote
BR ˈhiːθkət, ˈhɛθkət
AM ˈhiθˌkoʊt
heathen
BR ˈhiːðn, -z
AM ˈhiðən, -z
heathendom
BR ˈhiːðndəm
AM ˈhiðəndəm
heathenish
BR ˈhiːðnɪʃ, ˈhiːðənɪʃ
AM ˈhiðənɪʃ
heathenishly
BR ˈhiːðnɪʃli,
ˈhiːðənɪʃli
AM ˈhiðənɪʃli
heathenishness
BR ˈhiːðnɪʃnɪs,
ˈhiːðənɪʃnɪs
AM ˈhiðənɪʃnɪs
heathenism
BR ˈhiːðnɪz(ə)m

AM ˈhiðəˌnɪzəm
heathenry
BR ˈhiːðnri
AM ˈhiðənri
heather
BR ˈhɛðə(r), -z
AM ˈhɛðər, -z
heathery
BR ˈhɛð(ə)ri
AM ˈhɛðəri
Heathfield
BR ˈhiːθfiːld
AM ˈhiθˌfild
heathland
BR ˈhiːθlənd, ˈhiːθland,
-z
AM ˈhiθˌlænd, -z
heathless
BR ˈhiːθlɪs
AM ˈhiθlɪs
heathlike
BR ˈhiːθlʌɪk
AM ˈhiθˌlaɪk
Heathrow
BR ˌhiːθˈrəʊ
AM ˈhiθˌroʊ
heathy
BR ˈhiːθi
AM ˈhiθi
Heaton
BR ˈhiːtn
AM ˈhitn
heatproof
BR ˈhiːtpruːf
AM ˈhitˌpruf
heatstroke
BR ˈhiːtstrəʊk
AM ˈhitˌstroʊk
heatwave
BR ˈhiːtweɪv, -z
AM ˈhitˌweɪv, -z
heave
BR hiːv, -z, -ɪŋ, -d
AM hiv, -z, -ɪŋ, -d
heave-ho
BR ˌhiːvˈhəʊ
AM ˈhivˈhoʊ
heaven
BR ˈhɛvn, -z
AM ˈhɛvən, -z
heavenliness
BR ˈhɛvnlɪnɪs
AM ˈhɛvənlinɪs
heavenly
BR ˈhɛvnli
AM ˈhɛvənli
heavenward
BR ˈhɛvnwəd, -z
AM ˈhɛvənwərd, -z
heaver
BR ˈhiːvə(r), -z
AM ˈhivər, -z
heavily
BR ˈhɛvɪli
AM ˈhɛvəli
heaviness
BR ˈhɛvɪnɪs

AM ˈhɛvɪnɪs
Heaviside
BR ˈhɛvɪsʌɪd
AM ˈhɛviˌsaɪd
heavy
BR ˈhɛv|i, -ɪə(r), -ɪɪst
AM ˈhɛvi, -ər, -ɪst
heavy-footed
BR ˌhɛvɪˈfʊtɪd
AM ˈhɛviˈfʊdəd
heavy-handed
BR ˌhɛvɪˈhandɪd
AM ˌhɛviˈhændəd
heavy-handedly
BR ˌhɛvɪˈhandɪdli
AM ˌhɛviˈhændədli
heavy-
handedness
BR ˌhɛvɪˈhandɪdnɪs
AM ˌhɛviˈhændədnəs
heavy-hearted
BR ˌhɛvɪˈhɑːtɪd
AM ˌhɛviˈhɑrdəd
heavyish
BR ˈhɛvɪɪʃ
AM ˈhɛvɪɪʃ
heavyset
BR ˌhɛvɪˈsɛt
AM ˌhɛviˈsɛt
heavyweight
BR ˈhɛvɪweɪt, -s
AM ˈhɛviˌweɪt, -s
Hebburn
BR ˈhɛb(əː)n
AM ˈhɛbərn
Hebden
BR ˈhɛbd(ə)n
AM ˈhɛbdən
hebdomadal
BR hɛbˈdɒmədl
AM hɛbˈdamədəl
hebdomadally
BR hɛbˈdɒmədli
AM hɛbˈdamədli
Hebe
BR ˈhiːbi
AM ˈhibi
Hebert
BR ˈhiːbət, ˈhɛbət
AM ˈhɛbərt, ˈeɪˌbɛ(ə)r
hebetude
BR ˈhɛbɪtjuːd,
ˈhɛbɪtʃuːd
AM ˈhɛbəˌt(j)ud
Hebraic
BR hɪˈbreɪk,
hiːˈbreɪk
AM hiˈbreɪk
Hebraically
BR hɪˈbreɪkli,
hiːˈbreɪkli
AM hiˈbreɪk(ə)li
Hebraise
BR ˈhiːbreɪʌɪz, -ɪz, -ɪŋ,
-d
AM ˈhiˌbreɪˌaɪz, -ɪz, -ɪŋ,
-d

AM ˈhɛvɪnɪs
Hebraism
BR ˈhiːbreɪɪz(ə)m, -z
AM ˈhiˌbreɪˌɪzəm, -z
Hebraist
BR ˈhiːbreɪɪst, -s
AM ˈhiˌbreɪɪst, -s
Hebraistic
BR ˌhiːbreɪˈɪstɪk
AM ˌhibreɪˈɪstɪk
Hebraize
BR ˈhiːbreɪʌɪz, -ɪz, -ɪŋ,
-d
AM ˈhiˌbreɪˌaɪz, -ɪz, -ɪŋ,
-d
Hebrew
BR ˈhiːbruː, -z
AM ˈhiˌbru, -z
Hebridean
BR ˌhɛbrɪˈdiːən, -z
AM ˌhɛbrəˈdiən, -z
Hebrides
BR ˈhɛbrɪdiːz
AM ˈhɛbrədiz
Hebron
BR ˈhiːbrɒn, ˈhɛbrɒn
AM ˈhibrən, ˈhiˌbran
Hecate¹
Shakespearean
BR ˈhɛkəti, ˈhɛkət
AM ˈhɛkədi
Hecate²
BR ˈhɛkəti
AM ˈhɛkədi
hecatomb
BR ˈhɛkətuːm, -z
AM ˈhɛkəˌtoʊm, -z
heck
BR hɛk
AM hɛk
heckelphone
BR ˈhɛklfəʊn, -z
AM ˈhɛkəlˌfoʊn, -z
heckle
BR ˈhɛk|l, -lz, -lɪŋ \-lɪŋ,
-ld
AM ˈhɛk|əl, -əlz, -(ə)lɪŋ,
-əld
heckler
BR ˈhɛklə(r),
ˈhɛklə(r), -z
AM ˈhɛk(ə)lər, -z
Heckmondwike
BR ˈhɛkmən(d)wʌɪk
AM ˈhɛkmən(d)ˌwaɪk
hectarage
BR ˈhɛkt(ə)rɪdʒ
AM ˈhɛktərɪdʒ
hectare
BR ˈhɛktɛː(r), -z
AM ˈhɛkˌtɛ(ə)r, -z
hectic
BR ˈhɛktɪk
AM ˈhɛktɪk
hectically
BR ˈhɛktɪkli
AM ˈhɛktək(ə)li

hectogram
BR 'hektəgram, -z
AM 'hektə,græm, -z

hectograph
BR 'hektəgrɑːf,
'hektəgraf, -s
AM 'hektə,græf, -s

hectoliter
BR 'hektə,liːtə(r), -z
AM 'hektə,lidər, -z

hectolitre
BR 'hektə,liːtə(r), -z
AM 'hektə,lidər, -z

hectometer
BR 'hektə,miːtə(r), -z
AM 'hektə,midər, -z

hectometre
BR 'hektə,miːtə(r), -z
AM 'hektə,midər, -z

hector
BR 'hekt|ə(r), -əz,
-(ə)rɪŋ, -əd
AM 'hekt|ər, -ərz,
-(ə)rɪŋ, -ərd

hectoringly
BR 'hekt(ə)rɪŋli
AM 'hekt(ə)rɪŋli

Hecuba
BR 'hekjʊbə(r)
AM 'hekjəbə

he'd¹
strong form
BR hiːd
AM hid

he'd²
weak form
BR (h)ɪd
AM (h)ɪd

heddle
BR 'hedl, -z
AM 'hedəl, -z

Hedex®
BR 'hedeks
AM 'hedeks

hedge
BR hedʒ, -ɪz, -ɪŋ, -d
AM hedʒ, -əz, -ɪŋ, -d

hedgehog
BR 'hedʒ(h)ɒg, -z
AM 'hedʒ,(h)ɔg,
'hedʒ,(h)ɑg, -z

hedgehop
BR 'hedʒhɒp, -s, -ɪŋ, -t
AM 'hedʒ,(h)ɑp, -s, -ɪŋ,
-t

hedgehopper
BR 'hedʒ,hɒpə(r), -z
AM 'hedʒ,(h)ɑpər, -z

hedger
BR 'hedʒə(r), -z
AM 'hedʒər, -z

hedgerow
BR 'hedʒrəʊ, -z
AM 'hedʒ,roʊ, -z

Hedges
BR 'hedʒɪz
AM 'hedʒəs

Hedley
BR 'hedli
AM 'hedli

hedonic
BR hi:'dɒnɪk, hɪ'dɒnɪk
AM hi'dɑnɪk

hedonism
BR 'hiːdn̩ɪz(ə)m,
'hiːdənɪz(ə)m,
'hedn̩ɪz(ə)m,
'hedənɪz(ə)m
AM 'hidn̩,ɪzəm,
'hidə,nɪzəm

hedonist
BR 'hiːdn̩ɪst, 'hiːdənɪst,
'hedn̩ɪst, 'hedənɪst, -s
AM 'hidn̩əst, 'hidənəst,
-s

hedonistic
BR ,hiːdə'nɪstɪk,
,hedə'nɪstɪk
AM ,hidn̩'ɪstɪk

hedonistically
BR ,hiːdə'nɪstɪkli,
,hedə'nɪstɪkli
AM ,hidn̩'ɪstək(ə)li,
,hidə'nɪstək(ə)li

heebie-jeebies
BR ,hiːbɪ'dʒiːbɪz
AM ,hibi'dʒibɪz

heed
BR hiːd, -z, -ɪŋ, -ɪd
AM hid, -z, -ɪŋ, -ɪd

heedful
BR 'hiːdf(ʊ)l
AM 'hidfəl

heedfully
BR 'hiːdfəli, 'hiːdfl̩i
AM 'hidfəli

heedfulness
BR 'hiːdf(ʊ)lnəs
AM 'hidfəlnəs

heedless
BR 'hiːdlɪs
AM 'hidlɪs

heedlessly
BR 'hiːdlɪsli
AM 'hidlɪsli

heedlessness
BR 'hiːdlɪsnɪs
AM 'hidlɪsnɪs

hee-haw
BR 'hiːhɔː(r),
,hiː'hɔː(r), -z, -ɪŋ, -d
AM 'hi,hɔ, 'hi,hɑ, -z, -ɪŋ,
-d

heel
BR hiːl, -z, -ɪŋ, -d
AM hil, -z, -ɪŋ, -d

heelball
BR 'hiːlbɔːl
AM 'hil,bɔl, 'hil,bɑl

heelbar
BR 'hiːlbɑː(r), -z
AM 'hil,bar, -z

heelless
BR 'hiː(l)lɪs
AM 'hi(l)lɪs

heeltap
BR 'hiːltap, -s
AM 'hil,tæp, -s

Heep
BR hiːp
AM hip

Heffernan
BR 'hefənən
AM 'hefərnən

heft
BR heft, -s, -ɪŋ, -ɪd
AM heft, -s, -ɪŋ, -əd

heftily
BR 'heftɪli
AM 'heftəli

heftiness
BR 'heftɪnɪs
AM 'heftɪnɪs

hefty
BR 'heft|i, -ɪə(r), -ɪɪst
AM 'hefti, -ər, -ɪst

Hegarty
BR 'hegəti
AM 'hegərdi

Hegel
BR 'heɪgl
AM 'heɪgəl

Hegelian
BR hɪ'geɪlɪən,
her'geɪlɪən, -z
AM hə'geɪlɪən, -z

Hegelianism
BR hɪ'geɪlɪənɪz(ə)m,
her'geɪlɪənɪz(ə)m
AM hə'geɪlɪə,nɪzəm

hegemonic
BR ,hegɪ'mɒnɪk,
,hedʒɪ'mɒnɪk
AM ,hegə'mɑnɪk

hegemony
BR hɪ'geməni,
hɪ'dʒeməni,
'hegɪməni,
'hedʒɪməni
AM hə'dʒeməni,
'hedʒə,moʊni

Hegira
BR hɪ'dʒʌɪrə(r)
AM hə'dʒʌɪrə, 'hedʒərə

Heidegger
BR 'hʌɪdegə(r),
'hʌɪdɪgə(r)
AM 'hʌɪdəgər

Heidelberg
BR 'hʌɪdlbɜːg
AM 'hʌɪdl,bərg

Heidi
BR 'hʌɪdi
AM 'haɪdi

heifer
BR 'hefə(r), -z
AM 'hefər, -z

heigh
BR heɪ
AM haɪ, heɪ

heigh-ho
BR ,heɪ'həʊ, 'heɪhəʊ
AM 'heɪ'hoʊ

height
BR hʌɪt, -s
AM haɪt, -s

heighten
BR 'hʌɪtn̩, -z, -ɪŋ, -d
AM 'haɪtn̩, -z, -ɪŋ, -d

Heilbronn
BR 'hʌɪlbron
AM 'haɪl,bran
GER haɪl'brɔn

Heilong
BR ,hʌɪ'lɒŋ
AM 'haɪ'lɔŋ, 'haɪ'laŋ

Heimlich
BR 'hʌɪmlɪç
AM 'haɪmlɪk

Heine
BR 'hʌɪni, 'hʌɪnə(r)
AM 'haɪnə, 'haɪni

Heineken®
BR 'hʌɪnɪk(ə)n
AM 'haɪnəkən

Heinemann
BR 'hʌɪnɪmən
AM 'haɪnəmən

Heiney
BR 'hʌɪni
AM 'haɪni

Heinkel
BR 'hʌɪŋkl
AM 'haɪŋkəl

Heinlein
BR 'hʌɪnlʌɪn
AM 'haɪn,laɪn

heinous
BR 'heɪnəs, 'hiːnəs
AM 'heɪnəs

heinously
BR 'heɪnəsli, 'hiːnəsli
AM 'heɪnəsli

heinousness
BR 'heɪnəsnəs,
'hiːnəsnəs
AM 'heɪnəsnəs

Heinz
BR hʌɪnz, hʌɪns
AM haɪn(t)s

heir
BR ɛː(r), -z
AM ɛ(ə)r, -z

heirdom
BR 'ɛːdəm
AM 'ɛrdəm

heiress
BR 'ɛːrɪs, 'ɛːrɛs, ,ɛːˈrɛs,
-ɪz
AM 'ɛrəs, -əz

heirless
BR 'ɛːləs
AM 'ɛrləs

heirloom
BR 'ɛːluːm, -z
AM 'ɛr,lum, -z

heirship
BR 'ɛːʃɪp
AM 'ɛr,ʃɪp

Heisenberg
BR ˈhaɪznbəːg
AM ˈhaɪzənˌbɜrg

heist
BR haɪst, -s, -ɪŋ, -ɪd
AM haɪst, -s, -ɪŋ, -ɪd

hei-tiki
BR ˌheɪˈtɪk|i, -ɪz
AM ˌheɪˈtiˌki, -z

Hejira
BR hɪˈdʒʌɪrə(r)
AM həˈdʒaɪrə, ˈhɛdʒərə

Hekla
BR ˈhɛklə(r)
AM ˈhɛklə

HeLa
BR ˈhiːlə(r)
AM ˈhɛlə

held
BR hɛld
AM hɛld

Heldentenor
BR ˌhɛldnˈtɛnə(r), -z
AM ˈhɛldənˌtɛnər, -z

hele
BR hiːl, -z, -ɪŋ, -d
AM hil, -z, -ɪŋ, -d

Helen
BR ˈhɛlɪn
AM ˈhɛlən

Helena
BR ˈhɛlɪnə(r)
AM ˈhɛlənə

helenium
BR hɪˈliːnɪəm
AM həˈliniəm

Helga
BR ˈhɛlgə(r)
AM ˈhɛlgə

Helgoland
BR ˈhɛlgəland
AM ˈhɛlgəˌlænd

heliacal
BR hɪˈlʌɪəkl, hɛˈlʌɪəkl
AM həˈlaɪəkəl, hiˈlaɪəkəl

helianthemum
BR ˌhiːlɪˈanθɪməm, -z
AM ˌhiliˈænθəməm, -z

helianthus
BR ˌhiːlɪˈanθəs, -ɪz
AM ˌhiliˈænθəs, -əz

helical
BR ˈhɛlɪkl
AM ˈhilɪkəl, ˈhɛləkəl

helically
BR ˈhɛlɪkli
AM ˈhilɪk(ə)li, ˈhɛlək(ə)li

helices
BR ˈhɛlɪsiːz
AM ˈhiləˌsiz, ˈhɛləˌsiz

helichrysum
BR ˌhɛlɪˈkrʌɪsəm, -z
AM ˌhɛləˈkraɪsəm, -z

helicity
BR hiːˈlɪsɪti

AM ˌhiˈlɪsɪdi
helicoid
BR ˈhɛlɪkɔɪd, -z
AM ˈhɛləˌkɔɪd, -z

Helicon
BR ˈhɛlɪk(ə)n,
ˈhɛlɪkɒn, -z
AM ˈhɛləˌkɑn,
ˈhɛləkən, -z

helicopter
BR ˈhɛlɪkɒptə(r), -z
AM ˈhɛləˌkɑptər, -z

helideck
BR ˈhɛlɪdɛk, -s
AM ˈhɛləˌdɛk, -s

Heligoland
BR ˈhɛlɪgə(ʊ)land
AM ˈhɛləgoʊˌlænd

heliocentric
BR ˌhiːlɪə(ʊ)ˈsɛntrɪk
AM ˌhiliəˈsɛntrɪk

heliocentrically
BR ˌhiːlɪə(ʊ)ˈsɛntrɪkli
AM ˌhiliəˈsɛntrək(ə)li

Heliogabalus
BR ˌhiːlɪə(ʊ)ˈgabələs,
ˌhiːlɪə(ʊ)ˈgab|əs
AM ˌhiliəˈgæbələs

heliogram
BR ˈhiːlɪəgram, -z
AM ˈhilioʊˌgræm, -z

heliograph
BR ˈhiːlɪəgrɑːf,
ˈhiːlɪəgraf, -s, -ɪŋ, -t
AM ˈhilioʊˌgræf, -s, -ɪŋ,
-t

heliography
BR ˌhiːlɪˈɒgrəfi
AM ˌhiliˈɑgrəfi

heliogravure
BR ˌhiːlɪəʊgrəˈvjʊə(r)
AM ˌhilioʊgrəˈvjʊ(ə)r

heliolithic
BR ˌhiːlɪəˈlɪθɪk
AM ˌhiliəˈlɪθɪk

heliometer
BR ˌhiːlɪˈɒmɪtə(r), -z
AM ˌhiliˈɑmədər, -z

Heliopolis
BR ˌhiːlɪˈɒpəlɪs,
ˌhiːlɪˈɒplɪs
AM ˌhiliˈɑpələs

Helios
BR ˈhiːlɪɒs
AM ˈhiliˌɑs, ˈhiliəs

heliostat
BR ˈhiːlɪəstat, -s
AM ˈhiliəˌstæt,
ˈhiljəˌstæt, -s

heliostatic
BR ˌhiːlɪəˈstatɪk
AM ˌhiliəˈstædɪk

heliotherapy
BR ˌhiːlɪəʊˈθɛrəpi
AM ˌhiliəˈθɛrəpi,
ˌhiljəˈθɛrəpi

heliotrope
BR ˈhiːlɪətrəʊp, -s
AM ˈhiliəˌtroʊp,
ˈhiljəˌtroʊp, -s

heliotropic
BR ˌhiːlɪə(ʊ)ˈtrɒpɪk,
ˌhiːlɪəˈtrəʊpɪk
AM ˌhiliəˈtrɑpɪk

heliotropically
BR ˌhiːlɪə(ʊ)ˈtrəʊpɪkli,
ˌhiːlɪəˈtrɒpɪkli
AM ˌhiliəˈtrɑpək(ə)li

heliotropism
BR ˌhiːlɪə(ʊ)ˈtrəʊp-
ɪz(ə)m,
ˌhiːlɪˈɒtrəpɪz(ə)m
AM ˌhiliəˈtrɑˌpɪzəm

heliotype
BR ˈhiːlɪətʌɪp, -s
AM ˈhiliəˌtaɪp,
ˈhiljəˌtaɪp, -s

helipad
BR ˈhɛlɪpad, -z
AM ˈhɛləˌpæd, -z

heliport
BR ˈhɛlɪpɔːt, -s
AM ˈhɛləˌpɔ(ə)rt, -s

heli-skiing
BR ˈhɛlɪˌskɪɪŋ
AM ˈhɛliˌskɪɪŋ

helium
BR ˈhiːlɪəm
AM ˈhiliəm

helix
BR ˈhiːlɪks, -ɪz
AM ˈhilɪks, -ɪz

hell
BR hɛl
AM hɛl

he'll
BR hiːl
AM hil

hellacious
BR hɛˈleɪʃəs
AM hɛˈleɪʃəs

hellaciously
BR hɛˈleɪʃəsli
AM hɛˈleɪʃəsli

Helladic
BR hɛˈladɪk, -s
AM hɛˈlædɪk, -s

Hellas
BR ˈhɛlas
AM ˈhɛləs

hellcat
BR ˈhɛlkat, -s
AM ˈhɛlˌkæt, -s

hellebore
BR ˈhɛlɪbɔː(r)
AM ˈhɛləˌbɔ(ə)r

helleborine
BR ˈhɛlɪbəriːn,
ˈhɛlɪbərʌɪn, -z
AM ˈhɛləbəˌraɪn,
ˈhɛləbəˌrin, -z

Hellene
BR ˈhɛliːn, -z
AM ˈhɛˌlin, -z

Hellenic
BR hɪˈlɛnɪk, hɛˈlɛnɪk
AM hɛˈlɛnɪk

Hellenisation
BR ˌhɛlɪnʌɪˈzeɪʃn
AM ˌhɛlənəˈzeɪʃən,
ˌhɛləˌnaɪˈzeɪʃən

Hellenise
BR ˈhɛlɪnʌɪz, -ɪz, -ɪŋ, -d
AM ˈhɛləˌnaɪz, -ɪz, -ɪŋ, -d

Hellenism
BR ˈhɛlɪnɪz(ə)m, -z
AM ˈhɛləˌnɪzəm, -z

Hellenist
BR ˈhɛlɪnɪst, -s
AM ˈhɛlənəst, -s

Hellenistic
BR ˌhɛlɪˈnɪstɪk
AM ˌhɛləˈnɪstɪk

Hellenization
BR ˌhɛlɪnʌɪˈzeɪʃn
AM ˌhɛlənəˈzeɪʃən,
ˌhɛləˌnaɪˈzeɪʃən

Hellenize
BR ˈhɛlɪnʌɪz, -ɪz, -ɪŋ, -d
AM ˈhɛləˌnaɪz, -ɪz, -ɪŋ, -d

Heller
BR ˈhɛlə(r)
AM ˈhɛlər

Hellespont
BR ˈhɛlɪspɒnt
AM ˈhɛləˌspɑnt

hellfire
BR ˌhɛlˈfʌɪə(r),
ˈhɛlfʌɪə(r)
AM ˈhɛlˌfaɪ(ə)r

hell-for-leather
BR ˌhɛlfəˈlɛðə(r)
AM ˌhɛlfərˈlɛðər

hellgrammite
BR ˈhɛlgrəmʌɪt, -s
AM ˈhɛlgrəˌmaɪt, -s

hellhole
BR ˈhɛlhəʊl, -z
AM ˈhɛlˌ(h)oʊl, -z

hellhound
BR ˈhɛlhaʊnd, -z
AM ˈhɛlˌ(h)aʊnd, -z

hellion
BR ˈhɛljən, -z
AM ˈhɛljən, -z

hellish
BR ˈhɛlɪʃ
AM ˈhɛlɪʃ

hellishly
BR ˈhɛlɪʃli
AM ˈhɛlɪʃli

hellishness
BR ˈhɛlɪʃnɪs
AM ˈhɛlɪʃnɪs

hell-like
BR ˈhɛllʌɪk
AM ˈhɛlˌlaɪk

Hellman
BR ˈhɛlmən
AM ˈhɛlmən

hello
BR həˈləʊ, hɛˈləʊ, -z
AM həˈloʊ, hɛˈloʊ, -z
hellraiser
BR ˈhɛlˌreɪzə(r), -z
AM ˈhɛlˌreɪzər, -z
hellraising
BR ˈhɛlˌreɪzɪŋ
AM ˈhɛlˌreɪzɪŋ
helluva
BR ˈhɛləvə(r)
AM ˈhɛləvə
hellward
BR ˈhɛlwəd
AM ˈhɛlwərd
helm
BR hɛlm, -z
AM hɛlm, -z
helmet
BR ˈhɛlmɪt, -s, -ɪd
AM ˈhɛlməlt, -ts, -dəd
Helmholtz
BR ˈhɛlmhɒlts,
ˈhɛlmhəʊlts
AM ˈhɛlm,(h)oʊlts
helminth
BR ˈhɛlmɪnθ, -s
AM ˈhɛlmənθ, -s
helminthiasis
BR ˌhɛlmɪnˈθʌɪəsɪs
AM ˌhɛlmənˈθaɪəsəs
helminthic
BR hɛlˈmɪnθɪk
AM hɛlˈmɪnθɪk
helminthoid
BR ˈhɛlmɪnθɔɪd
AM hɛlˈmɪnˌθɔɪd, ˈhɛlmənˌθɔɪd
helminthologist
BR ˌhɛlmɪnˈθɒlədʒɪst, -s
AM ˌhɛlmənˈθɑlədʒəst, -s
helminthology
BR ˌhɛlmɪnˈθɒlədʒi
AM ˌhɛlmənˈθɑlədʒi
Helms
BR hɛlmz
AM hɛlmz
helmsman
BR ˈhɛlmzmən
AM ˈhɛlmzmən
helmsmen
BR ˈhɛlmzmən
AM ˈhɛlmzmən
Héloïse
BR ˈɛləʊiːz, ˌɛləʊˈiːz
AM ˈ(h)ɛləˌwiz
Helot
BR ˈhɛlət, -s
AM ˈhɛlət, -s
helotism
BR ˈhɛlətɪz(ə)m
AM ˈhɛləˌtɪzəm
helotry
BR ˈhɛlətri
AM ˈhɛlətri

help
BR hɛlp, -s, -ɪŋ, -t
AM hɛlp, -s, -ɪŋ, -t
helper
BR ˈhɛlpə(r), -z
AM ˈhɛlpər, -z
helpful
BR ˈhɛlpf(ʊ)l
AM ˈhɛlpfəl
helpfully
BR ˈhɛlpfəli, ˈhɛlpfḷi
AM ˈhɛlpfəli
helpfulness
BR ˈhɛlpf(ʊ)nəs
AM ˈhɛlpfəlnəs
helping
BR ˈhɛlpɪŋ, -z
AM ˈhɛlpɪŋ, -z
helpless
BR ˈhɛlpləs
AM ˈhɛlpləs
helplessly
BR ˈhɛlpləsli
AM ˈhɛlpləsli
helplessness
BR ˈhɛlpləsnəs
AM ˈhɛlpləsnəs
helpline
BR ˈhɛlplʌɪn, -z
AM ˈhɛlpˌlaɪn, -z
Helpmann
BR ˈhɛlpmən
AM ˈhɛlpmən
helpmate
BR ˈhɛlpmeɪt, -s
AM ˈhɛlpˌmeɪt, -s
helpmeet
BR ˈhɛlpmiːt, -s
AM ˈhɛlpˌmit, -s
Helsingborg
BR ˈhɛlsɪŋbɔːg
AM ˈhɛlsɪŋˌbɔ(ə)rg
Helsingfors
BR ˈhɛlsɪŋfɔːz
AM ˈhɛlsɪŋˌfɔ(ə)rz
Helsingør
BR ˈhɛlsɪŋə(r)
AM ˈhɛlsɪŋər
DAN ˌhɛlseŋˈœːˈʌ
Helsinki
BR hɛlˈsɪŋki, ˈhɛlsɪŋki
AM hɛlˈsɪŋki, ˈhɛlsɪŋki
helter-skelter
BR ˌhɛltəˈskɛltə(r), -z
AM ˌhɛltərˈskɛltər, -z
helve
BR hɛlv, -z
AM hɛlv, -z
Helvellyn
BR hɛlˈvɛlɪn
AM hɛlˈvɛlən
Helvetia
BR hɛlˈviːʃ(ɪ)ə(r)
AM hɛlˈviːʃə
Helvetian
BR hɛlˈviːʃ(ə)n, -z
AM hɛlˈviːʃən, -z

Helvetic
BR hɛlˈvɛtɪk
AM hɛlˈvɛdɪk
hem
BR hɛm, -z, -ɪŋ, -d
AM hɛm, -z, -ɪŋ, -d
hemal
BR ˈhiːml
AM ˈhiməl
he-man
BR ˈhiːman
AM ˈhiˌmæn
hematic
BR hiːˈmatɪk
AM hiˈmædɪk
hematin
BR ˈhiːmətɪn
AM ˈhiməˌtɪn
hematite
BR ˈhiːmətʌɪt
AM ˈhiməˌtaɪt
hematocele
BR hɪˈmatəsiːl
AM hiˈmædoʊˌsil
hematocrit
BR hɪˈmatəkrɪt, ˈhiːmətə(ʊ)krɪt, -s
AM hiˈmædəˌkrɪt, -s
hematologic
BR ˌhiːmətəˈlɒdʒɪk
AM ˌhiˌmədoʊˈlɑdʒɪk
hematological
BR ˌhiːmətəˈlɒdʒɪkl
AM ˌhiˌmədoʊˈlɑdʒəkəl
hematologist
BR ˌhiːməˈtɒlədʒɪst, -s
AM ˌhiməˈtɑlədʒəst, -s
hematology
BR ˌhiːməˈtɒlədʒi
AM ˌhiməˈtɑlədʒi
hematoma
BR ˌhiːməˈtəʊmə(r), -z
AM ˌhiməˈtoʊmə, -z
hematuria
BR ˌhiːməˈtjʊərɪə(r), ˌhiːməˈtʃʊərɪə(r)
AM ˌhiməˈtʊriə
heme
BR hiːm
AM him
Hemel Hempstead
BR ˌhɛml ˈhɛm(p)stɛd
AM ˈhɛməl ˈhɛm(p)ˌstɛd
he-men
BR ˈhiːmɛn
AM ˈhiˌmɛn
hemerocallis
BR ˌhɛm(ə)rəʊˈkalɪs
AM ˌhɛməroʊˈkæləs
hemianopia
BR ˌhɛmɪəˈnəʊpɪə(r)
AM ˌhimiəˈnoʊpiə
hemianopsia
BR ˌhɛmɪəˈnɒpsɪə(r)
AM ˌhimiəˈnɑpsiə

hemicellulose
BR ˌhɛmɪˈsɛljələʊs, ˌhɛmɪˈsɛljələʊz, -ɪz
AM ˈhɛməˈsɛl(j)əloʊs, ˈhɛməˈsɛl(j)əloʊz, -əz
hemicycle
BR ˈhɛmɪˌsʌɪkl, -z
AM ˈhɛməˌsaɪkəl, -z
hemidemisemiquaver
BR ˌhɛmɪˌdɛmɪˈsɛmɪˌkweɪvə -z
AM ˌhɛmɪˌdɛmɪˌsɛmaɪˈkweɪv -z
hemihedral
BR ˌhɛmɪˈhiːdr(ə)l
AM ˈhɛməˌhidrəl
Hemingway
BR ˈhɛmɪŋweɪ
AM ˈhɛmɪŋweɪ
hemiplegia
BR ˌhɛmɪˈpliːdʒ(ɪ)ə(r)
AM ˌhɛməˈpli(d)ʒə
hemiplegic
BR ˌhɛmɪˈpliːdʒɪk, -s
AM ˌhɛməˈplidʒɪk, -s
Hemiptera
BR hɪˈmɪpt(ə)rə(r)
AM həˈmɪptərə
hemipteran
BR hɪˈmɪpt(ə)rən, hɪˈmɪpt(ə)rn, -z
AM həˈmɪptərən, -z
hemipterous
BR hɪˈmɪpt(ə)rəs
AM həˈmɪptərəs
hemisphere
BR ˈhɛmɪsfɪə(r), -z
AM ˈhɛməˌsfɪ(ə)r, -z
hemispheric
BR ˌhɛmɪˈsfɛrɪk
AM ˌhɛməˈsfɪrɪk, ˈhɛməˈsfɛrɪk
hemispherical
BR ˌhɛmɪˈsfɛrɪkl
AM ˌhɛməˈsfɪrɪkəl, ˈhɛməˈsfɛrəkəl
hemispherically
BR ˌhɛmɪˈsfɛrɪkli
AM ˌhɛməˈsfɪrɪk(ə)li, ˈhɛməˈsfɛrək(ə)li
hemistich
BR ˈhɛmɪstɪk, -s
AM ˈhɛməstɪk, -s
hemline
BR ˈhɛmlʌɪn, -z
AM ˈhɛmˌlaɪn, -z
hemlock
BR ˈhɛmlɒk
AM ˈhɛmˌlɑk
hemocyanin
BR ˌhiːmə(ʊ)ˈsʌɪənɪn, -z
AM ˌhiməˈsaɪənən, -z
hemodialysis
BR ˌhiːmə(ʊ)dʌɪˈalɪsɪs, -ɪz
AM ˌhimoʊˌdaɪˈæləsəs, -əs

hemodynamic
BR ˌhiːmə(ʊ)daɪˈnamɪk
AM ˌhiːmoʊdaɪˈnæmɪk

hemoglobin
BR ˈhiːməˈgləʊbɪn
AM ˈhiːməˌgloʊbən

hemolysis
BR hiːˈmɒlɪsɪs
AM hiːˈmɑləsəs

hemolytic
BR ˌhiːməˈlɪtɪk
AM ˌhiːməˈlɪdɪk

hemophilia
BR ˌhiːməˈfɪliə(r)
AM ˌhiːməˈfɪljə,
ˌhiːməˈfɪliə

hemophiliac
BR ˌhiːməˈfɪlɪak, -s
AM ˌhiːməˈfɪliˌæk, -s

hemophilic
BR ˌhiːməˈfɪlɪk, -s
AM ˌhiːməˈfɪlɪk, -s

hemophyliac
BR ˌhiːməˈfɪlɪak, -s
AM ˌhiːməˈfɪliˌæk, -s

hemorrhage
BR ˈhɛm(ə)r|ɪdʒ, -ɪdʒɪz,
-ɪdʒɪŋ, -ɪdʒd
AM ˈhɛm(ə)rɪdʒ, -ɪz,
-ɪŋ, -d

hemorrhagic
BR ˌhɛməˈradʒɪk
AM ˌhɛməˈrædʒɪk

hemorrhoid
BR ˈhɛmərɔɪd, -z
AM ˈhɛm(ə)ˌrɔɪd, -z

hemorrhoidal
BR ˌhɛməˈrɔɪdl
AM ˌhɛm(ə)ˈrɔɪdəl

hemostasis
BR ˌhiːmə(ʊ)ˈsteɪsɪs
AM ˌhiːməˈsteɪsəs

hemostat
BR ˈhiːməstat, -s
AM ˈhiːməˌstæt, -s

hemostatic
BR ˌhiːməˈstatɪk
AM ˌhiːməˈstædɪk

hemp
BR hɛmp
AM hɛmp

hempen
BR ˈhɛmpən
AM ˈhɛmpən

hemp-nettle
BR ˈhɛmpˌnɛtl, -z
AM ˈhɛmpˌnɛdəl, -z

hemstitch
BR ˈhɛmstɪtʃ
AM ˈhɛmˌstɪtʃ

hen
BR hɛn, -z
AM hɛn, -z

Henan
BR ˈhiːnən
AM ˈhinən

henbane
BR ˈhɛnbeɪn
AM ˈhɛnˌbeɪn

hence
BR hɛns
AM hɛns

henceforth
BR ˌhɛnsˈfɔːθ, ˈhɛnsfɔːθ
AM ˌhɛnsˈfɔ(ə)rθ

henceforward
BR ˌhɛnsˈfɔːwəd
AM ˌhɛnsˈfɔrwərd

henchman
BR ˈhɛn(t)ʃmən
AM ˈhɛn(t)ʃmən

henchmen
BR ˈhɛn(t)ʃmən
AM ˈhɛn(t)ʃmən

hencoop
BR ˈhɛnkuːp, -s
AM ˈhɛnˌkup, -s

hendecagon
BR hɛnˈdekəg(ə)n,
hɛnˈdekəgɒn, -z
AM hɛnˈdɛkəˌgɑn, -z

hendecasyllabic
BR ˌhɛndɛkəsɪˈlabɪk,
-s
AM hɛnˌdɛkəsəˈlæbɪk,
-s

hendecasyllable
BR ˌhɛndɛkəˈsɪləbl,
hɛnˌdɛkəˈsɪləbl, -z
AM hɛnˈdɛkəˌsɪləbəl,
hɛnˌdɛkəˈsɪləbəl, -z

Henderson
BR ˈhɛndəs(ə)n
AM ˈhɛndərsən

hendiadys
BR hɛnˈdʌɪədɪs
AM hɛnˈdaɪədəs

Hendon
BR ˈhɛnd(ə)n
AM ˈhɛndən

Hendricks
BR ˈhɛndrɪks
AM ˈhɛndrɪks

Hendrickson
BR ˈhɛndrɪks(ə)n
AM ˈhɛndrɪksən

Hendrix
BR ˈhɛndrɪks
AM ˈhɛndrɪks

Hendry
BR ˈhɛndri
AM ˈhɛndri

Hendy
BR ˈhɛndi
AM ˈhɛndi

henequen
BR ˈhɛnɪken
AM ˈhɛnəkən

henge
BR hɛn(d)ʒ, -ɪz
AM hɛndʒ, -əz

Hengist
BR ˈhɛŋgɪst

AM ˈhɛŋgəst

henhouse
BR ˈhɛnhaʊ|s, -zɪz
AM ˈhɛnˌ(h)aʊ|s, -zəz

Henley
BR ˈhɛnli
AM ˈhɛnli

henna
BR ˈhɛnə(r), -d
AM ˈhɛnə, -d

Hennessey
BR ˈhɛnɪsi
AM ˈhɛnəsi

Hennessy
BR ˈhɛnɪsi
AM ˈhɛnəsi

henotheism
BR ˈhɛnəʊˌθiːɪz(ə)m,
ˌhɛnəʊˈθiːɪz(ə)m
AM ˈhɛnoʊθiˌɪzəm,
ˌhɛnoʊˈθiˌɪzəm

henpeck
BR ˈhɛnpɛk, -s, -ɪŋ, -t
AM ˈhɛnˌpɛk, -s, -ɪŋ, -t

Henri
English surname
BR ˈhɛnri
AM ˈhɛnri

Henrietta
BR ˌhɛnrɪˈɛtə(r)
AM ˌhɛnriˈɛdə

Henriques
BR hɛnˈriːkɪz
AM hɛnˈrikɪz

henry
BR ˈhɛnr|i, -ɪz
AM ˈhɛnri, -z

Henshaw
BR ˈhɛnʃɔː(r)
AM ˈhɛnˌʃɔ

Hensley
BR ˈhɛnzli
AM ˈhɛnzli

Henson
BR ˈhɛnsn
AM ˈhɛnsən

Henty
BR ˈhɛnti
AM ˈhɛn(t)i

Henze
BR ˈhɛntsə(r)
AM ˈhɛn(t)sə

heortologist
BR ˌhiːɔːˈtɒlədʒɪst, -s
AM hiˌɔrˈtɑlədʒəst, -s

heortology
BR ˌhiːɔːˈtɒlədʒi
AM hiˌɔrˈtɑlədʒi

hep
BR hɛp
AM hɛp, həp

heparin
BR ˈhɛpərɪn
AM ˈhɛpərən

heparinise
BR ˈhɛp(ə)rɪnʌɪz, -ɪz,
-ɪŋ, -d

AM ˈhɛŋgəst

heparinize
BR ˈhɛp(ə)rɪnʌɪz, -ɪz,
-ɪŋ, -d
AM ˈhɛpərəˌnaɪz, -ɪz,
-ɪŋ, -d

hepatic
BR hɪˈpatɪk, hɛˈpatɪk
AM həˈpædɪk

hepatica
BR hɪˈpatɪkə(r),
hɛˈpatɪkə(r)
AM həˈpædɪkə

hepatitis
BR ˌhɛpəˈtʌɪtɪs
AM ˌhɛpəˈtaɪdɪs

hepatocyte
BR ˈhɛpətə(ʊ)sʌɪt,
hɪˈpatə(ʊ)sʌɪt,
hɛˈpatəʊsʌɪt, -s
AM həˈpædəˌsaɪt, -s

hepatomegaly
BR ˌhɛpətəʊˈmɛgəli,
ˌhɛpətəʊˈmɛgli
AM hɛˌpædəˈmɛgəli,
ˌhɛpədoʊˈmɛgəli

hepatotoxic
BR ˌhɛpətəʊˈtɒksɪk,
hɪˌpatəʊˈtɒksɪk,
hɛˌpatəʊˈtɒksɪk
AM həˌpædəˈtɑksɪk

Hepburn
BR ˈhɛ(p)bəːn,
ˈhɛb(ə)n
AM ˈhɛpbərn

Hephaestus
BR hɪˈfiːstəs
AM hɪˈfɛstəs

Hephzibah
BR ˈhɛfzɪbɑː(r),
ˈhɛpsɪbɑː(r)
AM ˈhɛpzəˌbɑ

Hepplewhite
BR ˈhɛplwʌɪt
AM ˈhɛpəl(h)waɪt

heptachord
BR ˈhɛptəkɔːd, -z
AM ˈhɛptəˌkɔ(ə)rd, -z

heptad
BR ˈhɛptad, -z
AM ˈhɛpˌtæd, -z

heptaglot
BR ˈhɛptəglɒt, -s
AM ˈhɛptəˌglɑt, -s

heptagon
BR ˈhɛptəg(ə)n,
ˈhɛptəgɒn, -z
AM ˈhɛptəˌgɑn, -z

heptagonal
BR hɛpˈtagənl,
hɛpˈtagn̩l
AM hɛpˈtægənəl

heptahedra
BR ˌhɛptəˈhiːdrə(r)
AM ˌhɛptəˈhidrə

heptahedral
BR ˌhɛptəˈhiːdr(ə)l

AM ˌheptəˈhidrəl
heptahedron
BR ˈheptəˌhiːdr(ə)n, -z
AM ˌheptəˈhidˌrɑn,
ˌheptəˈhidrən, -z
heptameter
BR hepˈtamɪtə(r), -z
AM hepˈtæmədər, -z
heptane
BR ˈhepteɪn, -z
AM ˈhepˌteɪn, -z
heptarchic
BR hepˈtɑːkɪk
AM hepˈtɑrkɪk
heptarchical
BR hepˈtɑːkɪkl
AM hepˈtɑrkəkəl
heptarchy
BR ˈheptɑːki, -ɪz
AM ˈhepˌtɑrki, -z
heptasyllabic
BR ˌheptəsɪˈlabɪk
AM ˌheptəsəˈlæbɪk
Heptateuch
BR ˈheptətjuːk
AM ˈheptəˌt(j)uk
heptathlete
BR hepˈtaθliːt, -s
AM hepˈtæθlit, -s
heptathlon
BR hepˈtaθlən,
hepˈtaθlɒn, -z
AM hepˈtæθˌlɑn, -z
heptavalent
BR ˌheptəˈveɪlənt,
ˌheptəˈveɪln̩t
AM ˈheptəˈveɪlənt
Hepworth
BR ˈhepwəːθ, ˈhepwəθ
AM ˈhepˌwərθ
her¹
strong form
BR həː(r)
AM hər
her²
weak form
BR (h)ə(r)
AM (h)ər
Hera
BR ˈhɪərə(r)
AM ˈhɛrə
Heracles
BR ˈhɛrəkliːz
AM ˈhɛrəkliz
Heraclitus
BR ˌhɛrəˈklʌɪtəs
AM ˌhɛrəˈklaɪdəs
Heraklion
BR hɛˈraklɪən
AM hɛˈræklɪən
herald
BR ˈhɛrəld, ˈhɛrḷd, -z,
-ɪŋ, -ɪd
AM ˈhɛrəld, -z, -ɪŋ, -əd
heraldic
BR hɪˈraldɪk,
hɛˈraldɪk

AM hɛˈrældɪk,
həˈrældɪk
heraldically
BR hɪˈraldɪkli,
hɛˈraldɪkli
AM hɛˈrældək(ə)li,
həˈrældək(ə)li
heraldist
BR ˈhɛrəldɪst,
ˈhɛrḷdɪst, -s
AM ˈhɛrəldəst, -s
heraldry
BR ˈhɛrəldri, ˈhɛrḷdri
AM ˈhɛrəldri
herb
BR həːb, -z
AM (h)ərb, -z
herbaceous
BR hə(ː)ˈbeɪʃəs
AM (h)ərˈbeɪʃəs
herbage
BR ˈhəːbɪdʒ
AM ˈ(h)ərbɪdʒ
herbal
BR ˈhəːbl
AM ˈ(h)ərbəl
herbalism
BR ˈhəːbəlɪz(ə)m,
ˈhəːbḷɪz(ə)m
AM ˈ(h)ərbəˌlɪzəm
herbalist
BR ˈhəːbəlɪst, ˈhəːbḷɪst,
-s
AM ˈ(h)ərbələst, -s
herbaria
BR həːˈbɛːrɪə(r)
AM (h)ərˈbɛrɪə
herbarium
BR həːˈbɛːrɪəm, -z
AM (h)ərˈbɛrɪəm, -z
Herbert
BR ˈhəːbət
AM ˈhərbərt
herbicidal
BR ˌhəːbɪˈsʌɪdl
AM ˈ(h)ərbəˌsaɪdəl
herbicide
BR ˈhəːbɪsʌɪd, -z
AM ˈ(h)ərbəˌsaɪd, -z
Herbie
BR ˈhəːbi
AM ˈhərbi
herbiferous
BR həːˈbɪf(ə)rəs,
həˈbɪf(ə)rəs
AM (h)ərˈbɪfərəs
herbivore
BR ˈhəːbɪvɔː(r), -z
AM ˈ(h)ərbəˌvɔ(ə)r, -z
herbivorous
BR həːˈbɪv(ə)rəs,
həˈbɪv(ə)rəs
AM (h)ərˈbɪvərəs
herbless
BR ˈhəːbləs
AM ˈ(h)ərbləs

herblike
BR ˈhəːblʌɪk
AM ˈ(h)ərbˌlaɪk
herb Paris
BR ˌhəːb ˈparɪs
AM ˈ(h)ərb ˈpɛrəs
herb Robert
BR ˌhəːb ˈrɒbət
AM ˈ(h)ərb ˈrɑbərt
herb tea
BR ˌhəːb ˈtiː, -z
AM ˈ(h)ərb ˈti, -z
herb tobacco
BR ˌhəːb təˈbakəʊ
AM ˈ(h)ərb təˈbækoʊ
herby
BR ˈhəːbˌi, -ɪə(r), -ɪɪst
AM ˈ(h)ərbi, -ər, -ɪst
Hercegovina
BR ˌhəːtsəˈgɒvɪnə(r),
ˌhəːtsəgəˈviːnə(r)
AM ˌhərtsəˈgoʊvɪnə
Herculaneum
BR ˌhəːkjəˈleɪnɪəm
AM ˌhərkjəˈleɪnɪəm
Herculean
BR ˌhəːkjəˈliːən
AM ˌhərkjəˈliən,
hərˈkjuliən
Hercules
BR ˈhəːkjəliːz, -ɪz
AM ˈhərkjəˌliz, -ɪz
Hercynian
BR həːˈsɪnɪən
AM hərˈsɪnɪən
herd
BR həːd, -z, -ɪŋ, -ɪd
AM hərd, -z, -ɪŋ, -əd
herder
BR ˈhəːdə(r), -z
AM ˈhərdər, -z
herdsman
BR ˈhəːdzmən
AM ˈhərdzmən
herdsmen
BR ˈhəːdzmən
AM ˈhərdzmən
Herdwick
BR ˈhəːdwɪk, -s
AM ˈhərdˌwɪk, -s
here
BR hɪə(r)
AM hɪ(ə)r
hereabout
BR ˈhɪərəbaʊt,
ˌhɪərəˈbaʊt, -s
AM ˌhɪrəˈbaʊt, -s
hereafter
BR ˌhɪərˈɑːftə(r),
ˌhɪərˈaftə(r)
AM hɪrˈæftər
hereat
BR ˌhɪərˈat
AM ˈhɪrˈæt
hereby
BR ˌhɪəˈbʌɪ, ˈhɪəbʌɪ
AM ˈhɪrˈbaɪ

hereditable
BR hɪˈredɪtəbl
AM həˈrɛdədəbəl
hereditament
BR ˌhɛrɪˈdɪtəm(ə)nt, -s
AM ˌhɛrəˈdɪdəmənt, -s
hereditarily
BR hɪˈredɪt(ə)rəli,
hɪˈredɪt(ə)rḷi
AM həˌredəˈtɛrəli
hereditariness
BR hɪˈredɪt(ə)rɪnɪs
AM həˌredəˌtɛrinəs
hereditary
BR hɪˈredɪt(ə)ri
AM həˈredəˌtɛri
heredity
BR hɪˈredɪti
AM həˈredədi
Hereford
English town
BR ˈhɛrɪfəd
AM ˈhɛrəfərd
Herefordshire
BR ˈhɛrɪfədʃ(ɪ)ə(r)
AM ˈhɛrəfərdˌʃɪ(ə)r
herein
BR ˌhɪərˈɪn
AM ˈhɪrˈɪn
hereinafter
BR ˌhɪərɪnˈɑːftə(r),
ˌhɪərɪnˈaftə(r)
AM ˈhɪrɪnˈæftər
hereinbefore
BR ˌhɪərɪnbɪˈfɔː(r)
AM ˈhɪrɪnbəˈfɔ(ə)r
hereof
BR ˌhɪərˈɒv
AM ˈhɪrˈəv
Herero
BR hɛˈrɛːrəʊ,
həˈrɛːrəʊ, həˈrɪərəʊ,
-z
AM həˈrɛroʊ, -z
heresiarch
BR hɪˈriːzɪɑːk,
hɛˈriːzɪɑːk, -s
AM həˈriziˌɑrk,
hɛˈriziˌɑrk, -s
heresiology
BR hɪˌriːzɪˈɒlədʒi,
hɛˌriːzɪˈɒlədʒi
AM həˌriziˈɑlədʒi,
hɛˌriziˈɑlədʒi
heresy
BR ˈhɛrɪsˌi, -ɪz
AM ˈhɛrəsi, -z
heretic
BR ˈhɛrɪtɪk, -s
AM ˈhɛrəˌtɪk, -s
heretical
BR hɪˈretɪkl, hɛˈretɪkl
AM həˈredəkəl,
hɛˈredəkəl
heretically
BR hɪˈretɪkli,
hɛˈretɪkli

AM həˈrɛdək(ə)li,
hɛˈrɛdək(ə)li

hereto
BR ˌhɪəˈtuː
AM ˈhɪrˈtu

heretofore
BR ˌhɪətəˈfɔː(r)
AM ˌhɪrdəˈfɔ(ə)r

hereunder
BR ˌhɪərˈʌndə(r)
AM ˌhɪrˈəndər

hereunto
BR ˌhɪərˈʌntuː
AM ˈhɪrˈənˌtu

hereupon
BR ˌhɪərəˈpɒn
AM ˈhɪrəˈpɑn

Hereward
BR ˈhɛrɪwəd
AM ˈhɛrəˌwɑrd

herewith
BR ˌhɪəˈwɪð
AM ˌhɪrˈwɪθ, ˌhɪrˈwɪð

Herford
BR ˈhəːfəd
AM ˈhərfərd

heriot
BR ˈhɛrɪət, -s
AM ˈhɛriət, -s

Heriott
BR ˈhɛrɪət
AM ˈhɛriət

heritability
BR ˌhɛrɪtəˈbɪlɪti
AM ˌhɛrədəˈbɪlɪdi

heritable
BR ˈhɛrɪtəbl
AM ˈhɛrədəbəl

heritably
BR ˈhɛrɪtəbli
AM ˈhɛrədəbli

heritage
BR ˈhɛrɪt|ɪdʒ, -ɪdʒɪz
AM ˈhɛrədɪdʒ, -ɪz

heritor
BR ˈhɛrɪtə(r), -z
AM ˈhɛrədər, -z

herky-jerky
BR ˌhəːkɪˈdʒəːki
AM ˈhɛrkiˈdʒɛrki

herl
BR həːl
AM hərl

herm
BR həːm, -z
AM hərm, -z

Herman
BR ˈhəːmən
AM ˈhərmən

hermaphrodite
BR həˈ(ː)mæfrədʌɪt, -s
AM hərˈmæfrədaɪt, -s

hermaphroditic
BR həˈ(ː)ˌmæfrəˈdɪtɪk
AM hərˌmæfrəˈdɪdɪk

hermaphroditical
BR həˈ(ː)ˌmæfrəˈdɪtɪkl

AM hərˌmæfrəˈdɪdəkəl

hermaphroditism
BR həˈ(ː)ˈmæfrədɪtɪz(ə)m
AM hərˈmæfrədɪˌtɪzəm

hermeneutic
adjective
BR ˌhəːməˈnjuːtɪk, -s
AM ˌhərməˈn(j)udɪk, -s

hermeneutical
BR ˌhəːməˈnjuːtɪkl
AM ˌhərməˈn(j)udəkəl

hermeneutically
BR ˌhəːməˈnjuːtɪkli
AM ˌhərməˈn(j)udək(ə)li

Hermes
BR ˈhəːmiːz
AM ˈhərmiz

hermetic
BR həˈ(ː)mɛtɪk
AM hərˈmɛdɪk

hermetically
BR həˈ(ː)ˈmɛtɪkli
AM hərˈmɛdək(ə)li

hermetism
BR ˈhəːmɪtɪz(ə)m
AM ˈhərməˌtɪzəm

Hermia
BR ˈhəːmɪə(r)
AM ˈhərmiə

Hermione
BR həˈmʌɪəni,
həˈmʌɪəni
AM hərˈmaɪəni

hermit
BR ˈhəːmɪt, -s
AM ˈhərmət, -s

hermitage
BR ˈhəːmɪt|ɪdʒ, -ɪdʒɪz
AM ˈhərmədɪdʒ, -ɪz

Hermitian
BR həˈ(ː)ˈmɪʃn
AM hərˈmɪʃən

hermitic
BR həˈ(ː)ˈmɪtɪk
AM hərˈmɪdɪk

Hermon
BR ˈhəːmən
AM ˈhərmən

Hern
BR həːn
AM hərn

Hernández
BR həˈnandɛz
AM hərˈnæn,dɛz

Herne
BR həːn
AM hərn

hernia
BR ˈhəːnɪə(r), -z
AM ˈhərniə, -z

hernial
BR ˈhəːnɪəl
AM ˈhərniəl

herniary
BR ˈhəːnɪəri
AM ˈhərnɪɛri

herniated
BR ˈhəːnɪeɪtɪd
AM ˈhərniˌeɪdɪd

Herning
BR ˈhəːnɪŋ
AM ˈhərnɪŋ

hero
BR ˈhɪərəʊ, -z
AM ˈhiroʊ, -z

Herod
BR ˈhɛrəd
AM ˈhɛrəd

Herodias
BR hɪˈrəʊdɪəs,
hɪˈrəʊdɪəs,
hɛˈrəʊdɪəs,
hɛˈrəʊdiəs
AM həˈroʊdiəs

Herodotus
BR hɪˈrɒdətəs,
hɛˈrɒdətəs
AM hɛˈrɑdədəs

heroic
BR hɪˈrəʊɪk, -s
AM həˈroʊɪk, -s

heroically
BR hɪˈrəʊɪkli
AM həˈroʊək(ə)li

heroi-comic
BR hɪˌrəʊɪˈkɒmɪk
AM həˈroʊəˈkɑmɪk,
hɛˈroʊəˈkɑmɪk

heroi-comical
BR hɪˌrəʊɪˈkɒmɪkl
AM həˈroʊəˈkɑməkəl,
hɛˈroʊəˈkɑməkəl

heroin
BR ˈhɛrəʊɪn
AM ˈhɛrəwən

heroine
BR ˈhɛrəʊɪn, -z
AM ˈhɛrəwən, -z

heroise
BR ˈhɪərəʊʌɪz, -ɪz, -ɪŋ,
-d
AM ˈhirəˌwaɪz, -ɪz, -ɪŋ,
-d

heroism
BR ˈhɛrəʊɪz(ə)m
AM ˈhɛrəˌwɪzəm

heroize
BR ˈhɪərəʊʌɪz, -ɪz, -ɪŋ,
-d
AM ˈhirəˌwaɪz, -ɪz, -ɪŋ,
-d

heron
BR ˈhɛrən, ˈhɛrn̩, -z
AM ˈhɛrən, -z

heronry
BR ˈhɛrənr|i, ˈhɛrn̩r|i,
-ɪz
AM ˈhɛrənri, -z

herpes
BR ˈhəːpiːz
AM ˈhərpiz

herpes simplex
BR ˌhəːpiːz ˈsɪmplɛks
AM ˈhərpiz ˈsɪmˌplɛks

herpes zoster
BR ˌhəːpiːz ˈzɒstə(r)
AM ˈhərpiz ˈzɑstər

herpetic
BR həˈpɛtɪk
AM hərˈpɛdɪk

herpetological
BR ˌhəːpɪtəˈlɒdʒɪkl
AM ˈhərpədəˈlɑdʒəkəl

herpetologically
BR ˌhəːpɪtəˈlɒdʒɪkli
AM ˈhərpədəˈlɑdʒək(ə)li

herpetologist
BR ˌhəːpɪˈtɒlədʒɪst, -s
AM ˌhərpəˈtɑlədʒəst, -s

herpetology
BR ˌhəːpɪˈtɒlədʒi
AM ˌhərpəˈtɑlədʒi

Herr
BR hɛː(r)
AM hɛ(ə)r

Herrera
BR hɪˈrɛːrə(r)
AM həˈrɛrə

Herrick
BR ˈhɛrɪk
AM ˈhɛrɪk

herring
BR ˈhɛrɪŋ, -z
AM ˈhɛrɪŋ, -z

herringbone
BR ˈhɛrɪŋbəʊn
AM ˈhɛrɪŋˌboʊn

Herriot
BR ˈhɛrɪət
AM ˈhɛriət

Herrnhuter
BR ˈhɛːnˌhuːtə(r),
ˈhɛːnˌhuːtə(r),
ˈhɛrənˌhuːtə(r),
ˈhɛrənˌhuːtə(r), -z
AM ˈhɛrn̩ˌ(h)udər, -z

hers
BR həːz
AM hərz

Herschel
BR ˈhəːʃl
AM ˈhərʃəl

herself¹
strong form
BR həːˈsɛlf
AM hərˈsɛlf

herself²
weak form
BR (h)əˈsɛlf
AM (h)ərˈsɛlf

Hersey
BR ˈhəːsi
AM ˈhərsi

Hershey
BR ˈhəːʃi
AM ˈhərʃi

Herstmonceaux
BR ˌhəːs(t)mənˈs(j)uː
AM ˌhərs(t)mənˈsu

Hertford
BR ˈhɑːtfəd

AM ˈhɑːtfərd
Hertfordshire
BR ˈhɑːtfədʃ(ɪ)ə(r)
AM ˈhɑːrtfərdˌʃɪ(ə)r
Herts.
Hertfordshire
BR hɑːts
AM hɑrts
Hertz
BR hɜːts
AM hɜrts
hertz
BR hɜːts
AM hɜrts
Hertzog
BR ˈhɜːtspɡ, ˈhɜːzpɡ
AM ˈhɜrtˌspɡ, ˈhɜrˌzpɡ,
ˈhɜrtˌsaɡ, ˈhɜrˌzaɡ
Herzegovina
BR ˌhɜːtsəˈɡpvɪnə(r),
ˌhɜːtsəɡəˈviːnə(r)
AM ˌhɜrtsəˈɡouvinə
Herzl
BR ˈhɜːtsl
AM ˈhɜrtsəl
Herzog
BR ˈhɜːzpɡ, ˈhɜːtspɡ
AM ˈhɜrˌzpɡ, ˈhɜrˌzaɡ
he's[1]
strong form
BR hiːz
AM hiz
he's[2]
weak form
BR (h)ɪz
AM (h)ɪz
Heseltine
BR ˈhɛsltʌɪn, ˈhɛzltʌɪn
AM ˈhɛsəlˌtaɪn
Heshvan
BR ˈhɛʃvən
AM ˈhɛʃvən
Hesiod
BR ˈhɛsjəd
AM ˈhɛsiəd, ˈhɛsjəd
hesitance
BR ˈhɛzɪt(ə)ns
AM ˈhɛzədns
hesitancy
BR ˈhɛzɪt(ə)nsi
AM ˈhɛzədnsi
hesitant
BR ˈhɛzɪt(ə)nt
AM ˈhɛzədənt
hesitantly
BR ˈhɛzɪt(ə)ntli
AM ˈhɛzədən(t)li
hesitate
BR ˈhɛzɪteɪt, -s, -ɪŋ, -ɪd
AM ˈhɛzəˌteɪlt, -ts, -dɪŋ,
-dɪd
hesitater
BR ˈhɛzɪteɪtə(r), -z
AM ˈhɛzəˌteɪdər, -z
hesitatingly
BR ˈhɛzɪteɪtɪŋli
AM ˈhɛzəˌteɪdɪŋli

hesitation
BR ˌhɛzɪˈteɪʃn, -z
AM ˌhɛzəˈteɪʃən, -z
hesitative
BR ˈhɛzɪtətɪv,
ˈhɛzɪteɪtɪv
AM ˈhɛzəˌteɪdɪv
Hesketh
BR ˈhɛskɪθ
AM ˈhɛskəθ
Hesperian
BR hɛˈspɪərɪən
AM hɛˈspɪriən
Hesperides
BR hɛˈspɛrɪdiːz
AM hɛˈspɛrədiz
hesperidia
BR ˌhɛspɪˈrɪdɪə(r)
AM ˌhɛspəˈrɪdiə
hesperidium
BR ˌhɛspɪˈrɪdɪəm
AM ˌhɛspəˈrɪdiəm
Hesperus
BR ˈhɛsp(ə)rəs
AM ˈhɛspərəs
Hess
BR hɛs
AM hɛs
Hesse
BR hɛs, ˈhɛsə(r)
AM hɛs
Hessen
BR ˈhɛsn
AM ˈhɛsən
Hessian
BR ˈhɛsɪən, -z
AM ˈhɛʃən, -z
Hessle
BR ˈhɛzl
AM ˈhɛsəl
hest
BR hɛst
AM hɛst
Hester
BR ˈhɛstə(r)
AM ˈhɛstər
Heston
BR ˈhɛst(ə)n
AM ˈhɛstən
Hesvan
BR ˈhɛsvən
AM ˈhɛsvən
het
BR hɛt, -s
AM hɛt, -s
hetaera
BR hɪˈtɪərə(r), -z
AM həˈtɪrə, -z
hetaerae
BR hɪˈtɪəriː, hɪˈtɪərʌɪ
AM həˈtɪri, həˈtɛˌraɪ
hetaerism
BR hɪˈtɪərɪz(ə)m
AM həˈtɪˌrɪzəm
hetaira
BR hɪˈtʌɪrə(r), -z
AM həˈtaɪrə, -z

hetairai
BR hɪˈtʌɪrʌɪ
AM həˈtaɪˌraɪ
hetairism
BR hɪˈtʌɪrɪz(ə)m
AM həˈtaɪˌrɪzəm
hetero
BR ˈhɛt(ə)rəʊ, -z
AM ˈhɛdərou, -z
heterochromatic
BR ˌhɛt(ə)rəʊkrəˈmatɪk
AM ˌhɛdərəkrəˈmædɪk
heteroclite
BR ˈhɛt(ə)rəklʌɪt, -s
AM ˈhɛdərəˌklaɪt, -s
heterocyclic
BR ˌhɛt(ə)rə(ʊ)ˈsʌɪklɪk
AM ˌhɛdərəˈsaɪklɪk
heterodox
BR ˈhɛt(ə)rədɒks
AM ˈhɛdərəˌdaks,
ˈhɛtrəˌdaks
heterodoxy
BR ˈhɛt(ə)rədɒksi
AM ˈhɛdərəˌdaksi,
ˈhɛtrəˌdaksi
heterodyne
BR ˈhɛt(ə)rədʌɪn, -z,
-ɪŋ, -d
AM ˈhɛdərəˌdaɪn, -z,
-ɪŋ, -d
heterogamous
BR ˌhɛtəˈrɒɡəməs
AM ˌhɛdəˈraɡəməs
heterogamy
BR ˌhɛtəˈrɒɡəmi
AM ˌhɛdəˈraɡəmi
heterogeneity
BR ˌhɛt(ə)rə(ʊ)dʒɪˈniːɪti,
ˌhɛt(ə)rə(ʊ)dʒɪˈneɪti
AM ˌhɛdərədʒəˈniːdi,
ˌhɛdərədʒəˈneɪdi
heterogeneous
BR ˌhɛt(ə)rəˈdʒiːnɪəs
AM ˌhɛdərəˈdʒiniəs,
ˌhɛdərəˈdʒinjəs
heterogeneously
BR ˌhɛt(ə)rəˈdʒiːnɪəsli
AM ˌhɛdərəˈdʒiniəsli,
ˌhɛdərəˈdʒinjəsli
heterogeneous-
ness
BR ˌhɛt(ə)rəˈdʒiːnɪəsnəs
AM ˌhɛdərəˈdʒiniəsnəs,
ˌhɛdərəˈdʒinjəsnəs
heterogeneses
BR ˌhɛt(ə)rə(ʊ)ˈdʒɛnɪsiːz
AM ˌhɛdərəˈdʒɛnəˌsiz
heterogenesis
BR ˌhɛt(ə)rə(ʊ)ˈdʒɛnɪsɪs
AM ˌhɛdərəˈdʒɛnəsəs
heterogenetic
BR ˌhɛt(ə)rə(ʊ)dʒɪˈnɛtɪk
AM ˌhɛdərədʒəˈnɛdɪk
heterogeny
BR ˌhɛtəˈrɒdʒɪni
AM ˌhɛdəˈradʒəni

heterogonous
BR ˌhɛtəˈrɒɡənəs
AM ˌhɛdəˈraɡənəs
heterogony
BR ˌhɛtəˈrɒɡəni
AM ˌhɛdəˈraɡəni
heterograft
BR ˈhɛt(ə)rəɡrɑːft,
ˈhɛt(ə)rəɡraft, -s
AM ˈhɛdərouˌɡræft, -s
heterologous
BR ˌhɛtəˈrɒləɡəs
AM ˌhɛdəˈraləɡəs
heterology
BR ˌhɛtəˈrɒlədʒi
AM ˌhɛdəˈralədʒi
heteromerous
BR ˌhɛtəˈrɒm(ə)rəs
AM ˌhɛdəˈram(ə)rəs
heteromorphic
BR ˌhɛt(ə)rəˈmɔːfɪk
AM ˌhɛdərəˈmɔrfɪk
heteromorphism
BR ˌhɛt(ə)rəˈmɔːfɪz(ə)m
AM ˌhɛdərəˈmɔrˌfɪzəm
heteronomous
BR ˌhɛtəˈrɒnəməs
AM ˌhɛdəˈranəməs
heteronomy
BR ˌhɛtəˈrɒnəmi
AM ˌhɛdəˈranəmi
heteropathic
BR ˌhɛt(ə)rəˈpaθɪk
AM ˌhɛdərəˈpæθɪk
heterophony
BR ˌhɛtəˈrɒfənˌi,
ˌhɛtəˈrɒfni, -ɪz
AM ˌhɛdəˈrafəni, -z
heterophyllous
BR ˌhɛtəˈrɒfɪləs
AM ˌhɛdəˈrafələs
heterophylly
BR ˌhɛtəˈrɒfɪli
AM ˌhɛdəˈrafəli
heteroplastic
BR ˌhɛt(ə)rəˈplastɪk
AM ˌhɛdərəˈplæstɪk
heteroploid
BR ˈhɛt(ə)rəplɔɪd
AM ˈhɛdərəˌplɔɪd
heteropolar
BR ˌhɛt(ə)rə(ʊ)ˈpəʊlə(r)
AM ˌhɛdərəˈpoulər
Heteroptera
BR ˌhɛtəˈrɒpt(ə)rə(r)
AM ˌhɛdəˈraptərə
heteropteran
BR ˌhɛtəˈrɒpt(ə)rən,
ˌhɛtəˈrɒpt(ə)rn, -z
AM ˌhɛdəˈraptərən, -z
heteropterous
BR ˌhɛtəˈrɒpt(ə)rəs
AM ˌhɛdəˈraptərəs
heterosexism
BR ˌhɛt(ə)rəʊˈsɛksɪz(ə)m
AM ˌhɛdərəˈsɛkˌsɪzəm

heterosexist
BR ˌhet(ə)rəʊ'seksɪst
AM ˌhedərə'seksəst

heterosexual
BR ˌhet(ə)rə(ʊ)'sekʃʊəl,
ˌhet(ə)rə(ʊ)'sekʃ(ʊ)l,
ˌhet(ə)rə(ʊ)'seksjʊ(ə)l
AM ˌhedərə'sekʃ(əw)əl

heterosexuality
BR ˌhet(ə)rə(ʊ)ˌsekʃʊ-
'alɪti,
ˌhet(ə)rə(ʊ)ˌseksjʊ'alɪti-
AM ˌhedərəʊˌsekʃə'wæl-
ədi

heterosexually
BR ˌhet(ə)rə(ʊ)'sekʃʊəli,
ˌhet(ə)rə(ʊ)'sekʃʊli,
ˌhet(ə)rə(ʊ)'sekʃli,
ˌhet(ə)rə(ʊ)'seksjʊ(ə)li
AM ˌhedərə'sekʃ(əw)əli

heterosis
BR ˌhetə'rəʊsɪs, -ɪz
AM ˌhedə'rəʊsəs, -əz

heterotaxy
BR ˈhet(ə)rə(ʊ)ˌtaksi
AM ˈhedərəʊˌtæksi

heterotransplant
BR ˌhet(ə)rəʊ'trans-
plɑ:nt,
ˌhet(ə)rəʊ'trɑ:nsplɑ:nt,
ˌhet(ə)rəʊ'transplant,
-s
AM ˈhedərəʊ'træns-
ˌplænt, -s

heterotrophic
BR ˌhet(ə)rə(ʊ)'trɒfɪk,
ˌhet(ə)rə(ʊ)'trəʊfɪk
AM ˌhedərə'trɑfɪk

heterozygote
BR ˌhet(ə)rə(ʊ)'zaɪgəʊt,
-s
AM ˈhedərəʊ'zaɪgoʊt,
-s

heterozygotic
BR ˌhet(ə)rəzʌɪ'gɒtɪk
AM ˈhedərəʊˌzaɪ'gɑdɪk

heterozygous
BR ˌhet(ə)rə(ʊ)'zʌɪgəs
AM ˈhedərəʊ'zaɪgəs

Hetherington
BR 'heð(ə)rɪŋt(ə)n
AM 'heðərɪŋtən

hetman
BR 'hetmən
AM 'hetmən

hetmen
BR 'hetmən
AM 'hetmən

Hettie
BR 'heti
AM 'hedi

Hetton-le-Hole
BR ˌhetnlɪ'həʊl
AM ˌhedənlə'hoʊl

het up
BR ˌhet 'ʌp
AM ˌhet 'əp

heuchera
BR 'hju:k(ə)rə(r),
'hɔɪk(ə)rə(r), -z
AM 'hjukərə, -z

Heugh [1]
place in UK
BR hju:f
AM hjuf

Heugh [2]
surname
BR hju:
AM hju

heuristic
BR hjʊə'rɪstɪk, -s
AM hju'rɪstɪk, -s

heuristically
BR hjʊə'rɪstɪkli
AM hju'rɪstək(ə)li

hevea
BR 'hi:vɪə(r), -z
AM 'hiviə, -z

hew
BR hju:, -z, -ɪŋ, -d
AM hju, -z, -ɪŋ, -d

hewer
BR 'hju:ə(r), -z
AM 'hjuər, -z

Hewett
BR 'hju:ɪt
AM 'hjuɪt

Hewitt
BR 'hju:ɪt
AM 'hjuɪt

Hewlett
BR 'hju:lɪt
AM 'hjulɪt

hex
BR heks, -ɪz, -ɪŋ, -t
AM heks, -əz, -ɪŋ, -t

hexachord
BR 'heksəkɔ:d, -z
AM 'heksəˌkɔ(ə)rd, -z

hexad
BR 'heksad, -z
AM 'hekˌsæd, -z

hexadecimal
BR ˌheksə'desɪml
AM ˌheksə'des(ə)məl

hexadecimally
BR ˌheksə'desɪməli,
ˌheksə'desɪmli̩
AM ˌheksə'des(ə)məli

hexagon
BR 'heksəg(ə)n, -z
AM 'heksəˌgɑn, -z

hexagonal
BR hek'sagənl,
hek'sagn̩l
AM hek'sægənəl

hexagonally
BR hek'sagənəli,
hek'sagənl̩i,
hek'sagnəli,
hek'sagn̩li
AM hek'sægənəli

hexagram
BR 'heksəgram, -z
AM 'heksəˌgræm, -z

hexahedra
BR ˌheksə'hi:drə(r)
AM ˌheksə'hidrə

hexahedral
BR ˌheksə'hi:dr(ə)l
AM ˌheksə'hidrəl

hexahedron
BR ˌheksə'hi:dr(ə)n, -z
AM ˌheksə'hidrən, -z

hexameron
BR hek'sam(ə)rən,
hek'sam(ə)rn̩
AM hek'sæmərən

hexameter
BR hek'samɪtə(r), -z
AM hek'sæmədər, -z

hexametric
BR ˌheksə'metrɪk
AM ˌheksə'metrɪk

hexametrist
BR hek'samɪtrɪst, -s
AM ˌheksə'metrəst, -s

hexane
BR 'heksein
AM 'hekˌsein

hexapla
BR 'heksəplə(r)
AM 'heksəplə

hexapod
BR 'heksəpɒd, -z
AM 'heksəˌpad, -z

Hexapoda
BR ˌheksə'pəʊdə(r)
AM ˌheksə'poʊdə

hexapody
BR hek'sapədˌi, -ɪz
AM hek'sapədi, -z

hexastyle
BR 'heksəstʌɪl, -z
AM 'heksəˌstaɪl, -z

hexasyllabic
BR ˌheksəsɪ'labɪk
AM ˌheksəsə'læbɪk

Hexateuch
BR 'heksətju:k,
'heksətʃu:k
AM 'heksəˌtɔɪk

hexavalent
BR ˌheksə'veilənt,
ˌheksə'veiln̩t
AM ˌheksə'veilənt

hexode
BR 'heksəʊd, -z
AM 'heksoʊd, -z

hexose
BR 'heksəʊz, 'heksəʊs,
-ɪz
AM 'hekˌsoʊs, -əz

hey
BR hei
AM hei

heyday
BR 'heidei
AM 'heiˌdei

Heyerdahl
BR 'hʌɪədɑ:l
AM 'haɪərˌdɑl

Heyes
BR heiz
AM heiz

Heyford
BR 'heifəd
AM 'heifərd

Heyhoe
BR 'heihəʊ
AM 'heiˌ(h)oʊ

hey presto
BR ˌhei 'prestəʊ
AM ˌhei 'prestoʊ

Heysham
BR 'hi:ʃ(ə)m
AM 'hiʃəm

Heythrop
BR 'hi:θrɒp
AM 'hiθrəp

Heywood
BR 'heiwʊd
AM 'heiˌwʊd

Hezbollah
BR ˌhez'bɒlə(r),
ˌhezbə'lɑ:(r)
AM ˌhezbə'lɑ, hez'bɑlə

Hezekiah
BR ˌhezɪ'kʌɪə(r)
AM ˌhezə'kaɪə

hi
BR hʌɪ
AM hai

Hialeah
BR ˌhʌɪə'li:ə(r)
AM ˌhaɪə'liə

hiatal
BR hʌɪ'eɪtl
AM haɪ'eɪdəl

hiatus
BR hʌɪ'eɪtəs, -ɪz
AM haɪ'eɪdəs, -əz

Hiawatha
BR ˌhʌɪə'wɒθə(r)
AM ˌhaɪə'wɑθə

hibachi
BR hɪ'bɑ:tʃˌi, -ɪz
AM hə'bɑtʃi, -z

hibernal
BR hʌɪ'bə:nl
AM haɪ'bɜrnəl

hibernate
BR 'hʌɪbəneit, -s, -ɪŋ,
-ɪd
AM 'haɪbərˌneiˌt, -ts,
-dɪŋ, -dɪd

hibernation
BR ˌhʌɪbə'neiʃn
AM ˌhaɪbər'neiʃən

hibernator
BR 'hʌɪbəneɪtə(r), -z
AM 'haɪbərˌneɪdər, -z

Hibernia
BR hʌɪ'bə:nɪə(r),
hɪ'bə:nɪə(r)
AM haɪ'bɜrnɪə

Hibernian
BR hʌɪ'bə:nɪən,
hɪ'bə:nɪən, -z

AM haɪ'bɜːnɪən, -z
Hibernicism
BR hʌɪ'bɜːnɪsɪz(ə)m,
hɪ'bɜːnɪsɪz(ə)m, -z
AM haɪ'bɜːnəˌsɪzəm, -z
hibiscus
BR hɪ'bɪskəs
AM haɪ'bɪskəs
Hibs
BR hɪbz
AM hɪbz
hic
BR hɪk
AM hɪk
hiccough
BR 'hɪkʌp, -s, -ɪŋ, -t
AM 'hɪkəp, -s, -ɪŋ, -t
hiccoughy
BR 'hɪkʌpi
AM 'hɪkəpi
hiccup
BR 'hɪkʌp, -s, -ɪŋ, -t
AM 'hɪkəp, -s, -ɪŋ, -t
hiccupy
BR 'hɪkʌpi
AM 'hɪkəpi
hic jacet
BR ˌhɪk 'dʒeɪsɛt,
+ 'jakɛt, -s
AM ˌhɪk 'dʒeɪsət, -s
hick
BR hɪk, -s
AM hɪk, -s
hickey
BR 'hɪk|i, -ɪz
AM 'hɪki, -z
Hickling
BR 'hɪklɪŋ
AM 'hɪklɪŋ
Hickman
BR 'hɪkmən
AM 'hɪkmən
Hickok
BR 'hɪkɒk
AM 'hɪkɑk
hickory
BR 'hɪk(ə)r|i, -ɪz
AM 'hɪk(ə)ri, -z
Hicks
BR hɪks
AM hɪks
Hickson
BR 'hɪks(ə)n
AM 'hɪksən
hid
BR hɪd
AM hɪd
Hidalgo
BR hɪ'dalgəʊ
AM hə'dalgoʊ
Hidcote
BR 'hɪdkət
AM 'hɪdkət
hidden
BR 'hɪdn
AM 'hɪd(ə)n

hiddenness
BR 'hɪdnnəs
AM 'hɪd(ɪn)nɪs
hide
BR hʌɪd, -z, -ɪŋ
AM haɪd, -z, -ɪŋ
hide-and-seek
BR ˌhʌɪd(ə)n(d)'siːk
AM ˌhaɪdən'sik
hideaway
BR 'hʌɪdəweɪ, -z
AM 'haɪdˌəweɪ, -z
hidebound
BR 'hʌɪdbaʊnd
AM 'haɪdˌbaʊnd
hi-de-hi
BR ˌhʌɪdɪ'hʌɪ
AM ˌhaɪdi'haɪ
hideosity
BR ˌhɪdɪ'ɒsɪt|i, -ɪz
AM ˌhɪdi'ɑsədi, -z
hideous
BR 'hɪdɪəs
AM 'hɪdiəs
hideously
BR 'hɪdɪəsli
AM 'hɪdiəsli
hideousness
BR 'hɪdɪəsnəs
AM 'hɪdiəsnəs
hideout
BR 'hʌɪdaʊt, -s
AM 'haɪdˌaʊt, -s
hider
BR 'hʌɪdə(r), -z
AM 'haɪdər, -z
hidey-hole
BR 'hʌɪdɪhəʊl, -z
AM 'haɪdiˌ(h)oʊl, -z
hiding
BR 'hʌɪdɪŋ, -z
AM 'haɪdɪŋ, -z
hidrosis
BR hʌɪ'drəʊsɪs
AM hɪ'droʊsəs,
haɪ'droʊsəs
hidrotic
BR hʌɪ'drɒtɪk
AM hɪ'drɑtɪk
haɪ'drɑtɪk
hie
BR hʌɪ, -z, -ɪŋ, -d
AM haɪ, -z, -ɪŋ, -d
hierarch
BR 'hʌɪ(ə)rɑːk, -s
AM 'haɪ(ə)ˌrɑrk, -s
hierarchal
BR ˌhʌɪ(ə)'rɑːkl
AM ˌhaɪ(ə)'rɑrkəl
hierarchic
BR ˌhʌɪ(ə)'rɑːkɪk
AM ˌhaɪ(ə)'rɑrkɪk
hierarchical
BR ˌhʌɪ(ə)'rɑːkɪkl
AM ˌhaɪ(ə)'rɑrkəkəl
hierarchically
BR ˌhʌɪ(ə)'rɑːkɪkli

AM ˌhaɪ(ə)'rɑrkək(ə)li
hierarchise
BR 'hʌɪ(ə)rɑːkʌɪz, -ɪz,
-ɪŋ, -d
AM 'haɪ(ə)ˌrɑrˌkaɪz,
-ɪz, -ɪŋ, -d
hierarchism
BR 'hʌɪ(ə)rɑːkɪz(ə)m
AM 'haɪ(ə)ˌrɑrˌkɪzəm
hierarchize
BR 'hʌɪ(ə)rɑːkʌɪz, -ɪz,
-ɪŋ, -d
AM 'haɪ(ə)ˌrɑrˌkaɪz,
-ɪz, -ɪŋ, -d
hierarchy
BR 'hʌɪ(ə)rɑːk|i, -ɪz
AM 'haɪ(ə)ˌrɑrki, -z
hieratic
BR hʌɪ(ə)'ratɪk
AM ˌhaɪ(ə)'rædɪk
hieratically
BR hʌɪ(ə)'ratɪkli
AM ˌhaɪ(ə)'rædək(ə)li
hierocracy
BR hʌɪ(ə)'rɒkrəs|i, -ɪz
AM ˌhaɪ(ə)'rɑkrəsi, -z
hieroglyph
BR 'hʌɪ(ə)rəglɪf, -s
AM 'haɪrəˌglɪf,
'haɪroʊˌglɪf, -s
hieroglyphic
BR ˌhʌɪ(ə)rə'glɪfɪk, -s
AM ˌhaɪrə'glɪfɪk,
ˌhaɪroʊ'glɪfɪk, -s
hieroglyphical
BR ˌhʌɪ(ə)rə'glɪfɪkl
AM ˌhaɪrə'glɪfəkəl,
ˌhaɪroʊ'glɪfəkəl
hieroglyphically
BR ˌhʌɪ(ə)rə'glɪfɪkli
AM ˌhaɪrə'glɪfək(ə)li,
ˌhaɪ(ə)roʊ'glɪfək(ə)li
hierogram
BR 'hʌɪ(ə)rəgram, -z
AM 'haɪrəˌgræm,
'haɪroʊˌgræm, -z
hierograph
BR 'hʌɪ(ə)rəgrɑːf,
'hʌɪ(ə)rəgraf, -s
AM 'haɪrəˌgræf,
'haɪroʊˌgræf, -s
hierolatry
BR hʌɪ(ə)'rɒlətri
AM ˌhaɪ(ə)'ralətri
hierology
BR hʌɪ(ə)'rɒlədʒi
AM ˌhaɪ(ə)'ralədʒi
Hieronymus
BR hʌɪ'rɒnɪməs,
hɪ'rɒnɪməs
AM h(ɪ)ə'rɑnəməs
hierophant
BR 'hʌɪ(ə)rəfant, -s
AM 'haɪrəˌfænt, -s
hierophantic
BR ˌhʌɪ(ə)rə'fantɪk
AM ˌhaɪrə'fæn(t)ɪk

AM ˌhaɪ(ə)'rɑrkək(ə)li
hifalutin
BR ˌhʌɪfə'luːt(ɪ)n
AM ˌhaɪfə'lutn
hifalutin'
BR ˌhʌɪfə'luːt(ɪ)n
AM ˌhaɪfə'lutn
hi-fi
BR 'hʌɪfʌɪ, -z
AM 'haɪˌfaɪ, -z
Higginbotham
BR 'hɪg(ɪ)nˌbɒtəm
AM 'hɪgɪnˌbɑθəm,
'hɪgɪnˌbadəm
Higginbottom
BR 'hɪg(ɪ)nˌbɒtəm
AM 'hɪgɪnˌbadəm
Higgins
BR 'hɪgɪnz
AM 'hɪgɪnz
higgle
BR 'hɪg|l, -lz, -lɪŋ \-lɪŋ,
-ld
AM 'hɪg|əl, -əlz, -(ə)lɪŋ,
-əld
higgledy-piggledy
BR ˌhɪgldɪ'pɪgldi
AM ˌhɪgəldi'pɪgəldi
Higgs
BR hɪgz
AM hɪgz
high
BR hʌɪ, -z, -ə(r), -ɪst
AM haɪ, -z, -ər, -ɪst
Higham
BR 'hʌɪəm
AM 'haɪəm
high-and-dry
BR ˌhʌɪən'drʌɪ,
ˌhʌɪŋ'drʌɪ
AM ˌhaɪən'draɪ
high-and-mighty
BR ˌhʌɪən(d)'mʌɪti,
ˌhʌɪŋ(d)'mʌɪti
AM ˌhaɪən'maɪdi
highball
BR 'hʌɪbɔːl, -z
AM 'haɪˌbɔl, 'haɪˌbɑl, -z
highbinder
BR 'hʌɪˌbʌɪndə(r), -z
AM 'haɪˌbaɪndər, -z
highborn
BR 'hʌɪbɔːn, ˌhʌɪ'bɔːn
AM 'haɪˌbɔ(ə)rn
highboy
BR 'hʌɪbɔɪ, -z
AM 'haɪˌbɔɪ, -z
highbrow
BR 'hʌɪbraʊ
AM 'haɪˌbraʊ
Highclere
BR 'hʌɪklɪə(r)
AM 'haɪˌklɪ(ə)r
Highcliffe
BR 'hʌɪklɪf
AM 'haɪˌklɪf

highfalutin
BR ˌhʌɪfəˈluːt(ɪ)n
AM ˈhaɪfəˈlutn

highfalutin'
BR ˌhʌɪfəˈluːt(ɪ)n
AM ˈhaɪfəˈlutn

highfaluting
BR ˌhʌɪfəˈluːtɪŋ
AM ˈhaɪfəˈlutn

Highgate
BR ˈhʌɪgeɪt, ˈhʌɪgət
AM ˈhaɪˌgeɪt

high-handed
BR ˌhʌɪˈhandɪd
AM ˈhaɪˈhæn(d)əd

high-handedly
BR ˌhʌɪˈhandɪdli
AM ˈhaɪˈhæn(d)ədli

high-handedness
BR ˌhʌɪˈhandɪdnɪs
AM ˈhaɪˈhæn(d)ədnəs

high-hat
BR ˌhʌɪˈhat, -s, -ɪŋ, -ɪd
AM ˈhaɪˈhæ|t, -ts, -dɪŋ, -dəd

highland
BR ˈhʌɪlənd, -z
AM ˈhaɪlənd, -z

Highlander
BR ˈhʌɪləndə(r), -z
AM ˈhaɪləndər, -z

Highlandman
BR ˈhʌɪləndmən
AM ˈhaɪlən(d)ˌmæn

Highlandmen
BR ˈhʌɪləndmən
AM ˈhaɪlən(d)ˌmɛn

highlight
BR ˈhʌɪlʌɪt, -s, -ɪŋ, -ɪd
AM ˈhaɪˌlaɪ|t, -ts, -dɪŋ, -dɪd

highlighter
BR ˈhʌɪlʌɪtə(r), -z
AM ˈhaɪˌlaɪdər, -z

highly
BR ˈhʌɪli
AM ˈhaɪli

high-muck-a-muck
BR ˈhʌɪmʌkəˌmʌk, -s
AM ˈhaɪˈməkəˌmək, ˌˈhaɪˈməkiˌmək, -s

highness
BR ˈhʌɪnɪs, -ɪz
AM ˈhaɪnɪs, -ɪz

highrise
BR ˈhʌɪrʌɪz, ˌhʌɪˈrʌɪz, -ɪz
AM ˈhaɪˌraɪz, -ɪz

highroad
BR ˈhʌɪrəʊd, -z
AM ˈhaɪˌroʊd, -z

high-stepper
BR ˌhʌɪˈstɛpə(r), -z
AM ˈhaɪˈstɛpər, -z

hight
BR hʌɪt

AM haɪt

hightail
BR ˈhʌɪteɪl, -z, -ɪŋ, -d
AM ˈhaɪˌteɪl, -z, -ɪŋ, -d

highway
BR ˈhʌɪweɪ, -z
AM ˈhaɪˌweɪ, -z

highwayman
BR ˈhʌɪweɪmən
AM ˈhaɪˌweɪmən

highwaymen
BR ˈhʌɪweɪmən
AM ˈhaɪweɪmən, ˈhaɪweɪˌmɛn

hijack
BR ˈhʌɪdʒak, -s, -ɪŋ, -t
AM ˈhaɪˌdʒæk, -s, -ɪŋ, -t

hijacker
BR ˈhʌɪdʒakə(r), -z
AM ˈhaɪˌdʒækər, -z

hijinks
BR ˈhʌɪdʒɪŋks
AM ˈhaɪˌdʒɪŋks

Hijra
BR ˈhɪdʒrə(r)
AM ˈhɪdʒrə

hike
BR hʌɪk, -s, -ɪŋ, -t
AM haɪk, -s, -ɪŋ, -t

hiker
BR ˈhʌɪkə(r), -z
AM ˈhaɪkər, -z

hila
BR ˈhʌɪlə(r)
AM ˈhaɪlə

hilarious
BR hɪˈlɛːrɪəs
AM həˈlɛrɪəs

hilariously
BR hɪˈlɛːrɪəsli
AM həˈlɛrɪəsli

hilariousness
BR hɪˈlɛːrɪəsnəs
AM həˈlɛrɪəsnəs

hilarity
BR hɪˈlarɪti
AM həˈlɛrədi

Hilary
BR ˈhɪləri
AM ˈhɪləri

Hilbert
BR ˈhɪlbət
AM ˈhɪlbərt

Hilda
BR ˈhɪldə(r)
AM ˈhɪldə

Hildesheim
BR ˈhɪldəshʌɪm
AM ˈhɪldəsˌhaɪm

hill
BR hɪl, -z
AM hɪl, -z

Hillary
BR ˈhɪləri
AM ˈhɪləri

hillbilly
BR ˈhɪlˌbɪl|i, -iz

AM ˈhɪlˌbɪli, -z

hillcrest
BR ˈhɪlkrɛst, -s
AM ˈhɪlˌkrɛst, -s

Hillel
BR ˈhɪlɛl, ˈhɪləl
AM ˈhɪlˈɛl

Hiller
BR ˈhɪlə(r)
AM ˈhɪlər

Hillhead
BR ˌhɪlˈhɛd
AM ˈhɪlˈhɛd

Hilliard
BR ˈhɪlɑːd, ˈhɪlɪəd
AM ˈhɪljərd, ˈhɪliərd

Hillier
BR ˈhɪlɪə(r)
AM ˈhɪliər

hilliness
BR ˈhɪlɪnɪs
AM ˈhɪlɪnɪs

Hillingdon
BR ˈhɪlɪŋdən
AM ˈhɪlɪŋdən

Hillman
BR ˈhɪlmən
AM ˈhɪlmən

hillmen
BR ˈhɪlmən
AM ˈhɪlmən

hillock
BR ˈhɪlək, -s
AM ˈhɪlək, -s

hillocky
BR ˈhɪləki
AM ˈhɪləki

Hills
BR hɪlz
AM hɪlz

Hillsboro
BR ˈhɪlzb(ə)rə(r)
AM ˈhɪlzˌbərə

Hillsborough
BR ˈhɪlzb(ə)rə(r)
AM ˈhɪlzˌbərə

hillside
BR ˈhɪlsʌɪd, -z
AM ˈhɪlˌsaɪd, -z

hilltop
BR ˈhɪltɒp, -s
AM ˈhɪlˌtɑp, -s

hillwalker
BR ˈhɪlˌwɔːkə(r), -z
AM ˈhɪlˌwɔkər, ˈhɪlˌwɑkər, -z

hillwalking
BR ˈhɪlˌwɔːkɪŋ
AM ˈhɪlˌwɔkɪŋ, ˈhɪlˌwɑkɪŋ

hilly
BR ˈhɪl|i, -ɪə(r), -ɪɪst
AM ˈhɪli, -ər, -ɪst

Hilo
BR ˈhiːləʊ, ˈhʌɪləʊ
AM ˈhaɪloʊ, ˈhiloʊ

hilt
BR hɪlt, -s
AM hɪlt, -s

Hilton
BR ˈhɪlt(ə)n
AM ˈhɪlt(ə)n

hilum
BR ˈhʌɪləm
AM ˈhaɪləm

Hilversum
BR ˈhɪlvəs(ə)m
AM ˈhɪlvərsəm

him¹
strong form
BR hɪm
AM hɪm

him²
weak form
BR ɪm
AM ɪm

Himalaya
BR ˌhɪməˈleɪə(r), hɪˈmɑːlɪə(r), -z
AM ˌhɪməˈleɪə, -z

Himalayan
BR ˌhɪməˈleɪən, hɪˈmɑːlɪən
AM ˌhɪməˈleɪən

himation
BR hɪˈmatɪən, hɪˈmatɪɒn
AM həˈmædɪən, həˈmædiˌɑn

Himmler
BR ˈhɪmlə(r)
AM ˈhɪmlər

himself¹
strong form
BR hɪmˈsɛlf
AM hɪmˈsɛlf

himself²
weak form
BR ɪmˈsɛlf
AM ɪmˈsɛlf

Hinayana
BR ˌhiːnəˈjɑːnə(r)
AM ˌhinəˈjɑnə

Hinchcliffe
BR ˈhɪn(t)ʃklɪf
AM ˈhɪn(t)ʃˌklɪf

Hinchingbrooke
BR ˈhɪn(t)ʃɪŋbrʊk
AM ˈhɪn(t)ʃɪŋˌbrʊk

Hinchliffe
BR ˈhɪn(t)ʃlɪf
AM ˈhɪn(t)ʃlɪf

Hinckley
BR ˈhɪŋkli
AM ˈhɪŋkli

hind
BR hʌɪnd, -z
AM haɪnd, -z

hindbrain
BR ˈhʌɪn(d)breɪn, -z
AM ˈhaɪn(d)ˌbreɪn, -z

Hinde
BR hʌɪnd
AM haɪnd

Hindemith
BR 'hɪndəmɪt,
'hɪndəmɪθ
AM 'hɪndə,mɪθ

Hindenburg
BR 'hɪndənbə:g
AM 'hɪndən,bɜrg

hinder¹
adjective
BR 'hʌɪndə(r)
AM 'haɪndər

hinder²
verb, delay
BR 'hɪndə(r), -əz,
-(ə)rɪŋ, -əd
AM 'hɪnd|ər, -ərz,
-(ə)rɪŋ, -ərd

Hindhead
BR 'hʌɪndhɛd
AM 'haɪnd,(h)ɛd

Hindi
BR 'hɪndi, 'hɪndi:
AM 'hɪndi

Hindle
BR 'hɪndl
AM 'hɪndəl

Hindley
BR 'hɪndli, 'hʌɪndli
AM 'hɪn(d)li

Hindmarsh
BR 'hʌɪn(d)maːʃ
AM 'haɪn(d),marʃ

hindmost
BR 'hʌɪn(d)məʊst
AM 'haɪn(d),moʊst

Hindoo
BR ,hɪn'du:, 'hɪndu:, -z
AM 'hɪndu, -z

hindquarters
BR ,hʌɪn(d)'kwɔːtəz,
'hʌɪn(d),kwɔːtəz
AM 'haɪn(d),kwɔrdərz

hindrance
BR 'hɪndr(ə)ns, -ɪz
AM 'hɪndrəns, -əz

hindsight
BR 'hʌɪn(d)sʌɪt
AM 'haɪn(d),saɪt

Hindu
BR ,hɪn'du:, 'hɪndu:, -z
AM 'hɪndu, -z

Hinduise
BR 'hɪndu:ʌɪz, -ɪz, -ɪŋ,
-d
AM 'hɪndu,aɪz, -ɪz, -ɪŋ,
-d

Hinduism
BR 'hɪndu:ɪz(ə)m
AM 'hɪndu,ɪzəm

Hinduize
BR 'hɪndu:ʌɪz, -ɪz, -ɪŋ,
-d
AM 'hɪndu,aɪz, -ɪz, -ɪŋ,
-d

Hindu Kush
BR ,hɪndu: 'kʊʃ
AM 'hɪndu 'kʊʃ

Hindustan
BR ,hɪndʊ'staːn,
,hɪndʊ'stan
AM 'hɪndu,stæn

Hindustani
BR ,hɪndʊ'staːni
AM ,hɪndu'stani

hindwing
BR 'hʌɪndwɪŋ, -z
AM 'haɪn(d),wɪŋ, -z

Hines
BR hʌɪnz
AM haɪnz

hinge
BR hɪn(d)ʒ, -ɪz, -ɪŋ, -d
AM hɪndʒ, -ɪz, -ɪŋ, -d

hingeless
BR 'hɪn(d)ʒlɪs
AM 'hɪndʒlɪs

hingewise
BR 'hɪn(d)ʒwʌɪz
AM 'hɪndʒ,waɪz

hinny
BR 'hɪn|i, -ɪz
AM 'hɪni, -z

Hinshelwood
BR 'hɪnʃlwʊd
AM 'hɪnʃəl,wʊd

hint
BR hɪnt, -s, -ɪŋ, -ɪd
AM hɪn|t, -ts, -(t)ɪŋ,
-(t)ɪd

hinterland
BR 'hɪntəland, -z
AM 'hɪn(t)ər,lænd, -z

Hinton
BR 'hɪnt(ə)n
AM 'hɪn(t)ən

hip
BR hɪp, -s, -t
AM hɪp, -s, -t

hipbath
BR 'hɪp|baːθ, 'hɪp|baθ,
-baːðz \ -baːθs \ -baθs
AM 'hɪp,bæ|θ, -θs \ -ðz

hipbone
BR 'hɪpbəʊn, -z
AM 'hɪp,boʊn, -z

hip-hip-hooray
BR ,hɪp,hɪp'reɪ
AM ,hɪp,(h)ɪpə'reɪ

hiphop
noun
BR 'hɪphɒp
AM 'hɪp,(h)ɑp

hipless
BR 'hɪplɪs
AM 'hɪpləs

hipline
BR 'hɪplʌɪn, -z
AM 'hɪp,laɪn, -z

hipness
BR 'hɪpnɪs
AM 'hɪpnɪs

Hipparchus
BR hɪ'paːkəs
AM 'hɪ,parkəs

hippeastrum
BR ,hɪpɪ'astrəm, -z
AM ,hɪpə'æstrəm, -z

hipped
BR hɪpt
AM hɪpt

hipper
BR 'hɪpə(r), -z
AM 'hɪpər, -z

hippety-hop
BR ,hɪpɪtɪ'hɒp
AM ,hɪpədi,hap

hippie
BR 'hɪp|i, -ɪz
AM 'hɪpi, -z

hippo
BR 'hɪpəʊ, -z
AM 'hɪpoʊ, -z

hippocampi
BR ,hɪpə(ʊ)'kampʌɪ
AM ,hɪpə'kæm,paɪ

hippocampus
BR ,hɪpə(ʊ)'kampəs
AM ,hɪpə'kæmpəs

hippocentaur
BR ,hɪpə(ʊ)'sɛntɔː(r),
-z
AM ,hɪpə'sɛn,tɔ(ə)r, -z

hippocras
BR 'hɪpəkras
AM 'hɪpə,kræs

Hippocrates
BR hɪ'pɒkrəti:z
AM hɪ'pɑkrədiz

Hippocratic
BR ,hɪpə'kratɪk
AM ,hɪpə'krædɪk

Hippocrene
BR 'hɪpəkriːn
AM 'hɪpə,krin

hippodrome
BR 'hɪpədrəʊm, -z
AM 'hɪpə,droʊm, -z

hippogriff
BR 'hɪpə(ʊ)grɪf, -s
AM 'hɪpə,grɪf, -s

hippogryph
BR 'hɪpə(ʊ)grɪf, -s
AM 'hɪpə,grɪf, -s

Hippolyta
BR hɪ'pɒlɪtə(r)
AM hə'palədə

Hippolytus
BR hɪ'pɒlɪtəs
AM hɪ'palədəs

hippophagy
BR hɪ'pɒfədʒi
AM hɪ'pafədʒi

hippophile
BR 'hɪpəfʌɪl, -z
AM 'hɪpə,faɪl, -z

hippophobia
BR ,hɪpə(ʊ)'fəʊbɪə(r)
AM ,hɪpə,foʊbiə

hippopotamus
BR ,hɪpə'pɒtəməs, -ɪz
AM ,hɪpə'padəməs, -əz

Hippo Regius
BR ,hɪpəʊ 'riːdʒɪəs
AM ,hɪpoʊ 'ridʒ(i)əs

hippy
BR 'hɪp|i, -ɪz
AM 'hɪpi, -z

hipster
BR 'hɪpstə(r), -z
AM 'hɪpstər, -z

hipsterism
BR 'hɪpstərɪz(ə)m
AM 'hɪpstə,rɪzəm

hiragana
BR ,hɪrə'gaːnə(r),
,hɪrə'gaːnə(r)
AM ,hɪrə'ganə

Hiram
BR 'hʌɪrəm
AM 'haɪrəm

hircine
BR 'həːsʌɪn, 'həːsɪn
AM 'hər,saɪn, 'hərsən

hire
BR 'hʌɪə(r), -z, -ɪŋ, -d
AM 'haɪ(ə)r, -z, -ɪŋ, -d

hireable
BR 'hʌɪərəbl
AM 'haɪrəbəl

hireling
BR 'hʌɪəlɪŋ, -z
AM 'haɪrlɪŋ, -z

hirer
BR 'hʌɪərə(r), -z
AM 'haɪrər, -z

Hirohito
BR ,hɪrə'hiːtəʊ
AM ,hɪroʊ'hɪdoʊ

Hiroshima
BR hɪ'rɒʃɪmə(r),
,hɪrə'ʃiːmə(r)
AM ,hɪroʊ'ʃimə,
hɪ'roʊʃəmə

Hirst
BR həːst
AM hərst

hirsute
BR 'həːsjuːt, həː'sjuːt
AM 'hər,sut, hər'sut,
'hɪr,sut, hɪr'sut

hirsuteness
BR 'həːsjuːtnəs,
həː'sjuːtnəs
AM 'hər,sutnəs,
hər'sutnəs,
'hɪr,sutnəs,
hɪr'sutnəs

hirsutism
BR 'həːsjuːtɪz(ə)m,
həː'sjuːtɪz(ə)m
AM 'hər,su,tɪzəm,
hər'su,tɪzəm,
'hɪr,su,tɪzəm,
hɪr'su,tɪzəm

hirundine
BR 'hɪrʌndʌɪn,
hɪ'rʌndʌɪn, -z
AM hɪ'rəndən,
hɪ'rən,daɪn, -z

Hirwaun
BR ˈhɪrʊʌɪn
AM ˈhɪrʊaɪn
WE ˈhɪrwaɪn

his¹
strong form
BR hɪz
AM hɪz

his²
weak form
BR ɪz
AM ɪz

Hislop
BR ˈhɪzlɒp, ˈhɪzləp
AM ˈhɪzləp

Hispanic
BR hɪˈspanɪk, -s
AM hɪˈspænɪk, -s

Hispanicise
BR hɪˈspanɪsʌɪz, -ɪz,
-ɪŋ, -d
AM hɪˈspænəˌsaɪz, -ɪz,
-ɪŋ, -d

Hispanicist
BR hɪˈspanɪsɪst, -s
AM hɪˈspænəsəst, -s

Hispanicize
BR hɪˈspanɪsʌɪz, -ɪz,
-ɪŋ, -d
AM hɪˈspænəˌsaɪz, -ɪz,
-ɪŋ, -d

Hispaniola
BR ˌhɪspanɪˈəʊlə(r),
hɪˌspanɪˈəʊlə(r),
ˌhɪspanˈjəʊlə(r)
AM ˌhɪspənˈjoʊlə

Hispanist
BR hɪˈspanɪst, -s
AM ˈhɪspənəst, -s

Hispano-Suiza
BR hɪˌspanəʊˈswiːzə(r)
AM hɪˌspænoʊˈswizə

hispid
BR ˈhɪspɪd
AM ˈhɪspɪd

hiss
BR hɪs, -ɪz, -ɪŋ, -t
AM hɪs, -ɪz, -ɪŋ, -t

hist
BR hɪst
AM hɪst

histamine
BR ˈhɪstəmiːn,
ˈhɪstəmɪn
AM ˈhɪstəˌmin

histaminic
BR ˌhɪstəˈmɪnɪk
AM ˌhɪstəˈmɪnɪk

histidine
BR ˈhɪstədiːn
AM ˈhɪstəˌdin

histiocyte
BR ˈhɪstɪəsʌɪt, -s
AM ˈhɪstiəˌsaɪt, -s

histochemical
BR ˌhɪstəʊˈkɛmɪkl
AM ˌhɪstəˈkɛməkəl

histochemistry
BR ˌhɪstəʊˈkɛmɪstri
AM ˌhɪstəˈkɛməstri

histogenesis
BR ˌhɪstə(ʊ)ˈdʒɛnɪsɪs
AM ˌhɪstəˈdʒɛnəsəs

histogenetic
BR ˌhɪstəʊdʒɪˈnɛtɪk
AM ˌhɪstədʒəˈnɛdɪk

histogenic
BR ˌhɪstəˈdʒɛnɪk
AM ˌhɪstəˈdʒɛnɪk

histogeny
BR hɪˈstɒdʒɪni
AM hɪˈstadʒəni

histogram
BR ˈhɪstəgram, -z
AM ˈhɪstəˌgræm, -z

histological
BR ˌhɪstəˈlɒdʒɪkl
AM ˌhɪstəˈladʒəkəl

histologist
BR hɪˈstɒlədʒɪst, -s
AM hɪˈstalədʒəst, -s

histology
BR hɪˈstɒlədʒi
AM hɪˈstalədʒi

histolysis
BR hɪˈstɒlɪsɪs
AM hɪˈstaləsəs

histolytic
BR ˌhɪstəˈlɪtɪk
AM ˌhɪstəˈlɪdɪk

histone
BR ˈhɪstəʊn, -z
AM ˈhɪˌstoʊn, -z

histopathology
BR ˌhɪstəʊpəˈθɒlədʒi
AM ˈhɪstəpəˈθalədʒi

historian
BR hɪˈstɔːrɪən, -z
AM hɪˈstɔriən, -z

historiated
BR hɪˈstɔːrɪeɪtɪd
AM hɪˈstɔriˌeɪdɪd

historic
BR hɪˈstɒrɪk
AM hɪˈstɔrɪk

historical
BR hɪˈstɒrɪkl
AM hɪˈstɔrəkəl

historically
BR hɪˈstɒrɪkli
AM hɪˈstɔrək(ə)li

historicism
BR hɪˈstɒrɪsɪz(ə)m
AM hɪˈstɔrəˌsɪzəm

historicist
BR hɪˈstɒrɪsɪst, -s
AM hɪˈstɔrəsəst, -s

historicity
BR ˌhɪstəˈrɪsɪti
AM ˌhɪstəˈrɪsɪdi

historiographer
BR hɪˌstɒrɪˈɒgrəfə(r),
hɪˌstɔːrɪˈɒgrəfə(r),

ˌhɪstɒrɪˈɒgrəfə(r),
ˌhɪstɔːrɪˈɒgrəfə(r), -z
AM hɪˌstɔriˈagrəfər, -z

historiographic
BR hɪˌstɒrɪəˈgrafɪk,
hɪˌstɔːrɪəˈgrafɪk
AM hɪˌstɔriəˈgræfɪk

historiographical
BR hɪˌstɒrɪəˈgrafɪkl,
hɪˌstɔːrɪəˈgrafɪkl
AM hɪˌstɔriəˈgræfəkəl

historiography
BR hɪˌstɒrɪˈɒgrəfi,
hɪˌstɔːrɪˈɒgrəfi,
ˌhɪstɒrɪˈɒgrəfi,
ˌhɪstɔːrɪˈɒgrəfi
AM hɪˌstɔriˈagrəfi

history
BR ˈhɪst(ə)r|i, -ɪz
AM ˈhɪst(ə)ri, -z

histrionic
BR ˌhɪstrɪˈɒnɪk, -s
AM ˌhɪstriˈanɪk, -s

histrionically
BR ˌhɪstrɪˈɒnɪkli
AM ˌhɪstriˈanək(ə)li

histrionicism
BR ˌhɪstrɪˈɒnɪsɪz(ə)m
AM ˌhɪstriˈanəˌsɪzəm

histrionism
BR ˈhɪstrɪənɪz(ə)m
AM ˈhɪstriəˌnɪzəm

hit
BR hɪt, -s, -ɪŋ
AM hɪ|t, -ts, -dɪŋ

hit-and-miss
BR ˌhɪt(ə)n(d)ˈmɪs
AM ˈhɪtnˈmɪs

hit-and-run
BR ˌhɪt(ə)n(d)ˈrʌn
AM ˈhɪtnˈrən

hitch
BR hɪtʃ, -ɪz, -ɪŋ, -t
AM hɪtʃ, -ɪz, -ɪŋ, -t

Hitchcock
BR ˈhɪtʃkɒk
AM ˈhɪtʃˌkak

Hitchen
BR ˈhɪtʃɪn
AM ˈhɪtʃɪn

Hitchens
BR ˈhɪtʃ(ɪ)nz
AM ˈhɪtʃənz

hitcher
BR ˈhɪtʃə(r), -z
AM ˈhɪtʃər, -z

hitchhike
BR ˈhɪtʃhʌɪk, -s, -ɪŋ, -t
AM ˈhɪtʃˌhaɪk, -s, -ɪŋ, -t

Hitchin
BR ˈhɪtʃɪn
AM ˈhɪtʃɪn

hitech
BR ˌhʌɪˈtɛk
AM ˈhaɪˌtɛk

hither
BR ˈhɪðə(r)

AM ˈhɪðər

hitherto
BR ˌhɪðəˈtuː, ˈhɪðətuː
AM ˈhɪðərˌtu, ˌhɪðərˈtu

hitherward
BR ˈhɪðəwəd, -z
AM ˈhɪðərwərd, -z

Hitler
BR ˈhɪtlə(r)
AM ˈhɪtlər

Hitlerian
BR hɪtˈlɪərɪən
AM hɪtˈlɪriən

Hitlerism
BR ˈhɪtlərɪz(ə)m
AM ˈhɪtləˌrɪzəm

Hitlerite
BR ˈhɪtlərʌɪt, -s
AM ˈhɪtləˌraɪt, -s

hitman
BR ˈhɪtman
AM ˈhɪtˌmæn

hitmen
BR ˈhɪtmɛn
AM ˈhɪtˌmɛn

hitter
BR ˈhɪtə(r), -z
AM ˈhɪdər, -z

Hittite
BR ˈhɪtʌɪt, -s
AM ˈhɪˌtaɪt, -s

hive
BR hʌɪv, -z, -ɪŋ, -d
AM haɪv, -z, -ɪŋ, -d

hiya!
BR ˈhʌɪə(r)
AM ˈhaɪə

Hizbollah
BR ˌhɛzbəˈlɑː(r),
ˌhɪzbəˈlɑː(r)
AM ˌhɛzbəˈlɑ

h'm
BR (h)m
AM (h)m

hmm
BR (h)m, -z
AM (h)m, -z

ho
BR həʊ
AM hoʊ

hoagie
BR ˈhəʊɡ|i, -ɪz
AM ˈhouɡi, -z

hoar
BR hɔː(r)
AM hɔ(ə)r

hoard
BR hɔːd, -z, -ɪŋ, -ɪd
AM hɔ(ə)rd, -z, -ɪŋ, -əd

hoarder
BR ˈhɔːdə(r), -z
AM ˈhɔrdər, -z

hoarding
BR ˈhɔːdɪŋ, -z
AM ˈhɔrdɪŋ, -z

Hoare
BR hɔː(r)

AM hɔ(ə)r

hoarfrost
BR ˈhɔːfrɒst
AM ˈhɔrˌfrɔst,
ˈhɔrˌfrɑst

hoarhound
BR ˈhɔːhaʊnd
AM ˈhɔrˌ(h)aʊnd

hoarily
BR ˈhɔːrɪli
AM ˈhɔrəli

hoariness
BR ˈhɔːrɪnɪs
AM ˈhɔrɪnɪs

hoarse
BR hɔːs, -ə(r), -ɪst
AM hɔ(ə)rs, -ər, -əst

hoarsely
BR ˈhɔːsli
AM ˈhɔrsli

hoarsen
BR ˈhɔːs|n̩, -nz,
-n̩ɪŋ \-nɪŋ, -nd
AM ˈhɔrsən, -z, -ɪŋ, -d

hoarseness
BR ˈhɔːsnəs
AM ˈhɔrsnəs

hoarstone
BR ˈhɔːstəʊn, -z
AM ˈhɔrˌstoʊn, -z

hoary
BR ˈhɔːr|i, -ɪə(r), -ɪɪst
AM ˈhɔri, -ər, -ɪst

hoatzin
BR həʊˈatsɪn,
ˌwɑːtˈsiːn, -z
AM ˌwɑtˈsin, -z

hoax
BR həʊks, -ɪz, -ɪŋ, -t
AM hoʊks, -əz, -ɪŋ, -t

hoaxer
BR ˈhəʊksə(r), -z
AM ˈhoʊksər, -z

hob
BR hɒb, -z
AM hɑb, -z

Hobart
BR ˈhəʊbɑːt
AM ˈhoʊbərt

Hobbes
BR hɒbz
AM hɑbz

hobbit
BR ˈhɒbɪt, -s
AM ˈhɑbət, -s

hobbitry
BR ˈhɒbɪtri
AM ˈhɑbətri

hobble
BR ˈhɒb|l̩, -lz, -l̩ɪŋ \-lɪŋ,
-ld
AM ˈhɑb|əl, -əlz, -(ə)lɪŋ,
-əld

hobbledehoy
BR ˈhɒbldɪˌhɔɪ, -z
AM ˈhɑbəldiˌhɔɪ, -z

hobbler
BR ˈhɒblə(r),
ˈhɒblə(r), -z
AM ˈhab(ə)lər, -z

Hobbs
BR hɒbz
AM hɑbz

hobby
BR ˈhɒb|i, -ɪz
AM ˈhɑbi, -z

hobbyhorse
BR ˈhɒbɪhɔːs
AM ˈhɑbiˌhɔ(ə)rs

hobbyist
BR ˈhɒbɪɪst, -s
AM ˈhɑbiɪst, -s

Hobday
BR ˈhɒbdeɪ
AM ˈhɑbˌdeɪ

hobday
BR ˈhɒbdeɪ, -z, -ɪŋ, -d
AM ˈhɑbˌdeɪ, -z, -ɪŋ, -d

hobgoblin
BR ˈhɒbˈgɒblɪn,
ˈhɒbˌgɒblɪn, -z
AM ˈhɑbˌgɑblən, -z

Hobley
BR ˈhəʊbli
AM ˈhoʊbli

hobnail
BR ˈhɒbneɪl, -z, -d
AM ˈhɑbˌneɪl, -z, -d

hobnob
BR ˈhɒbnɒb, -z, -ɪŋ, -d
AM ˈhɑbˌnɑb, -z, -ɪŋ, -d

hobo
BR ˈhəʊbəʊ, -z
AM ˈhoʊˌboʊ, -z

Hoboken
BR ˈhəʊbəʊk(ə)n
AM ˈhoʊˌboʊkən

Hobsbawm
BR ˈhɒbzbɔːm
AM ˈhɑbz,bɔm,
ˈhɑbz,bɑm

Hobson
BR ˈhɒbsn
AM ˈhɑbsən

Hobson-Jobson
BR ˌhɒbsnˈdʒɒbsn
AM ˌhɑbsənˈdʒɑbsən

Ho Chi Minh
BR ˌhəʊ ˌ(t)ʃiː ˈmɪn
AM ˌhoʊ ˌ(t)ʃi ˈmɪn

hock
BR hɒk, -s, -ɪŋ, -t
AM hɑk, -s, -ɪŋ, -t

hockey
BR ˈhɒki
AM ˈhɑki

hockeyist
BR ˈhɒkiɪst, -s
AM ˈhɑkiɪst, -s

hockney
BR ˈhɒkni
AM ˈhɑkni

hockshop
BR ˈhɒkʃɒp, -s
AM ˈhakˌʃɑp, -s

Hocktide
BR ˈhɒktaɪd
AM ˈhakˌtaɪd

hocus
BR ˈhəʊkəs, -ɪz, -ɪŋ, -t
AM ˈhoʊkəs, -əz, -ɪŋ, -t

hocus-pocus
BR ˌhəʊkəsˈpəʊkəs
AM ˌhoʊkəsˈpoʊkəs

hod
BR hɒd, -z
AM hɑd, -z

hodden
BR ˈhɒdn
AM ˈhɑdən

Hodder
BR ˈhɒdə(r)
AM ˈhɑdər

Hoddesdon
BR ˈhɒdzd(ə)n
AM ˈhɑdzdən

hoddie
BR ˈhɒd|i, -ɪz
AM ˈhɑdi, -z

Hoddinott
BR ˈhɒdɪnɒt
AM ˈhɑdənat

Hoddle
BR ˈhɒdl
AM ˈhɑdəl

Hodeida
BR hə(ʊ)ˈdeɪdə(r)
AM hoʊˈdeɪdə

Hodge
BR hɒdʒ, -ɪz
AM hɑdʒ, -əz

hodgepodge
BR ˈhɒdʒpɒdʒ
AM ˈhɑdʒˌpɑdʒ

Hodges
BR ˈhɒdʒɪz
AM ˈhɑdʒəz

Hodgetts
BR ˈhɒdʒɪts
AM ˈhɑdʒəts

Hodgkin
BR ˈhɒdʒkɪn
AM ˈhɑdʒkən

Hodgkinson
BR ˈhɒdʒkɪns(ə)n
AM ˈhɑdʒkənsən

Hodgson
BR ˈhɒdʒsn
AM ˈhɑdʒsən

hodiernal
BR ˌhɒdɪˈɜːnl,
ˌhəʊdɪˈɜːnl
AM ˌhoʊdiˈɜrnəl,
ˌhɑdiˈɜrnəl

hodman
BR ˈhɒdmən
AM ˈhɑdmən

hodmen
BR ˈhɒdmən

AM ˈhadmən

hodograph
BR ˈhɒdəgrɑːf,
ˈhɒdəgraf, -s
AM ˈhɑdəˌgræf,
ˈhoʊdəˌgræf, -s

hodometer
BR hɒˈdɒmɪtə(r)
AM hɑˈdɑmədər,
hoʊˈdɑmədər

Hodson
BR ˈhɒdsn
AM ˈhɑdsən

hoe
BR həʊ, -z, -ɪŋ, -d
AM hoʊ, -z, -ɪŋ, -d

hoedown
BR ˈhəʊdaʊn, -z
AM ˈhoʊˌdaʊn, -z

hoer
BR ˈhəʊə(r), -z
AM ˈhoʊər, -z

Hoey
BR ˈhəʊi
AM ˈhoʊi

Hoffman
BR ˈhɒfmən
AM ˈhɑfmən, ˈhafmən

Hoffnung
BR ˈhɒfnʊŋ, ˈhɒfnʌŋ
AM ˈhɑfnəŋ, ˈhafnəŋ

Hofmannsthal
BR ˈhɒfmənˌʃtɑːl
AM ˈhɑfmənˌstɔl,
ˈhafmənˌstal

Hofmeister
BR ˈhɒfˌmaɪstə(r)
AM ˈhɑfˌmaɪstər,
ˈhafˌmaɪstər

hog
BR hɒg, -z, -ɪŋ, -d
AM hɔg, hag, -z, -ɪŋ, -d

hogan
BR ˈhəʊg(ə)n, -z
AM ˈhoʊgən, ˈhoʊˌgan,
-z

Hogarth
BR ˈhəʊgɑːθ
AM ˈhoʊˌgarθ

Hogarthian
BR həʊˈgɑːθɪən
AM hoʊˈgarθiən

hogback
BR ˈhɒgbak, -s
AM ˈhɔgˌbæk,
ˈhagˌbæk, -s

Hogben
BR ˈhɒgbən
AM ˈhɔgbən, ˈhagbən

Hogg
BR hɒg
AM hag

**Hoggar
Mountains**
BR ˌhɒgə ˈmaʊntɪnz
AM ˌhagər ˈmaʊntnz

Hoggart
BR 'hɒgət
AM 'hɔgərt, 'hagərt

hogger
BR 'hɒgə(r), -z
AM 'hɔgər, 'hagər, -z

hoggery
BR 'hɒg(ə)r|i, -ɪz
AM 'hɔgəri, 'hagəri, -z

hogget
BR 'hɒgɪt, -s
AM 'hɔgət, 'hagət, -s

hoggin
BR 'hɒgɪn
AM 'hɔgən, 'hagən

hoggish
BR 'hɒgɪʃ
AM 'hɔgɪʃ, 'hagɪʃ

hoggishly
BR 'hɒgɪʃli
AM 'hɔgɪʃli, 'hagɪʃli

hoggishness
BR 'hɒgɪʃnɪs
AM 'hɔgɪʃnɪs, 'hagɪʃnɪs

hoglike
BR 'hɒglaɪk
AM 'hɔg,laɪk, 'hag,laɪk

Hogmanay
BR 'hɒgmənei, ,hɒgmə'nei, -z
AM 'hagmə,nei, -z

hogshead
BR 'hɒgzhɛd, -z
AM 'hɔgz,(h)ɛd, 'hagz,(h)ɛd, -z

hogtie
BR 'hɒgtʌɪ, -z, -ɪŋ, -d
AM 'hɔg,taɪ, 'hag,taɪ, -z, -ɪŋ, -d

hogwash
BR 'hɒgwɒʃ
AM 'hɔg,wɔʃ, 'hag,waʃ

hogweed
BR 'hɒgwiːd
AM 'hɔg,wid, 'hag,wid

Hohenstaufen
BR 'həʊən,staʊfn, 'həʊən,ʃtaʊfn
AM 'hoʊən,staʊfən, 'hoʊən,ʃtaʊfən

Hohenzollern
BR ,həʊən'zɒlən
AM ,hoʊən'zalərn

ho-ho
BR ,həʊ'həʊ
AM ,hoʊ'hoʊ

ho-hum
BR ,həʊ'hʌm
AM 'hoʊ'həm

hoick
BR hɔɪk, -s, -ɪŋ, -t
AM hɔɪk, -s, -ɪŋ, -t

hoi polloi
BR ,hɔɪ pə'lɔɪ
AM ,hɔɪ pə'lɔɪ

hoisin
BR 'hɔɪzɪn
AM 'hɔɪzɪn

hoist
BR hɔɪst, -s, -ɪŋ, -ɪd
AM hɔɪst, -s, -ɪŋ, -ɪd

hoister
BR 'hɔɪstə(r), -z
AM 'hɔɪstər, -z

hoity-toity
BR ,hɔɪtɪ'tɔɪti
AM ,hɔɪdi'tɔɪdi

hokey
BR 'həʊki
AM 'hoʊki

hokey-cokey
BR ,həʊkɪ'kəʊki
AM 'hoʊki'koʊki

hokeyness
BR 'həʊkɪnɪs
AM 'hoʊkɪnɪs

hokey-pokey
BR ,həʊkɪ'pəʊki
AM 'hoʊki'poʊki

hoki
BR 'həʊki
AM 'hoʊki

hokily
BR 'həʊkɪli
AM 'hoʊkəli

Hokkaido
BR hɒ'kʌɪdəʊ
AM ha'kaɪ,doʊ

hokku
BR 'hɒkuː, -z
AM 'hɔ,ku, 'ha,ku, -z

hokonui
BR 'hɒkənʊi
AM 'hakənui

hokum
BR 'həʊkəm
AM 'hoʊkəm

hoky
BR 'həʊk|i, -ɪə(r), -ɪɪst
AM 'hoʊki, -ər, -ɪst

Holarctic
BR hɒl'ɑːktɪk
AM ,hal'ɑrktɪk, ,hɒl'ɑrktɪk, 'hoʊl'ɑrktɪk, 'hal'ɑrdɪk, ,hɒl'ɑrdɪk, 'hoʊl'ɑrdɪk

Holbeach
BR 'hɒlbiːtʃ
AM 'hɔl,bɪtʃ, 'hal,bɪtʃ

Holbech
BR 'hɒlbɪtʃ
AM 'hɔl,bɛk, 'hal,bɛk

Holbeche
BR 'hɒlbiːtʃ
AM 'hɔl,bɛk, 'hal,bɛk

Holbein
BR 'hɒlbʌɪn
AM 'hoʊl,baɪn

Holborn
BR 'həʊbn
AM 'hoʊ(l),bɔ(ə)rn

Holborne
BR 'həʊ(l)bn
AM 'hoʊ(l),bə(ə)rn

Holbrook
BR 'həʊlbrʊk
AM 'hoʊl,brʊk

Holbrooke
BR 'həʊlbrʊk
AM 'hoʊl,brʊk

Holcomb
BR 'həʊ(l)kəm
AM 'hoʊ(l)kəm

Holcombe
BR 'həʊ(l)kəm
AM 'hoʊ(l)kəm

hold
BR həʊld, -z, -ɪŋ
AM hoʊld, -z, -ɪŋ

holdable
BR 'həʊldəbl
AM 'hoʊldəbəl

holdall
BR 'həʊldɔːl, -z
AM 'hoʊld,ɔl, 'hoʊld,al, -z

holdback
BR 'həʊl(d)bak, -s
AM 'hoʊl(d),bæk, -s

hold-down
BR 'həʊl(d)daʊn, -z
AM 'hoʊl,daʊn, -z

Holden
BR 'həʊld(ə)n
AM 'hoʊldən

holder
BR 'həʊldə(r), -z
AM 'hoʊldər, -z

Hölderlin
BR 'həːldəliːn
AM 'həldərlin

Holderness
BR 'həʊldənɪs
AM 'hoʊldərnəs

holdfast
BR 'həʊl(d)fɑːst, 'həʊl(d)fast, -s
AM 'hoʊl(d),fæst, -s

holding
BR 'həʊldɪŋ, -z
AM 'hoʊldɪŋ, -z

holdout
BR 'həʊl(d)daʊt, -s
AM 'hoʊl,daʊt, -s

holdover
BR 'həʊld,əʊvə(r), -z
AM 'hoʊl,doʊvər, -z

Holdsworth
BR 'həʊl(d)zwɜːθ, 'həʊl(d)zwəθ
AM 'hoʊl(d)z,wərθ

holdup
BR 'həʊldʌp, -s
AM 'hoʊl,dəp, -s

hole
BR həʊl, -z, -ɪŋ, -d
AM hoʊl, -z, -ɪŋ, -d

holey
BR 'həʊli
AM 'hoʊli

Holford
BR 'həʊlfəd, 'hɒlfəd
AM 'hoʊ(l)fərd

Holi
BR 'həʊliː
AM 'hoʊli

holibut
BR 'hɒlɪbʌt, -s
AM 'haləbət, -s

holiday
BR 'hɒlɪd|eɪ, 'hɒlɪd|i, -eɪz\-ɪz
AM 'halə,deɪ, -z

holidaymaker
BR 'hɒlɪdɪ,meɪkə(r), -z
AM 'halədeɪ,meɪkər, -z

holily
BR 'həʊlɪli
AM 'hoʊləli

holiness
BR 'həʊlɪnɪs
AM 'hoʊlɪnɪs

Holinshed
BR 'hɒlɪnʃɛd, 'hɒlɪnzhɛd
AM 'halənz,(h)ɛd, 'halənʃɛd

holism
BR 'həʊlɪz(ə)m
AM 'hoʊl,ɪzəm

holist
BR 'həʊlɪst, -s
AM 'hoʊləst, -s

holistic
BR hə(ʊ)'lɪstɪk, hɒ'lɪstɪk
AM hoʊ'lɪstɪk

holistically
BR hə(ʊ)'lɪstɪkli, hɒ'lɪstɪkli
AM hoʊ'lɪstək(ə)li

holla
BR 'hɒlə(r), -z, -ɪŋ, -d
AM 'halə, -z, -ɪŋ, -d

Holland
BR 'hɒlənd, -z
AM 'halən(d), -z

hollandaise
BR ,hɒlən'deɪz
AM ,halən'deɪz

Hollander
BR 'hɒləndə(r), -z
AM 'haləndər, -z

Hollands
BR 'hɒlən(d)z
AM 'halən(d)z

holler
BR 'hɒl|ə(r), -əz, -(ə)rɪŋ, -əd
AM 'halər, -z, -ɪŋ, -d

Hollerith
BR 'hɒlərɪθ
AM 'halərɪθ

Holley
BR ˈhɒli
AM ˈhɑli

Holliday
BR ˈhɒlɪdeɪ
AM ˈhɑləˌdeɪ

Hollingsworth
BR ˈhɒlɪŋzwəːθ,
ˈhɒlɪŋzwəθ
AM ˈhɑlɪŋzˌwɚθ

Hollins
BR ˈhɒlɪnz
AM ˈhɑlənz

Hollis
BR ˈhɒlɪs
AM ˈhɑləs

hollo
BR ˈhɒləʊ, -z, -ɪŋ, -d
AM ˈhɑlˌoʊ, -oʊz, -əwɪŋ,
-oʊd

hollow
BR ˈhɒləʊ, -z, -ɪŋ, -d
AM ˈhɑlˌoʊ, -oʊz, -əwɪŋ,
-oʊd

holloware
BR ˈhɒlə(ʊ)wɛː(r)
AM ˈhɑləˌwɛ(ə)r

Holloway
BR ˈhɒləweɪ
AM ˈhɑləˌweɪ

hollow-cheeked
BR ˌhɒlə(ʊ)ˈtʃiːkt
AM ˈhɑloʊˈtʃikt

hollow-eyed
BR ˌhɒləʊˈaɪd
AM ˈhɑloʊˈaɪd

hollow-hearted
BR ˌhɒləʊˈhɑːtɪd
AM ˈhɑloʊˈhɑrdəd

hollowly
BR ˈhɒləʊli
AM ˈhɑloʊli

hollowness
BR ˈhɒləʊnəs
AM ˈhɑloʊnəs

hollowware
BR ˈhɒlə(ʊ)wɛː(r)
AM ˈhɑloʊˌwɛ(ə)r

holly
BR ˈhɒli
AM ˈhɑli

hollyhock
BR ˈhɒlihɒk, -s
AM ˈhɑliˌhɑk, -s

Hollywood
BR ˈhɒlɪwʊd
AM ˈhɑliˌwʊd

holm
BR həʊm, -z
AM hoʊm, -z

Holman
BR ˈhəʊlmən
AM ˈhoʊ(l)mən

Holme
BR həʊm
AM hoʊm

Holmes
BR həʊmz
AM hoʊmz

Holmesian
BR ˈhəʊmziən
AM ˈhoʊmziən

Holmfirth
BR ˈhəʊmfəːθ,
ˌhəʊmˈfəːθ
AM ˈhoʊ(l)mˌfɚθ

holmium
BR ˈhəʊlmiəm,
ˈhɒlmiəm
AM ˈhoʊ(l)miəm

holmoak
BR ˈhəʊməʊk, -s
AM ˈhoʊmˌoʊk, -s

Holmwood
BR ˈhəʊmwʊd
AM ˈhoʊ(l)mˌwʊd

holocaust
BR ˈhɒləkɔːst, -s
AM ˈhɑləˌkɔst,
ˈhoʊləˌkɔst,
ˈhɑləˌkɑst,
ˈhoʊləˌkɑst, -s

Holocene
BR ˈhɒləsiːn
AM ˈhɑləˌsin,
ˈhoʊləˌsin

holoenzyme
BR ˌhɒləʊˈɛnzaɪm, -z
AM ˈhɑloʊˈɛnˌzaɪm,
ˈhoʊloʊˈɛnˌzaɪm, -z

Holofernes
BR ˌhɒləˈfəːniːz,
həˈlɒfəniːz
AM ˌhɑləˈfɚniz

hologram
BR ˈhɒləgram, -z
AM ˈhɑləˌgræm,
ˈhoʊləˌgræm, -z

holograph
BR ˈhɒləgrɑːf,
ˈhɒləgraf, -s
AM ˈhɑləˌgræf,
ˈhoʊləˌgræf, -s

holographic
BR ˌhɒləˈgrafɪk
AM ˌhɑləˈgræfɪk,
ˌhoʊləˈgræfɪk

holographically
BR ˌhɒləˈgrafɪkli
AM ˌhɑləˈgræfək(ə)li,
ˌhoʊləˈgræfək(ə)li

holography
BR hɒˈlɒgrəfi
AM hoʊˈlɑgrəfi

holohedral
BR ˌhɒləˈhiːdr(ə)l
AM ˌhɑləˈhidrəl,
ˌhoʊləˈhidrəl

holometabolous
BR ˌhɒlə(ʊ)mɪˌtabələs
AM ˌhɑloʊməˈtæbələs,
ˈhoʊloʊməˈtæbələs

holophote
BR ˈhɒləfəʊt, -s

AM ˈhɑləˌfoʊt,
ˈhoʊləˌfoʊt, -s

holophyte
BR ˈhɒləfʌɪt, -s
AM ˈhɑləˌfaɪt,
ˈhoʊləˌfaɪt, -s

holophytic
BR ˌhɒləˈfɪtɪk
AM ˌhɑləˈfɪdɪk,
ˌhoʊləˈfɪdɪk

holothurian
BR ˌhɒləˈθ(j)ʊəriən,
ˌhɒləˈθjɔːriən, -z
AM ˌhɑləˈθʊriən,
ˈhoʊləˈθʊriən, -z

holotype
BR ˈhɒlətʌɪp, -s
AM ˈhɑləˌtaɪp,
ˈhoʊləˌtaɪp, -s

Holroyd
BR ˈhɒlrɔɪd, ˈhəʊlrɔɪd
AM ˈhɑlrɔɪd, ˈhoʊlrɔɪd

hols
holidays
BR hɒlz
AM hɑlz

Holst
BR həʊlst
AM hoʊlst

Holstein
BR ˈhɒlsteɪn, -z
AM ˈhoʊlˌsteɪn,
ˈhoʊlˌstin, -z
GER ˈhɔlʃtaɪn

holster
BR ˈhəʊlstə(r),
ˈhɒlstə(r), -z
AM ˈhoʊlstər, -z

holt
BR həʊlt, -s
AM hoʊlt, -s

holus-bolus
BR ˌhəʊləsˈbəʊləs
AM ˈhoʊləsˈboʊləs

holy
BR ˈhəʊl|i, -ɪə(r), -ɪɪst
AM ˈhoʊli, -ər, -ɪst

Holyhead
BR ˈhɒlihɛd
AM ˈhɑliˌhɛd,
ˈhoʊliˌ(h)ɛd

Holyoake
BR ˈhəʊliəʊk
AM ˈhoʊliˌoʊk

Holyrood
BR ˈhɒlɪruːd
AM ˈhɑliˌrud,
ˈhoʊliˌrud

holystone
BR ˈhəʊlɪstəʊn, -z, -ɪŋ,
-d
AM ˈhoʊliˌstoʊn, -z, -ɪŋ,
-d

Holywell
BR ˈhɒlɪwɛl
AM ˈhɑliˌwɛl,
ˈhoʊliˌwɛl

hom
BR həʊm
AM hoʊm

homa
BR ˈhəʊmə(r)
AM ˈhoʊmə

homage
BR ˈhɒmɪdʒ
AM ˈ(h)ɑmɪdʒ

hombre
BR ˈɒmbr|eɪ, ˈɒmbr|i,
-eɪz\-ɪz
AM ˈɑmbreɪ, ˈɑmbri, -z

homburg
BR ˈhɒmbəːg, -z
AM ˈhɑmˌbɚg, -z

home
BR həʊm, -z, -ɪŋ, -d
AM hoʊm, -z, -ɪŋ, -d

homebody
BR ˈhəʊmˌbɒd|i, -ɪz
AM ˈhoʊmˌbɑdi, -z

homebound
BR ˈhəʊmbaʊnd
AM ˈhoʊmˌbaʊnd

homeboy
BR ˈhəʊmbɔɪ, -z
AM ˈhoʊmˌbɔɪ, -z

homebuyer
BR ˈhəʊmˌbʌɪə(r), -z
AM ˈhoʊmˌbaɪər, -z

homecoming
BR ˈhəʊmˌkʌmɪŋ, -z
AM ˈhoʊmˌkəmɪŋ, -z

homegrown
BR ˌhəʊmˈgrəʊn
AM ˈhoʊmˈgroʊn

homeland
BR ˈhəʊmland, -z
AM ˈhoʊmˌlænd, -z

homeless
BR ˈhəʊmləs
AM ˈhoʊmləs

homelessness
BR ˈhəʊmləsnəs
AM ˈhoʊmləsnəs

homelike
BR ˈhəʊmlʌɪk
AM ˈhoʊmˌlaɪk

homeliness
BR ˈhəʊmlɪnɪs
AM ˈhoʊmlɪnɪs

homely
BR ˈhəʊml|i, -ɪə(r), -ɪɪst
AM ˈhoʊmli, -ər, -ɪst

homemade
BR ˌhəʊmˈmeɪd
AM ˈhoʊ(m)ˈmeɪd

homemaker
BR ˈhəʊmˌmeɪkə(r), -z
AM ˈhoʊ(m)ˌmeɪkər, -z

home-making
BR ˈhəʊmˌmeɪkɪŋ
AM ˈhoʊ(m)ˌmeɪkɪŋ

homeomorphism
BR ˌhɒmɪə(ʊ)ˈmɔːf-
ɪz(ə)m,

ˌhəʊmɪə(ʊ)'mɔːfɪz(ə)m
AM ˌhoʊmiə'mɔrfɪzəm
homeopath
BR 'həʊmɪəpaθ,
'hɒmɪəpaθ, -s
AM 'hoʊmiə,pæθ, -s
homeopathic
BR ˌhəʊmɪə'paθɪk,
ˌhɒmɪə'paθɪk
AM ˌhoʊmiə'pæθɪk
homeopathically
BR ˌhəʊmɪə'paθɪkli,
ˌhɒmɪə'paθɪkli
AM ˌhoʊmiə'pæθək(ə)li
homeopathist
BR ˌhəʊmɪ'ɒpəθɪst,
ˌhɒmɪ'ɒpəθɪst, -s
AM ˌhoʊmi'ɑpəθəst, -s
homeopathy
BR ˌhəʊmɪ'ɒpəθi,
ˌhɒmɪ'ɒpəθi
AM ˌhoʊmi'ɑpəθi
homeostasis
BR ˌhəʊmɪə(ʊ)'steɪsɪs,
ˌhɒmɪə(ʊ)'steɪsɪs
AM ˌhoʊmiə'steɪsɪs,
'hoʊmiə'stæsəs
homeostatic
BR ˌhəʊmɪə(ʊ)'statɪk,
ˌhɒmɪə(ʊ)'statɪk
AM ˌhoʊmiə'stædɪk
homeostatically
BR ˌhəʊmɪə(ʊ)'statɪkli,
ˌhɒmɪə(ʊ)'statɪkli
AM ˌhoʊmiə'stædək(ə)li
homeotherm
BR 'həʊmɪə(ʊ)θəːm, -z
AM 'hoʊmiə,θɜrm, -z
homeothermal
BR ˌhəʊmɪə(ʊ)'θəːml
AM ˌhoʊmiə'θɜrməl
homeothermic
BR ˌhəʊmɪə(ʊ)'θəːmɪk,
ˌhɒmɪə(ʊ)'θəːmɪk
AM ˌhoʊmiə'θɜrmɪk
homeothermy
BR 'həʊmɪə(ʊ)θəːmi
AM 'hoʊmiə,θɜrmi
homeowner
BR 'həʊm,əʊnə(r), -z
AM 'hoʊm,oʊnər, -z
Homer
BR 'həʊmə(r), -z
AM 'hoʊmər, -z
Homeric
BR hə(ʊ)'mɛrɪk
AM hoʊ'mɛrɪk
homeroom
BR 'həʊmruːm,
'həʊmrʊm, -z
AM 'hoʊm,rum,
'hoʊm,rʊm, -z
Homerton
BR 'hɒmət(ə)n
AM 'hamərtən,
'hoʊmərtən
homesick
BR 'həʊmsɪk

AM 'hoʊm,sɪk
homesickness
BR 'həʊm,sɪknɪs
AM 'hoʊm,sɪknɪs
homespun
BR 'həʊmspʌn
AM 'hoʊm,spən
homestead
BR 'həʊmstɛd, -z, -ɪŋ
AM 'hoʊm,stɛd, -z, -ɪŋ
homesteader
BR 'həʊmstɛdə(r), -z
AM 'hoʊm,stɛdər, -z
homestyle
BR 'həʊmstʌɪl
AM 'hoʊm,staɪl
hometown
BR 'həʊmtaʊn,
ˌhəʊm'taʊn
AM ˌhoʊm'taʊn
homeward
BR 'həʊmwəd, -z
AM 'hoʊmwərd, -z
homework
BR 'həʊmwəːk
AM 'hoʊm,wɜrk
homeworker
BR 'həʊm,wəːkə(r), -z
AM 'hoʊm,wɜrkər, -z
homey
BR 'həʊm|i, -ɪə(r), -ɪɪst
AM 'hoʊmi, -ər, -ɪst
homeyly
BR 'həʊmɪli
AM 'hoʊməli
homeyness
BR 'həʊmɪnɪs
AM 'hoʊmɪnɪs
homicidal
BR ˌhɒmɪ'sʌɪdl
AM ˌhamə'saɪdəl
homicidally
BR ˌhɒmɪ'sʌɪdļi
AM ˌhamə'saɪdļi
homicide
BR 'hɒmɪsʌɪd, -z
AM 'hamə,saɪd, -z
homiletic
BR ˌhɒmɪ'lɛtɪk, -s
AM ˌhamə'lɛdɪk, -s
homiliary
BR hɒ'mɪlɪər|i, -ɪz
AM hɑ'mɪli,ɛri, -z
homilist
BR 'hɒmɪlɪst,
'hɒmļɪst, -s
AM 'hamə021əst, -s
homily
BR 'hɒmɪl|i, 'hɒmļ|i,
-ɪz
AM 'haməli, -z
homing
BR 'həʊmɪŋ
AM 'hoʊmɪŋ
hominid
BR 'hɒmɪnɪd, -z

AM 'hamənəd,
'hamə,nɪd, -z
hominoid
BR 'hɒmɪnɔɪd, -z
AM 'hamə,nɔɪd, -z
hominy
BR 'hɒmɪni
AM 'haməni
Homo
BR 'həʊməʊ, 'hɒməʊ
AM 'hoʊ,moʊ
homo
BR 'həʊməʊ, -z
AM 'hoʊ,moʊ, -z
homocentric
BR ˌhəʊmə(ʊ)'sɛntrɪk,
ˌhɒmə(ʊ)'sɛntrɪk
AM ˌhoʊmoʊ'sɛntrɪk
homoeopath
BR 'həʊmɪəpaθ,
'hɒmɪəpaθ, -s
AM 'hoʊmiə,pæθ, -s
homoeopathic
BR ˌhəʊmɪə'paθɪk,
ˌhɒmɪə'paθɪk
AM ˌhoʊmiə'pæθɪk
homoeopathically
BR ˌhəʊmɪə'paθɪkli,
ˌhɒmɪə'paθɪkli
AM ˌhoʊmiə'pæθək(ə)li
homoeopathist
BR ˌhəʊmɪ'ɒpəθɪst,
ˌhɒmɪ'ɒpəθɪst, -s
AM ˌhoʊmi'ɑpəθəst, -s
homoeopathy
BR ˌhəʊmɪ'ɒpəθi,
ˌhɒmɪ'ɒpəθi
AM ˌhoʊmi'ɑpəθi
homoeostasis
BR ˌhəʊmɪə(ʊ)'steɪsɪs,
ˌhɒmɪə(ʊ)'steɪsɪs
AM ˌhoʊmiə'steɪsɪs,
'hoʊmiə'stæsəs
homoeostatic
BR ˌhəʊmɪə(ʊ)'statɪk,
ˌhɒmɪə(ʊ)'statɪk
AM ˌhoʊmiə'stædɪk
homoeostatically
BR ˌhəʊmɪə(ʊ)'statɪkli,
ˌhɒmɪə(ʊ)'statɪkli
AM ˌhoʊmiə'stædək(ə)li
homoeotherm
BR 'həʊmɪə(ʊ)θəːm,
'hɒmɪə(ʊ)θəːm, -z
AM 'hoʊmiə,θɜrm, -z
homoeothermal
BR ˌhəʊmɪə(ʊ)'θəːml,
ˌhɒmɪə(ʊ)'θəːml
AM ˌhoʊmiə'θɜrməl
homoeothermic
BR ˌhəʊmɪə(ʊ)'θəːmɪk,
ˌhɒmɪə(ʊ)'θəːmɪk
AM ˌhoʊmiə'θɜrmɪk
homoeothermy
BR 'həʊmɪə(ʊ)θəːmi,
'hɒmɪə(ʊ)θəːmi
AM 'hoʊmiə,θɜrmi

homoerotic
BR ˌhəʊməʊɪ'rɒtɪk,
ˌhɒməʊɪ'rɒtɪk
AM ˌhoʊmoʊə'rɑdɪk
homogametic
BR ˌhəʊməʊgə'mɛtɪk,
ˌhɒməʊgə'mɛtɪk
AM ˌhoʊmoʊgə'mɛdɪk
homogamous
BR hə(ʊ)'mɒgəməs,
hɒ'mɒgəməs
AM hoʊ'magəməs,
ha'magəməs
homogamy
BR hə(ʊ)'mɒgəmi,
hɒ'mɒgəmi
AM hoʊ'magəmi,
ha'magəmi
homogenate
BR hə(ʊ)'mɒdʒɪneɪt,
hɒ'mɒdʒɪnert, -s
AM hoʊ'madʒə,neɪt,
hə'madʒə,neɪt,
hoʊ'madʒənət,
hə'madʒənət, -s
homogeneity
BR ˌhəʊmə(ʊ)dʒɪ'niːɪti,
ˌhɒmə(ʊ)dʒɪ'niːɪti,
ˌhəʊmə(ʊ)dʒɪ'neɪti,
ˌhɒmɪə(ʊ)dʒɪ'neɪti
AM ˌhoʊmədʒə'niːɪdi,
ˌhoʊmoʊdʒə'niːdi,
ˌhoʊmədʒə'neɪɪdi,
ˌhoʊmoʊdʒə'neɪɪdi
homogeneous
BR ˌhəʊmə(ʊ)'dʒiːnɪəs,
ˌhɒmə(ʊ)'dʒiːnɪəs
AM ˌhoʊmə'dʒiniəs,
ˌhoʊmoʊ'dʒiniəs
homogeneously
BR ˌhəʊmə(ʊ)'dʒiːnɪəsli,
ˌhɒmə(ʊ)'dʒiːnɪəsli
AM ˌhoʊmə'dʒiniəsli,
ˌhoʊmoʊ'dʒiniəsli
homogeneousness
BR ˌhəʊmə(ʊ)'dʒiːnɪəsnəs,
ˌhɒmə(ʊ)'dʒiːnɪəsnəs
AM ˌhoʊmə'dʒiniəsnəs,
ˌhoʊmoʊ'dʒiniəsnəs
homogenetic
BR ˌhəʊmə(ʊ)dʒɪ'nɛtɪk,
ˌhɒmə(ʊ)dʒɪ'nɛtɪk
AM ˌhoʊmədʒə'nɛdɪk,
ˌhoʊmoʊdʒə'nɛdɪk
homogenisation
BR hə,mɒdʒɪnʌɪ'zeɪʃn,
hə,mɒdʒɪʌɪ'zeɪʃn,
hɒ,mɒdʒɪʌɪ'zeɪʃn,
hɒ,mɒdʒɪʌɪ'zeɪʃn
AM hə,madʒənə'zeɪʃən,
hə,madʒə,naɪ'zeɪʃən
homogenise
BR hə'mɒdʒɪnʌɪz,
hə'mɒdʒɪʌɪz,
hɒ'mɒdʒɪʌɪz,
hɒ'mɒdʒɪʌɪz, -ɪz, -ɪŋ,
-d
AM hə'madʒə,naɪz, -ɪz,
-ɪŋ, -d

homogeniser
BR həˈmɒdʒɪnʌɪzə(r),
həˈmɒdʒnʌɪzə(r),
hɒˈmɒdʒɪnʌɪzə(r),
hɒˈmɒdʒnʌɪzə(r), -z
AM həˈmɑdʒəˌnaɪzər,
-z

homogenization
BR həˌmɒdʒɪnʌɪˈzeɪʃn,
həˌmɒdʒnʌɪˈzeɪʃn,
hɒˌmɒdʒɪnʌɪˈzeɪʃn,
hɒˌmɒdʒnʌɪˈzeɪʃn
AM həˌmadʒənəˈzeɪʃən,
həˌmadʒəˌnaɪˈzeɪʃən

homogenize
BR həˈmɒdʒɪnʌɪz,
həˈmɒdʒnʌɪz,
hɒˈmɒdʒɪnʌɪz,
hɒˈmɒdʒnʌɪz, -ɪz, -ɪŋ,
-d
AM həˈmadʒəˌnaɪz, -ɪz,
-ɪŋ, -d

homogenizer
BR həˈmɒdʒɪnʌɪzə(r),
həˈmɒdʒnʌɪzə(r),
hɒˈmɒdʒɪnʌɪzə(r),
hɒˈmɒdʒnʌɪzə(r), -z
AM həˈmadʒəˌnaɪzər,
-z

homogenous
BR həˈmɒdʒɪnəs,
həˈmɒdʒnəs,
hɒˈmɒdʒɪnəs,
hɒˈmɒdʒnəs
AM həˈmadʒənəs

homogeny
BR həˈmɒdʒɪni,
həˈmɒdʒni,
hɒˈmɒdʒɪni,
hɒˈmɒdʒni
AM həˈmadʒəni

homograft
BR ˈhɒməɡrɑːft,
ˈhɒməɡraft,
ˈhəʊməɡrɑːft,
ˈhəʊməɡraft, -s
AM ˈhaməˌɡræft,
ˈhoʊməˌɡræft, -s

homograph
BR ˈhɒməɡrɑːf,
ˈhɒməɡraf,
ˈhəʊməɡrɑːf,
ˈhəʊməɡraf, -s
AM ˈhaməˌɡræf,
ˈhoʊməˌɡræf, -s

homographic
BR ˌhɒməˈɡrafɪk,
ˌhəʊməˈɡrafɪk
AM ˌhaməˈɡræfɪk,
ˌhoʊməˈɡræfɪk

homoiotherm
BR ˈhəʊmɔɪə(ʊ)θəːm,
ˈhɒmɔɪə(ʊ)θəːm, -z
AM ˈhoʊˌmɔɪəˌθərm, -z

homoiothermal
BR ˌhəʊmɔɪə(ʊ)ˈθəːml,
ˌhɒmɔɪə(ʊ)ˈθəːml
AM ˌhoʊˌmɔɪəˈθərməl

homoiothermic
BR ˌhəʊmɔɪə(ʊ)ˈθəːmɪk,
ˌhɒmɔɪə(ʊ)ˈθəːmɪk
AM ˌhoʊˌmɔɪəˈθərmɪk

homoiothermy
BR ˈhəʊmɔɪə(ʊ)θəːmi,
ˈhɒmɔɪə(ʊ)θəːmi
AM ˌhoʊˈmɔɪəˌθərmi

homoiousian
BR ˌhɒmɔɪˈuːsɪən,
ˌhəʊmɔɪˈuːsɪən,
ˌhɒmɔɪˈaʊsɪən,
ˌhəʊmɔɪˈaʊsɪən,
ˌhɒmɔɪˈuːzɪən,
ˌhəʊmɔɪˈuːzɪən,
ˌhɒmɔɪˈaʊzɪən,
ˌhəʊmɔɪˈaʊzɪən, -z
AM ˌhoʊˌmɔɪˈusɪən,
ˌhoʊˌmɔɪˈuzɪən, -z

homolog
BR ˈhɒməlɒɡ, -z
AM ˈhaməˌlaɡ,
ˈhoʊməˌlaɡ,
ˈhoʊməˌlɔɡ, -z

homologate
BR hɒˈmɒləɡeɪt,
həˈmɒləɡeɪt, -s, -ɪŋ, -ɪd
AM hoʊˈmaləˌɡeɪt,
həˈmaləˌɡeɪt, -ts, -dɪŋ,
-dɪd

homologation
BR hɒˌmɒləˈɡeɪʃn,
həˌmɒləˈɡeɪʃn,
ˌhɒmə(ʊ)ləˈɡeɪʃn
AM hoʊˌmaləˈɡeɪʃən,
həˌmaləˈɡeɪʃən

homological
BR ˌhɒməˈlɒdʒɪkl
AM ˌhaməˈladʒəkəl,
ˌhoʊməˈladʒəkəl

homologise
BR həˈmɒlədʒʌɪz,
hɒˈmɒlədʒʌɪz, -ɪz, -ɪŋ,
-d
AM hoʊˈmaləˌdʒaɪz,
həˈmaləˌdʒaɪz, -ɪz, -ɪŋ,
-d

homologize
BR həˈmɒlədʒʌɪz,
hɒˈmɒlədʒʌɪz, -ɪz, -ɪŋ,
-d
AM hoʊˈmaləˌdʒaɪz,
həˈmaləˌdʒaɪz, -ɪz, -ɪŋ,
-d

homologous
BR həˈmɒləɡəs,
hɒˈmɒləɡəs
AM hoʊˈmaləɡəs,
həˈmaləɡəs

homologue
BR ˈhɒməlɒɡ, -z
AM ˈhaməˌlaɡ,
ˈhoʊməˌlaɡ,
ˈhoʊməˌlɔɡ, -z

homology
BR həˈmɒlədʒi,
hɒˈmɒlədʒi, -ɪz
AM həˈmalədʒi,
hoʊˈmalədʒi, -z

homomorph
BR ˈhəʊmə(ʊ)mɔːf,
ˈhɒmə(ʊ)mɔːf, -s
AM ˈhoʊməˌmɔ(ə)rf,
ˈhaməˌmɔ(ə)rf, -s

homomorphic
BR ˌhəʊmə(ʊ)ˈmɔːfɪk,
ˌhɒmə(ʊ)ˈmɔːfɪk
AM ˌhoʊməˈmɔrfɪk,
ˌhaməˈmɔrfɪk

homomorphically
BR ˌhəʊmə(ʊ)ˈmɔːfɪkli,
ˌhɒmə(ʊ)ˈmɔːfɪkli
AM ˌhoʊməˈmɔrfək(ə)li,
ˌhaməˈmɔrfək(ə)li

homomorphism
BR ˌhəʊmə(ʊ)ˈmɔːf-
ɪz(ə)m,
ˌhɒmə(ʊ)ˈmɔːfɪz(ə)m,
-z
AM ˌhoʊməˈmɔrˌfɪzəm,
ˌhaməˈmɔrˌfɪzəm, -z

homomorphous
BR ˌhəʊmə(ʊ)ˈmɔːfəs,
ˌhɒmə(ʊ)ˈmɔːfəs
AM ˌhoʊməˈmɔrfəs,
ˈhaməˈmɔrfəs

homomorphy
BR ˈhəʊmə(ʊ)ˌmɔːfi,
ˈhɒmə(ʊ)ˌmɔːfi
AM ˈhoʊməˌmɔrfi,
ˈhaməˌmɔrfi

homonym
BR ˈhɒmənɪm, -z
AM ˈhaməˌnɪm, -z

homonymic
BR ˌhɒməˈnɪmɪk,
AM ˌhaməˈnɪmɪk,
ˌhoʊməˈnɪmɪk

homonymous
BR həˈmɒnɪməs,
hɒˈmɒnɪməs
AM həˈmanəməs,
hoʊˈmanəməs

homonymously
BR həˈmɒnɪməsli,
hɒˈmɒnɪməsli
AM həˈmanəməsli,
hoʊˈmanəməsli

homonymy
BR həˈmɒnɪmi,
hɒˈmɒnɪmi
AM həˈmanəmi,
hoʊˈmanəmi

homoousian
BR ˌhɒməʊˈuːsɪən,
ˌhəʊməʊˈuːsɪən,
ˌhɒməʊˈaʊsɪən,
ˌhəʊməʊˈaʊsɪən,
ˌhɒməʊˈuːzɪən,
ˌhɒməʊˈaʊzɪən,
ˌhəʊməʊˈaʊzɪən, -z
AM ˌhoʊmoʊˈusɪən,
ˌhoʊmoʊˈuzɪən, -z

homophile
BR ˈhəʊməfʌɪl,
ˈhɒməfʌɪl, -z

homophobe
AM ˈhoʊməˌfaɪl, -z

homophobe
BR ˈhəʊməfəʊb,
ˈhɒməfəʊb, -z
AM ˈhoʊməˌfoʊb, -z

homophobia
BR ˌhəʊməˈfəʊbɪə(r),
ˌhɒməˈfəʊbɪə(r)
AM ˌhoʊməˈfoʊbɪə

homophobic
BR ˌhəʊməˈfəʊbɪk,
ˌhɒməˈfəʊbɪk
AM ˌhoʊməˈfoʊbɪk

homophone
BR ˈhɒməfəʊn, -z
AM ˈhaməˌfoʊn,
ˈhoʊməˌfoʊn, -z

homophonic
BR ˌhɒməˈfɒnɪk,
ˌhəʊməˈfɒnɪk
AM ˌhaməˈfanɪk,
ˌhoʊməˈfanɪk

homophonically
BR ˌhɒməˈfɒnɪkli
AM ˌhaməˈfanək(ə)li,
ˌhoʊməˈfanək(ə)li

homophonous
BR həˈmɒfənəs,
həˈmɒfnəs,
hɒˈmɒfənəs,
hɒˈmɒfnəs
AM hoʊˈmafənəs,
həˈmafənəs

homophony
BR həˈmɒfəni
AM həˈmafəni, hɒˈmɒfəni,
hɒˈmɒfni
AM hoʊˈmafəni,
həˈmafəni

homoplastic
BR ˌhəʊmə(ʊ)ˈplastɪk,
ˌhɒmə(ʊ)ˈplastɪk
AM ˌhaməˈplæstɪk,
ˈhoʊməˈplæstɪk

homopolar
BR ˌhəʊmə(ʊ)ˈpəʊlə(r),
ˌhɒmə(ʊ)ˈpəʊlə(r)
AM ˈhaməˈpoʊlər,
ˈhoʊməˈpoʊlər

Homoptera
BR həˈmɒpt(ə)rə(r),
hɒˈmɒpt(ə)rə(r)
AM hoʊˈmaptərə

homopteran
BR həˈmɒpt(ə)rən,
həˈmɒpt(ə)rn,
hɒˈmɒpt(ə)rən,
hɒˈmɒpt(ə)rn, -z
AM hoʊˈmaptərən, -z

homopterous
BR həˈmɒpt(ə)rəs,
hɒˈmɒpt(ə)rəs
AM hoʊˈmaptərəs

Homo sapiens
BR ˌhəʊməʊ ˈsapɪɛnz,
ˌhɒməʊ +, + ˈsapɪənz,
+ ˈseɪpɪɛnz,
+ ˈseɪpɪənz

AM ˈhoʊmoʊ ˈseɪpiənz,
+ ˈsæpiənz
homosexual
BR ˌhəʊmə(ʊ)ˈsekʃʊəl,
ˌhəʊmə(ʊ)ˈsekʃ(ʊ)l,
ˌhəʊmə(ʊ)ˈseksjʊ(ə)l,
ˌhɒmə(ʊ)ˈsekʃʊəl,
ˌhɒmə(ʊ)ˈsekʃ(ʊ)l,
ˌhɒmə(ʊ)ˈseksjʊ(ə)l,
-z
AM ˈhoʊməˈsekʃ(əw)əl,
ˈhoʊmoʊˈsekʃ(əw)əl,
-z
homosexuality
BR ˌhəʊmə(ʊ)ˌsekʃʊˈalɪti,
ˌhəʊmə(ʊ)ˌseksjʊˈalɪti,
ˌhɒmə(ʊ)ˌsekʃʊˈalɪti,
ˌhɒmə(ʊ)ˌseksjʊˈalɪti
AM ˌhoʊməˌsekʃəˈwæl-
ədi,
ˌhoʊmoʊˌsekʃəˈwælədi
homosexually
BR ˌhəʊmə(ʊ)ˈsekʃʊəli,
ˌhəʊmə(ʊ)ˈsekʃʊli,
ˌhəʊmə(ʊ)ˈsekʃli,
ˌhəʊmə(ʊ)ˈseksjʊ(ə)li,
ˌhɒmə(ʊ)ˈsekʃʊəli,
ˌhɒmə(ʊ)ˈsekʃʊli,
ˌhɒmə(ʊ)ˈsekʃli,
ˌhɒmə(ʊ)ˈseksjʊ(ə)li
AM ˈhoʊməˈsekʃ(əw)əli,
ˈhoʊmoʊˈsekʃ(əw)əli
homotransplant
BR ˌhəʊməʊˈtrans-
plɑːnt,
ˌhəʊməʊˈtrɑːnsplɑːnt,
ˌhəʊməʊˈtransplant,
ˌhɒməʊˈtransplɑːnt,
ˌhɒməʊˈtrɑːnsplɑːnt,
ˌhɒməʊˈtransplant, -s
AM ˈhoʊmoʊˈtræns-
ˌplænt, -s
homousian
BR hɒˈmuːsɪən,
hɒˈmaʊsɪən,
hɒˈmuːzɪən,
hɒˈmaʊzɪən, -z
AM ˈhoʊmoʊˈusian,
ˈhoʊmoʊˈuzɪən, -z
homozygote
BR ˌhəʊməʊˈzaɪgəʊt,
ˌhɒməʊˈzaɪgəʊt, -s
AM ˈhoʊmoʊˈzaɪgoʊt,
-s
homozygous
BR ˌhəʊməʊˈzaɪgəs,
ˌhɒməʊˈzaɪgəs
AM ˈhoʊmoʊˈzaɪgəs
homuncule
BR hɒˈmʌŋkjuːl,
həˈmʌŋkjuːl, -z
AM həˈməŋkjul, -z
homunculus
BR hɒˈmʌŋkjʊləs,
həˈmʌŋkjʊləs, -ɪz
AM hoʊˈməŋkjələs, -əz
homy
BR ˈhəʊmi

AM ˈhoʊmi
Hon.
Honorary,
Honourable
BR ɒn
AM ɑn
hon
honey
BR hʌn
AM hən
Honan
BR ˈhəʊˈnan
AM ˈhoʊˈnæn
honcho
BR ˈhɒntʃəʊ, -z
AM ˈhɑn(t)ʃoʊ, -z
Honda®
BR ˈhɒndə(r), -z
AM ˈhɑndə, -z
Honddu
BR ˈhɒnði
AM ˈhɒnði, ˈhɑnði
Honduran
BR hɒnˈdjʊərən,
hɒnˈdjʊərn,
hɒnˈdʒʊərən,
hɒnˈdʒʊərn, -z
AM hɑnˈd(j)ʊrən, -z
Honduras
BR hɒnˈdjʊərəs,
hɒnˈdʒʊərəs
AM hɑnˈd(j)ʊrəs
hone
BR həʊn, -z, -ɪŋ, -d
AM hoʊn, -z, -ɪŋ, -d
Honecker
BR ˈhɒnɪkə(r)
AM ˈhɑnəkər
Honegger
BR ˈhɒnɪgə(r)
AM ˈhɑnəgər
honest
BR ˈɒnɪst
AM ˈɑnəst
honestly
BR ˈɒnɪstli
AM ˈɑnəs(t)li
honesty
BR ˈɒnɪsti
AM ˈɑnəsti
honey
BR ˈhʌnˌli, -ɪz, -d
AM ˈhəni, -z, -d
honeybee
BR ˈhʌnɪbiː, -z
AM ˈhəniˌbi, -z
honeybun
BR ˈhʌnɪbʌn, -z
AM ˈhəniˌbən, -z
honeybunch
BR ˈhʌnɪbʌn(t)ʃ, -ɪz
AM ˈhəniˌbən(t)ʃ, -ɪz
honeycomb
BR ˈhʌnɪkəʊm, -z, -d
AM ˈhəniˌkoʊm, -z, -d

honeydew
BR ˈhʌnɪdjuː,
ˈhʌnɪdʒuː:
AM ˈhəniˌd(j)u
honeyguide
BR ˈhʌnɪgʌɪd, -z
AM ˈhəniˌgaɪd, -z
honeymoon
BR ˈhʌnɪmuːn, -z
AM ˈhəniˌmun, -z
honeymooner
BR ˈhʌnɪmuːnə(r), -z
AM ˈhəniˌmunər, -z
honeysuckle
BR ˈhʌnɪˌsʌkl
AM ˈhəniˌsəkəl
Hong Kong
BR ˌhɒŋ ˈkɒŋ
AM ˈhɑŋˈkɔŋ, ˈhɑŋˈkɑŋ
Honiara
BR ˌhɒnɪˈɑːrə(r)
AM ˌhoʊniˈɑrə
honied
BR ˈhʌnɪd
AM ˈhənid
Honiton
BR ˈhʌnɪt(ə)n,
ˈhɒnɪt(ə)n
AM ˈhɑnətn, ˈhənətn
honk
BR hɒŋ|k, -ks, -kɪŋ,
-(k)t
AM hɔŋ|k, hɑŋ|k, -ks,
-kɪŋ, -(k)t
honkie
BR ˈhɒŋk|i, -ɪz
AM ˈhɔŋki, ˈhɑŋki, -z
honky
BR ˈhɒŋk|i, -ɪz
AM ˈhɔŋki, ˈhɑŋki, -z
honky-tonk
BR ˈhɒŋkɪtɒŋk, -s
AM ˈhɔŋkiˌtɔŋk,
ˈhɑŋkiˌtɑŋk, -s
honnête homme
BR ɒˌnet ˈɒm, -z
AM ɔːˈnet ˈɒm, ɑˈnet
ˈɑm, -z
Honolulu
BR ˌhɒnəˈluːluː
AM ˌhɑnəˈlulu
honor
BR ˈɒn|ə(r), -əz, -(ə)rɪŋ,
-əd
AM ˈɑnər, -z, -ɪŋ, -d
honorable
BR ˈɒn(ə)rəbl
AM ˈɑnər(ə)bəl,
ˈɑnrəbəl
honorableness
BR ˈɒn(ə)rəblnəs
AM ˈɑnər(ə)bəlnəs,
ˈɑnrəbəlnəs
honorably
BR ˈɒn(ə)rəbli
AM ˈɑnər(ə)bli,
ˈɑnrəbli

honorand
BR ˈɒnərand, -z
AM ˈɑnərənd, -z
honoraria
BR ˌɒnəˈreːrɪə(r)
AM ˌɑnəˈreːrɪə
honorarium
BR ˌɒnəˈreːrɪəm, -z
AM ˌɑnəˈreːriəm, -z
honorary
BR ˈɒn(ə)rəri
AM ˈɑnəˌreri
honorific
BR ˌɒnəˈrɪfɪk
AM ˌɑnəˈrɪfɪk
honorifically
BR ˌɒnəˈrɪfɪkli
AM ˌɑnəˈrɪfɪk(ə)li
honoris causa
BR (h)ɒˌnɔːrɪs
ˈkaʊzə(r)
AM (h)əˈnɔrəs ˈkɔzə,
+ ˈkɑzə
honour
BR ˈɒn|ə(r), -əz, -(ə)rɪŋ,
-əd
AM ˈɑnər, -z, -ɪŋ, -d
honourable
BR ˈɒn(ə)rəbl
AM ˈɑn(ə)r(ə)bəl
honourableness
BR ˈɒn(ə)rəblnəs
AM ˈɑnər(ə)bəlnəs,
ˈɑnrəbəlnəs
honourably
BR ˈɒn(ə)rəbli
AM ˈɑnər(ə)bli,
ˈɑnrəbli
Hon. Sec.
Honorary Secretary
BR ˌɒn ˈsek, -s
AM ˌɑn ˈsek, -s
Honshu
BR ˈhɒnʃuː
AM ˈhɑnˌʃu
hooch
BR huːtʃ
AM hutʃ
hood
BR hʊd, -z, -ɪŋ, -ɪd
AM hʊd, -z, -ɪŋ, -əd
hoodie
BR ˈhʊd|i, -ɪz
AM ˈhʊdi, -z
hoodless
BR ˈhʊdləs
AM ˈhʊdləs
hoodlike
BR ˈhʊdlʌɪk
AM ˈhʊdˌlaɪk
hoodlum
BR ˈhuːdləm, -z
AM ˈhudləm, ˈhʊdləm,
-z
hoodoo
BR ˈhuːduː, -z
AM ˈhuˌdu, -z

hoodwink
BR ˈhʊdwɪŋ|k, -ks,
-kɪŋ, -(k)t
AM ˈhʊˌdwɪŋ|k, -ks,
-kɪŋ, -(k)t

hooey
BR ˈhuːi
AM ˈhui

hoof
BR huːf, hʊf, -s, -ɪŋ, -t
AM hʊf, huf, -s, -ɪŋ, -t

hoofbeat
BR ˈhuːfbiːt, ˈhʊfbiːt, -s
AM ˈhʊfˌbit, ˈhufˌbit, -s

hoofer
BR ˈhuːfə(r), ˈhʊfə(r),
-z
AM ˈhʊfər, ˈhufər, -z

hoofmark
BR ˈhuːfmɑːk,
ˈhʊfmɑːk, -s
AM ˈhʊfˌmɑrk,
ˈhufˌmɑrk, -s

Hooghly
BR ˈhuːgli
AM ˈhugli

hoo-ha
BR ˈhuːhɑː(r), -z
AM ˈhuˌhɑ, -z

hoo-hah
BR ˈhuːhɑː(r), -z
AM ˈhuˌhɑ, -z

hook
BR hʊk, -s, -ɪŋ, -t
AM hʊk, -s, -ɪŋ, -t

hooka
BR ˈhʊkə(r),
ˈhuːkɑː(r), -z
AM ˈhʊkə, ˈhukə, -z

hookah
BR ˈhʊkə(r),
ˈhuːkɑː(r), -z
AM ˈhʊkə, ˈhukə, -z

Hooke
BR hʊk
AM hʊk

hooker
BR ˈhʊkə(r), -z
AM ˈhʊkər, -z

hookey
BR ˈhʊki
AM ˈhʊki

hookless
BR ˈhʊkləs
AM ˈhʊkləs

hooklet
BR ˈhʊklɪt, -s
AM ˈhʊklət, -s

hooklike
BR ˈhʊklʌɪk
AM ˈhʊkˌlaɪk

hookup
BR ˈhʊkʌp, -s
AM ˈhʊˌkəp, -s

hookworm
BR ˈhʊkwəːm, -z
AM ˈhʊkˌwərm, -z

hooky
BR ˈhʊki
AM ˈhʊki

Hooley
BR ˈhuːli
AM ˈhuli

hooligan
BR ˈhuːlɪg(ə)n, -z
AM ˈhuləgən, -z

hooliganism
BR ˈhuːlɪgənɪz(ə)m,
ˈhuːlɪgnɪz(ə)m
AM ˈhuləgəˌnɪzəm

hoon
BR huːn, -z, -ɪŋ, -d
AM hun, -z, -ɪŋ, -d

hoop
BR huːp, -s
AM hup, -s

Hooper
BR ˈhuːpə(r)
AM ˈhupər

hoopla
BR ˈhuːplɑː(r),
ˈhʊplɑː(r), -z
AM ˈhuˌplɑ, ˈhʊˌplɑ, -z

hoopoe
BR ˈhuːpuː, ˈhuːpəʊ, -z
AM ˈhuˌpoʊ, ˈhuˌpu, -z

hooray
BR hʊˈreɪ
AM həˈreɪ, huˈreɪ

hooroo
BR hʊˈruː, -z
AM ˌhuˈru, -z

hoosegow
BR ˈhuːsgaʊ, -z
AM ˈhusˌgaʊ, -z

Hoosier
BR ˈhuːʒə(r),
ˈhuːzɪə(r), -z
AM ˈhuʒər, -z

Hooson
BR ˈhuːsn
AM ˈhusən

hoot
BR huːt, -s, -ɪŋ, -ɪd
AM hu|t, -ts, -dɪŋ, -dəd

hootch
BR huːtʃ
AM hutʃ

hootenanny
BR ˈhuːtn̩anˌi,
ˌhuːtn̩ˈanˌi, -ɪz
AM ˈhutn̩ˌæni, -z

hooter
BR ˈhuːtə(r), -z
AM ˈhudər, -z

hoover
BR ˈhuːv|ə(r), -əz,
-(ə)rɪŋ, -əd
AM ˈhuvər, -z, -ɪŋ, -d

Hooverville
BR ˈhuːvəvɪl
AM ˈhuvərˌvɪl,
ˈhuvərvəl

hooves
BR huːvz
AM hʊvz, huvz

hop
BR hɒp, -s, -ɪŋ, -t
AM hɑp, -s, -ɪŋ, -t

hop-bine
BR ˈhɒpbaɪn, -z
AM ˈhɑ(p)ˌbaɪn, -z

Hopcraft
BR ˈhɒpkrɑːft,
ˈhɒpkraft
AM ˈhɑpˌkræft

Hopcroft
BR ˈhɒpkrɒft
AM ˈhɑpˌkrɔft,
ˈhɑpˌkrɑft

hope
BR həʊp, -s, -ɪŋ, -t
AM hoʊp, -s, -ɪŋ, -t

hopeful
BR ˈhəʊpf(ʊ)l
AM ˈhoʊpfəl

hopefully
BR ˈhəʊpfʊli, ˈhəʊpfl̩i
AM ˈhoʊpfəli

hopefulness
BR ˈhəʊpf(ʊ)lnəs
AM ˈhoʊpfəlnəs

hopeless
BR ˈhəʊpləs
AM ˈhoʊpləs

hopelessly
BR ˈhəʊpləsli
AM ˈhoʊpləsli

hopelessness
BR ˈhəʊpləsnəs
AM ˈhoʊpləsnəs

hoper
BR ˈhəʊpə(r), -z
AM ˈhoʊpər, -z

hophead
BR ˈhɒphɛd, -z
AM ˈhɑpˌ(h)ɛd, -z

Hopi
BR ˈhəʊp|i, -ɪz
AM ˈhoʊpi, -z

Hopkin
BR ˈhɒpkɪn
AM ˈhɑpkən

Hopkins
BR ˈhɒpkɪnz
AM ˈhɑpkənz

Hopkinson
BR ˈhɒpkɪns(ə)n
AM ˈhɑpkənsən

hoplite
BR ˈhɒplʌɪt, -s
AM ˈhɑˌplaɪt, -s

hop-o'-my-thumb
BR ˌhɒpəməˈθʌm, -z
AM ˌhɑpəməˈθəm,
ˌhɑpəˌmaɪˈθəm, -z

hopper
BR ˈhɒpə(r), -z
AM ˈhɑpər, -z

hopple
BR ˈhɒp|l, -lz, -l̩ɪŋ \-l-ɪŋ,
-ld
AM ˈhɑp|əl, -əlz, -(ə)lɪŋ,
-əld

hopsack
BR ˈhɒpsak
AM ˈhɑpˌsæk

hopsacking
BR ˈhɒpˌsakɪŋ
AM ˈhɑpˌsækɪŋ

hopscotch
BR ˈhɒpskɒtʃ
AM ˈhɑpˌskatʃ

Hopwood
BR ˈhɒpwʊd
AM ˈhɑpˌwʊd

Horabin
BR ˈhɒrəbɪn
AM ˈhɔrəbən

Horace
BR ˈhɒrɪs
AM ˈhɔrəs

Horan
BR ˈhɔːrən, ˈhɔːrn̩
AM ˈhɔrən

horary
BR ˈhɔːrər|i, -ɪz
AM ˈhɔrəri, -z

Horatia
BR həˈreɪʃ(ɪ)ə(r)
AM həˈreɪʃə

Horatian
BR həˈreɪʃn
AM həˈreɪʃən

Horatio
BR həˈreɪʃ(ɪ)əʊ
AM həˈreɪʃ(i)oʊ

Horbury
BR ˈhɔːb(ə)ri
AM ˈhɔrˌbɛri

horde
BR hɔːd, -z
AM hɔ(ə)rd, -z

Hordern
BR ˈhɔːdn
AM ˈhɔrdərn

Horeb
BR ˈhɔːrɛb
AM ˈhɔrəb

horehound
BR ˈhɔːhaʊnd, -z
AM ˈhɔrˌ(h)aʊnd, -z

Horgan
BR ˈhɔːg(ə)n
AM ˈhɔrgən

horizon
BR həˈrʌɪzn, -z
AM həˈraɪzn, -z

horizontal
BR ˌhɒrɪˈzɒntl
AM ˌhɔrəˈzɑn(t)l

horizontality
BR ˌhɒrɪzɒnˈtalɪti
AM ˌhɔrəˌzɑnˈtælədi

horizontally
BR ˌhɒrɪˈzɒntl̩i,
hɒrɪˈzɒntəli
AM ˌhɔːrəˈzæn(t)l̩i

horizontalness
BR ˌhɒrɪˈzɒntlnəs
AM ˌhɔːrəˈzæn(t)lnəs

Horkheimer
BR ˈhɔːkˌhʌɪmə(r)
AM ˈhɔːrkˌ(h)aɪmər

Horlicks®
BR ˈhɔːlɪks
AM ˈhɔːrˌlɪks

hormonal
BR hɔːˈməʊnl
AM hɔrˈmoʊnəl

hormonally
BR hɔːˈməʊnl̩i
AM hɔrˈmoʊnəli

hormone
BR ˈhɔːməʊn, -z
AM ˈhɔrˌmoʊn, -z

Hormuz
BR ˌhɔːˈmʊz, ˌhɔːˈmuːz
AM ˌhɔrˈmuz

horn
BR hɔːn, -z, -d
AM hɔ(ə)rn, -z, -d

hornbeam
BR ˈhɔːnbiːm, -z
AM ˈhɔrnˌbim, -z

hornbill
BR ˈhɔːnbɪl, -z
AM ˈhɔrnˌbɪl, -z

hornblende
BR ˈhɔːnblend, -z
AM ˈhɔrnˌblend, -z

Hornblower
BR ˈhɔːnˌbləʊə(r)
AM ˈhɔrnˌbloʊər

hornbook
BR ˈhɔːnbʊk, -s
AM ˈhɔrnˌbʊk, -s

Hornby
BR ˈhɔːnbi
AM ˈhɔrnbi

Horncastle
BR ˈhɔːnˌkɑːsl,
ˈhɔːnˌkasl
AM ˈhɔrnˌkæsəl

Hornchurch
BR ˈhɔːntʃəːtʃ
AM ˈhɔrnˌtʃərtʃ

Horne
BR hɔːn
AM hɔ(ə)rn

Horner
BR ˈhɔːnə(r)
AM ˈhɔrnər

horner
BR ˈhɔːnə(r), -z
AM ˈhɔrnər, -z

hornet
BR ˈhɔːnɪt, -s
AM ˈhɔrnət, -s

horniness
BR ˈhɔːnɪnɪs

AM ˈhɔːnɪnɪs

hornist
BR ˈhɔːnɪst, -s
AM ˈhɔrnəst, -s

hornless
BR ˈhɔːnləs
AM ˈhɔrnləs

hornlike
BR ˈhɔːnlʌɪk
AM ˈhɔrnˌlaɪk

hornpipe
BR ˈhɔːnpʌɪp, -s
AM ˈhɔrnˌpaɪp, -s

Hornsby
BR ˈhɔːnzbi
AM ˈhɔrnzbi

hornstone
BR ˈhɔːnstəʊn
AM ˈhɔrnˌstoʊn

hornswoggle
BR ˈhɔːnˌswɒgl̩, -lz,
-l̩ɪŋ \-l̩ɪŋ, -ld
AM ˈhɔrnˌswagləl, -əlz,
-(ə)lɪŋ, -əld

Hornung
BR ˈhɔːnʊŋ
AM ˈhɔrnɪŋ, ˈhɔrnʊŋ

hornwort
BR ˈhɔːnwəːt, -s
AM ˈhɔrnˌwərt,
ˈhɔrnˌwɔ(ə)rt, -s

horny
BR ˈhɔːn|i, -ɪə(r), -ɪɪst
AM ˈhɔrni, -ər, -ɪɪst

horologe
BR ˈhɒrəlɒdʒ, -ɪz
AM ˈhɔrəˌlɑdʒ, -əz

horologer
BR həˈrɒlədʒə(r),
hɒˈrɒlədʒə(r), -z
AM həˈrɑlədʒər, -z

horologic
BR ˌhɒrəˈlɒdʒɪk
AM ˌhɔrəˈlɑdʒɪk

horological
BR ˌhɒrəˈlɒdʒɪkl
AM ˌhɔrəˈlɑdʒəkəl

horologist
BR həˈrɒlədʒɪst,
hɒˈrɒlədʒɪst, -s
AM həˈrɑlədʒəst, -s

horology
BR həˈrɒlədʒi,
hɒˈrɒlədʒi
AM həˈrɑlədʒi

horoscope
BR ˈhɒrəskəʊp, -s
AM ˈhɔrəˌskoʊp, -s

horoscopic
BR ˌhɒrəˈskɒpɪk
AM ˌhɔrəˈskɑpɪk

horoscopical
BR ˌhɒrəˈskɒpɪkl
AM ˌhɔrəˈskɑpəkəl

horoscopy
BR həˈrɒskəpi,
hɒˈrɒskəpi

AM həˈrɑskəpi

Horowitz
BR ˈhɒrəwɪts,
ˈhɒrəvɪts
AM ˈhɔrəˌwɪts
RUS ˈgorəvits

horrendous
BR həˈrendəs,
hɒˈrendəs
AM həˈrendəs,
hɔˈrendəs

horrendously
BR həˈrendəsli,
hɒˈrendəsli
AM həˈrendəsli,
hɔˈrendəsli

horrendousness
BR həˈrendəsnəs,
hɒˈrendəsnəs
AM həˈrendəsnəs,
hɔˈrendəsnəs

horrent
BR ˈhɒrənt, ˈhɒrn̩t
AM ˈhɔrənt

horrible
BR ˈhɒrɪbl
AM ˈhɔrəbəl

horribleness
BR ˈhɒrɪblnəs
AM ˈhɔrəbəlnəs

horribly
BR ˈhɒrɪbli
AM ˈhɔrəbli

horrid
BR ˈhɒrɪd
AM ˈhɔrəd

horridly
BR ˈhɒrɪdli
AM ˈhɔrədli

horridness
BR ˈhɒrɪdnɪs
AM ˈhɔrədnəs

horrific
BR həˈrɪfɪk
AM hɔˈrɪfɪk, həˈrɪfɪk

horrifically
BR həˈrɪfɪkli
AM hɔˈrɪfək(ə)li,
həˈrɪfək(ə)li

horrification
BR ˌhɒrɪfɪˈkeɪʃn
AM hɔˌrɪfəˈkeɪʃən

horrifiedly
BR ˈhɒrɪfʌɪdli
AM ˈhɔrəˌfaɪdli

horrify
BR ˈhɒrɪfʌɪ, -z, -ɪŋ, -d
AM ˈhɔrəˌfaɪ, -z, -ɪŋ, -d

horrifyingly
BR ˈhɒrɪfʌɪɪŋli
AM ˈhɔrəˌfaɪɪŋli

horripilation
BR həˌrɪpɪˈleɪʃn,
hɒˌrɪpɪˈleɪʃn
AM hɔˌrɪpəˈleɪʃən

horror
BR ˈhɒrə(r), -z
AM ˈhɔrər, -z

AM həˈrɑskəpi

Horowitz

Horsa
BR ˈhɔːsə(r)
AM ˈhɔrsə

hors concours
BR ˌɔː ˈkɒ̃kʊə(r)
AM ˌɔ(ə)r kɔnˈkʊ(ə)r

hors de combat
BR ˌɔː də ˈkɒmbɑː(r)
AM ˌɔr də ˈkɑmˈbɑ

hors-d'œuvre
BR ˌɔːˈdəːv, -z
AM ˌɔrˈdərv, -z

horse
BR hɔːs, -ɪz, -ɪŋ, -t
AM hɔ(ə)rs, -ɪz, -ɪŋ, -t

horseback
BR ˈhɔːsbak
AM ˈhɔrsˌbæk

horsebean
BR ˈhɔːsbiːn, -z
AM ˈhɔrsˌbin, -z

horsebox
BR ˈhɔːsbɒks, -ɪz
AM ˈhɔrsˌbaks, -əz

horsebreaker
BR ˈhɔːsˌbreɪkə(r), -z
AM ˈhɔrsˌbreɪkər, -z

horse-coper
BR ˈhɔːsˌkəʊpə(r), -z
AM ˈhɔrsˌkoʊpər, -z

Horseferry
BR ˈhɔːsˌfɛri
AM ˈhɔrsˌfɛri

horseflesh
BR ˈhɔːsflɛʃ
AM ˈhɔrsˌflɛʃ

horsefly
BR ˈhɔːsflʌɪ, -z
AM ˈhɔrsˌflaɪ, -z

Horseforth
BR ˈhɔːsfəθ
AM ˈhɔrsˌfɔ(ə)rθ

Horseguard
BR ˈhɔːsgɑːd, -z
AM ˈhɔrsˌgard, -z

horsehair
BR ˈhɔːshɛː(r)
AM ˈhɔrsˌ(h)ɛ(ə)r

horsehide
BR ˈhɔːshʌɪd
AM ˈhɔrsˌ(h)aɪd

horseleech
BR ˈhɔːsliːtʃ, -ɪz
AM ˈhɔrsˌlitʃ, -ɪz

horseless
BR ˈhɔːsləs
AM ˈhɔrsləs

horselike
BR ˈhɔːslʌɪk
AM ˈhɔrsˌlaɪk

horseman
BR ˈhɔːsmən
AM ˈhɔrsmən

horsemanship
BR ˈhɔːsmənʃɪp
AM ˈhɔrsmənˌʃɪp

horsemeat
BR ˈhɔːsmiːt
AM ˈhɔrsˌmit

horseplay
BR ˈhɔːspleɪ
AM ˈhɔrsˌpleɪ

horsepower
BR ˈhɔːsˌpaʊə(r)
AM ˈhɔrsˌpaʊər

horseradish
BR ˈhɔːsˌrædɪʃ, -ɪʃɪz
AM ˈhɔrsˌrædɪʃ, -ɪz

horseshit
BR ˈhɔː(s)ʃɪt
AM ˈhɔr(s)ˌʃɪt

horseshoe
BR ˈhɔː(s)ʃuː, ˈhɔːʃʃuː, -z
AM ˈhɔr(s)ˌʃu, -z

horsetail
BR ˈhɔːsteɪl, -z
AM ˈhɔrsˌteɪl, -z

horsewhip
BR ˈhɔːswɪp, -s, -ɪŋ, -t
AM ˈhɔrsˌ(h)wɪp, -s, -ɪŋ, -t

horsewoman
BR ˈhɔːsˌwʊmən
AM ˈhɔrsˌwʊmən

horsewomen
BR ˈhɔːsˌwɪmɪn
AM ˈhɔrsˌwɪmɪn

horsey
BR ˈhɔːsi
AM ˈhɔrsi

Horsham
BR ˈhɔːʃəm
AM ˈhɔrʃəm

horsily
BR ˈhɔːsɪli
AM ˈhɔrsəli

horsiness
BR ˈhɔːsɪnɪs
AM ˈhɔrsɪnɪs

horst
BR hɔːst, -s
AM hɔ(ə)rst, -s

horsy
BR ˈhɔːsɪi, -ɪə(r), -ɪɪst
AM ˈhɔrsi, -ər, -ɪst

Horta
BR ˈhɔːtə(r)
AM ˈhɔrdə

hortation
BR hɔːˈteɪʃn, -z
AM ˌhɔrˈteɪʃən, -z

hortative
BR ˈhɔːtətɪv
AM ˈhɔrdədɪv

hortatory
BR ˈhɔːtət(ə)ri,
hɔːˈteɪt(ə)ri
AM ˈhɔdəˌtɔri

Hortense
BR hɔːˈtens
AM ˈhɔrˌtens

hortensia
BR hɔːˈtensɪə(r)
AM hɔrˈtensɪə

horticultural
BR ˌhɔːtɪˈkʌltʃ(ə)rəl,
ˌhɔːtɪˈkʌltʃ(ə)rl
AM ˈhɔrdəˈkəltʃ(ə)rəl

horticulturalist
BR ˌhɔːtɪˈkʌltʃ(ə)rəlɪst,
ˌhɔːtɪˈkʌltʃ(ə)rlɪst, -s
AM ˈhɔrdəˈkəltʃ(ə)rəl-
əst, -s

horticulturally
BR ˌhɔːtɪˈkʌltʃ(ə)rəli,
ˌhɔːtɪˈkʌltʃ(ə)rli
AM ˈhɔrdəˈkəltʃ(ə)rəli

horticulture
BR ˈhɔːtɪˈkʌltʃə(r)
AM ˈhɔrdəˌkəltʃər

horticulturist
BR ˌhɔːtɪˈkʌltʃ(ə)rɪst,
-s
AM ˈhɔrdəˈkəltʃərə()st,
-s

horti sicci
BR ˌhɔːtaɪ ˈsɪkaɪ, ˌhɔːtiː
ˈsɪkiː
AM ˈhɔrdaɪ ˈsɪˌkaɪ

Horton
BR ˈhɔːtn
AM ˈhɔrt(ə)n

hortus siccus
BR ˌhɔːtəs ˈsɪkəs
AM ˈhɔrdəs ˈsɪkəs

Horus
BR ˈhɔːrəs
AM ˈhɔrəs

hosanna
BR hə(ʊ)ˈzanə(r), -z
AM hoʊˈzænə, -z

hose
BR həʊz, -ɪz, -ɪŋ, -d
AM hoʊz, -ɪz, -ɪŋ, -d

Hosea
BR hə(ʊ)ˈzɪə(r)
AM hoʊˈzeɪə

Hoseason
BR həʊˈsiːzn
AM hoʊˈsizn

hosepipe
BR ˈhəʊzpaɪp, -s
AM ˈhoʊzˌpaɪp, -s

hosier
BR ˈhəʊzɪə(r), -z
AM ˈhoʊʒər, -z

hosiery
BR ˈhəʊz(ɪ)əri
AM ˈhoʊʒ(ə)ri

hospice
BR ˈhɒspɪs, -ɪsɪz
AM ˈhɑspəs, -əz

hospitable
BR hɒˈspɪtəbl,
həˈspɪtəbl, ˈhɒspɪtəbl
AM hɑˈspɪdəbəl,
ˈhɑspɪdəbəl

hospitably
BR hɒˈspɪtəbli,
həˈspɪtəbli,
ˈhɒspɪtəbli
AM hɑˈspɪdɪbli,
ˈhɑspɪdɪbli

hospital
BR ˈhɒspɪtl, -z
AM ˈhɑspɪdl, -z

hospitaler
BR ˈhɒspɪtələ(r)
AM ˈhɑˌspɪdlər

hospitalisation
BR ˌhɒspɪtlaɪˈzeɪʃn
AM ˌhɑˌspɪdələˈzeɪʃən,
ˌhɑˌspɪdəlˌaɪˈzeɪʃən

hospitalise
BR ˈhɒspɪtlaɪz,
ˈhɒspɪtəlaɪz, -ɪz, -ɪŋ, -d
AM ˈhɑˌspædəˌlaɪz, -ɪz,
-ɪŋ, -d

hospitalism
BR ˈhɒspɪtlɪz(ə)m,
ˈhɒspɪtəlɪz(ə)m
AM ˈhɑˌspædəˌlɪzəm

hospitality
BR ˌhɒspɪˈtaliti
AM ˌhɑspəˈtælədi

hospitalization
BR ˌhɒspɪtlaɪˈzeɪʃn
AM ˌhɑˌspɪdələˈzeɪʃən,
ˌhɑˌspɪdəlˌaɪˈzeɪʃən

hospitalize
BR ˈhɒspɪtlaɪz,
ˈhɒspɪtəlaɪz, -ɪz, -ɪŋ, -d
AM ˈhɑˌspædəˌlaɪz, -ɪz,
-ɪŋ, -d

hospitaller
BR ˈhɒspɪtlə(r)
AM ˈhɑˌspɪdlər

host
BR həʊst, -s, -ɪŋ, -ɪd
AM hoʊst, -s, -ɪŋ, -əd

hosta
BR ˈhɒstə(r), -z
AM ˈhɑstə, -z

hostage
BR ˈhɒstɪdʒ, -ɪdʒɪz
AM ˈhɑstɪdʒ, -ɪz

hostageship
BR ˈhɒstɪdʒʃɪp
AM ˈhɑstɪdʒˌʃɪp

hostel
BR ˈhɒstl̩, -z, -ɪŋ
AM ˈhɑstl̩, -lz, -l̩ɪŋ

hosteller
BR ˈhɒstlə(r),
ˈhɒstələ(r), -z
AM ˈhɑstələr, -z

hostelry
BR ˈhɒstlr̩i, -ɪz
AM ˈhɑstlri, -z

hostess
BR ˈhəʊstəs, həʊˈstes,
-ɪz
AM ˈhoʊstəs, -əz

hostile
BR ˈhɒstaɪl

hostlely
AM ˈhɑstl̩, ˈhɑˌstaɪl

hostilely
BR ˈhɒstaɪlli
AM ˈhɑstl̩li,
ˈhɑˌstaɪl)li

hostility
BR hɒˈstɪlɪti, -ɪz
AM hɑˈstɪlɪdi, -z

hostler
BR ˈ(h)ɒslə(r), -z
AM ˈ(h)ɑslər, -z

hot
BR hɒt, -ə(r), -ɪst
AM hɑt, -dər, -dəst

hotbed
BR ˈhɒtbed, -z
AM ˈhɑtˌbed, -z

hot-blooded
BR ˈhɒtˈblʌdɪd
AM ˈhɑtˈblədəd

hot-bloodedly
BR ˈhɒtˈblʌdɪdli
AM ˈhɑtˈblədədli

hot cake
BR ˌhɒt ˈkeɪk, -s
AM ˈhɑt ˌkeɪk, -s

Hotchkiss
BR ˈhɒtʃkɪs, -z
AM ˈhɑtʃˌkɪs, -z

hotchpot
BR ˈhɒtʃpɒt
AM ˈhɑtʃˌpɑt

hotchpotch
BR ˈhɒtʃpɒtʃ
AM ˈhɑtʃˌpɑtʃ

hotdog
BR ˌhɒtˈdɒg, -z, -ɪŋ
AM ˈhɑtˌdɔg, ˈhɑtˌdɑg,
-z, -ɪŋ

hotel
BR ˌhəʊˈtel, hə(ʊ)ˈtel, -z
AM hoʊˈtel, -z

hotelier
BR hə(ʊ)ˈtelɪə(r),
hə(ʊ)ˈtelɪeɪ, -z
AM hoʊˈteljər, ˌoʊtelˈjeɪ,
-z

hotelkeeper
BR hə(ʊ)ˈtelˌkiːpə(r),
-z
AM hoʊˈtelˌkipər, -z

hotfoot[1]
adverb
BR ˌhɒtˈfʊt
AM ˈhɑtˌfʊt

hotfoot[2]
verb
BR ˈhɒtfʊt, ˌhɒtˈfʊt, -s,
-ɪŋ, -ɪd
AM ˈhɑtˌfʊ|t, -ts, -dɪŋ,
-dəd

hot gospeler
BR ˌhɒt ˈgɒsplə(r),
+ ˈgɒsplə(r), -z
AM ˈhɑt ˈgɑspələr, -z

hot gospeller
BR ˌhɒt ˈgɒsplə(r),
+ ˈgɒsp(ə)lə(r), -z

AM ˌhɑt ˈgɑspələr, -z

hothead
BR ˈhɒthɛd, -z
AM ˈhɑt͡ˌ(h)ɛd, -z

hotheaded
BR ˌhɒtˈhɛdɪd
AM ˈhɑt͡ˌhɛdəd

hotheadedly
BR ˌhɒtˈhɛdɪdli
AM ˈhɑt͡ˌhɛdədli

hotheadedness
BR ˌhɒtˈhɛdɪdnɪs
AM ˈhɑt͡ˌhɛdədnəs

hothouse
BR ˈhɒthaʊs, -zɪz
AM ˈhɑt͡ˌ(h)aʊs, -zəz

hotline
BR ˈhɒtlʌm, -z
AM ˈhɑt͡ˌlaɪn, -z

hotly
BR ˈhɒtli
AM ˈhɑtli

hotness
BR ˈhɒtnəs
AM ˈhɑtnəs

hotplate
BR ˈhɒtpleɪt, -s
AM ˈhɑt͡ˌpleɪt, -s

hotpot
BR ˈhɒtpɒt, -s
AM ˈhɑt͡ˌpɑt, -s

hotrod
BR ˈhɒtrɒd, -z
AM ˈhɑt͡ˌrɑd, -z

hot-rodder
BR ˈhɒtˌrɒdə(r), -z
AM ˈhɑt͡ˌrɑdər, -z

hot-rodding
BR ˈhɒtˌrɒdɪŋ
AM ˈhɑt͡ˌrɑdɪŋ

hotshot
BR ˈhɒtʃɒt, -s
AM ˈhɑt͡ˌʃɑt, -s

hotspot
BR ˈhɒtspɒt, -s
AM ˈhɑt͡ˌspɑt, -s

hotspur
BR ˈhɒtspə:(r), -z
AM ˈhɑt͡ˌspər, -z

Hottentot
BR ˈhɒtntɒt, -s
AM ˈhɑtn͡ˌtɑt, -s

hotter
BR ˈhɒtə(r), -z
AM ˈhɑdər, -z

hottie
BR ˈhɒt|i, -ɪz
AM ˈhɑdi, -z

hottish
BR ˈhɒtɪʃ
AM ˈhɑdɪʃ

hotty
BR ˈhɒt|i, -ɪz
AM ˈhɑdi, -z

Houdini
BR huːˈdiːni, hʊˈdiːni
AM huːˈdini

Hough
BR haʊ, hʌf, hɒf
AM haʊ, hɔf

hough
BR hɒk, -s, -ɪŋ, -t
AM hɑk, -s, -ɪŋ, -t

hougher
BR ˈhɒkə(r), -z
AM ˈhɑkər, -z

Houghton
BR ˈhaʊtn, ˈhəʊtn, ˈhɔːtn
AM ˈhoʊtn

Houghton-le-Spring
BR ˌhəʊtnlɪˈsprɪŋ
AM ˌhoʊtnləˈsprɪŋ

Houlihan
BR ˈhuːlɪhən
AM ˈhuːləˌhæn

hoummos
BR ˈhʊməs, ˈhuːməs
AM ˈ(h)juməs

hound
BR haʊnd, -z, -ɪŋ, -ɪd
AM haʊnd, -z, -ɪŋ, -əd

hounder
BR ˈhaʊndə(r), -z
AM ˈhaʊndər, -z

houndish
BR ˈhaʊndɪʃ
AM ˈhaʊndɪʃ

Houndsditch
BR ˈhaʊn(d)zdɪtʃ
AM ˈhaʊn(d)z͡ˌdɪtʃ

houndstooth
BR ˈhaʊn(d)ztuːθ
AM ˈhaʊn(d)z͡ˌtuθ

hour
BR ˈaʊə(r), -z
AM ˈaʊ(ə)r, -z

hourglass
BR ˈaʊəglɑːs, ˈaʊəglɑs, -ɪz
AM ˈaʊ(ə)r͡ˌglæs, -əz

houri
BR ˈhʊər|i, -ɪz
AM ˈhuri, -z

hourly
BR ˈaʊəli
AM ˈaʊ(ə)rli

house ¹
BR haʊs, -zɪz
AM haʊs, -zəz

house ²
verb
BR haʊz, -ɪz, -ɪŋ, -d
AM haʊz, -əz, -ɪŋ, -t

houseboat
BR ˈhaʊsbəʊt, -s
AM ˈhaʊs͡ˌboʊt, -s

housebound
BR ˈhaʊsbaʊnd
AM ˈhaʊs͡ˌbaʊnd

houseboy
BR ˈhaʊsbɔɪ, -z
AM ˈhaʊs͡ˌbɔɪ, -z

housebreaker
BR ˈhaʊs͡ˌbreɪkə(r), -z
AM ˈhaʊs͡ˌbreɪkər, -z

housebreaking
BR ˈhaʊs͡ˌbreɪkɪŋ
AM ˈhaʊs͡ˌbreɪkɪŋ

housebuilder
BR ˈhaʊs͡ˌbɪldə(r), -z
AM ˈhaʊs͡ˌbɪldər, -z

housebuilding
BR ˈhaʊs͡ˌbɪldɪŋ
AM ˈhaʊs͡ˌbɪldɪŋ

housebuyer
BR ˈhaʊs͡ˌbʌɪə(r), -z
AM ˈhaʊs͡ˌbaɪər, -z

housebuying
BR ˈhaʊs͡ˌbʌɪɪŋ
AM ˈhaʊs͡ˌbaɪɪŋ

housecarl
BR ˈhaʊskɑːl, -z
AM ˈhaʊs͡ˌkɑrl, -z

housecarle
BR ˈhaʊskɑːl, -z
AM ˈhaʊs͡ˌkɑrl, -z

housecoat
BR ˈhaʊskəʊt, -s
AM ˈhaʊs͡ˌkoʊt, -s

housecraft
BR ˈhaʊskrɑːft, ˈhaʊskraft
AM ˈhaʊs͡ˌkræft

housedog
BR ˈhaʊsdɒg, -z
AM ˈhaʊs͡ˌdɔg, ˈhaʊs͡ˌdɑg, -z

housedress
BR ˈhaʊsdrɛs, -ɪz
AM ˈhaʊs͡ˌdrɛs, -əz

housefly
BR ˈhaʊsflʌɪ, -z
AM ˈhaʊs͡ˌflaɪ, -z

houseful
BR ˈhaʊsfʊl, -z
AM ˈhaʊsfʊl, -z

Housego
BR ˈhaʊsgəʊ
AM ˈhaʊsgoʊ

housegroup
BR ˈhaʊsgruːp, -s
AM ˈhaʊs͡ˌgrup, -s

houseguest
BR ˈhaʊsgɛst, -s
AM ˈhaʊs͡ˌgɛst, -s

household
BR ˈhaʊs(h)əʊld, -z
AM ˈhaʊs͡ˌ(h)oʊld, -z

householder
BR ˈhaʊs(h)əʊldə(r), -z
AM ˈhaʊs͡ˌ(h)oʊldər, -z

househusband
BR ˈhaʊs͡ˌhʌzbənd, -z
AM ˈhaʊs͡ˌ(h)əzbənd, -z

housekeep
BR ˈhaʊskiːp, -s
AM ˈhaʊs͡ˌkip, -s

housekeeper
BR ˈhaʊs͡ˌkiːpə(r), -z
AM ˈhaʊs͡ˌkipər, -z

housekeeping
BR ˈhaʊs͡ˌkiːpɪŋ
AM ˈhaʊs͡ˌkipɪŋ

housekept
BR ˈhaʊskɛpt
AM ˈhaʊs͡ˌkɛpt

houseleek
BR ˈhaʊsliːk, -s
AM ˈhaʊs͡ˌlik, -s

houseless
BR ˈhaʊsləs
AM ˈhaʊsləs

houselights
BR ˈhaʊslʌɪts
AM ˈhaʊs͡ˌlaɪts

housemaid
BR ˈhaʊsmeɪd, -z
AM ˈhaʊs͡ˌmeɪd, -z

houseman
BR ˈhaʊsmən
AM ˈhaʊsmən

housemaster
BR ˈhaʊs͡ˌmɑːstə(r), ˈhaʊs͡ˌmɑstə(r), -z
AM ˈhaʊs͡ˌmæstər, -z

housemate
BR ˈhaʊsmeɪt, -s
AM ˈhaʊs͡ˌmeɪt, -s

housemistress
BR ˈhaʊs͡ˌmɪstrɪs, -ɪz
AM ˈhaʊs͡ˌmɪstrɪs, -ɪz

housemother
BR ˈhaʊs͡ˌmʌðə(r), -z
AM ˈhaʊs͡ˌməðər, -z

housepainter
BR ˈhaʊs͡ˌpeɪntə(r), -z
AM ˈhaʊs͡ˌpeɪn(t)ər, -z

houseparent
BR ˈhaʊs͡ˌpɛːrənt, ˈhaʊs͡ˌpɛːrnt, -s
AM ˈhaʊs͡ˌpɛrənt, -s

houseplant
BR ˈhaʊsplɑːnt, ˈhaʊsplant, -s
AM ˈhaʊs͡ˌplænt, -s

houseroom
BR ˈhaʊsruːm, ˈhaʊsrom
AM ˈhaʊs͡ˌrum, ˈhaʊs͡ˌrom

housesitter
BR ˈhaʊs͡ˌsɪtə(r), -z
AM ˈhaʊ(s)͡ˌsɪdər, -z

housetop
BR ˈhaʊstɒp, -s
AM ˈhaʊs͡ˌtɑp, -s

housewares
BR ˈhaʊswɛːz
AM ˈhaʊs͡ˌwɛrz

housewarming
BR ˈhaʊs͡ˌwɔːmɪŋ, -z
AM ˈhaʊs͡ˌwɔrmɪŋ, -z

housewife
BR ˈhaʊswʌɪf

AM ˈhaʊsˌwaɪf
housewifeliness
BR ˈhaʊswʌɪflɪnɪs
AM ˈhaʊsˌwaɪflɪnɪs
housewifely
BR ˈhaʊswʌɪfli
AM ˈhaʊsˌwaɪfli
housewifery
BR ˈhaʊswɪf(ə)ri
AM ˈhaʊsˌwaɪfəri
housewives
BR ˈhaʊswʌɪvz
AM ˈhaʊsˌwaɪvz
housework
BR ˈhaʊswəːk
AM ˈhaʊsˌwərk
housey-housey
BR ˌhaʊziˈhaʊzi
AM ˌhaʊziˈhaʊzi
housing
BR ˈhaʊzɪŋ
AM ˈhaʊzɪŋ
Housman
BR ˈhaʊsmən
AM ˈhaʊsmən
Houston
BR ˈh(j)uːst(ə)n
AM ˈ(h)justən, ˈhʊstən
Houyhnhnm
BR ˈwɪnɪm, hʊˈɪnɪm, -z
AM ˈwɪnɪm, ˈhʊɪn(ɪ)m, -z
hove
BR həʊv
AM hoʊv
hovel
BR ˈhɒvl, -z
AM ˈhəvəl, -z
hover
BR ˈhɒv|ə(r), -əz, -(ə)rɪŋ, -əd
AM ˈhəv|ər, -ərz, -(ə)rɪŋ, -ərd
hovercraft
BR ˈhɒvəkrɑːft, ˈhɒvəkraft, -s
AM ˈhəvərˌkræft, -s
hoverer
BR ˈhɒv(ə)rə(r), -z
AM ˈhəvərər, -z
hoverfly
BR ˈhɒvəflʌɪ, -z
AM ˈhəvərˌflaɪ, -z
hoverport
BR ˈhɒvəpɔːt, -s
AM ˈhəvərˌpɔ(ə)rt, -s
hovertrain
BR ˈhɒvətreɪn, -z
AM ˈhəvərˌtreɪn, -z
Hovis®
BR ˈhəʊvɪs
AM ˈhoʊvəs
how
BR haʊ
AM haʊ
Howard
BR ˈhaʊəd

AM ˈhaʊərd
Howarth
BR ˈhaʊəθ
AM ˈhaʊərθ
howbeit
BR haʊˈbiːɪt
AM haʊˈbiːt
howdah
BR ˈhaʊdə(r), -z
AM ˈhaʊdə, -z
Howden
BR ˈhaʊdn
AM ˈhaʊdən
how-do-you-do
BR ˌhaʊdʒəˈduː, ˌhaʊd(ə)jəˈduː, -z
AM ˌhaʊdəjəˈdu, ˌhaʊdiˈdu, -z
howdy
BR ˈhaʊdi
AM ˈhaʊdi
how-d'ye-do
BR ˌhaʊdjəˈduː, ˌhaʊdʒəˈduː, -z
AM ˌhaʊdəjəˈdu, ˌhaʊdiˈdu, -z
Howe
BR haʊ
AM haʊ
Howell
BR ˈhaʊ(ə)l
AM ˈhaʊəl
Howells
BR ˈhaʊəlz
AM ˈhaʊəlz
Howerd
BR ˈhaʊəd
AM ˈhaʊərd
Howes
BR haʊz
AM haʊz
however
BR haʊˈɛvə(r)
AM haʊˈɛvər
Howie
BR ˈhaʊi
AM ˈhaʊi
howitzer
BR ˈhaʊɪtsə(r), -z
AM ˈhaʊətsər, -z
howl
BR haʊl, -z, -ɪŋ, -d
AM haʊl, -z, -ɪŋ, -d
howler
BR ˈhaʊlə(r), -z
AM ˈhaʊlər, -z
Howlett
BR ˈhaʊlɪt
AM ˈhaʊlət
howsoever
BR ˌhaʊsəʊˈɛvə(r)
AM ˈhaʊsəˈwɛvər, ˌhaʊsoʊˈɛvər
howzat
BR (ˌ)haʊˈzat
AM haʊˈzæt

Hoxton
BR ˈhɒkst(ə)n
AM ˈhɑkstən
hoy
BR hɔɪ, -z, -ɪŋ, -d
AM hɔɪ, -z, -ɪŋ, -d
hoya
BR ˈhɔɪə(r), -z
AM ˈhɔɪə, -z
hoyden
BR ˈhɔɪdn, -z
AM ˈhɔɪdn, -z
hoydenish
BR ˈhɔɪdənɪʃ, ˈhɔɪdn̩ɪʃ
AM ˈhɔɪdn̩ɪʃ
Hoylake
BR ˈhɔɪleɪk
AM ˈhɔɪˌleɪk
Hoyle
BR hɔɪl
AM hɔɪl
Hsing-king
BR ˈʃɪnˈdʒɪŋ
AM ˈʃɪnˈdʒɪŋ
Huascarán
BR ˌwɑːskəˈrɑːn
AM ˌwɑskəˈrɑn
hub
BR hʌb, -z
AM həb, -z
Hubbard
BR ˈhʌbəd
AM ˈhəbərd
Hubble
BR ˈhʌbl
AM ˈhəbəl
hubbub
BR ˈhʌbʌb
AM ˈhəbəb
hubby
BR ˈhʌb|i, -ɪz
AM ˈhəbi, -z
hubcap
BR ˈhʌbkap, -s
AM ˈhəbˌkæp, -s
Hubei
BR ˈhuːˈbeɪ
AM ˈhuˈbeɪ
Huber
BR ˈhjuːbə(r)
AM ˈhjubər
Hubert
BR ˈhjuːbət
AM ˈ(h)jubərt
hubris
BR ˈh(j)uːbrɪs
AM ˈ(h)jubrəs
hubristic
BR h(j)uːˈbrɪstɪk
AM (h)juˈbrɪstɪk
Huck
BR hʌk
AM hək
huckaback
BR ˈhʌkəbak
AM ˈhəkəˌbæk

huckle
BR ˈhʌkl, -z
AM ˈhəkəl, -z
huckle-back
BR ˈhʌklbak, -s
AM ˈhəkəlˌbæk, -s
huckleberry
BR ˈhʌklb(ə)r|i, -ɪz
AM ˈhəkəlˌbɛri, -z
huckster
BR ˈhʌkstə(r), -z
AM ˈhəkstər, -z
huckstery
BR ˈhʌkstəri
AM ˈhəkstəri
huckterism
BR ˈhʌkstərɪz(ə)m
AM ˈhəkstəˌrɪzəm
Huddersfield
BR ˈhʌdəzfiːld
AM ˈhədərsˌfild
huddle
BR ˈhʌdl̩, -əlz, -(ə)lɪŋ, -əld
AM ˈhəd|əl, -əlz, -(ə)lɪŋ, -əld
Huddleston
BR ˈhʌdlst(ə)n
AM ˈhədlstən
Hudibras
BR ˈhjuːdɪbras
AM ˈhjudəˌbræs
Hudibrastic
BR ˌhjuːdɪˈbrastɪk
AM ˌhjudəˈbræstɪk
Hudson
BR ˈhʌdsn
AM ˈhədsən
Hué
BR ˈ(h)weɪ
AM ˈ(h)weɪ
hue
BR hjuː, -z
AM (h)ju, -z
hueless
BR ˈhjuːləs
AM ˈhjuləs
Huey
BR ˈhjuːi
AM ˈhjui
huff
BR hʌf, -s, -ɪŋ, -t
AM həf, -s, -ɪŋ, -t
huffily
BR ˈhʌfɪli
AM ˈhəfəli
huffiness
BR ˈhʌfɪnɪs
AM ˈhəfinɪs
huffish
BR ˈhʌfɪʃ
AM ˈhəfɪʃ
huffishly
BR ˈhʌfɪʃli
AM ˈhəfɪʃli
huffishness
BR ˈhʌfɪʃnɪs

AM 'həfɪʃnɪs
Huffman
BR 'hʌfmən
AM 'həfmən
huffy
BR 'hʌf|i, -ɪə(r), -ɪɪst
AM 'həfi, -ər, -ɪst
hug
BR hʌg, -z, -ɪŋ, -d
AM həg, -z, -ɪŋ, -d
huge
BR hju:dʒ, -ə(r), -ɪst
AM (h)judʒ, -ər, -əst
hugely
BR 'hju:dʒli
AM '(h)judʒli
hugeness
BR 'hju:dʒnəs
AM '(h)judʒnəs
huggable
BR 'hʌgəbl
AM 'həgəbəl
hugger
BR 'hʌgə(r), -z
AM 'həgər, -z
hugger-mugger
BR 'hʌgə,mʌgə(r)
AM 'həgər,məgər
Huggins
BR 'hʌgɪnz
AM 'həgənz
Hugh
BR hju:
AM (h)ju
Hughenden
BR 'hju:ənd(ə)n
AM 'hjuəndən
Hughes
BR hju:z
AM (h)juz
Hughey
BR 'hju:i
AM '(h)jui
Hughie
BR 'hju:i
AM '(h)jui
Hugo
BR 'hju:gəʊ
AM '(h)jugoʊ
Huguenot
BR 'hju:gənəʊ, -z
AM 'hjugə,nɑt, -s
huh
BR hʌ(r)
AM hə
hula
BR 'hu:lə(r), -z, -ɪŋ, -d
AM 'hulə, -z, -ɪŋ, -d
hula-hoop
BR 'hu:ləhu:p, -s
AM 'hulə,hup, -s
hula-hula
BR ,hu:lə'hu:lə(r), -z,
-ɪŋ, -d
AM ,hulə'hulə, -z, -ɪŋ, -d
hulk
BR hʌlk, -s, -ɪŋ

AM həlk, -s, -ɪŋ
hull
BR hʌl, -z, -ɪŋ, -d
AM həl, -z, -ɪŋ, -d
hullabaloo
BR ,hʌləbə'lu:, -z
AM ,hələbə'lu, -z
hullo
BR hə'ləʊ, -z
AM hə'loʊ, -z
Hulme
BR hju:m, hʌlm
AM hjum
Hulot
BR 'u:ləʊ
AM 'uloʊ, 'hjulət
Hulse
BR hʌls
AM həls
hum
BR hʌm, -z, -ɪŋ, -d
AM həm, -z, -ɪŋ, -d
human
BR 'hju:mən, -z
AM '(h)jumən, -z
humane
BR 'hju:meɪn,
,hju:'meɪn, -ə(r), -ɪst
AM hju'meɪn, -ər, -ɪst
humanely
BR hju'meɪnli,
,hju:'meɪnli
AM hju'meɪnli
humaneness
BR hju'meɪnnɪs,
hju:'meɪnnɪs
AM hju'meɪ(n)nɪs
humanisation
BR ,hju:mənaɪ'zeɪʃn
AM ,hjumənə,zeɪʃən,
,(h)jumə,naɪ'zeɪʃən
humanise
BR 'hju:mənʌɪz, -ɪz,
-ɪŋ, -d
AM 'hjumə,naɪz, -ɪz,
-ɪŋ, -d
humanism
BR 'hju:mənɪz(ə)m
AM 'hjumə,nɪzəm
humanist
BR 'hju:mənɪst, -s
AM 'hjumənəst, -s
humanistic
BR ,hju:mə'nɪstɪk
AM ,hjumə'nɪstɪk
humanistically
BR ,hju:mə'nɪstɪkli
AM ,hjumə'nɪstək(ə)li
humanitarian
BR hju:,manɪ'tɛːrɪən,
,hju:manɪ'tɛːrɪən, -z
AM hju,mænə'tɛrɪən,
-z
humanitarianism
BR hju:,manɪ'tɛːrɪən-
ɪz(ə)m,
,hju:manɪ'tɛːrɪən-
ɪz(ə)m

AM hju,mænə'tɛrɪə-
,nɪzəm
humanity
BR hju'manɪt|i, -ɪz
AM hju'mænədi, -z
humanization
BR ,hju:mənʌɪ'zeɪʃn
AM ,hjumənə,zeɪʃən,
,(h)jumə,naɪ'zeɪʃən
humanize
BR 'hju:mənʌɪz, -ɪz,
-ɪŋ, -d
AM '(h)jumə,naɪz, -ɪz,
-ɪŋ, -d
humankind
BR ,hju:mən'kʌɪnd,
'hju:mənkʌɪnd
AM ,(h)jumən'kaɪnd
humanly
BR 'hju:mənli
AM 'hjumənli
humanness
BR 'hju:mənnəs
AM 'hjumə(n)nəs
humanoid
BR 'hju:mənɔɪd, -z
AM 'hjumə,nɔɪd, -z
Humber
BR 'hʌmbə(r)
AM 'həmbər
Humberside
BR 'hʌmbəsʌɪd
AM 'həmbər,saɪd
Humbert
BR 'hʌmbət
AM 'həmbərt
humble
BR 'hʌmb|l, -lz,
-|ɪŋ \-lɪŋ, -ld, -lə(r),
-lɪst
AM 'həmb|əl, -əlz,
-(ə)lɪŋ, -əld, -lər, -ləst
humbleness
BR 'hʌmblnəs
AM 'həmbəlnəs
humbly
BR 'hʌmbli
AM 'həmbli
Humboldt
BR 'hʌmbəʊlt
AM 'həm,boʊlt
humbug
BR 'hʌmbʌg, -z, -ɪŋ, -d
AM 'həm,bəg, -z, -ɪŋ, -d
humbuggery
BR 'hʌmbʌg(ə)ri
AM 'həm,bəgəri
humdinger
BR 'hʌm'dɪŋə(r), -z
AM 'həm'dɪŋgər, -z
humdrum
BR 'hʌmdrʌm
AM 'həm,drəm
Hume
BR hju:m
AM hjum

humectant
BR hju'mɛkt(ə)nt, -s
AM hju'mɛktnt, -s
humeral
BR 'hju:m(ə)rəl,
'hju:m(ə)r|
AM 'hjumərəl
humerus
BR 'hju:m(ə)rəs, -ɪz
AM 'hjumərəs, -əz
humic
BR 'hju:mɪk
AM 'hjumɪk
humid
BR 'hju:mɪd
AM '(h)juməd
humidification
BR hjʊ,mɪdɪfɪ'keɪʃn
AM hju,mɪdəfə'keɪʃən
humidifier
BR hjʊ'mɪdɪfʌɪə(r), -z
AM hju'mɪdə,faɪər, -z
humidify
BR hjʊ'mɪdɪfʌɪ, -z, -ɪŋ,
-d
AM hju'mɪdə,faɪ, -z, -ɪŋ,
-d
humidity
BR hjʊ'mɪdɪti
AM (h)ju'mɪdɪdi
humidly
BR 'hju:mɪdli
AM 'hjumədli
humidness
BR 'hju:mɪdnəs
AM 'hjumədnəs
humidor
BR 'hju:mɪdɔː(r), -z
AM 'hjumə,dɔ(ə)r, -z
humification
BR ,hju:mɪfɪ'keɪʃn
AM hju,mɪfə'keɪʃən
humify
BR 'hju:mɪfʌɪ, -z, -ɪŋ, -d
AM 'hjumə,faɪ, -z, -ɪŋ, -d
humiliate
BR hjʊ'mɪlieɪt, -s, -ɪŋ,
-ɪd
AM (h)ju'mɪli,eɪ|t, -ts,
-dɪŋ, -dɪd
humiliatingly
BR hjʊ'mɪlieɪtɪŋli
AM hju'mɪli,eɪdɪŋli
humiliation
BR hjʊ,mɪlɪ'eɪʃn,
,hju:mɪlɪ'eɪʃn, -z
AM hju,mɪlɪ'eɪʃən, -z
humiliator
BR hjʊ'mɪlieɪtə(r), -z
AM hju'mɪli,eɪdər, -z
humility
BR hjʊ'mɪlɪti
AM hju'mɪlɪdi
hummable
BR 'hʌməbl
AM 'həməbəl

hummer
BR ˈhʌmə(r), -z
AM ˈhəmər, -z

hummingbird
BR ˈhʌmɪŋbɜːd, -z
AM ˈhəmɪŋˌbɜrd, -z

hummock
BR ˈhʌmək, -s
AM ˈhəmək, -s

hummocky
BR ˈhʌməki
AM ˈhəməki

hummus
BR ˈhjuːməs
AM ˈhəməs, ˈhuməs

humongous
BR hjuːˈmʌŋgəs
AM hjuˈmʌŋgəs

humor
BR ˈhjuːm|ə(r), -əz,
-(ə)rɪŋ, -əd
AM ˈ(h)jumər, -z, -ɪŋ, -d

humoral
BR ˈhjuːm(ə)rəl,
ˈhjuːm(ə)rl̩
AM ˈhjumərəl

humoresque
BR ˌhjuːməˈrɛsk, -s
AM ˌhjuməˈrɛsk, -s

humorist
BR ˈhjuːmərɪst, -s
AM ˈhjumərəst, -s

humoristic
BR ˌhjuːməˈrɪstɪk
AM ˌhjuməˈrɪstɪk

humorless
BR ˈhjuːmələs
AM ˈhjumərləs

humorlessly
BR ˈhjuːmələsli
AM ˈhjumərləsli

humorlessness
BR ˈhjuːmələsnəs
AM ˈhjumərləsnəs

humorous
BR ˈhjuːm(ə)rəs
AM ˈhjumərəs

humorously
BR ˈhjuːm(ə)rəsli
AM ˈhjumərəsli

humorousness
BR ˈhjuːm(ə)rəsnəs
AM ˈhjumərəsnəs

humorsome
BR ˈhjuːməs(ə)m
AM ˈhjumərsəm

humorsomely
BR ˈhjuːməs(ə)mli
AM ˈhjumərsəmli

humorsomeness
BR ˈhjuːməs(ə)mnəs
AM ˈhjumərsəmnəs

humour
BR ˈhjuːm|ə(r), -əz,
-(ə)rɪŋ, -əd
AM ˈ(h)jumər, -z, -ɪŋ, -d

humourist
BR ˈhjuːm(ə)rɪst, -s
AM ˈhjumərəst, -s

humourless
BR ˈhjuːmələs
AM ˈhjumərləs

humourlessly
BR ˈhjuːmələsli
AM ˈhjumərləsli

humourlessness
BR ˈhjuːmələsnəs
AM ˈhjumərləsnəs

humoursome
BR ˈhjuːməs(ə)m
AM ˈhjumərsəm

humous
BR ˈhjuːməs
AM ˈhjuməs

hump
BR hʌm|p, -ps, -pɪŋ,
-(p)t
AM həmp, -s, -ɪŋ, -t

humpback
BR ˈhʌmpbak, -s
AM ˈhəmpˌbæk, -s

humpbacked
BR ˌhʌmpˈbakt
AM ˈhəmpˌbækt

humper
BR ˈhʌmpə(r), -z
AM ˈhəmpər, -z

Humperdinck
BR ˈhʊmpədɪŋk,
ˈhʌmpədɪŋk
AM ˈhəmpərˌdɪŋk

humph
BR hʌmf, hõh
AM həm(p)f

Humphrey
BR ˈhʌmfri
AM ˈhəm(p)fri

Humphreys
BR ˈhʌmfriz
AM ˈhəm(p)friz

Humphries
BR ˈhʌmfrɪz
AM ˈhəm(p)friz

humpiness
BR ˈhʌmpɪnɪs
AM ˈhəmpinɪs

humpless
BR ˈhʌmpləs
AM ˈhəmpləs

humpty
BR ˈhʌm(p)t|i, -ɪz
AM ˈhəmti, -z

humpty-dumpty
BR ˌhʌm(p)tɪˈdʌm(p)t|i,
-ɪz
AM ˈhəmtiˈdəmti, -z

humpy
BR ˈhʌmp|i, -ɪə(r), -ɪɪst
AM ˈhəmpi, -ər, -ɪɪst

humus
BR ˈhjuːməs
AM ˈhjuməs

humusify
BR ˈhjuːməsɪfʌɪ, -z, -ɪŋ,
-d
AM ˈhjuməsəˌfaɪ, -z, -ɪŋ,
-d

Hun
BR hʌn, -z
AM hən, -z

Hunan
BR ˌhuːˈnan
AM ˈhuˈnɑn

hunch
BR hʌn(t)ʃ, -ɪz, -ɪŋ, -t
AM hən(t)ʃ, -əz, -ɪŋ, -t

hunchback
BR ˈhʌn(t)ʃbak, -s
AM ˈhən(t)ʃˌbæk, -s

hunchbacked
BR ˌhʌn(t)ʃˈbakt
AM ˈhən(t)ʃˌbækt

hundred
BR ˈhʌndrəd, -z
AM ˈhəndrəd, -z

hundredfold
BR ˈhʌndrədfəʊld
AM ˈhəndrədˌfoʊld

hundredth
BR ˈhʌndrədθ,
ˈhʌndrətθ
AM ˈhəndrədθ,
ˈhəndrətθ

hundredweight
BR ˈhʌndrədweɪt, -s
AM ˈhəndrədˌweɪt, -s

hung
BR hʌŋ
AM hən

Hungarian
BR hʌŋˈgɛːrɪən, -z
AM həŋˈgɛrɪən, -z

Hungary
BR ˈhʌŋg(ə)ri
AM ˈhəŋgəri

hunger
BR ˈhʌŋg|ə(r), -əz,
-(ə)rɪŋ, -əd
AM ˈhəŋgər, -z, -ɪŋ, -d

Hungerford
BR ˈhʌŋgəfəd
AM ˈhəŋgərfərd

hungrily
BR ˈhʌŋgrɪli
AM ˈhəŋgrəli

hungriness
BR ˈhʌŋgrɪnɪs
AM ˈhəŋgrinɪs

hungry
BR ˈhʌŋgr|i, -ɪə(r), -ɪɪst
AM ˈhəŋgri, -ər, -ɪɪst

hunk
BR hʌŋk, -s
AM həŋk, -s

hunker
BR ˈhʌŋk|ə(r), -əz,
-(ə)rɪŋ, -əd
AM ˈhəŋkər, -z, -ɪŋ, -d

Hunkpapa
BR ˈhʌŋkˌpɑːpə(r), -z
AM ˈhəŋkˌpɑpə, -z

hunky
BR ˈhʌŋk|i, -ɪz
AM ˈhəŋki, -z

hunky-dory
BR ˌhʌŋkɪˈdɔːri
AM ˌhəŋkiˈdɔri

Hunniford
BR ˈhʌnɪfəd
AM ˈhənəfərd

Hunnish
BR ˈhʌnɪʃ
AM ˈhənɪʃ

Hunslet
BR ˈhʌnzlɪt
AM ˈhənzlət

Hunstanton
BR hʌnˈstant(ə)n,
ˈhʌnst(ə)n
AM ˈhənstən(t)ən

hunt
BR hʌnt, -s, -ɪŋ, -ɪd
AM hən|t, -ts, -(t)ɪŋ,
-(t)əd

huntaway
BR ˈhʌntəweɪ, -z
AM ˈhən(t)əˌweɪ, -z

hunter
BR ˈhʌntə(r), -z
AM ˈhən(t)ər, -z

Huntingdon
BR ˈhʌntɪŋd(ə)n
AM ˈhən(t)ɪŋdən

Huntingdonshire
BR ˈhʌntɪŋd(ə)nʃ(ɪ)ə(r)
AM ˈhən(t)ɪŋdənˌʃɪ(ə)r

Huntington
BR ˈhʌntɪŋt(ə)n
AM ˈhən(t)ɪŋtən

Huntley
BR ˈhʌntli
AM ˈhən(t)li

huntress
BR ˈhʌntrɪs, -ɪz
AM ˈhəntrəs, -əz

huntsman
BR ˈhʌn(t)smən
AM ˈhən(t)smən

huntsmen
BR ˈhʌn(t)smən
AM ˈhən(t)smən

Huntsville
BR ˈhʌn(t)svɪl
AM ˈhən(t)sˌvɪl

hup
BR hʌp, -s
AM həp, -s

Hupeh
BR ˌhuːˈpeɪ
AM ˈhuˈpeɪ

hurdle
BR ˈhɜːd|l̩, -lz, -l̩ɪŋ \-lɪŋ,
-ld
AM ˈhɜrd|əl, -əlz,
-(ə)lɪŋ, -əld

hurdler
BR ˈhɜːdlə(r),
ˈhɜːdlə(r), -z
AM ˈhɜrd(ə)lər, -z

hurdy-gurdy
BR ˌhɜːdɪˈgɜːd|i,
ˈhɜːdɪˌgɜːd|i, -ɪz
AM ˌhɜrdiˈgɜrdi, -z

Hurford
BR ˈhɜːfəd
AM ˈhɜrfərd

hurl
BR hɜːl, -z, -ɪŋ, -d
AM hɜrl, -z, -ɪŋ, -d

hurley
BR ˈhɜːli
AM ˈhɜrli

Hurlingham
BR ˈhɜːlɪŋəm
AM ˈhɜrlɪŋəm

hurly-burly
BR ˌhɜːlɪˈbɜːli,
ˈhɜːlɪˌbɜːli
AM ˌhɜrliˈbɜrli

Hurn
BR hɜːn
AM hɜrn

Huron
BR ˈhjʊərɒn
AM ˈhjʊˌrɑn

hurrah
BR hʊˈrɑː(r), -z
AM həˈrɑ, -z

hurray
BR hʊˈreɪ, -z
AM həˈreɪ, hʊˈreɪ, -z

Hurri
BR ˈhʊr|i, -ɪz
AM ˈhʊri, -z

hurricane
BR ˈhʌrɪk(ə)n, -z
AM ˈhɜrəˌkeɪn, -z

hurried
BR ˈhʌrɪd
AM ˈhɜrid

hurriedly
BR ˈhʌrɪdli
AM ˈhɜridli, ˈhɜrədli

hurriedness
BR ˈhʌrɪdnɪs
AM ˈhɜridnɪs

hurroo
BR hʊˈruː, -z
AM ˌhɜˈru, -z

hurry
BR ˈhʌr|i, -ɪz, -ɪɪŋ, -ɪd
AM ˈhɜri, -z, -ɪŋ, -d

hurry-scurry
BR ˌhʌrɪˈskʌri
AM ˌhɜriˈskɜri

Hurst
BR hɜːst
AM hɜrst

hurst
BR hɜːst, -s
AM hɜrst, -s

Hurstmonceux
BR ˌhɜːs(t)mənˈs(j)uː
AM ˌhɜrs(t)mənˈsu

Hurston
BR ˈhɜːst(ə)n
AM ˈhɜrstən

Hurstpierpoint
BR ˌhɜːs(t)pɪəˈpɔɪnt
AM ˌhɜrs(t)pɪrˈpɔɪnt

hurt
BR hɜːt, -s, -ɪŋ
AM hɜr|t, -ts, -dɪŋ

hurtful
BR ˈhɜːtf(ʊ)l
AM ˈhɜrtfəl

hurtfully
BR ˈhɜːtfʊli, ˈhɜːtfli
AM ˈhɜrtfəli

hurtfulness
BR ˈhɜːtf(ʊ)lnəs
AM ˈhɜrtfəlnəs

hurtle
BR ˈhɜːt|l, -lz, -lɪŋ \-lɪŋ,
-ld
AM ˈhɜrdəl, -z, -ɪŋ, -d

hurtless
BR ˈhɜːtləs
AM ˈhɜrtləs

Husain
BR hʊˈseɪn
AM hʊˈseɪn

Husák
BR ˈhuːsak
AM ˈhusæk

husband
BR ˈhʌzbənd, -z, -ɪŋ, -ɪd
AM ˈhəzbən(d), -z, -ɪŋ,
-əd

husbander
BR ˈhʌzbəndə(r), -z
AM ˈhəzbəndər, -z

husbandhood
BR ˈhʌzbəndhʊd
AM ˈhəzbən(dh)ʊd

husbandless
BR ˈhʌzbəndləs
AM ˈhəzbən(d)ləs

husbandlike
BR ˈhʌzbəndlaɪk
AM ˈhəzbəndˌlaɪk

husbandly
BR ˈhʌzbəndli
AM ˈhəzbən(d)li

husbandman
BR ˈhʌzbən(d)mən
AM ˈhəzbən(d)mən

husbandmen
BR ˈhʌzbən(d)mən
AM ˈhəzbən(d)mən

husbandry
BR ˈhʌzbəndri
AM ˈhəzbəndri

husbandship
BR ˈhʌzbən(d)ʃɪp
AM ˈhəzbən(d)ˌʃɪp

hush
BR hʌʃ, -ɪz, -ɪŋ, -t

AM həʃ, -əz, -ɪŋ, -t

hushaby
BR ˈhʌʃəbaɪ
AM ˈhəʃəˌbaɪ

hushabye
BR ˈhʌʃəbaɪ
AM ˈhəʃəˌbaɪ

hush-hush
BR ˌhʌʃˈhʌʃ
AM ˌhəʃˈhəʃ

hush money
BR ˈhʌʃ ˌmʌni
AM ˈhəʃ ˌməni

hush-up
BR ˈhʌʃʌp
AM ˈhəʃəp

husk
BR hʌsk, -s, -ɪŋ, -t
AM həsk, -s, -ɪŋ, -t

huskily
BR ˈhʌskɪli
AM ˈhəskəli

huskiness
BR ˈhʌskɪnɪs
AM ˈhəskɪnɪs

Huskisson
BR ˈhʌskɪs(ə)n
AM ˈhəskənsən

husky
BR ˈhʌsk|i, -ɪz, -ɪə(r),
-ɪɪst
AM ˈhəski, -z, -ər, -ɪst

huss
BR hʌs, -ɪz
AM həs, -əz

Hussain
BR hʊˈseɪn
AM həˈseɪn

hussar
BR hʊˈzɑː(r), -z
AM həˈzɑr, -z

Hussein
BR hʊˈseɪn
AM hʊˈseɪn

Husserl
BR ˈhʊsəːl
AM ˈhʊsərl

Hussey
BR ˈhʌsi
AM ˈhəsi

Hussite
BR ˈhʌsaɪt, ˈhʊsaɪt, -s
AM ˈhəˌsaɪt, ˈhʊˌsaɪt, -s

Hussitism
BR ˈhʌsʌɪtɪz(ə)m,
ˈhʊsʌɪtɪz(ə)m
AM ˈhəˌsaɪˌtɪzəm,
ˈhʊˌsaɪˌtɪzəm

hussy
BR ˈhʌs|i, ˈhʌz|i, -ɪz
AM ˈhəzi, ˈhəsi, -z

hustings
BR ˈhʌstɪŋz
AM ˈhəstɪŋz

hustle
BR ˈhʌs|l, -lz, -lɪŋ \-lɪŋ,
-ld

AM ˈhəs|əl, -əlz, -(ə)lɪŋ,
-əld

hustler
BR ˈhʌslə(r), -z
AM ˈhəs(ə)lər, -z

Huston
BR ˈhjuːst(ə)n
AM ˈhjustən

hut
BR hʌt, -s
AM hət, -s

hutch
BR hʌtʃ, -ɪz
AM hətʃ, -əz

Hutcheson
BR ˈhʌtʃɪs(ə)n
AM ˈhətʃəsən

Hutchings
BR ˈhʌtʃɪŋz
AM ˈhətʃɪŋz

Hutchins
BR ˈhʌtʃɪnz
AM ˈhətʃənz

Hutchinson
BR ˈhʌtʃ(ɪ)ns(ə)n
AM ˈhətʃənsən

Hutchison
BR ˈhʌtʃɪs(ə)n
AM ˈhətʃəsən

hutia
BR hʌˈtiː(r), -z
AM həˈtiə, -z

hutlike
BR ˈhʌtlʌɪk
AM ˈhətˌlaɪk

hutment
BR ˈhʌtm(ə)nt, -s
AM ˈhətmənt, -s

Hutterite
BR ˈhʌtərʌɪt, ˈhʊtərʌɪt
AM ˈhədəˌraɪt

Hutton
BR ˈhʌtn
AM ˈhətn

Hutu
BR ˈhuːtuː, -z
AM ˈhuˌtu, -z

Huw
BR hju:
AM hju
WE hɪʊ

Huxley
BR ˈhʌksli
AM ˈhəksli

Huxtable
BR ˈhʌkstəbl
AM ˈhəkstəbəl

Huygens
BR ˈhɔɪgənz
AM ˈhɔɪgənz
DU ˈhœyxəns

Huyton
BR ˈhaɪtn
AM ˈhaɪtn

huzza
BR hʊˈzɑː(r)
AM həˈzɑ

huzzah
BR hʊˈzɑː(r)
AM həˈzɑ
huzzy
BR ˈhʌz|i, -ɪz
AM ˈhəzi, -z
Hwange
BR ˈhwaŋgi, ˈhwaŋgeɪ
AM ˈ(h)waŋi
Hwang-Ho
BR ˈhwaŋˈhəʊ
AM ˈ(h)waŋˈhoʊ
hwyl
BR ˈhuːɪl, hwiːl
AM ˈhuɪl, (h)wil
WE hwɪl
hyacinth
BR ˈhaɪəsɪnθ, -s
AM ˈhaɪəˌsɪnθ, -s
hyacinthine
BR ˌhaɪəˈsɪnθʌɪn
AM ˈhaɪəˈsɪnθən, ˌhaɪəˈsɪnˌθaɪn
Hyacinthus
BR ˌhaɪəˈsɪnθəs
AM ˌhaɪəˈsɪnθəs
Hyades
BR ˈhʌɪədiːz
AM ˈhaɪˌdiz
hyaena
BR hʌɪˈiːnə(r), -z
AM haɪˈinə, -z
hyalin
BR ˈhʌɪəlɪn
AM ˈhaɪələn, ˈhaɪəˌlaɪn
hyaline
BR ˈhʌɪəlɪn, ˈhʌɪəliːn, ˈhʌɪəlʌɪn
AM ˈhaɪələn, ˈhaɪəˌlaɪn
hyalite
BR ˈhʌɪəlʌɪt
AM ˈhaɪəˌlaɪt
hyaloid
BR ˈhʌɪəlɔɪd
AM ˈhaɪəˌlɔɪd
Hyatt
BR ˈhʌɪət
AM ˈhaɪət
hybrid
BR ˈhʌɪbrɪd, -z
AM ˈhaɪˌbrɪd, -z
hybridisable
BR ˈhʌɪbrɪdʌɪzəbl
AM ˈhaɪbrəˌdaɪzəbəl, ˌhaɪbrəˈdaɪzəbəl
hybridisation
BR ˌhʌɪbrɪdʌɪˈzeɪʃn
AM ˌhaɪbrədəˈzeɪʃən, ˌhaɪbrəˌdaɪˈzeɪʃən
hybridise
BR ˈhʌɪbrɪdʌɪz, -ɪz, -ɪŋ, -d
AM ˈhaɪbrəˌdaɪz, -ɪz, -ɪŋ, -d
hybridism
BR ˈhʌɪbrɪdɪz(ə)m
AM ˈhaɪbrəˌdɪzəm

hybridity
BR hʌɪˈbrɪdɪti
AM haɪˈbrɪdɪdi
hybridizable
BR ˈhʌɪbrɪdʌɪzəbl
AM ˈhaɪbrəˌdaɪzəbəl, ˌhaɪbrəˈdaɪzəbəl
hybridization
BR ˌhʌɪbrɪdʌɪˈzeɪʃn
AM ˌhaɪbrədəˈzeɪʃən, ˌhaɪbrəˌdaɪˈzeɪʃən
hybridize
BR ˈhʌɪbrɪdʌɪz, -ɪz, -ɪŋ, -d
AM ˈhaɪbrəˌdaɪz, -ɪz, -ɪŋ, -d
hydantoin
BR hʌɪˈdantəʊɪn
AM haɪˈdæn,toʊən, haɪˈdæn(t)oʊən
hydathode
BR ˈhʌɪdəθəʊd, -z
AM ˈhaɪdəˌθoʊd, -z
hydatid
BR ˈhʌɪdətɪd, hʌɪˈdatɪd, -z
AM ˈhaɪdədəd, -z
hydatidiform
BR ˌhʌɪdəˈtɪdɪfɔːm
AM ˌhaɪdəˈtɪdəˌfɔ(ə)rm
Hyde
BR hʌɪd
AM haɪd
Hyderabad
BR ˈhʌɪd(ə)rəbad, ˈhʌɪd(ə)rəbɑːd
AM ˈhaɪd(ə)rəˌbɑd, ˈhaɪd(ə)rəˌbæd
Hydra
BR ˈhʌɪdrə(r)
AM ˈhaɪdrə
hydra
BR ˈhʌɪdrə(r), -z
AM ˈhaɪdrə, -z
hydrangea
BR hʌɪˈdreɪn(d)ʒə(r), -z
AM haɪˈdrændʒə, -z
hydrant
BR ˈhʌɪdr(ə)nt, -s
AM ˈhaɪdrənt, -s
hydratable
BR hʌɪˈdreɪtəbl
AM ˈhaɪˌdreɪdəbəl
hydrate¹
noun
BR ˈhʌɪdreɪt, -s
AM ˈhaɪˌdreɪt, -s
hydrate²
verb
BR hʌɪˈdreɪt, -s, -ɪŋ, -ɪd
AM ˈhaɪˌdreɪ|t, -ts, -dɪŋ, -dɪd
hydration
BR hʌɪˈdreɪʃn
AM haɪˈdreɪʃən
hydrator
BR hʌɪˈdreɪtə(r), -z

AM ˈhaɪˌdreɪdər, -z
hydraulic
BR hʌɪˈdrɒlɪk, -s
AM haɪˈdrɔlɪk, haɪˈdrɑlɪk, -s
hydraulically
BR hʌɪˈdrɒlɪkli
AM haɪˈdrɒlək(ə)li, haɪˈdrɑlək(ə)li
hydraulicity
BR ˌhʌɪdrəˈlɪsɪti
AM ˌhaɪdrəˈlɪsɪdi
hydrazine
BR ˈhʌɪdrəzɪːn
AM ˈhaɪdərəzən, ˈhaɪdrəˌzin
hydric
BR ˈhʌɪdrɪk
AM ˈhaɪdrɪk
hydride
BR ˈhʌɪdrʌɪd, -z
AM ˈhaɪˌdraɪd, -z
hydriodic acid
BR ˌhʌɪdrɪˈɒdɪk ˈasɪd
AM ˌhaɪdriˌɑdɪk ˈæsəd
hydro
BR ˈhʌɪdrəʊ, -z
AM ˈhaɪdroʊ, -z
hydrobromic acid
BR ˌhʌɪdrəbrəʊmɪk ˈasɪd
AM ˌhaɪdroʊˌbrɑmɪk ˈæsəd
hydrocarbon
BR ˌhʌɪdrə(ʊ)ˈkɑːb(ə)n, -z
AM ˈhaɪdroʊˌkɑrbən, -z
hydrocele
BR ˈhʌɪdrə(ʊ)siːl, -z
AM ˈhaɪdroʊˌsil, -z
hydrocephalic
BR ˌhʌɪdrə(ʊ)sɪˈfalɪk, ˌhaɪdrəʊkeˈfalɪk
AM ˌhaɪdroʊsəˈfælɪk
hydrocephalus
BR ˌhʌɪdrə(ʊ)ˈsefələs, ˌhʌɪdrə(ʊ)ˈsefləs, ˌhʌɪdrə(ʊ)ˈkefələs, ˌhʌɪdrə(ʊ)ˈkefləs
AM ˌhaɪdroʊˈsefələs
hydrochloric acid
BR ˌhʌɪdrəklɒrɪk ˈasɪd
AM ˈhaɪdroʊˌklɔrɪk ˈæsəd
hydrochloride
BR ˌhʌɪdrə(ʊ)ˈklɔːrʌɪd, -z
AM ˈhaɪdroʊˈklɔˌraɪd, -z
hydrocortisone
BR ˌhʌɪdrəʊˈkɔːtɪzəʊn
AM ˈhaɪdroʊˈkɔrdəˌzoʊn
hydrocyanic acid
BR ˌhʌɪdrə(ʊ)sʌɪˌanɪk ˈasɪd
AM ˈhaɪdroʊˌsaɪˌænɪk ˈæsəd

hydrodynamic
BR ˌhʌɪdrə(ʊ)dʌɪˈnamɪk, -s
AM ˈhaɪdroʊˌdaɪˈnæmɪk, -s
hydrodynamical
BR ˌhʌɪdrə(ʊ)dʌɪˈnam-ɪkl
AM ˈhaɪdroʊˌdaɪˈnæm-əkəl
hydrodynamicist
BR ˌhʌɪdrə(ʊ)dʌɪˈnam-sɪst, -s
AM ˈhaɪdroʊˌdaɪˈnæməsəst, -s
hydroelectric
BR ˌhʌɪdrəʊɪˈlektrɪk
AM ˈhaɪdroʊɪˈlektrɪk, ˌhaɪdroʊiˈlektrɪk
hydroelectrically
BR ˌhʌɪdrəʊɪˈlektrɪkli
AM ˈhaɪdroʊəˈlektrək(ə)li, ˌhaɪdroʊiˈlektrək(ə)li
hydroelectricity
BR ˌhʌɪdrəʊɪlekˈtrɪsɪti
AM ˈhaɪdroʊəˌlekˈtrɪsɪdi, ˌhaɪdroʊiˌlekˈtrɪsɪdi
hydrofined
BR ˈhʌɪdrəfʌɪnd
AM ˈhaɪdrəˌfaɪnd, ˈhaɪdrəˌfaɪnd
hydrofining
BR ˈhʌɪdrəˌfʌɪnɪŋ
AM ˈhaɪdroʊˌfaɪnɪŋ, ˈhaɪdrəˌfaɪnɪŋ
hydrofluoric acid
BR ˌhʌɪdrəflʊərɪk ˈasɪd, ˌhʌɪdrəflɔːrɪk +
AM ˈhaɪdroʊˌflʊrɪk ˈæsəd
hydrofoil
BR ˈhʌɪdrəfɔɪl, -z
AM ˈhaɪdroʊˌfɔɪl, ˈhaɪdrəˌfɔɪl, -z
hydrogen
BR ˈhʌɪdrədʒ(ə)n
AM ˈhaɪdrədʒən
hydrogenase
BR hʌɪˈdrɒdʒɪneɪz, hʌɪˈdrɒdʒɪneɪs, -ɪz
AM ˈhaɪdrədʒəˌneɪz, haɪˈdrɑdʒəˌneɪz, ˈhaɪdrədʒəˌneɪs, haɪˈdrɑdʒəˌneɪs, -ɪz
hydrogenate
BR ˈhʌɪdrədʒɪneɪt, hʌɪˈdrɒdʒɪneɪt, -s, -ɪŋ, -ɪd
AM ˈhaɪdrədʒəˌneɪ|t, haɪˈdrɑdʒəneɪ|t, -ts, -dɪŋ, -dɪd
hydrogenation
BR ˌhʌɪdrədʒɪˈneɪʃn, hʌɪˌdrɒdʒɪˈneɪʃən
AM ˌhaɪdrədʒɪˈneɪʃən, haɪˌdrɑdʒəˈneɪʃən
hydrogenous
BR hʌɪˈdrɒdʒɪnəs

AM haɪˈdrɑdʒənəs
hydrogeological
BR ˌhaɪdrəʊˌdʒiəˈlɒdʒɪkl
AM ˌhaɪdrəˌdʒiəˈlɑdʒəkəl
hydrogeologist
BR ˌhaɪdrəʊdʒɪˈɒlədʒɪst, -s
AM ˌhaɪdrədʒiˈɑlədʒəst, -s
hydrogeology
BR ˌhaɪdrəʊdʒɪˈɒlədʒi
AM ˌhaɪdrədʒiˈɑlədʒi
hydrographer
BR haɪˈdrɒgrəfə(r), -z
AM haɪˈdrɑgrəfər, -z
hydrographic
BR ˌhaɪdrəˈgrafɪk
AM ˌhaɪdrəˈgræfɪk
hydrographical
BR ˌhaɪdrəˈgrafɪkl
AM ˌhaɪdrəˈgræfəkəl
hydrographically
BR ˌhaɪdrəˈgrafɪkli
AM ˌhaɪdrəˈgræfək(ə)li
hydrography
BR haɪˈdrɒgrəfi
AM haɪˈdrɑgrəfi
hydroid
BR ˈhaɪdrɔɪd, -z
AM ˈhaɪˌdrɔɪd, -z
hydrolase
BR ˈhaɪdrəleɪz, -ɪz
AM ˈhaɪd(ə)rəˌleɪs, ˈhaɪd(ə)rəˌleɪz, -ɪz
hydrologic
BR ˌhaɪdrəˈlɒdʒɪk
AM ˌhaɪdrəˈlɑdʒɪk
hydrological
BR ˌhaɪdrəˈlɒdʒɪkl
AM ˌhaɪdrəˈlɑdʒəkəl
hydrologically
BR ˌhaɪdrəˈlɒdʒɪkli
AM ˌhaɪdrəˈlɑdʒək(ə)li
hydrologist
BR haɪˈdrɒlədʒɪst, -s
AM haɪˈdrɑlədʒəst, -s
hydrology
BR haɪˈdrɒlədʒi
AM haɪˈdrɑlədʒi
hydrolyse
BR ˈhaɪdrəlʌɪz, -ɪz, -ɪŋ, -d
AM ˈhaɪdrəˌlaɪz, -ɪz, -ɪŋ, -d
hydrolysis
BR haɪˈdrɒlɪsɪs
AM haɪˈdrɑləsəs
hydrolytic
BR ˌhaɪdrəˈlɪtɪk
AM ˌhaɪdrəˈlɪdɪk
hydrolytically
BR ˌhaɪdrəˈlɪtɪkli
AM ˌhaɪdrəˈlɪdək(ə)li
hydrolyze
BR ˈhaɪdrəlʌɪz, -ɪz, -ɪŋ, -d

AM ˈhaɪdrəˌlaɪz, -ɪz, -ɪŋ, -d
hydromagnetic
BR ˌhaɪdrəʊmagˈnɛtɪk, -s
AM ˌhaɪdrəmægˈnɛdɪk, -s
hydromania
BR ˈhaɪdrəˌmeɪniə(r)
AM ˌhaɪdrəˈmeɪniə
hydromechanics
BR ˌhaɪdrəʊmɪˈkanɪks
AM ˌhaɪdrəməˈkænɪks
hydromel
BR ˈhaɪdrəmɛl
AM ˈhaɪdrəˌmɛl
hydrometer
BR haɪˈdrɒmɪtə(r), -z
AM haɪˈdrɑmədər, -z
hydrometric
BR ˌhaɪdrəˈmɛtrɪk
AM ˌhaɪdrəˈmɛtrɪk
hydrometrical
BR ˌhaɪdrəˈmɛtrɪkl
AM ˌhaɪdrəˈmɛtrəkəl
hydrometrically
BR ˌhaɪdrəˈmɛtrɪkli
AM ˌhaɪdrəˈmɛtrək(ə)li
hydrometry
BR haɪˈdrɒmɪtri
AM haɪˈdrɑmətri
hydronium ion
BR haɪˈdrəʊniəm ˌʌɪən, -z
AM haɪˈdrʊoniəm ˌaɪən, -z
hydropathic
BR ˌhaɪdrəˈpaθɪk, -s
AM ˌhaɪdrəˈpæθɪk, -s
hydropathically
BR ˌhaɪdrəˈpaθɪkli
AM ˌhaɪdrəˈpæθək(ə)li
hydropathist
BR haɪˈdrɒpəθɪst, -s
AM haɪˈdrɑpəθəst, -s
hydropathy
BR haɪˈdrɒpəθi
AM haɪˈdrɑpəθi
hydrophane
BR ˈhaɪdrəfeɪn
AM ˈhaɪdrəˌfeɪn
hydrophil
BR ˈhaɪdrəfɪl
AM ˈhaɪdrəˌfɪl
hydrophile
BR ˈhaɪdrəfʌɪl
AM ˈhaɪdrəˌfaɪl
hydrophilic
BR ˌhaɪdrəˈfɪlɪk
AM ˌhaɪdrəˈfɪlɪk
hydrophobia
BR ˌhaɪdrəˈfəʊbiə(r)
AM ˌhaɪdrəˈfoʊbiə
hydrophobic
BR ˌhaɪdrəˈfəʊbɪk
AM ˌhaɪdrəˈfoʊbɪk

hydrophone
BR ˈhaɪdrəfəʊn, -z
AM ˈhaɪdrəˌfoʊn, -z
hydrophyte
BR ˈhaɪdrəfʌɪt, -s
AM ˈhaɪdrəˌfaɪt, -s
hydropic
BR haɪˈdrɒpɪk
AM haɪˈdrɑpɪk
hydroplane
BR ˈhaɪdrəpleɪn, -z
AM ˈhaɪdrəˌpleɪn, -z
hydropneumatic
BR ˌhaɪdrəʊnjuːˈmatɪk, ˌhaɪdrəʊnjəˈmatɪk
AM ˌhaɪdrəˌnjuˈmædɪk
hydroponic
BR ˌhaɪdrəˈpɒnɪk, -s
AM ˌhaɪdrəˈpɑnɪk, -s
hydroponically
BR ˌhaɪdrəˈpɒnɪkli
AM ˌhaɪdrəˈpɑnək(ə)li
hydroquinone
BR ˌhaɪdrəʊˈkwɪməʊn
AM ˈhaɪdrəˈkwɪˌnoʊn
hydrosphere
BR ˈhaɪdrə(ʊ)sfɪə(r)
AM ˈhaɪdrəˌsfɪ(ə)r
hydrostatic
BR ˌhaɪdrəˈstatɪk, -s
AM ˌhaɪdrəˈstædɪk, -s
hydrostatical
BR ˌhaɪdrəˈstatɪkl
AM ˌhaɪdrəˈstædəkəl
hydrostatically
BR ˌhaɪdrəˈstatɪkli
AM ˌhaɪdrəˈstædək(ə)li
hydrotherapist
BR ˌhaɪdrə(ʊ)ˈθɛrəpɪst, -s
AM ˌhaɪdroʊˈθɛrəpəst, -s
hydrotherapy
BR ˌhaɪdrə(ʊ)ˈθɛrəpi
AM ˌhaɪdroʊˈθɛrəpi
hydrothermal
BR ˌhaɪdrə(ʊ)ˈθəːml
AM ˌhaɪdroʊˈθərməl
hydrothermally
BR ˌhaɪdrə(ʊ)ˈθəːmļi, ˌhaɪdrə(ʊ)ˈθəːməli
AM ˌhaɪdroʊˈθərməli
hydrothorax
BR ˌhaɪdrə(ʊ)ˈθɔːraks
AM ˌhaɪdrəˈθɔˌræks
hydrotropism
BR ˌhaɪdrəʊˈtrəʊpɪz(ə)m
AM ˈhaɪdroʊˈtrɑˌpɪzəm
hydrous
BR ˈhaɪdrəs
AM ˈhaɪdrəs
hydroxide
BR haɪˈdrɒksʌɪd, -z
AM haɪˈdrɑkˌsaɪd, -z

hydroxonium ion
BR ˌhaɪdrɒkˈsəʊniəm ˌʌɪən, -z
AM haɪˌdrɑkˈsoʊniəm ˌaɪən, -z
hydroxy
BR haɪˈdrɒksi
AM haɪˈdrɑksi
hydroxyl
BR haɪˈdrɒksɪl, haɪˈdrɒksʌɪl, -z
AM haɪˈdrɑksəl, -z
hydrozoan
BR ˌhaɪdrəˈzəʊən, -z
AM ˌhaɪdrəˈzoʊən, -z
hyena
BR haɪˈiːnə(r), -z
AM haɪˈinə, -z
Hygeia
BR haɪˈdʒiːə(r)
AM haɪˈdʒiə
hygeian
BR haɪˈdʒiːən
AM haɪˈdʒiən
Hygena
BR haɪˈdʒiːnə(r)
AM haɪˈdʒinə
hygiene
BR ˈhaɪdʒiːn
AM ˈhaɪˌdʒin
hygienic
BR haɪˈdʒiːnɪk, -s
AM ˌhaɪˈdʒɛnɪk, ˌhaɪˈdʒinɪk, -s
hygienically
BR haɪˈdʒiːnɪkli
AM ˌhaɪˈdʒɛnək(ə)li, ˌhaɪˈdʒinək(ə)li
hygienist
BR ˈhaɪdʒiːnɪst, haɪˈdʒiːnɪst, -s
AM ˈhaɪˌdʒinɪst, ˈhaɪˌdʒɛnəst, -s
hygrology
BR haɪˈgrɒlədʒi
AM haɪˈgrɑlədʒi
hygrometer
BR haɪˈgrɒmɪtə(r), -z
AM haɪˈgrɑmədər, -z
hygrometric
BR ˌhaɪgrəˈmɛtrɪk
AM ˌhaɪgrəˈmɛtrɪk
hygrometrically
BR ˌhaɪgrəˈmɛtrɪkli
AM ˌhaɪgrəˈmɛtrək(ə)li
hygrometry
BR haɪˈgrɒmɪtri
AM haɪˈgrɑmətri
hygrophilous
BR haɪˈgrɒfɪləs, haɪˈgrɒfləs
AM haɪˈgrɑfələs
hygrophyte
BR ˈhaɪgrəfʌɪt, -s
AM ˈhaɪgrəˌfaɪt, -s
hygrophytic
BR ˌhaɪgrəˈfɪtɪk
AM ˌhaɪgrəˈfɪdɪk

hygroscope
BR 'haɪgrəskəʊp, -s
AM 'haɪgrə,skoʊp, -s
hygroscopic
BR ,haɪgrə'skɒpɪk
AM ,haɪgrə'skɑpɪk
hygroscopically
BR ,haɪgrə'skɒpɪkli
AM ,haɪgrə'skɑpək(ə)li
hying
BR 'haɪɪŋ
AM 'haɪɪŋ
Hyksos
BR 'hɪksɒs
AM 'hɪk,sɒs, 'hɪk,sɑs
Hyland
BR 'haɪlənd
AM 'haɪlənd
Hylda
BR 'hɪldə(r)
AM 'hɪldə
hylic
BR 'haɪlɪk
AM 'haɪlɪk
hylomorphism
BR ,haɪlə(ʊ)'mɔːfɪz(ə)m
AM ,haɪlə'mɔr,fɪzəm
hylotheism
BR ,haɪlə(ʊ)'θiːɪz(ə)m
AM ,haɪlə'θi,ɪzəm
hylozoism
BR ,haɪlə(ʊ)'zəʊɪz(ə)m
AM ,haɪlə'zoʊ,ɪzəm
hylozoist
BR ,haɪlə(ʊ)'zəʊɪst, -s
AM ,haɪlə'zoʊəst, -s
Hylton
BR 'hɪlt(ə)n
AM 'hɪlt(ə)n
Hyman
BR 'haɪmən
AM 'haɪmən
hymen
BR 'haɪmɛn, 'haɪmən, -z
AM 'haɪmən, -z
hymenal
BR 'haɪmənl
AM 'haɪmənəl
hymeneal
BR ,haɪmɪ'niːəl, ,haɪmɛ'niːəl
AM ,haɪmə'niəl
hymenia
BR haɪ'miːnɪə(r)
AM haɪ'miniə
hymenium
BR haɪ'miːnɪəm
AM haɪ'miniəm
Hymenoptera
BR ,haɪmɪ'nɒpt(ə)rə(r), ,haɪmɛ'nɒpt(ə)rə(r)
AM ,haɪmə'nɑptərə
hymenopteran
BR ,haɪmɪ'nɒpt(ə)rən, ,haɪmɪ'nɒpt(ə)rn̩

,haɪmɛ'nɒpt(ə)rən, ,haɪmɛ'nɒpt(ə)rn̩, -z
AM ,haɪmə'nɑptərən, -z
hymenopterous
BR ,haɪmɪ'nɒpt(ə)rəs, ,haɪmɛ'nɒpt(ə)rəs
AM ,haɪmə'nɑptərəs
hymn
BR hɪm, -z, -ɪŋ, -d
AM hɪm, -z, -ɪŋ, -d
hymnal
BR 'hɪmn(ə)l, -z
AM 'hɪmnəl, -z
hymnary
BR 'hɪmnər|i, -ɪz
AM 'hɪmnəri, -z
hymnbook
BR 'hɪmbʊk, -s
AM 'hɪm,bʊk, -s
hymnic
BR 'hɪmnɪk
AM 'hɪmnɪk
hymnist
BR 'hɪmnɪst, -s
AM 'hɪmnɪst, -s
hymnodist
BR 'hɪmnədɪst, -s
AM 'hɪmnədəst, -s
hymnody
BR 'hɪmnəd|i, -ɪz
AM 'hɪmnədi, -z
hymnographer
BR hɪm'nɒgrəfə(r), -z
AM hɪm'nɑgrəfər, -z
hymnography
BR hɪm'nɒgrəfi
AM hɪm'nɑgrəfi
hymnologist
BR hɪm'nɒlədʒɪst, -s
AM hɪm'nɑlədʒəst, -s
hymnology
BR hɪm'nɒlədʒi
AM hɪm'nɑlədʒi
Hynes
BR haɪnz
AM haɪnz
hyoid
BR 'haɪɔɪd
AM 'haɪ,ɔɪd
hyoscine
BR 'haɪəsiːn
AM 'haɪə,sin
hyoscyamine
BR ,haɪə(ʊ)'saɪəmiːn, ,haɪə(ʊ)'saɪəmɪn
AM ,haɪə'saɪəmən, ,haɪə'saɪə,min
hypaesthesia
BR ,haɪpɪs'θiːzɪə(r), ,haɪpɪs'θiːʒə(r)
AM ,haɪpəs'θiʒ(i)ə, ,haɪpəs'θiʒ(i)ə, ,haɪpəs'θiziə, ,haɪpəs'θiziə
hypaesthetic
BR ,haɪpɪs'θɛtɪk

AM ,haɪpəs'θɛdɪk, ,haɪpəs'θɛdɪk
hypaethral
BR haɪ'piːθr(ə)l
AM haɪ'piθrəl, hə'piθrəl
hypallage
BR haɪ'pælədʒ|i, -ɪz
AM haɪ'pælədʒi, hɪ'pælədʒi, -z
Hypatia
BR haɪ'peɪʃ(ɪ)ə(r)
AM ,haɪ'peɪʃə, ,haɪ'peɪdiə
hype
BR haɪp, -s, -ɪŋ, -t
AM haɪp, -s, -ɪŋ, -t
hyperactive
BR ,haɪpər'aktɪv
AM 'haɪpər'æktɪv
hyperactivity
BR ,haɪpərak'tɪvɪti
AM ,haɪpər,æk'tɪvɪdi
hyperaemia
BR ,haɪpə'riːmɪə(r)
AM ,haɪpə'rimiə
hyperaemic
BR ,haɪpə'riːmɪk
AM ,haɪpə'rimɪk
hyperaesthesia
BR ,haɪp(ə)rɪs'θiːzɪə(r), ,haɪp(ə)rɪs'θiːʒə(r)
AM ,haɪpərəs'θiʒ(i)ə, ,haɪpərəs'θiziə
hyperaesthetic
BR ,haɪp(ə)rɪs'θɛtɪk
AM ,haɪpərəs'θɛdɪk
hyperbaric
BR ,haɪpə'barɪk
AM ,haɪpər'bɛrɪk
hyperbaton
BR haɪ'pə:bət(ə)n, haɪ'pə:bətɒn
AM haɪ'pərbə,tan
hyperbola
BR haɪ'pə:bələ(r), haɪ'pə:b|ə(r), -z
AM haɪ'pərbələ, -z
hyperbole
BR haɪ'pə:bəl|i, haɪ'pə:b|li, -ɪz
AM haɪ'pərbəli, -z
hyperbolic
BR ,haɪpə'bɒlɪk
AM ,haɪpər'balɪk
hyperbolical
BR ,haɪpə'bɒlɪkl
AM 'haɪpər'baləkəl
hyperbolically
BR ,haɪpə'bɒlɪkli
AM ,haɪpər'balək(ə)li
hyperbolism
BR haɪ'pə:bəlɪz(ə)m, haɪ'pə:b|ɪz(ə)m
AM haɪ'pərbə,lɪzəm
hyperbolist
BR haɪ'pə:bəlɪst, haɪ'pə:b|ɪst, -s

AM ,haɪpəs'θɛdɪk, ,haɪpəs'θɛdɪk
hyperboloid
BR haɪ'pə:bəlɔɪd, haɪ'pə:b|ɔɪd, -z
AM haɪ'pərbə,lɔɪd, -z
hyperboloidal
BR haɪ,pə:bə'lɔɪdl
AM haɪ'pərbə,lɔɪdəl
Hyperborean
BR ,haɪpə'bɔːrɪən, ,haɪpəbə'riːən, -z
AM ,haɪpə(r)'bɔriən, 'haɪpərbə'riən, -z
hypercatalectic
BR ,haɪpə,katə'lɛktɪk, ,haɪpə,kat|'ɛktɪk
AM 'haɪpər,kædə'lɛktɪk
hyperconscious
BR ,haɪpə'kɒnʃəs
AM 'haɪpər'kɑnʃəs
hypercorrect
BR ,haɪpəkə'rɛkt
AM ,haɪpərkə'rɛk(t)
hypercorrection
BR ,haɪpəkə'rɛkʃn
AM ,haɪpərkə'rɛkʃən
hypercritical
BR ,haɪpə'krɪtɪkl
AM 'haɪpər'krɪdəkəl
hypercritically
BR ,haɪpə'krɪtɪkli
AM 'haɪpər'krɪdək(ə)li
hypercriticism
BR ,haɪpə'krɪtɪsɪz(ə)m
AM 'haɪpər'krɪdə,sɪzəm
hypercube
BR 'haɪpəkjuːb, -z
AM 'haɪpər,kjub, -z
hyperdulia
BR ,haɪpədjuː'lʌɪə(r), ,haɪpədʒuː'lʌɪə(r)
AM 'haɪpər,d(j)u'laɪə
hyperemia
BR ,haɪpə'riːmɪə(r)
AM ,haɪpə'rimiə
hyperemic
BR ,haɪpə'riːmɪk
AM ,haɪpə'rimɪk
hyperesthesia
BR ,haɪp(ə)rɪs'θiːzɪə(r), ,haɪp(ə)rɪs'θiːʒə(r)
AM ,haɪpərəs'θiʒ(i)ə, ,haɪpərəs'θiziə
hyperesthetic
BR ,haɪp(ə)rɪs'θɛtɪk
AM ,haɪpərəs'θɛdɪk
hyperfocal
BR ,haɪpə'fəʊkl
AM ,haɪpər'foʊkəl
hypergamy
BR haɪ'pə:gəmi
AM haɪ'pərgəmi
hyperglycaemia
BR ,haɪpəglʌɪ'siːmɪə(r)
AM ,haɪpərglaɪ'simiə
hyperglycaemic
BR ,haɪpəglʌɪ'siːmɪk

AM ˈhaɪpərglaɪˈsimɪk
hyperglycemia
BR ˌhaɪpəglaɪˈsiːmɪə(r)
AM ˌhaɪpərglaɪˈsimiə
hyperglycemic
BR ˌhaɪpəglaɪˈsiːmɪk
AM ˈhaɪpərglaɪˈsimɪk
hypergolic
BR ˌhaɪpəˈgɒlɪk
AM ˌhaɪpərˈgɑlɪk
hypericum
BR hʌɪˈpɛrɪkəm, -z
AM haɪˈpɛrəkəm, -z
Hyperion
BR hʌɪˈpɪərɪən
AM haɪˈpɪriən
hyperkinetic
BR ˌhʌɪpəkʌɪˈnɛtɪk,
ˌhʌɪpəkɪˈnɛtɪk
AM ˌhaɪpərkəˈnɛdɪk
hyperlipidaemia
BR ˌhʌɪpəˌlɪpɪˈdiːmɪə(r)
AM ˈhaɪpəˌlɪpəˈdimiə
hyperlipidaemic
BR ˌhʌɪpəˌlɪpɪˈdiːmɪk
AM ˈhaɪpəˌlɪpəˈdimɪk
hyperlipidemia
BR ˌhʌɪpəˌlɪpɪˈdiːmɪə(r)
AM ˈhaɪpəˌlɪpəˈdimiə
hyperlipidemic
BR ˌhʌɪpəˌlɪpɪˈdiːmɪk
AM ˈhaɪpəˌlɪpəˈdimɪk
hypermarket
BR ˈhʌɪpəˌmɑːkɪt, -s
AM ˈhaɪpərˌmarkət, -s
hypermetric
BR ˌhʌɪpəˈmɛtrɪk
AM ˈhaɪpərˈmɛtrɪk
hypermetrical
BR ˌhʌɪpəˈmɛtrɪkl
AM ˈhaɪpərˈmɛtrəkəl
hypermetropia
BR ˌhʌɪpəmɪˈtrəʊpɪə(r)
AM ˌhaɪpərməˈtroʊpiə
hypermetropic
BR ˌhʌɪpəmɪˈtrɒpɪk,
ˌhʌɪpəmɪˈtrəʊpɪk
AM ˌhaɪpərməˈtrɑpɪk
hypernym
BR ˈhʌɪpənɪm, -z
AM ˈhaɪpərˌnɪm, -z
hyperon
BR ˈhʌɪpərɒn, -z
AM ˈhaɪpəˌrɑn, -z
hyperonic
BR ˌhʌɪpəˈrɒnɪk
AM ˈhaɪpəˈrɑnɪk
hyperopia
BR ˌhʌɪpəˈrəʊpɪə(r)
AM ˈhaɪpəˈroʊpiə
hyperopic
BR ˌhʌɪpəˈrɒpɪk
AM ˈhaɪpəˈrɑpɪk
hyperphysical
BR ˌhʌɪpəˈfɪzɪkl
AM ˈhaɪpərˈfɪzɪkəl

hyperphysically
BR ˌhʌɪpəˈfɪzɪkli
AM ˈhaɪpərˈfɪzɪk(ə)li
hyperplasia
BR ˌhʌɪpəˈpleɪzɪə(r),
ˌhʌɪpəˈpleɪʒə(r)
AM ˈhaɪpərˈpleɪʒ(i)ə,
ˈhaɪpərˈpleɪziə
hypersensitive
BR ˌhʌɪpəˈsɛnsɪtɪv
AM ˈhaɪpərˈsɛnsədɪv
**hypersensitive-
ness**
BR ˌhʌɪpəˈsɛnsɪtɪvnɪs
AM ˈhaɪpərˈsɛnsədɪvnɪs
hypersensitivity
BR ˌhʌɪpəˌsɛnsɪˈtɪvɪti
AM ˈhaɪpərˌsɛnsəˈtɪvɪdi
hypersonic
BR ˌhʌɪpəˈsɒnɪk
AM ˈhaɪpərˈsɑnɪk
hypersonically
BR ˌhʌɪpəˈsɒnɪkli
AM ˈhaɪpərˈsɑnək(ə)li
hyperspace
BR ˈhʌɪpəspeɪs
AM ˈhaɪpərˌspeɪs
hypersthene
BR ˈhʌɪpəsθiːn
AM ˈhaɪpərˌsθin
hypertension
BR ˌhʌɪpəˈtɛnʃn
AM ˈhaɪpərˈtɛnʃən
hypertensive
BR ˌhʌɪpəˈtɛnsɪv
AM ˈhaɪpərˈtɛnsɪv
hypertext
BR ˈhʌɪpətɛkst, -s
AM ˈhaɪpərˌtɛkst, -s
hyperthermia
BR ˌhʌɪpəˈθəːmɪə(r)
AM ˈhaɪpərˈθɛrmiə
hyperthermic
BR ˌhʌɪpəˈθəːmɪk
AM ˈhaɪpərˈθɛrmɪk
hyperthyroid
BR ˌhʌɪpəˈθʌɪrɔɪd
AM ˈhaɪpərˈθaɪˌrɔɪd
hyperthyroidic
BR ˌhʌɪpəθʌɪˈrɔɪdɪk
AM ˈhaɪpərˈθaɪˈrɔɪdɪk
hyperthyroidism
BR ˌhʌɪpəˈθʌɪrɔɪdɪz(ə)m
AM ˈhaɪpərˈθaɪˌrɔɪˌdɪz-
əm
hypertonia
BR ˌhʌɪpəˈtəʊnɪə(r)
AM ˈhaɪpərˈtoʊniə
hypertonic
BR ˌhʌɪpəˈtɒnɪk
AM ˈhaɪpərˈtɑnɪk
hypertonicity
BR ˌhʌɪpətə(ʊ)ˈnɪsɪti
AM ˈhaɪpərtəˈnɪsɪdi
hypertrophic
BR ˌhʌɪpəˈtrɒfɪk,
ˌhʌɪpəˈtrəʊfɪk

AM ˌhaɪpərˈtrɑfɪk
hypertrophied
BR hʌɪˈpəːtrəfɪd
AM haɪˈpərtrəfɪd
hypertrophy
BR hʌɪˈpəːtrəfi
AM haɪˈpərtrəfi
hyperventilate
BR ˌhʌɪpəˈvɛntɪleɪt, -s,
-ɪŋ, -ɪd
AM ˈhaɪpərˈvɛn(t)əˌleɪlt,
-ts, -dɪŋ, -dɪd
hyperventilation
BR ˌhʌɪpəˌvɛntɪˈleɪʃn
AM ˈhaɪpərˌvɛn(t)əˈleɪ-
ʃən
hypesthesia
BR ˌhʌɪpɪsˈθiːzɪə(r),
ˌhʌɪpɪsˈθiːʒə(r)
AM ˈhɪpəsˈθiʒ(i)ə,
ˈhaɪpəsˈθiʒ(i)ə,
ˈhɪpəsˈθiziə,
ˈhaɪpəsˈθiziə
hypesthetic
BR ˌhʌɪpɪsˈθɛtɪk
AM ˈhɪpəsˈθɛdɪk,
ˈhaɪpəsˈθɛdɪk
hypethral
BR hʌɪˈpiːθr(ə)l
AM haɪˈpiθrəl,
həˈpiθrəl
hypha
BR ˈhʌɪfə(r)
AM ˈhaɪfə
hyphae
BR ˈhʌɪfiː
AM ˈhaɪfi, ˈhaɪˌfaɪ
hyphal
BR ˈhʌɪfl
AM ˈhaɪfəl
hyphen
BR ˈhʌɪfn, -z
AM ˈhaɪfən, -z
hyphenate
BR ˈhʌɪfəneɪt,
ˈhʌɪfneɪt, -s, -ɪŋ, -ɪd
AM ˈhaɪfəˌneɪlt, -ts,
-dɪŋ, -dɪd
hyphenation
BR ˌhʌɪfəˈneɪʃn
AM ˌhaɪfəˈneɪʃən
hypnogenesis
BR ˌhɪpnə(ʊ)ˈdʒɛnɪsɪs
AM ˌhɪpnoʊˈdʒɛnəsəs
hypnologist
BR hɪpˈnɒlədʒɪst, -s
AM hɪpˈnɑlədʒəst, -s
hypnology
BR hɪpˈnɒlədʒi
AM hɪpˈnɑlədʒi
hypnopaedia
BR ˌhɪpnə(ʊ)ˈpiːdɪə(r)
AM ˈhɪpnoʊˈpidiə
hypnopedia
BR ˌhɪpnə(ʊ)ˈpiːdɪə(r)
AM ˈhɪpnoʊˈpidiə
Hypnos
BR ˈhɪpnɒs

AM ˈhɪpnɒs, ˈhɪpˌnɑs
hypnoses
BR hɪpˈnəʊsiːz
AM hɪpˈnoʊsiz
hypnosis
BR hɪpˈnəʊsɪs
AM hɪpˈnoʊsəs
hypnotherapist
BR ˌhɪpnə(ʊ)ˈθɛrəpɪst,
-s
AM ˌhɪpnoʊˈθɛrəpəst,
-s
hypnotherapy
BR ˌhɪpnə(ʊ)ˈθɛrəpi
AM ˌhɪpnoʊˈθɛrəpi
hypnotic
BR hɪpˈnɒtɪk
AM hɪpˈnɑdɪk
hypnotically
BR hɪpˈnɒtɪkli
AM hɪpˈnɑdək(ə)li
hypnotisable
BR ˈhɪpnətʌɪzəbl
AM ˈhɪpnəˌtaɪzəbəl
hypnotise
BR ˈhɪpnətʌɪz, -ɪz, -ɪŋ,
-d
AM ˈhɪpnəˌtaɪz, -ɪz, -ɪŋ,
-d
hypnotism
BR ˈhɪpnətɪz(ə)m
AM ˈhɪpnəˌtɪzəm
hypnotist
BR ˈhɪpnətɪst, -s
AM ˈhɪpnədəst, -s
hypnotizable
BR ˈhɪpnətʌɪzəbl
AM ˈhɪpnəˌtaɪzəbəl
hypnotize
BR ˈhɪpnətʌɪz, -ɪz, -ɪŋ,
-d
AM ˈhɪpnəˌtaɪz, -ɪz, -ɪŋ,
-d
hypo
BR ˈhʌɪpəʊ
AM ˈhaɪpoʊ
hypoaesthesia
BR ˌhʌɪpəʊɪsˈθiːzɪə(r),
ˌhʌɪpəʊɪsˈθiːʒə(r)
AM ˌhaɪp(oʊ)əˈsθiʒ(i)ə,
ˌhaɪp(oʊ)əˈsθiziə
hypo-allergenic
BR ˌhʌɪpəʊˌaləˈdʒɛnɪk
AM ˈhaɪpoʊˌælərˈdʒɛnɪk
hypoblast
BR ˈhʌɪpə(ʊ)blɑːst,
ˈhʌɪpə(ʊ)blast
AM ˈhaɪpəˌblæst
hypocaust
BR ˈhʌɪpə(ʊ)kɔːst, -s
AM ˈhaɪpəˌkɔst,
ˈhaɪpəˌkast, -s
hypochlorite
BR ˌhʌɪpə(ʊ)ˈklɔːrʌɪt,
-s
AM ˌhaɪpəˈklɔˌraɪt, -s

hypochlorous acid
BR ˌhaɪpəˈklɔːrəs ˈasɪd
AM ˌhaɪpəˌklɔrəs ˈæsəd

hypochondria
BR ˌhaɪpəˈkɒndrɪə(r)
AM ˌhaɪpəˈkɑndrɪə

hypochondriac
BR ˌhaɪpəˈkɒndrɪak, -s
AM ˌhaɪpəˈkɑndriˌæk, -s

hypocoristic
BR ˌhaɪpə(ʊ)kəˈrɪstɪk
AM ˌhaɪpəkəˈrɪstɪk

hypocotyl
BR ˈhʌɪpə(ʊ)ˌkɒtl, -z
AM ˈhaɪpəˌkɑdl,
ˌhaɪpəˈkɑdl, -z

hypocrisy
BR hɪˈpɒkrəsǀi, -ɪz
AM həˈpɑkrəsi, -z

hypocrite
BR ˈhɪpəkrɪt, -s
AM ˈhɪpəˌkrɪt, -s

hypocritical
BR ˌhɪpəˈkrɪtɪkl
AM ˌhɪpəˈkrɪdəkəl

hypocritically
BR ˌhɪpəˈkrɪtɪkli
AM ˌhɪpəˈkrɪdək(ə)li

hypocycloid
BR ˌhaɪpə(ʊ)ˈsʌɪklɔɪd, -z
AM ˌhaɪpəˈsaɪˌklɔɪd, -z

hypocycloidal
BR ˌhaɪpə(ʊ)sʌɪˈklɔɪdl
AM ˌhaɪpəˌsaɪˈklɔɪdəl

hypoderma
BR ˌhʌɪpəˈdəːmə(r)
AM ˌhaɪpəˈdərmə

hypodermal
BR ˌhʌɪpəˈdəːml
AM ˌhaɪpəˈdərməl

hypodermata
BR ˌhʌɪpə(ʊ)ˈdəːmətə(r)
AM ˌhaɪpəˈdərmədə

hypodermic
BR ˌhʌɪpəˈdəːmɪk, -s
AM ˌhaɪpəˈdərmɪk, -s

hypodermically
BR ˌhʌɪpəˈdəːmɪkli
AM ˌhaɪpəˈdərmək(ə)li

hypodermis
BR ˌhʌɪpə(ʊ)ˈdəːmɪs
AM ˌhaɪpəˈdərməs

hypoesthesia
BR ˌhʌɪpəʊɪsˈθiːzɪə(r),
ˌhʌɪpəʊɪsˈθiːʒə(r)
AM ˌhaɪp(oʊ)əˈsθiːʒ(i)ə,
ˌhaɪp(oʊ)əˈsθiːʒiə

hypogastria
BR ˌhʌɪpə(ʊ)ˈgastrɪə(r)
AM ˌhaɪpəˈgæstriə

hypogastric
BR ˌhʌɪpə(ʊ)ˈgastrɪk
AM ˌhaɪpəˈgæstrɪk

hypogastrium
BR ˌhʌɪpə(ʊ)ˈgastrɪəm
AM ˌhaɪpəˈgæstriəm

hypogea
BR ˌhʌɪpə(ʊ)ˈdʒiːə(r)
AM ˌhaɪpəˈdʒiə

hypogeal
BR ˌhʌɪpə(ʊ)ˈdʒiːəl
AM ˌhaɪpəˈdʒiəl

hypogean
BR ˌhʌɪpə(ʊ)ˈdʒiːən
AM ˌhaɪpəˈdʒiən

hypogene
BR ˈhʌɪpə(ʊ)dʒiːn
AM ˈhaɪpəˌdʒin

hypogeum
BR ˌhʌɪpə(ʊ)ˈdʒiːəm
AM ˌhaɪpəˈdʒiəm

hypoglycaemia
BR ˌhʌɪpə(ʊ)glʌɪˈsiːm-
ɪə(r)
AM ˌhaɪpoʊglaɪˈsimiə

hypoglycaemic
BR ˌhʌɪpə(ʊ)glʌɪˈsiːmɪk
AM ˌhaɪpoʊglaɪˈsimɪk

hypoglycemia
BR ˌhʌɪpə(ʊ)glʌɪˈsiːm-
ɪə(r)
AM ˌhaɪpoʊglaɪˈsimiə

hypoglycemic
BR ˌhʌɪpə(ʊ)glʌɪˈsiːmɪk
AM ˌhaɪpoʊglaɪˈsimɪk

hypoid
BR ˈhʌɪpɔɪd, -z
AM ˈhaɪˌpɔɪd, -z

hypolimnia
BR ˌhʌɪpəˈlɪmnɪə(r)
AM ˌhaɪpəˈlɪmnɪə

hypolimnion
BR ˌhʌɪpəˈlɪmnɪˌɑn,
ˌhaɪpəˈlɪmnɪən

hypomania
BR ˌhʌɪpə(ʊ)ˈmeɪnɪə(r)
AM ˌhaɪpəˈmeɪniə

hypomaniac
BR ˌhʌɪpə(ʊ)ˈmeɪnɪak
AM ˌhaɪpəˈmeɪniˌæk,
-s

hypomanic
BR ˌhʌɪpə(ʊ)ˈmanɪk, -s
AM ˌhaɪpəˈmænɪk, -s

hyponastic
BR ˌhʌɪpəˈnastɪk
AM ˌhaɪpəˈnæstɪk

hyponasty
BR ˈhʌɪpə(ʊ)ˌnasti
AM ˈhaɪpəˌnasti

hyponym
BR ˈhʌɪpənɪm, -z
AM ˈhaɪpəˌnɪm, -z

hyponymous
BR hʌɪˈpɒnɪməs
AM haɪˈpɑnəməs,
həˈpɑnəməs

hyponymy
BR hʌɪˈpɒnɪmi

hypophyseal
BR ˌhʌɪpə(ʊ)ˈfɪzɪəl
AM ˌhaɪpəˈfɪzɪəl

hypophysial
BR ˌhʌɪpə(ʊ)ˈfɪzɪəl
AM ˌhaɪpəˈfɪzɪəl

hypophysis
BR hʌɪˈpɒfɪsɪs, -ɪz
AM ˌhaɪˈpɑfəsəs, -əz

hypostases
BR hʌɪˈpɒstəsɪs
AM haɪˈpɑstəsiz

hypostasis
BR hʌɪˈpɒstəsɪs
AM haɪˈpɑstəsəs

hypostasise
BR hʌɪˈpɒstəsʌɪz, -ɪz,
-ɪŋ, -d
AM haɪˈpɑstəˌsaɪz, -ɪz,
-ɪŋ, -d

hypostasize
BR hʌɪˈpɒstəsʌɪz, -ɪz,
-ɪŋ, -d
AM haɪˈpɑstəˌsaɪz, -ɪz,
-ɪŋ, -d

hypostatic
BR ˌhʌɪpə(ʊ)ˈstatɪk
AM ˌhaɪpəˈstædɪk

hypostatical
BR ˌhʌɪpə(ʊ)ˈstatɪkl
AM ˌhaɪpəˈstædəkəl

hypostatically
BR ˌhʌɪpə(ʊ)ˈstatɪkli
AM ˌhaɪpəˈstædək(ə)li

hypostatise
BR hʌɪˈpɒstətʌɪz, -ɪz,
-ɪŋ, -d
AM haɪˈpɑstəˌtaɪz, -ɪz,
-ɪŋ, -d

hypostatize
BR hʌɪˈpɒstətʌɪz, -ɪz,
-ɪŋ, -d
AM haɪˈpɑstəˌtaɪz, -ɪz,
-ɪŋ, -d

hypostyle
BR ˈhʌɪpəstʌɪl
AM ˈhaɪpəˌstaɪl

hyposulfite
BR ˌhʌɪpə(ʊ)ˈsʌlfaɪt, -s
AM ˈhaɪpəˈsəlˌfaɪt, -s

hyposulphite
BR ˌhʌɪpə(ʊ)ˈsʌlfaɪt, -s
AM ˈhaɪpəˈsəlˌfaɪt, -s

hypotactic
BR ˌhʌɪpə(ʊ)ˈtaktɪk
AM ˌhaɪpoʊˈtæktɪk

hypotaxes
BR ˌhʌɪpə(ʊ)ˈtaksiːz
AM ˌhaɪpəˈtæksiz

hypotaxis
BR ˌhʌɪpə(ʊ)ˈtaksɪs
AM ˌhaɪpəˈtæksəs

hypotension
BR ˌhʌɪpə(ʊ)ˈtɛnʃn
AM ˈhaɪpəˈtɛn(t)ʃən

hypotensive
BR ˌhʌɪpə(ʊ)ˈtɛnsɪv
AM ˌhaɪpouˈtɛnsɪv

hypotenuse
BR hʌɪˈpɒtɪnjuːs,
hʌɪˈpɒtɪnjuːz, -ɪz
AM haɪˈpatnˌ(j)us, -əz

hypothalami
BR ˌhʌɪpə(ʊ)ˈθaləmʌɪ,
ˌhʌɪpə(ʊ)ˈθaləmiː
AM ˈhaɪpəˈθælˌmaɪ

hypothalamic
BR ˌhʌɪpə(ʊ)ˈθaləmɪk
AM ˈhaɪpəˈθælmɪk

hypothalamus
BR ˌhʌɪpə(ʊ)ˈθaləməs
AM ˈhaɪpəˈθælməs

hypothec
BR hʌɪˈpɒθɪk
AM həˈpaθək,
haɪˈpaθək

hypothecary
BR hʌɪˈpɒθɪk(ə)rǀi, -ɪz
AM həˈpaθəˌkɛri,
haɪˈpaθəˌkɛri, -z

hypothecate
BR hʌɪˈpɒθɪkeɪt, -s, -ɪŋ,
-ɪd
AM həˈpaθəˌkeɪǀt,
haɪˈpaθəˌkeɪǀt, -ts,
-dɪŋ, -dɪd

hypothecation
BR hʌɪˌpɒθɪˈkeɪʃn
AM həˌpaθəˈkeɪʃən,
haɪˌpaθəˈkeɪʃən

hypothecator
BR hʌɪˈpɒθɪkeɪtə(r), -z
AM həˈpaθəˌkeɪdər,
haɪˈpaθəˌkeɪdər, -z

hypothermia
BR ˌhʌɪpə(ʊ)ˈθəːmɪə(r)
AM ˌhaɪpəˈθɜrmiə

hypotheses
BR hʌɪˈpɒθɪsiːz
AM haɪˈpaθəˌsiz

hypothesis
BR hʌɪˈpɒθɪsɪs
AM haɪˈpaθəsəs

hypothesise
BR hʌɪˈpɒθɪsʌɪz, -ɪz,
-ɪŋ, -d
AM haɪˈpaθəˌsaɪz, -ɪz,
-ɪŋ, -d

hypothesiser
BR hʌɪˈpɒθɪsʌɪzə(r), -z
AM haɪˈpaθəˌsaɪzər, -z

hypothesist
BR hʌɪˈpɒθɪsɪst, -s
AM haɪˈpaθəsəst, -s

hypothesize
BR hʌɪˈpɒθɪsʌɪz, -ɪz,
-ɪŋ, -d
AM haɪˈpaθəˌsaɪz, -ɪz,
-ɪŋ, -d

hypothesizer
BR hʌɪˈpɒθɪsʌɪzə(r), -z
AM haɪˈpaθəˌsaɪzər, -z

hypothetical
BR ˌhaɪpəˈθetɪkl
AM ˌhaɪpəˈθedəkəl

hypothetically
BR ˌhaɪpəˈθetɪkli
AM ˌhaɪpəˈθedək(ə)li

hypothyroid
BR ˌhaɪpə(ʊ)ˈθaɪrɔɪd
AM ˌhaɪpoʊˈθaɪˌrɔɪd

hypothyroidic
BR ˌhaɪpə(ʊ)θaɪˈrɔɪdɪk
AM ˌhaɪpərˌθaɪˈrɔɪdɪk

hypothyroidism
BR ˌhaɪpə(ʊ)ˈθaɪrɔɪd-
ɪz(ə)m
AM ˌhaɪpoʊˈθaɪˌrɔɪˌd-
ɪzəm

hypoventilation
BR ˌhaɪpə(ʊ)ˌventɪˈleɪʃn
AM ˌhaɪpoʊˌven(t)əˈleɪ-
ʃən

hypoxaemia
BR ˌhaɪpɒkˈsiːmɪə(r)
AM haɪˌpakˈsimiə

hypoxemia
BR ˌhaɪpɒkˈsiːmɪə(r)
AM haɪˌpakˈsimiə

hypoxia
BR haɪˈpɒksɪə(r)
AM haɪˈpɒksɪə,
haɪˈpaksɪə

hypoxic
BR haɪˈpɒksɪk
AM haɪˈpɒksɪk,
haɪˈpaksɪk

hypsilophodont
BR ˌhɪpsɪˈlɒfədɒnt, -s
AM ˌhɪpsəˈlɑfəˌdɑnt, -s

hypsographic
BR ˌhɪpsə(ʊ)ˈgræfɪk
AM ˌhɪpsoʊˈgræfɪk

hypsographical
BR ˌhɪpsə(ʊ)ˈgrafɪkl
AM ˌhɪpsoʊˈgræfəkəl

hypsography
BR hɪpˈsɒgrəfi
AM hɪpˈsɑgrəfi

hypsometer
BR hɪpˈsɒmɪtə(r), -z
AM hɪpˈsamədər, -z

hypsometric
BR ˌhɪpsə(ʊ)ˈmetrɪk
AM ˌhɪpsoʊˈmetrɪk

hypsometry
BR hɪpˈsɒmɪtri
AM hɪpˈsamətri

hyracotherium
BR ˌhaɪrəkəˈθɪərɪəm,
-z
AM ˌhaɪrəkəˈθɜriəm,
ˌhaɪrəkəˈθɪriəm, -z

hyrax
BR ˈhaɪraks, -ɪz
AM ˈhaɪˌræks, -əz

Hyrcania
BR həːˈkeɪnɪə(r)
AM hərˈkeɪnɪə

hyson
BR ˈhaɪsn
AM ˈhaɪsən

hyssop
BR ˈhɪsəp
AM ˈhɪsəp

hysterectomise
BR ˌhɪstəˈrektəmʌɪz,
-ɪz, -ɪŋ, -d
AM ˌhɪstəˈrektəˌmaɪz,
-ɪz, -ɪŋ, -d

hysterectomize
BR ˌhɪstəˈrektəmʌɪz,
-ɪz, -ɪŋ, -d
AM ˌhɪstəˈrektəˌmaɪz,
-ɪz, -ɪŋ, -d

hysterectomy
BR ˌhɪstəˈrektəmǀi, -ɪz
AM ˌhɪstəˈrektəmi, -z

hysteresis
BR ˌhɪstəˈriːsɪs
AM ˌhɪstəˈrisɪs

hysteria
BR hɪˈstɪərɪə(r)
AM həˈstɛriə, həˈstɪriə

hysteric
BR hɪˈsterɪk, -s
AM həˈsterɪk, -s

hysterical
BR hɪˈsterɪkl
AM həˈsterəkəl

hysterically
BR hɪˈsterɪkli
AM həˈsterək(ə)li

**hysteron
proteron**
BR ˌhɪstərɒn
ˈprəʊtərɒn
AM ˈhɪstəˌran
ˈproʊdəˌran

Hythe
BR hʌɪð
AM haɪð

Hyundai®
BR ˈhʌɪəndʌɪ,
hʌɪˈʌndʌɪ
AM ˈhaɪənˌdaɪ

Hywel
BR ˈhəwəl, ˈhaʊəl
AM ˈhəwəl
WE ˈhʌwel

Ii

i
BR ʌɪ, -z
AM aɪ, -z

Iain
BR 'iːən
AM 'iən

iamb
BR 'ʌɪam(b), -z
AM 'aɪˌæm(b), -z

iambic
BR ʌɪ'ambɪk
AM aɪ'æmbɪk

iambus
BR ʌɪ'ambəs, -ɪz
AM aɪ'æmbəs, -əz

Ian
BR 'iːən
AM 'iən

Iapetus
BR ʌɪ'apɪtəs
AM aɪə'pɛdəs

Iasi
BR 'jɑːsi
AM 'jaʃi, 'jasi

IATA
BR ɪ'ɑːtə(r), ʌɪ'ɑːtə(r)
AM aɪ'ɑdə

iatrogenic
BR ʌɪˌatrə'dʒɛnɪk
AM aɪˌætrə'dʒɛnɪk

Ibadan
BR ɪ'badn
AM i'badɑn

Iban
BR ɪ'bɑːn
AM i'ban, ɪ'ban

Ibbotson
BR 'ɪbəts(ə)n
AM 'ɪbɪtsən

Ibcol
BR 'ɪbkɒl
AM 'ɪbˌkɔl, 'ɪbˌkɑl

I-beam
BR 'ʌɪbiːm, -z
AM 'aɪˌbim, -z

Iberia
BR ʌɪ'bɪərɪə(r)
AM aɪ'bɪriə
SP i'βerja

Iberian
BR ʌɪ'bɪərɪən, -z
AM aɪ'bɪriən, -z

Ibero-American
BR ʌɪˌbɪərəʊə'mɛrɪk(ə)n, -z
AM aɪˌbɪroʊə'mɛrəkən, -z

ibex
BR 'ʌɪbɛks, -ɪz
AM 'aɪˌbɛks, -əz

ibid
BR 'ɪbɪd
AM 'ɪbɪd

ibidem
BR 'ɪbɪdɛm
AM 'ɪbəˌdɛm

ibis
BR 'ʌɪb|ɪs, -ɪsɪz
AM 'aɪbɪs, -ɪz

Ibiza
BR ɪ'biːθə(r)
AM ə'biθə
SP i'βiθa, i'βisa

IBM®
BR ˌʌɪbiː'ɛm
AM ˌaɪbiː'ɛm

Ibo
BR 'iːbəʊ, -z
AM 'iˌboʊ, -z

ibogaine
BR ɪ'bəʊɡəiːn
AM ə'boʊˌɡeɪn

Ibrahim
BR 'ɪbrəhɪm,
'ɪbrəhiːm
AM 'ɪbrəˌhim

Ibrox
BR 'ʌɪbrɒks
AM 'aɪbrɑks

Ibsen
BR 'ɪbs(ə)n
AM 'ɪbsən

ibuprofen
BR ˌʌɪbjuː'prəʊf(ə)n
AM ˌaɪbjuː'proʊfən

Icarus
BR 'ɪk(ə)rəs
AM 'ɪkərəs

ICBM
BR ˌʌɪsiːbiː'ɛm, -z
AM ˌaɪˌsiˌbi'ɛm, -z

ice
BR ʌɪs, -ɪz, -ɪŋ, -t
AM aɪs, -ɪz, -ɪŋ, -t

iceberg
BR 'ʌɪsbəːɡ, -z
AM 'aɪsˌbərɡ, -z

iceblink
BR 'ʌɪsblɪŋk, -s
AM 'aɪsˌblɪŋk, -s

iceboat
BR 'ʌɪsbəʊt, -s
AM 'aɪsˌboʊt, -s

icebound
BR 'ʌɪsbaʊnd
AM 'aɪsˌbaʊnd

icebox
BR 'ʌɪsbɒks, -ɪz
AM 'aɪsˌbaks, -əz

icebreaker
BR 'ʌɪsˌbreɪkə(r), -z
AM 'aɪsˌbreɪkər, -z

ice cream
BR ˌʌɪs 'kriːm, 'ʌɪs
kriːm, -z
AM 'aɪs ˌkrim, ˌaɪs
'krim, -z

icefall
BR 'ʌɪsfɔːl, -z
AM 'aɪsˌfɔl, 'aɪsˌfɑl, -z

icehouse
BR 'ʌɪshaʊ|s, -zɪz
AM 'aɪs(h)aʊ|s, -zəz

Iceland
BR 'ʌɪslənd
AM 'aɪslənd

Icelander
BR 'ʌɪsləndə(r), -z
AM 'aɪsləndər, -z

Icelandic
BR ʌɪs'landɪk
AM aɪs'lændɪk

iceman
BR 'ʌɪsman
AM 'aɪsmən

icemen
BR 'ʌɪsmɛn
AM 'aɪsmən

Iceni
BR ʌɪ'siːnʌɪ
AM aɪ'siˌnaɪ

Ichabod
BR 'ɪkəbɒd, 'ɪxəbɒd
AM 'ɪkəˌbad

I Ching
BR 'ʌɪ 'tʃɪŋ
AM 'i 'tʃɪŋ

ichneumon
BR ɪk'njuːmən
AM ɪk'n(j)umən

ichnography
BR ɪk'nɒɡrəfi
AM ɪk'nɑɡrəfi

ichor
BR 'ʌɪkɔː(r)
AM 'aɪˌkɔ(ə)r

ichorous
BR 'ʌɪk(ə)rəs
AM 'aɪkərəs

ichthyographer
BR ˌɪkθɪ'ɒɡrəfə(r), -z
AM ˌɪkθi'ɑɡrəfər, -z

ichthyography
BR ˌɪkθɪ'ɒɡrəfi
AM ˌɪkθi'ɑɡrəfi

ichthyoid
BR 'ɪkθɪɔɪd, -z
AM 'ɪkθiˌɔɪd, -z

ichthyolatry
BR ˌɪkθɪ'ɒlətri
AM ˌɪkθiə'ɑlətri

ichthyolite
BR 'ɪkθɪəlʌɪt, -s
AM 'ɪkθiəˌlaɪt, -s

ichthyological
BR ˌɪkθɪə'lɒdʒɪkl
AM ˌɪkθiə'lɑdʒəkəl

ichthyologist
BR ˌɪkθɪ'ɒlədʒɪst, -s
AM ˌɪkθi'ɑlədʒəst, -s

ichthyology
BR ˌɪkθɪ'ɒlədʒi
AM ˌɪkθi'ɑlədʒi

ichthyophagous
BR ˌɪkθɪ'ɒfəɡəs
AM ˌɪkθi'ɑfəɡəs

ichthyophagy
BR ˌɪkθɪ'ɒfədʒi
AM ˌɪkθi'ɑfədʒi

ichthyosaur
BR 'ɪkθɪəsɔː(r), -z
AM 'ɪkθiəˌs(ə)ɔ)r, -z

ichthyosauri
BR ˌɪkθɪə'sɔːrʌɪ
AM ˌɪkθiə'sɔˌraɪ

ichthyosaurus
BR ˌɪkθɪə'sɔːrəs, -ɪz
AM ˌɪkθiə'sɔrəs, -əz

ichthyosis
BR ˌɪkθɪ'əʊsɪs
AM ˌɪkθi'oʊsəs

ichthyotic
BR ˌɪkθɪ'ɒtɪk
AM ˌɪkθi'ɑdɪk

icicle
BR 'ʌɪsɪkl, -z
AM 'aɪˌsɪkəl, 'aɪskəl, -z

icily
BR 'ʌɪsɪli
AM 'aɪsɪli

iciness
BR 'ʌɪsɪnɪs
AM 'aɪsɪnɪs

icing
BR 'ʌɪsɪŋ
AM 'aɪsɪŋ

Icknield Way
BR ˌɪkniːld 'weɪ
AM ˌɪknild 'weɪ

icky
BR 'ɪki
AM 'ɪki

icon
BR 'ʌɪkɒn, -z
AM 'aɪˌkan, -z

iconic
BR ʌɪ'kɒnɪk
AM aɪ'kanɪk

iconicity
BR ˌʌɪkə'nɪsɪti
AM ˌaɪkə'nɪsɪdi

iconium
BR ʌɪ'kəʊnɪəm
AM aɪ'koʊniəm

iconoclasm
BR ʌɪ'kɒnəklaz(ə)m
AM aɪ'kanəˌklæzəm

iconoclast
BR ʌɪ'kɒnəklast,
ʌɪ'kɒnəklɑːst, -s
AM aɪ'kanəˌklæst, -s

iconoclastic
BR ʌɪˌkɒnə'klastɪk,
ˌʌɪkɒnə'klastɪk
AM aɪˌkanə'klæstɪk

iconoclastically
BR ʌɪˌkɒnə'klastɪkli,
ˌʌɪkɒnə'klastɪkli
AM aɪˌkanə'klæstək(ə)li

iconographer
BR ˌaɪkəˈnɒɡrəfə(r), -z
AM ˌaɪkəˈnɑɡrəfər, -z

iconographic
BR ˌaɪkənəˈɡræfɪk,
ˌaɪkn̩əˈɡrafɪk
AM ˌaɪkənəˈɡræfɪk

iconographical
BR ˌaɪkənəˈɡrafɪkl,
ˌaɪkn̩əˈɡrafɪkl
AM ˌaɪkənəˈɡræfəkəl

iconographically
BR ˌaɪkənəˈɡrafɪkli,
ˌaɪkn̩əˈɡrafɪkli
AM ˌaɪkənəˈɡræfək(ə)li

iconography
BR ˌaɪkəˈnɒɡrəfi
AM ˌaɪkəˈnɑɡrəfi

iconolater
BR ˌaɪkəˈnɒlətə(r), -z
AM ˌaɪkəˈnɑlədər, -z

iconolatry
BR ˌaɪkəˈnɒlətri
AM ˌaɪkəˈnɑlətri

iconology
BR ˌaɪkəˈnɒlədʒi
AM ˌaɪkəˈnɑlədʒi

iconometer
BR ˌaɪkəˈnɒmɪtə(r), -z
AM ˌaɪkəˈnɑmədər, -z

iconometry
BR ˌaɪkəˈnɒmɪtri
AM ˌaɪkəˈnɑmətri

iconostases
BR ˌaɪkəˈnɒstəsiːz
AM ˌaɪkəˈnɑstəsiz

iconostasis
BR ˌaɪkəˈnɒstəsɪs
AM ˌaɪkəˈnɑstəsəs

icosahedral
BR ˌaɪkɒsəˈhiːdr(ə)l,
ˌaɪˌkɒsəˈhiːdr(ə)l
AM aɪˌkoʊsəˈhidrəl

icosahedron
BR ˌaɪkɒsəˈhiːdr(ə)n,
ˌaɪˌkɒsəˈhiːdr(ə)n, -z
AM aɪˌkoʊsəˈhidrən, -z

icosidodecahedra
BR ˌaɪkɒsɪˌdəʊdɛkə-
ˈhiːdrə(r)
AM aɪˌkoʊsəˌdoʊˌdɛkə-
ˈhidrə

icosidodecahedron
BR ˌaɪkɒsɪˌdəʊdɛkə-
ˈhiːdr(ə)n
AM aɪˌkoʊsəˌdoʊˌdɛkə-
ˈhidrən

ictal
BR ˈɪktl
AM ˈɪktl

icteric
BR ɪkˈtɛrɪk
AM ɪkˈtɛrɪk

icterus
BR ˈɪkt(ə)rəs
AM ˈɪktərəs

ictus
BR ˈɪktəs, -ɪz

AM ˈɪktəs, -əz

icy
BR ˈaɪs|i, -iə(r), -ɪɪst
AM ˈaɪsi, -ər, -ɪst

ID
BR ˌaɪ ˈdiː
AM ˌaɪ ˈdi

I'd
BR ʌɪd
AM aɪd

id
BR ɪd
AM ɪd

Ida
BR ˈʌɪdə(r)
AM ˈaɪdə

Idaho
BR ˈʌɪdəhəʊ
AM ˈaɪdə,hoʊ

Idahoan
BR ˈʌɪdəhəʊən, -z
AM ˈaɪdə,hoʊən, -z

ide
BR ʌɪd, -z
AM aɪd, -z

idea
BR ʌɪˈdɪə(r), -z, -d
AM aɪˈdiə, -z, -d

ideal
BR ʌɪˈdɪəl, ʌɪˈdiː(ə)l, -z
AM aɪˈdi(ə)l, -z

idealess
BR ʌɪˈdɪələs
AM aɪˈdiələs

idealisation
BR ʌɪˌdɪəlʌɪˈzeɪʃn,
ʌɪˌdiːəlʌɪˈzeɪʃn,
ˌʌɪdɪəlʌɪˈzeɪʃn
AM aɪˌdi(ə)ləˈzeɪʃən,
aɪˌdi(ə),laɪˈzeɪʃən

idealise
BR ʌɪˈdɪəlʌɪz,
ʌɪˈdiːəlʌɪz, -ɪz, -ɪŋ, -d
AM aɪˈdi(ə),laɪz, -ɪz, -ɪŋ,
-d

idealiser
BR ʌɪˈdɪəlʌɪzə(r),
ʌɪˈdiːəlʌɪzə(r), -z
AM aɪˈdi(ə),laɪzər, -z

idealism
BR ʌɪˈdɪəlɪz(ə)m,
ʌɪˈdiːəlɪz(ə)m
AM ˌʌɪˈdi(ə),lɪzəm

idealist
BR ʌɪˈdɪəlɪst,
ʌɪˈdiːəlɪst, -s
AM aɪˈdi(ə)ləst, -s

idealistic
BR ʌɪˌdɪəˈlɪstɪk,
ʌɪˌdiːəˈlɪstɪk,
ˌʌɪdɪəˈlɪstɪk
AM ˌʌɪˈdi(ə)ˈlɪstɪk

idealistically
BR ʌɪˌdɪəˈlɪstɪkli,
ʌɪˌdiːəˈlɪstɪkli,
ˌʌɪdɪə(ə)ˈlɪstɪkli
AM ˌʌɪˈdi(ə)ˈlɪstək(ə)li

ideality
BR ˌʌɪdɪˈalɪt|i, -ɪz
AM ˌaɪdiˈælədi, -z

idealization
BR ʌɪˌdɪəlʌɪˈzeɪʃn,
ʌɪˌdiːəlʌɪˈzeɪʃn,
ˌʌɪdɪəlʌɪˈzeɪʃn
AM aɪˌdi(ə)ləˈzeɪʃən,
aɪˌdi(ə),laɪˈzeɪʃən

idealize
BR ʌɪˈdɪəlʌɪz,
ʌɪˈdiːəlʌɪz, -ɪz, -ɪŋ, -d
AM aɪˈdi(ə),laɪz, -ɪz, -ɪŋ,
-d

idealizer
BR ʌɪˈdɪəlʌɪzə(r),
ʌɪˈdiːəlʌɪzə(r), -z
AM aɪˈdi(ə),laɪzər, -z

ideally
BR ʌɪˈdɪəl(l)i,
ʌɪˈdiːəl(l)i
AM aɪˈdi(ə)li

ideate
BR ˈʌɪdɪeɪt, -s, -ɪŋ, -ɪd
AM ˈaɪdiˌeɪ|t, -ts, -dɪŋ,
-dɪd

ideation
BR ˌʌɪdɪˈeɪʃn, -z
AM ˌaɪdiˈeɪʃən, -z

ideational
BR ˌʌɪdɪˈeɪʃn̩,
ˌʌɪdɪˈeɪʃən(ə)l
AM ˌaɪdiˈeɪʃ(ə)nəl

ideationally
BR ˌʌɪdɪˈeɪʃn̩əli,
ˌʌɪdɪˈeɪʃn̩li,
ˌʌɪdɪˈeɪʃ(ə)nəli
AM ˌaɪdiˈeɪʃ(ə)nəli

idée fixe
BR ˌiːdeɪ ˈfiːks
AM ˌiˌdeɪ ˈfiks

idée reçue
BR ˌiːdeɪ rəˈsjuː, -z
AM ˌiˌdeɪ rəˈsu, -z

idées fixes
BR ˌiːdeɪ ˈfiːks
AM ˌiˌdeɪ ˈfiks

idem
BR ˈɪdɛm, ˈʌɪdɛm
AM ˈaɪˌdɛm, ˈiˌdɛm

identic
BR ʌɪˈdɛntɪk
AM aɪˈdɛn(t)ɪk,
əˈdɛn(t)ɪk

identical
BR ʌɪˈdɛntɪkl
AM aɪˈdɛn(t)əkəl,
əˈdɛn(t)əkəl

identically
BR ʌɪˈdɛntɪkli
AM aɪˈdɛn(t)ək(ə)li,
əˈdɛn(t)ək(ə)li

identicalness
BR ʌɪˈdɛntɪklnəs
AM aɪˈdɛn(t)əkəlnəs,
əˈdɛn(t)əkəlnəs

identifiable
BR ʌɪˈdɛntɪfʌɪəbl
AM aɪˌdɛn(t)əˈfaɪəbəl,
əˌdɛn(t)əˈfaɪəbəl

identifiably
BR ʌɪˈdɛntɪfʌɪəbli
AM aɪˌdɛn(t)əˈfaɪəbli,
əˌdɛn(t)əˈfaɪəbli

identification
BR ʌɪˌdɛntɪfɪˈkeɪʃn
AM aɪˌdɛn(t)əfəˈkeɪʃən

identifier
BR ʌɪˈdɛntɪfʌɪə(r), -z
AM aɪˈdɛn(t)əˌfaɪər,
əˈdɛn(t)əˌfaɪər, -z

identify
BR ʌɪˈdɛntɪfʌɪ, -z, -ɪŋ, -d
AM aɪˈdɛn(t)əˌfaɪ,
əˈdɛn(t)əˌfaɪ, -z, -ɪŋ, -d

identikit®
BR ʌɪˈdɛntɪkɪt, -s
AM aɪˈdɛn(t)əˌkɪt, -s

identity
BR ʌɪˈdɛntɪt|i, -ɪz
AM aɪˈdɛn(t)ədi, -z

ideogram
BR ˈɪdɪəɡram,
ˈʌɪdɪəɡram, -z
AM ˈɪdiəˌɡræm,
ˈaɪdiəˌɡræm, -z

ideograph
BR ˈɪdɪəɡrɑːf, ˈɪdɪəɡraf,
ˈʌɪdɪəɡrɑːf,
ˈʌɪdɪəɡraf, -s
AM ˈɪdiəˌɡræf,
ˈaɪdiəˌɡræf, -s

ideographic
BR ˌɪdɪəˈɡrafɪk,
ˌʌɪdɪəˈɡrafɪk
AM ˌɪdiəˈɡræfɪk,
ˌaɪdiəˈɡræfɪk

ideographical
BR ˌɪdɪəˈɡrafɪkl,
ˌʌɪdɪəˈɡrafɪkl
AM ˌɪdiəˈɡræfəkəl,
ˌaɪdiəˈɡræfəkəl

ideological
BR ˌʌɪdɪəˈlɒdʒɪkl,
ˌɪdɪəˈlɒdʒɪkl
AM ˌɪdiəˈlɑdʒəkəl,
ˌaɪdiəˈlɑdʒəkəl

ideologically
BR ˌʌɪdɪəˈlɒdʒɪkli,
ˌɪdɪəˈlɒdʒɪkli
AM ˌɪdiəˈlɑdʒək(ə)li,
ˌaɪdiəˈlɑdʒək(ə)li

ideologist
BR ˌʌɪdɪˈɒlədʒɪst,
ˌɪdɪˈɒlədʒɪst, -s
AM ˌaɪdiˈɑlədʒəst,
ˌɪdiˈɑlədʒəst, -s

ideologue
BR ˈʌɪdɪəlɒɡ, ˈɪdɪəlɒɡ,
-z
AM ˈɪdiəˌlɔɡ, ˈaɪdiəˌlɔɡ,
ˈɪdiəˌlɑɡ, ˈaɪdiəˌlɑɡ, -z

ideology
BR ˌʌɪdɪˈɒlədʒ|i,
ˌɪdɪˈɒlədʒ|i, -ɪz
AM ˌɪdiˈɑlədʒi,
ˌaɪdiˈɑlədʒi, -z

ides
BR ʌɪdz
AM aɪdz

idiocy
BR ˈɪdɪəs|i, -ɪz
AM ˈɪdiəsi, -z

idiolect
BR ˈɪdɪəlɛkt, -s
AM ˈɪdiəˌlɛk|(t), -(t)s

idiom
BR ˈɪdɪəm, -z
AM ˈɪdiəm, -z

idiomatic
BR ˌɪdɪəˈmatɪk
AM ˌɪdiəˈmædɪk

idiomatically
BR ˌɪdɪəˈmatɪkli
AM ˌɪdiəˈmædək(ə)li

idiopathic
BR ˌɪdɪəˈpaθɪk
AM ˌɪdiəˈpæθɪk

idiopathy
BR ˌɪdɪˈɒpəθ|i, -ɪz
AM ˌɪdiˈɑpəθi, -z

idiosyncrasy
BR ˌɪdɪə(ʊ)ˈsɪŋkrəs|i,
-ɪz
AM ˌɪdiəˈsɪŋkrəsi, -z

idiosyncratic
BR ˌɪdɪə(ʊ)sɪŋˈkratɪk
AM ˌɪdiəsɪŋˈkrædɪk

idiosyncratically
BR ˌɪdɪə(ʊ)sɪŋˈkratɪkli
AM ˌɪdiəsɪŋˈkrædək(ə)li

idiot
BR ˈɪdɪət, -s
AM ˈɪdiət, -s

idiotic
BR ˌɪdɪˈɒtɪk
AM ˌɪdiˈɑdɪk

idiotically
BR ˌɪdɪˈɒtɪkli
AM ˌɪdiˈɑdək(ə)li

Iditarod
BR ʌɪˈdɪtərɒd
AM aɪˈdɪdəˌrɑd

idle
BR ˈʌɪd|l, -lz, -l̩ɪŋ \-l-ɪŋ,
-ld
AM ˈaɪd|əl, -əlz, -(ə)l-ɪŋ,
-əld

idleness
BR ˈʌɪdlnəs
AM ˈaɪdlnəs

idler
BR ˈʌɪdlə(r), ˈʌɪd|lə(r),
-z
AM ˈaɪd(ə)lər, -z

idly
BR ˈʌɪdli
AM ˈaɪdli, ˈaɪd|li

Ido
BR ˈiːdəʊ
AM ˈiˌdoʊ

idol
BR ˈʌɪdl, -z
AM ˈaɪdəl, -z

idola
BR ʌɪˈdəʊlə(r)
AM aɪˈdoʊlə

idolater
BR ʌɪˈdɒlətə(r), -z
AM aɪˈdɑlədər, -z

idolatress
BR ʌɪˈdɒlətrəs, -ɪz
AM aɪˈdɑlətrəs, -əz

idolatrous
BR ʌɪˈdɒlətrəs
AM aɪˈdɑlətrəs

idolatrously
BR ʌɪˈdɒlətrəsli
AM aɪˈdɑlətrəsli

idolatry
BR ʌɪˈdɒlətri
AM aɪˈdɑlətri

idolisation
BR ˌʌɪdəlʌɪˈzeɪʃn,
ˌʌɪdl̩ʌɪˈzeɪʃn
AM ˌaɪdləˈzeɪʃən,
ˌaɪdlaɪˈzeɪʃən

idolise
BR ˈʌɪdəlʌɪz, ˈʌɪd|ʌɪz,
-ɪz, -ɪŋ, -d
AM ˈaɪdlˌaɪz, -ɪz, -ɪŋ, -d

idoliser
BR ˈʌɪdəlʌɪzə(r),
ˈʌɪd|ʌɪzə(r), -z
AM ˈaɪdlˌaɪzər, -z

idolization
BR ˌʌɪdəlʌɪˈzeɪʃn,
ˌʌɪdl̩ʌɪˈzeɪʃn
AM ˌaɪdləˈzeɪʃən,
ˌaɪdlaɪˈzeɪʃən

idolize
BR ˈʌɪdəlʌɪz, ˈʌɪd|ʌɪz,
-ɪz, -ɪŋ, -d
AM ˈaɪdlˌaɪz, -ɪz, -ɪŋ, -d

idolizer
BR ˈʌɪdəlʌɪzə(r),
ˈʌɪd|ʌɪzə(r), -z
AM ˈaɪdlˌaɪzər, -z

idolum
BR ʌɪˈdəʊləm
AM aɪˈdoʊləm

Idomeneus
BR ʌɪˈdɒmɪnjuːs,
ɪˈdɒmɪnjuːs
AM ˌaɪˈdɑmən(j)us

idyl
BR ˈɪd(ɪ)l, ˈʌɪd(ɪ)l, -z
AM ˈaɪdl, -z

idyll
BR ˈɪd(ɪ)l, ˈʌɪd(ɪ)l, -z
AM ˈaɪdl, -z

idyllic
BR ɪˈdɪlɪk, ʌɪˈdɪlɪk
AM aɪˈdɪlɪk

idyllically
BR ɪˈdɪlɪkli, ʌɪˈdɪlɪkli

idyllise
BR ˈɪdl̩ʌɪz, ˈɪdɪlʌɪz,
ˈʌɪdl̩ʌɪz, ˈʌɪdɪlʌɪz, -ɪz,
-ɪŋ, -d
AM ˈaɪdlˌaɪz, -ɪz, -ɪŋ, -d

idyllist
BR ˈɪdl̩ɪst, ˈɪdɪlɪst,
ˈʌɪdl̩ɪst, ˈʌɪdɪlɪst, -s
AM ˈaɪdl̩əst, -s

idyllize
BR ˈɪdl̩ʌɪz, ˈɪdɪlʌɪz,
ˈʌɪdl̩ʌɪz, ˈʌɪdɪlʌɪz, -ɪz,
-ɪŋ, -d
AM ˈaɪdlˌaɪz, -ɪz, -ɪŋ, -d

i.e.
BR ˌʌɪ ˈiː
AM ˌaɪ ˈi

Iestyn
BR ˈjɛstɪn
AM ˈjɛstən

Ieuan
BR ˈjʌɪən
AM ˈjaɪən

if
BR ɪf, -s
AM ɪf, -s

iff
BR ɪf
AM ɪf

iffy
BR ˈɪfi
AM ˈɪfi

Ifni
BR ˈɪfni
AM ˈɪfni

Ifor
BR ˈiːvɔː(r), ˈʌɪvɔː(r),
ˈʌɪvə(r)
AM ˈivɔ(ə)r, ˈaɪvɔ(ə)r
WE ˈɪvɒr

Igbo
BR ˈɪgbəʊ, -z
AM ˈɪgˌboʊ, -z

Ightham
BR ˈʌɪtəm
AM ˈaɪdəm

igloo
BR ˈɪgluː, -z
AM ˈɪglu, -z

Ignatius
BR ɪgˈneɪʃəs
AM ɪgˈneɪʃəs

igneous
BR ˈɪgnɪəs
AM ˈɪgniəs

ignis fatuus
BR ˌɪgnɪs ˈfatjʊəs,
+ ˈfatʃʊəs
AM ˌɪgnəs ˈfætʃ(əw)əs

ignitability
BR ɪgˌnʌɪtəˈbɪlɪti
AM ɪgˌnaɪdəˈbɪlɪdi

ignitable
BR ɪgˈnʌɪtəbl
AM ɪgˈnaɪdəbəl

ai'drɪlək(ə)li

idyllise
BR ˈɪdl̩ʌɪz, ˈɪdɪlʌɪz,
ˈʌɪdl̩ʌɪz, ˈʌɪdɪlʌɪz, -ɪz,
-ɪŋ, -d
AM ˈaɪdlˌaɪz, -ɪz, -ɪŋ, -d

ignite
BR ɪgˈnʌɪt, -s, -ɪŋ, -ɪd
AM ɪgˈnaɪ|t, -ts, -dɪŋ,
-dɪd

igniter
BR ɪgˈnʌɪtə(r), -z
AM ɪgˈnaɪdər, -z

ignitibility
BR ɪgˌnʌɪtɪˈbɪlɪti
AM ɪgˌnaɪdəˈbɪlɪdi

ignitible
BR ɪgˈnʌɪtɪbl
AM ɪgˈnaɪdəbəl

ignition
BR ɪgˈnɪʃn
AM ɪgˈnɪʃən

ignitron
BR ɪgˈnʌɪtrɒn,
ˈɪgnɪtrɒn, -z
AM ˈɪgnəˌtrɑn, -z

ignobility
BR ˌɪgnə(ʊ)ˈbɪlɪti
AM ˌɪgˌnoʊˈbɪlɪdi

ignoble
BR ɪgˈnəʊbl
AM ɪgˈnoʊbəl

ignobly
BR ɪgˈnəʊbli
AM ɪgˈnoʊbli

ignominious
BR ˌɪgnəˈmɪnɪəs
AM ˌɪgnəˈmɪniəs

ignominiously
BR ˌɪgnəˈmɪnɪəsli
AM ˌɪgnəˈmɪniəsli

ignominiousness
BR ˌɪgnəˈmɪnɪəsnəs
AM ˌɪgnəˈmɪniəsnəs

ignominy
BR ˈɪgnəmɪni
AM ˈɪgnəˌmɪni,
ˌɪgˈnɑmɪni

ignoramus
BR ˌɪgnəˈreɪməs, -ɪz
AM ˌɪgnəˈreɪməs,
ˌɪgnəˈræməs, -əz

ignorance
BR ˈɪgn(ə)rəns,
ˈɪgn(ə)r|n̩s
AM ˈɪgnərəns

ignorant
BR ˈɪgn(ə)rənt,
ˈɪgn(ə)r|n̩t
AM ˈɪgnərənt

ignorantly
BR ˈɪgn(ə)rəntli,
ˈɪgn(ə)r|n̩tli
AM ˈɪgnərən(t)li

ignore
BR ɪgˈnɔː(r), -z, -ɪŋ, -d
AM ɪgˈnɔ(ə)r, -z, -ɪŋ, -d

ignorer
BR ɪgˈnɔːrə(r), -z
AM ɪgˈnɔrər, -z

ignotum per ignotius
BR ɪɡˌnəʊtəm pər ɪɡˈnəʊtɪəs,
+ ɪɡˈnəʊʃəs
AM ɪɡˈnoʊdəm pər ɪɡˈnoʊʃəs

Igor
BR ˈiːɡɔː(r)
AM ˈiɡɔ(ə)r

Iguaçu
BR ɪˈɡwɑːsuː
AM ɪˈɡwɑˌsu

iguana
BR ˌɪɡjʊˈɑːnə(r),
ɪˈɡwɑːnə(r), -z
AM əˈɡwɑnə, ɪˈɡwɑnə,
-z

iguanodon
BR ˌɪɡjʊˈɑːnədɒn,
ɪˈɡwɑːnədɒn, -z
AM əˈɡwɑnəˌdɑn,
ɪˈɡwɑnəˌdɑn, -z

IKEA®
BR ʌɪˈkiːə(r)
AM aɪˈkiə

ikebana
BR ˌɪkɪˈbɑːnə(r),
ˌiːkeɪˈbɑːnə(r)
AM ˌɪkəˈbɑnə

Ikhnaton
BR ɪkˈnɑːtɒn,
ɪkˈnɑːt(ə)n
AM ɪkˈnɑtn

ikky
BR ˈɪki
AM ˈɪki

ikon
BR ˈʌɪkɒn, -z
AM ˈaɪˌkɑn, -z

ilang-ilang
BR ˈiːlaŋˈiːlaŋ
AM ˈilæŋˈilæŋ

Ilchester
BR ˈɪltʃɪstə(r)
AM ˈɪltʃɪstər

ILEA
BR ˈɪlɪə(r), ˌʌɪɛlɪˈeɪ
AM ˌaɪˌɛl͵iˈeɪ

ileac
BR ˈɪlɪak
AM ˈɪliˌæk

ileal
BR ˈɪlɪəl
AM ˈɪlɪəl

Île-de-France
BR ˌiːldəˈfrɑːns,
ˌiːldəˈfrans
AM ˈildəˈfrans

ileitis
BR ˌɪlɪˈʌɪtɪs
AM ˌɪliˈaɪdɪs

ileostomy
BR ˌɪlɪˈɒstəmˌi, -ɪz
AM ˌɪliˈɑstəmi, -z

Iles
BR ʌɪlz
AM aɪlz

ileum
BR ˈɪlɪəm, -z
AM ˈɪliəm, -z

ileus
BR ˈɪlɪəs, -ɪz
AM ˈɪliəs, -ɪz

ilex
BR ˈʌɪlɛks, -ɪz
AM ˈaɪˌlɛks, -əz

ilia
BR ˈɪlɪə(r)
AM ˈɪljə, ˈɪliə

iliac
BR ˈɪlɪak
AM ˈɪliˌæk

Iliad
BR ˈɪlɪəd, ˈɪlɪad
AM ˈɪliəd

ilium
BR ˈɪlɪəm
AM ˈɪliəm

ilk
BR ɪlk
AM ɪlk

I'll
BR ʌɪl
AM aɪl

ill
BR ɪl
AM ɪl

illation
BR ɪˈleɪʃn, -z
AM əˈleɪʃən, -z

illative
BR ɪˈleɪtɪv, ˈɪlətɪv
AM ˈɪlədɪv, əˈleɪdɪv

illatively
BR ɪˈleɪtɪvli, ˈɪlətɪvli
AM ˈɪlədɪvli, əˈleɪdɪvli

illegal
BR ɪˈliːɡl
AM ɪ(l)ˈliɡəl, əˈliɡəl

illegality
BR ˌɪlɪˈɡalɪt͵i, -ɪz
AM ͵ɪ(l)ləˈɡælədi, -z

illegally
BR ɪˈliːɡl͵i, ɪˈliːɡəli
AM ɪ(l)ˈliɡ(ə)li,
əˈliɡ(ə)li

illegibility
BR ɪˌlɛdʒɪˈbɪlɪti
AM ͵ɪ(l)͵lɛdʒəˈbɪlɪdi,
əˌlɛdʒəˈbɪlɪdi

illegible
BR ɪˈlɛdʒɪbl
AM ɪ(l)ˈlɛdʒəbəl,
əˈlɛdʒəbəl

illegibly
BR ɪˈlɛdʒɪbli
AM ɪ(l)ˈlɛdʒəbli,
əˈlɛdʒəbli

illegitimacy
BR ˌɪlɪˈdʒɪtɪməsi
AM ͵ɪ(l)ləˈdʒɪdəməsi

illegitimate
BR ˌɪlɪˈdʒɪtɪmət
AM ͵ɪ(l)ləˈdʒɪdəmət

illegitimately
BR ˌɪlɪˈdʒɪtɪmətli
AM ͵ɪ(l)ləˈdʒɪdəmətli

illegitimation
BR ˌɪlɪˌdʒɪtɪˈmeɪʃn
AM ͵ɪ(l)ləˌdʒɪdəˈmeɪʃən

illegitimise
BR ɪˈlɪˈdʒɪtɪmʌɪz, -ɪz,
-ɪŋ, -d
AM ͵ɪ(l)ləˈdʒɪdəˌmaɪz,
-ɪz, -ɪŋ, -d

illegitimize
BR ɪˈlɪˈdʒɪtɪmʌɪz, -ɪz,
-ɪŋ, -d
AM ͵ɪ(l)ləˈdʒɪdəˌmaɪz,
-ɪz, -ɪŋ, -d

ill-gotten
BR ͵ɪlˈɡɒtn
AM ˈɪl͵ɡɑtn

ill-humored
BR ͵ɪlˈhjuːməd
AM ˈɪl͵(h)jumərd

ill-humoured
BR ͵ɪlˈhjuːməd
AM ˈɪl͵(h)jumərd

illiberal
BR ɪˈlɪb(ə)rəl,
ɪˈlɪb(ə)rl̩
AM ɪ(l)ˈlɪb(ə)rəl

illiberality
BR ɪˌlɪbəˈralɪti
AM ͵ɪ(l)͵lɪbəˈrælədi

illiberally
BR ɪˈlɪb(ə)rəli,
ɪˈlɪb(ə)r͵li
AM ɪ(l)ˈlɪb(ə)rəli

illicit
BR ɪˈlɪsɪt
AM ɪ(l)ˈlɪsɪt

illicitly
BR ɪˈlɪsɪtli
AM ɪ(l)ˈlɪsɪtli

illicitness
BR ɪˈlɪsɪtnɪs
AM ɪ(l)ˈlɪsɪtnɪs

illimitability
BR ɪˌlɪmɪtəˈbɪlɪti
AM ɪ(l)͵lɪmədəˈbɪlɪdi

illimitable
BR ɪˈlɪmɪtəbl
AM ɪ(l)ˈlɪmədəbəl

illimitableness
BR ɪˈlɪmɪtəblnəs
AM ɪ(l)ˈlɪmədəbəlnəs

illimitably
BR ɪˈlɪmɪtəbli
AM ɪ(l)ˈlɪmədəbli

Illingworth
BR ˈɪlɪŋwəːθ, ˈɪlɪŋwəθ
AM ˈɪlɪŋˌwərθ

Illinois
BR ˌɪlɪˈnɔɪ
AM ˌɪləˈnɔɪ

Illinoisan
BR ˌɪlɪˈnɔɪən, -z
AM ˌɪləˈnɔɪən, -z

illiquid
BR ɪˈlɪkwɪd
AM ɪ(l)ˈlɪkwɪd

illiquidity
BR ˌɪlɪˈkwɪdɪti
AM ɪ(l)͵ləˈkwɪdɪdi

illiteracy
BR ɪˈlɪt(ə)rəsi
AM ɪ(l)ˈlɪtrəsi,
ɪ(l)ˈlɪdərəsi

illiterate
BR ɪˈlɪt(ə)rət
AM ɪ(l)ˈlɪdərət

illiterately
BR ɪˈlɪt(ə)rətli
AM ɪ(l)ˈlɪdərətli

illiterateness
BR ɪˈlɪt(ə)rətnəs
AM ɪ(l)ˈlɪdərətnəs

ill-natured
BR ͵ɪlˈneɪtʃəd
AM ˈɪl͵neɪtʃərd

ill-naturedly
BR ͵ɪlˈneɪtʃədli
AM ˈɪl͵neɪtʃərdli

illness
BR ˈɪlnɪs, -ɪz
AM ˈɪlnəs, -əz

illogical
BR ɪˈlɒdʒɪkl
AM ɪ(l)ˈlɑdʒəkəl

illogicality
BR ɪˌlɒdʒɪˈkalɪti
AM ɪ(l)͵lɑdʒəˈkælədi

illogically
BR ɪˈlɒdʒɪkli
AM ɪ(l)ˈlɑdʒək(ə)li

ill-omened
BR ͵ɪlˈəʊmɛnd,
͵ɪlˈəʊmənd
AM ˈɪl͵oʊmənd

ill-starred
BR ͵ɪlˈstɑːd
AM ˈɪl͵stɑrd

illude
BR ɪˈl(j)uːd, -z, -ɪŋ, -ɪd
AM ɪˈlud, -z, -ɪŋ, -əd

illume
BR ɪˈl(j)uːm, -z, -ɪŋ, -d
AM ɪˈlum, -z, -ɪŋ, -d

illuminance
BR ɪˈl(j)uːmɪnəns, -ɪz
AM ɪˈlumənəns, -əz

illuminant
BR ɪˈl(j)uːmɪnənt, -s
AM ɪˈlumənənt, -s

illuminate
BR ɪˈl(j)uːmɪneɪt, -s,
-ɪŋ, -ɪd
AM ɪˈluməˌneɪt, -ts,
-dɪŋ, -dɪd

illuminati
BR ɪˌl(j)uːmɪˈnɑːti:
AM ɪˌluməˈnadi

illuminatingly
BR ɪˈl(j)uːmɪneɪtɪŋli
AM ɪˈluməˌneɪdɪŋli

illumination
BR ɪˌl(j)uːmɪˈneɪʃn, -z
AM ɪˌluːməˈneɪʃən, -z
illuminative
BR ɪˈl(j)uːmɪnətɪv
AM ɪˈluːməˌneɪdɪv
illuminator
BR ɪˈl(j)uːmɪneɪtə(r),
-z
AM ɪˈluːməˌneɪdər, -z
illumine
BR ɪˈl(j)uːm|ɪn, -ɪnz,
-mɪŋ, -ɪnd
AM ɪˈluːmən, -z, -ɪŋ, -d
illuminism
BR ɪˈl(j)uːmɪnɪz(ə)m
AM ɪˈluːmə,nɪzəm
illuminist
BR ɪˈl(j)uːmɪnɪst, -s
AM ɪˈluːmənəst, -s
ill-use
BR ˌɪlˈjuːz, -ɪz, -ɪŋ, -d
AM ˈɪlˌjuz, -əz, -ɪŋ, -d
illusion
BR ɪˈl(j)uːʒn, -z
AM ɪˈluʒən, -z
illusional
BR ɪˈl(j)uːʒn(ə)l,
ɪˈl(j)uːʒən(ə)l
AM ɪˈluʒ(ə)nəl
illusionism
BR ɪˈl(j)uːʒnɪz(ə)m,
ɪˈl(j)uːʒənɪz(ə)m
AM ɪˈluʒə,nɪzəm
illusionist
BR ɪˈl(j)uːʒnɪst,
ɪˈl(j)uːʒənɪst, -s
AM ɪˈluʒənəst, -s
illusionistic
BR ɪˌl(j)uːʒəˈnɪstɪk,
ɪˌl(j)uːʒnˈɪstɪk
AM ɪˌluʒəˈnɪstɪk
illusive
BR ɪˈl(j)uːsɪv
AM ɪˈlusɪv
illusively
BR ɪˈl(j)uːsɪvli
AM ɪˈlusɪvli
illusiveness
BR ɪˈl(j)uːsɪvnɪs
AM ɪˈlusɪvnɪs
illusorily
BR ɪˈl(j)uːs(ə)rɪli,
ɪˈl(j)uːz(ə)rɪli
AM ɪˈlus(ə)rəli,
ɪˈluz(ə)rəli
illusoriness
BR ɪˈl(j)uːs(ə)rɪnɪs,
ɪˈl(j)uːz(ə)rɪnɪs
AM ɪˈlus(ə)rɪnɪs,
ɪˈluz(ə)rɪnɪs
illusory
BR ɪˈl(j)uːs(ə)ri,
ɪˈl(j)uːz(ə)ri
AM ɪˈlus(ə)ri, ɪˈluz(ə)ri
illustrate
BR ˈɪləstreɪt, -s, -ɪŋ, -ɪd

AM ˈɪlə,streɪ|t, -ts, -dɪŋ,
-dɪd
illustration
BR ˌɪləˈstreɪʃn, -z
AM ˌɪləˈstreɪʃən, -z
illustrational
BR ˌɪləˈstreɪʃn(ə)l,
ˌɪləˈstreɪʃən(ə)l
AM ˌɪləˈstreɪʃ(ə)nəl
illustrative
BR ˈɪləstrətɪv,
ˈɪləstreɪtɪv,
ɪˈlʌstrətɪv
AM ɪˈlʌstrədɪv,
ˈɪlə,streɪdɪv
illustratively
BR ˈɪləstrətɪvli,
ˈɪləstreɪtɪvli,
ɪˈlʌstrətɪvli
AM ɪˈlʌstrədɪvli,
ˈɪlə,streɪdɪvli
illustrator
BR ˈɪləstreɪtə(r), -z
AM ˈɪlə,streɪdər, -z
illustrious
BR ɪˈlʌstrɪəs
AM ɪˈləstrɪəs
illustriously
BR ɪˈlʌstrɪəsli
AM ɪˈləstrɪəsli
illustriousness
BR ɪˈlʌstrɪəsnəs
AM ɪˈləstrɪəsnəs
Illyria
BR ɪˈlɪrɪə(r)
AM ɪˈlɪrɪə
Illyrian
BR ɪˈlɪrɪən, -z
AM ɪˈlɪrɪən, -z
Illyricum
BR ɪˈlɪrɪkəm
AM ɪˈlɪrɪkəm
illywhacker
BR ˈɪlɪˌwakə(r), -z
AM ˈɪlɪˌ(h)wækər, -z
ilmenite
BR ˈɪlmɪnʌɪt, -s
AM ˈɪlmə,naɪt, -s
Ilminster
BR ˈɪlmɪnstə(r)
AM ˈɪl,mɪnstər
Ilona
BR ɪˈləʊnə(r)
AM ɪˈloʊnə
Ilson
BR ˈɪls(ə)n
AM ˈɪlsən
Ilyushin
BR ɪˈljuːʃ(ɪ)n
AM ɪlˈjuʃɪn
I'm
BR ʌɪm
AM aɪm
image
BR ˈɪm|ɪdʒ, -ɪdʒɪz,
-ɪdʒɪŋ, -ɪdʒd
AM ˈɪmɪdʒ, -ɪz, -ɪŋ, -d

imageable
BR ˈɪmɪdʒəbl
AM ˈɪmɪdʒəbəl
imageless
BR ˈɪmɪdʒlɪs
AM ˈɪmɪdʒlɪs
imagery
BR ˈɪmɪdʒ(ə)ri
AM ˈɪmɪdʒ(ə)ri
imaginable
BR ɪˈmadʒɪnəbl,
ɪˈmadʒnəbl
AM ɪˈmædʒ(ə)nəbəl
imaginably
BR ɪˈmadʒɪnəbli,
ɪˈmadʒnəbli
AM ɪˈmædʒ(ə)nəbli
imaginal
BR ɪˈmadʒɪnl, ɪˈmadʒnl
AM ɪˈmædʒ(ə)nəl
imaginarily
BR ɪˈmadʒɪn(ə)rɪli,
ɪˈmadʒɪn(ə)rli,
ɪˈmadʒn(ə)rɪli,
ɪˈmadʒn(ə)rli
AM ɪˌmædʒəˈnɛrəli
imaginary
BR ɪˈmadʒɪn(ə)ri,
ɪˈmadʒn(ə)ri
AM ɪˈmædʒə,nɛri
imagination
BR ɪˌmadʒɪˈneɪʃn
AM ɪˌmædʒəˈneɪʃən
imaginative
BR ɪˈmadʒɪnətɪv,
ɪˈmadʒnətɪv
AM ɪˈmædʒ(ə)nədɪv
imaginatively
BR ɪˈmadʒɪnətɪvli,
ɪˈmadʒnətɪvli
AM ɪˈmædʒ(ə)nədɪvli
imaginativeness
BR ɪˈmadʒɪnətɪvnɪs,
ɪˈmadʒnətɪvnɪs
AM ɪˈmædʒ(ə)nədɪvnɪs
imagine
verb
BR ɪˈmadʒɪn, ɪˈmadʒn,
-z, -ɪŋ, -d
AM ɪˈmædʒən, -z, -ɪŋ, -d
imaginer
BR ɪˈmadʒɪnə(r),
ɪˈmadʒnə(r), -z
AM ɪˈmædʒənər, -z
imagines[1]
from imagine
BR ɪˈmadʒɪnz,
ɪˈmadʒnz
AM ɪˈmædʒənz
imagines[2]
plural of imago
BR ɪˈmeɪdʒɪniːz,
ɪˈmɑːdʒɪniːz
AM ɪˈmeɪgə,niz,
ɪˈmɑgə,niz,
ɪˈmeɪdʒə,niz,
ɪˈmædʒə,niz

imaginings
BR ɪˈmadʒɪnɪŋz,
ɪˈmadʒnɪŋz
AM ɪˈmædʒənɪŋz
imagism
BR ˈɪmɪdʒɪz(ə)m
AM ˈɪmə,dʒɪzəm
imagist
BR ˈɪmɪdʒɪst, -s
AM ˈɪmədʒəst, -s
imagistic
BR ˌɪmɪˈdʒɪstɪk
AM ˌɪməˈdʒɪstɪk
imago
BR ɪˈmeɪgəʊ, ɪˈmɑːgəʊ,
-z
AM ɪˈmeɪgoʊ, ɪˈmɑgoʊ,
-z
imam
BR ɪˈmɑːm, ɪˈmam, -z
AM ɪˈmɑm, ɪˈmæm, -z
imamate
BR ɪˈmɑːmət, ɪˈmamət,
-s
AM ɪˈmɑ,meɪt,
ɪˈmæ,meɪt, -s
IMAX®
BR ˈʌɪmaks
AM ˈaɪˌmæks
imbalance
BR (,)ɪmˈbaləns,
(,)ɪmˈbalns
AM ɪmˈbæləns
imbecile
BR ˈɪmbɪsiːl, -z
AM ˈɪmbəsəl,
ˈɪmbə,saɪl, -z
imbecilely
BR ˈɪmbɪsiːlli
AM ˈɪmbəsə(l)li,
ˈɪmbə,saɪ(l)li
imbecilic
BR ˌɪmbɪˈsɪlɪk
AM ˌɪmbəˈsɪlɪk
imbecility
BR ˌɪmbɪˈsɪlɪti
AM ˌɪmbəˈsɪlɪdi
imbed
BR ɪmˈbɛd, -z, -ɪŋ, -ɪd
AM ɪmˈbɛd, -z, -ɪŋ, -əd
Imbert
BR ˈɪmbət
AM ˈɪmbərt
imbibe
BR ɪmˈbʌɪb, -z, -ɪŋ, -d
AM ɪmˈbaɪb, -z, -ɪŋ, -d
imbiber
BR ɪmˈbʌɪbə(r), -z
AM ɪmˈbaɪbər, -z
imbibition
BR ˌɪmbɪˈbɪʃn, -z
AM ɪm,baɪˈbɪʃən, -z
imbricate
BR ˈɪmbrɪkeɪt, -s, -ɪŋ,
-ɪd
AM ˈɪmbrə,keɪ|t, -ts,
-dɪŋ, -dɪd

imbrication
BR ˌɪmbrɪˈkeɪʃn
AM ˌɪmbrəˈkeɪʃən

imbroglio
BR ɪmˈbrəʊlɪəʊ, -z
AM ɪmˈbroʊljoʊ,
ɪmˈbrɔljoʊ, -z

Imbros
BR ˈɪmbrɒs
AM ˈɪm.brɒs, ˈɪm.brɑs

imbrue
BR ɪmˈbruː, -z, -ɪŋ, -d
AM ɪmˈbru, -z, -ɪŋ, -d

imbrute
BR ɪmˈbruːt, -s, -ɪŋ, -ɪd
AM ɪmˈbru|t, -ts, -dɪŋ,
-dəd

imbue
BR ɪmˈbjuː, -z, -ɪŋ, -d
AM ɪmˈbju, -z, -ɪŋ, -d

Imhotep
BR ˈɪmhəʊtɛp
AM ɪmˈhoʊˌtɛp

imide
BR ˈɪmʌɪd, -z
AM ˈɪˌmaɪd, -z

imidozole
BR ˌɪmɪˈdeɪzəʊl,
ɪˈmɪdəzəʊl
AM əˈmɪdəˌzoʊl

imine
BR ˈɪmiːn, ɪˈmiːn, -z
AM ˈɪˌmin, ˈɪmɪn, -z

imitability
BR ˌɪmɪtəˈbɪlɪti
AM ˌɪmədəˈbɪlɪdi

imitable
BR ˈɪmɪtəbl
AM ˈɪmədəbəl

imitate
BR ˈɪmɪteɪt, -s, -ɪŋ, -ɪd
AM ˈɪməˌteɪ|t, -ts, -dɪŋ,
-dɪd

imitation
BR ˌɪmɪˈteɪʃn, -z
AM ˌɪməˈteɪʃən, -z

imitative
BR ˈɪmɪtətɪv
AM ˈɪməˌteɪdɪv,
ˈɪmədədɪv

imitatively
BR ˈɪmɪtətɪvli
AM ˈɪməˌteɪdɪvli,
ˈɪmədədəvli

imitativeness
BR ˈɪmɪtətɪvnɪs
AM ˈɪməˌteɪdɪvnɪs,
ˈɪmədədɪvnɪs

imitator
BR ˈɪmɪteɪtə(r), -z
AM ˈɪməˌteɪdər, -z

immaculacy
BR ɪˈmakjʊləsi
AM ɪˈmækjələsi

immaculate
BR ɪˈmakjʊlət
AM ɪˈmækjələt

immaculately
BR ɪˈmakjʊlətli
AM ɪˈmækjələtli

immaculateness
BR ɪˈmakjʊlətnəs
AM ɪˈmækjələtnəs

immanence
BR ˈɪmənəns
AM ˈɪmənəns

immanency
BR ˈɪmənənsi
AM ˈɪmənənsi

immanent
BR ˈɪmənənt
AM ˈɪmənənt

immanentism
BR ˈɪmənəntɪz(ə)m
AM ˈɪmənənˌtɪzəm

immanentist
BR ˈɪmənəntɪst, -s
AM ˈɪmənən(t)əst, -s

Immanuel
BR ɪˈmanjʊəl,
ɪˈmanjʊl
AM ɪˈmænjəwəl

immaterial
BR ˌɪməˈtɪərɪəl
AM ˌɪ(m)məˈtɪriəl

immaterialise
BR ˌɪməˈtɪərɪəlʌɪz, -ɪz,
-ɪŋ, -d
AM ˌɪ(m)məˈtɪriəˌlaɪz,
-ɪz, -ɪŋ, -d

immaterialism
BR ˌɪməˈtɪərɪəlɪz(ə)m
AM ˌɪ(m)məˈtɪriəˌlɪzəm

immaterialist
BR ˌɪməˈtɪərɪəlɪst, -s
AM ˌɪ(m)məˈtɪriələst,
-s

immateriality
BR ˌɪməˌtɪərɪˈalɪti
AM ˌɪ(m)məˌtɪriˈælədi

immaterialize
BR ˌɪməˈtɪərɪəlʌɪz, -ɪz,
-ɪŋ, -d
AM ˌɪ(m)məˈtɪriəˌlaɪz,
-ɪz, -ɪŋ, -d

immaterially
BR ˌɪməˈtɪərɪəli
AM ˌɪ(m)məˈtɪriəli

immature
BR ˌɪməˈtjʊə(r),
ˌɪməˈtʃʊə(r),
ˌɪməˈtjɔː(r),
ˌɪməˈtʃɔː(r)
AM ˌɪ(m)məˈtʊ(ə)r,
ˌɪ(m)məˈtʃʊ(ə)r,
ˌɪ(m)məˈtʃər

immaturely
BR ˌɪməˈtjʊəli,
ˌɪməˈtʃʊəli,
ˌɪməˈtjɔːli, ˌɪməˈtʃɔːli
AM ˌɪ(m)məˈtʊrli,
ˌɪ(m)məˈtʃʊrli,
ˌɪ(m)məˈtʃərli

immaturity
BR ˌɪməˈtjʊərɪti,
ˌɪməˈtʃʊərɪti,
ˌɪməˈtjɔːrɪti,
ˌɪməˈtʃɔːrɪti
AM ˌɪ(m)məˈtʊrədi,
ˌɪ(m)məˈtʃʊrədi,
ˌɪ(m)məˈtʃərədi

immeasurability
BR ɪˌmɛʒ(ə)rəˈbɪlɪti
AM ɪ(m)ˌmɛʒ(ə)rəˈbɪlɪdi

immeasurable
BR (ˌ)ɪˈmɛʒ(ə)rəbl
AM ɪ(m)ˈmɛʒ(ə)r(ə)bəl

**immeasurable-
ness**
BR (ˌ)ɪˈmɛʒ(ə)rəblnəs
AM ɪ(m)ˈmɛʒ(ə)rəbəl-
nəs

immeasurably
BR (ˌ)ɪˈmɛʒ(ə)rəbli
AM ɪ(m)ˈmɛʒ(ə)rəbli

immediacy
BR ɪˈmiːdɪəsi
AM ɪˈmidiəsi

immediate
BR ɪˈmiːdɪət
AM ɪˈmidiət

immediately
BR ɪˈmiːdɪətli
AM ɪˈmidiətli

immediateness
BR ɪˈmiːdɪətnəs
AM ɪˈmidiətnəs

immedicable
BR ɪˈmɛdɪkəbl
AM ɪˈmɛdəkəbəl

immedicably
BR ɪˈmɛdɪkəbli
AM ɪˈmɛdəkəbli

immemorial
BR ˌɪməˈmɔːrɪəl
AM ˌɪ(m)məˈmɔriəl

immemorially
BR ˌɪməˈmɔːrɪəli
AM ˌɪ(m)məˈmɔriəli

immense
BR ɪˈmɛns
AM ɪˈmɛns

immensely
BR ɪˈmɛnsli
AM ɪˈmɛnsli

immenseness
BR ɪˈmɛnsnəs
AM ɪˈmɛnsnəs

immensity
BR ɪˈmɛnsɪti
AM ɪˈmɛnsədi

immerse
BR ɪˈməːs, -ɪz, -ɪŋ, -t
AM ɪˈmərs, -əz, -ɪŋ, -t

immersion
BR ɪˈməːʃn, ɪˈməːʒn
AM ɪˈmərʒən, ɪˈmərʃən

immigrant
BR ˈɪmɪgr(ə)nt, -s
AM ˈɪməgrənt, -s

immigrate
BR ˈɪmɪgreɪt, -s, -ɪŋ, -ɪd
AM ˈɪməˌgreɪ|t, -ts, -dɪŋ,
-dɪd

immigration
BR ˌɪmɪˈgreɪʃn
AM ˌɪməˈgreɪʃən

immigratory
BR ˈɪmɪgrət(ə)ri
AM ˈɪməgrəˌtɔri

imminence
BR ˈɪmɪnəns
AM ˈɪmənəns

imminent
BR ˈɪmɪnənt
AM ˈɪmənənt

imminently
BR ˈɪmɪnəntli
AM ˈɪmənən(t)li

immiscibility
BR ɪˌmɪsɪˈbɪlɪti
AM ɪ(m)ˌmɪsəˈbɪlɪdi

immiscible
BR (ˌ)ɪˈmɪsɪbl
AM ɪ(m)ˈmɪsɪbəl

immiscibly
BR (ˌ)ɪˈmɪsɪbli
AM ɪ(m)ˈmɪsɪbli

immitigable
BR (ˌ)ɪˈmɪtɪgəbl
AM ɪ(m)ˈmɪdəgəbəl

immitigably
BR (ˌ)ɪˈmɪtɪgəbli
AM ɪ(m)ˈmɪdəgəbli

immittance
BR ɪˈmɪt(ə)ns, -ɪz
AM ɪ(m)ˈmɪtns, -ɪz

immixture
BR ɪˈmɪkstʃə(r), -z
AM ɪ(m)ˈmɪkstʃər, -z

immobile
BR ɪˈməʊbʌɪl
AM ɪ(m)ˈmoʊbəl,
ɪ(m)ˌmoʊbail

immobilisation
BR ɪˌməʊbɪlʌɪˈzeɪʃn,
ɪˌməʊblʌɪˈzeɪʃn
AM ɪ(m)ˌmoʊbələˈzeɪʃən,
ˌɪ(m)ˌmoʊbəˌlaɪˈzeɪʃən,
əmoʊbələˈzeɪʃən,
əˌmoʊbəˌlaɪˈzeɪʃən

immobilise
BR ɪˈməʊbɪlʌɪz,
ɪˈməʊblʌɪz, -ɪz, -ɪŋ, -d
AM ɪ(m)ˈmoʊbəˌlaɪz,
əˈmoʊbəˌlaɪz, -ɪz, -ɪŋ,
-d

immobiliser
BR ɪˈməʊbɪlʌɪzə(r),
ɪˈməʊblʌɪzə(r), -z
AM ɪ(m)ˈmoʊbəˌlaɪzər,
əˈmoʊbəˌlaɪzər, -z

immobilism
BR ɪˈməʊbɪlɪz(ə)m,
ɪˈməʊblɪz(ə)m
AM ɪ(m)ˈmoʊbəˌlɪzəm,
əˈmoʊbəˌlɪzəm

immobility
BR ˌɪməʊ(ʊ)'bɪlɪti
AM 'ɪ(m)moʊ'bɪlɪdi

immobilization
BR ɪ,məʊbɪlaɪ'zeɪʃn,
ɪ,məʊblaɪ'zeɪʃn
AM 'ɪ(m),moʊbələ'zeɪ-
ʃən,
'ɪ(m),moʊbə,laɪ'zeɪʃən,
əmoʊbələ'zeɪʃən,
ə,moʊbə,laɪ'zeɪʃən

immobilize
BR ɪ'məʊbɪlaɪz,
ɪ'məʊblaɪz, -ɪz, -ɪŋ, -d
AM ɪ(m)'moʊbə,laɪz,
ə'moʊbə,laɪz, -ɪz, -ɪŋ,
-d

immobilizer
BR ɪ'məʊbɪlaɪzə(r),
ɪ'məʊblaɪzə(r), -z
AM ɪ(m)'moʊbə,laɪzər,
ə'moʊbə,laɪzər, -z

immoderacy
BR (ˌ)ɪ'mɒd(ə)rəsi
AM ɪ(m)'mad(ə)rəsi,
ə'mad(ə)rəsi

immoderate
BR (ˌ)ɪ'mɒd(ə)rət
AM ɪ(m)'mad(ə)rət,
ə'mad(ə)rət

immoderately
BR ɪ'mɒd(ə)rətli
AM ɪ(m)'mad(ə)rətli,
ə'mad(ə)rətli

immoderateness
BR (ˌ)ɪ'mɒd(ə)rətnəs
AM ɪ(m)'mad(ə)rətnəs,
ə'mad(ə)rətnəs

immoderation
BR ɪ,mɒd(ə)'reɪʃn
AM ɪ(m),mad(ə)'reɪʃən,
ə,mad(ə)'reɪʃən

immodest
BR (ˌ)ɪ'mɒdɪst
AM ɪ(m)'madəst,
ə'madəst

immodestly
BR (ˌ)ɪ'mɒdɪstli
AM ɪ(m)'madəs(t)li,
ə'madəs(t)li

immodesty
BR (ˌ)ɪ'mɒdɪsti
AM ɪ(m)'madəsti,
ə'madəsti

immolate
BR 'ɪmələɪt, -s, -ɪŋ, -ɪd
AM 'ɪmə,leɪ|t, -ts, -dɪŋ,
-dɪd

immolation
BR ,ɪmə'leɪʃn
AM ,ɪmə'leɪʃən

immolator
BR 'ɪmələɪtə(r), -z
AM 'ɪmə,leɪdər, -z

immoral
BR (ˌ)ɪ'mɒrəl,
(ˌ)ɪ'mɒrl̩

AM ɪ(m)'mɔrəl,
ə'mɔrəl

immorality
BR ,ɪmə'ralɪti
AM ,ɪmə'rælədi,
,ɪmɔ'rælədi

immorally
BR (ˌ)ɪ'mɒrəli,
(ˌ)ɪ'mɒrl̩i
AM ɪ(m)'mɔrəli,
ə'mɔrəli

immortal
BR (ˌ)ɪ'mɔ:tl, -z
AM ɪ(m)'mɔrdl
ə'mɔrdl, -z

immortalisation
BR ɪ,mɔ:tl̩aɪ'zeɪʃn,
ɪ,mɔ:tələɪ'zeɪʃn, -z
AM ɪ(m),mɔrdl̩,aɪ'zeɪʃən,
ɪ(m),mɔrdlə'zeɪʃən,
-z

immortalise
BR ɪ'mɔ:tl̩aɪz,
ɪ'mɔ:tələɪz, -ɪz, -ɪŋ, -d
AM ɪ(m)'mɔrdl̩,aɪz, -ɪz,
-ɪŋ, -d

immortality
BR ,ɪmɔ:'talɪti
AM 'ɪ(m),mɔr'tælədi

immortalization
BR ɪ'mɔ:tl̩aɪ'zeɪʃn,
ɪ,mɔ:tələɪ'zeɪʃn, -z
AM ɪ(m),mɔrdl̩,aɪ'zeɪʃən,
ɪ(m),mɔrdlə'zeɪʃən,
-z

immortalize
BR ɪ'mɔ:tl̩aɪz,
ɪ'mɔ:tələɪz, -ɪz, -ɪŋ, -d
AM ɪ(m)'mɔrdl̩,aɪz, -ɪz,
-ɪŋ, -d

immortally
BR ɪ'mɔ:tl̩i
AM ɪ(m)'mɔrdl̩i,
ə'mɔrdl̩i

immortelle
BR ,ɪmɔ:'tɛl, -z
AM 'ɪ,mɔr'tɛl,
ə,mɔr'tɛl, -z

immovability
BR ɪ,mu:və'bɪlɪti
AM ɪ(m),muvə'bɪlɪdi,
ə,muvə'bɪlɪdi

immovable
BR (ˌ)ɪ'mu:vəbl, -z
AM ɪ(m)'muvəbəl,
ə'muvəbəl, -z

immovableness
BR (ˌ)ɪ'mu:vəblnəs
AM ɪ(m)'muvəbəlnəs,
ə'muvəbəlnəs

immovably
BR (ˌ)ɪ'mu:vəbli
AM ɪ(m)'muvəbli,
ə'muvəbli

immoveable
BR (ˌ)ɪ'mu:vəbl, -z
AM ɪ(m)'muvəbəl,
ə'muvəbəl, -z

immoveableness
BR (ˌ)ɪ'mu:vəblnəs
AM ɪ(m)'muvəbəlnəs,
ə'muvəbəlnəs

immoveably
BR (ˌ)ɪ'mu:vəbli
AM ɪ(m)'muvəbli,
ə'muvəbli

immune
BR ɪ'mju:n
AM ɪ'mjun

immunisation
BR ,ɪmjʊnʌɪ'zeɪʃn
AM ,ɪmjənə'zeɪʃən,
,ɪmjə,naɪ'zeɪʃən

immunise
BR 'ɪmjʊnʌɪz, -ɪz, -ɪŋ,
-d
AM 'ɪmjə,naɪz, -ɪz, -ɪŋ,
-d

immuniser
BR 'ɪmjʊnʌɪzə(r), -z
AM 'ɪmjə,naɪzər, -z

immunity
BR ɪ'mju:nɪti
AM ɪ'mjunədi, -z

immunization
BR ,ɪmjʊnʌɪ'zeɪʃn
AM ,ɪmjənə'zeɪʃən,
,ɪmjə,naɪ'zeɪʃən

immunize
BR 'ɪmjʊnʌɪz, -ɪz, -ɪŋ,
-d
AM 'ɪmjə,naɪz, -ɪz, -ɪŋ,
-d

immunizer
BR 'ɪmjʊnʌɪzə(r), -z
AM 'ɪmjə,naɪzər, -z

immunoassay
BR ,ɪmjənəʊ'seɪ,
,ɪmjənəʊ'aseɪ, -z
AM ,ɪmjənoʊ'æ,seɪ, -z

immunochemistry
BR ,ɪmjənəʊ'kɛmɪstri
AM ,ɪmjənoʊ'kɛməstri

immunocompetence
BR ,ɪmjənəʊ'kɒmpɪ-
t(ə)ns
AM ,ɪmjənoʊ'kampə-
dəns

immunocompetent
BR ,ɪmjənəʊ'kɒmpɪ-
t(ə)nt
AM ,ɪmjənoʊ'kampədnt

immunocompromised
BR ,ɪmjənəʊ'kɒmprə-
maɪzd
AM ,ɪmjənoʊ'kamprə-
,maɪzd

immunodeficiency
BR ,ɪmjʊnəʊdɪ'fɪʃnsi
AM ,ɪmjənoʊdə'fɪʃənsi

immunodeficient
BR ,ɪmjʊnəʊdɪ'fɪʃnt
AM ,ɪmjənoʊdə'fɪʃənt

immunodepressed
BR ,ɪmjʊnəʊdɪ'prɛst
AM ,ɪmjənoʊdə'prɛst

immunodepression
BR ,ɪmjʊnəʊdɪ'prɛʃn
AM ,ɪmjənoʊdə'prɛʃən

immunogenic
BR ,ɪmjənəʊ'dʒɛnɪk
AM ,ɪmjənoʊ'dʒɛnɪk

immunoglobulin
BR ,ɪmjʊnəʊ'glɒbjʊlɪn,
-z
AM ,ɪmjənoʊ'glɑbjələn,
-z

immunologic
BR ,ɪmjənə'lɒdʒɪk
AM 'ɪmjənə'lɑdʒɪk

immunological
BR ,ɪmjənə'lɒdʒɪkl
AM ,ɪmjənə'lɑdʒəkəl

immunologically
BR ,ɪmjənə'lɒdʒɪkli
AM ,ɪmjənə'lɑdʒək(ə)li

immunologist
BR ,ɪmjʊ'nɒlədʒɪst, -s
AM ,ɪmjə'nɑlədʒəst, -s

immunology
BR ,ɪmjʊ'nɒlədʒi
AM ,ɪmjə'nɑlədʒi

immunosuppressant
BR ,ɪmjʊnəʊsə'prɛsnt,
-s
AM ,ɪmjənoʊsə'prɛsənt,
-s

immunosuppressed
BR ,ɪmjʊnəʊsə'prɛst
AM ,ɪmjənoʊsə'prɛst

immunosuppression
BR ,ɪmjʊnəʊsə'prɛʃn
AM ,ɪmjənoʊsə'prɛʃən

immunosuppressive
BR ,ɪmjʊnəʊsə'prɛsɪv,
-z
AM ,ɪmjənoʊsə'prɛsɪv,
-z

immunotherapy
BR ɪ,mju:nə(ʊ)'θɛrəpi,
,ɪmjʊnəʊ'θɛrəpi
AM ,ɪmjənoʊ'θɛrəpi,
ə'mjunoʊ'θɛrəpi

immure
BR ɪ'mjʊə(r), ɪ'mjɔ:(r),
-z, -ɪŋ, -d
AM ɪ'mjʊ(ə)r, -z, -ɪŋ, -d

immurement
BR ɪ'mjʊəm(ə)nt,
ɪ'mjɔ:m(ə)nt, -s
AM ɪ'mjʊrmənt, -s

immutability
BR ɪ,mju:tə'bɪlɪti
AM ɪ(m),mjudə'bɪlɪdi,
ə,mjudə'bɪlɪdi

immutable
BR (ˌ)ɪ'mju:təbl
AM ɪ(m)'mjudəbəl,
ə'mjudəbəl

immutably
BR (ˌ)ɪ'mju:təbli

AM ɪ(m)'mjudəbli,
ə'mjudəbli

Imogen
BR 'ɪmədʒ(ə)n
AM 'ɪmədʒən

imp
BR ɪmp, -s
AM ɪmp, -s

impact¹
noun
BR 'ɪmpakt, -s
AM 'ɪm,pæk(t), -s

impact²
verb
BR ɪm'pakt, -s, -ɪŋ, -ɪd
AM ɪm'pæk|(t), -(t)s,
-tɪŋ, -təd

impaction
BR ɪm'pakʃn, -z
AM ɪm'pækʃən, -z

impair
BR ɪm'pɛː(r), -z, -ɪŋ, -d
AM ɪm'pɛ(ə)r, -z, -ɪŋ, -d

impairment
BR ɪm'pɛːm(ə)nt
AM ɪm'pɛrmənt

impala
BR ɪm'pɑːlə(r), -z
AM ɪm'pælə, ɪm'pɑlə,
-z

impale
BR ɪm'peɪl, -z, -ɪŋ, -d
AM ɪm'peɪl, -z, -ɪŋ, -d

impalement
BR ɪm'peɪlm(ə)nt
AM ɪm'peɪlmənt

impalpability
BR ɪm,palpə'bɪlɪti
AM ɪm,pælpə'bɪlɪdi

impalpable
BR (,)ɪm'palpəbl
AM ɪm'pælpəbəl

impalpably
BR (,)ɪm'palpəbli
AM ɪm'pælpəbli

impanel
BR ɪm'panl̩, -z, -ɪŋ, -d
AM ɪm'pænəl, -z, -ɪŋ, -d

imparisyllabic
BR ɪm,parɪsɪ'labɪk
AM ,ɪm,pɛrəsə'læbɪk

impark
BR ɪm'pɑːk, -s, -ɪŋ, -t
AM ɪm'park, -s, -ɪŋ, -t

impart
BR ɪm'pɑːt, -s, -ɪŋ, -ɪd
AM ɪm'par|t, -ts, -dɪŋ,
-dəd

impartable
BR ɪm'pɑːtəbl
AM ɪm'pardəbəl

impartation
BR ,ɪmpɑː'teɪʃn, -z
AM ɪm,par'teɪʃən, -z

impartial
BR (,)ɪm'pɑːʃl
AM ɪm'parʃəl

impartiality
BR ,ɪmpɑːʃɪ'alɪti,
ɪm,pɑːʃɪ'alɪti
AM ɪm,parʃi'æɫədi

impartially
BR ɪm'pɑːʃl̩i,
ɪm'pɑːʃəli
AM ɪm'parʃəli

impartialness
BR ɪm'pɑːʃlnəs
AM ɪm'parʃəlnəs

impartible
BR ɪm'pɑːtɪbl
AM ɪm'pardəbəl

impartment
BR ɪm'pɑːtm(ə)nt, -s
AM ɪm'partmənt, -s

impassability
BR ɪm,pɑːsə'bɪlɪti,
ɪm,pasə'bɪlɪti
AM ɪm,pæsə'bɪlɪdi

impassable
BR (,)ɪm'pɑːsəbl,
(,)ɪm'pasəbl
AM ɪm'pæsəbəl

impassableness
BR (,)ɪm'pɑːsəblnəs,
(,)ɪm'pasəblnəs
AM ɪm'pæsəbəlnəs

impassably
BR (,)ɪm'pɑːsəbli,
(,)ɪm'pasəbli
AM ɪm'pæsəbli

impasse
BR ɪm'pɑːs, ɪm'pɑːs,
ɒm'pɑːs, am'pas,
ɪm'pas, ɒm'pas,
'ampɑːs, 'ɪmpɑːs,
'ɒmpɑːs, 'ampas,
'ɪmpas, 'ɒmpas, -ɪz
AM 'ɪm,pæs, ɪm'pæs,
-əz

impassibility
BR ɪm,pɑːsɪ'bɪlɪti,
ɪm,pasɪ'bɪlɪti
AM ɪm,pæsə'bɪlɪdi

impassible
BR (,)ɪm'pɑːsɪbl,
(,)ɪm'pasɪbl
AM ɪm'pæsəbl

impassibleness
BR (,)ɪm'pɑːsɪblnəs,
(,)ɪm'pasɪblnəs
AM ɪm'pæsəbəlnəs

impassibly
BR (,)ɪm'pɑːsɪbli,
(,)ɪm'pasɪbli
AM ɪm'pæsəbli

impassion
BR ɪm'paʃ|n, -nz,
-nɪŋ\-nɪŋ, -nd
AM ɪm'pæʃən, -z, -ɪŋ, -d

impassive
BR ɪm'pasɪv
AM ɪm'pæsɪv

impassively
BR ɪm'pasɪvli
AM ɪm'pæsəvli

impassiveness
BR ɪm'pasɪvnɪs
AM ɪm'pæsɪvnɪs

impassivity
BR ,ɪmpa'sɪvɪti,
,ɪmpə'sɪvɪti
AM ,ɪmpə'sɪvɪdi

impasto
BR ɪm'pastəʊ,
ɪm'pɑːstəʊ, -z
AM ɪm'pæstoʊ,
ɪm'pastoʊ, -z

impatience
BR ɪm'peɪʃns
AM ɪm'peɪʃəns

impatiens
BR ɪm'peɪʃɪɛnz,
ɪm'patɪɛnz
AM ɪm'peɪʃəns

impatient
BR ɪm'peɪʃnt
AM ɪm'peɪʃənt

impatiently
BR ɪm'peɪʃntli
AM ɪm'peɪʃən(t)li

impeach
BR ɪm'piːtʃ, -ɪz, -ɪŋ, -t
AM ɪm'pitʃ, -ɪz, -ɪŋ, -t

impeachable
BR ɪm'piːtʃəbl
AM ɪm'pitʃəbəl

impeachment
BR ɪm'piːtʃm(ə)nt, -s
AM ɪm'pitʃmənt, -s

impeccability
BR ɪm,pɛkə'bɪlɪti
AM ɪm,pɛkə'bɪlɪdi

impeccable
BR ɪm'pɛkəbl
AM ɪm'pɛkəbəl

impeccably
BR ɪm'pɛkəbli
AM ɪm'pɛkəbli

impeccancy
BR ɪm'pɛk(ə)nsi
AM ɪm'pɛkənsi

impeccant
BR ɪm'pɛk(ə)nt
AM ɪm'pɛkənt

impecuniosity
BR ,ɪmpɪ,kjuːnɪ'ɒsɪti
AM ,ɪmpə,kjuni'ɑsədi,
,ɪmpi,kjuni'ɑsədi

impecunious
BR ,ɪmpɪ'kjuːnɪəs
AM ,ɪmpə'kjuniəs

impecuniously
BR ,ɪmpɪ'kjuːnɪəsli
AM ,ɪmpə'kjuniəsli

impecuniousness
BR ,ɪmpɪ'kjuːnɪəsnəs
AM ,ɪmpə'kjuniəsnəs

impedance
BR ɪm'piːdns
AM ɪm'pidns

impede
BR ɪm'piːd, -z, -ɪŋ, -ɪd

AM ɪm'pid, -z, -ɪŋ, -ɪd

impediment
BR ɪm'pɛdɪm(ə)nt, -s
AM ɪm'pɛdəmənt, -s

impedimenta
BR ɪm,pɛdɪ'mɛntə(r)
AM əm,pɛdə'mɛn(t)ə,
,ɪm,pɛdə'mɛn(t)ə

impedimental
BR ɪm,pɛdɪ'mɛntl
AM əm,pɛdə'mɛn(t)l,
,ɪm,pɛdə'mɛn(t)l

impel
BR ɪm'pɛl, -z, -ɪŋ, -d
AM ɪm'pɛl, -z, -ɪŋ, -d

impellent
BR ɪm'pɛlənt, ɪm'pɛlnt,
-s
AM ɪm'pɛlənt, -s

impeller
BR ɪm'pɛlə(r), -z
AM ɪm'pɛlər, -z

impend
BR ɪm'pɛnd, -z, -ɪŋ, -ɪd
AM ɪm'pɛnd, -z, -ɪŋ, -əd

impendence
BR ɪm'pɛnd(ə)ns
AM ɪm'pɛndns

impendency
BR ɪm'pɛnd(ə)nsi
AM ɪm'pɛndnsi

impendent
BR ɪm'pɛnd(ə)nt, -s
AM ɪm'pɛndnt, -s

impending
BR ɪm'pɛndɪŋ
AM ɪm'pɛndɪŋ

impenetrability
BR ɪm,pɛnɪtrə'bɪlɪti
AM ɪm,pɛnətrə'bɪlɪdi

impenetrable
BR (,)ɪm'pɛnɪtrəbl
AM ɪm'pɛnətrəbəl

impenetrablness
BR (,)ɪm'pɛnɪtrəblnəs
AM ɪm'pɛnətrəbəlnəs

impenetrably
BR (,)ɪm'pɛnɪtrəbli
AM ɪm'pɛnətrəbli

impenetrate
BR (,)ɪm'pɛnɪtreɪt, -s,
-ɪŋ, -ɪd
AM ɪm'pɛnə,treɪ|t, -ts,
-dɪŋ, -dɪd

impenitence
BR (,)ɪm'pɛnɪt(ə)ns
AM ɪm'pɛnədəns,
ɪm'pɛnətns

impenitency
BR (,)ɪm'pɛnɪt(ə)nsi
AM ɪm'pɛnədənsi,
ɪm'pɛnətnsi

impenitent
BR (,)ɪm'pɛnɪt(ə)nt
AM ɪm'pɛnədnt

impenitently
BR (,)ɪm'pɛnɪt(ə)ntli

AM ɪmˈpɛnədən(t)li,
ɪmˈpɛnətn(t)li
imperatival
BR ɪmˌpɛrəˈtaɪvl
AM ɪmˌpɛrəˈtaɪvəl
imperative
BR ɪmˈpɛrətɪv, -z
AM əmˈpɛrədɪv, -z
imperatively
BR ɪmˈpɛrətɪvli
AM əmˈpɛrədəvli
imperativeness
BR ɪmˈpɛrətɪvnɪs
AM əmˈpɛrədɪvnɪs
imperator
BR ˌɪmpəˈrɑːtɔː(r), -z
AM ˌɪmpəˈreɪdər,
ˌɪmpəˈrɑːtɔ(ə)r, -z
imperatorial
BR ɪmˌpɛrəˈtɔːriəl,
ˌɪmpɛrəˌtɔːriəl
AM ɪmˈpɛrəˈtɔriəl
imperceptibility
BR ˌɪmpəˌsɛptɪˈbɪlɪti
AM ˌɪmpərˌsɛptəˈbɪlɪdi
imperceptible
BR ˌɪmpəˈsɛptɪbl
AM ˌɪmpərˈsɛptəbəl
imperceptibly
BR ˌɪmpəˈsɛptɪbli
AM ˌɪmpərˈsɛptəbli
impercipience
BR ˌɪmpəˈsɪpiəns
AM ˌɪmpərˈsɪpiəns
impercipient
BR ˌɪmpəˈsɪpiənt
AM ˌɪmpərˈsɪpiənt
imperfect
BR (ˌ)ɪmˈpəːfɪkt, -s
AM ɪmˈpərfək|(t), -(t)s
imperfection
BR ˌɪmpəˈfɛkʃn, -z
AM ˌɪmpərˈfɛkʃən, -z
imperfective
BR ˌɪmpəˈfɛktɪv, -z
AM ˌɪmpərˈfɛktɪv, -z
imperfectly
BR (ˌ)ɪmˈpəːfɪktli
AM ɪmˈpərfək(t)li
imperfectness
BR (ˌ)ɪmˈpəːfɪk(t)nəs
AM ɪmˈpərfək(t)nəs
imperforate
BR (ˌ)ɪmˈpəːf(ə)rət
AM ɪmˈpərfərət
imperia
BR ɪmˈpɪəriə(r)
AM ɪmˈpɪriə
imperial
BR ɪmˈpɪəriəl
AM ɪmˈpɪriəl
imperialise
BR ɪmˈpɪəriəlʌɪz, -ɪz,
-ɪŋ, -d
AM ɪmˈpɪriəˌlaɪz, -ɪz,
-ɪŋ, -d

imperialism
BR ɪmˈpɪəriəlɪz(ə)m
AM ɪmˈpɪriəˌlɪzəm
imperialist
BR ɪmˈpɪəriəlɪst, -s
AM ɪmˈpɪriələst, -s
imperialistic
BR ɪmˌpɪəriəˈlɪstɪk
AM ɪmˌpɪriəˈlɪstɪk
imperialistically
BR ɪmˌpɪəriəˈlɪstɪkli
AM ɪmˌpɪriəˈlɪstək(ə)li
imperialize
BR ɪmˈpɪəriəlʌɪz, -ɪz,
-ɪŋ, -d
AM ɪmˈpɪriəˌlaɪz, -ɪz,
-ɪŋ, -d
imperially
BR ɪmˈpɪəriəli
AM ɪmˈpɪriəli
imperil
BR ɪmˈpɛrɪl, ɪmˈpɛrl,
-z, -ɪŋ, -d
AM ɪmˈpɛrəl, -z, -ɪŋ, -d
imperious
BR ɪmˈpɪəriəs
AM ɪmˈpɪriəs
imperiously
BR ɪmˈpɪəriəsli
AM ɪmˈpɪriəsli
imperiousness
BR ɪmˈpɪəriəsnəs
AM ɪmˈpɪriəsnəs
imperishability
BR ɪmˌpɛrɪʃəˈbɪlɪti,
ˌɪmpɛrɪʃəˈbɪlɪti
AM ɪmˌpɛrəʃəˈbɪlɪdi
imperishable
BR ɪmˈpɛrɪʃəbl
AM ɪmˈpɛrəʃəbəl
imperishableness
BR ɪmˈpɛrɪʃəbli
AM ɪmˈpɛrɪʃəbli
imperishably
BR ɪmˈpɛrɪʃəblnəs
AM ɪmˈpɛrəʃəbəlnəs
imperium
BR ɪmˈpɪəriəm
AM ɪmˈpɪriəm
impermanence
BR (ˌ)ɪmˈpəːmənəns
AM ɪmˈpərmənəns
impermanency
BR (ˌ)ɪmˈpəːmənəns|i,
-ɪz
AM ɪmˈpərmənənsi, -z
impermanent
BR (ˌ)ɪmˈpəːmənənt
AM ɪmˈpərmənənt
impermanently
BR (ˌ)ɪmˈpəːmənəntli
AM ɪmˈpərmənən(t)li
impermeability
BR ɪmˌpəːmɪəˈbɪlɪti,
ˌɪmpəːmɪəˈbɪlɪti
AM ɪmˌpərmɪəˈbɪlɪdi

impermeable
BR (ˌ)ɪmˈpəːmɪəbl
AM ɪmˈpərmiəbəl
impermeableness
BR (ˌ)ɪmˈpəːmɪəblnəs
AM ɪmˈpərmiəbəlnəs
impermeably
BR (ˌ)ɪmˈpəːmɪəbli
AM ɪmˈpərmiəbli
impermissibility
BR ɪmˌpəˌmɪsɪˈbɪlɪti
AM ɪmˌpərmɪsəˈbɪlɪdi
impermissible
BR ˌɪmpəˈmɪsɪbl
AM ɪmˌpərˈmɪsɪbəl
imperscriptible
BR ˌɪmpəˈskrɪptɪbl
AM ˌɪmpərˈskrɪptɪbəl
impersonal
BR (ˌ)ɪmˈpəːs(ə)nl
(ˌ)ɪmˈpəːsn̩l
AM ɪmˈpərs(ə)nəl
impersonality
BR ɪmˌpəːsəˈnalɪti
AM ɪmˌpərsn̩ˈælədi
impersonally
BR (ˌ)ɪmˈpəːs(ə)nəli,
(ˌ)ɪmˈpəːsn̩əli
AM ɪmˈpərs(ə)nəli
impersonate
BR ɪmˈpəːsəneɪt,
ɪmˈpəːsn̩eɪt, -s, -ɪŋ, -ɪd
AM ɪmˈpərsn̩ˌeɪ|t, -ts,
-dɪŋ, -dɪd
impersonation
BR ɪmˌpəːsəˈneɪʃn,
ɪmˌpəːsn̩ˈeɪʃn, -z
AM əmˌpərsn̩ˈeɪʃən,
ˌɪmˌpərsəˈneɪʃən, -z
impersonator
BR ɪmˈpəːsəneɪtə(r),
ɪmˈpəːsn̩eɪtə(r), -z
AM ɪmˈpərsn̩ˌeɪdər, -z
impertinence
BR ɪmˈpəːtɪnəns,
ɪmˈpəːtn̩əns
AM ɪmˈpərtn̩əns
impertinent
BR ɪmˈpəːtɪnənt,
ɪmˈpəːtn̩ənt
AM ɪmˈpərtn̩ənt
impertinently
BR ɪmˈpəːtɪnəntli,
ɪmˈpəːtn̩əntli
AM ɪmˈpərtn̩ən(t)li
imperturbability
BR ɪmˌpəˌtəːbəˈbɪlɪti
AM ˌɪmpərtərbəˈbɪlɪdi
imperturbable
BR ˌɪmpəˈtəːbəbl
AM ˌɪmpərˈtərbəbəl
imperturbableness
BR ˌɪmpəˈtəːbəblnəs
AM ˌɪmpərˈtərbəbəlnəs
imperturbably
BR ˌɪmpəˈtəːbəbli
AM ˌɪmpərˈtərbəbli

impervious
BR ɪmˈpəːvɪəs
AM ɪmˈpərviəs
imperviously
BR ɪmˈpəːvɪəsli
AM ɪmˈpərviəsli
imperviousness
BR ɪmˈpəːvɪəsnəs
AM ɪmˈpərviəsnəs
impetiginous
BR ˌɪmpɪˈtɪdʒɪnəs
AM ˌɪmpəˈtɪdʒɪnəs
impetigo
BR ˌɪmpɪˈtʌɪɡəʊ
AM ˌɪmpəˈtiɡoʊ,
ˌɪmpəˈtaɪɡoʊ
impetrate
BR ˈɪmpɪtreɪt, -s, -ɪŋ, -ɪd
AM ˈɪmpəˌtreɪ|t, -ts,
-dɪŋ, -dɪd
impetration
BR ˌɪmpɪˈtreɪʃn, -z
AM ˌɪmpəˈtreɪʃən, -z
impetratory
BR ˈɪmpɪtrət(ə)ri
AM ˈɪmpətrəˌtɔri
impetuosity
BR ɪmˌpɛtjʊˈɒsɪti,
ɪmˌpɛtʃʊˈɒsɪti
AM ɪmˌpɛtʃəˈwɑsədi
impetuous
BR ɪmˈpɛtjʊəs,
ɪmˈpɛtʃʊəs
AM ɪmˈpɛtʃ(əw)əs
impetuously
BR ɪmˈpɛtjʊəsl̩,
ɪmˈpɛtʃʊəsli
AM ɪmˈpɛtʃ(əw)əsli
impetuousness
BR ɪmˈpɛtjʊəsnəs,
ɪmˈpɛtʃʊəsnəs
AM ɪmˈpɛtʃ(əw)əsnəs
impetus
BR ˈɪmpɪtəs
AM ˈɪmpədəs
impi
BR ˈɪmp|i, -ɪz
AM ˈɪmpi, -z
impiety
BR (ˌ)ɪmˈpʌɪɪt|i, -ɪz
AM ɪmˈpaɪədi, -z
impinge
BR ɪmˈpɪn(d)ʒ, -ɪz, -ɪŋ,
-d
AM ɪmˈpɪndʒ, -ɪz, -ɪŋ, -d
impingement
BR ɪmˈpɪn(d)ʒm(ə)nt,
-s
AM ɪmˈpɪndʒmənt, -s
impinger
BR ɪmˈpɪn(d)ʒə(r), -z
AM ɪmˈpɪndʒər, -z
impious
BR ˈɪmpiəs, (ˌ)ɪmˈpʌɪəs
AM ˈɪmpiəs, ɪmˈpaɪəs
impiously
BR ˈɪmpɪəsli,
(ˌ)ɪmˈpʌɪəsli

AM ˈɪmpiəsli,
ɪmˈpaɪəsli

impiousness
BR ˈɪmpiəsnəs,
(ˌ)ɪmˈpʌɪəsnəs
AM ˈɪmpiəsnəs,
ɪmˈpaɪəsnəs

impish
BR ˈɪmpɪʃ
AM ˈɪmpɪʃ

impishly
BR ˈɪmpɪʃli
AM ˈɪmpɪʃli

impishness
BR ˈɪmpɪʃnɪs
AM ˈɪmpɪʃnɪs

implacability
BR ɪmˌplakəˈbɪlɪti
AM ɪmˌplækəˈbɪlɪdi

implacable
BR ɪmˈplakəbl
AM ɪmˈplækəbəl

implacableness
BR ɪmˈplakəblnəs
AM ɪmˈplækəbəlnəs

implacably
BR ɪmˈplakəbli
AM ɪmˈplækəbli

implant[1]
noun
BR ˈɪmplɑːnt,
ˈɪmplant, -s
AM ˈɪm‚plænt, -s

implant[2]
verb
BR ɪmˈplɑːnt,
ɪmˈplant, -s, -ɪŋ, -ɪd
AM ɪmˈplæn|t, -ts,
-(t)ɪŋ, -(t)əd

implantation
BR ‚ɪmplɑːnˈteɪʃn,
‚ɪmplanˈteɪʃn, -z
AM ‚ɪmplənˈteɪʃən,
ɪmˌplænˈteɪʃən, -z

implausibility
BR ɪmˌplɔːziˈbɪlɪti
AM ɪmˌplɔːzəˈbɪlɪdi,
ɪmˌplazəˈbɪlɪdi

implausible
BR (ˌ)ɪmˈplɔːzɪbl
AM ɪmˈplɔzəbəl,
ɪmˈplazəbəl

implausibly
BR (ˌ)ɪmˈplɔːzɪbli
AM ɪmˈplɔzəbli,
ɪmˈplazəbli

implead
BR ɪmˈpliːd, -z, -ɪŋ, -ɪd
AM ɪmˈplid, -z, -ɪŋ, -ɪd

implement[1]
noun
BR ˈɪmplɪm(ə)nt, -s
AM ˈɪmpləmənt, -s

implement[2]
verb
BR ˈɪmplɪmɛnt, -s, -ɪŋ,
-ɪd

AM ˈɪmpləˌmɛn|t, -ts,
-(t)ɪŋ, -(t)əd

implementation
BR ‚ɪmplɪmɛnˈteɪʃn,
‚ɪmplɪm(ə)nˈteɪʃn, -z
AM ‚ɪmpləmənˈteɪʃən,
-z

implementer
BR ˈɪmplɪmɛntə(r), -z
AM ˈɪmpləˌmɛn(t)ər, -z

implicate
BR ˈɪmplɪkeɪt, -s, -ɪŋ,
-ɪd
AM ˈɪmpləˌkeɪ|t, -ts,
-dɪŋ, -dɪd

implication
BR ‚ɪmplɪˈkeɪʃn, -z
AM ‚ɪmpləˈkeɪʃən, -z

implicative
BR ɪmˈplɪkətɪv,
ˈɪmplɪkeɪtɪv
AM ˈɪmpləˌkeɪdɪv,
ɪmˈplɪkədɪv

implicatively
BR ɪmˈplɪkətɪvli,
ˈɪmplɪkeɪtɪvli
AM ˈɪmpləˌkeɪdɪvli,
ɪmˈplɪkədəvli

implicature
BR ɪmˈplɪkətʃə(r), -z
AM ˈɪmplɪkəˌtʃər, -z

implicit
BR ɪmˈplɪsɪt
AM ɪmˈplɪsɪt

implicitly
BR ɪmˈplɪsɪtli
AM ɪmˈplɪsɪtli

implicitness
BR ɪmˈplɪsɪtnɪs
AM ɪmˈplɪsɪtnɪs

implied
BR ɪmˈplʌɪd
AM ɪmˈplaɪd

impliedly
BR ɪmˈplʌɪ(ɪ)dli
AM ɪmˈplaɪ(ə)dli

implode
BR ɪmˈpləʊd, -z, -ɪŋ, -ɪd
AM ɪmˈploʊd, -z, -ɪŋ, -ɪd

implore
BR ɪmˈplɔː(r), -z, -ɪŋ, -d
AM ɪmˈplɔ(ə)r, -z, -ɪŋ, -d

imploringly
BR ɪmˈplɔːrɪŋli
AM ɪmˈplɔrɪŋli

implosion
BR ɪmˈpləʊʒn, -z
AM ɪmˈploʊʒən, -z

implosive
BR ɪmˈpləʊsɪv,
ɪmˈpləʊzɪv, -z
AM ɪmˈploʊzɪv, -z

imply
BR ɪmˈplʌɪ, -z, -ɪŋ, -d
AM ɪmˈplaɪ, -z, -ɪŋ, -d

impolder
BR ɪmˈpəʊld|ə(r), -əz,
-(ə)rɪŋ, -əd

AM ɪmˈpoʊldər, -d, -ɪŋ,
-d

impolicy
BR ɪmˈpɒlɪs|i, -ɪz
AM ɪmˈpɑləsi, -z

impolite
BR ‚ɪmpəˈlʌɪt
AM ‚ɪmpəˈlaɪt

impolitely
BR ‚ɪmpəˈlʌɪtli
AM ‚ɪmpəˈlaɪtli

impoliteness
BR ‚ɪmpəˈlʌɪtnɪs
AM ‚ɪmpəˈlaɪtnəs

impolitic
BR (ˌ)ɪmˈpɒlɪtɪk
AM ɪmˈpɑləˌtɪk

imponderability
BR ɪmˌpɒnd(ə)rəˈbɪlɪt|i,
‚ɪmpɒnd(ə)rəˈbɪlɪti,
-ɪz
AM ɪmˌpɑndərəˈbɪlɪdi,
-z

imponderable
BR (ˌ)ɪmˈpɒnd(ə)rəbl,
-z
AM ɪmˈpɑndərəbəl, -z

imponderably
BR (ˌ)ɪmˈpɒnd(ə)rəbli
AM ɪmˈpɑndərəbli

imponent
BR ɪmˈpəʊnənt, -s
AM ˈɪm‚pounənt,
ɪmˈpounənt, -s

import[1]
noun
BR ˈɪmpɔːt, -s
AM ˈɪm‚pɔ(ə)rt, -s

import[2]
verb
BR ɪmˈpɔːt, -s, -ɪŋ, -ɪd
AM ɪmˈpɔ(ə)rt, -ts,
-ˈpɔrdɪŋ, -ˈpɔrdɪd

importable
BR ɪmˈpɔːtəbl
AM ɪmˈpɔrdəbəl

importance
BR ɪmˈpɔːtns
AM ɪmˈpɔrtns

important
BR ɪmˈpɔːtnt
AM ɪmˈpɔrtnt

importantly
BR ɪmˈpɔːtntli
AM ɪmˈpɔrtn(t)li

importation
BR ‚ɪmpɔːˈteɪʃn, -z
AM ‚ɪmpɔrˈteɪʃən, -z

importer
BR ɪmˈpɔːtə(r), -z
AM ɪmˈpɔrdər, -z

importunate
BR ɪmˈpɔːtjʊnət,
ɪmˈpɔːtʃʊnət,
ɪmˈpɔːtʃ‚nət
AM əmˈpɔrtʃənət

AM ɪmˈpoʊldər, -d, -ɪŋ,
-d

importunately
BR ɪmˈpɔːtʃnətli,
ɪmˈpɔːtʃ(ə)nətli,
ɪmˈpɔːtjənətli
AM əmˈpɔrtʃənətli

importune
BR ‚ɪmpəˈtjuːn,
‚ɪmpɔːˈtjuːn,
ɪmpəˈtʃuːn,
ɪmpɔːˈtʃuːn, -z, -ɪŋ, -d
AM ‚ɪmpərˈt(j)un,
‚ɪmpɔrˈt(j)un, -z, -ɪŋ,
-d

importunity
BR ‚ɪmpəˈtjuːnɪti,
‚ɪmpɔːˈtjuːnɪti,
ɪmpəˈtʃuːnɪti,
‚ɪmpɔːˈtʃuːnɪti
AM ‚ɪmpərˈt(j)unədi,
‚ɪmpɔrˈt(j)unədi

impose
BR ɪmˈpəʊz, -ɪz, -ɪŋ, -d
AM ɪmˈpoʊz, -əz, -ɪŋ, -t

imposingly
BR ɪmˈpəʊzɪŋli
AM ɪmˈpoʊzɪŋli

imposingness
BR ɪmˈpəʊzɪŋnɪs
AM ɪmˈpoʊzɪŋnɪs

imposition
BR ‚ɪmpəˈzɪʃn, -z
AM ‚ɪmpəˈzɪʃən, -z

impossibility
BR ɪmˌpɒsɪˈbɪlɪt|i,
‚ɪmpɒsɪˈbɪlɪti, -ɪz
AM ‚ɪm‚pɑsəˈbɪlɪdi,
əm‚pɑsəˈbɪlɪdi, -z

impossible
BR ɪmˈpɒsɪbl
AM ɪmˈpɑsəbəl

impossibly
BR ɪmˈpɒsɪbli
AM ɪmˈpɑsəbli

impost
BR ˈɪmpəʊst, ˈɪmpɒst,
-s
AM ˈɪm‚poʊst, -s

imposter
BR ɪmˈpɒstə(r), -z
AM ɪmˈpɑstər, -z

impostor
BR ɪmˈpɒstə(r), -z
AM ɪmˈpɑstər, -z

impostorous
BR ɪmˈpɒst(ə)rəs
AM ɪmˈpɑst(ə)rəs

impostrous
BR ɪmˈpɒstrəs
AM ɪmˈpɑstrəs

imposture
BR ɪmˈpɒstʃə(r), -z
AM ɪmˈpɑstʃər, -z

impotence
BR ˈɪmpət(ə)ns
AM ˈɪmpədəns,
ˈɪmpətns

impotency
BR ˈɪmpət(ə)nsi

AM 'ɪmpədənsi,
'ɪmpətnsi
impotent
BR 'ɪmpət(ə)nt
AM 'ɪmpədənt,
'ɪmpədnt
impotently
BR 'ɪmpət(ə)ntli
AM 'ɪmpədən(t)li,
'ɪmpətn(t)li
impound
BR ɪm'paʊnd, -z, -ɪŋ, -ɪd
AM ɪm'paʊnd, -z, -ɪŋ,
-əd
impoundable
BR ɪm'paʊndəbl
AM ɪm'paʊndəbəl
impounder
BR ɪm'paʊndə(r), -z
AM ɪm'paʊndər, -z
impoundment
BR ɪm'paʊndm(ə)nt,
-s
AM ɪm'paʊndmənt, -s
impoverish
BR ɪm'pɒv(ə)r|ɪʃ, -ɪʃɪz,
-ɪʃɪŋ, -ɪʃt
AM ɪm'pɑv(ə)r|ɪʃ, -ɪz,
-ɪŋ, -t
impoverishment
BR ɪm'pɒv(ə)rɪʃm(ə)nt,
-s
AM ɪm'pɑv(ə)rɪʃmənt,
-s
impracticability
BR ɪm,præktɪkə'bɪlɪti,
,ɪmpræktɪkə'bɪlɪti
AM 'ɪm,præktəkə'bɪlɪdi,
əm,præktəkə'bɪlɪdi
impracticable
BR (,)ɪm'præktɪkəbl
AM ɪm'præktəkəbəl
impracticableness
BR (,)ɪm'præktɪkəblnəs
AM ɪm'præktəkəbəlnəs
impracticably
BR (,)ɪm'præktɪkəbli
AM ɪm'præktəkəbli
impractical
BR (,)ɪm'præktɪkl
AM ɪm'præktəkəl
impracticality
BR ɪm,præktɪ'kælɪti,
,ɪmpræktɪ'kælɪti
AM 'ɪm,præktə'kælədi,
əm,præktə'kælədi
impractically
BR (,)ɪm'præktɪk(ə)li,
(,)ɪm'præktɪk]i
AM ɪm'præktək(ə)li
imprecate
BR 'ɪmprɪkeɪt, -s, -ɪŋ,
-ɪd
AM 'ɪmprə,keɪ|t, -ts,
-dɪŋ, -dɪd
imprecation
BR ,ɪmprɪ'keɪʃn, -z
AM ,ɪmprə'keɪʃən, -z

imprecatory
BR 'ɪmprɪkeɪt(ə)ri,
ɪm'prɛkət(ə)ri
AM 'ɪmprəkə,tɔri
imprecise
BR ,ɪmprɪ'sʌɪs
AM 'ɪmprə'saɪs
imprecisely
BR ,ɪmprɪ'sʌɪsli
AM 'ɪmprə'saɪsli
impreciseness
BR ,ɪmprɪ'sʌɪsnɪs
AM 'ɪmprə'saɪsnɪs
imprecision
BR ,ɪmprɪ'sɪʒn, -z
AM ,ɪmprə'sɪʒən, -z
impregnability
BR ɪm,prɛgnə'bɪlɪti
AM əm,prɛgnə'bɪlɪdi,
ɪm,prɛgnə'bɪlɪdi
impregnable
BR (,)ɪm'prɛgnəbl
AM əm'prɛgnəbəl,
ɪm'prɛgnəbəl
impregnably
BR (,)ɪm'prɛgnəbli
AM əm'prɛgnəbli,
ɪm'prɛgnəbli
impregnatable
BR 'ɪmprɛgneɪtəbl,
,ɪmprɛg'neɪtəbl
AM ɪm,prɛg'neɪdəbəl
impregnate¹
adjective
BR (,)ɪm'prɛgnət
AM ɪm'prɛgnət
impregnate²
verb
BR 'ɪmprɛgneɪt, -s, -ɪŋ,
-ɪd
AM ɪm'prɛg,neɪ|t, -ts,
-dɪŋ, -dɪd
impregnation
BR ,ɪmprɛg'neɪʃn, -z
AM ,ɪm,prɛg'neɪʃən, -z
impresario
BR ,ɪmprɪ'sɑːrɪəʊ, -z
AM ,ɪmprə'sɑriou,
,ɪmprə'sɛriou, -z
imprescriptible
BR ,ɪmprɪ'skrɪptɪbl
AM ,ɪmprɪ'skrɪptəbəl
impress¹
noun
BR 'ɪmprɛs, -ɪz
AM 'ɪm,prɛs, -əz
impress²
verb
BR ɪm'prɛs, -ɪz, -ɪŋ, -t
AM ɪm'prɛs, -əz, -ɪŋ, -t
impressible
BR ɪm'prɛsɪbl
AM 'ɪm,prɛsəbəl
impression
BR ɪm'prɛʃn, -z
AM ɪm'prɛʃən, -z

impressionability
BR ɪm,prɛʃ(ə)nə'bɪlɪti,
ɪm,prɛʃnə'bɪlɪti
AM ɪmprəʃ(ə)nə'bɪlɪdi
impressionable
BR ɪm'prɛʃ(ə)nəbl,
ɪm'prɛʃnəbl
AM ɪm'prɛʃ(ə)nəbəl
impressionably
BR ɪm'prɛʃ(ə)nəbli,
ɪm'prɛʃnəbli
AM ɪm'prɛʃ(ə)nəbli
impressional
BR ɪm'prɛʃn(ə)l,
ɪm'prɛʃən(ə)l
AM ɪm'prɛʃ(ə)nəl
impressionism
BR ɪm'prɛʃnɪz(ə)m,
ɪm'prɛʃənɪz(ə)m
AM ɪm'prɛʃə,nɪzəm
impressionist
BR ɪm'prɛʃnɪst,
ɪm'prɛʃənɪst, -s
AM ɪm'prɛʃ(ə)nəst, -s
impressionistic
BR ɪm,prɛʃə'nɪstɪk,
ɪm,prɛʃn'ɪstɪk
AM ɪm,prɛʃə'nɪstɪk,
əm,prɛʃə'nɪstɪk
**impressionistic-
ally**
BR ɪm,prɛʃə'nɪstɪkli
AM (')ɪm'prɛʃə'nɪstək-
(ə)li,
əm,prɛʃə'nɪstək(ə)li
impressive
BR ɪm'prɛsɪv
AM əm'prɛsɪv,
'ɪm,prɛsɪv
impressively
BR ɪm'prɛsɪvli
AM əm'prɛsəvli,
'ɪm,prɛsəvli
impressiveness
BR ɪm'prɛsɪvnɪs
AM əm'prɛsɪvnɪs
impressment
BR ɪm'prɛsm(ə)nt
AM ɪm'prɛsmənt
imprest
BR 'ɪmprɛst, -s
AM 'ɪm,prɛst, -s
imprimatur
BR ,ɪmprɪ'mɑːtə(r),
,ɪmprɪ'meɪtə(r), -z
AM ,ɪmprə'mɑdər,
ɪm'prɪmə,t(j)ʊ(ə)r, -z
imprimatura
BR ,ɪmpriːmə'tʊərə(r),
-z
AM ɪm,primə'tʊrə, -z
imprint¹
noun
BR 'ɪmprɪnt, -s
AM 'ɪm,prɪnt, -s
imprint²
verb
BR ɪm'prɪnt, -s, -ɪŋ, -ɪd

AM ɪm'prɪn|t, -ts, -(t)ɪŋ,
-(t)əd
imprison
BR ɪm'prɪzn, -z, -ɪŋ, -d
AM ɪm'prɪzn̩, -z, -ɪŋ, -d
imprisonment
BR ɪm'prɪznm(ə)nt, -s
AM ɪm'prɪznmənt, -s
impro
BR 'ɪmprəʊ, -z
AM 'ɪm,prou, -z
improbability
BR ɪm,prɒbə'bɪlɪt|i, -ɪz
AM 'ɪm,prabə'bɪlɪdi,
əm,prabə'bɪlɪdi, -z
improbable
BR (,)ɪm'prɒbəbl
AM ɪm'prabəbəl
improbably
BR (,)ɪm'prɒbəbli
AM ɪm'prabəbli
improbity
BR (,)ɪm'prəʊbɪti
AM ɪm'proʊbədi,
ɪm'prabədi
impromptu
BR ɪm'prɒm(p)tjuː,
ɪm'prɒm(p)tʃuː, -z
AM ɪm'pram(p),t(j)u,
-z
improper
BR (,)ɪm'prɒpə(r)
AM ɪm'prɑpər
improperly
BR (,)ɪm'prɒpəli
AM ɪm'prɑpərli
impropriate
BR (,)ɪm'prəʊprɪeɪt, -s,
-ɪŋ, -ɪd
AM ɪm'proʊpri,eɪ|t, -ts,
-dɪŋ, -dɪd
impropriation
BR ɪm,prəʊprɪ'eɪʃn, -z
AM ɪm,proʊpri'eɪʃən,
-z
impropriator
BR (,)ɪm'prəʊprɪeɪtə(r),
-z
AM ɪm'proʊpri,eɪdər,
-z
impropriety
BR ,ɪmprə'prʌɪt|i, -ɪz
AM 'ɪmprə'praɪədi,
'ɪmproʊ'praɪədi, -z
improv
BR 'ɪmprɒv, -z
AM 'ɪm,prav, -z
improvability
BR ɪm,pruːvə'bɪlɪt|i,
-ɪz
AM ɪm,pruvə'bɪlɪdi, -z
improvable
BR ɪm'pruːvəbl
AM ɪm'pruvəbəl
improve
BR ɪm'pruːv, -z, -ɪŋ, -d
AM ɪm'pruv, -z, -ɪŋ, -d

improvement
BR ɪmˈpruːvm(ə)nt, -s
AM ɪmˈpruːvmənt, -s

improver
BR ɪmˈpruːvə(r), -z
AM ɪmˈpruːvər, -z

improvidence
BR (ˌ)ɪmˈprɒvɪd(ə)ns
AM ɪmˈprɑvədns

improvident
BR (ˌ)ɪmˈprɒvɪd(ə)nt
AM ɪmˈprɑvədnt

improvidently
BR (ˌ)ɪmˈprɒvɪd(ə)ntli
AM ɪmˈprɑvəd(ə)n(t)li

improvisation
BR ˌɪmprəvʌɪˈzeɪʃn, -z
AM ɪmˌprɑvəˈzeɪʃən,
ˌɪmprəvəˈzeɪʃən, -z

improvisational
BR ˌɪmprəvʌɪˈzeɪʃn̩(ə)l,
ˌɪmprəvʌɪˈzeɪʃən(ə)l
AM ɪmˌprɑvəˈzeɪʃ(ə)nəl,
ˌɪmprəvəˈzeɪʃ(ə)nəl

improvisatorial
BR ˌɪmprəvʌɪzəˈtɔːrɪəl,
ɪmˌprɒvɪzəˈtɔːrɪəl
AM ɪmˌprɑvəzəˈtɔriəl

improvisatory
BR ˌɪmprəˈvʌɪzət(ə)ri
AM ɪmˈprɑvəzəˌtɔri,
ˌɪmprəˈvaɪzəˌtɔri

improvise
BR ˈɪmprəvʌɪz, -ɪz, -ɪŋ,
-d
AM ˈɪmprəˌvaɪz, -ɪz, -ɪŋ,
-d

improviser
BR ˈɪmprəvʌɪzə(r), -z
AM ˈɪmprəˌvaɪzər, -z

imprudence
BR (ˌ)ɪmˈpruːd(ə)ns
AM ɪmˈprudns

imprudent
BR (ˌ)ɪmˈpruːd(ə)nt
AM ɪmˈprudnt

imprudently
BR (ˌ)ɪmˈpruːd(ə)ntli
AM ɪmˈprudn(t)li

impudence
BR ˈɪmpjʊd(ə)ns
AM ˈɪmpjədns

impudent
BR ˈɪmpjʊd(ə)nt
AM ˈɪmpjədnt

impudently
BR ˈɪmpjʊd(ə)ntli
AM ˈɪmpjəd(ə)n(t)li

impudicity
BR ˌɪmpjəˈdɪsɪti
AM ˌɪmpjəˈdɪsɪdi,
ˌɪmpjʊˈdɪsɪdi

impugn
BR ɪmˈpjuːn, -z, -ɪŋ, -d
AM ɪmˈpjun, -z, -ɪŋ, -d

impugnable
BR ɪmˈpjuːnəbl
AM ɪmˈpjunəbəl

impugnment
BR ɪmˈpjuːnm(ə)nt, -s
AM ɪmˈpjunmənt, -s

impuissance
BR (ˌ)ɪmˈpwɪsns,
(ˌ)ɪmˈpjuːɪsns
AM ɪmˈpjusəns,
ɪmˈpwɪsəns

impuissant
BR (ˌ)ɪmˈpwɪsnt,
(ˌ)ɪmˈpjuːɪsnt
AM ɪmˈpjusənt,
ɪmˈpwɪsənt

impulse
BR ˈɪmpʌls, -ɪz
AM ˈɪmˌpəls, -əz

impulsion
BR ɪmˈpʌlʃn, -z
AM ɪmˈpəlʃən, -z

impulsive
BR ɪmˈpʌlsɪv
AM ɪmˈpəlsɪv

impulsively
BR ɪmˈpʌlsɪvli
AM ɪmˈpəlsəvli

impulsiveness
BR ɪmˈpʌlsɪvnɪs
AM ɪmˈpəlsɪvnɪs

impunity
BR ɪmˈpjuːnɪti
AM ɪmˈpjunədi

impure
BR (ˌ)ɪmˈpjʊə(r),
(ˌ)ɪmˈpjɔː(r)
AM ɪmˈpjʊ(ə)r

impurely
BR (ˌ)ɪmˈpjʊəli,
(ˌ)ɪmˈpjɔːli
AM ɪmˈpjʊrli

impureness
BR (ˌ)ɪmˈpjʊənəs,
(ˌ)ɪmˈpjɔːnəs
AM ɪmˈpjʊrnəs

impurity
BR (ˌ)ɪmˈpjʊərɪt|i,
ˌɪmˈpjɔːrɪt|i, -ɪz
AM ɪmˈpjʊrədi, -z

imputable
BR ɪmˈpjuːtəbl
AM ɪmˈpjʊdəbəl

imputation
BR ˌɪmpjəˈteɪʃn, -z
AM ˌɪmpjəˈteɪʃən, -z

imputative
BR ɪmˈpjuːtətɪv
AM ɪmˈpjʊdədɪv

impute
BR ɪmˈpjuːt, -s, -ɪŋ, -ɪd
AM ɪmˈpju|t, -ts, -dɪŋ,
-dəd

imshi
BR ˈɪmʃi
AM ˈɪm͵ʃi

in
BR ɪn
AM ɪn

Ina
BR ˈiːnə(r), ˈʌɪnə(r)

AM ˈaɪnə, ˈinə

inability
BR ˌɪnəˈbɪlɪti
AM ˌɪnəˈbɪlɪdi

in absentia
BR ˌɪn əbˈsɛntɪə(r),
+ əbˈsɛnʃ(ɪ)ə(r)
AM ˌɪn əbˈsɛnʃə, ˌɪn
ˌæbˈsɛnʃə

inaccessibility
BR ˌɪnəkˌsɛsɪˈbɪlɪti,
ˌɪnakˌsɛsɪˈbɪlɪti
AM ˌɪnəkˌsɛsəˈbɪlɪdi,
ˈɪnəkˌsɛsəˈbɪlɪdi

inaccessible
BR ˌɪnəkˈsɛsɪbl,
ˌɪnakˈsɛsɪbl
AM ˌɪnækˈsɛsəbəl,
ˈɪnəkˈsɛsəbəl

inaccessibleness
BR ˌɪnəkˈsɛsɪblnəs,
ˌɪnakˈsɛsɪblnəs
AM ˌɪnækˈsɛsəbələs,
ˈɪnəkˈsɛsəbəlnəs

inaccessibly
BR ˌɪnəkˈsɛsɪbli,
ˌɪnakˈsɛsɪbli
AM ˌɪnækˈsɛsəbli,
ˈɪnəkˈsɛsəbli

inaccuracy
BR (ˌ)ɪnˈakjʊrəs|i, -ɪz
AM ɪnˈækjərəsi, -z

inaccurate
BR (ˌ)ɪnˈakjʊrət
AM ɪnˈækjərət

inaccurately
BR (ˌ)ɪnˈakjʊrətli
AM ɪnˈækjərətli

inaction
BR ɪnˈakʃn
AM ɪnˈækʃən

inactivate
BR ɪnˈaktɪveɪt, -s, -ɪŋ,
-ɪd
AM ɪnˈæktəˌveɪ|t, -ts,
-dɪŋ, -dɪd

inactivation
BR ɪnˌaktɪˈveɪʃn,
ˌɪnaktɪˈveɪʃn, -z
AM ɪnˌæktəˈveɪʃən, -z

inactive
BR (ˌ)ɪnˈaktɪv
AM ɪnˈæktɪv

inactively
BR (ˌ)ɪnˈaktɪvli
AM ɪnˈæktəvli

inactivity
BR ˌɪnakˈtɪvɪti
AM ˌɪnækˈtɪvɪdi

inadequacy
BR (ˌ)ɪnˈadɪkwəs|i, -ɪz
AM ɪnˈædəkwəsi, -z

inadequate
BR (ˌ)ɪnˈadɪkwət
AM ɪnˈædəkwət

inadequately
BR (ˌ)ɪnˈadɪkwətli
AM ɪnˈædəkwətli

inadmissibility
BR ˌɪnədˌmɪsɪˈbɪlɪti
AM ˌɪnədˌmɪsəˈbɪlɪdi

inadmissible
BR ˌɪnədˈmɪsɪbl
AM ˌɪnədˈmɪsəbəl

inadmissibly
BR ˌɪnədˈmɪsɪbli
AM ˌɪnədˈmɪsɪbli

inadvertence
BR ˌɪnədˈvɜː(t)(ə)ns
AM ˌɪnədˈvɜrtns,
ˌɪˌnædˈvɜrtns

inadvertency
BR ˌɪnədˈvɜː(t)(ə)nsi
AM ˌɪnədˈvɜrtnsi,
ˌɪˌnædˈvɜrtnsi

inadvertent
BR ˌɪnədˈvɜː(t)(ə)nt
AM ˌɪnədˈvɜrtnt

inadvertently
BR ˌɪnədˈvɜː(t)(ə)ntli
AM ˌɪnədˈvɜrtn(t)li

inadvisability
BR ˌɪnəd͵vʌɪzəˈbɪlɪti
AM ˌɪnəd͵vaɪzəˈbɪlɪdi

inadvisable
BR ˌɪnədˈvʌɪzəbl
AM ˌɪnədˈvaɪzəbəl

inalienability
BR ɪnˌeɪlɪənəˈbɪlɪti
AM ɪnˌeɪlɪənəˈbɪlɪdi

inalienable
BR (ˌ)ɪnˈeɪlɪənəbl
AM ɪnˈeɪlɪənəbəl

inalienableness
BR (ˌ)ɪnˈeɪlɪənəblnəs
AM ɪnˈeɪlɪənəbəlnəs

inalienably
BR (ˌ)ɪnˈeɪlɪənəbli
AM ɪnˈeɪlɪənəbli

inalterability
BR ɪnˌɔːlt(ə)rəˈbɪlɪti,
ˌɪnɒːlt(ə)rəˈbɪlɪti,
ɪnˌɒlt(ə)rəˈbɪlɪti
AM ɪnˌɔlt(ə)rəˈbɪlɪdi,
ɪnˌɑlt(ə)rəˈbɪlɪdi

inalterable
BR (ˌ)ɪnˈɔːlt(ə)rəbl,
(ˌ)ɪnˈɒlt(ə)rəbl
AM ɪnˈɔlt(ə)rəbəl,
ɪnˈɑlt(ə)rəbəl

inalterably
BR (ˌ)ɪnˈɔːlt(ə)rəbli,
(ˌ)ɪnˈɒlt(ə)rəbli
AM ɪnˈɔlt(ə)rəbli,
ɪnˈɑlt(ə)rəbli

inamorata
BR ɪnˌaməˈrɑːtə(r),
ˌɪnaməˈrɑːtə(r), -z
AM ɪˌnæməˈrɑdə, -z

inamorato
BR ɪnˌaməˈrɑːtəʊ,
ˌɪnaməˈrɑːtəʊ, -z
AM ɪˌnæməˈrɑdoʊ, -z

inane
BR ɪˈneɪn

AM ɪˈneɪn
inanely
BR ɪˈneɪmli
AM ɪˈneɪmli
inaneness
BR ɪˈneɪnnɪs
AM ɪˈneɪ(n)nɪs
inanga
BR ˈiːnaŋgə(r), -z
AM ˈiˌnaŋgə, -z
inanimate
BR ɪnˈanɪmət
AM ɪnˈænəmət
inanimately
BR ɪnˈanɪmətli
AM ɪnˈænəmətli
inanimation
BR ɪnˌanɪˈmeɪʃn
AM ɪnˌænəˈmeɪʃən
inanition
BR ˌɪnəˈnɪʃn
AM ˌɪnəˈnɪʃən
inanity
BR ɪˈnanɪt|i, -ɪz
AM ɪˈnænədi, -z
inappeasable
BR ˌɪnəˈpiːzəbl
AM ˌɪnəˈpizəbəl
inappellable
BR ˌɪnəˈpɛləbl
AM ˌɪnəˈpɛləbəl
inappetence
BR (ˌ)ɪnˈapɪt(ə)ns
AM ɪnˈæpədəns,
ɪnˈæpətns
inappetency
BR (ˌ)ɪnˈapɪt(ə)nsi
AM ɪnˈæpədənsi,
ɪnˈæpətnsi
inappetent
BR (ˌ)ɪnˈapɪt(ə)nt
AM ɪnˈæpədənt,
ɪnˈæpədnt
inapplicability
BR ˌɪnəˌplɪkəˈbɪlɪti,
ɪnˌaplɪkəˈbrlɪti
AM ˌɪnˌæpləkəˈbɪlɪdi,
ənˌæpləkəˈbɪlɪdi
inapplicable
BR ɪnˈplɪkəbl,
(ˌ)ɪnˈaplɪkəbl
AM ɪnˈæpləkəbəl,
ənˈæpləkəbəl
inapplicably
BR ˌɪnəˈplɪkəbli,
(ˌ)ɪnˈaplɪkəbli
AM ɪnˈæpləkəbli,
ənˈæpləkəbli
inapposite
BR (ˌ)ɪnˈapəzɪt
AM ɪnˈæpəzət
inappositely
BR (ˌ)ɪnˈapəzɪtli
AM ɪnˈæpəzətli
inappositeness
BR (ˌ)ɪnˈapəzɪtnɪs
AM ɪnˈæpəzətnəs

inappreciable
BR ˌɪnəˈpriːʃ(ɪ)əbl
AM ˌɪnəˈpriʃəbəl
inappreciably
BR ˌɪnəˈpriːʃ(ɪ)əbli
AM ˌɪnəˈpriʃəbli
inappreciation
BR ˌɪnəˌpriːʃɪˈeɪʃn,
ˌɪnəˌpriːsɪˈeɪʃn
AM ˌɪnəprɪˈʃiˈeɪʃən
inappreciative
BR ˌɪnəˈpriːʃ(ɪ)ətɪv,
ˌɪnəˈpriːsɪətɪv
AM ˌɪnəˈpriʃədɪv
inapprehensible
BR ɪnˌaprɪˈhɛnsɪbl,
ˌɪnaprɪˈhɛnsɪbl
AM ɪnˈæprəˈhɛnsəbəl
inappropriate
BR ˌɪnəˈprəʊprɪət
AM ˌɪnəˈproʊpriət
inappropriately
BR ˌɪnəˈprəʊprɪətli
AM ˌɪnəˈproʊpriətli
inappropriateness
BR ˌɪnəˈprəʊprɪətnəs
AM ˌɪnəˈproʊpriətnəs
inapt
BR (ˌ)ɪnˈapt
AM ɪnˈæpt
inaptitude
BR (ˌ)ɪnˈaptɪtjuːd,
(ˌ)ɪnˈaptɪtʃuːd
AM ɪnˈæptəˌt(j)ud
inaptly
BR (ˌ)ɪnˈaptli
AM ɪnˈæp(t)li
inaptness
BR (ˌ)ɪnˈap(t)nəs
AM ɪnˈæp(t)nəs
inarch
BR ɪnˈɑːtʃ, -ɪz, -ɪŋ, -t
AM ɪnˈɑrtʃ, -əz, -ɪŋ, -t
inarguable
BR (ˌ)ɪnˈɑːɡjʊəbl
AM ɪnˈɑrgjə(wə)bəl
inarguably
BR (ˌ)ɪnˈɑːɡjʊəbli
AM ɪnˈɑrgjə(wə)bli
inarticulacy
BR ˌɪnɑːˈtɪkjʊləsi
AM ˌɪnɑrˈtɪkjələsi
inarticulate
BR ˌɪnɑːˈtɪkjʊlət
AM ˌɪnɑrˈtɪkjələt
inarticulately
BR ˌɪnɑːˈtɪkjʊlətli
AM ˌɪnɑrˈtɪkjələtli
inarticulateness
BR ˌɪnɑːˈtɪkjʊlətnəs
AM ˌɪnɑrˈtɪkjələtnəs
inartistic
BR ˌɪnɑːˈtɪstɪk
AM ˌɪnɑrˈtɪstɪk
inartistically
BR ˌɪnɑːˈtɪstɪkli
AM ˌɪnɑrˈtɪstək(ə)li

inasmuch
BR ˌɪnəzˈmʌtʃ
AM ˌɪnəzˈmətʃ
inattention
BR ˌɪnəˈtɛnʃn
AM ˌɪnəˈtɛn(t)ʃən
inattentive
BR ˌɪnəˈtɛntɪv
AM ˌɪnəˈtɛn(t)ɪv
inattentively
BR ˌɪnəˈtɛntɪvli
AM ˌɪnəˈtɛn(t)əvli
inattentiveness
BR ˌɪnəˈtɛntɪvnɪs
AM ˌɪnəˈtɛn(t)ɪvnɪs
inaudibility
BR ɪnˌɔːdɪˈbɪlɪti,
ˌɪnɔːdɪˈbɪlɪti
AM ˌɪnədəˈbɪlɪdi,
ˌɪnɔdəˈbɪlɪdi,
ɪˌnɔdəˈbɪlɪdi
inaudible
BR (ˌ)ɪnˈɔːdɪbl
AM ɪnˈɔdəbəl,
ɪnˈadəbəl
inaudibly
BR (ˌ)ɪnˈɔːdɪbli
AM ɪnˈɔdəbli, ɪnˈadəbli
inaugural
BR ɪˈnɔːɡjʊrəl,
ɪˈnɔːɡjʊrl, -z
AM ɪˈnɔɡjʊrəl,
ɪˈnɔɡ(ə)rəl,
ɪˈnɑɡjʊrəl,
ɪˈnɑɡ(ə)rəl, -z
inaugurate
BR ɪˈnɔːɡjʊreɪt, -s, -ɪŋ,
-ɪd
AM ɪˈnɔɡ(j)əˌreɪ|t,
ɪˈnɑɡ(j)əˌreɪ|t, -ts,
-dɪŋ, -dɪd
inauguration
BR ɪˌnɔːɡjʊˈreɪʃn, -z
AM ɪˌnɔɡ(j)əˈreɪʃən,
ɪˌnɑɡ(j)əˈreɪʃən, -z
inaugurator
BR ɪˈnɔːɡjʊreɪtə(r), -z
AM ɪˈnɔɡ(j)əˌreɪdər,
ɪˈnɑɡ(j)əˌreɪdər, -z
inauguratory
BR ɪˈnɔːɡjʊrət(ə)ri
AM ɪˈnɔɡ(j)ərəˌtɔri,
ɪˈnɑɡ(j)ərəˌtɔri
inauspicious
BR ˌɪnɔːˈspɪʃəs
AM ˌɪnɔˈspɪʃəs,
ˌɪnɑˈspɪʃəs
inauspiciously
BR ˌɪnɔːˈspɪʃəsli
AM ˌɪnɔˈspɪʃəsli,
ˌɪnɑˈspɪʃəsli
inauspiciousness
BR ˌɪnɔːˈspɪʃəsnəs
AM ˌɪnɔˈspɪʃəsnəs,
ˌɪnɑˈspɪʃəsnəs
inauthentic
BR ˌɪnɔːˈθɛntɪk
AM ˌɪnɔːˈθɛntɪk,
ˌɪnənˈθentɪk

AM ˌɪnɔːˈθɛn(t)ɪk,
ˌɪnɑˈθɛn(t)ɪk
inauthenticity
BR ˌɪnɔːθɛnˈtɪsɪti
AM ˌɪnɔθənˈtɪsɪdi,
ˌɪnɑθənˈtɪsɪdi
in-between
BR ˌɪnbɪˈtwiːn
AM ˌɪnbəˈtwin
inboard
BR ˈɪnbɔːd
AM ˈɪnˌbɔ(ə)rd
inborn
BR ˌɪnˈbɔːn
AM ˈɪnˌbɔ(ə)rn
inbound
BR ˈɪnbaʊnd
AM ˈɪnˌbaʊnd
inbreathe
BR ˌɪnˈbriːð, -z, -ɪŋ, -d
AM ɪnˈbrið, -z, -ɪŋ, -d
inbred
BR ˌɪnˈbrɛd
AM ˈɪnˌbrɛd
inbreed
BR ˌɪnˈbriːd, -z, -ɪŋ
AM ˈɪnˌbrid, -z, -ɪŋ
inbreeding
BR ˈɪnˌbriːdɪŋ,
ˌɪnˈbriːdɪŋ
AM ˈɪnˌbridɪŋ
inbuilt
BR ˌɪnˈbɪlt
AM ˈɪnˌbɪlt
Inc.
BR ɪŋk
AM ɪŋk
Inca
BR ˈɪŋkə(r), -z
AM ˈɪŋkə, -z
Incaic
BR ɪŋˈkeɪɪk
AM ɪnˈkeɪɪk, ɪŋˈkeɪɪk
incalculability
BR ɪnˌkalkjʊləˈbɪlɪti,
ɪŋˌkalkjʊləˈbɪlɪti
AM ˌɪŋˌkælkjələˈbɪlɪdi,
ɪnˌkælkjələˈbɪlɪdi,
ˌɪnˌkælkjələˈbɪlɪdi
incalculable
BR (ˌ)ɪnˈkalkjʊləbl,
(ˌ)ɪŋˈkalkjʊləbl
AM ɪnˈkælkjələbəl,
ɪŋˈkælkjələbəl
incalculably
BR (ˌ)ɪnˈkalkjʊləbli,
(ˌ)ɪŋˈkalkjʊləbli
AM ɪnˈkælkjələbli,
ɪŋˈkælkjələbli
in camera
BR ˌɪn ˈkam(ə)rə(r)
AM ˌɪn ˈkæm(ə)rə
Incan
BR ˈɪŋkən
AM ˈɪŋkən
incandesce
BR ˌɪnkænˈdɛs,
ˌɪnkənˈdɛs,

,ɪŋkan'dɛs,
,ɪŋkən'dɛs, -ɪz, -ɪŋ, -t
AM ,ɪŋkən'dɛs,
,ɪŋkən'dɛs, -əz, -ɪŋ, -t

incandescence
BR ,ɪnkan'dɛsns,
,ɪŋkan'dɛsns,
,ɪŋkan'dɛsns,
AM ,ɪŋkən'dɛsəns,
,ɪŋkan'dɛsəns

incandescent
BR ,ɪnkan'dɛsnt,
,ɪŋkan'dɛsnt,
,ɪŋkan'dɛsnt,
,ɪŋkan'dɛsnt
AM ,ɪŋkən'dɛsənt,
,ɪŋkan'dɛsənt

incandescently
BR ,ɪnkan'dɛsntli,
,ɪŋkan'dɛsntli,
,ɪŋkan'dɛsntli,
,ɪŋkan'dɛsntli
AM ,ɪŋkən'dɛsn(t)li,
,ɪŋkan'dɛsn(t)li

incantation
BR ,ɪnkan'teɪʃn,
,ɪŋkan'teɪʃn, -z
AM ,ɪn,kæn'teɪʃən,
,ɪŋ,kæn'teɪʃən, -z

incantational
BR ,ɪnkan'teɪʃn(ə)l,
,ɪŋkan'teɪʃn(ə)l,
,ɪŋkan'teɪʃn(ə)l,
,ɪŋkan'teɪʃən(ə)l
AM ,ɪn,kæn'teɪʃ(ə)nəl,
,ɪŋ,kæn'teɪʃ(ə)nəl

incantatory
BR ,ɪnkan'teɪt(ə)ri,
ɪn'kantət(ə)ri,
,ɪŋkan'teɪt(ə)ri
ɪŋ'kantət(ə)ri
AM ,ɪn'kæn(t)ə,tɔri,
,ɪŋ'kæn(t)ə,tɔri

incapability
BR ɪn,keɪpə'bɪlɪti,
,ɪnkeɪpə'bɪlɪti,
ɪŋ,keɪpə'bɪlɪti,
,ɪŋkeɪpə'bɪlɪti
AM ɪn,keɪpə'bɪlɪdi,
ɪn,keɪpə'bɪlɪdi,
,ɪŋ,keɪpə'bɪlɪdi

incapable
BR ɪn'keɪpəbl,
ɪŋ'keɪpəbl
AM ɪn'keɪpəbəl,
ɪŋ'keɪpəbəl

incapably
BR ɪn'keɪpəbli,
ɪŋ'keɪpəbli
AM ɪn'keɪpəbli,
ɪŋ'keɪpəbli

incapacitant
BR ,ɪnkə'pasɪtnt,
,ɪŋkə'pasɪtnt, -s
AM ,ɪnkə'pæsətnt,
,ɪŋkə'pæsətnt, -s

incapacitate
BR ,ɪnkə'pasɪteɪt,
,ɪŋkə'pasɪteɪt, -s, -ɪŋ,
-ɪd
AM ,ɪnkə'pæsə,teɪt,
,ɪŋkə'pæsə,teɪt, -ts,
-dɪŋ, -dɪd

incapacitation
BR ,ɪnkə,pasɪ'teɪʃn,
,ɪŋkə,pasɪ'teɪʃn
AM ,ɪnkə,pæsə'teɪʃən,
,ɪŋkə,pæsə'teɪʃən

incapacity
BR ,ɪnkə'pasɪti,
,ɪŋkə'pasɪti
AM ,ɪnkə'pæsədi,
,ɪŋkə'pæsədi

in-car
BR ɪn'kɑː(r), ɪŋ'kɑː(r)
AM ,ɪn'kɑr

incarcerate
BR ɪn'kɑːsəreɪt,
ɪŋ'kɑːsəreɪt, -s, -ɪŋ, -ɪd
AM ɪn'kɑrsə,reɪt,
ɪŋ'kɑrsə,reɪt, -ts,
-dɪŋ, -dɪd

incarceration
BR ɪn,kɑːsə'reɪʃn,
ɪŋ,kɑːsə'reɪʃn
AM ɪn,kɑrsə'reɪʃən,
ɪŋ,kɑrsə'reɪʃən

incarcerator
BR ɪn'kɑːsəreɪtə(r),
ɪŋ'kɑːsəreɪtə(r), -z
AM ɪn'kɑrsə,reɪdər,
ɪŋ'kɑrsə,reɪdər, -z

incarnadine
BR ɪn'kɑːnədʌɪn,
ɪŋ'kɑːnədʌɪn, -z, -ɪŋ,
-d
AM ɪn'kɑrnə,daɪn,
ɪŋ'kɑrnə,daɪn, -z, -ɪŋ,
-d

incarnate¹
adjective
BR ɪn'kɑːnət,
ɪŋ'kɑːnət
AM ən'kɑrnət,
ɪn'kɑrnət, ɪŋ'kɑrnət

incarnate²
verb
BR ɪn'kɑːneɪt,
ɪŋ'kɑːneɪt, -s, -ɪŋ, -ɪd
AM ɪn'kɑr,neɪt,
'ɪn,kɑrn,eɪt,
'ɪŋ,kɑrn,eɪt, -ts, -dɪŋ,
-dɪd

incarnation
BR ,ɪnkɑː'neɪʃn,
,ɪŋkɑː'neɪʃn, -z
AM ,ɪn,kɑr'neɪʃən,
,ɪŋ,kɑr'neɪʃən, -z

incase
BR ɪn'keɪs, ɪŋ'keɪs, -ɪz,
-ɪŋ, -t
AM ɪn'keɪs, ɪŋ'keɪs, -ɪz,
-ɪŋ, -t

incaution
BR ɪn'kɔːʃn, ɪŋ'kɔːʃn,
-z
AM ɪn'kɔʃən, ɪŋ'kɔʃən,
ɪn'kɑʃən, ɪŋ'kɑʃən, -z

incautious
BR (,)ɪn'kɔːʃəs,
(,)ɪŋ'kɔːʃəs
AM ɪn'kɔʃəs, ɪŋ'kɔʃəs,
ɪn'kɑʃəs, ɪŋ'kɑʃəs

incautiously
BR (,)ɪn'kɔːʃəsli,
(,)ɪŋ'kɔːʃəsli
AM ɪn'kɔʃəsli,
ɪŋ'kɔʃəsli, ɪn'kɑʃəsli,
ɪŋ'kɑʃəsli

incautiousness
BR (,)ɪn'kɔːʃəsnəs,
(,)ɪŋ'kɔːʃəsnəs
AM ɪn'kɔʃəsnəs,
ɪŋ'kɔʃəsnəs,
ɪn'kɑʃəsnəs,
ɪŋ'kɑʃəsnəs

incendiarism
BR ɪn'sɛndɪərɪz(ə)m,
ɪn'sɛndʒərɪz(ə)m
AM ɪn'sɛndɪə,rɪzəm

incendiary
BR ɪn'sɛndɪər|i,
ɪn'sɛndʒ(ə)r|i, -ɪz
AM ɪn'sɛndi,ɛri, -z

incensation
BR ,ɪnsɛn'seɪʃn, -z
AM ,ɪn,sɛn'seɪʃən, -z

incense¹
noun
BR 'ɪnsɛns
AM 'ɪn,sɛns

incense²
verb
BR ɪn'sɛns, -ɪz, -ɪŋ, -t
AM ɪn'sɛns, -əz, -ɪŋ, -t

incensory
BR ɪn'sɛns(ə)r|i, -ɪz
AM ɪn'sɛns(ə)ri, -z

incentive
BR ɪn'sɛntɪv, -z
AM ɪn'sɛn(t)ɪv, -z

incept
BR ɪn'sɛpt, -s, -ɪŋ, -ɪd
AM ɪn'sɛpt, -s, -ɪŋ, -əd

inception
BR ɪn'sɛpʃn
AM ɪn'sɛpʃən

inceptive
BR ɪn'sɛptɪv
AM ɪn'sɛptɪv

inceptor
BR ɪn'sɛptə(r), -z
AM ɪn'sɛptər, -z

incertitude
BR (,)ɪn'səːtɪtjuːd,
(,)ɪn'səːtɪtʃuːd
AM ɪn'sərdə,t(j)ud

incessancy
BR ɪn'sɛsnsi
AM ɪn'sɛsənsi

incessant
BR ɪn'sɛsnt
AM ɪn'sɛsnt

incessantly
BR ɪn'sɛsntli
AM ɪn'sɛsn(t)li

incessantness
BR ɪn'sɛsntnəs
AM ɪn'sɛsn(t)nəs

incest
BR 'ɪnsɛst
AM 'ɪn,sɛst

incestuous
BR ɪn'sɛstjʊəs,
ɪn'sɛstʃʊəs
AM ɪn'sɛstʃ(əw)əs

incestuously
BR ɪn'sɛstjʊəsli,
ɪn'sɛstʃʊəsli
AM ɪn'sɛstʃ(əw)əsli

incestuousness
BR ɪn'sɛstjʊəsnəs,
ɪn'sɛstʃʊəsnəs
AM ɪn'sɛstʃ(əw)əsnəs

inch
BR ɪn(t)ʃ, -ɪz, -ɪŋ, -t
AM ɪn(t)ʃ, -ɪz, -ɪŋ, -t

Inchcape
BR 'ɪn(t)ʃkeɪp
AM 'ɪn(t)ʃ,keɪp

inchmeal
BR 'ɪn(t)ʃmiːl
AM 'ɪn(t)ʃ,mil

inchoate¹
adjective
BR ɪn'kəʊət, ɪn'kəʊeɪt,
'ɪnkəʊət, 'ɪnkəʊeɪt,
ɪŋ'kəʊət, ɪŋ'kəʊeɪt,
'ɪŋkəʊət, 'ɪŋkəʊeɪt
AM ɪn'koʊət,
'ɪnkə,weɪt, ɪŋ'koʊət,
'ɪŋkə,weɪt

inchoate²
verb
BR 'ɪnkəʊeɪt,
'ɪŋkəʊeɪt, -s, -ɪŋ, -ɪd
AM 'ɪnkə,weɪt,
'ɪŋkə,weɪt, -ts, -dɪŋ,
-dɪd

inchoately
BR ɪn'kəʊətli,
ɪn'kəʊeɪtli,
'ɪnkəʊətli, 'ɪnkəʊeɪtli,
ɪŋ'kəʊətli,
ɪŋ'kəʊeɪtli, 'ɪŋkəʊeɪtli,
'ɪŋkəʊeɪtli
AM ɪn'koʊətli,
'ɪnkə,weɪtli,
ɪŋ'koʊətli,
'ɪŋkə,weɪtli

inchoateness
BR ɪn'kəʊətnəs,
ɪn'kəʊeɪtnɪs,
'ɪnkəʊətnəs,
'ɪnkəʊeɪtnɪs,
ɪŋ'kəʊətnəs,
ɪŋ'kəʊeɪtnɪs,

'ɪŋkəʊətnəs,
'ɪŋkəʊeɪtnɪs
AM ɪn'koʊətnəs,
'ɪnkə,weɪtnɪs,
ɪŋ'koʊətnəs,
'ɪŋkə,weɪtnɪs
inchoation
BR ,ɪnkəʊ'eɪʃn,
,ɪŋkəʊ'eɪʃn, -z
AM ,ɪnkə'weɪʃən,
,ɪŋkə'weɪʃən, -z
inchoative
BR 'ɪnkəʊeɪtɪv,
'ɪŋkəʊeɪtɪv
AM 'ɪnkə,weɪdɪv,
'ɪŋkə,weɪdɪv
Inchon
BR 'ɪn'tʃɒn
AM 'ɪn'tʃɑn
inchworm
BR 'ɪn(t)ʃwɜːm, -z
AM 'ɪn(t)ʃ,wɜrm, -z
incidence
BR 'ɪnsɪd(ə)ns
AM 'ɪnsədns
incident
BR 'ɪnsɪd(ə)nt, -s
AM 'ɪnsədnt, -s
incidental
BR ,ɪnsɪ'dɛntl, -z
AM ,ɪnsə'dɛn(t)l, -z
incidentally
BR ,ɪnsɪ'dɛntḷi,
,ɪnsɪ'dɛntli
AM ,ɪnsə'dɛn(t)li
incidentalness
BR ,ɪnsɪ'dɛntlnəs
AM ,ɪnsə'dɛn(t)lnəs
incinerate
BR ɪn'sɪnəreɪt, -s, -ɪŋ,
-ɪd
AM ɪn'sɪnə,reɪ|t, -ts,
-dɪŋ, -dɪd
incineration
BR ɪn,sɪnə'reɪʃn
AM ɪn,sɪnə'reɪʃən
incinerator
BR ɪn'sɪnəreɪtə(r), -z
AM ɪn'sɪnə,reɪdər, -z
incipience
BR ɪn'sɪpɪəns
AM ɪn'sɪpɪəns
incipiency
BR ɪn'sɪpɪəns|i, -ɪz
AM ɪn'sɪpɪənsi, -z
incipient
BR ɪn'sɪpɪənt
AM ɪn'sɪpɪənt
incipiently
BR ɪn'sɪpɪəntli
AM ɪn'sɪpɪən(t)li
incipit
BR 'ɪnsɪpɪt, -s
AM 'ɪnsɪpɪt, -s
incise
BR ɪn'sʌɪz, -ɪz, -ɪŋ, -d
AM ɪn'saɪz, -ɪz, -ɪŋ, -d

incision
BR ɪn'sɪʒn, -z
AM ɪn'sɪʒən, -z
incisive
BR ɪn'sʌɪsɪv
AM ɪn'saɪsɪv
incisively
BR ɪn'sʌɪsɪvli
AM ɪn'saɪsɪvli
incisiveness
BR ɪn'sʌɪsɪvnɪs
AM ɪn'saɪsɪvnɪs
incisor
BR ɪn'sʌɪzə(r), -z
AM ɪn'saɪzər,
,ɪn'saɪzər, -z
incitation
BR ,ɪnsʌɪ'teɪʃn,
,ɪnsɪ'teɪʃn, -z
AM ɪn,saɪ'teɪʃən,
,ɪnsə'teɪʃən, -z
incite
BR ɪn'sʌɪt, -s, -ɪŋ, -ɪd
AM ɪn'saɪ|t, -ts, -dɪŋ,
-dɪd
incitement
BR ɪn'sʌɪtm(ə)nt, -s
AM ɪn'saɪtmənt, -s
inciter
BR ɪn'sʌɪtə(r), -z
AM ɪn'saɪdər, -z
incivility
BR ,ɪnsɪ'vɪlɪt|i, -ɪz
AM 'ɪnsə'vɪlɪdi, -z
incivism
BR 'ɪnsɪvɪz(ə)m
AM ɪn'sɪ,vɪzəm
inclemency
BR (,)ɪn'klɛm(ə)nsi,
(,)ɪŋ'klɛm(ə)nsi
AM ɪn'klɛmənsi,
ɪŋ'klɛmənsi
inclement
BR (,)ɪn'klɛm(ə)nt,
(,)ɪŋ'klɛm(ə)nt
AM ɪn'klɛmənt,
ɪŋ'klɛmənt
inclemently
BR (,)ɪn'klɛm(ə)ntli,
(,)ɪŋ'klɛm(ə)ntli
AM ɪn'klɛmən(t)li,
ɪŋ'klɛmən(t)li
inclinable
BR ɪn'klʌɪnəbl,
ɪŋ'klʌɪnəbl
AM ɪn'klaɪnəbəl,
ɪŋ'klaɪnəbəl
inclination
BR ,ɪnklɪ'neɪʃn,
,ɪŋklɪ'neɪʃn, -z
AM ,ɪnklə'neɪʃən,
,ɪŋklə'neɪʃən, -z
incline¹
noun
BR 'ɪnklʌɪn, 'ɪŋklʌɪn,
-z
AM 'ɪn,klaɪn, 'ɪŋ,klaɪn,
-z

incline²
verb
BR ɪn'klʌɪn, ɪŋ'klʌɪn,
-z, -ɪŋ, -d
AM ɪn'klaɪn, ɪŋ'klaɪn,
-z, -ɪŋ, -d
incliner
BR ɪn'klʌɪnə(r),
ɪŋ'klʌɪnə(r), -z
AM ɪn'klaɪnər,
ɪŋ'klaɪnər, -z
inclinometer
BR ,ɪnklɪ'nɒmɪtə(r),
,ɪŋklɪ'nɒmɪtə(r), -z
AM ɪn,klaɪ'nɑmədər,
ɪŋ,klaɪ'nɑmədər, -z
inclose
BR ɪn'kləʊz, ɪŋ'kləʊz,
-ɪz, -ɪŋ, -d
AM ɪn'kloʊz, ɪŋ'kloʊz,
-əz, -ɪŋ, -t
inclosure
BR ɪn'kləʊʒə(r),
ɪŋ'kləʊʒə(r), -z
AM ɪn'kloʊʒər,
ɪŋ'kloʊʒər, -z
includable
BR ɪn'kluːdəbl,
ɪŋ'kluːdəbl
AM ɪn'kludəbəl,
ɪŋ'kludəbəl
include
BR ɪn'kluːd, ɪŋ'kluːd,
-z, -ɪŋ, -ɪd
AM ɪn'klud, ɪŋ'klud, -z,
-ɪŋ, -əd
includible
BR ɪn'kluːdɪbl,
ɪŋ'kluːdɪbl
AM ɪn'kludəbəl,
ɪŋ'kludəbəl
inclusion
BR ɪn'kluːʒn,
ɪŋ'kluːʒn, -z
AM ɪn'kluʒən,
ɪŋ'kluʒən, -z
inclusive
BR ɪn'kluːsɪv,
ɪŋ'kluːsɪv
AM ɪn'klusɪv,
ɪŋ'klusɪv
inclusively
BR ɪn'kluːsɪvli,
ɪŋ'kluːsɪvli
AM ɪn'klusɪvli,
ɪŋ'klusɪvli
inclusiveness
BR ɪn'kluːsɪvnɪs,
ɪŋ'kluːsɪvnɪs,
AM ɪn'klusɪvnɪs,
ɪŋ'klusɪvnɪs
incog
incognito
BR ɪn'kɒg, ɪŋ'kɒg
AM ɪn'kɑg, ɪŋ'kɑg
incognisance
BR ɪn'kɒgnɪz(ə)ns,
ɪŋ'kɒgnɪz(ə)ns

AM ɪn'kɑgnəzns,
ɪŋ'kɑgnəzns
incognisant
BR ɪn'kɒgnɪz(ə)nt,
ɪŋ'kɒgnɪz(ə)nt
AM ɪn'kɑgnəznt,
ɪŋ'kɑgnəznt
incognito
BR ,ɪnkɒg'niːtəʊ,
,ɪŋkɒg'niːtəʊ
AM ,ɪn,kɑg'nidoʊ,
,ɪŋ,kɑg'nidoʊ
incognizance
BR ɪn'kɒgnɪz(ə)ns,
ɪŋ'kɒgnɪz(ə)ns
AM ɪn'kɑgnəzns,
ɪŋ'kɑgnəzns
incognizant
BR ɪn'kɒgnɪz(ə)nt,
ɪŋ'kɒgnɪz(ə)nt
AM ɪn'kɑgnəznt,
ɪŋ'kɑgnəznt
incoherence
BR ,ɪnkə(ʊ)'hɪərəns,
,ɪnkə(ʊ)'hɪərn̩s,
,ɪŋkə(ʊ)'hɪərəns,
,ɪŋkə(ʊ)'hɪərn̩s
AM ,ɪnkoʊ'hɪrəns,
'ɪnkoʊ'hɛrəns,
'ɪŋkoʊ'hɪrəns,
'ɪŋkoʊ'hɛrəns
incoherency
BR ,ɪnkə(ʊ)'hɪərəns|i,
,ɪnkə(ʊ)'hɪərn̩s|i,
,ɪŋkə(ʊ)'hɪərəns|i,
,ɪŋkə(ʊ)'hɪərn̩s|i, -ɪz
AM ,ɪnkoʊ'hɪrəns,
'ɪnkoʊ'hɛrənsi,
'ɪnkoʊ'hɪrənsi,
'ɪŋkoʊ'hɛrənsi, -z
incoherent
BR ,ɪnkə(ʊ)'hɪərənt,
,ɪnkə(ʊ)'hɪərn̩t,
,ɪŋkə(ʊ)'hɪərənt,
,ɪŋkə(ʊ)'hɪərn̩t
AM ,ɪnkoʊ'hɪrənt,
'ɪnkoʊ'hɪrənt,
'ɪŋkoʊ'hɛrənt
incoherently
BR ,ɪnkə(ʊ)'hɪərəntli,
,ɪnkə(ʊ)'hɪərn̩tli,
,ɪŋkə(ʊ)'hɪərəntli,
,ɪŋkə(ʊ)'hɪərn̩tli
AM 'ɪnkoʊ'hɪrən(t)li,
'ɪnkoʊ'hɛrən(t)li,
'ɪŋkoʊ'hɪrən(t)li,
'ɪŋkoʊ'hɛrən(t)li
incombustibility
BR ,ɪnkəm,bʌstɪ'bɪlɪti,
,ɪŋkəm,bʌstɪ'bɪlɪti
AM ,ɪnkəm,bəstə'bɪlɪdi,
'ɪŋkəm,bəstə'bɪlɪdi
incombustible
BR ,ɪnkəm'bʌstɪbl,
,ɪŋkəm'bʌstɪbl
AM ,ɪnkəm'bəstəbəl,
'ɪŋkəm'bəstəbəl

incombustibleness
BR ˌɪnkəm'bʌstɪblnəs,
ˌɪŋkəm'bʌstɪblnəs
AM ˈɪnkəm'bəstəbəlnəs,
ˈɪŋkəm'bəstəbəlnəs

income
BR 'ɪŋkʌm, 'ɪnkʌm,
'ɪŋkəm, 'ɪnkəm, -z
AM 'ɪn,kʌm, 'ɪŋ,kəm, -z

incomer
BR 'ɪn,kʌmə(r),
'ɪŋ,kʌmə(r), -z
AM 'ɪn,kəmər,
'ɪŋ,kəmər, -z

incoming
BR 'ɪn,kʌmɪŋ,
'ɪŋ,kʌmɪŋ
AM 'ɪn,kəmɪŋ,
'ɪŋ,kəmɪŋ

incommensurability
BR ˌɪnkə,menʃ(ə)rə'bɪlɪti,
ˌɪnkə,mens(ə)rə'bɪlɪti,
ˌɪnkə,mensjərə'bɪlɪti,
ˌɪŋkə,mens(ə)rə'bɪlɪti,
ˌɪŋkə,mens(ə)rə'bɪlɪti,
ˌɪŋkə,mensjərə'bɪlɪti
AM ˈɪnkə,mens(ə)rə'bɪlɪdi,
ˈɪnkə,mens(ə)rə'bɪlɪdi,
ˈɪnkə,menʃ(ə)rə'bɪlɪdi,
ˈɪŋkə,menʃ(ə)rə'bɪlɪdi

incommensurable
BR ˌɪnkə'menʃ(ə)rəbl,
ˌɪnkə'mens(ə)rəbl,
ˌɪnkə'mensjərəbl,
ˌɪŋkə'menʃ(ə)rəbl,
ˌɪŋkə'mens(ə)rəbl,
ˌɪŋkə'mensjərəbl
AM ˈɪnkə'mens(ə)rəbəl,
ˈɪŋkə'mens(ə)rəbəl,
ˈɪnkə'men(t)ʃ(ə)rəbəl,
ˈɪŋkə'men(t)ʃ(ə)rəbəl

incommensurably
BR ˌɪnkə'menʃ(ə)rəbli,
ˌɪnkə'mens(ə)rəbli,
ˌɪnkə'mensjərəbli,
ˌɪŋkə'menʃ(ə)rəbli,
ˌɪŋkə'mens(ə)rəbli,
ˌɪŋkə'mensjərəbli
AM ˈɪnkə'mens(ə)rəbli,
ˈɪnkə'mens(ə)rəbli,
ˈɪnkə'menʃ(ə)rəbli,
ˈɪŋkə'menʃ(ə)rəbli

incommensurate
BR ˌɪnkə'menʃ(ə)rət,
ˌɪnkə'mens(ə)rət,
ˌɪnkə'mensjərət,
ˌɪŋkə'menʃ(ə)rət,
ˌɪŋkə'mens(ə)rət,
ˌɪŋkə'mensjərət
AM ˈɪnkə'mens(ə)rət,
ˈɪŋkə'mens(ə)rət,
ˈɪnkə'menʃ(ə)rət,
ˈɪŋkə'menʃ(ə)rət

incommensurately
BR ˌɪnkə'menʃ(ə)rətli,
ˌɪnkə'mens(ə)rətli,

ˌɪŋkə'mensjərətli,
ˌɪŋkə'menʃ(ə)rətli,
ˌɪŋkə'mens(ə)rətli,
ˌɪŋkə'mensjərətli
AM ˈɪnkə'mens(ə)rətli,
ˈɪŋkə'mens(ə)rətli,
ˈɪnkə'menʃ(ə)rətli,
ˈɪŋkə'menʃ(ə)rətli

incommensurateness
BR ˌɪnkə'menʃ(ə)rətnəs,
ˌɪnkə'mens(ə)rətnəs,
ˌɪnkə'mensjərətnəs,
ˌɪŋkə'menʃ(ə)rətnəs,
ˌɪŋkə'mens(ə)rətnəs,
ˌɪŋkə'mensjərətnəs
AM ˈɪnkə'mens(ə)rətnəs,
ˈɪŋkə'mens(ə)rətnəs,
ˈɪnkə'menʃ(ə)rətnəs,
ˈɪŋkə'menʃ(ə)rətnəs

incommode
BR ˌɪnkə'məʊd,
ˌɪŋkə'məʊd, -z, -ɪŋ, -ɪd
AM ˈɪnkə'moʊd,
ˈɪŋkə'moʊd, -z, -ɪŋ, -əd

incommodious
BR ˌɪnkə'məʊdɪəs,
ˌɪŋkə'məʊdɪəs
AM ˈɪnkə'moʊdiəs,
ˈɪŋkə'moʊdiəs

incommodiously
BR ˌɪnkə'məʊdɪəsli,
ˌɪŋkə'məʊdɪəsli
AM ˈɪnkə'moʊdiəsli,
ˈɪŋkə'moʊdiəsli

incommodiousness
BR ˌɪnkə'məʊdɪəsnəs,
ˌɪŋkə'məʊdɪəsnəs
AM ˈɪnkə'moʊdiəsnəs,
ˈɪŋkə'moʊdiəsnəs

incommunicability
BR ˌɪnkə,mju:nɪkə'bɪlɪti,
ˌɪŋkə,mju:nɪkə'bɪlɪti
AM ˈɪnkə,mjunəkə'bɪlɪdi,
ˈɪŋkə,mjunəkə'bɪlɪdi

incommunicable
BR ˌɪnkə'mju:nɪkəbl,
ˌɪŋkə'mju:nɪkəbl
AM ˈɪnkə'mjunəkəbəl,
ˈɪŋkə'mjunəkəbəl

incommunicableness
BR ˌɪnkə'mju:nɪkəblnəs,
ˌɪŋkə'mju:nɪkəblnəs
AM ˈɪnkə'mjunəkəbəlnəs,
ˈɪŋkə'mjunəkəbəlnəs

incommunicably
BR ˌɪnkə'mju:nɪkəbli,
ˌɪŋkə'mju:nɪkəbli
AM ˈɪnkə'mjunəkəbli,
ˈɪŋkə'mjunəkəbli

incommunicado
BR ˌɪnkə,mju:nɪ'kɑ:dəʊ,
ˌɪŋkə,mju:nɪ'kɑ:dəʊ

AM ˌɪnkə,mjunə'kɑdoʊ,
ˈɪŋkə,mjunə'kɑdoʊ

incommunicative
BR ˌɪnkə'mju:nɪkətɪv,
ˌɪŋkə'mju:nɪkətɪv
AM ˈɪnkə'mjunə,keɪdɪv,
ˈɪnkə'mjunəkədɪv,
ˈɪŋkə'mjunə,keɪdɪv,
ˈɪŋkə'mjunəkədɪv

incommunicatively
BR ˌɪnkə'mju:nɪkətɪvli,
ˌɪŋkə'mju:nɪkətɪvli
AM ˈɪnkə'mjunə,keɪd-
ɪvli,
ˈɪnkə'mjunəkədəvli,
ˈɪŋkə'mjunə,keɪdɪvli,
ˈɪŋkə'mjunəkədəvli

incommunicativeness
BR ˌɪnkə'mju:nɪkətɪv-
nɪs,
ˌɪŋkə'mju:nɪkətɪvnɪs
AM ˈɪnkə'mjunə,keɪdɪv-
nɪs,
ˈɪnkə'mjunəkədɪvnɪs,
ˈɪŋkə'mjunə,keɪdɪvnɪs,
ˈɪŋkə'mjunəkədɪvnɪs

incommutable
BR ˌɪnkə'mju:təbl,
ˌɪŋkə'mju:təbl
AM ˈɪnkə'mjudəbəl,
ˈɪŋkə'mjudəbəl

incommutably
BR ˌɪnkə'mju:təbli,
ˌɪŋkə'mju:təbli
AM ˈɪnkə'mjudəbli,
ˈɪŋkə'mjudəbli

incomparability
BR ɪn,kɒmp(ə)rə'bɪlɪti,
ˌɪnkəm,pærə'bɪlɪti,
ɪŋ,kɒmp(ə)rə'bɪlɪti,
ˌɪŋkəm,pærə'bɪlɪti
AM ˈɪn,kamp(ə)rə'bɪl-
ɪdi,
ɪn,kamp(ə)rə'bɪlɪdi,
ˈɪŋ,kamp(ə)rə'bɪlɪdi

incomparable
BR ɪn'kɒmp(ə)rəbl,
ˌɪnkəm'pærəbl,
ɪŋ'kɒmp(ə)rəbl,
ˌɪŋkəm'pærəbl
AM ˈɪn'kamp(ə)rəbəl,
ɪn'kamp(ə)rəbəl,
ˈɪŋ'kamp(ə)rəbəl

incomparableness
BR ɪn'kɒmp(ə)rəblnəs,
ˌɪnkəm'pærəblnəs,
ɪŋ'kɒmp(ə)rəblnəs,
ˌɪŋkəm'pærəblnəs
AM ˈɪn'kamp(ə)rəbəl-
nəs,
ɪn'kamp(ə)rəbəlnəs,
ˈɪŋ'kamp(ə)rəbəlnəs

incomparably
BR ɪn'kɒmp(ə)rəbli,
ˌɪnkəm'pærəbli,
ɪŋ'kɒmp(ə)rəbli,
ˌɪŋkəm'pærəbli

incompatibility
BR ˌɪnkəm,patɪ'bɪlɪti,
ˌɪŋkəmpatɪ'bɪlɪti
AM ˈɪnkəm,pædə'bɪlɪdi,
ˈɪŋkəm,pædə'bɪlɪdi

incompatible
BR ˌɪnkəm'patɪbl,
ˌɪŋkəm'patɪbl
AM ˈɪnkəm'pædəbəl,
ˈɪŋkəm'pædəbəl

incompatibleness
BR ˌɪnkəm'patɪblnəs,
ˌɪŋkəm'patɪblnəs
AM ˈɪnkəm'pædəbəlnəs,
ˈɪŋkəm'pædəbəlnəs

incompatibly
BR ˌɪnkəm'patɪbli,
ˌɪŋkəm'patɪbli
AM ˈɪnkəm'pædəbli,
ˈɪŋkəm'pædəbli

incompetence
BR ɪn'kɒmpɪt(ə)ns,
ɪŋ'kɒmpɪt(ə)ns
AM ɪn'kampədns,
ɪŋ'kampədns

incompetency
BR ɪn'kɒmpɪt(ə)nsi,
ɪŋ'kɒmpɪt(ə)nsi
AM ɪn'kampədənsi,
ɪŋ'kampədənsi

incompetent
BR ɪn'kɒmpɪt(ə)nt,
ɪŋ'kɒmpɪt(ə)nt
AM ɪn'kampədnt,
ɪŋ'kampədnt

incompetently
BR ɪn'kɒmpɪt(ə)ntli,
ɪŋ'kɒmpɪt(ə)ntli
AM ɪn'kampədən(t)li,
ɪŋ'kampədən(t)li

incomplete
BR ˌɪnkəm'pli:t,
ˌɪŋkəm'pli:t
AM ˈɪnkəm'plit,
ˈɪŋkəm'plit

incompletely
BR ˌɪnkəm'pli:tli,
ˌɪŋkəm'pli:tli
AM ˈɪnkəm'plitli,
ˈɪŋkəm'plitli

incompleteness
BR ˌɪnkəm'pli:tnɪs,
ˌɪŋkəm'pli:tnɪs
AM ˈɪnkəm'plitnɪs,
ˈɪŋkəm'plitnɪs

incomprehensibility
BR ɪn,kɒmprɪ,hensɪ'bɪlɪti,
ˌɪnkɒmprɪ,hensɪ'bɪlɪti,
ɪŋ,kɒmprɪ,hensɪ'bɪlɪti,
ˌɪŋkɒmprɪ,hensɪ'bɪlɪti
AM ˈɪn,kamprə,hensə'bɪlɪdi,
ɪn,kamprə,hensə'bɪlɪdi,
ˈɪŋ,kamprə,hensə'bɪlɪdi

incomprehensible
BR ɪn,kɒmprɪˈhensɪbl,
,ɪnkɒmprɪˈhensɪbl,
ɪŋ,kɒmprɪˈhensɪbl,
,ɪŋkɒmprɪˈhensɪbl
AM ˈɪnˌkɑmprəˈhen-
səbəl,
ˈɪŋˌkɑmprəˈhensəbəl

**incomprehensible-
ness**
BR ɪn,kɒmprɪˈhensɪbl-
nəs,
,ɪnkɒmprɪˈhensɪblnəs,
ɪŋ,kɒmprɪˈhensɪblnəs,
,ɪŋkɒmprɪˈhensɪblnəs
AM ˈɪnˌkɑmprəˈhens-
əbəlnəs,
ˈɪŋˌkɑmprəˈhensəbəl-
nəs

incomprehensibly
BR ɪn,kɒmprɪˈhensɪbli,
,ɪnkɒmprɪˈhensɪbli,
ɪŋ,kɒmprɪˈhensɪbli,
,ɪŋkɒmprɪˈhensɪbli
AM ˈɪnˌkɑmprəˈhens-
əbli,
ˈɪŋˌkɑmprəˈhensəbli

incomprehension
BR ɪn,kɒmprɪˈhenʃn,
,ɪnkɒmprɪˈhenʃn,
ɪŋ,kɒmprɪˈhenʃn,
,ɪŋkɒmprɪˈhenʃn
AM ˈɪnˌkɑmprəˈhen-
(t)ʃən,
ɪn,kɑmprəˈhen(t)ʃən,
ˈɪŋˌkɑmprəˈhen(t)ʃən

incompressibility
BR ,ɪnkəm,presɪˈbɪlɪti,
,ɪŋkəm,presɪˈbɪlɪti
AM ˈɪnkəm,presəˈbɪlɪdi,
ˈɪŋkəm,presəˈbɪlɪdi

incompressible
BR ,ɪnkəmˈpresɪbl,
,ɪŋkəmˈpresɪbl
AM ˈɪnkəmˈpresəbəl,
,ɪŋkəmˈpresəbəl

inconceivability
BR ,ɪnkən,siːvəˈbɪlɪti,
,ɪŋkən,siːvəˈbɪlɪti
AM ˈɪnkən,siːvəˈbɪlɪdi,
,ɪŋkən,siːvəˈbɪlɪdi

inconceivable
BR ,ɪnkənˈsiːvəbl,
,ɪŋkənˈsiːvəbl
AM ˈɪnkənˈsivəbəl,
,ɪŋkənˈsivəbəl

inconceivableness
BR ,ɪnkənˈsiːvəblnəs,
,ɪŋkənˈsiːvəblnəs
AM ˈɪnkənˈsivəbəlnəs,
,ɪŋkənˈsivəbəlnəs

inconceivably
BR ,ɪnkənˈsiːvəbli,
,ɪŋkənˈsiːvəbli
AM ˈɪnkənˈsivəbli,
,ɪŋkənˈsivəbli

inconclusive
BR ,ɪnkənˈkluːsɪv,
,ɪŋkənˈkluːsɪv

AM ˈɪnkənˈkluːsɪv,
ˈɪŋkənˈkluːsɪv

inconclusively
BR ,ɪnkənˈkluːsɪvli,
,ɪŋkənˈkluːsɪvli
AM ˈɪnkənˈkluːsəvli,
ˈɪŋkənˈklusəvli

inconclusiveness
BR ,ɪnkənˈkluːsɪvnɪs,
,ɪŋkənˈkluːsɪvnɪs
AM ˈɪnkənˈklusɪvnɪs,
ˈɪŋkənˈklusɪvnɪs

incondensable
BR ,ɪnkənˈdensəbl,
,ɪŋkənˈdensəbl
AM ˈɪnkənˈdensəbəl,
ˈɪŋkənˈdensəbəl

incondite
BR ɪnˈkɒndɪt,
ɪnˈkɒndʌɪt,
ɪŋˈkɒndɪt, ɪŋˈkɒndʌɪt
AM ɪnˈkɑn,daɪt,
ɪŋˈkɑn,daɪt,
ɪnˈkɑndət, ɪŋˈkɑndət

incongruity
BR ,ɪnkənˈgruːɪti,
,ɪŋkənˈgruːɪti,
,ɪŋkəŋˈgruːɪti
AM ˈɪnkənˈgruədi,
ˈɪŋkəŋˈgruədi,
ˈɪnkənˈgruədi,
ˈɪŋkəŋˈgruədi

incongruous
BR ɪnˈkɒŋgrʊəs,
ɪŋˈkɒŋgrʊəs
AM ɪnˈkɑŋgrʊəs,
ɪŋˈkɑŋgrʊəs

incongruously
BR ɪnˈkɒŋgrʊəsli,
ɪŋˈkɒŋgrʊəsli
AM ɪnˈkɑŋgrʊəsli,
ɪŋˈkɑŋgrʊəsli

incongruousness
BR ɪnˈkɒŋgrʊəsnəs,
ɪŋˈkɒŋgrʊəsnəs
AM ɪnˈkɑŋgrʊəsnəs,
ɪŋˈkɑŋgrʊəsnəs

inconsecutive
BR ,ɪnkənˈsekjʊtɪv,
,ɪŋkənˈsekjʊtɪv
AM ˈɪnkənˈsekjədɪv,
ˈɪŋkənˈsekjədɪv

inconsecutively
BR ,ɪnkənˈsekjʊtɪvli,
,ɪŋkənˈsekjʊtɪvli
AM ˈɪnkənˈsekjədəvli,
ˈɪŋkənˈsekjədəvli

**inconsecutive-
ness**
BR ,ɪnkənˈsekjʊtɪvnɪs,
,ɪŋkənˈsekjʊtɪvnɪs
AM ˈɪnkənˈsekjədɪvnɪs,
ˈɪŋkənˈsekjədɪvnɪs

inconsequence
BR ɪnˈkɒnsɪkw(ə)ns,
ɪŋˈkɒnsɪkw(ə)ns
AM ɪnˈkɑnsəˌkwens,
ɪŋˈkɑnsəˌkwens

inconsequent
BR ɪnˈkɒnsɪkw(ə)nt,
ɪŋˈkɒnsɪkw(ə)nt
AM ɪnˈkɑnsə(ˌ)kwent,
ɪŋˈkɑnsə(ˌ)kwent

inconsequential
BR ɪn,kɒnsɪˈkwenʃl,
,ɪnkɒnsɪˈkwenʃl,
ɪŋ,kɒnsɪˈkwenʃl,
,ɪŋkɒnsɪˈkwenʃl
AM ˈɪnˌkɑnsəˈkwen-
(t)ʃəl,
ˈɪŋˌkɑnsəˈkwen(t)ʃəl

inconsequentiality
BR ɪn,kɒnsɪˌkwenʃi-
ˈalɪt|i,
,ɪnkɒnsɪˌkwenʃrˈalɪt|i,
ɪŋ,kɒnsɪˌkwenʃrˈalɪt|i,
,ɪŋkɒnsɪˌkwenʃrˈalɪt|i,
-ɪz
AM ˈɪnˌkɑnsəˌkwen(t)ʃi-
ˈælədi,
ˈɪŋˌkɑnsəˌkwen(t)ʃiˈæl-
ədi, -z

inconsequentially
BR ɪn,kɒnsɪˈkwenʃli,
ɪn,kɒnsɪˈkwenʃəli,
,ɪnkɒnsɪˈkwenʃli,
,ɪnkɒnsɪˈkwenʃəli,
ɪŋ,kɒnsɪˈkwenʃli,
ɪŋ,kɒnsɪˈkwenʃəli,
,ɪŋkɒnsɪˈkwenʃli,
,ɪŋkɒnsɪˈkwenʃəli
AM ˈɪnˌkɑnsəˈkwen-
(t)ʃəli,
ˈɪŋˌkɑnsəˈkwen(t)ʃəli

**inconsequential-
ness**
BR ɪn,kɒnsɪˈkwenʃlnəs,
,ɪnkɒnsɪˈkwenʃlnəs,
ɪŋ,kɒnsɪˈkwenʃlnəs,
,ɪŋkɒnsɪˈkwenʃlnəs
AM ˈɪnˌkɑnsəˈkwen-
(t)ʃəlnəs,
ˈɪŋˌkɑnsəˈkwen(t)ʃəl-
nəs

inconsequently
BR ɪnˈkɒnsɪkw(ə)ntli,
ɪŋˈkɒnsɪkw(ə)ntli
AM ɪnˈkɑnsə(ˌ)kwen-
(t)li,
ɪŋˈkɑnsə(ˌ)kwen(t)li

inconsiderable
BR ,ɪnkənˈsɪd(ə)rəbl,
,ɪŋkənˈsɪd(ə)rəbl
AM ˈɪnkənˈsɪdər(ə)bəl,
ˈɪnkənˈsɪdrəbəl,
ˈɪŋkənˈsɪdər(ə)bəl,
ˈɪŋkənˈsɪdrəbəl

**inconsiderable-
ness**
BR ,ɪnkənˈsɪd(ə)rəbl-
nəs,
,ɪŋkənˈsɪd(ə)rəblnəs
AM ˈɪnkənˈsɪdər(ə)bəl-
nəs,
ˈɪnkənˈsɪdrəbəlnəs,
ˈɪŋkənˈsɪdər(ə)bəlnəs,
ˈɪŋkənˈsɪdrəbəlnəs

inconsiderably
BR ,ɪnkənˈsɪd(ə)rəbli,
,ɪŋkənˈsɪd(ə)rəbli
AM ˈɪnkənˈsɪdər(ə)bli,
ˈɪnkənˈsɪdrəbli,
ˈɪŋkənˈsɪdər(ə)bli,
ˈɪŋkənˈsɪdrəbli

inconsiderate
BR ,ɪnkənˈsɪd(ə)rət,
,ɪŋkənˈsɪd(ə)rət
AM ˈɪnkənˈsɪd(ə)rət,
ˈɪŋkənˈsɪd(ə)rət

inconsiderately
BR ,ɪnkənˈsɪd(ə)rətli,
,ɪŋkənˈsɪd(ə)rətli
AM ˈɪnkənˈsɪd(ə)rətli,
ˈɪŋkənˈsɪd(ə)rətli

inconsiderateness
BR ,ɪnkənˈsɪd(ə)rətnəs,
,ɪŋkənˈsɪd(ə)rətnəs
AM ˈɪnkənˈsɪd(ə)rətnəs,
ˈɪŋkənˈsɪd(ə)rətnəs

inconsideration
BR ,ɪnkən,sɪdəˈreɪʃn,
,ɪŋkən,sɪdəˈreɪʃn, -z
AM ,ɪnkən,sɪd(ə)ˈreɪʃən,
ˈɪŋkən,sɪd(ə)ˈreɪʃən,
-z

inconsistency
BR ,ɪnkənˈsɪst(ə)ns|i,
,ɪŋkənˈsɪst(ə)ns|i, -ɪz
AM ˈɪnkənˈsɪstnsi,
ˈɪŋkənˈsɪstnsi, -z

inconsistent
BR ,ɪnkənˈsɪst(ə)nt,
,ɪŋkənˈsɪst(ə)nt
AM ˈɪnkənˈsɪstənt,
ˈɪŋkənˈsɪstənt

inconsistently
BR ,ɪnkənˈsɪst(ə)ntli,
,ɪŋkənˈsɪst(ə)ntli
AM ˈɪnkənˈsɪstən(t)li,
ˈɪŋkənˈsɪstən(t)li

inconsolability
BR ,ɪnkən,səʊləˈbɪlɪti,
,ɪŋkən,səʊləˈbɪlɪti
AM ˈɪnkən,soʊləˈbɪlɪdi,
ˈɪŋkən,soʊləˈbɪlɪdi

inconsolable
BR ,ɪnkənˈsəʊləbl,
,ɪŋkənˈsəʊləbl
AM ˈɪnkənˈsoʊləbəl,
ˈɪŋkənˈsoʊləbəl

inconsolableness
BR ,ɪnkənˈsəʊləblnəs,
,ɪŋkənˈsəʊləblnəs
AM ˈɪnkənˈsoʊləbəlnəs,
ˈɪŋkənˈsoʊləbəlnəs

inconsolably
BR ,ɪnkənˈsəʊləbli,
,ɪŋkənˈsəʊləbli
AM ˈɪnkənˈsoʊləbəli,
ˈɪŋkənˈsoʊləbəli

inconsonance
BR ɪnˈkɒnsənəns,
ɪnˈkɒnsnəns,
ɪŋˈkɒnsənəns,
ɪŋˈkɒnsnəns, -ɪz

AM ɪnˈkɑnsənəns,
ɪŋˈkɑnsənəns, -əz

inconsonant
BR ɪnˈkɒnsənənt,
ɪnˈkɒnsn̩ənt,
ɪŋˈkɒnsənənt,
ɪŋˈkɒnsn̩ənt
AM ɪnˈkɑnsənənt,
ɪŋˈkɑnsənənt

inconsonantly
BR ɪnˈkɒnsənəntli,
ɪnˈkɒnsn̩əntli,
ɪŋˈkɒnsənəntli,
ɪŋˈkɒnsn̩əntli
AM ɪnˈkɑnsənən(t)li,
ɪŋˈkɑnsənən(t)li

inconspicuous
BR ˌɪnkənˈspɪkjuəs,
ˌɪŋkənˈspɪkjuəs
AM ˌɪnkənzˈpɪkjəwəs,
ˈɪnkənˈspɪkjəwəs,
ˌɪŋkənzˈpɪkjəwəs,
ˈɪŋkənˈspɪkjəwəs

inconspicuously
BR ˌɪnkənˈspɪkjuəsli,
ˌɪŋkənˈspɪkjuəsli
AM ˌɪnkənzˈpɪkjəwəsli,
ˈɪnkənˈspɪkjəwəsli,
ˌɪŋkənzˈpɪkjəwəsli,
ˈɪŋkənˈspɪkjəwəsli

**inconspicuous-
ness**
BR ˌɪnkənˈspɪkjuəsnəs,
ˌɪŋkənˈspɪkjuəsnəs
AM ˌɪnkənzˈpɪkjəwəs-
nəs,
ˈɪnkənˈspɪkjəwəsnəs,
ˌɪŋkənzˈpɪkjəwəsnəs,
ˈɪŋkənˈspɪkjəwəsnəs

inconstancy
BR ɪnˈkɒnst(ə)nsi,
ɪŋˈkɒnst(ə)nsi
AM ɪnˈkɑnztnsi,
ɪnˈkɑnstnsi,
ɪŋˈkɑnztnsi,
ɪŋˈkɑnstnsi

inconstant
BR ɪnˈkɒnst(ə)nt,
ɪŋˈkɒnst(ə)nt
AM ɪnˈkɑnztənt,
ɪnˈkɑnstənt,
ɪŋˈkɑnztənt,
ɪŋˈkɑnstənt

inconstantly
BR ɪnˈkɒnst(ə)ntli,
ɪŋˈkɒnst(ə)ntli
AM ɪnˈkɑnztən(t)li,
ɪnˈkɑnstən(t)li,
ɪŋˈkɑnztən(t)li,
ɪŋˈkɑnstən(t)li

incontestability
BR ˌɪnkənˌtestəˈbɪlɪti,
ˌɪŋkənˌtestəˈbɪlɪti
AM ˌɪnkənˌtestəˈbɪlɪdi,
ˌɪŋkənˌtestəˈbɪlɪdi

incontestable
BR ˌɪnkənˈtestəbl,
ˌɪŋkənˈtestəbl

AM ˌɪnkənˈtestəbəl,
ˈɪŋkənˈtestəbəl

incontestably
BR ˌɪnkənˈtestəbli,
ˌɪŋkənˈtestəbli
AM ˌɪnkənˈtestəbli,
ˈɪŋkənˈtestəbli

incontinence
BR ɪnˈkɒntɪnəns,
ɪŋˈkɒntɪnəns
AM ɪnˈkɑnt(ə)nəns,
ɪŋˈkɑnt(ə)nəns

incontinent
BR ɪnˈkɒntɪnənt,
ɪŋˈkɒntɪnənt
AM ɪnˈkɑnt(ə)nənt,
ɪŋˈkɑnt(ə)nənt

incontinently
BR ɪnˈkɒntɪnəntli,
ɪŋˈkɒntɪnəntli
AM ɪnˈkɑnt(ə)nən(t)li,
ɪŋˈkɑnt(ə)nən(t)li

incontrovertibility
BR ɪnˌkɒntrəˌvɜːtəˈbɪl-
ɪti,
ˌɪnkɒntrəˌvɜːtəˈbɪlɪti,
ɪŋˌkɒntrəˌvɜːtəˈbɪlɪti,
ˌɪŋkɒntrəˌvɜːtəˈbɪlɪti
AM ˌɪnˌkɑntrəˌvɜrdəˈbɪl-
ɪdi,
ɪnˌkɑntrəˌvɜrdəˈbɪlɪdi,
ˈɪŋˌkɑntrəˌvɜrdəˈbɪlɪdi

incontrovertible
BR ɪnˌkɒntrəˈvɜːtəbl,
ˌɪnkɒntrəˈvɜːtəbl,
ɪŋˌkɒntrəˈvɜːtəbl,
ˌɪŋkɒntrəˈvɜːtəbl
AM ˌɪnˌkɑntrəˈvɜrdəbəl,
ɪnˌkɑntrəˈvɜrdəbəl,
ˈɪŋˌkɑntrəˈvɜrdəbəl

incontrovertibly
BR ɪnˌkɒntrəˈvɜːtəbli,
ˌɪnkɒntrəˈvɜːtəbli,
ɪŋˌkɒntrəˈvɜːtəbli,
ˌɪŋkɒntrəˈvɜːtəbli
AM ˌɪnˌkɑntrəˈvɜrdəbli,
ənˌkɑntrəˈvɜrdəbli,
ˈɪŋˌkɑntrəˈvɜrdəbli

inconvenience
BR ˌɪnkənˈviːnɪəns,
ˌɪŋkənˈviːnɪəns, -ɪz
AM ˌɪnkənˈvinjəns,
ˈɪŋkənˈvinjəns, -əz

inconvenient
BR ˌɪnkənˈviːnɪənt,
ˌɪŋkənˈviːnɪənt
AM ˌɪnkənˈvinjənt,
ˈɪŋkənˈvinjənt

inconveniently
BR ˌɪnkənˈviːnɪəntli,
ˌɪŋkənˈviːnɪəntli
AM ˌɪnkənˈvinjən(t)li,
ˈɪŋkənˈvinjən(t)li

inconvertibility
BR ˌɪnkənˌvɜːtɪˈbɪlɪti,
ˌɪŋkənˌvɜːtɪˈbɪlɪti
AM ˌɪnˌkɑnˌvɜrdəˈbɪlɪdi,
ɪnˌkɑnˌvɜrdəˈbɪlɪdi,
ˈɪŋˌkɑnˌvɜrdəˈbɪlɪdi

inconvertible
BR ˌɪnkənˈvɜːtɪbl,
ˌɪŋkənˈvɜːtɪbl
AM ˌɪnˌkɑnˈvɜrdəbəl,
ɪnˌkɑnˈvɜrdəbəl,
ˈɪŋˌkɑnˈvɜrdəbəl

inconvertibly
BR ˌɪnkənˈvɜːtɪbli,
ˌɪŋkənˈvɜːtɪbli
AM ˌɪnˌkɑnˈvɜrdəbli,
ɪnˌkɑnˈvɜrdəbli,
ˈɪŋˌkɑnˈvɜrdəbli

incoordination
BR ˌɪnkəʊˌɔːdɪˈneɪʃn,
ˌɪŋkəʊˌɔːdɪˈneɪʃn
AM ˌɪnkoʊˌɔrdəˈneɪʃən,
ˈɪŋkoʊˌɔrdəˈneɪʃən

incorporate¹
adjective
BR ɪnˈkɔːp(ə)rət,
ɪŋˈkɔːp(ə)rət
AM ɪnˈkɔrp(ə)rət,
ɪŋˈkɔrp(ə)rət

incorporate²
verb
BR ɪnˈkɔːpəreɪt,
ɪŋˈkɔːpəreɪt, -s, -ɪŋ, -ɪd
AM ɪnˈkɔrpəˌreɪt,
ɪŋˈkɔrpəˌreɪt, -ts,
-dɪŋ, -dɪd

incorporation
BR ɪnˌkɔːpəˈreɪʃn,
ɪŋˌkɔːpəˈreɪʃn, -z
AM ɪnˌkɔrpəˈreɪʃən,
ɪŋˌkɔrpəˈreɪʃən, -z

incorporator
BR ɪnˈkɔːpəreɪtə(r),
ɪŋˈkɔːpəreɪtə(r), -z
AM ɪnˈkɔrpəˌreɪdər,
ɪŋˈkɔrpəˌreɪdər, -z

incorporeal
BR ˌɪnkɔːˈpɔːrɪəl,
ˌɪŋkɔːˈpɔːrɪəl
AM ˌɪnˌkɔrˈpɔrɪəl,
ˈɪŋˌkɔrˈpɔrɪəl

incorporeality
BR ˌɪnkɔːˌpɔːrɪˈalɪti,
ˌɪŋkɔːˌpɔːrɪˈalɪti
AM ˌɪnˌkɔrˌpɔriˈælədi,
ˈɪŋˌkɔrˌpɔriˈælədi

incorporeally
BR ˌɪnkɔːˈpɔːrɪəli,
ˌɪŋkɔːˈpɔːrɪəli
AM ˌɪnˌkɔrˈpɔrɪəli,
ˈɪŋˌkɔrˈpɔrɪəli

incorporeity
BR ˌɪnkɔːpəˈriːɪti,
ˌɪŋkɔːpəˈriːɪti,
ˌɪŋkɔːpəˈriːɪti
AM ˌɪnˌkɔrpəˈriɪdi,
ˈɪŋˌkɔrpəˈreɪdi,
ˈɪŋˌkɔrpəˈreɪdi

incorporial
BR ˌɪnkɔːˈpɔːrɪəl,
ˌɪŋkɔːˈpɔːrɪəl
AM ˌɪnˌkɔrˈpɔrɪəl,
ˈɪŋˌkɔrˈpɔrɪəl

incorrect
BR ˌɪnkəˈrekt,
ˌɪŋkəˈrekt
AM ˌɪnkəˈrek(t),
ˈɪŋkəˈrek(t)

incorrectly
BR ˌɪnkəˈrektli,
ˌɪŋkəˈrektli
AM ˌɪnkəˈrek(t)li,
ˈɪŋkəˈrek(t)li

incorrectness
BR ˌɪnkəˈrek(t)nəs,
ˌɪŋkəˈrek(t)nəs
AM ˌɪnkəˈrek(t)nəs,
ˈɪŋkəˈrek(t)nəs

incorrigibility
BR ɪnˌkɒrɪdʒəˈbɪlɪti,
ˌɪnkɒrɪdʒəˈbɪlɪti,
ɪŋˌkɒrɪdʒəˈbɪlɪti,
AM ˈɪnˌkɔrədʒəˈbɪlɪdi,
ɪnˌkɔrədʒəˈbɪlɪdi,
ɪŋˌkɔrədʒəˈbɪlɪdi

incorrigible
BR ɪnˈkɒrɪdʒəbl,
ɪŋˈkɒrɪdʒəbl
AM ɪnˈkɔrədʒəbəl,
ɪnˈkɔrədʒəbəl,
ɪŋˈkɔrədʒəbəl

incorrigibleness
BR ɪnˈkɒrɪdʒəblnəs,
ɪŋˈkɒrɪdʒəblnəs
AM ɪnˈkɔrədʒəbəlnəs,
ɪnˈkɔrədʒəbəlnəs,
ɪŋˈkɔrədʒəbəlnəs

incorrigibly
BR ɪnˈkɒrɪdʒəbli,
ɪŋˈkɒrɪdʒəbli
AM ɪnˈkɔrədʒəbli,
ɪnˈkɔrədʒəbli,
ɪŋˈkɔrədʒəbli

incorruptibility
BR ˌɪnkəˌrʌptəˈbɪlɪti,
ˌɪŋkəˌrʌptəˈbɪlɪti
AM ˌɪnkəˌrəptəˈbɪlɪdi,
ˈɪŋkəˌrəptəˈbɪlɪdi

incorruptible
BR ˌɪnkəˈrʌptɪbl,
ˌɪŋkəˈrʌptɪbl
AM ˌɪnkəˈrəptəbəl,
ˈɪŋkəˈrəptəbəl

incorruptibly
BR ˌɪnkəˈrʌptɪbli,
ˌɪŋkəˈrʌptɪbli
AM ˌɪnkəˈrəptəbli,
ˈɪŋkəˈrəptəbli

incorruption
BR ˌɪnkəˈrʌpʃn,
ˌɪŋkəˈrʌpʃn
AM ˌɪnkəˈrəpʃən,
ˈɪŋkəˈrəpʃən

incrassate
BR ɪnˈkraseɪt,
ɪŋˈkraseɪt, -s, -ɪŋ, -ɪd
AM ɪnˈkræˌseɪt,
ɪŋˈkræˌseɪt, -ts, -dɪŋ,
-dɪd

increasable
BR ɪnˈkriːsəbl,
ɪŋˈkriːsəbl
AM ɪnˈkrisəbəl,
ɪŋˈkrisəbəl

increase¹
noun
BR ˈɪnkriːs, ˈɪŋkriːs, -ɪz
AM ˈɪnˌkris, ˈɪŋˌkris, -ɪz

increase²
verb
BR ɪnˈkriːs, ɪŋˈkriːs,
-ɪz, -ɪŋ, -t
AM ɪnˈkris, ɪŋˈkris, -ɪz,
-ɪŋ, -t

increaser
BR ɪnˈkriːsə(r),
ɪŋˈkriːsə(r), -z
AM ɪnˈkrisər,
ɪŋˈkrisər, -z

increasingly
BR ɪnˈkriːsɪŋli,
ɪŋˈkriːsɪŋli
AM ɪnˈkrisɪŋli,
ɪŋˈkrisɪŋli

incredibility
BR ɪnˌkredɪˈbɪlɪti,
ɪŋˌkredɪˈbɪlɪti
AM ɪnˌkredəˈbɪlɪdi,
ɪnˌkredəˈbɪlɪdi,
ˌɪŋˌkredəˈbɪlɪdi

incredible
BR ɪnˈkredɪbl,
ɪŋˈkredɪbl
AM ɪnˈkredəbəl,
ɪŋˈkredəbəl

incredibleness
BR ɪnˈkredɪblnəs,
ɪŋˈkredɪblnəs
AM ɪnˈkredəbəlnəs,
ɪŋˈkredəbəlnəs

incredibly
BR ɪnˈkredɪbli,
ɪŋˈkredɪbli
AM ɪnˈkredəbli,
ɪŋˈkredəbli

incredulity
BR ˌɪnkrɪˈdjuːlɪti,
ˌɪnkrɪˈdʒuːlɪti,
ˌɪŋkrɪˈdjuːlɪti,
ˌɪŋkrɪˈdʒuːlɪti
AM ˌɪnkrəˈd(j)uːlədi,
ˌɪŋkrəˈd(j)uːlədi

incredulous
BR ɪnˈkredjʊləs,
ɪnˈkredʒʊləs,
ɪŋˈkredjʊləs,
ɪŋˈkredʒʊləs
AM ɪnˈkredʒələs,
ɪŋˈkredʒələs

incredulously
BR ɪnˈkredjʊləsli,
ɪnˈkredʒʊləsli,
ɪŋˈkredjʊləsli,
ɪŋˈkredʒʊləsli
AM ɪnˈkredʒələsli,
ɪŋˈkredʒələsli

incredulousness
BR ɪnˈkredjʊləsnəs,
ɪnˈkredʒʊləsnəs,
ɪŋˈkredjʊləsnəs,
ɪŋˈkredʒʊləsnəs
AM ɪnˈkredʒələsnəs,
ɪŋˈkredʒələsnəs

increment
BR ˈɪnkrɪm(ə)nt,
ˈɪŋkrɪm(ə)nt, -s
AM ˈɪŋkrəmənt,
ˈɪnkrəmənt, -s

incremental
BR ˌɪnkrɪˈmentl,
ˌɪŋkrɪˈmentl
AM ˌɪŋkrəˈmen(t)l,
ˌɪnkrəˈmen(t)l

incrementally
BR ˌɪnkrɪˈmentli,
ˌɪŋkrɪˈmentli
AM ˌɪŋkrəˈmen(t)li,
ˌɪnkrəˈmen(t)li

incriminate
BR ɪnˈkrɪmɪneɪt,
ɪŋˈkrɪmɪneɪt, -s, -ɪŋ,
-ɪd
AM ɪnˈkrɪməˌneɪ|t,
ɪŋˈkrɪməˌneɪ|t, -ts,
-dɪŋ, -dɪd

incriminatingly
BR ɪnˈkrɪmɪneɪtɪŋli,
ɪŋˈkrɪmɪneɪtɪŋli
AM ɪnˈkrɪməˌneɪdɪŋli,
ɪŋˈkrɪməˌneɪdɪŋli

incrimination
BR ɪnˌkrɪmɪˈneɪʃn,
ɪŋˌkrɪmɪˈneɪʃn
AM ɪnˌkrɪməˈneɪʃən,
ɪŋˌkrɪməˈneɪʃən

incriminatory
BR ɪnˈkrɪmɪnət(ə)ri,
ɪŋˈkrɪmɪnət(ə)ri
AM ɪnˈkrɪmənəˌtori,
ɪŋˈkrɪmənəˌtori

in-crowd
BR ˈɪnkraʊd, ˈɪŋkraʊd,
-z
AM ˈɪnˌkraʊd, -z

incrust
BR ɪnˈkrʌst, ɪŋˈkrʌst,
-s, -ɪŋ, -ɪd
AM ɪnˈkrəst, ɪŋˈkrəst,
-s, -ɪŋ, -əd

incrustation
BR ˌɪnkrʌˈsteɪʃn,
ˌɪnkrʌˈsteɪʃn, -z
AM ˌɪnˌkrəˈsteɪʃən,
ˌɪŋˌkrəˈsteɪʃən, -z

incubate
BR ˈɪŋkjʊbeɪt,
ˈɪnkjʊbeɪt, -s, -ɪŋ, -ɪd
AM ˈɪnkjəˌbeɪ|t,
ˈɪŋkjəˌbeɪ|t, -ts, -dɪŋ,
-dɪd

incubation
BR ˌɪŋkjʊˈbeɪʃn,
ˌɪnkjʊˈbeɪʃn

AM ˌɪnkjəˈbeɪʃən,
ˌɪŋkjəˈbeɪʃən

incubational
BR ˌɪŋkjʊˈbeɪʃn(ə)l,
ˌɪŋkjʊˈbeɪʃən(ə)l,
ˌɪnkjʊˈbeɪʃn(ə)l,
ˌɪnkjʊˈbeɪʃən(ə)l
AM ˌɪnkjəˈbeɪʃ(ə)nəl,
ˌɪŋkjəˈbeɪʃ(ə)nəl

incubative
BR ˈɪŋkjʊbeɪtɪv,
ˈɪnkjʊbeɪtɪv
AM ˈɪnkjəˌbeɪdɪv,
ˈɪŋkjəˌbeɪdɪv

incubator
BR ˈɪŋkjʊbeɪtə(r),
ˈɪnkjʊbeɪtə(r), -z
AM ˈɪnkjəˌbeɪdər,
ˈɪŋkjəˌbeɪdər, -z

incubatory
BR ˌɪŋkjʊˈbeɪt(ə)ri,
ˌɪnkjʊˈbeɪt(ə)ri
AM ɪnˈkjubəˌtori,
ɪŋˈkjubətri

incubi
BR ˈɪŋkjʊbʌɪ,
ˈɪnkjʊbʌɪ
AM ˈɪŋkjəˌbaɪ,
ˈɪnkjəˌbaɪ

incubus
BR ˈɪŋkjʊbəs,
ˈɪnkjʊbəs, -ɪz
AM ˈɪŋkjəbəs,
ˈɪnkjəbəs, -əz

incudes
BR ˈɪŋkjʊdiːz,
ɪŋˈkjuːdiːz
ɪnˈkjuːdiːz
AM ɪnˈk(j)uˌdiz

inculcate
BR ˈɪnk(ʌ)lkeɪt,
ˈɪŋk(ʌ)lkeɪt, -s, -ɪŋ, -ɪd
AM ɪnˈkəlˌkeɪ|t,
ˈɪnkəlˌkeɪt
ˈɪŋkəlˌkeɪ|t, -ts, -dɪŋ,
-dɪd

inculcation
BR ˌɪnk(ʌ)lˈkeɪʃn,
ˌɪŋk(ʌ)lˈkeɪʃn
AM ˌɪnkəlˈkeɪʃən,
ˌɪŋkəlˈkeɪʃən

inculcator
BR ˈɪnk(ʌ)lkeɪtə(r),
ˈɪŋk(ʌ)lkeɪtə(r), -z
AM ɪnˈkəlˌkeɪdər,
ˈɪnkəlˌkeɪdər,
ˈɪŋkəlˌkeɪdər, -z

inculpate
BR ˈɪnkʌlpert,
ˈɪŋkʌlpert, -s, -ɪŋ, -ɪd
AM ɪnˈkəlˌpeɪ|t,
ˈɪnkəlˌpeɪ|t,
ˈɪŋkəlˌpeɪ|t, -ts, -dɪŋ,
-dɪd

inculpation
BR ˌɪnkʌlˈpeɪʃn,
ˌɪŋkʌlˈpeɪʃn

AM ˌɪnkjəˈbeɪʃən,
ˌɪŋkjəˈbeɪʃən

inculpative
BR ɪnˈkʌlpətɪv,
ɪŋˈkʌlpətɪv
AM ɪnˈkəlˌpeɪdɪv,
ˈɪnkəlˌpeɪdɪv,
ˈɪŋkəlˌpeɪdɪv

inculpatory
BR ɪnˈkʌlpət(ə)ri,
ɪŋˈkʌlpət(ə)ri
AM ɪnˈkəlpəˌtori,
ɪŋˈkəlpəˌtori

incult
BR ɪnˈkʌlt, ɪŋˈkʌlt
AM ɪnˈkəlt, ɪŋˈkəlt

inculturation
BR ɪnˌkʌltʃəˈreɪʃn
AM ɪnˌkəltʃəˈreɪʃ(ə)n

incumbency
BR ɪnˈkʌmbəns|i,
ɪŋˈkʌmbəns|i, -ɪz
AM ɪnˈkəmbənsi,
ɪŋˈkəmbənsi, -z

incumbent
BR ɪnˈkʌmbənt,
ɪŋˈkʌmbənt, -s
AM ɪnˈkəmbənt,
ɪŋˈkəmbənt, -s

incunable
BR ɪnˈkjuːnəbl,
ɪŋˈkjuːnəbl
AM ɪnˈkjunəbəl,
ɪŋˈkjunəbəl

incunabula
BR ˌɪnkjʊˈnabjʊlə(r),
ˌɪnkjʊˈnabjʊlə(r)
AM ˌɪnkjəˈnæbjʊlə,
ˌɪŋkjəˈnæbjələ

incunabular
BR ˌɪnkjʊˈnabjʊlə(r),
ˌɪŋkjʊˈnabjʊlə(r)
AM ˌɪnkjəˈnæbjələr,
ˌɪŋkjəˈnæbjələr

incunabulum
BR ˌɪnkjʊˈnabjʊləm,
ˌɪŋkjʊˈnabjʊləm
AM ˌɪnkjəˈnæbjələm,
ˌɪŋkjəˈnæbjələm

incur
BR ɪnˈkəː(r), ɪŋˈkəː(r),
-z, -ɪŋ, -d
AM ɪnˈkər, ɪŋˈkər, -z,
-ɪŋ, -d

incurability
BR ɪnˌkjʊərəˈbɪlɪti,
ɪnˌkjʊərəˈbɪlɪti,
ɪŋˌkjʊərəˈbɪlɪti,
ˌɪnˌkjʊrəˈbɪlɪdi,
ənˌkjʊrəˈbɪlɪdi,
ˌɪŋˌkjʊrəˈbɪlɪdi

incurable
BR ɪnˈkjʊərəbl,
ɪnˈkjɔːrəbl
ɪŋˈkjʊərəbl,
ɪŋˈkjɔːrəbl

AM ɪn'kjʊərəbəl,
ɪŋ'kjʊərəbəl

incurableness
BR ɪn'kjʊərəblnəs,
ɪn'kjɔːrəblnəs,
ɪŋ'kjʊərəblnəs,
ɪŋ'kjɔːrəblnəs
AM ɪn'kjʊrəbəlnəs,
ɪŋ'kjʊrəbəlnəs

incurably
BR ɪn'kjʊərəbli,
ɪn'kjɔːrəbli,
ɪŋ'kjʊərəbli,
ɪŋ'kjɔːrəbli
AM ɪn'kjʊrəbli,
ɪŋ'kjʊrəbli

incuriosity
BR ɪn,kjʊərɪ'ɒsɪti,
ɪn,kjɔː'rɪ'ɒsɪti,
ɪŋ,kjʊərɪ'ɒsɪti,
ɪŋ,kjɔː'rɪ'ɒsɪti,
,ɪnkjʊərɪ'ɒsɪti,
,ɪnkjɔː'rɪ'ɒsɪti,
,ɪŋkjʊərɪ'ɒsɪti,
,ɪŋkjɔː'rɪ'ɒsɪti
AM ɪn,kjʊri'ɑsədi,
ɪn,kjʊri'ɑsədi,
,ɪŋ,kjʊri'ɑsədi

incurious
BR ɪn'kjʊərɪəs,
ɪn'kjɔːrɪəs,
ɪŋ'kjʊərɪəs,
ɪŋ'kjɔːrɪəs
AM ɪn'kjʊriəs,
ɪn'kjʊriəs, ɪŋ'kjʊriəs

incuriously
BR ɪn'kjʊərɪəsli,
ɪn'kjɔːrɪəsli,
ɪŋ'kjʊərɪəsli,
ɪŋ'kjɔːrɪəsli
AM ɪn'kjʊriəsli,
ɪn'kjʊriəsli,
ɪŋ'kjʊriəsli

incuriousness
BR ɪn'kjʊərɪəsnəs,
ɪn'kjɔːrɪəsnəs,
ɪŋ'kjʊərɪəsnəs,
ɪŋ'kjɔːrɪəsnəs
AM ɪn'kjʊriəsnəs,
ɪn'kjʊriəsnəs,
ɪŋ'kjʊriəsnəs

incurrable
BR ɪn'kɜːrəbl,
ɪŋ'kɜːrəbl
AM ɪn'kɜːrəbəl,
ɪŋ'kɜːrəbəl

incursion
BR ɪn'kɜːʃn, ɪn'kɜːʒn,
ɪŋ'kɜːʃn, ɪŋ'kɜːʒn, -z
AM ɪn'kɜːʒən,
ɪŋ'kɜːʒən, -z

incursive
BR ɪn'kɜːsɪv, ɪŋ'kɜːsɪv
AM ɪn'kɜːsɪv,
ɪŋ'kɜːsɪv

incurvation
BR ,ɪnkɜː'veɪʃn,
,ɪŋkɜː'veɪʃn, -z

AM ,ɪnkər'veɪʃən,
,ɪŋkər'veɪʃən, -z

incurve
BR ɪn'kɜːv, ɪŋ'kɜːv, -z,
-ɪŋ, -d
AM ɪn'kɜːrv, ɪŋ'kɜːrv, -z,
-ɪŋ, -d

incus
BR 'ɪŋkəs
AM 'ɪŋkəs

incuse
BR ɪn'kjuːz, ɪŋ'kjuːz,
-ɪz, -ɪŋ, -d
AM ɪn'kjuz, ɪŋ'kjuz,
-əz, -ɪŋ, -d

indaba
BR ɪn'dɑːbə(r), -z
AM ɪn'dɑbə, -z

Indebele
BR ,ɪndə'biːli,
,ɪndə'beɪli
AM ,ɪndə'bili

indebted
BR ɪn'detɪd
AM ɪn'dedəd

indebtedness
BR ɪn'detɪdnɪs
AM ɪn'dedədnəs

indecency
BR ɪn'diːsns|i, -ɪz
AM ɪn'disənsi, -z

indecent
BR ɪn'diːsnt
AM ɪn'disənt

indecently
BR ɪn'diːsntli
AM ɪn'disn(t)li

indecipherability
BR ,ɪndɪ,sʌɪf(ə)rə'bɪlɪti
AM ,ɪndə,saɪf(ə)rə'bɪlɪdi

indecipherable
BR ,ɪndɪ'sʌɪf(ə)rəbl
AM ,ɪndə'saɪf(ə)rəbəl

indecipherably
BR ,ɪndɪ'sʌɪf(ə)rəbli
AM ,ɪndə'saɪf(ə)rəbli

indecision
BR ,ɪndɪ'sɪʒn
AM ,ɪndɪ'sɪʒən

indecisive
BR ,ɪndɪ'sʌɪsɪv
AM ,ɪndə'saɪsɪv

indecisively
BR ,ɪndɪ'sʌɪsɪvli
AM ,ɪndə'saɪsɪvli

indecisiveness
BR ,ɪndɪ'sʌɪsɪvnɪs
AM ,ɪndə'saɪsɪvnɪs

indeclinable
BR ,ɪndɪ'klʌɪnəbl
AM ,ɪndə'klaɪnəbəl

indecorous
BR (,)ɪn'dek(ə)rəs
AM ɪn'dekərəs

indecorously
BR (,)ɪn'dek(ə)rəsli
AM ɪn'dekərəsli

indecorousness
BR (,)ɪn'dek(ə)rəsnəs
AM ɪn'dekərəsnəs

indecorum
BR ,ɪndɪ'kɔːrəm
AM ,ɪndə'kɔrəm

indeed
BR ɪn'diːd
AM ɪn'diːd

indefatigability
BR ,ɪndɪ,fatɪgə'bɪlɪti
AM ,ɪndə,fædəgə'bɪlɪdi

indefatigable
BR ,ɪndɪ'fatɪgəbl
AM ,ɪndə'fædəgəbəl

indefatigableness
BR ,ɪndɪ'fatɪgəblnəs
AM ,ɪndə'fædəgəbəlnəs

indefatigably
BR ,ɪndɪ'fatɪgəbli
AM ,ɪndə'fædəgəbli

indefeasibility
BR ,ɪndɪ,fiːzɪ,bɪlɪti
AM ,ɪndə,fizə'bɪlɪdi

indefeasible
BR ,ɪndɪ'fiːzɪbl
AM ,ɪndə'fizəbəl

indefeasibly
BR ,ɪndɪ'fiːzɪbli
AM ,ɪndə'fizəbli

indefectible
BR ,ɪndɪ'fektɪbl
AM ,ɪndə'fektəbəl

indefensibility
BR ,ɪndɪ,fensɪ'bɪlɪti
AM ,ɪndə,fensə'bɪlɪdi

indefensible
BR ,ɪndɪ'fensɪbl
AM ,ɪndə'fensəbəl

indefensibly
BR ,ɪndɪ'fensɪbli
AM ,ɪndə'fensəbli

indefinable
BR ,ɪndɪ'fʌɪnəbl
AM ,ɪndə'faɪnəbəl

indefinably
BR ,ɪndɪ'fʌɪnəbli
AM ,ɪndə'faɪnəbli

indefinite
BR (,)ɪn'def(ɪ)nɪt,
(,)ɪn'defnɪt
AM ɪn'def(ə)nət

indefinitely
BR (,)ɪn,def(ɪ)nɪtli,
(,)ɪn'defnɪtli
AM ɪn'def(ə)nətli

indefiniteness
BR (,)ɪn'def(ɪ)nɪtnəs,
(,)ɪn'defnɪtnɪs
AM ɪn'def(ə)nətnəs

indehiscence
BR ,ɪndɪ'hɪsns
AM ,ɪndə'hɪsəns,
,ɪndi'hɪsəns

indehiscent
BR ,ɪndɪ'hɪsnt

indecorousness
BR (,)ɪn'dek(ə)rəsnəs
AM ɪn'dekərəsnəs

AM ,ɪndə'hɪsənt,
,ɪndi'hɪsənt

indelibility
BR ɪn,delɪ'bɪlɪti
AM ɪn,delə'bɪlɪdi

indelible
BR (,)ɪn'delɪbl
AM ɪn'deləbəl

indelibly
BR (,)ɪn'delɪbli
AM ɪn'deləbli

indelicacy
BR (,)ɪn'delɪkəs|i, -ɪz
AM ɪn'deləkəsi, -z

indelicate
BR (,)ɪn'delɪkət
AM ɪn'deləkət

indelicately
BR (,)ɪn'delɪkətli
AM ɪn'deləkətli

indelicateness
BR (,)ɪn'delɪkətnəs
AM ɪn'deləkətnəs

indeminify
BR ɪn'demnɪfʌɪ, -z, -ɪŋ,
-d
AM ɪn'demnə,faɪ, -z,
-ɪŋ, -d

indemnification
BR ɪn,demnɪfɪ'keɪʃn
AM ɪn,demnəfə'keɪʃən

indemnifier
BR ɪn'demnɪfʌɪə(r), -z
AM ɪn'demnə,faɪər, -z

indemnity
BR ɪn'demnɪti
AM ɪn'demnədi, -z

indemonstrable
BR ,ɪndɪ'mɒnstrəbl,
ɪn'demənstrəbl
AM ,ɪndə'mɑnstrəbəl,
ɪn'demənstrəbəl

indene
BR 'ɪndiːn, -z
AM 'ɪn,din, -z

indent¹
noun
BR 'ɪndent, -s
AM 'ɪn,dent, -s

indent²
verb
BR ɪn'dent, -s, -ɪŋ, -ɪd
AM ɪn'den|t, -ts, -ts, -(t)ɪŋ,
-(t)əd

indentation
BR ,ɪnden'teɪʃn, -z
AM ,ɪn,den'teɪʃən, -z

indenter
BR ɪn'dentə(r), -z
AM ɪn'den(t)ər, -z

indentor
BR ɪn'dentə(r), -z
AM ɪn'den(t)ər, -z

indenture
BR ɪn'dentʃ|ə(r), -əz,
-(ə)rɪŋ, -əd
AM ɪn'den(t)ʃər, -z, -ɪŋ,
-d

indentureship
BR ɪnˈdɛntʃəʃɪp, -s
AM ɪnˈdɛn(t)ʃərˌʃɪp, -s
independence
BR ˌɪndɪˈpɛnd(ə)ns
AM ˌɪndəˈpɛndəns
independency
BR ˌɪndɪˈpɛnd(ə)ns|i,
-ɪz
AM ˌɪndəˈpɛndnsi, -z
independent
BR ˌɪndɪˈpɛnd(ə)nt, -s
AM ˌɪndəˈpɛndənt, -s
independently
BR ˌɪndɪˈpɛnd(ə)ntli
AM ˌɪndəˈpɛndən(t)li
in-depth
BR ˌɪnˈdɛpθ
AM ˈɪnˈdɛpθ
indescribability
BR ˌɪndɪˌskrʌɪbəˈbɪlɪti
AM ˌɪndəˌskraɪbəˈbɪlɪdi
indescribable
BR ˌɪndɪˈskrʌɪbəbl
AM ˌɪndəˈskraɪbəbəl
indescribably
BR ˌɪndɪˈskrʌɪbəbli
AM ˌɪndəˈskraɪbəbli
indestructibility
BR ˌɪndɪˌstrʌktɪˈbɪlɪti
AM ˌɪndəˌstrəktəˈbɪlɪdi
indestructible
BR ˌɪndɪˈstrʌktɪbl
AM ˌɪndəˈstrəktəbəl
indestructibly
BR ˌɪndɪˈstrʌktɪbli
AM ˌɪndəˈstrəktəbli
indeterminable
BR ˌɪndɪˈtəːmɪnəbl
AM ˌɪndəˈtɜrmənəbəl
indeterminably
BR ˌɪndɪˈtəːmənɪbli
AM ˌɪndəˈtɜrmənəbli
indeterminacy
BR ˌɪndɪˈtəːmɪnəsi
AM ˌɪndəˈtɜrmənəsi
indeterminate
BR ˌɪndɪˈtəːmɪnət
AM ˌɪndəˈtɜrmənət
indeterminately
BR ˌɪndɪˈtəːmɪnətli
AM ˌɪndəˈtɜrmənətli
indeterminateness
BR ˌɪndɪˈtəːmɪnətnəs
AM ˌɪndəˈtɜrmənətnəs
indetermination
BR ˌɪndɪˌtəːmɪˈneɪʃn
AM ˌɪndəˌtɜrməˈneɪʃən
indeterminism
BR ˌɪndɪˈtəːmɪnɪz(ə)m
AM ˌɪndəˈtɜrməˌnɪzəm
indeterminist
BR ˌɪndɪˈtəːmɪnɪst, -s
AM ˌɪndəˈtɜrmənəst, -s
indeterministic
BR ˌɪndɪˌtəːmɪˈnɪstɪk
AM ˌɪndəˌtɜrməˈnɪstɪk

index
BR ˈɪndɛks, -ɪz, -ɪŋ, -t
AM ˈɪnˌdɛks, -əz, -ɪŋ, -t
indexation
BR ˌɪndɛkˈseɪʃn
AM ˌɪnˌdɛkˈseɪʃən
indexer
BR ˈɪndɛksə(r), -z
AM ˈɪnˌdɛksər, -z
indexible
BR ˈɪndɛksɪbl,
ɪnˈdɛksɪbl
AM ˈɪnˌdɛksəbəl
indexical
BR ɪnˈdɛksɪkl
AM ˈɪnˌdɛksəkəl
indexless
BR ˈɪndɛksləs
AM ˈɪnˌdɛksləs
India
BR ˈɪndɪə(r)
AM ˈɪndiə
Indiaman
BR ˈɪndɪəman
AM ˈɪndiəˌmæn
Indiamen
BR ˈɪndɪəmɛn
AM ˈɪndiəˌmɛn
Indian
BR ˈɪndɪən, -z
AM ˈɪndiən, -z
Indiana
BR ˌɪndɪˈanə(r)
AM ˌɪndiˈænə
Indianapolis
BR ˌɪndɪəˈnapəlɪs,
ˌɪndiəˈnapļɪs
AM ˌɪndiəˈnæp(ə)ləs
Indic
BR ˈɪndɪk, -s
AM ˈɪndɪk, -s
indicate
BR ˈɪndɪkeɪt, -s, -ɪŋ, -ɪd
AM ˈɪndəˌkeɪt, -ts, -dɪŋ,
-dɪd
indication
BR ˌɪndɪˈkeɪʃn, -z
AM ˌɪndəˈkeɪʃən, -z
indicative
BR ɪnˈdɪkətɪv, -z
AM ɪnˈdɪkədɪv, -z
indicatively
BR ɪnˈdɪkətɪvli
AM ɪnˈdɪkədəvli
indicator
BR ˈɪndɪkeɪtə(r), -z
AM ˈɪndəˌkeɪdər, -z
indicatory
BR ɪnˈdɪkət(ə)ri,
ˈɪndɪkeɪt(ə)ri
AM ˈɪndɪkəˌtɔri
indices
BR ˈɪndɪsiːz
AM ˈɪndəˌsiz
indicia
BR ɪnˈdɪsɪə(r),
ɪnˈdɪʃɪə(r)

AM ɪnˈdɪʃ(i)ə
indicial
BR ɪnˈdɪʃ(ə)l
AM ɪnˈdɪʃ(i)əl
indicium
BR ɪnˈdɪsɪəm,
ɪnˈdɪʃɪəm
AM ɪnˈdɪʃ(i)əm
indict
BR ɪnˈdʌɪt, -s, -ɪŋ, -ɪd
AM ɪnˈdaɪ|t, -ts, -dɪŋ,
-dɪd
indictable
BR ɪnˈdʌɪtəbl
AM ɪnˈdaɪdəbəl
indictee
BR ˌɪndʌɪˈtiː, -z
AM ɪnˌdaɪˈti, -z
indicter
BR ɪnˈdʌɪtə(r), -z
AM ɪnˈdaɪdər, -z
indiction
BR ɪnˈdɪkʃn, -z
AM ɪnˈdɪkʃən, -z
indictment
BR ɪnˈdʌɪtm(ə)nt, -s
AM ɪnˈdaɪtmənt, -s
indie
BR ˈɪnd|i, -ɪz
AM ˈɪndi, -z
Indies
BR ˈɪndɪz
AM ˈɪndiz
indifference
BR ɪnˈdɪf(ə)rəns,
ɪnˈdɪf(ə)r̩s
AM ɪnˈdɪf(ə)rəns
indifferent
BR ɪnˈdɪf(ə)rənt,
ɪnˈdɪf(ə)r̩t
AM ɪnˈdɪf(ə)rənt,
ɪnˈdɪfərnt
indifferentism
BR ɪnˈdɪf(ə)rəntɪz(ə)m,
ɪnˈdɪf(ə)r̩tɪz(ə)m
AM ɪnˈdɪfər̩ˌtɪzəm,
ɪnˈdɪf(ə)rənˌtɪzəm
indifferentist
BR ɪnˈdɪf(ə)rəntɪst,
ɪnˈdɪf(ə)r̩tɪst, -s
AM ɪnˈdɪfərntəst,
ɪnˈdɪf(ə)rən(t)əst, -s
indifferently
BR ɪnˈdɪf(ə)rəntli,
ɪnˈdɪf(ə)r̩tli
AM ɪnˈdɪfərntli,
ɪnˈdɪf(ə)rən(t)li
indigence
BR ˈɪndɪdʒ(ə)ns
AM ˈɪndədʒəns
indigene
BR ˈɪndɪdʒiːn, -z
AM ˈɪndəˌdʒin, -z
indigenisation
BR ɪnˌdɪdʒɪnʌɪˈzeɪʃn,
ɪnˌdɪdʒ̩ʌɪˈzeɪʃn
AM ɪnˌdɪdʒənəˈzeɪʃən,
ɪnˌdɪdʒəˌnaɪˈzeɪʃən

indigenise
BR ɪnˈdɪdʒɪnʌɪz,
ɪnˈdɪdʒ̩ʌɪz, -ɪz, -ɪŋ, -d
AM ɪnˈdɪdʒəˌnaɪz, -ɪz,
-ɪŋ, -d
indigenization
BR ɪnˌdɪdʒɪnʌɪˈzeɪʃn,
ɪnˌdɪdʒ̩ʌɪˈzeɪʃn
AM ɪnˌdɪdʒənəˈzeɪʃən,
ɪnˌdɪdʒəˌnaɪˈzeɪʃən
indigenize
BR ɪnˈdɪdʒɪnʌɪz,
ɪnˈdɪdʒ̩ʌɪz, -ɪz, -ɪŋ, -d
AM ɪnˈdɪdʒəˌnaɪz, -ɪz,
-ɪŋ, -d
indigenous
BR ɪnˈdɪdʒɪnəs,
ɪnˈdɪdʒ̩nəs
AM ɪnˈdɪdʒənəs
indigenously
BR ɪnˈdɪdʒɪnəsli,
ɪnˈdɪdʒ̩nəsli
AM ɪnˈdɪdʒənəsli
indigenousness
BR ɪnˈdɪdʒɪnəsnəs,
ɪnˈdɪdʒ̩nəsnəs
AM ɪnˈdɪdʒənəsnəs
indigent
BR ˈɪndɪdʒ(ə)nt
AM ˈɪndədʒənt
indigently
BR ˈɪndɪdʒ(ə)ntli
AM ˈɪndədʒən(t)li
indigested
BR ˌɪndɪˈdʒɛstɪd,
ˌɪndʌɪˈdʒɛstɪd
AM ˌɪndəˈdʒɛstəd
indigestibility
BR ˌɪndɪˌdʒɛstɪˈbɪlɪti,
ˌɪndʌɪˌdʒɛstɪˈbɪlɪti
AM ˌɪndəˌdʒɛstəˈbɪlɪdi
indigestible
BR ˌɪndɪˈdʒɛstɪbl,
ˌɪndʌɪˈdʒɛstɪbl
AM ˌɪndəˈdʒɛstəbəl
indigestibly
BR ˌɪndɪˈdʒɛstɪbli,
ˌɪndʌɪˈdʒɛstɪbli
AM ˌɪndəˈdʒɛstəbli
indigestion
BR ˌɪndɪˈdʒɛstʃ(ə)n
AM ˌɪndɪˈdʒɛstʃən,
ˌɪnˌdaɪˈdʒɛstʃən
indigestive
BR ˌɪndɪˈdʒɛstɪv
AM ˌɪndəˈdʒɛstɪv
indignant
BR ɪnˈdɪgnənt
AM ɪnˈdɪgnənt
indignantly
BR ɪnˈdɪgnəntli
AM ɪnˈdɪgnən(t)li
indignation
BR ˌɪndɪgˈneɪʃn
AM ˌɪndɪgˈneɪʃən
indignity
BR ɪnˈdɪgnɪt|i, -ɪz
AM ɪnˈdɪgnɪdi, -z

indigo
BR 'ɪndɪgəʊ
AM 'ɪndə‚goʊ
indigotic
BR ‚ɪndɪ'gɒtɪk
AM ‚ɪndə'gɑdɪk
Indira
BR 'ɪndɪrə(r),
ɪn'dɪərə(r)
AM ɪn'dɪrə
indirect
BR ‚ɪndɪ'rɛkt,
‚ɪndʌɪ'rɛkt
AM ‚ɪndə'rɛk(t)
indirection
BR ‚ɪndɪ'rɛkʃn,
‚ɪndʌɪ'rɛkʃn
AM ‚ɪndə'rɛkʃən
indirectly
BR ‚ɪndɪ'rɛktli,
‚ɪndʌɪ'rɛktli
AM ‚ɪndə'rɛk(t)li
indirectness
BR ‚ɪndɪ'rɛk(t)nəs,
‚ɪndʌɪ'rɛk(t)nəs
AM ‚ɪndə'rɛktnəs
indiscernibility
BR ‚ɪndɪ‚sə:nɪ'bɪlɪti
AM ‚ɪndə‚sɜrnə'bɪlɪdi
indiscernible
BR ‚ɪndɪ'sə:nɪbl
AM ‚ɪndə'sɜrnəbəl
indiscernibly
BR ‚ɪndɪ'sə:nɪbli
AM ‚ɪndə'sɜrnəbli
indiscipline
BR (‚)ɪn'dɪsɪplɪn
AM ɪn'dɪsəplən
indiscreet
BR ‚ɪndɪ'skri:t
AM ‚ɪndə'skrit
indiscreetly
BR ‚ɪndɪ'skri:tli
AM ‚ɪndə'skritli
indiscreetness
BR ‚ɪndɪ'skri:tnɪs
AM ‚ɪndə'skritnɪs
indiscrete
BR ‚ɪndɪ'skri:t
AM ‚ɪndə'skrit
indiscretion
BR ‚ɪndɪ'skrɛʃn, -z
AM ‚ɪndə'skrɛʃən, -z
indiscriminate
BR ‚ɪndɪ'skrɪmɪnət
AM ‚ɪndə'skrɪm(ə)nət
indiscriminately
BR ‚ɪndɪ'skrɪmɪnətli
AM ‚ɪndə'skrɪm(ə)nətli
**indiscriminate-
ness**
BR ‚ɪndɪ'skrɪmɪnətnəs
AM ‚ɪndə'skrɪm(ə)nət-
nəs
indiscrimination
BR ‚ɪndɪ‚skrɪmɪ'neɪʃn,
-z

indiscriminative
BR ‚ɪndɪ'skrɪmɪnətɪv
AM ‚ɪndə'skrɪmə‚neɪdɪv
indispensability
BR ‚ɪndɪ‚spɛnsə'bɪlɪti
AM ‚ɪndə‚spɛnsə'bɪlɪdi
indispensable
BR ‚ɪndɪ'spɛnsəbl
AM ‚ɪndə'spɛnsəbəl
indispensableness
BR ‚ɪndɪ'spɛnsəblnəs
AM ‚ɪndə'spɛnsəbəlnəs
indispensably
BR ‚ɪndɪ'spɛnsəbli
AM ‚ɪndə'spɛnsəbli
indispose
BR ‚ɪndɪ'spəʊz, -ɪz, -ɪŋ,
-d
AM ‚ɪndə'spoʊz, -əz, -ɪŋ,
-d
indisposition
BR ‚ɪndɪspə'zɪʃn,
ɪn‚dɪspə'zɪʃn, -z
AM ‚ɪn‚dɪspə'zɪʃən,
ɪn‚dɪspə'zɪʃən, -z
indisputability
BR ‚ɪndɪ‚spju:tə'bɪlɪti
AM ‚ɪndə‚spjudə'bɪlɪdi,
ɪndə‚spjudə'bɪlɪdi
indisputable
BR ‚ɪndɪ'spju:təbl
AM ‚ɪndə'spjudəbəl,
ɪndə'spjudəbəl
indisputableness
BR ‚ɪndɪ'spju:təblnəs
AM ‚ɪndə'spjudəbəlnəs,
ɪndə'spjudəbəlnəs
indisputably
BR ‚ɪndɪ'spju:təbli
AM ‚ɪndə'spjudəbli,
ɪndə'spjudəbli
indissolubilist
BR ‚ɪndɪ'sɒljəbɪlɪst,
‚ɪndɪ'sɒljəbl̩ɪst, -s
AM ‚ɪndə'saljə‚bɪlɪst,
‚ɪndə'saljə‚bɪlɪst, -s
indissolubility
BR ‚ɪndɪ‚sɒljə'bɪlɪti
AM ‚ɪndə‚saljə'bɪlɪdi,
ɪndə‚saljə'bɪlɪdi
indissoluble
BR ‚ɪndɪ'sɒljəbl
AM ‚ɪndə'saljəbəl,
ɪndə'saljəbəl
indissolubly
BR ‚ɪndɪ'sɒljəbli
AM ‚ɪndə'saljəbli,
ɪndə'saljəbli
indistinct
BR ‚ɪndɪ'stɪŋ(k)t
AM ‚ɪndɪ'stɪŋ(k)t,
'ɪndə'stɪŋk(t)
indistinctive
BR ‚ɪndɪ'stɪŋ(k)tɪv
AM ‚ɪndə'stɪŋ(k)tɪv

indistinctively
BR ‚ɪndɪ'stɪŋ(k)tɪvli
AM ‚ɪndə'stɪŋ(k)tɪvli
indistinctiveness
BR ‚ɪndɪ'stɪŋ(k)tɪvnɪs
AM ‚ɪndə'stɪŋ(k)tɪvnəs
indistinctly
BR ‚ɪndɪ'stɪŋ(k)tli
AM ‚ɪndə'stɪŋ(k)tli,
'‚ɪndə'stɪŋkli
indistinctness
BR ‚ɪndɪ'stɪŋ(k)tnɪs,
‚ɪndɪ'stɪŋk(t)nɪs
AM ‚ɪndə'stɪŋ(k)tnəs,
'ɪndə'stɪŋk(t)nəs
indistinguishable
BR ‚ɪndɪ'stɪŋgwɪʃəbl
AM ‚ɪndə'stɪŋgwəʃəbəl
**indistinguishable-
ness**
BR ‚ɪndɪ'stɪŋgwɪʃəblnəs
AM ‚ɪndə'stɪŋgwəʃəbəl-
nəs
indistinguishably
BR ‚ɪndɪ'stɪŋgwɪʃəbli
AM ‚ɪndə'stɪŋgwəʃəbli
indite
BR ɪn'dʌɪt, -s, -ɪŋ, -ɪd
AM ɪn'daɪt, -ts, -dɪŋ,
-dɪd
indium
BR 'ɪndɪəm
AM 'ɪndɪəm
indivertible
BR ‚ɪndʌɪ'və:tɪbl,
‚ɪndɪ'və:tɪbl
AM ‚ɪndə'vərdəbəl,
‚ɪn‚daɪ'vərdəbəl
indivertibly
BR ‚ɪndɪ'və:tɪbli,
‚ɪndɪ'və:tɪbli
AM ‚ɪndə'vərdəbli,
'ɪn‚daɪ'vərdəbli
individual
BR ‚ɪndɪ'vɪdʒʊəl,
‚ɪndɪ'vɪdʒ(ʊ)l,
‚ɪndɪ'vɪdʒʊəl,
‚ɪndɪ'vɪdʒʊl, -z
AM ‚ɪndə'vɪdʒ(ə)wəl,
'ɪndə'vɪdʒəl, -z
individualisation
BR ‚ɪndɪ‚vɪdʒʊəlʌɪ'zeɪʃn,
‚ɪndɪ‚vɪdʒʊlʌɪ'zeɪʃn,
‚ɪndɪ‚vɪdʒʌɪ'zeɪʃn,
‚ɪndɪ‚vɪdʒʊəlʌɪ'zeɪʃn,
‚ɪndɪ‚vɪdʒʊlʌɪ'zeɪʃn,
-z
AM ‚ɪndə‚vɪdʒ(ə)wə‚laɪ-
'zeɪʃən,
‚ɪndə‚vɪdʒə‚laɪ'zeɪʃən,
'ɪndə‚vɪdʒ(ə)wələ'zeɪ-
ʃən,
'ɪndə‚vɪdʒələ'zeɪʃən,
-z
individualise
BR ‚ɪndɪ'vɪdʒʊəlʌɪz,
‚ɪndɪ'vɪdʒʊlʌɪz,
‚ɪndɪ'vɪdʒlʌɪz,

individualize
BR ‚ɪndɪ'vɪdʒʊəlʌɪz, -s
ɪndɪ'vɪdʒʊlʌɪz, -ɪz, -ɪŋ,
-d
AM ‚ɪndə'vɪdʒ(ə)wə‚laɪz,
‚ɪndə'vɪdʒə‚laɪz, -ɪz,
-ɪŋ, -d
individualism
BR ‚ɪndɪ'vɪdʒʊəlɪz(ə)m,
‚ɪndɪ'vɪdʒʊlɪz(ə)m,
‚ɪndɪ'vɪdʒlɪz(ə)m,
‚ɪndɪ'vɪdʒʊəlɪz(ə)m,
‚ɪndɪ'vɪdʒʊlɪz(ə)m
AM ‚ɪndə'vɪdʒ(ə)wə-
‚lɪzəm, ‚ɪndə'vɪdʒə-
‚lɪzəm
individualist
BR ‚ɪndɪ'vɪdʒʊəlɪst,
‚ɪndɪ'vɪdʒʊlɪst,
‚ɪndɪ'vɪdʒlɪst,
‚ɪndɪ'vɪdʒʊəlɪst,
‚ɪndɪ'vɪdʒʊlɪst, -s
AM ‚ɪndə'vɪdʒ(ə)wələst,
'ɪndə'vɪdʒələst, -s
individualistic
BR ‚ɪndɪ‚vɪdʒʊə'lɪstɪk,
‚ɪndɪ‚vɪdʒʊ'lɪstɪk,
‚ɪndɪ‚vɪdʒl'ɪstɪk,
‚ɪndɪ‚vɪdʒʊə'lɪstɪk,
‚ɪndɪ‚vɪdʒʊ'lɪstɪk
AM ‚ɪndə‚vɪdʒ(ə)wə'lɪs-
tɪk, ‚ɪndə‚vɪdʒə'lɪstɪk
individualistically
BR ‚ɪndɪ‚vɪdʒʊə'lɪstɪkli,
‚ɪndɪ‚vɪdʒʊ'lɪstɪkli,
‚ɪndɪ‚vɪdʒl'ɪstɪkli,
‚ɪndɪ‚vɪdʒʊə'lɪstɪkli,
‚ɪndɪ‚vɪdʒʊ'lɪstɪkli
AM ‚ɪndə‚vɪdʒ(ə)wə-
'lɪstək(ə)li,
'ɪndə‚vɪdʒə'lɪstək(ə)li
individuality
BR ‚ɪndɪ‚vɪdʒʊ'alɪti,
‚ɪndɪ‚vɪdʒʊ'alɪti
AM ‚ɪndə‚vɪdʒə'wælədi
individualization
BR ‚ɪndɪ‚vɪdʒʊəlʌɪ'zeɪ-
ʃn,
‚ɪndɪ‚vɪdʒʊlʌɪ'zeɪʃn,
‚ɪndɪ‚vɪdʒlʌɪ'zeɪʃn,
‚ɪndɪ‚vɪdʒʊəlʌɪ'zeɪʃn,
‚ɪndɪ‚vɪdʒʊlʌɪ'zeɪʃn,
-z
AM ‚ɪndə‚vɪdʒ(ə)wə‚laɪ-
'zeɪʃən,
‚ɪndə‚vɪdʒə‚laɪ'zeɪʃən,
'ɪndə‚vɪdʒ(ə)wələ'zeɪ-
ʃən,
'ɪndə‚vɪdʒələ'zeɪʃən,
-z
individualize
BR ‚ɪndɪ'vɪdʒʊəlʌɪz,
ɪndɪ'vɪdʒʊlʌɪz,
‚ɪndɪ'vɪdʒlʌɪz,
‚ɪndɪ'vɪdʒʊəlʌɪz,
ɪndɪ'vɪdʒʊlʌɪz, -ɪz, -ɪŋ,
-d
AM ‚ɪndə'vɪdʒ(ə)wə‚laɪz,
‚ɪndə'vɪdʒə‚laɪz, -ɪz,
-ɪŋ, -d

individually
BR ˌɪndɪˈvɪdʒʊəli,
ˌɪndɪˈvɪdʒʉli,
ˌɪndɪˈvɪdʒḷi,
ˌɪndɪˈvɪdjʊəli,
ˌɪndɪˈvɪdjʉli,
AM ˈɪndəˈvɪdʒ(ə)wəli,
ˌɪndəˈvɪdʒəli

individuate
BR ˌɪndɪˈvɪdʒʊeɪt,
ˌɪndɪˈvɪdjʊeɪt, -s, -ɪŋ,
-ɪd
AM ˈɪndəˈvɪdʒə,weɪ|t.
-ts, -dɪŋ, -dɪd

individuation
BR ˌɪndɪˌvɪdʒʊˈeɪʃn,
ˌɪndɪˌvɪdjʊˈeɪʃn, -z
AM ˈɪndəˌvɪdʒəˈweɪʃən,
-z

indivisibility
BR ˌɪndɪˌvɪzɪˈbɪlɪti
AM ˈɪndəˌvɪzəˈbɪlɪdi

indivisible
BR ˌɪndɪˈvɪzɪbl̩
AM ˈɪndəˈvɪzəbəl

indivisibly
BR ˌɪndɪˈvɪzɪbli
AM ˈɪndəˈvɪzəbli

Indo-Aryan
BR ˌɪndəʊˈɛːrɪən,
ˌɪndəʊˈɑːrɪən,
ˌɪndəʊˈɑrɪən, -z
AM ˌɪndoʊˈɛrɪən, -z

Indo-China
BR ˌɪndəʊˈtʃʌɪnə(r)
AM ˌɪndoʊˈtʃaɪnə

Indo-Chinese
BR ˌɪndəʊˌtʃʌɪˈniːz
AM ˌɪndoʊˌtʃaɪˈniz

indocile
BR (ˌ)ɪnˈdəʊsʌɪl
AM ɪnˈdɑsəl

indocility
BR ˌɪndəˈsɪlɪti
AM ˌɪnˌdɑˈsɪlɪdi,
ˈɪndəˈsɪlɪdi

indoctrinate
BR ɪnˈdɒktrɪneɪt, -s,
-ɪŋ, -ɪd
AM ɪnˈdɑktrəˌneɪ|t, -ts,
-dɪŋ, -dɪd

indoctrination
BR ɪnˌdɒktrɪˈneɪʃn
AM ɪnˌdɑktrəˈneɪʃən

indoctrinator
BR ɪnˈdɒktrɪmeɪtə(r),
-z
AM ɪnˈdɑktrəˌneɪdər,
-z

Indo-European
BR ˌɪndəʊˌjʊərəˈpiːən,
ˌɪndəʊˌjɔːrəˈpiːən, -z
AM ˌɪndoˌjʊrəˈpiən,
ˌɪndoʊˌjʊərəˈpiən, -z

Indo-Germanic
BR ˌɪndəʊˌdʒəːˈmanɪk,
ˌɪndəʊdʒəˈmanɪk, -s

AM ˌɪndoʊdʒərˈmænɪk,
-s

Indo-Iranian
BR ˌɪndəʊɪˌreɪnɪən, -z
AM ˌɪndoʊəˈreɪnɪən, -z

indole
BR ˈɪndəʊl, -z
AM ˈɪnˌdoʊl, -z

indoleacetic acid
BR ˌɪndəʊləˌsiˈtɪk
ˈasɪd, ˌɪndəʊləˌsetɪk +,
-z
AM ɪnˌdoʊliəˌsedɪk
ˈæsəd, -z

indolence
BR ˈɪndələns, ˈɪndəlns,
ˈɪndl̩(ə)ns
AM ˈɪndələns

indolent
BR ˈɪndələnt, ˈɪndəlnt,
ˈɪndl̩(ə)nt
AM ˈɪndələnt

indolently
BR ˈɪndələntli,
ˈɪndəlntli, ˈɪndl̩(ə)ntli
AM ˈɪndələn(t)li

Indologist
BR ɪnˈdɒlədʒɪst, -s
AM ɪnˈdɑlədʒəst, -s

Indology
BR ɪnˈdɒlədʒi
AM ɪnˈdɑlədʒi

indomitability
BR ɪnˌdɒmɪtəˈbɪlɪti
AM ɪnˌdɑmədəˈbɪlɪdi

indomitable
BR ɪnˈdɒmɪtəbl̩
AM ɪnˈdɑmədəbəl

indomitableness
BR ɪnˈdɒmɪtəblnəs
AM ɪnˈdɑmədəbəlnəs

indomitably
BR ɪnˈdɒmɪtəbli
AM ɪnˈdɑmədəbəli

Indonesia
BR ˌɪndəˈniːzɪə(r),
ˌɪndəˈniːʒə(r)
AM ˌɪndəˈniʒə,
ˌɪndəˈniʃə,
ˌɪndoʊˈniʒə,
ˌɪndoʊˈniʃə

Indonesian
BR ˌɪndəˈniːzɪən,
ˌɪndəˈniːʒn, -z
AM ˌɪndəˈniʒən,
ˌɪndəˈniʃən,
ˌɪndəˈniziən,
ˌɪndoʊˈniʒən,
ˌɪndoʊˈniʃən,
ˌɪndoʊˈniziən, -z

indoor
BR ˌɪnˈdɔː(r)
AM ˈɪnˌdɔ(ə)r

indoors
BR ˌɪnˈdɔːz
AM ˌɪnˈdɔ(ə)rz,
ɪnˈdɔ(ə)rz

Indo-Pacific
BR ˌɪndəʊpəˈsɪfɪk
AM ˌɪndoʊpəˈsɪfɪk

Indore
BR (ˌ)ɪnˈdɔː(r)
AM ɪnˈdɔ(ə)r

indorse
BR ɪnˈdɔːs, -ɪz, -ɪŋ, -t
AM ɪnˈdɔ(ə)rs, -əz, -ɪŋ,
-t

indorsement
BR ɪnˈdɔːsm(ə)nt, -s
AM ɪnˈdɔrsmənt, -s

Indra
BR ˈɪndrə(r)
AM ˈɪndrə

indraft
BR ˈɪndrɑːft, ˈɪndraft,
-s
AM ˈɪnˌdræft, -s

indraught
BR ˈɪndrɑːft, ˈɪndraft,
-s
AM ˈɪnˌdræft, -s

indrawn
BR ˌɪnˈdrɔːn
AM ˈɪnˌdrɔn, ˈɪnˌdrɑn

indri
BR ˈɪndr|i, -ɪz
AM ˈɪndri, -z

indubitable
BR ɪnˈdjuːbɪtəbl̩,
ɪnˈdʒuːbɪtəbl̩
AM ɪnˈd(j)ubədəbəl

indubitably
BR ɪnˈdjuːbɪtəbli,
ɪnˈdʒuːbɪtəbli
AM ɪnˈd(j)ubədəbli

induce
BR ɪnˈdjuːs, ɪnˈdʒuːs,
-ɪz, -ɪŋ, -t
AM ənˈd(j)us,
ɪnˈd(j)us, -əz, -ɪŋ, -t

inducement
BR ɪnˈdjuːsm(ə)nt,
ɪnˈdʒuːsm(ə)nt, -s
AM ɪnˈd(j)usmənt,
ɪnˈd(j)usmənt, -s

inducer
BR ɪnˈdjuːsə(r),
ɪnˈdʒuːsə(r), -z
AM ɪnˈd(j)usər,
ɪnˈd(j)usər, -z

inducible
BR ɪnˈdjuːsɪbl̩,
ɪnˈdʒuːsɪbl
AM ɪnˈd(j)usəbəl,
ɪnˈd(j)usəbəl

induct
BR ɪnˈdʌkt, -s, -ɪŋ, -ɪd
AM ɪnˈdək|(t), -(t)s,
-tɪŋ, -təd

inductance
BR ɪnˈdʌkt(ə)ns, -ɪz
AM ɪnˈdəktns, -əz

inductee
BR ˌɪndəkˈtiː, -z
AM ɪnˌdəkˈti, -z

induction
BR ɪnˈdʌkʃn, -z
AM ɪnˈdəkʃən, -z

inductive
BR ɪnˈdʌktɪv
AM ɪnˈdəktɪv

inductively
BR ɪnˈdʌktɪvli
AM ɪnˈdəktəvli

inductiveness
BR ɪnˈdʌktɪvnɪs
AM ɪnˈdəktɪvnɪs

inductor
BR ɪnˈdʌktə(r), -z
AM ɪnˈdəktər, -z

indue
BR ɪnˈdjuː, ɪnˈdʒuː, -z,
-ɪŋ, -d
AM ɪnˈd(j)u, -z, -ɪŋ, -d

indulge
BR ɪnˈdʌldʒ, -ɪz, -ɪŋ, -d
AM ɪnˈdəldʒ, -əz, -ɪŋ, -t

indulgence
BR ɪnˈdʌldʒ(ə)ns, -ɪz, -t
AM ɪnˈdəldʒəns, -əz, -t

indulgent
BR ɪnˈdʌldʒ(ə)nt
AM ɪnˈdəldʒənt

indulgently
BR ɪnˈdʌldʒ(ə)ntli
AM ɪnˈdəldʒən(t)li

indulger
BR ɪnˈdʌldʒə(r), -z
AM ɪnˈdəldʒər, -z

indult
BR ɪnˈdʌlt, -s
AM ɪnˈdəlt, -s

indumenta
BR ˌɪndjʉˈmɛntə(r),
ˌɪndʒʉˈmɛntə(r)
AM ˌɪnd(j)əˈmɛn(t)ə

indumentum
BR ˌɪndjʉˈmɛntəm,
ˌɪndʒʉˈmɛntəm
AM ˌɪnd(j)əˈmɛn(t)əm

induna
BR ɪnˈduːnə(r), -z
AM ɪnˈdunə, -z

indurate[1]
adjective
BR ˈɪndjʉrət,
ˈɪndʒʉrət
AM ˈɪnd(j)ərət

indurate[2]
verb
BR ˈɪndjʉreɪt,
ˈɪndʒʉreɪt, -s, -ɪŋ, -ɪd
AM ˈɪnd(j)əˌreɪ|t, -ts,
-dɪŋ, -dɪd

induration
BR ˌɪndjʉˈreɪʃn,
ˌɪndʒʉˈreɪʃn, -z
AM ˌɪnd(j)əˈreɪʃən, -z

indurative
BR ˈɪndjʉrətɪv,
ˈɪndʒʉrətɪv
AM ˈɪnd(j)əˌreɪdɪv

Indus
BR ˈɪndəs
AM ˈɪndəs
indusia
BR ɪnˈdjuːzɪə(r),
ɪnˈdʒuːzɪə(r)
AM ɪnˈd(j)uːʒ(i)ə,
ɪnˈd(j)uːzɪə
indusial
BR ɪnˈdjuːzɪəl,
ɪnˈdʒuːzɪəl
AM ɪnˈd(j)uːʒ(i)əl,
ɪnˈd(j)uːzɪəl
indusium
BR ɪnˈdjuːzɪəm,
ɪnˈdʒuːzɪəm
AM ɪnˈd(j)uːʒ(i)əm,
ɪnˈd(j)uːzɪəm
industrial
BR ɪnˈdʌstrɪəl, -z
AM ɪnˈdəstrɪəl, -z
industrialisation
BR ɪnˌdʌstrɪəlʌɪˈzeɪʃn
AM ɪnˌdəstrɪələˈzeɪʃən,
ɪnˌdəstrɪəˌlaɪˈzeɪʃən
industrialise
BR ɪnˈdʌstrɪəlʌɪz, -ɪz,
-ɪŋ, -d
AM ɪnˈdəstrɪəˌlaɪz, -ɪz,
-ɪŋ, -d
industrialism
BR ɪnˈdʌstrɪəlɪz(ə)m
AM ɪnˈdəstrɪəˌlɪzəm
industrialist
BR ɪnˈdʌstrɪəlɪst, -s
AM ɪnˈdəstrɪələst, -s
industrialization
BR ɪnˌdʌstrɪəlʌɪˈzeɪʃn
AM ɪnˌdəstrɪələˈzeɪʃən,
ɪnˌdəstrɪəˌlaɪˈzeɪʃən
industrialize
BR ɪnˈdʌstrɪəlʌɪz, -ɪz,
-ɪŋ, -d
AM ɪnˈdəstrɪəˌlaɪz, -ɪz,
-ɪŋ, -d
industrially
BR ɪnˈdʌstrɪəli
AM ɪnˈdəstrɪəli
industrious
BR ɪnˈdʌstrɪəs
AM ɪnˈdəstrɪəs
industriously
BR ɪnˈdʌstrɪəsli
AM ɪnˈdəstrɪəsli
industriousness
BR ɪnˈdʌstrɪəsnəs
AM ɪnˈdəstrɪəsnəs
industry
BR ˈɪndəstr|i, -ɪz
AM ˈɪndəstri, -z
indwell
BR (ˌ)ɪnˈdwɛl, -z, -ɪŋ, -d
AM ɪnˈdwɛl, -z, -ɪŋ, -d
indweller
BR (ˌ)ɪnˈdwɛlə(r), -z
AM ɪnˈdwɛlər, -z

Indy
Indianapolis
BR ˈɪndi
AM ˈɪndi
Indycar
BR ˈɪndɪkɑː(r), -z
AM ˈɪndiˌkɑr, -z
inebriate[1]
noun
BR ɪˈniːbrɪət, -s
AM ɪˈnibrɪət,
ɪˈnibriˌeɪt, ɪˈnibrɪət,
ɪˈnibriˌeɪt, -s
inebriate[2]
verb
BR ɪˈniːbrɪeɪt, -s, -ɪŋ, -ɪd
AM ɪˈnibriˌeɪt,
ɪˈnibriˌeɪt, -ts, -dɪŋ,
-dɪd
inebriation
BR ɪˌniːbrɪˈeɪʃn
AM ɪˌnibriˈeɪʃən
inebriety
BR ˌɪnɪˈbrʌɪti
AM ˌɪnəˈbraɪədi
inedibility
BR ɪnˌɛdɪˈbɪlɪti
AM ˈɪnˌɛdəˈbɪlɪdi,
ɪnˌɛdəˈbɪlɪdi
inedible
BR (ˌ)ɪnˈɛdɪbl
AM ɪnˈɛdəbəl
inedibly
BR (ˌ)ɪnˈɛdɪbli
AM ɪnˈɛdəbli
ineducability
BR ɪnˌɛdjʊkəˈbɪlɪti,
ɪnˌɛdʒʊkəˈbɪlɪti
AM ˈɪnˌɛdʒəkəˈbɪlɪdi
ineducable
BR (ˌ)ɪnˈɛdjʊkəbl,
(ˌ)ɪnˈɛdʒʊkəbl
AM ɪnˈɛdʒəkəbəl
ineducably
BR (ˌ)ɪnˈɛdjʊkəbli,
(ˌ)ɪnˈɛdʒʊkəbli
AM ɪnˈɛdʒəkəbli
ineffability
BR ɪnˌɛfəˈbɪlɪti
AM ɪˌnɛfəˈbɪlɪdi
ineffable
BR ɪnˈɛfəbl
AM ɪnˈɛfəbəl
ineffably
BR ɪnˈɛfəbli
AM ɪnˈɛfəbli
ineffaceability
BR ˌɪnɪˌfeɪsəˈbɪlɪti
AM ˈɪnəˌfeɪsəˈbɪlɪdi,
ˈɪniˌfeɪsəˈbɪlɪdi
ineffaceable
BR ˌɪnɪˈfeɪsəbl
AM ˈɪnəˈfeɪsəbəl,
ˈɪniˈfeɪsəbəl
ineffaceably
BR ˌɪnɪˈfeɪsəbli
AM ˈɪnəˈfeɪsəbli,
ˈɪniˈfeɪsəbli

ineffective
BR ˌɪnɪˈfɛktɪv
AM ˈɪnəˈfɛktɪv,
ˈɪniˈfɛktɪv
ineffectively
BR ˌɪnɪˈfɛktɪvli
AM ˈɪnəˈfɛktəvli,
ˈɪniˈfɛktəvli
ineffectiveness
BR ˌɪnɪˈfɛktɪvnɪs
AM ˈɪnəˈfɛktɪvnɪs,
ˈɪniˈfɛktɪvnɪs
ineffectual
BR ˌɪnɪˈfɛktʃʊəl,
ˌɪnɪˈfɛktʃ(ʊ)l,
ˌɪnɪˈfɛktjʊəl,
ˌɪnɪˈfɛktjəl
AM ˈɪnəˈfɛk(t)ʃ(əw)əl
ineffectuality
BR ˌɪnɪˌfɛktʃʊˈalɪt|i,
ˌɪnɪˌfɛktjʊˈalɪt|i, -ɪz
AM ˈɪnəˈfɛk(t)ʃəˈwælədi,
-z
ineffectually
BR ˌɪnɪˈfɛktʃʊəli,
ˌɪnɪˈfɛktʃəli,
ˌɪnɪˈfɛktʃli,
ˌɪnɪˈfɛktjʊəli,
ˌɪnɪˈfɛktjəli
AM ˈɪnəˈfɛk(t)ʃ(əw)əli
ineffectualness
BR ˌɪnɪˈfɛktʃʊəlnəs,
ˌɪnɪˈfɛktʃ(ʊ)lnəs,
ˌɪnɪˈfɛktjʊəlnəs,
ˌɪnɪˈfɛktjəlnəs
AM ˈɪnəˈfɛk(t)ʃ(əw)əl-
nəs
inefficacious
BR ˌɪnɛfɪˈkeɪʃəs,
ɪnˌɛfɪˈkeɪʃəs
AM ˈɪnɛfəˈkeɪʃəs
inefficaciously
BR ˌɪnɛfɪˈkeɪʃəsli,
ɪnˌɛfɪˈkeɪʃəsli
AM ˈɪnɛfəˈkeɪʃəsli
inefficaciousness
BR ˌɪnɛfɪˈkeɪʃəsnəs,
ɪnˌɛfɪˈkeɪʃəsnəs
AM ˈɪnɛfəˈkeɪʃəsnəs
inefficacy
BR ɪnˈɛfɪkəs|i, -ɪz
AM ɪnˈɛfəkəsi, -z
inefficiency
BR ˌɪnɪˈfɪʃnsi
AM ˈɪnəˈfɪʃənsi,
ˈɪniˈfɪʃənsi
inefficient
BR ˌɪnɪˈfɪʃnt
AM ˈɪnəˈfɪʃənt,
ˈɪniˈfɪʃənt
inefficiently
BR ˌɪnɪˈfɪʃntli
AM ˈɪnəˈfɪʃən(t)li,
ˈɪniˈfɪʃən(t)li
inegalitarian
BR ˌɪnɪˌgalɪˈtɛːrɪən, -z
AM ˈɪnɪˌgæləˈtɛrɪən,
ˈɪnəˌgæləˈtɛrɪən, -z

inelastic
BR ˌɪnɪˈlastɪk
AM ˈɪnəˈlæstɪk
inelastically
BR ˌɪnɪˈlastɪkli
AM ˈɪnəˈlæstək(ə)li
inelasticity
BR ˌɪnɪlaˈstɪsɪti,
ˌmiːlaˈstɪsɪti
AM ˈɪnəˌlæˈstɪsɪdi,
ˈɪniˌlæˈstɪsɪdi
inelegance
BR (ˌ)ɪnˈɛlɪg(ə)ns
AM ɪnˈɛləgəns
inelegant
BR (ˌ)ɪnˈɛlɪg(ə)nt
AM ɪnˈɛləgənt
inelegantly
BR (ˌ)ɪnˈɛlɪg(ə)ntli
AM ɪnˈɛləgən(t)li
ineligibility
BR ɪnˌɛlɪdʒɪˈbɪlɪti
AM ˈɪnˌɛlədʒəˈbɪlɪdi,
ɪnˌɛlədʒəˈbɪlɪdi
ineligible
BR (ˌ)ɪnˈɛlɪdʒɪbl
AM ɪnˈɛlədʒəbəl
ineligibly
BR (ˌ)ɪnˈɛlɪdʒɪbli
AM ɪnˈɛlədʒəbli
ineluctability
BR ˌɪnɪˌlʌktəˈbɪlɪti
AM ˈɪnəˌləktəˈbɪlɪdi
ineluctable
BR ˌɪnɪˈlʌktəbl
AM ˈɪnəˈləktəbəl
ineluctably
BR ˌɪnɪˈlʌktəbli
AM ˈɪnəˈləktəbli
inept
BR ɪˈnɛpt, ˌɪnˈɛpt
AM ɪˈnɛpt
ineptitude
BR ɪˈnɛptɪtjuːd,
ɪˈnɛptɪtʃuːd
AM ɪˈnɛptəˌt(j)ud
ineptly
BR ɪˈnɛptli
AM ɪˈnɛp(t)li
ineptness
BR ɪˈnɛp(t)nəs
AM ɪˈnɛp(t)nəs
inequable
BR (ˌ)ɪnˈɛkwəbl
AM ɪnˈɛkwəbəl
inequality
BR ˌɪnɪˈkwɒlɪt|i, -ɪz
AM ˈɪnəˈkwɑlədi,
ˈɪnəˈkwɑlədi,
ˈɪniˈkwɑlədi,
ˈɪniˈkwɑlədi, -z
inequitable
BR (ˌ)ɪnˈɛkwɪtəbl
AM ɪnˈɛkwədəbəl
inequitably
BR (ˌ)ɪnˈɛkwɪtəbli
AM ɪnˈɛkwədəbli

inequity
BR (ˌ)ɪnˈɛkwɪt|i, -ɪz
AM ɪnˈɛkwədi, -z

ineradicable
BR ˌɪnɪˈrædɪkəbl
AM ˌɪnəˈrædəkəbəl

ineradicably
BR ˌɪnɪˈradɪkəbli
AM ˌɪnəˈrædəkəbli

inerrability
BR ɪnˌəːrəˈbɪlɪti
AM ˌɪnˌɛrəˈbɪlɪdi

inerrable
BR (ˌ)ɪnˈəːrəbl
AM ɪˈnɛrəbəl

inerrably
BR (ˌ)ɪnˈəːrəbli
AM ɪˈnɛrəbli

inerrancy
BR (ˌ)ɪnˈɛrənsi,
(ˌ)ɪnˈɛrn̩si
AM ɪˈnɛrənsi

inerrant
BR (ˌ)ɪnˈɛrənt,
(ˌ)ɪnˈɛrn̩t
AM ɪˈnɛrənt

inert
BR ɪˈnəːt
AM ɪˈnɚt

inertia
BR ɪˈnəːʃə(r)
AM ɪˈnɚʃə

inertial
BR ɪˈnəːʃl, ɪˈnəːʃɪəl
AM ɪˈnɚʃəl

inertialess
BR ɪˈnəːʃələs
AM ɪˈnɚʃələs

inertly
BR ɪˈnəːtli
AM ɪˈnɚtli

inertness
BR ɪˈnəːtnəs
AM ɪˈnɚtnəs

inescapability
BR ˌɪnɪˌskeɪpəˈbɪlɪti
AM ˌɪnəˌskeɪpəˈbɪlɪdi

inescapable
BR ˌɪnɪˈskeɪpəbl
AM ˌɪnəˈskeɪpəbəl

inescapably
BR ˌɪnɪˈskeɪpəbli
AM ˌɪnəˈskeɪpəbli

inescutcheon
BR ˌɪnɪˈskʌtʃ(ə)n
AM ˌɪnəˈskətʃən,
ˌɪnɛˈskətʃən

in essence
BR ˌɪn ˈɛsns
AM ɪ ˈnɛsəns

inessential
BR ˌɪnɪˈsenʃl, -z
AM ˌɪnəˈsɛn(t)ʃəl,
ˌɪniˈsɛn(t)ʃəl, -z

inestimable
BR ˌɪnˈɛstɪməbl

AM ɪnˈɛstəməbəl,
ɪnˈɛstəməbəl

inestimably
BR ˌɪnˈɛstɪməbli
AM ɪnˈɛstəməbli,
ɪnˈɛstəməbli

inevitability
BR ɪnˌɛvɪtəˈbɪlɪti,
ɪˌnɛvɪtəˈbɪlɪti
AM ɪˌnɛvədəˈbɪlɪdi,
ɪˌnɛvtəˈbɪlɪdi

inevitable
BR ɪnˈɛvɪtəbl,
ɪˈnɛvɪtəbl
AM ɪˈnɛvədəbəl,
ɪˈnɛvtəbəl

inevitableness
BR ɪnˈɛvɪtəblnəs,
ɪˈnɛvɪtəblnəs
AM ɪˈnɛvədəbəlnəs,
ɪˈnɛvtəbəlnəs

inevitably
BR ɪnˈɛvɪtəbli,
ɪˈnɛvɪtəbli
AM ɪˈnɛvədəbli,
ɪˈnɛvtəbli

inexact
BR ˌɪnɪɡˈzakt,
ˌɪnɛɡˈzakt
AM ˌɪnɪɡˈzæk(t),
ˌɪnɛɡˈzæk(t)

inexactitude
BR ˌɪnɪɡˈzaktɪtjuːd,
ˌɪnɛɡˈzaktɪtjuːd,
ˌɪnɪɡˈzaktɪtʃuːd,
ˌɪnɛɡˈzaktɪtʃuːd, -z
AM ˌɪnɪɡˈzæktəˌt(j)ud,
ˌɪnɛɡˈzæktət(j)ud, -z

inexactly
BR ˌɪnɪɡˈzak(t)li,
ˌɪnɛɡˈzak(t)li
AM ˌɪnɪɡˈzæk(t)li,
ˌɪnɛɡˈzæk(t)li

inexactness
BR ˌɪnɪɡˈzak(t)nəs,
ˌɪnɛɡˈzak(t)nəs
AM ˌɪnɪɡˈzæk(t)nəs,
ˌɪnɛɡˈzæk(t)nəs

inexcusable
BR ˌɪnɪkˈskjuːzəbl,
ˌɪnɛkˈskjuːzəbl
AM ˌɪnɪkˈskjuzəbəl,
ˌɪnɛkˈskjuzəbəl

inexcusably
BR ˌɪnɪkˈskjuːzəbli,
ˌɪnɛkˈskjuːzəbli
AM ˌɪnɪkˈskjuzəbli,
ˌɪnɛkˈskjuzəbli

inexhaustibility
BR ˌɪnɪɡˌzɔːstɪˈbɪlɪti,
ˌɪnɛɡˌzɔːstɪˈbɪlɪti
AM ˌɪnɪɡˌzɔstəˈbɪlɪdi,
ˌɪnɛɡˌzɔstəˈbɪlɪdi,
ˌɪnɪɡˌzastəˈbɪlɪdi,
ˌɪnɛɡˌzastəˈbɪlɪdi

inexhaustible
BR ˌɪnɪɡˈzɔːstɪbl,
ˌɪnɛɡˈzɔːstɪbl

AM ˌɪnɪɡˈzɔstəbəl,
ˌɪnɛɡˈzɔstəbəl,
ˌɪnɪɡˈzastəbəl,
ˌɪnɛɡˈzastəbəl

inexhaustibly
BR ˌɪnɪɡˈzɔːstɪbli,
ˌɪnɛɡˈzɔːstɪbli

inexplicability
AM ˌɪnɪɡˈzɔstəbli,
ˌɪnɛɡˈzɔstəbli,
ˌɪnɪɡˈzastəbli,
ˌɪnɛɡˈzastəbli

inexorability
BR ɪnˌɛks(ə)rəˈbɪlɪti
AM ɪˌnɛks(ə)rəˈbɪlɪdi

inexorable
BR ɪnˈɛks(ə)rəbl
AM ɪˈnɛks(ə)rəbəl

inexorably
BR ɪnˈɛks(ə)rəbli
AM ɪˈnɛks(ə)rəbli

inexpedience
BR ˌɪnɪkˈspiːdɪəns,
ˌɪnɛkˈspiːdɪəns
AM ˌɪnɪkˈspidiəns,
ˌɪnɛkˈspidiəns

inexpediency
BR ˌɪnɪkˈspiːdɪənsi,
ˌɪnɛkˈspiːdɪənsi
AM ˌɪnɪkˈspidiənsi,
ˌɪnɛkˈspidiənsi

inexpedient
BR ˌɪnɪkˈspiːdɪənt,
ˌɪnɛkˈspiːdɪənt
AM ˌɪnɪkˈspidiənt,
ˌɪnɛkˈspidiənt

inexpensive
BR ˌɪnɪkˈspensɪv,
ˌɪnɛkˈspensɪv
AM ˌɪnɪkˈspensɪv,
ˌɪniɛkˈspensɪv

inexpensively
BR ˌɪnɪkˈspensɪvli,
ˌɪnɛkˈspensɪvli
AM ˌɪnɪkˈspensəvli,
ˌɪniɛkˈspensəvli

inexpensiveness
BR ˌɪnɪkˈspensɪvnɪs,
ˌɪnɛkˈspensɪvnɪs
AM ˌɪnɪkˈspensɪvnɪs,
ˌɪniɛkˈspensɪvnɪs

inexperience
BR ˌɪnɪkˈspɪərɪəns,
ˌɪnɛkˈspɪərɪəns, -t
AM ˌɪnɪkˈspiriəns,
ˌɪnɛkˈspiriəns, -t

inexpert
BR (ˌ)ɪnˈɛkspəːt
AM ɪnˈɛkspərt,
ˌɪnəkˈspərt

inexpertly
BR (ˌ)ɪnˈɛkspəːtli
AM ɪnˈɛkspərtli,
ˌɪnəkˈspərtli

inexpertness
BR (ˌ)ɪnˈɛkspəːtnəs
AM ɪnˈɛkspərtnəs,
ˌɪnəkˈspərtnəs

inexpiable
BR (ˌ)ɪnˈɛkspɪəbl
AM ɪnˈɛkspɪəbəl

inexpiably
BR (ˌ)ɪnˈɛkspɪəbli
AM ɪnˈɛkspɪəbli

inexplicability
BR ˌɪnɪkˌsplɪkəˈbɪlɪti,
ˌɪnɛkˌsplɪkəˈbɪlɪti,
ɪnˌɛksplɪkəˈbɪlɪti
AM ˌɪnɛkˌsplɪkəˈbɪlɪdi,
ɪnˌɛkˌsplɪkəˈbɪlɪdi

inexplicable
BR ˌɪnɪkˈsplɪkəbl,
ˌɪnɛkˈsplɪkəbl,
ɪnˈɛksplɪkəbl
AM ˌɪnɛkˈsplɪkəbəl,
ɪnˌɛkˈsplɪkəbəl,
ˌɪnˈɛkspləkəbəl,
ɪnˈɛkspləkəbəl

inexplicably
BR ˌɪnɪkˈsplɪkəbli,
ˌɪnɛkˈsplɪkəbli,
ɪnˈɛksplɪkəbli
AM ˌɪnɛkˈsplɪkəbli,
ɪnˌɛkˈsplɪkəbli,
ˌɪnˈɛkspləkəbli,
ɪnˈɛkspləkəbli

inexplicit
BR ˌɪnɪkˈsplɪsɪt,
ˌɪnɛkˈsplɪsɪt
AM ˌɪnɪkˈsplɪsɪt,
ˌɪnɛkˈsplɪsɪt

inexplicitly
BR ˌɪnɪkˈsplɪsɪtli,
ˌɪnɛkˈsplɪsɪtli
AM ˌɪnɪkˈsplɪsɪtli,
ˌɪnɛkˈsplɪsɪtli

inexplicitness
BR ˌɪnɪkˈsplɪsɪtnɪs,
ˌɪnɛkˈsplɪsɪtnɪs
AM ˌɪnɪkˈsplɪsɪtnɪs,
ˌɪnɛkˈsplɪsɪtnɪs

inexpressible
BR ˌɪnɪkˈspresɪbl,
ˌɪnɛkˈspresɪbl
AM ˌɪnɪkˈspresəbəl,
ˌɪnəkˈspresəbəl,
ɪnɪkˈspresəbəl,
ɪnɛkˈspresəbəl

inexpressibly
BR ˌɪnɪkˈspresɪbli,
ˌɪnɛkˈspresɪbli
AM ˌɪnɪkˈspresəbli,
ˌɪnəkˈspresəbli,
ɪnɪkˈspresəbli,
ɪnɛkˈspresəbli

inexpressive
BR ˌɪnɪkˈspresɪv,
ˌɪnɛkˈspresɪv
AM ˌɪnɪkˈspresɪv,
ˌɪnɛkˈspresɪv

inexpressively
BR ˌɪnɪkˈspresɪvli,
ˌɪnɛkˈspresɪvli
AM ˌɪnɪkˈspresəvli,
ˌɪnɛkˈspresəvli

inexpressiveness
BR ˌɪnɪk'sprɛsɪvnɪs,
ˌɪnɛk'sprɛsɪvnɪs
AM ˌɪnɪk'sprɛsɪvnɪs,
ˌɪnɛk'sprɛsɪvnɪs

inexpugnable
BR ˌɪnɪk'spʌgnəbl,
ˌɪnɛk'spʌgnəbl
AM ˌɪnɛk'spjunəbəl,
ˌɪnɛk'spənəbəl

inexpungible
BR ˌɪnɪk'spʌn(d)ʒɪbl,
ˌɪnɛk'spʌn(d)ʒɪbl
AM ˌɪnɪk'spəndʒəbəl,
ˌɪnɛk'spəndʒəbəl

in extenso
BR ˌɪn ɪk'stɛnsəʊ,
+ ɛk'stɛnsəʊ
AM ˌɪ nək'stɛnˌsəʊ

inextinguishable
BR ˌɪnɪk'stɪŋgwɪʃəbl,
ˌɪnɛk'stɪŋgwɪʃəbl
AM ˌɪnɪk'stɪŋgwɪʃəbəl

inextinguishably
BR ˌɪnɪk'stɪŋgwɪʃəbli,
ˌɪnɛk'stɪŋgwɪʃəbli
AM ˌɪnɪk'stɪŋgwɪʃəbli

in extremis
BR ˌɪn ɪk'striːmɪs,
+ ɛk'striːmɪs
AM ˌɪn ɪk'streɪməs,
+ ɛk'streɪməs,
+ ɪk'strɪməs,
+ ɛk'strɪməs

inextricability
BR ˌɪnɪkˌstrɪkə'bɪlɪti,
ˌɪnɛkˌstrɪkə'bɪlɪti,
ɪnˌɛkstrɪkə'bɪlɪti
AM ˌɪnɛk'strɪkə'bɪlɪdi,
ˌɪnɪk'strɪkə'bɪlɪdi,
ˌɪn'ɛkstrəkə'bɪlɪdi,
ɪnɪk'strɪkə'bɪlɪdi,
ɪnˌɛk'strɪkə'bɪlɪdi,
ɪn'ɛkstrəkə'bɪlɪdi

inextricable
BR ˌɪnɪk'strɪkəbl,
ˌɪnɛk'strɪkəbl,
ɪn'ɛkstrɪkəbl
AM ˌɪnɛk'strɪkəbəl,
ˌɪnɪk'strɪkəbəl,
ˌɪn'ɛkstrəkəbəl,
ɪnɪk'strɪkəbəl,
ɪnˌɛk'strɪkəbəl,
ɪn'ɛkstrəkəbəl

inextricably
BR ˌɪnɪk'strɪkəbli,
ˌɪnɛk'strɪkəbli,
ɪn'ɛkstrɪkəbli
AM ˌɪnɛk'strɪkəbli,
ˌɪnɪk'strɪkəbli,
ˌɪn'ɛkstrəkəbli,
ɪnɪk'strɪkəbli,
ɪnˌɛk'strɪkəbli,
ɪn'ɛkstrəkəbli

Inez
BR 'iːnɛz, 'ʌɪnɛz
AM aɪ'nɛz

infallibility
BR ɪnˌfalɪ'bɪlɪti,
ˌɪnfalɪ'bɪlɪti
AM ˌɪnˌfælə'bɪlɪdi

infallible
BR ɪn'falɪbl
AM ɪn'fæləbəl

infallibly
BR ɪn'falɪbli
AM ɪn'fæləbli

infamous
BR 'ɪnfəməs
AM 'ɪnfəməs

infamously
BR 'ɪnfəməsli
AM 'ɪnfəməsli

infamy
BR 'ɪnfəmi
AM 'ɪnfəmi

infancy
BR 'ɪnf(ə)nsi
AM 'ɪnfənsi

infant
BR 'ɪnf(ə)nt, -s
AM 'ɪnfənt, -s

infanta
BR ɪn'fantə(r), -z
AM ɪn'fæn(t)ə, -z

infante
BR ɪn'fantǀi, -ɪz
AM ɪn'fænˌteɪ, -z

infanticidal
BR ɪnˌfantɪ'sʌɪdl
AM ɪnˌfæn(t)ə'saɪdəl

infanticide
BR ɪn'fantɪsʌɪd, -z
AM ɪn'fæn(t)ə,saɪd, -z

infantile
BR 'ɪnf(ə)ntʌɪl
AM 'ɪnfənˌtaɪl, 'ɪnfəntl

infantilism
BR ɪn'fantɪlɪz(ə)m
AM 'ɪnfən(t)lˌɪzəm,
ɪn'fæn(t)lˌɪzəm

infantility
BR ˌɪnf(ə)n'tɪlɪti, -ɪz
AM ˌɪnfən'tɪlɪdi, -z

infantine
BR 'ɪnf(ə)ntʌɪn
AM 'ɪnfənˌtaɪn,
'ɪnfənˌtin

infantry
BR 'ɪnf(ə)ntri
AM 'ɪnfəntri

infantryman
BR 'ɪnf(ə)ntrɪmən
AM 'ɪnfəntrɪmən

infantrymen
BR 'ɪnf(ə)ntrɪmən
AM 'ɪnfəntrɪmən

infarct
BR 'ɪnfɑːkt, ɪn'fɑːkt, -s
AM 'ɪnˌfɑrkǀ(t), -(t)s

infarction
BR ɪn'fɑːkʃn
AM ɪn'fɑrkʃən

infatuate
BR ɪn'fatjʊeɪt,
ɪn'fatʃʊeɪt, -s, -ɪŋ, -ɪd
AM ɪn'fætʃəˌweɪǀt, -ts,
-dɪŋ, -dɪd

infatuation
BR ɪnˌfatjʊ'eɪʃn,
ɪnˌfatʃʊ'eɪʃn, -z
AM ɪnˌfætʃə'weɪʃən, -z

infauna
BR 'ɪnˌfɔːnə(r)
AM ɪn'fɔːnə, ɪn'fɑnə

infeasibility
BR ɪnˌfiːzɪ'bɪlɪti,
ɪnˌfiːzɪ'bɪlɪti
AM ɪnˌfizə'bɪlɪdi

infeasible
BR ɪn'fiːzɪbl
AM ɪn'fizɪbəl

infect
BR ɪn'fɛkt, -s, -ɪŋ, -ɪd
AM ɪn'fɛkǀ(t), -(t)s, -tɪŋ, -təd

infection
BR ɪn'fɛkʃn, -z
AM ɪn'fɛkʃən, -z

infectious
BR ɪn'fɛkʃəs
AM ɪn'fɛkʃəs

infectiously
BR ɪn'fɛkʃəsli
AM ɪn'fɛkʃəsli

infectiousness
BR ɪn'fɛkʃəsnəs
AM ɪn'fɛkʃəsnəs

infective
BR ɪn'fɛktɪv
AM ɪn'fɛktɪv

infectiveness
BR ɪn'fɛktɪvnɪs
AM ɪn'fɛktɪvnɪs

infector
BR ɪn'fɛktə(r), -z
AM ɪn'fɛktər, -z

infelicitous
BR ˌɪnfɪ'lɪsɪtəs
AM ˌɪnfə'lɪsədəs

infelicitously
BR ˌɪnfɪ'lɪsɪtəsli
AM ˌɪnfə'lɪsədəsli

infelicity
BR ˌɪnfɪ'lɪsɪtǀi, -ɪz
AM ˌɪnfə'lɪsɪdi, -z

infer
BR ɪn'fəː(r), -z, -ɪŋ, -d
AM ɪn'fɚ, -z, -ɪŋ, -d

inferable
BR ɪn'fəːrəbl
AM ɪn'fɚrəbəl

inference
BR 'ɪnf(ə)rəns,
'ɪnf(ə)rn̩s, -ɪz
AM 'ɪnf(ə)rəns, -əz

inferential
BR ˌɪnfə'rɛnʃl
AM ˌɪnfə'rɛn(t)ʃəl

inferentially
BR ˌɪnfə'rɛnʃli,
ˌɪnfə'rɛnʃəli
AM ˌɪnfə'rɛn(t)ʃəli

inferior
BR ɪn'fɪərɪə(r), -z
AM ɪn'fɪriər, -z

inferiority
BR ɪnˌfɪərɪ'ɒrɪti
AM ɪnˌfɪri'ɔːrədi,
ɪnˌfɪri'ɑrədi

inferiorly
BR ɪn'fɪərɪəli
AM ɪn'fɪriərli

infernal
BR ɪn'fəːnl
AM ɪn'fɚnəl

infernally
BR ɪn'fəːnǀi, ɪn'fəːnəli
AM ɪn'fɚnəli

inferno
BR ɪn'fəːnəʊ, -z
AM ɪn'fɚnoʊ, -z

infertile
BR ɪn'fəːtʌɪl
AM ɪn'fɚdl

infertility
BR ˌɪnfə'tɪlɪti
AM ˌɪnfər'tɪlɪdi

infest
BR ɪn'fɛst, -s, -ɪŋ, -ɪd
AM ɪn'fɛst, -s, -ɪŋ, -əd

infestation
BR ˌɪnfɛ'steɪʃn, -z
AM ˌɪnfə'steɪʃən, -z

infeudation
BR ˌɪnfjuː'deɪʃn
AM ˌɪnfju'deɪʃ(ə)n

infibulate
BR ɪn'fɪbjʊleɪt, -s, -ɪŋ,
-ɪd
AM ɪn'fɪbjəˌleɪǀt, -ts,
-dɪŋ, -dɪd

infibulation
BR ɪnˌfɪbjʊ'leɪʃn
AM ɪnˌfɪbjə'leɪʃən

infidel
BR 'ɪnfɪd(ɛ)l, -z
AM 'ɪnfədəl, 'ɪnfəˌdɛl, -z

infidelity
BR ˌɪnfɪ'dɛlɪtǀi, -ɪz
AM ˌɪnfə'dɛlədi, -z

infield
BR 'ɪnfiːld, -z
AM 'ɪnˌfild, -z

infielder
BR 'ɪnˌfiːldə(r), -z
AM 'ɪnˌfildər, -z

infighter
BR 'ɪnˌfʌɪtə(r), -z
AM 'ɪnˌfaɪdər, -z

infighting
BR 'ɪnˌfʌɪtɪŋ
AM 'ɪnˌfaɪdɪŋ

infill
BR 'ɪnfɪl, -z, -ɪŋ, -d
AM 'ɪnˌfɪl, -z, -ɪŋ, -d

infiltrate
BR ˈɪnf(ɪ)ltreɪt, -s, -ɪŋ,
-ɪd
AM ɪnˈfɪlˌtreɪ|t,
ˈɪnfɪlˌtreɪ|t, -ts, -dɪŋ,
-dɪd

infiltration
BR ˌɪnf(ɪ)lˈtreɪʃn
AM ˌɪnfɪlˈtreɪʃən

infiltrator
BR ˈɪnf(ɪ)ltreɪtə(r), -z
AM ənˈfɪlˌtreɪdər,
ˈɪnfɪlˌtreɪdər, -z

infinite
BR ˈɪnfɪnət
AM ˈɪnfənət

infinitely
BR ˈɪnfɪnətli
AM ˈɪnfənətli

infiniteness
BR ˈɪnfɪnətnəs
AM ˈɪnfənətnəs

infinitesimal
BR ˌɪnfɪnɪˈtesɪml
AM ˌɪnˌfɪnəˈtɛs(ə)məl,
ˌɪnˌfɪnəˈtez(ə)məl

infinitesimally
BR ˌɪnfɪnɪˈtesɪmļi,
ˌɪnfɪnɪˈtesɪməli
AM ˌɪnˌfɪnəˈtes(ə)məli,
ˌɪnˌfɪnəˈtez(ə)məli

infinitival
BR ˌɪnfɪnɪˈtaɪvl,
ɪnˌfɪnɪˈtaɪvl
AM ˌɪnˌfɪnəˈtaɪvəl

infinitivally
BR ˌɪnfɪnɪˈtaɪvļi,
ˌɪnfɪnɪˈtaɪvəli,
ɪnˌfɪnɪˈtaɪvļi,
ɪnˌfɪnɪˈtaɪvəli
AM ˌɪnˌfɪnəˈtaɪvəli

infinitive
BR ɪnˈfɪnɪtɪv, -z
AM ɪnˈfɪnədɪv, -z

infinitude
BR ɪnˈfɪnɪtjuːd,
ɪnˈfɪnɪtʃuːd, -z
AM ɪnˈfɪnəˌt(j)ud, -z

infinity
BR ɪnˈfɪnɪt|i, -ɪz
AM ɪnˈfɪnɪdi, -z

infirm
BR ɪnˈfɜːm
AM ɪnˈfɜrm

infirmary
BR ɪnˈfɜːm(ə)r|i, -ɪz
AM ɪnˈfɜrm(ə)ri, -z

infirmity
BR ɪnˈfɜːmɪt|i, -ɪz
AM ɪnˈfɜrmədi, -z

infirmly
BR ɪnˈfɜːmli
AM ɪnˈfɜrmli

infix¹
noun
BR ˈɪnfɪks, -ɪz
AM ˈɪnˌfɪks, -ɪz

infix²
verb
BR (ˌ)ɪnˈfɪks, -ɪz, -ɪŋ, -t
AM ɪnˈfɪks, -ɪz, -ɪŋ, -t

infixation
BR ˌɪnfɪkˈseɪʃn, -z
AM ˌɪnˌfɪkˈseɪʃən, -z

in flagrante delicto
BR ˌɪn fləˌgrantɪ
dɪˈlɪktəʊ
AM ˌɪn fləˈgrɑnˌteɪ
dəˈlɪkˌtoʊ

inflame
BR ɪnˈfleɪm, -z, -ɪŋ, -d
AM ɪnˈfleɪm, -z, -ɪŋ, -d

inflamer
BR ɪnˈfleɪmə(r), -z
AM ɪnˈfleɪmər, -z

inflammability
BR ɪnˌflaməˈbɪlɪti
AM ɪnˌflæməˈbɪlɪdi

inflammable
BR ɪnˈflaməbl
AM ɪnˈflæməbəl

inflammableness
BR ɪnˈflaməblnəs
AM ɪnˈflæməbəlnəs

inflammably
BR ɪnˈflaməbli
AM ɪnˈflæməbli

inflammation
BR ˌɪnfləˈmeɪʃn, -z
AM ˌɪnfləˈmeɪʃən, -z

inflammatory
BR ɪnˈflamət(ə)ri
AM ɪnˈflæməˌtɔri

inflatable
BR ɪnˈfleɪtəbl, -z
AM ɪnˈfleɪdəbəl, -z

inflate
BR ɪnˈfleɪt, -s, -ɪŋ, -ɪd
AM ɪnˈfleɪ|t, -ts, -dɪŋ, -dɪd

inflatedly
BR ɪnˈfleɪtɪdli
AM ɪnˈfleɪdɪdli

inflatedness
BR ɪnˈfleɪtɪdnɪs
AM ɪnˈfleɪdɪdnɪs

inflater
BR ɪnˈfleɪtə(r), -z
AM ɪnˈfleɪdər, -z

inflation
BR ɪnˈfleɪʃn
AM ɪnˈfleɪʃən

inflationary
BR ɪnˈfleɪʃn(ə)ri
AM ɪnˈfleɪʃəˌneri

inflationism
BR ɪnˈfleɪʃnɪz(ə)m,
ɪnˈfleɪʃənɪz(ə)m
AM ɪnˈfleɪʃəˌnɪzəm

inflationist
BR ɪnˈfleɪʃnɪst,
ɪnˈfleɪʃənɪst, -s
AM ɪnˈfleɪʃənəst, -s

inflator
BR ɪnˈfleɪtə(r), -z
AM ɪnˈfleɪdər, -z

inflect
BR ɪnˈflɛkt, -s, -ɪŋ, -ɪd
AM ɪnˈflɛk|(t), -(t)s,
-tɪŋ, -təd

inflection
BR ɪnˈflɛkʃn, -z
AM ɪnˈflɛkʃən, -z

inflectional
BR ɪnˈflɛkʃn(ə)l,
ɪnˈflɛkʃən(ə)l
AM ɪnˈflɛkʃ(ə)nəl

inflectionally
BR ɪnˈflɛkʃnəli,
ɪnˈflɛkʃnļi,
ɪnˈflɛkʃ(ə)nəli
AM ɪnˈflɛkʃ(ə)nəli

inflectionless
BR ɪnˈflɛkʃnləs
AM ɪnˈflɛkʃənləs

inflective
BR ɪnˈflɛktɪv
AM ɪnˈflɛktɪv

inflexibility
BR ɪnˌflɛksɪˈbɪlɪti
AM ˌɪnˌflɛksəˈbɪlɪdi,
ɪnˌflɛksəˈbɪlɪdi

inflexible
BR ɪnˈflɛksɪbl
AM ɪnˈflɛksəbəl

inflexibly
BR ɪnˈflɛksɪbli
AM ɪnˈflɛksəbli

inflexion
BR ɪnˈflɛkʃn, -z
AM ɪnˈflɛkʃən, -z

inflexional
BR ɪnˈflɛkʃn(ə)l,
ɪnˈflɛkʃən(ə)l
AM ɪnˈflɛkʃ(ə)nəl

inflexionally
BR ɪnˈflɛkʃnəli,
ɪnˈflɛkʃnļi,
ɪnˈflɛkʃənļi,
ɪnˈflɛkʃ(ə)nəli
AM ɪnˈflɛkʃ(ə)nəli

inflexionless
BR ɪnˈflɛkʃnləs
AM ɪnˈflɛkʃənləs

inflict
BR ɪnˈflɪkt, -s, -ɪŋ, -ɪd
AM ɪnˈflɪk|(t), -(t)s, -tɪŋ, -tɪd

inflictable
BR ɪnˈflɪktəbl
AM ɪnˈflɪktɪbəl

inflicter
BR ɪnˈflɪktə(r), -z
AM ɪnˈflɪktər, -z

infliction
BR ɪnˈflɪkʃn, -z
AM ɪnˈflɪkʃən, -z

inflictor
BR ɪnˈflɪktə(r), -z
AM ɪnˈflɪktər, -z

inflator
BR ɪnˈfleɪtə(r), -z
AM ɪnˈfleɪdər, -z

in-flight
BR ˌɪnˈflʌɪt
AM ˈɪnˈflaɪt

inflorescence
BR ˌɪnfləˈrɛsns
AM ˌɪnfloʊˈrɛsəns,
ˌɪnfləˈrɛsəns

inflow
BR ˈɪnfləʊ, -z
AM ˈɪnˌfloʊ, -z

inflowing
BR ˈɪnˌfləʊɪŋ, -z
AM ˈɪnˌfloʊɪŋ, -z

influence
BR ˈɪnfluəns, -ɪz, -ɪŋ, -t
AM ˈɪnfluəns, -əz, -ɪŋ, -t

influenceable
BR ˈɪnfluənsəbl
AM ˈɪnfluənsəbəl

influencer
BR ˈɪnfluənsə(r), -z
AM ˈɪnfluənsər, -z

influent
BR ˈɪnfluənt, -s
AM ˈɪnfluənt, -s

influential
BR ˌɪnfluˈɛnʃl
AM ˌɪnˌfluˈɛn(t)ʃəl

influentially
BR ˌɪnfluˈɛnʃļi,
ˌɪnfluˈɛnʃəli
AM ˌɪnˌfluˈɛn(t)ʃəli

influenza
BR ˌɪnfluˈɛnzə(r)
AM ˌɪnˌfluˈɛnzə

influenzal
BR ˌɪnfluˈɛnzl
AM ˌɪnˌfluˈɛnzəl

influx
BR ˈɪnflʌks, -ɪz
AM ˈɪnˌflʌks, -əz

info
BR ˈɪnfəʊ
AM ˈɪnfoʊ

infobit
BR ˈɪnfəʊbɪt, -s
AM ˈɪnfoʊˌbɪt, -s

infold
BR (ˌ)ɪnˈfəʊld, -z, -ɪŋ, -ɪd
AM ɪnˈfoʊld, -z, -ɪŋ, -ɪd

in folio
BR ɪn ˈfəʊlɪəʊ
AM ɪn ˈfoʊlioʊ

infomania
BR ˌɪnfə(ʊ)ˈmeɪnɪə(r), -z
AM ˌɪnfoʊˈmeɪnɪə, -z

infomercial
BR ˌɪnfə(ʊ)ˈmɜː.ʃl, -z
AM ˌɪnfoʊˌmɜrʃəl, -z

infopreneur
BR ˌɪnfə(ʊ)prəˈnɜː(r), -z
AM ˌɪnfoʊprəˈnɜr,
ˌɪnfoʊprəˈnʊ(ə)r, -z

inform
BR ɪnˈfɔːm, -z, -ɪŋ, -d
AM ɪnˈfɔ(ə)rm, -z, -ɪŋ, -d
informal
BR ɪnˈfɔːml
AM ɪnˈfɔrməl
informality
BR ˌɪnfɔːˈmælɪti
AM ˌɪnfərˈmælədi
informally
BR ɪnˈfɔːmḷi,
ɪnˈfɔːməli
AM ɪnˈfɔrməli
informant
BR ɪnˈfɔːm(ə)nt, -s
AM ɪnˈfɔrmənt, -s
informatics
BR ˌɪnfəˈmatɪks
AM ˌɪnfərˈmædɪks
information
BR ˌɪnfəˈmeɪʃn
AM ˌɪnfərˈmeɪʃən
informational
BR ˌɪnfəˈmeɪʃṇ(ə)l,
ˌɪnfəˈmeɪʃən(ə)l
AM ˌɪnfərˈmeɪʃ(ə)nəl
informationally
BR ˌɪnfəˈmeɪʃṇəli,
ˌɪnfəˈmeɪʃṇḷi,
ˌɪnfəˈmeɪʃənḷi,
ˌɪnfəˈmeɪʃ(ə)nəli
AM ˌɪnfərˈmeɪʃ(ə)nəli
informative
BR ɪnˈfɔːmətɪv
AM ɪnˈfɔrmədɪv
informatively
BR ɪnˈfɔːmətɪvli
AM ɪnˈfɔrmədəvli
informativeness
BR ɪnˈfɔːmətɪvnɪs
AM ɪnˈfɔrmədɪvnɪs
informatory
BR ɪnˈfɔːmət(ə)ri
AM ɪnˈfɔrməˌtɔri
informedly
BR ɪnˈfɔːmɪdli
AM ɪnˈfɔrm(ə)dli
informedness
BR ɪnˈfɔːmɪdnɪs
AM ɪnˈfɔrm(əd)nəs
informer
BR ɪnˈfɔːmə(r), -z
AM ɪnˈfɔrmər, -z
infosphere
BR ˈɪnfə(ʊ)sfɪə(r), -z
AM ˈɪnfoʊˌsfɪ(ə)r, -z
infotainment
BR ˌɪnfə(ʊ)ˈteɪmm(ə)nt
AM ˌɪnfoʊˈteɪ(n)mənt
infotech
BR ˈɪnfəʊtɛk
AM ˈɪnfoʊˌtɛk
infra
BR ˈɪnfrə(r)
AM ˈɪnfrə

infraclass
BR ˈɪnfrəklɑːs,
ˈɪnfrəklas, -ɪz
AM ˈɪnfrəˌklæs, -əz
infract
BR ɪnˈfrakt, -s, -ɪŋ, -ɪd
AM ɪnˈfræk|(t), -(t)s,
-tɪŋ, -təd
infraction
BR ɪnˈfrakʃn, -z
AM ɪnˈfrækʃən, -z
infractor
BR ɪnˈfraktə(r), -z
AM ɪnˈfræktər, -z
infradian
BR ɪnˈfreɪdɪən
AM ɪnˈfreɪdiən
infra dig
BR ˌɪnfrə ˈdɪg
AM ˌɪnfrə ˈdɪg
infralapsarian
BR ˌɪnfrəlapˈsɛːrɪən, -z
AM ˌɪnfrəˌlæpˈsɛriən,
-z
infrangibility
BR ɪnˌfran(d)ʒɪˈbɪlɪti
AM ɪnˌfrænd ʒəˈbɪlɪdi
infrangible
BR ɪnˈfran(d)ʒɪbl
AM ɪnˈfrændʒəbəl
infrangibleness
BR ɪnˈfran(d)ʒɪblnəs
AM ɪnˈfrændʒəbəlnəs
infrangibly
BR ɪnˈfran(d)ʒɪbli
AM ɪnˈfrændʒəbli
infrared
BR ˌɪnfrəˈrɛd
AM ˌɪnfrəˈrɛd
infrarenal
BR ˌɪnfrəˈriːnl
AM ˌɪnfrəˈrinəl
infrasonic
BR ˌɪnfrəˈsɒnɪk
AM ˌɪnfrəˈsɑnɪk
infrasonically
BR ˌɪnfrəˈsɒnɪkli
AM ˌɪnfrəˈsɑnək(ə)li
infrasound
BR ˈɪnfrəsaʊnd
AM ˈɪnfrəˈsaʊnd
infrastructural
BR ˌɪnfrəˈstrʌktʃ(ə)rəl,
ˌɪnfrəˈstrʌktʃ(ə)rḷ
AM ˌɪnfrəˈstrək(t)ʃ(ə)-
rəl
infrastructure
BR ˈɪnfrəˌstrʌktʃə(r),
-z
AM ˈɪnfrəˌstrək(t)ʃər,
-z
infrequency
BR ɪnˈfriːkw(ə)nsi
AM ɪnˈfrikwənsi
infrequent
BR ɪnˈfriːkw(ə)nt
AM ɪnˈfrikwənt

infrequently
BR ɪnˈfriːkw(ə)ntli
AM ɪnˈfrikwən(t)li
infringe
BR ɪnˈfrɪn(d)ʒ, -ɪz, -ɪŋ,
-d
AM ɪnˈfrɪndʒ, -ɪz, -ɪŋ, -d
infringement
BR ɪnˈfrɪn(d)ʒm(ə)nt,
-s
AM ɪnˈfrɪndʒmənt, -s
infringer
BR ɪnˈfrɪn(d)ʒə(r), -z
AM ɪnˈfrɪndʒər, -z
infructescence
BR ˌɪnfrʌkˈtɛsns, -ɪz
AM ɪnˌfrəkˈtɛsəns, -əz
infula
BR ˈɪnfjʊlə(r)
AM ˈɪnfjələ
infulae
BR ˈɪnfjʊli:
AM ˈɪnfjəli, ˈɪnf(j)əˌlaɪ
infundibular
BR ˌɪnfʌnˈdɪbjʊlə(r)
AM ˈɪnfənˈdɪbjələr
infuriate
BR ɪnˈfjʊərɪeɪt,
ɪnˈfjɔːrɪeɪt, -s, -ɪŋ, -ɪd
AM ɪnˈfjuriˌeɪ|t, -ts,
-dɪŋ, -dɪd
infuriatingly
BR ɪnˈfjʊərɪeɪtɪŋli,
ɪnˈfjɔːrɪeɪtɪŋli
AM ɪnˈfjuriˌeɪdɪŋli
infuriation
BR ɪnˌfjʊərɪˈeɪʃn,
ɪnˌfjɔːrɪˈeɪʃn, -z
AM ɪnˌfjuriˈeɪʃən, -z
infusable
BR ɪnˈfjuːzəbl
AM ɪnˈfjuzəbəl
infuse
BR ɪnˈfjuːz, -ɪz, -ɪŋ, -d
AM ɪnˈfjuz, -ɪz, -ɪŋ, -d
infuser
BR ɪnˈfjuːzə(r), -z
AM ɪnˈfjuzər, -z
infusibility
BR ɪnˌfjuːzɪˈbɪlɪti
AM ɪnˌfjuzəˈbɪlɪdi
infusible
BR ɪnˈfjuːzɪbl
AM ɪnˈfjuzəbəl
infusion
BR ɪnˈfjuːʒn, -z
AM ɪnˈfjuʒən, -z
infusive
BR ɪnˈfjuːzɪv
AM ɪnˈfjuzɪv
infusorial earth
BR ˌɪnfjʊˌzɔːrɪəl ˈəːθ,
ˌɪnfjʊˌsɔːrɪəl +, -s
AM ˌɪnfjəˌzɔrɪəl ˈərθ, -s
Inga
BR ˈɪŋə(r)
AM ˈɪŋ(g)ə

Ingatestone
BR ˈɪŋgətstəʊn,
ˈɪŋgeɪtstəʊn
AM ˈɪŋgeɪtsˌtoʊn
ingather
BR ˌɪnˈgaðlə(r), -əz,
-(ə)rɪŋ, -əd
AM ˈɪnˌgæð|ər, -ərz,
-(ə)rɪŋ, -ərd
ingathering
noun
BR ˈɪnˌgað(ə)rɪŋ, -z
AM ˈɪnˌgæð(ə)rɪŋ, -z
ingeminate
BR ɪnˈdʒɛmɪneɪt, -s, -ɪŋ,
-ɪd
AM ɪnˈdʒɛməˌneɪ|t, -ts,
-dɪŋ, -dɪd
ingenious
BR ɪnˈdʒiːnɪəs
AM ɪnˈdʒinjəs,
ɪnˈdʒiniəs
ingeniously
BR ɪnˈdʒiːnɪəsli
AM ɪnˈdʒinjəsli,
ɪnˈdʒiniəsli
ingeniousness
BR ɪnˈdʒiːnɪəsnəs
AM ɪnˈdʒinjəsnəs,
ɪnˈdʒiniəsnəs
ingénue
BR ˈanʒənj(j)uː,
ˈanʒeɪn(j)uː,
ˌanʒəˈn(j)uː,
ˌanʒeɪˈn(j)uː, -z
AM ˈændʒəˌnu,
ˈɑndʒəˌnu, -z
ingenuity
BR ˌɪndʒɪˈnjuːɪti
AM ˌɪndʒəˈn(j)uədi
ingenuous
BR ɪnˈdʒɛnjʊəs
AM ɪnˈdʒɛnjəwəs
ingenuously
BR ɪnˈdʒɛnjʊəsli
AM ɪnˈdʒɛnjəwəsli
ingenuousness
BR ɪnˈdʒɛnjʊəsnəs
AM ɪnˈdʒɛnjəwəsnəs
Ingersoll®
BR ˈɪŋgəsɒl
AM ˈɪŋgərˌsɒl,
ˈɪŋgərˌsɑl
ingest
BR ɪnˈdʒɛst, -s, -ɪŋ, -ɪd
AM ɪnˈdʒɛst, -s, -ɪŋ, -əd
ingestion
BR ɪnˈdʒɛstʃn
AM ɪnˈdʒɛstʃən
ingestive
BR ɪnˈdʒɛstɪv
AM ɪnˈdʒɛstɪv
Ingham
BR ˈɪŋəm
AM ˈɪŋəm
inglenook
BR ˈɪŋglnʊk, -s
AM ˈɪŋgəlˌnʊk, -s

Ingleton
BR 'ɪŋglt(ə)n
AM 'ɪŋgəltən

Inglewood
BR 'ɪŋglwʊd
AM 'ɪŋgəl,wʊd

Inglis
BR 'ɪŋglɪs
AM 'ɪŋglɪs

inglorious
BR (,)ɪn'glɔːrɪəs,
(,)ɪŋ'glɔːrɪəs
AM ɪn'glɔːrɪəs,
ɪŋ'glɔːrɪəs

ingloriously
BR (,)ɪn'glɔːrɪəsli,
(,)ɪŋ'glɔːrɪəsli
AM ɪn'glɔːrɪəsli,
ɪŋ'glɔːrɪəsli

ingloriousness
BR (,)ɪn'glɔːrɪəsnəs,
(,)ɪŋ'glɔːrɪəsnəs
AM ɪn'glɔːrɪəsnəs,
ɪŋ'glɔːrɪəsnəs

Ingmar
BR 'ɪŋmɑː(r)
AM 'ɪŋmɑr

ingoing
BR 'ɪn,gəʊɪŋ, 'ɪŋ,gəʊɪŋ
AM 'ɪn,goʊɪŋ,
,ɪn'goʊɪŋ, 'ɪŋ,goʊɪŋ,
,ɪŋ'goʊɪŋ

Ingoldsby
BR 'ɪŋgl(d)zbi
AM 'ɪŋgəl(d)zbi

ingot
BR 'ɪŋgət, -s
AM 'ɪŋgət, -s

ingraft
BR ɪn'grɑːft, ɪn'graft,
ɪŋ'grɑːft, ɪŋ'graft, -s,
-ɪŋ, -ɪd
AM ɪn'græft, ɪŋ'græft,
-s, -ɪŋ, -əd

ingrain
adjective
BR 'ɪngreɪn,
(,)ɪn'greɪn, 'ɪŋgreɪn,
(,)ɪŋ'greɪn
AM ɪn'greɪn, 'ɪn'greɪn,
'ɪŋ'greɪn

ingrained
BR (,)ɪn'greɪnd,
(,)ɪŋ'greɪnd
AM ɪn'greɪnd,
'ɪn'greɪnd, 'ɪŋ'greɪnd

ingrainedly
BR (,)ɪn'greɪnɪdli,
(,)ɪŋ'greɪnɪdli
AM ɪn'greɪnɪdli,
'ɪn'greɪnɪdli,
'ɪŋ'greɪnɪdli

Ingram
BR 'ɪŋgrəm
AM 'ɪŋgrəm

Ingrams
BR 'ɪŋgrəmz
AM 'ɪŋgrəmz

ingrate
BR 'ɪŋgreɪt, ɪn'greɪt,
'ɪŋgreɪt, ɪŋ'greɪt, -s,
-ɪŋ, -ɪd
AM 'ɪn,greɪ|t, 'ɪŋ,greɪ|t,
ɪn'greɪ|t, ɪŋ'greɪ|t, -ts,
-dɪŋ, -dɪd

ingratiate
BR ɪn'greɪʃɪeɪt,
ɪŋ'greɪʃɪeɪt, -s, -ɪŋ, -ɪd
AM ɪn'greɪʃi,eɪ|t,
ɪŋ'greɪʃi,eɪ|t, -ts, -dɪŋ,
-dɪd

ingratiatingly
BR ɪn'greɪʃɪeɪtɪŋli,
ɪŋ'greɪʃɪeɪtɪŋli
AM ɪn'greɪʃi,eɪdɪŋli,
ɪŋ'greɪʃi,eɪdɪŋli

ingratiation
BR ɪn,greɪʃɪ'eɪʃn,
ɪŋ,greɪʃɪ'eɪʃn, -z
AM ɪn,greɪʃi'eɪʃən,
ɪŋ,greɪʃi'eɪʃən, -z

ingratitude
BR ɪn'grætɪtjuːd,
ɪn'grætɪtʃuːd,
ɪŋ'grætɪtjuːd,
ɪŋ'grætɪtʃuːd
AM ɪn'grædə,t(j)ud,
ɪŋ'grædə,t(j)ud

ingravescence
BR ,ɪngrə,vesns,
,ɪŋgrə'vesns, -ɪz
AM ,ɪngrə'vesəns,
,ɪŋgrə'vesəns, -əz

ingravescent
BR ,ɪngrə,vesnt,
,ɪŋgrə'vesnt
AM ,ɪngrə'vesənt,
,ɪŋgrə'vesənt

ingredient
BR ɪn'griːdɪənt,
ɪŋ'griːdɪənt, -s
AM ɪn'gridiənt,
ɪŋ'gridiənt, -s

Ingres
BR 'æŋgr(ər)
AM 'æŋgr(əs)

ingress
BR 'ɪngres, 'ɪŋgres
AM 'ɪn,gres, 'ɪŋ,gres

ingression
BR (,)ɪn'greʃn,
(,)ɪŋ'greʃn, -z
AM ɪn'greʃən,
ɪŋ'greʃən, -z

ingressive
BR (,)ɪn'gresɪv,
(,)ɪŋ'gresɪv
AM ɪn'gresɪv, ɪŋ'gresɪv

ingressively
BR (,)ɪn'gresɪvli,
(,)ɪŋ'gresɪvli
AM ɪn'gresɪvli,
ɪŋ'gresɪvli

ingressiveness
BR (,)ɪn'gresɪvnɪs,
(,)ɪŋ'gresɪvnɪs

AM ɪn'gresɪvli,
ɪŋ'gresɪvnɪs

Ingrid
BR 'ɪngrɪd
AM 'ɪŋgrɪd

in-group
BR 'ɪngruːp, 'ɪŋgruːp,
-s
AM 'ɪn,grup, -s

ingrowing
BR ,ɪn'grəʊɪŋ,
,ɪŋ'grəʊɪŋ
AM 'ɪn,groʊɪŋ

ingrown
BR ,ɪn'grəʊn, ,ɪŋ'grəʊn
AM 'ɪn,groʊn

ingrowth
BR 'ɪngrəʊθ, 'ɪŋgrəʊθ,
-s
AM 'ɪn,groʊθ, -s

inguinal
BR 'ɪŋgwɪnl
AM 'ɪŋgwənəl

inguinally
BR 'ɪŋgwɪnļi,
'ɪŋgwɪnəli
AM 'ɪŋgwənəli

ingulf
BR ɪn'gʌlf, ɪŋ'gʌlf
AM ɪn'gəlf, ɪŋ'gəlf

ingurgitate
BR (,)ɪn'gɜːdʒɪteɪt,
(,)ɪŋ'gɜːdʒɪteɪt, -s, -ɪŋ,
-ɪd
AM ɪŋ'gərdʒə,teɪ|t, -ts,
-dɪŋ, -dɪd

ingurgitation
BR ɪn,gɜːdʒɪ'teɪʃn,
ɪŋ,gɜːdʒɪ'teɪʃn, -z
AM ɪŋ,gərdʒə,teɪʃən, -z

inhabit
BR ɪn'hab|ɪt, -ɪts, -ɪtɪŋ,
-ɪtɪd
AM ɪn'hæbə|t, -ts, -dɪŋ,
-dəd

inhabitability
BR ɪn,habɪtə'bɪlɪti
AM ɪn,(h)æbədə'bɪlɪdi

inhabitable
BR ɪn'habɪtəbl
AM ɪn'hæbədəbəl

inhabitance
BR ɪn'habɪt(ə)ns, -ɪz
AM ɪn'hæbədəns,
ɪn'hæbətns, -əz

inhabitancy
BR ɪn'habɪt(ə)ns|i, -ɪz
AM ɪn'hæbədnsi,
ɪn'hæbətnsi, -z

inhabitant
BR ɪn'habɪt(ə)nt, -s
AM ɪn'hæbədnt, -s

inhabitation
BR ɪn,habɪ'teɪʃn, -z
AM ɪn,(h)æbə'teɪʃən,
-z

inhalant
BR ɪn'heɪlənt,
ɪn'heɪlņt, -s
AM ɪn'heɪlənt, -s

inhalation
BR ,ɪnhə'leɪʃn, -z
AM ,ɪnhə'leɪʃən, -z

inhale
BR ɪn'heɪl, -z, -ɪŋ, -d
AM ɪn'heɪl, -z, -ɪŋ, -d

inhaler
BR ɪn'heɪlə(r), -z
AM ɪn'heɪlər, -z

inharmonic
BR ,ɪnhɑː'mɒnɪk
AM ,ɪnhɑr'mɑnɪk

inharmonious
BR ,ɪnhɑː'məʊnɪəs
AM ,ɪnhɑr'moʊnɪəs

inharmoniously
BR ,ɪnhɑː'məʊnɪəsli
AM ,ɪnhɑr'moʊnɪəsli

inharmoniousness
BR ,ɪnhɑː'məʊnɪəsnəs
AM ,ɪnhɑr'moʊnɪəsnəs

inhere
BR ɪn'hɪə(r), -z, -ɪŋ, -d
AM ɪn'hɪ(ə)r, -z, -ɪŋ, -d

inherence
BR ɪn'hɪərəns, ɪn'herņs,
ɪn'hɪərņs
AM ɪn'hɪrəns,
ɪn'herəns

inherent
BR ɪn'hɪərənt, ɪn'herņt,
ɪn'hɪərņt, ɪn'hɪərņt
AM ɪn'hɪrənt,
ɪn'herənt

inherently
BR ɪn'hɪərəntli,
ɪn'herņtli,
ɪn'hɪərəntli,
ɪn'hɪərņtli
AM ɪn'hɪrən(t)li,
ɪn'herən(t)li

inherit
BR ɪn'her|ɪt, -ɪts, -ɪtɪŋ,
-ɪtɪd
AM ɪn'herə|t, -ts, -dɪŋ,
-dəd

inheritability
BR ɪn,herɪtə'bɪlɪti
AM ɪn,(h)erədə'bɪlɪdi

inheritable
BR ɪn'herɪtəbl
AM ɪn'herədəbəl

inheritance
BR ɪn'herɪt(ə)ns, -ɪz
AM ɪn'herədəns,
ɪn'herətns, -əz

inheritor
BR ɪn'herɪtə(r), -z
AM ɪn'herədər, -z

inheritress
BR ɪn'herɪtrɪs, -ɪz
AM ɪn'herətrəs, -əz

inheritrices
BR ɪn'herɪtrɪsiːz

AM ɪnˈhɛrətrəsiz
inheritrix
  BR ɪnˈhɛrɪtrɪks, -ɪz
  AM ɪnˈhɛrəˌtrɪks, -ɪz
inhesion
  BR ɪnˈhiːʒn, -z
  AM ɪnˈhiʒən, -z
inhibit
  BR ɪnˈhɪb|ɪt, -ɪts, -ɪtɪŋ,
  -ɪtɪd
  AM ɪnˈhɪbɪ|t, -ts, -dɪŋ,
  -dɪd
inhibition
  BR ˌɪn(h)ɪˈbɪʃn, -z
  AM ˌɪnəˈbɪʃən,
  ˌɪnhəˈbɪʃən,
  ˌɪn(h)ɪˈbɪʃən, -z
inhibitive
  BR ɪnˈhɪbɪtɪv
  AM ɪnˈhɪbɪdɪv
inhibitor
  BR ɪnˈhɪbɪtə(r), -z
  AM ɪnˈhɪbədər, -z
inhibitory
  BR ɪnˈhɪbɪt(ə)ri
  AM ɪnˈhɪbəˌtɔri
inhomogeneity
  BR ɪnˌhəʊmə(ʊ)dʒɪˈniː-
  ɪti,
  ɪnˌhɒmə(ʊ)dʒɪˈniːɪti,
  ɪnˌhəʊmə(ʊ)dʒɪˈneɪti,
  ɪnˌhɒmə(ʊ)dʒɪˈneɪti
  AM ɪnˌ(h)oʊmədʒəˈniːdi,
  ɪnˌ(h)oʊmoʊdʒəˈniːdi,
  ɪnˌ(h)oʊmədʒəˈneɪdi,
  ɪnˌ(h)oʊmoʊdʒəˈneɪdi
inhomogeneous
  BR ɪnˌhəʊmə(ʊ)ˈdʒiːn-
  ɪəs,
  ɪnˌhɒmə(ʊ)ˈdʒiːnɪəs
  AM ɪnˌ(h)oʊməˈdʒiniəs,
  ɪnˌ(h)oʊmoʊˈdʒiniəs
inhospitable
  BR ˌɪnhɒˈspɪtəbl,
  ɪnˈhɒspɪtəbl
  AM ˌɪnhɑˈspɪdəbəl,
  ˌɪnˈhɑspɪdəbəl,
  ɪnhɑˈspɪdəbəl,
  ɪnˈhɑspɪdəbəl
inhospitableness
  BR ˌɪnhɒˈspɪtəblnəs,
  (ˌ)ɪnˈhɒspɪtəblnəs
  AM ˌɪnhɑˈspɪdəbəlnəs,
  ˌɪnˈhɑspɪdəbəlnəs,
  ɪnhɑˈspɪdəbəlnəs,
  ɪnˈhɑspɪdəbəlnəs
inhospitably
  BR ˌɪnhɒˈspɪtəbli,
  (ˌ)ɪnˈhɒspɪtəbli
  AM ˌɪnhɑˈspɪdəbli,
  ˌɪnˈhɑspɪdəbli,
  ɪnhɑˈspɪdəbli,
  ɪnˈhɑspɪdəbli
inhospitality
  BR ˌɪnhɒspɪˈtælɪti,
  ɪnˌhɒspɪˈtælɪti
  AM ɪnˌ(h)ɑspəˈtælədi

in-house
  BR ˌɪnˈhaʊs
  AM ˈɪnˈhaʊs
inhuman
  BR (ˌ)ɪnˈhjuːmən
  AM ɪnˈ(h)jumən
inhumane
  BR ˌɪnhjʊˈmeɪn
  AM ˌɪn(h)juˈmeɪn,
  ɪn(h)juˈmeɪn
inhumanely
  BR ˌɪnhjʊˈmeɪnli
  AM ˌɪn(h)juˈmeɪnli,
  ɪn(h)juˈmeɪnli
inhumanity
  BR ˌɪnhjʊˈmanɪti
  AM ˈɪn(h)juˈmænədi,
  -z
inhumanly
  BR ɪnˈhjuːmənli
  AM ɪnˈ(h)jumənli
inhumanness
  BR ɪnˈhjuːmənnəs
  AM ɪnˈ(h)jumənnəs
inhumation
  BR ˌɪnhjʊˈmeɪʃn, -z
  AM ˌɪn(h)juˈmeɪʃən, -z
inhume
  BR (ˌ)ɪnˈhjuːm, -z, -ɪŋ,
  -d
  AM ɪnˈ(h)jum, -z, -ɪŋ, -d
Inigo
  BR ˈɪnɪgəʊ
  AM ˈɪnɪgoʊ
inimical
  BR ɪˈnɪmɪkl
  AM ɪˈnɪməkəl
inimically
  BR ɪˈnɪmɪkli
  AM ɪˈnɪmək(ə)li
inimitability
  BR ɪˌnɪmɪtəˈbɪlɪti
  AM ɪˌnɪmədəˈbɪlɪdi
inimitable
  BR ɪˈnɪmɪtəbl
  AM ɪˈnɪmədəbəl
inimitableness
  BR ɪˈnɪmɪtəblnəs
  AM ɪˈnɪmədəbəlnəs
inimitably
  BR ɪˈnɪmɪtəbli
  AM ɪˈnɪmədəbli
iniquitous
  BR ɪˈnɪkwɪtəs
  AM ɪˈnɪkwədəs
iniquitously
  BR ɪˈnɪkwɪtəsli
  AM ɪˈnɪkwədəsli
iniquitousness
  BR ɪˈnɪkwɪtəsnəs
  AM ɪˈnɪkwədəsnəs
iniquity
  BR ɪˈnɪkwɪt|i, -ɪz
  AM ɪˈnɪkwɪdi, -z
initial
  BR ɪˈnɪʃ|l, -lz, -|ɪŋ\-əlɪŋ,
  -ld

AM ɪˈnɪʃəl, -əlz, -(ə)lɪŋ,
  -əld
initialisation
  BR ɪˌnɪʃəlaɪˈzeɪʃn,
  ɪˌnɪʃlaɪˈzeɪʃn, -z
  AM ɪˌnɪʃələˈzeɪʃən,
  ɪˌnɪʃəˌlaɪˈzeɪʃən, -z
initialise
  BR ɪˈnɪʃəlʌɪz,
  ɪˈnɪʃlʌɪz, -ɪz, -ɪŋ, -d
  AM ɪˈnɪʃəˌlaɪz, -ɪz, -ɪŋ,
  -d
initialism
  BR ɪˈnɪʃəlɪz(ə)m,
  ɪˈnɪʃlɪz(ə)m, -z
  AM ɪˈnɪʃəˌlɪzəm, -z
initialization
  BR ɪˌnɪʃəlʌɪˈzeɪʃn,
  ɪˌnɪʃlʌɪˈzeɪʃn, -z
  AM ɪˌnɪʃələˈzeɪʃən,
  ɪˌnɪʃəˌlaɪˈzeɪʃən|, -z
initialize
  BR ɪˈnɪʃəlʌɪz,
  ɪˈnɪʃlʌɪz, -ɪz, -ɪŋ, -d
  AM ɪˈnɪʃəˌlaɪz, -ɪz, -ɪŋ,
  -d
initially
  BR ɪˈnɪʃli, ɪˈnɪʃəli
  AM ɪˈnɪʃ(ə)li
initiate¹
  noun
  BR ɪˈnɪʃɪət, -s
  AM ɪˈnɪʃɪət, -s
initiate²
  verb
  BR ɪˈnɪʃɪeɪt, -s, -ɪŋ, -ɪd
  AM ɪˈnɪʃiˌeɪ|t, -ts, -dɪŋ,
  -dɪd
initiation
  BR ɪˌnɪʃɪˈeɪʃn, -z
  AM ɪˈnɪʃiˌeɪʃən, -z
initiative
  BR ɪˈnɪʃətɪv, -z
  AM ɪˈnɪʃədɪv, -z
initiator
  BR ɪˈnɪʃɪeɪtə(r), -z
  AM ɪˈnɪʃiˌeɪdər, -z
initiatory
  BR ɪˈnɪʃ(ɪ)ət(ə)ri
  AM ɪˈnɪʃ(i)əˌtɔri
inject
  BR ɪnˈdʒɛkt, -s, -ɪŋ, -ɪd
  AM ɪnˈdʒɛk|(t), -(t)s,
  -tɪŋ, -təd
injectable
  BR ɪnˈdʒɛktəbl, -z
  AM ɪnˈdʒɛktəbəl, -z
injection
  BR ɪnˈdʒɛkʃn, -z
  AM ɪnˈdʒɛkʃən, -z
injector
  BR ɪnˈdʒɛktə(r), -z
  AM ɪnˈdʒɛktər, -z
in-joke
  BR ˈɪndʒəʊk, -s
  AM ˈɪnˌdʒoʊk, -s
injudicious
  BR ˌɪndʒʊˈdɪʃəs

AM ˈɪndʒuˈdɪʃəs
injudiciously
  BR ˌɪndʒʊˈdɪʃəsli
  AM ˈɪndʒuˈdɪʃəsli
injudiciousness
  BR ˌɪndʒʊˈdɪʃəsnəs
  AM ˈɪndʒuˈdɪʃəsnəs
Injun
  BR ˈɪndʒ(ə)n, -z
  AM ˈɪndʒən, -z
injunct
  BR ɪnˈdʒʌŋ(k)t
  AM ɪnˈdʒəŋ(k)t,
  ɪnˈdʒəŋk(t)
injunction
  BR ɪnˈdʒʌŋ(k)ʃn, -z
  AM ɪnˈdʒəŋ(k)ʃən, -z
injunctive
  BR ɪnˈdʒʌŋ(k)tɪv
  AM ɪnˈdʒəŋ(k)tɪv
injure
  BR ˈɪn(d)ʒə(r), -əz,
  -(ə)rɪŋ, -əd
  AM ˈɪndʒər, -ərz,
  -(ə)rɪŋ, -ərd
injurer
  BR ˈɪn(d)ʒ(ə)rə(r), -z
  AM ˈɪndʒərər, -z
injuria
  BR ɪnˈdʒʊərɪə(r)
  AM ɪnˈdʒʊriə
injuriae
  BR ɪnˈdʒʊəriiː,
  ɪnˈdʒʊərɪʌɪ
  AM ɪnˈdʒʊriˌi,
  ɪnˈdʒʊriˌaɪ
injurious
  BR ɪnˈdʒʊərɪəs
  AM ɪnˈdʒʊriəs
injuriously
  BR ɪnˈdʒʊərɪəsli
  AM ɪnˈdʒʊriəsli
injuriousness
  BR ɪnˈdʒʊərɪəsnəs
  AM ɪnˈdʒʊriəsnəs
injury
  BR ˈɪn(d)ʒ(ə)r|i, -ɪz
  AM ˈɪndʒ(ə)ri, -z
injustice
  BR ɪnˈdʒʌst|ɪs, -ɪsɪz
  AM ɪnˈdʒəstəs, -əz
ink
  BR ɪŋ|k, -ks, -kɪŋ, -(k)t
  AM ɪŋ|k, -ks, -kɪŋ, -(k)t
Inkatha
  BR ɪnˈkɑːtə(r),
  ɪŋˈkɑːtə(r)
  AM ɪnˈkɑdə, ɪŋˈkɑdə
inkblot
  BR ˈɪŋkblɒt, -s
  AM ˈɪŋkˌblɑt, -s
inkbottle
  BR ˈɪŋkˌbɒtl, -z
  AM ˈɪŋkˌbɑdəl, -z
inker
  BR ˈɪŋkə(r), -z
  AM ˈɪŋkər, -z

inkhorn
BR 'ɪŋkhɔːn, -z
AM 'ɪŋk,(h)ɔ(ə)rn, -z

inkily
BR 'ɪŋkɪli
AM 'ɪŋkɪli

inkiness
BR 'ɪŋkɪnɪs
AM 'ɪŋkɪnɪs

inkling
BR 'ɪŋklɪŋ, -z
AM 'ɪŋklɪŋ, -z

inkpad
BR 'ɪŋkpad, -z
AM 'ɪŋk,pæd, -z

Inkpen
BR 'ɪŋkpɛn
AM 'ɪŋk,pɛn

inkpot
BR 'ɪŋkpɒt, -s
AM 'ɪŋk,pat, -s

inkstand
BR 'ɪŋkstand, -z
AM 'ɪŋk,stænd, -z

inkwell
BR 'ɪŋkwɛl, -z
AM 'ɪŋk,wɛl, -z

inky
BR 'ɪŋk|i, -ɪə(r), -ɪɪst
AM 'ɪŋki, -ər, -ɪst

INLA
BR ,ʌɪɛnɛl'eɪ
AM ,aɪ,ɛn,ɛl'eɪ

inlaid
BR ,ɪn'leɪd
AM ,ɪn,leɪd

inland¹
adjective
BR 'ɪnland, 'ɪnlənd
AM 'ɪn,lænd, 'ɪnlənd

inland²
adverb
BR ɪn'land, 'ɪnland
AM 'ɪn,lænd, 'ɪnlənd

inlander
BR 'ɪnlandə(r),
'ɪnləndə(r), -z
AM 'ɪn,lændər,
'ɪnləndər, -z

inlandish
BR 'ɪnlandɪʃ, 'ɪnləndɪʃ
AM 'ɪn,lændɪʃ,
'ɪnləndɪʃ

in-law
BR 'ɪnlɔː(r), -z
AM 'ɪn,lɔ, 'ɪn,lɑ, -z

inlay¹
noun
BR 'ɪnleɪ, -z
AM 'ɪn,leɪ, -z

inlay²
verb
BR ,ɪn'leɪ, -z, -ɪŋ, -d
AM ,ɪn'leɪ, -z, -ɪŋ, -d

inlayer
BR ,ɪn'leɪə(r),
'ɪnleɪə(r), -z
AM ,ɪn'leɪər, 'ɪn,leɪər, -z

inlet
BR 'ɪnlɪt, 'ɪnlɛt, -s
AM 'ɪn,lɛt, 'ɪnlət, -s

inlier
BR 'ɪn,lʌɪə(r), -z
AM 'ɪn,laɪər, -z

in loco parentis
BR ɪn ,ləʊkəʊ
pə'rɛntis
AM ,ɪn ,loʊkoʊ
pə'rɛn(t)əs

inly
BR 'ɪnli
AM 'ɪnli

inlying
BR 'ɪn,lʌɪɪŋ
AM 'ɪn,laɪɪŋ

Inmarsat
BR 'ɪnmɑːsat
AM 'ɪnmɑr,sæt

inmate
BR 'ɪnmeɪt, -s
AM 'ɪn,meɪt, -s

in medias res
BR ɪn ,miːdɪas 'reɪz,
+ ,miːdɪɑːs +,
+ ,mɛdɪas +,
+ ,mɛdɪɑːs +,
+ 'reɪs
AM ,ɪn ,meɪdiˌɑs 'reɪs,
,ɪn ,midiˌɑs 'reɪs

in memoriam
BR ,ɪn mɪ'mɔːrɪam,
+ mɪ'mɔːrɪəm
AM ,ɪn mə'mɔriəm,
,ɪn mə'mɔriˌæm

inmost
BR 'ɪnməʊst
AM 'ɪn,moʊst

inn
BR ɪn, -z
AM ɪn, -z

innards
BR 'ɪnədz
AM 'ɪnərdz

innate
BR ɪ'neɪt
AM ɪ'neɪt

innately
BR ɪ'neɪtli
AM ɪ'neɪtli

innateness
BR ɪ'neɪtnɪs
AM ɪ'neɪtnɪs

inner
BR 'ɪnə(r)
AM 'ɪnər

innerly
BR 'ɪnəli
AM 'ɪnərli

innermost
BR 'ɪnəməʊst
AM 'ɪnər,moʊst

innerness
BR 'ɪnənəs
AM 'ɪnərnəs

innervate
BR 'ɪnəːveɪt, 'ɪnəveɪt,
ɪ'nəːveɪt, -s, -ɪŋ, -ɪd
AM ɪ'nər,veɪ|t,
'ɪnər,veɪ|t, -ts, -dɪŋ,
-dɪd

innervation
BR ,ɪnəː'veɪʃn,
,ɪnə'veɪʃn
AM ,ɪnər'veɪʃən

Innes
BR 'ɪnɪs, 'ɪnɪz
AM 'ɪnɪs

inning
BR 'ɪnɪŋ, -z
AM 'ɪnɪŋ, -z

Innisfail
BR ,ɪnɪs'feɪl
AM ,ɪnɪs'feɪl

innkeeper
BR 'ɪn,kiːpə(r), -z
AM 'ɪn,kipər, -z

innocence
BR 'ɪnəs(ə)ns
AM 'ɪnəsəns

innocency
BR 'ɪnəs(ə)nsi
AM 'ɪnəsənsi

innocent
BR 'ɪnəs(ə)nt, -s
AM 'ɪnəsənt, -s

innocently
BR 'ɪnəs(ə)ntli
AM 'ɪnəsən(t)li

innocuity
BR ,ɪnɒ'kjuːɪti
AM ɪ,nɑ'kjuədi

innocuous
BR ɪ'nɒkjʊəs
AM ɪ'nakjəwəs

innocuously
BR ɪ'nɒkjʊəsli
AM ɪ'nakjəwəsli

innocuousness
BR ɪ'nɒkjʊəsnəs
AM ɪ'nakjəwəsnəs

innominate
BR ɪ'nɒmɪnət
AM ɪ'namənət

innovate
BR 'ɪnəveɪt, -s, -ɪŋ, -ɪd
AM 'ɪnə,veɪ|t,
'ɪnoʊ,veɪ|t, -ts, -dɪŋ,
-dɪd

innovation
BR ,ɪnə'veɪʃn, -z
AM ,ɪnə'veɪʃən,
,ɪnoʊ'veɪʃən, -z

innovational
BR ,ɪnə'veɪʃ|n̩l,
,ɪnə'veɪʃən(ə)l
AM ,ɪnə'veɪʃ(ə)nəl,
,ɪnoʊ'veɪʃ(ə)nəl

innovative
BR 'ɪnəveɪtɪv,
'ɪnəvətɪv
AM 'ɪnə,veɪdɪv

innovatively
BR 'ɪnəveɪtɪvli,
'ɪnəvətɪvli
AM 'ɪnə,veɪdɪvli

innovativeness
BR 'ɪnəveɪtɪvnɪs,
'ɪnəvətɪvnɪs
AM 'ɪnə,veɪdɪvnɪs

innovator
BR 'ɪnəveɪtə(r), -z
AM 'ɪnə,veɪdər,
'ɪnoʊ,veɪdər, -z

innovatory
BR 'ɪnəveɪt(ə)ri,
'ɪnəvət(ə)ri
AM 'ɪnəvə,tɔri,
'ɪnoʊvə,tɔri

innoxious
BR ɪ'nɒkʃəs
AM ɪ(n)'nakʃəs,
ɪ'nakʃəs

innoxiously
BR ɪ'nɒkʃəsli
AM ɪ(n)'nakʃəsli,
ɪ'nakʃəsli

innoxiousness
BR ɪ'nɒkʃəsnəs
AM ɪ(n)'nakʃəsnəs,
ɪ'nakʃəsnəs

Innsbruck
BR 'ɪnzbrʊk
AM 'ɪnz,brʊk

Inns of Court
BR ,ɪnz əv 'kɔːt
AM ,ɪnz əv 'kɔ(ə)rt

innuendo
BR ,ɪnjuː'ɛndəʊ, -z
AM ,ɪnjə'wɛndoʊ, -z

Innuit
BR 'ɪn(j)ʊɪt
AM 'ɪn(j)uɪt

innumerability
BR ɪ,njuːm(ə)rə'bɪlɪti
AM ɪ,n(j)um(ə)rə'bɪlɪdi

innumerable
BR ɪ'njuːm(ə)rəbl
AM ɪ'n(j)um(ə)rəbəl

innumerably
BR ɪ'njuːm(ə)rəbli
AM ɪ'n(j)um(ə)rəbli

innumeracy
BR ɪ'njuːm(ə)rəsi
AM ɪ'n(j)um(ə)rəsi

innumerate
BR ɪ'njuːm(ə)rət
AM ɪ'n(j)umərət

innutrition
BR ,ɪnjuː'trɪʃn
AM ,ɪn(j)u'trɪʃən,
ɪ(n),n(j)u'trɪʃən

innutritious
BR ,ɪnjʊ'trɪʃəs
AM ɪ'n(j)u'trɪʃəs,
ɪ(n)'n(j)utrɪʃəs

inobservance
BR ,ɪnəb'zɜːvns
AM ,ɪnəb'zɜrvəns

inobservant
BR ˌɪnəbˈzɜːvnt
AM ˌɪnəbˈzɜrvənt

inocula
BR ɪˈnɒkjələ(r)
AM ɪˈnɑkjələ

inoculable
BR ɪˈnɒkjələbl
AM ɪˈnɑkjələbəl

inoculate
BR ɪˈnɒkjəleɪt, -s, -ɪŋ, -ɪd
AM ɪˈnɑkjəˌleɪ|t, -ts, -dɪŋ, -dɪd

inoculation
BR ɪˌnɒkjʊˈleɪʃn, -z
AM ɪˌnɑkjəˈleɪʃən, -z

inoculative
BR ɪˈnɒkjələtɪv
AM ɪˈnɑkjəˌleɪdɪv

inoculator
BR ɪˈnɒkjəleɪtə(r), -z
AM ɪˈnɑkjəˌleɪdər, -z

inoculum
BR ɪˈnɒkjələm
AM ɪˈnɑkjələm

inodorous
BR ɪnˈəʊd(ə)rəs
AM ɪnˈoʊdərəs

in-off
BR ˌɪnˈɒf, -s
AM ˈɪnˌɑf, -s

inoffensive
BR ˌɪnəˈfensɪv
AM ˌɪnəˈfensɪv

inoffensively
BR ˌɪnəˈfensɪvli
AM ˌɪnəˈfensəvli

inoffensiveness
BR ˌɪnəˈfensɪvnɪs
AM ˌɪnəˈfensɪvnɪs

inofficious
BR ˌɪnəˈfɪʃəs
AM ˌɪnəˈfɪʃəs

inoperability
BR ɪnˌɒp(ə)rəˈbɪlɪti
AM ɪnˌɑp(ə)rəˈbɪlɪdi

inoperable
BR (ˌ)ɪnˈɒp(ə)rəbl
AM ɪnˈɑp(ə)rəbəl

inoperably
BR (ˌ)ɪnˈɒp(ə)rəbli
AM ɪnˈɑp(ə)rəbli

inoperative
BR (ˌ)ɪnˈɒp(ə)rətɪv
AM ɪnˈɑp(ə)rədɪv

inoperativeness
BR (ˌ)ɪnˈɒp(ə)rətɪvnɪs
AM ɪnˈɑp(ə)rədɪvnɪs

inopportune
BR (ˌ)ɪnˈɒpətjuːn, ˌɪnɒpəˈtjuːn, (ˌ)ɪnˈɒpətʃuːn, ˌɪnɒpəˈtʃuːn
AM ˈɪnˌɑpərˌt(j)un, ɪnˈɑpərˌt(j)un

inopportunely
BR (ˌ)ɪnˈɒpətjuːnli, ˌɪnɒpəˈtjuːnli, (ˌ)ɪnˈɒpətʃuːnli, ˌɪnɒpəˈtʃuːnli
AM ˈɪnˌɑpərˌt(j)unli, ɪnˈɑpərˌt(j)unli

inopportuneness
BR (ˌ)ɪnˈɒpətjuːnnəs, ˌɪnɒpəˈtjuːnnəs, (ˌ)ɪnˈɒpətʃuːnnəs, ˌɪnɒpəˈtʃuːnnəs
AM ˈɪnˌɑpərˌt(j)u(n)nəs, ɪnˈɑpərˌt(j)u(n)nəs

inordinate
BR ɪnˈɔːdɪnət, ɪnˈɔːdn̩ət
AM ɪˈnɔrdn̩ət

inordinately
BR ɪnˈɔːdɪnətli, ɪnˈɔːdn̩ətli
AM ɪˈnɔrdn̩ətli

inordinateness
BR ɪnˈɔːdɪnətnəs, ɪnˈɔːdn̩ətnəs
AM ɪˈnɔrdn̩ətnəs

inorganic
BR ˌɪnɔːˈɡanɪk
AM ˌɪnɔrˈɡænɪk

inorganically
BR ˌɪnɔːˈɡanɪkli
AM ˌɪnɔrˈɡænək(ə)li

inosculate
BR ɪnˈɒskjʊleɪt, -s, -ɪŋ, -ɪd
AM ɪnˈɑskjəˌleɪ|t, -ts, -dɪŋ, -dɪd

inosculation
BR ɪnˌɒskjʊˈleɪʃn, -z
AM ɪnˌɑskjəˈleɪʃən, -z

inositol
BR ʌɪˈnəʊsɪtɒl
AM ɑɪˈnoʊsədɒl, ɑɪˈnoʊsədɑl

in-patient
BR ˈɪnˌpeɪʃnt, -s
AM ˈɪnˌpeɪʃənt, -s

in propria persona
BR ɪn ˌprəʊpriə pəˈsəʊnə(r), + pəˈsəʊnə(r)
AM ˌɪn ˈproʊpriə pərˈsoʊnə

input
BR ˈɪnpʊt, -s, -ɪŋ, -ɪd
AM ˈɪnˌpʊ|t, -ts, -dɪŋ, -dəd

inputter
BR ˈɪnpʊtə(r), -z
AM ˈɪnˌpʊdər, -z

inquest
BR ˈɪŋkwest, ˈɪnkwest, -s
AM ˈɪnˌkwest, ˈɪŋˌkwest, -s

inquietude
BR ɪnˈkwʌɪɪtjuːd, ɪŋˈkwʌɪɪtjuːd,

**in'kwʌɪtʃuːd,
ɪŋ'kwʌɪtʃuːd**
AM ɪnˈkwaɪə,t(j)ud,
ɪŋˈkwaɪə,t(j)ud

inquiline
BR ˈɪnkwɪlʌɪn, ˈɪŋkwɪlʌɪn, -z
AM ˈɪŋkwə,laɪn, ˈɪŋkwələn, -z

inquire
BR ɪnˈkwʌɪə(r), ɪŋˈkwʌɪə(r), -z, -ɪŋ, -d
AM ɪnˈkwaɪ(ə)r, ɪŋˈkwaɪ(ə)r, -z, -ɪŋ, -d

inquirer
BR ɪnˈkwʌɪərə(r), ɪŋˈkwʌɪərə(r), -z
AM ɪnˈkwaɪ(ə)rər, ɪŋˈkwaɪ(ə)rər, -z

inquiry
BR ɪnˈkwʌɪ(ə)r|i, ɪŋˈkwʌɪ(ə)r|i, -ɪz
AM ˈɪnˌkwaɪri, ɪnˈkwaɪri, ˈɪnkwəri, ˈɪŋˌkwaɪri, ˈɪŋkwəri, -z

inquisition
BR ˌɪnkwɪˈzɪʃn, ˌɪŋkwɪˈzɪʃn, -z
AM ˌɪnkwəˈzɪʃən, ˌɪŋkwəˈzɪʃən, -z

inquisitional
BR ˌɪnkwɪˈzɪʃn̩(ə)l, ˌɪŋkwɪˈzɪʃən(ə)l
AM ˌɪnkwəˈzɪʃ(ə)nəl, ˌɪŋkwəˈzɪʃ(ə)nəl

inquisitive
BR ɪnˈkwɪzɪtɪv, ɪŋˈkwɪzɪtɪv
AM ɪnˈkwɪzədɪv, ɪŋˈkwɪzədɪv

inquisitively
BR ɪnˈkwɪzɪtɪvli, ɪŋˈkwɪzɪtɪvli
AM ɪnˈkwɪzədəvli, ɪŋˈkwɪzədəvli

inquisitiveness
BR ɪnˈkwɪzɪtɪvnɪs, ɪŋˈkwɪzɪtɪvnɪs
AM ɪnˈkwɪzədɪvnɪs, ɪŋˈkwɪzədɪvnɪs

inquisitor
BR ɪnˈkwɪzɪtə(r), ɪŋˈkwɪzɪtə(r), -z
AM ɪnˈkwɪzədər, ɪŋˈkwɪzədər, -z

inquisitorial
BR ɪnˌkwɪzɪˈtɔːriəl, ɪŋˌkwɪzɪˈtɔːriəl, ˌɪnkwɪzɪˈtɔːriəl, ˌɪŋkwɪzɪˈtɔːriəl
AM ɪnˌkwɪzəˈtɔriəl, ɪŋˌkwɪzəˈtɔriəl

inquisitorially
BR ɪnˌkwɪzɪˈtɔːriəli, ɪŋˌkwɪzɪˈtɔːriəli, ˌɪnkwɪzɪˈtɔːriəli, ˌɪŋkwɪzɪˈtɔːriəli

AM ɪnˌkwɪzəˈtɔriəli, ɪŋˌkwɪzəˈtɔriəli

inquorate
BR ˌɪnˈkwɔːreɪt, ˌɪŋˈkwɔːreɪt
AM ɪnˈkwɔˌreɪt, ɪŋˈkwɔˌreɪt

in re
BR ˌɪn ˈreɪ, + ˈriː
AM ˌɪn ˈreɪ

in rem
BR ɪn ˈrɛm
AM ɪn ˈrɛm

inroad
BR ˈɪnrəʊd, -z
AM ˈɪnˌroʊd, -z

inrush
BR ˈɪnrʌʃ, -ɪz
AM ˈɪnˌrəʃ, -əz

inrushing
BR ˈɪnˌrʌʃɪŋ, -z
AM ˈɪnˌrəʃɪŋ, -z

insalubrious
BR ˌɪnsəˈl(j)uːbriəs
AM ˌɪnsəˈlubriəs

insalubrity
BR ˌɪnsəˈl(j)uːbrɪti
AM ˌɪnsəˈlubrədi

insane
BR ɪnˈseɪn
AM ɪnˈseɪn

insanely
BR ɪnˈseɪnli
AM ɪnˈseɪnli

insaneness
BR ɪnˈseɪnnɪs
AM ɪnˈseɪ(n)nɪs

insanitarily
BR ɪnˈsanɪt(ə)rɪli
AM ɪnˈsænəˌtɛrəli

insanitariness
BR ɪnˈsanɪt(ə)rɪnɪs
AM ɪnˈsænəˌtɛrɪnɪs

insanitary
BR ɪnˈsanɪt(ə)ri
AM ɪnˈsænəˌtɛri

insanity
BR ɪnˈsanɪti
AM ɪnˈsænədi

insatiability
BR ɪnˌseɪʃəˈbɪlɪti
AM ˌɪnˌseɪʃə,bɪlɪdi, ənˌseɪʃəˈbɪlɪdi

insatiable
BR ɪnˈseɪʃ(ɪ)əbl
AM ɪnˈseɪʃəbəl

insatiably
BR ɪnˈseɪʃ(ɪ)əbli
AM ɪnˈseɪʃəbli

insatiate
BR ɪnˈseɪʃɪət
AM ɪnˈseɪʃ(i)ɪt

inscape
BR ˈɪnskeɪp, -s
AM ˈɪnzˌkeɪp, ˈɪnˌskeɪp, -s

inscribable
BR ɪnˈskrʌɪbəbl
AM ɪnzˈkraɪbəbəl,
ɪnˈskraɪbəbəl

inscribe
BR ɪnˈskrʌɪb, -z, -ɪŋ, -d
AM ɪnzˈkraɪb,
ɪnˈskraɪb, -z, -ɪŋ, -d

inscriber
BR ɪnˈskrʌɪbə(r), -z
AM ɪnzˈkraɪbər,
ɪnˈskraɪbər, -z

inscription
BR ɪnˈskrɪpʃn, -z
AM ɪnzˈkrɪpʃən,
ɪnˈskrɪpʃən, -z

inscriptional
BR ɪnˈskrɪpʃn(ə)l,
ɪnˈskrɪpʃən(ə)l
AM ɪnzˈkrɪpʃ(ə)nəl,
ɪnˈskrɪpʃ(ə)nəl

inscriptive
BR ɪnˈskrɪptɪv
AM ɪnzˈkrɪptɪv,
ɪnˈskrɪptɪv

inscrutability
BR ɪnˌskruːtəˈbɪlɪti
AM ɪnzˌkrudəˈbɪlɪdi,
ənˌskrudəˈbɪlɪdi

inscrutable
BR ɪnˈskruːtəbl
AM ɪnzˈkrudəbəl,
ənˈskrudəbəl

inscrutableness
BR ɪnˈskruːtəblnəs
AM ɪnzˈkrudəbəlnəs,
ənˈskrudəbəlnəs

inscrutably
BR ɪnˈskruːtəbli
AM ɪnzˈkrudəbli,
ənˈskrudəbli

inscrutibility
BR ɪnˌskruːtəˈbɪlɪti
AM ɪnzˌkrudəˈbɪlɪti,
ənˌskrudəˈbɪlɪdi

inseam
BR ˈɪnsiːm, -z
AM ˈɪnˌsim, -z

insect
BR ˈɪnsɛkt, -s
AM ˈɪnˌsɛk|(t), -(t)s

insectaria
BR ˌɪnsɛkˈtɛːrɪə(r)
AM ɪnˌsɛkˈtɛrɪə

insectarium
BR ˌɪnsɛkˈtɛːrɪəm, -z
AM ɪnˌsɛkˈtɛrɪəm, -z

insectary
BR ˈɪnsɛkt(ə)r|i, -ɪz
AM ˈɪnˌsɛkˌtɛri, -z

insecticidal
BR ɪnˌsɛktɪˈsʌɪdl
AM ɪnˈsɛktəˌsaɪdəl

insecticide
BR ɪnˈsɛktɪsʌɪd, -z
AM ɪnˈsɛktəˌsaɪd, -z

insectile
BR ɪnˈsɛktʌɪl

inscribable
AM ɪnˈsɛktl, ɪnˈsɛkˌtaɪl

insectivore
BR ɪnˈsɛktɪvɔː(r), -z
AM ɪnˈsɛktəˌvɔ(ə)r, -z

insectivorous
BR ˌɪnsɛkˈtɪv(ə)rəs
AM ˌɪnˌsɛkˈtɪv(ə)rəs

insectology
BR ˌɪnsɛkˈtɒlədʒi
AM ˌɪnˌsɛkˈtɑlədʒi

insecure
BR ˌɪnsɪˈkjʊə(r),
ˌɪnsɪˈkjɔː(r)
AM ˌɪnsəˈkjʊ(ə)r

insecurely
BR ˌɪnsɪˈkjʊəli,
ˌɪnsɪˈkjɔːli
AM ˌɪnsəˈkjʊrli

insecurity
BR ˌɪnsɪˈkjʊərɪti,
ˌɪnsɪˈkjɔːrɪti
AM ˌɪnsəˈkjʊrədi

Inselberg
BR ˈɪnslbəːg, -z
AM ˈɪnsəlˌbɛrg, -z

inseminate
BR ɪnˈsɛmɪneɪt, -s, -ɪŋ,
-ɪd
AM ɪnˈsɛməˌneɪ|t, -ts,
-dɪŋ, -dɪd

insemination
BR ɪnˌsɛmɪˈneɪʃn
AM ɪnˌsɛməˈneɪʃən

inseminator
BR ɪnˈsɛmɪneɪtə(r), -z
AM ɪnˈsɛməˌneɪdər, -z

insensate
BR ɪnˈsɛnseɪt,
ɪnˈsɛnsət
AM ɪnˈsɛnˌseɪt,
ˈɪnˌsɛnˌseɪt

insensately
BR ɪnˈsɛnseɪtli,
ɪnˈsɛnsətli
AM ɪnˈsɛnˌseɪtli,
ˈɪnˌsɛnˌseɪtli

insensibility
BR ɪnˌsɛnsɪˈbɪlɪti
AM ˌɪnˌsɛnsəˈbɪlɪdi,
ənˌsɛnsəˈbɪlɪdi

insensible
BR ɪnˈsɛnsɪbl
AM ɪnˈsɛnsəbəl

insensibleness
BR ɪnˈsɛnsɪblnəs
AM ɪnˈsɛnsəbəlnəs

insensibly
BR ɪnˈsɛnsɪbli
AM ɪnˈsɛnsəbli

insensitive
BR ɪnˈsɛnsɪtɪv
AM ɪnˈsɛnsədɪv

insensitively
BR ɪnˈsɛnsɪtɪvli
AM ɪnˈsɛnsədəvli

insensitiveness
BR ɪnˈsɛnsɪtɪvnɪs
AM ɪnˈsɛnsədɪvnɪs

insensitivity
BR ˌɪnsɛnsɪˈtɪvɪti,
ɪnˌsɛnsɪˈtɪvɪti
AM ˌɪnˌsɛnsəˈtɪvɪdi,
ənˌsɛnsəˈtɪvɪdi

insentience
BR ɪnˈsɛnʃns,
ɪnˈsɛnʃɪəns,
ɪnˈsɛntɪəns
AM ɪnˈsɛnʃ(i)əns

insentient
BR ɪnˈsɛnʃnt,
ɪnˈsɛnʃɪənt,
ɪnˈsɛntɪənt
AM ɪnˈsɛnʃ(i)ənt

inseparability
BR ɪnˌsɛp(ə)rəˈbɪlɪti,
ˌɪnsɛp(ə)rəˈbɪlɪti
AM ɪnˌsɛp(ə)rəˈbɪlɪdi,
ɪnˌsɛp(ə)rəˈbɪlɪdi

inseparable
BR ɪnˈsɛp(ə)rəbl
AM ɪnˈsɛpərəbəl

inseparably
BR ɪnˈsɛp(ə)rəbli
AM ɪnˈsɛpərəbli

insert[1]
noun
BR ˈɪnsəːt, -s
AM ˈɪnˌsərt, -s

insert[2]
verb
BR ɪnˈsəːt, -s, -ɪŋ, -ɪd
AM ɪnˈsər|t, -ts, -dɪŋ,
-dəd

insertable
BR ɪnˈsəːtəbl
AM ɪnˈsərdəbəl

inserter
BR ɪnˈsəːtə(r), -z
AM ɪnˈsərdər, -z

insertion
BR ɪnˈsəːʃn, -z
AM ɪnˈsərʃən, -z

inset[1]
noun
BR ˈɪnsɛt, -s
AM ˈɪnˌsɛt, -s

inset[2]
verb
BR ɪnˈsɛt, ˈɪnsɛt, -s, -ɪŋ
AM ɪnˈsɛ|t, -ts, -dɪŋ

insetter
BR ˈɪnˌsɛtə(r), -z
AM ˈɪnˌsɛdər, -z

inshallah
BR ɪnˈʃalə(r)
AM ɪnˈʃɑlə

inshore
BR ˌɪnˈʃɔː(r)
AM ˌɪnˈʃɔ(ə)r, ɪnˈʃɔ(ə)r

inside
BR ɪnˈsʌɪd, -z
AM ɪnˈsaɪd, -z

insider
BR (ˌ)ɪnˈsʌɪdə(r), -z
AM ɪnˈsaɪdər, -z

insidious
BR ɪnˈsɪdɪəs
AM ɪnˈsɪdiəs

insidiously
BR ɪnˈsɪdɪəsli
AM ɪnˈsɪdiəsli

insidiousness
BR ɪnˈsɪdɪəsnəs
AM ɪnˈsɪdiəsnəs

insight
BR ˈɪnsʌɪt, -s
AM ˈɪnˌsaɪt, -s

insightful
BR ˈɪnsʌɪtf(ə)l
AM ɪnˈsaɪtfəl

insightfully
BR ˈɪnsʌɪtfəli,
ˈɪnsʌɪtfli
AM ɪnˈsaɪtfəli

insignia
BR ɪnˈsɪgnɪə(r)
AM ɪnˈsɪgniə

insignificance
BR ˌɪnsɪgˈnɪfɪk(ə)ns
AM ˌɪnsɪgˈnɪfəkəns

insignificancy
BR ˌɪnsɪgˈnɪfɪk(ə)nsi
AM ˌɪnsɪgˈnɪfəkənsi

insignificant
BR ˌɪnsɪgˈnɪfɪk(ə)nt
AM ˌɪnsɪgˈnɪfəkənt

insignificantly
BR ˌɪnsɪgˈnɪfɪk(ə)ntli
AM ˌɪnsɪgˈnɪfəkən(t)li

insincere
BR ˌɪns(ɪ)nˈsɪə(r)
AM ˌɪnsɪnˈsɪ(ə)r

insincerely
BR ˌɪns(ɪ)nˈsɪəli
AM ˌɪnsɪnˈsɪrli

insincerity
BR ˌɪns(ɪ)nˈsɛrɪti
AM ˌɪnsɪnˈsɛrədi

insinuate
BR ɪnˈsɪnjʊeɪt, -s, -ɪŋ,
-ɪd
AM ɪnˈsɪnjəˌweɪ|t, -ts,
-dɪŋ, -dɪd

insinuatingly
BR ɪnˈsɪnjʊeɪtɪŋli
AM ɪnˈsɪnjəˌweɪdɪŋli

insinuation
BR ɪnˌsɪnjʊˈeɪʃn, -z
AM ɪnˌsɪnjəˈweɪʃən, -z

insinuative
BR ɪnˈsɪnjʊətɪv,
ɪnˈsɪnjʊeɪtɪv
AM ɪnˈsɪnjəˌweɪdɪv

insinuator
BR ɪnˈsɪnjʊeɪtə(r), -z
AM ɪnˈsɪnjəˌweɪdər, -z

insinuatory
BR ɪnˈsɪnjʊət(ə)ri
AM ɪnˈsɪnjəwəˌtɔri

insipid
BR ɪnˈsɪpɪd
AM ɪnˈsɪpɪd

insipidity
BR ˌɪnsɪˈpɪdɪti, -ɪz
AM ˌɪnsəˈpɪdɪdi, -z

insipidly
BR ɪnˈsɪpɪdli
AM ɪnˈsɪpɪdli

insipidness
BR ɪnˈsɪpɪdnɪs
AM ɪnˈsɪpɪdnɪs

insist
BR ɪnˈsɪst, -s, -ɪŋ, -ɪd
AM ɪnˈsɪst, -s, -ɪŋ, -ɪd

insistence
BR ɪnˈsɪst(ə)ns
AM ɪnˈsɪstns

insistency
BR ɪnˈsɪst(ə)nsi
AM ɪnˈsɪstənsi

insistent
BR ɪnˈsɪst(ə)nt
AM ɪnˈsɪstənt

insistently
BR ɪnˈsɪst(ə)ntli
AM ɪnˈsɪstən(t)li

insister
BR ɪnˈsɪstə(r), -z
AM ɪnˈsɪstər, -z

insistingly
BR ɪnˈsɪstɪŋli
AM ɪnˈsɪstɪŋli

in situ
BR ˌɪn ˈsɪtjuː, + ˈsɪtʃuː
AM ˌɪn ˈsaɪtu, + ˈsɪtu

insobriety
BR ˌɪnsə(ʊ)ˈbrʌɪɪti
AM ˌɪnsəˈbraɪɪdi,
ˌɪnsoʊˈbraɪədi

insofar
BR ˌɪnsə(ʊ)ˈfɑː(r)
AM ˌɪnsoʊˈfar

insolation
BR ˌɪnsə(ʊ)ˈleɪʃn
AM ˌɪnsəˈleɪʃən,
ˌɪnˌsoʊˈleɪʃən

insole
BR ˈɪnsəʊl, -z
AM ˈɪnˌsoʊl, -z

insolence
BR ˈɪnsələns, ˈɪnsəlns,
ˈɪnsl̩(ə)ns
AM ˈɪnsələns

insolent
BR ˈɪnsələnt, ˈɪnsəlnt,
ˈɪnsl̩(ə)nt
AM ˈɪnsələnt

insolently
BR ˈɪnsələntli,
ˈɪnsəlntli, ˈɪnsl̩(ə)ntli
AM ˈɪnsələn(t)li

insolubilise
BR ɪnˈsɒljʊblʌɪz,
ɪnˈsɒljʊbɪlʌɪz, -ɪz, -ɪŋ,
-d
AM ˌɪnˈsaljəbəˌlaɪz,
ɪnˈsaljəbəˌlaɪz, -ɪz, -ɪŋ,
-d

insolubility
BR ɪnˌsɒljʊˈbɪlɪti,
ˌɪnsɒljʊˈbɪlɪti
AM ˌɪnˌsaljəˈbɪlɪdi,
ɪnˌsaljəˈbɪlɪdi

insolubilize
BR ɪnˈsɒljʊblʌɪz,
ɪnˈsɒljʊbɪlʌɪz, -ɪz, -ɪŋ,
-d
AM ˌɪnˈsaljəbəˌlaɪz,
ɪnˈsaljəbəˌlaɪz, -ɪz, -ɪŋ,
-d

insoluble
BR (ˌ)ɪnˈsɒljʊbl
AM ˌɪnˈsaljəbəl,
ɪnˈsaljəbəl

insolubleness
BR (ˌ)ɪnˈsɒljʊblnəs
AM ˌɪnˈsaljəbəlnəs,
ɪnˈsaljəbəlnəs

insolubly
BR (ˌ)ɪnˈsɒljʊbli
AM ˌɪnˈsaljəbli,
ɪnˈsaljəbli

insolvable
BR (ˌ)ɪnˈsɒlvəbl
AM ɪnˈsalvəbəl

insolvency
BR (ˌ)ɪnˈsɒlv(ə)nsi
AM ɪnˈsalvənsi

insolvent
BR (ˌ)ɪnˈsɒlv(ə)nt
AM ɪnˈsalvənt

insomnia
BR ɪnˈsɒmnɪə(r)
AM ɪnˈsamniə

insomniac
BR ɪnˈsɒmnɪak, -s
AM ɪnˈsamniˌæk, -s

insomuch
BR ˌɪnsə(ʊ)ˈmʌtʃ
AM ˌɪnsoʊˈmətʃ

insouciance
BR ɪnˈsuːsɪəns,
ɪnˈsuːsɪɒs
AM ɪnˈsusiəns,
ɪnˈsuʃəns

insouciant
BR ɪnˈsuːsɪənt,
ɪnˈsuːsɪɒs
AM ɪnˈsusiənt,
ɪnˈsuʃənt

insouciantly
BR ɪnˈsuːsɪəntli
AM ɪnˈsusiən(t)li,
ɪnˈsuʃən(t)li

insousiant
BR ɪnˈsuːsɪənt,
ɪnˈsuːsɪɒs
AM ɪnˈsusiənt,
ɪnˈsuʃənt

inspan
BR ˈɪnspan, ɪnˈspan, -z,
-ɪŋ, -d
AM ɪnzˈpæn, ɪnˈspæn,
-z, -ɪŋ, -d

inspect
BR ɪnˈspɛkt, -s, -ɪŋ, -ɪd

AM ɪnzˈpɛk|(t),
ɪnˈspɛk|(t), -(t)s, -tɪŋ,
-təd

inspection
BR ɪnˈspɛkʃn, -z
AM ɪnzˈpɛkʃən,
ɪnˈspɛkʃən, -z

inspector
BR ɪnˈspɛktə(r), -z
AM ɪnzˈpɛktər,
ɪnˈspɛktər, -z

inspectorate
BR ɪnˈspɛkt(ə)rət, -s
AM ɪnzˈpɛktərət,
ɪnˈspɛktərət, -s

inspectorial
BR ˌɪnspɛkˈtɔːrɪəl
AM ɪnzˌpɛkˈtɔriəl,
ɪnˌspɛkˈtɔriəl

inspectorship
BR ɪnˈspɛktəʃɪp, -s
AM ɪnzˈpɛktərˌʃɪp,
ɪnˈspɛktərˌʃɪp, -s

inspiration
BR ˌɪnspɪˈreɪʃn, -z
AM ˌɪnspəˈreɪʃən, -z

inspirational
BR ˌɪnspɪˈreɪʃn(ə)l,
ˌɪnspɪˈreɪʃən(ə)l
AM ˌɪnspəˈreɪʃ(ə)nəl

inspirationally
BR ˌɪnspɪˈreɪʃnəli,
ˌɪnspɪˈreɪʃn̩li,
ˌɪnspɪˈreɪʃən̩li,
ˌɪnspɪˈreɪʃ(ə)nəli
AM ˌɪnspəˈreɪʃ(ə)nəli

inspirationism
BR ˌɪnspɪˈreɪʃnɪz(ə)m,
ˌɪnspɪˈreɪʃənɪz(ə)m
AM ˌɪnspəˈreɪʃəˌnɪzəm,
ˌɪnspəˈreɪʃn̩ˌɪzəm

inspirationist
BR ˌɪnspɪˈreɪʃn̩ɪst,
ˌɪnspɪˈreɪʃənɪst, -s
AM ˌɪnspəˈreɪʃənəst,
ˌɪnspəˈreɪʃn̩ɪst, -s

inspirator
BR ˈɪnspɪreɪtə(r), -z
AM ˈɪnspəˌreɪdər, -z

inspiratory
BR ɪnˈspɪrət(ə)ri,
ɪnˈspʌɪ(ə)rət(ə)ri
AM ˈɪnspərəˌtɔri

inspire
BR ɪnˈspʌɪə(r), -z, -ɪŋ,
-d
AM ɪnzˈpaɪ(ə)r,
ɪnˈspaɪ(ə)r, -z, -ɪŋ, -d

inspiredly
BR ɪnˈspʌɪədli
AM ɪnzˈpaɪ(ə)rdli,
ɪnˈspaɪ(ə)rdli

inspirer
BR ɪnˈspʌɪərə(r), -z
AM ɪnzˈpaɪ(ə)rər,
ɪnˈspaɪ(ə)rər, -z

inspiringly
BR ɪnˈspʌɪərɪŋli

AM ɪnzˈpæk|(t),
ɪnˈspæk|(t), -(t)s, -tɪŋ,
-təd

inspirit
BR ɪnˈspɪr|ɪt, -ɪts, -ɪtɪŋ,
-ɪtɪd
AM ɪnzˈpɪrɪ|t,
ɪnˈspɪrɪ|t, -ts, -dɪŋ, -dɪd

inspiritingly
BR ɪnˈspɪrɪtɪŋli
AM ɪnzˈpɪrɪdɪŋli,
ɪnˈspɪrɪdɪŋli

inspissate
BR ɪnˈspɪseɪt,
ˈɪnspɪseɪt, -s, -ɪŋ, -ɪd
AM ˈɪnspəˌseɪt
ɪnzˈpɪˌseɪt,
ɪnˈspɪˌseɪt, -ts, -dɪŋ,
-dɪd

inspissation
BR ˌɪnspɪˈseɪʃn, -z
AM ˌɪnspəˈseɪʃən
ɪnzˌpɪˈseɪʃən,
ɪnˌspɪˈseɪʃən, -z

inspissator
BR ˈɪnspɪseɪtə(r), -z
AM ˈɪnspəˌseɪdər
ɪnzˈpɪˌseɪdər,
ɪnˈspɪˌseɪdər, -z

inst.
BR ɪnst
AM ɪnst

instability
BR ˌɪnstəˈbɪlɪti
AM ˌɪnztəˈbɪlɪdi,
ˌɪnstəˈbɪlɪdi

instal
BR ɪnˈstɔːl, -z, -ɪŋ, d
AM ɪnzˈtɔl, ɪnˈstɔl,
ɪnzˈtal, ɪnˈstal, -z, -ɪŋ,
-d

install
BR ɪnˈstɔːl, -z, -ɪŋ, d
AM ɪnzˈtɔl, ɪnˈstɔl,
ɪnzˈtal, ɪnˈstal, -z, -ɪŋ,
-d

installant
BR ɪnˈstɔːlənt,
ɪnˈstɔːlnt, -s
AM ɪnzˈtɔlənt,
ɪnˈstɔlənt, ɪnzˈtalənt,
ɪnˈstalənt, -s

installation
BR ˌɪnstəˈleɪʃn, -z
AM ˌɪnztəˈleɪʃən,
ˌɪnstəˈleɪʃən, -z

installer
BR ɪnˈstɔːlə(r), -z
AM ɪnzˈtɔlər, ɪnˈstɔlər,
ɪnzˈtalər, ɪnˈstalər, -z

installment
BR ɪnˈstɔːlm(ə)nt, -s
AM ɪnzˈtɔlmənt,
ɪnˈstɔlmənt,
ɪnzˈtalmənt,
ɪnˈstalmənt, -s

instalment
BR ɪnˈstɔːlm(ə)nt, -s

AM ɪnz'tɒlmənt,
ɪn'stɒlmənt,
ɪnz'tɑlmənt,
ɪn'stɑlmənt, -s

instance
BR 'ɪnst(ə)ns, -ɪz, -ɪŋ, -t
AM 'ɪnztəns, 'ɪnstəns,
-əz, -ɪŋ, -t

instancy
BR 'ɪnst(ə)ns|i, -ɪz
AM 'ɪnztənsi, 'ɪnstənsi,
-z

instant
BR 'ɪnst(ə)nt, -s
AM 'ɪnztənt, 'ɪnstənt, -s

instantaneity
BR ɪn,stantə'niːɪti,
ɪn,stantə'neɪti
AM ɪnz,tæntn̩'iɪdi,
ɪn,stæntn̩'iɪdi,
ɪnz,tæntn̩'eɪdi,
ɪn,stæntn̩'eɪdi

instantaneous
BR ,ɪnst(ə)n'teɪmɪəs
AM ,ɪnztən'teɪmɪəs,
,ɪnstən'teɪmɪəs,
,ɪnztən'teɪnjəs,
,ɪnstən'teɪnjəs

instantaneously
BR ,ɪnst(ə)n'teɪmɪəsli
AM ,ɪnztən'teɪmɪəsli,
,ɪnstən'teɪmɪəsli,
,ɪnztən'teɪnjəsli,
,ɪnstən'teɪnjəsli

**instantaneous-
ness**
BR ,ɪnst(ə)n'teɪmɪəsnəs
AM ,ɪnztən'teɪmɪəsnəs,
,ɪnstən'teɪmɪəsnəs,
,ɪnztən'teɪnjəsnəs,
,ɪnstən'teɪnjəsnəs

instanter
adverb
BR ɪn'stantə(r)
AM ɪnz'tæn(t)ər,
ɪn'stæn(t)ər

instantiate
BR ɪn'stanʃɪeɪt, -s, -ɪŋ,
-ɪd
AM ɪnz'tæn(t)ʃi,eɪ|t,
ɪn'stæn(t)ʃi,eɪ|t, -ts,
-dɪŋ, -dɪd

instantiation
BR ɪn,stanʃɪ'eɪʃn, -z
AM ɪnz,tæn(t)ʃi'eɪʃən,
ɪn,stæn(t)ʃi'eɪʃən, -z

instantly
BR 'ɪnst(ə)ntli
AM 'ɪnztən(t)li,
'ɪnstən(t)li

instar
BR 'ɪnstɑː(r), -z
AM 'ɪnz,tɑr, 'ɪn,stɑr, -z

instate
BR ɪn'steɪt, -s, -ɪŋ, -ɪd
AM ɪnz'teɪ|t, ɪn'steɪ|t,
-ts, -dɪŋ, -dɪd

in statu pupillari
BR ɪn ,statju:
,pju:pɪ'lɑːri
AM ,ɪn ,steɪ,tu
'pjupə,lɛri, ,ɪn ,stɑ,tu
'pjupə,lɛri, ,ɪn ,stædu
'pjupə,lɛri

instauration
BR ,ɪnstɔː'reɪʃn, -z
AM ,ɪnz,tɔ'reɪʃən,
,ɪn,stɔ'reɪʃən, -z

instaurator
BR 'ɪnstɔː,reɪtə(r), -z
AM 'ɪnztə,reɪdər,
'ɪnstə,reɪdər, -z

instead
BR ɪn'stɛd
AM ɪnz'tɛd, ɪn'stɛd

instep
BR 'ɪnstɛp, -s
AM 'ɪnz,tɛp, 'ɪn,stɛp, -s

instigate
BR 'ɪnstɪgeɪt, -s, -ɪŋ, -ɪd
AM 'ɪnztə,geɪ|t,
'ɪnstə,geɪ|t, -ts, -dɪŋ,
-dɪd

instigation
BR ,ɪnstɪ'geɪʃn
AM ,ɪnztə'geɪʃən,
,ɪnstə'geɪʃən

instigative
BR 'ɪnstɪgətɪv
AM 'ɪnztə,geɪdɪv,
'ɪnstə,geɪdɪv

instigator
BR 'ɪnstɪgeɪtə(r), -z
AM 'ɪnztə,geɪdər,
'ɪnstə,geɪdər, -z

instil
BR ɪn'stɪl, -z, -ɪŋ, -d
AM ɪnz'tɪl, ɪn'stɪl, -z,
-ɪŋ, -d

instill
BR ɪn'stɪl, -z, -ɪŋ, -d
AM ɪnz'tɪl, ɪn'stɪl, -z,
-ɪŋ, -d

instillation
BR ,ɪnstɪ'leɪʃn, -z
AM ,ɪnztə'leɪʃən,
,ɪnstə'leɪʃən, -z

instiller
BR ɪn'stɪlə(r), -z
AM ɪnz'tɪlər, ɪn'stɪlər,
-z

instillment
BR ɪn'stɪlm(ə)nt, -s
AM ɪnz'tɪlmənt,
ɪn'stɪlmənt, -s

instilment
BR ɪn'stɪlm(ə)nt, -s
AM ɪnz'tɪlmənt,
ɪn'stɪlmənt, -s

instinct
BR 'ɪnstɪŋ(k)t, -s
AM 'ɪnztɪŋ(k)t,
'ɪnstɪŋ(k)t,
'ɪnztɪŋk(t),
'ɪnstɪŋk(t), -(t)s

instinctive
BR ɪn'stɪŋ(k)tɪv
AM ɪnz'tɪŋ(k)tɪv,
ɪn'stɪŋ(k)tɪv

instinctively
BR ɪn'stɪŋ(k)tɪvli
AM ɪnz'tɪŋ(k)tɪvli,
ɪn'stɪŋ(k)tɪvli

instinctual
BR ɪn'stɪŋ(k)tʃʊəl,
ɪn'stɪŋ(k)tʃʊəl,
ɪn'stɪŋ(k)tjʊəl,
ɪn'stɪŋ(k)tjəl
AM ɪnz'tɪŋ(k)tʃə(wə)l,
ɪn'stɪŋ(k)tʃə(wə)l

instinctually
BR ɪn'stɪŋ(k)tʃʊəli,
ɪn'stɪŋ(k)tʃʊəli,
ɪn'stɪŋ(k)tʃʃi,
ɪn'stɪŋ(k)tjʊəli,
ɪn'stɪŋktjəli
AM ɪnz'tɪŋ(k)tʃə(wə)li,
ɪn'stɪŋ(k)tʃə(wə)li

institute
BR 'ɪnstɪtju:t,
'ɪnstɪtʃuːt, -s
AM 'ɪnztə,t(j)ut,
'ɪnstə,t(j)ut, -s

institution
BR ,ɪnstɪ'tju:ʃn,
,ɪnstɪ'tʃuːʃn, -z
AM ,ɪnztə't(j)uʃən,
,ɪnstə't(j)uʃən, -z

institutional
BR ,ɪnstɪ'tju:ʃn(ə)l,
,ɪnstɪ'tju:ʃən(ə)l,
,ɪnstɪ'tʃu:ʃn(ə)l,
,ɪnstɪ'tʃu:ʃən(ə)l
AM ,ɪnztə't(j)uʃ(ə)nəl,
,ɪnstə't(j)uʃ(ə)nəl

institutionalisation
BR ,ɪnstɪ,tju:ʃnəlʌɪ-
'zeɪʃn,
,ɪnstɪ,tju:ʃn̩lʌɪ'zeɪʃn,
,ɪnstɪ,tju:ʃənlʌɪ'zeɪʃn,
,ɪnstɪ,tʃu:ʃnəlʌɪ'zeɪʃn,
,ɪnstɪ,tʃu:ʃn̩lʌɪ'zeɪʃn,
,ɪnstɪ,tʃu:ʃənlʌɪ'zeɪʃn,
,ɪnstɪ,tʃu:ʃ(ə)nəlʌɪ-
'zeɪʃn
AM ,ɪnztə't(j)uʃənələ-
'zeɪʃən,
,ɪnztə't(j)uʃnələ'zeɪʃən,
,ɪnstə't(j)uʃənələ'zeɪʃən,
,ɪnstə't(j)uʃnələ'zeɪʃən,
,ɪnztə't(j)uʃənl,aɪ-
'zeɪʃən,
,ɪnztə't(j)uʃnə,laɪ-
'zeɪʃən,
,ɪnstə't(j)uʃənl,aɪ-
'zeɪʃən,
,ɪnstə't(j)uʃnə,laɪ-
'zeɪʃən

institutionalize
BR ,ɪnstɪ'tju:ʃnəlʌɪz,
,ɪnstɪ'tju:ʃn̩lʌɪz,
,ɪnstɪ'tju:ʃ(ə)nəlʌɪz,
,ɪnstɪ'tʃu:ʃnəlʌɪz,
,ɪnstɪ'tʃu:ʃn̩lʌɪz,
,ɪnstɪ'tʃu:ʃ(ə)nəlʌɪz,
-ɪz, -ɪŋ, -d
AM ,ɪnztə'tu)uʃənl,aɪz,
,ɪnztə'tu)uʃnə,laɪz,
,ɪnstə'tu)uʃənl,aɪz,
,ɪnstə'tu)uʃnə,laɪz, -ɪz,
-ɪŋ, -d

institutionally
BR ,ɪnstɪ'tju:ʃnəli,
,ɪnstɪ'tju:ʃn̩li,
,ɪnstɪ'tju:ʃənli,

instinctual (right col continued)

institutionalism
BR ,ɪnstɪ'tju:ʃnəlɪz(ə)m,
,ɪnstɪ'tju:ʃn̩lɪz(ə)m,
,ɪnstɪ'tju:ʃənlɪz(ə)m,
,ɪnstɪ'tʃu:ʃnəlɪz(ə)m,
,ɪnstɪ'tʃu:ʃn̩lɪz(ə)m,
,ɪnstɪ'tʃu:ʃənlɪz(ə)m,
,ɪnstɪ'tʃu:ʃ(ə)nəlɪz(ə)m
AM ,ɪnztə't(j)uʃənl,ɪzəm,
,ɪnztə't(j)uʃnə,lɪzəm,
,ɪnstə't(j)uʃənl,ɪzəm,
,ɪnstə't(j)uʃnə,lɪzəm

**institutionaliz-
ation**
BR ,ɪnstɪ,tju:ʃnəlʌɪ-
'zeɪʃn,
,ɪnstɪ,tju:ʃn̩lʌɪ'zeɪʃn,
,ɪnstɪ,tju:ʃənlʌɪ-
'zeɪʃn,
,ɪnstɪ,tʃu:ʃnəlʌɪ'zeɪʃn,
,ɪnstɪ,tʃu:ʃn̩lʌɪ'zeɪʃn,
,ɪnstɪ,tʃu:ʃənlʌɪ'zeɪʃn,
,ɪnstɪ,tʃu:ʃ(ə)nəlʌɪ-
'zeɪʃn
AM ,ɪnztə't(j)uʃənlə-
'zeɪʃən,
,ɪnztə't(j)uʃnələ'zeɪʃən,
,ɪnstə't(j)uʃənlə'zeɪʃən,
,ɪnstə't(j)uʃnələ'zeɪʃən,
,ɪnztə't(j)uʃənl,aɪ-
'zeɪʃən,
,ɪnztə't(j)uʃnə,laɪ-
'zeɪʃən,
,ɪnstə't(j)uʃənl,aɪ-
'zeɪʃən,
,ɪnstə't(j)uʃnə,laɪ-
'zeɪʃən

institutionalise
BR ,ɪnstɪ'tju:ʃnəlʌɪz,
,ɪnstɪ'tju:ʃn̩lʌɪz,
,ɪnstɪ'tju:ʃənlʌɪz,

ˌɪnstɪˈtjuːʃ(ə)nəli,
ˌɪnstɪˈtʃuːʃn̩əli,
ˌɪnstɪˈtʃuːʃnl̩i,
ˌɪnstɪˈtʃuːʃənl̩i,
ˌɪnstɪˈtʃuːʃ(ə)nəli
AM ˌɪnztəˈt(j)uʃ(ə)nəli,
ˌɪnstəˈt(j)uʃ(ə)nəli

in-store
BR ˌɪnˈstɔː(r)
AM ¦ɪnˈstɔ(ə)r

INSTRAW
BR ˈɪnstrɔː(r)
AM ˈɪnzˌtrɔ, ˈɪnˌstrɔ,
ˈɪnzˌtrɑ, ˈɪnˌstrɑ

instruct
BR ɪnˈstrʌkt, -s, -ɪŋ, -ɪd
AM ɪnzˈtrək|(t),
ɪnˈstrək|(t), -(t)s, -tɪŋ,
-təd

instruction
BR ɪnˈstrʌkʃn, -z
AM ɪnzˈtrəkʃən,
ɪnˈstrəkʃən, -z

instructional
BR ɪnˈstrʌkʃn̩(ə)l,
ɪnˈstrʌkʃən(ə)l
AM ɪnˈstrəkʃ(ə)nəl

instructive
BR ɪnˈstrʌktɪv
AM ɪnˈstrəktɪv

instructively
BR ɪnˈstrʌktɪvli
AM ɪnˈstrəktəvli

instructiveness
BR ɪnˈstrʌktɪvnɪs
AM ɪnˈstrəktɪvnɪs

instructor
BR ɪnˈstrʌktə(r), -z
AM ɪnˈstrəktər, -z

instructorship
BR ɪnˈstrʌktəʃɪp
AM ɪnˈstrəktərˌʃɪp

instructress
BR ɪnˈstrʌktrɪs, -ɪz
AM ɪnˈstrəktrəs, -əz

instrument
BR ˈɪnstrʊm(ə)nt, -s
AM ˈɪnztrəmənt,
ˈɪnstrəmənt, -s

instrumental
BR ˌɪnstrʊˈmɛntl
AM ¦ɪnztrəˌmɛn(t)l,
¦ɪnstrəˌmɛn(t)l

instrumentalist
BR ˌɪnstrʊˈmɛntl̩ɪst, -s
AM ¦ɪnztrəˈmɛn(t)ləst,
¦ɪnstrəˈmɛn(t)ləst, -s

instrumentality
BR ˌɪnstrʊmɛnˈtalɪti
AM ˌɪnztrəmənˈtælədi,
ˌɪnztrəˌmɛnˈtælədi,
ˌɪnstrəmənˈtælədi,
ˌɪnstrəˌmɛnˈtælədi

instrumentally
BR ˌɪnstrʊˈmɛntl̩i
AM ¦ɪnztrəˌmɛn(t)l̩i,
¦ɪnstrəˌmɛn(t)l̩i

instrumentation
BR ˌɪnstrʊmɛnˈteɪʃn,
ˌɪnstrʊm(ə)nˈteɪʃn
AM ˌɪnztrəmənˈteɪʃən,
ˌɪnztrəˌmɛnˈteɪʃən,
ˌɪnstrəmənˈteɪʃən,
ˌɪnstrəˌmɛnˈteɪʃən

insubordinate
BR ˌɪnsəˈbɔːdɪnət,
ˌɪnsəˈbɔːdn̩ət
AM ¦ɪnsəˈbɔrdn̩ət

insubordinately
BR ˌɪnsəˈbɔːdɪnətli,
ˌɪnsəˈbɔːdn̩ətli
AM ¦ɪnsəˈbɔrdn̩ətli

insubordination
BR ˌɪnsəˌbɔːdɪˈneɪʃn
AM ¦ɪnsəˌbɔrdəˈneɪʃən

insubstantial
BR ˌɪnsəbˈstanʃl
AM ¦ɪnsəbˈstæn(t)ʃəl

insubstantiality
BR ˌɪnsəbˌstanʃɪˈalɪt|i,
-ɪz
AM ¦ɪnsəbˌstæn(t)ʃi-
ˈælədi, -z

insubstantially
BR ˌɪnsəbˈstanʃl̩i,
ˌɪnsəbˈstanʃəli
AM ¦ɪnsəbˈstæn(t)ʃəli

insufferable
BR ɪnˈsʌf(ə)rəbl
AM ɪnˈsəf(ə)rəbəl

insufferableness
BR ɪnˈsʌf(ə)rəblnəs
AM ɪnˈsəf(ə)rəbəlnəs

insufferably
BR ɪnˈsʌf(ə)rəbli
AM ɪnˈsəf(ə)rəbli

insufficiency
BR ˌɪnsəˈfɪʃns|i, -ɪz
AM ¦ɪnsəˈfɪʃənsi, -z

insufficient
BR ˌɪnsəˈfɪʃnt
AM ¦ɪnsəˈfɪʃənt

insufficiently
BR ˌɪnsəˈfɪʃntli
AM ¦ɪnsəˈfɪʃən(t)li

insufflate
BR ˈɪnsəfleɪt,
ɪnˈsʌfleɪt, -s, -ɪŋ, -ɪd
AM ˈɪnsəˌfleɪ|t, -ts, -dɪŋ,
-dɪd

insufflation
BR ˌɪnsəˈfleɪʃn, -z
AM ˌɪnsəˈfleɪʃən, -z

insufflator
BR ˈɪnsəˌfleɪtə(r), -z
AM ˈɪnsəˌfleɪdər, -z

insular
BR ˈɪnsjʊlə(r)
AM ˈɪns(j)ələr

insularism
BR ˈɪnsjʊlərɪz(ə)m
AM ˈɪns(j)ələˌrɪzəm

insularity
BR ˌɪnsjʊˈlarɪti
AM ˌɪns(j)əˈlɛrədi

insularly
BR ˈɪnsjʊləli
AM ˈɪns(j)ələrli

insulate
BR ˈɪnsjʊleɪt, -s, -ɪŋ, -ɪd
AM ˈɪnsəˌleɪ|t, -ts, -dɪŋ,
-dɪd

insulation
BR ˌɪnsjʊˈleɪʃn
AM ˌɪnsəˈleɪʃən

insulator
BR ˈɪnsjʊleɪtə(r), -z
AM ˈɪnsəˌleɪdər, -z

insulin
BR ˈɪnsjʊlɪn
AM ˈɪnsələn

insult[1]
noun
BR ˈɪnsʌlt, -s
AM ˈɪnˌsəlt, -s

insult[2]
verb
BR ɪnˈsʌlt, -s, -ɪŋ, -ɪd
AM ɪnˈsəlt, -s, -ɪŋ, -əd

insulter
BR ɪnˈsʌltə(r), -z
AM ɪnˈsəltər, -z

insultingly
BR ɪnˈsʌltɪŋli
AM ɪnˈsəltɪŋli

insuperability
BR ɪnˌs(j)uːp(ə)rəˈbɪlɪti
AM ¦ɪnˌsup(ə)rəˈbɪlɪdi,
ənˌsup(ə)rəˈbɪlɪdi

insuperable
BR ɪnˈs(j)uːp(ə)rəbl
AM ɪnˈsup(ə)rəbəl

insuperably
BR ɪnˈs(j)uːp(ə)rəbli
AM ɪnˈsup(ə)rəbli

insupportable
BR ˌɪnsəˈpɔːtəbl
AM ¦ɪnsəˈpɔrdəbəl

insupportableness
BR ˌɪnsəˈpɔːtəblnəs
AM ¦ɪnsəˈpɔrdəbəlnəs

insupportably
BR ˌɪnsəˈpɔːtəbli
AM ¦ɪnsəˈpɔrdəbli

insurability
BR ɪnˌʃʊərəˈbɪlɪti,
ɪnˌʃɔːrəˈbɪlɪti
AM ɪnˌʃʊrəˈbɪlɪdi

insurable
BR ɪnˈʃʊərəbl,
ɪnˈʃɔːrəbl
AM ɪnˈʃʊrəbəl

insurance
BR ɪnˈʃʊərəns,
ɪnˈʃʊərn̩s, ɪnˈʃɔːrəns,
ɪnˈʃɔːrn̩s, -ɪz
AM ɪnˈʃʊrəns, -əz

insurant
BR ɪnˈʃʊərənt,
ɪnˈʃʊərn̩t, ɪnˈʃɔːrənt,
ɪnˈʃɔːrn̩t, -s
AM ɪnˈʃʊrənt, -s

insure
BR ɪnˈʃʊə(r), ɪnˈʃɔː(r),
-z, -ɪŋ, -d
AM ɪnˈʃʊ(ə)r, -z, -ɪŋ, -d

insurer
BR ɪnˈʃʊərə(r),
ɪnˈʃɔːrə(r), -z
AM ɪnˈʃʊrər, -z

insurgence
BR ɪnˈsəːdʒ(ə)ns, -ɪz
AM ɪnˈsərdʒəns, -əz

insurgency
BR ɪnˈsəːdʒ(ə)ns|i, -ɪz
AM ɪnˈsərdʒənsi, -z

insurgent
BR ɪnˈsəːdʒ(ə)nt, -s
AM ɪnˈsərdʒənt, -s

insurmountability
BR ˌɪnsəˌmaʊntəˈbɪlɪti
AM ¦ɪnsərˌmaʊn(t)əˈbɪl-
ɪdi

insurmountable
BR ˌɪnsəˈmaʊntəbl
AM ¦ɪnsərˈmaʊn(t)əbəl

insurmountably
BR ˌɪnsəˈmaʊntəbli
AM ¦ɪnsərˈmaʊn(t)əbli

insurrection
BR ˌɪnsəˈrɛkʃn, -z
AM ˌɪnsəˈrɛkʃən, -z

insurrectional
BR ˌɪnsəˈrɛkʃn̩(ə)l,
ˌɪnsəˈrɛkʃən(ə)l
AM ˌɪnsəˈrɛkʃ(ə)nəl

insurrectionary
BR ˌɪnsəˈrɛkʃn̩(ə)r|i,
-ɪz
AM ˌɪnsəˈrɛkʃəˌnɛri, -z

insurrectionism
BR ˌɪnsəˈrɛkʃn̩ɪz(ə)m,
ˌɪnsəˈrɛkʃənɪz(ə)m
AM ˌɪnsəˈrɛkʃəˌnɪzəm

insurrectionist
BR ˌɪnsəˈrɛkʃn̩ɪst,
ˌɪnsəˈrɛkʃənɪst, -s
AM ˌɪnsəˈrɛkʃənəst, -s

insusceptibility
BR ˌɪnsəˌsɛptɪˈbɪlɪti
AM ¦ɪnsəˌsɛptəˈbɪlɪdi

insusceptible
BR ˌɪnsəˈsɛptɪbl
AM ˌɪnsəˈsɛptəbəl

inswing
BR ˈɪnswɪŋ, -z
AM ˈɪnˌswɪŋ, -z

inswinger
BR ˈɪnˌswɪŋə(r), -z
AM ˈɪnˌswɪŋər, -z

intact
BR (ˌ)ɪnˈtakt
AM ɪnˈtæk(t)

intactness
BR (ˌ)ɪnˈtak(t)nəs
AM ɪnˈtæk(t)nəs

intaglio
BR ɪnˈtalɪəʊ, ɪnˈtɑːlɪəʊ
AM ɪnˈtæljoʊ,
ɪnˈtɑljoʊ, ɪnˈtægliou

intake
BR 'ɪnteɪk, -s
AM 'ɪn,teɪk, -s

intangibility
BR ɪn,tan(d)ʒɪ'bɪlɪti
AM ,ɪn,tændʒə'bɪlɪdi,
ɪn,tændʒə'bɪlɪdi

intangible
BR ɪn'tan(d)ʒɪbl
AM ɪn'tændʒəbəl

intangibly
BR ɪn'tan(d)ʒɪbli
AM ɪn'tændʒəbli

intarsia
BR ɪn'tɑːsɪə(r)
AM ɪn'tɑrsiə

Intasun
BR 'ɪntəsʌn
AM 'ɪn(t)ə,sən

integer
BR 'ɪntɪdʒə(r), -z
AM 'ɪn(t)ədʒər, -z

integrability
BR ,ɪntɪgrə'bɪlɪti
AM ,ɪn(t)əgrə'bɪlɪdi

integrable
BR 'ɪntɪgrəbl,
ɪn'tɛgrəbl
AM 'ɪn(t)əgrəbəl

integral¹
general use
BR 'ɪntɪgr(ə)l,
ɪn'tɛgr(ə)l
AM 'ɪn(t)əgrəl

integral²
mathematical
BR 'ɪntɪgr(ə)l, -z
AM 'ɪn(t)əgrəl, -z

integrality
BR ,ɪntɪ'gralɪt|i, -ɪz
AM ,ɪn(t)ə'grælədi, -z

integrally
BR 'ɪntɪgrəli, 'ɪntɪgrḷi,
ɪn'tɛgrəli, ɪn'tɛgrḷi
AM 'ɪn(t)əgrəli,
ɪn'tɛgrəli

integrand
BR 'ɪntɪgrand, -z
AM 'ɪn(t)əgrænd, -z

integrant
BR 'ɪntɪgr(ə)nt, -s
AM 'ɪn(t)əgrənt, -s

integrate
BR 'ɪntɪgreɪt, -s, -ɪŋ, -ɪd
AM 'ɪn(t)ə,greɪ|t, -ts,
-dɪŋ, -dɪd

integration
BR ,ɪntɪ'greɪʃn
AM ,ɪn(t)ə'greɪʃən

integrationist
BR ,ɪntɪ'greɪʃnɪst,
,ɪntɪ'greɪʃənɪst, -s
AM ,ɪn(t)ə'greɪʃənəst,
-s

integrative
BR 'ɪntɪgrətɪv
AM 'ɪn(t)ə,greɪdɪv

integrator
BR 'ɪntɪgreɪtə(r), -z
AM 'ɪn(t)ə,greɪdər, -z

integrity
BR ɪn'tɛgrɪti
AM ɪn'tɛgrədi

integument
BR ɪn'tɛgjʊm(ə)nt, -s
AM ɪn'tɛgjəmənt, -s

integumental
BR ɪn,tɛgjʊ'mɛntl
AM ɪn,tɛgjə'mɛn(t)l

integumentary
BR ɪn,tɛgjʊ'ment(ə)ri
AM ɪn,tɛgjə'mɛn(t)əri

intellect
BR 'ɪntɪlɛkt, -s
AM 'ɪn(t)l,ɛk|(t), -(t)s

intellection
BR ,ɪntɪ'lɛkʃn, -z
AM ,ɪn(t)l'ɛkʃən, -z

intellective
BR ,ɪntɪ'lɛktɪv
AM 'ɪn(t)l,ɛktɪv

intellectual
BR ,ɪntɪ'lɛktʃʊəl,
,ɪntɪ'lɛktʃ(ʊ)l,
,ɪntɪ'lɛktjʊəl,
,ɪntɪ'lɛktjʊl, -z
AM ,ɪn(t)ə'lɛk(t)ʃ(əw)əl,
-z

intellectualise
BR ,ɪntɪ'lɛktʃʊəlʌɪz,
,ɪntɪ'lɛktʃʊlʌɪz,
,ɪntɪ'lɛktʃlʌɪz,
,ɪntɪ'lɛktjʊəlʌɪz,
,ɪntɪ'lɛktjʊlʌɪz, -ɪz,
-ɪŋ, -d
AM ,ɪn(t)ə'lɛk(t)ʃ(əw)-
ə,lʌɪz, -ɪz, -ɪŋ, -d

intellectualism
BR ,ɪntɪ'lɛktʃʊəlɪz(ə)m,
,ɪntɪ'lɛktʃʊlɪz(ə)m,
,ɪntɪ'lɛktʃlɪz(ə)m,
,ɪntɪ'lɛktjʊəlɪz(ə)m,
,ɪntɪ'lɛktjʊlɪz(ə)m
AM ,ɪn(t)ə'lɛk(t)ʃ(əw)-
ə,lɪzəm

intellectualist
BR ,ɪntɪ'lɛktʃʊəlɪst,
,ɪntɪ'lɛktʃʊlɪst,
,ɪntɪ'lɛktʃlɪst,
,ɪntɪ'lɛktjʊəlɪst,
,ɪntɪ'lɛktjʊlɪst, -s
AM ,ɪn(t)ə'lɛk(t)ʃ(əw)-
ələst, -s

intellectuality
BR ,ɪntɪ'lɛktʃʊ'alɪti,
,ɪntɪ,lɛktjʊ'alɪti
AM ,ɪn(t)ə,lɛk(t)ʃə-
'wælədi

intellectualize
BR ,ɪntɪ'lɛktʃʊəlʌɪz,
,ɪntɪ'lɛktʃʊlʌɪz,
,ɪntɪ'lɛktʃlʌɪz,
,ɪntɪ'lɛktjʊəlʌɪz,
,ɪntɪ'lɛktjʊlʌɪz, -ɪz,
-ɪŋ, -d

AM ,ɪn(t)ə'lɛk(t)ʃ(əw)-
ə,lʌɪz, -ɪz, -ɪŋ, -d

intellectually
BR ,ɪntɪ'lɛktʃʊəli,
,ɪntɪ'lɛktʃʊli,
,ɪntɪ'lɛktʃli,
,ɪntɪ'lɛktjʊəli,
,ɪntɪ'lɛktjʊli
AM ,ɪn(t)ə'lɛk(t)ʃ(əw)-
əli

intelligence
BR ɪn'tɛlɪdʒ(ə)ns, -ɪz
AM ɪn'tɛlədʒəns, -əz

intelligent
BR ɪn'tɛlɪdʒ(ə)nt
AM ɪn'tɛlədʒənt

intelligential
BR ɪn,tɛlɪ'dʒɛnʃl
AM ɪn,tɛlə'dʒɛnʃəl

intelligently
BR ɪn'tɛlɪdʒ(ə)ntli
AM ɪn'tɛlədʒən(t)li

intelligentsia
BR ɪn,tɛlɪ'dʒɛnsɪə(r),
,ɪntɛlɪ'dʒɛnsɪə(r)
AM ɪn,tɛlə'dʒɛn(t)sɪə

intelligibility
BR ɪn,tɛlɪdʒɪ'bɪlɪti
AM ɪn,tɛlədʒə'bɪlɪdi

intelligible
BR ɪn'tɛlɪdʒɪbl
AM ɪn'tɛlədʒəbəl

intelligibly
BR ɪn'tɛlɪdʒɪbli
AM ɪn'tɛlədʒəbli

Intelpost
BR 'ɪntɛlpəʊst
AM 'ɪn,tɛl'pəʊst

Intelsat
BR 'ɪntɛlsat
AM 'ɪn,tɛl'sæt

intemperance
BR ɪn'tɛmp(ə)rəns,
ɪn'tɛmp(ə)rns
AM ɪn'tɛmp(ə)rəns

intemperate
BR ɪn'tɛmp(ə)rət
AM ɪn'tɛmp(ə)rət

intemperately
BR ɪn'tɛmp(ə)rətli
AM ɪn'tɛmp(ə)rətli

intemperateness
BR ɪn'tɛmp(ə)rətnəs
AM ɪn'tɛmp(ə)rətnəs

intend
BR ɪn'tɛnd, -z, -ɪŋ, -ɪd
AM ɪn'tɛnd, -z, -ɪŋ, -əd

intendancy
BR ɪn'tɛnd(ə)ns|i, -ɪz
AM ɪn'tɛndnsi, -z

intendant
BR ɪn'tɛnd(ə)nt, -s
AM ɪn'tɛndnt, -s

intended
BR ɪn'tɛndɪd, -z
AM ɪn'tɛndəd, -z

integrator
AM ,ɪn(t)ə'lɛk(t)ʃ(əw)-
ə,laɪz, -ɪz, -ɪŋ, -d

intendedly
BR ɪn'tɛndɪdli
AM ɪn'tɛndədli

intendment
BR ɪn'tɛn(d)m(ə)nt, -s
AM ɪn'tɛn(d)mənt, -s

intense
BR ɪn'tɛns, -ə(r), -ɪst
AM ɪn'tɛns, -ər, -əst

intensely
BR ɪn'tɛnsli
AM ɪn'tɛnsli

intenseness
BR ɪn'tɛnsnəs
AM ɪn'tɛnsnəs

intensification
BR ɪn,tɛnsɪfɪ'keɪʃn
AM ɪn,tɛnsəfə'keɪʃən

intensifier
BR ɪn'tɛnsɪfʌɪə(r), -z
AM ɪn'tɛnsə,faɪər, -z

intensify
BR ɪn'tɛnsɪfʌɪ, -z, -ɪŋ, -d
AM ɪn'tɛnsə,faɪ, -z, -ɪŋ,
-d

intension
BR ɪn'tɛnʃn, -z
AM ɪn'tɛnʃən, -z

intensional
BR ɪn'tɛnʃn(ə)l,
ɪn'tɛnʃən(ə)l
AM ɪn'tɛn(t)ʃ(ə)nəl

intensionally
BR ɪn'tɛnʃnəli,
ɪn'tɛnʃn̩li,
ɪn'tɛnʃ(ə)nəli
AM ɪn'tɛn(t)ʃ(ə)nəli

intensity
BR ɪn'tɛnsɪti
AM ɪn'tɛnsədi

intensive
BR ɪn'tɛnsɪv
AM ɪn'tɛnsɪv

intensively
BR ɪn'tɛnsɪvli
AM ɪn'tɛnsəvli

intensiveness
BR ɪn'tɛnsɪvnɪs
AM ɪn'tɛnsɪvnɪs

intent
BR ɪn'tɛnt, -s
AM ɪn'tɛnt, -s

intention
BR ɪn'tɛnʃn, -z, -d
AM ɪn'tɛn(t)ʃən, -z, -d

intentional
BR ɪn'tɛnʃn(ə)l,
ɪn'tɛnʃən(ə)l
AM ɪn'tɛn(t)ʃ(ə)nəl

intentionality
BR ɪn,tɛnʃə'nalɪt|i, -ɪz
AM ɪn,tɛn(t)ʃə'nælədi,
-z

intentionally
BR ɪn'tɛnʃnəli,
ɪn'tɛnʃn̩li,

ɪnˈtenʃən|i,
ɪnˈtenʃ(ə)nəli
AM ɪnˈten(t)ʃ(ə)nəli
intentioned
BR ɪnˈtenʃ(ə)nd
AM ɪnˈten(t)ʃənd
intently
BR ɪnˈtentli
AM ɪnˈten(t)li
intentness
BR ɪnˈtentnəs
AM ɪnˈtentnəs
inter
verb
BR ɪnˈtɜː(r), -z, -ɪŋ, -d
AM ɪnˈtɜr, -z, -ɪŋ, -d
interact
BR ˌɪntərˈakt, -s, -ɪŋ, -ɪd
AM ˌɪn(t)ərˈæk|(t),
-(t)s, -tɪŋ, -təd
interactant
BR ˌɪntərˈaktnt, -s
AM ˌɪn(t)ərˈæktnt, -s
interaction
BR ˌɪntərˈakʃn
AM ˌɪn(t)ərˈækʃən
interactional
BR ˌɪntərˈakʃn(ə)l,
ˌɪntərˈakʃən(ə)l
AM ˌɪn(t)ərˈækʃ(ə)nəl
interactive
BR ˌɪntərˈaktɪv
AM ˌɪn(t)ərˈæktɪv
interactively
BR ˌɪntərˈaktɪvli
AM ˌɪn(t)ərˈæktəvli
inter alia
BR ˌɪntər ˈeɪliə(r),
+ ˈɑːliə(r), + ˈaliə(r)
AM ˌɪntəˈrɑljə,
ˌɪntəˈreɪljə,
ˌɪntəˈrɑliə, ˌɪntəˈreɪliə
interAmerican
BR ˌɪntər(ə)rəˈmerɪk(ə)n
AM ˌɪn(t)ərəˈmerəkən
interarticular
BR ˌɪnt(ə)rɑːˈtɪkjələ(r)
AM ˌɪn(t)ərˌɑrˈtɪkjələr
interatomic
BR ˌɪnt(ə)rəˈtɒmɪk
AM ˌɪn(t)ərəˈtɑmɪk
interbank
BR ˌɪntəˈbaŋk
AM ˈɪn(t)ərˌbæŋk
interbed
BR ˌɪntəˈbed, -z, -ɪŋ, -ɪd
AM ˈɪn(t)ərˌbed, -z, -ɪŋ,
-əd
interblend
BR ˌɪntəˈblend, -z, -ɪŋ,
-ɪd
AM ˈɪn(t)ərˌblend, -z,
-ɪŋ, -əd
interbred
BR ˌɪntəˈbred
AM ˈɪn(t)ərˈbred
interbreed
BR ˌɪntəˈbriːd, -z, -ɪŋ

AM ˈɪn(t)ərˈbrid, -z, -ɪŋ
intercalary
BR ɪnˈtɜːkəl(ə)ri,
ɪnˈtɜːk|(ə)ri,
ˌɪntəˈkal(ə)ri
AM ɪnˈtɜrkəˌleri,
ˈɪn(t)ərˈkæləri
intercalate
BR ɪnˈtɜːkəleɪt,
ɪnˈtɜːk|leɪt,
ˌɪntəkəˈleɪt, -s, -ɪŋ, -ɪd
AM ɪnˈtɜrkəˌleɪ|t, -ts,
-dɪŋ, -dɪd
intercalation
BR ɪnˌtɜːkəˈleɪʃn,
ˌɪntəkəˈleɪʃn, -z
AM ɪnˌtɜrkəˈleɪʃən, -z
intercede
BR ˌɪntəˈsiːd, -z, -ɪŋ, -ɪd
AM ˌɪn(t)ərˈsid, -z, -ɪŋ,
-ɪd
interceder
BR ˌɪntəˈsiːdə(r), -z
AM ˌɪn(t)ərˈsidər, -z
intercellular
BR ˌɪntəˈseljʊlə(r)
AM ˌɪn(t)ərˈseljələr
intercensal
BR ˌɪntəˈsensl
AM ˌɪn(t)ərˈsensəl
intercept
BR ˌɪntəˈsept, -s, -ɪŋ, -ɪd
AM ˌɪn(t)ərˈsept, -s, -ɪŋ,
-əd
interception
BR ˌɪntəˈsepʃn, -z
AM ˌɪn(t)ərˈsepʃən, -z
interceptive
BR ˌɪntəˈseptɪv
AM ˌɪn(t)ərˈseptɪv
interceptor
BR ˈɪntəˌseptə(r),
ˌɪntəˈseptə(r), -z
AM ˌɪn(t)ərˈseptər, -z
intercession
BR ˌɪntəˈseʃn, -z
AM ˌɪn(t)ərˈseʃən, -z
intercessional
BR ˌɪntəˈseʃn(ə)l,
ˌɪntəˈseʃən(ə)l
AM ˌɪn(t)ərˈseʃ(ə)nəl
intercessor
BR ˌɪntəˈsesə(r),
ˈɪntəˌsesə(r), -z
AM ˈɪn(t)ərˈsesər, -z
intercessorial
BR ˌɪntəsɜːˈsɔːriəl,
ˌɪntəsəˈsɔːriəl
AM ˌɪn(t)ərsəˈsɔriəl
intercessory
BR ˌɪntəˈsesə(r)i
AM ˌɪn(t)ərˈsesəri
interchange¹
noun
BR ˈɪntətʃeɪn(d)ʒ, -ɪz
AM ˈɪn(t)ərˌtʃeɪndʒ, -ɪz

AM ˈɪn(t)ərˈbrid, -z, -ɪŋ
interchange²
verb
BR ˌɪntəˈtʃeɪn(d)ʒ, -ɪz,
-ɪŋ, -d
AM ˌɪn(t)ərˈtʃeɪndʒ, -ɪz,
-ɪŋ, -d
interchangeability
BR ˌɪntəˌtʃeɪn(d)ʒəˈbɪlɪti
AM ˌɪn(t)ərˌtʃeɪndʒə-
ˈbɪlɪdi
interchangeable
BR ˌɪntəˈtʃeɪn(d)ʒəbl
AM ˌɪn(t)ərˈtʃeɪndʒəbəl
**interchangeable-
ness**
BR ˌɪntəˈtʃeɪn(d)ʒəblnəs
AM ˌɪn(t)ərˈtʃeɪndʒəbəl-
nəs
interchangeably
BR ˌɪntəˈtʃeɪn(d)ʒəbli
AM ˌɪn(t)ərˈtʃeɪndʒəbli
inter-city
BR ˌɪntəˈsɪti
AM ˌɪn(t)ərˈsɪdi
inter-class
BR ˌɪntəˈklɑːs,
ˌɪntəˈklas
AM ˌɪn(t)ərˈklæs
intercollegiate
BR ˌɪntəkəˈliːdʒɪət
AM ˌɪn(t)ərkəˈlidʒ(i)ət
intercolonial
BR ˌɪntəkəˈləʊnɪəl
AM ˌɪn(t)ərkəˈloʊnɪəl
intercom
BR ˈɪntəkɒm, -z
AM ˈɪn(t)ərˌkɑm, -z
intercommunicate
BR ˌɪntəkəˈmjuːnɪkeɪt,
-s, -ɪŋ, -ɪd
AM ˌɪn(t)ərkə-
ˈmjunəˌkeɪ|t, -ts, -dɪŋ,
-dɪd
**intercommunica-
tion**
BR ˌɪntəkəˌmjuːnɪˈkeɪʃn
AM ˌɪn(t)ərkəˌmjunə-
ˈkeɪʃən
**intercommunica-
tive**
BR ˌɪntəkəˈmjuːnɪkətɪv
AM ˌɪn(t)ərkəˈmjunə-
ˌkeɪdɪv,
ˈɪn(t)ərkəˈmjunəkədɪv
intercommunion
BR ˌɪntəkəˈmjuːnɪən
AM ˌɪn(t)ərkəˈmjunjən
intercommunity
BR ˌɪntəkəˈmjuːnɪti
AM ˌɪn(t)ərkəˈmjunədi
interconnect
BR ˌɪntəkəˈnekt, -s, -ɪŋ,
-ɪd
AM ˌɪn(t)ərkəˈnek|(t),
-(t)s, -tɪŋ, -təd
interconnection
BR ˌɪntəkəˈnekʃn, -z

AM ˌɪn(t)ərkəˈnekʃən,
-z
intercontinental
BR ˌɪntəˌkɒntrɪˈnentl
AM ˌɪn(t)ərˌkɑntn'ɛn(t)l,
ˈɪn(t)ərˈkɑn(t)əˈnen(t)l
intercontinentally
BR ˌɪntəˌkɒntrɪˈnentļi
AM ˌɪn(t)ərˈkɑntn-
'ɛn(t)li,
ˈɪn(t)ərˈkɑn(t)ə-
ˈnen(t)li
interconversion
BR ˌɪntəkənˈvɜːʃn, -z
AM ˌɪn(t)ərkənˈvɜrʒən,
-z
interconvert
BR ˌɪntəkənˈvɜːt, -s, -ɪŋ,
-ɪd
AM ˌɪn(t)ərkənˈvɜr|t,
-ts, -dɪŋ, -dəd
interconvertible
BR ˌɪntəkənˈvɜːtbl
AM ˌɪn(t)ərkənˈvɜrdə-
bəl
intercool
BR ˈɪntəkuːl, -z, -ɪŋ, -d
AM ˈɪn(t)ərˈkul, -z, -ɪŋ,
-d
intercooler
BR ˈɪntəˌkuːlə(r), -z
AM ˈɪn(t)ərˌkulər, -z
intercooling
BR ˈɪntəˌkuːlɪŋ, -z
AM ˈɪn(t)ərˌkulɪŋ, -z
intercorrelate
BR ˌɪntəˈkɒrɪleɪt, -s,
-ɪŋ, -ɪd
AM ˌɪn(t)ərˈkɔrəˌleɪ|t,
-ts, -dɪŋ, -dɪd
intercorrelation
BR ˌɪntəˌkɒrɪˈleɪʃn, -z
AM ˌɪn(t)ərˌkɔrəˈleɪʃən,
-z
intercostal
BR ˌɪntəˈkɒstl
AM ˌɪn(t)ərˈkɑstəl
intercostally
BR ˌɪntəˈkɒstļi,
ˌɪntəˈkɒstəli
AM ˌɪn(t)ərˈkɑstəli
intercounty
BR ˌɪntəˈkaʊnti
AM ˌɪn(t)ərˈkaʊn(t)i
intercourse
BR ˈɪntəkɔːs
AM ˈɪn(t)ərˌkɔ(ə)rs
intercrop
BR ˌɪntəˈkrɒp, -s, -ɪŋ, -t
AM ˈɪn(t)ərˈkrɑp, -s, -ɪŋ,
-t
intercross
BR ˌɪntəˈkrɒs, -ɪz, -ɪŋ, -t
AM ˈɪn(t)ərˈkrɔs,
ˈɪn(t)ərˈkrɑs, -əz, -ɪŋ,
-t

intercrural
BR ˌɪntəˈkrʊərəl,
ˌɪntəˈkrʊərl̩
AM ˈɪn(t)ərˈkrʊrəl
intercurrence
BR ˌɪntəˈkʌrəns,
ˌɪntəˈkʌrn̩s, -ɪz
AM ˈɪn(t)ərˈkərəns, -əz
intercurrent
BR ˌɪntəˈkʌrənt,
ˌɪntəˈkʌrn̩t
AM ˈɪn(t)ərˈkərənt
intercut
BR ˌɪntəˈkʌt, -s, -ɪŋ
AM ˈɪn(t)ərˈkəlt, -ts,
-dɪŋ
interdenomina-
tional
BR ˌɪntədɪˌnɒmɪˈneɪ-
ʃn̩(ə)l,
ˌɪntədɪˌnɒmɪˈneɪʃə-
n(ə)l
AM ˈɪn(t)ərdəˌnɑməˈneɪ-
ʃ(ə)nəl
interdenomination-
ally
BR ˌɪntədɪˌnɒmɪˈneɪʃn̩-
əli,
ˌɪntədɪˌnɒmɪˈneɪʃn̩li,
ˌɪntədɪˌnɒmɪˈneɪʃənl̩i,
ˌɪntədɪˌnɒmɪˈneɪʃ(ə)n-
əli
AM ˈɪn(t)ərdəˌnɑməˈneɪ-
ʃ(ə)nəli
interdepartmental
BR ˌɪntəˌdiːpɑːˈtmentl,
ˌɪntədɪˌpɑːˈtmentl
AM ˈɪn(t)ərdəˌpɑrt-
ˈmen(t)l,
ˈɪn(t)ərdiˌpɑrtˈmen(t)l
interdepartment-
ally
BR ˌɪntəˌdiːpɑːˈtmentl̩i,
ˌɪntədɪˌpɑːˈtmentl̩i
AM ˈɪn(t)ərdəˌpɑrtˈmen-
(t)li,
ˈɪn(t)ərdiˌpɑrtˈmen(t)li
interdepend
BR ˌɪntədɪˈpend, -z, -ɪŋ,
-ɪd
AM ˈɪn(t)ərdəˈpend, -z,
-ɪŋ, -əd
interdependence
BR ˌɪntədɪˈpend(ə)ns
AM ˈɪn(t)ərdəˈpendns
interdependency
BR ˌɪntədɪˈpend(ə)ns|i,
-ɪz
AM ˈɪn(t)ərdəˈpendnsi,
-z
interdependent
BR ˌɪntədɪˈpend(ə)nt
AM ˈɪn(t)ərdəˈpendənt
interdependently
BR ˌɪntədɪˈpend(ə)ntli
AM ˈɪn(t)ərdəˈpend-
ən(t)li

interdict¹
noun
BR ˈɪntədɪkt, -s
AM ˈɪn(t)ərˌdɪk(t), -s
interdict²
verb
BR ˌɪntəˈdɪkt, -s, -ɪŋ, -ɪd
AM ˈɪn(t)ərˈdɪk|(t),
-(t)s, -tɪŋ, -tɪd
interdiction
BR ˌɪntəˈdɪkʃn, -z
AM ˈɪn(t)ərˈdɪkʃən, -z
interdictory
BR ˌɪntəˈdɪkt(ə)ri
AM ˈɪn(t)ərˈdɪkˌtɔri
interdigital
BR ˌɪntəˈdɪdʒɪtl
AM ˈɪn(t)ərˈdɪdʒɪdl
interdigitally
BR ˌɪntəˈdɪdʒɪtl̩i
AM ˈɪn(t)ərˈdɪdʒɪdl̩i
interdigitate
BR ˌɪntəˈdɪdʒɪteɪt, -s,
-ɪŋ, -ɪd
AM ˈɪn(t)ərˈdɪdʒɪˌteɪt,
-ts, -dɪŋ, -dɪd
interdisciplinary
BR ˌɪntəˌdɪsɪˈplɪn(ə)ri,
ˌɪntəˈdɪsɪplɪn(ə)ri
AM ˈɪn(t)ərˈdɪs(ə)plə-
ˌneri
interest
BR ˈɪntrɪst, ˈɪnt(ə)rest,
-s, -ɪŋ, -ɪd
AM ˈɪnt(ə)rəst, -s, -ɪŋ,
-əd
interestedly
BR ˈɪntrɪstɪdli,
ˈɪnt(ə)restɪdli
AM ˈɪnt(ə)rəstəd
interestedness
BR ˈɪntrɪstɪdnɪs,
ˈɪnt(ə)restɪdnɪs
AM ˈɪnt(ə)rəstədnəs,
ˈɪnt(ə)ˌrestədnəs
interestingly
BR ˈɪntrɪstɪŋli,
ˈɪnt(ə)restɪŋli
AM ˈɪnt(ə)rəstɪŋli
interestingness
BR ˈɪntrɪstɪŋnɪs,
ˈɪnt(ə)restɪŋnɪs
AM ˈɪnt(ə)rəstɪŋnɪs
interface
BR ˈɪntəfeɪs, -ɪz, -ɪŋ, -t
AM ˈɪn(t)ərˌfeɪs, -ɪz, -ɪŋ,
-t
interfacial
BR ˌɪntəˈfeɪʃl
AM ˈɪn(t)ərˈfeɪʃəl
interfacially
BR ˌɪntəˈfeɪʃl̩i,
ˌɪntəˈfeɪʃəli
AM ˈɪn(t)ərˈfeɪʃəli
interfacing
BR ˈɪntəˌfeɪsɪŋ, -z
AM ˈɪn(t)ərˌfeɪsɪŋ, -z

inter-faith
BR ˌɪntəˈfeɪθ
AM ˈɪn(t)ərˈfeɪθ
interfemoral
BR ˌɪntəˈfem(ə)rəl,
ˌɪntəˈfem(ə)rl̩
AM ˈɪn(t)ərˈfem(ə)rəl
interfere
BR ˌɪntəˈfɪə(r), -z, -ɪŋ, -d
AM ˈɪn(t)ərˈfɪ(ə)r, -z,
-ɪŋ, -d
interference
BR ˌɪntəˈfɪərəns,
ˌɪntəˈfɪərns
AM ˈɪn(t)ərˈfɪrəns
interferential
BR ˌɪntəfəˈrenʃl
AM ˈɪn(t)ərfəˈren(t)ʃəl
interferer
BR ˌɪntəˈfɪərə(r), -z
AM ˈɪn(t)ərˈfɪrər, -z
interferingly
BR ˌɪntəˈfɪərɪŋli
AM ˈɪn(t)ərˈfɪrɪŋli
interferometer
BR ˌɪntəfəˈrɒmɪtə(r),
-z
AM ˈɪn(t)ərfəˈrɑmədər,
-z
interferometric
BR ˌɪntəˌferə(ʊ)ˈmetrɪk,
ˌɪntəˌfɪərə(ʊ)ˈmetrɪk
AM ˈɪn(t)ərˌfɪrəˈmetrɪk
interferometric-
ally
BR ˌɪntəˌferəˈmetrɪkli,
ˌɪntəˌfɪərəˈmetrɪkli
AM ˈɪn(t)ərˌfɪrəˈmetrək-
(ə)li
interferometry
BR ˌɪntəfɪˈrɒmɪtri
AM ˈɪn(t)ərfəˈrɑmətri
interferon
BR ˌɪntəˈfɪərɒn
AM ˈɪn(t)ərˈfɪrˌɑn
interfile
BR ˌɪntəˈfaɪl, -z, -ɪŋ, -d
AM ˈɪn(t)ərˈfaɪl, -z, -ɪŋ,
-d
interflow
BR ˌɪntəˈfləʊ, -z, -ɪŋ, -d
AM ˈɪn(t)ərˈfloʊ, -z, -ɪŋ,
-d
interfluent
BR ˌɪntəˈflʊənt
AM ˈɪn(t)ərˈflʊənt
interfluve
BR ˈɪntəfluːv, -z
AM ˈɪn(t)ərˌfluv, -z
interfuse
BR ˌɪntəˈfjuːz, -ɪz, -ɪŋ, -d
AM ˈɪn(t)ərˈfjuz, -əz,
-ɪŋ, -d
interfusion
BR ˌɪntəˈfjuːʒn, -z
AM ˈɪn(t)ərˈfjuʒən, -z
intergalactic
BR ˌɪntəgəˈlaktɪk

intergalactically
AM ˈɪn(t)ərgəˈlæktɪk
intergalactically
BR ˌɪntəgəˈlaktɪkli
AM ˈɪn(t)ərgəˈlæktək-
(ə)li
interglacial
BR ˌɪntəˈgleɪʃl,
ˌɪntəˈgleɪsɪəl, -z
AM ˈɪn(t)ərˈgleɪʃəl, -z
intergovernmental
BR ˌɪntəˌgʌvnˈmentl,
ˌɪntəˌgʌvəˈmentl
AM ˈɪn(t)ərˌgəvər(n)-
ˈmen(t)l
intergovernment-
ally
BR ˌɪntəˌgʌvnˈmentl̩i,
ˌɪntəˌgʌvnˈmentl̩i,
ˌɪntəˌgʌvnˈmentəli,
ˌɪntəˌgʌvəˈmentəli
AM ˈɪn(t)ərˌgəvər(n)-
ˈmen(t)li
intergradation
BR ˌɪntəgrəˈdeɪʃn, -z
AM ˈɪn(t)ərgrəˈdeɪʃən,
-z
intergrade
BR ˌɪntəˈgreɪd, -z, -ɪŋ,
-ɪd
AM ˈɪn(t)ərˈgreɪd, -z,
-ɪŋ, -ɪd
intergrowth
BR ˈɪntəgrəʊθ, -s
AM ˈɪn(t)ərˌgroʊθ, -s
interim
BR ˈɪnt(ə)rɪm
AM ˈɪn(t)ərəm
interior
BR ɪnˈtɪərɪə(r), -z
AM ɪnˈtɪriər, -z
interiorise
BR ɪnˈtɪərɪərʌɪz, -ɪz,
-ɪŋ, -d
AM ɪnˈtɪriəˌraɪz, -ɪz, -ɪŋ,
-d
interiorize
BR ɪnˈtɪərɪərʌɪz, -ɪz,
-ɪŋ, -d
AM ɪnˈtɪriəˌraɪz, -ɪz, -ɪŋ,
-d
interiorly
BR ɪnˈtɪərɪəli
AM ɪnˈtɪriərli
interject
BR ˌɪntəˈdʒekt, -s, -ɪŋ,
-ɪd
AM ˈɪn(t)ərˈdʒek|(t),
-(t)s, -tɪŋ, -təd
interjection
BR ˌɪntəˈdʒekʃn, -z
AM ˈɪn(t)ərˈdʒekʃən, -z
interjectional
BR ˌɪntəˈdʒekʃn̩(ə)l,
ˌɪntəˈdʒekʃən(ə)l
AM ˈɪn(t)ərˈdʒekʃ(ə)nəl
interjectionary
BR ˌɪntəˈdʒekʃn̩(ə)ri
AM ˈɪn(t)ərˈdʒekʃəˌneri

interjectory
BR ˌɪntə'dʒekt(ə)ri
AM ˌɪn(t)ər'dʒekt(ə)ri
interknit
BR ˌɪntə'nɪt, -s, -ɪŋ, -ɪd
AM ˌɪn(t)ər'nɪ|t, -ts, -dɪŋ, -dəd
interlace
BR ˌɪntə'leɪs, -ɪz, -ɪŋ, -t
AM ˌɪn(t)ər'leɪs, -ɪz, -ɪŋ, -t
interlacement
BR ˌɪntə'leɪsm(ə)nt, -s
AM ˌɪn(t)ər'leɪsmənt, -s
Interlaken
BR ˌɪntəˌlɑːk(ə)n
AM ˌɪn(t)ərˌlɑkən
interlanguage
BR ˌɪntəˌlaŋ(g)wˌɪdʒ, -ɪdʒɪz
AM ˌɪn(t)ər'læŋ(g)wədʒ, -z
interlap
BR ˌɪntə'lap, -s, -ɪŋ, -t
AM ˌɪn(t)ər'læp, -s, -ɪŋ, -t
interlard
BR ˌɪntə'lɑːd, -z, -ɪŋ, -ɪd
AM ˌɪn(t)ər'lɑrd, -z, -ɪŋ, -ɪd
interleaf
BR ˌɪntə'liːf, -s, -ɪŋ, -t
AM ˌɪn(t)ər'lif, -s, -ɪŋ, -t
interleave
BR ˌɪntə'liːv, -z, -ɪŋ, -d
AM ˌɪn(t)ər'liv, -z, -ɪŋ, -d
interleukin
BR ˌɪntə'luːkɪn, -z
AM ˌɪn(t)ər'lukən, -z
interlibrary
BR ˌɪntə'lʌɪbr(ər)i
AM ˌɪn(t)ər'laɪb(r)əri
interline
BR ˌɪntə'lʌɪn, -z, -ɪŋ, -d
AM ˌɪn(t)ər'laɪn, -z, -ɪŋ, -d
interlinear
BR ˌɪntə'lɪnɪə(r)
AM ˌɪn(t)ər'lɪniər
interlineation
BR ˌɪntəˌlɪnɪ'eɪʃn, -z
AM ˌɪn(t)ərˌlɪni'eɪʃən, -z
Interlingua
BR ˌɪntə'lɪŋgwə(r)
AM ˌɪn(t)ər'lɪŋgwə
interlining[1]
interlineation
BR ˌɪntə'lʌɪnɪŋ, -z
AM ˌɪn(t)ər'laɪnɪŋ, -z
interlining[2]
layer between two others
BR 'ɪntəˌlʌɪnɪŋ, -z
AM ˌɪn(t)ərˌlaɪnɪŋ, -z

interlink
BR ˌɪntə'lɪŋ|k, -ks, -kɪŋ, -(k)t
AM ˌɪn(t)ər'lɪŋ|k, -ks, -kɪŋ, -(k)t
interlobular
BR ˌɪntə'lɒbjʉlə(r)
AM ˌɪn(t)ər'labjələr
interlock[1]
noun
BR 'ɪntəlɒk, -s
AM 'ɪn(t)ərˌlak, -s
interlock[2]
verb
BR ˌɪntə'lɒk, -s, -ɪŋ, -t
AM ˌɪn(t)ər'lak, -s, -ɪŋ, -t
interlocker
BR ˌɪntə'lɒkə(r), -z
AM ˌɪn(t)ər'lakər, -z
interlocution
BR ˌɪntələ'kjuːʃn, -z
AM ˌɪn(t)ərˌlou'kjuʃən, -z
interlocutor
BR ˌɪntə'lɒkjʉtə(r), -z
AM ˌɪn(t)ər'lakjədər, -z
interlocutory
BR ˌɪntə'lɒkjʉt(ə)r|i, -ɪz
AM ˌɪn(t)ər'lakjəˌtɔri, -z
interlocutrix
BR ˌɪntə'lɒkjʉtrɪks, -ɪz
AM ˌɪn(t)ər'lakjəˌtrɪks, -ɪz
interlope
BR ˌɪntə'ləʊp, -s, -ɪŋ, -t
AM 'ɪn(t)ərˌloup, ˌɪn(t)ər'loup, -s, -ɪŋ, -t
interloper
BR 'ɪntəˌləʊpə(r), -z
AM 'ɪn(t)ərˌloupər, ˌɪn(t)ər'loupər, -z
interlude
BR 'ɪntəl(j)uːd, -z
AM 'ɪn(t)ərˌlud, -z
intermarriage
BR ˌɪntə'marɪdʒ
AM ˌɪn(t)ər'merɪdʒ
intermarry
BR ˌɪntə'mar|i, -ɪz, -ɪɪŋ, -ɪd
AM ˌɪn(t)ər'meri, -z, -ɪŋ, -d
intermedia
BR ˌɪntə'miːdɪə(r)
AM ˌɪn(t)ər'midiə
intermediacy
BR ˌɪntə'miːdɪəs|i, -ɪz
AM ˌɪn(t)ər'midiəsi, -z
intermediary
BR ˌɪntə'miːdɪər|i, -ɪz
AM ˌɪn(t)ər'midiˌɛri, -z
intermediate
BR ˌɪntə'miːdɪət, -s
AM ˌɪn(t)ər'midiət, -s

intermediately
BR ˌɪntə'miːdɪətli
AM ˌɪn(t)ər'midiətli
intermediateness
BR ˌɪntə'miːdɪətnəs
AM ˌɪn(t)ər'midiətnəs
intermediation
BR ˌɪntəˌmiːdɪ'eɪʃn, -z
AM ˌɪn(t)ərˌmidi'eɪʃən, -z
intermediator
BR ˌɪntə'miːdɪeɪtə(r), -z
AM ˌɪn(t)ər'midiˌeɪdər, -z
intermedium
BR ˌɪntə'miːdɪəm
AM ˌɪn(t)ər'midiəm
interment
BR ɪn'təːm(ə)nt, -s
AM ɪn'tərmənt, -s
intermesh
BR ˌɪntə'meʃ, -ɪz, -ɪŋ, -t
AM ˌɪn(t)ər'meʃ, -əz, -ɪŋ, -t
intermezzo
BR ˌɪntə'metsəʊ, -z
AM ˌɪn(t)ər'metsou, -z
interminable
BR ɪn'təːmɪnəbl
AM ɪn'tərmənəbəl
interminableness
BR ɪn'təːmɪnəblnəs
AM ɪn'tərmənəbəlnəs
interminably
BR ɪn'təːmɪnəbli
AM ɪn'tərmənəbli
intermingle
BR ˌɪntə'mɪŋgl, -z, -ɪŋ, -d
AM ˌɪn(t)ər'mɪŋgəl, -əlz, -(ə)lɪŋ, -əld
intermission
BR ˌɪntə'mɪʃn, -z
AM ˌɪn(t)ər'mɪʃən, -z
intermit
BR ˌɪntə'mɪt, -s, -ɪŋ, -ɪd
AM ˌɪn(t)ər'mɪ|t, -ts, -dɪŋ, -dɪd
intermittence
BR ˌɪntə'mɪt(ə)ns, -ɪz
AM ˌɪn(t)ər'mɪtns, -əz
intermittency
BR ˌɪntə'mɪt(ə)nsi
AM ˌɪn(t)ər'mɪtnsi
intermittent
BR ˌɪntə'mɪt(ə)nt
AM ˌɪn(t)ər'mɪtnt
intermittently
BR ˌɪntə'mɪt(ə)ntli
AM ˌɪn(t)ər'mɪtn(t)li
intermix
BR ˌɪntə'mɪks, -ɪz, -ɪŋ, -t
AM ˌɪn(t)ər'mɪks, -ɪz, -ɪŋ, -t
intermixable
BR ˌɪntə'mɪksəbl
AM ˌɪn(t)ər'mɪksəbəl

intermixture
BR ˌɪntə'mɪkstʃə(r), -z
AM ˌɪn(t)ər'mɪkstʃər, -z
intermolecular
BR ˌɪntəmə'lekjʉlə(r)
AM ˌɪn(t)ərmə'lekjələr
intern[1]
noun
BR 'ɪntəːn, -z
AM 'ɪnˌtərn, -z
intern[2]
verb
BR ɪn'təːn, -z, -ɪŋ, -d
AM ɪn'tərn, -z, -ɪŋ, -d
internal
BR ɪn'təːnl
AM ɪn'tərnəl
internalisation
BR ɪnˌtəːnl̩ʌɪ'zeɪʃn, ɪnˌtəːnəlʌɪ'zeɪʃn
AM ɪnˌtərnl̩ə'zeɪʃən, ɪnˌtərnlˌaɪ'zeɪʃən
internalise
BR ɪn'təːnl̩ʌɪz, ɪn'təːnəlʌɪz, -ɪz, -ɪŋ, -d
AM ɪn'tərnl̩ˌaɪz, -ɪz, -ɪŋ, -d
internality
BR ˌɪntəː'nalɪti
AM ˌɪntər'nælədi
internalization
BR ɪnˌtəːnl̩ʌɪ'zeɪʃn, ɪnˌtəːnəlʌɪ'zeɪʃn
AM ɪnˌtərnl̩ə'zeɪʃən, ɪnˌtərnlˌaɪ'zeɪʃən
internalize
BR ɪn'təːnl̩ʌɪz, ɪn'təːnəlʌɪz, -ɪz, -ɪŋ, -d
AM ɪn'tərnl̩ˌaɪz, -ɪz, -ɪŋ, -d
internally
BR ɪn'təːnl̩i, ɪn'təːnəli
AM ɪn'tərnəli
international
BR ˌɪntə'naʃn(ə)l, ˌɪntə'naʃən(ə)l, -z
AM ˌɪn(t)ər'næʃ(ə)nəl, -z
Internationale
BR ˌɪntəˌnaʃ(ɪ)ə'nɑːl, ˌɪntəˌnaʃ(ɪ)ə'nal
AM ˌɪn(t)ərˌnæʃə'næl, ˌɪn(t)ərˌnæʃə'nal
FR ɛ̃tɛʁnasjɔnal
internationalisation
BR ˌɪntəˌnaʃnəlʌɪ'zeɪʃn, ˌɪntəˌnaʃn̩lʌɪ'zeɪʃn, ˌɪntəˌnaʃənlʌɪ'zeɪʃn, ˌɪntəˌnaʃ(ə)nəlʌɪ'zeɪʃn
AM ˌɪn(t)ər'næʃənlə'zeɪʃən, ˌɪn(t)ər'næʃnələ'zeɪʃən, ˌɪn(t)ər'næʃnl̩ˌaɪ'zeɪʃən,

,ın(t)ər,næʃnəl‚aɪ-
'zeɪʃən

internationalise
BR ,ıntə'naʃnəlʌɪz,
,ıntə'naʃn̩ʌɪz,
,ıntə'naʃənlʌɪz,
,ıntə'naʃ(ə)nəlʌɪz, -ɪz,
-ıŋ, -d
AM ,ın(t)ər'næʃənl‚aɪz,
,ın(t)ər'næʃnəl‚aɪz,
-ɪz, -ıŋ, -d

internationalism
BR ,ıntə'naʃnəlɪz(ə)m,
,ıntə'naʃn̩ɪz(ə)m,
,ıntə'naʃənlɪz(ə)m,
,ıntə'naʃ(ə)nəlɪz(ə)m
AM ,ın(t)ər'næʃənl‚ızəm,
,ın(t)ər'næʃnəl‚ızəm

internationalist
BR ,ıntə'naʃnəlıst,
,ıntə'naʃn̩ıst,
,ıntə'naʃənlıst,
,ıntə'naʃ(ə)nəlıst, -s
AM ,ın(t)ər'næʃənl‚əst,
,ın(t)ər'næʃnələst, -s

internationality
BR ,ıntə,naʃə'nalıti
AM ,ın(t)ər,næʃ(ə)'næl-
ədi

**internationaliz-
ation**
BR ,ıntə,naʃnəlʌɪ'zeɪʃn,
,ıntə,naʃn̩ʌɪ'zeɪʃn,
,ıntə,naʃənlʌɪ'zeɪʃn,
,ıntə,naʃ(ə)nəlʌɪ'zeɪʃn
AM ,ın(t)ər,næʃənlə-
'zeɪʃn,
,ın(t)ər,næʃnələ'zeɪʃən,
,ın(t)ər,næʃnl‚aɪ-
'zeɪʃən,
,ın(t)ər,næʃnəl‚aɪ-
'zeɪʃən

internationalize
BR ,ıntə'naʃnəlʌɪz,
,ıntə'naʃn̩ʌɪz,
,ıntə'naʃənlʌɪz,
,ıntə'naʃ(ə)nəlʌɪz, -ɪz,
-ıŋ, -d
AM ,ın(t)ər'næʃənl‚aɪz,
,ın(t)ər'næʃnəl‚aɪz,
-ɪz, -ıŋ, -d

internationally
BR ,ıntə'naʃn̩əli,
,ıntə'naʃn̩li,
,ıntə'naʃənli,
,ıntə'naʃ(ə)nəli
AM ,ın(t)ər'næʃ(ə)nəli

interne
BR 'ıntə:n, -z
AM 'ın‚tərn, -z

internecine
BR ,ıntə'ni:sʌɪn
AM ,ın(t)ər'nɛ‚sin,
,ın(t)ər'nisɪn

internee
BR ,ıntə:'ni:, -z
AM ,ın‚tər'ni:, -z

internist
BR ın'tə:nıst, -s

internment
BR ın'tə:nm(ə)nt, -s
AM ın'tərnmənt, -s

internode
BR 'ıntənəʊd, -z
AM 'ın(t)ər‚noʊd, -z

internship
BR 'ıntə:nʃıp, -s
AM 'ın‚tərn‚ʃıp, -s

internuclear
BR ,ıntə'nju:klıə(r)
AM ,ın(t)ər'n(j)ʊkliər

internuncial
BR ,ıntə'nʌnsıəl
AM ,ın(t)ər'nənsiəl

internuncio
BR ,ıntə'nʌnsıəʊ, -z
AM ,ın(t)ər'nənsioʊ, -z

interoceanic
BR ,ıntər‚əʊʃı'anık,
,ıntər‚əʊsı'anık
AM ,ın(t)ər‚oʊʃi'ænık

interoceptive
BR ,ınt(ə)rə'sɛptıv
AM ,ın(t)ərə-
'sɛptıv

interoperability
BR ,ıntər‚ɒp(ə)rə'bılıti
AM ,ın(t)ər‚ɑp(ə)rə'bıl-
ɪdi

interoperable
BR ,ıntər'ɒp(ə)rəbl
AM ,ın(t)ər'ɑp(ə)rəbəl

interosculate
BR ,ıntər'ɒskjʊleıt, -s,
-ıŋ, -ɪd
AM ,ın(t)ər'ɑskjə‚leı|t,
-ts, -dıŋ, -dıd

interosseous
BR ,ıntər'ɒsıəs
AM ,ın(t)ər'ɑsiəs

interpage
BR ,ıntə'peıdʒ, -ız, -ıŋ,
-d
AM ,ın(t)ər'peıdʒ, -ız,
-ıŋ, -d

interparietal
BR ,ıntəpə'rʌɪtl
AM ,ın(t)ərpə'raıdl

interparietally
BR ,ıntəpə'rʌɪtļi
AM ,ın(t)ərpə'raıdļi

interpellate
BR ın'tə:pəleıt,
,ıntə'pɛleıt, -s, -ıŋ, -ɪd
AM ,ın(t)ər'pɛ‚leı|t,
ın'tərpə‚leı|t, -ts, -dıŋ,
-dɪd

interpellation
BR ın,tə:pə'leıʃn,
,ıntəpə'leıʃn, -z
AM ın‚tərpə'leıʃən,
,ın(t)ərpə'leıʃən, -z

interpellator
BR ın'tə:pəleıtə(r), -z
AM ,ın(t)ər'pɛ‚leıdər,
ın'tərpə‚leıdər, -z

interpenetrate
BR ,ıntə'pɛnıtreıt, -s,
-ıŋ, -ɪd
AM ,ın(t)ər'pɛnə‚treı|t,
-ts, -dıŋ, -dıd

interpenetration
BR ,ıntə,penı'treıʃn
AM ,ın(t)ər,pɛnə'treıʃən

interpenetrative
BR ,ıntə'pɛnıtrətıv
AM ,ın(t)ər'pɛnə‚treıdıv,
,ın(t)ər'pɛnətrədıv

interpersonal
BR ,ıntə'pə:sn̩(ə)l,
,ıntə'pə:sən(ə)l
AM ,ın(t)ər'pərs(ə)nəl

interpersonally
BR ,ıntə'pə:sn̩əli,
,ıntə'pə:sn̩li,
,ıntə'pə:sən̩li,
,ıntə'pə:s(ə)nəli
AM ,ın(t)ər'pərs(ə)nəli

interplait
BR ,ıntə'plat, -s, -ıŋ, -ɪd
AM ,ın(t)ər'pl|eıt,
,ın(t)ər'l|æt,
-eıts \-æts,
-eıdıŋ \-ædıŋ,
-eıdıd \-ædəd

interplanetary
BR ,ıntə'planıt(ə)ri
AM ,ın(t)ər'plænə‚tɛri

interplay
BR 'ıntəpleı
AM 'ın(t)ər‚pleı

interplead
BR ,ıntə'pli:d, -z, -ıŋ, -ɪd
AM ,ın(t)ər'plid, -z, -ıŋ,
-ɪd

interpleader
BR ,ıntə'pli:də(r), -z
AM ,ın(t)ər'plidər, -z

Interpol
BR 'ıntəpɒl
AM 'ın(t)ər‚poʊl

interpolate
BR ın'tə:pəleıt, -s, -ıŋ,
-ɪd
AM ın'tərpə‚leı|t, -ts,
-dıŋ, -dıd

interpolation
BR ın,tə:pə'leıʃn, -z
AM ın‚tərpə'leıʃən, -z

interpolative
BR ın'tə:pəlatıv
AM ın'tərpə‚leıdıv,
ın'tərpələdıv

interpolator
BR ın'tə:pəleıtə(r), -z
AM ın'tərpə‚leıdər, -z

interposal
BR ,ıntə'pəʊzl, -z
AM ,ın(t)ər'poʊzəl, -z

interpose
BR ,ıntə'pəʊz, -ız, -ıŋ, -d
AM ,ın(t)ər'poʊz, -əz,
-ıŋ, -t

interposition
BR ,ıntəpə'zıʃn
AM ,ın(t)ərpə'zıʃən

interpret
BR ın'tə:prıt, -s, -ıŋ, -ɪd
AM ın'tərprə|t, -ts, -dıŋ,
-dəd

interpretability
BR ın,tə:prıtə'bılıti
AM ın,tərprədə'bılıdi

interpretable
BR ın'tə:prıtəbl
AM ın'tərprədəbəl

interpretation
BR ın,tə:prı'teıʃn, -z
AM ın,tərprə'teıʃən, -z

interpretational
BR ın,tə:prı'teıʃn(ə)l,
ın,tə:prı'teıʃ(ə)n(ə)l
AM ın,tərprə'teıʃ(ə)nəl

interpretative
BR ın'tə:prıtətıv
AM ın'tərprə‚teıdıv,
ın'tərprədədıv

interpreter
BR ın'tə:prıtə(r), -z
AM ın'tərprədər, -z

interpretive
BR ın'tə:prıtıv
AM ın'tərprədıv

interpretively
BR ın'tə:prıtıvli
AM ın'tərprədıvli

interprovincial
BR ,ıntəprə'vınʃl
AM ,ın(t)ərprə'vınʃəl

interracial
BR ,ıntə'reıʃl
AM ,ın(t)ər'reıʃəl

interracially
BR ,ıntə'reıʃļi,
,ıntə'reıʃəli
AM ,ın(t)ər'reıʃəli

interregna
BR ,ıntə'rɛgnə(r)
AM ,ın(t)ər'rɛgnə

interregnum
BR ,ıntə'rɛgnəm, -z
AM ,ın(t)ər'rɛgnəm, -z

interrelate
BR ,ıntərı'leıt, -s, -ıŋ,
-ɪd
AM ,ın(t)ərə'leı|t, -ts,
-dıŋ, -dɪd

interrelation
BR ,ıntərı'leıʃn, -z
AM ,ın(t)ərə'leıʃən, -z

interrelationship
BR ,ıntərı'leıʃnʃıp, -s
AM ,ın(t)ərə'leıʃən‚ʃıp,
-s

interrogate
BR ın'tɛrəgeıt, -s, -ıŋ,
-ɪd
AM ın'tɛrə‚geı|t, -ts,
-dıŋ, -dɪd

interrogation
BR ın,tɛrə'geıʃn, -z

interrogational
AM ɪn‚tɛrə'geɪʃən, -z

interrogational
BR ɪn‚tɛrə'geɪʃɳ(ə)l,
ɪn‚tɛrə'geɪʃən(ə)l
AM ɪn‚tɛrə'geɪʃ(ə)nəl

interrogative
BR ‚ɪntə'rɒgətɪv, -z
AM ‚ɪn(t)ə'rɑgədɪv, -z

interrogatively
BR ‚ɪntə'rɒgətɪvli
AM ‚ɪn(t)ə'rɑgədəvli

interrogator
BR ɪn'tɛrəgeɪtə(r), -z
AM ɪn'tɛrə‚geɪdər, -z

interrogatory
BR ‚ɪntə'rɒgət(ə)ri
AM ‚ɪn(t)ə'rɑgə‚tɔri

interrupt
BR ‚ɪntə'rʌpt, -s, -ɪŋ, -ɪd
AM ‚ɪn(t)ə'rəpt, -s, -ɪŋ, -əd

interrupter
BR ‚ɪntə'rʌptə(r), -z
AM ‚ɪn(t)ə'rəptər, -z

interruptible
BR ‚ɪntə'rʌptɪbl
AM ‚ɪn(t)ə'rəptəbəl

interruption
BR ‚ɪntə'rʌpʃn, -z
AM ‚ɪn(t)ə'rəpʃən, -z

interruptive
BR ‚ɪntə'rʌptɪv
AM ‚ɪn(t)ə'rəptɪv

interruptor
BR ‚ɪntə'rʌptə(r), -z
AM ‚ɪn(t)ə'rəptər, -z

interruptory
BR ‚ɪntə'rʌpt(ə)ri
AM ‚ɪn(t)ə'rəpt(ə)ri

intersect
BR ‚ɪntə'sɛkt, -s, -ɪŋ, -ɪd
AM ‚ɪn(t)ər'sɛk|(t),
-(t)s, -tɪŋ, -təd

intersection[1]
dividing
BR ‚ɪntə'sɛkʃn, -z
AM ‚ɪn(t)ər'sɛkʃən, -z

intersection[2]
road
BR 'ɪntə‚sɛkʃn, -z
AM 'ɪn(t)ər‚sɛkʃən, -z

intersectional
BR ‚ɪntə'sɛkʃɳ(ə)l,
‚ɪntə'sɛkʃən(ə)l
AM ‚ɪn(t)ər'sɛkʃ(ə)nəl

interseptal
BR ‚ɪntə'sɛptl
AM ‚ɪn(t)ər'sɛptl

intersex
BR 'ɪntəsɛks, -ɪz
AM 'ɪn(t)ər'sɛks, -əz

intersexual
BR ‚ɪntə'sɛkʃuəl,
‚ɪntə'sɛkʃ(ʉ)l,
‚ɪntə'sɛksjʊ(ə)l
AM ‚ɪn(t)ər'sɛkʃ(əw)əl

intersexuality
BR ‚ɪntə‚sɛkʃu'alɪt|i,
‚ɪntə‚sɛksju'alɪt|i, -ɪz
AM ‚ɪn(t)ər‚sɛkʃə'wæl-
ədi, -z

intersexually
BR ‚ɪntə'sɛkʃuəli,
‚ɪntə'sɛkʃʉli,
‚ɪntə'sɛkʃli,
‚ɪntə'sɛksjʊ(ə)li
AM ‚ɪn(t)ər'sɛkʃ(əw)əli

interspace[1]
noun
BR 'ɪntəspeɪs, -ɪz
AM 'ɪn(t)ər‚speɪs, -ɪz

interspace[2]
verb
BR ‚ɪntə'speɪs, -ɪz, -ɪŋ, -t
AM ‚ɪn(t)ər'speɪs, -ɪz, -ɪŋ, -t

interspecific
BR ‚ɪntəspɪ'sɪfɪk
AM ‚ɪn(t)ərspə'sɪfɪk

intersperse
BR ‚ɪntə'spə:s, -ɪz, -ɪŋ, -t
AM ‚ɪn(t)ər'spərs, -ɪz, -ɪŋ, -t

interspersion
BR ‚ɪntə'spə:ʃn
AM ‚ɪn(t)ər'spərʒən

interspinal
BR ‚ɪntə'spʌɪnl
AM ‚ɪn(t)ər'spaɪnəl

interspinous
BR ‚ɪntə'sɛptl
AM ‚ɪn(t)ər'spaɪnəs

interstate
BR ‚ɪntə'steɪt
AM ‚ɪn(t)ər'steɪt

interstellar
BR ‚ɪntə'stɛlə(r)
AM ‚ɪn(t)ər'stɛlər

interstice
BR ɪn'tə:stɪs, -ɪz
AM ɪn'tərstəs, -əz

interstitial
BR ‚ɪntə'stɪʃl
AM ‚ɪn(t)ər'stɪʃəl

interstitially
BR ‚ɪntə'stɪʃli,
‚ɪntə'stɪʃəli
AM ‚ɪn(t)ər'stɪʃəli

intertextuality
BR ‚ɪntə‚tɛkstjʊ'alɪti,
‚ɪntə‚tɛkstʃʊ'alɪt|i, -ɪz
AM ‚ɪn(t)ər‚tɛk(st)ʃə-
'wælədi, -z

intertidal
BR ‚ɪntə'tʌɪdl
AM ‚ɪn(t)ər'taɪdəl

intertribal
BR ‚ɪntə'trʌɪbl
AM ‚ɪn(t)ər'traɪbəl

intertrigo
BR ‚ɪntə'trʌɪgəʊ, -z
AM ‚ɪn(t)ər'traɪ‚goʊ, -z

intertwine
BR ‚ɪntə'twʌɪn, -z, -ɪŋ, -d
AM ‚ɪn(t)ər'twaɪn, -z, -ɪŋ, -d

intertwinement
BR ‚ɪntə'twʌɪnm(ə)nt, -s
AM ‚ɪn(t)ər'twaɪnmənt, -s

intertwist
BR ‚ɪntə'twɪst, -s, -ɪŋ, -ɪd
AM ‚ɪn(t)ər'twɪst, -s, -ɪŋ, -əd

interval
BR 'ɪntəvl, -z
AM 'ɪn(t)ərvəl, -z

intervallic
BR ‚ɪntə'valɪk
AM ‚ɪn(t)ər'vælɪk

intervene
BR ‚ɪntə'vi:n, -z, -ɪŋ, -d
AM ‚ɪn(t)ər'vin, -z, -ɪŋ, -d

intervener
BR ‚ɪntə'vi:nə(r), -z
AM ‚ɪn(t)ər'vinər, -z

intervenient
BR ‚ɪntə'vi:nɪənt
AM ‚ɪn(t)ər'vinɪənt

intervenor
BR ‚ɪntə'vi:nə(r), -z
AM ‚ɪn(t)ər'vinər, -z

intervention
BR ‚ɪntə'vɛnʃn, -z
AM ‚ɪn(t)ər'vɛn(t)ʃən, -z

interventionism
BR ‚ɪntə'vɛnʃɳɪz(ə)m
AM ‚ɪn(t)ər'vɛn(t)ʃə‚nɪzəm

interventionist
BR ‚ɪntə'vɛnʃɳɪst, -s
AM ‚ɪn(t)ər'vɛn(t)ʃən-əst, -s

intervertebral
BR ‚ɪntə'və:tɪbr(ə)l
AM ‚ɪn(t)ər'vɜrdəbrəl

interview
BR 'ɪntəvju:, -z, -ɪŋ, -d
AM 'ɪn(t)ər‚vju, -z, -ɪŋ, -d

interviewee
BR ‚ɪntəvju:'i:, -z
AM ‚ɪn(t)ər‚vju'i, -z

interviewer
BR 'ɪntəvju:ə(r), -z
AM 'ɪn(t)ər‚vjuər, -z

inter vivos
BR ‚ɪntə 'vi:vəʊs
AM ‚ɪn(t)ər ‚vi‚voʊs,
+ ‚vaɪ‚voʊs

interwar
BR ‚ɪntə'wɔ:(r)
AM ‚ɪn(t)ər'wɔ(ə)r

interweave
BR ‚ɪntə'wi:v, -z, -ɪŋ

interweave (cont.)
AM ‚ɪn(t)ər'wiv, -z, -ɪŋ

interwind
BR ‚ɪntə'wʌɪnd, -z, -ɪŋ
AM ‚ɪn(t)ər'waɪnd, -z, -ɪŋ

interwork
BR ‚ɪntə'wə:k, -s, -ɪŋ, -t
AM ‚ɪn(t)ər'wərk, -s, -ɪŋ, -t

interwound
BR ‚ɪntə'waʊnd
AM ‚ɪn(t)ər'waʊnd

interwove
BR ‚ɪntə'wəʊv
AM ‚ɪn(t)ər'woʊv

interwoven
BR ‚ɪntə'wəʊvn
AM ‚ɪn(t)ər'woʊvən

intestacy
BR ɪn'tɛstəsi
AM ɪn'tɛstəsi

intestate
BR ɪn'tɛsteɪt, ɪn'tɛstət
AM ɪn'tɛ‚steɪt, ɪn'tɛstət

intestinal
BR ɪn'tɛstɪnl,
‚ɪntɛ'staɪnl
AM ɪn'tɛstənəl

intestine
BR ɪn'tɛst(ɪ)n, -z
AM ɪn'tɛstən, -z

inthrall
BR ɪn'θrɔ:l
AM ɪn'θrɔl, ɪn'θrɑl

intifada
BR ‚ɪntɪ'fɑ:də(r), -z
AM ‚ɪn(t)ə'fɑdə, -z

intimacy
BR 'ɪntɪməs|i, -ɪz
AM 'ɪn(t)əməsi, -z

intimate[1]
noun, adjective
BR 'ɪntɪmət, -s
AM 'ɪn(t)əmət, -s

intimate[2]
verb
BR 'ɪntɪmeɪt, -s, -ɪŋ, -ɪd
AM 'ɪn(t)ə‚meɪ|t, -ts, -dɪŋ, -dɪd

intimately
BR 'ɪntɪmətli
AM 'ɪn(t)əmətli

intimater
BR 'ɪntɪmeɪtə(r), -z
AM 'ɪn(t)ə‚meɪdər, -z

intimation
BR ‚ɪntɪ'meɪʃn, -z
AM ‚ɪn(t)ə'meɪʃən, -z

intimidate
BR ɪn'tɪmɪdeɪt, -s, -ɪŋ, -ɪd
AM ɪn'tɪmə‚deɪ|t, -ts, -dɪŋ, -dɪd

intimidatingly
BR ɪn'tɪmɪdeɪtɪŋli
AM ɪn'tɪmə‚deɪdɪŋli

intimidation
BR ɪnˌtɪmɪˈdeɪʃn
AM ɪnˌtɪməˈdeɪʃən

intimidator
BR ɪnˈtɪmɪdeɪtə(r), -z
AM ɪnˈtɪməˌdeɪdər, -z

intimidatory
BR ɪnˌtɪmɪˈdeɪt(ə)ri
AM ɪnˈtɪmədəˌtɔri

intinction
BR ɪnˈtɪŋ(k)ʃn, -z
AM ɪnˈstɪŋ(k)ʃən, -z

intitule
BR ɪnˈtɪtjuːl, ɪnˈtɪtʃuːl,
-z, -ɪŋ, -d
AM ɪnˈtɪˌtʃʊl, ɪnˈtɪtʃəl,
-z, -ɪŋ, -d

into¹
strong form
BR ˈɪntuː
AM ˈɪntu

into²
*weak form, before
consonants*
BR ˈɪntə
AM ˈɪn(t)ə

into³
*weak form, before
vowels*
BR ˈɪntʊ
AM ˈɪn(t)ʊ

intolerable
BR ɪnˈtɒl(ə)rəbl
AM ɪnˈtɑl(ə)rəbəl,
ɪnˈtɑlərbəl

intolerableness
BR ɪnˈtɒl(ə)rəblnəs
AM ɪnˈtɑl(ə)rəbəlnəs,
ɪnˈtɑlərbəlnəs

intolerably
BR ɪnˈtɒl(ə)rəbli
AM ɪnˈtɑl(ə)rəbli,
ɪnˈtɑlərbli

intolerance
BR ɪnˈtɒl(ə)rəns,
ɪnˈtɒl(ə)rn̩s
AM ɪnˈtɑl(ə)rəns

intolerant
BR ɪnˈtɒl(ə)rənt,
ɪnˈtɒl(ə)rn̩t
AM ɪnˈtɑl(ə)rənt

intolerantly
BR ɪnˈtɒl(ə)rəntli,
ɪnˈtɒl(ə)rn̩tli
AM ɪnˈtɑl(ə)rən(t)li

intonate
BR ˈɪntəneɪt, -s, -ɪŋ, -ɪd
AM ˈɪn(t)əˌneɪt, -ts,
-dɪŋ, -dɪd

intonation
BR ˌɪntəˈneɪʃn, -z
AM ˌɪn(t)əˈneɪʃən,
ˌɪntoʊˈneɪʃən, -z

intonational
BR ˌɪntəˈneɪʃn̩(ə)l,
ˌɪntəˈneɪʃən(ə)l
AM ˌɪn(t)əˈneɪʃ(ə)nəl,
ˌɪntoʊˈneɪʃ(ə)nəl

intone
BR ɪnˈtəʊn, -z, -ɪŋ, -d
AM ɪnˈtoʊn, -z, -ɪŋ, -d

intoner
BR ɪnˈtəʊnə(r), -z
AM ɪnˈtoʊnər, -z

in toto
BR ˌɪn ˈtəʊtəʊ
AM ˌɪn ˈtoʊdoʊ

intoxicant
BR ɪnˈtɒksɪk(ə)nt, -s
AM ɪnˈtɑksəkənt, -s

intoxicate
BR ɪnˈtɒksɪkeɪt, -s, -ɪŋ,
-ɪd
AM ɪnˈtɑksəkeɪ|t, -ts,
-dɪŋ, -dɪd

intoxicatingly
BR ɪnˈtɒksɪkeɪtɪŋli
AM ɪnˈtɑksəkeɪdɪŋli

intoxication
BR ɪnˌtɒksɪˈkeɪʃn
AM ɪnˌtɑksəˈkeɪʃən

intracellular
BR ˌɪntrəˈseljʊlə(r)
AM ˌɪntrəˈseljələr

intracranial
BR ˌɪntrəˈkreɪniəl
AM ˌɪntrəˈkreɪniəl

intracranially
BR ˌɪntrəˈkreɪniəli
AM ˌɪntrəˈkreɪniəli

intractability
BR ɪnˌtræktəˈbɪlɪti
AM ˌɪnˌtræktəˈbɪlɪdi,
ɪnˌtræktəˈbɪlɪdi

intractable
BR ɪnˈtræktəbl
AM ˌɪnˈtræktəbəl,
ɪnˈtræktəbəl

intractableness
BR ɪnˈtræktəblnəs
AM ˌɪnˈtræktəbəlnəs,
ɪnˈtræktəbəlnəs

intractably
BR ɪnˈtræktəbli
AM ˌɪnˈtræktəbli,
ɪnˈtræktəbli

intrados
BR ˈɪntrɑdɒs, -ɪz
AM ˈɪntrəˌdɑs,
ˈɪntrəˌdoʊs, -əz

intramolecular
BR ˌɪntrəməˈlekjʊlə(r)
AM ˌɪntrəməˈlekjələr

intramural
BR ˌɪntrəˈmjʊərəl,
ˌɪntrəˈmjʊər̩l,
ˌɪntrəˈmjɔːrəl,
AM ˌɪntrəˈmjur(ə)l

intramurally
BR ˌɪntrəˈmjʊərəli,
ˌɪntrəˈmjʊər̩li,
ˌɪntrəˈmjɔːrəli,
ˌɪntrəˈmjɔːr̩li
AM ˌɪntrəˈmjur(ə)li

intramuscular
BR ˌɪntrəˈmʌskjʊlə(r)
AM ˌɪntrəˈməskjələr

intranational
BR ˌɪntrəˈnaʃn̩(ə)l,
ˌɪntrəˈnaʃən(ə)l
AM ˌɪntrəˈnæʃ(ə)nəl

Intranet
BR ˈɪntrənet
AM ˈɪntrəˌnet

intransigence
BR ɪnˈtransɪdʒ(ə)ns,
ɪnˈtranzɪdʒ(ə)ns,
ɪnˈtrɑːnsɪdʒ(ə)ns,
ɪnˈtrɑːnzɪdʒ(ə)ns
AM ɪnˈtrænsədʒəns,
ɪnˈtrænzədʒəns

intransigency
BR ɪnˈtransɪdʒ(ə)ns|i,
ɪnˈtranzɪdʒ(ə)ns|i,
ɪnˈtrɑːnsɪdʒ(ə)ns|i,
ɪnˈtrɑːnzɪdʒ(ə)ns|i,
-ɪz
AM ɪnˈtrænsədʒənsi,
ɪnˈtrænzədʒənsi, -z

intransigent
BR ɪnˈtransɪdʒ(ə)nt,
ɪnˈtranzɪdʒ(ə)nt,
ɪnˈtrɑːnsɪdʒ(ə)nt,
ɪnˈtrɑːnzɪdʒ(ə)nt
AM ɪnˈtrænsədʒənt,
ɪnˈtrænzədʒənt

intransigently
BR ɪnˈtransɪdʒ(ə)ntli,
ɪnˈtranzɪdʒ(ə)ntli,
ɪnˈtrɑːnsɪdʒ(ə)ntli,
ɪnˈtrɑːnzɪdʒ(ə)ntli
AM ɪnˈtrænsədʒən(t)li,
ɪnˈtrænzədʒən(t)li

intransitive
BR ɪnˈtransɪtɪv,
ɪnˈtranzɪtɪv,
ɪnˈtrɑːnsɪtɪv,
ɪnˈtrɑːnzɪtɪv
AM ɪnˈtrænzədɪv

intransitively
BR ɪnˈtransɪtɪvli,
ɪnˈtranzɪtɪvli,
ɪnˈtrɑːnsɪtɪvli,
ɪnˈtrɑːnzɪtɪvli
AM ɪnˈtrænzədəvli

intransitivity
BR ɪnˌtransɪˈtɪvɪti,
ɪnˌtranzɪˈtɪvɪti,
ɪnˌtrɑːnsɪˈtɪvɪti,
ɪnˌtrɑːnzɪˈtɪvɪti
AM ɪnˌtrænzəˈtɪvɪdi

intrapreneur
BR ˌɪntrəprəˈnəː(r)
AM ˌɪntrəprəˈnər,
ˌɪntrəprəˈnʊ(ə)r

intrauterine
BR ˌɪntrəˈjuːtərʌɪn
AM ˌɪntrəˈjudərən,
ˈɪntrəˈjudəraɪn

intravasate
BR ɪnˈtravəseɪt, -s, -ɪŋ,
-ɪd

AM ɪnˈtrævəˌseɪ|t, -ts,
-dɪŋ, -dɪd

intravasation
BR ɪnˌtravəˈseɪʃn, -z
AM ɪnˌtrævəˈseɪʃən, -z

intravenous
BR ˌɪntrəˈviːnəs
AM ˌɪntrəˈvinəs

intravenously
BR ˌɪntrəˈviːnəsli
AM ˌɪntrəˈvinəsli

in-tray
BR ˈɪntreɪ, -z
AM ˈɪnˌtreɪ, -z

intrench
BR ɪnˈtren(t)ʃ, -ɪz, -ɪŋ,
-t
AM ɪnˈtren(t)ʃ, -əz, -ɪŋ,
-t

intrenchment
BR ɪnˈtren(t)ʃm(ə)nt,
-s
AM ɪnˈtren(t)ʃmənt, -s

intrepid
BR ɪnˈtrepɪd
AM ɪnˈtrepəd

intrepidity
BR ˌɪntrɪˈpɪdɪti,
ˌɪntrɛˈpɪdɪti
AM ˌɪntrəˈpɪdɪdi,
ˌɪntrɛˈpɪdɪdi

intrepidly
BR ɪnˈtrepɪdli
AM ɪnˈtrepədli

intricacy
BR ˈɪntrɪkəs|i, -ɪz
AM ˈɪntrəkəsi, -z

intricate
BR ˈɪntrɪkət
AM ˈɪntrəkət

intricately
BR ˈɪntrɪkətli
AM ˈɪntrəkətli

intrigant
BR ˈɪntrɪg(ə)nt, -s
AM ˈɪntrəˌgɑnt, -s

intrigante
BR ˈɪntrɪg(ə)nt, -s
AM ˈɪntrəˌgɑnt, -s

intrigue¹
noun
BR ˈɪntriːg, -z
AM ˈɪnˌtrig, ɪnˈtrig, -z

intrigue²
verb
BR ɪnˈtriːg, -z, -ɪŋ, -d
AM ɪnˈtrig, -z, -ɪŋ, -d

intriguer
BR ɪnˈtriːgə(r), -z
AM ɪnˈtrigər, -z

intriguingly
BR ɪnˈtriːgɪŋli
AM ɪnˈtrigɪŋli

intrinsic
BR ɪnˈtrɪnsɪk,
ɪnˈtrɪnzɪk
AM ɪnˈtrɪnzɪk,
ɪnˈtrɪnsɪk

intrinsically
BR ɪnˈtrɪnsɪkli,
ɪnˈtrɪnzɪkli
AM ɪnˈtrɪnzək(ə)li,
ɪnˈtrɪnsək(ə)li
intro
BR ˈɪntrəʊ, -z
AM ˈɪntroʊ, -z
introduce
BR ˌɪntrəˈdjuːs,
ˌɪntrəˈdʒuːs, -ɪz, -ɪŋ, -t
AM ˈɪntrəˈd(j)us,
ˈɪntroʊˈd(j)us, -əz, -ɪŋ,
-t
introducer
BR ˌɪntrəˈdjuːsə(r),
ˌɪntrəˈdʒuːsə(r), -z
AM ˈɪntrəˈd(j)usər,
ˈɪntroʊˈd(j)usər, -z
introducible
BR ˌɪntrəˈdjuːsɪbl,
ˌɪntrəˈdʒuːsɪbl
AM ˈɪntrəˈd(j)usəbəl,
ˈɪntroʊˈd(j)usəbəl
introduction
BR ˌɪntrəˈdʌkʃn, -z
AM ˈɪntrəˈdəkʃən,
ˈɪntroʊˈdəkʃən, -z
introductory
BR ˌɪntrəˈdʌkt(ə)ri
AM ˈɪntrəˈdəkt(ə)ri,
ˈɪntroʊˈdəkt(ə)ri
introflexion
BR ˌɪntrə(ʊ)ˈflɛkʃn, -z
AM ˈɪntrəˈflɛkʃən,
ˈɪntroʊˈflɛkʃən, -z
introgression
BR ˌɪntrə(ʊ)ˈgrɛʃn, -z
AM ˈɪntrəˈgrɛʃən,
ˈɪntroʊˈgrɛʃən, -z
introit
BR ˈɪntrɔɪt, -s
AM ˈɪnˌtrɔɪt, ɪnˈtrɔɪt, -s
introjection
BR ˌɪntrə(ʊ)ˈdʒɛkʃn, -z
AM ˈɪntrəˈdʒɛkʃən,
ˈɪntroʊˈdʒɛkʃən, -z
intromission
BR ˌɪntrə(ʊ)ˈmɪʃn, -z
AM ˈɪntrəˈmɪʃən,
ˈɪntroʊˈmɪʃən, -z
intromit
BR ˌɪntrə(ʊ)ˈmɪt, -s, -ɪŋ,
-ɪd
AM ˈɪntrəˈmɪ|t,
ˈɪntroʊˈmɪ|t, -ts, -dɪŋ,
-dɪd
intromittent
BR ˌɪntrə(ʊ)ˈmɪtnt
AM ˈɪntrəˈmɪtnt,
ˈɪntroʊˈmɪtnt
introrse
BR ɪnˈtrɔːs
AM ɪnˈtrɔ(ə)rs
introspect
BR ˌɪntrə(ʊ)ˈspɛkt, -s,
-ɪŋ, -ɪd

AM ˈɪntrəˈspɛk|(t),
ˈɪntroʊˈspɛk|(t), -(t)s,
-tɪŋ, -təd
introspection
BR ˌɪntrə(ʊ)ˈspɛkʃn
AM ˈɪntrəˈspɛkʃən,
ˈɪntroʊˈspɛkʃən
introspective
BR ˌɪntrə(ʊ)ˈspɛktɪv
AM ˈɪntrəˈspɛktɪv,
ˈɪntroʊˈspɛktɪv
introspectively
BR ˌɪntrə(ʊ)ˈspɛktɪvli
AM ˈɪntrəˈspɛktəvli,
ˈɪntroʊˈspɛktəvli
introspectiveness
BR ˌɪntrə(ʊ)ˈspɛktɪvnɪs
AM ˈɪntrəˈspɛktɪvnɪs,
ˈɪntroʊˈspɛktɪvnɪs
introsusception
BR ˌɪntrə(ʊ)səˈsɛpʃn,
-z
AM ˌɪntrəsəˈsɛpʃən, -z
introversible
BR ˌɪntrə(ʊ)ˈvəːsɪbl
AM ˈɪntrəˌvərsəbəl,
ˈɪntroʊˌvərsəbəl
introversion
BR ˌɪntrə(ʊ)ˈvəːʃn
AM ˈɪntrəˈvərʒən,
ˈɪntroʊˈvərʒən
introversive
BR ˌɪntrə(ʊ)ˈvəːsɪv
AM ˈɪntrəˈvərsɪv,
ˈɪntroʊˈvərsɪv
introvert[1]
noun
BR ˈɪntrəvəːt, -s
AM ˈɪntrəˌvərt,
ˈɪntroʊˌvərt, -s
introvert[2]
verb
BR ˌɪntrə(ʊ)ˈvəːt, -s, -ɪŋ,
-ɪd
AM ˈɪntrəˌvər|t,
ˈɪntroʊˌvər|t, -ts, -dɪŋ,
-dəd
introverted
adjective
BR ˈɪntrəvəːtɪd
AM ˈɪntrəˌvərdəd,
ˈɪntroʊˌvərdəd
introvertive
BR ˌɪntrə(ʊ)ˈvəːtɪv
AM ˈɪntrəˌvərdɪv,
ˈɪntroʊˌvərdɪv
intrude
BR ɪnˈtruːd, -z, -ɪŋ, -ɪd
AM ɪnˈtrud, -z, -ɪŋ, -əd
intruder
BR ɪnˈtruːdə(r), -z
AM ɪnˈtrudər, -z
intrudingly
BR ɪnˈtruːdɪŋli
AM ɪnˈtrudɪŋli
intrusion
BR ɪnˈtruːʒn, -z
AM ɪnˈtruʒən, -z

intrusionist
BR ɪnˈtruːʒnɪst, -s
AM ɪnˈtruʒənəst, -s
intrusive
BR ɪnˈtruːsɪv
AM ɪnˈtrusɪv
intrusively
BR ɪnˈtruːsɪvli
AM ɪnˈtrusəvli
intrusiveness
BR ɪnˈtruːsɪvnɪs
AM ɪnˈtrusɪvnɪs
intrust
BR ɪnˈtrʌst, -s, -ɪŋ, -ɪd
AM ɪnˈtrəst, -s, -ɪŋ, -əd
intubate
BR ˈɪntjʉbeɪt,
ˈɪntʃʉbeɪt, -s, -ɪŋ, -ɪd
AM ˈɪntjəˌbeɪ|t, -ts, -dɪŋ,
-dɪd
intubation
BR ˌɪntjʉˈbeɪʃn,
ˌɪntʃʉˈbeɪʃn, -z
AM ˌɪntjəˈbeɪʃən, -z
intuit
BR ɪnˈtjuː|ɪt, ɪnˈtʃuː|ɪt,
-ɪts, -ɪtɪŋ, -ɪtɪd
AM ɪnˈt(j)uə|t, -ts, -dɪŋ,
-dɪd
intuitable
BR ɪnˈtjuːɪtəbl,
ɪnˈtʃuːɪtəbl
AM ɪnˈt(j)uədəbəl
intuition
BR ˌɪntjʊˈɪʃn,
ˌɪntʃʊˈɪʃn, -z
AM ˌɪnt(j)uˈɪʃən,
ˌɪntəˈwɪʃən, -z
intuitional
BR ˌɪntjʊˈɪʃn(ə)l,
ˌɪntjʊˈɪʃən(ə)l,
ˌɪntʃʊˈɪʃn(ə)l,
ˌɪntʃʊˈɪʃən(ə)l
AM ˌɪnt(j)uˈɪʃ(ə)nəl,
ˌɪntəˈwɪʃ(ə)nəl
intuitionalism
BR ˌɪntjʊˈɪʃnəlɪz(ə)m,
ˌɪntjʊˈɪʃn̩ɪz(ə)m,
ˌɪntjʊˈɪʃənlɪz(ə)m,
ˌɪntʃʊˈɪʃ(ə)nəlɪz(ə)m,
ˌɪntʃʊˈɪʃn̩ɪz(ə)m,
ˌɪntʃʊˈɪʃənlɪz(ə)m,
ˌɪntʃʊˈɪʃ(ə)nəlɪz(ə)m
AM ˌɪnt(j)uˈɪʃənlˌɪzəm,
ˌɪntəˈwɪʃənlˌɪzəm,
ˌɪnt(j)uˈɪʃnəˌlɪzəm,
ˌɪntəˈwɪʃnəˌlɪzəm
intuitionalist
BR ˌɪntjʊˈɪʃnəlɪst,
ˌɪntjʊˈɪʃn̩lɪst,
ˌɪntjʊˈɪʃənlɪst,
ˌɪntʃʊˈɪʃnəlɪst,
ˌɪntʃʊˈɪʃn̩lɪst,
ˌɪntʃʊˈɪʃənlɪst,
ˌɪntʃʊˈɪʃ(ə)nəlɪst, -s

AM ˌɪnt(j)uˈɪʃənləst,
ˌɪntəˈwɪʃənləst,
ˌɪnt(j)uˈɪʃnələst,
ˌɪntəˈwɪʃnələst, -s
intuitionism
BR ˌɪntjʊˈɪʃnɪz(ə)m,
ˌɪntjʊˈɪʃənɪz(ə)m,
ˌɪntʃʊˈɪʃnɪz(ə)m,
ˌɪntʃʊˈɪʃənɪz(ə)m
AM ˌɪnt(j)uˈɪʃəˌnɪzəm,
ˌɪntəˈwɪʃəˌnɪzəm
intuitionist
BR ˌɪntjʊˈɪʃnɪst,
ˌɪntjʊˈɪʃənɪst,
ˌɪntʃʊˈɪʃnɪst,
ˌɪntʃʊˈɪʃənɪst, -s
AM ˌɪnt(j)uˈɪʃənəst,
ˌɪntəˈwɪʃənəst, -s
intuitive
BR ɪnˈtjuːɪtɪv,
ɪnˈtʃuːɪtɪv
AM ɪnˈt(j)uədɪv
intuitively
BR ɪnˈtjuːɪtɪvli,
ɪnˈtʃuːɪtɪvli
AM ɪnˈt(j)uədəvli
intuitiveness
BR ɪnˈtjuːɪtɪvnɪs,
ɪnˈtʃuːɪtɪvnɪs
AM ɪnˈt(j)uədɪvnɪs
intuitivism
BR ɪnˈtjuːɪtɪvɪz(ə)m,
ɪnˈtʃuːɪtɪvɪz(ə)m
AM ɪnˈt(j)uədɪˌvɪzəm
intuitivist
BR ɪnˈtjuːɪtɪvɪst,
ɪnˈtʃuːɪtɪvɪst, -s
AM ɪnˈt(j)uədɪvɪst, -s
intumesce
BR ˌɪntjʉˈmɛs,
ˌɪntʃʉˈmɛs, -ɪz, -ɪŋ, -t
AM ˌɪnt(j)uˈmɛs, -əz,
-ɪŋ, -t
intumescence
BR ˌɪntjʉˈmɛsns,
ˌɪntʃʉˈmɛsns
AM ˌɪnt(j)uˈmɛsəns
intumescent
BR ˌɪntjʉˈmɛsnt,
ˌɪntʃʉˈmɛsnt
AM ˌɪnt(j)uˈmɛsənt
intumescently
BR ˌɪntjʉˈmɛsntli,
ˌɪntʃʉˈmɛsntli
AM ˌɪnt(j)uˈmɛsn(t)li
intussusception
BR ˌɪntəsəˈsɛpʃn, -z
AM ˌɪn(t)əsəˈsɛpʃən, -z
intwine
BR ɪnˈtwʌɪn, -z, -ɪŋ, -d
AM ɪnˈtwaɪn, -z, -ɪŋ, -d
Inuit
BR ˈɪn(j)ʊɪt, -s
AM ˈɪn(j)ʊɪt, -s
Inuk
BR ˈɪnʊk, -s
AM ˈɪˌnək, -s

Inuktitut
BR ɪˈnʊktɪtʊt
AM ɪˈnʊktəˌtʊt

inunction
BR ɪˈnʌŋ(k)ʃn, -z
AM ɪˈnəŋkʃən, -z

inundate
BR ˈɪnʌndeɪt, -s, -ɪŋ, -ɪd
AM ˈɪnənˌdeɪ|t, -ts, -dɪŋ, -dɪd

inundation
BR ˌɪnʌnˈdeɪʃn, -z
AM ˌɪnənˈdeɪʃən, -z

Inupik
BR ɪˈnuːpɪk, -s
AM ɪˈnuˌpɪk, -s

inure
BR ɪˈnjʊə(r), ɪˈnjɔː(r), -z, -ɪŋ, -d
AM ɪˈn(j)ʊə)r, -z, -ɪŋ, -d

inurement
BR ɪˈnjʊəm(ə)nt, ɪˈnjɔːm(ə)nt, -s
AM ɪˈn(j)ʊrmənt, -s

in utero
BR ɪn ˈjuːt(ə)rəʊ
AM ɪn ˈjudəroʊ

in vacuo
BR ɪn ˈvakjʊəʊ
AM ɪn ˈvækjəˌwoʊ

invade
BR ɪnˈveɪd, -z, -ɪŋ, -ɪd
AM ɪnˈveɪd, -z, -ɪŋ, -ɪd

invader
BR ɪnˈveɪdə(r), -z
AM ɪnˈveɪdər, -z

invaginate
BR ɪnˈvadʒɪneɪt, ɪnˈvadʒɪneɪt, -s, -ɪŋ, -ɪd
AM ɪnˈvædʒəˌneɪ|t, -ts, -dɪŋ, -dɪd

invagination
BR ɪnˌvadʒɪˈneɪʃn, -z
AM ɪnˌvædʒəˈneɪʃən, -z

invalid[1]
adjective, not valid
BR (ˌ)ɪnˈvalɪd
AM ɪnˈvæləd

invalid[2]
noun
BR ˈɪnvəlɪd, ˈɪnvəliːd, -z
AM ˈɪnvələd, -z

invalid[3]
verb
BR ˈɪnvəliːd, ˈɪnvəlɪd, -z, -ɪŋ, -ɪd
AM ˈɪnvələd, -z, -ɪŋ, -əd

invalidate
BR ɪnˈvalɪdeɪt, -s, -ɪŋ, -ɪd
AM ɪnˈvæləˌdeɪ|t, -ts, -dɪŋ, -dɪd

invalidation
BR ɪnˌvalɪˈdeɪʃn
AM ɪnˌvæləˈdeɪʃən

invalidism
BR ˌɪnvəˈliːdɪz(ə)m
AM ˌɪnvələˌdɪzəm

invalidity
BR ˌɪnvəˈlɪdɪti
AM ˌɪnvəˈlɪdɪdi, ˌɪnvæˈlɪdɪdi

invalidly
BR (ˌ)ɪnˈvalɪdli
AM ɪnˈvælədli

invaluable
BR ɪnˈvaljʊəbl, ɪnˈvaljəbl
AM ɪnˈvæljəbəl

invaluableness
BR ɪnˈvaljʊəblnəs, ɪnˈvaljəblnəs
AM ɪnˈvæljəbəlnəs

invaluably
BR ɪnˈvaljʊəbli, ɪnˈvaljəbli
AM ɪnˈvæljəbli

Invar®
BR ɪnˈvɑː(r), ˈɪnvɑː(r)
AM ˈɪnˌvɑr

invariability
BR ɪnˌvɛːrɪəˈbɪlɪti
AM ˌɪnˌvɛrɪəˈbɪlɪdi, ɪnˌvɛrɪəˈbɪlɪdi

invariable
BR (ˌ)ɪnˈvɛːrɪəbl
AM ɪnˈvɛrɪəbəl, ɪnˈvɛrɪəbəl

invariableness
BR (ˌ)ɪnˈvɛːrɪəblnəs
AM ɪnˈvɛrɪəbəlnəs, ɪnˈvɛrɪəbəlnəs

invariably
BR (ˌ)ɪnˈvɛːrɪəbli
AM ɪnˈvɛrɪəbli, ɪnˈvɛrɪəbli

invariance
BR (ˌ)ɪnˈvɛːrɪəns, -ɪz
AM ˌɪnˈvɛrɪəns, ɪnˈvɛrɪəns, -əz

invariant
BR (ˌ)ɪnˈvɛːrɪənt, -s
AM ˌɪnˈvɛrɪənt, ɪnˈvɛrɪənt, -s

invasion
BR ɪnˈveɪʒn, -z
AM ɪnˈveɪʒən, -z

invasive
BR ɪnˈveɪsɪv, ɪnˈveɪzɪv
AM ɪnˈveɪsɪv, ɪnˈveɪzɪv

invasively
BR ɪnˈveɪsɪvli, ɪnˈveɪzɪvli
AM ɪnˈveɪsɪvli, ɪnˈveɪzɪvli

invasiveness
BR ɪnˈveɪsɪvnɪs, ɪnˈveɪzɪvnɪs
AM ɪnˈveɪsɪvnɪs, ɪnˈveɪzɪvnɪs

invected
BR ɪnˈvɛktɪd
AM ɪnˈvɛktəd

invective
BR ɪnˈvɛktɪv
AM ɪnˈvɛktɪv

invectively
BR ɪnˈvɛktɪvli
AM ɪnˈvɛktəvli

invectiveness
BR ɪnˈvɛktɪvnɪs
AM ɪnˈvɛktɪvnɪs

inveigh
BR ɪnˈveɪ, -z, -ɪŋ, -d
AM ɪnˈveɪ, -z, -ɪŋ, -d

inveigle
BR ɪnˈveɪg‖l, ɪnˈviːg‖l, -lz, -lɪŋ‖-lɪŋ, -ld
AM ɪnˈveɪgəl, -əlz, -(ə)lɪŋ, -əld

inveiglement
BR ɪnˈveɪglm(ə)nt, ɪnˈviːglm(ə)nt, -s
AM ɪnˈveɪgəlmənt, -s

invent
BR ɪnˈvɛnt, -s, -ɪŋ, -ɪd
AM ɪnˈvɛn|t, -ts, -(t)ɪŋ, -(t)əd

inventable
BR ɪnˈvɛntəbl
AM ɪnˈvɛn(t)əbəl

invention
BR ɪnˈvɛnʃn, -z
AM ɪnˈvɛnʃən, -z

inventive
BR ɪnˈvɛntɪv
AM ɪnˈvɛn(t)ɪv

inventively
BR ɪnˈvɛntɪvli
AM ɪnˈvɛn(t)əvli

inventiveness
BR ɪnˈvɛntɪvnɪs
AM ɪnˈvɛn(t)ɪvnɪs

inventor
BR ɪnˈvɛntə(r), -z
AM ɪnˈvɛn(t)ər, -z

inventory
BR ˈɪnv(ə)nt(ə)r|i, -ɪz
AM ˈɪnvənˌtɔri, -z

inventress
BR ɪnˈvɛntrɪs, -ɪz
AM ɪnˈvɛntrəs, -əz

Inveraray
BR ˌɪnvəˈrɛːri
AM ˌɪnvəˈrɛri

Invercargill
BR ˌɪnvəˈkɑːg(ɪ)l
AM ˌɪnvərˈkɑrgəl

Invergordon
BR ˌɪnvəˈgɔːdn
AM ˌɪnvərˈgordən

Inverness
BR ˌɪnvəˈnɛs
AM ˌɪnvərˈnɛs

Inverness-shire
BR ˌɪnvəˈnɛsʃ(ɪ)ə(r)
AM ˌɪnvərˈnɛsˌʃɪ(ə)r

inverse
BR ˈɪnvəːs, ɪnˈvəːs, -ɪz
AM ˈɪnvərs, ɪnˈvərs, -əz

inversely
BR ˈɪnvəːsli, ɪnˈvəːsli
AM ˈɪnvərsli, ɪnˈvərsli

inversion
BR ɪnˈvəːʃn, -z
AM ɪnˈvərʒən, -z

inversive
BR ɪnˈvəːsɪv
AM ɪnˈvərsɪv

invert[1]
noun
BR ˈɪnvəːt, -s
AM ˈɪnvərt, -s

invert[2]
verb
BR ɪnˈvəːt, -s, -ɪŋ, -ɪd
AM ɪnˈvər|t, -ts, -dɪŋ, -dəd

invertase
BR ˈɪnvəteɪz, ɪnˈvəːteɪz
AM ˈɪnvərˌteɪz, ɪnˈvərˌteɪz

invertebrate
BR ɪnˈvəːtɪbrət, ɪnˈvəːtɪbreɪt, -s
AM ɪnˈvərdəbrət, ɪnˈvərdəˌbreɪt, -s

inverter
BR ɪnˈvəːtə(r), -z
AM ɪnˈvərdər, -z

invertibility
BR ɪnˌvəːtɪˈbɪlɪti
AM ɪnˌvərdəˈbɪlɪdi

invertible
BR ɪnˈvəːtɪbl
AM ɪnˈvərdəbəl

Inverurie
BR ˌɪnvəˈrʊəri
AM ˌɪnvəˈrʊri

invest
BR ɪnˈvɛst, -s, -ɪŋ, -ɪd
AM ɪnˈvɛst, -s, -ɪŋ, -əd

investable
BR ɪnˈvɛstəbl
AM ɪnˈvɛstəbəl

investible
BR ɪnˈvɛstɪbl
AM ɪnˈvɛstəbəl

investigate
BR ɪnˈvɛstɪgeɪt, -s, -ɪŋ, -ɪd
AM ɪnˈvɛstəˌgeɪ|t, -ts, -dɪŋ, -dɪd

investigation
BR ɪnˌvɛstɪˈgeɪʃn, -z
AM ɪnˌvɛstəˈgeɪʃən, -z

investigational
BR ɪnˌvɛstɪˈgeɪʃn(ə)l, ɪnˌvɛstɪˈgeɪʃən(ə)l
AM ɪnˌvɛstəˈgeɪʃ(ə)nəl

investigative
BR ɪnˈvɛstɪgətɪv
AM ɪnˈvɛstəˌgeɪdɪv

investigator
BR ɪnˈvɛstɪgeɪtə(r), -z
AM ɪnˈvɛstəˌgeɪdər, -z

investigatory
BR ɪnˈvɛstɪgət(ə)ri

AM ɪnˈvɛstəgəˌtɔri
investiture
BR ɪnˈvɛstɪtʃə(r),
ɪnˈvɛstɪtjʊə(r), -z
AM ɪnˈvɛstətʃʊ(ə)r,
ɪnˈvɛstətʃər, -z
investment
BR ɪnˈvɛs(t)m(ə)nt, -s
AM ɪnˈvɛs(t)mənt, -s
investor
BR ɪnˈvɛstə(r), -z
AM ɪnˈvɛstər, -z
inveteracy
BR ɪnˈvɛt(ə)rəs|i, -ɪz
AM ɪnˈvɛdərəsi, -z
inveterate
BR ɪnˈvɛt(ə)rət
AM ɪnˈvɛdərət
inveterately
BR ɪnˈvɛt(ə)rətli
AM ɪnˈvɛdərətli
inveterateness
BR ɪnˈvɛt(ə)rətnəs
AM ɪnˈvɛdərətnəs
invidious
BR ɪnˈvɪdiəs
AM ɪnˈvɪdiəs
invidiously
BR ɪnˈvɪdiəsli
AM ɪnˈvɪdiəsli
invidiousness
BR ɪnˈvɪdiəsnəs
AM ɪnˈvɪdiəsnəs
invigilate
BR ɪnˈvɪdʒɪleɪt, -s, -ɪŋ,
-ɪd
AM ɪnˈvɪdʒəˌleɪ|t, -ts,
-dɪŋ, -dɪd
invigilation
BR ɪnˌvɪdʒɪˈleɪʃn
AM ɪnˌvɪdʒəˈleɪʃən
invigilator
BR ɪnˈvɪdʒɪleɪtə(r), -z
AM ɪnˈvɪdʒəˌleɪdər, -z
invigorate
BR ɪnˈvɪgəreɪt, -s, -ɪŋ,
-ɪd
AM ɪnˈvɪgəˌreɪ|t, -ts,
-dɪŋ, -dɪd
invigoratingly
BR ɪnˈvɪgəreɪtɪŋli
AM ɪnˈvɪgəˌreɪdɪŋli
invigoration
BR ɪnˌvɪgəˈreɪʃn
AM ɪnˌvɪgəˈreɪʃən
invigorative
BR ɪnˈvɪg(ə)rətɪv
AM ɪnˈvɪgəˌreɪdɪv
invigorator
BR ɪnˈvɪgəreɪtə(r), -z
AM ɪnˈvɪgəˌreɪdər, -z
invincibility
BR ɪnˌvɪnsɪˈbɪlɪti,
ˌɪnvɪnsɪˈbɪlɪti
AM ɪnˌvɪnsəˈbɪlɪdi
invincible
BR ɪnˈvɪnsɪbl

AM ɪnˈvɪnsəbəl
invincibleness
BR ɪnˈvɪnsɪblnəs
AM ɪnˈvɪnsəbəlnəs
invincibly
BR ɪnˈvɪnsɪbli
AM ɪnˈvɪnsəbli
inviolability
BR ɪnˌvaɪələˈbɪlɪti,
ˌɪnvaɪələˈbɪlɪti
AM ɪnˌvaɪələˈbɪlɪdi,
ɪnˌvaɪələˈbɪlɪdi
inviolable
BR ɪnˈvaɪələbl
AM ɪnˈvaɪələbəl
inviolableness
BR ɪnˈvaɪələblnəs
AM ɪnˈvaɪələbəlnəs
inviolably
BR ɪnˈvaɪələbli
AM ɪnˈvaɪələbli
inviolacy
BR ɪnˈvaɪələsi
AM ɪnˈvaɪələsi
inviolate
BR ɪnˈvaɪələt
AM ɪnˈvaɪələt
inviolately
BR ɪnˈvaɪələtli
AM ɪnˈvaɪələtli
inviolateness
BR ɪnˈvaɪələtnəs
AM ɪnˈvaɪələtnəs
inviscid
BR ɪnˈvɪsɪd
AM ɪnˈvɪsɪd
invisibility
BR ɪnˌvɪzɪˈbɪlɪti,
ˌɪnvɪzɪˈbɪlɪti
AM ɪnˌvɪzəˈbɪlɪdi,
ɪnˌvɪzəˈbɪlɪdi
invisible
BR ɪnˈvɪzɪbl
AM ɪnˈvɪzəbəl
invisibleness
BR ɪnˈvɪzɪblnəs
AM ɪnˈvɪzəbəlnəs
invisibly
BR ɪnˈvɪzɪbli
AM ɪnˈvɪzəbli
invitation
BR ˌɪnvɪˈteɪʃn, -z
AM ˌɪnvəˈteɪʃən, -z
invitatory
BR ɪnˈvaɪtət(ə)ri
AM ɪnˈvaɪdəˌtɔri
invite
BR ɪnˈvaɪt, -s, -ɪŋ, -ɪd
AM ɪnˈvaɪ|t, -ts, -dɪŋ,
-dɪd
invitee
BR ˌɪnvaɪˈtiː, ɪnˌvaɪˈtiː,
-z
AM ɪnˌvaɪˈti, -z
inviter
BR ɪnˈvaɪtə(r), -z
AM ɪnˈvaɪdər, -z

invitingly
BR ɪnˈvaɪtɪŋli
AM ɪnˈvaɪdɪŋli
invitingness
BR ɪnˈvaɪtɪŋnɪs
AM ɪnˈvaɪdɪŋnɪs
in vitro
BR ɪn ˈviːtrəʊ,
+ ˈvɪtrəʊ
AM ɪn ˈviˌtroʊ
in vivo
BR ɪn ˈviːvəʊ,
+ ˈvaɪvəʊ
AM ɪn ˈviˌvoʊ
invocable
BR ˈɪnvəkəbl,
ɪnˈvəʊkəbl
AM ɪnˈvoʊkəbəl,
ˈɪnvəkəbəl
invocation
BR ˌɪnvə(ʊ)ˈkeɪʃn, -z
AM ˌɪnvəˈkeɪʃən,
ˌɪnvoʊˈkeɪʃən, -z
invocatory
BR ɪnˈvɒkət(ə)ri
AM ɪnˈvɑkəˌtɔri
invoice
BR ˈɪnvɔɪs, -ɪz, -ɪŋ, -t
AM ˈɪnˌvɔɪs, -ɪz, -ɪŋ, -t
invoke
BR ɪnˈvəʊk, -s, -ɪŋ, -t
AM ɪnˈvoʊk, -s, -ɪŋ, -t
invoker
BR ɪnˈvəʊkə(r), -z
AM ɪnˈvoʊkər, -z
involucral
BR ˌɪnvəˈl(j)uːkr(ə)l
AM ˌɪnvəˈlukrəl
involucre
BR ˈɪnvəˌl(j)uːkə(r), -z
AM ˈɪnvəˌlukər, -z
involuntarily
BR (ˌ)ɪnˈvɒləntrɪli,
(ˌ)ɪnˈvɒlntrɪli
AM ɪnˈvɑlənˌterəli
involuntariness
BR (ˌ)ɪnˈvɒlənt(ə)rɪnɪs,
(ˌ)ɪnˈvɒlntrɪnɪs
AM ɪnˈvɑlənˌterɪnɪs
involuntary
BR (ˌ)ɪnˈvɒlənt(ə)ri,
(ˌ)ɪnˈvɒlnt(ə)ri
AM ɪnˈvɑlənˌteri
involute
BR ˈɪnvəl(j)uːt, -s, -ɪd
AM ˈɪnvəˌl(j)u|t, -ts,
-dəd
involution
BR ˌɪnvəˈl(j)uːʃn, -z
AM ˌɪnvəˈl(j)uʃən, -z
involutional
BR ˌɪnvəˈl(j)uːʃ(ə)l,
ˌɪnvəˈl(j)uːʃən(ə)l
AM ˌɪnvəˈl(j)uʃ(ə)nəl
involve
BR ɪnˈvɒlv, -z, -ɪŋ, -d
AM ɪnˈvɑ(l)v, ɪnˈvɔ(l)v,
-z, -ɪŋ, -d

involvement
BR ɪnˈvɒlvm(ə)nt, -s
AM ɪnˈvɑ(l)vmənt,
ɪnˈvɔ(l)vmənt, -s
invulnerability
BR ɪnˌvʌln(ə)rəˈbɪlɪti,
ˌɪnvʌln(ə)rəˈbɪlɪti
AM ɪnˌvəln(ə)rəˈbɪlɪdi,
ɪnˌvəln(ə)rəˈbɪlɪdi
invulnerable
BR (ˌ)ɪnˈvʌln(ə)rəbl
AM ɪnˈvəlnər(ə)bəl
invulnerably
BR (ˌ)ɪnˈvʌln(ə)rəbli
AM ɪnˈvəlnər(ə)bli
inward
BR ˈɪnwəd, -z
AM ˈɪnwərd, -z
inwardly
BR ˈɪnwədli
AM ˈɪnwərdli
inwardness
BR ˈɪnwədnəs
AM ˈɪnwərdnəs
inweave
BR ˌɪnˈwiːv, -z, -ɪŋ
AM ˌɪnˈwiv, ɪnˈwiv, -z,
-ɪŋ
inwove
BR ˌɪnˈwəʊv
AM ˌɪnˈwoʊv, ɪnˈwoʊv
inwoven
BR ˌɪnˈwəʊvn
AM ˌɪnˈwoʊvən,
ɪnˈwoʊvən
inwrap
BR ˌɪnˈrap, -s, -ɪŋ, -t
AM ˌɪnˈræp, ɪnˈræp, -s,
-ɪŋ, -t
inwreathe
BR ˌɪnˈriːð, -z, -ɪŋ, -d
AM ˌɪnˈrið, ɪnˈrið, -z, -ɪŋ,
-d
inwrought
BR ˌɪnˈrɔːt
AM ˌɪnˈrɔt, ɪnˈrɔt,
ˌɪnˈrɑt, ɪnˈrɑt
inyala
BR ɪnˈjɑːlə(r), -z
AM ɪnˈjɑlə, -z
in-your-face
adjective
BR ˌɪnjəˈfeɪs
AM ˌɪnjərˈfeɪs
Io
BR ˈaɪəʊ
AM ˈaɪˌoʊ
iodate
BR ˈaɪədeɪt, -s
AM ˈaɪəˌdeɪt, -s
iodic
BR aɪˈɒdɪk
AM aɪˈɑdɪk
iodide
BR ˈaɪədaɪd, -z
AM ˈaɪəˌdaɪd, -z
iodin
BR ˈaɪədɪn, -z

iodinate
AM 'aɪə,daɪn, -z

iodinate
BR 'ʌɪədɪneɪt,
ʌɪ'ɒdɪneɪt, -s, -ɪŋ, -ɪd
AM 'aɪədə,neɪ|t, -ts,
-dɪŋ, -dɪd

iodination
BR ,ʌɪədɪ'neɪʃn,
ʌɪ,ɒdɪ'neɪʃn, -z
AM 'aɪədə'neɪʃən, -z

iodine
BR 'ʌɪədiːn, -z
AM 'aɪə,daɪn, -z

iodinise
BR 'ʌɪədɪnʌɪz, -ɪz, -ɪŋ,
-d
AM 'aɪədə,naɪz, -ɪz, -ɪŋ,
-d

iodinize
BR 'ʌɪədɪnʌɪz, -ɪz, -ɪŋ,
-d
AM 'aɪədə,naɪz, -ɪz, -ɪŋ,
-d

iodisation
BR ,ʌɪədʌɪ'zeɪʃn
AM ,aɪədə'zeɪʃən,
,aɪə,daɪ'zeɪʃən

iodise
BR 'ʌɪədʌɪz, -ɪz, -ɪŋ, -d
AM 'aɪə,daɪz, -ɪz, -ɪŋ, -d

iodism
BR 'ʌɪədɪz(ə)m
AM 'aɪə,dɪzəm

iodization
BR ,ʌɪədʌɪ'zeɪʃn
AM ,aɪədə'zeɪʃən,
,aɪə,daɪ'zeɪʃən

iodize
BR 'ʌɪədʌɪz, -ɪz, -ɪŋ, -d
AM 'aɪə,daɪz, -ɪz, -ɪŋ, -d

iodoform
BR ʌɪ'ɒdə(ʊ)fɔːm,
ʌɪ'əʊdə(ʊ)fɔːm,
'ʌɪədəfəːm, -z
AM aɪ'oʊdə,fɔ(ə)rm,
aɪ'ɑdə,fɔ(ə)rm, -z

Iolanthe
BR ,ʌɪə'lanθi
AM ,aɪə'lænθi

Iolo
BR 'jəʊləʊ
AM 'joʊloʊ
WE 'jɒlɒ

ion
BR 'ʌɪən, 'ʌɪɒn, -z
AM 'aɪən, 'aɪ,ɑn, -z

Iona
BR ʌɪ'əʊnə(r)
AM aɪ'oʊnə

Ionesco
BR, iːə'nɛskəʊ,
jɒ'nɛskəʊ
AM jɒ'nɛskoʊ

Ionia
BR ʌɪ'əʊnɪə(r)
AM aɪ'oʊnɪə

Ionian
BR ʌɪ'əʊnɪən, -z

AM aɪ'oʊnɪən, -z

ionic
BR ʌɪ'ɒnɪk
AM aɪ'ɑnɪk

ionically
BR ʌɪ'ɒnɪkli
AM aɪ'ɑnək(ə)li

ionisable
BR 'ʌɪənʌɪzəbl
AM 'aɪə,naɪzəbəl

ionisation
BR ,ʌɪənʌɪ'zeɪʃn
AM ,aɪənə'zeɪʃən,
,aɪə,naɪ'zeɪʃən

ionise
BR 'ʌɪənʌɪz, -ɪz, -ɪŋ, -d
AM 'aɪə,naɪz, -ɪz, -ɪŋ, -d

ioniser
BR 'ʌɪənʌɪzə(r), -z
AM 'aɪə,naɪzər, -z

ionium
BR ʌɪ'əʊnɪəm, -z
AM aɪ'oʊnɪəm, -z

ionizable
BR 'ʌɪənʌɪzəbl
AM 'aɪə,naɪzəbəl

ionization
BR ,ʌɪənʌɪ'zeɪʃn
AM ,aɪənə'zeɪʃən,
,aɪə,naɪ'zeɪʃən

ionize
BR 'ʌɪənʌɪz, -ɪz, -ɪŋ, -d
AM 'aɪə,naɪz, -ɪz, -ɪŋ, -d

ionizer
BR 'ʌɪənʌɪzə(r), -z
AM 'aɪə,naɪzər, -z

ionophore
BR ʌɪ'ɒnə(ʊ)fɔː(r), -z
AM aɪ'ɑnə,fɔ(ə)r, -z

ionosphere
BR ʌɪ'ɒnəsfɪə(r)
AM aɪ'ɑnə,sfɪ(ə)r

ionospheric
BR ,ʌɪ,ɒnə(ʊ)'sfɛrɪk
AM ,aɪ,ɑnə'sfɪrɪk

iontophoresis
BR ʌɪ,ɒntə(ʊ)fə'riːsɪs
AM aɪ'ɑn(t)əfə'risis

Iorwerth
BR 'jɔːwəːθ, 'jɔːwəθ
AM 'jɔr,wərθ
WE 'jɒrwerθ

iota
BR ʌɪ'əʊtə(r), -z
AM aɪ'oʊdə, -z

IOU
BR ,ʌɪəʊ'juː, -z
AM ,aɪ,oʊ'ju, -z

Iowa
BR 'ʌɪəwə(r)
AM 'aɪəwə

Iowan
BR 'ʌɪəwən, -z
AM 'aɪəwən, -z

Ipatieff
BR ɪ'patɪɛf
AM ɪ'pæt,jɛf

ipecac
BR 'ɪpɪkak
AM 'ɪpəkæk

ipecacuanha
BR ,ɪpɪkakjʊ'anə(r),
,ɪpɪkakjʊ'ɑːnə(r)
AM ,ɪpə,kækjə'wɑn(j)ə,
i,peɪkə'kwɑnjə

Iphigenia
BR ɪ,fɪdʒɪ'niːə(r),
,ʌɪfɪdʒɪ'nʌɪə(r)
AM ,ɪfədʒə'niə

Ipoh
BR 'iːpəʊ
AM 'ɪ,poʊ

ipomoea
BR ,ɪpə'miːə(r), -z
AM ,ɪpə'miə, -z

ipse dixit
BR ,ɪpsɪ 'dɪksɪt,
,ɪpseɪ +
AM 'ɪpsi 'dɪksɪt

ipsilateral
BR ,ɪpsɪ'lat(ə)rəl,
,ɪpsɪ'lat(ə)r|
AM 'ɪpsɪ'læd(ə)rəl

ipsissima verba
BR ɪp,sɪsɪmə 'vəːbə(r)
AM ɪp'sɪsəmə 'vərbə

ipso facto
BR ,ɪpsəʊ 'faktəʊ
AM 'ɪpsoʊ 'fæktoʊ

Ipswich
BR 'ɪpswɪtʃ
AM 'ɪpswɪtʃ

Iqbal
BR 'ɪkbal, 'ɪkbɑːl
AM 'ɪk,bɑl

IRA[1]
banking
BR 'ʌɪrə(r)
AM 'aɪrə, ,aɪ,ɑr'eɪ

IRA[2]
*Irish Republican
Army*
BR ,ʌɪɑː'r'eɪ
AM ,aɪ,ɑr'eɪ

Ira
BR 'ʌɪrə(r)
AM 'aɪrə

irade
BR ɪ'rɑːd|i, -ɪz
AM ɪ'rɑdi, -z

Iran
BR ɪ'rɑːn, ɪ'ran
AM ɪ'rɑn, ɪ'ræn

Iran-Contra
BR ɪ,rɑːn'kɒntrə(r),
ɪ,ran'kɒntrə(r)
AM ɪ,ran'kɑntrə,
ɪ,ræn'kɑntrə

Irangate
BR ɪ'rɑːngeɪt, ɪ'rangeɪt
AM ɪ'ran,geɪt,
ɪ'ræn,geɪt

Iranian
BR ɪ'reɪnɪən, -z

AM ɪ'reɪnɪən, ɪ'rɑnɪən,
-z

Iraq
BR ɪ'rɑːk, ɪ'rak
AM ɪ'rɑk, ɪ'ræk

Iraqi
BR ɪ'rɑːk|i, ɪ'rak|i, -ɪz
AM ɪ'rɑki, ɪ'ræki, -z

IRAS
BR 'ʌɪras
AM 'aɪ,ræs

irascibility
BR ɪ,rasɪ'bɪlɪti
AM ɪ,ræsə'bɪlɪdi

irascible
BR ɪ'rasɪbl
AM ɪ'ræsəbəl

irascibleness
BR ɪ'rasɪblnəs
AM ɪ'ræsəbəlnəs

irascibly
BR ɪ'rasɪbli
AM ɪ'ræsəbli

irate
BR ʌɪ'reɪt
AM aɪ'reɪt

irately
BR ʌɪ'reɪtli
AM aɪ'reɪtli

irateness
BR ʌɪ'reɪtnɪs
AM aɪ'reɪtnɪs

ire
BR 'ʌɪə(r)
AM 'aɪ(ə)r

ireful
BR 'ʌɪəf(ʊ)l
AM 'aɪrfəl

irefully
BR 'ʌɪəfʊli, 'ʌɪəfʃi
AM 'aɪrfəli

irefulness
BR 'ʌɪəf(ʊ)lnəs
AM 'aɪrfəlnəs

Ireland
BR 'ʌɪələnd
AM 'aɪrlən(d)

Irenaeus
BR ʌɪ'riːnɪəs
AM aɪ'riniəs

Irene
BR ʌɪ'riːn, ʌɪ'riːn
AM aɪ'rin, 'aɪ,rin

irenic
BR ʌɪ'riːnɪk, ʌɪ'rɛnɪk
AM aɪ'rɛnɪk, aɪ'rinɪk

irenical
BR ʌɪ'riːnɪkl, ʌɪ'rɛnɪkl
AM aɪ'rɛnəkəl,
aɪ'rinɪkəl

irenicon
BR ʌɪ'riːnɪkɒn,
ʌɪ'rɛnɪkɒn, -z
AM aɪ'rinə,kɑn, -z

Ireton
BR 'ʌɪət(ə)n

AM ˈaɪ(ə)rtən

Irgun
BR əːˈguːn
AM ərˈgun

Irian
BR ˈɪriən
AM ˈiriən

Irian Jaya
BR ˌɪriən ˈdʒʌɪə(r)
AM ˈɪriən ˈdʒaɪə

iridaceous
BR ˌɪrɪˈdeɪʃəs
AM ˌɪrəˈdeɪʃəs

iridescence
BR ˌɪrɪˈdɛsns
AM ˌɪrəˈdɛsəns

iridescent
BR ˌɪrɪˈdɛsnt
AM ˌɪrəˈdɛsənt

iridescently
BR ˌɪrɪˈdɛsntli
AM ˌɪrəˈdɛsn(t)li

iridium
BR ɪˈrɪdiəm
AM ɪˈrɪdiəm

iridologist
BR ˌɪrɪˈdɒlədʒɪst, -s
AM ˌɪrəˈdɑlədʒəst, -s

iridology
BR ˌɪrɪˈdɒlədʒi
AM ˌɪrəˈdɑlədʒi

iris
BR ˈʌɪr|ɪs, -ɪsɪz
AM ˈaɪrɪs, -ɪz

Irish
BR ˈʌɪrɪʃ
AM ˈaɪrɪʃ

Irishman
BR ˈʌɪrɪʃmən
AM ˈaɪrɪʃmən

Irishmen
BR ˈʌɪrɪʃmən
AM ˈaɪrɪʃmən

Irishness
BR ˈʌɪrɪʃnɪs
AM ˈaɪrɪʃnɪs

Irishwoman
BR ˈʌɪrɪʃˌwʊmən
AM ˈaɪrɪʃˌwʊmən

Irishwomen
BR ˈʌɪrɪʃˌwɪmɪn
AM ˈaɪrɪʃˌwɪmɪn

iritis
BR ʌɪˈrʌɪtɪs
AM aɪˈraɪdɪs

irk
BR əːk, -s, -ɪŋ, -t
AM ərk, -s, -ɪŋ, -t

irksome
BR ˈəːks(ə)m
AM ˈərksəm

irksomely
BR ˈəːks(ə)mli
AM ˈərksəmli

irksomeness
BR ˈəːks(ə)mnəs
AM ˈərksəmnəs

Irkutsk
BR əːˈkʊtsk, ɪəˈkʊtsk
AM ˈɪrˌkʊ(t)sk

Irlam
BR ˈəːləm
AM ˈərləm

Irma
BR ˈəːmə(r)
AM ˈərmə

Irnbru
BR ˈʌɪənbruː
AM ˈaɪ(ə)rnˌbru

iroko
BR ɪˈrəʊkəʊ, iːˈrəʊkəʊ, -z
AM ɪˈroʊˌkoʊ, -z

iron
BR ˈʌɪən, -z, -ɪŋ, -d
AM ˈaɪ(ə)rn, -z, -ɪŋ, -d

Iron Age
BR ˈʌɪən eɪdʒ
AM ˈaɪ(ə)rn ˌeɪdʒ

ironbark
BR ˈʌɪənbɑːk, -s
AM ˈaɪ(ə)rnˌbɑrk, -s

ironclad
BR ˈʌɪənklad, -z
AM ˈaɪ(ə)rnˌklæd, -z

ironer
BR ˈʌɪənə(r), -z
AM ˈaɪ(ə)rnər, -z

ironic
BR ʌɪˈrɒnɪk
AM aɪˈrɑnɪk

ironical
BR ʌɪˈrɒnɪkl
AM aɪˈranəkəl

ironically
BR ʌɪˈrɒnɪkli
AM aɪˈranək(ə)li

ironise
BR ˈʌɪrənʌɪz, -ɪz, -ɪŋ, -d
AM ˈaɪrəˌnaɪz, -ɪz, -ɪŋ, -d

ironist
BR ˈʌɪrənɪst, -s
AM ˈaɪrənəst, -s

ironize
BR ˈʌɪrənʌɪz, -ɪz, -ɪŋ, -d
AM ˈaɪrəˌnaɪz, -ɪz, -ɪŋ, -d

ironless
BR ˈʌɪənləs
AM ˈaɪ(ə)rnləs

ironmaster
BR ˈʌɪənˌmɑːstə(r),
ˈʌɪənˌmɑstə(r), -z
AM ˈaɪ(ə)rnˌmæstər, -z

ironmonger
BR ˈʌɪənˌmʌŋɡə(r), -z
AM ˈaɪ(ə)rnˌmɑŋɡər,
ˈaɪ(ə)rnˌməŋɡər, -z

ironmongery
BR ˈʌɪənˌmʌŋɡ(ə)ri
AM ˈaɪ(ə)rnˌmɑŋɡ(ə)ri,
ˈaɪ(ə)rnˌmʌŋɡ(ə)ri

Ironside
BR ˈʌɪənsʌɪd, -z
AM ˈaɪ(ə)rnˌsaɪd, -z

ironstone
BR ˈʌɪənstəʊn
AM ˈaɪ(ə)rnˌstoʊn

ironware
BR ˈʌɪənwɛː(r)
AM ˈaɪ(ə)rnˌwɛ(ə)r

ironwood
BR ˈʌɪənwʊd
AM ˈaɪ(ə)rnˌwʊd

ironwork
BR ˈʌɪənwəːk, -s
AM ˈaɪ(ə)rnˌwərk, -s

irony
BR ˈʌɪrən|i, -ɪz
AM ˈaɪrəni, ˈaɪərni, -z

Iroquoian
BR ˌɪrəˈkwɔɪən, -z
AM ˌɪrəˌk(w)ɔɪən, -z

Iroquois
BR ˈɪrəkwɔɪ, -z
AM ˈɪrəˌk(w)ɔɪ, -z

irradiance
BR ɪˈreɪdɪəns, -ɪz
AM ɪˈreɪdiəns, -əz

irradiant
BR ɪˈreɪdɪənt
AM ɪˈreɪdiənt

irradiate
BR ɪˈreɪdɪeɪt, -s, -ɪŋ, -ɪd
AM ɪˈreɪdiˌeɪ|t, -ts, -dɪŋ, -dɪd

irradiation
BR ɪˌreɪdɪˈeɪʃn
AM ɪˌreɪdiˈeɪʃən

irradiative
BR ɪˈreɪdɪətɪv
AM ɪˌreɪdiˌeɪdɪv

irrational
BR (ˌ)ɪˈraʃn(ə)l,
(ˌ)ɪˈraʃən(ə)l
AM ɪ(r)ˈræʃ(ə)nəl

irrationalise
BR (ˌ)ɪˈraʃnəlʌɪz,
(ˌ)ɪˈraʃn̩lʌɪz,
(ˌ)ɪˈraʃənlʌɪz,
(ˌ)ɪˈraʃ(ə)nəlʌɪz, -ɪz,
-ɪŋ, -d
AM ɪ(r)ˈræʃənlˌaɪz,
ɪ(r)ˈræʃnəˌlaɪz, -ɪz,
-ɪŋ, -d

irrationality
BR ɪˌraʃəˈnalɪti
AM ɪ(r)ˌræʃəˈnælədi,
əˌræʃəˈnælədi

irrationalize
BR (ˌ)ɪˈraʃnəlʌɪz,
(ˌ)ɪˈraʃn̩lʌɪz,
(ˌ)ɪˈraʃənlʌɪz,
(ˌ)ɪˈraʃ(ə)nəlʌɪz, -ɪz,
-ɪŋ, -d
AM ɪ(r)ˈræʃənlˌaɪz,
ɪ(r)ˈræʃnəˌlaɪz, -ɪz,
-ɪŋ, -d

irrationally
BR (ˌ)ɪˈraʃnəli,
(ˌ)ɪˈraʃn̩li,
(ˌ)ɪˈraʃənli,
(ˌ)ɪˈraʃ(ə)nəli

irreconcilability
BR ɪˌrɛk(ə)nˌsʌɪləˈbɪlɪti,
ˌɪrɛk(ə)nˌsʌɪləˈbɪlɪti
AM ˈɪ(r)ˌrɛkənˌsaɪləˈbɪl-
ɪdi,
ɪˈrɛkənˌsaɪləˈbɪlɪdi

irreconcilable
BR ˌɪrɛk(ə)nˈsʌɪləbl,
ɪˌrɛk(ə)nˈsʌɪləbl,
ɪˈrɛk(ə)nsʌɪləbl
AM ˈɪ(r)ˌrɛkənˈsaɪləbəl,
ɪˌrɛkənˈsaɪləbəl

irreconcilableness
BR ˌɪrɛk(ə)nˈsʌɪləblnəs,
ɪˌrɛk(ə)nˈsʌɪləblnəs,
ɪˈrɛk(ə)nsʌɪləblnəs
AM ˈɪ(r)ˌrɛkənˈsaɪləbəl-
nəs,
ɪˌrɛkənˈsaɪləbəlnəs

irreconcilably
BR ˌɪrɛk(ə)nˈsʌɪləbli,
ɪˌrɛk(ə)nˈsʌɪləbli,
ɪˈrɛk(ə)nsʌɪləbli
AM ˈɪ(r)ˌrɛkənˈsaɪləbli,
ɪˌrɛkənˈsaɪləbli

irrecoverable
BR ˌɪrɪˈkʌv(ə)rəbl
AM ˈɪ(r)rəˈkəv(ə)rəbəl

irrecoverably
BR ˌɪrɪˈkʌv(ə)rəbli
AM ˈɪ(r)rəˈkəv(ə)rəbli

irrecusable
BR ˌɪrɪˈkjuːzəbl
AM ˈɪ(r)rəˈkjuzəbəl

irredeemability
BR ɪrɪˌdiːməˈbɪlɪti
AM ˈɪ(r)rəˌdiməˈbɪlɪdi

irredeemable
BR ˌɪrɪˈdiːməbl
AM ˈɪ(r)rəˈdiməbəl

irredeemably
BR ˌɪrɪˈdiːməbli
AM ˈɪ(r)rəˈdiməbli

irredentism
BR ˌɪrɪˈdɛntɪz(ə)m
AM ˈɪ(r)rəˈdɛnˌtɪzəm

irredentist
BR ˌɪrɪˈdɛntɪst, -s
AM ˈɪ(r)rəˈdɛn(t)əst, -s

irreducibility
BR ˌɪrɪˌdjuːsɪˈbɪlɪti,
ˌɪrɪˌdʒuːsɪˈbɪlɪti
AM ˈɪ(r)rəˌd(j)usəˈbɪlɪdi

irreducible
BR ˌɪrɪˈdjuːsɪbl,
ˌɪrɪˈdʒuːsɪbl
AM ˈɪ(r)rəˈd(j)usəbəl

irreducibly
BR ˌɪrɪˈdjuːsɪbli,
ˌɪrɪˈdʒuːsɪbli
AM ˈɪ(r)rəˈd(j)usəbli

irrefragability
BR ɪˌrɛfrəgəˈbɪlɪti
AM ˈi(r)ˌrɛfrəgəˈbɪlɪdi

irrefragable
BR ˌ)ɪˈrɛfrəgəbl
AM ɪ(r)ˈrɛfrəgəbəl,
ɪˈrɛfrəgəbəl

irrefragableness
BR ˌ)ɪˈrɛfrəgəblnəs
AM ɪ(r)ˈrɛfrəgəbəlnəs,
ɪˈrɛfrəgəbəlnəs

irrefragably
BR ˌ)ɪˈrɛfrəgəbli
AM ɪ(r)ˈrɛfrəgəbli,
ɪˈrɛfrəgəbli

irrefrangible
BR ˌɪrɪˈfran(d)ʒɪbl
AM ɪ(r)rəˈfrændʒəbəl

irrefutability
BR ɪrɪˌfjuːtəˈbɪlɪti,
ɪˌrɛfjʊtəˈbɪlɪti
AM ˈɪ(r)rəˌfjudəˈbɪlɪdi,
ˈɪ(r)ˌrɛfjədəˈbɪlɪdi,
ɪˌrɛfjədəˈbɪlɪdi

irrefutable
BR ɪrɪˈfjuːtəbl,
ɪˈrɛfjʊtəbl
AM ɪ(r)rəˈfjudəbəl,
ˈɪ(r)ˈrɛfjədəbəl,
ɪˈrɛfjədəbəl

irrefutably
BR ɪrɪˈfjuːtəbli,
ɪˈrɛfjʊtəbli
AM ˈɪ(r)rəˈfjudəbli,
ˈɪ(r)ˈrɛfjədəbli,
ɪˈrɛfjədəbli

irregardless
BR ɪrɪˈgɑːdləs
AM ˈɪ(r)rəˈgɑrdləs

irregular
BR ˌ)ɪˈrɛgjʊlə(r)
AM ɪ(r)ˈrɛgjələr

irregularity
BR ɪˌrɛgjʊˈlærɪt‖i, -ɪz
AM ˈɪ(r)ˌrɛgjəˈlɛrədi,
ɪˌrɛgjəˈlɛrədi, -z

irregularly
BR ˌ)ɪˈrɛgjʊləli
AM ɪ(r)ˈrɛgjələrli

irrelative
BR ˌ)ɪˈrɛlətɪv
AM ˈɪ(r)ˈrɛlədɪv,
ɪˈrɛlədɪv

irrelatively
BR ˌ)ɪˈrɛlətɪvli
AM ˈɪ(r)ˈrɛlədəvli,
ɪˈrɛlədəvli

irrelevance
BR ˌ)ɪˈrɛlɪv(ə)ns, -ɪz

irrelevances,
ɪˈrɛləvəns, -əz

irrelevancy
BR ˌ)ɪˈrɛlɪv(ə)ns‖i, -ɪz
AM ɪ(r)ˈrɛləvənsi,
ɪˈrɛləvənsi, -z

irrelevant
BR ˌ)ɪˈrɛlɪv(ə)nt
AM ˈɪ(r)ˈrɛləvənt,
ɪˈrɛləvənt

irrelevantly
BR ˌ)ɪˈrɛlɪv(ə)ntli
AM ˈɪ(r)ˈrɛləvən(t)li,
ɪˈrɛləvən(t)li

irreligion
BR ɪrɪˈlɪdʒ(ə)n
AM ˈɪ(r)rəˈlɪdʒən

irreligionist
BR ɪrɪˈlɪdʒənɪst,
ˌɪrɪˈlɪdʒnɪst, -s
AM ˈɪ(r)rəˈlɪdʒənəst, -s

irreligious
BR ɪrɪˈlɪdʒəs
AM ˈɪ(r)rəˈlɪdʒəs

irreligiously
BR ɪrɪˈlɪdʒəsli
AM ˈɪ(r)rəˈlɪdʒəsli

irreligiousness
BR ɪrɪˈlɪdʒəsnəs
AM ˈɪ(r)rəˈlɪdʒəsnəs

irremediable
BR ɪrɪˈmiːdɪəbl
AM ˈɪ(r)rəˈmidiəbəl

irremediably
BR ɪrɪˈmiːdɪəbli
AM ˈɪ(r)rəˈmidiəbli

irremissible
BR ɪrɪˈmɪsɪbl
AM ˈɪ(r)rəˈmɪsɪbəl

irremissibly
BR ɪrɪˈmɪsɪbli
AM ˈɪ(r)rəˈmɪsɪbli

irremovability
BR ɪrɪˌmuːvəˈbɪlɪt‖i,
-ɪz
AM ˈɪ(r)rəˌmuvəˈbɪlɪdi,
-z

irremovable
BR ɪrɪˈmuːvəbl
AM ˈɪ(r)rəˈmuvəbəl

irremovably
BR ɪrɪˈmuːvəbli
AM ˈɪ(r)rəˈmuvəbli

irremoveability
BR ɪrɪˌmuːvəˈbɪlɪti
AM ˈɪ(r)rəˌmuvəˈbɪlɪdi

irremoveable
BR ɪrɪˈmuːvəbl
AM ˈɪ(r)rəˈmuvəbəl

irreparability
BR ɪˌrɛp(ə)rəˈbɪlɪti
AM ˈɪ(r)ˌrɛp(ə)rəˈbɪlɪdi

irreparable
BR ˌ)ɪˈrɛp(ə)rəbl
AM ˈɪˈrɛp(ə)rəbəl,
ɪˈrɛp(ə)rəbəl

irreparableness
BR ˌ)ɪˈrɛp(ə)rəblnəs
AM ˈɪˈrɛp(ə)rəbəlnəs,
ɪˈrɛp(ə)rəbəlnəs

irreparably
BR ˌ)ɪˈrɛp(ə)rəbli
AM ˈɪˈrɛp(ə)rəbli,
ɪˈrɛp(ə)rəbli

irreplaceable
BR ɪrɪˈpleɪsəbl
AM ˈɪ(r)rəˈpleɪsəbəl

irreplaceably
BR ɪrɪˈpleɪsəbli
AM ˈɪ(r)rəˈpleɪsəbli

irrepressibility
BR ɪrɪˌpresɪˈbɪlɪti
AM ˈɪ(r)rəˌpresəˈbɪlɪdi

irrepressible
BR ɪrɪˈpresɪbl
AM ˈɪ(r)rəˈpresəbəl

irrepressibleness
BR ɪrɪˈpresɪblnəs
AM ˈɪ(r)rəˈpresəbəlnəs

irrepressibly
BR ɪrɪˈpresɪbli
AM ˈɪ(r)rəˈpresəbli

irreproachability
BR ɪrɪˌprəʊtʃəˈbɪlɪti
AM ˈɪ(r)rəˌproʊtʃəˈbɪlɪdi

irreproachable
BR ɪrɪˈprəʊtʃəbl
AM ˈɪ(r)rəˈproʊtʃəbəl

**irreproachable-
ness**
BR ɪrɪˈprəʊtʃəblnəs
AM ˈɪ(r)rəˈproʊtʃəbəln-
nəs

irreproachably
BR ɪrɪˈprəʊtʃəbli
AM ˈɪ(r)rəˈproʊtʃəbli

irresistibility
BR ɪrɪˌzɪstɪˈbɪlɪti
AM ˈɪ(r)rəˌzɪstəˈbɪlɪdi

irresistible
BR ɪrɪˈzɪstɪbl
AM ˈɪ(r)rəˈzɪstəbəl

irresistibleness
BR ɪrɪˈzɪstɪblnəs
AM ˈɪ(r)rəˈzɪstəbəlnəs

irresistibly
BR ɪrɪˈzɪstɪbli
AM ˈɪ(r)rəˈzɪstəbli

irresolute
BR ˌ)ɪˈrɛzəl(j)uːt
AM ɪ(r)ˈrɛzəˌlut

irresolutely
BR ˌ)ɪˈrɛzəl(j)uːtli
AM ɪ(r)ˈrɛzəˌlutli

irresoluteness
BR ˌ)ɪˈrɛzəl(j)uːtnəs
AM ɪ(r)ˈrɛzəˌlutnəs

irresolution
BR ɪˌrɛzəˈl(j)uːˌʃn,
ˌɪrɛzəˈl(j)uːˌʃn
AM ɪ(r)ˌrɛzəˈluʃən

irresolvability
BR ˌɪrɪˌzɒlvəˈbɪlɪti

irresolvable
BR ɪrɪˈzɒlvəbl
AM ˈɪ(r)rəˈzɑlvəbəl

irrespective
BR ɪrɪˈspɛktɪv
AM ˈɪ(r)rəˈspɛktɪv

irrespectively
BR ɪrɪˈspɛktɪvli
AM ˈɪ(r)rəˈspɛktəvli

irresponsibility
BR ɪrɪˌspɒnsɪˈbɪlɪti
AM ˈɪ(r)rəˌspɑnsəˈbɪlɪdi

irresponsible
BR ɪrɪˈspɒnsɪbl
AM ˈɪ(r)rəˈspɑnsəbəl

irresponsibly
BR ɪrɪˈspɒnsɪbli
AM ˈɪ(r)rəˈspɑnsəbli

irresponsive
BR ɪrɪˈspɒnsɪv
AM ˈɪ(r)rəˈspɑnsɪv

irresponsively
BR ɪrɪˈspɒnsɪvli
AM ˈɪ(r)rəˈspɑnsəvli

irresponsiveness
BR ɪrɪˈspɒnsɪvnɪs
AM ˈɪ(r)rəˈspɑnsɪvnɪs

irretentive
BR ɪrɪˈtɛntɪv
AM ˈɪ(r)rəˈtɛn(t)ɪv

irretrievability
BR ɪrɪˌtriːvəˈbɪlɪti
AM ˈɪ(r)rəˌtrivəˈbɪlɪdi

irretrievable
BR ɪrɪˈtriːvəbl
AM ˈɪ(r)rəˈtrivəbəl

irretrievably
BR ɪrɪˈtriːvəbli
AM ˈɪ(r)rəˈtrivəbli

irreverence
BR ɪˈrɛv(ə)rəns,
ɪˈrɛv(ə)rns
AM ɪ(r)ˈrɛv(ə)rəns

irreverent
BR ɪˈrɛv(ə)rənt,
ɪˈrɛv(ə)rnt
AM ɪ(r)ˈrɛv(ə)rənt

irreverential
BR ɪˌrɛvəˈrɛnʃl,
ˌɪrɛvəˈrɛnʃl
AM ɪ(r)ˌrɛvəˈrɛn(t)ʃəl

irreverently
BR ɪˈrɛv(ə)rəntli,
ɪˈrɛv(ə)rntli
AM ɪ(r)ˈrɛv(ə)rən(t)li

irreversibility
BR ɪrɪˌvəːsɪˈbɪlɪti
AM ˈɪ(r)rəˌvərsəˈbɪlɪdi

irreversible
BR ɪrɪˈvəːsɪbl
AM ˈɪ(r)rəˈvərsəbəl

irreversibly
BR ɪrɪˈvəːsɪbli
AM ˈɪ(r)rəˈvərsəbli

irrevocability
BR ɪˌrɛvəkəˈbɪlɪti

irrevocable
AM ˈɪ(r)ˌrɛvəkəˈbɪlɪdi,
ɪˌrɛvəkəˈbɪlɪdi

irrevocable
BR ɪˈrɛvəkəbl
AM ˈɪ(r)ˈrɛvəkəbəl,
ɪˈrɛvəkəbəl,
ˈɪ(r)rəˈvoʊkəbəl

irrevocably
BR ɪˈrɛvəkəbli
AM ˈɪ(r)ˈrɛvəkəbli,
ɪˈrɛvəkəbli,
ˈɪ(r)rəˈvoʊkəbli

irrigable
BR ˈɪrɪgəbl
AM ˈɪrəgəbəl

irrigate
BR ˈɪrɪgeɪt, -s, -ɪŋ, -ɪd
AM ˈɪrəgeɪ|t, -ts, -dɪŋ, -dɪd

irrigation
BR ˌɪrɪˈgeɪʃn
AM ˌɪrəˈgeɪʃən

irrigative
BR ˈɪrɪgətɪv
AM ˈɪrəˌgeɪdɪv

irrigator
BR ˈɪrɪgeɪtə(r), -z
AM ˈɪrəˌgeɪdər, -z

irritability
BR ˌɪrɪtəˈbɪlɪti
AM ˌɪrədəˈbɪlɪdi

irritable
BR ˈɪrɪtəbl
AM ˈɪrədəbəl

irritably
BR ˈɪrɪtəbli
AM ˈɪrədəbli

irritancy
BR ˈɪrɪt(ə)nsi
AM ˈɪrədnsi

irritant
BR ˈɪrɪt(ə)nt, -s
AM ˈɪrədnt, -s

irritate
BR ˈɪrɪteɪt, -s, -ɪŋ, -ɪd
AM ˈɪrəˌteɪ|t, -ts, -dɪŋ, -dɪd

irritatedly
BR ˈɪrɪteɪtɪdli
AM ˈɪrəˌteɪdɪdli

irritatingly
BR ˈɪrɪteɪtɪŋli
AM ˈɪrəˌteɪdɪŋli

irritation
BR ˌɪrɪˈteɪʃn, -z
AM ˌɪrəˈteɪʃən, -z

irritative
BR ˈɪrɪtətɪv
AM ˈɪrəˌteɪdɪv

irritator
BR ˈɪrɪteɪtə(r), -z
AM ˈɪrəˌteɪdər, -z

irrupt
BR ɪˈrʌpt, -s, -ɪŋ, -ɪd
AM ɪˈrəpt, -s, -ɪŋ, -əd

irruption
BR ɪˈrʌpʃn, -z

AM ɪˈrəpʃən, -z

irruptive
BR ɪˈrʌptɪv
AM ɪˈrəptɪv

Irvine¹
placename in UK
BR ˈəːvɪn
AM ˈərvən

Irvine²
placename in USA
BR ˈəːvaɪn
AM ˈərˌvaɪn

Irvine³
surname
BR ˈəːvɪn
AM ˈərvən

Irving
BR ˈəːvɪŋ
AM ˈərvɪŋ

Irvingite
BR ˈəːvɪŋʌɪt, -s
AM ˈərvɪŋˌgaɪt, -s

Irwell
BR ˈəːwɛl
AM ˈərˌwɛl

Irwin
BR ˈəːwɪn
AM ˈərwən

is¹
strong
BR ɪz
AM ɪz

is²
weak
BR s, z
AM s, z

Isaac
BR ˈaɪzək
AM ˈaɪzək

Isaacs
BR ˈaɪzəks
AM ˈaɪzəks

Isabel
BR ˈɪzəbɛl
AM ˈɪzəˌbɛl

Isabella
BR ˌɪzəˈbɛlə(r)
AM ˌɪzəˈbɛlə

Isabelle
BR ˈɪzəbɛl, ˌɪzəˈbɛl
AM ˈɪzəˌbɛl, ˌɪzəˈbɛl

isabelline
BR ˌɪzəˈbɛliːn,
ˌɪzəˈbɛlɪn, ˌɪzəˈbɛlʌɪn
AM ˌɪzəˈbɛlən,
ˈɪzəˈbɛˌlaɪn, ˈɪzəˈbɛˌlin

Isadora
BR ˌɪzəˈdɔːrə(r)
AM ˌɪzəˈdorə

Isadore
BR ˈɪzədɔː(r)
AM ˈɪzəˌdɔː(ə)r

isagogic
BR ˌʌɪsəˈgɒdʒɪk, -s
AM ˌaɪsəˈgɑdʒɪk, -s

Isaiah
BR ʌɪˈzʌɪə(r)

AM aɪˈzeɪə

Isambard
BR ˈɪz(ə)mbɑːd
AM ˈɪzəmˌbɑrd

isatin
BR ˈaɪsətɪn
AM ˈaɪsədən, ˈaɪsneɪtn

Iscariot
BR ɪˈskarɪət
AM ɪsˈkeriət

ischaemia
BR ɪˈskiːmɪə(r)
AM ɪsˈkimiə

ischaemic
BR ɪˈskiːmɪk
AM ɪsˈkimɪk

ischemia
BR ɪˈskiːmɪə(r)
AM ɪsˈkimiə

ischemic
BR ɪˈskiːmɪk
AM ɪsˈkimɪk

Ischia
BR ˈɪskɪə(r)
AM ˈɪskiə

ischiadic
BR ˌɪskɪˈadɪk
AM ˌɪskiˈædɪk

ischial
BR ˈɪskɪəl
AM ˈɪskiəl

ischiatic
BR ˌɪskɪˈatɪk
AM ˌɪskiˈædɪk

ischium
BR ˈɪskɪəm
AM ˈɪskiə

isentropic
BR ˌʌɪsɛnˈtrɒpɪk,
ˌʌɪzɛnˈtrɒpɪk,
ˌʌɪs(ɪ)nˈtrɒpɪk,
ˌʌɪz(ɪ)nˈtrɒpɪk,
ˌʌɪsɛnˈtrəʊpɪk,
ˌʌɪzɛnˈtrəʊpɪk,
ˌʌɪs(ɪ)nˈtrəʊpɪk,
ˌʌɪz(ɪ)nˈtrəʊpɪk
AM ˌaɪsənˈtrɑpɪk,
ˌaɪzənˈtrɑpɪk

Iseult
BR ɪˈzuːlt, ɪˈsuːlt
AM ˌɪˈsɔlt, ˌɪˈzɔlt

Isfahan
BR ˌɪsfəˈhɑːn, ˈɪsfəhɑːn
AM ˈɪsfəˈhɑn

Isherwood
BR ˈɪʃəwʊd
AM ˈɪʃərˌwʊd

Ishiguro
BR ˌɪʃɪˈgʊərəʊ
AM ˌɪʃiˈguˌroʊ

Ishmael
BR ˈɪʃmeɪl, ˈɪʃmɪəl
AM ˈɪʃˌmeɪl, ˈɪʃmiəl

Ishmaelite
BR ˈɪʃməlʌɪt,
ˈɪʃmeɪlʌɪt, ˈɪʃmɪəlʌɪt,
-s

Islamite
AM ˈɪʃˌmeɪˌlaɪt,
ˈɪʃmiəˌlaɪt, -s

Ishtar
BR ˈɪʃtɑː(r)
AM ˈɪʃˌtɑr

Isidore
BR ˈɪzɪdɔː(r)
AM ˈɪzəˌdɔ(ə)r

isinglass
BR ˈʌɪzɪŋglɑːs,
ˈʌɪzɪŋglas,
AM ˈaɪznˌglæs,
ˈaɪzɪŋˌglæs

Isis
BR ˈʌɪsɪs
AM ˈaɪsɪs

Isla
BR ˈaɪlə(r)
AM ˈaɪlə

Islam
BR ˈɪzlɑːm, ˈɪslɑːm,
ˈɪzlam, ˈɪslam, ɪzˈlɑːm,
ɪsˈlɑːm, ɪzˈlam, ɪsˈlam
AM ɪˈslɑm, ɪzˈlɑm,
ˈɪsˌlam, ˈɪzˌlam

Islamabad
BR ɪzˈlɑːməbad,
ɪsˈlɑːməbad,
ɪzˈlaməbad,
ɪsˈləmabad,
ɪzˈlɑːməbɑːd,
ɪzˈləmabɑːd,
ɪsˈlɑːməbɑːd
AM ɪˌslaməˈbad,
ɪˌzlaməˈbad,
ɪˌslæməˈbæd,
ɪˌzlæməˈbæd

Islamic
BR ɪzˈlamɪk, ɪsˈlamɪk
AM ɪˈslamɪk, ɪzˈlamɪk

Islamisation
BR ɪzˌlaːmʌɪˈzeɪʃn,
ɪsˌlaːmʌɪˈzeɪʃn,
ɪzˌlamʌɪˈzeɪʃn,
ɪsˌlamʌɪˈzeɪʃn
AM ɪˌslaməˈzeɪʃən,
ɪˌzlaməˈzeɪʃən,
ɪˌslamˌaɪˈzeɪʃən,
ɪˌzlamˌaɪˈzeɪʃən

Islamise
BR ˈɪzləmʌɪz,
ˈɪsləmʌɪz, -ɪz, -ɪŋ, -d
AM ˈɪsləˌmaɪz,
ˈɪzləˌmaɪz, -ɪz, -ɪŋ, -d

Islamism
BR ˈɪzləmɪz(ə)m,
ˈɪsləmɪz(ə)m
AM ˈɪsləˌmɪzəm,
ˈɪzləˌmɪzəm

Islamist
BR ˈɪzləmɪst, ˈɪsləmɪst,
-s
AM ˈɪsləməst,
ˈɪzləməst, -s

Islamite
BR ˈɪzləmʌɪt,
ˈɪsləmʌɪt, -s

AM ˈɪslə,maɪt, ˈɪzlə,maɪt, -s

Islamitic
BR ˌɪzləˈmɪtɪk, ˌɪsləˈmɪtɪk
AM ˌɪsləˈmɪdɪk, ˌɪzləˈmɪdɪk

Islamization
BR ɪz,lɑːmʌɪˈzeɪʃn, ɪs,lɑːmʌɪˈzeɪʃn, ɪz,lamʌɪˈzeɪʃn, ɪs,lamʌɪˈzeɪʃn
AM ɪ,slɑməˈzeɪʃən, ɪ,zlɑməˈzeɪʃən, ɪ,slɑm,aɪˈzeɪʃən, ɪ,zlɑm,aɪˈzeɪʃən

Islamize
BR ˈɪzləmʌɪz, ˈɪsləmʌɪz, -ɨz, -ɪŋ, -d
AM ˈɪslə,maɪz, ˈɪzlə,maɪz, -ɨz, -ɪŋ, -d

island
BR ˈʌɪlən|d, -(d)z
AM ˈaɪlən|d, -(d)z

islander
BR ˈʌɪləndə(r), -z
AM ˈaɪləndər, -z

isle
BR ʌɪl, -z
AM aɪl, -z

Isle of Man
BR ˌʌɪl əv ˈman
AM ¦aɪl əv ˈmæn

Isle of Wight
BR ˌʌɪl əv ˈwʌɪt
AM ¦aɪl əv ˈwaɪt

islet
BR ˈʌɪlɨt, -s
AM ˈaɪlət, -s

Isleworth
BR ˈʌɪzlwəːθ, ˈʌɪzlwəθ
AM ˈaɪl,wərθ

Islington
BR ˈɪzlɪŋt(ə)n
AM ˈaɪlɪŋtən

Islwyn
BR ˈɪslʊɪn
AM ˈɪslʊɨn
WE ˈɪslwɪn

ism
BR ˈɪz(ə)m, -z
AM ˈɪzəm, -z

Ismaili
BR ˌɪzməˈiːl|i, ˌɪzmɑːˈiːl|i, -ɪz
AM ˌɪzməˈili, ˌɪzmɑˈili, -z

Ismailia
BR ˌɪzmʌɪˈliːə(r), ˌɪsmʌɪˈliːə(r)
AM ˌɪzmaɪˈliə, ˌɪsmaɪˈliə

Ismay
BR ˈɪzmeɪ
AM ˈɪzmaɪ

isn't
BR ˈɪznt
AM ˈɪznt

isobar
BR ˈʌɪsə(ʊ)bɑː(r), -z
AM ˈaɪsə,bɑr, ˈaɪsoʊ,bɑr, -z

isobaric
BR ˌʌɪsə(ʊ)ˈbarɪk
AM ¦aɪsəˈbɛrɪk, ¦aɪsoʊˈbɛrɪk

Isobel
BR ˈɪzəbɛl
AM ˈɪzə,bɛl

isocheim
BR ˈʌɪsə(ʊ)kʌɪm, -z
AM ˈaɪsə,kaɪm, ˈaɪsoʊ,kaɪm, -z

isochromatic
BR ˌʌɪsə(ʊ)krəˈmatɪk
AM ¦aɪsəkrəˈmædɪk

isochronal
BR ʌɪˈsɒkrənl, ʌɪˈsɒkrn̩l
AM aɪˈsɑkrənəl

isochronally
BR ʌɪˈsɒkrənl̩i, ʌɪˈsɒkrn̩l̩i
AM aɪˈsɑkrənəli

isochronicity
BR ʌɪ,sɒkrəˈnɪsɨt|i, -ɪz
AM aɪ,sɑkrəˈnɪsɨdi, -z

isochronize
BR ʌɪˈsɒkrənʌɪz, -ɨz, -ɪŋ, -d
AM aɪˈsɑkrə,naɪz, -ɨz, -ɪŋ, -d

isochronous
BR ʌɪˈsɒkrənəs
AM aɪˈsɑkrənəs

isochronously
BR ʌɪˈsɒkrənəsli
AM aɪˈsɑkrənəsli

isochrony
BR ʌɪˈsɒkrəni
AM aɪˈsɑkrəni

isoclinal
BR ˌʌɪsə(ʊ)ˈklʌɪnl
AM ¦aɪsəˈklaɪnəl, ¦aɪsoʊˈklaɪnl

isoclinic
BR ˌʌɪsə(ʊ)ˈklɪnɪk
AM ¦aɪsəˈklɪnɪk, ¦aɪsoʊˈklɪnɪk

isocracy
BR ʌɪˈsɒkrəs|i, -ɪz
AM aɪˈsɑkrəsi, -z

Isocrates
BR ʌɪˈsɒkrətiːz
AM aɪˈsɑkrə,tiz

isocratic
BR ˌʌɪsə(ʊ)ˈkratɪk
AM ¦aɪsəˈkrædɪk, ¦aɪsoʊˈkrædɪk

isocyclic
BR ˌʌɪsə(ʊ)ˈsʌɪklɪk
AM ¦aɪsəˈsaɪklɪk, ¦aɪsoʊˈsaɪklɪk

isodynamic
BR ˌʌɪsə(ʊ)dʌɪˈnamɪk
AM ¦aɪsə,daɪˈnæmɪk, ¦aɪsoʊ,daɪˈnæmɪk

isoenzyme
BR ˈʌɪsəʊ,ɛnzʌɪm, -z
AM ¦aɪsəˈɛn,zaɪm, ¦aɪsoʊˈɛn,zaɪm, -z

isogeotherm
BR ˌʌɪsə(ʊ)ˈdʒɪə(ʊ)θəːm, -z
AM ¦aɪsəˈdʒiə,θərm, ¦aɪsoʊˈdʒiə,θərm, -z

isogeothermal
BR ˌʌɪsəʊ,dʒiːə(ʊ)ˈθəːml
AM ¦aɪsə,dʒiəˈθərməl, ¦aɪsoʊ,dʒiəˈθərməl

isogloss
BR ˈʌɪsəglɒs, -ɨz
AM ˈaɪsə,glɔs, ˈaɪsə,glɑs, ˈaɪsoʊ,glɔs, ˈaɪsoʊ,glɑs, -əz

isogonic
BR ˌʌɪsə(ʊ)ˈgɒnɪk
AM ¦aɪsəˈgɑnɪk

isohel
BR ˈʌɪsə(ʊ)hɛl, -z
AM ˈaɪsə,hɛl, ˈaɪsoʊ,hɛl, -z

isohyet
BR ˌʌɪsə(ʊ)ˈhʌɪɨt, -s
AM ¦aɪsə¦haɪət, ¦aɪsoʊ¦haɪət, -s

isolable
BR ˈʌɪs(ə)ləbl
AM ˈaɪsələbəl

isolatable
BR ˈʌɪsəleɪtəbl
AM ˈaɪsə,leɪdəbəl

isolate[1]
noun, adjective
BR ˈʌɪs(ə)lət, -s
AM ˈaɪsələt, -s

isolate[2]
verb
BR ˈʌɪsəleɪt, -s, -ɪŋ, -ɨd
AM ˈaɪsə,leɪ|t, -ts, -dɪŋ, -dɨd

isolation
BR ˌʌɪsəˈleɪʃn
AM ˌaɪsəˈleɪʃən

isolationism
BR ˌʌɪsəˈleɪʃn̩ɪz(ə)m, ˌʌɪsəˈleɪʃənɪz(ə)m
AM ˌaɪsəˈleɪʃə,nɪzəm

isolationist
BR ˌʌɪsəˈleɪʃn̩ɪst, ˌʌɪsəˈleɪʃənɪst, -s
AM ˌaɪsəˈleɪʃənəst, -s

isolative
BR ˈʌɪs(ə)lətɪv
AM ˈaɪsə,leɪdɪv

isolatively
BR ˈʌɪs(ə)lətɪvli
AM ˈaɪsə,leɪdɪvli

isolator
BR ˈʌɪsəleɪtə(r), -z
AM ˈaɪsə,leɪdər, -z

Isolde
BR ɪˈzɒldə(r)
AM ɪˈsɔld, ɪˈzɔld

isolette
BR ˌʌɪsəˈlɛt
AM ˌaɪsəˈlɛt

isoleucine
BR ˌʌɪsə(ʊ)ˈluːsiːn
AM ¦aɪsəˈlusən, ¦aɪsoʊˈlusən

isomer
BR ˈʌɪsəmə(r), -z
AM ˈaɪsəmər, -z

isomerase
BR ʌɪˈsɒməreɪz
AM aɪˈsɑmə,reɪz

isomeric
BR ˌʌɪsəˈmɛrɪk
AM ˌaɪsoʊˈmɛrɪk, ˌaɪzəˈmɛrɪk

isomerise
BR ʌɪˈsɒmərʌɪz, -ɨz, -ɪŋ, -d
AM aɪˈsɑmə,raɪz, -ɨz, -ɪŋ, -d

isomerism
BR ʌɪˈsɒmərɪz(ə)m
AM aɪˈsɑmə,rɪzəm

isomerize
BR ʌɪˈsɒmərʌɪz, -ɨz, -ɪŋ, -d
AM aɪˈsɑmə,raɪz, -ɨz, -ɪŋ, -d

isomerous
BR ʌɪˈsɒm(ə)rəs
AM aɪˈsɑmərəs

isometric
BR ˌʌɪsə(ʊ)ˈmɛtrɪk, -s
AM ˌaɪsoʊˈmɛtrɪk, ˌaɪzəˈmɛtrɪk, -s

isometrically
BR ˌʌɪsə(ʊ)ˈmɛtrɪkli
AM ˌaɪsoʊˈmɛtrək(ə)li, ˌaɪzəˈmɛtrək(ə)li

isometry
BR ʌɪˈsɒmɨtri
AM aɪˈsɑmətri

isomorph
BR ˈʌɪsə(ʊ)mɔːf, -s
AM ˈaɪsə,mɔ(ə)rf, ˈaɪsoʊ,mɔ(ə)rf, -s

isomorphic
BR ˌʌɪsə(ʊ)ˈmɔːfɪk
AM ˌaɪsoʊˈmɔrfɪk

isomorphically
BR ˌʌɪsə(ʊ)ˈmɔːfɨkli
AM ˌaɪsoʊˈmɔrfək(ə)li

isomorphism
BR ˌʌɪsə(ʊ)ˈmɔːfɪz(ə)m
AM ˌaɪsoʊˈmɔr,fɪzəm

isomorphous
BR ˌʌɪsə(ʊ)ˈmɔːfəs
AM ˌaɪsoʊˈmɔrfəs

isonomy
BR ʌɪˈsɒnəmi
AM aɪˈsɑnəmi

isooctane
BR ˌʌɪsəʊˈɒkteɪn
AM ˌaɪsoʊˈɑkteɪn

isophote
BR 'ʌɪsə(ʊ)fəʊt, -s
AM 'aɪsə‚foʊt, -s

isopleth
BR 'ʌɪsə(ʊ)plɛθ, -s
AM 'aɪsə‚plɛθ,
'aɪsoʊ‚plɛθ, -s

isopod
BR 'ʌɪsə(ʊ)pɒd, -z
AM 'aɪsə‚pɑd, -z

isopropyl
BR ‚ʌɪsəʊ'prəʊpʌɪl,
‚ʌɪsəʊ'prəʊpɪl
AM ‚aɪsə'proʊpəl,
‚aɪsoʊ‚proʊpəl

isoproterenol
BR ‚ʌɪsə(ʊ)‚prəʊtə'riː-
nɒl
AM ‚aɪsə‚proʊdə'rinal,
‚aɪsoʊ‚proʊdə'rinal,
‚aɪsə‚proʊdə'rinɒl,
‚aɪsoʊ‚proʊdə'rinɒl

isosceles
BR ʌɪ'sɒsɪliːz,
ʌɪ'sɒsḷiːz
AM aɪ'sɑsə‚liz

isoseismal
BR ‚ʌɪsə(ʊ)'sʌɪzml
AM 'aɪsə'saɪzməl,
'aɪsoʊ'saɪzməl

isoseismic
BR ‚ʌɪsə(ʊ)'sʌɪzmɪk
AM 'aɪsə'saɪzmɪk,
'aɪsoʊ'saɪzmɪk

isospin
BR 'ʌɪsə(ʊ)spɪn
AM 'aɪsə‚spɪn,
'aɪsəʊ‚spɪn

isostasy
BR ʌɪ'sɒstəs|i, -ɪz
AM aɪ'sɑstəsi, -z

isostatic
BR ‚ʌɪsə(ʊ)'statɪk
AM 'aɪsə'stædɪk,
'aɪsoʊ'stædɪk

isothere
BR 'ʌɪsə(ʊ)θɪə(r), -z
AM 'aɪsə‚θɪ(ə)r, -z

isotherm
BR 'ʌɪsə(ʊ)θəːm, -z
AM 'aɪsə‚θərm,
'aɪsoʊ‚θərm, -z

isothermal
BR ‚ʌɪsə(ʊ)'θəːml
AM 'aɪsə'θərməl,
'aɪsoʊ'θərməl

isothermally
BR ‚ʌɪsə(ʊ)'θəːm‚li,
‚ʌɪsə(ʊ)'θəːməli
AM 'aɪsə'θərməli,
'aɪsoʊ'θərməli

isotonic
BR ‚ʌɪsə(ʊ)'tɒnɪk
AM 'aɪsə'tanɪk,
'aɪsoʊ'tanɪk

isotonically
BR ‚ʌɪsə(ʊ)'tɒnɪkli

AM 'aɪsə'tanək(ə)li,
'aɪsoʊ'tanək(ə)li

isotonicity
BR ‚ʌɪsə(ʊ)tə'nɪsɪti
AM 'aɪsətə'nɪsɪdi,
'aɪsoʊtə'nɪsɪdi

isotope
BR 'ʌɪsətəʊp, -s
AM 'aɪsə‚toʊp,
'aɪsoʊ‚toʊp, -s

isotopic
BR ‚ʌɪsə(ʊ)'tɒpɪk
AM 'aɪsə'tapɪk,
'aɪsoʊ'tapɪk

isotopically
BR ‚ʌɪsə(ʊ)'tɒpɪkli
AM 'aɪsə'tapək(ə)li,
'aɪsoʊ'tapək(ə)li

isotopy
BR ʌɪ'sɒtəpi
AM 'aɪsə‚tapi,
'aɪsə‚toʊpi, aɪ'sadəpi

isotropic
BR ‚ʌɪsə(ʊ)'trɒpɪk,
‚ʌɪsə(ʊ)'trəʊpɪk
AM 'aɪsə'trapɪk,
'aɪsoʊ'trapɪk

isotropically
BR ‚ʌɪsə(ʊ)'trɒpɪkli,
‚ʌɪsə(ʊ)'trəʊpɪkli
AM 'aɪsə'trapək(ə)li,
'aɪsoʊ'trapək(ə)li

isotropy
BR ʌɪ'sɒtrəpi
AM aɪ'satrəpi

Ispahan
BR ‚ɪspə'haːn,
'ɪspəhaːn
AM ‚ɪspə'han

I-spy
BR ‚ʌɪ'spʌɪ
AM ‚aɪ'spaɪ

Israel
BR 'ɪzreɪl
AM 'ɪzrɪəl, 'ɪz‚reɪl

Israeli
BR ɪz'reɪl|i, -ɪz
AM ɪz'reɪli, -z

Israelite
BR 'ɪzrəlʌɪt, -s
AM 'ɪzrɪə‚laɪt, -s

Issachar
BR 'ɪsəkɑː(r)
AM 'ɪsə‚kɑr

Issigonis
BR ‚ɪsɪ'gəʊnɪs,
‚ɪzɪ'gəʊnɪs
AM ‚ɪsɪ'goʊnəs

issuable
BR 'ɪʃ(j)ʊəbl, 'ɪsjʊəbl
AM 'ɪʃ(j)u(w)əbəl

issuance
BR 'ɪʃ(j)ʊəns, 'ɪsjʊəns,
-ɪz
AM 'ɪʃ(j)u(w)əns, -əz

issuant
BR 'ɪʃ(j)ʊənt, 'ɪsjʊənt
AM 'ɪʃ(j)u(w)ənt

issue
BR 'ɪʃ(j)uː, 'ɪsjuː, -z, -ɪŋ,
-d
AM 'ɪʃ(j)u, -z, -ɪŋ, -d

issueless
BR 'ɪʃ(j)uːləs, 'ɪsjuːləs
AM 'ɪʃ(j)uləs

issuer
BR 'ɪʃ(j)uːə(r),
'ɪsjuːə(r), -z
AM 'ɪʃ(j)u(w)ər, -z

Istanbul
BR ‚ɪstan'bʊl
AM ‚ɪstæn'bʊl,
'ɪstæm‚bʊl

isthmian
BR 'ɪs(θ)mɪən
AM 'ɪsmɪən

isthmus
BR 'ɪs(θ)məs, -ɪz
AM 'ɪsməs, -əz

istle
BR 'ɪstli
AM 'ɪs(t)li

Istria
BR 'ɪstrɪə(r)
AM 'ɪstrɪə

Istrian
BR 'ɪstrɪən, -z
AM 'ɪstrɪən, -z

it
BR ɪt
AM ɪt

Italian
BR ɪ'taljən, -z
AM ɪ'tæljən, -z

Italianate
BR ɪ'taljəneɪt
AM ɪ'tæljə‚neɪt

italic
BR ɪ'talɪk, -s
AM ɪ'tælɪk, aɪ'tælɪk, -s

italicisation
BR ɪ‚talɪsʌɪ'zeɪʃn
AM ‚tæləsə'zeɪʃən,
aɪ‚tæləsə'zeɪʃən,
ɪ‚tælə‚saɪ'zeɪʃən,
aɪ‚tælə‚saɪ'zeɪʃən

italicise
BR ɪ'talɪsʌɪz, -ɪz, -ɪŋ, -d
AM ɪ'tælə‚saɪz,
aɪ'tælə‚saɪz, -ɪz, -ɪŋ, -d

italicization
BR ɪ‚talɪsʌɪ'zeɪʃn
AM ə‚tæləsə'zeɪʃən,
aɪ‚tæləsə'zeɪʃən,
ɪ‚tælə‚saɪ'zeɪʃən,
aɪ‚tælə‚saɪ'zeɪʃən

italicize
BR ɪ'talɪsʌɪz, -ɪz, -ɪŋ, -d
AM ɪ'tælə‚saɪz,
aɪ'tælə‚saɪz, -ɪz, -ɪŋ, -d

Italiot
BR ɪ'talɪət, -s
AM ɪ'tæli‚ɑt, ɪ'tæliət, -s

Italy
BR 'ɪtəli, 'ɪtḷi

AM 'ɪdəli

itch
BR ɪtʃ, -ɪz, -ɪŋ, -t
AM ɪtʃ, -ɪz, -ɪŋ, -t

Itchen
BR 'ɪtʃ(ɪ)n
AM 'ɪtʃɪn

itchiness
BR 'ɪtʃɪnɪs
AM 'ɪtʃɪnɪs

itchy
BR 'ɪtʃ|i, -ɪə(r), -ɪɪst
AM 'ɪtʃi, -ər, -ɪst

it'd
BR 'ɪtəd
AM 'ɪdɪd

item
BR 'ʌɪtɪm, -z
AM 'aɪdəm, -z

itemisation
BR ‚ʌɪtɪmʌɪ'zeɪʃn
AM ‚aɪdəmə'zeɪʃən,
‚aɪdə‚maɪ'zeɪʃən

itemise
BR 'ʌɪtɪmʌɪz, -ɪz, -ɪŋ, -d
AM 'aɪdə‚maɪz, -ɪz, -ɪŋ,
-d

itemiser
BR 'ʌɪtɪmʌɪzə(r), -z
AM 'aɪdə‚maɪzər, -z

itemization
BR ‚ʌɪtɪmʌɪ'zeɪʃn
AM ‚aɪdəmə'zeɪʃən,
‚aɪdə‚maɪ'zeɪʃən

itemize
BR 'ʌɪtɪmʌɪz, -ɪz, -ɪŋ, -d
AM 'aɪdə‚maɪz, -ɪz, -ɪŋ,
-d

itemizer
BR 'ʌɪtɪmʌɪzə(r), -z
AM 'aɪdə‚maɪzər, -z

iterance
BR 'ɪt(ə)rəns, 'ɪt(ə)rn̩s,
-ɪz
AM 'ɪdərəns, -əz

iterancy
BR 'ɪt(ə)rənsi,
'ɪt(ə)rn̩si
AM 'ɪdərənsi

iterate
BR 'ɪtəreɪt, -s, -ɪŋ, -ɪd
AM 'ɪdə‚reɪ|t, -ts, -dɪŋ,
-dɪd

iteration
BR ‚ɪtə'reɪʃn, -z
AM ‚ɪdə'reɪʃən, -z

iterative
BR 'ɪt(ə)rətɪv
AM 'ɪdə‚reɪdɪv,
'ɪdərədɪv

iteratively
BR 'ɪt(ə)rətɪvli
AM 'ɪdə‚reɪdɪvli,
'ɪdərədɪvli

iterativeness
BR 'ɪt(ə)rətɪvnɪs
AM 'ɪdə‚reɪdɪvnɪs,
'ɪdərədɪvnɪs

iterativity
BR ˌɪt(ə)rəˈtɪvɪti
AM ˌɪd(ə)rəˈtɪvɪdi

Ithaca
BR ˈɪθəkə(r)
AM ˈɪθəkə

ithyphallic
BR ˌɪθɪˈfalɪk
AM ˌɪθəˈfælɪk

itineracy
BR ʌɪˈtɪn(ə)rəsi
AM aɪˈtɪn(ə)rəsi,
ɪˈtɪn(ə)rəsi

itinerancy
BR ʌɪˈtɪn(ə)rənsi,
ʌɪˈtɪn(ə)rn̩si
AM aɪˈtɪn(ə)rənsi,
ɪˈtɪn(ə)rənsi

itinerant
BR ʌɪˈtɪn(ə)rənt,
ʌɪˈtɪn(ə)rn̩t, -s
AM aɪˈtɪn(ə)rənt,
ɪˈtɪn(ə)rənt, -s

itinerary
BR ʌɪˈtɪn(ə)rər|i, -ɪz
AM aɪˈtɪnəˌrɛri,
ɪˈtɪnəˌrɛri, -z

itinerate
BR ʌɪˈtɪn(ə)reɪt, -s, -ɪŋ,
-ɪd
AM aɪˈtɪnəˌreɪ|t,
ɪˈtɪnəˌreɪ|t, -ts, -dɪŋ,
-dɪd

itineration
BR ʌɪˌtɪnəˈreɪʃn, -z

AM aɪˌtɪnəˈreɪʃən,
ɪˌtɪnəˈreɪʃən, -z

it'll
BR ˈɪtl
AM ˈɪdl

Ito
BR ˈiːtəʊ
AM ˈiˌdoʊ

its
BR ɪts
AM ɪts

it's
BR ɪts
AM ɪts

itself
BR ɪtˈsɛlf
AM ɪtˈsɛlf

itsy-bitsy
BR ˌɪtsɪˈbɪtsi
AM ˌɪtsiˈbɪtsi

itty-bitty
BR ˌɪtɪˈbɪti
AM ˌɪdiˈbɪdi

Ivan¹
BR ˈʌɪvn̩
AM ˈaɪvən

Ivan²
foreign
BR ɪˈvan, ɪˈvɑːn
AM ˈaɪvən

Ivanhoe
BR ˈʌɪvnhəʊ
AM ˈaɪvənˌ(h)oʊ

I've
BR ʌɪv

AM aɪv

Iveagh
BR ˈʌɪvi, ˈʌɪveɪ
AM ˈaɪvi, ˈaɪveɪ

Iveco®
BR ɪˈveɪkəʊ
AM ɪˈveɪkoʊ

Ivens
BR ˈʌɪvn̩z
AM ˈaɪvənz

Iver
BR ˈʌɪvə(r)
AM ˈaɪvər

Ives
BR ʌɪvz
AM aɪvz

ivied
BR ˈʌɪvid
AM ˈaɪvid

Ivor
BR ˈʌɪvə(r)
AM ˈaɪvər

ivoried
BR ˈʌɪv(ə)rɪd
AM ˈaɪv(ə)rid

ivory
BR ˈʌɪv(ə)r|i, -ɪz
AM ˈaɪv(ə)ri, -z

ivy
BR ˈʌɪv|i, -ɪz, -ɪd
AM ˈaɪvi, -z, -d

Iwo Jima
BR ˌiwə(ʊ) ˈdʒiːmə(r)

AM ˌiwoʊ ˈdʒimə

ixia
BR ˈɪksɪə(r), -z
AM ˈɪksiə, -z

Ixion
BR ɪkˈsʌɪən
AM ˈɪksiˌɑn, ˈɪksiən

Iyar
BR ˈiːjɑː(r)
AM ˈiˌjɑr, ˈijər

Iyyar
BR ˈiːjɑː(r)
AM ˈiˌjɑr, ˈijər

izard
BR ˈɪzəd, -z
AM iˈzərd, -z

Izmir
BR ɪzˈmɪə(r)
AM ɪzˈmɪ(ə)r

Iznik
BR ˈɪznɪk
AM ˈɪznɪk
TU ɪzˈnɪk

Izvestia
BR ɪzˈvɛstɪə(r)
AM ɪzˈvɛstiə
RUS ɪzˈvʲestʲijə

Izzard
BR ˈɪzɑːd, bɛd
AM ˈɪzərd

Izzy
BR ˈɪzi
AM ˈɪzi

Jj

j
BR dʒeɪ, -z
AM dʒeɪ, -z

jab
BR dʒab, -z, -ɪŋ, -d
AM dʒæb, -z, -ɪŋ, -d

Jabalpur
BR 'dʒablpʊə(r),
'dʒablpɔ:(r)
AM 'dʒabəl,pʊ(ə)r

jabber
BR 'dʒablə(r), -əz,
-(ə)rɪŋ, -əd
AM 'dʒæbər, -z, -ɪŋ, -d

jabberer
BR 'dʒab(ə)rə(r), -z
AM 'dʒæbərər, -z

jabberwock
BR 'dʒabəwɒk
AM 'dʒæbər,wɒk,
'dʒæbər,wɑk

jabberwocky
BR 'dʒabə,wɒki
AM 'dʒæbər,wɒki,
'dʒæbər,wɑki

Jabez
BR 'dʒeɪbez, 'dʒeɪbɪz
AM 'dʒeɪbez

jabiru
BR 'dʒabɪru:,
,dʒabɪ'ru:, -z
AM 'dʒæbə,ru:, -z

jaborandi
BR ,dʒabə'rand|i, -ɪz
AM ,dʒæbə'rændi, -z

jabot
BR 'ʒabəʊ, -z
AM ʒæ'bəʊ, 'ʒæ,bəʊ, -z

jacana
BR 'dʒakənə(r),
,dʒasə'nɑ:(r), -z
AM 'dʒækənə, -z

jacaranda
BR ,dʒakə'randə(r), -z
AM 'dʒækə'rændə, -z

Jacinta
BR dʒə'sɪntə(r)
AM dʒə'sɪn(t)ə

jacinth
BR 'dʒasɪnθ, 'dʒeɪsɪnθ,
-s
AM 'dʒeɪsənθ,
'dʒæsənθ, -s

Jacintha
BR dʒə'sɪnθə(r)
AM dʒə'sɪnθə

jack
BR dʒak, -s, -ɪŋ, -t
AM dʒæk, -s, -ɪŋ, -t

jackal
BR 'dʒakl, -z

AM 'dʒækəl, -z
jackanapes
BR 'dʒakəneɪps
AM 'dʒækə,neɪps

jackaroo
BR ,dʒakə'ru:, -z
AM ,dʒækə'ru, -z

jackass
BR 'dʒakas, -ɪz
AM 'dʒæ,kæs, -əz

jackboot
BR 'dʒakbu:t, -s, -ɪd
AM 'dʒæk,bu|t, -ts, -dəd

jackdaw
BR 'dʒakdɔ:(r), -z
AM 'dʒæk,dɔ,
'dʒæk,dɑ, -z

jackeroo
BR ,dʒakə'ru:, -z
AM ,dʒækə'ru, -z

jacket
BR 'dʒak|ɪt, -ɪts, -ɪtɪd
AM 'dʒækə|t, -ts, -dəd

jackfish
BR 'dʒakfɪʃ
AM 'dʒæk,fɪʃ

Jack Frost
BR ,dʒak 'frɒst
AM 'dʒæk 'frɒst, ,dʒæk
'frɑst

jackfruit
BR 'dʒakfru:t
AM 'dʒæk,frut

jackhammer
BR 'dʒak,hamə(r), -z
AM 'dʒæk,(h)æmər, -z

Jackie
BR 'dʒaki
AM 'dʒæki

jackknife
noun
BR 'dʒaknʌɪf
AM 'dʒæk,naɪf

jack-knife
verb
BR 'dʒaknʌɪf, -s, -ɪŋ, -t
AM 'dʒæk,naɪf, -s, -ɪŋ, -t

jackknives
noun
BR 'dʒaknʌɪvz
AM 'dʒæk,naɪvz

jackleg
BR 'dʒaklɛg, -z
AM 'dʒæk,lɛg, -z

jacklight
BR 'dʒaklʌɪt, -s
AM 'dʒæk,laɪt, -s

Jacklin
BR 'dʒaklɪn
AM 'dʒæklɪn

jack-o'-lantern
BR ,dʒakə'lantən, -z
AM 'dʒækə,læn(t)ərn,
-z

jackpot
BR 'dʒakpɒt, -s
AM 'dʒæk,pɑt, -s

jackrabbit
BR 'dʒak,rabɪt, -s
AM 'dʒæk,ræbət, -s

Jack Russell
BR ,dʒak 'rʌsl, -z
AM ,dʒæk 'rəsəl, -z

jackscrew
BR 'dʒakskru:, -z
AM 'dʒæk,skru, -z

jackshaft
BR 'dʒakʃɑ:ft,
'dʒak,ʃaft, -s
AM 'dʒæk,ʃæf|t, -(t)s

jacksnipe
BR 'dʒaksnʌɪp, -s
AM 'dʒæk,snaɪp, -s

Jackson
BR 'dʒaksn
AM 'dʒæksən

Jacksonville
BR 'dʒaksnvɪl
AM 'dʒæksən,vɪl,
'dʒæksənvəl

jackstaff
BR 'dʒaksta:f,
'dʒakstaf, -s
AM 'dʒæk,stæf, -s

jackstaves
BR 'dʒaksteɪvz
AM 'dʒæk,steɪvz

jackstone
BR 'dʒakstəʊn, -z
AM 'dʒæk,stoʊn, -z

jackstraw
BR 'dʒakstrɔ:(r), -z
AM 'dʒæk,strɔ,
'dʒæk,strɑ, -z

Jacky
BR 'dʒaki
AM 'dʒæki

Jacob
BR 'dʒeɪkəb
AM 'dʒeɪkəb

Jacobean
BR ,dʒakə'bi:ən, -z
AM 'dʒækə'biən,
'dʒeɪkə'biən, -z

Jacobi
BR 'dʒakəbi, dʒə'kəʊbi
AM dʒə'koʊbi

Jacobin
BR 'dʒakəbɪn, -z
AM 'dʒækəbən, -z
'dʒeɪkəbən, -z

Jacobinic
BR ,dʒakə'bɪnɪk
AM 'dʒækə'bɪnɪk

Jacobinical
BR ,dʒakə'bɪnɪkl
AM 'dʒækə'bɪnɪkəl

Jacobinism
BR 'dʒakəbɪnɪz(ə)m
AM 'dʒækəbə,nɪzəm

Jacobite
BR 'dʒakəbʌɪt, -s
AM 'dʒækə,baɪt,
'dʒeɪkə,baɪt, -s

Jacobitical
BR ,dʒakə'bɪtɪkl
AM 'dʒækə'bɪdɪkəl

Jacobitism
BR 'dʒakəbɪtɪz(ə)m
AM 'dʒækə,baɪt,ɪzəm

Jacobs
BR 'dʒeɪkəbz
AM 'dʒeɪkəbz

Jacobson
BR 'dʒeɪkəbs(ə)n,
'jɑ:kəbs(ə)n
AM 'dʒeɪkəbsən

jaconet
BR 'dʒakənɛt, -s
AM 'dʒækə,nɛt,
,dʒækə'nɛt, -s

Jacquard
BR 'dʒakɑ:d, -z
AM 'dʒæ,kɑrd,
dʒə'kɑrd, -z

Jacqueline
BR 'dʒak(ə)li:n,
'dʒakli:n, 'dʒak(ə)lɪn,
'dʒaklɪn
AM 'dʒæk(ə)lən,
'dʒækwələn

Jacquelyn
BR 'dʒak(ə)lɪn,
'dʒaklɪn
AM 'dʒæk(ə)lən,
'dʒækwələn

jacquerie
BR 'dʒeɪk(ə)r|i, -ɪz
AM ,(d)ʒakə'ri, -z

Jacques
BR dʒeɪks, dʒaks, ʒak
AM ʒak, dʒæk

Jacqui
BR 'dʒaki
AM 'dʒæki, 'dʒeɪ,kwi

jactation
BR dʒak'teɪʃn
AM dʒæk'teɪʃən

jactitation
BR ,dʒaktɪ'teɪʃn
AM ,dʒæktə'teɪʃən

jacuzzi
BR dʒə'ku:z|i, -ɪz
AM dʒə'kuzi, -z

jade
BR dʒeɪd, -z, -ɪd
AM dʒeɪd, -z, -ɪd

jadedly
BR 'dʒeɪdɪdli
AM 'dʒeɪdɪdli

jadedness
BR 'dʒeɪdɪdnɪs
AM 'dʒeɪdɪdnɪs

jadeite
BR 'dʒeɪdʌɪt, -s
AM 'dʒeɪd,aɪt, -s

j'adoube
BR ʒa'du:b, ʒə'du:b
AM ʒɑ'dub

Jaeger®
BR 'jeɪgə(r)
AM 'jeɪgər, 'dʒægər

Jaffa
BR 'dʒafə(r), -z
AM 'dʒæfə, -z

Jaffna
BR 'dʒafnə(r)
AM 'dʒæfnə

jag
BR dʒag, -z, -ɪŋ, -d
AM dʒæg, -z, -ɪŋ, -d

jagged¹
adjective
BR 'dʒagɪd
AM 'dʒægəd

jagged²
verb
BR dʒagd
AM dʒægd

jaggedly
BR 'dʒagɪdli
AM 'dʒægədli

jaggedness
BR 'dʒagɪdnɪs
AM 'dʒægədnəs

Jagger
BR 'dʒagə(r)
AM 'dʒægər

jagger
BR 'dʒagə(r), -z
AM 'dʒægər, -z

jagginess
BR 'dʒagɪnɪs
AM 'dʒægɪnɪs

jaggy
BR 'dʒag|i, -ɪə(r), -ɪɪst
AM 'dʒægi, -ər, -ɪst

Jago
BR 'dʒeɪgəʊ, 'jeɪgəʊ
AM 'dʒeɪˌgoʊ

jaguar
BR 'dʒagjʊə(r), -z
AM 'dʒægˌwɑr, -z

jaguarundi
BR ˌdʒagwə'rʌnd|i,
ˌdʒagwɑː'rʌnd|i, -ɪz
AM ˌdʒægwə'rəndi, -z

jail
BR dʒeɪl, -z, -ɪŋ, -d
AM dʒeɪl, -z, -ɪŋ, -d

jailbait
BR 'dʒeɪlbeɪt
AM 'dʒeɪlˌbeɪt

jailbird
BR 'dʒeɪlbəːd, -z
AM 'dʒeɪlˌbərd, -z

jailbreak
BR 'dʒeɪlbreɪk, -s
AM 'dʒeɪlˌbreɪk, -s

jailer
BR 'dʒeɪlə(r), -z
AM 'dʒeɪlər, -z

jailhouse
BR 'dʒeɪlhaʊ|s, -zɪz
AM 'dʒeɪlˌ(h)aʊ|s, -zəz

Jain
BR dʒeɪn, -z
AM dʒeɪn, -z

Jainism
BR 'dʒeɪnɪz(ə)m
AM 'dʒeɪˌnɪzəm

Jainist
BR 'dʒeɪnɪst, -s
AM 'dʒeɪnɪst, -s

Jaipur
BR ˌdʒaɪ'pʊə(r),
ˌdʒaɪ'pɔː(r)
AM 'dʒaɪˌpʊ(ə)r

Jakarta
BR dʒə'kaːtə(r)
AM dʒə'kɑrdə

Jake
BR dʒeɪk
AM dʒeɪk

jake
BR dʒeɪk, -s
AM dʒeɪk, -s

Jalalabad
BR dʒə'lɑːləbad,
dʒə'laləbad,
dʒə'lɑːləbɑːd,
dʒə'laləbɑːd
AM dʒə'lɑləˌbad,
dʒə'læləˌbæd

jalap
BR 'dʒaləp, 'dʒɒləp
AM 'dʒɑləp

jalapeño
BR ˌhalə'peɪnjəʊ,
ˌhalə'piːnjəʊ, -z
AM ˌhɑlə'peɪnjoʊ,
ˌhɑlə'pinjoʊ, -z

jalopy
BR dʒə'lɒp|i, -ɪz
AM dʒə'lɑpi, -z

jalousie
BR 'ʒaluːzi:, -z
AM 'dʒælə,si, -z

jam
BR dʒam, -z, -ɪŋ, -d
AM dʒæm, -z, -ɪŋ, -d

Jamaica
BR dʒə'meɪkə(r)
AM dʒə'meɪkə

Jamaican
BR dʒə'meɪk(ə)n, -z
AM dʒə'meɪkən, -z

Jamal
BR dʒə'mɑːl
AM dʒə'mɑl

jamb
BR dʒam, -z
AM dʒæm, -z

jambalaya
BR ˌdʒambə'lʌɪə(r), -z
AM ˌdʒæmbə'laɪə, -z

jamberoo
BR ˌdʒambə'ruː, -z
AM ˌdʒæmbə'ru, -z

jamboree
BR ˌdʒambə'riː, -z
AM ˌdʒæmbə'ri, -z

James
BR dʒeɪmz
AM dʒeɪmz

Jameson
BR 'dʒeɪms(ə)n
AM 'dʒeɪm(ə)sən

Jamestown
BR 'dʒeɪmztaʊn
AM 'dʒeɪmˌstaʊn

Jamie
BR 'dʒeɪmi
AM 'dʒeɪmi

Jamieson
BR 'dʒeɪmɪs(ə)n
AM 'dʒeɪməsən

jammer
BR 'dʒamə(r), -z
AM 'dʒæmər, -z

jammies
BR 'dʒamɪz
AM 'dʒæmiz

jamminess
BR 'dʒamɪnɪs
AM 'dʒæmɪnɪs

Jammu
BR 'dʒamuː, 'dʒʌmuː
AM 'dʒəmu

jammy
BR 'dʒam|i, -ɪə(r), -ɪɪst
AM 'dʒæmi, -ər, -ɪst

Jamshid
BR ˌdʒam'ʃiːd,
'dʒamʃiːd, ˌdʒam'ʃɪd,
'dʒamʃɪd
AM 'dʒæmˌʃɪd

Jan¹
*English female
forename*
BR dʒan
AM dʒæn

Jan²
*non-English male
forename*
BR jan
AM jɑn

Janáček
BR 'janətʃɛk,
'jaːnətʃɛk
AM 'jɑnəˌtʃɛk,
'jænəˌtʃɛk
CZ 'jʌnɑːtʃɛk

Jancis
BR 'dʒansɪs
AM 'dʒænsəs

Jane
BR dʒeɪn
AM dʒeɪn

jane
BR dʒeɪn, -z
AM dʒeɪn, -z

Janet
BR 'dʒanɪt
AM 'dʒænət

Janette
BR dʒə'nɛt
AM dʒə'nɛt

Janey
BR 'dʒeɪni
AM 'dʒeɪni

jangle
BR 'dʒaŋg|l, -lz,
-lɪŋ \-lɪŋ, -ld
AM 'dʒæŋg|əl, -əlz,
-(ə)lɪŋ, -əld

Janglish
BR 'dʒaŋglɪʃ
AM 'dʒæŋglɪʃ

Janice
BR 'dʒanɪs
AM 'dʒænəs

Janine
BR dʒə'niːn
AM dʒə'nin

Janis
BR 'dʒanɪs
AM 'dʒænəs

janissary
BR 'dʒanɪs(ə)r|i, -ɪz
AM 'dʒænəˌsɛri, -z

janitor
BR 'dʒanɪtə(r), -z
AM 'dʒænədər, -z

janitorial
BR ˌdʒanɪ'tɔːrɪəl
AM ˌdʒænə'tɔriəl

janizary
BR 'dʒanɪz(ə)r|i, -ɪz
AM 'dʒænəˌzɛri, -z

jankers
BR 'dʒaŋkəz
AM 'dʒæŋkərz

Jansen
BR 'dʒans(ə)n
AM 'dʒænsən

Jansenism
BR 'dʒansənɪz(ə)m,
'dʒansnɪz(ə)m
AM 'dʒænsəˌnɪzəm

Jansenist
BR 'dʒansənɪst,
'dʒansnɪst, -s
AM 'dʒænsənəst, -s

January
BR 'dʒanjʊər|i,
'dʒanjʊr|i, -ɪz
AM 'dʒænjəˌwɛri, -z

Janus
BR 'dʒeɪnəs
AM 'dʒeɪnəs

Jap
BR dʒap, -s
AM dʒæp, -s

Japan
BR dʒə'pan, -z, -ɪŋ, -d
AM dʒə'pæn, -z, -ɪŋ, -d

Japanese
BR ˌdʒapə'niːz
AM ˌdʒæpə'niz

jape
BR dʒeɪp, -s
AM dʒeɪp, -s

japery
BR 'dʒeɪp(ə)ri
AM 'dʒeɪp(ə)ri

Japheth
BR 'dʒeɪfɛθ, 'dʒeɪfɪθ

AM 'dʒeɪˌfɛθ
Japhetic
BR dʒəˈfɛtɪk
AM dʒəˈfɛdɪk
japonica
BR dʒəˈpɒnɪkə(r), -z
AM dʒəˈpɑnəkə, -z
Jaques¹
general name
BR dʒeɪks
AM dʒeɪks
Jaques²
Shakespearian name
BR ˈdʒeɪkwɪz
AM ˈdʒeɪkwɪz
Jaques-Dalcroze
BR dʒeɪks ˌdalˈkrəʊz
AM dʒeɪks ˌdælˈkroʊz
FR ʒak dalkʀoz
jar
BR dʒɑː(r), -z, -ɪŋ, -d
AM dʒɑr, -z, -ɪŋ, -d
Jardine
BR ˈdʒɑːdiːn, ˈdʒɑːdʌɪn
AM dʒɑrˈdin
jardinière
BR ˌʒɑːdɪˈnjɛː(r), -z
AM ˌdʒɑrdnˈɪ(ə)r, -z
jarful
BR ˈdʒɑːfʊl, -z
AM ˈdʒɑrˌfʊl, -z
jargon
BR ˈdʒɑːg(ə)n
AM ˈdʒɑrgən
jargonelle
BR ˌdʒɑːgəˈnɛl, -z
AM ˌdʒɑrgəˈnɛl, -z
jargonise
BR ˈdʒɑːgənʌɪz,
ˈdʒɑːgnʌɪz, -ɪz, -ɪŋ, -d
AM ˈdʒɑrgəˌnaɪz, -ɪz,
-ɪŋ, -d
jargonistic
BR ˌdʒɑːgəˈnɪstɪk
AM ˌdʒɑrgəˈnɪstɪk
jargonize
BR ˈdʒɑːgənʌɪz,
ˈdʒɑːgnʌɪz, -ɪz, -ɪŋ, -d
AM ˈdʒɑrgəˌnaɪz, -ɪz,
-ɪŋ, -d
jargoon
BR dʒɑːˈguːn, -z
AM dʒɑrˈgun, -z
Jarman
BR ˈdʒɑːmən
AM ˈdʒɑrmən
Jarndyce
BR ˈdʒɑːndʌɪs
AM ˈdʒɑrndəs,
ˈdʒɑrnˌdaɪs
jarrah
BR ˈdʒɑrə(r), -z
AM ˈdʒɛrə, -z
Jarratt
BR ˈdʒɑrət
AM ˈdʒɛrət

Jarrett
BR ˈdʒɑrət
AM ˈdʒɛrət
Jarrold
BR ˈdʒɑrəld, ˈdʒarl̩d
AM ˈdʒɛrəld
Jarrow
BR ˈdʒɑrəʊ
AM ˈdʒɛroʊ
Jarvis
BR ˈdʒɑːvɪs
AM ˈdʒɑrvəs
jasmin
BR ˈdʒasmɪn,
ˈdʒazmɪn, -z
AM ˈdʒæzmən, -z
jasmine
BR ˈdʒasmɪn,
ˈdʒazmɪn, -z
AM ˈdʒæzmən, -z
Jason
BR ˈdʒeɪsn
AM ˈdʒeɪsən
jaspé
BR ˈ(d)ʒaspeɪ
AM ʒæˈspeɪ
jasper
BR ˈdʒaspə(r)
AM ˈdʒæspər
Jat
BR dʒɑːt, -s
AM dʒɑt, -s
Jataka
BR ˈdʒɑːtəkə(r)
AM ˈdʒɑdəkə
jati
BR ˈdʒɑːt|i, -ɪz
AM ˈdʒɑdi, -ɪz
JATO
BR ˈdʒeɪtəʊ
AM ˈdʒeɪdoʊ, ˈdʒeɪˌtoʊ
jaundice
BR ˈdʒɔːndɪs, -t
AM ˈdʒɔndəs, ˈdʒɑndəs,
-t
jaunt
BR dʒɔːnt, -s, -ɪŋ, -ɪd
AM dʒɔn|t, dʒɑn|t, -ts,
-(t)ɪŋ, -(t)əd
jauntily
BR ˈdʒɔːntɪli
AM ˈdʒɔn(t)əli,
ˈdʒɑn(t)əli
jauntiness
BR ˈdʒɔːntɪnɪs
AM ˈdʒɔn(t)inɪs,
ˈdʒɑn(t)inɪs
jaunty
BR ˈdʒɔːnt|i, -ɪə(r), -ɪɪst
AM ˈdʒɔn(t)i, ˈdʒɑn(t)i,
-ər, -ɪst
Java
BR ˈdʒɑːvə(r)
AM ˈdʒɑvə
Javan
BR ˈdʒɑːvn, -z
AM ˈdʒɑvən, -z

Javanese
BR ˌdʒɑːvəˈniːz
AM ˌdʒɑvəˈniz
javelin
BR ˈdʒav(ə)lɪn, -z
AM ˈdʒæv(ə)lən, -z
Javelle water
BR dʒəˈvɛl ˌwɔːtə(r)
AM dʒəˈvɛl ˌwɔdər,
+ ˌwadər
jaw
BR dʒɔː(r), -z, -ɪŋ, -d
AM dʒɔ, dʒɑ, -z, -ɪŋ, -d
jawbone
BR ˈdʒɔːbəʊn, -z
AM ˈdʒɔˌboʊn,
ˈdʒɑˌboʊn, -z
jawbreaker
BR ˈdʒɔːˌbreɪkə(r), -z
AM ˈdʒɔˌbreɪkər,
ˈdʒɑˌbreɪkər, -z
jawline
BR ˈdʒɔːlʌɪn, -z
AM ˈdʒɔˌlaɪn, ˈdʒɑˌlaɪn,
-z
jay
BR dʒeɪ, -z
AM dʒeɪ, -z
jaybird
BR ˈdʒeɪbɜːd, -z
AM ˈdʒeɪˌbərd, -z
Jaycee
BR ˌdʒeɪˈsiː, -z
AM ˌdʒeɪˈsi, -z
Jayne
BR dʒeɪn
AM dʒeɪn
jaywalk
BR ˈdʒeɪwɔːk, -s, -ɪŋ, -d
AM ˈdʒeɪˌwɔk,
ˈdʒeɪˌwɑk, -s, -ɪŋ, -d
jaywalker
BR ˈdʒeɪˌwɔːkə(r), -z
AM ˈdʒeɪˌwɔkər,
ˈdʒeɪˌwɑkər, -z
jazz
BR dʒaz, -ɪz, -ɪŋ, -d
AM dʒæz, -əz, -ɪŋ, -t
jazzband
BR ˈdʒazband, -z
AM ˈdʒæzˌbænd, -z
jazzer
BR ˈdʒazə(r), -z
AM ˈdʒæzər, -z
jazzily
BR ˈdʒazɪli
AM ˈdʒæzəli
jazziness
BR ˈdʒazɪnɪs
AM ˈdʒæzinɪs
jazzman
BR ˈdʒazman
AM ˈdʒæzmən,
ˈdʒæzˌmæn
jazzmen
BR ˈdʒazmɛn
AM ˈdʒæzmən,
ˈdʒæzˌmɛn

jazzy
BR ˈdʒaz|i, -ɪə(r), -ɪɪst
AM ˈdʒæzi, -ər, -ɪst
J-cloth®
BR ˈdʒeɪ klɒ|θ, -θs\-ðz
AM ˈdʒeɪ ˌklɑ|θ, ˈdʒeɪ
ˌklɑ|θ, -θs\-ðz
jealous
BR ˈdʒɛləs
AM ˈdʒɛləs
jealously
BR ˈdʒɛləsli
AM ˈdʒɛləsli
jealousness
BR ˈdʒɛləsnəs
AM ˈdʒɛləsnəs
jealousy
BR ˈdʒɛləs|i, -ɪz
AM ˈdʒɛləsi, -z
Jean¹
female forename
BR dʒiːn
AM dʒin
Jean²
male forename
BR ʒɒ̃
AM dʒin, ʒɒn, ʒɑn
jean
BR dʒiːn, -z
AM dʒin, -z
Jeanette
BR dʒɪˈnɛt
AM dʒəˈnɛt
Jeanie
BR ˈdʒiːni
AM ˈdʒini
Jeanne d'Arc
BR (d)ʒan ˈdɑːk
AM (d)ʒan ˈdɑrk
Jeannette
BR dʒɪˈnɛt
AM dʒəˈnɛt
Jeannie
BR ˈdʒiːni
AM ˈdʒini
Jeannine
BR dʒɪˈniːn
AM dʒəˈnin
Jeans
BR ˈdʒiːnz
AM ˈdʒinz
Jeavons
BR ˈdʒɛvnz
AM ˈdʒɛvəns
Jedah
BR ˈdʒɛdə(r)
AM ˈdʒɛdə
Jedburgh
BR ˈdʒɛdb(ə)rə(r)
AM ˈdʒɛdbərə
Jeddah
BR ˈdʒɛdə(r)
AM ˈdʒɛdə
Jeep®
BR dʒiːp, -s
AM dʒip, -s

jeepers
BR 'dʒiːpəz
AM 'dʒipərz

jeer
BR dʒɪə(r), -z, -ɪŋ, -d
AM dʒɪ(ə)r, -z, -ɪŋ, -d

jeeringly
BR 'dʒɪərɪŋli
AM 'dʒɪrɪŋli

Jeeves
BR dʒiːvz
AM dʒivz

jeez
BR dʒiːz
AM dʒiz

Jeff
BR dʒɛf
AM dʒɛf

Jefferies
BR 'dʒɛfrɪz
AM 'dʒɛfriz

Jefferson
BR 'dʒɛfəs(ə)n
AM 'dʒɛfərsən

Jeffery
BR 'dʒɛfri
AM 'dʒɛfri

Jeffrey
BR 'dʒɛfri
AM 'dʒɛfri

Jeffreys
BR 'dʒɛfriz
AM 'dʒɛfriz

jehad
BR dʒɪ'had, dʒɪ'hɑːd, -z
AM dʒə'hæd, dʒə'hɑd, -z

Jehoshaphat
BR dʒɪ'hɒʃəfat, dʒɪ'hɒsəfat
AM dʒə'hɑsə,fæt

Jehovah
BR dʒɪ'həʊvə(r)
AM dʒə'hoʊvə

Jehovist
BR dʒɪ'həʊvɪst, -s
AM dʒə'hoʊvəst, -s

Jehu
BR 'dʒiːhjuː
AM 'dʒi,h(j)u

jejune
BR dʒɪ'dʒuːn
AM dʒə'dʒun

jejunely
BR dʒɪ'dʒuːnli
AM dʒə'dʒunli

jejuneness
BR dʒɪ'dʒuːnnəs
AM dʒə'dʒu(n)nəs

jejunum
BR dʒɪ'dʒuːnəm
AM dʒə'dʒunəm

Jekyll
BR 'dʒɛkl, 'dʒiːk(ɪ)l
AM 'dʒɛkəl

jell
BR dʒɛl, -z, -ɪŋ, -d

jellaba
BR 'dʒɛləbə(r), dʒɪ'lɑːbə(r), -z
AM 'dʒɛləbə, -z

jellabah
BR 'dʒɛləbə(r), dʒɪ'lɑːbə(r), -z
AM 'dʒɛləbə, -z

Jellicoe
BR 'dʒɛlɪkəʊ
AM 'dʒɛləkoʊ

jellification
BR ,dʒɛlɪfɪ'keɪʃn
AM ,dʒɛləfə'keɪʃən

jellify
BR 'dʒɛlɪfʌɪ, -z, -ɪŋ, -d
AM 'dʒɛlə,faɪ, -z, -ɪŋ, -d

jello
BR 'dʒɛləʊ
AM 'dʒɛloʊ

jelly
BR 'dʒɛl|i, -ɪz, -ɪɪŋ, -ɪd
AM 'dʒɛli, -z, -ɪŋ, -d

jellyfish
BR 'dʒɛlɪfɪʃ, -ɪz
AM 'dʒɛli,fɪʃ, -ɪz

Jem
BR dʒɛm
AM dʒɛm

Jemima
BR dʒɪ'mʌɪmə(r)
AM dʒə'maɪmə

Jemma
BR 'dʒɛmə(r)
AM 'dʒɛmə

jemmy
BR 'dʒɛm|i, -ɪz, -ɪɪŋ, -ɪd
AM 'dʒɛmi, -z, -ɪŋ, -d

Jena
BR 'jeɪnə(r)
AM 'jeɪnə

je ne sais quoi
BR ,ʒə nə seɪ 'kwɑː(r)
AM ,ʒə nə seɪ 'kwɑ

Jenifer
BR 'dʒɛnɪfə(r)
AM 'dʒɛnəfər

Jenkin
BR 'dʒɛŋkɪn
AM 'dʒɛŋkən

Jenkins
BR 'dʒɛŋkɪnz
AM 'dʒɛŋkənz

Jenkinson
BR 'dʒɛŋkɪns(ə)n
AM 'dʒɛŋkənsən

Jenna
BR 'dʒɛnə(r)
AM 'dʒɛnə

Jenner
BR 'dʒɛnə(r)
AM 'dʒɛnər

jennet
BR 'dʒɛnɪt, -s
AM 'dʒɛnət, -s

Jennifer
BR 'dʒɛnɪfə(r)
AM 'dʒɛnəfər

Jennings
BR 'dʒɛnɪŋz
AM 'dʒɛnɪŋz

jenny
BR 'dʒɛn|i, -ɪz
AM 'dʒɛni, -z

Jensen¹
foreign name
BR 'jɛnsn
AM 'jɛnsən

Jensen²
BR 'dʒɛnsn
AM 'dʒɛnsən

jeon
BR 'dʒiːɒn
AM 'dʒi,ɑn

jeopardise
BR 'dʒɛpədʌɪz, -ɪz, -ɪŋ, -d
AM 'dʒɛpər,daɪz, -ɪz, -ɪŋ, -d

jeopardize
BR 'dʒɛpədʌɪz, -ɪz, -ɪŋ, -d
AM 'dʒɛpər,daɪz, -ɪz, -ɪŋ, -d

jeopardy
BR 'dʒɛpədi
AM 'dʒɛpərdi

Jephthah
BR 'dʒɛfθə(r)
AM 'dʒɛf,tɑ

jequirity
BR dʒɪ'kwɪrɪti, -ɪz
AM dʒə'kwɪrɪdi, -z

Jerba
BR 'dʒɜː,bə(r)
AM 'dʒɜrbə

jerbil
BR 'dʒɜː,b(ɪ)l, -z
AM 'dʒɜrbəl, -z

jerboa
BR dʒɜː'bəʊə(r), dʒə'bəʊə(r), -z
AM dʒər'boʊə, -z

jeremiad
BR ,dʒɛrɪ'mʌɪəd, ,dʒɛrɪ'mʌɪad, -z
AM ,dʒɛrə'maɪəd, ,dʒɛrə'maɪ,æd, -z

Jeremiah
BR ,dʒɛrɪ'mʌɪə(r), -z
AM ,dʒɛrə'maɪə, -z

Jeremy
BR 'dʒɛrɪmi
AM 'dʒɛrəmi

Jerez
BR hɛ'rɛθ
AM hɛ'rɛs, hɛ'rɛθ
SP xe'reθ, xe'res

Jericho
BR 'dʒɛrɪkəʊ
AM 'dʒɛrə,koʊ

jerk
BR dʒɜːk, -s, -ɪŋ, -t

Jennifer right column —

jerk
AM dʒɜrk, -s, -ɪŋ, -t

jerker
BR 'dʒɜːkə(r), -z
AM 'dʒɜrkər, -z

jerkily
BR 'dʒɜːkɪli
AM 'dʒɜrkəli

jerkin
BR 'dʒɜːkɪn, -z
AM 'dʒɜrkən, -z

jerkiness
BR 'dʒɜːkɪnɪs
AM 'dʒɜrkinɪs

jerky
BR 'dʒɜːk|i, -ɪə(r), -ɪɪst
AM 'dʒɜrki, -ər, -ɪst

Jermaine
BR dʒə'meɪn
AM dʒər'meɪn

Jermyn
BR 'dʒɜː,mɪn
AM 'dʒɜrmən

jeroboam
BR ,dʒɛrə'bəʊəm, -z
AM ,dʒɛrə'boʊəm, -z

Jerome
BR dʒɪ'rəʊm, dʒɛ'rəʊm
AM dʒə'roʊm

jerry
BR 'dʒɛr|i, -ɪz
AM 'dʒɛri, -z

jerrycan
BR 'dʒɛrɪkan, -z
AM 'dʒɛri,kæn, -z

jerrymander
BR 'dʒɛrɪmandə(r), ,dʒɛrɪ'mandə(r), -əz, -(ə)rɪŋ, -əd
AM 'dʒɛri'mændər, -ərz, -(ə)rɪŋ, -ərd

jersey
BR 'dʒɜː,z|i, -ɪz
AM 'dʒɜrzi, -z

Jerusalem
BR dʒɪ'ruːs(ə)ləm
AM dʒə'rus(ə)ləm

Jervaulx¹
placename
BR 'dʒɜː,vəʊ
AM 'dʒɜrvoʊ

Jervaulx²
surname
BR 'dʒɜːvɪs
AM 'dʒɜrvəs

Jervis
BR 'dʒɜːvɪs
AM 'dʒɜrvəs

Jespersen
BR 'jɛspəs(ə)n, 'dʒɛspəs(ə)n
AM 'dʒɛspərsən, 'jɛspərsən

jess
BR dʒɛs, -ɪz, -ɪŋ, -t
AM dʒɛs, -əz, -ɪŋ, -t

jessamin
BR 'dʒɛsəmɪn, -z
AM 'dʒɛz(ə)mən, -z

jesse
BR 'dʒɛs|i, -ɪz
AM 'dʒɛs, -z

Jessel
BR 'dʒɛsl
AM 'dʒɛsəl

Jessica
BR 'dʒɛsɪkə(r)
AM 'dʒɛsəkə

Jessie
BR 'dʒɛsi
AM 'dʒɛsi

Jessop
BR 'dʒɛsəp
AM 'dʒɛsəp

jest
BR dʒɛst, -s, -ɪŋ, -ɪd
AM dʒɛst, -s, -ɪŋ, -əd

jester
BR 'dʒɛstə(r), -z
AM 'dʒɛstər, -z

jestful
BR 'dʒɛs(t)fʊl
AM 'dʒɛs(t)fəl

Jesu¹
when singing
BR 'dʒiːzjuː, 'jeɪzuː,
'jeɪsuː
AM 'dʒeɪzu

Jesu²
BR 'dʒiːzjuː
AM 'dʒizu

Jesuit
BR 'dʒɛzjʊɪt, 'dʒɛzʊɪt,
-s
AM 'dʒɛzəwət,
'dʒɛzəwət, -s

jesuitic
BR ,dʒɛzjʊ'ɪtɪk,
,dʒɛzʊ'ɪtɪk
AM ,dʒɛzʒə'wɪdɪk

Jesuitical
BR ,dʒɛzjʊ'ɪtɪkl,
,dʒɛzʊ'ɪtɪkl
AM ,dʒɛzʒə'wɪdɪkəl

Jesuitically
BR ,dʒɛzjʊ'ɪtɪkli,
,dʒɛzʊ'ɪtɪkli
AM ,dʒɛzʒə'wɪdɪk(ə)li

Jesus
BR 'dʒiːzəs
AM 'dʒizəs

jet
BR dʒɛt, -s, -ɪŋ, -ɪd
AM 'dʒɛ|t, -ts, -dɪŋ, -dəd

jeté
BR 'ʒɛteɪ, -z
AM ʒə'teɪ, -z

jetfoil
BR 'dʒɛtfɔɪl, -z
AM 'dʒɛt,fɔɪl, -z

Jethro
BR 'dʒɛθrəʊ
AM 'dʒɛθroʊ

jetlag
BR 'dʒɛtlag, -d
AM 'dʒɛt,læg, -d

jetliner
BR 'dʒɛt,lʌɪnə(r), -z
AM 'dʒɛt,laɪnə(r), -z

jeton
BR 'dʒɛt(ə)n, -z
AM 'dʒɛtn, ʒə'tɑn, -z

jetsam
BR 'dʒɛts(ə)m
AM 'dʒɛtsəm

jetstream
BR 'dʒɛtstriːm
AM 'dʒɛt,strim

jettison
BR 'dʒɛtɪs|(ə)n,
'dʒɛtɪz|(ə)n, -(ə)nz,
-nɪŋ \-ənɪŋ, -(ə)nd
AM 'dʒɛdəsən,
'dʒɛdəzən, -z, -ɪŋ, -d

jetton
BR 'dʒɛt(ə)n, -z
AM 'dʒɛtn, ʒə'tɑn, -z

jetty
BR 'dʒɛt|i, -ɪz
AM 'dʒɛdi, -z

jeu
BR ʒɜː(r), -z
AM ʒə, -z

jeu d'esprit
BR ,ʒɜː dɛ'spri:
AM ,ʒə də'spri

jeunesse dorée
BR ʒɜː,nɛs dɔː'reɪ,
,ʒɜːnɛs 'dɔːreɪ
AM ʒə,nɛs də'reɪ,
+ də'reɪ

jeux d'esprit
BR ,ʒɜː dɛ'spri:
AM ,ʒə(z) də'spri

Jevons
BR 'dʒɛvnz
AM 'dʒɛvənz

Jew
BR dʒuː, -z
AM dʒu, -z

jewel
BR 'dʒuː(ə)l, -z, -d
AM 'dʒu(ə)l, -z, -d

jeweler
BR 'dʒuː(ə)lə(r), -z
AM 'dʒu(ə)lər, -z

Jewell
BR 'dʒuː(ə)l
AM 'dʒu(ə)l

jeweller
BR 'dʒuː(ə)lə(r), -z
AM 'dʒu(ə)lər, -z

jewellery
BR 'dʒuː(ə)lri
AM 'dʒu(ə)lri

jewelly
BR 'dʒuː:əli
AM 'dʒu(ə)li

jewelry
BR 'dʒuː(ə)lri

AM 'dʒu(ə)lri

Jewess
BR 'dʒuːɛs, 'dʒuːɪs,
dʒuː'ɛs, -ɪz
AM 'dʒuəs, -əz

jewfish
BR 'dʒuːfɪʃ, -ɪz
AM 'dʒu,fɪʃ, -ɪz

Jewish
BR 'dʒuːɪʃ
AM 'dʒuɪʃ

Jewishly
BR 'dʒuːɪʃli
AM 'dʒuəʃli

Jewishness
BR 'dʒuːɪʃnɪs
AM 'dʒuɪʃnɪs

Jewry
BR 'dʒʊəri
AM 'dʒuri

Jewson
BR 'dʒuːsn
AM 'dʒusən

Jeyes
BR dʒeɪz
AM dʒeɪz

jezail
BR dʒɪ'zʌɪl, dʒɪ'zeɪl, -z
AM dʒə'zaɪ(ə)l,
dʒə'zeɪl, -z

Jezebel
BR 'dʒɛzəbɛl, -z
AM 'dʒɛzə,bɛl,
'dʒɛzəbəl, -z

Jezreel
BR 'dʒɛzrɪəl, dʒɛz'ri:l
AM 'dʒɛz,'ril

jib
BR dʒɪb, -z, -ɪŋ, -d
AM dʒɪb, -z, -ɪŋ, -d

jibba
BR 'dʒɪbə(r), -z
AM 'dʒɪbə, -z

jibbah
BR 'dʒɪbə(r), -z
AM 'dʒɪbə, -z

jibber
BR 'dʒɪb|ə(r), -əz,
-(ə)rɪŋ, -əd
AM 'dʒɪb|ər, -ərz,
-(ə)rɪŋ, -ərd

jibe
BR dʒʌɪb, -z, -ɪŋ, -d
AM dʒaɪb, -z, -ɪŋ, -d

Jibuti
BR dʒɪ'buːti
AM dʒɪ'budi

JICTAR
BR 'dʒɪktɑː(r)
AM 'dʒɪk,tɑr

Jiddah
BR 'dʒɪdə(r)
AM 'dʒɪdə

Jif®
BR dʒɪf
AM dʒɪf

jiff
BR dʒɪf, -s
AM dʒɪf, -s

jiffy
BR 'dʒɪf|i, -ɪz
AM 'dʒɪfi, -z

jig
BR dʒɪg, -z, -ɪŋ, -d
AM dʒɪg, -z, -ɪŋ, -d

jigaboo
BR 'dʒɪgəbuː, -z
AM 'dʒɪgə,bu, -z

jigger
BR 'dʒɪgə(r), -z, -d
AM 'dʒɪgər, -z, -d

jiggery-pokery
BR ,dʒɪg(ə)rɪ'pəʊk(ə)ri
AM ,dʒɪgəri'poʊkəri

jiggle
BR 'dʒɪg|l, -lz, -lɪŋ \-lɪŋ,
-ld
AM 'dʒɪg|əl, -əlz, -(ə)lɪŋ,
-əld

jiggly
BR 'dʒɪgli, 'dʒɪgli
AM 'dʒɪg(ə)li

jigot
BR 'dʒɪgət, -s
AM 'dʒɪgət, -s

jigsaw
BR 'dʒɪgsɔː(r), -z
AM 'dʒɪg,sɔ, 'dʒɪg,sɑ, -z

jihad
BR dʒɪ'had, dʒɪ'hɑːd, -z
AM dʒə'hæd, dʒə'had,
-z

jill
BR dʒɪl, -z
AM dʒɪl, -z

jillaroo
BR ,dʒɪlə'ruː, -z
AM ,dʒɪlə'ru, -z

jilleroo
BR ,dʒɪlə'ruː, -z
AM ,dʒɪlə'ru, -z

Jillian
BR 'dʒɪlɪən
AM 'dʒɪliən, 'dʒɪljən

jillion
BR 'dʒɪljən, -z
AM 'dʒɪljən, -z

jilt
BR dʒɪlt, -s, -ɪŋ, -ɪd
AM dʒɪlt, -s, -ɪŋ, -ɪd

Jim
BR dʒɪm
AM dʒɪm

Jim Crowism
BR ,dʒɪm 'krəʊɪz(ə)m
AM ,dʒɪm 'kroʊ,ɪzəm

jim-dandy
BR ,dʒɪm'dandi
AM 'dʒɪm'dændi

Jiménez
BR 'hɪmɪnɛz, hɪ'mɛnɛz
AM hɪ'mænɛz,
'hɪmənɛz

SP xi'meneθ, xi'menes

jiminy
BR 'dʒɪmɪni
AM 'dʒɪməni

jimjams
BR 'dʒɪmdʒamz
AM 'dʒɪm,dʒæmz

Jimmi
BR 'dʒɪmi
AM 'dʒɪmi

Jimmie
BR 'dʒɪmi
AM 'dʒɪmi

jimmy
BR 'dʒɪm|i, -ɪz, -ɪŋ, -ɪd
AM 'dʒɪmi, -z, -ɪŋ, -d

jimmygrant
BR 'dʒɪmɪɡrɑːnt,
'dʒɪmɪɡrant, -s
AM 'dʒɪmi,ɡrænt, -s

jimpson
BR 'dʒɪm(p)s(ə)n, -z
AM 'dʒɪmsən, -z

jimson
BR 'dʒɪms(ə)n, -z
AM 'dʒɪmsən, -z

Jin
BR dʒɪn
AM dʒɪn

Jinan
BR ,dʒɪ'nan
AM ,dʒɪ'næn

jingle
BR 'dʒɪŋɡ|l, -lz,
-|ɪŋ\-lɪŋ, -ld
AM 'dʒɪŋɡ|əl, -əlz,
-(ə)lɪŋ, -əld

jingly
BR 'dʒɪŋɡl|i, -ɪə(r), -ɪɪst
AM 'dʒɪŋli, -ər, -ɪst

jingo
BR 'dʒɪŋɡəʊ
AM 'dʒɪŋɡoʊ

jingoism
BR 'dʒɪŋɡəʊɪz(ə)m
AM 'dʒɪŋɡoʊ,ɪzəm

jingoist
BR 'dʒɪŋɡəʊɪst, -s
AM 'dʒɪŋɡoʊəst, -s

jingoistic
BR ,dʒɪŋɡəʊ'ɪstɪk
AM ,dʒɪŋɡoʊ'ɪstɪk

jink
BR 'dʒɪŋ|k, -ks, -kɪŋ,
-(k)t
AM 'dʒɪŋ|k, -ks, -kɪŋ,
-(k)t

jinker
BR 'dʒɪŋkə(r), -z
AM 'dʒɪŋkər, -z

jinks
BR dʒɪŋks
AM dʒɪŋks

jinn
BR dʒɪn, -z
AM dʒɪn, -z

Jinnah
BR 'dʒɪnə(r)
AM 'dʒɪnə

jinnee
BR 'dʒɪn|i, -ɪz
AM 'dʒɪni, -z

jinni
BR 'dʒɪn|i, -ɪz
AM 'dʒɪni, -z

Jinnie
BR 'dʒɪni
AM 'dʒɪni

Jinny
BR 'dʒɪni
AM 'dʒɪni

jinricksha
BR dʒɪn'rɪkʃə(r),
dʒɪn'rɪkʃɔː(r), -z
AM ,dʒɪn'rɪkʃə,
,dʒɪn'rɪkʃɑ, -z

jinrickshaw
BR dʒɪn'rɪkʃɔː(r), -z
AM ,dʒɪn'rɪkʃə,
,dʒɪn'rɪkʃɑ, -z

jinx
BR dʒɪŋks, -ɪz, -ɪŋ, -t
AM dʒɪŋks, -ɪz, -ɪŋ, -t

jipijapa
BR ,hiːpɪ'hɑːpə(r), -z
AM ,hipi'hɑpə, -z

jitney
BR 'dʒɪtn|i, -ɪz
AM 'dʒɪtni, -z

jitter
BR 'dʒɪt|ə(r), -əz,
-(ə)rɪŋ, -əd
AM 'dʒɪtər, -z, -ɪŋ, -d

jitterbug
BR 'dʒɪtəbʌɡ, -z, -ɪŋ, -d
AM 'dʒɪtər,bəɡ, -z, -ɪŋ,
-d

jitteriness
BR 'dʒɪt(ə)rɪnɪs
AM 'dʒɪdərinɪs

jittery
BR 'dʒɪt(ə)ri
AM 'dʒɪdəri

jiujitsu
BR ,dʒuː'dʒɪtsuː
AM ,dʒuː'dʒɪtsu

Jivaro
BR 'hiːvərəʊ, -z
AM 'jivərou, -z

jive
BR dʒʌɪv, -z, -ɪŋ, -d
AM dʒaɪv, -z, -ɪŋ, -d

jiver
BR 'dʒʌɪvə(r), -z
AM 'dʒaɪvər, -z

jizz
BR dʒɪz
AM dʒɪz

Jnr
BR 'dʒuːnɪə(r)
AM 'dʒunjər

jo
BR dʒəʊ, -z

AM dʒoʊ, -z

Joachim
BR 'dʒəʊəkɪm
AM wɑ'kim,
'dʒoʊə,kɪm

Joan
BR dʒəʊn
AM dʒoʊn

Joanna
BR dʒəʊ'anə(r)
AM dʒoʊ'ænə,
dʒə'wænə

Joanne
BR dʒəʊ'an
AM dʒoʊ'æn, dʒə'wæn

Joan of Arc
BR ,dʒəʊn əv 'ɑːk
AM 'dʒoʊn əv 'ɑrk

Job
name
BR dʒəʊb
AM dʒoʊb

job
BR dʒɒb, -z, -ɪŋ
AM dʒab, -z, -ɪŋ

jobber
BR 'dʒɒbə(r), -z
AM 'dʒabər, -z

jobbery
BR 'dʒɒb(ə)ri
AM 'dʒabəri

jobcentre
BR 'dʒɒb,sentə(r), -z
AM 'dʒab,sen(t)ər, -z

jobholder
BR 'dʒɒb,həʊldə(r), -z
AM 'dʒab,(h)oʊldər, -z

jobless
BR 'dʒɒbləs
AM 'dʒabləs

joblessness
BR 'dʒɒbləsnəs
AM 'dʒabləsnəs

Jobling
BR 'dʒɒblɪŋ
AM 'dʒablɪŋ

Job's comforter
BR ,dʒəʊbz
'kʌmfətə(r), -z
AM ,dʒoʊbz
'kəmfərdər, -z

jobsheet
BR 'dʒɒbʃiːt, -s
AM 'dʒab,ʃit, -s

jobsworth
BR 'dʒɒbzwə:θ,
'dʒɒbzwəθ, -s
AM 'dʒabz,wər|θ,
-θs\-ðz

Jo'burg
BR 'dʒəʊbə:ɡ
AM 'dʒoʊ,bərɡ

jobwork
BR 'dʒɒbwəːk
AM 'dʒab,wərk

Jocasta
BR dʒə(ʊ)'kastə(r)

AM dʒoʊ, -z

Jocelyn
BR 'dʒɒs(ə)lɪn,
'dʒɒslɪn
AM 'dʒɑs(ə)lən

jock
BR dʒɒk, -s
AM dʒɑk, -s

jockey
BR 'dʒɒk|i, -ɪz, -ɪɪŋ, -ɪd
AM 'dʒɑki, -z, -ɪŋ, -d

jockeydom
BR 'dʒɒkɪdəm
AM 'dʒɑkidəm

jockeyship
BR 'dʒɒkɪʃɪp
AM 'dʒɑki,ʃɪp

jockstrap
BR 'dʒɒkstrap, -s
AM 'dʒɑk,stræp, -s

jocose
BR dʒə(ʊ)'kəʊs
AM dʒoʊ'koʊs

jocosely
BR dʒə(ʊ)'kəʊsli
AM dʒoʊ'koʊsli

jocoseness
BR dʒə(ʊ)'kəʊsnəs
AM dʒoʊ'koʊsnəs

jocosity
BR dʒə(ʊ)'kɒsɪti
AM dʒoʊ'kasədi

jocular
BR 'dʒɒkjʉlə(r)
AM 'dʒɑkjələr

jocularity
BR ,dʒɒkjʉ'larɪt|i, -ɪz
AM ,dʒɑkjə'lɛrədi, -z

jocularly
BR 'dʒɒkjʉləli
AM 'dʒɑkjələrli

jocund
BR 'dʒɒk(ə)nd,
'dʒəʊk(ə)nd,
'dʒəʊkʌnd
AM 'dʒɑkənd,
'dʒoʊkənd

jocundity
BR dʒə'kʌndɪti,
dʒɒ'kʌndɪti,
dʒəʊ'kʌndɪti
AM dʒɑ'kəndədi,
dʒoʊ'kəndədi

jocundly
BR 'dʒɒk(ə)ndli,
'dʒɒkʌndli,
'dʒəʊk(ə)ndli,
'dʒəʊkʌndli
AM 'dʒɑkən(d)li,
'dʒoʊkən(d)li

jocundness
BR 'dʒɒk(ə)n(d)nəs,
'dʒɒkʌn(d)nəs,
'dʒəʊk(ə)n(d)nəs,
'dʒəʊkʌn(d)nəs
AM 'dʒɑkən(d)nəs,
'dʒoʊkən(d)nəs

jodel
BR ˈjəʊd|l, -lz, -lɪŋ\-lɪŋ,
-ld
AM ˈjoʊd|əl, -əlz,
-(ə)lɪŋ, -əld
Jodhpur
BR ˈdʒɒdpʊə(r),
ˈdʒɒdpɔː(r)
AM ˈdʒadpər
jodhpurs
BR ˈdʒɒdpəz
AM ˈdʒadpərz
Jodie
BR ˈdʒəʊdi
AM ˈdʒoʊdi
Jodrell Bank
BR ˌdʒɒdr(ə)l ˈbaŋk
AM ˈdʒadrəl ˈbæŋk
Jody
BR ˈdʒəʊdi
AM ˈdʒoʊdi
Joe
BR dʒəʊ
AM dʒoʊ
Joe Bloggs
BR ˌdʒəʊ ˈblɒgz
AM ˌdʒoʊ ˈblagz
Joe Blow
BR ˌdʒəʊ ˈbləʊ
AM ˈdʒoʊ ˈbloʊ
Joel
BR dʒəʊl
AM dʒoʊ(ə)l
joey
BR ˈdʒəʊ|i, -ɪz
AM ˈdʒoʊi, -z
jog
BR dʒɒg, -z, -ɪŋ, -d
AM dʒag, -z, -ɪŋ, -d
jogger
BR ˈdʒɒgə(r), -z
AM ˈdʒagər, -z
joggle
BR ˈdʒɒg|l, -lz,
-lɪŋ\-lɪŋ, -ld
AM ˈdʒag|əl, -əlz,
-(ə)lɪŋ, -əld
Jogjakarta
BR ˌdʒɒgdʒəˈkaːtə(r)
AM ˌdʒagdʒəˈkardə
jogtrot
BR ˈdʒɒgtrɒt, -s, -ɪŋ, -ɪd
AM ˈdʒag,traɪt, -ts, -dɪŋ,
-dəd
Johanna
BR dʒəʊˈanə(r)
AM dʒoʊˈænə
Johannesburg
BR dʒə(ʊ)ˈhanɪzbəːg,
dʒə(ʊ)ˈhanɪsbəːg
AM dʒoʊˈhanəs,bərg
john
BR dʒɒn, -z
AM dʒan, -z
Johnnie
BR ˈdʒɒni
AM ˈdʒani

johnny
BR ˈdʒɒn|i, -ɪz
AM ˈdʒani, -z
johnnycake
BR ˈdʒɒnɪkeɪk, -s
AM ˈdʒani,keɪk, -s
John o'Groats
BR ˌdʒɒn əˈgrəʊts
AM ˌdʒan əˈgroʊts
Johns
BR dʒɒnz
AM dʒanz
Johnson
BR ˈdʒɒnsn
AM ˈdʒansən
Johnsonian
BR ˌdʒɒnˈsəʊnɪən
AM ˌdʒanˈsoʊnɪən
Johnston
BR ˈdʒɒnst(ə)n,
ˈdʒɒnsn
AM ˈdʒanstən
Johnstone
BR ˈdʒɒnst(ə)n,
ˈdʒɒnsn, ˈdʒɒnstəʊn
AM ˈdʒanstən,
ˈdʒan,stoʊn
Johor
BR dʒəˈhɔː(r)
AM dʒəˈhɔ(ə)r
Johore
BR dʒəˈhɔː(r)
AM dʒəˈhɔ(ə)r
joie de vivre
BR ˌʒwaː də ˈviːvr(ər)
AM ˌʒwa də ˈvivrə
join
BR dʒɔɪn, -z, -ɪŋ, -d
AM dʒɔɪn, -z, -ɪŋ, -d
joinable
BR ˈdʒɔɪnəbl
AM ˈdʒɔɪnəbəl
joinder
BR ˈdʒɔɪndə(r)
AM ˈdʒɔɪndər
joiner
BR ˈdʒɔɪnə(r), -z
AM ˈdʒɔɪnər, -z
joinery
BR ˈdʒɔɪn(ə)ri
AM ˈdʒɔɪnəri
joint
BR dʒɔɪnt, -s, -ɪŋ, -ɪd
AM dʒɔɪn|t, -ts, -(t)ɪŋ,
-(t)ɪd
jointedly
BR ˈdʒɔɪntɪdli
AM ˈdʒɔɪn(t)ɪdli
jointedness
BR ˈdʒɔɪntɪdnɪs
AM ˈdʒɔɪn(t)ɪdnɪs
jointer
BR ˈdʒɔɪntə(r), -z
AM ˈdʒɔɪn(t)ər, -z
jointless
BR ˈdʒɔɪntlɪs
AM ˈdʒɔɪntləs

jointly
BR ˈdʒɔɪntli
AM ˈdʒɔɪn(t)li
jointress
BR ˈdʒɔɪntrɪs, -ɪz
AM ˈdʒɔɪntrəs, -əz
jointure
BR ˈdʒɔɪntʃə(r), -z
AM ˈdʒɔɪn(t)ʃər, -z
joist
BR dʒɔɪst, -s
AM dʒɔɪst, -s
jojoba
BR hə(ʊ)ˈhəʊbə(r)
AM hoʊˈhoʊbə
joke
BR dʒəʊk, -s, -ɪŋ, -t
AM dʒoʊk, -s, -ɪŋ, -t
joker
BR ˈdʒəʊkə(r), -z
AM ˈdʒoʊkər, -z
jokesmith
BR ˈdʒəʊksmɪθ, -s
AM ˈdʒoʊk,smɪ|θ,
-θs\-ðz
jokey
BR ˈdʒəʊki
AM ˈdʒoʊki
jokily
BR ˈdʒəʊkɪli
AM ˈdʒoʊkəli
jokiness
BR ˈdʒəʊkɪnɪs
AM ˈdʒoʊkinɪs
jokingly
BR ˈdʒəʊkɪŋli
AM ˈdʒoʊkɪŋli
joky
BR ˈdʒəʊki
AM ˈdʒoʊki
Jolene
BR dʒəʊˈliːn
AM dʒoʊˈlin
Jolley
BR ˈdʒɒli
AM ˈdʒali
Jollie
BR ˈdʒɒli
AM ˈdʒali
jollification
BR ˌdʒɒlɪfɪˈkeɪʃn, -z
AM ˌdʒaləfəˈkeɪʃən, -z
jollify
BR ˈdʒɒlɪfʌɪ, -z, -ɪŋ, -d
AM ˈdʒalə,faɪ, -z, -ɪŋ, -d
jollily
BR ˈdʒɒlɪli
AM ˈdʒaləli
jolliness
BR ˈdʒɒlɪnɪs
AM ˈdʒalinɪs
jollity
BR ˈdʒɒlɪti
AM ˈdʒalədi
jollo
BR ˈdʒɒləʊ, -z
AM ˈdʒa,loʊ, -z

jolly
BR ˈdʒɒl|i, -ɪz, -ɪɪŋ, -ɪd,
-ɪə(r), -ɪɪst
AM ˈdʒali, -z, -ɪŋ, -d, -ər,
-ɪst
jollyboat
BR ˈdʒɒlɪbəʊt, -s
AM ˈdʒali,boʊt, -s
Jolson
BR ˈdʒəʊls(ə)n
AM ˈdʒoʊlsən
jolt
BR dʒəʊlt, -s, -ɪŋ, -ɪd
AM dʒoʊlt, -s, -ɪŋ, -ɪd
joltily
BR ˈdʒəʊltɪli
AM ˈdʒoʊltəli
joltiness
BR ˈdʒəʊltɪnɪs
AM ˈdʒoʊltinɪs
jolty
BR ˈdʒəʊlt|i, -ɪə(r), -ɪɪst
AM ˈdʒoʊlti, -ər, -ɪst
Jolyon
BR ˈdʒəʊlɪən, ˈdʒɒlɪən
AM ˈdʒaliən
Jomon
BR ˈdʒəʊmɒn
AM ˈdʒoʊman
Jon
BR dʒɒn
AM dʒan
Jonah
BR ˈdʒəʊnə(r), -z
AM ˈdʒoʊnə, -z
Jonas
BR ˈdʒəʊnəs
AM ˈdʒoʊnəs
Jonathan
BR ˈdʒɒnəθ(ə)n
AM ˈdʒanəθən
Jones
BR dʒəʊnz
AM dʒoʊnz
Joneses
BR ˈdʒəʊnzɪz
AM ˈdʒoʊnzəz
Jong
BR jɒŋ
AM jɒŋ, jaŋ
jongleur
BR ʒɔ̃ˈgləː(r),
ʒɒŋˈgləː(r), -z
AM ʒɒnˈglər, ˈdʒaŋglər,
-z
jonquil
BR ˈdʒɒŋkw(ɪ)l, -z
AM ˈdʒankwəl, -z
Jonson
BR ˈdʒɒns(ə)n
AM ˈdʒansən
Jools
BR dʒuːlz
AM dʒulz
Joplin
BR ˈdʒɒplɪn
AM ˈdʒaplən

Jopling
BR ˈdʒɒplɪŋ
AM ˈdʒɑplɪŋ

Joppa
BR ˈdʒɒpə(r)
AM ˈdʒɑpə

Jordan
BR ˈdʒɔːdn
AM ˈdʒɔrdən

Jordanhill
BR ˌdʒɔːdnˈhɪl
AM ˌdʒɔrdənˈhɪl

Jordanian
BR dʒɔːˈdeɪniən, -z
AM dʒɔrˈdeɪniən, -z

jorum
BR ˈdʒɔːrəm, -z
AM ˈdʒɔrəm, -z

Jorvik
BR ˈjɔːvɪk
AM ˈjɔrˌvɪk

Josceline
BR ˈdʒɒs(ə)lɪn
AM ˈdʒɑslən

José
BR həʊˈzeɪ, həʊˈseɪ
AM hoʊˈzeɪ, hoʊˈseɪ

Joseph
BR ˈdʒəʊzɪf
AM ˈdʒoʊzəf, ˈdʒoʊsəf

Josephine
BR ˈdʒəʊzfiːn
AM ˈdʒoʊzəfin

Josephus
BR dʒə(ʊ)ˈsiːfəs
AM ˌdʒoʊˈsifəs

josh
BR dʒɒʃ, -ɪz, -ɪŋ, -t
AM dʒɑʃ, -əz, -ɪŋ, -t

josher
BR ˈdʒɒʃə(r), -z
AM ˈdʒɑʃər, -z

Joshua
BR ˈdʒɒʃ(j)ʊə(r)
AM ˈdʒɑʃ(ə)wə

Josiah
BR dʒə(ʊ)ˈzʌɪə(r),
dʒə(ʊ)ˈsʌɪə(r)
AM ˌdʒoʊˈsaɪə,
ˌdʒoʊˈzaɪə

Josie
BR ˈdʒəʊzi, ˈdʒəʊsi
AM ˈdʒoʊzi

joss
BR dʒɒs
AM dʒɔs, dʒɑs

josser
BR ˈdʒɒsə(r), -z
AM ˈdʒɔsər, ˈdʒɑsər, -z

jostle
BR ˈdʒɒs|l, -lz, -ɪŋ \-l|ŋ,
-ld
AM ˈdʒɑs|əl, -əlz,
-(ə)lŋ, -əld

jot
BR dʒɒt, -s, -ɪŋ, -ɪd
AM dʒɑ|t, -ts, -dɪŋ, -dəd

jota
BR ˈxəʊtə(r), -z
AM ˈhoʊdə, -z

jotter
BR ˈdʒɒtə(r), -z
AM ˈdʒɑdər, -z

jougs
BR dʒuːgz
AM dʒugz

Joule
BR dʒuːl
AM dʒul

joule
BR dʒuːl, -z
AM dʒul, -z

jounce
BR dʒaʊns, -ɪz, -ɪŋ, -t
AM dʒaʊns, -əz, -ɪŋ, -t

journal
BR ˈdʒɜːnl, -z
AM ˈdʒɜrnəl, -z

journalese
BR ˌdʒɜːnəˈliːz,
ˌdʒɜːnlˈiːz
AM ˌdʒɜrnlˈiz

journalise
BR ˈdʒɜːnəlʌɪz,
ˈdʒɜːn| lʌɪz, -ɪz, -ɪŋ, -d
AM ˈdʒɜrnlˌaɪz, -ɪz, -ɪŋ,
-d

journalism
BR ˈdʒɜːnəlɪz(ə)m,
ˈdʒɜːn|lɪz(ə)m
AM ˈdʒɜrnlˌɪzəm

journalist
BR ˈdʒɜːnəlɪst,
ˈdʒɜːn|lɪst, -s
AM ˈdʒɜrn|ləst -s

journalistic
BR ˌdʒɜːnəˈlɪstɪk,
ˌdʒɜːn|lˈɪstɪk
AM ˌdʒɜrnlˈɪstɪk

journalistically
BR ˌdʒɜːnəˈlɪstɪkli,
ˌdʒɜːn|lˈɪstɪkli
AM ˌdʒɜrnlˈɪstək(ə)li

journalize
BR ˈdʒɜːnəlʌɪz,
ˈdʒɜːn|lʌɪz, -ɪz, -ɪŋ, -d
AM ˈdʒɜrnlˌaɪz, -ɪz, -ɪŋ,
-d

journey
BR ˈdʒɜːn|i, -ɪz, -ɪŋ, -ɪd
AM ˈdʒɜrni, -z, -ɪŋ, -d

journeyer
BR ˈdʒɜːnɪə(r), -z
AM ˈdʒɜrniər, -z

journeyman
BR ˈdʒɜːnɪmən
AM ˈdʒɜrnɪmən

journeymen
BR ˈdʒɜːnɪmən
AM ˈdʒɜrnɪmən

journo
BR ˈdʒɜːnəʊ, -z
AM ˈdʒɜrnoʊ, -z

joust
BR dʒaʊst, -s, -ɪŋ, -ɪd

jouster
BR ˈdʒaʊstə(r), -z
AM ˈdʒaʊstər, -z

Jove
BR dʒəʊv
AM dʒoʊv

jovial
BR ˈdʒəʊviəl
AM ˈdʒoʊviəl

joviality
BR ˌdʒəʊviˈalɪti
AM ˌdʒoʊviˈælədi

jovially
BR ˈdʒəʊviəli
AM ˈdʒoʊviəli

Jovian
BR ˈdʒəʊviən
AM ˈdʒoʊviən

jowar
BR dʒaʊˈwɑː(r)
AM dʒəˈwɑr

Jowett
BR ˈdʒaʊɪt, ˈdʒəʊɪt, -s
AM ˈdʒaʊət, ˈdʒoʊət, -s

Jowitt
BR ˈdʒaʊɪt, ˈdʒəʊɪt
AM ˈdʒaʊət, ˈdʒoʊət

jowl
BR dʒaʊl, -z, -d
AM dʒaʊl, -z, -d

jowly
BR ˈdʒaʊli
AM ˈdʒaʊli, ˈdʒaʊəli

joy
BR dʒɔɪ, -z
AM dʒɔɪ, -z

Joyce
BR dʒɔɪs
AM dʒɔɪs

Joycean
BR ˈdʒɔɪsiən
AM ˈdʒɔɪsiən

joyful
BR ˈdʒɔɪf(ʊ)l
AM ˈdʒɔɪfəl

joyfully
BR ˈdʒɔɪfʊli, ˈdʒɔɪfli
AM ˈdʒɔɪfəli

joyfulness
BR ˈdʒɔɪf(ʊ)lnəs
AM ˈdʒɔɪfəlnəs

joyless
BR ˈdʒɔɪlɪs
AM ˈdʒɔɪlɪs

joylessly
BR ˈdʒɔɪlɪsli
AM ˈdʒɔɪlɪsli

joylessness
BR ˈdʒɔɪlɪsnɪs
AM ˈdʒɔɪlɪsnɪs

joyous
BR ˈdʒɔɪəs
AM ˈdʒɔɪəs

joyously
BR ˈdʒɔɪəsli
AM ˈdʒɔɪəsli

joyousness
BR ˈdʒɔɪəsnəs
AM ˈdʒɔɪəsnəs

joyride
BR ˈdʒɔɪrʌɪd, -z, -ɪŋ
AM ˈdʒɔɪˌraɪd, -z, -ɪŋ

joyrider
BR ˈdʒɔɪrʌɪdə(r), -z
AM ˈdʒɔɪˌraɪdər, -z

joystick
BR ˈdʒɔɪstɪk, -s
AM ˈdʒɔɪˌstɪk, -s

JPEG
BR ˈdʒeɪpɛg
AM ˈdʒeɪˌpɛg

Jr
BR ˈdʒuniə(r)
AM ˈdʒunjər

Juan
BR hwɑːn
AM (h)wɑn

Juanita
BR (h)wəˈniːtə(r)
AM (h)wəˈnidə

Juárez
BR ˈhwɑːrɛz
AM ˌ(h)wɑˈrɛz

Juba
BR ˈdʒuːbə(r)
AM ˈdʒubə

jube[1]
in a church
BR ˈdʒuːb|i, -ɪz
AM ˈjuˌbeɪ, -z

jube[2]
watercourse
BR dʒuːb, -z
AM dʒub, -z

jubilance
BR ˈdʒuːbɪləns,
ˈdʒuːbɪlns,
ˈdʒuːbl(ə)ns
AM ˈdʒubələns

jubilant
BR ˈdʒuːbɪlənt,
ˈdʒuːbɪlnt,
ˈdʒuːbl(ə)nt
AM ˈdʒubələnt

jubilantly
BR ˈdʒuːbɪləntli,
ˈdʒuːbɪlntli,
ˈdʒuːbl(ə)ntli
AM ˈdʒubələn(t)li

Jubilate
noun
BR ˌdʒuːbɪˈlɑːteɪ
AM ˌdʒubəˈladeɪ

jubilate
verb
BR ˈdʒuːbɪleɪt, -s, -ɪŋ,
-ɪd
AM ˈdʒubəˌleɪ|t, -ts,
-dɪŋ, -dɪd

jubilation
BR ˌdʒuːbɪˈleɪʃn
AM ˌdʒubəˈleɪʃən

jubilee
BR 'dʒuːbɪliː, -z
AM 'dʒubə,li, ,dʒubə'li,
-z

Judaea
BR dʒuː'dɪə(r),
dʒʊ'dɪə(r)
AM dʒu'diə

Judaean
BR dʒuː'dɪən, dʒʊ'dɪən
AM dʒu'diən

Judaeo-Christian
BR dʒʊ,deɪəʊ'krɪstʃ(ə)n
AM dʒu'deɪoʊ'krɪstʃən

Judah
BR 'dʒuːdə(r)
AM 'dʒudə

Judaic
BR dʒuː'deɪɪk,
dʒʊ'deɪɪk
AM dʒu'deɪɪk

Judaism
BR 'dʒuːdeɪɪz(ə)m
AM 'dʒudə,ɪzəm,
'dʒudi,ɪzəm

Judaization
BR ,dʒuːdə(r)ʌɪ'zeɪʃn
AM ,dʒudeɪɪ'zeɪʃən,
,dʒudiː'zeɪʃən

Judaize
BR 'dʒuːdə(r)ʌɪz, -ɪz,
-ɪŋ, -d
AM 'dʒudə,aɪz,
'dʒudi,aɪz, -ɪz, -ɪŋ, -d

Judas
BR 'dʒuːdəs, -ɪz
AM 'dʒudəs, -əz

Judas Iscariot
BR ,dʒuːdəs ɪ'skarɪət
AM 'dʒudəs ɪs'kɛriət

Judas Maccabaeus
BR ,dʒuːdəs
,makə'biːəs
AM 'dʒudəs
,mækə'biəs

Judd
BR dʒʌd
AM dʒəd

judder
BR 'dʒʌd|ə(r), -əz,
-(ə)rɪŋ, -əd
AM 'dʒədər, -z, -ɪŋ, -d

Jude
BR dʒuːd
AM dʒud

Judea
BR dʒuː'dɪə(r),
dʒʊ'dɪə(r)
AM dʒu'diə

Judean
BR dʒuː'dɪən, dʒʊ'dɪən
AM dʒu'diən

Judeo-Christian
BR dʒʊ,deɪəʊ'krɪstʃ(ə)n
AM dʒu'deɪoʊ'krɪstʃən

judge
BR dʒʌdʒ, -ɪz, -ɪŋ, -d

AM dʒədʒ, -əz, -ɪŋ, -d

judgelike
BR 'dʒʌdʒlʌɪk
AM 'dʒədʒ,laɪk

judgematic
BR dʒʌdʒ'matɪk
AM dʒədʒ'mædɪk

judgematical
BR dʒʌdʒ'matɪkl
AM dʒədʒ'mædəkəl

judgematically
BR dʒʌdʒ'matɪkli
AM dʒədʒ'mædək(ə)li

judgement
BR 'dʒʌdʒm(ə)nt, -s
AM 'dʒədʒmənt, -s

judgemental
BR dʒʌdʒ'mɛntl
AM dʒədʒ'mɛn(t)l

judgementally
BR dʒʌdʒ'mɛntli,
dʒʌdʒ'mɛntəli
AM dʒədʒ'mɛn(t)li

Judges
BR 'dʒʌdʒɪz
AM 'dʒədʒəz

judgeship
BR 'dʒʌdʒʃɪp, -s
AM 'dʒədʒ,ʃɪp, -s

judgment
BR 'dʒʌdʒm(ə)nt, -s
AM 'dʒədʒmənt, -s

judgmental
BR dʒʌdʒ'mɛntl
AM dʒədʒ'mɛn(t)l

judgmentally
BR dʒʌdʒ'mɛntli,
dʒʌdʒ'mɛntəli
AM dʒədʒ'mɛn(t)li

Judi
BR 'dʒuːd|i, -ɪz
AM 'dʒudi, -z

judicative
BR 'dʒuːdɪkətɪv
AM 'dʒudə,keɪdɪv

judicatory
BR 'dʒuːdɪkət(ə)r|i,
dʒʊ'dɪkət(ə)r|i, -ɪz
AM 'dʒudəkə,tɔri, -z

judicature
BR 'dʒuːdɪkətʃə(r),
dʒʊ'dɪkətʃə(r)
AM 'dʒudəkə,tʃʊ(ə)r,
dʒudəkətʃər,
'dʒudə,keɪtʃər

judicial
BR dʒʊ'dɪʃl
AM dʒu'dɪʃəl

judicially
BR dʒʊ'dɪʃli,
dʒʊ'dɪʃəli
AM dʒu'dɪʃ(ə)li

judiciary
BR dʒʊ'dɪʃ(ə)ri
AM dʒu'dɪʃi,ɛri,
dʒu'dɪʃəri

judicious
BR dʒʊ'dɪʃəs
AM dʒu'dɪʃəs

judiciously
BR dʒʊ'dɪʃəsli
AM dʒu'dɪʃəsli

judiciousness
BR dʒʊ'dɪʃəsnəs
AM dʒu'dɪʃəsnəs

Judith
BR 'dʒuːdɪθ
AM 'dʒudəθ

judo
BR 'dʒuːdəʊ
AM 'dʒudoʊ

judoist
BR 'dʒuːdəʊɪst, -s
AM 'dʒudoʊəst, -s

judoka
BR 'dʒuːdəʊkə(r), -z
AM 'dʒudoʊ,ka,
,dʒudoʊ'ka, -z

Judy
BR 'dʒuːd|i, -ɪz
AM 'dʒudi, -z

jug
BR dʒʌg, -z, -ɪŋ, -d
AM dʒəg, -z, -ɪŋ, -d

Jugendstil
BR 'juː.gənt-ʃtiːl
AM 'jugənt,stil

jugful
BR 'dʒʌgfʊl, -z
AM 'dʒəg,fʊl, -z

juggernaut
BR 'dʒʌgənɔːt, -s
AM 'dʒəgər,nɔt,
'dʒəgər,nat, -s

juggins
BR 'dʒʌgɪnz, -ɪz
AM 'dʒəgənz, -əz

juggle
BR 'dʒʌg|l, -lz,
-lɪŋ \ -lɪŋ, -ld
AM 'dʒəg|əl, -əlz,
-(ə)lɪŋ, -əld

juggler
BR 'dʒʌglə(r), -z
AM 'dʒəg(ə)lər, -z

jugglery
BR 'dʒʌglər|i, -ɪz
AM 'dʒəgləri, -z

Jugoslav
BR 'juːgə(ʊ)slɑːv, -z
AM 'jugoʊ,slav,
'jugə,slav, -z

Jugoslavia
BR ,juːgə(ʊ)'slɑːvɪə(r)
AM ,jugoʊ'slaviə,
,jugə'slaviə

Jugoslavian
BR ,juːgə(ʊ)'slɑːvɪən,
-z
AM ,jugoʊ'slaviən,
,jugə'slaviən, -z

jugular
BR 'dʒʌgjʊlə(r), -z
AM 'dʒəgjələr, -z

jugulate
BR 'dʒʌgjʊleɪt, -s, -ɪŋ,
-ɪd
AM 'dʒəgjə,leɪ|t, -ts,
-dɪŋ, -dɪd

Jugurtha
BR dʒʊ'gɜːθə(r)
AM dʒu'gərθə

Jugurthine
BR dʒʊ'gɜːθʌɪn
AM dʒu'gərθən,
dʒu'gər,θin

juice
BR dʒuːs, -ɪz
AM dʒus, -əz

juiceless
BR 'dʒuːsləs
AM 'dʒusləs

juicer
BR 'dʒuːsə(r), -z
AM 'dʒusər, -z

juicily
BR 'dʒuːsɪli
AM 'dʒusəli

juiciness
BR 'dʒuːsɪnɪs
AM 'dʒusɪnɪs

juicy
BR 'dʒuːs|i, -ɪə(r), -ɪɪst
AM 'dʒusi, -ər, -ɪst

jujitsu
BR ,dʒuː'dʒɪtsuː
AM ,dʒu'dʒɪtsu

juju
BR 'dʒuːdʒuː, -z
AM 'dʒudʒu, -z

jujube
BR 'dʒuːdʒuːb, -z
AM 'dʒu,dʒub,
'dʒudʒəbi, -z

jujutsu
BR ,dʒuː'dʒʌtsuː
AM ,dʒu'dʒɪtsu

jukebox
BR 'dʒuːkbɒks, -ɪz
AM 'dʒuk,baks, -əz

Jukes
BR dʒuːks
AM dʒuks

juku
BR 'dʒʊkuː, -z
AM 'dʒʊku, -z

julep
BR 'dʒuːlɪp, 'dʒuːlɛp, -s
AM 'dʒuləp, -s

Jules
BR dʒuːlz
AM dʒulz

Julia
BR 'dʒuːlɪə(r)
AM 'dʒuljə, 'dʒuliə

Julian
BR 'dʒuːlɪən
AM 'dʒuliən

Julie
BR 'dʒuːli
AM 'dʒuli

Julien
BR 'dʒuːliən
AM 'dʒuliən

julienne
BR ˌdʒuːliˈɛn
AM ˌ(d)ʒuliˈɛn,
(d)ʒulˈjɛn

Juliet
BR 'dʒuːliət, ˌdʒuːlɪˈɛt
AM ˌdʒuliˈɛt, 'dʒuljət

Julius
BR 'dʒuːliəs
AM 'dʒuliəs

July
BR dʒʊˈlaɪ, -z
AM dʒəˈlaɪ, dʒuˈlaɪ, -z

jumble
BR 'dʒʌmb|l, -lz,
-lɪŋ\-lɪŋ, -ld
AM 'dʒəmb|əl, -əlz,
-(ə)lɪŋ, -əld

jumbly
BR 'dʒʌmbl|i, -iə(r),
-ɪɪst
AM 'dʒəmbli,
'dʒəmbəli, -ər, -ɪst

jumbo
BR 'dʒʌmbəʊ, -z
AM 'dʒəmboʊ, -z

jumboise
BR 'dʒʌmbəʊʌɪz, -ɪz,
-ɪŋ, -d
AM 'dʒəmboʊˌaɪz, -ɪz,
-ɪŋ, -d

jumboize
BR 'dʒʌmbəʊʌɪz, -ɪz,
-ɪŋ, -d
AM 'dʒəmboʊˌaɪz, -ɪz,
-ɪŋ, -d

jumbuck
BR 'dʒʌmbʌk, -s
AM 'dʒəmbək, -s

jump
BR dʒʌm|p, -ps, -pɪŋ,
-(p)t
AM dʒəmp, -s, -ɪŋ, -t

jumpable
BR 'dʒʌmpəbl
AM 'dʒəmpəbəl

jumper
BR 'dʒʌmpə(r), -z
AM 'dʒəmpər, -z

jumpily
BR 'dʒʌmpɪli
AM 'dʒəmpəli

jumpiness
BR 'dʒʌmpɪnɪs
AM 'dʒəmpɪnɪs

jumpsuit
BR 'dʒʌmps(j)uːt, -s
AM 'dʒəm(p)ˌsut, -s

jumpy
BR 'dʒʌmp|i, -iə(r),
-ɪɪst
AM 'dʒəmpi, -ər, -ɪst

Jun.
BR 'dʒuːniə(r)
AM 'dʒunjər

junco
BR 'dʒʌŋkəʊ, -z
AM 'dʒəŋkoʊ, -z

junction
BR 'dʒʌŋ(k)ʃn, -z
AM 'dʒəŋ(k)ʃən, -z

juncture
BR 'dʒʌŋ(k)tʃə(r), -z
AM 'dʒəŋ(k)(t)ʃər, -z

June
BR dʒuːn, -z
AM dʒun, -z

Juneau
BR 'dʒuːnəʊ
AM 'dʒuˌnoʊ

Jung
BR jʊŋ
AM jʊŋ

Jungfrau
BR 'jʊŋfraʊ
AM 'jʊŋˌfraʊ

Jungian
BR 'jʊŋgiən
AM 'jʊŋgiən

jungle
BR 'dʒʌŋgl, -z, -d
AM 'dʒəŋgəl, -z, -d

jungly
BR 'dʒʌŋgl|i, -iə(r),
-ɪɪst
AM 'dʒəŋgli, 'dʒəŋgəli,
-ər, -ɪst

junior
BR 'dʒuːniə(r), -z
AM 'dʒunjər, -z

juniorate
BR 'dʒuːniərət, -s
AM 'dʒunjərət,
'dʒunjəˌreɪt, -s

juniority
BR dʒuːnɪˈɒrɪti
AM dʒunˈjorədi

juniper
BR 'dʒuːnɪpə(r), -z
AM 'dʒunəpər, -z

junk
BR dʒʌŋ|k, -ks, -kɪŋ,
-(k)t
AM dʒəŋ|k, -ks, -kɪŋ,
-(k)t

Junker
BR 'jʊŋkə(r), -z
AM 'jʊŋkər, -z

junkerdom
BR 'jʊŋkədəm
AM 'jʊŋkərdəm

junket
BR 'dʒʌŋk|ɪt, -ɪts, -ɪtɪŋ,
-ɪtɪd
AM 'dʒəŋkə|t, -ts, -dɪŋ,
-dəd

junkie
BR 'dʒʌŋk|i, -iz
AM 'dʒəŋki, -z

Junkin
BR 'dʒʌŋkɪn
AM 'dʒəŋkən

junk mail
BR 'dʒʌŋk meɪl,
ˌdʒʌŋk 'meɪl
AM 'dʒəŋk ˌmeɪl

junky
BR 'dʒʌŋk|i, -ɪz
AM 'dʒəŋki, -z

junkyard
BR 'dʒʌŋkjɑːd, -z
AM 'dʒəŋkˌjɑrd, -z

Juno
BR 'dʒuːnəʊ
AM 'dʒunoʊ

Junoesque
BR ˌdʒuːnəʊˈɛsk
AM 'dʒunoʊˈɛsk

Junor
BR 'dʒuːnə(r)
AM 'dʒunər

junta
BR 'dʒʌntə(r),
'hʊntə(r), -z
AM 'hʊntə, 'huntə,
'dʒəntə, -z

Jupiter
BR 'dʒuːpɪtə(r)
AM 'dʒupədər

Jura
BR 'dʒʊərə(r)
AM 'dʒurə

jural
BR 'dʒʊərəl, 'dʒʊərl̩
AM 'dʒurəl

Jurassic
BR dʒʊˈrasɪk
AM dʒəˈræsɪk

jurat
BR 'dʒʊərat, -s
AM 'dʒʊræt, -s

juridical
BR dʒʊˈrɪdɪkl
AM dʒəˈrɪdəkəl,
dʒuˈrɪdəkəl

juridically
BR dʒʊˈrɪdɪkli
AM dʒəˈrɪdək(ə)li
dʒuˈrɪdək(ə)li

jurisconsult
BR ˌdʒʊərɪskənˈsʌlt, -s
AM ˌdʒʊrəˈskənsəlt,
ˌdʒʊrəskənˈsəlt, -s

jurisdiction
BR ˌdʒʊərɪsˈdɪkʃn,
ˌdʒʊərɪsˈdɪkʃn, -z
AM ˌdʒʊrəsˈdɪkʃən,
ˌdʒʊrəzˈdɪkʃən, -z

jurisdictional
BR ˌdʒʊərɪzˈdɪkʃn(ə)l,
ˌdʒʊərɪzˈdɪkʃən(ə)l,
ˌdʒʊərɪsˈdɪkʃn(ə)l,
ˌdʒʊərɪsˈdɪkʃən(ə)l
AM ˌdʒʊrəsˈdɪkʃ(ə)nəl,
ˌdʒʊrəzˈdɪkʃ(ə)nəl

jurisprudence
BR ˌdʒʊərɪsˈpruːd(ə)ns
AM ˌdʒʊrəˈsprudns,

jurisprudent
BR ˌdʒʊərɪsˈpruːd(ə)nt
AM ˌdʒʊrəˈsprudnt,
'dʒʊrəˌsprudnt,
ˌdʒʊrəˈsprudnt,
'dʒʊrəˌsprudnt

jurisprudential
BR ˌdʒʊərɪsprʊˈdɛnʃl
AM ˌdʒʊrəˌspruˈdɛn(t)ʃəl,
ˌdʒʊrəˌspruˈdɛn(t)ʃəl

jurist
BR 'dʒʊərɪst, -s
AM 'dʒʊrəst, 'dʒurəst,
-s

juristic
BR dʒʊˈrɪstɪk
AM dʒʊˈrɪstɪk,
dʒuˈrɪstɪk

juristical
BR dʒʊˈrɪstɪkl
AM dʒʊˈrɪstɪkəl,
dʒuˈrɪstɪkəl

juror
BR 'dʒʊərə(r), -z
AM 'dʒʊrər, 'dʒurər,
'dʒʊˌrɔ(ə)r,
'dʒuˌrɔ(ə)r, -z

jury
BR 'dʒʊər|i, -ɪz
AM 'dʒʊri, 'dʒuri, -z

juryman
BR 'dʒʊərɪmən
AM 'dʒʊrimən,
'dʒurimən

jurymen
BR 'dʒʊərɪmən
AM 'dʒʊrimən,
'dʒurimən

jurywoman
BR 'dʒʊərɪˌwʊmən
AM 'dʒʊriˌwʊmən,
'dʒuriˌwʊmən

jurywomen
BR 'dʒʊərɪˌwɪmɪn
AM 'dʒʊriˌwɪmɪn,
'dʒuriˌwɪmɪn

jussive
BR 'dʒʌsɪv, -z
AM 'dʒəsɪv, -z

just¹
adjective, adverb
strong form
BR dʒʌst
AM dʒəst

just²
adverb weak form
BR dʒəst
AM dʒəst

juste milieu
BR ʒuːst 'miːljə(r),
+ mɪlˈjə(r)
AM 'ʒust mɪlˈju, 'ʒəst
mɪlˈjə

justice
BR ˈdʒʌst|ɪs, -ɪsɪz
AM ˈdʒəstəs, -əz
justiceship
BR ˈdʒʌstɪs|ʃɪp
AM ˈdʒəstə(s)ˌʃɪp
justiciable
BR dʒʌˈstɪʃ(ɪ)əbl,
dʒəˈstɪʃ(ɪ)əbl
AM ˌdʒəˈstɪʃ(i)əbəl
justiciar
BR dʒʌˈstɪʃə(r),
dʒəˈstɪʃə(r)
AM ˌdʒəˈstɪʃ(i)ər
justiciary
BR dʒʌˈstɪʃɪər|i,
dʒəˈstɪʃɪər|i,
dʒʌˈstɪʃ(ə)r|i,
dʒəˈstɪʃ(ə)r|i, -ɪz
AM ˌdʒəˈstɪʃi,ɛri, -z
justifiability
BR ˌdʒʌstɪfaɪə'bɪlɪti
AM ˌdʒəstəˌfaɪə'bɪlɪdi
justifiable
BR ˈdʒʌstɪfʌɪəbl,
ˌdʒʌstɪ'faɪəbl
AM ˈdʒəstəˌfaɪəbəl,
ˌdʒəstə'faɪəbəl
justifiableness
BR ˈdʒʌstɪfʌɪəblnəs,

ˌdʒʌstɪ'fʌɪəblnəs
AM ˈdʒəstəˌfaɪəbəlnəs,
ˌdʒəstə'faɪəbəlnəs
justifiably
BR ˈdʒʌstɪfʌɪəbli,
ˌdʒʌstɪ'fʌɪəbli
AM ˈdʒəstəˌfaɪəbli,
ˌdʒəstə'faɪəbli
justification
BR ˌdʒʌstɪfɪ'keɪʃn, -z
AM ˌdʒəstəfə'keɪʃən, -z
justificatory
BR ˈdʒʌstɪfɪkeɪt(ə)ri,
ˈdʒʌstɪfɪkət(ə)ri,
ˌdʒʌstɪfɪ'keɪt(ə)ri
AM dʒə'stɪfəkəˌtɔri,
ˌdʒəstə'fɪkəˌtɔri
justifier
BR ˈdʒʌstɪfʌɪə(r)
AM ˈdʒəstəˌfaɪər
justify
BR ˈdʒʌstɪfʌɪ, -z, -ɪŋ, -d
AM ˈdʒəstəˌfaɪ, -z, -ɪŋ, -d
Justin
BR ˈdʒʌstɪn
AM ˈdʒəstən
Justine
BR ˈdʒʌsti:n, dʒʌ'sti:n
AM ˈdʒəstin

Justinian
BR dʒʌs'tɪnɪən,
dʒəs'tɪnɪən
AM dʒəs'tɪniən
justly
BR ˈdʒʌs(t)li
AM ˈdʒəs(t)li
justness
BR ˈdʒʌs(t)nəs
AM ˈdʒəs(t)nəs
jut
BR dʒʌt, -s, -ɪŋ, -ɪd
AM dʒə|t, -ts, -dɪŋ, -dəd
jute
BR dʒu:t, -s
AM dʒut, -s
Jutish
BR ˈdʒu:tɪʃ
AM ˈdʒudɪʃ
Jutland
BR ˈdʒʌtlənd
AM ˈdʒətlənd
Juvenal
BR ˈdʒu:vɪnl, ˈdʒu:vn̩l
AM ˈdʒuvənəl
juvenescence
BR ˌdʒu:vɪ'nɛsns
AM ˌdʒuvə'nɛsəns
juvenescent
BR ˌdʒu:vɪ'nɛsnt

AM ˌdʒuvə'nɛsənt
juvenile
BR ˈdʒu:vɪnʌɪl, -z
AM ˈdʒuvə,naɪl,
ˈdʒuvənl, -z
juvenilely
BR ˈdʒu:vɪnʌɪlli
AM ˈdʒuvəˌnaɪ(l)li,
ˈdʒuvənli
juvenilia
BR ˌdʒu:vɪ'nɪlɪə(r)
AM ˌdʒuvə'nɪljə,
ˌdʒuvə'nɪliə
juvenility
BR ˌdʒu:vɪ'nɪlɪti
AM ˌdʒuvə'nɪlɪdi
juxtapose
BR ˌdʒʌkstə'pəʊz,
ˈdʒʌkstəpəʊz, -ɪz, -ɪŋ, -d
AM ˈdʒəkstə,pouz,
ˌdʒəkstə'pouz, -əz, -ɪŋ, -t
juxtaposition
BR ˌdʒʌkstəpə'zɪʃn
AM ˌdʒəkstəpə'zɪʃən
juxtapositional
BR ˌdʒʌkstəpə'zɪʃn(ə)l,
ˌdʒʌkstəpə'zɪʃən(ə)l
AM ˌdʒəkstəpə'zɪʃ(ə)nəl

Kk

k
BR keɪ, -z
AM keɪ, -z

ka
BR kɑː(r)
AM kɑ

Kaaba
BR 'kɑːbə(r)
AM 'kɑbə, 'kæbə

kabaddi
BR kə'badi
AM kə'bɑdi

Kabaka
BR kə'bɑːkə(r)
AM kə'bɑkə

kabala
BR kə'bɑːlə(r), ka'bɑːlə(r)
AM kə'bɑlə, 'kabələ

Kabalega
BR ˌkabə'leɪgə(r)
AM ˌkæbə'lɛgə

kabbala
BR kə'bɑːlə(r), ka'bɑːlə(r)
AM kə'bɑlə, 'kæbələ

kabbalism
BR 'kabəlɪz(ə)m, 'kabˌlɪz(ə)m
AM 'kæbəˌlɪzm, kə'bɑˌlɪzəm

kabbalist
BR 'kabəlɪst, 'kabˌlɪst, -s
AM 'kæbələst, kə'baləst, -s

kabob
BR kə'bɑːb, -z
AM kə'bɑb, -z

kabuki
BR kə'buːki
AM kə'buki

Kabul
BR 'kɑːb(ʊ)l, kə'bʊl
AM 'kabʊl, kə'bʊl

Kabwe
BR 'kabweɪ, 'kabwi
AM 'kabweɪ

Kabyle
BR kə'bʌɪl, -z
AM kə'baɪ(ə)l, -z

kachina
BR kə'tʃiːnə(r), -z
AM kə'tʃinə, -z

Kádáar
BR 'kɑːdɑː(r)
AM 'kɑˌdar
HU 'kɑːdɑːr

Kaddafi
BR kə'dafi, kə'dɑːfi
AM kə'dɑfi

kaddish
BR 'kadlɪʃ, -ɪʃɪz
AM 'kɑdɪʃ, -ɪz

kadi
BR 'kɑːdli, -ɪz
AM 'kɑdi, -z

kaffir
BR 'kafə(r), -z
AM 'kæfər, -z

kaffiyeh
BR kə'fiː(j)ə(r), ka'fiː(j)ə(r), -z
AM kə'fi(j)ə, -z

kafir
BR 'kafə(r), -z
AM 'kæfər, -z

Kafka
BR 'kafkə(r)
AM 'kɑfkə

Kafkaesque
BR ˌkafkə(r)'ɛsk
AM ˌkafkə'ɛsk

kaftan
BR ˌkaftan, -z
AM 'kæftən, 'kæfˌtæn, -z

Kagan
BR 'keɪg(ə)n
AM 'keɪgən

Kagoshima
BR 'kagə'ʃiːmə(r)
AM 'kɑgə'ʃimə

kagoul
BR kə'guːl, -z
AM kə'gul, -z

kagoule
BR kə'guːl, -z
AM kə'gul, -z

Kahlua®
BR kə'luːə(r)
AM kə'luə

Kahn
BR kɑːn
AM kɑn

kahuna
BR kə'huːnə(r)
AM kə'hunə

kai
BR kʌɪ
AM kaɪ

Kaifeng
BR ˌkʌɪ'fɛŋ
AM ˌkaɪ'fɛŋ

kail
BR keɪl, -z
AM keɪl, -z

kailyard
BR 'keɪljɑːd
AM 'keɪlˌjard

kainite
BR 'kʌɪnʌɪt, 'keɪnʌɪt
AM 'kaɪnaɪt, 'keɪnaɪt

Kaiser
BR 'kʌɪzə(r), -z
AM 'kaɪzər, -z

kaisership
BR kʌɪzəʃɪp, -s

AM 'kaɪzərˌʃɪp, -s

Kai Tak
BR ˌkʌɪ 'tak
AM ˌkaɪ 'tɑk

kaizen
BR 'kʌɪzn
AM 'kaɪzən

kaka
BR 'kɑːkɑː(r), 'kɑːkə(r), -z
AM 'kɑkɑ, -z

kakapo
BR 'kɑːkəpəʊ, -z
AM 'kɑkəˌpoʊ, -z

kakemono
BR ˌkɑːkɪ'məʊnəʊ, -z
AM ˌkɑkə'moʊnoʊ, ˌkækə'moʊnoʊ, -z

kala-azar
BR ˌkɑːlə(r)ə'zɑː(r)
AM ˌkɑlə'zar

Kalahari
BR ˌkalə'hɑːri
AM 'kɑlə'hɑri

Kalamazoo
BR ˌkaləmə'zuː
AM ˌkæləmə'zu

Kalashnikov
BR kə'laʃnɪkɒf, -s
AM kə'læʃnəˌkaf, -s

kale
BR keɪl, -z
AM keɪl, -z

kaleidoscope
BR kə'lʌɪdəskəʊp, -s
AM kə'laɪdəˌskoʊp, -s

kaleidoscopic
BR kə̩lʌɪdə'skɒpɪk
AM kə̩laɪdə'skɑpɪk

kaleidoscopical
BR kə̩lʌɪdə'skɒpɪkl
AM kə̩laɪdə'skɑpəkəl

kaleidoscopically
BR kə̩lʌɪdə'skɒpɪkli
AM kə̩laɪdə'skɑpək(ə)li

kalenchoe
BR ˌkalən'kəʊi, ˌkalən'kəʊi
AM ˌkælən'koʊi

kalends
BR 'kalɛndz, 'kalɪndz
AM 'kælən(d)z

kaleyard
BR 'keɪljɑːd, -z
AM 'keɪlˌjard, -z

Kalgoorlie
BR kal'gʊəli
AM kal'gʊrli

Kali
BR 'kɑːli
AM 'kɑli

kali
BR 'kɑli, 'keɪli, 'keɪlʌɪ
AM 'keɪli

Kalinin
BR kə'liːnɪn
AM kə'linɪn

Kalgoorlie
AM 'kaɪzərˌʃɪp, -s

Kai Tak
RUS ka'lʲinʲin

Kaliningrad
BR kə'liːnɪngrad
AM kə'linɪnˌgræd
RUS kəlʲinʲinʲin'grat

Kalmar
BR 'kalmɑː(r), 'kɑːlmə(r)
AM 'kalmar

kalmia
BR 'kalmɪə(r), -z
AM 'kalmɪə, -z

Kalmuck
BR 'kalmʌk, -s
AM 'kalmək, -s

Kalmuk
BR 'kalmʌk, -s
AM 'kalmək, -s

Kalmyk
BR 'kalmɪk, -s
AM 'kælmɪk, -s

kalong
BR 'kalɒŋ, 'kɑːlɒŋ, -z
AM 'kalɒŋ, 'kalaŋ, -z

kalpa
BR 'kʌlpə(r), 'kalpə(r), -z
AM 'kəlpə, -z

Kaluga
BR kə'luːgə(r)
AM kə'lugə

Kama
BR 'kɑːmə(r)
AM 'kɑmə

Kama Sutra
BR ˌkɑːmə 'suːtrə(r)
AM ˌkɑmə 'sutrə

Kamchatka
BR kam'tʃatkə(r)
AM kam'tʃatkə

kame
BR keɪm, -z
AM keɪm, -z

Kamenskoye
BR kə'mɛnskɔɪə(r)
AM kə'mɛnˌskɔɪə
RUS 'kamʲinskəji

Kamensk-Uralski
BR ˌkamɛnsk jʊ'ralski
AM ˌkamɛnsk jʊ'ralski

kamikaze
BR ˌkamɪ'kɑːzi
AM ˌkɑmə'kazi

Kampala
BR kam'pɑːlə(r)
AM kam'pɑlə

kampong
BR 'kampɒn, 'kampʊŋ, -z
AM ˌkam'pɒŋ, 'kamˌpaŋ, -z

Kampuchea
BR ˌkampʊ'tʃiːə(r)
AM ˌkampə'tʃiə

Kampuchean
BR ˌkæmpʊˈtʃiːən, -z
AM ˌkæmpəˈtʃiən, -z

kana
BR ˈkɑːnə(r)
AM ˈkɑnə

kanaka
BR kəˈnɑːkə(r), -z
AM kəˈnɑkə, -z

Kanarese
BR ˌkɑnəˈriːz
AM ˌkɑnəˈriz

Kanawa
BR ˈkænəwə(r),
kəˈnɑːwə(r)
AM kəˈnɑwə, ˈkænəwə

kanban
BR ˈkænbæn, -z
AM ˈkanˌbæn, -z

Kanchenjunga
BR ˌkæntʃ(ə)nˈdʒʊŋgə(r)
AM ˌkæn(t)ʃənˈdʒʊŋgə

Kandahar
BR ˌkændəˈhɑː(r)
AM ˈkændəˈhɑr

Kandinsky
BR kænˈdɪnski
AM kænˈdɪnski

Kandy
BR ˈkændi
AM ˈkændi

Kandyan
BR ˈkændiən, -z
AM ˈkændiən, -z

Kane
BR keɪn
AM keɪn

kanga
BR ˈkæŋgə(r), -z
AM ˈkæŋgə, -z

kangaroo
BR ˌkæŋgəˈruː, -z
AM ˌkæŋgəˈruː, -z

Kangchenjunga
BR ˌkæntʃ(ə)nˈdʒʊŋgə(r)
AM ˌkæntʃənˈdʒʊŋgə

kanji
BR ˈkændʒi
AM ˈkændʒi

Kannada
BR ˈkɑːnədə(r),
ˈkænədə(r)
AM ˈkɑnədə, ˈkænədə

Kano
BR ˈkɑːnəʊ
AM ˈkɑnoʊ

kanoon
BR kəˈnuːn, -z
AM kɑˈnun, -z

Kansan
BR ˈkænz(ə)n, -z
AM ˈkænzn, -z

Kansas
BR ˈkænzəs
AM ˈkænzəs

Kant
BR kænt

AM kænt

Kantian
BR ˈkæntiən, -z
AM ˈkæn(t)iən, -z

KANU
BR ˈkɑːnuː
AM ˈkɑnu

kaolin
BR ˈkeɪəlɪn
AM ˈkeɪələn

kaolinic
BR ˌkeɪəˈlɪnɪk
AM ˌkeɪəˈlɪnɪk

kaolinise
BR ˈkeɪəlɪnʌɪz, -ɪz, -ɪŋ,
-d
AM ˈkeɪələˌnaɪz, -ɪz, -ɪŋ,
-d

kaolinite
BR ˈkeɪəlɪnʌɪt
AM ˈkeɪələˌnaɪt

kaolinize
BR ˈkeɪəlɪnʌɪz, -ɪz, -ɪŋ,
-d
AM ˈkeɪələˌnaɪz, -ɪz, -ɪŋ,
-d

kaon
BR ˈkeɪɒn, -z
AM ˈkeɪˌɑn, ˈkeɪən, -z

Kapellmeister
BR kəˈpɛlmʌɪstə(r), -z
AM kəˈpɛlˌmaɪstər, -z

Kap Farvel
BR ˌkap fɑːˈvɛl
AM ˌkæp farˈvɛl

Kaplan
BR ˈkæplən
AM ˈkæplən

kapok
BR ˈkeɪpɒk
AM ˈkeɪˌpɑk

kappa
BR ˈkapə(r)
AM ˈkæpə

kaput
BR kəˈpʊt
AM kəˈpʊt, kɑˈpʊt

Karabiner
BR ˌkærəˈbiːnə(r), -z
AM ˌkɛrəˈbinər, -z

Karachi
BR kəˈrɑːtʃi
AM kəˈrɑtʃi

Karaite
BR ˈkɛrəʌɪt, -s
AM ˈkɛrəˌaɪt, -s

Karajan
BR ˈkærəjɑːn
AM ˈkɛrəˌjɑn

Karakoram
BR ˌkærəˈkɔːrəm
AM ˌkɛrəˈkɔrəm

Karakorum
BR ˌkærəˈkɔːrəm
AM ˌkɛrəˈkɔrəm

karakul
BR ˈkærək(ʊ)l, -z

AM ˈkɛrəkəl, -z

Kara Kum
BR ˌkɑrə ˈkʌm
AM ˌkɛrə ˈkəm

karaoke
BR ˌkærɪˈəʊki
AM ˌkɛriˈoʊki

karat
BR ˈkærət, -s
AM ˈkɛrət, -s

karate
BR kəˈrɑːti
AM kəˈrɑdi

Kardomah
BR kɑːˈdəʊmə(r)
AM karˈdoʊmə

karela
BR kəˈrɛlə(r),
kəˈreɪlə(r), -z
AM kəˈrɛlə, -z

Karelia
BR kəˈriːliə(r)
AM kəˈriljə, kəˈriliə

Karelian
BR kəˈriːliən, -z
AM kəˈriliən, -z

Karen[1]
Burmese people
BR kəˈrɛn, kaˈrɛn, -z
AM kəˈrɛn, -z

Karen[2]
forename
BR ˈkɑːrən, ˈkɑːrn̩
AM ˈkɛrən

Kariba
BR kəˈriːbə(r)
AM kəˈribə

Karin
BR ˈkɑːrɪn, ˈkɑːrn̩
AM ˈkɛrən, ˈkɑːrən

Karl
BR kɑːl
AM karl

Karloff
BR ˈkɑːlɒf
AM ˈkarˌlɔf, ˈkarˌlɑf

Karlsbad
BR ˈkɑːlzbad
AM ˈkarlzˌbad,
ˈkarlzˌbæd

Karlsruhe
BR ˈkɑːlzrʊə(r)
AM ˈkarlzˌrʊə

karma
BR ˈkɑːmə(r)
AM ˈkarmə

karmic
BR ˈkɑːmɪk
AM ˈkarmɪk

Karnak
BR ˈkɑːnak
AM ˈkarˌnæk

Karnataka
BR kəˈnɑːtəkə(r)
AM ˌkarˈnɑdəkə

Karno
BR ˈkɑːnəʊ

Katanga
AM ˈkarnoʊ

karoo
BR kəˈruː, -z
AM kəˈru, -z

Karpov
BR ˈkɑːpɒv
AM ˈkarˌpɔv, ˈkarˌpɑv

karri
BR ˈkarˌi, -ɪz
AM ˈkɛri, -z

Karroo
BR kəˈruː
AM kəˈru

Kars
BR kɑːs
AM kars

karst
BR kɑːst
AM karst

kart
BR kɑːt, -s, -ɪŋ, -ɪd
AM kart, -ts, -dɪŋ, -dɪd

karyokinesis
BR ˌkærɪəʊkɪˈniːsɪs
AM ˌkɛriəkəˈnisɪs

karyotype
BR ˈkærɪə(ʊ)tʌɪp, -s
AM ˈkɛrioʊˌtaɪp,
ˈkɛriəˌtaɪp, -s

kasbah
BR ˈkazbɑː(r), -z
AM ˈkæzˌbɑ, ˈkæsˌbɑ, -z

Kashmir
BR ˌkaʃˈmɪə(r)
AM ˈkæʃˌmɪ(ə)r,
ˈkæʒˌmɪ(ə)r

Kashmiri
BR ˌkaʃˈmɪərˌi, -ɪz
AM ˌkæʃˈmɪri,
ˌkæʒˈmɪri, -z

Kasparov
BR ˈkaspərɒv,
kaˈspaːrɒv
AM ˈkæspəˌrɔv,
ˈkæspəˌrɑv,
kæsˈpɛrɒv,
kæsˈpɛrɑv

Kassel
BR ˈkasl
AM ˈkæsəl

Kassite
BR ˈkasʌɪt, -s
AM ˈkæˌsaɪt, -s

katabatic
BR ˌkatəˈbatɪk, -s
AM ˈkædəˈbædɪk, -s

katabolism
BR kəˈtabəlɪz(ə)m
AM kəˈtæbəˌlɪzm

katakana
BR ˌkatəˈkɑːnə(r), -z
AM ˌkadəˈkɑnə, -z

Katanga
BR kəˈtaŋgə(r)
AM kəˈtæŋ(g)ə

katathermometer
BR ˌkatəθə'mɒmɪtə(r),
-z
AM ˌkædəθər'mɑmədər,
-z

Kate
BR keɪt
AM keɪt

Kath
BR kaθ
AM kæθ

katharevousa
BR ˌkaθə'revu:sə(r)
AM ˌkɑθə'rɛvəsə

Katharine
BR 'kaθ(ə)rɪn,
'kaθ(ə)rn̩
AM 'kæθ(ə)rən

Katherine
BR 'kaθ(ə)rɪn,
'kaθ(ə)rn̩
AM 'kæθ(ə)rən

Kathie
BR 'kaθi
AM 'kæθi

Kathleen
BR 'kaθli:n
AM kæθ'lin

Kathmandu
BR ˌkatman'du:
AM ˌkatman'du,
ˌkætmæn'du

kathode
BR 'kaθəʊd, -z
AM 'kæθoʊd, -z

Kathryn
BR 'kaθr(ɪ)n
AM 'kæθrən

Kathy
BR 'kaθi
AM 'kæθi

Katia
BR 'katɪə(r)
AM 'kɑdiə, 'katjə

Katie
BR 'keɪti
AM 'keɪdi

Katmandu
BR ˌkatman'du:
AM ˌkatman'du,
ˌkætmæn'du

Katowice
BR ˌkatə'vi:tʃə(r),
ˌkatə'vi:tsə(r)
AM ˌkadə'vɪtsə

Katrina
BR kə'tri:nə(r)
AM kə'trinə

Katrine
BR 'katrɪn
AM 'kætrɪn, kə'trin(ə)

Kattegat
BR 'katɪgat
AM 'kædəˌgæt

Katy
BR 'keɪti
AM 'keɪdi

Katya
BR 'katjə(r)
AM 'kɑdiə, 'katjə

katydid
BR 'keɪtɪdɪd, -z
AM 'keɪdiˌdɪd, -z

Katz
BR kats
AM kætz

Kauffmann
BR 'kɔ:fmən,
'kaʊfmən
AM 'kɔfmən, 'kɑfmən

Kaufman
BR 'kɔ:fmən,
'kaʊfmən
AM 'kɔfmən, 'kɑfmən

Kaunas
BR 'kaʊnəs
AM 'kaʊnəs

Kaunda
BR kaʊ'ʊndə(r)
AM kə'wʊndə

kauri
BR 'kaʊr|i, -ɪz
AM 'kaʊri, -z

kava
BR 'kɑ:və(r)
AM 'kɑvə

Kavanagh
BR 'kavənə(r),
'kavnə(r), kə'vanə(r)
AM 'kævəˌnɑ

kawakawa
BR 'kɑ:wə,kɑ:wə(r), -z
AM 'kawə'kawə, -z

Kawasaki
BR ˌkawə'sɑ:k|i,
ˌkɑ:wə'sɑ:k|i,
ˌkawə'sak|i, -ɪz
AM ˌkawə'sɑki, -z

Kawthulei
BR kɔ:'θu:leɪ
AM kɔ'θuleɪ, kɑ'θuleɪ

Kay
BR keɪ
AM keɪ

kayak
BR 'kʌɪak, -s
AM 'kaɪˌæk, -s

Kaye
BR keɪ
AM keɪ

kayo
BR ˌkeɪ'əʊ, -z, -ɪŋ, -d
AM ˌkeɪ'oʊ, -z, -ɪŋ, -d

Kazakh
BR kə'zak, 'kazak, -s
AM kə'zak, -s

Kazakhstan
BR ˌkazək'stɑ:n,
ˌkazək'stan
AM ˌkazak'stan,
'kazəkˌstan

Kazan
BR kə'zan
AM kə'zæn

kazoo
BR kə'zu:, -z
AM kə'zu, -z

kea
BR 'ki:ə(r), 'keɪə(r), -z
AM 'kiə, -z

Kean
BR ki:n
AM kin

Keane
BR ki:n
AM kin

Kearney
BR 'kɑ:ni, 'kə:ni
AM 'kərni

Kearns
BR kə:nz
AM kərnz

Kearny
BR 'kɑ:ni, 'kə:ni
AM 'kərni

Keating
BR 'ki:tɪŋ
AM 'kidɪŋ

Keaton
BR 'ki:tn̩
AM 'kitn̩

Keats
BR ki:ts
AM kits

Keatsian
BR 'ki:tsɪən, -z
AM 'kitsiən, -z

Keays
BR ki:z
AM kiz

kebab
BR kɪ'bab, -z
AM kə'bab, -z

Keble
BR 'ki:bl
AM 'kibəl

keck
BR kɛk, -s, -ɪŋ, -t
AM kɛk, -s, -ɪŋ, -t

ked
BR kɛd, -z
AM kɛd, -z

Kedah
BR 'kɛdə(r)
AM 'kɛdə, kə'dɑ

kedge
BR kɛdʒ, -ɪz, -ɪŋ, -d
AM kɛdʒ, -əz, -ɪŋ, -d

kedgeree
BR 'kɛdʒəri:, ˌkɛdʒə'ri:
AM 'kɛdʒəˌri, ˌkɛdʒə'ri

Keeble
BR 'ki:bl
AM 'kibəl

Keefe
BR ki:f
AM kif

Keegan
BR 'ki:g(ə)n
AM 'kigən

keek
BR ki:k, -s, -ɪŋ, -t
AM kik, -s, -ɪŋ, -t

keel
BR ki:l, -z, -ɪŋ, -d
AM kil, -z, -ɪŋ, -d

keelboat
BR 'ki:lbəʊt, -s
AM 'kilˌboʊt, -s

Keele
BR ki:l
AM kil

Keeler
BR 'ki:lə(r)
AM 'kilər

Keeley
BR 'ki:li
AM 'kili

keelhaul
BR 'ki:lhɔ:l, -z, -ɪŋ, -d
AM 'kil,(h)ɔl, 'kil,(h)ɑl,
-z, -ɪŋ, -d

Keeling
BR 'ki:lɪŋ
AM 'kilɪŋ

keelless
BR 'ki:llɪs
AM 'ki(l)lɪs

keelson
BR 'kɛlsn, 'ki:lsn, -z
AM 'kilsən, -z

keen
BR ki:n, -z, -ɪŋ, -d, -ə(r),
-ɪst
AM kin, -z, -ɪŋ, -d, -ər,
-ɪst

Keenan
BR 'ki:nən
AM 'kinən

Keene
BR ki:n
AM kin

keenly
BR 'ki:nli
AM 'kinli

keenness
BR 'ki:nnɪs
AM 'ki(n)nɪs

keep
BR ki:p, -s, -ɪŋ
AM kip, -s, -ɪŋ

keepable
BR 'ki:pəbl
AM 'kipəbəl

keeper
BR 'ki:pə(r), -z
AM 'kipər, -z

keepnet
BR 'ki:pnɛt, -s
AM 'kip,nɛt, -s

keepsake
BR 'ki:pseɪk, -s
AM 'kip,seɪk, -s

keeshond
BR 'keɪshɒnd, -z
AM 'keɪs,(h)ɑnd, -z

kef
BR kɛf
AM kɛf
keffiyeh
BR kəˈfiː(j)ə(r), -z
AM kəˈfi(j)ə, -z
Keflavik
BR ˈkɛfləvɪk
AM ˈkɛfləvɪk
keg
BR kɛg, -z
AM kɛg, -z
kegler
BR ˈkɛglə(r), -z
AM ˈkɛglər, -z
Kehoe
BR ˈkiːəʊ
AM ˈki,(h)oʊ
Keighley[1]
place in UK
BR ˈkiːθli
AM ˈkiθli
Keighley[2]
surname
BR ˈkiːθli, ˈkiːli
AM ˈkili
Keillor
BR ˈkiːlə(r)
AM ˈkilər
Keir
BR kɪə(r)
AM kɛ(ə)r
keiretsu
BR keɪˈrɛtsuː, -z
AM keɪˈrɛtsu, -z
keister
BR ˈkiːstə(r), -z
AM ˈkistər, -z
Keith
BR kiːθ
AM kiθ
kelim
BR kɛˈliːm, -z
AM kəˈlim, -z
Kelleher
BR ˈkɛləhə(r)
AM ˈkɛləhər
Keller
BR ˈkɛlə(r)
AM ˈkɛlər
Kellet
BR ˈkɛlɪt
AM ˈkɛlət
Kellett
BR ˈkɛlɪt
AM ˈkɛlət
Kelley
BR ˈkɛli
AM ˈkɛli
Kellogg
BR ˈkɛlɒg
AM ˈkɛlɔg, ˈkɛlɑg
Kells
BR kɛlz
AM kɛlz
kelly
BR ˈkɛlɪi, -ɪz

AM ˈkɛli, -z
keloid
BR ˈkiːlɔɪd, -z
AM ˈki,lɔɪd, -z
kelp
BR kɛlp
AM kɛlp
kelpie
BR ˈkɛlpɪi, -ɪz
AM ˈkɛlpi, -z
kelpy
BR ˈkɛlpɪi, -ɪz
AM ˈkɛlpi, -z
Kelso
BR ˈkɛlsəʊ
AM ˈkɛl,soʊ
kelson
BR ˈkɛlsn, -z
AM ˈkɛlsən, -z
kelt
BR kɛlt, -s
AM kɛlt, -s
kelter
BR ˈkɛltə(r)
AM ˈkɛltər
kelvin
BR ˈkɛlvɪn, -z
AM ˈkɛlvən, -z
Kelvinator
BR ˈkɛlvɪneɪtə(r)
AM ˈkɛlvə,neɪdər
Kelvinside
BR ,kɛlv(ɪ)nˈsʌɪd
AM ˈkɛlvən,saɪd
Kemble
BR ˈkɛmbl
AM ˈkɛmbəl
kemp
BR kɛmp
AM kɛmp
Kempis
BR ˈkɛmpɪs
AM ˈkɛmpəs
kempt
BR kɛm(p)t
AM kɛm(p)t
kempy
BR ˈkɛmpi
AM ˈkɛmpi
ken
BR kɛn, -z, -ɪŋ, -d
AM kɛn, -z, -ɪŋ, -d
Kenco
BR ˈkɛnkəʊ, ˈkɛŋkəʊ
AM ˈkɛŋkoʊ
Kendall
BR ˈkɛndl
AM ˈkɛndl
kendo
BR ˈkɛndəʊ
AM ˈkɛndoʊ
Kendrick
BR ˈkɛndrɪk
AM ˈkɛndrɪk
Keneally
BR kɪˈniːli
AM kəˈnili

Kenelm
BR ˈkɛnɛlm
AM ˈkɛnɛlm
Kenilworth
BR ˈkɛn(ɪ)lwəːθ, ˈkɛn(ɪ)lwəθ
AM ˈkɛnəl,wərθ
Kennebunkport
BR ,kɛnɪˈbʌŋkpɔːt
AM ,kɛnəˈbəŋk,pɔ(ə)rt
Kennedy
BR ˈkɛnɪdi
AM ˈkɛnədi
kennel
BR ˈkɛnl, -z
AM ˈkɛnəl, -z
Kennelly
BR ˈkɛnəli, ˈkɛnḷi
AM ˈkɛnəli
Kennet
BR ˈkɛnɪt
AM ˈkɛnət
Kenneth
BR ˈkɛnɪθ
AM ˈkɛnəθ
Kenney
BR ˈkɛni
AM ˈkɛni
kenning
BR ˈkɛnɪŋ, -z
AM ˈkɛnɪŋ, -z
Kennington
BR ˈkɛnɪŋt(ə)n
AM ˈkɛnɪŋtən
Kenny
BR ˈkɛni
AM ˈkɛni
keno
BR ˈkiːnəʊ
AM ˈkinoʊ
kenosis
BR kɪˈnəʊsɪs
AM kəˈnoʊsəs, kiˈnoʊsəs
kenotic
BR kɪˈnɒtɪk
AM kɪˈnɑdɪk, kiˈnɑdɪk
kenotron
BR ˈkɛnətrɒn
AM ˈkɛnə,trɑn
Kenrick
BR ˈkɛnrɪk
AM ˈkɛnrɪk
Kensal
BR ˈkɛnsl
AM ˈkɛnsəl
Kensington
BR ˈkɛnzɪŋt(ə)n
AM ˈkɛnsɪŋtən
Kensitas
BR ˈkɛnzɪtas, ˈkɛnzɪtəs
AM ˈkɛnzədəs
kent
BR kɛnt, -s, -ɪŋ, -ɪd
AM kɛn|t, -ts, -(t)ɪŋ, -(t)ɪd

Kentigern
BR ˈkɛntɪgəːn, ˈkɛntɪg(ə)n
AM ˈkɛn(t)ə,gərn
Kentish
BR ˈkɛntɪʃ
AM ˈkɛn(t)ɪʃ
kentledge
BR ˈkɛntlɪdʒ
AM ˈkɛnt,lɛdʒ
Kenton
BR ˈkɛntən
AM ˈkɛn(t)ən
Kentuckian
BR kɛnˈtʌkɪən, -z
AM kənˈtəkiən, -z
Kentucky
BR kɛnˈtʌki, kənˈtʌki
AM kənˈtəki
Kenwood®
BR ˈkɛnwʊd
AM ˈkɛn,wʊd
Kenya[1]
before independence
BR ˈkiːnjə(r)
AM ˈkinjə, ˈkɛnjə
Kenya[2]
BR ˈkɛnjə(r)
AM ˈkinjə, ˈkɛnjə
Kenyan[1]
before independence
BR ˈkiːnjən, -z
AM ˈkinjən, ˈkɛnjən, -z
Kenyan[2]
BR ˈkɛnjən, -z
AM ˈkinjən, ˈkɛnjən, -z
Kenyatta
BR kɛnˈjatə(r)
AM kɛˈnjɑdə
Kenyon
BR ˈkɛnjən
AM ˈkɛnjən
Keogh
BR ˈkiːəʊ
AM ˈkioʊ
Keough
BR ˈkiːəʊ
AM ˈkioʊ
kepi
BR ˈkeɪpɪi, ˈkɛpɪi, -ɪz
AM ˈkeɪpi, ˈkɛpi, -z
Kepler
BR ˈkɛplə(r)
AM ˈkɛplər
Keplerian
BR kɛˈplɪərɪən
AM kɛˈplɪəriən
Keppel
BR ˈkɛpl
AM ˈkɛpəl
kept
BR kɛpt
AM kɛp(t)
Kerala
BR ˈkɛrələ(r)
AM ˈkɛrələ

Keralite
BR ˈkerəlʌɪt, -s
AM ˈkerəˌlaɪt, -s

keratin
BR ˈkerətɪn
AM ˈkerətən

keratinisation
BR ˌkerətɪnʌɪˈzeɪʃn,
ˌkerətn̩ʌɪˈzeɪʃn
AM ˌkerəˌtɪnɪˈzeɪʃən,
ˌkerətnˌaɪˈzeɪʃən

keratinise
BR ˈkerətɪnʌɪz,
ˈkerətn̩ʌɪz, -ɪz, -ɪŋ, -d
AM ˈkerətnˌaɪz, -ɪz, -ɪŋ, -d

keratinization
BR ˌkerətɪnʌɪˈzeɪʃn,
ˌkerətn̩ʌɪˈzeɪʃn
AM ˌkerəˌtɪnɪˈzeɪʃən,
ˌkerətnˌaɪˈzeɪʃən

keratinize
BR ˈkerətɪnʌɪz,
ˈkerətn̩ʌɪz, -ɪz, -ɪŋ, -d
AM ˈkerətnˌaɪz, -ɪz, -ɪŋ, -d

keratose
BR ˈkerətəʊs,
ˈkerətəʊz
AM ˈkerəˌtoʊs,
ˈkerəˌtoʊz

keratosis
BR ˌkerəˈtəʊsɪs
AM ˌkerəˈtoʊsəs

kerb
BR kəːb, -z
AM kɜrb, -z

kerbside
BR ˈkəːbsʌɪd
AM ˈkɜrbˌsaɪd

kerbstone
BR ˈkəːbstəʊn, -z
AM ˈkɜrbˌstoʊn, -z

kerchief
BR ˈkəːtʃɪf, ˈkəːtʃiːf, -s
AM ˈkɜrtʃəf, ˈkərˌtʃif, -s, -t

Kerensky
BR kəˈrenski
AM kəˈrenski

kerf
BR kəːf, -s
AM kɜrf, -s

kerfuffle
BR kəˈfʌfl, -z
AM kərˈfəfəl, -z

Kerguelen
BR ˈkəːgɪlɪn, ˈkəːgl̩ɪn
AM kərˈgjulən

kermes
BR ˈkəːmɪz, ˈkəːmiːz
AM ˈkɜrmiz, ˈkɜrməs

kermess
BR ˈkəːmɛs, kəˈmɛs, -ɪz
AM ˈkɜrməs, -əz

kermesse
BR ˈkəːmɛs, kəˈmɛs, -ɪz
AM ˈkɜrməs, -əz

kermis
BR ˈkəːm|ɪs, -ɪsɪz
AM ˈkɜrməs, -əz

Kermit
BR ˈkəːmɪt
AM ˈkɜrmɪt

Kermode
BR kəˈməʊd, ˈkəːməʊd
AM ˈkərˌmoʊd, ˈkɜrmədi

kern
BR kəːn, -z, -ɪŋ, -d
AM kɜrn, -z, -ɪŋ, -d

kernel
BR ˈkəːnl, -z
AM ˈkɜrnəl, -z

kero
BR ˈkerəʊ
AM ˈkeˌroʊ

kerosene
BR ˈkerəsiːn
AM ˈkerəˌsin

kerosine
BR ˈkerəsiːn
AM ˈkerəˌsin

Kerouac
BR ˈkeruak
AM ˈkerəˌwæk

kerplunk
BR kəˈplʌŋk
AM kərˈplʌŋk

Kerr
BR kəː(r), kɛː(r), kɑː(r)
AM kɜr, kɑr

Kerrigan
BR ˈkerɪg(ə)n
AM ˈkerəgən

Kerry
BR ˈker|i, -ɪz
AM ˈkeri, -ɪz

kersey
BR ˈkəːzi
AM ˈkɜrzi

kerseymere
BR ˈkəːzɪmɪə(r), -z
AM ˈkɜrziˌmɪ(ə)r, -z

Kershaw
BR ˈkəːʃɔː(r)
AM ˈkɜrˌʃɔ

kerygma
BR kəˈrɪgmə(r)
AM kəˈrɪgmə

kerygmata
BR kəˈrɪgmətə(r)
AM kəˈrɪgmədə

kerygmatic
BR ˌkerɪgˈmatɪk
AM ˌkerɪgˈmædɪk

Kes
BR kez, kes
AM kes, kez

Kesey
BR ˈkiːzi
AM ˈkizi

Kesh
BR keʃ

kermis AM keʃ

kesh
BR keɪʃ
AM keɪʃ

keskidee
BR ˈkeskɪdiː, -z
AM ˈkeskəˌdi, -z

Kessler
BR ˈkeslə(r)
AM ˈkeslər

Kesteven
BR kɪˈstiːvn, kɛˈstiːvn, ˈkestɪvn
AM kəˈstivn, ˈkestəvn

Keston
BR ˈkest(ə)n
AM ˈkestən

kestrel
BR ˈkestr(ə)l, -z
AM ˈkestrəl, -z

Keswick
BR ˈkezɪk
AM ˈkesˌwɪk

ketch
BR ketʃ, -ɪz
AM ketʃ, -əz

ketchup
BR ˈketʃəp, ˈketʃʌp, -s
AM ˈketʃəp, -s

ketoacidosis
BR ˌkiːtəʊˌasɪˈdəʊsɪs
AM ˌkidoʊˌæsəˈdoʊsəs

ketone
BR ˈkiːtəʊn, -z
AM ˈkiˌtoʊn, -z

ketonic
BR kiːˈtɒnɪk
AM kiˈtɑnɪk

ketonuria
BR ˌkiːtəˈnjʊərɪə(r)
AM ˌkidəˈn(j)uriə

ketosis
BR kiːˈtəʊsɪs
AM kiˈtoʊsəs

ketotic
BR kiːˈtɒtɪk
AM kiˈtɑdɪk

Kettering
BR ˈket(ə)rɪŋ
AM ˈkedərɪŋ

kettle
BR ˈketl, -z
AM ˈkedəl, -z

kettledrum
BR ˈketldrʌm, -z
AM ˈkedlˌdrəm, -z

kettledrummer
BR ˈketlˌdrʌmə(r), -z
AM ˈkedlˌdrəmər, -z

kettleful
BR ˈketlfʊl, -z
AM ˈkedlˌfʊl, -z

keuper
BR ˈkɔɪpə(r)
AM ˈkɔɪpər

kevel
BR ˈkevl, -z

kermis AM ˈkevəl, -z

Kevin
BR ˈkevɪn
AM ˈkevən

kevlar
BR ˈkevlɑː(r)
AM ˈkevˌlɑr

Kew
BR kjuː
AM kju

Kewpie®
BR ˈkjuːp|i, -ɪz
AM ˈkjupi, -z

kex
BR keks
AM keks

key
BR kiː, -z, -ɪŋ, -d
AM ki, -z, -ɪŋ, -d

keyboard
BR ˈkiːbɔːd, -z, -ɪŋ, -ɪd
AM ˈkiˌbɔ(ə)rd, -z, -ɪŋ, -əd

keyboarder
BR ˈkiːbɔːdə(r), -z
AM ˈkiˌbɔrdər, -z

keyboardist
BR ˈkiːbɔːdɪst, -s
AM ˈkiˌbɔrdəst, -s

keyer
BR ˈkiːə(r), -z
AM ˈkiər, -z

Keyes
BR ˈkiːz
AM kiz

keyholder
BR ˈkiːˌhəʊldə(r), -z
AM ˈkiˌ(h)oʊldər, -z

keyhole
BR ˈkiːhəʊl, -z
AM ˈkiˌ(h)oʊl, -z

Key Largo
BR ˌkiː ˈlɑːgəʊ
AM ˌki ˈlɑrˌgoʊ

keyless
BR ˈkiːlɪs
AM ˈkilɪs

Keynes
BR keɪnz, kiːnz
AM kinz, keɪnz

Keynesian
BR ˈkeɪnzɪən, -z
AM ˈkeɪnzɪən, -z

Keynesianism
BR ˈkeɪnzɪənɪz(ə)m
AM ˈkeɪnziəˌnɪzəm

keynote
BR ˈkiːnəʊt, -s, -ɪŋ, -ɪd
AM ˈkiˌnoʊ|t, -ts, -dɪŋ, -dəd

Keynsham
BR ˈkeɪnʃ(ə)m
AM ˈkeɪnʃəm

keypad
BR ˈkiːpad, -z
AM ˈkiˌpæd, -z

keypunch
BR ˈkiːpʌn(t)ʃ, -ɪz
AM ˈkiˌpən(t)ʃ, -əz

keypuncher
BR ˈkiːˌpʌn(t)ʃə(r), -z
AM ˈkiˌpən(t)ʃər, -z

keyring
BR ˈkiːrɪŋ, -z
AM ˈkiˌrɪŋ, -z

Keys
BR kiːz
AM kiz

Keyser
BR ˈkʌɪzə(r), ˈkiːzə(r)
AM ˈkaɪzər

keystone
BR ˈkiːstəʊn, -z
AM ˈkiˌstoʊn, -z

Keystone Kops
BR ˈkiːstəʊn ˈkɒps
AM ˈkiˌstoʊn ˈkɑps

keystroke
BR ˈkiːstrəʊk, -s
AM ˈkiˌstroʊk, -s

keyway
BR ˈkiːweɪ, -z
AM ˈkiˌweɪ, -z

Key West
BR ˌkiː ˈwest
AM ˌki ˈwest

keyword
BR ˈkiːwəːd, -z
AM ˈkiˌwərd, -z

KGB
BR ˌkeɪdʒiːˈbiː
AM ˌkeɪˌdʒiˈbi

Khabarovsk
BR ˈkɑːbərɒfsk,
ˌkɑːbəˈrɒfsk
AM ˈkɑbəˌrɑfsk
RUS xɑˈbarəfsk

Khachaturian
BR ˌkatʃəˈtjʊərɪən,
ˌkatʃəˈtʃʊərɪən
AM ˌkɑtʃəˈtʊrɪən
RUS xətʃətuˈrjɑn

khaddar
BR ˈkadə(r)
AM ˈkɑdər

khaki
BR ˈkɑːki
AM ˈkæki

khalif
BR ˈkeɪlɪf, -s
AM ˈkeɪlɪf, -s

khalifate
BR ˈkeɪlɪfeɪt, -s
AM ˈkeɪləˌfeɪt,
ˈkeɪləfət, -s

Khalki
BR ˈkalki
AM ˈkɑlki

khamsin
BR ˈkamsɪn, -z
AM ˌkamˈsin, -z

khan
BR kɑːn, -z

AM kɑn, -z

khanate
BR ˈkɑːneɪt, -s
AM ˈkɑneɪt, -s

Kharg
BR kɑːg
AM kɑrg

Kharkov
BR ˈkɑːkɒv
AM ˈkɑrˌkɒv, ˈkɑrˌkɑv

Khartoum
BR kɑːˈtuːm
AM kɑrˈtum

Khayyam
BR kʌɪˈam, kʌɪˈɑːm
AM kaɪˈæm

khazi
BR ˈkɑːzˌi, -ɪz
AM ˈkɑzi, -z

Khedival
BR kɪˈdiːvl, kɛˈdiːvl
AM kəˈdivəl, kɛˈdivəl

khedive
BR kɪˈdiːv, kɛˈdiːv, -z
AM kəˈdiv, kɛˈdiv, -z

Khedivial
BR kɪˈdiːvɪəl,
kɛˈdiːvɪəl
AM kəˈdivɪəl, kɛˈdivɪəl

Khíos
BR ˈkʌɪɒs
AM ˈkaɪɒs, ˈkaɪɑs
GR ˈhiːɔs

Khitai
BR ˌkiːˈtʌɪ
AM ˈkiˈtaɪ

Khmer
BR kmɛː(r), kəˈmɛː(r)
AM k(ə)ˈmɛ(ə)r

Khmer Rouge
BR ˌkmɛː ˈruːʒ,
kəˌmɛː +
AM k(ə)ˈmɛ(ə)r ˈruʒ

Khoikhoi
BR ˈkɔɪkɔɪ
AM ˈkɔɪˈkɔɪ

Khoisan
BR ˈkɔɪsɑːn
AM ˈkɔɪˌsan

Khomeini
BR kəˈmeɪni, kɒˈmeɪni
AM koʊˈmeɪni,
hoʊˈmeɪni

Khorramshahr
BR ˌkɒrəmˈʃɑː(r)
AM ˌkɔrəmˈʃɑr

khoum
BR kuːm, -z
AM kum, -z

Khrushchev
BR ˈkrʊstʃɒf, ˈkrʊʃtʃɒf
AM ˈkrʊʃˌ(t)ʃev,
ˈkrʊʃˌ(t)ʃɒf,
ˈkrʊʃˌ(t)ʃev,
ˈkrʊʃˌ(t)ʃɑf
RUS xruʃˈtʃʲof

Khufu
BR ˈkuːfuː
AM ˈkuˌfu

Khyber Pass
BR ˌkʌɪbə ˈpɑːs,
ˌxʌɪbə +, + ˈpas
AM ˈkaɪbər ˈpæs

kHz
BR ˈkɪləhəːts
AM ˈkɪləˌhərts

kiang
BR kɪˈaŋ, -z
AM ki'(j)æŋ, -z

Kiangsu
BR kɪˌaŋˈsuː
AM ki,(j)æŋˈsu

Kia-Ora®
BR ˌkiːəˈɔːrə(r)
AM ˌkiəˈɔrə

kibble
BR ˈkɪb|l, -lz, -l̩ŋ \-lŋ,
-ld
AM ˈkɪb|əl, -əlz, -(ə)lɪŋ,
-əld

kibbutz
BR kɪˈbʊts, -ɪz
AM kɪˈbʊts, -əz

kibbutzim
BR kɪˈbʊtsɪm
AM kɪˌbʊtˈsim

kibbutznik
BR kɪˈbʊtsnɪk, -s
AM kɪˈbʊtsnɪk, -s

kibe
BR kʌɪb, -z
AM kaɪb, -z

kibitka
BR kɪˈbɪtkə(r), -z
AM kəˈbɪ(t)kə, -z

kibits
BR ˈkɪb|ɪts, -ɪtsɪz,
-ɪtsɪŋ, -ɪtst
AM ˈkɪbəts, -əz, -ɪŋ, -t

kibitzer
BR ˈkɪbɪtsə(r), -z
AM ˈkɪbətsər, -z

kiblah
BR ˈkɪblə(r)
AM ˈkɪblə

kibosh
BR ˈkʌɪbɒʃ
AM kəˈbɑʃ, ˈkaɪˌbɑʃ

kick
BR kɪk, -s, -ɪŋ, -t
AM kɪk, -s, -ɪŋ, -t

kickable
BR ˈkɪkəbl
AM ˈkɪkəbəl

kick-ass
BR ˌkɪkˈɑːs, ˌkɪkˈas
AM ˈkɪkˈæs

kickback
BR ˈkɪkbak, -s
AM ˈkɪkˌbæk, -s

kick-boxer
BR ˈkɪkˌbɒksə(r), -z
AM ˈkɪkˌbaksər, -z

kick-boxing
BR ˈkɪkˌbɒksɪŋ
AM ˈkɪkˌbaksɪŋ

kickdown
BR ˈkɪkdaʊn
AM ˈkɪkˌdaʊn

kicker
BR ˈkɪkə(r), -z
AM ˈkɪkər, -z

kickoff
BR ˈkɪkɒf, -s
AM ˈkɪkˌɔf, ˈkɪkˌɑf, -s

kick-pleat
BR ˈkɪkpliːt, -s
AM ˈkɪkˌplit, -s

kickshaw
BR ˈkɪkʃɔː(r), -z
AM ˈkɪkˌʃɔ, ˈkɪkˌʃɑ, -z

kicksorter
BR ˈkɪkˌsɔːtə(r), -z
AM ˈkɪkˌsɔrdər, -z

kickstand
BR ˈkɪkstand, -z
AM ˈkɪkˌstænd, -z

kickstart
BR ˈkɪkstɑːt, ˌkɪkˈstɑːt,
-s, -ɪŋ, -ɪd
AM ˈkɪkˈstɑr|t, -ts, -dɪŋ,
-dəd

kid
BR kɪd, -z, -ɪŋ, -ɪd
AM kɪd, -z, -ɪŋ, -ɪd

Kidd
BR kɪd
AM kɪd

kidder
BR ˈkɪdə(r), -z
AM ˈkɪdər, -z

Kidderminster
BR ˈkɪdəˌmɪnstə(r)
AM ˈkɪdərˌmɪnstər

kiddie
BR ˈkɪd|i, -ɪz
AM ˈkɪdi, -z

kiddiewink
BR ˈkɪdɪwɪŋk, -s
AM ˈkɪdiˌwɪŋk, -s

kiddingly
BR ˈkɪdɪŋli
AM ˈkɪdɪŋli

kiddle
BR ˈkɪdl, -z
AM ˈkɪdəl, -z

kiddo
BR ˈkɪdəʊ
AM ˈkɪdoʊ

kiddush
BR ˈkɪdʊʃ
AM ˈkɪdəʃ

kiddy
BR ˈkɪd|i, -ɪz
AM ˈkɪdi, -z

kidnap
BR ˈkɪdnap, -s, -ɪŋ, -t
AM ˈkɪdˌnæp, -s, -ɪŋ, -t

kidnaper
BR ˈkɪdnapə(r), -z

AM ˈkɪdˌnæpər, -z
kidnaping
BR ˈkɪdnapɪŋ, -z
AM ˈkɪdˌnæpɪŋ, -z
kidnapper
BR ˈkɪdnapə(r), -z
AM ˈkɪdˌnæpər, -z
kidnapping
BR ˈkɪdnapɪŋ, -z
AM ˈkɪdˌnæpɪŋ, -z
kidney
BR ˈkɪdn|i, -ɪz
AM ˈkɪdni, -z
kidology
BR kɪˈdɒlədʒi
AM kɪˈdɑlədʒi
kidskin
BR ˈkɪdskɪn
AM ˈkɪdˌskɪn
Kidwelly
BR kɪdˈwɛli
AM kɪdˈwɛli
Kiel
BR kiːl
AM kil
Kielce
BR ˈkjɛl(t)sə(r)
AM ˈkjɛl(t)sə
Kielder
BR ˈkiːldə(r)
AM ˈkildər
Kiely
BR ˈkiːli
AM ˈkili
kier
BR kɪə(r), -z
AM kɪ(ə)r, -z
Kieran
BR ˈkɪərən, ˈkɪərn̩
AM ˈkɪran
Kierkegaard
BR ˈkɪəkəgɑːd
AM ˈkɪrkɛˌgard
DAN ˈkiʌgəˌgɒːˈ
Kieron
BR ˈkɪərən, ˈkɪərn̩
AM ˈkɪrən
kieselguhr
BR ˈkiːzlguə(r)
AM ˈkizɛlgər
Kiev
BR ˌkiːˈɛf, ˌkiːˈɛv, ˈkiːɛf, ˈkiːɛv
AM ˌkiˈɛv, ˈkiɛv
kif
BR kɪf, -s
AM kɪf, -s
Kigali
BR kɪˈgɑːli
AM kɪˈgali
kike
BR kʌɪk, -s
AM kaɪk, -s
Kikuyu
BR kɪˈkuːjuː, -z
AM kɪˈkuju, -z

Kilbracken
BR kɪlˈbrak(ə)n
AM kɪlˈbrækən
Kilbride
BR kɪlˈbrʌɪd
AM kɪlˈbraɪd
Kilburn
BR ˈkɪlb(ə)n, ˈkɪlbəːn
AM ˈkɪlbərn
Kildare
BR kɪlˈdɛː(r)
AM ˌkɪlˈdɛ(ə)r
kilderkin
BR ˈkɪldəkɪn, -z
AM ˈkɪldərkən, -z
Kilfedder
BR kɪlˈfɛdə(r)
AM kɪlˈfɛdər
kilim
BR kɪˈliːm, -z
AM kəˈlim, -z
Kilimanjaro
BR ˌkɪlɪmənˈdʒɑːrəʊ, ˌkɪlɪmanˈdʒɑːrəʊ
AM ˌkɪləmənˈdʒɑroʊ
Kilkenny
BR kɪlˈkɛni
AM kɪlˈkɛnni
kill
BR kɪl, -z, -ɪŋ, -d
AM kɪl, -z, -ɪŋ, -d
Killamarsh
BR ˈkɪləmɑːʃ
AM ˈkɪləˌmɑrʃ
Killanin
BR kɪˈlanɪn
AM kɪˈlænən
Killarney
BR kɪˈlɑːni
AM kɪˈlɑrni
killdeer
BR ˈkɪldɪə(r), -z
AM ˈkɪldɪ(ə)r, -z
killer
BR ˈkɪlə(r), -z
AM ˈkɪlər, -z
killick
BR ˈkɪlɪk, -s
AM ˈkɪlɪk, -s
Killiecranckie
BR ˌkɪlɪˈkraŋki
AM ˌkɪliˈkrænki
killifish
BR ˈkɪlɪfɪʃ, -ɪz
AM ˈkɪliˌfɪʃ, -ɪz
killing
BR ˈkɪlɪŋ, -z
AM ˈkɪlɪŋ, -z
killingly
BR ˈkɪlɪŋli
AM ˈkɪlɪŋli
killjoy
BR ˈkɪldʒɔɪ, -z
AM ˈkɪlˌdʒɔɪ, -z
Kilmarnock
BR kɪlˈmɑːnək, kɪlˈmɑːnɒk

AM kɪlˈmɑrnək
Kilmuir
BR kɪlˈmjʊə(r)
AM kɪlˈmjʊ(ə)r
kiln
BR kɪln, -z
AM kɪln, -z
Kilner®
BR ˈkɪlnə(r)
AM ˈkɪlnər
kilo
BR ˈkiːləʊ, -z
AM ˈkiloʊ, -z
kilobyte
BR ˈkɪlə(ʊ)bʌɪt, -s
AM ˈkɪləˌbaɪt, -s
kilocalorie
BR ˈkɪlə(ʊ)ˌkal(ə)r|i, -ɪz
AM ˈkɪləˌkæl(ə)ri, -z
kilocycle
BR ˈkɪlə(ʊ)ˌsʌɪkl, -z
AM ˈkɪləˌsaɪkəl, -z
kilogram
BR ˈkɪləgram, -z
AM ˈkɪləˌgræm, -z
kilogramme
BR ˈkɪləgram, -z
AM ˈkɪləˌgræm, -z
kilohertz
BR ˈkɪlə(ʊ)həːts
AM ˈkɪləˌhərts
kilojoule
BR ˈkɪlə(ʊ)dʒuːl, -z
AM ˈkɪləˌdʒul, -z
kiloliter
BR ˈkɪlə(ʊ)ˌliːtə(r)
AM ˈkɪləˌlidər
Killarney
BR ˈkɪlə(ʊ)ˌliːtə(r)
AM ˈkɪləˌlidər
kilometer
BR ˈkɪləˌmiːtə(r), kɪˈlɒmɪtə(r), -z
AM kəˈlɑmədər, ˈkɪləˌmidər, -z
kilometre
BR ˈkɪləˌmiːtə(r), kɪˈlɒmɪtə(r), -z
AM kəˈlɑmədər, ˈkɪləˌmidər, -z
kilometric
BR ˌkɪləˈmɛtrɪk
AM ˌkɪləˈmɛtrɪk
kiloton
BR ˈkɪlə(ʊ)tʌn, -z
AM ˈkɪləˌtən, ˈkɪləˌtɑn, -z
kilotonne
BR ˈkɪlə(ʊ)tʌn, -z
AM ˈkɪləˌtən, -z
kilovolt
BR ˈkɪlə(ʊ)vəʊlt, -s
AM ˈkɪləˌvoʊlt, -s
kilowatt
BR ˈkɪləwɒt, -s
AM ˈkɪləˌwat, -s

Kilpatrick
BR kɪlˈpatrɪk
AM kɪlˈpætrɪk
Kilroy
BR ˈkɪlrɔɪ, ˌkɪlˈrɔɪ
AM ˈkɪlˌrɔɪ
kilt
BR kɪlt, -s, -ɪd
AM kɪlt, -s, -ɪd
kilter
BR ˈkɪltə(r)
AM ˈkɪltər
kiltie
BR ˈkɪlt|i, -ɪz
AM ˈkɪlti, -z
Kim
BR kɪm
AM kɪm
Kimber
BR ˈkɪmbə(r)
AM ˈkɪmbər
Kimberley
BR ˈkɪmbəli
AM ˈkɪmbərli
kimberlite
BR ˈkɪmbəlʌɪt
AM ˈkɪmbərˌlaɪt
Kimberly
BR ˈkɪmbəli
AM ˈkɪmbərli
Kimbolton
BR kɪmˈbəʊlt(ə)n
AM kɪmˈboʊltən
kimchi
BR ˈkɪmtʃi
AM kɪmˈtʃi
kimono
BR kɪˈməʊnəʊ, -z, -d
AM kəˈmoʊnoʊ, kəˈmoʊnə, -z, -d
kin
BR kɪm
AM kɪn
kina
BR ˈkiːnə(r), -z
AM ˈkinə, -z
Kinabalu
BR ˌkiːnəˈbɑːluː
AM ˌkinəˈbɑˌlu
kinaesthesia
BR ˌkɪnɪsˈθiːzɪə(r), ˌkɪnɪsˈθiːʒə(r), ˌkʌɪnɪsˈθiːzɪə(r), ˌkʌɪnɪsˈθiːʒə(r)
AM ˌkɪnəsˈθiʒ(i)ə, ˌkɪnəsˈθiziə
kinaesthetic
BR ˌkɪnɪsˈθɛtɪk, ˌkʌɪnɪsˈθɛtɪk
AM ˌkɪnəsˈθɛdɪk
kinaesthetically
BR ˌkɪnɪsˈθɛtɪkli, ˌkʌɪnɪsˈθɛtɪkli
AM ˌkɪnəsˈθɛdək(ə)li
Kincaid
BR kɪnˈkeɪd
AM kɪnˈkeɪd

Kincardine
BR kɪn'kɑːd(ɪ)n
AM kɪn'kɑrdən
Kinchinjunga
BR ˌkɪntʃ(ɪ)n'dʒʊŋgə(r)
AM ˌkɪn(t)ʃən'dʒʊŋgə
kincob
BR 'kɪŋkəb
AM 'kɪnˌkɑb, 'kɪŋˌkɑb
kind
BR kʌɪnd, -ə(r), -ɪst
AM kaɪnd, -ər, -ɪst
kinda
kind of
BR 'kʌɪndə(r)
AM 'kaɪndə
Kinder
BR 'kɪndə(r)
AM 'kɪndər
kindergarten
BR 'kɪndəˌgɑːtn, -z
AM 'kɪndərˌgɑrtən, 'kɪndərˌgɑrdən, -z
kind-hearted
BR ˌkʌɪnd'hɑːtɪd
AM ˌkaɪn(d)ˌhɑrdəd
kind-heartedly
BR ˌkʌɪnd'hɑːtɪdli
AM ˌkaɪn(d)ˌhɑrdədli
kind-heartedness
BR ˌkʌɪnd'hɑːtɪdnɪs
AM ˌkaɪn(d)ˌhɑrdədnəs
kindle
BR 'kɪndl̩, -lz, -lɪŋ\-l̩ɪŋ, -ld
AM 'kɪn|dəl, -dəlz, -(d)(ə)lɪŋ, -dəld
kindler
BR 'kɪndlə(r), 'kɪndlə(r), -z
AM 'kɪn(də)lər, -z
kindlily
BR 'kʌɪndlɪli
AM 'kaɪn(d)lɪli
kindliness
BR 'kʌɪndlɪnɪs
AM 'kaɪn(d)linɪs
kindling
BR 'kɪndlɪŋ
AM 'kɪn(d)lɪŋ
kindly
BR 'kʌɪndl|i, -ɪə(r), -ɪst
AM 'kaɪn(d)li, -ər, -ɪst
kindness
BR 'kʌɪn(d)nɪs, -ɪz
AM 'kaɪn(d)nɪs, -ɪz
kindred
BR 'kɪndrɪd
AM 'kɪndrɪd
kine
BR kʌɪn
AM kaɪn
kinematic
BR ˌkɪnɪ'matɪk, ˌkʌɪnɪ'matɪk, -s
AM ˌkɪnə'mædɪk, -s

kinematical
BR ˌkɪnɪ'matɪkl, ˌkʌɪnɪ'matɪkl
AM ˌkɪnə'mædəkəl
kinematically
BR ˌkɪnɪ'matɪkli, ˌkʌɪnɪ'matɪkli
AM ˌkɪnə'mædək(ə)li
kinematograph
BR ˌkɪnɪ'matəgrɑːf, ˌkɪnɪ'matəgraf, -s
AM ˌkɪnə'mædəˌgræf, -s
kinescope
BR 'kɪnɪskəʊp, -s
AM 'kɪnəˌskoʊp, -s
kinesics
BR kɪ'niːsɪks, kʌɪ'niːsɪks
AM kə'nisɪks
kinesiology
BR kɪˌniːsɪ'ɒlədʒi, kɪˌniːzɪ'ɒlədʒi, kʌɪˌniːsɪ'ɒlədʒi, kʌɪˌniːzɪ'ɒlədʒi
AM kəˌnisi'ɑlədʒi, kəˌnizi'ɑlədʒi
kinesthesia
BR ˌkɪnɪs'θiːzɪə(r), ˌkɪnɪs'θiːʒə(r), ˌkʌɪnɪs'θiːzɪə(r), ˌkʌɪnɪs'θiːʒə(r)
AM ˌkɪnəs'θiːʒ(i)ə, ˌkɪnəs'θiziə
kinesthetic
BR ˌkɪnɪs'θɛtɪk, ˌkʌɪnɪs'θɛtɪk
AM ˌkɪnəs'θɛdɪk
kinesthetically
BR ˌkɪnɪs'θɛtɪkli, ˌkʌɪnɪs'θɛtɪkli
AM ˌkɪnəs'θɛdək(ə)li
kinetic
BR kɪ'nɛtɪk, kʌɪ'nɛtɪk, -s
AM kə'nɛdɪk, -s
kinetically
BR kɪ'nɛtɪkli, kʌɪ'nɛtɪkli
AM kə'nɛdək(ə)li
kinetin
BR 'kʌɪnɪtɪn, -z
AM 'kɪnətn, -z
kinfolk
BR 'kɪnfəʊk
AM 'kɪnˌfoʊk
king
BR kɪŋ, -z
AM kɪŋ, -z
kingbird
BR 'kɪŋbɜːd, -z
AM 'kɪŋˌbɜrd, -z
kingbolt
BR 'kɪŋbəʊlt
AM 'kɪŋˌboʊlt
kingcraft
BR 'kɪŋkrɑːft, 'kɪŋkraft

kingcup
BR 'kɪŋkʌp, -s
AM 'kɪŋˌkəp, -s
kingdom
BR 'kɪŋdəm, -z, -d
AM 'kɪŋdəm, -z, -d
kingfish
BR 'kɪŋfɪʃ, -ɪz
AM 'kɪŋˌfɪʃ, -ɪz
kingfisher
BR 'kɪŋˌfɪʃə(r), -z
AM 'kɪŋˌfɪʃər, -z
kinghood
BR 'kɪŋhʊd, -z
AM 'kɪŋˌ(h)ʊd, -z
King Kong
BR ˌkɪŋ 'kɒŋ
AM ˌkɪŋ 'kɔŋ, ˌkɪŋ 'kɑŋ
kingless
BR 'kɪŋlɪs
AM 'kɪŋlɪs
kinglet
BR 'kɪŋlɪt, -s
AM 'kɪŋlɪt, -s
kinglike
BR 'kɪŋlʌɪk
AM 'kɪŋˌlaɪk
kingliness
BR 'kɪŋlɪnɪs
AM 'kɪŋlinɪs
kingling
BR 'kɪŋlɪŋ, -z
AM 'kɪŋlɪŋ, -z
kingly
BR 'kɪŋl|i, -ɪə(r), -ɪst
AM 'kɪŋli, -ər, -ɪst
kingmaker
BR 'kɪŋˌmeɪkə(r), -z
AM 'kɪŋˌmeɪkər, -z
kingpin
BR 'kɪŋpɪn, -z
AM 'kɪŋˌpɪn, -z
Kingsbridge
BR 'kɪŋzbrɪdʒ
AM 'kɪŋzˌbrɪdʒ
Kingsbury
BR 'kɪŋzb(ə)ri
AM 'kɪŋzˌbɛri
kingship
BR 'kɪŋʃɪp
AM 'kɪŋˌʃɪp
Kingsley
BR 'kɪŋzli
AM 'kɪŋzli
Kingston
BR 'kɪŋst(ə)n
AM 'kɪŋstən
Kingstown
BR 'kɪŋstaʊn
AM 'kɪŋˌstoʊn
Kingsway
BR 'kɪŋzweɪ
AM 'kɪŋzˌweɪ
Kingswear
BR 'kɪŋzwɪə(r)
AM 'kɪŋzˌwɪ(ə)r

Kingswinford
BR kɪŋ'swɪnfəd, kɪŋz'wɪnfəd
AM kɪŋz'wɪnfərd
Kingswood
BR 'kɪŋzwʊd
AM 'kɪŋzˌwʊd
kinin
BR 'kʌɪnɪn, -z
AM 'kaɪnɪn, -z
kink
BR kɪŋ|k, -ks, -kɪŋ, -(k)t
AM kɪŋ|k, -ks, -kɪŋ, -(k)t
kinkajou
BR 'kɪŋkədʒuː, -z
AM 'kɪŋkəˌdʒu, -z
Kinki
BR 'kɪŋki
AM 'kɪŋki
kinkily
BR 'kɪŋkɪli
AM 'kɪŋkɪli
kinkiness
BR 'kɪŋkɪnɪs
AM 'kɪŋkɪnɪs
kinky
BR 'kɪŋk|i, -ɪə(r), -ɪst
AM 'kɪŋki, -ər, -ɪst
kinless
BR 'kɪnlɪs
AM 'kɪnlɪs
Kinloch
BR kɪn'lɒx, kɪn'lɒk
AM 'kɪnlɑk, kɪn'lɑk
Kinloss
BR kɪn'lɒs
AM kɪn'lɔs, kɪn'lɑs
Kinnear
BR kɪ'nɪə(r)
AM kɪ'nɪ(ə)r
Kinney
BR 'kɪni
AM 'kɪni
Kinnock
BR 'kɪnək
AM 'kɪnək
kino
BR 'kiːnəʊ, -z
AM 'kinoʊ, -z
Kinross
BR kɪn'rɒs
AM 'kɪnˌrɑs, 'kɪnˌrɔs, ˌkɪn'rɑs, ˌkɪn'rɑs
Kinsale
BR kɪn'seɪl
AM kɪn'seɪl
Kinsella
BR kɪn'sɛlə(r), 'kɪns(ə)lə(r)
AM kɪn'sɛlə
Kinsey
BR 'kɪnzi
AM 'kɪnzi
kinsfolk
BR 'kɪnzfəʊk
AM 'kɪnzˌfoʊk

Kinshasa
BR kɪnˈʃɑːsə(r),
kɪnˈʃɑːsə(r)
AM kənˈʃɑːsə

kinship
BR ˈkɪnʃɪp
AM ˈkɪnˌʃɪp

kinsman
BR ˈkɪnzmən
AM ˈkɪnzmən

kinsmen
BR ˈkɪnzmən
AM ˈkɪnzmən

kinswoman
BR ˈkɪnzˌwʊmən
AM ˈkɪnzˌwʊmən

kinswomen
BR ˈkɪnzˌwɪmɪn
AM ˈkɪnzˌwɪmɪn

Kintyre
BR kɪnˈtʌɪə(r)
AM kɪnˈtaɪ(ə)r

kiosk
BR ˈkiːɒsk, -s
AM ˈkiɑsk, -s

Kiowa
BR ˈkʌɪəwə(r), -z
AM ˈkaɪəwə, -z

kip
BR kɪp, -s, -ɪŋ, -t
AM kɪp, -s, -ɪŋ, -t

Kipling
BR ˈkɪplɪŋ
AM ˈkɪplɪŋ

Kippax
BR ˈkɪpaks
AM ˈkɪpæks

kipper
BR ˈkɪp|ə(r), -əz,
-(ə)rɪŋ, -əd
AM ˈkɪpər, -z, -ɪŋ, -d

kipsie
BR ˈkɪps|i, -ɪz
AM ˈkɪpsi, -z

kipsy
BR ˈkɪps|i, -ɪz
AM ˈkɪpsi, -z

kir
BR kɪə(r)
AM kɪ(ə)r

Kirbigrip®
BR ˈkəːbɪgrɪp, -s
AM ˈkərbiˌgrɪp, -s

Kirby
BR ˈkəːbi
AM ˈkərbi

kirby-grip
BR ˈkəːbɪgrɪp, -s
AM ˈkərbiˌgrɪp, -s

Kirchhoff
BR ˈkəːkɒf
AM ˈkərk,(h)ɔf,
ˈkərk,(h)af, ˈkərˌtʃɔf,
ˈkərˌtʃaf
GER ˈkɪrçhɔf

Kirghiz
BR ˈkəːgɪz, ˈkɪəgɪz,
kɪəˈgɪz
AM kɪrˈgiz

Kirghizia
BR kəːˈgɪzɪə(r),
kɪəˈgɪzɪə(r)
AM kərˈgɪzɪə

Kirgiz
BR ˈkəːgɪz, ˈkɪəgɪz,
kɪəˈgɪz
AM kɪrˈgiz

Kirgizia
BR kəːˈgɪzɪə(r),
kɪəˈgɪzɪə(r)
AM kərˈgɪzɪə

Kiribati
BR ˌkɪrɪˈbɑːti, ˌkɪrɪˈbas
AM ˌkɪrəˈbadi,
ˌkɪrəˈbas

Kirin
BR ˈkɪərɪn
AM ˈkɪrɪn

kirk
BR kəːk, -s
AM kərk, -s

Kirkbride
BR kəːkˈbrʌɪd
AM ˌkərkˈbraɪd

Kirkby
BR ˈkəː(k)bi
AM ˈkərkbi

Kirkcaldy
BR kəˈkɒdi, kəːˈkɒdi,
kəˈkɔːdi, kəːˈkɔːdi
AM kərˈkɔ(l)di,
kərˈkɑ(l)di

Kirkcudbright
BR kəˈkuːbri,
kəːˈkuːbri
AM kərˈkubri

Kirkgate
BR ˈkəːgət
AM ˈkər(k)ˌgeɪt

Kirkham
BR ˈkəːkəm
AM ˈkərkəm

Kirkland
BR ˈkəːklənd
AM ˈkərklən(d)

Kirklees
BR kəːkˈliːz
AM kərkˈliz

kirkman
BR ˈkəːkmən
AM ˈkərkmən

kirkmen
BR ˈkəːkmən
AM ˈkərkmən

Kirkpatrick
BR kəːkˈpatrɪk
AM ˌkərkˈpætrɪk

Kirkstall
BR ˈkəːkst(ə)l,
ˈkəːkstɔːl
AM ˈkərkstɔl,
ˈkərkˌstal

Kirkstone
BR ˈkəːkst(ə)n
AM ˈkərkˌstoʊn

Kirkwall
BR ˈkəːkwɔːl
AM kərˈkwɔl,
kərˈkwal

Kirkwood
BR kəˈkwʊd
AM ˈkərkˌwʊd

Kirov
BR ˈkɪərɒv, ˈkɪərɒf
AM ˈkɪˌrɔv, ˈkɪˌrɑv
RUS ˈkʲirəf

Kirriemuir
BR ˌkɪrɪˈmjʊə(r)
AM ˌkɪrɪˈmjʊ(ə)r

kirsch
BR kɪəʃ, kəːʃ
AM kɪrʃ

kirschwasser
BR ˈkɪəʃˌvasə(r),
ˈkəːʃˌvasə(r), -z
AM ˈkɪrʃˌvasər, -z

Kirsten
BR ˈkəːst(ɪ)n
AM ˈkərstən

Kirstie
BR ˈkəːsti
AM ˈkərsti

kirtle
BR ˈkəːtl, -z
AM ˈkərdəl, -z

Kirundi
BR kɪˈrʊndi
AM kiˈrʊndi

Kirwan
BR ˈkəːw(ə)n
AM ˈkərwən

kishke
BR ˈkɪʃkə(r), -z
AM ˈkɪʃkə, -z

kiskadee
BR ˌkɪskəˈdiː, -z
AM ˌkɪskəˌdi, -z

Kislev
BR ˈkɪslɛf
AM ˈkɪsləv, ˈkɪsləf

Kislew
BR ˈkɪslɛf
AM ˈkɪsləv, ˈkɪsləf

kismet
BR ˈkɪzmɪt, ˈkɪzmɛt
AM ˈkɪzmət, ˈkɪzˌmɛt,
ˌkɪzˈmɛt

kiss
BR kɪs, -ɪz, -ɪŋ, -t
AM kɪs, -ɪz, -ɪŋ, -t

kissable
BR ˈkɪsəbl
AM ˈkɪsəbəl

kissagram
BR ˈkɪsəgram, -z
AM ˈkɪsəˌgræm, -z

kisser
BR ˈkɪsə(r), -z
AM ˈkɪsər, -z

Kissinger
BR ˈkɪs(ɪ)ndʒə(r)
AM ˈkɪsəndʒər

kissogram
BR ˈkɪsəgram, -z
AM ˈkɪsəˌgræm, -z

kissy
BR ˈkɪsi
AM ˈkɪsi

kist
BR kɪst, -s
AM kɪst, -s

Kiswahili
BR ˌkiːswɑːˈhiːli,
ˌkiːswəˈhiːli
AM ˌkiswɑˈhili

kit
BR kɪt, -s, -ɪŋ, -ɪd
AM kɪ|t, -ts, -dɪŋ, -dɪd

kitbag
BR ˈkɪtbag, -z
AM ˈkɪtˌbæg, -z

kitchen
BR ˈkɪtʃ(ɪ)n, -z
AM ˈkɪtʃən, -z

Kitchener
BR ˈkɪtʃɪnə(r)
AM ˈkɪtʃ(ə)nər

kitchenette
BR ˌkɪtʃɪˈnɛt, -s
AM ˌkɪtʃəˈnɛt, -s

kitchenware
BR ˈkɪtʃ(ɪ)nwɛː(r)
AM ˈkɪtʃənˌwɛ(ə)r

kite
BR kʌɪt, -s
AM kaɪt, -s

Kitemark®
BR ˈkʌɪtmɑːk, -s
AM ˈkaɪtˌmɑrk, -s

kith
BR kɪθ
AM kɪθ

Kit-Kat
BR ˈkɪtkat, -s
AM ˈkɪ(t)ˌkæt, -s

kitsch
BR kɪtʃ
AM kɪtʃ

kitschiness
BR ˈkɪtʃɪnɪs
AM ˈkɪtʃinɪs

kitschy
BR ˈkɪtʃ|i, -ɪə(r), -ɪɪst
AM ˈkɪtʃi, -ər, -ɪst

Kitson
BR ˈkɪts(ə)n
AM ˈkɪtsən

kitten
BR ˈkɪtn, -z, -ɪŋ, -d
AM ˈkɪtn, -z, -ɪŋ, -d

kittenish
BR ˈkɪtnɪʃ
AM ˈkɪtnɪʃ

kittenishly
BR ˈkɪtnɪʃli
AM ˈkɪtnɪʃli

kittenishness
BR ˈkɪtn̩ɪʃnɪs
AM ˈkɪtn̩ɪʃnɪs

kittiwake
BR ˈkɪtɪweɪk, -s
AM ˈkɪdi,weɪk, -s

kittle
BR ˈkɪtl̩
AM ˈkɪdəl

kitty
BR ˈkɪt|i, -ɪz
AM ˈkɪdi, -z

Kitwe
BR ˈkɪtweɪ
AM ˈkɪt,weɪ

Kivu
BR ˈkiːvuː
AM ˈki,vu

Kiwanis
BR kɪˈwɑːnɪs
AM kəˈwɑnəs

kiwi
BR ˈkiːwiː, -z
AM ˈkiwi, -z

Klan
BR klan
AM klæn

Klansman
BR ˈklanzmən
AM ˈklænzmən

Klansmen
BR ˈklanzmən
AM ˈklænzmən

Klaus
BR klaʊs
AM klaʊs

klavier
BR kləˈvɪə(r),
klaˈvɪə(r), -z
AM kləˈvɪ(ə)r, -z

klaxon
BR ˈklaksn̩, -z
AM ˈklæksən, -z

klebsiella
BR ˌklɛbzɪˈelə(r)
AM ˌklɛbsiˈelə,
ˌklɛbzɪˈelə

Klee
BR kleɪ
AM kleɪ

Kleenex®
BR ˈkliːnɛks, -ɪz
AM ˈkli,nɛks, -əz

Klein
BR klʌɪn
AM klaɪn

Kleinwort
BR ˈklʌɪnwɔːt
AM ˈklaɪnwərt,
ˈklaɪn,wɔ(ə)rt

Kleist
BR klʌɪst
AM klaɪst

Klemperer
BR ˈklɛmp(ə)rə(r)
AM ˈklɛmpərər

klepht
BR klɛft, -s
AM klɛft, -s

kleptomania
BR ˌklɛptə(ʊ)ˈmeɪnɪə(r)
AM ˌklɛptəˈmeɪnɪə

kleptomaniac
BR ˌklɛptə(ʊ)ˈmeɪnɪak,
-s
AM ˌklɛptəˈmeɪniˌæk,
-s

Klerksdorp
BR ˈkləːksdɔːp
AM ˈklərksˌdɔ(ə)rp

klieg
BR kliːg, -z
AM klig, -z

Klimt
BR klɪmt
AM klɪmt

Kline
BR klʌɪn
AM klaɪn

klipspringer
BR ˈklɪpˌsprɪŋə(r), -z
AM ˈklɪpˌsprɪŋər, -z

Klondike
BR ˈklɒndʌɪk
AM ˈklɑnˌdaɪk

kloof
BR kluːf, -s
AM kluf, -s

Klosters
BR ˈkləʊstəz, ˈklɒstəz
AM ˈklɒstərz, ˈklɑstərz

kludge
BR kluːdʒ
AM klʊdʒ, kludʒ

klutz
BR klʌts, -ɪz
AM klʌts, -əz

klutzy
BR ˈklʌtz|i, -ɪə(r), -ɪɪst
AM ˈklʌtzi, -ər, -ɪst

klystron
BR ˈklʌɪstrɒn, -z
AM ˈklaɪ,strɑn, -z

K-meson
BR ˌkeɪˈmɛzɒn,
ˌkeɪˈmiːzɒn
AM ˈkeɪˌmeɪˌzɑn,
ˈkeɪˌmɛzn̩

knack
BR nak, -s
AM næk, -s

knacker
BR ˈnakə(r), -z, -d
AM ˈnækər, -z, -d

knackery
BR ˈnak(ə)r|i, -ɪz
AM ˈnæk(ə)ri, -z

knackwurst
BR ˈnakwəːst,
ˈnakvʊəst
AM ˈnɑkˌwərst,
ˈnɑkˌwʊrst

knag
BR nag, -z
AM næg, -z

knaggy
BR ˈnag|i, -ɪə(r), -ɪɪst
AM ˈnægi, -ər, -ɪst

knap
BR nap, -s, -ɪŋ, -t
AM næp, -s, -ɪŋ, -t

Knapp
BR nap
AM næp

knapper
BR ˈnapə(r), -z
AM ˈnæpər, -z

knapsack
BR ˈnapsak, -s
AM ˈnæp,sæk, -s

knapweed
BR ˈnapwiːd, -z
AM ˈnæp,wid, -z

knar
BR nɑː(r), -z
AM nɑr, -z

Knaresborough
BR ˈnɛːzb(ə)rə(r)
AM ˈnɛrz,bərə

Knatchbull
BR ˈnatʃbʊl
AM ˈnætʃ,bʊl

knave
BR neɪv, -z
AM neɪv, -z

knavery
BR ˈneɪv(ə)ri
AM ˈneɪvəri

knavish
BR ˈneɪvɪʃ
AM ˈneɪvɪʃ

knavishly
BR ˈneɪvɪʃli
AM ˈneɪvɪʃli

knavishness
BR ˈneɪvɪʃnɪs
AM ˈneɪvɪʃnɪs

knawel
BR nɔː(ə)l
AM nɔl, nɑl

knead
BR niːd, -z, -ɪŋ, -ɪd
AM nid, -z, -ɪŋ, -ɪd

kneadable
BR ˈniːdəbl
AM ˈnidəbəl

kneader
BR ˈniːdə(r), -z
AM ˈnidər, -z

Knebworth
BR ˈnɛbwəːθ
AM ˈnɛb,wərθ

knee
BR niː, -z, -ɪŋ, -d
AM ni, -z, -ɪŋ, -d

kneecap
BR ˈniːkap, -s, -ɪŋ, -t
AM ˈni,kæp, -s, -ɪŋ, -t

kneecapping
BR ˈniːˌkapɪŋ, -z
AM ˈni,kæpɪŋ, -z

kneehole
BR ˈniːhəʊl, -z
AM ˈni,hoʊl, -z

kneel
BR niːl, -z, -ɪŋ
AM nil, -z, -ɪŋ

kneeler
BR ˈniːlə(r), -z
AM ˈnilər, -z

knee-trembler
BR ˈniːˌtremblə(r), -z
AM ˈni,tremb(ə)lər, -z

knell
BR nɛl, -z, -ɪŋ, -d
AM nɛl, -z, -ɪŋ, -d

Kneller
BR ˈnɛlə(r)
AM ˈnɛlər

knelt
BR nɛlt
AM nɛlt

Knesset
BR (kə)ˈnɛsɪt
AM (kə)ˈnɛsət

knew
BR njuː
AM n(j)u

knicker
BR ˈnɪkə(r), -z
AM ˈnɪkər, -z

Knickerbocker
BR ˈnɪkəˌbɒkə(r), -z
AM ˈnɪkərˌbɑkər, -z

knick-knack
BR ˈnɪknak, -s
AM ˈnɪk,næk, -s

knick-knackery
BR ˈnɪkˌnak(ə)ri
AM ˈnɪk,nækəri

knick-knackish
BR ˈnɪkˌnakɪʃ
AM ˈnɪk,nækɪʃ

knife
BR nʌɪf
AM naɪf

knifelike
BR ˈnʌɪflʌɪk
AM ˈnaɪf,laɪk

knifepoint
BR ˈnʌɪfpɔɪnt
AM ˈnaɪf,pɔɪnt

knifer
BR ˈnʌɪfə(r), -z
AM ˈnaɪfər, -z

knight
BR nʌɪt, -s, -ɪŋ, -ɪd
AM naɪt, -ts, -dɪŋ, -dɪd

knightage
BR ˈnʌɪt|ɪdʒ, -ɪdʒɪz
AM ˈnaɪdɪdʒ, -ɪz

knight-errant
BR ˌnʌɪtˈɛrənt,
ˌnʌɪtˈɛrn̩t
AM ˌnaɪtˈɛrənt

knight-errantry
BR ˈnaɪtˈɛrəntri,
ˌnaɪtˈɛrn̩tri
AM ˈnaɪtˈɛrəntri

knighthood
BR ˈnaɪthʊd, -z
AM ˈnaɪt‚(h)ʊd, -z

Knight Hospitaller
BR ˌnaɪt ˈhɒspɪtlə(r)
AM ˈnaɪt ˈhɑ‚spɪtlər

knightlike
BR ˈnaɪtlaɪk
AM ˈnaɪt‚laɪk

knightliness
BR ˈnaɪtlɪnɪs
AM ˈnaɪtlɪnɪs

knightly
BR ˈnaɪtl̩i, -ɪə(r), -ɪst
AM ˈnaɪtli, -ər, -ɪst

Knighton
BR ˈnaɪt(ə)n
AM ˈnaɪtn̩

Knights
BR naɪts
AM naɪts

Knightsbridge
BR ˈnaɪtsbrɪdʒ
AM ˈnaɪts‚brɪdʒ

knights-errant
BR ˌnaɪtsˈɛrənt,
ˌnaɪtsˈern̩t
AM ˈnaɪtsˈɛrənt

Knights Hospitaller
BR ˌnaɪts ˈhɒspɪtlə(r)
AM ˈnaɪts ˈhɑ‚spɪtlər

Knights Templar
BR ˌnaɪts ˈtemplə(r)
AM ˈnaɪts ˈtemplər

Knight Templar
BR ˌnaɪt ˈtemplə(r)
AM ˈnaɪt ˈtemplər

kniphofia
BR nɪˈfəʊfɪə(r),
nʌɪˈfəʊfɪə(r),
nɪpˈhəʊfɪə(r)
AM nəˈfoʊfɪə

knish
BR kəˈnɪʃ, knɪʃ, -ɪz
AM kəˈnɪʃ, -ɪz

knit
BR nɪt, -s, -ɪŋ, -ɪd
AM nɪ|t, -ts, -dɪŋ, -dɪd

knitter
BR ˈnɪtə(r), -z
AM ˈnɪdər, -z

knitwear
BR ˈnɪtweː(r)
AM ˈnɪt‚we(ə)r

knives
BR naɪvz
AM naɪvz

knob
BR nɒb, -z
AM nɑb, -z

knobbiness
BR ˈnɒbɪnɪs
AM ˈnabɪnɪs

knobble
BR ˈnɒbl̩, -z
AM ˈnabəl, -z

knobbliness
BR ˈnɒblɪnɪs
AM ˈnab(ə)lɪnɪs

knobbly
BR ˈnɒbl̩i, ˈnɒbl̩i,
-ɪə(r), -ɪst
AM ˈnab(ə)li, -ər, -ɪst

knobby
BR ˈnɒb|i, -ɪə(r), -ɪst
AM ˈnabi, -ər, -ɪst

knobkerrie
BR ˈnɒb‚ker|i, -ɪz
AM ˈnab‚keri, -z

knoblike
BR ˈnɒblaɪk
AM ˈnab‚laɪk

knobstick
BR ˈnɒbstɪk, -s
AM ˈnab‚stɪk, -s

knock
BR nɒk, -s, -ɪŋ, -t
AM nak, -s, -ɪŋ, -t

knockabout
BR ˈnɒkəbaʊt
AM ˈnakə‚baʊt

knocker
BR ˈnɒkə(r), -z
AM ˈnakər, -z

knockout
BR ˈnɒkaʊt, -s
AM ˈnɑ‚kaʊt, -s

knockwurst
BR ˈnɒkwɜːst,
ˈnɒkvʊəst
AM ˈnak‚wɜrst,
ˈnak‚wʊrst

knoll
BR nəʊl, nɒl, -z
AM noʊl, -z

Knollys
BR nəʊlz
AM noʊlz

knop
BR nɒp, -s
AM nɑp, -s

knopkierie
BR ˈknɒp‚kɪər|i, -ɪz
AM ˈ(k)nap‚kiri, -z

Knossos
BR ˈ(k)nɒsɒs
AM ˈ(k)nasɔs,
ˈ(k)nasas

knot
BR nɒt, -s, -ɪŋ, -ɪd
AM nɑ|t, -ts, -dɪŋ, -dəd

knotgrass
BR ˈnɒtgrɑːs, ˈnɒtgras
AM ˈnat‚græs

knothole
BR ˈnɒthəʊl, -z
AM ˈnat‚(h)oʊl, -z

knotless
BR ˈnɒtləs
AM ˈnatləs

Knott
BR nɒt
AM nɑt

knotter
BR ˈnɒtə(r), -z
AM ˈnadər, -z

knottily
BR ˈnɒtɪli
AM ˈnadəli

knottiness
BR ˈnɒtɪnɪs
AM ˈnadɪnɪs

knotting
BR ˈnɒtɪŋ, -z
AM ˈnadɪŋ, -z

knotty
BR ˈnɒt|i, -ɪə(r), -ɪst
AM ˈnadi, -ər, -ɪst

knotweed
BR ˈnɒtwiːd
AM ˈnat‚wid

knotwork
BR ˈnɒtwɜːk
AM ˈnat‚wɜrk

knout
BR naʊt, nuːt, -s, -ɪŋ, -ɪd
AM naʊ|t, -ts, -dɪŋ, -dəd

know
BR nəʊ, -z, -ɪŋ
AM noʊ, -z, -ɪŋ

knowable
BR ˈnəʊəbl
AM ˈnoʊəbəl

knower
BR ˈnəʊə(r), -z
AM ˈnoʊər, -z

know-how
BR ˈnəʊhaʊ
AM ˈnoʊ‚haʊ

knowing
BR ˈnəʊɪŋ
AM ˈnoʊɪŋ

knowingly
BR ˈnəʊɪŋli
AM ˈnoʊɪŋli

knowingness
BR ˈnəʊɪŋnɪs
AM ˈnoʊɪŋnɪs

Knowle
BR nəʊl
AM noʊl

knowledgability
BR ˌnɒlɪdʒəˈbɪlɪti
AM ˌnalədʒəˈbɪlɪdi

knowledgable
BR ˈnɒlɪdʒəbl
AM ˈnalədʒəbəl

knowledgableness
BR ˈnɒlɪdʒəblnəs
AM ˈnalədʒəbəlnəs

knowledgably
BR ˈnɒlɪdʒəbli
AM ˈnalədʒəbli

knowledge
BR ˈnɒlɪdʒ
AM ˈnalədʒ

knowledgeability
BR ˌnɒlɪdʒəˈbɪlɪti
AM ˌnalədʒəˈbɪlɪdi

knowledgeable
BR ˈnɒlɪdʒəbl
AM ˈnalədʒəbəl

knowledgeableness
BR ˈnɒlɪdʒəblnəs
AM ˈnalədʒəbəlnəs

knowledgeably
BR ˈnɒlɪdʒəbli
AM ˈnalədʒəbli

Knowles
BR nəʊlz
AM noʊlz

known
BR nəʊn
AM noʊn

Knox
BR nɒks
AM naks

Knoxville
BR ˈnɒksvɪl
AM ˈnaks‚vɪl, ˈnaksvəl

knuckle
BR ˈnʌk|l, -lz, -lɪŋ \-lɪŋ, -ld
AM ˈnək|əl, -əlz, -(ə)lɪŋ, -əld

knuckleball
BR ˈnʌklbɔːl, -z
AM ˈnəkəl‚bɔl, ˈnəkəl‚bal, -z

knucklebone
BR ˈnʌklbəʊn, -z
AM ˈnəkəl‚boʊn, -z

knucklehead
BR ˈnʌklhed, -z
AM ˈnəkəl‚(h)ɛd, -z

knuckly
BR ˈnʌkl̩i, ˈnʌkli
AM ˈnəkli

knur
BR nɜː(r), -z
AM nɜr, -z

knurl
BR nɜːl, -d
AM nɜrl, -d

knurr
BR nɜː(r), -z
AM nɜr, -z

Knut
BR knʌt, kəˈnuːt
AM kəˈnut

Knutsford
BR ˈnʌtsfəd
AM ˈnʌtsfərd

KO
BR ˌkeɪˈəʊ, -z, -ɪŋ, -d
AM ˌkeɪˈoʊ, -z, -ɪŋ, -d

koa
BR ˈkəʊə(r), -z
AM ˈkoʊə, -z

koala
BR kəʊˈɑːlə(r), -z
AM koʊˈɑlə, kəˈwɑlə, -z

koan
BR ˈkəʊan, -z
AM ˈkoʊˌɑn, -z

Kobe
BR ˈkəʊbi, ˈkəʊbeɪ
AM ˈkoʊbi

kobold
BR ˈkəʊb(ə)ld
AM ˈkoʊˌbɒld, ˈkoʊˌbald

Koch
BR kəʊk, kɒtʃ, kɒk, kɒx
AM kɔk, kʊk, kak

Köchel
BR ˈkɜːkl, ˈkɜːxl
AM ˈkoʊkəl

Kodachrome
BR ˈkəʊdəkrəʊm
AM ˈkoʊdəˌkroʊm

Kodak®
BR ˈkəʊdak, -s
AM ˈkoʊˌdæk, -s

Kodály
BR ˈkəʊdʌɪ
AM ˌkoʊˈdaɪ(i)
HU ˈkɔdɑːj

Kodiak
BR ˈkəʊdɪak, -s
AM ˈkoʊdiˌæk, -s

koel
BR ˈkəʊəl, -z
AM ˈkoʊəl, -z

Koestler
BR ˈkɜːs(t)lə(r)
AM ˈkɛs(t)lər

Koh-i-noor
BR ˌkəʊɪˈnʊə(r), ˌkəʊɪˈnɔː(r)
AM ˈkoʊəˌnʊ(ə)r

kohl
BR kəʊl
AM koʊl

kohlrabi
BR ˌkəʊlˈrɑːbˌi, -ɪz
AM ˌkoʊlˈrɑbi, -z

koi
BR kɔɪ
AM kɔɪ

Koil
BR kɔɪl
AM kɔɪl

koiné
BR ˈkɔɪneɪ, ˈkɔɪniː, ˈkɔɪni
AM kɔɪˈneɪ

Kojak
BR ˈkəʊdʒak
AM ˈkoʊˌdʒæk

Kokoschka
BR kəˈkɒʃkə(r)
AM kəˈkɔʃkə, kəˈkɑʃkə

kola
BR ˈkəʊlə(r)

koʊlə
Kolhapur
BR ˈkɒləpʊə(r)
AM ˈkɔləˌpʊ(ə)r, ˈkaləˌpʊ(ə)r

kolinsky
BR kəˈlɪnskˌi, -ɪz
AM kəˈlɪnski, -z

kolkhoz
BR ˌkɒlˈkɒz, ˌkɒlˈkɔːz, ˌkʌlkˈhɔːz
AM kəlˈkɔz, kəlˈkaz

Köln
BR kɜːln, kəʊln
AM kəln

Koluma
BR kəˈluːmə(r)
AM kəˈluːmə
RUS kəlɪˈma

komitadji
BR ˌkɒmɪˈtadʒˌi, -ɪz
AM ˌkɑməˈtɑdʒi, ˌkoʊməˈtɑdʒi, -z

Komodo
BR kəˈməʊdəʊ
AM kəˈmoʊˌdoʊ

Kompong Cham
BR ˌkɒmpɒŋ ˈtʃam
AM ˌkamˈpɔŋ ˈtʃɑm, ˈkamˌpaŋ ˈtʃɑm

Kompong Som
BR ˌkɒmpɒŋ ˈsɒm
AM ˌkamˈpɔŋ ˈsɑm, ˈkamˌpaŋ ˈsɑm

Komsomol
BR ˈkɒmsəmɒl
AM ˌkamsəˈmɔl, ˈkamsəˌmɑl
RUS kəmsaˈmol

Komsomolsk
BR ˈkɒmsəmɒlsk
AM ˈkamsəˌmalsk
RUS kəmsaˈmolsk

Kongo
BR ˈkɒŋgəʊ
AM ˈkaŋgoʊ

Königsberg
BR ˈkɜːnɪgzbɜːg
AM ˈkɜːnɪgzˌbɜrg
GER ˈkœːnɪçsbɛrk

Konika
BR ˈkɒnɪkə(r), ˈkəʊnɪkə(r)
AM ˈkanəkə

Konopka
BR kəˈnɒpkə(r)
AM kəˈnapkə

Konrad
BR ˈkɒnrad
AM ˈkanˌræd

Kon-Tiki
BR ˌkɒnˈtiːki
AM ˌkanˈtiki

koodoo
BR ˈkuːduː, -z
AM ˈkuˌdu, -z

kook
BR kuːk, -s

kuk, -s

kookaburra
BR ˈkʊkəˌbʌrə(r), -z
AM ˈkʊkəˌbɜrə, -z

kookily
BR ˈkʊkɪli
AM ˈkukəli

kookiness
BR ˈkʊkɪnɪs
AM ˈkukɪnɪs

kooky
BR ˈkuːkˌi, ˈkʊkˌi, -ɪə(r), -ɪɪst
AM ˈkuki, -ər, -ɪɪst

kop
BR kɒp, -s
AM kɑp, -s

kopeck
BR ˈkəʊpɛk, -s
AM ˈkoʊˌpɛk, -s

kopek
BR ˈkəʊpɛk, -s
AM ˈkoʊˌpɛk, -s

kopi
BR ˈkəʊpi
AM ˈkoʊpi

kopje
BR ˈkɒpˌi, -ɪz
AM ˈkɑpi, -z

koppa
BR ˈkɒpə(r), -z
AM ˈkɑpə, -z

koppie
BR ˈkɒpˌi, -ɪz
AM ˈkɑpi, -z

koradji
BR ˈkɒrədʒˌi, kəˈradʒˌi, -ɪz
AM kəˈradʒi, -z

Koran
BR kəˈrɑːn, kɔːˈrɑːn
AM kəˈran, kɔˈran

Koranic
BR kəˈranɪk
AM kəˈranɪk, kɔˈranɪk

Korda
BR ˈkɔːdə(r)
AM ˈkɔrdə

Kordofan
BR ˌkɔːdə(ʊ)ˈfan, ˌkɔːdə(ʊ)ˈfɑːn
AM ˌkɔrdoʊˈfan

Korea
BR kəˈrɪə(r)
AM kəˈriə

Korean
BR kəˈrɪən, -z
AM kəˈrɪən, -z

korfball
BR ˈkɔːfbɔːl
AM ˈkɔrfˌbɔl, ˈkɔrfˌbal

Kórinthos
BR ˈkɔːrɪnθɒs
AM kəˈrɪnθɔs, ˌkɔˈrɪnθəs, kəˈrɪnθəs, ˌkɔˈrɪnθɑs
GR ˈkɔriːnθɔs

korma
BR ˈkɔːmə(r), -z
AM ˈkɔrmə, -z

Korsakoff
BR ˈkɔːsəkɒf
AM ˈkɔrsəˌkɔf, ˈkɔrsəˌkaf

koruna
BR ˈkɒrɜnə(r), -z
AM ˈkɔrənə, -z
CZ ˈkɔrunʌ

Kos
BR kɒs
AM kɔs, kɑs

Kościuszko
BR ˌkɒsɪˈʌskəʊ, ˌkɒsɪˈʊskəʊ
AM ˌkɑsiˈəsˌkoʊ
POL kɒʃiˈtʃuʃkɒ

kosher
BR ˈkəʊʃə(r)
AM ˈkoʊʃər

Kosovo
BR ˈkɒsəvəʊ
AM ˈkɔsəˌvə, ˈkɑsəˌvə

Kostroma
BR ˈkɒstrəmɑː(r)
AM ˈkastrəˌma
RUS kəstraˈma

Kosygin
BR kəˈsiːgɪn
AM kəˈsigɪn, kəˈsidʒɪn

Kota
BR ˈkəʊtə(r)
AM ˈkoʊdə

Kota Baharu
BR ˌkəʊtə bəˈhɑːruː, + ˈbɑːruː
AM ˈkoʊdə bəˈhɑˌru

Kota Kinabalu
BR ˌkəʊtə ˌkɪnəˈbɑːluː
AM ˈkoʊdə ˌkɪnəˈbɑˌlu

Kotka
BR ˈkɒtkə(r)
AM ˈkatkə

koto
BR ˈkəʊtəʊ, -z
AM ˈkoʊdoʊ, -z

kotow
BR ˌkəʊˈtaʊ, ˌkaʊˈtaʊ, -z, -ɪŋ, -d
AM ˈkaʊˌtaʊ, -z, -ɪŋ, -d

koulan
BR ˈkuːlən, -z
AM ˈkuˌlan, -z

koumis
BR ˈkuːmɪs
AM kuˈmɪs, ˈkuməs

koumiss
BR ˈkuːmɪs
AM kuˈmɪs, ˈkuməs

kouprey
BR ˈkuːpreɪ, -z
AM ˈkuˌpreɪ, -z

kourbash
BR ˈkʊəbaʃ, -ɪz
AM ˈkʊrˌbaʃ, ˈkurˈbaʃ, -əz

kowhai
BR ˈkəʊwʌɪ, ˈkɔːfʌɪ, -z
AM ˈkoʊˌwaɪ, -z

Kowloon
BR ˌkaʊˈluːn
AM ˌkaʊˈlun

kowtow
BR ˌkaʊˈtaʊ, -z, -ɪŋ, -d
AM ˌkaʊˈtaʊ, -z, -ɪŋ, -d

Kra
BR krɑː(r)
AM krɑ

kraal
BR krɑːl, -z
AM krɑl, -z

kraft
BR krɑːft, kraft
AM kræft

krait
BR krʌɪt, -s
AM krʌɪt, -s

Krakatoa
BR ˌkrakəˈtəʊə(r)
AM ˌkrækəˈtoʊə

kraken
BR ˈkrɑːk(ə)n, -z
AM ˈkrɑkən, -z

Kraków
BR ˈkrakaʊ, ˈkrakɒf
AM ˈkrɑˌkaʊ, ˈkrɑkɔf, ˈkrɑkɑf
POL ˈkrakʊf

Kramer
BR ˈkreɪmə(r)
AM ˈkreɪmər

krans
BR krɑːns, krans
AM kræns

krantz
BR krɑːns, krans
AM kræn(t)s

Krasnodar
BR ˌkraznə(ʊ)ˈdɑː(r)
AM ˈkrɑsnəˌdɑr

Krasnoyarsk
BR ˌkrasnəˈjɑːsk
AM ˈkrɑsnəˌjɑrsk

krater
BR ˈkreɪtə(r), -z, -d
AM ˈkreɪdər, -z, -d

K-ration
BR ˈkeɪˌraʃn, -z
AM ˈkeɪˌræʃən, ˈkeɪˌreɪʃən, -z

Kraus
BR kraʊs
AM kraʊs

Krause
BR kraʊs
AM kraʊs
GER ˈkraʊzə

Krauss
BR kraʊs
AM kraʊs

Kraut
BR kraʊt, -s
AM kraʊt, -s

Kray
BR kreɪ
AM kreɪ

Krebs
BR krɛbz
AM krɛbz

Krefeld
BR ˈkreɪfɛld
AM ˈkreɪˌfɛld

Kreisler
BR ˈkrʌɪzlə(r)
AM ˈkraɪslər

Kremlin
BR ˈkrɛmlɪn
AM ˈkrɛmlən

Kremlinologist
BR ˌkrɛmlɪˈnɒlədʒɪst, -s
AM ˌkrɛmləˈnɑlədʒəst, -s

Kremlinology
BR ˌkrɛmlɪˈnɒlədʒi
AM ˌkrɛmləˈnɑlədʒi

Kretzschmar
BR ˈkrɛtʃmɑː(r)
AM ˈkrɛtʃˌmɑr

kriegspiel
BR ˈkriːgspiːl
AM ˈkriɡˌʃpil, ˈkriɡzˌpil

krill
BR krɪl
AM krɪl

krimmer
BR ˈkrɪmə(r)
AM ˈkrɪmər

Krio
BR ˈkriːəʊ, -z
AM ˈkrioʊ, -z

kris
BR kriːs, -ɪz
AM krɪs, kris, -ɪz

Krishna
BR ˈkrɪʃnə(r)
AM ˈkrɪʃnə

Krishnaism
BR ˈkrɪʃnə(r)ɪz(ə)m
AM ˈkrɪʃnəˌɪzəm

Krishnamurti
BR ˌkrɪʃnəˈmʊəti, ˌkrɪʃnəˈməːti
AM ˌkrɪʃnəˈmərdi

Krista
BR ˈkrɪstə(r)
AM ˈkrɪstə

Kristallnacht
BR ˈkrɪstlnaxt
AM ˈkrɪstlˌnɑkt
GER krɪsˈtalnaxt

Kroeber
BR ˈkrəʊbə(r)
AM ˈkroʊbər

kromesky
BR krə(ʊ)ˈmɛskli, ˈkrɒmɛskli, -ɪz
AM kroʊˈmɛski, -z

krona
BR ˈkrəʊnə(r)
AM ˈkroʊnə
SW ˈkroːna

krone
BR ˈkrəʊnə(r)
AM ˈkroʊnə
DAN ˈkroːnə
NO ˈkruːne

kroner
BR ˈkrəʊnə(r)
AM ˈkroʊnər
DAN ˈkroːnʌ
NO ˈkruːner

kronor
BR ˈkrəʊnə(r)
AM ˈkroʊnər
SW ˈkroːnɒr

Kronos
BR ˈkrɒnɒs
AM ˈkroʊˌnɒs, ˈkroʊˌnɑs

Kronstadt
BR ˈkrɒnstat
AM ˈkrɑnˌstad

kronur
BR ˈkrəʊnə(r)
AM ˈkroʊnər

Kroo
BR kruː
AM kru

Kropotkin
BR krəˈpɒtkɪn
AM krəˈpɑtkən

Kru
BR kruː
AM kru

Krueger
BR ˈkruːɡə(r)
AM ˈkruɡər

Kruger
BR ˈkruːɡə(r)
AM ˈkruɡər
AFK ˈkryər

Krugerrand
BR ˈkruːɡərand, -z
AM ˈkruɡərænd, -(d)z
AFK ˈkryəˌrant

krumhorn
BR ˈkrʌmhɔːn, -z
AM ˈkrʊm, (h)ɔ(ə)rn, -z

krummholz
BR ˈkrʌmhɒlts
AM ˈkrəm, (h)ɒlts, ˈkrəm, (h)alts

krummhorn
BR ˈkrʌmhɔːn, -z
AM ˈkrʊm, (h)ɔ(ə)rn, -z

Krupp
BR krʊp, krʌp
AM krʊp

krypton
BR ˈkrɪptɒn
AM ˈkrɪpˌtɑn

Kshatriya
BR ˈkʃatrɪə(r), -z
AM (kə)ˈʃatri(j)ə, -z

krona
BR ˈkrəʊnə(r)
AM ˈkroʊnə
SW ˈkroːna

K2
BR ˌkeɪˈtuː
AM ˌkeɪˈtu

Kuala Lumpur
BR ˌkwɑːlə ˈlʊmpʊə(r), + ˈlʌmpə(r)
AM ˌkwɑlə lʊmˈpʊ(ə)r

Kublai Khan
BR ˌkuːblə ˈkɑːn, ˌkuːblʌɪ +
AM ˌkʊblə ˈkɑn

Kubrick
BR ˈk(j)uːbrɪk
AM ˈkʊbrɪk

kuccha
BR ˈkʌtʃə(r)
AM ˈkətʃə

kudos
BR ˈkjuːdɒs
AM ˈkuˌdoʊs

kudu
BR ˈkuːduː, -z
AM ˈkudu, -z

kudzu
BR ˈkʊdzuː
AM ˈkədˌzu

Kufic
BR ˈk(j)uːfɪk
AM ˈk(j)ufɪk

Kuhn
BR kuːn
AM k(j)un

Ku Klux Klan
BR ˌkuː klʌks ˈklan
AM ˌku ˌkləks ˈklæn

Ku Klux Klansman
BR ˌkuː klʌks ˈklanzmən
AM ˌku ˌkləks ˈklænzmən

Ku Klux Klansmen
BR ˌkuː klʌks ˈklanzmən
AM ˌku ˌkləks ˈklænzmən

kukri
BR ˈkʊkrˌli, -ɪz
AM ˈkʊkri, -z

kulak
BR ˈkuːlak, -s
AM ˈkulæk, kuˈlak, -s
RUS kuˈlak

kulan
BR ˈkuːlən, -z
AM ˈkulɑn, -z

Kultur
BR kʊlˈtʊə(r)
AM kʊlˈtʊ(ə)r

Kulturkampf
BR kʊlˈtʊəkam(p)f
AM kʊlˈtʊrˌkam(p)f

Kumamoto
BR ˌkuːməˈməʊtəʊ
AM ˌkuməˈmoʊdoʊ

kumara
BR ˈkuːmərə(r), -z

kumis
AM ˈkuːmərə, -z

kumis
BR ˈkuːmɪs
AM kuˈmɪs, ˈkuməs

kumiss
BR ˈkuːmɪs
AM kuˈmɪs, ˈkuməs

Kümmel
BR ˈkʊml
AM ˈkɪməl

kumquat
BR ˈkʌmkwɒt, -s
AM ˈkəmˌkwɑt, -s

Kundera
BR ˈkʊndərə(r)
AM ˈkʊndərə

Kung
BR kʊŋ
AM kʊŋ

kung fu
BR ˌkʊŋ ˈfuː, ˌkʌŋ +
AM ˌkʊŋ ˈfu

Kunlun Shan
BR ˌkʊnlʊn ˈʃan
AM ˈkʊnˌlʊn ˈʃʌn

Kunming
BR ˌkʊnˈmɪn
AM ˈkʊnˈmɪŋ

Kuomintang
BR ˌkwəʊmɪnˈtaŋ
AM ˌkwɔˈmɪnˈtæŋ

Kuoni
BR kʊˈəʊni
AM kʊˈoʊni

kurbash
BR ˈkʊəbaʃ, -ɪz
AM ˈkʊrˌbaʃ, ˌkʊrˈbaʃ, -əz

kurchatovium
BR ˌkɜːtʃəˈtəʊviəm
AM ˌkɜrtʃəˈtoʊviəm

Kurd
BR kɜːd, -z
AM kɜrd, -z

kurdaitcha
BR kəˈdʌɪtʃə(r), -z
AM kərˈdaɪtʃə, -z

Kurdish
BR ˈkɜːdɪʃ
AM ˈkɜrdɪʃ

Kurdistan
BR ˌkɜːdɪˈstaːn, ˌkɜːdɪˈstaːn
AM ˈkɜrdəˌstæn

Kurgan
BR kʊəˈgaːn
AM kʊrˈgan

Kurile
BR kjʊˈriːl

Kurosawa
BR ˌkʊrəˈsaːwə(r)
AM ˌkʊrəˈsawə

kurrajong
BR ˈkʌrədʒɒŋ, -z
AM ˈkɜrəˌdʒɔŋ, ˈkɜrəˌdʒaŋ, -z

Kursaal
BR ˈkʊəzaːl, ˈkʊəsaːl, ˈkɜːzl, ˈkɜːsl, -z
AM ˈkʊrˌzal, -z

Kurt
BR kɜːt
AM kɜrt

kurta
BR ˈkɜːtə(r), -z
AM ˈkɜrdə, -z

kurtosis
BR kɜːˈtəʊsɪs
AM kərˈtoʊsəs

kurus
BR kʊˈrʊʃ, kʊˈruːʃ
AM kəˈrʊʃ

Kurzweil
BR ˈkɜːtswʌɪl, ˈkɜːtsvʌɪl
AM ˈkɜrts,waɪl

Kush
BR kʊʃ
AM kʊʃ

Kuwait
BR k(j)ʊˈweɪt, -i
AM ˌkuˈweɪ|t, kəˈweɪ|t, -di

Kuwaiti
BR k(j)ʊˈweɪt|i, -ɪz
AM kəˈweɪdi, -z

Kuznetz Basin
BR kʊzˌnɛts ˈbeɪsn
AM ˈkʊzˌnɛts ˈbeɪsən

kvas
BR kvɑːs
AM kəˈvas, kvas

kvass
BR kvɑːs
AM kəˈvas, kvas

kvetch
BR kvɛtʃ, -ɪz, -ɪŋ, -t
AM kəˈvɛtʃ, kvɛtʃ, -əz, -ɪŋ, -t

kvetcher
BR ˈkvɛtʃə(r), -z
AM ˈkvɛtʃər, -z

Kwa
BR kwɑː(r)
AM kwɑ

KWAC
BR kwak
AM kwæk

kwacha
BR ˈkwaːtʃə(r), ˈkwatʃə(r), -z
AM ˈkwɑtʃə, -z

KwaNdebele
BR ˌkwaːŋdɪˈbiːli, ˌkwaːŋdɪˈbeɪli
AM ˈkwandəˈbiˌli

kwanza
BR ˈkwanzə(r), -z
AM ˈkwan,za, -z

kwashiorkor
BR ˈkwɒʃɪəkɔː(r), ˌkwɒʃɪˈɔːkɔː(r)
AM ˌkwaˈʃiˌɔrˈkɔ(ə)r

KwaZulu
BR ˌkwaːˈzuːluː
AM ˌkwaˈzulu

Kweilin
BR ˌkweɪˈlɪn
AM ˈkweɪˈlɪn

Kweiyang
BR ˌkweɪˈjaŋ
AM ˈkweɪˈjæŋ

kwela
BR ˈkweɪlə(r)
AM ˈkweɪlə

Kwells
BR kwɛlz
AM kwɛlz

KWIC
BR kwɪk
AM kwɪk

Kwik-Fit
BR ˈkwɪkfɪt
AM ˈkwɪkˌfɪt

KWOC
BR kwɒk
AM kwak

kyanise
BR ˈkʌɪənʌɪz, -ɪz, -ɪŋ, -d
AM ˈkaɪəˌnaɪz, -ɪz, -ɪŋ, -d

kyanite
BR ˈkʌɪənʌɪt
AM ˈkaɪəˌnaɪt

kyanitic
BR ˌkʌɪəˈnɪtɪk
AM ˌkaɪəˈnɪdɪk

kyanize
BR ˈkʌɪənʌɪz, -ɪz, -ɪŋ, -d
AM ˈkaɪəˌnaɪz, -ɪz, -ɪŋ, -d

kyat
BR kiːˈɑːt, -s
AM ki·(j)ɑt, -s

kybosh
BR ˈkʌɪbɒʃ
AM ˈkaɪˌbɒʃ, kəˈbaʃ

Kyd
BR kɪd

AM kɪd

kyle
BR kʌɪl, -z
AM kaɪl, -z

kylie
BR ˈkʌɪl|i, -ɪz
AM ˈkaɪli, -z

kylin
BR ˈkiːlɪn, -z
AM ˈkilɪn, -z

kylix
BR ˈkʌɪlɪks
AM ˈkaɪlɪks

kyloe
BR ˈkʌɪləʊ, -z
AM ˈkaɪloʊ, -z

kymogram
BR ˈkʌɪmə(ʊ)gram, -z
AM ˈkaɪməˌgræm, -z

kymograph
BR ˈkʌɪmə(ʊ)grɑːf, ˈkʌɪmə(ʊ)graf, -s
AM ˈkaɪməˌgræf, -s

kymographic
BR ˌkʌɪmə(ʊ)ˈgrafɪk
AM ˈkaɪməˈgræfɪk

kymographically
BR ˌkʌɪmə(ʊ)ˈgrafɪkli
AM ˈkaɪmə·ˈgræfək(ə)li

Kyoto
BR kɪˈəʊtəʊ
AM ki·(j)oʊdoʊ, ki·(j)oʊˌtoʊ

kyphosis
BR kʌɪˈfəʊsɪs
AM kaɪˈfoʊsəs

kyphotic
BR kʌɪˈfɒtɪk
AM kaɪˈfadɪk

Kyrenia
BR kʌɪˈriːnɪə(r)
AM kəˈriniə

Kyrgyz
BR ˈkɜːgɪz, ˈkɪəgɪz, kɪəˈgɪz
AM kɪrˈgɪz
RUS kʲirˈgʲis

Kyrgyzstan
BR ˌkɜːgɪˈstaːn, ˈkɪəgɪˈstaːn, ˌkɪəgɪˈstɑn
AM ˈkɪrgəˌstæn
RUS kʲirgʲiˈstan

kyrie
BR ˈkɪrɪeɪ, -z
AM ˈkɪriˌeɪ, -z

Kyushu
BR kɪˈuːʃuː, ˈkjuːʃuː
AM kiˈjuʃu

L l

l
BR ɛl, -z
AM ɛl, -z

la
BR lɑː(r)
AM lɑ

laager
BR 'lɑːgə(r), -z
AM 'lɑgər, -z

lab
BR læb, -z
AM læb, -z

Laban[1]
dancer/choreographer
BR 'lɑːb(ə)n
AM 'lɑbən

Laban[2]
in Bible
BR 'leɪb(ə)n, 'leɪban
AM 'leɪbən

labara
BR 'lab(ə)rə(r), 'leɪb(ə)rə(r)
AM 'læbərə

labarum
BR 'lab(ə)rəm, 'leɪb(ə)rəm, -z
AM 'læbərəm, -z

labdanum
BR 'labdənəm, -z
AM 'læbdənəm, -z

labefaction
BR ˌlabɪ'fakʃn, -z
AM ˌlæbə'fækʃən, -z

label
BR 'leɪbl, -lz, -ˌlɪŋ \-lɪŋ, -ld
AM 'leɪbəl, -əlz, -(ə)lɪŋ, -əld

labeler
BR 'leɪblə(r), 'leɪblə(r), -z
AM 'leɪb(ə)lər, -z

labeller
BR 'leɪblə(r), 'leɪblə(r), -z
AM 'leɪb(ə)lər, -z

labia
BR 'leɪbɪə(r)
AM 'leɪbɪə

labial
BR 'leɪbɪəl, -z
AM 'leɪbɪəl, -z

labialisation
BR ˌleɪbɪəlaɪ'zeɪʃn, -z
AM ˌleɪbɪələ'zeɪʃən, ˌleɪbɪəˌlaɪ'zeɪʃən, -z

labialise
BR 'leɪbɪəlʌɪz, -ɪz, -ɪŋ, -d

labialism
BR 'leɪbɪəlɪz(ə)m, -z
AM 'leɪbɪəˌlɪzəm, -z

labiality
BR ˌleɪbɪ'alɪti
AM ˌleɪbi'ælədi

labialization
BR ˌleɪbɪəlʌɪ'zeɪʃn, -z
AM ˌleɪbɪələ'zeɪʃən, ˌleɪbɪəˌlaɪ'zeɪʃən, -z

labialize
BR 'leɪbɪəlʌɪz, -ɪz, -ɪŋ, -d
AM 'leɪbɪəˌlaɪz, -ɪz, -ɪŋ, -d

labially
BR 'leɪbɪəli
AM 'leɪbɪəli

labia majora
BR ˌleɪbɪə məˈdʒɔːrə(r)
AM 'leɪbɪə məˈdʒɔrə

labia minora
BR ˌleɪbɪə mɪˈnɔːrə(r)
AM 'leɪbɪə məˈnɔrə

labiate
BR 'leɪbɪeɪt, 'leɪbɪət, -s
AM 'leɪbiɪt, 'leɪbiˌeɪt, -s

labile
BR 'leɪbʌɪl
AM 'leɪbəl, 'leɪˌbaɪl

lability
BR leɪ'bɪlɪti, lə'bɪlɪti
AM leɪ'bɪlɪdi, lə'bɪlɪdi

labiodental
BR ˌleɪbɪə(ʊ)'dɛntl
AM ˌleɪbioʊ'dɛn(t)l

labiovelar
BR ˌleɪbɪə(ʊ)'viːlə(r)
AM ˌleɪbioʊ'vilər

labium
BR 'leɪbɪəm
AM 'leɪbɪəm

La Bohème
BR ˌlɑː bəʊ'ɛm, ˌla +
AM ˌlɑ boʊ'ɛm

labor
BR 'leɪb|ə(r), -əz, -(ə)rɪŋ, -əd
AM 'leɪb|ər, -ərz, -(ə)rɪŋ, -ərd

laboratory
BR lə'bɒrət(ə)r|i, -ɪz
AM 'læbrəˌtɔri, -z

laborer
BR 'lab(ə)rə(r), -z
AM 'leɪb(ə)rər, -z

laborious
BR lə'bɔːrɪəs
AM lə'bɔriəs

laboriously
BR lə'bɔːrɪəsli
AM lə'bɔriəsli

laboriousness
BR lə'bɔːrɪəsnəs
AM lə'bɔriəsnəs

laborism
BR 'leɪbərɪz(ə)m
AM 'leɪbəˌrɪzəm

Laborite
BR 'leɪbərʌɪt, -s
AM 'leɪbəˌraɪt, -s

Labouchere
BR ˌlabuː'ʃɛː(r)
AM ˌlabu'ʃɛ(ə)r

labour
BR 'leɪb|ə(r), -əz, -(ə)rɪŋ, -əd
AM 'leɪb|ər, -ərz, -(ə)rɪŋ, -ərd

labourer
BR 'lab(ə)rə(r), -z
AM 'leɪb(ə)rər, -z

labourism
BR 'leɪbərɪz(ə)m
AM 'leɪbəˌrɪzəm

Labourite
BR 'leɪbərʌɪt, -s
AM 'leɪbəˌraɪt, -s

Labov
BR lə'bɒv, lə'bəʊv
AM lə'bɒv, lə'boʊv, lə'bav

Labovian
BR lə'bɒvɪən, lə'bəʊvɪən
AM lə'bɒvɪən, lə'boʊvɪən, lə'bavɪən

labra
BR 'leɪbrə(r), 'labrə(r)
AM 'leɪbrə, 'læbrə

Labrador
BR 'labrədɔː(r), -z
AM 'læbrəˌdɔ(ə)r, -z

labret
BR 'leɪbrɪt, -s
AM 'leɪbˌbrɛt, -s

labrum
BR 'leɪbrəm, 'labrəm
AM 'leɪbrəm, 'læbrəm

La Bruyère
BR ˌla brʊ'jɛː(r)
AM ˌla brʊ'jɛ(ə)r

Labuan
BR lə'buːən
AM 'labjəwən

laburnum
BR lə'bəːnəm, -z
AM lə'bərnəm, -z

labyrinth
BR 'lab(ə)rɪnθ, -s
AM 'læb(ə)ˌrɪnθ, -s

labyrinthian
BR ˌlabə'rɪnθɪən
AM ˌlæb(ə)'rɪnθɪən

labyrinthine
BR ˌlabə'rɪnθʌɪn
AM ˌlæb(ə)'rɪnˌθin, ˌlæb(ə)'rɪnθən, ˌlæb(ə)'rɪnˌθaɪn

lac
BR lak, -s

Lacan
BR la'kan
AM lɑ'kɑn

Laccadive
BR 'lakədɪv, 'lakədiːv
AM 'lɑkədɪv

laccolith
BR 'lakəlɪθ, -s
AM 'lækəˌlɪθ, -s

lace
BR leɪs, -ɪz, -ɪŋ, -t
AM leɪs, -ɪz, -ɪŋ, -t

lacemaker
BR 'leɪsˌmeɪkə(r), -z
AM 'leɪsˌmeɪkər, -z

lacemaking
BR 'leɪsˌmeɪkɪŋ
AM 'leɪsˌmeɪkɪŋ

lacerable
BR 'las(ə)rəbl
AM 'læsərəbəl

lacerate
BR 'lasəreɪt, -s, -ɪŋ, -ɪd
AM 'læsəˌreɪ|t, -ts, -dɪŋ, -dɪd

laceration
BR ˌlasə'reɪʃn, -z
AM ˌlæsə'reɪʃən, -z

lacertian
BR lə'səːtɪən, lə'səːʃn, -z
AM lə'sərʃ(i)ən, -z

lacertilian
BR ˌlasə'tɪlɪən, -z
AM ˌlæsər'tɪljən, ˌlæsər'tɪliən, -z

lacertine
BR lə'səːtʌɪn
AM 'læsərˌtaɪn

lacewing
BR 'leɪswɪŋ, -z
AM 'leɪsˌwɪŋ, -z

lacewood
BR 'leɪswʊd
AM 'leɪsˌwʊd

lacework
BR 'leɪswəːk
AM 'leɪswərk

lacey
BR 'leɪsi
AM 'leɪsi

laches
BR 'latʃɪz, 'leɪtʃɪz
AM 'lætʃəz

Lachesis
BR 'lakɪsɪs
AM 'lakəsəs

Lachlan
BR 'lɒklən, 'laklən
AM 'lɑklən

lachryma Christi
BR 'lakrɪmə 'krɪsti
AM 'lɑkrəmə 'krɪsti

lachrymal
BR 'lakrɪml
AM 'lækrəməl

lachrymation
BR ˌlakrɪ'meɪʃn, -z
AM ˌlækrə'meɪʃən, -z

lachrymator
BR 'lakrɪmeɪtə(r), -z
AM 'lækrəˌmeɪdər, -z

lachrymatory
BR 'lakrɪmət(ə)r|i, -ɪz
AM 'lækrəməˌtɔri, -z

lachrymose
BR 'lakrɪməʊs,
'lakrɪməʊz
AM 'lækrəˌmoʊs,
'lækrəˌmoʊz

lachrymosely
BR 'lakrɪməʊsli,
'lakrɪməʊzli
AM 'lækrəˌmoʊsli,
'lækrəˌmoʊzli

lacily
BR 'leɪsɪli
AM 'leɪsɪli

laciness
BR 'leɪsɪnɪs
AM 'leɪsɪnɪs

lacing
BR 'leɪsɪŋ, -z
AM 'leɪsɪŋ, -z

laciniate
BR lə'sɪnɪət
AM lə'sɪniˌeɪt

laciniated
BR lə'sɪnɪeɪtɪd
AM lə'sɪniˌeɪdɪd

laciniation
BR lə,sɪnɪ'eɪʃn, -z
AM lə,sɪni'eɪʃən, -z

lack
BR lak, -s, -ɪŋ, -t
AM læk, -s, -ɪŋ, -t

lackadaisical
BR ˌlakə'deɪzɪkl
AM ˌlækə'deɪzɪkəl

lackadaisically
BR ˌlakə'deɪzɪkli
AM ˌlækə'deɪzɪk(ə)li

lackadaisicalness
BR ˌlakə'deɪzɪklnəs
AM ˌlækə'deɪzɪkəlnəs

lacker
BR 'lak|ə(r), -əz,
-(ə)rɪŋ, -əd
AM 'lækər, -z, -ɪŋ, -d

lackey
BR 'lak|i, -ɪz
AM 'læki, -z

lackland
BR 'lak,land, 'laklənd,
-z
AM 'læklənd,
'læk,lænd, -z

lackluster
BR 'lak,lʌstə(r)
AM 'læk,ləstər

lacklustre
BR 'lak,lʌstə(r)
AM 'læk,ləstər

Lacock
BR 'leɪkɒk
AM 'leɪ,kɑk

Laconia
BR lə'kəʊnɪə(r)
AM lə'koʊniə

Laconian
BR lə'kəʊnɪən, -z
AM lə'koʊniən, -z

laconic
BR lə'kɒnɪk
AM lə'kɑnɪk

laconically
BR lə'kɒnɪkli
AM lə'kɑnək(ə)li

laconicism
BR lə'kɒnɪsɪz(ə)m, -z
AM lə'kɑnəˌsɪzəm, -z

laconism
BR 'lakənɪz(ə)m
AM 'lakəˌnɪzəm

La Coruña
BR ˌlɑː kə'ru:njə(r),
ˌla +
AM ˌlɑ kə'runə

lacquer
BR 'lak|ə(r), -əz,
-(ə)rɪŋ, -əd
AM 'lækər, -z, -ɪŋ, -d

lacquerer
BR 'lak(ə)rə(r), -z
AM 'lækərər, -z

lacquerware
BR 'lakəwɛ:(r)
AM 'lækərˌwɛ(ə)r

lacquey
BR 'lak|i, -ɪz
AM 'læki, -z

lacrimal
BR 'lakrɪml, -z
AM 'lækrəməl, -z

lacrimation
BR ˌlakrɪ'meɪʃn
AM ˌlækrə'meɪʃən

lacrosse
BR lə'krɒs
AM lə'krɔs, lə'krɑs

lacrymal
BR 'lakrɪml, -z
AM 'lækrəməl, -z

lacrymation
BR ˌlakrɪ'meɪʃn
AM ˌlækrə'meɪʃən

lactase
BR 'lakteɪz, -ɪz
AM 'læk,teɪs, 'læk,teɪz,
-ɪz

lactate[1]
noun
BR 'lakteɪt, -s
AM 'læk,teɪt, -s

lactate[2]
verb
BR lak'teɪt, -s, -ɪŋ, -ɪd
AM læk'teɪ|t, -ts, -dɪŋ,
-dɪd

lactation
BR lak'teɪʃn
AM læk'teɪʃən

lacteal
BR 'laktɪəl, -z
AM 'læktiəl, -z

lactescence
BR lak'tɛsns, -ɪz
AM læk'tɛsəns, -əz

lactescent
BR lak'tɛsnt
AM læk'tɛsənt

lactic
BR 'laktɪk
AM 'læktɪk

lactiferous
BR lak'tɪf(ə)rəs
AM læk'tɪf(ə)rəs

lactobacilli
BR ˌlaktəʊbə'sɪlʌɪ
AM ˌlæktoʊbə'sɪˌlaɪ

lactobacillus
BR ˌlaktəʊbə'sɪləs
AM ˌlæktoʊbə'sɪləs

lactometer
BR lak'tɒmɪtə(r), -z
AM læk'tɑmədər, -z

lactone
BR 'laktəʊn, -z
AM 'læk,toʊn, -z

lactoprotein
BR ˌlaktə(ʊ)'prəʊti:n,
-z
AM ˌlæktoʊ'proʊˌtin,
-z

lactose
BR 'laktəʊs, 'laktəʊz
AM 'læk,toʊs,
'læk,toʊz

lacuna
BR lə'kju:nə(r), -z
AM lə'k(j)unə, -z

lacunae
BR lə'kju:ni:,
lə'kju:nʌɪ
AM lə'k(j)uˌnaɪ,
lə'k(j)uni

lacunal
BR lə'kju:nl
AM lə'k(j)unəl

lacunar
BR lə'kju:nə(r)
AM 'læk(j)ənər

lacunary
BR 'lakjʊn(ə)ri,
lə'kju:n(ə)ri
AM 'lækjəˌnɛri,
lə'k(j)unɑri

lacunose
BR lə'kju:nəʊs
AM 'lækjəˌnoʊs,
'lakjəˌnoʊz

lacustrine
BR lə'kʌstrʌɪn,
lə'kʌstrɪn
AM lə'kəstrən

lacy
BR 'leɪsi

AM 'leɪsi

lad
BR lad, -z
AM læd, -z

Lada®
BR 'lɑːdə(r), -z
AM 'lɑdə, -z

Ladakh
BR lə'dɑːk, lə'dak
AM lə'dak

ladanum
BR 'ladənəm, 'ladŋəm
AM 'ladənəm

Ladbroke
BR 'ladbrʊk, -s
AM 'læd,brʊk, -s

ladder
BR 'lad|ə(r), -əz,
-(ə)rɪŋ, -əd
AM 'lædər, -z, -ɪŋ, -d

laddie
BR 'lad|i, -ɪz
AM 'lædi, -z

laddish
BR 'ladɪʃ
AM 'lædɪʃ

laddishness
BR 'ladɪʃnɪs
AM 'lædɪʃnɪs

laddy
BR 'lad|i, -ɪz
AM 'lædi, -z

lade
BR leɪd, -z, -ɪŋ, -ɪd
AM leɪd, -z, -ɪŋ, -ɪd

Ladefoged
BR 'ladɪfəʊgɪd
AM 'lædəˌfoʊgəd

laden
BR 'leɪdn
AM 'leɪdən

la-di-da
BR ˌlɑːdɪ'dɑ:(r), -z
AM ˌladi'dɑ, -z

ladify
BR 'leɪdɪfʌɪ, -z, -ɪŋ, -d
AM 'leɪdiˌfaɪ, -z, -ɪŋ, -d

Ladin
BR la'di:n, lə'di:n
AM lə'din

lading
BR 'leɪdɪŋ
AM 'leɪdɪŋ

Ladino
BR la'di:nəʊ, lə'di:nəʊ,
-z
AM lə'dinoʊ, -z

ladle
BR 'leɪd|l, -lz, -lɪŋ \-lɪŋ,
-ld
AM 'leɪd|əl, -əlz, -(ə)lɪŋ,
-əld

ladleful
BR 'leɪdlfʊl, -z
AM 'leɪdəlˌfʊl, -z

ladler
BR ˈleɪdlə(r),
ˈleɪdlə(r), -z
AM ˈleɪd(ə)lər, -z

Ladoga
BR lə'dəʊgə(r),
la'dəʊgə(r)
AM lɑ'doʊgə, lɑ'dɔgə

lady
BR ˈleɪd|i, -ɪz
AM ˈleɪdi, -z

ladybird
BR ˈleɪdɪbɜːd, -z
AM ˈleɪdi,bɜrd, -z

ladybug
BR ˈleɪdɪbʌg, -z
AM ˈleɪdi,bəg, -z

lady-fern
BR ˈleɪdɪfɜːn, -z
AM ˈleɪdi,fɜrn, -z

ladyfinger
BR ˈleɪdɪ,fɪŋgə(r)
AM ˈleɪdi,fɪŋgər

ladyfy
BR ˈleɪdɪfʌɪ, -z, -ɪŋ, -d
AM ˈleɪdi,faɪ, -z, -ɪŋ, -d

ladyhood
BR ˈleɪdɪhʊd
AM ˈleɪdi,(h)ʊd

ladykiller
BR ˈleɪdɪ,kɪlə(r), -z
AM ˈleɪdi,kɪlər, -z

ladylike
BR ˈleɪdɪlʌɪk
AM ˈleɪdi,laɪk

ladyship
BR ˈleɪdɪʃɪp, -s
AM ˈleɪdi,ʃɪp, -s

Ladysmith
BR ˈleɪdɪsmɪθ
AM ˈleɪdi,smɪθ

Lae
BR leɪ
AM leɪ

Laertes
BR leɪ'ɜːtiːz
AM leɪ'ɜrtiz

Laetitia
BR lɪ'tɪʃə(r)
AM lə'tɪʃə

laetrile
BR ˈleɪtrʌɪl, ˈleɪtr(ɪ)l
AM ˈleɪə,trɪl

laevodopa
BR ˈliːvə,dəʊpə(r)
AM ˈliːvoʊ,doupə

laevorotatory
BR ˌliːvəʊˈrəʊtət(ə)ri
AM ˌliːvəˈroʊdə,tɔri

laevotartaric
BR ˌliːvəʊtɑːˈtarɪk
AM ˌliːvoʊˌtɑrˈtɛrɪk

laevulose
BR ˈliːvjʊləʊs,
ˈliːvjələʊz, ˈlɛvjʊləʊs,
ˈlɛvjʊləʊz

AM ˈlɛvjəlous,
ˈlɛvjəlouz

La Fayette
BR ˌlaː fʌɪˈjɛt, ˌlaː +
+ feˈjɛt
AM lɑ fəˈjɛt, lɑˌfaɪˈjɛt,
lɑˌferˈjɛt

La Fontaine
BR ˌlaː fɒnˈteɪn, ˌlaː +
AM lɑ fɑnˈteɪn

lag
BR lag, -z, -ɪŋ, -d
AM læg, -z, -ɪŋ, -d

lagan
BR ˈlag(ə)n, -z
AM ˈlægən, -z

lager
BR ˈlaːgə(r), -z
AM ˈlɑgər, -z

Lagerkvist
BR ˈlaːgəkfɪst
AM ˈlagər,kvist

Lagerlöf
BR ˈlaːgələʊf
AM ˈlagər,loof
SW ˈlaːgər,lə:v

lagerphone
BR ˈlaːgəfəʊn, -z
AM ˈlagər,foun, -z

laggard
BR ˈlagəd, -z
AM ˈlægərd, -z

laggardly
BR ˈlagədli
AM ˈlægərdli

laggardness
BR ˈlagədnəs
AM ˈlægərdnəs

lagger
BR ˈlagə(r), -z
AM ˈlægər, -z

lagging
BR ˈlagɪŋ, -z
AM ˈlægɪŋ, -z

lagniappe
BR ˈlanjap, ˌlanˈjap, -s
AM ˌlænˈjæp, -s

lagomorph
BR ˈlagəmɔːf, -s
AM ˈlægə,mɔ(ə)rf, -s

Lagonda
BR lə'gɒndə(r)
AM lə'gandə

lagoon
BR lə'guːn, -z
AM lə'gun, -z

lagoonal
BR lə'guːnl
AM lə'gunəl

Lagos
BR ˈleɪgɒs
AM ˈlagoʊs

Lagrange
BR lə'greɪn(d)ʒ
AM lə'greɪndʒ

La Guardia
BR lə ˈgwaːdɪə(r)

AM lə ˈgwɑrdiə

lah
BR lɑː(r)
AM lɑ

lahar
BR ˈlɑːhɑː(r), -z
AM lə'hɑr, ˈlahɑr, -z

lah-di-dah
BR ˌlɑːdɪˈdɑː(r)
AM ˌladiˈda

Lahnda
BR ˈlɑːndə(r)
AM ˈlandə

Lahore
BR lə'hɔː(r)
AM lə'hɔ(ə)r

Lahu
BR ˈlɑːhuː, -z
AM ˈlɑhu, -z

laic
BR ˈleɪɪk
AM ˈleɪɪk

laical
BR ˈleɪɪkl
AM ˈleɪɪkəl

laically
BR ˈleɪɪkli
AM ˈleɪɪk(ə)li

laicisation
BR ˌleɪɪsʌɪˈzeɪʃn, -z
AM ˌleɪəsəˈzeɪʃən,
ˌleɪə,saɪˈzeɪʃən, -z

laicise
BR ˈleɪɪsaɪz, -ɪz, -ɪŋ, -d
AM ˈleɪə,saɪz, -ɪz, -ɪŋ, -d

laicity
BR leɪˈɪsɪti
AM leɪˈɪsɪdi

laicization
BR ˌleɪɪsʌɪˈzeɪʃn, -z
AM ˌleɪəsəˈzeɪʃən,
ˌleɪə,saɪˈzeɪʃən, -z

laicize
BR ˈleɪɪsʌɪz, -ɪz, -ɪŋ, -d
AM ˈleɪə,saɪz, -ɪz, -ɪŋ, -d

laid
BR leɪd
AM leɪd

Laidlaw
BR ˈleɪdlɔː(r)
AM ˈleɪd,lɔ

lain
BR leɪn
AM leɪn

Laing
BR laŋ
AM læŋ

lair
BR lɛː(r), -z
AM lɛ(ə)r, -z

lairage
BR ˈlɛːrɪdʒ, -ɪdʒɪz
AM ˈlɛrɪdʒ, -ɪz

laird
BR lɛːd, -z
AM lɛ(ə)rd, -z

lairdship
BR ˈlɛːdʃɪp, -s
AM ˈlɛrd,ʃɪp, -s

lairy
BR ˈlɛːri
AM ˈlɛri

laisser-aller
BR ˌleɪseɪˈaleɪ
AM ˌlɛseɪəˈleɪ,
ˌlɛzeɪəˈleɪ

laisser-faire
BR ˌleɪseɪˈfɛː(r)
AM ˌlɛseɪˈfɛ(ə)r,
ˌlɛzeɪˈfɛ(ə)r

laissez-faire
BR ˌleɪseɪˈfɛː(r)
AM ˌlɛseɪˈfɛ(ə)r,
ˌlɛzeɪˈfɛ(ə)r

laissez-passer
BR ˌleɪseɪˈpaseɪ
AM ˌlɛseɪpəˈseɪ,
ˌlɛzeɪpəˈseɪ

laity
BR ˈleɪɪti
AM ˈleɪɪdi

Laius
BR ˈleɪəs
AM ˈleɪəs

La Jolla
BR lə ˈhɔɪə(r)
AM lə ˈhɔɪə

lake
BR leɪk, -s
AM leɪk, -s

lakefront
BR ˈleɪkfrʌnt
AM ˈleɪk,frənt

Lakeland
BR ˈleɪklənd
AM ˈleɪklənd

lakeless
BR ˈleɪklɪs
AM ˈleɪklɪs

lakelet
BR ˈleɪklɪt, -s
AM ˈleɪklət, -s

Lakenheath
BR ˈleɪk(ə)nhiː:θ
AM ˈleɪkən,(h)iθ

Laker
BR ˈleɪkə(r)
AM ˈleɪkər

lakeshore
BR ˈleɪkʃɔː(r)
AM ˈleɪk,ʃɔ(ə)r

lakeside
BR ˈleɪksʌɪd
AM ˈleɪk,saɪd

lakh
BR lak, -s
AM lɑk, -s

Lakshmi
BR ˈlakʃmi
AM ˈlakʃmi

Lalage
BR ˈlaləgi, ˈlalədʒi
AM ˈlæləgi, ˈlælədʒi

lalapalooza
BR ˌlaləpəˈluːzə(r)
AM ˌlaləpəˈluːzə

Lalique®
BR laˈliːk, ləˈliːk
AM lɑˈlik

Lallan
BR ˈlalən, -z
AM ˈlɑlən, -z

lallation
BR laˈleɪʃn
AM ləˈleɪʃən

lalling
BR ˈlalɪŋ
AM ˈlɑlɪŋ

lallygag
BR ˈlalɪgag, -z, -ɪŋ, -d
AM ˈlɑliˌgæg, -z, -ɪŋ, -d

Lalo
BR ˈlɑːləʊ
AM ˈlɑˌloʊ

lam
BR lam, -z, -ɪŋ, -d
AM læm, -z, -ɪŋ, -d

lama
BR ˈlɑːmə(r), -z
AM ˈlɑmə, -z

Lamaism
BR ˈlɑːmə(r)ɪz(ə)m
AM ˈlɑməˌɪzəm

Lamaist
BR ˈlɑːmə(r)ɪst
AM ˈlɑmə(j)əst

Lamarck
BR ləˈmɑːk, laˈmɑːk
AM lɑˈmɑrk

Lamarckian
BR ləˈmɑːkɪən,
laˈmɑːkɪən, -z
AM ləˈmɑrkɪən, -z

Lamarckism
BR ləˈmɑːkɪz(ə)m,
laˈmɑːkɪz(ə)m
AM ləˈmɑrˌkɪzəm

lamasery
BR ˈlɑːməs(ə)r|i, -ɪz
AM ˈlɑməˌsɛri, -z

Lamaze
BR ləˈmɑːz, ləˈmeɪz
AM ləˈmɑz

lamb
BR lam, -z, -ɪŋ, -d
AM læm, -z, -ɪŋ, -d

lambada
BR lamˈbɑːdə(r), -z
AM læmˈbɑdə, -z

lambast
BR lamˈbast, -s, -ɪŋ, -ɪd
AM ˈlæmˈbæst, -s, -ɪŋ, -əd

lambaste
BR lamˈbeɪst, -s, -ɪŋ, -ɪd
AM læmˈbeɪst, -s, -ɪŋ, -ɪd

lambda
BR ˈlamdə(r), -z
AM ˈlæmdə, -z

lambdacism
BR ˈlamdəsɪz(ə)m
AM ˈlæmdəˌsɪzəm

lambency
BR ˈlamb(ə)nsi
AM ˈlæmbənsi

lambent
BR ˈlambənt
AM ˈlæmbənt

lambently
BR ˈlambəntli
AM ˈlæmbən(t)li

lamber
BR ˈlamə(r), -z
AM ˈlæmər, -z

lambert
BR ˈlambət, -s
AM ˈlæmbərt, -s

Lambeth
BR ˈlambəθ
AM ˈlæmbəθ

lambhood
BR ˈlamhʊd
AM ˈlæmˌ(h)ʊd

lambkin
BR ˈlamkɪn, -z
AM ˈlæmkən, -z

lamblike
BR ˈlamlʌɪk
AM ˈlæmˌlaɪk

Lamborghini®
BR ˌlambəˈgiːn|i, -ɪz
AM ˌlɑmbərˈgini, -z

lambrequin
BR ˈlamb(r)əkɪn, -z
AM ˈlæmbərkən,
ˈlæmbrəkən, -z

Lambretta®
BR lamˈbrɛtə(r)
AM læmˈbrɛdə

Lambrusco
BR lamˈbrʊskəʊ
AM lamˈbrʊskoʊ

lambskin
BR ˈlamskɪn, -z
AM ˈlæmˌskɪn, -z

lambswool
BR ˈlamzwʊl, -z
AM ˈlæmzˌwʊl, -z

Lambton
BR ˈlamtən
AM ˈlæmtən

LAMDA
BR ˈlamdə(r)
AM ˈlæmdə

lame
BR ˈleɪm
AM ˈleɪm

lamé
BR ˈlɑːmeɪ
AM lɑˈmeɪ

lamebrain
BR ˈleɪmbreɪn, -z
AM ˈleɪmˌbreɪn, -z

lamella
BR ləˈmɛlə(r)

AM ləˈmɛlə

lamellae
BR ləˈmɛliː
AM ləˈmɛli, ləˈmɛˌlaɪ

lamellar
BR ləˈmɛlə(r)
AM ləˈmɛlər

lamellate
BR ˈlaməlɛt, ˈlamlət
AM ˈlæmələt, ləˈmɛlət,
ˈlæməˌleɪt

lamellibranch
BR ləˈmɛlɪbraŋk, -s
AM ləˈmɛləˌbræŋk, -s

lamellicorn
BR ləˈmɛlɪkɔːn, -z
AM ləˈmɛləˌkɔ(ə)rn, -z

lamelliform
BR ləˈmɛlɪfɔːm
AM ləˈmɛləˌfɔ(ə)rm

lamellose
BR ləˈmɛləʊs
AM ləˈmɛˌloʊs,
ˈlæməˌloʊs,
ləˈmɛˌloʊz,
ˈlæməˌloʊz

lamely
BR ˈleɪmli
AM ˈleɪmli

lameness
BR ˈleɪmnɪs
AM ˈleɪmnɪs

lament
BR ləˈmɛnt, -s, -ɪŋ, -ɪd
AM ləˈmɛn|t, -ts, -(t)ɪŋ,
-(t)əd

lamentable
BR ˈlam(ɪ)ntəbl,
ləˈmɛntəbl
AM ˈlæmən(t)əbəl,
ləˈmɛn(t)əbəl

lamentably
BR ˈlam(ɪ)ntəbli,
ləˈmɛntəbli
AM ˈlæmən(t)əbli,
ləˈmɛn(t)əbli

lamentation
BR ˌlam(ɪ)nˈteɪʃn, -z
AM ˌlæmənˈteɪʃən, -z

Lamentations
BR ˌlam(ɪ)nˈteɪʃnz
AM ˌlæmənˈteɪʃənz

lamenter
BR ləˈmɛntə(r), -z
AM ləˈmɛn(t)ər, -z

lamentingly
BR ləˈmɛntɪŋli
AM ləˈmɛn(t)ɪŋli

lamina
BR ˈlamɪnə(r),
ˈlamnə(r), -z
AM ˈlæmənə, -z

laminae
BR ˈlamɪniː, ˈlamɲiː,
ˈlamɪnʌɪ, ˈlamɲʌɪ
AM ˈlæməˌni,
ˈlæməˌnaɪ

laminar
BR ˈlamɪnə(r),
ˈlamnə(r)
AM ˈlæmənər

laminate¹
noun
BR ˈlamɪnət, ˈlamɲət, -s
AM ˈlæmənət,
ˈlæməˌneɪt, -s

laminate²
verb
BR ˈlamɪneɪt, ˈlamɲeɪt,
-s, -ɪŋ, -ɪd
AM ˈlæməˌneɪ|t, -ts,
-dɪŋ, -dɪd

lamination
BR ˌlamɪˈneɪʃn, -z
AM ˌlæməˈneɪʃən, -z

laminator
BR ˈlamɪneɪtə(r),
ˈlamɲeɪtə(r), -z
AM ˈlæməˌneɪdər, -z

lamington
BR ˈlamɪŋt(ə)n, -z
AM ˈlæmɪŋtən, -z

laminose
BR ˈlamɪnəʊs,
ˈlamɲəʊs
AM ˈlæməˌnoʊs,
ˈlæməˌnoʊz

lamish
BR ˈleɪmɪʃ
AM ˈleɪmɪʃ

Lammas
BR ˈlaməs
AM ˈlæməs

lammergeier
BR ˈlaməˌgʌɪə(r), -z
AM ˈlɑmərˌgaɪ(ə)r, -z

lammergeyer
BR ˈlaməˌgʌɪə(r), -z
AM ˈlɑmərˌgaɪ(ə)r, -z

Lammermuir
BR ˈlaməmjʊə(r),
ˈlaməmjɔː(r)
AM ˈlæmərˌmjʊ(ə)r

Lamont
BR ləˈmɒnt, ˈlam(ə)nt
AM ləˈmɑnt

lamp
BR lamp, -s
AM læmp, -s

lampblack
BR ˈlampblak
AM ˈlæm(p)ˌblæk

lampern
BR ˈlampən, -z
AM ˈlæmpərn, -z

Lampeter
BR ˈlampɪtə(r)
AM ˈlæmpədər

lampless
BR ˈlampləs
AM ˈlæmpləs

lamplight
BR ˈlamplʌɪt
AM ˈlæmpˌlaɪt

lamplighter
BR ˈlampˌlʌɪtə(r), -z
AM ˈlæmpˌlaɪdər, -z
lamplit
BR ˈlamplɪt
AM ˈlæmpˌlɪt
Lamplugh
BR ˈlampluː
AM ˈlæmplu
lampoon
BR lamˈpuːn, -z, -ɪŋ, -d
AM læmˈpun, -z, -ɪŋ, -d
lampooner
BR lamˈpuːnə(r), -z
AM læmˈpunər, -z
lampoonery
BR lamˈpuːn(ə)ri
AM læmˈpun(ə)ri
lampoonist
BR lamˈpuːnɪst, -s
AM læmˈpunəst, -s
lamp-post
BR ˈlam(p)pəʊst, -s
AM ˈlæm(p)ˌpoʊst, -s
lamprey
BR ˈlamprǀi, -ɪz
AM ˈlæmpri, -z
lampshade
BR ˈlampʃeɪd, -z
AM ˈlæm(p)ˌʃeɪd, -z
Lana
BR ˈlɑːnə(r)
AM ˈlɑnə
Lanark
BR ˈlanək
AM ˈlænərk
Lanarkshire
BR ˈlanəkʃ(ɪ)ə(r)
AM ˈlænərkʃ(ɪ)ər
Lancashire
BR ˈlaŋkəʃ(ɪ)ə(r)
AM ˈlæŋkəʃɪ(ə)r
Lancaster
BR ˈlaŋkəstə(r),
ˈlaŋkastə(r),
ˈlaŋkɑːstə(r)
AM ˈlæŋˌkæstər,
ˈlæŋkəstər
Lancastrian
BR laŋˈkastrɪən, -z
AM læŋˈkæstriən, -z
lance
BR lɑːns, lans, -ɪz, -ɪŋ, -t
AM læns, -əz, -ɪŋ, -t
lancelet
BR ˈlɑːnslɪt, ˈlanslɪt, -s
AM ˈlænslət, -s
Lancelot
BR ˈlɑːnsəlɒt,
ˈlɑːns(ə)lət, ˈlansəlɒt,
ˈlans(ə)lət
AM ˈlænsəˌlɑt
lanceolate
BR ˈlɑːnsɪəleɪt,
ˈlɑːnsɪələt, ˈlansɪəleɪt,
ˈlansɪələt
AM ˈlænsɪələt,
ˈlænsɪəˌleɪt

lancer
BR ˈlɑːnsə(r),
ˈlansə(r), -z
AM ˈlænsər, -z
lancet
BR ˈlɑːnsɪt, ˈlansɪt, -s,
-ɪd
AM ˈlænsəǀt, -ts, -dəd
lancewood
BR ˈlɑːnswʊd,
ˈlanswʊd, -z
AM ˈlænsˌwʊd, -z
Lanchester
BR ˈlɑːntʃɪstə(r),
ˈlantʃɪstə(r)
AM ˈlæn(t)ʃɪstər
Lanchow
BR ˌlanˈtʃaʊ
AM ˌlɑnˈtʃaʊ
Lancia®
BR ˈlɑːnsɪə(r),
ˈlansɪə(r), -z
AM ˈlɑnsɪə, -z
lancinate
BR ˈlɑːnsɪneɪt,
ˈlansɪneɪt, -s, -ɪŋ, -ɪd
AM ˈlænsəˌneɪǀt, -ts,
-dɪŋ, -dɪd
Lancing
BR ˈlɑːnsɪŋ, ˈlansɪŋ
AM ˈlænsɪŋ
Lancôme®
BR ˈlɒŋkəʊm
AM ˌlɑŋˈkoʊm
Lancs.
Lancashire
BR laŋks
AM læŋks
Land
German province
BR land, lant
AM lɑnd, lɑnt
land
BR land, -z, -ɪŋ, -ɪd
AM lænd, -z, -ɪŋ, -ɪd
landau
BR ˈlandɔː(r), ˈlandaʊ,
-z
AM ˈlænˌdaʊ, -z
landaulet
BR ˌlandɔːˈlɛt, -s
AM ˌlændɔːˈlɛt,
ˌlændɑˈlɛt, -s
landaulette
BR ˌlandɔːˈlɛt, -s
AM ˌlændɔːˈlɛt,
ˌlændɑˈlɛt, -s
Länder
BR ˈlɛndə(r)
AM ˈlɛndər
Landers
BR ˈlandəz
AM ˈlændərz
Landes
BR lɒd
AM ˈlæn(d)z
landfall
BR ˈlan(d)fɔːl

landfill
BR ˈlan(d)fɪl, -z
AM ˈlæn(d)ˌfɪl, -z
landform
BR ˈlan(d)fɔːm, -z
AM ˈlæn(d)ˌfɔ(ə)rm, -z
landgrave
BR ˈlan(d)greɪv, -z
AM ˈlæn(d)ˌgreɪv, -z
landgraviate
BR lan(d)ˈgreɪvɪət, -s
AM læn(d)ˈgreɪviˌeɪt,
-s
landgravine
BR ˈlan(d)grəviːn, -z
AM ˈlæn(d)grəˌvin, -z
landholder
BR ˈlandˌhəʊldə(r), -z
AM ˈlæn(d)ˌ(h)oʊldər,
-z
landholding
BR ˈlandˌhəʊldɪŋ, -z
AM ˈlæn(d)ˌ(h)oʊldɪŋ,
-z
landing
BR ˈlandɪŋ, -z
AM ˈlændɪŋ, -z
Landis
BR ˈlandɪs
AM ˈlændəs
landlady
BR ˈlan(d)ˌleɪdǀi, -ɪz
AM ˈlæn(d)ˌleɪdi, -z
Ländler
BR ˈlɛndlə(r), -z
AM ˈlɛn(d)lər, -z
landless
BR ˈlan(d)ləs
AM ˈlæn(d)ləs
landline
BR ˈlan(d)lʌɪn, -z
AM ˈlæn(d)ˌlaɪn, -z
landlocked
BR ˈlan(d)lɒkt
AM ˈlæn(d)ˌlɑkt
landloper
BR ˈlan(d)ˌləʊpə(r), -z
AM ˈlæn(d)ˌloʊpər, -z
landlord
BR ˈlan(d)lɔːd, -z
AM ˈlæn(d)ˌlɔ(ə)rd, -z
landlubber
BR ˈlan(d)ˌlʌbə(r), -z
AM ˈlæn(d)ˌləbər, -z
landmark
BR ˈlan(d)mɑːk, -s
AM ˈlæn(d)ˌmɑrk, -s
landmass
BR ˈlan(d)mas, -ɪz
AM ˈlæn(d)ˌmæs, -əz
landmine
BR ˈlan(d)mʌɪn, -z
AM ˈlæn(d)ˌmaɪn, -z
landocracy
BR lanˈdɒkrəsǀi, -ɪz

AM lænˈdɑkræsi, -z
landocrat
BR ˈlandə(ʊ)krat, -s
AM ˈlændəˌkræt, -s
Landon
BR ˈlandən
AM ˈlændən
Landor
BR ˈlandɔː(r),
ˈlandə(r)
AM ˈlændər
landowner
BR ˈlandəʊnə(r), -z
AM ˈlænˌdoʊnər, -z
landownership
BR ˈlandˌəʊnəʃɪp, -s
AM ˈlænˌdoʊnərˌʃɪp
landowning
BR ˈlandəʊnɪŋ
AM ˈlænˌdoʊnɪŋ
landrail
BR ˈlandreɪl, -z
AM ˈlæn(d)ˌreɪl, -z
Land-Rover®
BR ˈlandˌrəʊvə(r), -z
AM ˈlæn(d)ˌroʊvər, -z
Landry
BR ˈlandri
AM ˈlændri
landscape
BR ˈlan(d)skeɪp, -s, -ɪŋ,
-t
AM ˈlænzˌkeɪp,
ˈlæn(d)ˌskeɪp, -s, -ɪŋ, -t
landscapist
BR ˈlan(d)skeɪpɪst, -s
AM ˈlæn(d)ˌskeɪpɪst, -s
Landseer
BR ˈlan(d)sɪə(r)
AM ˈlæn(d)ˌsɪ(ə)r
Landshut
BR ˈlandzhʊt
AM ˈlɑndzˌ(h)ʊt
landslide
BR ˈlan(d)slʌɪd, -z
AM ˈlæn(d)ˌslaɪd, -z
landslip
BR ˈlan(d)slɪp, -s
AM ˈlæn(d)ˌslɪp, -s
Landsmål
BR ˈlan(d)zmɔːl
AM ˈlandzˌmɔl,
ˈlandzˌmɑl
landsman
BR ˈlan(d)zmən
AM ˈlæn(d)zmən
landsmen
BR ˈlan(d)zmən
AM ˈlæn(d)zmən
Landsteiner
BR ˈlan(d)ˌʃtʌɪnə(r)
AM ˈlɑn(d)ˌstaɪnər
landward
AM ˈlæn(d)wərd,
ˈlændərd, -z

lane
BR leɪn, -z
AM leɪn, -z
Lang
BR laŋ
AM læŋ
Langbaurgh
BR ˈlɑnbaːf
AM ˈlæŋbæf
Langdale
BR ˈlaŋdeɪl
AM ˈlæŋˌdeɪl
Lange[1]
*New Zealand
politician*
BR ˈlɒŋi
AM ˈlæŋi, læŋ
Lange[2]
BR laŋ
AM ˈlæŋi, læŋ
Langerhans
BR ˈlaŋəhanz
AM ˈlæŋərˌhænz
Langford
BR ˈlaŋfəd
AM ˈlæŋfərd
Langland
BR ˈlaŋlənd
AM ˈlæŋlənd
langlauf
BR ˈlaŋlaʊf, -s
AM ˈlaŋˌlaʊf, -s
Langley
BR ˈlaŋli
AM ˈlæŋli
Langmuir
BR ˈlaŋmjʊə(r)
AM ˈlæŋˌmjuər
Lango
BR ˈlaŋgəʊ
AM ˈlæŋgoʊ
Langobardic
BR ˌlaŋgə(ʊ)ˈbaːdɪk
AM ˌlæŋgoʊˈbɑrdək
langouste
BR ˌlɒŋˈguːst,
ˈlɒŋguːst, -s
AM laŋˈgust, -s
langoustine
BR ˌlɒŋguˈstiːn,
ˈlɒŋgʊstiːn, -z
AM ˈlæŋgəˌstiːn, -z
Langton
BR ˈlaŋt(ə)n
AM ˈlæŋtən
Langtry
BR ˈlaŋtri
AM ˈlæŋtri
language
BR ˈlaŋgw|ɪdʒ, -ɪdʒɪz
AM ˈlæŋgwɪdʒ, -ɪz
langue
BR lɒŋ(g), lɒ̃g, laːŋ(g)
AM laŋ(g)
langue de chat
BR ˌlɒŋ də ˈʃaː(r),
ˌlɒ̃g +, ˌlaːŋ +

AM ˌlaŋ də ˈʃɑ
Languedoc
BR ˈlɒŋgədɒk,
ˈlaːŋgədɒk
AM ˌlaŋ(gə)ˈdɒk,
ˈlaŋ(gə)ˈdak
langue d'oc
BR ˌlɒŋ ˈdɒk, ˌlɒ̃g +,
ˌlaːŋ +
AM ˌlaŋ(gə) ˈdɒk,
ˈlaŋ(gə) ˈdak
langue d'oïl
BR ˌlɒŋ ˈdɔɪ(l), ˌlɒ̃g +,
ˌlaːŋ +
AM ˌlaŋ(gə) ˈdɔɪl
langues de chat
BR ˌlɒŋ də ˈʃaː(r),
ˌlɒ̃g +, ˌlaːŋ +
AM ˌlaŋ də ˈʃɑ
languid
BR ˈlaŋgwɪd
AM ˈlæŋgwəd
languidly
BR ˈlaŋgwɪdli
AM ˈlæŋgwədli
languidness
BR ˈlaŋgwɪdnɪs
AM ˈlæŋgwədnəs
languish
BR ˈlaŋgw|ɪʃ, -ɪʃɪz,
-ɪʃɪŋ, -ɪʃt
AM ˈlæŋgwɪʃ, -ɪz, -ɪŋ, -t
languisher
BR ˈlaŋgwɪʃə(r), -z
AM ˈlæŋgwɪʃər, -z
languishingly
BR ˈlaŋgwɪʃɪŋli
AM ˈlæŋgwɪʃɪŋli
languishment
BR ˈlaŋgwɪʃm(ə)nt
AM ˈlæŋgwɪʃmənt
languor
BR ˈlaŋgə(r)
AM ˈlaŋg(g)ər
languorous
BR ˈlaŋg(ə)rəs
AM ˈlæŋ(g)(ə)rəs
languorously
BR ˈlaŋg(ə)rəsli
AM ˈlæŋ(g)(ə)rəsli
langur
BR ˈlaŋgəː(r),
laŋˈgʊə(r),
lʌŋˈgʊə(r), -z
AM lʊŋˈgʊr, -z
laniary
BR ˈlanɪər|i, -ɪz
AM ˈleɪniˌeri, -z
laniferous
BR laˈnɪf(ə)rəs,
ləˈnɪf(ə)rəs
AM ləˈnɪfərəs
lanigerous
BR laˈnɪdʒ(ə)rəs,
ləˈnɪdʒ(ə)rəs
AM ləˈnɪdʒ(ə)rəs
lank
BR laŋk, -ə(r), -ɪst

AM læŋk, -ər, -əst
Lankester
BR ˈlaŋkɪstə(r)
AM ˈlæŋkəstər
lankily
BR ˈlaŋkɪli
AM ˈlæŋkəli
lankiness
BR ˈlaŋkɪnɪs
AM ˈlæŋkinɪs
lankly
BR ˈlaŋkli
AM ˈlæŋkli
lankness
BR ˈlaŋknəs
AM ˈlæŋknəs
lanky
BR ˈlaŋk|i, -ɪə(r), -ɪɪst
AM ˈlæŋki, -ər, -ɪst
lanner
BR ˈlanə(r), -z
AM ˈlænər, -z
lanneret
BR ˈlanərɪt, -s
AM ˈlænəˌrɛt,
ˌlænəˈrɛt, -s
lanolin
BR ˈlanəlɪn, ˈlanlɪn
AM ˈlænlən
lanoline
BR ˈlanəliːn, ˈlanliːn
AM ˈlænəˌlin
Lansbury
BR ˈlanzb(ə)ri
AM ˈlænzˌberi
Lansdown
BR ˈlanzdaʊn
AM ˈlænzˌdaʊn
Lansdowne
BR ˈlanzdaʊn
AM ˈlænzˌdaʊn
Lansing
BR ˈlaːnsɪŋ, ˈlansɪŋ
AM ˈlænsɪŋ
lansker
BR ˈlanskə(r)
AM ˈlænskər
lansquenet
BR ˈlaːnskənɛt,
ˈlanskənɛt, -s
AM ˈlænskəˈnɛt, -s
lantana
BR lanˈtɑːnə(r),
lanˈteɪnə(r), -z
AM lænˈtænə, -z
lantern
BR ˈlantən, -z
AM ˈlæn(t)ərn, -z
lanthanide
BR ˈlanθənʌɪd, -z
AM ˈlænθəˌnaɪd, -z
lanthanum
BR ˈlanθənʌm
AM ˈlænθənəm
lanugo
BR ləˈnjuːgəʊ
AM ləˈn(j)ugoʊ

lanyard
BR ˈlanjəd, ˈlanjaːd, -z
AM ˈlænjərd, -z
Lanza
BR ˈlanzə(r)
AM ˈlænzə, ˈlɑnzə
Lanzarote
BR ˌlanzəˈrɒti
AM ˌlɑnsəˈroʊdi
SP ˌlanθaˈrote,
ˌlansaˈrote
Lanzhou
BR ˌlanˈʒuː
AM ˈlænˈʒu
Lao
BR laʊ
AM laʊ
Laocoon
BR leɪˈɒkəʊɒn,
leɪˈɒkəʊən
AM leɪˈɑkəˌwɑn
Laodicean
BR ˌleɪə(ʊ)dɪˈsiːən, -z
AM leɪˈɑdiˈsiən, -z
Laois
BR liːʃ
AM liʃ
Laos
BR ˈlaːɒs, laʊs
AM ˈlaoʊs
Laotian
BR leɪˈəʊʃn, -z
AM leɪˈoʊʃən, -z
Lao-tzu
BR ˌlaʊˈtsuː
AM ˈlaoʊˈtsu
lap
BR lap, -s, -ɪŋ, -t
AM læp, -s, -ɪŋ, -t
laparoscope
BR ˈlap(ə)rəskəʊp, -s
AM ˈlæpərəˌskoʊp, -s
laparoscopy
BR ˌlapəˈrɒskəp|i, -ɪz
AM ˌlæpəˈrɑskəpi, -z
laparotomy
BR ˌlapəˈrɒtəm|i, -ɪz
AM ˌlæpəˈrɑdəmi, -z
La Paz
BR la ˈpaz
AM lə ˈpɑz
lapdog
BR ˈlapdɒg, -z
AM ˈlæpˌdɔg, ˈlæpˌdɑg,
-z
lapel
BR ləˈpɛl, -z
AM ləˈpɛl, -z, -d
lapful
BR ˈlapfʊl, -z
AM ˈlæpˌfʊl, -z
lapicide
BR ˈlapɪsʌɪd, -z
AM ˈlæpəˌsaɪd, -z
lapidary
BR ˈlapɪd(ə)r|i, -ɪz
AM ˈlæpəˌderi, -z

lapidate
BR 'læpɪdeɪt, -s, -ɪŋ, -ɪd
AM 'læpə,deɪ|t, -ts, -dɪŋ, -dɪd

lapidation
BR ,læpɪ'deɪʃn
AM ,læpə'deɪʃən

lapilli
BR lə'pɪlʌɪ
AM lə'pɪˌlaɪ

lapis lazuli
BR ,lapɪs 'lazjʊlʌɪ, + 'lazjʊli:
AM 'læpəs 'læzjələɪ, + 'læʒəlaɪ, + 'læzjəli

Lapith
BR 'lapɪθ, -s
AM 'læpəθ, -s

Laplace
BR lə'plɑːs, lə'plas, la'plɑːs, la'plas
AM lə'plɑs

Lapland
BR 'lapland
AM 'læp,lænd

Laplander
BR 'lap,landə(r), -z
AM 'læp,lændər, -z

Lapotaire
BR ,lapə'tɛː(r), ,lapɒ'tɛː(r)
AM ,lapə'tɛ(ə)r

Lapp
BR lap, -s
AM læp, -s

Lappard
BR 'lɛpɑːd
AM 'lɛ,pɑrd, 'læpərd

lappet
BR 'lap|ɪt, -s, -ɪtɪŋ, -ɪtɪd
AM 'læpə|t, -ts, -dəd

Lappish
BR 'lapɪʃ
AM 'læpɪʃ

Lapsang Souchong
BR ,lapsaŋ 'suːʃɒŋ, + suːˈʃɒŋ
AM ,lapsaŋ su'tʃaŋ

lapse
BR laps, -ɪz, -ɪŋ, -t
AM læps, -əz, -ɪŋ, -t

lapser
BR 'lapsə(r), -z
AM 'læpsər, -z

lapstone
BR 'lapstəʊn, -z
AM 'læp,stoʊn, -z

lapsus calami
BR ,lapsəs 'kaləmʌɪ
AM 'læpsəs 'kalə,maɪ, + 'kaləmi

lapsus linguae
BR ,lapsəs 'lɪŋgwʌɪ
AM 'lapsəs 'lɪŋgwaɪ

Laptev
BR 'laptɛv
AM 'lap,tɛv

RUS 'laptʲif

laptop
BR 'laptɒp, -s
AM 'læp,tɑp, -s

Laputa
BR lə'pjuːtə(r)
AM lə'p(j)udə

Laputan
BR lə'pjuːtn, -z
AM lə'pjutn, -z

lapwing
BR 'lapwɪŋ, -z
AM 'læp,wɪŋ, -z

Lara
BR 'lɑːrə(r)
AM 'lɑrə

Laramie
BR 'larəmi
AM 'lɛrəˌmi

larboard
BR 'lɑːbɔːd, 'labəd
AM 'lɑr,bɔ(ə)rd, 'læbərd

larcener
BR 'lɑːsmə(r), 'lɑːsnə(r), -z
AM 'lɑrsənər, 'lɑrsn̩ər, -z

larcenist
BR 'lɑːsmɪst, 'lɑːsn̩ɪst, -s
AM 'lɑrsənəst, 'lɑrsn̩əst, -s

larcenous
BR 'lɑːsmənəs, 'lɑːsn̩əs
AM 'lɑrsənənəs, 'lɑrsn̩əs

larcenously
BR 'lɑːsmənəsli, 'lɑːsn̩əsli
AM 'lɑrsənənəsli, 'lɑrsn̩əsli

larceny
BR 'lɑːsn̩|i, 'lɑːsn̩|i, -ɪz
AM 'lɑrsən̩i, 'lɑrsn̩i, -z

larch
BR lɑːtʃ, -ɪz
AM lɑrtʃ, -əz

larchwood
BR 'lɑːtʃwʊd, -z
AM 'lɑrtʃ,wʊd, -z

lard
BR lɑːd, -z, -ɪŋ, -ɪd
AM lɑrd, -z, -ɪŋ, -əd

lardass
BR 'lɑːdɑːs, 'lɑːdas, -ɪz
AM 'lɑrdæs, -əz

larder
BR 'lɑːdə(r), -z
AM 'lɑrdər, -z

Lardner
BR 'lɑːdnə(r)
AM 'lɑrdnər

lardon
BR 'lɑːdn
AM 'lɑrdən

lardoon
BR lɑː'duːn, -z

AM lɑr'dun, -z

lardy
BR 'lɑːdi
AM 'lɑrdi

lardy-dardy
BR ,lɑːdɪ'dɑːdi
AM 'lɑrdi'dɑrdi

Laredo
BR lə'reɪdəʊ
AM lə'reɪdoʊ

lares
BR 'lɑːriːz, 'lɑːreɪz, 'lɛːriːz
AM 'leɪˌriz, 'lɛriz

Largactil®
BR lɑːˈgaktɪl
AM lɑrˈgæktəl

large
BR lɑːdʒ, -ə(r), -ɪst
AM lɑrdʒ, -ər, -əst

largely
BR 'lɑːdʒli
AM 'lɑrdʒli

largen
BR 'lɑːdʒ|(ə)n, -(ə)nz, -ɪŋ\-(ə)nɪŋ, -(ə)nd
AM 'lɑrdʒən, -z, -ɪŋ, -d

largeness
BR 'lɑːdʒnəs
AM 'lɑrdʒnəs

largess
BR lɑːˈ(d)ʒes
AM lɑrˈ(d)ʒes

largesse
BR lɑːˈ(d)ʒes
AM lɑrˈ(d)ʒes

larghetto
BR lɑːˈgɛtəʊ, -z
AM lɑrˈgɛdoʊ, -z

largish
BR 'lɑːdʒɪʃ
AM 'lɑrdʒɪʃ

largo
BR 'lɑːgəʊ, -z
AM 'lɑrgoʊ, -z

Largs
BR lɑːgz
AM lɑrgz

lariat
BR 'larɪət, -s
AM 'lɛrɪət, -s

Larissa
BR lə'rɪsə(r)
AM lə'rɪsə

lark
BR lɑːk, -s, -ɪŋ, -t
AM lɑrk, -s, -ɪŋ, -t

Larkin
BR 'lɑːkɪn
AM 'lɑrkən

larkiness
BR 'lɑːkɪnɪs
AM 'lɑrkɪnɪs

larkspur
BR 'lɑːkspə:(r), -z
AM 'lɑrk,spər, -z

larky
BR 'lɑːki
AM 'lɑrki

larn
BR lɑːn, -z, -ɪŋ, -d
AM lɑrn, -z, -ɪŋ, -d

La Rochelle
BR ,lɑː rɒ'ʃɛl, ,la +
AM la rə'ʃɛl

Larousse
BR lə'ruːs, la'ruːs
AM lə'rus

larrikin
BR 'larɪkɪn, -z
AM 'lɛrəkən, -z

larrup
BR 'larəp, -s, -ɪŋ, -t
AM 'lɛrəp, -s, -ɪŋ, -t

Larry
BR 'lari
AM 'lɛri

Lars
BR lɑːz
AM lɑrz

Larsen
BR 'lɑːsn
AM 'lɑrsən
DAN 'lɑːsən
SW 'lɑːʃɛn

Larson
BR 'lɑːsn
AM 'lɑrsən

larva
BR 'lɑːvə(r), -z
AM 'lɑrvə, -z

larvae
BR 'lɑːviː
AM 'lɑrvi, 'lɑr,vaɪ, 'lɑrveɪ

larval
BR 'lɑːvl
AM 'lɑrvəl

larvicide
BR 'lɑːvɪsʌɪd, -z
AM 'lɑrvə,saɪd, -z

Larwood
BR 'lɑːwʊd
AM 'lɑr,wʊd

laryngeal
BR lə'rɪn(d)ʒɪəl, ,larɪn'dʒiːəl, ,larɪn'dʒiːəl
AM lə'rɪndʒ(i)əl, ,lɛrən'dʒiəl

larynges
BR lə'rɪn(d)ʒiːz, la'rɪn(d)ʒiːz
AM lə'rɪn,dʒiz

laryngic
BR lə'rɪndʒɪk, la'rɪndʒɪk
AM lə'rɪndʒɪk

laryngitic
BR ,larɪn'dʒɪtɪk, ,larɪn'dʒɪtɪk
AM ,lɛrən'dʒɪdɪk

laryngitis
BR ˌlærɪn'dʒʌɪtɪs,
ˌlærŋ'dʒʌɪtɪs
AM ˌlɛrən'dʒaɪdɪs

laryngology
BR ˌlærɪŋ'gɒlədʒi
AM ˌlɛrən'gɑlədʒi

laryngoscope
BR lə'rɪŋgəskəʊp,
lə'rɪŋgəskəʊp, -s
AM lə'rɪŋgəˌskoʊp,
lə'rɪndʒəˌskoʊp, -s

laryngoscopic
BR ləˌrɪŋgə'skɒpɪk,
laˌrɪŋgə'skɒpɪk
AM lə'rɪŋgə'skɑpɪk,
ləˌrɪndʒə'skɑpɪk

laryngoscopically
BR ləˌrɪŋgə'skɒpɪkli,
laˌrɪŋgə'skɒpɪkli
AM lə'rɪŋgə'skɑpək(ə)li,
lə'rɪndʒə'skɑpək(ə)li

laryngoscopy
BR ˌlærɪŋ'gɒskəp|i, -ɪz
AM ˌlɛrən'gɑskəpi, -z

laryngotomy
BR ˌlærɪŋ'gɒtəm|i, -ɪz
AM ˌlɛrən'gɑdəmi, -z

larynx
BR 'lærɪŋks, -ɪz
AM 'lɛrɪŋks, -ɪz

lasagna
BR lə'zanjə(r)
AM lə'zɑnjə

lasagne
BR lə'zanjə(r)
AM lə'zɑnjə

La Salle
BR la 'sal
AM lə 'sɑl

La Scala
BR la 'skɑːlə(r)
AM lɑ 'skɑlə

lascar
BR 'laskə(r), -z
AM 'læskər, -z

lascivious
BR lə'sɪvɪəs
AM lə'sɪvɪəs

lasciviously
BR lə'sɪvɪəsli
AM lə'sɪvɪəsli

lasciviousness
BR lə'sɪvɪəsnəs
AM lə'sɪvɪəsnəs

laser
BR 'leɪzə(r), -z
AM 'leɪzər, -z

laserdisc
BR 'leɪzədɪsk, -s
AM 'leɪzərˌdɪsk, -s

LaserVision®
BR 'leɪzəˌvɪʒn
AM 'leɪzərˌvɪʒən

lash
BR laʃ, -ɪz, -ɪŋ, -t
AM læʃ, -əz, -ɪŋ, -t

lasher
BR 'laʃə(r), -z
AM 'læʃər, -z

lashing
BR 'laʃɪŋ, -z
AM 'læʃɪŋ, -z

lashingly
BR 'laʃɪŋli
AM 'læʃɪŋli

lashkar
BR 'laʃkɑː(r),
'laʃkə(r), -z
AM 'læʃkər, -z

lashless
BR 'laʃləs
AM 'læʃləs

Lasker
BR 'laskə(r), -z
AM 'læskər, -z

Laski
BR 'laski
AM 'læski

Las Palmas
BR las 'palməs,
+ 'pɑː(l)məs
AM ˌlas 'pɑlməs

lasque
BR lɑːsk, lask, -s
AM læsk, -s

lass
BR las, -ɪz
AM læs, -əz

Lassa fever
BR 'lasə ˌfiːvə(r)
AM ˌlasə 'fivər

lassie
BR 'las|i, -ɪz
AM 'læsi, -z

lassitude
BR 'lasɪtjuːd,
'lasɪtʃuːd
AM 'læsəˌt(j)ud

lasso
BR lə'suː, la'suː, 'lasəʊ,
-z, -ɪŋ, -d
AM 'læsoʊ, 'læsu,
læ'su, -z, -ɪŋ, -d

lassoer
BR lə'suːə(r),
la'su:ə(r), 'lasəʊə(r),
-z
AM 'læsəwər, -z

Lassus
BR 'lasəs
AM 'lasəs

last
BR lɑːst, last, -s, -ɪŋ, -ɪd
AM læst, -s, -ɪŋ, -əd

lasting
BR 'lɑːstɪŋ, 'lastɪŋ
AM 'læstɪŋ

lastingly
BR 'lɑːstɪŋli, 'lastɪŋli
AM 'læstɪŋli

lastingness
BR 'lɑːstɪŋnɪs,
'lastɪŋnɪs
AM 'læstɪŋnɪs

lastly
BR 'lɑːstli, 'lastli
AM 'læs(t)li

Las Vegas
BR las 'veɪgəs
AM las 'veɪgəs

lat
BR lat, -s
AM læt, -s

Latakia
BR ˌlatə'kiːə(r)
AM ˌladə'kiə

latch
BR latʃ, -ɪz, -ɪŋ, -t
AM lætʃ, -əz, -ɪŋ, -t

latchet
BR 'latʃɪt, -s
AM 'lætʃət, -s

latchkey
BR 'latʃkiː, -z
AM 'lætʃˌki, -z

late
BR leɪt, -ə(r), -ɪst
AM leɪ|t, -dər, -dɪst

latecomer
BR 'leɪtˌkʌmə(r), -z
AM 'leɪtˌkəmər, -z

lateen
BR lə'tiːn, la'tiːn
AM lə'tin, læ'tin

lateish
BR 'leɪtɪʃ
AM 'leɪdɪʃ

lately
BR 'leɪtli
AM 'leɪtli

laten
BR 'leɪt|n, -nz,
-ŋn\-ənɪŋ, -nd
AM 'leɪtn, -z, -ɪŋ, -d

latency
BR 'leɪt(ə)nsi
AM 'leɪtnsi

La Tène
BR lə 'tɛn
AM lə 'tɛn

lateness
BR 'leɪtnɪs
AM 'leɪtnɪs

latent
BR 'leɪt(ə)nt
AM 'leɪtnt

latently
BR 'leɪt(ə)ntli
AM 'leɪtn(t)li

later
BR 'leɪtə(r)
AM 'leɪdər

lateral
BR 'lat(ə)rəl, 'lat(ə)r̩l,
-z
AM 'lædərəl, 'lætrəl, -z

laterally
BR 'lat(ə)rəli,
'lat(ə)r̩li
AM 'lædərəli, 'lætrəli

Lateran
BR 'lat(ə)rən, 'lat(ə)r̩n
AM 'læd(ə)rən

laterite
BR 'latərʌɪt
AM 'lædəˌraɪt

lateritic
BR ˌlatə'rɪtɪk
AM ˌlædə'rɪdɪk

latex
BR 'leɪtɛks
AM 'leɪˌtɛks

lath
BR lɑː|θ, la|θ,
lɑːðz\lɑːθs\laθs
AM læ|θ, -ðz\-θs

Latham
BR 'leɪθ(ə)m, 'leɪð(ə)m
AM 'leɪθəm

lathe
BR leɪð, -z
AM leɪð, -z

lather
BR 'lɑːð|ə(r), 'lað|ə(r),
-əz, -(ə)rɪŋ, -əd
AM 'læð|ər, -ərz,
-(ə)rɪŋ, -ərd

lathery
BR 'lɑːð(ə)ri, 'lað(ə)ri
AM 'læðəri

lathi
BR 'lɑːt|i, -ɪz
AM 'ladi, -z

lathy
BR 'leɪði
AM 'leɪði

latices
BR 'latɪsiːz
AM 'lædəˌsiz

latifundia
BR ˌlatɪ'fʌndɪə(r)
AM ˌlædə'fəndɪə

latifundium
BR ˌlatɪ'fʌndɪəm
AM ˌlædə'fəndɪəm

Latimer
BR 'latɪmə(r)
AM 'lædəmər

Latin
BR 'latɪn, -z
AM 'lætn, -z

Latinate
BR 'latɪneɪt
AM 'lætnˌeɪt

Latinisation
BR ˌlatɪnʌɪ'zeɪʃn
AM ˌlætnaɪ'zeɪʃən,
ˌlætnˌaɪ'zeɪʃən

Latinise
BR 'latɪnʌɪz, -ɪz, -ɪŋ, -d
AM 'lætnˌaɪz, -ɪz, -ɪŋ, -d

Latiniser
BR 'latɪnʌɪzə(r), -z
AM 'lætnˌaɪzər, -z

Latinism
BR 'latɪnɪz(ə)m, -z
AM 'lætnˌɪzəm, -z

Latinist
BR ˈlatɪnɪst, -s
AM ˈlætnəst, -s

Latinization
BR ˌlatɪnʌɪˈzeɪʃn
AM ˌlætnəˈzeɪʃən,
ˌlætn̩ˌarˈzeɪʃən

Latinize
BR ˈlatɪnʌɪz, -ɪz, -ɪŋ, -d
AM ˈlætn̩ˌaɪz, -ɪz, -ɪŋ, -d

Latinizer
BR ˈlatɪnʌɪzə(r), -z
AM ˈlætn̩ˌaɪzər, -z

Latino
BR laˈtiːnəʊ, ləˈtiːnəʊ, -z
AM ləˈtiˌnoʊ, -z

latish
BR ˈleɪtɪʃ
AM ˈleɪdɪʃ

latitude
BR ˈlatɪtjuːd,
ˈlatɪtʃuːd, -z
AM ˈlædəˌt(j)ud, -z

latitudinal
BR ˌlatɪˈtjuːdɪnl,
ˌlatɪˈtʃuːdɪnl
AM ˌlædəˈt(j)udn̩əl

latitudinally
BR ˌlatɪˈtjuːdɪnl̩i,
ˌlatɪˈtjuːdɪnəli,
ˌlatɪˈtʃuːdɪnl̩i,
ˌlatɪˈtʃuːdɪnəli
AM ˌlædəˈt(j)udn̩əli

latitudinarian
BR ˌlatɪˌtjuːdɪˈnɛːrɪən,
ˌlatɪˌtʃuːdɪˈnɛːrɪən, -z
AM ˌlædəˌt(j)udn̩ˈɛrɪən, -z

latitudinarianism
BR ˌlatɪˌtjuːdɪˈnɛːrɪən-
ɪz(ə)m,
ˌlatɪˌtʃuːdɪˈnɛːrɪən-
ɪz(ə)m
AM ˌlædəˌt(j)udn̩ˈɛrɪə-
ˌnɪzəm

Latium
BR ˈleɪʃ(ɪ)əm, ˈlaːtɪəm
AM ˈleɪʃ(i)əm

latke
BR ˈlʌtkə(r), -z
AM ˈlatkə, -z

Latona
BR ləˈtəʊnə(r)
AM ləˈtoʊnə

Latoya
BR ləˈtɔɪə(r)
AM ləˈtɔɪə

latria
BR ləˈtrʌɪə(r)
AM ləˈtraɪə

latrine
BR ləˈtriːn, -z
AM ləˈtrin, -z

Latrobe
BR ləˈtrəʊb
AM ləˈtroʊb

latten
BR ˈlatn, -z
AM ˈlætn, -z

latter
BR ˈlatə(r)
AM ˈlædər

latterly
BR ˈlatəli
AM ˈlædərli

lattice
BR ˈlatɪs, -ɪz, -t
AM ˈlædəs, -əz, -t

latticing
BR ˈlatɪsɪŋ
AM ˈlædəsɪŋ

Latvia
BR ˈlatvɪə(r)
AM ˈlætvɪə

Latvian
BR ˈlatvɪən, -z
AM ˈlætvɪən, -z

laud
BR lɔːd, -z, -ɪŋ, -ɪd
AM lɔd, lad, -z, -ɪŋ, -əd

Lauda
BR ˈlaʊdə(r)
AM ˈlaʊdə

laudability
BR ˌlɔːdəˈbɪlɪti
AM ˌlɔdəˈbɪlɪdi, ˌladəˈbɪlɪdi

laudable
BR ˈlɔːdəbl
AM ˈlɔdəbəl, ˈladəbəl

laudably
BR ˈlɔːdəbli
AM ˈlɔdəbli, ˈladəbli

laudanum
BR ˈlɔːd(ə)nəm, ˈlɔːdnəm
AM ˈlɔdnəm, ˈladnəm

laudation
BR lɔːˈdeɪʃn, -z
AM lɔˈdeɪʃən, laˈdeɪʃən, -z

laudative
BR ˈlɔːdətɪv
AM ˈlɔdədɪv, ˈladədɪv

laudatory
BR ˈlɔːdət(ə)ri
AM ˈlɔdəˌtori, ˈladəˌtori

Lauderdale
BR ˈlɔːdədeɪl
AM ˈlɔdərˌdeɪl, ˈladərˌdeɪl

laugh
BR laːf, laf, -s, -ɪŋ, -t
AM læf, -s, -ɪŋ, -t

laughable
BR ˈlaːfəbl, ˈlafəbl
AM ˈlæfəbəl

laughably
BR ˈlaːfəbli, ˈlafəbli
AM ˈlæfəbli

Laugharne
BR laːn

AM lɑrn

laugher
BR ˈlaːfə(r), ˈlafə(r), -z
AM ˈlæfər, -z

laughingly
BR ˈlaːfɪŋli, ˈlafɪŋli
AM ˈlæfɪŋli

laughingstock
BR ˈlaːfɪŋstɒk,
ˈlafɪŋstɒk, -s
AM ˈlæfɪŋˌstak, -s

laughter
BR ˈlaːftə(r), ˈlaftə(r)
AM ˈlæftər

Laughton
BR ˈlɔːtn
AM ˈlɔtn, ˈlatn

launce
BR lɔːns, -ɪz
AM lɔns, lans, -əz

Launceston
BR ˈlɔːnst(ə)n,
ˈlaːnst(ə)n
AM ˈlɔnstən, ˈlanstən

launch
BR lɔːn(t)ʃ, -ɪz, -ɪŋ, -t
AM lɔːn(t)ʃ, lan(t)ʃ, -əz,
-ɪŋ, -t

launcher
BR ˈlɔːn(t)ʃə(r), -z
AM ˈlɔn(t)ʃər,
ˈlan(t)ʃər, -z

launchpad
BR ˈlɔːn(t)ʃpad, -z
AM ˈlɔn(t)ʃˌpæd,
ˈlan(t)ʃˌpæd, -z

launder
BR ˈlɔːnd|ə(r), -əz,
-(ə)rɪŋ, -əd
AM ˈlɔnd|ər, ˈland|ər,
-ərz, -(ə)rɪŋ, -ərd

launderer
BR ˈlɔːnd(ə)rə(r), -z
AM ˈlɔndərər,
ˈlandərər, -z

launderette
BR ˌlɔːnˈdrɛt,
ˌlɔːndəˈrɛt, -s
AM ˌlɔndəˈrɛt,
ˌlandəˈrɛt, -s

laundress
BR ˈlɔːndrɪs, lɔːnˈdrɛs,
-ɪz
AM ˈlɔndrəs, ˈlandrəs,
-əz

laundromat
BR ˈlɔːndrəmat, -s
AM ˈlɔndrəˌmæt,
ˈlandrəˌmæt, -s

laundry
BR ˈlɔːndr|i, -ɪz
AM ˈlɔndri, ˈlandri, -z

Laura
BR ˈlɔːrə(r)
AM ˈlɔrə

Laurasia
BR lɔːˈreɪʃə(r),
lɔːˈreɪʒə(r)

AM ləˈreɪʒə, lɔˈreɪʃə

laureate
BR ˈlɔːrɪət, ˈlɒrɪət, -s
AM ˈlɔriət, -s

laureateship
BR ˈlɔːrɪətʃɪp,
ˈlɒrɪətʃɪp, -s
AM ˈlɔriətˌʃɪp, -s

laurel
BR ˈlɒrəl, ˈlɒrl̩, -z
AM ˈlɔrəl, -z

Lauren
BR ˈlɔːrən, ˈlɔːrn̩,
ˈlɒrən, ˈlɒrn̩
AM ˈlɔrən

Laurence
BR ˈlɒrəns, ˈlɒrn̩s
AM ˈlɔrəns

Laurentian
adjective
BR lɒˈrɛnʃn, lɔːˈrɛnʃn,
ləˈrɛnʃn
AM lɔˈrɛn(t)ʃən

Laurie
BR ˈlɒri
AM ˈlɔri

Laurier
BR ˈlɒrɪə(r), ˈlɒrɪeɪ
AM ˈlɔriər

Lauriston
BR ˈlɒrɪst(ə)n
AM ˈlɔrəstən

laurustinus
BR ˌlɒrəˈstʌɪnəs, -ɪz
AM ˌlɔrəstənəs, -əz

Lausanne
BR ləʊˈzan
AM lɔˈzan, laˈzan

LAUTRO
BR ˈlaʊtrəʊ
AM ˈlɔˌtroʊ, ˈlaˌtroʊ

lav
BR lav, -z
AM læv, -z

lava
BR ˈlaːvə(r)
AM ˈlavə

lavabo
BR ləˈvaːbəʊ,
ləˈveɪbəʊ, -z
AM ləˈvaboʊ,
ləˈveɪboʊ, -z

lavage
BR ˈlavɪdʒ
AM ləˈvaʒ, ˈlævɪdʒ

Laval
BR laˈval, laˈval
AM laˈval

lavaliere
BR ləˌvalɪˈɛː(r),
ləˈvaljɛː(r)
AM ˌlavəˈlɪ(ə)r,
ˌlævəˈlɪ(ə)r

lavation
BR ləˈveɪʃn
AM ləˈveɪʃən

lavatorial
BR ˌlævəˈtɔːriəl
AM ˌlævəˈtɔriəl

lavatory
BR ˈlavət(ə)r|i, -ɪz
AM ˈlævəˌtɔri, -z

lave
BR leɪv, -z, -ɪŋ, -d
AM leɪv, -z, -ɪŋ, -d

lavender
BR ˈlav(ɪ)ndə(r)
AM ˈlævəndər

laver
BR ˈleɪvə(r), -z
AM ˈleɪvər, -z

Laverick
BR ˈlav(ə)rɪk
AM ˈlæv(ə)rək

laverock
BR ˈlav(ə)rək, -s
AM ˈlæv(ə)rək, -s

Lavery
BR ˈleɪv(ə)ri
AM ˈleɪvəri

Lavinia
BR ləˈvɪnɪə(r)
AM ləˈvɪnɪə, ləˈvɪnjə

lavish
BR ˈlavɪʃ
AM ˈlævɪʃ

lavishly
BR ˈlavɪʃli
AM ˈlævɪʃli

lavishness
BR ˈlavɪʃnɪs
AM ˈlævɪʃnɪs

Lavoisier
BR ləˈvwɑːzieɪ,
laˈvwɑːzieɪ,
ləˈvwazieɪ, laˈvwazieɪ
AM ləˌvwɑˈzieɪ

lavvy
BR ˈlav|i, -ɪz
AM ˈlævi, -z

law
BR lɔː(r), -z
AM lɔ, lɑ, -z

Lawes
BR lɔːz
AM lɔz, lɑz

Lawford
BR ˈlɔːfəd
AM ˈlɔfərd, ˈlɑfərd

lawful
BR ˈlɔːf(ʊ)l
AM ˈlɔfəl, ˈlɑfəl

lawfully
BR ˈlɔːfʊli, ˈlɔːfʃi
AM ˈlɔf(ə)li, ˈlɑf(ə)li

lawfulness
BR ˈlɔːf(ʊ)lnəs
AM ˈlɔfəlnəs, ˈlɑfəlnəs

lawgiver
BR ˈlɔːˌgɪvə(r), -z
AM ˈlɔˌgɪvər, ˈlɑˌgɪvər,
-z

Lawler
BR ˈlɔːlə(r)
AM ˈlɔlər, ˈlɑlər

lawless
BR ˈlɔːləs
AM ˈlɔləs, ˈlɑləs

lawlessly
BR ˈlɔːləsli
AM ˈlɔləsli, ˈlɑləsli

lawlessness
BR ˈlɔːləsnəs
AM ˈlɔləsnəs, ˈlɑləsnəs

Lawley
BR ˈlɔːli
AM ˈlɔli, ˈlɑli

Lawlor
BR ˈlɔːlə(r)
AM ˈlɔlər, ˈlɑlər

lawmaker
BR ˈlɔːˌmeɪkə(r), -z
AM ˈlɔˌmeɪkər,
ˈlɑˌmeɪkər, -z

lawman
BR ˈlɔːman, ˈlɔːmən
AM ˈlɔˌmæn, ˈlɔmən,
ˈlɑˌmæn, ˈlɑmən

lawmen
BR ˈlɔːmɛn, ˈlɔːmən
AM ˈlɔˌmɛn, ˈlɔmən,
ˈlɑˌmɛn, ˈlɑmən

lawn
BR lɔːn, -z
AM lɔn, lɑn, -z, -d

lawnmower
BR ˈlɔːnˌməʊə(r), -z
AM ˈlɔnˌmoʊ(ə)r,
ˈlɑnˌmoʊ(ə)r, -z

lawny
BR ˈlɔːni
AM ˈlɔni, ˈlɑni

Lawrence
BR ˈlɒrəns, ˈlɒrn̩s
AM ˈlɔrəns

lawrencium
BR ləˈrɛnsɪəm
AM lɔˈrɛn(t)sɪəm,
lɑˈrɛn(t)sɪəm

Lawrey
BR ˈlɒri
AM ˈlɑuri

Lawrie
BR ˈlɒri
AM ˈlɑuri, ˈlɔri

Laws
BR lɔːz
AM lɔz, lɑz

Lawson
BR ˈlɔːsn
AM ˈlɔsən, ˈlɑsən

lawsuit
BR ˈlɔːs(j)uːt, -s
AM ˈlɔˌsut, ˈlɑˌsut, -s

Lawton
BR ˈlɔːtn
AM ˈlɔtn, ˈlɑtn

lawyer
BR ˈlɔɪə(r), ˈlɔːjə(r), -z

AM ˈlɔɪər, ˈlɔjər, ˈlɑjər,
-z

lawyerly
BR ˈlɔːɪəli, ˈlɔːjəli
AM ˈlɔɪərli, ˈlɔjərli,
ˈlɑjərli

lax
BR laks, -ə(r), -ɪst
AM læks, -ər, -əst

laxative
BR ˈlaksətɪv, -z
AM ˈlæksədɪv, -z

Laxey
BR ˈlaksi
AM ˈlæksi

laxity
BR ˈlaksɪti
AM ˈlæksədi

laxly
BR ˈlaksli
AM ˈlæksli

laxness
BR ˈlaksnəs
AM ˈlæksnəs

lay
BR leɪ, -z, -ɪŋ, -d
AM leɪ, -z, -ɪŋ, -d

layabout
BR ˈleɪəbaʊt, -s
AM ˈleɪəˌbaʊt, -s

Layamon
BR ˈleɪəmən
AM ˈleɪəˌman,
ˈleɪəmən

lay-by
BR ˈleɪbʌɪ, -z
AM ˈleɪˌbaɪ, -z

Laycock
BR ˈleɪkɒk
AM ˈleɪkak

layer
BR ˈleɪə(r), -z, -ɪŋ, -d
AM ˈleɪər, ˈlɛ(ə)r, -z, -ɪŋ,
-d

layette
BR leɪˈɛt, -s
AM leɪˈɛt, -s

layman
BR ˈleɪmən
AM ˈleɪmən

laymen
BR ˈleɪmən
AM ˈleɪmən

lay-off
noun
BR ˈleɪɒf, -s
AM ˈleɪˌɔf, ˈleɪˌɑf, -s

layout
BR ˈleɪaʊt, -s
AM ˈleɪˌaʊt, -s

layover
BR ˈleɪˌəʊvə(r), -z
AM ˈleɪˌoʊvər, -z

layperson
BR ˈleɪˌpəːsn, -z
AM ˈleɪˌpərsən, -z

layshaft
BR ˈleɪʃɑːft, ˈleɪʃaft, -s
AM ˈleɪˌʃæft, -s

laystall
BR ˈleɪstɔːl, -z
AM ˈleɪˌstɔl, ˈleɪˌstɑl, -z

Layton
BR ˈleɪtn
AM ˈleɪtn

laywoman
BR ˈleɪˌwʊmən
AM ˈleɪˌwʊmən

laywomen
BR ˈleɪˌwɪmɪn
AM ˈleɪˌwɪmɪn

lazar
BR ˈlazə(r), -z
AM ˈlæzər, ˈleɪzər, -z

lazaret
BR ˌlazəˈrɛt, -s
AM ˌlæzəˈrɛt, -s

lazaretto
BR ˌlazəˈrɛtəʊ, -z
AM ˌlæzəˈrɛdoʊ, -z

Lazarist
BR ˈlaz(ə)rɪst, -s
AM ˈlæzərəst, -s

Lazarus
BR ˈlaz(ə)rəs
AM ˈlæzərəs

laze
BR leɪz, -ɪz, -ɪŋ, -d
AM leɪz, -ɪz, -ɪŋ, -d

lazily
BR ˈleɪzɪli
AM ˈleɪzɪli

laziness
BR ˈleɪzɪnɪs
AM ˈleɪzɪnɪs

Lazio
BR ˈlatsɪəʊ
AM ˈlatsɪoʊ

Lazonby
BR ˈleɪznbi
AM ˈleɪzənbi

lazuli
BR ˈlazjʊlʌɪ, ˈlazjʊliː
AM ˈlæzjəlaɪ, ˈlaʒəlaɪ,
ˈlæzjəli

lazy
BR ˈleɪz|i, -ɪə(r), -ɪɪst
AM ˈleɪzi, -ər, -ɪst

lazybones
BR ˈleɪzibəʊnz
AM ˈleɪziˌboʊnz

L-dopa
BR ˌɛlˈdəʊpə(r)
AM ˌɛlˈdoʊpə

LEA
BR ˌɛliːˈeɪ, -z
AM ˌɛlˌiˈeɪ, -z

Lea
BR liː
AM ˈli(ə), ˈleɪə

lea
BR liː, -z
AM li, -z

leach
BR liːtʃ, -ɪz, -ɪŋ, -t
AM litʃ, -ɪz, -ɪŋ, -t
leacher
BR 'liːtʃə(r), -z
AM 'litʃər, -z
Leacock
BR 'liːkɒk
AM 'liˌkɑk, 'leɪˌkɑk
lead¹
noun, verb present,
guide etc
BR liːd, -z, -ɪŋ
AM lid, -z, -ɪŋ
lead²
noun, verb past,
metal
BR lɛd, -z, -ɪŋ, -ɪd
AM lɛd, -z, -ɪŋ, -ɪd
leadable
BR 'liːdəbl
AM 'lidəbəl
Leadbelly
BR 'lɛdˌbɛli
AM 'lɛdˌbɛli
Leadbetter
BR 'lɛdˌbɛtə(r)
AM 'lɛdˌbədər
leaden
BR 'lɛdn
AM 'lɛdən
Leadenhall
BR 'lɛdnhɔːl
AM 'lɛdənˌ(h)ɔl,
'lɛdənˌ(h)ɑl
leadenly
BR 'lɛdnli
AM 'lɛdnli
leadenness
BR 'lɛdnnəs
AM 'lɛd(n)nəs
leader
BR 'liːdə(r), -z
AM 'lidər, -z
leaderene
BR ˌliːdə'riːn, -z
AM 'lidəˌrin, -z
leaderless
BR 'liːdələs
AM 'lidərləs
leadership
BR 'liːdəʃɪp
AM 'lidərˌʃɪp
lead-free
BR ˌlɛd'friː
AM ˌlɛd'fri
lead-in
BR 'liːdɪn, -z
AM 'liˌdɪn, -z
leading
BR 'liːdɪŋ, -z
AM 'lidɪŋ, -z
leadless
BR 'liːdlɪs
AM 'lidlɪs
leadwort
BR 'lɛdwɜːt

AM 'lɛdwərt,
'lɛdwɔ(ə)rt
leaf¹
noun
BR liːf
AM lif
leaf²
verb
BR liːf, -s, -ɪŋ, -t
AM lif, -s, -ɪŋ, -t
leafage
BR 'liːfɪdʒ
AM 'lifɪdʒ
leafcutter
BR 'liːfˌkʌtə(r), -z
AM 'lifˌkədər, -z
leafhopper
BR 'liːfˌhɒpə(r), -z
AM 'lif(h)ɑpər, -z
leafiness
BR 'liːfɪnɪs
AM 'lifɪnɪs
leafless
BR 'liːflɪs
AM 'liflɪs
leaflessness
BR 'liːflɪsnɪs
AM 'liflɪsnɪs
leaflet
BR 'liːflɪt, -s, -ɪŋ, -ɪd
AM 'liflɪ|t, -ts, -dɪŋ, -dɪd
leaflike
BR 'liːflʌɪk
AM 'lifˌlaɪk
leafy
BR 'liːfʲi, -ɪə(r), -ɪɪst
AM 'lifi, -ər, -ɪst
league
BR liːg, -z, -ɪŋ, -d
AM lig, -z, -ɪŋ, -d
leaguer
BR 'liːgə(r), -z
AM 'ligər, -z
Leah
BR 'liːə(r)
AM 'liə, 'leɪə
Leahy
BR 'liːhi, 'leɪhi
AM 'leɪ(h)i, 'lihi
leak
BR liːk, -s, -ɪŋ, -t
AM lik, -s, -ɪŋ, -t
leakage
BR 'liːkɪdʒ, -ɪdʒɪz
AM 'likɪdʒ, -ɪz
leaker
BR 'liːkə(r), -z
AM 'likər, -z
Leakey
BR 'liːki
AM 'liki
leakiness
BR 'liːkɪnɪs
AM 'likɪnɪs
leakproof
BR 'liːkpruːf
AM 'likˌpruf

leaky
BR 'liːk|i, -ɪə(r), -ɪɪst
AM 'liki, -ər, -ɪst
leal
BR liːl
AM lil
Leamington Spa
BR ˌlɛmɪŋt(ə)n
'spɑː(r)
AM ˌlɛmɪŋtən 'spɑ
lean
BR liːn, -z, -ɪŋ, -d, -ə(r),
-ɪst
AM lin, -z, -ɪŋ, -d, -ər, -ɪst
lean-burn
BR ˌliːn'bɜːn
AM 'linˌbɜrn
Leander
BR lɪ'andə(r)
AM li'ændər
leaning
BR 'liːnɪŋ, -z
AM 'linɪŋ, -z
leanly
BR 'liːnli
AM 'linli
Leanne
BR liː'an
AM li'æn
leanness
BR 'liːnnɪs
AM 'li(n)nɪs
leant
BR lɛnt
AM lɛnt
lean-to
BR 'liːntuː, -z
AM 'linˌtu, -z
leap
BR liːp, -s, -ɪŋ, -t
AM lip, -s, -ɪŋ, -t
leaper
BR 'liːpə(r), -z
AM 'lipər, -z
leapfrog
BR 'liːpfrɒg
AM 'lipˌfrɔg, 'lipˌfrɑg
leapt
BR lɛpt
AM lɛpt
Lear
BR lɪə(r)
AM lɪ(ə)r
learn
BR lɜːn, -z, -ɪŋ
AM lɜrn, -z, -ɪŋ
learnability
BR ˌlɜːnə'bɪlɪti
AM ˌlɜrnə'bɪlɪdi
learnable
BR 'lɜːnəbl
AM 'lɜrnəbəl
learned¹
adjective
BR 'lɜːnɪd
AM 'lɜrnəd

learned²
verb
BR lɜːnd, lɜːnt
AM lɜrnd, lɜrnt
learnedly
BR 'lɜːnɪdli
AM 'lɜrnədli
learnedness
BR 'lɜːnɪdnɪs
AM 'lɜrnədnəs
learner
BR 'lɜːnə(r), -z
AM 'lɜrnər, -z
learnt
BR lɜːnt
AM lɜrnt
leasable
BR 'liːsəbl
AM 'lisəbəl
lease
BR liːs, -ɪz, -ɪŋ, -t
AM lis, -ɪz, -ɪŋ, -t
leaseback
BR 'liːsbak, -s
AM 'lisˌbæk, -s
leasehold
BR 'liːshəʊld, -z
AM 'lisˌ(h)oʊld, -z
leaseholder
BR 'liːsˌhəʊldə(r), -z
AM 'lisˌ(h)oʊldər, -z
leaser
BR 'liːsə(r), -z
AM 'lisər, -z
leash
BR liːʃ, -ɪz
AM liʃ, -ɪz
least
BR liːst
AM list
leastways
BR 'liːstweɪz
AM 'listˌweɪz
leastwise
BR 'liːstwʌɪz
AM 'listˌwaɪz
leat
BR liːt, -s
AM lit, -s
leather
BR 'lɛð|ə(r), -əz, -(ə)rɪŋ,
-əd
AM 'lɛðər, -z, -ɪŋ, -d
leatherback
BR 'lɛðəbak, -s
AM 'lɛðərˌbæk, -s
leathercloth
BR 'lɛðəklʊθ, -θs\-ðz
AM 'lɛðərˌklɔ|θ,
'lɛðərˌklɑ|θ, -θs\-ðz
leatherette
BR ˌlɛðə'rɛt
AM ˌlɛðər'ɛt
Leatherhead
BR 'lɛðəhɛd
AM 'lɛðərˌ(h)ɛd

leatheriness
BR ˈleð(ə)rɪnɪs
AM ˈleð(ə)rɪnɪs

leatherjacket
BR ˈleðəˌdʒakɪt, -s
AM ˈleðərˌdʒækət, -s

leathern
BR ˈleðn
AM ˈleðərn

leatherneck
BR ˈleðənek, -s
AM ˈleðərˌnek, -s

leatheroid
BR ˈleðərɔɪd
AM ˈleðəˌrɔɪd

leatherwear
BR ˈleðəweː(r)
AM ˈleðərˌwe(ə)r

leathery
BR ˈleð(ə)ri
AM ˈleð(ə)ri

leave
BR liːv, -z, -ɪŋ
AM liv, -z, -ɪŋ

leaven
BR ˈlevn̩, -z, -ɪŋ, -d
AM ˈlevən, -ənz,
-(ə)nɪŋ, -ənd

leaver
BR ˈliːvə(r), -z
AM ˈlivər, -z

leaves
BR liːvz
AM livz

leavings
BR ˈliːvɪŋz
AM ˈlivɪŋz

Leavis
BR ˈliːvɪs
AM ˈlivɪs

Lebanese
BR ˌlebəˈniːz
AM ˌlebəˈniz

Lebanon
BR ˈlebənən
AM ˈlebəˌnɑn, ˈlebənən

Le Bardo
BR lə ˈbɑːdəʊ
AM lə ˈbɑrdoʊ

Lebensraum
BR ˈleɪb(ə)nzraʊm,
ˈleɪb(ə)nsraʊm
AM ˈleɪbənˌsraʊm,
ˈleɪbənzˌraʊm

Leblanc
BR ləˈblɒŋk, ləˈblɑːŋk,
ləˈblɒ̃
AM ləˈblɑŋk

Lebowa
BR ləˈbəʊə(r)
AM ləˈboʊə

Lec®
BR lek
AM lek

Le Carré
BR lə ˈkareɪ
AM lə kəˈreɪ

lech
BR letʃ, -ɪz, -ɪŋ, -t
AM letʃ, -əz, -ɪŋ, -t

lecher
BR ˈletʃə(r), -z
AM ˈletʃər, -z

lecherous
BR ˈletʃ(ə)rəs
AM ˈletʃ(ə)rəs

lecherously
BR ˈletʃ(ə)rəsli
AM ˈletʃ(ə)rəsli

lecherousness
BR ˈletʃ(ə)rəsnəs
AM ˈletʃ(ə)rəsnəs

lechery
BR ˈletʃ(ə)r|i, -ɪz
AM ˈletʃ(ə)ri, -z

Lechlade
BR ˈletʃleɪd
AM ˈletʃˌleɪd

lecithin
BR ˈlesɪθ(ɪ)n
AM ˈlesəθən

Leclanché
BR ləˈklɑːnʃeɪ,
ləˈklɒʃeɪ
AM ləˈklɑnʃ

Leconfield
BR ˈlek(ə)nfiːld
AM ˈlekənˌfild

Le Corbusier
BR lə ˌkɔːˈb(j)uːzɪeɪ
AM lə ˌkɔrbəˈzjeɪ
FR lə kɔrbyzje

lectern
BR ˈlekt(ə)n, ˈlektəːn,
-z
AM ˈlektərn, -z

lection
BR ˈlekʃn, -z
AM ˈlekʃən, -z

lectionary
BR ˈlekʃn̩(ə)ri, -ɪz
AM ˈlekʃəˌneri, -z

lector
BR ˈlektɔː(r), -z
AM ˈlektər, ˈlekˌtɔ(ə)r,
-z

lectrice
BR lekˈtriːs, ˈlektriːs,
-ɪz
AM ˈlektrəs, -əz

lecture
BR ˈlektʃə(r), -əz,
-(ə)rɪŋ, -əd
AM ˈlek(t)ʃər, -(t)ʃərz,
-tʃərɪŋ\-ʃ(ə)rɪŋ,
-(t)ʃərd

lecturer
BR ˈlektʃ(ə)rə(r), -z
AM ˈlek(t)ʃərər, -z

lecturership
BR ˈlektʃ(ə)rəˌʃɪp, -s
AM ˈlek(t)ʃərərˌʃɪp, -s

lectureship
BR ˈlektʃəˌʃɪp, -s
AM ˈlek(t)ʃərˌʃɪp, -s

lecythi
BR ˈlesɪθaɪ
AM ˈlesəθaɪ

lecythus
BR ˈlesɪθəs
AM ˈlesəθəs

LED
BR ˌeliːˈdiː
AM ˌelˌiˈdi

led
BR led
AM led

Leda
BR ˈliːdə(r)
AM ˈlidə

Ledbetter
BR ˈledbetə(r)
AM ˈledˌbedər

Ledbury
BR ˈledb(ə)ri
AM ˈledˌberi

Lederhosen
BR ˈleɪdəˌhəʊzn
AM ˈleɪdərˌ(h)oʊzn

ledge
BR ledʒ, -ɪz
AM ledʒ, -əz, -d

ledger
BR ˈledʒə(r), -z
AM ˈledʒər, -z

ledgy
BR ˈledʒ|i, -ɪə(r), -ɪɪst
AM ˈledʒi, -ər, -ɪst

Led Zeppelin
BR ˌled ˈzepəlɪn,
+ ˈzepl̩ɪn
AM ˌled ˈzep(ə)lən

lee
BR liː, -z
AM li, -z

leech
BR liːtʃ, -ɪz
AM litʃ, -ɪz

leechcraft
BR ˈliːtʃkrɑːft,
ˈliːtʃkraft
AM ˈlitʃˌkræft

Leeds
BR liːdz
AM lidz

Lee-Enfield
BR ˈliːˈenfiːld, -z
AM ˈliˈenˌfild, -z

leek
BR liːk, -s
AM lik, -s

leer
BR lɪə(r), -z, -ɪŋ, -d
AM lɪ(ə)r, -z, -ɪŋ, -d

leeriness
BR ˈlɪərɪnɪs
AM ˈlɪrɪnɪs

leeringly
BR ˈlɪərɪŋli
AM ˈlɪrɪŋli

leery
BR ˈlɪəri

lecythi (continued)
AM ˈlɪri

lees
BR liːz
AM liz

leet
BR liːt, -s
AM lit, -s

leeward¹
non-technical
BR ˈliːwəd
AM ˈliwərd

leeward²
technical, shipping
BR ˈluːəd
AM ˈluərd

Leeward Islands
BR ˈliːwəd ˌaɪlən(d)z
AM ˈliwərd ˌaɪlən(d)z

leewardly¹
non-technical
BR ˈliːwədli
AM ˈliwərdli

leewardly²
technical, shipping
BR ˈluːədli
AM ˈluərdli

leeway
BR ˈliːweɪ
AM ˈliˌweɪ

left
BR left, -s
AM left, -s

leftie
BR ˈleft|i, -ɪz
AM ˈlefti, -z

leftish
BR ˈleftɪʃ
AM ˈleftɪʃ

leftism
BR ˈleftɪz(ə)m
AM ˈlefˌtɪzəm

leftist
BR ˈleftɪst, -s
AM ˈleftəst, -s

leftmost
BR ˈlef(t)məʊst
AM ˈlef(t)ˌmoʊst

leftover
noun
BR ˈleftəʊvə(r), -z
AM ˈleftˌoʊvər, -z

left-over
adjective
BR ˌleftˈəʊvə(r)
AM ˈleftˌoʊvər

leftward
BR ˈleftwəd, -z
AM ˈleft(t)wərd, -z

lefty
BR ˈleft|i, -ɪz
AM ˈlefti, -z

leg
BR leg, -z, -ɪŋ, -d
AM leg, -z, -ɪŋ, -d

legacy
BR ˈlegəs|i, -ɪz
AM ˈlegəsi, -z

legal
BR ˈliːgl
AM ˈliːgəl

legalese
BR ˌliːgəˈliːz, ˌliːglˈiːz
AM ˌliːgəˈliz

legalisation
BR ˌliːgəlaɪˈzeɪʃn, ˌliːglaɪˈzeɪʃn
AM ˌliːgələˈzeɪʃən, ˌliːgəˌlaɪˈzeɪʃən

legalise
BR ˈliːgəlʌɪz, ˈliːglʌɪz, -ɪz, -ɪŋ, -d
AM ˈliːgəˌlaɪz, -ɪz, -ɪŋ, -d

legalism
BR ˈliːgəlɪz(ə)m, ˈliːglɪz(ə)m
AM ˈliːgəˌlɪzəm

legalist
BR ˈliːgəlɪst, ˈliːglɪst, -s
AM ˈliːgələst, -s

legalistic
BR ˌliːgəˈlɪstɪk, ˌlɪglˈɪstɪk
AM ˌliːgəˈlɪstɪk

legalistically
BR ˌliːgəˈlɪstɪkli, ˌliːglˈɪstɪkli
AM ˌliːgəˈlɪstək(ə)li

legality
BR liːˈgalɪt|i, lɪˈgalɪt|i, -ɪz
AM ləˈgælədi, lɪˈgælədi, -z

legalization
BR ˌliːgəlaɪˈzeɪʃn, ˌliːglʌɪˈzeɪʃn
AM ˌliːgələˈzeɪʃən, ˌliːgəˌlaɪˈzeɪʃən

legalize
BR ˈliːgəlʌɪz, ˈliːglʌɪz, -ɪz, -ɪŋ, -d
AM ˈliːgəˌlaɪz, -ɪz, -ɪŋ, -d

legally
BR ˈliːgli, ˈliːgəli
AM ˈliːgəli

legate
BR ˈlɛgət, -s
AM ˈlɛgət, -s

legatee
BR ˌlɛgəˈtiː, -z
AM ˌlɛgəˈti, -z

legateship
BR ˈlɛgətʃɪp, -s
AM ˈlɛgətˌʃɪp, -s

legatine
BR ˈlɛgətɪn
AM ˈlɛgəˌtin

legation
BR lɪˈgeɪʃn, -z
AM ləˈgeɪʃən, -z

legato
BR lɪˈgɑːtəʊ
AM ləˈgɑdoʊ

legator
BR lɪˈgeɪtə(r), -z
AM ləˈgeɪdər, -z

legend
BR ˈlɛdʒ(ə)nd, -z
AM ˈlɛdʒənd, -z

legendarily
BR ˈlɛdʒ(ə)ndrɪli
AM ˈlɛdʒənˌdɛrəli

legendary
BR ˈlɛdʒ(ə)nd(ə)ri
AM ˈlɛdʒənˌdɛri

legendry
BR ˈlɛdʒ(ə)ndri
AM ˈlɛdʒəndri

leger
BR ˈlɛdʒə(r), -z
AM ˈlɛdʒər, -z

legerdemain
BR ˌlɛdʒədəˈmeɪn
AM ˌlɛdʒərdəˈmeɪn

leger line
BR ˈlɛdʒə lʌɪn, -z
AM ˈlɛdʒər ˌlaɪn, -z

Legg
BR lɛg
AM lɛg

Leggatt
BR ˈlɛgət
AM ˈlɛgət

Legge
BR lɛg
AM ˈlɛg(gi)

legged
BR ˈlɛg(ɪ)d
AM ˈlɛg(ə)d

legger
BR ˈlɛgə(r), -z
AM ˈlɛgər, -z

legginess
BR ˈlɛgɪnɪs
AM ˈlɛgɪnɪs

legging
BR ˈlɛgɪŋ, -z
AM ˈlɛgɪŋ, -z

leggy
BR ˈlɛgi
AM ˈlɛgi

leghorn
BR ˈlɛghɔːn, -z
AM ˈlɛg,(h)ɔ(ə)rn, -z

legibility
BR ˌlɛdʒɪˈbɪlɪti
AM ˌlɛdʒəˈbɪlɪdi

legible
BR ˈlɛdʒɪbl
AM ˈlɛdʒəbəl

legibly
BR ˈlɛdʒɪbli
AM ˈlɛdʒəbli

legion
BR ˈliːdʒ(ə)n, -z
AM ˈliːdʒən, -z, -d

legionary
BR ˈliːdʒən(ə)r|i, ˈliːdʒn(ə)ri, -ɪz
AM ˈliːdʒəˌnɛri, -z

legionella
BR ˌliːdʒəˈnɛlə(r), -z
AM ˌliːdʒəˈnɛlə, -z

legionellae
BR ˌliːdʒəˈnɛliː
AM ˌlidʒəˈnɛli

legionnaire
BR ˌliːdʒəˈnɛː(r), -z
AM ˌlidʒəˈnɛ(ə)r, -z

legislate
BR ˈlɛdʒɪsleɪt, -s, -ɪŋ, -ɪd
AM ˈlɛdʒəˌsleɪ|t, -ts, -dɪŋ, -dɪd

legislation
BR ˌlɛdʒɪˈsleɪʃn
AM ˌlɛdʒəˈsleɪʃən

legislative
BR ˈlɛdʒɪslətɪv
AM ˈlɛdʒəˌsleɪdɪv

legislatively
BR ˈlɛdʒɪslətɪvli
AM ˈlɛdʒəˌsleɪdɪvli

legislator
BR ˈlɛdʒɪsleɪtə(r), -z
AM ˈlɛdʒəˌsleɪdər, -z

legislature
BR ˈlɛdʒɪslətʃə(r), -z
AM ˈlɛdʒəˌsleɪtʃər, -z

legit
BR lɪˈdʒɪt
AM ləˈdʒɪt

legitimacy
BR lɪˈdʒɪtɪməsi
AM ləˈdʒɪdəməsi

legitimate
BR lɪˈdʒɪtɪmət
AM ləˈdʒɪdəmət

legitimately
BR ləˈdʒɪtɪmətli
AM ləˈdʒɪdəmətli

legitimation
BR lɪˌdʒɪtɪˈmeɪʃn
AM ləˌdʒɪtɪˈmeɪʃən

legitimatisation
BR lɪˌdʒɪtɪmətʌɪˈzeɪʃn
AM ləˌdʒɪdəmədəˈzeɪʃən, ləˌdʒɪdəməˌtaɪˈzeɪʃən

legitimatise
BR lɪˈdʒɪtɪmətʌɪz, -ɪz, -ɪŋ, -d
AM ləˈdʒɪdəməˌtaɪz, -ɪz, -ɪŋ, -d

legitimatization
BR lɪˌdʒɪtɪmətʌɪˈzeɪʃn
AM ləˌdʒɪdəmədəˈzeɪʃən, ləˌdʒɪdəməˌtaɪˈzeɪʃən

legitimatize
BR lɪˈdʒɪtɪmətʌɪz, -ɪz, -ɪŋ, -d
AM ləˈdʒɪdəməˌtaɪz, -ɪz, -ɪŋ, -d

legitimisation
BR lɪˌdʒɪtɪmʌɪˈzeɪʃn
AM ləˌdʒɪdəməˈzeɪʃən, ləˌdʒɪdəˌmaɪˈzeɪʃən

legitimise
BR lɪˈdʒɪtɪmʌɪz, -ɪz, -ɪŋ, -d
AM ləˈdʒɪdəˌmaɪz, -ɪz, -ɪŋ, -d

legitimism
BR ləˈdʒɪtɪmɪz(ə)m
AM ləˈdʒɪdəˌmɪzəm

legitimist
BR ləˈdʒɪtɪmɪst, -s
AM ləˈdʒɪdəmɪst, -s

legitimization
BR lɪˌdʒɪtɪmʌɪˈzeɪʃn
AM ləˌdʒɪdəməˈzeɪʃən, ləˌdʒɪdəˌmaɪˈzeɪʃən

legitimize
BR lɪˈdʒɪtɪmʌɪz, -ɪz, -ɪŋ, -d
AM ləˈdʒɪdəˌmaɪz, -ɪz, -ɪŋ, -d

legless
BR ˈlɛgləs
AM ˈlɛgləs

legman
BR ˈlɛgman
AM ˈlɛgˌmæn

legmen
BR ˈlɛgmen
AM ˈlɛgˌmɛn

Lego®
BR ˈlɛgəʊ
AM ˈlɛgoʊ

legroom
BR ˈlɛgruːm, ˈlɛgrʊm
AM ˈlɛgˌrum, ˈlɛgˌrʊm

legume
BR ˈlɛgjuːm, -z
AM ˈlɛg(j)um, -z

leguminous
BR lɪˈgjuːmɪnəs
AM ləˈg(j)umənəs

legwork
BR ˈlɛgwəːk
AM ˈlɛgˌwərk

Lehár
BR leɪˈhɑː(r), ləˈhɑː(r), ˈleɪhɑː(r)
AM ˈleɪˌhɑr

Le Havre
BR lə ˈɑːvrə(r)
AM lə ˈhɑvrə

Lehman
BR ˈleɪmən, ˈliːmən
AM ˈleɪmən, ˈlimən

Lehmann
BR ˈleɪmən, ˈliːmən
AM ˈleɪmən, ˈlimən

lehr
BR lɪə(r), leː(r), -z
AM lɛ(ə)r, -z

Lehrer
BR ˈlɛːrə(r), ˈlɪərə(r)
AM ˈlɛrər

lei
BR leɪ, -z
AM leɪ, -z

Leibniz
BR ˈlʌɪbnɪts, ˈliːbnɪts
AM ˈlaɪbˌnɪts

Leibnizian
BR lʌɪbˈnɪtsɪən, liːbˈnɪtsɪən, -z

Leica AM laɪbˈnɪtsiən, -z
Leica®
BR ˈlʌɪkə(r)
AM ˈlaɪkə
Leicester
BR ˈlɛstə(r)
AM ˈlɛstər
Leicestershire
BR ˈlɛstəʃ(ɪ)ə(r)
AM ˈlɛstərʃɪ(ə)r
Leichhardt
BR ˈlʌɪkhɑːt
AM ˈlaɪk͵(h)ɑrd
Leiden
BR ˈlʌɪdn, ˈleɪdn
AM ˈlaɪdən, ˈleɪdn
Leif
BR liːf
AM lif
Leigh
BR liː
AM li
Leighton
BR ˈleɪtn
AM ˈleɪtn
Leila
BR ˈliːlə(r), ˈleɪlə(r)
AM ˈlilə
Leinster
BR ˈlɛnstə(r)
AM ˈlɛnstər
Leipzig
BR ˈlʌɪpsɪg
AM ˈlaɪpsɪg, ˈlaɪpzɪg
GER ˈlaɪptsɪç
Leishman
BR ˈliːʃmən, ˈlɪʃmən
AM ˈliʃmən
leishmaniasis
BR ͵liːʃməˈnʌɪəsɪs
AM ͵liʃməˈnaɪəsəs
Leister
BR ˈlɛstə(r)
AM ˈlɛstər, ˈlɪstər
leister
BR ˈliːstə(r), -z
AM ˈlistər, -z
leisure
BR ˈlɛʒə(r), -d
AM ˈliʒər, ˈlɛʒər, -d
leisureless
BR ˈlɛʒələs
AM ˈliʒərləs, ˈlɛʒərləs
leisureliness
BR ˈlɛʒəlɪnɪs
AM ˈliʒərlɪnɪs, ˈlɛʒərlɪnɪs
leisurely
BR ˈlɛʒəli
AM ˈliʒərli, ˈlɛʒərli
leisurewear
BR ˈlɛʒəwɛː(r)
AM ˈliʒər͵wɛ(ə)r, ˈlɛʒər͵wɛ(ə)r
Leitch
BR liːtʃ
AM litʃ

Leith
BR liːθ
AM liθ
leitmotif
BR ˈlʌɪtməʊ͵tiːf, -s
AM ͵laɪtmoʊˈtif, -s
leitmotiv
BR ˈlʌɪtməʊ͵tiːf, -s
AM ͵laɪtmoʊˈtif, -s
leitmotive
BR ˈlʌɪt|məʊ͵tiːf, ˈlʌɪt|͵məʊtɪv, -məʊ͵tiːfs \ -͵məʊtɪvz
AM ͵laɪtmoʊˈtif, -s
Leitrim
BR ˈliːtrɪm
AM ˈlitrəm
Leix
BR liːʃ, leɪʃ
AM leɪʃ, liʃ
lek
BR lɛk, -s, -ɪŋ, -t
AM lɛk, -s, -ɪŋ, -t
Leland
BR ˈliːlənd
AM ˈlilənd
Lely
BR ˈliːli
AM ˈlili
LEM
BR lɛm, -z
AM lɛm, -z
leman
BR ˈlɛmən, ˈliːmən, -z
AM ˈlɛmən, -z
Le Mans
BR lə ˈmɒ̃
AM lə ˈmɑn(z)
Lemesurier
BR ləˈmɛʒ(ə)rə(r)
AM lə͵mɛʒəriˈeɪ
lemma
BR ˈlɛmə(r), -z
AM ˈlɛmə, -z
lemmatisation
BR ͵lɛmətʌɪˈzeɪʃn, -z
AM ͵lɛmədəˈzeɪʃən, ͵lɛmə͵taɪˈzeɪʃən, -z
lemmatise
BR ˈlɛmətʌɪz, -ɪz, -ɪŋ, -d
AM ˈlɛmə͵taɪz, -ɪz, -ɪŋ, -d
lemmatization
BR ͵lɛmətʌɪˈzeɪʃn, -z
AM ͵lɛmədəˈzeɪʃən, ͵lɛmə͵taɪˈzeɪʃən, -z
lemmatize
BR ˈlɛmətʌɪz, -ɪz, -ɪŋ, -d
AM ˈlɛmə͵taɪz, -ɪz, -ɪŋ, -d
lemme
BR ˈlɛmi
AM ˈlɛmi
lemming
BR ˈlɛmɪŋ, -z
AM ˈlɛmɪŋ, -z

Lemmon
BR ˈlɛmən
AM ˈlɛmən
Lemnos
BR ˈlɛmnɒs
AM ˈlɛmnoʊs, ˈlɛm͵nɑs
lemon
BR ˈlɛmən, -z
AM ˈlɛmən, -z
lemonade
BR ͵lɛməˈneɪd, -z
AM ͵lɛməˈneɪd, -z
lemony
BR ˈlɛməni
AM ˈlɛməni
lempira
BR lɛmˈpɪərə(r), -z
AM lɛmˈpɪrə, -z
Lemuel
BR ˈlɛmjʊəl, ˈlɛmjʉl
AM ˈlɛmjəwəl
lemur
BR ˈliːmə(r), -z
AM ˈlimər, -z
lemurine
BR ˈliːmjʉrʌɪn, ˈlɛmjʉrʌɪn
AM ˈlim(j)ə͵raɪn, ˈlɛm(j)ə͵raɪn,
lemuroid
BR ˈliːmjʉrɔɪd, ˈlɛmjʉrɔɪd
AM ˈlimjə͵rɔɪd, ˈlɛmjə͵rɔɪd
Len
BR lɛn
AM lɛn
Lena¹
forename
BR ˈliːnə(r)
AM ˈlinə
Lena²
river
BR ˈleɪnə(r), ˈliːnə(r)
AM ˈleɪnə
lend
BR lɛnd, -z, -ɪŋ
AM lɛnd, -z, -ɪŋ
lendable
BR ˈlɛndəbl
AM ˈlɛndəbəl
lender
BR ˈlɛndə(r), -z
AM ˈlɛndər, -z
Lendl
BR ˈlɛndl
AM ˈlɛndl
length
BR lɛŋ(k)θ, -s
AM lɛŋθ, -s
lengthen
BR ˈlɛŋ(k)θ|(ə)n, -(ə)nz, -(ə)nɪŋ \ -ŋɪŋ, -(ə)nd
AM ˈlɛŋθ|ən, -ənz, -(ə)nɪŋ, -ənd

lengthener
BR ˈlɛŋ(k)θ(ə)nə(r), ˈlɛŋ(k)θŋə(r), -z
AM ˈlɛŋθ(ə)nər, -z
lengthily
BR ˈlɛŋ(k)θɪli
AM ˈlɛŋθəli
lengthiness
BR ˈlɛŋ(k)θɪnɪs
AM ˈlɛŋθinɪs
lengthman
BR ˈlɛŋ(k)θmən
AM ˈlɛŋθ͵mæn, ˈlɛŋθmən
lengthmen
BR ˈlɛŋ(k)θmən
AM ˈlɛŋθ͵mɛn, ˈlɛŋθmən
lengthways
BR ˈlɛŋ(k)θweɪz
AM ˈlɛŋθ͵weɪz
lengthwise
BR ˈlɛŋ(k)θwʌɪz
AM ˈlɛŋθ͵waɪz
lengthy
BR ˈlɛŋ(k)θ|i, -ɪə(r), -ɪɪst
AM ˈlɛŋθi, -ər, -ɪɪst
lenience
BR ˈliːnɪəns
AM ˈliniəns, ˈlinjəns
leniency
BR ˈliːnɪənsi
AM ˈliniənsi, ˈlinjənsi
lenient
BR ˈliːnɪənt
AM ˈliniənt, ˈlinjənt
leniently
BR ˈliːnɪəntli
AM ˈliniən(t)li, ˈlinjən(t)li
Lenihan
BR ˈlɛnəhən
AM ˈlɛnə͵hæn
Lenin
BR ˈlɛnɪn
AM ˈlɛnən
RUS lʲenʲin
Leninakan
BR ləˈnɪnəkan
AM ˈlɛnənəˈkan
RUS lʲinʲinaˈkan
Leningrad
BR ˈlɛnɪngrad
AM ˈlɛnən͵græd
RUS lʲinʲinˈgrat
Leninism
BR ˈlɛnɪnɪz(ə)m
AM ˈlɛnən͵ɪzəm
Leninist
BR ˈlɛnɪnɪst, -s
AM ˈlɛnənəst, -s
Leninite
BR ˈlɛnɪnʌɪt, -s
AM ˈlɛnə͵naɪt, -s
lenis
BR ˈliːnɪs
AM ˈlinɪs, ˈleɪnɪs

lenite
BR lɪˈnaɪt, -s, -ɪŋ, -ɪd
AM ˈliˌnaɪ|t, -ts, -dɪŋ, -dɪd

lenition
BR lɪˈnɪʃn, -z
AM ləˈnɪʃən, -z

lenitive
BR ˈlenɪtɪv, -z
AM ˈlenədɪv, -z

lenity
BR ˈlenɪti
AM ˈlenədi

Lennie
BR ˈleni
AM ˈleni

Lennon
BR ˈlenən
AM ˈlenən

Lennox
BR ˈlenəks
AM ˈlenəks

Lenny
BR ˈleni
AM ˈleni

Leno
BR ˈliːnəʊ
AM ˈlenoʊ

leno
BR ˈliːnəʊ, -z
AM ˈlinoʊ, ˈleɪnoʊ, -z

Lenor®
BR lɪˈnɔː(r)
AM ləˈnɔ(ə)r

Lenora
BR lɪˈnɔːrə(r)
AM ləˈnɔrə

Lenore
BR lɪˈnɔː(r)
AM ləˈnɔ(ə)r

Le Nôtre
BR lə ˈnʊtrə(r)
AM lə ˈnɔtrə

Lenox
BR ˈlenəks
AM ˈlenəks

lens
BR lenz, -ɪz, -d
AM lenz, -əz, -d

lensless
BR ˈlenzləs
AM ˈlenzləs

lensman
BR ˈlenzmən
AM ˈlenzmən

lensmen
BR ˈlenzmən
AM ˈlenzmən

lent
BR lent
AM lent

Lenten
BR ˈlent(ə)n
AM ˈlen(t)ən

lenticel
BR ˈlentɪsel, -z
AM ˈlen(t)əˌsel, -z

lenticular
BR lenˈtɪkjələ(r)
AM lenˈtɪkjələr

lentigo
BR lenˈtaɪgəʊ
AM lenˈtaɪgoʊ

lentil
BR ˈlent(ɪ)l, -z
AM ˈlen(t)l, -z

lentisc
BR lenˈtɪsk, -s
AM ˈlenˌtɪsk, -s

lentisk
BR lenˈtɪsk, -s
AM ˈlenˌtɪsk, -s

lento
BR ˈlentəʊ
AM ˈlen(t)oʊ

lentoid
BR ˈlentɔɪd
AM ˈlenˌtɔɪd

Leo
BR ˈliːəʊ
AM ˈlioʊ

Leofric
BR ˈleɪəfrɪk, ˈliːəfrɪk, ˈlefrɪk
AM ˈleɪəfrɪk, ˈliəfrɪk, ˈlefrɪk

Leominster
BR ˈlemstə(r)
AM ˈlemstər

Leon
forename
BR ˈliːɒn, ˈliːən, ˈleɪɒn, ˈleɪən
AM ˈliˌɑn

León
place in Spain
BR leɪˈɒn
AM leɪˈoʊn

Leona
BR lɪˈəʊnə(r)
AM liˈoʊnə

Leonard
BR ˈlenəd
AM ˈlenərd

Leonardo
BR ˌliːəˈnɑːdəʊ, ˌleɪəˈnɑːdəʊ
AM liəˈnɑrdoʊ

leone
BR liːˈəʊn, -z
AM liˈoʊn, -z

Leonid
BR ˈliːənɪd, ˈleɪənɪd
AM ˈliəˌnɪd, ˈleɪəˌnɪd
RUS lʲiaˈnʲit

Léonie
BR ˈliːəni, lɪˈəʊni
AM ˈleɪəni

leonine
BR ˈliːənaɪn
AM ˈliəˌnaɪn

Leonora
BR ˌliːəˈnɔːrə(r)
AM l(i)əˈnɔrə

leopard
BR ˈlepəd, -z
AM ˈlepərd, -z

leopardess
BR ˈlepədes, ˌlepəˈdes, -ɪz
AM ˈlepərdəs, -əz

Leopold
BR ˈliːəpəʊld
AM ˈliəˌpoʊld

Léopoldville
BR ˈliːəpəʊldˌvɪl
AM ˈliəˌpoʊl(d)ˌvɪl

leotard
BR ˈliːə(ʊ)tɑːd, -z
AM ˈliəˌtɑrd, -z

leper
BR ˈlepə(r), -z
AM ˈlepər, -z

lepidolite
BR ˈlepɪdəlaɪt, lɪˈpɪdəlaɪt
AM ləˈpɪdəˌlaɪt, ˈlepədəˌlaɪt

Lepidoptera
BR ˌlepɪˈdɒpt(ə)rə(r)
AM ˌlepəˈdɑptərə

lepidopteran
BR ˌlepɪˈdɒpt(ə)rən, ˌlepɪˈdɒpt(ə)rŋ, -z
AM ˌlepəˈdɑptərən, -z

lepidopterist
BR ˌlepɪˈdɒpt(ə)rɪst, -s
AM ˌlepəˈdɑpt(ə)rəst, -s

lepidopterous
BR ˌlepɪˈdɒpt(ə)rəs
AM ˌlepəˈdɑptərəs

Lepidus
BR ˈlepɪdəs
AM ˈlepədəs

leporine
BR ˈlepərʌɪn
AM ˈlepəˌraɪn, ˈlepərən

leprechaun
BR ˈleprɪkɔːn, -z
AM ˈleprəˌkɑn, ˈleprəˌkɔn, -z

leprosaria
BR ˌleprəˈseːrɪə(r)
AM ˌleprəˈseriə

leprosarium
BR ˌleprəˈseːrɪəm
AM ˌleprəˈseriəm

leprosy
BR ˈleprəsi
AM ˈleprəsi

leprous
BR ˈleprəs
AM ˈleprəs

lepta
BR ˈleptə(r)
AM ˈleptə

Leptis Magna
BR ˌleptɪs ˈmagnə(r)
AM ˈleptəs ˈmɑgnə

leptocephalic
BR ˌleptəʊsɪˈfalɪk, ˌleptəʊkeˈfalɪk
AM ˌleptəsəˈfælɪk

leptocephalous
BR ˌleptəʊˈsef(ə)ləs, ˌleptəʊˈsefləs, ˌleptəʊˈkef(ə)ləs, ˌleptəʊˈkefləs
AM ˌleptəˈsefələs

leptodactyl
BR ˌleptəʊˈdakt(ɪ)l, -z
AM ˌleptəˈdæktl, -z

lepton
BR ˈleptɒn
AM ˈlepˌtɑn, ˈleptən

leptonic
BR lepˈtɒnɪk
AM lepˈtɑnɪk

leptospirosis
BR ˌleptə(ʊ)spaɪˈrəʊsɪs, ˌleptə(ʊ)spɪˈrəʊsɪs
AM ˌleptəˌspaɪˈroʊsəs

leptotene
BR ˈleptə(ʊ)tiːn, -z
AM ˈleptəˌtin, -z

Lepus
BR ˈliːpəs, ˈlepəs
AM ˈlepəs, ˈlipəs

Lermontov
BR ˈleːm(ə)ntɒv
AM lərˈmɑnˌtɔv, ˈlərmɑnˌtɔv, lərˈmɑnˌtɑv, ˈlərmɑnˌtɑv

Leroy
BR ˈliːrɔɪ, ləˈrɔɪ
AM ˈliˌrɔɪ

Lerwick
BR ˈleːwɪk
AM ˈlər(w)ɪk

Les
BR lez
AM les

Lesage
BR ləˈsɑːʒ
AM ləˈsɑʒ

lesbian
BR ˈlezbɪən, -z
AM ˈlezbiən, -z

lesbianism
BR ˈlezbɪənɪz(ə)m
AM ˈlezbiənˌɪzəm

Lesbos
BR ˈlezbɒs
AM ˈlezbɔs, ˈlezˌboʊs

lèse-majesté
BR ˌliːzˈmadʒɪsti
AM ˌlezˌmɑdʒəsˈteɪ

lesion
BR ˈliːʒn, -z
AM ˈliʒən, -z

Lesley
BR ˈlezli
AM ˈlezli, ˈlesli

Leslie
BR ˈlezli

AM ˈlɛzli, ˈlɛsli

Lesney
BR ˈlɛzni
AM ˈlɛzni

Lesotho
BR lɪˈsuːtuː, lɪˈsəʊtəʊ
AM ləˈsut,(h)u,
ləˈsoʊ,ðoʊ

less
BR lɛs, -ə(r)
AM lɛs, -ər

lessee
BR lɛˈsiː, -z
AM lɛˈsi, -z

lesseeship
BR lɛˈsiːˌʃɪp, -s
AM lɛˈsiˌʃɪp, -s

lessen
BR ˈlɛs|n, -nz,
-ŋɪŋ\-nɪŋ, -nd
AM ˈlɛsən, -z, -ɪŋ, -d

Lesseps
BR ˈlɛsɛps, ˈlɛsəps
AM ləˈsɛps

lesser
BR ˈlɛsə(r)
AM ˈlɛsər

Lessing
BR ˈlɛsɪŋ
AM ˈlɛsɪŋ

lesson
BR ˈlɛsn, -z
AM ˈlɛsən, -z

lessor
BR lɛˈsɔː(r), ˈlɛsɔː(r), -z
AM ˈlɛˌsɔ(ə)r, -z

lest
BR lɛst
AM lɛst

Lester
BR ˈlɛstə(r)
AM ˈlɛstər

let
BR lɛt, -s, -ɪŋ
AM lɛ|t, -ts, -dɪŋ

letch
BR lɛtʃ, -ɪz, -ɪŋ, -t
AM lɛtʃ, -əz, -ɪŋ, -t

Letchworth
BR ˈlɛtʃwəθ
AM ˈlɛtʃˌwərθ

letdown
BR ˈlɛtdaʊn, -z
AM ˈlɛtˌdaʊn, -z

lethal
BR ˈliːθl
AM ˈliːθəl

lethality
BR liːˈθalɪti
AM liˈθælədi

lethally
BR ˈliːθl̩i, ˈliːθəli
AM ˈliːθəli

lethargic
BR lɪˈθɑːdʒɪk
AM ləˈθɑːrdʒɪk

lethargically
BR lɪˈθɑːdʒɪkli
AM ləˈθɑːrdʒək(ə)li

lethargy
BR ˈlɛθədʒi
AM ˈlɛθərdʒi

Lethbridge
BR ˈlɛθbrɪdʒ
AM ˈlɛθˌbrɪdʒ

Lethe
BR ˈliːθi
AM ˈliθi

Lethean
BR ˈliːθɪən
AM ˈliθiən

Leticia
BR lɪˈtɪʃ(ɪ)ə(r)
AM ləˈtɪʃə

Letitia
BR lɪˈtɪʃ(ɪ)ə(r)
AM ləˈtɪʃə

Letraset®
BR ˈlɛtrəset
AM ˈlɛtrəˌset

Lett
BR lɛt, -s
AM lɛt, -s

letter
BR ˈlɛt|ə(r), -əz, -(ə)rɪŋ,
-əd
AM ˈlɛdər, -z, -ɪŋ, -d

letterbox
BR ˈlɛtəbɒks, -ɪz
AM ˈlɛdərˌbaks, -əz

letterer
BR ˈlɛt(ə)rə(r), -z
AM ˈlɛdərər, -z

letterhead
BR ˈlɛtəhɛd, -z
AM ˈlɛdərˌ(h)ɛd, -z

letterless
BR ˈlɛtələs
AM ˈlɛdərləs

Letterman
BR ˈlɛtəmən
AM ˈlɛdərmən

letterpress
BR ˈlɛtəprɛs, -ɪz
AM ˈlɛdərˌprɛs, -əz

Lettic
BR ˈlɛtɪk, -s
AM ˈlɛdɪk, -s

Lettice
BR ˈlɛtɪs
AM ˈlɛdɪs

letting
BR ˈlɛtɪŋ, -z
AM ˈlɛdɪŋ, -z

Lettish
BR ˈlɛtɪʃ
AM ˈlɛdɪʃ

lettuce
BR ˈlɛtɪs, -ɪz
AM ˈlɛdəs, -ɪz

letup
BR ˈlɛtʌp, -s
AM ˈlɛdˌəp, -s

leu
BR ˈleɪuː
AM ˈlɛʊ

Leuchars¹
place in UK
BR ˈluːxəz, ˈluːkəz
AM ˈlukərz

Leuchars²
surname
BR ˈluːkəz
AM ˈlukərz

leucine
BR ˈl(j)uːsiːn, -z
AM ˈlusən, ˈluˌsin, -z

leucoblast
BR ˈl(j)uːkə(ʊ)blɑːst,
ˈl(j)uːkə(ʊ)blast, -s
AM ˈlukəˌblæst, -s

leucocyte
BR ˈl(j)uːkə(ʊ)saɪt, -s
AM ˈlukəˌsaɪt, -s

leucocytic
BR ˌl(j)uːkə(ʊ)ˈsɪtɪk
AM ˌlukəˈsɪtɪk

leucoderma
BR ˌluːkə(ʊ)ˈdəːmə(r)
AM ˌlukəˈdərmə

leucoma
BR l(j)uːˈkəʊmə(r), -z
AM luˈkoumə, -z

leucopathy
BR l(j)uːˈkɒpəθi
AM luˈkɑpəθi

leucopenia
BR ˌluːkə(ʊ)piːnɪə(r)
AM ˌlukəˈpiniə

leucoplast
BR ˈluːkəplast,
ˈl(j)uːkəplɑːst
AM ˈlukəˌplæst

leucorrhoea
BR ˌl(j)uːkə(ʊ)ˈriːə(r)
AM ˌlukəˈrɪə

leucotome
BR ˈl(j)uːkətəʊm, -z
AM ˈlukəˌtoum, -z

leucotomize
BR l(j)uːˈkɒtəmʌɪz, -ɪz,
-ɪŋ, -d
AM luˈkadəˌmaɪz, -ɪz,
-ɪŋ, -d

leucotomy
BR l(j)uːˈkɒtəm|i, -ɪz
AM luˈkadəmi, -z

leukaemia
BR l(j)uːˈkiːmɪə(r)
AM luˈkimiə

leukaemic
BR l(j)uːˈkiːmɪk
AM luˈkimɪk

leukaemogen
BR luːˈkiːmədʒ(ə)n, -z
AM luˈkiməˌdʒɛn,
luˈkiməˌdʒɛn, -z

leukaemogenic
BR luːˌkiːməˈdʒɛnɪk
AM luˌkiməˈdʒɛnɪk

leukemia
BR l(j)uːˈkiːmɪə(r)
AM luˈkimiə

leukemic
BR l(j)uːˈkiːmɪk
AM luˈkimɪk

leukemogen
BR luːˈkiːmədʒ(ə)n, -z
AM luˈkiməˌdʒɛn,
luˈkiməˌdʒɛn, -z

leukemogenic
BR luːˌkiːməˈdʒɛnɪk
AM luˌkiməˈdʒɛnɪk

leukocyte
BR ˈl(j)uːkəsʌɪt, -s
AM ˈlukəˌsaɪt, -s

leukotriene
BR ˌluːkə(ʊ)ˈtrʌɪn, -z
AM ˌlukəˈtraɪin, -z

Leuven
BR ˈluːvɛn
AM ˈlʊˌvɛn
FL ˈløvə(n)

lev
BR lɛv, -z
AM lɛv, -z

leva
BR ˈlɛvə(r), -z
AM ˈlɛvə, ˈlɛˌvɑ, -z

Levalloisean
BR ˌləvəˈlwɑːzɪən
AM ˌlɛvəˈlɔɪziən

levant
BR lɪˈvant, -s, -ɪŋ, -ɪd
AM ləˈvænt, ləˈvant, -s,
-ɪŋ, -ɪd

levanter
BR ləˈvantə(r), -z
AM ləˈvæn(t)ər,
ləˈvan(t)ər, -z

Levantine
BR ˈlɛvntʌɪn
AM ləˈvæn(t)ən,
ˈlɛvənˌtaɪn

levator
BR lɪˈveɪtə(r), -z
AM ləˈveɪdər, -z

levee
BR ˈlɛv|i, ˈlɛv|eɪ,
-ɪz\-eɪz
AM ˈlɛvi, -z

level
BR ˈlɛv|l, -lz,
-lɪŋ\-(ə)lɪŋ, -ld
AM ˈlɛv|əl, -əlz, -(ə)lɪŋ,
-əld

leveller
BR ˈlɛvlə(r),
ˈlɛv(ə)lə(r), -z
AM ˈlɛv(ə)lər, -z

levelly
BR ˈlɛvl̩i
AM ˈlɛvəli

levelness
BR ˈlɛvlnəs
AM ˈlɛvəlnəs

lever
BR ˈliːv|ə(r), -əz,
-(ə)rɪŋ, -əd
AM ˈlɛv|ər, ˈlɪv|ər, -ərz,
-(ə)rɪŋ, -ərd

leverage
BR ˈliːv(ə)rɪdʒ,
ˈlɛv(ə)rɪdʒ
AM ˈlɛv(ə)rɪdʒ

leveret
BR ˈlɛv(ə)rɪt, -s
AM ˈlɛv(ə)rət, -s

Leverhulme
BR ˈliːvəhjuːm
AM ˈlɛvərˌhjum

Le Verrier
BR lə ˈvɛrɪeɪ
AM lə verˈjeɪ

Levi¹
Biblical name
BR ˈliːvʌɪ
AM ˈliːˌvaɪ

Levi²
surname
BR ˈlɛvi, ˈliːvi
AM ˈlɛvi

leviable
BR ˈlɛvɪəbl
AM ˈlɛvɪəbəl

leviathan
BR lɪˈvʌɪəθn, -z
AM ləˈvaɪəθən, -z

levigate
BR ˈlɛvɪgeɪt, -s, -ɪŋ, -ɪd
AM ˈlɛvəˌgeɪ|t, -ts, -dɪŋ,
-dɪd

levigation
BR ˌlɛvɪˈgeɪʃn, -z
AM ˌlɛvəˈgeɪʃən, -z

levin
BR ˈlɛvɪn, -z
AM ˈlɛvən, -z

Levine
BR lɪˈviːn
AM ləˈvin, ləˈvaɪn

levirate
BR ˈliːvɪrət, ˈlɛvɪrət, -s
AM ˈlɛvərət, ˈlɛvəˌreɪt,
-s

leviratic
BR ˌliːvɪˈratɪk,
ˌlɛvɪˈratɪk
AM ˌlɛvəˈrædɪk

leviratical
BR ˌliːvɪˈratɪkl,
ˌlɛvɪˈratɪkl
AM ˌlɛvəˈrædəkəl

Levi's®
BR ˈliːvʌɪz
AM ˈliːˌvaɪz

levitate
BR ˈlɛvɪteɪt, -s, -ɪŋ, -ɪd
AM ˈlɛvəˌteɪ|t, -ts, -dɪŋ,
-dɪd

levitation
BR ˌlɛvɪˈteɪʃn
AM ˌlɛvəˈteɪʃən

levitator
BR ˈlɛvɪteɪtə(r), -z
AM ˈlɛvɪˌteɪdər, -z

Levite
BR ˈliːvʌɪt, -s
AM ˈliˌvaɪt, -s

Levitical
BR lɪˈvɪtɪkl
AM ləˈvɪdəkəl

Leviticus
BR lɪˈvɪtɪkəs
AM ləˈvɪdəkəs

Levittown
BR ˈlɛvɪttaʊn
AM ˈlɛvə(t)ˌtaʊn

levity
BR ˈlɛvɪti
AM ˈlɛvədi

levodopa
BR ˌliːvəˈdəʊpə(r),
ˌlɛvəˈdəʊpə(r)
AM ˌlɛvəˈdoʊpə

levorotatory
BR ˌliːvəʊˈrəʊtət(ə)ri
AM ˈliːvoʊˈroʊdəˌtɔri

levulose
BR ˈliːvjʊləʊs,
ˈliːvjʊləʊz, ˈlɛvjʊləʊs,
ˈlɛvjʊləʊz
AM ˈlɛvjələʊs,
ˈlɛvjələʊz

levy
BR ˈlɛv|i, -ɪz, -ɪɪŋ, -ɪd
AM ˈlɛvi, -z, -ɪŋ, -d

lewd
BR l(j)uːd, -ə(r), -ɪst
AM lud, -ər, -əst

lewdly
BR ˈl(j)uːdli
AM ˈludli

lewdness
BR ˈl(j)uːdnəs
AM ˈludnəs

Lewes
BR ˈluːɪs
AM ˈluwəs

lewis
BR ˈluːɪs, -ɪz
AM ˈluwəs, -ɪz

Lewisham
BR ˈluːɪʃ(ə)m
AM ˈluwəʃəm

lewisite
BR ˈluːɪsʌɪt
AM ˈluəˌsaɪt

lex
BR lɛks
AM lɛks

lex domicilii
BR ˌlɛks dɒmɪˈsɪlɪʌɪ
AM ˌlɛks ˌdɑməˈsɪliˌi

lexeme
BR ˈlɛksiːm, -z
AM ˈlɛkˌsim, -z

lexemic
BR lɛkˈsiːmɪk
AM lɛkˈsimɪk

lex fori
BR ˌlɛks ˈfɔːrʌɪ
AM ˌlɛks ˈfɔri

lexical
BR ˈlɛksɪkl
AM ˈlɛksəkəl

lexically
BR ˈlɛksɪkli
AM ˈlɛksək(ə)li

lexicographer
BR ˌlɛksɪˈkɒɡrəfə(r), -z
AM ˌlɛksəˈkɑɡrəfər, -z

lexicographic
BR ˌlɛksɪkəˈɡrafɪk
AM ˌlɛksəkəˈɡræfɪk

lexicographical
BR ˌlɛksɪkəˈɡrafɪkl
AM ˌlɛksəkəˈɡræfəkəl

lexicographically
BR ˌlɛksɪkəˈɡrafɪkli
AM ˌlɛksəkəˈɡræfək(ə)li

lexicography
BR ˌlɛksɪˈkɒɡrəfi
AM ˌlɛksəˈkɑɡrəfi

lexicological
BR ˌlɛksɪkəˈlɒdʒɪkl
AM ˌlɛksəkəˈlɑdʒəkəl

lexicologically
BR ˌlɛksɪkəˈlɒdʒɪkli
AM ˌlɛksəkəˈlɑdʒək(ə)li

lexicologist
BR ˌlɛksɪˈkɒlədʒɪst, -s
AM ˌlɛksəˈkɑlədʒəst, -s

lexicology
BR ˌlɛksɪˈkɒlədʒi
AM ˌlɛksəˈkɑlədʒi

lexicon
BR ˈlɛksɪk(ə)n, -z
AM ˈlɛksəˌkɑn,
ˈlɛksəkən, -z

lexicostatistics
BR ˌlɛksɪkəʊstəˈtɪstɪks
AM ˌlɛksəkoʊstəˈtɪstɪks

lexigraphy
BR lɛkˈsɪɡrəfi
AM lɛkˈsɪɡrəfi

Lexington
BR ˈlɛksɪŋt(ə)n
AM ˈlɛksɪŋtən

lexis
BR ˈlɛksɪs
AM ˈlɛksəs

lex loci
BR ˌlɛks ˈləʊsʌɪ
AM ˌlɛks ˈloʊsi

lex talionis
BR ˌlɛks talɪˈəʊnɪs
AM ˌlɛks ˌtaliˈoʊnəs

Ley
BR liː, leɪ
AM leɪ, li

ley
BR liː, leɪ, -z
AM leɪ, -z

Leyburn
BR ˈleɪbəːn
AM ˈleɪbərn

Leyden
BR ˈlʌɪdn
AM ˈlaɪdən

Leyland
BR ˈleɪlənd
AM ˈleɪlənd, ˈlilənd

leylandii
BR leɪˈlandɪʌɪ
AM leɪˈlændiaɪ

Leyte
BR ˈleɪti
AM ˈleɪˌti

Leyton
BR ˈleɪtn
AM ˈleɪtn

Leytonstone
BR ˈleɪtnstəʊn
AM ˈleɪtnˌstoʊn

Lhasa
BR ˈlɑːsə(r), ˈlasə(r)
AM ˈlɑsə

lhasa apso
BR ˌlɑːsə(r)ˈapsəʊ,
ˌlasə(r) +, -z
AM ˌlɑsə ˈapsoʊ, -z

liability
BR ˌlʌɪəˈbɪlɪt|i, -ɪz
AM ˌlaɪəˈbɪlɪdi, -z

liable
BR ˈlʌɪəbl
AM ˈlaɪəbəl

liaise
BR lɪˈeɪz, -ɪz, -ɪŋ, -d
AM liˈeɪz, -ɪz, -ɪŋ, -d

liaison
BR lɪˈeɪzn, lɪˈeɪzɒn,
lɪˈeɪzõ
AM ˈliəˌzɑn, liˈeɪˌzɑn

Liam
BR ˈliːəm
AM ˈlaɪəm, ˈliəm

liana
BR lɪˈɑːnə(r), -z
AM liˈɑnə, liˈænə, -z

liane
BR lɪˈɑːn, lɪˈan, -z
AM liˈɑn, liˈæn, -z

Lianne
BR lɪˈan
AM liˈæn

Liao
BR lɪˈaʊ
AM lɪˈaʊ

liar
BR ˈlʌɪə(r), -z
AM ˈlaɪ(ə)r, -z

Lias
BR ˈlʌɪəs
AM ˈlaɪəs

liassic
BR lʌɪˈasɪk
AM laɪˈæsɪk

lib
BR lɪb
AM lɪb

libation
BR lʌɪˈbeɪʃn, -z

AM laɪ'beɪʃən, -z
libber
BR 'lɪbə(r), -z
AM 'lɪbər, -z
Libby
BR 'lɪbi
AM 'lɪbi
LibDem
BR ˌlɪb'dɛm, -z
AM ˌlɪb'dɛm, -z
libel
BR 'laɪbl̩, -lz, -lɪŋ \-əlɪŋ, -ld
AM 'laɪbəl, -əlz, -(ə)lɪŋ, -əld
libelant
BR 'laɪbələnt, 'laɪbəln̩t, 'laɪbl̩(ə)nt, -s
AM 'laɪbələnt, -s
libelee
BR ˌlaɪbə'li:, -z
AM ˌlaɪbə'li, -z
libeler
BR 'laɪbl̩ə(r), 'laɪbələ(r), -z
AM 'laɪbələr, -z
libelist
BR 'laɪbl̩ɪst, 'laɪbəlɪst, -s
AM 'laɪbələst, -s
libellant
BR 'laɪbələnt, 'laɪbəln̩t, 'laɪbl̩(ə)nt, -s
AM 'laɪbələnt, -s
libellee
BR ˌlaɪbə'li:, -z
AM ˌlaɪbə'li, -z
libeller
BR 'laɪbl̩ə(r), 'laɪbələ(r), -z
AM 'laɪbələr, -z
libellist
BR 'laɪbl̩ɪst, 'laɪbəlɪst, -s
AM 'laɪbələst, -s
libellous
BR 'laɪbl̩əs, 'laɪbələs
AM 'laɪbələs
libellously
BR 'laɪbl̩əsli, 'laɪbələsli
AM 'laɪbələsli
libelous
BR 'laɪbl̩əs, 'laɪbələs
AM 'laɪbələs
libelously
BR 'laɪbl̩əsli, 'laɪbələsli
AM 'laɪbələsli
liber
BR 'laɪbə(r)
AM 'laɪbər, 'lɪbər
Liberace
BR ˌlɪbə'rɑːtʃi
AM ˌlɪbə'rɑtʃi

liberal
BR 'lɪb(ə)rəl, 'lɪb(ə)rl̩, -z
AM 'lɪb(ə)rəl, -z
liberalisation
BR ˌlɪb(ə)rəlaɪ'zeɪʃn, ˌlɪb(ə)rl̩aɪ'zeɪʃn
AM ˌlɪb(ə)rələ'zeɪʃən, ˌlɪb(ə)rəˌlaɪ'zeɪʃən
liberalise
BR 'lɪb(ə)rəlaɪz, 'lɪb(ə)rl̩aɪz, -ɪz, -ɪŋ, -d
AM 'lɪb(ə)rəˌlaɪz, -ɪz, -ɪŋ, -d
liberaliser
BR 'lɪb(ə)rəlaɪzə(r), 'lɪb(ə)rl̩aɪzə(r), -z
AM 'lɪb(ə)rəˌlaɪzər, -z
liberalism
BR 'lɪb(ə)rəlɪz(ə)m, 'lɪb(ə)rl̩ɪz(ə)m
AM 'lɪb(ə)rəˌlɪzəm
liberalist
BR 'lɪb(ə)rəlɪst, 'lɪb(ə)rl̩ɪst, -s
AM 'lɪb(ə)rələst, -s
liberalistic
BR ˌlɪb(ə)rə'lɪstɪk, ˌlɪb(ə)rl̩'ɪstɪk
AM ˌlɪb(ə)rə'lɪstɪk
liberality
BR ˌlɪbə'ralɪti
AM ˌlɪbə'rælədi
liberalization
BR ˌlɪb(ə)rəlaɪ'zeɪʃn, ˌlɪb(ə)rl̩aɪ'zeɪʃn
AM ˌlɪb(ə)rələ'zeɪʃən, ˌlɪb(ə)rəˌlaɪ'zeɪʃən
liberalize
BR 'lɪb(ə)rəlaɪz, 'lɪb(ə)rl̩aɪz, -ɪz, -ɪŋ, -d
AM 'lɪb(ə)rəˌlaɪz, -ɪz, -ɪŋ, -d
liberalizer
BR 'lɪb(ə)rəlaɪzə(r), 'lɪb(ə)rl̩aɪzə(r), -z
AM 'lɪb(ə)rəˌlaɪzər, -z
liberally
BR 'lɪb(ə)rəli, 'lɪb(ə)rl̩i
AM 'lɪb(ə)rəli
liberalness
BR 'lɪb(ə)rəlnəs, 'lɪb(ə)rl̩nəs
AM 'lɪb(ə)rəlnəs
liberate
BR 'lɪbəreɪt, -s, -ɪŋ, -ɪd
AM 'lɪbəˌreɪt, -ts, -dɪŋ, -dɪd
liberation
BR ˌlɪbə'reɪʃn
AM ˌlɪbə'reɪʃən
liberationist
BR ˌlɪbə'reɪʃnɪst, ˌlɪbə'reɪʃənɪst, -s
AM ˌlɪbə'reɪʃənəst, -s
liberator
BR 'lɪbəreɪtə(r), -z

AM 'lɪbəˌreɪdər, -z
Liberia
BR laɪ'bɪərɪə(r)
AM laɪ'bɪriə
Liberian
BR laɪ'bɪərɪən, -z
AM laɪ'bɪriən, -z
libertarian
BR ˌlɪbə'tɛːrɪən, -z
AM ˌlɪbər'tɛriən, -z
libertarianism
BR ˌlɪbə'tɛːrɪənɪz(ə)m
AM ˌlɪbər'tɛriəˌnɪzəm
libertinage
BR 'lɪbətɪnɪdʒ
AM 'lɪbərˌtinɪdʒ
libertine
BR 'lɪbəti:n, -z
AM 'lɪbərˌtin, -z
libertinism
BR 'lɪbətɪnɪz(ə)m
AM 'lɪbərˌtiˌnɪzəm
liberty
BR 'lɪbətˌi, -ɪz
AM 'lɪbərdi, -z
libidinal
BR lɪ'bɪdɪn(ə)l, lɪ'bɪdn̩(ə)l
AM lə'bɪdn̩əl
libidinally
BR lɪ'bɪdɪnəli, lɪ'bɪdɪnl̩i, lɪ'bɪdn̩əli, lɪ'bɪdn̩l̩i
AM lə'bɪd(ə)nəli
libidinous
BR lɪ'bɪdɪnəs, lɪ'bɪdn̩əs
AM lə'bɪdn̩əs
libidinously
BR lɪ'bɪdɪnəsli, lɪ'bɪdn̩əsli
AM lə'bɪdn̩əsli
libidinousness
BR lɪ'bɪdɪnəsnəs, lɪ'bɪdn̩əsnəs
AM lə'bɪdn̩əsnəs
libido
BR lɪ'bi:dəʊ, -z
AM lə'bidoʊ, -z
libitum
BR 'lɪbɪtəm
AM 'lɪbɪdəm
Lib-Lab
BR ˌlɪb'lab
AM ˌlɪbˌlæb
Li Bo
BR ˌli: 'bəʊ
AM 'li 'boʊ
LIBOR
BR 'laɪbɔː(r)
AM 'laɪbɔ(ə)r
Libra
BR 'li:brə(r), -z
AM 'librə, -z
Libran
BR 'li:brən, 'lɪbrən, -z
AM 'laɪbrən, -z

librarian
BR laɪ'brɛːrɪən, -z
AM laɪ'brɛriən, -z
librarianship
BR laɪ'brɛːrɪənˌʃɪp, -s
AM laɪ'brɛriənˌʃɪp, -s
library
BR 'laɪb(rə)r|i, -ɪz
AM 'laɪˌbrɛri, -z
librate
BR laɪ'breɪt, 'laɪbreɪt, -s, -ɪŋ, -ɪd
AM 'laɪˌbreɪ|t, -ts, -dɪŋ, -dɪd
libration
BR laɪ'breɪʃn, -z
AM laɪ'breɪʃən, -z
libratory
BR 'laɪbrət(ə)ri
AM 'laɪbrəˌtori
librettist
BR lɪ'brɛtɪst, -s
AM lə'brɛdəst, -s
libretto
BR lɪ'brɛtəʊ, -z
AM lə'brɛdoʊ, -z
Libreville
BR 'li:brəvɪl
AM 'librəˌvɪl
Librium®
BR 'lɪbrɪəm
AM 'lɪbriəm
Libya
BR 'lɪbɪə(r), 'lɪbjə(r)
AM 'lɪbiə
Libyan
BR 'lɪbɪən, 'lɪbjən, -z
AM 'lɪbiən, -z
lice
BR laɪs
AM laɪs
licence
BR 'laɪs(ə)ns, -ɪz, -ɪŋ, -t
AM 'laɪsns, -ɪz, -ɪŋ, -t
licensable
BR 'laɪs(ə)nsəbl̩
AM 'laɪsnsəbəl
license
BR 'laɪs(ə)ns, -ɪz, -ɪŋ, -t
AM 'laɪsns, -ɪz, -ɪŋ, -t
licensee
BR ˌlaɪs(ə)n'si:, -z
AM ˌlaɪsn̩'si, -z
licenser
BR 'laɪs(ə)nsə(r), -z
AM 'laɪsnsər, -z
licensor
BR 'laɪs(ə)nsə(r), -z
AM 'laɪsnsər, -z
licentiate
BR laɪ'sɛnʃɪət, -s
AM laɪ'sɛnʃ(i)ɪt, -s
licentious
BR laɪ'sɛnʃəs
AM laɪ'sɛnʃəs
licentiously
BR laɪ'sɛnʃəsli

AM laɪˈsɛnʃəsli
licentiousness
BR ˌlʌɪˈsɛnʃəsnəs
AM laɪˈsɛnʃəsnəs
lichee
BR lʌɪˈtʃiː, ˈlʌɪtʃiː,
'liːtʃiː, 'lɪtʃiː, -z
AM ˈliːtʃi, -z
lichen
BR ˈlɪtʃ(ɪ)n, ˈlʌɪk(ə)n,
-z, -d
AM ˈlaɪkən, -z, -d
lichenology
BR ˌlɪtʃɪˈnɒlədʒi,
ˌlʌɪkəˈnɒlədʒi
AM ˌlaɪkəˈnɑlədʒi
lichenous
BR ˈlɪtʃɪnəs, ˈlʌɪkənəs
AM ˈlaɪkənəs
Lichfield
BR ˈlɪtʃfiːld
AM ˈlɪtʃˌfild
lich-gate
BR ˈlɪtʃgeɪt, -s
AM ˈlɪtʃˌgeɪt, -s
Lichtenstein
BR ˈlɪkt(ə)nstʌɪn,
ˈlɪxt(ə)nstʌɪn
AM ˈlɪktənˌstaɪn
licit
BR ˈlɪsɪt
AM ˈlɪsɪt
licitly
BR ˈlɪsɪtli
AM ˈlɪsɪtli
lick
BR lɪk, -s, -ɪŋ, -t
AM lɪk, -s, -ɪŋ, -t
licker
BR ˈlɪkə(r), -z
AM ˈlɪkər, -z
lickerish
BR ˈlɪk(ə)rɪʃ
AM ˈlɪk(ə)rɪʃ
lickety-split
BR ˌlɪkɪtɪˈsplɪt
AM ˌlɪkədiˈsplɪt
licking
BR ˈlɪkɪŋ, -z
AM ˈlɪkɪŋ, -z
lickspittle
BR ˈlɪkˌspɪtl, -z
AM ˈlɪkˌspɪdəl, -z
licorice
BR ˈlɪk(ə)rɪʃ, ˈlɪk(ə)rɪs
AM ˈlɪk(ə)rɪʃ
lictor
BR ˈlɪktə(r), ˈlɪktɔː(r),
-z
AM ˈlɪktər, -z
lid
BR lɪd, -z, -ɪd
AM lɪd, -z, -ɪd
lidar
BR ˈlʌɪdɑː(r)
AM ˈlaɪˌdɑr

Liddell
BR ˈlɪdl
AM ˈlɪdəl, lɪˈdɛl
lidless
BR ˈlɪdlɪs
AM ˈlɪdləs
lido
BR ˈliːdəʊ, ˈlʌɪdəʊ, -z
AM ˈlidoʊ, -z
lidocaine
BR ˈlʌɪdəkeɪn
AM ˈlaɪdəˌkeɪn
lie
BR lʌɪ, -z, -ɪŋ, -d
AM laɪ, -z, -ɪŋ, -d
Liebfraumilch
BR ˈliːbfraʊmɪlk,
ˈliːbfraʊmɪlʃ,
ˈliːbfraʊmɪlx
AM ˈlibˌfraʊˌmɪltʃ
Liebig
BR ˈliːbɪg
AM ˈlibɪg
Liechtenstein
BR ˈlɪkt(ə)nstʌɪn,
ˈlɪxt(ə)nstʌɪn
AM ˈlɪktənˌstaɪn
Liechtensteiner
BR ˈlɪkt(ə)nstʌɪnə(r),
ˈlɪxt(ə)nstʌɪnə(r), -z
AM ˈlɪktənˌstaɪnər, -z
Lied
song
BR liːd
AM lid
lied
past tense
BR lʌɪd
AM laɪd
Lieder
BR ˈliːdə(r)
AM ˈlidər
Liederkrantz
BR ˈliːdəkranz,
ˈliːdəkrants
AM ˈlidərˌkrænz,
ˈlidərˌkræn(t)s
lief
BR liːf
AM lif
Liège
BR lɪˈeɪʒ
AM liˈɛʒ
liege
BR liːdʒ, -ɪz
AM li(d)ʒ, -ɪz
liegeman
BR ˈliːdʒmən
AM ˈli(d)ʒˌmæn,
ˈli(d)ʒmən
liegemen
BR ˈliːdʒmən
AM ˈli(d)ʒˌmɛn,
ˈli(d)ʒmən
lie-in
BR ˈlʌɪɪn, ˌlʌɪˈɪn, -z
AM ˈlaɪˌɪn, -z

lien
BR ˈliː(ə)n, -z
AM ˈli(ə)n, -z
lierne
BR lɪˈəːn, -z
AM liˈərn, -z
lieu
BR l(j)uː
AM l(j)u
lieutenancy
BR lɛfˈtɛnəns|i,
ləfˈtɛnəns|i, -ɪz
AM luˈtɛnənsi, -z
lieutenant
BR lɛfˈtɛnənt,
ləfˈtɛnənt, -s
AM luˈtɛnənt, -s
lieux
BR l(j)uː
AM l(j)u
life
BR lʌɪf
AM laɪf
lifebelt
BR ˈlʌɪfbɛlt, -s
AM ˈlaɪfˌbɛlt, -s
lifeblood
BR ˈlʌɪfblʌd
AM ˈlaɪfˌbləd
lifeboat
BR ˈlʌɪfbəʊt, -s
AM ˈlaɪfˌboʊt, -s
lifeboatman
BR ˈlʌɪfbəʊtmən
AM ˈlaɪfˌboʊtmən
lifeboatmen
BR ˈlʌɪfbəʊtmən
AM ˈlaɪfˌboʊtmən
lifebuoy
BR ˈlʌɪfbɔɪ, -z
AM ˈlaɪfˌbɔɪ, ˈlaɪfˌbui, -z
lifeguard
BR ˈlʌɪfgɑːd, -z
AM ˈlaɪfˌgɑrd, -z
lifejacket
BR ˈlʌɪfˌdʒakɪt, -s
AM ˈlaɪfˌdʒækət, -s
lifeless
BR ˈlʌɪflɪs
AM ˈlaɪflɪs
lifelessly
BR ˈlʌɪflɪsli
AM ˈlaɪflɪsli
lifelessness
BR ˈlʌɪflɪsnɪs
AM ˈlaɪflɪsnɪs
lifelike
BR ˈlʌɪflʌɪk
AM ˈlaɪfˌlaɪk
lifelikeness
BR ˈlʌɪflʌɪknɪs
AM ˈlaɪfˌlaɪknɪs
lifeline
BR ˈlʌɪflʌɪn, -z
AM ˈlaɪfˌlaɪn, -z
lifelong
BR ˈlʌɪflɒŋ, ˌlʌɪfˈlɒŋ

AM ˈlaɪfˌlɒŋ, ˈlaɪfˌlɑŋ
lifer
BR ˈlʌɪfə(r), -z
AM ˈlaɪfər, -z
lifesaver
BR ˈlʌɪfˌseɪvə(r), -z
AM ˈlaɪfˌseɪvər, -z
lifespan
BR ˈlʌɪfspan, -z
AM ˈlaɪfˌspæn, -z
lifestyle
BR ˈlʌɪfstʌɪl, -z
AM ˈlaɪfˌstaɪl, -z
lifetime
BR ˈlʌɪftʌɪm, -z
AM ˈlaɪfˌtaɪm, -z
Liffey
BR ˈlɪfi
AM ˈlɪfi
Lifford
BR ˈlɪfəd
AM ˈlɪfərd
LIFO
last in, first out
BR ˈliːfəʊ
AM ˈlifoʊ
lift
BR lɪft, -s, -ɪŋ, -ɪd
AM lɪft, -s, -ɪŋ, -ɪd
liftable
BR ˈlɪftəbl
AM ˈlɪftəbəl
liftboy
BR ˈlɪf(t)bɔɪ, -z
AM ˈlɪf(t)ˌbɔɪ, -z
lifter
BR ˈlɪftə(r), -z
AM ˈlɪftər, -z
liftgate
BR ˈlɪf(t)geɪt, -s
AM ˈlɪf(t)ˌgeɪt, -s
liftman
BR ˈlɪf(t)man
AM ˈlɪf(t)ˌmæn
liftmen
BR ˈlɪf(t)mɛn
AM ˈlɪf(t)ˌmɛn
lig
BR lɪg, -z, -ɪŋ, -d
AM lɪg, -z, -ɪŋ, -d
ligament
BR ˈlɪgəm(ə)nt, -s
AM ˈlɪgəmənt, -s
ligamental
BR ˌlɪgəˈmɛntl
AM ˌlɪgəˈmɛn(t)l
ligamentary
BR ˌlɪgəˈmɛnt(ə)ri
AM ˌlɪgəˈmɛn(t)əri
ligamentous
BR ˌlɪgəˈmɛntəs
AM ˌlɪgəˈmɛn(t)əs
ligand
BR ˈlɪg(ə)nd, -z
AM ˈlɪgənd, ˈlaɪgənd, -z

ligate
BR ˈlaɪgeɪt, lɪˈgeɪt, -s,
-ɪŋ, -d
AM ˈlaɪˌgeɪt, -ts, -dɪŋ,
-dɪd

ligation
BR laɪˈgeɪʃn, lɪˈgeɪʃn,
-z
AM laɪˈgeɪʃən, -z

ligature
BR ˈlɪgətʃə(r),
ˈlɪgətʃʊə(r),
ˈlɪgɪtjʊə(r), -z
AM ˈlɪgətʃər,
ˈlɪgəˌtʃʊ(ə)r, -z

liger
BR ˈlaɪgə(r), -z
AM ˈlaɪgər, -z

ligger
BR ˈlɪgə(r), -z
AM ˈlɪgər, -z

light
BR laɪt, -s, -ɪŋ, -ə(r), -ɪst
AM laɪt, -ts, -dɪŋ, -dər,
-dɪst

lighten
BR ˈlaɪt|n, -nz,
-ɪŋ\-nɪŋ, -nd
AM ˈlaɪtn, -z, -ɪŋ, -d

lightening
BR ˈlaɪtnɪŋ, ˈlaɪtnɪŋ, -z
AM ˈlaɪtnɪŋ, ˈlaɪtnɪŋ, -z

lighter
BR ˈlaɪtə(r), -z
AM ˈlaɪdər, -z

lighterage
BR ˈlaɪt(ə)rɪdʒ
AM ˈlaɪdərɪdʒ

lighterman
BR ˈlaɪtəmən
AM ˈlaɪdərmən

lightermen
BR ˈlaɪtəmən
AM ˈlaɪdərmən

lightfast
BR ˈlaɪtfɑːst, ˈlaɪtfast
AM ˈlaɪtˌfæst

lightfoot
BR ˈlaɪtfʊt, -s
AM ˈlaɪtˌfʊt, -s

light-footed
BR ˈlaɪtˈfʊtɪd
AM ˈlaɪtˈfʊdəd

light-footedly
BR ˈlaɪtˈfʊtɪdli
AM ˈlaɪtˈfʊdədli

light-footedness
BR ˈlaɪtˈfʊtɪdnɪs
AM ˈlaɪtˈfʊdədnəs

light-handed
BR ˈlaɪtˈhandɪd
AM ˈlaɪtˈhæn(d)əd

light-handedly
BR ˈlaɪtˈhandɪdli
AM ˈlaɪtˈhæn(d)ədli

light-handedness
BR ˈlaɪtˈhandɪdnɪs
AM ˈlaɪtˈhæn(d)ədnəs

light-headed
BR ˌlaɪtˈhedɪd
AM ˈlaɪtˈhedəd

light-headedly
BR ˌlaɪtˈhedɪdli
AM ˈlaɪtˈhedədli

light-headedness
BR ˌlaɪtˈhedɪdnɪs
AM ˈlaɪtˈhedədnəs

light-hearted
BR ˌlaɪtˈhɑːtɪd
AM ˈlaɪtˈhɑrdəd

light-heartedly
BR ˌlaɪtˈhɑːtɪdli
AM ˈlaɪtˈhɑrdədli

light-heartedness
BR ˌlaɪtˈhɑːtɪdnɪs
AM ˈlaɪtˈhɑrdədnəs

lighthouse
BR ˈlaɪthaʊ|s, -zɪz
AM ˈlaɪt,(h)aʊ|s, -zəz

lighting
BR ˈlaɪtɪŋ
AM ˈlaɪdɪŋ

lightish
BR ˈlaɪtɪʃ
AM ˈlaɪdɪʃ

lightless
BR ˈlaɪtlɪs
AM ˈlaɪtlɪs

lightly
BR ˈlaɪtli
AM ˈlaɪtli

lightness
BR ˈlaɪtnɪs
AM ˈlaɪtnɪs

lightning
BR ˈlaɪtnɪŋ
AM ˈlaɪtnɪŋ

light of day
BR ˌlaɪt əv ˈdeɪ
AM ˈlaɪt əv ˈdeɪ

light-o'-love
BR ˈlaɪtəˈlʌv
AM ˈlaɪdəˈləv

lightproof
BR ˈlaɪtpruːf
AM ˈlaɪtˌpruf

lightship
BR ˈlaɪtˈʃɪp, -s
AM ˈlaɪtˌʃɪp, -s

lightsome
BR ˈlaɪts(ə)m
AM ˈlaɪtsəm

lightsomely
BR ˈlaɪts(ə)mli
AM ˈlaɪtsəmli

lightsomeness
BR ˈlaɪts(ə)mnəs
AM ˈlaɪtsəmnəs

lightweight
BR ˈlaɪtweɪt, -s
AM ˈlaɪtˌweɪt, -s

lightwood
BR ˈlaɪtwʊd, -z
AM ˈlaɪtˌwʊd, -z

lign-aloe
BR ˌlaɪnˈaləʊ, -z
AM ˈlaɪnˌæloʊ, -z

ligneous
BR ˈlɪgnɪəs
AM ˈlɪgnɪəs

ligniferous
BR lɪgˈnɪf(ə)rəs
AM lɪgˈnɪfərəs

lignification
BR ˌlɪgnɪfɪˈkeɪʃn
AM ˌlɪgnəfəˈkeɪʃən

ligniform
BR ˈlɪgnɪfɔːm
AM ˈlɪgnəˌfɔ(ə)rm

lignify
BR ˈlɪgnɪfaɪ, -z, -ɪŋ, -d
AM ˈlɪgnəˌfaɪ, -z, -ɪŋ, -d

lignin
BR ˈlɪgnɪn
AM ˈlɪgnən

lignite
BR ˈlɪgnaɪt
AM ˈlɪgˌnaɪt

lignitic
BR lɪgˈnɪtɪk
AM lɪgˈnɪdɪk

lignocaine
BR ˈlɪgnə(ʊ)keɪn
AM ˈlɪgnəˌkeɪn

lignum
BR ˈlɪgnəm
AM ˈlɪgnəm

lignum vitae
BR ˌlɪgnəm ˈvʌitiː,
+ ˈviːtaɪ
AM ˈlɪgnəm ˈvaɪˌdi,
+ ˈviˌtaɪ

ligroin
BR ˈlɪgrəʊɪn
AM ˈlɪgroʊwən

ligroine
BR ˈlɪgrəʊiːn
AM ˈlɪgroʊwən

ligulate
BR ˈlɪgjʊleɪt
AM ˈlɪgjəˌleɪt

ligule
BR ˈlɪgjuːl, -z
AM ˈlɪˌgjul, -z

Liguria
BR lɪˈgjʊərɪə(r)
AM ləˈgʊriə

Ligurian
BR lɪˈgjʊərɪən, -z
AM ləˈgurɪən, -z

ligustrum
BR lɪˈgʌstrəm, -z
AM ləˈgəstrəm, -z

likability
BR ˌlaɪkəˈbɪlɪti
AM ˌlaɪkəˈbɪlɪdi

likable
BR ˈlaɪkəbl
AM ˈlaɪkəbəl

likableness
BR ˈlaɪkəblnəs

like
BR laɪk, -s, -ɪŋ, -t
AM laɪk, -s, -ɪŋ, -t

likeability
BR ˌlaɪkəˈbɪlɪti
AM ˌlɪkəˈbɪlɪdi

likeable
BR ˈlaɪkəbl
AM ˈlaɪkəbəl

likeableness
BR ˈlaɪkəblnəs
AM ˈlaɪkəbəlnəs

likeably
BR ˈlaɪkəbli
AM ˈlaɪkəbli

likelihood
BR ˈlaɪklɪhʊd
AM ˈlaɪkli,(h)ʊd

likeliness
BR ˈlaɪklɪnɪs
AM ˈlaɪklɪnɪs

likely
BR ˈlaɪkl|i, -ɪə(r), -ɪɪst
AM ˈlaɪkli, -ər, -ɪst

like-minded
BR ˌlaɪkˈmaɪndɪd
AM ˈlaɪkˈmaɪndɪd

like-mindedly
BR ˌlaɪkˈmaɪndɪdli
AM ˈlaɪkˈmaɪndɪdli

like-mindedness
BR ˌlaɪkˈmaɪndɪdnɪs
AM ˈlaɪkˈmaɪndɪdnɪs

liken
BR ˈlaɪk|(ə)n, -(ə)nz,
-ɪŋ\-(ə)nɪŋ, -(ə)nd
AM ˈlaɪk|ən, -ənz,
-(ə)nɪŋ, -ənd

likeness
BR ˈlaɪknɪs, -ɪz
AM ˈlaɪknɪs, -ɪz

likewise
BR ˈlaɪkwʌɪz
AM ˈlaɪkˌwaɪz

liking
BR ˈlaɪkɪŋ, -z
AM ˈlaɪkɪŋ, -z

Likud
BR lɪˈkʊd
AM lɪˈkʊd

likuta
BR lɪˈkuːtə(r)
AM lɪˈkudə

lilac
BR ˈlaɪlək, -s
AM ˈlaɪˌlak, ˈlaɪlək, -s

lilangeni
BR ˌliːlaŋˈgeɪni
AM ˌlɪlaŋˈgeɪni

liliaceous
BR ˌlɪlɪˈeɪʃəs
AM ˌlɪliˈeɪʃəs

Lilian
BR ˈlɪlɪən
AM ˈlɪlɪən

Lilienthal
BR ˈlɪliəntɑːl
AM ˈlɪliən‚tɑl

Lilith
BR ˈlɪlɪθ
AM ˈlɪlɪθ

Lille
BR liːl
AM lɪl

Lillee
BR ˈlɪli
AM ˈlɪli

Lil-lets®
BR lɪˈlɛts
AM lɪˈlɛts

Lilley
BR ˈlɪli
AM ˈlɪli

Lillian
BR ˈlɪliən
AM ˈlɪljən, ˈlɪliən

Lilliburlero
BR ‚lɪlɪbəˈlɛːrəʊ
AM ‚lɪlibərˈlɛroʊ

Lillie
BR ˈlɪli
AM ˈlɪli

Lilliput
BR ˈlɪlɪpʌt, ˈlɪlɪpʊt
AM ˈlɪlɪpʊt, ˈlɪlɪpət

Lilliputian
BR ‚lɪlɪˈpjuːʃn
AM ‚lɪləˈpjuʃən

Lilly
BR ˈlɪli
AM ˈlɪli

lillywhite
BR ˈlɪlɪˈwʌɪt
AM ˈlɪliˈ(h)waɪt

lilo
BR ˈlʌɪləʊ, -z
AM ˈlaɪloʊ, -z

Lilongwe
BR lɪˈlɒŋwi, lɪˈlɒŋwei
AM ləˈlɑŋwi, ləˈlɑŋwei

lilt
BR lɪlt, -s, -ɪŋ, -ɪd
AM lɪlt, -s, -ɪŋ, -ɪd

lily
BR ˈlɪl|i, -ɪz, -ɪd
AM ˈlɪli, -z, -d

lily-livered
BR ˈlɪlɪˈlɪvəd
AM ˈlɪli‚lɪvərd

Lima
Peru
BR ˈliːmə(r)
AM ˈliːmə

lima bean
BR ˈliːmə ‚biːn,
ˈlaɪmə +, -z
AM ˈlaɪmə ‚bin, -z

Limassol
BR ˈlɪməsɒl
AM ˈlɪmə‚sɔl, ˈlɪmə‚sɑl

limb
BR lɪm, -z, -d

AM lɪm, -z, -(b)d

limber¹
BR ˈlɪmbə(r)
AM ˈlɪmər, -z

limber²
verb, adjective, noun
'gun carriage'
BR ˈlɪmb|ə(r), -əz,
-(ə)rɪŋ, -əd
AM ˈlɪmb|ər, -ərz,
-(ə)rɪŋ, -ərd

limberness
BR ˈlɪmbənəs
AM ˈlɪmbərnəs

limbi
BR ˈlɪmbʌɪ
AM ˈlɪm‚baɪ

limbic
BR ˈlɪmbɪk
AM ˈlɪmbɪk

limbless
BR ˈlɪmlɪs
AM ˈlɪmlɪs

limbo
BR ˈlɪmbəʊ, -z
AM ˈlɪmboʊ, -z

Limburg
BR ˈlɪmbəːg
AM ˈlɪm‚bɜrg

Limburger
BR ˈlɪmbəːgə(r), -z
AM ˈlɪm‚bɜrgər, -z

limbus
BR ˈlɪmbəs
AM ˈlɪmbəs

lime
BR lʌɪm, -z, -ɪŋ, -d
AM laɪm, -z, -ɪŋ, -d

limeade
BR ‚lʌɪmˈeɪd, -z
AM ˈlaɪmˈeɪd, -z

Limehouse
BR ˈlʌɪmhaʊs
AM ˈlaɪm‚(h)aʊs

limejuice
BR ˈlʌɪmdʒuːs, -ɪz
AM ˈlaɪm‚dʒus, -əz

limekiln
BR ˈlʌɪmkɪln, -z
AM ˈlaɪm‚kɪl(n), -z

limeless
BR ˈlʌɪmlɪs
AM ˈlaɪmlɪs

limelight
BR ˈlʌɪmlʌɪt, -s
AM ˈlaɪm‚laɪt, -s

limen
BR ˈlʌɪmɛn, ˈlʌɪmən
AM ˈlaɪmən

limepit
BR ˈlʌɪmpɪt, -s
AM ˈlaɪm‚pɪt, -s

limerick
BR ˈlɪm(ə)rɪk, -s
AM ˈlɪm(ə)rɪk, -s

limestone
BR ˈlʌɪmstəʊn
AM ˈlaɪm‚stoʊn

limewash
BR ˈlʌɪmwɒʃ, -ɪz
AM ˈlaɪm‚wɑʃ,
ˈlaɪm‚wɒʃ, -əz

lime-wort
BR ˈlʌɪmwəːt, -s
AM ˈlaɪm‚wərt,
ˈlaɪm‚wɔ(ə)rt, -s

limey
BR ˈlʌɪm|i, -ɪz
AM ˈlaɪmi, -z

limina
BR ˈlɪmɪnə(r)
AM ˈlɪmɪnə

liminal
BR ˈlɪmɪnl
AM ˈlɪmɪnəl

liminality
BR ‚lɪmɪˈnalɪti
AM ‚lɪməˈnælədi

limit
BR ˈlɪm|ɪt, -ɪts, -ɪtɪŋ,
-ɪtɪd
AM ˈlɪmɪ|t, -ts, -dɪŋ, -dɪd

limitable
BR ˈlɪmɪtəbl
AM ˈlɪmɪdəbəl

limitary
BR ˈlɪmɪt(ə)ri
AM ˈlɪmə‚teri

limitation
BR ‚lɪmɪˈteɪʃn, -z
AM ‚lɪməˈteɪʃən, -z

limitative
BR ˈlɪmɪtətɪv
AM ˈlɪmə‚teɪdɪv

limitedly
BR ˈlɪmɪtɪdli
AM ˈlɪmɪdɪdli

limitedness
BR ˈlɪmɪtɪdnɪs
AM ˈlɪmɪdɪdnɪs

limiter
BR ˈlɪmɪtə(r), -z
AM ˈlɪmɪdər, -z

limitless
BR ˈlɪmɪtlɪs
AM ˈlɪmɪtlɪs

limitlessly
BR ˈlɪmɪtlɪsli
AM ˈlɪmɪtlɪsli

limitlessness
BR ˈlɪmɪtlɪsnɪs
AM ˈlɪmɪtlɪsnɪs

limn
BR lɪm, -z, -ɪŋ, -d
AM lɪm, -z, -ɪŋ, -d

limner
BR ˈlɪm(n)ə(r), -z
AM ˈlɪm(n)ər, -z

limnological
BR ‚lɪmnəˈlɒdʒɪkl
AM ‚lɪmnəˈlɑdʒəkəl

limnologist
BR lɪmˈnɒlədʒɪst, -s
AM lɪmˈnɑlədʒəst, -s

limnology
BR lɪmˈnɒlədʒi
AM lɪmˈnɑlədʒi

limo
BR ˈlɪməʊ, -z
AM ˈlɪmoʊ, -z

Limoges
BR lɪˈməʊʒ
AM ləˈmoʊʒ

Limousin
BR ‚lɪməˈzɑ̃, -z
AM ‚lɪmə‚zin, ‚lɪməˈzin,
-z

limousine
BR ‚lɪməˈziːn,
ˈlɪməziːn, -z
AM ‚lɪmə‚zin, ‚lɪməˈzin,
-z

limp
BR lɪm|p, -ps, -pɪŋ, -(p)t
AM lɪmp, -s, -ɪŋ, -t

limpet
BR ˈlɪmpɪt, -s
AM ˈlɪmpɪt, -s

limpid
BR ˈlɪmpɪd
AM ˈlɪmpɪd

limpidity
BR lɪmˈpɪdɪti
AM lɪmˈpɪdɪdi

limpidly
BR ˈlɪmpɪdli
AM ˈlɪmpɪdli

limpidness
BR ˈlɪmpɪdnɪs
AM ˈlɪmpɪdnɪs

limpingly
BR ˈlɪmpɪŋli
AM ˈlɪmpɪŋli

limpkin
BR ˈlɪm(p)kɪn
AM ˈlɪm(p)kɪn

limply
BR ˈlɪmpli
AM ˈlɪmpli

limpness
BR ˈlɪmpnɪs
AM ˈlɪmpnɪs

Limpopo
BR lɪmˈpəʊpəʊ
AM lɪmˈpoʊpoʊ

limpwort
BR ˈlɪmpwəːt, -s
AM ˈlɪmpwərt,
ˈlɪmpwɔ(ə)rt, -s

limp-wristed
BR ˈlɪmpˈrɪstɪd
AM ˈlɪmp‚rɪstɪd

limuli
BR ˈlɪmjʊlʌɪ
AM ˈlɪmjə‚laɪ

limulus
BR ˈlɪmjʊləs
AM ˈlɪmjələs

limy
BR 'laɪm|i, -ɪə(r), -ɪst
AM 'laɪmi, -ər, -ɪst

Linacre
BR 'lɪnəkə(r)
AM 'lɪnəkər

linage
BR 'laɪn|ɪdʒ, -ɪdʒɪz
AM 'laɪnɪdʒ, -ɪz

Linch
BR lɪn(t)ʃ
AM lɪn(t)ʃ

linchpin
BR 'lɪn(t)ʃpɪn, -z
AM 'lɪn(t)ʃˌpɪn, -z

Lincoln
BR 'lɪŋk(ə)n
AM 'lɪŋkən

Lincolnshire
BR 'lɪŋk(ə)nʃ(ɪ)ə(r)
AM 'lɪŋkənʃɪ(ə)r

Lincrusta®
BR ˌlɪŋ'krʌstə(r)
AM ˌlɪn'krəstə,
ˌlɪŋ'krəstə

Lincs.
Lincolnshire
BR lɪŋks
AM lɪŋks

linctus
BR 'lɪŋ(k)təs
AM 'lɪŋktəs

Lind
BR lɪnd
AM lɪnd

Linda
BR 'lɪndə(r)
AM 'lɪndə

lindane
BR 'lɪndeɪn
AM 'lɪnˌdeɪn

Lindbergh
BR 'lɪn(d)bəːg
AM 'lɪn(d)ˌbɜrg

Lindemann
BR 'lɪndɪmən
AM 'lɪndəmən

linden
BR 'lɪndən, -z
AM 'lɪndən, -z

Lindisfarne
BR 'lɪndɪsfɑːn
AM 'lɪndɪsˌfɑrn

Lindley
BR 'lɪn(d)li
AM 'lɪn(d)li

Lindon
BR 'lɪndən
AM 'lɪndən

Lindsay
BR 'lɪn(d)zi
AM 'lɪnzi

Lindsey
BR 'lɪn(d)zi
AM 'lɪnzi

Lindwall
BR 'lɪndwɔːl

AM 'lɪn(d)ˌwɔl,
'lɪn(d)ˌwɑl

Lindy
BR 'lɪndi
AM 'lɪndi

line
BR lʌɪn, -z, -ɪŋ, -d
AM laɪn, -z, -ɪŋ, -d

lineage
BR 'lɪnɪ|ɪdʒ, -ɪdʒɪz
AM 'laɪnɪdʒ, -ɪz

lineal
BR 'lɪnɪəl
AM 'lɪniəl

lineally
BR 'lɪnɪəli
AM 'lɪniəli

lineament
BR 'lɪnɪəm(ə)nt, -s
AM 'lɪn(i)əmənt, -s

linear
BR 'lɪnɪə(r)
AM 'lɪniər

linearise
BR 'lɪnɪərʌɪz, -ɪz, -ɪŋ, -d
AM 'lɪniəˌraɪz, -ɪz, -ɪŋ,
-d

linearity
BR ˌlɪnɪ'arɪt|i, -ɪz
AM ˌlɪni'ɛrədi, -z

linearize
BR 'lɪnɪərʌɪz, -ɪz, -ɪŋ, -d
AM 'lɪniəˌraɪz, -ɪz, -ɪŋ,
-d

linearly
BR 'lɪnɪəli
AM 'lɪniərli

lineation
BR ˌlɪnɪ'eɪʃn, -z
AM ˌlɪni'eɪʃən, -z

linebacker
BR 'lʌɪnˌbakə(r), -z
AM 'laɪnˌbækər, -z

linefeed
BR 'lʌɪnfiːd
AM 'laɪnˌfid

Linehan
BR 'lɪnɪhən
AM 'lɪnəhæn

Lineker
BR 'lɪnɪkə(r)
AM 'lɪnəkər

lineman
BR 'lʌɪnmən
AM 'laɪnmən

linemen
BR 'lʌɪnmən
AM 'laɪnmən

linen
BR 'lɪnɪn
AM 'lɪnɪn

linenfold
BR 'lɪnɪnfəʊld
AM 'lɪnənˌfoʊld

lineout
BR 'lʌɪnaʊt, -s
AM 'laɪnˌaʊt, -s

liner
BR 'lʌɪnə(r), -z
AM 'laɪnər, -z

linertrain
BR 'lʌɪnətreɪn, -z
AM 'laɪnərˌtreɪn, -z

lineshooter
BR 'lʌɪnˌʃuːtə(r), -z
AM 'laɪnˌʃudər, -z

lineside
BR 'lʌɪnsʌɪd
AM 'laɪnˌsaɪd

linesman
BR 'lʌɪnzmən
AM 'laɪnzmən

linesmen
BR 'lʌɪnzmən
AM 'laɪnzmən

lineup
BR 'lʌɪnʌp, -s
AM 'laɪnˌəp, -s

Linford
BR 'lɪnfəd
AM 'lɪnfərd

ling
BR lɪŋ, -z
AM lɪŋ, -z

linga
BR 'lɪŋgə(r), -z
AM 'lɪŋgə, -z

Lingala
BR lɪŋ'gɑːlə(r)
AM lɪŋ'gɑlə

lingam
BR 'lɪŋgəm, -z
AM 'lɪŋgəm, -z

linger
BR 'lɪŋg|ə(r), -əz,
-(ə)rɪŋ, -əd
AM 'lɪŋg|ər, -ərz,
-(ə)rɪŋ, -ərd

lingerer
BR 'lɪŋg(ə)rə(r), -z
AM 'lɪŋgərər, -z

lingerie
BR 'lãʒ(ə)ri, 'lɔ̃ʒ(ə)ri,
'lɒn(d)ʒ(ə)ri,
'lɑːn(d)ʒ(ə)ri
AM ˌlɑn(d)ʒə'reɪ

lingeringly
BR 'lɪŋg(ə)rɪŋli
AM 'lɪŋg(ə)rɪŋli

Lingfield
BR 'lɪŋfiːld
AM 'lɪŋˌfild

lingo
BR 'lɪŋgəʊ, -z
AM 'lɪŋgoʊ, -z

lingua franca
BR ˌlɪŋgwə 'fraŋkə(r),
-z
AM ˌlɪŋgwə 'fræŋkə, -z

lingual
BR 'lɪŋgw(ə)l
AM 'lɪŋgwəl

lingualise
BR 'lɪŋgwəlʌɪz,
'lɪŋgw|ʌɪz, -ɪz, -ɪŋ, -d
AM 'lɪŋgwəˌlaɪz, -ɪz, -ɪŋ,
-d

lingualize
BR 'lɪŋgwəlʌɪz,
'lɪŋgw|ʌɪz, -ɪz, -ɪŋ, -d
AM 'lɪŋgwəˌlaɪz, -ɪz, -ɪŋ,
-d

lingually
BR 'lɪŋgwəli, 'lɪŋgw|i
AM 'lɪŋgwəli

Linguaphone®
BR 'lɪŋgwəfəʊn
AM 'lɪŋgwəˌfoʊn

linguiform
BR 'lɪŋgwɪfɔːm
AM 'lɪŋgwəˌfɔ(ə)rm

linguine
BR lɪŋ'gwiːni
AM lɪŋ'gwini

linguist
BR 'lɪŋgwɪst, -s
AM 'lɪŋgwɪst, -s

linguistic
BR lɪŋ'gwɪstɪk, -s
AM lɪŋ'gwɪstɪk, -s

linguistically
BR lɪŋ'gwɪstɪkli
AM lɪŋ'gwɪstək(ə)li

linguistician
BR ˌlɪŋgwɪ'stɪʃn, -z
AM ˌlɪŋgwə'stɪʃən, -z

linguodental
BR ˌlɪŋgwəʊ'dɛntl
AM ˌlɪŋgwoʊ'dɛn(t)l

lingy
BR 'lɪŋi
AM 'lɪŋi

liniment
BR 'lɪnɪm(ə)nt, -s
AM 'lɪnəmənt, -s

lining
BR 'lʌɪnɪŋ, -z
AM 'laɪnɪŋ, -z

link
BR lɪŋ|k, -ks, -kɪŋ, -(k)t
AM lɪŋ|k, -ks, -kɪŋ, -(k)t

linkage
BR 'lɪŋk|ɪdʒ, -ɪdʒɪz
AM 'lɪŋkɪdʒ, -ɪz

Linklater
BR 'lɪŋkˌleɪtə(r),
'lɪŋklətə(r)
AM 'lɪŋkˌlɛdər

linkman
BR 'lɪŋkman
AM 'lɪŋkmən

linkmen
BR 'lɪŋkmɛn
AM 'lɪŋkmən

linkup
BR 'lɪŋkʌp, -s
AM 'lɪŋkˌəp, -s

Linley
BR 'lɪnli

AM 'lɪnli
Linlithgow
BR lɪn'lɪθgəʊ
AM lɪn'lɪθˌgoʊ
linn
BR lɪn, -z
AM lɪn, -z
Linnaean
BR lɪ'niːən, lɪ'neɪən, -z
AM lɪ'niən, lɪ'neɪən, -z
Linnaeus
BR lɪ'niːəs, lɪ'neɪəs
AM lɪ'niəs
linnet
BR 'lɪnɪt, -s
AM 'lɪnɪt, -s
Linnhe
BR 'lɪni
AM 'lɪni
lino
BR 'lʌɪnəʊ
AM 'laɪnoʊ
linocut
BR 'lʌɪnəʊkʌt, -s
AM 'laɪnoʊˌkət, -s
linocutting
BR 'lʌɪnəʊˌkʌtɪŋ, -z
AM 'laɪnoʊˌkədɪŋ, -z
linoleic acid
BR ˌlɪnəliːɪk 'asɪd,
ˌlɪnələɪk +
AM ˌlɪnə'liɪk 'æsəd,
lə'noʊlɪɪk +
linolenic acid
BR ˌlɪnəlenɪk 'asɪd
AM ˌlɪnə'liːnɪk 'æsəd,
ˌlɪnə'lɛnɪk +
linoleum
BR lɪ'nəʊlɪəm, -d
AM lɪ'noʊlɪəm, -d
linotype
BR 'lʌɪnə(ʊ)tʌɪp
AM 'laɪnəˌtaɪp
linsang
BR 'lɪnsaŋ, -z
AM 'lɪnˌsæŋ, -z
linseed
BR 'lɪnsiːd
AM 'lɪnˌsid
linsey-woolsey
BR ˌlɪnzɪ'wʊlzi
AM ˌlɪnzɪ'wʊlzi
linstock
BR 'lɪnstɒk, -s
AM 'lɪnzˌtɑk, 'lɪnˌstɑk, -s
lint
BR lɪnt
AM lɪnt
lintel
BR 'lɪntl, -z
AM 'lɪn(t)l, -z, -d
linter
BR 'lɪntə(r), -z
AM 'lɪn(t)ər, -z
Linton
BR 'lɪntən

AM 'lɪn(t)ən
linty
BR 'lɪnti
AM 'lɪn(t)i
Linus
BR 'lʌɪnəs
AM 'laɪnəs
Linwood
BR 'lɪnwʊd
AM 'lɪnˌwʊd
liny
BR 'lʌɪn|i, -ɪə(r), -ɪɪst
AM 'laɪni, -ər, -ɪst
Linz
BR lɪn(t)s
AM lɪn(t)s
lion
BR 'lʌɪən, -z
AM 'laɪən, -z
Lionel
BR 'lʌɪənl
AM 'laɪ(ə)nl, ˌlaɪə'nɛl
lioness
BR 'lʌɪənɛs, 'lʌɪənɪs,
ˌlʌɪə'nɛs, -ɪz
AM 'laɪənɪs, -ɪz
lionet
BR 'lʌɪənɪt, -s
AM 'laɪənət, -s
lion-hearted
BR ˌlʌɪən'hɑːtɪd
AM 'laɪənˌ(h)ɑrdəd
lionhood
BR 'lʌɪənhʊd
AM 'lɪən,(h)ʊd
lionisation
BR ˌlʌɪənʌɪ'zeɪʃn
AM ˌlɪənə'zeɪʃən,
ˌlɪənˌaɪ'zeɪʃən
lionise
BR 'lʌɪənʌɪz, -ɪz, -ɪŋ, -d
AM 'laɪəˌnaɪz, -ɪz, -ɪŋ, -d
lioniser
BR ˌlʌɪənʌɪzə(r), -z
AM 'laɪəˌnaɪzər, -z
lionization
BR ˌlʌɪənʌɪ'zeɪʃn
AM ˌlaɪənə'zeɪʃən,
ˌlɪənˌaɪ'zeɪʃən
lionize
BR 'lʌɪənʌɪz, -ɪz, -ɪŋ, -d
AM 'laɪəˌnaɪz, -ɪz, -ɪŋ, -d
lionizer
BR ˌlʌɪənʌɪzə(r), -z
AM 'laɪəˌnaɪzər, -z
lion-like
BR 'lʌɪənlʌɪk
AM 'laɪənˌlaɪk
Lions
BR 'lʌɪənz
AM 'laɪənz
lion-tamer
BR ˌlʌɪənˌteɪmə(r), -z
AM 'laɪənˌteɪmər, -z
lip
BR lɪp, -s, -t
AM lɪp, -s, -t

lipase
BR 'lʌɪpeɪz, 'lʌɪpeɪs,
'lɪpeɪz, 'lɪpeɪs
AM 'lɪˌpeɪs, 'laɪˌpeɪs
lipid
BR 'lɪpɪd, -z
AM 'lɪpɪd, -z
lipidoses
BR ˌlɪpɪ'dəʊsiːz
AM ˌlɪpə'doʊsiz
lipidosis
BR ˌlɪpɪ'dəʊsɪs, -ɪz
AM ˌlɪpə'doʊsəs, -əz
Lipizzaner
BR ˌlɪpɪt'sɑːnə(r), -z
AM 'lɪpəˌzanər,
ˌlɪpə'tsɑnər, -z
lipless
BR 'lɪplɪs
AM 'lɪpləs
liplike
BR 'lɪplʌɪk
AM 'lɪpˌlaɪk
Li Po
BR ˌli: 'pəʊ
AM ˌli 'poʊ
lipography
BR lɪ'pɒgrəfi
AM lə'pɑgrəfi
lipoid
BR 'lɪpɔɪd, 'lʌɪpɔɪd, -z
AM 'lɪˌpɔɪd, 'laɪˌpɔɪd, -z
lipoma
BR lɪ'pəʊmə(r),
lʌɪ'pəʊmə(r), -z
AM laɪ'poʊmə, -z
lipomata
BR lɪ'pəʊmətə(r),
lʌɪ'pəʊmətə(r)
AM laɪ'poʊmədə
lipoprotein
BR ˌlɪpəʊ'prəʊtiːn, -z
AM ˌlɪpə'proʊˌtin, -z
liposome
BR 'lɪpə(ʊ)səʊm, -z
AM 'lɪpəˌsoʊm, -z
liposuction
BR 'lɪpəʊˌsʌkʃn,
'lʌɪpəʊˌsʌkʃn
AM 'laɪpoʊˌsəkʃən,
'lɪpoʊˌsəkʃən
Lippi
BR 'lɪpi
AM 'lɪpi
Lippizaner
BR ˌlɪpɪt'sɑːnə(r), -z.
AM 'lɪpəˌzanər,
ˌlɪpə'tsɑnər, -z
Lippmann
BR 'lɪpmən
AM 'lɪpmən
lippy
BR 'lɪp|i, -ɪə(r), -ɪɪst
AM 'lɪpi, -ər, -ɪst
lipsalve
BR 'lɪpsalv, -z
AM 'lɪpˌsæ(l)v, -z

lipstick
BR 'lɪpstɪk, -s
AM 'lɪpˌstɪk, -s
lip-sync
BR 'lɪpsɪŋ|k, -ks, -kɪŋ,
-(k)t
AM 'lɪpˌsɪŋk, -s, -ɪŋ, -t
lip-syncer
BR 'lɪpˌsɪŋkə(r), -z
AM 'lɪpˌsɪŋkər, -z
lip-synch
BR 'lɪpsɪŋ|k, -ks, -kɪŋ,
-(k)t
AM 'lɪpˌsɪŋk, -s, -ɪŋ, -t
lip-syncher
BR 'lɪpˌsɪŋkə(r), -z
AM 'lɪpˌsɪŋkər, -z
Lipton
BR 'lɪpt(ə)n
AM 'lɪptən
liquate
BR lɪ'kweɪt, -s, -ɪŋ, -ɪd
AM 'laɪˌkweɪ|t,
'lɪˌkweɪ|t, -ts, -dɪŋ, -dɪd
liquation
BR lɪ'kweɪʃn
AM laɪ'kweɪʃən,
lə'kweɪʃən
liquefacient
BR ˌlɪkwɪ'feɪʃnt
AM ˌlɪkwə'feɪʃənt
liquefaction
BR ˌlɪkwɪ'fakʃn
AM ˌlɪkwə'fækʃən
liquefactive
BR ˌlɪkwɪ'faktɪv
AM ˌlɪkwə'fæktɪv
liquefiable
BR 'lɪkwɪfʌɪəbl
AM 'lɪkwəˌfaɪəbəl
liquefier
BR 'lɪkwɪfʌɪə(r), -z
AM 'lɪkwəˌfaɪər, -z
liquefy
BR 'lɪkwɪfʌɪ, -z, -ɪŋ, -d
AM 'lɪkwəˌfaɪ, -z, -ɪŋ, -d
liquescent
BR lɪ'kwɛsnt
AM lɪ'kwɛsənt
liqueur
BR lɪ'kjʊə(r), lɪ'kjɔː(r),
lɪ'kjɜː(r), -z
AM lɪ'kɜr, -z
liquid
BR 'lɪkwɪd, -z
AM 'lɪkwɪd, -z
liquidambar
BR 'lɪkwɪd'ambə(r), -z
AM 'lɪkwə'dæmbər, -z
liquidate
BR 'lɪkwɪdeɪt, -s, -ɪŋ, -ɪd
AM 'lɪkwəˌdeɪ|t, -ts,
-dɪŋ, -dɪd
liquidation
BR ˌlɪkwɪ'deɪʃn
AM ˌlɪkwə'deɪʃən

liquidator
BR ˈlɪkwɪdeɪtə(r), -z
AM ˈlɪkwəˌdeɪdər, -z

liquidise
BR ˈlɪkwɪdʌɪz, -ɪz, -ɪŋ, -d
AM ˈlɪkwəˌdaɪz, -ɪz, -ɪŋ, -d

liquidiser
BR ˈlɪkwɪdʌɪzə(r), -z
AM ˈlɪkwəˌdaɪzər, -z

liquidity
BR lɪˈkwɪdɪti
AM lɪˈkwɪdɪdi

liquidize
BR ˈlɪkwɪdʌɪz, -ɪz, -ɪŋ, -d
AM ˈlɪkwəˌdaɪz, -ɪz, -ɪŋ, -d

liquidizer
BR ˈlɪkwɪdʌɪzə(r), -z
AM ˈlɪkwəˌdaɪzər, -z

liquidly
BR ˈlɪkwɪdli
AM ˈlɪkwɪdli

liquidness
BR ˈlɪkwɪdnɪs
AM ˈlɪkwɪdnɪs

liquidus
BR ˈlɪkwɪdəs, -ɪz
AM ˈlɪkwɪdəs, -əz

liquify
BR ˈlɪkwɪfʌɪ, -z, -ɪŋ, -d
AM ˈlɪkwəˌfaɪ, -z, -ɪŋ, -d

liquor
BR ˈlɪkə(r), -z
AM ˈlɪkər, -z

liquorice
BR ˈlɪk(ə)rɪʃ, ˈlɪk(ə)rɪs
AM ˈlɪk(ə)rɪʃ

liquorish
BR ˈlɪk(ə)rɪʃ
AM ˈlɪk(ə)rɪʃ

liquorishly
BR ˈlɪk(ə)rɪʃli
AM ˈlɪk(ə)rɪʃli

liquorishness
BR ˈlɪk(ə)rɪʃnɪs
AM ˈlɪk(ə)rɪʃnɪs

lira
BR ˈlɪərə(r), -z
AM ˈlɪrə, -z

lire
BR ˈlɪərə(r), -z
AM ˈlɪrə, -z

liripipe
BR ˈlɪrɪpʌɪp, -s
AM ˈlɪrəˌpaɪp, -s

Lisa
BR ˈliːsə(r), ˈliːzə(r), ˈlʌɪzə(r)
AM ˈlɪsə, ˈlaɪzə

Lisbeth
BR ˈlɪzbəθ, ˈlɪzbɛθ
AM ˈlɪzbəθ, ˈlɪzbɛθ

Lisbon
BR ˈlɪzbən

AM ˈlɪzbən

Lisburn
BR ˈlɪzbəːn
AM ˈlɪzbərn

lisente
BR lɪˈsɛnti
AM ləˈsɛn(t)i

Liskeard
BR lɪˈskɑːd
AM lɪˈskɑrd

lisle
BR lʌɪl
AM laɪl

lisp
BR lɪsp, -s, -ɪŋ, -t
AM lɪsp, -s, -ɪŋ, -t

lisper
BR ˈlɪspə(r), -z
AM ˈlɪspər, -z

lispingly
BR ˈlɪspɪŋli
AM ˈlɪspɪŋli

lissom
BR ˈlɪs(ə)m
AM ˈlɪsəm

lissome
BR ˈlɪs(ə)m
AM ˈlɪsəm

lissomly
BR ˈlɪs(ə)mli
AM ˈlɪsəmli

lissomness
BR ˈlɪs(ə)mnəs
AM ˈlɪsəmnəs

list
BR lɪst, -s, -ɪŋ, -ɪd
AM lɪst, -s, -ɪŋ, -ɪd

listable
BR ˈlɪstəbl
AM ˈlɪstəbəl

listel
BR ˈlɪstl, -z
AM ˈlɪstəl, -z

listen
BR ˈlɪsˌn, -nz, -n̩ɪŋ\-nɪŋ, -nd
AM ˈlɪsˌn, -nz, -n̩ɪŋ, -nd

listenability
BR ˌlɪsnəˈbɪlɪti, ˌlɪsnəˈbɪlɪdi
AM ˌlɪsnəˈbɪlɪdi, ˌlɪsnəˈbɪlɪdi

listenable
BR ˈlɪsnəbl, ˈlɪsnəbl
AM ˈlɪsnəbəl, ˈlɪsnəbəl

listener
BR ˈlɪsnə(r), ˈlɪsnə(r), -z
AM ˈlɪsnər, ˈlɪsnər, -z

lister
BR ˈlɪstə(r), -z
AM ˈlɪstər, -z

listeria
BR lɪˈstɪərɪə(r)
AM ləˈstɪrɪə

Listerine®
BR ˈlɪstərɪːn

AM ˈlɪstərˈin

listeriosis
BR lɪˌstɪərɪˈəʊsɪs
AM ləˌstɪriˈoʊsəs

listing
BR ˈlɪstɪŋ, -z
AM ˈlɪstɪŋ, -z

listless
BR ˈlɪs(t)lɪs
AM ˈlɪs(t)lɪs

listlessly
BR ˈlɪs(t)lɪsli
AM ˈlɪs(t)lɪsli

listlessness
BR ˈlɪs(t)lɪsnɪs
AM ˈlɪs(t)lɪsnɪs

Liston
BR ˈlɪst(ə)n
AM ˈlɪstən

Liszt
BR lɪst
AM lɪst

lit
BR lɪt
AM lɪt

Li T'ai Po
BR ˌliː taɪ ˈpəʊ
AM ˌli ˈtaɪ ˈpoʊ

litany
BR ˈlɪtən|i, ˈlɪtn̩|i, -ɪz
AM ˈlɪtn̩i, -z

Litchfield
BR ˈlɪtʃfiːld
AM ˈlɪtʃˌfild

litchi
BR lʌɪˈtʃiː, ˈlʌɪtʃiː, ˈliːtʃiː, ˈlɪtʃiː, -z
AM ˈlitʃi, -z

lite
BR lʌɪt
AM laɪt

liter
BR ˈliːtə(r), -z
AM ˈlidər, -z

literacy
BR ˈlɪt(ə)rəsi
AM ˈlɪdərəsi, ˈlɪtrəsi

literae humaniores
BR ˌlɪtərʌɪ hjuːˌmænɪˈɔːriːz
AM ˌlɪdəreɪ (h)juˌmæniˈoʊˌreɪs

literal
BR ˈlɪt(ə)rəl, ˈlɪt(ə)rl
AM ˈlɪdərəl, ˈlɪtrəl

literalise
BR ˈlɪt(ə)rəlʌɪz, ˈlɪt(ə)rlʌɪz, -ɪz, -ɪŋ, -d
AM ˈlɪdərəˌlaɪz, ˈlɪtrəˌlaɪz, -ɪz, -ɪŋ, -d

literalism
BR ˈlɪt(ə)rəlɪz(ə)m, ˈlɪt(ə)rlɪz(ə)m
AM ˈlɪdərəˌlɪzəm, ˈlɪtrəˌlɪzəm

literalist
BR ˈlɪt(ə)rəlɪst, ˈlɪt(ə)rlɪst, -s
AM ˈlɪdərələst, ˈlɪtrələst, -s

literalistic
BR ˌlɪt(ə)rəˈlɪstɪk, ˌlɪt(ə)rlˈɪstɪk
AM ˌlɪdərəˈlɪstɪk, ˌlɪtrəˈlɪstɪk

literality
BR ˌlɪtəˈralɪti
AM ˌlɪtəˈrælədi

literalize
BR ˈlɪt(ə)rəlʌɪz, ˈlɪt(ə)rlʌɪz, -ɪz, -ɪŋ, -d
AM ˈlɪdərəˌlaɪz, ˈlɪtrəˌlaɪz, -ɪz, -ɪŋ, -d

literally
BR ˈlɪt(ə)rəli, ˈlɪt(ə)rl̩i
AM ˈlɪdərəli, ˈlɪtrəli

literal-minded
BR ˌlɪt(ə)rəlˈmʌɪndɪd, ˌlɪt(ə)rl̩ˈmʌɪndɪd
AM ˈlɪdərəlˌmaɪndɪd, ˈlɪtrəlˌmaɪndɪd

literalness
BR ˈlɪt(ə)rəlnəs, ˈlɪt(ə)rl̩nəs
AM ˈlɪdərəlnəs, ˈlɪtrəlnəs

literarily
BR ˈlɪt(ə)rərɪli
AM ˈlɪdəˌrɛrəli

literariness
BR ˈlɪt(ə)rərɪnɪs
AM ˈlɪdəˌrɛrɪnɪs

literary
BR ˈlɪt(ə)rəri
AM ˈlɪdəˌrɛri

literate
BR ˈlɪt(ə)rət
AM ˈlɪdərət

literately
BR ˈlɪt(ə)rətli
AM ˈlɪdərətli

literateness
BR ˈlɪt(ə)rətnəs
AM ˈlɪdərətnəs

literati
BR ˌlɪtəˈrɑːti
AM ˌlɪdəˈrɑdi

literatim
BR ˌlɪtəˈrɑːtɪm
AM ˌlɪdəˈrɑdɪm

literation
BR ˌlɪtəˈreɪʃn
AM ˌlɪdəˈreɪʃən

literator
BR ˈlɪtəreɪtə(r), -z
AM ˈlɪdəˌreɪtər, -z

literature
BR ˈlɪt(ə)rɪtʃə(r)
AM ˈlɪdər(ə)tʃər, ˈlɪdərəˌtʃʊ(ə)r, ˈlɪtrəˌtʃʊ(ə)r, ˈlɪdərəˌt(j)ʊ(ə)r

litharge
BR ˈlɪθɑːdʒ, -ɪz
AM ˈlɪˌθɑrdʒ, lɪˈθɑrdʒ, -əz

lithe
BR lʌɪð, -ə(r), -ɪst
AM laɪð, -ər, -ɪst

lithely
BR ˈlʌɪðli
AM ˈlaɪðli

litheness
BR ˈlʌɪðnɪs
AM ˈlaɪðnɪs

lithesome
BR ˈlʌɪðs(ə)m
AM ˈlaɪθsəm

Lithgow
BR ˈlɪθgəʊ
AM ˈlɪθgaʊ, ˈlɪθgoʊ

lithia
BR ˈlɪθɪə(r)
AM ˈlɪθɪə

lithic
BR ˈlɪθɪk
AM ˈlɪθɪk

lithium
BR ˈlɪθɪəm
AM ˈlɪθɪəm

litho
BR ˈlʌɪθəʊ, -z
AM ˈlɪθoʊ, -z

lithograph
BR ˈlɪθə(ʊ)grɑːf, ˈlɪθə(ʊ)graf, -s, -ɪŋ, -t
AM ˈlɪθəˌgræf, -s, -ɪŋ, -t

lithographer
BR lɪˈθɒgrəfə(r), -z
AM ləˈθɑgrəfər, -z

lithographic
BR ˌlɪθə(ʊ)ˈgrafɪk
AM ˌlɪθəˈgræfɪk

lithographically
BR ˌlɪθə(ʊ)ˈgrafɪkli
AM ˌlɪθəˈgræfək(ə)li

lithography
BR lɪˈθɒgrəfi
AM ləˈθɑgrəfi

lithological
BR ˌlɪθə(ʊ)ˈlɒdʒɪkl
AM ˌlɪθəˈlɑdʒəkəl

lithologist
BR lɪˈθɒlədʒɪst, -s
AM ləˈθɑlədʒəst, -s

lithology
BR lɪˈθɒlədʒi
AM ləˈθɑlədʒi

lithophyte
BR ˈlɪθə(ʊ)fʌɪt, -s
AM ˈlɪθəˌfaɪt, -s

lithopone
BR ˈlɪθə(ʊ)pəʊn, -z
AM ˈlɪθəˌpoʊn, -z

lithosphere
BR ˈlɪθə(ʊ)sfɪə(r), -z
AM ˈlɪθəˌsfɪ(ə)r, -z

lithospheric
BR ˌlɪθə(ʊ)ˈsfɛrɪk

AM ˌlɪθəˈsfɛrɪk

lithotomise
BR lɪˈθɒtəmʌɪz, -ɪz, -ɪŋ, -d
AM ləˈθɑdəˌmaɪz, -ɪz, -ɪŋ, -d

lithotomist
BR lɪˈθɒtəmɪst, -s
AM ləˈθɑdəməst, -s

lithotomize
BR lɪˈθɒtəmʌɪz, -ɪz, -ɪŋ, -d
AM ləˈθɑdəˌmaɪz, -ɪz, -ɪŋ, -d

lithotomy
BR lɪˈθɒtəmˌli, -ɪz
AM ləˈθɑdəmi, -z

lithotripsy
BR ˈlɪθə(ʊ)ˌtrɪpsˌli, -ɪz
AM ˈlɪθəˌtrɪpsi, -z

lithotripter
BR ˈlɪθə(ʊ)ˌtrɪptə(r), -z
AM ˈlɪθəˌtrɪptər, -z

lithotriptic
BR ˌlɪθə(ʊ)ˈtrɪptɪk
AM ˌlɪθəˈtrɪptɪk

lithotrity
BR lɪˈθɒtrɪti
AM ləˈθɑˌtrədi

Lithuania
BR ˌlɪθjʊˈeɪnɪə(r)
AM ˌlɪθəˈweɪnɪə

Lithuanian
BR ˌlɪθjʊˈeɪnɪən, -z
AM ˌlɪθəˈweɪnɪən, -z

litigable
BR ˈlɪtɪgəbl
AM ˈlɪdəgəbəl

litigant
BR ˈlɪtɪg(ə)nt, -s
AM ˈlɪdəgənt, -s

litigate
BR ˈlɪtɪgeɪt, -s, -ɪŋ, -ɪd
AM ˈlɪdəˌgeɪt, -ts, -dɪŋ, -dɪd

litigation
BR ˌlɪtɪˈgeɪʃn, -z
AM ˌlɪdəˈgeɪʃən, -z

litigator
BR ˈlɪtɪgeɪtə(r), -z
AM ˈlɪdəˌgeɪdər, -z

litigious
BR lɪˈtɪdʒəs
AM ləˈtɪdʒəs

litigiously
BR lɪˈtɪdʒəsli
AM ləˈtɪdʒəsli

litigiousness
BR lɪˈtɪdʒəsnəs
AM ləˈtɪdʒəsnəs

litmus
BR ˈlɪtməs
AM ˈlɪtməs

litotes
BR ˈlʌɪtətiːz, lʌɪˈtəʊtiːz
AM ˈlaɪdəˌtiz, ˈlɪdəˌtiz, laɪˈtoʊdiz

litre
BR ˈliːtə(r), -z
AM ˈlidər, -z

litreage
BR ˈliːt(ə)rˌɪdʒ, -ɪdʒɪz
AM ˈlidərɪdʒ, ˈlitrɪdʒ, -ɪz

Litt.D.
Doctor of Letters
BR ˌlɪtˈdiː
AM ˈlɪt ˈdi

litter
BR ˈlɪt|ə(r), -əz, -(ə)rɪŋ, -əd
AM ˈlɪdər, -z, -ɪŋ, -d

littérateur
BR ˌlɪt(ə)rəˈtəː(r), -z
AM ˌlɪdərəˈtər, -z

litterbag
BR ˈlɪtəbag, -z
AM ˈlɪdərˌbæg, -z

litterbin
BR ˈlɪtəbɪn, -z
AM ˈlɪdərˌbɪn, -z

litterbug
BR ˈlɪtəbʌg, -z
AM ˈlɪdərˌbəg, -z

litterlout
BR ˈlɪtəlaʊt, -s
AM ˈlɪdərˌlaʊt, -s

littery
adjective
BR ˈlɪt(ə)ri
AM ˈlɪdəri

little
BR ˈlɪt|l, -lə(r)\-lə(r), -lɪst\-lɪst
AM ˈlɪdəl, -ər, -ɪst

Little Bighorn
BR ˌlɪtl ˈbɪghɔːn
AM ˌlɪdəl
'bɪg,(h)ɔ(ə)rn

Little Englander
BR ˌlɪtl ˈɪŋgləndə(r), -z
AM ˌlɪdəl ˈɪŋ(g)ləndər, -z

Littlehampton
BR ˌlɪtlˈham(p)t(ə)n, ˈlɪtlˌham(p)t(ə)n
AM ˈlɪdlˈhæm(p)tən

Littlejohn
BR ˈlɪtldʒɒn
AM ˈlɪdlˌdʒɑn

littleness
BR ˈlɪtlnəs
AM ˈlɪdlnɪs

Littler
BR ˈlɪtlə(r)
AM ˈlɪtlər, ˈlɪdələr

Littleton
BR ˈlɪtlt(ə)n
AM ˈlɪdltən

Littlewood
BR ˈlɪtlwʊd, -z
AM ˈlɪdlˌwʊd, -z

Litton
BR ˈlɪtn
AM ˈlɪtn

littoral
BR ˈlɪt(ə)rəl, ˈlɪt(ə)rl̩, -z
AM ˈlɪdərəl, -z

Littré
BR lɪˈtreɪ
AM ləˈtreɪ

liturgic
BR lɪˈtəːdʒɪk, -s
AM ləˈtərdʒɪk, -s

liturgical
BR lɪˈtəːdʒɪkl
AM ləˈtərdʒəkəl

liturgically
BR lɪˈtəːdʒɪkli
AM ləˈtərdʒək(ə)li

liturgiology
BR lɪˌtəːdʒɪˈɒlədʒi
AM ləˌtərdʒiˈɑlədʒi

liturgist
BR ˈlɪtədʒɪst, -s
AM ˈlɪdərdʒəst, -s

liturgy
BR ˈlɪtədʒ|i, -ɪz
AM ˈlɪdərdʒi, -z

livable
BR ˈlɪvəbl
AM ˈlɪvəbəl

live¹
adjective
BR lʌɪv
AM laɪv

live²
verb
BR lɪv, -z, -ɪŋ, -d
AM lɪv, -z, -ɪŋ, -d

liveability
BR ˌlɪvəˈbɪlɪti
AM ˌlɪvəˈbɪlɪdi

liveable
BR ˈlɪvəbl
AM ˈlɪvəbəl

liveableness
BR ˈlɪvəblnəs
AM ˈlɪvəbəlnəs

livelihood
BR ˈlʌɪvlɪhʊd, -z
AM ˈlaɪvliˌ(h)ʊd, -z

livelily
BR ˈlʌɪvlɪli
AM ˈlaɪvlɪli

liveliness
BR ˈlʌɪvlɪnɪs
AM ˈlaɪvlinɪs

livelong
BR ˈlɪvlɒŋ
AM ˈlɪvˌlɔŋ, ˈlɪvˌlɑŋ

lively
BR ˈlʌɪvl|i, -ɪə(r), -ɪɪst
AM ˈlaɪvli-, -ər, -ɪst

liven
BR ˈlʌɪv|n, -nz, -ŋɪŋ\-nɪŋ, -nd
AM ˈlaɪv|ən, -ənz, -(ə)nɪŋ, -ənd

Liver
connected with
Liverpool
BR 'lʌɪvə(r)
AM 'laɪvər

liver
BR 'lɪvə(r), -z
AM 'lɪvər, -z

liveried
BR 'lɪv(ə)rɪd
AM lɪv(ə)rɪd

liverish
BR 'lɪv(ə)rɪʃ
AM 'lɪv(ə)rɪʃ

liverishly
BR 'lɪv(ə)rɪʃli
AM 'lɪv(ə)rɪʃli

liverishness
BR 'lɪv(ə)rɪʃnɪs
AM 'lɪv(ə)rɪʃnɪs

liverless
BR 'lɪvələs
AM 'lɪvərləs

Liverpool
BR 'lɪvəpuːl
AM 'lɪvər,pul

Liverpudlian
BR ,lɪvə'pʌdliən, -z
AM ,lɪvər'pədliən, -z

liverwort
BR 'lɪvəwəːt
AM 'lɪvər,wərt,
'lɪvər,wɔ(ə)rt

liverwurst
BR 'lɪvəwəːst
AM 'lɪvər,wərst

livery
BR 'lɪv(ə)r|i, -ɪz
AM 'lɪv(ə)ri, -z

liveryman
BR 'lɪv(ə)rɪmən
AM 'lɪv(ə)rɪmən

liverymen
BR 'lɪv(ə)rɪmən
AM 'lɪv(ə)rɪmən

lives[1]
from verb live
BR lɪvz
AM lɪvz

lives[2]
plural of life
BR lʌɪvz
AM laɪvz

Livesey
BR 'lɪvzi, 'lɪvsi
AM 'lɪvzi, 'lɪvsi

livestock
BR 'lʌɪvstɒk
AM 'laɪv,stɑk

Livia
BR 'lɪvɪə(r)
AM 'lɪvɪə

livid
BR 'lɪvɪd
AM 'lɪvɪd

lividity
BR lɪ'vɪdɪti

AM lə'vɪdɪdi

lividly
BR 'lɪvɪdli
AM 'lɪvɪdli

lividness
BR 'lɪvɪdnɪs
AM 'lɪvɪdnɪs

living
BR 'lɪvɪŋ, -z
AM 'lɪvɪŋ, -z

Livings
BR 'lɪvɪŋz
AM 'lɪvɪŋz

Livingston
BR 'lɪvɪŋst(ə)n
AM 'lɪvɪŋstən

Livingstone
BR 'lɪvɪŋstən
AM 'lɪvɪŋstən

Livonia
BR lɪ'vəʊnɪə(r)
AM lə'voʊnɪə

Livorno
BR lɪ'vɔːnəʊ
AM lə'vɔr,noʊ

Livy
BR 'lɪvi
AM 'lɪvi

lixiviate
BR lɪk'sɪvɪeɪt, -s, -ɪŋ, -ɪd
AM lɪk'sɪvɪ,eɪ|t, -ts,
-dɪŋ, -dɪd

lixiviation
BR lɪk,sɪvɪ'eɪʃn
AM lɪk,sɪvɪ'eɪʃən

Liz
BR lɪz
AM lɪz

Liza
BR 'lʌɪzə(r), 'liːzə(r)
AM 'laɪzə, 'lizə

lizard
BR 'lɪzəd, -z
AM 'lɪzərd, -z

Lizzie
BR 'lɪzi
AM 'lɪzi

Lizzy
BR 'lɪzi
AM 'lɪzi

Ljubljana
BR ,l(j)uːblɪ'ɑːnə(r)
AM ,l(j)ʊbli'ɑnə

llama
BR 'lɑːmə(r), -z
AM 'lɑmə, -z

Llan
BR ɬan, lan
AM ɬæn
WE ɬan

Llanberis
BR ɬan'bɛrɪs, lan'bɛrɪs
AM ɬæn'bɛrəs

Llandaff
BR 'ɬandaf, ɬan'daf,
'landaf, lan'daf
AM 'læn,dæf

Llandeilo
BR ɬan'dʌɪləʊ,
lan'dʌɪləʊ
AM læn'daɪloʊ

Llandovery
BR ɬan'dʌv(ə)ri,
lan'dʌv(ə)ri
AM læn'dəvəri

Llandrindod
Wells
BR ɬan,drɪndɒd 'wɛlz,
lan,drɪndɒd +
AM læn,drɪndɑd 'wɛlz

Llandudno
BR ɬan'dɪdnəʊ,
lan'dɪdnəʊ,
lan'dʌdnəʊ
AM læn'dədnoʊ

Llanelli
BR ɬa'nɛɬi, ɬə'nɛɬi,
lə'nɛɬli, la'nɛθli
AM lə'nɛθli

llanero
BR l(j)ɑ:'nɛːrəʊ, -z
AM lɑ'nɛroʊ, -z

Llangollen
BR ɬan'gɒɬən,
lan'gɒθlən
AM læŋ'goʊlən

llano
BR 'l(j)ɑːnəʊ, -z
AM 'lɑ,noʊ, -z

Llanwrtyd
BR ɬan'ʊətɪd, ɬan'əːtɪd,
lan'əːtɪd
AM læn'ərdəd
WE ɬan'wrtɪd

Llewellyn
BR ɬʊ'ɛlɪn, lʊ'ɛlɪn,
lə'wɛlɪn
AM lʊ'wɛlɪn

Llewelyn
BR ɬʊ'ɛlɪn, lʊ'ɛlɪn,
lə'wɛlɪn
AM lʊ'(w)ɛlən
WE ɬe'welɪn

Lleyn
BR ɬiːn, liːn
AM lin

Lloyd
BR lɔɪd
AM lɔɪd

Lloyd's
BR lɔɪdz
AM lɔɪdz

llyn
BR ɬɪn, lɪn, -z
AM lɪn, -z

Llywelyn
BR ɬʊ'ɛlɪn, lʊ'ɛlɪn,
lə'wɛlɪn
AM lʊ'wɛlən
WE ɬʌ'welɪn

lo
BR ləʊ
AM loʊ

loa
BR 'ləʊə(r), -z

Llandeilo
AM lə'wɑ, -z

loach
BR ləʊtʃ, -ɪz
AM loʊ(t)ʃ, -əz

load
BR ləʊd, -z, -ɪŋ, -ɪd
AM loʊd, -z, -ɪŋ, -əd

loader
BR 'ləʊdə(r), -z
AM 'loʊdər, -z

loading
BR 'ləʊdɪŋ, -z
AM 'loʊdɪŋ, -z

loadsamoney
BR 'ləʊdzə,mʌni,
,ləʊdzə'mʌni
AM 'loʊdzə,məni

loadstar
BR 'ləʊdstɑː(r), -z
AM 'loʊd,stɑr, -z

loadstone
BR 'ləʊdstəʊn, -z
AM 'loʊd,stoʊn, -z

loaf
BR ləʊf, -s, -ɪŋ, -t
AM loʊf, -s, -ɪŋ, -t

loafer
BR 'ləʊfə(r), -z
AM 'loʊfər, -z

loam
BR ləʊm
AM loʊm

loaminess
BR 'ləʊmɪnɪs
AM 'loʊmɪnɪs

loamy
BR 'ləʊmi
AM 'loʊmi

loan
BR ləʊn, -z, -ɪŋ, -d
AM loʊn, -z, -ɪŋ, -d

loanable
BR 'ləʊnəbl
AM 'loʊnəbəl

lo and behold
BR ,ləʊ ən(d) bɪ'həʊld,
+ ŋ(d) +
AM ,loʊ (ə)n bə'hoʊld

loanee
BR ,ləʊn'iː, -z
AM ,loʊ'ni, -z

loaner
BR 'ləʊnə(r), -z
AM 'loʊnər, -z

loanholder
BR 'ləʊn,həʊldə(r), -z
AM 'loʊn,(h)oʊldər, -z

loanshark
BR 'ləʊnʃɑːk, -s
AM 'loʊn,ʃɑrk, -s

loanword
BR 'ləʊnwəːd, -z
AM 'loʊn,wərd, -z

loath
BR ləʊθ
AM loʊθ

loathe
BR ləʊð, -z, -ɪŋ, -d
AM loʊð, -z, -ɪŋ, -d

loather
BR 'ləʊðə(r), -z
AM 'loʊðər, -z

loathsome
BR 'ləʊðs(ə)m,
'ləʊθs(ə)m
AM 'loʊðsəm, 'loʊðsəm

loathsomely
BR 'ləʊðs(ə)mli,
'ləʊθs(ə)mli
AM 'loʊðsəmli,
'loʊðsəmli

loathsomeness
BR 'ləʊðs(ə)mnəs,
'ləʊθs(ə)mnəs
AM 'loʊðsəmnəs,
'loʊðsəmnəs

loaves
BR ləʊvz
AM loʊvz

lob
BR lɒb, -z, -ɪŋ, -d
AM lab, -z, -ɪŋ, -d

lobar
BR 'ləʊbə(r), -z
AM 'loʊˌbar, -z

lobate
BR 'ləʊbeɪt
AM 'loʊˌbeɪt

lobation
BR lə(ʊ)'beɪʃn, -z
AM loʊ'beɪʃən, -z

lobby
BR 'lɒb|i, -ɪz, -ɪɪŋ, -ɪd
AM 'labi, -z, -ɪŋ, -d

lobbyer
BR 'lɒbɪə(r), -z
AM 'labiər, -z

lobbyism
BR 'lɒbɪɪz(ə)m
AM 'labiˌɪzəm

lobbyist
BR 'lɒbɪɪst, -s
AM 'labiɪst, -s

lobe
BR ləʊb, -z, -d
AM loʊb, -z, -d

lobectomy
BR ləʊ'bɛktəm|i, -ɪz
AM loʊ'bɛktəmi, -z

lobeless
BR 'ləʊbləs
AM 'loʊbləs

lobelia
BR lə'biːlɪə(r)
AM loʊ'biljə, loʊ'biliə

lobeline
BR 'ləʊbəliːn
AM 'loʊbəˌlin

Lobito
BR lə'biːtəʊ
AM lə'bidoʊ

loblolly
BR 'lɒbˌlɒl|i, -ɪz

loathe
AM 'lab,lali, -z
lobo
BR 'ləʊbəʊ, -z
AM 'loʊboʊ, -z

lobotomise
BR lə'bɒtəmAɪz, -ɪz, -ɪŋ, -d
AM lə'badəˌmaɪz, -ɪz, -ɪŋ, -d

lobotomize
BR lə'bɒtəmAɪz, -ɪz, -ɪŋ, -d
AM lə'badəˌmaɪz, -ɪŋ, -d

lobotomy
BR lə'bɒtəm|i, -ɪz
AM lə'badəmi, -z

lobscouse
BR 'lɒbskaʊs
AM 'lab,skaʊs

lobster
BR 'lɒbstə(r), -z
AM 'labstər, -z

lobsterman
BR 'lɒbstəmən
AM 'labstərmən

lobstermen
BR 'lɒbstəmən
AM 'labstərmən

lobsterpot
BR 'lɒbstəpɒt, -s
AM 'labstər,pat, -s

lobster thermidor
BR ˌlɒbstə 'θəːmɪdɔː(r)
AM ˌlabstər 'θərməˌdɔ(ə)r

lobular
BR 'lɒbjʊlə(r)
AM 'labjələr

lobulate
BR 'lɒbjʊlət
AM 'labjəˌleɪt

lobule
BR 'lɒbjuːl, -z
AM 'labjul, -z

lobworm
BR 'lɒbwəːm, -z
AM 'labwɜrm, -z

local
BR 'ləʊkl, -z
AM 'loʊkəl, -z

locale
BR ləʊ'kaːl, -z
AM loʊ'kæl, -z

localisable
BR 'ləʊkəlAɪzəbl, 'ləʊklAɪzəbl
AM 'loʊkəˌlaɪzəbəl

localisation
BR ˌləʊkəlAɪ'zeɪʃn, ˌləʊklAɪ'zeɪʃn
AM ˌloʊkələ'zeɪʃən, ˌloʊkəˌlaɪ'zeɪʃən

localise
BR 'ləʊkəlAɪz, 'ləʊklAɪz, -ɪz, -ɪŋ, -d

AM 'loʊkəˌlaɪz, -ɪz, -ɪŋ, -d
localism
BR 'ləʊkəlɪz(ə)m, 'ləʊklɪz(ə)m, -z
AM 'loʊkəˌlɪzəm, -z

locality
BR lə(ʊ)'kalɪt|i, -ɪz
AM loʊ'kælədi, -z

localizable
BR 'ləʊkəlAɪzəbl, 'ləʊklAɪzəbl
AM 'loʊkəˌlaɪzəbəl

localization
BR ˌləʊkəlAɪ'zeɪʃn, ˌləʊklAɪ'zeɪʃn
AM ˌloʊkələ'zeɪʃən, ˌloʊkəˌlaɪ'zeɪʃən

localize
BR 'ləʊkəlAɪz, 'ləʊklAɪz, -ɪz, -ɪŋ, -d
AM 'loʊkəˌlaɪz, -ɪz, -ɪŋ, -d

locally
BR 'ləʊkl̩i, 'ləʊkəli
AM 'loʊkəli

localness
BR 'ləʊklnəs
AM 'loʊkəlnəs

Locarno
BR lə(ʊ)'kaːnəʊ
AM loʊ'kar,noʊ

locatable
BR lə(ʊ)'keɪtəbl
AM ˌloʊˈkeɪdəbəl

locate
BR lə(ʊ)'keɪt, -s, -ɪŋ, -ɪd
AM 'loʊˌkeɪt, loʊ'keɪ|t, -ts, -dɪŋ, -dɪd

location
BR lə(ʊ)'keɪʃn, -z
AM loʊ'keɪʃən, -z

locational
BR lə(ʊ)'keɪʃn(ə)l, lə(ʊ)'keɪʃən(ə)l
AM loʊ'keɪʃ(ə)nəl

locative
BR 'lɒkətɪv, -z
AM 'lakədɪv, -z

locator
BR lə(ʊ)'keɪtə(r), -z
AM 'loʊˌkeɪdər, -z

loc. cit.
loco citato
BR ˌlɒk 'sɪt
AM 'lak 'sɪt

loch
BR lɒx, lɒk, -s
AM lak, -s

lochan
BR 'lɒx(ə)n, 'lɒk(ə)n, -z
AM 'lakən, -z

Lochgilphead
BR lɒx'gɪlphɛd, lɒk'gɪlphɛd
AM lak'gɪlfɛd

lochia
BR 'lɒkɪə(r), 'ləʊkɪə(r), -z
AM 'loʊkiə, 'lakiə, -z

lochial
BR 'lɒkɪəl, 'ləʊkɪəl
AM 'loʊkiəl, 'lakiəl

Lochinvar
BR ˌlɒxɪn'vaː(r), ˌlɒkɪn'vaː(r)
AM ˌlakən'var

lochside
BR 'lɒxsʌɪd, 'lɒksʌɪd
AM 'lak,saɪd

loci
BR 'ləʊsʌɪ, 'ləʊkʌɪ, 'lɒkʌɪ, 'ləʊsiː, 'ləʊki:, 'lɒki:
AM 'loʊˌsaɪ, 'loʊˌsi, 'loʊˌki

loci classici
BR ˌləʊsʌɪ 'klasɪsʌɪ, ˌləʊkʌɪ +, ˌləʊsiː 'klasɪsiː, ˌləʊki: +, ˌlɒki: +
AM ˌloʊˌsaɪ 'klæsəˌsaɪ, ˌloʊˌsi 'klæsəˌsi, ˌloʊˌki 'klæsəˌki

lock
BR lɒk, -s, -ɪŋ, -t
AM lak, -s, -ɪŋ, -t

lockable
BR 'lɒkəbl
AM 'lakəbəl

lockage
BR 'lɒkɪdʒ
AM 'lakɪdʒ

lockbox
BR 'lɒkbɒks, -ɪz
AM 'lak,baks, -əz

Locke
BR lɒk
AM lak

locker
BR 'lɒkə(r), -z
AM 'lakər, -z

Lockerbie
BR 'lɒkəbi
AM 'lakərbi

locket
BR 'lɒkɪt, -s
AM 'lakət, -s

lockfast
BR 'lɒkfaːst, 'lɒkfast
AM 'lakˌfæst

lockgate
BR ˌlɒk'geɪt, 'lɒkgeɪt, -s
AM 'lak,geɪt, -s

Lockhart
BR 'lɒkhaːt, 'lɒkət
AM 'lak,(h)art

Lockheed
BR 'lɒkhiːd
AM 'lak,(h)id

lockjaw
BR 'lɒkdʒɔː(r)
AM 'lak,dʒɔ

lockless
BR ˈlɒkləs
AM ˈlɑkləs

locknut
BR ˈlɒknʌt, -s
AM ˈlɑkˌnət, -s

lockout
BR ˈlɒkaʊt, -s
AM ˈlɑkˌaʊt, ˈlɑkaʊt, -s

Locksley
BR ˈlɒksli
AM ˈlɑksli

locksman
BR ˈlɒksmən
AM ˈlɑksmən

locksmen
BR ˈlɒksmən
AM ˈlɑksmən

locksmith
BR ˈlɒksmɪθ, -s
AM ˈlɑkˌsmɪθ, -s

lockstitch
BR ˈlɒkstɪtʃ
AM ˈlɑkˌstɪtʃ

lockup
BR ˈlɒkʌp, -s
AM ˈlɑkəp, -s

Lockwood
BR ˈlɒkwʊd
AM ˈlɑkˌwʊd

Lockyer
BR ˈlɒkjə(r)
AM ˈlɑkjər

loco
BR ˈləʊkəʊ, -z
AM ˈloʊkoʊ, -z

locomotion
BR ˌləʊkəˈməʊʃn
AM ˌloʊkəˈmoʊʃən

locomotive
BR ˌləʊkəˈməʊtɪv, -z
AM ˌloʊkəˈmoʊdɪv, -z

locomotor
BR ˌləʊkə(ʊ)ˈməʊtə(r), -z
AM ˌloʊkəˈmoʊdər, -z

locomotory
BR ˌləʊkə(ʊ)ˈməʊt(ə)ri
AM ˌloʊkəˈmoʊdəri

locoweed
BR ˈləʊkəʊwiːd
AM ˈloʊkoʊˌwid

locular
BR ˈlɒkjʊlə(r)
AM ˈlɑkjələr

loculi
BR ˈlɒkjʊlʌɪ, ˈlɒkjʊliː
AM ˈlɑkjəˌlaɪ

loculus
BR ˈlɒkjʊləs
AM ˈlɑkjələs

locum
BR ˈləʊkəm, -z
AM ˈloʊkəm, -z

locum tenency
BR ˌləʊkəm ˈtɛnəns|i, -ɪz

AM ˈloʊkəm ˈtɛnɛnsi, -z

locum tenens
BR ˌləʊkəm ˈtɛnɛnz
AM ˈloʊkəm ˈtɛnɛnz

locus
BR ˈləʊkəs, ˈlɒkəs
AM ˈloʊkəs

locus classicus
BR ˌləʊkəs ˈklasɪkəs, ˌlɒkəs +
AM ˈloʊkəs ˈklæsəkəs

locus standi
BR ˌlɒkəs ˈstandʌɪ, ˌlɒkəs +, + ˈstandiː
AM ˈloʊkəs ˈstanˌdaɪ, + ˈstandi

locust
BR ˈləʊkəst, -s
AM ˈloʊkəst, -s

locution
BR ləˈkjuːʃn, -z
AM ləˈkjuʃən, -z

locutory
BR ˈlɒkjʊt(ə)r|i, -ɪz
AM ˈlɑkjəˌtɔri, -z

lode
BR ləʊd, -z
AM loʊd, -z

loden
BR ˈləʊdn, -z
AM ˈloʊdən, -z

lodestar
BR ˈləʊdstɑː(r), -z
AM ˈloʊdˌstar, -z

lodestone
BR ˈləʊdstəʊn, -z
AM ˈloʊdˌstoʊn, -z

lodge
BR lɒdʒ, -ɪz, -ɪŋ, -d
AM lɑdʒ, -əz, -ɪŋ, -d

lodgement
BR ˈlɒdʒm(ə)nt, -s
AM ˈlɑdʒmənt, -s

lodger
BR ˈlɒdʒə(r), -z
AM ˈlɑdʒər, -z

lodging
BR ˈlɒdʒɪŋ, -z
AM ˈlɑdʒɪŋ, -z

lodgment
BR ˈlɒdʒm(ə)nt, -s
AM ˈlɑdʒmənt, -s

lodicule
BR ˈlɒdɪkjuːl, -z
AM ˈlɑdəˌkjul, -z

Łódź
BR wʊtʃ
AM ladz
POL wʊtɕ

Loeb
BR ləʊb, ləːb
AM loʊb

loess
BR ˈləʊɪs, ˈləʊɛs, ləːs
AM lɛs, ləs, ˈloʊˌɛs

loessial
BR ləʊˈɛsɪəl, ˈləːsɪəl
AM ˈlɛsɪəl, ˈləsɪəl, loʊˈɛsɪəl

Loew
BR ləʊ
AM loʊ

Loewe
BR ləʊ
AM loʊ

Lofoten
BR ləˈfəʊtn
AM loˈfutn
NO ˈluːfuːten

loft
BR lɒft, -s, -ɪŋ, -ɪd
AM lɑft, laft, -s, -ɪŋ, -əd

lofter
BR ˈlɒftə(r), -z
AM ˈlɔfdər, ˈlafdər, -z

Lofthouse
BR ˈlɒfthaʊs, ˈlɒftəs
AM ˈlɔftˌ(h)aʊs, ˈlaftˌ(h)aʊs

loftily
BR ˈlɒftɪli
AM ˈlɔfdəli, ˈlafdəli

loftiness
BR ˈlɔːftɪnɪs
AM ˈlɔfdinɪs, ˈlafdinɪs

Loftus
BR ˈlɒftəs
AM ˈlɔfdəs, ˈlafdəs

lofty
BR ˈlɒft|i, -ɪə(r), -ɪst
AM ˈlɔfdi, ˈlafdi, -ər, -ɪst

log
BR lɒg, -z, -ɪŋ, -d
AM lɔg, lag, -z, -ɪŋ, -d

Logan
BR ˈləʊg(ə)n
AM ˈloʊgən

logan[1]
BR ˈlɒg(ə)n, -z
AM ˈlɔgən, -z

logan[2]
BR ˈlɒg(ə)n, -z
AM ˈlɔgən, ˈlagən, -z

loganberry
BR ˈləʊg(ə)nb(ə)r|i, ˈləʊg(ə)nˌbɛr|i, -ɪz
AM ˈloʊgənˌbɛri, -z

logaoedic
BR ˌlɒgə(r)ˈiːdɪk
AM ˌlagəˈidɪk

logarithm
BR ˈlɒgərɪð(ə)m, -z
AM ˈlɔgəˌrɪðəm, ˈlagəˌrɪðəm, -z

logarithmic
BR ˌlɒgəˈrɪðmɪk
AM ˌlɔgəˈrɪðmɪk, ˌlagəˈrɪðmɪk

logarithmically
BR ˌlɒgəˈrɪðmɪkli
AM ˌlɔgəˈrɪðmɪk(ə)li, ˌlagəˈrɪðmɪk(ə)li

logbook
BR ˈlɒgbʊk, -s
AM ˈlɔgˌbʊk, ˈlagˌbʊk, -s

loge
BR ləʊʒ, -ɪz
AM loʊʒ, -əz

logger
BR ˈlɒgə(r), -z
AM ˈlɔgər, ˈlagər, -z

loggerhead
BR ˈlɒgəhɛd, -z
AM ˈlɔgərˌ(h)ɛd, ˈlagərˌ(h)ɛd, -z

loggia
BR ˈlɒdʒ(ɪ)ə(r), ˈləʊdʒ(ɪ)ə(r), -z
AM ˈlɔdʒ(i)ə, ˈloʊdʒ(i)ə, -z

logia
BR ˈləʊgɪə(r), ˈlɒgɪə(r), -z
AM ˈloʊdʒ(i)ə, -z

logic
BR ˈlɒdʒɪk
AM ˈladʒɪk

logical
BR ˈlɒdʒɪkl
AM ˈladʒəkəl

logicality
BR ˌlɒdʒɪˈkalti
AM ˌladʒəˈkælədi

logically
BR ˈlɒdʒɪkli
AM ˈladʒək(ə)li

logical positivism
BR ˌlɒdʒɪkl ˈpɒzɪtɪvɪz(ə)m
AM ˌladʒəkəl ˈpazədəˌvɪzəm

logical positivist
BR ˌlɒdʒɪkl ˈpɒzɪtɪvɪst, -s
AM ˌladʒəkəl ˈpazədəvəst, -s

logician
BR ləˈ(ʊ)dʒɪʃn, lɒˈdʒɪʃn, -z
AM ləˈdʒɪʃən, loʊˈdʒɪʃən, -z

logion
BR ˈləʊgɪən, ˈlɒgɪən, ˈlɒgɪɒn
AM ˈloʊdʒɪən

logistic
BR ləˈdʒɪstɪk, lɒˈdʒɪstɪk, -s
AM ləˈdʒɪstɪk, loʊˈdʒɪstɪk, -s

logistical
BR ləˈdʒɪstɪkl, lɒˈdʒɪstɪkl
AM ləˈdʒɪstɪkəl

logistically
BR ləˈdʒɪstɪkli, lɒˈdʒɪstɪkli
AM ˌloʊˈdʒɪstɪk(ə)li

logjam
BR 'lɒgdʒam, -z
AM 'lɔg,dʒæm,
'lɑg,dʒæm, -z

logo
BR 'lɒgəʊ, 'ləʊgəʊ, -z
AM 'loʊgoʊ, -z

logogram
BR 'lɒgəgram, -z
AM 'loʊgə,græm, -z

logographer
BR lɒ'gɒgrəfə(r),
lə'gɒgrəfə(r), -z
AM loʊ'gɑgrəfər, -z

logomachy
BR lə(ʊ)'gɒməkǀi, -ɪz
AM loʊ'gaməki, -z

logon
BR 'lɒgɒn, ,lɒg'ɒn, -z
AM 'lɔg,ɑn, 'lɑg,ɑn, -z

logopaedic
BR ,lɒgə'piːdɪk, -s
AM ,lɒgə'pidɪk,
,loʊgə'pidɪk, -s

logopedic
BR ,lɒgə'piːdɪk, -s
AM ,lɒgə'pidɪk,
,loʊgə'pidɪk, -s

logorrhea
BR ,lɒgə'riːə(r)
AM ,lɒgə'riə, ,loʊgə'riə

logorrheic
BR ,lɒgə'riːɪk
AM ,lɒgə'riɪk,
,loʊgə'riɪk

logorrhoea
BR ,lɒgə'riːə(r)
AM ,lɒgə'riə, ,loʊgə'riə

logorrhoeic
BR ,lɒgə'riːɪk
AM ,lɒgə'riɪk,
,loʊgə'riɪk

logos
BR 'lɒgɒs
AM 'loʊ,goʊs

logotype
BR 'lɒgə(ʊ)tʌɪp, -s
AM 'lɒgə,tʌɪp,
'loʊgə,tʌɪp, -s

logroll
BR 'lɒgrəʊl, -z, -ɪŋ, -d
AM 'lɔg,roʊl, 'lɑg,roʊl,
-z, -ɪŋ, -d

logroller
BR 'lɒg,rəʊlə(r), -z
AM 'lɔg,roʊlər,
'lɑg,roʊlər, -z

Logue
BR ləʊg
AM loʊg

logwood
BR 'lɒgwʊd
AM 'lɔg,wʊd, 'lɑg,wʊd

Lohengrin
BR 'ləʊəngrɪn
AM 'loʊən,grɪn

loin
BR lɔɪn, -z

AM lɔɪn, -z

loincloth
BR 'lɔɪnklɒǀθ, -θsǀ-ðz
AM 'lɔɪn,klɔǀθ,
'lɔɪn,klɑǀθ, -θsǀ-ðz

loir
BR 'lɔɪə(r), lwɑː(r)
AM 'lɔɪ(ə)r, l(ə)'wɑr

Loire
BR lwɑː(r)
AM l(ə)'wɑr

Lois
BR 'ləʊɪs
AM 'loʊwəs

loiter
BR 'lɔɪtǀə(r), -əz,
-(ə)rɪŋ, -əd
AM 'lɔɪdər, -z, -ɪŋ, -d

loiterer
BR 'lɔɪt(ə)rə(r), -z
AM 'lɔɪdərər, -z

Loki
BR 'ləʊki
AM 'loʊ,ki

Lola
BR 'ləʊlə(r)
AM 'loʊlə

Lolita
BR lɒ'liːtə(r),
lə(ʊ)'liːtə(r)
AM loʊ'lidə

loll
BR lɒl, -z, -ɪŋ, -d
AM lɑl, -z, -ɪŋ, -d

Lolland
BR 'lɒlənd
AM 'laland

lollapalooza
BR ,lɒləpə'luːzə(r)
AM ,laləpə'luzə

Lollard
BR 'lɒləd, 'lɒlɑːd, -z
AM 'lalərd, -z

Lollardism
BR 'lɒlədɪz(ə)m,
'lɒlɑːdɪz(ə)m
AM 'lalər,dɪzəm

Lollardy
BR 'lɒlədi, 'lɒlɑːdi
AM 'lalərdi

loller
BR 'lɒlə(r), -z
AM 'lalər, -z

lollipop
BR 'lɒlɪpɒp, -s
AM 'lali,pap, -s

lollop
BR 'lɒləp, -s, -ɪŋ, -t
AM 'laləp, -s, -ɪŋ, -t

lolly
BR 'lɒlǀi, -ɪz
AM 'lali, -z

Lomas
BR 'ləʊmas, 'ləʊməs
AM 'loʊməs

Lomax
BR 'ləʊmaks

AM lɔm, -z

Lombard
BR 'lɒmbɑːd, -z
AM 'lam,bard, -z

Lombardi
BR ləm'bɑːdi
AM ləm'bardi

Lombardic
BR (,)lɒm'bɑːdɪk
AM ,lam'bardɪk

Lombardy
BR 'lɒmbədi
AM 'lam,bardi,
'lambərdi

Lombok
BR 'lɒmbɒk
AM 'lam,bak

Lomé
BR 'ləʊmeɪ
AM loʊ'meɪ

loment
BR 'ləʊment,
'ləʊm(ə)nt, -s
AM 'loʊment, -s

lomentaceous
BR ,ləʊm(ə)n'teɪʃəs
AM ,loʊmən'teɪʃəs

London
BR 'lʌndən
AM 'ləndən

Londonderry
BR 'lʌndʌn,dɛri,
,lʌndʌn'dɛri
AM 'ləndən,dɛri,
,ləndən'dɛri

Londoner
BR 'lʌndənə(r), -z
AM 'ləndənər, -z

lone
BR ləʊn
AM loʊn

loneliness
BR 'ləʊnlɪnɪs
AM 'loʊnlinɪs

lonely
BR 'ləʊnlǀi, -ɪə(r), -ɪɪst
AM 'loʊnli, -ər, -ɪst

loner
BR 'ləʊnə(r), -z
AM 'loʊnər, -z

lonesome
BR 'ləʊns(ə)m
AM 'loʊnsəm

lonesomely
BR 'ləʊns(ə)mli
AM 'loʊnsəmli

lonesomeness
BR 'ləʊns(ə)mnəs
AM 'loʊnsəmnəs

long
BR lɒǀŋ, -ŋz, -ŋɪŋ, -ŋd,
-ŋgə(r), -ŋgɪst
AM lɔǀŋ, -ŋz, -ŋɪŋ, -ŋd,
-ŋgər, -ŋgəst

longanimity
BR ,lɒŋgə'nɪmɪti

AM ,lɒŋgə'nɪmɪdi,
,laŋgə'nɪmɪdi

long-awaited
BR 'lɒŋə,weɪtɪd
AM 'lɔŋə,weɪdɪd,
'laŋə,weɪdɪd

Long Beach
BR 'lɒŋ biːtʃ
AM 'lɔŋ ,bitʃ, 'laŋ +

longboard
BR 'lɒŋbɔːd, -z
AM 'lɔŋ,bɔ(ə)rd,
'laŋ,bɔ(ə)rd, -z

longboat
BR 'lɒŋbəʊt, -s
AM 'lɔŋ,boʊt,
'laŋ,boʊt, -s

Longbottom
BR 'lɒŋ,bɒtəm
AM 'lɔŋ,badəm,
'laŋ,badəm

longbow
BR 'lɒŋbəʊ, -z
AM 'lɔŋ,boʊ, 'laŋ,boʊ,
-z

Longbridge
BR 'lɒŋbrɪdʒ
AM 'lɔŋ,brɪdʒ,
'laŋ,brɪdʒ

Longden
BR 'lɒŋdən
AM 'lɔŋdən, 'laŋdən

longe
BR lʌn(d)ʒ, lɒn(d)ʒ, -ɪz,
-ɪŋ, -d
AM ləndʒ, -əz, -ɪŋ, -d

longeron
BR 'lɒn(d)ʒ(ə)rən,
'lɒn(d)ʒ(ə)rŋ,
'lɒn(d)ʒ(ə)rɒn, -z
AM 'land3ərən,
'land3ə,ran, -z

longevity
BR lɒn'dʒɛvɪti
AM lɑn'dʒɛvədi,
lan'dʒɛvədi

Longfellow
BR 'lɒŋ,fɛləʊ
AM 'lɔŋ,fɛloʊ,
'laŋ,fɛloʊ

Longford
BR 'lɒŋfəd
AM 'lɔŋfərd, 'laŋfərd

longhair
BR 'lɒŋhɛː(r), -z
AM 'lɔŋ,(h)ɛ(ə)r,
'laŋ,(h)ɛ(ə)r, -z

longhand
BR 'lɒŋhand
AM 'lɔŋ,(h)ænd,
'laŋ,(h)ænd

longhop
BR 'lɒŋhɒp, -s
AM 'lɔŋ,(h)ap,
'laŋ,(h)ap, -s

longhorn
BR 'lɒŋhɔːn, -z

AM 'lɒŋ,(h)ɔ:(ə)rn,
'laŋ,(h)ɔ:(ə)rn, -z

longhouse
BR 'lɒŋhaʊ|s, -zɪz
AM 'lɔ:ŋ,(h)aʊ|s,
'laŋ,(h)aʊ|s, -zəz

longicorn
BR 'lɒn(d)ʒɪkɔ:n, -z
AM 'lɑːndʒə,kɔ(ə)rn, -z

longing
BR 'lɒŋɪŋ, -z
AM 'lɔ:ŋɪŋ, 'lɑːŋɪŋ, -z

longingly
BR 'lɒŋɪŋli
AM 'lɔ:ŋɪŋli, 'lɑːŋɪŋli

Longinus
BR lɒn'dʒaɪnəs,
lɒŋ'giːnəs
AM lɑn'dʒaɪnəs

longish
BR 'lɒŋɪʃ
AM 'lɔ:ŋɪʃ, 'lɑːŋɪʃ

longitude
BR 'lɒŋgɪtjuːd,
'lɒŋgɪtʃuːd,
'lɒn(d)ʒɪtjuːd,
'lɒn(d)ʒɪtʃuːd, -z
AM 'lɑːndʒɪ,t(j)ud,
'lɑːndʒɪ,t(j)ud, -z

longitudinal
BR ,lɒŋgɪ'tjuːdɪnl,
,lɒŋgɪ'tʃuːdɪnl,
,lɒn(d)ʒɪ'tjuːdɪnl,
,lɒn(d)ʒɪ'tʃuːdɪnl
AM ,lɑːndʒə't(j)udṇəl,
,lɑːndʒə't(j)udṇəl

longitudinally
BR ,lɒŋgɪ'tjuːdɪnḷi,
,lɒŋgɪ'tʃuːdɪnḷi,
,lɒn(d)ʒɪ'tjuːdɪnḷi,
,lɒn(d)ʒɪ'tʃuːdɪnḷi,
,lɒŋgɪ'tjuːdɪnəli,
,lɒŋgɪ'tʃuːdɪnəli,
,lɒn(d)ʒɪ'tjuːdɪnəli,
,lɒn(d)ʒɪ'tʃuːdɪnəli
AM ,lɑːndʒə't(j)udṇəli,
,lɑːndʒə't(j)udṇəli

long jump
BR 'lɒŋ dʒʌmp
AM 'lɔ:ŋ ,dʒəmp, 'lɑŋ
,dʒəmp

Longleat
BR 'lɒŋliːt
AM 'lɔ:ŋlit, 'lɑŋlit

Longman
BR 'lɒŋmən
AM 'lɔ:ŋmən, 'lɑŋmən

longship
BR 'lɒŋʃɪp, -s
AM 'lɔ:ŋ,ʃɪp, 'lɑŋ,ʃɪp, -s

longshore
BR 'lɒŋʃɔ:(r)
AM 'lɔ:ŋ,ʃɔ(ə)r,
'lɑŋ,ʃɔ(ə)r

longshoreman
BR 'lɒŋʃɔ:mən
AM ,lɔ:ŋ'ʃɔrmən,
,lɑŋ'ʃɔrmən

longshoremen
BR 'lɒŋʃɔ:mən
AM ,lɔ:ŋ'ʃɔrmən,
,lɑŋ'ʃɔrmən

longstop
BR 'lɒŋstɒp, -s
AM 'lɔ:ŋ,stɑp, 'lɑŋ,stɑp,
-s

Longton
BR 'lɒŋt(ə)n
AM 'lɔ:ŋtən, 'lɑŋtən

Longtown
BR 'lɒŋtaʊn
AM 'lɔ:ŋ,taʊn, 'lɑŋ,taʊn

longueur
BR (,)lɒŋ'gəː(r), -z
AM lɔ:ŋ'(g)ər, lɑŋ'(g)ər,
-z

longways
BR 'lɒŋweɪz
AM 'lɔ:ŋ,weɪz, 'lɑŋ,weɪz

longwise
BR 'lɒŋwaɪz
AM 'lɔ:ŋ,waɪz,
'lɑŋ,waɪz

Ionicera
BR lə'nɪs(ə)rə(r),
lɒ'nɪs(ə)rə(r)
AM loʊ'nɪsərə

Lonnie
BR 'lɒni
AM 'lɑni

Lonrho®
BR 'lɒnrəʊ
AM 'lɑnroʊ

Lonsdale
BR 'lɒnzdeɪl
AM 'lɑnz,deɪl

loo
BR lu:, -z
AM lu, -z

Looe
BR lu:
AM lu

loof
BR lu:f, -s, -ɪŋ, -d
AM luf, -s, -ɪŋ, -d

loofa
BR 'lu:fə(r), -z
AM 'lufə, -z

loofah
BR 'lu:fə(r), -z
AM 'lufə, -z

look
BR lʊk, -s, -ɪŋ, -t
AM lʊk, -s, -ɪŋ, -t

lookalike
BR 'lʊkəlʌɪk, -s
AM 'lʊkə,laɪk, -s

looker
BR 'lʊkə(r), -z
AM 'lʊkər, -z

lookout
BR 'lʊkaʊt, -s
AM 'lʊk,aʊt, 'lʊkaʊt, -s

look-see
BR 'lʊksi:

AM 'lʊk,si

lookup
BR 'lʊkʌp, -s
AM 'lʊk,əp, -s

loom
BR lu:m, -z, -ɪŋ, -d
AM lum, -z, -ɪŋ, -d

loon
BR lu:n, -z
AM lun, -z

looniness
BR 'lu:nɪnɪs
AM 'luninɪs

loony
BR 'lu:n|i, -ɪz
AM 'luni, -z

loop
BR lu:p, -s, -ɪŋ, -t
AM lup, -s, -ɪŋ, -t

looper
BR 'lu:pə(r), -z
AM 'lupər, -z

loophole
BR 'lu:phəʊl, -z
AM 'lup,(h)oʊl, -z

loopiness
BR 'lu:pɪnɪs
AM 'lupinɪs

loopy
BR 'lu:p|i, -ɪə(r), -ɪɪst
AM 'lupi, -ər, -ɪst

loose
BR lu:s, -ɪz, -ɪŋ, -t, -ə(r),
-ɪst
AM lus, -əz, -ɪŋ, -t, -ər,
-əst

loosebox
BR 'lu:sbɒks, -ɪz
AM 'lus,bɑks, -əz

loosely
BR 'lu:sli
AM 'lusli

loosen
BR 'lu:s|n, -nz,
-ṇɪŋ \-nɪŋ, -nd
AM 'lusən, -z, -ɪŋ, -d

loosener
BR 'lu:sṇə(r),
'lu:snə(r), -z
AM 'lusnər, -z

looseness
BR 'lu:snəs
AM 'lusnəs

loosestrife
BR 'lu:sstrʌɪf, -s
AM 'lu(s),straɪf, -s

loosish
BR 'lu:sɪʃ
AM 'lusɪʃ

loot
BR lu:t, -s, -ɪŋ, -ɪd
AM lu|t, -ts, -dɪŋ, -dəd

looter
BR 'lu:tə(r), -z
AM 'ludər, -z

lop
BR lɒp, -s, -ɪŋ, -t

lope
BR ləʊp, -s, -ɪŋ, -t
AM loʊp, -s, -ɪŋ, -t

López
BR 'ləʊpɛz
AM 'loʊpez
SP 'lopeθ, 'lopes

lophobranch
BR 'ləʊfə(ʊ)braŋk,
'lɒfə(ʊ)braŋk, -s
AM 'lɑfə,braŋk,
'loʊfə,braŋk, -s

lophodont
BR 'ləʊfə(ʊ)dɒnt,
'lɒfə(ʊ)dɒnt, -s
AM 'lɑfə,dɑnt,
'loʊfə,dɑnt, -s

lophophore
BR 'ləʊfə(ʊ)fɔ:(r),
'lɒfə(ʊ)fɔ:(r), -z
AM 'lɑfə,fɔ(ə)r,
'loʊfə,fɔ(ə)r, -z

lopolith
BR 'lɒpəlɪθ, 'lɒplɪθ, -s
AM 'lɑpə,lɪθ, -s

lopper
BR 'lɒpə(r), -z
AM 'lɑpər, -z

loppy
BR 'lɒp|i, -ɪə(r), -ɪɪst
AM 'lɑpi, -ər, -ɪst

lopsided
BR ,lɒp'saɪdɪd
AM 'lɑp,saɪdɪd

lopsidedly
BR ,lɒp'saɪdɪdli
AM 'lɑp,saɪdɪdli

lopsidedness
BR ,lɒp'saɪdɪdnɪs
AM 'lɑp,saɪdɪdnɪs

loquacious
BR lə'kweɪʃəs
AM loʊ'kweɪʃəs

loquaciously
BR lə'kweɪʃəsli
AM loʊ'kweɪʃəsli

loquaciousness
BR lə'kweɪʃəsnəs
AM loʊ'kweɪʃəsnəs

loquacity
BR lə(ʊ)'kwasɪti
AM loʊ'kwæsədi

loquat
BR 'ləʊkwɒt, 'ləʊkwət,
-s
AM 'loʊ,kwɑt,
'loʊkwɑt, -s

loquitur
BR 'lɒkwɪtə(r)
AM 'lɑkwədər,
'loʊkwədər

lor
BR lɔ:(r)
AM lɔ(ə)r

loral
BR 'lɔ:rəl, 'lɔ:rḷ, -z
AM 'lɔrəl, -z

loran
BR ˈlɔːrən, ˈlɔːr̩n, -z
AM ˈlɔrən, -z

Lorca
BR ˈlɔːkə(r)
AM ˈlɔrkə

Lorcan
BR ˈlɔːk(ə)n
AM ˈlɔrkən

lorch
BR lɔːtʃ, -ɪz
AM lɔrtʃ, -əz

lorcha
BR ˈlɔːtʃə(r), -z
AM ˈlɔr(t)ʃə, -z

lord
BR lɔːd, -z, -ɪŋ, -ɪd
AM lɔ(ə)rd, -z, -ɪŋ, -əd

lordless
BR ˈlɔːdləs
AM ˈlɔrdləs

lordlike
BR ˈlɔːdlʌɪk
AM ˈlɔrd,lɑɪk

lordliness
BR ˈlɔːdlɪnɪs
AM ˈlɔrdlɪnɪs

lordling
BR ˈlɔːdlɪŋ, -z
AM ˈlɔrdlɪŋ, -z

lordly
BR ˈlɔːdl|i, -ɪə(r), -ɪɪst
AM ˈlɔrdli, -ər, -ɪst

lordosis
BR lɔːˈdəʊsɪs
AM lɔrˈdoʊsəs

lordotic
BR lɔːˈdɒtɪk
AM lɔrˈdɑdɪk

lordship
BR ˈlɔːdʃɪp, -s
AM ˈlɔrdˌʃɪp, -s

Lordy
BR ˈlɔːdi
AM ˈlɔrdi

lore
BR lɔː(r)
AM lɔ(ə)r

L'Oréal®
BR ˈlɒrɪal
AM ˌlɔriˈæl

Lorelei
BR ˈlɒrəlʌɪ, ˈlɔːrəlʌɪ, -z
AM ˈlɔrəˌlaɪ, -z

Loren
BR ləˈrɛn, ˈlɔːrən, ˈlɔːrn̩
AM ləˈrɛn

Lorentz
BR ˈlɒrən(t)s, ˈlɒrn̩(t)s
AM lɔˈrənz

Lorenz
BR ˈlɒrənz, ˈlɒrn̩z
AM lɔˈrənz

Lorenzo
BR ləˈrɛnzəʊ
AM ləˈrɛnˌzoʊ

Loreto
BR ləˈreɪtəʊ
AM ləˈredoʊ

Loretta
BR ləˈɛtə(r)
AM ləˈredə

lorgnette
BR lɔːˈnjɛt, -s
AM lɔrnˈjɛt, -s

lorgnon
BR ˈlɔːnj(ə)n, -z
AM lɔrnˈjɒn, -z

loricate
BR ˈlɒrɪkeɪt, -s
AM ˈlɔrəˌkeɪt, -s

lorikeet
BR ˈlɒrɪkiːt, ˌlɒrɪˈkiːt, -s
AM ˈlɔrəˌkit, -s

lorimer
BR ˈlɒrɪmə(r), -z
AM ˈlɔrəmər, -z

loris
BR ˈlɔːrɪs, -ɪz
AM ˈlɔrəs, -əz

lorn
BR lɔːn
AM lɔ(ə)rn

Lorna
BR ˈlɔːnə(r)
AM ˈlɔrnə

Lorraine
BR ləˈreɪn
AM ləˈreɪn

lorry
BR ˈlɒr|i, -ɪz
AM ˈlɔri, -z

lorryload
BR ˈlɒrɪləʊd, -z
AM ˈlɔriˌloʊd, -z

lory
BR ˈlɔːr|i, -ɪz
AM ˈlɔri, -z

losable
BR ˈluːzəbl
AM ˈluzəbəl

Los Alamos
BR lɒs ˈaləmɒs
AM lɔ ˈsæləmoʊs, lɑ ˈsæləmoʊs

Los Angeles
BR lɒs ˈan(d)ʒɪliːz
AM lɔ ˈsændʒələs, lɑ ˈsændʒələs

lose
BR luːz, -ɪz, -ɪŋ
AM luz, -əz, -ɪŋ

loser
BR ˈluːzə(r), -z
AM ˈluzər, -z

Losey
BR ˈləʊzi
AM ˈloʊzi

loss
BR lɒs, -ɪz
AM lɔs, lɑs, -əz

löss
BR ˈləʊɪs, ˈləʊɛs, ləːs
AM lɛs, ləs, ˈloʊˌɛs

Lossiemouth
BR ˈlɒsɪmaʊθ, ˌlɒsɪˈmaʊθ
AM ˌlɔsiˈmaʊθ, ˌlɑsiˈmaʊθ

lost
BR lɒst
AM lɔst, lɑst

Lostwithiel
BR lɒs(t)ˈwɪθɪəl
AM ˌlɔstˈwɪθɪəl, ˌlɑstˈwɪθɪəl

lot
BR lɒt, -s
AM lɑt, -s

loth
BR ləʊθ
AM loʊθ

Lothario
BR ləˈθɑːrɪəʊ, ləˈθɛːrɪəʊ, -z
AM loʊˈθɛrioʊ, loʊˈθɑrioʊ, -z

Lothian
BR ˈləʊðɪən
AM ˈloʊðiən

loti
BR ˈləʊt|i, ˈluːt|i, -ɪz
AM ˈloʊdi, -z

lotic
BR ˈləʊtɪk
AM ˈloʊdɪk

lotion
BR ˈləʊʃn, -z
AM ˈloʊʃən, -z

lotsa
lots of
BR ˈlɒtsə(r)
AM ˈlɑtsə

lotta
lot of
BR ˈlɒtə(r)
AM ˈlɑdə

lottery
BR ˈlɒt(ə)r|i, -ɪz
AM ˈlɑdəri, -z

Lottie
BR ˈlɒti
AM ˈlɑdi

lotto
BR ˈlɒtəʊ
AM ˈlɑdoʊ

lotus
BR ˈləʊtəs, -ɪz
AM ˈloʊdəs, -əz

Lou
BR luː
AM lu

louche
BR luːʃ
AM luʃ

loud
BR laʊd, -ə(r), -ɪst
AM laʊd, -ər, -əst

louden
BR ˈlaʊd|n, -nz, -n̩ɪŋ \ -nɪŋ, -nd
AM ˈlaʊdən, -z, -ɪŋ, -d

loudhailer
BR ˌlaʊdˈheɪlə(r), -z
AM ˈlaʊdˌheɪlər, -z

loudish
BR ˈlaʊdɪʃ
AM ˈlaʊdɪʃ

loudly
BR ˈlaʊdli
AM ˈlaʊdli

loudmouth
BR ˈlaʊdmaʊθ, -ðz \ -θs
AM ˈlaʊdˌmaʊθ, -ðz

loudmouthed
BR ˌlaʊdˈmaʊðd
AM ˈlaʊdˌmaʊðd

loudness
BR ˈlaʊdnəs
AM ˈlaʊdnəs

loudspeaker
BR ˌlaʊdˈspiːkə(r), -z
AM ˈlaʊdˌspikər, -z

Louella
BR luˈɛlə(r)
AM luˈɛlə

lough
BR lɒx, lɒk, -s
AM lɑk, -s

Loughborough
BR ˈlʌfb(ə)rə(r)
AM ˈləfbərə

Loughlin
BR ˈlɒxlɪn, ˈlɒklɪn
AM ˈlɑklən

Lough Neagh
BR ˌlɒx ˈneɪ, ˌlɒk +
AM ˌlɑk ˈneɪ

Loughor
BR ˈlʌxə(r), ˈlʌkə(r)
AM ˈlɑkər

Louie
BR ˈluːi
AM ˈluwi

Louis
BR ˈluːiː, ˈluːɪs
AM ˈluwəs, ˈluwi

louis¹
coin
BR ˈluːi
AM ˈluwəs, ˈluwi

louis²
coins
BR ˈluːiz
AM ˈluwiz

Louisa
BR luˈiːzə(r)
AM ləˈwizə

Louisburg
BR ˈluːɪsbəːg
AM ˈləwəsˌbərg

Louise
BR luˈiːz
AM ləˈwiz

Louisiana
BR lʊ,iːzɪˈanə(r)
AM ˌluwiziˈænə

Louisianan
BR lʊ,iːzɪˈanən, -z
AM ˌluwiziˈænən, -z

Louisville
BR ˈluːɪvɪl
AM ˈluwi,vɪl, ˈlu(wə)vəl

lounge
BR laʊn(d)ʒ, -ɪz, -ɪŋ, -d
AM laʊndʒ, -əz, -ɪŋ, -d

lounger
BR ˈlaʊn(d)ʒə(r), -z
AM ˈlaʊndʒər, -z

Lounsbury
BR ˈlaʊnzb(ə)ri
AM ˈlaʊnz,bɛri

loupe
BR luːp, -s
AM lup, -s

lour
BR ˈlaʊə(r), -z, -ɪŋ, -d
AM ˈlaʊ(ə)r, -z, -ɪŋ, -d

Lourdes
BR lʊəd(z), lɔːdz
AM lʊ(ə)rd
FR luʀd

Lourenço Marques
BR lə,rɛnsəʊ ˈmaːks
AM lə,rɛn(t)soʊ ˈmɑrˈkɛs
B PORT lo,rẽsu ˈmarkis
L PORT lo,rẽsu ˈmarkəʃ

louringly
BR ˈlaʊərɪŋli
AM ˈlaʊrɪŋli

loury
BR ˈlaʊəri
AM ˈlaʊri

louse
BR laʊs, -ɪz, -ɪŋ, -t
AM laʊs, -əz, -ɪŋ, -t

lousewort
BR ˈlaʊswəːt, -s
AM ˈlaʊswərt, ˈlaʊswɔ(ə)rt, -s

lousily
BR ˈlaʊzɪli
AM ˈlaʊzəli

lousiness
BR ˈlaʊzɪnɪs
AM ˈlaʊzɪnɪs

lousy
BR ˈlaʊz|i, -ɪə(r), -ɪɪst
AM ˈlaʊzi, -ər, -ɪɪst

lout
BR laʊt, -s
AM laʊt, -s

Louth
BR laʊθ
AM laʊθ

loutish
BR ˈlaʊtɪʃ
AM ˈlaʊdɪʃ

loutishly
BR ˈlaʊtɪʃli
AM ˈlaʊdɪʃli

loutishness
BR ˈlaʊtɪʃnɪs
AM ˈlaʊdɪʃnɪs

Louvain
BR lʊˈvã, lʊˈvan
AM luˈvæn

louver
BR ˈluːvə(r), -z
AM ˈluvər, -z, -d

Louvre
BR ˈluːvrə(r), luːv
AM ˈluːv(rə)

louvre
BR ˈluːvə(r), -z, -d
AM ˈluvər, -z, -d

lovability
BR ˌlʌvəˈbɪlɪti
AM ˌləvəˈbɪlɪdi

lovable
BR ˈlʌvbl
AM ˈləvəbəl

lovableness
BR ˈlʌvblnəs
AM ˈləvəbəlnəs

lovably
BR ˈlʌvəbli
AM ˈləvəbli

lovage
BR ˈlʌvɪdʒ
AM ˈləvɪdʒ

lovat
BR ˈlʌvət
AM ˈləvət

love
BR lʌv, -z, -ɪŋ, -d
AM ləv, -z, -ɪŋ, -d

loveable
BR ˈlʌvəbl
AM ˈləvəbəl

loveably
BR ˈlʌvəbli
AM ˈləvəbli

lovebird
BR ˈlʌvbəːd, -z
AM ˈləv,bərd, -z

lovebite
BR ˈlʌvbaɪt, -s
AM ˈləv,baɪt, -s

lovechild
BR ˈlʌvtʃaɪld
AM ˈləv,tʃaɪld

lovechildren
BR ˈlʌv,tʃɪldr(ə)n
AM ˈləv,tʃɪldrən

Loveday
BR ˈlʌvdeɪ
AM ˈləv,deɪ

Lovejoy
BR ˈlʌvdʒɔɪ
AM ˈləv,dʒɔɪ

Lovelace
BR ˈlʌvleɪs
AM ˈləvləs

loveless
BR ˈlʌvləs
AM ˈləvləs

lovelessly
BR ˈlʌvləsli
AM ˈləvləsli

lovelessness
BR ˈlʌvləsnəs
AM ˈləvləsnəs

lovelily
BR ˈlʌvlɪli
AM ˈləvləli

loveliness
BR ˈlʌvlɪnɪs
AM ˈləvlinɪs

Lovell
BR ˈlʌvl
AM ləˈvɛl

lovelock
BR ˈlʌvlɒk, -s
AM ˈləv,lɑk, -s

lovelorn
BR ˈlʌvlɔːn
AM ˈləv,lɔ(ə)rn

lovely
BR ˈlʌvl|i, -ɪz, -ɪə(r), -ɪɪst
AM ˈləvli, -z, -ər, -ɪɪst

lovemaking
BR ˈlʌv,meɪkɪŋ
AM ˈləv,meɪkɪŋ

lover
BR ˈlʌvə(r), -z
AM ˈləvər, -z

Loveridge
BR ˈlʌv(ə)rɪdʒ
AM ˈləv,rɪdʒ

loverless
BR ˈlʌvələs
AM ˈləvərləs

loverlike
BR ˈlʌvəlʌɪk
AM ˈləvər,laɪk

lovesick
BR ˈlʌvsɪk
AM ˈləv,sɪk

lovesickness
BR ˈlʌv,sɪknɪs
AM ˈləv,sɪknɪs

lovesome
BR ˈlʌvs(ə)m
AM ˈləvsəm

loveworthy
BR ˈlʌv,wəːði
AM ˈləv,wərði

lovey
BR ˈlʌv|i, -ɪz
AM ˈləvi, -z

lovey-dovey
BR ˌlʌvɪˈdʌvi
AM ˌləviˈdəvi

lovingly
BR ˈlʌvɪŋli
AM ˈləvɪŋli

lovingness
BR ˈlʌvɪŋnɪs
AM ˈləvɪŋnɪs

low
BR ləʊ, -z, -ɪŋ, -d, -ə(r), -ɪst
AM loʊ, -z, -ɪŋ, d, -(ə)r, -əst

lowball
BR ˈləʊbɔːl, -z
AM ˈloʊ,bɔl, ˈloʊ,bɑl, -z

lowboy
BR ˈləʊbɔɪ, -z
AM ˈloʊ,bɔɪ, -z

lowbrow
BR ˈləʊbraʊ, -z
AM ˈloʊ,braʊ, -z

lowbrowed
BR ˌləʊˈbraʊd
AM ˈloʊbraʊd

low-cal
BR ˌləʊˈkal
AM ˌloʊˈkæl

low-calorie
BR ˌləʊˈkaləri
AM ˌloʊˈkæl(ə)ri

low-down[1]
adjective
BR ˌləʊˈdaʊn
AM ˈloʊˈdaʊn

low-down[2]
noun
BR ˈləʊdaʊn
AM ˈloʊ,daʊn

Lowell
BR ˈləʊəl
AM ˈloʊəl

Löwenbräu
BR ˈləʊənbraʊ
AM ˈloʊən,braʊ
GER ˈlœːvɪnbrɔy

lower[1]
lour
BR ˈlaʊə(r), -z, -ɪŋ, -d
AM ˈloʊər, ˈlaʊər, -z, -(ə)rɪŋ, -d

lower[2]
position
BR ˈləʊə(r), -z, -ɪŋ, -d
AM ˈloʊ(ə)r, -z, -ɪŋ, -d

lowermost
BR ˈləʊəməʊst
AM ˈloʊ(ə)r,moʊst

Lowery
BR ˈlaʊ(ə)ri
AM ˈlaʊri

Lowestoft
BR ˈləʊ(ɪ)stɒft
AM ˈloʊ(ə),stɔft, ˈloʊ(ə),staft

lowish
BR ˈləʊɪʃ
AM ˈloʊɪʃ

lowland
BR ˈləʊlənd, -z
AM ˈloʊlənd, ˈloʊ,lænd, -z

lowlander
BR ˈləʊləndə(r), -z
AM ˈloʊləndər, ˈloʊ,lændər, -z

lowlife
BR ˈləʊlʌɪf
AM ˈloʊˌlaɪf
lowlight
BR ˈləʊlʌɪt, -s
AM ˈloʊˌlaɪt, -s
lowlily
BR ˈləʊlɪli
AM ˈloʊlɪli
lowliness
BR ˈləʊlɪnɪs
AM ˈloʊlinɪs
lowly
BR ˈləʊl|i, -ɪə(r), -ɪɪst
AM ˈloʊli, -ər, -ɪst
Lowman
BR ˈləʊmən
AM ˈloʊmən
Lowndes
BR laʊn(d)z
AM ˈlaʊndəs
lowness
BR ˈləʊnəs, -ɪz
AM ˈloʊnəs, -əz
Lowrie
BR ˈlaʊri
AM ˈlaʊri
low-rise¹
adjective
BR ˌləʊˈrʌɪz
AM ˈloʊˌraɪz
low-rise²
noun
BR ˈləʊrʌɪz, -ɪz
AM ˈloʊˌraɪz, -ɪz
Lowry
BR ˈlaʊri
AM ˈlaʊri
low season¹
adjective
BR ˌləʊ ˈsiːzn
AM ˈloʊ ˌsizn
low season²
noun
BR ˈləʊ ˌsiːzn, -z
AM ˈloʊ ˌsizn, -z
lox
BR lɒks
AM lɑks
Loxene
BR ˈlɒksiːn
AM ˈlɑkˌsin
Loxley
BR ˈlɒksli
AM ˈlɑksli
loxodrome
BR ˈlɒksədrəʊm, -z
AM ˈlɑksəˌdroʊm, -z
loxodromic
BR ˌlɒksəˈdrɒmɪk
AM ˌlɑksəˈdrɑmɪk
loyal
BR ˈlɔɪəl
AM ˈlɔɪ(ə)l
loyalism
BR ˈlɔɪəlɪz(ə)m
AM ˈlɔɪ(ə)lˌɪzəm

loyalist
BR ˈlɔɪəlɪst, -s
AM ˈlɔɪ(ə)ləst, -s
loyally
BR ˈlɔɪəli
AM ˈlɔɪ(ə)li
loyalty
BR ˈlɔɪəlt|i, -ɪz
AM ˈlɔɪ(ə)lti, -z
lozenge
BR ˈlɒz(ɪ)n(d)ʒ, -ɪz, -d
AM ˈlɑzəndʒ, -əz, -d
lozengy
BR ˈlɒz(ɪ)ndʒi
AM ˈlɑzəndʒi
Ltd
BR ˈlɪmɪtɪd
AM ˈlɪmɪdɪd
Lualaba
BR ˌluːəˈlɑːbə(r)
AM ˌluəˈlɑbə
Luanda
BR lʊˈandə(r)
AM ləˈwɑndə
Luandan
BR lʊˈandən, -z
AM ləˈwɑndən, -z
Luang Prabang
BR lʊˌaŋ prəˈbaŋ
AM luˈæŋ prəˈbæŋ
luau
BR ˈluːaʊ, -z
AM ˈluˌaʊ, -z
lubber
BR ˈlʌbə(r), -z
AM ˈləbər, -z
lubberlike
BR ˈlʌbəlʌɪk
AM ˈləbərˌlaɪk
lubberly
BR ˈlʌbəli
AM ˈləbərli
Lubbock
BR ˈlʌbək
AM ˈləbək
lube
BR luːb, -z, -ɪŋ, -d
AM lub, -z, -ɪŋ, -d
Lübeck
BR ˈluːbɛk
AM ˈluˌbɛk
Lublin
BR ˈluːblɪn
AM ˈluˌblɪn
lubra
BR ˈl(j)uːbrə(r), -z
AM ˈlubrə, -z
lubricant
BR ˈl(j)uːbrɪk(ə)nt, -s
AM ˈlubrəkənt, -s
lubricate
BR ˈl(j)uːbrɪkeɪt, -s, -ɪŋ, -ɪd
AM ˈlubrəˌkeɪt, -ts, -dɪŋ, -dɪd
lubrication
BR ˌl(j)uːbrɪˈkeɪʃn

AM ˌlubrəˈkeɪʃən
lubricative
BR ˈl(j)uːbrɪkətɪv
AM ˈlubrəˌkeɪdɪv
lubricator
BR ˈl(j)uːbrɪkeɪtə(r), -z
AM ˈlubrəˌkeɪdər, -z
lubricious
BR l(j)uːˈbrɪʃəs
AM luˈbrɪʃəs
lubricity
BR l(j)uːˈbrɪsɪti
AM luˈbrɪsɪdi
Lubumbashi
BR ˌlʊbʊmˈbaʃi
AM ˌlubumˈbɑʃi
Lubyanka
BR ˌlʊbɪˈaŋkə(r)
AM lʊˈbjaŋkə
RUS lʲuˈbʲankə
Lucan
BR ˈluːk(ə)n
AM ˈlukən
Lucania
BR luːˈkeɪnɪə(r)
AM luˈkeɪnɪə
lucarne
BR ˈl(j)uːkɑːn, -z
AM luˈkɑrn, -z
Lucas
BR ˈluːkəs
AM ˈlukəs
luce
BR luːs
AM lus
lucency
BR ˈluːsnsi
AM ˈlusənsi
lucent
BR ˈluːsnt
AM ˈlusənt
lucently
BR ˈluːsntli
AM ˈlusn(t)li
Lucerne
BR luːˈsəːn
AM luˈsərn
Lucey
BR ˈluːsi
AM ˈlusi
Lucia¹
Italian
BR lʊˈtʃiːə(r)
AM lʊˈtʃiə
Lucia²
BR ˈluːsɪə(r), ˈluːʃ(ɪə)(r)
AM ˈluʃə
Lucian
BR ˈluːʃɪən, ˈluːsɪən, ˈluːʃ(ə)n
AM ˈluʃən
lucid
BR ˈl(j)uːsɪd
AM ˈlusəd
lucidity
BR l(j)uːˈsɪdɪti

AM ˌlubrəˈkeɪʃən
lucidly
BR ˈl(j)uːsɪdli
AM ˈlusədli
lucidness
BR ˈl(j)uːsɪdnɪs
AM ˈlusədnəs
Lucie
BR ˈluːsi
AM ˈlusi
Lucifer
BR ˈl(j)uːsɪfə(r), -z
AM ˈlusəfər, -z
lucifer
BR ˈl(j)uːsɪfə(r), -z
AM ˈlusəfər, -z
luciferin
BR l(j)uːˈsɪf(ə)rɪn
AM luˈsɪf(ə)rən
Lucille
BR luːˈsiːl
AM luˈsil
Lucinda
BR luːˈsɪndə(r)
AM luˈsɪndə
Lucite®
BR ˈluːsʌɪt
AM ˈluˌsaɪt
Lucius
BR ˈluːsɪəs, ˈluːʃəs
AM ˈluʃəs
luck
BR lʌk
AM lək
luckily
BR ˈlʌkɪli
AM ˈləkəli
luckiness
BR ˈlʌkɪnɪs
AM ˈləkinɪs
luckless
BR ˈlʌkləs
AM ˈləkləs
lucklessly
BR ˈlʌkləsli
AM ˈləkləsli
lucklessness
BR ˈlʌkləsnəs
AM ˈləkləsənəs
Lucknow
BR ˈlʌknaʊ
AM ˈləknaʊ
lucky
BR ˈlʌk|i, -ɪə(r), -ɪɪst
AM ˈləki, -ər, -ɪst
Lucozade®
BR ˈluːkəzeɪd
AM ˈlukəˌzeɪd
lucrative
BR ˈl(j)uːkrətɪv
AM ˈlukrədɪv
lucratively
BR ˈl(j)uːkrətɪvli
AM ˈlukrədəvli
lucrativeness
BR ˈl(j)uːkrətɪvnɪs
AM ˈlukrədɪvnɪs

lucre
BR ˈl(j)uːkə(r)
AM ˈlukər

Lucrece
BR l(j)uːˈkriːs
AM luˈkris

Lucretia
BR l(j)uːˈkriːʃə(r)
AM luˈkriʃə

Lucretius
BR l(j)uːˈkriːʃəs
AM luˈkriʃəs

lucubrate
BR ˈl(j)uːkjʊbreɪt, -s,
-ɪŋ, -ɪd
AM ˈluk(j)əˌbreɪ|t, -ts,
-dɪŋ, -dɪd

lucubration
BR ˌl(j)uːkjʊˈbreɪʃn
AM ˌluk(j)əˈbreɪʃən

lucubrator
BR ˈl(j)uːkjʊbreɪtə(r),
-z
AM ˈluk(j)əˌbreɪdər, -z

luculent
BR ˈluːkjʊl(ə)nt
AM ˈlukjələnt

luculently
BR ˈluːkjʊl(ə)ntli
AM ˈlukjələn(t)li

Lucullan
adjective
BR l(j)uːˈkʌlən
AM luˈkələn

Lucy
BR ˈluːsi
AM ˈlusi

Lūda
BR ˈluːdə(r)
AM ˈludə

Luddism
BR ˈlʌdɪz(ə)m
AM ˈləˌdɪzəm

Luddite
BR ˈlʌdʌɪt, -s
AM ˈləˌdaɪt, -s

Ludditism
BR ˈlʌdʌɪtɪz(ə)m
AM ˈlədəˌtɪzəm

lude
BR luːd, -z
AM lud, -z

Ludendorff
BR ˈluːdndɔːf
AM ˈludnˌdɔ(ə)rf

Ludgate
BR ˈlʌdgət, ˈlʌdgeɪt
AM ˈlədgət, ˈlədˌgeɪt

ludic
BR ˈl(j)uːdɪk
AM ˈl(j)udɪk

ludicrous
BR ˈl(j)uːdɪkrəs
AM ˈludəkrəs

ludicrously
BR ˈl(j)uːdɪkrəsli
AM ˈludəkrəsli

ludicrousness
BR ˈl(j)uːdɪkrəsnəs
AM ˈludəkrəsnəs

Ludlow
BR ˈlʌdləʊ
AM ˈlədˌloʊ

Ludlum
BR ˈlʌdləm
AM ˈlədləm

ludo
BR ˈl(j)uːdəʊ
AM ˈluˌdoʊ

Ludovic
BR ˈluːdəvɪk
AM ˈludəˌvɪk

Ludwig
BR ˈlʊdwɪg, ˈlʊdvɪg
AM ˈlʊdˌwɪg

lues
BR ˈl(j)uːiːz
AM ˈluiz
lues venerea

luetic
BR l(j)uːˈiːtɪk,
l(j)uːˈetɪk
AM luˈidɪk

luff
BR lʌf, -s, -ɪŋ, -t
AM ləf, -s, -ɪŋ, -t

luffa
BR ˈlʌfə(r), -z
AM ˈləfə, -z

Luftwaffe
BR ˈlʊftˌwafə(r),
ˈlʊftˌvafə(r),
ˈlʊftˌwɑːfə(r),
ˈlʊftˌvɑːfə(r)
AM ˈlʊf(t)ˌwafə

lug
BR lʌg, -z, -ɪŋ, -d
AM ləg, -z, -ɪŋ, -d

Lugano
BR luːˈgɑːnəʊ
AM luˈganoʊ

Lugard
BR ˈluːgɑːd
AM ˈluˌgard

luge
BR luː(d)ʒ, -ɪz, -ɪŋ, -d
AM luʒ, -əz, -ɪŋ, -d

Luger®
BR ˈluːgə(r), -z
AM ˈlugər, -z

luggable
BR ˈlʌgəbl
AM ˈləgəbəl

luggage
BR ˈlʌgɪdʒ
AM ˈləgɪdʒ

lugger
BR ˈlʌgə(r), -z
AM ˈləgər, -z

lughole
BR ˈlʌghəʊl, -z
AM ˈləg,(h)oʊl, -z

lugsail
BR ˈlʌgseɪl, ˈlʌgsl, -z

ludicrousness
AM ˈləgsəl, ˈləgˌseɪl, -z

lugubrious
BR ləˈg(j)uːbrɪəs
AM luˈgubriəs,
ləˈgubriəs

lugubriously
BR ləˈg(j)uːbrɪəsli
AM luˈgubriəsli

lugubriousness
BR ləˈg(j)uːbrɪəsnəs
AM luˈgubriəsnəs

lugworm
BR ˈlʌgwəːm, -z
AM ˈləgˌwərm, -z

Luick
BR ˈluːɪk
AM ˈluwɪk

Lukács
BR ˈluːkatʃ
AM ˈluˌkatʃ

Luke
BR luːk
AM luk

lukewarm
BR ˌluːkˈwɔːm
AM ˈlukˌwɔ(ə)rm

lukewarmly
BR ˌluːkˈwɔːmli
AM ˈlukˌwɔrmli

lukewarmness
BR ˌluːkˈwɔːmnəs
AM ˈlukˌwɔrmnəs

lull
BR lʌl, -z, -ɪŋ, -d
AM ləl, -z, -ɪŋ, -d

lullaby
BR ˈlʌləbʌɪ, -z
AM ˈlələˌbaɪ, -z

Lully
BR ˈlʊli
AM lʊˈli

lulu
BR ˈluːluː, -z
AM ˈluˌlu, -z

Lulworth
BR ˈlʌlwəθ, ˈlʌlwəːθ
AM ˈləlˌwərθ

lum
BR lʌm, -z
AM ləm, -z

Lumb
BR lʌm
AM ləm

lumbago
BR lʌmˈbeɪgəʊ
AM ˌləmˈbeɪˌgoʊ

lumbar
BR ˈlʌmbə(r)
AM ˈləmˌbar, ˈləmbər

lumber
BR ˈlʌmb|ə(r), -əz,
-(ə)rɪŋ, -əd
AM ˈləmb|ər, -ərz,
-(ə)rɪŋ, -ərd

lumberer
BR ˈlʌmb(ə)rə(r), -z
AM ˈləmbərər, -z

lumberjack
BR ˈlʌmbədʒak, -s
AM ˈləmbərˌdʒæk, -s

lumberman
BR ˈlʌmbəmən,
ˈlʌmbəman
AM ˈləmbərmən

lumbermen
BR ˈlʌmbəmən,
ˈlʌmbəmɛn
AM ˈləmbərmən

lumbersome
BR ˈlʌmbəs(ə)m
AM ˈləmbərsəm

lumberyard
BR ˈlʌmbəjɑːd, -z
AM ˈləmbərˌjard, -z

lumbrical
BR ˈlʌmbrɪkl
AM ˈləmbrəkəl

lumen
BR ˈl(j)uːmɪn,
ˈl(j)uːmɛn, -z
AM ˈlumən, -z

lumière
BR ˈluːmɪɛː(r),
ˌluːmɪˈɛː(r)
AM ˌlumiˈɛ(ə)r

luminaire
BR ˌl(j)uːmɪˈnɛː(r), -z
AM ˌluməˈnɛ(ə)r, -z

luminal
BR ˈl(j)uːmɪnl
AM ˈlumənəl

luminance
BR ˈl(j)uːmɪnəns
AM ˈlumənəns

luminary
BR ˈl(j)uːmɪn(ə)r|i, -ɪz
AM ˈluməˌnɛri, -z

luminesce
BR ˌl(j)uːmɪˈnɛs, -ɪz,
-ɪŋ, -t
AM ˌluməˈnɛs, -əz, -ɪŋ, -t

luminescence
BR ˌl(j)uːmɪˈnɛsns
AM ˌluməˈnɛsəns

luminescent
BR ˌl(j)uːmɪˈnɛsnt
AM ˌluməˈnɛsənt

luminiferous
BR ˌl(j)uːmɪˈnɪf(ə)rəs
AM ˌluməˈnɪf(ə)rəs

luminosity
BR ˌl(j)uːmɪˈnɒsɪti
AM ˌluməˈnasədi

luminous
BR ˈl(j)uːmɪnəs
AM ˈlumənəs

luminously
BR ˈl(j)uːmɪnəsli
AM ˈlumənəsli

luminousness
BR ˈl(j)uːmɪnəsnəs
AM ˈlumənəsnəs

Lumley
BR ˈlʌmli

AM 'ləmli

lumme
BR 'lʌmi
AM 'ləmi

lummox
BR 'lʌməks, -ɪz
AM 'ləməks, -əz

lummy
BR 'lʌmi
AM 'ləmi

lump
BR lʌmp, -ps, -pɪŋ, -(p)t
AM lʌmp, -s, -ɪŋ, -t

lumpectomy
BR ,lʌm'pektəm|i, -ɪz
AM ,ləm'pektəmi, -z

lumpen
BR 'lʌmpən
AM 'ləmpən

lumpenproletariat
BR ,lʌmpən,prəʊlɪ-'teːriət
AM ,ləmpən,proʊlə-'teriət

lumper
BR 'lʌmpə(r), -z
AM 'ləmpər, -z

lumpfish
BR 'lʌmpfɪʃ, -ɪz
AM 'ləm(p),fɪʃ, -ɪz

lumpily
BR 'lʌmp|li
AM 'ləmpəli

lumpiness
BR 'lʌmpinɪs
AM 'ləmpinɪs

lumpish
BR 'lʌmpɪʃ
AM 'ləmpɪʃ

lumpishly
BR 'lʌmpɪʃli
AM 'ləmpɪʃli

lumpishness
BR 'lʌmpɪʃnɪs
AM 'ləmpɪʃnɪs

lumpsucker
BR 'lʌmp,sʌkə(r), -z
AM 'ləm(p),səkər, -z

lumpy
BR 'lʌmp|i, -iə(r), -iist
AM 'ləmpi, -ər, -ist

Lumsden
BR 'lʌmzd(ə)n
AM 'ləmzdən

Luna
BR 'luːnə(r)
AM 'lunə

lunacy
BR 'luːnəs|i, -ɪz
AM 'lunəsi, -z

lunar
BR 'luːnə(r)
AM 'lunər

lunate
BR 'luːneɪt, 'luːnət
AM 'lu,neɪt

lunatic
BR 'luːnətɪk, -s
AM 'luːnə,tɪk, -s

lunation
BR luː'neɪʃn, -z
AM lu'neɪʃən, -z

lunch
BR lʌn(t)ʃ, -ɪz, -ɪŋ, -t
AM lən(t)ʃ, -əz, -ɪŋ, -t

luncheon
BR 'lʌn(t)ʃ(ə)n, -z
AM 'lən(t)ʃən, -z

luncheonette
BR ,lʌn(t)ʃə'net,
,lʌn(t)ʃə'nɛt, -s
AM ,lən(t)ʃə'net, -s

luncher
BR 'lʌn(t)ʃə(r), -z
AM 'lən(t)ʃər, -z

lunchroom
BR 'lʌn(t)ʃruːm,
'lʌn(t)ʃrʊm, -z
AM 'lən(t)ʃ,rum,
'lən(t)ʃ,rʊm, -z

lunchtime
BR 'lʌn(t)ʃtaɪm, -z
AM 'lən(t)ʃ,taɪm, -z

Lund¹
place in Sweden
BR lʊnd
AM lʊnd

Lund²
surname
BR lʌnd
AM lənd

Lundy
BR 'lʌndi
AM 'ləndi

lune
BR luːn, -z
AM lun, -z

lunette
BR luː'nɛt, -s
AM lu'nɛt, -s

lung
BR lʌŋ, -z, -d
AM ləŋ, -z, -d

lunge
BR lʌn(d)ʒ, -ɪz, -ɪŋ, -d
AM ləndʒ, -əz, -ɪŋ, -d

lungfish
BR 'lʌŋfɪʃ, -ɪz
AM 'ləŋ,fɪʃ, -ɪz

lungful
BR 'lʌŋfʊl, -z
AM 'ləŋ,fʊl, -z

lungi
BR 'lʌŋ|i, 'lʊŋ|i, -ɪz
AM 'ləŋgi, -z

lungless
BR 'lʌŋləs
AM 'ləŋləs

lungworm
BR 'lʌŋwɜːm, -z
AM 'ləŋwɜrm, -z

lungwort
BR 'lʌŋwɜːt, -s

AM 'lʌŋwɜrt,
'ləŋw(ə)rt, -s

lunisolar
BR ,luːnɪ'səʊlə(r)
AM 'luni'soʊlər

lunker
BR 'lʌŋkə(r), -z
AM 'ləŋkər, -z

lunkhead
BR 'lʌŋkhɛd, -z
AM 'ləŋk,(h)ɛd, -z

Lunn
BR lʌn
AM lən

Lunt
BR lʌnt
AM lənt

lunula
BR 'luːnjələ(r)
AM 'lunjələ

lunulae
BR 'luːnjəli
AM 'lunjə,li, 'lunjə,laɪ

Luo
BR 'luːəʊ
AM 'lu,oʊ

Lupercalia
BR ,luːpə'keɪliə(r)
AM ,lupər'keɪljə,
,lupər'keɪliə

lupiform
BR 'luːpɪfɔːm
AM 'lupə,fɔ(ə)rm

lupin
BR 'luːpɪn, -z
AM 'lupən, -z

lupine¹
flower
BR 'luːpɪn, -z
AM 'lupən, -z

lupine²
wolf-like
BR 'l(j)uːpʌɪn
AM 'lu,paɪn

lupoid
BR 'l(j)uːpɔɪd
AM 'lu,pɔɪd

lupous
BR 'l(j)uːpəs
AM 'lupəs

lupus
BR 'l(j)uːpəs
AM 'lupəs

lupus vulgaris
BR ,l(j)uːpəs
vʌl'gɑːrɪs,
+ vʌl'gɛːrɪs
AM 'lupəs vəl'gɛrəs

lur
BR lʊə(r), lɜː(r), -z
AM lʊ(ə)r, -z

lurch
BR lɜːtʃ, -ɪz, -ɪŋ, -t
AM lɜrtʃ, -əz, -ɪŋ, -t

lurcher
BR 'lɜːtʃə(r), -z
AM 'lɜrtʃər, -z

lure
BR l(j)ʊə(r), ljɔː(r), -z, -ɪŋ, -d
AM lʊ(ə)r, -z, -ɪŋ, -d

Lurex®
BR 'l(j)ʊərɛks, 'ljɔːrɛks
AM 'lʊ,rɛks

lurgy
BR 'lɜːg|i, -ɪz
AM 'lɜrgi, -z

lurid
BR 'l(j)ʊərɪd, 'ljɔːrɪd
AM 'lʊrəd

luridly
BR 'l(j)ʊərɪdli,
'ljɔːrɪdli
AM 'lʊrədli

luridness
BR 'l(j)ʊərɪdnɪs,
'ljɔːrɪdnɪs
AM 'lʊrədnəs

luringly
BR 'l(j)ʊərɪŋli,
'ljɔːrɪŋli
AM 'lʊrɪŋli

lurk
BR lɜːk, -s, -ɪŋ, -t
AM lɜrk, -s, -ɪŋ, -t

lurker
BR 'lɜːkə(r), -z
AM 'lɜrkər, -z

Lurpak®
BR 'lɜːpak
AM 'lɜr,pæk

Lusaka
BR lʊ'sɑːkə(r)
AM lʊ'sɑkə

luscious
BR 'lʌʃəs
AM 'ləʃəs

lusciously
BR 'lʌʃəsli
AM 'ləʃəsli

lusciousness
BR 'lʌʃəsnəs
AM 'ləʃəsnəs

lush
BR lʌʃ, -ɪz
AM ləʃ, -əz

lushly
BR 'lʌʃli
AM 'ləʃli

lushness
BR 'lʌʃnəs
AM 'ləʃnəs

Lusiad
BR 'l(j)uːsiad
AM 'luzi,æd

Lusitania
BR ,luːsɪ'teɪnɪə(r)
AM ,lusə'teɪnɪə,
,luzə'teɪnɪə

lust
BR lʌst, -s, -ɪŋ, -ɪd
AM ləst, -s, -ɪŋ, -əd

luster
BR ˈlʌstə(r), -z
AM ˈləstər, -z

lustful
BR ˈlʌs(t)fʊl
AM ˈləs(t)fəl

lustfully
BR ˈlʌs(t)fʊli, ˈlʌs(t)fl̩i
AM ˈləs(t)fəli

lustfulness
BR ˈlʌs(t)f(ʊ)lnəs
AM ˈləs(t)fəlnəs

lustily
BR ˈlʌstɪli
AM ˈləstəli

lustiness
BR ˈlʌstɪnɪs
AM ˈləstɪnɪs

lustra
BR ˈlʌstrə(r)
AM ˈləstrə

lustral
BR ˈlʌstr(ə)l
AM ˈləstrəl

lustrate
BR lʌˈstreɪt, ˈlʌstreɪt, -s, -ɪŋ, -ɪd
AM ˈlə͵streɪ|t, -ts, -dɪŋ, -dɪd

lustration
BR lʌˈstreɪʃn, -z
AM ləˈstreɪʃən, -z

lustre
BR ˈlʌstə(r), -z
AM ˈləstər, -z

lustreless
BR ˈlʌstələs
AM ˈləstərləs

lustreware
BR ˈlʌstəwɛː(r), -z
AM ˈləstər͵wɛ(ə)r, -z

lustrous
BR ˈlʌstrəs
AM ˈləstrəs

lustrously
BR ˈlʌstrəsli
AM ˈləstrəsli

lustrousness
BR ˈlʌstrəsnəs
AM ˈləstrəsnəs

lustrum
BR ˈlʌstrəm, -z
AM ˈləstrəm, -z

lusty
BR ˈlʌst|i, -ɪə(r), -ɪɪst
AM ˈləsti, -ər, -ɪst

lusus
BR ˈl(j)uːsəs
AM ˈlusəs

lutanist
BR ˈl(j)uːtənɪst, ˈl(j)uːtn̩ɪst, -s
AM ˈlutn̩əst, -s

lute
BR l(j)uːt, -s
AM lut, -s

luteal
BR ˈl(j)uːtɪəl
AM ˈludiəl

lutecium
BR l(j)uːˈteʃ(ɪ)əm, l(j)uːˈtiːsɪəm
AM luˈtiʃ(i)əm, luˈtisiəm

lutein
BR ˈl(j)uːtiːn, -z
AM ˈludiən, -z

luteinize
BR ˈl(j)uːtiːnʌɪz, -ɪz, -ɪŋ, -d
AM ˈludiə͵naɪz, -ɪz, -ɪŋ, -d

lutenist
BR ˈl(j)uːtɪnɪst, ˈl(j)uːtn̩ɪst, -s
AM ˈlutn̩əst, -s

luteofulvous
BR ˌl(j)uːtɪəʊˈfʌlvəs
AM ˌludioʊˈfəlvəs

luteous
BR ˈl(j)uːtɪəs
AM ˈludiəs

lutestring
BR ˈl(j)uːtstrɪŋ, -z
AM ˈlut͵strɪŋ, -z

lutetium
BR l(j)uːˈtiːʃəm, l(j)uːˈtiːsɪəm
AM luˈtiʃ(i)əm, luˈtisiəm

Luther
BR ˈluːθə(r)
AM ˈluθər

Lutheran
BR ˈluːθ(ə)rən, ˈluːθ(ə)rn̩, -z
AM ˈluθ(ə)rən, ˈluθərn, -z

Lutheranise
BR ˈluːθ(ə)rənʌɪz, ˈluːθ(ə)rn̩ʌɪz, -ɪz, -ɪŋ, -d
AM ˈluθ(ə)rə͵naɪz, -ɪz, -ɪŋ, -d

Lutheranism
BR ˈluːθ(ə)rənɪz(ə)m, ˈluːθ(ə)rn̩ɪz(ə)m
AM ˈluθ(ə)rə͵nɪzəm

Lutheranize
BR ˈluːθ(ə)rənʌɪz, ˈluːθ(ə)rn̩ʌɪz, -ɪz, -ɪŋ, -d
AM ˈluθ(ə)rə͵naɪz, -ɪz, -ɪŋ, -d

Lutine Bell
BR ˌluːtiːn ˈbɛl
AM ˈlu͵tin ˈbɛl

luting
BR ˈl(j)uːtɪŋ, -z
AM ˈludɪŋ, -z

Luton
BR ˈluːtn
AM ˈlutn

Lutterworth
BR ˈlʌtəwəθ, ˈlʌtəwəːθ
AM ˈlədər͵wərθ

Lutyens
BR ˈlʌtjənz
AM ˈlətjɛnz

Lutz
BR lʊts, luːts, -ɪz
AM luts, -əz

luv
BR lʌv, -z
AM ləv, -z

luvvie
BR ˈlʌv|i, -ɪz
AM ˈləvi, -z

luvvy
BR ˈlʌv|i, -ɪz
AM ˈləvi, -z

lux
BR lʌks
AM ləks

luxate
BR lʌkˈseɪt, ˈlʌkseɪt, -s, -ɪŋ, -ɪd
AM ˈlək͵seɪ|t, -ts, -dɪŋ, -dɪd

luxation
BR lʌkˈseɪʃn
AM ləkˈseɪʃən

luxe
BR lʌks, lʊks
AM ləks

Luxembourg
BR ˈlʌks(ə)mbəːg
AM ˈləksəm͵bərg

Luxembourger
BR ˈlʌks(ə)mbəːgə(r), -z
AM ˈləksəm͵bərgər, -z

Luxemburg
BR ˈlʌks(ə)mbəːg
AM ˈləksəm͵bərg

Luxemburger
BR ˈlʌks(ə)mbəːgə(r), -z
AM ˈləksəm͵bərgər, -z

Luxemburgish
BR ˈluːks(ə)mbəːgɪʃ
AM ˈləksəm͵bərgɪʃ

Luxor
BR ˈlʌksɔː(r)
AM ˈlək͵sɔ(ə)r

luxuriance
BR lʌɡˈʒʊərɪəns, ləɡˈʒʊərɪəns, lʌɡˈzjʊərɪəns, ləɡˈzjʊərɪəns, lʌkˈsjʊərɪəns, ləkˈsjʊərɪəns
AM ləɡˈʒʊrɪəns, ləkˈʃʊrɪəns

luxuriant
BR lʌɡˈʒʊərɪənt, ləɡˈʒʊərɪənt, lʌɡˈzjʊərɪənt, ləɡˈzjʊərɪənt, lʌkˈsjʊərɪənt, ləkˈsjʊərɪənt
AM ləɡˈʒʊrɪənt, ləkˈʃʊrɪənt

luxuriantly
BR lʌɡˈʒʊərɪəntli, ləɡˈʒʊərɪəntli, lʌɡˈzjʊərɪəntli, ləɡˈzjʊərɪəntli, lʌkˈsjʊərɪəntli, ləkˈsjʊərɪəntli
AM ləɡˈʒʊrɪən(t)li, ləkˈʃʊrɪən(t)li

luxuriate
BR lʌɡˈʒʊərɪeɪt, ləɡˈʒʊərɪeɪt, lʌɡˈzjʊərɪeɪt, ləɡˈzjʊərɪeɪt, lʌkˈsjʊərɪeɪt, ləkˈsjʊərɪeɪt, -s, -ɪŋ, -ɪd
AM ləɡˈʒʊri͵eɪ|t, ləkˈʃʊri͵eɪ|t, -ts, -dɪŋ, -dɪd

luxurious
BR lʌɡˈʒʊərɪəs, ləɡˈʒʊərɪəs, lʌɡˈzjʊərɪəs, ləɡˈzjʊərɪəs, lʌkˈsjʊərɪəs, ləkˈsjʊərɪəs
AM ləɡˈʒʊrɪəs, ləkˈʃʊrɪəs

luxuriously
BR lʌɡˈʒʊərɪəsli, ləɡˈʒʊərɪəsli, lʌɡˈzjʊərɪəsli, ləɡˈzjʊərɪəsli, lʌkˈsjʊərɪəsli, ləkˈsjʊərɪəsli
AM ləɡˈʒʊrɪəsli, ləkˈʃʊrɪəsli

luxuriousness
BR lʌɡˈʒʊərɪəsnəs, ləɡˈʒʊərɪəsnəs, lʌɡˈzjʊərɪəsnəs, ləɡˈzjʊərɪəsnəs, lʌkˈsjʊərɪəsnəs, ləkˈsjʊərɪəsnəs
AM ləɡˈʒʊrɪəsnəs, ləkˈʃʊrɪəsnəs

luxury
BR ˈlʌkʃ(ə)r|i, -ɪz
AM ˈləkʃ(ə)ri, ˈləɡʒ(ə)ri, -z

Luzon
BR ˌluːˈzɒn
AM ˌluˈzɑn

Lvov
BR lvɒv
AM ˈl(ə)vɒv, ˈl(ə)vɑv

lwei
BR lweɪ, ləˈweɪ, -z
AM ləˈweɪ, -z

Lyall
BR ˈlʌɪ(ə)l
AM ˈlaɪəl

lycanthrope
BR ˈlʌɪk(ə)nθrəʊp, -s
AM ˈlaɪkən͵θroʊp, -s

lycanthropy
BR lʌɪˈkanθrəpi
AM laɪˈkænθrəpi

lycée
BR 'li:seɪ, -z
AM li'seɪ, -z

lyceum
BR lʌɪ'si:əm, -z
AM 'lʌɪ,siəm, -z

lychee
BR lʌɪ'tʃi:, 'lʌɪtʃi:,
'li:tʃi:, 'lɪtʃi:, -z
AM 'litʃi, -z

lychgate
BR 'lɪtʃgeɪt, -s
AM 'lɪtʃ,geɪt, -s

lychnis
BR 'lɪknɪs
AM 'lɪknɪs

Lycia
BR 'lɪsɪə(r)
AM 'lɪʃə, 'lɪʃɪə

Lycian
BR 'lɪsɪən, -z
AM 'lɪʃən, 'lɪʃɪən, -z

Lycidas
BR 'lɪsɪdas
AM 'lɪsɪdəs

lycopene
BR 'lʌɪkə(ʊ)pi:n
AM 'laɪkə,pin

lycopod
BR 'lʌɪkəpɒd, -z
AM 'laɪkə,pad, -z

lycopodium
BR ,lʌɪkə(ʊ)'pəʊdɪəm
AM ,laɪkə'poʊdiəm

Lycra®
BR 'lʌɪkrə(r)
AM 'laɪkrə

Lycurgus
BR lʌɪ'kə:gəs
AM laɪ'kərgəs

Lydd
BR lɪd
AM lɪd

lyddite
BR 'lɪdʌɪt
AM 'lɪ,daɪt

Lydgate
BR 'lɪdgeɪt
AM 'lɪd,geɪt, 'lɪdgət

Lydia
BR 'lɪdɪə(r)
AM 'lɪdiə

Lydian
BR 'lɪdɪən, -z
AM 'lɪdiən, -z

lye
BR lʌɪ
AM laɪ

Lyell
BR 'lʌɪ(ə)l
AM 'laɪ(ə)l

Lygon
BR 'lɪg(ə)n
AM 'lɪgən

lying
BR 'lʌɪɪŋ
AM 'laɪɪŋ

lyingly
BR 'lʌɪɪŋli
AM 'laɪɪŋli

lyke wake
BR 'lʌɪk weɪk, -s
AM 'laɪk ,weɪk, -s

Lyle
BR lʌɪl
AM laɪl

Lyly
BR 'lɪli
AM 'lɪli

Lyme disease
BR 'lʌɪm dɪ,zi:z
AM 'laɪm də,ziz

lyme-grass
BR 'lʌɪmgrɑ:s,
'lʌɪmgras
AM 'laɪm,græs

Lyme Regis
BR ,lʌɪm 'ri:dʒɪs
AM ,laɪm 'ridʒɪs

Lymington
BR 'lɪmɪŋt(ə)n
AM 'lɪmɪŋtən

Lymm
BR lɪm
AM lɪm

lymph
BR lɪmf
AM lɪmf

lymphadenitis
BR ,lɪmfadɪ'nʌɪtɪs
AM ,lɪmfædn̩'aɪdɪs

lymphadenopathy syndrome
BR ,lɪmfadɪ'nɒpəθɪ ,sɪndrəʊm
AM ,lɪm,fædn̩'apəθi ,sɪn,droʊm

lymphangitis
BR ,lɪmfan'dʒʌɪtɪs
AM ,lɪmfændʒaɪdɪs

lymphatic
BR lɪm'fatɪk
AM lɪm'fædɪk

lymphocyte
BR 'lɪmfə(ʊ)sʌɪt, -s
AM 'lɪmfə,saɪt, -s

lymphocytic
BR ,lɪmfə(ʊ)'sɪtɪk
AM ,lɪmfə'sɪdɪk

lymphoid
BR 'lɪmfɔɪd
AM 'lɪm,fɔɪd

lymphoma
BR lɪm'fəʊmə(r), -z
AM lɪm'foʊmə, -z

lymphomata
BR lɪm'fəʊmətə(r)
AM lɪm'foʊmədə

lymphopathy
BR lɪm'fɒpəθ|i, -ɪz
AM lɪm'fɑpəθi, -z

lymphous
BR 'lɪmfəs
AM 'lɪmfəs

Lympne
BR lɪm
AM lɪm

Lyn
BR lɪn
AM lɪn

Lynam
BR 'lʌɪnəm
AM 'laɪnəm

lyncean
BR lɪn'si:ən
AM lɪn'siən, 'lɪnsiən

lynch
BR lɪn(t)ʃ, -ɪz, -ɪŋ, -t
AM lɪn(t)ʃ, -ɪz, -ɪŋ, -t

lyncher
BR 'lɪn(t)ʃə(r), -z
AM 'lɪn(t)ʃər, -z

lynchet
BR 'lɪn(t)ʃɪt, -s
AM 'lɪn(t)ʃɪt, -s

lynching
BR 'lɪn(t)ʃɪŋ, -z
AM 'lɪn(t)ʃɪŋ, -z

lynchpin
BR 'lɪn(t)ʃpɪn, -z
AM 'lɪn(t)ʃ,pɪn, -z

Lynda
BR 'lɪndə(r)
AM 'lɪndə

Lynette
BR lɪ'nɛt
AM lɪ'nɛt

Lynmouth
BR 'lɪnməθ
AM 'lɪnməθ

Lynn
BR lɪn
AM lɪn

Lynne
BR lɪn
AM lɪn

Lynsey
BR 'lɪnzi
AM 'lɪnzi

Lynton
BR 'lɪntən
AM 'lɪn(t)ən

lynx
BR lɪŋks, -ɪz
AM lɪŋks, -ɪz

lynxlike
BR 'lɪŋkslʌɪk
AM 'lɪŋks,laɪk

Lyon
BR 'lʌɪən
AM 'laɪən

Lyonnais
BR ,li:ə'neɪz, ,lʌɪə'neɪz
AM ,laɪə'neɪz, ,liə'neɪz

lyonnaise
BR ,li:ə'neɪz, ,lʌɪə'neɪz
AM ,laɪə'neɪz, ,liə'neɪz

Lyonnesse
BR ,lʌɪə'nɛs

Lyons
AM ,laɪə'nɛs

Lyons[1]
place in France
BR 'li:ɒ̃
AM li'ɔn, li'ɑn

Lyons[2]
surname
BR 'lʌɪənz
AM 'laɪənz

lyophilic
BR ,lʌɪə(ʊ)'fɪlɪk
AM ,laɪə'fɪlɪk

lyophilise
BR lʌɪ'ɒfɪlʌɪz, -ɪz, -ɪŋ, -d
AM 'laɪ'afɪlaɪz, -z, -ɪŋ, -d

lyophilize
BR lʌɪ'ɒfɪlʌɪz, -ɪz, -ɪŋ, -d
AM 'laɪ'afɪlaɪz, -z, -ɪŋ, -d

lyophobic
BR ,lʌɪə(ʊ)'fəʊbɪk
AM ,laɪə'fo'bɪk

Lyra
BR 'lʌɪrə(r)
AM 'laɪrə

lyrate
BR 'lʌɪreɪt, 'lʌɪrət
AM 'laɪ,reɪt, 'laɪrət

lyre
BR 'lʌɪə(r), -z
AM 'laɪ(ə)r, -z

lyrebird
BR 'lʌɪəbə:d, -z
AM 'laɪr,bərd, -z

lyric
BR 'lɪrɪk, -s
AM 'lɪrɪk, -s

lyrical
BR 'lɪrɪkl
AM 'lɪrɪkəl

lyrically
BR 'lɪrɪkli
AM 'lɪrɪk(ə)li

lyricism
BR 'lɪrɪsɪz(ə)m
AM 'lɪrə,sɪzəm

lyricist
BR 'lɪrɪsɪst, -s
AM 'lɪrəsəst, -s

lyrist[1]
lyre player
BR 'lʌɪ(ə)rɪst, -s
AM 'laɪ(ə)rɪst, -s

lyrist[2]
lyricist
BR 'lɪrɪst, -s
AM 'lɪrɪst, -s

Lysander
BR lʌɪ'sandə(r)
AM laɪ'sændər

lyse
BR lʌɪz, -ɪz, -ɪŋ, -d
AM laɪs, laɪz, -ɪz, -ɪŋ, -d

Lysenko
BR lɪ'sɛŋkəʊ, lʌɪ'sɛŋkəʊ
AM laɪ'sɛnkoʊ

lysergic
BR lʌɪˈsəːdʒɪk
AM laɪˈsərdʒɪk

Lysippus
BR lʌɪˈsɪpəs
AM laɪˈsɪpəs

lysosome
BR ˈlʌɪsə(ʊ)səʊm, -z
AM ˈlaɪsəˌsoʊm, -z

lytta
BR ˈlɪtə(r)
AM ˈlɪdə

Lysias
BR ˈlɪsɪas
AM ˈlɪsɪəs

lysis
BR ˈlʌɪsɪs
AM ˈlaɪsɪs

lysozyme
BR ˈlʌɪsə(ʊ)zʌɪm
AM ˈlaɪzəˌzaɪm

lyttae
BR ˈlɪtiː
AM ˈlɪdi, ˈliˌtaɪ

lysin
BR ˈlʌɪsɪn
AM ˈlaɪsn

Lysistrata
BR lʌɪˈsɪstrətə(r)
AM ˌlɪsɪˈstrɑdə

Lytham
BR ˈlɪð(ə)m
AM ˈlɪθəm

Lyttleton
BR ˈlɪtlt(ə)n
AM ˈlɪdltən

lysine
BR ˈlʌɪsiːn
AM ˈlaɪˌsin

Lysol®
BR ˈlʌɪsɒl
AM ˈlaɪˌsol, ˈlaɪˌsɑl

lytic
BR ˈlɪtɪk
AM ˈlɪdɪk

Lytton
BR ˈlɪtn
AM ˈlɪtn

Mm

m
BR ɛm, -z
AM ɛm, -z

M.A.
BR ˌɛm'eɪ, -z
AM ɛ'meɪ, -z

ma
BR mɑː(r), -z
AM mɑ, -z

ma'am
BR mɑːm, mam, məm
AM mæm

maar
BR mɑː(r), -z
AM mɑr, -z

Maas
BR mɑːs
AM mɑs

Maastricht
BR 'mɑːstrɪxt,
'mɑːstrɪkt
AM 'mɑstrɪk(t)

Maat
BR mɑːt
AM mɑt

Mabel
BR 'meɪbl
AM 'meɪbəl

Mabinogion
BR ˌmabɪ'nɒgɪɒn
AM ˌmæbə'noʊgiən

mac
BR mak, -s
AM mæk, -s

macabre
BR mə'kɑːbrə(r)
AM mə'kɑbrə,
mə'kɑbr

macaco
BR mə'keɪkəʊ, -z
AM mə'kɑˌkoʊ, -z

macadam
BR mə'kadəm
AM mə'kædəm

macadamia
BR ˌmakə'deɪmɪə(r)
AM ˌmækə'deɪmiə

macadamise
BR mə'kadəmʌɪz, -ɪz,
-ɪŋ, -d
AM mə'kædəˌmaɪz, -ɪz,
-ɪŋ, -d

macadamization
BR məˌkadəmʌɪ'zeɪʃn
AM məˌkædəmə'zeɪʃən,
məˌkædəˌmaɪ'zeɪʃən

macadamize
BR mə'kadəmʌɪz, -ɪz,
-ɪŋ, -d
AM mə'kædəˌmaɪz, -ɪz,
-ɪŋ, -d

Macanese
BR ˌmakə'niːz
AM ˌmækə'niz

Macao
BR mə'kaʊ
AM mə'kaʊ

macaque
BR mə'kɑːk, mə'kak, -s
AM mə'kɑk, mə'kæk, -s

macaroni
BR ˌmakə'rəʊni
AM ˌmækə'roʊni

macaronic
BR ˌmakə'rɒnɪk, -s
AM ˌmækə'rɑnɪk, -s

macaroon
BR ˌmakə'ruːn, -z
AM ˌmækə'run, -z

MacArthur
BR mə'kɑːθə(r)
AM mə'kɑrθər

macassar
BR mə'kasə(r)
AM mə'kæsər

Macau
BR mə'kaʊ
AM mə'kaʊ

Macaulay
BR mə'kɔːli
AM mə'kɔli, mə'kɑli

macaw
BR mə'kɔː(r), -z
AM mə'kɔ, mə'kɑ, -z

Macbeth
BR mək'bɛθ, mak'bɛθ
AM mək'bɛθ, ˌmæk'bɛθ

Maccabean
BR ˌmakə'biːən
AM ˌmækə'biən

Maccabees
BR 'makəbiːz
AM 'mækəbiz

MacDiarmid
BR mək'dəːmɪd
AM mək'dɛrməd

Macdonald
BR mək'dɒnld
AM mək'dɑnəl(d)

MacDonnell
BR mək'dɒnl
AM mək'dɑnl

mace
BR meɪs, -ɪz
AM meɪs, -ɪz

mace-bearer
BR 'meɪsˌbɛːrə(r), -z
AM 'meɪsˌbɛrər, -z

macédoine
BR ˌmasɪ'dwɑːn,
'masɪdwɑːn, -z
AM ˌmasə'dwɑn, -z

Macedon
BR 'masɪd(ə)n
AM 'mæsədn,
'mæsəˌdɒn

Macedonia
BR ˌmasɪ'dəʊnɪə(r)

AM ˌmæsə'doʊniə

Macedonian
BR ˌmasɪ'dəʊnɪən, -z
AM ˌmæsə'doʊniən, -z

macer
BR 'meɪsə(r), -z
AM 'meɪsər, -z

macerate
BR 'masəreɪt, -s, -ɪŋ, -ɪd
AM 'mæsəˌreɪ|t, -ts,
-dɪŋ, -dɪd

maceration
BR ˌmasə'reɪʃn, -z
AM ˌmæsə'reɪʃən, -z

macerator
BR 'masəreɪtə(r), -z
AM 'mæsəˌreɪdər, -z

**Macgillicuddy's
Reeks**
BR məˌgɪlɪkʌdɪz 'riːks
AM mə'gɪləkədiz ˌriks

mach
BR mak, mɑːk
AM mɑk

machete
BR mə'(t)ʃɛt|i, -ɪz
AM mə'(t)ʃɛdi, -z

Machiavelli
BR ˌmakjə'vɛli
AM ˌmɑkiə'vɛli

Machiavellian
BR ˌmakjə'vɛlɪən
AM ˌmɑkiə'vɛljən,
ˌmɑkiə'vɛliən

Machiavellianism
BR ˌmakjə'vɛlɪənɪz(ə)m
AM ˌmɑkiə'vɛljəˌnɪzəm,
ˌmɑkiə'veliəˌnɪzəm

machicolate
BR mə'tʃɪkəleɪt, -s, -ɪŋ,
-ɪd
AM mə'tʃɪkəˌleɪ|t, -ts,
-dɪŋ, -dɪd

machicolation
BR məˌtʃɪkə'leɪʃn, -z
AM məˌtʃɪkə'leɪʃən, -z

Machin
BR 'meɪtʃɪn
AM 'meɪtʃ(ɪ)n

machinability
BR məˌʃiːnə'bɪlɪti
AM məˌʃinə'bɪlɪdi

machinable
BR mə'ʃiːnəbl
AM mə'ʃinəbəl

machinate
BR 'makɪneɪt,
'maʃɪneɪt, -s, -ɪŋ, -ɪd
AM 'mæʃəˌneɪ|t,
'mæʃəˌneɪ|t, -ts, -dɪŋ,
-dɪd

machination
BR ˌmakɪ'neɪʃn,
ˌmaʃɪ'neɪʃn, -z
AM ˌmækə'neɪʃən,
ˌmæʃə'neɪʃən, -z

machinator
BR 'makɪneɪtə(r),
'maʃɪneɪtə(r), -z
AM 'mækəˌneɪdər,
'mæʃəˌneɪdər, -z

machine
BR mə'ʃiːn, -z, -ɪŋ, -d
AM mə'ʃin, -z, -ɪŋ, -d

machinelike
BR mə'ʃiːnlʌɪk
AM mə'ʃinˌlaɪk

machinery
BR mə'ʃiːn(ə)ri
AM mə'ʃin(ə)ri

machinist
BR mə'ʃiːnɪst, -s
AM mə'ʃinɪst, -s

machismo
BR mə'kɪzməʊ,
mə'tʃɪzməʊ
AM mə'kɪzmoʊ,
mə'tʃɪzmoʊ

Machmeter
BR 'makˌmiːtə(r),
'mɑːkˌmiːtə(r), -z
AM 'mɑkˌmidər, -z

macho
BR 'matʃəʊ
AM 'mɑtʃoʊ

Machu Picchu
BR ˌmatʃuː 'pɪtʃuː
AM 'mɑtʃu 'pɪ(k)tʃu

Machynlleth
BR mə'xʌnɬəθ,
mə'kʌnɬəθ
AM mə'kənləθ

macintosh
BR 'makɪntɒʃ, -ɪz
AM 'mækənˌtɑʃ, -əz

mack
BR mak
AM mæk

Mackay
BR mə'kʌɪ
AM mə'keɪ

Mackenzie
BR mə'kɛnzi
AM mə'kɛnzi

mackerel
BR 'mak(ə)rəl,
'mak(ə)r|, -z
AM 'mæk(ə)rəl, -z

Mackeson
BR 'makɪs(ə)n
AM 'mækəsən

Mackey
BR 'maki
AM 'mæki

Mackie
BR 'maki
AM 'mæki

Mackin
BR 'mak(ɪ)n
AM 'mækən

Mackinac
BR 'makɪnɔː(r), -z
AM 'makəˌnɔ,
'makəˌnɑ, -z

mackinaw
BR ˈmakɪnɔː(r)
AM ˈmækəˌnɔ, ˈmækəˌnɑ

mackintosh
BR ˈmakɪntɒʃ, -ɪz
AM ˈmækənˌtɑʃ, -əz

mackle
BR ˈmakl, -z
AM ˈmækəl, -z

Maclaren
BR məˈklarən, məˈklarn̩
AM məˈklɛrən

macle
BR ˈmakl, -z
AM ˈmækəl, -z

Maclean
BR məˈkliːn, məˈkleɪn
AM məˈklin

Macleans®
BR məˈkliːnz
AM məˈklinz

MacLehose
BR ˈmaklhəʊz
AM ˈmækl̩ˌ(h)oʊz

Macleod
BR məˈklaʊd
AM məˈklaʊd

Macmillan
BR məkˈmɪlən
AM məkˈmɪlən

MacNeice
BR məkˈniːs
AM məkˈnis

Macon
city in Georgia, US
BR ˈmeɪk(ə)n
AM ˈmeɪkən

Mâcon
BR ˈmakɔ̃, ˈmɑːkɔ̃
AM mɑˈkɔn

Maconachie
BR məˈkɒnəki, məˈkɒnəxi
AM məˈkɑnəki

Maconochie
BR məˈkɒnəki, məˈkɒnəxi
AM məˈkɑnəki

Macquarie
BR məˈkwɒri
AM məˈkweri, məˈkwɒri

macrame
BR məˈkrɑːmi, məˈkrɑːmeɪ
AM ˈmækrəˌmeɪ

macramé
BR məˈkrɑːmi, məˈkrɑːmeɪ
AM ˈmækrəˌmeɪ

Macready
BR məˈkriːdi
AM məˈkridi, məkˈridi

macro
BR ˈmakrəʊ, -z
AM ˈmækroʊ, -z

macrobiotic
BR ˌmakrə(ʊ)bʌɪˈɒtɪk
AM ˌmækroʊbaɪˈɑdɪk

macrobiotically
BR ˌmakrə(ʊ)bʌɪˈɒtɪkli
AM ˌmækroʊbaɪˈɑdək(ə)li

macrocarpa
BR ˈmakrə(ʊ)ˌkɑːpə(r), -z
AM ˈmækrəˌkɑrpə, -z

macrocephalic
BR ˌmakrə(ʊ)sɪˈfalɪk, ˌmakrə(ʊ)kɛˈfalɪk
AM ˌmækroʊsəˈfælɪk

macrocephalous
BR ˌmakrə(ʊ)ˈsɛfələs, ˌmakrə(ʊ)ˈsɛfl̩əs, ˌmakrə(ʊ)ˈkɛfələs, ˌmakrə(ʊ)ˈkɛfl̩əs
AM ˈmækroʊˈsɛfələs

macrocephaly
BR ˌmakrə(ʊ)ˈsɛfəli, ˌmakrə(ʊ)ˈsɛfl̩i, ˌmakrə(ʊ)ˈkɛfəli, ˌmakrə(ʊ)ˈkɛfl̩i
AM ˈmækroʊˈsɛfəli

macrocosm
BR ˈmakrə(ʊ)kɒz(ə)m, -z
AM ˈmækrəˌkɑzəm, ˈmækroʊˌkɑzəm, -z

macrocosmic
BR ˌmakrə(ʊ)ˈkɒzmɪk
AM ˌmækrəˈkɑzmɪk

macrocosmically
BR ˌmakrə(ʊ)ˈkɒzmɪkli
AM ˌmækrəˈkɑzmək(ə)li

macroeconomic
BR ˌmakrəʊˌiːkəˈnɒmɪk, ˌmakrəʊˌɛkəˈnɒmɪk, -s
AM ˈmækroʊˌɛkəˈnɑmɪk, ˈmækroʊˌikəˈnɑmɪk, -s

macro-instruction
BR ˌmakrəʊɪnˈstrʌkʃn, -z
AM ˈmækroʊˌɪnˈstrək-ʃən, -z

macromolecular
BR ˌmakrəʊməˈlɛkjʊlə(r)
AM ˌmækroʊməˈlɛkjələr

macromolecule
BR ˌmakrəʊˈmɒlɪkjuːl, -z
AM ˈmækroʊˈmɑləˌkjul, -z

macron
BR ˈmakrɒn, ˈmakr(ə)n, ˈmeɪkrɒn, ˈmeɪkr(ə)n, -z
AM ˈmeɪˌkrɑn, ˈmæˌkrɑn, ˈmeɪkrən, -z

macrophage
BR ˈmakrə(ʊ)feɪdʒ, -ɪz
AM ˈmækrəˌfeɪdʒ, -ɪz

macrophotography
BR ˌmakrə(ʊ)fəˈtɒgrəfi
AM ˈmækroʊfəˈtɑgrəfi

macropod
BR ˈmakrəpɒd, -z
AM ˈmækrəˌpɑd, -z

macroscopic
BR ˌmakrə(ʊ)ˈskɒpɪk
AM ˈmækrəˈskɑpɪk

macroscopically
BR ˌmakrə(ʊ)ˈskɒpɪkli
AM ˈmækrəˈskɑpək(ə)li

macula
BR ˈmakjʊlə(r), -z
AM ˈmækjələ, -z

maculae
BR ˈmakjʊliː
AM ˈmækjəˌli, ˈmækjəˌlaɪ

maculae luteae
BR ˌmakjʊli: ˈl(j)uːtiːi
AM ˈmækjəli ˈludiˌi, ˈmækjəˌlaɪ ˈludiˌaɪ

macula lutea
BR ˈmakjʊlə ˈl(j)uːtɪə(r)
AM ˈmækjələ ˈludiə

macular
BR ˈmakjʊlə(r)
AM ˈmækjələr

maculation
BR ˌmakjʊˈleɪʃn, -z
AM ˌmækjəˈleɪʃən, -z

mad
BR mad, -ə(r), -ɪst
AM mæd, -ər, -əst

Madagascan
BR ˌmadəˈgask(ə)n, -z
AM ˌmædəˈgæskən, -z

Madagascar
BR ˌmadəˈgaskə(r)
AM ˌmædəˈgæskər

madam
BR ˈmadəm, -z
AM ˈmædəm, -z

Madame
BR ˈmadəm, -z
AM ˈmædəm, məˈdam, -z

Madang
BR məˈdaŋ
AM məˈdæŋ

madcap
BR ˈmadkap, -s
AM ˈmædˌkæp, -s

madden
BR ˈmadn, -z, -ɪŋ, -d
AM ˈmædn, -z, -ɪŋ, -d

maddeningly
BR ˈmadn̩ɪŋli

AM ˈmædn̩ɪŋli

madder
BR ˈmadə(r), -z
AM ˈmædər, -z

Maddie
BR ˈmadi
AM ˈmædi

Maddison
BR ˈmadɪsn
AM ˈmædəsən

Maddock
BR ˈmadək
AM ˈmædək

Maddocks
BR ˈmadəks
AM ˈmædəks

Maddox
BR ˈmadəks
AM ˈmædəks

Maddy
BR ˈmadi
AM ˈmædi

made
BR meɪd
AM meɪd

Madeira
BR məˈdɪərə(r)
AM məˈdɛrə, məˈdɪrə

Madeiran
BR məˈdɪərən, -z
AM məˈdɛrən, məˈdɪrən, -z

Madelaine
BR ˈmadl̩ɪn, ˈmad(ə)lɪn, ˈmadleɪn, ˈmad(ə)leɪn
AM ˈmædlən, ˈmadl̩eɪn

madeleine
BR ˈmadl̩ɪn, ˈmad(ə)lɪn, ˈmadleɪn, ˈmad(ə)leɪn, -z
AM ˈmædlən, ˈmadl̩eɪn, -z

Madeley
BR ˈmeɪdli
AM ˈmeɪdli

Madeline
BR ˈmadl̩ɪn, ˈmad(ə)lɪn
AM ˈmædlən

mademoiselle
BR ˌmadəm(w)əˈzɛl, ˌmam(wə)ˈzɛl, -z
AM ˌmæd(ə)m(w)əˈzɛl, -z

made-to-measure
BR ˌmeɪdtəˈmɛʒə(r)
AM ˌmeɪdtəˈmɛʒər

Madge
BR madʒ
AM mædʒ

madhouse
BR ˈmadhaʊs, -zɪz
AM ˈmædˌ(h)aʊs, -zəz

Madhya Pradesh
BR ˌmadɪə prəˈdɛʃ

AM ˌmɑdiə prəˈdɛʃ
Madison
BR ˈmædɪs(ə)n
AM ˈmædəsən
madly
BR ˈmædli
AM ˈmædli
madman
BR ˈmædmən
AM ˈmædˌmæn, ˈmædmən
madmen
BR ˈmædmən
AM ˈmædˌmɛn, ˈmædmən
madness
BR ˈmædnəs, -ɪz
AM ˈmædnəs, -əz
madonna
BR məˈdɒnə(r), -z
AM məˈdɑnə, -z
Madras
BR məˈdrɑːs, məˈdras
AM ˈmædrəs, məˈdræs, məˈdras
madrasa
BR məˈdrasə(r), -z
AM məˈdrɑsə, -z
madrepore
BR ˈmædrɪpɔː(r), -z
AM ˈmædrəˌpɔ(ə)r, -z
madreporic
BR ˌmadrɪˈpɒrɪk
AM ˌmædrəˈpɔrɪk
Madrid
BR məˈdrɪd
AM məˈdrɪd
madrigal
BR ˈmædrɪɡl, -z
AM ˈmædrəɡəl, -z
madrigalesque
BR ˌmadrɪɡəˈlɛsk, ˌmadrɪɡlɛsk
AM ˌmædrəɡəˈlɛsk
madrigalian
BR ˌmadrɪˈɡeɪlɪən
AM ˌmædrəˈɡeɪljən, ˌmædrəˈɡeɪlɪən
madrigalist
BR ˈmadrɪɡəlɪst, ˈmadrɪɡlɪst, -s
AM ˈmædrəɡələst, -s
madrona
BR məˈdrəʊnə(r), -z
AM məˈdroʊnə, -z
madrone
BR məˈdrəʊnə(r), -z
AM məˈdroʊnə, -z
Madura
BR məˈd(j)ʊərə(r)
AM ˈmædʒərə
Madurese
BR ˌmadjʊˈriːz, ˌmadʒʊˈriːz
AM ˌmædəˈriz
madwoman
BR ˈmadˌwʊmən

AM ˈmædˌwʊmən
madwomen
BR ˈmadˌwɪmɪn
AM ˈmædˌwɪmɪn
Mae
BR meɪ
AM meɪ
Maecenas
BR mʌɪˈsiːnəs
AM maɪˈsinəs
maelstrom
BR ˈmeɪlstrəm, ˈmeɪlstrɒm, -z
AM ˈmaɪlˌstrɑm, ˈmeɪlztrəm, -z
maenad
BR ˈmiːnad, ˈmʌɪnad, -z
AM ˈmiˌnæd, -z
maenadic
BR miːˈnadɪk, mʌɪˈnadɪk
AM miˈnædɪk
Maendy
BR ˈmeɪndi
AM ˈmeɪndi
Maerdy
BR ˈmɑːdi
AM ˈmɑrdi, ˈmɛrdi
Maesteg
BR ˌmʌɪˈsteɪɡ
AM ˌmaɪˌsteɪɡ
maestoso
BR mʌɪˈstəʊsəʊ, mʌɪˈstəʊzəʊ, -z
AM maɪˈstoʊˌsoʊ, maɪˈstoʊzoʊ, -z
maestro
BR ˈmʌɪstrəʊ, -z
AM ˈmaɪstroʊ, -z
Maeterlinck
BR ˈmɛtəlɪŋk
AM ˈmɛdərˌlɪŋk
Maeve
BR meɪv
AM meɪv
Mae West
BR ˌmeɪ ˈwɛst, -s
AM ˌmeɪ ˈwɛst, -s
Mafeking
BR ˈmafɪkɪŋ
AM ˈmæfəˌkɪŋ
MAFF
BR maf
AM mæf
maffick
BR ˈmafɪk, -ɪks, -ɪkɪŋ, -ɪkt
AM ˈmæfɪk, -s, -ɪŋ, -t
Mafia
BR ˈmafiə(r)
AM ˈmɑfiə
mafiosi
BR ˌmafɪˈəʊziː, ˌmafɪˈəʊsi
AM ˌmɑfiˈoʊzi, ˌmɑfiˈousi

mafioso
BR ˌmafɪˈəʊzəʊ, ˌmafɪˈəʊsəʊ
AM ˌmɑfiˈoʊzoʊ, mɑfiˈousoʊ
mag
BR mag, -z
AM mæg, -z
magalogue
BR ˈmagəlɒɡ, -z
AM ˈmægəˌlɔɡ, ˈmægəˌlɑɡ, -z
magazine
BR ˌmagəˈziːn, -z
AM ˌmægəˈzin, -z
Magda
BR ˈmagdə(r)
AM ˈmægdə
Magdala
BR ˈmagdələ(r)
AM ˈmægdələ
Magdalen
Oxford college
BR ˈmɔːdlɪn
AM ˈmɔdlən, ˈmægdələn
Magdalena
BR ˌmagdəˈliːnə(r)
AM ˌmægdəˈlinə
Magdalene[1]
biblical name
BR ˌmagdəˈliːni, ˈmagdəlɪn
AM ˈmægdələn, ˈmægdəˌlin
Magdalene[2]
Cambridge college
BR ˈmɔːdlɪn
AM ˈmɔdlən, ˈmægdələn
Magdalenian
BR ˌmagdəˈliːnɪən, -z
AM ˌmægdəˈlinɪən, -z
Magdeburg
BR ˈmagdəbəːɡ
AM ˈmægdəˌbərɡ
magdelen
BR ˈmagdəlɪn, -z
AM ˈmægdələn, -z
mage
BR meɪdʒ, -ɪz
AM meɪdʒ, -ɪz
Magee
BR məˈɡiː
AM məˈɡi
Magellan
BR məˈɡɛlən, məˈdʒɛlən
AM məˈdʒɛlən
Magellanic clouds
BR ˌmagdʒɪlanɪk ˈklaʊdz
AM ˌmægdʒəˌlænɪk ˈklaʊdz
magenta
BR məˈdʒɛntə(r), -z
AM məˈdʒɛn(t)ə, -z

Maggie
BR ˈmagi
AM ˈmægi
Maggiore
BR ˌmadʒɪˈɔːri
AM məˈdʒɔri
IT madˈdʒore
maggot
BR ˈmagət, -s
AM ˈmægət, -s
maggoty
BR ˈmagəti
AM ˈmægədi
Magherafelt
BR ˌmak(ə)rəˈfɛlt
AM ˌmak(ə)rəˈfɛlt
Maghrib
BR maˈɡriːb
AM ˈmæˌɡrɪb
magi
BR ˈmeɪdʒʌɪ
AM ˈmeɪˌdʒaɪ, ˈmæˌdʒaɪ
magian
BR ˈmeɪdʒɪən
AM ˈmeɪdʒ(i)ən
magianism
BR ˈmeɪdʒɪənɪz(ə)m
AM ˈmeɪdʒəˌnɪzəm
magic
BR ˈmadʒɪk
AM ˈmædʒɪk
magical
BR ˈmadʒɪkl
AM ˈmædʒəkəl
magically
BR ˈmadʒɪkli
AM ˈmædʒək(ə)li
magician
BR məˈdʒɪʃn, -z
AM məˈdʒɪʃən, -z
Maginnis
BR məˈɡɪnɪs
AM məˈɡɪnɪs
Magilligan
BR məˈɡɪlɪɡ(ə)n
AM məˈɡɪlɪɡ(ɪ)n
magilp
BR məˈɡɪlp
AM məˈɡɪlp
Maginot Line
BR ˈma(d)ʒɪnəʊ lʌɪn
AM ˈmɑ(d)ʒənoʊ ˌlaɪn
magisterial
BR ˌmadʒɪˈstɪərɪəl
AM ˌmædʒəˈstɪriəl, ˌmædʒəˈstɛriəl
magisterially
BR ˌmadʒɪˈstɪərɪəli
AM ˌmædʒəˈstɪriəli, ˌmædʒəˈstɛriəli
magisterium
BR ˌmadʒɪˈstɪərɪəm
AM ˌmædʒəˈstɪriəm, ˌmædʒəˈstɛriəm
magistracy
BR ˈmadʒɪstrəsˌi, -ɪz

AM 'mædʒəstrəsi, -z
magistral
BR 'madʒɪstr(ə)l
AM 'mædʒəstrəl
magistrand
BR 'madʒɪstrand, -z
AM 'mædʒə,straend, -z
magistrate
BR 'madʒɪstreɪt,
'madʒɪstrət, -s
AM 'mædʒə,streɪt, -s
magistrateship
BR 'madʒɪstreɪtʃɪp,
'madʒɪstrətʃɪp, -s
AM 'mædʒə,streɪt,ʃɪp,
-s
magistrature
BR 'madʒɪstreɪtʃə(r),
'madʒɪstrətʃə(r), -z
AM 'mædʒə,streɪtʃər,
'mædʒəstrə,tʃʊ(ə)r,
-z
Maglemosian
BR ,maglə'məʊsɪən,
,maglə'məʊzɪən, -z
AM ,maglə'məʊsɪən,
,malə'məʊzən, -z
maglev
BR 'maglɛv, -z
AM 'mæg,lɛv, -z
magma
BR 'magmə(r)
AM 'mægmə
magmatic
BR mag'matɪk
AM mæg'mædɪk
Magna Carta
BR ,magnə 'kɑːtə(r)
AM 'mægnə 'kɑrdə
magna cum laude
BR ,magnə kʊm
'laʊdeɪ, + 'lɔːdi
AM ,mægnə kəm
'laʊdə, + 'laʊdi
Magna Graecia
BR ,magnə 'griːsɪə(r)
AM 'mægnə 'greɪʃ(i)ə
magnanimity
BR ,magnə'nɪmɪti
AM ,mægnə'nɪmɪdi
magnanimous
BR mag'nanɪməs
AM mæg'nænəməs
magnanimously
BR mag'nanɪməsli
AM mæg'nænəməsli
magnate
BR 'magneɪt, 'magnət, -s
AM 'mæg,neɪt, 'mægnət, -s
magnesia
BR mag'niːʃə(r), mag'niːʒ(r), mag'niːzɪə(r)
AM mæg'niːʒə, mæg'niʃə

magnesian
BR mag'niːʃn, mag'niːʒn, mag'niːzɪən
AM mæg'niʒən, mæg'niʃən
magnesite
BR 'magnɪsʌɪt
AM 'mægnɪsaɪt
magnesium
BR mag'niːzɪəm
AM mæg'niziəm
magnet
BR 'magnɪt, -s
AM 'mægnət, -s
magnetic
BR mag'nɛtɪk, -s
AM mæg'nɛdɪk, -s
magnetically
BR mag'nɛtɪkli
AM mæg'nɛdək(ə)li
magnetisable
BR 'magnɪtʌɪzəbl
AM 'mægnə,taɪzəbəl
magnetisation
BR ,magnɪtʌɪ'zeɪʃn, -z
AM ,mægnədə'zeɪʃən, ,mægnə,taɪ'zeɪʃən, -z
magnetise
BR 'magnɪtʌɪz, -ɪz, -ɪŋ, -d
AM 'mægnə,taɪz, -ɪz, -ɪŋ, -d
magnetiser
BR 'magnɪtʌɪzə(r), -z
AM 'mægnə,taɪzər, -z
magnetism
BR 'magnɪtɪz(ə)m
AM 'mægnə,tɪzəm
magnetite
BR 'magnɪtʌɪt
AM 'mægnə,taɪt
magnetizable
BR 'magnɪtʌɪzəbl
AM 'mægnə,taɪzəbəl
magnetization
BR ,magnɪtʌɪ'zeɪʃn, -z
AM ,mægnədə'zeɪʃən, ,mægnə,taɪ'zeɪʃən, -z
magnetize
BR 'magnɪtʌɪz, -ɪz, -ɪŋ, -d
AM 'mægnə,taɪz, -ɪz, -ɪŋ, -d
magnetizer
BR 'magnɪtʌɪzə(r), -z
AM 'mægnə,taɪzər, -z
magneto
BR mag'niːtəʊ, -z
AM mæg'nidoʊ, -z
magnetograph
BR mag'niːtə(ʊ)grɑːf, mag'niːtə(ʊ)graf, -s
AM mæg'nɛdə,græf, -s
magnetohydro-dynamic
BR mag,niːtəʊ-,hʌɪdrə(ʊ)dʌɪ'namɪk

AM mæg'nɛdoʊ-,haɪdroʊ,daɪ'næmɪk
magnetometer
BR ,magnɪ'tɒmɪtə(r), -z
AM ,mægnə'tɑmədər, -z
magnetometry
BR ,magnɪ'tɒmɪtri
AM ,mægnə'tɑmətri
magnetomotive
BR mag,niːtə(ʊ)'məʊtɪv
AM mæg,nɛdoʊ'moʊdɪv
magneton
BR 'magnɪtɒn, -z
AM 'mægnətən, 'mægnə,tan, -z
magnetosphere
BR mag'niːtə(ʊ)sfɪə(r)
AM ,mæg'nɛdə,sfɪ(ə)r, ,mæg'nidɪ,sfɪ(ə)r
magnetostriction
BR mag,niːtə(ʊ)-'strɪkʃn, -z
AM mæg'nɛdoʊ-'strɪkʃən, -z
magnetron
BR 'magnɪtrɒn, -z
AM 'mægnə,tran, -z
magnifiable
BR 'magnɪfʌɪəbl
AM 'mægnəfaɪəbəl
Magnificat
BR mag'nɪfɪkat, məg'nɪfɪkat, -s
AM mæg'nɪfə,kat, -s
magnification
BR ,magnɪfɪ'keɪʃn, -z
AM ,mægnəfə'keɪʃən, -z
magnificence
BR mag'nɪfɪs(ə)ns, məg'nɪfɪs(ə)ns
AM mæg'nɪfəsəns
magnificent
BR mag'nɪfɪs(ə)nt, məg'nɪfɪs(ə)nt
AM mæg'nɪfəsənt
magnificently
BR mag'nɪfɪs(ə)ntli, məg'nɪfɪs(ə)ntli
AM mæg'nɪfəsən(t)li
magnifico
BR mag'nɪfɪkəʊ, məg'nɪfɪkəʊ, -z
AM mæg'nɪfə,koʊ, -z
magnifier
BR 'magnɪfʌɪə(r), -z
AM 'mægnə,faɪər, -z
magnify
BR 'magnɪfʌɪ, -z, -ɪŋ, -d
AM 'mægnə,faɪ, -z, -ɪŋ, -d
magniloquence
BR mag'nɪləkw(ə)ns
AM mæg'nɪləkwəns
magniloquent
BR mag'nɪləkw(ə)nt

AM mæg'nɪləkwənt
magniloquently
BR mag'nɪlɒkw(ə)ntli
AM mæg'nɪləkwən(t)li
magnitude
BR 'magnɪtʃuːd, 'magnɪtjuːd
AM 'mægnə,t(j)ud
magnolia
BR mag'nəʊlɪə(r), məg'nəʊlɪə(r), -z
AM mæg'noʊljə, mæg'noʊliə, -z
Magnox
BR 'magnɒks
AM 'mæg,naks
magnum
BR 'magnəm, -z
AM 'mægnəm, -z
magnum opus
BR ,magnəm 'əʊpəs
AM ,mægnəm 'oʊpəs
Magnus
BR 'magnəs
AM 'mægnəs
Magog
BR 'meɪgɒg
AM mə'gag
Magoo
BR mə'guː
AM mə'gu
Magowan
BR mə'gaʊən
AM mə'gaʊən
magpie
BR 'magpʌɪ, -z
AM 'mæg,paɪ, -z
Magrath
BR mə'grɑː θ, mə'graθ
AM mə'græθ
Magraw
BR mə'grɔː(r)
AM mə'grɔ, mə'grɑ
Magritte
BR mə'griːt, mə'grɪt
AM mə'grit
Magruder
BR mə'gruːdə(r)
AM mə'grudər
magsman
BR 'magzmən
AM 'mægzmən
magsmen
BR 'magzmən
AM 'mægzmən
maguey
BR mə'geɪ, 'magweɪ, -z
AM mə'geɪ, -z
Maguire
BR mə'gwʌɪə(r)
AM mə'gwaɪər
magus
BR 'meɪgəs
AM 'meɪgəs
Magwitch
BR 'magwɪtʃ
AM 'mæg,wɪtʃ

Magyar
BR ˈmægjɑ:(r), -z
AM ˈmægˌjɑr, -z
HU ˈmɔʒar

Mahabharata
BR mə,hɑ:ˈbɑːrətə(r)
AM ,məhəˈbɑrədə,
mə,hɑːˈbɑrədə

mahaleb
BR ˈmɑːhələb, -z
AM ˈmɑ(h)əˌlɛb, -z

Mahalia
BR məˈheɪlɪə(r)
AM məˈheɪljə,
məˈheɪlɪə

mahant
BR məˈhʌnt, -s
AM məˈhənt, -s

maharaja
BR ,mɑ:(h)əˈrɑ:dʒə(r),
-z
AM ,mɑ(h)əˈrɑ(d)ʒə, -z

maharajah
BR ,mɑ:(h)əˈrɑ:dʒə(r),
-z
AM ,mɑ(h)əˈrɑ(d)ʒə, -z

maharanee
BR ,mɑ:(h)əˈrɑ:nˌi, -ız
AM ,mɑ(h)əˈrɑni, -z

maharani
BR ,mɑ:(h)əˈrɑ:nˌi, -ız
AM ,mɑ(h)əˈrɑni, -z

Maharashtra
BR ,mɑ:(h)əˈrɑ:ʃtrə(r)
AM ,mɑ(h)əˈrɑʃtrə

Maharashtrian
BR ,mɑ:(h)əˈrɑ:ʃtrɪən,
-z
AM ,mɑ(h)əˈrɑʃtrɪən,
-z

maharishi
BR ,mɑ:(h)əˈrɪʃ|i, -ız
AM ,mɑ(h)əˈrɪʃi, -z

mahatma
BR məˈhɑtmə(r),
məˈhɑːtmə(r), -z
AM məˈhɑtmə,
məˈhætmə, -z

Mahaweli
BR ,mɑ:həˈwɛli
AM ,mɑ(h)əˈwɛli

Mahayana
BR ,mɑ:həˈjɑ:nə(r)
AM ,mɑ(h)əˈjɑnə

Mahdi
BR ˈmɑːdⱼi, -ız
AM ˈmɑdi, -z

Mahdism
BR ˈmɑːdɪz(ə)m
AM ˈmɑˌdɪzəm

Mahdist
BR ˈmɑːdɪst, -s
AM ˈmɑdəst, -s

Maher
BR mɑ:(r), ˈmeɪə(r)
AM ˈmeɪər

Mahfouz
BR mɑːˈfuːz

AM mɑːˈfuz

mah-jong
BR ,mɑ:ˈdʒɒŋ
AM ,mɑ:ˈ(d)ʒɒŋ,
,mɑ:ˈ(d)ʒɑŋ

mah-jongg
BR ,mɑ:ˈdʒɒŋ
AM ,mɑ:ˈ(d)ʒɒŋ,
,mɑ:ˈ(d)ʒɑŋ

Mahler
BR ˈmɑːlə(r)
AM ˈmɑlər

mahlstick
BR ˈmɔːlstɪk, -s
AM ˈmɑlˌstɪk,
ˈmɔlˌstɪk, -s

mahogany
BR məˈhɒgəni
AM məˈhɑgəni

Mahomet
BR məˈhɒmɪt
AM məˈhɑmət

Mahometan
BR məˈhɒmɪt(ə)n, -z
AM məˈhɑmədən, -z

Mahommed
BR məˈhɒmɪd
AM məˈhɑməd

Mahommedan
BR məˈhɒmɪd(ə)n, -z
AM məˈhɑmədən, -z

Mahon
BR mɑ:n
AM mæn, ˈmeɪən

Mahoney
BR ˈmɑːni, məˈhəʊni
AM məˈhoʊni

mahonia
BR məˈhəʊnɪə(r), -z
AM məˈhoʊnɪə, -z

Mahony
BR ˈmɑːni, məˈhəʊni
AM məˈhoʊni

mahout
BR məˈhaʊt, məˈhuːt,
-s
AM məˈhaʊt, -s

Mahratta
BR məˈrɑːtə(r),
məˈrɑtə(r), -z
AM məˈrɑdə, -z

Mahratti
BR məˈrɑːti, məˈrɑti
AM məˈrɑdi

mahseer
BR ˈmɑːsɪə(r), -z
AM ,mɑˌsɪ(ə)r, -z

Maia
BR ˈmʌɪə(r), ˈmeɪə(r)
AM ˈmaɪə, ˈmeɪ(j)ə

maid
BR meɪd, -z
AM meɪd, -z

maidan
BR mʌɪˈdɑːn,
ˈmʌɪdɑːn, -z
AM maɪˈdɑn, -z

Maida Vale
BR ,meɪdə ˈveɪl
AM ,meɪdə ˈveɪl

maiden
BR ˈmeɪdn, -z
AM ˈmeɪdən, -z

maidenhair
BR ˈmeɪdnhɛ:(r), -z
AM ˈmeɪdn,(h)ɛ(ə)r, -z

maidenhead
BR ˈmeɪdnhɛd, -z
AM ˈmeɪdn,(h)ɛd, -z

maidenhood
BR ˈmeɪdnhʊd
AM ˈmeɪdn,(h)ʊd

maidenish
BR ˈmeɪdnɪʃ
AM ˈmeɪdnɪʃ

maidenlike
BR ˈmeɪdnlʌɪk
AM ˈmeɪdnˌlaɪk

maidenly
BR ˈmeɪdnli
AM ˈmeɪdnli

maidish
BR ˈmeɪdɪʃ
AM ˈmeɪdɪʃ

maidservant
BR ˈmeɪdˌsəːv(ə)nt, -s
AM ˈmeɪdˌsərvənt, -s

Maidstone
BR ˈmeɪdstən
AM ˈmeɪdˌstoʊn

maieutic
BR meɪˈjuːtɪk,
mʌɪˈjuːtɪk
AM meɪˈjudək

maigre
BR ˈmeɪgə(r)
AM ˈmeɪgər

Maigret
BR ˈmeɪgreɪ
AM meɪˈgreɪ

maihem
BR ˈmeɪhɛm
AM ˈmeɪ,(h)ɛm

mail
BR meɪl, -z, -ıŋ, -d
AM meɪl, -z, -ıŋ, -d

mailable
BR ˈmeɪləbl
AM ˈmeɪləbəl

mailbag
BR ˈmeɪlbag, -z
AM ˈmeɪlˌbæg, -z

mailboat
BR ˈmeɪlbəʊt, -s
AM ˈmeɪlˌbout, -s

mailbox
BR ˈmeɪlbɒks, -ız
AM ˈmeɪlˌbɑks, -əz

mailer
BR ˈmeɪlə(r), -z
AM ˈmeɪlər, -z

mailing
BR ˈmeɪlıŋ, -z
AM ˈmeɪlıŋ, -z

maillot
BR mʌɪˈəʊ, -z
AM maɪˈ(j)ou, -z

mailman
BR ˈmeɪlman
AM ˈmeɪlˌmæn

mailmen
BR ˈmeɪlmɛn
AM ˈmeɪlˌmɛn

mail order
BR ,meɪl ˈɔːdə(r)
AM ˈmeɪl ˌɔrdər

mailshot
BR ˈmeɪlˌʃɒt, -s
AM ˈmeɪlˌʃɑt, -s

maim
BR meɪm, -z, -ıŋ, -d
AM meɪm, -z, -ıŋ, -d

Maimonides
BR mʌɪˈmɒnɪdi:z
AM maɪˈmɑnədiz

Main
German river
BR mʌɪn
AM maɪn

main
BR meɪm, -z
AM meɪm, -z

maincrop
BR ˈmeɪnkrɒp
AM ˈmeɪnˌkrɑp

Maine
BR meɪn
AM meɪn

mainframe
BR ˈmeɪnfreɪm, -z
AM ˈmeɪnˌfreɪm, -z

mainland
BR ˈmeɪnlənd,
ˈmeɪnland
AM ˈmeɪnˌlænd,
ˈmeɪnland

mainlander
BR ˈmeɪnləndə(r),
ˈmeɪnləndə(r), -z
AM ˈmeɪnˌlændər,
ˈmeɪnləndər, -z

mainline
BR ˈmeɪnlʌɪn, -z, -ıŋ, -d
AM ˈmeɪnˌlaɪn, -z, -ıŋ, -d

mainliner
BR ˈmeɪnlʌɪnə(r), -z
AM ˈmeɪnˌlaɪnər, -z

mainly
BR ˈmeɪnli
AM ˈmeɪnli

mainmast
BR ˈmeɪnmɑːst,
ˈmeɪnmast, -s
AM ˈmeɪnˌmæst, -s

mainplane
BR ˈmeɪnpleɪn, -z
AM ˈmeɪnˌpleɪn, -z

mainsail
BR ˈmeɪnsl, ˈmeɪnseɪl,
-z
AM ˈmeɪnsəl,
ˈmeɪnˌseɪl, -z

mainsheet
BR ˈmeɪnʃiːt, -s
AM ˈmeɪnˌʃit, -s

mainspring
BR ˈmeɪnsprɪŋ, -z
AM ˈmeɪnˌsprɪŋ, -z

mainstay
BR ˈmeɪnsteɪ, -z
AM ˈmeɪnˌsteɪ, -z

mainstream
BR ˈmeɪnstriːm
AM ˈmeɪnˌstrim

maintain
BR meɪnˈteɪn,
mənˈteɪn, -z, -ɪŋ, -d
AM meɪnˈteɪn, -z, -ɪŋ, -d

maintainability
BR ˌmeɪnteɪnəˈbɪlɪti,
mənˌteɪnəˈbɪlɪti
AM ˌmeɪnteɪnəˈbɪlɪdi

maintainable
BR meɪnˈteɪnəbl̩,
mənˈteɪnəbl
AM meɪnˈteɪnəbəl

maintainer
BR meɪnˈteɪnə(r),
mənˈteɪnə(r), -z
AM meɪnˈteɪnər, -z

maintainor
BR meɪnˈteɪnə(r),
mənˈteɪnə(r), -z
AM meɪnˈteɪnər, -z

maintenance
BR ˈmeɪnt(ɪ)nəns,
ˈmeɪntnəns
AM ˈmeɪnt(ə)nəns,
ˈmeɪntnəns

Maintenon
BR ˈmantənɒn
AM ˌmænt(ə)ˈnɒn
FR mɛ̃tnɔ̃

maintop
BR ˈmeɪntɒp, -s
AM ˈmeɪnˌtɑp, -s

maintopmast
BR ˌmeɪnˈtɒpmɑːst,
ˌmeɪnˈtɒpmast, -s
AM ˌmeɪnˈtɑpˌmæst, -s

Mainwaring
BR ˈmanərɪŋ,
ˈmeɪnˌwɛːrɪŋ
AM ˈmeɪnˌwɛrɪŋ

Mainz
BR mʌɪnts
AM maɪn(t)s

maiolica
BR məˈjɒlɪkə(r)
AM məˈjɑləkə

Mair
BR mʌɪə(r)
AM ˈmaɪər

Mairead
BR məˈreɪd
AM ˈmeɪˌrid

Maisie
BR ˈmeɪzi
AM ˈmeɪzi

maisonette
BR ˌmeɪzəˈnɛt, -s
AM ˌmeɪzəˈnɛt, -s

maisonnette
BR ˌmeɪzəˈnɛt, -s
AM ˌmeɪzəˈnɛt, -s

Maithili
BR ˈmʌɪtɪli
AM ˈmaɪdəli

Maitland
BR ˈmeɪtlənd
AM ˈmeɪtlən(d)

maître d'
BR ˌmeɪtrə ˈdiː,
ˌmɛtrə +, -z
AM ˌmeɪdər ˈdi,
ˌmeɪtrə +, -z

maître d'hôtel
BR ˌmeɪtrə dəʊˈtɛl,
ˌmɛtrə +
AM ˌmeɪtrə ˌdoʊˈtɛl

maîtres d'
BR ˌmeɪtrə ˈdiː,
ˌmɛtrə +
AM ˌmeɪdər ˈdiz,
ˌmeɪtrə +

maîtres d'hôtel
BR ˌmeɪtrə dəʊˈtɛl,
ˌmɛtrə +
AM ˌmeɪtrə ˌdoʊˈtɛl

maize
BR meɪz
AM meɪz

majestic
BR məˈdʒɛstɪk
AM məˈdʒɛstɪk

majestically
BR məˈdʒɛstɪkli
AM məˈdʒɛstək(ə)li

majesty
BR ˈmadʒɪst|i, -ɪz
AM ˈmædʒ|esti, -z

Maj.-Gen.
BR ˌmeɪdʒə
ˈdʒɛn(ə)rəl,
+ ˈdʒɛn(ə)rl̩
AM ˌmeɪdʒər
ˈdʒɛn(ə)rəl

Majlis
BR madʒˈlɪs, ˈmadʒlɪs
AM mædʒˈlɪs

majolica
BR məˈdʒɒlɪkə(r)
AM məˈdʒɑləkə

major
BR ˈmeɪdʒə(r), -z, -ɪŋ, -d
AM ˈmeɪdʒər, -z, -ɪŋ, -d

Majorca
BR məˈjɔːkə(r),
məˈdʒɔːkə(r)
AM məˈjorkə

Majorcan
BR məˈjɔːkən,
məˈdʒɔːkən
AM məˈjorkən

majordomo
BR ˌmeɪdʒəˈdəʊməʊ, -z

majorette
BR ˌmeɪdʒəˈrɛt, -s
AM ˌmeɪdʒəˈrɛt, -s

major general
BR ˌmeɪdʒə
ˈdʒɛn(ə)rəl,
+ ˈdʒɛn(ə)rl̩
AM ˌmeɪdʒər
ˈdʒɛn(ə)rəl, -z

Majorism
BR ˈmeɪdʒərɪz(ə)m
AM ˈmeɪdʒəˌrɪzəm

majoritarian
BR məˌdʒɒrɪˈtɛːrɪən, -z
AM məˌdʒɔrəˈtɛrɪən, -z

majority
BR məˈdʒɒrɪt|i, -ɪz
AM məˈdʒɔrədi, -z

majorship
BR ˈmeɪdʒəʃɪp, -s
AM ˈmeɪdʒərˌʃɪp, -s

majuscular
BR məˈdʒʌskjʊlə(r)
AM məˈdʒəskjələr

majuscule
BR ˈmadʒəskjuːl
AM ˈmædʒəsˌkjuˌ(ə)l

makable
BR ˈmeɪkəbl̩
AM ˈmeɪkəbəl

Makarios
BR məˈkarɪɒs,
məˈkɑːrɪɒs
AM məˈkeriəs

Makassar
BR məˈkasə(r)
AM məˈkasər

make
BR meɪk, -s, -ɪŋ
AM meɪk, -s, -ɪŋ

make-believe
BR ˈmeɪkbɪliːv
AM ˈmeɪkbəˌliv

make-or-break
BR ˌmeɪkɔːˈbreɪk
AM ˈmeɪkɔrˈbreɪk

Makepeace
BR ˈmeɪkpiːs
AM ˈmeɪkˌpis

maker
BR ˈmeɪkə(r), -z
AM ˈmeɪkər, -z

makeready
BR ˈmeɪkˌrɛd|i, -ɪz
AM ˈmeɪkˌrɛdi, -z

Makerere
BR məˈkɛrəri
AM məˈkɛrəri

makeshift
BR ˈmeɪkʃɪft
AM ˈmeɪkˌʃɪft

makeup
BR ˈmeɪkʌp, -s

AM ˈmeɪˌkəp, -s

makeweight
BR ˈmeɪkweɪt, -s
AM ˈmeɪkˌweɪt, -s

Makgadikgadi
BR məˈ(k)ˈgadɪ(k)ˌgɑːdi
AM məˈgædiˌgædi

making
BR ˈmeɪkɪŋ, -z
AM ˈmeɪkɪŋ, -z

mako¹
shark
BR ˈmɑːkəʊ, ˈmeɪkəʊ,
-z
AM ˈmeɪkoʊ, -z

mako²
tree
BR ˈmɑːkəʊ, ˈmakəʊ,
ˈmeɪkəʊ, -z
AM ˈmeɪkoʊ, ˈmakoʊ, -z

Maksutov
BR ˈmaksʊtɒv,
makˈsuːtɒv, -z
AM ˈmaksəˌtɒv,
makˈsudɒv,
ˌmaksəˌtɑv,
makˈsudɑv, -z

Malabar
BR ˈmaləbɑː(r)
AM ˈmæləbɑr

Malabo
BR ˈmaləbəʊ
AM ˈmæləˌboʊ

malabsorption
BR ˌmaləbˈsɔːpʃn̩, -z
AM ˌmæləbˈsɔrpʃən,
ˌmæləbˈzɔrpʃən, -z

malacca
BR məˈlakə(r), -z
AM məˈlakə, -z

Malachi
BR ˈmaləkʌɪ
AM ˈmæləˌkaɪ

malachite
BR ˈmaləkʌɪt
AM ˈmæləˌkaɪt

Malachy
BR ˈmaləki
AM ˈmæləki

malacoderm
BR ˈmaləkə(ʊ)dəːm, -z
AM ˈmæləkoʊˌdərm, -z

malacology
BR ˌmaləˈkɒlədʒi
AM ˌmæləˈkɑlədʒi

malacostracan
BR ˌmaləˈkɒstrək(ə)n,
-z
AM ˌmæləˈkastrəkən,
-z

maladaptation
BR ˌmaladəpˈteɪʃn, -z
AM ˌmælˌædəpˈteɪʃən,
-z

maladaptive
BR ˌmaləˈdaptɪv
AM ˌmæləˈdæptɪv

maladjusted
BR ˌmæləˈdʒʌstɪd
AM ˈmæləˈdʒəstəd
maladjustment
BR ˌmæləˈdʒʌs(t)m(ə)nt,
-s
AM ˈmæləˈdʒəstmənt,
-s
maladminister
BR ˌmælədˈmɪnɪstjə(r),
-əz, -(ə)rɪŋ, -əd
AM ˈmælˌædˈmɪnɪstər,
-z, -ɪŋ, -d
maladministration
BR ˌmælədˌmɪnɪˈstreɪʃn
AM ˈmælədˌmɪnəˈstreɪ-
ʃən
maladroit
BR ˌmæləˈdrɔɪt
AM ˈmæləˈdrɔɪt
maladroitly
BR ˌmæləˈdrɔɪtli
AM ˈmæləˈdrɔɪtli
maladroitness
BR ˌmæləˈdrɔɪtnɪs
AM ˈmæləˈdrɔɪtnɪs
malady
BR ˈmælədli, -ɪz
AM ˈmælədi, -z
mala fide
BR ˌmælə ˈfʌɪdi,
ˌmeɪlə +, + ˈfiːdeɪ
AM ˌmɑlə ˈfaɪdi
Málaga
BR ˈmæləgə(r)
AM ˈmæləgə
Malagasy
BR ˌmæləˈgasi
AM ˈmæləˈgæsi
malagueña
BR ˌmæləˈgeɪnjə(r), -z
AM ˌmæləˈg(w)eɪnjə, -z
malaise
BR məˈleɪz, maˈleɪz
AM məˈleɪz, mɑˈleɪz,
məˈlɛz, mɑˈlɛz
Malamud
BR ˈmaləmʊd
AM ˈmæləməd
malamute
BR ˈmaləmjuːt, -s
AM ˈmæləˌmjut, -s
malanders
BR ˈmaləndəz,
ˈmalndəz
AM ˈmæləndərz
malapert
BR ˌmæləˈpəːt,
ˈmaləpəːt, -s
AM ˈmæləˈpərt, -s
malaprop
BR ˈmaləprɒp, -s
AM ˈmæləˈprɑp, -s
malapropism
BR ˈmaləprəpɪz(ə)m,
-z
AM ˈmæləˈprɑˌpɪzəm,
-z

malapropos
BR ˌmalaprəˈpəʊ
AM ˌmæˌlaprəˈpoʊ,
ˌmæˈlaprəˌpoʊ
malar
BR ˈmeɪlə(r), -z
AM ˈmeɪlər, -z
malaria
BR məˈlɛːrɪə(r)
AM məˈlɛrɪə
malarial
BR məˈlɛːrɪəl
AM məˈlɛrɪəl
malarian
BR məˈlɛːrɪən
AM məˈlɛrɪən
malarious
BR məˈlɛːrɪəs
AM məˈlɛrɪəs
malarkey
BR məˈlɑːki
AM məˈlɑrki
malarky
BR məˈlɑːki
AM məˈlɑrki
malathion
BR ˌmaləˈθʌɪən
AM ˌmæləˈθaɪən
Malawi
BR məˈlɑːwi
AM məˈlɑwi
Malawian
BR məˈlɑːwɪən, -z
AM məˈlɑwɪən, -z
Malay
BR məˈleɪ
AM ˈmeɪˌleɪ, məˈleɪ
Malaya
BR məˈleɪə(r)
AM məˈleɪə
Malayalam
BR ˌmaləˈjɑːləm
AM ˌmæləˈjaləm
Malayan
BR məˈleɪən, -z
AM məˈleɪən, -z
Malayo-Chinese
BR məˌleɪəʊtʃʌɪˈniːz
AM məˈleɪoʊˌtʃaɪˈniz
Malayo-Polynesian
BR məˌleɪəʊˌpɒlɪ-
ˈniːzj(ə)n,
məˌleɪəʊˌpɒlɪˈniːʒn, -z
AM məˈleɪoʊˌpɑləˈniʒən,
meˈleɪoʊˌpɑləˈniʃən,
-z
Malaysia
BR məˈleɪzɪə(r),
məˈleɪʒə(r)
AM məˈleɪʒə
Malaysian
BR məˈleɪzɪən,
məˈleɪʒ(ə)n, -z
AM məˈleɪʒən, -z
Malcolm
BR ˈmalkəm
AM ˈmælkəm

malcontent
BR ˈmalkəntɛnt, -s
AM ˈmælkənˈtɛnt,
ˈmælkənˌtɛnt, -s
malcontented
BR ˌmalkənˈtɛntɪd
AM ˌmælkənˈtɛn(t)əd
mal de mer
BR ˌmal də ˈmɛː(r)
AM ˌmɑl də ˈmɛ(ə)r
Malden
BR ˈmɔːld(ə)n,
ˈmɒld(ə)n
AM ˈmɔldən, ˈmaldən
maldistributed
BR ˌmaldɪˈstrɪbjʊtɪd,
ˌmalˈdɪstrɪbjuːtɪd
AM ˈmældəˈstrɪbjʊdəd
maldistribution
BR ˌmaldɪstrɪˈbjuːʃn
AM ˈmælˌdɪstrəˈbjuʃən
Maldive
BR ˈmɔːldiːv, ˈmɒldiːv,
-z
AM ˈmɑldaɪv, ˈmɑldiv,
-z
Maldivian
BR mɔːlˈdɪvɪən,
mɒlˈdɪvɪən, -z
AM mɑlˈdɪvɪən, -z
Maldon
BR ˈmɔːld(ə)n,
ˈmɒld(ə)n
AM ˈmɔldən, ˈmaldən
male
BR meɪl, -z
AM meɪl, -z
malediction
BR ˌmalɪˈdɪkʃn, -z
AM ˌmæləˈdɪkʃən, -z
maledictive
BR ˌmalɪˈdɪktɪv
AM ˌmæləˈdɪktɪv
maledictory
BR ˌmalɪˈdɪkt(ə)ri
AM ˈmæləˈdɪkt(ə)ri
malefaction
BR ˌmalɪˈfakʃn, -z
AM ˈmæləˈfækʃən, -z
malefactor
BR ˈmalɪfaktə(r), -z
AM ˈmæləˈfæktər, -z
malefic
BR məˈlɛfɪk
AM məˈlɛfɪk
maleficence
BR məˈlɛfɪs(ə)ns
AM məˈlɛfəsəns
maleficent
BR məˈlɛfɪs(ə)nt
AM məˈlɛfəsənt
maleic
BR məˈliːɪk
AM məˈliɪk, məˈleɪɪk
malemute
BR ˈmaləmjuːt, -s
AM ˈmæləˌmjut, -s

maleness
BR ˈmeɪlnɪs
AM ˈmeɪlnɪs
Malet
BR ˈmalɪt
AM ˈmælət
malevolence
BR məˈlɛvələns,
məˈlɛvələs,
məˈlɛvl(ə)ns
AM məˈlɛvələns
malevolent
BR məˈlɛvələnt,
məˈlɛvəlnt,
məˈlɛvl(ə)nt
AM məˈlɛvələnt
malevolently
BR məˈlɛvələntli,
məˈlɛvələntli,
məˈlɛvl(ə)ntli
AM məˈlɛvələn(t)li
malfeasance
BR malˈfiːzns
AM mælˈfizns
malfeasant
BR malˈfiːznt, -s
AM mælˈfiznt, -s
Malfi
BR ˈmalfi
AM ˈmælfi
malformation
BR ˌmalfɔːˈmeɪʃn,
ˌmalfəˈmeɪʃn, -z
AM ˈmælfɔrˈmeɪʃən,
ˈmælfərˈmeɪʃən, -z
malformed
BR ˌmalˈfɔːmd
AM ˈmælˈfɔrmd
malfunction
BR ˌmalˈfʌŋ(k)ʃn, -z,
-ɪŋ, -d
AM ˈmælˈfəŋ(k)ʃən, -z,
-ɪŋ, -d
Malham
BR ˈmaləm
AM ˈmæləm
Malherbe
BR malˈɛːb
AM ˌmɑˈlɛrb
Mali
BR ˈmɑːli
AM ˈmɑli
Malian
BR ˈmɑːlɪən, -z
AM ˈmaljən, ˈmɑlɪən, -z
Malibu
BR ˈmalɪbuː
AM ˈmæləˌbu
malic
BR ˈmalɪk, ˈmeɪlɪk
AM ˈmælɪk
malice
BR ˈmalɪs
AM ˈmæləs
malice aforethought
BR ˌmalɪs əˈfɔːθɔːt

malicious
AM ˌmæləs əˌfɔːˈθɔt,
ˌmæləs əˌfɔːˈθɑːt
malicious
BR məˈlɪʃəs
AM məˈlɪʃəs
maliciously
BR məˈlɪʃəsli
AM məˈlɪʃəsli
maliciousness
BR məˈlɪʃəsnəs
AM məˈlɪʃəsnəs
malign
BR məˈlaɪn, -z, -ɪŋ, -d
AM məˈlaɪn, -z, -ɪŋ, -d
malignancy
BR məˈlɪɡnəns|i, -ɪz
AM məˈlɪɡnənsi, -z
malignant
BR məˈlɪɡnənt
AM məˈlɪɡnənt
malignantly
BR məˈlɪɡnəntli
AM məˈlɪɡnən(t)li
maligner
BR məˈlaɪnə(r), -z
AM məˈlaɪnər, -z
malignity
BR məˈlɪɡnɪt|i, -ɪz
AM məˈlɪɡnɪdi, -z
malignly
BR məˈlaɪnli
AM məˈlaɪnli
Malin
BR ˈmalɪn
AM ˈmælən
Malines
BR maˈliːn, məˈliːn
AM məˈlin
malinger
BR məˈlɪŋɡlə(r), -əz,
-(ə)rɪŋ, -əz
AM məˈlɪŋɡlər, -ərz,
-(ə)rɪŋ, -ərd
malingerer
BR məˈlɪŋɡ(ə)rə(r), -z
AM məˈlɪŋɡərər, -z
Malinowski
BR ˌmalɪˈnɒfski
AM ˌmaləˈnɑfski
malism
BR ˈmeɪlɪz(ə)m
AM ˈmeɪˌlɪzəm
malison
BR ˈmalɪz(ə)n,
ˈmalɪs(ə)n, -z
AM ˈmæləzən,
ˈmæləsən, -z
mall
BR mal, mɔːl, -z
AM mɔl, mal, -z
Mallaig
BR ˈmaleɪɡ, maˈleɪɡ
AM ˈmæˌleɪɡ
Mallalieu
BR ˈmaləlju:
AM ˈmæləˌlju

mallam
BR ˈmaləm, -z
AM ˈmæləm, -z
mallard
BR ˈmaːlɑːd, ˈmaləd, -z
AM ˈmælərd, -z
Mallarmé
BR ˌmalaːˈmeɪ
AM ˌmɑˌlarˌmeɪ
malleability
BR ˌmalɪəˈbɪlɪti
AM ˌmæl(j)əˈbɪlɪdi,
ˌmæliəˈbɪlɪdi
malleable
BR ˈmalɪəbl
AM ˈmæl(j)əbəl,
ˈmæliəbəl
malleableness
BR ˈmalɪəblnəs
AM ˈmæl(j)əbəlnəs,
ˈmæliəbəlnəs
malleably
BR ˈmalɪəbli
AM ˈmæl(j)əbli,
ˈmæliəbli
mallee
BR ˈmali
AM ˈmæli
mallei
BR ˈmalɪaɪ
AM ˈmæliˌaɪ
mallemuck
BR ˈmalɪmʌk, -s
AM ˈmæləˌmək, -s
mallenders
BR ˈmaləndəz,
ˈmaln̩dəz
AM ˈmæləndərz
malleoli
BR məˈliːəlaɪ
AM məˈliəˌlaɪ
malleolus
BR məˈliːələs
AM məˈliələs
mallet
BR ˈmalɪt, -s
AM ˈmælət, -s
malleus
BR ˈmalɪəs
AM ˈmæliəs
Mallorca
BR məˈjɔːkə(r)
AM məˈjɔrkə
Mallorcan
BR məˈjɔːk(ə)n, -z
AM məˈjɔrkən, -z
mallow
BR ˈmaləʊ, -z
AM ˈmæloʊ, -z
malm
BR mɑːm, -z
AM mɑm, -z
Malmesbury
BR ˈmɑːmzb(ə)ri
AM ˈmɑmzˌbɛri,
ˈmæmzˌbɛri

Malmö
BR ˈmɑːlməʊ, ˈmalməʊ
AM ˈmalˌmoʊ
SW ˈmalmə:
malmsey
BR ˈmɑːmzi
AM ˈmamzi
malnourished
BR ˌmalˈnʌrɪʃt
AM ˌmælˈnərɪʃt
malnourishment
BR ˌmalˈnʌrɪʃm(ə)nt
AM ˌmælˈnərɪʃmənt
malnutrition
BR ˌmalnjuˈtrɪʃn
AM ˌmæln(j)uˈtrɪʃən
malodorous
BR malˈəʊd(ə)rəs
AM mælˈoʊdərəs
malodorously
BR malˈəʊd(ə)rəsli
AM mælˈoʊdərəsli
malodorousness
BR malˈəʊd(ə)rəsnəs
AM mælˈoʊdərəsnəs
Malone
BR məˈləʊn
AM məˈloʊn
Maloney
BR məˈləʊni
AM məˈloʊni
malope
BR ˈmaləp|i, -ɪz
AM ˈmæləpi, -z
Malory
BR ˈmaləri
AM ˈmæləri
maloti
BR məˈləʊti, məˈluːti
AM məˈladi
Malpas¹
place in Cheshire, UK
BR ˈmɔː(l)pəs, ˈmalpəs
AM ˈmalˌpas
Malpas²
place in Cornwall, UK
BR ˈməʊpəs
AM ˈmalˌpas
Malpas³
place in Gwent, UK
BR ˈmalpas, ˈmalpəs
AM ˈmalˌpas
Malpighi
BR malˈpiːɡi
AM ˌmælˈpɪɡi
Malpighian layer
BR malˈpɪɡɪən ˌleɪə(r),
-z
AM ˌmælˈpɪɡiən
ˌleɪ(ə)r, -z
Malplaquet
BR ˈmalpləkeɪ
AM ˈmælplə,kɛt
malpractice
BR ˌmalˈpraktɪs, -ɪsɪz
AM mælˈpræktəs, -əz

malt
BR mɔːlt, mɒlt, -s, -ɪŋ,
-ɪd
AM mɒlt, malt, -s, -ɪŋ,
-əd
Malta
BR ˈmɔːltə(r),
ˈmɒltə(r)
AM ˈmɒltə, ˈmaltə
Maltese
BR mɔːlˈtiːz, mɒlˈtiːz
AM mɒlˈtiz, malˈtiz
Malteser
BR mɔːlˈtiːzə(r),
mɒlˈtiːzə(r)
AM ˌmɒlˈtizər,
ˌmalˈtizər
maltha
BR ˈmalθə(r), -z
AM ˈmɒlθə, ˈmalθə, -z
malthouse
BR ˈmɔːlthaʊ|s,
ˈmɒlthaʊ|s, -zɪz
AM ˈmɒltˌ(h)aʊ|s,
ˈmaltˌ(h)aʊ|s, -zəz
Malthus
BR ˈmalθəs
AM ˈmɒlθəs, ˈmalθəs
Malthusian
BR malˈθjuːzɪən
AM mɒlˈθuziən,
mɒlˈθuʒən
maltiness
BR ˈmɔːltɪnɪs,
ˌmɒltɪnɪs
AM ˌmɒltinɪs,
ˈmaltinɪs
malting
BR ˈmɔːltɪŋ, ˈmɒltɪŋ, -z
AM ˈmɒltɪŋ, ˈmaltɪŋ, -z
maltose
BR ˈmɔːltəʊz,
ˌmɔːltəʊs, ˌmɒltəʊz,
ˈmɒltəʊs
AM ˈmɒlˌtoʊs,
ˈmɒlˌtoʊz, ˈmalˌtoʊs,
ˈmalˌtoʊz
maltreat
BR malˈtriːt, -s, -ɪŋ, -ɪd
AM mælˈtri|t, -ts, -dɪŋ,
-dɪd
maltreater
BR malˈtriːtə(r), -z
AM mælˈtridər, -z
maltreatment
BR malˈtriːtm(ə)nt
AM mælˈtritmənt
maltster
BR ˈmɔːltstə(r),
ˈmɒltstə(r), -z
AM ˈmɒltstər,
ˈmaltstər, -z
malty
BR ˈmɔːlt|i, -ɪə(r), -ɪɪst
AM ˈmɒlti, ˈmalti, -ər,
-ɪst
malvaceous
BR malˈveɪʃəs

AM mæl'veɪʃəs

Malvern
BR 'mɔːlv(ə)n, 'mɒlv(ə)n
AM 'mɔlvərn, 'mɑlvərn

malversation
BR ˌmalvə'seɪʃn
AM ˌmælvər'seɪʃən

Malvinas
BR mal'viːnəs
AM mɑl'vinəs

malvoisie
BR 'malvɔɪzi, ˌmalvɔɪ'ziː
AM ˌmɑl,vwɑ'zi, 'mælvəzi

Malvolio
BR mal'vəʊlɪəʊ
AM mæl'voʊlioʊ

mam
BR mam, -z
AM mæm, -z

mama
BR mə'mɑː(r), 'mamə(r), -z
AM 'mɑmɑ, -z

mamaguy
BR 'mamagʌɪ, -z, -ɪŋ, -d
AM 'mɑməgaɪ, -z, -ɪŋ, -d

mamba
BR 'mambə(r), -z
AM 'mɑmbə, -z

mambo
BR 'mambəʊ, -z
AM 'mɑmboʊ, -z

mamelon
BR 'mamɪlən, -z
AM 'mæmələn, -z

Mameluke
BR 'mamɪl(j)uːk, -s
AM 'mæmə,luk, -s

Mamet
BR 'mamɪt
AM 'mæmət

Mamie
BR 'meɪmi
AM 'meɪmi

mamilla
BR ma'mɪlə(r), mə'mɪlə(r)
AM mə'mɪlə

mamillae
BR ma'mɪliː, mə'mɪliː
AM mə'mɪli, mə'mɪ,laɪ

mamillary
BR 'mamɪləri
AM 'mæmə,lɛri

mamillate
BR 'mamɪleɪt
AM 'mæmə,leɪt

mamma¹
gland
BR 'mamə(r)
AM 'mæmə

mamma²
mother
BR mə'mɑː(r), 'mamə(r), -z
AM 'mamə, mə'mɑ, -z

mammae
BR 'mami:
AM 'mæmi, 'mæ,maɪ

mammal
BR 'maml, -z
AM 'mæməl, -z

mammalian
BR mə'meɪlɪən, ma'meɪlən, -z
AM mə'meɪljən, mə'meɪlɪən, -z

mammaliferous
BR ˌmamə'lɪf(ə)rəs
AM ˌmæmə'lɪfərəs

mammalogy
BR mə'malədʒi, ma'malədʒi
AM mə'mælədʒi

mammary
BR 'mam(ə)ri
AM 'mæm(ə)ri

mammee
BR 'mam|i, -ɪz
AM 'mæmi, -z

mammiform
BR 'mamɪfɔːm
AM 'mæmə,fɔ(ə)rm

mammilla
BR ma'mɪlə(r), mə'mɪlə(r)
AM mə'mɪlə

mammillae
BR ma'mɪliː, mə'mɪliː
AM mə'mɪli, mə'mɪ,laɪ

mammogram
BR 'mamə(ʊ)gram, -z
AM 'mæmə,græm, -z

mammography
BR ma'mɒgrəfi, mə'mɒgrəfi
AM mæ'mɑgrəfi

Mammon
BR 'mamən
AM 'mæmən

Mammonish
BR 'mamənɪʃ
AM 'mæmənɪʃ

Mammonism
BR 'mamənɪz(ə)m
AM 'mæmə,nɪzəm

Mammonist
BR 'mamənɪst, -s
AM 'mæmənəst, -s

Mammonite
BR 'mamənaɪt, -s
AM 'mæmə,naɪt, -s

mammoth
BR 'maməθ, -s
AM 'mæməθ, -s

mammy
BR 'mam|i, -ɪz
AM 'mæmi, -z

man
BR man, -z, -ɪŋ, -d
AM mæn, -z, -ɪŋ, -d

mana
BR 'mɑːnə(r), -z
AM 'mɑnə, -z

manacle
BR 'manək|l, -lz,
-lɪŋ \ -lɪŋ, -ld
AM 'mænək|əl, -əlz,
-(ə)lɪŋ, -əld

manage
BR 'man|ɪdʒ, -ɪdʒɪz,
-ɪdʒɪŋ, -ɪdʒd
AM 'mænɪdʒ, -ɪz, -ɪŋ, -d

manageability
BR ˌmanɪdʒə'bɪlɪti
AM ˌmænɪdʒə'bɪlɪdi

manageable
BR 'manɪdʒəbl
AM 'mænɪdʒəbəl

manageableness
BR 'manɪdʒəblnəs
AM 'mænɪdʒəbəlnəs

manageably
BR 'manɪdʒəbli
AM 'mænɪdʒəbli

management
BR 'manɪdʒm(ə)nt, -s
AM 'mænɪdʒmənt, -s

manager
BR 'manɪdʒə(r), -z
AM 'mænɪdʒər, -z

manageress
BR ˌmanɪdʒə'rɛs, -ɪz
AM 'mænɪdʒ(ə)rəs, -əz

managerial
BR ˌmanɪ'dʒɪərɪəl
AM ˌmænə'dʒɪriəl,
ˌmænə'dʒɪriəl

managerially
BR ˌmanɪ'dʒɪərɪəli
AM ˌmænə'dʒɪriəli,
ˌmænə'dʒɪriəli

managership
BR 'manɪdʒəˌʃɪp, -s
AM 'mænɪdʒərˌʃɪp, -s

managing
BR 'manɪdʒɪŋ
AM 'mænɪdʒɪŋ

Managua
BR mə'nagjʊə(r),
mə'nagwə(r)
AM mə'nɑgwə

manakin
BR 'manəkɪn, -z
AM 'mænəˌkɪn, -z

mañana
BR ma'njɑːnə(r),
mə'njɑːnə(r)
AM mə'njɑnə

Manasseh
BR mə'nasi,
mə'nasə(r)
AM mə'næsə

man-at-arms
BR ˌmanət'ɑːmz
AM 'mænəd'ɑrmz

manatee
BR ˌmanə'tiː, 'manəti:, -z
AM 'mænəˌti, -z

Manaus
BR ma'naʊs
AM mɑ'naʊs

Manawatu
BR ˌmanə'wɑtuː
AM 'mɑnə'wɑˌtu

Manchester
BR 'mantʃɪstə(r),
'mantʃɛstə(r)
AM 'mæn(t)ʃɛstər

manchineel
BR ˌman(t)ʃɪ'niːl, -z
AM ˌmæn(t)ʃə'ni(ə)l,
-z

Manchu
BR man'tʃuː, -z
AM mæn'tʃu, -z

Manchuria
BR man'tʃʊərɪə(r)
AM mæn'tʃʊriə

Manchurian
BR man'tʃʊərɪən, -z
AM mæn'tʃurɪən, -z

manciple
BR 'mansɪpl, -z
AM 'mænsəpəl, -z

Mancunian
BR man'kjuːnɪən,
maŋ'kjuːnɪən,
AM mæn'kjuniən, -z

Mandaean
BR man'diːən, -z
AM mæn'diən, -z

mandala
BR 'mandələ(r),
'mʌndələ(r), -z
AM 'mændələ, -z

Mandalay
BR ˌmandə'leɪ,
'mandəleɪ
AM 'mændəleɪ

mandamus
BR man'deɪməs, -ɪz
AM mæn'deɪməs, -ɪz

mandarin
BR 'mand(ə)rɪn, -z
AM 'mændərən, -z

mandarinate
BR 'mand(ə)rɪneɪt, -s
AM 'mændərəˌneɪt, -s

mandatary
BR 'mandət(ə)r|i, -ɪz
AM 'mændəˌtɛri, -z

mandate¹
noun
BR 'mandeɪt, -s
AM 'mænˌdeɪt, -s

mandate²
verb
BR ˌman'deɪt,
'mandeɪt, -s, -ɪŋ, -ɪd
AM 'mænˌdeɪt, -ts,
-dɪŋ, -dɪd

mandator
BR ˌmanˈdeɪtə(r),
ˈmandeɪtə(r), -z
AM ˈmænˌdeɪdər, -z
mandatorily
BR ˈmandət(ə)rɪli
AM ˈmændəˌtɔrəli
mandatory
BR ˈmandət(ə)ri
AM ˈmændəˌtɔri
man-day
BR ˈmandeɪ, -z
AM ˈmænˌdeɪ, -z
Mandela
BR manˈdɛlə(r)
AM mænˈdɛlə
Mandelbaum
BR ˈmandlbaʊm
AM ˈmændlbɑm
Mandelstam
BR ˈmandlstam
AM ˈmɑndlˌstam
RUS mændʲɪlʲˈstam
Mandeville
BR ˈmandɪvɪl
AM ˈmændəvəl,
ˈmændəˌvɪl
mandible
BR ˈmandɪbl, -z
AM ˈmændəbəl, -z
mandibular
BR manˈdɪbjʉlə(r)
AM mænˈdɪbjələr
mandibulate
BR manˈdɪbjʉleɪt
AM mænˈdɪbjəˌleɪt
Mandingo
BR manˈdɪŋɡəʊ
AM mænˈdɪŋɡoʊ
mandola
BR manˈdəʊlə(r), -z
AM mænˈdoʊlə, -z
mandolin
BR ˌmandəˈlɪn,
ˈmandəlɪn, ˈmandl̩ɪn,
-z
AM ˌmændəˈlɪn, -z
mandoline
BR ˌmandəˈlɪn,
ˈmandəlɪn, ˈmandl̩ɪn,
-z
AM ˌmændəˈlɪn, -z
mandolinist
BR ˌmandəˈlɪnɪst,
ˈmandəlɪnɪst,
ˈmandl̩ɪnɪst, -s
AM ˌmændəˈlɪnɪst, -s
mandorla
BR manˈdɔːlə(r), -z
AM ˈmɑndɔrˌlɑ, -z
mandragora
BR manˈdrag(ə)rə(r),
-z
AM mænˈdrægərə, -z
mandrake
BR ˈmandreɪk, -s
AM ˈmænˌdreɪk, -s

mandrel
BR ˈmandr(ɪ)l, -z
AM ˈmændrəl, -z
mandril
BR ˈmandr(ɪ)l, -z
AM ˈmændrəl, -z
mandrill
BR ˈmandr(ɪ)l, -z
AM ˈmændrəl, -z
manducate
BR ˈmandjʉkeɪt,
ˈmandʒʉkeɪt, -s, -ɪŋ,
-ɪd
AM ˈmændʒəˌkeɪ|t, -ts,
-dɪŋ, -dɪd
manducation
BR ˌmandjʉˈkeɪʃn,
ˌmandʒʊˈkeɪʃn
AM ˌmændʒəˈkeɪʃən
manducatory
BR ˈmandjʉkət(ə)ri,
ˈmandʒʉkət(ə)ri
AM ˈmændʒəkəˌtɔri
Mandy
BR ˈmandi
AM ˈmændi
mane
BR meɪn, -z
AM meɪn, -z
maned
BR meɪnd
AM meɪnd
manège
BR maˈneɪʒ, maˈnɛʒ,
-ɪz
AM məˈnɛʒ, -əz
maneless
BR ˈmeɪnlɪs
AM ˈmeɪnlɪs
manes
spirit, spirits
BR ˈmɑːneɪz, ˈmeɪniːz
AM ˈmɑˌneɪz, ˈmeɪˌniz
Manet
BR ˈmaneɪ
AM mɑˈneɪ
maneuver
BR məˈnuːv|ə(r), -əz,
-(ə)rɪŋ, -əd
AM mə(n)juv|ər, -ərz,
-(ə)rɪŋ, -ərd
maneuverability
BR məˌnuːv(ə)rəˈbɪlɪti
AM mə(n)juv(ə)rəˈbɪl-
ɪdi
maneuverable
BR məˈnuːv(ə)rəbl
AM mə(n)juv(ə)rəbəl
maneuverer
BR məˈnuːv(ə)rə(r), -z
AM mə(n)juv(ə)rər, -z
maneuvering
BR məˈnuːv(ə)rɪŋ, -z
AM mə(n)juv(ə)rɪŋ, -z
Manfred
BR ˈmanfrɪd
AM ˈmænfrəd,
ˈmænˌfrɛd

manful
BR ˈmanf(ʊ)l
AM ˈmænfəl
manfully
BR ˈmanfʊli, ˈmanfl̩i
AM ˈmænfəli
manfulness
BR ˈmanf(ʊ)lnəs
AM ˈmænfəlnəs
mangabey
BR ˈmaŋɡəbeɪ, -z
AM ˈmæŋɡəˌbeɪ, -z
Mangan
BR ˈmaŋɡən
AM ˈmæŋɡən
manganese
BR ˈmaŋɡəniːz,
ˌmaŋɡəˈniːz
AM ˈmæŋɡəˌniz,
ˈmæŋɡəˌniz
manganic
BR manˈɡanɪk,
maŋˈɡanɪk
AM mænˈɡænɪk,
mæŋˈɡænɪk
manganite
BR ˈmaŋɡənʌɪt
AM ˈmæŋɡənaɪt
manganous
BR ˈmaŋɡənəs
AM ˈmæŋɡənəs
mange
BR meɪn(d)ʒ
AM meɪndʒ
mangel
BR ˈmaŋɡl, -z
AM ˈmæŋɡəl, -z
mangel-wurzel
BR ˈmaŋɡl̩ˌwəːzl, -z
AM ˈmæŋɡəlˌwərzəl, -z
manger
BR ˈmeɪn(d)ʒə(r), -z
AM ˈmeɪndʒər, -z
mangetout
BR ˌmɒn(d)ʒˈtuː,
ˌmɒ̃ʒˈtuː, -z
AM ˌmɑnʒˈtu, -z
mangey
BR ˈmeɪn(d)ʒ|i, -ɪə(r),
-ɪɪst
AM ˈmeɪndʒi, -ər, -ɪst
mangily
BR ˈmeɪn(d)ʒɪli
AM ˈmeɪndʒɪli
manginess
BR ˈmeɪn(d)ʒɪnɪs
AM ˈmeɪndʒɪnɪs
mangle
BR ˈmaŋɡl̩, -lz
-lɪŋ\-lŋ, -ld
AM ˈmæŋɡl̩əl, -əlz,
-(ə)lɪŋ, -əld
mangler
BR ˈmaŋɡlə(r),
ˈmaŋɡlə(r), -z
AM ˈmæŋɡ(ə)lər, -z
mango
BR ˈmaŋɡəʊ, -z

AM ˈmæŋɡoʊ, -z
mangold
BR ˈmaŋɡəʊld, -z
AM ˈmæŋɡoʊld, -z
mangonel
BR ˈmaŋɡən(ɛ)l, -z
AM ˈmæŋɡəˌnɛl, -z
mangosteen
BR ˈmaŋɡəstiːn, -z
AM ˈmæŋɡəˌstin, -z
mangrove
BR ˈmaŋɡrəʊv, -z
AM ˈmæŋɡroʊv, -z
mangy
BR ˈmeɪn(d)ʒ|i, -ɪə(r),
-ɪɪst
AM ˈmeɪndʒi, -ər, -ɪst
manhandle
BR ˈmanhand|l,
ˌmanˈhand|l, -lz,
-lɪŋ\-lŋ, -ld
AM ˈmæn,(h)æn|dəl,
-dəlz, -(d)(ə)lɪŋ, -dəld
Manhattan
BR manˈhatn
AM mænˈhætn,
mənˈhætn
manhole
BR ˈmanhəʊl, -z
AM ˈmæn,(h)oʊl, -z
manhood
BR ˈmanhʊd
AM ˈmæn,(h)ʊd
man-hour
BR ˈmanˌaʊə(r), -z
AM ˈmænˌaʊ(ə)r, -z
manhunt
BR ˈmanhʌnt, -s
AM ˈmæn,(h)ənt, -s
mania
BR ˈmeɪnɪə(r),
ˈmeɪnjə(r), -z
AM ˈmeɪnɪə, -z
maniac
BR ˈmeɪnɪak, -s
AM ˈmeɪniˌæk, -s
maniacal
BR məˈnʌɪəkl
AM məˈnaɪəkəl
maniacally
BR məˈnʌɪəkli
AM məˈnaɪək(ə)li
manic
BR ˈmanɪk
AM ˈmænɪk
Manicaland
BR məˈniːkəland
AM məˈnikəˌlænd
manically
BR ˈmanɪkli
AM ˈmænək(ə)li
Manichaean
BR ˌmanɪˈkiːən, -z
AM ˌmænəˈkiən, -z
Manichaeism
BR ˌmanɪˈkiːɪz(ə)m
AM ˌmænəˈkiɪzəm

Manichean
BR ˌmanɪˈkiːən, -z
AM ˌmænəˈkiən, -z
Manichee
BR ˌmanɪˈkiː, -z
AM ˈmænəˌki, -z
Manicheism
BR ˌmanɪˈkiːɪz(ə)m
AM ˈmænəˈkiːzəm
manicotti
BR ˌmanɪˈkɒti
AM ˌmænəˈkɑdi
manicure
BR ˈmanɪkjʊə(r),
ˈmanɪkjɔː(r), -z, -ɪŋ, -d
AM ˈmænəˌkjʊ(ə)r, -z,
-ɪŋ, -d
manicurist
BR ˈmanɪkjʊərɪst,
ˈmanɪkjɔːrɪst, -s
AM ˈmænəˌkjʊrəst, -s
manifest
BR ˈmanɪfɛst, -s, -ɪŋ, -ɪd
AM ˈmænəˌfɛst, -s, -ɪŋ,
-ɪd
manifestation
BR ˌmanɪfɛˈsteɪʃn,
ˌmanɪfəˈsteɪʃn, -z
AM ˌmænəfəˈsteɪʃən,
ˌmænəˌfɛˈsteɪʃən, -z
manifestative
BR ˌmanɪˈfɛstətɪv
AM ˌmænəˈfɛstədɪv
manifestly
BR ˈmanɪfɛstli,
ˈmanɪfəstli
AM ˈmænəˌfɛs(t)li
manifesto
BR ˌmanɪˈfɛstəʊ, -z
AM ˌmænəˈfɛstoʊ, -z
manifold
BR ˈmanɪfəʊld, -z
AM ˈmænəˌfoʊld, -z
manifoldly
BR ˈmanɪfəʊldli
AM ˈmænəˌfoʊl(dl)i
manifoldness
BR ˈmanɪfəʊldnəs
AM ˈmænəˌfoʊl(d)nəs
manikin
BR ˈmanɪkɪn, -z
AM ˈmænəkən, -z
manila
BR məˈnɪlə(r)
AM məˈnɪlə
manilla
BR məˈnɪlə(r)
AM məˈnɪlə
manille
BR məˈnɪl, -z
AM məˈnil, -z
Manilow
BR ˈmanɪləʊ
AM ˈmænəˌloʊ
manioc
BR ˈmanɪɒk
AM ˈmæniˌɑk

maniple
BR ˈmanɪpl, -z
AM ˈmænəpəl, -z
manipulability
BR məˌnɪpjʊləˈbɪlɪti
AM məˌnɪpjələˈbɪlɪdi
manipulable
BR məˈnɪpjʊləbl
AM məˈnɪpjələbəl
manipulatable
BR məˈnɪpjʊleɪtəbl
AM məˈnɪpjəˌleɪdəbəl
manipulate
BR məˈnɪpjʊleɪt, -s, -ɪŋ,
-ɪd
AM məˈnɪpjəˌleɪ|t, -ts,
-dɪŋ, -dɪd
manipulation
BR məˌnɪpjʊˈleɪʃn
AM məˌnɪpjəˈleɪʃən
manipulative
BR məˈnɪpjʊlətɪv
AM məˈnɪpjələdɪv,
məˈnɪpjəˌleɪdɪv
manipulatively
BR məˈnɪpjʊlətɪvli
AM məˈnɪpjəˌleɪdɪvli
manipulativeness
BR məˈnɪpjʊlətɪvnɪs
AM məˈnɪpjəˌleɪdɪvnɪs
manipulator
BR məˈnɪpjʊleɪtə(r), -z
AM məˈnɪpjəˌleɪdər, -z
manipulatory
BR məˈnɪpjʊlət(ə)ri
AM məˈnɪpjələˌtɔri
Manipur
BR ˈmanɪpʊə(r),
ˈmʌnɪpʊə(r),
ˈmanɪpɔː(r),
ˈmʌnɪpɔː(r)
AM ˌmænəˌpʊ(ə)r
Manipuri
BR ˌmanɪˈpʊəri,
ˌmʌnɪˈpʊəri,
ˌmanɪˈpɔːri,
ˌmʌnɪˈpɔːri, -ɪz
AM ˌmænəˈpʊri, -z
Manitoba
BR ˌmanɪˈtəʊbə(r)
AM ˌmænəˈtoʊbə
Manitoban
BR ˌmanɪˈtəʊbən, -z
AM ˌmænəˈtoʊbən, -z
manitou
BR ˈmanɪtuː
AM ˈmænəˌtu
mankind
BR ˌmanˈkʌɪnd
AM ˌmænˈkaɪnd,
ˈmænˌkaɪnd
manky
BR ˈmaŋk|i, -ɪə(r), -ɪɪst
AM ˈmæŋki, -ər, -ɪst
manless
BR ˈmanləs
AM ˈmænləs

Manley
BR ˈmanli
AM ˈmænli
manlike
BR ˈmanlʌɪk
AM ˈmænˌlaɪk
manliness
BR ˈmanlɪnɪs
AM ˈmænlinɪs
manly
BR ˈmanl|i, -ɪə(r), -ɪɪst
AM ˈmænli, -ər, -ɪst
man-made
BR ˌmanˈmeɪd
AM ˌmænˈmeɪd
Mann
BR man
AM mæn, mɑn
manna
BR ˈmanə(r)
AM ˈmænə
manna-ash
BR ˈmanə(r)aʃ, -ɪz
AM ˈmænəˌæʃ, -əz
manned
BR mand
AM mænd
mannequin
BR ˈmanɪkɪn, -z
AM ˈmænəkən, -z
manner
BR ˈmanə(r), -z, -d
AM ˈmænər, -z, -d
mannerism
BR ˈmanərɪz(ə)m, -z
AM ˈmænəˌrɪzəm, -z
mannerist
BR ˈmanərɪst, -s
AM ˈmænərəst, -s
manneristic
BR ˌmanəˈrɪstɪk
AM ˌmænəˈrɪstɪk
manneristical
BR ˌmanəˈrɪstɪkl
AM ˌmænəˈrɪstəkəl
manneristically
BR ˌmanəˈrɪstɪkli
AM ˌmænəˈrɪstək(ə)li
mannerless
BR ˈmanələs
AM ˈmænərləs
mannerliness
BR ˈmanəlɪnɪs
AM ˈmænərlinɪs
mannerly
BR ˈmanəli
AM ˈmænərli
Mannheim
BR ˈmanhʌɪm
AM ˈmæn,(h)aɪm
mannikin
BR ˈmanɪkɪn, -z
AM ˈmænəkən, -z
Manning
BR ˈmanɪŋ
AM ˈmænɪŋ

Mannion
BR ˈmanɪən, ˈmanjən
AM ˈmænjən, ˈmænɪən
mannish
BR ˈmanɪʃ
AM ˈmænɪʃ
mannishly
BR ˈmanɪʃli
AM ˈmænɪʃli
mannishness
BR ˈmanɪʃnɪs
AM ˈmænɪʃnɪs
Mano
BR ˈmanəʊ
AM ˈmæˌnoʊ
manoeuvrability
BR məˌnuːv(ə)rəˈbɪlɪti
AM məˌn(j)uv(ə)rəˈbɪlɪdi
manoeuvrable
BR məˈnuːv(ə)rəbl
AM məˈn(j)uv(ə)rəbəl
manoeuvre
BR məˈnuːv|ə(r), -əz,
-(ə)rɪŋ, -əd
AM məˈn(j)uv|ər, -ərz,
-(ə)rɪŋ, -ərd
manoeuvrer
BR məˈnuːv(ə)rə(r)
AM məˈn(j)uv(ə)rər
manoeuvring
BR məˈnuːv(ə)rɪŋ, -z
AM məˈn(j)uv(ə)rɪŋ, -z
manometer
BR məˈnɒmɪtə(r), -z
AM məˈnɑmədər, -z
manometric
BR ˌmanə(ʊ)ˈmɛtrɪk
AM ˌmænəˈmɛtrɪk
manometrical
BR ˌmanə(ʊ)ˈmɛtrɪkl
AM ˌmænəˈmɛtrəkəl
manometrically
BR ˌmanə(ʊ)ˈmɛtrɪkli
AM ˌmænəˈmɛtrək(ə)li
ma non troppo
BR ˌmɑː nɒn ˈtrɒpəʊ
AM ˌmɑ nɑn ˈtrɑpoʊ
manor
BR ˈmanə(r), -z
AM ˈmænər, -z
Manorbier
BR ˌmanəˈbɪə(r)
AM ˌmænəˈbɪ(ə)r
manorial
BR məˈnɔːrɪəl
AM məˈnɔriəl
man-o'-war
BR ˌmanəˈwɔː(r)
AM ˌmænəˈwɔ(ə)r
manpower
BR ˈmanpaʊə(r)
AM ˈmænˌpaʊ(ə)r
manqué
BR ˈmɒŋkeɪ
AM ˈmɑŋˌkeɪ
Man Ray
BR ˌman ˈreɪ

AM 'mæn 'reɪ
mansard
BR 'mansɑːd, -z
AM 'mæn,sɑrd, -z
Mansart
BR ,mɔ̃'sɑːt, ,mɒn'sɑːt
AM mɑn'sɑr(t)
manse
BR mans, -ɪz
AM mæns, -əz
Mansell
BR 'mansl
AM 'mænsəl
manservant
BR 'man,səːv(ə)nt, -s
AM 'mæn,sɜrvənt, -s
Mansfield
BR 'mansfiːld
AM 'mæns,fild
mansion
BR 'manʃn, -z
AM 'mæn(t)ʃən, -z
manslaughter
BR 'man,slɔːtə(r)
AM 'mæn,slɔdər,
'mæn,slɑdər
Manson
BR 'mansn
AM 'mænsən
mansuetude
BR 'manswɪtjuːd,
'manswɪtʃuːd
AM mæn'suə,t(j)ud
manta
BR 'mantə(r), -z
AM 'mæn(t)ə, -z
manteau
BR 'mantəʊ, -z
AM mæn'toʊ, -z
manteaux
BR 'mantəʊz
AM mæn'toʊ
Mantegna
BR man'tɛnjə(r),
man'teɪnjə(r)
AM ,mɑn'teɪnjə
mantel
BR 'mantl, -z
AM 'mæn(t)l, -z
mantelet
BR 'mantlɪt, 'matlɪt, -s
AM 'mæn(t)lət, -s
mantelletta
BR ,mantɪ'lɛtə(r), -z
AM ,mæn(t)ə'lɛdə, -z
mantellette
BR ,mantɪ'lɛteɪ
AM ,mæn(t)ə'lɛdeɪ
mantelpiece
BR 'mantlpiːs, -ɪz
AM 'mæn(t)l,pis, -ɪz
mantelshelf
BR 'mantlʃɛlf
AM 'mæn(t)l,ʃɛlf
mantelshelves
BR 'mantlʃɛlvz
AM 'mæn(t)l,ʃɛlvz

mantic
BR 'mantɪk
AM 'mæn(t)ɪk
manticore
BR 'mantɪkɔː(r), -z
AM 'mæn(t)ə,kɔ(ə)r, -z
mantid
BR 'mantɪd, -z
AM 'mæn(t)əd, -z
mantilla
BR man'tɪlə(r), -z
AM mæn'ti(j)ə,
mæn'tɪlə, -z
mantis
BR 'mantɪs, -ɪz
AM 'mæn(t)əs, -əz
mantissa
BR man'tɪsə(r), -z
AM mæn'tɪsə, -z
mantle
BR 'mantḷl, -lz,
-lɪŋ\-lŋ, -ld
AM 'mæn(t)əl, -z, -ɪŋ, -d
mantlet
BR 'mantlɪt
AM 'mæn(t)lɛt
mantling
BR 'mantlɪŋ, -z
AM 'mæn(t)lɪŋ, -z
man-to-man
BR ,mantə'man
AM 'mæn(t)ə'mæn
Mantovani
BR ,mantə'vɑːni
AM ,mɑn(t)ə'vɑni
mantra
BR 'mantrə(r), -z
AM 'mæntrə, -z
mantrap
BR 'mantrap, -s
AM 'mæn,træp, -s
mantua
BR 'mantjʊə(r),
'mantʃʊə(r), -z
AM 'mæn(t)ʃəwə, -z
Manu
BR 'manuː
AM 'mɑ,nu
manual
BR 'manjʊəl, 'manjʊl,
-z
AM 'mænjə(wə)l, -z
manually
BR 'manjʊəli,
'manjʊli
AM 'mænjə(wə)li
Manuel
BR man'wɛl
AM mæn'wɛl
manufactory
BR ,manjʊ'fakt(ə)r|i,
-ɪz
AM ,mæn(j)ə'fækt(ə)ri,
-z
manufacturability
BR ,manjʊ,faktʃ(ə)rə-
'bɪlɪti

AM ,mænjə,fæktʃərə-
'bɪlɪdi,
,manjə,fækʃ(ə)rə'bɪlɪdi
manufacturable
BR ,manjʊ'faktʃ(ə)rəbl
AM ,mænjə'fæktʃərəbəl,
,mænjə'fækʃ(ə)rəbəl
manufacture
BR ,manjʊ'faktʃ|ə(r),
-əz, -(ə)rɪŋ, -əd
AM ,mæn(j)ə'fæk|(t)ʃər,
-(t)ʃərz,
-tʃərɪŋ\-ʃ(ə)rɪŋ,
-(t)ʃərd
manufacturer
BR ,manjʊ'faktʃ(ə)rə(r),
-z
AM ,mænjə'fæktʃərər,
,mænjə'fækʃ(ə)rər, -z
manuka
BR 'mɑːnɵkə(r),
'manɵkə(r),
ma'nuːkə(r), -z
AM 'mɑnəkə, -z
manumission
BR ,manjʊ'mɪʃn
AM ,mænjə'mɪʃən
manumit
BR ,manjʊ'mɪt, -s, -ɪŋ,
-ɪd
AM ,mænjə'mɪ|t, -ts,
-dɪŋ, -dɪd
manure
BR mə'njʊə(r),
mə'njɔː(r), -z, -ɪŋ, -d
AM mə'n(j)ʊ(ə)r, -z, -ɪŋ,
-d
manurial
BR mə'njʊərɪəl,
mə'njɔːrɪəl
AM mə'n(j)ʊrɪəl
manuscript
BR 'manjʊskrɪpt, -s
AM 'mænjə,skrɪp(t), -s
Manx
BR manks
AM mæŋks
Manxman
BR 'manksmən
AM 'mæŋksmən
Manxmen
BR 'manksmən
AM 'mæŋksmən
Manxwoman
BR 'manks,wʊmən
AM 'mæŋks,wʊmən
Manxwomen
BR 'manks,wɪmɪn
AM 'mæŋks,wɪmɪn
many
BR 'mɛni
AM 'mɛni
manyfold
BR 'mɛnɪfəʊld
AM 'mɛni,foʊld
manyplies
BR 'mɛnɪplaɪz
AM 'mɛni,plaɪz

manzanilla
BR ,manzə'nɪlə(r),
,manzə'niːljə(r), -z
AM ,mænzə'ni(j)ə, -z
manzanita
BR ,manzə'niːtə(r), -z
AM ,mænzə'nidə, -z
Manzoni
BR man'zəʊni
AM mɑn'zoʊni
Maoism
BR 'maʊɪz(ə)m
AM 'maʊ,ɪzəm
Maoist
BR 'maʊɪst, -s
AM 'maʊəst, -s
Maori
BR 'maʊr|i, -ɪz
AM 'maʊri, -z
Maoriland
BR 'maʊrɪland
AM 'maʊri,lænd
Mao Tse-tung
BR ,maʊ tseɪ'tʊŋ
AM 'maʊ ,(t)seɪ'tʊŋ
Mao Zedong
BR ,maʊ zeɪ'dɒŋ
AM 'maʊ ,zeɪ'dɔŋ, 'maʊ
,zeɪ'daŋ
map
BR map, -s, -ɪŋ, -t
AM mæp, -s, -ɪŋ, -t
maple
BR 'meɪpl, -z
AM 'meɪpəl, -z
mapless
BR 'mapləs
AM 'mæpləs
mappable
BR 'mapəbl
AM 'mæpəbəl
Mappa Mundi
BR ,mapə 'mʊndi
AM ,mɑpə 'mʊndi
mapper
BR 'mapə(r), -z
AM 'mæpər, -z
Maputo
BR mə'puːtəʊ
AM mə'pudoʊ
maquette
BR ma'kɛt, -s
AM mæ'kɛt, -s
maquilladora
BR mə,kɪlə'dɔːrə(r)
AM mə,kɪlə'dɔrə
maquillage
BR ,makɪ'(j)ɑːʒ
AM ,mɑki'jɑʒ
maquis
BR ma'kiː, 'makiː,
'mɑːkiː
AM mɑ'ki
maquisard
BR ,makɪ'zɑː(r), -z
AM ,mɑkə'zɑr, -z

mar
BR mɑː(r), -z, -ɪŋ, -d
AM mɑr, -z, -ɪŋ, -d
marabou
BR ˈmarəbuː, -z
AM ˈmɛrəˌbu, -z
marabout¹
stork, silk
BR ˈmarəbuː, -z
AM ˈmɛrəˌbu, -z
marabout²
holy man, shrine
BR ˈmarəbuːt, -s
AM ˈmɛrəˌbut, -z
maraca
BR məˈrakə(r), -z
AM məˈrakə, -z
Maracaibo
BR ˌmarəˈkʌɪbəʊ
AM ˌmɛrəˈkaɪbou
Maradona
BR ˌmarəˈdɒnə(r)
AM ˌmɛrəˈdɒnə,
ˌmɛrəˈdanə
Maramba
BR məˈrambə(r)
AM məˈrambə
maranta
BR məˈrantə(r), -z
AM məˈræn(t)ə, -z
maraschino
BR ˌmarəˈskiːnəʊ,
ˌmarəˈʃiːnəʊ, -z
AM ˌmɛrəˈʃiːˌnou,
ˌmɛrəˈskiˌnou, -z
marasmic
BR məˈrazmɪk
AM məˈræzmɪk
marasmus
BR məˈrazməs
AM məˈræzməs
Marat
BR ˈmarɑː(r)
AM məˈrɑ(t)
Maratha
BR məˈrɑːtə(r),
məˈratə(r), -z
AM məˈrɑdə, -z
Marathi
BR məˈrɑːti, məˈrati
AM məˈrɑdi
marathon
BR ˈmarəθ(ə)n, -z
AM ˈmɛrəˌθɑn, -z
marathoner
BR ˈmarəθənə(r),
ˈmarəˌθnə(r), -z
AM ˈmɛrəˌθɑnər, -z
maraud
BR məˈrɔːd, -z, -ɪŋ, -ɪd
AM məˈrɑd, məˈrad, -z,
-ɪŋ, -əd
marauder
BR məˈrɔːdə(r), -z
AM məˈrɑdər,
məˈradər, -z
maravedi
BR ˌmarəˈveɪd|i, -ɪz

AM ˌmɛrəˈveɪd|i, -z
Marazion
BR ˌmarəˈzʌɪən
AM ˌmɛrəˈzaɪən
Marbella
BR mɑːˈbeɪə(r)
AM mɑrˈbeɪə
marble
BR ˈmɑːb|l, -lz,
-lɪŋ\-lɪŋ, -ld
AM ˈmɑrb|əl, -əlz,
-(ə)lɪŋ, -əld
marbling
BR ˈmɑːblɪŋ, ˈmɑːblɪŋ,
-z
AM ˈmɑrb(ə)lɪŋ, -z
marbly
BR ˈmɑːb|i
AM ˈmɑrb(ə)li
marc
BR mɑːk
AM mɑrk
Marcan
BR ˈmɑːk(ə)n
AM ˈmɑrkən
marcasite
BR ˈmɑːkəsʌɪt,
ˈmɑːkəziːt
AM ˈmɑrkəˌsaɪt
marcato
BR mɑːˈkɑːtəʊ
AM mɑrˈkɑdou
Marceau
BR mɑːˈsəʊ
AM mɑrˈsou
marcel
BR mɑːˈsɛl, -z, -ɪŋ, -d
AM mɑrˈsɛl, -z, -ɪŋ, -d
Marcella
BR mɑːˈsɛlə(r)
AM mɑrˈsɛlə
Marcellus
BR mɑːˈsɛləs
AM mɑrˈsɛləs
marcescence
BR mɑːˈsɛsns, -ɪz
AM mɑrˈsɛsəns, -əz
marcescent
BR mɑːˈsɛsnt
AM mɑrˈsɛsənt
march
BR mɑːtʃ, -ɪz, -ɪŋ, -t
AM mɑrtʃ, -əz, -ɪŋ, -t
Marchant
BR ˈmɑːtʃ(ə)nt
AM ˈmɑrtʃənt
Marche
BR mɑːtʃ
AM mɑrtʃ
marcher
BR ˈmɑːtʃə(r), -z
AM ˈmɑrtʃər, -z
Marches
BR ˈmɑːtʃɪz
AM ˈmɑrtʃəz
marchioness
BR ˌmɑːtʃəˈnɛs, -ɪz

AM ˌmɛrəˈveɪdi, -z
marchpane
BR ˈmɑːtʃpeɪn
AM ˈmɑrtʃˌpeɪn
Marcia
BR ˈmɑːsɪə(r),
ˈmɑːʃə(r)
AM ˈmɑrʃə
Marciano
BR ˌmɑːsɪˈɑːnəʊ
AM mɑrˈsianou
Marconi
BR mɑːˈkəʊni
AM mɑrˈkouni
Marco Polo
BR ˌmɑːkəʊ ˈpəʊləʊ
AM ˌmɑrkou ˈpouˌlou
Marcos
BR ˈmɑːkɒs
AM ˈmɑrkous
marcottage
BR ˌmɑːkɒˈtɑːʒ,
mɑːˈkɒtɪdʒ
AM ˌmɑrkəˈtɑʒ,
ˌmɑrˈkɑdɪdʒ
Marcus
BR ˈmɑːkəs
AM ˈmɑrkəs
Marcus Aurelius
BR ˌmɑːkəs ɔːˈriːlɪəs
AM ˌmɑrkəs ɔːˈreɪlɪəs,
+ ɔːˈrilɪəs
Marcuse
BR mɑːˈkuːzə(r)
AM mɑrˈkuzə
Mar del Plata
BR ˌmɑː dɛl ˈplɑtə(r)
AM ˌmɑr dəl ˈplɑdə
Mardi Gras
BR ˌmɑːdɪ ˈgrɑː(r), -z
AM ˌmɑrdiˈgrɑ, -z
Marduk
BR ˈmɑːdək
AM ˈmɑrdək
mardy
BR ˈmɑːdi
AM ˈmɑrdi
mare¹
horse
BR mɛː(r), -z
AM mɛ(ə)r, -z
mare²
on moon
BR ˈmɑːr|eɪ, ˈmɑr|i,
-eɪz\-ɪz
AM ˈmɑreɪ, ˈmɑri, -z
maremma
BR məˈrɛmə(r)
AM məˈrɛmə
maremme
BR məˈrɛmi
AM məˈrɛmi
Marengo
BR məˈrɛŋɡəʊ
AM məˈrɛŋɡou
marg
BR mɑːdʒ

AM ˌmɑːrʃ(ə)nəs, -əz
Margam
BR ˈmɑːɡəm
AM ˈmɑrɡəm
Margaret
BR ˈmɑːɡ(ə)rɪt
AM ˈmɑrɡ(ə)rət
margarine
BR ˌmɑːdʒəˈriːn,
ˌmɑːɡəˈriːn
AM ˈmɑrdʒ(ə)rən
margarita
BR ˌmɑːɡəˈriːtə(r), -z
AM ˌmɑrɡəˈridə, -z
margarite
BR ˈmɑːɡərʌɪt
AM ˈmɑrɡəˌraɪt
Margate
BR ˈmɑːɡeɪt
AM ˈmɑrˌɡeɪt
margate
fish
BR ˈmɑːɡɪt, -s
AM ˈmɑrɡət, -s
margay
BR ˈmɑːɡeɪ, -z
AM ˈmɑrˌɡeɪ, -z
marge
BR mɑːdʒ
AM mɑrdʒ
Margerison
BR məˈdʒɛrɪs(ə)n,
ˈmɑːdʒ(ə)rɪs(ə)n
AM ˈmɑrˈdʒɛrəsən
Margery
BR ˈmɑːdʒ(ə)ri
AM ˈmɑrdʒ(ə)ri
Margeurite
BR ˌmɑːɡəˈriːt
AM ˌmɑrɡ(j)əˈrit
margin
BR ˈmɑːdʒɪn, -z
AM ˈmɑrdʒən, -z
marginal
BR ˈmɑːdʒɪnl, ˈmɑːdʒnl
AM ˈmɑrdʒənəl
marginalia
BR ˌmɑːdʒɪˈneɪlɪə(r)
AM ˈmɑrdʒəˈneɪljə,
ˌmɑrdʒəˈneɪlɪə
marginalisation
BR ˌmɑːdʒɪnəlʌɪˈzeɪʃn,
ˌmɑːdʒn̩ˌlʌɪˈzeɪʃn,
ˌmɑːdʒnəlʌɪˈzeɪʃn,
ˌmɑːdʒn̩ˌlʌɪˈzeɪʃn
AM ˌmɑrdʒənələˈzeɪʃən,
ˌmɑrdʒənəˌlaɪˈzeɪʃən
marginalise
BR ˈmɑːdʒɪnəlʌɪz,
ˈmɑːdʒn̩lʌɪz,
ˈmɑːdʒnəlʌɪz,
ˈmɑːdʒn̩ˌlʌɪz, -ɪz, -ɪŋ, -d
AM ˈmɑrdʒənəˌlaɪz, -ɪz,
-ɪŋ, -d
marginality
BR ˌmɑːdʒɪˈnalɪti
AM ˌmɑrdʒəˈnælədi

marginalization
BR ˌmɑːdʒɪnəlʌɪˈzeɪʃn,
ˌmɑːdʒɪnlʌɪˈzeɪʃn,
ˌmɑːdʒŋəlʌɪˈzeɪʃn,
ˌmɑːdʒŋlʌɪˈzeɪʃn
AM ˌmɑrdʒənələˈzeɪʃən,
ˌmɑrdʒənəˌlaɪˈzeɪʃən

marginalize
BR ˈmɑːdʒɪnəlʌɪz,
ˈmɑːdʒɪnl̩ʌɪz,
ˈmɑːdʒŋəlʌɪz,
ˈmɑːdʒŋl̩ʌɪz, -ɪz, -ɪŋ, -d
AM ˈmɑrdʒənəˌlaɪz, -ɪz,
-ɪŋ, -d

marginally
BR ˈmɑːdʒɪnəli,
ˈmɑːdʒɪnl̩i,
ˈmɑːdʒŋəli, ˈmɑːdʒŋl̩i
AM ˈmɑrdʒənl̩i

marginate
BR ˈmɑːdʒɪneɪt, -s, -ɪŋ,
-ɪd
AM ˈmɑrdʒɪˌneɪt, -ts,
-dɪŋ, -dɪd

margination
BR ˌmɑːdʒɪˈneɪʃn, -z
AM ˌmɑrdʒəˈneɪʃən, -z

Margo
BR ˈmɑːgəʊ
AM ˈmɑrgoʊ

Margolis
BR mɑːˈgəʊlɪs
AM mɑrˈgoʊlɪs

Margot
BR ˈmɑːgəʊ
AM ˈmɑrgoʊ

margravate
BR ˈmɑːgrəveɪt, -s
AM ˈmɑrgrəˌveɪt, -s

margrave
BR ˈmɑːgreɪv, -z
AM ˈmɑrgreɪv, -z

margravine
BR ˈmɑːgrəviːn, -z
AM ˈmɑrgrəˌvin, -z

marguerite
BR ˌmɑːgəˈriːt, -s
AM ˌmɑrg(j)əˈrit, -s

Mari
BR ˈmɑːri
AM ˈmɑri

Maria
BR məˈrɪə(r),
məˈrʌɪə(r)
AM məˈriə

maria
plural of mare
BR ˈmɑːrɪə(r)
AM ˈmɑriə

**mariage de
convenance**
BR marɪˌɑːʒ də
ˌkɒvəˈnɒs
AM ˌmɑriˈɑʒ də
ˌkɔnvəˈnɑns

**mariages de
convenance**
BR marɪˌɑːʒ də
ˌkɒvəˈnɒs
AM ˌmɑriˈɑʒ də
ˌkɔnvəˈnɑns

Marian¹
adjective
BR ˈmɛːrɪən
AM ˈmɛriən

Marian²
forename
BR ˈmarɪən
AM ˈmɛriən

Mariana
BR ˌmarɪˈɑːnə(r)
AM ˌmɛriˈɑnə

Marianas
BR ˌmarɪˈɑːnəz
AM ˌmɛriˈɑnəz

Marianne
BR ˌmarɪˈan
AM ˌmɛriˈæn

Maria Theresa
BR məˌrɪə təˈreɪzə(r)
AM məˈriə təˈreɪsə

Marie
BR məˈriː
AM məˈri

Marie-Antoinette
BR məˌriː antwəˈnɛt
AM məˌri ˌantwəˈnɛt

Marienbad
BR ˈmarɪənbad
AM ˈmɛrɪənˌbad,
ˈmɛrɪənˌbæd

marigold
BR ˈmarɪgəʊld, -z
AM ˈmɛrəˌgoʊld, -z

marihuana
BR ˌmarɪˈ(h)wɑːnə(r)
AM ˌmɛrəˈ(h)wɑnə

marijuana
BR ˌmarɪˈ(h)wɑːnə(r)
AM ˌmɛrəˈ(h)wɑnə

Marilyn
BR ˈmarɪlɪn, ˈmarl̩ɪn
AM ˈmɛrələn

marimba
BR məˈrɪmbə(r), -z
AM məˈrɪmbə, -z

marina
BR məˈriːnə(r), -z
AM məˈrinə, -z

marinade
BR ˌmarɪˈneɪd, -z
AM ˌmɛrəˈneɪd, -z

marinara
BR ˌmarɪˈnɑːrə(r)
AM ˌmɛrəˈnɛrə

marinate
BR ˈmarɪneɪt, -s, -ɪŋ, -ɪd
AM ˈmɛrəˌneɪt, -ts,
-dɪŋ, -dɪd

marination
BR ˌmarɪˈneɪʃn, -z
AM ˌmɛrəˈneɪʃən, -z

marine
BR məˈriːn, -z
AM məˈrin, -z

mariner
BR ˈmarɪnə(r), -z
AM ˈmɛrənər, -z

Marinetti
BR ˌmarɪˈnɛti:
AM ˌmɛrəˈnɛdi

Marino
BR məˈriːnəʊ
AM məˈrinoʊ

Mario
BR ˈmarɪəʊ
AM ˈmarioʊ, ˈmɛrioʊ

mariolatry
BR ˌmɛːrɪˈɒlətri,
ˌmarɪˈɒlətri
AM ˌmɛriˈɑlətri

Mariology
BR ˌmɛːrɪˈɒlədʒi,
ˌmarɪˈɒlədʒi
AM ˌmɛriˈɑlədʒi

Marion
BR ˈmarɪən
AM ˈmɛriən

marionette
BR ˌmarɪəˈnɛt, -s
AM ˌmɛriəˈnɛt, -s

Marisa
BR məˈrɪsə(r)
AM məˈrisə, məˈrɪsə

Marischal
BR ˈmɑːʃl
AM ˈmɛrəˌʃæl

Marist
BR ˈmɛːrɪst, ˈmarɪst, -s
AM ˈmɛrəst, -s

marital
BR ˈmarɪtl
AM ˈmɛrədl

maritally
BR ˈmarɪtl̩i
AM ˈmɛrədl̩i

maritime
BR ˈmarɪtʌɪm
AM ˈmɛrəˌtaɪm

Maritimes
BR ˈmarɪtʌɪmz
AM ˈmɛrəˌtaɪmz

Maritsa
BR məˈrɪtsə(r)
AM məˈrɪtsə

Marius
BR ˈmarɪəs
AM ˈmɛriəs, ˈmariəs

marjoram
BR ˈmɑːdʒ(ə)rəm
AM ˈmɑrdʒərəm

Marjoribanks
BR ˈmɑːtʃbaŋks
AM ˈmɑrtʃˌbaŋks

Marjorie
BR ˈmɑːdʒ(ə)ri
AM ˈmɑrdʒ(ə)ri

mark
BR mɑːk, -s, -ɪŋ, -t

mark
AM mɑrk, -s, -ɪŋ, -t

markdown
BR ˈmɑːkdaʊn, -z
AM ˈmɑrkˌdaʊn, -z

marked
adjective
BR mɑːkt, ˈmɑːkɪd
AM ˈmɑrkəd

markedly
BR ˈmɑːkɪdli
AM ˈmɑrkədli

markedness
BR ˈmɑːkɪdnɪs
AM ˈmɑrkədnəs

marker
BR ˈmɑːkə(r), -z
AM ˈmɑrkər, -z

market
BR ˈmɑːk|ɪt, -ɪts, -ɪtɪŋ,
-ɪtɪd
AM ˈmɑrkə|t, -ts, -dɪŋ,
-dɪd

marketability
BR ˌmɑːkɪtəˈbɪlɪti
AM ˌmɑrkədəˈbɪlɪdi

marketable
BR ˈmɑːkɪtəbl
AM ˈmɑrkədəbəl

marketeer
BR ˌmɑːkɪˈtɪə(r), -z
AM ˌmɑrkəˈti(ə)r, -z

marketer
BR ˈmɑːkɪtə(r), -z
AM ˈmɑrkədər, -z

marketing
BR ˈmɑːkɪtɪŋ, -z
AM ˈmɑrkədɪŋ, -z

marketplace
BR ˈmɑːkɪtpleɪs, -ɪz
AM ˈmɑrkətˌpleɪs, -ɪz

markhor
BR ˈmɑːkɔː(r), -z
AM ˈmɑrkɔː(ə)r, -z

marking
BR ˈmɑːkɪŋ, -z
AM ˈmɑrkɪŋ, -z

markka
BR ˈmɑːkɑː(r),
ˈmɑːkə(r), -z
AM ˈmɑrkə, -z

Markova
BR mɑːˈkəʊvə(r)
AM mɑrˈkoʊvə

Marks
BR mɑːks
AM mɑrks

marksman
BR ˈmɑːksmən
AM ˈmɑrksmən

marksmanship
BR ˈmɑːksmənʃɪp
AM ˈmɑrksmənˌʃɪp

marksmen
BR ˈmɑːksmən
AM ˈmɑrksmən

markup
BR ˈmɑːkʌp, -s

AM 'mɑːˌkəp, -s

marl
BR mɑːl
AM mɑrl

Marlboro
BR 'mɑːlb(ə)rə(r)
AM 'mɑrl(ˌ),b(ə)rou

Marlborough
BR 'mɑːlb(ə)rə(r)
AM 'mɑrl(ˌ)b(ə)rou

Marlburian
BR ˌmɑːl'bjuəriən, -z
AM ˌmɑrl'bɛriən, -z

Marlene¹
English name
BR 'mɑːliːn
AM mɑr'lin

Marlene²
German name
BR mɑː'leinə(r)
AM mɑr'leinə

Marley
BR 'mɑːli
AM 'mɑrli

marlin
BR 'mɑːlin, -z
AM 'mɑrlən, -z

marline
BR 'mɑːlin, -z
AM 'mɑrlən, -z

marlinespike
BR 'mɑːlinspʌik, -s
AM 'mɑrlən,spɑik, -s

marlinspike
BR 'mɑːlinspʌik, -s
AM 'mɑrlən,spɑik, -s

marlite
BR 'mɑːlʌit, -s
AM 'mɑrˌlait, -s

Marlon
BR 'mɑːlən, 'mɑːlɒn
AM 'mɑrlən

Marlow
BR 'mɑːləu
AM 'mɑrlou

Marlowe
BR 'mɑːləu
AM 'mɑrlou

marly
BR 'mɑːli, -iə(r), -iist
AM 'mɑrli, -ər, -ist

Marmaduke
BR 'mɑːmədjuːk, 'mɑːmədʒuːk
AM 'mɑrməˌd(j)uk

marmalade
BR 'mɑːməleid
AM 'mɑrməˌleid

Marmara
BR 'mɑːm(ə)rə(r)
AM 'mɑrmərə

Marmion
BR 'mɑːmiən
AM 'mɑrmiən

marmite
BR 'mɑːmʌit, -s
AM 'mɑrˌmait, -s

marmolite
BR 'mɑːmələit, -s
AM 'mɑrməˌlait, -s

Marmora
BR 'mɑːm(ə)rə(r)
AM 'mɑrmərə

marmoreal
BR mɑː'mɔːriəl
AM mɑr'mɔriəl

marmoreally
BR mɑː'mɔːriəli
AM mɑr'mɔriəli

marmoset
BR 'mɑːməzɛt, ˌmɑːmə'zɛt, -s
AM 'mɑrməˌsɛt, 'mɑrməˌzɛt, -s

marmot
BR 'mɑːmət, -s
AM 'mɑrmət, -s

Marne
BR mɑːn
AM mɑrn

Marner
BR 'mɑːnə(r)
AM 'mɑrnər

marocain
BR 'mɑrəkein, ˌmɑrə'kem
AM ˌmɑrəˌkein

Maronite
BR 'mɑrənʌit, -s
AM 'mɛrəˌnait, -s

maroon
BR mə'ruːn, -z, -iŋ, -d
AM mə'run, -z, -iŋ, -d

Marple
BR 'mɑːpl
AM 'mɑrpl

marplot
BR 'mɑːplɒt, -s
AM 'mɑrˌplat, -s

marque
BR mɑːk, -s
AM mɑrk, -s

marquee
BR mɑː'kiː, -z
AM mɑr'ki, -z

Marquesas
BR mɑː'keizəz, mɑː'keisəs
AM ˌmɑr'keizəz

marquess
BR 'mɑːkwis, -iz
AM 'mɑrkwəs, -əz

marquessate
BR 'mɑːkwisət, -s
AM 'mɑrkwəseit, 'mɑrkwəsət, -s

marquetry
BR 'mɑːkitri
AM 'mɑrkətri

Marquette
BR mɑː'kɛt
AM mɑr'kɛt

marquis
BR 'mɑːkwis, mɑː'kiː

AM mɑr'ki, 'mɑrkwəs

marquisate
BR 'mɑːkwisət, -s
AM 'mɑrkwəseit, 'mɑrkwəsət, -s

marquise
BR mɑː'kiːz, -iz
AM mɑr'kiz, -iz

marquises
plural
BR 'mɑːkwisiz, mɑː'kiːz
AM mɑr'kiz, 'mɑrkwəsəz

marquisette
BR ˌmɑːkɪ'zɛt, -s
AM ˌmɑrkwə'zɛt, ˌmɑrki'zɛt, -s

Marr
BR mɑː(r)
AM mɑr

Marrakesh
BR ˌmɑrə'kɛʃ
AM ˌmɛrə'kɛʃ

marram
BR 'mɑrəm
AM 'mɛrəm

Marrano
BR mə'rɑːnəu, -z
AM mə'ranou, -z

marriage
BR 'mɑr|idʒ, -idʒiz
AM 'mɛridʒ, -iz

marriageability
BR ˌmɑridʒə'biliti
AM ˌmɛridʒə'bilidi

marriageable
BR 'mɑridʒəbl
AM 'mɛridʒəbəl

married
BR 'mɑrid, -z
AM 'mɛrid, -z

Marriott
BR 'mɑriət
AM 'mɛriˌɑt

marron glacé
BR ˌmɑrɒn 'glɑsei, -z
AM mə'ran glɑ'sei, -z

marrow
BR 'mɑrəu, -z
AM 'mɛrou, -z

marrowbone
BR 'mɑrə(u)bəun, -z
AM 'mɛrouˌboun, -z

marrowfat
BR 'mɑrə(u)fat
AM 'mɛrouˌfæt

marry
BR 'mɑr|i, -iz, -iiŋ, -id
AM 'mɛri, -z, -iŋ, -id

Marryat
BR 'mɑriət
AM 'mɛriət

Mars
BR mɑːz
AM mɑrz

Marsala
BR mɑː'sɑːlə(r)
AM mɑr'sɑlə

Marsden
BR 'mɑːzd(ə)n
AM 'mɑrzdən

Marseillaise
BR ˌmɑːsei'jeiz, ˌmɑːsə'leiz, ˌmɑːsl'eiz
AM ˌmɑrsə'jei(z), ˌmɑrsə'jɛz

Marseille
BR mɑː'sei
AM mɑr'sei

Marseilles
BR mɑː'sei
AM mɑr'sei

marsh
BR mɑːʃ, -iz
AM mɑrʃ, -iz

Marsha
BR 'mɑːʃə(r)
AM 'mɑrʃə

marshal
BR 'mɑːʃl, -lz, -liŋ\-əliŋ, -ld
AM 'mɑrʃ[əl, -əlz, -(ə)liŋ, -əld

marshalship
BR 'mɑːʃʃip, -s
AM 'mɑrʃəlˌʃip, -s

marshiness
BR 'mɑːʃinis
AM 'mɑrʃinis

marshland
BR 'mɑːʃland, 'mɑːʃlənd, -z
AM 'mɑrʃˌlænd, -z

marshmallow
BR ˌmɑːʃ'maləu, -z
AM 'mɑrʃˌmɛlou, -z

marshy
BR 'mɑːʃi, -iə(r), -iist
AM 'mɑrʃi, -ər, -ist

Marston Moor
BR ˌmɑːst(ə)n 'muə(r), + 'mɔː(r)
AM ˌmɑrstən 'mɔ(ə)r

marsupial
BR mɑː's(j)uːpiəl, -z
AM mɑr'supiəl, -z

mart
BR mɑːt, -s
AM mɑrt, -s

Martaban
BR 'mɑːtəban
AM 'mɑrdəˌbæn

martagon
BR 'mɑːtəg(ə)n, -z
AM 'mɑrdəgən, -z

martello
BR mɑː'tɛləu, -z
AM mɑr'tɛlou, -z

marten
BR 'mɑːt(ɪ)n, -z
AM 'mɑrtən, -z

Martens
BR ˈmɑːt(ɪ)nz
AM ˈmɑːrtənz
martensite
BR ˈmɑːtɪnzaɪt
AM ˈmɑːrtn̩ˌsaɪt
Martha
BR ˈmɑːθə(r)
AM ˈmɑːrθə
martial
BR ˈmɑːʃl
AM ˈmɑːrʃəl
martialise
BR ˈmɑːʃlʌɪz,
ˈmɑːʃəlʌɪz, -ɪz, -ɪŋ, -d
AM ˈmɑːrʃəˌlaɪz, -ɪz, -ɪŋ,
-d
martialize
BR ˈmɑːʃlʌɪz,
ˈmɑːʃəlʌɪz, -ɪz, -ɪŋ, -d
AM ˈmɑːrʃəˌlaɪz, -ɪz, -ɪŋ,
-d
martially
BR ˈmɑːʃli
AM ˈmɑːrʃəli
Martian
BR ˈmɑːʃn, -z
AM ˈmɑːrʃən, -z
martin
BR ˈmɑːtɪn, -z
AM ˈmɑːrtn, -z
Martina
BR mɑːˈtiːnə(r)
AM mɑːrˈtinə
Martine
BR mɑːˈtiːn
AM mɑːrˈtin
Martineau
BR ˈmɑːtɪnəʊ
AM ˈmɑːrtəˌnoʊ,
ˈmɑːrtn̩ˌoʊ
martinet
BR ˌmɑːtɪˈnɛt, -s
AM ˌmɑːrtn̩ˈɛt, -s
Martínez
BR mɑːˈtiːnɛz
AM mɑːrˈtinəz,
ˈmɑːrtəˌnɛz
martingale
BR ˈmɑːtɪŋgeɪl, -z
AM ˈmɑːrtn̩ˌgeɪl, -z
martini
BR mɑːˈtiːnǀi, -ɪz
AM mɑːrˈtini, -z
Martinique
BR ˌmɑːtɪˈniːk
AM ˌmɑːrtn̩ˈik
Martinmas
BR ˈmɑːtɪnməs,
ˈmɑːtɪnmæs
AM ˈmɑːrtnməs
Martinmass
BR ˈmɑːtɪnməs,
ˈmɑːtɪnmæs
AM ˈmɑːrtnməs
martlet
BR ˈmɑːtlɪt, -s
AM ˈmɑːrtlət, -s

Martyn
BR ˈmɑːtɪn
AM ˈmɑːrtn
martyr
BR ˈmɑːtǀə(r), -əz,
-(ə)rɪŋ, -əd
AM ˈmɑːrdər, -z, -ɪŋ, -d
martyrdom
BR ˈmɑːtədəm, -z
AM ˈmɑːrdərdəm, -z
martyrisation
BR ˌmɑːt(ə)rʌɪˈzeɪʃn
AM ˌmɑːrdərəˈzeɪʃən,
ˌmɑːrdəˌraɪˈzeɪʃən
martyrise
BR ˈmɑːtərʌɪz, -ɪz, -ɪŋ,
-d
AM ˈmɑːrdəˌraɪz, -ɪz, -ɪŋ,
-d
martyrization
BR ˌmɑːt(ə)rʌɪˈzeɪʃn
AM ˌmɑːrdərəˈzeɪʃən,
ˌmɑːrdəˌraɪˈzeɪʃən
martyrize
BR ˈmɑːtərʌɪz, -ɪz, -ɪŋ,
-d
AM ˈmɑːrdəˌraɪz, -ɪz, -ɪŋ,
-d
martyrological
BR ˌmɑːt(ə)rəˈlɒdʒɪkl
AM ˌmɑːrdərəˈlɑdʒəkəl
martyrologist
BR ˌmɑːtəˈrɒlədʒɪst, -s
AM ˌmɑːrdəˈrɑlədʒəst,
-s
martyrology
BR ˌmɑːtəˈrɒlədʒǀi, -ɪz
AM ˌmɑːrdəˈrɑlədʒi, -z
martyry
BR ˈmɑːtərǀi, -ɪz
AM ˈmɑːrdəri, -z
marvel
BR ˈmɑːvǀl, -lz,
-ǀɪŋ \-əlɪŋ, -ld
AM ˈmɑːrvǀəl, -əlz,
-(ə)lɪŋ, -əld
marveler
BR ˈmɑːvǀlə(r),
ˈmɑːvələ(r), -z
AM ˈmɑːrv(ə)lər, -z
Marvell
BR ˈmɑːvl
AM ˈmɑːrvəl
marveller
BR ˈmɑːvǀlə(r),
ˈmɑːvələ(r), -z
AM ˈmɑːrv(ə)lər, -z
marvellous
BR ˈmɑːv(ə)ləs,
ˈmɑːvǀəs
AM ˈmɑːrv(ə)ləs
marvellously
BR ˈmɑːv(ə)ləsli,
ˈmɑːvǀəsli
AM ˈmɑːrv(ə)ləsli
marvellousness
BR ˈmɑːv(ə)ləsnəs,
ˈmɑːvǀəsnəs

AM ˈmɑːrv(ə)ləsnəs
marvelous
BR ˈmɑːv(ə)ləs,
ˈmɑːvǀəs
AM ˈmɑːrv(ə)ləs
marvelously
BR ˈmɑːv(ə)ləsli,
ˈmɑːvǀəsli
AM ˈmɑːrv(ə)ləsli
marvelousness
BR ˈmɑːv(ə)ləsnəs,
ˈmɑːvǀəsnəs
AM ˈmɑːrv(ə)ləsnəs
Marvin
BR ˈmɑːvɪn
AM ˈmɑːrv(ə)n
Marx
BR mɑːks
AM mɑːrks
Marxian
BR ˈmɑːksɪən
AM ˈmɑːrksiən
Marxism
BR ˈmɑːksɪz(ə)m
AM ˈmɑːrkˌsɪzəm
**Marxism-
Leninism**
BR ˌmɑːksɪz(ə)mˈlɛnɪn-
ɪz(ə)m
AM ˈmɑːrkˌsɪzəmˈlɛnə-
ˌnɪzəm
Marxist
BR ˈmɑːksɪst, -s
AM ˈmɑːrksəst, -s
Marxist-Leninist
BR ˌmɑːksɪstˈlɛnɪnɪst,
-s
AM ˈmɑːrksəstˈlɛnənəst,
-s
Mary
BR ˈmɛːri
AM ˈmɛri
Mary Celeste
BR ˌmɛːrɪ sɪˈlɛst
AM ˈmɛri səˈlɛst
Maryland
BR ˈmɛːrɪlənd
AM ˈmɛrələn(d)
Marylebone
BR ˈmɑːrɪlɪb(ə)n,
ˈmɑːrǀɪb(ə)n,
ˈmɑːrɪlɪbəʊn,
ˈmɑːrǀɪbəʊn
AM ˈmɛrɪləˌboʊn
Mary Magdalene
BR ˌmɛːrɪ ˈmagdəlɪn
AM ˈmɛri ˈmægdələn
Maryport
BR ˈmɛːrɪpɔːt
AM ˈmɛriˌpɔ(ə)rt
marzipan
BR ˈmɑːzɪpan
AM ˈmɑːrtsəˌpan,
ˈmɑːrtsəˌpæn,
ˈmɑːrzəˌpæn
Masada
BR məˈsɑːdə(r)
AM məˈsadə

Masai
BR ˈmɑːsʌɪ, ˌmɑːˈsʌɪ,
ˈmasʌɪ, ˌmaˈsʌɪ,
məˈsʌɪ
AM ˈmɑsaɪ, mɑˈsaɪ
masala
BR məˈsɑːlə(r), -z
AM məˈsalə, -z
Masaryk
BR ˈmazərɪk
AM ˈmasəˌrɪk
Mascagni
BR maˈskanji
AM məˈskan(j)i
Mascall
BR ˈmaskl
AM ˈmæskl
mascara
BR maˈskɑːrə(r),
məˈskɑːrə(r)
AM mæˈskɛrə,
məˈskɛrə
**Mascarene
Islands**
BR ˌmaskəˈriːn
ˌʌɪlən(d)z,
ˈmaskəriːn +
AM ˌmæskəˈrin
ˌaɪlən(d)z
mascaron
BR ˈmaskərən,
ˈmaskərn̩, -z
AM ˈmaskəˌran, -z
mascarpone
BR ˌmaskəˈpəʊnǀi, -ɪz
AM ˌmaskarˈpoʊn(i),
-z
mascle
BR ˈmaskl, ˈmɑːskl, -z
AM ˈmæskəl, -z
mascon
BR ˈmaskɒn, -z
AM ˈmæskɑn, -z
mascot
BR ˈmaskɒt, ˈmaskət,
-s
AM ˈmæˌskɑt,
ˈmæskət, -s
masculine
BR ˈmaskjʉlɪn
AM ˈmæskjələn
masculinely
BR ˈmaskjʉlɪnli
AM ˈmæskjələnli
masculineness
BR ˈmaskjʉlɪnnɪs
AM ˈmæskjələ(n)nəs
masculinisation
BR ˌmaskjʉlɪnʌɪˈzeɪʃn
AM ˌmæskjələnəˈzeɪʃən,
ˌmæskjələˌnaɪˈzeɪʃən
masculinise
BR ˈmaskjʉlɪnʌɪz, -ɪz,
-ɪŋ, -d
AM ˈmæskjələˌnaɪz,
-ɪz, -ɪŋ, -d
masculinity
BR ˌmaskjʉˈlɪnɪti

AM ˌmæskjəˈlɪnɪdi
masculinization
BR ˌmaskjʊlɪnʌɪˈzeɪʃn
AM ˌmæskjələnəˈzeɪʃən,
ˌmæskjələˌnɑɪˈzeɪʃən
masculinize
BR ˈmaskjʊlɪnʌɪz, -ɪz,
-ɪŋ, -d
AM ˈmæskjələˌnɑɪz,
-ɪz, -ɪŋ, -d
masculist
BR ˈmaskjʊlɪst, -s
AM ˈmæskjələst, -s
Masefield
BR ˈmeɪsfiːld
AM ˈmeɪsˌfild
maser
BR ˈmeɪzə(r), -z
AM ˈmeɪzər, -z
Maserati®
BR ˌmazəˈrɑːt|i, -iz
AM ˌmazəˈradi,
ˌmæzəˈradi, -z
Maseru
BR məˈsɛːruː,
məˈsɪəruː
AM ˈmæzəˌru,
ˈmasəˌru
MASH
BR maʃ
AM mæʃ
mash
BR maʃ, -ɪz, -ɪŋ, -t
AM mæʃ, -əz, -ɪŋ, -t
Masham[1]
place in Yorkshire
BR ˈmas(ə)m
AM ˈmæʃəm
Masham[2]
surname, sheep
BR ˈmaʃ(ə)m
AM ˈmæʃəm
masher
BR ˈmaʃə(r), -z
AM ˈmæʃər, -z
mashie
BR ˈmaʃ|i, -ɪz
AM ˈmæʃ|i, -z
Mashona
BR məˈʃɒnə(r),
məˈʃʊnə(r)
AM məˈʃoʊnə,
məˈʃanə
Mashonaland
BR məˈʃɒnəland,
məˈʃəʊnəland
AM məˈʃoʊnəlænd,
məˈʃanəlænd
mask
BR mɑːsk, mask, -s, -ɪŋ,
-t
AM mæsk, -s, -ɪŋ, -t
Maskall
BR ˈmaskl
AM ˈmæskl
Maskell
BR ˈmaskl
AM ˈmæskl

masker
BR ˈmɑːskə(r),
ˈmaskə(r), -z
AM ˈmæskər, -z
maskinonge
BR ˈmaskɪnɒn(d)ʒ, -ɪz
AM ˈmæskəˌnɑndʒ, -əz
masochism
BR ˈmasəkɪz(ə)m,
ˈmazəkɪz(ə)m
AM ˈmæzəˌkɪzəm,
ˈmæsəˌkɪzəm
masochist
BR ˈmasəkɪst,
ˈmazəkɪst, -s
AM ˈmæzəkəst,
ˈmæsəkəst, -s
masochistic
BR ˌmasəˈkɪstɪk,
ˌmazəˈkɪstɪk
AM ˌmæzəˈkɪstɪk,
ˌmæsəˈkɪstɪk
masochistically
BR ˌmasəˈkɪstɪkli,
ˌmazəˈkɪstɪkli
AM ˌmæzəˈkɪstək(ə)li,
ˌmæsəˈkɪstək(ə)li
mason
BR ˈmeɪsn, -z
AM ˈmeɪs(ə)n, -z
**Mason-Dixon
Line**
BR ˌmeɪsnˈdɪksn lʌɪn
AM ˈmeɪsnˈdɪksənˌlaɪn
Masonic
BR məˈsɒnɪk
AM məˈsɑnɪk
masonry
BR ˈmeɪsnri
AM ˈmeɪsnri
Masorah
BR məˈsɔːrə(r)
AM məˈsɔrə
Masorete
BR ˈmasəriːt, -s
AM ˈmæsəˌrit, -s
Masoretic
BR ˌmasəˈrɛtɪk
AM ˌmæsəˈrɛdɪk
masque
BR mɑːsk, mask, -s
AM mæsk, -s
masquer
BR ˈmɑːskə(r),
ˈmaskə(r), -z
AM ˈmæskər, -z
masquerade
BR ˌmɑːskəˈreɪd,
ˌmaskəˈreɪd, -z, -ɪŋ, -ɪd
AM ˌmæskəˈreɪd, -z, -ɪŋ,
-ɪd
masquerader
BR ˌmɑːskəˈreɪdə(r),
ˌmaskəˈreɪdə(r), -z
AM ˈmæskəˈreɪdər, -z
mass
BR mas, -ɪz, -ɪŋ, -t
AM mæs, -əz, -ɪŋ, -t

Massachusetts
BR ˌmasəˈtʃuːsɪts
AM ˌmæsəˈtʃusəts
massacre
BR ˈmasək|ə(r), -əz,
-(ə)rɪŋ, -əd
AM ˈmæsəkər, -ərz,
-(ə)rɪŋ, -ərd
massage
BR ˈmasɑː(d)ʒ, -ɪz, -ɪŋ,
-d
AM məˈsɑ(d)ʒ, -əz, -ɪŋ,
-d
massager
BR ˈmasə(d)ʒə(r), -z
AM məˈsɑ(d)ʒər, -z
massasauga
BR ˌmasəˈsɔːɡə(r), -z
AM ˌmæsəˈsɔɡə,
ˌmæsəˈsaɡə, -z
Massawa
BR məˈsɑːwə(r)
AM məˈsawə
massé
BR ˈmas|i, -ɪz
AM mæˈseɪ, -z
Massenet
BR ˈmasəneɪ
AM ˌmasəˈneɪ
masseter
BR maˈsiːtə(r),
məˈsiːtə(r),
ˈmasɪtə(r), -z
AM məˈsidər, -z
masseur
BR maˈsɜː(r),
məˈsɜː(r), -z
AM mæˈsər, məˈsər, -z
masseuse
BR maˈsɜːz, məˈsɜːz, -ɪz
AM mæˈsus, məˈsus,
-əz
Massey
BR ˈmasi
AM ˈmæsi
massicot
BR ˈmasɪkɒt
AM ˈmæsəˌkɑt
massif
BR ˈmasiːf, maˈsiːf, -s
AM mæˈsif, -s
Massif Central
BR ˌmasiːf sɒnˈtrɑːl,
maˌsiːf +
AM mɑˈsif ˌsanˈtral
Massine
BR maˈsiːn
AM maˈsin
massiness
BR ˈmasɪnɪs
AM ˈmæsɪnɪs
Massinger
BR ˈmasɪn(d)ʒə(r)
AM ˈmæsɪndʒər
massive
BR ˈmasɪv
AM ˈmæsɪv

massively
BR ˈmasɪvli
AM ˈmæsɪvli
massiveness
BR ˈmasɪvnɪs
AM ˈmæsɪvnɪs
massless
BR ˈmasləs
AM ˈmæsləs
Masson
BR ˈmasn
AM məˈsɑn
Massorah
BR məˈsɔːrə(r)
AM məˈsɔrə
Massorete
BR ˈmasəriːt, -s
AM ˈmæsəˌrit, -s
Massoretic
BR ˌmasəˈrɛtɪk
AM ˌmæsəˈrɛdɪk
massy
BR ˈmasi
AM ˈmæsi
mast
BR mɑːst, mast, -s, -ɪd
AM mæst, -s, -əd
mastaba
BR ˈmastəbə(r), -z
AM ˈmæstəbə, -z
mastectomy
BR maˈstɛktəm|i,
məˈstɛktəm|i, -iz
AM mæˈstɛktəmi, -z
master
BR ˈmɑːst|ə(r),
ˈmast|ə(r), -əz, -(ə)rɪŋ,
-əd
AM ˈmæst|ər, -ərz,
-(ə)rɪŋ, -ərd
masterclass
BR ˈmɑːstəklɑːs,
ˈmastəklas, -ɪz
AM ˈmæstərˌklæs, -əz
masterdom
BR ˈmɑːstədəm,
ˈmastədəm, -z
AM ˈmæstərdəm, -z
masterful
BR ˈmɑːstəf(ʊ)l,
ˈmastəf(ʊ)l
AM ˈmæstərfəl
masterfully
BR ˈmɑːstəfʊli,
ˈmɑːstəfli,
ˈmastəfʊli, ˈmastəfli
AM ˈmæstərf(ə)li
masterfulness
BR ˈmɑːstəf(ʊ)lnəs,
ˈmastəf(ʊ)lnəs
AM ˈmæstərfəlnəs
masterhood
BR ˈmɑːstəhʊd,
ˈmastəhʊd, -z
AM ˈmæstərˌ(h)ʊd, -z
masterless
BR ˈmɑːstələs,
ˈmastələs

AM 'mæstərləs

masterliness
BR 'mɑːstəlɪnɪs,
'mɑstəlɪnɪs
AM 'mæstərlinɪs

masterly
BR 'mɑːstəli, 'mɑstəli
AM 'mæstərli

mastermind
BR 'mɑːstəmaɪnd,
'mɑstəmaɪnd, -z, -ɪŋ,
-ɪd
AM 'mæstərˌmaɪnd, -z,
-ɪŋ, -ɪd

masterpiece
BR 'mɑːstəpiːs,
'mɑstəpiːs, -ɪz
AM 'mæstərˌpis, -ɪz

Masters
BR 'mɑːstəz, 'mɑstəz
AM 'mæstərz

mastership
BR 'mɑːstəʃɪp,
'mɑstəʃɪp, -s
AM 'mæstərˌʃɪp, -s

mastersinger
BR 'mɑːstəˌsɪŋə(r),
'mɑstəˌsɪŋə(r), -z
AM 'mæstərˌsɪŋər, -z

masterstroke
BR 'mɑːstəstrəʊk,
'mɑstəstrəʊk, -s
AM 'mæstərˌstrəʊk, -s

masterwork
BR 'mɑːstəwɜːk,
'mɑstəwɜːk, -s
AM 'mæstərˌwɜrk, -s

mastery
BR 'mɑːst(ə)ri,
'mɑst(ə)ri
AM 'mæst(ə)ri

masthead
BR 'mɑːsthɛd,
'mɑsthɛd, -z
AM 'mæstˌ(h)ɛd, -z

mastic
BR 'mæstɪk
AM 'mæstɪk

masticate
BR 'mæstɪkeɪt, -s, -ɪŋ,
-ɪd
AM 'mæstəˌkeɪt, -ts,
-dɪŋ, -dɪd

mastication
BR ˌmæstɪ'keɪʃn
AM ˌmæstə'keɪʃən

masticator
BR 'mæstɪkeɪtə(r), -z
AM 'mæstəˌkeɪdər, -z

masticatory
BR 'mæstɪkət(ə)ri,
ˌmæstɪ'keɪt(ə)ri
AM 'mæstəkəˌtɔri

mastiff
BR 'mæstɪf, -s
AM 'mæstəf, -s

mastitis
BR mæ'staɪtɪs,
mə'staɪtɪs
AM mæ'staɪdɪs

mastodon
BR 'mæstədɒn,
'mæstəd(ə)n, -z
AM 'mæstəˌdɑn, -z

mastodontic
BR ˌmæstə'dɒntɪk
AM ˌmæstə'dɑn(t)ɪk

mastoid
BR 'mæstɔɪd, -z
AM 'mæˌstɔɪd, -z

mastoiditis
BR ˌmæstɔɪ'daɪtɪs
AM ˌmæstɔɪ'daɪdəs

masturbate
BR 'mæstəbeɪt, -s, -ɪŋ,
-ɪd
AM 'mæstərˌbeɪt, -ts,
-dɪŋ, -dɪd

masturbation
BR ˌmæstə'beɪʃn
AM ˌmæstər'beɪʃən

masturbator
BR 'mæstəbeɪtə(r), -z
AM 'mæstərˌbeɪdər, -z

masturbatory
BR 'mæstəbeɪtri
AM 'mæstərbəˌtɔri

mat
BR mæt, -s, -ɪŋ, -ɪd
AM mæ|t, -ts, -dɪŋ, -dəd

Matabele
BR ˌmætə'biːli
AM ˌmædə'bili

Matabeleland
BR ˌmætə'biːlɪlænd
AM ˌmædə'biliˌlænd

matador
BR 'mætədɔː(r), -z
AM 'mædəˌdɔ(ə)r, -z

Mata Hari
BR ˌmɑːtə 'hɑːri
AM ˌmɑdə 'hɑri

matamata
BR ˌmætə'mætə(r), -z
AM ˌmædə'mædə, -z

Matapan
BR 'mætəpan,
ˌmætə'pan
AM 'mædəˌpæn

match
BR mætʃ, -ɪz, -ɪŋ, -t
AM mætʃ, -ɪz, -ɪŋ, -t

matchable
BR 'mætʃəbl
AM 'mætʃəbəl

matchboard
BR 'mætʃbɔːd
AM 'mætʃˌbɔ(ə)rd

matchbook
BR 'mætʃbʊk, -s
AM 'mætʃˌbʊk, -s

matchbox
BR 'mætʃbɒks, -ɪz
AM 'mætʃˌbɑks, -ɪz

matchet
BR 'mætʃɪt, -s
AM 'mætʃət, -s

matchless
BR 'mætʃləs
AM 'mætʃləs

matchlessly
BR 'mætʃləsli
AM 'mætʃləsli

matchlock
BR 'mætʃlɒk, -s
AM 'mætʃˌlɑk, -s

matchmaker
BR 'mætʃˌmeɪkə(r), -z
AM 'mætʃˌmeɪkər, -z

matchmaking
BR 'mætʃˌmeɪkɪŋ
AM 'mætʃˌmeɪkɪŋ

matchplay
BR 'mætʃpleɪ
AM 'mætʃˌpleɪ

matchstick
BR 'mætʃstɪk, -s
AM 'mætʃˌstɪk, -s

matchup
BR 'mætʃʌp, -s
AM 'mætʃˌəp, -s

matchwood
BR 'mætʃwʊd
AM 'mætʃˌwʊd

mate
BR meɪt, -s, -ɪŋ, -ɪd
AM meɪ|t, -ts, -ɪŋ, -dɪd

maté
BR 'mateɪ, 'mɑːteɪ
AM 'mɑˌteɪ

mateless
BR 'meɪtlɪs
AM 'meɪtlɪs

matelot
BR 'matləʊ, 'matʃəʊ,
'matələʊ, -z
AM 'mætˌloʊ,
'mædlˌoʊ, -z

matelote
BR 'matələʊt,
'matʃəʊt, 'matələʊt
AM 'mædlˌoʊt,
'mætˌloʊt

mater
BR 'meɪtə(r)
AM 'meɪdər, 'mɑˌtər

materfamilias
BR ˌmeɪtəfə'mɪliəs
AM ˌmeɪdərfə'mɪliəs,
ˌmɑˌtərfə'mɪliəs

material
BR mə'tɪəriəl, -z
AM mə'tɪriəl, -z

materialisation
BR məˌtɪəriəlaɪ'zeɪʃn
AM məˌtɪriələ'zeɪʃən,
məˌtɪriəlaɪ'zeɪʃən

materialise
BR mə'tɪəriəlaɪz, -ɪz,
-ɪŋ, -d
AM mə'tɪriəˌlaɪz, -ɪz,
-ɪŋ, -d

materialism
BR mə'tɪəriəlɪz(ə)m
AM mə'tɪriəˌlɪzəm

materialist
BR mə'tɪəriəlɪst
AM mə'tɪriələst

materialistic
BR məˌtɪəriə'lɪstɪk
AM məˌtɪriə'lɪstɪk

materialistically
BR məˌtɪəriə'lɪstɪkli
AM məˌtɪriə'lɪstək(ə)li

materiality
BR məˌtɪərɪ'alɪti
AM məˌtɪri'ælədi

materialization
BR məˌtɪəriəlaɪ'zeɪʃn
AM məˌtɪriələ'zeɪʃən,
məˌtɪriəˌlaɪ'zeɪʃən

materialize
BR mə'tɪəriəlaɪz, -ɪz,
-ɪŋ, -d
AM mə'tɪriəˌlaɪz, -ɪz,
-ɪŋ, -d

materially
BR mə'tɪəriəli
AM mə'tɪriəli

materia medica
BR məˌtɪəriə
'mɛdɪkə(r)
AM mə'tɪriə 'mɛdəkə

matériel
BR məˌtɪərɪ'ɛl
AM məˌtɪri'ɛl

maternal
BR mə'tɜːnl
AM mə'tɜrnəl

maternalism
BR mə'tɜːnəlɪz(ə)m,
mə'tɜːnlɪz(ə)m
AM mə'tɜrnlˌɪzəm

maternalistic
BR məˌtɜːnə'lɪstɪk,
məˌtɜːnl'ɪstɪk
AM məˌtɜrnl'ɪstɪk

maternally
BR mə'tɜːnəli,
mə'tɜːnli
AM mə'tɜrnli

maternity
BR mə'tɜːnɪti
AM mə'tɜrnədi

mateship
BR 'meɪtʃɪp, -s
AM 'meɪtˌʃɪp, -s

matey
BR 'meɪti, -iə(r), -ɪɪst
AM 'meɪdi, -ər, -ɪst

mateyness
BR 'meɪtɪnɪs
AM 'meɪdɪnɪs

math
BR mæθ, -s

mathematical
AM mæθ, -s
mathematical
BR ˌmaθ(ə)'matɪkl
AM ˌmæθ(ə)'mædəkəl
mathematically
BR maθ(ə)'matɪkli
AM ˌmæθ(ə)'mædək(ə)li
mathematician
BR ˌmaθ(ə)mə'tɪʃn, -z
AM ˌmæθ(ə)mə'tɪʃən,
-z
mathematics
BR ˌmaθ(ə)'matɪks
AM ˌmæθ(ə)'mædɪks
Mather
BR 'meɪðə(r), 'maðə(r)
AM 'mæðər
Matheson
BR 'maθɪs(ə)n
AM 'maθəsən
Mathew
BR 'maθjuː
AM 'mæθju
Mathews
BR 'maθjuːz
AM 'mæθjuz
Mathias
BR mə'θʌɪəs
AM mə'θaɪəs
Mathieson
BR 'maθɪs(ə)n
AM 'maθəsən
Mathilda
BR mə'tɪldə(r)
AM mə'tɪldə
Mathis
BR 'maθɪs
AM 'mæθəs
maths
BR maθs
AM mæθs
matico
BR mə'tiːkəʊ, -z
AM mə'tiˌkoʊ, -z
Matilda
BR mə'tɪldə(r), -z
AM mə'tɪldə, -z
matily
BR 'meɪtɪli
AM 'meɪdɪli
matinée
BR 'matɪneɪ, -z
AM 'mætnˌeɪ, -z
matiness
BR 'meɪtɪnɪs
AM 'meɪdɪnɪs
matins
BR 'matɪnz
AM 'mætnz
Matisse
BR ma'tiːs
AM mə'tis
matlo
BR 'matləʊ, -z
AM 'mætˌloʊ, -z
Matlock
BR 'matlɒk

AM 'mætˌlɑk
matlow
BR 'matləʊ, -z
AM 'mætˌloʊ, -z
Matmata
BR mat'mata(r)
AM mɑt'mɑdə
Mato Grosso
BR ˌmataʊ 'grɒsəʊ
AM ˌmɑdə 'groʊsoʊ
PORT ˌmatu 'grosu
matrass
BR 'matrəs, -ɪz
AM 'mætrəs, -əz
matriarch
BR 'meɪtrɪɑːk, -s
AM 'meɪtriˌɑrk, -s
matriarchal
BR ˌmeɪtrɪ'ɑːkl
AM ˌmeɪtri'ɑrkəl
matriarchy
BR 'meɪtrɪɑːk|i, -ɪz
AM 'meɪtriˌɑrki, -z
matric
BR mə'trɪk
AM mə'trɪk
matrices
BR 'meɪtrɪsiːz
AM 'meɪtrəˌsiz
matricidal
BR ˌmatrɪ'sʌɪdl
AM ˌmætrə'saɪdəl
matricide
BR 'matrɪsʌɪd, -z
AM 'mætrəˌsaɪd, -z
matriculant
BR mə'trɪkjʊlənt,
mə'trɪkjʊlnt, -s
AM mə'trɪkjələnt, -s
matriculate
BR mə'trɪkjʊleɪt, -s,
-ɪŋ, -ɪd
AM mə'trɪkjəˌleɪ|t, -ts,
-dɪŋ, -dɪd
matriculation
BR mə,trɪkjʊ'leɪʃn
AM mə,trɪkjə'leɪʃən
matriculatory
BR mə'trɪkjʊlət(ə)ri
AM mə'trɪkjələˌtɔri
matrilineal
BR ˌmatrɪ'lɪnɪəl
AM ˌmætrə'lɪnɪəl
matrilineally
BR ˌmatrɪ'lɪnɪəli
AM ˌmætrə'lɪnɪəli
matrilocal
BR ˌmatrɪ'ləʊkl
AM ˌmætrə'loʊkəl
matrimonial
BR ˌmatrɪ'məʊnɪəl
AM ˌmætrə'moʊnɪəl
matrimonially
BR ˌmatrɪ'məʊnɪəli
AM ˌmætrə'moʊnɪəli
matrimony
BR 'matrɪməni

AM 'mætrəˌmoʊni
matrix
BR 'meɪtrɪks, -ɪz
AM 'meɪtrɪks, -ɪz
matron
BR 'meɪtr(ə)n, -z
AM 'meɪtrən, -z
matronal
BR 'meɪtr(ə)nl
AM 'meɪtrənəl
matronhood
BR 'meɪtr(ə)nhʊd, -z
AM 'meɪtrən,(h)ʊd, -z
matronly
BR 'meɪtr(ə)nli
AM 'meɪtr(ə)nli
Matsui®
BR mat'suːi
AM mæt'sui
matsuri
BR mat'suːr|i, -ɪz
AM ˌmæt'suri, -z
Matsushita®
BR ˌmatsʊ'ʃiːtə(r)
AM ˌmæt'sʊʃidə
Matsuyama
BR ˌmatsʊ'jaːmə(r)
AM ˌmatsə'jamə
matt
BR mat, -s, -ɪŋ, -ɪd
AM mæt|t, -ts, -dɪŋ, -dəd
mattamore
BR 'matəmɔː(r), -z
AM ˌmædə'mɔ(ə)r, -z
matte
BR mat, -s
AM mæt, -s
matted
BR 'matɪd
AM 'mædəd
mattedly
BR 'matɪdli
AM 'mædədli
mattedness
BR 'matɪdnɪs
AM 'mædədnəs
matter
BR 'mat|ə(r), -əz,
-(ə)rɪŋ, -əd
AM 'mædər, -z, -ɪŋ, -d
Matterhorn
BR 'matəhɔːn
AM 'mædər,(h)ɔ(ə)rn
matter-of-fact
BR ˌmat(ə)rəv'fakt
AM ˌmædərə(v)'fækt
matter-of-factly
BR ˌmat(ə)rəv'faktli
AM ˌmædərə(v)'fæk(t)li
matter-of-
factness
BR ˌmat(ə)rəv'fak(t)nəs
AM ˌmædərə(v)'fæk(t)-
nəs
mattery
BR 'mat(ə)ri

AM 'mædəri
Matthew
BR 'maθjuː
AM 'mæθju
Matthews
BR 'maθjuːz
AM 'mæθjuz
Matthias
BR mə'θʌɪəs
AM mə,θaɪəs
matting
BR 'matɪŋ
AM 'mædɪŋ
mattins
BR 'matɪnz
AM 'mætnz
mattock
BR 'matək, -s
AM 'mædək, -s
mattoid
BR 'matɔɪd, -z
AM 'mædˌɔɪd, -z
mattress
BR 'matrɪs, -ɪz
AM 'mætrəs, -əz
maturate
BR 'matʃʊreɪt,
'matjʊreɪt, -s, -ɪŋ, -ɪd
AM 'mætʃəˌreɪ|t, -ts,
-dɪŋ, -dɪd
maturation
BR ˌmatʃʊ'reɪʃn,
ˌmatjʊ'reɪʃn
AM ˌmætʃə'reɪʃən
maturational
BR ˌmatʃə'reɪʃn(ə)l,
ˌmatʃʊ'reɪʃən(ə)l,
matjʊ'reɪʃn(ə)l,
ˌmatjʊ'reɪʃən(ə)l
AM ˌmætʃə'reɪʃ(ə)nəl
maturative
BR mə'tʃʊərətɪv,
mə'tjʊərətɪv,
mə'tʃɔːrətɪv,
mə'tjɔːrətɪv
AM 'mætʃəˌreɪdɪv,
mə'tʃərədɪv,
mə'tʃʊrədɪv
mature
BR mə'tʃʊə(r),
mə'tjʊə(r), mə'tʃɔː(r),
mə'tjɔː(r), -z, -ɪŋ, -d
AM mə'tʃər,
mə'tʃʊ(ə)r,
mə't(j)ʊ(ə)r, -z, -ɪŋ, -d
maturely
BR mə'tʃʊəli,
mə'tjʊəli, mə'tʃɔːli,
mə'tjɔːli
AM mə'tʃərli,
mə'tʃʊrli, mə't(j)ʊrli
matureness
BR mə'tʃʊənəs,
mə'tjʊənəs,
mə'tʃɔːnəs,
mə'tjɔːnəs
AM mə'tʃərnəs,
mə'tʃʊrnəs,
mə't(j)ʊrnəs

maturity
BR məˈtʃʊərɪti,
məˈtjʊərɪti,
məˈtʃɔːrɪti,
məˈtjɔːrɪti
AM məˈtʃərədi,
məˈtʃʊrədi,
məˈt(j)ʊrədi

matutinal
BR ˌmatjʉˈtʌɪnl,
ˌmatʃʉˈtʌɪnl,
məˈtjuːtɪnl,
məˈtʃuːtɪnl
AM məˈt(j)uːtnəl,
ˌmætʃəˈtaɪnəl

maty
BR ˈmeɪti
AM ˈmeɪdi

matza
BR ˈmɒtsə(r),
ˈmatsə(r), ˈmʌtsə(r),
-z
AM ˈmɑtzə, ˈmatsə, -z

matzah
BR ˈmɒtsə(r),
ˈmatsə(r), ˈmʌtsə(r),
-z
AM ˈmɑtzə, ˈmatsə, -z

matzo
BR ˈmɒtsə(r),
ˈmatsə(r), ˈmʌtsə(r),
ˈmatsəʊ, -z
AM ˈmɑtzə, ˈmatsə, -z

matzoh
BR ˈmɒtsə(r),
ˈmatsə(r), ˈmʌtsə(r),
ˈmatsəʊ, -z
AM ˈmɑtzə, ˈmatsə, -z

mauby
BR ˈmaʊbi, ˈmɔːbi
AM ˈmɒbi, ˈmabi

maud
BR mɔːd, -z
AM mɒd, mad, -z

Maude
BR mɔːd
AM mɒd, mad

maudlin
BR ˈmɔːdlɪn
AM ˈmɒdlən, ˈmadlən

Maudling
BR ˈmɔːdlɪŋ
AM ˈmɒdlɪŋ, ˈmadlɪŋ

Maudsley
BR ˈmɔːdzli
AM ˈmɒdzli, ˈmadzli

Maugham
BR mɔːm
AM mɒm, mam

Maughan
BR mɔːn
AM mɔː(ə)n

maul
BR mɔːl, -z, -ɪŋ, -d
AM mɒl, mal, -z, -ɪŋ, -d

mauler
BR ˈmɔːlə(r), -z
AM ˈmɒlər, ˈmalər, -z

Mauleverer
BR məˈlev(ə)rə(r)
AM mɔːˈlevərər,
maˈlevərər

maulstick
BR ˈmɔːlstɪk, -s
AM ˈmɒlˌstɪk,
ˈmalˌstɪk, -s

Mau Mau
BR ˈmaʊ maʊ
AM ˈmaʊ ˈmaʊ

Mauna Kea
BR ˌmaʊnə ˈkeɪə(r)
AM ˌmaʊnə ˈkeɪə

Mauna Loa
BR ˌmaʊnə ˈləʊə(r)
AM ˌmaʊnə ˈloʊə

maunder
BR ˈmɔːnd|ə(r), -əz,
-(ə)rɪŋ, -əd
AM ˈmɒndər, ˈmandər,
-z, -ɪŋ, -d

maundering
BR ˈmɔːnd(ə)rɪŋ, -z
AM ˈmɒnd(ə)rɪŋ,
ˈmand(ə)rɪŋ, -z

Maundy
BR ˈmɔːndi
AM ˈmɒndi, ˈmandi

Maupassant
BR ˈməʊpasɒ̃
AM ˌmopəˈsɑn

Maura
BR ˈmɔːrə(r)
AM ˈmɔːrə

Maureen
BR ˈmɔːriːn
AM mɔːˈrin

Mauretania
BR ˌmɒrɪˈteɪnɪə(r),
ˌmɔːrɪˈteɪnɪə(r)
AM ˌmɔːrəˈteɪnɪə

Mauretanian
BR ˌmɒrɪˈteɪnɪən,
ˌmɔːrɪˈteɪnɪən, -z
AM ˌmɔːrəˈteɪnɪən, -z

Mauriac
BR ˈmɔːrɪak
AM ˌmɔːriˈ(j)ak

Maurice
BR ˈmɒrɪs
AM mɔːˈris

Maurist
BR ˈmɔːrɪst, -s
AM ˈmɔːrəst, -s

Mauritania
BR ˌmɒrɪˈteɪnɪə(r),
ˌmɔːrɪˈteɪnɪə(r)
AM ˌmɔːrəˈteɪnɪə

Mauritanian
BR ˌmɒrɪˈteɪnɪən,
ˌmɔːrɪˈteɪnɪən, -z
AM ˌmɔːrəˈteɪnɪən, -z

Mauritian
BR məˈrɪʃn, -z
AM mɔːˈrɪʃən, -z

Mauritius
BR məˈrɪʃəs

AM mɔːˈrɪʃəs

Maury
BR ˈmɔːri
AM ˈmɔːri

Maurya
BR ˈmaʊrɪə(r)
AM ˈmaʊrɪə

Mauser®
BR ˈmaʊzə(r), -z
AM ˈmaʊzər, -z

mausolea
BR ˌmɔːsəˈliːə(r),
ˌmɔːzəˈliːə(r)
AM ˌmɔːzəˈliə,
ˌmɔsəˈliə, ˌmazəˈliə,
ˌmasəˈliə

mausoleum
BR ˌmɔːsəˈliːəm,
ˌmɔːzəˈliːəm, -z
AM ˌmɔːzəˈliəm,
ˌmɔsəˈliəm,
ˌmazəˈliəm,
ˌmasəˈliəm, -z

mauve
BR məʊv
AM mɔv, moʊv, mav

mauvish
BR ˈməʊvɪʃ
AM ˈmɔvɪʃ, ˈmoʊvɪʃ,
ˈmavɪʃ

maven
BR ˈmeɪvn, -z
AM ˈmeɪvən, -z

maverick
BR ˈmav(ə)rɪk, -s
AM ˈmæv(ə)rɪk, -s

mavis
BR ˈmeɪv|ɪs, -ɪsɪz
AM ˈmeɪvɪs, -ɪz

maw
BR mɔː(r), -z
AM mɔː, mɑ, -z

Mawddach
BR ˈmaʊðax, ˈmɔːðak
AM ˈmɒðak, ˈmaðak

Mawdesley
BR ˈmɔːdzli
AM ˈmɒdzli, ˈmadzli

Mawer
BR mɔː(r), ˈmɔːə(r)
AM ˈmɒwər

Mawgan
BR ˈmɔːg(ə)n
AM ˈmɒgən, ˈmagən

Mawhinny
BR məˈwɪni
AM mɑˈwɪni

mawkish
BR ˈmɔːkɪʃ
AM ˈmɒkɪʃ, ˈmakɪʃ

mawkishly
BR ˈmɔːkɪʃli
AM ˈmɒkɪʃli, ˈmakɪʃli

mawkishness
BR ˈmɔːkɪʃnɪs
AM ˈmɒkɪʃnɪs,
ˈmakɪʃnɪs

Mawson
BR ˈmɔːsn
AM ˈmɒsən, ˈmasən

mawworm
BR ˈmɔːwəːm, -z
AM ˈmɒˌwərm,
ˈmɑˌwərm, -z

max
BR maks
AM mæks

maxi
BR ˈmaksi
AM ˈmæksi

maxilla
BR makˈsɪlə(r), -z
AM mækˈsɪlə, -z

maxillae
BR makˈsɪliː
AM mækˈsɪli,
mækˈsɪlaɪ

maxillary
BR makˈsɪl(ə)ri
AM ˈmæksəˌlɛri

maxim
BR ˈmaksɪm, -z
AM ˈmæksəm, -z

maxima
BR ˈmaksɪmə(r)
AM ˈmæksəmə

maximal
BR ˈmaksɪml
AM ˈmæksəməl

maximalist
BR ˈmaksɪmlɪst,
ˈmaksɪmələst, -s
AM ˈmæksəmələst, -s

maximally
BR ˈmaksɪmlˌi,
ˈmaksɪməli
AM ˈmæksəməli

Maximilian
BR ˌmaksɪˈmɪlɪən
AM ˌmæksəˈmɪlɪən

maximin
BR ˈmaksɪmɪn,
ˌmaksɪˈmɪn
AM ˈmæksiˌmɪn

maximisation
BR ˌmaksɪmʌɪˈzeɪʃn
AM ˌmæksəməˈzeɪʃən,
ˌmæksəˌmaɪˈzeɪʃən

maximise
BR ˈmaksɪmʌɪz, -ɪz, -ɪŋ,
-d
AM ˈmæksəˌmaɪz, -ɪz,
-ɪŋ, -d

maximiser
BR ˈmaksɪmʌɪzə(r), -z
AM ˈmæksəˌmaɪzər, -z

maximization
BR ˌmaksɪmʌɪˈzeɪʃn
AM ˌmæksəməˈzeɪʃən,
ˌmæksəˌmaɪˈzeɪʃən

maximize
BR ˈmaksɪmʌɪz, -ɪz, -ɪŋ,
-d
AM ˈmæksəˌmaɪz, -ɪz,
-ɪŋ, -d

maximizer
BR ˈmaksɪmʌɪzə(r), -z
AM ˈmæksə‚maɪzər, -z

maximum
BR ˈmaksɪməm, -z
AM ˈmæksəməm, -z

maximus
BR ˈmaksɪməs
AM ˈmæksəməs

Maxine
BR makˈsiːn
AM məkˈsin

maxixe
BR makˈsiːks,
məˈʃiːʃə(r),
makˈsiːksɪz\məˈsiːʃəz
AM mækˈsiks, məˈʃiʃə,
mæksˈiksz\məˈʃiʃɪz

Maxwell
BR ˈmaksw(ɛ)l
AM ˈmæks‚wɛl

may
BR meɪ
AM meɪ

Maya[1]
American people
BR ˈmʌɪə(r)
AM ˈmaɪə

Maya[2]
forename
BR ˈmeɪə(r), ˈmʌɪə(r)
AM ˈmaɪə

Mayall
BR ˈmeɪəl, ˈmeɪɔːl
AM ˈmeɪ‚ɔl, ˈmeɪ‚ɑl

Mayan
BR ˈmʌɪən, -z
AM ˈmaɪən, -z

maybe
BR ˈmeɪbiː
AM ˈmeɪbi

maybeetle
BR ˈmeɪ‚biːtl, -z
AM ˈmeɪ‚bidəl, -z

mayday
BR ˈmeɪdeɪ, -z
AM ˈmeɪ‚deɪ, -z

Mayer[1]
German
BR ˈmʌɪə(r)
AM ˈmaɪər

Mayer[2]
BR ˈmeɪə(r)
AM ˈmeɪər

mayest
BR ˈmeɪɪst
AM ˈmeɪɪst

Mayfair
BR ˈmeɪfɛː(r), -z
AM ˈmeɪ‚fɛ(ə)r, -z

Mayfield
BR ˈmeɪfiːld
AM ˈmeɪ‚fild

mayflower
BR ˈmeɪ‚flaʊə(r), -z
AM ˈmeɪ‚flaʊər, -z

mayfly
BR ˈmeɪflʌɪ, -z
AM ˈmeɪ‚flaɪ, -z

mayhap
BR ˈmeɪhap
AM ˈmeɪ‚hæp

mayhem
BR ˈmeɪhɛm
AM ˈmeɪ‚hɛm

Mayhew
BR ˈmeɪhjuː
AM ˈmeɪ‚hju

maying
BR ˈmeɪɪŋ, -z
AM ˈmeɪɪŋ, -z

Maynard
BR ˈmeɪnɑːd
AM ˈmeɪnərd

Mayne
BR meɪn
AM meɪn

Maynooth
BR məˈnuːθ, meɪˈnuːθ
AM meɪˈnuθ

mayn't
BR ˈmeɪ(ə)nt, meɪn̩t
AM ˈmeɪ(ə)nt

Mayo
BR ˈmeɪəʊ
AM ˈmeɪoʊ

mayonnaise
BR ‚meɪəˈneɪz
AM ˈmeɪə‚neɪz,
‚meɪəˈneɪz

mayor
BR mɛː(r), -z
AM ˈmeɪ(ə)r, -z

mayoral
BR ˈmɛːrəl, ˈmɛːr̩l
AM ˈmeɪˈɔrəl, ˈmeɪərəl

mayoralty
BR ˈmɛːrəlt|i, ˈmɛːr|t|i,
-ɪz
AM ˈmeɪərəlti, -z

mayoress
BR ˈmɛːrəs, ‚mɛːˈrɛs, -ɪz
AM ˈmeɪərəs, -əz

mayorship
BR ˈmɛːˈʃɪp, -s
AM ˈmeɪər‚ʃɪp, -s

Mayotte
BR maˈjɒt
AM mɑˈjɒt, mɑˈjɑt

maypole
BR ˈmeɪpəʊl, -z
AM ˈmeɪ‚poʊl, -z

Mays
BR meɪz
AM meɪz

mayst
BR meɪst
AM meɪst

mayweed
BR ˈmeɪwiːd, -z
AM ˈmeɪ‚wid, -z

mazard
BR ˈmazəd, -z

AM ˈmæzərd, -z

Mazar-e-Sharif
BR mə‚zɑːrəʃəˈriːf,
mə‚zɑːrəʃəˈriːf
AM məˈzɑrəʃəˈrif

Mazarin
BR ˈmazərɪn,
ˈmazəran
AM ˈmæzərən

mazarine
BR ‚mazəˈriːn,
ˈmazəriːn, -z
AM ‚mæzəˈriːn,
ˈmæzərən, -z

Mazda®
BR ˈmazdə(r), -z
AM ˈmɑzdə, -z

Mazdaism
BR ˈmazdə(r)ɪz(ə)m
AM ˈmɑzdə‚ɪzəm

maze
BR meɪz, -ɪz, -d
AM meɪz, -ɪz, -d

mazer
BR ˈmeɪzə(r), -z
AM ˈmeɪzər, -z

mazily
BR ˈmeɪzɪli
AM ˈmeɪzɪli

maziness
BR ˈmeɪzɪnɪs
AM ˈmeɪzɪnɪs

mazurka
BR məˈzɜːkə(r),
məˈzʊəkə(r), -z
AM məˈzɜrkə,
məˈzʊrkə, -z

mazy
BR ˈmeɪz|i, -ɪə(r), -ɪɪst
AM ˈmeɪzi, -ər, -ɪst

mazzard
BR ˈmazəd, -z
AM ˈmæzərd, -z

Mazzini
BR matˈsiːni
AM məˈzini

Mb
BR ˈmɛgəbʌɪt, -s
AM ˈmɛgə‚baɪt, -s

Mbabane
BR mbaˈbɑːni
AM mbɑˈbani

McAfee
BR ‚makəˈfiː, məˈkafi
AM ‚mækəˈfi, məˈkæfi

McAleese
BR ‚makəˈliːs
AM ‚mækəˈlis

McAlister
BR məˈkalɪstə(r)
AM məˈkæləstər

McAllister
BR mək'alɪstə(r)
AM məˈkæləstər

McAlpine
BR məˈkalpʌɪn
AM məˈkæl‚paɪn

McAnally
BR ‚makəˈnali
AM ‚mækə‚næli

McArdle
BR məˈkɑːdl
AM məˈkardəl

McArthur
BR məkˈɑːθə(r)
AM məˈkarθər

McAteer
BR ‚makəˈtɪə(r)
AM ‚mækə‚tɪər

McAuliffe
BR məˈkɔːlɪf
AM məˈkɔlɪf, məˈkɑlɪf

McAvoy
BR ˈmakəvɔɪ
AM ˈmækə‚vɔɪ

McBain
BR məkˈbeɪn
AM məkˈbeɪn

McBrain
BR məkˈbreɪn
AM məkˈbreɪn

McBride
BR məkˈbrʌɪd
AM məkˈbraɪd

McCabe
BR məˈkeɪb
AM məˈkeɪb

McCain
BR məˈkeɪn
AM məˈkeɪn

McCall
BR məˈkɔːl
AM məˈkɔl, məˈkɑl

McCallum
BR məˈkaləm
AM məˈkæləm

McCann
BR məˈkan
AM məˈkæn

McCarthy
BR məˈkɑːθi
AM məˈkarθi

McCarthyism
BR məˈkɑːθɪɪz(ə)m
AM məˈkarθi‚ɪzəm

McCarthyite
BR məˈkɑːθɪʌɪt
AM məˈkarθi‚aɪt

McCartney
BR məˈkɑːtni
AM məˈkartni

McCarty
BR məˈkɑːti
AM məˈkardi

McCaskill
BR məˈkaskɪl
AM məˈkæskəl

McClain
BR məˈkleɪn
AM məˈkleɪn

McClellan
BR məˈklɛlən
AM məˈklɛlən

McClelland
BR məˈklɛlənd
AM məˈklɛlən(d)

McClintock
BR məˈklɪntɒk
AM məˈklɪn.tɑk,
məˈklɪn(t)ək

McClure
BR məˈkluə(r)
AM məˈklu(ə)r

McCluskie
BR məˈklʌski
AM məˈkləski

McColl
BR məˈkɒl
AM məˈkɔl, məˈkɑl

McConachie
BR məˈkɒnəki
AM məˈkɑnəki

McConachy
BR məˈkɒnəki
AM məˈkɑnəki

McConnell
BR məˈkɒn(ə)l
AM məˈkɑnəl

McCormack
BR məˈkɔːmak
AM məˈkɔrmək

McCormick
BR məˈkɔːmɪk
AM məˈkɔrmək

McCorquodale
BR məˈkɔːkədeɪl
AM məˈkɔrkə.deɪl

McCowan
BR məˈkaʊən
AM məˈkaʊən

McCoy
BR məˈkɔɪ, -z
AM məˈkɔɪ, -z

McCracken
BR məˈkrak(ə)n
AM məˈkrækən

McCrae
BR məˈkreɪ
AM məˈkreɪ

McCrea
BR məˈkreɪ
AM məˈkreɪ

McCready
BR məˈkriːdi
AM məˈkridi

McCrindle
BR məˈkrɪndl
AM məˈkrɪndəl

McCrum
BR məˈkrʌm
AM məˈkrəm

McCulloch
BR məˈkʌlɒk,
məˈkʌləx
AM məˈkələ(k)

McCullogh
BR məˈkʌlɒk,
məˈkʌləx
AM məˈkələ(k)

McCullough
BR məˈkʌlək,
məˈkʌləx
AM məˈkələ(k)

McCusker
BR məˈkʌskə(r)
AM məˈkəskər

McDade
BR məkˈdeɪd
AM məkˈdeɪd

McDaniel
BR məkˈdanjəl
AM məkˈdænjəl

McDermot
BR məkˈdəːmət
AM məkˈdərmət

McDermott
BR məkˈdəːmət
AM məkˈdərmət

McDonagh
BR məkˈdɒnə(r)
AM məkˈdɑnə

McDonald
BR məkˈdɒnld
AM məkˈdɑnəld

McDonnell
BR məkˈdɒnl
AM məkˈdɑnəl

McDougal
BR məkˈduːgl
AM məkˈdugl

McDougall
BR məkˈduːgl
AM məkˈdugl

McDowall
BR məkˈdaʊəl
AM məkˈdaʊəl

McDowell
BR məkˈdaʊəl
AM məkˈdaʊəl

McDuff
BR məkˈdʌf
AM məkˈdəf

McElroy
BR ˈmaklrɔɪ
AM ˈmækl.rɔɪ

McElwain
BR ˈmaklweɪn,
məˈkɛlweɪn
AM ˈmækl.weɪn,
məˈkɛl.weɪn

McElwie
BR məkˈɛlwi
AM məkˈɛlwi

McEnroe
BR ˈmak(ɪ)nrəʊ
AM ˈmækən.roʊ

McEvoy
BR ˈmakɪvɔɪ
AM ˈmækə.vɔɪ

McEwan
BR məˈkjuːən
AM məkˈjuwən

McFadden
BR məkˈfadn
AM məkˈfædən

McFadyean
BR məkˈfadɪən,
məkˈfadjən
AM məkˈfædɪən,
məkˈfædjən

McFadyen
BR məkˈfadɪən,
məkˈfadjən
AM məkˈfædɪən,
məkˈfædjən

McFadzean
BR məkˈfadɪən,
məkˈfadjən
AM məkˈfædɪən,
məkˈfædjən

McFarland
BR məkˈfɑːlənd
AM məkˈfɑrlən(d)

McFarlane
BR məkˈfɑːlən
AM məkˈfɑrlən

McFee
BR məkˈfiː
AM məkˈfi

McGahey
BR məˈgɑːhi, məˈgaxi,
məˈgahi
AM məˈgɑhi

McGee
BR məˈgiː
AM məˈgi

McGhee
BR məˈgiː
AM məˈgi

McGill
BR məˈgɪl
AM məˈgɪl

McGilligan
BR məˈgɪlɪg(ə)n
AM məˈgɪlɪgən

McGillivray
BR məˈgɪlɪvreɪ,
məˈgɪlɪvri
AM məˈgɪlɪvreɪ

McGinn
BR məˈgɪn
AM məˈgɪn

McGinnis
BR məˈgɪnɪs
AM məˈgɪnɪs

McGinty
BR məˈgɪnti
AM məˈgɪn(t)i

McGoldrick
BR məˈgəʊldrɪk
AM məˈgoʊldrɪk

McGonagall
BR məˈgɒnəgl
AM məˈgɑnəgəl

McGoohan
BR məˈguːən
AM məˈguən

McGough
BR məˈgɒf
AM məˈgɒf, məˈgəf,
məˈgɑf

McGovern
BR məˈgʌvn

McGavern
AM məˈgəvərn

McGowan
BR məˈgaʊən
AM məˈgaʊən

McGrath[1]
BR məˈgrɑːθ, məˈgraθ
AM məˈgræθ

McGrath[2]
in Ireland
BR məˈgrah
AM məˈgræθ

McGraw
BR məˈgrɔː(r)
AM məˈgrɔ, məˈgrɑ

McGregor
BR məˈgrɛgə(r)
AM məˈgrɛgər

McGuigan
BR məˈgwɪg(ə)n
AM məˈgwɪgn

McGuinness
BR məˈgɪnɪs
AM məˈgɪnəs

McGuire
BR məˈgwʌɪə(r)
AM məˈgwaɪər

McGurk
BR məˈgəːk
AM məˈgərk

McHenry
BR məkˈhɛnri
AM məkˈhɛnri

McHugh
BR məkˈhjuː
AM məkˈ(h)ju

McIlroy
BR ˈmak(ɪ)lrɔɪ
AM ˈmækl.rɔɪ

McIlvaney
BR ˌmaklˈveɪni
AM ˈmækl.veɪni

McIlvenny
BR ˌmaklˈvɛni
AM ˈmækl.vɛni

McIlwain
BR ˈmaklweɪn
AM ˈmækl.weɪn

McInerney
BR ˌmakɪˈnəːni
AM ˈmækə.nərni

McInnes
BR məkˈɪnɪs
AM məkˈɪnɪs

McInnis
BR məkˈɪnɪs
AM məkˈɪnɪs

McIntosh
BR ˈmak(ɪ)ntɒʃ
AM ˈmækən.tɑʃ

McIntyre
BR ˈmakɪntʌɪə(r)
AM ˈmækən.taɪər

McIver
BR məkˈʌɪvə(r)
AM məˈkaɪvər

McKay
BR məˈkeɪ

AM məˈkeɪ
McKechnie
BR məˈkɛkni,
məˈkɛxni
AM məˈkɛkni
McKee
BR məˈkiː
AM məˈki
McKellar
BR məˈkɛlə(r)
AM məˈkɛlər
McKellen
BR məˈkɛlən
AM məˈkɛlən
McKendrick
BR məˈkɛndrɪk
AM məˈkɛndrɪk
McKenna
BR məˈkɛnə(r)
AM məˈkɛnə
McKenzie
BR məˈkɛnzi
AM məˈkɛnzi
McKeon
BR məˈkjəʊn
AM məˈkiən
McKeown
BR məˈkjəʊn
AM məˈkiən
McKie
BR məˈkʌɪ, məˈkiː
AM məˈki
McKinlay
BR məˈkɪnli
AM məˈkɪnli
McKinley
BR məˈkɪnli
AM məˈkɪnli
McKinney
BR məˈkɪni
AM məˈkɪni
McKinnon
BR məˈkɪnən
AM məˈkɪnɪn
McKittrick
BR məˈkɪtrɪk
AM məˈkɪtrɪk
McKnight
BR məkˈnʌɪt
AM məkˈnaɪt
McLachlan
BR məˈklɒxlən,
məˈklʊklən
AM məˈklaklən
McLaughlin
BR məˈklɒxlɪn,
məˈklʊklɪn
AM məˈklaklən,
məˈklaflən,
məˈklɒklən,
məˈklɒflən
McLean
BR məˈkleɪn, məˈkliːn
AM məˈklin
McLeish
BR məˈkliːʃ
AM məˈkliʃ

McLellan
BR məˈklɛlən
AM məˈklɛlən
McLennan
BR məˈklɛnən
AM məˈklɛnən
McLeod
BR məˈklaʊd
AM məˈklaʊd
McLoughlin
BR məˈklɒxlɪn,
məˈklʊklɪn
AM məˈklaklən,
məˈklaflən,
məˈklɒklən,
məˈklɒflən
McLuhan
BR məˈkluːən
AM məˈkluwən
McMahon
BR məkˈmɑːn
AM məkˈmæn
McManus
BR məkˈmanəs
AM məkˈmænəs
McMaster
BR məkˈmɑːstə(r),
məkˈmastə(r)
AM məkˈmæstər
McMenemey
BR məkˈmɛnəmi
AM məkˈmɛnəmi
McMenemy
BR məkˈmɛnəmi
AM məkˈmɛnəmi
McMillan
BR məkˈmɪlən
AM məkˈmɪlən
McMurdo
BR məkˈməːdəʊ
AM məkˈmərdoʊ
McMurtry
BR məkˈməːtri
AM məkˈmərtri
McNab
BR məkˈnab
AM məkˈnæb
McNaghten
BR məkˈnɔːt(ə)n
AM məkˈnotn̩,
məkˈnatn̩
McNaghten rules
BR məkˈnɔːtn̩ ruːlz
AM məkˈnotn̩ ˌrulz,
məkˈnatn̩ ˌrulz
McNaghton
BR məkˈnɔːt(ə)n
AM məkˈnotn̩,
məkˈnatn̩
McNair
BR məkˈnɛː(r)
AM məkˈnɛ(ə)r
McNally
BR məkˈnali
AM məkˈnæli
McNamara
BR ˌmaknəˈmɑːrə(r)
AM ˈmæknəˌmɛrə

McNamee
BR ˌmaknəˈmiː
AM ˈmæknəˌmi
McNaughten
BR məkˈnɔːt(ə)n
AM məkˈnotn̩,
məkˈnatn̩
McNaughton
BR məkˈnɔːt(ə)n
AM məkˈnotn̩,
məkˈnatn̩
McNeil
BR məkˈniːl
AM məkˈnil
McNeill
BR məkˈniːl
AM məkˈnil
McNestry
BR məkˈnɛstri
AM məkˈnɛstri
McNulty
BR məkˈnʌlti
AM məkˈnəlti
McPhail
BR məkˈfeɪl
AM məkˈfeɪl
McPhee
BR məkˈfiː
AM məkˈfi
McPherson
BR məkˈfəːsn̩
AM məkˈfərsən,
məkˈfɪrsən
McQueen
BR məˈkwiːn
AM məˈkwin
McRae
BR məˈkreɪ
AM məˈkreɪ
McReady
BR məˈkriːdi
AM məˈkridi, məkˈridi
McShane
BR məkˈʃeɪn
AM məkˈʃeɪn
McShea
BR məkˈʃeɪ
AM məkˈʃeɪ
McSweeney
BR məkˈswiːni
AM məkˈswini
McTaggart
BR məkˈtagət
AM məkˈtægərt
McTavish
BR məkˈtavɪʃ
AM məkˈtævɪʃ
McTeer
BR məkˈtɪə(r)
AM məkˈtɪ(ə)r
McVay
BR məkˈveɪ
AM məkˈveɪ
McVey
BR məkˈveɪ
AM məkˈveɪ

McVicar
BR məkˈvɪkə(r)
AM məkˈvɪkər
McVitie
BR məkˈvɪti
AM məkˈvɪdi
McWhirter
BR məkˈwəːtə(r)
AM məkˈwərdər
McWhorter
BR məkˈwɔːtə(r)
AM məkˈwərdər
McWilliam
BR məkˈwɪljəm
AM məkˈwɪljəm,
məkˈwɪliəm
McWilliams
BR məkˈwɪljəmz
AM məkˈwɪljəmz,
məkˈwɪliəmz
me[1]
strong pronoun,
musical note
BR miː
AM mi
me[2]
weak pronoun
BR mi
AM mi
Meacham
BR ˈmiːtʃ(ə)m
AM ˈmitʃəm
Meacher
BR ˈmiːtʃə(r)
AM ˈmitʃər
mea culpa
BR ˌmeɪə ˈkʊlpə(r),
ˌmiːə +, + ˈkʌlpə(r)
AM ˌmeɪə ˈkʊlpə
mead
BR miːd
AM mid
meadow
BR ˈmɛdəʊ, -z
AM ˈmɛdoʊ, -z
meadowland
BR ˈmɛdəʊland, -z
AM ˈmɛdoʊˌlænd, -z
meadowlark
BR ˈmɛdəʊlɑːk, -s
AM ˈmɛdoʊˌlark, -s
meadowsweet
BR ˈmɛdəʊswiːt
AM ˈmɛdoʊˌswit
meadowy
BR ˈmɛdəʊi
AM ˈmɛdoʊi
meager
BR ˈmiːgə(r)
AM ˈmigər
meagerly
BR ˈmiːgəli
AM ˈmigərli
meagerness
BR ˈmiːgənəs
AM ˈmigərnəs

meagre
BR 'miːgə(r)
AM 'migər

meagrely
BR 'miːgəli
AM 'migərli

meagreness
BR 'miːgənəs
AM 'migərnəs

Meakin
BR 'miːkɪn
AM 'mikɪn

meal
BR miːl, -z
AM mil, -z

mealie
BR 'miːl| i, -ɪz
AM 'mili, -z

mealiness
BR 'miːlɪnɪs
AM 'milinɪs

mealtime
BR 'miːltʌɪm, -z
AM 'mil,taɪm, -z

mealworm
BR 'miːlwəːm, -z
AM 'mil,wərm, -z

mealy
BR 'miːl| i, -ɪə(r), -ɪɪst
AM 'mili, -ər, -ɪst

mealybug
BR 'miːlɪbʌg, -z
AM 'mili,bəg, -z

mealy-mouthed
BR ,miːlɪˈmaʊðd
AM 'mili,maʊðd,
'mili,maʊθt

mean
BR miːn, -z, -ɪŋ, -ə(r),
-ɪst
AM min, -z, -ɪŋ, -ə(r),
-ɪst

meander
BR mɪˈand| ə(r), -əz,
-(ə)rɪŋ, -əd
AM mɪˈænd| ər, -ərz,
-(ə)rɪŋ, -ərd

meandering
BR mɪˈand(ə)rɪŋ, -z
AM mɪˈænd(ə)rɪŋ, -z

meandrine
BR mɪˈandrʌɪn,
mɪˈandrɪn
AM mɪˈændrin,
mɪˈæn,draɪn,
mɪˈændrən

meanie
BR 'miːn| i, -ɪz
AM 'mini, -z

meaning
BR 'miːnɪŋ, -z
AM 'minɪŋ, -z

meaningful
BR 'miːnɪŋf(ʊ)l
AM 'minɪŋfəl

meaningfully
BR 'miːnɪŋfʊli,
'miːnɪŋfli

AM 'minɪŋf(ə)li

meaningfulness
BR 'miːnɪŋf(ʊ)lnəs
AM 'minɪŋfəlnəs

meaningless
BR 'miːnɪŋlɪs
AM 'minɪŋlɪs

meaninglessly
BR 'miːnɪŋlɪsli
AM 'minɪŋglɪsli

meaninglessness
BR 'miːnɪŋlɪsnɪs
AM 'minɪŋglɪsnɪs

meaningly
BR 'miːnɪŋli
AM 'minɪŋli

meanly
BR 'miːnli
AM 'minli

meanness
BR 'miːnnɪs
AM 'mi(n)nɪs

means
BR miːnz
AM minz

meant
BR mɛnt
AM mɛnt

meantime
BR 'miːntʌɪm
AM 'min,taɪm

meanwhile
BR 'miːnwʌɪl
AM 'min,(h)waɪl

meany
BR 'miːn| i, -ɪz
AM 'mini, -z

Mearns
BR mɛːnz
AM mərnz

Measham
BR 'miːʃ(ə)m
AM 'miʃəm

measles
BR 'miːzlz
AM 'mizəlz

measliness
BR 'miːzlɪnɪs
AM 'mizlinɪs

measly
BR 'miːzli
AM 'mizli

measurability
BR ,mɛʒ(ə)rəˈbɪlɪti
AM ,mɛʒ(ə)rəˈbɪlɪdi,
,mɛʒərˈbɪlɪdi

measurable
BR 'mɛʒ(ə)rəbl
AM 'mɛʒ(ə)r(ə)bəl

measurableness
BR 'mɛʒ(ə)rəblnəs
AM 'mɛʒ(ə)rəbəlnəs,
'mɛʒərbəlnəs

measurably
BR 'mɛʒ(ə)rəbli
AM 'mɛʒ(ə)rəbli,
'mɛʒərbli

measure
BR 'mɛʒ| ə(r), -əz,
-(ə)rɪŋ, -əd
AM 'mɛʒ| ər, -ərz,
-(ə)rɪŋ, -ərd

measuredly
BR 'mɛʒədli
AM 'mɛʒərdli

measureless
BR 'mɛʒələs
AM 'mɛʒərləs

measurelessly
BR 'mɛʒələsli
AM 'mɛʒərləsli

measurement
BR 'mɛʒəm(ə)nt, -s
AM 'mɛʒərmənt, -s

meat
BR miːt, -s
AM mit, -s

meatball
BR 'miːtbɔːl, -z
AM 'mit,bɔl, 'mit,bɑl, -z

Meath
BR miːð, miːθ
AM miθ

meathead
BR 'miːthɛd, -z
AM 'mit,(h)ɛd, 'midɛd,
-z

meatily
BR 'miːtɪli
AM 'midɪli

meatiness
BR 'miːtɪnɪs
AM 'midinɪs

meatless
BR 'miːtlɪs
AM 'mitlɪs

meatus
BR mɪˈeɪtəs, -ɪz
AM mɪˈeɪdəs, -əz

meaty
BR 'miːt| i, -ɪə(r), -ɪɪst
AM 'midi, -ər, -ɪst

Mebyon Kernow
BR ,mɛbɪən ˈkəːnəʊ
AM 'mɛbɪən ˈkər,noʊ

mecca
BR 'mɛkə(r)
AM 'mɛkə

meccano
BR mɪˈkɑːnəʊ
AM mɪˈkænoʊ,
məˈkɑnoʊ

mechanic
BR mɪˈkanɪk, -s
AM məˈkænɪk, -s

mechanical
BR mɪˈkanɪkl
AM məˈkænəkəl

mechanicalism
BR mɪˈkanɪkl̩ɪz(ə)m,
mɪˈkanɪkəlɪz(ə)m
AM məˈkænəkə,lɪzəm

mechanically
BR mɪˈkanɪkli

meconium AM məˈkænək(ə)li

mechanicalness
BR mɪˈkanɪklnəs
AM məˈkænɪklnəs

mechanician
BR ,mɛkəˈnɪʃn, -z
AM ,mɛkəˈnɪʃən, -z

mechanisation
BR ,mɛkənʌɪˈzeɪʃn,
,mɛkn̩ʌɪˈzeɪʃn
AM ,mɛkənəˈzeɪʃən,
,mɛkə,naɪˈzeɪʃən

mechanise
BR 'mɛkənʌɪz,
'mɛkn̩ʌɪz, -ɪz, -ɪŋ, -d
AM 'mɛkə,naɪz, -ɪz, -ɪŋ,
-d

mechaniser
BR 'mɛkənʌɪzə(r),
'mɛkn̩ʌɪzə(r), -z
AM 'mɛkə,naɪzər, -z

mechanism
BR 'mɛkənɪz(ə)m,
'mɛkn̩ɪz(ə)m
AM 'mɛkə,nɪzəm

mechanist
BR 'mɛkənɪst,
'mɛkn̩ɪst, -s
AM 'mɛkənəst, -s

mechanistic
BR ,mɛkəˈnɪstɪk,
,mɛkn̩ˈɪstɪk
AM ,mɛkəˈnɪstɪk

mechanistically
BR ,mɛkəˈnɪstɪkli,
,mɛkn̩ˈɪstɪkli
AM ,mɛkəˈnɪstək(ə)li

mechanization
BR ,mɛkənʌɪˈzeɪʃn,
,mɛkn̩ʌɪˈzeɪʃn
AM ,mɛkənəˈzeɪʃən,
,mɛkə,naɪˈzeɪʃən

mechanize
BR 'mɛkənʌɪz,
'mɛkn̩ʌɪz, -ɪz, -ɪŋ, -d
AM 'mɛkə,naɪz, -ɪz, -ɪŋ,
-d

mechanizer
BR 'mɛkənʌɪzə(r),
'mɛkn̩ʌɪzə(r), -z
AM 'mɛkə,naɪzər, -z

mechanoreceptor
BR ,mɛkənəʊrɪˈsɛptə(r),
,mɛkn̩əʊrɪˈsɛptə(r), -z
AM ,mɛkənoʊrəˈsɛptər,
,mɛkənoʊrɪˈsɛptər, -z

mechatronics
BR ,mɛkəˌtrɒnɪks
AM ,mɛkəˌtrɑnɪks

Mechlin
BR 'mɛklɪn, -z
AM 'mɛklən, -z

Mecklenburg
BR 'mɛklənbəːg
AM 'mɛklən,bərg

meconium
BR mɪˈkəʊnɪəm
AM məˈkoʊnɪəm

Med
BR mɛd
AM mɛd

medal
BR 'mɛdl̩, -z, -d
AM 'mɛdəl, -əlz, -(ə)lɪŋ, -əld

medalist
BR 'mɛdl̩ɪst, -s
AM 'mɛdl̩əst, -s

medallic
BR mɪ'dalɪk
AM mə'dælɪk

medallion
BR mɪ'dalɪən, mɪ'daljən, -z
AM mə'dæljən, mɛ'dæljən, -z

medallist
BR 'mɛdl̩ɪst, -s
AM 'mɛdl̩əst, -s

Medawar
BR 'mɛdəwə(r)
AM 'mɛdəwər

meddle
BR 'mɛdl̩, -lz, -lɪŋ \-lɪŋ, -ld
AM 'mɛdl̩əl, -əlz, -(ə)lɪŋ, -əld

meddler
BR 'mɛdlə(r), 'mɛdlə(r), -z
AM 'mɛd(ə)lər, -z

meddlesome
BR 'mɛdls(ə)m
AM 'mɛdlsəm

meddlesomely
BR 'mɛdls(ə)mli
AM 'mɛdlsəmli

meddlesomeness
BR 'mɛdls(ə)mnəs
AM 'mɛdlsəmnəs

Mede
BR miːd, -z
AM mid, -z

Medea
BR mɪ'dɪə(r)
AM mɪ'diə

Medellín
BR ,mɛdɪ'jiːn
AM ,mɛdə'jin

Medevac
BR 'mɛdɪvak
AM 'mɛdə,væk

media
BR 'miːdɪə(r)
AM 'midiə

mediaeval
BR ,mɛdɪ'iːvl
AM ,mɛd(i)'ivəl, mə'divəl

mediaevalist
BR ,mɛdɪ'iːvl̩ɪst, ,mɛdɪ'iːvəlɪst, -s
AM ,mɛd(i)'ivələst, mə'dɪvələst, -s

mediagenic
BR ,miːdɪə'dʒɛnɪk

AM ,midiə'dʒɛnɪk

medial
BR 'miːdɪəl
AM 'midiəl

medially
BR 'miːdɪəli
AM 'midiəli

median
BR 'miːdɪən, -z
AM 'midiən, -z

medianly
BR 'miːdɪənli
AM 'midiənli

mediant
BR 'miːdɪənt, -s
AM 'midiənt, -s

mediastina
BR ,miːdɪə'staɪnə(r)
AM ,midiə'staɪnə

mediastinal
BR ,miːdɪə'staɪnl
AM 'midiə'staɪnəl

mediastinum
BR ,miːdɪə'staɪnəm
AM ,midiə'staɪnəm

mediate
BR 'miːdɪeɪt, -s, -ɪŋ, -ɪd
AM 'midi,eɪ|t, -ts, -dɪŋ, -dɪd

mediately
BR 'miːdɪətli
AM 'midiətli

mediation
BR ,miːdɪ'eɪʃn
AM ,midi'eɪʃən

mediatisation
BR ,miːdɪətaɪ'zeɪʃn, -z
AM ,midiədə'zeɪʃən, ,midiə,taɪ'zeɪʃən, -z

mediatise
BR 'miːdɪətaɪz, -ɪz, -ɪŋ, -d
AM 'midiə,taɪz, -ɪz, -ɪŋ, -d

mediatization
BR ,miːdɪətaɪ'zeɪʃn, -z
AM ,midiədə'zeɪʃən, ,midiə,taɪ'zeɪʃən, -z

mediatize
BR 'miːdɪətaɪz, -ɪz, -ɪŋ, -d
AM 'midiə,taɪz, -ɪz, -ɪŋ, -d

mediator
BR 'miːdɪeɪtə(r), -z
AM 'midi,eɪdər, -z

mediatorial
BR ,miːdɪə'tɔːrɪəl
AM 'midiə'tɔriəl

mediatory
BR 'miːdɪət(ə)ri
AM 'midiə,tɔri

mediatrices
BR ,miːdɪ'eɪtrɪsiːz
AM ,midi'eɪtɪsiz

mediatrix
BR 'miːdɪətrɪks, -ɪz

medic
BR 'mɛdɪk, -s
AM 'mɛdɪk, -s

medicable
BR 'mɛdɪkəbl
AM 'mɛdəkəbəl

Medicaid
BR 'mɛdɪkeɪd
AM 'mɛdə,keɪd

medical
BR 'mɛdɪkl
AM 'mɛdəkəl

medically
BR 'mɛdɪkli
AM 'mɛdək(ə)li

medicament
BR mɪ'dɪkəm(ə)nt, -s
AM mə'dɪkəmənt, 'mɛdəkə,mɛnt, -s

Medicare
BR 'mɛdɪkɛː(r)
AM 'mɛdə,kɛ(ə)r

medicate
BR 'mɛdɪkeɪt, -s, -ɪŋ, -ɪd
AM 'mɛdə,keɪ|t, -ts, -dɪŋ, -dɪd

medication
BR ,mɛdɪ'keɪʃn, -z
AM ,mɛdə'keɪʃən, -z

medicative
BR 'mɛdɪkətɪv
AM 'mɛdə,keɪdɪv

Medicean
BR ,mɛdɪ'tʃiːən
AM ,mɛdə'tʃiən, 'mɛdə'siən

Medici
BR 'mɛdɪtʃiː, mɪ'diːtʃiː
AM 'mɛdətʃi

medicinal
BR mɪ'dɪsɪn(ə)l, mɪ'dɪsɪn(ə)l
AM mə'dɪsn̩l, mɛ'dɪsnəl

medicinally
BR mɪ'dɪsn̩li, mɪ'dɪsnəli, mɪ'dɪsn̩li, mɪ'dɪsɪnəli
AM mɛ'dɪsn̩əli, mə'dɪsnəli

medicine
BR 'mɛd(ɪ)s(ɪ)n, -z
AM 'mɛd(ə)s(ə)n, -z

medick
plant
BR 'miːdɪk, -s
AM 'midɪk, -s

medico
BR 'mɛdɪkəʊ, -z
AM 'mɛdɪkoʊ, -z

medieval
BR ,mɛdɪ'iːvl
AM ,mɛd(i)'ivəl, mə'divəl

medievalise
BR ,mɛdɪ'iːvl̩ʌɪz, ,mɛdɪ'i:vəlʌɪz, -ɪz, -ɪŋ, -d
AM ,mɛd(i)'ivə,laɪz, mə'divə,laɪz, -ɪz, -ɪŋ, -d

medievalism
BR ,mɛdɪ'iːvl̩ɪz(ə)m, ,mɛdɪ'iːvəlɪz(ə)m
AM ,mɛd(i)'ivə,lɪzəm, , mə'divə,lɪzəm

medievalist
BR ,mɛdɪ'iːvl̩ɪst, ,mɛdɪ'iːvəlɪst, -s
AM ,mɛd(i)'ivələst, mə'divələst, -s

medievalize
BR ,mɛdɪ'iːvl̩ʌɪz, ,mɛdɪ'iːvəlʌɪz, -ɪz, -ɪŋ, -d
AM ,mɛd(i)'ivə,laɪz, mə'divə,laɪz, -ɪz, -ɪŋ, -d

medievally
BR ,mɛdɪ'iːvl̩i, ,mɛdɪ'iːvəli
AM ,mɛd(i)'ivəli, mə'divəli

Medina[1]
place in Saudi Arabia
BR mɛ'diːnə(r), mɪ'diːnə(r)
AM mə'dinə

Medina[2]
place in US
BR mɪ'dʌɪnə(r)
AM mə'daɪnə

mediocre
BR ,miːdɪ'əʊkə(r)
AM ,midi'oʊkər

mediocrity
BR ,miːdɪ'ɒkrɪt|i, -ɪz
AM ,midi'ɑkrədi, -z

meditate
BR 'mɛdɪteɪt, -s, -ɪŋ, -ɪd
AM 'mɛdə,teɪ|t, -ts, -dɪŋ, -dɪd

meditation
BR ,mɛdɪ'teɪʃn, -z
AM ,mɛdə'teɪʃən, -z

meditative
BR 'mɛdɪtətɪv
AM 'mɛdə,teɪdɪv

meditatively
BR 'mɛdɪtətɪvli
AM 'mɛdə,teɪdɪvli

meditativeness
BR 'mɛdɪtətɪvnɪs
AM 'mɛdə,teɪdɪvnɪs

meditator
BR 'mɛdɪteɪtə(r), -z
AM 'mɛdə,teɪdər, -z

Mediterranean
BR ,mɛdɪtə'reɪnɪən
AM ,mɛdətə'reɪnɪən, ,mɛdətə'reɪnjən

medium
BR ˈmiːdɪəm, -z
AM ˈmidiəm, -z

mediumism
BR ˈmiːdɪəmɪz(ə)m
AM ˈmidiə,mɪzəm

mediumistic
BR ˌmiːdɪəˈmɪstɪk
AM ˌmidiəˈmɪstɪk

mediumship
BR ˈmiːdɪəmʃɪp, -s
AM ˈmidiəm,ʃɪp, -s

medlar
BR ˈmɛdlə(r), -z
AM ˈmɛdlər, -z

medley
BR ˈmɛdl|i, -ɪz
AM ˈmɛdli, -z

Médoc
BR ˌmeɪˈdɒk
AM ˌmeɪˈdɑk, ˌmeɪˈdɔk

medrese
BR mɛˈdrɛseɪ, -z
AM mɛˈdrɛseɪ, -z

medulla
BR mɛˈdʌlə(r),
mɪˈdʌlə(r), -z
AM məˈdələ, -z

**medulla
oblongata**
BR mɛ,dʌlə
,ɒblɒŋˈgɑːtə(r),
mɪ,dʌlə +
AM məˈdələ
ɑ,blɒŋˈgɑdə,
+ ɔ,blɒŋˈgɑdə

medullary
BR mɛˈdʌl(ə)ri,
mɪˈdʌl(ə)ri
AM məˈdəl(ə)ri,
ˈmɛdʒələri

medusa
BR mɪˈdjuːzə(r),
mɪˈdjuːsə(r),
mɪˈdʒuːzə(r),
mɪˈdʒuːsə(r), -z
AM məˈd(j)uːzə,
məˈd(j)usə, -z

medusae
BR mɪˈdjuːziː,
mɪˈdjuːsiː, mɪˈdʒuːziː,
mɪˈdʒuːsiː
AM məˈd(j)uzi,
məˈd(j)usi,
məˈd(j)uzaɪ,
məˈd(j)u,saɪ

medusan
BR mɪˈdjuːz(ə)n,
mɪˈdjuːs(ə)n,
mɪˈdʒuːz(ə)n,
mɪˈdʒuːs(ə)n
AM məˈd(j)uzən,
məˈd(j)usən

Medway
BR ˈmɛdweɪ
AM ˈmɛdweɪ

Medwin
BR ˈmɛdwɪn

AM ˈmɛdwɪn

Mee
BR miː
AM mi

meed
BR miːd
AM mid

Meehan
BR ˈmiːən
AM ˈmiən, ˈmi,hæn

meek
BR miːk
AM mik

meekly
BR ˈmiːkli
AM ˈmikli

meekness
BR ˈmiːknɪs
AM ˈmiknɪs

meerkat
BR ˈmɪəkat, -s
AM ˈmɪr,kæt, -s

meerschaum
BR ˈmɪəʃ(ə)m,
ˈmɪəʃɔːm, -z
AM ˈmɪr,ʃɔm, ˈmɪrʃəm,
ˈmɪr,ʃɑm, -z

Meerut
BR ˈmɪərət
AM ˈmeɪrət, ˈmɪrət

meet
BR miːt, -s, -ɪŋ
AM mi|t, -ts, -dɪŋ

meeter
BR ˈmiːtə(r), -z
AM ˈmidər, -z

meeting
BR ˈmiːtɪŋ, -z
AM ˈmidɪŋ, -z

meetinghouse
BR ˈmiːtɪŋhaʊ|s, -zɪz
AM ˈmidɪŋ,(h)aʊ|s, -zəz

meetly
BR ˈmiːtli
AM ˈmitli

meetness
BR ˈmiːtnɪs
AM ˈmitnɪs

Meg
BR mɛg
AM mɛg

mega
BR ˈmɛgə(r)
AM ˈmɛgə

megabuck
BR ˈmɛgəbʌk, -s
AM ˈmɛgə,bək, -s

megabyte
BR ˈmɛgəbaɪt, -s
AM ˈmɛgə,baɪt, -s

megacephalic
BR ˌmɛgəsɪˈfalɪk,
ˌmɛgəkɛˈfalɪk
AM ˌmɛgəsəˈfælɪk

megacycle
BR ˈmɛgə,saɪkl, -z
AM ˈmɛgə,saɪkəl, -z

megadeath
BR ˈmɛgədɛθ, -s
AM ˈmɛgə,dɛθ, -s

Megaera
BR mɪˈdʒɪərə(r)
AM məˈdʒirə

megaflop
BR ˈmɛgəflɒp, -s
AM ˈmɛgə,flɑp, -s

megahertz
BR ˈmɛgəhəːts
AM ˈmɛgə,hərts

megalith
BR ˈmɛgəlɪθ, -s
AM ˈmɛgə,lɪθ, -s

megalithic
BR ˌmɛgəˈlɪθɪk
AM ˌmɛgəˈlɪθɪk

megalomania
BR ˌmɛg(ə)lə(ʊ)ˈmeɪ-
nɪə(r),
ˌmɛglə(ʊ)ˈmeɪnɪə(r)
AM ˌmɛg(ə)loʊˈmeɪniə,
ˌmɛg(ə)ləˈmeɪniə

megalomaniac
BR ˌmɛg(ə)lə(ʊ)ˈmeɪ-
nɪak,
ˌmɛglə(ʊ)ˈmeɪnɪak, -s
AM ˌmɛg(ə)loʊˈmeɪni-
,æk,
ˌmɛg(ə)ləˈmeɪni,æk,
-s

megalomaniacal
BR ˌmɛgləməˈnʌɪəkl
AM ˌmɛg(ə)ləməˈnaɪəkəl

megalopolis
BR ˌmɛgəˈlɒpəlɪs, -ɪz
AM ˌmɛgəˈlɑpələs, -əz

megalopolitan
BR ˌmɛgəˈlɒpʊlɪt(ə)n,
ˈmɛglɒˈpɒlɪt(ə)n
AM ˌmɛgələˈpalədən,
ˌmɛgələˈpalətn

megalosaur
BR ˈmɛg(ə)ləsɔː(r),
ˈmɛgləsɔː(r), -z
AM ˈmɛgələ,sɔ(ə)r, -z

megalosaurus
BR ˌmɛg(ə)ləˈsɔːrəs,
ˌmɛgləˈsɔːrəs, -ɪz
AM ˌmɛgələˈsɔrəs, -əz

Megan
BR ˈmɛg(ə)n
AM ˈmɛgən, ˈmeɪgən

megaphone
BR ˈmɛgəfəʊn, -z
AM ˈmɛgə,foʊn, -z

megapod
BR ˈmɛgəpɒd, -z
AM ˈmɛgə,pɑd, -z

megapode
BR ˈmɛgəpəʊd, -z
AM ˈmɛgə,poʊd, -z

megaron
BR ˈmɛgərɒn,
ˈmɛgərən, ˈmɛgərn, -z
AM ˈmɛgə,rɑn, -z

megascopic
BR ˌmɛgəˈskɒpɪk
AM ˌmɛgəˈskɑpɪk

megaspore
BR ˈmɛgəspɔː(r), -z
AM ˈmɛgə,spɔ(ə)r, -z

megastar
BR ˈmɛgəstɑː(r), -z
AM ˈmɛgə,stɑr, -z

megastore
BR ˈmɛgəstɔː(r), -z
AM ˈmɛgə,stɔ(ə)r, -z

megatheria
BR ˌmɛgəˈθɪərɪə(r)
AM ˌmɛgəˈθɪriə

megatherium
BR ˌmɛgəˈθɪərɪəm
AM ˌmɛgəˈθɪriəm

megaton
BR ˈmɛgətʌn, -z
AM ˈmɛgə,tən,
ˈmɛgə,tɑn, -z

megatonne
BR ˈmɛgətʌn, -z
AM ˈmɛgə,tən,
ˈmɛgə,tɑn, -z

megavolt
BR ˈmɛgəvəʊlt,
ˈmɛgəvɒlt, -s
AM ˈmɛgə,voʊlt, -s

megawatt
BR ˈmɛgəwɒt, -s
AM ˈmɛgə,wɑt, -s

Megger®
BR ˈmɛgə(r), -z
AM ˈmɛgər, -z

megillah
BR mɪˈgɪlə(r), -z
AM məˈgɪlə, -z

megilp
BR məˈgɪlp
AM məˈgɪlp

megohm
BR ˈmɛgəʊm, -z
AM ˈmɛg,oʊm, -z

megrim
BR ˈmiːgrɪm, -z
AM ˈmigrɪm, -z

Mehmet
BR ˈmɛmɛt
AM ˈmɛmɛt

Meier
BR ˈmʌɪə(r)
AM ˈmaɪər

Meiji Tenno
BR ˌmeɪdʒɪ ˈtɛnəʊ
AM ˌmeɪˈidʒi ˈtɛ,noʊ

Meikle
BR ˈmiːkl
AM ˈmikl

Meiklejohn
BR ˈmiːkldʒɒn
AM ˈmikl,dʒɑn,
ˈmɪkl,dʒɑn

meioses
BR mʌɪˈəʊsiːz
AM maɪˈoʊsiz

meiosis
BR maɪˈəʊsɪs
AM maɪˈoʊsəs
meiotic
BR maɪˈɒtɪk
AM meiˈɑdɪk
meiotically
BR maɪˈɒtɪkli
AM maɪˈɒdək(ə)li
Meir
BR meɪˈrɪə(r)
AM meɪˈrɪ(ə)r
Meissen
BR ˈmaɪsn
AM ˈmaɪsən
Meistersinger
BR ˈmaɪstəˌsɪŋə(r),
ˈmaɪstəˌzɪŋə(r), -z
AM ˈmaɪstərˌsɪŋər, -z
Mekong
BR ˌmiːˈkɒŋ
AM ˈmeɪˈkɒŋ, ˌmiˈkɒŋ,
ˌmeɪˈkɑŋ, ˌmiˈkɑŋ
mel
BR mɛl, -z
AM mɛl, -z
melamine
BR ˈmɛləmaɪn,
ˈmɛləmiːn
AM ˈmɛləˌmin
melancholia
BR ˌmɛlənˈkəʊlɪə(r),
ˌmɛləŋˈkəʊlɪə(r)
AM ˌmɛlənˈkoʊljə,
ˌmɛlənˈkaljə,
ˌmɛlənˈkoʊlɪə,
ˌmɛlənˈkalɪə
melancholic
BR ˌmɛlənˈkɒlɪk,
ˌmɛləŋˈkɒlɪk
AM ˈmɛlənˌkalɪk
melancholically
BR ˌmɛlənˈkɒlɪkli,
ˌmɛləŋˈkɒlɪkli
AM ˌmɛlənˈkalək(ə)li
melancholy
BR ˈmɛlənk(ə)li,
ˈmɛləŋk(ə)li
AM ˈmɛlənˌkali
Melanchthon
BR maˈlaŋkθən
AM məˈlæŋkˌθan
Melanesia
BR ˌmɛləˈniːzjə(r),
ˌmɛləˈniːʒə(r)
AM ˌmɛləˈniʒə,
ˌmɛləˈniʃə
Melanesian
BR ˌmɛləˈniːzj(ə)n,
ˌmɛləˈniːʒn, -z
AM ˌmɛləˈniʒən,
ˌmɛləˈniʃən, -z
mélange
BR meɪˈlɒ̃ʒ, meɪˈlɑːnʒ,
-ɪz
AM meɪˈlan(d)ʒ, -əz
Melanie
BR ˈmɛləni

AM ˈmɛləni
melanin
BR ˈmɛlənɪn
AM ˈmɛlənən
melanism
BR ˈmɛlənɪz(ə)m
AM ˈmɛləˌnɪzəm
melanoma
BR ˌmɛləˈnəʊmə(r), -z
AM ˌmɛləˈnoʊmə, -z
melanoses
BR ˌmɛləˈnəʊsiːz
AM ˌmɛləˈnoʊsiz
melanosis
BR ˌmɛləˈnəʊsɪs
AM ˌmɛləˈnoʊsəs
melanotic
BR ˌmɛləˈnɒtɪk
AM ˌmɛləˈnadɪk
melba
BR ˈmɛlbə(r)
AM ˈmɛlbə
Melbourne
BR ˈmɛlbən, ˈmɛlbɔːn
AM ˈmɛlbərn
Melchett
BR ˈmɛltʃɪt
AM ˈmɛltʃət
Melchior
BR ˈmɛlkɪɔː(r)
AM ˈmɛlkiˌɔ(ə)r
Melchite
BR ˈmɛlkʌɪt, -s
AM ˈmɛlˌkaɪt, -s
Melchizedek
BR mɛlˈkɪzədɛk
AM mɛlˈkɪzəˌdɛk
meld
BR mɛld, -z, -ɪŋ, -ɪd
AM mɛld, -z, -ɪŋ, -əd
Meldrum
BR ˈmɛldrəm
AM ˈmɛldrəm
Meleager
BR ˌmɛlɪˈeɪgə(r)
AM ˌmɛliˈeɪgər
melee
BR ˈmɛleɪ, mɛˈleɪ, -z
AM ˈmeɪleɪ, -z
Melhuish
BR mɛlˈhjuːɪʃ,
ˈmɛlhjʊɪʃ, ˈmɛlɪʃ
AM mɛlˈhjuɪʃ
Melia
BR ˈmiːlɪə(r)
AM ˈmiljə, ˈmiliə
melic
BR ˈmɛlɪk
AM ˈmɛlɪk
melick
BR ˈmɛlɪk
AM ˈmɛlɪk
Melilla
BR mɪˈlɪə(r)
AM məˈlɪjə
melilot
BR ˈmɛlɪlɒt, -s

AM ˈmɛləˌlat, -s
Melina
BR mɪˈliːnə(r)
AM məˈlinə
Melinda
BR mɪˈlɪndə(r)
AM məˈlɪndə
meliorate
BR ˈmiːlɪəreɪt, -s, -ɪŋ,
-ɪd
AM ˈmiljəˌreɪt,
ˈmiliəˌreɪt, -ts, -dɪŋ,
-dɪd
melioration
BR ˌmiːlɪəˈreɪʃn
AM ˌmiljəˈreɪʃən,
ˌmiliəˈreɪʃən
meliorative
BR ˈmiːlɪərətɪv
AM ˈmiljəˌreɪdɪv,
ˈmiliəˌreɪdɪv
meliorism
BR ˈmiːlɪərɪz(ə)m
AM ˈmiljəˌrɪzəm,
ˈmiliəˌrɪzəm
meliorist
BR ˈmiːlɪərɪst, -s
AM ˈmiljərəst,
ˈmiliərəst, -s
melisma
BR mɪˈlɪzmə(r), -z
AM məˈlɪzmə, -z
melismata
BR mɪˈlɪzmətə(r)
AM məˈlɪzmədə
melismatic
BR ˌmɛlɪzˈmatɪk
AM ˌmɛləzˈmædɪk
Melissa
BR mɪˈlɪsə(r)
AM məˈlɪsə
Melksham
BR ˈmɛlkʃ(ə)m
AM ˈmɛlkˌʃəm
melliferous
BR mɪˈlɪf(ə)rəs
AM məˈlɪf(ə)rəs
mellifluence
BR mɪˈlɪflʊəns
AM məˈlɪflʊəns
mellifluent
BR mɪˈlɪflʊənt
AM məˈlɪflʊənt
mellifluous
BR mɪˈlɪflʊəs
AM məˈlɪfləwəs
mellifluously
BR mɪˈlɪflʊəsli
AM məˈlɪfləwəsli
mellifluousness
BR mɪˈlɪflʊəsnəs
AM məˈlɪfləwəsnəs
Mellish
BR ˈmɛlɪʃ
AM ˈmɛlɪʃ
Mellon
BR ˈmɛlən

AM ˈmɛlən
Mellor
BR ˈmɛlə(r)
AM ˈmɛlər
Mellors
BR ˈmɛləz
AM ˈmɛlərz
mellotron
BR ˈmɛlətrɒn, -z
AM ˈmɛləˌtran, -z
mellow
BR ˈmɛləʊ, -z, -ɪŋ, -d,
-ə(r), -ɪst
AM ˈmɛloʊ, -z, -ɪŋ, -d,
-ər, -əst
mellowly
BR ˈmɛləʊli
AM ˈmɛloʊli
mellowness
BR ˈmɛləʊnəs
AM ˈmɛloʊnəs
Melly
BR ˈmɛli
AM ˈmɛli
melodeon
BR mɪˈləʊdɪən, -z
AM məˈloʊdiən, -z
melodic
BR mɪˈlɒdɪk
AM məˈladɪk
melodica
BR mɪˈlɒdɪkə(r), -z
AM məˈladəkə, -z
melodically
BR mɪˈlɒdɪkli
AM məˈladək(ə)li
melodious
BR mɪˈləʊdɪəs
AM məˈloʊdiəs
melodiously
BR mɪˈləʊdɪəsli
AM məˈloʊdiəsli
melodiousness
BR mɪˈləʊdɪəsnəs
AM məˈloʊdiəsnəs
melodise
BR ˈmɛlədʌɪz, -ɪz, -ɪŋ, -d
AM ˈmɛləˌdaɪz, -ɪz, -ɪŋ,
-d
melodiser
BR ˈmɛlədʌɪzə(r), -z
AM ˈmɛləˌdaɪzər, -z
melodist
BR ˈmɛlədɪst, -s
AM ˈmɛlədəst, -s
melodize
BR ˈmɛlədʌɪz, -ɪz, -ɪŋ, -d
AM ˈmɛləˌdaɪz, -ɪz, -ɪŋ,
-d
melodizer
BR ˈmɛlədʌɪzə(r), -z
AM ˈmɛləˌdaɪzər, -z
melodrama
BR ˈmɛlədrɑːmə(r), -z
AM ˈmɛləˌdramə, -z
melodramatic
BR ˌmɛlədrəˈmatɪk, -s

AM ˌmelədrəˈmædɪk, -s

melodramatically
BR ˌmelədrəˈmatɪkli
AM ˌmelədrəˈmædək(ə)li

melodramatise
BR ˌmelə(ʊ)ˈdramətʌɪz, -ɪz, -ɪŋ, -d
AM ˌmeləˈdramə.taɪz, -ɪz, -ɪŋ, -d

melodramatist
BR ˌmelə(ʊ)ˈdramətɪst, -s
AM ˌmeləˈdramədəst, -s

melodramatize
BR ˌmelə(ʊ)ˈdramətʌɪz, -ɪz, -ɪŋ, -d
AM ˌmeləˈdramə.taɪz, -ɪz, -ɪŋ, -d

melody
BR ˈmeləd|i, -ɪz
AM ˈmelədi, -z

melon
BR ˈmelən, -z
AM ˈmelən, -z

Melos
BR ˈmiːlɒs, ˈmelɒs
AM ˈmilas

Melpomene
BR melˈpɒmɪni
AM melˈpɑməni

Melrose
BR ˈmelrəʊz
AM ˈmelˌrouz

melt
BR melt, -s, -ɪŋ, -ɪd
AM melt, -s, -ɪŋ, -əd

meltable
BR ˈmeltəbl
AM ˈmeltəbəl

meltage
BR ˈmelt|ɪdʒ, -ɪdʒɪz
AM ˈmeltɪdʒ, -ɪz

meltdown
BR ˈmeltdaʊn, -z
AM ˈmeltˌdaʊn, -z

melter
BR ˈmeltə(r), -z
AM ˈmeltər, -z

meltingly
BR ˈmeltɪŋli
AM ˈmeltɪŋli

melton
BR ˈmeltn, -z
AM ˈmeltən, -z

Meltonian®
BR melˈtəʊnɪən
AM melˈtouniən

Melton Mowbray
BR ˌmelt(ə)n ˈməʊbri, + ˈməʊbreɪ
AM ˈmeltn ˈmoubri

meltwater
BR ˈmeltˌwɔːtə(r), -z
AM ˈmeltˌwɔdər, ˈmeltˌwɑdər, -z

Melville
BR ˈmelvɪl
AM ˈmelvəl, ˈmelˌvɪl

Melvin
BR ˈmelvɪn
AM ˈmelvən

member
BR ˈmembə(r), -z, -d
AM ˈmembər, -z, -d

memberless
BR ˈmembələs
AM ˈmembərləs

membership
BR ˈmembəʃɪp, -s
AM ˈmembərˌʃɪp, -s

member state
BR ˌmembə ˈsteɪt, -s
AM ˈmembər ˌsteɪt, -s

membranaceous
BR ˌmembrəˈneɪʃəs
AM ˌmembrəˈneɪʃəs

membrane
BR ˈmembreɪn, -z
AM ˈmemˌbreɪn, -z

membraneous
BR memˈbreɪnɪəs
AM memˈbreɪnɪəs

membranous
BR ˈmembrənəs
AM ˈmembrənəs, memˈbreɪnəs

membrum virile
BR ˌmembrəm vɪˈrʌɪli, + vɪˈriːli, -z
AM ˈmembrəm ˈvɪrɪl, -z

memento
BR mɪˈmentəʊ, -z
AM məˈmenˌtoʊ, məˈmenoʊ, -z

memento mori
BR mɪˈmentəʊ ˈmɔːrʌɪ, + ˈmɔːri
AM məˈmenˌtoʊ ˈmɔri, məˈmenoʊ +

Memnon
BR ˈmemnɒn, ˈmemnən
AM ˈmemnən, ˈmemnɑn

memo
BR ˈmeməʊ, -z
AM ˈmemoʊ, -z

memoir
BR ˈmemwɑː(r), -z
AM ˈmemˌwar, -z

memoirist
BR ˈmemwɑːrɪst, -s
AM ˈmemwɑrəst, -s

memorabilia
BR ˌmem(ə)rəˈbɪlɪə(r)
AM ˌmem(ə)rəˈbɪljə, ˌmem(ə)rəˈbɪliə

memorability
BR ˌmem(ə)rˈbɪlɪti
AM ˌmem(ə)rəˈbɪlɪdi

memorable
BR ˈmem(ə)rəbl

AM ˈmem(ə)rəbəl, ˈmemərbəl

memorableness
BR ˈmem(ə)rəblnəs
AM ˈmem(ə)rəbəlnəs, ˈmemərbəlnəs

memorably
BR ˈmem(ə)rəbli
AM ˈmem(ə)rəbli, ˈmemərbli

memoranda
BR ˌmeməˈrandə(r)
AM ˌmeməˈrændə

memorandum
BR ˌmeməˈrandəm, -z
AM ˌmeməˈrændəm, -z

memorial
BR mɪˈmɔːrɪəl, -z
AM məˈmɔriəl, -z

memorialise
BR mɪˈmɔːrɪəlʌɪz, -ɪz, -ɪŋ, -d
AM məˈmɔriəˌlaɪz, -ɪz, -ɪŋ, -d

memorialist
BR mɪˈmɔːrɪəlɪst, -s
AM məˈmɔriələst, -s

memorialize
BR mɪˈmɔːrɪəlʌɪz, -ɪz, -ɪŋ, -d
AM məˈmɔriəˌlaɪz, -ɪz, -ɪŋ, -d

memoria technica
BR mɪˌmɔːrɪə ˈteknɪkə(r), -z
AM məˌmɔriə ˈteknəkə, -z

memorisable
BR ˈmemərʌɪzəbl
AM ˈmeməˌraɪzəbəl

memorisation
BR ˌmemərʌɪˈzeɪʃn
AM ˌmemərəˈzeɪʃən, ˌmeməˌraɪˈzeɪʃən

memorise
BR ˈmemərʌɪz, -ɪz, -ɪŋ, -d
AM ˈmeməˌraɪz, -ɪz, -ɪŋ, -d

memoriser
BR ˈmemərʌɪzə(r), -z
AM ˈmeməˌraɪzər, -z

memorizable
BR ˈmemərʌɪzəbl
AM ˈmeməˌraɪzəbəl

memorization
BR ˌmemərʌɪˈzeɪʃn
AM ˌmemərəˈzeɪʃən, ˌmeməˌraɪˈzeɪʃən

memorize
BR ˈmemərʌɪz, -ɪz, -ɪŋ, -d
AM ˈmeməˌraɪz, -ɪz, -ɪŋ, -d

memorizer
BR ˈmemərʌɪzə(r), -z
AM ˈmeməˌraɪzər, -z

memory
BR ˈmem(ə)r|i, -ɪz
AM ˈmem(ə)ri, -z

Memphis
BR ˈmemfɪs
AM ˈmem(p)fəs

memsahib
BR ˈmemsɑː(ɪ)b, -z
AM ˈmemˌsa(h)ɪb, ˈmemˌsab, -z

men
BR men
AM men

menace
BR ˈmenɪs, -ɪz, -ɪŋ, -t
AM ˈmenəs, -əz, -ɪŋ, -t

menacer
BR ˈmenɪsə(r), -z
AM ˈmenəsər, -z

menacingly
BR ˈmenɪsɪŋli
AM ˈmenəsɪŋli

ménage
BR meɪˈnɑːʒ, meˈnɑːʒ, məˈnɑːʒ, -ɪz
AM meɪˈnɑʒ, məˈnɑʒ, -əz

ménage à trois
BR ˌmenɑːʒ ɑː ˈtrwɑː(r), ˌmenɑːʒ +, məˌnɑːʒ +, -z
AM meɪˈnɑʒ ə ˈt(r)wɑ, məˈnɑʒ +, -z

menagerie
BR mɪˈnadʒ(ə)r|i, -ɪz
AM məˈnæ(d)ʒəri, -z

Menai Strait
BR ˌmenʌɪ ˈstreɪt
AM ˈmeˌnaɪ ˈstreɪt

Menander
BR mɪˈnandə(r)
AM məˈnændər

menaquinone
BR ˌmenəˈkwɪnəʊn, -z
AM ˌmenəˈkwɪnoun, -z

menarche
BR meˈnɑːki, mɪˈnɑːki
AM məˈnɑrki, ˈmenɑrki

Mencken
BR ˈmeŋk(ə)n
AM ˈmeŋkən

mend
BR mend, -z, -ɪŋ, -ɪd
AM mend, -z, -ɪŋ, -əd

mendable
BR ˈmendəbl
AM ˈmendəbəl

mendacious
BR menˈdeɪʃəs
AM menˈdeɪʃəs

mendaciously
BR menˈdeɪʃəsli
AM menˈdeɪʃəsli

mendaciousness
BR menˈdeɪʃəsnəs
AM menˈdeɪʃəsnəs

mendacity
BR mɛnˈdasɪti
AM mɛnˈdæsədi
Mendel
BR ˈmɛndl
AM ˈmɛnd(ə)l
Mendeleev
BR ˌmɛndəˈleɪɛv
AM ˌmɛndəˈleɪɛv
mendelevium
BR ˌmɛndəˈliːvɪəm,
ˌmɛndəˈleɪvɪəm
AM ˌmɛndəˈliviəm,
ˌmɛndəˈleɪvɪəm
Mendelian
BR mɛnˈdiːlɪən
AM mɛnˈdiliən
Mendelism
BR ˈmɛndlɪz(ə)m
AM ˈmɛndl.ɪzəm
Mendelssohn
BR ˈmɛndls(ə)n
AM ˈmɛndlsən
mender
BR ˈmɛndə(r), -z
AM ˈmɛndər, -z
Méndez
BR ˈmɛndɛz
AM ˈmɛn.dɛz
SP ˈmendeθ, ˈmendes
mendicancy
BR ˈmɛndɪk(ə)nsi
AM ˈmɛndəkənsi
mendicant
BR ˈmɛndɪk(ə)nt, -s
AM ˈmɛndəkənt, -s
mendicity
BR mɛnˈdɪsɪti
AM mɛnˈdɪsɪdi
Mendip
BR ˈmɛndɪp, -s
AM ˈmɛndɪp, -s
Mendoza
BR mɛnˈdəʊzə(r)
AM mɛnˈdoʊzə
SP menˈdoθa,
menˈdosa
Menelaus
BR ˌmɛnɪˈleɪəs
AM ˌmɛnəˈleɪəs
Menes
BR ˈmiːniːz
AM ˈmiˌniz
menfolk
BR ˈmɛnfəʊk
AM ˈmɛnˌfoʊk
Meng-tzu
BR ˌmɛŋˈtsuː
AM ˌmɛŋˈtsu
menhaden
BR mɛnˈheɪdn, -z
AM mɛnˈheɪdən, -z
menhir
BR ˈmɛnhɪə(r), -z
AM ˈmɛn,(h)ɪ(ə)r, -z
menial
BR ˈmiːnɪəl, -z

AM ˈminiəl, -z
menially
BR ˈmiːnɪəli
AM ˈminiəli
Meniere
BR ˈmɛnɪɛː(r),
ˌmɛnɪˈɛː(r)
AM ˌmeɪnˈjɛ(ə)r
meningeal
BR mɪˈnɪn(d)ʒɪəl
AM məˈnɪndʒɪəl
meninges
BR mɪˈnɪn(d)ʒiːz
AM məˈnɪndʒiz
meningitic
BR ˌmɛnɪnˈdʒɪtɪk
AM ˌmɛnənˈdʒɪdɪk
meningitis
BR ˌmɛnɪnˈdʒʌɪtɪs
AM ˌmɛnənˈdʒaɪdɪs
meningocele
BR mɪˈnɪŋɡə(ʊ)siːl, -z
AM məˈnɪŋɡoʊˌsil, -z
meningococcal
BR məˌnɪŋɡə(ʊ)ˈkɒkl
AM məˌnɪŋɡoʊˈkakəl
meningococcus
BR məˌnɪŋɡə(ʊ)ˈkɒkəs
AM məˌnɪŋɡoʊˈkakəs
meninx
BR ˈmiːnɪŋks, -ɪz
AM ˈmɪnɪŋ(k)s, -ɪz
meniscoid
BR mɪˈnɪskɔɪd
AM məˈnɪs.kɔɪd
meniscus
BR mɪˈnɪskəs, -ɪz
AM məˈnɪskəs, -əz
Menlo Park
BR ˌmɛnləʊ ˈpaːk
AM ˌmɛnloʊ ˈpark
Mennonite
BR ˈmɛnənʌɪt, -s
AM ˈmɛnəˌnaɪt, -s
menologia
BR ˌmɛnə(ʊ)ˈləʊdʒɪə(r)
AM ˌmɛnəˈloʊdʒə
menologist
BR mɪˈnɒlədʒɪst, -s
AM məˈnalədʒəst, -s
menologium
BR ˌmɛnə(ʊ)ˈləʊdʒɪəm,
-z
AM ˌmɛnəˈloʊdʒɪəm, -z
menology
BR mɪˈnɒlədʒi, -ɪz
AM məˈnalədʒi, -z
menopausal
BR ˌmɛnə(ʊ)ˈpɔːzl
AM ˌmɛnəˈpɔzəl,
ˌmɛnəˈpazəl
menopause
BR ˈmɛnə(ʊ)pɔːz, -ɪz
AM ˈmɛnəˌpɔz,
ˈmɛnəˌpaz, -ɪz
menorah
BR mɪˈnɔːrə(r), -z

AM məˈnɔrə, -z
Menorca
BR mɪˈnɔːkə(r)
AM məˈnɔrkə
Menorcan
BR mɪˈnɔːk(ə)n, -z
AM məˈnɔrkən, -z
menorrhagia
BR ˌmɛnəˈreɪdʒɪə(r)
AM ˌmɛnəˈreɪdʒ(i)ə
menorrhoea
BR ˌmɛnəˈriːə(r)
AM ˌmɛnəˈriə
Menotti
BR mɪˈnɒti
AM məˈnɑdi
mens
BR mɛnz
AM mɛnz
Mensa
BR ˈmɛnsə(r)
AM ˈmɛnsə
menses
BR ˈmɛnsiːz
AM ˈmɛnsiz
Menshevik
BR ˈmɛnʃəvɪk, -s
AM ˈmɛn(t)ʃəˌvɪk, -s
RUS mʲinʃɪˈvʲik
mens rea
BR ˌmɛnz ˈriːə(r),
+ ˈreɪə(r)
AM ˌmɛnz ˈriə
Menston
BR ˈmɛnst(ə)n
AM ˈmɛnstən
menstrua
BR ˈmɛnstrʊə(r)
AM ˈmɛnstr(əw)ə,
ˈmɛnztr(əw)ə
menstrual
BR ˈmɛnstrʊəl,
ˈmɛnstrəl
AM ˈmɛnstr(əw)əl,
ˈmɛnztr(əw)əl
menstrual cycle
BR ˌmɛnstrəl ˈsʌɪkl, -z
AM ˈmɛnstr(əw)əl
ˌsaɪkəl,
ˈmɛnztr(əw)əl +, -z
menstruate
BR ˈmɛnstrʊeɪt, -s, -ɪŋ,
-ɪd
AM ˈmɛnsˌtreɪt,
ˈmɛnzˌtreɪt,
ˈmɛnstrəˌweɪt,
ˈmɛnztrəˌweɪt, -ts,
-dɪŋ, -dɪd
menstruation
BR ˌmɛnstrʊˈeɪʃn
AM ˌmɛnsˈtreɪʃən,
ˌmɛnzˈtreɪʃən,
ˌmɛnztrəˈweɪʃən,
ˌmɛnstrəˈweɪʃən
menstruous
BR ˈmɛnstrʊəs
AM ˈmɛnstr(əw)əs,
ˈmɛnztr(əw)əs

menstruum
BR ˈmɛnstrʊəm
AM ˈmɛnstr(əw)əm,
ˈmɛnztr(əw)əm
mensurability
BR ˌmɛnʃ(ʊ)rəˈbɪlɪti,
ˌmɛnsjʊrəˈbɪlɪti,
ˌmɛns(ə)rəˈbɪlɪti
AM ˌmɛnʃərəˈbɪlɪdi,
ˌmɛnsərəˈbɪlɪdi
mensurable
BR ˈmɛnʃ(ʊ)rəbl,
ˈmɛnsjʊrəbl,
ˈmɛns(ə)rəbl
AM ˈmɛn(t)ʃ(ə)rəbəl,
ˈmɛns(ə)rəbəl
mensural
BR ˈmɛnʃ(ʊ)rəl,
ˈmɛnʃ(ʊ)rl,
ˈmɛnsjʊrəl,
ˈmɛnsjʊrl,
ˈmɛns(ə)rəl,
ˈmɛns(ə)rl
AM ˈmɛn(t)ʃ(ə)rəl,
ˈmɛnsərəl
mensuration
BR ˌmɛnʃʊˈreɪʃn,
ˌmɛnsjʊˈreɪʃn,
ˌmɛnsəˈreɪʃn
AM ˌmɛn(t)ʃəˈreɪʃən,
ˌmɛnsəˈreɪʃən
menswear
BR ˈmɛnzwɛː(r)
AM ˈmɛnzˌwɛ(ə)r
Mentadent®
BR ˈmɛntədɛnt
AM ˈmɛn(t)əˌdɛnt
mental
BR ˈmɛntl
AM ˈmɛn(t)l
mentalism
BR ˈmɛntlɪz(ə)m
AM ˈmɛn(t)lˌɪzəm
mentalist
BR ˈmɛntlɪst, -s
AM ˈmɛn(t)ləst, -s
mentalistic
BR ˌmɛntəˈlɪstɪk,
ˌmɛntlˈɪstɪk
AM ˌmɛn(t)lˈɪstɪk
mentalistically
BR ˌmɛntəˈlɪstɪkli,
ˌmɛntlˈɪstɪkli
AM ˌmɛn(t)lˈɪstɪk(ə)li
mentality
BR mɛnˈtalɪti, -ɪz
AM mɛnˈtælədi, -z
mentally
BR ˈmɛntli, ˈmɛntəli
AM ˈmɛn(t)li
mentation
BR mɛnˈteɪʃn, -z
AM mɛnˈteɪʃən, -z
menthol
BR ˈmɛnθɒl
AM ˈmɛnˌθɒl, ˈmɛnˌθɑl
mentholated
BR ˈmɛnθəleɪtɪd

mention AM 'mɛnθə,leɪdɪd
mention
BR 'mɛnʃ|n, -nz,
-ŋɪŋ \-ənɪŋ, -nd
AM 'mɛn(t)ʃ|ən, -ənz,
-(ə)nɪŋ, -ənd
mentionable
BR 'mɛnʃnəbl,
'mɛnʃ(ə)nəbl
AM 'mɛn(t)ʃənəbəl,
'mɛnʃnəbəl
mentor
BR 'mɛntɔ:(r), -z
AM 'mɛn,tɔ(ə)r,
'mɛn(t)ər, -z
menu
BR 'mɛnju:, -z
AM 'mɛnju, -z
Menuhin
BR 'mɛnjʊɪn
AM 'mɛnuɪn
Menzies
BR 'mɛnzɪz, 'mɪŋgɪz,
'mɪŋgɪs
AM 'mɛnziz
Meon
BR 'mi:ən
AM 'mi,ɑn
Meopham
BR 'mɛp(ə)m
AM 'miəpəm
meow
BR mɪ'aʊ, -z, -ɪŋ, -d
AM mi'aʊ, -z, -ɪŋ, -d
mepacrine
BR 'mɛpəkrɪn
AM 'mɛpə,krɪn
Mephistophelean
BR ,mɛfɪstə'fi:lɪən,
mɪ,fɪstə'fi:lɪən
AM mə,fɪstə,filiən,
,mɛfə,stəfə'liən
Mephistopheles
BR ,mɛfɪ'stɒfɪli:z
AM ,mɛfə'stafəliz
Mephistophelian
BR ,mɛfɪstə'fi:lɪən,
mɪ,fɪstə'fi:lɪən
AM mə,fɪstə,filiən,
,mɛfə,stəfə'liən
mephitic
BR mɪ'fɪtɪk
AM mə'fɪdɪk
mephitis
BR mɪ'fʌɪtɪs, -ɪz
AM mə'faɪdɪs, -ɪz
meranti
BR mə'rant|i, -ɪz
AM mə'ræn(t)i, -z
mercantile
BR 'mɜ:k(ə)ntʌɪl
AM 'mɜrkən,til,
'mɜrkən,taɪl
mercantilism
BR 'mɜ:k(ə)ntɪlɪz(ə)m,
'mɜ:k(ə)ntʌɪlɪz(ə)m
AM 'mɜrkən(t)ə,lɪz(ə)m

mercantilist
BR 'mɜ:k(ə)ntɪlɪst,
'mɜ:k(ə)ntʌɪlɪst,
mə:'kantɪlɪst, -s
AM 'mɜrkən(t)ələst, -s
mercaptan
BR mə:'kapt(ə)n,
mə:'kaptan
AM mər'kæp,tæn
Mercator
BR mə:'keɪtə(r),
mə'keɪtə(r)
AM mər'keɪdər
Mercedes
BR mə'seɪdi:z
AM mər'seɪdiz
mercenariness
BR 'mɜ:s(ɪ)n(ə)rɪnɪs,
'mɜ:snrɪnɪs
AM 'mɜrsn,ɛrinɪs
mercenary
BR 'mɜ:s(ɪ)n(ə)r|i,
'mɜ:snr|i, -ɪz
AM 'mɜrsn,ɛri, -z
mercer
BR 'mɜ:sə(r), -z
AM 'mɜrsər, -z
mercerise
BR 'mɜ:sərʌɪz, -ɪz, -ɪŋ,
-d
AM 'mɜrsə,raɪz, -ɪz, -ɪŋ,
-d
mercerize
BR 'mɜ:sərʌɪz, -z, -ɪŋ, -d
AM 'mɜrsər,aɪz, -z, -ɪŋ,
-d
mercery
BR 'mɜ:s(ə)r|i, -ɪz
AM 'mɜrsəri, -z
merchandisable
BR 'mɜ:tʃ(ə)ndʌɪzəbl
AM 'mɜrtʃən,daɪzəbəl
merchandise[1]
noun
BR 'mɜ:tʃ(ə)ndʌɪs,
'mɜ:tʃ(ə)ndʌɪz
AM 'mɜrtʃən,daɪz,
'mɜrtʃən,daɪs
merchandise[2]
verb
BR 'mɜ:tʃ(ə)ndʌɪz, -ɪz,
-ɪŋ, -d
AM 'mɜrtʃən,daɪz, -ɪz,
-ɪŋ, -d
merchandiser
BR 'mɜ:tʃ(ə)ndʌɪzə(r),
-z
AM 'mɜrtʃən,daɪzər, -z
merchandizable
BR 'mɜ:tʃ(ə)ndʌɪzəbl
AM 'mɜrtʃən,daɪzəbəl
merchandize[1]
noun
BR 'mɜ:tʃ(ə)ndʌɪs,
'mɜ:tʃ(ə)ndʌɪz
AM 'mɜrtʃən,daɪz

merchandize[2]
verb
BR 'mɜ:tʃ(ə)ndʌɪz, -ɪz,
-ɪŋ, -d
AM 'mɜrtʃən,daɪz, -ɪz,
-ɪŋ, -d
merchandizer
BR 'mɜ:tʃ(ə)ndʌɪzə(r),
-z
AM 'mɜrtʃən,daɪzər, -z
merchant
BR 'mɜ:tʃ(ə)nt, -s
AM 'mɜrtʃənt, -s
merchantable
BR 'mɜ:tʃ(ə)ntəbl
AM 'mɜrtʃən(t)əbəl
merchantman
BR 'mɜ:tʃ(ə)ntmən
AM 'mɜrtʃən(t)mən
merchantmen
BR 'mɜ:tʃ(ə)ntmən
AM 'mɜrtʃəntmən
Mercia
BR 'mɜ:sɪə(r),
'mə:ʃ(ɪ)ə(r)
AM 'mɜrʃ(i)ə
Mercian
BR 'mɜ:sɪən,
'mə:ʃ(ɪə)n, -z
AM 'mɜrʃ(i)ən, -z
merciful
BR 'mɜ:sɪf(ʊ)l
AM 'mɜrsəfəl
mercifully
BR 'mɜ:sɪfəli,
'mə:sɪf|i
AM 'mɜrsəf(ə)li
mercifulness
BR 'mɜ:sɪf(ʊ)lnəs
AM 'mɜrsəfəlnəs
merciless
BR 'mɜ:sɪlɪs
AM 'mɜrsələs
mercilessly
BR 'mɜ:sɪlɪsli
AM 'mɜrsələsli
mercilessness
BR 'mɜ:sɪlɪnɪs
AM 'mɜrsələsnəs
Merck
BR mɜ:k
AM mɜrk
Merckx
BR mɜ:ks
AM mɜrks
mercurial
BR mə:'kjʊərɪəl
AM ,mər'kjʊriəl
mercurialism
BR mə:'kjʊərɪəlɪz(ə)m
AM ,mər'kjʊriə,lɪzəm
mercuriality
BR mə:,kjʊərɪ'alɪti
AM ,mər'kjʊri'ælədi
mercurially
BR mə:'kjʊərɪəli
AM ,mər'kjʊriəli
mercuric
BR mə:'kjʊərɪk

merchandize[2]
verb
BR 'mɜ:tʃ(ə)ndʌɪz, -ɪz,
-ɪŋ, -d
AM 'mɜrtʃən,daɪz, -ɪz,
-ɪŋ, -d
merchandizer
BR 'mɜ:tʃ(ə)ndʌɪzə(r),
-z
AM 'mɜrtʃən,daɪzər, -z
Mercurochrome®
BR mə:'kjʊərəkrəʊm
AM mə(r)'kjʊrə,krəʊm
mercurous
BR 'mɜ:kjərəs
AM 'mɜrkjərəs
mercury
BR 'mɜ:kjʊri
AM 'mɜrkjəri
Mercutio
BR mə(:)'kju:ʃɪəʊ
AM mər'kjuʃiʊ
mercy
BR 'mɜ:s|i, -ɪz
AM 'mɜrsi, -z
mere
BR mɪə(r)
AM mɪ(ə)r
Meredith
BR 'mɛrədɪθ, mɛ'rɛdɪθ,
mɪ'rɛdɪθ
AM 'mɛrədəθ
Meredydd
BR mə'rɛdɪð
AM 'mɛrə,dɪd
WE me'redɪð
merely
BR 'mɪəli
AM 'mɪrli
meretricious
BR ,mɛrɪ'trɪʃəs
AM ,mɛrə'trɪʃəs
meretriciously
BR ,mɛrɪ'trɪʃəsli
AM ,mɛrə'trɪʃəsli
meretriciousness
BR ,mɛrɪ'trɪʃəsnəs
AM ,mɛrə'trɪʃəsnəs
Merfyn
BR 'mɜ:vɪn
AM 'mɜrfən
merganser
BR mə:'gansə(r),
mə:'ganzə(r), -z
AM mər'gænsər, -z
merge
BR mɜ:dʒ, -ɪz, -ɪŋ, -d
AM mɜrdʒ, -əz, -ɪŋ, -d
mergence
BR 'mɜ:dʒns, -ɪz
AM 'mɜrdʒəns, -əz
Mergenthaler
BR 'mɜ:g(ə)n,tɑ:lə(r)
AM 'mɜrgən,tɑlər
merger
BR 'mɜ:dʒə(r), -z
AM 'mɜrdʒər, -z
Mérida
BR 'mɛrɪdə(r)
AM 'mɛridə
Meriden
BR 'mɛrɪd(ə)n
AM 'mɛrədən
meridian
BR mɪ'rɪdɪən, -z
AM mə'rɪdiən, -z

meridional
BR mɪˈrɪdiənl
AM məˈrɪdiənəl

Meriel
BR ˈmɛriəl
AM ˈmɛriəl

meringue
BR məˈraŋ, -z
AM məˈræŋ, -z

merino
BR məˈriːnəʊ, -z
AM məˈrinoʊ, -z

Merioneth
BR ˌmɛriˈɒnɪθ
AM ˌmɛriˈɑnəθ

meristem
BR ˈmɛrɪstɛm, -z
AM ˈmɛriˌstɛm, -z

meristematic
BR ˌmɛrɪstəˈmatɪk
AM ˌmɛrəstəˈmædɪk

merit
BR ˈmɛrɪt, -ɪts, -ɪtɪŋ,
-ɪtɪd
AM ˈmɛrəlt, -ts, -dɪŋ,
-dəd

meritocracy
BR ˌmɛrɪˈtɒkrəs|i, -ɪz
AM ˌmɛrəˈtakrəsi, -z

meritocratic
BR ˌmɛrɪtəˈkratɪk
AM ˌmɛrədəˈkrædɪk

meritorious
BR ˌmɛrɪˈtɔːriəs
AM ˌmɛrəˈtɔriəs

meritoriously
BR ˌmɛrɪˈtɔːriəsli
AM ˌmɛrəˈtɔriəsli

meritoriousness
BR ˌmɛrɪˈtɔːriəsnəs
AM ˌmɛrəˈtɔriəsnəs

merkin
BR ˈməːkɪn, -z
AM ˈmərkən, -z

merle
BR məːl, -z
AM ˈmər(ə)l, -z

merlin
BR ˈməːlɪn, -z
AM ˈmərlən, -z

merlon
BR ˈməːlən, -z
AM ˈmərlən, -z

Merlot
BR ˈməːlət, -s
AM mərˈloʊ, -s

Merlyn
BR ˈməːlɪn
AM ˈmərlən

mermaid
BR ˈməːmeɪd, -z
AM ˈmərˌmeɪd, -z

merman
BR ˈməːman
AM ˈmərˌmæn

mermen
BR ˈməːmɛn

AM ˈmərˌmɛn

meroblast
BR ˈmɛrə(ʊ)blɑːst,
ˈmɛrə(ʊ)blast, -s
AM ˈmɛrəˌblæst, -s

Meroe
BR ˈmɛrəʊ
AM ˈmɛroʊ

merohedral
BR ˌmɛrə(ʊ)ˈhiːdr(ə)l
AM ˌmɛroʊˈhidrəl

meronymy
BR mɪˈrɒnɪmi
AM məˈrɑnəmi

Merovingian
BR ˌmɛrə(ʊ)ˈvɪn(d)ʒiən,
-z
AM ˌmɛrəˈvɪndʒ(i)ən,
-z

Merrick
BR ˈmɛrɪk
AM ˈmɛrɪk

Merrill
BR ˈmɛrɪl, ˈmɛrḷ
AM ˈmɛrəl

merrily
BR ˈmɛrɪli
AM ˈmɛrəli

Merrimac
BR ˈmɛrɪmak
AM ˈmɛrəˌmæk

Merrimack
BR ˈmɛrɪmak
AM ˈmɛrəˌmæk

merriment
BR ˈmɛrɪm(ə)nt
AM ˈmɛrɪmənt

merriness
BR ˈmɛrɪnɪs
AM ˈmɛrinɪs

Merrion
BR ˈmɛriən
AM ˈmɛriən

Merritt
BR ˈmɛrɪt
AM ˈmɛrət

merry
BR ˈmɛr|i, -iə(r), -ɪɪst
AM ˈmɛri, -ər, -ɪst

merry-go-round
BR ˈmɛrɪgə(ʊ)ˌraʊnd,
-z
AM ˈmɛrigoʊˌraʊnd, -z

merrymaker
BR ˈmɛrɪˌmeɪkə(r), -z
AM ˈmɛriˌmeɪkər, -z

merrymaking
BR ˈmɛrɪˌmeɪkɪŋ
AM ˈmɛriˌmeɪkɪŋ

Merryweather
BR ˈmɛriˌwɛðə(r)
AM ˈmɛriˌwɛðər

Mersa Matruh
BR ˌməːsə məˈtru:
AM ˌmərsə məˈtru

Mersey
BR ˈməːzi

AM ˈmərzi

Merseyside
BR ˈməːzɪsʌɪd
AM ˈmərziˌsaɪd

Merthiolate®
BR məːˈθʌɪəleɪt
AM mə(r)ˈθaɪəˌleɪt

Merthyr Tydfil
BR ˌməːθə ˈtɪdv(ɪ)l
AM ˈmərθər ˈtɪdvɪl
WE ˈmerθɪr ˈtɪdvɪl

Merton
BR ˈməːtn
AM ˈmərt(ə)n

Mervin
BR ˈməːvɪn
AM ˈmərvən

Mervyn
BR ˈməːvɪn
AM ˈmərvən

Meryl
BR ˈmɛrɪl, ˈmɛrḷ
AM ˈmərəl

mesa
BR ˈmeɪsə(r), -z
AM ˈmeɪsə, -z

mésalliance
BR mɛˈzalɪəns
AM ˌmeɪzəˈlaɪəns

Mesa Verde
BR ˌmeɪsə ˈvɛːdi,
+ ˈvəːdi
AM ˈmeɪsə ˈverdi

mescal
BR ˈmɛskal, mɛˈskal,
məˈskal
AM mɛˈskæl, məˈskæl

mescalin
BR ˈmɛskəlɪn
AM ˈmɛskələn,
ˈmɛskəˌlin

mescaline
BR ˈmɛskəlɪn,
ˈmɛskəli:n
AM ˈmɛskəˌlin,
ˈmɛskələn

mesdames
BR meɪˈdam
AM meɪˈdɑm

mesdemoiselles
BR ˌmeɪd(ə)mwəˈzɛl
AM ˌmeɪdəm(w)əˈzɛl,
ˌmeɪdˌmwɑˈzɛl

meseemed
BR mɪˈsiːmd
AM miˈsimd, məˈsimd

meseems
BR mɪˈsiːmz
AM miˈsimz, məˈsimz

**mesembryanthe-
mum**
BR mɪˌzɛmbrɪˈanθɪməm,
-z
AM məˌzɛmbriˈænθə-
məm, -z

mesencephalon
BR ˌmɛsɛnˈsɛfəlɒn,
ˌmɛsɛnˈsɛfḷɒn,

Merzi
AM ˈmərzi

ˌmɛzɛnˈsɛfəlɒn,
ˌmɛzɛnˈsɛfḷɒn,
ˌmɛsɛnˈkɛfəlɒn,
ˌmɛsɛnˈkɛfḷɒn,
ˌmɛzɛnˈkɛfəlɒn,
ˌmɛzɛnˈkɛfḷɒn,
AM ˌmɛzənˈsɛfələn,
ˌmɛzənˈsɛfələn

mesenterial
BR ˌmɛs(ə)nˈtɪəriəl,
ˌmɛz(ə)nˈtɪəriəl
AM ˌmɛzənˈtɛriəl,
ˌmɛsənˈtɛriəl

mesenteric
BR ˌmɛs(ə)nˈtɛrɪk,
ˌmɛz(ə)nˈtɛrɪk
AM ˌmɛzənˈtɛrɪk,
ˌmɛsənˈtɛrɪk

mesenteritis
BR ˌmɛs(ə)ntəˈrʌɪtɪs,
ˌmɛz(ə)ntəˈrʌɪtɪs,
mɪˌsɛntəˈrʌɪtɪs,
mɪˌzɛntəˈrʌɪtɪs
AM ˌmɛzən(t)əˈraɪdɪs,
ˌmɛsən(t)əˈraɪdɪs

mesentery
BR ˈmɛs(ə)nt(ə)ri,
ˈmɛz(ə)nt(ə)r|i, -ɪz
AM ˈmɛzənˌtɛri, -z

mesh
BR mɛʃ, -ɪz, -ɪŋ, -t
AM mɛʃ, -əz, -ɪŋ, -t

Meshach
BR ˈmiːʃak
AM ˈmiʃæk

mesial
BR ˈmiːzɪəl, ˈmiːsɪəl,
ˈmɛsɪəl
AM ˈmeɪzɪəl, ˈmɛsɪəl,
ˈmiziəl, ˈmisiəl

mesially
BR ˈmiːzɪəli, ˈmiːsɪəli,
ˈmɛsɪəli
AM ˈmeɪzɪəli, ˈmɛsɪəli,
ˈmiziəli, ˈmisiəli

mesic
BR ˈmiːzɪk, ˈmɛzɪk
AM ˈmɛsɪk, ˈmɛsɪk,
ˈmizɪk, ˈmɪsɪk

Mesmer
BR ˈmɛzmə(r)
AM ˈmɛsmər, ˈmɛzmər

mesmeric
BR mɛzˈmɛrɪk
AM mɛzˈmɛrɪk,
mɛsˈmɛrɪk

mesmerically
BR mɛzˈmɛrɪkli
AM mɛzˈmɛrək(ə)li,
mɛsˈmɛrək(ə)li

mesmerisation
BR ˌmɛzmərʌɪˈzeɪʃn
AM ˌmɛzmərəˈzeɪʃən,
ˌmɛzmərˌaɪˈzeɪʃən,
ˌmɛsmərˌaɪˈzeɪʃən

mesmerise
BR ˈmɛzmərʌɪz, -ɪz, -ɪŋ,
-d
AM ˈmɛzmə͵raɪz,
ˈmɛsmə͵raɪz, -ɪz, -ɪŋ,
-d
mesmeriser
BR ˈmɛzmərʌɪzə(r), -z
AM ˈmɛzmə͵raɪzər,
ˈmɛsmə͵raɪzər, -z
mesmerisingly
BR ˈmɛzmərʌɪzɪŋli
AM ˈmɛzmə͵raɪzɪŋli,
ˈmɛsmə͵raɪzɪŋli
mesmerism
BR ˈmɛzmərɪz(ə)m
AM ˈmɛzmə͵rɪzəm,
ˈmɛsmə͵rɪzəm
mesmerist
BR ˈmɛzm(ə)rɪst, -s
AM ˈmɛzmərəst,
ˈmɛsmərəst, -s
mesmerization
BR ͵mɛzmərʌɪˈzeɪʃn
AM ͵mɛzmərəˈzeɪʃən,
͵mɛsmərəˈzeɪʃən,
͵mɛzmə͵raɪˈzeɪʃən,
͵mɛsmə͵raɪˈzeɪʃən
mesmerize
BR ˈmɛzmərʌɪz, -ɪz, -ɪŋ,
-d
AM ˈmɛzmə͵raɪz,
ˈmɛsmə͵raɪz, -ɪz, -ɪŋ,
-d
mesmerizer
BR ˈmɛzmərʌɪzə(r), -z
AM ˈmɛzmə͵raɪzər,
ˈmɛsmə͵raɪzər, -z
mesmerizingly
BR ˈmɛzmərʌɪzɪŋli
AM ˈmɛzmə͵raɪzɪŋli,
ˈmɛsmə͵raɪzɪŋli
mesne
BR miːn
AM min
Meso-America
BR ͵mɛsəʊəˈmɛrɪkə(r),
͵mɛzəʊəˈmɛrɪkə(r),
͵miːsəʊəˈmɛrɪkə(r),
͵miːzəʊəˈmɛrɪkə(r)
AM ͵mɛzəʊəˈmɛrəkə,
͵mɛsəʊəˈmɛrəkə
Meso-American
BR ͵mɛsəʊəˈmɛrɪk(ə)n,
͵mɛzəʊəˈmɛrɪk(ə)n,
͵miːsəʊəˈmɛrɪk(ə)n,
͵miːzəʊəˈmɛrɪk(ə)n,
-z
AM ͵mɛzəʊəˈmɛrəkən,
͵mɛsəʊəˈmɛrəkən, -z
mesoblast
BR ˈmɛsə(ʊ)blɑːst,
ˈmɛsə(ʊ)blast,
ˈmɛzə(ʊ)blɑːst,
ˈmɛzə(ʊ)blast,
ˈmiːsə(ʊ)blɑːst,
ˈmiːsəʊblast,

ˈmiːzə(ʊ)blɑːst,
ˈmiːzə(ʊ)blast
AM ˈmɛzoʊ͵blæst,
ˈmɛsoʊ͵blæst
mesocarp
BR ˈmɛsə(ʊ)kɑːp
ˈmɛzə(ʊ)kɑːp,
ˈmiːsə(ʊ)kɑːp,
ˈmiːzə(ʊ)kɑːp
AM ˈmɛzə͵kɑrp,
ˈmɛsə͵kɑrp
mesocephalic
BR ͵mɛsəʊsɪˈfalɪk,
͵mɛsəʊkɛˈfalɪk,
͵mɛzəʊsɪˈfalɪk,
͵mɛzəʊkɛˈfalɪk,
͵miːsəʊsɪˈfalɪk,
͵miːsəʊkɛˈfalɪk,
͵miːzəʊsɪˈfalɪk,
͵miːzəʊkɛˈfalɪk
AM ͵mɛzoʊsəˈfælɪk,
͵mɛsoʊsəˈfælɪk
mesoderm
BR ˈmɛsə(ʊ)dəːm,
ˈmɛzə(ʊ)dəːm,
ˈmiːsə(ʊ)dəːm,
ˈmiːzə(ʊ)dəːm
AM ˈmɛzə͵dərm,
ˈmɛsə͵dərm
mesogaster
BR ˈmɛsə(ʊ)͵gastə(r),
ˈmɛzə(ʊ)͵gastə(r),
ˈmiːsə(ʊ)͵gastə(r),
ˈmiːzə(ʊ)͵gastə(r), -z
AM ˈmɛzoʊ͵gæstər,
ˈmɛsoʊ͵gæstər, -z
mesolect
BR ˈmɛsə(ʊ)lɛkt,
ˈmɛzə(ʊ)lɛkt,
ˈmiːsə(ʊ)lɛkt,
ˈmiːzə(ʊ)lɛkt, -s
AM ˈmɛzə͵lɛk|(t),
ˈmɛsə͵lɛk|(t), -(t)s
mesolectal
BR ͵mɛsə(ʊ)ˈlɛktl,
͵mɛzə(ʊ)ˈlɛktl,
͵miːsə(ʊ)ˈlɛktl,
͵miːzə(ʊ)ˈlɛktl
AM ͵mɛzəˈlɛktəl,
ˈmɛsəˈlɛktəl
Mesolithic
BR ͵mɛsə(ʊ)ˈlɪθɪk,
͵mɛzə(ʊ)ˈlɪθɪk,
͵miːsə(ʊ)ˈlɪθɪk,
͵miːzə(ʊ)ˈlɪθɪk
AM ͵mɛzəˈlɪθɪk,
ˈmɛsəˈlɪθɪk
mesomorph
BR ˈmɛsə(ʊ)mɔːf,
ˈmɛzə(ʊ)mɔːf,
ˈmiːsə(ʊ)mɔːf,
ˈmiːzə(ʊ)mɔːf, -s
AM ˈmɛzə͵mɔ(ə)rf,
ˈmɛsə͵mɔ(ə)rf, -s
mesomorphic
BR ͵mɛsə(ʊ)ˈmɔːfɪk,
͵mɛzə(ʊ)ˈmɔːfɪk,
͵miːsə(ʊ)ˈmɔːfɪk,
͵miːzə(ʊ)ˈmɔːfɪk

AM ͵mɛzəˈmɔrfɪk,
ˈmɛsəˈmɔrfɪk
mesomorphy
BR ˈmɛsə(ʊ)͵mɔːfi,
ˈmɛzə(ʊ)͵mɔːfi,
ˈmiːsə(ʊ)͵mɔːfi,
ˈmiːzə(ʊ)͵mɔːfi
AM ˈmɛzə͵mɔrfi,
ˈmɛsə͵mɔrfi
meson
BR ˈmiːzɒn, ˈmiːsɒn,
ˈmɛzɒn, ˈmɛsɒn,
ˈmeɪzɒn, -z
AM ˈmiˌzɑn, ˈmeɪˌzɑn,
ˈmiˌsɑn, ˈmeɪˌsɑn, -z
mesonic
BR mɪˈzɒnɪk, mɪˈsɒnɪk
AM mɪˈzɑnɪk,
məˈzɑnɪk, meɪˈzɑnɪk,
mɪˈsɑnɪk, məˈsɑnɪk,
meɪˈsɑnɪk
mesopause
BR ˈmɛsə(ʊ)pɔːz,
ˈmɛzə(ʊ)pɔːz,
ˈmiːsə(ʊ)pɔːz,
ˈmiːzə(ʊ)pɔːz, -z
AM ˈmɛzə͵pɔz,
ˈmɛsə͵pɔz, ˈmɛzə͵pɑz,
ˈmɛsə͵pɑz, -z
mesophyll
BR ˈmɛsə(ʊ)fɪl,
ˈmɛzə(ʊ)fɪl,
ˈmiːsə(ʊ)fɪl,
ˈmiːzə(ʊ)fɪl, -z
AM ˈmɛzə͵fɪl, ˈmɛsə͵fɪl,
-z
mesophyte
BR ˈmɛsə(ʊ)fʌɪt,
ˈmɛzə(ʊ)fʌɪt,
ˈmiːsə(ʊ)fʌɪt,
ˈmiːzə(ʊ)fʌɪt, -s
AM ˈmɛzə͵faɪt,
ˈmɛzə͵faɪt, -s
Mesopotamia
BR ͵mɛsəpəˈteɪmɪə(r)
AM ͵mɛsəpəˈteɪmɪə
Mesopotamian
BR ͵mɛsəpəˈteɪmɪən, -z
AM ͵mɛsəpəˈteɪmɪən,
-z
mesosphere
BR ˈmɛsə(ʊ)sfɪə(r),
ˈmɛzə(ʊ)sfɪə(r),
ˈmiːsə(ʊ)sfɪə(r),
ˈmiːzə(ʊ)sfɪə(r), -z
AM ˈmɛzə͵sfɪ(ə)r,
ˈmɛsə͵sfɪ(ə)r, -z
mesothelium
BR ͵mɛsə(ʊ)ˈθiːlɪəm,
͵mɛzə(ʊ)ˈθiːlɪəm,
͵miːsə(ʊ)ˈθiːlɪəm,
͵miːzə(ʊ)ˈθiːlɪəm
AM ͵mɛzəˈθiːlɪəm,
͵mɛsəˈθiːlɪəm,
͵mizəˈθiːlɪəm,
͵misəˈθiːlɪəm
mesotron
BR ˈmɛsətrɒn,
ˈmɛzətrɒn,

ˈmiːsətrɒn,
ˈmiːzətrɒn, -z
AM ˈmɛzə͵trɑn,
ˈmizə͵trɑn,
ˈmɛsə͵trɑn,
ˈmisə͵trɑn, -z
Mesozoic
BR ͵mɛsə(ʊ)ˈzəʊɪk,
͵mɛzə(ʊ)ˈzəʊɪk,
͵miːsə(ʊ)ˈzəʊɪk,
͵miːzə(ʊ)ˈzəʊɪk, -s
AM ͵mɛzəˈzoʊɪk,
͵mizəˈzoʊɪk,
͵mɛsəˈzoʊɪk,
͵misəˈzoʊɪk, -s
mesquit
BR mɛˈskiːt, -s
AM mɛˈskit, -s
mesquite
BR mɛˈskiːt
AM mɛˈskit
mess
BR mɛs, -ɪz, -ɪŋ, -t
AM mɛs, -əz, -ɪŋ, -t
message
BR ˈmɛsɪdʒ, -ɪdʒɪz
AM ˈmɛsɪdʒ, -ɪz
Messalina
BR ͵mɛsəˈliːnə(r)
AM ͵mɛsəˈlinə
messenger
BR ˈmɛs(ɪ)ndʒə(r), -z
AM ˈmɛsndʒər, -z
Messerschmitt
BR ˈmɛsˌ∫mɪt, -s
AM ˈmɛsər͵∫mɪt, -s
Messiaen
BR ˈmɛsjɒ̃
AM məˈsaɪən
messiah
BR mɪˈsʌɪə(r), -z
AM məˈsaɪə, -z
Messiahship
BR mɪˈsʌɪə∫ɪp, -s
AM məˈsaɪə͵∫ɪp, -s
messianic
BR ͵mɛsɪˈanɪk,
͵mɛsʌɪˈanɪk
AM ͵mɛsiˈænɪk,
ˈmɛsiˈɑnɪk
messianically
BR ͵mɛsɪˈanɪkli,
͵mɛsʌɪˈanɪkli
AM ͵mɛsiˈænək(ə)li,
ˈmɛsiˈɑnək(ə)li
Messianism
BR mɪˈsʌɪənɪz(ə)m
AM məˈsaɪə͵nɪzəm
messieurs
BR meˈsjəːz, məˈsjəːz,
ˈmɛsəz
AM meɪˈsjərz
messily
BR ˈmɛsɪli
AM ˈmɛsəli
Messina
BR mɛˈsiːnə(r),
mɪˈsiːnə(r)

AM məˈsinə

messiness
BR ˈmɛsɪnɪs
AM ˈmɛsɪnɪs

messmate
BR ˈmɛsmeɪt, -s
AM ˈmɛsˌmeɪt, -s

Messrs
BR ˈmɛsəz
AM ˈmɛsərz

messuage
BR ˈmɛswɪdʒ, -ɪdʒɪz
AM ˈmɛswɪdʒ, -ɪz

messy
BR ˈmɛs|i, -ɪə(r), -ɪɪst
AM ˈmɛsi, -ər, -ɪst

mestiza
BR mɛˈstiːzə(r),
mɪˈstiːzə(r), -z
AM məˈstizə, məˈstisə,
-z

mestizo
BR mɛˈstiːzəʊ,
mɪˈstiːzəʊ, -z
AM mɛˈstizoʊ,
məˈstizoʊ, -z

met
BR mɛt
AM mɛt

metabisulfite
BR ˌmɛtəbaɪˈsʌlfʌɪt, -s
AM ˌmɛdəˌbaɪˈsəlˌfaɪt,
-s

metabisulphite
BR ˌmɛtəbaɪˈsʌlfʌɪt, -s
AM ˌmɛdəˌbaɪˈsəlˌfaɪt,
-s

metabolic
BR ˌmɛtəˈbɒlɪk
AM ˌmɛdəˈbɑlɪk

metabolically
BR ˌmɛtəˈbɒlɪkli
AM ˌmɛdəˈbɑlək(ə)li

metabolisable
BR mɪˈtabəlʌɪzəbl,
mɛˈtabəlʌɪzəbl
AM məˈtæbəˌlaɪzəbəl

metabolise
BR mɪˈtabəlʌɪz,
mɛˈtabəlʌɪz, -ɪz, -ɪŋ, -d
AM məˈtæbəˌlaɪz, -ɪz,
-ɪŋ, -d

metabolism
BR mɪˈtabəlɪz(ə)m,
mɛˈtabəlɪz(ə)m
AM məˈtæbəˌlɪzəm

metabolite
BR mɪˈtabəlʌɪt,
mɛˈtabəlʌɪt
AM məˈtæbəˌlaɪt

metabolizable
BR mɪˈtabəlʌɪzəbl,
mɛˈtabəlʌɪzəbl
AM məˈtæbəˌlaɪzəbəl

metabolize
BR mɪˈtabəlʌɪz,
mɛˈtabəlʌɪz, -ɪz, -ɪŋ, -d

AM məˈtæbəˌlaɪz, -ɪz,
-ɪŋ, -d

metacarpal
BR ˌmɛtəˈkɑːpl,
ˈmɛtəˌkɑːpl, -z
AM ˈmɛdəˈkɑrpəl, -z

metacarpus
BR ˌmɛtəˈkɑːpəs,
ˈmɛtəˌkɑːpəs
AM ˈmɛdəˈkɑrpəs

metacenter
BR ˈmɛtəˌsɛntə(r), -z
AM ˈmɛdəˌsɛn(t)ər, -z

metacentre
BR ˈmɛtəˌsɛntə(r), -z
AM ˈmɛdəˌsɛn(t)ər, -z

metacentric
BR ˌmɛtəˈsɛntrɪk
AM ˌmɛdəˈsɛntrɪk

metage
BR ˈmiːt|ɪdʒ, ˈmɛt|ɪdʒ,
-ɪdʒɪz
AM ˈmɛdɪdʒ, -ɪz

metageneses
BR ˌmɛtəˈdʒɛnɪsiːz
AM ˌmɛdəˈdʒɛnəsiz

metagenesis
BR ˌmɛtəˈdʒɛnɪsɪs
AM ˌmɛdəˈdʒɛnəsəs

metagenetic
BR ˌmɛtədʒɪˈnɛtɪk
AM ˈmɛdədʒəˈnɛdɪk

metal
BR ˈmɛt|, -z, -ɪŋ, -d
AM ˈmɛdl, -z, -ɪŋ, -d

metalanguage
BR ˈmɛtəˌlaŋgw|ɪdʒ,
-ɪdʒɪz
AM ˈmɛdəˌlæŋgwɪdʒ,
-ɪz

metalinguistic
BR ˌmɛtəlɪŋˈgwɪstɪk
AM ˌmɛdəˌlɪŋˈgwɪstɪk

metalize
BR ˈmɛtlʌɪz, -ɪz, -ɪŋ, -d
AM ˈmɛdlˌaɪz, -ɪz, -ɪŋ, -d

metallic
BR mɪˈtalɪk
AM məˈtælɪk

metallically
BR mɪˈtalɪkli
AM məˈtælək(ə)li

metalliferous
BR ˌmɛtəˈlɪf(ə)rəs,
ˌmɛtlˈɪf(ə)rəs
AM ˌmɛdlˈɪf(ə)rəs

metalline
BR ˈmɛtəlʌɪn,
ˈmɛtlʌɪn
AM ˈmɛdlən, ˈmɛdlɪn

metallisation
BR ˌmɛtlʌɪˈzeɪʃn
AM ˌmɛdləˈzeɪʃən,
ˌmɛdəˌlaɪˈzeɪʃən

metallise
BR ˈmɛtlʌɪz, -ɪz, -ɪŋ, -d
AM ˈmɛdlˌaɪz, -ɪz, -ɪŋ, -d

metallization
BR ˌmɛtlʌɪˈzeɪʃn
AM ˌmɛdləˈzeɪʃən,
ˌmɛdəˌlaɪˈzeɪʃən

metallize
BR ˈmɛtlʌɪz, -ɪz, -ɪŋ, -d
AM ˈmɛdlˌaɪz, -ɪz, -ɪŋ, -d

metallographic
BR ˌmɛtləˈgrafɪk
AM ˌmɛdləˈgræfɪk

metallographical
BR ˌmɛtləˈgrafɪkl
AM ˌmɛdləˈgræfəkəl

**metallographic-
ally**
BR ˌmɛtləˈgrafɪkli
AM ˌmɛdləˈgræfək(ə)li

metallography
BR ˌmɛtəˈlɒgrəfi,
ˌmɛtlˈɒgrəfi
AM ˌmɛdəˈlɑgrəfi

metalloid
BR ˈmɛtəlɔɪd,
ˈmɛtlˌɔɪd
AM ˈmɛdlˌɔɪd, -z

metallophone
BR ˈmɛtləfəʊn, -z
AM ˈmɛdləˌfoʊn, -z

metallurgic
BR mɛtəˈləːdʒɪk
AM ˈmɛdlˈərdʒɪk

metallurgical
BR ˌmɛtəˈləːdʒɪkl
AM ˈmɛdlˈərdʒəkəl

metallurgically
BR ˌmɛtəˈləːdʒɪkli
AM ˈmɛdlˈərdʒək(ə)li

metallurgist
BR mɪˈtalədʒɪst,
ˈmɛtələːdʒɪst, -s
AM ˈmɛdlˌərdʒəst, -s

metallurgy
BR mɪˈtalədʒi,
ˈmɛtələːdʒi
AM ˈmɛdlˌərdʒi

metalwork
BR ˈmɛtlwəːk
AM ˈmɛdlˌwərk

metalworker
BR ˈmɛtlˌwəːkə(r), -z
AM ˈmɛdlˌwərkər, -z

metalworking
BR ˈmɛtlˌwəːkɪŋ
AM ˈmɛdlˌwərkɪŋ

metamer
BR ˈmɛtəmə(r), -z
AM ˈmɛdəmər, -z

metamere
BR ˈmɛtəmɪə(r), -z
AM ˈmɛdəmɪ(ə)r, -z

metameric
BR ˌmɛtəˈmɛrɪk
AM ˈmɛdəˈmɛrɪk

metamerism
BR mɪˈtamərɪz(ə)m
AM məˈtæməˌrɪzəm

metamorphic
BR ˌmɛtəˈmɔːfɪk
AM ˌmɛdəˈmɔrfɪk

metamorphism
BR ˌmɛtəˈmɔːfɪz(ə)m
AM ˌmɛdəˈmɔrˌfɪzəm

metamorphose
BR ˌmɛtəˈmɔːfəʊz, -ɪz,
-ɪŋ, -d
AM ˌmɛdəˈmɔrˌfoʊz,
-əz, -ɪŋ, -d

metamorphoses
plural of
metamorphosis
BR ˌmɛtəˈmɔːfəsiːz
AM ˌmɛdəˈmɔrfəsiz

metamorphosis
BR ˌmɛtəˈmɔːfəsɪs
AM ˌmɛdəˈmɔrfəsəs

metaphase
BR ˈmɛtəfeɪz, -ɪz
AM ˈmɛdəˌfeɪz, -ɪz

metaphor
BR ˈmɛtəfə(r),
ˈmɛtəfɔː(r), -z
AM ˈmɛdəˌfɔ(ə)r, -z

metaphoric
BR ˌmɛtəˈfɒrɪk
AM ˈmɛdəˈfɔrɪk

metaphorical
BR ˌmɛtəˈfɒrɪkl
AM ˈmɛdəˈfɔrəkəl

metaphorically
BR ˌmɛtəˈfɒrɪkli
AM ˈmɛdəˈfɔrək(ə)li

metaphrase
BR ˈmɛtəfreɪz, -ɪz, -ɪŋ,
-d
AM ˈmɛdəˌfreɪz, -ɪz, -ɪŋ,
-d

metaphrastic
BR ˌmɛtəˈfrastɪk
AM ˈmɛdəˈfræstɪk

metaphysic
BR ˌmɛtəˈfɪzɪk, -s
AM ˈmɛdəˈfɪzɪk, -s

metaphysical
BR ˌmɛtəˈfɪzɪkl
AM ˈmɛdəˈfɪzɪkəl

metaphysically
BR ˌmɛtəˈfɪzɪkli
AM ˈmɛdəˈfɪzɪk(ə)li

metaphysician
BR ˌmɛtəfɪˈzɪʃn, -z
AM ˈmɛdəfəˈzɪʃən, -z

metaphysicise
BR ˌmɛtəˈfɪzɪsʌɪz, -ɪz,
-ɪŋ, -d
AM ˈmɛdəˈfɪzəˌsaɪz, -ɪz,
-ɪŋ, -d

metaphysicize
BR ˌmɛtəˈfɪzɪsʌɪz, -ɪz,
-ɪŋ, -d
AM ˈmɛdəˈfɪzəˌsaɪz, -ɪz,
-ɪŋ, -d

metaplasia
BR ˌmɛtəˈpleɪzɪə(r),
ˌmɛtəˈpleɪʒə(r), -z

AM ˌmɛdəˈpleɪʒ(i)ə,
ˌmɛdəˈpleɪzɪə ,-z
metaplasm
BR ˈmɛtəplaz(ə)m, -z
AM ˈmɛdəˌplæzəm, -z
metaplastic
BR ˌmɛtəˈplastɪk
AM ˌmɛdəˈplæstɪk
metapolitics
BR ˌmɛtəˈpɒlɪtɪks
AM ˈmɛdəˈpɑləˌtɪks
**metapsychologic-
al**
BR ˌmɛtəˌsaɪkəˈlɒdʒɪkl
AM ˈmɛdəˌsaɪkəˈlɑdʒək-
əl
metapsychology
BR ˌmɛtəsaɪˈkɒlədʒi
AM ˈmɛdəˌsaɪˈkɑlədʒi
metastability
BR ˌmɛtəstəˈbɪlɪti
AM ˈmɛdəstəˈbɪlɪdi
metastable
BR ˌmɛtəˈsteɪbl
AM ˈmɛdəˈsteɪbəl
metastases
BR mɪˈtastəsiːz
AM məˈtæstəsiz
metastasis
BR mɪˈtastəsɪs
AM məˈtæstəsəs
metastasise
BR mɪˈtastəsʌɪz, -ɪz,
-ɪŋ, -d
AM məˈtæstəˌsaɪz, -ɪz,
-ɪŋ, -d
metastasize
BR mɪˈtastəsʌɪz, -ɪz,
-ɪŋ, -d
AM məˈtæstəˌsaɪz, -ɪz,
-ɪŋ, -d
metastatic
BR ˌmɛtəˈstatɪk
AM ˈmɛdəˈstædɪk
metatarsal
BR ˌmɛtəˈtɑːsl,
ˈmɛtəˌtɑːsl, -z
AM ˈmɛdəˈtarsəl, -z
metatarsus
BR ˌmɛtəˈtɑːsəs,
ˈmɛtəˌtɑːsəs
AM ˈmɛdəˈtarsəs
metatherian
BR ˌmɛtəˈθɪərɪən, -z
AM ˈmɛdəˈθɪrɪən, -z
metathesis
BR mɪˈtaθɪsɪs
AM məˈtæθəsəs
metathetic
BR ˌmɛtəˈθɛtɪk
AM ˈmɛdəˈθɛdɪk
metathetical
BR ˌmɛtəˈθɛtɪkl
AM ˈmɛdəˈθɛdəkəl
metazoan
BR ˌmɛtəˈzəʊən, -z
AM ˈmɛdəˈzoʊən, -z

Metcalf
BR ˈmɛtkɑːf
AM ˈmɛtkæf
Metcalfe
BR ˈmɛtkɑːf
AM ˈmɛtkæf
mete
BR miːt, -s, -ɪŋ, -ɪd
AM mi|t, -ts, -dɪŋ, -dɪd
metempsychosis
BR ˌmɛtəmsʌɪˈkəʊsɪs
AM ˌmɛdəmˌsaɪˈkoʊsəs,
məˌtɛmsəˈkoʊsəs
metempsychosist
BR ˌmɛtəmsʌɪˈkəʊsɪst,
-s
AM ˌmɛdəmˌsaɪˈkoʊsəst,
məˌtɛmsəˈkoʊsəst, -s
meteor
BR ˈmiːtɪə(r), -z
AM ˈmidiər, -z
meteoric
BR ˌmiːtɪˈɒrɪk
AM ˈmidiˈɔrɪk
meteorically
BR ˌmiːtɪˈɒrɪkli
AM ˈmidiˈɔrək(ə)li
meteorite
BR ˈmiːtɪərʌɪt, -s
AM ˈmidiəˌraɪt, -s
meteoritic
BR ˌmiːtɪəˈrɪtɪk
AM ˈmidiəˈrɪdɪk
meteorograph
BR ˈmiːtɪərəˌɡrɑːf,
ˈmiːtɪərəˌɡraf, -s
AM ˈmidiˈɔrəˌɡræf, -s
meteoroid
BR ˈmiːtɪərɔɪd, -z
AM ˈmidiəˌrɔɪd, -z
meteoroidal
BR ˌmiːtɪəˈrɔɪdl
AM ˈmidiəˈrɔɪdəl
meteorological
BR ˌmiːtɪərəˈlɒdʒɪkl
AM ˈmidiər(ə)ˈlɑdʒəkəl
meteorologically
BR ˌmiːtɪərəˈlɒdʒɪkli
AM ˈmidiər(ə)ˈlɑdʒə-
k(ə)li
meteorologist
BR ˌmiːtɪəˈrɒlədʒɪst, -s
AM ˈmidiəˈrɑlədʒəst, -s
meteorology
BR ˌmiːtɪəˈrɒlədʒi
AM ˈmidiəˈrɑlədʒi
meter
BR ˈmiːt|ə(r), -əz,
-(ə)rɪŋ, -əd
AM ˈmi|dər, -dərz,
-dərɪŋ \-trɪŋ, -dərd
metermaid
BR ˈmiːtəmeɪd, -z
AM ˈmidərˌmeɪd, -z
mete-wand
BR ˈmiːtwɒnd, -z
AM ˈmitˌwɒnd,
ˈmitˌwand, -z

methadone
BR ˈmɛθədəʊn
AM ˈmɛθəˌdoʊn
methamphetamine
BR ˌmɛθəmˈfɛtəmiːn,
ˌmɛθəmˈfɛtəmɪn, -z
AM ˌmɛθəmˈfɛdəmin,
ˌmɛθəmˈfɛdəmən, -z
methanal
BR ˈmɛθənal
AM ˈmɛθəˌnæl
methane
BR ˈmiːθeɪn
AM ˈmɛˌθeɪn
methanoic acid
BR mɛθəˌnəʊɪk ˈasɪd
AM ˌmɛθəˌnoʊɪk ˈæsəd
methanol
BR ˈmɛθənɒl
AM ˈmɛθəˌnɔl,
ˈmɛθəˌnal
Methedrine®
BR ˈmɛθədriːn,
ˈmɛθədrɪn
AM ˈmɛθəˌdrin,
ˈmɛθədrən
metheglin
BR mɪˈθɛɡlɪn,
mɛˈθɛɡlɪn
AM məˈθɛɡlən
methinks
BR mɪˈθɪŋks
AM mɪˈθɪŋks, məˈθɪŋks
methionine
BR mɪˈθʌɪəniːn,
mɪˈθʌɪənɪn
AM məˈθaɪəˌnin,
məˈθaɪənən
metho
BR ˈmɛθəʊ, -z
AM ˈmɛθoʊ, -z
method
BR ˈmɛθəd, -z
AM ˈmɛθəd, -z
methodic
BR mɪˈθɒdɪk
AM məˈθadɪk
methodical
BR mɪˈθɒdɪkl
AM məˈθadəkəl
methodically
BR mɪˈθɒdɪkli
AM məˈθadək(ə)li
methodise
BR ˈmɛθədʌɪz, -ɪz, -ɪŋ,
-d
AM ˈmɛθəˌdaɪz, -ɪz, -ɪŋ,
-d
methodiser
BR ˈmɛθədʌɪzə(r)
AM ˈmɛθəˌdaɪzər
Methodism
BR ˈmɛθədɪz(ə)m
AM ˈmɛθəˌdɪzəm
Methodist
BR ˈmɛθədɪst, -s
AM ˈmɛθədəst, -s

Methodistic
BR ˌmɛθəˈdɪstɪk
AM ˌmɛθəˈdɪstɪk
Methodistical
BR ˌmɛθəˈdɪstɪkl
AM ˌmɛθəˈdɪstəkəl
Methodius
BR mɪˈθəʊdɪəs
AM məˈθoʊdiəs
methodize
BR ˈmɛθədʌɪz, -ɪz, -ɪŋ,
-d
AM ˈmɛθəˌdaɪz, -ɪz, -ɪŋ,
-d
methodizer
BR ˈmɛθədʌɪzə(r), -z
AM ˈmɛθəˌdaɪzər, -z
methodological
BR ˌmɛθədəˈlɒdʒɪkl
AM ˈmɛθədəˈladʒəkəl
methodologically
BR ˌmɛθədəˈlɒdʒɪkli
AM ˈmɛθədəˈladʒək(ə)li
methodologist
BR ˌmɛθəˈdɒlədʒɪst, -s
AM ˌmɛθəˈdalədʒəst, -s
methodology
BR ˌmɛθəˈdɒlədʒ|i, -ɪz
AM ˌmɛθəˈdalədʒi, -z
methotrexate
BR ˌmɛθə(ʊ)ˈtrɛkseɪt,
ˌmiːθə(ʊ)ˈtrɛkseɪt
AM ˌmɛθəˈtrɛkseɪt
methought
BR mɪˈθɔːt
AM mɪˈθɔt, məˈθɔt,
mɪˈθat, məˈθat
meths
BR mɛθs
AM mɛθs
Methuen¹
place in US
BR mɪˈθjuːən
AM məˈθ(j)uən
Methuen²
surname
BR ˈmɛθjʊən
AM ˈmɛθ(j)ʊən
methuselah
BR mɪˈθjuːzələ(r), -z
AM məˈθ(j)uzə(ə)lə,
məˈθ(j)us(ə)lə, -z
methyl¹
non-technical
BR ˈmɛθ(ɪ)l
AM ˈmɛθəl
methyl²
technical
BR ˈmiːθʌɪl, ˈmɛθʌɪl,
ˈmɛθ(ɪ)l
AM ˈmɛθəl
methylate
BR ˈmɛθɪleɪt, -s, -ɪŋ, -ɪd
AM ˈmɛθəˌleɪ|t, -ts, -dɪŋ,
-dɪd
methylated spirit
BR ˌmɛθɪleɪtɪd ˈspɪrɪt,
-s

methylation
AM 'meθə,leɪdɪd
'spɪrɪt, -s
methylation
BR ,meθɪ'leɪʃn, -z
AM ,meθə'leɪʃən, -z
methylene
BR 'meθɪliːn
AM 'meθə,liːn
methylic
BR mɪ'θɪlɪk
AM mə'θɪlɪk
metic
BR 'metɪk, -s
AM 'medɪk, -s
metical
BR 'metɪkl, -z
AM 'medəkəl, -z
meticulous
BR mɪ'tɪkjʊləs
AM mə'tɪkjələs
meticulously
BR mɪ'tɪkjʊləsli
AM mə'tɪkjələsli
meticulousness
BR mɪ'tɪkjʊləsnəs
AM mə'tɪkjələsnəs
métier
BR 'meɪtɪeɪ, 'metɪeɪ, -z
AM mer'tjeɪ, me'tjeɪ,
'meɪ,tjeɪ, 'me,tjeɪ,
'meɪdieɪ, -z
metif
BR meɪ'tiːf, -s
AM meɪ'tif, -s
metis
BR meɪ'tiː(s), 'meɪtiː,
meɪ'tiː(s)\'meɪtiː:\
'meɪtɪz
AM meɪ'tiː|(s), -z\-s
metisse
BR meɪ'tiːs, 'meɪtiːs, -ɪz
AM meɪ'tis, -ɪz
metol
BR 'metɒl, -z
AM 'mi,tɒl, 'mi,tal, -z
Metonic
BR me'tɒnɪk, mɪ'tɒnɪk
AM me'tanɪk
metonym
BR 'metənɪm, -z
AM 'medə,nɪm, -z
metonymic
BR ,metə'nɪmɪk
AM ,medə'nɪmɪk
metonymical
BR ,metə'nɪmɪkl
AM ,medə'nɪmɪkəl
metonymically
BR ,metə'nɪmɪkli
AM ,medə'nɪmɪk(ə)li
metonymy
BR mɪ'tɒnəmi
AM mə'tanəmi
metope
BR 'met|əʊp, 'met|əpi,
-əʊps\-əpɪz
AM 'medoʊpi, -z

metoposcopy
BR ,metə'pɒskəp|i, -ɪz
AM ,medə'paskəpi, -z
metre
BR 'miːtə(r), -z
AM 'midər, -z
metreage
BR 'miːtərɪdʒ,
'miːtrɪdʒ
AM 'midərɪdʒ
metric
BR 'metrɪk
AM 'metrɪk
metrical
BR 'metrɪkl
AM 'metrəkəl
metrically
BR 'metrɪkli
AM 'metrək(ə)li
metricate
BR 'metrɪkeɪt, -s, -ɪŋ,
-ɪd
AM 'metrə,keɪ|t, -ts,
-dɪŋ, -dɪd
metrication
BR ,metrɪ'keɪʃn
AM ,metrə'keɪʃən
metrician
BR me'trɪʃn, mɪ'trɪʃn,
-z
AM me'trɪʃən,
mə'trɪʃən, -z
metricise
BR 'metrɪsʌɪz, -ɪz, -ɪŋ,
-d
AM 'metrə,saɪz, -ɪz, -ɪŋ,
-d
metricize
BR 'metrɪsʌɪz, -ɪz, -ɪŋ,
-d
AM 'metrə,saɪz, -ɪz, -ɪŋ,
-d
metrist
BR 'metrɪst, -s
AM 'metrəst, -s
metritis
BR mɪ'trʌɪtɪs
AM mə'traɪdɪs
metro
BR 'metrəʊ, -z
AM 'metroʊ, -z
metrologic
BR ,metrə'lɒdʒɪk
AM ,metrə'ladʒɪk
metrological
BR ,metrə'lɒdʒɪkl
AM ,metrə'ladʒəkəl
metrology
BR mɪ'trɒlədʒi,
me'trɒlədʒi
AM mə'tralədʒi
metronidazole
BR ,metrə'nʌɪdəzəʊl
AM ,metrə'naɪdəzoʊl
metronome
BR 'metrənəʊm, -z
AM 'metrə,noʊm, -z

metronomic
BR ,metrə'nɒmɪk
AM ,metrə'namɪk
metronymic
BR ,metrə'nɪmɪk, -s
AM ,metrə'nɪmɪk, -s
Metropole
BR 'metrəpəʊl
AM 'metrə,poʊl
metropolis
BR mɪ'trɒpəlɪs,
mɪ'trɒp|ɪs, -ɪz
AM mə'trɑp(ə)ləs,
me'trɑp(ə)ləs, -əz
metropolitan
BR ,metrə'pɒlɪt(ə)n, -z
AM 'metrə'palətn,
'metrə'palədən, -z
metropolitanate
BR ,metrə'pɒlɪtəneɪt,
,metrə'pɒlɪtn̩eɪt, -s
AM 'metrə'palətn̩eɪt,
'metrə'palədə,neɪt, -s
metropolitanism
BR ,metrə'pɒlɪtən-
ɪz(ə)m,
,metrə'pɒlɪtn̩ɪz(ə)m,
-z
AM 'metrə'palətn̩,ɪzəm,
'metrə'palədə,nɪzəm,
-z
metrorrhagia
BR ,miːtrə'reɪdʒɪə(r),
,metrə'reɪdʒɪə(r)
AM ,mitrə'reɪdʒ(i)ə,
,metrə'reɪdʒ(i)ə
Metternich
BR 'metənɪk, 'metənɪx
AM 'medər,nɪk
mettle
BR 'metl, -d
AM 'medəl, -d
mettlesome
BR 'metls(ə)m
AM 'medlsəm
Mettoy®
BR 'metɔɪ
AM 'medɔɪ
Metz
BR mets
AM mets
meu
BR mjuː, -z
AM mju, -z
meunière
BR ,məː'njɛː(r)
AM mən'jɛ(ə)r
Meurig
BR 'mʌɪrɪg
AM 'mɔɪrɪg
Meuse
BR məːz
AM mjuz
mew
BR mjuː, -z, -ɪŋ, -d
AM mju, -z, -ɪŋ, -d
mewl
BR mjuːl, -z, -ɪŋ, -d

Mexborough
BR 'meksb(ə)rə(r)
AM 'meks,bərə,
'meks,bəroʊ
Mexicali
BR ,meksɪ'kali,
,meksɪ'kɑːli
AM ,meksə'kæli
Mexican
BR 'meksɪk(ə)n, -z
AM 'meksəkən, -z
Mexico
BR 'meksɪkəʊ
AM 'meksəkoʊ
Meyer
BR 'mʌɪə(r), 'meɪə(r)
AM 'maɪər, 'meɪər
Meyerbeer
BR 'mʌɪə,bɪə(r)
AM 'meɪərbɪ(ə)r
Meyerhof
BR 'mʌɪəhɒf
AM 'meɪərhɒf,
'meɪərhaf
Meyers
BR 'mʌɪəz, 'meɪəz
AM 'maɪərz, 'meɪərz
Meynell
BR 'meɪnl, 'menl
AM 'meɪnl
Meyrick
BR 'merɪk
AM 'meɪrɪk
mezereon
BR mɪ'zɪərɪən, -z
AM mə'zɪriən,
mə'ziriən, -z
mezuzah
BR mə'zuː:zə(r),
mə'zuzə(r), -z
AM mə'zuzə, -z
mezuzoth
BR mə'zuː:zəʊt
AM mə'zuzoʊθ
mezzanine
BR 'mezəniːn,
'metsəniːn, -z
AM 'mezn̩'jin, -z
mezza voce
BR ,metsə 'vəʊtʃeɪ
AM ,metsə 'voʊ,tʃeɪ
mezzo
BR 'metsəʊ, -z
AM 'metsoʊ, -z
mezzo forte
BR ,metsəʊ 'fɔːteɪ
AM ,metsoʊ 'fɔrteɪ
Mezzogiorno
BR ,metsəʊ'dʒ(ɪ)ɔːnəʊ
AM ,metsoʊ'dʒ(i)ɔrnoʊ
mezzo piano
BR ,metsəʊ 'pjɑːnəʊ,
+ 'pjanəʊ

AM ˌmɛtsoʊ ˈpjɑːnoʊ

mezzorilievo
BR ˌmɛtsəʊriˈliːvəʊ, -z
AM ˌmɛtsoʊrəˈlivoʊ, -z

mezzo soprano
BR ˌmɛtsəʊ
səˈprɑːnəʊ, -z
AM ˌmɛtsoʊ səˈprɑnoʊ,
ˌmɛtsoʊ səˈprænoʊ, -z

mezzotint
BR ˈmɛtsəʊtɪnt,
ˈmɛzəʊtɪnt, -s
AM ˈmɛtsoʊˌtɪnt, -s

mezzotinter
BR ˈmɛtsəʊˌtɪntə(r),
ˈmɛzəʊˌtɪntə(r), -z
AM ˈmɛtsoʊˌtɪn(t)ər, -z

mho
BR məʊ, -z
AM moʊ, -z

Mhz
BR ˈmɛgəhəːts
AM ˈmɛgəˌhɜrts

mi
BR miː
AM mi

Mia
BR ˈmiə(r)
AM ˈmiə

Miami
BR mʌɪˈami
AM maɪˈæmi

miaow
BR miˈaʊ, -z, -ɪŋ, -d
AM miˈaʊ, -z, -ɪŋ, -d

miasma
BR miˈazmə(r),
mʌɪˈazmə(r), -z
AM maɪˈæzmə,
miˈæzmə, -z

miasmal
BR miˈazml, mʌɪˈazml
AM maɪˈæzməl,
miˈæzməl

miasmatic
BR ˌmiəzˈmatɪk,
ˌmʌɪəzˈmatɪk
AM ˌmiəzˈmædɪk,
ˌmaɪəzˈmædɪk

miasmic
BR miˈazmɪk,
mʌɪˈazmɪk
AM maɪˈæzmɪk,
miˈæzmɪk

miasmically
BR miˈazmɪkli,
mʌɪˈazmɪkli
AM maɪˈæzmək(ə)li

miaul
BR miˈɔːl, -z, -ɪŋ, -d
AM miˈaʊl, -z, -ɪŋ, -d

mica
BR ˈmʌɪkə(r)
AM ˈmaɪkə

micaceous
BR mʌɪˈkeɪʃəs
AM maɪˈkeɪʃəs

mica-schist
BR ˈmʌɪkəˌʃɪst, -s
AM ˈmaɪkəˌʃɪst, -s

Micawber
BR mɪˈkɔːbə(r), -z
AM məˈkɔbər,
məˈkɑbər, -z

Micawberish
BR mɪˈkɔːb(ə)rɪʃ
AM məˈkɔbərɪʃ,
məˈkɑbərɪʃ

Micawberism
BR mɪˈkɔːbərɪz(ə)m
AM məˈkɔbəˌrɪzəm,
məˈkɑbəˌrɪzəm

mice
BR mʌɪs
AM maɪs

micelle
BR mɪˈsɛl, mʌɪˈsɛl, -z
AM məˈsɛl, maɪˈsɛl, -z

Michael
BR ˈmʌɪkl
AM ˈmaɪkəl

Michaela
BR mɪˈkeɪlə(r)
AM məˈkeɪlə

Michaelmas
BR ˈmɪklməs
AM ˈmɪkəlməs

Michel
BR mɪˈʃɛl
AM məˈʃɛl

Michelangelo
BR ˌmʌɪklˈan(d)ʒələʊ
AM ˈmɪkəlˈændʒəloʊ,
ˈmaɪkəlˈændʒəloʊ

Micheldever
BR ˈmɪtʃlˌdɛvə(r)
AM ˈmɪtʃlˌdɛvər

Michèle
BR mɪˈʃɛl
AM məˈʃɛl

Michelin®
BR ˈmɪtʃəlɪn, ˈmɪtʃlɪn
AM ˈmɪʃələn

Michelle
BR mɪˈʃɛl
AM məˈʃɛl

Michelmore
BR ˈmɪtʃlmɔː(r)
AM ˈmɪtʃlˌmɔ(ə)r

Michelson
BR ˈmʌɪkls(ə)n
AM ˈmaɪkəlsən

Michener
BR ˈmɪtʃənə(r),
ˈmɪtʃnə(r), ˈmɪʃnə(r)
AM ˈmɪtʃ(ə)nər,
ˈmɪʃnər

Michigan
BR ˈmɪʃɪg(ə)n
AM ˈmɪʃɪgən

Michoacán
BR ˌmɪtʃəʊəˈkɑːn
AM ˌmɪtʃoʊəˈkɑn

mick
BR mɪk, -s
AM mɪk, -s

mickerie
BR ˈmɪk(ə)r|i, -ɪz
AM ˈmɪk(ə)ri, -z

mickery
BR ˈmɪk(ə)r|i, -ɪz
AM ˈmɪk(ə)ri, -z

mickey
BR ˈmɪk|i, -ɪz
AM ˈmɪki, -z

mickey finn
BR ˌmɪki ˈfɪn, -z
AM ˌmɪki ˈfɪn, -z

Mickiewicz
BR ˈmɪ(t)sˈkjɛvɪtʃ
AM ˈmɪkiˌwɪtʃ

mickle
BR ˈmɪkl
AM ˈmɪkəl

Mickleover
BR ˈmɪklˌəʊvə(r)
AM ˈmɪkəlˌoʊvər

Micklethwaite
BR ˈmɪklθweɪt
AM ˈmɪkəlˌθweɪt

Micklewhite
BR ˈmɪklwʌɪt
AM ˈmɪkəlˌwaɪt

micky
BR ˈmɪki
AM ˈmɪki

micro
BR ˈmʌɪkrəʊ, -z
AM ˈmaɪˌkroʊ, -z

microanalyses
plural noun
BR ˌmʌɪkrəʊəˈnalɪsiːz
AM ˌmaɪkroʊəˈnæləsiz

microanalysis
BR ˌmʌɪkrəʊəˈnalɪsɪs
AM ˈmaɪkroʊəˈnæləsəs

microbe
BR ˈmʌɪkrəʊb, -z
AM ˈmaɪˌkroʊb, -z

microbial
BR mʌɪˈkrəʊbiəl
AM maɪˈkroʊbiəl

microbic
BR mʌɪˈkrəʊbɪk
AM maɪˈkroʊbɪk

microbiological
BR ˌmʌɪkrə(ʊ)ˌbʌɪə-
ˈlɒdʒɪkl
AM ˈmaɪkroʊˌbaɪə-
ˈlɑdʒəkəl

microbiologically
BR ˌmʌɪkrə(ʊ)ˌbʌɪə-
ˈlɒdʒɪkli
AM ˈmaɪkroʊˌbaɪə-
ˈlɑdʒək(ə)li

microbiologist
BR ˌmʌɪkrə(ʊ)bʌɪˈɒləd-
ʒɪst, -s
AM ˈmaɪkroʊˌbaɪˈɑləd-
ʒəst, -s

microbiology
BR ˌmʌɪkrə(ʊ)bʌɪˈɒlədʒi
AM ˈmaɪkroʊˌbaɪˈɑlədʒi

microburst
BR ˈmʌɪkrə(ʊ)bəːst, -s
AM ˈmaɪkroʊˌbɜrst, -s

Microcard®
BR ˈmʌɪkrə(ʊ)kɑːd
AM ˈmaɪkroʊˌkɑrd

microcephalic
BR ˌmʌɪkrə(ʊ)sɪˈfalɪk,
ˌmʌɪkrə(ʊ)kɛˈfalɪk
AM ˈmaɪkroʊsəˈfælɪk

microcephalous
BR ˌmʌɪkrə(ʊ)ˈsɛfələs,
ˌmʌɪkrə(ʊ)ˈsɛfləs,
ˌmʌɪkrə(ʊ)ˈkɛfələs,
ˌmʌɪkrə(ʊ)ˈkɛfləs
AM ˈmaɪkroʊˈsɛfələs

microcephaly
BR ˌmʌɪkrə(ʊ)ˈsɛfəli,
ˌmʌɪkrə(ʊ)ˈsɛfli,
ˌmʌɪkrə(ʊ)ˈkɛfəli,
ˌmʌɪkrə(ʊ)ˈkɛfli
AM ˈmaɪkroʊˈsɛfəli

microchip
BR ˈmʌɪkrə(ʊ)tʃɪp, -s
AM ˈmaɪkroʊˌtʃɪp, -s

microcircuit
BR ˈmʌɪkrə(ʊ)ˌsəːkɪt,
-s
AM ˈmaɪkroʊˌsɜrkət, -s

microcircuitry
BR ˈmʌɪkrə(ʊ)ˌsəːkɪtri
AM ˈmaɪkroʊˈsɜrkətri

microclimate
BR ˈmʌɪkrə(ʊ)ˌklʌɪmɪt,
-s
AM ˈmaɪkroʊˌklaɪmɪt,
-s

microclimatic
BR ˌmʌɪkrə(ʊ)klʌɪ-
ˈmatɪk
AM ˈmaɪkroʊˌklaɪ-
ˈmædɪk

microclimatically
BR ˌmʌɪkrə(ʊ)klʌɪ-
ˈmatɪkli
AM ˈmaɪkroʊˌklaɪ-
ˈmædək(ə)li

microcline
BR ˈmʌɪkrə(ʊ)klʌɪn, -z
AM ˈmaɪkroʊˌklaɪn, -z

microcode
BR ˈmʌɪkrə(ʊ)kəʊd, -z
AM ˈmaɪkrəˌkoʊd, -z

microcomputer
BR ˈmʌɪkrə(ʊ)kəm-
ˌpjuːtə(r), -z
AM ˈmaɪkroʊkəm-
ˈpjudər, -z

microcopy
BR ˈmʌɪkrə(ʊ)ˌkɒp|i,
-ɪz, -ɪŋ, -ɪd
AM ˈmaɪkrəˌkɑpi, -z,
-ɪŋ, -d

microcosm
BR 'mʌɪkrə(ʊ)ˌkɒz(ə)m,
-z
AM 'maɪkrəˌkazəm, -z

microcosmic
BR ˌmʌɪkrə(ʊ)'kɒzmɪk
AM ˌmaɪkrə'kazmɪk

microcosmically
BR ˌmʌɪkrə(ʊ)'kɒzmɪk-
li
AM ˌmaɪkrə'kazmək-
(ə)li

microcrystalline
BR ˌmʌɪkrə(ʊ)'krɪstəl-
ʌɪn,
ˌmʌɪkrə(ʊ)'krɪstlʌɪn
AM ˌmaɪkroʊ'krɪstələn,
ˌmaɪkroʊ'krɪstəˌlaɪn

microdot
BR 'mʌɪkrə(ʊ)dɒt, -s
AM 'maɪkrəˌdat, -s

microeconomic
BR ˌmʌɪkrəʊ,i:kə'nɒm-
ɪk,
ˌmʌɪkrəʊˌɛkə'nɒmɪk,
-s
AM ˌmaɪkroʊˌɛkə'nam-
ɪk,
ˌmaɪkroʊˌikə'namɪk,
-s

microelectronic
BR ˌmʌɪkrəʊɪˌlɛk'trɒn-
ɪk,
ˌmʌɪkrəʊˌɛlɛk'trɒnɪk,
ˌmʌɪkrəʊˌɛlɪk'trɒnɪk,
ˌmʌɪkrəʊˌɪlɛk'trɒnɪk,
ˌmʌɪkrəʊˌi:lɛk'trɒnɪk,
-s
AM ˌmaɪkroʊəˌlɛk'tran-
ɪk,
ˌmaɪkroʊiˌlɛk'tranɪk,
-s

microelectronics
BR ˌmʌɪkrəʊɪˌlɛk'trɒn-
ɪks,
ˌmʌɪkrəʊˌɛlɛk'trɒnɪks,
ˌmʌɪkrəʊˌɛlɪk'trɒnɪks,
ˌmʌɪkrəʊˌɪlɛk'trɒnɪks,
ˌmʌɪkrəʊˌi:lɛk'trɒnɪks
AM ˌmaɪkroʊəˌlɛk'tran-
ɪks,
ˌmaɪkroʊiˌlɛk'tranɪks

microfiche
BR 'mʌɪkrə(ʊ)fi:ʃ, -ɪz
AM 'maɪkrəˌfiʃ, -ɪz

microfilm
BR 'mʌɪkrə(ʊ)fɪlm, -z
AM 'maɪkrəˌfɪlm, -z

microfloppy
BR 'mʌɪkrə(ʊ)ˌflɒp|i,
-ɪz
AM 'maɪkrəˌflapi, -z

microform
BR 'mʌɪkrə(ʊ)fɔ:m, -z
AM 'maɪkrəˌfɔ(ə)rm, -z

microgram
BR 'mʌɪkrə(ʊ)gram, -z
AM 'maɪkrəˌgræm, -z

micrograph
BR 'mʌɪkrə(ʊ)grɑ:f,
'mʌɪkrə(ʊ)graf, -s
AM 'maɪkrəˌgræf, -s

microgroove
BR 'mʌɪkrə(ʊ)gru:v, -z
AM 'maɪkrəˌgruv, -z

microinstruction
BR ˌmʌɪkrəʊɪn'strʌkʃn,
-z
AM 'maɪkroʊɪnz'trək-
ʃən,
'maɪkroʊɪn'strəkʃən,
-z

microlight
BR 'mʌɪkrə(ʊ)lʌɪt, -s
AM 'maɪkrəˌlaɪt, -s

microlith
BR 'mʌɪkrə(ʊ)lɪθ, -s
AM 'mʌɪkrəˌlɪθ, -s

microlithic
BR ˌmʌɪkrə(ʊ)'lɪθɪk
AM ˌmɪkrə'lɪθɪk

micromesh
BR 'mʌɪkrə(ʊ)mɛʃ
AM 'maɪkrəˌmɛʃ

micrometer¹
measurement
BR 'mʌɪkrəʊˌmi:tə(r),
-z
AM 'maɪkroʊˌmidər, -z

micrometer²
*measuring
instrument*
BR maɪ'krɒmɪtə(r), -z
AM maɪ'kramədər, -z

micrometre
measurement
BR 'mʌɪkrəʊˌmi:tə(r),
-z
AM 'maɪkroʊˌmidər, -z

micrometry
BR maɪ'krɒmɪtri
AM maɪ'kramətri

**microminiaturis-
ation**
BR ˌmʌɪkrəʊˌmɪnɪtʃ(ə)-
rʌɪ'zeɪʃn, -z
AM ˌmaɪkroʊˌmɪnɪtʃə-
rə'zeɪʃən,
ˌmaɪkroʊˌmɪnɪtʃəˌraɪ-
'zeɪʃən, -z

**microminiaturiz-
ation**
BR ˌmʌɪkrəʊˌmɪnɪtʃ(ə)-
rʌɪ'zeɪʃn, -z
AM ˌmaɪkroʊˌmɪnɪtʃə-
rə'zeɪʃən,
ˌmaɪkroʊˌmɪnɪtʃəˌraɪ-
'zeɪʃən, -z

micron
BR 'mʌɪkrɒn, -z
AM 'maɪˌkrɑn, -z

Micronesia
BR ˌmʌɪkrə(ʊ)'ni:zjə(r),
ˌmʌɪkrə'ni:ʒə(r)
AM ˌmaɪkrə'niʒə,
ˌmaɪkrə'niʃə

Micronesian
BR ˌmʌɪkrə(ʊ)'ni:zj(ə)n,
ˌmʌɪkrə(ʊ)'ni:ʒn, -z
AM ˌmaɪkrə'niʒən,
ˌmaɪkrə'nɪʃən, -z

microorganism
BR ˌmʌɪkrəʊ'ɔ:gən-
ɪz(ə)m,
ˌmʌɪkrəʊ'ɔ:gnɪz(ə)m,
-z
AM ˌmaɪkroʊ'ɔrgə-
ˌnɪzəm, -z

micro-organism
BR ˌmʌɪkrəʊ'ɔ:gən-
ɪz(ə)m,
ˌmʌɪkrəʊ'ɔ:gnɪz(ə)m,
-z
AM ˌmaɪkroʊ'ɔrgə-
ˌnɪzəm, -z

microphone
BR 'mʌɪkrəfəʊn, -z
AM 'maɪkrəˌfoʊn, -z

microphonic
BR ˌmʌɪkrə'fɒnɪk
AM ˌmaɪkrə'fanɪk

microphotograph
BR ˌmʌɪkrəʊ'fəʊtəgrɑ:f,
ˌmʌɪkrəʊ'fəʊtəgraf,
-s
AM ˌmaɪkrə'foʊdəˌgræf,
-s

microphyte
BR 'mʌɪkrə(ʊ)fʌɪt, -s
AM 'maɪkrəˌfaɪt, -s

microprocessor
BR ˌmʌɪkrəʊ'prəʊ-
sɛsə(r), -z
AM ˌmaɪkroʊ'prasəsər,
-z

microprogram
BR 'mʌɪkrə(ʊ)ˌprəʊ-
gram, -z
AM 'maɪkrəˌproʊgrəm,
-z

micropyle
BR 'mʌɪkrə(ʊ)pʌɪl, -z
AM 'maɪkrəˌpaɪl, -z

microscope
BR 'mʌɪkrəskəʊp, -s
AM 'maɪkrəˌskoʊp, -s

microscopic
BR ˌmʌɪkrə'skɒpɪk
AM ˌmaɪkrə'skapɪk

microscopical
BR ˌmʌɪkrə'skɒpɪkl
AM ˌmaɪkrə'skapəkəl

microscopically
BR ˌmʌɪkrə'skɒpɪkli
AM ˌmaɪkrə'skapək-
(ə)li

microscopist
BR maɪ'krɒskəpɪst, -s
AM maɪ'kraskəpəst, -s

microscopy
BR maɪ'krɒskəpi
AM maɪ'kraskəpi

microsecond
BR 'mʌɪkrə(ʊ)ˌsɛknd,
-z
AM 'maɪkroʊˌsɛkənd,
-z

microseism
BR 'mʌɪkrə(ʊ)ˌsʌɪz-
(ə)m, -z
AM 'maɪkroʊˌsaɪzəm,
-z

Microsoft®
BR 'mʌɪkrəsɒft
AM 'maɪkrəˌsɔft,
'maɪkrəˌsaft

microsome
BR 'mʌɪkrəsəʊm, -z
AM 'maɪkrəˌsoʊm, -z

microspore
BR 'mʌɪkrə(ʊ)spɔ:(r),
-z
AM 'maɪkrəˌspɔ(ə)r, -z

microstructure
BR 'mʌɪkrə(ʊ)ˌstrʌktʃə(r),
-z
AM 'maɪkrə'strək(t)ʃər,
-z

microsurgery
BR 'mʌɪkrə(ʊ)ˌsə:dʒ(ə)ri,
ˌmʌɪkrə(ʊ)'sə:dʒ(ə)ri
AM 'maɪkrə'sərdʒ(ə)ri

microsurgical
BR ˌmʌɪkrə(ʊ)'sə:dʒɪkl
AM 'maɪkrə'sərdʒəkəl

microswitch
BR 'mʌɪkrə(ʊ)swɪtʃ,
-ɪz
AM 'maɪkrəˌswɪtʃ, -ɪz

microtechnique
BR 'mʌɪkrə(ʊ)tɛkˌni:k,
-s
AM 'maɪkroʊˌtɛk'nik,
-s

microtome
BR 'mʌɪkrə(ʊ)təʊm, -z
AM 'maɪkrəˌtoʊm, -z

microtone
BR 'mʌɪkrə(ʊ)təʊn, -z
AM 'maɪkrəˌtoʊn, -z

microtubule
BR ˌmʌɪkrəʊˌtju:bju:l,
'mʌɪkrəʊˌtʃu:bju:l, -z
AM 'maɪkrəˌt(j)ubjul,
-z

microwave
BR 'mʌɪkrə(ʊ)weɪv, -z,
-ɪŋ, -d
AM 'maɪkrəˌweɪv, -z,
-ɪŋ, -d

micrurgy
BR 'mʌɪkrə:dʒi
AM maɪ'krərdʒi

micturition
BR ˌmɪktjʊ'rɪʃn,
ˌmɪktʃə'rɪʃn
AM ˌmɪktʃə'rɪʃən

mid
BR mɪd
AM mɪd

midair
BR ˌmɪdˈeː(r)
AM ˈmɪdˈe(ə)r

Midas
BR ˈmaɪdəs
AM ˈmaɪdəs

midbrain
BR ˈmɪdbreɪn, -z
AM ˈmɪdˌbreɪn, -z

midcourse
BR ˌmɪdˈkɔːs
AM ˈmɪdˈkɔ(ə)rs

midday
BR ˌmɪdˈdeɪ
AM ˈmɪdˈdeɪ

midden
BR ˈmɪdn, -z
AM ˈmɪdən, -z

middle
BR ˈmɪdl, -z
AM ˈmɪd(ə)l, -z

middlebrow
BR ˈmɪdlbraʊ, -z
AM ˈmɪdlˌbraʊ, -z

middleman
BR ˈmɪdlman
AM ˈmɪdlˌmæn

middlemen
BR ˈmɪdlmen
AM ˈmɪdlˌmɛn

middle-of-the-road
BR ˌmɪdlə(v)ðəˈrəʊd
AM ˈmɪdələ(v)ðəˈroʊd

Middlesboro
BR ˈmɪdlzb(ə)rə(r)
AM ˈmɪdlzˌbərə, ˈmɪdlzˌbəroʊ

Middlesborough
BR ˈmɪdlzb(ə)rə(r)
AM ˈmɪdlzˌbərə, ˈmɪdlzˌbəroʊ

Middlesbrough
BR ˈmɪdlzbrə(r)
AM ˈmɪdlzb(ə)rə

Middlesex
BR ˈmɪdlsɛks
AM ˈmɪdlˌsɛks

Middleton
BR ˈmɪdlt(ə)n
AM ˈmɪdltən

middleweight
BR ˈmɪdlweɪt, -s
AM ˈmɪdlˌweɪt, -s

Middlewich
BR ˈmɪdlwɪtʃ
AM ˈmɪdlˌwɪtʃ

middling
BR ˈmɪdlɪŋ, ˈmɪdlɪŋ
AM ˈmɪdlɪŋ, ˈmɪdlɪŋ

middlingly
BR ˈmɪdlɪŋli, ˈmɪdlɪŋli
AM ˈmɪdlɪŋli, ˈmɪdlɪŋli

middy
BR ˈmɪdˌi, -ɪz
AM ˈmɪdi, -z

Mideast
BR ˌmɪdˈiːst
AM ˈmɪdˈist

midfield
BR ˌmɪdˈfiːld, ˈmɪdfiːld
AM ˈmɪdˈfild

midfielder
BR ˌmɪdˈfiːldə(r), -z
AM ˈmɪdˈfildər, -z

Midgard
BR ˈmɪdgɑːd
AM ˈmɪdˌgɑrd

midge
BR ˈmɪdʒ, -ɪz
AM ˈmɪdʒ, -ɪz

midget
BR ˈmɪdʒɪt, -s
AM ˈmɪdʒɪt, -s

Midgley
BR ˈmɪdʒli
AM ˈmɪdʒli

midgut
BR ˈmɪdgʌt, -s
AM ˈmɪdˌgət, -s

Midhurst
BR ˈmɪdhəːst
AM ˈmɪd(h)ərst

MIDI
BR ˈmɪdˌi, -ɪz
AM ˈmɪdi, -z

Midi
south of France
BR mɪˈdiː
AM miˈdi

midi
BR ˈmɪdˌi, -ɪz
AM ˈmɪdi, -z

Midian
BR ˈmɪdiən
AM ˈmɪdiən

Midianite
BR ˈmɪdiənʌɪt, -s
AM ˈmɪdiəˌnaɪt, -s

midibus
BR ˈmɪdibʌs, -ɪz
AM ˈmɪdiˌbəs, -əz

midinette
BR ˌmɪdɪˈnɛt, -s
AM ˌmɪdnˈɛt, ˌmɪdiˈnɛt, -s

midiron
BR ˈmɪdˌʌɪən, -z
AM ˈmɪdˌaɪ(ə)rn, -z

midland
BR ˈmɪdlənd, -z
AM ˈmɪdlənd, ˈmidˌlænd, -z

midlander
BR ˈmɪdləndə(r), -z
AM ˈmɪdləndər, ˈmidˌlændər, -z

midline
BR ˈmɪdlʌɪn, -z
AM ˈmɪdˌlaɪn, -z

Midlothian
BR mɪdˈləʊðiən
AM mɪdˈloʊðiən

midmost
BR ˈmɪdməʊst
AM ˈmɪdˌmoʊst

midnight
BR ˈmɪdnʌɪt
AM ˈmɪdˌnaɪt

midpoint
BR ˈmɪdpɔɪnt, -s
AM ˈmɪdˌpɔɪnt, -s

Midrash
BR ˈmɪdraʃ, ˈmɪdrʌʃ
AM ˈmɪˌdrɑʃ

Midrashim
BR mɪˈdrɑʃɪm, ˌmɪdraˈʃɪm, ˌmɪdrʌˈʃɪm
AM mɪˌdrɑˈʃim

midrib
BR ˈmɪdrɪb, -z
AM ˈmɪdˌrɪb, -z

midriff
BR ˈmɪdrɪf, -s
AM ˈmɪˌdrɪf(t), -s

midsection
BR ˈmɪdˌsɛkʃn, -z
AM ˈmɪdˌsɛkʃən, -z

midship
BR ˈmɪdʃɪp, -s
AM ˈmɪdˌʃɪp, -s

midshipman
BR ˈmɪdʃɪpmən
AM ˈmɪdˌʃɪpmən, ˌmɪdˈʃɪpmən

midshipmen
BR ˈmɪdʃɪpmən
AM ˈmɪdˌʃɪpmən, ˌmɪdˈʃɪpmən

midships
BR ˈmɪdʃɪps
AM ˈmɪdˌʃɪps

midst
BR mɪdst
AM mɪdst

midstream
BR ˌmɪdˈstriːm
AM ˈmɪdˈstrim

midsummer
BR ˌmɪdˈsʌmə(r)
AM ˈmɪdˈsəmər

midterm
BR ˌmɪdˈtəːm, -z
AM ˈmɪdˈtərm, -z

midtown
BR ˈmɪdtaʊn
AM ˈmɪdˌtaʊn

Midway
BR ˈmɪdweɪ
AM ˈmɪdˌweɪ

midway
BR ˌmɪdˈweɪ
AM ˈmɪdˈweɪ

midweek
BR ˌmɪdˈwiːk
AM ˈmɪdˈwik

Midwest
BR ˌmɪdˈwɛst
AM ˈmɪdˈwɛst

Midwestern
BR ˌmɪdˈwɛst(ə)n
AM ˌmɪdˈwɛstərn

Midwesterner
BR ˌmɪdˈwɛstənə(r), ˌmɪdˈwɛstnə(r), -z
AM ˌmɪdˈwɛstərnər, -z

midwicket
BR ˌmɪdˈwɪkɪt, -s
AM ˈmɪdˈwɪkɪt, -s

midwife
BR ˈmɪdwʌɪf
AM ˈmɪdˌwaɪf

midwifery
BR ˌmɪdˈwɪf(ə)ri, ˈmɪdwɪf(ə)ri
AM ˌmɪdˈwaɪf(ə)ri

midwinter
BR ˌmɪdˈwɪntə(r)
AM ˌmɪdˈwɪn(t)ər

midwives
BR ˈmɪdwʌɪvz
AM ˈmɪdˌwaɪvz

Miele
BR ˈmiːlə(r)
AM ˈmilə

mielie
BR ˈmiːlˌi, -ɪz
AM ˈmili, -z

mien
BR miːn, -z
AM min, -z

Miesian
BR ˈmiːziən
AM ˈmisiən, ˈmiziən

Mies van der Rohe
BR ˌmiːz van də ˈrəʊə(r)
AM ˌmiz væn dər ˈroʊə, ˈmis +

miff
BR mɪf, -s, -ɪŋ, -t
AM mɪf, -s, -ɪŋ, -t

MI5
BR ˌɛmʌɪˈfʌɪv
AM ˌɛmˌaɪˈfaɪv

MiG
BR mɪg, -z
AM mɪg, -z

might
BR mʌɪt
AM maɪt

mightest
BR ˈmʌɪtɪst
AM ˈmaɪdɪst

might-have-been
BR ˈmʌɪtəvbiːn, -z
AM ˈmaɪdə(v)ˌbɪn, -z

mightily
BR ˈmʌɪtɪli
AM ˈmaɪdɪli

mightiness
BR ˈmʌɪtɪnɪs
AM ˈmaɪdinɪs

mightn't
BR ˈmʌɪtnt

AM ˈmaɪtn(t)

mighty
BR ˈmaɪtǀi, -ɪə(r), -ɪɪst
AM ˈmaɪdi, -ər, -ɪst

migmatite
BR ˈmɪɡmətʌɪt
AM ˈmɪɡməˌtaɪt

mignon
BR ˈmiːnjɒn, ˈmɪnjɒn,
ˌmɪnˈjɒn
AM mɪnˈjɒn, mɪnˈjɑn

mignonette
BR ˌmɪnjəˈnɛt, -s
AM ˌmɪnjəˈnɛt, -s

migraine
BR ˈmiːɡreɪn,
ˈmʌɪɡreɪn, -z
AM ˈmaɪˌɡreɪn, -z

migrainous
BR miːˈɡreɪnəs,
mʌɪˈɡreɪnəs
AM maɪˈɡreɪnəs

migrant
BR ˈmʌɪɡr(ə)nt, -s
AM ˈmaɪɡrənt, -s

migrate
BR mʌɪˈɡreɪt, -s, -ɪŋ, -ɪd
AM ˈmaɪˌɡreɪǀt, -ts, -dɪŋ,
-dɪd

migration
BR mʌɪˈɡreɪʃn, -z
AM maɪˈɡreɪʃən, -z

migrational
BR mʌɪˈɡreɪʃn̩(ə)l,
mʌɪˈɡreɪʃən(ə)l
AM maɪˈɡreɪʃ(ə)nəl

migrator
BR ˈmʌɪɡreɪtə(r),
mʌɪˈɡreɪtə(r), -z
AM ˈmaɪˌɡreɪdər, -z

migratory
BR ˈmʌɪɡrət(ə)ri,
mʌɪˈɡreɪt(ə)ri
AM ˈmaɪɡrəˌtɔri

Miguel
BR mɪˈɡɛl
AM məˈɡ(w)ɛl

mihrab
BR ˈmiːrɑːb, -z
AM ˈmirəb, -z

Mikado
BR mɪˈkɑːdəʊ, -z
AM məˈkɑdoʊ, -z

mike
BR mʌɪk, -s
AM maɪk, -s

Mikhail
BR mɪˈkʌɪl, mɪˈxʌɪl
AM məˈkaɪl
RUS mʲixaˈil

Míkonos
BR ˈmɪkənɒs
AM ˈmɪkəˌnɒs,
ˈmɪkəˌnɑs

mil
BR mɪl, -z
AM mɪl, -z

milady
BR mɪˈleɪdǀi, -ɪz
AM məˈleɪdi, maɪˈleɪdi,
-z

milage
BR ˈmʌɪlǀɪdʒ, -ɪdʒɪz
AM ˈmaɪlɪdʒ, -ɪz

Milan
BR mɪˈlan
AM məˈlan, məˈlæn

Milanese
BR ˌmɪləˈniːz
AM ˌmɪləˈniz

Milburn
BR ˈmɪlbəːn
AM ˈmɪlbərn

milch
BR mɪl(t)ʃ
AM mɪltʃ, mɪlk

mild
BR mʌɪld, -ə(r), -ɪst
AM maɪld, -ər, -ɪst

milden
BR ˈmʌɪldǀn, -nz,
-n̩ɪŋ \-nɪŋ, -nd
AM ˈmaɪldən, -z, -ɪŋ, -d

Mildenhall
BR ˈmɪld(ə)nhɔːl
AM ˈmɪldən,(h)ɔl,
ˈmɪldən,(h)ɑl

mildew
BR ˈmɪldjuː, ˈmɪldʒuː,
-d
AM ˈmɪl,d(j)u, -d

mildewy
BR ˈmɪldjuːi, ˈmɪldʒuːi
AM ˈmɪl,d(j)ui

mildish
BR ˈmʌɪldɪʃ
AM ˈmaɪldɪʃ

mildly
BR ˈmʌɪldli
AM ˈmaɪl(d)li

mildness
BR ˈmʌɪldnɪs
AM ˈmaɪl(d)nɪs

Mildred
BR ˈmɪldrɪd
AM ˈmɪldrɪd

mile
BR mʌɪl, -z
AM maɪl, -z

mileage
BR ˈmʌɪlǀɪdʒ, -ɪdʒɪz
AM ˈmaɪlɪdʒ, -ɪz

mileometer
BR mʌɪˈlɒmɪtə(r), -z
AM maɪˈlɑmədər, -z

milepost
BR ˈmʌɪlpəʊst, -s
AM ˈmaɪl,poʊst, -s

miler
BR ˈmʌɪlə(r), -z
AM ˈmaɪlər, -z

Miles
BR mʌɪlz
AM maɪlz

Milesian
BR mʌɪˈliːzɪən,
mʌɪˈliːʒn, mɪˈliːzɪən,
mɪˈliːʒn, -z
AM məˈliʒən,
maɪˈliʒən, -z

milestone
BR ˈmʌɪlstəʊn, -z
AM ˈmaɪlˌstoʊn, -z

Miletus
BR mʌɪˈliːtəs
AM maɪˈlidəs

milfoil
BR ˈmɪlfɔɪl, -z
AM ˈmɪlˌfɔɪl, -z

Milford Haven
BR ˌmɪlfəd ˈheɪvn
AM ˈmɪlfərd ˈheɪvən

Milhaud
BR ˈmiː(j)əʊ
AM miˈ(j)oʊ
FR milo

miliaria
BR ˌmɪlɪˈɛːrɪə(r)
AM ˌmɪliˈɛriə

miliary
BR ˈmɪliəri
AM ˈmɪli,ɛri

milieu
BR ˈmiːljəː(r),
mɪˈljəː(r), -z
AM mɪˈlju, mɪlˈjə, -z

milieux
BR ˈmiːljəː(r),
ˈmiːljəːz, mɪˈljəː(r),
mɪˈljəːz
AM mɪˈlju, mɪlˈjə

militancy
BR ˈmɪlɪt(ə)nsi
AM ˈmɪlədənsi,
ˈmɪlətnsi

militant
BR ˈmɪlɪt(ə)nt, -s
AM ˈmɪlədənt,
ˈmɪlətnt, -s

militantly
BR ˈmɪlɪt(ə)ntli
AM ˈmɪlədəntli,
ˈmɪlətn(t)li

militaria
BR ˌmɪlɪˈtɛːrɪə(r)
AM ˌmɪləˈtɛriə

militarily
BR ˈmɪlɪt(ə)rɪli,
ˌmɪlɪˈtɛrɪli
AM ˌmɪləˈtɛrəli

militariness
BR ˈmɪlɪt(ə)rɪnɪs
AM ˈmɪləˌtɛrinɪs

militarisation
BR ˌmɪlɪt(ə)rʌɪˈzeɪʃn
AM ˌmɪlədərəˈzeɪʃən,
ˌmɪlədəˌraɪˈzeɪʃən

militarise
BR ˈmɪlɪtərʌɪz, -ɪz, -ɪŋ,
-d
AM ˈmɪlədəˌraɪz, -ɪz,
-ɪŋ, -d

militarism
BR ˈmɪlɪtərɪz(ə)m
AM ˈmɪlədəˌrɪzəm

militarist
BR ˈmɪlɪt(ə)rɪst, -s
AM ˈmɪlədərəst, -s

militaristic
BR ˌmɪlɪtəˈrɪstɪk
AM ˌmɪlədəˈrɪstɪk

militaristically
BR ˌmɪlɪtəˈrɪstɪkli
AM ˌmɪlədəˈrɪstək(ə)li

militarization
BR ˌmɪlɪt(ə)rʌɪˈzeɪʃn
AM ˌmɪlədərəˈzeɪʃən,
ˌmɪlədəˌraɪˈzeɪʃən

militarize
BR ˈmɪlɪtərʌɪz, -ɪz, -ɪŋ,
-d
AM ˈmɪlədəˌraɪz, -ɪz,
-ɪŋ, -d

military
BR ˈmɪlɪt(ə)ri
AM ˈmɪləˌtɛri

militate
BR ˈmɪlɪteɪt, -s, -ɪŋ, -ɪd
AM ˈmɪləˌteɪǀt, -ts, -dɪŋ,
-dɪd

militerist
BR ˈmɪlɪt(ə)rɪst, -s
AM ˈmɪlədərəst, -s

militeristically
BR ˌmɪlɪtəˈrɪstɪkli
AM ˌmɪlədəˈrɪstək(ə)li

militerization
BR ˌmɪlɪt(ə)rʌɪˈzeɪʃn
AM ˌmɪlədərəˈzeɪʃən,
ˌmɪlədərərˈzeɪʃən

militerize
BR ˈmɪlɪtərʌɪz, -ɪz, -ɪŋ,
-d
AM ˈmɪlədəˌraɪz, -ɪz,
-ɪŋ, -d

militia
BR mɪˈlɪʃə(r), -z
AM məˈlɪʃə, -z

militiaman
BR mɪˈlɪʃəmən
AM məˈlɪʃəmən

militiamen
BR mɪˈlɪʃəmən
AM məˈlɪʃəmən

milk
BR mɪlk, -s, -ɪŋ, -t
AM mɪlk, -s, -ɪŋ, -t

milker
BR ˈmɪlkə(r), -z
AM ˈmɪlkər, -z

milkily
BR ˈmɪlkɪli
AM ˈmɪlkɪli

milkiness
BR ˈmɪlkɪnɪs
AM ˈmɪlkɪnɪs

milkmaid
BR ˈmɪlkmeɪd, -z
AM ˈmɪlkˌmeɪd, -z

milkman
BR 'mɪlkmən
AM 'mɪlkˌmæn,
'mɪlkmən

milkmen
BR 'mɪlkmɛn,
'mɪlkmən
AM 'mɪlkˌmɛn,
'mɪlkmən

Milk of Magnesia®
BR ˌmɪlk əv
magˈniːʃə(r),
+ magˈniːʒə(r),
+ magˈniːzɪə(r)
AM ˌmɪlk ə(v)
mægˈniːʒə,
+ mægˈniʃə

milksop
BR 'mɪlksɒp, -s
AM 'mɪlkˌsɑp, -s

milkwort
BR 'mɪlkwɜːt, -s
AM 'mɪlkwɜrt,
'mɪlkwɔ(ə)rt, -s

milky
BR 'mɪlk|i, -ɪə(r), -ɪɪst
AM 'mɪlki, -ər, -ɪst

mill
BR mɪl, -z, -ɪŋ, -d
AM mɪl, -z, -ɪŋ, -d

millable
BR 'mɪləbl
AM 'mɪləbəl

millage
BR 'mɪlɪdʒ
AM 'mɪlɪdʒ

Millais
BR 'mɪleɪ
AM məˈleɪ

Millar
BR 'mɪlə(r)
AM 'mɪlər

Millard
BR 'mɪlɑːd
AM 'mɪlərd

Millay
BR 'mɪleɪ
AM məˈleɪ

Millbank
BR 'mɪlbaŋk
AM 'mɪlˌbæŋk

millboard
BR 'mɪlbɔːd, -z
AM 'mɪlˌbɔ(ə)rd, -z

milldam
BR 'mɪldam, -z
AM 'mɪlˌdæm, -z

millefeuille
BR ˌmiːlˈfɜːj, -z
AM ˌmilˈfɜɪ, -z

millenarian
BR ˌmɪlɪˈnɛːrɪən, -z
AM ˌmɪləˈnɛrɪən, -z

millenarianism
BR ˌmɪlɪˈnɛːrɪənɪz(ə)m
AM ˌmɪləˈnɛrɪəˌnɪzəm

millenarianist
BR ˌmɪlɪˈnɛːrɪənɪst, -s
AM ˌmɪləˈnɛrɪənəst, -s

millenary
BR mɪˈlɛnər|i,
'mɪlɪn(ə)r|i, -ɪz
AM 'mɪləˌnɛri, -z

millenia
BR mɪˈlɛnɪə(r)
AM məˈlɛnɪə

millenium
BR mɪˈlɛnɪəm, -z
AM məˈlɛnɪəm, -z

millennial
BR mɪˈlɛnɪəl
AM məˈlɛnɪəl

millennialist
BR mɪˈlɛnɪəlɪst, -s
AM məˈlɛnɪələst, -s

millennium
BR mɪˈlɛnɪəm, -z
AM məˈlɛnɪəm, -z

millepede
BR 'mɪlɪpiːd, -z
AM 'mɪləˌpid, -z

millepore
BR 'mɪlɪpɔː(r), -z
AM 'mɪləˌpɔ(ə)r, -z

miller
BR 'mɪlə(r), -z
AM 'mɪlər, -z

millesimal
BR mɪˈlɛsɪml
AM məˈlɛsəməl

millesimally
BR mɪˈlɛsɪml̩i,
mɪˈlɛsɪməli
AM məˈlɛsəməli

millet
BR 'mɪlɪt
AM 'mɪlɪt

millhand
BR 'mɪlhand, -z
AM 'mɪlˌ(h)ænd, -z

milliammeter
BR ˌmɪlɪˈamɪtə(r), -z
AM ˌmili'æ(m)ˌmidər, -z

milliampere
BR ˌmɪlɪˈampɛː(r), -z
AM ˌmili'æmpɪ(ə)r, -z

milliard
BR 'mɪlɪɑːd, -z
AM 'mɪliˌjɑrd, -z
'mɪliˌɑrd, -z

millibar
BR 'mɪlɪbɑː(r), -z
AM 'mɪləˌbɑr, -z

Millicent
BR 'mɪlɪs(ə)nt
AM 'mɪləsənt

Millie
BR 'mɪli
AM 'mɪli

Milligan
BR 'mɪlɪg(ə)n
AM 'mɪləgən

milligram
BR 'mɪlɪgram, -z
AM 'mɪləˌgræm, -z

milligramme
BR 'mɪlɪgram, -z
AM 'mɪləˌgræm, -z

Millikan
BR 'mɪlɪk(ə)n
AM 'mɪləkən

milliliter
BR 'mɪlɪˌliːtə(r), -z
AM 'mɪləˌlidər, -z

millilitre
BR 'mɪlɪˌliːtə(r), -z
AM 'mɪləˌlidər, -z

millimeter
BR 'mɪlɪˌmiːtə(r), -z
AM 'mɪləˌmidər, -z

millimetre
BR 'mɪlɪˌmiːtə(r), -z
AM 'mɪləˌmidər, -z

millimicron
BR 'mɪlɪˌmʌɪkrɒn, -z
AM ˌmɪləˈmaɪˌkrɑn, -z

milliner
BR 'mɪlɪnə(r), -z
AM 'mɪlənər, -z

millinery
BR 'mɪlɪn(ə)ri
AM 'mɪləˌnɛri

million
BR 'mɪljən, -z
AM 'mɪljən, -z

millionaire
BR ˌmɪljəˈnɛː(r), -z
AM ˌmɪljəˈnɛ(ə)r,
'mɪljəˌnɛ(ə)r, -z

millionairess
BR ˌmɪljəˈnɛːrɪs,
ˌmɪljəˈnɛːrɛs, -ɪz
AM ˌmɪljəˈnɛrəs, -əz

millionfold
BR 'mɪljənfəʊld
AM 'mɪljənˌfoʊld

millionth
BR 'mɪljənθ, -s
AM 'mɪljənθ, -s

millipede
BR 'mɪlɪpiːd, -z
AM 'mɪləˌpid, -z

millisecond
BR 'mɪlɪˌsɛk(ə)nd, -z
AM 'mɪləˌsɛkənd, -z

millivolt
BR 'mɪlɪvəʊlt,
'mɪlɪvɒlt, -s
AM 'mɪləˌvoʊlt, -s

milliwatt
BR 'mɪlɪwɒt, -s
AM 'mɪliˌwat, -s

millpond
BR 'mɪlpɒnd, -z
AM 'mɪlˌpand, -z

millrace
BR 'mɪlreɪs, -ɪz
AM 'mɪlˌreɪs, -ɪz

Mills
BR mɪlz
AM mɪlz

millstone
BR 'mɪlstəʊn, -z
AM 'mɪlˌstoʊn, -z

millstream
BR 'mɪlstriːm, -z
AM 'mɪlˌstrim, -z

Millwall
BR 'mɪlwɔːl, 'mɪlw(ə)l
AM 'mɪlˌwɔl, 'mɪlˌwɑl

millwheel
BR 'mɪlwiːl, -z
AM 'mɪlˌ(h)wil, -z

millworker
BR 'mɪlˌwɜːkə(r), -z
AM 'mɪlˌwɜrkər, -z

millwright
BR 'mɪlrʌɪt, -s
AM 'mɪlˌraɪt, -s

Milne
BR mɪln
AM mɪln

Milner
BR 'mɪlnə(r)
AM 'mɪlnər

Milngavie
BR mɪlˈgʌɪ
AM mɪlˈgaɪ

milo
BR 'mʌɪləʊ
AM 'maɪloʊ

milometer
BR mʌɪˈlɒmɪtə(r), -z
AM maɪˈlamədər, -z

milord
BR mɪˈlɔːd, -z
AM məˈlɔ(ə)rd,
maɪˈlɔ(ə)rd, -z

Milosz
BR 'miːlɒʃ
AM 'miləʃ, 'milaʃ

milquetoast
BR 'mɪlktəʊst, -s
AM 'mɪlkˌtoʊst, -s

milt
BR mɪlt, -s, -ɪŋ, -ɪd
AM mɪlt, -s, -ɪŋ, -ɪd

milter
BR 'mɪltə(r), -z
AM 'mɪltər, -z

Milton
BR 'mɪlt(ə)n
AM 'mɪltən

Miltonian
BR mɪlˈtəʊnɪən, -z
AM mɪlˈtoʊnɪən, -z

Miltonic
BR mɪlˈtɒnɪk
AM mɪlˈtɑnɪk

Milwaukee
BR mɪlˈwɔːki
AM mɪlˈwaki,
mɪlˈwɔki

Mimas
BR 'mʌɪməs, 'mʌɪmas

AM 'maɪməs, 'mɪməs
mimbar
BR 'mɪmbɑː(r), -z
AM 'mɪm,bɑr, -z
mime
BR mAɪm, -z, -ɪŋ, -d
AM maɪm, -z, -ɪŋ, -d
mimeo
BR 'mɪmɪəʊ, -z, -ɪŋ, -d
AM 'mɪmioʊ, -z, -ɪŋ, -d
mimeograph
BR 'mɪmɪəɡrɑːf,
'mɪmɪəɡraf, -s, -ɪŋ, -t
AM 'mɪmɪə,ɡræf, -s, -ɪŋ, -t
mimer
BR 'mAɪmə(r), -z
AM 'maɪmər, -z
mimesis
BR mɪ'miːsɪs,
mAɪ'miːsɪs
AM mə'misɪs
mimetic
BR mɪ'metɪk,
mAɪ'metɪk
AM mə'medɪk
mimetically
BR mɪ'metɪkli,
mAɪ'metɪkli
AM mə'medək(ə)li
Mimi
BR 'miːmi
AM 'mimi
mimic
BR 'mɪmɪk, -s, -ɪŋ, -t
AM 'mɪmɪk, -s, -ɪŋ, -t
mimicker
BR 'mɪmɪkə(r), -z
AM 'mɪmɪkər, -z
mimicry
BR 'mɪmɪkri
AM 'mɪmɪkri
miminy-piminy
BR ,mɪmɪnɪ'pɪmɪni
AM 'mɪmɪni'pɪmɪni
mimosa
BR mɪ'məʊzə(r),
mɪ'məʊsə(r)
AM mə'moʊsə,
mə'moʊzə
mimulus
BR 'mɪmjʉləs
AM 'mɪmjələs
Min
BR mɪn
AM mɪn
mina
BR 'mAɪnə(r), -z
AM 'maɪnə, -z
minacious
BR mɪ'neɪʃəs
AM mə'neɪʃəs
minacity
BR mɪ'nasɪt|i, -ɪz
AM mə'næsədi, -z
minae
BR 'mAɪniː

AM 'maɪni
Minaean
BR mɪ'niːən, -z
AM mə'niən, -z
minaret
BR ,mɪnə'ret, -s
AM 'mɪnə'ret, -s
minareted
BR ,mɪnə'retɪd
AM 'mɪnə'redəd
minatory
BR 'mɪnət(ə)ri
AM 'mɪnə,tɔri,
'maɪnə,tɔri
minbar
BR 'mɪnbɑː(r), -z
AM 'mɪn,bɑr, -z
mince
BR mɪns, -ɪz, -ɪŋ, -t
AM mɪns, -ɪz, -ɪŋ, -t
mincemeat
BR 'mɪnsmiːt
AM 'mɪns,mit
mincer
BR 'mɪnsə(r), -z
AM 'mɪnsər, -z
Minch
BR mɪn(t)ʃ
AM mɪn(t)ʃ
mincingly
BR 'mɪnsɪŋli
AM 'mɪnsɪŋli
mind
BR mAɪnd, -z, -ɪŋ, -ɪd
AM maɪnd, -z, -ɪŋ, -ɪd
Mindanao
BR ,mɪndə'naʊ
AM ,mɪndə'naoʊ
minder
BR 'mAɪndə(r), -z
AM 'maɪndər, -z
mindful
BR 'mAɪn(d)f(ʉ)l
AM 'maɪn(d)fəl
mindfully
BR 'mAɪn(d)fʉli,
'mAɪn(d)f|i
AM 'maɪn(d)fəli
mindfulness
BR 'mAɪn(d)f(ʉ)lnəs
AM 'maɪn(d)fəlnəs
mindless
BR 'mAɪndlɪs
AM 'maɪn(d)lɪs
mindlessly
BR 'mAɪndlɪsli
AM 'maɪn(d)lɪsli
mindlessness
BR 'mAɪndlɪsnɪs
AM 'maɪn(d)lɪnɪs
mind-numbing
BR 'mAɪn(d),nʌmɪŋ
AM 'maɪn(d),nəmɪŋ
Mindoro
BR 'mɪndɔːrəʊ
AM mɪn'dɔroʊ

mind-read[1]
present tense
BR 'mAɪndriːd, -z, -ɪŋ
AM 'maɪn(d),rid, -z, -ɪŋ
mind-read[2]
past tense
BR 'mAɪndred
AM 'maɪn(d),red
mind-reader
BR 'mAɪnd,riːdə(r), -z
AM 'maɪn(d),ridər, -z
mindset
BR 'mAɪn(d)set, -s
AM 'maɪn(d)set, -s
Mindy
BR 'mɪndi
AM 'mɪndi
mine
BR mAɪn, -z, -ɪŋ, -d
AM maɪn, -z, -ɪŋ, -d
minefield
BR 'mAɪnfiːld, -z
AM 'maɪn,fild, -z
Minehead
BR 'mAɪnhed
AM 'maɪn,(h)ed
minelayer
BR 'mAɪn,leɪə(r), -z
AM 'maɪn,leɪ(ə)r, -z
minelaying
BR 'mAɪn,leɪɪŋ
AM 'maɪn,leɪɪŋ
Minelli
BR mɪ'neli
AM mə'neli
miner
BR 'mAɪnə(r), -z
AM 'maɪnər, -z
mineral
BR 'mɪn(ə)rəl,
'mɪn(ə)r|, -z
AM 'mɪn(ə)rəl, -z
mineralisation
BR ,mɪn(ə)rəlAɪ'zeɪʃn,
,mɪn(ə)r|Aɪ'zeɪʃn
AM ,mɪn(ə)rələ'zeɪʃən,
,mɪn(ə)rə,laɪ'zeɪʃən
mineralise
BR 'mɪn(ə)rəlAɪz,
'mɪn(ə)r|Aɪz, -ɪz, -ɪŋ,
-d
AM 'mɪn(ə)rə,laɪz, -ɪz,
-ɪŋ, -d
mineralization
BR ,mɪn(ə)rəlAɪ'zeɪʃn,
,mɪn(ə)r|Aɪ'zeɪʃn
AM ,mɪn(ə)rələ'zeɪʃən,
,mɪn(ə)rə,laɪ'zeɪʃən
mineralize
BR 'mɪn(ə)rəlAɪz,
'mɪn(ə)r|Aɪz, -ɪz, -ɪŋ,
-d
AM 'mɪn(ə)rə,laɪz, -ɪz,
-ɪŋ, -d
mineralogical
BR ,mɪn(ə)rə'lɒdʒɪkl
AM 'mɪn(ə)rə'lɑdʒəkəl

mineralogist
BR ,mɪnə'ralədʒɪst, -s
AM ,mɪnə'ralədʒəst, -s
mineralogy
BR ,mɪnə'ralədʒi
AM ,mɪnə'ralədʒi
Minerva
BR mɪ'nɜːvə(r)
AM mə'nərvə
minestrone
BR ,mɪnɪ'strəʊni
AM ,mɪnə'strooni
minesweeper
BR 'mAɪn,swiːpə(r), -z
AM 'maɪn,swipər, -z
minesweeping
BR 'mAɪn,swiːpɪŋ
AM 'maɪn,swipɪŋ
minever
BR 'mɪnɪvə(r), -z
AM 'mɪnəvər, -z
mineworker
BR 'mAɪn,wɜːkə(r), -z
AM 'maɪn,wərkər, -z
Ming
BR mɪŋ
AM mɪŋ
mingily
BR 'mɪn(d)ʒɪli
AM 'mɪndʒɪli
mingle
BR 'mɪŋɡl, -lz,
-lɪŋ \-l-lŋ, -ld
AM 'mɪŋɡəl, -əlz,
-(ə)lɪŋ, -əld
mingler
BR 'mɪŋɡlə(r),
'mɪŋɡl|ə(r), -z
AM 'mɪŋɡ(ə)lər, -z
Mingulay
BR 'mɪŋɡʉleɪ
AM 'mɪŋɡə,leɪ
Mingus
BR 'mɪŋɡəs
AM 'mɪŋɡəs
mingy
BR 'mɪn(d)ʒ|i, -ɪə(r),
-ɪɪst
AM 'mɪndʒi, -ər, -ɪst
mini
BR 'mɪn|i, -ɪz
AM 'mɪni, -z
miniate
BR 'mɪnɪeɪt, -s, -ɪŋ, -ɪd
AM 'mɪni,eɪ|t, -ts, -dɪŋ,
-dɪd
miniature
BR 'mɪnɪtʃə(r), -z
AM 'mɪn(i)ə,tʃʊ(ə)r,
'mɪn(i)ətʃər, -z
miniaturisation
BR ,mɪnɪtʃ(ə)rAɪ'zeɪʃn
AM ,mɪn(i)ə,tʃʊrə'zeɪ-
ʃən,
,mɪn(i)ətʃərə'zeɪʃən,
,mɪn(i)ətʃə,raɪ'zeɪʃən

miniaturise
BR ˈmɪnɪtʃərʌɪz, -ɪz, -ɪŋ, -d
AM ˈmɪn(i)ətʃʊˌraɪz, ˈmɪn(i)ətʃəˌraɪz, -ɪz, -ɪŋ, -d

miniaturist
BR ˈmɪnɪtʃ(ə)rɪst, -s
AM ˈmɪn(i)əˌtʃʊrəst, ˈmɪn(i)ətʃərəst, -s

miniaturization
BR ˌmɪnɪtʃ(ə)rʌɪˈzeɪʃn
AM ˌmɪn(i)əˌtʃʊrəˈzeɪʃən, ˌmɪn(i)ətʃərəˈzeɪʃən, ˌmɪn(i)ətʃəˌraɪˈzeɪʃən

miniaturize
BR ˈmɪnɪtʃərʌɪz, -ɪz, -ɪŋ, -d
AM ˈmɪn(i)əˌtʃʊˌraɪz, ˈmɪn(i)ətʃəˌraɪz, -ɪz, -ɪŋ, -d

minibar
BR ˈmɪnɪbɑː(r), -z
AM ˈmɪniˌbɑr, -z

minibike
BR ˈmɪnɪbʌɪk, -s
AM ˈmɪniˌbaɪk, -s

minibus
BR ˈmɪnɪbʌs, -ɪz
AM ˈmɪniˌbəs, -əz

minicab
BR ˈmɪnɪkab, -z
AM ˈmɪniˌkæb, -z

minicam
BR ˈmɪnɪkam, -z
AM ˈmɪniˌkæm, -z

Minicom
BR ˈmɪnɪkɒm, -z
AM ˈmɪniˌkɑm, -z

minicomputer
BR ˈmɪnɪkəmˌpjuːtə(r), -z
AM ˈmɪnɪkəmˌpjudər, -z

minicourse
BR ˈmɪnɪkɔːs, -ɪz
AM ˈmɪniˌkɔ(ə)rs, -ɪz

minidress
BR ˈmɪnɪdrɛs, -ɪz
AM ˈmɪniˌdrɛs, -əz

minify
BR ˈmɪnɪfʌɪ, -z, -ɪŋ, -d
AM ˈmɪnəˌfaɪ, -z, -ɪŋ, -d

minikin
BR ˈmɪnɪkɪn, -z
AM ˈmɪnɪkɪn, -z

minim
BR ˈmɪnɪm, -z
AM ˈmɪnɪm, -z

minima
BR ˈmɪnɪmə(r)
AM ˈmɪnəmə

minimal
BR ˈmɪnɪml
AM ˈmɪnəməl

minimalism
BR ˈmɪnɪmlɪz(ə)m
AM ˈmɪnəməlˌɪzəm

minimalist
BR ˈmɪnɪməmlɪst, -s
AM ˈmɪnəmələst, -s

minimally
BR ˈmɪnɪməli, ˈmɪnɪmli
AM ˈmɪnəməli

minimax
BR ˈmɪnɪmaks
AM ˈminiˌmæks

minimisation
BR ˌmɪnɪmʌɪˈzeɪʃn
AM ˈmɪnəməˈzeɪʃən, ˌmɪnəˌmaɪˈzeɪʃən

minimise
BR ˈmɪnɪmʌɪz, -ɪz, -ɪŋ, -d
AM ˈmɪnəˌmaɪz, -ɪz, -ɪŋ, -d

minimiser
BR ˈmɪnɪmʌɪzə(r), -z
AM ˈmɪnəˌmaɪzər, -z

minimization
BR ˌmɪnɪmʌɪˈzeɪʃn
AM ˈmɪnəməˈzeɪʃən, ˌmɪnəˌmaɪˈzeɪʃən

minimize
BR ˈmɪnɪmʌɪz, -ɪz, -ɪŋ, -d
AM ˈmɪnəˌmaɪz, -ɪz, -ɪŋ, -d

minimizer
BR ˈmɪnɪmʌɪzə(r), -z
AM ˈmɪnəˌmaɪzər, -z

minimum
BR ˈmɪnɪməm, -z
AM ˈmɪnəməm, -z

minion
BR ˈmɪnjən, ˈmɪnɪən, -z
AM ˈmɪnjən, -z

minipill
BR ˈmɪnɪpɪl, -z
AM ˈmɪniˌpɪl, -z

miniscule
BR ˈmɪnɪskjuːl
AM ˈmɪnɪskjul

miniseries
BR ˈmɪnɪˌsɪərɪz
AM ˈmɪniˌsɪrɪz

miniskirt
BR ˈmɪnɪskəːt, -s
AM ˈmɪniˌskərt, -s

minister
BR ˈmɪnɪst|ə(r), -əz, -(ə)rɪŋ, -əd
AM ˈmɪnəst|ər, -ərz, -(ə)rɪŋ, -ərd

ministerial
BR ˌmɪnɪˈstɪərɪəl
AM ˌmɪnəˌstɪriəl, ˌmɪnəˌstɛrɪəl

ministerialist
BR ˌmɪnɪˈstɪərɪəlɪst, -s
AM ˌmɪnəˈstɪriələst, -s

ministerially
BR ˌmɪnɪˈstɪərɪəli
AM ˌmɪnəˈstɪriəli

ministership
BR ˈmɪnɪstəʃɪp, -s
AM ˈmɪnəstərˌʃɪp, -s

ministrable
BR ˈmɪnɪstrəbl
AM ˈmɪnəstrəbəl

ministrant
BR ˈmɪnɪstr(ə)nt, -s
AM ˈmɪnəstrənt, -s

ministration
BR ˌmɪnɪˈstreɪʃn
AM ˌmɪnəˈstreɪʃən

ministrative
BR ˈmɪnɪstrətɪv
AM ˈmɪnəˌstreɪdɪv

ministry
BR ˈmɪnɪstr|i, -ɪz
AM ˈmɪnəstri, -z

minium
BR ˈmɪnɪəm
AM ˈmɪniəm

minivan
BR ˈmɪnɪvan
AM ˈmɪnɪˌvæn

miniver
BR ˈmɪnɪvə(r)
AM ˈmɪnəvər

mink
BR mɪŋk, -s
AM mɪŋk, -s

minke
BR ˈmɪŋk|i, ˈmɪŋk|ə(r), -ɪz\-əz
AM ˈmɪŋki, -z

Minkowski
BR mɪŋˈkɒfski
AM ˈmɪŋkaʊski
RUS mʲinˈkofskʲij

Minna
BR ˈmɪnə(r)
AM ˈmɪnə

Minneapolis
BR ˌmɪnɪˈapəlɪs
AM ˌmɪniˈæpələs

Minnehaha
BR ˌmɪnɪˈhɑːhɑː(r)
AM ˌmɪnɪˈhɑhɑ

Minnelli
BR mɪˈnɛli
AM məˈnɛli

Minnesinger
BR ˈmɪnɪˌsɪŋgə(r), -z
AM ˈmɪnɪˌsɪŋər, ˈmɪnɪˌzɪŋər, -z

Minnesota
BR ˌmɪnɪˈsəʊtə(r)
AM ˌmɪnəˈsoʊdə

Minnesotan
BR ˌmɪnɪˈsəʊt(ə)n, -z
AM ˌmɪnəˈsoʊtn, -z

Minnie
BR ˈmɪni
AM ˈmɪni

minnow
BR ˈmɪnəʊ, -z
AM ˈmɪnoʊ, -z

Minoan
BR mɪˈnəʊən, mʌɪˈnəʊən, -z
AM məˈnoʊn, maɪˈnoʊən, -z

Minogue
BR mɪˈnəʊg
AM məˈnoʊg

Minolta®
BR mɪˈnɒltə(r)
AM məˈnoʊltə

minor
BR ˈmʌɪnə(r), -z
AM ˈmaɪnər, -z

Minorca
BR mɪˈnɔːkə(r)
AM məˈnɔrkə

Minorcan
BR mɪˈnɔːk(ə)n, -z
AM məˈnɔrkən, -z

Minories
BR ˈmɪn(ə)rɪz
AM ˈmɪnərɪz

Minorite
BR ˈmʌɪnərʌɪt, -s
AM ˈmaɪnəˌraɪt, -s

minority
BR mʌɪˈnɒrɪt|i, mɪˈnɒrɪt|i, -ɪz
AM məˈnɔrədi, -z

Minos
BR ˈmʌɪnɒs
AM ˈmaɪnəs, ˈmaɪnɑs, ˈmaɪnɔs

Minotaur
BR ˈmʌɪnətɔː(r)
AM ˈmɪnəˌtɔ(ə)r

minoxidil
BR mɪˈnɒksɪdɪl
AM məˈnɑksəˌdɪl

Minsk
BR mɪnsk
AM mɪnsk

minster
BR ˈmɪnstə(r), -z
AM ˈmɪnstər, -z

minstrel
BR ˈmɪnstr(ə)l, -z
AM ˈmɪnstrəl, -z

minstrelsy
BR ˈmɪnstr(ə)lsi
AM ˈmɪnstrəlsi

mint
BR mɪnt, -s, -ɪŋ, -ɪd
AM mɪnt, -s, -ɪŋ, -ɪd

mintage
BR ˈmɪnt|ɪdʒ, -ɪdʒɪz
AM ˈmɪn(t)ɪdʒ, -ɪz

Minter
BR ˈmɪntə(r)
AM ˈmɪn(t)ər

mintiness
BR ˈmɪntɪnɪs
AM ˈmɪn(t)ɪnɪs

Minto®
BR ˈmɪntəʊ
AM ˈmɪn(t)oʊ

Minton
BR 'mɪnt(ə)n
AM 'mɪn(t)ən, 'mɪntn

minty
BR 'mɪnt|i, -ɪə(r), -ɪst
AM 'mɪn(t)i, -ər, -ɪst

minuend
BR 'mɪnjʊɛnd, -z
AM 'mɪnjə,wɛnd, -z

minuet
BR ,mɪnju'ɛt, -s
AM ,mɪnjə'wɛt, -s

minus
BR 'maɪnəs, -ɪz
AM 'maɪnəs, -ɪz

minuscular
BR mɪ'nʌskjələ(r)
AM mə'nəskjələr

minuscule
BR 'mɪnɪskju:l
AM 'mɪnə,skjul

minute¹
adjective
BR maɪ'nju:t
AM maɪ'n(j)ut

minute²
noun, verb
BR 'mɪn|ɪt, -ɪts, -ɪtɪŋ, -ɪtɪd
AM 'mɪnɪ|t, -ts, -dɪŋ, -dɪd

minutely
BR maɪ'nju:tli
AM maɪ'n(j)utli, mə'n(j)utli

Minuteman
BR 'mɪnɪtman
AM 'mɪnɪt,mæn

Minutemen
BR 'mɪnɪtmɛn
AM 'mɪnɪt,mɛn

minuteness
BR maɪ'nju:tnəs
AM maɪ'n(j)utnəs, mə'n(j)utnəs

minutia
BR maɪ'nju:ʃ(ɪ)ə(r), mɪ'nju:ʃ(ɪ)ə(r)
AM mə'n(j)uʃ(i)ə

minutiae
BR maɪ'nju:ʃɪaɪ, mɪ'nju:ʃɪaɪ, maɪ'nju:ʃii:, mɪ'nju:ʃii:
AM mə'n(j)uʃi,i, mə'n(j)uʃi,aɪ

minx
BR mɪŋks, -ɪz
AM mɪŋks, -ɪz

minxish
BR 'mɪŋksɪʃ
AM 'mɪŋksɪʃ

minxishly
BR 'mɪŋksɪʃli
AM 'mɪŋksɪʃli

Minya Konka
BR ,mɪnjə 'kʌŋkə(r)
AM ,mɪnjə 'kəŋkə

Miocene
BR 'maɪəsi:n
AM 'maɪə,sin

mioses
BR maɪ'əʊsi:z
AM maɪ'oʊsiz

miosis
BR maɪ'əʊsɪs
AM maɪ'oʊsəs

miotic
BR maɪ'ɒtɪk
AM maɪ'ɑdɪk

Miquelon
BR 'mi:kəlɒn
AM 'mikə,lɑn

Mir
BR mɪə(r)
AM mɪ(ə)r

Mira
BR 'maɪrə(r)
AM 'maɪrə

Mirabeau
BR 'mɪrəbəʊ
AM ,mɪrə'boʊ

Mirabel
BR 'mɪrəbɛl
AM 'mɪrə,bɛl

mirabelle
BR 'mɪrəbɛl, -z
AM 'mɪrə,bɛl, -z

miracle
BR 'mɪrɪkl, -z
AM 'mɪrɪkəl, -z

miraculous
BR mɪ'rakjʊləs
AM mə'rækjələs

miraculously
BR mɪ'rakjʊləsli
AM mə'rækjələsli

miraculousness
BR mɪ'rakjʊləsnəs
AM mə'rækjələsnəs

mirador
BR ,mɪrə'dɔ:(r), 'mɪrədɔ:(r), -z
AM ,mɪrə'dɔ(ə)r, -z

mirage
BR 'mɪrɑ:ʒ, -ɪz
AM mə'rɑʒ, -əz

Miranda
BR mɪ'randə(r)
AM mə'rændə

MIRAS
BR 'maɪrəs
AM 'maɪrəs

mire
BR 'maɪ|ə(r), -əz, -(ə)rɪŋ, -əd
AM 'maɪ(ə)r, -z, -ɪŋ, -d

mirepoix
BR ,mɪə'pwɑ:(r)
AM mɪr'pwɑ

Mirfield
BR 'mə:fi:ld
AM 'mər,fild

Miriam
BR 'mɪrɪəm

AM 'mɪriəm

mirid
BR 'mɪrɪd, 'maɪrɪd, -z
AM 'maɪrɪd, 'mɪrɪd, -z

miriness
BR 'maɪərɪnɪs
AM 'maɪrinɪs

mirk
BR mə:k
AM mərk

mirkily
BR 'mə:kɪli
AM 'mərkəli

mirkiness
BR 'mə:kɪnɪs
AM 'mərkinɪs

mirky
BR 'mə:k|i, -ɪə(r), -ɪst
AM 'mərki, -ər, -ɪst

Miró
BR mɪ'rəʊ
AM mɪ'roʊ

Mirren
BR 'mɪrən, 'mɪrn̩
AM 'mɪrən, 'mərən

mirror
BR 'mɪrə(r), -z, -ɪŋ, -d
AM 'mɪrər, -z, -ɪŋ, -d

mirth
BR mə:θ
AM mərθ

mirthful
BR 'mə:θf(ʊ)l
AM 'mərθfəl

mirthfully
BR 'mə:θfəli, 'mə:θfli
AM 'mərθfəli

mirthfulness
BR 'mə:θf(ʊ)lnəs
AM 'mərθfəlnəs

mirthless
BR 'mə:θləs
AM 'mərθləs

mirthlessly
BR 'mə:θləsli
AM 'mərθləsli

mirthlessness
BR 'mə:θləsnəs
AM 'mərθləsnəs

MIRV
BR mə:v, -z, -ɪŋ, -d
AM mərv, -z, -ɪŋ, -d

miry
BR 'maɪ(ə)ri
AM 'maɪri

misaddress
BR ,mɪsə'drɛs, -ɪz, -ɪŋ, -t
AM ,mɪsə'drɛs, -əz, -ɪŋ, -t

misadventure
BR ,mɪsəd'vɛntʃə(r), -z
AM ,mɪsəd'vɛn(t)ʃər, -z

misadvise
BR ,mɪsəd'vʌɪz, -ɪz, -ɪŋ, -d

AM ,mɪsəd'vaɪz, -ɪz, -ɪŋ, -d

misalign
BR ,mɪsə'lʌɪn, -z, -ɪŋ, -d
AM ,mɪsə'lain, -z, -ɪŋ, -d

misalignment
BR ,mɪsə'lʌɪnm(ə)nt, -s
AM ,mɪsə'lainmənt, -s

misalliance
BR ,mɪsə'lʌɪəns, -ɪz
AM ,mɪsə'laɪəns, -əz

misally
BR ,mɪsə'lʌɪ, -z, -ɪŋ, -d
AM ,mɪsə'laɪ, -z, -ɪŋ, -d

misanthrope
BR 'mɪs(ə)nθrəʊp, 'mɪz(ə)nθrəʊp, -s
AM 'mɪsn̩,θroʊp, -s

misanthropic
BR ,mɪs(ə)n'θrɒpɪk, ,mɪz(ə)n'θrɒpɪk
AM 'mɪsn̩'θrɑpɪk

misanthropical
BR ,mɪs(ə)n'θrɒpɪkl, ,mɪz(ə)n'θrɒpɪkl
AM 'mɪsn̩'θrɑpəkəl

misanthropically
BR ,mɪs(ə)n'θrɒpɪkli, ,mɪz(ə)n'θrɒpɪkli
AM 'mɪsn̩'θrɑpək(ə)li

misanthropise
BR mɪ'sanθrəpʌɪz, mɪ'zanθrəpʌɪz, -ɪz, -ɪŋ, -d
AM mə'sænθrə,paɪz, -ɪz, -ɪŋ, -d

misanthropist
BR mɪ'sanθrəpɪst, mɪ'zanθrəpɪst, -s
AM mə'sænθrəpəst, -s

misanthropize
BR mɪ'sanθrəpʌɪz, mɪ'zanθrəpʌɪz, -ɪz, -ɪŋ, -d
AM mə'sænθrə,paɪz, -ɪz, -ɪŋ, -d

misanthropy
BR mɪ'sanθrəpi, mɪ'zanθrəpi
AM mə'sænθrəpi

misapplication
BR ,mɪsaplɪ'keɪʃn, -z
AM ,mɪs,æplə'keɪʃən, -z

misapply
BR ,mɪsə'plʌɪ, -z, -ɪŋ, -d
AM ,mɪsə'plaɪ, -z, -ɪŋ, -d

misapprehend
BR ,mɪsaprɪ'hɛnd, -z, -ɪŋ, -ɪd
AM ,mɪs,æprə'hɛnd, -z, -ɪŋ, -ɪd

misapprehension
BR ,mɪsaprɪ'hɛnʃn, -z
AM ,mɪs,æprə'hɛnʃən, -z

misapprehensive
BR ˌmɪsæprɪˈhensɪv
AM ˌmɪsˌæprəˈhensɪv

misappropriate
BR ˌmɪsəˈprəʊprɪeɪt,
-s, -ɪŋ, -ɪd
AM ˌmɪsəˈprəʊpriˌeɪ|t,
-ts, -dɪŋ, -dɪd

misappropriation
BR ˌmɪsəˌprəʊprɪˈeɪʃn
AM ˌmɪsəˌprəʊpriˈeɪʃən

misbecame
BR ˌmɪsbɪˈkeɪm
AM ˌmɪsbəˈkeɪm,
ˈmɪsbiˈkeɪm

misbecome
BR ˌmɪsbɪˈkʌm, -z, -ɪŋ
AM ˈmɪsbəˈkəm,
ˈmɪsbiˈkəm, -z, -ɪŋ

misbegotten
BR ˌmɪsbɪˈgɒtn
AM ˈmɪsbəˈgɑtn

misbehave
BR ˌmɪsbɪˈheɪv, -z, -ɪŋ,
-d
AM ˈmɪsbəˈheɪv,
ˈmɪsbiˈheɪv, -z, -ɪŋ, -d

misbehaver
BR ˌmɪsbɪˈheɪvə(r), -z
AM ˈmɪsbəˈheɪvər,
ˈmɪsbiˈheɪvər, -z

misbehavior
BR ˌmɪsbɪˈheɪvjə(r)
AM ˈmɪsbəˈheɪvjər,
ˈmɪsbiˈheɪvjər

misbehaviour
BR ˌmɪsbɪˈheɪvjə(r)
AM ˈmɪsbəˈheɪvjər,
ˈmɪsbiˈheɪvjər

misbelief
BR ˌmɪsbɪˈliːf
AM ˈmɪsbəˈlif,
ˈmɪsbiˈlif

miscalculate
BR ˌmɪsˈkælkjəleɪt, -s,
-ɪŋ, -ɪd
AM ˈmɪsˈkælkjəˌleɪ|t,
-ts, -dɪŋ, -dɪd

miscalculation
BR ˌmɪskælkjəˈleɪʃn,
ˌmɪsˌkælkjəˈleɪʃn, -z
AM ˈmɪsˌkælkjəˈleɪʃən,
-z

miscall
BR ˌmɪsˈkɔːl, -z, -ɪŋ, -d
AM ˈmɪsˈkɔl, mɪsˈkɑl, -z,
-ɪŋ, -d

miscarriage
of f(o)etus
BR ˈmɪskar|ɪdʒ, -ɪdʒɪz
AM ˈmɪsˌkerɪdʒ, -ɪz

miscarriage[1]
of foetus/fetus
BR ˈmɪskar|ɪdʒ, -ɪdʒɪz
AM ˈmɪsˌkerɪdʒ, -ɪz

miscarriage[2]

miscarry
BR (ˌ)mɪsˈkar|ɪdʒ,
-ɪdʒɪz
AM məsˈkerɪdʒ,
ˈmɪsˌkerɪdʒ, -ɪz

miscarry
BR (ˌ)mɪsˈkar|i, -ɪz,
-ɪŋ, -ɪd
AM ˈmɪsˈkeri, -z, -ɪŋ, -d

miscast
BR ˌmɪsˈkɑːst,
ˌmɪsˈkast, -s, -ɪŋ
AM ˈmɪsˈkæst, -s, -ɪŋ

miscegenation
BR ˌmɪsɪdʒɪˈneɪʃn,
mɪˌsedʒɪˈneɪʃn
AM məˌsedʒəˈneɪʃən,
ˌmɪsədʒəˈneɪʃən

miscellanea
BR ˌmɪsəˈleɪnɪə(r)
AM ˈmɪsəˈleɪniə,
ˈmɪsəˈleɪnjə

miscellaneous
BR ˌmɪsəˈleɪnɪəs
AM ˈmɪsəˈleɪnɪəs,
ˈmɪsəˈleɪnjəs

miscellaneously
BR ˌmɪsəˈleɪnɪəsli
AM ˈmɪsəˈleɪnɪəsli,
ˈmɪsəˈleɪnjəsli

**miscellaneous-
ness**
BR ˌmɪsəˈleɪnɪəsnəs
AM ˈmɪsəˈleɪnɪəsnəs,
ˈmɪsəˈleɪnjəsnəs

miscellanist
BR mɪˈselənɪst, -s
AM ˈmɪsəˈleɪnɪst,
ˈmɪsəˈleɪnɪst, -s

miscellany
BR mɪˈselən|i, -ɪz
AM ˈmɪsəˌleɪni,
məˈseləni, -z

mischance
BR ˌmɪsˈtʃɑːns,
ˌmɪsˈtʃans, -ɪz
AM mɪsˈtʃæns,
mɪʃˈtʃæns, -əz

mischief
BR ˈmɪstʃɪf
AM ˈmɪstʃɪf

mischiefmaker
BR ˈmɪstʃɪfˌmeɪkə(r),
-z
AM ˈmɪstʃɪfˌmeɪkər, -z

mischievous
BR ˈmɪstʃɪvəs
AM ˈmɪstʃɪvəs,
ˈmɪʃtʃɪvəs

mischievously
BR ˈmɪstʃɪvəsli
AM ˈmɪstʃɪvəsli

mischievousness
BR ˈmɪstʃɪvəsnəs
AM ˈmɪstʃɪvəsnəs

misch metal
BR ˈmɪʃˌmetl, -z
AM ˈmɪʃˌmedl, -z

miscibility
BR ˌmɪsɪˈbɪlɪti
AM ˌmɪsəˈbɪlɪdi

miscible
BR ˈmɪsɪbl
AM ˈmɪsəbəl

**miscommunica-
tion**
BR ˌmɪskəˌmjuːnɪˈkeɪʃn
AM ˌmɪskəˌmjunəˈkeɪ-
ʃən

misconceive
BR ˌmɪskənˈsiːv, -z, -ɪŋ,
-d
AM ˈmɪskənˈsiv, -z, -ɪŋ,
-d

misconceiver
BR ˌmɪskənˈsiːvə(r), -z
AM ˈmɪskənˈsivər, -z

misconception
BR ˌmɪskənˈsepʃn, -z
AM ˈmɪskənˈsepʃən, -z

misconduct[1]
noun
BR ˌmɪsˈkɒndʌkt
AM mɪsˈkandək(t)

misconduct[2]
verb
BR ˌmɪskənˈdʌkt, -s,
-ɪŋ, -ɪd
AM ˌmɪskənˈdək|(t),
-(t)s, -tɪŋ, -təd

misconstruction
BR ˌmɪskənˈstrʌkʃn, -z
AM ˌmɪskənˈstrəkʃən,
-z

misconstrue
BR ˌmɪskənˈstruː, -z,
-ɪŋ, -d
AM ˌmɪskənˈstru, -z,
-ɪŋ, -d

miscopy
BR ˌmɪsˈkɒp|i, -ɪz, -ɪɪŋ,
-ɪd
AM ˌmɪsˈkɑpi, -z, -ɪŋ, -d

miscount[1]
noun
BR ˈmɪskaʊnt, -s
AM ˈmɪsˌkaʊnt, -s

miscount[2]
verb
BR ˌmɪsˈkaʊnt, -s, -ɪŋ,
-ɪd
AM ˌmɪsˈkaʊn|t, -ts,
-(t)ɪŋ, -(t)əd

miscreant
BR ˈmɪskrɪənt, -s
AM ˈmɪskriənt, -s

miscue[1]
noun
BR ˈmɪsˌkjuː, -z
AM ˈmɪsˌkju, -z

miscue[2]
verb
BR ˌmɪsˈkjuː, -z, -ɪŋ, -d
AM ˌmɪsˈkju, -z, -ɪŋ, -d

misdate
BR ˌmɪsˈdeɪt, -s, -ɪŋ, -ɪd

misdeal[1]
noun
BR ˈmɪsdiːl, -z
AM ˈmɪsˌdil, -z

misdeal[2]
verb
BR ˌmɪsˈdiːl, -z, -ɪŋ
AM ˌmɪsˈdil, -z, -ɪŋ

misdealt
BR ˌmɪsˈdelt
AM ˌmɪsˈdelt

misdeclaration
BR ˌmɪsdekləˈreɪʃn, -z
AM ˈmɪsˌdekləˈreɪʃən,
-z

misdeed
BR ˌmɪsˈdiːd, -z
AM ˌmɪsˈdid, -z

misdemeanant
BR ˌmɪsdɪˈmiːnənt, -s
AM ˌmɪsdəˈminənt, -s

misdemeanor
BR ˌmɪsdɪˈmiːnə(r), -z
AM ˌmɪsdəˈminər, -z

misdemeanour
BR ˌmɪsdɪˈmiːnə(r), -z
AM ˌmɪsdəˈminər, -z

misdescribe
BR ˌmɪsdɪˈskrʌɪb, -z,
-ɪŋ, -d
AM ˌmɪsdəˈskraɪb,
ˈmɪsdiˈskraɪb, -z, -ɪŋ,
-d

misdescription
BR ˌmɪsdɪˈskrɪpʃn, -z
AM ˌmɪsdəˈskrɪpʃən, -z
ˈmɪsdiˈskrɪpʃən, -z

misdiagnose
BR ˌmɪsˈdʌɪəgnəʊz,
ˌmɪsdʌɪəgˈnəʊz, -ɪz,
-ɪŋ, -d
AM ˌmɪsˈdaɪəgˈnoʊz,
-əz, -ɪŋ, -d

misdiagnoses
BR ˌmɪsdʌɪəgˈnəʊsiːz
AM ˈmɪsˌdaɪəgˈnoʊsiz

misdiagnosis
BR ˌmɪsdʌɪəgˈnəʊsɪs
AM ˈmɪsˌdaɪəgˈnoʊsəs

misdial
BR ˌmɪsˈdʌɪəl, -z, -ɪŋ, -d
AM ˌmɪsˈdaɪəl, -z, -ɪŋ, -d

misdirect
BR ˌmɪsdʌɪˈrɛkt,
ˌmɪsdɪˈrɛkt, -s, -ɪŋ, -ɪd
AM ˈmɪsdəˈrɛk|(t),
-(t)s, -tɪŋ, -təd

misdirection
BR ˌmɪsdʌɪˈrɛkʃn,
ˌmɪsdɪˈrɛkʃn
AM ˌmɪsdəˈrɛkʃən

misdoing
BR ˌmɪsˈduːɪŋ, -z
AM ˌmɪsˈduɪŋ, -z

misdoubt
BR ˌmɪsˈdaʊt, -s, -ɪŋ, -ɪd

AM ˌmɪsˈdaʊ|t, -ts, -dɪŋ,
-dəd

mise au point
BR ˌmiːz əʊ ˈpwã
AM ˌmiːz oʊ ˈpwɑnt

miseducate
BR ˌmɪsˈɛdjʊkeɪt,
ˌmɪsˈɛdʒʊkeɪt, -s, -ɪŋ,
-ɪd
AM ˌmɪsˈɛdʒəˌkeɪ|t, -ts,
-dɪŋ, -dɪd

miseducation
BR ˌmɪsɛdjʊˈkeɪʃn,
ˌmɪsɛdʒʊˈkeɪʃn
AM ˌmɪsˌɛdʒəˈkeɪʃən

mise en scène
BR ˌmiːz ɒn ˈseɪn, ˌmiːz
ɒn ˈsen
AM ˌmiːz ɑn ˈsen

misemploy
BR ˌmɪsɪmˈplɔɪ,
ˌmɪsɛmˈplɔɪ, -z, -ɪŋ, -d
AM ˌmɪsˌɛmˈplɔɪ, -z, -ɪŋ,
-d

misemployment
BR ˌmɪsɪmˈplɔɪm(ə)nt,
ˌmɪsɛmˈplɔɪm(ə)nt, -s
AM ˌmɪsɛmˈplɔɪmənt,
-s

miser
BR ˈmaɪzə(r), -z
AM ˈmaɪzər, -z

miserable
BR ˈmɪz(ə)rəbl
AM ˈmɪzərbəl,
ˈmɪz(ə)r(ə)bəl

miserableness
BR ˈmɪz(ə)rəblnəs
AM ˈmɪzərbəlnəs,
ˈmɪz(ə)r(ə)bəlnəs

miserably
BR ˈmɪz(ə)rəbli
AM ˈmɪzərbli,
ˈmɪz(ə)rəbli

misère
BR mɪˈzɛː(r), -z
AM məˈzeɪr, -z

miserere
BR ˌmɪzɪˈrɛːr|i,
ˌmɪzəˈrɪər|i, -iz
AM ˌmɪzəˈreri,
ˌmɪzəˈrɪri, -z

misericord
BR mɪˈzɛ(ə)rɪkɔːd, -z
AM ˈmɪzərəˌkɔ(ə)rd,
məˈzɛ(ə)rəˌkɔ(ə)rd, -z

miserliness
BR ˈmaɪzəlɪnɪs
AM ˈmaɪzərlɪnɪs

miserly
BR ˈmaɪzəli
AM ˈmaɪzərli

misery
BR ˈmɪz(ə)ri, -ɪz
AM ˈmɪz(ə)ri, -z

misfeasance
BR ˌmɪsˈfiːz(ə)ns
AM ˌmɪsˈfizns

misfield
BR ˌmɪsˈfiːld, -z, -ɪŋ, -ɪd
AM ˈmɪsˈfild, -z, -ɪŋ, -ɪd

misfire[1]
noun
BR ˈmɪsfʌɪə(r), -z
AM ˈmɪsˌfaɪər, -z

misfire[2]
verb
BR ˌmɪsˈfʌɪə(r), -z, -ɪŋ,
-d
AM ˌmɪsˈfaɪər, -z, -ɪŋ, -d

misfit
BR ˈmɪsfɪt, -s
AM ˈmɪsˌfɪt, -s

misfortune
BR ˌmɪsˈfɔːtʃuːn,
ˌmɪsˈfɔːtʃ(ə)n,
ˌmɪsˈfɔːtjuːn, -z
AM ˌmɪsˈfɔrtʃən, -z

misgave
BR ˌmɪsˈgeɪv, -z
AM ˌmɪsˈgeɪv, -z

misgive
BR ˌmɪsˈgɪv, -z
AM ˌmɪsˈgɪv, -z

misgiven
BR ˌmɪsˈgɪvn, -z
AM ˌmɪsˈgɪvən, -z

misgiving
BR (ˌ)mɪsˈgɪvɪŋ, -z
AM ˌmɪsˈgɪvɪŋ, -z

misgovern
BR ˌmɪsˈgʌvn, -z, -ɪŋ, -d
AM ˌmɪsˈgəvərn, -z, -ɪŋ,
-d

misgovernment
BR ˌmɪsˈgʌvnm(ə)nt,
ˌmɪsˈgʌvəm(ə)nt
AM ˌmɪsˈgəvər(n)mənt,
ˌmɪsˈgəvə(r)mənt

misguidance
BR ˌmɪsˈgʌɪdns
AM ˌmɪsˌgaɪdns

misguide
BR ˌmɪsˈgʌɪd, -z, -ɪŋ, -ɪd
AM ˌmɪsˈgaɪd, -z, -ɪŋ, -ɪd

misguided
BR (ˌ)mɪsˈgʌɪdɪd
AM ˌmɪsˈgaɪdɪd

misguidedly
BR (ˌ)mɪsˈgʌɪdɪdli
AM ˌmɪsˈgaɪdɪdli

misguidedness
BR (ˌ)mɪsˈgʌɪdɪdnɪs
AM ˌmɪsˈgaɪdɪdnɪs

mishandle
BR ˌmɪsˈhand|l, -lz,
-|ɪŋ\-l.ɪŋ, -ld
AM ˌmɪsˈhæn|dəl,
-dəlz, -(d)(ə)lɪŋ, -dəld

mishap
BR ˈmɪshap, -s
AM ˈmɪs.(h)æp, -s

mishear
BR ˌmɪsˈhɪə(r), -z, -ɪŋ
AM ˌmɪsˈhɪ|(ə)r, -(ə)rz,
-rɪŋ

misheard
BR ˌmɪsˈhəːd
AM ˌmɪsˈhərd

mishit
BR ˌmɪsˈhɪt, -s, -ɪŋ
AM ˌmɪsˈhɪ|t, -ts, -dɪŋ

mishmash
BR ˈmɪʃmaʃ
AM ˈmɪʃˌmæʃ,
ˈmɪʃˌmɑʃ

Mishna
BR ˈmɪʃnə(r)
AM ˈmɪʃnə

Mishnah
BR ˈmɪʃnə(r)
AM ˈmɪʃnə

Mishnaic
BR mɪʃˈneɪɪk
AM mɪʃˈneɪɪk

misidentification
BR ˌmɪsʌɪˌdɛntɪfɪˈkeɪʃn,
-z
AM ˈmɪsaɪˌdɛn(t)əfəˈkeɪ-
ʃən, -z

misidentify
BR ˌmɪsʌɪˈdɛntɪfʌɪ, -z,
-ɪŋ, -d
AM ˈmɪsaɪˈdɛn(t)əˌfaɪ,
-z, -ɪŋ, -d

misinform
BR ˌmɪsɪnˈfɔːm, -z, -ɪŋ,
-d
AM ˈmɪsɪnˈfɔ(ə)rm, -z,
-ɪŋ, -d

misinformation
BR ˌmɪsɪnfəˈmeɪʃn
AM ˌmɪsɪnfərˈmeɪʃən

misinterpret
BR ˌmɪsɪnˈtəːprɪt, -s,
-ɪŋ, -ɪd
AM ˌmɪsɪnˈtərprə|t, -ts,
-dɪŋ, -dəd

misinterpretation
BR ˌmɪsɪnˌtəːprɪˈteɪʃn,
-z
AM ˌmɪsɪnˌtərprəˈteɪ-
ʃən, -z

misinterpreter
BR ˌmɪsɪnˈtəːprɪtə(r),
-z
AM ˌmɪsɪnˈtərprədər,
-z

MI6
BR ˌɛmʌɪˈsɪks
AM ˌɛmˌaɪˈsɪks

misjudge
BR ˌmɪsˈdʒʌdʒ, -ɪz, -ɪŋ,
-d
AM ˌmɪsˈdʒədʒ, -əz, -ɪŋ,
-d

misjudgement
BR (ˌ)mɪsˈdʒʌdʒm(ə)nt,
-s
AM ˌmɪsˈdʒədʒmənt, -s

misjudgment
BR (ˌ)mɪsˈdʒʌdʒm(ə)nt,
-s
AM ˌmɪsˈdʒədʒmənt, -s

miskey
BR ˌmɪsˈkiː, -z, -ɪŋ, -d
AM ˌmɪsˈki, -z, -ɪŋ, -d

miskick
BR ˌmɪsˈkɪk, -s, -ɪŋ, -d
AM ˌmɪsˈkɪk, -s, -ɪŋ, -d

Miskin
BR ˈmɪskɪn
AM ˈmɪskɪn

Miskito
BR mɪˈskiːtəʊ, -z
AM məˈskidoʊ,
məˈskiˌtoʊ, -z

mislay
BR (ˌ)mɪsˈleɪ, -z, -ɪŋ, -d
AM ˌmɪsˈleɪ, -z, -ɪŋ, -d

mislead
BR (ˌ)mɪsˈliːd, -z, -ɪŋ
AM ˌmɪsˈlid, -z, -ɪŋ

misleader
BR (ˌ)mɪsˈliːdə(r), -z
AM ˌmɪsˈlidər, -z

misleading
BR (ˌ)mɪsˈliːdɪŋ
AM ˌmɪsˈlidɪŋ

misleadingly
BR (ˌ)mɪsliːdɪŋli
AM ˌmɪsˈlidɪŋli

misleadingness
BR (ˌ)mɪsˈliːdɪŋnɪs
AM ˌmɪsˈlidɪŋnɪs

misled
BR (ˌ)mɪsˈlɛd
AM ˌmɪsˈlɛd

mislike
BR (ˌ)mɪsˈlʌɪk, -s, -ɪŋ, -d
AM ˌmɪsˈlaɪk, -s, -ɪŋ, -d

mismanage
BR ˌmɪsˈman|ɪdʒ,
-ɪdʒɪz, -ɪdʒɪŋ, -ɪdʒd
AM ˌmɪsˈmænɪdʒ, -ɪz,
-ɪŋ, -d

mismanagement
BR ˌmɪsˈmanɪdʒm(ə)nt
AM ˌmɪsˈmænədʒmənt

mismarriage
BR ˌmɪsˈmar|ɪdʒ, -ɪdʒɪz
AM ˌmɪsˈmerɪdʒ, -ɪz

mismatch[1]
noun
BR ˈmɪsmatʃ, -ɪz
AM ˈmɪsˌmætʃ, -əz

mismatch[2]
verb
BR ˌmɪsˈmatʃ, -ɪz, -ɪŋ, -t
AM ˌmɪsˈmætʃ, -əz, -ɪŋ,
-t

mismated
BR ˌmɪsˈmeɪtɪd
AM ˌmɪsˈmeɪdɪd

mismeasure
BR ˌmɪsˈmɛʒə(r), -əz,
-(ə)rɪŋ, -əd
AM ˌmɪsˈmɛʒ|ər, -ərz,
-(ə)rɪŋ, -ərd

mismeasurement
BR ˌmɪsˈmɛʒəm(ə)nt,
-s

AM ˌmɪsˈmeʒəmənt, -s

misname
BR ˌmɪsˈneɪm, -z, -ɪŋ, -d
AM ˌmɪsˈneɪm, -z, -ɪŋ, -d

misnomer
BR ˌmɪsˈnəʊmə(r), -z
AM mɪsˈnoʊmər, -z

misogamist
BR mɪˈsɒgəmɪst,
mʌɪˈsɒgəmɪst,
AM məˈsagəməst, -s

misogamy
BR mɪˈsɒgəmi,
mʌɪˈsɒgəmi
AM məˈsagəmi

misogynist
BR mɪˈsɒdʒɪnɪst,
mʌɪˈsɒdʒɪnɪst, -s
AM məˈsadʒənəst, -s

misogynistic
BR mɪˌsɒdʒɪˈnɪstɪk,
mʌɪˌsɒdʒɪˈnɪstɪk
AM məˌsadʒəˈnɪstɪk

misogynous
BR mɪˈsɒdʒɪnəs,
mʌɪˈsɒdʒɪnəs
AM məˈsadʒənəs

misogyny
BR mɪˈsɒdʒɪni,
mʌɪˈsɒdʒɪni
AM məˈsadʒəni

misologist
BR mɪˈsɒlədʒɪst,
mʌɪˈsɒlədʒɪst, -s
AM məˈsalədʒəst, -s

misology
BR mɪˈsɒlədʒi,
mʌɪˈsɒlədʒi
AM məˈsalədʒi

misoneism
BR ˌmɪsə(ʊ)ˈniːɪz(ə)m, -z
AM ˌmɪsəˈniˌɪzəm, -z

misoneist
BR ˌmɪsə(ʊ)ˈniːɪst, -s
AM ˌmɪsəˈniɪst, -s

mispickel
BR ˈmɪsˌpɪkl, -z
AM ˈmɪsˌpɪkəl, -z

misplace
BR ˌmɪsˈpleɪs, -ɪz, -ɪŋ, -t
AM ˌmɪsˈpleɪs, -ɪz, -ɪŋ, -t

misplacement
BR ˌmɪsˈpleɪsm(ə)nt
AM ˌmɪsˈpleɪsmənt

misplay[1]
noun
BR ˈmɪspleɪ, -z, -ɪŋ, -d
AM ˈmɪsˌpleɪ, -z, -ɪŋ, -d

misplay[2]
verb
BR ˌmɪsˈpleɪ, -z, -ɪŋ, -d
AM ˌmɪsˈpleɪ, -z, -ɪŋ, -d

misprint[1]
noun
BR ˈmɪsprɪnt, -s
AM ˈmɪsˌprɪnt, -s

misprint[2]
verb
BR ˌmɪsˈprɪnt, -s, -ɪŋ, -ɪd
AM ˈmɪsˈprɪn|t, -ts, -(t)ɪŋ, -(t)ɪd

misprision
BR ˌmɪsˈprɪʒn
AM ˌmɪsˈprɪʒən

misprize
BR ˌmɪsˈprʌɪz, -ɪz, -ɪŋ, -d
AM ˌmɪsˈpraɪz, -ɪz, -ɪŋ, -d

mispronounce
BR ˌmɪsprəˈnaʊns, -ɪz, -ɪŋ, -t
AM ˌmɪsprəˈnaʊns, -əz, -ɪŋ, -t

mispronunciation
BR ˌmɪsprəˌnʌnsiˈeɪʃn, -z
AM ˌmɪsprəˌnənsiˈeɪʃən, -z

misquotation
BR ˌmɪskwə(ʊ)ˈteɪʃn, -z
AM ˌmɪskwoʊˈteɪʃən, -z

misquote
BR ˌmɪsˈkwəʊt, -s, -ɪŋ, -ɪd
AM ˌmɪsˈkwoʊ|t, -ts, -dɪŋ, -dəd

misread[1]
present tense
BR ˌmɪsˈriːd, -z, -ɪŋ
AM ˌmɪsˈrid, -z, -ɪŋ

misread[2]
past tense
BR ˌmɪsˈrɛd
AM ˌmɪsˈrɛd

misremember
BR ˌmɪsrɪˈmɛmb|ə(r), -əz, -(ə)rɪŋ, -əd
AM ˌmɪsrəˈmɛmb|ər, ˈmɪsriˈmɛmb|ər, -ərz, -(ə)rɪŋ, -ərd

misreport
BR ˌmɪsrɪˈpɔːt, -s, -ɪŋ, -ɪd
AM ˈmɪsrəˈpɔ(ə)rt, -ts, -ˈpɔrdɪŋ, -ˈpɔrdəd

misrepresent
BR ˌmɪsrɛprɪˈzɛnt, -s, -ɪŋ, -ɪd
AM ˌmɪsˈrɛprəˈzɛn|t, -ts, -(t)ɪŋ, -(t)əd

misrepresentation
BR ˌmɪsˌrɛprɪzɛnˈteɪʃn, mɪsˌrɛprɪzɛnˈteɪʃən, -z
AM ˈmɪsˌrɛprəˌzɛnˈteɪʃən, -z

misrepresentative
BR ˌmɪsrɛprɪˈzɛntətɪv
AM ˈmɪsˌrɛprəˈzɛn(t)ədɪv

misrule
BR ˌmɪsˈruːl, -z, -ɪŋ, -d
AM ˌmɪsˈrul, -z, -ɪŋ, -d

miss
BR mɪs, -ɪz, -ɪŋ, -t
AM mɪs, -ɪz, -ɪŋ, -t

missable
BR ˈmɪsəbl
AM ˈmɪsəbəl

missal
BR ˈmɪsl, -z
AM ˈmɪsəl, -z

missel thrush
BR ˈmɪsl θrʌʃ, ˈmɪzl +, -ɪz
AM ˈmɪsəl ˌθrəʃ, -əz

Missenden
BR ˈmɪsndən
AM ˈmɪsəndən

misshape[1]
noun
BR ˈmɪsˌʃeɪp, ˈmɪʃʃeɪp, -s
AM ˈmɪsˌʃeɪp, ˈmɪʃʃeɪp, -s

misshape[2]
verb
BR ˌmɪsˈʃeɪp, ˌmɪʃˈʃeɪp, -s, -ɪŋ, -t
AM ˌmɪsˈʃeɪp, ˌmɪʃˈʃeɪp, -s, -ɪŋ, -t

misshapen
BR ˌmɪsˈʃeɪp(ə)n, ˌmɪʃˈʃeɪp(ə)n
AM ˌmɪsˈʃeɪpən, ˌmɪʃˈʃeɪpən

misshapenly
BR ˌmɪsˈʃeɪp(ə)nli, ˌmɪʃˈʃeɪp(ə)nli
AM ˌmɪsˈʃeɪpənli, ˌmɪʃˈʃeɪpənli

misshapenness
BR ˌmɪsˈʃeɪp(ə)nnəs, ˌmɪʃˈʃeɪp(ə)nnəs
AM ˌmɪsˈʃeɪpə(n)nəs, ˌmɪʃˈʃeɪpə(n)nəs

missile
BR ˈmɪsʌɪl, -z
AM ˈmɪsəl, -z

missilery
BR ˈmɪsʌɪlri
AM ˈmɪsəlri

mission
BR ˈmɪʃn, -z
AM ˈmɪʃən, -z

missionary
BR ˈmɪʃn(ə)r|i, -ɪz
AM ˈmɪʃəˌnɛri, -z

missioner
BR ˈmɪʃ(ə)nə(r), ˈmɪʃnə(r), -z
AM ˈmɪʃənər, -z

missis
BR ˈmɪsɪz
AM ˈmɪsɪz

missish
BR ˈmɪsɪʃ
AM ˈmɪsɪʃ

Mississauga
BR ˌmɪsɪˈsɔːgə(r)
AM ˌmɪsɪˈsɔgə, ˌmɪsɪˈsagə

Mississippi
BR ˌmɪsɪˈsɪpi
AM ˌmɪsɪˈsɪpi

Mississippian
BR ˌmɪsɪˈsɪpiən, -z
AM ˌmɪsɪˈsɪpiən, -z

missive
BR ˈmɪsɪv, -z
AM ˈmɪsɪv, -z

Missolonghi
BR ˌmɪsəˈlɒŋi
AM ˌmɪsəˈlɒŋi, ˌmɪsəˈlaŋi

Missouri
BR mɪˈzʊəri
AM məˈzʊri, məˈzʊrə

Missourian
BR mɪˈzʊəriən, -z
AM məˈzʊriən, -z

misspell
BR ˌmɪsˈspɛl, -z, -ɪŋ, -t
AM ˌmɪ(s)ˈspɛl, -z, -ɪŋ, -t

misspelling
BR ˌmɪsˈspɛlɪŋ, -z
AM ˌmɪ(s)ˈspɛlɪŋ, -z

misspend
BR ˌmɪsˈspɛnd, -z, -ɪŋ
AM ˌmɪ(s)ˈspɛnd, -z, -ɪŋ

misspent
BR ˌmɪsˈspɛnt
AM ˌmɪ(s)ˈspɛnt

misstate
BR ˌmɪsˈsteɪt, -s, -ɪŋ, -ɪd
AM ˌmɪ(s)ˈsteɪ|t, -ts, -dɪŋ, -dɪd

misstatement
BR ˌmɪ(s)ˈsteɪtm(ə)nt, -s
AM ˌmɪ(s)ˈsteɪtmənt, -s

misstep
BR ˌmɪsˈstɛp, -s, -ɪŋ, -t
AM ˌmɪ(s)ˈstɛp, -s, -ɪŋ, -t

missus
BR ˈmɪsɪz
AM ˈmɪsɪz

missy
BR ˈmɪs|i, -ɪz
AM ˈmɪsi, -z

mist
BR mɪst, -s, -ɪŋ, -ɪd
AM mɪst, -s, -ɪŋ, -ɪd

mistakable
BR mɪˈsteɪkəbl
AM məˈsteɪkəbəl

mistakably
BR mɪˈsteɪkəbli
AM məˈsteɪkəbli

mistake
BR mɪˈsteɪk, -s, -ɪŋ
AM məˈsteɪk, -s, -ɪŋ

mistaken
BR mɪˈsteɪk(ə)n
AM məˈsteɪkən

mistakenly
BR mɪ'steɪk(ə)nli
AM mə'steɪkənli

mistakenness
BR mɪ'steɪk(ə)nnəs
AM mə'steɪkə(n)nəs

mistaught
BR ˌmɪs'tɔːt
AM ˌmɪs'tɔt, ˌmɪs'tɑt

misteach
BR ˌmɪs'tiːtʃ, -z
AM ˌmɪs'titʃ, -z

misteaching
BR ˌmɪs'tiːtʃɪŋ, -z
AM ˌmɪs'titʃɪŋ, -z

mister
BR 'mɪstə(r), -z
AM 'mɪstər, -z

mistful
BR 'mɪstf(ʊ)l
AM 'mɪst(f)əl

mistigris
BR 'mɪstɪgrɪs
AM 'mɪstɪˌgrɪs

mistily
BR 'mɪstɪli
AM 'mɪstɪli

mistime
BR ˌmɪs'tʌɪm, -z, -ɪŋ, -d
AM ˌmɪs'taɪm, -z, -ɪŋ, -d

mistiness
BR 'mɪstɪnɪs
AM 'mɪstɪnɪs

mistitle
BR ˌmɪs'tʌɪt|l, -lz,
-|ɪŋ\-lɪŋ, -ld
AM ˌmɪs'taɪdəl, -z, -ɪŋ,
-d

mistle thrush
BR 'mɪsl θrʌʃ, 'mɪzl +,
-ɪz
AM 'mɪsəl ˌθrəʃ, -əz

mistletoe
BR 'mɪsltəʊ, 'mɪzltəʊ
AM 'mɪsəlˌtoʊ

mistlike
BR 'mɪstlʌɪk
AM 'mɪs(t)ˌlaɪk

mistook
BR mɪ'stʊk
AM mə'stʊk

mistral
BR 'mɪstr(ə)l,
mɪ'strɑːl
AM 'mɪstrəl, mə'strɑl

mistranslate
BR ˌmɪstrans'leɪt,
ˌmɪstrɑːns'leɪt,
ˌmɪstranz'leɪt,
ˌmɪstrɑːnz'leɪt, -s, -ɪŋ,
-ɪd
AM ˌmɪsˈtrænz'leɪ|t,
ˌmɪsˈtræns'leɪ|t, -ts,
-dɪŋ, -dɪd

mistranslation
BR ˌmɪstrans'leɪʃn,
ˌmɪstrɑːns'leɪʃn,

ˌmɪstranz'leɪʃn,
ˌmɪstrɑːnz'leɪʃn, -z
AM ˌmɪsˌtrænz'leɪʃən,
ˌmɪsˌtræns'leɪʃən, -z

mistreat
BR ˌmɪs'triːt, -s, -ɪŋ, -ɪd
AM ˌmɪs'tri|t, -ts, -dɪŋ,
-dɪd

mistreatment
BR ˌmɪs'triːtm(ə)nt
AM ˌmɪs'tritmənt

mistress
BR 'mɪstrɪs, -ɪz
AM 'mɪstrɪs, -ɪz

mistrial
BR ˌmɪs'trʌɪəl,
'mɪsˌtrʌɪəl, -z
AM ˌmɪs'traɪəl, -z

mistrust
BR ˌmɪs'trʌst, -s, -ɪŋ, -ɪd
AM ˌmɪs'trəst, -s, -ɪŋ, -ɪd

mistrustful
BR ˌmɪs'trʌs(t)f(ʊ)l
AM ˌmɪs'trəs(t)fəl

mistrustfully
BR ˌmɪs'trʌs(t)fʊli,
ˌmɪs'trʌs(t)fli
AM ˌmɪs'trəs(t)fəli

mistrustfulness
BR ˌmɪs'trʌstf(ʊ)lnəs
AM ˌmɪs'trəs(t)fəlnəs

misty
BR 'mɪst|i, -ɪə(r), -ɪɪst
AM 'mɪsti, -ər, -ɪst

mistype
BR ˌmɪs'tʌɪp, -s, -ɪŋ, -t
AM ˌmɪs'taɪp, -s, -ɪŋ, -t

misunderstand
BR ˌmɪsʌndə'stand, -z,
-ɪŋ
AM ˌmɪsˌəndər'stænd,
-z, -ɪŋ

misunderstanding
BR ˌmɪsʌndə'standɪŋ,
-z
AM ˌmɪsˌəndər'stændɪŋ,
-z

misunderstood
BR ˌmɪsʌndə'stʊd
AM ˌmɪsˌəndər'stʊd

misusage
BR ˌmɪs'juːs|ɪdʒ, -ɪdʒɪz
AM ˌmɪs'jusɪdʒ, -ɪz

misuse¹
noun
BR ˌmɪs'juːs
AM ˌmɪs'jus

misuse²
verb
BR ˌmɪs'juːz, -ɪz, -ɪŋ, -d
AM ˌmɪs'juz, -əz, -ɪŋ, -d

misuser
BR ˌmɪs'juːzə(r), -z
AM ˌmɪs'juzər, -z

Mitanni
BR mɪ'tani
AM mə'tæni

Mitannian
BR mɪ'taniən, -z
AM mə'tæniən,
mə'tænjən, -z

Mitch
BR mɪtʃ
AM mɪtʃ

Mitcham
BR 'mɪtʃ(ə)m
AM 'mɪtʃəm

Mitchell
BR 'mɪtʃ(ə)l
AM 'mɪtʃəl

Mitchum
BR 'mɪtʃ(ə)m
AM 'mɪtʃəm

mite
BR mʌɪt, -s
AM maɪt, -s

miter
BR 'mʌɪtə(r), -z
AM 'maɪdər, -z

Mitford
BR 'mɪtfəd
AM 'mɪtfərd

Mithraic
BR mɪ'θreɪk
AM mə'θreɪk

Mithraism
BR 'mɪθreɪɪz(ə)m,
'mɪθrə-ɪz(ə)m
AM 'mɪθreɪˌɪzəm

Mithraist
BR 'mɪθreɪɪst,
'mɪθrə-ɪst, -s
AM 'mɪθreɪɪst, -s

Mithras
BR 'mɪθras
AM 'mɪθras

Mithridates
BR ˌmɪθrɪ'deɪtiːz
AM ˌmɪθrə'deɪdiz

mithridatic
BR ˌmɪθrɪ'datɪk
AM ˌmɪθrə'deɪdɪk

mithridatise
BR 'mɪθrɪˌdeɪtʌɪz,
mɪ'θrɪdətʌɪz, -ɪz, -ɪŋ,
-d
AM ˌmɪθrə'deɪdaɪz, -ɪz,
-ɪŋ, -d

mithridatism
BR 'mɪθrɪdeɪtɪz(ə)m,
mɪ'θrɪdətɪz(ə)m
AM ˌmɪθrə'deɪˌtɪzəm

mithridatize
BR 'mɪθrɪˌdeɪtʌɪz,
mɪ'θrɪdətʌɪz, -ɪz, -ɪŋ,
-d
AM ˌmɪθrə'deɪdaɪz, -ɪz,
-ɪŋ, -d

mitigable
BR 'mɪtɪgəbl
AM 'mɪdəgəbəl

mitigate
BR 'mɪtɪgeɪt, -s, -ɪŋ, -ɪd
AM 'mɪdəˌgeɪ|t, -ts,
-dɪŋ, -dɪd

mitigation
BR ˌmɪtɪ'geɪʃn
AM ˌmɪdə'geɪʃən

mitigator
BR 'mɪtɪgeɪtə(r), -z
AM 'mɪdəˌgeɪdər, -z

mitigatory
BR 'mɪtɪgeɪt(ə)ri
AM 'mɪdəgəˌtɔri

Mitilini
BR ˌmiːtɪ'liːni
AM ˌmɪdɪ'lini

Mitla
BR 'mɪtlə(r)
AM 'mɪtlə

mitochondria
BR ˌmʌɪtə(ʊ)'kɒndrɪə(r)
AM ˌmaɪdə'kandriə

mitochondrion
BR ˌmʌɪtə(ʊ)'kɒndrɪən
AM ˌmaɪdə'kandriən

mitosis
BR mʌɪ'təʊsɪs
AM maɪ'toʊsəs

mitotic
BR mʌɪ'tɒtɪk
AM maɪ'tadɪk

mitrailleuse
BR ˌmɪtrʌɪ'əːz, -ɪz
AM 'mitrə'jəz, -əz

mitral
BR 'mʌɪtr(ə)l
AM 'maɪtrəl

mitre
BR 'mʌɪtə(r), -z, -d
AM 'maɪdər, -z, -d

Mitsubishi®
BR ˌmɪtsə'bɪʃi
AM ˌmɪtsʊ'biʃi

mitt
BR mɪt, -s
AM mɪt, -s

mitten
BR mɪtn, -z, -d
AM mɪtn, -z, -d

Mitterrand
BR 'mɪtərɒ̃
AM 'mɪtəran(d)

mittimus
BR 'mɪtɪməs, -ɪz
AM 'mɪdəməs, -əz

Mitty
BR 'mɪt|i, -ɪz
AM 'mɪdi, -z

mity
BR 'mʌɪti
AM 'maɪdi

Mitylene
BR ˌmɪtɪ'liːni,
ˌmɪtl'iːni
AM ˌmɪdɪ'lini

Mitzi
BR 'mɪtsi
AM 'mɪtsi

mitzvah
BR 'mɪtsvə(r)
AM 'mɪtsvə

mitzvoth
BR ˈmɪtsvəʊt
AM ˌmɪtsˈvoʊt

mix
BR mɪks, -ɪz, -ɪŋ, -t
AM mɪks, -ɪz, -ɪŋ, -t

mixable
BR ˈmɪksəbl
AM ˈmɪksəbəl

mixedness
BR ˈmɪksɪdnɪs
AM ˈmɪksɪdnɪs

mixer
BR ˈmɪksə(r), -z
AM ˈmɪksər, -z

Mixtec
BR ˈmiːstɛk, -s
AM ˈmiˌstɛk, -s

mixture
BR ˈmɪkstʃə(r), -z
AM ˈmɪk(st)ʃər, -z

mizen
BR ˈmɪzn, -z
AM ˈmɪzən, -z

mizenmast
BR ˈmɪznmɑːst,
ˈmɪznmast,
ˈmɪznməst, -s
AM ˈmɪzənˌmæst,
ˈmɪzənməst, -s

mizen-sail
BR ˈmɪznseɪl, ˈmɪznsl,
-z
AM ˈmɪzənˌseɪl,
ˈmɪzənsəl, -z

Mizoram
BR mɪˈzɔːrəm
AM məˈzɔrəm

mizuna
BR mɪˈzuːnə(r)
AM məˈzunə

mizzen
BR ˈmɪzn, -z
AM ˈmɪzən, -z

mizzenmast
BR ˈmɪznmɑːst,
ˈmɪznmast,
ˈmɪznməst, -s
AM ˈmɪzənˌmæst,
ˈmɪznməst, -s

mizzle
BR ˈmɪz|l, -lz, -lɪŋ\-lɪŋ,
-ld
AM ˈmɪz|əl, -əlz, -(ə)lɪŋ,
-əld

mizzly
BR ˈmɪzli
AM ˈmɪzli

M.Litt.
BR ˌɛm ˈlɪt, -s
AM ˌɛm ˈlɪt, -s

Mlle
Mademoiselle
BR ˌmadəm(w)əˈzɛl,
ˌmam(wə)ˈzɛl, -z
AM ˌmæd(ə)m(w)əˈzɛl,
-z

m'lud
BR məˈlʌd, ˈmlʌd
AM ˈmləd

Mme
Madame
BR məˈdɑːm, ˈmadəm,
-z
AM məˈdam, ˈmædəm,
-z

M.Mus.
Master of Music
BR ˌɛm ˈmʌz, -ɪz
AM ˌɛm ˈmjuz, -əz

mnemonic
BR nɪˈmɒnɪk,
niːˈmɒnɪk, -s
AM nəˈmanɪk, -s

mnemonically
BR nɪˈmɒnɪkli,
niːˈmɒnɪkli
AM nəˈmanək(ə)li

mnemonist
BR nɪˈmɒnɪst,
ˈniːmɒnɪst, -s
AM nəˈmanəst, -s

Mnemosyne
BR nɪˈmɒzɪni,
niːˈmɒzɪni,
nɪˈmɒsɪni, niːˈmɒsɪni
AM nəˈmasəni,
nəˈmazəni

MO
BR ˌɛmˈəʊ, -z
AM ˌɛmˈoʊ, -z

mo
BR məʊ
AM moʊ

moa
BR ˈməʊə(r), -z
AM ˈmoʊə, -z

Moab
BR ˈməʊab
AM ˈmoʊæb

Moabite
BR ˈməʊəbʌɪt, -s
AM ˈmoʊəˌbaɪt, -s

moan
BR məʊn, -z, -ɪŋ, -d
AM moʊn, -z, -ɪŋ, -d

moaner
BR ˈməʊnə(r), -z
AM ˈmoʊnər, -z

moanful
BR ˈməʊnf(ʊ)l
AM ˈmoʊnfəl

moaningly
BR ˈməʊnɪŋli
AM ˈmoʊnɪŋli

moat
BR məʊt, -s, -ɪd
AM moʊ|t, -ts, -dəd

mob
BR mɒb, -z, -ɪŋ, -d
AM mab, -z, -ɪŋ, -d

mobber
BR ˈmɒbə(r), -z
AM ˈmabər, -z

Mobberley
BR ˈmɒbəli
AM ˈmabərli

mobbish
BR ˈmɒbɪʃ
AM ˈmabɪʃ

Moberly
BR ˈməʊbəli
AM ˈmoʊbərli

Mobil®
BR ˈməʊb(ɪ)l
AM ˈmoʊbəl

Mobile
place in US
BR məʊˈbiːl
AM moʊˈbil

mobile
noun
BR ˈməʊbʌɪl, -z
AM ˈmoʊˌbil, -z

mobiliary
BR məʊˈbɪliəri
AM moʊˈbɪliˌɛri,
moʊˈbɪljəri

mobilisable
BR ˈməʊbɪlʌɪzəbl,
ˈməʊblʌɪzəbl
AM ˈmoʊbəˌlaɪzəbəl

mobilisation
BR ˌməʊbɪlʌɪˈzeɪʃn,
ˌməʊblʌɪˈzeɪʃn, -z
AM ˌmoʊbələˈzeɪʃən,
ˌmoʊbəˌlaɪˈzeɪʃən, -z

mobilise
BR ˈməʊbɪlʌɪz,
ˈməʊblʌɪz, -ɪz, -ɪŋ, -d
AM ˈmoʊbəˌlaɪz, -ɪz, -ɪŋ,
-d

mobiliser
BR ˈməʊbɪlʌɪzə(r),
ˈməʊblʌɪzə(r), -z
AM ˈmoʊbəˌlaɪzər, -z

mobility
BR məʊ(ʊ)ˈbɪlɪti
AM moʊˈbɪlɪdi

mobilizable
BR ˈməʊbɪlʌɪzəbl,
ˈməʊblʌɪzəbl
AM ˈmoʊbəˌlaɪzəbəl

mobilization
BR ˌməʊbɪlʌɪˈzeɪʃn,
ˌməʊblʌɪˈzeɪʃn, -z
AM ˌmoʊbələˈzeɪʃən,
ˌmoʊbəˌlaɪˈzeɪʃən, -z

mobilize
BR ˈməʊbɪlʌɪz,
ˈməʊblʌɪz, -ɪz, -ɪŋ, -d
AM ˈmoʊbəˌlaɪz, -ɪz, -ɪŋ,
-d

mobilizer
BR ˈməʊbɪlʌɪzə(r),
ˈməʊblʌɪzə(r), -z
AM ˈmoʊbəˌlaɪzər, -z

Möbius strip
BR ˈməːbɪəs ˌstrɪp,
ˈməʊbɪəs +
AM ˈmoʊbiəs ˌstrɪp,
ˈmibiəs +

mobocracy
BR mɒbˈɒkrəs|i, -ɪz
AM mɑˈbakrəsi, -z

mobster
BR ˈmɒbstə(r), -z
AM ˈmabstər, -z

Mobutu
BR məˈbuːtu:
AM məˈbudu

Moby Dick
BR ˌməʊbi ˈdɪk
AM ˌmoʊbi ˈdɪk

Mocatta
BR mə(ʊ)ˈkatə(r)
AM moʊˈkadə

moccasin
BR ˈmɒkəsɪn, -z
AM ˈmakəsən, -z

mocha
BR ˈmɒkə(r)
AM ˈmoʊkə

Mochica
BR mə(ʊ)ˈtʃiːkə(r)
AM moʊˈtʃikə

mock
BR mɒk, -s, -ɪŋ, -t
AM mak, -s, -ɪŋ, -t

mockable
BR ˈmɒkəbl
AM ˈmakəbəl

mocker
BR ˈmɒkə(r), -z
AM ˈmakər, -z

mockery
BR ˈmɒk(ə)r|i, -ɪz
AM ˈmak(ə)ri, -z

mockingbird
BR ˈmɒkɪŋbəːd, -z
AM ˈmakɪŋˌbərd, -z

mockingly
BR ˈmɒkɪŋli
AM ˈmakɪŋli

mod
BR mɒd, -z
AM mad, -z

modal
BR ˈməʊdl
AM ˈmoʊdəl

modality
BR mə(ʊ)ˈdalɪti
AM moʊˈdælədi

modally
BR ˈməʊdli, ˈməʊdəli
AM ˈmoʊdli

mod cons
modern conveniences
BR ˌmɒd ˈkɒnz
AM ˌmad ˈkɑnz

mode
BR məʊd, -z
AM moʊd, -z

model
BR ˈmɒd|l, -lz, -lɪŋ\-lɪŋ,
-ld
AM ˈmadəl, -əlz, -(ə)lɪŋ,
-əld

modeler
BR ˈmɒdlə(r), -z
AM ˈmɑd(ə)lər, -z

modeller
BR ˈmɒdlə(r), -z
AM ˈmɑd(ə)lər, -z

modem
BR ˈməʊdɛm, -z
AM ˈmoʊdəm,
ˈmoʊˌdɛm, -z

Modena
BR ˈmɒdɪnə(r),
ˈmɒdnə(r)
AM ˈmoʊdənə

moderate[1]
noun, adjective
BR ˈmɒd(ə)rət, -s
AM ˈmɑd(ə)rət, -s

moderate[2]
verb
BR ˈmɒdəreɪt, -s, -ɪŋ, -ɪd
AM ˈmɑdəˌreɪ|t, -ts,
-dɪŋ, -dɪd

moderately
BR ˈmɒd(ə)rətli
AM ˈmɑd(ə)rətli

moderateness
BR ˈmɒd(ə)rətnəs
AM ˈmɑd(ə)rətnəs

moderation
BR ˌmɒdəˈreɪʃn, -z
AM ˌmɑdəˈreɪʃən, -z

moderatism
BR ˈmɒd(ə)rətɪz(ə)m
AM ˈmɑd(ə)rəˌtɪzəm

moderato
BR ˌmɒdəˈrɑːtəʊ, -z
AM ˌmɑdəˈrɑdoʊ, -z

moderator
BR ˈmɒdəreɪtə(r), -z
AM ˈmɑdəˌreɪdər, -z

moderatorship
BR ˈmɒdəreɪtəʃɪp, -s
AM ˈmɑdəˌreɪdərˌʃɪp,
-s

modern
BR ˈmɒdn, -z
AM ˈmɑdərn, -z

modernisation
BR ˌmɒdənʌɪˈzeɪʃn,
ˌmɒdṇʌɪˈzeɪʃn, -z
AM ˌmɑdərnəˈzeɪʃən,
ˌmɑdərˌnaɪˈzeɪʃən, -z

modernise
BR ˈmɒdənʌɪz,
ˈmɒdṇʌɪz, -ɪz, -ɪŋ, -d
AM ˈmɑdərˌnaɪz, -ɪz,
-ɪŋ, -d

moderniser
BR ˈmɒdənʌɪzə(r),
ˈmɒdṇʌɪzə(r), -z
AM ˈmɑdərˌnaɪzər, -z

modernism
BR ˈmɒdnɪz(ə)m,
ˈmɒdənɪz(ə)m
AM ˈmɑdərnˌɪzəm

modernist
BR ˈmɒdənɪst,
ˈmɒdnɪst, -s
AM ˈmɑdərnəst, -s

modernistic
BR ˌmɒdəˈnɪstɪk,
ˌmɒdnˈɪstɪk
AM ˌmɑdərˈnɪstɪk

modernistically
BR ˌmɒdəˈnɪstɪkli,
ˌmɒdṇˈɪstɪkli
AM ˌmɑdərˈnɪstək(ə)li

modernity
BR məˈdəːnɪti
AM mɑˈdərnədi,
məˈdərnədi,
mɑˈdɛrnədi,
məˈdɛrnədi

modernization
BR ˌmɒdənʌɪˈzeɪʃn,
ˌmɒdṇʌɪˈzeɪʃn, -z
AM ˌmɑdərnəˈzeɪʃən,
ˌmɑdərˌnaɪˈzeɪʃən, -z

modernize
BR ˈmɒdənʌɪz,
ˈmɒdṇʌɪz, -ɪz, -ɪŋ, -d
AM ˈmɑdərˌnaɪz, -ɪz,
-ɪŋ, -d

modernizer
BR ˈmɒdənʌɪzə(r),
ˈmɒdṇʌɪzə(r), -z
AM ˈmɑdərˌnaɪzər, -z

modernly
BR ˈmɒdnli
AM ˈmɑdərnli

modernness
BR ˈmɒdṇnəs
AM ˈmɑdər(n)nəs

modest
BR ˈmɒdɪst
AM ˈmɑdəst

Modestine
BR ˈmɒdɪstiːn,
ˌmɒdɪˈstiːn
AM ˈmɑdəˌstin

modestly
BR ˈmɒdɪstli
AM ˈmɑdəs(t)li

Modesto
BR mɒˈdɛstəʊ
AM məˈdɛstoʊ

modesty
BR ˈmɒdɪsti
AM ˈmɑdəsti

modicum
BR ˈmɒdɪkəm, -z
AM ˈmɑdəkəm, -z

modifiable
BR ˈmɒdɪfʌɪəbl
AM ˈmɑdəˈfaɪəbəl

modification
BR ˌmɒdɪfɪˈkeɪʃn, -z
AM ˌmɑdəfəˈkeɪʃən, -z

modificatory
BR ˈmɒdɪfrˈkeɪt(ə)ri
AM ˌmɑdəfəkəˌtɔri,
ˌmɑdəˈfɪkəˌtɔri

modifier
BR ˈmɒdɪfʌɪə(r), -z
AM ˈmɑdəˌfaɪər, -z

modify
BR ˈmɒdɪfʌɪ, -z, -ɪŋ, -d
AM ˈmɑdəˌfaɪ, -z, -ɪŋ, -d

Modigliani
BR ˌmɒdɪlˈjɑːni
AM ˌmɒdɪlˈjɑni,
ˌmɑdɪlˈjɑni

modillion
BR məˈ(ʊ)dɪljən, -z
AM moʊˈdɪljən, -z

modi operandi
BR ˌməʊdiː
ˌɒpəˈrandiː, ˌməʊdʌɪ
ˌɒpəˈrandʌɪ
AM ˈmoʊˌdi
ˌɑpəˈrændi, ˈmoʊˌdaɪ
ˌɑpəˈrænˌdaɪ

modish
BR ˈməʊdɪʃ
AM ˈmoʊdɪʃ, ˈmɑdɪʃ

modishly
BR ˈməʊdɪʃli
AM ˈmoʊdɪʃli, ˈmɑdɪʃli

modishness
BR ˈməʊdɪʃnɪs
AM ˈmoʊdɪʃnɪs,
ˈmɑdɪʃnɪs

modiste
BR məʊˈdiːst, -s
AM moʊˈdist, -s

modi vivendi
BR ˌməʊdiː vɪˈvɛndiː,
ˌməʊdʌɪ vɪˈvɛndʌɪ
AM ˈmoʊˌdi vəˈvɛndi,
ˈmoʊˌdaɪ vəˈvɛnˌdaɪ

Mods
BR mɒdz
AM mɑdz

modular
BR ˈmɒdjʊlə(r),
ˈmɒdʒʊlə(r)
AM ˈmɑdʒələr

modularisation
BR ˌmɒdjʊlərʌɪˈzeɪʃn,
ˌmɒdʒʊlərʌɪˈzeɪʃn
AM ˌmɑdʒələrəˈzeɪʃən,
ˌmɑdʒələˌraɪˈzeɪʃən

modularise
BR ˈmɒdjʊlərʌɪz,
ˈmɒdʒʊlərʌɪz, -ɪz, -ɪŋ,
-d
AM ˈmɑdʒələˌraɪz, -ɪz,
-ɪŋ, -d

modularity
BR ˌmɒdjʊˈlarɪti,
ˌmɒdʒʊˈlarɪti
AM ˌmɑdʒəˈlɛrədi

modularization
BR ˌmɒdjʊlərʌɪˈzeɪʃn,
ˌmɒdʒʊlərʌɪˈzeɪʃn
AM ˌmɑdʒələrəˈzeɪʃən,
ˌmɑdʒələˌraɪˈzeɪʃən

modularize
BR ˈmɒdjʊlərʌɪz,
ˈmɒdʒʊlərʌɪz, -ɪz, -ɪŋ,
-d
AM ˈmɑdʒələˌraɪz, -ɪz,
-ɪŋ, -d

modulate
BR ˈmɒdjʊleɪt,
ˈmɒdʒʊleɪt, -s, -ɪŋ, -ɪd
AM ˈmɑdʒəˌleɪ|t, -ts,
-dɪŋ, -dɪd

modulation
BR ˌmɒdjʊˈleɪʃn,
ˌmɒdʒʊˈleɪʃn, -z
AM ˌmɑdʒəˈleɪʃən, -z

modulator
BR ˈmɒdjʊleɪtə(r),
ˈmɒdʒʊleɪtə(r), -z
AM ˈmɑdʒəˌleɪdər, -z

module
BR ˈmɒdjuːl, ˈmɒdʒuːl,
-z
AM ˈmɑdʒul, -z

moduli
BR ˈmɒdjʊlʌɪ,
ˈmɒdʒʊlʌɪ, ˈmɒdʒʊliː,
ˈmɒdʒʊliː
AM ˈmɑdʒəˌlaɪ

modulo
BR ˈmɒdjʊləʊ,
ˈmɒdʒʊləʊ
AM ˈmɑdʒəˌloʊ

modulus
BR ˈmɒdjʊləs,
ˈmɒdʒʊləs
AM ˈmɑdʒələs

modus operandi
BR ˌməʊdəs
ˌɒpəˈrandiː,
+ ˌɒpəˈrandʌɪ
AM ˈmoʊdəs
ˌɑpəˈrændi,
+ ˌɑpərænˌdaɪ

modus vivendi
BR ˌməʊdəs vɪˈvɛndiː,
+ vɪˈvɛndʌɪ
AM ˈmoʊdəs vəˈvɛndi,
+ vəˈvɛnˌdaɪ

Moesia
BR ˈmiːsɪə(r),
ˈmiːzɪə(r)
AM ˈmiziə, ˈmiʃɪə

mofette
BR mɒˈfɛt, -s
AM moʊˈfɛt, -s

Moffat
BR ˈmɒfət
AM ˈmɑfət

Moffatt
BR ˈmɒfət
AM ˈmɑfət

mog
BR mɒg, -z
AM mɑg, -z

Mogadishu
BR ˌmɒgəˈdɪʃuː
AM ˈmoʊgəˈdiʃu,
ˈmɑgəˈdiʃu

Mogadon®
BR 'mɒgədɒn, -z
AM 'magədn,
'magə,dan, -z

Mogen David
BR ,məʊg(ə)n 'deɪvɪd
AM ,moʊgən 'deɪvɪd

Mogford
BR 'mɒgfəd
AM 'magfərd

Mogg
BR mɒg
AM mag

moggie
BR 'mɒg|i, -ɪz
AM 'magi, -z

moggy
BR 'mɒg|i, -ɪz
AM 'magi, -z

mogul
BR 'məʊgl, -z
AM 'moʊgəl, -z

mohair
BR 'məʊheː(r)
AM 'moʊ,hɛ(ə)r

Mohammed
BR mə(ʊ)'hamɪd
AM moʊ'haməd

Mohammedan
BR mə(ʊ)'hamɪd(ə)n,
-z
AM moʊ'hamədən, -z

Mohammedanism
BR mə(ʊ)'hamɪdən-
ɪz(ə)m,
mə(ʊ)'hamɪdnɪz(ə)m
AM moʊ'hamədn,ɪzəm,
moʊ'hamədə,nɪzəm

Mohave
BR mə'ha:v|i, -ɪz
AM moʊ'havi,
mə'havi, -z

mohawk
BR 'məʊhɔːk, -s
AM 'moʊ,hak,
'moʊ,hak, -s

Mohican
BR mə(ʊ)'hi:k(ə)n, -z
AM moʊ'hikən, -z

Moho
BR 'məʊhəʊ
AM 'moʊ,hoʊ

Mohock
BR 'məʊhɒk, -s
AM 'moʊ,hak, -s

Mohole
BR 'məʊhəʊl
AM 'moʊ,hoʊl

Mohs
BR məʊ(z)
AM moʊ(s)

moidore
BR 'mɔɪdɔː(r),
,mɔɪ'dɔː(r), -z
AM 'mɔɪdɔ(ə)r, -z

moiety
BR 'mɔɪt|i, -ɪz
AM 'mɔɪədi, -z

moil
BR mɔɪl, -z, -ɪŋ, -d
AM mɔɪl, -z, -ɪŋ, -d

Moir
BR 'mɔɪə(r)
AM 'mɔɪər

Moira
BR 'mɔɪrə(r)
AM 'mɔɪrə

moire
BR mwaː(r)
AM mwar

moiré
BR 'mwaːreɪ
AM mɔ'reɪ, mwa'reɪ,
ma'reɪ

moist
BR mɔɪst, -ə(r), -ɪst
AM mɔɪst, -ər, -ɪst

moisten
BR 'mɔɪs|n, -nz,
-nɪŋ \-nɪŋ, -nd
AM 'mɔɪs|n, -nz,
-(ə)nɪŋ, -nd

moistly
BR 'mɔɪstli
AM 'mɔɪs(t)li

moistness
BR 'mɔɪs(t)nɪs
AM 'mɔɪs(t)nɪs

moisture
BR 'mɔɪstʃə(r)
AM 'mɔɪstʃər

moistureless
BR 'mɔɪstʃələs
AM 'mɔɪstʃərləs

moisturise
BR 'mɔɪstʃərʌɪz, -ɪz,
-ɪŋ, -d
AM 'mɔɪstʃə,raɪz, -ɪz,
-ɪŋ, -d

moisturiser
BR 'mɔɪstʃərʌɪzə(r), -z
AM 'mɔɪstʃə,raɪzər, -z

moisturize
BR 'mɔɪstʃərʌɪz, -ɪz,
-ɪŋ, -d
AM 'mɔɪstʃə,raɪz, -ɪz,
-ɪŋ, -d

moisturizer
BR 'mɔɪstʃərʌɪzə(r), -z
AM 'mɔɪstʃə,raɪzər, -z

Mojave
BR mə(ʊ)'ha:vi
AM moʊ'havi, mə'havi

moke
BR məʊk, -s
AM moʊk, -s

moko
BR 'məʊkəʊ, -z
AM 'moʊ,koʊ, -z

moksha
BR 'mɒkʃə(r)
AM 'makʃə

mol
BR məʊl
AM moʊl

molal
BR 'məʊləl
AM 'moʊləl

molality
BR mə(ʊ)'lalɪt|i, -ɪz
AM moʊ'lælədi, -z

molar
BR 'məʊlə(r), -z
AM 'moʊlər, -z

molarity
BR mə(ʊ)'larɪt|i, -ɪz
AM moʊ'lɛrədi, -z

molasses
BR mə(ʊ)'lasɪz
AM mə'læsəz

mold
BR məʊld, -z
AM moʊld, -z

Moldau
BR 'mɒldaʊ
AM 'mɔl,daʊ,
'moʊl,daʊ

Moldavia
BR mɒl'deɪvɪə(r)
AM mal'deɪvɪə,
mɔl'deɪvɪə,
moʊl'deɪvɪə

Moldavian
BR mɒl'deɪvɪən, -z
AM mal'deɪvɪən,
mɔl'deɪvɪən,
moʊl'deɪvɪən, -z

moldboard
BR 'məʊl(d)bɔːd, -z
AM 'moʊl(d),bɔ(ə)rd,
-z

molder
BR 'məʊld|ə(r), -əz,
-(ə)rɪŋ, -əd
AM 'moʊldər, -z, -ɪŋ, -d

moldiness
BR 'məʊldɪnɪs
AM 'moʊldɪnɪs

molding
BR 'məʊldɪŋ, -z
AM 'moʊldɪŋ, -z

Moldova
BR mɒl'dəʊvə(r)
AM mal'doʊvə,
mɔl'doʊvə,
moʊl'doʊvə

moldy
BR 'məʊld|i, -ɪə(r), -ɪɪst
AM 'moʊldi, -ər, -ɪst

mole
BR məʊl, -z
AM moʊl, -z

molecular
BR mə'lɛkjələ(r)
AM mə'lɛkjələr

molecularity
BR mə,lɛkjʊ'larɪti
AM mə,lɛkjə'lɛrədi

molecularly
BR mə'lɛkjʊləli
AM mə'lɛkjələrli

molecule
BR 'mɒlɪkjuːl, -z

AM 'malə,kjuːl, -z

molehill
BR 'məʊlhɪl, -z
AM 'moʊl,(h)ɪl, -z

Molesey
BR 'məʊlzi
AM 'moʊlzi

moleskin
BR 'məʊlskɪn
AM 'moʊl,skɪn

molest
BR mə'lɛst, -s, -ɪŋ, -ɪd
AM mə'lɛst, -s, -ɪŋ, -əd

molestation
BR ,məʊlɛ'steɪʃn,
məʊlɪ'steɪʃn,
mɒlɛ'steɪʃn,
mɒlɪ'steɪʃn
AM ,moʊ,lɛ'steɪʃən,
,moʊlə'steɪʃən

molester
BR mə'lɛstə(r), -z
AM mə'lɛstər, -z

Molesworth
BR 'məʊlzwəːθ
AM 'moʊlz,wərθ

Molière
BR 'mɒliɛː(r)
AM mɔl'jɛ(ə)r

Moline
BR məʊ'liːn
AM moʊ'lin

moline
BR mə'lʌɪn
AM 'moʊlən, moʊ'laɪn

moll
BR mɒl, -z
AM mal, -z

Mollie
BR 'mɒli
AM 'mali

mollification
BR ,mɒlɪfɪ'keɪʃn
AM ,maləfə'keɪʃən

mollifier
BR 'mɒlɪfʌɪə(r), -z
AM 'malə,faɪər, -z

mollify
BR 'mɒlɪfʌɪ, -z, -ɪŋ, -d
AM 'malə,faɪ, -z, -ɪŋ, -d

Molloy
BR mə'lɔɪ
AM mə'lɔɪ

mollusc
BR 'mɒləsk, -s
AM 'maləsk, -s

molluscan
BR mə'lʌsk(ə)n
AM mə'ləskən

molluscoid
BR mə'lʌskɔɪd
AM mə'ləs,kɔɪd

molluscous
BR mə'lʌskəs
AM mə'ləskəs

mollusk
BR 'mɒləsk, -s

AM 'mɑləsk, -s

molly
BR 'mɒl‖i, -ɪz
AM 'mɑli, -z

mollycoddle
BR 'mɒlɪˌkɒd‖l, -lz,
-lɪŋ\-l.ɪŋ, -ld
AM 'mɑliˌkɑd‖əl, -əlz,
-(ə)lɪŋ, -əld

mollymawk
BR 'mɒlɪmɔːk, -s
AM 'mɑliˌmɔk,
'mɑliˌmɑk, -s

moloch
BR 'məʊlɒk, -s
AM 'mɑlək, -s

Moloney
BR mə'ləʊni
AM mə'loʊni

Molony
BR mə'ləʊni
AM mə'loʊni

molossi
BR mə'lɒsʌɪ
AM mə'lɑˌsaɪ

molossus
BR mə'lɒsəs
AM mə'lɑsəs

Molotov
BR 'mɒlətɒf, 'mɒlətɒv
AM 'mɑləˌtɔf,
'moʊləˌtɒv, 'mɑləˌtɑf,
'moʊləˌtɑv

molt
BR məʊlt, -s, -ɪŋ, -ɪd
AM moʊlt, -s, -ɪŋ, -əd

molten
BR 'məʊlt(ə)n
AM 'moʊlt(ə)n

molto
BR 'mɒltəʊ
AM 'moʊlˌtoʊ, 'mɒlˌtoʊ

Molton
BR 'məʊlt(ə)n
AM 'moʊlt(ə)n

Moluccas
BR mə'lʌkəz
AM mə'ləkəz

moly
BR 'məʊl‖i, -ɪz
AM 'moʊli, -z

molybdate
BR mə'lɪbdeɪt
AM mə'lɪbdeɪt

molybdenite
BR mə'lɪbdənʌɪt, -s
AM mə'lɪbdəˌnaɪt, -s

molybdenum
BR mə'lɪbdənəm
AM mə'lɪbdənəm

molybdic
BR mə'lɪbdɪk
AM mə'lɪbdɪk

Molyneaux
BR 'mɒlɪnəʊ
AM 'mɑlənoʊ

Molyneux
BR 'mɒlɪnjuː
AM 'mɑlənju

mom
BR mɒm, -z
AM mɑm, -z

mom-and-pop
BR ˌmɒm(ə)n(d)'pɒp
AM ˌmɑmən'pɑp

Mombasa
BR mɒm'bɑsə(r)
AM mɑm'bɑsə

moment
BR 'məʊm(ə)nt, -s
AM 'moʊmənt, -s

momenta
BR mə(ʊ)'mɛntə(r)
AM moʊ'men(t)ə

momentarily
BR 'məʊm(ə)nt(ə)rɪli,
ˌməʊm(ə)n'tɛrɪli
AM ˌmoʊmən'tɛrəli

momentariness
BR 'məʊm(ə)nt(ə)rmɪs
AM 'moʊmənˌterɪnɪs

momentary
BR 'məʊm(ə)nt(ə)ri
AM 'moʊmənˌtɛri

momently
BR 'məʊm(ə)ntli
AM 'moʊmən(t)li

momentous
BR mə'mɛntəs
AM moʊ'men(t)əs,
mə'men(t)əs

momentously
BR mə'mɛntəsli
AM moʊ'men(t)əsli,
mə'men(t)əsli

momentousness
BR mə'mɛntəsnəs
AM moʊ'men(t)əsnəs,
mə'men(t)əsnəs

momentum
BR mə(ʊ)'mɛntəm
AM moʊ'men(t)əm,
mə'men(t)əm

Momi
BR 'məʊmʌɪ
AM 'moʊˌmaɪ

momma
BR 'mɒmə(r), -z
AM 'mɑmə, -z

Mommsen
BR 'mɒms(ə)n
AM 'mɑmsən

mommy
BR 'mɒm‖i, -ɪz
AM 'mɑmi, -z

Momus
BR 'məʊməs, -ɪz
AM 'moʊməs, -əz

Mon
BR məʊn, mɒn
AM moʊn

Mona
BR 'məʊnə(r)

AM 'moʊnə

monacal
BR 'mɒnəkl
AM 'mɑnəkəl

Monacan
BR 'mɒnək(ə)n,
mə'nɑːk(ə)n, -z
AM 'mɑnəkən, -z

monachal
BR 'mɒnəkl
AM 'mɑnəkəl

monachism
BR 'mɒnəkɪz(ə)m
AM 'mɑnəˌkɪzəm

Monaco
BR 'mɒnəkəʊ,
mə'nɑːkəʊ
AM 'mɑnəkoʊ

monad
BR 'mɒnad, 'məʊnad,
-z
AM 'moʊˌnæd, -z

monadelphous
BR ˌmɒnə'dɛlfəs
AM ˌmɑnə'dɛlfəs

monadic
BR mɒ'nadɪk,
mə(ʊ)'nadɪk
AM moʊ'nædɪk

monadism
BR 'mɒnədɪz(ə)m,
'məʊnədɪz(ə)m
AM 'moʊnædˌɪzəm

monadnock
BR mə'nadnɒk, -s
AM mə'nædˌnɑk, -s

Monaghan
BR 'mɒnəhən
AM 'mɑnəˌhæn,
'mɑnəgən

Monahan
BR 'mɒnəhən
AM 'mɑnəˌhæn

monandrous
BR mɒ'nandrəs,
mə'nandrəs
AM mə'nændrəs

monandry
BR mɒ'nandri,
mə'nandri
AM mə'nændri

monarch
BR 'mɒnək, -s
AM 'mɑnərk,
'mɑˌnɑrk, -s

monarchal
BR mə'nɑːkl
AM mə'nɑrkəl

monarchial
BR mə'nɑːkɪəl
AM mə'nɑrkiəl

monarchic
BR mə'nɑːkɪk
AM mə'nɑrkɪk

monarchical
BR mə'nɑːkɪkl
AM mə'nɑrkəkəl

monarchically
BR mə'nɑːkɪkli
AM mə'nɑrkəkə(ə)li

monarchism
BR 'mɒnəkɪz(ə)m
AM 'mɑnərˌkɪzəm

monarchist
BR 'mɒnəkɪst, -s
AM 'mɑnərkəst, -s

monarchy
BR 'mɒnək‖i, -ɪz
AM 'mɑnərki, -z

Monash
BR 'mɒnaʃ
AM 'moʊˌnæʃ

monastery
BR 'mɒnəst(ə)r‖i, -ɪz
AM 'mɑnəˌsteri, -z

monastic
BR mə'nastɪk
AM mə'næstɪk

monastically
BR mə'nastɪkli
AM mə'næstək(ə)li

monasticise
BR mə'nastɪsʌɪz, -ɪz,
-ɪŋ, -d
AM mə'næstəˌsaɪz, -ɪz,
-ɪŋ, -d

monasticism
BR mə'nastɪsɪz(ə)m
AM mə'næstəˌsɪzəm

monasticize
BR mə'nastɪsʌɪz, -ɪz,
-ɪŋ, -d
AM mə'næstəˌsaɪz, -ɪz,
-ɪŋ, -d

Monastir
BR ˌmɒnə'stɪə(r)
AM 'mɑnəˌstɪ(ə)r,
'mɑnəˌstɪ(ə)r

monatomic
BR ˌmɒnə'tɒmɪk
AM ˌmɑnə'tɑmɪk

monaural
BR ˌmɒn'ɔːrəl,
ˌmɒn'ɔːr‖
AM ˌmɑn'ɔrəl

monaurally
BR ˌmɒn'ɔːrəli,
ˌmɒn'ɔːr‖i
AM ˌmɑn'ɔrəli

monazite
BR 'mɒnəzʌɪt, -s
AM 'mɑnəˌzaɪt, -s

Monck
BR mʌŋk
AM məŋk

Monckton
BR 'mʌŋ(k)t(ə)n
AM 'məŋ(k)tən

Moncreiff
BR mɒn'kriːf,
mən'kriːf
AM 'mɑnˌkrif

Moncrieff
BR mɒn'kriːf,
mən'kriːf

AM ˈmɑnˌkrif
Moncton
BR ˈmʌŋ(k)t(ə)n
AM ˈmɑŋ(k)tən
mondaine
BR ˈmɒndeɪn, -z
AM ˈmɑnˈdeɪn, -z
Mondale
BR ˈmɒndeɪl
AM ˈmɑnˌdeɪl
Monday
BR ˈmʌndeɪ, ˈmʌndi,
-eɪz\-ɪz
AM ˈmʌndeɪ, ˈmʌndi, -z
mondial
BR ˈmɒndɪəl
AM ˈmɑndɪəl
Mondriaan
BR ˈmɒndrɪən
AM ˈmɒndri,ɑn,
ˈmɒndrɪən,
ˈmɑndri,ɑn,
ˈmɑndrɪən
monecious
BR mɒˈniːʃəs,
məˈniːʃəs
AM məˈnɪʃəs
Monégasque
BR ˌmɒnɪˈgɑsk, -s
AM ˌmɑnəˈgɑsk, -s
Monel®
BR ˈməʊn(ə)l, -z
AM moʊˈnɛl, -z
moneme
BR ˈmɒniːm,
ˈməʊniːm, -z
AM ˈmoʊˌnim, -z
Monet
BR ˈmɒneɪ
AM ˌmoʊˈneɪ
monetarily
BR ˈmʌnɪt(ə)rɪli
AM ˌmɑnəˈtɛrəli
monetarism
BR ˈmʌnɪt(ə)rɪz(ə)m
AM ˈmɑnədəˌrɪzəm
monetarist
BR ˈmʌnɪt(ə)rɪst, -s
AM ˈmɑnədərəst, -s
monetary
BR ˈmʌnɪt(ə)ri
AM ˈmɑnəˌteri
monetisation
BR ˌmʌnɪtʌɪˈzeɪʃn
AM ˌmɑnədəˈzeɪʃən,
ˌmɑnəˌtarˈzeɪʃən
monetise
BR ˈmʌnɪtʌɪz, -ɪz, -ɪŋ, -d
AM ˈmɑnəˌtaɪz, -ɪz, -ɪŋ,
-d
monetization
BR ˌmʌnɪtʌɪˈzeɪʃn
AM ˌmɑnədəˈzeɪʃən,
ˌmɑnəˌtarˈzeɪʃən
monetize
BR ˈmʌnɪtʌɪz, -ɪz, -ɪŋ, -d
AM ˈmɑnəˌtaɪz, -ɪz, -ɪŋ,
-d

money
BR ˈmʌnˌli, -ɪz, -d
AM ˈməni, -z, -d
moneybags
BR ˈmʌnɪbagz
AM ˈməniˌbægz
moneybox
BR ˈmʌnɪbɒks, -ɪz
AM ˈməniˌbɑks, -əz
moneychanger
BR ˈmʌnɪˌtʃeɪn(d)ʒə(r),
-z
AM ˈməniˌtʃeɪndʒər, -z
moneyer
BR ˈmʌnɪə(r), -z
AM ˈməniər, -z
moneylender
BR ˈmʌnɪˌlɛndə(r), -z
AM ˈməniˌlɛndər, -z
moneylending
BR ˈmʌnɪˌlɛndɪŋ
AM ˈməniˌlɛndɪŋ
moneyless
BR ˈmʌnɪlɪs
AM ˈmənɪlɪs
moneymaker
BR ˈmʌnɪˌmeɪkə(r), -z
AM ˈməniˌmeɪkər, -z
moneymaking
BR ˈmʌnɪˌmeɪkɪŋ
AM ˈməniˌmeɪkɪŋ
moneywort
BR ˈmʌnɪwɜːt
AM ˈməniwərt,
ˈməniwɔ(ə)rt
monger
BR ˈmʌŋɡə(r), -əz,
-(ə)rɪŋ
AM ˈmʌŋɡər,
ˈməŋɡər, -ərz, -(ə)rɪŋ
mongo
BR ˈmɒŋɡəʊ, -z
AM ˈmɑŋɡoʊ, -z
Mongol
BR ˈmɒŋɡl, -z
AM ˈmɑŋɡəl,
ˈmɑŋˌɡoʊl, -z
Mongolia
BR mɒŋˈɡəʊlɪə(r)
AM mɑŋˈɡoʊljə,
mɑŋˈɡoʊlɪə
Mongolian
BR mɒŋˈɡəʊlɪən, -z
AM mɑŋˈɡoʊljən,
mɑŋˈɡoʊlɪən, -z
mongolism
BR ˈmɒŋɡəlɪz(ə)m
AM ˈmɑŋɡəˌlɪzəm
mongoloid
BR ˈmɒŋɡəlɔɪd, -z
AM ˈmɑŋɡəˌlɔɪd, -z
mongoose
BR ˈmɒŋɡuːs, -ɪz
AM ˈmɑŋˌɡus, -əz
mongrel
BR ˈmʌŋɡr(ə)l, -z
AM ˈmɑŋɡrəl,
ˈməŋɡrəl, -z

mongrelisation
BR ˌmʌŋɡrəlʌɪˈzeɪʃn,
ˌmʌŋɡrlʌɪˈzeɪʃn, -z
AM ˌmɑŋɡrələˈzeɪʃən,
ˌməŋɡrələˈzeɪʃən,
ˌməŋɡrəˌlaɪˈzeɪʃən,
ˌməŋɡrəˌlaɪˈzeɪʃən, -z
mongrelise
BR ˈmʌŋɡrəlʌɪz,
ˈmʌŋɡrlʌɪz, -ɪz, -ɪŋ, -d
AM ˈmɑŋɡrəˌlaɪz,
ˈməŋɡrəˌlaɪz, -ɪz, -ɪŋ,
-d
mongrelism
BR ˈmʌŋɡrəlɪz(ə)m,
ˈmʌŋɡrlɪz(ə)m
AM ˈmɑŋɡrəˌlɪzəm,
ˈməŋɡrəˌlɪzəm
mongrelization
BR ˌmʌŋɡrəlʌɪˈzeɪʃn,
ˌmʌŋɡrlʌɪˈzeɪʃn, -z
AM ˌmɑŋɡrələˈzeɪʃən,
ˌməŋɡrələˈzeɪʃən,
ˌməŋɡrəˌlaɪˈzeɪʃən,
ˌməŋɡrəˌlaɪˈzeɪʃən, -z
mongrelize
BR ˈmʌŋɡrəlʌɪz,
ˈmʌŋɡrlʌɪz, -ɪz, -ɪŋ, -d
AM ˈmɑŋɡrəˌlaɪz,
ˈməŋɡrəˌlaɪz, -ɪz, -ɪŋ,
-d
mongrelly
BR ˈmʌŋɡrəli,
ˈmʌŋɡrli
AM ˈmɑŋɡrəli,
ˈməŋɡrəli
'mongst
BR mʌŋst
AM məŋst
monial
BR ˈməʊnɪəl, -z
AM ˈmoʊnɪəl, -z
Monica
BR ˈmɒnɪkə(r)
AM ˈmɑnɪkə
monicker
BR ˈmɒnɪkə(r), -z
AM ˈmɑnəkər, -z
monies
BR ˈmʌnɪz
AM ˈmənɪz
moniker
BR ˈmɒnɪkə(r), -z
AM ˈmɑnəkər, -z
moniliform
BR məˈnɪlɪfɔːm
AM məˈnɪləˌfɔ(ə)rm
Monique
BR mɒˈniːk
AM məˈnik, moʊˈnik
monism
BR ˈmɒnɪz(ə)m
AM ˈmɑˌnɪzəm,
ˈmoʊˌnɪzəm
monist
BR ˈmɒnɪst, -s
AM ˈmɑnəst, ˈmoʊnəst,
-s

monistic
BR mɒˈnɪstɪk,
məˈnɪstɪk
AM məˈnɪstɪk,
moʊˈnɪstɪk
monition
BR mɒˈnɪʃn, məˈnɪʃn,
-z
AM məˈnɪʃən, -z
monitor
BR ˈmɒnɪtə(r), -əz,
-(ə)rɪŋ, -əd
AM ˈmɑnəˌdər, -dərz,
-dərɪŋ\-trɪŋ, -dərd
monitorial
BR ˌmɒnɪˈtɔːrɪəl
AM ˌmɑnəˈtɔriəl
monitorship
BR ˈmɒnɪtəˌʃɪp, -s
AM ˈmɑnədərˌʃɪp, -s
monitory
BR ˈmɒnɪt(ə)r|i, -ɪz
AM ˈmɑnəˌtɔri, -z
monk
BR mʌŋk, -s
AM məŋk, -s
monkery
BR ˈmʌŋk(ə)ri
AM ˈməŋkəri
monkey
BR ˈmʌŋk|i, -ɪz, -ɪŋ, -ɪd
AM ˈməŋki, -z, -ɪŋ, -d
monkeyish
BR ˈmʌŋkiɪʃ
AM ˈməŋkiɪʃ
monkeyshine
BR ˈmʌŋkɪʃʌɪn, -z
AM ˈməŋkiˌʃaɪn, -z
monkfish
BR ˈmʌŋkfɪʃ
AM ˈməŋkˌfɪʃ
Mon-Khmer
BR ˌməʊnˈkmɛː(r),
ˌmɒnˈkmɛː(r),
ˌməʊnkəˈmɛː(r),
ˌmɒnkəˈmɛː(r)
AM ˌmoʊnkəˈmɛ(ə)r
monkhood
BR ˈmʌŋkhʊd
AM ˈməŋkˌ(h)ʊd
Monkhouse
BR ˈmʌŋkhaʊs
AM ˈməŋkˌ(h)aʊs
monkish
BR ˈmʌŋkɪʃ
AM ˈməŋkɪʃ
monkishly
BR ˈmʌŋkɪʃli
AM ˈməŋkɪʃli
monkishness
BR ˈmʌŋkɪʃnɪs
AM ˈməŋkɪʃnɪs
Monks
BR mʌŋks
AM məŋks
monkshood
BR ˈmʌŋkshʊd
AM ˈməŋkˌ(h)ʊd

Monkton
BR ˈmʌŋ(k)t(ə)n
AM ˈməŋ(k)tən

Monmouth
BR ˈmɒnməθ,
ˈmʌnməθ
AM ˈmɑnməθ

Monmouthshire
BR ˈmɒnməθʃ(ɪ)ə(r),
ˈmʌnməθʃ(ɪ)ə(r)
AM ˈmɑnməθʃɪ(ə)r

monniker
BR ˈmɒnɪkə(r), -z
AM ˈmɑnəkər, -z

Mono
lake in US
BR ˈməʊnəʊ
AM ˈmoʊnoʊ

mono
BR ˈmɒnəʊ
AM ˈmɑnoʊ

monoacid
BR ˈmɒnəʊˌasɪd
AM ˌmɑnoʊˈæsəd

monobasic
BR ˌmɒnə(ʊ)ˈbeɪsɪk
AM ˌmɑnoʊˈbeɪsɪk

monocarpic
BR ˌmɒnə(ʊ)ˈkɑːpɪk
AM ˌmɑnoʊˈkɑrpɪk

monocarpous
BR ˌmɒnə(ʊ)ˈkɑːpəs
AM ˌmɑnoʊˈkɑrpəs

monocausal
BR ˌmɒnə(ʊ)ˈkɔːzl
AM ˌmɑnoʊˈkɔzəl,
ˌmɑnoʊˈkazəl

monocephalous
BR ˌmɒnə(ʊ)ˈsefələs,
ˌmɒnə(ʊ)ˈsefləs,
ˌmɒnə(ʊ)ˈkefələs,
ˌmɒnə(ʊ)ˈkefləs
AM ˌmɑnoʊˈsefələs

Monoceros
BR məˈnɒs(ə)rəs
AM məˈnɑsərəs

monochasia
BR ˌmɒnəˈkeɪzɪə(r)
AM ˌmɑnəˈkeɪzɪə,
ˌmɑnəˈkeɪʒə

monochasium
BR ˌmɒnəˈkeɪzɪəm
AM ˌmɑnəˈkeɪzɪəm

monochord
BR ˈmɒnə(ʊ)kɔːd, -z
AM ˈmɑnoʊˌkɔ(ə)rd, -z

monochromatic
BR ˌmɒnə(ʊ)krəˈmatɪk
AM ˌmɑnoʊkrəˈmædɪk

**monochromatic-
ally**
BR ˌmɒnə(ʊ)krəˈmat-
ɪkli
AM ˌmɑnoʊkrəˈmæd-
ək(ə)li

monochromatism
BR ˌmɒnə(ʊ)ˈkrəʊmət-
ɪz(ə)m

AM ˈmɑnəˈkrəʊməˌtɪz-
əm

monochromator
BR ˈmɒnə(ʊ)krəmeɪ-
tə(r),
ˌmɒnə(ʊ)ˈkrɒmɪtə(r),
-z
AM ˌmɑnəˈkroʊmeɪ-
də(r),
ˈmɑnəˌkroʊmeɪdər, -z

monochrome
BR ˈmɒnə(ʊ)krəʊm,
ˌmɒnə(ʊ)ˈkrəʊm
AM ˈmɑnəˌkroʊm

monochromic
BR ˌmɒnə(ʊ)ˈkrəʊmɪk
AM ˌmɑnəˈkroʊmɪk

monocle
BR ˈmɒnəkl, -z, -d
AM ˈmɑnəkəl, -z, -d

monoclinal
BR ˌmɒnə(ʊ)ˈklʌɪnl
AM ˌmɑnəˈklaɪnəl

monocline
BR ˈmɒnə(ʊ)klʌɪn, -z
AM ˈmɑnəˌklaɪn, -z

monoclinic
BR ˌmɒnə(ʊ)ˈklɪnɪk
AM ˌmɑnəˈklɪnɪk

monoclonal
BR ˌmɒnə(ʊ)ˈkləʊnl
AM ˌmɑnəˈkloʊnəl

monocoque
BR ˈmɒnə(ʊ)kɒk, -s
AM ˈmɑnəˌkak, -s
FR mɔnɔcɔk

monocot
BR ˈmɒnə(ʊ)kɒt, -s
AM ˈmɑnəˌkat, -s

monocotyledon
BR ˌmɒnə(ʊ)ˌkɒtɪˈliːdn,
-z
AM ˌmɑnəˌkadlˈidn, -z

**monocotyledon-
ous**
BR ˌmɒnə(ʊ)ˌkɒtɪˈliːdə-
nəs
AM ˌmɑnəˌkadlˈid(ə)nəs

monocracy
BR mɒˈnɒkrəsi,
məˈnɒkrəsi, -ɪz
AM məˈnɑkrəsi, -z

monocratic
BR ˌmɒnə(ʊ)ˈkratɪk
AM ˌmɑnəˈkrædɪk

monocrotic
BR ˌmɒnə(ʊ)ˈkrɒtɪk
AM ˌmɑnəˈkradɪk

monocular
BR mɒˈnɒkjʊlə(r),
məˈnɒkjʊlə(r)
AM məˈnɑkjələr

monocularly
BR mɒˈnɒkjʊləli,
məˈnɒkjʊləli
AM məˈnɑkjələrli

monoculture
BR ˈmɒnə(ʊ)ˌkʌltʃə(r)

AM ˈmɑnəˈkroʊməˌtɪz-
əm

monochromator
BR ˈmɒnə(ʊ)krəmeɪ-
tə(r),
ˌmɒnə(ʊ)ˈkrɒmɪtə(r),
-z

AM ˈmɑnəˌkɔltʃər

monocycle
BR ˈmɒnə(ʊ)ˌsʌɪkl, -z
AM ˈmɑnəˌsaɪkəl, -z

monocyte
BR ˈmɒnə(ʊ)sʌɪt, -s
AM ˈmɑnəˌsaɪt, -s

monodactylous
BR ˌmɒnə(ʊ)ˈdaktɪləs,
ˌmɒnə(ʊ)ˈdaktləs
AM ˌmɑnəˈdæktləs

monodic
BR mɒˈnɒdɪk,
məˈnɒdɪk
AM məˈnɑdɪk

monodisperse
BR ˌmɒnə(ʊ)ˈdɪspəːs
AM ˌmɑnədɪsˈpərs

monodist
BR ˈmɒnədɪst, -s
AM ˈmɑnədəst, -s

monodrama
BR ˈmɒnə(ʊ)ˌdrɑːmə(r),
ˌmɒnə(ʊ)ˈdrɑːmə(r),
-z
AM ˈmɑnoʊˌdrɑmə, -z

monody
BR ˈmɒnəd|i, -ɪz
AM ˈmɑnədi, -z

monoecious
BR mɒˈniːʃəs,
məˈniːʃəs
AM məˈniʃəs

monofil
BR ˈmɒnə(ʊ)fɪl
AM ˈmɑnəˌfɪl

monofilament
BR ˈmɒnə(ʊ)ˌfɪləm(ə)nt
AM ˈmɑnəˈfɪləmənt

monogamist
BR məˈnɒgəmɪst,
mɒˈnɒgəmɪst, -s
AM məˈnɑgəˌməst, -s

monogamous
BR məˈnɒgəməs,
mɒˈnɒgəməs
AM məˈnɑgəməs

monogamously
BR məˈnɒgəməsli,
mɒˈnɒgəməsli
AM məˈnɑgəməsli

monogamy
BR məˈnɒgəmi,
mɒˈnɒgəmi
AM məˈnɑgəmi

monogenean
BR ˌmɒnə(ʊ)dʒɪˈniːən,
ˌmɒnə(ʊ)dʒɛnɪən
AM ˌmɑnədʒəˈniən,
ˌmɑnəˈdʒɛnɪən

monogenesis
BR ˌmɒnə(ʊ)ˈdʒɛnɪsɪs
AM ˌmɑnoʊˈdʒɛnəsəs

monogenetic
BR ˌmɒnə(ʊ)dʒɪˈnɛtɪk
AM ˌmɑnədʒəˈnɛdɪk

AM ˈmɑnəˌkəltʃər

monogeny
BR məˈnɒdʒɪni,
mɒˈnɒdʒɪni
AM məˈnɑdʒəni

monoglot
BR ˈmɒnə(ʊ)glɒt, -s
AM ˈmɑnəˌglɑt, -s

monogram
BR ˈmɒnəgram, -z, -d
AM ˈmɑnəˌgræm, -z, -d

monogrammatic
BR ˌmɒnə(ʊ)grəˈmatɪk
AM ˌmɑnəgrəˈmædɪk

monograph
BR ˈmɒnəgrɑːf,
ˈmɒnəgraf, -s
AM ˈmɑnəˌgræf, -s

monographer
BR məˈnɒgrəfə(r),
mɒˈnɒgrəfə(r), -z
AM məˈnɑgrəfər, -z

monographic
BR ˌmɒnə(ʊ)ˈgrafɪk
AM ˌmɑnəˈgræfɪk

monographist
BR məˈnɒgrəfɪst,
mɒˈnɒgrəfɪst, -s
AM məˈnɑgrəfəst, -s

monogynous
BR məˈnɒdʒɪnəs,
mɒˈnɒdʒɪnəs
AM məˈnɑdʒənəs

monogyny
BR məˈnɒdʒɪni,
mɒˈnɒdʒɪni
AM məˈnɑdʒəni

monohull
BR ˈmɒnəʊhʌl, -z
AM ˈmɑnoʊˌhəl, -z

monohybrid
BR ˌmɒnə(ʊ)ˈhʌɪbrɪd,
-z
AM ˌmɑnəˈhaɪbrɪd, -z

monohydric
BR ˌmɒnə(ʊ)ˈhʌɪdrɪk
AM ˌmɑnəˈhaɪdrɪk

monokini
BR ˈmɒnə(ʊ)ˌkiːn|i,
ˌmɒnə(ʊ)ˈkiːn|i, -ɪz
AM ˈmɑnoʊˌkɪni, -z

monolatry
BR məˈnɒlətri,
mɒˈnɒlətri
AM məˈnɑlətri

monolayer
BR ˈmɒnə(ʊ)ˌleɪə(r), -z
AM ˈmɑnəˈleɪər,
ˈmɑnəˈlɛ(ə)r, -z

monolingual
BR ˌmɒnə(ʊ)ˈlɪŋgw(ə)l
AM ˌmɑnəˈlɪŋgwəl

monolith
BR ˈmɒnəlɪθ, ˈmɒnlɪθ, -s
AM ˈmɑnəˌlɪθ, -s

monolithic
BR ˌmɒnəˈlɪθɪk
AM ˌmɑnəˈlɪθɪk

monolithically
BR ˌmɒnəˈlɪθɪkli
AM ˌmɑnəˈlɪθək(ə)li

monolog
BR ˈmɒnəlɒg, -z
AM ˈmɑnəlɔg, ˈmɑnəlɑg, -z

monologic
BR ˌmɒnəˈlɒdʒɪk
AM ˌmɑnəˈlɑdʒɪk

monological
BR ˌmɒnəˈlɒdʒɪkl
AM ˌmɑnəˈlɑdʒəkəl

monologise
BR ˈmɒnəlɒdʒaɪz, məˈnɒlədʒaɪz, -ɪz, -ɪŋ, -d
AM məˈnɑləˌdʒaɪz, -ɪz, -ɪŋ, -d

monologist
BR məˈnɒlədʒɪst, -s
AM məˈnɑlədʒəst, -s

monologize
BR ˈmɒnəlɒdʒaɪz, məˈnɒlədʒaɪz, -ɪz, -ɪŋ, -d
AM məˈnɑləˌdʒaɪz, -ɪz, -ɪŋ, -d

monologue
BR ˈmɒnəlɒg, -z
AM ˈmɑnəlɔg, ˈmɑnəlɑg, -z

monomania
BR ˌmɒnə(ʊ)ˈmeɪnɪə(r)
AM ˌmɑnoʊˈmeɪniə

monomaniac
BR ˌmɒnə(ʊ)ˈmeɪnɪæk, -s
AM ˌmɑnoʊˈmeɪniæk, -s

monomaniacal
BR ˌmɒnə(ʊ)məˈnaɪəkl
AM ˌmɑnoʊməˈnaɪəkəl

monomark
BR ˈmɒnə(ʊ)mɑːk, -s
AM ˈmɑnoʊˌmɑrk, -s

monomer
BR ˈmɒnəmə(r), -z
AM ˈmɑnəmər, -z

monomeric
BR ˌmɒnəˈmɛrɪk
AM ˌmɑnəˈmɛrɪk

monometallism
BR ˌmɒnə(ʊ)ˈmɛtˌlɪz(ə)m
AM ˌmɑnoʊˈmɛdlˌɪzəm

monomial
BR mɒˈnəʊmiəl, məˈnəʊmiəl,
AM məˈnoʊmiəl, -z

monomolecular
BR ˌmɒnə(ʊ)məˈlɛkjʊlə(r)
AM ˌmɑnoʊməˈlɛkjələr

monomorphic
BR ˌmɒnə(ʊ)ˈmɔːfɪk
AM ˌmɑnəˈmɔrfɪk

monomorphism
BR ˌmɒnə(ʊ)ˈmɔːfˌɪz(ə)m, -z
AM ˌmɑnəˈmɔrˌfɪzəm, -z

monomorphous
BR ˌmɒnə(ʊ)ˈmɔːfəs
AM ˌmɑnəˈmɔrfəs

Monongahela
BR məˌnɒŋgəˈhiːlə(r)
AM məˌnɑŋgəˈhilə

mononucleosis
BR ˌmɒnəʊˌnjuːklɪˈəʊsɪs
AM ˌmɑnoʊˌn(j)ukliˈoʊsəs

monopetalous
BR ˌmɒnə(ʊ)ˈpɛtləs
AM ˌmɑnəˈpɛdləs

monophagous
BR məˈnɒfəgəs
AM məˈnɑfəgəs

monophonic
BR ˌmɒnə(ʊ)ˈfɒnɪk
AM ˌmɑnəˈfɑnɪk

monophonically
BR ˌmɒnə(ʊ)ˈfɒnɪkli
AM ˌmɑnəˈfɑnək(ə)li

monophthong
BR ˈmɒnə(f)θɒŋ, -z
AM ˈmɑnə(f)ˌθɔŋ, məˈnapˌθɒŋ, ˈmɑnə(f)ˌθɑŋ, məˈnapˌθɑŋ, -z

monophthongal
BR ˌmɒnə(f)ˈθɒŋgl
AM ˌmɑnə(f)ˈθɑŋ(g)əl, ˈmɑnəpˈθɑŋ(g)əl

monophthongally
BR ˌmɒnə(f)ˈθɒŋgli, ˌmɒnə(f)ˈθɒŋgəli
AM ˌmɑnə(f)ˈθɑŋ(g)əli, ˈmɑnəpˈθɑŋ(g)əli

Monophysite
BR məˈnɒfɪsaɪt, -s
AM məˈnɑfəˌsaɪt, -s

monoplane
BR ˈmɒnəpleɪn, -z
AM ˈmɑnəˌpleɪn, -z

monopod
BR ˈmɒnəpɒd, -z
AM ˈmɑnəˌpad, -z

Monopole
BR ˈmɒnə(ʊ)pəʊl
AM ˈmɑnəˌpoʊl

monopolisation
BR məˌnɒpəlaɪˈzeɪʃn, məˌnɒpələˈzeɪʃən, məˌnɒpəˌlaɪˈzeɪʃən

monopolise
BR məˈnɒpəlaɪz, -ɪz, -ɪŋ, -d
AM məˈnɑpəˌlaɪz, -ɪz, -ɪŋ, -d

monopoliser
BR məˈnɒpəlaɪzə(r), -z
AM məˈnɑpəˌlaɪzər, -z

monopolist
BR məˈnɒpəlɪst, -s

monopolistic
BR məˌnɒpəˈlɪstɪk
AM məˌnɑpəˈlɪstɪk

monopolization
BR məˌnɒpəlaɪˈzeɪʃn
AM məˌnɑpələˈzeɪʃən, məˌnɑpəˌlaɪˈzeɪʃən

monopolize
BR məˈnɒpəlaɪz, -ɪz, -ɪŋ, -d
AM məˈnɑpəˌlaɪz, -ɪz, -ɪŋ, -d

monopolizer
BR məˈnɒpəlaɪzə(r), -z
AM məˈnɑpəˌlaɪzər, -z

monopoly
BR məˈnɒpəlˌi, məˈnɒplˌi, -ɪz
AM məˈnɑpəli, -z

monopsony
BR məˈnɒpsənˌi, məˈnɑpsnˌi, -ɪz
AM məˈnɑpsəni, -z

monopsychism
BR ˌmɒnə(ʊ)ˈsaɪkɪz(ə)m
AM ˌmɑnəˈsaɪˌkɪzəm

monopteros
BR məˈnɒptərɒs, -ɪz
AM məˈnɑptərəs, -əz

monorail
BR ˈmɒnəreɪl, -z
AM ˈmɑnəˌreɪl, -z

monorhyme
BR ˈmɒnə(ʊ)rʌɪm, -z
AM ˈmɑnəˌraɪm, -z

monosaccharide
BR ˌmɒnə(ʊ)ˈsakərʌɪd, -z
AM ˌmɑnəˈsækəˌraɪd, -z

monosodium glutamate
BR ˌmɒnə(ʊ)səʊdɪəm ˈgluːtəmeɪt
AM ˌmɑnəˌsoʊdiəm ˈgludəˌmeɪt

monospermous
BR ˌmɒnə(ʊ)ˈspɜːməs
AM ˌmɑnəˈspɜrməs

monostichous
BR məˈnɒstɪkəs, ˌmɒnə(ʊ)ˈstʌɪkəs
AM ˌmɑnəˈstɪkəs

monostrophic
BR ˌmɒnə(ʊ)ˈstrɒfɪk, ˌmɒnə(ʊ)ˈstrəʊfɪk
AM ˌmɑnəˈstrɑfɪk

monosyllabic
BR ˌmɒnə(ʊ)sɪˈlabɪk
AM ˌmɑnəsəˈlæbɪk

monosyllabically
BR ˌmɒnə(ʊ)sɪˈlabɪkli
AM ˌmɑnəsəˈlæbək(ə)li

monosyllable
BR ˈmɒnə(ʊ)ˌsɪləbl, -z
AM ˈmɑnəˌsɪləbəl, -z

monotheism
BR ˈmɒnə(ʊ)θiːɪz(ə)m, ˈmɒnə(ʊ)ˌθiːɪz(ə)m
AM ˈmɑnəθiˌɪzəm, ˌmɑnəˈθiˌɪzəm

monotheist
BR ˈmɒnə(ʊ)θiɪst, ˈmɒnə(ʊ)ˌθiːɪst, -s
AM ˈmɑnəˈθiɪst, -s

monotheistic
BR ˌmɒnə(ʊ)θiˈɪstɪk
AM ˌmɑnəθiˈɪstɪk

monotheistically
BR ˌmɒnə(ʊ)θiˈɪstɪkli
AM ˌmɑnəθiˈɪstɪk(ə)li

Monothelite
BR məˈnɒθɪlʌɪt, -s
AM məˈnɑθəˌlaɪt, -s

monotint
BR ˈmɒnə(ʊ)tɪnt, -s
AM ˈmɑnəˌtɪnt, -s

monotone
BR ˈmɒnətəʊn, -z
AM ˈmɑnəˌtoʊn, -z

monotonic
BR ˌmɒnəˈtɒnɪk
AM ˌmɑnəˈtanɪk

monotonically
BR ˌmɒnəˈtɒnɪkli
AM ˌmɑnəˈtanək(ə)li

monotonise
BR məˈnɒtənʌɪz, məˈnɒtnʌɪz, -ɪz, -ɪŋ, -d
AM məˈnɑtnˌaɪz, məˈnɑdəˌnaɪz, -ɪz, -ɪŋ, -d

monotonize
BR məˈnɒtənʌɪz, məˈnɒtnʌɪz, -ɪz, -ɪŋ, -d
AM məˈnɑtnˌaɪz, məˈnɑdəˌnaɪz, -ɪz, -ɪŋ, -d

monotonous
BR məˈnɒtənəs, məˈnɒtnəs
AM məˈnɑtnəs, məˈnɑdənəs

monotonously
BR məˈnɒtənəsli, məˈnɒtnəsli
AM məˈnɑtnəsli, məˈnɑdənəsli

monotonousness
BR məˈnɒtənəsnəs, məˈnɒtnəsnəs
AM məˈnɑtnəsnəs, məˈnɑdənəsnəs

monotony
BR məˈnɒt(ə)ni, məˈnɒtnˌi
AM məˈnɑtnˌi, məˈnɑdəni

monotreme
BR ˈmɒnətriːm, -z
AM ˈmɑnəˌtrim, -z

Monotype®
BR ˈmɒnə(ʊ)tʌɪp, -s
AM ˈmɑnəˌtaɪp, -s

monotypic
BR ˌmɒnə(ʊ)'tɪpɪk
AM ˌmɑnə'tɪpɪk

monounsaturate
BR ˌmɒnəʊʌn'satʃʊrət,
ˌmɒnəʊʌn'stjʊrət, -s
AM ˌmɑnoʊən'sætʃərət,
-s

monounsaturated
BR ˌmɒnəʊʌn'satʃʊreɪtɪd,
ˌmɒnəʊʌn'satjʊreɪtɪd
AM ˌmɑnoʊən'sætʃəˌreɪdɪd

monovalence
BR ˌmɒnə(ʊ)'veɪləns,
ˌmɒnə(ʊ)'veɪlns̩, -ɪz
AM ˌmɑnə'veɪləns, -əz

monovalency
BR ˌmɒnə(ʊ)'veɪləns|i,
ˌmɒnə(ʊ)'veɪlns̩|i, -ɪz
AM ˌmɑnə'veɪlənsi, -z

monovalent
BR ˌmɒnə(ʊ)'veɪlənt,
ˌmɒnə(ʊ)'veɪlnt̩
AM ˌmɑnə'veɪlənt

monoxide
BR mə'nɒksʌɪd, -z
AM mə'nɑkˌsaɪd, -z

Monroe
BR mən'rəʊ, mʌn'rəʊ
AM mən'roʊ

Monroe doctrine
BR ˌmənrəʊ
'dɒktr(ɪ)n, ˌmʌnrəʊ +
AM mən'roʊ 'dɑktrən

Monrovia
BR mən'rəʊvɪə(r),
mɒn'rəʊvɪə(r)
AM mən'roʊvɪə,
mɑn'roʊvɪə

Monrovian
BR mən'rəʊvɪən,
mɒn'rəʊvɪən, -z
AM mən'roʊvɪən,
mɑn'roʊvɪən, -z

Mons
BR mɒnz
AM mɔnz

Monsarrat
BR 'mɒnsərat,
ˌmɒnsə'rat
AM ˌmɑnsə'rɑt

Monseigneur
BR ˌmɒnsɛ'njə:(r)
AM ˌmɑnˌseɪ'njɜr

monsieur
BR mə'sjə:(r)
AM mə'sjɜr, mə'ʃər

Monsignor
BR mɒn'si:njə(r),
ˌmɒnsi:'njɔ:(r), -z
AM mɑn'sinjər, -z

monsignore
BR ˌmɒnsi:'njɔ:ri
AM ˌmɑnˌsin'jɔri

monsignori
BR ˌmɒnsi:'njɔ:ri:

AM ˌmɑnˌsin'jɔri

monsoon
BR mɒn'su:n, -z
AM mɑn'sun, -z

monsoonal
BR mɒn'su:nl
AM mɑn'sunəl

mons pubis
BR ˌmɒnz 'pju:bɪs, -ɪz
AM 'mɑnz 'pjubəs, -əz

monster
BR 'mɒnstə(r), -z
AM 'mɑnstər, -z

monstera
BR mɒn'stɪərə(r),
'mɒnst(ə)rə(r), -z
AM 'mɑnstərə, -z

monstrance
BR 'mɒnstr(ə)ns, -ɪz
AM 'mɑnztrəns,
'mɑnstrəns, -əz

monstrosity
BR mɒn'strɒsɪt|i, -ɪz
AM mɑnz'trɑsədi,
mɑn'strɑsədi, -z

monstrous
BR 'mɒnstrəs
AM 'mɑnztrəs,
'mɑnstrəs

monstrously
BR 'mɒnstrəsli
AM 'mɑnztrəsli,
'mɑnstrəsli

monstrousness
BR 'mɒnstrəsnəs
AM 'mɑnztrəsnəs,
'mɑnstrəsnəs

mons veneris
BR ˌmɒnz 'vɛnər|ɪs,
-ɪsɪz
AM ˌmɑnz 'vɛnərəs, -əz

montage
BR 'mɒntɑːʒ, -ɪz
AM mɑn'tɑʒ, -əz

Montagna
BR mɒn'teɪnjə(r)
AM mɔn'teɪnjə

Montagnard
BR ˌmɒntə'njɑ:d, -z
AM ˌmɑntə'njɑrd, -z
FR mɔ̃taɲaʀ

Montague
BR 'mɒntəgju:
AM 'mɑn(t)əgju

Montaigne
BR mɒn'teɪn
AM mɑn'teɪn

Montana
BR mɒn'tanə(r)
AM mɑn'tænə

Montanan
BR mɒn'tanən, -z
AM mɑn'tænən, -z

montane
BR 'mɒnteɪn
AM mɑn'teɪn

Montanism
BR 'mɒntənɪz(ə)m

AM 'mɑn(t)əˌnɪzəm

Montanist
BR 'mɒntənɪst, -s
AM 'mɑn(t)ənəst, -s

Mont Blanc
BR ˌmɔ̃ 'blɔ̃
AM ˌmɑn 'blɑŋk

montbretia
BR ˌmɒn(t)'bri:ʃə(r),
-z
AM ˌmɑnt'briʃ(i)ə, -z

Montcalm
BR ˌmɒnt'kɑ:m
AM ˌmɑn(t)'kɑm

Monte
BR 'mɒnti
AM 'mɑn(t)i

Monte Carlo
BR ˌmɒntɪ 'kɑːləʊ
AM ˌmɑn(t)ə 'kɑrˌloʊ,
ˌmɑn(t)i +

Monte Cassino
BR ˌmɒntɪ kə'si:nəʊ
AM ˌmɑn(t)ə kə'siˌnoʊ,
ˌmɑn(t)i +

Montefiore
BR ˌmɒntɪfɪ'ɔ:ri,
ˌmɒntɪ'fjɔ:ri
AM ˌmɑn(t)əfi'ɔri

Montego Bay
BR ˌmɒnˌtiːgəʊ 'beɪ
AM mən'tigoʊ 'beɪ

Monteith
BR mɒn'ti:θ
AM mɑn'tiθ

Montenegrin
BR ˌmɒntɪ'ni:grɪn,
ˌmɒntɪ'neɪgrɪn, -z
AM ˌmɑn(t)ə'neɪgrɪn,
-z

Montenegro
BR ˌmɒntɪ'ni:grəʊ,
ˌmɒntɪ'neɪgrəʊ
AM ˌmɑn(t)ə'neɪˌgroʊ

Monterrey
BR ˌmɒntə'reɪ
AM ˌmɑn(t)ə'reɪ

Montesquieu
BR ˌmɒntɛ'skjə:(r),
ˌmɒntɛ'skju:,
'mɒntɛskju:
AM ˌmɑntəˌskju

Montessori
BR ˌmɒntɪ'sɔ:ri
AM ˌmən(t)ə'sɔri

Monteverdi
BR ˌmɒntɪ'vɛ:di,
ˌmɒntɪ'və:di
AM ˌmɑn(t)ə'vɛrdi

Montevideo
BR ˌmɒntɪvɪ'deɪəʊ
AM ˌmɑn(t)əvə'deɪoʊ

Montez
BR mɒn'tɛz
AM mɑn'tɛz

Montezuma
BR ˌmɒntɪ'z(j)u:mə(r)
AM ˌmɑn(t)ə'zumə

Montfort
BR 'mɒntfət
AM 'mɑn(t)fərt

Montgolfier
BR ˌmɒnt'gɒlfɪə(r),
ˌmɒnt'gɒlfɪeɪ
AM ˌmɑn'gɔlfɪər,
ˌmɑn'gɔlfɪeɪ

Montgomery
BR m(ə)nt'gʌm(ə)ri
AM mɑn(t)'gəm(ə)ri

month
BR mʌnθ, -s
AM mʌnθ, -s

monthly
BR 'mʌnθl|i, -ɪz
AM 'mənθli, -z

Monticello
BR ˌmɒntɪ'tʃɛləʊ,
ˌmɒntɪ'sɛləʊ
AM ˌmɑn(t)ə'tʃɛloʊ,
ˌmɑn(t)ə'sɛloʊ

monticule
BR 'mɒntɪkju:l, -z
AM 'mɑn(t)əˌkjul, -z

Montmartre
BR ˌmɔ̃'mɑ:tr(ər)
AM ˌmɑn'mɑrtrə

Montmorency
BR ˌmɒntmə'rɛnsi
AM ˌmɑntmə'rɛnsi

montmorillonite
BR ˌmɒntmə'rɪlənʌɪt
AM ˌmɑntmə'rɪlənaɪt

Mont Pelée
BR ˌmɒnt 'pɛleɪ
AM ˌmɑn(t) pɛ'leɪ

Montpelier
BR ˌmɒnt'pi:lɪə(r)
AM ˌmɑn(t)'piliər

Montpellier
BR ˌmɒnt'pɛlɪə(r),
ˌmɒnt'pɛlɪeɪ
AM ˌmɑnpəl'jeɪ
FR mɔ̃pəlje

Montreal
BR ˌmɒntrɪ'ɔ:l
AM ˌmɑntri'ɔl

Montreux
BR mɒn'trə:(r)
AM mən'tru
FR mɔ̃tʀø

Montrose
BR mɒn'trəʊz
AM 'mɑnˌtroʊz,
mɑn'troʊz

Mont-Saint-Michel
BR ˌmɒntsanmɪ'ʃɛl,
ˌmɔ̃sanmɪ'ʃɛl
AM ˌmɑnsanmə'ʃɛl

Montserrat
BR ˌmɒn(t)sə'rat
AM ˌmɑn(t)sə'rɑt

Montserratian
BR ˌmɒn(t)sə'ratɪən, -z
AM ˌmɑn(t)sə'radiən,
-z

Monty
BR ˈmɒnti
AM ˈmɑn(t)i

monument
BR ˈmɒnjʊm(ə)nt, -s
AM ˈmɑnjəmənt, -s

monumental
BR ˌmɒnjʊˈmɛntl
AM ˌmɑnjəˈmɛn(t)l

monumentalise
BR ˌmɒnjʊˈmɛntlʌɪz,
-ɪz, -ɪŋ, -d
AM ˌmɑnjəˈmɛn(t)l͵aɪz,
-ɪz, -ɪŋ, -d

monumentalism
BR ˌmɒnjʊˈmɛntlɪz(ə)m
AM ˌmɑnjəˈmɛn(t)l͵ɪzəm

monumentality
BR ˌmʌnjʊmɛnˈtalɪti
AM ˌmɑnjə͵mɛnˈtælədi

monumentalize
BR ˌmɒnjʊˈmɛntlʌɪz,
-ɪz, -ɪŋ, -d
AM ˌmɑnjəˈmɛn(t)l͵aɪz,
-ɪz, -ɪŋ, -d

monumentally
BR ˌmɒnjʊˈmɛntl̩i
AM ˌmɑnjəˈmɛn(t)l̩i

Monza
BR ˈmɒnzə(r)
AM ˈmɑnzə, ˈmɔn(t)sə

moo
BR muː, -z, -ɪŋ, -d
AM mu, -z, -ɪŋ, -d

mooch
BR muːtʃ, -ɪz, -ɪŋ, -t
AM mutʃ, -əz, -ɪŋ, -t

moocher
BR ˈmuːtʃə(r), -z
AM ˈmutʃər, -z

moocow
BR ˈmuːkaʊ, -z
AM ˈmu͵kaʊ, -z

mood
BR muːd, -z
AM mud, -z

Moodie
BR ˈmuːdi
AM ˈmudi

moodily
BR ˈmuːdɪli
AM ˈmudəli

moodiness
BR ˈmuːdɪnɪs
AM ˈmudɪnɪs

moody
BR ˈmuːd|i, -ɪə(r), -ɪɪst
AM ˈmudi, -ər, -ɪst

Moog
BR muːg, -z
AM mug, -z

moola
BR ˈmuːlə(r)
AM ˈmu͵lɑ

moolah
BR ˈmuːlə(r)
AM ˈmu͵lɑ

mooli
BR ˈmuːl|i, -ɪz
AM ˈmuli, -z

moolvi
BR ˈmuːlv|i, -ɪz
AM ˈmulvi, -z

moolvie
BR ˈmuːlv|i, -ɪz
AM ˈmulvi, -z

moon
BR muːn, -z, -ɪŋ, -d
AM mun, -z, -ɪŋ, -d

moonbeam
BR ˈmuːnbiːm, -z
AM ˈmun͵bim, -z

mooncalf
BR ˈmuːnkɑːf
AM ˈmun͵kæf

mooncalves
BR ˈmuːnkɑːvz
AM ˈmun͵kævz

Mooney
BR ˈmuːni
AM ˈmuni

moonfish
BR ˈmuːnfɪʃ
AM ˈmun͵fɪʃ

Moonie
BR ˈmuːn|i, -ɪz
AM ˈmuni, -z

moonily
BR ˈmuːnɪli
AM ˈmunəli

moonless
BR ˈmuːnləs
AM ˈmunləs

moonlight
BR ˈmuːnlʌɪt, -s, -ɪŋ, -ɪd
AM ˈmun͵laɪ|t, -ts, -dɪŋ,
-dɪd

moonlighter
BR ˈmuːnlʌɪtə(r), -z
AM ˈmun͵laɪdər, -z

moonlit
BR ˈmuːnlɪt
AM ˈmun͵lɪt

moonquake
BR ˈmuːnkweɪk, -s
AM ˈmun͵kweɪk, -s

moonrise
BR ˈmuːnrʌɪz, -ɪz
AM ˈmun͵raɪz, -ɪz

moonscape
BR ˈmuːnskeɪp, -s
AM ˈmun͵skeɪp, -s

moonset
BR ˈmuːnsɛt, -s
AM ˈmun͵sɛt, -s

moonshee
BR ˈmuːnʃiː, -z
AM ˈmun͵ʃi, -z

moonshine
BR ˈmuːnʃʌɪn
AM ˈmun͵ʃaɪn

moonshiner
BR ˈmuːnʃʌɪnə(r), -z
AM ˈmun͵ʃaɪnər, -z

moonshot
BR ˈmuːnʃɒt, -s
AM ˈmun͵ʃɑt, -s

moonstone
BR ˈmuːnstəʊn, -z
AM ˈmun͵stoʊn, -z

moonstruck
BR ˈmuːnstrʌk
AM ˈmun͵strʌk

moony
BR ˈmuːn|i, -ɪz, -ɪə(r),
-ɪɪst
AM ˈmuni, -z, -ər, -ɪst

moor
BR mʊə(r), mɔː(r), -z,
-ɪŋ, -d
AM mʊ|(ə)r, -(ə)rz, -rɪŋ,
-(ə)rd

moorage
BR ˈmʊər|ɪdʒ,
ˈmɔːr|ɪdʒ, -ɪdʒɪz
AM ˈmʊrɪdʒ, -ɪz

moorcock
BR ˈmʊəkɒk, ˈmɔːkɒk,
-s
AM ˈmʊr͵kɑk, -s

Moorcroft
BR ˈmʊəkrɒft,
ˈmɔːkrɒft
AM ˈmʊr͵krɔft,
ˈmɔr͵krɔft

Moore
BR mʊə(r), mɔː(r)
AM mʊ(ə)r, mɔ(ə)r

moorfowl
BR ˈmʊəfaʊl, ˈmɔːfaʊl
AM ˈmʊr͵faʊl

Moorhead
BR ˈmʊəhɛd, ˈmɔːhɛd
AM ˈmʊr͵(h)ɛd,
ˈmɔr͵(h)ɛd

moorhen
BR ˈmʊəhɛn, ˈmɔːhɛn,
-z
AM ˈmʊr͵(h)ɛn, -z

Moorhouse
BR ˈmʊəhaʊs,
ˈmɔːhaʊs
AM ˈmʊr͵(h)aʊs,
ˈmɔr͵(h)aʊs

mooring
BR ˈmʊərɪŋ, ˈmɔːrɪŋ, -z
AM ˈmʊrɪŋ, -z

Moorish
BR ˈmʊərɪʃ, ˈmɔːrɪʃ
AM ˈmʊrɪʃ

Moorish idol
BR ˌmʊərɪʃ ˈʌɪdl,
ˌmɔːrɪʃ +,
AM ˌmʊrɪʃ ˈaɪdəl, -z

moorland
BR ˈmʊələnd, ˈmɔːlənd
AM ˈmʊr͵lænd,
ˈmʊrlənd

Moorman
BR ˈmʊəmən, ˈmɔːmən
AM ˈmʊrmən

moory
BR ˈmʊəri, ˈmɔːri
AM ˈmʊri

moose
BR muːs, -ɪz
AM mus, -əz

moot
BR muːt, -s, -ɪŋ, -ɪd
AM mu|t, -ts, -dɪŋ, -dəd

mop
BR mɒp, -s, -ɪŋ, -t
AM mɑp, -s, -ɪŋ, -t

mope
BR məʊp, -s, -ɪŋ, -t
AM moʊp, -s, -ɪŋ, -t

moped
BR ˈməʊpɛd, -z
AM ˈmoʊ͵pɛd, -z

moper
BR ˈməʊpə(r), -z
AM ˈmoʊpər, -z

mophead
BR ˈmɒphɛd, -z
AM ˈmɑp͵(h)ɛd, -z

mopily
BR ˈməʊpɪli
AM ˈmoʊpəli

mopiness
BR ˈməʊpɪnɪs
AM ˈmoʊpɪnɪs

mopish
BR ˈməʊpɪʃ
AM ˈmoʊpɪʃ

mopoke
BR ˈməʊpəʊk, -s
AM ˈmoʊ͵poʊk, -s

moppet
BR ˈmɒpɪt, -s
AM ˈmɑpət, -s

moppy
BR ˈmɒp|i, -ɪə(r), -ɪɪst
AM ˈmɑpi, -ər, -əst

Mopti
BR ˈmɒpti
AM ˈmɑpti

mopy
BR ˈməʊp|i, -ɪə(r), -ɪɪst
AM ˈmoʊpi, -ər, -əst

moquette
BR mɒˈkɛt, mə(ʊ)ˈkɛt
AM moʊˈkɛt

mor
BR mɔː(r)
AM mɔ(ə)r

Morag
BR ˈmɔːrag
AM ˈmɔræg

morainal
BR məˈreɪnl
AM məˈreɪnəl

moraine
BR məˈreɪn, -z
AM məˈreɪn, -z

morainic
BR məˈreɪnɪk
AM məˈreɪnɪk

moral
BR ˈmɒrəl, ˈmɒrl̩, -z
AM ˈmɔːrəl, -z
morale
BR məˈrɑːl
AM məˈræl, mɔˈræl
Morales
BR məˈrɑːliz
AM məˈræləs
moralisation
BR ˌmɒrəlaɪˈzeɪʃn,
ˌmɒrl̩aɪˈzeɪʃn, -z
AM ˌmɔrələˈzeɪʃən,
ˌmɔrəlaɪˈzeɪʃən, -z
moralise
BR ˈmɒrəlaɪz,
ˈmɒrl̩aɪz, -ɪz, -ɪŋ, -d
AM ˈmɔrəˌlaɪz, -ɪz, -ɪŋ,
-d
moraliser
BR ˈmɒrəlaɪzə(r),
ˈmɒrl̩aɪzə(r), -z
AM ˈmɔrəˌlaɪzər, -z
moralisingly
BR ˈmɒrəlaɪzɪŋli,
ˈmɒrl̩aɪzɪŋli
AM ˈmɔrəˌlaɪzɪŋli
moralism
BR ˈmɒrəliz(ə)m,
ˈmɒrl̩ɪz(ə)m
AM ˈmɔrəˌlɪzəm
moralist
BR ˈmɒrəlɪst, ˈmɒrl̩ɪst,
-s
AM ˈmɔrələst, -s
moralistic
BR ˌmɒrəˈlɪstɪk,
ˌmɒrl̩ˈɪstɪk
AM ˌmɔrəˈlɪstɪk
moralistically
BR ˌmɒrəˈlɪstɪkli,
ˌmɒrl̩ˈɪstɪkli
AM ˌmɔrəˈlɪstək(ə)li
morality
BR məˈralɪti
AM məˈrælədi,
mɔˈrælədi
moralization
BR ˌmɒrəlaɪˈzeɪʃn,
ˌmɒrl̩aɪˈzeɪʃn, -z
AM ˌmɔrələˈzeɪʃən,
ˌmɔrəlaɪˈzeɪʃən, -z
moralize
BR ˈmɒrəlaɪz,
ˈmɒrl̩aɪz, -ɪz, -ɪŋ, -d
AM ˈmɔrəˌlaɪz, -ɪz, -ɪŋ,
-d
moralizer
BR ˈmɒrəlaɪzə(r),
ˈmɒrl̩aɪzə(r), -z
AM ˈmɔrəˌlaɪzər, -z
moralizingly
BR ˈmɒrəlaɪzɪŋli,
ˈmɒrl̩aɪzɪŋli
AM ˈmɔrəˌlaɪzɪŋli
morally
BR ˈmɒrəli, ˈmɒrl̩i
AM ˈmɔrəli

Moran
BR məˈran, ˈmɔːrən,
ˈmɔːrn̩
AM məˈræn
Morant
BR məˈrant
AM məˈrænt
morass
BR məˈras, -ɪz
AM məˈræs, mɔˈræs,
-əz
moratoria
BR ˌmɒrəˈtɔːriə(r)
AM ˌmɔrəˈtɔriə
moratorium
BR ˌmɒrəˈtɔːriəm, -z
AM ˌmɔrəˈtɔriəm, -z
Moravia
BR məˈreɪviə(r)
AM məˈreɪviə
Moravian
BR məˈreɪviən, -z
AM məˈreɪviən, -z
moray
BR ˈmɒreɪ, ˈmɔːreɪ,
mʊˈreɪ, məˈreɪ, -z
AM ˈmɔːreɪ, məˈreɪ, -z
Moray Firth
BR ˌmʌrɪ ˈfəːθ
AM ˈmɔˌreɪ ˈfərθ
məˈreɪ +
morbid
BR ˈmɔːbɪd
AM ˈmɔrbəd
morbidity
BR ˈmɔːˈbɪdɪti
AM mɔrˈbɪdɪdi
morbidly
BR ˈmɔːbɪdli
AM ˈmɔrbədli
morbidness
BR ˈmɔːbɪdnɪs
AM ˈmɔrbədnəs
morbific
BR ˈmɔːˈbɪfɪk
AM mɔrˈbɪfɪk
morbilli
BR mɔːˈbɪlaɪ, mɔːˈbɪliː
AM mɔrˈbɪˌlaɪ
morbillivirus
BR mɔːˈbɪlɪvaɪrəs, -ɪz
AM mɔrˈbɪləˌvaɪrəs,
-əz
mordacious
BR mɔːˈdeɪʃəs
AM mɔrˈdeɪʃəs
mordacity
BR mɔːˈdasɪti
AM mɔrˈdæsədi
mordancy
BR ˈmɔːdnsi
AM ˈmɔrdnsi
mordant
BR ˈmɔːdnt, -s
AM ˈmɔrdnt, -s
mordantly
BR ˈmɔːdntli

AM ˈmɔrdn(t)li
Mordecai
BR ˈmɔːdɪkaɪ
AM ˈmɔrdəˌkaɪ
mordent
BR ˈmɔːdnt, -s
AM ˈmɔrdnt, -s
Mordred
BR ˈmɔːdrɪd
AM ˈmɔrdrəd
Mordvin
BR ˈmɔːdvɪn
AM ˈmɔrdvən
more
BR mɔː(r)
AM mɔ(ə)r
moreen
BR mʊˈriːn
AM məˈrin
moreish
BR ˈmɔːrɪʃ
AM ˈmɔrɪʃ
morel
BR məˈrɛl, mʊˈrɛl
AM məˈrɛl, mɔˈrɛl
morello
BR məˈrɛləʊ, mʊˈrɛləʊ,
-z
AM məˈrɛloʊ, -z
Moreno
BR məˈriːnəʊ,
məˈreɪnəʊ
AM məˈrinoʊ,
məˈreɪnoʊ
moreover
BR mɔːrˈəʊvə(r)
AM mɔˈroʊvər
morepork
BR ˈmɔːpɔːk, -s
AM ˈmɔrˌpɔ(ə)rk, -s
mores
BR ˈmɔːreɪz
AM ˈmɔreɪz
Moresby¹
place in UK
BR ˈmʊrɪsbi
AM ˈmɔrzbi
Moresby²
Port Moresby
BR ˈmɔːzbi
AM ˈmɔrzbi
Moresco
BR məˈrɛskəʊ
AM məˈrɛskoʊ
Moresque
BR məˈrɛsk, mɔːˈrɛsk
AM məˈrɛsk
**Moretonhamp-
stead**
BR ˌmɔːtn̩ˈham(p)stɪd,
ˌmɔːtn̩ˈham(p)stɛd
AM ˌmɔr(ə)tən̩ˈhæm(p)-
stɛd
Morfa
BR ˈmɔːvə(r)
AM ˈmɔrfə
WE ˈmɒrva

Morgan
BR ˈmɔːg(ə)n
AM ˈmɔrgən
morganatic
BR ˌmɔːgəˈnatɪk
AM ˌmɔrgəˈnædɪk
morganatically
BR ˌmɔːgəˈnatɪkli
AM ˌmɔrgəˈnædək(ə)li
Morgan le Fay
BR ˌmɔːg(ə)n lə ˈfeɪ
AM ˌmɔrgən lə ˈfeɪ
morgen
BR ˈmɔːg(ə)n, -z
AM ˈmɔrgən, -z
morgue
BR mɔːg, -z
AM mɔ(ə)rg, -z
Moriarty
BR ˌmɒrɪˈɑːti
AM ˌmɔriˈɑrdi
moribund
BR ˈmɒrɪbʌnd
AM ˈmɔrəˌbənd
moribundity
BR ˌmɒrɪˈbʌndɪti
AM ˌmɔrəˈbəndədi
morion
BR ˈmɒrɪən, -z
AM ˈmɔriən, -z
Morisco
BR məˈrɪskəʊ, -z
AM məˈrɪskoʊ, -z
morish
BR ˈmɔːrɪʃ
AM ˈmɔrɪʃ
Morison
BR ˈmɒrɪs(ə)n
AM ˈmɔrəsən
Morland
BR ˈmɔːlənd
AM ˈmɔrlənd
Morley
BR ˈmɔːli
AM ˈmɔrli
Mormon
BR ˈmɔːmən, -z
AM ˈmɔrmən, -z
Mormonism
BR ˈmɔːmənɪz(ə)m
AM ˈmɔrməˌnɪzəm
morn
BR mɔːn, -z
AM mɔ(ə)rn, -z
Morna
BR ˈmɔːnə(r)
AM ˈmɔrnə
Mornay
BR ˈmɔːneɪ, -z
AM mɔrˈneɪ, -z
morning
BR ˈmɔːnɪŋ, -z
AM ˈmɔrnɪŋ, -z
Mornington
BR ˈmɔːnɪŋt(ə)n
AM ˈmɔrnɪŋtən

Moro
BR 'mɔːrəʊ, -z
AM 'mɔːroʊ, -z

Moroccan
BR məˈrɒk(ə)n, -z
AM məˈrɑːkən, -z

Morocco
BR məˈrɒkəʊ
AM məˈrɑːkoʊ

moron
BR 'mɔːrɒn, -z
AM 'mɔːrɑːn, 'moʊrɑːn, -z

Moroni
BR məˈrəʊni
AM məˈrɑːni, mɔːˈrɑːni

moronic
BR məˈrɒnɪk
AM məˈrɑːnɪk, mɔːˈrɑːnɪk

moronically
BR məˈrɒnɪkli
AM məˈrɑːnək(ə)li, mɔːˈrɑːnək(ə)li

moronism
BR 'mɔːrɒnɪz(ə)m
AM 'mɔːrəˌnɪzəm, 'mɔːrɑːnˌɪzəm

morose
BR məˈrəʊs
AM məˈroʊs, mɔːˈrəʊs

morosely
BR məˈrəʊsli
AM məˈroʊsli, mɔːˈroʊsli

moroseness
BR məˈrəʊsnəs
AM məˈroʊsnəs, mɔːˈroʊsnəs

Morpeth
BR 'mɔːpəθ
AM 'mɔːrpəθ

morph
BR mɔːf, -s
AM mɔː(ə)rf, -s

morpheme
BR 'mɔːfiːm, -z
AM 'mɔːrˌfiːm, -z

morphemic
BR mɔːˈfiːmɪk, -s
AM mɔːrˈfiːmɪk, -s

morphemically
BR mɔːˈfiːmɪkli
AM mɔːrˈfiːmɪk(ə)li

Morpheus
BR 'mɔːfiəs
AM 'mɔːrfiəs, 'mɔːrˌfjuːs

morphia
BR 'mɔːfiə(r)
AM 'mɔːrfiə

morphine
BR 'mɔːfiːn
AM 'mɔːrfin

morphing
BR 'mɔːfɪŋ, -z
AM 'mɔːrfɪŋ, -z

morphinism
BR 'mɔːfɪnɪz(ə)m
AM 'mɔːrfəˌnɪzəm

morphogenesis
BR ˌmɔːfə(ʊ)ˈdʒenɪsɪs
AM ˌmɔːrfəˈdʒenəsəs

morphogenetic
BR ˌmɔːfə(ʊ)dʒɪˈnetɪk
AM ˌmɔːrfədʒəˈnedɪk

morphogenic
BR ˌmɔːfə(ʊ)ˈdʒenɪk
AM ˌmɔːrfəˈdʒenɪk

morphological
BR ˌmɔːfəˈlɒdʒɪkl
AM ˌmɔːrfəˈlɑdʒəkəl

morphologically
BR ˌmɔːfəˈlɒdʒɪkli
AM ˌmɔːrfəˈlɑdʒək(ə)li

morphologist
BR mɔːˈfɒlədʒɪst, -s
AM mɔːrˈfɑːlədʒəst, -s

morphology
BR mɔːˈfɒlədʒi
AM mɔːrˈfɑːlədʒi

morphometrics
BR ˌmɔːfəˈmetrɪks
AM ˌmɔːrfəˈmetrɪks

morphometry
BR mɔːˈfɒmɪtri
AM mɔːrˈfɑmətri

morphophonemic
BR ˌmɔːfəʊfəˈniːmɪk
AM ˌmɔːrfoʊfəˈnimɪk

morphophonemically
BR ˌmɔːfəʊfəˈniːmɪkli
AM ˌmɔːrfoʊfəˈnimək(ə)li

Morphy
BR 'mɔːfi
AM 'mɔːrfi

morris
BR 'mɒrɪs, -ɪsɪz
AM 'mɔːrəs, 'mɑrəs, -əz

Morrison
BR 'mɒrɪs(ə)n
AM 'mɔːrəsən, 'mɑrəsən

Morrissey
BR 'mɒrɪsi
AM 'mɔːrəsi

morrow
BR 'mɒrəʊ, -z
AM 'mɔːroʊ, 'mɑroʊ, -z

morse
BR mɔːs, -ɪz, -ɪŋ, -t
AM mɔː(ə)rs, -əz, -ɪŋ, -t

Morse code
BR ˌmɔːs ˈkəʊd
AM ˌmɔːrs ˈkoʊd

morsel
BR 'mɔːsl, -z
AM 'mɔːrsəl, -z

mort
BR mɔːt, -s
AM mɔː(ə)rt, -s

mortadella
BR ˌmɔːtəˈdelə(r)
AM ˌmɔːrdəˈdelə

mortal
BR 'mɔːtl, -z
AM 'mɔːrdl, -z

mortality
BR mɔːˈtalɪti
AM mɔːrˈtælədi

mortally
BR 'mɔːtli, 'mɔːtəli
AM 'mɔːrdli

mortar
BR 'mɔːtə(r), -z
AM 'mɔːrdər, -z

mortarboard
BR 'mɔːtəbɔːd, -z
AM 'mɔːrdərˌbɔ(ə)rd, -z

mortarless
BR 'mɔːtələs
AM 'mɔːrdərləs

mortary
BR 'mɔːtəri
AM 'mɔːrdəri

mortgage
BR 'mɔːgɪdʒ, -ɪdʒɪz, -ɪdʒɪŋ, -ɪdʒd
AM 'mɔːrgɪdʒ, -ɪz, -ɪŋ, -d

mortgageable
BR 'mɔːgɪdʒəbl
AM 'mɔːrgədʒəbəl

mortgagee
BR ˌmɔːgɪˈdʒiː, -z
AM ˌmɔːrgəˈdʒi, -z

mortgager
BR 'mɔːgɪdʒə(r), -z
AM 'mɔːrgədʒər, -z

mortgagor
BR ˌmɔːgɪˈdʒɔː(r), 'mɔːgɪdʒə(r), -z
AM ˌmɔːrgəˈdʒɔ(ə)r, 'mɔːrgədʒər, -z

mortice
BR 'mɔːtɪs, -ɪsɪz, -ɪsɪŋ, -ɪst
AM 'mɔːrdəs, -əz, -ɪŋ, -t

mortician
BR mɔːˈtɪʃn, -z
AM mɔːrˈtɪʃən, -z

mortification
BR ˌmɔːtɪfɪˈkeɪʃn
AM ˌmɔːrdəfəˈkeɪʃən

mortify
BR 'mɔːtɪfaɪ, -z, -ɪŋ, -d
AM 'mɔːrdəˌfaɪ, -z, -ɪŋ, -d

mortifyingly
BR 'mɔːtɪfaɪɪŋli
AM 'mɔːrdəˌfaɪɪŋli

Mortimer
BR 'mɔːtɪmə(r)
AM 'mɔːrdəmər

mortise
BR 'mɔːtɪs, -ɪsɪz, -ɪsɪŋ, -ɪst
AM 'mɔːrdəs, -əz, -ɪŋ, -t

Mortlake
BR 'mɔːtleɪk

AM 'mɔːrtˌleɪk

mortmain
BR 'mɔːtmeɪn
AM 'mɔːrtˌmeɪn

Morton
BR 'mɔːtn
AM 'mɔːrt(ə)n

mortuary
BR 'mɔːtjʊər|i, 'mɔːtjʊər|i, 'mɔːtʃ(ə)r|i, -iz
AM 'mɔːrtʃəˌweri, -z

morula
BR 'mɔːr(j)ələ(r), 'mɒr(j)ələ(r)
AM 'mɔːrələ, 'mɑrələ

morulae
BR 'mɔːr(j)əli:, 'mɒr(j)əli:
AM 'mɔːrəli, 'mɑrəli, 'mɑrəˌlaɪ, 'mɔːrəlaɪ

Morwenna
BR mɔːˈwenə(r)
AM 'mɔːrˈwenə

morwong
BR 'mɔːwɒŋ, -z
AM 'mɔːrˌwɒŋ, 'mɑrˌwɑŋ, -z

mosaic
BR mə(ʊ)ˈzeɪɪk, -s
AM moʊˈzeɪɪk, -s

mosaic gold
BR mə(ʊ)ˌzeɪɪk ˈgəʊld
AM moʊˌzeɪɪk ˈgoʊld

mosaicist
BR mə(ʊ)ˈzeɪɪsɪst, -s
AM moʊˈzeɪəsəst, -s

Mosaic Law
BR mə(ʊ)ˌzeɪɪk ˈlɔː(r)
AM moʊˌzeɪɪk ˈlɔ

mosasaur
BR 'məʊsəsɔː(r), -z
AM 'moʊsəˌsɔ(ə)r, -z

mosasauri
BR ˌməʊsəˈsɔːraɪ
AM ˌmoʊsəˈsɔraɪ

mosasaurus
BR ˌməʊsəˈsɔːrəs, -iz
AM ˌmoʊsəˈsɔrəs, -əz

moschatel
BR ˌmɒskəˈtel
AM ˌmɑːskəˈtel, ˌmɑːskəˈtel

Moscow
BR 'mɒskəʊ
AM 'mɑːsˌkaʊ, 'mɑːsˌkoʊ

Moseley
BR 'məʊzli
AM 'moʊzli

Moselle
BR mə(ʊ)ˈzel, -z
AM moʊˈzel, -z

Moser
BR 'məʊzə(r)
AM 'moʊzər

Moses
BR 'məʊzɪz
AM 'moʊzəs

mosey
BR 'məʊz|i, -ɪz, -ɪŋ, -ɪd
AM 'moʊzi, -z, -ɪŋ, -d

moshav
BR 'məʊʃɑːv, məʊ'ʃɑːv
AM moʊ'ʃɑv

moshavim
BR mə(ʊ)'ʃɑːvɪm,
ˌməʊʃə'vɪm
AM ˌmoʊʃə'vɪm

Moskva
BR 'mɒskvə(r)
AM 'mɑskvə
RUS ma'skva

Moslem
BR 'mɒzlɪm, 'mʊzlɪm,
-z
AM 'mɑzləm, -z

Mosley
BR 'məʊzli, 'mɒzli
AM 'moʊzli

mosque
BR mɒsk, -s
AM mɑsk, -s

mosquito
BR mə'skiːtəʊ,
mɒ'skiːtəʊ, -z
AM mə'skidoʊ, -z

moss
BR mɒs, -ɪz
AM mɔs, mɑs, -əz

Mossad
BR 'mɒsad
AM ˌmɔ'sɑd, ˌmɑ'sɑd

mossback
BR 'mɒsbak, -s
AM 'mɔs,bæk,
'mɑs,bæk, -s

Mossel Bay
BR ˌmɒsl 'beɪ
AM ˌmɔsəl 'beɪ, ˌmɑsəl
'beɪ

mossgrown
BR ˌmɒs'grəʊn
AM 'mɔs,groʊn,
'mɑs,groʊn

mossie
BR 'mɒz|i, 'mɒs|i, -ɪz
AM 'mɔsi, 'mɑsi, -z

mossiness
BR 'mɒsɪnɪs
AM 'mɔsɪnɪs, 'mɑsɪnɪs

mosslike
BR 'mɒslaɪk
AM 'mɔs,laɪk,
'mɑs,laɪk

mosso
BR 'mɒsəʊ
AM 'moʊ,soʊ

Mossop
BR 'mɒsəp
AM 'mɑsəp

mosstrooper
BR 'mɒs,truːpə(r), -z

AM 'mɔs,truːpər,
'mɑs,truːpər, -z

mossy
BR 'mɒs|i, -ɪə(r), -ɪɪst
AM 'mɔsi, 'mɑsi, -ər,
-ɪst

most
BR məʊst
AM moʊst

mostly
BR 'məʊs(t)li
AM 'moʊs(t)li

Mostyn
BR 'mɒstɪn
AM 'mɑstən

Mosul
BR 'məʊs(ə)l
AM mə'suːl

MOT
BR ˌeməʊ'tiː, -z, -ɪŋ, -d
AM ˌem,oʊ'ti, -z, -ɪŋ, -d

mot
BR məʊ, -z
AM moʊ, -z

mote
BR məʊt, -s
AM moʊt, -s

motel
BR məʊ'tel, -z
AM moʊ'tel, -z

motet
BR məʊ'tet, -s
AM moʊ'tet, -s

moth
BR mɒθ, -s
AM mɔ|θ, mɑ|θ, -ðz

mothball
BR 'mɒθbɔːl, -z, -ɪŋ, -d
AM 'mɔθ,bɔl, 'mɑθ,bɑl,
-z, -ɪŋ, -d

mother
BR 'mʌðə(r), -əz,
-(ə)rɪŋ, -əd
AM 'mʌðər, -ərz,
-(ə)rɪŋ, -ərd

motherboard
BR 'mʌðəbɔːd, -z
AM 'mʌðər,bɔ(ə)rd, -z

mothercraft
BR 'mʌðəkrɑːft,
'mʌðəkraft
AM 'mʌðər,kræft

motherfucker
BR 'mʌðəˌfʌkə(r), -z
AM 'mʌðərˌfəkər, -z

motherfucking
BR 'mʌðəˌfʌkɪŋ
AM 'mʌðərˌfəkɪŋ

motherhood
BR 'mʌðəhʊd
AM 'mʌðər,(h)ʊd

motherland
BR 'mʌðəland, -z
AM 'mʌðərˌlænd, -z

motherless
BR 'mʌðələs
AM 'mʌðərləs

motherlessness
BR 'mʌðələsnəs
AM 'mʌðərləsnəs

motherlike
BR 'mʌðəlʌɪk
AM 'mʌðər,laɪk

motherliness
BR 'mʌðəlɪnɪs
AM 'mʌðərlɪnɪs

motherly
BR 'mʌðəli
AM 'mʌðərli

Motherwell
BR 'mʌðəwel,
'mʌðəw(ə)l
AM 'mʌðər,wel

mothproof
BR 'mɒθpruːf, -s, -ɪŋ, -t
AM 'mɔθ,pruf,
'mɑθ,pruf, -s, -ɪŋ, -t

mothy
BR 'mɒθ|i, -ɪə(r), -ɪɪst
AM 'mɑθi, -ər, -ɪst

motif
BR məʊ'tiːf, -s
AM moʊ'tif, -s

motile
BR 'məʊtʌɪl
AM 'moʊtl, 'moʊ,taɪl

motility
BR məʊ'tɪlɪti
AM moʊ'tɪlɪdi

motion
BR 'məʊʃ|n, -nz,
-ŋɪŋ\-ənɪŋ, -nd
AM 'moʊʃ|ən, -ənz,
-(ə)nɪŋ, -ənd

motional
BR 'məʊʃnl
AM 'moʊʃənl,
'moʊʃnəl

motionless
BR 'məʊʃnləs
AM 'moʊʃənləs

motionlessly
BR 'məʊʃnləsli
AM 'moʊʃənləsli

motionlessness
BR 'məʊʃnləsnəs
AM 'moʊʃənləsnəs

motivate
BR 'məʊtɪveɪt, -s, -ɪŋ,
-ɪd
AM 'moʊdə,veɪt, -ts,
-dɪŋ, -dɪd

motivation
BR ˌməʊtɪ'veɪʃn
AM ˌmoʊdə'veɪʃən

motivational
BR ˌməʊtɪ'veɪʃn(ə)l,
ˌməʊtɪ'veɪʃən(ə)l
AM ˌmoʊdə'veɪʃ(ə)nəl

motivationally
BR ˌməʊtɪ'veɪʃnəli,
ˌməʊtɪ'veɪʃn̩li,
ˌməʊtɪ'veɪʃən|i,
ˌməʊtɪ'veɪʃ(ə)nəli
AM ˌmoʊdə'veɪʃ(ə)nəli

motivator
BR 'məʊtɪveɪtə(r), -z
AM 'moʊdə,veɪdər, -z

motive
BR 'məʊtɪv, -z
AM 'moʊdɪv, -z

motiveless
BR 'məʊtɪvlɪs
AM 'moʊdɪvlɪs

motivelessly
BR 'məʊtɪvlɪsli
AM 'moʊdɪvlɪsli

motivelessness
BR 'məʊtɪvlɪsnɪs
AM 'moʊdɪvlɪsnɪs

motivity
BR məʊ'tɪvɪti
AM moʊ'tɪvɪdi

mot juste
BR ˌməʊ 'ʒuːst
AM ˌmoʊ 'ʒust

motley
BR 'mɒtli
AM 'mɑtli

motmot
BR 'mɒtmɒt, -s
AM 'mɑt,mɑt, -s

motocross
BR 'məʊtə(ʊ)krɒs
AM 'moʊdoʊ,krɔs,
'moʊdoʊ,krɑs

moto perpetuo
BR ˌməʊtəʊ
pə'petjuəʊ,
+ pə'petʃuəʊ
AM 'moʊ,doʊ
pər'pedə,woʊ

motor
BR 'məʊtə(r), -əz,
-(ə)rɪŋ, -əd
AM 'moʊdər, -z, -ɪŋ, -d

motorable
BR 'məʊt(ə)rəbl
AM 'moʊdərəbəl

motorbike
BR 'məʊtəbʌɪk, -s
AM 'moʊdər,baɪk, -s

motorboat
BR 'məʊtəbəʊt, -s
AM 'moʊdər,boʊt, -s

motorcade
BR 'məʊtəkeɪd, -z
AM 'moʊdər,keɪd, -z

motorcar
BR 'məʊtəkɑː(r), -z
AM 'moʊdər,kar, -z

motorcoach
BR 'məʊtəkəʊtʃ, -ɪz
AM 'moʊdər,koʊtʃ, -ɪz

motorcycle
BR 'məʊtəˌsʌɪk|l, -lz,
-lɪŋ\-lɪŋ, -ld
AM 'moʊdər,saɪk|əl,
-əlz, -(ə)lɪŋ, -əld

motorcycling
BR 'məʊtəˌsʌɪklɪŋ
AM 'moʊdər,saɪk(ə)lɪŋ

motorcyclist
BR ˈməʊtəˌsʌɪklɪst, -s
AM ˈmoʊdərˌsaɪklɪst,
-s

motorhome
BR ˈməʊtəhəʊm, -z
AM ˈmoʊdərˌ(h)oʊm,
-z

motorial
BR məʊˈtɔːrɪəl
AM moʊˈtorɪəl

motorisation
BR ˌməʊt(ə)rʌɪˈzeɪʃn
AM ˌmoʊdərəˈzeɪʃən,
ˌmoʊdəˌraɪˈzeɪʃən

motorise
BR ˈməʊtərʌɪz, -ɪz, -ɪŋ,
-d
AM ˈmoʊdərˌraɪz, -ɪz,
-ɪŋ, -d

motorist
BR ˈməʊt(ə)rɪst, -s
AM ˈmoʊdərəst, -s

motorization
BR ˌməʊt(ə)rʌɪˈzeɪʃn
AM ˌmoʊdərəˈzeɪʃən,
ˌmoʊdəˌraɪˈzeɪʃən

motorize
BR ˈməʊtərʌɪz, -ɪz, -ɪŋ,
-d
AM ˈmoʊdərˌraɪz, -ɪz,
-ɪŋ, -d

motorman
BR ˈməʊtəmən
AM ˈmoʊdərˌmæn

motormen
BR ˈməʊtəmɛn
AM ˈmoʊdərˌmɛn

motormouth
BR ˈməʊtəmaʊθ, -ðz
AM ˈmoʊdərˌmaʊθ, -ðz

motorway
BR ˈməʊtəweɪ, -z
AM ˈmoʊdərˌweɪ, -z

motory
BR ˈməʊt(ə)ri
AM ˈmoʊdəri

Motown®
BR ˈməʊtaʊn
AM ˈmoʊˌtaʊn

mots justes
BR ˌməʊ ˈʒuːst
AM ˌmoʊ ˈʒust

Mott
BR mɒt
AM mɑt

motte
BR mɒt, -s
AM mɑt, -s

mottle
BR ˈmɒtl̩, -z, -ɪŋ, -d
AM ˈmɑdəl, -z, -ɪŋ, -d

motto
BR ˈmɒtəʊ, -z
AM ˈmɑdoʊ, -z

Mottram
BR ˈmɒtrəm
AM ˈmɑtrəm

Motu
BR ˈməʊtuː
AM ˈmoʊdu

moue
BR muː, -z
AM mu, -z

moufflon
BR ˈmuːflɒn, -z
AM ˈmuflɑn, -z

mouflon
BR ˈmuːflɒn, -z
AM ˈmuflɑn, -z

mouillé
BR ˈmuːjeɪ, ˈmwiːeɪ
AM muˈjeɪ

moujik
BR ˌmuːˈʒɪk, -s
AM ˈmuʒɪk, -s

mould
BR məʊld, -z, -ɪŋ, -ɪd
AM moʊld, -z, -ɪŋ, -əd

mouldable
BR ˈməʊldəbl
AM ˈmoʊldəbəl

mouldboard
BR ˈməʊl(d)bɔːd, -z
AM ˈmoʊl(d)ˌbɔ(ə)rd,
-z

moulder
BR ˈməʊldə(r), -əz,
-(ə)rɪŋ, -əd
AM ˈmoʊldər, -z, -ɪŋ, -d

mouldiness
BR ˈməʊldɪnɪs
AM ˈmoʊldɪnɪs

moulding
BR ˈməʊldɪŋ, -z
AM ˈmoʊldɪŋ, -z

mouldy
BR ˈməʊld|i, -ɪə(r), -ɪɪst
AM ˈmoʊldi, -ər, -ɪst

moulin
BR ˈmuːlɪn, -z
AM muˈlɛn, -z

Moulinex®
BR ˈmuːlɪnɛks
AM ˈmulənɛks

Moulin Rouge
BR ˌmuːlɑ̃ ˈruːʒ
AM muˈlɛn ˈru(d)ʒ

Moulmein
BR ˈmuːlmeɪn
AM ˈmulˌmeɪn

moult
BR məʊlt, -s, -ɪŋ, -ɪd
AM moʊlt, -s, -ɪŋ, -əd

moulter
BR ˈməʊltə(r), -z
AM ˈmoʊltər, -z

Moulton
BR ˈməʊlt(ə)n
AM ˈmoʊltən, ˈmʊltən

mound
BR maʊnd, -z
AM maʊnd, -z

mount
BR maʊnt, -s, -ɪŋ, -ɪd

Mount
BR maʊn|t, -ts, -(t)ɪŋ,
-(t)əd

mountable
BR ˈmaʊntəbl
AM ˈmaʊnt(ə)bəl

mountain
BR ˈmaʊntɪn, -z
AM ˈmaʊnt(ə)n, -z

mountaineer
BR ˌmaʊntɪˈnɪə(r), -z,
-ɪŋ
AM ˌmaʊnt(ə)nˈɪ(ə)r,
-z, -ɪŋ

mountainous
BR ˈmaʊntɪnəs
AM ˈmaʊntnəs,
ˈmaʊn(t)ənəs

mountainside
BR ˈmaʊntɪnsʌɪd, -z
AM ˈmaʊntnˌsaɪd,
ˈmaʊn(t)ənˌsaɪd, -z

mountaintop
BR ˈmaʊntɪntɒp, -s
AM ˈmaʊntnˌtɑp,
ˈmaʊn(t)ənˌtɑp, -s

mountainy
BR ˈmaʊntɪni
AM ˈmaʊntni,
ˈmaʊn(t)əni

Mountbatten
BR ˌmaʊntˈbatn
AM ˌmaʊn(t)ˈbætn

mountebank
BR ˈmaʊntɪbaŋk, -s
AM ˈmaʊn(t)əˌbæŋk, -s

mountebankery
BR ˈmaʊntɪˌbaŋk(ə)ri
AM ˈmaʊn(t)əˌbæŋkəri

mounter
BR ˈmaʊntə(r), -z
AM ˈmaʊn(t)ər, -z

Mountie
BR ˈmaʊnt|i, -ɪz
AM ˈmaʊn(t)i, -z

mounting
BR ˈmaʊntɪŋ, -z
AM ˈmaʊn(t)ɪŋ, -z

Mount Isa
BR ˌmaʊnt ˈʌɪzə(r)
AM ˌmaʊn(t) ˈaɪzə

Mountjoy
BR ˈmaʊntdʒɔɪ,
ˌmaʊntˈdʒɔɪ
AM ˈmaʊn(t)ˈdʒɔɪ

Mounty
BR ˈmaʊnt|i, -ɪz
AM ˈmaʊn(t)i, -z

mourn
BR mɔːn, -z, -ɪŋ, -d
AM mɔ(ə)rn, -z, -ɪŋ, -d

Mourne
BR mɔːn
AM mɔ(ə)rn

mourner
BR ˈmɔːnə(r), -z
AM ˈmɔrnər, -z

mournful
BR ˈmɔːnf(ʊ)l
AM ˈmɔrnfəl

mournfully
BR ˈmɔːnfʊli, ˈmɔːnfˌli
AM ˈmɔrnfəli

mournfulness
BR ˈmɔːnf(ʊ)lnəs
AM ˈmɔrnfəlnəs

mourning
BR ˈmɔːnɪŋ
AM ˈmɔrnɪŋ

mousaka
BR mʊˈsɑːkə(r),
muːˈsɑːkə(r), -z
AM muˈsɑkə,
ˌmusəˈkɑ, -z

mouse
BR maʊs
AM maʊs

mousehole
BR ˈmaʊshəʊl, -z
AM ˈmaʊsˌ(h)oʊl, -z

Mousehoule
BR ˈmaʊzl
AM ˈmaʊsˌ(h)oʊl

mouselike
BR ˈmaʊslʌɪk
AM ˈmaʊsˌlaɪk

mouser
BR ˈmaʊsə(r), -z
AM ˈmaʊsər, -z

mousetrap
BR ˈmaʊstrap, -s
AM ˈmaʊsˌtræp, -s

mousey
BR ˈmaʊs|i, -ɪə(r), -ɪɪst
AM ˈmaʊsi, -ər, -ɪst

mousily
BR ˈmaʊsɪli
AM ˈmaʊsəli

mousiness
BR ˈmaʊsɪnɪs
AM ˈmaʊsɪnɪs

moussaka
BR mʊˈsɑːkə(r),
muːˈsɑːkə(r), -z
AM muˈsɑkə,
ˌmusəˈkɑ, -z

mousse
BR muːs, -ɪz
AM mus, -əz

mousseline
BR ˈmuːsliːn, muːˈsliːn
AM ˌmusəˈlin, muˈslin

moustache
BR məˈstɑːʃ, -ɪz, -t
AM ˈməˌstæʃ, məˈstæʃ,
-əz, -t

moustachio
BR məˈstɑːʃ(ɪ)əʊ,
məˈstɑʃ(ɪ)əʊ, -z, -d
AM məˈstæʃioʊ, -z, -d

Mousterian
BR muːˈstɪərɪən, -z
AM muˈstɪriən, -z

mousy
BR ˈmaʊs|i, -iə(r), -ɪst
AM ˈmaʊsi, -ər, -ɪst

mouth¹
noun
BR maʊθ, -ðz
AM maʊθ, -ðz

mouth²
verb
BR maʊð, -z, -ɪŋ, -d
AM maʊð, -z, -ɪŋ, -d

mouthbrooder
BR ˈmaʊθˌbruːdə(r), -z
AM ˈmaʊθˌbrudər, -z

mouther
BR ˈmaʊðə(r), -z
AM ˈmaʊðər, -z

mouthful
BR ˈmaʊθfʊl, -z
AM ˈmaʊθˌfʊl, -z

mouthless
BR ˈmaʊθləs
AM ˈmaʊθləs

mouthpart
BR ˈmaʊθpɑːt, -s
AM ˈmaʊθˌpart, -s

mouthpiece
BR ˈmaʊθpiːs, -ɪz
AM ˈmaʊθˌpis, -ɪz

mouth-to-mouth
BR ˌmaʊθtəˈmaʊθ
AM ˌmaʊθtəˈmaʊθ

mouthwash
BR ˈmaʊθwɒʃ, -ɪz
AM ˈmaʊʃˌwɔʃ, ˈmaʊʃˌwɑʃ, -əz

mouthy
BR ˈmaʊð|i, -iə(r), -ɪst
AM ˈmaʊði, ˈmaʊθi, -ər, -əst

movability
BR ˌmuːvəˈbɪlɪti
AM ˌmuːvəˈbɪlɪdi

movable
BR ˈmuːvəbl, -z
AM ˈmuːvəbəl, -z

movableness
BR ˈmuːvəblnəs
AM ˈmuːvəbəlnəs

movably
BR ˈmuːvəbli
AM ˈmuːvəbli

move
BR muːv, -z, -ɪŋ, -d
AM muːv, -z, -ɪŋ, -d

moveable
BR ˈmuːvəbl, -z
AM ˈmuːvəbəl, -z

movement
BR ˈmuːvm(ə)nt, -s
AM ˈmuːvmənt, -s

mover
BR ˈmuːvə(r), -z
AM ˈmuːvər, -z

movie
BR ˈmuːv|i, -ɪz
AM ˈmuːvi, -z

moviegoer
BR ˈmuːvɪˌɡəʊə(r), -z
AM ˈmuːviˌɡoʊər, -z

movie house
BR ˈmuːvɪ haʊ|s, -zɪz
AM ˈmuːvi haʊ|s, -zəz

moviemaker
BR ˈmuːvɪˌmeɪkə(r), -z
AM ˈmuːviˌmeɪkər, -z

Movietone®
BR ˈmuːvɪtəʊn
AM ˈmuːviˌtoʊn

movingly
BR ˈmuːvɪŋli
AM ˈmuːvɪŋli

mow¹
noun, in barley mow
BR məʊ, -z
AM moʊ, -z

mow²
noun, verb, stack
BR maʊ, -z, -ɪŋ, -d
AM maʊ, -z, -ɪŋ, -d

mow³
verb, to cut
BR məʊ, -z, -ɪŋ, -d
AM moʊ, -z, -ɪŋ, -d

mowable
BR ˈməʊəbl
AM ˈmoʊəbəl

Mowbray
BR ˈməʊbri, ˈməʊbreɪ
AM ˈmoʊbri, ˈmoʊˌbreɪ

mowburnt
BR ˈməʊbɜːnt
AM ˈmoʊˌbərnt

mower
BR ˈməʊə(r), -z
AM ˈmoʊər, -z

Mowgli
BR ˈmaʊgli
AM ˈmoʊgli

mowing
BR ˈməʊɪŋ, -z
AM ˈmoʊɪŋ, -z

mowlem
BR ˈməʊləm, -z
AM ˈmoʊləm, -z

mown
BR məʊn
AM moʊn

moxa
BR ˈmɒksə(r)
AM ˈmɑksə

moxibustion
BR ˌmɒksɪˈbʌstʃ(ə)n
AM ˌmɑksəˈbəstʃən

moxie
BR ˈmɒksi
AM ˈmɑksi

Moy
BR mɔɪ
AM mɔɪ

Moya
BR ˈmɔɪə(r)
AM ˈmɔɪə

Moyer
BR ˈmɔɪə(r)
AM ˈmɔɪər

Moyers
BR ˈmɔɪəz
AM ˈmɔɪərz

Moynahan
BR ˈmɔɪnəhən, ˈmɔɪnəhan
AM ˈmɔɪnəˌhæn

Moyne
BR mɔɪn
AM mɔɪn

Moynihan
BR ˈmɔɪnɪən, ˈmɔɪnɪhən, ˈmɔɪnɪhan
AM ˈmɔɪnɪˌhæn

Moyra
BR ˈmɔɪrə(r)
AM ˈmɔɪrə

Mozambican
BR ˌməʊz(ə)mˈbiːk(ə)n, ˌməʊzamˈbiːk(ə)n, -z
AM ˈmoʊzæmˈbikən, -z

Mozambiquan
BR ˌməʊz(ə)mˈbiːk(ə)n, ˌməʊzamˈbiːk(ə)n, -z
AM ˈmoʊzæmˈbikən, -z

Mozambique
BR ˌməʊz(ə)mˈbiːk, ˌməʊzamˈbiːk
AM ˌmoʊzæmˈbik

Mozarab
BR məʊˈzarəb, -z
AM moʊˈzɛrəb, -z

Mozarabic
BR məʊˈzarəbɪk
AM moʊˈzɛrəbɪk

Mozart
BR ˈməʊtsɑːt
AM ˈmoʊˌtsɑrt

Mozartian
BR məʊtˈsɑːtɪən, -z
AM moʊˈtsɑrdiən, -z

mozz
BR mɒz
AM mɑz

mozzarella
BR ˌmɒtsəˈrɛlə(r)
AM ˌmɑtsəˈrɛlə

mozzle
BR ˈmɒzl, -z
AM ˈmɑzəl, -z

MP
BR ˌɛmˈpiː, -z
AM ˌɛmˈpi, -z

mph
BR ˌɛmpiˈeɪtʃ
AM ˌɛmˌpiˈeɪtʃ

M.Phil.
BR ˌɛmˈfɪl, -z
AM ˌɛmˈfɪl, -z

Mr
BR ˈmɪstə(r)
AM ˈmɪstər

Mrs
BR ˈmɪsɪz
AM ˈmɪsɪz, ˈmɪsɪs

Ms
BR mɪz
AM mɪz

MSc
BR ˌɛmɛsˈsiː, -z
AM ˌɛmˌɛsˈsi, -z

MS-DOS®
BR ˌɛmɛsˈdɒs
AM ˌɛmˌɛsˈdɑs, ˌɛmˌɛsˈdɑs

M.Tech.
BR ˌɛmˈtɛk, -s
AM ˌɛmˈtɛk, -s

mu
BR mjuː, -z
AM mju, -z

Mubarak
BR məˈbarak
AM məˈbɑrak

much
BR mʌtʃ
AM mətʃ

Muchinga
BR muˈtʃɪŋɡə(r)
AM muˈtʃɪŋɡə

muchly
BR ˈmʌtʃli
AM ˈmətʃli

muchness
BR ˈmʌtʃnəs
AM ˈmətʃnəs

mucilage
BR ˈmjuːsɪlɪdʒ, ˈmjuːsˌlɪdʒ
AM ˈmjus(ə)lɪdʒ

mucilaginous
BR ˌmjuːsɪˈladʒɪnəs
AM ˌmjusəˈlædʒənəs

mucin
BR ˈmjuːsɪn, -z
AM ˈmjusən, -z

muck
BR mʌk, -s, -ɪŋ, -t
AM mək, -s, -ɪŋ, -t

mucker
BR ˈmʌkə(r), -z
AM ˈməkər, -z

muckerish
BR ˈmʌk(ə)rɪʃ
AM ˈmək(ə)rɪʃ

muckheap
BR ˈmʌkhiːp, -s
AM ˈmək(h)ip, -s

muckily
BR ˈmʌkɪli
AM ˈməkəli

muckiness
BR ˈmʌkɪnɪs
AM ˈməkɪnɪs

muckle
BR ˈmʌkl, -z
AM ˈməkəl, -z

muckrake
BR ˈmʌkreɪk, -s, -ɪŋ, -t

AM 'mək‚reɪk, -s, -ɪŋ, -t
muckraker
BR 'mʌk‚reɪkə(r), -z
AM 'mək‚reɪkər, -z
muckworm
BR 'mʌkwɜːm, -z
AM 'mək‚wɜrm, -z
mucky
BR 'mʌk|i, -ɪə(r), -ɪɪst
AM 'məki, -ər, -ɪst
mucopoly-saccharide
BR ‚mjuːkəʊ‚pɒlɪ-'sakəraɪd, -z
AM ‚mjukoʊ‚pɑli-'sækə‚raɪd, -z
mucosa
BR mjuː'kəʊzə(r)
AM mju'koʊzə
mucosity
BR mjuː'kɒsɪti
AM ‚mju'kɑsədi
mucous
BR 'mjuːkəs
AM 'mjukəs
mucro
BR 'mjuːkrəʊ, -z
AM 'mjukroʊ, -z
mucronate
BR 'mjuːkrəneɪt, 'mjuːkrənət
AM 'mjukrənət, 'mjukrə‚neɪt
mucus
BR 'mjuːkəs
AM 'mjukəs
mud
BR mʌd
AM məd
mudbank
BR 'mʌdbaŋk, -s
AM 'məd‚bæŋk, -s
mudbath
BR 'mʌd|bɑːθ, 'mʌd|baθ, -bɑːðz\-bɑːθs\-baθs
AM 'məd‚bæ|θ, -θs\-ðz
mudbrick
BR 'mʌdbrɪk, -s
AM 'məd‚brɪk, -s
muddily
BR 'mʌdɪli
AM 'mədəli
muddiness
BR 'mʌdɪnɪs
AM 'mədɪnɪs
muddle
BR 'mʌd|l, -lz, -l̩ɪŋ\-lɪŋ, -ld
AM 'məd|əl, -əlz, -(ə)lɪŋ, -əld
muddler
BR 'mʌd|ə(r), 'mʌd|ə(r), -z
AM 'məd(ə)lər, -z
muddlingly
BR 'mʌdɪŋli, 'mʌdɪŋli

AM 'mədl̩ɪŋli
muddy
BR 'mʌd|i, -ɪz, -ɪɪŋ, -ɪd, -ɪə(r), -ɪɪst
AM 'mədi, -z, -ɪŋ, -d, -ər, -ɪst
Mudeford
BR 'mʌdɪfəd
AM 'mədəfərd
Mudéjar
BR ‚muː'deɪhɑː(r)
AM mu'dɛ‚hɑr
Mudéjares
BR ‚muː'deɪhɑːrɛs
AM mu'dɛhɑr‚ɛs
mudfish
BR 'mʌdfɪʃ, -ɪz
AM 'məd‚fɪʃ, -ɪz
mudflap
BR 'mʌdflap, -s
AM 'məd‚flæp, -s
mudflat
BR 'mʌdflat, -s
AM 'məd‚flæt, -s
mudflow
BR 'mʌdfləʊ, -z
AM 'məd‚floʊ, -z
Mudge
BR mʌdʒ
AM mədʒ
mudguard
BR 'mʌdgɑːd, -z
AM 'məd‚gɑrd, -z
Mudie
BR 'mjuːdi
AM 'm(j)udi
mudlark
BR 'mʌdlɑːk, -s
AM 'məd‚lɑrk, -s
mudpack
BR 'mʌdpak, -s
AM 'məd‚pæk, -s
mudroom
BR 'mʌdruːm, 'mʌdrʊm, -z
AM 'məd‚rum, 'məd‚rʊm, -z
mudskipper
BR 'mʌd‚skɪpə(r), -z
AM 'məd‚skɪpər, -z
mudslinger
BR 'mʌd‚slɪŋə(r), -z
AM 'məd‚slɪŋər, -z
mudslinging
BR 'mʌd‚slɪŋɪŋ
AM 'məd‚slɪŋɪŋ
mudstone
BR 'mʌdstəʊn, -z
AM 'məd‚stoʊn, -z
mud volcano
BR ‚mʌd vɒl'keɪnəʊ
AM 'məd vɑl'keɪnoʊ
Mueller
BR 'mʊlə(r), 'm(j)uːlə(r)
AM 'm(j)ulər

Muenster
BR 'mʌnstə(r)
AM 'mənstər
muesli
BR 'm(j)uːzli
AM 'mjuzli
muezzin
BR mu'ɛzɪn, -z
AM m(j)u'ɛzn, 'muəzən, -z
muff
BR mʌf, -s, -ɪŋ, -t
AM məf, -s, -ɪŋ, -t
muffetee
BR ‚mʌfɪ'tiː, -z
AM 'məfiti, -z
muffin
BR 'mʌfɪn, -z
AM 'məfən, -z
muffineer
BR ‚mʌfɪ'nɪə(r), -z
AM 'məfə'nɪ(ə)r, -z
muffish
BR 'mʌfɪʃ
AM 'məfɪʃ
muffle
BR 'mʌf|l, -lz, -l̩ɪŋ\-lɪŋ, -ld
AM 'məf|əl, -əlz, -(ə)lɪŋ, -əld
muffler
BR 'mʌflə(r), -z
AM 'məf(ə)lər, -z
mufti
BR 'mʌfti
AM 'məfti
mug
BR mʌg, -z, -ɪŋ, -d
AM məg, -z, -ɪŋ, -d
Mugabe
BR mʊ'gɑːbi
AM mu'gɑbi
mugful
BR 'mʌgfʊl, -z
AM 'məg‚fʊl, -z
mugger
BR 'mʌgə(r), -z
AM 'məgər, -z
Muggeridge
BR 'mʌg‚ərɪdʒ
AM 'məgərɪdʒ
mugginess
BR 'mʌgɪnɪs
AM 'məgɪnɪs
mugging
BR 'mʌgɪŋ, -z
AM 'məgɪŋ, -z
muggins
BR 'mʌgɪnz, -ɪz
AM 'məgɪnz, -ɪz
muggy
BR 'mʌg|i, -ɪə(r), -ɪɪst
AM 'məgi, -ər, -ɪst
Mughal
BR 'mʊg(ə)l, 'muːg(ə)l, -z
AM 'məgəl, -z

mugshot
BR 'mʌgʃɒt, -s
AM 'məg‚ʃɑt, -s
mugwort
BR 'mʌgwɜːt, -s
AM 'məg‚wɜrt, 'məg‚wɔ(ə)rt, -s
mugwump
BR 'mʌgwʌmp, -s
AM 'məg‚wəmp, -s
Muhammad
BR mə'hamɪd
AM moʊ'hamɪd, mə'hamɪd
Muhammadanism
BR mə'hamədənɪz(ə)m
AM moʊ'hamədn̩‚ɪzəm, moʊ'hamədə‚nɪzəm, mə'hamədn̩‚ɪzəm, mə'hamədə‚nɪzəm
Muhammed
BR mə'hamɪd
AM moʊ'hamɪd, mə'hamɪd
Muhammedan
BR mə'hamɪd(ə)n, -z
AM moʊ'hamədən, mə'hamədən, -z
Muir
BR 'mjʊə(r), mjɔː(r)
AM 'mjʊ(ə)r
Muirhead
BR 'mjʊəhɛd, 'mjɔːhɛd
AM 'mjʊ(ə)r‚hɛd
mujahadeen
BR ‚mʊdʒəhə'diːn, ‚muːdʒəhə'diːn
AM ‚mʊdʒəhə'din, ‚mudʒəhə'din
mujaheddin
BR ‚mʊdʒəhɪ'diːn, ‚muːdʒəhɪ'diːn
AM ‚mʊdʒəhə'din, ‚mudʒəhə'din
mujahedin
BR ‚mʊdʒəhɪ'diːn, ‚muːdʒəhɪ'diːn
AM ‚mʊdʒəhə'din, ‚mudʒəhə'din
mujahidin
BR ‚mʊdʒəhə'diːn, ‚muːdʒəhə'diːn
AM ‚mʊdʒəhɪ'din, ‚mudʒəhɪ'din
Mukden
BR 'mʊkdən
AM 'mʊkdən
mukluk
BR 'mʌklʌk, -s
AM 'mək‚lək, -s
mulatto
BR mjuː'latəʊ, mjʊ'latəʊ, -z
AM 'm(j)ʊ'latoʊ, m(j)ʊ'lædoʊ, -z
mulberry
BR 'mʌlb(ə)r|i, -ɪz
AM 'məl‚bɛri, -z

Mulcaghey
BR mʌl'kaxi,
mʌl'kahi
AM məl'keɪhi

Mulcahy
BR mʌl'kahi
AM məl'keɪhi

mulch
BR mʌl(t)ʃ, -ɪz, -ɪŋ, -t
AM məltʃ, -əz, -ɪŋ, -t

mulct
BR mʌlkt, -s, -ɪŋ, -ɪd
AM məlk|(t), -(t)s, -tɪŋ, -təd

Muldoon
BR mʌl'duːn
AM məl'dun

mule
BR mjuːl, -z
AM mjul, -z

muleteer
BR ˌmjuːlɪˈtɪə(r), -z
AM ˌmjul(ə)'tɪ(ə)r, -z

mulga
BR 'mʌlgə(r), -z
AM 'məlgə, -z

Mulhearn
BR mʌl'həːn
AM məl'hərn

Mulholland
BR mʌl'hɒlənd
AM məl'hɑlən(d)

muli
BR 'muːlʲi, -ɪz
AM 'mjuli, -z

muliebrity
BR ˌmjuːlɪˈɛbrɪti
AM ˌmjuli'ɛbrədi

mulish
BR 'mjuːlɪʃ
AM 'mjulɪʃ

mulishly
BR 'mjuːlɪʃli
AM 'mjulɪʃli

mulishness
BR 'mjuːlɪʃnɪs
AM 'mjulɪʃnɪs

mull
BR mʌl, -z, -ɪŋ, -d
AM mʌl, -z, -ɪŋ, -d

mulla
BR 'mʌlə(r), 'mʊlə(r),
-z
AM 'mʊlə, 'mulə, -z

mullah
BR 'mʌlə(r), 'mʊlə(r),
-z
AM 'mʊlə, 'mulə, -z

Mullan
BR 'mʌlən
AM 'mələn

mullein
BR 'mʌlɪn, 'mʌleɪn, -z
AM 'mələn, -z

Mullen
BR 'mʌlən
AM 'mələn

Muller
BR 'mʌlə(r)
AM 'mələr

Müller
BR 'mʊlə(r)
AM 'm(j)ʊlər
GER 'mylɐ

muller
BR 'mʌlə(r), -z
AM 'mələr, -z

mullet
BR 'mʌlɪt, -s
AM 'mələt, -s

Mulley
BR 'mʌli
AM 'məli

mulligan
BR 'mʌlɪg(ə)n, -z
AM 'mələgən, -z

mulligatawny
BR ˌmʌlɪgəˈtɔːni
AM ˌmələgə'tɔni,
'mələgə'tɑni

mulligrubs
BR 'mʌlɪgrʌbz
AM 'məli,grəbz

Mullins
BR 'mʌlɪnz
AM 'mələnz

mullion
BR 'mʌliən, -z, -d
AM 'məljən, 'məliən, -z,
-d

mullock
BR 'mʌlək
AM 'mələk

mulloway
BR 'mʌləweɪ, -z
AM 'mələˌweɪ, -z

Mulroney
BR mʌl'rəʊni
AM məl'roʊni

se**multangular**
BR mʌl'taŋgjələ(r)
AM ˌməl'tæŋ(g)jələr

multiaxial
BR ˌmʌltɪ'aksɪəl
AM 'məlti'æksɪəl,
'məlˌtaɪ'æksɪəl

multicellular
BR ˌmʌltɪ'sɛljələ(r)
AM 'məlti'sɛljələr,
'məltə'sɛljələr,
'məlˌtaɪ'sɛljələr

multichannel
BR ˌmʌltɪ't'ʃanl
AM 'məlti't'ʃænl,
'məltə't'ʃænəl,
'məlˌtaɪ't'ʃænəl

multicolor
BR 'mʌltɪˌkʌlə(r),
ˌmʌltɪ'kʌlə(r)
AM 'məlti'kələr,
'məltə'kələr,
'məlˌtaɪ'kələr

multicolored
BR ˌmʌltɪ'kʌləd
AM 'məlti'kələrd,

'məltə'kələrd,
'məlˌtaɪ'kələrd

multicolour
BR 'mʌltɪˌkʌlə(r),
ˌmʌltɪ'kʌlə(r)
AM 'məlti'kələr,
'məltə'kələr,
'məlˌtaɪ'kələr

multicoloured
BR ˌmʌltɪ'kʌləd
AM 'məlti'kələrd,
'məltə'kələrd,
'məlˌtaɪ'kələrd

multicultural
BR ˌmʌltɪ'kʌltʃ(ə)rəl,
ˌmʌltɪ'kʌltʃ(ə)r|l
AM 'məlti'kəl(t)ʃ(ə)rəl,
'məltə'kəl(t)ʃ(ə)rəl,
'məlˌtaɪ'kəl(t)ʃ(ə)rəl

multiculturalism
BR ˌmʌltɪ'kʌltʃ(ə)rəl-
ɪz(ə)m,
ˌmʌltɪ'kʌltʃ(ə)r|ɪz(ə)m
AM 'məlti'kəl(t)ʃ(ə)rə-
ˌlɪzəm,
'məltə'kəl(t)ʃ(ə)rə-
ˌlɪzəm,
'məlˌtaɪ'kəl(t)ʃ(ə)rə-
ˌlɪzəm

multiculturalist
BR ˌmʌltɪ'kʌltʃ(ə)rəlɪst,
ˌmʌltɪ'kʌltʃ(ə)r|ɪst,
-s
AM 'məlti'kəl(t)ʃ(ə)rəl-
əst,
'məltə'kəl(t)ʃ(ə)rələst,
'məlˌtaɪ'kəl(t)ʃ(ə)rələst,
-s

multiculturally
BR ˌmʌltɪ'kʌltʃ(ə)rəli,
ˌmʌltɪ'kʌltʃ(ə)r|li
AM 'məlti'kəl(t)ʃ(ə)rəli,
'məltə'kəl(t)ʃ(ə)rəli,
'məlˌtaɪ'kəl(t)ʃ(ə)rəli

multidimensional
BR ˌmʌltɪdaɪ'mɛnʃn(ə)l,
ˌmʌltɪdaɪ'mɛnʃən(ə)l,
ˌmʌltɪdɪ'mɛnʃŋəl,
ˌmʌltɪdɪ'mɛnʃənəl
AM 'məltidə'mɛn(t)ʃ(ə)-
nəl,
'məltədə'mɛn(t)ʃ(ə)nəl,
'məlti,daɪ'mɛn(t)ʃ(ə)-
nəl,
'məltə,daɪ'mɛn(t)ʃ(ə)-
nəl,
'məlˌtaɪdə'mɛn(t)ʃ(ə)-
nəl

**multidimensional-
ity**
BR ˌmʌltɪdaɪˌmɛnʃə-
'nalɪti,
ˌmʌltɪdɪˌmɛnʃə'nalɪti
AM 'məltidə,mɛn(t)ʃə-
'næl ədi,
'məltidə,mɛn(t)ʃŋ-
'æl ədi,
'məlti,daɪ,mɛn(t)ʃə-
'næl ədi,

'məlti,daɪ,mɛn(t)ʃŋ-
'æl ədi,
'məltə,daɪ,mɛn(t)ʃə-
'næl ədi,
'məltə,daɪ,mɛn(t)ʃŋ-
'æl ədi,
'məltədə,mɛn(t)ʃə-
'næl ədi,
'məltədə,mɛn(t)ʃŋ-
'æl ədi,
'məl,taɪdə,mɛn(t)ʃə-
'næl ədi,
'məl,taɪdə,mɛn(t)ʃŋ-
'æl ədi

multidimensionally
BR ˌmʌltɪdaɪ'mɛnʃŋəli,
ˌmʌltɪdaɪ'mɛnʃ(ə)nəli,
ˌmʌltɪdɪ'mɛnʃŋəli,
ˌmʌltɪdɪ'mɛnʃ(ə)nəli,
ˌmʌltɪdaɪ'mɛnʃŋli,
ˌmʌltɪdaɪ'mɛnʃənli
AM 'məltidə'mɛn(t)ʃ(ə)-
nəli,
'məlti,daɪ'mɛn(t)ʃ(ə)-
nəli,
'məltədə'mɛn(t)ʃ(ə)-
nəli,
'məltə,daɪ'mɛn(t)ʃ(ə)-
nəli,
'məl,taɪdə'mɛn(t)ʃ(ə)-
nəli

multidirectional
BR ˌmʌltɪdɪ'rɛkʃ n(ə)l,
ˌmʌltɪdɪ'rɛkʃən(ə)l,
ˌmʌltɪdaɪ'rɛkʃ n(ə)l,
ˌmʌltɪdaɪ'rɛkʃən(ə)l
AM 'məltidə'rɛkʃ(ə)nəl,
'məlti,daɪ'rɛkʃ(ə)nəl,
'məltədə'rɛkʃ(ə)nəl,
'məltə,daɪ'rɛkʃ(ə)nəl,
'məl,taɪdə'rɛkʃ(ə)nəl

multi-ethnic
BR ˌmʌltɪ'ɛθnɪk
AM 'məlti'ɛθnɪk,
'məlˌtaɪ'ɛθnɪk

multifaceted
BR ˌmʌltɪ'fasɪtɪd
AM 'məlti'fæsədəd,
'məltə'fæsədəd,
'məlˌtaɪ'fæsədəd

multifarious
BR ˌmʌltɪ'fɛːrɪəs
AM 'məlti'fɛrɪəs,
'məltə'fɛrɪəs

multifariously
BR ˌmʌltɪ'fɛːrɪəsli
AM 'məlti'fɛrɪəsli,
'məltə'fɛrɪəsli

multifariousness
BR ˌmʌltɪ'fɛːrɪəsnəs
AM 'məlti'fɛrɪəsnəs,
'məltə'fɛrɪəsnəs

multifid
BR 'mʌltɪfɪd
AM 'məltɪ,fɪd,
'məltə,fɪd, 'məlˌtaɪ,fɪd

multifoil
BR 'mʌltɪfɔɪl

multiform
AM ˈmʌlti̩fɔːrl,
ˈmʌltə̩fɔːl,
ˈməl̩taɪ̩fɔːl

multiform
BR ˈmʌltɪfɔːm
AM ˈmʌlti̩fɔ(ə)rm,
ˈmʌltə̩fɔ(ə)rm,
ˈməl̩taɪ̩fɔ(ə)rm

multiformity
BR ˌmʌltɪˈfɔːmɪtˌli, -ɪz
AM ˌmʌlti̩fɔːrmədi,
ˌmʌltəˈfɔːmədi, -z

multifunction
BR ˌmʌltɪˈfʌŋ(k)ʃn
AM ˈmʌlti̩fəŋkʃən,
ˈmʌltəˈfəŋkʃən,
ˈməl̩taɪˈfəŋkʃən

multifunctional
BR ˌmʌltɪˈfʌŋ(k)ʃn̩(ə)l,
ˌmʌltɪˈfʌŋ(k)ʃən(ə)l
AM ˈmʌlti̩fəŋkʃ(ə)nəl,
ˈmʌltəˈfəŋkʃ(ə)nəl,
ˈməl̩taɪˈfəŋkʃ(ə)nəl

multigrade
BR ˈmʌltɪgreɪd, -z
AM ˈmʌlti̩greɪd,
ˈmʌltə̩greɪd,
ˈməl̩taɪ̩greɪd, -z

multihull
BR ˈmʌltɪhʌl, -z
AM ˈmʌlti̩həl,
ˈmʌltə̩həl,
ˈməl̩taɪ̩həl, -z

multilateral
BR ˌmʌltɪˈlat(ə)rəl,
ˌmʌltɪˈlat(ə)rl̩
AM ˈmʌltiˈlædərəl,
ˈmʌltiˈlætrəl,
ˈmʌltəˈlædərəl,
ˈmʌltəˈlætrəl,
ˈməl̩taɪˈlædərəl,
ˈməl̩taɪˈlætrəl

multilateralism
BR ˌmʌltɪˈlat(ə)rəl-
ɪz(ə)m,
ˌmʌltɪˈlat(ə)rl̩ɪz(ə)m
AM ˈmʌltiˈlætərəlɪzəm,
ˈmʌltələtərəlɪzəm,
ˈməl̩taɪlætərəlɪzəm

multilateralist
BR ˌmʌltɪˈlat(ə)rəlɪst,
ˌmʌltɪˈlatrl̩ɪst, -s
AM ˈmʌltiˈlætərələst,
ˈmʌltələtərələst,
ˈməl̩taɪlætərələst, -s

multilaterally
BR ˌmʌltɪˈlat(ə)rəli,
ˌmʌltɪˈlat(ə)rl̩i
AM ˈmʌltiˈlædərəli,
ˈmʌltiˈlætrəli,
ˈmʌltəˈlædərəli,
ˈmʌltəˈlætrəli,
ˈməl̩taɪˈlædərəli,
ˈməl̩taɪˈlætrəli

multi-layered
BR ˌmʌltɪˈleɪəd
AM ˈmʌltiˈleɪərd,
ˈmʌltəˈleɪərd,
ˈməl̩taɪˈleɪərd

multilevel
BR ˌmʌltɪˈlɛvl
AM ˈmʌlti̩lɛvəl,
ˈmʌltəˈlɛvəl,
ˈməl̩taɪˈlɛvəl

multilingual
BR ˌmʌltɪˈlɪŋgw(ə)l
AM ˈmʌlti̩lɪŋgwəl,
ˈmʌltəˈlɪŋgwəl,
ˈməl̩taɪˈlɪŋgwəl

multilingualism
BR ˌmʌltɪˈlɪŋgwəl-
ɪz(ə)m,
ˌmʌltɪˈlɪŋgwl̩ɪz(ə)m
AM ˈmʌlti̩lɪŋgwə̩lɪzəm,
ˈmʌltəˈlɪŋgwə̩lɪzəm,
ˈməl̩taɪˈlɪŋgwə̩lɪzəm

multilingually
BR ˌmʌltɪˈlɪŋgwəli,
ˌmʌltɪˈlɪŋgwl̩i
AM ˈmʌlti̩lɪŋgwəli,
ˈmʌltəˈlɪŋgwəli,
ˈməl̩taɪˈlɪŋgwəli

multimedia
BR ˌmʌltɪˈmiːdɪə(r)
AM ˈmʌlti̩midiə,
ˈmʌltəˈmidiə

multimillion
BR ˌmʌltɪˈmɪljən, -z
AM ˈmʌlti̩mɪljən,
ˈmʌltəˈmɪljən, -z

multimillionaire
BR ˌmʌltɪ̩mɪljəˈnɛː(r),
-z
AM ˈmʌlti̩mɪljəˈnɛ(ə)r,
ˈmʌltə̩mɪljəˈnɛ(ə)r,
ˈməl̩taɪ̩mɪljəˈnɛ(ə)r,
-z

multimillionnaire
BR ˌmʌltɪ̩mɪljəˈnɛː(r),
-z
AM ˈmʌlti̩mɪljəˈnɛ(ə)r,
ˈmʌltə̩mɪljəˈnɛ(ə)r,
ˈməl̩taɪ̩mɪljəˈnɛ(ə)r,
-z

multinational
BR ˌmʌltɪˈnaʃn̩(ə)l,
ˌmʌltɪˈnaʃən(ə)l, -z
AM ˈmʌlti̩næʃ(ə)nəl,
ˈmʌltəˈnæʃ(ə)nəl,
ˈməl̩taɪˈnæʃ(ə)nəl, -z

multinationally
BR ˌmʌltɪˈnaʃn̩əli,
ˌmʌltɪˈnaʃn̩l̩i,
ˌmʌltɪˈnaʃən̩l̩i,
ˌmʌltɪˈnaʃ(ə)nəli
AM ˈmʌlti̩næʃ(ə)nəli,
ˈmʌltəˈnæʃ(ə)nəli,
ˈməl̩taɪˈnæʃ(ə)nəli

multinomial
BR ˌmʌltɪˈnəʊmɪəl, -z
AM ˈmʌlti̩noʊmiəl,
ˈmʌltəˈnoʊmiəl, -z

multiparous
BR mʌlˈtɪp(ə)rəs
AM ˈməlˈtɪpərəs

multipartite
BR ˌmʌltɪˈpɑːtaɪt

multilevel
AM ˌmʌltiˈpɑːr̩taɪt,
ˈmʌltəˈpɑːr̩taɪt,
ˈməl̩taɪˈpɑːr̩taɪt

multi-party
BR ˌmʌltɪˈpɑːti
AM ˈmʌlti̩pɑːrdi,
ˈmʌltəˈpɑːrdi,
ˈməl̩taɪˈpɑːrdi

multiphase
BR ˈmʌltɪfeɪz, -ɪz
AM ˈmʌlti̩feɪz,
ˈmʌltəˈfeɪz,
ˈməl̩taɪˈfeɪz, -ɪz

multiple
BR ˈmʌltɪpl, -z
AM ˈmʌltəpəl, -z

multiplex
BR ˈmʌltɪplɛks
AM ˈmʌlti̩plɛks,
ˈmʌltə̩plɛks

multiplexer
BR ˈmʌltɪplɛksə(r), -z
AM ˈmʌlti̩plɛksər,
ˈmʌltə̩plɛksər, -z

multiplexor
BR ˈmʌltɪplɛksə(r), -z
AM ˈmʌlti̩plɛksər,
ˈmʌltə̩plɛksər, -z

multipliable
BR ˈmʌltɪplaɪəbl
AM ˈmʌltəplaɪəbəl,
ˈmʌltɪplaɪəbəl

multiplicable
BR ˈmʌltɪplɪkəbl
AM ˈmʌltiˈplɪkəbəl,
ˈmʌltiˈplɪkəbəl

multiplicand
BR ˌmʌltɪplɪˈkand,
ˈmʌltɪplɪkand, -z
AM ˈmʌltəpləˈkænd, -z

multiplication
BR ˌmʌltɪplɪˈkeɪʃn
AM ˈmʌltəpləˈkeɪʃən

multiplicative
BR ˈmʌltɪplɪkətɪv
AM ˈmʌltəpləˌkeɪdɪv,
ˈmʌltəˈplɪkədɪv

multiplicity
BR ˌmʌltɪˈplɪsɪti
AM ˈmʌltəˈplɪsɪdi

multiplier
BR ˈmʌltɪplaɪə(r), -z
AM ˈmʌltə̩plaɪər, -z

multiply
BR ˈmʌltɪplaɪ, -z, -ɪŋ, -d
AM ˈmʌltə̩plaɪ, -z, -ɪŋ,
-d

multipolar
BR ˌmʌltɪˈpəʊlə(r)
AM ˈmʌlti̩poʊlər,
ˈmʌltəˈpoʊlər,
ˈməl̩taɪˈpoʊlər

multiprocessing
BR ˌmʌltɪˈprəʊsɛsɪŋ, -z
AM ˈmʌlti̩prasəsɪŋ,
ˈmʌltəˈprasəsɪŋ,
ˈməl̩taɪˈprasəsɪŋ,
ˈmɛlti̩prɑ̩sɛsɪŋ,

multiprocessing
ˈməltə̩prɑ̩sɛsɪŋ,
ˈməltaɪ̩prɑ̩sɛsɪŋ-z

multiprocessor
BR ˌmʌltɪˈprəʊsɛsə(r),
-z
AM ˈmʌlti̩prasəsər,
ˈmʌltəˈprasəsər,
ˈmʌlti̩prɑ̩sɛsər,
ˈmʌltəˈprɑ̩sɛsər, -z

multiprogramming
BR ˌmʌltɪˈprəʊgramɪŋ,
-z
AM ˈmʌlti̩proʊ̩græmɪŋ,
ˈmʌltəˈproʊ̩græmɪŋ,
ˈməl̩taɪˈproʊ̩græmɪŋ,
-z

multipurpose
BR ˌmʌltɪˈpɜːpəs
AM ˈmʌlti̩pərpəs,
ˈmʌltəˈpərpəs,
ˈməl̩taɪˈpərpəs

multiracial
BR ˌmʌltɪˈreɪʃl
AM ˈmʌlti̩reɪʃəl,
ˈmʌltəˈreɪʃəl,
ˈməl̩taɪˈreɪʃəl

multiracially
BR ˌmʌltɪˈreɪʃli,
ˌmʌltɪˈreɪʃəli
AM ˈmʌlti̩reɪʃəli,
ˈmʌltəˈreɪʃəli,
ˈməl̩taɪˈreɪʃəli

multistage
BR ˌmʌltɪˈsteɪdʒ
AM ˈmʌlti̩steɪdʒ,
ˈmʌltəˈsteɪdʒ,
ˈməl̩taɪˈsteɪdʒ

multistorey
BR ˌmʌltɪˈstɔːri
AM ˈmʌlti̩stɔːri,
ˈmʌltəˈstɔːri,
ˈməl̩taɪˈstɔːri

multitude
BR ˈmʌltɪtjuːd,
ˈmʌltɪtʃuːd, -z
AM ˈmʌltə̩t(j)ud, -z

multitudinous
BR ˌmʌltɪˈtjuːdɪnəs,
ˌmʌltɪˈtʃuːdɪnəs
AM ˈmʌltəˈt(j)udn̩əs

multitudinously
BR ˌmʌltɪˈtjuːdɪnəsli,
ˌmʌltɪˈtʃuːdɪnəsli
AM ˈmʌltəˈt(j)udn̩əsli

multitudinousness
BR ˌmʌltɪˈtjuːdɪnəsnəs,
ˌmʌltɪˈtʃuːdɪnəsnəs
AM ˈmʌltəˈt(j)udn̩əsnəs

multivalency
BR ˌmʌltɪˈveɪlənsˌli,
ˌmʌltɪˈveɪln̩sˌli, -ɪz
AM ˈmʌlti̩veɪlənsi,
ˈmʌltəˈveɪlənsi,
ˈməl̩taɪˈveɪlənsi, -z

multivalent
BR ˌmʌltɪˈveɪlənt,
ˌmʌltɪˈveɪln̩t

AM ˌmʌlti'veɪlənt,
ˌmʌltə'veɪlənt,
ˌməl.taɪ'veɪlənt
multivalve
BR 'mʌltɪ'vælv
AM ˌmʌlti'vælv,
ˌmʌltə'vælv,
ˌməl.taɪ'vælv
multivariate
BR ˌmʌltɪ'veːriət
AM ˌmʌlti'veriət,
ˌmʌltə'veriət,
ˌməl.taɪ'veriət
multiversity
BR ˌmʌltɪ'vəːsɪt|i, -ɪz
AM ˌmʌlti'vərsədi,
ˌmʌltə'vərsədi, -z
multivocal
BR ˌmʌltɪ'vəʊkl
AM ˌmʌlti'voʊkəl,
ˌmʌltə'voʊkəl,
ˌməl.taɪ'voʊkəl
multum in parvo
BR ˌmʌltəm ɪn 'pɑːvəʊ
AM ˌmʌltəm ɪn 'parvoʊ
multure
BR 'mʌltʃə(r), -z
AM 'mʌltʃər, -z
mum
BR mʌm, -z, -ɪŋ, -d
AM mʌm, -z, -ɪŋ, -d
mumble
BR 'mʌmb|l̩, -lz,
-|ɪŋ\-lɪŋ, -ld
AM 'mʌmbəl, -əlz,
-(ə)lɪŋ, -əld
mumbler
BR 'mʌmblə(r),
'mʌmblə(r), -z
AM 'mʌmb(ə)lər, -z
Mumbles
BR 'mʌmblz
AM 'mʌmblz
mumbling
BR 'mʌmblɪŋ,
'mʌmblɪŋ, -z
AM 'mʌmb(ə)lɪŋ, -z
mumblingly
BR 'mʌmblɪŋli,
'mʌmblɪŋli
AM 'mʌmbəlɪŋli
mumbo-jumbo
BR ˌmʌmbəʊ'dʒʌmbəʊ,
-z
AM 'mʌmboʊ'dʒəmboʊ,
-z
mumchance
BR 'mʌmtʃɑːns,
'mʌmtʃans, -ɪz
AM 'məm.tʃæns, -əz
mu-meson
BR ˌmjuː'miːzɒn,
ˌmju:'mi:sɒn,
ˌmju:'mezɒn,
ˌmju:'mesɒn,
ˌmju:'meɪzɒn, -z

AM ˌmju'meɪˌzɑn,
'mju'meɪˌsɑn, -z
Mumford
BR 'mʌmfəd
AM 'mʌmfərd
mummer
BR 'mʌmə(r), -z
AM 'məmər, -z
mummery
BR 'mʌm(ə)ri
AM 'məməri
mummification
BR ˌmʌmɪfɪ'keɪʃn
AM ˌməməfə'keɪʃən
mummify
BR 'mʌmɪfaɪ, -z, -ɪŋ, -d
AM 'məməˌfaɪ, -z, -ɪŋ, -d
mumming
BR 'mʌmɪŋ
AM 'məmɪŋ
mummy
BR 'mʌm|i, -ɪz
AM 'məmi, -z
mumpish
BR 'mʌmpɪʃ
AM 'məmpɪʃ
mumps
BR mʌmps
AM məmps
Munch
BR mʊŋk
AM məŋk, mʊŋk
munch
BR mʌn(t)ʃ, -ɪz, -ɪŋ, -t
AM mən(t)ʃ, -əz, -ɪŋ, -t
Munchausen
BR 'mʊntʃaʊzn
AM 'mʊn,(t)ʃaʊzn
München
BR 'mʊn(t)ʃ(ə)n
AM 'mʊntʃən
GER 'mʏnçn̩
munchies
BR 'mʌn(t)ʃɪz
AM 'mən(t)ʃiz
Muncie
BR 'mʌnsi
AM 'mənsi
Munda
BR 'mʊndə(r), -z
AM 'mʊndə, -z
mundane
BR mʌn'deɪn
AM ˌmən'deɪn
mundanely
BR ˌmʌn'deɪnli
AM ˌmən'deɪnli
mundaneness
BR ˌmʌn'deɪnnɪs
AM ˌmən'deɪ(n)nɪs
mundanity
BR ˌmʌn'deɪnɪt|i, -ɪz
AM ˌmən'deɪnɪdi, -z
mung
BR mʌŋ, mu:ŋ
AM məŋ

mungo
BR 'mʌŋgəʊ
AM 'məŋgoʊ
Munich
BR 'mju:nɪk, 'mju:nɪx
AM 'mjunɪk
municipal
BR mjʊ'nɪsɪpl
AM mju'nɪsəpəl,
mjə'nɪsəpəl
municipalisation
BR mjʊˌnɪsɪpəlaɪ'zeɪʃn,
mjʊˌnɪsɪplʌɪ'zeɪʃn
AM mju,nɪsəpələ'zeɪ-
ʃən,
mjə,nɪsəpələ'zeɪʃən,
mju,nɪsəpəˌlaɪ'zeɪʃən,
mjə,nɪsəpəˌlaɪ'zeɪʃən
municipalise
BR mjʊ'nɪsɪpəlaɪz,
mjʊ'nɪsɪplʌɪz, -ɪz, -ɪŋ,
-d
AM mju'nɪsəpəˌlaɪz,
mjə'nɪsəpəˌlaɪz, -ɪz,
-ɪŋ, -d
municipality
BR mjʊˌnɪsɪ'palɪt|i,
ˌmju:nɪsɪ'palɪt|i, -ɪz
AM mju,nɪsə'pælədi,
mjə,nɪsə'pælədi, -z
municipalization
BR mjʊˌnɪsɪpəlaɪ'zeɪʃn,
mjʊ,nɪsɪplʌɪ'zeɪʃn
AM mju,nɪsəpələ'zeɪ-
ʃən,
mjə,nɪsəpələ'zeɪʃən,
mju,nɪsəpəˌlaɪ'zeɪʃən,
mjə,nɪsəpəˌlaɪ'zeɪʃən
municipalize
BR mjʊ'nɪsɪpəlaɪz,
mjʊ'nɪsɪplʌɪz, -ɪz, -ɪŋ,
-d
AM mju'nɪsəpəˌlaɪz,
mjə'nɪsəpəˌlaɪz, -ɪz,
-ɪŋ, -d
municipally
BR mjʊ'nɪsɪpli,
mjʊ'nɪsɪpəli
AM mju'nɪsəpəli,
mjə'nɪsəpəli
munificence
BR mjʊ'nɪfɪsns
AM mju'nɪfəsəns,
mjə'nɪfəsəns
munificent
BR mjʊ'nɪfɪsnt
AM mju'nɪfəsənt,
mjə'nɪfəsənt
munificently
BR mjʊ'nɪfɪsntli
AM mju'nɪfəsəntli,
mjə'nɪfəsən(t)li
muniment
BR mju:nɪm(ə)nt, -s
AM 'mjunəmənt, -s
munition
BR mjʊ'nɪʃn, -z

AM mju'nɪʃən,
mjə'nɪʃən, -z
munitioner
BR mjʊ'nɪʃŋə(r),
mjʊ'nɪʃənə(r), -z
AM mju'nɪʃənər,
mjə'nɪʃənər, -z
munnion
BR 'mʌnjən, -z
AM 'mʌnjən, -z
Muñoz
BR 'mu:njəʊz
AM 'munjoʊz
SP mu'ɲoθ, mu'ɲos
Munro
BR mən'rəʊ, mʌn'rəʊ
AM mən'roʊ
munshi
BR 'mu:nʃiː, -z
AM 'mənʃi, -z
Munster
BR 'mʌnstə(r)
AM 'mənstər
Münster
BR 'mʊnstə(r)
AM 'mʊnstər
GER 'mʏnstɐ
munt
BR mʊnt, -s
AM mʊnt, -s
muntjac
BR 'mʌntdʒak, -s
AM 'mənt.dʒæk, -s
muntjak
BR 'mʌntdʒak, -s
AM 'mənt.dʒæk, -s
Muntz metal
BR 'mʌnts ˌmetl
AM 'mən(t)s ˌmedl
muon
BR 'mju:ɒn, -z
AM 'mju.ɑn, -z
muonic
BR mju:'ɒnɪk
AM mju'ɑnɪk
mjə'wɑnɪk
murage
BR 'mjʊər|ɪdʒ,
'mjɔːr|ɪdʒ, -ɪdʒɪz
AM 'mjʊrɪdʒ, -ɪz
mural
BR 'mjʊərəl, 'mjʊər|,
'mjɔːrəl, 'mjɔːr|, -z
AM 'mjʊrəl, -z
muralist
BR 'mjʊər|ɪst,
'mjʊərəlɪst,
'mjɔːr|ɪst, 'mjɔːrəlɪst,
-s
AM 'mjʊrələst, -s
Murchison
BR 'məːtʃɪs(ə)n
AM 'mərtʃəzən
murder
BR 'məːd|ə(r), -əz,
-(ə)rɪŋ, -əd
AM 'mərdər, -z, -ɪŋ, -d

murderer
BR 'mɜːd(ə)rə(r), -z
AM 'mɝdərər, -z

murderess
BR 'mɜːdərɛs,
'mɜːd(ə)rɪs,
ˌmɜːdə'rɛs, -ɪz
AM 'mɝdərəs, -əz

murderous
BR 'mɜːd(ə)rəs
AM 'mɝd(ə)rəs

murderously
BR 'mɜːd(ə)rəsli
AM 'mɝd(ə)rəsli

murderousness
BR 'mɜːd(ə)rəsnəs
AM 'mɝd(ə)rəsnəs

Murdo
BR 'mɜːdəʊ
AM 'mɝdoʊ

Murdoch
BR 'mɜːdɒk, 'mɜːdəx
AM 'mɝdak, 'mɝdək

mure
BR mjʊə(r), mjɔː(r), -z,
-ɪŋ, -d
AM mjʊ(ə)r, -z, -ɪŋ, -d

murex
BR 'mjʊərɛks,
'mjɔːrɛks
AM 'mjʊˌrɛks

Murgatroyd
BR 'mɜːgətrɔɪd
AM 'mɝgəˌtrɔɪd

muriatic
BR ˌmjʊərɪ'atɪk,
ˌmjɔːrɪ'atɪk
AM ˌmjʊri'ædɪk

Muriel
BR 'mjʊərɪəl, 'mjɔːrɪəl
AM 'mjʊriəl

Murillo
BR mjʊ'rɪləʊ
AM m(j)ʊ'rɪljoʊ
SP mu'rijo

murine
BR 'mjʊərʌɪn,
'mjʊərɪn, 'mjɔːrʌɪn,
'mjɔːrɪn
AM 'mjuˌraɪn,
'mjurən, 'mjuˌrin

murk
BR mɜːk
AM mɝk

murkily
BR 'mɜːkɪli
AM 'mɝkəli

murkiness
BR 'mɜːkɪnɪs
AM 'mɝkɪnɪs

murky
BR 'mɜːk|i, -ɪə(r), -ɪɪst
AM 'mɝki, -ər, -ɪst

Murmansk
BR mɜː'mansk
AM mʊr'mænsk,
'mʊrˌmænsk
RUS 'murmənsk

murmur
BR 'mɜːm|ə(r), -əz,
-(ə)rɪŋ, -əd
AM 'mɝm|ər, -ərz,
-(ə)rɪŋ, -ərd

murmurer
BR 'mɜːm(ə)rə(r), -z
AM 'mɝmərər, -z

murmuringly
BR 'mɜːm(ə)rɪŋli
AM 'mɝm(ə)rɪŋli

murmurous
BR 'mɜːm(ə)rəs
AM 'mɝm(ə)rəs

murphy
BR 'mɜːfli, -ɪz
AM 'mɝfi, -z

murrain
BR 'mʌrɪn, 'mʌrn̩,
'mʌreɪn, -z
AM 'mɝən, -z

Murray
BR 'mʌri
AM 'mɝi

murre
BR mɜː(r), -z
AM mɝ, -z

murrelet
BR 'mɜːlɪt, -s
AM 'mɝlət, -s

murrey
BR 'mʌri, -ɪz
AM 'mɝi, -z

murrhine
BR 'mʌrɪn, 'mʌrn̩,
'mʌrʌɪn, -z
AM 'mɝən, 'məˌraɪn, -z

Murrow
BR 'mʌrəʊ
AM 'mɝoʊ

Murrumbidgee
BR ˌmʌrəm'bɪdʒiː
AM ˌmɝəm'bɪdʒi

Murtagh
BR 'mɜːtə(r)
AM 'mɝˌtɔ

murther
BR 'mɜːð|ə(r), -əz,
-(ə)rɪŋ, -əd
AM 'mɝð|ər, -ərz,
-(ə)rɪŋ, -ərd

Mururoa
BR ˌm(j)ʊərə'rəʊə(r)
AM ˌmjʊrə'roʊə

musaceous
BR mjuː'zeɪʃəs,
mjʊ'zeɪʃəs
AM mju'zeɪʃəs

Musala
BR mjuː'sɑːlə(r)
AM mju'sɑlə

muscadel
BR ˌmʌskə'dɛl, -z
AM ˌmʌskə'dɛl, -z

Muscadet
BR 'mʌskədeɪ,
ˌmʌskə'deɪ, -z
AM ˌmʌskə'dɛt, -s

muscadine
BR 'mʌskədʌɪn,
'mʌskədɪn, -z
AM 'məskəˌdaɪn, -z

muscarine
BR 'mʌskəriːn,
'mʌskərɪn, -z
AM 'məskərən,
'məskəˌrin, -z

muscat
BR 'mʌskat, -s
AM 'məˌskæt, -s

muscatel
BR ˌmʌskə'tɛl, -z
AM ˌməskə'tɛl, -z

muscle
BR 'mʌs|l̩, -lz, -l̩ɪŋ \-lɪŋ,
-ld
AM 'məs|əl, -əlz, -(ə)lɪŋ,
-əld

muscleless
BR 'mʌsl̩ləs
AM 'məs(l)ləs

muscly
BR 'mʌsl̩i
AM 'məsl̩i

muscologist
BR mʌ'skɒlədʒɪst, -s
AM məs'kɑlədʒəst, -s

muscology
BR mʌ'skɒlədʒi
AM məs'kɑlədʒi

muscovado
BR ˌmʌskə'vɑːdəʊ, -z
AM ˌməskə'veɪdoʊ,
ˌməskə'vadoʊ, -z

Muscovite
BR 'mʌskəvʌɪt, -s
AM 'məskəˌvaɪt, -s

Muscovy
BR 'mʌskəvi
AM 'məskəvi

muscular
BR 'mʌskjʊlə(r)
AM 'məskjələr

muscularity
BR ˌmʌskjʊ'larɪti
AM ˌməskjə'lɛrədi

muscularly
BR 'mʌskjʊləli
AM 'məskjələrli

musculature
BR 'mʌskjʊlətʃə(r)
AM 'məskjələtʃər

musculoskeletal
BR ˌmʌskjʊləʊ'skɛlɪtl̩
AM ˌməskjələ'skɛlətl̩

muse
BR mjuːz, -ɪz, -ɪŋ, -d
AM mjuz, -əz, -ɪŋ, -d

museology
BR ˌmjuːzɪ'ɒlədʒi
AM ˌmjuzi'ɑlədʒi

musette
BR mjuː'zɛt, mjʊ'zɛt, -s
AM mju'zɛt, -s

museum
BR mju:'ziːəm,
mjʊ'ziːəm, -z
AM mju'ziəm, -z

Musgrave
BR 'mʌzgreɪv
AM 'məsgreɪv

Musgrove
BR 'mʌzgrəʊv
AM 'məsgroʊv

mush¹
noun, man
BR mʊʃ, -ɪz
AM məʃ, -əz

mush²
verb
BR mʌʃ, -ɪz, -ɪŋ, -t
AM məʃ, -əz, -ɪŋ, -t

mushily
BR 'mʌʃɪli
AM 'məʃəli

mushiness
BR 'mʌʃɪnɪs
AM 'məʃɪnɪs

mushroom
BR 'mʌʃruːm,
'mʌʃrʊm, -z
AM 'məʃˌrum,
'məʃˌrʊm, -z

mushroomy
BR 'mʌʃruːmi,
'mʌʃrʊmi
AM 'məʃˌrumi,
'məʃˌrʊmi

mushy
BR 'mʌʃ|i, -ɪə(r), -ɪɪst
AM 'məʃi, -ər, -ɪst

music
BR 'mjuːzɪk
AM 'mjuzɪk

musical
BR 'mjuːzɪkl̩, -z
AM 'mjuzəkəl, -z

musicale
BR ˌmjuːzɪ'kɑːl,
ˌmjuːzɪ'kal, -z
AM ˌmjuzə'kæl, -z

musicalise
BR 'mjuːzɪkəlʌɪz,
'mjuːzɪkl̩ʌɪz, -ɪz, -ɪŋ,
-d
AM 'mjuzəkəˌlaɪz, -ɪz,
-ɪŋ, -d

musicality
BR ˌmjuːzɪ'kalɪti
AM ˌmjuzɪ'kælədi

musicalize
BR 'mjuːzɪkəlʌɪz,
'mjuːzɪkl̩ʌɪz, -ɪz, -ɪŋ,
-d
AM 'mjuzəkəˌlaɪz, -ɪz,
-ɪŋ, -d

musically
BR 'mjuːzɪkli,
'mjuːzɪkli
AM 'mjuzək(ə)li

musicalness
BR 'mjuːzɪklnəs

AM 'mjuzəkəlnəs
musician
BR mju:'zɪʃn,
mjʊ'zɪʃn, -z
AM mju'zɪʃən, -z
musicianly
BR mju:'zɪʃnli,
mjʊ'zɪʃnli
AM mju'zɪʃənli
musicianship
BR mju:'zɪʃnʃɪp,
mjʊ'zɪʃnʃɪp
AM mju'zɪʃən.ʃɪp
musicological
BR ,mju:zɪkə'lɒdʒɪkl
AM 'mjuzəkə'lɑdʒəkl
musicologically
BR ,mju:zɪkə'lɒdʒɪkli
AM ,mjuzəkə'lɑdʒ(ə)kli
musicologist
BR ,mju:zɪ'kɒlədʒɪst,
-s
AM ,mjuzə'kɑlədʒəst,
-s
musicology
BR ,mju:zɪ'kɒlədʒi
AM ,mjuzə'kɑlədʒi
musing
BR 'mju:zɪŋ, -z
AM 'mjuzɪŋ, -z
musingly
BR 'mju:zɪŋli
AM 'mjuzɪŋli
**musique
concrète**
BR mju:,zi:k kɒŋ'krɛt,
mjʊ,zi:k +
AM mʊ'zik kan'krɛt
musk
BR mʌsk
AM məsk
muskeg
BR 'mʌskɛg
AM 'məs,kɛg
muskellunge
BR 'mʌskələn(d)ʒ, -ɪz
AM 'məskə,ləndʒ, -əz
musket
BR 'mʌskɪt, -s
AM 'məskət, -s
musketeer
BR ,mʌskɪ'tɪə(r), -z
AM ,məskə'tɪ(ə)r, -z
musketoon
BR ,mʌskɪ'tu:n, -z
AM ,məskə'tun, -z
musketry
BR 'mʌskɪtri
AM 'məskətri
muskie
BR 'mʌski
AM 'məski
muskiness
BR 'mʌskɪnɪs
AM 'məskɪnɪs
muskmelon
BR 'mʌsk,mɛlən, -z

AM 'məsk,mɛlən,
'məʃ,mɛlən, -z
Muskogean
BR mʌ'skəʊgɪən, -z
AM mə'skoʊgɪən,
,mə'skoʊgɪən, -z
muskrat
BR 'mʌskrat, -s
AM 'mə,skræt, -s
muskwood
BR 'mʌskwʊd
AM 'məsk,wʊd
musky
BR 'mʌski
AM 'məski
Muslim
BR 'mʊzlɪm, 'mʌzlɪm,
'mʊslɪm, -z
AM 'məzləm, 'mʊzləm,
-z
muslin
BR 'mʌzlɪn, -d
AM 'məzlən, -d
musmon
BR 'mʌsmən,
'mʌzmən, -z
AM 'məzmən, -z
muso
BR 'mju:zəʊ, -z
AM 'mjuzoʊ, -z
musquash
BR 'mʌskwɒʃ, -ɪz
AM 'mə,skwɑʃ,
'mə,skwɑʃ, -əz
muss
BR mʌs, -ɪz, -ɪŋ, -t
AM məs, -əz, -ɪŋ, -t
mussel
BR 'mʌsl, -z
AM 'məsəl, -z
Musselburgh
BR 'mʌslb(ə)rə(r)
AM 'məsl,bərg,
'məsl,bərə
Mussolini
BR ,mʊsə'li:ni,
,mʌsə'li:ni
AM ,musə'lini
Mussorgsky
BR mʊ'sɔ:gski,
mʊ'zɔ:gski
AM mə'sɔrgski
RUS 'musərkskⁱij
Mussulman
BR 'mʌs(ə)lmən, -z
AM 'məsəlmən, -z
Mussulmen
BR 'mʌs(ə)lmən
AM 'məsəlmən
mussy
BR 'mʌsi
AM 'məsi
must
BR mʌst
AM məst
mustache
BR mə'stɑ:ʃ, -ɪz, -t

AM 'mə,stæʃ, mə'stæʃ,
-əz, -t
mustachio
BR mə'stɑ:ʃ(ɪ)əʊ,
mə'staʃ(ɪ)əʊ, -z, -d
AM mə'stæʃɪoʊ, -z, -d
Mustafa
BR 'mʊstəfə(r),
'mʌstəfə(r),
mʊ'stɑ:fə(r),
mʊ'stafə(r)
AM 'mʊstəfə, mʊs'tɑfə
mustang
BR 'mʌstaŋ, -z
AM 'mə,stæŋ, -z
Mustapha
BR 'mʊstəfə(r),
'mʌstəfə(r),
mʊ'stɑ:fə(r),
mʊ'stafə(r)
AM 'mʊstəfə, mʊs'tɑfə
mustard
BR 'mʌstəd
AM 'məstərd
muster
BR 'mʌst|ə(r), -əz,
-(ə)rɪŋ, -əd
AM 'məst|ər, -ərz,
-(ə)rɪŋ, -ərd
musterer
BR 'mʌst(ə)rə(r), -z
AM 'məst(ə)rər, -z
musth
BR mʌst
AM məst
mustily
BR 'mʌstɪli
AM 'məstəli
mustiness
BR 'mʌstɪnɪs
AM 'məstɪnɪs
Mustique
BR mʊ'sti:k
AM mə'stik
mustn't
BR 'mʌsnt
AM 'məsnt
musty
BR 'mʌst|i, -ɪə(r), -ɪɪst
AM 'məsti, -ər, -ɪst
Mut
BR mʌt
AM mət
mutability
BR ,mju:tə'bɪlɪti
AM ,mjudə'bɪlɪdi
mutable
BR 'mju:təbl
AM 'mjudəbəl
mutagen
BR 'mju:tədʒ(ə)n
AM 'mjudə,dʒɛn,
'mjudədʒən
mutagenesis
BR ,mju:tə'dʒɛnɪsɪs
AM ,mjudə'dʒɛnəsəs
mutagenic
BR ,mju:tə'dʒɛnɪk

AM ,mjudə'dʒɛnɪk
mutant
BR 'mju:t(ə)nt, -s
AM 'mjutnt, -s
mutate
BR mju:'teɪt, -s, -ɪŋ, -ɪd
AM 'mju,teɪ|t, -ts, -dɪŋ,
-dɪd
mutation
BR mju:'teɪʃn, -z
AM mju'teɪʃən, -z
mutational
BR mju:'teɪʃn(ə)l,
mju:'teɪʃən(ə)l
AM ,mju'teɪʃ(ə)nəl
mutationally
BR mju:'teɪʃnəli,
mju:'teɪʃnli,
mju:'teɪʃənli,
mju:'teɪʃ(ə)nəli
AM mju'teɪʃ(ə)nəli
**mutatis
mutandis**
BR m(j)u:,tɑ:tɪs
m(j)u:'tandɪs
AM m(j)u,tadəs
m(j)u'tandəs,
+ m(j)u'tændəs
mutch
BR mʌtʃ, -ɪz
AM mətʃ, -əz
mute
BR mju:t, -s, -ɪŋ, -ɪd
AM mju|t, -ts, -dɪŋ, -dəd
mutely
BR 'mju:tli
AM 'mjutli
muteness
BR 'mju:tnəs
AM 'mjutnəs
mutilate
BR 'mju:tɪleɪt,
'mju:tɪeɪt, -s, -ɪŋ, -ɪd
AM 'mjudl,eɪ|t, -ts, -dɪŋ,
-dɪd
mutilation
BR ,mju:tɪ'leɪʃn,
,mju:tl'eɪʃn, -z
AM ,mjudl'eɪʃən, -z
mutilative
BR 'mju:tɪlətɪv,
'mju:tlətɪv
AM 'mjudl,eɪdɪv
mutilator
BR 'mju:tɪleɪtə(r),
'mju:tleɪtə(r), -z
AM 'mjudl,eɪdər, -z
mutineer
BR ,mju:tɪ'nɪə(r), -z
AM ,mjutn'ɪ(ə)r, -z
mutinous
BR 'mju:tɪnəs
AM 'mjutnəs
mutinously
BR 'mju:tɪnəsli
AM 'mjutnəsli

mutiny
BR ˈmjuːtɪn|i, -ɪz, -ɪŋ,
-ɪd
AM ˈmjuːtn̩i, -z, -ɪŋ, -d
mutism
BR ˈmjuːtɪz(ə)m
AM ˈmjuˌtɪzəm,
ˈmjudɪzəm
muton
BR ˈmjuːtɒn, -z
AM ˈmjutn̩, -z
mutt
BR mʌt, -s
AM mət, -s
mutter
BR ˈmʌt|ə(r), -əz,
-(ə)rɪŋ, -əd
AM ˈmə|dər, -dərz,
-dərɪŋ\-trɪŋ, -dərd
mutterer
BR ˈmʌt(ə)rə(r), -z
AM ˈmədərər, -z
muttering
BR ˈmʌt(ə)rɪŋ, -z
AM ˈmədərɪŋ, ˈmətrɪŋ,
-z
mutteringly
BR ˈmʌt(ə)rɪŋli
AM ˈmədərɪŋli,
ˈmətrɪŋli
mutton
BR ˈmʌtn̩
AM ˈmətn̩
muttonchop
BR ˌmʌtn̩ˈtʃɒp, -s
AM ˌmətn̩ˌtʃɑp, -s
muttonhead
BR ˈmʌtn̩hɛd, -z
AM ˈmətn̩ˌ(h)ɛd, -z
muttony
BR ˈmʌtn̩i
AM ˈmətn̩i
mutual
BR ˈmjuːtʃʊəl,
ˈmjuːtʃ(ʊ)l,
ˈmjuːtjʊəl, ˈmjuːtjʊl
AM ˈmjutʃ(əw)əl
mutualism
BR ˈmjuːtʃʊəlɪz(ə)m,
ˈmjuːtʃʊlɪz(ə)m,
ˈmjuːtʃlɪz(ə)m,
ˈmjuːtjʊəlɪz(ə)m,
ˈmjuːtjʊlɪz(ə)m
AM ˈmjutʃ(u)wəˌlɪzəm
mutualist
BR ˈmjuːtʃʊəlɪst,
ˈmjuːtʃʊlɪst,
ˈmjuːtʃlɪst,
ˈmjuːtjʊəlɪst,
ˈmjuːtjʊlɪst, -s
AM ˈmjutʃ(əw)ələst, -s
mutualistic
BR ˌmjuːtʃʊəˈlɪstɪk,
ˌmjuːtʃʊˈlɪstɪk,
ˌmjuːtʃlˈɪstɪk,
ˌmjuːtjʊəˈlɪstɪk,
ˌmjuːtjʊˈlɪstɪk
AM ˌmjutʃ(u)wəˈlɪstɪk

mutualistically
BR ˌmjuːtʃʊəˈlɪstɪkli,
ˌmjuːtʃʊˈlɪstɪkli,
ˌmjuːtʃlˈɪstɪkli,
ˌmjuːtjʊəˈlɪstɪkli,
ˌmjuːtjʊˈlɪstɪkli
AM ˌmjutʃ(u)wəˈlɪstək-
(ə)li
mutuality
BR ˌmjuːtʃʊˈalɪti,
ˌmjuːtjʊˈalɪti
AM ˌmjutʃəˈwælədi
mutually
BR ˈmjuːtʃʊəli,
ˈmjuːtʃʊli, ˈmjuːtʃli,
ˈmjuːtjʊəli, ˈmjuːtjʊli
AM ˈmjutʃ(əw)əli
mutuel
BR ˈmjuːtʃʊəl,
ˈmjuːtjʊəl, -z
AM ˈmjutʃ(ə)wəl, -z
mutule
BR ˈmjuːtʃuːl,
ˈmjuːtjuːl, -z
AM ˈmjuˌtʃul, -z
muu-muu
BR ˈmuːmuː, -z
AM ˈmuˌmu, -z
Muzak®
BR ˈmjuːzak
AM ˈmjuzæk
muzhik
BR ˈmuː(d)ʒɪk, -s
AM muˈʒɪk, -s
RUS muˈʒɪk
muzz
BR mʌz, -ɪz, -ɪŋ, -d
AM məz, -əz, -ɪŋ, -d
muzzily
BR ˈmʌzɪli
AM ˈməzəli
muzziness
BR ˈmʌzɪnɪs
AM ˈməzɪnɪs
muzzle
BR ˈmʌz|l̩, -lz, -lɪŋ\-lɪŋ,
-ld
AM ˈməz|əl, -əlz, -(ə)lɪŋ,
-əld
muzzler
BR ˈmʌzlə(r),
ˈmʌzlə(r), -z
AM ˈməz(ə)lər, -z
muzzy
BR ˈmʌz|i, -ɪə(r), -ɪɪst
AM ˈməzi, -ər, -ɪst
my
BR mʌɪ
AM maɪ
myalgia
BR mʌɪˈaldʒ(ɪ)ə(r)
AM maɪˈældʒ(i)ə
myalgic
BR mʌɪˈaldʒɪk
AM maɪˈældʒɪk
myalism
BR ˈmʌɪəlɪz(ə)m
AM ˈmaɪəlɪzəm

myall
BR ˈmʌɪəl, -z
AM ˈmaɪˌɔl, ˈmaɪˌɑl, -z
myasthenia
BR ˌmʌɪəsˈθiːnɪə(r)
AM ˌmaɪəsˈθiniə
myasthenic
BR ˌmʌɪəsˈθɛnɪk
AM ˌmaɪəsˈθɛnɪk
mycelia
BR mʌɪˈsiːlɪə(r)
AM maɪˈsiljə, maɪˈsiliə
mycelial
BR mʌɪˈsiːlɪəl
AM maɪˈsiliəl
mycelium
BR mʌɪˈsiːlɪəm
AM maɪˈsiliəm
Mycenae
BR mʌɪˈsiːniː
AM maɪˈsini
Mycenaean
BR mʌɪˈsiːnɪən, -z
AM maɪˈsiniən, -z
mycological
BR ˌmʌɪkəˈlɒdʒɪkl̩
AM ˌmaɪkəˈladʒəkəl
mycologically
BR ˌmʌɪkəˈlɒdʒɪkli
AM ˌmaɪkəˈladʒək(ə)li
mycologist
BR mʌɪˈkɒlədʒɪst, -s
AM maɪˈkɑlədʒəst, -s
mycology
BR mʌɪˈkɒlədʒi
AM maɪˈkɑlədʒi
mycorrhiza
BR ˌmʌɪkə(ʊ)ˈrʌɪzə(r)
AM ˌmaɪkəˈraɪzə
mycorrhizae
BR ˌmʌɪkə(ʊ)ˈrʌɪziː
AM ˌmaɪkəˈraɪzi
mycorrhizal
BR ˌmʌɪkə(ʊ)ˈrʌɪzl̩
AM ˌmaɪkəˈraɪzəl
mycosis
BR mʌɪˈkəʊsɪs
AM maɪˈkoʊsəs
mycotic
BR mʌɪˈkɒtɪk
AM maɪˈkɑdɪk
mycotoxin
BR ˌmʌɪkə(ʊ)ˈtɒksɪn,
-z
AM ˌmaɪkəˈtɑksən, -z
mycotrophy
BR mʌɪˈkɒtrəfi
AM maɪˈkɑtrəfi
mydriasis
BR mʌɪˈdrʌɪəsɪs,
mɪˈdrʌɪəsɪs,
ˌmɪdrɪˈeɪsɪs
AM maɪˈdraɪəsəs
myelin
BR ˈmʌɪɪlɪn
AM ˈmaɪələn

myelination
BR ˌmʌɪɪlɪˈneɪʃn̩
AM ˌmaɪələˈneɪʃən
myelitis
BR ˌmʌɪəˈlʌɪtɪs
AM ˌmaɪəˈlaɪdɪs
myeloid
BR ˈmʌɪəlɔɪd
AM ˈmaɪəˌlɔɪd
myeloma
BR ˌmʌɪəˈləʊmə(r), -z
AM ˌmaɪəˈloʊmə, -z
myelomata
BR ˌmʌɪəˈləʊmətə(r)
AM ˌmaɪəˈloʊmədə
Myers
BR ˈmʌɪəz
AM ˈmaɪərz
Myfanwy
BR mɪˈvanwi
AM məˈvɑnwi
WE mʌˈvanwi
Mykonos
BR ˈmɪkənɒs
AM ˈmɪkəˌnɑs,
ˈmɪkəˌnɑs
Mylar
BR ˈmʌɪlɑː(r)
AM ˈmaɪˌlɑr
Myles
BR mʌɪlz
AM maɪlz
mylodon
BR ˈmʌɪlədɒn,
ˈmʌɪləd(ə)n, -z
AM ˈmaɪləˌdɑn, -z
mylonite
BR ˈmʌɪlənʌɪt,
ˈmɪlənʌɪt
AM ˈmaɪləˌnaɪt,
ˈmɪləˌnaɪt
myna
BR ˈmʌɪnə(r), -z
AM ˈmaɪnə, -z
mynah
BR ˈmʌɪnə(r), -z
AM ˈmaɪnə, -z
Mynd
BR mɪnd
AM mɪnd
Mynett
BR ˈmʌɪnɪt, mʌɪˈnɛt
AM ˈmaɪnət, ˈmɪnət
Mynott
BR ˈmʌɪnət
AM ˈmaɪnət, ˈmaɪˌnɑt
Mynwy
BR ˈmʌnwi
AM ˈmɑnwi
myocardia
BR ˌmʌɪə(ʊ)ˈkɑːdɪə(r)
AM ˌmaɪəˈkɑrdiə
myocardial
BR ˌmʌɪə(ʊ)ˈkɑːdɪəl
AM ˌmaɪəˈkɑrdiəl

myocardiogram
BR ˌmaɪə(ʊ)ˈkɑːdɪəgram,
-z
AM ˌmaɪəˈkɑrdiəˌgræm,
-z

myocarditis
BR ˌmaɪə(ʊ)kɑːˈdaɪtɪs
AM ˌmaɪəˌkɑrˈdaɪdɪs

myocardium
BR ˌmaɪə(ʊ)ˈkɑːdɪəm
AM ˌmaɪəˈkɑrdiəm

myofibril
BR ˌmaɪə(ʊ)ˈfaɪbrɪl,
ˌmaɪə(ʊ)ˈfɪbrɪl, -z
AM ˌmaɪəˈfɪbrəl, -z

myogenic
BR ˌmaɪə(ʊ)ˈdʒɛnɪk
AM ˌmaɪəˈdʒɛnɪk

myoglobin
BR ˌmaɪə(ʊ)ˈgləʊbɪn,
-z
AM ˌmaɪəˈgloʊbən, -z

myology
BR maɪˈɒlədʒi
AM maɪˈɑlədʒi

myope
BR ˈmaɪəʊp, -s
AM ˈmaɪˌoʊp, -s

myopia
BR maɪˈəʊpɪə(r)
AM maɪˈoʊpiə

myopic
BR maɪˈɒpɪk
AM maɪˈɑpɪk

myopically
BR maɪˈɒpɪkli
AM maɪˈɑpək(ə)li

myosis
BR maɪˈəʊsɪs
AM maɪˈoʊsəs

myositis
BR ˌmaɪəˈsaɪtɪs
AM ˌmaɪəˈsaɪdɪs

myosote
BR ˈmaɪə(ʊ)səʊt, -s
AM ˈmaɪəˌsoʊt, -s

myosotis
BR ˌmaɪə(ʊ)ˈsəʊtɪs, -ɪz
AM ˌmaɪəˈsoʊdəs, -əz

myotonia
BR ˌmaɪə(ʊ)ˈtəʊnɪə(r)
AM ˌmaɪəˈtoʊniə

myotonic
BR maɪə(ʊ)ˈtɒnɪk
AM ˌmaɪəˈtɑnɪk

Myra
BR ˈmaɪrə(r)
AM ˈmaɪrə

Myrdal
BR ˈmɪədɑːl
AM ˈmɪrˌdɑl

myriad
BR ˈmɪrɪəd, -z
AM ˈmɪriəd, -z

myriapod
BR ˈmɪrɪəpɒd, -z
AM ˈmɪriəˌpɑd, -z

myrmecology
BR ˌmɜːmɪˈkɒlədʒi
AM ˌmɜrməˈkɑlədʒi

myrmecophile
BR ˈmɜːmɪkəfʌɪl,
məˈmɪkəfʌɪl, -z
AM ˈmɜrməkəˌfaɪl, -z

Myrmidon
BR ˈmɜːmɪd(ə)n, -z
AM ˈmɜrməˌdɑn, -z

Myrna
BR ˈmɜːnə(r)
AM ˈmɜrnə

myrobalan
BR maɪˈrɒbələn,
maɪˈrɒblən, -z
AM maɪˈrɑbələn,
məˈrɑbələn, -z

Myron
BR ˈmaɪrən, ˈmaɪrn̩
AM ˈmaɪrən

myrrh
BR mɜː(r)
AM mɜr

myrrhic
BR ˈmɜːrɪk
AM ˈmɜrɪk

myrrhy
BR ˈmɜːri
AM ˈmɜri

myrtaceous
BR mɜːˈteɪʃəs
AM mɜrˈteɪʃəs

myrtle
BR ˈmɜːtl
AM ˈmɜrdəl

myself
BR maɪˈsɛlf, məˈsɛlf
AM maɪˈsɛlf, məˈsɛlf

Mysia
BR ˈmɪsɪə(r)
AM ˈmɪʃ iə

Mysian
BR ˈmɪsɪən, -z
AM ˈmɪʃiən, -z

Mysore
BR (ˌ)maɪˈsɔː(r)
AM maɪˈsɔ(ə)r

mystagogic
BR ˌmɪstəˈgɒdʒɪk
AM ˌmɪstəˈgɑdʒɪk

mystagogical
BR ˌmɪstəˈgɒdʒɪkl
AM ˌmɪstəˈgɑdʒəkəl

mystagogue
BR ˈmɪstəgɒg, -z
AM ˈmɪstəˌgɑg, -z

mysterious
BR mɪˈstɪərɪəs
AM məˈstɪriəs

mysteriously
BR mɪˈstɪərɪəsli
AM məˈstɪriəsli

mysteriousness
BR mɪˈstɪərɪəsnəs
AM məˈstɪriəsnəs

mystery
BR ˈmɪst(ə)r|i, -ɪz
AM ˈmɪst(ə)ri, -z

mystic
BR ˈmɪstɪk, -s
AM ˈmɪstɪk, -s

mystical
BR ˈmɪstɪkl
AM ˈmɪstəkəl

mystically
BR ˈmɪstɪkli
AM ˈmɪstək(ə)li

mysticism
BR ˈmɪstɪsɪz(ə)m
AM ˈmɪstəˌsɪzəm

mystification
BR ˌmɪstɪfɪˈkeɪʃn
AM ˌmɪstəfəˈkeɪʃən

mystify
BR ˈmɪstɪfʌɪ, -z, -ɪŋ, -d
AM ˈmɪstəˌfaɪ, -z, -ɪŋ, -d

mystifyingly
BR ˈmɪstɪfʌɪɪŋli
AM ˈmɪstəˌfaɪɪŋli

mystique
BR mɪˈstiːk
AM mɪˈstik

myth
BR mɪθ, -s
AM mɪθ, -s

mythi
BR ˈmʌɪθʌɪ, ˈmɪθiː
AM ˈmaɪθi

mythic
BR ˈmɪθɪk
AM ˈmɪθɪk

mythical
BR ˈmɪθɪkl
AM ˈmɪθəkəl

mythically
BR ˈmɪθɪkli
AM ˈmɪθək(ə)li

mythicise
BR ˈmɪθɪsʌɪz, -ɪz, -ɪŋ, -d
AM ˈmɪθəˌsaɪz, -ɪz, -ɪŋ, -d

mythicism
BR ˈmɪθɪsɪz(ə)m
AM ˈmɪθəˌsɪzəm

mythicist
BR ˈmɪθɪsɪst, -s
AM ˈmɪθəsəst, -s

mythicize
BR ˈmɪθɪsʌɪz, -ɪz, -ɪŋ, -d
AM ˈmɪθəˌsaɪz, -ɪz, -ɪŋ, -d

mythogenesis
BR ˌmɪθə(ʊ)ˈdʒɛnɪsɪs
AM ˌmɪθəˈdʒɛnəsəs

mythographer
BR mɪˈθɒgrəfə(r), -z
AM məˈθɑgrəfər, -z

mythography
BR mɪˈθɒgrəfi
AM məˈθɑgrəfi

Mytholmroyd
BR ˈmʌɪð(ə)mrɔɪd

AM ˈmɪðəmˌrɔɪd

mythologer
BR mɪˈθɒlədʒə(r), -z
AM məˈθɑlədʒər, -z

mythologic
BR ˌmɪθəˈlɒdʒɪk
AM ˌmɪθəˈlɑdʒɪk

mythological
BR ˌmɪθəˈlɒdʒɪkl
AM ˌmɪθəˈlɑdʒəkəl

mythologically
BR ˌmɪθəˈlɒdʒɪkli
AM ˌmɪθəˈlɑdʒək(ə)li

mythologise
BR mɪˈθɒlədʒʌɪz, -ɪz,
-ɪŋ, -d
AM məˈθɑləˌdʒaɪz, -ɪz,
-ɪŋ, -d

mythologiser
BR mɪˈθɒlədʒʌɪzə(r),
-z
AM məˈθɑləˌdʒaɪzər, -z

mythologist
BR mɪˈθɒlədʒɪst, -s
AM məˈθɑlədʒəst, -s

mythologize
BR mɪˈθɒlədʒʌɪz, -ɪz,
-ɪŋ, -d
AM məˈθɑləˌdʒaɪz, -ɪz,
-ɪŋ, -d

mythologizer
BR mɪˈθɒlədʒʌɪzə(r),
-z
AM məˈθɑləˌdʒaɪzər, -z

mythology
BR mɪˈθɒlədʒ|i, -ɪz
AM məˈθɑlədʒi, -z

mythomania
BR ˌmɪθə(ʊ)ˈmeɪnɪə(r),
-z
AM ˌmɪθəˈmeɪniə, -z

mythomaniac
BR ˌmɪθə(ʊ)ˈmeɪnɪak,
-s
AM ˌmɪθəˈmeɪniˌæk, -s

mythopoeia
BR ˌmɪθə(ʊ)ˈpiːə(r), -z
AM ˌmɪθəˈpiə, -z

mythopoeic
BR ˌmɪθə(ʊ)ˈpiːɪk
AM ˌmɪθəˈpiɪk

mythus
BR ˈmʌɪθəs, ˈmɪθəs
AM ˈmaɪθəs, ˈmɪθəʃ

Mytilene
BR ˈmɪtɪliːn, ˈmɪtɫiːn
AM ˈmɪtlɪn

myxedema
BR ˌmɪksɪˈdiːmə(r)
AM ˌmɪksəˈdimə

myxoedema
BR ˌmɪksɪˈdiːmə(r)
AM ˌmɪksəˈdimə

myxoma
BR mɪkˈsəʊmə(r), -z
AM mɪkˈsoʊmə, -z

myxomata
BR mɪkˈsəʊmətə(r)
AM mɪkˈsoʊmədə

myxomatosis
BR ˌmɪksəməˈtəʊsɪs
AM mɪkˌsoʊməˈtoʊsəs

myxomycete
BR ˌmɪksə(ʊ)ˈmʌɪsiːt,
-s
AM ˌmɪksəˈmaɪˌsiːt, -s

myxovirus
BR ˈmɪksəʊˌvʌɪrəs, -zɪ-
AM ˈmɪksoʊˌvaɪrəs, -zɪ-

Nn

n
BR ɛn, -z
AM ɛn, -z

'n
and
BR (ə)n
AM (ə)n

na
BR nə(r)
AM nə

NAAFI
BR 'nafʃi, -ɪz
AM 'næ,fi, 'nɑ,fi, -z

nab
BR nab, -z, -ɪŋ, -d
AM næb, -z, -ɪŋ, -d

Nabarro
BR nə'bɑ:rəʊ
AM nə'baroʊ

Nabataean
BR ,nabə'ti:ən, -z
AM ,næbə'tiən, -z

Nabi
BR 'nɑ:bi:, -z
AM 'nɑbi, -z

Nabisco®
BR nə'bɪskəʊ
AM nə'bɪskoʊ

Nablus
BR 'nabləs, 'nɑ:bləs
AM 'nabləs, 'næbləs

nabob
BR 'neɪbɒb, -z
AM 'neɪ,bab, -z

Nabokov
BR 'nabəkɒv
AM 'nabə,kɔv,
nə'bɔ,kɔf, 'nabə,kav,
nə'bɑ,kaf

Naboth
BR 'neɪbɒθ
AM 'neɪbɑθ

nacarat
BR 'nakərat
AM 'nækə,ræt

nacelle
BR nə'sɛl, -z
AM nə'sɛl, neɪ'sɛl, -z

nacho
BR 'nɑ:tʃəʊ, 'natʃəʊ, -z
AM 'natʃoʊ, -z

NACODS
BR 'neɪkɒdz
AM 'neɪ,kɑdz

nacre
BR 'neɪkə(r)
AM 'neɪkər

nacred
BR 'neɪkəd
AM 'neɪkərd

nacreous
BR 'neɪkrɪəs
AM 'neɪkriəs

NACRO
BR 'nakrəʊ
AM 'nækroʊ

nacrous
BR 'neɪkrəs
AM 'neɪkrəs

Na-Dene
BR ,nɑ:'deɪ'neɪ,
,nɑ:'deɪneɪ,
,nɑ:'deɪni, ,nɑ:'dɛni
AM ,nɑ'deɪ'neɪ,
,nɑ'dɛ,ni

Nader
BR 'neɪdə(r)
AM 'neɪdər

Nadia
BR 'nɑ:dɪə(r),
'neɪdɪə(r)
AM 'nɑdiə

Nadine
BR neɪ'di:n, nə'di:n
AM neɪ'din, nə'din

nadir
BR 'neɪdɪə(r), -z
AM 'neɪdər, 'neɪ,dɪ(ə)r,
-z

nae
BR neɪ
AM neɪ

naevae
BR 'ni:vʌɪ
AM 'ni,vaɪ

naevoid
BR 'ni:vɔɪd
AM 'ni,vɔɪd

naevus
BR 'ni:vəs
AM 'nivəs

naff
BR naf
AM næf

Naffy
BR 'nafi
AM 'næfi

nag
BR nag, -z, -ɪŋ, -d
AM næg, -z, -ɪŋ, -d

naga
BR 'nɑ:gə(r), -z
AM 'nɑgə, -z

Nagaland
BR 'nɑ:gəland
AM 'nɑgə,lænd

nagana
BR nə'gɑ:nə(r)
AM nə'gɑnə

Nagasaki
BR ,nagə'sɑ:ki
AM ,nɑgə'saki

nagger
BR 'nagə(r), -z
AM 'nægər, -z

naggingly
BR 'nagɪŋli

Nagle
BR 'neɪgl
AM 'neɪgəl

nagor
BR 'neɪgɔ:(r), -z
AM 'nægər, -z

Nagorno-Karabakh
BR nə,gɔ:nəʊ,karə'bak
AM nə'gɔrnoʊ,kɛrə'bak

Nagoya
BR nə'gɔɪə(r)
AM nə'gɔɪə

Nagpur
BR ,nag'pʊə(r)
AM ,næg'pʊ(ə)r

Nahuatl
BR 'nɑ:wɑ:tl, nɑ:'wɑ:tl, -z
AM ,nɑ'wɑtl, -z

Nahuatlan
BR 'nɑ:wɑ:tlən, nɑ:'wɑ:tlən
AM nɑ'wɑtlən

Nahum
BR 'neɪhəm
AM 'neɪhəm

naiad
BR 'nʌɪad, -z
AM 'neɪ,æd, 'nɑɪ,æd, 'neɪəd, 'nɑɪəd, -z

naiant
BR 'neɪənt
AM 'neɪənt

naif
BR nʌɪ'i:f, nɑ:'i:f, -s
AM nɑɪ'if, nɑ'if, -s

nail
BR neɪl, -z, -ɪŋ, -d
AM neɪl, -z, -ɪŋ, -d

nailbrush
BR 'neɪlbrʌʃ, -ɪz
AM 'neɪl,brəʃ, -əz

nailer
BR 'neɪlə(r), -z
AM 'neɪlər, -z

nailery
BR 'neɪlər|i, -ɪz
AM 'neɪləri, -z

nailless
BR 'neɪlɪs
AM 'neɪlɪs

nainsook
BR 'neɪnsʊk, -s
AM 'neɪn,sʊk, -s

Naipaul
BR 'nʌɪpɔ:l, 'nʌɪpɔ:l
AM 'nɑɪ,pɔl, 'nɑɪ,pɑl

naira
BR 'nʌɪrə(r)
AM 'nɑɪrə

Nairn
BR nɛ:n
AM nɛrn

Nairobi
BR nʌɪ'rəʊbi
AM nɑɪ'roʊbi

Naismith
BR 'neɪsmɪθ
AM 'neɪ,smɪθ

naive
BR nɑɪ'i:v, nɑ:'i:v
AM nɑ'iv

naively
BR nɑɪ'i:vli, nɑ:'i:vli
AM nɑ'ivli

naiveness
BR nʌɪ'i:vnɪs, nɑ:'i:vnɪs
AM nɑ'ivnɪs

naiveté
BR nʌɪ'i:v(ɪ)teɪ, nɑ:'i:v(ɪ)teɪ
AM ,nɑ,iv(ə)'teɪ, nɑ'iv(ə),teɪ

naivety
BR nʌɪ'i:v(ɪ)ti, nɑ:'i:v(ɪ)ti
AM nɑ'ivədi, nɑ'ivti

Najaf
BR nɑ'dʒaf
AM nə'dʒaf

naked
BR 'neɪkɪd
AM 'neɪkɪd

nakedly
BR 'neɪkɪdli
AM 'neɪkɪdli

nakedness
BR 'neɪkɪdnɪs
AM 'neɪkɪdnɪs

naker
BR 'neɪkə(r), -z
AM 'neɪkər, -z

Nakuru
BR nɑ'ku:ru:
AM nə'kuru

NALGO
BR 'nalgəʊ
AM 'næl,goʊ

'Nam
BR nam, nɑ:m
AM nam, næm

Namaqualand
BR nə'mɑ:kwəland
AM nə'makwə,lænd

namby-pamby
BR ,nambi'pambi
AM 'næmbi'pæmbi

name
BR neɪm, -z, -ɪŋ, -d
AM neɪm, -z, -ɪŋ, -d

nameable
BR 'neɪməbl
AM 'neɪməbəl

namedrop
BR 'neɪmdrɒp, -s, -ɪŋ, -t
AM 'neɪm,drɑp, -s, -ɪŋ, -t

name-dropper
BR 'neɪm,drɒpə(r), -z
AM 'neɪm,drɑpər, -z

nameless
BR ˈneɪmlɪs
AM ˈneɪmlɪs

namelessly
BR ˈneɪmlɪsli
AM ˈneɪmlɪsli

namelessness
BR ˈneɪmlɪsnɪs
AM ˈneɪmlɪnɪs

namely
BR ˈneɪmli
AM ˈneɪmli

nameplate
BR ˈneɪmpleɪt, -s
AM ˈneɪm,pleɪt, -s

namesake
BR ˈneɪmseɪk, -s
AM ˈneɪm,seɪk, -s

Namibia
BR nəˈmɪbɪə(r)
AM nəˈmɪbɪə

Namibian
BR nəˈmɪbɪən, -z
AM nəˈmɪbɪən, -z

namma
BR ˈnamə(r), -z
AM ˈnamə, -z

Namur
BR nəˈmjʊə(r)
AM nəˈm(j)ʊ(ə)r
FR namyʀ

nan
BR nan, -z
AM næn, -z

nana[1]
foolish person
BR ˈnɑːnə(r), -z
AM ˈnɑːnə, -z

nana[2]
grandmother
BR ˈnanə(r), -z
AM ˈnɑːnə, ˈnænə, -z

Nanaimo
BR nəˈnʌɪməʊ
AM nəˈnaɪˌmoʊ

Nanak
BR ˈnɑːnak
AM ˈnɑːnək, ˈnɑˌnæk

Nancarrow
BR nanˈkarəʊ
AM nænˈkɛroʊ

nance
BR nans, -ɪz
AM næns, -əz

Nanchang
BR nanˈtʃaŋ
AM nænˈtʃæŋ

Nancy
city
BR ˈnansi
AM ˈnɑːnsi, nɑnˈsi
FR nɑ̃si

nancy
BR ˈnans|i, -ɪz
AM ˈnænsi, -z

NAND
BR nand

AM nænd

Nandi
BR ˈnandi
AM ˈnɑndi

Nanette
BR naˈnɛt
AM nəˈnɛt

Nanga Parbat
BR ˌnaŋgə ˈpɑːbat
AM ˌnɑŋgə ˈpɑrbət

Nanjing
BR nanˈdʒɪŋ
AM nænˈdʒɪŋ

nankeen
BR nanˈkiːn, naŋˈkiːn
AM nænˈkin

Nanking
BR nanˈkɪŋ, naŋˈkɪŋ
AM nænˈkɪŋ

nanna
BR ˈnanə(r), -z
AM ˈnænə, ˈnɑnə, -z

nanny
BR ˈnan|i, -ɪz, -ɪɪŋ, -ɪd
AM ˈnæni, -z, -ɪŋ, -d

nannygoat
BR ˈnanɪgəʊt, -s
AM ˈnæniˌgoʊt, -s

nannyish
BR ˈnanɪɪʃ
AM ˈnæniɪʃ

nanogram
BR ˈnanə(ʊ)gram, -z
AM ˈnænəˌgræm, -z

nanometer
BR ˈnanə(ʊ)ˌmiːtə(r), -z
AM ˈnænəˌmidər, -z

nanometre
BR ˈnanə(ʊ)ˌmiːtə(r), -z
AM ˈnænəˌmidər, -z

nanosecond
BR ˈnanə(ʊ)ˌsɛknd, -z
AM ˈnænəˌsɛkənd, -z

nanotechnology
BR ˌnanə(ʊ)tɛkˈnɒlədʒi
AM ˌnænoʊˌtɛkˈnɑlədʒi

Nansen
BR ˈnansn
AM ˈnænsən

Nantes
BR nɑːnt, nɒnt
AM nɑnt

Nantgaredig
BR ˌnantgəˈrɛdɪg
AM ˌnæntgəˈrɛdɪg

Nantucket
BR nanˈtʌkɪt
AM nænˈtəkət

Nantwich
BR ˈnantwɪtʃ
AM ˈnæntwɪtʃ

Nant-y-glo
BR ˌnantəˈɡləʊ
AM ˌnæn(t)əˈɡloʊ
WE ˌnant ʌ ˈɡlɒ

naoi
BR ˈneɪɔɪ
AM ˈneɪˌɔɪ

Naomi
BR neɪˈəʊmi
AM neɪˈoʊmi,
naɪˈoʊmi

naos
BR ˈneɪɒs
AM ˈneɪˌɑs

nap
BR nap, -s, -ɪŋ, -t
AM næp, -s, -ɪŋ, -t

napa
BR ˈnapə(r), -z
AM ˈnæpə, -z

napalm
BR ˈneɪpɑːm
AM ˈneɪˌpɑ(l)m

Napa Valley
BR ˌnapə ˈvali
AM ˌnæpə ˈvæli

nape
BR neɪp, -s
AM neɪp, -s

napery
BR ˈneɪp(ə)ri
AM ˈneɪp(ə)ri

Naphtali
BR ˈnaftəlʌɪ
AM ˈnæftəˌlaɪ,
ˈnæptəˌlaɪ

naphtha
BR ˈnafθə(r), ˈnapθə(r)
AM ˈnæpθə, ˈnæfθə

naphthalene
BR ˈnafθəliːn,
ˈnapθəliːn
AM ˈnæpθəˌlin,
ˈnæfθəˌlin

naphthalic
BR nafˈθalɪk,
napˈθalɪk
AM næpˈθælɪk,
næfˈθælɪk

naphthene
BR ˈnafθiːn, ˈnapθiːn, -z
AM ˈnæpˌθin, ˈnæfˌθin,
-z

naphthenic
BR nafˈθiːnɪk,
napˈθiːnɪk, nafˈθɛnɪk,
napˈθɛnɪk
AM næpˈθɛnɪk,
næpˈθinɪk, næfˈθɛnɪk,
næfˈθinɪk

naphthol
BR ˈnafθɒl, ˈnapθɒl
AM ˈnæpˌθɔl, ˈnæpˌθɑl,
ˈnæpˌθoʊl, ˈnæfˌθɔl,
ˈnæfˌθɑl, ˈnæfˌθoʊl

Napier
BR ˈneɪpɪə(r)
AM ˈneɪpi(ə)r

Napierian
BR neɪˈpɪərɪən,
nəˈpɪərɪən
AM neɪˈpɪriən

napkin
BR ˈnapkɪn, -z
AM ˈnæpkɪn, -z

Naples
BR ˈneɪplz
AM ˈneɪpəlz

napoleon
BR nəˈpəʊlɪən, -z
AM nəˈpoʊlɪən,
nəˈpoʊljən, -z

Napoleonic
BR nəˌpəʊlɪˈɒnɪk
AM nəˌpoʊliˈɑnɪk

nappa
BR ˈnapə(r), -z
AM ˈnæpə, -z

nappe
BR nap, -s
AM næp, -s

napper
BR ˈnapə(r), -z
AM ˈnæpər, -z

nappy
BR ˈnap|i, -ɪz
AM ˈnæpi, -z

Nara
BR ˈnɑːrə(r)
AM ˈnɑrə

Narayan
BR nəˈrʌɪən
AM nəˈraɪən

Narberth
BR ˈnɑːbəθ
AM ˈnɑrˌbərθ

Narbonne
BR nɑːˈbɒn
AM nɑrˈbən

narc
BR nɑːk, -s
AM nɑrk, -s

narcissi
BR nɑːˈsɪsʌɪ
AM nɑrˈsɪˌsaɪ

narcissism
BR ˈnɑːsɪsɪz(ə)m
AM ˈnɑrsəˌsɪzəm

narcissist
BR ˈnɑːsɪsɪst, -s
AM ˈnɑrsəsəst, -s

narcissistic
BR ˌnɑːsɪˈsɪstɪk
AM ˌnɑrsəˈsɪstɪk

narcissistically
BR ˌnɑːsɪˈsɪstɪkli
AM ˌnɑrsəˈsɪstək(ə)li

narcissus
BR nɑːˈsɪsəs, -ɪz
AM nɑrˈsɪsəs, -əz

narcolepsy
BR ˈnɑːkə(ʊ)lɛpsi
AM ˈnɑrkəˌlɛpsi

narcoleptic
BR ˌnɑːkə(ʊ)ˈlɛptɪk
AM ˌnɑrkəˈlɛptɪk

narcosis
BR nɑːˈkəʊsɪs
AM nɑrˈkoʊsəs

narcoterrorism
BR ˌnɑːkəʊˈtɛrərɪz(ə)m
AM ˈnɑrkoʊˈtɛrəˌrɪzəm

narcoterrorist
BR ˌnɑːkəʊˈtɛrərɪst, -s
AM ˈnɑrkoʊˈtɛrərəst, -s

narcotic
BR nɑːˈkɒtɪk, -s
AM nɑrˈkɑdɪk, -s

narcotically
BR nɑːˈkɒtɪkli
AM nɑrˈkɑdək(ə)li

narcotisation
BR ˌnɑːkɑːtʌɪˈzeɪʃn
AM ˌnɑrkədəˈzeɪʃən,
ˌnɑrkəˌtaɪˈzeɪʃən

narcotise
BR ˈnɑːkətʌɪz, -ɪz, -ɪŋ,
-d
AM ˈnɑrkəˌtaɪz, -ɪz, -ɪŋ,
-d

narcotism
BR ˈnɑːkətɪz(ə)m
AM ˈnɑrkəˌtɪzəm

narcotization
BR ˌnɑːkətʌɪˈzeɪʃn
AM ˌnɑrkədəˈzeɪʃən,
ˌnɑrkəˌtaɪˈzeɪʃən

narcotize
BR ˈnɑːkətʌɪz, -ɪz, -ɪŋ,
-d
AM ˈnɑrkəˌtaɪz, -ɪz, -ɪŋ,
-d

nard
BR nɑːd
AM nɑrd

nardoo
BR ˌnɑːˈduː, ˈnɑːduː, -z
AM ˈnɑrˌdu, -z

nareal
BR ˈnɛːrɪəl
AM ˈnɛrɪəl

nares
BR ˈnɛːriːz
AM ˈnɛriz, nɛrz

nargile
BR ˈnɑːɡɪl|eɪ, ˈnɑːɡɪl|i,
-eɪz\-ɪz
AM ˈnɑrɡəli, -ɪz

nargileh
BR ˈnɑːɡɪl|eɪ, ˈnɑːɡɪl|i,
-eɪz\-ɪz
AM ˈnɑrɡəli, -ɪz

narial
BR ˈnɛːrɪəl
AM ˈnɛrɪəl

nark
BR nɑːk, -s, -ɪŋ, -t
AM nɑrk, -s, -ɪŋ, -t

narky
BR ˈnɑːk|i, -ɪə(r), -ɪɪst
AM ˈnɑrki, -ər, -ɪst

Narnia
BR ˈnɑːnɪə(r)
AM ˈnɑrnɪə

Narragansett
BR ˌnaraˈɡansɪt

AM ˌnɛrəˈɡænsət

narratable
BR nəˈreɪtəbl
AM nəˈreɪdəbəl

narrate
BR nəˈreɪt, -s, -ɪŋ, -ɪd
AM ˈnɛˌreɪ|t, -ts, -dɪŋ,
-dɪd

narration
BR nəˈreɪʃn, -z
AM nɛˈreɪʃən, -z

narrational
BR nəˈreɪʃn(ə)l,
nəˈreɪʃən(ə)l
AM nəˈreɪʃ(ə)nəl

narrative
BR ˈnarətɪv, -z
AM ˈnɛrədɪv, -z

narratively
BR ˈnarətɪvli
AM ˈnɛrədəvli

narrator
BR nəˈreɪtə(r), -z
AM ˈnɛˌreɪdər, -z

narrow
BR ˈnarəʊ, -z, -ɪŋ, -d,
-ə(r), -ɪst
AM ˈnɛr|oʊ, -oʊz, -əwɪŋ,
-oʊd, -əwər, -əwəst

narrowcast
BR ˈnarəʊkɑːst,
ˈnarəʊkast, -s
AM ˈnɛroʊˌkæst, -s

narrowcaster
BR ˈnarəʊˌkɑːstə(r),
ˈnarəʊˌkastə(r), -z
AM ˈnæroʊˌkæstər, -z

narrowcasting
BR ˈnarəʊˌkɑːstɪŋ,
ˈnarəʊˌkastɪŋ
AM ˈnɛroʊˌkæstɪŋ

narrowish
BR ˈnarəʊɪʃ
AM ˈnɛrəwɪʃ

narrowly
BR ˈnarəʊli
AM ˈnɛroʊli

narrowness
BR ˈnarəʊnəs
AM ˈnɛroʊnəs

narthex
BR ˈnɑːθeks, -ɪz
AM ˈnɑrˌθeks, -əz

Narvik
BR ˈnɑːvɪk
AM ˈnɑrˌvɪk

narwhal
BR ˈnɑːw(ə)l, -z
AM ˈnɑrˌ(h)wɑl,
ˈnɑrwəl, -z

nary
BR ˈnɛːri
AM ˈnɛri

NASA
BR ˈnasə(r)
AM ˈnæsə

nasal
BR ˈneɪzl
AM ˈneɪzəl

nasalisation
BR ˌneɪzəlʌɪˈzeɪʃn,
ˌneɪzˌlʌɪˈzeɪʃn, -z
AM ˌneɪzələˈzeɪʃən,
ˌneɪzəˌlaɪˈzeɪʃən, -z

nasalise
BR ˈneɪzəlʌɪz,
ˈneɪzˌlʌɪz, -ɪz, -ɪŋ, -d
AM ˈneɪzəˌlaɪz, -ɪz, -ɪŋ,
-d

nasality
BR neɪˈzalɪti
AM ˌneɪˈzælədi

nasalization
BR ˌneɪzəlʌɪˈzeɪʃn,
ˌneɪzˌlʌɪˈzeɪʃn, -z
AM ˌneɪzələˈzeɪʃən,
ˌneɪzəˌlaɪˈzeɪʃən, -z

nasalize
BR ˈneɪzəlʌɪz,
ˈneɪzˌlʌɪz, -ɪz, -ɪŋ, -d
AM ˈneɪzəˌlaɪz, -ɪz, -ɪŋ,
-d

nasally
BR ˈneɪzli, ˈneɪzəli
AM ˈneɪzəli

NASCAR
BR ˈnaskɑː(r)
AM ˈnæsˌkɑr

nascency
BR ˈnasnsi, ˈneɪsnsi
AM ˈneɪsənsi

nascent
BR ˈnasnt, ˈneɪsnt
AM ˈneɪsənt

NASDAQ
BR ˈnazdak
AM ˈnæzˌdæk

naseberry
BR ˈneɪzb(ə)r|i, -ɪz
AM ˈneɪsˌbɛri, -z

Naseby
BR ˈneɪzbi
AM ˈneɪzbi

Nash
BR naʃ
AM næʃ

Nashe
BR naʃ
AM næʃ

Nashua
BR ˈnaʃʊə(r)
AM ˈnæʃəwə

Nashville
BR ˈnaʃvɪl
AM ˈnæʃˌvɪl, ˈnæʃvəl

nasion
BR ˈneɪzɪən, -z
AM ˈneɪˌzaɪən, -z

Nasmyth
BR ˈneɪsmɪθ
AM ˈneɪˌsmɪθ

naso-frontal
BR ˈneɪzəʊˈfrʌntl
AM ˈneɪzoʊˈfrʌn(t)l

Nassau[1]
Bahamas
BR ˈnasɔː(r)
AM ˈnæˌsɔ

Nassau[2]
Germany
BR ˈnasaʊ
AM ˈnɑˌsaʊ

Nasser
BR ˈnasə(r)
AM ˈnæsər

Nastase
BR nəˈstɑːzi
AM nəˈstazi, nəˈstasi

nastic
BR ˈnastɪk
AM ˈnæstɪk

nastily
BR ˈnɑːstɪli, ˈnastɪli
AM ˈnæstəli

nastiness
BR ˈnɑːstɪnɪs,
ˈnastɪnɪs
AM ˈnæstɪnɪs

nasturtium
BR nəˈstəːʃ(ə)m, -z
AM næˈstərʃəm,
nəˈstərʃəm, -z

nasty
BR ˈnɑːst|i, ˈnast|i,
-ɪə(r), -ɪɪst
AM ˈnæsti, -ər, -ɪst

Nat
BR nat
AM næt

Natal
BR nəˈtal, nəˈtɑːl
AM nəˈtɑl

natal
BR ˈneɪtl
AM ˈneɪdl

Natalie
BR ˈnatəli
AM ˈnædli

natality
BR nəˈtalɪt|i, -ɪz
AM nəˈtælədi,
neɪˈtælədi, -z

Natasha
BR nəˈtaʃə(r)
AM nəˈtaʃə, nəˈtæʃə

natation
BR nəˈteɪʃn
AM nɑˈteɪʃən,
neɪˈteɪʃən

natatoria
BR ˌneɪtəˈtɔːrɪə(r)
AM ˌneɪdəˈtɔriə,
ˌnædəˈtɔriə

natatorial
BR ˌneɪtəˈtɔːrɪəl
AM ˌneɪdəˈtɔriəl,
ˌnædəˈtɔriəl

natatorium
BR ˌneɪtəˈtɔːrɪʌm, -z
AM ˌneɪdəˈtɔriəm,
ˌnædəˈtɔriəm, -z

natatory
BR 'neɪtətri
AM 'neɪdə,tɔːri,
'nædə,tɔːri

natch
BR natʃ
AM nætʃ

nates
plural noun
BR 'neɪtiːz
AM 'neɪ,tiz

Nathalie
BR 'natəli
AM 'nædli

Nathan
BR 'neɪθn
AM 'neɪθən

Nathaniel
BR nə'θanɪəl
AM nə'θænjəl

nation
BR 'neɪʃn, -z
AM 'neɪʃən, -z

national
BR 'naʃn(ə)l,
'naʃən(ə)l
AM 'næʃ(ə)nəl

nationalisation
BR ,naʃnəlaɪ'zeɪʃn,
,naʃnlʌɪ'zeɪʃn,
,naʃənlʌɪ'zeɪʃn,
,naʃ(ə)nəlʌɪ'zeɪʃn,
AM ,næʃ(ə)nələ'zeɪʃən,
,næʃ(ə)nə,laɪ'zeɪʃən

nationalise
BR 'naʃnəlʌɪz,
'naʃnlʌɪz, 'naʃənlʌɪz,
'naʃ(ə)nəlʌɪz, -ɪz, -ɪŋ,
-d
AM 'næʃ(ə)nə,laɪz, -ɪz,
-ɪŋ, -d

nationaliser
BR 'naʃnəlʌɪzə(r),
'naʃnlʌɪzə(r),
'naʃənlʌɪzə(r),
'naʃ(ə)nəlʌɪzə(r), -z
AM 'næʃ(ə)nə,laɪzər, -z

nationalism
BR 'naʃnəlɪz(ə)m,
'naʃnlɪz(ə)m,
'naʃənlɪz(ə)m,
'naʃ(ə)nəlɪz(ə)m
AM 'næʃ(ə)nə,lɪzəm

nationalist
BR 'naʃnəlɪst,
'naʃnlɪst, 'naʃənlɪst,
'naʃ(ə)nəlɪst, -s
AM 'næʃ(ə)nələst, -s

nationalistic
BR ,naʃnə'lɪstɪk,
,naʃnl'ɪstɪk,
,naʃənl'ɪstɪk,
,naʃ(ə)nə'lɪstɪk
AM ,næʃ(ə)nə'lɪstɪk

nationalistically
BR ,naʃnə'lɪstɪkli,
,naʃnl'ɪstɪkli,
,naʃənl'ɪstɪkli,

,naʃ(ə)nə'lɪstɪkli,
,naʃnə'lɪstɪkli,
,naʃnl'ɪstɪkli
AM ,næʃ(ə)nə'lɪstək-
(ə)li

nationality
BR ,naʃ(ə)'nalɪt|i, -ɪz
AM ,næʃə'nælədi, -z

nationalization
BR ,naʃnəlʌɪ'zeɪʃn,
,naʃnlʌɪ'zeɪʃn,
,naʃənlʌɪ'zeɪʃn,
,naʃ(ə)nəlʌɪ'zeɪʃn
AM ,næʃ(ə)nələ'zeɪʃən,
,næʃ(ə)nə,laɪ'zeɪʃən

nationalize
BR 'naʃnəlʌɪz,
'naʃnlʌɪz, 'naʃənlʌɪz,
'naʃ(ə)nəlʌɪz, -ɪz, -ɪŋ,
-d
AM 'næʃ(ə)nə,laɪz, -ɪz,
-ɪŋ, -d

nationalizer
BR 'naʃnəlʌɪzə(r),
'nasnlʌɪzə(r),
'naʃənlʌɪzə(r),
'naʃ(ə)nəlʌɪzə(r), -z
AM 'næʃ(ə)nə,laɪzər, -z

nationally
BR 'naʃnəli, 'naʃnli,
'naʃənli, 'naʃ(ə)nəli
AM 'næʃ(ə)nəli

nationhood
BR 'neɪʃnhʊd
AM 'neɪʃən,(h)ʊd

nationwide
BR ,neɪʃn'wʌɪd
AM 'neɪʃən,waɪd

native
BR 'neɪtɪv, -z
AM 'neɪdɪv, -z

natively
BR 'neɪtɪvli
AM 'neɪdɪvli

nativeness
BR 'neɪtɪvnɪs
AM 'neɪdɪvnɪs

nativism
BR 'neɪtɪvɪz(ə)m
AM 'neɪdə,vɪzəm

nativist
BR 'neɪtɪvɪst, -s
AM 'neɪdəvəst, -s

nativity
BR nə'tɪvɪt|i, -ɪz
AM nə'tɪvɪdi, -z

NATO
BR 'neɪtəʊ
AM 'neɪ,doʊ

natriuresis
BR ,neɪtrijʊ(ə)'riːsɪs,
,natrijʊ(ə)'riːsɪs
AM ,neɪtriju'risɪs

natriuretic
BR ,neɪtrijʊ(ə)'retɪk,
,natrijʊ(ə)'retɪk
AM ,neɪtriju'redɪk

natron
BR 'neɪtrɒn, 'neɪtr(ə)n
AM 'neɪ,trɑn, 'neɪtrən

NATSOPA
BR nat'səʊpə(r)
AM næt'soʊpə

natter
BR 'nat|ə(r), -əz,
-(ə)rɪŋ, -əd
AM 'nædər, -z, -ɪŋ, -d

natterer
BR 'nat(ə)rə(r), -z
AM 'nædərər, -z

natterjack
BR 'natədʒak, -s
AM 'nædər,dʒæk, -s

nattier blue
BR ,natjeɪ 'bluː
AM ,nædiər 'blu

nattily
BR 'natɪli
AM 'nædəli

nattiness
BR 'natnɪs
AM 'nædinɪs

natty
BR 'nat|i, -ɪə(r), -ɪɪst
AM 'nædi, -ər, -ɪst

Natufian
BR nɑː'tuːfɪən, -z
AM nə'tufɪən, -z

natural
BR 'natʃ(ə)rəl,
'natʃ(ə)r|, -z
AM 'natʃ(ə)rəl, -z

naturalisation
BR ,natʃ(ə)rəlʌɪ'zeɪʃn,
,natʃ(ə)r|ʌɪ'zeɪʃn
AM ,nætʃ(ə)rələ'zeɪʃən,
,nætʃ(ə)rə,laɪ'zeɪʃən

naturalise
BR 'natʃ(ə)rəlʌɪz,
'natʃ(ə)r|ʌɪz, -ɪz, -ɪŋ,
-d
AM 'nætʃ(ə)rə,laɪz, -ɪz,
-ɪŋ, -d

naturalism
BR 'natʃ(ə)rəlɪz(ə)m,
'natʃ(ə)r|ɪz(ə)m
AM 'nætʃ(ə)rə,lɪzəm

naturalist
BR 'natʃ(ə)rəlɪst,
'natʃ(ə)r|ɪst, -s
AM 'nætʃ(ə)rələst, -s

naturalistic
BR ,natʃ(ə)rə'lɪstɪk,
,natʃ(ə)r|'ɪstɪk
AM ,nætʃ(ə)rə'lɪstɪk

naturalistically
BR ,natʃ(ə)rə'lɪstɪkli,
,natʃ(ə)r|'ɪstɪkli
AM ,nætʃ(ə)rə'lɪstək-
(ə)li

naturalization
BR ,natʃ(ə)rəlʌɪ'zeɪʃn,
,natʃ(ə)r|ʌɪ'zeɪʃn
AM ,nætʃ(ə)rələ'zeɪʃən,
,nætʃ(ə)rə,laɪ'zeɪʃən

naturalize
BR 'natʃ(ə)rəlʌɪz,
'natʃ(ə)r|ʌɪz, -ɪz, -ɪŋ,
-d
AM 'nætʃ(ə)rə,laɪz, -ɪz,
-ɪŋ, -d

naturally
BR 'natʃ(ə)rəli,
'natʃ(ə)r|i
AM 'nætʃ(ə)rəli

naturalness
BR 'natʃ(ə)rəlnəs,
'natʃ(ə)r|nəs
AM 'nætʃ(ə)rəlnəs

nature
BR 'neɪtʃə(r), -z
AM 'neɪtʃər, -z

natured
BR 'neɪtʃəd
AM 'neɪtʃərd

naturism
BR 'neɪtʃ(ə)rɪz(ə)m
AM 'neɪtʃə,rɪzəm

naturist
BR 'neɪtʃ(ə)rɪst, -s
AM 'neɪtʃərəst, -s

naturopath
BR 'neɪtʃ(ə)rəpaθ,
'natʃ(ə)rəpaθ, -s
AM 'neɪtʃərə,pæθ,
'nætʃərə,pæθ, -s

naturopathic
BR ,neɪtʃ(ə)rə'paθɪk,
,natʃ(ə)rə'paθɪk
AM ,neɪtʃərə'pæθɪk,
'nætʃərə'pæθɪk

naturopathically
BR ,neɪtʃ(ə)rə'paθɪkli,
,natʃ(ə)rə'paθɪkli
AM ,neɪtʃərə'pæθək(ə)li,
'nætʃərə'pæθək(ə)li

naturopathy
BR ,neɪtʃə'rɒpəθi,
,natʃə'rɒpəθi
AM ,neɪtʃə'rɑpəθi,
,nætʃə'rɑpəθi

NatWest®
BR ,nat'west
AM ,næt'west

naugahyde
BR 'nɔːgəhʌɪd
AM 'nɔgə,haɪd,
'nɑgə,haɪd

naught
BR nɔːt, -s
AM nɔt, nɑt, -s

Naughtie
BR 'nɒxti
AM 'nɔdi, 'nɑdi

naughtily
BR 'nɔːtɪli
AM 'nɔdəli, 'nɑdəli

naughtiness
BR 'nɔːtɪnɪs, -ɪz
AM 'nɔdinɪs, 'nɑdinɪs,
-ɪz

Naughton
BR 'nɔːt(ə)n

AM 'nɔtn, 'nɑtn

naughty
BR 'nɔːt|i, -ɪə(r), -ɪɪst
AM 'nɔdi, 'nɑdi, -ər, -ɪst

nauplii
BR 'nɔːplɪʌɪ, 'nɔːplɪiː
AM 'nɔpliˌɑɪ, 'nɑpliˌɑɪ

nauplius
BR 'nɔːplɪəs
AM 'nɔpliəs, 'nɑpliəs

Nauru
BR nɑːˈuːruː, nauˈruː, nɑːˈruː
AM nɑˈuru

Nauruan
BR nɑːˈuːruːən, nauˈruːən, nɑːˈruːən, -z
AM nɑˈuruwən, -z

nausea
BR 'nɔːsɪə(r), 'nɔːzɪə(r)
AM 'nɔziə, 'nɔʒə, 'naziə, 'naʒə

nauseate
BR 'nɔːsɪeɪt, 'nɔːzɪeɪt, -s, -ɪŋ, -ɪd
AM 'nɔziˌeɪ|t, 'nɔʒiˌeɪ|t, 'naziˌeɪ|t, 'naʒiˌeɪ|t, -ts, -dɪŋ, -dɪd

nauseatingly
BR 'nɔːsɪeɪtɪŋli, 'nɔːzɪeɪtɪŋli
AM 'nɔziˌeɪdɪŋli, 'nɔʒiˌeɪdɪŋli, 'naziˌeɪdɪŋli, 'naʒiˌeɪdɪŋli

nauseous
BR 'nɔːsɪəs, 'nɔːzɪəs
AM 'nɔʃəs, 'nɔʒəs, 'naʃəs, 'naʒəs

nauseously
BR 'nɔːsɪəsli, 'nɔːzɪəsli
AM 'nɔʃəsli, 'nɔʒəsli, 'naʃəsli, 'naʒəsli

nauseousness
BR 'nɔːsɪəsnəs, 'nɔːzɪəsnəs
AM 'nɔʃəsnəs, 'nɔʒəsnəs, 'naʃəsnəs, 'naʒəsnəs

Nausicaa
BR nɔːˈsɪkɪə(r), nɔːˈsɪkeɪə(r)
AM nɔːˈsɪkiə, nɔːˈsɪkeɪə, nɑˈsɪkiə, nɑˈsɪkeɪə

nautch
BR nɔːtʃ, -ɪz
AM nɔtʃ, nɑtʃ, -əz

nautical
BR 'nɔːtɪkl
AM 'nɔdəkəl, 'nɑdəkəl

nautically
BR 'nɔːtɪkli
AM 'nɔdək(ə)li, 'nɑdək(ə)li

nautilus
BR 'nɔːtɪləs, 'nɔːt|əs, -ɪz
AM 'nɑdləs, 'nɑd|əs, -əz

Navaho
BR 'navəhəʊ, -z
AM 'navəˌhoʊ, 'nævəˌhoʊ, -z

Navajo
BR 'navəhəʊ, -z
AM 'navəˌhoʊ, 'nævəˌhoʊ, -z

naval
BR 'neɪvl
AM 'neɪvəl

navally
BR 'neɪv|li, 'neɪvəli
AM 'neɪvəli

navarin
BR 'nav(ə)rɪn, 'nav(ə)rn̩
AM 'nævərən

Navarino
BR ˌnavəˈriːnəʊ
AM ˌnævəˈrinoʊ

Navarone
BR ˌnavəˈrəʊn
AM ˌnævəˈroʊn

Navarre
BR nəˈvɑː(r)
AM nəˈvɑr

nave
BR neɪv, -z
AM neɪv, -z

navel
BR 'neɪvl, -z
AM 'neɪvəl, -z

navelwort
BR 'neɪvlwɜːt, -s
AM 'neɪvəlˌwɜrt, 'neɪvəlˌwɔ(ə)rt, -s

navicular
BR nəˈvɪkjələ(r), -z
AM nəˈvɪkjələr, -z

navigability
BR ˌnavɪɡəˈbɪlɪti
AM ˌnævəɡəˈbɪlɪdi

navigable
BR 'navɪɡəbl
AM 'nævəɡəbəl

navigableness
BR 'navɪɡəblnəs
AM 'nævəɡəbəlnəs

navigate
BR 'navɪɡeɪt, -s, -ɪŋ, -ɪd
AM 'nævəˌɡeɪ|t, -ts, -dɪŋ, -dɪd

navigation
BR ˌnavɪˈɡeɪʃn̩, -z
AM ˌnævəˈɡeɪʃən, -z

navigational
BR ˌnavɪˈɡeɪʃn̩(ə)l, ˌnavɪˈɡeɪʃən(ə)l
AM ˌnævəˈɡeɪʃ(ə)nəl

navigator
BR 'navɪɡeɪtə(r), -z
AM 'nævəˌɡeɪdər, -z

Navrátilová
BR ˌnavratrˈləʊvə(r)
AM ˌnavrədəˈloʊvə
CZ 'nʌvrɑːtjlovɑː

navvy
BR 'nav|i, -ɪz
AM 'nævi, -z

navy
BR 'neɪv|i, -ɪz
AM 'neɪvi, -z

nawab
BR nəˈwɑːb, nəˈwɔːb, -z
AM nəˈwɔb, nəˈwɑb, -z

Náxos
BR 'naksɒs
AM 'nækˌsɒs, 'nækˌsɑs

nay
BR neɪ, -z
AM neɪ, -z

Nayland
BR 'neɪlənd
AM 'neɪlənd

Naylor
BR 'neɪlə(r)
AM 'neɪlər

naysay
BR 'neɪseɪ, -z, -ɪŋ, -d
AM 'neɪˌseɪ, -z, -ɪŋ, -d

naysayer
BR 'neɪˌseɪə(r), -z
AM 'neɪˌseɪər, -z

Nazarene
BR ˌnazəˈriːn, 'nazəriːn, -z
AM 'næzəˌrin, -z

Nazareth
BR 'naz(ə)rəθ
AM 'næz(ə)rəθ

Nazarite
BR 'nazərʌɪt, -s
AM 'næzəˌraɪt, -s

Nazca Lines
BR 'nazkə lʌɪnz, 'naskə +
AM 'naskə ˌlaɪnz

naze
BR neɪz, -ɪz
AM neɪz, -ɪz

Nazi
BR 'nɑːts|i, 'nats|i, -ɪz
AM 'nɑtsi, 'nætsi, -z

Nazidom
BR 'nɑːtsɪdəm, 'natsɪdəm
AM 'natsidəm, 'nætsidəm

Nazification
BR ˌnɑːtsɪfɪˈkeɪʃn, ˌnatsɪfɪˈkeɪʃn
AM ˌnatsəfəˈkeɪʃən, ˌnætsəfəˈkeɪʃən

Nazify
BR 'nɑːtsɪfʌɪ, 'natsɪfʌɪ, -z, -ɪŋ, -d
AM 'natʃəˌfaɪ, 'nætsəˌfaɪ, -z, -ɪŋ, -d

Naziism
BR 'nɑːtsɪɪz(ə)m, 'natsiːz(ə)m
AM 'natsiˌɪzəm, 'nætsiˌɪzəm

Nazirite
BR 'nazɪrʌɪt
AM 'næzəˌraɪt

Nazism
BR 'nɑːtsɪz(ə)m, 'natsɪz(ə)m
AM 'natˌsɪzəm, 'nætˌsɪzəm

Ndebele
BR n̩dɪˈbiːli, (n)dɪˈbeɪli
AM (n)dəˈbili

N'Djamena
BR n̩dʒəˈmeɪnə(r)
AM (n)ˈdʒamənə

Ndola
BR n̩ˈdəʊlə(r)
AM ˈ(n)doʊlə

né
BR neɪ
AM neɪ

Neagh
BR neɪ
AM neɪ

Neal
BR niːl
AM nil

Neale
BR niːl
AM nil

neanderthal
BR nɪˈandətɑːl, -z
AM niˈændərˌθɒl, niˈændərˌθɑl, -z

neap
BR niːp, -s
AM nip, -s

Neapolitan
BR nɪəˈpɒlɪt(ə)n, ˌniːəˈpɒlɪt(ə)n, -z
AM ˌniəˈpɑlətn̩, ˌniəˈpɑlədən, -z

near
BR nɪə(r)
AM nɪ(ə)r

nearby
BR ˌnɪəˈbʌɪ
AM ˌnɪrˈbaɪ

Nearctic
BR ˌniːˈɑːktɪk
AM niˈɑr(k)tɪk, niˈɑrdɪk

nearish
BR 'nɪərɪʃ
AM 'nɪrɪʃ

nearly
BR 'nɪəli
AM 'nɪrli

nearness
BR 'nɪənəs
AM 'nɪrnəs

nearside
BR 'nɪəsʌɪd
AM 'nɪrˌsaɪd

Neasden
BR 'niːzd(ə)n
AM 'nizdən

neat
BR niːt, -ə(r), -ɪst
AM niǀt, -dər, -dɪst

neaten
BR 'niːtn̩, -z, -ɪŋ, -d
AM 'nitn̩, -z, -ɪŋ, -d

neath
BR niːθ
AM niθ

neatly
BR 'niːtli
AM 'nitli

neatness
BR 'niːtnɪs
AM 'nitnɪs

Neave
BR niːv
AM niv

nebbish
BR 'nebɪʃ, -ɪʃɪz
AM 'nebɪʃ, -ɪz

Nebraska
BR nə'braskə(r)
AM nə'bræskə

Nebraskan
BR nɪ'braskən, -z
AM nə'bræskən, -z

Nebuchadnezzar
BR ˌnebjəkəd'nezə(r), -z
AM ˌneb(j)əkə(d)'nezər, -z

nebula
BR 'nebjələ(r), -z
AM 'nebjələ, -z

nebulae
BR 'nebjəliː
AM 'nebjəli, 'nebjəˌlaɪ

nebular
BR 'nebjələ(r)
AM 'nebjələr

nebuliser
BR 'nebjəlʌɪzə(r), -z
AM 'nebjəˌlaɪzər, -z

nebulizer
BR 'nebjəlʌɪzə(r), -z
AM 'nebjəˌlaɪzər, -z

nebulosity
BR ˌnebjə'lɒsɪti
AM ˌnebjə'lasədi

nebulous
BR 'nebjələs
AM 'nebjələs

nebulously
BR 'nebjələsli
AM 'nebjələsli

nebulousness
BR 'nebjələsnəs
AM 'nebjələsnəs

nebuly
BR 'nebjəli
AM 'nebjəli

necessarian
BR ˌnesɪ'seːrɪən, -z

necessarianism
BR ˌnesɪ'seːrɪənɪz(ə)m
AM ˌnesə'seːrɪəˌnɪzəm

necessarily
BR 'nesɪs(ə)rɪli, ˌnesə'serɪli
AM ˌnesə'serəli

necessariness
BR 'nesɪs(ə)rɪnɪs
AM 'nesəˌserɪnɪs

necessary
BR 'nesɪs(ə)rǀi, -ɪz
AM 'nesəˌseri, -z

necessitarian
BR nɪˌsesɪ'teːrɪən, -z
AM nəˌsesə'terɪən, -z

necessitarianism
BR nɪˌsesɪ'teːrɪənɪz(ə)m
AM nəˌsesə'terɪəˌnɪzəm

necessitate
BR nɪ'sesɪteɪt, -s, -ɪŋ, -ɪd
AM nə'sesəˌteɪǀt, -ts, -dɪŋ, -dɪd

necessitous
BR nɪ'sesɪtəs
AM nə'sesədəs

necessitously
BR nɪ'sesɪtəsli
AM nə'sesədəsli

necessitousness
BR nɪ'sesɪtəsnəs
AM nə'sesədəsnəs

necessity
BR nɪ'sesɪtǀi, -ɪz
AM nə'sesədi, -z

neck
BR nek, -s, -ɪŋ, -t
AM nek, -s, -ɪŋ, -t

neck-and-neck
BR ˌnek(ə)n(d)'nek
AM 'nekən'nek

Neckar
BR 'nekə(r), 'nekɑː(r)
AM 'nekər

neckband
BR 'nekband, -z
AM 'nekˌbænd, -z

Necker
BR 'nekə(r)
AM 'nekər

neckerchief
BR 'nekətʃɪf, 'nekətʃiːf, -s
AM 'nekərˌtʃɪf, 'nekərˌtʃif, -s

necklace
BR 'neklɪs, -ɪz
AM 'nekləs, -əz

necklet
BR 'neklɪt, -s
AM 'neklət, -s

neckline
BR 'neklʌɪn, -z
AM 'nekˌlaɪn, -z

necktie
BR 'nektʌɪ, -z
AM 'nekˌtaɪ, -z

neckwear
BR 'nekweː(r)
AM 'nekˌwe(ə)r

necrobiosis
BR ˌnekrə(ʊ)bʌɪ'əʊsɪs
AM ˌnekrə'baɪəsəs

necrobiotic
BR ˌnekrə(ʊ)bʌɪ'ɒtɪk
AM ˌnekrəˌbaɪ'ɑdɪk

necrogenic
BR ˌnekrə(ʊ)'dʒenɪk
AM ˌnekrə'dʒenɪk

necrolatry
BR nɪ'krɒlətri, ne'krɒlətri
AM nə'krɑlətri, ne'kralətri

necrological
BR ˌnekrə'lɒdʒɪkl
AM ˌnekrə'lɑdʒəkəl

necrologist
BR nɪ'krɒlədʒɪst, ne'krɒlədʒɪst, -s
AM nə'krɑlədʒəst, ne'kralədʒəst, -s

necrology
BR nɪ'krɒlədʒǀi, ne'krɒlədʒǀi, -ɪz
AM nə'krɑlədʒi, ne'kralədʒi, -z

necromancer
BR 'nekrə(ʊ)mansə(r), -z
AM 'nekrəˌmænsər, -z

necromancy
BR 'nekrə(ʊ)mansi
AM 'nekrəˌmænsi

necromantic
BR ˌnekrə(ʊ)'mantɪk, -s
AM ˌnekrə'mæn(t)ɪk, -s

necrophagous
BR nɪ'krɒfəgəs, ne'krɒfəgəs
AM nə'krɑfəgəs, ne'krafəgəs

necrophil
BR ˌnekrə(ʊ)fɪl, -z
AM 'nekrəˌfɪl, -z

necrophile
BR ˌnekrə(ʊ)fʌɪl, -z
AM 'nekrəˌfaɪl, -z

necrophilia
BR ˌnekrə(ʊ)'fɪlɪə(r)
AM ˌnekrə'fɪljə, ˌnekrə'fɪlɪə

necrophiliac
BR ˌnekrə(ʊ)'fɪlɪak, -s
AM ˌnekrə'fɪliˌæk, -s

necrophilic
BR ˌnekrə(ʊ)'fɪlɪk
AM ˌnekrə'fɪlɪk

necrophilism
BR nɪ'krɒfɪlɪz(ə)m, ne'krɒfɪlɪz(ə)m
AM nə'krɑfəˌlɪzəm, ne'krafəˌlɪzəm

necrophilist
BR nɪ'krɒfɪlɪst, ne'krɒfɪlɪst, -s
AM nə'krɑfələst, ne'krafələst, -s

necrophily
BR nɪ'krɒfɪli, ne'krɒfɪli
AM nə'krɑfəli, ne'krafəli

necrophobia
BR ˌnekrə(ʊ)'fəʊbɪə(r)
AM ˌnekrə'foʊbiə

necropolis
BR nɪ'krɒpəlɪs, nɪ'krɒp‖ɪs, ne'krɒpəlɪs, ne'krɒp‖ɪs, -ɪz
AM nə'krɑpələs, ne'krapələs, -əz

necropsy
BR 'nekrɒpsi, nɪ'krɒpsi, ne'krɒpsi
AM nə'krɑpsi, 'neˌkrɑpsi

necroscopic
BR ˌnekrə(ʊ)'skɒpɪk
AM ˌnekrə'skɑpɪk

necroscopy
BR nɪ'krɒskəp‖i, ne'krɒskəpi, -ɪz
AM nə'kraskəpi, ne'kraskɑpi, -z

necrose
BR 'nekrəʊs, nɪ'krəʊs, ne'krəʊs
AM 'neˌkrous, nə'krous, ne'krous

necrosis
BR nɪ'krəʊsɪs, ne'krəʊsɪs
AM nə'krousəs, ne'krousəs

necrotic
BR nɪ'krɒtɪk, ne'krɒtɪk
AM nə'krɑdɪk, ne'kradɪk

necrotise
BR 'nekrə(ʊ)tʌɪz, -ɪz, -ɪŋ, -d
AM 'nekrəˌtaɪz, -ɪz, -ɪŋ, -d

necrotize
BR 'nekrə(ʊ)tʌɪz, -ɪz, -ɪŋ, -d
AM 'nekrəˌtaɪz, -ɪz, -ɪŋ, -d

nectar
BR 'nektə(r)
AM 'nektər

nectarean
BR nek'teːrɪən

AM nɛkˈtɛriən
nectared
BR ˈnɛktəd
AM ˈnɛktərd
nectareous
BR nɛkˈtɛːriəs
AM nɛkˈtɛriəs
nectariferous
BR ˌnɛktəˈrɪf(ə)rəs
AM ˌnɛktəˈrɪf(ə)rəs
nectarine
BR ˈnɛktəriːn,
ˈnɛktərɪn, -z
AM ˌnɛktəˈriːn, -z
nectarous
BR ˈnɛkt(ə)rəs
AM ˈnɛktərəs
nectary
BR ˈnɛkt(ə)r|i, -ɪz
AM ˈnɛktəri, -z
Ned
BR nɛd
AM nɛd
neddy
BR ˈnɛd|i, -ɪz
AM ˈnɛdi, -z
nee
BR neɪ
AM neɪ
née
BR neɪ
AM neɪ
need
BR niːd, -z, -ɪŋ, -ɪd
AM nid, -z, -ɪŋ, -ɪd
needful
BR ˈniːdf(ʊ)l
AM ˈnidfəl
needfully
BR ˈniːdfəli, ˈniːdfl̩i
AM ˈnidfəli
needfulness
BR ˈniːdf(ʊ)lnəs
AM ˈnidfəlnəs
Needham
BR ˈniːdəm
AM ˈnidəm
needily
BR ˈniːdɪli
AM ˈnidɪli
neediness
BR ˈniːdɪnɪs
AM ˈnidɪnɪs
needle
BR ˈniːd|l, -lz, -l̩ɪŋ \ -lɪŋ,
-ld
AM ˈnid|əl, -əlz, -(ə)lɪŋ,
-əld
needlecord
BR ˈniːdlkɔːd
AM ˈnidl̩kɔrd
needlecraft
BR ˈniːdlkrɑːft,
ˈniːdlkraft
AM ˈnidl̩kræft
needleful
BR ˈniːdlfʊl, -z

AM ˈnidl̩fʊl, -z
needlepoint
BR ˈniːdlpɔɪnt
AM ˈnidl̩pɔɪnt
Needles
BR ˈniːdlz
AM ˈnidlz
needless
BR ˈniːdlɪs
AM ˈnidlɪs
needlessly
BR ˈniːdlɪsli
AM ˈnidlɪsli
needlessness
BR ˈniːdlɪsnɪs
AM ˈnidlɪnɪs
needlewoman
BR ˈniːdl̩ˌwʊmən
AM ˈnidl̩ˌwʊmən
needlewomen
BR ˈniːdl̩ˌwɪmɪn
AM ˈnidl̩ˌwɪmɪn
needlework
BR ˈniːdlwəːk
AM ˈnidl̩wərk
needn't
BR ˈniːdnt
AM ˈnidnt
needy
BR ˈniːd|i, -iə(r), -ɪɪst
AM ˈnidi, -ər, -ɪst
neep
BR niːp, -s
AM nip, -s
ne'er
BR nɛː(r)
AM nɛ(ə)r
ne'er-do-well
BR ˈnɛːdəwɛl, -z
AM ˈnɛrduˌwɛl,
ˈnɛrdəˌwɛl, -z
nefarious
BR nɪˈfɛːriəs
AM nəˈfɛriəs
nefariously
BR nɪˈfɛːriəsli
AM nəˈfɛriəsli
nefariousness
BR nɪˈfɛːriəsnəs
AM nəˈfɛriəsnəs
Nefertiti
BR ˌnɛfəˈtiːti
AM ˌnɛfərˈtidi
Neff®
BR nɛf
AM nɛf
Nefyn
BR ˈnɛv(ɪ)n
AM ˈnɛvən
neg.
negative
BR nɛg
AM nɛg
negate
BR nɪˈgeɪt, -s, -ɪŋ, -ɪd
AM nəˈgeɪt, -ts, -dɪŋ,
-dɪd

negation
BR nɪˈgeɪʃn, -z
AM nəˈgeɪʃən, -z
negationist
BR nɪˈgeɪʃn̩ɪst, -s
AM nəˈgeɪʃ(ə)nəst, -s
negative
BR ˈnɛgətɪv, -z
AM ˈnɛgədɪv, -z
negatively
BR ˈnɛgətɪvli
AM ˈnɛgədɪvli
negativeness
BR ˈnɛgətɪvnɪs
AM ˈnɛgədɪvnɪs
negativism
BR ˈnɛgətɪvɪz(ə)m
AM ˈnɛgədəvˌɪzəm
negativist
BR ˈnɛgətɪvɪst, -s
AM ˈnɛgədəvəst, -s
negativistic
BR ˌnɛgətɪˈvɪstɪk
AM ˌnɛgədəˈvɪstɪk
negativity
BR ˌnɛgəˈtɪvɪti
AM ˌnɛgəˈtɪvɪdi
negator
BR nɪˈgeɪtə(r), -z
AM nəˈgeɪdər, -z
negatory
BR ˈnɛgət(ə)ri
AM ˈnɛgəˌtɔri
Negev
BR ˈnɛgɛv
AM ˈnɛˌgɛv
neglect
BR nɪˈglɛkt, -s, -ɪŋ, -ɪd
AM nəˈglɛk|(t), -(t)s,
-tɪŋ, -təd
neglectful
BR nɪˈglɛk(t)f(ʊ)l
AM nəˈglɛk(t)fəl
neglectfully
BR nɪˈglɛk(t)fəli,
nɪˈglɛk(t)fl̩i
AM nəˈglɛk(t)fəli
neglectfulness
BR nɪˈglɛk(t)f(ʊ)lnəs
AM nəˈglɛk(t)fəlnəs
negligee
BR ˈnɛglɪʒeɪ, -z
AM ˈnɛgləˌʒeɪ,
ˌnɛgləˈʒeɪ, -z
negligence
BR ˈnɛglɪdʒ(ə)ns
AM ˈnɛglədʒəns
negligent
BR ˈnɛglɪdʒ(ə)nt
AM ˈnɛglədʒənt
negligently
BR ˈnɛglɪdʒ(ə)ntli
AM ˈnɛglədʒən(t)li
negligibility
BR ˌnɛglɪdʒɪˈbɪlɪti
AM ˌnɛglədʒəˈbɪlɪdi

negligible
BR ˈnɛglɪdʒɪbl
AM ˈnɛglədʒəbəl
negligibly
BR ˈnɛglɪdʒɪbli
AM ˈnɛglədʒəbli
Negombo
BR nɪˈgɒmbəʊ
AM nəˈgɑm,boʊ,
nəˈgɑm,boʊ
negotiability
BR nɪ,gəʊʃ(ɪ)əˈbɪlɪti
AM nə,goʊʃ(i)əˈbɪlɪdi
negotiable
BR nɪˈgəʊʃ(ɪ)əbl
AM nəˈgoʊʃ(i)əbəl
negotiant
BR nɪˈgəʊʃɪənt,
nɪˈgəʊʃ(ə)nt, -s
AM nəˈgoʊʃ(i)ənt, -s
negotiate
BR nɪˈgəʊʃieɪt,
nɪˈgəʊsieɪt, -s, -ɪŋ, -ɪd
AM nəˈgoʊʃiˌeɪ|t,
nəˈgoʊsiˌeɪ|t, -ts, -dɪŋ,
-dɪd
negotiation
BR nɪ,gəʊʃiˈeɪʃn,
nɪ,gəʊsiˈeɪʃn, -z
AM nə,goʊʃiˈeɪʃən,
nə,goʊsiˈeɪʃən, -z
negotiator
BR nɪˈgəʊʃieɪtə(r),
nɪˈgəʊsieɪtə(r), -z
AM nəˈgoʊʃiˌeɪdər,
nəˈgoʊsiˌeɪdər, -z
Negress
BR ˈniːgrɪs, ˈniːgrɛs, -ɪz
AM ˈnigrɪs, -əz
Negrillo
BR nɪˈgrɪləʊ, -z
AM nəˈgrɪloʊ, -z
Negrito
BR nɪˈgriːtəʊ, -z
AM nəˈgridoʊ, -z
negritude
BR ˈnɛgrɪtjuːd,
ˈnɛgrɪtʃuːd
AM ˈnɛgrəˌt(j)ud
Negro
BR ˈniːgrəʊ, -z
AM ˈnigroʊ, -z
negroid
BR ˈniːgrɔɪd
AM ˈniˌgrɔɪd
Negroism
BR ˈniːgrəʊɪz(ə)m
AM ˈnigrəˌwɪzəm
Negrophobia
BR ˌniːgrə(ʊ)ˈfəʊbiə(r)
AM ˌnigrəˈfoʊbiə
Negrophobic
BR ˌniːgrə(ʊ)ˈfəʊbɪk
AM ˌnigrəˈfoʊbɪk
negus
BR ˈniːgəs
AM ˈnigəs

Nehemiah
BR niːɪˈmʌɪə(r)
AM ˌniːəˈmaɪə

Nehru
BR ˈnɛːruː
AM ˈneɪru

neigh
BR neɪ, -z, -ɪŋ, -d
AM neɪ, -z, -ɪŋ, -d

neighbor
BR ˈneɪb|ə(r), -əz,
-(ə)rɪŋ, -əd
AM ˈneɪbər, -z, -ɪŋ, -d

neighborhood
BR ˈneɪbəhʊd, -z
AM ˈneɪbər,(h)ʊd, -z

neighborliness
BR ˈneɪbəlɪnɪs
AM ˈneɪbərlɪnɪs

neighborly
BR ˈneɪbəli
AM ˈneɪbərli

neighbour
BR ˈneɪb|ə(r), -əz,
-(ə)rɪŋ, -əd
AM ˈneɪbər, -z, -ɪŋ, -d

neighbourhood
BR ˈneɪbəhʊd, -z
AM ˈneɪbər,(h)ʊd, -z

neighbourliness
BR ˈneɪbəlɪnɪs
AM ˈneɪbərlɪnɪs

neighbourly
BR ˈneɪbəli
AM ˈneɪbərli

Neil
BR niːl
AM nil

Neill
BR niːl
AM nil

Neilson
BR ˈniːls(ə)n
AM ˈnilsən

neither
BR ˈnʌɪðə(r), ˈniːðə(r)
AM ˈniðər, ˈnaɪðər

nekton
BR ˈnɛkt(ə)n, ˈnɛktɒn
AM ˈnɛktən, ˈnɛk,tan

Nell
BR nɛl
AM nɛl

Nellie
BR ˈnɛli
AM ˈnɛli

nelly
BR ˈnɛl|i, -ɪz
AM ˈnɛli, -z

Nelson
BR ˈnɛlsn
AM ˈnɛlsən

nelumbo
BR nɪˈlʌmbəʊ, -z
AM nəˈləmboʊ, -z

nematocyst
BR nɪˈmatə(ʊ)sɪst,
ˈnɛmətəsɪst, -s
AM ˈnimədə,sɪst,
nəˈmædə,sɪst, -s

nematode
BR ˈnɛmətəʊd, -z
AM ˈnimə,toʊd, -z

Nembutal®
BR ˈnɛmbjʊtal,
ˈnɛmbjʊtbl
AM ˈnɛmbjə,tɔl,
ˈnɛmbjə,tal,
ˈnɛmbjə,tæl

nem con
BR ˌnɛm ˈkɒn
AM ˌnɛm ˈkan

nemertean
BR nɪˈməːtɪən,
ˌnɛməˈtiːən,
ˈnɛmətiːn, -z
AM nəˈmərdiən, -z

nemertine
BR nɪˈməːtʌɪn,
nɪˈmətiːn, ˈnɛmətʌɪn,
ˈnɛmətiːn
AM ˈnɛmər,tin

nemeses
BR ˈnɛmɪsiːz
AM ˈnɛmə,siz

nemesia
BR nɪˈmiːʒ(ɪ)ə(r)
AM nəˈmiʒ(i)ə,
nəˈmiziə

nemesis
BR ˈnɛmɪsɪs
AM ˈnɛməsəs

Nemo
BR ˈniːməʊ
AM ˈnimoʊ

Nene[1]
*river at
Northampton, UK*
BR nɛn
AM nɛn

Nene[2]
*river at
Peterborough,
Norfolk and
Lincolnshire, UK*
BR niːn
AM nin

nene
BR ˈneɪneɪ, -z
AM ˈneɪ,neɪ, -z

Nennius
BR ˈnɛnɪəs
AM ˈnɛnɪəs

nenuphar
BR ˈnɛnjʊfɑː(r), -z
AM ˈnɛnjə,far, -z

neo-Cambrian
BR ˌniːə(ʊ)ˈkambrɪən
AM ˈnioʊˈkæmbriən

Neocene
BR ˈnɪə(ʊ)siːn
AM ˈnɪəˌsin

neoclassic
BR ˌniːə(ʊ)ˈklasɪk
AM ˈnioʊˈklæsɪk

neoclassical
BR ˌniːə(ʊ)ˈklasɪkl
AM ˈnioʊˈklæsəkəl

neoclassicism
BR ˌniːə(ʊ)ˈklasɪsɪz(ə)m
AM ˈnioʊˈklæsə,sɪzəm

neoclassicist
BR ˌniːə(ʊ)ˈklasɪsɪst, -s
AM ˈnioʊˈklæsəsəst, -s

neocolonial
BR ˌniːəʊkəˈləʊnɪəl
AM ˈnioʊkəˈloʊnjəl,
ˌnioʊkəˈloʊniəl

neocolonialism
BR ˌniːəʊkəˈləʊnɪəliz-
(ə)m
AM ˈnioʊkəˈloʊnjə,lɪ-
zəm,
ˈnioʊkəˈloʊniə,lɪzəm

neocolonialist
BR ˌniːəʊkəˈləʊnɪəlɪst,
-s
AM ˈnioʊkəˈloʊnjələst,
ˈnioʊkəˈloʊniələst, -s

neodymium
BR ˌnɪə(ʊ)ˈdɪmɪəm
AM ˌnioʊˈdɪmiəm

neolithic
BR ˌniːəˈlɪθɪk
AM ˈnɪəˌlɪθɪk

neologian
BR ˌniːəˈləʊdʒɪən,
ˌniːəˈləʊdʒ(ə)n, -z
AM ˈnioʊˈloʊdʒ(i)ən, -z

neologise
BR nɪˈɒlədʒʌɪz, -ɪz, -ɪŋ,
-d
AM niˈalə,dʒaɪz, -ɪz, -ɪŋ,
-d

neologism
BR nɪˈɒlədʒɪz(ə)m, -z
AM niˈalə,dʒɪzəm, -z

neologist
BR nɪˈɒlədʒɪst, -s
AM niˈalədʒəst, -s

neologize
BR nɪˈɒlədʒʌɪz, -ɪz, -ɪŋ,
-d
AM niˈalə,dʒaɪz, -ɪz, -ɪŋ,
-d

neology
BR nɪˈɒlədʒ|i, -ɪz
AM niˈalədʒi, -z

neomycin
BR ˌnɪə(ʊ)ˈmʌɪsɪn
AM ˌnioʊˈmaɪsən

neon
BR ˈniːɒn
AM ˈni,ɑn

neonatal
BR ˌnɪə(ʊ)ˈneɪtl
AM ˌnioʊˈneɪdəl

neonate
BR ˌnɪə(ʊ)ˈneɪt, -s
AM ˈnɪəˌneɪt, -s

neonatology
BR ˌnɪə(ʊ)neɪˈtɒlədʒi
AM ˌnioʊˌneɪˈtalədʒi

neontologist
BR ˌnɪɒnˈtɒlədʒɪst, -s
AM ˌni,anˈtalədʒəst, -s

neontology
BR ˌnɪɒnˈtɒlədʒi
AM ˌni,anˈtalədʒi

neopentane
BR ˌniːə(ʊ)ˈpɛnteɪn
AM ˈnioʊˈpɛn,teɪn

neophobia
BR ˌniːə(ʊ)ˈfəʊbɪə(r)
AM ˈnioʊˈfoʊbiə

neophron
BR ˈnɪə(ʊ)frɒn, -z
AM ˈnɪəˌfran, -z

neophyte
BR ˈnɪə(ʊ)fʌɪt, -s
AM ˈnɪəˌfaɪt, -s

neoplasm
BR ˈnɪə(ʊ)plaz(ə)m, -z
AM ˈnɪəˌplæzəm, -z

neoplastic
BR ˌniːə(ʊ)ˈplastɪk
AM ˈnɪəˈplæstɪk

neo-plasticism
BR ˌniːə(ʊ)ˈplastɪsɪz(ə)m
AM ˈnɪəˈplæstəˌsɪzəm

Neoplatonic
BR ˌniːə(ʊ)pləˈtɒnɪk
AM ˈnioʊpləˈtanɪk

Neoplatonism
BR ˌniːə(ʊ)ˈpleɪtənɪz(ə)m,
ˌniːəʊˈpleɪtnɪz(ə)m
AM ˈnɪəˈpleɪtn̩ˌɪzəm

Neoplatonist
BR ˌniːə(ʊ)ˈpleɪtənɪst,
ˌniːəʊˈpleɪtnɪst, -s
AM ˈnɪəˈpleɪtnəst, -s

neoprene
BR ˈnɪə(ʊ)priːn
AM ˈnɪəˌprin

neostigmine
BR ˌniːə(ʊ)ˈstɪgmiːn
AM ˈnioʊˈstɪgmin

neotenic
BR ˌniːə(ʊ)ˈtɛnɪk
AM ˌnioʊˈtɛnɪk,
ˌnioʊˈtinɪk

neotenous
BR nɪˈɒtɪnəs, nɪˈɒtnəs
AM ˌnioʊˈtinəs

neoteny
BR nɪˈɒtɪni, nɪˈɒtni
AM niˈat(ɪ)ni

neoteric
BR ˌniːə(ʊ)ˈtɛrɪk
AM ˌnɪəˈtɛrɪk

neotropical
BR ˌniːə(ʊ)ˈtrɒpɪkl
AM ˈnioʊˈtrapəkəl

Neozoic
BR ˌniːə(ʊ)ˈzəʊɪk
AM ˌnɪəˈzoʊɪk

Nepal
BR nɪˈpɔːl
AM ˌneɪˈpɑl

Nepalese
BR ˌnepəˈliːz
AM ˌnepəˈliz

Nepali
BR nɪˈpɔːl|i, -ɪz
AM nəˈpɑli, nəˈpɑli, -z

nepenthe
BR nɪˈpenθi
AM nəˈpenθi

nepenthes
BR nɪˈpenθiːz
AM nəˈpenθiz

nepeta
BR nɪˈpiːtə(r), -z
AM nəˈpidə, -z

nepheline
BR ˈnefəliːn, ˈnefˌliːn
AM ˈnefəˌlin

nephelometer
BR ˌnefɪˈlɒmɪtə(r), -z
AM ˌnefəˈlɑmədər, -z

nephelometric
BR ˌnefələ(ʊ)ˈmetrɪk,
ˌneflə(ʊ)ˈmetrɪk
AM ˌnefəloʊˈmetrɪk

nephelometry
BR ˌnefəˈlɒmɪtri
AM ˌnefəˈlɑmətri

nephew
BR ˈnefjuː, ˈnevjuː, -z
AM ˈnefju, -z

nephology
BR nɪˈfɒlədʒi,
neˈfɒlədʒi
AM nəˈfɑlədʒi,
neˈfɑlədʒi

nephrectomy
BR nɪˈfrektəm|i,
neˈfrektəmi, -ɪz
AM nəˈfrektəmi, -z

nephridia
BR nɪˈfrɪdɪə(r)
AM nəˈfrɪdɪə

nephridiopore
BR nɪˈfrɪdɪəpɔː(r), -z
AM nəˈfrɪdɪəˌpɔː(ə)r, -z

nephridium
BR nɪˈfrɪdɪəm
AM nəˈfrɪdɪəm

nephrite
BR ˈnefrʌɪt
AM ˈnefˌraɪt

nephritic
BR nɪˈfrɪtɪk, neˈfrɪtɪk
AM nəˈfrɪdɪk

nephritis
BR nɪˈfrʌɪtɪs,
neˈfrʌɪtɪs
AM nəˈfraɪdɪs

nephrology
BR nɪˈfrɒlədʒi,
neˈfrɒlədʒi,
AM nəˈfrɑlədʒi,
neˈfrɑlədʒi

nephron
BR ˈnefrɒn, -z
AM ˈneˌfrɑn, -z

nephropathy
BR nɪˈfrɒpəθi,
neˈfrɒpəθi
AM nəˈfrɑpəθi,
neˈfrɑpəθi

nephrosis
BR nɪˈfrəʊsɪs
AM nəˈfroʊsəs

nephrotomy
BR nɪˈfrɒtəm|i,
neˈfrɒtəmi, -ɪz
AM nəˈfrɑdəmi,
neˈfrɑdəmi, -z

ne plus ultra
BR ˌneɪ plʌs ˈʌltrə(r),
ˌniː +, + plʌs +,
+ ˈʊltrɑː(r)
AM ˌni ˌpləs ˈəltrə, ˌneɪ
ˌplʊs ˈʊltrɑ

nepotism
BR ˈnepətɪz(ə)m
AM ˈnepəˌtɪzəm

nepotist
BR ˈnepətɪst, -s
AM ˈnepədəst, -s

nepotistic
BR ˌnepəˈtɪstɪk
AM ˌnepəˈtɪstɪk

Neptune
BR ˈneptjuːn,
ˈneptʃuːn
AM ˈnepˌt(j)un

Neptunian
BR nepˈtjuːnɪən,
nepˈtʃuːnɪən
AM nepˈt(j)unɪən

Neptunist
BR ˈneptjuːnɪst,
ˈneptʃuːnɪst, -s
AM ˈnepˈt(j)unəst, -s

neptunium
BR nepˈtjuːnɪəm,
nepˈtʃuːnɪəm
AM nepˈt(j)unɪəm

nerd
BR nɜːd, -z
AM nɜrd, -z

nerdy
BR ˈnɜːd|i, -ɪə(r), -ɪɪst
AM ˈnɜrdi, -ər, -əst

nereid
BR ˈnɪərɪɪd, -z
AM ˈnɪriɪd, ˈnɛriɪd, -z

Nereus
BR ˈnɪərɪəs
AM ˈnɛriəs, ˈnɪ(ə)rjəs

nerine
BR nɪˈrʌɪn|i, nɪˈriːn|i,
-ɪz
AM nəˈrini, -z

Nerissa
BR nɪˈriːsə(r)
AM nəˈrisə, nəˈrɪsə

nerka
BR ˈnɜːkə(r), -z

AM ˈnɜːkə, -z

Nernst
BR nəːnst
AM nɜrnst

Nero
BR ˈnɪərəʊ
AM ˈnɪroʊ, ˈnɪroʊ

neroli
BR ˈnɪərəli
AM ˈnɛrəli

Neronian
BR nɪˈrəʊnɪən
AM nəˈroʊnɪən

Neruda
BR nəˈruːdə(r)
AM nəˈrudə

Nerva
BR ˈnɜːvə(r)
AM ˈnɜrvə

nervate
BR ˈnɜːveɪt
AM ˈnɜrˌveɪt

nervation
BR nɜː(ː)ˈveɪʃn, -z
AM ˌnɜrˈveɪʃən, -z

nerve
BR nɜːv, -z, -ɪŋ, -d
AM nɜrv, -z, -ɪŋ, -d

nerveless
BR ˈnɜːvləs
AM ˈnɜrvləs

nervelessly
BR ˈnɜːvləsli
AM ˈnɜrvləsli

nervelessness
BR ˈnɜːvləsnəs
AM ˈnɜrvləsnəs

nerve-racking
BR ˈnɜːvˌrakɪŋ
AM ˈnɜrvˌrækɪŋ

nerve-wracking
BR ˈnɜːvˌrakɪŋ
AM ˈnɜrvˌrækɪŋ

Nervi
BR ˈnɜːvi
AM ˈnɜrvi

nervily
BR ˈnɜːvɪli
AM ˈnɜrvəli

nervine
BR ˈnɜːvʌm, ˈnɜːviːn, -z
AM ˈnɜrˌvin, -z

nerviness
BR ˈnɜːvɪnɪs
AM ˈnɜrvinɪs

nervous
BR ˈnɜːvəs
AM ˈnɜrvəs

nervously
BR ˈnɜːvəsli
AM ˈnɜrvəsli

nervousness
BR ˈnɜːvəsnəs
AM ˈnɜrvəsnəs

nervure
BR ˈnɜːvj(ʊ)ə(r), -z

nervjər,
ˈnərˌvjʊ(ə)r, -z

nervy
BR ˈnɜːv|i, -ɪə(r), -ɪɪst
AM ˈnɜrvi, -ər, -ɪst

Nerys
BR ˈnɛrɪs
AM ˈnɛrɪs

Nesbit
BR ˈnezbɪt
AM ˈnezbət

Nesbitt
BR ˈnezbɪt
AM ˈnezbət

Nescafé®
BR ˈneskəfeɪ
AM ˈneskəˌfeɪ

nescience
BR ˈnesɪəns
AM ˈneʃ(i)əns,
ˈnesɪəns

nescient
BR ˈnesɪənt
AM ˈneʃ(i)ənt, ˈnesɪənt

nesh
BR neʃ
AM neʃ

ness
BR nes, -ɪz
AM nes, -ɪz

Nessa
BR ˈnesə(r)
AM ˈnesə

Nessie
BR ˈnesi
AM ˈnesi

nest
BR nest, -s, -ɪŋ, -ɪd
AM nest, -s, -ɪŋ, -əd

Nesta
BR ˈnestə(r)
AM ˈnestə

nestful
BR ˈnestfʊl, -z
AM ˈnes(t)ˌfʊl, -z

Nestlé®
BR ˈnesleɪ, ˈnesl
AM ˈnesli

nestle
BR ˈnes|l, -lz, -lɪŋ \ -lɪŋ,
-ld
AM ˈnesˌləl, -əlz, -(ə)lɪŋ,
-əld

nestlike
BR ˈnes(t)lʌɪk
AM ˈnes(t)ˌlaɪk

nestling
BR ˈnes(t)lɪŋ, -z
AM ˈnes(t)lɪŋ, -z

Nestor
BR ˈnestə(r)
AM ˈnestər

Nestorian
BR neˈstɔːrɪən
AM nesˈtɔriən

Nestorianism
BR neˈstɔːrɪənɪz(ə)m

AM nɛsˈtɔːriəˌnɪzəm

Nestorius
BR nɛˈstɔːriəs
AM nɛˈstɔːriəs

net
BR nɛt, -s, -ɪŋ, -ɪd
AM nɛ|t, -ts, -dɪŋ, -dəd

netball
BR ˈnɛtbɔːl
AM ˈnɛtˌbɔl, ˈnɛtˌbɑl

netful
BR ˈnɛtfʊl, -z
AM ˈnɛtˌfʊl, -z

nether
BR ˈnɛðə(r)
AM ˈnɛðər

Netherlander
BR ˈnɛðəˌlandə(r), -z
AM ˈnɛðərˌlændər, -z

Netherlandish
BR ˈnɛðəˌlandɪʃ
AM ˈnɛðərˌlændɪʃ

Netherlands
BR ðə ˈnɛðəːlən(d)z
AM ˈnɛðərlən(d)z

nethermost
BR ˈnɛðəməʊst
AM ˈnɛðərˌmoʊst

netherworld
BR ˈnɛðəwəːld
AM ˈnɛðərˌwərld

netsuke
BR ˈnɛts(ʊ)k|i, -ɪz
AM ˈnɛts(ʊ)ki, -z

nett
BR nɛt
AM nɛt

Nettie
BR ˈnɛti
AM ˈnɛdi

nettle
BR ˈnɛt|l, -lz, -|ɪŋ \-lɪŋ, -ld
AM ˈnɛdəl, -z, -ɪŋ, -d

Nettlefold
BR ˈnɛtlfəʊld
AM ˈnɛdlˌfoʊld

nettlesome
BR ˈnɛtls(ə)m
AM ˈnɛdlsəm

network
BR ˈnɛtwəːk, -s, -ɪŋ, -t
AM ˈnɛtˌwərk, -s, -ɪŋ, -t

networker
BR ˈnɛtwəːkə(r), -z
AM ˈnɛtˌwərkər, -z

neum
BR njuːm, -z
AM n(j)um, -z

Neumann
BR ˈnjuːmən
AM ˈn(j)umən

neume
BR njuːm, -z
AM n(j)um, -z

neural
BR ˈnjʊərəl, ˈnjʊərl̩

AM ˈn(j)ʊrəl, ˈn(j)urəl

neuralgia
BR njʉˈraldʒə(r),
njʊəˈraldʒə(r)
AM n(j)uˈrældʒə,
n(j)əˈrældʒə

neuralgic
BR njʉˈraldʒɪk,
njʊəˈraldʒɪk
AM n(j)uˈrældʒɪk,
n(j)əˈrældʒɪk

neurally
BR ˈnjʊərl̩i, ˈnjʊərəli
AM ˈn(j)ʊrəli,
ˈn(j)urəli

neurasthenia
BR ˌnjʊərəsˈθiːnɪə(r)
AM ˌn(j)ʊrəsˈθiniə

neurasthenic
BR ˌnjʊərəsˈθɛnɪk, -s
AM ˌn(j)ʊrəsˈθɛnɪk, -s

neuration
BR njʉˈreɪʃn,
njʊəˈreɪʃn, -z
AM njuˈreɪʃən,
njəˈreɪʃən, -z

neuritic
BR njʉˈrɪtɪk,
njʊəˈrɪtɪk
AM n(j)uˈrɪdɪk,
n(j)əˈrɪdɪk

neuritis
BR njʉˈrʌɪtɪs
njʊəˈrʌɪtɪs
AM n(j)uˈraɪdɪs,
n(j)əˈraɪdɪs

neuroanatomical
BR ˌnjʊərəʊˌanəˈtɒmɪkl
AM ˈn(j)uroʊˌænəˈtaməˌkəl,
ˈn(j)əroʊˌænəˈtaməkəl

neuroanatomy
BR ˌnjʊərəʊəˈnatəmi
AM ˈn(j)uroʊəˈnædəmi,
ˌn(j)əroʊəˈnædəmi

neurobiological
BR ˌnjʊərəʊˌbʌɪəˈlɒdʒ-
ɪkl
AM ˈn(j)uroʊbaɪəˈladʒə-
kəl,
ˈn(j)ərəbaɪəˈladʒəkəl

neurobiology
BR ˌnjʊərəʊbʌɪˈɒlədʒi
AM ˈn(j)uroʊbaɪˈalədʒi,
ˌn(j)ərəbaɪˈalədʒi

neurofibroma
BR ˌnjʊərəʊfʌɪˈbrəʊ-
mə(r), -z
AM ˈn(j)ʊroʊfaɪˈbroʊ-
mə, -z

neurofibromata
BR ˌnjʊərəʊfʌɪˈbrəʊ-
mətə(r)
AM ˈn(j)ʊroʊfaɪbroʊ-
ˈmədə

neurofibromatosis
BR ˌnjʊərəʊfʌɪˌbrəʊmə-
ˈtəʊsɪs

AM ˌn(j)ʊroʊˌfaɪbroʊmə-
ˈtoʊsəs

neurogenesis
BR ˌnjʊərə(ʊ)ˈdʒɛnɪsɪs,
-ɪz
AM ˌn(j)ʊroʊˈdʒɛnəsəs,
ˌn(j)ərəˈdʒɛnəsəs, -əz

neurogenic
BR ˌnjʊərə(ʊ)ˈdʒɛnɪk
AM ˌn(j)ʊroʊˈdʒɛnɪk,
ˌn(j)ərəˈdʒɛnɪk

neuroglia
BR njʉˈrɒglɪə(r),
njʊəˈrɒglɪə(r)
AM n(j)uˈrɑgliə,
n(j)əˈrɑgliə

neurohormone
BR ˌnjʊərəˈhɔːməʊn,
ˈnjʊərə(ʊ)ˌhɔːməʊn,
-z
AM ˌn(j)ʊroʊˈhɔrˌmoʊn,
ˌn(j)ərəˈhɔrˌmoʊn, -z

neurolinguistic
BR ˌnjʊərəʊlɪŋˈgwɪstɪk
AM ˌn(j)ʊroʊˌlɪŋˈgwɪst-
ɪk,
ˌn(j)ərəˌlɪŋˈgwɪstɪk

neurological
BR ˌnjʊərəˈlɒdʒɪkl
AM ˌn(j)ʊrəˈladʒəkəl,
ˌn(j)ərəˈladʒəkəl

neurologically
BR ˌnjʊərəˈlɒdʒɪkli
AM ˌn(j)ʊrəˈladʒək(ə)li,
ˌn(j)ərəˈladʒək(ə)li

neurologist
BR njʉˈrɒlədʒɪst,
njʊəˈrɒlədʒɪst, -s
AM n(j)uˈralədʒəst,
n(j)əˈralədʒəst, -s

neurology
BR njʉˈrɒlədʒi,
njʊəˈrɒlədʒi
AM n(j)uˈralədʒi,
n(j)əˈralədʒi

neuroma
BR njʉˈrəʊmə(r),
njʊəˈrəʊmə(r), -z
AM n(j)uˈroʊmə, -z

neuromata
BR njʉˈrəʊmətə(r),
njʊəˈrəʊmətə(r)
AM n(j)uˈroʊmədə

neuromuscular
BR ˌnjʊərəʊˈmʌskjʉ-
lə(r)
AM ˌn(j)ʊroʊˈmaskjələr,
ˌn(j)ərəˈmaskjələr

neuron
BR ˈnjʊərɒn, -z
AM ˈn(j)uˌrɑn,
ˈn(j)uˌrɑn, -z

neuronal
BR ˈnjʊərənl,
njʉˈrəʊnl, njʊəˈrəʊnl
AM ˈn(j)uroʊnl,
ˈn(j)ʊrənl,
n(j)uˈroʊnəl

AM ˌn(j)ʊroʊˌfaɪbroʊmə-
ˈtoʊsəs

neurone
BR ˈnjʊərəʊn, -z
AM ˈn(j)uˌroʊn,
ˈn(j)uˌroʊn, -z

neuronic
BR njʉˈrɒnɪk,
njʊəˈrɒnɪk
AM n(j)uˈrɑnɪk

neuropath
BR ˈnjʊərəpaθ, -s
AM ˈn(j)ʊroʊˌpæθ,
ˈn(j)ərəˌpæθ, -s

neuropathic
BR ˌnjʊərə(ʊ)ˈpaθɪk
AM ˌn(j)ʊroʊˈpæθɪk,
ˌn(j)ərəˈpæθɪk

neuropathologist
BR ˌnjʊərəʊpəˈθɒlədʒɪst,
-s
AM ˌn(j)ʊroʊpəˈθɑlədʒəst,
ˌn(j)ərəpəˈθalədʒəst, -s

neuropathology
BR ˌnjʊərəʊpəˈθɒlədʒi
AM ˌn(j)ʊroʊpəˈθalədʒi,
ˌn(j)ərəpəˈθalədʒi

neuropathy
BR njʉˈrɒpəθi,
njʊəˈrɒpəθi
AM n(j)uˈrɑpəθi,
n(j)əˈrɑpəθi

neurophysiological
BR ˌnjʊərəʊfɪzɪəˈlɒdʒɪkl
AM ˌn(j)ʊroʊˌfɪziəˈladʒəkəl,
ˌn(j)ərəˌfɪziəˈladʒəkəl

neurophysiologist
BR ˌnjʊərəʊfɪzɪˈɒlədʒɪst,
-s
AM ˌn(j)ʊroʊˌfɪziˈalədʒəst,
ˌn(j)ərəˌfɪziˈalədʒəst,
-s

neurophysiology
BR ˌnjʊərəʊfɪzɪˈɒlədʒi
AM ˌn(j)ʊroʊˌfɪziˈalədʒi,
ˌn(j)ərəˌfɪziˈalədʒi

neuropsychological
BR ˌnjʊərəʊsʌɪkəˈlɒdʒɪkl
AM ˌn(j)ərəˌsaɪkəˈladʒəkəl

neuropsychology
BR ˌnjʊərəʊsʌɪˈkɒlədʒi
AM ˌn(j)ʊroʊˌsaɪˈkalədʒi,
ˌn(j)ərəˌsaɪˈkalədʒi

Neuroptera
BR njʉˈrɒpt(ə)rə(r),
njʊəˈrɒpt(ə)rə(r)
AM n(j)uˈraptərə,
n(j)ʊˈraptərə

neuropteran
BR njʉˈrɒpt(ə)rən,
njʊəˈrɒpt(ə)rən, -z
AM n(j)uˈraptərən,
n(j)ʊˈraptərən, -z

neuropterous
BR njʉˈrɒpt(ə)rəs,
njʊəˈrɒpt(ə)rəs
AM n(j)uˈraptərəs,
n(j)ʊˈraptərəs

neuroscience
BR ˌnjʊərəʊ'saɪəns,
'njʊərə(ʊ)ˌsaɪəns
AM 'n(j)ʊroʊˌsaɪəns,
'n(j)ərəˌsaɪəns

neuroscientist
BR ˌnjʊərəʊ'saɪəntɪst,
'njʊərə(ʊ)ˌsaɪəntɪst,
-s
AM 'n(j)ʊroʊˌsaɪən-
(t)əst,
'n(j)ərəˌsaɪən(t)əst,
-s

neuroses
BR njʉ'rəʊsi:z,
njʊə'rəʊsi:z
AM n(j)ʊ'roʊsiz,
n(j)ə'rousiz

neurosis
BR njʉ'rəʊsɪs,
njʊə'rəʊsɪs
AM n(j)ʊ'roʊsəz,
n(j)ə'rousəz

neurosurgeon
BR 'njʊərə(ʊ)ˌsə:dʒ(ə)n,
-z
AM 'n(j)ʊroʊˌsərdʒən,
'n(j)ərəˌsərdʒən, -z

neurosurgery
BR 'njʊərə(ʊ)ˌsə:dʒ(ə)ri,
-ɪz
AM ˌn(j)ʊroʊˈsərdʒəri,
ˌn(j)ərə'sərdʒəri, -z

neurosurgical
BR ˌnjʊərə(ʊ)'sə:dʒɪkl
AM ˌn(j)ʊroʊˈsərdʒəkəl,
ˌn(j)ərə'sərdʒəkəl

neurotic
BR njʉ'rɒtɪk,
njʊə'rɒtɪk, -s
AM n(j)ʊ'radɪk,
n(j)ə'radɪk, -s

neurotically
BR njʉ'rɒtɪkli,
njʊə'rɒtɪkli
AM n(j)ʊ'radək(ə)li,
n(j)ə'radək(ə)li

neuroticism
BR njʉ'rɒtɪsɪz(ə)m,
njʊə'rɒtɪsɪz(ə)m
AM n(j)ʊ'radəˌsɪzəm,
n(j)ə'radəˌsɪzəm

neurotomy
BR njʉ'rɒtəm|i,
njʊə'rɒtəm|i, -ɪz
AM n(j)ʊ'radəmi,
n(j)ə'radəmi, -z

neurotoxin
BR 'njʊərəʊˌtɒksɪn, -z
AM ˌn(j)ʊroʊ'taksən,
ˌn(j)ərə'taksən, -z

neurotransmitter
BR ˌnjʊərəʊtranz'mɪ-
tə(r), -z
AM ˌn(j)ʊroʊ'trænzmɪ-
dər,
ˌn(j)ərə'trænzmɪdər,
-z

neuston
BR 'nju:stɒn
AM 'n(j)ustən

neuter
BR 'nju:t|ə(r), -əz,
-(ə)rɪŋ, -əd
AM 'n(j)udər, -z, -ɪŋ, -d

neutral
BR 'nju:tr(ə)l, -z
AM 'n(j)utrəl, -z

neutralisation
BR ˌnju:trəlaɪ'zeɪʃn,
ˌnju:trˌlaɪ'zeɪʃn, -z
AM ˌnjutrələ'zeɪʃən,
ˌnjutrəˌlaɪ'zeɪʃən, -z

neutralise
BR 'nju:trəlaɪz,
'nju:trˌlaɪz, -ɪz, -ɪŋ, -d
AM 'n(j)utrəˌlaɪz, -ɪz,
-ɪŋ, -d

neutraliser
BR 'nju:trəlaɪzə(r),
'nju:trˌlaɪzə(r), -z
AM 'n(j)utrəˌlaɪzər, -z

neutralism
BR 'nju:trəlɪz(ə)m,
'nju:trˌlɪz(ə)m
AM 'n(j)utrəˌlɪzəm

neutralist
BR 'nju:trəlɪst,
'nju:trˌlɪst, -s
AM 'n(j)utrələst, -s

neutrality
BR nju:'tralɪti
AM n(j)u'trælədi

neutralization
BR ˌnju:trəlaɪ'zeɪʃən,
ˌnju:trˌlaɪ'zeɪʃn, -z
AM ˌn(j)utrələ'zeɪʃən,
ˌn(j)utrəˌlaɪ'zeɪʃən, -z

neutralize
BR 'nju:trəlaɪz,
'nju:trˌlaɪz, -ɪz, -ɪŋ, -d
AM 'n(j)utrəˌlaɪz, -ɪz,
-ɪŋ, -d

neutralizer
BR 'nju:trəlaɪzə(r),
'nju:trˌlaɪzə(r), -z
AM 'n(j)utrəˌlaɪzər, -z

neutrally
BR 'nju:trəli
AM 'n(j)utrəli

neutrino
BR nju:'tri:nəʊ, -z
AM n(j)u'trinoʊ, -z

neutron
BR 'nju:trɒn, -z
AM 'n(j)uˌtran, -z

neutropenia
BR ˌnju:trə(ʊ)'pi:nɪə(r)
AM ˌn(j)utrə'piniə

neutrophil
BR 'nju:trəfɪl, -z
AM 'n(j)utrəˌfɪl, -z

Neva
BR 'ni:və(r), 'neɪvə(r)
AM 'nivə
RUS nʲi'va

Nevada
BR nɪ'va:də(r)
AM nə'væda

Nevadan
BR nɪ'va:d(ə)n, -z
AM nə'vædən, -z

Neve
BR ni:v
AM niv

névé
BR 'nevei
AM nei'vei

never
BR 'nevə(r)
AM 'nevər

nevermore
BR ˌnevə'mɔ:(r),
'nevəmɔ:(r)
AM 'nevər'mɔ(ə)r

never-never
BR ˌnevə'nevə(r)
AM 'nevər'nevər

nevertheless
BR ˌnevəðə'les
AM ˌnevərðə'les

nevi
BR 'ni:vʌɪ
AM 'ni,vai

Neville
BR 'nevɪl
AM 'nevəl

Nevin
BR 'nev(ɪ)n
AM 'nevən

Nevis[1]
Scotland
BR 'nevɪs
AM 'nevəs

Nevis[2]
West Indies
BR 'ni:vɪs
AM 'nivəs, 'nevəs

nevoid
BR 'nevɔɪd
AM 'nevɔɪd

Nevsky
BR 'nevski
AM 'nevski
RUS 'nʲefskʲij

nevus
BR 'ni:vəs
AM 'nivəs

new
BR nju:, -ə(r), -ɪst
AM n(j)u|u, -uər\-ʊ(ə)r,
-uəst

Newark[1]
New Jersey
BR 'nju:ək
AM 'n(j)uwərk

Newark[2]
Delaware
BR nju:'a:k
AM n(j)u'ark

Newbiggin
BR 'nju:bɪg(ɪ)n
AM 'n(j)uˌbɪgɪn

Newbold
BR 'nju:bəʊld
AM 'n(j)uˌboʊld

Newbolt
BR 'nju:bəʊlt
AM 'n(j)uˌboʊlt

newborn[1]
adjective
BR ˌnju:'bɔ:n
AM 'n(j)uˌbɔ(ə)rn

newborn[2]
noun
BR 'nju:bɔ:n, -z
AM 'n(j)uˌbɔ(ə)rn, -z

Newborough
BR 'nju:b(ə)rə(r)
AM 'n(j)uˌbərə

Newbould
BR 'nju:bəʊld
AM 'n(j)uˌboʊld

Newbridge
BR 'nju:brɪdʒ
AM 'n(j)uˌbrɪdʒ

Newburg
BR 'nju:bə:g
AM 'n(j)uˌbərg

Newburgh
BR 'nju:b(ə)rə(r)
AM 'n(j)uˌbərə

Newbury
BR 'nju:b(ə)ri
AM 'n(j)uˌberi

Newby
BR 'nju:bi
AM 'n(j)ubi

Newcastle
BR 'nju:ka:sl,
'nju:kasl
AM 'n(j)uˌkæsəl

Newcastle upon Tyne
BR 'nju:kasl əˌpɒn
'tʌɪn, njʉ'kasl +,
'nju:ka:sl +
AM 'n(j)uˌkæsəl əˌpɑn
'tain

Newcomb
BR 'nju:kəm
AM 'n(j)ukəm

Newcombe
BR 'nju:kəm
AM 'n(j)ukəm

Newcome
BR 'nju:kəm
AM 'n(j)ukəm

Newcomen
BR 'nju:kʌmən
AM 'n(j)uˌkəmən

newcomer
BR 'nju:kʌmə(r), -z
AM 'n(j)uˌkəmər, -z

Newdigate
BR 'nju:dɪgeɪt
AM 'n(j)udəˌgeɪt

newel
BR 'nju:əl, -z
AM 'n(j)uwəl, -z

Newell
BR 'nju:əl
AM 'n(j)uəl

newelpost
BR 'nju:əlpəʊst, -s
AM 'n(j)uwəl,poʊst, -s

newfangled
BR ˌnju:'faŋgld
AM ˌn(j)u'fæŋgəld

Newfoundland
BR 'nju:fn(d)lənd,
ˌnju:'faʊn(d)lənd
AM 'n(j)ufən(d)lən(d),
'n(j)ufən(d),lænd,
ˌn(j)u'faʊn(d)lənd,
ˌn(j)ufən'lænd

Newfoundlander
BR 'nju:fn(d)ləndə(r),
ˌnju:'faʊn(d)ləndə(r),
-z
AM 'n(j)ufən(d)ləndər,
'n(j)ufən(d),lændər,
ˌn(j)u'faʊn(d)ləndər,
ˌn(j)ufən'lændər, -z

Newgate
BR 'nju:geɪt
AM 'n(j)u,geɪt

Newham
BR 'nju:əm
AM 'n(j)uəm

Newhaven
BR 'nju:,heɪvn
AM 'n(j)u'heɪvən

Ne Win
BR ,neɪ 'wɪn
AM ,neɪ 'wɪn

Newington
BR 'nju:ɪŋt(ə)n
AM 'n(j)uɪŋtən

newish
BR 'nju:ɪʃ
AM 'n(j)uɪʃ

newlaid
BR ˌnju:'leɪd
AM ˌn(j)u'leɪd

Newlands
BR 'nju:lən(d)z
AM 'n(j)ulən(d)z

newly
BR 'nju:li
AM 'n(j)uli

Newlyn
BR 'nju:lɪn
AM 'n(j)ulən

newlywed
BR 'nju:lɪwɛd, -z
AM 'n(j)uli,wɛd, -z

Newman
BR 'nju:mən
AM 'n(j)umən

Newmark
BR 'nju:mɑ:k
AM 'n(j)u,mɑrk

Newmarket
BR 'nju:,mɑ:kɪt
AM 'n(j)u,mɑrkət

new-mown
BR ˌnju:'məʊn

'n(j)u'məʊn

Newnes
BR nju:nz
AM 'n(j)unəs

newness
BR 'nju:nəs
AM 'n(j)unəs

Newnham
BR 'nju:nəm
AM 'n(j)unəm

New Orleans
BR ˌnju: ɔ:'li:ənz
AM ˌn(j)u 'ɔrlənz,
ˌn(j)u ər'linz

Newport
BR 'nju:pɔ:t
AM 'n(j)u,pɔ(ə)rt

Newquay
BR 'nju:ki:
AM 'n(j)u,ki

Newry
BR 'njʊəri
AM 'n(j)uri

news
BR nju:z
AM n(j)uz

newsagent
BR 'nju:z,eɪdʒ(ə)nt, -s
AM 'n(j)uz,eɪdʒənt, -s

newsboy
BR 'nju:zbɔɪ, -z
AM 'n(j)uz,bɔɪ, -z

newsbrief
BR 'nju:zbri:f, -s
AM 'n(j)uz,brif, -s

newscast
BR 'nju:zkɑ:st,
'nju:zkast, -s, -ɪŋ
AM 'n(j)uz,kæst, -s, -ɪŋ

newscaster
BR 'nju:z,kɑ:stə(r),
'nju:z,kastə(r), -z
AM 'n(j)uz,kæstər, -z

newsdealer
BR 'nju:z,di:lə(r), -z
AM 'n(j)uz,dilər, -z

newsflash
BR 'nju:zflaʃ, -ɪz
AM 'n(j)uz,flæʃ, -əz

newsgirl
BR 'nju:zgɜ:l, -z
AM 'n(j)uz,gərl, -z

newshound
BR 'nju:zhaʊnd, -z
AM 'n(j)uz,(h)aʊnd, -z

newsiness
BR 'nju:zɪnɪs
AM 'n(j)uzinɪs

newsless
BR 'nju:zləs
AM 'n(j)uzləs

newsletter
BR 'nju:z,lɛtə(r), -z
AM 'n(j)uz,lɛdər, -z

newsman
BR 'nju:zman
AM 'n(j)uz,mæn

newsmen
BR 'nju:zmɛn
AM 'n(j)uz,mɛn

newsmonger
BR 'nju:z,mʌŋgə(r), -z
AM 'n(j)uz,mɑŋgər,
'n(j)uz,məŋgər, -z

Newsom
BR 'nju:s(ə)m
AM 'n(j)usəm

Newsome[1]
place in UK
BR 'nju:z(ə)m
AM 'n(j)uzəm

Newsome[2]
surname
BR 'nju:s(ə)m
AM 'n(j)usəm

New South Wales
BR ˌnju: saʊθ 'weɪlz
AM ˌn(j)u ˌsaʊθ 'weɪlz

newspaper
BR 'nju:z,peɪpə(r), -z
AM 'n(j)uz,peɪpər, -z

newspaperman
BR 'nju:z,peɪpə,man
AM 'n(j)uz,peɪpər,mæn

newspapermen
BR 'nju:z,peɪpə,mɛn
AM 'n(j)uz,peɪpər,mɛn

newspeak
BR 'nju:spi:k
AM 'n(j)u,spik

newsprint
BR 'nju:zprɪnt
AM 'n(j)uz,prɪnt

newsreader
BR 'nju:z,ri:də(r), -z
AM 'n(j)uz,ridər, -z

newsreel
BR 'nju:zri:l, -z
AM 'n(j)uz,ril, -z

newsroom
BR 'nju:zru:m,
'nju:zrʊm
AM 'n(j)uz,rum,
'n(j)uz,rʊm

newssheet
BR 'nju:zʃi:t, -s
AM 'n(j)uz,ʃit, -s

newsstand
BR 'nju:zstand, -z
AM 'n(j)uz,stænd, -z

Newstead
BR 'nju:stɪd, 'nju:stɛd
AM 'n(j)u,stɛd

newsvendor
BR 'nju:z,vɛndə(r), -z
AM 'n(j)uz,vɛndər, -z

newsworthiness
BR 'nju:z,wə:ðɪnɪs
AM 'n(j)uz,wərðinɪs

newsworthy
BR 'nju:z,wə:ði
AM 'n(j)uz,wərði

newsy
BR 'nju:zi

Newell   AM 'n(j)u'moʊn

AM 'n(j)uzi

newt
BR nju:t, -s
AM n(j)ut, -s

newton
BR 'nju:tn, -z
AM 'n(j)utn, -z

Newton Abbott
BR ˌnju:tn 'abət
AM ˌn(j)utn 'æbət

Newtonian
BR nju:'təʊniən,
nju:'təʊniən
AM n(j)u'toʊniən

Newtonmore
BR ˌnju:tn'mɔ:(r)
AM ˌn(j)utn'mɔ(ə)r

Newtown
BR 'nju:taʊn
AM 'n(j)u,taʊn

Newtownabbey
BR ˌnju:tn'abi
AM ˌn(j)utn'æbi

next
BR nɛkst
AM nɛkst

nexus
BR 'nɛksəs, -ɪz
AM 'nɛksəs, -ɪz

Ney
BR neɪ

Nez Percé
BR ˌnɛz 'pə:s
AM ˌnɛz 'pərs

ngaio
BR 'nʌɪəʊ, -z
AM 'naɪoʊ, -z

Ngamiland
BR (ə)ŋ'gɑ:mɪland
AM (ə)ŋ'gɑmi,lænd

Ngorungoro Crater
BR (ə)ŋ,gʊrəŋgʊrə(ʊ)
'kreɪtə(r)
AM (ə)ŋ,gɔrəŋ'gɔroʊ
ˌkreɪdər

Nguni
BR (ə)ŋ'gu:ni
AM (ə)ŋ'guni

Nguyen
BR ˌnɔɪ'ɛn
AM ˌnu'jɛn

niacin
BR 'nʌɪəsɪn
AM 'naɪəsən

Niagara
BR nʌɪ'agrə(r)
AM naɪ'æg(ə)rə

Niall
BR 'nʌɪəl
AM 'naɪəl

Niamey
BR nɪ'ɑ:meɪ, ˌnɪə'meɪ
AM ni'ɑ,meɪ

nib
BR nɪb, -z

AM nɪb, -z

nibble
BR 'nɪb|l, -lz, -lɪŋ\-lɪŋ,
-ld
AM 'nɪbəl, -əlz, -(ə)lɪŋ,
-əld

nibbler
BR 'nɪblə(r), 'nɪblə(r),
-z
AM 'nɪb(ə)lər, -z

Nibelung
BR 'ni:bəlʊŋ
AM 'nibə,lʊŋ

Nibelungenlied
BR 'ni:bəlʊŋ(g)ən,li:d
AM 'nibə'lʊŋ(g)ən,lid

niblick
BR 'nɪblɪk, -s
AM 'nɪblɪk, -s

nicad
BR 'nʌɪkad
AM 'naɪ,kæd

Nicaea
BR nʌɪ'si:ə(r)
AM naɪ'siə

Nicam
BR 'nʌɪkam
AM 'naɪ,kæm

Nicaragua
BR ,nɪkə'ragjʊə(r)
AM ,nɪkə'ragwə

Nicaraguan
BR ,nɪkə'ragjʊən, -z
AM ,nɪkə'ragwən, -z

Nice
place in France
BR ni:s
AM nis

nice
BR nʌɪs, -ə(r), -ɪst
AM naɪs, -ər, -ɪst

niceish
BR 'nʌɪsɪʃ
AM 'naɪsɪʃ

nicely
BR 'nʌɪsli
AM 'naɪsli

Nicene
BR ,nʌɪ'si:n
AM 'naɪ,sin, ,naɪ'sin

niceness
BR 'nʌɪsnɪs
AM 'naɪsnɪs

nicety
BR 'nʌɪsɪt|i, -ɪz
AM 'naɪsɪdi, -z

niche
BR ni:ʃ, nɪtʃ, -ɪz
AM nɪtʃ, -ɪz

Nichol
BR 'nɪkl
AM 'nɪkəl

Nichola
BR 'nɪkələ(r),
'nɪklə(r)
AM 'nɪkələ

Nicholas
BR 'nɪk(ə)ləs, 'nɪkləs
AM 'nɪk(ə)ləs

Nicholls
BR 'nɪklz
AM 'nɪkəlz

Nichols
BR 'nɪklz
AM 'nɪkəlz

Nicholson
BR 'nɪkls(ə)n
AM 'nɪkəlsən

Nichrome®
BR 'nʌɪkrəʊm
AM 'naɪ,kroʊm

nicish
BR 'nʌɪsɪʃ
AM 'naɪsɪʃ

nick
BR nɪk, -s, -ɪŋ, -t
AM nɪk, -s, -ɪŋ, -t

nickel
BR 'nɪkl, -z
AM 'nɪkəl, -z

nickelic
BR 'nɪkəlɪk
AM nɪ'kelɪk, 'nɪkəlɪk

nickelodeon
BR ,nɪkə'ləʊdɪən,
,nɪkl'əʊdɪən, -z
AM ,nɪkə'loʊdiən, -z

nickelous
BR 'nɪk|əs, 'nɪkələs
AM 'nɪkələs

nicker
BR 'nɪk|ə(r), -əz,
-(ə)rɪŋ, -əd
AM 'nɪkər, -z, -ɪŋ, -d

Nicki
BR 'nɪki
AM 'nɪki

Nicklaus
BR 'nɪkləs
AM 'nɪkləs

Nickleby
BR 'nɪklbi
AM 'nɪkəlbi

nicknack
BR 'nɪknak, -s
AM 'nɪk,næk, -s

nickname
BR 'nɪkneɪm, -z
AM 'nɪk,neɪm, -z

Nicky
BR 'nɪki
AM 'nɪki

Nicobar Islands
BR 'nɪkə(ʊ)bɑːr
,ʌɪlən(d)z
AM 'nɪkəbɑr ¦aɪlən(d)z

Nicodemus
BR ,nɪkə'di:məs
AM ,nɪkə'diməs

nicol
BR 'nɪkl, -z
AM 'nɪkəl, -z

Nicola
BR 'nɪkələ(r),
'nɪklə(r)
AM 'nɪkələ

Nicole
BR nɪ'kəʊl
AM nə'koʊl

Nicolet
BR ,nɪkə'leɪ
AM ,nɪkə'leɪ

Nicolette
BR ,nɪkə'lɛt
AM ,nɪkə'lɛt

Nicoll
BR 'nɪkl
AM 'nɪkəl

Nicolson
BR 'nɪkls(ə)n
AM 'nɪkəlsən

Nicomachean
BR nʌɪ,kɒmə'ki:ən,
,nʌɪkəmə'ki:ən
AM ,nɪkəmə'kiən

Nicomachus
BR nʌɪ'kɒməkəs
AM ,nɪkə'makəs

Nicosia
BR ,nɪkə'si:ə(r)
AM ,nɪkə'siə

nicotiana
BR nɪ,kɒtɪ'ɑːnə(r),
nɪ,kəʊʃɪ'ɑːnə(r),
,nɪkɒtɪ'ɑːnə(r),
,nɪkəʊʃɪ'ɑːnə(r)
AM nɪ,koʊʃi'ɑnə,
nɪ,kɑdi'ɑnə

nicotinamide
BR ,nɪkə'tɪnəmʌɪd
AM ,nɪkə'tɪnə,maɪd

nicotine
BR 'nɪkəti:n
AM 'nɪkə,tin, ,nɪkə'tin

nicotinic
BR ,nɪkə'tɪnɪk
AM ,nɪkə'tɪnɪk

nicotinise
BR 'nɪkətɪnʌɪz, -ɪz, -ɪŋ,
-d
AM 'nɪkədn,aɪz, -ɪz, -ɪŋ,
-d

nicotinism
BR 'nɪkətɪnɪz(ə)m
AM 'nɪkədn,ɪzəm

nicotinize
BR 'nɪkətɪnʌɪz, -ɪz, -ɪŋ,
-d
AM 'nɪkədn,aɪz, -ɪz, -ɪŋ,
-d

nictitate
BR 'nɪktɪteɪt, -s, -ɪŋ, -ɪd
AM 'nɪktə,teɪt, -ts, -dɪŋ,
-dɪd

nictitation
BR ,nɪktɪ'teɪʃn
AM ,nɪktə'teɪʃən

nidamental
BR ,nʌɪdə'mentl
AM ,naɪdə'men(t)l

Nicola
BR 'nɪkələ(r),
'nɪklə(r)
AM 'nɪkələ

nide
BR nʌɪd, -z
AM naɪd, -z

nidi
BR 'nʌɪdʌɪ
AM 'naɪ,daɪ

nidificate
BR 'nɪdɪfɪkeɪt, -s, -ɪŋ,
-ɪd
AM 'nɪdəfə,keɪt, -ts,
-dɪŋ, -dɪd

nidification
BR ,nɪdɪfɪ'keɪʃn
AM ,nɪdəfə'keɪʃən

nidifugous
BR nɪ'dɪfjʊgəs
AM nə'dɪfjəgəs

nidify
BR 'nɪdɪfʌɪ, -z, -ɪŋ, -d
AM 'nɪdə,faɪ, -z, -ɪŋ, -d

nidus
BR 'nʌɪdəs, -ɪz
AM 'naɪdəs, -əz

niece
BR ni:s, -ɪz
AM nis, -ɪz

niello
BR nɪ'ɛləʊ, -z, -ɪŋ, -d
AM ni'ɛloʊ, -z, -ɪŋ, -d

nielsbohrium
BR ,ni:lz'bɔ:rɪəm
AM ,nilz'bɔriəm

Nielsen
BR 'ni:ls(ə)n
AM 'nilsən

Niemann
BR 'ni:mən
AM 'nimən

Niemeyer
BR 'ni:mʌɪə(r)
AM 'ni,maɪər

Niemöller
BR 'ni:mʊlə(r)
AM 'ni,moʊlər
GER 'ni:mœlɐ

Niersteiner
BR 'nɪəstʌɪnə(r),
'nɪəʃtʌɪnə(r)
AM 'nɪr,staɪnər

Nietzsche
BR 'ni:tʃə(r)
AM 'nitʃə

Nietzschean
BR 'ni:tʃɪən
AM 'nitʃiən

niff
BR nɪf, -s, -ɪŋ, -t
AM nɪf, -s, -ɪŋ, -t

niffy
BR 'nɪf|i, -ɪə(r), -ɪɪst
AM 'nɪfi, -ər, -ɪst

Niflheim
BR 'nɪflhʌɪm
AM 'nɪfəl,(h)aɪm

niftily
BR 'nɪftɪli
AM 'nɪftɪli

niftiness
BR ˈnɪftɪnɪs
AM ˈnɪftinɪs
nifty
BR ˈnɪftǀi, -ɪə(r), -ɪɪst
AM ˈnɪfti, -ər, -ɪst
Nigel
BR ˈnaɪdʒl
AM ˈnaɪdʒəl
Nigella
BR naɪˈdʒɛlə(r)
AM naɪˈgɛlə
Niger[1]
country
BR niːˈʒɛː(r), nɪˈʒɛː(r), ˈnaɪdʒə(r)
AM ˈnaɪdʒər
Niger[2]
river
BR ˈnaɪdʒə(r)
AM ˈnaɪdʒər
Niger-Congo
BR ˈnaɪdʒəˈkɒŋgəʊ
AM ˈnaɪdʒərˈkɒŋ,goʊ, ˈnaɪdʒərˈkɑŋ,goʊ
Nigeria
BR naɪˈdʒɪərɪə(r)
AM naɪˈdʒɪriə
Nigerian
BR naɪˈdʒɪərɪən, -z
AM naɪˈdʒɪriən, -z
Nigerien
BR naɪˈdʒɪərɪən, -z
AM naɪˈdʒɪriən, -z
niggard
BR ˈnɪgəd, -z
AM ˈnɪgərd, -z
niggardliness
BR ˈnɪgədlɪnɪs
AM ˈnɪgərdlɪnɪs
niggardly
BR ˈnɪgədli
AM ˈnɪgərdli
nigger
BR ˈnɪgə(r), -z
AM ˈnɪgər, -z
niggle
BR ˈnɪglǀl, -lz, -l̩ɪŋ \-lɪŋ, -ld
AM ˈnɪgǀəl, -əlz, -(ə)lɪŋ, -əld
niggler
BR ˈnɪglə(r), ˈnɪglə(r), -z
AM ˈnɪg(ə)lər, -z
niggliness
BR ˈnɪglɪnɪs
AM ˈnɪglɪnɪs, ˈnɪgl̩ɪnɪs
nigglingly
BR ˈnɪgl̩ɪŋli, ˈnɪglɪŋli
AM ˈnɪg(ə)lɪŋli
niggly
BR ˈnɪgli
AM ˈnɪgli, ˈnɪgl̩i
nigh
BR naɪ
AM naɪ

night
BR naɪt, -s
AM naɪt, -s
nightbird
BR ˈnaɪtbəːd, -z
AM ˈnaɪt,bərd, -z
nightcap
BR ˈnaɪtkap, -s
AM ˈnaɪt,kæp, -s
nightclothes
BR ˈnaɪtkləʊ(ð)z
AM ˈnaɪt,kloʊðz
nightclub
BR ˈnaɪtklʌb, -z, -ɪŋ, -d
AM ˈnaɪt,kləb, -z, -ɪŋ, -d
nightcrawler
BR ˈnaɪt,krɔːlə(r), -z
AM ˈnaɪt,krɔlər, ˈnaɪt,krɑlər, -z
nightdress
BR ˈnaɪtdrɛs, -ɪz
AM ˈnaɪt,drɛs, -əz
nightfall
BR ˈnaɪtfɔːl
AM ˈnaɪt,fɔl, ˈnaɪt,fɑl
nightgown
BR ˈnaɪtgaʊn, -z
AM ˈnaɪt,gaʊn, -z
nighthawk
BR ˈnaɪthɔːk, -s
AM ˈnaɪt,(h)ɔk, ˈnaɪt,(h)ɑk, -s
nightie
BR ˈnaɪtǀi, -ɪz
AM ˈnaɪdi, -z
nightingale
BR ˈnaɪtɪŋgeɪl, -z
AM ˈnaɪtn̩,geɪl, -z
nightjar
BR ˈnaɪtdʒɑː(r), -z
AM ˈnaɪt,dʒɑr, -z
nightlife
BR ˈnaɪtlaɪf
AM ˈnaɪt,laɪf
nightlight
BR ˈnaɪtlaɪt, -s
AM ˈnaɪt,laɪt, -s
nightline
BR ˈnaɪtlaɪn, -z
AM ˈnaɪt,laɪn, -z
nightlong
BR ˌnaɪtˈlɒŋ
AM ˈnaɪt,lɔŋ, ˈnaɪt,lɑŋ
nightly
BR ˈnaɪtli
AM ˈnaɪtli
nightman
BR ˈnaɪtman
AM ˈnaɪt,mæn
nightmare
BR ˈnaɪtmɛː(r), -z
AM ˈnaɪt,mɛ(ə)r, -z
nightmarish
BR ˈnaɪtmɛːrɪʃ
AM ˈnaɪt,mɛrɪʃ
nightmarishly
BR ˈnaɪtmɛːrɪʃli

AM ˈnaɪt,mɛrɪʃli
nightmarishness
BR ˈnaɪtmɛːrɪʃnɪs
AM ˈnaɪt,mɛrɪʃnɪs
nightmen
BR ˈnaɪtmen
AM ˈnaɪt,mɛn
nightrider
BR ˈnaɪt,raɪdə(r), -z
AM ˈnaɪt,raɪdər, -z
nightshade
BR ˈnaɪtʃeɪd
AM ˈnaɪt,ʃeɪd
nightshirt
BR ˈnaɪtʃəːt, -s
AM ˈnaɪt,ʃərt, -s
nightspot
BR ˈnaɪtspɒt, -s
AM ˈnaɪt,spɑt, -s
nightstick
BR ˈnaɪtstɪk, -s
AM ˈnaɪt,stɪk, -s
nighttime
BR ˈnaɪttaɪm
AM ˈnaɪt,taɪm
nightwear
BR ˈnaɪtwɛː(r)
AM ˈnaɪt,wɛ(ə)r
nigrescence
BR nɪˈgrɛsns
AM naɪˈgrɛsəns
nigrescent
BR nɪˈgrɛsnt
AM naɪˈgrɛsənt
nigritude
BR ˈnɪgrɪtjuːd, ˈnɪgrɪtʃuːd
AM ˈnɪgrə,t(j)ud
nihilism
BR ˈnaɪ(h)ɪlɪz(ə)m, ˈniː(h)ɪlɪz(ə)m, ˈnɪhɪlɪz(ə)m
AM ˈnaɪə,lɪzəm, ˈniə,lɪzəm, ˈnɪhɪ,lɪzəm
nihilist
BR ˈnaɪ(h)ɪlɪst, ˈniː(h)ɪlɪst, ˈnɪhɪlɪst, -s
AM ˈnaɪələst, ˈniəlɪst, ˈnɪhɪlɪst, -s
nihilistic
BR ˌnaɪ(h)ɪˈlɪstɪk, ˌniː(h)ɪˈlɪstɪk, ˌnɪhɪˈlɪstɪk
AM ˌnaɪəˈlɪstɪk, ˌniəˈlɪstɪk, ˌnɪhɪˈlɪstɪk
nihility
BR naɪˈ(h)ɪlɪtǀi, niːˈ(h)ɪlɪti, nɪˈhɪlɪti, -ɪz
AM naɪˈhɪlɪdi, -z
nihilo
BR ˈnaɪ(h)ɪləʊ, ˈniː(h)ɪləʊ, ˈnɪhɪləʊ
AM ˈnaɪhə,loʊ

nihil obstat
BR ˌnaɪhɪl ˈɒbstat, ˌnɪhɪl +
AM ˈnaɪhɪl ˈɑbz,tæt, + ˈɑb,stæt
Nijinsky
BR nɪˈʒɪnski
AM nəˈʒɪnski
Nijmegen
BR ˈnaɪmeɪg(ə)n
AM ˈnaɪ,meɪgən
DU ˈnɛimexə(n)
Nike
BR ˈnaɪki
AM ˈnaɪki
Nikkei index
BR ˌnɪkeɪ ˈɪndɛks
AM ˈnɪ,keɪ ˈɪndɛks
Nikki
BR ˈnɪki
AM ˈnɪki
Nikon®
BR ˈnɪkɒn
AM ˈnaɪ,kɑn
nil
BR nɪl
AM nɪl
nil desperandum
BR ˌnɪl ˌdɛspəˈrandəm
AM ˌnɪl ˌdɛspəˈrɑndəm
Nile
BR naɪl
AM naɪl
nilgai
BR ˈnɪlgʌɪ, -z
AM ˈnɪl,gaɪ, -z
Nilotic
BR naɪˈlɒtɪk
AM naɪˈlɑdɪk
Nilsson
BR ˈnɪls(ə)n
AM ˈnɪlsən
nim
BR nɪm
AM nɪm
nimbi
BR ˈnɪmbʌɪ
AM ˈnɪm,baɪ
nimble
BR ˈnɪmbl̩, -ə(r), -ɪst
AM ˈnɪmbǀəl, -(ə)lər, -(ə)ləst
nimbleness
BR ˈnɪmblnəs
AM ˈnɪmbəlnəs
nimbly
BR ˈnɪmbli
AM ˈnɪmbli, ˈnɪmbl̩i
nimbostrati
BR ˌnɪmbəʊˈstrɑːtʌɪ, ˌnɪmbəʊˈstreɪtʌɪ
AM ˌnɪmboʊˈstræd,aɪ
nimbostratus
BR ˌnɪmbəʊˈstrɑːtəs, ˌnɪmbəʊˈstreɪtəs
AM ˈnɪmboʊˈstrædəs

nimbus
BR 'nɪmbəs, -ɪz, -t
AM 'nɪmbəs, -əz, -t
nimby
BR 'nɪmb|i, -ɪz
AM 'nɪmbi, -z
Nîmes
BR niːm
AM nim
niminy-piminy
BR ,nɪmɪnɪ'pɪmɪni
AM ,nɪmɪni'pɪmɪni
Nimitz
BR 'nɪmɪts
AM 'nɪmɪts
Nimmo
BR 'nɪməʊ
AM 'nɪmoʊ
Nimrod
BR 'nɪmrɒd
AM 'nɪm,rɑd
Nina
BR 'niːnə(r)
AM 'ninə
nincompoop
BR 'nɪŋkəmpuːp, -s
AM 'nɪnkəm,pup,
'nɪŋkəm,pup, -s
nine
BR naɪn, -z
AM naɪn, -z
ninefold
BR 'naɪnfəʊld
AM 'naɪn,foʊld
ninepin
BR 'naɪnpɪn, -z
AM 'naɪn,pɪn, -z
nineteen
BR ,naɪn'tiːn
AM 'naɪn,tin
nineteenth
BR ,naɪn'tiːnθ, -s
AM 'naɪn,tinθ, -s
ninetieth
BR 'naɪntɪɪθ
AM 'naɪn(t)iɪθ
ninety
BR 'naɪnt|i, -ɪz
AM 'naɪn(t)i, -z
ninetyfold
BR 'naɪntɪfəʊld
AM 'naɪn(t)i,foʊld
Nineveh
BR 'nɪnɪvə(r)
AM 'nɪnɪvə
Ninian
BR 'nɪnɪən
AM 'nɪnjən, 'nɪnɪən
ninja
BR 'nɪndʒə(r), -z
AM 'nɪndʒə, -z
ninjutsu
BR nɪn'dʒʌtsu:
AM nɪn'dʒət,su
ninny
BR 'nɪn|i, -ɪz
AM 'nɪni, -z

ninon
BR 'niːnɒn
AM 'ni,nɑn
Nintendo®
BR nɪn'tendəʊ
AM nɪn'tendoʊ
ninth
BR naɪnθ
AM naɪnθ
ninthly
BR 'naɪnθli
AM 'naɪnθli
Niobe
BR 'naɪəbi
AM naɪ'oʊbi
niobic
BR naɪ'əʊbɪk
AM naɪ'oʊbɪk
niobium
BR naɪ'əʊbɪəm
AM naɪ'oʊbɪəm
niobous
BR 'naɪəbəs
AM 'naɪəbəs
nip
BR nɪp, -s, -ɪŋ, -t
AM nɪp, -s, -ɪŋ, -t
nipa
BR 'niːpə(r), 'naɪpə(r),
-z
AM 'nipə, -z
nipper
BR 'nɪpə(r), -z
AM 'nɪpər, -z
nippily
BR 'nɪpɪli
AM 'nɪpɪli
nippiness
BR 'nɪpɪnɪs
AM 'nɪpɪnɪs
nipple
BR 'nɪpl, -z
AM 'nɪpl, -z
nipplewort
BR 'nɪplwəːt, -s
AM 'nɪpl,wərt,
'nɪpl,wɔ(ə)rt, -s
Nippon
BR 'nɪpɒn
AM 'nɪ,pɑn
Nipponese
BR ,nɪpə'niːz
AM ,nɪpə'niz
nippy
BR 'nɪp|i, -ɪə(r), -ɪɪst
AM 'nɪpi, -ər, -ɪst
NIREX
BR 'naɪrɛks
AM 'naɪ,rɛks
nirvana
BR nɪə'vɑːnə(r),
nə(ː)'vɑːnə(r)
AM nər'vɑnə, nɪr'vɑnə
Nisan
BR 'niːsɑːn, 'nɪsɑːn,
'naɪsan, 'nɪs(ə)n
AM 'nɪsɑn, ni'sɑn

Nisbet
BR 'nɪzbɪt
AM 'nɪzbət
Nisbett
BR 'nɪzbɪt
AM 'nɪzbət
nisei
BR 'niːseɪ, -z
AM ni'seɪ, -z
nisi
BR 'naɪsaɪ
AM 'naɪ,saɪ
Nissan®
BR 'nɪsan, -z
AM 'nɪ,sɑn, -z
Nissen
BR 'nɪsn
AM 'nɪsən
nit
BR nɪt, -s
AM nɪt, -s
nite
BR naɪt, -s
AM naɪt, -s
niter
BR 'naɪtə(r)
AM 'naɪdər
niterie
BR 'naɪt(ə)r|i, -ɪz
AM 'naɪdəri, -z
nitid
BR 'nɪtɪd
AM 'nɪdɪd
nitinol
BR 'nɪtɪnɒl
AM 'naɪdə,nɑl, 'nɪtn̩,ɑl
nitpick
BR 'nɪtpɪk, -s, -ɪŋ, -t
AM 'nɪt,pɪk, -s, -ɪŋ, -t
nitrate
BR 'naɪtreɪt, -s
AM 'naɪ,treɪt, -s
nitration
BR naɪ'treɪʃn, -z
AM naɪ'treɪʃən, -z
nitrazepam
BR naɪ'treɪzɪpam,
naɪ'trazɪpam
AM naɪ'træzə,pæm
nitre
BR 'naɪtə(r)
AM 'naɪdər
nitric
BR 'naɪtrɪk
AM 'naɪtrɪk
nitride
BR 'naɪtraɪd, -z
AM 'naɪ,traɪd, -z
nitrifiable
BR 'naɪtrɪfaɪəbl
AM 'naɪtrə,faɪəbəl
nitrification
BR ,naɪtrɪfɪ'keɪʃn, -z
AM ,naɪtrəfə'keɪʃən, -z
nitrify
BR 'naɪtrɪfaɪ, -z, -ɪŋ, -d
AM 'naɪtrə,faɪ, -z, -ɪŋ, -d

nitrile
BR 'naɪtrʌɪl, -z
AM 'naɪtrl̩, 'naɪ,traɪl,
-z
nitrite
BR 'naɪtrʌɪt, -s
AM 'naɪ,traɪt, -s
nitro
BR 'naɪtrəʊ
AM 'naɪtroʊ
nitrobenzene
BR ,naɪtrəʊ'benzi:n
AM 'naɪtroʊ'benzin
nitrocellulose
BR ,naɪtrəʊ'sɛljʊləʊs,
,naɪtrəʊ'sɛljələʊz
AM 'naɪtroʊ'sɛljə,loʊs,
'naɪtroʊ'sɛljə,loʊz
nitrogen
BR 'naɪtrədʒ(ə)n
AM 'naɪtrədʒən
nitrogenous
BR naɪ'trɒdʒɪnəs
AM naɪ'trɑdʒənəs
nitroglycerin
BR ,naɪtrəʊ'glɪs(ə)ri:n,
,naɪtrəʊ'glɪs(ə)rɪn
AM 'naɪtroʊ'glɪsərən
nitroglycerine
BR ,naɪtrəʊ'glɪs(ə)ri:n,
,naɪtrəʊ'glɪs(ə)rɪn
AM 'naɪtroʊ'glɪsərən
nitrosamine
BR naɪ'trəʊsəmi:n
AM naɪ'troʊsə,min
nitrous
BR 'naɪtrəs
AM 'naɪtrəs
nitty-gritty
BR ,nɪtɪ'grɪti
AM 'nɪdi'grɪdi
nitwit
BR 'nɪtwɪt, -s
AM 'nɪt,wɪt, -s
nitwitted
BR 'nɪt'wɪtɪd
AM 'nɪt,wɪdɪd
nitwittedness
BR ,nɪt'wɪtɪdnɪs
AM 'nɪt'wɪdɪdnɪs
nitwittery
BR 'nɪt,wɪt(ə)ri
AM ,nɪt'wɪdəri
Niue
BR 'njuːeɪ
AM 'nju,(w)eɪ
Niu Gini
BR ,nju: 'gɪmi
AM ,nu 'gɪmi
nival
BR 'naɪvl
AM 'naɪvəl
nivation
BR naɪ'veɪʃn
AM naɪ'veɪʃən
Nivea®
BR 'nɪviːə(r)

AM 'nɪviə

Niven
BR 'nɪvn
AM 'nɪvən

niveous
BR 'nɪviəs
AM 'nɪviəs

nix
BR nɪks, -ɪz-, -ɪŋ, -t
AM nɪks, -ɪz-, -ɪŋ, -t

Nixdorf®
BR 'nɪksdɔːf
AM 'nɪks͵dɔ(ə)rf

Nixon
BR 'nɪks(ə)n
AM 'nɪksən

Nizari
BR nɪ'zɑːr|i, -ɪz
AM nə'zɑri, -z

Nizhni Novgorod
BR ͵nɪʒni 'nɒvgərɒd
AM ͵nɪʒni 'nɑv͵gɔrəd, ͵nɪʒni 'nav͵gɔrəd

Njanja
BR nɪ'an(d)ʒə(r), 'njan(d)ʒə(r)
AM nə'jændʒə

Nkomo
BR (ə)ŋ'kəʊməʊ
AM (ə)ŋ'kɔmoʊ, (ə)ŋ'koʊmoʊ

Nkrumah
BR (ə)ŋ'kruːmə(r)
AM (ə)ŋ'krumə

no
BR nəʊ, -z
AM noʊ, -z

no-account
BR ͵nəʊə'kaʊnt, -s
AM 'noʊə͵kaʊnt, -s

Noah
BR 'nəʊə(r), nɔː(r)
AM 'noʊə

Noakes
BR nəʊks
AM noʊks

Noam
BR 'nəʊ(ə)m
AM 'noʊəm

nob
BR nɒb, -z
AM nɑb, -z

no-ball
BR 'nəʊbɔːl, -z, -ɪŋ, -d
AM 'noʊ͵bɔl, 'noʊ͵bɑl, -z, -ɪŋ, -d

nobble
BR 'nɒb|l, -lz, -l̩ɪŋ \-lɪŋ, -ld
AM 'nɑbəl, -əlz, -(ə)lɪŋ, -əld

nobbler
BR 'nɒblə(r), 'nɒblə(r), -z
AM 'nɑb(ə)lər, -z

nobbut
BR 'nɒbət

AM 'nabət

Nobel
BR nəʊ'bɛl
AM noʊ'bɛl

nobelium
BR nə(ʊ)'biːliəm, nə(ʊ)'bɛliəm
AM noʊ'bɛliəm

Nobel prize
BR ͵nəʊbɛl 'prʌɪz, -ɪz
AM noʊ'bɛl 'praɪz, 'noʊbɛl +, -ɪz

nobiliary
BR nə(ʊ)'bɪliəri
AM noʊ'bɪli͵ɛri, noʊ'bɪljəri

nobility
BR nə(ʊ)'bɪlɪti
AM noʊ'bɪlɪdi

noble
BR 'nəʊbl, -z, -ə(r), -ɪst
AM 'noʊb|əl, -əlz, -lər, -ləst

nobleman
BR 'nəʊblmən
AM 'noʊbəlmən

noblemen
BR 'nəʊblmən
AM 'noʊbəlmən

nobleness
BR 'nəʊblnəs
AM 'noʊbəlnəs

noblesse
BR nə(ʊ)'blɛs
AM noʊ'blɛs

noblesse oblige
BR nə(ʊ)͵blɛs ə(ʊ)'bliːʒ, + ɒ'bliːʒ
AM noʊ'blɛs ə'bliʒ

noblewoman
BR 'nəʊbl͵wʊmən
AM 'noʊbəl͵wʊmən

noblewomen
BR 'nəʊbl͵wɪmɪn
AM 'noʊbəl͵wɪmɪn

nobly
BR 'nəʊbli
AM 'noʊbli

nobody
BR 'nəʊbəd|i, -ɪz
AM 'noʊ͵badi, 'noʊbədi, -z

nociceptor
BR 'nəʊsɪsɛptə(r), -z
AM 'noʊsə͵sɛptər, -z

nock
BR nɒk, -s
AM nɑk, -s

no-claim bonus
BR ͵nəʊkleɪm 'bəʊnəs, -ɪz
AM ͵noʊ͵kleɪm 'boʊnəs, -əz

no-claims bonus
BR ͵nəʊkleɪmz 'bəʊnəs, -ɪz
AM ͵noʊ͵kleɪmz 'boʊnəs, -əz

noctambulism
BR nɒk'tambjʊlɪz(ə)m
AM nak'tæmbjə͵lɪzəm

noctambulist
BR nɒk'tambjʊlɪst, -s
AM nak'tæmbjələst, -s

noctiluca
BR ͵nɒktɪ'luːkə(r)
AM ͵naktə'lukə

noctilucae
BR ͵nɒktɪ'luːkiː
AM ͵naktə'luki

noctilucent
BR ͵nɒktɪ'luːsnt
AM ͵naktə'lusnt

noctivagant
BR nɒk'tɪvəg(ə)nt
AM nak'tɪvəgənt

noctivagous
BR nɒk'tɪvəgəs
AM nak'tɪvəgəs

noctuid
BR 'nɒktjʊɪd, 'nɒktʃʊɪd, -z
AM 'nak͵tʃuɪd, -z

noctule
BR 'nɒktjuːl, 'nɒktʃuːl, -z
AM 'nak͵tʃul, -z

nocturn
BR 'nɒktɜːn, ͵nɒk'tɜːn, -z
AM 'naktərn, -z

nocturnal
BR nɒk'tɜːnl
AM nak'tɜrnəl

nocturnally
BR nɒk'tɜːn|li, nɒk'tɜːnəli
AM nak'tɜrnəli

nocturne
BR 'nɒktɜːn, ͵nɒk'tɜːn, -z
AM 'naktərn, -z

nocuous
BR 'nɒkjʊəs
AM 'nakjəwəs

nod
BR nɒd, -z, -ɪŋ, -ɪd
AM nad, -z, -ɪŋ, -əd

nodal
BR 'nəʊdl
AM 'noʊdəl

noddle
BR 'nɒdl, -z
AM 'nadəl, -z

noddy
BR 'nɒd|i, -ɪz
AM 'nadi, -z

node
BR nəʊd, -z
AM noʊd, -z

nodi
BR 'nəʊdʌɪ
AM 'noʊ͵daɪ

nodical
BR 'nəʊdɪkl

AM 'nadəkəl, 'noʊdəkəl

nodose
BR nə(ʊ)'dəʊs
AM 'noʊ͵doʊs, 'noʊ͵doʊz

nodosity
BR nə(ʊ)'dɒsɪti
AM noʊ'dɑsədi

nodular
BR 'nɒdjʊlə(r), 'nɒdʒələ(r)
AM 'nadʒələr, 'nadjələr

nodulated
BR 'nɒdjʊleɪtɪd, 'nɒdʒəleɪtɪd
AM 'nadʒə͵leɪdɪd, 'nadjə͵leɪdɪd

nodulation
BR ͵nɒdjʊ'leɪʃn, ͵nɒdʒə'leɪʃn
AM ͵nadʒə'leɪʃən, ͵nadjə'leɪʃən

nodule
BR 'nɒdjuːl, 'nɒdʒuːl, 'nɒdʒəl, -z
AM 'na͵dʒul, 'na͵djul, -z

nodulose
BR 'nɒdjʊləʊs, 'nɒdʒələʊs
AM 'nadʒəloʊs, 'nadʒəloʊz

nodulous
BR 'nɒdjʊləʊs, 'nɒdʒələʊs
AM 'nadʒəloʊs

nodus
BR 'nəʊdəs
AM 'noʊdəs

Noel[1]
Christmas
BR nəʊ'ɛl
AM noʊ'ɛl

Noel[2]
forename
BR 'nəʊ(ə)l
AM 'noʊ(ə)l

Noelle
BR nəʊ'ɛl
AM noʊ'ɛl

noes
BR nəʊz
AM noʊz

noesis
BR nəʊ'iːsɪs
AM noʊ'isɪs

noetic
BR nəʊ'ɛtɪk
AM noʊ'ɛdɪk

nog
BR nɒg
AM nag

noggin
BR 'nɒgɪn, -z
AM 'nagən, -z

nogging
BR 'nɒgɪŋ, -z
AM 'nɑgɪŋ, -z

Noguchi
BR nɒ'gu:tʃi, nə'gu:tʃi
AM noʊ'gutʃi

Noh
BR nəʊ
AM noʊ

no-hoper
BR ˌnəʊ'həʊpə(r), -z
AM ˌnoʊ'hoʊpər, -z

nohow
BR 'nəʊhaʊ
AM 'noʊˌhaʊ

noil
BR nɔɪl, -z
AM nɔɪl, -z

noise
BR nɔɪz, -ɪz, -ɪŋ, -d
AM nɔɪz, -ɪz, -ɪŋ, -d

noiseless
BR 'nɔɪzlɪs
AM 'nɔɪzlɪs

noiselessly
BR 'nɔɪzlɪsli
AM 'nɔɪzlɪsli

noiselessness
BR 'nɔɪzlɪsnɪs
AM 'nɔɪzlɪsnɪs

noisemaker
BR 'nɔɪzˌmeɪkə(r), -z
AM 'nɔɪzˌmeɪkər, -z

noisette
BR nwɑ:'zɛt, nwɒ'zɛt, -s
AM nwɑ'zɛt, -s

noisily
BR 'nɔɪzɪli
AM 'nɔɪzɪli

noisiness
BR 'nɔɪzɪnɪs
AM 'nɔɪzɪnɪs

noisome
BR 'nɔɪs(ə)m
AM 'nɔɪsəm

noisomely
BR 'nɔɪs(ə)mli
AM 'nɔɪsəmli

noisomeness
BR 'nɔɪs(ə)mnəs
AM 'nɔɪsəmnəs

noisy
BR 'nɔɪz|i, -iə(r), -ɪɪst
AM 'nɔɪzi, -ər, -ɪst

Nok
BR nɒk
AM nɑk

Nola
BR 'nəʊlə(r)
AM 'noʊlə

Nolan
BR 'nəʊlən
AM 'noʊl(ə)n

nolens volens
BR ˌnəʊlɛnz 'vəʊlɛnz
AM ˌnoʊlənz 'voʊlɛnz

nolle prosequi
BR ˌnɒli 'prɒsɪkwʌɪ
AM 'noʊli 'prɑsəˌkwaɪ

nomad
BR 'nəʊmad, -z
AM 'noʊˌmæd, -z

nomadic
BR nə(ʊ)'madɪk
AM noʊ'mædɪk

nomadically
BR nə(ʊ)'madɪkli
AM noʊ'mædək(ə)li

nomadise
BR 'nəʊmədʌɪz, -ɪz, -ɪŋ, -d
AM 'noʊˌmædˌaɪz, 'noʊməˌdaɪz, -ɪz, -ɪŋ, -d

nomadism
BR 'nəʊmədɪz(ə)m
AM 'noʊməˌdɪzəm

nomadize
BR 'nəʊmədʌɪz, -ɪz, -ɪŋ, -d
AM 'noʊˌmædˌaɪz, 'noʊməˌdaɪz, -ɪz, -ɪŋ, -d

no-man's-land
BR 'nəʊmanzland
AM 'noʊˌmænzˌlæn(d)

nombril
BR 'nɒmbrɪl, -z
AM 'nɑmbrəl, -z

nom de guerre
BR ˌnɒm də 'gɛː(r)
AM ˌnɑm də 'gɛ(ə)r

nom de plume
BR ˌnɒm də 'plu:m
AM ˌnɑm də 'plum

Nome
BR nəʊm
AM noʊm

nomen
BR 'nəʊmɛn, 'nəʊmən
AM 'noʊmən

nomenclative
BR 'nəʊmənˌkleɪtɪv
AM 'noʊmənˌkleɪdɪv

nomenclatural
BR ˌnəʊmən'klatʃ(ə)rəl, ˌnəʊmən'klatʃ(ə)r̩l
AM ˌnoʊmən'kleɪtʃ(ə)rəl

nomenclature
BR nə(ʊ)'mɛŋklətʃə(r), -z
AM 'noʊmənˌkleɪtʃər, -z

nomenklatura
BR nɒˌmɛnklə'tjʊərə(r), nɒˌmɛŋklə'tʃʊərə(r)
AM ˌnoʊmənˌklə't(j)ʊrə
RUS naˌmjɛnklə'tura

nomina
BR 'nɒmɪnə(r)
AM 'nɑmənə

nominal
BR 'nɒmɪnl

nolle prosequi
AM 'nɑmənəl

nominalisation
BR ˌnɒmɪnlʌɪ'zeɪʃn, ˌnɒmɪnəlʌɪ'zeɪʃn, -z
AM 'nɑmənlə'zeɪʃən, 'nɑmənələ'zeɪʃən, 'nɑmənlˌaɪ'zeɪʃən, 'nɑmənəˌlaɪ'zeɪʃən, -z

nominalise
BR 'nɒmɪnlʌɪz, 'nɒmɪnəlʌɪz, -ɪz, -ɪŋ, -d
AM 'nɑmənlˌaɪz, 'nɑmənəˌlaɪz, -ɪz, -ɪŋ, -d

nominalism
BR 'nɒmɪnlɪz(ə)m, 'nɒmɪnəlɪz(ə)m
AM 'nɑmənlˌɪzəm, 'nɑmənəˌlɪzəm

nominalist
BR 'nɒmɪnlɪst, 'nɒmɪnəlɪst, -s
AM 'nɑmənləst, 'nɑmənələst, -s

nominalistic
BR ˌnɒmɪnl'ɪstɪk, ˌnɒmɪnə'lɪstɪk
AM ˌnɑmənə'lɪstɪk

nominalization
BR ˌnɒmɪnlʌɪ'zeɪʃn, ˌnɒmɪnəlʌɪ'zeɪʃn, -z
AM 'nɑmənlə'zeɪʃən, 'nɑmənələ'zeɪʃən, 'nɑmənlˌaɪ'zeɪʃən, 'nɑmənəˌlaɪ'zeɪʃən, -z

nominalize
BR 'nɒmɪnlʌɪz, 'nɒmɪnəlʌɪz, -ɪz, -ɪŋ, -d
AM 'nɑmənlˌaɪz, 'nɑmənəˌlaɪz, -ɪz, -ɪŋ, -d

nominally
BR 'nɒmɪnli, 'nɒmɪnəli
AM 'nɑmənli, 'nɑmənəli

nominate
BR 'nɒmɪneɪt, -s, -ɪŋ, -ɪd
AM 'nɑməˌneɪ|t, -ts, -dɪŋ, -dɪd

nomination
BR ˌnɒmɪ'neɪʃn, -z
AM ˌnɑmə'neɪʃən, -z

nominatival
BR ˌnɒm(ɪ)nə'tʌɪvl, ˌnɒmnə'tʌɪvl
AM 'nɑm(ə)nəˌtaɪvəl

nominative
BR 'nɒm(ɪ)nətɪv, 'nɒmnətɪv, -z
AM 'nɑm(ə)nədɪv, -z

nominator
BR 'nɒmɪneɪtə(r), 'nɒmneɪtə(r), -z
AM 'nɑməˌneɪdər, -z

nominee
BR ˌnɒmɪ'ni:, -z

AM ˌnɑmə'ni, -z

nomogram
BR 'nɒməgram, 'nəʊməgram, -z
AM 'nɑməˌgræm, 'noʊməˌgræm, -z

nomograph
BR 'nɒməgrɑ:f, 'nɒməgraf, 'nəʊməgrɑ:f, 'nəʊməgraf, -s
AM 'nɑməˌgræf, 'noʊməˌgræf, -s

nomographic
BR ˌnɒmə'grafɪk, ˌnəʊmə'grafɪk
AM ˌnɑmə'græfɪk, ˌnoʊmə'græf

nomographically
BR ˌnɒmə'grafɪkli, ˌnəʊmə'grafɪkli
AM ˌnɑmə'græfək(ə)li, ˌnoʊmə'græfək(ə)li

nomography
BR nə'mɒgrəfi
AM nə'mɑgrəfi

nomothetic
BR ˌnɒmə'θɛtɪk, ˌnəʊmə'θɛtɪk
AM ˌnɑmə'θɛdɪk, ˌnoʊmə'θɛdɪk

noms de guerre
BR ˌnɒm(z) də 'gɛː(r)
AM ˌnɑm(z) də 'gɛ(ə)r

noms de plume
BR ˌnɒm(z) də 'plu:m
AM ˌnɑm(z) də 'plum

non
BR nɒn
AM nɑn

nonacceptance
BR ˌnɒnək'sɛpt(ə)ns
AM ˌnɑnək'sɛptns

nonage
BR 'nəʊnɪdʒ, 'nɒnɪdʒ
AM 'nɑnɪdʒ, 'noʊnɪdʒ

nonagenarian
BR ˌnɒnədʒɪ'nɛːrɪən, ˌnəʊnədʒɪ'nɛːrɪən, -z
AM ˌnɑnədʒə'nɛrɪən, ˌnoʊnədʒə'nɛrɪən, -z

nonaggressive
BR ˌnɒnə'grɛsɪv
AM ˌnɑnə'grɛsɪv

nonagon
BR 'nɒnəgɒn, 'nɒnəg(ə)n, -z
AM 'nɑnəˌgɑn, 'noʊnəˌgɑn, -z

nonaggression
BR ˌnɒnə'grɛʃn
AM ˌnɑnə'grɛʃən

nonalcoholic
BR ˌnɒnalkə'hɒlɪk
AM ˌnɑnˌælkə'hɔlɪk, ˌnɑnˌælkə'hɑlɪk

nonaligned
BR ˌnɒnə'lʌɪnd

AM ˌnɑnəˈlaɪnd

nonalignment
BR ˌnɒnəˈlaɪnm(ə)nt
AM ˌnɑnəˈlaɪnmənt

nonappearance
BR ˌnɒnəˈpɪərəns,
ˌnɒnəˈpɪərns
AM ˌnɑnəˈpɪrəns

nonary
BR ˈnəʊnəri
AM ˈnoʊnəri

nonassertive
BR ˌnɒnəˈsɜːtɪv
AM ˌnɑnəˈsɜrdɪv

nonassertively
BR ˌnɒnəˈsɜːtɪvli
AM ˌnɑnəˈsɜrdɪvli

nonattendance
BR ˌnɒnəˈtend(ə)ns
AM ˌnɑnəˈtɛndns

nonavailability
BR ˌnɒnəveɪləˈbɪlɪti
AM ˌnɑnəveɪləˈbɪlɪdi

nonbelligerency
BR ˌnɒnbɪˈlɪdʒ(ə)rənsi,
ˌnɒnbɪˈlɪdʒ(ə)rnsi
AM ˌnɑnbəˈlɪdʒərənsi

nonbelligerent
BR ˌnɒnbɪˈlɪdʒ(ə)rənt,
ˌnɒnbɪˈlɪdʒ(ə)rnt, -s
AM ˌnɑnbəˈlɪdʒərənt,
-s

nonbiodegradable
BR ˌnɒnˌbaɪə(ʊ)dɪˈɡreɪd-
əbl
AM ˌnɑnˌbaɪoʊdəˈɡreɪd-
əbəl

non-biological
BR ˌnɒnbaɪəˈlɒdʒɪkl
AM ˌnɑnˌbaɪəˈlɑdʒəkəl

nonce
BR nɒns
AM nɑns

nonchalance
BR ˈnɒnʃəl(ə)ns,
ˈnɒnʃl(ə)ns
AM ˈnɑnʃəˌlɑns

nonchalant
BR ˈnɒnʃəl(ə)nt,
ˈnɒnʃl(ə)nt
AM ˈnɑnʃəˈlɑnt

nonchalantly
BR ˈnɒntʃəl(ə)ntli,
ˈnɒnʃl(ə)ntli
AM ˈnɑn(t)ʃəˈlɑn(t)li

non-com
BR ˈnɒnˌkɒm, -z
AM ˈnɑnˌkɑm, -z

**non compos
mentis**
BR ˌnɒn ˌkɒmpəs
ˈmɛntɪs
AM ˌnɑn ˌkɑmpəs
ˈmɛn(t)əs

nonconformism
BR ˌnɒnkənˈfɔːmɪz(ə)m
AM ˌnɑnkənˈfɔrˌmɪzəm

nonconformist
BR ˌnɒnkənˈfɔːmɪst, -s
AM ˌnɑnkənˈfɔrməst,
-s

nonconformity
BR ˌnɒnkənˈfɔːmɪti
AM ˌnɑnkənˈfɔrmədi

nonda
BR ˈnɒndə(r), -z
AM ˈnɑndə, -z

**nondescrimin-
atory**
BR ˌnɒndɪˈskrɪmɪnətri
AM ˈnɑndəˈskrɪmɪnə-
ˌtɔri

nondescript
BR ˈnɒndɪskrɪpt
AM ˈnɑndəˈskrɪpt

nondescriptly
BR ˈnɒndɪskrɪp(t)li
AM ˈnɑndəˈskrɪp(t)li

nondescriptness
BR ˈnɒndɪskrɪp(t)nɪs
AM ˈnɑndəˈskrɪp(t)nɪs

none
BR nʌn
AM nən

nonentity
BR nɒˈnɛntɪt|i,
nəˈnɛntɪti, -ɪz
AM nɑnˈɛn(t)ədi, -z

nones
BR nəʊnz
AM noʊnz

nonessential
BR ˌnɒnɪˈsɛnʃl, -z
AM ˈnɑnəˈsɛn(t)ʃəl,
ˈnɑnɪˈsɛn(t)ʃəl, -z

nonesuch
BR ˈnʌnsʌtʃ, -ɪz
AM ˈnən.sətʃ, -əz

nonet
BR nəʊˈnɛt, nɒˈnɛt, -s
AM noʊˈnɛt, -s

nonetheless
BR ˌnʌnðəˈlɛs
AM ˌnənðəˈlɛs

nonexistent
BR ˌnɒnɪɡˈzɪst(ə)nt
AM ˈnɑnəɡˈzɪstənt

nonfeasance
BR ˌnɒnˈfiːz(ə)ns
AM nɑnˈfizəns

nonfiction
BR ˌnɒnˈfɪkʃn
AM ˌnɑnˈfɪkʃən

nong
BR nɒŋ, -z
AM nɔŋ, nɑŋ, -z

noninvolvement
BR ˌnɒnɪnˈvɒlvm(ə)nt
AM ˌnɑnənˈvɑlvmənt,
ˈnɑnənˈvɑlvmənt

nonjoinder
BR ˌnɒnˈdʒɔɪmdə(r), -z
AM ˈnɑnˈdʒɔɪndər, -z

nonjuring
BR ˌnɒnˈdʒʊərɪŋ
AM ˈnɑnˈdʒʊrɪŋ

nonjuror
BR ˌnɒnˈdʒʊərə(r), -z
AM ˈnɑnˈdʒʊrər,
ˈnɑnˈdʒʊˌrɔ(ə)r,
ˈnɑnˈdʒʊrər,
ˈnɑnˈdʒʊrˌɔ(ə)r, -z

non-jury
BR ˌnɒnˈdʒʊəri
AM ˈnɑnˈdʒʊri,
ˈnɑnˈdʒʊri

non-material
BR ˌnɒnməˈtɪərɪəl
AM ˈnɑnməˈtɪriəl

no-no
BR ˈnəʊnəʊ, -z
AM ˈnoʊˌnoʊ, -z

nonpareil
BR ˌnɒnpəˈreɪl,
ˈnɒnp(ə)rəl,
ˈnɒnp(ə)rl
ˈnɒmp(ə)rəl,
ˈnɒnp(ə)rl̩
AM ˈnɑnpəˌrel

non placet
BR ˌnɒn ˈpleɪset,
+ ˈplakɛt, -s
AM ˌnɑn ˈpleɪsɪt, -s

nonplus
BR ˌnɒnˈplʌs, -ɪz, -ɪŋ, -t
AM ˌnɑnˈpləs, -əz, -ɪŋ, -t

non possumus
BR ˌnɒn ˈpɒsjəməs
AM ˌnɑn ˈpɑs(j)əməs

nonrestrictive
BR ˌnɒnrɪˈstrɪktɪv
AM ˈnɑnrəˈstrɪktɪv,
ˈnɑnriˈstrɪktɪv

nonreturnable
BR ˌnɒnrɪˈtəːnəbl
AM ˈnɑnrəˈtɜrnəbəl,
ˈnɑnriˈtɜrnəbəl

nonsense
BR ˈnɒns(ə)ns, -ɪz
AM ˈnɑnˌsɛns,
ˈnɑnsəns, -əz

nonsensical
BR nɒnˈsɛnsɪkl
AM nɑnˈsɛnsəkəl

nonsensicality
BR ˌnɒnsɛnsɪˈkalɪt|i,
-ɪz
AM ˌnɑnˌsɛnsəˈkælədi,
-z

nonsensically
BR nɒnˈsɛnsɪkli
AM nɑnˈsɛnsək(ə)li

non sequitur
BR ˌnɒn ˈsɛkwɪtə(r), -z
AM ˌnɑn ˈsɛkwədər, -z

nonstandard
BR ˌnɒnˈstandəd
AM ˈnɑnˈstændərd

nonstick
BR ˌnɒnˈstɪk
AM ˈnɑnˈstɪk

nonstop
BR ˌnɒnˈstɒp
AM ˈnɑnˈstɑp

nonsuch
BR ˈnɒnsʌtʃ, ˈnʌnsʌtʃ,
-ɪz
AM ˈnən.sətʃ, -əz

nonsuit
BR ˌnɒnˈsuːt,
ˌnɒnˈsjuːt, -s, -ɪŋ, -ɪd
AM ˈnɑnˈs(j)u|t, -ts,
-dɪŋ, -dəd

nontheless
BR ˌnʌnðəˈlɛs
AM ˌnənðəˈlɛs

non-U
BR ˌnɒnˈjuː
AM ˈnɑnˈju

nonviolence
BR ˌnɒnˈvaɪəl(ə)ns
AM nɑnˈvaɪələns

nonviolent
BR ˌnɒnˈvaɪəl(ə)nt
AM ˈnɑnˈvaɪələnt

noodle
BR ˈnuːdl, -z
AM ˈnudəl, -z

nook
BR nʊk, -s
AM nʊk, -s

nookie
BR ˈnʊki
AM ˈnʊki

nooky
BR ˈnʊki
AM ˈnʊki

noon
BR nuːn, -z
AM nun, -z

Noonan
BR ˈnuːnən
AM ˈnunən

noonday
BR ˈnuːndeɪ
AM ˈnunˌdeɪ

no one
BR ˈnəʊ wʌn
AM ˈnoʊ ˌwən

noontide
BR ˈnuːntaɪd
AM ˈnunˌtaɪd

noontime
BR ˈnuːntaɪm
AM ˈnunˌtaɪm

noose
BR nuːs, -ɪz
AM nus, -əz

Nootka
BR ˈnuːtkə(r),
ˈnʊtkə(r), -z
AM ˈnutkə, -z

nopal
BR ˈnəʊpl, -z
AM ˈnoʊpəl, -z

nope
BR nəʊp
AM noʊp

noplace
BR 'nəʊpleɪs
AM 'noʊ,pleɪs

nor
BR nɔː(r)
AM nɔ(ə)r

Nora
BR 'nɔːrə(r)
AM 'nɔrə

NORAD
BR 'nɔːrad
AM 'nɔr,æd

noradrenalin
BR ,nɔːrə'drɛnəlɪn, ,nɔːrə'drɛnlɪn
AM ,nɔrə'drɛnələn

noradrenaline
BR ,nɔːrə'drɛnəlɪn, ,nɔːrə'drɛnlɪn
AM ,nɔrə'drɛnələn

Norah
BR 'nɔːrə(r)
AM 'nɔrə

Noraid
BR 'nɔːreɪd
AM 'nɔ,reɪd

Norbert
BR 'nɔːbət
AM 'nɔrbərt

Norden
BR 'nɔːdn
AM 'nɔrdən

Nordic
BR 'nɔːdɪk
AM 'nɔrdɪk

Nordkinn
BR 'nɔːdkɪn
AM 'nɔrdkɪn
NO 'nuːrçɪn

Nore
BR nɔː(r)
AM nɔ(ə)r

Noreen
BR 'nɔːriːn
AM nɔ'rin

Norfolk
BR 'nɔːfək
AM 'nɔrfək

Noriega
BR ,nɒrɪ'eɪgə(r)
AM ,nɔri'eɪgə

nork
BR nɔːk, -s
AM nɔ(ə)rk, -s

norland
BR 'nɔːlənd, -z
AM 'nɔrlən(d), -z

norm
BR nɔːm, -z
AM nɔ(ə)rm, -z

Norma
BR 'nɔːmə(r)
AM 'nɔrmə

normal
BR 'nɔːml
AM 'nɔrməl

normalcy
BR 'nɔːmlsi
AM 'nɔrməlsi

normalisation
BR ,nɔːməlaɪ'zeɪʃn, ,nɔːmlaɪ'zeɪʃn
AM ,nɔrmələ'zeɪʃən, ,nɔrmə,laɪ'zeɪʃən

normalise
BR 'nɔːməlaɪz, 'nɔːmlaɪz, -ɪz, -ɪŋ, -d
AM 'nɔrmə,laɪz, -ɪz, -ɪŋ, -d

normaliser
BR 'nɔːməlaɪzə(r), 'nɔːmlaɪz, -z
AM 'nɔrmə,laɪzər, -z

normality
BR nɔː'malɪti
AM nɔr'mælədi

normalization
BR ,nɔːməlaɪ'zeɪʃn, ,nɔːmlaɪ'zeɪʃn
AM ,nɔrmələ'zeɪʃən, ,nɔrmə,laɪ'zeɪʃən

normalize
BR 'nɔːməlaɪz, 'nɔːmlaɪzə(r), -ɪz, -ɪŋ, -d
AM 'nɔrmə,laɪz, -ɪz, -ɪŋ, -d

normalizer
BR 'nɔːməlaɪzə(r), 'nɔːmlaɪzə(r), -z
AM 'nɔrmə,laɪzər, -z

normally
BR 'nɔːməli, 'nɔːmli
AM 'nɔrməli

Norman
BR 'nɔːmən, -z
AM 'nɔrmən, -z

Normandy
BR 'nɔːməndi
AM 'nɔrməndi

Normanesque
BR ,nɔːmə'nɛsk
AM ,nɔrmə'nɛsk

Normanise
BR 'nɔːmənaɪz, -ɪz, -ɪŋ, -d
AM 'nɔrmə,naɪz, -ɪz, -ɪŋ, -d

Normanism
BR 'nɔːmənɪz(ə)m, -z
AM 'nɔrmə,nɪzəm, -z

Normanize
BR 'nɔːmənaɪz, -ɪz, -ɪŋ, -d
AM 'nɔrmə,naɪz, -ɪz, -ɪŋ, -d

Normanton
BR 'nɔːməntən
AM 'nɔrməntən

normative
BR 'nɔːmətɪv
AM 'nɔrmədɪv

normatively
BR 'nɔːmətɪvli
AM 'nɔrmədɪvli

normativeness
BR 'nɔːmətɪvnɪs
AM 'nɔrmədɪvnɪs

Norn
BR nɔːn, -z
AM nɔ(ə)rn, -z

Norris
BR 'nɒrɪs
AM 'nɔrəs

Norrköping
BR 'nɔːkəpɪŋ
AM 'nɔrkəpɪŋ
sw nɒr'ʃəpɪŋ

Norroy
BR 'nɒrɔɪ
AM 'nɔ,rɔɪ

Norse
BR nɔːs
AM nɔ(ə)rs

Norseman
BR 'nɔːsmən
AM 'nɔrsmən

Norsemen
BR 'nɔːsmən, 'nɔːsmɛn
AM 'nɔrsmən, 'nɔrs,mɛn

north
BR nɔːθ
AM nɔrθ

Northallerton
BR nɔː'θalət(ə)n
AM nɔr'θælərtən

Northampton
BR nɔː'θam(p)t(ə)n
AM nɔr'θæm(p)tən

Northamptonshire
BR nɔː'θam(p)tən-ʃ(ɪ)ə(r)
AM nɔr'θæm(p)tən-ʃɪ(ə)r

Northanger
BR 'nɔːθaŋgə(r), nɔː'θaŋgə(r)
AM 'nɔrθæŋər, nɔr'θæŋər

Northants
BR nɔː'θants, 'nɔːθants
AM nɔr'θæn(t)s

northbound
BR 'nɔːθbaʊnd
AM 'nɔrθ,baʊnd

Northcliffe
BR 'nɔːθklɪf
AM 'nɔrθ,klɪf

North Dakota
BR ,nɔːθ də'kəʊtə(r)
AM ,nɔrθ də'koʊdə

northeast
BR ,nɔːθ'iːst
AM ,nɔrθ'ist

northeaster
BR ,nɔːθ'iːstə(r), -z
AM ,nɔrθ'istər, -z

northeasterly
BR ,nɔːθ'iːstəli, -ɪz
AM ,nɔrθ'istərli, -z

northeastern
BR ,nɔːθ'iːst(ə)n
AM ,nɔrθ'istərn

northeastward
BR ,nɔːθ'iːstwəd, -z
AM ,nɔrθ'istwərd, -z

Northenden
BR 'nɔːðndən
AM 'nɔrðəndən

norther
BR 'nɔːðə(r), -z
AM 'nɔrðər, -z

northerly
BR 'nɔːðəlji, -ɪz
AM 'nɔrðərli, -z

northern
BR 'nɔːðn
AM 'nɔrðərn

northerner
BR 'nɔːðnə(r), 'nɔːðənə(r), -z
AM 'nɔrðərnər, -z

northernmost
BR 'nɔːðnməʊst
AM 'nɔrðərn,moʊst

Northfleet
BR 'nɔːθfliːt
AM 'nɔrθ,flit

northing
BR 'nɔːθɪŋ, 'nɔːðɪŋ, -z
AM 'nɔrθɪŋ, 'nɔrðɪŋ, -z

Northland
BR 'nɔːθlənd
AM 'nɔrθlən(d), 'nɔrθ,lænd

Northman
BR 'nɔːθmən
AM 'nɔrθmən

Northmen
BR 'nɔːθmɛn, 'nɔːθmən
AM 'nɔrθmən

north-northeast[1]
BR ,nɔːθnɔː'θiːst
AM ,nɔrθ,nɔrθ'ist

north-northeast[2]
nautical use
BR ,nɔːnɔː'riːst
AM ,nɔr,nɔr'ist

north-northwest[1]
BR ,nɔːθnɔː'θwɛst
AM ,nɔrθ,nɔrθ'wɛst

north-northwest[2]
nautical use
BR ,nɔːnɔː'wɛst
AM ,nɔr,nɔr'wɛst

Northolt
BR 'nɔːθəʊlt
AM 'nɔrθ,(h)oʊlt

North Pole
BR ,nɔːθ 'pəʊl
AM ,nɔrθ 'poʊl

North Rhine-Westphalia
BR ,nɔːθ 'raɪnwɛst'feɪlɪə(r)
AM ,nɔrθ 'raɪn,wɛst'fɑːljə, ,nɔrθ 'raɪn,wɛst'fɑːliə

Northrop
BR ˈnɔːθrəp
AM ˈnɔrθrəp

Northrup
BR ˈnɔːθrəp
AM ˈnɔrθrəp

Northumberland
BR nɔːˈθʌmbələnd
AM nɔrˈθəmbərlən(d)

Northumbria
BR nɔːˈθʌmbriə(r)
AM nɔrˈθəmbriə

Northumbrian
BR nɔːˈθʌmbriən, -z
AM nɔrˈθəmbriən, -z

North Utsire
BR ˌnɔːθ ʊtˈsiərə(r)
AM ˌnɔrθ ʊtˈsi(ə)r

northward
BR ˈnɔːθwəd, -z
AM ˈnɔrθwərd, -z

northwest
BR ˌnɔːθˈwest
AM ˌnɔrθˈwest

northwester
BR ˌnɔːθˈwestə(r), -z
AM ˌnɔrθˈwestər, -z

northwesterly
BR ˌnɔːθˈwestəl|i, -ɪz
AM ˌnɔrθˈwestərli, -z

northwestern
BR ˌnɔːθˈwest(ə)n
AM ˌnɔrθˈwestərn

North-West Frontier
BR ˌnɔːθwest ˈfrʌntiə(r), + frʌnˈtiə(r)
AM ˌnɔrθˌwest frənˈtiər

northwestward
BR ˌnɔːθˈwestwəd, -z
AM ˌnɔrθˈwes(t)wərd, -z

Northwich
BR ˈnɔːθwɪtʃ
AM ˈnɔrθwɪtʃ

Norton
BR ˈnɔːtn
AM ˈnɔrtən

Norvic
BR ˈnɔːvɪk
AM ˈnɔrvɪk

Norway
BR ˈnɔːweɪ
AM ˈnɔrweɪ

Norwegian
BR nɔːˈwiːdʒ(ə)n, -z
AM ˌnɔrˈwidʒən, -z

nor'-wester
BR ˌnɔːˈwestə(r), -z
AM ˌnɔrˈwestər, -z

Norwich
BR ˈnɒrɪdʒ, ˈnɒrɪtʃ
AM ˈnɔr(w)ɪtʃ, ˈnɒrɪdʒ

Norwood
BR ˈnɔːwʊd

AM ˈnɔrˌwʊd

nos
numbers
BR ˈnʌmbəz
AM ˈnəmbərz

nose
BR nəʊz, -ɪz, -ɪŋ, -d
AM noʊz, -əz, -ɪŋ, -d

nosebag
BR ˈnəʊzbag, -z
AM ˈnoʊz‚bæg, -z

noseband
BR ˈnəʊzband, -z
AM ˈnoʊz‚bænd, -z

nosebleed
BR ˈnəʊzbliːd, -z
AM ˈnoʊz‚blid, -z

nosecone
BR ˈnəʊzkəʊn, -z
AM ˈnoʊz‚koʊn, -z

nosedive
BR ˈnəʊzdʌɪv, -z, -ɪŋ, -d
AM ˈnoʊz‚daɪv, -z, -ɪŋ, -d

nosegay
BR ˈnəʊzgeɪ, -z
AM ˈnoʊz‚geɪ, -z

noseless
BR ˈnəʊzləs
AM ˈnoʊzləs

nosepipe
BR ˈnəʊzpʌɪp, -s
AM ˈnoʊz‚paɪp, -s

nosering
BR ˈnəʊzrɪŋ, -z
AM ˈnoʊz‚rɪŋ, -z

nosey
BR ˈnəʊz|i, -iə(r), -ɪɪst
AM ˈnoʊzi, -ər, -ɪst

nosey parker
BR ˌnəʊzi ˈpɑːkə(r), -z
AM ˌnoʊzi ˈpɑrkər, -z

Nosferatu
BR ˌnɒsfəˈrɑːtuː
AM ˌnɒsfəˈrɑtu, ˌnɑsfəˈrɑtu

nosh
BR nɒʃ, -ɪz, -ɪŋ, -t
AM nɑʃ, -əz, -ɪŋ, -t

noshery
BR ˈnɒʃ(ə)r|i, -ɪz
AM ˈnɑʃəri, -z

no-show
BR ˌnəʊˈʃəʊ, ˈnəʊʃəʊ, -z
AM ˌnoʊˈʃoʊ, -z

nosh-up
BR ˈnɒʃʌp, -s
AM ˈnɑʃəp, -s

nosily
BR ˈnəʊzɪli
AM ˈnoʊzɪli

nosiness
BR ˈnəʊzɪnɪs
AM ˈnoʊzɪnɪs

nosocomial
BR ˌnɒsə(ʊ)ˈkəʊmɪəl
AM ˌnoʊzoʊˈkoʊmɪəl

nosography
BR nəʊˈsɒgrəfi
AM noʊˈsɑgrəfi

nosological
BR ˌnɒsəˈlɒdʒɪkl
AM ˌnɑsəˈlɑdʒəkəl

nosology
BR nɒˈsɒlədʒi
AM noʊˈsɑlədʒi

nostalgia
BR nɒˈstaldʒ(ɪ)ə(r)
AM nəˈstældʒə, nɒsˈtældʒə, nɑsˈtældʒə

nostalgic
BR nɒˈstaldʒɪk
AM nəˈstældʒɪk, nɒsˈtældʒɪk, nɑsˈtældʒɪk

nostalgically
BR nɒˈstaldʒɪkli
AM nəˈstældʒək(ə)li, nɒsˈtældʒək(ə)li, nɑsˈtældʒək(ə)li

nostoc
BR ˈnɒstɒk, -s
AM ˈnɑ‚stak, -s

Nostradamus
BR ˌnɒstrəˈdɑːməs
AM ˌnɒstrəˈdaməs, ˌnastrəˈdaməs

nostril
BR ˈnɒstr(ɪ)l, -z
AM ˈnɑstrəl, -z

nostrum
BR ˈnɒstrəm, -z
AM ˈnastrəm, -z

nosy
BR ˈnəʊz|i, -iə(r), -ɪɪst
AM ˈnoʊzi, -ər, -ɪst

nosy parker
BR ˌnəʊzi ˈpɑːkə(r), -z
AM ˌnoʊzi ˈpɑrkər, -z

not
BR nɒt
AM nɑt

nota bene
BR ˌnəʊtə ˈbeneɪ, + ˈbeni
AM ˌnoʊdə ˈbeni, + ˈbeneɪ

notability
BR ˌnəʊtəˈbɪlɪt|i, -ɪz
AM ˌnoʊdəˈbɪlɪdi, -z

notable
BR ˈnəʊtəbl
AM ˈnoʊdəbəl

notableness
BR ˈnəʊtəblnəs
AM ˈnoʊdəbəlnəs

notably
BR ˈnəʊtəbli
AM ˈnoʊdəbli

notarial
BR nəʊˈtɛːrɪəl
AM noʊˈterɪəl

notarially
BR nəʊˈtɛːrɪəli

AM noʊˈterɪəli

notarise
BR ˈnəʊtərʌɪz, -ɪz, -ɪŋ, -d
AM ˈnoʊdə‚raɪz, -ɪz, -ɪŋ, -d

notarization
BR ˌnəʊtərʌɪˈzeɪʃn
AM ˌnoʊdərəˈzeɪʃən, ˌnoʊdəraɪˈzeɪʃən

notarize
BR ˈnəʊtərʌɪz, -ɪz, -ɪŋ, -d
AM ˈnoʊdə‚raɪz, -ɪz, -ɪŋ, -d

notary
BR ˈnəʊt(ə)r|i, -ɪz
AM ˈnoʊdəri, -z

notate
BR nə(ʊ)ˈteɪt, -s, -ɪŋ, -ɪd
AM ˈnoʊ‚teɪt, -ts, -dɪŋ, -dɪd

notation
BR nə(ʊ)ˈteɪʃn, -z
AM noʊˈteɪʃən, -z

notational
BR nə(ʊ)ˈteɪʃn(ə)l, nə(ʊ)ˈteɪʃən(ə)l
AM noʊˈteɪʃ(ə)nəl

notch
BR nɒtʃ, -ɪz, -ɪŋ, -t
AM nɑtʃ, -əz, -ɪŋ, -t

notcher
BR ˈnɒtʃə(r), -z
AM ˈnɑtʃər, -z

notchy
BR ˈnɒtʃ|i, -iə(r), -ɪɪst
AM ˈnɑtʃi, -ər, -əst

note
BR nəʊt, -s, -ɪŋ, -ɪd
AM noʊt, -ts, -dɪŋ, -dəd

notebook
BR ˈnəʊtbʊk, -s
AM ˈnoʊt‚bʊk, -s

notecase
BR ˈnəʊtkeɪs, -ɪz
AM ˈnoʊt‚keɪs, -ɪz

noteless
BR ˈnəʊtləs
AM ˈnoʊtləs

notelet
BR ˈnəʊtlɪt, -s
AM ˈnoʊtlət, -s

notepad
BR ˈnəʊtpad, -z
AM ˈnoʊt‚pæd, -z

notepaper
BR ˈnəʊtpeɪpə(r)
AM ˈnoʊt‚peɪpər

note-row
BR ˈnəʊtrəʊ, -z
AM ˈnoʊt‚roʊ, -z

noteworthiness
BR ˈnəʊtˌwəːðɪnɪs
AM ˈnoʊtˌwərðɪnɪs

noteworthy
BR ˈnəʊtˌwəːði

AM ˈnəʊt͵wɜːði

nothing
BR ˈnʌθɪŋ, -z
AM ˈnəθɪŋ, -z

nothingness
BR ˈnʌθɪŋnɪs
AM ˈnəθɪŋnɪs

notice
BR ˈnəʊtɪs, -ɪz, -ɪŋ, -t
AM ˈnoʊdəs, -əz, -ɪŋ, -t

noticeable
BR ˈnəʊtɪsəbl
AM ˈnoʊdəsəbəl

noticeably
BR ˈnəʊtɪsəbli
AM ˈnoʊdəsəbli

noticeboard
BR ˈnəʊtɪsbɔːd, -z
AM ˈnoʊdəs͵bɔː(ə)rd, -z

notifiable
BR ˈnəʊtɪfʌɪəbl
AM ˈnoʊdəˈfaɪəbəl

notification
BR ˌnəʊtɪfɪˈkeɪʃn
AM ˌnoʊdəfəˈkeɪʃən

notify
BR ˈnəʊtɪfʌɪ, -z, -ɪŋ, -d
AM ˈnoʊdə͵faɪ, -z, -ɪŋ, -d

notion
BR ˈnəʊʃn, -z
AM ˈnoʊʃən, -z

notional
BR ˈnəʊʃn(ə)l,
ˈnəʊʃən(ə)l
AM ˈnoʊʃ(ə)nəl

notionalist
BR ˈnəʊʃnəlɪst,
ˈnəʊʃnlɪst,
ˈnəʊʃənlɪst,
ˈnəʊʃ(ə)nəlɪst, -s
AM ˈnoʊʃənələst,
ˈnoʊʃnələst, -s

notionally
BR ˈnəʊʃnəli, ˈnəʊʃnlʲi,
ˈnəʊʃnlʲi,
ˈnəʊʃ(ə)nəli
AM ˈnoʊʃ(ə)nəli

notochord
BR ˈnəʊtəkɔːd, -z
AM ˈnoʊdə͵kɔː(ə)rd, -z

notoriety
BR ˌnəʊtəˈrʌɪti
AM ˌnoʊdəˈraɪɪti

notorious
BR nə(ʊ)ˈtɔːriəs
AM nəˈtɔriəs,
noʊˈtɔriəs

notoriously
BR nə(ʊ)ˈtɔːriəsli
AM nəˈtɔriəsli,
noʊˈtɔriəsli

notoriousness
BR nə(ʊ)ˈtɔːriəsnəs
AM nəˈtɔriəsnəs,
noʊˈtɔriəsnəs

Notre-Dame[1]
church in Paris
BR ˌnɒtrə ˈdɑːm,
ˌnəʊtrə +
AM ˌnəʊtrə ˈdɑm,
ˈnoʊdər ˈdɑm

Notre Dame[2]
US university
BR ˌnɒtrə ˈdɑːm,
ˈnəʊtrə +, + ˈdeɪm
AM ˈnoʊdər ˈdeɪm

no-trump
BR ˌnəʊˈtrʌmp
AM ˌnoʊˈtrʌmp

no-trumper
BR ˌnəʊˈtrʌmpə(r), -z
AM ˌnoʊˈtrʌmpər, -z

Nott
BR nɒt
AM nat

Nottingham
BR ˈnɒtɪŋəm
AM ˈnɑdɪŋ͵hæm,
ˈnɑdɪŋəm

Nottinghamshire
BR ˈnɒtɪŋəmʃ(ɪ)ə(r)
AM ˈnɑdɪŋəm͵ʃɪ(ə)r,
ˈnɑdɪŋ͵hæm͵ʃɪ(ə)r

Notting Hill
BR ˌnɒtɪŋ ˈhɪl
AM ˌnɑdɪŋ ˈhɪl

Notts.
Nottinghamshire
BR nɒts
AM nats

notwithstanding
BR ˌnɒtwɪðˈstandɪŋ,
ˌnɒtwɪθˈstandɪŋ
AM ˈnɑtwɪ(θ)ˈstændɪŋ,
ˈnɑtwɪðˈstændɪŋ

nougat
BR ˈnuːgɑː(r), ˈnʌgɪt
AM ˈnugət

nougatine
BR ˌnuːgəˈtiːn,
ˈnuːgətiːn
AM ˈnugə͵tin

nought
BR nɔːt, -s
AM nɔt, nat, -s

Nouméa
BR nuːˈmeɪə(r)
AM nuˈmeɪə

noumena
BR ˈnuːmɪnə(r),
ˈnaʊmɪnə(r)
AM ˈnumənə

noumenal
BR ˈnuːmɪnl, ˈnaʊmɪnl
AM ˈnumənəl

noumenally
BR ˈnuːmɪnlʲi,
ˈnuːmɪnəli,
ˈnaʊmɪnlʲi,
ˈnaʊmɪnəli
AM ˈnumənəli

noumenon
BR ˈnuːmɪnɒn,
ˈnaʊmɪnɒn

AM ˈnuːmə͵nɑn

noun
BR naʊn, -z
AM naʊn, -z

nounal
BR ˈnaʊnl
AM ˈnaʊnəl

nourish
BR ˈnʌr|ɪʃ, -ɪʃɪz, -ɪʃɪŋ,
-ɪʃt
AM ˈnərɪʃ, ˈnʊrɪʃ, -ɪz,
-ɪŋ, -t

nourisher
BR ˈnʌrɪʃə(r), -z
AM ˈnərɪʃər, ˈnʊrɪʃər,
-z

nourishingly
BR ˈnʌrɪʃɪŋli
AM ˈnərɪʃɪŋli,
ˈnʊrɪʃɪŋli

nourishment
BR ˈnʌrɪʃm(ə)nt, -s
AM ˈnərɪʃmənt,
ˈnʊrɪʃmənt, -s

nous
BR naʊs
AM nus

nouveau riche
BR ˌnuːvəʊ ˈriːʃ
AM ˌnuˌvoʊ ˈriʃ

nouveau roman
BR ˌnuːvəʊ
rə(ʊ)ˈmɑːn, -z
AM ˌnuˌvoʊ roʊˈmɑn,
-z

nouveaux riches
BR ˌnuːvəʊ ˈriːʃ
AM ˌnuˌvoʊ ˈriʃ

nova
BR ˈnəʊvə(r), -z
AM ˈnoʊvə, -z

novae
BR ˈnəʊviː
AM ˈnoʊvi

Novak
BR ˈnəʊvak
AM ˈnoʊvæk

Nova Lisboa
BR ˌnəʊvə lɪzˈbəʊə(r)
AM ˌnoʊvə lɪzˈboʊə

Nova Scotia
BR ˌnəʊvə ˈskəʊʃə(r)
AM ˌnoʊvə ˈskoʊʃə

Nova Scotian
BR ˌnəʊvə ˈskəʊʃ(ə)n,
-z
AM ˌnoʊvə ˈskoʊʃən, -z

Novaya Zemlya
BR ˌnəʊvʌɪə ˈzemlɪə(r)
AM ˌnoʊvəjə ˌzemˈl(j)ɑ
RUS ˌnovəjə zʲinˈlʲa

novel
BR ˈnɒvl, -z
AM ˈnɑvəl, -z

novelese
BR ˌnɒvəˈliːz, ˌnɒvlˈiːz
AM ˌnɑvəˈliz

novelesque
BR ˌnɒvəˈlesk,
ˌnɒvlˈesk
AM ˌnɑvəˈlesk

novelette
BR ˌnɒvəˈlet, ˌnɒvlˈet,
-s
AM ˌnɑvəˈlet, -s

novelettish
BR ˌnɒvəˈletɪʃ,
ˌnɒvlˈetɪʃ
AM ˌnɑvəˈledɪʃ

novelisation
BR ˌnɒvəlʌɪˈzeɪʃn,
ˌnɒvlʌɪˈzeɪʃn, -z
AM ˌnɑvələˈzeɪʃən,
ˌnɑvə͵laɪˈzeɪʃən, -z

novelise
BR ˈnɒvəlʌɪz,
ˈnɒvlʌɪz, -ɪz, -ɪŋ, -d
AM ˈnɑvə͵laɪz, -ɪz, -ɪŋ,
-d

novelist
BR ˈnɒvəlɪst, ˈnɒvlɪst,
-s
AM ˈnɑvələst, -s

novelistic
BR ˌnɒvəˈlɪstɪk,
ˌnɒvlˈɪstɪk
AM ˌnɑvəˈlɪstɪk

novelization
BR ˌnɒvəlʌɪˈzeɪʃn,
ˌnɒvlʌɪˈzeɪʃn, -z
AM ˌnɑvələˈzeɪʃən,
ˌnɑvə͵laɪˈzeɪʃən, -z

novelize
BR ˈnɒvəlʌɪz,
ˈnɒvlʌɪz, -ɪz, -ɪŋ, -d
AM ˈnɑvə͵laɪz, -ɪz, -ɪŋ,
-d

novella
BR nə(ʊ)ˈvelə(r), -z
AM noʊˈvelə, -z

novelle
BR nə(ʊ)ˈveliː
AM noʊˈveli

Novello
BR nəˈveləʊ
AM noʊˈveloʊ

novelty
BR ˈnɒvlt|i, -ɪz
AM ˈnɑvəlti, -z

November
BR nə(ʊ)ˈvembə(r), -z
AM noʊˈvembər,
nəˈvembər, -z

novena
BR nə(ʊ)ˈviːnə(r), -z
AM noʊˈvinə, -z

Novgorod
BR ˈnɒvgərod
AM ˈnɑvgə͵rad
RUS ˈnovgərət

novice
BR ˈnɒvɪs, -ɪz
AM ˈnɑvəs, -əz

Novi Sad
BR ˌnəʊvi ˈsad

AM ˌnoʊvi ˈsæd

novitiate
BR nəˈvɪʃɪət, -s
AM noʊˈvɪʃət, nəˈvɪʃət, -s

Novocain
BR ˈnəʊvə(ʊ)keɪn
AM ˈnoʊvəˌkeɪn

Novocaine®
BR ˈnəʊvə(ʊ)keɪn
AM ˈnoʊvəˌkeɪn

Novokuznetsk
BR ˌnəʊvə(ʊ)kʊz-ˈn(j)ɛtsk
AM ˌnoʊvəkʊzˈn(j)ɛtsk

Novosibirsk
BR ˌnəʊvə(ʊ)sɪˈbɪəsk
AM ˌnoʊvəsɪˈbərsk
RUS nəvəsʲiˈbʲirsk

Novotel
BR ˈnəʊvə(ʊ)tɛl
AM ˈnoʊvəˌtɛl

Novotný
BR nəˈvɒtni
AM nəˈvɒtni, nəˈvɑtni
CZ ˈnɔvɔtniː

now
BR naʊ
AM naʊ

nowaday
BR ˈnaʊədeɪ
AM ˈnaʊəˌdeɪ

nowadays
BR ˈnaʊədeɪz
AM ˈnaʊəˌdeɪz

noway
BR ˌnəʊˈweɪ, -z
AM ˈnoʊˌweɪ, -z

Nowel
BR nəʊˈɛl
AM ˈnoʊəl

Nowell¹
Christmas
BR nəʊˈɛl
AM noʊˈwɛl

Nowell²
forename
BR ˈnəʊ(ə)l
AM ˈnoʊ(ə)l

nowhere
BR ˈnəʊwɛː(r)
AM ˈnoʊˌ(h)wɛ(ə)r

no-win
BR ˌnəʊˈwɪn
AM ˈnoʊˈwɪn

nowise
BR ˈnəʊwʌɪz
AM ˈnoʊˌwaɪz

nowt
BR naʊt
AM naʊt

noxious
BR ˈnɒkʃəs
AM ˈnɒkʃəs, ˈnɑkʃəs

noxiously
BR ˈnɒkʃəsli

AM ˈnɒkʃəsli, ˈnakʃəsli

noxiousness
BR ˈnɒkʃəsnəs
AM ˈnɒkʃəsnəs, ˈnakʃəsnəs

noyau
BR ˌnwɑːˈjəʊ
AM ˌnwɑˈjoʊ

noyaux
BR ˌnwɑːˈjəʊ(z)
AM ˌnwɑˈjoʊ(z)

Noyes
BR nɔɪz
AM nɔɪz

nozzle
BR ˈnɒzl, -z
AM ˈnazəl, -z

n't
BR n̩t
AM n̩t

nth
BR ɛnθ
AM ɛnθ

nu
BR nju:
AM n(j)u

nuance
BR ˈnjuːɑːns, -ɪz
AM ˈn(j)uˌɑns, -əz

nub
BR nʌb, -z
AM nəb, -z

Nuba
BR ˈnjuːbə(r)
AM ˈnubə

nubble
BR ˈnʌbl, -z
AM ˈnəbəl, -z

nubbly
BR ˈnʌbli
AM ˈnəbl̩i

nubby
BR ˈnʌbi
AM ˈnəbi

Nubia
BR ˈnjuːbɪə(r)
AM ˈn(j)ubiə

Nubian
BR ˈnjuːbɪən, -z
AM ˈn(j)ubiən, -z

nubile
BR ˈnjuːbʌɪl
AM ˈn(j)uˌbaɪl, ˈn(j)ubəl

nubility
BR ˌnjuːˈbɪlɪti
AM ˌn(j)uˈbɪlɨdi

nuchal
BR ˈnjuːkl
AM ˈn(j)ukəl

nuciferous
BR njuːˈsɪf(ə)rəs
AM ˌn(j)uˈsɪf(ə)rəs

nucivorous
BR ˌnjuːˈsɪv(ə)rəs
AM ˌn(j)uˈsɪv(ə)rəs

nuclear
BR ˈnjuːklɪə(r)
AM ˈn(j)uklɪər, ˈn(j)ukjələr

nuclease
BR ˈnjuːklɪeɪz, -ɪz
AM ˈn(j)ukliˌeɪz, -ɪz

nucleate
BR ˈnjuːklɪeɪt, -s, -ɪŋ, -ɪd
AM ˈn(j)ukliˌeɪ|t, -ts, -dɪŋ, -dɪd

nucleation
BR ˌnjuːklɪˈeɪʃn, -z
AM ˌn(j)ukliˈeɪʃən, -z

nuclei
BR ˈnjuːklʌɪ
AM ˈn(j)ukliˌaɪ

nucleic
BR njuːˈkliːɪk, njuːˈkleɪɪk,
AM n(j)uˈkliːɪk, n(j)uˈkleɪɪk

nucleolar
BR njuːˈklɪələ(r), ˌnjuːklɪˈəʊlə(r)
AM ˌn(j)ukliˈoʊlər, ˌn(j)uˈklɪələr

nucleoli
BR njuːˈklɪəlʌɪ, ˌnjuːklɪˈəʊlʌɪ
AM ˌn(j)ukliˈoʊlaɪ, ˌn(j)uˈkliəˌlaɪ

nucleolus
BR njuːˈklɪələs, ˌnjuːklɪˈəʊləs
AM ˌn(j)ukliˈoʊləs, ˌn(j)uˈkliələs

nucleon
BR ˈnjuːklɪɒn, -z
AM ˈn(j)ukl:iəˌɑn, -z

nucleonic
BR ˌnjuːklɪˈɒnɪk, -s
AM ˌn(j)ukliˈɑnɪk, -s

nucleoprotein
BR ˌnjuːklɪəˈprəʊtiːn, -z
AM ˌn(j)uklioʊˈproʊˌtin, -z

nucleoside
BR ˈnjuːklɪəsʌɪd, -z
AM ˈn(j)ukliəˌsaɪd, -z

nucleotide
BR ˈnjuːklɪətʌɪd, -z
AM ˈn(j)ukliəˌtaɪd, -z

nucleus
BR ˈnjuːklɪəs
AM ˈn(j)ukliəs

nuclide
BR ˈnjuːklʌɪd, -z
AM ˈn(j)uˌklaɪd, -z

nuclidic
BR njuːˈklɪdɪk
AM n(j)uˈklɪdɪk

nuddy
BR ˈnʌdi
AM ˈnədi

nude
BR njuːd, -z
AM n(j)ud, -z

nudge
BR nʌdʒ, -ɪz, -ɪŋ, -d
AM nədʒ, -əz, -ɪŋ, -d

nudger
BR ˈnʌdʒə(r), -z
AM ˈnədʒər, -z

nudism
BR ˈnjuːdɪz(ə)m
AM ˈn(j)uˌdɪzəm

nudist
BR ˈnjuːdɪst, -s
AM ˈn(j)udəst, -s

nudity
BR ˈnjuːdɪti
AM ˈn(j)udədi

nudnik
BR ˈnʊdnɪk, -s
AM ˈnʊdˌnɪk, -s

nuée ardente
BR ˌnjʊeɪ ɑːˈdɒt
AM ˌnueɪ ˌɑrˈdɑnt

Nuer
BR ˈnuːə(r)
AM ˈnuər

Nuevo León
BR ˌnweɪvəʊ liːˈɒn
AM ˌnweɪvoʊ liˈoʊn
SP ˌnweβo leˈon

Nuffield
BR ˈnʌfiːld
AM ˈnəfild

nugatory
BR ˈnjuːgət(ə)ri, njuːˈgeɪt(ə)ri
AM ˈnugəˌtɔri

Nugent
BR ˈnjuːdʒ(ə)nt
AM ˈnudʒənt

nugget
BR ˈnʌgɪt, -s
AM ˈnəgət, -s

nuisance
BR ˈnjuːsns, -ɪz
AM ˈn(j)usns, -əz

Nuits-Saint-George
BR ˌnwiːsanˈʒɔːʒ
AM ˌnwisænˈ(d)ʒɔr(d)ʒ

nuke
BR njuːk, -s, -ɪŋ, -t
AM n(j)uk, -s, -ɪŋ, -t

Nuku'alofa
BR ˌnuːkuːəˈləʊfə(r)
AM ˌnukuəˈlɔfə, ˌnukuəˈloʊfə

null
BR nʌl
AM nəl

nullah
BR ˈnʌlə(r), -z
AM ˈnələ, -z

nulla-nulla
BR ˈnʌlənʌlə(r), -z
AM ˈnələˈnələ, -z

Nullarbor Plain
BR ˌnʌləbɔː 'pleɪn
AM nəlˌɑrbər 'pleɪn
nullification
BR ˌnʌlɪfɪ'keɪʃn
AM ˌnələfə'keɪʃən
nullifidian
BR ˌnʌlɪ'fɪdɪən, -z
AM ˌnələ'fɪdɪən, -z
nullifier
BR 'nʌlɪfʌɪə(r), -z
AM 'nələˌfaɪər, -z
nullify
BR 'nʌlɪfʌɪ, -z, -ɪŋ, -d
AM 'nələˌfaɪ, -z, -ɪŋ, -d
nullipara
BR nʌ'lɪp(ə)rə(r), -z
AM nə'lɪpərə, -z
nulliparous
BR nʌ'lɪp(ə)rəs
AM nə'lɪp(ə)rəs
nullipore
BR 'nʌlɪpɔː(r), -z
AM 'nələˌpɔ(ə)r, -z
nullity
BR 'nʌlɪt|i, -ɪz
AM 'nələdi, -z
numb
BR nʌm, -z, -ɪŋ, -d
AM nəm, -z, -ɪŋ, -d
numbat
BR 'nʌmbat, -s
AM 'nəmˌbæt, -s
number
BR 'nʌmb|ə(r), -əz,
-(ə)rɪŋ, -əd
AM 'nəmb|ər, -ərz,
-(ə)rɪŋ, -ərd
numberless
BR 'nʌmbələs
AM 'nəmbərləs
numberplate
BR 'nʌmbəpleɪt, -s
AM 'nəmbərˌpleɪt, -s
numbingly
BR 'nʌmɪŋli
AM 'nəmɪŋli
numbly
BR 'nʌmli
AM 'nəmli
numbness
BR 'nʌmnəs
AM 'nəmnəs
numbskull
BR 'nʌmskʌl, -z
AM 'nəmˌskəl, -z
numdah
BR 'nʌmdə(r), -z
AM 'nəmdə, -z
numen
BR 'nju:mən
AM 'n(j)umən
numerable
BR 'nju:m(ə)rəbl
AM 'n(j)um(ə)rəbəl
numerably
BR 'nju:m(ə)rəbli

AM 'n(j)um(ə)rəbli
numeracy
BR 'nju:m(ə)rəsi
AM 'n(j)um(ə)rəsi
numeral
BR 'nju:m(ə)rəl,
'nju:m(ə)r|, -z
AM 'n(j)um(ə)rəl, -z
numerate
BR 'nju:m(ə)rət
AM 'n(j)um(ə)rət
numeration
BR ˌnju:mə'reɪʃn
AM ˌn(j)umə'reɪʃən
numerative
BR 'nju:m(ə)rətɪv
AM 'n(j)uməˌreɪdɪv
numerator
BR 'nju:məreɪtə(r), -z
AM 'n(j)uməˌreɪdər, -z
numeric
BR nju:'mɛrɪk,
njʊ'mɛrɪk
AM n(j)u'mɛrɪk
numerical
BR nju:'mɛrɪkl,
njʊ'mɛrɪkl
AM n(j)u'mɛrɪkəl
numerically
BR nju:'mɛrɪkli,
njʊ'mɛrɪkli
AM n(j)u'mɛrək(ə)li
numerological
BR ˌnju:m(ə)rə'lɒdʒɪkl
AM ˌn(j)umərə'ladʒəkəl
numerologist
BR ˌnju:mə'rɒlədʒɪst,
-s
AM ˌn(j)umə'ralədʒəst,
-s
numerology
BR ˌnju:mə'rɒlədʒi
AM ˌn(j)umə'ralədʒi
numerous
BR 'nju:m(ə)rəs
AM 'n(j)um(ə)rəs
numerously
BR 'nju:m(ə)rəsli
AM 'n(j)um(ə)rəsli
numerousness
BR 'nju:m(ə)rəsnəs
AM 'n(j)um(ə)rəsnəs
numerus clausus
BR ˌnju:mərəs
'klausəs
AM ˌn(j)umərəs
'klausəs
Numidia
BR nju:'mɪdɪə(r),
njʊ'mɪdɪə(r)
AM n(j)u'mɪdɪə
Numidian
BR nju:'mɪdɪən,
njʊ'mɪdɪən,
AM n(j)u'mɪdɪən, -z
numina
BR 'nju:mɪnə(r)
AM 'n(j)umɪnə

numinous
BR 'nju:mɪnəs
AM 'n(j)umənəs
numinously
BR 'nju:mɪnəsli
AM 'n(j)umənəsli
numinousness
BR 'nju:mɪnəsnəs
AM 'n(j)umənəsnəs
numismatic
BR ˌnju:mɪz'matɪk, -s
AM ˌn(j)uməz'mædɪk,
ˌn(j)uməs'mædɪk, -s
numismatically
BR ˌnju:mɪz'matɪkli
AM ˌn(j)uməz'mædək-
(ə)li,
ˌn(j)uməs'mædək(ə)li
numismatist
BR nju:'mɪzmətɪst,
njʊ'mɪzmətɪst, -s
AM n(j)u'mɪzmədəst,
n(j)u'mɪsmədəst, -s
numismatology
BR nju:ˌmɪzmə'tɒlədʒi
njʊˌmɪzmə'tɒlədʒi
AM n(j)uˌmɪzmə'talədʒi,
n(j)uˌmɪsmə'talədʒi
nummary
BR 'nʌm(ə)ri
AM 'nəməri
nummular
BR 'nʌmjʊlə(r)
AM 'nəmjələr
nummulite
BR 'nʌmjʊlʌɪt, -s
AM 'nəmjəˌlaɪt, -s
numnah
BR 'nʌmnə(r), -z
AM 'nəmnə, -z
numskull
BR 'nʌmskʌl, -z
AM 'nəmˌskəl, -z
nun
BR nʌn, -z
AM nən, -z
nunatak
BR 'nʌnətak, -s
AM 'nənəˌtæk, -s
nun-buoy
BR 'nʌnbɔɪ, -z
AM 'nənˌbʊi, 'nənˌbɔɪ,
-z
Nunc Dimittis
BR ˌnʌŋk dɪ'mɪtɪs,
ˌnʊŋk +
AM ˌnəŋk də'mɪdəs
nunchaks
BR 'nʌntʃaks
AM 'nənˌtʃaks
nunchaku
BR nʌn'tʃaku:, -z
AM nən'tʃɑku, -z
nunciature
BR 'nʌnsɪətjʊə(r),
'nʌnsɪətʃə(r), -z
AM 'nənsiəˌtʃʊ(ə)r,
nənsiətʃər, -z

nuncio
BR 'nʌnsɪəʊ, -z
AM 'nənsiou, -z
nuncupate
BR 'nʌŋkjʊpeɪt, -s, -ɪŋ,
-ɪd
AM 'nəŋkjəˌpeɪ|t, -ts,
-dɪŋ, -dɪd
nuncupation
BR ˌnʌŋkjʊ'peɪʃn, -z
AM ˌnəŋkjə'peɪʃən, -z
nuncupative
BR 'nʌŋkjʊpətɪv
AM 'nəŋkjəˌpeɪdɪv
Nuneaton
BR nʌn'i:tn
AM nən'itn
nunhood
BR 'nʌnhʊd, -z
AM 'nən,(h)ʊd, -z
nunlike
BR 'nʌnlʌɪk
AM 'nənˌlaɪk
Nunn
BR nʌn
AM nən
nunnery
BR 'nʌn(ə)r|i, -ɪz
AM 'nənəri, -z
nunnish
BR 'nʌnɪʃ
AM 'nənɪʃ
NUPE
BR 'nju:pi
AM 'n(j)upi
Nupe
language
BR 'nu:peɪ
AM 'nupeɪ
nuptial
BR 'nʌpʃl, 'nʌptʃ(ə)l,
-z
AM 'nəp(t)ʃəl, -z
nurd
BR nɜːd, -z
AM nərd, -z
Nuremberg
BR 'njʊərəmbəːg
AM 'nʊr(ə)mˌbərg
Nureyev
BR 'njʊəreɪɛf,
'njʊəreɪɛv, njʊ'reɪɛf,
njʊ'reɪɛv
AM nʊ'reɪɛv, 'nʊrəjɛv
Nuristan
BR ˌnʊərɪ'stɑːn,
ˌnʊərɪ'stan
AM 'nʊrəˌstæn
Nurofen®
BR 'njʊərə(ʊ)fɛn
AM 'n(j)ʊrəˌfɛn
nurse
BR nɜːs, -ɪz, -ɪŋ, -t
AM nərs, -əz, -ɪŋ, -t
nurseling
BR 'nɜːslɪŋ, -z
AM 'nərslɪŋ, -z

nursemaid
BR ˈnɜːsmeɪd, -z
AM ˈnɜrsˌmeɪd, -z

nursery
BR ˈnɜːs(ə)r|i, -ɪz
AM ˈnɜrs(ə)ri, -z

nurseryman
BR ˈnɜːs(ə)rɪmən
AM ˈnɜrs(ə)rɪmæn,
ˈnɜrs(ə)rɪmən

nurserymen
BR ˈnɜːs(ə)rɪmən
AM ˈnɜrs(ə)rɪmən

nursling
BR ˈnɜːslɪŋ, -z
AM ˈnɜrslɪŋ, -z

nurture
BR ˈnɜːtʃ|ə(r), -əz,
-(ə)rɪŋ, -əd
AM ˈnɜrtʃər, -z, -ɪŋ, -d

nurturer
BR ˈnɜːtʃ(ə)rə(r), -z
AM ˈnɜrtʃərər, -z

NUT
BR ˌɛnjuːˈtiː
AM ˌɛnˌjuˈti

nut
BR nʌt, -s, -ɪŋ, -ɪd
AM nə|t, -ts, -dɪŋ, -dəd

nutant
BR ˈnjuːt(ə)nt
AM ˈn(j)utnt

nutation
BR njuːˈteɪʃn,
njʊˈteɪʃn, -z
AM n(j)uˈteɪʃən, -z

nutcase
BR ˈnʌtkeɪs, -ɪz
AM ˈnətˌkeɪs, -ɪz

nutcracker
BR ˈnʌtˌkrakə(r), -z
AM ˈnətˌkrækər, -z

nutgall
BR ˈnʌtgɔːl, -z
AM ˈnətˌgɔl, ˈnətˌgɑl, -z

nuthatch
BR ˈnʌthatʃ, -ɪz
AM ˈnətˌ(h)ætʃ, -əz

nuthouse
BR ˈnʌthaʊ|s, -zɪz
AM ˈnətˌ(h)aʊ|s, -zəz

nutlet
BR ˈnʌtlɪt, -s
AM ˈnətlət, -s

nutlike
BR ˈnʌtlʌɪk
AM ˈnətˌlaɪk

nutmeat
BR ˈnʌtmiːt, -s
AM ˈnətˌmit, -s

nutmeg
BR ˈnʌtmɛg, -z
AM ˈnətˌmɛg, -z

nutpick
BR ˈnʌtpɪk, -s
AM ˈnətˌpɪk, -s

Nutrasweet®
BR ˈnjuːtrəswiːt
AM ˈn(j)utrəˌswit

nutria
BR ˈnjuːtrɪə(r)
AM ˈn(j)utriə

nutrient
BR ˈnjuːtrɪənt, -s
AM ˈn(j)utriənt, -s

nutriment
BR ˈnjuːtrɪm(ə)nt
AM ˈn(j)utrəmənt

nutrimental
BR ˌnjuːtrɪˈmɛntl
AM ˌn(j)utrəˈmɛn(t)l

nutrition
BR njuːˈtrɪʃn,
njʊˈtrɪʃn
AM n(j)uˈtrɪʃən

nutritional
BR njuːˈtrɪʃn̩(ə)l,
njʊˈtrɪʃən(ə)l
AM n(j)uˈtrɪʃ(ə)nəl

nutritionally
BR njuːˈtrɪʃn̩əli,
njʊˈtrɪʃnəli,
njuːˈtrɪʃ(ə)nəli,
njʊˈtrɪʃ(ə)nəli
AM n(j)uˈtrɪʃ(ə)nəli

nutritionist
BR njuːˈtrɪʃn̩ɪst,
njʊˈtrɪʃn̩ɪst,
njuːˈtrɪʃənɪst,
njʊˈtrɪʃənɪst, -s
AM n(j)uˈtrɪʃənəst, -s

nutritious
BR njuːˈtrɪʃəs,
njʊˈtrɪʃəs
AM n(j)uˈtrɪʃəs

nutritiously
BR njuːˈtrɪʃəsli,
njʊˈtrɪʃəsli
AM n(j)uˈtrɪʃəsli

nutritiousness
BR njuːˈtrɪʃəsnəs,
njʊˈtrɪʃəsnəs
AM n(j)uˈtrɪʃəsnəs

nutritive
BR ˈnjuːtrətɪv
AM ˈn(j)utrədɪv

nutshell
BR ˈnʌtʃɛl, -z

AM ˈnətˌʃɛl, -z

Nuttall
BR ˈnʌtɔːl
AM ˈnədɔl, ˈnədɑl

nutter
BR ˈnʌtə(r), -z
AM ˈnədər, -z

nuttiness
BR ˈnʌtɪnɪs
AM ˈnədinɪs

Nutting
BR ˈnʌtɪŋ
AM ˈnədɪŋ

nutty
BR ˈnʌt|i, -ɪə(r), -ɪɪst
AM ˈnədi, -ər, -ɪst

nux vomica
BR ˌnʌks ˈvɒmɪkə(r),
-z
AM ˌnəks ˈvɑməkə, -z

nuzzle
BR ˈnʌz|l, -lz, -l̩ɪŋ \-lɪŋ,
-ld
AM ˈnəz|əl, -əlz, -(ə)lɪŋ,
-əld

nyala
BR ˈnjɑːlə(r), -z
AM ˈnjɑlə, -z

Nyasa
BR nʌɪˈasə(r),
nɪˈasə(r)
AM ˈnjɑsə, niˈɑsə

Nyasaland
BR nʌɪˈasəland,
nɪˈasələnd
AM ˈnjɑsələnd,
niˈɑsələnd

nyctalopia
BR ˌnɪktəˈlaʊpɪə(r)
AM ˌnɪktəˈloʊpiə

nyctitropic
BR ˌnɪktɪˈtrɒpɪk,
ˌnɪktɪˈtrəʊpɪk
AM ˌnɪktəˈtrɑpɪk

Nye
BR nʌɪ
AM naɪ

Nyerere
BR njəˈrɛːri
AM njəˈrɛri

nylghau
BR ˈnɪlgɔ:(r), -z
AM ˈnɪlˌgɔ, -z

nylon
BR nʌɪlɒn, -z
AM ˈnaɪˌlɑn, -z

nymph
BR nɪmf, -s
AM nɪmf, -s

nympha
BR ˈnɪmfə(r)
AM nɪmfə

nymphae
BR ˈnɪmfiː
AM ˈnɪmfi, ˈnɪmˌfaɪ

nymphal
BR ˈnɪmfl
AM ˈnɪmfəl

nymphean
BR ˈnɪmfɪən
AM ˈnɪmfɪən

nymphet
BR nɪmˈfɛt, -s
AM nɪmˈfɛt, -s

nymphlike
BR ˈnɪmflʌɪk
AM ˈnɪmfˌlaɪk

nympho
BR ˈnɪmfəʊ, -z
AM ˈnɪmˌfoʊ, -z

nympholepsy
BR ˌnɪmfəlɛpsi
AM ˈnɪmfəˌlɛpsi

nympholept
BR ˈnɪmfəlɛpt, -s
AM ˈnɪmfəˌlɛpt, -s

nympholeptic
BR ˌnɪmfəˈlɛptɪk
AM ˌnɪmfəˈlɛptɪk

nymphomania
BR ˌnɪmfəˈmeɪnɪə(r)
AM nɪmfəˈmeɪniə

nymphomaniac
BR ˌnɪmfəˈmeɪnɪak, -s
AM nɪmfəˈmeɪniˌæk, -s

Nynorsk
BR ˈnjuːnɔːsk,
ˈnʌɪnɔːsk
AM ˈn(j)uˌnɔrsk
NOR ˈnyːˌnɔrsk

Nyree
BR ˈnʌɪriː
AM ˈnaɪri

nystagmic
BR nɪˈstagmɪk
AM nəˈstægmɪk

nystagmus
BR nɪˈstagməs
AM nəˈstægməs

Nyx
BR nɪks
AM nɪks

Oo

O'
BR əʊ, ə
AM ə, oʊ

o
BR əʊ, -z
AM oʊ, -z

o'
BR ə
AM ə, oʊ

Oadby
BR 'əʊdbi
AM 'oʊdbi

oaf
BR əʊf, -s
AM oʊf, -s

oafish
BR 'əʊfɪʃ
AM 'oʊfɪʃ

oafishly
BR 'əʊfɪʃli
AM 'oʊfɪʃli

oafishness
BR 'əʊfɪʃnɪs
AM 'oʊfɪʃnɪs

Oahu
BR əʊ'ɑːhuː
AM oʊ'wɑhu

oak
BR əʊk, -s
AM oʊk, -s

oaken
BR 'əʊk(ə)n
AM 'oʊkən

Oakes
BR əʊks
AM oʊks

Oakham
BR 'əʊkəm
AM 'oʊkəm

Oakland
BR 'əʊklənd
AM 'oʊklən(d)

Oakley
BR 'əʊkli
AM 'oʊkli

Oaks
BR əʊks
AM oʊks

Oaksey
BR 'əʊksi
AM 'oʊksi

oakum
BR 'əʊkəm
AM 'oʊkəm

Oakville
BR 'əʊkvɪl
AM 'oʊk,vɪl

OAP
BR ,əʊeɪ'piː, -z
AM ,oʊ,eɪ'pi, -z

OAPEC
BR 'əʊpɛk
AM 'oʊ,pɛk

oar
BR ɔː(r), -z, -d
AM ɔ(ə)r, -z, -d

oarfish
BR 'ɔːfɪʃ
AM 'ɔr,fɪʃ

oarless
BR 'ɔːləs
AM 'ɔrləs

oarlock
BR 'ɔːlɒk, -s
AM 'ɔr,lɑk, -s

oarsman
BR 'ɔːzmən
AM 'ɔrzmən

oarsmanship
BR 'ɔːzmənʃɪp
AM 'ɔrzmən,ʃɪp

oarsmen
BR 'ɔːzmən
AM 'ɔrzmən

oarswoman
BR 'ɔːz,wʊmən
AM 'ɔrz,wʊmən

oarswomen
BR 'ɔːz,wɪmɪn
AM 'ɔrz,wɪmɪn

oarweed
BR 'ɔːwiːd
AM 'ɔr,wid

oases
BR əʊ'eɪsiːz
AM oʊ'eɪsiz

oasis
BR əʊ'eɪsɪs
AM oʊ'eɪsɪs

oast
BR əʊst, -s
AM oʊst, -s

oasthouse
BR 'əʊsthaʊ|s, -zɪz
AM 'oʊst,(h)aʊ|s, -zəz

oat
BR əʊt, -s
AM oʊt, -s

oatcake
BR 'əʊtkeɪk, -s
AM 'oʊt,keɪk, -s

oaten
BR 'əʊtn
AM 'oʊtn

Oates
BR əʊts
AM oʊts

oath
BR əʊ|θ, -ðz\-θs
AM oʊθ, -s

oatmeal
BR 'əʊtmiːl
AM 'oʊt,mil

oaty
BR 'əʊti
AM 'oʊdi

Oaxaca
BR wɑː'hɑːkə(r)
AM wɑ'hɑkə

Ob
BR ɒb
AM ɑb, ɔb

Obadiah
BR ,əʊbə'dʌɪə(r)
AM ,oʊbə'daɪə

obbligati
BR ,ɒblɪ'gɑːti(ː)
AM ,ɑblə'gɑdi

obbligato
BR ,ɒblɪ'gɑːtəʊ, -z
AM ,ɑblə'gɑdoʊ, -z

obconic
BR ɒb'kɒnɪk
AM ɑb'kɑnɪk

obconical
BR ɒb'kɒnɪkl
AM ɑb'kɑnəkəl

obcordate
BR ɒb'kɔːdeɪt
AM ɑb'kɔr,deɪt

obduracy
BR 'ɒbdjʊrəsi,
'ɒbdʒʊrəsi
AM 'ɑbd(j)ərəsi

obdurate
BR 'ɒbdjʊrət,
'ɒbdʒʊrət
AM 'ɑbd(j)ərət

obdurately
BR 'ɒbdjʊrətli,
'ɒbdʒʊrətli
AM 'ɑbd(j)ərətli

obdurateness
BR 'ɒbdjʊrətnəs,
'ɒbdʒʊrətnəs
AM 'ɑbd(j)ərətnəs

OBE
BR 'əʊbiː'iː, -z
AM ,oʊ,bi'i, -z

obeah
BR 'əʊbɪə(r)
AM 'oʊbiə

obeche
BR əʊ'biːtʃ|i, -ɪz
AM oʊ'bitʃi, -z

obedience
BR ə(ʊ)'biːdɪəns
AM ə'bidiəns,
oʊ'bidiəns

obedient
BR ə(ʊ)'biːdɪənt
AM ə'bidiənt,
oʊ'bidiənt

obediently
BR ə(ʊ)'biːdɪəntli
AM ə'bidiən(t)li,
oʊ'bidiən(t)li

obeisance
BR ə(ʊ)'beɪsns,
ə(ʊ)'biːsns, -ɪz
AM oʊ'beɪsəns,
ə'beɪsns, oʊ'bisəns,
ə'bisəns, -ɪz

obeisant
BR ə(ʊ)'beɪsnt,
ə(ʊ)'biːsnt
AM oʊ'beɪsənt,
ə'beɪsənt, oʊ'bisənt,
ə'bisənt

obeisantly
BR ə(ʊ)'beɪsntli,
ə(ʊ)'biːsntli
AM oʊ'beɪsntli,
ə'beɪsn(t)li,
oʊ'bisn(t)li,
ə'bisn(t)li

obeli
BR 'ɒbɪlʌɪ, 'ɒbḷʌɪ
AM 'abə,laɪ

obelise
BR 'ɒbɪlʌɪz, 'ɒbḷʌɪz,
-ɪz, -ɪŋ, -d
AM 'abə,laɪz, -ɪz, -ɪŋ, -d

obelisk
BR 'ɒbɪlɪsk, 'ɒbḷɪsk, -s
AM 'abə,lɪsk, -s

obelize
BR 'ɒbɪlʌɪz, 'ɒbḷʌɪz,
-ɪz, -ɪŋ, -d
AM 'abə,laɪz, -ɪz, -ɪŋ, -d

obelus
BR 'ɒbɪləs, 'ɒbḷəs
AM 'abələs

Oberammergau
BR ,əʊbər'aməgaʊ
AM ,oʊbər'amərgaʊ

Oberland
BR 'əʊbəland
AM 'oʊbər,lænd

Oberon
BR 'əʊbərɒn
AM 'oʊbə,rɑn

Oberösterreich
BR ,əʊbər'ɔːstərʌɪk,
,əʊbər'ɔːstərʌɪx
AM ,oʊbər'ɔstə,raɪk

obese
BR ə(ʊ)'biːs
AM oʊ'bis

obeseness
BR ə(ʊ)'biːsnɪs
AM oʊ'bisnɪs

obesity
BR ə(ʊ)'biːsɪti
AM oʊ'bisɪdi

obey
BR ə(ʊ)'beɪ, -z, -ɪŋ, -d
AM ə'beɪ, oʊ'beɪ, -z, -ɪŋ,
-d

obeyer
BR ə(ʊ)'beɪə(r), -z
AM ə'beɪər, oʊ'beɪər, -z

obfuscate
BR 'ɒbfʌskeɪt,
'ɒbfəskeɪt, -s, -ɪŋ, -ɪd
AM 'abfə,skeɪ|t, -ts,
-dɪŋ, -d

obfuscation
BR ,ɒbfʌ'skeɪʃn,
,ɒbfə'skeɪʃn, -z
AM ,abfə'skeɪʃən, -z

obfuscatory
BR ɒbˈfʌskət(ə)ri,
əbˈfʌskət(ə)ri
AM ɑbˈfəskəˌtɔri

obi
BR ˈəʊb|i, -ız
AM ˈoʊbi, -z

obit
BR ˈɒbɪt, ˈəʊbɪt, -s
AM ˈoʊbət, oʊˈbɪt, -s

obiter
BR ˈɒbɪtə(r), ˈəʊbɪtə(r)
AM ˈoʊbɪdər

obiter dicta
BR ˌɒbɪtə ˈdɪktə(r),
ˌəʊbɪtə +
AM ˈoʊbɪdər ˈdɪktə

obiter dictum
BR ˌɒbɪtə ˈdɪktəm,
ˌəʊbɪtə +
AM ˈoʊbɪdər ˈdɪktəm

obituarial
BR əˌbɪtʃʊˈɛːriəl,
əˌbɪtjʊˈɛːriəl
AM əˈbɪtʃəˌwɛriəl,
oʊˈbɪtʃəˌwɛriəl

obituarist
BR əˈbɪtʃ(ʊ)ərɪst,
əˈbɪtj(ʊ)ərɪst, -s
AM əˈbɪtʃəˌwɛrəst,
oʊˈbɪtʃəˌwɛrəst, -s

obituary
BR əˈbɪtʃʊər|i,
əˈbɪtʃ(ɵ)r|i,
əˈbɪtjʊər|i, əˈbɪtjʊr|i,
-ız
AM əˈbɪtʃəˌwɛri,
oʊˈbɪtʃəˌwɛri, -z

object[1]
noun
BR ˈɒbdʒɪkt, ˈɒbdʒɛkt,
-s
AM ˈɑbdʒək(t), -s

object[2]
verb
BR əbˈdʒɛkt, -s, -ɪŋ, -ɪd
AM əbˈdʒɛk|(t),
əbˈdʒɛk|(t), -(t)s, -tɪŋ,
-təd

objectification
BR əbˌdʒɛktɪfɪˈkeɪʃn,
-z
AM əbˌdʒɛktəfəˈkeɪʃən,
əbˌdʒɛktəfəˈkeɪʃən, -z

objectify
BR əbˈdʒɛktɪfʌɪ, -z, -ɪŋ,
-d
AM əbˈdʒɛktəˌfaɪ,
əbˈdʒɛktəˌfaɪ, -z, -ɪŋ, -d

objection
BR əbˈdʒɛkʃn, -z
AM əbˈdʒɛkʃən,
əbˈdʒɛkʃən, -z

objectionable
BR əbˈdʒɛkʃnəbl,
əbˈdʒɛkʃ(ə)nəbl
AM əbˈdʒɛkʃ(ə)nəbəl,
əbˈdʒɛkʃ(ə)nəbəl

objectionableness
BR əbˈdʒɛkʃnəblnəs,
əbˈdʒɛkʃ(ə)nəblnəs
AM əbˈdʒɛkʃ(ə)nəbəlnəs,
əbˈdʒɛkʃ(ə)nəbəlnəs

objectionably
BR əbˈdʒɛkʃnəbli,
əbˈdʒɛkʃ(ə)nəbli
AM əbˈdʒɛkʃ(ə)nəbli,
əbˈdʒɛkʃ(ə)nəbli

objectival
BR ˌɒbdʒɪkˈtʌɪvl,
ˌɒbdʒɛkˈtʌɪvl
AM ˌɑbdʒəkˈtaɪvəl

objective
BR əbˈdʒɛktɪv, -z
AM əbˈdʒɛktɪv,
əbˈdʒɛktɪv, -z

objectively
BR əbˈdʒɛktɪvli
AM əbˈdʒɛktɪvli,
əbˈdʒɛktɪvli

objectiveness
BR əbˈdʒɛktɪvnɪs
AM əbˈdʒɛktɪvnɪs,
əbˈdʒɛktɪvnɪs

objectivisation
BR əbˌdʒɛktɪvʌɪˈzeɪʃn
AM əbˈdʒɛktəvəˈzeɪʃən,
əbˌdʒɛktəvəˈzeɪʃən,
əbˌdʒɛktəˌvaɪˈzeɪʃən,
əbˌdʒɛktəˌvaɪˈzeɪʃən

objectivise
BR əbˈdʒɛktɪvʌɪz, -ɪz,
-ɪŋ, -d
AM əbˈdʒɛktəˌvaɪz,
əbˈdʒɛktəˌvaɪz, -ɪz,
-ɪŋ, -d

objectivism
BR əbˈdʒɛktɪvɪz(ə)m
AM əbˈdʒɛktəˌvɪzəm,
əbˈdʒɛktəˌvɪzəm

objectivist
BR əbˈdʒɛktɪvɪst, -s
AM əbˈdʒɛktəvəst,
əbˈdʒɛktəvəst, -s

objectivistic
BR əbˌdʒɛktɪˈvɪstɪk
AM əbˌdʒɛktəˈvɪstɪk,
əbˌdʒɛktəˈvɪstɪk

objectivity
BR ˌɒbdʒɛkˈtɪvɪti,
ˌɒbdʒɪkˈtɪvɪti
AM ˌɑbdʒɛkˈtɪvɪdi

objectivization
BR əbˌdʒɛktɪvʌɪˈzeɪʃn
AM əbˌdʒɛktəvəˈzeɪʃən,
əbˌdʒɛktəvəˈzeɪʃən,
əbˌdʒɛktəˌvaɪˈzeɪʃən,
əbˌdʒɛktəˌvaɪˈzeɪʃən

objectivize
BR əbˈdʒɛktɪvʌɪz, -ɪz,
-ɪŋ, -d
AM əbˈdʒɛktəˌvaɪz,
əbˈdʒɛktəˌvaɪz, -ɪz,
-ɪŋ, -d

objectless
BR ˈɒbdʒɪk(t)lɪs,
ˈɒbdʒɛk(t)ləs
AM ˈɑbdʒək(t)ləs

objector
BR əbˈdʒɛktə(r), -z
AM əbˈdʒɛktər,
əbˈdʒɛktər, -z

objet d'art
BR ˌɒbʒeɪ ˈdɑ:(r)
AM ˌɑbˌʒeɪ ˈdɑr

objets d'art
BR ˌɒbʒeɪ ˈdɑ:(r)
AM ˌɑbˌʒeɪ ˈdɑr

objurgate
BR ˈɒbdʒəgeɪt, -s, -ɪŋ,
-ɪd
AM ˈɑbdʒərˌgeɪ|t, -ts,
-dɪŋ, -dɪd

objurgation
BR ˌɒbdʒəˈgeɪʃn
AM ˌɑbdʒərˈgeɪʃən

objurgatory
BR əbˈdʒəːgət(ə)ri
AM əbˈdʒərgəˌtɔri,
əbˈdʒərgəˌtɔri

oblanceolate
BR əbˈlɑːnsɪəleɪt,
əbˈlansɪələt
AM əbˈlænsɪəˌleɪt,
əbˈlænsɪəˌleɪt

oblast
BR ˈɒblast, -s
AM ˈɑblæst, ˈɑblast, -s

oblate[1]
adjective
BR ˈɒbleɪt, ɒˈbleɪt,
ə(ʊ)ˈbleɪt, -s
AM ˈɑbˌleɪt, oʊˈbleɪt, -s

oblate[2]
person
BR ˈɒbleɪt, ɒˈbleɪt,
ə(ʊ)ˈbleɪt, -s
AM ˈɑbˌleɪt, -s

oblation
BR ə(ʊ)ˈbleɪʃn,
ɒˈbleɪʃn, -z
AM əˈbleɪʃən,
oʊˈbleɪʃən, -z

oblational
BR ə(ʊ)ˈbleɪʃn(ə)l,
ə(ʊ)ˈbleɪʃən(ə)l,
ɒˈbleɪʃn(ə)l,
ɒˈbleɪʃən(ə)l
AM əˈbleɪʃ(ə)nəl,
oʊˈbleɪʃ(ə)nəl

oblatory
BR ˈɒblət(ə)ri
AM ˈɑbləˌtɔri

obligate
BR ˈɒblɪgeɪt, -s, -ɪŋ, -ɪd
AM ˈɑbləˌgeɪt, -ts, -dɪŋ,
-dɪd

obligation
BR ˌɒblɪˈgeɪʃn, -z
AM ˌɑbləˈgeɪʃən, -z

obligational
BR ˌɒblɪˈgeɪʃn(ə)l,
ˌɒblɪˈgeɪʃən)l
AM ˌɑbləˈgeɪʃ(ə)nəl

obligator
BR ˈɒblɪgeɪtə(r), -z
AM ˈɑbləˌgeɪdər, -z

obligatorily
BR əˈblɪgət(ə)rɪli
AM əˈblɪgəˌtɔrəli

obligatory
BR əˈblɪgət(ə)ri
AM əˈblɪgəˌtɔri

oblige
BR əˈblʌɪdʒ, -ɪz, -ɪŋ, -d
AM əˈblaɪdʒ, -ɪz, -ɪŋ, -d

obligee
BR ˌɒblɪˈdʒiː, -z
AM ˌɑbləˈdʒi,
ˌɑbˌlaɪˈdʒi, -z

obliger
BR əˈblʌɪdʒə(r), -z
AM əˈblaɪdʒər, -z

obliging
BR əˈblʌɪdʒɪŋ
AM əˈblaɪdʒɪŋ

obligingly
BR əˈblʌɪdʒɪŋli
AM əˈblaɪdʒɪŋli

obligingness
BR əˈblʌɪdʒɪŋnɪs
AM əˈblaɪdʒɪŋnɪs

obligor
BR ˌɒblɪˈgɔː(r), -z
AM ˌɑbləˈgɔ(ə)r, -z

oblique
BR ə(ʊ)ˈbliːk
AM əˈblik, oʊˈblik

obliquely
BR ə(ʊ)ˈbliːkli
AM əˈblikli, oʊˈblikli

obliqueness
BR ə(ʊ)ˈbliːknɪs
AM əˈbliknɪs,
oʊˈbliknɪs

obliquity
BR ə(ʊ)ˈblɪkwɪt|i, -ɪz
AM əˈblɪkwɪdi,
oʊˈblɪkwɪdi, -z

obliterate
BR əˈblɪtəreɪt, -s, -ɪŋ,
-ɪd
AM əˈblɪdəˌreɪt,
oʊˈblɪdəˌreɪt, -ts, -dɪŋ,
-dɪd

obliteration
BR əˌblɪtəˈreɪʃn
AM əˌblɪdəˈreɪʃən,
oʊˌblɪdəˈreɪʃən

obliterative
BR əˈblɪt(ə)rətɪv
AM əˈblɪdəˌreɪdɪv,
oʊˈblɪdəˌreɪdɪv

obliterator
BR əˈblɪtəreɪtə(r), -z
AM əˈblɪdəˌreɪdər,
oʊˈblɪdəˌreɪdər, -z

oblivion
BR əˈblɪvɪən
AM əˈblɪvɪən,
oʊˈblɪvɪən

oblivious
BR əˈblɪvɪəs
AM əˈblɪvɪəs,
oʊˈblɪvɪəs

obliviously
BR əˈblɪvɪəsli
AM əˈblɪvɪəsli,
oʊˈblɪvɪəsli

obliviousness
BR əˈblɪvɪəsnəs
AM əˈblɪvɪəsnəs,
oʊˈblɪvɪəsnəs

oblong
BR ˈɒblɒŋ, -z
AM ˈɑb.lɒŋ, ˈɑb.lɑŋ, -z

obloquy
BR ˈɒbləkwi
AM ˈɑbləkwi

obnoxious
BR əbˈnɒkʃəs,
ɒbˈnɒkʃəs
AM əbˈnɑkʃəs

obnoxiously
BR əbˈnɒkʃəsli
ɒbˈnɒkʃəsli
AM əbˈnɑkʃəsli

obnoxiousness
BR əbˈnɒkʃəsnəs,
ɒbˈnɒkʃəsnəs
AM əbˈnɑkʃəsnəs

oboe
BR ˈəʊbəʊ, -z
AM ˈoʊboʊ, -z

oboe d'amore
BR ˌəʊbəʊ daˈmɔːreɪ
AM ˌoʊboʊ daˈmɔreɪ

oboes d'amore
BR ˌəʊbəʊz daˈmɔːreɪ
AM ˌoʊboʊz daˈmɔreɪ

oboist
BR ˈəʊbəʊɪst, -s
AM ˈoʊboʊwəst,
ˈoʊbəwəst, -s

obol
BR ˈɒb(ɒ)l, -z
AM ˈɔ,bɒl, ˈɑ,bɑl, -z

obovate
BR ɒbˈəʊveɪt
AM ɑbˈoʊ,veɪt

O'Boyle
BR əʊˈbɔɪl
AM oʊˈbɔɪl

O'Brady
BR ə(ʊ)ˈbreɪdi,
ə(ʊ)ˈbrɔːdi
AM oʊˈbreɪdi

O'Brien
BR ə(ʊ)ˈbrʌɪən
AM əˈbraɪən,
oʊˈbraɪən

obscene
BR əbˈsiːn
AM əbˈsin

obscenely
BR əbˈsiːnli
AM əbˈsinli

obsceneness
BR əbˈsiːnnɪs
AM əbˈsi(n)nɪs

obscenity
BR əbˈsenɪt‖i, -ɪz
AM əbˈsenədi,
ɑbˈsenədi, -z

obscurant
BR ˈɒbskjʊərənt, -s
AM ˈɑbskjʊrənt, -s

obscurantism
BR ˌɒbskjʊˈrantɪz(ə)m
AM əbˈskjʊrən,tɪzəm,
ɑbˈskjʊrən,tɪzəm,
ˌɑbskjəˈræn,tɪzəm

obscurantist
BR ˌɒbskjʊˈrantɪst, -s
AM əbˈskjʊrəntəst,
ɑbˈskjʊrəntəst,
ˌɑbskjəˈræntəst, -s

obscuration
BR ˌɒbskjʊˈreɪʃn, -z
AM ˌɑbskjʊˈreɪʃən, -z

obscure
BR əbˈskjʊə(r),
əbˈskjɔː(r), -z, -ɪŋ, -d,
-ə(r), -ɪst
AM əbˈskjʊ(ə)r,
ɑbˈskjʊ(ə)r, -z, -ɪŋ, -d,
-ər, -əst

obscurely
BR əbˈskjʊəli,
əbˈskjɔːli
AM əbˈskjʊrli,
ɑbˈskjʊrli

obscurity
BR əbˈskjʊərɪt‖i,
əbˈskjɔːrɪti, -ɪz
AM əbˈskjʊrədi,
ɑbˈskjʊrədi, -z

obsecrate
BR ˈɒbsɪkreɪt, -s, -ɪŋ, -ɪd
AM ˈɑbsə,kreɪ‖t, -ts,
-dɪŋ, -dɪd

obsecration
BR ˌɒbsɪˈkreɪʃn, -z
AM ˌɑbsəˈkreɪʃən, -z

obsequial
BR əbˈsiːkwɪəl
AM əbˈsikwɪəl

obsequies
BR ˈɒbsɪkwɪz
AM ˈɑbsəkwɪz

obsequious
BR əbˈsiːkwɪəs
AM əbˈsikwɪəs

obsequiously
BR əbˈsiːkwɪəsli
AM əbˈsikwɪəsli

obsequiousness
BR əbˈsiːkwɪəsnəs
AM əbˈsikwɪəsnəs

observable
BR əbˈzəːvəbl
AM əbˈzərvəbəl

observably
BR əbˈzəːvəbli
AM əbˈzərvəbli

observance
BR əbˈzəːvns, -ɪz
AM əbˈzərvəns, -əz

observant
BR əbˈzəːvnt
AM əbˈzərvənt

observantly
BR əbˈzəːvntli
AM əbˈzərvən(t)li

observation
BR ˌɒbzəˈveɪʃn, -z
AM ˌɑbzərˈveɪʃən, -z

observational
BR ˌɒbzəˈveɪʃn̩(ə)l,
ˌɒbzəˈveɪʃənəl
AM ˌɑbzərˈveɪʃ(ə)nəl

observationally
BR ˌɒbzəˈveɪʃnəli,
ˌɒbzəˈveɪʃn̩li,
ˌɒbzəˈveɪʃənli,
ˌɒbzəˈveɪʃ(ə)nəli
AM ˌɑbzərˈveɪʃ(ə)nəli

observatory
BR əbˈzəːvət(ə)r‖i, -ɪz
AM əbˈzərvə,tori, -z

observe
BR əbˈzəːv, -z, -ɪŋ, -d
AM əbˈzərv, -z, -ɪŋ, -d

observer
BR əbˈzəːvə(r), -z
AM əbˈzərvər, -z

obsess
BR əbˈses, -ɪz, -ɪŋ, -t
AM əbˈses, ɑbˈses, -əz,
-ɪŋ, -t

obsession
BR əbˈseʃn, -z
AM əbˈseʃən, ɑbˈseʃən,
-z

obsessional
BR əbˈseʃn̩(ə)l,
əbˈseʃən(ə)l, -z
AM əbˈseʃ(ə)nəl,
ɑbˈseʃ(ə)nəl, -z

obsessionalism
BR əbˈseʃn̩əlɪz(ə)m,
əbˈseʃn̩lɪz(ə)m,
əbˈseʃənlɪz(ə)m,
əbˈseʃ(ə)nəlɪz(ə)m
AM əbˈseʃənl,ɪzəm,
əbˈseʃnə,lɪzəm,
ɑbˈseʃənl,ɪzəm,
ɑbˈseʃnə,lɪzəm

obsessionally
BR əbˈseʃnəli,
əbˈseʃn̩li, əbˈseʃənli,
əbˈseʃ(ə)nəli
AM əbˈseʃ(ə)nəli,
ɑbˈseʃ(ə)nəli

obsessive
BR əbˈsesɪv, -z
AM əbˈsesɪv, ɑbˈsesɪv,
-z

obsessively
BR əbˈsesɪvli

AM əbˈsesɪvli,
ɑbˈsesɪvli

obsessiveness
BR əbˈsesɪvnɪs
AM əbˈsesɪvnɪs,
ɑbˈsesɪvnɪs

obsidian
BR əbˈsɪdɪən
AM əbˈsɪdɪən,
ɑbˈsɪdiən

obsolescence
BR ˌɒbsəˈlesns
AM ˌɑbsəˈlesəns

obsolescent
BR ˌɒbsəˈlesnt
AM ˌɑbsəˈlesənt

obsolete
BR ˈɒbsəliːt, ˌɒbsəˈliːt
AM ˌɑbsəˈlit

obsoletely
BR ˈɒbsəliːtli,
ˌɒbsəˈliːtli
AM ˌɑbsəˈlitli

obsoleteness
BR ˈɒbsəliːtnɪs,
ˌɒbsəˈliːtnɪs
AM ˌɑbsəˈlitnɪs

obsoletism
BR ˈɒbsəliːtɪz(ə)m,
ˌɒbsəˈliːtɪz(ə)m
AM ˌɑbsəˈli,tɪzəm

obstacle
BR ˈɒbstəkl, -z
AM ˈɑbstəkəl,
ˈɑbstəkəl, -z

obstetric
BR əbˈstetrɪk,
ɒbˈstetrɪk, -s
AM əbˈstetrɪk,
ɑbˈstetrɪk, -s

obstetrical
BR əbˈstetrɪkl,
ɒbˈstetrɪkl
AM əbˈstetrəkəl,
ɑbˈstetrəkəl

obstetrically
BR əbˈstetrɪkli,
ɒbˈstetrɪkli
AM əbˈstetrək(ə)li,
ɑbˈstetrək(ə)li

obstetrician
BR ˌɒbstɪˈtrɪʃn,
ˌɒbstəˈtrɪʃn, -z
AM ˌɑbztəˈtrɪʃən,
ˌɑbstəˈtrɪʃən, -z

obstinacy
BR ˈɒbstɪnəsi
AM ˈɑbztənəsi,
ˈɑbstənəsi

obstinate
BR ˈɒbstɪnət
AM ˈɑbztənət,
ˈɑbstənət

obstinately
BR ˈɒbstɪnətli
AM ˈɑbztənətli,
ˈɑbstənətli

obstreperous
BR əb'strɛp(ə)rəs,
ɒb'strɛp(ə)rəs
AM əb'strɛp(ə)rəs,
ab'strɛp(ə)rəs

obstreperously
BR əb'strɛp(ə)rəsli,
ɒb'strɛp(ə)rəsli
AM əb'strɛp(ə)rəsli,
ab'strɛp(ə)rəsli

obstreperousness
BR əb'strɛp(ə)rəsnəs,
ɒb'strɛp(ə)rəsnəs
AM əb'strɛp(ə)rəsnəs,
ab'strɛp(ə)rəsnəs

obstruct
BR əb'strʌkt, -s, -ɪŋ, -ɪd
AM əb'strək|(t),
ab'strək|(t), -(t)s, -tɪŋ,
-təd

obstruction
BR əb'strʌkʃn, -z
AM əb'strəkʃən,
əb'strəkʃən, -z

obstructionism
BR əb'strʌkʃnɪz(ə)m,
əb'strʌkʃənɪz(ə)m
AM əb'strəkʃə,nɪzəm,
ab'strəkʃə,nɪzəm

obstructionist
BR əb'strʌkʃnɪst,
əb'strʌkʃənɪst, -s
AM əb'strəkʃənəst,
əb'strəkʃənəst, -s

obstructive
BR əb'strʌktɪv
AM əb'strəktɪv,
ab'strəktɪv

obstructively
BR əb'strʌktɪvli
AM əb'strəktɪvli,
ab'strəktɪvli

obstructiveness
BR əb'strʌktɪvnɪs
AM əb'strəktɪvnɪs,
ab'strəktɪvnɪs

obstructor
BR əb'strʌktə(r), -z
AM əb'strəktər,
ab'strəktər, -z

obstupefaction
BR əb,stju:pɪ'fakʃn,
əb,stʃu:pɪ'fakʃn
AM əb,st(j)upə'fækʃən,
ab,st(j)upə'fækʃən

obstupefy
BR əb'stju:pɪfʌɪ,
əb'stʃu:pɪfʌɪ, -z, -ɪŋ, -d
AM əb'st(j)upə,fʌɪ,
ab'st(j)upə,fʌɪ, -z, -ɪŋ,
-d

obtain
BR əb'teɪn, -z, -ɪŋ, -d
AM əb'teɪn, ab'teɪn, -z,
-ɪŋ, -d

obtainability
BR əb,teɪnə'bɪlɪti

AM əb'teɪnə'bɪlɪdi,
ab'teɪnə'bɪlɪdi

obtainable
BR əb'teɪnəbl
AM əb'teɪnəbəl,
ab'teɪnəbəl

obtainer
BR əb'teɪnə(r), -z
AM əb'teɪnər,
ab'teɪnər, -z

obtainment
BR əb'teɪnm(ə)nt, -s
AM əb'teɪnmənt,
ab'teɪnmənt, -s

obtention
BR əb'tɛnʃn, -z
AM əb'tɛn(t)ʃən,
ab'tɛn(t)ʃən, -z

obtrude
BR əb'tru:d, ɒb'tru:d,
-z, -ɪŋ, -ɪd
AM əb'trud, ab'trud, -z,
-ɪŋ, -əd

obtruder
BR əb'tru:də(r),
ɒb'tru:də(r), -z
AM əb'trudər,
ab'trudər, -z

obtrusion
BR əb'tru:ʒn,
ɒb'tru:ʒn, -z
AM əb'truʒən,
ab'truʒən, -z

obtrusive
BR əb'tru:sɪv,
ɒb'tru:sɪv
AM əb'trusɪv,
ab'trusɪv

obtrusively
BR əb'tru:sɪvli,
ɒb'tru:sɪvli
AM əb'trusɪvli,
ab'trusɪvli

obtrusiveness
BR əb'tru:sɪvnɪs,
ɒb'tru:sɪvnɪs
AM əb'trusɪvnɪs,
ab'trusɪvnɪs

obtund
BR əb'tʌnd, ɒb'tʌnd, -z,
-ɪŋ, -ɪd
AM əb'tənd, ab'tənd, -z,
-ɪŋ, -əd

obturate
BR 'ɒbtjʊreɪt,
'ɒbtʃʊreɪt, -s, -ɪŋ, -ɪd
AM 'abt(j)ə,reɪ|t, -ts,
-dɪŋ, -dɪd

obturation
BR ,ɒbtjʊ'reɪʃn,
,ɒbtʃʊ'reɪʃn, -z
AM ,abt(j)ə'reɪʃən, -z

obturator
BR 'ɒbtjʊreɪtə(r),
'ɒbtʃʊreɪtə(r), -z
AM 'abt(j)ə,reɪdər, -z

obtuse
BR əb'tju:s, ɒb'tju:s,
əb'tʃu:s, ɒb'tʃu:s
AM əb't(j)us, ab't(j)us

obtusely
BR əb'tju:sli,
ɒb'tju:sli, əb'tʃu:sli,
ɒb'tʃu:sli
AM əb't(j)usli,
ab't(j)usli

obtuseness
BR əb'tju:snəs,
ɒb'tju:snəs,
əb'tʃu:snəs,
ɒb'tʃu:snəs
AM əb't(j)usnəs,
ab't(j)usnəs

obtusity
BR əb'tju:sɪti,
ɒb'tju:sɪti, əb'tʃu:sɪti,
ɒb'tʃu:sɪti
AM əb't(j)usədi,
ab't(j)usədi

obverse¹
adjective
BR 'ɒbvɑ:s
AM əb'vɜrs, ab'vɜrs

obverse²
noun
BR 'ɒbvɑ:s, -ɪz
AM 'ab,vɜrs, -əz

obversely
BR 'ɒbvɑ:sli
AM əb'vɜrsli, ab'vɜrsli

obversion
BR əb'vɑ:ʃn, ɒb'vɑ:ʃn,
-z
AM əb'vɜrʒən,
ab'vɜrʒən, əb'vɜrʃən,
ab'vɜrʃən, -z

obvert
BR əb'vɑ:t, ɒb'vɑ:t, -s,
-ɪŋ, -ɪd
AM əb'vɜrt, ab'vɜr|t,
-ts, -dɪŋ, -dəd

obviate
BR 'ɒbvɪeɪt, -s, -ɪŋ, -ɪd
AM 'abvi,eɪ|t, -ts, -dɪŋ,
-dɪd

obviation
BR ,ɒbvɪ'eɪʃn
AM ,abvi'eɪʃən

obvious
BR 'ɒbvɪəs
AM 'abvɪəs

obviously
BR 'ɒbvɪəsli
AM 'abvɪəsli

obviousness
BR 'ɒbvɪəsnəs
AM 'abvɪəsnəs

O'Byrne
BR ə(ʊ)'bɑ:n
AM oʊ'bɜrn

O'Callaghan
BR ə(ʊ)'kaləhən,
ə(ʊ)'kaləhan
AM oʊ'kæləhæn

ocarina
BR ,ɒkə'ri:nə(r), -z
AM ,akə'rinə, -z

O'Carroll
BR ə(ʊ)'karəl,
ə(ʊ)'karḷ
AM oʊ'kɛrəl

O'Casey
BR ə(ʊ)'keɪsi
AM ə'keɪsi, oʊ'keɪsi

Occam
BR 'ɒkəm, -z
AM 'akəm, -z

occasion
BR ə'keɪʒn, -z
AM ə'keɪʒən, -z

occasional
BR ə'keɪʒn(ə)l,
ə'keɪʒən(ə)l
AM ə'keɪʒ(ə)nəl

occasionalism
BR ə'keɪʒnəlɪz(ə)m,
ə'keɪʒn̩lɪz(ə)m,
ə'keɪʒənlɪz(ə)m,
ə'keɪʒ(ə)nəlɪz(ə)m
AM ə'keɪʒənl,ɪzəm,
ə'keɪʒnə,lɪzəm

occasionalist
BR ə'keɪʒnəlɪst,
ə'keɪʒn̩lɪst,
ə'keɪʒənlɪst,
ə'keɪʒ(ə)nəlɪst, -s
AM ə'keɪʒənl̩əst,
ə'keɪʒnələst, -s

occasionality
BR ə,keɪʒə'nalɪti
AM ə,keɪʒə'nælədi

occasionally
BR ə'keɪʒnəli,
ə'keɪʒn̩li, ə'keɪʒənli,
ə'keɪʒ(ə)nəli
AM ə'keɪʒ(ə)nəli

occident
BR 'ɒksɪd(ə)nt
AM 'aksədnt

occidental
BR ,ɒksɪ'dɛntl, -z
AM ,aksə'dɛn(t)l, -z

occidentalise
BR ,ɒksɪ'dɛntl̩ʌɪz, -ɪz,
-ɪŋ, -d
AM ,aksə'dɛn(t)l̩,ʌɪz,
-ɪz, -ɪŋ, -d

occidentalism
BR ,ɒksɪ'dɛntl̩ɪz(ə)m
AM ,aksə'dɛn(t)l̩,ɪzəm

occidentalist
BR ,ɒksɪ'dɛntl̩ɪst, -s
AM ,aksə'dɛn(t)ləst, -s

occidentalize
BR ,ɒksɪ'dɛntl̩ʌɪz, -ɪz,
-ɪŋ, -d
AM ,aksə'dɛn(t)l̩,ʌɪz,
-ɪz, -ɪŋ, -d

occidentally
BR ,ɒksɪ'dɛntl̩i,
,ɒksɪdɛnt(ə)li
AM ,aksə'dɛn(t)l̩i

occipital
BR ɒk'sɪpɪtl
AM ɑk'sɪpɪdl

occipitally
BR ɒk'sɪpɪtḷi,
ɒk'sɪpɪtəli
AM ɑk'sɪpɪdli

occiput
BR 'ɒksɪpʌt, 'ɒksɪpət,
-s
AM 'ɑksəpət, -s

Occitan
BR 'ɒksɪtn
AM 'ɑksə,tɑn, 'ɑksətn

Occitanian
BR ,ɒksɪ'teɪniən, -z
AM ,ɑksə'teɪniən, -z

occlude
BR ə'klu:d, -z, -ɪŋ, -ɪd
AM ə'klud, -z, -ɪŋ, -əd

occlusion
BR ə'klu:ʒn, -z
AM ə'kluʒən, -z

occlusive
BR ə'klu:sɪv, -z
AM ə'klusɪv, -z

occult
BR 'ɒkʌlt, ə'kʌlt
AM ə'kəlt

occultation
BR ,ɒk(ʌ)l'teɪʃn, -z
AM ,ɑkəl'teɪʃən, -z

occultism
BR 'ɒk(ʌ)ltɪz(ə)m
AM ə'kəl,tɪzəm

occultist
BR 'ɒk(ʌ)ltɪst, -s
AM ə'kəltəst, -s

occultly
BR 'ɒk(ʌ)ltli, ə'kʌltli
AM ə'kəltli

occultness
BR 'ɒk(ʌ)ltnəs,
ə'kʌltnəs
AM ə'kəltnəs

occupancy
BR 'ɒkjʉp(ə)nsi
AM 'ɑkjəpənsi

occupant
BR 'ɒkjʉp(ə)nt, -s
AM 'ɑkjəpənt, -s

occupation
BR ,ɒkjə'peɪʃn, -z
AM ,ɑkjə'peɪʃən, -z

occupational
BR ,ɒkjə'peɪʃṇ(ə)l,
,ɒkjə'peɪʃən(ə)l
AM ,ɑkjə'peɪʃ(ə)nəl

occupationally
BR ,ɒkjʉ'peɪʃṇəli,
,ɒkjʉ'peɪʃṇḷi,
,ɒkjʉ'peɪʃənḷi,
,ɒkjʉ'peɪʃ(ə)nəli
AM ,ɑkjə'peɪʃ(ə)nəli

occupier
BR 'ɒkjʉpʌɪə(r), -z
AM 'ɑkjə,paɪər, -z

occupy
BR 'ɒkjʉpʌɪ, -z, -ɪŋ, -d
AM 'ɑkjə,paɪ, -z, -ɪŋ, -d

occur
BR ə'kɜː(r), -z, -ɪŋ, -d
AM ə'kər, -z, -ɪŋ, -d

occurrence
BR ə'kʌrəns, ə'kʌrns,
-ɪz
AM ə'kərəns, -əz

occurrent
BR ə'kʌrənt, ə'kʌrnt
AM ə'kərənt

ocean
BR 'əʊʃn, -z
AM 'oʊʃən, -z

oceanaria
BR ,əʊʃə'nɛːrɪə(r)
AM ,oʊʃə'nɛriə

oceanarium
BR ,əʊʃə'nɛːrɪəm, -z
AM ,oʊʃə'nɛriəm, -z

oceanfront
BR 'əʊʃnfrʌnt
AM 'oʊʃən,frʌnt

ocean-going
BR ,əʊʃn'gəʊɪŋ
AM 'oʊʃən,goʊɪŋ

Oceania
BR ,əʊsɪ'ɑːnɪə(r),
,əʊʃɪ'ɑːnɪə(r),
,əʊsɪ'eɪnɪə(r),
,əʊʃɪ'eɪnɪə(r)
AM ,oʊʃi'ænɪə

Oceanian
BR ,əʊsɪ'ɑːnɪən,
,əʊʃɪ'ɑːnɪən,
,əʊsɪ'eɪnɪən,
,əʊʃɪ'eɪnɪən, -z
AM ,oʊʃi'æniən, -z

oceanic
BR ,əʊʃɪ'anɪk,
,əʊsɪ'anɪk
AM ,oʊʃi'ænɪk

Oceanid
BR əʊ'si:ənɪd, 'əʊʃṇɪd,
-z
AM oʊ'siənɪd, -z

oceanographer
BR ,əʊʃə'nɒgrəfə(r), -z
AM ,oʊʃə'nɑgrəfər, -z

oceanographic
BR ,əʊʃ(ə)nə'grafɪk,
,əʊʃṇə'grafɪk
AM ,oʊʃənə'græfɪk

oceanographical
BR ,əʊʃ(ə)nə'grafɪkl,
,əʊʃṇə'grafɪkl
AM ,oʊʃənə'græfəkəl

oceanography
BR ,əʊʃə'nɒgrəfi
AM ,oʊʃə'nɑgrəfi

Oceanus
BR əʊ'si:ənəs,
əʊ'ʃi:ənəs
AM oʊ'siənəs

oceanward
BR 'əʊʃnwəd

AM 'oʊʃənwərd

ocellar
BR ə(ʊ)'sɛlə(r),
ɒ'sɛlə(r)
AM oʊ'sɛlər

ocellate
BR 'ɒsɪlət
AM oʊ'sɛ,leɪt, oʊ'sɛlət,
'asələt

ocellated
BR 'ɒsɪleɪtɪd
AM 'asə,leɪdəd

ocelli
BR ə(ʊ)'sɛlʌɪ, ɒ'sɛlʌɪ
AM oʊ'sɛ,laɪ

ocellus
BR ə(ʊ)'sɛləs, ɒ'sɛləs
AM oʊ'sɛləs

ocelot
BR 'ɒsɪlɒt, 'ɒsɪɒt, -s
AM 'asə,lat, 'oʊsə,lat, -s

och
BR ɒx
AM ɑx

oche
BR 'ɒki, -ɪz
AM 'ɑki, -z

ocher
BR 'əʊkə(r)
AM 'oʊkər

Ochil
BR 'əʊxl, 'əʊkl
AM 'oʊkəl

ochlocracy
BR ɒk'lɒkrəsi, -ɪz
AM ɑk'lɑkrəsi, -z

ochlocrat
BR 'ɒkləkrat, -s
AM 'ɑklə,kræt, -s

ochlocratic
BR ,ɒklə'kratɪk
AM ,ɑklə'krædɪk

ochone
BR əʊ'həʊn, ɒ'xəʊn
AM oʊ'hoʊn

ochre
BR 'əʊkə(r)
AM 'oʊkər

ochrea
BR 'ɒkrɪə(r), -z
AM 'ɑkriə, -z

ochreae
BR 'ɒkrii:
AM 'ɑkrii

ochreish
BR 'əʊk(ə)rɪʃ
AM 'oʊk(ə)rɪʃ

ochreous
BR 'əʊkrɪəs,
'əʊk(ə)rəs
AM 'oʊk(ə)rəs

ochrous
BR 'əʊkrəs
AM 'oʊk(ə)rəs

ochry
BR 'əʊkri
AM 'oʊk(ə)ri

ocker
BR 'ɒkə(r), -z
AM 'ɑkər, -z

o'clock
BR ə'klɒk
AM ə'klɑk

O'Connell
BR ə(ʊ)'kɒnl
AM ə'kɑnəl, oʊ'kɑnəl

O'Connor
BR ə(ʊ)'kɒnə(r)
AM ə'kɑnər, oʊ'kɑnər

Ocrecoke
BR 'əʊkrəkəʊk
AM 'oʊkrə,koʊk

octachord
BR 'ɒktəkɔːd, -z
AM 'ɑktə,kɔ(ə)rd, -z

octad
BR 'ɒktad, -z
AM 'ɑk,tæd, -z

octagon
BR 'ɒktəg(ə)n, -z
AM 'ɑktə,gan,
'ɑktəgən, -z

octagonal
BR ɒk'tagṇ(ə)l
AM ɑk'tægənəl

octagonally
BR ɒk'tagṇḷi,
ɒk'tagṇəli
AM ɑk'tægənəli

octahedra
BR ,ɒktə'hi:drə(r)
AM ,ɑktə'hidrə

octahedral
BR ,ɒktə'hi:dr(ə)l
AM ,ɑktə'hidrəl

octahedron
BR ,ɒktə'hi:drən, -z
AM ,ɑktə'hidrən, -z

octal
BR 'ɒktl, -z
AM 'ɑktl, -z

octamerous
BR ɒk'tam(ə)rəs
AM ɑk'tæm(ə)rəs

octameter
BR ɒk'tamɪtə(r), -z
AM ɑk'tæmədər, -z

octane
BR 'ɒkteɪn
AM 'ɑk,teɪn

Octans
BR 'ɒktanz
AM 'ɑktənz

octant
BR 'ɒkt(ə)nt, -s
AM 'ɑktnt, -s

octarchy
BR 'ɒktɑːki, -ɪz
AM 'ɑk,tɑrki, -z

octaroon
BR ,ɒktə'ru:n, -z
AM ,ɑktə'run, -z

octastyle
BR 'ɒktəstʌɪl, -z

AM 'ɑktə‚staɪl, -z

Octateuch
BR 'ɒktətjuːk,
'ɒktətʃuːk
AM 'ɑktə‚t(j)uk

octavalent
BR ‚ɒktə'veɪlənt,
‚ɒktə'veɪlŋt
AM ‚ɑktə'veɪlənt

octave
BR 'ɒktɪv, 'ɒkteɪv, -z
AM 'ɑktəv, 'ɑk‚teɪv, -z

Octavia
BR ɒk'teɪvɪə(r)
AM ɑk'teɪvɪə

Octavian
BR ɒk'teɪvɪən
AM ɑk'teɪvɪən

Octavius
BR ɒk'teɪvɪəs
AM ɑk'teɪvɪəs

8vo
octavo
BR ɒk'tɑːvəʊ
AM ɑk'tɑvoʊ

octavo
BR ɒk'tɑːvəʊ,
ɒk'teɪvəʊ, -z
AM ɑk'tɑvoʊ, -z

octennial
BR ɒk'tenɪəl
AM ɑk'tɛnɪəl

octennially
BR ɒk'tɛnɪəli
AM ɑk'tɛnɪəli

octet
BR ɒk'tɛt, -s
AM ɑk'tɛt, -s

octette
BR ɒk'tɛt, -s
AM ɑk'tɛt, -s

October
BR ɒk'təʊbə(r), -z
AM ɑk'toʊbər, -z

Octobrist
BR ɒk'təʊbrɪst, -s
AM ɑk'toʊbrəst, -s

octocentenary
BR ‚ɒktəʊsɛn'tiːn(ə)r|i,
‚ɒktəʊsɛn'tɛn(ə)r|i,
-ɪz
AM ‚ɑktoʊ‚sɛn'tɛnəri,
-z

octodecimo
BR ‚ɒktəʊ'dɛsɪməʊ, -z
AM ‚ɑktoʊ'dɛsə‚moʊ, -z

octogenarian
BR ‚ɒktədʒɪ'nɛːrɪən, -z
AM ‚ɑktədʒə'nɛrɪən, -z

octonarian
BR ‚ɒktə(ʊ)'nɛːrɪən, -z
AM ‚ɑktə'nɛrɪən, -z

octonarii
BR ‚ɒktə(ʊ)'nɛːrɪʌɪ
AM ‚ɑktə'nɛri‚aɪ

octonarius
BR ‚ɒktə(ʊ)'nɛːrɪəs

AM ‚ɑktə'nɛrɪəs

octonary
BR 'ɒktə(ʊ)n(ə)r|i, -ɪz
AM 'ɑktə‚nɛri, -z

octopod
BR 'ɒktəpɒd, -z
AM 'ɑktə‚pad, -z

octopus
BR 'ɒktəpəs, -ɪz
AM 'ɑktəpəs, -əz

octoroon
BR ‚ɒktə'ruːn, -z
AM ‚ɑktə'run, -z

octosyllabic
BR ‚ɒktəʊsɪ'labɪk
AM ‚ɑktəsə'læbɪk,
‚ɑktoʊsə'læbɪk

octosyllable
BR 'ɒktəʊ‚sɪləbl,
‚ɒktəʊ'sɪləbl, -z
AM ‚ɑktə'sɪləbəl, -z

octroi
BR 'ɒktrwɑː, -z
AM ɑk'trwɑ, 'ɑk'trɔɪ, -z

octuple
BR 'ɒktjʊpl, ɒk'tjuːpl,
-z
AM ɑk't(j)əpəl, -z

octyl
BR 'ɒktʌɪl, 'ɒktɪl
AM 'ɑktl

ocular
BR 'ɒkjʊlə(r)
AM 'ɑkjələr

ocularist
BR 'ɒkjʊlərɪst, -s
AM 'ɑkjələrəst, -s

ocularly
BR 'ɒkjʊləli
AM 'ɑkjələrli

ocular spectra
BR ‚ɒkjʊlə 'spɛktrə(r)
AM ‚ɑkjələr 'spɛktrə

ocular spectrum
BR ‚ɒkjʊlə 'spɛktrəm
AM ‚ɑkjələr 'spɛktrəm

oculate
BR 'ɒkjʊlət
AM 'ɑkjələt, 'ɑkjə‚leɪt

oculist
BR 'ɒkjʊlɪst, -s
AM 'ɑkjələst, -s

oculistic
BR ‚ɒkjʊ'lɪstɪk
AM ‚ɑkjə'lɪstɪk

oculonasal
BR ‚ɒkjʊləʊ'neɪzl
AM ‚ɑkjələ'neɪzəl

OD
BR ‚əʊ'diː, -z, -ɪŋ, -d
AM ‚oʊ'di, -z, -ɪŋ, -d

od
God
BR ɒd
AM ɑd, ɔd

odal
BR 'əʊdl, -z

AM ‚ɑktə'nɛrɪəs

octonary
BR 'ɒkta(ʊ)n(ə)r|i, -ɪz
AM 'ɑktə‚nɛri, -z

odalisk
BR 'əʊdəlɪsk, 'əʊdˌlɪsk,
'ɒdəlɪsk, 'ɒdˌlɪsk, -s
AM 'oʊdlˌɪsk, ‚oʊdl'ɪsk,
-s

odalisque
BR 'əʊdəlɪsk, 'əʊdˌlɪsk,
'ɒdəlɪsk, 'ɒdˌlɪsk, -s
AM 'oʊdlˌɪsk, ‚oʊdl'ɪsk,
-s

odd
BR ɒd, -z, -ə(r), -ɪst
AM ɑd, -z, -ər, -əst

oddball
BR 'ɒdbɔːl, -z
AM 'ɔd‚bɔl, 'ɑd‚bal, -z

Oddfellow
BR 'ɒd‚fɛləʊ, -z
AM 'ɑd‚fɛloʊ, -z

Oddie
BR 'ɒdi
AM 'ɑdi

oddish
BR 'ɒdɪʃ
AM 'ɑdɪʃ

oddity
BR 'ɒdɪt|i, -ɪz
AM 'ɑdədi, -z

oddly
BR 'ɒdli
AM 'ɑdli

oddment
BR 'ɒdm(ə)nt, -s
AM 'ɑdmənt, -s

oddness
BR 'ɒdnəs
AM 'ɑdnəs

odds and ends
BR ‚ɒdz(ə)n(d)'ɛndz
AM ‚ɑdzən'ɛn(d)z

odds-on
BR ‚ɒdz'ɒn
AM ‚ɑdz'ɑn

ode
BR əʊd, -z
AM oʊd, -z

O'Dea
BR ə(ʊ)'deɪ, ə(ʊ)'diː
AM oʊ'deɪ

odea
BR 'əʊdɪə(r)
AM 'oʊdɪə

Odell
BR ə(ʊ)'dɛl, 'əʊdl
AM ə'dɛl, oʊ'dɛl

Odense
BR 'əʊdənsə(r)
AM 'oʊdənsə
DAN 'oːˈðənsə

Odeon
BR 'əʊdɪən, -z
AM 'oʊdi‚ɑn, -z

Oder
BR 'əʊdə(r)
AM 'oʊdər

Odessa
BR ə(ʊ)'dɛsə(r)
AM oʊ'dɛsə
RUS a'dʲesə

Odets
BR 'əʊdɛts
AM oʊ'dɛts

Odette
BR ə(ʊ)'dɛt
AM ɔ'dɛt, oʊ'dɛt

odeum
BR 'əʊdɪəm
AM 'oʊdiəm

Odham
BR 'ɒdəm
AM 'adəm

Odiham
BR 'əʊdɪ(h)əm
AM 'oʊdiəm

Odin
BR 'əʊdɪn
AM 'oʊdən

odious
BR 'əʊdɪəs
AM 'oʊdɪəs

odiously
BR 'əʊdɪəsli
AM 'oʊdɪəsli

odiousness
BR 'əʊdɪəsnəs
AM 'oʊdɪəsnəs

odium
BR 'əʊdɪəm
AM 'oʊdɪəm

Odo
BR 'əʊdəʊ
AM 'oʊdoʊ

O'Doherty
BR ə(ʊ)'dɒxəti,
ə(ʊ)'dɒhəti,
ə(ʊ)'dɒkəti
AM oʊ'dɔrdi

Odom
BR 'əʊdəm
AM 'oʊdəm

odometer
BR ə(ʊ)'dɒmɪtə(r), -z
AM oʊ'damədər, -z

odometry
BR ə(ʊ)'dɒmɪtri
AM oʊ'damətri

Odonata
BR ‚əʊdə'nɑːtə(r)
AM ‚oʊdn̩'adə,
oʊ'danədə

odonate
BR 'əʊdəneɪt, -s
AM 'oʊdn̩‚eɪt, 'oʊdn‚eɪt,
-s

O'Donnell
BR ə(ʊ)'dɒnl
AM ə'danəl, oʊ'danəl

O'Donoghue
BR ə(ʊ)'dɒnəhjuː
AM oʊ'danəhju

O'Donovan
BR əˈ(ʊ)ˈdɒnəv(ə)n,
əˈ(ʊ)ˈdʌnəv(ə)n
AM oʊˈdɑnəvən

odontoglossum
BR ɒˌdɒntəˈglɒsəm,
əʊˌdɒntəˈglɒsəm, -z
AM oʊˌdɑn(t)əˈglɑsəm,
-z

odontoid
BR ɒˈdɒntɔɪd,
əʊˈdɒntɔɪd
AM ouˈdɑnˌtɔɪd

odontological
BR ɒˌdɒntəˈlɒdʒɪkl̩,
əʊˌdɒntəˈlɒdʒɪkl̩
AM oʊˌdɑn(t)əˈlɑdʒəkəl

odontologist
BR ˌɒdɒnˈtɒlədʒɪst,
ˌəʊdɒnˈtɒlədʒɪst, -s
AM oʊdnˈtalədʒəst, -s

odontology
BR ˌɒdɒnˈtɒlədʒi,
ˌəʊdɒnˈtɒlədʒi
AM ˌoʊdnˈtalədʒi

odontorhynchous
BR ɒˌdɒntəˈrɪŋkəs,
əʊˌdɒntəˈrɪŋkəs
AM oʊˌdɑn(t)əˈrɪŋkəs

odor
BR ˈəʊdə(r), -z
AM ˈoʊdər, -z

odoriferous
BR ˌəʊdəˈrɪf(ə)rəs
AM ˌoʊdəˈrɪf(ə)rəs

odoriferously
BR ˌəʊdəˈrɪf(ə)rəsli
AM ˌoʊdəˈrɪf(ə)rəsli

odoriferousness
BR ˌəʊdəˈrɪf(ə)rəsnəs
AM ˌoʊdəˈrɪf(ə)rəsnəs

odorless
BR ˈəʊdələs
AM ˈoʊdərləs

Odo-Ro-No
BR ˌəʊdə(ʊ)ˈrəʊnəʊ
AM ˌoʊdouˈrounou

odorous
BR ˈəʊd(ə)rəs
AM ˈoʊdərəs

odorously
BR ˈəʊd(ə)rəsli
AM ˈoʊdərəsli

odorousness
BR ˈəʊd(ə)rəsnəs
AM ˈoʊdərəsnəs

odour
BR ˈəʊdə(r), -z
AM ˈoʊdər, -z

odourless
BR ˈəʊdələs
AM ˈoʊdərləs

O'Dowd
BR əˈ(ʊ)ˈdaʊd
AM oʊˈdaʊd

O'Driscoll
BR əˈ(ʊ)ˈdrɪskl̩
AM oʊˈdrɪskəl

O'Dwyer
BR əˈ(ʊ)ˈdwʌɪə(r)
AM oʊˈdwaɪər

Odyssean
BR əˈ(ʊ)ˈdɪsɪən,
ɒˈdɪsɪən
AM əˈdisiən

Odysseus
BR əˈ(ʊ)ˈdɪsjuːs,
ɒˈdɪsjuːs, əˈ(ʊ)ˈdɪsɪəs,
ɒˈdɪsɪəs
AM əˈdisiəs

odyssey
BR ˈɒdɪs|i, -ɪz
AM ˈadəsi, -z

oecist
BR ˈiːsɪst, ˈiːkɪst, -s
AM ˈisɪst, -s

oecumenical
BR ˌiːkjʊˈmɛnɪkl̩,
ˌɛkjʊˈmɛnɪkl̩
AM ˌɛkjəˈmɛnəkəl

oecumenicalism
BR ˌiːkjʊˈmɛnɪkəlɪz(ə)m,
ˌiːkjʊˈmɛnɪkl̩ɪz(ə)m,
ˌɛkjʊˈmɛnɪkəlɪz(ə)m,
ˌɛkjʊˈmɛnɪkl̩ɪz(ə)m
AM ˌɛkjəˈmɛnəkəˌlɪzəm

oecumenically
BR ˌiːkjʊˈmɛnɪkli,
ˌɛkjʊˈmɛnɪkli
AM ˌɛkjəˈmɛnək(ə)li

oecumenicity
BR ˌiːˌkjuːməˈnɪsɪti
AM ˌɛkjəməˈnɪsɪdi

oecumenism
BR ɪˈkjuːmənɪz(ə)m
AM ˈɛkjəməˌnɪzəm,
ɛˈkjʊməˌnɪzəm

oedema
BR ɪˈdiːmə(r),
iːˈdiːmə(r), -z
AM əˈdimə, iˈdimə, -z

oedematose
BR ɪˈdiːmətəʊs,
iːˈdiːmətəʊs
AM əˈdimaˌtous,
əˈdiməˌtouz

oedematous
BR ɪˈdiːmətəs,
iːˈdiːmətəs
AM əˈdɛmədəs

Oedipal
BR ˈiːdɪpl̩
AM ˈɛdəpəl, ˈidəpəl

Oedipus
BR ˈiːdɪpəs
AM ˈɛdəpəs, ˈidəpəs

œillade
BR əːˈjɑːd, -z
AM əˈjɑd, eɪˈjad, -z

oenological
BR ˌiːnəˈlɒdʒɪkl̩
AM ˌinəˈladʒəkəl

oenologist
BR iːˈnɒlədʒɪst
AM iˈnalədʒəst

oenology
BR iːˈnɒlədʒi
AM iˈnalədʒi

Oenone
BR ˈiːnəʊn
AM iˈnouni

oenophile
BR ˈiːnəfʌɪl
AM ˈinəˌfaɪl

oenophilist
BR iːˈnɒfɪlɪst
AM iˈnafələst

o'er
BR ˈəʊə(r)
AM ˈoʊ(ə)r

Oerlikon®
BR ˈəːlɪkɒn, ˈəːlɪk(ə)n
AM ˈərləkən, ˈərləˌkan

oersted
BR ˈəːstɪd, ˈəːstɛd, -z
AM ˈərˌstɛd, -z

oesophageal
BR ɪˌsɒfəˈdʒiːəl,
iːˌsɒfəˈdʒiːəl
AM əˈsafəˈdʒiəl

oesophagi
BR ɪˈsɒfəgʌɪ,
iːˈsɒfəgʌɪ, ɪˈsɒfədʒʌɪ,
iːˈsɒfədʒʌɪ
AM əˈsafəˌgaɪ,
əˈsafəˌdʒaɪ

oesophagus
BR ɪˈsɒfəgəs,
iːˈsɒfəgəs, -ɪz
AM əˈsafəgəs, -əz

oestral
BR ˈiːstr(ə)l, ˈɛstr(ə)l
AM ˈɛstrəl

oestrogen
BR ˈiːstrədʒ(ə)n,
ˈɛstrədʒ(ə)n
AM ˈɛstrədʒən

oestrogenic
BR ˌiːstrəˈdʒɛnɪk,
ˌɛstrəˈdʒɛnɪk
AM ˌɛstrəˈdʒɛnɪk

oestrogenically
BR ˌiːstrəˈdʒɛnɪkli,
ˌɛstrəˈdʒɛnɪkli
AM ˌɛstrəˈdʒɛnək(ə)li

oestrous
BR ˈiːstrəs, ˈɛstrəs
AM ˈɛstrəs

oestrum
BR ˈiːstrəm, ˈɛstrəm
AM ˈɛstrəm

oestrus
BR ˈiːstrəs, ˈɛstrəs
AM ˈɛstrəs

oeuvre
BR ˈəːvrə(r)
AM ˈoʊvrə

of¹
strong form
BR ɒv
AM əv

of²
weak form
BR əv, ə
AM əv, ə

O'Faolain
BR əˈ(ʊ)ˈfeɪlən,
əˈ(ʊ)ˈfalən
AM oʊˈfeɪlən

ofay
BR ˈəʊfeɪ, -z
AM ˈoʊˌfeɪ, -z

off
BR ɒf
AM ɔf, af

Offa
BR ˈɒfə(r)
AM ˈɔfə, ˈafə

offal
BR ˈɒfl̩
AM ˈɔfəl, ˈafəl

Offaly
BR ˈɒfl̩i, ˈɒfəli
AM ˈɔfəli, ˈafəli

off and on
BR ˈɒf (ə)n(d) ˈɒn
AM ˈɔf ən ˈɔn, ˈaf ən ˈan

offbeat
noun
BR ˈɒfbiːt, -s
AM ˈɔfˌbit, ˈafˌbit, -s

off-beat
adjective
BR ˈɒfbiːt
AM ˈɔfˌbit, ˈafˈbit

off-cast
BR ˈɒfkɑːst, ˈɒfkast, -s
AM ˈɔfˌkæst, ˈafˌkæst, -s

off-chance
BR ˈɒftʃɑːns, ˈɒftʃans
AM ˈɔfˌtʃæns, ˈafˌtʃæns

offcut
BR ˈɒfkʌt, -s
AM ˈɔfˌkət, ˈafˌkət, -s

Offenbach
BR ˈɒfnbɑːk
AM ˈɔfənˌbak, ˈafənˌbak

offence
BR əˈfɛns, -ɪz
AM əˈfɛns, ˈɔˌfɛns, ˈaˌfɛns, -əz

offenceless
BR əˈfɛnsləs
AM əˈfɛnsləs, ˈɔˌfɛnsləs, ˈaˌfɛnsləs

offend
BR əˈfɛnd, -z, -ɪd
AM əˈfɛnd, -z, -ɪŋ, -əd

offendedly
BR əˈfɛndɪdli
AM əˈfɛndədli

offender
BR əˈfɛndə(r), -z
AM əˈfɛndər, -z

offense
BR əˈfɛns, -ɪz

AM ə'fɛns, 'ɔ,fɛns,
'ɑ,fɛns, -əz

offenseless
BR ə'fɛnsləs
AM ə'fɛnsləs,
'ɔ,fɛnsləs, 'ɑ,fɛnsləs

offensive
BR ə'fɛnsɪv
AM ə'fɛnsɪv, 'ɔ,fɛnsɪv,
'ɑ,fɛnsɪv

offensively
BR ə'fɛnsɪvli
AM ə'fɛnsɪvli,
'ɔ,fɛnsɪvli, 'ɑ,fɛnsɪvli

offensiveness
BR ə'fɛnsɪvnɪs
AM ə'fɛnsɪvnɪs,
'ɔ,fɛnsɪvnɪs,
'ɑ,fɛnsɪvnɪs

offer
BR 'ɒf|ə(r), -əz, -(ə)rɪŋ,
-əd
AM 'ɒf|ər, 'ɑf|ər, -ərz,
-(ə)rɪŋ, -ərd

offerer
BR 'ɒf(ə)rə(r), -z
AM 'ɒf(ə)rər, 'ɑf(ə)rər,
-z

offering
BR 'ɒf(ə)rɪŋ, -z
AM 'ɒf(ə)rɪŋ, 'ɑf(ə)rɪŋ,
-z

offeror
BR 'ɒf(ə)rə(r), -z
AM 'ɒf(ə)rər, 'ɑf(ə)rər,
-z

offertory
BR 'ɒfət(ə)r|i, -ɪz
AM 'ɔfər,tɔri,
'ɑfər,tɔri, -z

offhand
BR ,ɒf'hænd
AM 'ɔf,hænd, 'ɑf,hænd

offhanded
BR ,ɒf'hændɪd
AM 'ɔf,hæn(d)əd,
'ɑf,hæn(d)əd

offhandedly
BR ,ɒf'hændɪdli
AM 'ɔf,hæn(d)ədli,
'ɑf,hæn(d)ədli

offhandedness
BR ,ɒf'hændɪdnɪs
AM 'ɔf,hæn(d)ədnəs,
'ɑf,hændə(d)nəs

office
BR 'ɒf|ɪs, -ɪsɪz
AM 'ɔfəs, 'ɑfəs, -əz

officeholder
BR 'ɒfɪs,həʊldə(r), -z
AM 'ɔfəs,(h)oʊldər,
'ɑfəs,(h)oʊldər, -z

officer
BR 'ɒfɪsə(r), -z
AM 'ɔfəsər, 'ɑfəsər, -z

official
BR ə'fɪʃ|l, -z
AM ə'fɪʃəl, oʊ'fɪʃəl, -z

officialdom
BR ə'fɪʃldəm
AM ə'fɪʃəldəm,
oʊ'fɪʃəldəm

officialese
BR ə,fɪʃə'li:z, ə,fɪʃl'i:z
AM ə,fɪʃə'liz, oʊ'fɪʃə'liz

officialism
BR ə'fɪʃlɪz(ə)m
AM ə'fɪʃə,lɪzəm,
oʊ'fɪʃə,lɪzəm

officially
BR ə'fɪʃli, ə'fɪʃəli
AM ə'fɪʃəli, oʊ'fɪʃəli

officiant
BR ə'fɪʃ|ənt, -s
AM ə'fɪʃ|ənt,
oʊ'fɪʃ|ənt, -s

officiate
BR ə'fɪʃi,eɪt, -s, -ɪŋ, -ɪd-
AM ə'fɪʃi,eɪt,
oʊ'fɪʃi,eɪ|t, -ts, -dɪŋ,
-dɪd

officiation
BR ə,fɪʃi'eɪʃn
AM ə,fɪʃi'eɪʃn,
oʊ,fɪʃi'eɪʃn

officiator
BR ə'fɪʃi,eɪtə(r), -z
AM ə'fɪʃi,eɪdər,
oʊ'fɪʃi,eɪdər, -z

officinal
BR ,ɒfɪ'si:nl, ə'fɪsɪnl
AM ə'fɪsənəl

officinally
BR ,ɒfɪ'si:nl,i,
,ɒfɪ'si:nəli, ə'fɪsɪnl,i,
ə'fɪsnəli
AM ə'fɪsənəli

officious
BR ə'fɪʃəs
AM ə'fɪʃəs

officiously
BR ə'fɪʃəsli
AM ə'fɪʃəsli

officiousness
BR ə'fɪʃəsnəs
AM ə'fɪʃəsnəs

offing
BR 'ɒfɪŋ
AM 'ɔfɪŋ, 'ɑfɪŋ

offish
BR 'ɒfɪʃ
AM 'ɔfɪʃ, 'ɑfɪʃ

offishly
BR 'ɒfɪʃli
AM 'ɔfɪʃli, 'ɑfɪʃli

offishness
BR 'ɒfɪʃnɪs
AM 'ɔfɪʃnɪs, 'ɑfɪʃnɪs

offload
BR ,ɒf'ləʊd, -z, -ɪŋ, -ɪd-
AM 'ɔf,loʊd, 'ɑf,loʊd, -z,
-ɪŋ, -əd

offprint
BR 'ɒfprɪnt, -s
AM 'ɔf,prɪnt, 'ɑf,prɪnt,
-s

off-putting
BR ,ɒf'pʊtɪŋ, ɒf'pʊtɪŋ
AM 'ɔf,pʊdɪŋ, 'ɑf,pʊdɪŋ

off-puttingly
BR ,ɒf'pʊtɪŋli,
,ɒf'pʊtɪŋli
AM 'ɔf,pʊdɪŋli,
'ɑf,pʊdɪŋli

offset¹
noun
BR 'ɒfsɛt, -s
AM 'ɔf,sɛt, 'ɑf,sɛt, -s

offset²
verb
BR 'ɒfsɛt, ,ɒf'sɛt, -s, -ɪŋ
AM ,ɔf'sɛ|t, ,ɑf'sɛ|t, -ts,
-dɪŋ

offshoot
BR 'ɒfʃu:t, -s
AM 'ɔf,ʃut, 'ɑf,ʃut, -s

offshore
BR ,ɒf'ʃɔ:(r)
AM ,ɔf,ʃɔ(ə)r, ,ɑf,ʃɔ(ə)r

offside
BR ,ɒf'sʌɪd, -z
AM 'ɔf,saɪd, 'ɑf,saɪd, -z

offsider
BR ,ɒ'fsʌɪdə(r), -z
AM 'ɔf,saɪdər,
'ɑf,saɪdər, -z

offspring
BR 'ɒfsprɪŋ, -z
AM 'ɔf,sprɪŋ, 'ɑf,sprɪŋ,
-z

offstage
BR ,ɒf'steɪdʒ
AM 'ɔf,steɪdʒ, 'ɑf,steɪdʒ

off stage
adverbial
BR ,ɒf'steɪdʒ
AM ,ɔf'steɪdʒ, ,ɑf +

Ofgas
BR 'ɒfgas
AM 'ɔf,gæs, 'ɑf,gæs

O'Flaherty
BR ə(ʊ)'flɑ:(h)əti
AM oʊ'flɛrdi

O'Flynn
BR ə(ʊ)'flɪn
AM oʊ'flɪn

oft
BR ɒft
AM ɔft, ɑft

Oftel
BR 'ɒftɛl
AM 'ɔf,tɛl, 'ɑf,tɛl

often
BR 'ɒf(t)ŋ, 'ɒftən, -ə-(r),
-ɪst
AM 'ɔf(t)ən, 'ɑf(t)ən,
-ər, -əst

oftentimes
BR 'ɒfntʌɪmz,
'ɒft(ə)ntʌɪmz
AM 'ɔf(t)ən,taɪmz,
'ɑf(t)ən,taɪmz

Ofwat
BR 'ɒfwɒt

AM 'ɔf,wɒt, 'ɑf,wɑt

Ogaden
BR ,ɒgə'dɛn
AM ,ɔgə'dɛn, ,ɑgə'dɛn

ogam
BR 'ɒgəm, -z
AM 'ɑgəm, -z

Ogden
BR 'ɒgdən
AM 'ɑgdən

ogdoad
BR 'ɒgdəʊad, -z
AM 'ɑgdə,wad, -z

Ogdon
BR 'ɒgdən
AM 'ɑgdən

ogee
BR 'əʊdʒi:, -z, -d
AM 'oʊdʒi, -z, -d

ogham
BR 'ɒgəm, -z
AM 'ɑgəm, -z

Ogilvie
BR 'əʊglvi
AM 'oʊgəlvi

Ogilvy
BR 'əʊglvi
AM 'oʊgəlvi

ogival
BR 'əʊdʒ,ʌɪvl
əʊ'dʒʌɪvl
AM oʊ'dʒaɪvəl

ogive
BR 'əʊdʒʌɪv, əʊ'dʒʌɪv,
-z
AM oʊ'dʒaɪv, -z

ogle
BR 'əʊg|l, -lz, -lɪŋ\-lɪŋ,
-ld
AM 'oʊg|əl, 'ɑg|əl, -əlz,
-(ə)lɪŋ, -əld

ogler
BR 'əʊglə(r), 'əʊg|ə(r),
-z
AM 'oʊg(ə)lər,
'ɑg(ə)lər, -z

Oglethorpe
BR 'əʊglθɔ:p
AM 'oʊgəl,θɔ(ə)rp

Ogmore
BR 'ɒgmɔ:(r)
AM 'ɑg,mɔ(ə)r

O'Gorman
BR ə(ʊ)'gɔ:mən
AM oʊ'gɔrmən

OGPU
BR ,əʊdʒi:pi:'ju:,
'ɒgpu:
AM ,oʊ,dʒi,pi'ju, 'ɑg,pu

O'Grady
BR ə(ʊ)'greɪdi
AM oʊ'greɪdi

ogre
BR 'əʊgə(r), -z
AM 'oʊgər, -z

ogreish
BR 'əʊg(ə)rɪʃ

ogreishly
AM 'oʊg(ə)rɪʃ
BR 'əʊg(ə)rɪʃli
AM 'oʊg(ə)rɪʃli

ogress
BR 'əʊgrɪs, 'əʊgres, -ɪz
AM 'oʊgrəs, -əz

ogrish
BR 'əʊg(ə)rɪʃ
AM 'oʊg(ə)rɪʃ

Ogwen
BR 'ɒgwɛn, 'ɒgwən
AM 'ɑgwən
WE 'ɒgwen

Ogygian
BR əʊ'dʒɪdʒɪən
AM oʊ'dʒɪdʒɪən

oh
BR əʊ
AM oʊ

O'Hagan
BR ə(ʊ)'heɪg(ə)n
AM oʊ'heɪgən

O'Halloran
BR ə(ʊ)'halərən,
ə(ʊ)'halərn̩
AM oʊ'hælərən

O'Hanlon
BR ə(ʊ)'hanlən
AM oʊ'hænlən

O'Hara
BR ə(ʊ)'hɑːrə(r)
AM oʊ'hɛrə

O'Hare
BR ə(ʊ)'hɛː(r)
AM oʊ'hɛ(ə)r

O'Higgins
BR ə(ʊ)'hɪgɪnz
AM oʊ'hɪgɪnz

Ohio
BR ə(ʊ)'hʌɪəʊ
AM oʊ'haɪoʊ

Ohioan
BR ə(ʊ)'hʌɪəʊən, -z
AM oʊ'haɪoʊən, -z

ohm
BR əʊm, -z
AM oʊm, -z

ohmage
BR 'əʊmɪdʒ
AM 'oʊmɪdʒ

ohmic
BR 'əʊmɪk
AM 'oʊmɪk

ohmmeter
BR 'əʊm‚miːtə(r), -z
AM 'oʊ(m)‚midər, -z

oho
BR ə(ʊ)'həʊ
AM oʊ'hoʊ

OHP
BR ‚əʊeɪtʃ'piː, -z
AM ‚oʊ‚eɪtʃ'pi, -z

oi
BR ɔɪ
AM ɔɪ

oick
BR ɔɪk, -s
AM ɔɪk, -s

oidia
BR əʊ'ɪdɪə(r)
AM oʊ'ɪdɪə

oidium
BR əʊ'ɪdɪəm
AM oʊ'ɪdɪəm

oik
BR ɔɪk, -s
AM ɔɪk, -s

oil
BR ɔɪl, -z, -ɪŋ, -d
AM ɔɪl, -z, -ɪŋ, -d

oilcake
BR 'ɔɪlkeɪk
AM 'ɔɪl‚keɪk

oilcan
BR 'ɔɪlkan, -z
AM 'ɔɪl‚kæn, -z

oilcloth
BR 'ɔɪlklɒθ
AM 'ɔɪl‚klɒθ, 'ɔɪl‚klɑθ

oiler
BR 'ɔɪlə(r), -z
AM 'ɔɪlər, -z

oilfield
BR 'ɔɪlfiːld, -z
AM 'ɔɪl‚fild, -z

oilily
BR 'ɔɪlɪli
AM 'ɔɪlɪli

oiliness
BR 'ɔɪlɪnɪs
AM 'ɔɪlɪnɪs

oilless
BR 'ɔɪlɪs
AM 'ɔɪ(l)lɪs

oilman
BR 'ɔɪlman
AM 'ɔɪl‚mæn, 'ɔɪlmən

oilmen
BR 'ɔɪlmen
AM 'ɔɪl‚men, 'ɔɪlmən

oilrig
BR 'ɔɪlrɪg, -z
AM 'ɔɪl‚rɪg, -z

oilseed
BR 'ɔɪlsiːd, -z
AM 'ɔɪl‚sid, -z

oilskin
BR 'ɔɪlskɪn, -z
AM 'ɔɪl‚skɪn, -z

oilstone
BR 'ɔɪlstəʊn, -z
AM 'ɔɪl‚stoʊn, -z

oily
BR 'ɔɪl|i, -ɪə(r), -ɪɪst
AM 'ɔɪli, -ər, -ɪɪst

oink
BR ɔɪŋ|k, -ks, -kɪŋ, -(k)t
AM ɔɪŋ|k, -ks, -kɪŋ, -(k)t

ointment
BR 'ɔɪntm(ə)nt, -s
AM 'ɔɪntmənt, -s

Oireachtas
BR 'ɛrəktəs, 'ɛrəxtəs
AM 'ɛrəkθəs
IR 'orʲəxtəs

Oistrakh
BR 'ɔɪstrɑːk, 'ɔɪstrɑːx
AM 'ɔɪstrɑk

Ojibwa
BR ə(ʊ)'dʒɪbwə(r), -z
AM ə'dʒɪbwə, -z

Ojibway
BR ə(ʊ)'dʒɪbweɪ, -z
AM oʊ'dʒɪbweɪ, -z

OK
BR (‚)əʊ'keɪ, -z, -ɪŋ, -d
AM 'oʊ'keɪ, -z, -ɪŋ, -d

okapi
BR ə(ʊ)'kɑːp|i, -ɪz
AM oʊ'kɑpi, -z

Okavango
BR ‚ɒkə'vaŋgəʊ
AM ‚oʊkə'vaŋgoʊ

okay
BR (‚)əʊ'keɪ, -z, -ɪŋ, -d
AM 'oʊ'keɪ, -z, -ɪŋ, -d

O'Keefe
BR ə(ʊ)'kiːf
AM oʊ'kif

O'Keeffe
BR ə(ʊ)'kiːf
AM oʊ'kif

Okefenokee
BR ‚əʊkɪfɪ'nəʊki
AM ‚oʊkɪfə'noʊki

Okehampton
BR ‚əʊk'ham(p)t(ə)n
AM ‚oʊk'hæm(p)tən

O'Kelly
BR ə(ʊ)'kɛli
AM oʊ'kɛli

okey-doke
BR ‚əʊkɪ'dəʊk
AM ‚oʊki'doʊk

okey-dokey
BR ‚əʊkɪ'dəʊki
AM ‚oʊki'doʊki

Okhotsk
BR əʊ'kɒtsk, 'əʊkɒtsk
AM ‚ɑ‚kɑtsk

Okie
BR 'əʊk|i, -ɪz
AM 'oʊki, -z

Okinawa
BR ‚ɒkɪ'nɑːwə(r),
‚əʊkɪ'nɑːwə(r)
AM ‚oʊkə'nɑwə

Oklahoma
BR ‚əʊklə'həʊmə(r)
AM ‚oʊklə'hoʊmə

Oklahoman
BR ‚əʊklə'həʊmən, -z
AM ‚oʊklə'hoʊmən, -z

okra
BR 'əʊkrə(r), 'ɒkrə(r)
AM 'oʊkrə

okta
BR 'ɒktə(r), -z

Olaf
BR 'əʊlaf, 'əʊlæf
AM 'oʊ‚laf

Öland
BR 'əː‚land
AM 'ə‚land
SW 'øːlʌnd

Olav
BR 'əʊlav, 'əʊləv
AM 'oʊləv

Olave
BR 'əʊləv, 'əʊleɪv
AM 'oʊlav, 'oʊleɪv

Olbers
BR 'ɒlbəz
AM 'ɔlbərz, 'ɑlbərz

old
BR əʊld, -ə(r), -ɪst
AM oʊld, -ər, -əst

Oldbury
BR 'əʊl(d)b(ə)ri
AM 'oʊl(d)‚beri

Oldcastle
BR 'əʊl(d)‚kɑːsl,
'əʊl(d)‚kasl
AM 'oʊl(d)‚kæsəl

Old Dominion
BR ‚əʊl(d) də'mɪnjən
AM ‚oʊl(d) də'mɪnjən

olden
BR 'əʊld(ə)n
AM 'oʊldən

Oldenburg
BR 'əʊld(ə)nbəːg
AM 'oʊldən‚bərg

olde worlde
BR ‚əʊldɪ 'wəːldi
AM ‚oʊl(d) 'wərld(i)

old-fashioned
BR ‚əʊl(d)'faʃnd
AM ‚oʊl(d)'fæʃənd

Oldfield
BR 'əʊl(d)fiːld
AM 'oʊl(d)‚fild

Oldham
BR 'əʊldəm
AM 'oʊld‚hæm,
'oʊldəm

oldie
BR 'əʊld|i, -ɪz
AM 'oʊldi, -z

oldish
BR 'əʊldɪʃ
AM 'oʊldɪʃ

old-maidish
BR ‚əʊl(d)'meɪdɪʃ
AM ‚oʊl(d)'meɪdɪʃ

oldness
BR 'əʊldnəs
AM 'oʊl(d)nəs

Old Sarum
BR ‚əʊl(d) 'sɛːrəm
AM ‚oʊl(d) 'sɛrəm

Oldsmobile
BR 'əʊl(d)zməbiːl, -z
AM 'oʊl(d)zmə‚bil, -z

old-stager
BR ˌəʊl(d)ˈsteɪdʒə(r),
-z
AM ˌoʊl(d)ˈsteɪdʒər, -z

oldster
BR ˈəʊldstə(r), -z
AM ˈoʊl(d)stər, -z

old-timer
BR ˌəʊl(d)ˈtaɪmə(r), -z
AM ˌoʊl(d)ˈtaɪmər, -z

Olduvai Gorge
BR ˌɒldʊvaɪ ˈgɔːdʒ
AM ˌɔːldəˌvaɪ ˈgɔː(ə)rdʒ,
ˌoʊldəˌvaɪ ˈgɔː(ə)rdʒ

Old Vic
BR ˌəʊl(d) ˈvɪk
AM ˌoʊl(d) vɪk

olé
BR əʊˈleɪ
AM oʊˈleɪ

olea
BR ˈəʊliə(r)
AM ˈoʊliə

oleaceous
BR ˌəʊlɪˈeɪʃəs
AM ˌoʊliˈeɪʃəs

oleaginous
BR ˌəʊlɪˈædʒɪnəs
AM ˌoʊliˈædʒənəs

oleander
BR ˌəʊlɪˈandə(r), -z
AM ˌoʊliˈændər, -z

O'Leary
BR ə(ʊ)ˈlɪəri
AM oʊˈlɪri

oleaster
BR ˌəʊlɪˈastə(r), -z
AM ˌoʊliˌæstər, -z

oleate
BR ˈəʊlieɪt, -s
AM ˈoʊliˌeɪt, -s

olecranon
BR əʊˈlɛkrənɒn,
ˌəʊlɪˈkreɪnɒn, -z
AM oʊˈlɛkrəˌnɑn,
ˌoʊləˈkreɪˌnɑn, -z

olefin
BR ˈəʊlɪfɪn, -z
AM ˈoʊləfən, -z

olefine
BR ˈəʊlɪfiːn, ˈəʊlɪfɪn, -z
AM ˈoʊləfən, -z

Oleg
BR ˈəʊlɛg
AM ˈoʊlɛg

oleiferous
BR ˌəʊlɪˈɪf(ə)rəs
AM ˌoʊliˈɪf(ə)rəs

oleo
BR ˈəʊliəʊ
AM ˈoʊlioʊ

oleograph
BR ˈəʊliəgrɑːf,
ˈəʊliəgraf, -s
AM ˈoʊlioʊˌgræf, -s

oleomargarine
BR ˌəʊliəʊˌmɑːˈdʒəˈriːn,
ˌəʊliəʊˌmɑːgəˈriːn
AM ˌoʊlioʊˈmɑrdʒ(ə)rən

oleometer
BR ˌəʊlɪˈɒmɪtə(r), -z
AM ˌoʊliˈɑmədər, -z

oleo-resin
BR ˌəʊliəʊˈrɛzɪn, -z
AM ˌoʊlioʊˈrɛzən, -z

oleum
BR ˈəʊliəm
AM ˈoʊliəm

olfaction
BR ɒlˈfakʃn
AM ɑlˈfækʃən,
oʊlˈfækʃən

olfactive
BR ɒlˈfaktɪv
AM ɑlˈfæktɪv,
oʊlˈfæktɪv

olfactometer
BR ˌɒlfakˈtɒmɪtə(r), -z
AM ˌɑlfækˈtamədər, -z

olfactory
BR ɒlˈfakt(ə)ri
AM ɑlˈfækt(ə)ri,
oʊlˈfækt(ə)ri

Olga
BR ˈɒlgə(r)
AM ˈoʊlgə

olibanum
BR ɒˈlɪbənəm
AM oʊˈlɪbənəm

Olifant
BR ˈɒlɪf(ə)nt
AM ˈɑləfənt

oligarch
BR ˈɒlɪgɑːk, -s
AM ˈɑləˌgɑrk,
ˈoʊləˌgɑrk, -s

oligarchic
BR ˌɒlɪˈgɑːkɪk
AM ˌɑləˈgɑrkɪk,
ˌoʊləˈgɑrkɪk

oligarchical
BR ˌɒlɪˈgɑːkɪkl
AM ˌɑləˈgɑrkəkəl,
ˌoʊləˈgɑrkəkəl

oligarchically
BR ˌɒlɪˈgɑːkɪkli
AM ˌɑləˈgɑrkək(ə)li,
ˌoʊləˈgɑrkək(ə)li

oligarchy
BR ˈɒlɪgɑːkˌli, -ɪz
AM ˈɑləˌgɑrki,
ˈoʊləˌgɑrki, -z

oligocarpous
BR ˌɒlɪgə(ʊ)ˈkɑːpəs
AM ˌɑləgoʊˈkɑrpəs

Oligocene
BR ˈɒlɪgə(ʊ)siːn,
ɒˈlɪgə(ʊ)siːn
AM ˈɑləgoʊˌsin,
əˈlɪgəˌsin

oligoclase
BR ˈɒlɪgə(ʊ)kleɪz
AM ˈɑləgoʊˌkleɪs

oligodendrocyte
BR ˌɒlɪgəʊˈdɛndrəsʌɪt,
-s
AM ˌɑləgoʊˈdɛndrəˌsaɪt,
-s

oligodendroglia
BR ˌɒlɪgə(ʊ)ˌdɛndrə-
ˈglʌɪə(r)
AM ˌɑləgoʊˌdɛndrəˈgliə

oligomer
BR ˈɒlɪˈgəʊmə(r),
əˈlɪgəmə(r),
ɒˈlɪgəmə(r),
ˈɒlɪgəmə(r), -z
AM ˈɑləgəˌmɛ(ə)r,
əˈlɪgəˌmɛ(ə)r, -z

oligomerise
BR əˈlɪgəmərˌʌɪz, -ɪz,
-ɪŋ, -d
AM əˈlɪgəməˌraɪz, -ɪz,
-ɪŋ, -d

oligomerize
BR əˈlɪgəmərˌʌɪz, -ɪz,
-ɪŋ, -d
AM əˈlɪgəməˌraɪz, -ɪz,
-ɪŋ, -d

oligomerous
BR ˌɒlɪˈgɒm(ə)rəs
AM ˌɑləˈgɑm(ə)rəs

oligonucleotide
BR ˌɒlɪgə(ʊ)ˈnjuːklɪə-
tʌɪd
AM ˌɑləgoʊˈn(j)ukliə-
ˌtaɪd

oligopeptide
BR ˌɒlɪgə(ʊ)ˈpɛptʌɪd
AM ˌɑləgoʊˈpɛpˌtaɪd

oligopolist
BR ɒˈlɪgɒpəlɪst, -s
AM ˌɑləˈgɑpələst, -s

oligopolistic
BR ˌɒlɪgɒpəˈlɪstɪk
AM ˌɑləgəpəˈlɪstɪk

oligopoly
BR ˈɒlɪˈgɒpəlˌli,
ˌɒlɪˈgɒpl̩ˌli, -ɪz
AM ˌɑləˈgɑpəli, -z

oligopsony
BR ˈɒlɪˈgɒpsənˌli,
ˌɒlɪˈgɒpsn̩ˌli, -ɪz
AM ˌɑləˈgɑpsəni, -z

oligosaccharide
BR ˌɒlɪgə(ʊ)ˈsakərˌʌɪd,
-z
AM ˌɑləgəˈsækəˌraɪd,
-z

oligotrophic
BR ˌɒlɪgəˈtrɒfɪk,
ˌɒlɪgəˈtrəʊfɪk
AM ˌɑləgəˈtrɑfɪk

oligotrophy
BR ˌɒlɪˈgɒtrəfi
AM ˌɑləˈgɑtrəfi

olingo
BR ɒˈlɪŋgəʊ, -z
AM əˈlɪŋgoʊ, -z

olio
BR ˈəʊliəʊ, -z

oligodendrocyte
AM ˈoʊlioʊ, -z

Oliphant
BR ˈɒlɪf(ə)nt
AM ˈɑləfənt

olivaceous
BR ˌɒlɪˈveɪʃəs
AM ˌɑləˈveɪʃəs

olivary
BR ˈɒlɪv(ə)ri
AM ˈɑləˌvɛri

olive
BR ˈɒlɪv, -z
AM ˈɑləv, -z

Oliver
BR ˈɒlɪvə(r)
AM ˈɑləvər

Olivet
BR ˈɒlɪvɛt, ˈɒlɪvɪt
AM ˌɑləˈvɛt

Olivetti®
BR ˌɒlɪˈvɛti
AM ˌɑləˈvɛdi

Olivia
BR əˈlɪvɪə(r), ɒˈlɪvɪə(r)
AM əˈlɪvɪə

Olivier
BR əˈlɪvɪeɪ, ɒˈlɪvɪeɪ,
əˈlɪvɪə(r), ɒˈlɪvɪə(r)
AM əˈlɪvɪeɪ, oʊˈlɪvɪeɪ

olivine
BR ˈɒlɪviːn, ˌɒlɪˈviːn, -z
AM ˈɑləˌvin, -z

olla podrida
BR ˌɒlə pəˈdriːdə(r), -z
AM ˌɑlə pəˈdridə,
ˌɔ(l)jə +, -z

Ollerenshaw
BR ˈɒl(ə)rənʃɔː(r),
ˈɒl(ə)rn̩ʃɔː(r)
AM ˈɑlərənˌʃɔ

Ollerton
BR ˈɒlət(ə)n
AM ˈɑlərtən

Ollie
BR ˈɒli
AM ˈɑli

olm
BR ɒlm, əʊlm, -z
AM ɑlm, oʊlm, -z

Olmec
BR ˈɒlmɛk
AM ˈɑlˌmɛk

Olmsted
BR ˈɒmstɛd
AM ˈoʊmˌstɛd

ology
BR ˈɒlədʒˌli, -ɪz
AM ˈɑlədʒi, -z

oloroso
BR ˌɒləˈrəʊsəʊ, -z
AM ˌoʊləˈroʊˌsoʊ, -z

O'Loughlin
BR ə(ʊ)ˈlɒxlɪn,
ə(ʊ)ˈlɒklɪn
AM oʊˈlɒflən, oʊˈlɑflən

Olsen
BR ˈɒls(ə)n

AM 'oʊlsən

Olson
BR 'ɒls(ə)n
AM 'oʊlsən

Olwen
BR 'ɒlwɪn
AM 'ɑlwən

Olympia
BR ə'lɪmpɪə(r)
AM ə'lɪmpiə

Olympiad
BR ə'lɪmpɪəd,
ə'lɪmpɪad, -z
AM oʊ'lɪmpi,æd,
ə'lɪmpiəd, -z

Olympian
BR ə'lɪmpɪən, -z
AM ə'lɪmpiən,
oʊ'lɪmpiən, -z

Olympic
BR ə'lɪmpɪk, -s
AM ə'lɪmpɪk,
oʊ'lɪmpɪk, -s

Olympus
BR ə'lɪmpəs
AM ə'lɪmpəs

om
BR əʊm, ɒm
AM ɔm, oʊm, ɑm

Omagh
BR 'əʊmə(r), əʊ'mɑː(r)
AM oʊ'mɑ

Omaha
BR 'əʊməhɑː(r)
AM 'oʊmə,hɑ

O'Mahoney
BR ə(ʊ)'mɑː(h)əni
AM ,oʊmə'hoʊni

O'Mahony
BR ə(ʊ)'mɑː(h)əni
AM ,oʊmə'hoʊni

O'Malley
BR ə(ʊ)'mali
AM oʊ'mæli

Oman¹
country
BR əʊ'mɑːn
AM oʊ'mɑn

Oman²
surname
BR 'əʊmən
AM 'oʊmən

Omani
BR əʊ'mɑːn|i, -ɪz
AM oʊ'mɑni, -z

O'Mara
BR ə(ʊ)'mɑːrə(r)
AM oʊ'mɛrə

Omar Khayyám
BR ,əʊmɑː kʌɪ'am,
+ kʌɪ'ɑːm
AM ,oʊmar kaɪ'am

omasa
BR əʊ'meɪsə(r)
AM oʊ'meɪsə

omasum
BR əʊ'meɪsəm

AM oʊ'meɪsəm

ombre
BR 'ɒmbə(r), -z
AM 'ambər, -z

ombré
BR 'ɒmbreɪ, 'ɔ̃breɪ, -z
AM 'am,breɪ, -z

ombrology
BR ɒm'brɒlədʒi
AM ɑm'brɑlədʒi

ombrometer
BR ɒm'brɒmɪtə(r), -z
AM ɑm'brɑmədər, -z

ombudsman
BR 'ɒmbʊdzmən
AM 'am,bədzmən,
'am,bʊdzmən

ombudsmen
BR 'ɒmbʊdzmən
AM 'am,bədzmən,
'am,bʊdzmən

Omdurman
BR 'ɒmdəmən,
,ɒmdə'mɑːn,
,ɒmdə'man
AM ,əmdər'man,
,amdər'man,
,əmdər'man,
,amdər'man

O'Meara
BR ə(ʊ)'mɑːrə(r),
ə(ʊ)'mɛːrə(r),
ə(ʊ)'mɪərə(r)
AM oʊ'mɪrə

omega
BR 'əʊmɪgə(r), -z
AM oʊ'meɪgə, oʊ'mɛgə,
-z

omelet
BR 'ɒmlɪt, -s
AM 'amlət, -s

omelette
BR 'ɒmlɪt, -s
AM 'amlət, -s

omen
BR 'əʊmən, -z
AM 'oʊmən, -z

omenta
BR əʊ'mɛntə(r)
AM oʊ'mɛn(t)ə

omental
BR əʊ'mɛntl
AM oʊ'mɛn(t)l

omentum
BR əʊ'mɛntəm
AM oʊ'mɛn(t)əm

omer
BR 'əʊmə(r), -z
AM 'oʊmər, -z

omicron
BR ə(ʊ)'mʌɪkrɒn,
ə(ʊ)'mʌɪkr(ə)n,
'ɒmɪkrɒn,
'ɒmɪkr(ə)n, -z
AM 'amə,krɑn,
'oʊmə,krɑn, -z

ominous
BR 'ɒmɪnəs

AM 'amənəs

ominously
BR 'ɒmɪnəsli
AM 'amənəsli

ominousness
BR 'ɒmɪnəsnəs
AM 'amənəsnəs

omissible
BR ə(ʊ)'mɪsɪbl
AM oʊ'mɪsəbəl

omission
BR ə(ʊ)'mɪʃn, -z
AM oʊ'mɪʃən, ə'mɪʃən,
-z

omissive
BR ə(ʊ)'mɪsɪv
AM oʊ'mɪsɪv, ə'mɪsɪv

omit
BR ə(ʊ)'mɪt, -s, -ɪŋ, -ɪd
AM oʊ'mɪ|t, ə'mɪ|t, -ts,
-dɪŋ, -dɪd

ommatidia
BR ,ɒmə'tɪdɪə(r)
AM ,amə'tɪdiə

ommatidium
BR ,ɒmə'tɪdɪəm
AM ,amə'tɪdiəm

omnibus
BR 'ɒmnɪbəs,
'ɒmnɪbʌs, -ɪz
AM 'amnə,bəs, -əz

omnicompetence
BR ,ɒmnɪ'kɒmpɪt(ə)ns
AM ,amnə'kampətns

omnicompetent
BR ,ɒmnɪ'kɒmpɪt(ə)nt
AM ,amnə'kampədnt

omnidirectional
BR ,ɒmnɪdɪ'rɛkʃn(ə)l,
,ɒmnɪdɪ'rɛkʃən(ə)l,
,ɒmnɪdʌɪ'rɛkʃn(ə)l,
,ɒmnɪdʌɪ'rɛkʃən(ə)l
AM ,amnə,daɪ'rɛkʃ(ə)-
nəl,
,amnədə'rɛkʃ(ə)nəl

omnifarious
BR ,ɒmnɪ'fɛːrɪəs
AM ,amnə'fɛriəs

omnific
BR ɒm'nɪfɪk
AM am'nɪfɪk

omnigenous
BR ɒm'nɪdʒɪnəs
AM am'nɪdʒənəs

omnipotence
BR ɒm'nɪpət(ə)ns
AM am'nɪpədəns,
əm'nɪpədəns,
am'nɪpətns,
əm'nɪpətns

omnipotent
BR ɒm'nɪpət(ə)nt
AM am'nɪpədnt,
əm'nɪpədnt

omnipotently
BR ɒm'nɪpət(ə)ntli
AM am'nɪpədən(t)li,
əm'nɪpədən(t)li,

am'nɪpətn(t)li,
əm'nɪpətn(t)li

omnipresence
BR ,ɒmnɪ'prɛzns
AM ,amnə'prɛzns

omnipresent
BR ,ɒmnɪ'prɛznt
AM ,amnə'prɛznt

omniscience
BR ɒm'nɪsɪəns
AM am'nɪʃəns

omniscient
BR ɒm'nɪsɪənt
AM am'nɪʃənt

omnisciently
BR ɒm'nɪsɪəntli
AM am'nɪʃən(t)li

omnivore
BR 'ɒmnɪvɔː(r), -z
AM 'amnə,vɔ(ə)r, -z

omnivorous
BR ɒm'nɪv(ə)rəs
AM am'nɪv(ə)rəs

omnivorously
BR ɒm'nɪv(ə)rəsli
AM am'nɪv(ə)rəsli

omnivorousness
BR ɒm'nɪv(ə)rəsnəs
AM am'nɪv(ə)rəsnəs

omphaloi
BR 'ɒmfəlɔɪ
AM 'amfə,lɔɪ

omphalos
BR 'ɒmfəlɒs
AM 'ɔmfələs, 'ɒmfələs,
'amfələs, 'amfələs

omphalotomy
BR ,ɒmfə'lɒtəm|i, -ɪz
AM ,amfə'lɑdəmi,
,ampə'lɑdəmi, -z

Omsk
BR ɒmsk
AM amsk

on
BR ɒn
AM ɔn, ɑn

onager
BR 'ɒnədʒə(r),
'ɒnəgə(r), -z
AM 'ɑnədʒər, 'anədʒər,
-z

Onan
BR 'əʊnən, 'əʊnan
AM 'oʊnən

onanism
BR 'əʊnənɪz(ə)m
AM 'oʊnə,nɪzəm

onanist
BR 'əʊnənɪst, -s
AM 'oʊnənəst, -s

onanistic
BR ,əʊnə'nɪstɪk
AM ,oʊnə'nɪstɪk

Onassis
BR ə(ʊ)'nasɪs
AM ə'næsəs, oʊ'næsəs

ONC
BR ˌəʊɛnˈsiː, -z
AM ˌoʊɛnˈsi, -z

once
BR wʌns
AM wəns

once-over
BR ˈwʌns,əʊvə(r)
AM ˈwəns,oʊvər

oncer
BR ˈwʌnsə(r), -z
AM ˈwənsər, -z

oncogene
BR ˈɒŋkə(ʊ)dʒiːn, -z
AM ˈɒnkoʊˌdʒin,
ˈɒŋkoʊˌdʒin,
ˈankoʊˌdʒin,
ˈaŋkoʊˌdʒin, -z

oncogenic
BR ˌɒŋkə(ʊ)ˈdʒɛnɪk
AM ˌɒnkoʊˈdʒɛnɪk,
ˌɒŋkoʊˈdʒɛnɪk,
ˌankoʊˈdʒɛnɪk,
ˌaŋkoʊˈdʒɛnɪk

oncogenous
BR ɒŋˈkɒdʒɪnəs
AM ɒnˈkadʒənəs,
ɒŋˈkadʒənəs,
anˈkadʒənəs,
aŋˈkadʒənəs

oncologist
BR ɒŋˈkɒlədʒɪst, -s
AM ɒnˈkalədʒəst,
ɒŋˈkalədʒəst,
anˈkalədʒəst,
aŋˈkalədʒəst, -s

oncology
BR ɒŋˈkɒlədʒi
AM ɒnˈkalədʒi,
ɒŋˈkalədʒi,
anˈkalədʒi,
aŋˈkalədʒi

oncoming
BR ˈɒn,kʌmɪŋ
AM ˈɒn,kəmɪŋ,
ˈan,kəmɪŋ

oncost
BR ˈɒnkɒst, -s
AM ɒnˈkɔst, anˈkast, -s

OND
BR ˌəʊɛnˈdiː, -z
AM ˌoʊɛnˈdi, -z

one
BR wʌn
AM wən

O'Neal
BR ə(ʊ)ˈniːl
AM oʊˈnil

onefold
BR ˈwʌnfəʊld
AM ˈwən,foʊld

Oneida
BR əʊˈnʌɪdə(r)
AM oʊˈnaɪdə

O'Neil
BR ə(ʊ)ˈniːl
AM oʊˈnil

O'Neill
BR ə(ʊ)ˈniːl
AM oʊˈnil

oneiric
BR ə(ʊ)ˈnʌɪrɪk
AM oʊˈnaɪrɪk

oneirocritic
BR ə(ʊ)ˌnʌɪrəˈkrɪtɪk,
-s
AM oʊˌnaɪroʊˈkrɪdɪk,
-s

oneirologist
BR ə(ʊ)ˌnʌɪˈrɒlədʒɪst,
-s
AM oʊˌnaɪˈralədʒəst, -s

oneirology
BR ə(ʊ)ˌnʌɪˈrɒlədʒi
AM oʊˌnaɪˈralədʒi

oneiromancer
BR ə(ʊ)ˈnʌɪrəmansə(r),
-z
AM oʊˈnaɪrəˌmænsər,
-z

oneiromancy
BR ə(ʊ)ˈnʌɪrəmansi
AM oʊˈnaɪrouˌmænsi

oneness
BR ˈwʌnnəs
AM ˈwə(n)nəs

oner
BR ˈwʌnə(r), -z
AM ˈwənər, -z

onerous
BR ˈəʊn(ə)rəs,
ˈɒn(ə)rəs
AM ˈoʊnərəs, ˈanərəs

onerously
BR ˈəʊn(ə)rəsli,
ˈɒn(ə)rəsli
AM ˈoʊnərəsli,
ˈanərəsli

onerousness
BR ˈəʊn(ə)rəsnəs,
ˈɒn(ə)rəsnəs
AM ˈoʊnərəsnəs,
ˈanərəsnəs

oneself
BR ˌwʌnˈsɛlf
AM ˌwənˈsɛlf

one-sided
BR ˌwʌnˈsʌɪdɪd
AM ˌwənˈsaɪdɪd

one-sidedly
BR ˌwʌnˈsʌɪdɪdli
AM ˌwənˈsaɪdɪdli

one-sidedness
BR ˌwʌnˈsʌɪdɪdnɪs
AM ˌwənˈsaɪdɪdnɪs

Onesimus
BR əʊˈniːsɪməs,
əʊˈnɛsɪməs
AM oʊˈnisɪməs,
oʊˈnɛsɪməs

one-step
BR ˈwʌnstɛp, -s, -ɪŋ, -t
AM ˈwənˌstɛp, -s, -ɪŋ, -t

one-time
adjective
BR ˈwʌntʌɪm
AM ˈwənˌtaɪm

one-to-one
BR ˌwʌntəˈwʌn
AM ˌwən(t)əˈwən

one-upmanship
BR (ˌ)wʌnˈʌpmənʃɪp
AM wənˈəp(s)mənˌʃɪp

onflow
BR ˈɒnfləʊ, -z
AM ˈɒnˌfloʊ, ˈan,floʊ, -z

onglaze
BR ˈɒnɡleɪz
AM ˈɔn,ɡleɪz, ˈan,ɡleɪz

ongoing
BR ˈɒnɡəʊɪŋ, ˌɒnˈɡəʊɪŋ
AM ˈɔn,ɡoʊɪŋ,
ˈan,ɡoʊɪŋ

ongoingness
BR ˈɒnɡəʊɪŋnɪs,
ˌɒnˈɡəʊɪŋnɪs
AM ˈɔnɡoʊɪŋnɪs,
ˈanɡoʊɪŋnɪs

onion
BR ˈʌnjən, -z
AM ˈənjən, -z

Onions
BR ˈʌnjənz,
ə(ʊ)ˈnʌɪənz
AM ˈənjənz

onionskin
BR ˈʌnjənskɪn, -z
AM ˈənjənˌskɪn, -z

oniony
BR ˈʌnjəni
AM ˈənjəni

on-line
BR ˈɒnlʌɪn
AM ˌɒnˈlaɪn, ˌanˈlaɪn

onlooker
BR ˈɒn,lʊkə(r), -z
AM ˈɔn,lʊkər,
ˈan,lʊkər, -z

onlooking
BR ˈɒn,lʊkɪŋ
AM ˈɔn,lʊkɪŋ, ˈan,lʊkɪŋ

only
BR ˈəʊnli
AM ˈoʊnli

only-begotten
BR ˈəʊnlɪbɪˈɡɒtn
AM ˈoʊnlɪbəˈɡatn,
ˈoʊnlibiˈɡatn

on-off
BR ˈɒnˈɒf
AM ˈɔnˈɔf, ˈanˈaf

onomasiology
BR ˌɒnəmeɪsɪˈɒlədʒi,
ˌɒnəmeɪzɪˈɒlədʒi
AM ˌɒnəˌmeɪsɪˈalədʒi,
ˌɒnəˌmeɪzɪˈalədʒi,
ˌanəˌmeɪsɪˈalədʒi,
ˌanəˌmeɪzɪˈalədʒi

onomast
BR ˈɒnəmast, -s
AM ˈanəˌmæst, -s

onomastic
BR ˌɒnəˈmastɪk, -s
AM ˌɒnəˈmæstɪk,
ˌanəˈmæstɪk, -s

onomatopoeia
BR ˌɒnəmatəˈpiːə(r)
AM ˌɒnəˌmædəˈpiə,
ˌanəˌmædəˈpiə

onomatopoeic
BR ˌɒnəmatəˈpiːɪk
AM ˌɒnəˌmædəˈpiɪk,
ˌanəˌmædəˈpiɪk

onomatopoeically
BR ˌɒnəmatəˈpiːɪkli
AM ˌanəˌmædəˈpiɪk(ə)li

onomatopoetic
BR ˌɒnəmatəˌpəʊˈɛtɪk
AM ˌɒnəˌmædəpoʊˈɛdɪk,
ˌanəˌmædəpoʊˈɛdɪk

Onondaga
BR ˌɒnənˈdɑːɡə(r), -z
AM ˌɒnənˈdaɡə,
ˌanənˈdaɡə, -z

onrush
BR ˈɒnrʌʃ, -ɪz
AM ˈɔn,rəʃ, ˈan,rəʃ, -əz

onrushing
BR ˈɒn,rʌʃɪŋ
AM ˈɔn,rəʃɪŋ, ˈan,rəʃɪŋ

onset
noun
BR ˈɒnsɛt, -s
AM ˈɔn,sɛt, ˈan,sɛt, -s

on-set
adjective, adverb
BR ˈɒnˈsɛt
AM ˈɒnˈsɛt, ˈanˈsɛt

onshore
BR ˈɒnˈʃɔː(r)
AM ˈɒnˈʃɔ(ə)r,
ˈanˈʃɔ(ə)r

onside
BR ˈɒnˈsʌɪd
AM ˈɔnˈsaɪd, ˈanˈsaɪd

onslaught
BR ˈɒnslɔːt, -s
AM ˈɔn,slɔt, ˈan,slɔt, -s

Onslow
BR ˈɒnzləʊ
AM ˈanzloʊ

onstream
BR ˈɒnˈstriːm
AM ˈɒnˈstrim,
ˈanˈstrim

Ontario
BR ɒnˈtɛːrɪəʊ
AM ɒnˈtɛrioʊ,
anˈtɛrioʊ

on-the-spot
BR ˌɒnðəˈspɒt
AM ˌɒnðəˈspat,
ˌanðəˈspat

onto
BR ˈɒntʊ
AM ˈɒn,tʊ, ˈan,tʊ

ontogenesis
BR ˌɒntə(ʊ)ˈdʒɛnɪsɪs

ontogenetic
AM ˌɒnˌtoʊˈdʒɛnəsəs,
ˌɑnˌtoʊˈdʒɛnəsəs
ontogenetic
BR ˌɒntəʊdʒɪˈnɛtɪk
AM ˌɒnˌtoʊdʒəˈnɛdɪk,
ˌɑnˌtoʊdʒəˈnɛdɪk
ontogenetically
BR ˌɒntəʊdʒɪˈnɛtɪkli
AM ˌɒnˌtoʊdʒəˈnɛdək-
(ə)li,
ˌɑnˌtoʊdʒəˈnɛdək(ə)li
ontogenic
BR ˌɒntə(ʊ)ˈdʒɛnɪk
AM ˌɒnˌtoʊˈdʒɛnɪk,
ˌɑnˌtoʊˈdʒɛnɪk
ontogenically
BR ˌɒntə(ʊ)ˈdʒɛnɪkli
AM ˌɒnˌtoʊˈdʒɛnək(ə)li,
ˌɑnˌtoʊˈdʒɛnək(ə)li
ontogeny
BR ɒnˈtɒdʒɪni,
ɒnˈtɒdʒni
AM ɒnˈtadʒəni,
ɑnˈtadʒəni
ontological
BR ˌɒntəˈlɒdʒɪkl
AM ˌɒn(t)əˈladʒəkəl,
ˌɑn(t)əˈladʒəkəl
ontologically
BR ˌɒntəˈlɒdʒɪkli
AM ˌɒn(t)əˈladʒək(ə)li,
ˌɑn(t)əˈladʒək(ə)li
ontologist
BR ɒnˈtɒlədʒɪst, -s
AM ɒnˈtalədʒəst,
ɑnˈtalədʒəst, -s
ontology
BR ɒnˈtɒlədʒi
AM ɒnˈtalədʒi,
ɑnˈtalədʒi
onus
BR ˈəʊnəs
AM ˈoʊnəs
onward
BR ˈɒnwəd, -z
AM ˈɒnwərd, ˈɑnwərd,
-z
onymous
BR ˈɒnɪməs
AM ˈɒnəməs, ˈɑnəməs
onyx
BR ˈɒnɪks, -ɪz
AM ˈɒnɪks, ˈɑnɪks, -ɪz
oocyte
BR ˈəʊəsʌɪt
AM ˈoʊəˌsaɪt
oodles
BR ˈuːdlz
AM ˈudlz
oof
BR uːf
AM uf
oofiness
BR ˈuːfɪnɪs
AM ˈufinɪs
oofy
BR ˈuːfʃi, -ɪə(r), -ɪɪst
AM ˈufi, -ər, -əst

oogamous
BR əʊˈɒgəməs
AM oʊˈ(w)agəməs
oogamy
BR əʊˈɒgəmi
AM oʊˈ(w)agəmi
oogenesis
BR əʊə(ʊ)ˈdʒɛnɪsɪs
AM ˌoʊəˈdʒɛnəsəs
oogenetic
BR ˌəʊə(ʊ)dʒɪˈnɛtɪk
AM ˌoʊədʒəˈnɛdɪk
ooh
BR uː, -z, -ɪŋ, -d
AM u, -z, -ɪŋ, -d
oolite
BR ˈəʊəlʌɪt, -s
AM ˈoʊəˌlaɪt, -s
oolith
BR ˈəʊəlɪθ, -s
AM ˈoʊəˌlɪθ, -s
oolitic
BR ˌəʊəˈlɪtɪk
AM ˌoʊəˈlɪdɪk
oological
BR ˌəʊəˈlɒdʒɪkl
AM ˌoʊəˈladʒəkəl
oologist
BR əʊˈɒlədʒɪst, -s
AM oʊˈ(w)alədʒəst, -s
oology
BR əʊˈɒlədʒi
AM oʊˈ(w)alədʒi
oolong
BR ˈuːlɒŋ
AM ˈuˌlɒŋ, ˈuˌlɑŋ
oomiak
BR ˈuːmɪak, -s
AM ˈumiək, ˈumiˌæk, -s
oompah
BR ˈʊmpɑː(r),
ˈuːmpɑː(r)
AM ˈʊmˌpɑ, ˈʊmˌpɑ
oomph
BR ʊmf, uːmf
AM ʊmf, umf
Oona
BR ˈuːnə(r)
AM ˈunə
Oonagh
BR ˈuːnə(r)
AM ˈunə
oophorectomy
BR ˌəʊəfəˈrɛktəmʃi, -ɪz
AM ˌoʊfəˈrɛktəmi, -z
oops
BR (w)ʊps
AM (w)ʊps, ups
oops-a-daisy
BR ˌ(w)ʊpsəˈdeɪzi,
ˌ(w)uːpsəˈdeɪzi
AM ˈ(w)ʊpsəˌdeɪzi,
ˈ(w)upsəˌdeɪzi
Oort
BR ɔːt, ʊət
AM ɔ(ə)rt

oosperm
BR ˈəʊə(ʊ)spəːm, -z
AM ˈoʊəˌspɛrm, -z
Oostende
BR ɒˈstɛnd
AM ˈɔˌstɛnd, ˈoʊˌstɛnd
FL oːstˈɛndə
Oosterhuis
BR ˈəʊstəhaʊs,
ˈuːstəhaʊs
AM ˈustərˌ(h)aʊs
ooze
BR uːz, -ɪz, -ɪŋ, -d
AM uz, -əz, -ɪŋ, -d
oozily
BR ˈuːzɪli
AM ˈuzəli
ooziness
BR ˈuːzɪnɪs
AM ˈuzɪnɪs
oozy
BR ˈuːzʃi, -ɪə(r), -ɪɪst
AM ˈuzi, -ər, -ɪst
op
BR ɒp, -s
AM ɑp, -s
op.
opus, operator
BR ɒp
AM ɑp
opacifier
BR əʊˈpasɪfʌɪə(r), -z
AM oʊˈpæsəˌfaɪər, -z
opacify
BR əʊˈpasɪfʌɪ, -z, -ɪŋ, -d
AM oʊˈpæsəˌfaɪ, -z, -ɪŋ,
-d
opacity
BR ə(ʊ)ˈpasɪti
AM oʊˈpæsədi
opah
BR ˈəʊpə(r), -z
AM ˈoʊpə, -z
opal
BR ˈəʊpl, -z
AM ˈoʊpəl, -z
opalesce
BR ˌəʊpəˈlɛs, -ɪz, -ɪŋ, -t
AM ˌoʊpəˈlɛs, -əz, -ɪŋ, -t
opalescence
BR ˌəʊpəˈlɛsns
AM ˌoʊpəˈlɛsəns
opalescent
BR ˌəʊpəˈlɛsnt
AM ˌoʊpəˈlɛsənt
opaline
BR ˈəʊpəlʌɪn
AM ˈoʊpəˌlin,
ˈoʊpəˌlaɪn
opaque
BR ə(ʊ)ˈpeɪk
AM oʊˈpeɪk
opaquely
BR ə(ʊ)ˈpeɪkli
AM oʊˈpeɪkli
opaqueness
BR ə(ʊ)ˈpeɪknɪs

opera buffa
AM oʊˈpeɪknɪs
op art
BR ˈɒp ɑːt
AM ˈɑp ˌɑrt
op. cit.
BR ˌɒp ˈsɪt
AM ˌɑp ˌsɪt
ope
BR əʊp, -s, -ɪŋ, -t
AM oʊp, -s, -ɪŋ, -t
OPEC
BR ˈəʊpɛk
AM ˈoʊpɛk
Op-Ed
BR ˌɒpˈɛd
AM ˌɑpˈɛd
Opel®
BR ˈəʊpl, -z
AM ˈoʊpɛl, -z
open
BR ˈəʊp|(ə)n, -(ə)nz,
-(ə)nɪŋ \-pɪŋ, -(ə)nd
AM ˈoʊp|ən, -ənz,
-(ə)nɪŋ, -ənd \-ɳd
openable
BR ˈəʊp(ə)nəbl,
ˈəʊpɳəbl
AM ˈoʊp(ə)nəbəl
opencast
BR ˈəʊp(ə)nkɑːst,
ˈəʊp(ə)nkast
AM ˈoʊpənˌkæst
opener
BR ˈəʊp(ə)nə(r),
ˈəʊpɳə(r), -z
AM ˈoʊp(ə)nər, -z
opening
BR ˈəʊp(ə)nɪŋ, ˈəʊpɳɪŋ,
-z
AM ˈoʊp(ə)nɪŋ, -z
openly
BR ˈəʊp(ə)nli
AM ˈoʊpənli
openness
BR ˈəʊp(ə)nnəs
AM ˈoʊpə(n)nəs
Openshaw
BR ˈəʊp(ə)nʃɔː(r)
AM ˈoʊpənˌʃɔ
openwork
BR ˈəʊp(ə)nwəːk
AM ˈoʊpənˌwərk
opera
BR ˈɒp(ə)rə(r), -z
AM ˈɑp(ə)rə, -z
operability
BR ˌɒp(ə)rəˈbɪlɪti
AM ˌɑp(ə)rəˈbɪlɪdi
operable
BR ˈɒp(ə)rəbl
AM ˈɑp(ə)rəbəl
operably
BR ˈɒp(ə)rəbli
AM ˈɑp(ə)rəbli
opera buffa
BR ˌɒp(ə)rə ˈbuːfə(r)
AM ˌoʊp(ə)rə ˈbufə

opéra comique
BR ˌɒp(ə)rə kɒˈmiːk, -s
AM ˌoʊp(ə)rə kɔˈmik, -s

operand
BR ˈɒpərand, ˈɒp(ə)rənd, ˈɒp(ə)rn̩d, -z
AM ˈɑpəˌrænd, -z

operant
BR ˈɒp(ə)rənt, ˈɒp(ə)rn̩t, -s
AM ˈɑpərənt, -s

operas buffa
BR ˌɒp(ə)rəz ˈbuːfə(r)
AM ˌoʊp(ə)rəz ˈbufə

opera seria
BR ˌɒp(ə)rə ˈsɪərɪə(r)
AM ˌoʊp(ə)rə ˈsɪriə

operas seria
BR ˌɒp(ə)rəz ˈsɪərɪə(r)
AM ˌoʊp(ə)rəz ˈsɪriə

operate
BR ˈɒpəreɪt, -s, -ɪŋ, -ɪd
AM ˈɑpəˌreɪ|t, -ts, -dɪŋ, -dɪd

operatic
BR ˌɒpəˈratɪk, -s
AM ˌɑpəˈrædɪk, -s

operatically
BR ˌɒpəˈratɪkli
AM ˌɑpəˈrædək(ə)li

operation
BR ˌɒpəˈreɪʃn, -z
AM ˌɑpəˈreɪʃən, -z

operational
BR ˌɒpəˈreɪʃn̩(ə)l, ˌɒpəˈreɪʃən(ə)l
AM ˌɑpəˈreɪʃ(ə)nəl

operationalise
BR ˌɒpəˈreɪʃn̩əlʌɪz, ˌɒpəˈreɪʃn̩lʌɪz, ˌɒpəˈreɪʃən̩lʌɪz, ˌɒpəˈreɪʃ(ə)nəlʌɪz, -ɪz, -ɪŋ, -d
AM ˌɑpəˈreɪʃən̩lˌaɪz, ˌɑpəˈreɪʃnəˌlaɪz, -ɪz, -ɪŋ, -d

operationalize
BR ˌɒpəˈreɪʃn̩əlʌɪz, ˌɒpəˈreɪʃn̩lʌɪz, ˌɒpəˈreɪʃən̩lʌɪz, ˌɒpəˈreɪʃ(ə)nəlʌɪz, -ɪz, -ɪŋ, -d
AM ˌɑpəˈreɪʃən̩lˌaɪz, ˌɑpəˈreɪʃnəˌlaɪz, -ɪz, -ɪŋ, -d

operationally
BR ˌɒpəˈreɪʃn̩əli, ˌɒpəˈreɪʃn̩li, ˌɒpəˈreɪʃən̩li, ˌɒpəˈreɪʃ(ə)nəli
AM ˌɑpəˈreɪʃ(ə)nəli

operative
BR ˈɒp(ə)rətɪv, -z
AM ˈɑp(ə)rədɪv, -z

operatively
BR ˈɒp(ə)rətɪvli

operativeness
BR ˈɒp(ə)rətɪvnɪs
AM ˈɑp(ə)rədɪvnɪs

operator
BR ˈɒpəreɪtə(r), -z
AM ˈɑpəˌreɪdər, -z

opercula
BR ə(ʊ)ˈpəːkjʊlə(r), ɒˈpəːkjʊlə(r)
AM oʊˈpərkjələ

opercular
BR ə(ʊ)ˈpəːkjʊlə(r), ɒˈpəːkjʊlə(r)
AM oʊˈpərkjələr

operculate
BR əʊˈpəːkjʊlət, ɒˈpəːkjʊlət
AM oʊˈpərkjəˌleɪt

operculum
BR ə(ʊ)ˈpəːkjʊləm, ɒˈpəːkjʊləm
AM oʊˈpərkjələm

opere buffe
BR ˌɒp(ə)reɪ ˈbuːfeɪ
AM ˌoʊp(ə)reɪ ˈbufeɪ

opere serie
BR ˌɒp(ə)reɪ ˈsɪərɪeɪ
AM ˌoʊp(ə)rə ˈsɪrieɪ

operetta
BR ˌɒpəˈrɛtə(r), -z
AM ˌɑpəˈrɛdə, -z

operon
BR ˈɒpərɒn, -z
AM ˈɑpərɑn, -z

Ophelia
BR ə(ʊ)ˈfiːlɪə(r), ɒˈfiːlɪə(r)
AM oʊˈfiljə, əˈfiljə, oʊˈfiliə, əˈfiliə

ophicleide
BR ˈɒfɪklʌɪd, -z
AM ˈɑfəˌklaɪd, ˈoʊfəˌklaɪd, -z

ophidia
BR ɒˈfɪdɪə(r), ə(ʊ)ˈfɪdɪə(r)
AM oʊˈfɪdiə

ophidian
BR ɒˈfɪdɪən, ə(ʊ)ˈfɪdɪən, -z
AM oʊˈfɪdiən, -z

ophiolatry
BR ˌɒfɪˈɒlətri
AM ˌɑfiˈɑlətri, ˌoʊfiˈɑlətri

ophiolite
BR ˈɒfɪəlʌɪt
AM ˈɑfiəˌlaɪt

ophiologist
BR ˌɒfɪˈɒlədʒɪst, -s
AM ˌɑfiˈɑlədʒəst, ˌoʊfiˈɑlədʒəst, -s

ophiology
BR ˌɒfɪˈɒlədʒi
AM ˌɑfiˈɑlədʒi, ˌoʊfiˈɑlədʒi

Ophir
BR ˈəʊfə(r)
AM ˈoʊfər

ophite
BR ˈɒfʌɪt, ˈəʊfʌɪt, -s
AM ˈoʊˌfaɪt, -s

ophitic
BR ɒˈfɪtɪk, əʊˈfɪtɪk
AM oʊˈfɪdɪk

Ophiuchus
BR ɒˈfjuːkəs, ˌɒfɪˈuːkəs
AM ɑˈfjukəs

ophthalmia
BR ɒfˈθalmɪə(r), ɒpˈθalmɪə(r)
AM ɑpˈθælmiə, ɑfˈθælmiə

ophthalmic
BR ɒfˈθalmɪk, ɒpˈθalmɪk
AM ɑpˈθælmɪk, ɑfˈθælmɪk

ophthalmitis
BR ˌɒfθalˈmʌɪtɪs, ˌɒpθalˈmʌɪtɪs
AM ˌɑpθə(l)ˈmaɪdɪs, ˌɑfθə(l)ˈmaɪdɪs

ophthalmological
BR ˌɒfθalməˈlɒdʒɪkl, ˌɒpθalməˈlɒdʒɪkl
AM ˌɑpθə(l)məˈlɑdʒəkəl, ˌɑfθə(l)məˈlɑdʒəkəl

ophthalmologist
BR ˌɒfθalˈmɒlədʒɪst, ˌɒpθalˈmɒlədʒɪst, -s
AM ˌɑpθə(l)ˈmɑlədʒəst, ˌɑfθə(l)ˈmɑlədʒəst-, ˌɑpθə(l)ˈmɑlədʒəst-, -s

ophthalmology
BR ˌɒfθalˈmɒlədʒi, ˌɒpθalˈmɒlədʒi
AM ˌɑpθə(l)ˈmɑlədʒi, ˌɑfθə(l)ˈmɑlədʒi

ophthalmoscope
BR ɒfˈθalməskəʊp, ɒpˈθalməskəʊp, -s
AM ɑpˈθælməˌskoʊp, ɑfˈθælməˌskoʊp, -s

ophthalmoscopic
BR ɒfˌθalməˈskɒpɪk, ɒpˌθalməˈskɒpɪk
AM ˌɑpθə(l)məˈskapɪk, ˌɑfθə(l)məˈskapɪk

ophthalmoscopic-ally
BR ɒfˌθalməˈskɒpɪkli, ɒpˌθalməˈskɒpɪkli
AM ˌɑpθə(l)məˈskapək-(ə)li, ˌɑfθə(l)məˈskapək(ə)li

ophthalmoscopy
BR ˌɒfθalˈmɒskəpi, ˌɒpθalˈmɒskəpi
AM ˌɑpθə(l)ˈmɑskəpi, ˌɑfθə(l)ˈmɑskəpi

opiate
BR ˈəʊpɪət, -s
AM ˈoʊpiɪt, -s

Opie
BR ˈəʊpi
AM ˈoʊpi

opine
BR ə(ʊ)ˈpʌɪn, -z, -ɪŋ, -d
AM oʊˈpaɪn, -z, -ɪŋ, -d

opinion
BR əˈpɪnjən, -z
AM əˈpɪnjən, -z

opinionated
BR əˈpɪnjəneɪtɪd
AM əˈpɪnjəˌneɪdɪd

opinionatedly
BR əˈpɪnjəneɪtɪdli
AM əˈpɪnjəˌneɪdɪdli

opinionatedness
BR əˈpɪnjəneɪtɪdnɪs
AM əˈpɪnjəˌneɪdɪdnɪs

opinionative
BR əˈpɪnjənətɪv
AM əˈpɪnjəˌneɪdɪv

opioid
BR ˈəʊpɪɔɪd, -z
AM ˈoʊpiɔɪd, -z

opisometer
BR ˌɒpɪˈsɒmɪtə(r), -z
AM ˌɑpəˈsamədər, -z

opisthograph
BR əˈpɪsθəɡrɑːf, əˈpɪsθəɡraf, -s
AM əˈpɪsθəˌɡræf, -s

opisthography
BR ˌɒpɪsˈθɒɡrəfi
AM ˌɑpəsˈθaɡrəfi

opisthosoma
BR əˌpɪsθəˈsəʊmə(r), -z
AM əˌpɪsθəˈsoʊmə, -z

opium
BR ˈəʊpɪəm
AM ˈoʊpiəm

opiumise
BR ˈəʊpɪəmʌɪz, -ɪz, -ɪŋ, -d
AM ˈoʊpiəˌmaɪz, -ɪz, -ɪŋ, -d

opiumize
BR ˈəʊpɪəmʌɪz, -ɪz, -ɪŋ, -d
AM ˈoʊpiəˌmaɪz, -ɪz, -ɪŋ, -d

opodeldoc
BR ˌɒpə(ʊ)ˈdɛldɒk
AM ˌɑpəˈdɛlˌdak

opopanax
BR ə(ʊ)ˈpɒpənaks
AM əˈpɑpəˌnæks

Oporto
BR ə(ʊ)ˈpɔːtəʊ, ɒˈpɔːtəʊ
AM əˈpɔrdoʊ, ɔˈpɔrˌtoʊ, ɑˈpɔrˌtoʊ

opossum
BR əˈpɒsəm, -z
AM (ə)ˈpasəm, -z

Oppenheim
BR ˈɒp(ə)nhʌɪm
AM ˈɑpənhaɪm

Oppenheimer
BR 'ɒp(ə)nhaɪmə(r)
AM 'ɑp(ə)n,(h)aɪmər
oppidan
BR 'ɒpɪd(ə)n, -z
AM 'ɑpədən, -z
oppo
BR 'ɒpəʊ, -z
AM 'ɑ,poʊ, -z
opponency
BR ə'pəʊnənsi
AM ə'poʊnənsi
opponent
BR ə'pəʊnənt, -s
AM ə'poʊnənt, -s
opportune
BR 'ɒpətjuːn,
'ɒpətʃuːn, ,ɒpə'tjuːn,
,ɒpə'tʃuːn
AM ,ɑpər̩'t(j)un
opportunely
BR 'ɒpətjuːnli,
'ɒpətʃuːnli,
,ɒpə'tjuːnli,
,ɒpə'tʃuːnli
AM ,ɑpər̩'t(j)unli
opportuneness
BR 'ɒpətjuːnnəs,
'ɒpətʃuːnnəs,
,ɒpə'tjuːnnəs,
,ɒpə'tʃuːnnəs
AM ,ɑpər̩'t(j)u(n)nəs
opportunism
BR 'ɒpətjuːnɪz(ə)m,
'ɒpətʃuːnɪz(ə)m,
,ɒpə'tjuːnɪz(ə)m,
,ɒpə'tʃuːnɪz(ə)m
AM ,ɑpər̩'t(j)u,nɪzəm
opportunist
BR 'ɒpətjuːnɪst,
'ɒpətʃuːnɪst,
,ɒpə'tjuːnɪst,
,ɒpə'tʃuːnɪst, -s
AM ,ɑpər̩'t(j)unəst, -s
opportunistic
BR ,ɒpətjuː'nɪstɪk,
,ɒpətʃuː'nɪstɪk
AM ,ɑpərt(j)u'nɪstɪk
opportunistically
BR ,ɒpətjuː'nɪstɪkli,
,ɒpətʃuː'nɪstɪkli
AM ,ɑpərt(j)u'nɪstək-
(ə)li
opportunity
BR ,ɒpə'tjuːnɪt|i,
,ɒpə'tʃuːnɪt|i, -ɪz
AM ,ɑpər̩'t(j)unədi, -z
opposable
BR ə'pəʊzəbl
AM ə'poʊzəbəl
oppose
BR ə'pəʊz, -ɪz, -ɪŋ, -d
AM ə'poʊz, -əz, -ɪŋ, -d
opposer
BR ə'pəʊzə(r), -z
AM ə'poʊzər, -z
opposite
BR 'ɒpəzɪt, 'ɒpəsɪt, -s

oppositely
BR 'ɒpəzɪtli, 'ɒpəsɪtli
AM 'ɑpəzətli
oppositeness
BR 'ɒpəzɪtnɪs,
'ɒpəsɪtnɪs
AM 'ɑpəzətnəs
opposition
BR ,ɒpə'zɪʃn, -z
AM ,ɑpə'zɪʃən, -z
oppositional
BR ,ɒpə'zɪʃŋ(ə)l,
,ɒpə'zɪʃən(ə)l
AM ,ɑpə'zɪʃ(ə)nəl
oppositive
BR ə'pɒzɪtɪv
AM ə'pazədɪv
oppress
BR ə'prɛs, -ɪz, -ɪŋ, -t
AM ə'prɛs, -əz, -ɪŋ, -t
oppression
BR ə'prɛʃn
AM ə'prɛʃən
oppressive
BR ə'prɛsɪv
AM ə'prɛsɪv
oppressively
BR ə'prɛsɪvli
AM ə'prɛsɪvli
oppressiveness
BR ə'prɛsɪvnɪs
AM ə'prɛsɪvnɪs
oppressor
BR ə'prɛsə(r), -z
AM ə'prɛsər, -z
opprobrious
BR ə'prəʊbrɪəs
AM ə'proʊbrɪəs
opprobriously
BR ə'prəʊbrɪəsli
AM ə'proʊbrɪəsli
opprobriousness
BR ə'prəʊbrɪəsnəs
AM ə'proʊbrɪəsnəs
opprobrium
BR ə'prəʊbrɪəm
AM ə'proʊbrɪəm
oppugn
BR ə'pjuːn, -z, -ɪŋ, -d
AM ə'pjun, -z, -ɪŋ, -d
oppugnance
BR ə'pʌgnəns
AM ə'pəgnəns
oppugnancy
BR ə'pʌgnənsi
AM ə'pəgnənsi
oppugnant
BR ə'pʌgnənt
AM ə'pəgnənt
oppugnation
BR ,ɒpʌg'neɪʃn
AM ,ɑpəg'neɪʃən
oppugner
BR ə'pjuːnə(r), -z
AM ə'pjunər, -z

Oprah
BR 'əʊprə(r)
AM 'oʊprə
Opren®
BR 'əʊpr(ə)n, 'əʊprɛn
AM 'oʊprən
opsimath
BR 'ɒpsɪmaθ, -s
AM 'ɑpsə,mæθ, -s
opsimathy
BR ɒp'sɪməθi
AM ɑp'sɪməθi
opsonic
BR ɒp'sɒnɪk
AM ɑp'sɑnɪk
opsonin
BR 'ɒpsənɪn, -z
AM 'ɑpsənən, -z
opt
BR ɒpt, -s, -ɪŋ, -ɪd
AM ɑpt, -s, -ɪŋ, -əd
Optacon
BR 'ɒptək(ə)n
AM 'ɑptə,kɑn
optant
BR 'ɒpt(ə)nt, -s
AM 'ɑptnt, -s
optative
BR 'ɒptətɪv, -z
AM 'ɑptədɪv, -z
optatively
BR 'ɒptətɪvli
AM 'ɑptədɪvli
optic
BR 'ɒptɪk, -s
AM 'ɑptɪk, -s
optical
BR 'ɒptɪkl
AM 'ɑptəkəl
optically
BR 'ɒptɪkli
AM 'ɑptək(ə)li
optician
BR ɒp'tɪʃn, -z
AM ɑp'tɪʃən, -z
optima
BR 'ɒptɪmə(r)
AM 'ɑptəmə
optimal
BR 'ɒptɪml
AM 'ɑptəməl
optimality
BR ,ɒptɪ'malɪti
AM ,ɑptə'mælədi
optimally
BR 'ɒptɪməli, 'ɒptɪml̩i
AM 'ɑptəm(ə)li
optimisation
BR ,ɒptɪmaɪ'zeɪʃn, -z
AM ,ɑptəmə'zeɪʃən,
,ɑptə,maɪ'zeɪʃən, -z
optimise
BR 'ɒptɪmaɪz, -ɪz, -ɪŋ, -d
AM 'ɑptə,maɪz, -ɪz, -ɪŋ,
-d
optimism
BR 'ɒptɪmɪz(ə)m

AM 'ɑptə,mɪzəm
optimist
BR 'ɒptɪmɪst, -s
AM 'ɑptəməst, -s
optimistic
BR ,ɒptɪ'mɪstɪk
AM ,ɑptə'mɪstɪk
optimistically
BR ,ɒptɪ'mɪstɪkli
AM ,ɑptə'mɪstɪk(ə)li
optimization
BR ,ɒptɪmaɪ'zeɪʃn, -z
AM ,ɑptəmə'zeɪʃən,
,ɑptə,maɪ'zeɪʃən, -z
optimize
BR 'ɒptɪmaɪz, -ɪz, -ɪŋ, -d
AM 'ɑptə,maɪz, -ɪz, -ɪŋ,
-d
optimum
BR 'ɒptɪməm, -z
AM 'ɑptəməm, -z
option
BR 'ɒpʃn, -z
AM 'ɑpʃən, -z
optional
BR 'ɒpʃŋ(ə)l,
'ɒpʃən(ə)l
AM 'ɑpʃ(ə)nəl
optionality
BR ,ɒpʃə'nalɪti
AM ,ɑpʃə'nælədi
optionally
BR 'ɒpʃŋəli, 'ɒpʃn̩li,
'ɒpʃən̩li, 'ɒpʃ(ə)nəli
AM 'ɑpʃ(ə)nəli
optometer
BR ɒp'tɒmɪtə(r), -z
AM ɑp'tɑmədər, -z
optometric
BR ,ɒptə'mɛtrɪk
AM ,ɑptə'mɛtrɪk
optometrist
BR ɒp'tɒmɪtrɪst, -s
AM ɑp'tɑmətrəst, -s
optometry
BR ɒp'tɒmɪtri
AM ɑp'tɑmətri
optophone
BR 'ɒptəfəʊn, -z
AM 'ɑptə,foʊn, -z
opt-out
BR 'ɒptaʊt, -s
AM 'ɑp,taʊt, -s
Optrex®
BR 'ɒptrɛks
AM 'ɑptrɛks
opulence
BR 'ɒpjʊləns, 'ɒpjʊl̩ns
AM 'ɑpjələns,
'oʊpjələns
opulent
BR 'ɒpjʊlənt, 'ɒpjʊl̩nt
AM 'ɑpjələnt,
'oʊpjələnt
opulently
BR 'ɒpjʊləntli,
'ɒpjʊl̩ntli

AM 'ɒpjələn(t)li,
'oʊpjələn(t)li

opuntia
BR ə(ʊ)'pʌnʃ(ɪ)ə(r),
ɒ'pʌnʃ(ɪ)ə(r), -z
AM oʊ'pənʃ(i)ə, -z

opus
BR 'əʊpəs, -ɪz
AM 'oʊpəs, -əz

opuscule
BR ə'pʌskjuːl, -z
AM oʊ'pəskjul, -z

or¹
strong
BR ɔː(r)
AM ɔ(ə)r

or²
weak
BR ə(r)
AM ə(r)

orach
BR 'ɒrətʃ, -ɪz
AM 'ɔrətʃ, 'ɑrətʃ, -əz

orache
BR 'ɒrətʃ, -ɪz
AM 'ɔrətʃ, 'ɑrətʃ, -əz

oracle
BR 'ɒrəkl, -z
AM 'ɔrəkəl, -z

oracular
BR ɒ'rakjələ(r),
ə'rakjʊlə(r),
ɔː'rakjʊlə(r)
AM ɔ'ræjkələr,
ə'ræjkələr

oracularity
BR ɒ,rakjə'larɪti,
ə,rakjʊ'larɪti,
ɔː,rakjʊ'larɪti
AM ɔ,ræjkjə'lɛrədi,
ə,ræjkjə'lɛrədi

oracularly
BR ə'rakjʊləli,
ɒ'rakjʊləli,
ɔː'rakjʊləli
AM ɔ'ræjkələrli,
ə'ræjkələrli

oracy
BR 'ɔːrəsi
AM 'ɔrəsi, 'oʊrəsi

oral
BR 'ɔːrəl, 'ɒrl̩, -z
AM 'ɔrəl, 'oʊrəl, -z

oralism
BR 'ɔːrəlɪz(ə)m,
'ɒːrlɪz(ə)m
AM 'ɔrə,lɪzəm,
'ɒrə,lɪzəm

oralist
BR 'ɔːrəlɪst, 'ɔːrl̩ɪst, -s
AM 'ɔrələst, 'oʊrələst,
-s

orality
BR ɔː'ralɪti
AM ɔ'ræjlədi,
oʊ'ræjlədi

orally
BR 'ɔːrəli, 'ɒrl̩i

AM 'ɔrəli, 'oʊrəli

Oran
BR ə'ran, ə'rɑːn
AM oʊ'rɑn

orange
BR 'ɒrɪn(d)ʒ, -ɪz
AM 'ɔrən(d)ʒ, -ɪz

orangeade
BR ,ɒrɪn(d)ʒ'eɪd, -z
AM 'ɔrən(d)ʒ,eɪd, -z

Orangeism
BR 'ɒrɪn(d)ʒɪz(ə)m
AM 'ɔrən(d)ʒ,ɪzm

Orangeman
BR 'ɒrɪn(d)ʒmən
AM 'ɔrən(d)ʒmən

Orangemen
BR 'ɒrɪn(d)ʒmən
AM 'ɔrən(d)ʒmən

orangery
BR 'ɒrɪn(d)ʒ(ə)r|i, -ɪz
AM 'ɔrən(d)ʒri, -z

orang-outang
BR ə'raŋətaŋ,
ɔː'raŋətaŋ,
ɒ'raŋətaŋ,
,ɔːraŋ'uːtaŋ, -z
AM ə'ræŋ(g)ə,tæŋ,
oʊ'ræŋ(g)ə,tæŋ, -z

orangutan
BR ə'raŋətan,
ə'raŋətaŋ, ɔː'raŋətan,
ɒ'raŋətaŋ,
,ɔːraŋ'uːtan, -z
AM ə'ræŋ(g)ə,tæŋ,
oʊ'ræŋ(g)ə,tæŋ, -z

orangutang
BR ə'raŋətaŋ,
ɔː'raŋətaŋ,
ɒ'raŋətaŋ,
,ɔːraŋ'uːtaŋ, -z
AM ə'ræŋ(g)ə,tæŋ,
oʊ'ræŋ(g)ə,tæŋ, -z

orate
BR ɔː'reɪt, ɒ'reɪt, ə'reɪt,
-s, -ɪŋ, -ɪd
AM ɔ'reɪ|t, 'ɔr,eɪ|t, -ts,
-dɪŋ, -dɪd

oration
BR ə'reɪʃn, ɒ'reɪʃn, -z
AM ɔ'reɪʃən, ə'reɪʃən,
-z

orator
BR 'ɒrətə(r), -z
AM 'ɔrədər, -z

oratorial
BR ,ɒrə'tɔːriəl
AM ,ɔrə'tɔriəl

oratorian
BR ,ɒrə'tɔːriən, -z
AM ,ɔrə'tɔriən, -z

oratorical
BR ,ɒrə'tɒrɪkl
AM ,ɔrə'tɔrəkəl

oratorically
BR ,ɒrə'tɒrɪkli
AM ,ɔrə'tɔrək(ə)li

oratorio
BR ,ɒrə'tɔːriəʊ, -z
AM ,ɔrə'tɔrioʊ, -z

oratory
BR 'ɒrət(ə)ri
AM 'ɔrə,tɔri

orb
BR ɔːb, -z
AM ɔ(ə)rb, -z

Orbach
BR 'ɔːbak
AM 'ɔr,bak

orbicular
BR ɔː'bɪkjələ(r)
AM ɔr'bɪkjələr

orbicularity
BR ɔː,bɪkjə'larɪti
AM ɔr,bɪkjə'lɛrədi

orbicularly
BR ɔː'bɪkjʊləli
AM ɔr'bɪkjələrli

orbiculate
BR ɔː'bɪkjələt
AM ɔr'bɪkjələt,
ɔr'bɪkjə,leɪt

orbit
BR 'ɔːb|ɪt, -ɪts, -ɪtɪŋ,
-ɪtɪd
AM 'ɔrbə|t, -ts, -dɪŋ,
-dəd

orbital
BR 'ɔːbɪtl
AM 'ɔrbədəl

orbiter
BR 'ɔːbɪtə(r), -z
AM 'ɔrbədər, -z

orc
BR ɔːk, -s
AM ɔ(ə)rk, -s

orca
BR 'ɔːkə(r), -z
AM 'ɔrkə, -z

Orcadian
BR ɔː'keɪdiən, -z
AM ɔr'keɪdiən, -z

orchard
BR 'ɔːtʃəd, -z
AM 'ɔrtʃərd, -z

orcharding
BR 'ɔːtʃədɪŋ
AM 'ɔrtʃərdɪŋ

orchardist
BR 'ɔːtʃədɪst, -s
AM 'ɔrtʃərdəst, -s

orchardman
BR 'ɔːtʃədmən
AM 'ɔrtʃərd,mæn

orchardmen
BR 'ɔːtʃədmən
AM 'ɔrtʃərd,mɛn

orchestic
BR ɔː'kɛstɪk
AM ɔr'kɛstɪk

orchestra
BR 'ɔːkɪstrə(r),
'ɔːkɛstrə(r), -z

AM 'ɔːkəstrə,
'ɔr,kɛstrə, -z

orchestral
BR ɔː'kɛstr(ə)l
AM ɔr'kɛstrəl

orchestrally
BR ɔː'kɛstrl̩i,
ɔː'kɛstrəli
AM ɔr'kɛstrəli

orchestrate
BR 'ɔːkɪstreɪt
'ɔː'kɛstreɪt, -s, -ɪŋ, -ɪd
AM 'ɔːkə,streɪ|t, -ts,
-dɪŋ, -dɪd

orchestration
BR ,ɔːkɪ'streɪʃn,
,ɔːke'streɪʃn, -z
AM ,ɔrkə'streɪʃən, -z

orchestrator
BR 'ɔːkɪstreɪtə(r),
'ɔː'kɛstreɪtə(r), -z
AM 'ɔːkə,streɪdər, -z

orchestrina
BR ,ɔːkɪ'striːnə(r),
,ɔːke'striːnə(r), -z
AM ,ɔrkə'strinə, -z

orchid
BR 'ɔːkɪd, -z
AM 'ɔrkəd, -z

orchidaceous
BR ,ɔːkɪ'deɪʃəs
AM ,ɔrkə'deɪʃəs

orchidist
BR 'ɔːkɪdɪst, -s
AM 'ɔrkədəst, -s

orchidology
BR ,ɔːkɪ'dɒlədʒi
AM ,ɔrkə'dɑlədʒi

orchil
BR 'ɔːkɪl, 'ɔːtʃɪl, -z
AM 'ɔrkəl, -z

orchilla
BR ɔː'kɪlə(r),
ɔː'tʃɪlə(r), -z
AM 'ɔrkələ, -z

orchis
BR 'ɔːk|ɪs, -ɪsɪz
AM 'ɔrkəs, -əz

orchitis
BR ɔː'kʌɪtɪs
AM ɔr'kaɪdəs

orcin
BR 'ɔːsɪn
AM 'ɔrsən

orcinol
BR 'ɔːsɪnɒl
AM 'ɔrsə,nɑl, 'ɔrsənəl

Orcus
BR 'ɔːkəs
AM 'ɔrkəs

Orczy
BR 'ɔːtsi, 'ɔːksi
AM 'ɔrtsi

ordain
BR ɔː'deɪn, -z, -ɪŋ, -d
AM ɔr'deɪn, -z, -ɪŋ, -d

ordainer
BR ɔːˈdeɪnə(r), -z
AM ɔrˈdeɪnər, -z

ordainment
BR ɔːˈdeɪm(ə)nt, -s
AM ɔrˈdeɪnmənt, -s

ordeal
BR ɔːˈdiːl, -z
AM ɔrˈdil, -z

order
BR ˈɔːd|ə(r), -əz, -(ə)rɪŋ,
-əd
AM ˈɔrdər, -z, -ɪŋ, -d

orderer
BR ˈɔːd(ə)rə(r), -z
AM ˈɔrdərər, -z

ordering
BR ˈɔːd(ə)rɪŋ, -z
AM ˈɔrd(ə)rɪŋ, -z

orderliness
BR ˈɔːdəlɪnɪs
AM ˈɔrdərlinɪs

orderly
BR ˈɔːdəl|i, -ɪz
AM ˈɔrdərli, -z

ordinaire
BR ˌɔːdiˈnɛː(r)
AM ˌɔrdəˈnɛ(ə)r

ordinal
BR ˈɔːdɪnl, ˈɔːdn̩l, -z
AM ˈɔrdnl, -z

ordinance
BR ˈɔːd(ɪ)nəns,
ˈɔːdn̩əns, -ɪz
AM ˈɔrdn̩əns, -əz

ordinand
BR ˈɔːdɪnand,
ˈɔːdɪmənd, -z
AM ˈɔrdəˌnænd, -z

ordinarily
BR ˈɔːdɪn(ə)rəli,
ˈɔːdn̩(ə)rəli
AM ˌɔrdn̩ˈɛrəli

ordinariness
BR ˈɔːdɪn(ə)rɪnɪs,
ˈɔːdn̩(ə)rɪnɪs
AM ˈɔrdn̩ˌɛrɪnɪs

ordinary
BR ˈɔːdɪn(ə)ri,
ˈɔːdn̩(ə)ri
AM ˈɔrdn̩ˌɛri

ordinate
BR ˈɔːdɪnət, ˈɔːdn̩ət, -s
AM ˈɔrdn̩ət, -s

ordination
BR ˌɔːdɪˈneɪʃn, -z
AM ˌɔrdn̩ˈeɪʃən, -z

ordnance
BR ˈɔːdnəns
AM ˈɔrdnəns

ordonnance
BR ˈɔːdənəns, -ɪz
AM ˈɔrdnəns, -əz

Ordovician
BR ˌɔːdə(ʊ)ˈvɪʃiən,
ˌɔːdə(ʊ)ˈvɪsɪən
AM ˌɔrdəˈvɪʃən

ordure
BR ˈɔːdj(ʊ)ə(r),
ˈɔːdʒə(r)
AM ˈɔrdʒər

ore
BR ɔː(r), -z
AM ɔ(ə)r, -z

öre
BR ˈəːrə(r)
AM ˈɛrə
SW ˈəːrɛ

øre
BR ˈəːrə(r)
AM ˈɛrə
DAN ˈœːʌ
NO ˈœːrə

oread
BR ˈɔːriad, -z
AM ˈɔriˌæd, -z

orectic
BR ɒˈrɛktɪk
AM oʊˈrɛktɪk

oregano
BR ˌɒrɪˈgɑːnəʊ,
əˈrɛgənəʊ
AM əˈrɛgəˌnoʊ

Oregon
BR ˈɒrɪg(ə)n
AM ˈɔrəˌgɑn, ˈɔrəgən

Oregonian
BR ˌɒrɪˈgəʊniən, -z
AM ˌɔrəˈgoʊniən, -z

O'Reilly
BR əˈ(ʊ)rʌɪli
AM oʊˈraɪli

Orenburg
BR ˈɒrənbəːg
AM ˈɔrənˌbɜrg

Oreo®
BR ˈɔːriəʊ, -z
AM ˈɔrioʊ, -z

oreography
BR ˌɒrɪˈɒgrəfi
AM ˌɔriˈɑgrəfi

Oresteia
BR ˌɒrɪˈstʌɪə(r),
ˌɒrɪˈstiːə(r),
ˌɒrɪˈsteɪə(r),
ˌɔːrɪˈstʌɪə(r),
ˌɔːrɪˈstiːə(r),
ˌɔːrɪˈsteɪə(r)
AM ˌɔrəsˈteɪə

Orestes
BR ɒˈrɛstiːz
AM ɔˈrɛstiz

oreweed
BR ˈɔːwiːd
AM ˈɔrˌwid

orfe
BR ɔːf, -s
AM ɔ(ə)rf, -s

Orff
BR ɔːf
AM ɔ(ə)rf

Orford
BR ˈɔːfəd
AM ˈɔrfərd

organ
BR ˈɔːg(ə)n, -z
AM ˈɔrgən, -z

organa
BR ˈɔːgənə(r), ˈɔːgnə(r)
AM ˈɔrgənə

organdie
BR ˈɔːg(ə)ndˌi, -ɪz
AM ˈɔrgəndi, -z

organdy
BR ˈɔːg(ə)ndˌi, -ɪz
AM ˈɔrgəndi, -z

organelle
BR ˌɔːgəˈnɛl, -z
AM ˌɔrgəˈnɛl, -z

organic
BR ɔːˈganɪk
AM ɔrˈgænɪk

organically
BR ɔːˈganɪkli
AM ɔrˈgænək(ə)li

organisable
BR ˈɔːgənʌɪzəbl,
ˈɔːgnʌɪzəbl
AM ˈɔrgəˌnaɪzəbəl

organisation
BR ˌɔːgənʌɪˈzeɪʃn,
ˌɔːgnʌɪˈzeɪʃn, -z
AM ˌɔrgənəˈzeɪʃən,
ˌɔrgəˌnaɪˈzeɪʃən, -z

organisational
BR ˌɔːgənʌɪˈzeɪʃn̩(ə)l,
ˌɔːgənʌɪˈzeɪʃən(ə)l,
ˌɔːgnʌɪˈzeɪʃn̩(ə)l,
ˌɔːgnʌɪˈzeɪʃən(ə)l
AM ˌɔrgənəˈzeɪʃ(ə)nəl,
ˌɔrgəˌnaɪˈzeɪʃ(ə)nəl

organisationally
BR ˌɔːgənʌɪˈzeɪʃn̩əli,
ˌɔːgənʌɪˈzeɪʃn̩li,
ˌɔːgənʌɪˈzeɪʃ(ə)nəli,
ˌɔːgnʌɪˈzeɪʃn̩əli,
ˌɔːgnʌɪˈzeɪʃn̩li,
ˌɔːgnʌɪˈzeɪʃ(ə)nəli
AM ˌɔrgənəˈzeɪʃ(ə)nəli,
ˌɔrgəˌnaɪˈzeɪʃ(ə)nəli

organise
BR ˈɔːgənʌɪz, ˈɔːgnʌɪz,
-ɪz, -ɪŋ, -d
AM ˈɔrgəˌnaɪz, -ɪz, -ɪŋ,
-d

organiser
BR ˈɔːgənʌɪzə(r),
ˈɔːgnʌɪzə(r), -z
AM ˈɔrgəˌnaɪzər, -z

organism
BR ˈɔːgənɪz(ə)m,
ˈɔːgnɪz(ə)m, -z
AM ˈɔrgəˌnɪzəm, -z

organist
BR ˈɔːgənɪst, ˈɔːgnɪst, -s
AM ˈɔrgənəst, -s

organizable
BR ˈɔːgənʌɪzəbl,
ˈɔːgnʌɪzəbl
AM ˈɔrgəˌnaɪzəbəl

organization
BR ˌɔːgənʌɪˈzeɪʃn,
ˌɔːgnʌɪˈzeɪʃn, -z
AM ˌɔrgənəˈzeɪʃən,
ˌɔrgəˌnaɪˈzeɪʃən, -z

organizational
BR ˌɔːgənʌɪˈzeɪʃn̩(ə)l,
ˌɔːgənʌɪˈzeɪʃən(ə)l,
ˌɔːgnʌɪˈzeɪʃn̩(ə)l,
ˌɔːgnʌɪˈzeɪʃən(ə)l
AM ˌɔrgənəˈzeɪʃ(ə)nəl,
ˌɔrgəˌnaɪˈzeɪʃ(ə)nəl

organizationally
BR ˌɔːgənʌɪˈzeɪʃn̩əli,
ˌɔːgənʌɪˈzeɪʃn̩li,
ˌɔːgənʌɪˈzeɪʃ(ə)nəli,
ˌɔːgnʌɪˈzeɪʃn̩əli,
ˌɔːgnʌɪˈzeɪʃn̩li,
ˌɔːgnʌɪˈzeɪʃ(ə)nəli
AM ˌɔrgənəˈzeɪʃ(ə)nəli,
ˌɔrgəˌnaɪˈzeɪʃ(ə)nəli

organize
BR ˈɔːgənʌɪz, ˈɔːgnʌɪz,
-ɪz, -ɪŋ, -d
AM ˈɔrgəˌnaɪz, -ɪz, -ɪŋ,
-d

organizer
BR ˈɔːgənʌɪzə(r),
ˈɔːgnʌɪzə(r), -z
AM ˈɔrgəˌnaɪzər, -z

organochlorine
BR ɔːˌganəʊˈklɔːriːn,
ˌɔːgənəʊˈklɔːriːn,
ˌɔːgnəʊˈklɔːriːn, -z
AM ˈɔrgənoʊˈklɔrin,
ɔrˌgænoʊˈklɔrin, -z

organoleptic
BR ɔːˌganə(ʊ)ˈlɛptɪk,
ˌɔːgənə(ʊ)ˈlɛptɪk,
ˌɔːgnə(ʊ)ˈlɛptɪk
AM ˈɔrgənoʊˈlɛptɪk

organometallic
BR ɔːˌganəʊmɪˈtalɪk,
ˌɔːgənəʊmɪˈtalɪk,
ˌɔːgnəʊmɪˈtalɪk
AM ˌɔrgənoʊməˈtælɪk

organon
BR ˈɔːgənɒn, ˈɔːgnɒn, -z
AM ˈɔrgəˌnɑn, -z

organophosphate
BR ɔːˌganəʊˈfɒsfeɪt,
ˌɔːgənəʊˈfɒsfeɪt,
ˌɔːgnəʊˈfɒsfeɪt, -s
AM ˌɔrgənəˈfɑsˌfeɪt,
ɔrˌgænoʊˈfɑsˌfeɪt, -s

organophosphorus
BR ɔːˌganəʊˈfɒsf(ə)rəs,
ˌɔːgənəʊˈfɒsf(ə)rəs,
ˌɔːgnəʊˈfɒsf(ə)rəs
AM ˈɔrgənəˈfɑsf(ə)rəs,
ɔrˌgænoʊˈfɑsf(ə)rəs

organotherapy
BR ɔːˌganəʊˈθɛrəpi,
ˌɔːgnəʊˈθɛrəpi
AM ˈɔrgənəˈθɛrəpi,
ɔrˌgænoʊˈθɛrəpi

organum
BR ˈɔːɡənəm, ˈɔːɡnəm
AM ˈɔrɡənəm
organza
BR ɔːˈɡænzə(r), -z
AM ɔrˈɡænzə, -z
organzine
BR ˈɔːɡ(ə)nziːn,
ɔːˈɡanziːn, -z
AM ˈɔrɡənˌzin, -z
orgasm
BR ˈɔːɡaz(ə)m, -z
AM ˈɔrˌɡæzəm, -z
orgasmic
BR ɔːˈɡazmɪk
AM ɔrˈɡæzmɪk
orgasmically
BR ɔːˈɡazmɪkli
AM ɔrˈɡæzmək(ə)li
orgastic
BR ɔːˈɡastɪk
AM ɔrˈɡæstɪk
orgastically
BR ɔːˈɡastɪkli
AM ɔrˈɡæstək(ə)li
orgeat
BR ˈɔːdʒɪət, -s
AM ˈɔrˌʒɑt, -s
orgiastic
BR ˌɔːdʒɪˈastɪk
AM ˌɔrdʒiˈæstɪk
orgiastically
BR ˌɔːdʒɪˈastɪkli
AM ˌɔrdʒiˈæstək(ə)li
orgone
BR ˈɔːɡəʊn
AM ˈɔrˌɡoʊn
Orgreave
BR ˈɔːɡriːv
AM ˈɔrˌɡriv
orgulous
BR ˈɔːɡjʉləs
AM ˈɔrɡ(j)ələs
orgy
BR ˈɔːdʒi, -ɪz
AM ˈɔrdʒi, -z
Oriana
BR ˌɒrɪˈɑːnə(r),
ˌɔːrɪˈɑːnə(r)
AM ˌɔriˈɑnə
oribi
BR ˈɒrɪb|i, -ɪz
AM ˈɔrəbi, -z
oriel
BR ˈɔːrɪəl, -z
AM ˈɔriəl, -z
Orient
BR ˈɔːrɪənt, ˈɒrɪənt
AM ˈɔriənt
orient
verb
BR ˈɔːrɪɛnt, ˈɒrɪɛnt, -s,
-ɪŋ, -ɪd
AM ˈɔriˌɛn|t, -ts, -(t)ɪŋ,
-(t)əd

Oriental
BR ˌɔːrɪˈɛntl, ˌɒrɪˈɛntl,
-z
AM ˌɔriˈɛn(t)l, -z
orientalise
BR ˌɔːrɪˈɛntlˌʌɪz,
ˌɔːrɪˈɛntəlˌʌɪz,
ˌɒrɪˈɛntlˌʌɪz,
ˌɒrɪˈɛntəlˌʌɪz, -ɪz, -ɪŋ, -d
AM ˈɔriˈɛn(t)lˌʌɪz, -ɪz,
-ɪŋ, -d
orientalism
BR ˌɔːrɪˈɛntlɪz(ə)m,
ˌɔːrɪˈɛntəlɪz(ə)m,
ˌɒrɪˈɛntlɪz(ə)m,
ˌɒrɪˈɛntəlɪz(ə)m
AM ˈɔriˈɛn(t)lˌɪzəm
orientalist
BR ˌɔːrɪˈɛntlɪst,
ˌɔːrɪˈɛntəlɪst,
ˌɒrɪˈɛntlɪst,
ˌɒrɪˈɛntəlɪst, -s
AM ˈɔriˈɛn(t)ləst, -s
orientalize
BR ˌɔːrɪˈɛntlˌʌɪz,
ˌɔːrɪˈɛntəlˌʌɪz,
ˌɒrɪˈɛntlˌʌɪz,
ˌɒrɪˈɛntəlˌʌɪz, -ɪz, -ɪŋ, -d
AM ˈɔriˈɛn(t)lˌʌɪz, -ɪz,
-ɪŋ, -d
orientally
BR ˌɔːrɪˈɛntli,
ˌɔːrɪˈɛntəli, ˌɒrɪˈɛntli,
ˌɒrɪˈɛntəli
AM ˈɔriˈɛn(t)li
orientate
BR ˈɔːrɪənteɪt,
ˈɔːrɪənteɪt, ˈɒrɪənteɪt,
ˈɒrɪənteɪt, -s
AM ˈɔriənˌteɪt, -s
orientation
BR ˌɔːrɪənˈteɪʃn,
ˌɔːrɪɛnˈteɪʃn,
ˌɒrɪənˈteɪʃn,
ˌɒrɪɛnˈteɪʃn, -z
AM ˌɔriənˈteɪʃən, -z
orientational
BR ˌɔːrɪənˈteɪʃn̩(ə)l,
ˌɔːrɪənˈteɪʃən(ə)l,
ˌɔːrɪɛnˈteɪʃn̩(ə)l,
ˌɔːrɪɛnˈteɪʃən(ə)l,
ˌɒrɪənˈteɪʃn̩(ə)l,
ˌɒrɪənˈteɪʃən(ə)l,
ˌɒrɪɛnˈteɪʃn̩(ə)l,
ˌɒrɪɛnˈteɪʃən(ə)l
AM ˌɔriənˈteɪʃ(ə)nəl
orienteer
BR ˌɔːrɪənˈtɪə(r),
ˌɔːrɪɛnˈtɪə(r),
ˌɒrɪənˈtɪə(r),
ˌɒrɪɛnˈtɪə(r), -z
AM ˌɔriənˈtɪ(ə)r, -z
orienteering
BR ˌɔːrɪənˈtɪərɪŋ,
ˌɔːrɪɛnˈtɪərɪŋ,
ˌɒrɪənˈtɪərɪŋ,
ˌɒrɪɛnˈtɪərɪŋ
AM ˌɔriənˈtɪrɪŋ

orifice
BR ˈɒrɪf|ɪs, -ɪsɪz
AM ˈɔrəfəs, -əz
oriflamme
BR ˈɒrɪflam, -z
AM ˈɔrəˌflæm, -z
origami
BR ˌɒrɪˈɡɑːmi
AM ˌɔrəˈɡɑmi
origan
BR ˈɒrɪɡ(ə)n, -z
AM ˈɔrəɡən, -z
origanum
BR əˈrɪɡənəm,
əˈrɪɡnəm, ɒˈrɪɡənəm,
ɒˈrɪɡnəm, -z
AM əˈrɪɡənəm, -z
Origen
BR ˈɒrɪdʒɛn
AM ˈɔriˌdʒɛn
origin
BR ˈɒrɪdʒ(ɪ)n, -z
AM ˈɔrədʒən, -z
original
BR əˈrɪdʒn̩l, əˈrɪdʒɪnl,
-z
AM əˈrɪdʒ(ə)nəl, -z
originality
BR əˌrɪdʒɪˈnalɪti
AM əˌrɪdʒəˈnælədi
originally
BR əˈrɪdʒn̩li,
əˈrɪdʒnəli, əˈrɪdʒɪnli,
əˈrɪdʒɪnəli
AM əˈrɪdʒ(ə)nəli
originate
BR əˈrɪdʒɪneɪt, -s, -ɪŋ,
-ɪd
AM əˈrɪdʒəˌneɪ|t, -ts,
-dɪŋ, -dɪd
origination
BR əˌrɪdʒɪˈneɪʃn, -z
AM əˌrɪdʒəˈneɪʃən, -z
originative
BR əˈrɪdʒɪnətɪv
AM əˈrɪdʒəˌneɪdɪv
originator
BR əˈrɪdʒɪneɪtə(r), -z
AM əˈrɪdʒəˌneɪdər, -z
orinasal
BR ˌɔːrɪˈneɪzl
AM ˌɔrəˈneɪzəl
O-ring
BR ˈəʊrɪŋ, -z
AM ˈoʊˌrɪŋ, -z
Orinoco
BR ˌɒrɪˈnəʊkəʊ
AM ˌɔrəˈnoʊkoʊ
Orinthia
BR əˈrɪnθɪə(r),
ɒˈrɪnθɪə(r)
AM əˈrɪnθɪə
oriole
BR ˈɔːrɪəʊl, -z
AM ˈɔriˌoʊl, -z
Orion
BR əˈrʌɪən
AM əˈraɪən, oʊˈraɪən

O'Riordan
BR ə(ʊ)ˈrɪədn
AM oʊˈrɪrdən
orison
BR ˈɒrɪzn, -z
AM ˈɔrəsən, ˈɔrəzn, -z
Orissa
BR ɒˈrɪsə(r)
AM ɔˈrɪsə
Oriya
BR ɒˈriːə(r), -z
AM ɔˈriə, -z
ork
BR ɔːk, -s
AM ɔ(ə)rk, -s
Orkney
BR ˈɔːkn|i, -ɪz
AM ˈɔrkni, -z
Orlando
BR ɔːˈlandəʊ
AM ɔrˈlændoʊ
orle
BR ɔːl, -z
AM ˈɔr(ə)l, -z
Orleanist
BR ɔːˈlɪənɪst, -s
AM ɔrˈlɪənəst, -s
Orléans
BR ɔːˈliːənz, ˈɔːlɪənz
AM ˈɔrliən(z),
ɔrˈliən(z)
FR ɔRleɑ̃
Orlon®
BR ˈɔːlɒn
AM ˈɔrˌlɑn
orlop
BR ˈɔːlɒp, -s
AM ˈɔrˌlɑp, -s
Orm
BR ɔːm
AM ɔ(ə)rm
DAN ˈɔːˈʌm
Orme
BR ɔːm
AM ɔ(ə)rm
ormer
BR ˈɔːmə(r), -z
AM ˈɔrmər, -z
Ormerod
BR ˈɔːm(ə)rɒd
AM ˈɔrmˌrɑd
Ormesby
BR ˈɔːmzbi
AM ˈɔrmzbi
ormolu
BR ˈɔːməluː
AM ˈɔrməˌlu
Ormond
BR ˈɔːm(ə)nd
AM ˈɔrmənd
Ormonde
BR ˈɔːm(ə)nd
AM ˈɔrmənd
Ormrod
BR ˈɔːmrɒd
AM ˈɔrmˌrɑd

Ormsby
BR ˈɔːmzbi
AM ˈɔrmzbi
Ormskirk
BR ˈɔːmzkəːk
AM ˈɔrmzˌkərk
Ormuz
BR ˈɔːmʌz
AM ˈɔrməz
ornament[1]
noun
BR ˈɔːnəm(ə)nt
AM ˈɔrnəmənt
ornament[2]
verb
BR ˈɔːnəmɛnt, -s, -ɪŋ, -ɪd
AM ˈɔrnəˌmɛn|t, -ts,
-(t)ɪŋ, -(t)əd
ornamental
BR ˌɔːnəˈmɛntl
AM ˌɔrnəˈmen(t)l
ornamentalism
BR ˌɔːnəˈmɛnt|ɪz(ə)m,
ˌɔːnəˈmɛntəlɪz(ə)m
AM ˌɔrnəˈmen(t)lˌɪzəm
ornamentalist
BR ˌɔːnəˈmɛntlɪst,
ˌɔːnəˈmɛntəlɪst, -s
AM ˌɔrnəˈmen(t)ləst,
-s
ornamentally
BR ˌɔːnəˈmɛntli,
ˌɔːnəˈmɛntəli
AM ˌɔrnəˈmen(t)li
ornamentation
BR ˌɔːnəmɛnˈteɪʃn,
ˌɔːnəm(ə)nˈteɪʃn
AM ˌɔrnəˌmenˈteɪʃən
ornate
BR ɔːˈneɪt
AM ɔrˈneɪt
ornately
BR ɔːˈneɪtli
AM ɔrˈneɪtli
ornateness
BR ɔːˈneɪtnɪs
AM ɔrˈneɪtnɪs
orneriness
BR ˈɔːn(ə)rɪnɪs
AM ˈɔrn(ə)rinɪs
ornery
BR ˈɔːn(ə)ri
AM ˈɔrn(ə)ri
ornithic
BR ɔːˈnɪθɪk
AM ɔrˈnɪθɪk
ornithischian
BR ˌɔːnɪˈθɪʃən,
ˌɔːnɪˈθɪskɪən, -z
AM ˌɔrnəˈθɪskɪən,
ˌɔrnəˈθɪʃ(i)ən, -z
ornithological
BR ˌɔːnɪθəˈlɒdʒɪkl
AM ɔrˈnɪθəˈlɑdʒəkəl
ornithologically
BR ˌɔːnɪθəˈlɒdʒɪkli
AM ɔrˈnɪθəˈlɑdʒək(ə)li

ornithologist
BR ˌɔːnɪˈθɒlədʒɪst, -s
AM ˌɔrnəˈθɑlədʒəst, -s
ornithology
BR ˌɔːnɪˈθɒlədʒi
AM ˌɔrnəˈθɑlədʒi
ornithorhynchus
BR ˌɔːnɪθə(ʊ)ˈrɪŋkəs,
-ɪz
AM ɔrˌnɪθəˈrɪŋkəs,
ˈɔrnəθəˈrɪŋkəs, -əz
ornithoscopy
BR ˌɔːnɪˈθɒskəpi
AM ˌɔrnəˈθɑskəpi
orogenesis
BR ˌɒrə(ʊ)ˈdʒɛnɪsɪs,
ˌɔːrə(ʊ)ˈdʒɛnɪsɪs
AM ˌɔrouˈdʒɛnəsəs
orogenetic
BR ˌɒrəʊdʒɪˈnɛtɪk,
ˌɔːrəʊdʒɪˈnɛtɪk
AM ˌɔrouˈdʒəˈnɛdɪk
orogenic
BR ˌɒrə(ʊ)ˈdʒɛnɪk,
ˌɔːrə(ʊ)ˈdʒɛnɪk
AM ˌɔrouˈdʒɛnɪk
orogeny
BR ɒˈrɒdʒɪni,
əˈrɒdʒɪni, ɔːˈrɒdʒɪni
AM əˈrɑdʒ(ə)ni
orographic
BR ˌɒrəˈɡrafɪk,
ˌɔːrəˈɡrafɪk
AM ˌɔrəˈɡræfɪk
orographical
BR ˌɒrəˈɡrafɪkl,
ˌɔːrəˈɡrafɪkl
AM ˌɔrəˈɡræfəkəl
orography
BR ɒˈrɒɡrəfi, əˈrɒɡrəfi,
ɔːˈrɒɡrəfi
AM ɔˈrɑɡrəfi
oroide
BR ˈɒrəʊʌɪd, -z
AM ˈɔrəˌwaɪd, -z
orological
BR ˌɒrəˈlɒdʒɪkl
AM ˌɔrəˈlɑdʒəkəl
orologist
BR ɒˈrɒlədʒɪst,
əˈrɒlədʒɪst,
ɔːˈrɒlədɪst, -s
AM ɔˈrɑlədʒəst, -s
orology
BR ɒˈrɒlədʒi,
əˈrɒlədʒi, ɔːˈrɒlədʒi
AM ɔˈrɑlədʒi
Oronsay
BR ˈɒrənseɪ, ˈɒrŋseɪ,
ˈɒrənzeɪ, ˈɒrŋzeɪ
AM ˈɔrənˌseɪ
Orontes
BR əˈrɒntiːz, ɒˈrɒntiːz
AM ɔˈrɑn(t)iz,
ɔˈrɑn(t)iz
oropendola
BR ˌɒrəˈpɛndələ(r),
ˌɒrəˈpɛndlə(r), -z

AM ˌɔrəˈpɛndələ, -z
oropharynges
BR ˌɔːrəʊfəˈrɪn(d)ʒiːz
AM ˌɔroufəˈrɪndʒiz
oropharynx
BR ˌɔːrəʊˈfarɪŋks, -ɪz
AM ˌɔrouˈfɛrɪŋks, -ɪz
orotund
BR ˈɒrətʌnd
AM ˈɔrəˌtənd
O'Rourke
BR əˈ(ʊ)ˈrɔːk
AM oʊˈrɔ(ə)rk
orphan
BR ˈɔːfn, -nz, -nɪŋ, -nd
AM ˈɔrfjən, -ənz,
-(ə)nɪŋ, -ənd
orphanage
BR ˈɔːfn|ɪdʒ, ˈɔːfən|ɪdʒ,
-ɪdʒɪz
AM ˈɔrf(ə)nɪdʒ, -ɪz
orphanhood
BR ˈɔːfnhʊd
AM ˈɔrfənˌ(h)ʊd
orphanise
BR ˈɔːfnʌɪz, ˈɔːfənʌɪz,
-ɪz, -ɪŋ, -d
AM ˈɔrfəˌnaɪz, -ɪz, -ɪŋ, -d
orphanize
BR ˈɔːfnʌɪz, ˈɔːfənʌɪz,
-ɪz, -ɪŋ, -d
AM ˈɔrfəˌnaɪz, -ɪz, -ɪŋ, -d
Orphean
BR ɔːˈfiːən, ˈɔːfɪən
AM ˈɔrfiən
Orpheus
BR ˈɔːfɪəs
AM ˈɔrfiəs
Orphic
BR ˈɔːfɪk
AM ˈɔrfɪk
Orphism
BR ˈɔːfɪz(ə)m
AM ˈɔrˌfɪzəm
orphrey
BR ˈɔːfr|i, -ɪz
AM ˈɔrfri, -z
orpiment
BR ˈɔːpɪm(ə)nt, -s
AM ˈɔrpəmənt, -s
orpin
BR ˈɔːpɪn, -z
AM ˈɔrpən, -z
orpine
BR ˈɔːpʌɪn, ˈɔːpɪn, -z
AM ˈɔrpən, -z
Orpington
BR ˈɔːpɪŋt(ə)n
AM ˈɔrpɪŋtən
Orr
BR ɔː(r)
AM ɔ(ə)r
orra
BR ˈɒrə(r)
AM ˈɒrə
Orrell
BR ˈɒrəl, ˈɒrl

AM ˈɔrəl
orrery
BR ˈɒrər|i, -ɪz
AM ˈɔrəri, -z
orris
BR ˈɒr|ɪs, -ɪsɪz
AM ˈɔrəs, -əz
Orsino
BR ɔːˈsiːnəʊ
AM ɔrˈsinoʊ
Orson
BR ˈɔːsn
AM ˈɔrsən
ortanique
BR ˌɔːtəˈniːk, -s
AM ˌɔrtəˈnik, -s
Ortega
BR ɔːˈteɪɡə(r),
ɔːˈtiːɡə(r)
AM ɔrˈteɪɡə
orthocephalic
BR ˌɔːθəʊsɪˈfalɪk,
ˌɔːθəʊkɛˈfalɪk
AM ˌɔrθoʊsəˈfælɪk
orthochromatic
BR ˌɔːθəʊkrəˈmatɪk
AM ˌɔrθoʊkrəˈmædɪk
orthoclase
BR ˈɔːθə(ʊ)kleɪz,
ˈɔːθə(ʊ)kleɪs, -ɪz
AM ˈɔrθəˌkleɪs,
ˈɔrθəˌkleɪz, -ɪz
orthodontia
BR ˌɔːθəˈdɒntɪə(r)
AM ˌɔrθəˈdɑn(t)ʃ(i)ə
orthodontic
BR ˌɔːθəˈdɒntɪk, -s
AM ˌɔrθəˈdɑn(t)ɪk, -s
orthodontist
BR ˌɔːθəˈdɒntɪst, -s
AM ˌɔrθəˈdɑn(t)əst, -s
orthodox
BR ˈɔːθədɒks
AM ˈɔrθəˌdɑks
orthodoxly
BR ˈɔːθədɒksli
AM ˈɔrθəˌdɑksli
orthodoxy
BR ˈɔːθədɒks|i, -ɪz
AM ˈɔrθəˌdɑksi, -z
orthoepic
BR ˌɔːθəʊˈɛpɪk
AM ˌɔrθoʊˈɛpɪk
orthoepist
BR ˈɔːθəʊˌɛpɪst,
ˌɔːθəʊˈɛpɪst,
ˈɔːθəʊiːpɪst,
ˌɔːθəʊiːpɪst,
ɔːˈθəʊɪpɪst, -s
AM ɔrˈθoʊəpəst, -s
orthoepy
BR ˈɔːθəʊiːpi,
ˈɔːθəʊˌɛpi, ɔːˈθəʊɪpi,
ɔːˈθəʊɪpi
AM ɔrˈθoʊəpi
orthogenesis
BR ˌɔːθə(ʊ)ˈdʒɛnɪsɪs
AM ˌɔrθoʊˈdʒɛnəsəs

orthogenetic
BR ˌɔːθəʊdʒɪˈnetɪk
AM ˌɔrθoʊdʒəˈnedɪk

orthogenetically
BR ˌɔːθəʊdʒɪˈnetɪkli
AM ˌɔrθoʊdʒəˈnedək(ə)li

orthognathous
BR ˈɔːθɒgnəθəs
AM ˈɔːθɑgnəθəs

orthogonal
BR ɔːˈθɒgənl, ɔˈθɒgnl
AM ˈɔːθagənəl

orthogonally
BR ɔːˈθɒg(ə)nli,
ɔːθɒgnḷi,
ɔːˈθɒg(ə)nəli,
ɔːθɒgnəli
AM ɔːˈθɑg(ə)nəli

orthographer
BR ɔːˈθɒgrəfə(r), -z
AM ɔːˈθɑgrəfər, -z

orthographic
BR ˌɔːθəˈgræfɪk
AM ˌɔrθəˈgræfɪk

orthographical
BR ˌɔːθəˈgræfɪkl
AM ˌɔrθəˈgræfəkəl

orthographically
BR ˌɔːθəˈgræfɪkli
AM ˌɔrθəˈgræfək(ə)li

orthography
BR ɔːˈθɒgrəfi
AM ɔːˈθɑgrəfi

ortho-hydrogen
BR ˌɔːθəʊˈhʌɪdrədʒ(ə)n
AM ˌɔrθoʊˈhaɪdrədʒən

orthopaedic
BR ˌɔːθəˈpiːdɪk, -s
AM ˌɔrθəˈpidɪk, -s

orthopaedist
BR ˌɔːθəˈpiːdɪst, -s
AM ˌɔrθəˈpidɪst, -s

orthopedic
BR ˌɔːθəˈpiːdɪk, -s
AM ˌɔrθəˈpidɪk, -s

orthopedist
BR ˌɔːθəˈpiːdɪst, -s
AM ˌɔrθəˈpidɪst, -s

Orthoptera
BR ɔːˈθɒpt(ə)rə(r)
AM ɔrˈθɑptərə

orthopteran
BR ɔːˈθɒpt(ə)rən,
ɔːˈθɒpt(ə)rṇ
AM ɔrˈθɑptərən

orthopterous
BR ɔːˈθɒpt(ə)rəs
AM ɔrˈθɑptərəs

orthoptic
BR ɔːˈθɒptɪk, -s
AM ɔrˈθɑptɪk, -s

orthoptist
BR ɔːˈθɒptɪst, -s
AM ɔrˈθɑptəst, -s

orthorhombic
BR ˌɔːθəˈrɒmbɪk
AM ˌɔrθəˈrɑmbɪk

orthostatic
BR ˌɔːθəˈstatɪk
AM ˌɔrθəˈstædɪk

orthotone
BR ˈɔːθətəʊn, -z
AM ˈɔrθəˌtoʊn, -z

Ortiz
BR ɔːˈtiːz
AM ɔrˈtiz
SP orˈtiθ, orˈtis

ortolan
BR ˈɔːtələn, ˈɔːtlən, -z
AM ˈɔrdlən, -z

Orton
BR ˈɔːtn
AM ˈɔrtən

orts
BR ɔːts
AM ɔ(ə)rts

Oruro
BR ɔːˈrʊərəʊ
AM ɔˈrʊroʊ

Orvieto
BR ɔːˈvjetəʊ
AM ɔrˈvjedoʊ

Orville
BR ˈɔːv(ɪ)l
AM ˈɔrvəl

Orwell
BR ˈɔːw(ɛ)l
AM ˈɔrˌwɛl

Orwellian
BR ɔːˈwelɪən
AM ɔrˈwelˌjən,
ɔrˈwelɪən

oryx
BR ˈɒrɪks, -ɪksɪz
AM ˈɔrɪks, -ɪz

Osage
BR əʊˈseɪdʒ, ˈəʊseɪdʒ
AM oʊˈseɪdʒ

Osaka
BR əʊˈsɑːkə(r)
AM oʊˈsɑːkə

Osbert
BR ˈɒzbət, ˈɒzbɜːt
AM ˈɑzbərt

Osborn
BR ˈɒzbɔːn
AM ˈɑzˌbɔ(ə)rn,
ˈɑzbərn

Osborne
BR ˈɒzbɔːn
AM ˈɑzˌbɔ(ə)rn,
ˈɑzbərn

Oscar
BR ˈɒskə(r), -z
AM ˈɑskər, -z

oscillate
BR ˈɒsɪleɪt, -s, -ɪŋ, -ɪd
AM ˈɑsəˌleɪ|t, -ts, -dɪŋ,
-dɪd

oscillation
BR ˌɒsɪˈleɪʃn, -z
AM ˌɑsəˈleɪʃən, -z

oscillator
BR ˈɒsɪleɪtə(r), -z

oscillatory
BR əˈsɪlət(ə)ri,
ɒˈsɪlət(ə)ri
AM əˈsɪləˌtɔri

oscillogram
BR əˈsɪləgram,
ɒˈsɪləgram, -z
AM əˈsɪləˌgræm, -z

oscillograph
BR əˈsɪləgrɑːf,
ɒˈsɪləgrɑːf, əˈsɪləgraf,
ɒˈsɪləgraf, -s
AM əˈsɪləˌgræf, -s

oscillographic
BR əˌsɪləˈgrafɪk,
ɒˌsɪləˈgrafɪk
AM əˌsɪləˈgræfɪk

oscillography
BR ˌɒsɪˈlɒgrəfi
AM ˌɑsəˈlɑgrəfi

oscilloscope
BR əˈsɪləskəʊp,
ɒˈsɪləskəʊp, -s
AM əˈsɪləˌskoʊp, -s

oscilloscopic
BR əˌsɪləˈskɒpɪk,
ɒˌsɪləˈskɒpɪk
AM əˌsɪləˈskɑpɪk

oscine
BR ˈɒsaɪn, ˈɒsɪn
AM ˈɑsn, ˈɑˌsaɪn

oscinine
BR ˈɒsɪnʌɪn, ˈɒsɪniːn
AM ˈɑsəˌnaɪn, ˈɑsənən

oscitation
BR ˌɒsɪˈteɪʃn, -z
AM ˌɑsəˈteɪʃən, -z

oscula
BR ˈɒskjələ(r)
AM ˈɑskjələ

osculant
BR ˈɒskjələnt,
ˈɒskjəlṇt
AM ˈɑskjələnt

oscular
BR ˈɒskjələ(r)
AM ˈɑskjələr

osculate
BR ˈɒskjəleɪt, -s, -ɪŋ, -ɪd
AM ˈɑskjəˌleɪ|t, -ts, -dɪŋ,
-dɪd

osculation
BR ˌɒskjəˈleɪʃn, -z
AM ˌɑskjəˈleɪʃən, -z

osculatory
BR ˈɒskjələt(ə)ri
AM ˈɑskjələˌtɔri

osculum
BR ˈɒskjələm
AM ˈɑskjələm

Osgood
BR ˈɒzgʊd
AM ˈɑzˌgʊd

OSHA
BR ˈəʊʃə(r)
AM ˈoʊʃə

O'Shaughnessy
BR ə(ʊ)ˈʃɔːnɪsi
AM oʊˈʃɒnəsi,
oʊˈʃɑnəsi

O'Shea
BR ə(ʊ)ˈʃeɪ, ə(ʊ)ˈʃiː
AM oʊˈʃeɪ

osier
BR ˈəʊzɪə(r),
ˈəʊʒ(ɪ)ə(r), -z
AM ˈoʊʒər, -z

Osiris
BR ə(ʊ)ˈsʌɪrɪs
AM oʊˈsaɪrɪs

Osler
BR ˈɒslə(r)
AM ˈɑslər

Oslo
BR ˈɒzləʊ
AM ˈɑzˌloʊ
NO ˈuslu

Osman
BR ˈɒzmən, ˈɒsmən
AM ˈɑzmən, ˈɑzˌmɑn

Osmanli
BR ɒzˈmanl|i,
ɒsˈmanl|i, ɒzˈmɑːnl|i,
ɒsˈmɑːnl|i, -ɪz
AM ˈɑzmənli,
ˈɑzˌmanli, -z

osmic
BR ˈɒzmɪk
AM ˈɑzmɪk

osmically
BR ˈɒzmɪkli
AM ˈɑzmək(ə)li

Osmiroid
BR ˈɒzmɪrɔɪd
AM ˈɑzmɪˌrɔɪd

osmium
BR ˈɒzmɪəm
AM ˈɑzmɪəm

osmolality
BR ˌɒzməˈlalɪti
AM ˌɑzməˈlælədi

osmolarity
BR ˌɒzməˈlarɪti
AM ˌɑzməˈlɛrədi

Osmond
BR ˈɒzmənd
AM ˈɑzmən(d)

osmosis
BR ɒzˈməʊsɪs
AM ɑzˈmoʊsəs,
ɑˈsmoʊsəs

Osmotherley
BR ɒzˈmʌðəli
AM ɑzˈməðərli

Osmotherly
BR ɒzˈmʌðəli
AM ɑzˈməðərli

osmotic
BR ɒzˈmɒtɪk
AM ɑzˈmɑdɪk,
ɑˈsmɑdɪk

osmotically
BR ɒzˈmɒtɪkli

osmund
AM ɑz'mɑdək(ə)li,
ɑ'smɑdək(ə)li
osmund
BR 'ɒzmənd, -z
AM 'ɑzmən(d), -z
osmunda
BR ɒz'mʌndə(r), -z
AM ɑz'məndə, -z
Osnabrück
BR 'ɒznəbrʊk
AM 'ɑsnə,brʊk
GER ɔsnə'brʏk
osnaburg
BR 'ɒznəbəːg
AM 'ɑznə,bərg
osprey
BR 'ɒspreɪ, -z
AM 'ɑspri, -z
Ossa
BR 'ɒsə(r)
AM 'ɑsə
ossein
BR 'ɒsiːn
AM 'ɑsiːn
osseous
BR 'ɒsɪəs
AM 'ɑsiəs
Ossetia
BR ɒ'sɛtɪə(r), ɒ'siː,ʃə(r)
AM ɔ'siʃə, ɔ'sɛdiə,
ɑ'siʃə, ɑ'sɛdiə
Ossetic
BR ɒ'sɛtɪk
AM ɔ'sɛdɪk, ɑ'sɛdɪk
Ossett
BR 'ɒsɪt
AM 'ɑsət
ossia
BR ɒ'siːə(r), 'ɒsjə(r)
AM oʊ'siə
Ossian
BR 'ɒsɪən
AM 'ɑsiən
Ossianic
BR ,ɒsi'anɪk
AM ,ɑsi'ænɪk,
,ɑʃi'ænɪk
ossicle
BR 'ɒsɪkl, -z
AM 'ɑsəkəl, -z
Ossie
BR 'ɒs|i, -ɪz
AM 'ɑsi, -z
ossific
BR ɒ'sɪfɪk
AM ɑ'sɪfɪk
ossification
BR ,ɒsɪfɪ'keɪʃn
AM ,ɑsəfə'keɪʃən
ossifrage
BR 'ɒsɪfr|ɪdʒ, -ɪdʒɪz
AM 'ɑsə,frɪdʒ, -ɪz
ossify
BR 'ɒsɪfaɪ, -z, -ɪŋ, -d
AM 'ɑsə,faɪ, -z, -ɪŋ, -d

osso buco
BR ,ɒsəʊ 'buːkəʊ,
+ 'buːkəʊ
AM ,ɑsoʊ 'buːko
ossuary
BR 'ɒsjʊər|i, -ɪz
AM 'ɑʃə,wɛri,
'ɑs(j)ə,wɛri, -z
Ostade
BR 'ɒstɑːd
AM 'ɑs,tɑd
osteitis
BR ,ɒstɪ'ʌɪtɪs
AM ,ɑsti'aɪdəs
Ostend
BR ɒ'stɛnd
AM ɔ'stɛnd, ɑ'stɛnd
ostensible
BR ɒ'stɛnsɪbl
AM ə'stɛnsəbəl
ostensibly
BR ɒ'stɛnsɪbli
AM ə'stɛnsɪbli
ostensive
BR ɒ'stɛnsɪv
AM ə'stɛnsɪv
ostensively
BR ɒ'stɛnsɪvli
AM ə'stɛnsɪvli
ostensiveness
BR ɒ'stɛnsɪvnɪs
AM ə'stɛnsɪvnɪs
ostensory
BR ɒ'stɛns(ə)r|i, -ɪz
AM ə'stɛnsəri, -z
ostentation
BR ,ɒstɛn'teɪʃn,
,ɒst(ə)n'teɪʃn
AM ,ɑstən'teɪʃən
ostentatious
BR ,ɒstɛn'teɪʃəs,
,ɒst(ə)n'teɪʃəs
AM ,ɑstən'teɪʃəs
ostentatiously
BR ,ɒstɛn'teɪʃəsli,
,ɒst(ə)n'teɪʃəsli
AM ,ɑstən'teɪʃəsli
osteoarthritic
BR ,ɒstɪəʊɑ:'θrɪtɪk
AM ,ɑstioʊ,ɑr'θrɪdɪk
osteoarthritis
BR ,ɒstɪəʊɑ:'θrʌɪtɪs
AM ,ɑstioʊ,ɑr'θraɪdɪs
osteogenesis
BR ,ɒstɪəʊ'dʒɛnɪsɪs
AM ,ɑstioʊ'dʒɛnəsəs
osteogenetic
BR ,ɒstɪəʊdʒɪ'nɛtɪk
AM ,ɑstioʊdʒə'nɛdɪk
osteogeny
BR ,ɒstɪ'ɒdʒɪni
AM ,ɑsti'ɑdʒɛni
osteography
BR ,ɒstɪ'ɒgrəfi
AM ,ɑsti'ɑgrəfi
osteological
BR ,ɒstɪə'lɒdʒɪkl

AM ,ɑstiə'lɑdʒəkəl
osteologically
BR ,ɒstɪə'lɒdʒɪkli
AM ,ɑstiə'lɑdʒək(ə)li
osteologist
BR ,ɒstɪ'ɒlədʒɪst, -s
AM ,ɑsti'ɑlədʒəst, -s
osteology
BR ,ɒstɪ'ɒlədʒi
AM ,ɑsti'ɑlədʒi
osteomalacia
BR ,ɒstɪəʊmə'leɪʃ(ɪ)ə(r)
AM ,ɑstioʊmə'leɪʃ(i)ə
osteomalacic
BR ,ɒstɪəʊmə'lasɪk
AM ,ɑstioʊmə'læsɪk
osteomyelitis
BR ,ɒstɪəʊ,mʌɪə'lʌɪtɪs
AM ,ɑstioʊ,maɪ(ə)'laɪdɪs
osteopath
BR 'ɒstɪəpaθ, -s
AM 'ɑstiə,pæθ, -s
osteopathic
BR ,ɒstɪə'paθɪk
AM ,ɑstiə'pæθɪk
osteopathically
BR ,ɒstɪə'paθɪkli
AM ,ɑstiə'pæθək(ə)li
osteopathy
BR ,ɒstɪ'ɒpəθi
AM ,ɑsti'ɑpəθi
osteophyte
BR 'ɒstɪəfʌɪt, -s
AM 'ɑstiə,faɪt, -s
osteoporosis
BR ,ɒstɪəʊpə'rəʊsɪs
AM ,ɑstioʊpə'roʊsəs
Ostermilk
BR 'ɒstəmɪlk
AM 'ɑstər,mɪlk,
'oʊstər,mɪlk
Österreich
BR 'əːstərʌɪk,
'əːstərʌɪx
AM 'østə,raɪk
Ostia
BR 'ɒstɪə(r)
AM 'ɑstiə
ostinato
BR ,ɒstɪ'nɑːtəʊ, -z
AM ,ɑstə'nɑdoʊ,
,ɑsti'nɑdoʊ, -z
ostler
BR 'ɒslə(r), -z
AM 'ɑslər, -z
Ostmark
BR 'ɒstmɑːk
AM 'ɑs(t),mɑrk
ostomy
BR 'ɒstəmi
AM 'ɑstəmi
Ostpolitik
BR 'ɒstpɒlɪ,tiːk
AM 'ɑs(t),pɑlə'tik
ostraca
BR 'ɒstrəkə(r)
AM 'ɑstrəkə

ostracise
BR 'ɒstrəsʌɪz, -ɪz, -ɪŋ, -d
AM 'ɑstrə,saɪz, -ɪz, -ɪŋ,
-d
ostracism
BR 'ɒstrəsɪz(ə)m
AM 'ɑstrə,sɪzəm
ostracize
BR 'ɒstrəsʌɪz, -ɪz, -ɪŋ, -d
AM 'ɑstrə,saɪz, -ɪz, -ɪŋ,
-d
ostracoderm
BR ɒ'strakədəːm, -z
AM ə'stækə,dərm, -z
ostracon
BR 'ɒstrəkɒn
AM 'ɑstrə,kɑn
Ostrava
BR 'ɒstrəvə(r)
AM 'ɔstrəvə, 'ɑstrəvə
ostrich
BR 'ɒstrɪtʃ, 'ɒstrɪdʒ, -ɪz
AM 'ɑstrɪtʃ, -ɪz
Ostrogoth
BR 'ɒstrəgɒθ, -s
AM 'ɑstrə,gɑθ, -s
Ostrogothic
BR ,ɒstrə'gɒθɪk
AM ,ɑstrə'gɑθɪk
Ostwald
BR 'ɒs(t)w(ə)ld
AM 'ɑs(t),wald
GER 'ɔstvalt
O'Sullivan
BR ə(ʊ)'sʌlɪv(ə)n
AM oʊ'sələvən
Oswald
BR 'ɒzw(ə)ld
AM 'ɑz,wald
Oswaldtwistle
BR 'ɒzw(ə)l(d),twɪsl
AM 'ɑzwəl(d),twɪsəl
Oswego
BR ɒs'wiːgəʊ
AM ɑs'wigoʊ
Oswestry
BR 'ɒzwɪstri
AM 'ɑzwəstri
Osyth
BR 'əʊzɪθ, 'əʊsɪθ
AM 'oʊzɪθ, 'oʊsɪθ
Otago
BR ə(ʊ)'tɑːgəʊ,
ɒ'tɑːgəʊ
AM oʊ'teɪgoʊ
otary
BR 'əʊt(ə)r|i, -ɪz
AM 'oʊdəri, -z
Otello
BR ə(ʊ)'tɛləʊ
AM oʊ'tɛloʊ, ə'tɛloʊ
Othello
BR ə'θɛləʊ
AM oʊ'θɛloʊ, ə'θɛloʊ
other
BR 'ʌðə(r), -z
AM 'əðər, -z

otherness
BR ˈʌðənəs
AM ˈeðərnəs
otherwhere
BR ˈʌðəwɛː(r)
AM ˈʌðəɹ,(h)wɛ(ə)r
otherwise
BR ˈʌðəwaɪz
AM ˈeðər,waɪz
Othman
BR ˈɒθmən, ɒθˈmɑːn
AM ˈɑθmən, ɑθˈmɑn
Otho
BR ˈəʊθəʊ
AM ˈoʊθoʊ
otic
BR ˈəʊtɪk, ˈɒtɪk
AM ˈoʊdɪk, ˈɑdɪk
otiose
BR ˈəʊtɪəʊs, ˈəʊʃɪəʊs,
ˈəʊtɪəʊz, ˈəʊʃɪəʊz
AM ˈoʊdi,oʊz,
ˈoʊʃi,oʊz, ˈoʊdi,oʊs,
ˈoʊʃi,oʊs
otiosely
BR ˈəʊtɪəʊsli,
ˈəʊʃɪəʊsli, ˈəʊtɪəʊzli,
ˈəʊʃɪəʊzli
AM ˈoʊdi,oʊzli,
ˈoʊʃi,oʊzli,
ˈoʊdi,oʊsli,
ˈoʊʃi,oʊsli
otioseness
BR ˈəʊtɪəʊsnəs,
ˈəʊʃɪəʊsnəs,
ˈəʊtɪəʊznəs,
ˈəʊʃɪəʊznəs
AM ˈoʊdi,oʊznəs,
ˈoʊʃi,oʊznəs,
ˈoʊdi,oʊsnəs,
ˈoʊʃi,oʊsnəs
Otis
BR ˈəʊtɪs
AM ˈoʊdəs
otitis
BR əʊˈtʌɪtɪs
AM oʊˈtaɪdɪs
Otley
BR ˈɒtli
AM ˈɑtli
otolaryngological
BR ˌəʊtəʊˌlarɪŋɡəˈlɒdʒɪkl
AM ˌoʊdoʊˌlɛrəŋɡəˈlɑdʒəkəl
otolaryngologist
BR ˌəʊtəʊˌlarɪŋˈɡɒlədʒɪst, -s
AM ˌoʊdoʊˌlɛrənˈɡɑlədʒəst, -s
otolaryngology
BR ˌəʊtəʊˌlarɪŋˈɡɒlədʒi
AM ˌoʊdoʊˌlɛrənˈɡɑlədʒi
otolith
BR ˈəʊtəlɪθ, -s
AM ˈoʊdl,ɪθ, -s
otolithic
BR ˌəʊtəˈlɪθɪk

otological
BR ˌəʊtəˈlɒdʒɪkl
AM ˌoʊdəˈlɑdʒəkəl
otologist
BR əʊˈtɒlədʒɪst, -s
AM oʊˈtɑlədʒəst, -s
otology
BR əʊˈtɒlədʒi
AM oʊˈtɑlədʒi
Otomi
BR ˌəʊtəˈmiː
AM ˌoʊdəˈmi
O'Toole
BR ə(ʊ)ˈtuːl
AM oʊˈtul
otoplasty
BR ˈəʊtə(ʊ)plastli, -ɪz
AM ˈoʊdou,plæsti, -z
otorhinolaryngol- ogist
BR ˌəʊtəʊˌrʌɪnəʊˌlarɪŋˈɡɒlədʒɪst, -s
AM ˌoʊdou,raɪnou,lɛrənˈɡalədʒəst, -s
otorhinolaryngol- ogy
BR ˌəʊtəʊˌrʌɪnəʊˌlarɪŋˈɡɒlədʒi
AM ˌoʊdou,raɪnou,lɛrənˈɡalədʒi
otoscope
BR ˈəʊtəskəʊp, -s
AM ˈoʊdə,skoʊp, -s
otoscopic
BR ˌəʊtəˈskɒpɪk
AM ˌoʊdəˈskɑpɪk
Otranto
BR əˈtrantəʊ
AM ˌoʊˈtræn(t)oʊ
Ott
BR ɒt
AM ɑt
ottar
BR ˈɒtə(r)
AM ˈɑdər
ottava rima
BR ə(ʊ)ˌtɑːvə ˈriːmə(r)
AM əˈtɑvə ˈrimə, oʊˈtɑvə +
Ottawa
BR ˈɒtəwə(r)
AM ˈɑdə,wɑ
otter
BR ˈɒtə(r), -z
AM ˈɑdər, -z
Otterburn
BR ˈɒtəbəːn
AM ˈɑdər,bərn
Ottery
BR ˈɒt(ə)ri
AM ˈɑdəri
Otto
BR ˈɒtəʊ, -z
AM ˈɑdoʊ, -z
Ottoline
BR ˈɒtəlɪn, ˈɒtl,ɪn

AM ˌoʊdlˈɪθɪk
ottoman
BR ˈɒtəmən, -z
AM ˈɑdəmən, -z
Otway
BR ˈɒtweɪ
AM ˈɑtweɪ
Ouagadougou
BR ˌwɑːɡəˈduːɡuː, ˌwɑɡəˈduːɡuː
AM ˌwɑɡəˈdugu
ouananiche
BR ˌwɑnəˈniːʃ
AM ˌwɑnəˈniʃ
oubliette
BR ˌuːblɪˈɛt, -s
AM ˌubliˈɛt, -s
ouch
BR aʊtʃ
AM aʊtʃ
oud
BR uːd, -z
AM ud, -z
Oudenarde
BR ˈuːdənɑːd, ˈʊdnɑːd
AM ˈudəˈnard
Oudh
BR uːd
AM ud
ought
BR ɔːt
AM ɔt, ɑt
oughtn't
BR ˈɔːtnt
AM ˈɔtnt, ˈɑtnt
ougiya
BR uːˈɡiːjə(r), -z
AM uˈdʒiə, -z
ouguiya
BR uːˈɡiːjə(r), -z
AM uˈɡiə, -z
Ouida
BR ˈwiːdə(r)
AM ˈwidə
ouija board
BR ˈwiːdʒə ˌbɔːd, ˈwiːdʒɪ +, -z
AM ˈwidʒə ˌbɔ(ə)rd, ˈwidʒɪ +, -z
Ould
BR əʊld, uːld
AM oʊld
Oulton
BR ˈəʊlt(ə)n
AM ˈoʊlt(ə)n
Oulu
BR ˈəʊluː
AM ˈoʊ,lu
ounce
BR aʊns, -ɪz
AM aʊns, -əz
Oundle
BR ˈaʊndl
AM ˈaʊndəl
our¹
strong form
BR ˈaʊə(r)

AM ˈaʊ(ə)r
our²
weak form
BR ɑː(r)
AM ɑr
ours¹
strong form
BR ˈaʊəz
AM ˈaʊ(ə)rz
ours²
weak form
BR ɑːz
AM ɑrz
ourself¹
strong form
BR aʊəˈsɛlf
AM aʊrˈsɛlf
ourself²
weak form
BR ɑːˈsɛlf
AM ɑrˈsɛlf
ourselves¹
strong form
BR aʊəˈsɛlvz
AM aʊrˈsɛlvz
ourselves²
weak form
BR ɑːˈsɛlvz
AM ɑrˈsɛlvz
Ouse
BR uːz
AM uz
ousel
BR ˈuːzl, -z
AM ˈuzəl, -z
oust
BR aʊst, -s, -ɪŋ, -ɪd
AM aʊst, -s, -ɪŋ, -əd
ouster
BR ˈaʊstə(r), -z
AM ˈaʊstər, -z
out
BR aʊt
AM aʊt
outact
BR ˌaʊtˈakt, -s, -ɪŋ, -ɪd
AM ˌaʊtˈæk|(t), -(t)s, -tɪŋ, -təd
outage
BR ˈaʊt|ɪdʒ, -ɪdʒɪz
AM ˈaʊdɪdʒ, -ɪz
out-and-out
BR ˌaʊt(ə)n(d)ˈaʊt
AM ˈaʊdən'aʊt, ˈaʊtn'aʊt
out-and-outer
BR ˌaʊt(ə)n(d)ˈaʊtə(r), -z
AM ˈaʊdən'aʊdər, ˈaʊtn'aʊdər-z
outback¹
BR ˈaʊtbak
AM ˈaʊt,bæk
outback²
Australia
AM ˈaʊtbak
BR ˈaʊt,bæk

outbacker
BR 'aʊtˌbakə(r), -z
AM 'aʊtˌbækər, -z

outbalance
BR 'aʊtˌbaləns,
ˌaʊtˈbalns, -ɪz, -ɪŋ, -t
AM 'aʊtˈbæləns, -əz,
-ɪŋ, -t

outbid
BR 'aʊtˈbɪd, -z, -ɪŋ
AM 'aʊtˈbɪd, -z, -ɪŋ

outbidder
BR 'aʊtˈbɪdə(r), -z
AM 'aʊtˈbɪdər, -z

outblaze
BR 'aʊtˈbleɪz, -ɪz, -ɪŋ, -d
AM 'aʊtˈbleɪz, -ɪz, -ɪŋ, -d

outboard
BR 'aʊtˈbɔːd, -z
AM 'aʊtˈbɔ(ə)rd, -z

outbound
BR 'aʊtbaʊnd
AM 'aʊtbaʊnd

outbrave
BR 'aʊtˈbreɪv, -z, -ɪŋ, -d
AM 'aʊtˈbreɪv, -z, -ɪŋ, -d

outbreak
BR 'aʊtˌbreɪk, -s
AM 'aʊtˌbreɪk, -s

outbred
BR 'aʊtˈbrɛd, -z, -ɪŋ
AM 'aʊtˈbrɛd, -z, -ɪŋ

outbreed
BR 'aʊtˈbriːd, -z, -ɪŋ
AM 'aʊtˈbriːd, -z, -ɪŋ

outbuilding
BR 'aʊtˌbɪldɪŋ, -z
AM 'aʊtˌbɪldɪŋ, -z

outburst
BR 'aʊtbəːst, -s
AM 'aʊtˌbɜrst, -s

outcast
BR 'aʊtkɑːst, 'aʊtkast,
-s
AM 'aʊtˌkæst, -s

outcaste
BR 'aʊtkɑːst, 'aʊtkast,
-s
AM 'aʊtˌkæst, -s

outclass
BR 'aʊtˈklɑːs, ˌaʊtˈklas,
-ɪz, -ɪŋ, -t
AM 'aʊtˈklæs, -əz, -ɪŋ, -t

outcome
BR 'aʊtkʌm, -z
AM 'aʊtˌkəm, -z

outcompete
BR ˌaʊtkəmˈpiːt, -s, -ɪŋ,
-ɪd
AM ˌaʊtkəmˈpiʃt, -ts,
-dɪŋ, -dɪd

outcrop
BR 'aʊtkrɒp, -s, -ɪŋ
AM 'aʊtˌkrɑp, -s, -ɪŋ

outcry
BR 'aʊtkrʌɪ, -z
AM 'aʊtˌkraɪ, -z

outdance
BR 'aʊtˈdɑːns,
ˌaʊtˈdans, -ɪz, -ɪŋ, -t
AM ˌaʊtˈdæns, -əz, -ɪŋ, -t

outdare
BR 'aʊtˈdɛː(r), -z, -ɪŋ, -d
AM 'aʊtˈdɛ(ə)r, -z, -ɪŋ, -d

outdated
BR 'aʊtˌdeɪtɪd
AM 'aʊtˌdeɪtɪd

outdatedness
BR 'aʊtˌdeɪtɪdnɪs
AM 'aʊtˌdeɪtɪdnɪs

outdid
BR 'aʊtˌdɪd
AM 'aʊtˌdɪd

outdistance
BR 'aʊtˈdɪst(ə)ns, -ɪz,
-ɪŋ, -t
AM ˌaʊtˈdɪstəns, -əz,
-ɪŋ, -t

outdo
BR 'aʊtˈduː, -ɪŋ
AM ˌaʊtˈdu, -ɪŋ

outdoes
BR ˌaʊtˈdʌz
AM ˌaʊtˈdəz

outdone
BR ˌaʊtˈdʌn
AM ˌaʊtˈdən

outdoor
BR 'aʊtˈdɔː(r), -z
AM ˌaʊtˈdɔ(ə)r, -z

outdoorsman
BR aʊtˈdɔːzmən
AM aʊtˈdɔrzmən

outdoorsmen
BR 'aʊtˈdɔːzmən
AM aʊtˈdɔrzmən

outer
BR 'aʊtə(r)
AM 'aʊdər

outermost
BR 'aʊtəməʊst
AM 'aʊdərˌmoʊst

outerwear
BR 'aʊtəwɛː(r)
AM 'aʊdərˌwɛ(ə)r

outface
BR 'aʊtˈfeɪs, -ɪz, -ɪŋ, -t
AM 'aʊtˈfeɪs, -ɪz, -ɪŋ, -t

outfall
BR 'aʊtfɔːl, -z
AM 'aʊtˌfɔl, 'aʊtˌfɑl, -z

outfield
BR 'aʊtfiːld, -z
AM 'aʊtˌfild, -z

outfielder
BR 'aʊtfiːldə(r), -z
AM 'aʊtˌfildər, -z

outfight
BR 'aʊtˈfʌɪt, -s, -ɪŋ
AM 'aʊtˈfaɪt, -ts, -dɪŋ

outfit
BR 'aʊtfɪt, -s, -ɪŋ, -ɪd
AM 'aʊtˌfɪ|t, -ts, -dɪŋ,
-dɪd

outfitter
BR 'aʊtfɪtə(r), -z
AM 'aʊtˌfɪdər, -z

outflank
BR 'aʊtˈflaŋ|k, -ks,
-kɪŋ, -(k)t
AM 'aʊtˈflæŋ|k, -ks,
-kɪŋ, -(k)t

outflew
BR 'aʊtˈfluː
AM 'aʊtˈflu

outflow
BR 'aʊtfləʊ, -z
AM 'aʊtˌfloʊ, -z

outflown
BR 'aʊtˈfləʊn
AM 'aʊtˈfloʊn

outflung
BR 'aʊtˈflʌŋ
AM 'aʊtˈfləŋ

outfly
BR 'aʊtˈflʌɪ, -z, -ɪŋ
AM 'aʊtˈflaɪ, -z, -ɪŋ

outfought
BR 'aʊtˈfɔːt
AM 'aʊtˈfɔt, 'aʊtˈfɑt

outfox
BR 'aʊtˈfɒks, -ɪz, -ɪŋ, -t
AM 'aʊtˈfɑks, -əz, -ɪŋ, -t

outgas
BR 'aʊtˌgas, -ɪz, -ɪŋ, -t
AM 'aʊtˈgæs, -əz, -ɪŋ, -t

outgeneral
BR 'aʊtˈdʒɛn(ə)rəl,
ˌaʊtˈdʒɛn(ə)r|, -z, -ɪŋ,
-d
AM ˌaʊtˈdʒɛn(ə)rəl, -z,
-ɪŋ, -d

outgo
BR 'aʊtˈgəʊ, -z, -ɪŋ
AM ˌaʊtˈgoʊ, -z, -ɪŋ

outgoing[1]
adjective
BR 'aʊtˌgəʊɪŋ
AM 'aʊtˌgoʊɪŋ

outgoing[2]
noun
BR 'aʊtˌgəʊɪŋ, -z
AM 'aʊtˌgoʊɪŋ, -z

outgone
BR 'aʊtˌgɒn
AM 'aʊtˌgɑn, 'aʊtˌgɑn

outgrew
BR 'aʊtˈgruː
AM 'aʊtˈgru

outgrow
BR 'aʊtˈgrəʊ, -z, -ɪŋ
AM 'aʊtˈgroʊ, -z, -ɪŋ

outgrown
BR 'aʊtˈgrəʊn
AM 'aʊtˈgroʊn

outgrowth
BR 'aʊtgrəʊθ, -s
AM 'aʊtˌgroʊθ, -s

outguess
BR 'aʊtˈgɛs, -ɪz, -ɪŋ, -t
AM 'aʊtˈgɛs, -əz, -ɪŋ, -t

outgun
BR 'aʊtˈgʌn, -z, -ɪŋ, -d
AM 'aʊtˈgən, -z, -ɪŋ, -d

outhouse
BR 'aʊthaʊ|s, -zɪz
AM 'aʊtˌ(h)aʊ|s, -zəz

outie
BR 'aʊt|i, -ɪz
AM 'aʊdi, -z

outing
BR 'aʊtɪŋ, -z
AM 'aʊdɪŋ, -z

outjockey
BR ˌaʊtˈdʒɒk|i, -ɪz, -ɪɪŋ,
-ɪd
AM ˌaʊtˈdʒɑki, -z, -ɪŋ, -d

outjump
BR ˌaʊtˈdʒʌmp, -s, -ɪŋ, -t
AM ˌaʊtˈdʒəmp, -s, -ɪŋ, -t

outlander
BR 'aʊtˌlandə(r), -z
AM 'aʊtˌlændər, -z

outlandish
BR (ˌ)aʊtˈlandɪʃ
AM aʊtˈlændɪʃ

outlandishly
BR (ˌ)aʊtˈlandɪʃli
AM aʊtˈlændɪʃli

outlandishness
BR (ˌ)aʊtˈlandɪʃnɪs
AM aʊtˈlændɪʃnɪs

outlast
BR 'aʊtˈlɑːst, 'aʊtˈlast,
-s, -ɪŋ, -ɪd
AM 'aʊtˈlæst, -s, -ɪŋ, -əd

outlaw
BR 'aʊtlɔː(r), -z, -ɪŋ, -d
AM 'aʊtˌlɔ, 'aʊtˌlɑ, -z,
-ɪŋ, -d

outlawry
BR 'aʊtlɔːri
AM 'aʊtˌlɔri

outlay[1]
noun
BR 'aʊtleɪ, -z
AM 'aʊtˌleɪ, -z

outlay[2]
verb
BR 'aʊtˈleɪ, -z, -ɪŋ, -d
AM 'aʊtˈleɪ, -z, -ɪŋ, -d

outlet
BR 'aʊtlɛt, -s
AM 'aʊtˌlɛt, 'aʊtˌlət, -s

outlier
BR 'aʊtˌlʌɪə(r), -z
AM 'aʊtˌlaɪ(ə)r, -z

outline
BR 'aʊtlʌɪn, -z, -ɪŋ, -d
AM 'aʊtˌlaɪn, -z, -ɪŋ, -d

outlive
BR 'aʊtˈlɪv, -z, -ɪŋ, -d
AM 'aʊtˈlɪv, -z, -ɪŋ, -d

outlook
BR 'aʊtlʊk, -s
AM 'aʊtˌlʊk, -s

outlying
BR 'aʊtˌlʌɪɪŋ

AM 'aʊt,laɪɪŋ

outmaneuver
BR ˌaʊtmə'nuːv|ə(r), -əz, -(ə)rɪŋ, -əd
AM ˌaʊtmə'n(j)uːv|ər, -ərz, -(ə)rɪŋ, -ərd

outmanoeuvre
BR ˌaʊtmə'nuːv|ə(r), -əz, -(ə)rɪŋ, -əd
AM ˌaʊtmə'n(j)uːv|ər, -ərz, -(ə)rɪŋ, -ərd

outmatch
BR ˌaʊt'mætʃ, -ɪz, -ɪŋ, -t
AM ˌaʊt'mætʃ, -əz, -ɪŋ, -t

outmeasure
BR ˌaʊt'meʒ|ə(r), -əz, -(ə)rɪŋ, -əd
AM ˌaʊt'meʒ|ər, -ərz, -(ə)rɪŋ, -ərd

outmoded
BR ˌaʊt'məʊdɪd
AM ˌaʊt'moʊdəd

outmodedly
BR ˌaʊt'məʊdɪdli
AM ˌaʊt'moʊdədli

outmodedness
BR ˌaʊt'məʊdɪdnɪs
AM ˌaʊt'moʊdədnəs

outmost
BR 'aʊtməʊst
AM 'aʊt,moʊst

outnumber
BR ˌaʊt'nʌmb|ə(r), -əz, -(ə)rɪŋ, -əd
AM ˌaʊt'nəmbər, -ərz, -(ə)rɪŋ, -ərd

outpace
BR ˌaʊt'peɪs, -ɪz, -ɪŋ, -t
AM ˌaʊt'peɪs, -ɪz, -ɪŋ, -t

outpatient
BR 'aʊt,peɪʃnt, -s
AM 'aʊt,peɪʃənt, -s

outperform
BR ˌaʊtpə'fɔːm, -z, -ɪŋ, -d
AM ˌaʊtpər'fɔ(ə)rm, -z, -ɪŋ, -d

outperformance
BR ˌaʊtpə'fɔːməns, -ɪz
AM ˌaʊtpər'fɔrməns, -əz

outplacement
BR 'aʊt,pleɪsm(ə)nt, -s
AM 'aʊt,pleɪsmənt, -s

outplay
BR ˌaʊt'pleɪ, -z, -ɪŋ, -d
AM ˌaʊt'pleɪ, -z, -ɪŋ, -d

outpoint
BR ˌaʊt'pɔɪnt, -s, -ɪŋ, -ɪd
AM ˌaʊt'pɔɪn|t, -ts, -(t)ɪŋ, -(t)ɪd

outport
BR 'aʊtpɔːt, -s
AM 'aʊt,pɔ(ə)rt, -s

outpost
BR 'aʊtpəʊst, -s
AM 'aʊt,poʊst, -s

outpouring
BR 'aʊt,pɔːrɪŋ, -z
AM 'aʊt,pɔrɪŋ, -z

output
BR 'aʊtpʊt, -s
AM 'aʊt,pʊt, -s

outrage
BR 'aʊtreɪdʒ, -ɪz, -ɪŋ, -d
AM 'aʊt,reɪdʒ, -ɪz, -ɪŋ, -d

outrageous
BR (ˌ)aʊt'reɪdʒəs
AM aʊt'reɪdʒəs

outrageously
BR (ˌ)aʊt'reɪdʒəsli
AM aʊt'reɪdʒəsli

outrageousness
BR (ˌ)aʊt'reɪdʒəsnəs
AM aʊt'reɪdʒəsnəs

Outram
BR 'uːtr(ə)m, 'aʊtr(ə)m
AM 'uːtrəm, 'aʊtrəm

outran
BR ˌaʊt'ran
AM ˌaʊt'ræn

outrange
BR ˌaʊt'reɪn(d)ʒ, -ɪz, -ɪŋ, -d
AM ˌaʊt'reɪndʒ, -ɪz, -ɪŋ, -d

outrank
BR ˌaʊt'raŋ|k, -ks, -kɪŋ, -(k)t
AM ˌaʊt'ræŋ|k, -ks, -kɪŋ, -(k)t

outré
BR 'uːtreɪ
AM u'treɪ

outreach¹
noun
BR 'aʊtriːtʃ
AM 'aʊt,ritʃ

outreach²
verb
BR ˌaʊt'riːtʃ, -ɪz, -ɪŋ, -t
AM ˌaʊt'ritʃ, -ɪz, -ɪŋ, -t

outridden
BR ˌaʊt'rɪdn
AM ˌaʊt'rɪdən

outride
BR ˌaʊt'raɪd, -z, -ɪŋ
AM ˌaʊt'raɪd, -z, -ɪŋ

outrider
BR ˌaʊt'rʌɪdə(r), -z
AM ˌaʊt'raɪdər, -z

outrigged
BR 'aʊtrɪgd
AM 'aʊt,rɪgd

outrigger
BR 'aʊt,rɪgə(r), -z
AM 'aʊt,rɪgər, -z

outright
BR (ˌ)aʊt'rʌɪt, 'aʊtrʌɪt
AM 'aʊt,raɪt

outrightness
BR 'aʊtrʌɪtnɪs
AM 'aʊt,raɪtnəs

outrival
BR ˌaʊt'rʌɪv|l, -lz,
-lɪŋ \ -əlɪŋ, -ld
AM ˌaʊt'raɪv|əl, -əlz,
-(ə)lɪŋ, -əld

outrode
BR ˌaʊt'rəʊd
AM ˌaʊt'roʊd

outrun¹
noun
BR 'aʊtrʌn, -z
AM 'aʊt,rən, -z

outrun²
verb
BR ˌaʊt'rʌn, -z, -ɪŋ
AM ˌaʊt'rən, -z, -ɪŋ

outrush
BR 'aʊtrʌʃ, -ɪz
AM ˌaʊt'rəʃ, -əz

outsail
BR ˌaʊt'seɪl, -z, -ɪŋ, -d
AM ˌaʊt'seɪl, -z, -ɪŋ, -d

outsat
BR ˌaʊt'sat
AM ˌaʊt'sæt

outsell
BR ˌaʊt'sel, -z, -ɪŋ
AM ˌaʊt'sel, -z, -ɪŋ

outset
BR 'aʊtset
AM 'aʊt,set

outshine
BR ˌaʊt'ʃaɪn
AM ˌaʊt'ʃaɪn

outshone
BR ˌaʊt'ʃɒn
AM ˌaʊt'ʃoʊn

outshoot
BR ˌaʊt'ʃuːt, -s, -ɪŋ
AM ˌaʊt'ʃu|t, -ts, -dɪŋ

outshot
BR ˌaʊt'ʃɒt
AM ˌaʊt'ʃat

outside
BR ˌaʊt'saɪd
AM ˌaʊt,saɪd

outsider
BR ˌaʊt'saɪdə(r), -z
AM ˌaʊt,saɪdər, -z

outsit
BR ˌaʊt'sɪt, -s, -ɪŋ
AM ˌaʊt'sɪ|t, -ts, -dɪŋ

outsize
BR ˌaʊt'saɪz, -ɪz, -ɪŋ, -d
AM ˌaʊt'saɪz, -ɪz, -ɪŋ, -d

outsizeness
BR 'aʊtsaɪznɪs
AM 'aʊt,saɪznɪs

outskirts
BR 'aʊtskəːts
AM 'aʊt,skərts

outsmart
BR ˌaʊt'smɑːt, -s, -ɪŋ, -ɪd
AM ˌaʊt'smɑr|t, -ts, -dɪŋ, -dəd

outsold
BR ˌaʊt'səʊld
AM ˌaʊt'soʊld

outsource
BR 'aʊtsɔːs, -ɪz, -ɪŋ, -t
AM 'aʊt,sɔ(ə)rs, -əz, -ɪŋ, -t

outspan¹
noun
BR 'aʊtspan, -z
AM 'aʊt,spæn, -z

outspan²
verb
BR ˌaʊt'span, -z, -ɪŋ, -d
AM ˌaʊt'spæn, -z, -ɪŋ, -d

outspend
BR ˌaʊt'spend, -z, -ɪŋ
AM ˌaʊt'spend, -z, -ɪŋ

outspent
BR ˌaʊt'spent
AM ˌaʊt'spent

outspoken
BR ˌaʊt'spəʊk(ə)n
AM ˌaʊt'spoʊkən

outspokenly
BR ˌaʊt'spəʊk(ə)nli
AM ˌaʊt'spoʊkənli

outspokenness
BR ˌaʊt'spəʊk(ə)nnəs
AM ˌaʊt'spoʊkə(n)nəs

outspread
BR ˌaʊt'spred
AM ˌaʊt'spred

outstanding¹
exceptional
BR (ˌ)aʊt'standɪŋ
AM ˌaʊt'stændɪŋ

outstanding²
sticking out
BR (ˌ)aʊt'standɪŋ
AM 'aʊt,stændɪŋ

outstandingly
BR ˌaʊt'standɪŋli
AM ˌaʊt'stændɪŋli

outstare
BR ˌaʊt'stɛː(r), -z, -ɪŋ, -d
AM ˌaʊt'stɛ(ə)r, -z, -ɪŋ, -d

outstation
BR 'aʊt,steɪʃn, -z
AM 'aʊt,steɪʃən, -z

outstay
BR ˌaʊt'steɪ, -z, -ɪŋ, -d
AM ˌaʊt'steɪ, -z, -ɪŋ, -d

outstep
BR ˌaʊt'step, -s, -ɪŋ, -t
AM ˌaʊt'step, -s, -ɪŋ, -t

outstretch
BR ˌaʊt'stretʃ, -ɪz, -ɪŋ
AM ˌaʊt'stretʃ, -ɪz, -ɪŋ

outstretched
BR ˌaʊt'stretʃt
AM ˌaʊt'stretʃt

outstrip
BR ˌaʊt'strɪp, -s, -ɪŋ, -t
AM ˌaʊt'strɪp, -s, -ɪŋ, -t

outswing
BR ˈaʊtswɪŋ, -z
AM ˈaʊtˌswɪŋ, -z

out-swinger
BR ˈaʊtˌswɪŋə(r), -z
AM ˈaʊtˌswɪŋər, -z

out-take
BR ˈaʊtteɪk, -s
AM ˈaʊtˌteɪk, -s

outtalk
BR ˌaʊtˈtɔːk, -s, -ɪŋ, -t
AM ˌaʊtˈtɔk, ˌaʊtˈtɑk, -s, -ɪŋ, -t

outvalue
BR ˌaʊtˈvæljuː, -z, -ɪŋ, -d
AM ˌaʊtˈvæljuː, -juz, -jəwɪŋ, -jud

outvote
BR ˌaʊtˈvəʊt, -s, -ɪŋ, -ɪd
AM ˌaʊtˈvoʊt, -ts, -dɪŋ, -dəd

outwalk
BR ˌaʊtˈwɔːk, -s, -ɪŋ, -t
AM ˌaʊtˈwɔk, ˌaʊtˈwɑk, -s, -ɪŋ, -t

outward
BR ˈaʊtwəd, -z
AM ˈaʊtwərd, -z

outwardly
BR ˈaʊtwədli
AM ˈaʊtwərdli

outwardness
BR ˈaʊtwədnəs
AM ˈaʊtwərdnəs

outwash
BR ˈaʊtwɒʃ, -ɪz
AM ˈaʊtˌwɒʃ, ˈaʊtˌwɑʃ, -əz

outwatch
BR ˌaʊtˈwɒtʃ, -ɪz, -ɪŋ, -t
AM ˌaʊtˈwɑtʃ, ˌaʊtˈwɒtʃ, -əz, -ɪŋ, -t

outwear
BR ˌaʊtˈweə(r), -z, -ɪŋ
AM ˌaʊtˈwe(ə)r, -z, -ɪŋ

outweigh
BR ˌaʊtˈweɪ, -z, -ɪŋ, -d
AM ˌaʊtˈweɪ, -z, -ɪŋ, -d

outwent
BR ˌaʊtˈwent
AM ˌaʊtˈwent

outwit
BR ˌaʊtˈwɪt, -s, -ɪŋ, -ɪd
AM ˌaʊtˈwɪt, -ts, -dɪŋ, -dɪd

outwith
BR ˌaʊtˈwɪθ, ˌaʊtˈwɪð
AM ˌaʊtˈwɪθ

outwore
BR ˌaʊtˈwɔː(r)
AM ˌaʊtˈwɔ(ə)r

outwork¹
noun
BR ˈaʊtwəːk, -s
AM ˈaʊtwɜrk, -s

outwork²
verb
BR ˌaʊtˈwəːk, -s, -ɪŋ, -t

AM ˌaʊtˈwɜrk, -s, -ɪŋ, -t

outworker
BR ˈaʊtˌwəːkə(r), -z
AM ˈaʊtˌwɜrkər, -z

outworking
noun
BR ˈaʊtˌwəːkɪŋ
AM ˈaʊtˌwɜrkɪŋ

outworn
BR ˌaʊtˈwɔːn
AM ˌaʊtˈwɔ(ə)rn

ouzel
BR ˈuːzl, -z
AM ˈuzəl, -z

ouzo
BR ˈuːzəʊ
AM ˈuzoʊ

ova
BR ˈəʊvə(r)
AM ˈoʊvə

oval
BR ˈəʊvl, -z
AM ˈoʊvəl, -z

ovality
BR əʊˈvalɪti
AM oʊˈvælədi

ovally
BR ˈəʊvl̩i
AM ˈoʊvəli

ovalness
BR ˈəʊvlnəs
AM ˈoʊvəlnəs

Ovaltine®
BR ˈəʊvltiːn
AM ˈoʊvəlˌtin

Ovambo
BR ə(ʊ)ˈvambəʊ, -z
AM oʊˈvæmboʊ, -z

Ovamboland
BR ə(ʊ)ˈvambəʊland
AM oʊˈvæmboʊˌlænd

ovarian
BR ə(ʊ)ˈveːrɪən
AM oʊˈverɪən

ovariectomy
BR ə(ʊ)ˌveːrɪˈektəm|i, -ɪz
AM oʊˌveriˈektəmi, -z

ovariotomy
BR ə(ʊ)ˌveːrɪˈɒtəm|i, -ɪz
AM oʊˌveriˈadəmi, -z

ovaritis
BR ˌəʊvəˈraɪtɪs
AM ˌoʊvəˈraɪdɪs

ovary
BR ˈəʊv(ə)r|i, -ɪz
AM ˈoʊv(ə)ri, -z

ovate
BR ˈəʊveɪt
AM ˈoʊˌveɪt

ovation
BR ə(ʊ)ˈveɪʃn, -z
AM oʊˈveɪʃən, -z

ovational
BR ə(ʊ)ˈveɪʃn̩(ə)l,
ə(ʊ)ˈveɪʃən(ə)l

AM oʊˈveɪʃ(ə)nəl

oven
BR ˈʌvn, -z
AM ˈəvən, -z

ovenbird
BR ˈʌvnbəːd, -z
AM ˈəvənˌbərd, -z

Ovenden
BR ˈɒvndən, ˈəʊvndən
AM ˈəvəndən

ovenproof
BR ˈʌvnpruːf
AM ˈəvənˌpruf

oven-ready
BR ˌʌvnˈredi
AM ˌəvənˈredi

Ovens
BR ˈʌvnz
AM ˈəvənz

ovenware
BR ˈʌvnweː(r)
AM ˈʌvnˌwe(ə)r

over
BR ˈəʊvə(r), -z
AM ˈoʊvər, -z

overabundance
BR ˌəʊv(ə)rəˈbʌnd(ə)ns, -ɪz
AM ˌoʊvərəˈbəndns, -əz

overabundant
BR ˌəʊv(ə)rəˈbʌnd(ə)nt
AM ˌoʊvərəˈbəndnt

overabundantly
BR ˌəʊv(ə)rəˈbʌnd(ə)ntli
AM ˌoʊvərəˈbəndən(t)li

overachieve
BR ˌəʊv(ə)rəˈtʃiːv, -z, -ɪŋ, -d
AM ˌoʊvərəˈtʃiv, -z, -ɪŋ, -d

overachievement
BR ˌəʊv(ə)rəˈtʃiːvm(ə)nt, -s
AM ˌoʊvərəˈtʃivmənt, -s

overachiever
BR ˌəʊv(ə)rəˈtʃiːvə(r), -z
AM ˌoʊvərəˈtʃivər, -z

overact
BR ˌəʊvərˈakt, -s, -ɪŋ, -ɪd
AM ˌoʊvərˈæk|(t), -(t)s, -tɪŋ, -təd

overactive
BR ˌəʊvərˈaktɪv
AM ˌoʊvərˈæktɪv

overactivity
BR ˌəʊv(ə)rakˈtɪvɪti
AM ˌoʊvərˌækˈtɪvɪdi

overage¹
adjective
BR ˌəʊvərˈeɪdʒ
AM ˌoʊvərˈeɪdʒ

overage²
noun
BR ˈəʊv(ə)r|ɪdʒ, -ɪdʒɪz
AM ˈoʊv(ə)rɪdʒ, -ɪz

overall¹
adjective, adverb
BR ˌəʊvərˈɔːl
AM ˈoʊvəˌrɔl, ˈoʊvəˈrɑl

overall²
noun
BR ˈəʊvərɔːl, -z, -d
AM ˈoʊvəˌrɔl, ˈoʊvəˌrɑl, -z, -d

overambition
BR ˌəʊv(ə)ramˈbɪʃn
AM ˌoʊvərəmˈbɪʃən, ˌoʊvərˌæmˈbɪʃən

overambitious
BR ˌəʊv(ə)ramˈbɪʃəs
AM ˌoʊvərəmˈbɪʃəs, ˈoʊvərˌæmˈbɪʃəs

overambitiously
BR ˌəʊv(ə)ramˈbɪʃəsli
AM ˌoʊvərəmˈbɪʃəsli, ˈoʊvərˌæmˈbɪʃəsli

over-and-over
BR ˌəʊv(ə)ran(d)ˈəʊvə(r), ˌəʊv(ə)rŋ(d)ˈəʊvə(r)
AM ˈoʊv(ə)rənˈoʊvər

overanxiety
BR ˌəʊv(ə)raŋˈzʌɪti
AM ˌoʊvərænˈzaɪdi

overanxious
BR ˌəʊvərˈaŋ(k)ʃəs
AM ˈoʊvərˈæŋ(k)ʃəs

overanxiously
BR ˌəʊvərˈaŋ(k)ʃəsli
AM ˈoʊvərˈæŋ(k)ʃəsli

overarch
BR ˌəʊvərˈɑːtʃ, -ɪz, -ɪŋ, -t
AM ˈoʊvərˈɑrtʃ, -əz, -ɪŋ, -t

overarm
BR ˈəʊvərɑːm
AM ˈoʊvərˌɑrm

overate
from verb 'overeat'
BR ˌəʊvərˈet, ˌoʊvərˈeɪt
AM ˌoʊvərˈeɪt

overattentive
BR ˌəʊv(ə)rəˈtentɪv
AM ˈoʊvərəˈten(t)ɪv

overawe
BR ˌəʊvərˈɔː(r), -z, -ɪŋ, -d
AM ˈoʊvərˈɔ, ˈoʊvərˈɑ, -z, -ɪŋ, -d

overbalance
BR ˌəʊvəˈbaləns, ˌəʊvəˈbalns, -ɪz, -ɪŋ, -t
AM ˌoʊvərˈbæləns, -ɪz, -ɪŋ, -t

overbear
BR ˌəʊvəˈbeː(r), -z, -ɪŋ
AM ˌoʊvərˈbe(ə)r, -z, -ɪŋ

overbearing
BR ˌəʊvəˈbeːrɪŋ
AM ˌoʊvərˈberɪŋ

overbearingly
BR ˌəʊvəˈbeːrɪŋli
AM ˌoʊvərˈberɪŋli

overbearingness
BR ˌəʊvəˈbeːrɪŋnɪs
AM ˌoʊvərˈberɪŋnɪs

overbid
BR ˌəʊvəˈbɪd, -z, -ɪŋ
AM ˌoʊvərˈbɪd, -z, -ɪŋ

overbidder
BR ˌəʊvəˈbɪdə(r), -z
AM ˌoʊvərˈbɪdər, -z

overblew
BR ˌəʊvəˈbluː
AM ˌoʊvərˈblu

overblouse
BR ˈəʊvəblaʊz, -ɪz
AM ˈoʊvərˌblaʊs,
ˈoʊvərˌblaʊz, -əz

overblow
BR ˌəʊvəˈbləʊ, -z, -ɪŋ
AM ˌoʊvərˈbloʊ, -z, -ɪŋ

overblown
BR ˌəʊvəˈbləʊn
AM ˌoʊvərˈbloʊn

overboard
BR ˈəʊvəbɔːd
AM ˈoʊvərˌbɔ(ə)rd

overbold
BR ˌəʊvəˈbəʊld
AM ˌoʊvərˈboʊld

overboldly
BR ˌəʊvəˈbəʊldli
AM ˌoʊvərˈboʊldli

overbook
BR ˌəʊvəˈbʊk, -s, -ɪŋ, -t
AM ˌoʊvərˈbʊk, -s, -ɪŋ, -t

overboot
BR ˈəʊvəbuːt, -s
AM ˈoʊvərˌbut, -s

overborne
BR ˌəʊvəˈbɔːn
AM ˌoʊvərˈbɔ(ə)rn

overbought
BR ˌəʊvəˈbɔːt,
AM ˌoʊvərˈbɔt,
ˈoʊvərˌbat

overbred
BR ˌəʊvəˈbred
AM ˌoʊvərˈbred

overbreed
BR ˌəʊvəˈbriːd, -z, -ɪŋ
AM ˌoʊvərˈbrid, -z, -ɪŋ

overbrim
BR ˌəʊvəˈbrɪm, -z, -ɪŋ,
-d
AM ˌoʊvərˈbrɪm, -z, -ɪŋ,
-d

overbuild
BR ˌəʊvəˈbɪld, -z, -ɪŋ
AM ˌoʊvərˈbɪld, -z, -ɪŋ

overbuilt
BR ˌəʊvəˈbɪlt
AM ˌoʊvərˈbɪlt

overburden
BR ˌəʊvəˈbəːd|n, -nz,
-nɪŋ\-nɪŋ, -nd
AM ˌoʊvərˈbərdən, -z,
-ɪŋ, -d

overburdensome
BR ˌəʊvəˈbəːdns(ə)m
AM ˌoʊvərˈbərdnsəm

Overbury
BR ˈəʊvəb(ə)ri
AM ˈoʊvərˌberi

overbusy
BR ˌəʊvəˈbɪzi
AM ˌoʊvərˈbɪzi

overbuy
BR ˌəʊvəˈbaɪ, -z, -ɪŋ
AM ˌoʊvərˈbaɪ, -z, -ɪŋ

overcall¹
noun
BR ˈəʊvəkɔːl, -z
AM ˈoʊvərˌkɔl,
ˈoʊvərˌkɑl, -z

overcall²
verb
BR ˌəʊvəˈkɔːl, -z, -ɪŋ, -d
AM ˌoʊvərˈkɔl,
ˌoʊvərˈkɑl, -z, -ɪŋ, -d

overcame
BR ˌəʊvəˈkeɪm
AM ˌoʊvərˈkeɪm

overcapacity
BR ˌəʊvəkəˈpasɪti
AM ˌoʊvərkəˈpæsədi

overcapitalize
BR ˌəʊvəˈkapɪtlʌɪz,
ˌəʊvəˈkapɪtəlʌɪz, -ɪz,
-ɪŋ, -d
AM ˌoʊvərˈkæpədlˌaɪz,
-ɪz, -ɪŋ, -d

overcareful
BR ˌəʊvəˈkeːf(ʊ)l
AM ˌoʊvərˈkerfəl

overcarefully
BR ˌəʊvəˈkeːfʊli,
ˌəʊvəˈkeːfli
AM ˌoʊvərˈkerfəli

overcast
BR ˌəʊvəˈkaːst,
ˌəʊvəˈkast,
ˈəʊvəkaːst, ˈəʊvəkast
AM ˈoʊvərˌkæst

overcaution
BR ˌəʊvəˈkɔːʃn
AM ˌoʊvərˈkɔʃən,
ˌoʊvərˈkaʃən

overcautious
BR ˌəʊvəˈkɔːʃəs
AM ˌoʊvərˈkɔʃəs,
ˌoʊvərˈkaʃəs

overcautiously
BR ˌəʊvəˈkɔːʃəsli
AM ˌoʊvərˈkɔʃəsli,
ˌoʊvərˈkaʃəsli

overcautiousness
BR ˌəʊvəˈkɔːʃəsnəs
AM ˌoʊvərˈkɔʃəsnəs,
ˌoʊvərˈkaʃəsnəs

overcharge¹
noun
BR ˈəʊvətʃaːdʒ
AM ˈoʊvərˌtʃɑrdʒ

overcharge²
verb
BR ˌəʊvəˈtʃaːdʒ, -ɪz, -ɪŋ,
-d
AM ˌoʊvərˈtʃɑrdʒ, -əz,
-ɪŋ, -d

overcheck
BR ˈəʊvətʃek, -s
AM ˈoʊvərˌtʃek, -s

overcloud
BR ˌəʊvəˈklaʊd, -z, -ɪŋ,
-ɪd
AM ˌoʊvərˈklaʊd, -z,
-ɪŋ, -ɪd

overcoat
BR ˈəʊvəkəʊt, -s
AM ˈoʊvərˌkoʊt, -s

overcome
BR ˌəʊvəˈkʌm, -z, -ɪŋ
AM ˌoʊvərˈkəm, -z, -ɪŋ

overcommit
BR ˌəʊvəkəˈmɪt, -s, -ɪŋ,
-ɪd
AM ˌoʊvərkəˈmɪ|t, -ts,
-dɪŋ, -dɪd

overcompensate
BR ˌəʊvəˈkɒmp(ə)nseɪt,
ˌəʊvəˈkɒmpenseɪt, -s,
-ɪŋ, -ɪd
AM ˌoʊvərˈkɑmpən.seɪ|t,
-ts, -dɪŋ, -dɪd

overcompensation
BR ˌəʊvəˌkɒmp(ə)n-
ˈseɪʃn,
ˌəʊvəˌkɒmpenˈseɪʃn
AM ˌoʊvərˌkɑmpən-
ˈseɪʃən

overcompensatory
BR ˌəʊvəˌkɒmp(ə)nˈseɪt-
(ə)ri,
ˌəʊvəˌkɒmpenˈseɪt(ə)ri
AM ˌoʊvərkəmˈpensə-
ˌtɔri

overconfidence
BR ˌəʊvəˈkɒnfɪd(ə)ns
AM ˌoʊvərˈkɑnfədəns

overconfident
BR ˌəʊvəˈkɒnfɪd(ə)nt
AM ˌoʊvərˈkɑnfədnt

overconfidently
BR ˌəʊvəˈkɒnfɪd(ə)ntli
AM ˌoʊvərˈkɑnfədən(t)li

overcook
BR ˌəʊvəˈkʊk, -s, -ɪŋ, -t
AM ˌoʊvərˈkʊk, -s, -ɪŋ, -t

overcritical
BR ˌəʊvəˈkrɪtɪkl
AM ˌoʊvərˈkrɪdəkəl

overcrop
BR ˌəʊvəˈkrɒp, -s, -ɪŋ, -t
AM ˌoʊvərˈkrɑp, -s, -ɪŋ,
-t

overcrowd
BR ˌəʊvəˈkraʊd, -z, -ɪŋ,
-ɪd
AM ˌoʊvərˈkraʊd, -z,
-ɪŋ, -əd

overdetermination
BR ˌəʊvədɪˌtəːmɪˈneɪʃn
AM ˌoʊvərdəˌtərmə-
ˈneɪʃən

overdetermine
BR ˌəʊvədɪˈtəːmɪn, -z,
-ɪŋ, -d
AM ˌoʊvərdəˈtərmən,
-z, -ɪŋ, -d

overdevelop
BR ˌəʊvədɪˈveləp, -s,
-ɪŋ, -t
AM ˌoʊvərdəˈveləp, -s,
-ɪŋ, -t

overdid
BR ˌəʊvəˈdɪd
AM ˌoʊvərˈdɪd

overdo
BR ˌəʊvəˈduː, -ɪŋ
AM ˌoʊvərˈdu, -ɪŋ

overdoes
BR ˌəʊvəˈdʌz
AM ˌoʊvərˈdəz

overdone
BR ˌəʊvəˈdʌn
AM ˌoʊvərˈdən

overdosage
BR ˌəʊvəˈdəʊs|ɪdʒ,
-ɪdʒɪz
AM ˌoʊvərˌdoʊsɪdʒ, -ɪz

overdose¹
*noun, verb, drug
abuse*
BR ˈəʊvədəʊs, -ɪz, -ɪŋ, -t
AM ˈoʊvərˌdoʊs, -ɪz, -ɪŋ,
-t

overdose²
verb, by mistake
BR ˌəʊvəˈdəʊs, -ɪz, -ɪŋ,
-t
AM ˌoʊvərˈdoʊs, -ɪz, -ɪŋ,
-t

overdraft
BR ˈəʊvədraːft,
ˈəʊvədraft, -s
AM ˈoʊvərˌdræft, -s

overdramatise
BR ˌəʊvəˈdramətʌɪz,
-ɪz, -ɪŋ, -d
AM ˌoʊvərˈdræməˌtaɪz,
ˌoʊvərˈdraməˌtaɪz,
-ɪz, -ɪŋ, -d

overdramatize
BR ˌəʊvəˈdramətʌɪz,
-ɪz, -ɪŋ, -d
AM ˌoʊvərˈdræməˌtaɪz,
ˌoʊvərˈdraməˌtaɪz,
-ɪz, -ɪŋ, -d

overdrank
BR ˌəʊvəˈdraŋk
AM ˌoʊvərˈdræŋk

overdraw
BR ˌəʊvəˈdrɔː(r), -z, -ɪŋ

AM ˌəʊvəˈdrɔː, ˌoʊvərˈdrɑ, -z, -ɪŋ

overdrawer
BR ˌəʊvəˈdrɔː(r)ə(r), -z
AM ˌoʊvərˈdrɔ(ə)r, -z

overdrawn
BR ˌəʊvəˈdrɔːn
AM ˌoʊvərˈdrɔn, ˌoʊvərˈdrɑn

overdress
BR ˌəʊvəˈdrɛs, -ɪz, -ɪŋ, -t
AM ˌoʊvərˈdrɛs, -əz, -ɪŋ, -t

overdrew
BR ˌəʊvəˈdruː
AM ˌoʊvərˈdru

overdrink
BR ˌəʊvəˈdrɪŋk, -s, -ɪŋ
AM ˌoʊvərˈdrɪŋk, -s, -ɪŋ

overdrive
BR ˈəʊvədrʌɪv, -z
AM ˈoʊvərˌdraɪv, -z

overdrunk
BR ˌəʊvəˈdrʌŋk
AM ˌoʊvərˈdrʌŋk

overdub
BR ˌəʊvəˈdʌb, -z, -ɪŋ, -d
AM ˌoʊvərˈdəb, -z, -ɪŋ, -d

overdue
BR ˌəʊvəˈdjuː, ˌəʊvəˈdʒuː
AM ˌoʊvərˈd(j)u

overeager
BR ˌəʊvərˈiːgə(r)
AM ˌoʊvərˈigər

overeagerly
BR ˌəʊvərˈiːgəli
AM ˌoʊvərˈigərli

overeagerness
BR ˌəʊvərˈiːgənəs
AM ˌoʊvərˈigərnəs

overeat
BR ˌəʊvərˈiːt, -s, -ɪŋ
AM ˌoʊvərˈiļt, -ts, -dɪŋ

overeaten
BR ˌəʊvərˈiːtn
AM ˌoʊvərˈitn

overemphases
BR ˌəʊvərˈɛmfəsiːz
AM ˌoʊvərˈɛmfəsiz

overemphasis
BR ˌəʊvərˈɛmfəsɪs
AM ˌoʊvərˈɛmfəsəs

overemphasise
BR ˌəʊvərˈɛmfəsʌɪz, -ɪz, -ɪŋ, -d
AM ˌoʊvərˈɛmfəˌsaɪz, -ɪz, -ɪŋ, -d

overemphasize
BR ˌəʊvərˈɛmfəsʌɪz, -ɪz, -ɪŋ, -d
AM ˌoʊvərˈɛmfəˌsaɪz, -ɪz, -ɪŋ, -d

overenthusiasm
BR ˌəʊv(ə)rɪnˈθjuːzɪaz(ə)m, ˌəʊv(ə)rɛnˈθjuːzɪaz(ə)m

AM ˌoʊvərənˈθ(j)uziˌæzəm

overenthusiastic
BR ˌəʊv(ə)rɪnˌθjuːzɪˈastɪk, ˌəʊv(ə)rɛnˌθjuːzɪˈastɪk
AM ˌoʊvərənˌθjuziˈæstɪk

overenthusiastically
BR ˌəʊv(ə)rɪnˌθjuːzɪˈastɪkli, ˌəʊv(ə)rɛnˌθjuːzɪˈastɪkli
AM ˌoʊvərənˌθjuziˈæstək(ə)li

overestimate¹
noun
BR ˌəʊvərˈɛstɪmət, -s
AM ˌoʊvərˈɛstəmət, -s

overestimate²
verb
BR ˌəʊvərˈɛstɪmeɪt, -s, -ɪŋ, -ɪd
AM ˌoʊvərˈɛstəˌmeɪļt, -ts, -dɪŋ, -dɪd

overestimation
BR ˌəʊvərˌɛstɪˈmeɪʃn
AM ˌoʊvərˌɛstəˈmeɪʃən

overexcite
BR ˌəʊv(ə)rɪkˈsʌɪt, ˌəʊv(ə)rɛkˈsʌɪt, -s, -ɪŋ, -ɪd
AM ˌoʊvərɪkˈsaɪļt, ˈoʊvərɛkˈsaɪļt, -ts, -dɪŋ, -dɪd

overexcitement
BR ˌəʊv(ə)rɪkˈsʌɪtm(ə)nt, ˌəʊv(ə)rɛkˈsʌɪtm(ə)nt
AM ˌoʊvərɪkˈsaɪtmənt, ˈoʊvərɛkˈsaɪtmənt

overexert
BR ˌəʊv(ə)rɪgˈzɜːt, ˌəʊv(ə)rɛgˈzɜːt, -s, -ɪŋ, -ɪd
AM ˌoʊvərɪgˈzərļt, ˈoʊvərɛgˈzərt, -ts, -dɪŋ, -dəd

overexertion
BR ˌəʊv(ə)rɪgˈzɜːʃn, ˌəʊv(ə)rɛgˈzɜːʃn
AM ˌoʊvərɪgˈzərʃən, ˈoʊvərɛgˈzərʃən

overexpose
BR ˌəʊv(ə)rɪkˈspəʊz, ˌəʊv(ə)rɛkˈspəʊz, -ɪz, -ɪŋ, -d
AM ˌoʊvərɪkˈspoʊz, ˈoʊvərɛkˈspoʊz, -ɪz, -ɪŋ, -d

overexposure
BR ˌəʊv(ə)rɪkˈspəʊʒə(r), ˌəʊv(ə)rɛkˈspəʊʒə(r)
AM ˌoʊvərɪkˈspoʊʒər, ˈoʊvərɛkˈspoʊʒər

overextend
BR ˌəʊvərɪkˈstɛnd, ˌəʊvərɛkˈstɛnd, -z, -ɪŋ, -ɪd
AM ˌoʊvərɪkˈstɛnd, ˈoʊvərɛkˈstɛnd, -z, -ɪŋ, -əd

overfall
BR ˈəʊvəfɔːl, -z
AM ˈoʊvərˌfɔl, ˈoʊvərˌfɑl, -z

overfamiliar
BR ˌəʊvəfəˈmɪlɪə(r)
AM ˌoʊvərfəˈmɪljər, ˌoʊvərfəˈmɪliər

overfamiliarity
BR ˌəʊvəfəˌmɪlɪˈarɪti
AM ˌoʊvərfəˌmɪliˈɛrədi

overfatigue
BR ˌəʊvəfəˈtiːg, -z, -ɪŋ, -d
AM ˌoʊvərfəˈtig, -z, -ɪŋ, -d

overfed
BR ˌəʊvəˈfɛd
AM ˌoʊvərˈfɛd

overfeed
BR ˌəʊvəˈfiːd, -z, -ɪŋ
AM ˌoʊvərˈfid, -z, -ɪŋ

overfill
BR ˌəʊvəˈfɪl, -z, -ɪŋ, -d
AM ˌoʊvərˈfɪl, -z, -ɪŋ, -d

overfine
BR ˌəʊvəˈfʌɪn
AM ˌoʊvərˈfaɪn

overfish
BR ˌəʊvəˈfɪʃ, -ɪz, -ɪŋ, -t
AM ˌoʊvərˈfɪʃ, -ɪz, -ɪŋ, -t

overflew
BR ˌəʊvəˈfluː
AM ˌoʊvərˈflu

overflight
BR ˈəʊvəflʌɪt, -s
AM ˈoʊvərˌflaɪt, -s

overflow¹
noun
BR ˈəʊvəfləʊ, -z
AM ˈoʊvərˌfloʊ, -z

overflow²
verb
BR ˌəʊvəˈfləʊ, -z, -ɪŋ, -d
AM ˌoʊvərˈfloʊ, -z, -ɪŋ, -d

overflown
BR ˌəʊvəˈfləʊn
AM ˌoʊvərˈfloʊn

overfly
BR ˌəʊvəˈflʌɪ, -z, -ɪŋ
AM ˌoʊvərˈflaɪ, -z, -ɪŋ

overfold
BR ˈəʊvəfəʊld, -z
AM ˈoʊvərˌfoʊld, -z

overfond
BR ˌəʊvəˈfɒnd
AM ˌoʊvərˈfɑnd

overfondly
BR ˌəʊvəˈfɒndli
AM ˌoʊvərˈfɑn(d)li

overfondness
BR ˌəʊvəˈfɒn(d)nəs
AM ˌoʊvərˈfɑn(d)nəs

overfulfil
BR ˌəʊvəfʊlˈfɪl, -z, -ɪŋ, -d
AM ˌoʊvərˌfʊ(l)ˈfɪl, -z, -ɪŋ, -d

overfulfill
BR ˌəʊvəfʊlˈfɪl, -z, -ɪŋ, -d
AM ˌoʊvərˌfʊ(l)ˈfɪl, -z, -ɪŋ, -d

overfulfillment
BR ˌəʊvəfʊlˈfɪlm(ə)nt
AM ˌoʊvərˌfʊ(l)ˈfɪlmənt

overfulfilment
BR ˌəʊvəfʊlˈfɪlm(ə)nt
AM ˌoʊvərˌfʊ(l)ˈfɪlmənt

overfull
BR ˌəʊvəˈfʊl
AM ˌoʊvərˈfʊl

overgarment
BR ˈəʊvəˌgɑːm(ə)nt, -s
AM ˈoʊvərˌgɑrmənt, -s

overgeneralisation
BR ˌəʊvəˌdʒɛn(ə)rəlʌɪˈzeɪʃn, ˌəʊvəˌdʒɛn(ə)rļʌɪˈzeɪʃn, -z
AM ˌoʊvərˌdʒɛn(ə)rələˈzeɪʃən, ˈoʊvərˌdʒɛn(ə)rəˌlaɪˈzeɪʃən, -z

overgeneralise
BR ˌəʊvəˈdʒɛn(ə)rəlʌɪz, ˌəʊvəˈdʒɛn(ə)rļʌɪz, -ɪz, -ɪŋ, -d
AM ˌoʊvərˈdʒɛn(ə)rəˌlaɪz, -ɪz, -ɪŋ, -d

overgeneralization
BR ˌəʊvəˌdʒɛn(ə)rəlʌɪˈzeɪʃn, ˌəʊvəˌdʒɛn(ə)rļʌɪˈzeɪʃn, -z
AM ˌoʊvərˌdʒɛn(ə)rələˈzeɪʃən, ˈoʊvərˌdʒɛn(ə)rəˌlaɪˈzeɪʃən, -z

overgeneralize
BR ˌəʊvəˈdʒɛn(ə)rəlʌɪz, ˌəʊvəˈdʒɛn(ə)rļʌɪz, -ɪz, -ɪŋ, -d
AM ˌoʊvərˈdʒɛn(ə)rəˌlaɪz, -ɪz, -ɪŋ, -d

overgenerous
BR ˌəʊvəˈdʒɛn(ə)rəs
AM ˌoʊvərˈdʒɛn(ə)rəs

overgenerously
BR ˌəʊvəˈdʒɛn(ə)rəsli
AM ˌoʊvərˈdʒɛn(ə)rəsli

overglaze
BR ˌəʊvəˈgleɪz, -ɪz, -ɪŋ, -d
AM ˌoʊvərˈgleɪz, -ɪz, -ɪŋ, -d

overgraze
BR ˌəʊvəˈgreɪz, -ɪz, -ɪŋ, -d
AM ˌoʊvərˈgreɪz, -ɪz, -ɪŋ, -d

overgrew
BR ˌəʊvəˈgruː
AM ˌoʊvərˈgru

overground
BR ˈəʊvəgraʊnd
AM ˈoʊvərˌgraʊnd

overgrow
BR ˌəʊvəˈgrəʊ, -z, -ɪŋ
AM ˌoʊvərˈgroʊ, -z, -ɪŋ

overgrown
BR ˌəʊvəˈgrəʊn
AM ˌoʊvərˈgroʊn

overgrowth
BR ˈəʊvəgrəʊθ
AM ˈoʊvərˌgroʊθ

overhand
BR ˈəʊvəhænd
AM ˈoʊvərˌ(h)ænd

overhang¹
noun
BR ˈəʊvəhæŋ, -z
AM ˈoʊvərˌ(h)æŋ, -z

overhang²
verb
BR ˌəʊvəˈhæŋ, -z, -ɪŋ
AM ˌoʊvərˈhæŋ, -z, -ɪŋ

overhanging
BR ˌəʊvəˈhæŋɪŋ
AM ˌoʊvərˈhæŋɪŋ

overhaste
BR ˌəʊvəˈheɪst
AM ˌoʊvərˈheɪst

overhastily
BR ˌəʊvəˈheɪstɪli
AM ˈoʊvərˈheɪstɪli

overhasty
BR ˌəʊvəˈheɪsti
AM ˌoʊvərˈheɪsti

overhaul¹
noun
BR ˈəʊvəhɔːl, -z
AM ˈoʊvərˌ(h)ɔl,
ˈoʊvərˌ(h)ɑl, -z

overhaul²
verb
BR ˈəʊvəhɔːl,
ˌəʊvəˈhɔːl, -z, -ɪŋ, -d
AM ˌoʊvərˈhɔl,
ˈoʊvərˌhɑl, -z, -ɪŋ, -d

overhead¹
adjective
BR ˌəʊvəˈhɛd
AM ˌoʊvərˈhɛd

overhead²
adverb
BR ˌəʊvəˈhɛd
AM ˌoʊvərˈhɛd

overhead³
noun
BR ˈəʊvəhɛd, -z
AM ˈoʊvərˌ(h)ɛd, -z

overhear
BR ˌəʊvəˈhɪə(r), -z, -ɪŋ
AM ˌoʊvərˈhɪ(ə)r, -z, -ɪŋ

overheard
BR ˌəʊvəˈhɜːd
AM ˌoʊvərˈhɜrd

overheat
BR ˌəʊvəˈhiːt, -s, -ɪŋ, -ɪd
AM ˌoʊvərˈhi|t, -ts, -dɪŋ, -dɪd

overhung
BR ˌəʊvəˈhʌŋ
AM ˌoʊvərˈhəŋ

overindulge
BR ˌəʊv(ə)rɪnˈdʌldʒ, -ɪz, -ɪŋ, -d
AM ˌoʊvərənˈdəldʒ, -əz, -ɪŋ, -d

overindulgence
BR ˌəʊv(ə)rɪnˈdʌldʒ(ə)ns
AM ˌoʊvərənˈdəldʒəns

overindulgent
BR ˌəʊv(ə)rɪnˈdʌldʒ(ə)nt
AM ˌoʊvərənˈdəldʒənt

overindulgently
BR ˌəʊv(ə)rɪnˈdʌldʒ-
(ə)ntli
AM ˌoʊvərənˈdəldʒ-
ən(t)li

over-inflated
BR ˌəʊv(ə)rɪnˈfleɪtɪd
AM ˌoʊvərənˈfleɪdɪd

overinsurance
BR ˌəʊv(ə)rɪnˈʃʊərəns,
ˌəʊvərɪnˈʃʊərns,
ˌəʊv(ə)rɪnˈʃɔːrəns,
ˌəʊvərɪnˈʃɔːrns
AM ˌoʊvərənˈʃʊrəns

overinsure
BR ˌəʊv(ə)rɪnˈʃʊə(r),
ˌəʊv(ə)rɪnˈʃɔː(r), -z, -ɪŋ, -d
AM ˌoʊvərənˈʃʊ(ə)r, -z, -ɪŋ, -d

overissue
BR ˌəʊvərˈɪʃ(j)uː,
ˌəʊvərˈɪsjuː, -z, -ɪŋ, -d
AM ˌoʊvərˈɪʃu, -z, -ɪŋ, -d

overjoyed
BR ˌəʊvəˈdʒɔɪd
AM ˌoʊvərˈjɔɪd

overkill
BR ˈəʊvəkɪl
AM ˈoʊvərˌkɪl

overladen
BR ˌəʊvəˈleɪdn
AM ˌoʊvərˈleɪdən

overlaid
BR ˌəʊvəˈleɪd
AM ˌoʊvərˈleɪd

overlain
BR ˌəʊvəˈleɪn
AM ˌoʊvərˈleɪn

overland
BR ˈəʊvəland,
ˌəʊvəˈland
AM ˈoʊvərˌlænd

overlander
BR ˈəʊvəˌlandə(r), -z
AM ˈoʊvərˌlændər, -z

overlap¹
noun
BR ˈəʊvəlap, -s
AM ˈoʊvərˌlæp, -s

overlap²
verb
BR ˌəʊvəˈlap, -s, -ɪŋ, -t
AM ˌoʊvərˈlæp, -s, -ɪŋ, -t

overlarge
BR ˌəʊvəˈlɑːdʒ
AM ˌoʊvərˈlɑrdʒ

overlay¹
noun
BR ˈəʊvəleɪ, -z
AM ˈoʊvərˌleɪ, -z

overlay²
verb
BR ˌəʊvəˈleɪ, -z, -ɪŋ, -d
AM ˌoʊvərˈleɪ, -z, -ɪŋ, -d

overleaf
BR ˌəʊvəˈliːf
AM ˈoʊvərˌlif

overleap
BR ˌəʊvəˈliːp, -s, -ɪŋ
AM ˌoʊvərˈlip, -s, -ɪŋ

overleaped
BR ˌəʊvəˈlɛpt
AM ˌoʊvərˈlipt

overlept
BR ˌəʊvəˈlɛpt
AM ˌoʊvərˈlɛpt

overlie
BR ˌəʊvəˈlaɪ, -z
AM ˌoʊvərˈlaɪ, -z

overload¹
noun
BR ˈəʊvələʊd, -z
AM ˈoʊvərˌloʊd, -z

overload²
verb
BR ˌəʊvəˈləʊd, -z, -ɪŋ, -ɪd
AM ˌoʊvərˈloʊd, -z, -ɪŋ, -əd

overlong
BR ˌəʊvəˈlɒŋ
AM ˌoʊvərˈlɔŋ,
ˈoʊvərˌlɑŋ

overlook
BR ˌəʊvəˈlʊk, -s, -ɪŋ, -t
AM ˌoʊvərˈlʊk, -s, -ɪŋ, -t

overlooker
BR ˌəʊvəˈlʊkə(r), -z
AM ˌoʊvərˈlʊkər, -z

overlord
BR ˈəʊvələːd, -z
AM ˈoʊvərˌlɔ(ə)rd, -z

overlordship
BR ˈəʊvələːdʃɪp, -s
AM ˈoʊvərˌlɔrdˌʃɪp, -s

overly
BR ˈəʊvəli
AM ˈoʊvərli

overlying
BR ˌəʊvəˈlaɪɪŋ
AM ˌoʊvərˈlaɪ(ɪ)ŋ

overman¹
noun
BR ˈəʊvəmən,
ˈəʊvəman
AM ˈoʊvərˌmæn

overman²
verb
BR ˌəʊvəˈman, -z, -ɪŋ, -d
AM ˌoʊvərˈmæn, -z, -ɪŋ, -d

overmantel
BR ˈəʊvəˌmantl, -z
AM ˈoʊvərˌmæn(t)l, -z

over-many
BR ˌəʊvəˈmɛni
AM ˌoʊvərˈmɛni

overmaster
BR ˌəʊvəˈmɑːstə(r),
ˌəʊvəˈmast|ə(r), -əz,
-(ə)rɪŋ, -əd
AM ˌoʊvərˈmæst|ər,
-ərz, -(ə)rɪŋ, -ərd

overmastery
BR ˌəʊvəˈmɑːst(ə)ri,
ˌəʊvəˈmast(ə)ri
AM ˌoʊvərˈmæstəri

overmatch
BR ˌəʊvəˈmatʃ, -ɪz, -ɪŋ, -t
AM ˌoʊvərˈmætʃ, -əz, -ɪŋ, -t

overmeasure
BR ˌəʊvəˈmɛʒə(r), -əz, -(ə)rɪŋ, -əd
AM ˌoʊvərˈmɛʒər, -z, -ɪŋ, -d

overmen
BR ˈəʊvəmən,
ˈəʊvəmɛn
AM ˈoʊvərˌmɛn

over-mighty
BR ˌəʊvəˈmʌɪti
AM ˌoʊvərˈmaɪdi

overmuch
BR ˌəʊvəˈmʌtʃ
AM ˌoʊvərˈmətʃ

overnight
BR ˌəʊvəˈnʌɪt
AM ˌoʊvərˈnaɪt

overnighter
BR ˌəʊvəˈnʌɪtə(r), -z
AM ˌoʊvərˈnaɪdər, -z

overpaid
BR ˌəʊvəˈpeɪd
AM ˌoʊvərˈpeɪd

overpaint
BR ˌəʊvəˈpeɪnt, -s, -ɪŋ, -ɪd
AM ˌoʊvərˈpeɪn|t, -ts, -dɪŋ, -dɪd

overparted
BR ˌəʊvəˈpɑːtɪd
AM ˌoʊvərˈpɑrdəd

overpass¹
noun
BR ˈəʊvəpɑːs,
ˈəʊvəpas, -ɪz
AM ˈoʊvərˌpæs, -əz

overpass²
verb
BR ˌəʊvəˈpɑːs,
ˌəʊvəˈpas, -ɪz, -ɪŋ, -t

AM ˈoʊvərˈpæs, -əz, -ɪŋ, -t

overpay
BR ˌəʊvəˈpeɪ, -z, -ɪŋ, -d
AM ˌoʊvərˈpeɪ, -z, -ɪŋ, -d

overpayed
adjective
BR ˌəʊvəˈpeɪd
AM ˌoʊvərˈpeɪd

overpayment
BR ˌəʊvəˈpeɪm(ə)nt, ˌəʊvəˈpeɪm(ə)nt, -s
AM ˌoʊvərˈpeɪmənt, -s

overpersuade
BR ˌəʊvəpəˈsweɪd, -z, -ɪŋ, -ɪd
AM ˌoʊvərpərˈsweɪd, -z, -ɪŋ, -ɪd

overpitch
BR ˌəʊvəˈpɪtʃ, -ɪz, -ɪŋ, -t
AM ˌoʊvərˈpɪtʃ, -ɪz, -ɪŋ, -t

overplay
BR ˌəʊvəˈpleɪ, -z, -ɪŋ, -d
AM ˌoʊvərˈpleɪ, -z, -ɪŋ, -d

overplus
BR ˈəʊvəplʌs, -ɪz
AM ˈoʊvərˌpləs, -əz

overpopulate
BR ˌəʊvəˈpɒpjʊleɪt, -s, -ɪŋ, -ɪd
AM ˌoʊvərˈpɑpjəˌleɪt, -ts, -dɪŋ, -dɪd

overpopulation
BR ˌəʊvəˌpɒpjʊˈleɪʃn
AM ˌoʊvərˌpɑpjəˈleɪʃən

overpower
BR ˌəʊvəˈpaʊə(r), -z, -ɪŋ, -d
AM ˌoʊvərˈpaʊ(ə)r, -z, -ɪŋ, -d

overpoweringly
BR ˌəʊvəˈpaʊərɪŋli
AM ˌoʊvərˈpaʊrɪŋli

overpraise
BR ˌəʊvəˈpreɪz, -ɪz, -ɪŋ, -d
AM ˌoʊvərˈpreɪz, -ɪz, -ɪŋ, -d

overprice
BR ˌəʊvəˈprʌɪs, -ɪz, -ɪŋ, -t
AM ˌoʊvərˈprʌɪs, -ɪz, -ɪŋ, -t

overprint[1]
noun
BR ˈəʊvəprɪnt, -s
AM ˈoʊvərˌprɪnt, -s

overprint[2]
verb
BR ˌəʊvəˈprɪnt, -s, -ɪŋ, -ɪd
AM ˌoʊvərˈprɪn|t, -ts, -(t)ɪŋ, -(t)əd

overproduce
BR ˌəʊvəprəˈdjuːs, ˌəʊvəprəˈdʒuːs, -ɪz, -ɪŋ, -t
AM ˌoʊvərprəˈd(j)uːs, -ɪz, -ɪŋ, -t

overproduction
BR ˌəʊvəprəˈdʌkʃn
AM ˌoʊvərprəˈdəkʃən

overproof
BR ˌəʊvəˈpruːf
AM ˌoʊvərˈpruf

overprotective
BR ˌəʊvəprəˈtɛktɪv
AM ˌoʊvərprəˈtɛktɪv

overqualified
BR ˌəʊvəˈkwɒlɪfʌɪd
AM ˌoʊvərˈkwɒləˌfaɪd, ˈoʊvərˈkwɑləˌfaɪd

overran
BR ˌəʊvəˈran
AM ˌoʊvə(r)ˈræn

overrate
BR ˌəʊvəˈreɪt, -s, -ɪŋ, -ɪd
AM ˌoʊvə(r)ˈreɪ|t, -ts, -dɪŋ, -dɪd

overreach
BR ˌəʊvəˈriːtʃ, -ɪz, -ɪŋ, -d
AM ˌoʊvə(r)ˈritʃ, -ɪz, -ɪŋ, -d

overreact
BR ˌəʊvərɪˈakt, -s, -ɪŋ, -d
AM ˌoʊvə(r)riˈæk|(t), -(t)s, -tɪŋ, -təd

overreaction
BR ˌəʊvərɪˈakʃn, -z
AM ˌoʊvə(r)riˈækʃən, -z

overridden
BR ˌəʊvəˈrɪdn
AM ˌoʊvə(r)ˈrɪdən

override
BR ˌəʊvəˈrʌɪd, -z, -ɪŋ
AM ˌoʊvə(r)ˈraɪd, -z, -ɪŋ

overrider
BR ˌəʊvəˈrʌɪdə(r), -z
AM ˌoʊvə(r)ˈraɪdər, -z

overripe
BR ˌəʊvəˈrʌɪp
AM ˌoʊvə(r)ˈraɪp

overripen
BR ˌəʊvəˈrʌɪp|n, -nz, -nɪŋ\-nɪŋ, -nd
AM ˌoʊvə(r)ˈraɪp|ən, -ənz, -(ə)nɪŋ, -ənd

overripeness
BR ˌəʊvəˈrʌɪpnɪs
AM ˌoʊvə(r)ˈraɪpnɪs

overrode
BR ˌəʊvəˈrəʊd
AM ˌoʊvə(r)ˈroʊd

overruff[1]
noun
BR ˈəʊvərʌf, -s
AM ˈoʊvə(r)ˌrəf, -s

overruff[2]
verb
BR ˌəʊvəˈrʌf, -s, -ɪŋ, -d
AM ˌoʊvə(r)ˈrəf, -s, -ɪŋ, -d

overrule
BR ˌəʊvəˈruːl, -z, -ɪŋ, -d
AM ˌoʊvə(r)ˈrul, -z, -ɪŋ, -d

overrun
BR ˌəʊvəˈrʌn, -z, -ɪŋ
AM ˌoʊvə(r)ˈrən, -z, -ɪŋ

oversailing
BR ˌəʊvəˈseɪlɪŋ
AM ˌoʊvərˈseɪlɪŋ

oversaw
BR ˌəʊvəˈsɔː(r)
AM ˌoʊvərˈsɔ

overscrupulous
BR ˌəʊvəˈskruːpjələs
AM ˌoʊvərˈskrupjələs

oversea
BR ˌəʊvəˈsiː, -z
AM ˌoʊvərˈsi, -z

oversee
BR ˌəʊvəˈsiː, -z, -ɪŋ
AM ˌoʊvərˈsi, -z, -ɪŋ

overseen
BR ˌəʊvəˈsiːn
AM ˌoʊvərˈsin

overseer
BR ˌəʊvəsɪə(r), -z
AM ˌoʊvərˈsɪ(ə)r, -z

oversell
BR ˌəʊvəˈsɛl, -z, -ɪŋ
AM ˌoʊvərˈsɛl, -z, -ɪŋ

overset
BR ˌəʊvəˈsɛt, -s, -ɪŋ
AM ˌoʊvərˈsɛ|t, -ts, -dɪŋ

oversew
BR ˌəʊvəˈsəʊ, -z, -ɪŋ, -d
AM ˌoʊvərˈsoʊ, -z, -ɪŋ, -d

oversexed
BR ˌəʊvəˈsɛkst
AM ˌoʊvərˈsɛkst

overshadow
BR ˌəʊvəˈʃadəʊ, -z, -ɪŋ, -d
AM ˌoʊvərˈʃæd|oʊ, -oʊz, -əwɪŋ, -oʊd

overshoe
BR ˈəʊvəʃuː, -z
AM ˈoʊvərˌʃu, -z

overshoot
BR ˌəʊvəˈʃuːt, -s, -ɪŋ
AM ˌoʊvərˈʃu|t, -ts, -dɪŋ

overshot
BR ˌəʊvəˈʃɒt
AM ˈoʊvərˈʃɑt

overside
BR ˈəʊvəsʌɪd
AM ˈoʊvərˌsaɪd

oversight
BR ˈəʊvəsʌɪt, -s
AM ˈoʊvərˌsaɪt, -s

oversimplification
BR ˌəʊvəˌsɪmplɪfɪˈkeɪʃn, -z
AM ˌoʊvərˌsɪmpləfəˈkeɪʃən, -z

oversimplify
BR ˌəʊvəˈsɪmplɪfʌɪ, -z, -ɪŋ, -d
AM ˌoʊvərˈsɪmpləˌfaɪ, -z, -ɪŋ, -d

oversize
BR ˌəʊvəˈsʌɪz, -d
AM ˈoʊvərˌsaɪz, -d

overskirt
BR ˈəʊvəskəːt, -s
AM ˈoʊvərˌskərt, -s

overslaugh
BR ˌəʊvəˈslɔː(r), -z, -ɪŋ, -d
AM ˌoʊvərˈslɔ, ˌoʊvərˈslɑ, -z, -ɪŋ, -d

oversleep
BR ˌəʊvəˈsliːp, -s, -ɪŋ
AM ˌoʊvərˈslip, -s, -ɪŋ

oversleeve
BR ˈəʊvəsliːv, -z
AM ˈoʊvərˌsliv, -z

overslept
BR ˌəʊvəˈslɛpt
AM ˌoʊvərˈslɛpt

oversold
BR ˌəʊvəˈsəʊld
AM ˌoʊvərˈsoʊld

oversolicitous
BR ˌəʊvəsəˈlɪsɪtəs
AM ˌoʊvərsəˈlɪsədəs

oversolicitude
BR ˌəʊvəsəˈlɪsɪtjuːd, ˌəʊvəsəˈlɪsɪtʃuːd
AM ˌoʊvərsəˈlɪsəˌt(j)ud

oversoul
BR ˈəʊvəsəʊl
AM ˈoʊvərˌsoʊl

overspecialisation
BR ˌəʊvəˌspɛʃəlʌɪˈzeɪʃn, ˌəʊvəˌspɛʃlʌɪˈzeɪʃn
AM ˌoʊvərˌspɛʃ(ə)ləˈzeɪʃən, ˌoʊvərˌspɛʃ(ə)ˌlaɪˈzeɪʃən

overspecialise
BR ˌəʊvəˈspɛʃəlʌɪz, ˌəʊvəˈspɛʃlʌɪz, -ɪz, -ɪŋ, -d
AM ˌoʊvərˈspɛʃ(ə)ˌlaɪz, -ɪz, -ɪŋ, -d

overspecialization
BR ˌəʊvəˌspɛʃəlʌɪˈzeɪʃn, ˌəʊvəˌspɛʃlʌɪˈzeɪʃn
AM ˌoʊvərˌspɛʃ(ə)ləˈzeɪʃən, ˌoʊvərˌspɛʃ(ə)ˌlaɪˈzeɪʃən

overspecialize
BR ˌəʊvəˈspɛʃəlʌɪz, ˌəʊvəˈspɛʃlʌɪz, -ɪz, -ɪŋ, -d
AM ˌoʊvərˈspɛʃ(ə)ˌlaɪz, -ɪz, -ɪŋ, -d

overspend[1]
noun
BR ˈəʊvəspɛnd, -z

overspend
AM ˈoʊvərˌspɛnd, -z

overspend²
verb
BR ˌəʊvəˈspɛnd, -z, -ɪŋ
AM ˌoʊvərˈspɛnd, -z, -ɪŋ

overspent
BR ˌəʊvəˈspɛnt
AM ˌoʊvərˈspɛnt

overspill
BR ˈəʊvəspɪl
AM ˈoʊvərˌspɪl

overspread
BR ˌəʊvəˈsprɛd, -z, -ɪŋ
AM ˌoʊvərˈsprɛd, -z, -ɪŋ

overstaff
BR ˌəʊvəˈstɑːf,
ˌəʊvəˈstaf, -s, -ɪŋ, -t
AM ˈoʊvərˈstæf, -s, -ɪŋ,
-t

overstate
BR ˌəʊvəˈsteɪt, -s, -ɪŋ,
-ɪd
AM ˌoʊvərˈsteɪ|t, -ts,
-dɪŋ, -dɪd

overstatement
BR ˌəʊvəˈsteɪtm(ə)nt,
ˈəʊvəˌsteɪtm(ə)nt, -s
AM ˈoʊvərˈsteɪtmənt,
-s

overstay
BR ˌəʊvəˈsteɪ, -z, -ɪŋ, -d
AM ˌoʊvərˈsteɪ, -z, -ɪŋ,
-d

oversteer¹
noun
BR ˈəʊvəstɪə(r)
AM ˈoʊvərˌstɪ(ə)r

oversteer²
verb
BR ˌəʊvəˈstɪə(r), -z, -ɪŋ,
-d
AM ˈoʊvərˈstɪ(ə)r, -z,
-ɪŋ, -d

overstep
BR ˌəʊvəˈstɛp, -s, -ɪŋ, -t
AM ˌoʊvərˈstɛp, -s, -ɪŋ,
-t

overstock
BR ˌəʊvəˈstɒk, -s, -ɪŋ, -t
AM ˌoʊvərˈstɑk, -s, -ɪŋ,
-t

overstrain
verb
BR ˌəʊvəˈstreɪn, -z, -ɪŋ,
-d
AM ˈoʊvərˈstreɪn, -z,
-ɪŋ, -d

overstress
BR ˌəʊvəˈstrɛs, -ɪz, -ɪŋ,
-t
AM ˈoʊvərˈstrɛs, -əz,
-ɪŋ, -t

overstretch
BR ˌəʊvəˈstretʃ, -ɪz, -ɪŋ,
-t
AM ˈoʊvərˈstretʃ, -əz,
-ɪŋ, -t

overstrong
BR ˌəʊvəˈstrɒŋ
AM ˈoʊvərˈstrɔŋ,
ˈoʊvərˌstrɑŋ

overstrung
BR ˌəʊvəˈstrʌŋ
AM ˈoʊvərˈstrəŋ

overstudy
BR ˌəʊvəˈstʌd|i, -ɪz,
-ɪŋ, -ɪd
AM ˌoʊvərˈstədi, -z, -ɪŋ,
-d

overstuff
BR ˌəʊvəˈstʌf, -s, -ɪŋ, -d
AM ˌoʊvərˈstəf, -s, -ɪŋ,
-d

oversubscribe
BR ˌəʊvəsəbˈskrʌɪb, -z,
-ɪŋ, -d
AM ˈoʊvərsəbˈskraɪb,
-z, -ɪŋ, -d

oversubtle
BR ˌəʊvəˈsʌtl
AM ˈoʊvərˈsədəl

oversupply
BR ˌəʊvəsəˈplʌɪ, -z, -ɪŋ,
-d
AM ˈoʊvərsəˈplaɪ, -z,
-ɪŋ, -d

oversusceptible
BR ˌəʊvəsəˈsɛptɪbl
AM ˈoʊvərsəˈsɛptəbəl

overt
BR əˈ(ʊ)ˈvəːt, ˈəʊvəːt
AM oʊˈvərt, ˈoʊvərt

overtake
BR ˌəʊvəˈteɪk, -s, -ɪŋ
AM ˈoʊvərˈteɪk, -s, -ɪŋ

overtaken
BR ˌəʊvəˈteɪk(ə)n
AM ˈoʊvərˈteɪkən

overtask
BR ˌəʊvəˈtɑːsk,
ˌəʊvəˈtask, -s, -ɪŋ, -t
AM ˈoʊvərˈtæsk, -s, -ɪŋ,
-t

overtax
BR ˌəʊvəˈtaks
AM ˈoʊvərˈtæks

over-the-counter
BR ˌəʊvəðəˈkaʊntə(r)
AM ˈoʊvərðəˈkaʊn(t)ər

over-the-top
BR ˌəʊvəðəˈtɒp
AM ˈoʊvərðəˈtɑp

overthrew
BR ˌəʊvəˈθruː
AM ˈoʊvərˈθru

overthrow¹
noun
BR ˈəʊvəθrəʊ, -z
AM ˈoʊvərˌθroʊ, -z

overthrow²
verb
BR ˌəʊvəˈθrəʊ, -z, -ɪŋ
AM ˈoʊvərˈθroʊ, -z, -ɪŋ

overthrown
BR ˌəʊvəˈθrəʊn

AM ˈoʊvərˈθroʊn

overthrust
BR ˈəʊvəθrʌst, -s
AM ˈoʊvərˌθrəst, -s

overtime
BR ˈəʊvətʌɪm
AM ˈoʊvərˌtaɪm

overtire
BR ˌəʊvəˈtʌɪə(r), -z, -ɪŋ,
-d
AM ˌoʊvərˈtaɪ(ə)r, -z,
-ɪŋ, -d

overtly
BR əˈ(ʊ)ˈvəːtli, ˈəʊvəːtli
AM oʊˈvərtli, ˈoʊvərtli

overtness
BR əˈ(ʊ)ˈvəːtnəs,
ˈəʊvəːtnəs
AM oʊˈvərtnəs,
ˈoʊvərtnəs

Overton
BR ˈəʊvət(ə)n
AM ˈoʊvərt(ə)n

overtone
BR ˈəʊvətəʊn, -z
AM ˈoʊvərˌtoʊn, -z

overtook
BR ˌəʊvəˈtʊk
AM ˈoʊvərˈtʊk

overtop
BR ˌəʊvəˈtɒp, -s, -ɪŋ, -t
AM ˈoʊvərˈtɑp, -s, -ɪŋ, -t

overtrain
BR ˌəʊvəˈtreɪn, -z, -ɪŋ,
-d
AM ˌoʊvərˈtreɪn, -z, -ɪŋ,
-d

overtrick
BR ˈəʊvətrɪk, -s
AM ˈoʊvərˌtrɪk, -s

overtrump
BR ˌəʊvəˈtrʌmp, -s, -ɪŋ,
AM ˈoʊvərˈtrəmp, -s,
-ɪŋ, -t

overture
BR ˈəʊvətjʊə(r),
ˈəʊvətʃ(ʊ)ə(r), -z
AM ˈoʊvərˌtʃʊ(ə)r,
ˈoʊvərˌtʃər, -z

overturn
BR ˌəʊvəˈtəːn, -z, -ɪŋ, -d
AM ˌoʊvərˈtərn, -z, -ɪŋ,
-d

overuse¹
noun
BR ˌəʊvəˈjuːs
AM ˌoʊvərˈjus

overuse²
verb
BR ˌəʊvəˈjuːz, -ɪz, -ɪŋ, -d
AM ˈoʊvərˈjuz, -əz, -ɪŋ,
-d

overvaluation
BR ˌəʊvəˌvaljʊˈeɪʃn, -z
AM ˈoʊvərəˌvæljəˈweɪ-
ʃən, -z

overvalue
BR ˌəʊvəˈvaljuː, -z, -ɪŋ,
-d
AM ˈoʊvərˈvælju, -z,
-ɪŋ, -d

overview
BR ˈəʊvəvjuː, -z
AM ˈoʊvərˌvju, -z

overwater
BR ˌəʊvəˈwɔːt|ə(r), -əz,
-(ə)rɪŋ, -əd
AM ˈoʊvərˈwɔdər,
ˈoʊvərˈwɑdər, -z, -ɪŋ,
-d

overweening
BR ˌəʊvəˈwiːnɪŋ
AM ˈoʊvərˈwinɪŋ

overweeningly
BR ˌəʊvəˈwiːnɪŋli
AM ˈoʊvərˈwinɪŋli

overweeningness
BR ˌəʊvəˈwiːnɪŋnɪs
AM ˈoʊvərˈwinɪŋnɪs

overweight
BR ˌəʊvəˈweɪt
AM ˈoʊvərˈweɪt

overwhelm
BR ˌəʊvəˈwɛlm, -z, -ɪŋ,
-d
AM ˈoʊvərˈ(h)wɛlm, -z,
-ɪŋ, -d

overwhelmingly
BR ˌəʊvəˈwɛlmɪŋli
AM ˈoʊvərˈ(h)wɛlmɪŋli

overwhelmingness
BR ˌəʊvəˈwɛlmɪŋnɪs
AM ˈoʊvərˈ(h)wɛlmɪŋnɪs

overwind
BR ˌəʊvəˈwʌɪnd, -z, -ɪŋ
AM ˈoʊvərˈwaɪnd, -z,
-ɪŋ

overwinter
BR ˌəʊvəˈwɪnt|ə(r), -əz,
-(ə)rɪŋ, -əd
AM ˈoʊvərˈwɪn(t)ər, -z,
-ɪŋ, -d

overwork
BR ˌəʊvəˈwəːk, -s, -ɪŋ, -t
AM ˈoʊvərˈwərk, -s, -ɪŋ,
-t

overwound
BR ˌəʊvəˈwaʊnd
AM ˈoʊvərˈwaʊnd

overwrite
BR ˌəʊvəˈrʌɪt, -s, -ɪŋ
AM ˈoʊvərˈraɪ|t, -ts, -dɪŋ

overwritten
BR ˌəʊvəˈrɪtn
AM ˈoʊvərˈrɪtn

overwrote
BR ˌəʊvəˈrəʊt
AM ˈoʊvəˈroʊt

overwrought
BR ˌəʊvəˈrɔːt
AM ˈoʊvərˈrɔt, ˈoʊvəˈrɑt

overzeal
BR ˌəʊvəˈziːl
AM ˈoʊvərˌzil

overzealous
BR ˌəʊvəˈzɛləs
AM ˈoʊvərˈzɛləs
Ovett
BR ˈəʊvɪt, ˈəʊvɛt,
əʊˈvɛt,
AM oʊˈvɛt, ˈoʊvət
ovibovine
BR ˌəʊviˈbəʊvʌɪn, -z
AM ˈoʊviˈboʊvaɪn, -z
ovicide
BR ˈəʊvɪsʌɪd, ˈɒvɪsʌɪd
AM ˈoʊvəˌsaɪd,
ˈɑvəˌsaɪd
Ovid
BR ˈɒvɪd
AM ˈɑvɪd
oviducal
BR ˌəʊviˈdjuːkl,
ˌəʊviˈdʒuːkl
AM ˌoʊvəˈdukəl
oviduct
BR ˈəʊvɪdʌkt, -s
AM ˈoʊvəˌdək(t), -(t)s
oviductal
BR ˌəʊviˈdʌktl
AM ˌoʊvəˈdəktəl
Oviedo
BR ˌɒviˈeɪdəʊ
AM ɔˈvjɛdoʊ, ɑˈvjɛdoʊ
SP oˈβjeðo
oviform
BR ˈəʊvifɔːm
AM ˈoʊvəˌfɔ(ə)rm
ovine
BR ˈəʊvʌɪn
AM ˈoʊˌvaɪn
oviparity
BR ˌəʊviˈpariti
AM ˌoʊvəˈpɛrədi
oviparous
BR əʊˈvɪp(ə)rəs
AM oʊˈvɪpərəs
oviparously
BR əʊˈvɪp(ə)rəsli
AM oʊˈvɪpərəsli
oviposit
BR ˌəʊviˈpɒzɪt, -ɪts,
-ɪtɪŋ, -ɪtɪd
AM ˌoʊvəˈpazəlt, -ts,
-dɪŋ, -dəd
oviposition
BR ˌəʊvipəˈzɪʃn
AM ˌoʊvəpəˈzɪʃən
ovipositor
BR ˌəʊviˈpɒzɪtə(r), -z
AM ˈoʊvəˈpazədər, -z
ovoid
BR ˈəʊvɔɪd
AM ˈoʊˌvɔɪd
ovoli
BR ˈəʊvəli:
AM ˈoʊvəlaɪ, ˈovəˌlaɪ
ovolo
BR ˈəʊvələʊ
AM ˈoʊvəloʊ, ˈovəˌloʊ

ovotestes
BR ˌəʊvəʊˈtɛstiːz
AM ˌoʊvoʊˈtɛstiz
ovotestis
BR ˌəʊvəʊˈtɛstɪs
AM ˌoʊvoʊˈtɛstəs
ovoviviparity
BR ˌəʊvəʊˌvɪvɪˈpariti
AM oʊˌvoʊˌvɪvɪˈpɛrədi
ovoviviparous
BR ˌəʊvəʊvɪˈvɪp(ə)rəs,
ˌəʊvəʊvʌɪˈvɪp(ə)rəs
AM oʊˌvoʊvəˈvɪp(ə)rəs
ovular
BR ˈɒvjʊlə(r)
AM ˈoʊvjələr, ˈavjələr
ovulate
BR ˈɒvjʊleɪt, -s, -ɪŋ, -ɪd
AM ˈoʊvjəˌleɪlt,
ˈavjəˌleɪlt, -ts, -dɪŋ,
-dɪd
ovulation
BR ˌɒvjʊˈleɪʃn, -z
AM ˌoʊvjəˈleɪʃən,
ˌavjəˈleɪʃən, -z
ovulatory
BR ˈɒvjʊlət(ə)ri
AM ˈoʊvjələˌtɔri,
ˈavjələˌtɔri
ovule
BR ˈɒvjuːl, -z
AM ˈoʊvjul, ˈavjul, -z
ovum
BR ˈəʊvəm
AM ˈoʊvəm
owl!
BR aʊ
AM aʊ
Owain
BR ˈəʊvʌɪn
AM ˈoʊweɪn
owe
BR əʊ, -z, -ɪŋ, -d
AM oʊ, -z, -(w)ɪŋ, -d
Owen
BR ˈəʊɪn
AM ˈoʊ(w)ən
Owens
BR ˈəʊɪnz
AM ˈoʊ(w)ənz
owl
BR aʊl, -z
AM aʊl, -z
owlery
BR ˈaʊlər|i, -ɪz
AM ˈaʊləri, -z
owlet
BR ˈaʊlɪt, -s
AM ˈaʊlət, -s
owlish
BR ˈaʊlɪʃ
AM ˈaʊlɪʃ
owlishly
BR ˈaʊlɪʃli
AM ˈaʊlɪʃli
owlishness
BR ˈaʊlɪʃnɪs

own
BR əʊn, -z, -ɪŋ, -d
AM oʊn, -z, -ɪŋ, -d
own brand
BR ˌəʊn ˈbrand, ˈəʊn
brand, -z
AM ˈoʊn ˌbrænd, -z
owner
BR ˈəʊnə(r), -z
AM ˈoʊnər, -z
ownerless
BR ˈəʊnələs
AM ˈoʊnərləs
ownership
BR ˈəʊnəʃɪp
AM ˈoʊnərˌʃɪp
owt
BR aʊt
AM aʊt
ox
BR ɒks
AM ɑks
oxalate
BR ˈɒksəleɪt, -s
AM ˈɑksəˌleɪt, -s
oxalic
BR ɒkˈsalɪk
AM ɑkˈsælɪk
oxalis
BR ˈɒksəlɪs, ɒkˈsalɪs,
ɒkˈsaːlɪs
AM ˈɑksələs, ɑkˈsæləs
oxbow
BR ˈɒksbəʊ, -z
AM ˈɑksˌboʊ, -z
Oxbridge
BR ˈɒksbrɪdʒ
AM ˈɑksˌbrɪdʒ
oxcart
BR ˈɒkskaːt, -s
AM ˈɑksˌkart, -s
oxen
BR ˈɒksn
AM ˈɑksən
Oxenden
BR ˈɒksndən
AM ˈɑksəndən
Oxenford
BR ˈɒksnfɔːd
AM ˈɑksənfərd
Oxenholme
BR ˈɒksnhəʊm
AM ˈɑksən,(h)oʊm
oxer
BR ˈɒksə(r), -z
AM ˈɑksər, -z
Oxfam
BR ˈɒksfam
AM ˈɑksfæm
Oxford
BR ˈɒksfəd
AM ˈɑksfərd
Oxfordshire
BR ˈɒksfədʃ(ɪ)ə(r)
AM ˈɑksfərdˌʃɪ(ə)r

oxheart
BR ˈɒkshaːt, -s
AM ˈɑks,(h)art, -s
oxherd
BR ˈɒkshəːd, -z
AM ˈɑks,(h)ərd, -z
Oxhey
BR ˈɒksi, ˈɒksheɪ
AM ˈɑksi
oxhide
BR ˈɒkshʌɪd
AM ˈɑks,(h)aɪd
oxidant
BR ˈɒksɪd(ə)nt, -s
AM ˈɑksədnt, -s
oxidate
BR ˈɒksɪdeɪt, -s, -ɪŋ, -ɪd
AM ˈɑksəˌdeɪlt, -ts, -dɪŋ,
-dɪd
oxidation
BR ˌɒksɪˈdeɪʃn
AM ˌɑksəˈdeɪʃən
oxidational
BR ˌɒksɪˈdeɪʃn(ə)l,
ˌɒksɪˈdeɪʃən(ə)l
AM ˌɑksəˈdeɪʃ(ə)nəl
oxidative
BR ˈɒksɪdeɪtɪv
AM ˈɑksəˌdeɪdɪv
oxide
BR ˈɒksʌɪd, -z
AM ˈɑkˌsaɪd, -z
oxidisable
BR ˈɒksɪdaɪzəbl
AM ˈɑksəˌdaɪzəbəl
oxidisation
BR ˌɒksɪdʌɪˈzeɪʃn
AM ˌɑksəˌdaɪˈzeɪʃən,
ˌɑksədəˈzeɪʃən
oxidise
BR ˈɒksɪdʌɪz, -ɪz, -ɪŋ, -d
AM ˈɑksəˌdaɪz, -ɪz, -ɪŋ,
-d
oxidiser
BR ˈɒksɪdʌɪzə(r), -z
AM ˈɑksəˌdaɪzər, -z
oxidizable
BR ˈɒksɪdaɪzəbl
AM ˈɑksəˌdaɪzəbəl
oxidization
BR ˌɒksɪdʌɪˈzeɪʃn
AM ˌɑksəˌdaɪˈzeɪʃən,
ˌɑksədəˈzeɪʃən
oxidize
BR ˈɒksɪdʌɪz, -ɪz, -ɪŋ, -d
AM ˈɑksəˌdaɪz, -ɪz, -ɪŋ,
-d
oxidizer
BR ˈɒksɪdʌɪzə(r), -z
AM ˈɑksəˌdaɪzər, -z
Oxley
BR ˈɒksli
AM ˈɑksli
oxlip
BR ˈɒkslɪp, -s
AM ˈɑks,lɪp, -s

Oxnard
BR ˈɒksnɑːd, ˈɒksnəd
AM ˈɑksˌnɑrd

oxo
BR ˈɒksəʊ
AM ˈɑksoʊ

Oxon
BR ˈɒks(ɒ)n
AM ˈɑksˌɑn

Oxonian
BR ɒkˈsəʊnɪən, -z
AM ɑkˈsoʊnɪən,
ɑkˈsoʊnjən, -z

oxonium
BR ɒkˈsəʊnɪəm
AM ɑkˈsoʊnɪəm

Oxshott
BR ˈɒk(s)ʃɒt
AM ˈɑkˌʃɑt

oxslip
BR ˈɒkslɪp, -s
AM ˈɑksˌlɪp, -s

oxtail
BR ˈɒksteɪl, -z
AM ˈɑksˌteɪl, -z

oxter
BR ˈɒkstə(r), -z
AM ˈɑkstər, -z

Oxton
BR ˈɒkst(ə)n
AM ˈɑkstən

oxtongue
BR ˈɒkstʌŋ, -z
AM ˈɑksˌtəŋ, -z

Oxus
BR ˈɒksəs
AM ˈɑksəs

oxyacetylene
BR ˌɒksɪəˈsɛtɪliːn,
ˌɒksɪəˈsɛtḷiːn,
ˌɒksɪəˈsɛtɪlɪn,
ˌɒksɪəˈsɛtḷɪn
AM ˌɑksɪəˈsɛdḷən,
ˌɑksɪəˈsɛdḷˌin

oxyacid
BR ˌɒksɪˈasɪd, -z

oxycarpous
BR ˌɒksɪˈkɑːpəs
AM ˌɑksɪˈkɑrpəs

Oxydol
BR ˈɒksɪdɒl
AM ˈɑksɪˌdɒl, ˈɑksɪˌdɑl

oxygen
BR ˈɒksɪdʒ(ə)n
AM ˈɑksədʒən

oxygenate
BR ˈɒksɪdʒneɪt,
ɒkˈsɪdʒəneɪt, -s, -ɪŋ,
-ɪd
AM ˈɑksədʒəˌneɪ|t, -ts,
-dɪŋ, -dɪd

oxygenation
BR ˌɒksɪdʒɪˈneɪʃn
AM ˌɑksədʒəˈneɪʃən

oxygenator
BR ˈɒksɪdʒneɪtə(r),
ɒkˈsɪdʒəneɪtə(r), -z
AM ˈɑksədʒəˌneɪdər, -z

oxygenise
BR ˈɒksɪdʒɪnaɪz, -ɪz,
-ɪŋ, -d
AM ˈɑksədʒəˌnaɪz, -ɪz,
-ɪŋ, -d

oxygenize
BR ˈɒksɪdʒɪnaɪz, -ɪz,
-ɪŋ, -d
AM ˈɑksədʒəˌnaɪz, -ɪz,
-ɪŋ, -d

oxygenous
BR ɒkˈsɪdʒɪnəs
AM ɑkˈsɪdʒənəs

oxyhaemoglobin
BR ˌɒksɪˌhiːməˈgləʊbɪn
AM ˌɑksɪˌhiməˈgloʊbən

oxyhemoglobin
BR ˌɒksɪˌhiːməˈgləʊbɪn
AM ˌɑksɪˌhiməˈgloʊbən

oxy-hydrogen
BR ˌɒksɪˈhʌɪdrədʒ(ə)n
AM ˌɑksɪˈhaɪdrədʒən

oxymoron
BR ˌɒksɪˈmɔːrɒn, -z
AM ˌɑksəˈmɔrˌɑn, -z

oxyopia
BR ˌɒksɪˈəʊpɪə(r)
AM ˌɑksɪˈoʊpɪə

Oxyrhynchus
BR ˌɒksɪˈrɪŋkəs
AM ˌɑksəˈrɪŋkəs

oxysalt
BR ˌɒksɪˈsɔːlt,
ˌɒksɪˈsɒlt, ˈɒksɪˌsɔːlt,
ˈɒksɪsɒlt, -s
AM ˈɑksɪˌsɔlt,
ˈɑksɪˌsɑlt, -s

oxytocin
BR ˌɒksɪˈtəʊsɪn, -z
AM ˌɑksəˈtoʊsn, -z

oxytone
BR ˈɒksɪtəʊn, -z
AM ˈɑksəˌtoʊn, -z

oyes
BR əʊˈjeɪ, əʊˈjɛz, əʊˈjɛs
AM oʊˈjeɪ, oʊˈjɛz

oyez
BR əʊˈjeɪ, əʊˈjɛz, əʊˈjɛs
AM oʊˈjeɪ, oʊˈjɛz

oyster
BR ˈɔɪstə(r), -z
AM ˈɔɪstər, -z

oystercatcher
BR ˈɔɪstəˌkatʃə(r), -z
AM ˈɔɪstərˌkætʃər, -z

Oystermouth
BR ˈɔɪstəmaʊθ
AM ˈɔɪstərməθ

oystershell
BR ˈɔɪstəʃɛl
AM ˈɔɪstərˌʃɛl

Oz
BR ɒz
AM ɑz

oz.
BR aʊns, -ɪz
AM aʊns, -ɪz

Ozalid®
BR ˈɒzælɪd, ˈɒzˌlɪd,
ˈəʊzæl, ˈəʊzæd
AM ˈoʊzəˌlɪd, ˈɑzə,lɪd

Ozark
BR ˈəʊzɑːk, -s
AM ˈoʊˌzɑrk, -s

Ozawa
BR ɒˈzɑːwə(r)
AM oʊˈzɑwə

ozocerite
BR əʊˈzɒsərʌɪt,
əʊˈzəʊsərʌɪt,
ˌəʊzə(ʊ)ˈsɪərʌɪt
AM oʊˈzoʊkəˌraɪt

ozokerite
BR əʊˈzɒkərʌɪt,
əʊˈzəʊkərʌɪt,
ˌəʊzə(ʊ)ˈkɪərʌɪt
AM oʊˈzoʊkəˌraɪt

ozone
BR ˈəʊzəʊn
AM ˈoʊˌzoʊn

ozonic
BR əʊˈzɒnɪk
AM oʊˈzɑnɪk

ozonisation
BR ˌəʊzə(ʊ)nʌɪˈzeɪʃn
AM ˌoʊzənəˈzeɪʃən,
ˌoʊzəˌnaɪˈzeɪʃən

ozonise
BR ˈəʊzə(ʊ)nʌɪz, -ɪz,
-ɪŋ, -d
AM ˈoʊzəˌnaɪz, -ɪz, -ɪŋ,
-d

ozonization
BR ˌəʊzə(ʊ)nʌɪˈzeɪʃn
AM ˌoʊzənəˈzeɪʃən,
ˌoʊzəˌnaɪˈzeɪʃən

ozonize
BR ˈəʊzə(ʊ)nʌɪz, -ɪz,
-ɪŋ, -d
AM ˈoʊzəˌnaɪz, -ɪz, -ɪŋ,
-d

Ozymandias
BR ˌɒzɪˈmandɪəs,
ˌɒzɪˈmandɪas
AM ˌoʊzəˈmændɪəs

Ozzie
BR ˈɒzi
AM ˈɑzi

Pp

p
BR piː, -z
AM pi, -z

PA
BR ˌpiːˈeɪ, -z
AM ˌpiˈeɪ, -z

pa
BR pɑː(r), -z
AM pɑ, -z

Paarl
BR pɑːl
AM pɑrl

Pablo
BR ˈpabləʊ
AM ˈpɑbloʊ

Pablum®
BR ˈpabləm
AM ˈpæbləm

pabulum
BR ˈpabjələm
AM ˈpæb(jə)ləm

paca
BR ˈpakə(r), ˈpɑːkə(r), -z
AM ˈpɑkə, ˈpækə, -z

pacarana
BR ˌpakəˈrɑːnə(r), -z
AM ˌpɑkəˈrɑnə, -z

pace¹
noun, verb
BR peɪs, -ɪz, -ɪŋ, -t
AM peɪs, -ɪz, -ɪŋ, -t

pace²
preposition, with respect to
BR ˈpeɪsi, ˈpɑːtʃeɪ, ˈpɑːkeɪ
AM ˈpeɪˌsi, ˈpɑˌtʃeɪ

pacemaker
BR ˈpeɪsˌmeɪkə(r), -z
AM ˈpeɪsˌmeɪkər, -z

pacemaking
BR ˈpeɪsˌmeɪkɪŋ
AM ˈpeɪsˌmeɪkɪŋ

paceman
BR ˈpeɪsmən, ˈpeɪsman
AM ˈpeɪsˌmæn, ˈpeɪsmən

pacemen
BR ˈpeɪsmən, ˈpeɪsmɛn
AM ˈpeɪsmən, ˈpeɪsˌmɛn

pacer
BR ˈpeɪsə(r), -z
AM ˈpeɪsər, -z

pacesetter
BR ˈpeɪsˌsɛtə(r), -z
AM ˈpeɪs(s)ˌsɛdər, -z

pace-setting
BR ˈpeɪsˌsɛtɪŋ
AM ˈpeɪs(s)ˌsɛdɪŋ

pacey
BR ˈpeɪsi
AM ˈpeɪsi

pacha
BR ˈpɑːʃə(r), ˈpaʃə(r), -z
AM ˈpɑʃə, -z

Pachelbel
BR ˈpaklbɛl, paxlbɛl
AM ˈpɑkəlˌbɛl

pachinko
BR pəˈtʃɪŋkəʊ
AM pəˈtʃɪŋkoʊ

pachisi
BR pəˈtʃiːzi
AM pəˈtʃizi

pachuco
BR pəˈtʃuːkəʊ, -z
AM pəˈtʃʊkoʊ, -z

pachyderm
BR ˈpakɪdɜːm, -z
AM ˈpækəˌdɜrm, -z

pachydermal
BR ˌpakɪˈdɜːml
AM ˌpækəˈdɜrməl

pachydermatous
BR ˌpakɪˈdɜːmətəs
AM ˌpækəˈdɜrmədəs

pachysandra
BR ˌpakɪˈsandrə(r)
AM ˌpækəˈsændrə

pachytene
BR ˈpakɪtiːn
AM ˈpækəˌtin

pacific
BR pəˈsɪfɪk
AM pəˈsɪfɪk

pacifically
BR pəˈsɪfɪkli
AM pəˈsɪfək(ə)li

pacification
BR ˌpasɪfɪˈkeɪʃn, -z
AM ˌpæsəfəˈkeɪʃən, -z

pacificatory
BR pəˈsɪfɪkət(ə)ri, ˌpasɪfɪˈkeɪt(ə)ri
AM pəˈsɪfɪkəˌtɔri

Pacific Ocean
BR pəˌsɪfɪk ˈəʊʃn
AM pəˌsɪfɪk ˈoʊʃən

pacifier
BR ˈpasɪfʌɪə(r), -z
AM ˈpæsəˌfaɪ(ə)r, -z

pacifism
BR ˈpasɪfɪz(ə)m
AM ˈpæsəˌfɪzəm

pacifist
BR ˈpasɪfɪst, -s
AM ˈpæsəfəst, -s

pacify
BR ˈpasɪfʌɪ, -z, -ɪŋ, -d
AM ˈpæsəˌfaɪ, -z, -ɪŋ, -d

Pacino
BR pəˈtʃiːnəʊ

AM pəˈtʃinoʊ

pack
BR pak, -s, -ɪŋ, -t
AM pæk, -s, -ɪŋ, -t

packable
BR ˈpakəbl
AM ˈpækəbəl

package
BR ˈpakɪdʒ, -ɪdʒɪz, -ɪdʒɪŋ, -ɪdʒd
AM ˈpækɪdʒ, -ɪz, -ɪŋ, -d

packager
BR ˈpakɪdʒə(r), -z
AM ˈpækɪdʒər, -z

Packard
BR ˈpakɑːd
AM ˈpækərd

packer
BR ˈpakə(r), -z
AM ˈpækər, -z

packet
BR ˈpakɪt, -ɪts, -ɪtɪŋ, -ɪtɪd
AM ˈpækəlt, -ts, -dɪŋ, -dəd

packhorse
BR ˈpakhɔːs, -ɪz
AM ˈpæk(h)ɔ(ə)rs, -əz

packice
BR ˈpakʌɪs
AM ˈpækˌaɪs

packing
BR ˈpakɪŋ, -z
AM ˈpækɪŋ, -z

packingcase
BR ˈpakɪŋkeɪs, -ɪz
AM ˈpækɪŋˌkeɪs, -ɪz

packman
BR ˈpakman, ˈpakmən
AM ˈpækˌmæn, ˈpækmən

packmen
BR ˈpakmɛn, ˈpakmən
AM ˈpækˌmɛn, ˈpækmən

packsaddle
BR ˈpakˌsadl, -z
AM ˈpækˌsædəl, -z

packthread
BR ˈpakθrɛd
AM ˈpækˌθrɛd

Pac-man®
BR ˈpakman
AM ˈpækˌmæn

pact
BR pakt, -s
AM pæk(t), -(t)s

pacy
BR ˈpeɪsi, -ɪə(r), -ɪɪst
AM ˈpeɪsi, -ər, -əst

pad
BR pad, -z, -ɪŋ, -ɪd
AM pæd, -z, -ɪŋ, -əd

Padbury
BR ˈpadb(ə)ri
AM ˈpædˌbɛri

AM pəˈtʃinoʊ

Paddington
BR ˈpadɪŋt(ə)n
AM ˈpædɪŋtən

paddle
BR ˈpadl, -lz, -lɪŋ\-əlɪŋ, -ld
AM ˈpædləl, -əlz, -(ə)lɪŋ, -əld

paddleball
BR ˈpadlbɔːl
AM ˈpædlˌbɔl, ˈpædlˌbɑl

paddler
BR ˈpadlə(r), -z
AM ˈpæd(ə)lər, -z

paddock
BR ˈpadək, -s
AM ˈpædək, -s

paddy
BR ˈpadi, -ɪz
AM ˈpædi, -z

paddywack
BR ˈpadɪwak, -s
AM ˈpædi,(h)wæk, -s

paddywhack
BR ˈpadɪwak, -s
AM ˈpædi,(h)wæk, -s

pademelon
BR ˈpadɪˌmɛlən, -z
AM ˈpædiˌmɛlən, -z

Paderewski
BR ˌpadəˈrɛfski, ˌpadəˈrɛvski
AM ˌpædəˈrɛfski

Padfield
BR ˈpadfiːld
AM ˈpædˌfild

Padiham
BR ˈpadɪəm
AM ˈpædiəm

Padilla
BR pəˈdɪlə(r)
AM pəˈdɪlə

padlock
BR ˈpadlɒk, -s, -ɪŋ, -t
AM ˈpædˌlɑk, -s, -ɪŋ, -t

padloper
BR ˈpatˌləʊpə(r), -z
AM ˈpædˌloʊpər, -z

Padma
BR ˈpadmə(r)
AM ˈpædmə

Padmore
BR ˈpadmɔː(r)
AM ˈpædˌmɔ(ə)r

padouk
BR pəˈdaʊk, -s
AM pəˈdaʊk, -s

padre
BR ˈpɑːdreɪ, -z
AM ˈpɑˌdreɪ, -z

padrone
BR pəˈdrəʊnli, -ɪz
AM pəˈdroʊn(eɪ), -z

padsaw
BR ˈpadsɔː(r), -z
AM ˈpædˌsɔ, ˈpædˌsɑ, -z

Padstow
BR 'padstəʊ
AM 'pæd,stoʊ
Padua
BR 'padjʊə(r),
'padʒʊə(r)
AM 'pædʒʊə
Paduan
BR 'padjʊən,
'padʒʊən, -z
AM 'pædʒʊən, -z
Paducah
BR pə'd(j)uːkə(r)
AM pə'd(j)ukə
paean
BR 'piːən, -z
AM 'piən, -z
paederast
BR 'pɛdərast, -s
AM 'pɛdə,ræst, -s
paederastic
BR ,pɛdə'rastɪk
AM ,pɛdə'ræstɪk
paederasty
BR 'pɛdərasti
AM 'pɛdə,ræsti
paediatric
BR ,piːdɪ'atrɪk, -s
AM ,pidi'ætrɪk, -s
paediatrician
BR ,piːdɪə'trɪʃn, -z
AM ,pidiə'trɪʃən, -z
paediatrist
BR ,piː'dʌɪətrɪst,
,piːdɪ'atrɪst, -s
AM ,pidi'ætrəst, -s
paedophile
BR 'piːdəfʌɪl
AM 'pɛdə,faɪl
paedophilia
BR ,piːdə'fɪlɪə(r)
AM ,pɛdə'fɪljə,
,pidə'fɪljə, ,pɛdə'fɪliə,
,pidə'fɪliə
paedophiliac
BR ,piːdə'fɪlɪak
AM ,pidə'fɪli,æk, -s
paella
BR pʌɪ'ɛlə(r)
AM pə'ɛlə, paɪ'ɛlə
paeon
BR 'piːən, -z
AM 'piən, -z
paeonic
BR ,piː'ɒnɪk
AM pi'ɑnɪk
paeony
BR 'piːən|i, -ɪz
AM 'piəni, -z
Pagalu
BR 'pagəlu:
AM 'pægəlu
pagan
BR 'peɪg(ə)n, -z
AM 'peɪgən, -z
Paganini
BR ,pagə'niːni

AM ,pægə'nini
paganise
BR 'peɪgənʌɪz,
'peɪgnʌɪz, -ɪz, -ɪŋ, -d
AM 'peɪgə,naɪz, -ɪz, -ɪŋ,
-d
paganish
BR 'peɪgənɪʃ, 'peɪgnɪʃ
AM 'peɪgənɪʃ
paganism
BR 'peɪgənɪz(ə)m,
'peɪgnɪz(ə)m
AM 'peɪgə,nɪzəm
paganize
BR 'peɪgənʌɪz,
'peɪgnʌɪz, -ɪz, -ɪŋ, -d
AM 'peɪgə,naɪz, -ɪz, -ɪŋ,
-d
page
BR peɪdʒ, -ɪz, -ɪŋ, -d
AM peɪdʒ, -ɪz, -ɪŋ, -d
pageant
BR 'padʒ(ə)nt, -s
AM 'pædʒənt, -s
pageantry
BR 'padʒ(ə)ntri
AM 'pædʒəntri
pageboy
BR 'peɪdʒbɔɪ, -z
AM 'peɪdʒ,bɔɪ, -z
pager
BR 'peɪdʒə(r), -z
AM 'peɪdʒər, -z
Paget
BR 'padʒɪt
AM 'pædʒət
paginal
BR 'padʒɪnl
AM 'pædʒənəl
paginary
BR 'padʒɪn(ə)ri
AM 'pædʒə,nɛri
paginate
BR 'padʒɪneɪt, -s, -ɪŋ,
-ɪd
AM 'pædʒə,neɪ|t, -ts,
-dɪŋ, -dɪd
pagination
BR ,padʒɪ'neɪʃn
AM ,pædʒə'neɪʃən
Pagliacci
BR ,palɪ'aːtʃi
AM ,pæ(g)li'atʃi
IT paʎ'ʎattʃi
Pagnell
BR 'pagnl
AM 'pægnəl
pagoda
BR pə'gəʊdə(r), -z
AM pə'goʊdə, -z
pah
BR pɑː(r)
AM pɑ
Pahang
BR pə'haŋ, pə'hʌŋ
AM pə'hæŋ

Pahlavi
BR 'pɑːləvi
AM 'pɑləvi
pahoehoe
BR pə'həʊɪ,həʊi
AM pə'hoʊ,i'hoʊ,i
paid
BR peɪd
AM peɪd
Paige
BR peɪdʒ
AM peɪdʒ
Paignton
BR 'peɪntən
AM 'peɪn(t)ən
pail
BR peɪl, -z
AM peɪl, -z
pailful
BR 'peɪlfʊl, -z
AM 'peɪl,fʊl, -z
paillasse
BR 'palɪas, ,palɪ'as, -ɪz
AM paɪ'(j)ɑs, 'pæli,æs,
pæl'jæs, -ɪəz
paillette
BR pal'jɛt, ,palɪ'ɛt, -s
AM paɪ'(j)ɛt, pɑ'(j)ɛt,
pə'lɛt, -s
pain
BR peɪn, -z, -ɪŋ, -d
AM peɪn, -z, -ɪŋ, -d
Paine
BR peɪn
AM peɪn
painful
BR 'peɪnf(ʊ)l
AM 'peɪnfəl
painfully
BR 'peɪnfəli, 'peɪnfḷi
AM 'peɪnfəli
painfulness
BR 'peɪnf(ʊ)lnəs
AM 'peɪnfəlnəs
painkiller
BR 'peɪn,kɪlə(r), -z
AM 'peɪn,kɪlər, -z
painkilling
BR 'peɪn,kɪlɪŋ
AM 'peɪn,kɪlɪŋ
painless
BR 'peɪnlɪs
AM 'peɪnlɪs
painlessly
BR 'peɪnlɪsli
AM 'peɪnlɪsli
painlessness
BR 'peɪnlɪsnɪs
AM 'peɪnlɪnɪs
painstaking
BR 'peɪnz,teɪkɪŋ
AM 'peɪn|,steɪkɪŋ
painstakingly
BR 'peɪnz,teɪkɪŋli
AM 'peɪn|,steɪkɪŋli
painstakingness
BR 'peɪnz,teɪkɪŋnɪs

Paiute
AM 'peɪn|,stækɪŋnɪs
paint
BR peɪnt, -s, -ɪŋ, -ɪd
AM peɪn|t, -ts, -s, -(t)ɪŋ,
-(t)əd
paintable
BR 'peɪntəbl
AM 'peɪn(t)əbəl
paintball
BR 'peɪntbɔːl
AM 'peɪnt,bɔl,
'peɪnt,bɑl
paintbox
BR 'peɪntbɒks, -ɪz
AM 'peɪnt,bɑks, -əz
paintbrush
BR 'peɪntbrʌʃ, -ɪz
AM 'peɪnt,brəʃ, -əz
painter
BR 'peɪntə(r), -z
AM 'peɪn(t)ər, -z
painterliness
BR 'peɪntəlɪnɪs
AM 'peɪn(t)ərlinɪs
painterly
BR 'peɪntəli
AM 'peɪn(t)ərli
painting
BR 'peɪntɪŋ, -z
AM 'peɪn(t)ɪŋ, -z
paintstick
BR 'peɪntstɪk, -s
AM 'peɪnt,stɪk, -s
paintwork
BR 'peɪntwəːk
AM 'peɪnt,wərk
painty
BR 'peɪnti
AM 'peɪn(t)i
pair
BR pɛː(r), -z, -ɪŋ, -d
AM pɛ(ə)r, -z, -ɪŋ, -d
pairing
BR 'pɛːrɪŋ, -z
AM 'pɛrɪŋ, -z
pairwork
BR 'pɛːwəːk
AM 'pɛr,wərk
paisa
BR 'pʌɪsɑː(r), 'pʌɪsə(r)
AM 'paɪsə
paise
BR 'pʌɪsə(r)
AM 'paɪsə
Paish
BR peɪʃ
AM peɪʃ
paisley
BR 'peɪzli
AM 'peɪzli
Paisleyite
BR 'peɪzlɪʌɪt, -s
AM 'peɪzli,aɪt, -s
Paiute
BR 'pʌɪuːt, ,pʌɪ'(j)uːt,
-s

pajama
AM 'paɪ,(j)ut,
,paɪ'(j)ut, -s

pajama
BR pə'dʒɑːmə(r), -z
AM pə'dʒɑmə,
pə'dʒæmə, -z

pakapoo
BR ,pakə'puː, 'pakəpuː
AM ,pækə'pu

pakapu
BR ,pakə'puː, 'pakəpuː
AM ,pækə'pu

pakeha
BR 'pɑːkɪhɑː(r), -z
AM 'pɑkə,hɑ, 'paki,ɑ, -z

Pakenham¹
surname
BR 'pak(ə)nəm,
'paknəm
AM 'pæknəm

Pakenham²
UK placename
BR 'peɪkənəm,
'peɪknəm
AM 'peɪknəm

Paki
BR 'pak|i, -ɪz
AM 'pæki, -z

Pakistan
BR ,pɑːkɪ'stɑːn,
,pakɪ'stan
AM 'pækə,stæn

Pakistani
BR ,pɑːkɪ'stɑːn|i,
,pakɪ'stan|i, -ɪz
AM ,pækə'stɑni, -z

pakora
BR pə'kɔːrə(r)
AM pə'kɔrə

pal
BR pal, -z, -ɪŋ, -d
AM pæl, -z, -ɪŋ, -d

palace
BR 'palɪs, -ɪz
AM 'pæləs, -əz

paladin
BR 'palədɪn, -z
AM 'pælədn, 'pælədən, -z

Palaearctic
BR ,palɪ'ɑːktɪk,
,peɪlɪ'ɑːktɪk
AM ,peɪli'ɑr(k)tɪk,
,pæli'ɑr(k)tɪk

palaeoanthropological
BR ,palɪəʊ,anθrəpə-'lɒdʒɪkl,
,peɪlɪəʊ,anθrəpə'lɒdʒ-ɪkl
AM ,peɪliʊʊ,ænθrəpə-'ladʒəkəl

palaeoanthropologist
BR ,palɪəʊ,anθrə'pɒlə-dʒɪst,
,peɪlɪəʊ,anθrə'pɒlə-dʒɪst, -s

palaeoanthropology
BR ,palɪəʊ,anθrə'pɒl-ədʒi,
,peɪlɪəʊ,anθrə'pɒlədʒi
AM ,peɪliʊʊ,ænθrə'pal-ədʒi

palaeobotany
BR ,palɪəʊ'bɒtəni,
,palɪəʊ'bɒtn̩i,
,peɪlɪəʊ'bɒtəni,
,peɪlɪəʊ'bɒtn̩i
AM ,peɪliʊʊ'batn̩i

Palaeocene
BR 'palɪə(ʊ)siːn,
'peɪlɪə(ʊ)siːn
AM 'peɪliə,sin

palaeoclimatology
BR ,palɪəʊ,klʌɪmə'tɒl-ədʒi,
,peɪlɪəʊ,klʌɪmə'tɒlədʒi
AM ,peɪliʊʊ,klaɪmə'tal-ədʒi

palaeoecological
BR ,palɪəʊ,iːkə'lɒdʒɪkl,
,palɪəʊ,ɛkə'lɒdʒɪkl,
,peɪlɪəʊ,iːkə'lɒdʒɪkl,
,peɪlɪəʊ,ɛkə'lɒdʒɪkl
AM ,peɪliʊʊ,ɛkə'ladʒə-kəl,
,peɪliʊʊ,ikə'ladʒəkəl

palaeoecologist
BR ,palɪəʊɪ'kɒlədʒɪst,
,peɪlɪəʊɪ'kɒlədʒɪst, -s
AM ,peɪliʊʊ,ɛ'kalədʒəst,
,peɪliʊʊ,i'kalədʒəst, -s

palaeoecology
BR ,palɪəʊɪ'kɒlədʒi,
,palɪəʊɛ'kɒlədʒi,
,peɪlɪəʊɪ'kɒlədʒi,
,peɪlɪəʊɛ'kɒlədʒi
AM ,peɪliʊʊ,ɛ'kalədʒi,
,peɪliʊʊ,i'kalədʒi

palaeogeography
BR ,palɪəʊdʒɪ'ɒgrəfi,
,palɪəʊ'dʒɒgrəfi,
,peɪlɪəʊdʒɪ'ɒgrəfi,
,peɪlɪəʊ'dʒɒgrəfi
AM ,peɪliʊʊdʒi'agrəfi

palaeographer
BR ,palɪ'ɒgrəfə(r),
,peɪlɪ'ɒgrəfə(r), -z
AM ,peɪli'agrəfər, -z

palaeographic
BR ,palɪə'grafɪk,
,peɪlɪə'grafɪk
AM ,peɪliə'græfɪk

palaeographical
BR ,palɪə'grafɪkl,
,peɪlɪə'grafɪkl
AM ,peɪliə'græfəkəl

palaeographically
BR ,palɪə'grafɪkli,
,peɪlɪə'grafɪkli

palaeography
BR ,palɪ'ɒgrəfi,
,peɪlɪ'ɒgrəfi
AM ,peɪli'agrəfi

Palaeolithic
BR ,palɪə'lɪθɪk,
,peɪlɪə'lɪθɪk
AM ,peɪliə'lɪθɪk

palaeomagnetism
BR ,palɪəʊ'magnɪt-ɪz(ə)m,
,peɪlɪəʊ'magnɪtɪz(ə)m
AM ,peɪliʊʊ'mægnə-,tɪzəm

palaeontological
BR ,palɪ,ɒntə'lɒdʒɪkl,
,peɪlɪ,ɒntə'lɒdʒɪkl
AM ,peɪli,antə'ladʒəkəl

palaeontologist
BR ,palɪən'tɒlədʒɪst,
,peɪlɪən'tɒlədʒɪst, -s
AM ,peɪli,ən'talədʒəst, -s

palaeontology
BR ,palɪən'tɒlədʒi,
,peɪlɪən'tɒlədʒi
AM ,peɪli,ən'talədʒi

Palaeozoic
BR ,palɪə'zəʊɪk,
,peɪlɪə'zəʊɪk
AM ,peɪliə'zoʊɪk

palaestra
BR pə'liːstrə(r),
pə'lʌɪstrə(r), -z
AM pə'lɛstrə, -z

palais
BR 'pal|eɪ, 'pal|i,
-eɪz\-ɪz
AM pæ'leɪ, -z

palankeen
BR ,palən'kiːn, -z
AM ,pælən'k(w)in,
,pæ'læŋk(w)ən, -z

palanquin
BR ,palən'kiːn,
'paləŋkwɪn, -z
AM ,pælən'k(w)in,
,pæ'læŋk(w)ən, -z

palapa
BR pə'lapə(r), -z
AM pə'lɑpə, -z

palatability
BR ,palɪtə'bɪlɪti
AM ,pælədə'bɪlɪdi

palatable
BR 'palɪtəbl
AM 'pælədəbəl

palatableness
BR 'palɪtəblnəs
AM 'pælədəbəlnəs

palatably
BR 'palɪtəbli
AM 'pælədəbli

palatal
BR 'palətl, pə'leɪtl, -z
AM 'pælədl, -z

palatalisation
BR ,palətəlʌɪ'zeɪʃn,
,palətɭʌɪ'zeɪʃn
AM ,pælədlə'zeɪʃən,
,pælədl,aɪ'zeɪʃən

palatalise
BR 'palətəlʌɪz,
'palətɭʌɪz, -ɪz, -ɪŋ, -d
AM 'pælədl,aɪz, -ɪz, -ɪŋ, -d

palatalization
BR ,palətəlʌɪ'zeɪʃn,
,palətɭʌɪ'zeɪʃn
AM ,pælədlə'zeɪʃən,
,pælədl,aɪ'zeɪʃən

palatalize
BR 'palətəlʌɪz,
'palətɭʌɪz, -ɪz, -ɪŋ, -d
AM 'pælədl,aɪz, -ɪz, -ɪŋ, -d

palatally
BR 'palətɭi, 'palətəli,
pə'leɪtɭi, pə'leɪtəli
AM 'pælədɭi

palate
BR 'palət, -s
AM 'pælət, -s

palatial
BR pə'leɪʃl
AM pə'leɪʃəl

palatially
BR pə'leɪʃɭi, pə'leɪʃəli
AM pə'leɪʃəli

Palatinate
BR pə'latɪnət,
pə'latn̩ət, -s
AM pə'lætn̩ət,
pə'lætn̩,eɪt, -s

Palatine
BR 'palətʌɪn
AM 'pælə,taɪn

Palau
BR pə'laʊ, pa'laʊ
AM pə'laʊ, pæ'laʊ

palaver
BR pə'lɑːv|ə(r), -əz,
-(ə)rɪŋ, -əd
AM pə'lævər, pə'lɑvər,
-z, -ɪŋ, -d

Palawan
BR pa'laʊən, -z
AM pə'laʊən, pɑ'laʊən,
-z

pale
BR peɪl, -z, -ɪŋ, -d
AM peɪl, -z, -ɪŋ, -d

palea
BR 'peɪlɪə(r), -z
AM 'peɪliə, -z

paleae
BR 'peɪliː
AM 'peɪli,i, 'peɪli,aɪ

Palearctic
BR ,palɪ'ɑːktɪk,
,peɪlɪ'ɑːktɪk
AM ,peɪli'ɑr(k)tɪk,
,pæli'ɑr(k)tɪk

paleface
BR ˈpeɪlfeɪs, -ɪz
AM ˈpeɪlˌfeɪs, -ɪz

pale-faced
BR ˌpeɪlˈfeɪst
AM ˈpeɪlˌfeɪst

Palekh
BR ˈpɑːlɛk
AM ˈpɑlɛk

palely
BR ˈpeɪl(l)li
AM ˈpeɪl(l)li

Palembang
BR pɑːˈlɛmbaŋ, pəˈlɛmbaŋ
AM pɑˈlɛmˌbæŋ

paleness
BR ˈpeɪlnɪs
AM ˈpeɪlnɪs

Palenque
BR pəˈlɛŋki
AM pəˈlɛŋki, pæˈlɛŋki

paleoanthropological
BR ˌpalɪəʊˌanθrəpəˈlɒdʒɪkl, ˌpeɪlɪəʊˌanθrəpəˈlɒdʒɪkl
AM ˌpeɪliouˌænθrəpəˈladʒəkəl

paleoanthropologist
BR ˌpalɪəʊˌanθrəˈpɒlədʒɪst, ˌpeɪlɪəʊˌanθrəˈpɒlədʒɪst, -s
AM ˌpeɪliouˌænθrəˈpalədʒəst, -s

paleoanthropology
BR ˌpalɪəʊˌanθrəˈpɒlədʒi, ˌpeɪlɪəʊˌanθrəˈpɒlədʒi
AM ˌpeɪliouˌænθrəˈpalədʒi

paleobotany
BR ˌpalɪəʊˈbɒtəni, ˌpalɪəʊˈbɒtṇi, ˌpeɪlɪəʊˈbɒtəni, ˌpeɪlɪəʊˈbɒtṇi
AM ˌpeɪliouˈbatni

Paleocene
BR ˈpalɪə(ʊ)siːn, ˈpeɪlɪə(ʊ)siːn
AM ˈpeɪliəˌsin

paleoclimatology
BR ˌpalɪəʊˌklʌɪməˈtɒlədʒi, ˌpeɪlɪəʊˌklaɪməˈtɒlədʒi
AM ˌpeɪliouˌklaɪməˈtalədʒi

paleoecological
BR ˌpalɪəʊˌiːkəˈlɒdʒɪkl, ˌpalɪəʊˌɛkəˈlɒdʒɪkl, ˌpeɪlɪəʊˌiːkəˈlɒdʒɪkl, ˌpeɪlɪəʊˌɛkəˈlɒdʒɪkl
AM ˌpeɪliouˌɛkəˈladʒəkəl, ˈpeɪliouˌikəˈladʒəkəl

paleoecologist
BR ˌpalɪəʊˈkɒlədʒɪst, ˌpalɪəʊɛˈkɒlədʒɪst, ˌpeɪlɪəʊˈkɒlədʒɪst, ˌpeɪlɪəʊɛˈkɒlədʒɪst, -s
AM ˌpeɪliouˌɛˈkalədʒəst, ˌpeɪliouˌiˈkalədʒəst, -s

paleoecology
BR ˌpalɪəʊˈkɒlədʒi, ˌpalɪəʊɛˈkɒlədʒi, ˌpeɪlɪəʊˈkɒlədʒi, ˌpeɪlɪəʊɛˈkɒlədʒi
AM ˌpeɪliouˌɛˈkalədʒi, ˌpeɪliouˌiˈkalədʒi

paleogeography
BR ˌpalɪəʊdʒɪˈɒgrəfi, ˌpalɪəʊˈdʒʊɡrəfi, ˌpeɪlɪəʊdʒɪˈɒgrəfi, ˌpeɪlɪəʊˈdʒʊɡrəfi
AM ˌpeɪliouˌdʒiˈagrəfi

paleographer
BR ˌpalɪˈɒgrəfə(r), ˌpeɪlɪˈɒgrəfə(r), -z
AM ˌpeɪliˈagrəfər, -z

paleographic
BR ˌpalɪəˈgrafɪk, ˌpeɪlɪəˈgrafɪk
AM ˌpeɪliəˈgræfɪk

paleographical
BR ˌpalɪəˈgrafɪkl, ˌpeɪlɪəˈgrafɪkl
AM ˌpeɪliəˈgræfəkəl

paleographically
BR ˌpalɪəˈgrafɪkli, ˌpeɪlɪəˈgrafɪkli
AM ˌpeɪliəˈgræfək(ə)li

paleography
BR ˌpalɪˈɒgrəfi, ˌpeɪlɪˈɒgrəfi
AM ˌpeɪliˈagrəfi

Paleolithic
BR ˌpalɪəˈlɪθɪk, ˌpeɪlɪəˈlɪθɪk
AM ˌpeɪliəˈlɪθɪk

paleomagnetism
BR ˌpalɪəʊˈmagnɪtˌɪz(ə)m, ˌpeɪlɪəʊˈmagnɪtɪz(ə)m
AM ˌpeɪliouˈmægnəˌtɪzəm

paleontological
BR ˌpalɪˌɒntəˈlɒdʒɪkl, ˌpeɪlɪˌɒntəˈlɒdʒɪkl
AM ˌpeɪliˌantəˈladʒəkəl

paleontologist
BR ˌpalɪənˈtɒlədʒɪst, ˌpeɪlɪənˈtɒlədʒɪst, -s
AM ˌpeɪliˌənˈtalədʒəst, -s

paleontology
BR ˌpalɪənˈtɒlədʒi, ˌpeɪlɪənˈtɒlədʒi
AM ˌpeɪliˌənˈtalədʒi

Paleozoic
BR ˌpalɪəˈzəʊɪk, ˌpeɪlɪəˈzəʊɪk
AM ˌpeɪliəˈzouɪk

Palermo
BR pəˈlɛːməʊ, pəˈləːməʊ
AM pəˈlərˌmoʊ, pəˈlɛrˌmoʊ

Palestine
BR ˈpalɪstʌɪn
AM ˈpæləˌstaɪn

Palestinian
BR ˌpalɪˈstɪnɪən, -z
AM ˌpæləˈstɪnɪən, -z

palestra
BR pəˈlɛstrə(r), -z
AM pəˈlɛstrə, -z

Palestrina
BR ˌpalɪˈstriːnə(r)
AM ˌpæləˈstrinə

Palethorp
BR ˈpeɪlθɔːp
AM ˈpeɪlˌθɔ(ə)rp

Palethorpe
BR ˈpeɪlθɔːp
AM ˈpeɪlˌθɔ(ə)rp

paletot
BR ˈpalɪtəʊ, -z
AM ˈpæl(ə)ˌtoʊ, -z

palette
BR ˈpalɪt, -s
AM ˈpælət, -s

palfrey
BR ˈpɔːlfr|i, ˈpɒlfr|i, -ɪz
AM ˈpɒlfri, ˈpalfri, -z

Palfreyman
BR ˈpɔːlfrɪmən, ˈpɒlfrɪmən
AM ˈpɒlfrɪmən, ˈpalfrɪmən

Palgrave
BR ˈpɔːlgreɪv, ˈpalgreɪv
AM ˈpɒlˌgreɪv, ˈpalˌgreɪv

Pali
BR ˈpɑːli
AM ˈpɑˌli

palilalia
BR ˌpalɪˈleɪlɪə(r)
AM ˌpaləˈleɪliə

palimony
BR ˈpalɪmən|i
AM ˈpæləˌmoʊni

palimpsest
BR ˈpalɪm(p)sɛst, -s
AM ˈpæləm(p)ˌsɛst, -s

Palin
BR ˈpeɪlɪn
AM ˈpeɪlən

palindrome
BR ˈpalɪndrəʊm, -z
AM ˈpælənˌdroʊm, -z

palindromic
BR ˌpalɪnˈdrɒmɪk
AM ˌpælənˈdramɪk

palindromist
BR pəˈlɪndrəmɪst, -s
AM pəˈlɪndrəməst, -s

paling
BR ˈpeɪlɪŋ, -z
AM ˈpeɪlɪŋ, -z

palingenesis
BR ˌpalɪnˈdʒɛnɪsɪs
AM ˌpælənˈdʒɛnəsəs

palingenetic
BR ˌpalɪndʒɪˈnɛtɪk
AM ˌpæləndʒəˈnɛdɪk

palinode
BR ˈpalɪnəʊd, -z
AM ˈpæləˌnoʊd, -z

palisade
BR ˌpalɪˈseɪd, -z, -ɪŋ, -ɪd
AM ˌpæləˈseɪd, -z, -ɪŋ, -əd

Palisades
BR ˌpalɪseɪdz
AM ˌpæləˈseɪdz

palish
BR ˈpeɪlɪʃ
AM ˈpeɪlɪʃ

Palissy
BR ˈpalɪsi
AM ˈpæləsi

pall
BR pɔːl, -z
AM pɒl, pal, -z

Palladian
BR pəˈleɪdɪən
AM pəˈleɪdɪən

Palladianism
BR pəˈleɪdɪənɪz(ə)m
AM pəˈleɪdɪəˌnɪzəm

Palladio
BR pəˈladɪəʊ, pəˈlɑːdɪəʊ
AM pəˈladiou

palladium
BR pəˈleɪdɪəm, -z
AM pəˈleɪdɪəm, -z

Pallas
BR ˈpaləs, ˈpalas
AM ˈpæləs

pallbearer
BR ˈpɔːlˌbɛːrə(r), -z
AM ˈpɒlˌbɛrər, ˈpalˌbɛrər, -z

pallet
BR ˈpalɪt, -s
AM ˈpælət, -s

palletisation
BR ˌpalɪtʌɪˈzeɪʃn
AM ˌpælədəˈzeɪʃən, ˌpæləˌtaɪˈzeɪʃən

palletise
BR ˈpalɪtʌɪz, -ɪz, -ɪŋ, -d
AM ˈpæləˌtaɪz, -ɪz, -ɪŋ, -d

palletization
BR ˌpalɪtʌɪˈzeɪʃn
AM ˌpælədəˈzeɪʃən, ˌpæləˌtaɪˈzeɪʃən

palletize
BR ˈpalɪtʌɪz, -ɪz, -ɪŋ, -d
AM ˈpæləˌtaɪz, -ɪz, -ɪŋ, -d

pallia
BR ˈpalɪə(r)
AM ˈpæljə, ˈpælɪə
pallial
BR ˈpalɪəl
AM ˈpæljəl, ˈpælɪəl
palliasse
BR ˈpalɪas, -ɪz
AM ˌpæliˈæs, pælˈjæs, -əz
palliate
BR ˈpalɪeɪt, -s, -ɪŋ, -ɪd
AM ˈpæliˌeɪt, -ts, -dɪŋ, -dɪd
palliation
BR ˌpalɪˈeɪʃn
AM ˌpæliˈeɪʃən
palliative
BR ˈpalɪətɪv, -z
AM ˈpæliˌeɪdɪv, ˈpæljədɪv, -z
palliatively
BR ˈpalɪətɪvli
AM ˈpæljədɪvli, ˈpæliˌeɪdɪvli
palliator
BR ˈpalɪeɪtə(r), -z
AM ˈpæliˌeɪdər, -z
pallid
BR ˈpalɪd
AM ˈpæləd
pallidity
BR pəˈlɪdɪti
AM pəˈlɪdɪdi, pæˈlɪdɪdi
pallidly
BR ˈpalɪdli
AM ˈpælədli
pallidness
BR ˈpalɪdnɪs
AM ˈpælədnəs
pallium
BR ˈpalɪəm, -z
AM ˈpæliəm, -z
Pall Mall
BR ˌpal ˈmal
AM ˌpal ˈmal
pall-mall
BR ˌpalˈmal
AM ˌpɛlˈmɛl, ˌpɔlˈmɔl, ˈpalˈmal
pallor
BR ˈpalə(r)
AM ˈpælər
pally
BR ˈpalⁱi, -ɪə(r), -ɪɪst
AM ˈpæli, -ər, -əst
palm
BR pɑːm, -z, -ɪŋ, -d
AM pɑ(l)m, -z, -ɪŋ, -d
Palma
BR ˈpalmə(r), ˈpɑːmə(r)
AM ˈpɑlmə
palmaceous
BR palˈmeɪʃəs, pɑːˈmeɪʃəs
AM pælˈmeɪʃəs, pɑˈmeɪʃəs

palmar
BR ˈpalmə(r), ˈpɑlmɑː(r), -z
AM ˈpælmɑr, ˈpɑ(l)mər, -z
palmate
BR ˈpalmeɪt, ˈpɑːmeɪt
AM ˈpælˌmeɪt, ˈpɑ(l)ˌmeɪt
palmer
BR ˈpɑːmə(r), -z
AM ˈpɑ(l)mər, -z
Palmerston
BR ˈpɑːməst(ə)n
AM ˈpɑ(l)mərstən
Palmerston North
BR ˌpɑːməst(ə)n ˈnɔːθ
AM ˈpɑ(l)mərstən ˈnɔː(ə)rθ
palmette
BR palˈmɛt, pɑːˈmɛt, -s
AM ˌpælˈmɛt, ˌpɑ(l)ˈmɛt, -s
palmetto
BR palˈmɛtəʊ, pɑːˈmɛtəʊ, -z
AM ˌpɑ(l)ˈmɛdoʊ, -z
palmful
BR ˈpɑːmfʊl, -z
AM ˈpɑ(l)mˌfʊl, -z
palmiped
BR ˈpalmɪpɛd, -z
AM ˈpælməˌpɛd, ˈpɑlməˌpɛd, ˈpɑlməˌpɛd, -z
palmipede
BR ˈpalmɪpiːd, -z
AM ˈpælməˌpid, ˈpɑlməˌpid, ˈpɑlməˌpid, -z
palmist
BR ˈpɑːmɪst, -s
AM ˈpɑ(l)məst, -s
palmistry
BR ˈpɑːmɪstri
AM ˈpɑ(l)məstri
palmitate
BR ˈpalmɪteɪt, ˈpɑːmɪteɪt, -s, -ɪŋ, -ɪd
AM ˈpɑ(l)məˌteɪt, -ts, -dɪŋ, -dɪd
palmitic
BR palˈmɪtɪk, pɑːˈmɪtɪk
AM ˌpɑ(l)ˈmɪdɪk
palm-oil
BR ˈpɑːmɔɪl
AM ˈpɑ(l)mˌɔɪl
Palmolive®
BR ˌpɑːmˈɒlɪv
AM pɑ(l)ˈmɑlɪv, pɑ(l)ˈmɑlɪv
Palm Springs
BR ˌpɑːm ˈsprɪŋz
AM ˌpɑ(l)m ˈsprɪŋz
palmtop
BR ˈpɑːmtɒp, -s

AM ˈpɑ(l)mˌtɑp, -s
palmy
BR ˈpɑːmⁱi, -ɪə(r), -ɪɪst
AM ˈpɑ(l)mi, -ər, -əst
palmyra
BR palˈmʌɪrə(r), -z
AM ˈpælˈmaɪrə, -z
Palo Alto
BR ˌpaləʊ ˈaltəʊ
AM ˌpæˌloʊ ˈælˌtoʊ
palolo
BR pəˈləʊləʊ, -z
AM pəˈloʊˌloʊ, -z
Palomar
BR ˈpaləmɑː(r)
AM ˈpæləˌmar
palomino
BR ˌpaləˈmiːnəʊ, -z
AM ˌpæləˈminoʊ, -z
palooka
BR pəˈluːkə(r), -z
AM pəˈlukə, -z
Palouse
BR pəˈluːs
AM pəˈlus
paloverde
BR ˌpalə(ʊ)ˈvɜːd|i, -ɪz
AM ˌpæloʊˈvɜrdi, -z
palp
BR palp, -s
AM pælp, -s
palpability
BR ˌpalpəˈbɪlɪti
AM ˌpælpəˈbɪlɪdi
palpable
BR ˈpalpəbl
AM ˈpælpəbəl
palpably
BR ˈpalpəbli
AM ˈpælpəbli
palpal
BR ˈpalpl
AM ˈpælpəl
palpate
BR ˈpalpeɪt, palˈpeɪt, -s, -ɪŋ, -ɪd
AM ˈpælˌpeɪt, -ts, -dɪŋ, -dɪd
palpation
BR palˈpeɪʃn
AM pælˈpeɪʃən
palpebral
BR ˈpalpəbr(ə)l
AM ˈpælpəbrəl, pælˈpibrəl
palpitant
BR ˈpalpɪt(ə)nt
AM ˈpælpədənt, ˈpælpətnt
palpitate
BR ˈpalpɪteɪt, -s, -ɪŋ, -ɪd
AM ˈpælpəˌteɪt, -ts, -dɪŋ, -dɪd
palpitation
BR ˌpalpɪˈteɪʃn
AM ˌpælpəˈteɪʃən

palpus
BR ˈpalpəs
AM ˈpælpəs
palsgrave
BR ˈpɔːlzgreɪv, ˈpɒlzgreɪv, -z
AM ˈpɒlzˌgreɪv, ˈpɑlzˌgreɪv, -z
palsied
BR ˈpɔːlzɪd, ˈpɒlzɪd
AM ˈpɒlzid, ˈpɑlzid
palstave
BR ˈpɔːlsteɪv, ˈpɒlsteɪv, -z
AM ˈpɒlˌsteɪv, ˈpɑlˌsteɪv, -z
palsy
BR ˈpɔːlz|i, ˈpɒlz|i, -ɪz
AM ˈpɒlzi, ˈpɑlzi, -z
palsy-walsy
BR ˌpalzɪˈwalzi
AM ˈpælziˈwælzi
palter
BR ˈpɔːlt|ə(r), ˈpɒlt|ə(r), -əz, -(ə)rɪŋ, -əd
AM ˈpɒltər, ˈpɑltər, -z, -ɪŋ, -d
palterer
BR ˈpɔːlt(ə)rə(r), ˈpɒlt(ə)rə(r), -z
AM ˈpɒltərər, ˈpɑltərər, -z
paltrily
BR ˈpɔːltrɪli, ˈpɒltrɪli
AM ˈpɒltrəli, ˈpɑltrəli
paltriness
BR ˈpɔːltrɪnɪs, ˈpɒltrɪnɪs
AM ˈpɒltrɪnɪs, ˈpɑltrɪnɪs
paltry
BR ˈpɔːltr|i, ˈpɒltr|i, -ɪə(r), -ɪɪst
AM ˈpɒltri, ˈpɑltri, -ər, -ɪst
paludism
BR ˈpaljʊdɪz(ə)m
AM ˈpæljəˌdɪzəm
Paludrine®
BR ˈpaljʊdrɪn
AM ˈpæljədrən
paly
BR ˈpeɪli
AM ˈpeɪli
palynological
BR ˌpalɪməˈlɒdʒɪkl
AM ˌpælənəˈladʒəkəl
palynologist
BR ˌpalɪˈnɒlədʒɪst, -s
AM ˌpæləˈnɑlədʒəst, -s
palynology
BR ˌpalɪˈnɒlədʒi
AM ˌpæləˈnɑlədʒi
Pam
BR pam
AM pæm

Pamela
BR 'pam(ɪ)lə(r),
'pamlə(r)
AM 'pæmələ

Pamirs
BR pə'mɪəz
AM pə'mɪərz

pampas
BR 'pampəs
AM 'pæmpəz, 'pɑmpəz

pamper
BR 'pamp|ə(r), -əz,
-(ə)rɪŋ, -əd
AM 'pæmp|ər, -ərz,
-(ə)rɪŋ, -ərd

pamperer
BR 'pamp(ə)rə(r), -z
AM 'pæmpərər, -z

pampero
BR pam'pɛːrəʊ, -z
AM pæm'pɛroʊ, -z

Pampers®
BR 'pampəz
AM 'pæmpərz

pamphlet
BR 'pamflɪt, -s
AM 'pæmflət, -s

pamphleteer
BR ,pamflɪ'tɪə(r), -z,
-ɪŋ, -d
AM ,pæmflə'tɪ(ə)r, -z,
-ɪŋ, -d

Pamphylia
BR pam'fɪlɪə(r)
AM pæm'fɪljə,
pæm'fɪlɪə

Pamphylian
BR pam'fɪlɪən, -z
AM pæm'fɪlɪən, -z

Pamplona
BR pam'pləʊnə(r)
AM pæm'ploʊnə

Pan
BR pan
AM pæn

pan¹
betel leaf
BR pɑːn
AM pɑn

pan²
noun, verb
BR pan, -z, -ɪŋ, -d
AM pæn, -z, -ɪŋ, -d

panacea
BR ,panə'sɪə(r),
,panə'siːə(r), -z
AM ,pænə'siə, -z

panacean
BR ,panə'sɪən,
,panə'siːən
AM ,pænə'siən

panache
BR pə'naʃ
AM pə'næʃ, pə'nɑʃ

panada
BR pə'nɑːdə(r)

Panadol®
BR 'panədɒl
AM 'pænə,dɒl,
'pænə,dɑl

Pan-African
BR ,pan'afrɪk(ə)n
AM ,pæn'æfrəkən

Panaji
BR pə'nɑːdʒi
AM pɑ'nɑdʒi

Pan-Am
BR ,pan'am
AM ,pæn'æm

Panama
BR ,panə'mɑː(r),
'panəmɑː(r)
AM 'pænə,mɑ

Panamanian
BR ,panə'meɪnɪən, -z
AM ,pænə'meɪnɪən, -z

Pan-American
BR ,panə'mɛrɪk(ə)n
AM ,pænə'mɛrəkən

Pan-Anglican
BR ,pan'aŋglɪk(ə)n
AM ,pæn'æŋgləkən

Panasonic
BR ,panə'sɒnɪk
AM ,pænə'sɑnɪk

panatela
BR ,panə'tɛlə(r), -z
AM ,pænə'tɛlə, -z

panatella
BR ,panə'tɛlə(r), -z
AM ,pænə'tɛlə, -z

pancake
BR 'pankeɪk, 'paŋkeɪk,
-s, -ɪŋ, -t
AM 'pæn,keɪk, -s, -ɪŋ, -t

panchayat
BR pʌn'tʃʌɪət, -s
AM pæn'tʃaɪət, -s

Panchen lama
BR ,pantʃən 'lɑːmə(r),
-z
AM 'pæn(t)ʃən ,lɑmə,
-z

panchromatic
BR ,pankrə'matɪk
AM 'pænkroʊ'mædɪk,
'pænkrə'mædɪk

pancosmism
BR ,pan'kɒzmɪz(ə)m
AM ,pæn'kɑz,mɪzəm

Pancras
BR 'paŋkrəs
AM 'pæŋkrəs,
'pæŋkrəs

pancreas
BR 'paŋkrɪəs, -ɪz
AM 'pæŋkriəs,
'pæŋkriəs, -əz

pancreatic
BR ,paŋkrɪ'atɪk
AM ,pæŋkri'ædɪk,
pæŋkri'ædɪk

pancreatin
BR 'paŋkrɪətɪn

AM 'pæŋkriətn,
'pæŋkriətn

pancreatitis
BR ,paŋkrɪə'tʌɪtɪs
AM ,pæŋkriə'taɪdɪs,
,pæŋkriə'taɪdɪs

panda
BR 'pandə(r), -z
AM 'pændə, -z

pandanus
BR pan'danəs, -ɪz
AM pæn'deɪnəs,
pæn'dænəs, -əz

Pandarus
BR 'pand(ə)rəs
AM 'pændərəs

pandean
BR 'pandɪən, -z
AM 'pændiən, -z

pandect
BR 'pandɛkt, -s
AM 'pæn,dɛk|(t), -(t)s

pandemic
BR (,)pan'dɛmɪk, -s
AM 'pæn'dɛmɪk, -s

pandemonium
BR ,pandɪ'məʊnɪəm, -z
AM ,pændə'moʊniəm,
-z

pander
BR 'pand|ə(r), -əz,
-(ə)rɪŋ, -əd
AM 'pænd|ər, -ərz,
-(ə)rɪŋ, -ərd

pandit
BR 'pandɪt, 'pʌndɪt, -s
AM 'pændət, 'pəndət, -s

Pandora
BR pan'dɔːrə(r)
AM pæn'dɔrə

pandowdy
BR pan'daʊd|i, -ɪz
AM pæn'daʊdi, -z

pane
BR peɪn, -z, -d
AM peɪn, -z, -d

paneer
BR pə'nɪə(r)
AM pə'nɪ(ə)r

panegyric
BR ,panɪ'dʒɪrɪk, -s
AM ,pænə'dʒɪrɪk, -s

panegyrical
BR ,panɪ'dʒɪrɪkl
AM ,pænə'dʒɪrəkəl

panegyrise
BR 'panɪdʒɪrʌɪz, -ɪz,
-ɪŋ, -d
AM 'pænədʒə,raɪz, -ɪz,
-ɪŋ, -d

panegyrist
BR ,panɪ'dʒɪrɪst, -s
AM ,pænə'dʒɪrɪst,
,pænə'dʒaɪrɪst, -s

panegyrize
BR 'panɪdʒɪrʌɪz, -ɪz,
-ɪŋ, -d

AM 'pænədʒə,raɪz, -ɪz,
-ɪŋ, -d

panel
BR 'panl, -lz,
-lɪŋ\-əlɪŋ, -ld
AM 'pænəl, -z, -ɪŋ, -d

panelist
BR 'panlɪst, -s
AM 'pænləst, -s

panellist
BR 'panlɪst, -s
AM 'pænləst, -s

panettone
BR ,panɪ'təʊn|eɪ,
,panɪ'təʊn|i, -ɪz
AM ,pænə'toʊni, -z

panettoni
BR ,panɪ'təʊni:
AM ,pænə'toʊni

pan-European
BR ,pan,jʊərə'pi:ən,
,pan,jɔːrə'pi:ən
AM ,pæn,jʊrə'piən,
'pæn,jʊrə'piən

panfish
BR 'panfɪʃ
AM 'pæn,fɪʃ

panforte
BR ,pan'fɔːteɪ,
,pan'fɔːti
AM ,pæn'fɔr,teɪ

pan-fried
BR ,pan'frʌɪd
AM ,pæn,fraɪd

panfry
BR 'panfrʌɪ, -z, -ɪŋ, -d
AM 'pæn,fraɪ, -z, -ɪŋ, -d

panful
BR 'panfʊl, -z
AM 'pæn,fʊl, -z

pang
BR paŋ, -z
AM pæŋ, -z

panga
BR 'paŋgə(r), -z
AM 'pæŋgə, -z

Pangaea
BR pan'dʒiːə(r)
AM pæn'dʒiə

Pangbourne
BR 'paŋbɔːn
AM 'pæŋ,bɔ(ə)rn

pangolin
BR paŋ'gəʊlɪn,
'paŋgəlɪn, -z
AM 'pæŋgələn,
pæŋ'goʊlən, -z

panhandle
BR 'pan,handl, -lz,
-lɪŋ\-əlɪŋ, -ld
AM 'pæn,(h)æn(d)əl,
-z, -ɪŋ, -d

panhandler
BR 'pan,handlə(r), -z
AM 'pæn,(h)æn(də)lər,
-z

pan-Hellenic
BR ˌpanhɛ'lɛnɪk,
ˌpanhɪ'lɛnɪk
AM ˈpæn,(h)ɛ'lɛnɪk

pan-Hellenism
BR ˌpan'hɛlɪnɪz(ə)m
AM ˈpæn'hɛlə,nɪzəm

panic
BR ˈpan|ɪk, -ɪks, -ɪkɪŋ,
-ɪkt
AM ˈpænɪk, -ɪks, -ɪkɪŋ,
-ɪkt

panicky
BR ˈpanɪki
AM ˈpænəki

panicle
BR ˈpanɪkl, -z, -d
AM ˈpænəkəl, -z, -d

Panini[1]
Italian name
BR pə'niːni
AM pə'nini

Panini[2]
Sanskrit name
BR ˈpaniniː
AM ˈpænmi

Panjabi
BR pʌn'dʒɑːb|i,
pən'dʒɑːb|i, -ɪz
AM pən'dʒɑbi, -z

panjandrum
BR pan'dʒandrəm, -z
AM pæn'dʒændrəm, -z

Pankhurst
BR ˈpaŋkhə:st
AM ˈpæŋk,(h)ərst

panlike
BR ˈpanlʌɪk
AM ˈpæn,lʌɪk

Panmunjom
BR ˌpanmʊn'dʒɒm
AM ˈpæn'mʊn'dʒɒm,
ˌpæn'mʊn'dʒɑm

pannage
BR ˈpanɪdʒ
AM ˈpænɪdʒ

Pannal
BR ˈpanl
AM ˈpænəl

panne
BR ˈpan
AM ˈpæn

Pannell
BR ˈpanl
AM ˈpænəl, pə'nɛl

panner
BR ˈpanə(r), -z
AM ˈpænər, -z

pannier
BR ˈpanɪə(r), -z
AM ˈpænjər, ˈpænɪər, -z

pannikin
BR ˈpanɪkɪn, -z
AM ˈpænəkən, -z

pannus
BR ˈpanəs
AM ˈpanəs

panoplied
BR ˈpanəplɪd
AM ˈpænəplɪd

panoply
BR ˈpanəpl|i, -ɪz
AM ˈpænəpli, -z

panoptic
BR pə'nɒptɪk,
(,)pan'ɒptɪk
AM pæ'nɑptɪk,
pə'nɑptɪk

panorama
BR ˌpanə'rɑːmə(r), -z
AM ˌpænə'ræmə,
ˌpænə'rɑmə, -z

panoramic
BR ˌpanə'ramɪk
AM ˌpænə'ræmɪk

panoramically
BR ˌpanə'ramɪkli
AM ˈpænə'ræmək(ə)li

panpipe
BR ˈpanpʌɪp, -s
AM ˈpæn,pʌɪp, -s

panpsychism
BR pan'sʌɪkɪz(ə)m
AM ˈpæn'sʌɪkɪzəm

panslavism
BR pan'slɑː'vɪz(ə)m
AM pæn'slavɪzəm

panspermia
BR pan'spəːmɪə(r)
AM pæn'spərmɪə

panstick
BR ˈpanstɪk
AM ˈpæn,stɪk

pansy
BR ˈpanz|i, -ɪz
AM ˈpænzi, -z

pant
BR ˈpant, -s, -ɪŋ, -ɪd
AM pæn|t, -(t)s, -(t)ɪŋ,
-(t)əd

pantagraph
BR ˈpantəgrɑːf,
ˈpantəgraf, -s
AM ˈpæn(t)ə,græf, -s

Pantagruel
BR ˌpantəgrʊ'ɛl,
ˈpantəgrʊəl
AM ˌpæn(t)əgrʊ'ɛl,
ˈpæn(t)ə,grʊəl

pantalets
BR ˌpantə'lɛts,
ˌpantl'ɛts
AM ˌpæn(t)l'ɛts

pantalettes
BR ˌpantə'lɛts,
ˌpantl'ɛts
AM ˌpæn(t)l'ɛts

pantaloon
BR ˌpantə'luːn, -z
AM ˌpæn(t)l'un,
ˌpæn(t)ə'lun, -z

pantechnicon
BR pan'tɛknɪk(ə)n, -z
AM pæn'tɛknəkən,
pæn'tɛknə,kɑn, -z

Pantelleria
BR ˌpantələ'riːə(r)
AM ˈpæn(t)ələ'riə

Panthalassa
BR ˌpanθə'lasə(r)
AM ˌpænθə'læsə

pantheism
BR ˈpanθiɪz(ə)m
AM ˈpænθi,ɪzəm

pantheist
BR ˈpanθiɪst, -s
AM ˈpænθiɪst, -s

pantheistic
BR ˌpanθi'ɪstɪk
AM ˌpænθi'ɪstɪk

pantheistical
BR ˌpanθi'ɪstɪkl
AM ˌpænθi'ɪstɪkəl

pantheistically
BR ˌpanθi:stɪkli
AM ˌpænθi'ɪstɪk(ə)li

pantheon
BR ˈpanθiən, -z
AM ˈpænθi,ɑn,
ˈpænθiən, -z

panther
BR ˈpanθə(r), -z
AM ˈpænθər, -z

pantie-girdle
BR ˈpantɪ,gəːdl, -z
AM ˈpæn(t)i,gərdəl, -z

panties
BR ˈpantɪz
AM ˈpæn(t)iz

pantihose
BR ˈpantɪhəʊz
AM ˈpæn(t)i,houz

pantile
BR ˈpantʌɪl, -z, -d
AM ˈpæn,tail, -z, -d

pantingly
BR ˈpantɪŋli
AM ˈpæn(t)ɪŋli

panto
BR ˈpantəʊ, -z
AM ˈpæn,tou, -z

pantograph
BR ˈpantəgrɑːf,
ˈpantəgraf, -s
AM ˈpæn(t)ə,græf, -s

pantographic
BR ˌpantə'grafɪk
AM ˌpæn(t)ə'græfɪk

pantologic
BR ˌpantə'lɒdʒɪk
AM ˌpæn(t)ə'ladʒɪk

pantology
BR pan'tɒlədʒi
AM pæn'talədʒi

pantomime
BR ˈpantəmʌɪm, -z
AM ˈpæn(t)ə,maim, -z

pantomimic
BR ˌpantə'mɪmɪk
AM ˌpæn(t)ə'mɪmɪk

pantomimist
BR ˈpantəmʌɪmɪst, -s

AM ˈpæn(t)ə,maimɪst,
-s

pantomorphic
BR ˌpantə(ʊ)'mɔːfɪk
AM ˌpæn(t)ə'mɔrfɪk

pantoscopic
BR ˌpantə'skɒpɪk
AM ˌpæn(t)ə'skapɪk

pantothenic
BR ˌpantə'θɛnɪk
AM ˌpæn(t)ə'θɛnɪk

pantry
BR ˈpantr|i, -ɪz
AM ˈpæntri, -z

pantryman
BR ˈpantrimən
AM ˈpæntrimən

pantrymen
BR ˈpantrimən
AM ˈpæntrimən

pants
BR pants
AM pæn(t)s

pantsuit
BR ˈpantsuːt, -s
AM ˈpænt,sut, -s

pantyhose
BR ˈpantihəʊz
AM ˈpæn(t)i,houz

pantywaist
BR ˈpantɪweist, -s
AM ˈpæn(t)i,weist, -s

Panzer
BR ˈpanzə(r), -z
AM ˈpænzər,
ˈpan(t)sər, -z

pap
BR pap, -s
AM pæp, -s

papa
BR pə'pɑː(r), -z
AM ˈpɑpə, -z

papabile
BR pə'pɑːbɪleɪ
AM pə'pɑbə,leɪ

papacy
BR ˈpeɪpəs|i, -ɪz
AM ˈpeɪpəsi, -z

papain
BR pə'peɪɪn, pə'pʌɪn
AM ˈpæ,peɪn, pə'peɪn

papal
BR ˈpeɪpl
AM ˈpeɪpəl

papalism
BR ˈpeɪpl,ɪz(ə)m,
ˈpeɪpəlɪz(ə)m
AM ˈpeɪpə,lɪzəm

papalist
BR ˈpeɪpl,ɪst,
ˈpeɪpəlɪst, -s
AM ˈpeɪpələst, -s

papally
BR ˈpeɪpli, ˈpeɪpəli
AM ˈpeɪpəli

paparazzi
BR ˌpapə'ratsiː

AM ˌpɑpəˈrɑtˌsi

paparazzo
BR ˌpæpəˈrɑtsəʊ
AM ˌpɑpəˈrɑtˌsoʊ

papaveraceous
BR pəˌpeɪvəˈreɪʃəs
AM pəˌpævəˈreɪʃəs

papaverine
BR pəˈpeɪvəriːn,
pəˈpævəriːn,
pəˈpeɪvərɪn,
pəˈpævərɪn
AM pəˈpævəˌriːn,
pəˈpævərən

papaw
BR ˈpɔːpɔː(r), pəˈpɔː(r),
-z
AM pəˈpɔ, pəˈpɑ, -z

papaya
BR pəˈpaɪə(r), -z
AM pəˈpaɪə, -z

Papeete
BR ˌpɑːpɪˈiːti,
ˌpɑːpɪˈeɪti, ˌpɑpɪˈiːti,
ˌpɑpɪˈeɪti, pəˈpiːti
AM ˌpɑpiˈiti, pəˈpidi

paper
BR ˈpeɪp|ə(r), -əz,
-(ə)rɪŋ, -əd
AM ˈpeɪp|ər, -ərz,
-(ə)rɪŋ, -ərd

paperback
BR ˈpeɪpəbak, -s
AM ˈpeɪpərˌbæk, -s

paperboy
BR ˈpeɪpəbɔɪ, -z
AM ˈpeɪpərˌbɔɪ, -z

paperchase
BR ˈpeɪpətʃeɪs, -ɪz
AM ˈpeɪpərˌtʃeɪs, -ɪz

paperclip
BR ˈpeɪpəklɪp, -s
AM ˈpeɪpərˌklɪp, -s

paperer
BR ˈpeɪp(ə)rə(r), -z
AM ˈpeɪpərər, -z

paperhanger
BR ˈpeɪpəˌhaŋə(r), -z
AM ˈpeɪpərˌ(h)æŋər, -z

paperknife
BR ˈpeɪpənaɪf
AM ˈpeɪpərˌnaɪf

paperknives
BR ˈpeɪpənʌɪvz
AM ˈpeɪpərˌnaɪvz

paperless
BR ˈpeɪpələs
AM ˈpeɪpərləs

papermaker
BR ˈpeɪpəˌmeɪkə(r), -z
AM ˈpeɪpərˌmeɪkər, -z

papermaking
BR ˈpeɪpəˌmeɪkɪŋ
AM ˈpeɪpərˌmeɪkɪŋ

paperweight
BR ˈpeɪpəweɪt, -s
AM ˈpeɪpərˌweɪt, -s

paperwork
BR ˈpeɪpəwɜːk
AM ˈpeɪpərˌwɜrk

papery
BR ˈpeɪp(ə)ri
AM ˈpeɪpəri

Paphlagonia
BR ˌpafləˈɡəʊniə(r)
AM ˌpæfləˈɡoʊniə

Paphlagonian
BR ˌpafləˈɡəʊniən, -z
AM ˌpæfləˈɡoʊniən, -z

papier-mâché
BR ˈpapjeɪˈmaʃeɪ
AM ˈpeɪpərməˈʃeɪ

papilionaceous
BR pəˌpɪliəˈneɪʃəs
AM pəˌpɪliəˈneɪʃəs

papilla
BR pəˈpɪlə(r)
AM pəˈpɪlə

papillae
BR pəˈpɪli
AM pəˈpɪlˌi, pəˈpɪlˌaɪ

papillary
BR pəˈpɪl(ə)ri,
ˈpapɪləri
AM ˈpæpəˌleri

papillate
BR ˈpapɪleɪt, pəˈpɪlət
AM ˈpæpəˌleɪt, pəˈpɪlɪt

papilloma
BR ˌpapɪˈləʊmə(r), -z
AM ˌpæpəˈloʊmə, -z

papillomata
BR ˌpapɪˈləʊmətə(r)
AM ˌpæpəˈloʊmədə

papillon
BR ˈpapɪlɒn, ˈpapɪjɒ̃, -z
AM ˈpæpiˈjɑn, -z

papillose
BR ˈpapɪləʊs, ˈpapɪləʊz
AM ˈpapəˈloʊs,
ˈpapəˌloʊz

papism
BR ˈpeɪpɪz(ə)m
AM ˈpeɪˌpɪzəm

papist
BR ˈpeɪpɪst, -s
AM ˈpeɪpɪst, -s

papistic
BR pəˈpɪstɪk
AM pəˈpɪstɪk

papistical
BR pəˈpɪstɪkl
AM pəˈpɪstəkəl

papistry
BR ˈpeɪpɪstri
AM ˈpeɪpɪstri

papoose
BR pəˈpuːs, -ɪz
AM pæˈpus, pəˈpus, -əz

Papp
BR pap, -s
AM pæp, -s

pappardelle
BR ˌpapɑːˈdɛleɪ

AM ˌpapəˈdɛli

pappi
BR ˈpapʌɪ
AM ˈpæˌpaɪ

pappose
BR paˈpəʊs
AM ˈpæˌpoʊs, ˈpæˌpoʊz

pappus
BR ˈpapəs
AM ˈpæpəs

pappy
BR ˈpap|i, -iə(r), -ɪɪst
AM ˈpæpi, -ər, -əst

paprika
BR ˈpaprɪkə(r),
pəˈpriːkə(r)
AM pəˈprikə, pæˈprikə

Papua
BR ˈpap(j)ʊə(r),
ˈpɑːpʊə(r)
AM ˈpapʊə, ˈpæpjʊə

Papuan
BR ˈpap(j)ʊən,
ˈpɑːp(j)ʊən, -z
AM ˈpapʊən, ˈpæpjʊən,
-z

**Papua New
Guinea**
BR ˌpap(j)ʊə njuː ˈɡɪni,
ˌpɑːp(j)ʊə +
AM ˌpapʊə ˌn(j)u ˈɡɪni,
ˌpæpjʊə +

**Papua New
Guinean**
BR ˌpap(j)ʊə njuː
ˈɡɪniən, ˌpɑːp(j)ʊə +,
-z
AM ˌpapʊə ˌn(j)u
ˈɡɪniən, ˌpæpjʊə +, -z

papula
BR ˈpapjʊlə(r)
AM ˈpæpjələ

papulae
BR ˈpapjʊli
AM ˈpæpjəˌli,
ˈpæpjəˌlaɪ

papular
BR ˈpapjʊlə(r)
AM ˈpæpjələr

papule
BR ˈpapjuːl, -z
AM ˈpæpˌjul, -z

papulose
BR ˈpapjʊləʊs,
ˈpapjʊləʊz
AM ˈpæpjəloʊs,
ˈpæpjəˌloʊz

papulous
BR ˈpapjʊləs
AM ˈpæpjələs

Papworth
BR ˈpapwəθ
AM ˈpæpˌwɜrθ

papyraceous
BR ˌpapɪˈreɪʃəs
AM ˌpæpəˈreɪʃəs

papyri
BR pəˈpʌɪrʌɪ

AM pəˈpaɪri, pəˈpaɪˌraɪ

papyrological
BR pəˌpʌɪrəˈlɒdʒɪkl,
pəˌpɪərəˈlɒdʒɪkl
AM pəˌpaɪrəˈlɑdʒəkl,
pəˌpaɪərəˈlɑdʒəkəl

papyrologist
BR ˌpapɪˈrɒlədʒɪst, -s
AM ˌpæpəˈrɑlədʒəst, -s

papyrology
BR ˌpapɪˈrɒlədʒi
AM ˌpæpəˈrɑlədʒi

papyrus
BR pəˈpʌɪrəs, -ɪz
AM pəˈpaɪrəs, -əz

par
BR pɑː(r)
AM pɑr

Pará
BR paˈrɑː(r)
AM pɑˈrɑ

para
*paratrooper,
paragraph*
BR ˈparə(r), -z
AM ˈpɛrə, -z

parabases
BR ˌparaˈbeɪsiːz
AM ˌpɛrəˈbeɪˌsiz

parabasis
BR ˌparaˈbeɪsɪs
AM ˌpɛrəˈbeɪsɪs

parabioses
BR ˌparəbʌɪˈəʊsiːz
AM ˌpɛrəˈbaɪəˌsiz

parabiosis
BR ˌparəbʌɪˈəʊsɪs
AM ˌpɛrəˈbaɪəsəs

parabiotic
BR ˌparəbʌɪˈɒtɪk
AM ˌpɛrəbaɪˈɑdɪk

parable
BR ˈparəbl, -z
AM ˈpɛrəbəl, -z

parabola
BR pəˈrabələ(r),
pəˈrablə(r), -z
AM pəˈræbələ, -z

parabolic
BR ˌparəˈbɒlɪk
AM ˌpɛrəˈbɑlɪk

parabolical
BR ˌparəˈbɒlɪkl
AM ˌpɛrəˈbɑləkəl

parabolically
BR ˌparəˈbɒlɪkli
AM ˌpɛrəˈbɑlək(ə)li

paraboloid
BR pəˈrabəlɔɪd,
pəˈrablɔɪd, -z
AM pəˈræbəˌlɔɪd, -z

paraboloidal
BR pəˈrabəˈlɔɪdl
AM pəˈræbəˈlɔɪdəl

Paracelsus
BR ˌparəˈsɛlsəs
AM ˌpɛrəˈsɛlsəs

paracetamol
BR ˌparəˈsiːtəmɒl,
ˌparəˈsɛtəmɒl, -z
AM ˌpɛrəˈsidəˌmɑl,
ˌpɛrəˈsɛdəˌmɑl, -z
parachronism
BR pəˈrakrəniz(ə)m, -z
AM ˌpɛrəˈkrɑˌnizəm, -z
parachute
BR ˈparəʃuːt, -s, -ɪŋ, -ɪd
AM ˈpɛrəˌʃu|t, -ts, -dɪŋ,
-dəd
parachutist
BR ˈparəʃuːtɪst, -s
AM ˈpɛrəˌʃudəst, -s
paraclete
BR ˈparəkliːt, -s
AM ˈpɛrəˌklit, -s
parade
BR pəˈreɪd, -z, -ɪŋ, -ɪd
AM pəˈreɪd, -z, -ɪŋ, -ɪd
parader
BR pəˈreɪdə(r), -z
AM pəˈreɪdər, -z
paradichloroben-
zene
BR ˌparədʌɪˌklɔːrəʊ-
ˈbenziːn
AM ˌpɛrəˌdʌɪˌklɔrə-
ˈbenzin
paradiddle
BR ˈparədɪdl,
ˌparəˈdɪdl, -z
AM ˈpɛrəˌdɪdəl, -z
paradigm
BR ˈparədʌɪm, -z
AM ˈpɛrəˌdaɪm, -z
paradigmatic
BR ˌparədɪɡˈmatɪk
AM ˌpɛrəˌdɪɡˈmædɪk
paradigmatical
BR ˌparədɪɡˈmatɪkl
AM ˌpɛrəˌdɪɡˈmædəkəl
paradigmatically
BR ˌparədɪɡˈmatɪkli
AM ˌpɛrəˌdɪɡˈmædək-
(ə)li
paradisaical
BR ˌparədɪˈsʌɪkl,
ˌparədɪˈzʌɪkl
AM ˌpɛrədəˈsaɪəkəl,
ˌpɛrədəˈzaɪəkəl
paradisal
BR ˌparəˈdʌɪsl,
ˌparəˈdʌɪzl
AM ˌpɛrəˈdaɪzəl
paradise
BR ˈparədʌɪs, -ɪz
AM ˈpɛrəˌdaɪs,
ˈpɛrəˌdaɪz, -ɪz
paradisiacal
BR ˌparədɪˈsʌɪkl,
ˌparədɪˈzʌɪkl
AM ˌpɛrədəˈsaɪəkəl,
ˌpɛrədəˈzaɪəkəl
paradisical
BR ˌparəˈdɪsɪkl,
ˌparəˈdɪzɪkl

paracetamol
AM ˈparəˈdɪsəkəl,
ˈparəˈdɪzəkəl
parador
BR ˈparədɔː(r), -z
AM ˈpɛ(ə)rəˌdɔ(ə)r, -z
parados
BR ˈparədɒs, -ɪz
AM ˈpɛrəˌdɑs, -əz
paradox
BR ˈparədɒks, -ɪz
AM ˈpɛrəˌdɑks, -əz
paradoxical
BR ˌparəˈdɒksɪkl
AM ˌpɛrəˈdɑksəkəl
paradoxically
BR ˌparəˈdɒksɪkli
AM ˌpɛrəˈdɑksək(ə)li
paradoxure
BR ˌparəˈdɒksjʊə(r), -z
AM ˈpɛrəˈdɑkʃər, -z
paradrop
BR ˈparədrɒp, -s
AM ˈpɛrəˌdrɑp, -s
paraffin
BR ˈparəfɪn
AM ˈpɛrəfən
paraglide
BR ˈparəɡlʌɪd
AM ˈpɛrəˌɡlaɪd
paraglider
BR ˈparəˌɡlʌɪdə(r), -z
AM ˈpɛrəˌɡlaɪdər, -z
paragliding
BR ˈparəˌɡlʌɪdɪŋ
AM ˈpɛrəˌɡlaɪdɪŋ
paragoge
BR ˌparəˈɡəʊdʒi
AM ˌpɛrəˈɡoʊdʒi
paragogic
BR ˌparəˈɡɒdʒɪk
AM ˌpɛrəˈɡɑdʒɪk
paragon
BR ˈparəɡ(ə)n, -z
AM ˈpɛrəˌɡɑn,
ˈpɛrəɡən, -z
paragraph
BR ˈparəɡrɑːf,
ˈparəɡraf, -s, -ɪŋ, -t
AM ˈpɛrəˌɡræf, -s, -ɪŋ, -t
paragraphic
BR ˌparəˈɡrafɪk
AM ˌpɛrəˈɡræfɪk
paragraphist
BR ˈparəˌɡrafɪst, -s
AM ˈpɛrəˌɡræfəst, -s
Paraguay
BR ˈparəɡwʌɪ,
ˌparəˈɡwʌɪ
AM ˈpɛrəˌɡwaɪ
SP para ˈɣwaj
Paraguayan
BR ˌparəˈɡwʌɪən, -z
AM ˌpɛrəˈɡwaɪən, -z
parahydrogen
BR ˌparəˈhʌɪdrədʒ(ə)n
AM ˈpɛrəˈhaɪdrədʒen

parakeet
BR ˈparəkiːt,
ˌparəˈkiːt, -s
AM ˈpɛrəˌkit, -s
paralanguage
BR ˈparəˌlaŋɡwɪdʒ
AM ˈpɛrəˌlæŋɡwɪdʒ
paraldehyde
BR pəˈraldɪhaɪd
AM pəˈrældəˌhaɪd
paralegal
BR ˌparəˈliːɡl
AM ˈpɛrəˈliɡəl
paraleipomena
BR ˌparəlʌɪˈpɒmɪnə(r),
ˌparəlɪˈpɒmɪnə(r)
AM ˌpɛrəˌlaɪˈpɑmənə,
ˈpɛrələˈpɑmənə
paraleipses
BR ˌparəˈlʌɪpsiːz
AM ˌpɛrəˈlaɪpsiz
paraleipsis
BR ˌparəˈlʌɪpsɪs
AM ˈpɛrəˈlaɪpsɪs
paralinguistic
BR ˌparəlɪŋˈɡwɪstɪk
AM ˌpɛrəˌlɪŋˈɡwɪstɪk
paralipomena
BR ˌparəlʌɪˈpɒmɪnə(r),
ˌparəlɪˈpɒmɪnə(r)
AM ˌpɛrəˌlaɪˈpɑmənə,
ˈpɛrələˈpɑmənə
paralipses
BR ˌparəˈlɪpsiːz
AM ˌpɛrəˈlɪpˌsiz
paralipsis
BR ˌparəˈlɪpsɪs
AM ˈpɛrəˈlɪpsɪs
parallactic
BR ˌparəˈlaktɪk
AM ˈpɛrəˈlæktɪk
parallax
BR ˈparəlaks, -ɪz
AM ˈpɛrəˌlæks, -əz
parallel
BR ˈparəlɛl, -z, -ɪŋ, -d
AM ˈpɛrəˌlɛl, -z, -ɪŋ, -d
parallelepiped
BR ˌparəlɛləˈpʌɪped, -z
AM ˌpɛrəˌlɛləˈpaɪpɪd, -z
parallelism
BR ˈparəlɛlɪz(ə)m
AM ˈpɛrəˌlɛlˌɪzəm
parallelogram
BR ˌparəˈlɛləɡram, -z
AM ˌpɛrəˈlɛləˌɡræm, -z
paralogise
BR pəˈralədʒʌɪz, -ɪz,
-ɪŋ, -d
AM pəˈrælədʒaɪz, -ɪz,
-ɪŋ, -d
paralogism
BR pəˈralədʒɪz(ə)m, -z
AM pəˈrælədʒɪzəm, -z
paralogist
BR pəˈralədʒɪst, -s
AM pəˈrælədʒəst, -s

paralogize
BR pəˈralədʒʌɪz, -ɪz,
-ɪŋ, -d
AM pəˈrælədʒaɪz, -ɪz,
-ɪŋ, -d
Paralympics
BR ˌparəˈlɪmpɪks
AM ˌpɛrəˈlɪmpɪks
paralysation
BR ˌparəlʌɪˈzeɪʃn,
ˌpɛrələˈzeɪʃən,
ˌpɛrəˌlaɪˈzeɪʃən
paralyse
BR ˈparəlʌɪz, -ɪz, -ɪŋ, -d
AM ˈpɛrəˌlaɪz, -ɪz, -ɪŋ, -d
paralyses
noun plural
BR pəˈralɪsiːz
AM pəˈræləˌsiz
paralysingly
BR ˈparəlʌɪzɪŋli
AM ˈpɛrəˌlaɪzɪŋli
paralysis
BR pəˈralɪsɪs
AM pəˈræləsəs
paralytic
BR ˌparəˈlɪtɪk
AM ˈpɛrəˈlɪdɪk
paralytically
BR ˌparəˈlɪtɪkli
AM ˈpɛrəˈlɪdək(ə)li
paralyzation
BR ˌparəlʌɪˈzeɪʃn
AM ˌpɛrələˈzeɪʃən,
ˌpɛrəˌlaɪˈzeɪʃən
paralyze
BR ˈparəlʌɪz, -ɪz, -ɪŋ, -d
AM ˈpɛrəˌlaɪz, -ɪz, -ɪŋ, -d
paralyzingly
BR ˈparəlʌɪzɪŋli
AM ˈpɛrəˌlaɪzɪŋli
paramagnetic
BR ˌparəmagˈnɛtɪk
AM ˈpɛrəmæɡˈnɛdɪk
paramagnetism
BR ˌparəˈmaɡnɪtɪz(ə)m
AM ˈpɛrəˈmæɡnəˌtɪzəm
paramatta
BR ˌparəˈmatə(r)
AM ˈpɛrəˈmædə
paramecia
BR ˌparəˈmiːsɪə(r)
AM ˌpɛrəˈmisiə
paramecium
BR ˌparəˈmiːsɪəm
AM ˈpɛrəˈmisiəm
paramedic
BR ˌparəˈmɛdɪk, -s
AM ˈpɛrəˈmɛdɪk, -s
paramedical
BR ˌparəˈmɛdɪkl
AM ˈpɛrəˈmɛdəkəl
parameter
BR pəˈramɪtə(r), -z
AM pəˈræmədər, -z
parametric
BR ˌparəˈmɛtrɪk

AM ˌperəˈmɛtrɪk
parametrise
BR pəˈræmɪtrʌɪz, -ɪz, -ɪŋ, -d
AM pəˈræməˌtraɪz, -ɪz, -ɪŋ, -d
parametrize
BR pəˈræmɪtrʌɪz, -ɪz, -ɪŋ, -d
AM pəˈræməˌtraɪz, -ɪz, -ɪŋ, -d
paramilitary
BR ˌparəˈmɪlɪt(ə)ri
AM ˌperəˈmɪləˌtɛri
paramnesia
BR ˌparəmˈniːzɪə(r), ˌparəmˈniːʒə(r)
AM ˌpɛˌræmˈniʒ(i)ə, ˌperəmˈniʒə, ˌpɛˌræmˈniziə, ˌperəmˈniziə
paramo
BR ˈparəməʊ, -z
AM ˈperəˌmoʊ, -z
paramoecia
BR ˌparəˈmiːʃ(i)ə(r), -z
AM ˌperəˈmiʃ(i)ə, -z
paramoecium
BR ˌparəˈmiːʃ(i)əm, -z
AM ˌperəˈmiʃ(i)əm, -z
paramount
BR ˈparəmaʊnt
AM ˈperəˌmaʊnt
paramountcy
BR ˈparəmaʊn(t)si
AM ˈperəˌmaʊn(t)si
paramountly
BR ˈparəmaʊntli
AM ˈperəˌmaʊn(t)li
paramour
BR ˈparəmʊə(r), ˈparəmɔː(r), -z
AM ˈperəˌmʊ(ə)r, ˈperəˌmɔ(ə)r, -z
Paraná
BR ˌparəˈnɑː(r)
AM ˌparəˈnɑ
parang
BR pəˈraŋ, -z
AM pəˈraŋ, -z
paranoia
BR ˌparəˈnɔɪə(r)
AM ˌperəˈnɔɪə
paranoiac
BR ˌparəˈnɔɪak, -s
AM ˌperəˈnɔɪk, -s
paranoiacally
BR ˌparəˈnɔɪəkli
AM ˌperəˈnɔɪk(ə)li
paranoic
BR ˌparəˈnɔɪk
AM ˌperəˈnɔɪk
paranoically
BR ˌparəˈnɔɪkli
AM ˌperəˈnɔɪk(ə)li
paranoid
BR ˈparənɔɪd
AM ˈperəˌnɔɪd

paranormal
BR ˌparəˈnɔːml
AM ˈperəˈnɔrməl
paranormally
BR ˌparəˈnɔːmˌli, ˌparəˈnɔːməli
AM ˈperəˈnɔrməli
Paranthropus
BR pəˈranθrəpəs, ˌparənˈθrəʊpəs
AM pəˈrænθrəpəs
parapet
BR ˈparəpɪt, -s, -ɪd
AM ˈperəpəlt, -ts, -dɪd
paraph
BR ˈparaf, ˈparəf, -s
AM ˈperəf, pəˈræf, -s
paraphernalia
BR ˌparəfəˈneɪlɪə(r)
AM ˌperəfə(r)ˈneɪljə, ˌperəfə(r)ˈneɪlɪə
paraphrase
BR ˈparəfreɪz, -ɪz, -ɪŋ, -d
AM ˈperəˌfreɪz, -ɪz, -ɪŋ, -d
paraphrastic
BR ˌparəˈfrastɪk
AM ˌperəˈfræstɪk
paraphrastically
BR ˌparəˈfrastɪkli
AM ˌperəˈfræstək(ə)li
paraplegia
BR ˌparəˈpliːdʒə(r)
AM ˌperəˈplidʒ(i)ə
paraplegic
BR ˌparəˈpliːdʒɪk, -s
AM ˌperəˈplidʒɪk, -s
paraprofessional
BR ˌparəprəˈfɛʃn(ə)l, ˌparəprəˈfɛʃən(ə)l
AM ˌperəprəˈfɛʃ(ə)nəl
parapsychological
BR ˌparəˌsʌɪkəˈlɒdʒɪkl
AM ˌperəˌsaɪkəˈlɑdʒəkəl
parapsychologic-ally
BR ˌparəˌsʌɪkəˈlɒdʒɪkli
AM ˌperəˌsaɪkəˈlɑdʒək-(ə)li
parapsychologist
BR ˌparəsʌɪˈkɒlədʒɪst, -s
AM ˌperəsaɪˈkɑlədʒəst, -s
parapsychology
BR ˌparəsʌɪˈkɒlədʒi
AM ˌperəsaɪˈkɑlədʒi
paraquat
BR ˈparəkwɒt, ˈparəkwat
AM ˈperəˌkwɑt
pararhyme
BR ˈparərʌɪm
AM ˈperəˌraɪm
parasailer
BR ˌparəˌseɪlə(r), -z
AM ˌperəˌseɪlər, -z

parasailing
BR ˌparəˌseɪlɪŋ
AM ˌperəˌseɪlɪŋ
parasailor
BR ˌparəˌseɪlə(r), -z
AM ˌperəˌseɪlər, -z
parasang
BR ˈparəsaŋ, -z
AM ˈperəˌsæŋ, -z
parascend
BR ˈparəsend, -z, -ɪŋ, -ɪd
AM ˈperəˌsend, -z, -ɪŋ, -əd
parascender
BR ˈparəˌsendə(r), -z
AM ˈperəˌsendər, -z
paraselenae
BR ˌparəsɪˈliːniː
AM ˌperəsəˈlini, ˌperəsəˈlinaɪ
paraselene
BR ˌparəsɪˈliːni
AM ˌperəsəˈlini
parasitaemia
BR ˌparəsɪˈtiːmɪə(r)
AM ˌperəsəˈtimiə
parasite
BR ˈparəsʌɪt, -s
AM ˈperəˌsaɪt, -s
parasitemia
BR ˌparəsɪˈtiːmɪə(r)
AM ˌperəsəˈtimiə
parasitic
BR ˌparəˈsɪtɪk
AM ˌperəˈsɪdɪk
parasitical
BR ˌparəˈsɪtɪkl
AM ˌperəˈsɪdɪkəl
parasitically
BR ˌparəˈsɪtɪkli
AM ˌperəˈsɪdɪk(ə)li
parasiticide
BR ˌparəˈsɪtɪsʌɪd
AM ˌperəˈsɪdɪˌsaɪd
parasitisation
BR ˌparəsɪtʌɪˈzeɪʃn
AM ˌperəsədəˈzeɪʃən, ˌperəsəˌtaɪˈzeɪʃən
parasitise
BR ˈparəsɪtʌɪz, -ɪz, -ɪŋ, -d
AM ˈperəsəˌtaɪz, ˈperəsaɪˌtaɪz, -ɪz, -ɪŋ, -d
parasitism
BR ˈparəsɪtɪz(ə)m
AM ˈperəsəˌtɪzəm, ˈperəˌsaɪˌtɪzəm
parasitization
BR ˌparəsɪtʌɪˈzeɪʃn
AM ˌperəsədəˈzeɪʃən, ˌperəsəˌtaɪˈzeɪʃən
parasitize
BR ˈparəsɪtʌɪz, -ɪz, -ɪŋ, -d

parasol
AM ˈperəˌsaɪˌtaɪz, ˈperəsaɪˌtaɪz, -ɪz, -ɪŋ, -d
parasitoid
BR ˈparəsɪtɔɪd, -z
AM ˈperəsəˌtɔɪd, ˈperəˌsaɪˌtɔɪd, -z
parasitologist
BR ˌparəsɪˈtɒlədʒɪst, ˌparəsʌɪˈtɒlədʒɪst, -s
AM ˌperəsaɪˈtalədʒəst, ˌperəsaɪˈtalədʒəst, -s
parasitology
BR ˌparəsɪˈtɒlədʒi, ˌparəsʌɪˈtɒlədʒi
AM ˌperəsəˈtalədʒi, ˌperəsaɪˈtalədʒi
parasol
BR ˈparəsɒl, -z
AM ˈperəˌsɒl, ˈperəˌsal, -z
parasuicide
BR ˌparəˈs(j)ʊɪsʌɪd, -z
AM ˌperəˈsʊ(w)əˌsaɪd, -z
parasympathetic
BR ˌparəˌsɪmpəˈθɛtɪk
AM ˌperəˌsɪmpəˈθɛdɪk
parasyntheses
BR ˌparəˈsɪnθɪsiːz
AM ˌperəˈsɪnθəsiz
parasynthesis
BR ˌparəˈsɪnθɪsɪs
AM ˌperəˈsɪnθəsəs
parasynthetic
BR ˌparəsɪnˈθɛtɪk
AM ˌperəˌsɪnˈθɛdɪk
paratactic
BR ˌparəˈtaktɪk
AM ˌperəˈtæktɪk
paratactically
BR ˌparəˈtaktɪkli
AM ˌperəˈtæktək(ə)li
parataxis
BR ˌparəˈtaksɪs
AM ˌperəˈtæksəs
parathion
BR ˌparəˈθʌɪɒn
AM ˌperəˈθaɪˌɑn
parathyroid
BR ˌparəˈθʌɪrɔɪd
AM ˌperəˈθaɪˌrɔɪd
paratroop
BR ˈparətruːp, -s
AM ˈperəˌtrup, -s
paratrooper
BR ˈparətruːpə(r), -z
AM ˈperəˌtrupər, -z
paratroops
BR ˈparətruːps
AM ˈperəˌtrups
paratyphoid
BR ˌparəˈtʌɪfɔɪd
AM ˌperəˈtaɪˌfɔɪd
paravane
BR ˈparəveɪn, -z
AM ˈperəˌveɪn, -z

par avion
BR ˌpɑːr ˈavjɵ̃
AM ˌpɑr ɑˈvjɔn

parboil
BR ˈpɑːbɔɪl, -z, -ɪŋ, -d
AM ˈpɑrˌbɔɪl, -z, -ɪŋ, -d

parbuckle
BR ˈpɑːˌbʌk|l̩, -lz,
-|ɪŋ\-lɪŋ, -ld
AM ˈpɑrˌbək|əl, -əlz,
-(ə)lɪŋ, -əld

Parcae
BR ˈpɑːsi
AM ˈpɑrsi, ˈpɑrˌkaɪ

parcel
BR ˈpɑːs|l̩, -lz,
-|ɪŋ\-əlɪŋ, -ld
AM ˈpɑrs|əl, -əlz,
-(ə)lɪŋ, -əld

parch
BR pɑːtʃ, -ɪz, -ɪŋ, -t
AM pɑrtʃ, -əz, -ɪŋ, -t

Parcheesi®
BR pɑːˈtʃiːzi
AM pɑrˈtʃizi

parchment
BR ˈpɑːtʃm(ə)nt, -s
AM ˈpɑrtʃmənt, -s

parclose
BR ˈpɑːkləʊz, -ɪz
AM ˈpɑrˌkloʊz, -əz

pard
BR pɑːd, -z
AM pɑrd, -z

pardalote
BR ˈpɑːdələʊt,
ˈpɑːdˌləʊt, -s
AM ˈpɑrdlˌoʊt, -s

pardner
BR ˈpɑːdnə(r), -z
AM ˈpɑrdnər, -z

Pardoe
BR ˈpɑːdəʊ
AM ˈpɑrdoʊ

pardon
BR ˈpɑːd|n̩, -nz,
-ŋɪn\-nɪŋ, -nd
AM ˈpɑrdən, -z, -ɪŋ, -d

pardonable
BR ˈpɑːdnəbl,
ˈpɑːdnəbl
AM ˈpɑrdnəbəl

pardonably
BR ˈpɑːdnəbli,
ˈpɑːdnəbli
AM ˈpɑrdnəbli

pardoner
BR ˈpɑːdnə(r),
ˈpɑːdnə(r), -z
AM ˈpɑrdnər, -z

pare
BR pɛː(r), -z, -ɪŋ, -d
AM pɛ(ə)r, -z, -ɪŋ, -d

paregoric
BR ˌparəˈgɒrɪk
AM ˌperəˈgɒrɪk

pareira
BR pəˈrɛːrə(r)

AM pəˈrɛːrə, pəˈreɪrə

paren
BR pəˈrɛn, -z
AM ˈpɛrɛn, ˈpɛrən, -z

parenchyma
BR pəˈrɛŋkɪmə(r)
AM pəˈrɛŋkəmə

parenchymal
BR pəˈrɛŋkɪml
AM pəˈrɛŋkəməl

parenchymatous
BR ˌparənˈkɪmətəs,
ˌpɑrnˈkɪmətəs
AM ˌpɛrənˈkɪmədəs

parent
BR ˈpɛːrənt, ˈpɛːrn̩t, -s,
-ɪŋ, -ɪd
AM ˈpɛrənt, -s, -ɪŋ, -ɪd

parentage
BR ˈpɛːrəntɪdʒ,
ˈpɛːrn̩tɪdʒ
AM ˈpɛrən(t)ədʒ

parental
BR pəˈrɛntl
AM pəˈrɛn(t)l

parentally
BR pəˈrɛntli,
pəˈrɛntəli
AM pəˈrɛn(t)li

parenteral
BR pəˈrɛnt(ə)rəl,
pəˈrɛnt(ə)rl̩
AM pəˈrɛn(t)ərəl

parenterally
BR pəˈrɛnt(ə)rəli,
pəˈrɛnt(ə)rl̩i
AM pəˈrɛn(t)ərəli

parentheses
BR pəˈrɛnθɪsiːz
AM pəˈrɛnθəsiz

parenthesis
BR pəˈrɛnθɪsɪs
AM pəˈrɛnθəsəs

parenthesise
BR pəˈrɛnθɪsʌɪz, -ɪz,
-ɪŋ, -d
AM pəˈrɛnθəˌsaɪz, -ɪz,
-ɪŋ, -d

parenthesize
BR pəˈrɛnθɪsʌɪz, -ɪz,
-ɪŋ, -d
AM pəˈrɛnθəˌsaɪz, -ɪz,
-ɪŋ, -d

parenthetic
BR ˌparənˈθɛtɪk,
ˌpɑrnˈθɛtɪk
AM ˌpɛrənˈθɛdɪk

parenthetical
BR ˌparənˈθɛtɪkl,
ˌpɑrnˈθɛtɪkl
AM ˌpɛrənˈθɛdəkəl

parenthetically
BR ˌparənˈθɛtɪkli,
ˌpɑrnˈθɛtɪkli
AM ˌpɛrənˈθɛdək(ə)li

parenthood
BR ˈpɛːrənthʊd,
ˈpɛːrn̩thʊd

AM ˈpɛrən(t)ˌ(h)ʊd

parentless
BR ˈpɛːrəntləs,
ˈpɛːrn̩tləs
AM ˈpɛrən(t)ləs

parer
BR ˈpɛːrə(r), -z
AM ˈpɛrər, -z

parerga
BR pəˈrəːgə(r)
AM pəˈrərgə

parergon
BR pəˈrəːgɒn
AM pəˈrərˌgɑn

paresis
BR pəˈriːsɪs
AM pəˈrisɪs

paresthesia
BR ˌparəsˈθiːzɪə(r),
ˌparəsˈθiːʒə(r)
AM ˌpɛrəsˈθiʒ(i)ə,
ˌpɛrəsˈθizɪə

paresthetic
BR ˌparəsˈθɛtɪk
AM ˌpɛrəsˈθɛdɪk

paretic
BR pəˈrɛtɪk
AM pəˈrɛdɪk

par excellence
BR ˌpɑːr ˌɛksəˈlɑːns,
+ ˈɛksəlɑːns, ˌɛksəˈlɒ̃s,
ˈɛksəlɒ̃s
AM ˌpɑr ˌɛksəˈlɑns

parfait
BR ˈpɑːfeɪ, -z
AM pɑrˈfeɪ, -z

Parfitt
BR ˈpɑːfɪt
AM ˈpɑrfɪt

parfleche
BR ˈpɑːflɛʃ
AM ˈpɑrˌflɛʃ

parfumerie
BR pɑːˈfjuːmər|i, -ɪz
AM pɑrˌfjuməˈri, -z

parget
BR ˈpɑːdʒ|ɪt, -ɪts, -ɪtɪŋ,
-ɪtɪd
AM ˈpɑrdʒət, -s, -ɪŋ, -əd

Pargiter
BR ˈpɑːdʒɪtə(r)
AM ˈpɑrdʒɪdər

parhelia
BR pɑːˈhiːlɪə(r)
AM pɑrˈhiljə, pɑrˈhiliə

parheliacal
BR ˌpɑːhɪˈlʌɪəkl,
ˌpɑːhɛˈlʌɪəkl
AM ˌpɑrhəˈlaɪəkəl,
ˌpɑrhiˈlaɪəkəl

parhelic
BR ˌpɑːˈhiːlɪk
AM ˌpɑrˈhɛlɪk,
ˈpɑrˈhilɪk

parhelical
BR ˌpɑːˈhiːlɪkl
AM ˈpɑrˈhɛləkəl,
ˈpɑrˈhilɪkəl

parhelion
BR pɑːˈhiːlɪən
AM pɑrˈhiliən,
pɑrˈhiliˌən

pariah
BR pəˈrʌɪə(r), -z
AM pəˈraɪə, -z

Parian
BR ˈpɛːrɪən, -z
AM ˈpɛriən, -z

parietal
BR pəˈrʌɪtl
AM pəˈraɪədəl

pari-mutuel
BR ˌparɪˈmjuːtʃʊəl,
ˌparɪˈmjuːtʃ(ʊ)l,
ˌparɪˈmjuːtjuəl,
ˌparɪˈmjuːtjəl
AM ˌpɛrəˈmjutʃə(wə)l

paring
BR ˈpɛːrɪŋ, -z
AM ˈpɛrɪŋ, -z

pari passu
BR ˌparɪ ˈpɑːsuː,
ˌpɑrɪ +
AM ˌpɑrɪ ˈpɑˌsu,
ˌpɑrə +

Paris
BR ˈparɪs
AM ˈpɛrəs

parish
BR ˈparɪʃ, -ɪʃɪz
AM ˈpɛrɪʃ, -ɪz

parishioner
BR pəˈrɪʃ(ə)nə(r),
pəˈrɪʃnə(r), -z
AM pəˈrɪʃ(ə)nər, -z

Parisian
BR pəˈrɪzɪən, -z
AM pəˈriʒən, -z

parison
BR ˈparɪsən, -z
AM ˈpɛrəsən, -z

parisyllabic
BR ˌparɪsɪˈlabɪk
AM ˌpɛrəsəˈlæbɪk

parity
BR ˈparɪti
AM ˈpɛrədi

park
BR pɑːk, -s, -ɪŋ, -t
AM pɑrk, -s, -ɪŋ, -t

parka
BR ˈpɑːkə(r), -z
AM ˈpɑrkə, -z

park and ride
BR ˌpɑːk (ə)n(d) ˈrʌɪd,
-z
AM ˈpɑrk ən ˌraɪd, -z

Parke
BR pɑːk
AM pɑrk

parker
BR ˈpɑːkə(r), -z
AM ˈpɑrkər, -z

Parkes
BR pɑːks
AM pɑrks

Parkeston
BR 'pɑːkst(ə)n
AM 'pɑrkstən
Parkhouse
BR 'pɑːkhaʊs
AM 'pɑrk,(h)aʊs
parkin
BR 'pɑːkɪn
AM 'pɑrkɪn
Parkinson
BR 'pɑːkɪns(ə)n
AM 'pɑrkənsən
Parkinsonism
BR 'pɑːkɪnsənɪz(ə)m,
'pɑːkɪnsn̩ɪz(ə)m
AM 'pɑrkənsə,nɪzəm
parkland
BR 'pɑːklənd,
'pɑːkland, -z
AM 'pɑrk,lænd, -z
Parks
BR pɑːks
AM pɑrks
Parkstone
BR 'pɑːkst(ə)n
AM 'pɑrk,stoʊn
parkway
BR 'pɑːkweɪ, -z
AM 'pɑrk,weɪ, -z
parky
BR 'pɑːk|i, -ɪə(r), -ɪɪst
AM 'pɑrki, -ər, -ɪst
parlance
BR 'pɑːləns, 'pɑːln̩s
AM 'pɑrləns
parlay
BR 'pɑːleɪ, -z, -ɪŋ, -d
AM 'pɑr,leɪ, -z, -ɪŋ, -d
parley
BR 'pɑːl|i, -ɪz, -ɪɪŋ, -ɪd
AM 'pɑrli, -z, -ɪŋ, -d
parliament
BR 'pɑːlɪm(ə)nt, -s
AM 'pɑrləmənt, -s
parliamentarian
BR ,pɑːləmen'tɛːrɪən,
,pɑːləm(ə)n'tɛːrɪən, -z
AM ,pɑrlə,men'terɪən,
,pɑrləmən'terɪən, -z
parliamentary
BR ,pɑːlə'ment(ə)ri
AM ,pɑrlə'ment(ə)ri,
,pɑrlə'menəri
Parlophone
BR 'pɑːləfəʊn
AM 'pɑrlə,fon
parlor
BR 'pɑːlə(r), -z
AM 'pɑrlər, -z
parlormaid
BR 'pɑːləmeɪd, -z
AM 'pɑrlər,meɪd, -z
parlour
BR 'pɑːlə(r), -z
AM 'pɑrlər, -z
parlourmaid
BR 'pɑːləmeɪd, -z

AM 'pɑrlər,meɪd, -z
parlous
BR 'pɑːləs
AM 'pɑrləs
parlously
BR 'pɑːləsli
AM 'pɑrləsli
parlousness
BR 'pɑːləsnəs
AM 'pɑrləsnəs
Parma
BR 'pɑːmə(r)
AM 'pɑrmə
Parmenides
BR pɑːˈmenɪdiːz
AM pɑrˈmenə,diz
Parmenter
BR 'pɑːmɪntə(r)
AM 'pɑrmən(t)ər
Parmentier
BR pɑːˈmentɪə(r),
pɑːˈmɒntɪeɪ
AM 'pɑrmən(t)ər,
,pɑrmən(t)i'eɪ
parmesan
BR ,pɑːmɪˈzan
AM ,pɑrmə,zɑn
Parmigianino
BR ,pɑːmɪdʒəˈniːnəʊ
AM ,pɑrmədʒəˈni,noʊ
Parmigiano
BR ,pɑːmɪˈdʒɑːnəʊ
AM ,pɑrmə'dʒɑnoʊ,
,pɑrmi'dʒɑ,noʊ
Parmiter
BR 'pɑːmɪtə(r)
AM 'pɑrmədər
Parnassian
BR pɑːˈnasɪən, -z
AM pɑrˈnæsɪən,
pɑrˈnæsjən, -z
Parnassus
BR pɑːˈnasəs
AM pɑrˈnæsəs
Parnell
BR pɑːˈnel
AM pɑrˈnel
Parnes
BR pɑːnz
AM pɑrnz
parochial
BR pəˈrəʊkɪəl
AM pəˈroʊkɪəl,
pəˈroʊkjəl
parochialism
BR pəˈrəʊkɪəlɪz(ə)m
AM pəˈroʊkɪə,lɪzəm,
pəˈroʊkjə,lɪzəm
parochiality
BR pə,rəʊkɪˈalɪti
AM pə,roʊki'ælədi
parochially
BR pəˈrəʊkɪəli
AM pəˈroʊkɪəli,
pəˈroʊkjəli
parodic
BR pəˈrɒdɪk

AM pəˈrɑdɪk
parodist
BR 'parədɪst, -s
AM 'perədəst, -s
parody
BR 'parəd|i, -ɪz
AM 'perədi, -z
paroecious
BR pəˈriːʃəs
AM pəˈriʃəs
parol
BR pəˈrəʊl, 'parəl,
'parl̩, -z
AM pəˈroʊl, 'perəl, -z
parole
BR pəˈrəʊl, -z, -ɪŋ, -d
AM pəˈroʊl, -z, -ɪŋ, -d
parolee
BR pəˈrəʊˈliː, -z
AM pə,roʊ'li, -z
paronomasia
BR ,parənə(ʊ)ˈmeɪzɪə(r),
,parn̩ə(ʊ)ˈmeɪzɪə(r)
AM ,perənoʊˈmeɪʒ(i)ə,
,perənoʊˈmeɪzɪə
paronym
BR 'parənɪm, -z
AM 'perə,nɪm, -z
paronymous
BR pəˈrɒnɪməs
AM pəˈrɑnəməs
parotid
BR pəˈrɒtɪd, -z
AM pəˈrɑdəd, -z
parotitis
BR ,parəˈtaɪtɪs
AM ,perəˈtaɪdəs
paroxysm
BR 'parəksɪz(ə)m, -z
AM 'perək,sɪzəm,
pəˈrak,sɪzəm, -z
paroxysmal
BR ,parəkˈsɪzm(ə)l
AM ,perəkˈsɪzməl,
pəˈrak,sɪzməl
paroxytone
BR pəˈrɒksɪtəʊn,
pa'rɒksɪtəʊn, -z
AM per'aksə,toʊn, -z
parozone
BR 'parəzəʊn
AM 'perə,zoʊn
parpen
BR 'pɑːp(ə)n, -z
AM 'pɑrpən, -z
parquet
BR 'pɑːkeɪ, -z
AM pɑr'keɪ, -z
parquetry
BR 'pɑːkɪtri
AM 'pɑrkətri
parr
BR pɑː(r)
AM pɑr
Parramatta
BR ,parəˈmatə(r)
AM ,perəˈmædə

parricidal
BR ,parɪˈsaɪdl
AM ,perəˈsaɪdəl
parricide
BR 'parɪsʌɪd, -z
AM 'perə,saɪd, -z
Parrish
BR 'parɪʃ
AM 'perɪʃ
parrot
BR 'parət, -s
AM 'perət, -s
parrotfish
BR 'parətfɪʃ, -ɪz
AM 'perət,fɪʃ, -ɪz
Parrott
BR 'parət
AM 'perət
parry
BR 'par|i, -ɪz, -ɪɪŋ, -ɪd
AM 'peri, -z, -ɪŋ, -d
parse
BR pɑːz, -ɪz, -ɪŋ, -d
AM pɑrs, -əz, -ɪŋ, -d
parsec
BR 'pɑːsek, -s
AM 'pɑr,sek, -s
Parsee
BR ,pɑːˈsiː, 'pɑːsiː, -z
AM ,pɑr'si, 'pɑrsi, -z
Parseeism
BR ,pɑːˈsiːɪz(ə)m,
'pɑːsiːɪz(ə)m
AM ,pɑr'si,ɪzəm,
'pɑrsi,ɪzəm
parser
BR 'pɑːzə(r), -z
AM 'pɑrsər, -z
Parsifal
BR 'pɑːsɪf(ə)l
AM 'pɑrsəfəl,
'pɑr(t)sə,fɑl
parsimonious
BR ,pɑːsɪˈməʊnɪəs
AM ,pɑrsəˈmoʊnɪəs,
'pɑrsəˈmoʊnjəs
parsimoniously
BR ,pɑːsɪˈməʊnɪəsli
AM ,pɑrsəˈmoʊnɪəsli,
'pɑrsəˈmoʊnjəsli
parsimoniousness
BR ,pɑːsɪˈməʊnɪəsnəs
AM ,pɑrsəˈmoʊnɪəsnəs,
'pɑrsəˈmoʊnjəsnəs
parsimony
BR 'pɑːsɪməni
AM 'pɑrsə,moʊni
Parsley
surname
BR 'pɑːzli
AM 'pɑrzli
parsley
BR 'pɑːsli
AM 'pɑrsli
parsley-piert
BR ,pɑːslɪ'pɪət, -s
AM 'pɑrsli,pɪ(ə)rt, -s

parsnip
BR 'pɑːsnɪp, -s
AM 'pɑrsnəp, -s

parson
BR 'pɑːsn, -z
AM 'pɑrsən, -z

parsonage
BR 'pɑːsn̩|ɪdʒ, -ɪdʒɪz
AM 'pɑrsn̩ɪdʒ, -ɪz

parsonical
BR pɑː'sɒnɪkl
AM pɑr'sɑnəkəl

Parsons
BR 'pɑːsnz
AM 'pɑrsənz

part
BR pɑːt, -s, -ɪŋ, -ɪd
AM pɑr|t, -ts, -dɪŋ, -dəd

partakable
BR pɑː'teɪkəbl
AM pɑr'teɪkəbəl

partake
BR pɑː'teɪk, -s, -ɪŋ
AM pɑr'teɪk, -s, -ɪŋ

partaken
BR pɑː'teɪk(ə)n
AM pɑr'teɪkən

partaker
BR pɑː'teɪkə(r), -z
AM pɑr'teɪkər, -z

partan
BR 'pɑːt(ə)n, -z
AM 'pɑrdn, -z

parterre
BR pɑː'tɛː(r), -z
AM pɑr'tɛ(ə)r, -z

part-exchange
BR ,pɑːtɪks'tʃeɪn(d)ʒ,
,pɑːtɛks'tʃeɪn(d)ʒ, -ɪz,
-ɪŋ, -d
AM 'pɑrdɪks'tʃeɪndʒ,
'pɑrdɛks'tʃeɪndʒ, -ɪz,
-ɪŋ, -d

parthenogenesis
BR ,pɑːθɪnə(ʊ)'dʒɛnɪsɪs
AM 'pɑrθənoʊ'dʒɛnəsəs

parthenogenetic
BR ,pɑːθɪnə(ʊ)dʒɪˈnɛtɪk,
,pɑːθn̩ə(ʊ)dʒɪˈnɛtɪk
AM 'pɑrθənoʊdʒə'nɛdɪk

parthenogenetically
BR ,pɑːθɪnə(ʊ)dʒɪ'nɛt-
ɪkli
AM 'pɑrθənoʊdʒə'nɛd-
ək(ə)li

Parthenon
BR 'pɑːθɪnən, 'pɑːθn̩ən,
'pɑːθɪnɒn, 'pɑːθn̩ɒn
AM 'pɑrθə,nɑn

Parthia
BR 'pɑːθɪə(r)
AM 'pɑrθiə

Parthian
BR 'pɑːθɪən, -z
AM 'pɑrθiən, -z

parti
BR 'pɑːt|i, -ɪz

partial
BR 'pɑːʃl
AM 'pɑrʃəl

partiality
BR ,pɑːʃɪ'alɪti
AM ,pɑrʃi'ælədi

partially
BR 'pɑːʃli, 'pɑːʃəli
AM 'pɑrʃəli

partialness
BR 'pɑːʃlnəs
AM 'pɑrʃəlnəs

partible
BR 'pɑːtɪbl
AM 'pɑrdəbəl

participant
BR pɑː'tɪsɪp(ə)nt, -s
AM pɑr'tɪsɪpənt, -s

participate
BR pɑː'tɪsɪpeɪt, -s, -ɪŋ,
-ɪd
AM pɑr'tɪsɪ,peɪ|t, -ts,
-dɪŋ, -dɪd

participation
BR pɑː,tɪsɪ'peɪʃn,
,pɑːtɪsɪ'peɪʃn
AM pɑr,tɪsɪ'peɪʃən

participative
BR pɑː'tɪsɪpətɪv
AM pɑr'tɪsɪ,peɪdɪv,
pɑr'tɪsɪpədɪv

participator
BR pɑː'tɪsɪpeɪtə(r), -z
AM pɑr'tɪsɪ,peɪdər, -z

participatory
BR pɑː'tɪsɪ'peɪt(ə)ri,
,pɑːtɪsɪ'peɪt(ə)ri,
pɑː'tɪsɪpət(ə)ri
AM pɑr'tɪsəpə,tɔri

participial
BR ,pɑːtɪ'sɪpɪəl
AM 'pɑrdə'sɪpiəl

participially
BR ,pɑːtɪ'sɪpɪəli
AM 'pɑrdə'sɪpiəli

participle
BR 'pɑːtɪsɪpl,
pɑː'tɪsɪpl, pə'tɪsɪpl, -z
AM 'pɑrdə,sɪpəl, -z

Partick
BR 'pɑːtɪk
AM 'pɑrdək

particle
BR 'pɑːtɪkl, -z
AM 'pɑrdəkəl, -z

particolored
BR ,pɑːtɪ'kʌləd
AM 'pɑrdi,kələrd

particoloured
BR ,pɑːtɪ'kʌləd
AM 'pɑrdi,kələrd

particular
BR pə'tɪkjələ(r), -z
AM pə(r)'tɪkjələr,
pɑr'tɪkjələr, -z

particularisation
BR pə,tɪkjələrʌɪ'zeɪʃn
AM pə(r),tɪkjələrə'zeɪ-
ʃən,
pə(r),tɪkjələ,rʌɪ'zeɪʃən

particularise
BR pə'tɪkjələrʌɪz, -ɪz,
-ɪŋ, -d
AM pə(r)'tɪkjələ,rʌɪz,
pɑr'tɪkjələ,rʌɪz, -ɪz,
-ɪŋ, -d

particularism
BR pə'tɪkjələrɪz(ə)m
AM pə(r)'tɪkjələ,rɪzəm

particularist
BR pə'tɪkjələrɪst, -s
AM pə(r)'tɪkjələrəst, -s

particularity
BR pə,tɪkjə'larɪti
AM pə(r),tɪkjə'lɛrədi,
pɑr,tɪkjə'lɛrədi

particularization
BR pə,tɪkjələrʌɪ'zeɪʃn
AM pə(r),tɪkjələrə'zeɪ-
ʃən,
pə(r),tɪkjələ,rʌɪ'zeɪʃən

particularize
BR pə'tɪkjələrʌɪz, -ɪz,
-ɪŋ, -d
AM pə(r)'tɪkjələ,rʌɪz,
pɑr'tɪkjələ,rʌɪz, -ɪz,
-ɪŋ, -d

particularly
BR pə'tɪkjələli
AM pə(r)'tɪkjələrli,
pɑr'tɪkjələrli

particulate
BR pɑː'tɪkjələɪt,
pɑː'tɪkjələt,
pə'tɪkjələɪt,
pə'tɪkjələt, -s
AM pə(r)'tɪkjələt,
pə(r)'tɪkjə,leɪt,
pɑr'tɪkjələt,
pɑr'tɪkjə,leɪt, -s

parting
BR 'pɑːtɪŋ, -z
AM 'pɑrdɪŋ, -z

Partington
BR 'pɑːtɪŋt(ə)n
AM 'pɑrdɪŋtən

parti pris
BR ,pɑːtɪ 'priː, -z
AM ,pɑrdi 'pri, -z

partisan
BR ,pɑːtɪ'zan,
'pɑːtɪz(ə)n, -z
AM 'pɑrdəzn,
'pɑrdə,zæn, -z

partisanship
BR ,pɑːtɪ'zanʃɪp,
'pɑːtɪz(ə)nʃɪp
AM 'pɑrdəzən,ʃɪp

partita
BR pɑː'tiːtə(r)
AM pɑr'tidə

partite
BR 'pɑːtʌɪt

partition
BR pɑː'tɪʃn, pə'tɪʃn, -z
AM pɑr'tɪʃən, -z

partitioner
BR pɑː'tɪʃnə(r),
pə'tɪʃnə(r), -z
AM pɑr'tɪʃənər, -z

partitionist
BR pɑː'tɪʃnɪst,
pə'tɪʃnɪst, -s
AM pɑr'tɪʃənəst, -s

partitive
BR 'pɑːtɪtɪv
AM 'pɑrdədɪv

partitively
BR 'pɑːtɪtɪvli
AM 'pɑrdədɪvli

partizan
BR ,pɑːtɪ'zan,
'pɑːtɪz(ə)n, -z
AM 'pɑrdəzən,
'pɑrdə,zæn, -z

partly
BR 'pɑːtli
AM 'pɑrtli

partner
BR 'pɑːtnə(r), -z
AM 'pɑrtnər, -z

partnerless
BR 'pɑːtnələs
AM 'pɑrtnərləs

partnership
BR 'pɑːtnəʃɪp, -s
AM 'pɑrtnər,ʃɪp, -s

Parton
BR 'pɑːtn
AM 'pɑrtn

partook
BR pɑː'tʊk
AM pɑr'tʊk

partridge
BR 'pɑːtr|ɪdʒ, -ɪdʒɪz
AM 'pɑrtrɪdʒ, -ɪz

part-singing
BR 'pɑːt,sɪŋɪŋ
AM 'pɑrt,sɪŋɪŋ

part-song
BR 'pɑːtsɒŋ, -z
AM 'pɑrt,sɔŋ,
'pɑrt,sɑŋ, -z

part-time
BR ,pɑːt'tʌɪm
AM 'pɑr(t),tʌɪm

part-timer
BR ,pɑːt'tʌɪmə(r), -z
AM 'pɑr(t),tʌɪmər, -z

parturient
BR pɑː'tjʊərɪənt
AM pɑr't(j)ʊriənt

parturition
BR ,pɑːtjə'rɪʃn,
,pɑːtʃə'rɪʃn
AM ,pɑrdə'rɪʃən,
,pɑr,tʊ'rɪʃən,
,pɑrtʃə'rɪʃən,
,pɑrtjə'rɪʃən

part-way
BR ˈpɑːtˈweɪ
AM ˈpɑrtˈweɪ

part-work
BR ˈpɑːtwɜːk
AM ˈpɑrtˌwɜrk

party
BR ˈpɑːt|i, -ɪz
AM ˈpɑrdi, -z

party line[1]
in politics
BR ˈpɑːtɪ ˈlaɪn, -z
AM ˈpɑrdi ˈlaɪn, -z

party line[2]
telephone
BR ˈpɑːtɪ laɪn, -z
AM ˈpɑrdi ˌlaɪn, -z

party-pooper
BR ˈpɑːtɪˌpuːpə(r), -z
AM ˈpɑrdiˌpupər, -z

parvenu
BR ˈpɑːvən(j)uː, -z
AM ˈpɑrvəˈn(j)u, -z

parvenue
BR ˈpɑːvən(j)uː, -z
AM ˈpɑrvəˈn(j)u, -z

parvis
BR ˈpɑːvɪs, -ɪz
AM ˈpɑrvəs, -əz

parvise
BR ˈpɑːvɪs, -ɪz
AM ˈpɑrvəs, -əz

parvovirus
BR ˈpɑːvəʊˌvaɪrəs, -ɪz
AM ˈpɑrvəˌvaɪrəs, -əz

pas
BR pɑː(r)
AM pɑ

Pasadena
BR ˌpæsəˈdiːnə(r)
AM ˌpæsəˈdinə

Pascal
BR pɑˈskɑːl, ˈpæskɑːl,
pɑˈskal, ˈpaskal
AM pəˈskæl, pæsˈkæl

pascal
BR pɑˈskɑːl, ˈpæskɑːl,
pɑˈskal, ˈpaskal, -z
AM pəˈskæl, pæsˈkæl,
-z

Pascale
BR pɑˈskɑːl
AM pæˈskæl

paschal
BR ˈpask(ə)l
AM ˈpæskəl, ˈpæʃəl

Pasco
BR ˈpaskəʊ
AM ˈpæskoʊ

Pascoe
BR ˈpaskəʊ
AM ˈpæskoʊ

pas de chat
BR ˌpɑː də ˈʃɑː(r)
AM ˌpɑ də ˈʃɑ

pas de deux
BR ˌpɑː də ˈdɜː(r), -z

AM ˌpɑdəˈdə, -z

paseo
BR pəˈseɪəʊ, -z
AM pəˈseɪoʊ, -z

pas glissé
BR ˌpɑː gliˈseɪ
AM ˌpɑ gliˈseɪ

pash
BR paʃ, -ɪz
AM pæʃ, -əz

pasha
BR ˈpɑʃə(r), -z
AM ˈpɑʃə, ˈpæʃə, -z

pashalic
BR ˈpɑːʃəlɪk, pəˈʃɑːlɪk,
-s
AM pəˈʃælɪk, -s

pashm
BR ˈpɑʃ(ə)m
AM ˈpæʃəm

Pashto
BR ˈpʌʃtəʊ, ˈpaʃtəʊ
AM ˈpæʃˌtoʊ

Pasiphaë
BR pəˈsɪfiː, pəˈsɪfeɪiː
AM pəˈsɪfəˌi

Pasmore
BR ˈpɑːsmɔː(r),
ˈpasmɔː(r)
AM ˈpæsˌmɔ(ə)r

paso doble
BR ˌpasə ˈdəʊbleɪ, -z
AM ˌpæsoʊ ˈdoʊbleɪ, -z

paspalum
BR ˈpaspələm
AM ˈpæspələm

pasque flower
BR ˈpask ˌflaʊə(r), -z
AM ˈpæsk ˌflaʊər, -z

pasquinade
BR ˌpaskwɪˈneɪd, -z
AM ˌpæskwəˈneɪd, -z

pass
BR pɑːs, pas, -ɪz, -ɪŋ, -t
AM pæs, -əz, -ɪŋ, -t

passable
BR ˈpɑːsəbl, ˈpasəbl
AM ˈpæsəbəl

passableness
BR ˈpɑːsəblnəs,
ˈpasəblnəs
AM ˈpæsəbəlnəs

passably
BR ˈpɑːsəbli, ˈpasəbli
AM ˈpæsəbli

passacaglia
BR ˌpasəˈkɑːlɪə(r), -z
AM ˌpɑsəˈkɑljə,
ˌpɑsəˈkɑliə, -z

passade
BR pəˈseɪd, pɑˈseɪd
AM pəˈseɪd

passage
BR ˈpas|ɪdʒ, -ɪdʒɪz
AM ˈpæsɪdʒ, -ɪz

passageway
BR ˈpasɪdʒweɪ, -z

Passamaquoddy
BR ˌpasəməˈkwɒdi
AM ˌpæsəməˈkwɑdi

passant[1]
chess
BR ˈpasɒt
AM pəˈsɑnt

passant[2]
heraldry
BR ˈpas(ə)nt
AM ˈpæsnt

Passat®
BR pɑˈsat
AM pəˈsat

passata
BR pəˈsɑːtə(r)
AM pəˈsɑdə

passband
BR ˈpɑːsband,
ˈpasband, -z
AM ˈpæsˌbænd, -z

passbook
BR ˈpɑːsbʊk, ˈpasbʊk,
-s
AM ˈpæsˌbʊk, -s

Passchendaele
BR ˈpaʃndeɪl
AM ˈpæʃənˌdeɪl
FL ˈpɑsxəndɑːlə

passé
BR ˈpɑːseɪ, ˈpaseɪ,
pɑˈseɪ
AM pæˈseɪ

passée
BR ˈpɑːseɪ, ˈpaseɪ,
pɑˈseɪ
AM pæˈseɪ

passel
BR ˈpasl, -z
AM ˈpæsəl, -z

passementerie
BR ˈpasm(ə)ntri
AM ˌpɑsəˌmənˈtri

passenger
BR ˈpas(ɪ)n(d)ʒə(r), -z
AM ˈpæsndʒər, -z

passe-partout
BR ˈpas pɑːtuː, ˈpas
pətuː, ˌpas pɑːˈtuː,
ˌpas pəˈtuː, -z
AM ˌpæs pərˈtu, ˌpɑs
pɑrˈtu, -z

passer
BR ˈpɑːsə(r), ˈpasə(r),
-z
AM ˈpæsər, -z

passer-by
BR ˌpɑːsəˈbʌɪ,
ˌpasəˈbʌɪ
AM ˈpæsərˈbaɪ

passerine
BR ˈpasərʌɪn
AM ˈpæsərən,
ˈpæsəˌraɪn, ˈpæsəˌrin

passers-by
BR ˌpɑːsəzˈbʌɪ,
ˌpasəzˈbʌɪ

AM ˌpæsərzˈbaɪ

pas seul
BR ˌpɑː ˈsəːl, -z
AM ˌpɑ ˈsəl, -z

passibility
BR ˌpasɪˈbɪlɪti
AM ˌpæsəˈbɪlɪdi

passible
BR ˈpasɪbl
AM ˈpæsəbəl

passim
BR ˈpasɪm
AM ˈpæsəm, ˈpæsˌɪm

passing
BR ˈpɑːsɪŋ, ˈpasɪŋ, -z
AM ˈpæsɪŋ, -z

passingly
BR ˈpɑːsɪŋli, ˈpasɪŋli
AM ˈpæsɪŋli

passing-out
BR ˌpɑːsɪŋˈaʊt,
ˌpasɪŋˈaʊt
AM ˌpæsɪŋˈaʊt

passion
BR ˈpaʃn, -z
AM ˈpæʃən, -z

passional
BR ˈpaʃn(ə)l,
ˈpaʃ(ə)n(ə)l, -z
AM ˈpæʃ(ə)nəl, -z

passionate
BR ˈpaʃnət, ˈpaʃənət
AM ˈpæʃ(ə)nət

passionately
BR ˈpaʃnətli,
ˈpaʃənətli
AM ˈpæʃ(ə)nətli

passionateness
BR ˈpaʃnətnəs,
ˈpaʃənətnəs
AM ˈpæʃ(ə)nətnəs

passionflower
BR ˈpaʃnˌflaʊə(r), -z
AM ˈpæʃənˌflaʊ(ə)r, -z

passionfruit
BR ˈpaʃnfruːt, -s
AM ˈpæʃənˌfrut, -s

Passionist
BR ˈpaʃnɪst, ˈpaʃənɪst,
-s
AM ˈpæʃənəst, -s

passionless
BR ˈpaʃnləs
AM ˈpæʃənləs

Passiontide
BR ˈpaʃnˌtaɪd
AM ˈpæʃənˌtaɪd

passivate
BR ˈpasɪveɪt, -s, -ɪŋ, -ɪd
AM ˈpæsəˌveɪ|t, -ts,
-dɪŋ, -dɪd

passivation
BR ˌpasɪˈveɪʃn
AM ˌpæsəˈveɪʃən

passive
BR ˈpasɪv
AM ˈpæsɪv

passively
BR ˈpasɪvli
AM ˈpæsɪvli

passiveness
BR ˈpasɪvnɪs
AM ˈpæsɪvnɪs

passivity
BR pəˈsɪvɪti
AM pæˈsɪvɪdi,
pəˈsɪvɪdi

passkey
BR ˈpɑːskiː, ˈpaskiː, -z
AM ˈpæsˌkiː, -z

Passover
BR ˈpɑːsˌəʊvə(r),
ˈpasˌəʊvə(r)
AM ˈpæsˌoʊvər

passport
BR ˈpɑːspɔːt, ˈpaspɔːt,
-s
AM ˈpæsˌpɔ(ə)rt, -s

password
BR ˈpɑːswəːd,
ˈpaswəːd, -z
AM ˈpæsˌwərd, -z

past
BR pɑːst, past
AM pæst

pasta
BR ˈpastə(r)
AM ˈpɑstə

paste
BR peɪst, -s, -ɪŋ, -ɪd
AM peɪst, -s, -ɪŋ, -ɪd

pasteboard
BR ˈpeɪs(t)bɔːd
AM ˈpeɪs(t)ˌbɔ(ə)rd

pastedown
BR ˈpeɪs(t)daʊn
AM ˈpeɪs(t)ˌdaʊn

pastel
BR ˈpastl
AM pæˈstɛl

pastelist
BR ˈpastəlɪst, ˈpastlɪst,
-s
AM pæˈstɛləst, -s

pastellist
BR ˈpastəlɪst, ˈpastlɪst,
-s
AM pæˈstɛləst, -s

pastern
BR ˈpastn, ˈpastəːn, -z
AM ˈpæstərn, -z

Pasternak
BR ˈpastənak
AM ˈpæstərˌnæk

Pasteur
BR paˈstəː(r)
AM pæsˈtər

pasteurisation
BR ˌpɑːst(ʃ)ərʌɪˈzeɪʃn,
ˌpast(ʃ)ərʌɪˈzeɪʃn,
ˌpɑːstjərʌɪˈzeɪʃn,
ˌpastjərʌɪˈzeɪʃn
AM ˈpæstʃərəˈzeɪʃən,
ˈpæstərəˈzeɪʃən,

ˌpæstʃəˌraɪˈzeɪʃən,
ˌpæstəˌraɪˈzeɪʃən

pasteurise
BR ˈpɑːst(ʃ)ərʌɪz,
ˈpast(ʃ)ərʌɪz,
ˈpɑːstjərʌɪz,
ˈpastjərʌɪz, -ɪz, -ɪŋ, -d
AM ˈpæstʃəˌraɪz,
ˈpæʃtʃəˌraɪz,
ˈpæstəˌraɪz, -ɪz, -ɪŋ, -d

pasteuriser
BR ˈpɑːst(ʃ)ərʌɪzə(r),
ˈpast(ʃ)ərʌɪzə(r),
ˈpɑːstjərʌɪzə(r),
ˈpastjərʌɪzə(r), -z
AM ˈpæstʃəˌraɪzər,
ˈpæʃtʃəˌraɪzər,
ˈpæstəˌraɪzər, -z

pasteurization
BR ˌpɑːst(ʃ)ərʌɪˈzeɪʃn,
ˌpast(ʃ)ərʌɪˈzeɪʃn,
ˌpɑːstjərʌɪˈzeɪʃn,
ˌpastjərʌɪˈzeɪʃn
AM ˈpæstʃərəˈzeɪʃən,
ˈpæstərəˈzeɪʃən,
ˌpæstʃəˌraɪˈzeɪʃən,
ˌpæstəˌraɪˈzeɪʃən

pasteurize
BR ˈpɑːst(ʃ)ərʌɪz,
ˈpast(ʃ)ərʌɪz,
ˈpɑːstjərʌɪz,
ˈpastjərʌɪz, -ɪz, -ɪŋ, -d
AM ˈpæstʃəˌraɪz,
ˈpæʃtʃəˌraɪz,
ˈpæstəˌraɪz, -ɪz, -ɪŋ, -d

pasteurizer
BR ˈpɑːst(ʃ)ərʌɪzə(r),
ˈpast(ʃ)ərʌɪzə(r),
ˈpɑːstjərʌɪzə(r),
ˈpastjərʌɪzə(r), -z
AM ˈpæstʃəˌraɪzər,
ˈpæʃtʃəˌraɪzər,
ˈpæstəˌraɪzər, -z

pasticcio
BR paˈstiːtʃəʊ, -z
AM pæˈstiː(t)ʃ(i)oʊ, -z

pastiche
BR paˈstiːʃ, -ɪz
AM pæˈstiːʃ, pɑˈstiːʃ, -ɪz

pastie
BR ˈpeɪsti, -ɪz
AM ˈpeɪsti, -ɪz

pastil
BR ˈpast(ɪ)l, -z
AM ˈpæstəl, -z

pastile
BR ˈpast(ɪ)l, -z
AM ˈpæstəl, -z

pastille
BR ˈpast(ɪ)l, -z
AM pæˈstil, -z

pastily
BR ˈpeɪstɪli
AM ˈpeɪstɪli

pastime
BR ˈpɑːstaɪm,
ˈpastaɪm, -z
AM ˈpæsˌtaɪm, -z

pastiness
BR ˈpeɪstɪnɪs
AM ˈpeɪstɪnɪs

pasting
BR ˈpeɪstɪŋ, -z
AM ˈpeɪstɪŋ, -z

pastis
BR ˈpastɪs, paˈstiːs
AM pɑˈstis

pastmaster
BR ˈpɑːs(t)ˌmɑːstə(r),
ˈpas(t)ˌmastə(r), -z
AM ˈpæstˌmæstər, -z

Paston[1]
BR ˈpast(ə)n
AM ˈpæstən

Paston[2]
BR ˈpast(ə)n
AM ˈpæstən

pastor
BR ˈpɑːstə(r),
ˈpastə(r), -z
AM ˈpæstər, -z

pastoral
BR ˈpɑːst(ə)rəl,
ˈpɑːst(ə)rl,
ˈpast(ə)rəl, ˈpast(ə)rl̩,
-z
AM ˈpæstərəl,
pæsˈtɔrəl, -z

pastorale
BR ˌpastəˈrɑːl,
ˌpastəˈrɑːˌli, -lz\-lɪz
AM ˌpæstəˈrɑl,
ˌpæstəˈræl, -z

pastoralism
BR ˈpɑːst(ə)rəlɪz(ə)m,
ˈpast(ə)rəlɪz(ə)m
AM ˈpæst(ə)rəˌlɪzəm

pastoralist
BR ˈpɑːst(ə)rəlɪst,
ˈpast(ə)rəlɪst, -s
AM ˈpæst(ə)rələst, -s

pastorality
BR ˌpastəˈralɪti
AM ˌpæstəˈrælədi

pastorally
BR ˈpɑːst(ə)rəli,
ˈpɑːst(ə)rl̩i,
ˈpast(ə)rəli,
ˈpast(ə)rl̩i
AM ˈpæstərəli,
pæsˈtɔrəli

pastorate
BR ˈpɑːst(ə)rət,
ˈpast(ə)rət, -s
AM ˈpæst(ə)rət, -s

pastorship
BR ˈpɑːstəˌʃɪp,
ˈpastəˌʃɪp, -s
AM ˈpæstərˌʃɪp, -s

pastrami
BR pəˈstrɑːmi
AM pəˈstrɑmi

pastry
BR ˈpeɪstr|i, -ɪz
AM ˈpeɪstri, -z

pastrycook
BR ˈpeɪstrɪkʊk, -s
AM ˈpeɪstriˌkʊk, -s

pasturage
BR ˈpɑːst(ʃ)(ə)rɪdʒ,
ˈpast(ʃ)(ə)rɪdʒ,
ˈpɑːstjərɪdʒ,
ˈpastjərɪdʒ
AM ˈpæstʃərədʒ,
ˈpæʃtʃərədʒ

pasture
BR ˈpɑːstʃə(r),
ˈpastʃə(r), -z, -ɪŋ, -d
AM ˈpæstʃər, ˈpæʃtʃər,
-z, -ɪŋ, -d

pastureland
BR ˈpɑːstʃəland,
ˈpastʃəland, -z
AM ˈpæstʃərˌlænd,
ˈpæʃtʃərˌlænd, -z

pasty[1]
adjective
BR ˈpeɪst|i, -ɪə(r), -ɪɪst
AM ˈpeɪsti, -ər, -ɪst

pasty[2]
noun
BR ˈpast|i, -ɪz
AM ˈpæsti, -z

pat
BR pat, -s, -ɪŋ, -ɪd
AM pæ|t, -ts, -dɪŋ, -dəd

pat-a-cake
BR ˈpatəkeɪk
AM ˈpædəˌkeɪk

patagia
BR ˌpatəˈdʒʌɪə(r)
AM pəˈteɪdʒiə

patagium
BR ˌpatəˈdʒʌɪəm
AM pəˈteɪdʒiəm

Patagonia
BR ˌpatəˈɡəʊnɪə(r)
AM ˌpædəˈɡoʊniə

Patagonian
BR ˌpatəˈɡəʊnɪən, -z
AM ˌpædəˈɡoʊnɪən, -z

Patavinity
BR ˌpatəˈvɪnɪti
AM ˌpædəˈvɪnɪdi

patball
BR ˈpatbɔːl
AM ˈpætˌbɔl, ˈpætˌbɑl

patch
BR patʃ, -ɪz, -ɪŋ, -t
AM pætʃ, -əz, -ɪŋ, -t

patchboard
BR ˈpatʃbɔːd, -z
AM ˈpætʃˌbɔ(ə)rd, -z

patcher
BR ˈpatʃə(r), -z
AM ˈpætʃər, -z

patchily
BR ˈpatʃɪli
AM ˈpætʃɪli

patchiness
BR ˈpatʃɪnɪs
AM ˈpætʃɪnɪs

patchouli
BR 'pætʃʊli, pəˈtʃuːli
AM pəˈtʃuli

patchwork
BR 'pætʃwɜːk, -s
AM 'pætʃˌwɜrk, -s

patchy
BR 'pætʃli, -ɪə(r), -ɪɪst
AM 'pætʃi, -ər, -ɪɪst

Pate
BR peɪt
AM peɪt

pate
top of head
BR peɪt, -s
AM peɪt, -s

paté
of a cross
BR 'pateɪ, 'pati
AM pəˈteɪ

pâte
BR pɑːt, -s
AM pɑt, -s

pâté
meat spread
BR 'pateɪ, -z
AM pɑˈteɪ, pæˈteɪ, -z

pâté de foie gras
BR ˌpateɪ də ˌfwɑː
'grɑː(r)
AM ˌpateɪ də ˌfwɑ 'grɑ

patée
of a cross
BR 'pateɪ, 'pati
AM pəˈteɪ

Patel
BR pəˈtɛl
AM pəˈtɛl

Pateley
BR 'peɪtli
AM 'peɪtli

patella
BR pəˈtɛlə(r), -z
AM pəˈtɛlə, -z

patellae
BR pəˈtɛliː
AM pəˈtɛˌli, pəˈtɛˌlaɪ

patellar
BR pəˈtɛlə(r)
AM pəˈtɛlər

patellate
BR pəˈtɛlət
AM pəˈtɛlət, pəˈtɛˌleɪt

paten
BR 'patn̩, -z
AM 'pætn̩, -z

patency
BR 'peɪtnsi
AM 'pætnsi, 'peɪtnsi

patent[1]
adjective, open
BR 'peɪtnt
AM 'peɪtnt

patent[2]
inventions, legal etc
BR 'patnt, 'peɪtnt, -s,
-ɪŋ, -ɪd
AM 'pætnt, -s, -ɪŋ, -əd

patent[3]
leather
BR 'peɪtnt
AM 'pætnt

patentable
BR 'patntəbl,
'peɪtntəbl
AM 'pætntəbəl,
'pætn̩əbəl

patentee
BR ˌpatn̩ˈtiː, ˌpeɪtn̩ˈtiː,
-z
AM ˌpætn̩ˈti, -z

patently
BR 'peɪtntli
AM 'pætn̩(t)li,
'peɪtn̩(t)li

patentor
BR 'patntə(r),
'peɪtntə(r), -z
AM 'pætntər, 'pætn̩ər,
-z

Pater
BR 'peɪtə(r)
AM 'peɪdər

pater
BR 'peɪtə(r), -z
AM 'peɪdər, 'pɑdər, -z

paterfamilias
BR ˌpeɪtəfəˈmɪlias,
ˌpatəfəˈmɪlias, -ɪz
AM ˌpædərfəˈmɪliəs,
ˌpɑdərfəˈmɪliəs, -əz

paternal
BR pəˈtɜːnl
AM pəˈtɜrnəl

paternalism
BR pəˈtɜːnəlɪz(ə)m,
pəˈtɜːnˌlɪz(ə)m
AM pəˈtɜrnlˌɪzəm

paternalist
BR pəˈtɜːnəlɪst,
pəˈtɜːnˌlɪst, -s
AM pəˈtɜrnləst, -s

paternalistic
BR pəˌtɜːnəˈlɪstɪk,
pəˌtɜːnlˈɪstɪk
AM pəˌtɜrnlˈɪstɪk

paternalistically
BR pəˌtɜːnəˈlɪstɪkli,
pəˌtɜːnlˈɪstɪkli
AM pəˈtɜrnlˈɪstək(ə)li

paternally
BR pəˈtɜːnəli, pəˈtɜːnˌli
AM pəˈtɜrnəli

paternity
BR pəˈtɜːnɪti
AM pəˈtɜrnədi

paternoster
BR ˌpatəˈnɒstə(r), -z
AM 'pædərˌnɑstər,
'pɑdərˌnɑstər, -z

Paterson
BR 'patəs(ə)n
AM 'pædərsən

path
BR pɑːθ, paθ,
pɑːðz\paðz\paθs

Pathan
BR pəˈtɑːn, -z
AM pəˈtɑn, -z

Pathé
BR 'paθeɪ
AM pɑˈteɪ

pathetic
BR pəˈθɛtɪk
AM pəˈθɛdɪk

pathetically
BR pəˈθɛtɪkli
AM pəˈθɛdək(ə)li

pathfinder
BR 'pɑːθˌfʌɪndə(r),
'paθˌfʌɪndə(r), -z
AM 'pæθˌfaɪndər, -z

pathic
BR 'paθɪk, -s
AM 'pæθɪk, -s

pathless
BR 'pɑːθləs, 'paθləs
AM 'pæθləs

pathogen
BR 'paθədʒen,
'paθədʒ(ə)n
AM 'pæθəˌdʒen,
'pæθədʒən

pathogenesis
BR ˌpaθəˈdʒenɪsɪs
AM ˌpæθəˈdʒenəsəs

pathogenetic
BR ˌpaθədʒɪˈnɛtɪk
AM 'pæθədʒəˈnedɪk

pathogenic
BR ˌpaθəˈdʒenɪk
AM 'pæθəˈdʒenɪk

pathogenous
BR pəˈθɒdʒɪnəs
AM pəˈθɑdʒenəs

pathogeny
BR pəˈθɒdʒɪni
AM 'pəˈθɑdʒəni

pathognomonic
BR ˌpaθəgnəˈmɒnɪk, -s
AM pəˌθɑgnəˈmɑnɪk,
ˌpæθəgnəˈmɑnɪk, -s

pathognomy
BR pəˈθɒgnəmi
AM pəˈθɑgnəmi

pathologic
BR ˌpaθəˈlɒdʒɪk
AM 'pæθəˈlɑdʒɪk

pathological
BR ˌpaθəˈlɒdʒɪkl
AM 'pæθəˈlɑdʒəkəl

pathologically
BR ˌpaθəˈlɒdʒɪkli
AM 'pæθəˈlɑdʒək(ə)li

pathologist
BR pəˈθɒlədʒɪst, -s
AM pəˈθɑlədʒəst, -s

pathology
BR pəˈθɒlədʒi
AM pəˈθɑlədʒi

pathos
BR 'peɪθɒs

Pathan
BR pæ|θ, -ðz\-θs
AM pæˈθɒs, 'peɪˌθɑs,
'pæˌθɑs, 'pæˌθɒs

pathway
BR 'pɑːθweɪ, 'paθweɪ,
-z
AM 'pæθˌweɪ, -z

patience
BR 'peɪʃns
AM 'peɪʃəns

patient
BR 'peɪʃnt
AM 'peɪʃənt

patiently
BR 'peɪʃntli
AM 'peɪʃən(t)li

patina
BR 'patɪnə(r),
pəˈtiːnə(r), -z
AM pəˈtinə, -z

patinaed
BR 'patɪnəd, pəˈtiːnəd
AM pəˈtinəd

patinated
BR 'patɪneɪtɪd
AM 'pædəˌneɪdɪd,
'pætn̩ˌeɪdɪd

patination
BR ˌpatɪˈneɪʃn
AM ˌpædəˈneɪʃən,
ˌpætn̩ˈeɪʃən

patinous
BR 'patɪnəs
AM 'pædənəs, 'pætn̩əs

patio
BR 'patɪəʊ, -z
AM 'pædioʊ, -z

pâtisserie
BR pəˈtɪs(ə)r|i, -ɪz
AM pəˈtɪsəri, -z

patly
BR 'patli
AM 'pætli

Patmore
BR 'patmɔː(r)
AM 'pætˌmɔ(ə)r

Pátmos
BR 'patmɒs
AM 'pætˌmɔs,
'pætˌmɑs

Patna
BR 'patnə(r)
AM 'pætnə

patness
BR 'patnəs
AM 'pætnəs

patois[1]
singular
BR 'patwɑː(r)
AM 'pæˌtwɑ, 'pɑˌtwɑ

patois[2]
plural
BR 'patwɑːz
AM 'pæˌtwɑz, 'pɑˌtwɑz

Paton
BR 'peɪtn
AM 'peɪtn

patrial
BR 'peɪtrɪəl, 'patrɪəl, -z
AM 'peɪtriəl, -z

patriality
BR ˌpeɪtrɪ'alɪti,
ˌpatrɪ'alɪti
AM ˌpeɪtri'ælədi

patriarch
BR 'peɪtrɪɑːk,
'patrɪɑːk, -s
AM 'peɪtriˌɑrk, -s

patriarchal
BR ˌpeɪtrɪ'ɑːkl,
ˌpatrɪ'ɑːkl
AM ˌpeɪtri'ɑrkəl

patriarchally
BR ˌpeɪtrɪ'ɑːkļi,
ˌpeɪtrɪ'ɑːkəli,
ˌpatrɪ'ɑːkļi,
ˌpatrɪ'ɑːkəli
AM ˌpeɪtri'ɑrkəli

patriarchate
BR 'peɪtrɪɑːkət,
'patrɪɑːkət, -s
AM 'peɪtri'ɑrkət,
'peɪtri'ɑrˌkeɪt, -s

patriarchism
BR 'peɪtrɪɑːkɪz(ə)m,
'patrɪɑːkɪz(ə)m
AM 'peɪtriˌɑrˌkɪzəm

patriarchy
BR 'peɪtrɪɑːkļi,
'patrɪɑːkļi, -ɪz
AM 'peɪtriˌɑrki, -z

Patrice
BR pa'triːs, pə'triːs
AM pə'tris

Patricia
BR pə'trɪʃə(r)
AM pə'trɪʃə

patrician
BR pə'trɪʃn, -z
AM pə'trɪʃən, -z

patriciate
BR pə'trɪʃɪət, -s
AM pə'trɪʃ(i)ɪt,
pə'trɪʃiˌeɪt, -s

patricidal
BR ˌpatrɪ'sʌɪdl
AM ˌpætrə'saɪdəl

patricide
BR 'patrɪsʌɪd, -z
AM 'pætrəˌsaɪd, -z

Patrick
BR 'patrɪk
AM 'pætrɪk

patrilineal
BR ˌpatrɪ'lɪnɪəl
AM ˌpætrə'lɪniəl,
ˌpætrə'lɪmjəl

patrimonial
BR ˌpatrɪ'məʊnɪəl
AM ˌpætrə'moʊniəl,
ˌpætrə'moʊnjəl

patrimonially
BR ˌpatrɪ'məʊnɪəli
AM ˌpætrə'moʊniəli,
ˌpætrə'moʊnjəli

patrimony
BR 'patrɪmən|i, -ɪz
AM 'pætrəˌmoʊni, -z

patriot
BR 'patrɪət, 'peɪtrɪət, -s
AM 'peɪtriət, -s

patriotic
BR ˌpatrɪ'ɒtɪk,
ˌpeɪtrɪ'ɒtɪk
AM ˌpeɪtri'ɑdɪk

patriotically
BR ˌpatrɪ'ɒtɪkli,
ˌpeɪtrɪ'ɒtɪkli
AM ˌpeɪtri'ɑdək(ə)li

patriotism
BR 'patrɪətɪz(ə)m,
'peɪtrɪətɪz(ə)m
AM 'peɪtriəˌtɪzəm

patristic
BR pə'trɪstɪk, -s
AM pə'trɪstɪk, -s

Patroclus
BR pə'trɒkləs
AM pə'trɑkləs

patrol
BR pə'trəʊl, -z, -ɪŋ, -d
AM pə'troʊl, -z, -ɪŋ, -d

patroller
BR pə'trəʊlə(r), -z
AM pə'troʊlər, -z

patrolman
BR pə'trəʊlman,
pə'trəʊlmən
AM pə'troʊlmən

patrolmen
BR pə'trəʊlmɛn,
pə'trəʊlmən
AM pə'troʊlmən

patrological
BR ˌpatrə'lɒdʒɪkl
AM ˌpætrə'lɑdʒəkəl

patrologist
BR pə'trɒlədʒɪst, -s
AM pə'trɑlədʒəst, -s

patrology
BR pə'trɒlədʒi
AM pə'trɑlədʒi

patron
BR 'peɪtr(ə)n, -z
AM 'peɪtrən, -z

patronage
BR 'patrənɪdʒ,
'patrņɪdʒ
AM 'pætrənədʒ,
'peɪtrənədʒ

patronal
BR pə'trəʊnl
AM 'peɪtrənəl

patroness
BR 'peɪtrənɪs,
'peɪtrņɪs, ˌpeɪtrə'nɛs,
-ɪz
AM 'peɪtrənəs, -əz

patronisation
BR ˌpatrənʌɪ'zeɪʃn
AM ˌpeɪtrənə'zeɪʃən,
ˌpeɪtrəˌnaɪ'zeɪʃən,

ˌpætrənə'zeɪʃən,
ˌpætrəˌnaɪ'zeɪʃən

patronise
BR 'patrənʌɪz, -ɪz, -ɪŋ,
-d
AM 'peɪtrəˌnaɪz,
'pætrəˌnaɪz, -ɪz, -ɪŋ, -d

patroniser
BR 'patrənʌɪzə(r), -z
AM 'peɪtrəˌnaɪzər,
'pætrəˌnaɪzər, -z

patronisingly
BR 'patrənʌɪzɪŋli
AM 'peɪtrəˌnaɪzɪŋli,
'pætrəˌnaɪzɪŋli

patronization
BR ˌpatrənʌɪ'zeɪʃn
AM ˌpeɪtrənə'zeɪʃən,
ˌpeɪtrəˌnaɪ'zeɪʃən,
ˌpætrənə'zeɪʃən,
ˌpætrəˌnaɪ'zeɪʃən

patronize
BR 'patrənʌɪz, -ɪz, -ɪŋ,
-d
AM 'peɪtrəˌnaɪz,
'pætrəˌnaɪz, -ɪz, -ɪŋ, -d

patronizer
BR 'patrənʌɪzə(r), -z
AM 'peɪtrəˌnaɪzər,
'pætrəˌnaɪzər, -z

patronizingly
BR 'patrənʌɪzɪŋli
AM 'peɪtrəˌnaɪzɪŋli,
'pætrəˌnaɪzɪŋli

patronymic
BR ˌpatrə'nɪmɪk, -s
AM ˌpætrə'nɪmɪk, -s

patronymically
BR ˌpatrə'nɪmɪkli
AM ˌpætrə'nɪmək(ə)li

patroon
BR pə'truːn, -z
AM pə'trun, -z

patsy
BR 'pats|i, -ɪz
AM 'pætsi, -z

pattée
of a cross
BR 'pateɪ, 'pati
AM pə'teɪ

patten
BR 'patn, -z
AM 'pætn, -z

patter
BR 'pat|ə(r), -əz,
-(ə)rɪŋ, -əd
AM 'pædər, -z, -ɪŋ, -d

Patterdale
BR 'patədeɪl
AM 'pædərˌdeɪl

pattern
BR 'patn, -nz,
-nɪŋ \-ənɪŋ, -nd
AM 'pædərn, -z, -ɪŋ, -d

Patterson
BR 'patəs(ə)n
AM 'pædərsən

Patti
BR 'pati
AM 'pædi

Pattie
BR 'pati
AM 'pædi

Pattison
BR 'patɪs(ə)n
AM 'pædəsən

Patton
BR 'patn
AM 'pætn

patty
BR 'pat|i, -ɪz
AM 'pædi, -z

pattypan
BR 'patɪpan, -z
AM 'pædiˌpæn, -z

patulous
BR 'patjʊləs
AM 'pætʃələs

patulously
BR 'patjʊləsli
AM 'pætʃələsli

patulousness
BR 'patjʊləsnəs,
'patʃʊləsnəs
AM 'pætʃələsnəs

Patuxent
BR pə'taksnt
AM pə'təksənt

paua
BR 'paʊə(r), -z
AM 'paʊə, -z

paucity
BR 'pɔːsɪti
AM 'pɑsədi, 'pɑsədi

Paul
BR pɔːl
AM pɔl, pɑl

Paula
BR 'pɔːlə(r)
AM 'pɒlə, 'pɑlə

Paulette
BR pɔː'lɛt
AM pɔ'lɛt, pɑ'lɛt

Pauli
BR 'paʊli
AM 'paʊli

Pauline[1]
of St Paul
BR 'pɔːlʌɪn
AM 'pɔˌlaɪn, 'pɔˌlin,
'pɑˌlaɪn, 'pɑˌlin

Pauline[2]
forename
BR 'pɔːliːn
AM pɔ'lin, pɑ'lin

Pauling
BR 'pɔːlɪŋ
AM 'pɔlɪŋ, 'pɑlɪŋ

paulownia
BR pɔː'ləʊnɪə(r), -z
AM pɔ'loʊniə,
pɑ'loʊniə, -z

paunch
BR pɔːn(t)ʃ, -ɪz, -ɪŋ, -t

AM pɒn(t)ʃ, pɑn(t)ʃ,
-əz, -ɪŋ, -t

paunchiness
BR 'pɔːn(t)ʃɪnɪs
AM 'pɒntʃɪnɪs,
'pɑntʃɪnɪs

paunchy
BR 'pɔːn(t)ʃ|i, -ɪə(r),
-ɪɪst
AM 'pɒntʃi, 'pɑntʃi, -ər,
-əst

pauper
BR 'pɔːpə(r), -z
AM 'pɒpər, 'pɑpər, -z

pauperdom
BR 'pɔːpədəm
AM 'pɒpərdəm,
'pɑpərdəm

pauperisation
BR ,pɔːp(ə)rʌɪ'zeɪʃn
AM ,pɒpərə'zeɪʃən,
,pɒpə,rɑɪ'zeɪʃən,
,pɑpərə'zeɪʃən,
,pɑpə,rɑɪ'zeɪʃən

pauperise
BR 'pɔːp(ə)rʌɪz, -ɪz, -ɪŋ,
-d
AM 'pɒpə,rɑɪz,
'pɑpə,rɑɪz, -ɪz, -ɪŋ, -d

pauperism
BR 'pɔːp(ə)rɪz(ə)m
AM 'pɒpə,rɪzəm,
'pɑpə,rɪzəm

pauperization
BR ,pɔːp(ə)rʌɪ'zeɪʃn
AM ,pɒpərə'zeɪʃən,
,pɒpə,rɑɪ'zeɪʃən,
,pɑpərə'zeɪʃən,
,pɑpə,rɑɪ'zeɪʃən

pauperize
BR 'pɔːp(ə)rʌɪz, -ɪz, -ɪŋ,
-d
AM 'pɒpə,rɑɪz,
'pɑpə,rɑɪz, -ɪz, -ɪŋ, -d

paupiette
BR pɔː'pjɛt, -s
AM pou'piɛt, -z

Pausanias
BR pɔː'seɪnɪəs
AM pɔː'seɪnɪəs,
pɑ'seɪnɪəs

pause
BR pɔːz, -ɪz, -ɪŋ, -d
AM pɔz, pɑz, -ɪz, -ɪŋ, -d

pavage
BR 'peɪvɪdʒ
AM 'peɪvɪdʒ

pavan
BR pə'van, pə'vɑːn,
'pavn, -z
AM pə'van, -z

pavane
BR pə'van, pə'vɑːn,
'pavn, -z
AM pə'van, -z

Pavarotti
BR ,pavə'rɒti

AM ,pavə'rɑdi,
,pævə'rɑdi

pave
BR peɪv, -z, -ɪŋ, -d
AM peɪv, -z, -ɪŋ, -d

pavé
noun
BR 'paveɪ, -z
AM pæ'veɪ, pæ'veɪ, -z

pavement
BR 'peɪvm(ə)nt, -s
AM 'peɪvmənt, -s

paver
BR 'peɪvə(r), -z
AM 'peɪvər, -z

Pavey
BR 'peɪvi
AM 'peɪvi

pavilion
BR pə'vɪlɪən, -z
AM pə'vɪljən, -z

paving
BR 'peɪvɪŋ, -z
AM 'peɪvɪŋ, -z

pavior
BR 'peɪvɪə(r), -z
AM 'peɪvɪər, -z

paviour
BR 'peɪvɪə(r), -z
AM 'peɪvɪər, -z

Pavlov
BR 'pavlɒv
AM 'pav,lɒv, 'pav,lav

Pavlova
BR pav'ləʊvə(r),
'pavləvə(r)
AM pav'loʊvə

Pavlovian
BR pav'ləʊvɪən
AM pav'loʊvɪən,
pav'lɒvɪən,
pav'lavɪən

pavonine
BR 'pavənʌɪn
AM 'pævə,nɑɪn

paw
BR pɔː(r), -z, -ɪŋ, -d
AM pɔ, pɑ, -z, -ɪŋ, -d

pawkily
BR 'pɔːkɪli
AM 'pɒkəli, 'pɑkəli

pawkiness
BR 'pɔːkɪnɪs
AM 'pɒkɪnɪs, 'pɑkɪnɪs

pawky
BR 'pɔːk|i, -ɪə(r), -ɪɪst
AM 'pɒki, 'pɑki, -ər, -ɪst

pawl
BR pɔːl, -z, -ɪŋ, -d
AM pɒl, pɑl, -z, -ɪŋ, -d

pawn
BR pɔːn, -z, -ɪŋ, -d
AM pɒn, pɑn, -z, -ɪŋ, -d

pawnbroker
BR 'pɔːn,brəʊkə(r), -z
AM 'pɒn,broʊkər,
'pɑn,broʊkər, -z

pawnbroking
BR 'pɔːn,brəʊkɪŋ
AM 'pɒn,broʊkɪŋ,
'pɑn,broʊkɪŋ

Pawnee
BR pɔː'niː, -z
AM pɔ'ni, pɑ'ni, -z

pawnshop
BR 'pɔːnʃɒp, -s
AM 'pɒn,ʃap, 'pɑn,ʃap,
-s

pawpaw
BR 'pɔːpɔː(r), -z
AM 'pɒpɔ, 'pɑpɑ, -z

pax
BR paks
AM pæks, pɑks

Paxo®
BR 'paksəʊ
AM 'pæksoʊ

Paxton
BR 'pakstən
AM 'pækstən

pay
BR peɪ, -z, -ɪŋ, -d
AM peɪ, -z, -ɪŋ, -d

payable
BR 'peɪəbl
AM 'peɪəbəl

pay-as-you-earn
BR ,peɪəzju:'əːn
AM ,peɪəz,ju'ərn

payback
BR 'peɪbak, -s
AM 'peɪ,bæk, -s

paycheck
BR 'peɪtʃɛk, -s
AM 'peɪ,tʃɛk, -s

paycheque
BR 'peɪtʃɛk, -s
AM 'peɪ,tʃɛk, -s

payday
BR 'peɪdeɪ, -z
AM 'peɪ,deɪ, -z

paydirt
BR 'peɪdəːt
AM 'peɪ,dərt

PAYE
BR ,piːeɪwʌɪ'iː
AM ,pi,eɪ,wɑɪ'i

payee
BR ,peɪ'iː, -z
AM peɪ'i, -z

payer
BR 'peɪə(r), -z
AM 'peɪər, -z

payload
BR 'peɪləʊd, -z
AM 'peɪ,loʊd, -z

paymaster
BR 'peɪ,mɑːstə(r),
'peɪ,mɑstə(r), -z
AM 'peɪ,mæstər, -z

payment
BR 'peɪm(ə)nt, -s
AM 'peɪmənt, -s

Payn
BR peɪn
AM peɪn

Payne
BR peɪn
AM peɪn

paynim
BR 'peɪnɪm
AM 'peɪnɪm

payoff
BR 'peɪɒf, -s
AM 'peɪ,ɔf, 'peɪ,ɑf, -s

payola
BR peɪ'əʊlə(r), -z
AM peɪ'oʊlə, -z

payout
BR 'peɪaʊt, -s
AM 'peɪ,aʊt, -s

paypacket
BR 'peɪ,pakɪt, -s
AM 'peɪ,pækət, -s

payphone
BR 'peɪfəʊn, -z
AM 'peɪ,foʊn, -z

payroll
BR 'peɪrəʊl, -z
AM 'peɪ,roʊl, -z

paysage
BR ,peɪ'zɑːʒ,
'peɪzɑː(d)ʒ, -ɪz
AM ,peɪ(i)'z|ɑʒ, -əz

payslip
BR 'peɪslɪp, -s
AM 'peɪ,slɪp, -s

Payton
BR 'peɪtn
AM 'peɪtn

Paz
BR pɑːz
AM pɑz

pea
BR piː, -z
AM pi, -z

Peabody
BR 'piː,bɒdi, 'piːbədi
AM 'pi,badi

peace
BR piːs
AM pis

peaceable
BR 'piːsəbl
AM 'pisəbəl

peaceableness
BR 'piːsəblnəs
AM 'pisəblnɪs

peaceably
BR 'piːsəbli
AM 'pisəbli

peaceful
BR 'piːsf(ʊ)l
AM 'pisfəl

peacefully
BR 'piːsfʊli, 'piːsfʃi
AM 'pisfəli

peacefulness
BR 'piːsf(ʊ)lnəs
AM 'pisfəlnəs

peacekeeper
BR ˈpiːsˌkiːpə(r), -z
AM ˈpisˌkipər, -z

peacekeeping
BR ˈpiːsˌkiːpɪŋ
AM ˈpisˌkipɪŋ

peacemaker
BR ˈpiːsˌmeɪkə(r), -z
AM ˈpisˌmeɪkər, -z

peacemaking
BR ˈpiːsˌmeɪkɪŋ
AM ˈpisˌmeɪkɪŋ

peacenik
BR ˈpiːsnɪk, -s
AM ˈpisˌnɪk, -s

peacetime
BR ˈpiːstaɪm
AM ˈpisˌtaɪm

peach
BR piːtʃ, -ɪz, -ɪŋ, -t
AM pitʃ, -ɪz, -ɪŋ, -t

Peachey
BR ˈpiːtʃi
AM ˈpitʃi

peachick
BR ˈpiːtʃɪk, -s
AM ˈpiːtʃɪk, -s

peachiness
BR ˈpiːtʃɪnɪs
AM ˈpitʃinɪs

peachy
BR ˈpiːtʃi, -ɪə(r), -ɪɪst
AM ˈpitʃi, -ər, -əst

peacock
BR ˈpiːkɒk, -s
AM ˈpiˌkak, -s

peacockery
BR ˈpiːkɒk(ə)ri
AM ˈpiˌkak(ə)ri

peafowl
BR ˈpiːfaʊl, -z
AM ˈpiˌfaʊl, -z

peahen
BR ˈpiːhɛn, -z
AM ˈpiˌhɛn, -z

peak
BR piːk, -s, -ɪŋ, -t
AM pik, -s, -ɪŋ, -t

Peak District
BR ˈpiːk ˌdɪstrɪkt
AM ˈpik ˌdɪstrɪk(t)

Peake
BR piːk
AM pik

peakiness
BR ˈpiːkɪnɪs
AM ˈpikɪnɪs

peakish
BR ˈpiːkɪʃ
AM ˈpikɪʃ

peakload
BR ˈpiːkləʊd, -z
AM ˈpikˈloʊd, -z

peaky
BR ˈpiːki
AM ˈpiki

peal
BR piːl, -z, -ɪŋ, -d
AM pil, -z, -ɪŋ, -d

pean
BR ˈpiːən
AM ˈpiən

peanut
BR ˈpiːnʌt, -s
AM ˈpinət, -s

pear
BR pɛː(r), -z
AM pɛ(ə)r, -z

Pearce
BR pɪəs
AM pɪ(ə)rs

pearl
BR pɜːl, -z, -ɪŋ, -d
AM pɜrl, -z, -ɪŋ, -d

pearler
BR ˈpɜːlə(r), -z
AM ˈpɜrlər, -z

pearlescent
BR pɜːˈlɛsnt
AM pɜrˈlɛsənt

Pearl Harbor
BR ˌpɜːl ˈhɑːbə(r)
AM ˌpɜrl ˈhɑrbər

pearliness
BR ˈpɜːlɪnɪs
AM ˈpɜrlɪnɪs

pearlised
BR ˈpɜːlʌɪzd
AM ˈpɜrˌlaɪzd

pearlite
BR ˈpɜːlʌɪt
AM ˈpɜrˌlaɪt

pearlized
BR ˈpɜːlʌɪzd
AM ˈpɜrˌlaɪzd

pearlware
BR ˈpɜːlwɛː(r)
AM ˈpɜrlˌwɛ(ə)r

pearlwort
BR ˈpɜːlwɔːt
AM ˈpɜrlˌwɔrt
ˈpɜrlˌwɔ(ə)rt

pearly
BR ˈpɜːl|i, -ɪz, -ɪə(r),
-ɪɪst
AM ˈpɜrli, -z, -ər, -ɪst

pearmain
BR ˈpɜːmeɪn, ˈpɛːmeɪn,
pəˈmeɪn
AM ˈpɛrˌmeɪn,
pərˈmeɪn

Pears[1]®
soap brand
BR pɛːz
AM pɛrz

Pears[2]
surname
BR pɪəz, pɛːz
AM pɛrz

Pearsall
BR ˈpɪəsl
AM ˈpɪrˌsɔl, ˈpɪrˌsɑl

pearshaped
BR ˈpɛːʃeɪpt
AM ˈpɛrˌʃeɪpt

Pearson
BR ˈpɪəsn
AM ˈpɪrsən

peart
BR ˈpɪət
AM ˈpɪ(ə)rt

Peary
BR ˈpɪəri
AM ˈpɪri

peasant
BR ˈpɛznt, -s
AM ˈpɛznt, -s

peasantry
BR ˈpɛzntri
AM ˈpɛzntri

peasanty
BR ˈpɛznti
AM ˈpɛzn(t)i

peascod
BR ˈpiːzkɒd, -z
AM ˈpizˌkad, -z

pease
BR piːz
AM piz

peasecod
BR ˈpiːzkɒd, -z
AM ˈpizˌkad, -z

peasepudding
BR ˌpiːzˈpʊdɪŋ
AM ˈpizˈpʊdɪŋ

peashooter
BR ˈpiːˌʃuːtə(r), -z
AM ˈpiˌʃudər, -z

pea-soup
BR ˌpiːˈsuːp
AM ˈpiˈsup

pea-souper
BR ˌpiːˈsuːpə(r), -z
AM ˈpiˈsupər, -z

pea stick
BR ˈpiː stɪk, -s
AM ˈpi ˌstɪk, -s

peat
BR piːt
AM pit

peatbog
BR ˈpiːtbɒg, -z
AM ˈpitˌbag, ˈpitˌbɔg, -z

peatiness
BR ˈpiːtɪnɪs
AM ˈpidɪnɪs

peatland
BR ˈpiːtland, -z
AM ˈpitˌlænd, -z

peatmoss
BR ˈpiːtmɒs, -ɪz
AM ˈpitˌmɔs, ˈpitˌmɑs,
-əz

peaty
BR ˈpiːt|i, -ɪə(r), -ɪɪst
AM ˈpidi, -ər, -ɪst

peau-de-soie
BR ˌpəʊdəˈswɑː(r)
AM ˈpoʊdəˈswɑ

Peaudouce®
BR pəʊˈd(j)uːs
AM poʊˈd(j)us

peavey
BR ˈpiːv|i, -ɪz
AM ˈpivi, -z

peavy
BR ˈpiːv|i, -ɪz
AM ˈpivi, -z

pebble
BR ˈpɛbl, -z, -d
AM ˈpɛbəl, -z, -d

pebbledash
BR ˈpɛbldaʃ, -t
AM ˈpɛbəlˌdæʃ, -t

pebbly
BR ˈpɛbli, ˈpɛbli
AM ˈpɛb(ə)li

pec
BR pɛk, -s
AM pɛk, -s

pecan
BR pɪˈkan, ˈpiːk(ə)n, -z
AM pəˈkan, pəˈkæn,
ˈpiˌkan, ˈpiˌkæn, -z

peccability
BR ˌpɛkəˈbɪlɪti
AM ˌpɛkəˈbɪlɪdi

peccable
BR ˈpɛkəbl
AM ˈpɛkəbəl

peccadillo
BR ˌpɛkəˈdɪləʊ, -z
AM ˌpɛkəˈdɪloʊ, -z

peccancy
BR ˈpɛk(ə)nsi
AM ˈpɛkənsi

peccant
BR ˈpɛk(ə)nt
AM ˈpɛkənt

peccary
BR ˈpɛk(ə)r|i, -ɪz
AM ˈpɛkəri, -z

peccavi
BR pɛˈkɑːviː, pəˈkɑːvi
AM pəˈkɑvi

pêche Melba
BR ˌpɛʃ ˈmɛlbə(r), -z
AM ˌpɛʃ ˈmɛlbə, -z

peck
BR pɛk, -s, -ɪŋ, -t
AM pɛk, -s, -ɪŋ, -t

pecker
BR ˈpɛkə(r), -z
AM ˈpɛkər, -z

Peckham
BR ˈpɛkəm
AM ˈpɛkəm

peckish
BR ˈpɛkɪʃ
AM ˈpɛkɪʃ

peckishly
BR ˈpɛkɪʃli
AM ˈpɛkɪʃli

peckishness
BR ˈpɛkɪʃnɪs
AM ˈpɛkɪʃnɪs

Pecksniff
BR 'pɛksnɪf
AM 'pɛk,snɪf

pecorino
BR ,pɛkə'riːnəʊ
AM ,pɛkə'riːnoʊ

Pecos
BR 'peɪkəs, 'peɪkɒs
AM 'peɪ,koʊs, 'peɪkəs

pecten
BR 'pɛktɪn, 'pɛktɛn, -z
AM 'pɛktən, -z

pectic
BR 'pɛktɪk
AM 'pɛktɪk

pectin
BR 'pɛktɪn
AM 'pɛktən

pectinate
BR 'pɛktɪnət
AM 'pɛktənət,
'pɛktə,neɪt

pectinated
BR 'pɛktɪneɪtɪd
AM 'pɛktə,neɪdɪd

pectination
BR ,pɛktɪ'neɪʃn
AM ,pɛktə'neɪʃən

pectines
BR 'pɛktɪniːz
AM 'pɛktə,niz

pectoral
BR 'pɛkt(ə)rəl,
'pɛkt(ə)r̩
AM 'pɛkt(ə)rəl

pectose
BR 'pɛktəʊs, 'pɛktəʊz
AM 'pɛktoʊs, 'pɛktoʊz

peculate
BR 'pɛkjʊleɪt, -s, -ɪŋ, -ɪd
AM 'pɛkjə,leɪ|t, -ts, -dɪŋ, -dɪd

peculation
BR ,pɛkjʊ'leɪʃn, -z
AM ,pɛkjə'leɪʃən, -z

peculator
BR 'pɛkjʊleɪtə(r), -z
AM 'pɛkjə,leɪdər, -z

peculiar
BR pɪ'kjuːlɪə(r)
AM pə'kjuljər

peculiarity
BR pɪ,kjuːlɪ'arɪt|i, -ɪz
AM pə,kjul'jɛrədi, pə,kjuli'ɛrədi, -z

peculiarly
BR pɪ'kjuːlɪəli
AM pə'kjuljərli

pecuniarily
BR pɪ'kjuːn(jə)rɪli
AM pə,kjuni'ɛrəli

pecuniary
BR pɪ'kjuːn(jə)ri
AM pə'kjuni,ɛri

pedagogic
BR ,pɛdə'gɒdʒɪk,
,pɛdə'gɒgɪk, -s

AM ,pɛdə'gɑdʒɪk, -s

pedagogical
BR ,pɛdə'gɒdʒɪkl,
,pɛdə'gɒgɪkl
AM ,pɛdə'gɑdʒəkəl

pedagogically
BR ,pɛdə'gɒdʒɪkli,
,pɛdə'gɒgɪkli
AM ,pɛdə'gɑdʒək(ə)li

pedagogism
BR 'pɛdəgɒgɪz(ə)m,
'pɛdəgɒdʒɪz(ə)m
AM 'pɛdə,gɑ,gɪzəm,
'pɛdə,gɑ,dʒɪzəm

pedagogue
BR 'pɛdəgɒg, -z
AM 'pɛdə,gɑg, -z

pedagoguism
BR 'pɛdəgɒgɪz(ə)m,
'pɛdəgɒdʒɪz(ə)m
AM 'pɛdə,gɑ,gɪzəm

pedagogy
BR 'pɛdəgɒdʒi,
'pɛdəgɒgi
AM 'pɛdə,gɑdʒi

pedal¹
adjective, of the foot
BR 'pɛdl, 'piːdl
AM 'pidəl, 'pɛdəl

pedal²
noun, verb
BR 'pɛd|l, -lz, -|ɪŋ \-lɪŋ,
-ld
AM 'pɛdəl, -z, -ɪŋ, -d

pedalo
BR 'pɛdələʊ, 'pɛdl̩əʊ, -z
AM 'pɛdl̩,oʊ, -z

pedant
BR 'pɛdnt, -s
AM 'pɛdnt, -s

pedantic
BR pɪ'dantɪk
AM pə'dæn(t)ɪk

pedantically
BR pɪ'dantɪkli
AM pə'dæn(t)ək(ə)li

pedantry
BR 'pɛdntri
AM 'pɛdntri

pedate
BR 'pɛdət, 'pɛdeɪt
AM 'pɛ,deɪt, 'pɛdət

peddle
BR 'pɛd|l, -lz, -|ɪŋ \-lɪŋ,
-ld
AM 'pɛd|əl, -əlz, -(ə)lɪŋ,
-əld

peddler
BR 'pɛdlə(r), -z
AM 'pɛd(ə)lər, -z

pederast
BR ,pɛdərast, -s
AM 'pɛdə,ræst, -s

pederastic
BR ,pɛdə'rastɪk
AM ,pɛdə'ræstɪk

pederasty
BR 'pɛdərasti

AM 'pɛdə,ræsti

pedestal
BR 'pɛdɪstl, -z
AM 'pɛdəstl, -z

pedestrian
BR pɪ'dɛstrɪən, -z
AM pə'dɛstrɪən, -z

pedestrianisation
BR pɪ,dɛstrɪənʌɪ'zeɪʃn
AM pə,dɛstrɪənə'zeɪʃən,
pə,dɛstriə,naɪ'zeɪʃən

pedestrianise
BR pɪ'dɛstrɪənʌɪz, -ɪz,
-ɪŋ, -d
AM pə'dɛstriə,naɪz, -ɪz,
-ɪŋ, -d

pedestrianism
BR pɪ'dɛstrɪənɪz(ə)m
AM pə'dɛstriə,nɪzəm

pedestrianization
BR pɪ,dɛstrɪənʌɪ'zeɪʃn
AM pə,dɛstriənə'zeɪʃən,
pə,dɛstriə,naɪ'zeɪʃən

pedestrianize
BR pɪ'dɛstrɪənʌɪz, -ɪz,
-ɪŋ, -d
AM pə'dɛstriə,naɪz, -ɪz,
-ɪŋ, -d

pediatric
BR ,piːdɪ'atrɪk, -s
AM 'pidi'ætrɪk, -s

pediatrician
BR ,piːdɪə'trɪʃn, -z
AM ,pidiə'trɪʃən, -z

pediatrist
BR ,piː'dʌɪətrɪst,
,piːdɪ'atrɪst
AM 'pidi'ætrəst

pedicab
BR 'pɛdɪkab, -z
AM 'pɛdɪkæb, -z

pedicel
BR 'pɛdɪs(ɛ)l, -z
AM 'pɛdə,sɛl, -z

pedicellate
BR 'pɛdɪsɪleɪt,
'pɛdɪsl̩eɪt
AM ,pɛdi'sɛlət,
,pɛdi'sɛ,leɪt

pedicle
BR 'pɛdɪkl, -z
AM 'pɛdəkəl, -z

pedicular
BR pɪ'dɪkjʊlə(r),
pɛ'dɪkjʊlə(r)
AM pə'dɪkjələr

pediculate
BR pɪ'dɪkjʊlət,
pɛ'dɪkjʊlət
AM pə'dɪkjə,leɪt,
pə'dɪkjə,leɪt

pediculosis
BR pɪ,dɪkjʊ'ləʊsɪs,
pɛ,dɪkjʊ'ləʊsɪs
AM pə,dɪkjʊ'loʊsəs

pediculous
BR pɪ'dɪkjʊləs,
pɛ'dɪkjʊləs

AM 'pɛdə,ræsti

pedicure
BR 'pɛdɪkjʊə(r),
'pɛdɪkjɔː(r), -z
AM 'pɛdə,kjʊ(ə)r, -z

pedicurist
BR 'pɛdɪkjʊərɪst,
'pɛdɪkjɔːrɪst, -s
AM 'pɛdə,kjʊrəst, -s

pediform
BR 'pɛdɪfɔːm
AM 'pɛdə,fɔ(ə)rm

pedigree
BR 'pɛdɪgri:, -z, -d
AM 'pɛdə,gri, -z, -d

pediment
BR 'pɛdɪm(ə)nt, -s, -ɪd
AM 'pɛdəmən|t, -ts, -ɪd

pedimental
BR ,pɛdɪ'mɛntl
AM ,pɛdə'mɛn(t)l

pedlar
BR 'pɛdlə(r), -z
AM 'pɛdlər, -z

pedlary
BR 'pɛdləri
AM 'pɛdləri

pedological¹
child study
BR ,pɛdə'lɒdʒɪkl
AM ,pɛdə'lɑdʒəkəl,
,pidə'lɑdʒəkəl

pedological²
soil science
BR ,pɛdə'lɒdʒɪkl
AM ,pɛdə'lɑdʒəkəl

pedologist
BR pɪ'dɒlədʒɪst,
pɛ'dɒlədʒɪst, -s
AM pə'dɑlədʒəst, -s

pedology
BR pɪ'dɒlədʒi,
pɛ'dɒlədʒi
AM pə'dɑlədʒi

pedometer
BR pɪ'dɒmɪtə(r),
pɛ'dɒmɪtə(r), -z
AM pə'dɑmədər, -z

pedophile
BR 'piːdəfʌɪl, -z
AM 'pɛdə,faɪl,
'pidə,faɪl, -z

pedophilia
BR ,piːdə'fɪlɪə(r)
AM ,pɛdə'fɪljə,
,pidə'fɪljə, ,pɛdə'fɪlɪə,
,pidə'fɪliə

pedophiliac
BR ,piːdə'fɪlɪak, -s
AM ,pɛdə'fɪli,æk,
,pidə'fɪli,æk, -s

pedophiliad
BR ,piːdə'fɪlɪad
AM ,pɛdə'fɪli,æd,
,pidə'fɪli,æd

Pedro
BR 'pɛdrəʊ
AM 'peɪdroʊ

peduncle
BR pɪˈdʌŋkl, -z
AM ˈpiːˌdəŋkəl,
pɪˈdəŋkəl, -z
peduncular
BR pɪˈdʌŋkjələ(r)
AM pəˈdəŋkjələr
pedunculate
BR pɪˈdʌŋkjʊleɪt,
pɪˈdʌŋkjələt
AM pəˈdəŋkjəˌleɪt,
pəˈdəŋkjələt
pee
BR piː, -z, -ɪŋ, -d
AM pi, -z, -ɪŋ, -d
Peebles
BR ˈpiːblz
AM ˈpibəlz
peek
BR piːk, -s, -ɪŋ, -t
AM pik, -s, -ɪŋ, -t
peekaboo
BR ˌpiːkəˈbuː
AM ˈpikəˌbu
peekily
BR ˈpiːkɪli
AM ˈpikɪli
peekiness
BR ˈpiːkɪnɪs
AM ˈpikinɪs
peeky
BR ˈpiːk|i, -iə(r), -iɪst
AM ˈpiki, -ər, -ɪst
peel
BR piːl, -z, -ɪŋ, -d
AM pil, -z, -ɪŋ, -d
peeler
BR ˈpiːlə(r), -z
AM ˈpilər, -z
peeling
BR ˈpiːlɪŋ, -z
AM ˈpilɪŋ, -z
Peelite
BR ˈpiːlʌɪt, -s
AM ˈpiˌlaɪt, -s
peen
BR piːn, -z
AM pin, -z
Peenemunde
BR ˈpiːnəˌmʊndə(r)
AM ˌpinəˈmʊndə
GER ˈpeːnəmʏndə
peep
BR piːp, -s, -ɪŋ, -t
AM pip, -s, -ɪŋ, -t
peep-bo
BR ˈpiːp(b)əʊ
AM ˈpipˌbou
peeper
BR ˈpiːpə(r), -z
AM ˈpipər, -z
peephole
BR ˈpiːphəʊl, -z
AM ˈpipˌ(h)oʊl, -z
peepshow
BR ˈpiːpʃəʊ, -z
AM ˈpipˌʃou, -z

peepul
BR ˈpiːpl, -z
AM ˈpipəl, -z
peer
BR pɪə(r), -z
AM pɪ(ə)r, -z
peerage
BR ˈpɪər|ɪdʒ, -ɪdʒɪz
AM ˈpɪrɪdʒ, -ɪz
peeress
BR ˈpɪərɪs, ˌpɪəˈrɛs, -ɪz
AM ˈpɪrɪs, -ɪz
peer-group
BR ˈpɪəgruːp
AM ˈpɪrˌgrup
peerless
BR ˈpɪələs
AM ˈpɪrlɪs
peerlessly
BR ˈpɪələsli
AM ˈpɪrlɪsli
peerlessness
BR ˈpɪələsnəs
AM ˈpɪrlɪsnɪs
peeve
BR piːv, -z, -ɪŋ, -d
AM piv, -z, -ɪŋ, -d
peevish
BR ˈpiːvɪʃ
AM ˈpivɪʃ
peevishly
BR ˈpiːvɪʃli
AM ˈpivɪʃli
peevishness
BR ˈpiːvɪʃnɪs
AM ˈpivɪʃnɪs
peewee
BR ˈpiːwiː, -z
AM ˈpiˌwi, -z
peewit
BR ˈpiːwɪt, -s
AM ˈpiwɪt, ˈpiˌwɪt, -s
peg
BR pɛg, -z, -ɪŋ, -d
AM pɛg, -z, -ɪŋ, -d
Pegasean
BR ˌpɛgəˈsiːən
AM ˌpɛgəˈsiən
Pegasus
BR ˈpɛgəsəs
AM ˈpɛgəsəs
pegboard
BR ˈpɛgbɔːd, -z
AM ˈpɛgˌbɔ(ə)rd, -z
Pegg
BR pɛg
AM pɛg
Peggie
BR ˈpɛgi
AM ˈpɛgi
Peggotty
BR ˈpɛgəti
AM ˈpɛgədi
Peggy
BR ˈpɛgi
AM ˈpɛgi

peg-leg
BR ˈpɛglɛg, -z
AM ˈpɛgˌlɛg, -z
pegmatite
BR ˈpɛgmətʌɪt
AM ˈpɛgməˌtaɪt
pegtop
BR ˈpɛgtɒp, -s
AM ˈpɛgˌtɑp, -s
Pegu
BR ˈpɛgjuː, -z
AM pɛˈgu, -z
Pei
BR peɪ
AM peɪ
peignoir
BR ˈpeɪnwɑː(r), -z
AM ˌpeɪnˈwɑr, -z
Peirce
BR pɪəs
AM pɪ(ə)rs
pejoration
BR ˌpɛdʒəˈreɪʃn
AM ˌpɛdʒəˈreɪʃən,
ˌpeɪəˈreɪʃən
pejorative
BR pɪˈdʒɒrətɪv, -z
AM pəˈdʒɔrədɪv,
ˈpɛdʒəˌreɪdɪv, -z
pejoratively
BR pɪˈdʒɒrətɪvli
AM pəˈdʒɔrədɪvli,
ˈpɛdʒəˌreɪdɪvli
pekan
BR ˈpɛk(ə)n
AM pəˈkɑn, pəˈkæn,
ˈpiˌkɑn, ˈpiˌkæn
peke
BR piːk, -s
AM pik, -s
Pekin
BR ˌpiːˈkɪn
AM ˈpikɪn
Pekinese
BR ˌpiːkɪˈniːz
AM ˈpikɪnˌiz
Peking
BR ˌpiːˈkɪŋ
AM ˈpiˈkɪŋ, ˈpeɪˈkɪŋ
pekingese
BR ˌpiːkɪˈniːz, -ɪz
AM ˈpikɪnˌiz, -ɪz
pekoe
BR ˈpiːkəʊ
AM ˈpiˌkou
pelage
BR ˈpɛl|ɪdʒ, -ɪdʒɪz
AM ˈpɛlɪdʒ, -ɪz
Pelagian
BR pɪˈleɪdʒən,
pɪˈleɪdʒ(ə)n, -z
AM pəˈleɪdʒən, -z
Pelagianism
BR pɪˈleɪdʒ(ɪ)ənɪz(ə)m,
pɪˈleɪdʒnɪz(ə)m
AM pəˈleɪdʒ(i)əˌnɪzəm

pelagic
BR pɪˈladʒɪk
AM pəˈlædʒɪk
Pelagius
BR pɪˈleɪdʒɪəs
AM pəˈleɪdʒ(i)əs
pelargonium
BR ˌpɛləˈgəʊnɪəm, -z
AM ˌpɛˌlɑrˈgouniəm,
ˌpɛlərˈgouniəm, -z
Pelasgian
BR pɪˈlazdʒɪən,
pɛˈlazdʒɪən,
pɪˈlazgɪən, pɛˈlazgɪən,
-z
AM pəˈlæzdʒɪən,
pəˈlæzgiən, -z
Pelasgic
BR pɪˈlazdʒɪk,
pɛˈlazdʒɪk, pɪˈlazgɪk,
pɛˈlazgɪk
AM pəˈlæzdʒɪk,
pəˈlæzgɪk
Pelé
BR ˈpɛleɪ
AM ˈpɛˌleɪ
pele
BR piːl, -z
AM pil, -z
pelerine
BR ˈpɛlərɪn, ˈpɛləriːn,
-z
AM ˌpɛləˈrin, -z
Peleus
BR ˈpɛljəs, ˈpiːljəs,
ˈpɛlɪəs, ˈpiːlɪəs
AM ˈpɛliəs, ˈpiliəs,
ˈpɛljəs, ˈpiljəs
pelf
BR pɛlf
AM pɛlf
pelham
BR ˈpɛləm, -z
AM ˈpɛləm, -z
Pelias
BR ˈpiːlɪas, ˈpɛlɪas
AM ˈpɛliəs
pelican
BR ˈpɛlɪk(ə)n, -z
AM ˈpɛləkən, -z
Pelion
BR ˈpiːlɪən, ˈpiːlɪɒn
AM ˈpiliən, ˈpiljən
pelisse
BR pɪˈliːs, -ɪz
AM pəˈlis, -ɪz
pelite
BR ˈpiːlʌɪt
AM ˈpiˌlait
pellagra
BR pɪˈlagrə(r),
pɛˈlagrə(r),
pɪˈleɪgrə(r),
pɛˈleɪgrə(r)
AM pəˈlægrə, pəˈlægrə
pellagrous
BR pɪˈlagrəs,
pɪˈleɪgrəs

pellet
AM pəˈleɪgrəs,
pəˈlægrəs
pellet
BR ˈpɛlɪt, -s
AM ˈpɛlət, -s
pelletise
BR ˈpɛlɪtʌɪz, -ɪz, -ɪŋ, -d
AM ˈpɛləˌtaɪz, -ɪz, -ɪŋ, -d
pelletize
BR ˈpɛlɪtʌɪz, -ɪz, -ɪŋ, -d
AM ˈpɛləˌtaɪz, -ɪz, -ɪŋ, -d
pellicle
BR ˈpɛlɪkl, -z
AM ˈpələkəl, -z
pellicular
BR pɪˈlɪkjʊlə(r)
AM pəˈlɪkjələr
pellitory
BR ˈpɛlɪt(ə)r|i, -ɪz
AM ˈpɛləˌtɔri, -z
pell-mell
BR ˌpɛlˈmɛl
AM ˌpɛlˈmɛl
pellucid
BR pɪˈl(j)uːsɪd,
pɛˈl(j)uːsɪd
AM pəˈlusəd, pəlˈjusəd
pellucidity
BR ˌpɛljʊˈsɪdɪti
AM ˌpɛljəˈsɪdɪdi
pellucidly
BR pɪˈl(j)uːsɪdli,
pɛˈl(j)uːsɪdli
AM pəˈlusədli,
pəlˈjusədli
pellucidness
BR pɪˈl(j)uːsɪdnɪs,
pɛˈl(j)uːsɪdnɪs
AM pəˈlusədnəs,
pəlˈjusədnəs
Pelmanise
BR ˈpɛlmənʌɪz, -ɪz, -ɪŋ,
-d
AM ˈpɛlməˌnaɪz, -ɪz, -ɪŋ,
-d
Pelmanism
BR ˈpɛlmənɪz(ə)m
AM ˈpɛlməˌnɪzəm
Pelmanize
BR ˈpɛlmənʌɪz, -ɪz, -ɪŋ,
-d
AM ˈpɛlməˌnaɪz, -ɪz, -ɪŋ,
-d
pelmet
BR ˈpɛlmɪt, -s
AM ˈpɛlmət, -s
Peloponnese
BR ˌpɛləpəˈniːz
AM ˌpɛləpəˈniz
Peloponnesian
BR ˌpɛləpəˈniːzj(ə)n,
ˌpɛləpəˈniːʒn, -z
AM ˌpɛləpəˈniʒən,
ˌpɛləpəˈniʃən, -z
Pelops
BR ˈpiːlɒps, ˈpɛlɒps
AM ˈpɛˌlɑps

pelorus
BR pɪˈlɔːrəs, -ɪz
AM pəˈlɔrəs, -əz
pelota
BR pɪˈlɒtə(r),
pɛˈlɒtə(r), pɪˈləʊtə(r),
pɛˈləʊtə(r)
AM pəˈloʊdə
pelt
BR pɛlt, -s, -ɪŋ, -ɪd
AM pɛlt, -s, -ɪŋ, -əd
pelta
BR ˈpɛltə(r)
AM ˈpɛltə
peltae
BR ˈpɛltiː
AM ˈpɛlti, ˈpɛlˌtaɪ
peltate
BR ˈpɛlteɪt
AM ˈpɛlˌteɪt
peltry
BR ˈpɛltri
AM ˈpɛltri
pelvic
BR ˈpɛlvɪk
AM ˈpɛlvɪk
pelvis
BR ˈpɛlvɪs, -ɪz
AM ˈpɛlvəs, -əz
Pemba
BR ˈpɛmbə(r)
AM ˈpɛmbə
Pemberton
BR ˈpɛmbət(ə)n
AM ˈpɛmbərtən
Pembroke
BR ˈpɛmbrʊk,
ˈpɛmbrəʊk
AM ˈpɛmˌbrʊk,
ˈpɛmˌbrʊk
pemican
BR ˈpɛmɪk(ə)n
AM ˈpɛməkən
pemmican
BR ˈpɛmɪk(ə)n
AM ˈpɛməkən
pemphigoid
BR ˈpɛmfɪɡɔɪd
AM ˈpɛm(p)fəˌɡɔɪd
pemphigous
BR ˈpɛmfɪɡəs
AM ˈpɛm(p)fəɡəs,
pɛmˈfaɪɡəs
pemphigus
BR ˈpɛmfɪɡəs
AM ˈpɛm(p)fəɡəs,
pɛmˈfaɪɡəs
pen
BR pɛn, -z, -ɪŋ, -d
AM pɛn, -z, -ɪŋ, -d
Peña
BR ˈpeɪnjə(r)
AM ˈpeɪnjə
penal
BR ˈpiːnl
AM ˈpinəl

penalisation
BR ˌpiːnəlʌɪˈzeɪʃn,
ˌpiːn|ʌɪˈzeɪʃn
AM ˌpɛnləˈzeɪʃən,
ˌpinləˈzeɪʃən,
ˌpɛnlˌaɪˈzeɪʃən,
ˌpinlˌaɪˈzeɪʃən
penalise
BR ˈpiːnəlʌɪz,
ˈpiːn|ʌɪz, -ɪz, -ɪŋ, -d
AM ˈpɛnlˌaɪz, ˈpinlˌaɪz,
-ɪz, -ɪŋ, -d
penalization
BR ˌpiːnəlʌɪˈzeɪʃn,
ˌpiːn|ʌɪˈzeɪʃn
AM ˌpɛnləˈzeɪʃən,
ˌpinləˈzeɪʃən,
ˌpɛnlˌaɪˈzeɪʃən,
ˌpinlˌaɪˈzeɪʃən
penalize
BR ˈpiːnəlʌɪz,
ˈpiːn|ʌɪz, -ɪz, -ɪŋ, -d
AM ˈpɛnlˌaɪz, ˈpinlˌaɪz,
-ɪz, -ɪŋ, -d
penally
BR ˈpiːnļi, ˈpiːnəli
AM ˈpinəli
penalty
BR ˈpɛnlt|i, -ɪz
AM ˈpɛnlti, -z
penance
BR ˈpɛnəns, -ɪz
AM ˈpɛnəns, -əz
pen-and-ink
BR ˌpɛnən(d)ˈɪŋk
AM ˌpɛnənˈɪŋk
Penang
BR pɪˈnaŋ, pɛˈnaŋ
AM pəˈnæŋ
penannular
BR pɛnˈanjʊlə(r)
AM pɛnˈænjələr
Penarth
BR pɛˈnɑːθ
AM pəˈnɑrθ
penates
BR pɪˈnɑːtiːz,
pɪˈnɑːteɪz, pɪˈneɪtiːz,
pɛˈnɑːtiːz, pɛˈnɑːteɪz,
pɛˈneɪtiːz
AM pəˈneɪdiz, pəˈnɑdiz
pence
BR pɛns
AM pɛns
penchant
BR ˈpɒ̃ʃ̃ʊ̃, -z
AM ˈpɛn(t)ʃənt, -s
pencil
BR ˈpɛns|l, -lz,
-lɪŋ\-əlɪŋ, -ld
AM ˈpɛnsļəl, -əlz,
-(ə)lɪŋ, -əld
penciller
BR ˈpɛnsļə(r),
ˈpɛnsələ(r), -z
AM ˈpɛnsələr, -z
pend
BR pɛnd, -z, -ɪŋ, -ɪd

pellet
AM pɛnd, -z, -ɪŋ, -əd
pendant
BR ˈpɛnd(ə)nt, -s
AM ˈpɛndnt, -s
pendency
BR ˈpɛnd(ə)nsi
AM ˈpɛndnsi
Pendennis
BR pɛnˈdɛnɪs
AM pɛnˈdɛnəs
pendent
BR ˈpɛnd(ə)nt, -s
AM ˈpɛndnt, -s
pendentive
BR pɛnˈdɛntɪv, -z
AM pɛnˈdɛn(t)ɪv, -z
Penderecki
BR ˌpɛndəˈrɛtski
AM ˌpɛndəˈrɛtski
Pendine
BR pɛnˈdʌɪn
AM pɛnˈdaɪn
Pendle
BR ˈpɛndl
AM ˈpɛndəl
Pendlebury
BR ˈpɛndlb(ə)ri
AM ˈpɛndəlˌbɛri
Pendleton
BR ˈpɛndlt(ə)n
AM ˈpɛn(d)əltən
pendragon
BR pɛnˈdraɡ(ə)n, -z
AM ˌpɛnˈdræɡən, -z
pendulate
BR ˈpɛndjʊleɪt,
ˈpɛndʒʊleɪt, -s, -ɪŋ, -ɪd
AM ˈpɛndʒəˌleɪ|t,
ˈpɛnd(j)əˌleɪ|t, -ts,
-dɪŋ, -dɪd
penduline
BR ˈpɛndjʊlʌɪn,
ˈpɛndʒʊlʌɪn
AM ˈpɛndʒələn,
ˈpɛndʒəˌlaɪn
pendulous
BR ˈpɛndjʊləs,
ˈpɛndʒʊləs
AM ˈpɛndʒələs,
ˈpɛndʒələs
pendulously
BR ˈpɛndjʊləsli,
ˈpɛndʒʊləsli
AM ˈpɛndʒələsli,
ˈpɛndʒələsli
pendulum
BR ˈpɛndjʊləm,
ˈpɛndʒʊləm, -z
AM ˈpɛndʒələm,
ˈpɛndʒələm, -z
Penelope
BR pɪˈnɛləpi
AM pəˈnɛləpi
peneplain
BR ˈpiːnɪpleɪn,
ˈpɛnɪpleɪn,
ˌpiːnɪˈpleɪn,
ˌpɛnɪˈpleɪn, -z

AM ˈpɪnəˌpleɪn, -z
penetrability
BR ˌpenɪtrəˈbɪlɪti
AM ˌpenətrəˈbɪlɪdi
penetrable
BR ˈpenɪtrəbl
AM ˈpenətrəbəl
penetralia
BR ˌpenɪˈtreɪlɪə(r)
AM ˌpenəˈtreɪljə,
ˌpenəˈtreɪliə
penetrance
BR ˈpenɪtr(ə)ns
AM ˈpenətrəns
penetrant
BR ˈpenɪtr(ə)nt, -s
AM ˈpenətrənt, -s
penetrate
BR ˈpenɪtreɪt, -s, -ɪŋ, -ɪd
AM ˈpenəˌtreɪ|t, -ts,
-dɪŋ, -dɪd
penetratingly
BR ˈpenɪˌtreɪtɪŋli
AM ˈpenəˌtreɪdɪŋli
penetration
BR ˌpenɪˈtreɪʃn, -z
AM ˌpenəˈtreɪʃən, -z
penetrative
BR ˈpenɪtrətɪv
AM ˈpenəˌtreɪdɪv,
ˈpenətrədɪv
penetratively
BR ˈpenɪtrətɪvli
AM ˈpenəˌtreɪdɪvli,
ˈpenətrədɪvli
penetrator
BR ˈpenɪtreɪtə(r), -z
AM ˈpenəˌtreɪdər, -z
pen-feather
BR ˈpenˌfeðə(r), -z
AM ˈpenˌfeðər, -z
Penfold
BR ˈpenfəʊld
AM ˈpenˌfoʊld
penfriend
BR ˈpenfrend, -z
AM ˈpenˌfrend, -z
Pengam
BR ˈpeŋgəm
AM ˈpenəm
Penge
BR ˈpen(d)ʒ
AM ˈpen(d)ʒ
Pengelly
BR penˈgeli
AM penˈgeli
penguin
BR ˈpeŋgwɪn, -z
AM ˈpeŋgwən, -z
Penhaligon
BR penˈhælɪg(ə)n
AM penˈhæləgən
penicillate
BR ˈpenɪˌsɪlət,
ˌpenɪˈsɪlət
AM ˈpenəˈsɪlɪt,
ˌpenəˈsɪleɪt

penicillia
BR ˌpenɪˈsɪlɪə(r)
AM ˌpenəˈsɪljə,
ˌpenəˈsɪliə
penicillin
BR ˌpenɪˈsɪlɪn
AM ˌpenəˈsɪlɪn
penicillium
BR ˌpenɪˈsɪlɪəm
AM ˌpenəˈsɪliəm
penile
BR ˈpiːnʌɪl
AM ˈpinaɪl, ˈpinl
penillion
BR peˈnɪɬən,
peˈnɪθlɪən
AM pəˈnɪljən
peninsula
BR pɪˈnɪnsjʊlə(r), -z
AM pəˈnɪns(ə)lə, -z
peninsular
BR pɪˈnɪnsjʊlə(r)
AM pəˈnɪns(ə)lər
penis
BR ˈpiːn|ɪs, -ɪsɪz
AM ˈpinɪs, -əs
Penistone
BR ˈpenɪst(ə)n
AM ˈpenəstən
penitence
BR ˈpenɪt(ə)ns
AM ˈpenədəns,
ˈpenətns
penitent
BR ˈpenɪt(ə)nt, -s
AM ˈpenədnt, -s
penitential
BR ˌpenɪˈtenʃl
AM ˌpenəˈten(t)ʃəl
penitentially
BR ˌpenɪˈtenʃli,
ˌpenɪˈtenʃəli
AM ˌpenəˈten(t)ʃəli
penitentiary
BR ˌpenɪˈtenʃ(ə)r|i, -ɪz
AM ˌpenəˈten(t)ʃ(ə)ri,
-z
penitently
BR ˈpenɪt(ə)ntli
AM ˈpenədən(t)li,
ˈpenətn̩(t)li
penknife
BR ˈpennʌɪf
AM ˈpenˌnaɪf
penknives
BR ˈpennʌɪvz
AM ˈpenˌnaɪvz
penlight
BR ˈpenlʌɪt, -s
AM ˈpenˌlaɪt, -s
Penmaenmawr
BR ˌpenmʌɪnˈmaʊə(r),
ˌpenmə(n)ˈmaʊə(r)
AM ˌpenmainˈmaʊ(ə)r
WE ˌpenmainˈmaʊr
penman
BR ˈpenmən
AM ˈpenˌmæn

penmanship
BR ˈpenmənʃɪp
AM ˈpenmənˌʃɪp
penmen
BR ˈpenmən
AM ˈpenˌmen
Penn
BR pen
AM pen
pennant
BR ˈpenənt, -s
AM ˈpenənt, -s
penne
BR ˈpeni
AM ˈpeneɪ, ˈpenə
penni
BR ˈpeni
AM ˈpeni
penniä
BR ˈpenɪɑː(r)
AM ˈpeniə
pennies
BR ˈpenɪz
AM ˈpeniz
penniless
BR ˈpenɪlɪs, ˈpenləs
AM ˈpenləs, ˈpenɪlɪs
pennilessly
BR ˈpenɪlsli, ˈpenləsli
AM ˈpenləsli, ˈpenɪlɪsli
pennilessness
BR ˈpenɪlɪsnɪs,
ˈpenləsnəs
AM ˈpenləsnəs,
ˈpenɪlɪsnɪs
pennill
BR ˈpenɪl
AM ˈpenˌnɪl
Pennine
BR ˈpenʌɪn, -z
AM ˈpeˌnain, -z
Pennington
BR ˈpenɪŋt(ə)n
AM ˈpenɪŋtən
pennon
BR ˈpenən, -z, -d
AM ˈpenən, -z, -d
penn'orth
BR ˈpenəθ
AM ˈpenərθ
Pennsylvania
BR ˌpens(ɪ)lˈveɪnɪə(r)
AM ˌpensəlˈveɪnjə
Pennsylvanian
BR ˌpens(ɪ)lˈveɪnɪən,
-z
AM ˌpensəlˈveɪnjən, -z
penny
BR ˈpen|i, -ɪz
AM ˈpeni, -z
penny-ante
BR ˈpenɪˈanti
AM ˈpeniˈæn(t)i
Pennycuick
BR ˈpenɪkʊk,
ˈpenɪkjuːk, ˈpenɪkwɪk

AM ˈpeniˌkʊk,
ˈpeniˌkwɪk
pennyfarthing
BR ˌpenɪˈfɑːθɪŋ, -z
AM ˈpeniˌfɑrðɪŋ, -z
Pennyfeather
BR ˈpenɪˌfeðə(r)
AM ˈpeniˌfeðər
pennyroyal
BR ˌpenɪˈrɔɪəl
AM ˈpeniˈrɔɪəl
pennyweight
BR ˈpenɪweɪt, -s
AM ˈpeniˌweɪt, -s
pennywort
BR ˈpenɪwəːt, -s
AM ˈpeniˌwɔrt,
ˈpeniwɔ(ə)rt, -s
pennyworth
BR ˈpenəθ, ˈpenɪwəθ,
ˈpenɪwəːθ
AM ˈpeniˌwɔrth
penological
BR ˌpiːnəˈlɒdʒɪkl
AM ˈpinlˈadʒəkəl
penologist
BR piˈnɒlədʒɪst,
pɪˈnɒlədʒɪst, -s
AM piˈnalədʒəst,
pəˈnalədʒəst, -s
penology
BR piːˈnɒlədʒi,
pɪˈnɒlədʒi
AM piˈnalədʒi,
pəˈnalədʒi
penpusher
BR ˈpenˌpʊʃə(r), -z
AM ˈpenˌpʊʃər, -z
Penrhos
BR (ˌ)penˈrəʊs,
ˈpenrəʊs
AM penˈroʊs, ˈpenˌroʊs
WE ˈpenrɔs
Penrhyn
BR (ˌ)penˈrɪn, ˈpenrɪn
AM penˈrɪn, ˈpenrən
Pensacola
BR ˌpensəˈkəʊlə(r)
AM ˌpensəˈkoʊlə
pensée
BR ˈpɒseɪ, pɒˈseɪ, -z
AM ˌpɑnˈseɪ, -z
Penshurst
BR ˈpenzhəːst
AM ˈpenzˌ(h)ərst
pensile
BR ˈpensʌɪl
AM ˈpensəl
pension[1]
hotel
BR ˈpɒsjɒ̃, -z
AM ˌpɑnsiˈɔn,
ˌpɑnsiˈɑn, -z
pension[2]
money
BR ˈpenʃ|n, -nz,
-nɪŋ\-ənɪŋ, -ənd

AM 'pɛnʃ|ən, -ənz,
-(ə)nɪŋ, -ənd
pensionability
BR ˌpɛnʃnə'bɪlɪti,
ˌpɛnʃənə'bɪlɪti
AM ˌpɛnʃ(ə)nə'bɪlɪdi
pensionable
BR 'pɛnʃnəbl,
'pɛnʃənəbl
AM 'pɛnʃ(ə)nəbəl
pensionary
BR 'pɛnʃn(ə)r|i,
'pɛnʃənə)ri, -ɪz
AM 'pɛnʃə,nɛri, -z
pensioner
BR 'pɛnʃnə(r),
'pɛnʃənə(r), -z
AM 'pɛnʃ(ə)nər, -z
pensionless
BR 'pɛnʃnləs
AM 'pɛnʃənləs
pensive
BR 'pɛnsɪv
AM 'pɛnsɪv
pensively
BR 'pɛnsɪvli
AM 'pɛnsɪvli
pensiveness
BR 'pɛnsɪvnɪs
AM 'pɛnsɪvnɪs
penstemon
BR pɛn'sti:mən,
'pɛn(t)stɪmən, -z
AM pɛn'stimən,
'pɛnstəmən, -z
penstock
BR 'pɛnstɒk, -s
AM 'pɛn,stɑk, -s
pent
BR pɛnt
AM pɛnt
pentachord
BR 'pɛntəkɔːd, -z
AM 'pɛn(t)ə,kɔ(ə)rd, -z
pentacle
BR 'pɛntəkl, -z
AM 'pɛn(t)əkəl, -z
pentad
BR 'pɛntad, -z
AM 'pɛn,tæd, -z
pentadactyl
BR ˌpɛntə'dakt(ɪ)l, -z
AM ˌpɛn(t)ə'dæktl, -z
pentagon
BR 'pɛntəɡ(ə)n, -z
AM 'pɛn(t)ə,ɡɑn, -z
pentagonal
BR pɛn'taɡənl,
pɛn'taɡnl
AM pɛn'tæɡənəl
pentagonally
BR pɛn'taɡənli,
pɛn'taɡnəli,
pɛn'taɡn̩li,
pɛn'taɡnəli
AM pɛn'tæɡ(ə)nəli
pentagram
BR 'pɛntəɡram, -z

AM 'pɛn(t)ə,ɡræm, -z
pentagynous
BR pɛn'tadʒɪnəs
AM pɛn'tædʒənəs
pentahedra
BR ˌpɛntə'hi:drə(r)
AM ˌpɛn(t)ə'hidrə
pentahedral
BR ˌpɛntə'hi:dr(ə)l
AM ˌpɛn(t)ə'hidrəl
pentahedron
BR ˌpɛntə'hi:drən
AM ˌpɛn(t)ə'hidrən
pentamerous
BR pɛn'tam(ə)rəs
AM pɛn'tæmərəs
pentameter
BR pɛn'tamɪtə(r), -z
AM pɛn'tæmədər, -z
pentamidine
BR pɛn'tamɪdi:n
AM pɛn'tæmə,din
pentandrous
BR pɛn'tandrəs
AM pɛn'tændrəs
pentane
BR 'pɛnteɪn
AM 'pɛn,teɪn
pentangle
BR 'pɛntaŋgl, -z
AM 'pɛn,tæŋgəl, -z
pentanoic acid
BR ˌpɛntənəʊɪk 'asɪd
AM ˌpɛn(t)ə'noʊɪk
'æsəd
pentaprism
BR 'pɛntə,prɪz(ə)m, -z
AM 'pɛn(t)ə,prɪzəm, -z
Pentateuch
BR 'pɛntətju:k,
'pɛntətʃu:k
AM 'pɛn(t)ə,t(j)uk
pentateuchal
BR ˌpɛntə'tju:kl,
ˌpɛntə'tʃu:kl
AM ˌpɛn(t)ə't(j)ukəl
pentathlete
BR pɛn'taθli:t, -s
AM pɛn'tæθ,lit, -s
pentathlon
BR pɛn'taθlən,
pɛn'taθlɒn, -z
AM pɛn'tæθ(ə)lən,
pɛn'tæθ(ə),lan, -z
pentatonic
BR ˌpɛntə'tɒnɪk
AM ˌpɛn(t)ə'tɑnɪk
pentavalent
BR ˌpɛntə'veɪlənt,
ˌpɛntə'veɪln̩t
AM ˌpɛn(t)ə'veɪlənt
Pentax®
BR 'pɛntaks
AM 'pɛntæks
Pentecost
BR 'pɛntɪkɒst

AM 'pɛn(t)ə,kɔst,
'pɛn(t)ə,kast
Pentecostal
BR ˌpɛntɪ'kɒstl, -z
AM ˌpɛn(t)ə'kɔstl,
'pɛn(t)ə'kastl, -z
Pentecostalism
BR ˌpɛntɪ'kɒstlɪz(ə)m
AM ˌpɛn(t)ə'kɔstl,ɪzəm,
'pɛn(t)ə'kastl,ɪzəm
Pentecostalist
BR ˌpɛntɪ'kɒstlɪst, -s
AM ˌpɛn(t)ə'kɔstləst,
'pɛn(t)ə'kastləst, -s
Pentel®
BR 'pɛntɛl
AM 'pɛn,tɛl
Penthesilea
BR ˌpɛnθɛsɪ'leɪə(r),
ˌpɛnθɪsɪ'leɪə(r)
AM ˌpɛnθə'sɪliə
penthouse
BR 'pɛnthaʊ|s, -zɪz
AM 'pɛn(t),(h)aʊ|s, -zəz
pentimenti
BR ˌpɛntɪ'mɛnti
AM ˌpɛn(t)ə'mɛn,ti
pentimento
BR ˌpɛntɪ'mɛntəʊ
AM ˌpɛn(t)ə'mɛn,toʊ
Pentire
BR pɛn'taɪə(r)
AM pɛn'taɪ(ə)r
Pentland
BR 'pɛntlənd
AM 'pɛn(t)lənd
pentobarbital
BR ˌpɛntə(ʊ)'baːbɪtl
AM ˌpɛn(t)ə'barbədl,
ˌpɛn(t)ə'barbə,tɔl,
ˌpɛn(t)ə'barbə,tal
pentobarbitol
BR ˌpɛntə(ʊ)'baːbɪtɒl
AM ˌpɛn(t)ə'barbədl,
ˌpɛn(t)ə'barbə,tɔl,
'pɛn(t)ə'barbə,tal
pentobarbitone
BR ˌpɛntə(ʊ)'baːbɪtəʊn
AM ˌpɛn(t)ə'barbə,toʊn
pentode
BR 'pɛntəʊd, -z
AM 'pɛn,toʊd, -z
Pentonville
BR 'pɛntənvɪl
AM 'pɛntn̩,vɪl
pentose
BR 'pɛntəʊz, 'pɛntəʊs,
-ɪz
AM 'pɛn,toʊs,
'pɛn,toʊz, -əz
Pentothal®
BR 'pɛntəθal
AM 'pɛn(t)ə,θɔl,
'pɛn(θ)ə,θal
pent-roof
BR 'pɛntru:f, 'pɛntrʊf,
-s
AM 'pɛn(t),ruf, -s

pentstemon
BR pɛn(t)'sti:mən,
'pɛn(t)stɪmən, -z
AM pɛn(t)'stimən,
'pɛn(t)stəmən, -z
pentyl
BR 'pɛntʌɪl
AM 'pɛn(t)əl
penuche
BR pɪ'nu:tʃi
AM pə'nutʃi
penult
BR pɪ'nʌlt, 'pɛnʌlt, -s
AM 'pi,nʌlt, pə'nʌlt, -s
penultimate
BR pɪ'nʌltɪmət,
pə'nʌltɪmət, -s
AM pə'nəltəmət, -s
penultimately
BR pɪ'nʌltɪmətli,
pə'nʌltɪmətli
AM pə'nəltəmətli
penumbra
BR pɪ'nʌmbrə(r),
pə'nʌmbrə(r), -z
AM pə'nəmbrə, -z
penumbrae
BR pɪ'nʌmbri:,
pə'nʌmbri:
AM pə'nəm,bri,
pə'nəm,braɪ
penumbral
BR pɪ'nʌmbr(ə)l,
pə'nʌmbr(ə)l
AM pə'nəmbrəl
penurious
BR pɪ'njʊərɪəs,
pə'njʊərɪəs,
pɪ'njɔːrɪəs,
pə'njɔːrɪəs
AM pə'n(j)ʊriəs
penuriously
BR pɪ'njʊərɪəsli,
pə'njʊərɪəsli,
pɪ'njɔːrɪəsli,
pə'njɔːrɪəsli
AM pə'n(j)ʊriəsli
penuriousness
BR pɪ'njʊərɪəsnəs,
pə'njʊərɪəsnəs,
pɪ'njɔːrɪəsnəs,
pə'njɔːrɪəsnəs
AM pə'n(j)ʊriəsnəs
penury
BR 'pɛnjəri
AM 'pɛnjəri
Penybont
BR ˌpɛnɪ'bɒnt
AM ˌpɛni'bɒnt,
ˌpɛni'bant
WE ˌpɛnʌ'bʊnt
Penyghent
BR ˌpɛnɪ'ɡɛnt
AM ˌpɛni'ɡɛnt
Penza
BR 'p(j)ɛnzə(r)
AM 'pɛnzə

Penzance
BR penˈzans
AM penˈzæns

peon
BR ˈpiːən, ˈpiːɒn, -z
AM ˈpiˌɑn, ˈpiən, -z

peonage
BR ˈpiːənɪdʒ
AM ˈpiənɪdʒ

peony
BR ˈpiːəni, -ɪz
AM ˈpiəni, -z

people
BR ˈpiːp|l, -lz, -l̩ɪŋ \-lɪŋ, -ld
AM ˈpipləl, -əlz, -(ə)lɪŋ, -əld

pep
BR pep, -s, -ɪŋ, -t
AM pep, -s, -ɪŋ, -t

Pepe
BR ˈpepeɪ
AM ˈpepeɪ

peperino
BR ˌpepəˈriːnəʊ
AM ˌpepəˈriˌnou

peperoni
BR ˌpepəˈrəʊn|i, -ɪz
AM ˌpepəˈrouni, -z

Pepin
BR ˈpepɪn
AM ˈpepən

pepla
BR ˈpeplə(r)
AM ˈpeplə

peplum
BR ˈpepləm, -z
AM ˈpepləm, -z

pepo
BR ˈpepəʊ, -z
AM ˈpeˌpou, -z

Peppard
BR ˈpepɑːd
AM pəˈpɑrd, ˈpepərd

pepper
BR ˈpep|ə(r), -əz, -(ə)rɪŋ, -əd
AM ˈpepər, -z, -ɪŋ, -d

pepperbox
BR ˈpepəbɒks, -ɪz
AM ˈpepərˌbɑks, -əz

peppercorn
BR ˈpepəkɔːn, -z
AM ˈpepərˌkɔ(ə)rn, -z

pepperiness
BR ˈpep(ə)rɪnɪs
AM ˈpep(ə)rɪnɪs

peppermint
BR ˈpepəmɪnt, -s
AM ˈpepərˌmɪnt, -s

pepperminty
BR ˈpepəmɪnti
AM ˈpepərˌmɪn(t)i

pepperoni
BR ˌpepəˈrəʊni
AM ˌpepəˈrouni

pepperpot
BR ˈpepəppt, -s
AM ˈpepərˌpɑt, -s

pepperwort
BR ˈpepəwɜːt, -s
AM ˈpepərwərt, ˈpepərwɔːt, -s

peppery
BR ˈpep(ə)ri
AM ˈpep(ə)ri

peppily
BR ˈpepɪli
AM ˈpepəli

peppiness
BR ˈpepɪnɪs
AM ˈpepɪnɪs

peppy
BR ˈpep|i, -ɪə(r), -ɪɪst
AM ˈpepi, -ər, -ɪst

Pepsi®
BR ˈpepsi
AM ˈpepsi

Pepsi-Cola®
BR ˌpepsɪˈkəʊlə(r)
AM ˌpepsəˈkoulə

pepsin
BR ˈpepsɪn, -z
AM ˈpepsən, -z

Pepsodent®
BR ˈpepsədent, ˈpepsəd(ə)nt
AM ˈpepsədnt

peptalk
BR ˈpeptɔːk, -s
AM ˈpepˌtɔk, ˈpepˌtɑk, -s

peptic
BR ˈpeptɪk
AM ˈpeptɪk

peptide
BR ˈpeptʌɪd
AM ˈpepˌtaɪd

peptone
BR ˈpeptəʊn, -z
AM ˈpepˌtoun, -z

peptonise
BR ˈpeptənʌɪz, -ɪz, -ɪŋ, -d
AM ˈpeptəˌnaɪz, -ɪz, -ɪŋ, -d

peptonize
BR ˈpeptənʌɪz, -ɪz, -ɪŋ, -d
AM ˈpeptəˌnaɪz, -ɪz, -ɪŋ, -d

Pepys
BR piːps, ˈpep(ɪ)s
AM pips

per¹
strong form
BR pɜː(r)
AM pɜr

per²
weak form
BR pə(r)
AM pər

peradventure
BR ˌpɜːrədˈventʃə(r), p(ə)rədˈventʃə(r)
AM ˈpərədˈven(t)ʃər, ˌpɜːrədˈven(t)ʃər

Perak
BR ˈpɛːrə(r), ˈpɪərə(r), pɛˈrak
AM ˈpɛræk, pəˈræk

perambulate
BR pəˈrambjʊleɪt, -s, -ɪŋ, -ɪd
AM pəˈræmbjəˌleɪt, -ts, -dɪŋ, -dɪd

perambulation
BR pəˌrambjʊˈleɪʃn, -z
AM pəˌræmbjʊˈleɪʃən, -z

perambulator
BR pəˈrambjʊleɪtə(r), -z
AM pəˈræmbjəˌleɪdər, -z

perambulatory
BR pəˈrambjʊlət(ə)ri
AM pəˈræmbjələˌtori

per annum
BR pər ˈanəm, pɜːr +
AM pə ˈrænəm

percale
BR pəˈkeɪl, pəˈkɑːl
AM pərˈkeɪ(ə)l

per capita
BR pə ˈkapɪtə(r), pɜː +
AM pər ˈkæpədə

per caput
BR pə ˈkapʊt, pɜː +
AM pər ˈkæpət

perceivable
BR pəˈsiːvəbl
AM pərˈsivəbəl

perceivably
BR pəˈsiːvəbli
AM pərˈsivəbli

perceive
BR pəˈsiːv, -z, -ɪŋ, -d
AM pərˈsiv, -z, -ɪŋ, -d

perceiver
BR pəˈsiːvə(r), -z
AM pərˈsivər, -z

percent
BR pəˈsent
AM pərˈsent

percentage
BR pəˈsent|ɪdʒ, -ɪdʒɪz
AM pərˈsen(t)ɪdʒ, -ɪz

percentile
BR pəˈsentʌɪl
AM pərˈsenˌtaɪl

percept
BR ˈpɜːsept, -s
AM ˈpɜrˌsept, -s

perceptibility
BR pəˌseptɪˈbɪlɪti
AM pərˌseptəˈbɪlɪdi

perceptible
BR pəˈseptɪbl
AM pərˈseptəbəl

perceptibly
BR pəˈseptɪbli
AM pərˈseptəbli

perception
BR pəˈsepʃn, -z
AM pərˈsepʃən, -z

perceptional
BR pəˈsepʃn̩(ə)l, pəˈsepʃən(ə)l
AM pərˈsepʃ(ə)nəl

perceptive
BR pəˈseptɪv
AM pərˈseptɪv

perceptively
BR pəˈseptɪvli
AM pərˈseptɪvli

perceptiveness
BR pəˈseptɪvnɪs
AM pərˈseptɪvnɪs

perceptivity
BR ˌpɜːsepˈtɪvɪti
AM ˌpərsepˈtɪvɪdi

perceptual
BR pəˈseptʃʊəl, pəˈseptʃ(ʊ)l, pəˈseptjʊəl, pəˈseptjʊl
AM pərˈsep(t)ʃ(əw)əl

perceptually
BR pəˈseptʃʊəli, pəˈseptʃʊli, pəˈseptʃli, pəˈseptjʊəli, pəˈseptjʊli
AM pərˈsep(t)ʃ(əw)əli

Perceval
BR ˈpɜːsɪvl
AM ˈpɜrsəvəl

perch
BR pɜːtʃ, -ɪz, -ɪŋ, -t
AM pɜrtʃ, -əz, -ɪŋ, -t

perchance
BR pəˈtʃɑːns, pəˈtʃans
AM pərˈtʃæns

percher
BR ˈpɜːtʃə(r), -z
AM ˈpɜrtʃər, -z

Percheron
BR ˈpɜːʃ(ə)rɒn, -z
AM ˈpɜr(t)ʃəˌrɑn, -z

perchlorate
BR pəˈklɔːreɪt, -s
AM pərˈklɔˌreɪt, -s

perchloric acid
BR pəˌklɔːrɪk ˈasɪd, pəˌklɒrɪk +
AM pərˌklɔrɪk ˈæsəd

perchloroethylene
BR pəˌklɔːrəʊˈeθɪliːn
AM pərˌklɔrouˈeθəˌlin

percipience
BR pəˈsɪpɪəns
AM pərˈsɪpɪəns

percipient
BR pəˈsɪpɪənt
AM pərˈsɪpɪənt

percipiently
BR pəˈsɪpɪəntli

AM pər'sɪpiən(t)li
Percival
BR 'pəːsɪvl
AM 'pərsəvəl
percoid
BR 'pəːkɔɪd, -z
AM 'pərkɔɪd, -z
percolate
BR 'pəːkələɪt, -s, -ɪŋ, -ɪd
AM 'pərkə,leɪ|t, -ts,
-dɪŋ, -dɪd
percolation
BR ,pəːkə'leɪʃn
AM ,pərkə'leɪʃən
percolator
BR 'pəːkələɪtə(r), -z
AM 'pərkə,leɪdər, -z
per contra
BR pəː 'kɒntrə(r)
AM pər 'kɒntrə, pər
'kɑntrə
percuss
BR pə'kʌs, -ɪz, -ɪŋ, -t
AM pər'kəs, -əz, -ɪŋ, -t
percussion
BR pə'kʌʃn
AM pər'kəʃən
percussionist
BR pə'kʌʃnɪst, -s
AM pər'kəʃənəst, -s
percussive
BR pə'kʌsɪv
AM pər'kəsɪv
percussively
BR pə'kʌsɪvli
AM pər'kəsɪvli
percussiveness
BR pə'kʌsɪvnɪs
AM pər'kəsɪvnɪs
percutaneous
BR ,pəːkjə'teɪniəs
AM ,pərkjə'teɪniəs
percutaneously
BR ,pəːkjə'teɪniəsli
AM ,pərkjə'teɪniəsli
Percy
BR 'pəːsi
AM 'pərsi
per diem
BR pəː 'diːεm, -z
AM pər 'diəm, -z
Perdita
BR 'pəːdɪtə(r)
AM pər'dɪdə
perdition
BR pə'dɪʃn
AM pər'dɪʃən
perdurability
BR pə,djʊərə'bɪlɪti,
pə,djɔːrə'bɪlɪti,
pə,dʒʊərə'bɪlɪti,
pə,dʒɔːrə'bɪlɪti
AM pər,d(j)ʊrə'bɪlɪdi
perdurable
BR pə'djʊərəbl,
pə'djɔːrəbl,

pə'dʒʊərəbl,
pə'dʒɔːrəbl
AM pər'd(j)ʊrəbəl
perdurably
BR pə'djʊərəbli,
pə'djɔːrəbli,
pə'dʒʊərəbli,
pə'dʒɔːrəbli
AM pər'd(j)ʊrəbli
père
BR pεː(r)
AM pε(ə)r
peregrinate
BR 'pεrɪgrɪneɪt, -s, -ɪŋ,
-ɪd
AM 'pεrəgrə,neɪ|t, -ts,
-dɪŋ, -dɪd
peregrination
BR ,pεrɪgrɪ'neɪʃn, -z
AM ,pεrəgrə'neɪʃən, -z
peregrinator
BR 'pεrɪgrɪneɪtə(r), -z
AM 'pεrəgrə,neɪdər, -z
peregrine
BR 'pεrɪgrɪn, -z
AM 'pεrəgrən, -z
pereira
BR pə'rεːrə(r),
pə'rɪərə(r)
AM pə'rεrə
Perelman
BR 'pəːlmən
AM 'pər(ə)lmən
peremptorily
BR pə'rεm(p)t(ə)rɪli
AM pə'rεm(p)t(ə)rəli
peremptoriness
BR pə'rεm(p)t(ə)rɪnɪs
AM pə'rεm(p)t(ə)rɪnɪs
peremptory
BR pə'rεm(p)t(ə)ri
AM pə'rεm(p)t(ə)ri
perennial
BR pə'rεniəl, -z
AM pə'rεnjəl,
pə'rεniəl, -z
perenniality
BR pə,rεni'alɪti
AM pə,rεni'ælədi
perennially
BR pə'rεniəli
AM pə'rεnjəli,
pə'rεniəli
Peres
BR 'pεrεz
AM 'pεrəs, 'pε,rεz
perestroika
BR ,pεrɪ'strɔɪ(ɪ)kə(r)
AM ,pεrə'strɔɪkə
Pérez
BR 'pεrεz
AM pə'rεz, 'pεrəz
SP 'pεrεθ, 'peres
perfect¹
adjective
BR 'pəːfɪkt
AM 'pərfək(t)

perfect²
verb
BR pə'fεkt, -s, -ɪŋ, -ɪd
AM pər'fεk|(t), -(t)s,
-tɪŋ, -təd
perfecta
BR pə'fεktə(r)
AM pər'fεktə
perfecter
BR pə'fεktə(r), -z
AM pər'fεktər, -z
perfectibility
BR pə,fεktɪ'bɪlɪti
AM pər,fεktə'bɪlɪdi
perfectible
BR pə'fεktɪbl
AM pər'fεktəbəl
perfection
BR pə'fεkʃn
AM pər'fεkʃən
perfectionism
BR pə'fεkʃnɪz(ə)m,
pə'fεkʃənɪz(ə)m
AM pər'fεkʃə,nɪzəm
perfectionist
BR pə'fεkʃnɪst,
pə'fεkʃənɪst, -s
AM pər'fεkʃ(ə)nəst, -s
perfective
BR pə'fεktɪv
AM pər'fεktɪv
perfectly
BR 'pəːfɪk(t)li
AM 'pərfək(t)li
perfectness
BR 'pəːfɪk(t)nɪs
AM 'pərfək(t)nəs
perfecto
BR pə'fεktəʊ
AM pər'fεk,toʊ
perfervid
BR pəː'fəːvɪd, pə'fəːvɪd
AM 'pər'fərvɪd
perfervidly
BR pəː'fəːvɪdli,
pə'fəːvɪdli
AM 'pər'fərvɪdli
perfervidness
BR pəː'fəːvɪdnɪs,
pə'fəːvɪdnɪs
AM 'pər'fərvɪdnɪs
perfidious
BR pə'fɪdiəs
AM pər'fɪdiəs
perfidiously
BR pə'fɪdiəsli
AM pər'fɪdiəsli
perfidiousness
BR pə'fɪdiəsnəs
AM pər'fɪdiəsnəs
perfidy
BR 'pəːfɪd|i, -ɪz
AM 'pərfədi, -z
perfin
BR 'pəːfɪn, -z
AM 'pərfɪn, -z

perfoliate
BR pə'fəʊliət
AM pər'foʊli,eɪt,
pər'foʊliət
perforate¹
adjective
BR 'pəːf(ə)rət
AM 'pərf(ə)rət,
'pərfə,reɪt
perforate²
verb
BR 'pəːfəreɪt, -s, -ɪŋ, -ɪd
AM 'pərfə,reɪ|t, -ts,
-dɪŋ, -dɪd
perforation
BR ,pəːfə'reɪʃn, -z
AM ,pərfə'reɪʃən, -z
perforative
BR 'pəːf(ə)rətɪv
AM 'pərfə,reɪdɪv,
'pərfərədɪv
perforator
BR 'pəːfəreɪtə(r), -z
AM 'pərfə,reɪdər, -z
perforce
BR pə'fɔːs
AM pər'fɔ(ə)rs
perforin
BR 'pəːf(ə)rɪn
AM 'pərfərɪn
perform
BR pə'fɔːm, -z, -ɪŋ, -d
AM pər'fɔ(ə)rm, -z, -ɪŋ,
-d
performability
BR pə,fɔːmə'bɪlɪti
AM pər,fɔrmə'bɪlɪdi
performable
BR pə'fɔːməbl
AM pər'fɔrməbəl
performance
BR pə'fɔːməns, -ɪz
AM pər'fɔrməns, -ɪz
performative
BR pə'fɔːmətɪv, -z
AM pər'fɔrmədɪv, -z
performatory
BR pə'fɔːmət(ə)r|i, -ɪz
AM pər'fɔrmə,tɔri, -z
performer
BR pə'fɔːmə(r), -z
AM pər'fɔrmər, -z
perfume¹
noun
BR 'pəːfjuːm, -z
AM 'pər,fjum,
,pər'fjum, -z
perfume²
verb
BR pə'fjuːm, 'pəːfjuːm,
-z, -ɪŋ, -d
AM ,pər'fjum,
'pər,fjum, -z, -ɪŋ, -d
perfumer
BR pə'fjuːmə(r), -z
AM pər'fjumər, -z
perfumery
BR pə'fjuːm(ə)r|i, -ɪz

AM pər'fjum(ə)ri, -z
perfumier
BR pə'fju:miə(r), -z
AM pər'fjumɪ(ə)r, -z
perfumy
BR 'pə:fju:mi
AM 'pər,fjumi,
,pər'fjumi
perfunctorily
BR pə'fʌŋ(k)t(ə)rɪli
AM pər'fəŋ(k)t(ə)rəli
perfunctoriness
BR pə'fʌŋ(k)t(ə)rɪnɪs
AM pər'fəŋ(k)t(ə)rinɪs
perfunctory
BR pə'fʌŋ(k)t(ə)ri
AM pər'fəŋ(k)t(ə)ri
perfuse
BR pə'fju:z, -ɪz, -ɪŋ, -d
AM pər'fjuz, -əz, -ɪŋ, -d
perfusion
BR pə'fju:ʒn, -z
AM pər'fjuʒən, -z
perfusive
BR pə'fju:zɪv
AM pər'fjuzɪv
Pergamene
BR 'pə:gəmi:n,
,pə:gə'mi:n, -z
AM 'pərgə,min, -z
Pergamon
BR 'pə:gəmən
AM 'pərgəmən
Pergamum
BR 'pə:gəməm
AM 'pərgəməm
pergola
BR 'pə:gələ(r),
'pə:glə(r), -z
AM 'pərgələ, -z
perhaps
BR pə'haps, praps
AM pər'(h)æps
peri
BR 'pɪər|i, -ɪz
AM 'pɪəri, -z
perianth
BR 'perɪanθ, -s
AM 'peri,ænθ, -s
periapses
BR ,perɪ'apsi:z
AM ,peri'æpsiz
periapsis
BR ,perɪ'apsɪs
AM ,peri'æpsɪs
periapt
BR 'perɪapt, -s
AM 'peri,æpt, -s
pericardia
BR ,perɪ'kɑ:dɪə(r)
AM ,perə'kardiə
pericardiac
BR ,perɪ'kɑ:dɪak
AM ,perə'kardi,æk
pericardial
BR ,perɪ'kɑ:dɪəl
AM ,perə'kardiəl

pericarditis
BR ,perɪkɑ:'dʌɪtɪs
AM ,perə,kar'daɪdɪs
pericardium
BR ,perɪ'kɑ:dɪəm, -z
AM ,perə'kardiəm, -z
pericarp
BR 'perɪkɑ:p, -s
AM 'perə,karp, -s
perichondria
BR ,perɪ'kɒndrɪə(r)
AM ,perə'kandriə
perichondrium
BR ,perɪ'kɒndrɪəm
AM ,perə'kandriəm
periclase
BR 'perɪkleɪz,
'perɪkleɪs
AM 'perə,kleɪs,
'perə,kleɪz
Periclean
BR ,perɪ'kli:ən
AM ,perə'kliən
Pericles
BR 'perɪkli:z
AM 'perə,kliz
periclinal
BR ,perɪ'klʌɪnl
AM ,perə'klaɪnəl
pericope
BR pɪ'rɪkəpi
AM pə'rɪkəpi
pericrania
BR ,perɪ'kreɪnɪə(r)
AM ,perə'kreɪniə
pericranium
BR ,perɪ'kreɪnɪəm, -z
AM ,perə'kreɪniəm, -z
peridia
BR pɪ'rɪdɪə(r)
AM pə'rɪdiə
peridium
BR pɪ'rɪdɪəm
AM pə'rɪdiəm
peridot
BR 'perɪdɒt
AM 'peri,dat
peridotite
BR 'perɪdətʌɪt
AM pə'rɪdə,taɪt
perigean
BR ,perɪ'dʒi:ən
AM ,perə'dʒiən
perigee
BR 'perɪdʒi:, -z
AM 'perədʒi, -z
periglacial
BR ,perɪ'gleɪʃl,
,perɪ'gleɪsɪəl
AM ,perə'gleɪʃəl
perigynous
BR pɪ'rɪdʒɪnəs
AM pə'rɪdʒənəs
perihelion
BR ,perɪ'hi:lɪən
AM ,perə'hiljən,
,perə'hiliən

peril
BR 'perɪl, perl̩, -z
AM 'perəl, -z
perilous
BR 'perɪləs, 'perl̩əs
AM 'perələs
perilously
BR 'perɪləsli, 'perl̩əsli
AM 'perələsli
perilousness
BR 'perɪləsnəs,
'perl̩əsnəs
AM 'perələsnəs
perilune
BR 'perɪl(j)u:n
AM 'perə,lun
perilymph
BR 'perɪlɪmf
AM 'perə,lɪmf
perimeter
BR pɪ'rɪmɪtə(r), -z
AM pə'rɪmɪdər, -z
perimetric
BR ,perɪ'metrɪk
AM ,perə'metrɪk
perimysium
BR ,perɪ'mɪsɪəm
AM ,perə'mɪʒ(i)əm
perinatal
BR ,perɪ'neɪtl
AM ,perə'neɪdl
perinea
BR ,perɪ'ni:ə(r)
AM ,perə'niə
perineal
BR ,perɪ'ni:əl
AM ,perə'niəl
perineum
BR ,perɪ'ni:əm, -z
AM ,perə'niəm, -z
period
BR 'pɪərɪəd, -z
AM 'pɪriəd, -z
periodate
BR pə'rʌɪədeɪt, -s
AM pər'aɪə,deɪt, -s
periodic
BR ,pɪərɪ'ɒdɪk
AM ,pɪri'adɪk
periodical
BR ,pɪərɪ'ɒdɪkl, -z
AM ,pɪri'adəkəl, -z
periodically
BR ,pɪərɪ'ɒdɪkli
AM ,pɪri'adək(ə)li
periodicity
BR ,pɪərɪə'dɪsɪti
AM ,pɪriə'dɪsɪdi
periodisation
BR ,pɪərɪədʌɪ'zeɪʃn
AM ,perɪədə'zeɪʃən,
,perɪə,daɪ'zeɪʃən
periodise
BR 'pɪərɪədʌɪz, -ɪz, -ɪŋ,
-d
AM 'pɪriədaɪz, -ɪz, -ɪŋ,
-d

periodization
BR ,pɪərɪədʌɪ'zeɪʃn
AM ,perɪədə'zeɪʃən,
,perɪə,daɪ'zeɪʃən
periodize
BR 'pɪərɪədʌɪz, -ɪz, -ɪŋ,
-d
AM 'pɪriədaɪz, -ɪz, -ɪŋ,
-d
periodontal
BR ,perɪə'dɒntl
AM ,perioʊ'dan(t)l
periodontics
BR ,perɪə'dɒntɪks
AM ,perioʊ'dan(t)ɪks
periodontist
BR ,perɪə'dɒntɪst, -s
AM ,perioʊ'dan(t)əst,
-s
periodontology
BR ,perɪədɒn'tɒlədʒi
AM ,perioʊ,dan'talədʒi
periostea
BR ,perɪ'ɒstɪə(r)
AM ,peri'astiə
periosteal
BR ,perɪ'ɒstɪəl
AM ,peri'astiəl
periosteum
BR ,perɪ'ɒstɪəm
AM ,peri'astiəm
periostitis
BR ,perɪə'stʌɪtɪs
AM ,peri,as'taɪdɪs,
,periə'staɪdɪs
peripatetic
BR ,perɪpə'tetɪk
AM ,perəpə'tedɪk
peripatetically
BR ,perɪpə'tetɪkli
AM ,perəpə'tedək(ə)li
peripateticism
BR ,perɪpə'tetɪsɪz(ə)m
AM ,perəpə'tedə,sɪzəm
peripeteia
BR ,perɪpɪ'tʌɪə(r),
,perɪpɪ'tɪə(r)
AM ,perəpə'ti(j)ə,
,perəpə'taɪə
peripheral
BR pɪ'rɪf(ə)rəl,
pɪ'rɪf(ə)rl̩
AM pə'rɪf(ə)rəl
peripherality
BR pɪ,rɪfə'ralɪti
AM pə,rɪfə'rælədi
peripherally
BR pɪ'rɪf(ə)rəli,
pɪ'rɪf(ə)rli
AM pə'rɪf(ə)rəli
periphery
BR pɪ'rɪf(ə)r|i, -ɪz
AM pə'rɪf(ə)ri, -z
periphrases
BR pɪ'rɪfrəsi:z
AM pə'rɪfrə,siz
periphrasis
BR pɪ'rɪfrəsɪs

AM pəˈrɪfrəsəz
periphrastic
  BR ˌperɪˈfrastɪk
  AM ˌperəˈfræstɪk
periphrastically
  BR ˌperɪˈfrastɪkli
  AM ˌperəˈfræstək(ə)li
peripteral
  BR pɪˈrɪpt(ə)rəl,
  pɪˈrɪpt(ə)r|
  AM pəˈrɪpt(ə)rəl
perique
  BR pəˈriːk
  AM pəˈrik
periscope
  BR ˈperɪskəʊp, -s
  AM ˈperəˌskoʊp, -s
periscopic
  BR ˌperɪˈskɒpɪk
  AM ˌperəˈskɑpɪk
periscopically
  BR ˌperɪˈskɒpɪkli
  AM ˌperəˈskɑpək(ə)li
perish
  BR ˈper|ɪʃ, -ɪʃɪz, -ɪʃɪŋ,
  -ɪʃt
  AM ˈperɪʃ, -ɪz, -ɪŋ, -t
perishability
  BR ˌperɪʃəˈbɪlɪti
  AM ˌperəʃəˈbɪlɪdi
perishable
  BR ˈperɪʃəbl, -z
  AM ˈperəʃəbəl, -z
perishableness
  BR ˈperɪʃəblnəs
  AM ˈperəʃəbəlnəs
perishably
  BR ˈperɪʃəbli
  AM ˈperəʃəbli
perisher
  BR ˈperɪʃə(r), -z
  AM ˈperɪʃər, -z
perishingly
  BR ˈperɪʃɪŋli
  AM ˈperɪʃɪŋli
perishless
  BR ˈperɪʃlɪs
  AM ˈperɪʃləs
perisperm
  BR ˈperɪspəːm, -z
  AM ˈperəˌspɜrm, -z
perissodactyl
  BR pɪˌrɪsə(ʊ)ˈdakt(ɪ)l,
  -z
  AM pəˌrɪsəˈdæktl, -z
Perissodactyla
  BR ˌperɪsəˈdaktɪlə(r)
  AM pəˌrɪsəˈdæktələ
peristalith
  BR pɪˈrɪstəlɪθ, -s
  AM pəˈrɪstəˌlɪθ, -s
peristalsis
  BR ˌperɪˈstalsɪs
  AM ˌperəˈstɒlsəs,
  ˌperəˈstalsəs
peristaltic
  BR ˌperɪˈstaltɪk

AM ˌperəˈstɒltɪk,
ˌperəˈstaltɪk
peristaltically
  BR ˌperɪˈstaltɪkli
  AM ˌperəˈstɒltək(ə)li,
  ˌperəˈstaltək(ə)li
peristome
  BR ˈperɪstəʊm, -z
  AM ˈperəˌstoʊm, -z
peristyle
  BR ˈperɪstʌɪl, -z
  AM ˈperəˌstaɪl, -z
peritonea
  BR ˌperɪtəˈniːə(r)
  AM ˌperətnˈiə
peritoneal
  BR ˌperɪtəˈniːəl
  AM ˌperətnˈiəl
peritoneum
  BR ˌperɪtəˈniːəm, -z
  AM ˌperətnˈiəm, -z
peritonitis
  BR ˌperɪtəˈnʌɪtɪs
  AM ˌperətnˈaɪdɪs
Perivale
  BR ˈperɪveɪl
  AM ˈperəˌveɪl
periwig
  BR ˈperɪwɪg, -z, -d
  AM ˈperəˌwɪg,
  ˈperɪˌwɪg, -z, -d
periwinkle
  BR ˈperɪˌwɪŋkl, -z
  AM ˈperəˌwɪŋkəl,
  ˈperɪˌwɪŋkəl, -z
perjure
  BR ˈpəːdʒə(r), -əz,
  -(ə)rɪŋ, -əd
  AM ˈpɜrdʒər, -ərz,
  -(ə)rɪŋ, -ərd
perjurer
  BR ˈpəːdʒ(ə)rə(r), -z
  AM ˈpɜrdʒərər, -z
perjurious
  BR pəːˈdʒʊərɪəs
  AM pərˈdʒʊriəs
perjury
  BR ˈpəːdʒ(ə)r|i, -ɪz
  AM ˈpɜrdʒ(ə)ri, -z
perk
  BR pəːk, -s, -ɪŋ, -t
  AM pɜrk, -s, -ɪŋ, -t
perkily
  BR ˈpəːkɪli
  AM ˈpɜrkəli
Perkin
  BR ˈpəːkɪn
  AM ˈpɜrkən
perkiness
  BR ˈpəːkɪnɪs
  AM ˈpɜrkɪnɪs
Perkins
  BR ˈpəːkɪnz
  AM ˈpɜrkənz
Perks
  BR pəːks
  AM pɜrks

perky
  BR ˈpəːk|i, -ɪə(r), -ɪɪst
  AM ˈpɜrki, -ər, -ɪst
Perlis
  BR ˈpəːlɪs
  AM ˈpɜrləs
perlite
  BR ˈpəːlʌɪt, -s
  AM ˈpɜrˌlaɪt, -s
perlocution
  BR ˌpəːləˈkjuːʃn
  AM ˌpɜrləˈkjuʃən
perm
  BR pəːm, -z, -ɪŋ, -d
  AM pɜrm, -z, -ɪŋ, -d
permafrost
  BR ˈpəːməfrɒst
  AM ˈpɜrməˌfrɒst,
  ˈpɜrməˌfrast
Permalloy
  BR ˈpəːməlɔɪ
  AM ˈpɜrməˌlɔɪ
permanence
  BR ˈpəːmənəns,
  ˈpəːmnəns
  AM ˈpɜrm(ə)nəns
permanency
  BR ˈpəːmənəns|i,
  ˈpəːmnəns|i, -ɪz
  AM ˈpɜrm(ə)nənsi, -z
permanent
  BR ˈpəːmənənt,
  ˈpəːmnənt
  AM ˈpɜrm(ə)nənt
permanentise
  BR ˈpəːmənəntʌɪz,
  ˈpəːmnəntʌɪz, -ɪz, -ɪŋ,
  -d
  AM ˈpɜrm(ə)nənˌtaɪz,
  -ɪz, -ɪŋ, -d
permanentize
  BR ˈpəːmənəntʌɪz,
  ˈpəːmnəntʌɪz, -ɪz, -ɪŋ,
  -d
  AM ˈpɜrm(ə)nənˌtaɪz,
  -ɪz, -ɪŋ, -d
permanently
  BR ˈpəːmənəntli,
  ˈpəːmnəntli
  AM ˈpɜrm(ə)nən(t)li
permanganate
  BR pəˈmaŋgəneɪt,
  pəˈmaŋgənət
  AM ˈpɜrˌmæŋgəˌneɪt,
  ˈpɜrˈmæŋgənət
**permanganic
acid**
  BR ˌpəːmaŋganɪk
  ˈasɪd
  AM ˌpɜrˌmænˈgænɪk
  ˈæsəd
permeability
  BR ˌpəːmɪəˈbɪlɪti
  AM ˌpɜrmiəˈbɪlɪdi
permeable
  BR ˈpəːmɪəbl
  AM ˈpɜrmiəbəl

permeance
  BR ˈpəːmɪəns
  AM ˈpɜrmiəns
permeant
  BR ˈpəːmɪənt
  AM ˈpɜrmiənt
permeate
  BR ˈpəːmɪeɪt, -s, -ɪŋ, -ɪd
  AM ˈpɜrmiˌeɪ|t, -ts, -dɪŋ,
  -dɪd
permeation
  BR ˌpəːmɪˈeɪʃn
  AM ˌpɜrmiˈeɪʃən
permeator
  BR ˈpəːmɪeɪtə(r), -z
  AM ˈpɜrmiˌeɪdər, -z
Permian
  BR ˈpəːmɪən
  AM ˈpɜrmiən
per mil
  BR pəː ˈmɪl
  AM pər ˈmɪl
per mille
  BR pəː ˈmɪl
  AM pər ˈmɪl
permissibility
  BR pəˌmɪsɪˈbɪlɪti
  AM pərˌmɪsəˈbɪlɪdi
permissible
  BR pəˈmɪsɪbl
  AM pərˈmɪsəbəl
permissibleness
  BR pəˈmɪsɪblnəs
  AM pərˈmɪsəbəlnəs
permissibly
  BR pəˈmɪsɪbli
  AM pərˈmɪsəbli
permission
  BR pəˈmɪʃn
  AM pərˈmɪʃən
permissive
  BR pəˈmɪsɪv
  AM pərˈmɪsɪv
permissively
  BR pəˈmɪsɪvli
  AM pərˈmɪsɪvli
permissiveness
  BR pəˈmɪsɪvnɪs
  AM pərˈmɪsɪvnɪs
permit[1]
  noun
  BR ˈpəːmɪt, -s
  AM ˈpɜrmɪt, -s
permit[2]
  verb
  BR pəˈmɪt, -s, -ɪŋ, -ɪd
  AM pərˈmɪ|t, -ts, -dɪŋ,
  -dɪd
permittee
  BR ˌpəːmɪˈtiː, -z
  AM ˌpɜrməˈti, -z
permitter
  BR pəˈmɪtə(r), -z
  AM pərˈmɪdər, -z
permittivity
  BR ˌpəːmɪˈtɪvɪti
  AM ˌpɜrməˈtɪvɪdi

permutable
BR pəˈmjuːtəbl
AM pərˈmjudəbəl

permutate
BR ˈpəːmjʉteɪt, -s, -ɪŋ, -ɪd
AM ˈpərmjəˌteɪ|t, -ts, -dɪŋ, -dɪd

permutation
BR ˌpəːmjʉˈteɪʃn, -z
AM ˌpərmjəˈteɪʃən, ˌpərmjuˈteɪʃən, -z

permutational
BR ˌpəːmjʉˈteɪʃn(ə)l, ˌpəːmjʉˈteɪʃən(ə)l
AM ˌpərmjəˈteɪʃ(ə)nəl

permute
BR pəˈmjuːt, -s, -ɪŋ, -ɪd
AM pərˈmju|t, -ts, -dɪŋ, -dəd

Pernambuco
BR ˌpəːnəmˈb(j)uːkəʊ, ˌpəːnamˈb(j)uːkəʊ
AM ˌpərnəmˈbjuˌkoʊ

pernicious
BR pəˈnɪʃəs
AM pərˈnɪʃəs

perniciously
BR pəˈnɪʃəsli
AM pərˈnɪʃəsli

perniciousness
BR pəˈnɪʃəsnəs
AM pərˈnɪʃəsnəs

pernicketiness
BR pəˈnɪkɪtɪnɪs
AM pərˈnɪkɪdɪnɪs

pernickety
BR pəˈnɪkɪti
AM pərˈnɪkɪdi

pernoctate
BR ˈpəːnɒkteɪt, -s, -ɪŋ, -d
AM pərˈnɑkˌteɪ|t, -ts, -dɪŋ, -dɪd

pernoctation
BR ˌpəːnɒkˈteɪʃn
AM ˌpərˌnɑkˈteɪʃən

Pernod®
BR ˈpɛːnəʊ, ˈpəːnəʊ
AM ˈpɛrˈnoʊ

Perón
BR pɛˈrɒn
AM pɛˈroʊn

peroneal
BR ˌpɛrə(ʊ)ˈniːəl
AM ˌpɛrəˈniəl

Peronism
BR ˈpɛrənɪz(ə)m
AM ˈpɛroʊnɪzəm

Peronist
BR ˈpɛrənɪst, -s
AM ˈpɛroʊnəst, -s

perorate
BR ˈpɛrəreɪt, -s, -ɪŋ, -ɪd
AM ˈpɛrəˌreɪ|t, -ts, -dɪŋ, -dɪd

peroration
BR ˌpɛrəˈreɪʃn, -z

Perot
BR pəˈrəʊ
AM pəˈroʊ

peroxidase
BR pəˈrɒksɪdeɪz, -ɪz
AM pəˈrɑksəˌdeɪz, -ɪz

peroxide
BR pəˈrɒksaɪd, -z
AM pəˈrɑkˌsaɪd, -z

perpend
BR pəˈpɛnd, -z, -ɪŋ, -ɪd
AM pərˈpɛnd, -z, -ɪŋ, -əd

perpendicular
BR ˌpəːp(ə)nˈdɪkjʉlə(r), -z
AM ˌpərpənˈdɪkjələr, -z

perpendicularity
BR ˌpəːp(ə)nˌdɪkjʉˈlarɪti
AM ˌpərpənˌdɪkjəˈlɛrədi

perpendicularly
BR ˌpəːp(ə)nˈdɪkjʉləli
AM ˌpərpənˈdɪkjələrli

perpetrable
BR ˈpəːpətrəbl
AM ˈpərpətrəbəl

perpetrate
BR ˈpəːpɪtreɪt, -s, -ɪŋ, -ɪd
AM ˈpərpəˌtreɪ|t, -ts, -dɪŋ, -dɪd

perpetration
BR ˌpəːpɪˈtreɪʃn
AM ˌpərpəˈtreɪʃən

perpetrator
BR ˈpəːpɪtreɪtə(r), -z
AM ˈpərpəˌtreɪdər, -z

perpetual
BR pəˈpɛtʃʊəl, pəˈpɛtʃ(ʉ)l, pəˈpɛtjʊəl, pəˈpɛtjʉl
AM pərˈpɛtʃ(əw)əl

perpetualism
BR pəˈpɛtʃʊəlɪz(ə)m, pəˈpɛtʃʉlɪz(ə)m, pəˈpɛtʃlɪz(ə)m, pəˈpɛtjʊəlɪz(ə)m, pəˈpɛtjʉlɪz(ə)m
AM pərˈpɛtʃ(əw)əˌlɪzəm

perpetually
BR pəˈpɛtʃʊəli, pəˈpɛtʃʉli, pəˈpɛtʃli, pəˈpɛtjʊəli, pəˈpɛtjʉli
AM pərˈpɛtʃ(əw)əli

perpetuance
BR pəˈpɛtʃʊəns, pəˈpɛtjʊəns
AM pərˈpɛtʃəwəns

perpetuate
BR pəˈpɛtʃʊeɪt, pəˈpɛtjʊeɪt, -s, -ɪŋ, -ɪd
AM pərˈpɛtʃəˌweɪ|t, -ts, -dɪŋ, -dɪd

perpetuation
BR pəˌpɛtʃʊˈeɪʃn, pəˌpɛtjʊˈeɪʃn
AM pərˌpɛtʃəˈweɪʃən

perpetuator
BR pəˈpɛtʃʊeɪtə(r), pəˈpɛtjʊeɪtə(r), -z
AM pərˈpɛtʃəˌweɪdər, -z

perpetuity
BR ˌpəːpɪˈtjuːti, ˌpəːpɪˈtʃuːti
AM ˌpərpəˈt(j)uədi

perpetuum mobile
BR pəˌpɛtjʊəm ˈməʊbɪli, pəˌpɛtʃʊəm +
AM pərˈpɛtʃəwəm ˈmoʊbəli, + ˈmoʊbəˌleɪ

perplex
BR pəˈplɛks, -ɪz, -ɪŋ, -t
AM pərˈplɛks, -əz, -ɪŋ, -t

perplexedly
BR pəˈplɛksɪdli
AM pərˈplɛksədli

perplexingly
BR pəˈplɛksɪŋli
AM pərˈplɛksɪŋli

perplexity
BR pəˈplɛksɪt|i, -ɪz
AM pərˈplɛksədi, -z

per pro.
BR pəː ˈprəʊ
AM pər ˈproʊ

perquisite
BR ˈpəːkwɪzɪt, -s
AM ˈpərkwəzət, -s

Perranporth
BR ˌpɛrənˈpɔːθ, ˌpɛrɳˈpɔːθ, ˈpɛrənpɔːθ, ˈpɛrɳpɔːθ
AM ˌpɛrənˈpɔ(ə)rθ

Perrault
BR pɛˈrəʊ, ˈpɛrəʊ
AM pəˈroʊ

Perrier®
BR ˈpɛrɪeɪ
AM ˈpɛriˌjeɪ, ˈpɛriˌjeɪ

Perrin¹
BR ˈpɛrɪn
AM ˈpɛrən

Perrin²
French
BR ˈpɛrã
AM ˈpɛrən

perron
BR ˈpɛrən, ˈpɛrɒ̃, -z
AM ˈpɛrən, pəˈrɔn, pəˈrɑn, -z

perruquier
BR pəˈruːkɪeɪ, pɛˈruːkɪeɪ, -z
AM pəˌruːkiˈeɪ, -z

perry
BR ˈpɛr|i, -ɪz
AM ˈpɛri, -z

perse
BR pəːs
AM pərs

per se
BR pəː ˈseɪ
AM pər ˈseɪ

persecute
BR ˈpəːsɪkjuːt, -s, -ɪŋ, -ɪd
AM ˈpərsəˌkju|t, -ts, -dɪŋ, -dəd

persecution
BR ˌpəːsɪˈkjuːʃn, -z
AM ˌpərsəˈkjuʃən, -z

persecutor
BR ˈpəːsɪkjuːtə(r), -z
AM ˈpərsəˌkjudər, -z

persecutory
BR ˈpəːsɪkjuːt(ə)ri
AM ˈpərsəkjəˌtɔri, pərˈsɛkjəˌtɔri

Perseids
BR ˈpəːsiɪdz
AM ˈpərsiidz

Persephone
BR pəˈsɛfəni, pəˈsɛfni
AM pərˈsɛfəni

Persepolis
BR pəˈsɛpəlɪs, pəˈsɛplɪs
AM pərˈsɛpələs

Perseus
BR ˈpəːsɪəs
AM ˈpərsiəs

perseverance
BR ˌpəːsɪˈvɪərəns, ˌpəːsɪˈvɪərɳs
AM ˌpərsəˈvɪrəns

perseverate
BR pəˈsɛvəreɪt, -s, -ɪŋ, -ɪd
AM pərˈsɛvəˌreɪ|t, -ts, -dɪŋ, -dɪd

perseveration
BR pəˌsɛvəˈreɪʃn
AM pərˌsɛvəˈreɪʃən

persevere
BR ˌpəːsɪˈvɪə(r), -z, -ɪŋ, -d
AM ˌpərsəˈvɪ(ə)r, -z, -ɪŋ, -d

Pershing
BR ˈpəːʃɪŋ
AM ˈpərˌʃɪŋ, ˈpərˌʒɪŋ

Persia
BR ˈpəːʃ(ə)r, ˈpəːʒə(r)
AM ˈpərʒə

Persian
BR ˈpəːʃn, ˈpəːʒn, -z
AM ˈpərʒən, -z

persiennes
BR ˌpəːsɪˈɛn(z)
AM ˌpərziˈɛn(z)

persiflage
BR ˈpəːsɪflɑːʒ, ˌpəːsɪˈflɑːʒ
AM ˈpərsəˌflɑʒ

Persil®
BR ˈpəːs(ɪ)l
AM ˈpərsəl

persimmon
BR pə'sɪmən, -z
AM pər'sɪmən, -z

persist
BR pə'sɪst, -s, -ɪŋ, -ɪd
AM pər'sɪst, -s, -ɪŋ, -ɪd

persistence
BR pə'sɪst(ə)ns
AM pər'sɪstəns

persistency
BR pə'sɪst(ə)nsi
AM pər'sɪstnsi

persistent
BR pə'sɪst(ə)nt
AM pər'sɪstənt

persistently
BR pə'sɪst(ə)ntli
AM pər'sɪst(ə)n(t)li

person
BR 'pəːsn, -z
AM 'pərsən, -z

persona
BR pə'səʊnə(r), -z
AM pər'soʊnə, -z

personable
BR 'pəːsŋəbl, 'pəːs(ə)nəbl
AM 'pərs(ə)nəbəl

personableness
BR 'pəːsŋəblnəs, 'pəːs(ə)nəblnəs
AM 'pərs(ə)nəbəlnəs

personably
BR 'pəːsŋəbli, 'pəːs(ə)nəbli
AM 'pərs(ə)nəbli

personae
BR pə'səʊnʌɪ, pə'səʊniː
AM ˌpər'soʊni, ˌpər'soʊˌnaɪ

personage
BR 'pəːsŋɪdʒ, 'pəːsənɪdʒ, -ɪdʒɪz
AM 'pərsənɪdʒ, -ɪz

persona grata
BR pəˌsəʊnə 'grɑːtə(r)
AM ˌpər'soʊnə 'grɑːdə

personal
BR 'pəːsŋ(ə)l, 'pəːsən(ə)l
AM 'pərs(ə)nəl

personalisation
BR ˌpəːsŋəlʌɪ'zeɪʃn, ˌpəːsŋlʌɪ'zeɪʃn, ˌpəːsənlʌɪ'zeɪʃn, ˌpəːs(ə)nəlʌɪ'zeɪʃn, ˌpərsn(ə)lə'zeɪʃən, ˌpərs(ə)nəˌlaɪ'zeɪʃən

personalise
BR 'pəːsŋəlʌɪz, 'pəːsŋlʌɪz, 'pəːsənlʌɪz, 'pəːs(ə)nəlʌɪz, -ɪz, -ɪŋ, -d
AM 'pərs(ə)nəˌlaɪz, -ɪz, -ɪŋ, -d

personality
BR ˌpəːsə'nalɪt|i, -ɪz
AM ˌpərsn'æLədi, -z

personalization
BR ˌpəːsŋəlʌɪ'zeɪʃn, ˌpəːsŋlʌɪ'zeɪʃn, ˌpəːsənlʌɪ'zeɪʃn, ˌpəːs(ə)nəlʌɪ'zeɪʃn, ˌpərsn(ə)lə'zeɪʃən, ˌpərs(ə)nəˌlaɪ'zeɪʃən

personalize
BR 'pəːsŋəlʌɪz, 'pəːsŋlʌɪz, 'pəːsənlʌɪz, 'pəːs(ə)nəlʌɪz, -ɪz, -ɪŋ, -d
AM 'pərs(ə)nəˌlaɪz, -ɪz, -ɪŋ, -d

personally
BR 'pəːsŋəli, 'pəːsŋli, 'pəːsənli, 'pəːs(ə)nəli
AM 'pərs(ə)nəli

personalty
BR 'pəːsŋlt|i, 'pəːsŋl]t|i, -ɪz
AM 'pərs(ə)nəlti, -z

persona non grata
BR pəˌsəʊnə nɒn 'grɑːtə(r)
AM ˌpər'soʊnə ˌnɑn 'grɑːdə, + ˌnoʊn 'grɑːdə

personate
BR 'pəːsŋeɪt, 'pəːsəneɪt, -s, -ɪŋ, -ɪd
AM 'pərsn͵eɪ|t, -ts, -dɪŋ, -dɪd

personation
BR ˌpəːsə'neɪʃn, ˌpəːsn'eɪʃn, -z
AM ˌpərsn'eɪʃən, -z

personator
BR 'pəːsəneɪtə(r), 'pəːsŋeɪtə(r)
AM 'pərsn͵eɪdər

personhood
BR 'pəːsnhʊd
AM 'pərsən,(h)ʊd

personification
BR pəˌsɒnɪfɪ'keɪʃn, -z
AM pərˌsɑnəfə'keɪʃən, -z

personifier
BR pə'sɒnɪfʌɪə(r), -z
AM pər'sɑnəˌfaɪ(ə)r, -z

personify
BR pə'sɒnɪfʌɪ, -z, -ɪŋ, -d
AM pər'sɑnəˌfaɪ, -z, -ɪŋ, -d

personnel
BR ˌpəːsə'nɛl, ˌpəːsn'ɛl
AM ˌpərsn'ɛl

person-to-person
BR ˌpəːsntə'pəːsn
AM ˌpərsn(t)ə'pərsən

perspectival
BR pə'spɛktɪvl
AM pər'spɛktɪvəl

perspective
BR pə'spɛktɪv, -z
AM pər'spɛktɪv, -z

perspectively
BR pə'spɛktɪvli
AM pər'spɛktɪvli

perspex
BR 'pəːspɛks
AM 'pərˌspɛks

perspicacious
BR ˌpəːspɪ'keɪʃəs
AM ˌpərspə'keɪʃəs

perspicaciously
BR ˌpəːspɪ'keɪʃəsli
AM ˌpərspə'keɪʃəsli

perspicacious-ness
BR ˌpəːspɪ'keɪʃəsnəs
AM ˌpərspə'keɪʃəsnəs

perspicacity
BR ˌpəːspɪ'kasɪti
AM ˌpərspə'kæsədi

perspicuity
BR ˌpəːspɪ'kjuːɪti
AM ˌpərspə'kjuədi

perspicuous
BR pə'spɪkjʊəs
AM pər'spɪkjəwəs

perspicuously
BR pə'spɪkjʊəsli
AM pər'spɪkjəwəsli

perspicuousness
BR pə'spɪkjʊəsnəs
AM pər'spɪkjəwəsnəs

perspiration
BR ˌpəːspə'reɪʃn
AM ˌpərspə'reɪʃən

perspiratory
BR pə'spʌɪrət(ə)ri
AM pər'spaɪrəˌtɔri

perspire
BR pə'spʌɪə(r), -z, -ɪŋ, -d
AM pər'spaɪ(ə)r, -z, -ɪŋ, -d

persuadability
BR pəˌsweɪdə'bɪlɪti
AM pərˌsweɪdə'bɪlɪdi

persuadable
BR pə'sweɪdəbl
AM pər'sweɪdəbəl

persuade
BR pə'sweɪd, -z, -ɪŋ, -ɪd
AM pər'sweɪd, -z, -ɪŋ, -ɪd

persuader
BR pə'sweɪdə(r), -z
AM pər'sweɪdər, -z

persuasible
BR pə'sweɪzɪbl
AM pər'sweɪzəbəl

persuasion
BR pə'sweɪʒn, -z
AM pər'sweɪʒən, -z

persuasive
BR pə'sweɪsɪv, pə'sweɪzɪv

AM pər'sweɪsɪv, pər'sweɪzɪv

persuasively
BR pə'sweɪsɪvli, pə'sweɪzɪvli
AM pər'sweɪsɪvli, pər'sweɪzɪvli

persuasiveness
BR pə'sweɪsɪvnɪs, pə'sweɪzɪvnɪs
AM pər'sweɪsɪvnɪs, pər'sweɪzɪvnɪs

pert
BR pəːt
AM pərt

pertain
BR pə'teɪn, -z, -ɪŋ, -d
AM pər'teɪn, -z, -ɪŋ, -d

Perth
BR pəːθ
AM pərθ

pertinacious
BR ˌpəːtɪ'neɪʃəs
AM ˌpərtn'eɪʃəs

pertinaciously
BR ˌpəːtɪ'neɪʃəsli
AM ˌpərtn'eɪʃəsli

pertinaciousness
BR ˌpəːtɪ'neɪʃəsnəs
AM ˌpərtn'eɪʃəsnəs

pertinacity
BR ˌpəːtɪ'nasɪti
AM ˌpərtn'æsədi

pertinence
BR 'pəːtɪnəns
AM 'pərtŋəns

pertinency
BR 'pəːtɪnənsi
AM 'pərtŋənsi

pertinent
BR 'pəːtɪnənt
AM 'pərtŋənt

pertinently
BR 'pəːtɪnəntli
AM 'pərtŋən(t)li

pertly
BR 'pəːtli
AM 'pərtli

pertness
BR 'pəːtnəs
AM 'pərtnəs

perturb
BR pə'təːb, -z, -ɪŋ, -d
AM pər'tərb, -z, -ɪŋ, -d

perturbable
BR pə'təːbəbl
AM pər'tərbəbəl

perturbation
BR ˌpəːtə'beɪʃn, -z
AM ˌpərdər'beɪʃən, -z

perturbative
BR pə'təːbətɪv
AM pər'tərbədɪv, 'pərdərˌbeɪdɪv

perturbingly
BR pə'təːbɪŋli
AM pər'tərbɪŋli

pertussis
BR pə'tʌsɪs
AM pər'təsəs

Pertwee
BR 'pɜːtwiː
AM 'pɜrt,wi

Peru
BR pə'ruː
AM pə'ru

Perugia
BR pə'ruːdʒ(ɪ)ə(r)
AM pə'rudʒə

peruke
BR pə'ruːk, -s
AM pə'ruk, -s

perusal
BR pə'ruːzl, -z
AM pə'ruzəl, -z

peruse
BR pə'ruːz, -ɪz, -ɪŋ, -d
AM pə'ruz, -əz, -ɪŋ, -d

peruser
BR pə'ruːzə(r), -z
AM pə'ruzər, -z

Perutz
BR pə'rʊts
AM pə'rʊtz

Peruvian
BR pə'ruːvɪən, -z
AM pə'ruvɪən, -z

perv
BR pɜːv, -z, -ɪŋ, -d
AM pɜrv, -z, -ɪŋ, -d

pervade
BR pə'veɪd, -z, -ɪŋ, -ɪd
AM pər'veɪd, -z, -ɪŋ, -ɪd

pervasion
BR pə'veɪʒn
AM pər'veɪʒən

pervasive
BR pə'veɪsɪv, pə'veɪzɪv
AM pər'veɪsɪv

pervasively
BR pə'veɪsɪvli,
pə'veɪzɪvli
AM pər'veɪsɪvli

pervasiveness
BR pə'veɪsɪvnɪs,
pə'veɪzɪvnɪs
AM pər'veɪsɪvnɪs

perve
BR pɜːv, -z, -ɪŋ, -d
AM pɜrv, -z, -ɪŋ, -d

perverse
BR pə'vɜːs
AM pər'vɜrs

perversely
BR pə'vɜːsli
AM pər'vɜrsli

perverseness
BR pə'vɜːsnəs
AM pər'vɜrsnəs

perversion
BR pə'vɜːʃn, pə'vɜːʒn,
-z
AM pər'vɜrʒən, -z

perversity
BR pə'vɜːsɪti
AM pər'vɜrsədi

perversive
BR pə'vɜːsɪv
AM pər'vɜrsɪv

pervert[1]
noun
BR 'pɜːvɜːt, -s
AM 'pɜr,vɜrt, -s

pervert[2]
verb
BR pə'vɜːt, -s, -ɪŋ, -ɪd
AM pər'vɜr|t, -ts, -dɪŋ,
-dəd

pervertedly
BR pə'vɜːtɪdli
AM pər'vɜrdədli

perverter
BR pə'vɜːtə(r), -z
AM pər'vɜrdər, -z

pervious
BR 'pɜːvɪəs
AM 'pɜrvɪəs

perviously
BR 'pɜːvɪəsli
AM 'pɜrvɪəsli

perviousness
BR 'pɜːvɪəsnəs
AM 'pɜrvɪəsnəs

Pery
BR 'pɪəri, 'pɛːri, 'pɛri
AM 'pɛri

Pesach
BR 'peɪsɑːk, 'peɪsɑːx
AM 'peɪ,sɑk

peseta
BR pə'seɪtə(r), -z
AM pə'seɪdə, -z

Peshitta
BR pə'ʃiːtə(r)
AM pə'ʃidə

peskily
BR 'pɛskɪli
AM 'pɛskəli

peskiness
BR 'pɛskɪnɪs
AM 'pɛskɪnɪs

pesky
BR 'pɛsk|i, -ɪə(r), -ɪɪst
AM 'pɛski, -ər, -ɪst

peso
BR 'peɪsəʊ, -z
AM 'peɪsoʊ, -z

pessary
BR 'pɛs(ə)r|i, -ɪz
AM 'pɛsəri, -z

pessimism
BR 'pɛsɪmɪz(ə)m
AM 'pɛsə,mɪzəm

pessimist
BR 'pɛsɪmɪst, -s
AM 'pɛsəməst, -s

pessimistic
BR ,pɛsɪ'mɪstɪk
AM ,pɛsə'mɪstɪk

pessimistically
BR ,pɛsɪ'mɪstɪkli
AM ,pɛsə'mɪstɪk(ə)li

pest
BR pɛst, -s
AM pɛst, -s

Pestalozzi
BR ,pɛstə'lɒtsi
AM ,pɛstə'lɑtsi

pester
BR 'pɛst|ə(r), -əz,
-(ə)rɪŋ, -əd
AM 'pɛstər, -z, -ɪŋ, -d

pesterer
BR 'pɛst(ə)rə(r), -z
AM 'pɛstərər, -z

pesthole
BR 'pɛsthəʊl, -z
AM 'pɛst,(h)oʊl, -z

pesticidal
BR ,pɛstɪ'sʌɪdl
AM ,pɛstə'saɪdəl

pesticide
BR 'pɛstɪsʌɪd, -z
AM 'pɛstə,saɪd, -z

pestiferous
BR pɛ'stɪf(ə)rəs
AM pɛ'stɪf(ə)rəs

pestiferously
BR pɛ'stɪf(ə)rəsli
AM pɛ'stɪf(ə)rəsli

pestilence
BR 'pɛstɪləns, 'pɛstɪlns,
-ɪz
AM 'pɛstələns, -ɪz

pestilent
BR 'pɛstɪlənt, 'pɛstɪlnt
AM 'pɛstələnt

pestilential
BR ,pɛstɪ'lenʃl
AM ,pɛstə'len(t)ʃəl

pestilentially
BR ,pɛstɪ'lenʃli,
,pɛstɪ'lenʃəli
AM ,pɛstə'len(t)ʃəli

pestilently
BR 'pɛstɪləntli,
'pɛstɪlntli
AM 'pɛstələn(t)li

pestle
BR 'pɛs(t)l, -z
AM 'pɛstəl, 'pɛsəl, -z

pesto
BR 'pɛstəʊ
AM 'pɛstoʊ

pestological
BR ,pɛstə'lɒdʒɪkl
AM ,pɛstə'lɑdʒəkəl

pestologist
BR pɛ'stɒlədʒɪst, -s
AM pɛs'tɑlədʒəst, -s

pestology
BR pɛ'stɒlədʒi
AM pɛs'tɑlədʒi

PET
*positron emission
tomography,*

*polyethylene
terephthalate*
BR ,piːiː'tiː, pɛt
AM ,pii'ti, pɛt

pet
BR pɛt, -s, -ɪŋ, -ɪd
AM pɛ|t, -ts, -dɪŋ, -dəd

Peta
BR 'piːtə(r)
AM 'peɪdə, 'pidə

Pétain
BR pɛ'tɑ̃
AM pɛ'tɛn

petal
BR 'pɛtl, -z, -d
AM 'pɛdl, -z, -d

petaline
BR 'pɛtəlʌɪn, 'pɛtlʌɪn
AM 'pɛdl,aɪn, 'pɛdlən

petal-like
BR 'pɛtllʌɪk
AM 'pɛdl,laɪk

petaloid
BR 'pɛtlɔɪd
AM 'pɛdl,ɔɪd

petalon
BR 'pɛtəlɒn, 'pɛtələn
AM 'pɛdl,ɑn

pétanque
BR ,peɪ'tɒŋk
AM ,peɪ'tɑŋk

petard
BR pɪ'tɑːd, -z
AM pə'tɑrd, -z

petasus
BR 'pɛtəsəs, -ɪz
AM 'pɛdəsəs, -əz

petaurist
BR pɪ'tɔːrɪst, -s
AM pə'tɔrəst, -s

petcock
BR 'pɛtkɒk, -s
AM 'pɛt,kɑk, -s

Pete
BR piːt
AM pit

petechia
BR pɪ'tiːkɪə(r)
AM pə'tikɪə

petechiae
BR pə'tiːkiː
AM pə'tiki,aɪ, pə'tiki,i

petechial
BR pɪ'tiːkɪəl
AM pə'tikiəl

peter
BR 'piːt|ə(r), -əz,
-(ə)rɪŋ, -əd
AM 'pidər, -z, -ɪŋ, -d

Peterborough
BR 'piːtəb(ə)rə(r)
AM 'pidər,bərə

Peterhead
BR ,piːtə'hɛd
AM ,pidər'hɛd

Peterkin
BR 'piːtəkɪn

AM ˈpidərkən
Peterlee
BR ˈpiːtəˈli
AM ˌpidərˈli
Peterloo
BR ˈpiːtəˈluː
AM ˌpidərˈlu
peterman
BR ˈpiːtəmən
AM ˈpidərmən
petermen
BR ˈpiːtəmən
AM ˈpidərmən
Peter Pan
BR ˈpiːtə ˈpan
AM ˌpidər ˈpæn
Peters
BR ˈpiːtəz
AM ˈpidərz
Petersburg
BR ˈpiːtəzbəːg
AM ˈpidərzˌbərg
Petersen
BR ˈpiːtəs(ə)n
AM ˈpidərsən
DAN ˈpeːˈdʌsən
Petersfield
BR ˈpiːtəzfiːld
AM ˈpidərzˌfild
petersham
BR ˈpiːtəʃ(ə)m, -z
AM ˈpidəˌrʃæm, -z
Peterson
BR ˈpiːtəs(ə)n
AM ˈpidərsən
Petherick
BR ˈpɛθ(ə)rɪk
AM ˈpɛθ(ə)rək
pethidine
BR ˈpɛθɪdiːn
AM ˈpɛθəˌdin
petiolar
BR ˈpɛtɪəʊlə(r)
AM ˌpidiˈoʊlər
petiolate
BR ˈpɛtɪəlæt
AM ˌpidiˈoʊlət,
ˈpidiəˌleɪt
petiole
BR ˈpɛtɪəʊl, -z
AM ˈpidiˌoʊl, -z
petit
BR ˈpɛti, pəˈti:
AM ˈpɛdi, pəˈti(t)
petit bourgeois
BR ˌpɛti ˈbʊəʒwɑ:(r),
pəˌti: +, + ˈbɔːʒwɑ:(r),
-z
AM ˌpɛdi bʊrˈʒwɑ,
pəˌti(t) +, -z
petite
BR pəˈti:t
AM pəˈtit
petite bourgeoisie
BR pəˌti:t ˌbʊəʒwɑːˈzi:,
+ ˌbɔːʒwɑːˈzi:

AM ˌpɛdi ˌbʊrˌʒwɑˈzi,
pəˌti(t) +
petit four
BR ˌpɛti ˈfɔː(r), -z
AM ˈpɛdi ˌfɔ(ə)r, -z
petition
BR pɪˈtɪʃ|n, -nz,
-n̩ɪŋ\-ənɪŋ, -nd
AM pəˈtɪʃən, -ənz,
-(ə)nɪŋ, -ənd
petitionable
BR pɪˈtɪʃn̩əbl,
pɪˈtɪʃənəbl
AM pəˈtɪʃ(ə)nəbəl
petitionary
BR pɪˈtɪʃ(ə)nər|i, -ɪz
AM pəˈtɪʃəˌnɛri, -z
petitioner
BR pəˈtɪʃn̩ə(r),
pəˈtɪʃənə(r), -z
AM pəˈtɪʃənər, -z
petitio principii
BR pɪˈtɪʃɪəʊ
prɪnˈsɪpɪʌɪ,
+ prɪŋˈkɪpɪʌɪ
AM pəˌtɪʃioʊ
prɪnˈsɪpi,i
petit jury
BR ˌpɛti ˈdʒʊər|i, -ɪz
AM ˈpɛdi ˌdʒʊri, -z
petit-maître
BR ˌpɛtɪˈmeɪtrə(r), -z
AM ˌpɛdiˈmeɪtrə, -z
petit mal
BR ˌpɛtɪ ˈmal
AM ˈpɛdi ˌmal
petit point
BR ˌpɛt ˈpɔɪnt
AM ˈpɛdi ˌpɔɪnt
petits pois
plural noun
BR ˌpɛti ˈpwɑ:(r)
AM ˌpɛdi ˈpwɑ
petnapper
BR ˈpɛtˌnapə(r), -z
AM ˈpɛtˌnæpər, -z
petnapping
BR ˈpɛtˌnapɪŋ
AM ˈpɛtˌnæpɪŋ
Peto
BR ˈpiːtəʊ
AM ˈpidoʊ
Petra
BR ˈpɛtrə(r)
AM ˈpɛtrə
Petrarch
BR ˈpɛtrɑːk
AM ˈpɛˌtrɑrk
Petrarchan
BR pɪˈtrɑːk(ə)n
AM pəˈtrɑrkən
petrel
BR ˈpɛtr(ə)l, -z
AM ˈpɛtrəl, -z
Petri dish
BR ˈpɛtrɪ ˌdɪʃ, ˈpiːtrɪ +,
-ɪz
AM ˈpitri ˌdɪʃ, -ɪz

Petrie
BR ˈpiːtri
AM ˈpɛtri, ˈpitri
petrifaction
BR ˌpɛtrɪˈfakʃn
AM ˌpɛtrəˈfækʃən
petrification
BR ˌpɛtrɪfɪˈkeɪʃn
AM ˌpɛtrəfəˈkeɪʃən
petrify
BR ˈpɛtrɪfʌɪ, -z, -ɪŋ, -d
AM ˈpɛtrəˌfaɪ, -z, -ɪŋ, -d
petrochemical
BR ˌpɛtrəʊˈkɛmɪkl
AM ˌpɛtroʊˈkɛməkəl
petrochemistry
BR ˌpɛtrəʊˈkɛmɪstri
AM ˌpɛtroʊˈkɛməstri
petrodollar
BR ˌpɛtrə(ʊ)ˌdɒlə(r), -z
AM ˈpɛtroʊˌdɑlər, -z
Petrofina
BR ˌpɛtrə(ʊ)ˈfiːnə(r)
AM ˌpɛtrəˈfinə
petrogenesis
BR ˌpɛtrə(ʊ)ˈdʒɛnɪsɪs
AM ˌpɛtroʊˈdʒɛnəsəs
petroglyph
BR ˌpɛtrə(ʊ)glɪf, -s
AM ˈpɛtrəˌglɪf, -s
Petrograd
BR ˈpɛtrəgrad
AM ˈpɛtrəˌgræd
RUS pʲitraˈgrat
petrographer
BR pɪˈtrɒgrəfə(r), -z
AM pəˈtrɑgrəfər, -z
petrographic
BR ˌpɛtrəˈgrafɪk
AM ˌpɛtrəˈgræfɪk
petrographical
BR ˌpɛtrəˈgrafɪkl
AM ˌpɛtrəˈgræfəkəl
petrography
BR pɪˈtrɒgrəfi
AM pəˈtrɑgrəfi
petrol
BR ˈpɛtr(ə)l
AM ˈpɛtrəl
petrolatum
BR ˌpɛtrəˈleɪtəm
AM ˌpɛtroʊˈleɪdəm
petroleum
BR pɪˈtrəʊlɪəm
AM pəˈtroʊliəm
petrolic
BR pɪˈtrɒlɪk
AM pəˈtrɑlɪk
petrologic
BR ˌpɛtrəˈlɒdʒɪk
AM ˌpɛtrəˈlɑdʒɪk
petrological
BR ˌpɛtrəˈlɒdʒɪkl
AM ˌpɛtrəˈlɑdʒəkəl
petrologist
BR pɪˈtrɒlədʒɪst, -s
AM pəˈtrɑlədʒəst, -s

petrology
BR pɪˈtrɒlədʒi
AM pəˈtrɑlədʒi
petronel
BR ˈpɛtrənl, -z
AM ˈpɛtrənəl, -z
Petronella
BR ˌpɛtrəˈnɛlə(r)
AM ˌpɛtrəˈnɛlə
Petronius
BR pɪˈtrəʊnɪəs
AM pəˈtroʊniəs
petrous
BR ˈpɛtrəs
AM ˈpɛtrəs, ˈpitrəs
petter
BR ˈpɛtə(r), -z
AM ˈpɛdər, -z
petticoat
BR ˈpɛtɪkəʊt, -s
AM ˈpɛdiˌkoʊt,
ˈpɛdəˌkoʊt, -ts
Pettifer
BR ˈpɛtɪfə(r)
AM ˈpɛdəfər
pettifog
BR ˈpɛtɪfɒg, -z, -ɪŋ, -d
AM ˈpɛdiˌfɑg, ˈpɛdiˌfɔg,
-z, -ɪŋ, -d
pettifogger
BR ˈpɛtɪˌfɒgə(r), -z
AM ˈpɛdiˌfɔgər,
ˈpɛdiˌfɑgər, -z
pettifoggery
BR ˈpɛtɪˌfɒg(ə)ri
AM ˈpɛdiˌfɔgəri,
ˈpɛdiˌfɑgəri
Pettigrew
BR ˈpɛtɪgruː
AM ˈpɛdəˌgru
pettily
BR ˈpɛtɪli
AM ˈpɛdəli
pettiness
BR ˈpɛtɪnɪs
AM ˈpɛdinɪs
pettish
BR ˈpɛtɪʃ
AM ˈpɛdɪʃ
pettishly
BR ˈpɛtɪʃli
AM ˈpɛdɪʃli
pettishness
BR ˈpɛtɪʃnɪs
AM ˈpɛdɪʃnɪs
Pettit
BR ˈpɛtɪt
AM ˈpɛdɪt
pettitoe
BR ˈpɛtɪtəʊ, -z
AM ˈpɛdiˌtoʊ, -z
Pettitt
BR ˈpɛtɪt
AM ˈpɛdɪt
petty
BR ˈpɛt|i, -ɪə(r), -ɪɪst
AM ˈpɛdi, -ər, -ɪst

petty bourgeois
BR ˌpeti ˈbʊəʒwɑː(r),
+ ˈbɔːʒwɑː(r), -z
AM ˌpedi bʊrˈʒwɑ, -z

petty bourgeoisie
BR ˌpeti ˌbʊəʒwɑːˈziː,
+ ˌbɔːʒwɑːˈziː
AM ˌpedi ˌbʊrˌʒwɑˈzi

Petula
BR pɪˈtjuːlə(r),
pɪˈtʃuːlə(r)
AM pəˈt(j)uːlə, pəˈtʃuːlə

petulance
BR ˈpetjʊləns,
ˈpetjʊlns, ˈpetʃʊləns,
ˈpetʃʊlns
AM ˈpetʃələns

petulant
BR ˈpetjʊlənt,
ˈpetjʊlnt, ˈpetʃʊlənt,
ˈpetʃʊlnt
AM ˈpetʃələnt

petulantly
BR ˈpetjʊləntli,
ˈpetjʊlntli,
ˈpetʃʊləntli,
ˈpetʃʊlntli
AM ˈpetʃələn(t)li

Petulengro
BR ˌpetjʊˈleŋgrəʊ,
ˌpetʃəˈleŋgrəʊ
AM ˌpet(j)əˈleŋgroʊ,
ˌpetʃəˈleŋgroʊ

petunia
BR pɪˈtjuːniə(r),
pɪˈtʃuːniə(r), -z
AM pəˈt(j)uniə,
pəˈt(j)unjə, -z

petuntse
BR peɪˈtʊntsə(r),
pɪˈtʌntsə(r)
AM pəˈtʊn(t)sə

Petworth
BR ˈpetwəːθ, ˈpetwəθ
AM ˈpet̬ˌwərθ

Peugeot®
BR ˈpəːʒəʊ, ˈpjuːʒəʊ, -z
AM p(j)əˈʒoʊ, ˈpjuˌʒoʊ,
-z

Pevensey
BR ˈpevnzi
AM ˈpevənsi

Peveril
BR ˈpev(ə)rɪl,
ˈpev(ə)rl̩
AM ˈpev(ə)rəl

Pevsner
BR ˈpevznə(r)
AM ˈpevznər

pew
BR pjuː, -z
AM pju, -z

pewage
BR ˈpjuːɪdʒ
AM ˈpjuɪdʒ

pewee
BR ˈpiːwiː, -z

AM ˈpiˌwi, -z

pewit
BR ˈpiːwɪt, -s
AM ˈpiwɪt, ˈpjuət, -s

pewless
BR ˈpjuːləs
AM ˈpjuləs

Pewsey
BR ˈpjuːzi
AM ˈpjuzi

pewter
BR ˈpjuːtə(r)
AM ˈpjudər

pewterer
BR ˈpjuːt(ə)rə(r), -z
AM ˈpjudərər, -z

peyote
BR peɪˈəʊti, pɪˈəʊti
AM peɪˈoʊdi

peyotism
BR peɪˈəʊtɪz(ə)m,
pɪˈəʊtɪz(ə)m
AM peɪˈoʊˌtizəm

Peyton
BR ˈpeɪtn
AM ˈpeɪtn

Pfennig
BR ˈ(p)fenɪg, -z
AM ˈ(p)fenɪg, -z

pH
BR ˌpiːˈeɪtʃ
AM ˌpiˈeɪtʃ

Phaedo
BR ˈfiːdəʊ
AM ˈfeɪdoʊ

Phaedra
BR ˈfeɪdrə(r)
AM ˈfeɪdrə

Phaedrus
BR ˈfiːdrəs
AM ˈfeɪdrəs

Phaethon
BR ˈfeɪθ(ə)n
AM ˈfeɪ(ə)tn

phaeton
BR ˈfeɪtn, -z
AM ˈfeɪ(ə)tn, -z

phage
BR feɪdʒ, -ɪz
AM feɪdʒ, -ɪz

phagedaena
BR ˌfadʒɪˈdiːnə(r)
AM ˌfædʒəˈdinə

phagedaenic
BR ˌfadʒɪˈdiːnɪk
AM ˌfædʒəˈdinɪk

phagedena
BR ˌfadʒɪˈdiːnə(r)
AM ˌfædʒəˈdinə

phagedenic
BR ˌfadʒɪˈdiːnɪk
AM ˌfædʒəˈdinɪk

phagocyte
BR ˈfagəsʌɪt, -s
AM ˈfægəˌsaɪt, -s

phagocytic
BR ˌfagəˈsɪtɪk

phagocytise
BR ˈfagəsʌɪtʌɪz, -ɪz, -ɪŋ,
-d
AM ˈfægəsəˌtaɪz, -ɪz, -ɪŋ,
-d

phagocytize
BR ˈfagəsʌɪtʌɪz, -ɪz, -ɪŋ,
-d
AM ˈfægəsəˌtaɪz, -ɪz, -ɪŋ,
-d

phagocytose
BR ˈfagəsʌɪtəʊz, -ɪz,
-ɪŋ, -d
AM ˈfægəˌsaɪˌtoʊs,
ˈfægəˌsaɪˌtoʊz, -əz, -ɪŋ,
-d

phagocytosis
BR ˌfagəsʌɪˈtəʊsɪs
AM ˌfægəˌsaɪˈtoʊsəs

Phaidon
BR ˈfaɪdn
AM ˈfaɪdən

Phalange
BR fəˈlan(d)ʒ
AM fəˈlændʒ

phalangeal
BR fəˈlan(d)ʒɪəl
AM ˈfeɪˌlændʒ(i)əl,
fəˈlændʒ(i)əl

phalanger
BR fəˈlan(d)ʒə(r), -z
AM ˈfeɪˌlændʒər,
fəˈlændʒər, -z

phalanges
bones, plural of
phalanx
BR fəˈlan(d)ʒiːz
AM fəˈlændʒiz,
feɪˈlændʒiz

phalangist
BR fəˈlan(d)ʒɪst, -s
AM fəˈlændʒəst,
feɪˈlændʒəst, -s

phalansterian
BR ˌfalənˈstɪərɪən,
ˌfaln̩ˈstɪərɪən
AM ˌfælənˈstɪriən

phalanstery
BR ˈfalənst(ə)r|i,
ˈfaln̩st(ə)r|i, -ɪz
AM ˈfælənˌsteri, -z

phalanx
BR ˈfalaŋks, -ɪz
AM ˈfeɪˌlæŋks, -əz

phalarope
BR ˈfalərəʊp, -s
AM ˈfæləˌroʊp, -s

phalli
BR ˈfalʌɪ, ˈfaliː
AM ˈfæˌlaɪ

phallic
BR ˈfalɪk
AM ˈfælɪk

phallically
BR ˈfalɪkli
AM ˈfælək(ə)li

phallicism
BR ˈfalɪsɪz(ə)m
AM ˈfæləˌsɪzəm

phallism
BR ˈfalɪz(ə)m
AM ˈfæˌlɪzəm

phallocentric
BR ˌfalə(ʊ)ˈsentrɪk
AM ˈfæloʊˈsentrɪk

phallocentricity
BR ˌfalə(ʊ)senˈtrɪsɪti
AM ˌfæloʊˌsenˈtrɪsədi

phallocentrism
BR ˌfalə(ʊ)ˈsentrɪz(ə)m
AM ˈfæloʊˈsenˌtrɪzəm

phallus
BR ˈfaləs, -ɪz
AM ˈfæləs, -əz

phanariot
BR fəˈnarɪət, -s
AM fəˈnɛrɪət,
fəˈnɛriˌɑt, -s

phanerogam
BR ˈfan(ə)rə(ʊ)gam, -z
AM ˈfænərəˌgæm, -z

phanerogamic
BR ˌfan(ə)rəˈgamɪk
AM ˈfænərəˈgæmɪk

phanerogamous
BR ˌfanəˈrɒgəməs
AM ˌfænəˈrɑgəməs

Phanerozoic
BR ˌfan(ə)rəˈzəʊɪk
AM ˌfæn(ə)rəˈzoʊɪk

phantasise
BR ˈfantəsʌɪz, -ɪz, -ɪŋ, -d
AM ˈfæn(t)əˌsaɪz, -ɪz,
-ɪŋ, -d

phantasize
BR ˈfantəsʌɪz, -ɪz, -ɪŋ, -d
AM ˈfæn(t)əˌsaɪz, -ɪz,
-ɪŋ, -d

phantasm
BR ˈfantaz(ə)m, -z
AM ˈfæn̩ˌtæzəm, -z

phantasmagoria
BR ˌfantazməˈgɔːrɪə(r),
fanˌtazməˈgɔːrɪə(r)
AM ˌfænˌtæzməˈgɔriə

phantasmagoric
BR ˌfantazməˈgɒrɪk,
fanˌtazməˈgɒrɪk
AM fænˈtæzməˈgɔrɪk

phantasmagorical
BR ˌfantazməˈgɒrɪkl,
fanˌtazməˈgɒrɪkl
AM fænˈtæzməˈgɔrəkəl

phantasmal
BR fanˈtazml
AM fænˈtæzməl

phantasmally
BR fanˈtazmļi,
fanˈtazməli
AM fænˈtæzməli

phantasmic
BR fanˈtazmɪk
AM fænˈtæzmɪk

phantast
BR ˈfantast, -s
AM ˈfæn.tæst, -s

phantasy
BR ˈfantəs|i, -ɪz
AM ˈfæn(t)əsi, -z

phantom
BR ˈfantəm, -z
AM ˈfæn(t)əm, -z

pharanges
BR fəˈran(d)ʒiːz
AM fəˈrandʒiz

Pharaoh
BR ˈfɛːrəʊ, -z
AM ˈfɛrəʊ, -z

Pharaonic
BR ˌfɛːreɪˈɒnɪk
AM ˌfɛreɪˈɑnɪk

Pharisaic
BR ˌfarɪˈseɪɪk
AM ˌfɛrəˈseɪɪk

Pharisaical
BR ˌfarɪˈseɪɪkl
AM ˌfɛrəˈseɪɪkəl

Pharisaically
BR ˌfarɪˈseɪɪkli
AM ˌfɛrəˈseɪɪk(ə)li

Pharisaicalness
BR ˌfarɪˈseɪɪklnɪs
AM ˌfɛrəˈseɪɪkəlnəs

Pharisaism
BR ˈfarɪseɪɪz(ə)m
AM ˈfɛrəˌseɪˌɪzəm

Pharisee
BR ˈfarɪsiː, -z
AM ˈfɛrəˌsi, -z

pharmaceutic
BR ˌfaːməˈs(j)uːtɪk, -s
AM ˌfaːrməˈsudɪk, -s

pharmaceutical
BR ˌfaːməˈs(j)uːtɪkl, -z
AM ˌfaːrməˈsudəkəl, -z

pharmaceutically
BR ˌfaːməˈs(j)uːtɪkli
AM ˌfaːrməˈsudək(ə)li

pharmacist
BR ˈfaːməsɪst, -s
AM ˈfaːrməsəst, -s

pharmacognosy
BR ˌfaːməˈkɒgnəsi
AM ˌfaːrməˈkagnəsi

pharmacological
BR ˌfaːməkəˈlɒdʒɪkl
AM ˌfaːrməkəˈladʒəkəl

pharmacologically
BR ˌfaːməkəˈlɒdʒɪkli
AM ˌfaːrməkəˈladʒək(ə)li

pharmacologist
BR ˌfaːməˈkɒlədʒɪst, -s
AM ˌfaːrməˈkalədʒəst, -s

pharmacology
BR ˌfaːməˈkɒlədʒi
AM ˌfaːrməˈkalədʒi

pharmacopeia
BR ˌfaːməkəˈpiːə(r), -z

AM ˌfaːrməkəˈpi(j)ə,
ˌfaːrməˈkoʊpi(j)ə, -z

pharmacopeial
BR ˌfaːməkəˈpiːəl, -z
AM ˌfaːrməkəˈpi(j)əl,
ˌfaːrməˈkoʊpi(j)əl, -z

pharmacopoeia
BR ˌfaːməkəˈpiːə(r), -z
AM ˌfaːrməkəˈpi(j)ə,
ˌfaːrməˈkoʊpi(j)ə, -z

pharmacopoeial
BR ˌfaːməkəˈpiːəl, -z
AM ˌfaːrməˈkoʊpi(j)əl,
-z

pharmacy
BR ˈfaːməs|i, -ɪz
AM ˈfaːrməsi, -z

Pharoah
BR ˈfɛːrəʊ, -z
AM ˈfɛrəʊ, -z

pharos
BR ˈfɛːrɒs, -ɪz
AM ˈfɛˌrɒs, ˈfɛras, -əz

Pharsala
BR faːˈsɑːlə(r),
faːˈseɪlə(r)
AM faːrˈsalə

pharyngal
BR fəˈrɪŋgl, -z
AM fəˈrɪŋgəl, -z

pharyngeal
BR fəˈrɪn(d)ʒɪəl,
ˌfarɪnˈdʒiːəl,
ˌfarɪnˈdʒiːəl
AM fəˈrɪndʒ(i)əl,
ˌfɛrənˈdʒiəl

pharyngitis
BR ˌfarɪnˈdʒʌɪtɪs,
ˌfarɪnˈdʒʌɪtɪs
AM ˌfɛrənˈdʒaɪdɪs

pharyngoscope
BR fəˈrɪŋgəskəʊp, -s
AM fəˈrɪŋgəˌskoʊp, -s

pharyngotomy
BR ˌfarɪŋˈgɒtəm|i, -ɪz
AM ˌfɛrɪŋˈgadəmi, -z

pharynx
BR ˈfarɪŋks, -ɪz
AM ˈfɛrɪŋ(k)s, -ɪz

phase
BR feɪz, -ɪz, -ɪŋ, -d
AM feɪz, -ɪz, -ɪŋ, -d

phasedown
BR ˈfeɪzdaʊn, -z
AM ˈfeɪzˌdaʊn, -z

phaseout
BR ˈfeɪzaʊt, -s
AM ˈfeɪzˌaʊt, -s

phasic
BR ˈfeɪzɪk
AM ˈfeɪzɪk

phasmid
BR ˈfazmɪd, -z
AM ˈfæzməd, -z

Phasmida
BR ˈfazmɪdə(r)
AM ˈfæzmədə

phatic
BR ˈfatɪk
AM ˈfædɪk

Ph.D.
BR ˌpiːeɪtʃˈdiː, -z
AM ˌpietʃˈdi, -z

pheasant
BR ˈfɛznt, -s
AM ˈfɛznt, -s

pheasantry
BR ˈfɛzntr|i, -ɪz
AM ˈfɛzntri, -z

Pheidippides
BR fʌɪˈdɪpɪdiːz
AM faɪˈdɪpəˌdiz

Phelan
BR ˈfiːlən
AM ˈfeɪlən

Phelps
BR fɛlps
AM fɛlps

phenacetin
BR fɪˈnasɪtɪn
AM fiˈnæsədən,
fɛˈnæsədən

phenobarbital
BR ˌfiːnə(ʊ)ˈbaːbɪtl
AM ˌfiːnoʊˈbaːbəˌtɔl,
ˈfiːnoʊˈbaːbəˌtal

phenobarbitone
BR ˌfiːnə(ʊ)ˈbaːbɪtəʊn
AM ˈfiːnoʊˈbaːbəˌtoʊn

phenocryst
BR ˈfiːnə(ʊ)krɪst,
ˈfɛnə(ʊ)krɪst, -s
AM ˈfinəˌkrɪst,
ˈfɛnəˌkrɪst, -s

phenol
BR ˈfiːnɒl
AM ˈfiˌnɔl, ˈfiˌnɑl

phenolic
BR fɪˈnɒlɪk
AM fəˈnɑlɪk, fiˈnɑlɪk

phenological
BR ˌfiːnəˈlɒdʒɪkl
AM ˌfinəˈladʒəkəl

phenologist
BR fɪˈnɒlədʒɪst, -s
AM fəˈnalədʒəst, -s

phenology
BR fɪˈnɒlədʒi
AM fəˈnalədʒi

phenolphthalein
BR ˌfiːnɒlˈ(f)θeɪlɪɪn,
ˌfiːnɒlˈ(f)θalɪn,
ˌfiːnɒlˈ(f)θeɪlriːin,
ˌfiːnɒlˈ(f)θalriːn
AM ˈfinəlˈθeɪˌli(ə)n

phenomena
BR fɪˈnɒmɪnə(r)
AM fəˈnamənə

phenomenal
BR fɪˈnɒmɪnl
AM fəˈnamənəl

phenomenalise
BR fɪˈnɒmɪnlʌɪz,
fɪˈnɒmɪnəlʌɪz, -ɪz, -ɪŋ,
-d

AM fəˈnamənəˌlaɪz, -ɪz,
-ɪŋ, -d

phenomenalism
BR fɪˈnɒmɪnlɪz(ə)m,
fɪˈnɒmɪnəlɪz(ə)m
AM fəˈnamənəˌlɪzəm

phenomenalist
BR fɪˈnɒmɪnlɪst,
fɪˈnɒmɪnəlɪst, -s
AM fəˈnamənələst, -s

phenomenalistic
BR fɪˌnɒmɪnəˈlɪstɪk,
fɪˌnɒmɪnlˈɪstɪk
AM fɪˌnamənəˈlɪstɪk

phenomenalize
BR fɪˈnɒmɪnlʌɪz,
fɪˈnɒmɪnəlʌɪz, -ɪz, -ɪŋ,
-d
AM fəˈnamənəˌlaɪz, -ɪz,
-ɪŋ, -d

phenomenally
BR fɪˈnɒmɪnl|i,
fɪˈnɒmɪnəli
AM fəˈnam(ə)n(ə)li

phenomenological
BR fɪˌnɒmɪnəˈlɒdʒɪkl
AM fəˈnamənəˈladʒəkəl

**phenomenologic-
ally**
BR fɪˌnɒmɪnəˈlɒdʒɪkli
AM fəˈnamənəˈladʒə-
k(ə)li

phenomenologist
BR fɪˌnɒmɪˈnɒlədʒɪst,
-s
AM fəˌnaməˈnalədʒəst,
-s

phenomenology
BR fɪˌnɒmɪˈnɒlədʒi
AM fəˌnaməˈnalədʒi

phenomenon
BR fɪˈnɒmɪnən
AM fəˈnaməˌnan,
fəˈnamənən

phenotype
BR ˈfiːnə(ʊ)tʌɪp, -s
AM ˈfinəˌtaɪp, -s

phenotypic
BR ˌfiːnə(ʊ)ˈtɪpɪk
AM ˌfinəˈtɪpɪk

phenotypical
BR ˌfiːnə(ʊ)ˈtɪpɪkl
AM ˌfinəˈtɪpɪkəl

phenotypically
BR ˌfiːnə(ʊ)ˈtɪpɪkli
AM ˌfinəˈtɪpɪk(ə)li

Phensic
BR ˈfɛnzɪk, ˈfɛnsɪk
AM ˈfɛnzɪk, ˈfɛnsɪk

phenyl
BR ˈfiːnʌɪl, ˈfɛnʌɪl,
ˈfiːn(ɪ)l, ˈfen(ɪ)l, -z
AM ˈfɛnəl, ˈfinəl, -z

phenylalanine
BR ˌfiːnʌɪlˈaləniːn,
ˌfiːn(ɪ)lˈaləniːn,
ˌfiːnʌɪlˈalənʌɪn
ˌfiːn(ɪ)lˈalənʌɪn

phenylalanine
AM ˌfenəlˈæləˌnin,
ˌfinəlˈæləˌnin
phenylketonuria
BR ˌfiːnaɪlˌkiːtəˈnjʊə-
rɪə(r),
ˌfiːn(ɪ)lˌkiːtəˈnjʊərɪə(r)
AM ˌfenəlˌkiːtəˈn(j)uriə,
ˌfinəlˌkiːtəˈn(j)uriə
pheromonal
BR ˌferəˈməʊnl,
ˈferəməʊnl
AM ˈferəˌmoʊnəl
pheromone
BR ˈferəməʊn, -z
AM ˈferəˌmoʊn, -z
phew
BR ɸː, fjuː
AM fju
phi
BR faɪ, -z
AM faɪ, -z
phial
BR ˈfaɪəl, -z
AM ˈfaɪ(ə)l, -z
Phi Beta Kappa
BR ˌfaɪ ˌbeɪtə ˈkapə(r),
+ ˌbiːtə +, -z
AM ˈfaɪ ˈbeɪdə ˈkæpə, -z
Phidias
BR ˈfɪdɪəs
AM ˈfɪdiəs
Phil
BR fɪl
AM fɪl
philabeg
BR ˈfɪləbeg, -z
AM ˈfɪləˌbeg, -z
Philadelphia
BR ˌfɪləˈdelfɪə(r)
AM ˌfɪləˈdelfiə
Philadelphian
BR ˌfɪləˈdelfɪən, -z
AM ˌfɪləˈdelfiən, -z
philadelphus
BR ˌfɪləˈdelfəs
AM ˌfɪləˈdelfəs
philander
BR frˈlandlə(r), -əz,
-(ə)rɪŋ, -əd
AM fəˈlændlər, -ərz,
-(ə)rɪŋ, -ərd
philanderer
BR frˈland(ə)rə(r), -z
AM fəˈlændərər, -z
philanthrope
BR ˈfɪlənθrəʊp, -s
AM ˈfɪlənˌθroʊp, -s
philanthropic
BR ˌfɪlənˈθrɒpɪk
AM ˌfɪlənˈθrɑpɪk
philanthropically
BR ˌfɪlənˈθrɒpɪkli
AM ˌfɪlənˈθrɑpək(ə)li
philanthropise
BR frˈlanθrəpaɪz, -ɪz,
-ɪŋ, -d
AM fəˈlænθrəˌpaɪz, -ɪz,
-ɪŋ, -d

philanthropism
BR frˈlanθrəpɪz(ə)m
AM fəˈlænθrəˌpɪzəm
philanthropist
BR frˈlanθrəpɪst, -s
AM fəˈlænθrəpəst, -s
philanthropize
BR frˈlanθrəpaɪz, -ɪz,
-ɪŋ, -d
philanthropy
BR frˈlanθrəpi
AM fəˈlænθrəpi
philatelic
BR ˌfɪləˈtelɪk
AM ˈfɪləˈtelɪk
philatelically
BR ˌfɪləˈtelɪkli
AM ˈfɪləˈtelək(ə)li
philatelist
BR frˈlatəlɪst, frˈlatlɪst,
-s
AM fəˈlædləst, -s
philately
BR frˈlatəli, frˈlatli
AM fəˈlædli
Philbin
BR ˈfɪlbɪn
AM ˈfɪlbɪn
Philby
BR ˈfɪlbi
AM ˈfɪlbi
Philemon
BR faɪˈliːmən
AM fəˈlimən, faɪˈlimən
philharmonia
BR ˌfɪl(h)ɑːˈməʊnɪə(r),
ˌfɪləˈməʊnɪə(r)
AM ˌfɪl(h)ɑrˈmoʊniə
philharmonic
BR ˌfɪl(h)ɑːˈmɒnɪk,
ˌfɪləˈmɒnɪk, -s
AM ˈfɪlɑrˈmɑnɪk,
ˈfɪl(h)ɑrˈmɑnɪk, -s
philhellene
BR fɪlˈheliːn, -z
AM fɪlˈhelɪn, -z
philhellenic
BR ˌfɪlheˈliːnɪk,
ˌfɪlhəˈliːnɪk,
ˌfɪlheˈlenɪk,
ˌfɪlhəˈlenɪk
AM ˌfɪl(h)eˈlenɪk
philhellenism
BR fɪlˈhelɪnɪz(ə)m
AM fɪlˈheləˌnɪzəm
philhellenist
BR fɪlˈhelɪnɪst, -s
AM fɪlˈhelənəst, -s
Philip
BR ˈfɪlɪp
AM ˈfɪlɪp
Philippa
BR ˈfɪlɪpə(r)
AM fəˈlɪpə
Philippi
BR ˈfɪlɪpaɪ

AM fəˈlɪpi
Philippian
BR frˈlɪpɪən, -z
AM fəˈlɪpiən, -z
philippic
BR frˈlɪpɪk, -s
AM fəˈlɪpɪk, -s
philippina
BR ˌfɪlɪˈpiːnə(r), -z
AM ˈfɪləˌpinə, -z
Philippine
BR ˈfɪlɪpiːn, -z
AM ˈfɪləˌpin, -z
Philippino
BR ˌfɪlɪˈpiːnəʊ, -z
AM ˌfɪləˈpinoʊ, -z
Philips
BR ˈfɪlɪps
AM ˈfɪlɪps
Philistine
BR ˈfɪlɪstaɪn, -z
AM ˈfɪləˌstin,
ˈfɪləˌstaɪn, -z
Philistinism
BR ˈfɪlɪstɪnɪz(ə)m
AM ˈfɪləˌstiˌnɪzəm,
ˈfɪləˌstaɪˌnɪzəm
Phillida
BR ˈfɪlɪdə(r)
AM ˈfɪlədə
Phillip
BR ˈfɪlɪp
AM ˈfɪlɪp
Phillipines
BR ˈfɪlɪpiːnz
AM ˈfɪləˌpinz
Phillips
BR ˈfɪlɪps
AM ˈfɪlɪps
Phillpot
BR ˈfɪlpɒt
AM ˈfɪlˌpɑt
Phillpott
BR ˈfɪlpɒt
AM ˈfɪlˌpɑt
phillumenist
BR frˈl(j)uːmɪnɪst, -s
AM fəˈl(j)uːmənəst, -s
phillumeny
BR frˈl(j)uːmɪni
AM fəˈl(j)uːməni
Philly
BR ˈfɪli
AM ˈfɪli
Philoctetes
BR ˌfɪləkˈtiːtiːz
AM ˌfɪləkˈtidiz
philodendron
BR ˌfɪləˈdendr(ə)n, -z
AM ˌfɪləˈdendrən, -z
philogynist
BR frˈlɒdʒɪnɪst, -s
AM fəˈlɑdʒənəst, -s
philologer
BR frˈlɒlədʒə(r), -z
AM fəˈlɑlədʒər, -z

philologian
BR ˌfɪləˈləʊdʒɪən, -z
AM ˌfɪləˈloʊdʒiən, -z
philologic
BR ˌfɪləˈlɒdʒɪk
AM ˈfɪləˈlɑdʒɪk
philological
BR ˌfɪləˈlɒdʒɪkl
AM ˈfɪləˈlɑdʒəkəl
philologically
BR ˌfɪləˈlɒdʒɪkli
AM ˈfɪləˈlɑdʒək(ə)li
philologise
BR frˈlɒlədʒaɪz, -ɪz, -ɪŋ,
-d
AM fəˈlaləˌdʒaɪz, -ɪz,
-ɪŋ, -d
philologist
BR frˈlɒlədʒɪst, -s
AM fəˈlalədʒəst, -s
philologize
BR frˈlɒlədʒaɪz, -ɪz, -ɪŋ,
-d
AM fəˈlaləˌdʒaɪz, -ɪz,
-ɪŋ, -d
philology
BR frˈlɒlədʒi
AM fəˈlalədʒi
philomel
BR ˈfɪləmel, -z
AM ˈfɪləˌmel, -z
Philomela
BR ˌfɪləˈmiːlə(r)
AM ˌfɪləˈmilə
Philomena
BR ˌfɪləˈmiːnə(r)
AM ˌfɪləˈminə
philoprogenitive
BR ˌfɪlə(ʊ)prə(ʊ)ˈdʒen-
ɪtɪv
AM ˌfɪləproʊˈdʒenədɪv
philosophaster
BR frˈlɒsəfastə(r),
fɪˌlɒsəˈfastə(r), -z
AM fəˈlasəˈfæstər, -z
philosopher
BR frˈlɒsəfə(r), -z
AM fəˈlɑs(ə)fər, -z
philosophic
BR ˌfɪləˈsɒfɪk
AM ˈfɪləˈsafɪk
philosophical
BR ˌfɪləˈsɒfɪkl
AM ˈfɪləˈsafəkəl
philosophically
BR ˌfɪləˈsɒfɪkli
AM ˈfɪləˈsafək(ə)li
philosophise
BR frˈlɒsəfaɪz, -ɪz, -ɪŋ,
-d
AM fəˈlɑsəˌfaɪz, -ɪz, -ɪŋ,
-d
philosophiser
BR frˈlɒsəfaɪzə(r), -z
AM fəˈlɑsəˌfaɪzər, -z
philosophize
BR frˈlɒsəfaɪz, -ɪz, -ɪŋ,
-d

AM fə'lɑsəˌfaɪz, -ɪz, -ɪŋ,
-d
philosophizer
BR fɪ'lɒsəfʌɪzə(r), -z
AM fə'lɑsəˌfaɪzər, -z
philosophy
BR fɪ'lɒsəf̬li, -ɪz
AM fə'lɑsəfi, -z
Philostratus
BR fɪ'lɒstrətəs
AM fr'lastrədəs,
ˌfɪlə'stradəs
Philpot
BR 'fɪlpɒt
AM 'fɪlˌpɑt
philter
BR 'fɪltə(r), -z
AM 'fɪltər, -z
philtre
BR 'fɪltə(r), -z
AM 'fɪltər, -z
phimosis
BR fʌɪ'məʊsɪs
AM faɪ'moʊsəs
phimotic
BR fʌɪ'mɒtɪk
AM faɪ'mɑdɪk
Phineas
BR 'fɪnɪəs
AM 'fɪniəs
Phipps
BR fɪps
AM fɪps
phiz
BR fɪz, -ɪz
AM fɪz, -ɪz
phizog
BR 'fɪzɒg, -z
AM 'fɪzˌɑg, -z
phlebitic
BR flɪ'bɪtɪk
AM flɛ'bɪdɪk
phlebitis
BR flɪ'bʌɪtɪs
AM flə'baɪdɪs
phlebotomise
BR flɪ'bɒtəmʌɪz, -ɪz,
-ɪŋ, -d
AM flə'badəˌmaɪz, -ɪz,
-ɪŋ, -d
phlebotomist
BR flɪ'bɒtəmɪst, -s
AM flə'badəməst, -s
phlebotomize
BR flɪ'bɒtəmʌɪz, -ɪz,
-ɪŋ, -d
AM flə'badəˌmaɪz, -ɪz,
-ɪŋ, -d
phlebotomy
BR flɪ'bɒtəm|i, -ɪz
AM flə'badəmi, -z
phlegm
BR flɛm
AM flɛm
phlegmatic
BR flɛg'matɪk
AM flɛg'mædɪk

phlegmatically
BR flɛg'matɪkli
AM flɛg'mædək(ə)li
phlegmy
BR 'flɛmi
AM 'flɛmi
phloem
BR 'fləʊɛm
AM 'floʊˌɛm, 'floʊəm
phlogistic
BR flə'dʒɪstɪk
AM flə'dʒɪstɪk
phlogiston
BR flə'dʒɪstɒn,
flə'dʒɪst(ə)n
AM flou'dʒɪstən
phlox
BR flɒks, -ɪz
AM flaks, -əz
Phnom Penh
BR ˌ(p)nɒm 'pɛn
AM ˌ(p)nɑm 'pɛn
phobia
BR 'fəʊbɪə(r), -z
AM 'foʊbiə, -z
phobic
BR 'fəʊbɪk
AM 'foʊbɪk
Phobos
BR 'fəʊbɒs
AM 'foʊˌbɒs, 'foʊˌbas
Phocaea
BR fə(ʊ)'siːə(r)
AM foʊ'siə
Phocian
BR 'fəʊʃɪən, 'fəʊsɪən
AM 'foʊsiən
Phocis
BR 'fəʊsɪs
AM 'foʊsəs
phoebe
BR 'fiːb|i, -ɪz
AM 'fiˌbi, -z
Phoebus
BR 'fiːbəs
AM 'fibəs
Phoenicia
BR fɪ'nɪʃə(r),
fɪ'niːʃə(r)
AM fə'nɪʃə, fə'niʃə
Phoenician
BR fɪ'nɪʃn, fɪ'niːʃn, -z
AM fə'nɪʃən, fə'niʃən,
-z
phoenix
BR 'fiːnɪks, -ɪz
AM 'finɪks, -ɪz
pholas
BR 'fəʊləs
AM 'foʊləs
phon
BR fɒn, -z
AM fɑn, -z
phonaesthesia
BR ˌfɒnəs'θiːzɪə(r),
ˌfɒnəs'θiːʒə(r)
AM ˌfoʊnəs'θiz(i)ə

phonate
BR fə'neɪt, -s, -ɪŋ, -ɪd
AM 'foʊˌneɪ|t, -ts, -dɪŋ,
-dɪd
phonation
BR fə'neɪʃn
AM foʊ'neɪʃən
phonatory
BR 'fəʊnət(ə)ri
AM 'foʊnəˌtɔri
phonautograph
BR fə(ʊ)'nɔːtəgrɑːf,
fə(ʊ)'nɔːtəgraf, -s
AM foʊ'nɑdəˌgræf,
foʊ'nɑdəˌgræf, -s
phone
BR fəʊn, -z, -ɪŋ, -d
AM foʊn, -z, -ɪŋ, -d
phonecard
BR 'fəʊnkɑːd, -z
AM 'foʊnˌkard, -z
phone-in
BR 'fəʊnɪn, -z
AM 'foʊn'ɪn, -z
phoneme
BR 'fəʊniːm, -z
AM 'foʊˌnim, -z
phonemic
BR fə'niːmɪk, -s
AM foʊ'nimɪk,
fə'nimɪk, -s
phonemicisation
BR fəˌniːmɪsʌɪ'zeɪʃn
AM foʊˌniməsə'zeɪʃən,
fəˌniməsə'zeɪʃən,
foʊˌniməˌsaɪ'zeɪʃən,
fəˌniməˌsaɪ'zeɪʃən
phonemicise
BR fə'niːmɪsʌɪz, -ɪz, -ɪŋ,
-d
AM foʊ'niməˌsaɪz,
fə'niməˌsaɪz, -ɪz, -ɪŋ, -d
phonemicist
BR fə'niːmɪsɪst, -s
AM foʊ'nimɪsəst, -s
phonemicization
BR fəˌniːmɪsʌɪ'zeɪʃn
AM foʊˌniməsə'zeɪʃən,
fəˌniməsə'zeɪʃən,
foʊˌniməˌsaɪ'zeɪʃən,
fəˌniməˌsaɪ'zeɪʃən
phonemicize
BR fə'niːmɪsʌɪz, -ɪz, -ɪŋ,
-d
AM foʊ'niməˌsaɪz,
fə'niməˌsaɪz, -ɪz, -ɪŋ, -d
phonendoscope
BR ˌfəʊn'ɛndəskəʊp, -s
AM ˌfoʊn'ɛndəˌskoʊp,
-s
phonesthesia
BR ˌfɒnəs'θiːzɪə(r),
ˌfɒnəs'θiːʒə(r)
AM ˌfoʊnəs'θiz(i)ə
phonetapping
BR 'fəʊnˌtapɪŋ, -z
AM 'foʊnˌtæpɪŋ, -z

phonetic
BR fə'nɛtɪk, -s
AM foʊ'nɛdɪk,
fə'nɛdɪk, -s
phonetically
BR fə'nɛtɪkli
AM foʊ'nɛdək(ə)li,
fə'nɛdək(ə)li
phonetician
BR ˌfɒnə'tɪʃn,
ˌfəʊnə'tɪʃn, -z
AM ˌfoʊnə'tɪʃən, -z
phoneticise
BR fə'nɛtɪsʌɪz, -ɪz, -ɪŋ,
-d
AM foʊ'nɛdəˌsaɪz,
fə'nɛdəˌsaɪz, -ɪz, -ɪŋ, -d
phoneticism
BR fə'nɛtɪsɪz(ə)m
AM foʊ'nɛdəˌsɪzəm,
fə'nɛdəˌsɪzəm
phoneticist
BR fə'nɛtɪsɪst, -s
AM foʊ'nɛdəsəst,
fə'nɛdəsəst, -s
phoneticization
BR fəˌnɛtɪsʌɪ'zeɪʃn
AM foʊˌnɛtəsə'zeɪʃən,
fəˌnɛtəsə'zeɪʃən,
foʊˌnɛtəˌsaɪ'zeɪʃən,
fəˌnɛtəˌsaɪ'zeɪʃən
phoneticize
BR fə'nɛtɪsʌɪz, -ɪz, -ɪŋ,
-d
AM foʊ'nɛdəˌsaɪz,
fə'nɛdəˌsaɪz, -ɪz, -ɪŋ, -d
phonetist
BR fə'nɛtɪst, -s
AM foʊ'nɛdəst,
fə'nɛdəst, -s
phoney
BR 'fəʊn|i, -ɪz
AM 'foʊni, -z
phonic
BR 'fɒnɪk, 'fəʊnɪk, -s
AM 'fɑnɪk, -s
phonically
BR 'fɒnɪkli, 'fəʊnɪkli
AM 'fɑnək(ə)li
phonily
BR 'fəʊnɪli
AM 'foʊnəli
phoniness
BR 'fəʊnɪnɪs
AM 'foʊnɪnɪs
phono
BR 'fəʊnə(ʊ), 'fɒnə(ʊ)
AM 'foʊnoʊ
phonogram
BR 'fəʊnəgram, -z
AM 'foʊnəˌgræm, -z
phonograph
BR 'fəʊnəgrɑːf,
'fəʊnəgraf, -s
AM 'foʊnəˌgræf, -s
phonographer
BR fə'nɒgrəfə(r), -z

AM fə'nɑgrəfər, foʊ'nɑgrəfər, -z

phonographic
BR ˌfəʊnə'grafɪk
AM ˌfoʊnə'græfɪk

phonographical
BR ˌfəʊnə'grafɪkl
AM ˌfoʊnə'græfəkəl

phonographically
BR ˌfəʊnə'grafɪkli
AM ˌfoʊnə'græfək(ə)li

phonography
BR fə'nɒgrəfi
AM fə'nɑgrəfi

phonolite
BR 'fəʊnəlʌɪt, -s
AM 'foʊnəˌlaɪt, -s

phonological
BR ˌfɒnə'lɒdʒɪkl, ˌfəʊnə'lɒdɪkl
AM ˌfɑnl'ɑdʒəkəl, ˌfoʊnl'ɑdʒəkəl

phonologically
BR ˌfɒnə'lɒdʒɪkli, ˌfəʊnə'lɒdʒɪkli
AM ˌfɑnl'ɑdʒək(ə)li, ˌfoʊnl'ɑdʒək(ə)li

phonologist
BR fə'nɒlədʒɪst, -s
AM fə'nɑlədʒəst, foʊ'nɑlədʒəst, -s

phonology
BR fə'nɒlədʒi
AM fə'nɑlədʒi, foʊ'nɑlədʒi

phonometer
BR fə(ʊ)'nɒmɪtə(r), -z
AM foʊ'nɑmədər, -z

phonon
BR 'fəʊnɒn, -z
AM 'foʊˌnɑn, -z

phonoscope
BR 'fəʊnəskəʊp, -s
AM 'foʊnəˌskoʊp, -s

phonotype
BR 'fəʊnətʌɪp, -s
AM 'foʊnəˌtaɪp, -s

phony
BR 'fəʊn|i, -ɪz
AM 'foʊni, -z

phooey
BR 'fu:i
AM 'fui

phoresy
BR 'fɔːrəsi
AM 'fɔrəsi

phoretic
BR fə'rɛtɪk
AM fə'rɛdɪk

phormium
BR 'fɔːmɪəm
AM 'fɔrmɪəm

phosgene
BR 'fɒzdʒiːn
AM 'faz,dʒin

phosphatase
BR 'fɒsfəteɪz, 'fɒsfəteɪs

AM 'fasfə,teɪs, 'fasfə,teɪz

phosphate
BR 'fɒsfeɪt, -s
AM 'fas,feɪt, -s

phosphatic
BR fɒs'fatɪk
AM fas'fædɪk

phosphene
BR 'fɒsfiːn
AM 'fas,fin

phosphide
BR 'fɒsfʌɪd, -z
AM 'fas,faɪd, -z

phosphine
BR 'fɒsfiːn
AM 'fas,fin

phosphinic
BR fɒs'fɪnɪk
AM fas'fɪnɪk

phosphite
BR 'fɒsfʌɪt, -s
AM 'fas,faɪt, -s

phospholipid
BR ˌfɒsfə(ʊ)'lɪpɪd, -z
AM ˌfasfoʊ'lɪpɪd, -z

phosphor
BR 'fɒsfə(r)
AM 'fasfər

phosphorate
BR 'fɒsfəreɪt, -s, -ɪŋ, -ɪd
AM 'fasfə,reɪ|t, -ts, -dɪŋ, -dɪd

phosphoresce
BR ˌfɒsfə'rɛs, -ɪz, -ɪŋ, -t
AM ˌfasfə'rɛs, -əz, -ɪŋ, -t

phosphorescence
BR ˌfɒsfə'rɛsns
AM ˌfasfə'rɛsəns

phosphorescent
BR ˌfɒsfə'rɛsnt
AM ˌfasfə'rɛsənt

phosphoric
BR fɒs'fɒrɪk
AM fas'fɔrɪk

phosphorite
BR 'fɒsfərʌɪt
AM 'fasfə,raɪt

phosphorous
BR 'fɒsf(ə)rəs
AM 'fasf(ə)rəs

phosphorus
BR 'fɒsf(ə)rəs
AM 'fasf(ə)rəs

phosphorylate
BR fɒs'fɒrɪleɪt, -s, -ɪŋ, -ɪd
AM fas'fɔrə,leɪ|t, -ts, -dɪŋ, -dɪd

phosphorylation
BR ˌfɒsfɒrɪ'leɪʃn
AM fas,fɔrə'leɪʃən

phossy
BR 'fɒsi
AM 'fɒsi, 'fasi

phot
BR fəʊt, -s

AM foʊt, fat, -s

photic
BR 'fəʊtɪk
AM 'foʊdɪk

photism
BR 'fəʊtɪz(ə)m, -z
AM 'foʊ,tɪzəm, -z

Photius
BR 'fəʊtɪəs
AM 'foʊdɪəs

photo
BR 'fəʊtəʊ, -z
AM 'foʊdoʊ, -z

photobiology
BR ˌfəʊtəʊbʌɪ'ɒlədʒi
AM ˌfoʊdoʊ,baɪ'ɑlədʒi

photocall
BR 'fəʊtə(ʊ)kɔːl
AM 'foʊdoʊ,kɔl, 'foʊdoʊ,kal

photocell
BR 'fəʊtə(ʊ)sɛl, -z
AM 'foʊdə,sɛl, -z

photochemical
BR ˌfəʊtə(ʊ)'kɛmɪkl
AM ˌfoʊdə'kɛməkəl

photochemistry
BR ˌfəʊtə(ʊ)'kɛmɪstri
AM ˌfoʊdə'kɛməstri

photochromic
BR ˌfəʊtə(ʊ)'krəʊmɪk
AM ˌfoʊdə'kroʊmɪk

photocomposition
BR ˌfəʊtəʊˌkɒmpə'zɪʃn
AM ˌfoʊdəˌkampə'zɪʃən

photoconductive
BR ˌfəʊtəʊkən'dʌktɪv
AM ˌfoʊdəkən'dəktɪv

photoconductivity
BR ˌfəʊtəʊˌkɒndʌk'tɪv-ɪti
AM ˌfoʊdoʊˌkandək'tɪv-ɪdi

photoconductor
BR ˌfəʊtə(ʊ)kən,dʌk-tə(r), -z
AM ˌfoʊdəkən'dəktər, -z

photocopiable
BR ˌfəʊtə(ʊ)ˌkʊpɪəbl
AM ˌfoʊdə,kapiəbəl

photocopier
BR ˌfəʊtə(ʊ)ˌkʊpɪə(r), -z
AM ˌfoʊdə,koʊpiər, -z

photocopy
BR ˌfəʊtə(ʊ)ˌkʊp|i, -ɪz, -ɪŋ, -ɪd
AM ˌfoʊdə,kapi, -z, -ɪŋ, -d

photodegradable
BR ˌfəʊtəʊdɪ'greɪdəbl
AM ˌfoʊdoʊdə'greɪdəbəl, ˌfoʊdoʊdi'greɪdəbəl

photodiode
BR ˌfəʊtəʊ,dʌɪəʊd, -z
AM ˌfoʊdoʊ,daɪoʊd, -z

photoduplicate
BR ˌfəʊtə(ʊ)'djuːplɪkeɪt, ˌfəʊtə(ʊ)'dʒuːplɪkeɪt, -s, -ɪŋ, -ɪd
AM ˌfoʊdə'd(j)uplə,keɪ|t, -ts, -dɪŋ, -dɪd

photoduplication
BR ˌfəʊtə(ʊ),djuː,plɪ'keɪʃn, ˌfəʊtə(ʊ),dʒuː,plɪ'keɪʃn
AM ˌfoʊdə,d(j)uplə'keɪʃən

photodynamic
BR ˌfəʊtə(ʊ)dʌɪ'namɪk
AM ˌfoʊdə,daɪ'næmɪk

photoelectric
BR ˌfəʊtəʊɪ'lɛktrɪk
AM ˌfoʊdoʊi'lɛktrɪk, 'foʊdoʊə'lɛktrɪk

photoelectricity
BR ˌfəʊtəʊɪ,lɛk'trɪsɪti, ˌfəʊtəʊ,ɛlɛk'trɪsɪti, ˌfəʊtəʊ,elɪk'trɪsɪti, ˌfəʊtəʊ,ɪlɛk'trɪsɪti, ˌfəʊtəʊ,iːlɛk'trɪsɪti
AM ˌfoʊdoʊə,lɛk'trɪsədi, ˌfoʊdoʊi,lɛk'trɪsədi

photoelectron
BR ˌfəʊtəʊɪ'lɛktrɒn
AM ˌfoʊdoʊə'lɛk,tran, ˌfoʊdoʊi'lɛk,tran, -z

photoemission
BR ˌfəʊtəʊɪ'mɪʃn, -z
AM ˌfoʊdoʊə'mɪʃən, ˌfoʊdoʊi'mɪʃən, -z

photoemitter
BR ˌfəʊtəʊɪ'mɪtə(r), -z
AM ˌfoʊdoʊə'mɪdər, ˌfoʊdoʊi'mɪdər, -z

photoengraving
BR ˌfəʊtəʊɪn'greɪvɪŋ, ˌfəʊtəʊɛn'greɪvɪŋ
AM ˌfoʊdoʊɪn'greɪvɪŋ, ˌfoʊdoʊɛn'greɪvɪŋ

photo finish
BR ˌfəʊtəʊ 'fɪnɪʃ
AM ˌfoʊdoʊ 'fɪnɪʃ

photofit
BR 'fəʊtə(ʊ)fɪt, -s
AM 'foʊdə,fɪt, -s

photogenic
BR ˌfəʊtə'dʒɛnɪk, ˌfəʊtə'dʒiːnɪk
AM ˌfoʊdə'dʒɛnɪk

photogenically
BR ˌfəʊtə'dʒɛnɪkli, ˌfəʊtə'dʒiːnɪkli
AM ˌfoʊdə'dʒɛnək(ə)li

photogram
BR 'fəʊtəgram, -z
AM 'foʊdə,græm, -z

photogrammetrist
BR ˌfəʊtə(ʊ)'gramɪtrɪst, -s
AM ˌfoʊdə'græmətrəst, -s

photogrammetry
BR ˌfəʊtə(ʊ)'gramɪtri
AM ˌfoʊdə'græmətri

photograph
BR ˈfəʊtəɡrɑːf,
ˈfəʊtəgraf, -s, -ɪŋ, -t
AM ˈfoʊdəˌgræf, -s, -ɪŋ,
-t

photographable
BR ˈfəʊtəgrɑːfəbl,
ˈfəʊtəgrafəbl
AM ˈfoʊdəˌgræfəbəl

photographer
BR fəˈtɒgrəfə(r), -z
AM fəˈtɑgrəfər, -z

photographic
BR ˌfəʊtəˈgrafɪk
AM ˌfoʊdəˈgræfɪk

photographical
BR ˌfəʊtəˈgrafɪkl
AM ˌfoʊdəˈgræfəkəl

photographically
BR ˌfəʊtəˈgrafɪkli
AM ˌfoʊdəˈgræfək(ə)li

photography
BR fəˈtɒgrəfi
AM fəˈtɑgrəfi

photogravure
BR ˌfəʊtə(ʊ)grəˈvjʊə(r),
-z
AM ˌfoʊdəgrəˈvju(ə)r,
-z

photojournalism
BR ˌfəʊtəʊˈdʒɜːnəl-
ɪz(ə)m,
ˌfəʊtəʊˈdʒɜːnl̩ɪz(ə)m
AM ˌfoʊdəˈdʒɜrnəˌlɪzəm

photojournalist
BR ˌfəʊtəʊˈjɜːnəlɪst,
ˌfəʊtəʊˈjɜːnl̩ɪst, -s
AM ˌfoʊdəˈdʒɜrnələst,
-s

photokinetic
BR ˌfəʊtə(ʊ)kɪˈnɛtɪk
AM ˌfoʊdəkəˈnɛdɪk

photolithographer
BR ˌfəʊtəʊlɪˈθɒɡrəfə(r),
-z
AM ˌfoʊdoʊˌlɪˈθɑgrəfər,
-z

photolithographic
BR ˌfəʊtəʊˌlɪθəˈgrafɪk
AM ˌfoʊdəˌlɪθəˈgræfɪk

**photolithograph-
ically**
BR ˌfəʊtəʊˌlɪθəˈgrafɪkli
AM ˌfoʊdəˌlɪθəˈgræf-
ək(ə)li

photolithography
BR ˌfəʊtə(ʊ)lɪˈθɒgrəfi
AM ˌfoʊdəˌlɪˈθɑgrəfi

photolyse
BR ˈfəʊtəlaɪz,
ˈfəʊtl̩aɪz, -ɪz, -ɪŋ, -d
AM ˈfoʊdl̩aɪz, -ɪz, -ɪŋ, -d

photolysis
BR fə(ʊ)ˈtɒlɪsɪs
AM foʊˈtɑləsəs

photolytic
BR ˌfəʊtəˈlɪtɪk
AM ˌfoʊdəˈlɪdɪk

photolyze
BR ˈfəʊtəlaɪz,
ˈfəʊtl̩aɪz, -ɪz, -ɪŋ, -d
AM ˈfoʊdl̩aɪz, -ɪz, -ɪŋ, -d

photomechanical
BR ˌfəʊtəʊmɪˈkanɪkl
AM ˌfoʊdəməˈkænəkəl

**photomechanic-
ally**
BR ˌfəʊtəʊmɪˈkanɪkli
AM ˌfoʊdoʊməˈkæn-
ək(ə)li

photometer
BR fə(ʊ)ˈtɒmɪtə(r), -z
AM fəˈtɑmədər, -z

photometric
BR ˌfəʊtəˈmɛtrɪk
AM ˌfoʊdəˈmɛtrɪk

photometry
BR fə(ʊ)ˈtɒmɪtri
AM fəˈtɑmətri

photomicrograph
BR ˌfəʊtəʊˈmʌɪkrəgrɑːf,
ˌfəʊtəʊˈmʌɪkrəgraf,
-s
AM ˌfoʊdəˈmaɪkroʊ-
ˌgræf, -s

photomicrography
BR ˌfəʊtə(ʊ)mʌɪˈkrɒg-
rəfi
AM ˌfoʊdəˌmaɪˈkrɑgrəfi

photomontage
BR ˌfəʊtəʊˈmɒntɑːʒ,
ˌfəʊtə(ʊ)mɒnˈtɑːʒ
AM ˌfoʊdoʊˌmɑnˈtɑʒ

photon
BR ˈfəʊtɒn, -z
AM ˈfoʊˌtɑn, -z

photonics
BR fəʊˈtɒnɪks
AM foʊˈtɑnɪks

photonovel
BR ˈfəʊtəˌnɒvl, -z
AM ˈfodoʊˌnɑvəl, -z

photo-offset
BR ˌfəʊtəʊˈɒfsɛt
AM ˌfoʊdoʊˈɔfˌsɛt,
ˌfoʊdoʊˈafˌsɛt

photoperiod
BR ˈfəʊtəʊˌpɪərɪəd, -z
AM ˈfoʊdoʊˌpɪriəd, -z

photoperiodic
BR ˌfəʊtəʊˌpɪərɪˈɒdɪk
AM ˌfoʊdoʊˌpɪriˈɑdɪk

photoperiodism
BR ˌfəʊtə(ʊ)ˈpɪərɪəd-
ɪz(ə)m
AM ˌfoʊdoʊˈpɪriəˌdɪzəm

photophobia
BR ˌfəʊtə(ʊ)ˈfəʊbɪə(r)
AM ˌfoʊdəˈfoʊbiə

photophobic
BR ˌfəʊtə(ʊ)ˈfəʊbɪk
AM ˌfoʊdəˈfoʊbɪk

photopic
BR fəʊˈtɒpɪk,
fəʊˈtəʊpɪk
AM fəˈtɑpɪk, foʊˈtɑpɪk

photorealism
BR ˌfəʊtəʊˈrɪəlɪz(ə)m
AM ˈfoʊdoʊˈri(ə)lɪzəm

photoreception
BR ˌfəʊtə(ʊ)rɪˈsɛpʃn
AM ˌfoʊdərəˈsɛpʃən

photoreceptor
BR ˌfəʊtə(ʊ)rɪˈsɛptə(r),
-z
AM ˌfoʊdərəˈsɛptər, -z

photosensitive
BR ˌfəʊtəʊˈsɛnsɪtɪv
AM ˈfoʊdəˈsɛnsədɪv

photosensitivity
BR ˌfəʊtəʊˌsɛnsɪˈtɪvɪti
AM ˌfoʊdəˌsɛnsəˈtɪvɪdi

photosensitize
BR ˌfəʊtəʊˈsɛnsɪtʌɪz,
-ɪz, -ɪŋ, -d
AM ˌfoʊdəˈsɛnsəˌtaɪz,
-ɪz, -ɪŋ, -d

photoset
BR ˈfəʊtə(ʊ)sɛt, -s, -ɪŋ
AM ˈfoʊdəˌsɛt̬, -ts, -dɪŋ

photosetter
BR ˈfəʊtə(ʊ)sɛtə(r), -z
AM ˈfoʊdəˌsɛdər, -z

photosetting
BR ˈfəʊtəʊˌsɛtɪŋ
AM ˈfoʊdəˌsɛdɪŋ

photosphere
BR ˈfəʊtəsfɪə(r), -z
AM ˈfoʊdəˌsfɪ(ə)r, -z

photospheric
BR ˌfəʊtəˈsfɛrɪk
AM ˌfoʊdəˈsfɛrɪk

photostat®
BR ˈfəʊtəstat, -s, -ɪŋ, -ɪd
AM ˈfoʊdəˌstæt̬, -ts,
-dɪŋ, -dəd

photostatic
BR ˌfəʊtəˈstatɪk
AM ˌfoʊdəˈstædɪk

photosynthesis
BR ˌfəʊtə(ʊ)ˈsɪnθɪsɪs
AM ˌfoʊdəˈsɪnθəsəs

photosynthesise
BR ˌfəʊtə(ʊ)ˈsɪnθɪsʌɪz,
-ɪz, -ɪŋ, -d
AM ˌfoʊdəˈsɪnθəˌsaɪz,
-ɪz, -ɪŋ, -d

photosynthesize
BR ˌfəʊtə(ʊ)ˈsɪnθɪsʌɪz,
-ɪz, -ɪŋ, -d
AM ˌfoʊdəˈsɪnθəˌsaɪz,
-ɪz, -ɪŋ, -d

photosynthetic
BR ˌfəʊtə(ʊ)sɪnˈθɛtɪk
AM ˌfoʊdəˌsɪnˈθɛdɪk

photosynthetically
BR ˌfəʊtə(ʊ)sɪnˈθɛtɪkli
AM ˌfoʊdəˌsɪnˈθɛdək(ə)li

phototransistor
BR ˌfəʊtə(ʊ)tranˈzɪstə(r),
ˌfəʊtə(ʊ)trɑːnˈzɪstə(r),
ˌfəʊtə(ʊ)tranˈsɪstə(r),

ˌfəʊtə(ʊ)trɑːnˈsɪstə(r), -z
AM ˌfoʊdou,trænˈzɪstər, -z

phototropic
BR ˌfəʊtə(ʊ)ˈtrɒpɪk,
ˌfəʊtə(ʊ)ˈtrəʊpɪk
AM ˌfoʊdəˈtrɑpɪk

phototropism
BR ˌfəʊtə(ʊ)ˈtrəʊpɪz(ə)m
AM ˌfoʊdəˈtroʊˌpɪzəm

phototypesetter
BR ˌfəʊtə(ʊ)ˈtʌɪpsɛtə(r), -z
AM ˈfoʊdoʊˈtaɪpˌsɛdər, -z

phototypesetting
BR ˌfəʊtə(ʊ)ˈtʌɪpsɛtɪŋ
AM ˈfoʊdoʊˈtaɪpˌsɛdɪŋ

photovoltaic
BR ˌfəʊtə(ʊ)vɒlˈteɪk
AM ˌfoʊdoʊˌvoʊlˈteɪk

phrasal
BR ˈfreɪzl
AM ˈfreɪzəl

phrase
BR freɪz, -ɪz, -ɪŋ, -d
AM freɪz, -ɪz, -ɪŋ, -d

phrasebook
BR ˈfreɪzbʊk, -s
AM ˈfreɪzˌbʊk, -s

phraseogram
BR ˈfreɪzɪəgram, -z
AM ˈfreɪziəˌgræm, -z

phraseological
BR ˌfreɪzɪəˈlɒdʒɪkl
AM ˌfreɪziəˈlɑdʒəkəl

phraseology
BR ˌfreɪzɪˈɒlədʒ|i, -ɪz
AM ˌfreɪziˈɑlədʒi, -z

phrasing
BR ˈfreɪzɪŋ, -z
AM ˈfreɪzɪŋ, -z

phratry
BR ˈfreɪtr|i, -ɪz
AM ˈfreɪtri, -z

phreatic
BR frɪˈatɪk
AM friˈædɪk

phrenetic
BR frɪˈnɛtɪk
AM frəˈnɛdɪk

phrenetically
BR frɪˈnɛtɪkli
AM frəˈnɛdək(ə)li

phrenic
BR ˈfrɛnɪk
AM ˈfrɛnɪk

phrenological
BR ˌfrɛnəˈlɒdʒɪkl
AM ˌfrɛnəˈlɑdʒəkəl

phrenologically
BR ˌfrɛnəˈlɒdʒɪkli
AM ˌfrɛnəˈlɑdʒək(ə)li

phrenologist
BR frɪˈnɒlədʒɪst, -s
AM frəˈnɑlədʒəst, -s

phrenology
BR frɪˈnɒlədʒi

AM frə'nɑlədʒi

Phrygia
BR 'frɪdʒɪə(r)
AM 'frɪdʒiə

Phrygian
BR 'frɪdʒɪən, -z
AM 'frɪdʒɪən, -z

phthalate
BR '(f)θaleɪt, -s
AM 'θæˌleɪt, -s

phthalic acid
BR ,(f)θalɪk 'asɪd
AM ,θælɪk 'æsəd

phthisic
BR '(f)θʌɪsɪk, 'tʌɪsɪk
AM 'tɪzɪk, 'θaɪsɪk,
'taɪsɪk

phthisical
BR '(f)θʌɪsɪkl, 'tʌɪsɪkl
AM 'tɪzɪkəl, 'θaɪsɪkəl,
'taɪsɪkəl

phthisis
BR '(f)θʌɪsɪs, 'tʌɪsɪs
AM 'θaɪsəs, 'taɪsəs

Phuket
BR ,pu:'kɛt
AM ,pu'kɛt

phut
BR fʌt
AM fət

phut-phut
BR 'fʌtfʌt
AM 'fətˌfət

phutt
BR fʌt
AM fət

phycological
BR ,fʌɪkə'lɒdʒɪkl
AM ,faɪkə'lɑdʒəkəl

phycologist
BR faɪ'kɒlədʒɪst, -s
AM 'faɪ'kɑlədʒəst, -s

phycology
BR faɪ'kɒlədʒi
AM faɪ'kɑlədʒi

phycomycete
BR ,fʌɪkə(ʊ)'mʌɪsi:t, -s
AM 'faɪkə'maɪˌsit, -s

phyla
BR 'fʌɪlə(r)
AM 'faɪlə

phylactery
BR fɪ'lakt(ə)r|i, -ɪz
AM fə'lækt(ə)ri, -z

phyletic
BR fʌɪ'lɛtɪk
AM faɪ'lɛdɪk

phyletically
BR fʌɪ'lɛtɪkli
AM faɪ'lɛdək(ə)li

Phyllida
BR 'fɪlɪdə(r)
AM 'fɪlədə

Phyllis
BR 'fɪlɪs
AM 'fɪlɪs

phyllite
BR 'fɪlʌɪt
AM 'fɪlaɪt

phyllode
BR 'fɪləʊd, -z
AM 'fɪˌloʊd, -z

phyllophagous
BR fɪ'lɒfəgəs
AM fə'lɑfəgəs

phyllopod
BR 'fɪləpɒd, -z
AM 'fɪlə,pɑd, -z

phylloquinone
BR ,fʌɪləʊ'kwɪnəʊn
AM 'fɪloʊ'kwaɪˌnoʊn

Phyllosan
BR 'fɪlə(ʊ)san
AM 'fɪləsən

phyllostome
BR 'fɪləstəʊm, -z
AM 'fɪlə,stoʊm, -z

phyllotactic
BR ,fɪlə(ʊ)'taktɪk
AM ,fɪlə'tæktɪk

phyllotaxis
BR ,fɪlə(ʊ)'taksɪs,
'fɪlə(ʊ),taksɪs
AM ,fɪlə'tæksəs

phyllotaxy
BR 'fɪlə(ʊ),taksi
AM 'fɪlə,tæksi

phylloxera
BR fɪ'lɒks(ə)rə(r),
,fɪlɒk'sɪərə(r)
AM fə'laksərə,
,fɪlək'sɪrə

phylogenesis
BR ,fʌɪlə(ʊ)'dʒɛnɪsɪs
AM 'faɪloʊ'dʒɛnəsəs

phylogenetic
BR ,fʌɪlə(ʊ)dʒɪ'nɛtɪk
AM 'faɪloʊdʒə'nɛdɪk

phylogenetically
BR ,fʌɪlə(ʊ)dʒɪ'nɛtɪkli
AM 'faɪloʊdʒə'nɛdək(ə)li

phylogenic
BR ,fʌɪlə(ʊ)'dʒɛnɪk
AM ,faɪloʊ'dʒɛnɪk

phylogeny
BR fʌɪ'lɒdʒɪni,
fʌɪ'lɒdʒ̩ni
AM 'faɪ'lɑdʒəni

phyloxera
BR fɪ'lɒks(ə)rə(r),
,fɪlɒk'sɪərə(r)
AM fə'laksərə,
,fɪlək'sɪrə

phylum
BR 'fʌɪləm
AM 'faɪləm

physalis
BR 'fʌɪsəlɪs, 'fɪsəlɪs,
fʌɪ'seɪlɪs
AM 'faɪsələs, 'fɪsələs,
faɪ'sæləs

physic
BR 'fɪzɪk, -s, -ɪŋ, -t
AM 'fɪzɪk, -s, -ɪŋ, -t

physical
BR 'fɪzɪkl
AM 'fɪzəkəl

physicalism
BR 'fɪzɪklɪz(ə)m,
'fɪzɪkəlɪz(ə)m
AM 'fɪzəkə,lɪzəm

physicalist
BR 'fɪzɪkl̩ɪst,
'fɪzɪkəlɪst, -s
AM 'fɪzəkələst, -s

physicalistic
BR ,fɪzɪkə'lɪstɪk,
,fɪzɪkl'ɪstɪk
AM ,fɪzəkə'lɪstɪk

physicality
BR ,fɪzɪ'kalɪti
AM ,fɪzə'kælədi

physically
BR 'fɪzɪkli
AM 'fɪzək(ə)li

physicalness
BR 'fɪzɪklnəs
AM 'fɪzəkəlnəs

physician
BR fɪ'zɪʃn, -z
AM fə'zɪʃən, -z

physicist
BR 'fɪzɪsɪst, -s
AM 'fɪzəsəst, -s

physicky
BR 'fɪzɪki
AM 'fɪzɪki

**physico-
chemical**
BR ,fɪzɪkəʊ'kɛmɪkl
AM 'fɪzəkoʊ'kɛməkəl

physio
BR 'fɪzɪəʊ, -z
AM 'fɪzioʊ, -z

physiocracy
BR ,fɪzɪ'ɒkrəs|i, -ɪz
AM ,fɪzi'ɑkrəsi, -z

physiocrat
BR 'fɪzɪəkrat, -s
AM 'fɪziə,kræt, -s

physiocratic
BR ,fɪzɪə'kratɪk
AM ,fɪziə'krædɪk

physiognomic
BR ,fɪzɪə'nɒmɪk
AM 'fɪziə'namɪk

physiognomical
BR ,fɪzɪə'nɒmɪkl
AM 'fɪziə'naməkəl

physiognomically
BR ,fɪzɪə'nɒmɪkli
AM 'fɪziə'namək(ə)li

physiognomist
BR ,fɪzɪ'ɒnəmɪst, -s
AM ,fɪzi'ɑ(g)nəməst, -s

physiognomy
BR ,fɪzɪ'ɒnəm|i, -ɪz
AM ,fɪzi'ɑ(g)nəmi, -z

physiographer
BR ,fɪzɪ'ɒgrəfə(r), -z
AM ,fɪzi'ɑgrəfər, -z

physiographic
BR ,fɪzɪə'grafɪk
AM 'fɪzɪə'græfɪk

physiographical
BR ,fɪzɪə'grafɪkl
AM 'fɪzɪə'græfəkəl

physiographically
BR ,fɪzɪə'grafɪkli
AM 'fɪzɪə'græfək(ə)li

physiography
BR ,fɪzɪ'ɒgrəfi
AM ,fɪzi'ɑgrəfi

physiological
BR ,fɪzɪə'lɒdʒɪkl
AM 'fɪzɪə'lɑdʒəkəl

physiologically
BR ,fɪzɪə'lɒdʒɪkli
AM 'fɪzɪə'lɑdʒək(ə)li

physiologist
BR ,fɪzɪ'ɒlədʒɪst, -s
AM ,fɪzi'ɑlədʒəst, -s

physiology
BR ,fɪzɪ'ɒlədʒi
AM ,fɪzi'ɑlədʒi

physiotherapist
BR ,fɪzɪə(ʊ)'θɛrəpɪst, -s
AM 'fɪzioʊ'θɛrəpɪst, -s

physiotherapy
BR ,fɪzɪə(ʊ)'θɛrəpi
AM 'fɪzioʊ'θɛrəpi

physique
BR fɪ'zi:k
AM fə'zik

physostigmine
BR ,fʌɪsəʊ'stɪgmi:n
AM 'faɪzə'stɪg,min

phytoalexin
BR ,fʌɪtəʊə'lɛksɪn
AM 'faɪtoʊə'lɛksɪn

phytochemical
BR ,fʌɪtəʊ'kɛmɪkl
AM 'faɪtə'kɛməkəl

phytochemist
BR ,fʌɪtəʊ'kɛmɪst
AM 'faɪtə'kɛməst

phytochemistry
BR ,fʌɪtəʊ'kɛmɪstri
AM 'faɪtə'kɛməstri

phytochrome
BR 'fʌɪtəkrəʊm
AM 'faɪtə,kroʊm

phytogenesis
BR ,fʌɪtəʊ'dʒɛnɪsɪs
AM 'faɪtə'dʒɛnəsəs

phytogeny
BR fʌɪ'tɒdʒɪni
AM faɪ'tɑdʒəni

phytogeography
BR ,fʌɪtəʊdʒi'ɒgrəfi,
,fʌɪtəʊ'dʒɒgrəfi
AM 'faɪtədʒi'ɑgrəfi

phytography
BR fʌɪ'tɒgrəfi
AM faɪ'tɑgrəfi

phytolith
BR 'fʌɪtəlɪθ, -s
AM 'faɪdə,lɪθ, -s

phytopathology
BR ˌfʌɪtəʊpə'θɒlədʒi
AM ˌfaɪdəpə'θɑlədʒi

phytophagous
BR fʌɪ'tɒfəgəs
AM faɪ'tɑfəgəs

phytoplankton
BR ˈfʌɪtəʊˌplaŋ(k)tən
AM ˈfaɪdə'plæŋktən

phytotomy
BR fʌɪ'tɒtəmi
AM faɪ'tɑdəmi

phytotoxic
BR ˌfʌɪtə(ʊ)'tɒksɪk
AM ˌfaɪdə'taksɪk

phytotoxin
BR ˈfʌɪtəˌtɒksɪn, -z
AM ˈfaɪdəˌtaksən, -z

pi
BR pʌɪ, -z
AM paɪ, -z

piacular
BR pʌɪ'akjələ(r)
AM paɪ'ækjələr

Piaf
BR 'piːaf
AM 'piaf

piaffe
BR pi'af, -s, -ɪŋ, -t
AM pi'æf, pjæf, -s, -ɪŋ, -t

Piaget
BR pɪ'aʒeɪ
AM ˌpiɑ'ʒeɪ

pia mater
BR ˌpʌɪə 'meɪtə(r), ˌpiːə +
AM ˌpiə 'madər, ˌpaɪə 'meɪdər

pianism
BR 'pɪənɪz(ə)m
AM ˈpiəˌnɪzəm

pianissimo
BR ˌpɪə'nɪsɪməʊ, -z
AM ˌpiə'nɪsəˌmoʊ, -z

pianist
BR 'pɪənɪst, -s
AM 'piənəst, -s

pianistic
BR ˌpɪə'nɪstɪk
AM ˌpiə'nɪstɪk

pianistically
BR ˌpɪə'nɪstɪkli
AM ˌpiə'nɪstək(ə)li

piano¹
instrument
BR pɪ'anəʊ, -z
AM pi'ænoʊ, -z

piano²
softly
BR pja:nəʊ, pɪ'a:nəʊ
AM pi'anoʊ

piano-accordion
BR pɪˌanəʊə'kɔːdɪən, -z
AM pɪ'ænoʊə'kɔrdiən, -z

pianoforte
BR pɪˌanəʊ'fɔːtli, pɪˌanəʊ'fɔːtlei, -ɪz\-eiz
AM pi'ænəˌfɔrdi, -z

pianola®
BR ˌpɪə'nəʊlə(r), -z
AM ˌpiə'noʊlə, -z

piano nobile
BR ˌpjɑːnəʊ 'nəʊbɪleɪ, -z
AM ˈpjɑˌnoʊ 'noʊbɪˌleɪ, -z

piasava
BR ˌpiːə'sɑːvə(r), -z
AM ˌpiə'savə, -z

piassava
BR ˌpiːə'sɑːvə(r), -z
AM ˌpiə'savə, -z

piaster
BR pɪ'astə(r), -z
AM pi'æstər, -z

piastre
BR pɪ'astə(r), -z
AM pi'æstər, -z

Piat
BR 'piːət, -s
AM 'piət, -s

piazza
BR pi'atsə(r), -z
AM pi'atsə, pi'æzə, -z

pibroch
BR 'piːbrɒk, 'piːbrɒx, -s
AM 'piˌbrax, 'piˌbrak, -s

PIBS
permanent interest-bearing share
BR pɪbz
AM pɪbz

pic
BR pɪk, -s
AM pɪk, -s

pica
BR 'pʌɪkə(r)
AM 'paɪkə

picador
BR 'pɪkədɔː(r), -z
AM 'pɪkəˌdɔ(ə)r, -z

picadore
BR 'pɪkədɔː(r), -z
AM 'pɪkəˌdɔ(ə)r, -z

picaninny
BR 'pɪkənɪn|i, ˌpɪkə'nɪn|i, -ɪz
AM 'pɪkəˌnɪni, -z

Picard
BR 'pɪkɑːd, pɪ'kɑːd
AM pə'kard

Picardy
BR 'pɪkədi
AM 'pɪkərdi

picaresque
BR ˌpɪkə'rɛsk
AM ˌpɪkə'rɛsk

picaroon
BR ˌpɪkə'ruːn, -z

AM 'pɪkə'run, -z

Picasso
BR pɪ'kasəʊ, pɪ'kɑːsəʊ
AM pə'kasoʊ

picayune
BR ˌpɪkə'juːn, -z
AM ˌpɪkə'jun, ˌpɪki'jun, -z

Piccadilly
BR ˌpɪkə'dɪli
AM ˌpɪkə'dɪli

piccalilli
BR ˌpɪkə'lɪli
AM ˌpɪkə'lɪli

piccaninny
BR 'pɪkənɪn|i, ˌpɪkə'nɪn|i, -ɪz
AM 'pɪkəˌnɪmi, -z

piccolo
BR 'pɪkələʊ, -z
AM 'pɪkəˌloʊ, -z

pice
BR pʌɪs
AM paɪs

pichiciago
BR ˌpɪtʃɪ'sjeɪgəʊ, -z
AM ˌpitʃisi'eɪgoʊ, -z

pick
BR pɪk, -s, -ɪŋ, -t
AM pɪk, -s, -ɪŋ, -t

pickaback
BR 'pɪkəbak, -s
AM 'pɪkəˌbæk, -s

pickable
BR 'pɪkəbl
AM 'pɪkəbəl

pickaninny
BR 'pɪkənɪn|i, ˌpɪkə'nɪm|i, -ɪz
AM 'pɪkəˌnɪmi, -z

pickax
BR 'pɪkaks, -ɪz, -ɪŋ, -t
AM 'pɪkˌæks, -əz, -ɪŋ, -t

pickaxe
BR 'pɪkaks, -ɪz, -ɪŋ, -t
AM 'pɪkˌæks, -əz, -ɪŋ, -t

Pickelhaube
BR 'pɪklˌhaʊbə(r), -z
AM 'pɪkl,(h)aʊbə, -z

picker
BR 'pɪkə(r), -z
AM 'pɪkər, -z

pickerel
BR 'pɪk(ə)rəl, 'pɪk(ə)r|, -z
AM 'pɪk(ə)rəl, -z

Pickering
BR 'pɪk(ə)rɪŋ
AM 'pɪk(ə)rɪŋ

picket
BR 'pɪk|ɪt, -ɪts, -ɪtɪŋ, -ɪtɪd
AM 'pɪkɪ|t, -ts, -dɪŋ, -dɪd

picketer
BR 'pɪkɪtə(r), -z
AM 'pɪkɪdər, -z

Pickett
BR 'pɪkɪt
AM 'pɪkɪt

Pickford
BR 'pɪkfəd
AM 'pɪkfərd

pickiness
BR 'pɪkɪnɪs
AM 'pɪkɪnɪs

pickings
BR 'pɪkɪŋz
AM 'pɪkɪŋz

pickle
BR 'pɪk|l, -lz, -lɪŋ\-lɪŋ, -ld
AM 'pɪk|əl, -əlz, -(ə)lɪŋ, -əld

pickler
BR 'pɪklə(r), 'pɪklə(r), -z
AM 'pɪk(ə)lər, -z

Pickles
BR 'pɪklz
AM 'pɪkəlz

picklock
BR 'pɪklɒk, -s
AM 'pɪkˌlak, -s

pick-me-up
BR 'pɪkmɪʌp, -s
AM 'pɪkmiˌəp, -s

pickoff
BR 'pɪkɒf, -s
AM 'pɪkˌɔf, 'pɪkˌaf, -s

pickpocket
BR 'pɪkˌpɒk|ɪt, -s, -ɪtɪŋ, -ɪdɪd
AM 'pɪkˌpakə|t, -ts, -dɪŋ, -dəd

pickpocketing
BR 'pɪkˌpɒkɪtɪŋ
AM 'pɪkˌpakədɪŋ

Pickthorne
BR 'pɪkθɔːn
AM 'pɪkˌθɔ(ə)rn

pickup
BR 'pɪkʌp, -s
AM 'pɪkˌəp, -s

Pickwick
BR 'pɪkwɪk
AM 'pɪkˌwɪk

Pickwickian
BR pɪk'wɪkɪən
AM pɪk'wɪkiən

picky
BR 'pɪk|i, -ɪə(r), -ɪɪst
AM 'pɪki, -ər, -ɪst

pick-your-own
BR ˌpɪkjər'əʊn, -z
AM ˌpɪkˌjə'roʊn, -z

picnic
BR 'pɪkn|ɪk, -ɪks, -ɪkɪŋ, -ɪkt
AM 'pɪkˌnɪk, -s, -ɪŋ, -t

picnicker
BR 'pɪknɪkə(r), -z
AM 'pɪkˌnɪkər, -z

picnicky
BR ˈpɪknɪki
AM ˈpɪkˌnɪki
Pico
BR ˈpiːkəʊ
AM ˈpikoʊ
picosecond
BR ˈpiːkəʊˌsɛk(ə)nd,
ˈpʌɪkəʊˌsek(ə)nd, -z
AM ˈpaɪkoʊˌsekənd, -z
picot
BR ˈpiːkəʊ, -z, -ɪŋ, -d
AM ˈpiˌkoʊ, -z, -ɪŋ, -d
picotee
BR ˌpɪkəˈtiː, -z
AM ˌpɪkəˈti, -z
picquet[1]
picket
BR ˈpɪkɪt, -s
AM ˈpɪkɪt, -s
picquet[2]
piquet
BR pɪˈkɛt
AM pəˈkeɪ
picrate
BR ˈpɪkreɪt, -s
AM ˈpɪˌkreɪt, -s
picric acid
BR ˌpɪkrɪk ˈasɪd
AM ˌpɪˌkrɪk ˈæsəd
Pict
BR pɪkt, -s
AM pɪk|(t), -(t)s
Pictish
BR ˈpɪktɪʃ
AM ˈpɪktɪʃ
pictogram
BR ˈpɪktəgram, -z
AM ˈpɪktəˌgræm, -z
pictograph
BR ˈpɪktəgrɑːf,
ˈpɪktəgraf, -s
AM ˈpɪktəˌgræf, -s
pictographic
BR ˌpɪktəˈgrafɪk
AM ˌpɪktəˈgræfɪk
pictography
BR pɪkˈtɒgrəfi
AM pɪkˈtɑgrəfi
pictorial
BR pɪkˈtɔːrɪəl
AM pɪkˈtoriəl
pictorially
BR pɪkˈtɔːrɪəli
AM pɪkˈtoriəli
picture
BR ˈpɪktʃ|ə(r), -əz,
-(ə)rɪŋ, -əd
AM ˈpɪk(t)ʃər, -z, -ɪŋ, -d
picturebook
BR ˈpɪktʃəbʊk, -s
AM ˈpɪk(t)ʃərˌbʊk, -s
picturegoer
BR ˈpɪktʃəˌgəʊə(r), -z
AM ˈpɪk(t)ʃərˌgoʊər, -z
picturesque
BR ˌpɪktʃəˈrɛsk

AM ˌpɪk(t)ʃəˈrɛsk
picturesquely
BR ˌpɪktʃəˈrɛskli
AM ˌpɪk(t)ʃəˈrɛskli
picturesqueness
BR ˌpɪktʃəˈrɛsknəs
AM ˌpɪk(t)ʃəˈrɛsknəs
piddle
BR ˈpɪd|l, -lz, -l̩ɪŋ \-lɪŋ,
-ld
AM ˈpɪd|əl, -əlz, -(ə)lɪŋ,
-əld
piddler
BR ˈpɪdlə(r), ˈpɪdlə(r),
-z
AM ˈpɪd(ə)lər, -z
piddock
BR ˈpɪdək, -s
AM ˈpɪdək, -s
pidgin
BR ˈpɪdʒ(ɪ)n, -z
AM ˈpɪdʒɪn, -z
pidginisation
BR ˌpɪdʒɪnʌɪˈzeɪʃn,
ˌpɪdʒnʌɪˈzeɪʃn
AM ˌpɪdʒɪnəˈzeɪʃən,
ˌpɪdʒɪˌnaɪˈzeɪʃən
pidginise
BR ˈpɪdʒɪnʌɪz,
ˈpɪdʒnʌɪz, -ɪz, -ɪŋ, -d
AM ˈpɪdʒɪnˌaɪz, -ɪz, -ɪŋ,
-d
pidginization
BR ˌpɪdʒɪnʌɪˈzeɪʃn,
ˌpɪdʒnʌɪˈzeɪʃn
AM ˌpɪdʒɪnəˈzeɪʃən,
ˌpɪdʒɪˌnaɪˈzeɪʃən
pidginize
BR ˈpɪdʒɪnʌɪz,
ˈpɪdʒnʌɪz, -ɪz, -ɪŋ, -d
AM ˈpɪdʒɪnˌaɪz, -ɪz, -ɪŋ,
-d
pi-dog
BR ˈpʌɪdɒg, -z
AM ˈpaiˌdɔg, ˈpaiˌdɑg,
-z
pie
BR pʌɪ, -z
AM paɪ, -z
piebald
BR ˈpʌɪbɔːld, -z
AM ˈpaɪˌbɔld, ˈpaɪˌbɑld,
-z
piece
BR piːs, -ɪz, -ɪŋ, -t
AM pis, -ɪz, -ɪŋ, -t
**pièce de
résistance**
BR piːˌɛs də rɪˈzɪstɒs,
+ rɛˈzɪstɒs,
+ ˌrɛziˈstɒs
AM piˌɛs də rəˌziˈstɑns
+ reɪˌziˈstɑns
piece-goods
BR ˈpiːsgʊdz
AM ˈpisˌgʊdz
piecemeal
BR ˈpiːsmiːl

AM ˈpisˌmil
piecer
BR ˈpiːsə(r), -z
AM ˈpisər, -z
piece-rate
BR ˈpiːsreɪt, -s
AM ˈpisˌreɪt, -s
**pièces de
résistance**
BR piːˌɛs də rɪˈzɪstɒs,
+ rɛˈzɪstɒs,
+ ˌrɛziˈstɒs
AM piˌɛs də rəˌziˈstɑns,
+ reɪˌziˈstɑns
piecework
BR ˈpiːswəːk
AM ˈpisˌwərk
piecrust
BR ˈpʌɪkrʌst, -s
AM ˈpaɪˌkrəst, -s
pied
BR pʌɪd
AM paɪd
pied-à-terre
BR ˌpjedəˈtɛ:(r),
ˌpjeɪdəˈtɛ:(r), -z
AM piˌeɪdəˈtɛ(ə)r, -z
piedmont
BR ˈpiːdmɒnt, -s
AM ˈpidˌmɑnt, -s
Piedmontese
BR ˌpiːdmɒnˈtiːz,
ˌpiːdmənˈtiːz
AM ˌpidmənˈtiz
pie-dog
BR ˈpʌɪdɒg, -z
AM ˈpaiˌdɔg, ˈpaiˌdɑg, -z
Pied Piper
BR ˌpʌɪd ˈpʌɪpə(r)
AM ˌpaɪd ˈpaɪpər
pie-eater
BR ˈpʌɪˌiːtə(r), -z
AM ˈpaɪˌidər, -z
pie-eyed
BR ˌpʌɪˈʌɪd
AM ˈpaɪˌaɪd
pie in the sky
BR ˌpʌɪ ɪn ðə ˈskʌɪ
AM ˌpaɪ ɪn ðə ˈskaɪ
pieman
BR ˈpʌɪmən
AM ˈpaɪmən, ˈpaɪˌmæn
piemen
BR ˈpʌɪmən
AM ˈpaɪmən, ˈpaɪˌmɛn
pier
BR pɪə(r), -z
AM pɪ(ə)r, -z
pierce
BR pɪəs, -ɪz, -ɪŋ, -t
AM pɪ(ə)rs, -ɪz, -ɪŋ, -t
piercer
BR ˈpɪəsə(r), -z
AM ˈpɪrsər, -z
piercingly
BR ˈpɪəsɪŋli
AM ˈpɪrsɪŋli

Piercy
BR ˈpɪəsi
AM ˈpɪrsi
Pierian
BR pʌɪˈɪərɪən,
pʌɪˈɛːrɪən
AM paɪˈɪriən
pierogi
BR pɪəˈrəʊgli,
pəˈrəʊgli, -ɪz
AM pəˈroʊgi, pɪrˈoʊgi,
-z
Pierre[1]
city in S. Dakota
BR ˈpɪə(r)
AM ˈpɪ(ə)r
Pierre[2]
French forename
BR pɪˈɛ:(r), pjɛ:(r)
AM pɪˈɛ(ə)r, ˈpjɛ(ə)r
Pierrot
BR ˈpɪərəʊ, -z
AM ˈpiəˌroʊ, ˈpɪˌroʊ, -z
Piers
BR pɪəz
AM pɪ(ə)rz
Pierson
BR ˈpɪəsn
AM ˈpɪrsən
pieta
BR ˌpiːɛˈtɑː(r),
ˌpiːeɪˈtɑː(r), -z
AM ˈpieɪˈtɑ, -z
pietà
BR ˌpiːɛˈtɑː(r),
ˌpiːeɪˈtɑː(r), -z
AM ˈpieɪˈtɑ, -z
Pietermaritzburg
BR ˌpiːtəˈmarɪtsbəːg
AM ˌpidərˈmɛrətsˌbərg
AFK ˌpiːtərmaˈrətsbərx
Pietism
BR ˈpʌɪtɪz(ə)m
AM ˈpaɪəˌtɪzəm
pietist
BR ˈpʌɪtɪst, -s
AM ˈpaɪədəst, -s
pietistic
BR ˌpʌɪˈtɪstɪk
AM ˌpaɪəˈtɪstɪk
pietistical
BR ˌpʌɪˈtɪstɪkl
AM ˌpaɪəˈtɪstəkəl
pietra dura
BR ˌpjɛtrə ˈduːrə(r)
AM ˌpiertrə ˈd(j)ʊrə
piety
BR ˈpʌɪti
AM ˈpaɪədi
piezoelectric
BR ˌpiːzəʊɪˈlɛktrɪk,
ˌpiːtsəʊɪˈlɛktrɪk,
pɪˌɛtsəʊɪˈlɛktrɪk,
pʌɪˌiːzəʊɪˈlɛktrɪk,
pʌɪˌiːtsəʊɪˈlɛktrɪk,
ˌpʌɪzəʊɪˈlɛktrɪk
AM piˈeɪzoʊəˈlɛktrɪk,
piˈeɪtsoʊəˈlɛktrɪk

piezoelectrically
BR ˌpiːzəʊɪˈlektrɪkli,
ˌpiːtsəʊɪˈlektrɪkli,
pɪˌetsəʊɪˈlektrɪkli,
pʌɪˌiːzəʊɪˈlektrɪkli,
pʌɪˌiːtsəʊɪˈlektrɪkli,
ˌpʌɪɪzəʊɪˈlektrɪkli
AM piˈeɪzoʊəˈlektrək-
(ə)li,
piˈeɪtsoʊəˈlektrək(ə)li

piezoelectricity
BR ˌpiːzəʊɪˌlekˈtrɪsɪti,
ˌpiːtsəʊɪlekˈtrɪsɪti,
pɪˌetsəʊɪlekˈtrɪsɪti,
pʌɪˌiːzəʊɪlekˈtrɪsɪti,
pʌɪˌiːtsəʊɪlekˈtrɪsɪti,
ˌpʌɪɪzəʊɪlekˈtrɪsɪti
AM piˈeɪzoʊˌelekˈtrɪsɪdi,
piˈeɪtsoʊˌelekˈtrɪsɪdi

piezometer
BR ˌpiːɪˈzɒmɪtə(r),
ˌpʌɪˈzɒmɪtə(r), -z
AM piəˈzɑmədər, -z

piffle
BR ˈpɪfl
AM ˈpɪfəl

piffler
BR ˈpɪflə(r), ˈpɪflə(r),
-z
AM ˈpɪf(ə)lər, -z

piffling
BR ˈpɪflɪŋ
AM ˈpɪf(ə)lɪŋ

pig
BR pɪg, -z
AM pɪg, -z

pigeon
BR ˈpɪdʒ(ɪ)n, -z
AM ˈpɪdʒən, -z

pigeonhole
BR ˈpɪdʒ(ɪ)nhəʊl, -z,
-ɪŋ, -d
AM ˈpɪdʒən,(h)oʊl, -z,
-ɪŋ, -d

pigeon pair
BR ˌpɪdʒ(ɪ)n ˈpɛː(r), -z
AM ˈpɪdʒən ˌpɛ(ə)r, -z

pigeonry
BR ˈpɪdʒ(ɪ)nr|i, -ɪz
AM ˈpɪdʒənri, -z

piggery
BR ˈpɪg(ə)r|i, -ɪz
AM ˈpɪg(ə)ri, -z

piggin
BR ˈpɪgɪn, -z
AM ˈpɪgɪn, -z

piggish
BR ˈpɪgɪʃ
AM ˈpɪgɪʃ

piggishly
BR ˈpɪgɪʃli
AM ˈpɪgɪʃli

piggishness
BR ˈpɪgɪʃnɪs
AM ˈpɪgɪʃnɪs

Piggott
BR ˈpɪgət
AM ˈpɪgət

piggy
BR ˈpɪg|i, -ɪz
AM ˈpɪgi, -z

piggyback
BR ˈpɪgɪbak, -s
AM ˈpɪgiˌbæk, -s

piggybank
BR ˈpɪgɪbaŋk, -s
AM ˈpɪgiˌbæŋk, -s

piggy in the middle
BR ˌpɪgɪ ɪn ðə ˈmɪdl
AM ˌpɪgi ɪn(ð)ə ˈmɪdəl

piggywig
BR ˈpɪgɪwɪg, -z
AM ˈpɪgiˌwɪg, -z

pigheaded
BR ˌpɪgˈhedɪd
AM ˈpɪgˌ(h)edəd

pig in the middle
BR ˌpɪg ɪn ðə ˈmɪdl
AM ˌpɪg ən(ð)ə ˈmɪdəl

piglet
BR ˈpɪglɪt, -s
AM ˈpɪglɪt, -s

piglike
BR ˈpɪglʌɪk
AM ˈpɪgˌlaɪk

pigling
BR ˈpɪglɪŋ, -z
AM ˈpɪg(ə)lɪŋ, -z

pigmaean
BR pɪgˈmiːən
AM ˈpɪgmiən, pɪgˈmiən

pigmean
BR pɪgˈmiːən
AM ˈpɪgmiən, pɪgˈmiən

pigmeat
BR ˈpɪgmiːt
AM ˈpɪgˌmit

pigment¹
noun
BR ˈpɪgm(ə)nt, -s
AM ˈpɪgmənt, -s

pigment²
verb
BR pɪgˈment,
ˈpɪgm(ə)nt, -s, -ɪŋ, -ɪd
AM pɪgˈment,
ˈpɪgmənt, -s, -ɪŋ, -ɪd

pigmental
BR pɪgˈmentl
AM pɪgˈmen(t)l

pigmentary
BR ˈpɪgmənt(ə)ri
AM ˈpɪgmənˌteri

pigmentation
BR ˌpɪgmənˈteɪʃn,
ˌpɪgm(ə)nˈteɪʃn
AM ˌpɪgmənˈteɪʃən,
ˌpɪgˌmenˈteɪʃən

pigmentosa
BR ˌpɪgm(ə)nˈtəʊsə(r)
AM ˌpɪgmənˈtoʊsə,
ˌpɪgˌmenˈtoʊsə

pigmy
BR ˈpɪgmi, -ɪz
AM ˈpɪgmi, -z

pignut
BR ˈpɪgnʌt, -s
AM ˈpɪgˌnət, -s

pig-out
BR ˌpɪgˈaʊt
AM ˈpɪgˈaʊt

pigpen
BR ˈpɪgpɛn, -z
AM ˈpɪgˌpɛn, -z

pigskin
BR ˈpɪgskɪn, -z
AM ˈpɪgˌskɪn, -z

pigsticker
BR ˈpɪgˌstɪkə(r), -z
AM ˈpɪgˌstɪkər, -z

pigsticking
BR ˈpɪgˌstɪkɪŋ
AM ˈpɪgˌstɪkɪŋ

pigsty
BR ˈpɪgstʌɪ, -z
AM ˈpɪgˌstaɪ, -z

pigswill
BR ˈpɪgswɪl
AM ˈpɪgˌswɪl

pigtail
BR ˈpɪgteɪl, -z, -d
AM ˈpɪgˌteɪl, -z, -d

pigwash
BR ˈpɪgwɒʃ
AM ˈpɪgˌwɔʃ, ˈpɪgˌwɑʃ

pigweed
BR ˈpɪgwiːd, -z
AM ˈpɪgˌwid, -z

pi jaw
BR ˈpʌɪ dʒɔː(r)
AM ˈpaɪ ˌdʒɔ, ˈpaɪˌdʒɑ

pika
BR ˈpʌɪkə(r), ˈpiːkə(r),
-z
AM ˈpaɪkə, ˈpikə, -z

pike
BR pʌɪk, -s
AM paɪk, -s

pikelet
BR ˈpʌɪklɪt, -s
AM ˈpaɪklət, -s

pikeman
BR ˈpʌɪkmən
AM ˈpaɪkmən

pikemen
BR ˈpʌɪkmən
AM ˈpaɪkmən

pikeperch
BR ˈpʌɪkpəːtʃ
AM ˈpaɪkˌpərtʃ

piker
BR ˈpʌɪkə(r), -z
AM ˈpaɪkər, -z

pikestaff
BR ˈpʌɪkstɑːf,
ˈpʌɪkstaf, -s
AM ˈpaɪkˌstæf, -s

pilaf
BR ˈpɪlaf, ˈpiːlaf, pɪˈlaf,
-s
AM ˈpiˌlɑf, pəˈlɑf, -s

pilaff
BR ˈpɪlaf, ˈpiːlaf, pɪˈlaf,
-s
AM ˈpiˌlɑf, pəˈlɑf, -s

pilaster
BR pɪˈlastə(r), -z, -d
AM pəˈlæstər, -z, -d

Pilate
BR ˈpʌɪlət
AM ˈpaɪlət

Pilatus
BR pɪˈlɑːtəs
AM pəˈlɑdəs

pilau
BR pɪˈlaʊ, ˈpiːlaʊ, -z
AM pəˈlaʊ, piˈlaʊ, -z

pilaw
BR pɪˈlaʊ, ˈpiːlaʊ, -z
AM pəˈlaʊ, piˈlaʊ, -z

pilch
BR pɪltʃ, -ɪz
AM pɪltʃ, -ɪz

pilchard
BR ˈpɪltʃəd, -z
AM ˈpɪltʃərd, -z

pile
BR pʌɪl, -z, -ɪŋ, -d
AM paɪl, -z, -ɪŋ, -d

pileate
BR ˈpɪlɪət, ˈpʌɪlɪət
AM ˈpaɪliət, ˈpɪliət

pileated
BR ˈpɪlɪeɪtɪd,
ˈpʌɪlɪeɪtɪd
AM ˈpaɪliˌeɪdɪd,
ˈpɪliˌeɪdɪd

piledriver
BR ˈpʌɪlˌdrʌɪvə(r), -z
AM ˈpaɪlˌdraɪvər, -z

piledriving
BR ˈpʌɪlˌdrʌɪvɪŋ
AM ˈpaɪlˌdrɪvɪŋ

pilei
BR ˈpʌɪlɪʌɪ
AM ˈpaɪliˌaɪ

pileup
BR ˈpʌɪlʌp, -s
AM ˈpaɪlˌəp, -s

pileus
BR ˈpʌɪlɪəs
AM ˈpaɪliəs

pilewort
BR ˈpʌɪlwəːt
AM ˈpaɪlwərt,
ˈpaɪlwɔ(ə)rt

pilfer
BR ˈpɪlf|ə(r), -əz,
-(ə)rɪŋ, -əd
AM ˈpɪlfər, -z, -ɪŋ, -d

pilferage
BR ˈpɪlf(ə)rɪdʒ
AM ˈpɪlf(ə)rɪdʒ

pilferer
BR ˈpɪlf(ə)rə(r), -z
AM ˈpɪlf(ə)rər, -z

pilgrim
BR ˈpɪlgrɪm, -z

AM ˈpɪlgrɪm, -z

pilgrimage
BR ˈpɪlgrɪm|ɪdʒ, -ɪdʒɪz
AM ˈpɪlgrəmɪdʒ, -ɪz

pilgrimise
BR ˈpɪlgrɪmʌɪz, -ɪz, -ɪŋ, -d
AM ˈpɪlgrə,maɪz, -ɪz, -ɪŋ, -d

pilgrimize
BR ˈpɪlgrɪmʌɪz, -ɪz, -ɪŋ, -d
AM ˈpɪlgrə,maɪz, -ɪz, -ɪŋ, -d

piliferous
BR pʌɪˈlɪf(ə)rəs
AM paɪˈlɪf(ə)rəs

piliform
BR ˈpʌɪlɪfɔːm
AM ˈpaɪlə,fɔ(ə)rm

piling
BR ˈpʌɪlɪŋ, -z
AM ˈpaɪlɪŋ, -z

Pilipino
BR ˌpɪlɪˈpiːnəʊ
AM ˌpɪləˈpɪˌnoʊ

Pilkington
BR ˈpɪlkɪŋt(ə)n
AM ˈpɪlkɪŋtən

pill
BR pɪl, -z, -ɪŋ, -d
AM pɪl, -z, -ɪŋ, -d

pillage
BR ˈpɪl|ɪdʒ, -ɪdʒɪz, -ɪdʒɪŋ, -ɪdʒd
AM ˈpɪlɪdʒ, -ɪz, -ɪŋ, -d

pillager
BR ˈpɪlɪdʒə(r), -z
AM ˈpɪlədʒər, -z

pillar
BR ˈpɪlə(r), -z, -d
AM ˈpɪlər, -z, -d

pillarbox
BR ˈpɪləbɒks, -ɪz
AM ˈpɪlər,bɑks, -əz

pillaret
BR ˌpɪləˈrɛt, -s
AM ˌpɪləˈrɛt, -s

pillbox
BR ˈpɪlbɒks, -ɪz
AM ˈpɪl,bɑks, -əz

Pilling
BR ˈpɪlɪŋ
AM ˈpɪlɪŋ

pillion
BR ˈpɪljən, ˈpɪlɪən, -z, -ɪŋ, -d
AM ˈpɪljən, -z, -ɪŋ, -d

pilliwinks
BR ˈpɪlɪwɪŋks
AM ˈpɪli,wɪŋks

pillock
BR ˈpɪlək, -s
AM ˈpɪlək, -s

pillory
BR ˈpɪl(ə)r|i, -ɪz, -ɪŋ, -ɪd

AM ˈpɪləri, -z, -ɪŋ, -d

pillow
BR ˈpɪləʊ, -z, -ɪŋ, -d
AM ˈpɪloʊ, -z, -ɪŋ, -d

pillowcase
BR ˈpɪlə(ʊ)keɪs, -ɪz
AM ˈpɪloʊ,keɪs, -ɪz

pillowslip
BR ˈpɪlə(ʊ)slɪp, -s
AM ˈpɪloʊ,slɪp, -s

pillowy
BR ˈpɪləʊi
AM ˈpɪloʊi

pillular
BR ˈpɪljələ(r)
AM ˈpɪljələr

pillule
BR ˈpɪljuːl, -z
AM ˈpɪl,jul, -z

pillwort
BR ˈpɪlwəːt, -s
AM ˈpɪlwərt, ˈpɪlwɔ(ə)rt, -s

pilose
BR ˈpʌɪləʊz, ˈpʌɪləʊs
AM ˈpaɪ,loʊs, ˈpaɪ,loʊz

pilosity
BR pʌɪˈlɒsɪti
AM paɪˈlɑsədi

pilot
BR ˈpʌɪlət, -s, -ɪŋ, -ɪd
AM ˈpaɪlə|t, -ts, -dɪŋ, -dəd

pilotage
BR ˈpʌɪlətɪdʒ
AM ˈpaɪlədɪdʒ

pilothouse
BR ˈpʌɪləthaʊ|s, -zɪz
AM ˈpaɪlət,(h)aʊ|s, -zəz

pilot-jacket
BR ˈpʌɪlət,dʒakɪt, -s
AM ˈpaɪlət,dʒækɛt, -s

pilotless
BR ˈpʌɪlətləs
AM ˈpaɪlətləs

pilous
BR ˈpʌɪləs
AM ˈpaɪləs

Pilsen
BR ˈpɪlzn, ˈpɪlsn
AM ˈpɪlzən, ˈpɪlsən

pilsener
BR ˈpɪlznə(r), ˈpɪlsnə(r)
AM ˈpɪlz(ə)nər, ˈpɪlsnər

pilsner
BR ˈpɪlznə(r), ˈpɪlsnə(r)
AM ˈpɪlz(ə)nər, ˈpɪlsnər

Piltdown
BR ˈpɪltdaʊn
AM ˈpɪlt,daʊn

Pilton
BR ˈpɪlt(ə)n
AM ˈpɪltən

pilular
BR ˈpɪljələ(r)
AM ˈpɪljələr

pilule
BR ˈpɪljuːl, -z
AM ˈpɪl,jul, -z

pilulous
BR ˈpɪljələs
AM ˈpɪljələs

Pima
BR ˈpiːmə(r), -z
AM ˈpimə, -z

Piman
BR ˈpiːmən
AM ˈpimən

pimento
BR pɪˈmɛntəʊ, -z
AM pəˈmɛn(t)oʊ, -z

pi-meson
BR ˌpʌɪˈmiːzɒn,
ˌpʌɪˈmiːsɒn,
ˌpʌɪˈmɛzɒn,
ˌpʌɪˈmɛsɒn,
ˌpʌɪˈmeɪzɒn
AM ˈpaɪ,meɪ,sɑn,
ˈpaɪ,meɪ,zɑn

pimiento
BR ˌpɪmiˈɛntəʊ,
pɪmˈjɛntəʊ, -z
AM pəˈm(j)ɛn(t)oʊ, -z

Pimlico
BR ˈpɪmlɪkəʊ
AM ˈpɪmlɪ,koʊ

Pimm
BR pɪm, -z
AM pɪm, -z

pimp
BR pɪm|p, -(p)s, -pɪŋ, -(p)t
AM pɪmp, -s, -ɪŋ, -t

pimpernel
BR ˈpɪmpənɛl, -z
AM ˈpɪmpər,nɛl, ˈpɪmpərnəl, -z

pimple
BR ˈpɪmpl, -z, -d
AM ˈpɪmpəl, -z, -d

pimpliness
BR ˈpɪmplɪnɪs
AM ˈpɪmp(ə)linɪs

pimply
BR ˈpɪmpli
AM ˈpɪmp(ə)li

PIN
BR pɪn
AM pɪn

pin
BR pɪn, -z, -ɪŋ, -d
AM pɪn, -z, -ɪŋ, -d

piña colada
BR ˌpiːnjə kəˈlɑːdə(r), ˌpiːnə +
AM ˈpinjə kəˈladə

pinafore
BR ˈpɪnəfɔː(r), -z
AM ˈpɪnə,fɔ(ə)r, -z

Pinang
BR pɪˈnaŋ

pilular
AM pəˈnæŋ

pinaster
BR pʌɪˈnastə(r),
pɪˈnastə(r), -z
AM paɪˈnæstər, -z

piñata
BR pɪˈn(j)ɑːtə(r), -z
AM pɪnˈjɑdə, -z

pinball
BR ˈpɪnbɔːl
AM ˈpɪn,bɔl, ˈpɪn,bɑl

PINC
BR pɪŋk
AM pɪŋk

pince-nez¹
singular
BR ˌpans'neɪ, ˌpãs'neɪ
AM ˌpɪn(t)'sneɪ

pince-nez²
plural
BR ˌpans'neɪz,
ˌpãs'neɪz
AM ˌpɪn(t)'sneɪz

pincer
BR ˈpɪnsə(r), -z
AM ˈpɪntʃər, ˈpɪn(t)sər, -z

pincette
BR pɪn'sɛt, pã'sɛt, -s
AM pɪn'sɛt, -s

pinch
BR pɪn(t)ʃ, -ɪz, -ɪŋ, -t
AM pɪn(t)ʃ, -ɪz, -ɪŋ, -t

pinchbeck
BR ˈpɪn(t)ʃbɛk, -s
AM ˈpɪn(t)ʃ,bɛk, -s

Pincher
BR ˈpɪn(t)ʃə(r)
AM ˈpɪn(t)ʃər

pinch-hit
BR ˈpɪn(t)ʃˈhɪt, -s, -ɪŋ
AM ˈpɪn(t)ʃˈhɪ|t, -ts, -dɪŋ

pinch-hitter
BR ˈpɪn(t)ʃˈhɪtə(r), -z
AM ˈpɪn(t)ʃˈhɪdər, -z

pinchpenny
BR ˈpɪn(t)ʃˌpɛn|i, -ɪz
AM ˈpɪn(t)ʃˌpɛni, -z

pinch-run
BR ˌpɪn(t)ʃˈrʌn, -z, -ɪŋ
AM ˌpɪn(t)ʃˈrən, -z, -ɪŋ

pinch-runner
BR ˌpɪn(t)ʃˈrʌnə(r), -z
AM ˌpɪn(t)ʃˈrənər, -z

Pincus
BR ˈpɪŋkəs
AM ˈpɪŋkəs

pincushion
BR ˈpɪn,kʊʃn
AM ˈpɪn,kʊʃən

Pindar
BR ˈpɪndɑː(r)
AM ˈpɪn,dɑr

Pindaric
BR (ˌ)pɪnˈdarɪk
AM pɪnˈdɛrɪk

pin-down
noun
BR ˈpɪndaʊn
AM ˈpɪnˌdaʊn

Pindus
BR ˈpɪndəs
AM ˈpɪndəs

pine
BR paɪn, -z, -ɪŋ, -d
AM paɪn, -z, -ɪŋ, -d

pineal
BR ˈpɪniəl, paɪˈniːəl
AM ˈpaɪniəl, paɪˈniəl

pineapple
BR ˈpaɪnˌæpl, -z
AM ˈpaɪˌnæpəl, -z

pinecone
BR ˈpaɪnkəʊn, -z
AM ˈpaɪnˌkoʊn, -z

pine marten
BR ˈpaɪn ˌmɑːt(ɪ)n, -z
AM ˈpaɪn ˌmɑrtən, -z

Pinero
BR pɪˈnɪərəʊ, pɪˈnɛːrəʊ
AM pəˈnɪroʊ, pəˈnɛroʊ

pinery
BR ˈpaɪn(ə)r|i, -ɪz
AM ˈpaɪnəri, -z

pineta
BR paɪˈniːtə(r)
AM paɪˈnidə

pinetree
BR ˈpaɪntriː, -z
AM ˈpaɪnˌtri, -z

pinetum
BR paɪˈniːtəm
AM paɪˈnidəm

pinewood
BR ˈpaɪnwʊd, -z
AM ˈpaɪnˌwʊd, -z

pinfeather
BR ˈpɪnˌfɛðə(r), -z
AM ˈpɪnˌfɛðər, -z

pinfold
BR ˈpɪnfəʊld, -z, -ɪŋ, -ɪd
AM ˈpɪnˌfoʊld, -z, -ɪŋ, -əd

ping
BR pɪŋ, -z, -ɪŋ, -d
AM pɪŋ, -z, -ɪŋ, -d

pinger
BR ˈpɪŋə(r), -z
AM ˈpɪŋ(g)ər, -z

pingo
BR ˈpɪŋgəʊ, -z
AM ˈpɪŋ(g)oʊ, -z

pingpong
BR ˈpɪŋpɒŋ
AM ˈpɪŋˌpɒŋ, ˈpɪŋˌpɑŋ

pinguid
BR ˈpɪŋgwɪd
AM ˈpɪŋgwɪd

pinguin
BR ˈpɪŋgwɪn, -z
AM ˈpɪŋgwɪn, -z

pinhead
BR ˈpɪnhɛd, -z
AM ˈpɪn(h)ɛd, -z

pinheaded
BR ˌpɪnˈhɛdɪd
AM ˈpɪnˌhɛdəd

pinheadedness
BR ˌpɪnˈhɛdɪdnɪs
AM ˈpɪnˌhɛdədnəs

pinhole
BR ˈpɪnhəʊl, -z
AM ˈpɪn(h)oʊl, -z

pinion
BR ˈpɪnjən, -z, -ɪŋ, -d
AM ˈpɪnjən, -z, -ɪŋ, -d

pink
BR pɪŋ|k, -ks, -kɪŋ, -(k)t
AM pɪŋ|k, -ks, -kɪŋ, -(k)t

Pinkerton
BR ˈpɪŋkət(ə)n
AM ˈpɪŋkərtən

pinkeye
BR ˈpɪŋkaɪ
AM ˈpɪŋkˌaɪ

Pink Floyd
BR ˌpɪŋk ˈflɔɪd
AM ˌpɪŋk ˈflɔɪd

pinkie
BR ˈpɪŋk|i, -ɪz
AM ˈpɪŋki, -z

pinkish
BR ˈpɪŋkɪʃ
AM ˈpɪŋkɪʃ

pinkly
BR ˈpɪŋkli
AM ˈpɪŋkli

pinkness
BR ˈpɪŋknɪs
AM ˈpɪŋknɪs

pinko
BR ˈpɪŋkəʊ, -z
AM ˈpɪŋkoʊ, -z

Pinkster
BR ˈpɪŋkstə(r)
AM ˈpɪŋkstər

pinky
BR ˈpɪŋk|i, -ɪz
AM ˈpɪŋki, -z

pinna
BR ˈpɪnə(r), -z
AM ˈpɪnə, -z

pinnace
BR ˈpɪnɪs, -ɪz
AM ˈpɪnɪs, -ɪz

pinnacle
BR ˈpɪnɪkl, -z
AM ˈpɪnɪkəl, -z

pinnae
BR ˈpɪniː
AM ˈpɪni, ˈpɪnaɪ

pinnate
BR ˈpɪneɪt, ˈpɪnət
AM ˈpɪˌneɪt, ˈpɪnɪt

pinnated
BR ˈpɪneɪtɪd, ˈpɪnətɪd
AM ˈpɪˌneɪdɪd, ˈpɪnɪdɪd

pinnately
BR ˈpɪneɪtli, ˈpɪnətli
AM ˈpɪˌneɪtli, ˈpɪnɪtli

pinnation
BR pɪˈneɪʃn
AM pəˈneɪʃən

Pinner
BR ˈpɪnə(r)
AM ˈpɪnər

Pinney
BR ˈpɪni
AM ˈpɪni

pinnigrade
BR ˈpɪnɪgreɪd
AM ˈpɪnəˌgreɪd

pinniped
BR ˈpɪnɪpɛd, -z
AM ˈpɪniˌpɛd, -z

pinnular
BR ˈpɪnjələ(r)
AM ˈpɪnjələr

pinnule
BR ˈpɪnjuːl, -z
AM ˈpɪnjul, -z

pinny
BR ˈpɪn|i, -ɪz
AM ˈpɪni, -z

Pinocchio
BR pɪˈnəʊkɪəʊ, pɪˈnɒkɪəʊ
AM pəˈnoʊkioʊ

Pinochet
BR ˈpɪnəʃeɪ
AM ˌpinəˈʃeɪ

pinochle
BR ˈpiːˌnʌkl, ˈpiːˌnɒkl
AM ˈpiˌnəkəl, ˈpiˌnɑkl

pinocle
BR ˈpiːˌnʌkl, ˈpiːˌnɒkl
AM ˈpiˌnəkəl, ˈpiˌnɑkl

pinol
BR ˈpɪnɒl, ˈpɪnəʊl
AM ˈpaɪˌnɔl, ˈpaɪˌnɑl

pinole¹
kind of flour
BR pɪˈnəʊli, pɪˈnəʊleɪ
AM pəˈnoʊli

pinole²
liquid ether
BR ˈpɪnəʊl
AM ˈpaɪˌnoʊl

piñon
BR piːˈnjɒn, ˈpɪnjən, -z
AM pinˈjɑn, ˈpɪnjən, -z

Pinot Blanc
BR ˌpiːnəʊ ˈblɒ, -z
AM ˌpinoʊ ˈblɑŋk, -s

Pinot Noir
BR ˌpiːnəʊ ˈnwɑː(r), -z
AM ˌpinoʊ ˈnwɑr, -z

pinpoint
BR ˈpɪnpɔɪnt, -s, -ɪŋ, -ɪd
AM ˈpɪnˌpɔɪn|t, -ts, -(t)ɪŋ, -(t)ɪd

pinprick
BR ˈpɪnprɪk, -s
AM ˈpɪnˌprɪk, -s

pinsetter
BR ˈpɪnˌsɛtə(r), -z
AM ˈpɪnˌsɛdər, -z

pinspotter
BR ˈpɪnˌspɒtə(r), -z
AM ˈpɪnˌspɑdər, -z

pinstripe
BR ˈpɪnstrʌɪp, -s, -t
AM ˈpɪnˌstraɪp, -s, -t

pint
BR paɪnt, -s
AM paɪnt, -s

Pinta
Columbus ship
BR ˈpɪntə(r)
AM ˈpɪn(t)ə

pinta¹
disease
BR ˈpɪntə(r)
AM ˈpɪn(t)ə

pinta²
pint of
BR ˈpʌɪntə(r), -z
AM ˈpaɪn(t)ə, -z

pintable
BR ˈpɪnˌteɪbl, -z
AM ˈpɪnˌteɪbəl, -z

pintado
BR pɪnˈtɑːdəʊ, -z
AM pɪnˈtɑˌdoʊ, -z

pintail
BR ˈpɪnteɪl, -z
AM ˈpɪnˌteɪl, -z

Pinter
BR ˈpɪntə(r)
AM ˈpɪn(t)ər

pintle
BR ˈpɪntl, -z
AM ˈpɪn(t)əl, -z

pinto
BR ˈpɪntəʊ, -z
AM ˈpɪn(t)oʊ, -z

pinup
BR ˈpɪnʌp, -s
AM ˈpɪnˌəp, -s

pinwheel
BR ˈpɪnwiːl, -z
AM ˈpɪnˌ(h)wil, -z

pinworm
BR ˈpɪnwəːm, -z
AM ˈpɪnˌwərm, -z

piny
BR ˈpʌɪni
AM ˈpaɪni

Pinyin
BR ˌpɪnˈjɪn
AM ˈpɪnˈjɪn

piolet
BR ˈpiːˌəleɪ, -z
AM ˌpiəˈleɪ, -z

pion
BR ˈpʌɪɒn, -z
AM ˈpaɪˌɑn, -z

pioneer
BR ˌpʌɪəˈnɪə(r), -z, -ɪŋ, -d
AM ˌpaɪəˈnɪ(ə)r, -z, -ɪŋ, -d

pionic
BR pʌɪˈɒnɪk
AM paɪˈɑnɪk

pious
BR ˈpʌɪəs
AM ˈpaɪəs

piously
BR ˈpʌɪəsli
AM ˈpaɪəsli

piousness
BR ˈpʌɪəsnəs
AM ˈpaɪəsnəs

pip
BR pɪp, -s, -ɪŋ, -t
AM pɪp, -s, -ɪŋ, -t

pipa
BR pɪˈpɑː(r), ˈpʌɪpə(r), -z
AM ˈpipə, -z

pipal
BR ˈpiːpl, -z
AM ˈpipəl, -z

pipe
BR pʌɪp, -s, -ɪŋ, -t
AM paɪp, -s, -ɪŋ, -t

pipeclay
BR ˈpʌɪpkleɪ
AM ˈpaɪpˌkleɪ

pipecleaner
BR ˈpʌɪpˌkliːnə(r), -z
AM ˈpaɪpˌklinər, -z

pipefish
BR ˈpʌɪpfɪʃ, -ɪz
AM ˈpaɪpˌfɪʃ, -ɪz

pipefitting
BR ˈpʌɪpˌfɪtɪŋ
AM ˈpaɪpˌfɪdɪŋ

pipeful
BR ˈpʌɪpfʊl, -z
AM ˈpaɪpˌfʊl, -z

pipeless
BR ˈpʌɪplɪs
AM ˈpaɪplɪs

pipeline
BR ˈpʌɪplʌɪn, -z
AM ˈpaɪpˌlaɪn, -z

pip emma
BR ˌpɪp ˈɛmə(r)
AM ˌpɪp ˈɛmə

piper
BR ˈpʌɪpə(r), -z
AM ˈpaɪpər, -z

piperade
BR ˌpɪpəˈrɑːd, ˌpiːpəˈrɑːd, -z
AM ˌpɪpəˈrɑd, -z

piperidine
BR pɪˈpɛrɪdiːn, pɪˈpɛrɪdɪn, pʌɪˈpɛrɪdiːn, pʌɪˈpɛrɪdɪn
AM pəˈpɛrəˌdin, paɪˈpɛrəˌdin, paɪˈpɛrədn, pəˈpɛrədn

pipette
BR pɪˈpɛt, -s
AM paɪˈpɛt, -s

pipework
BR ˈpʌɪpwəːk
AM ˈpaɪpˌwərk

pipistrelle
BR ˈpɪpɪstrɛl, -z
AM ˈpɪpəˌstrɛl, -z

pipit
BR ˈpɪpɪt, -s

pipkin
BR ˈpɪpkɪn, -z
AM ˈpɪpkɪn, -z

pipless
BR ˈpɪplɪs
AM ˈpɪplɪs

Pippa
BR ˈpɪpə(r)
AM ˈpɪpə

pippin
BR ˈpɪpɪn, -z
AM ˈpɪpɪn, -z

pipsqueak
BR ˈpɪpskwiːk, -s
AM ˈpɪpˌskwik, -s

pipy
BR ˈpʌɪpi
AM ˈpaɪpi

piquancy
BR ˈpiːk(ə)nsi
AM ˈpik(w)ənsi

piquant
BR ˈpiːk(ə)nt
AM ˈpik(w)ənt

piquantly
BR ˈpiːk(ə)ntli
AM ˈpik(w)ən(t)li

pique
BR piːk
AM pik

piqué
BR ˈpiːkeɪ, -z
AM piˈkeɪ, -z

piquet¹
card game
BR pɪˈkɛt, pɪˈkeɪ
AM piˈkeɪ, pəˈkeɪ

piquet²
group of people
BR ˈpɪkɪt, -s
AM ˈpɪkɪt, -s

piracy
BR ˈpʌɪrəsi
AM ˈpaɪrəsi

Piraeus
BR pʌɪˈriːəs, pɪˈreɪəs
AM pəˈreɪəs, paɪˈriəs

piragua
BR pɪˈragwə(r), -z
AM pɪˈragwə, -z

piraña
BR pɪˈrɑːnə(r), -z
AM pəˈran(j)ə, -z

Pirandello
BR ˌpɪrənˈdɛləʊ, ˌpɪrnˈdɛləʊ
AM ˌpɪrənˈdɛloʊ

Piranesi
BR ˌpɪrəˈneɪzi

AM ˌpɪrəˈnɛzi

piranha
BR pɪˈrɑːnə(r), -z
AM pəˈran(j)ə, -z

pirate
BR ˈpʌɪrət, -s, -ɪŋ, -ɪd
AM ˈpaɪrə|t, -ts, -dɪŋ, -dəd

piratic
BR pʌɪˈratɪk, pɪˈratɪk
AM paɪˈrædɪk, pəˈrædɪk

piratical
BR pʌɪˈratɪkl, pɪˈratɪkl
AM paɪˈrædəkəl, pəˈrædəkəl

piratically
BR pʌɪˈratɪkli, pɪˈratɪkli
AM paɪˈrædək(ə)li, pəˈrædək(ə)li

Pirie
BR ˈpɪri
AM ˈpɪri

piripiri
BR ˈpɪrɪˌpɪri
AM ˈpɪriˈpɪri

pirog
BR pɪˈrəʊg, -z
AM piˈroʊg, pɪˈroʊg, -z

pirogue
BR pɪˈrəʊg, -z
AM piˈroʊg, pɪˈroʊg, -z

pirouette
BR ˌpɪrʊˈɛt, -s, -ɪŋ, -ɪd
AM ˌpɪrəˈwɛ|t, -ts, -dɪŋ, -dəd

Pisa
BR ˈpiːzə(r)
AM ˈpizə

pis aller
BR ˌpiːz ˈaleɪ, -z
AM ˌpiz əˈleɪ, + æˈleɪ, -z

Pisan
BR ˈpiːzn, -z
AM ˈpizn, -z

Pisano
BR pɪˈzɑːnəʊ
AM pəˈzɑnoʊ

piscary
BR ˈpɪsk(ə)r|i, -ɪz
AM ˈpɪskəri, -z

piscatorial
BR ˌpɪskəˈtɔːrɪəl
AM ˌpɪskəˈtɔriəl

piscatorially
BR ˌpɪskəˈtɔːrɪəli
AM ˌpɪskəˈtɔriəli

piscatory
BR ˈpɪskət(ə)ri
AM ˈpɪskəˌtɔri

Piscean
astrology
BR ˈpʌɪsɪən
AM ˈpaɪsɪən

piscean
biology
BR pɪˈsiːən, ˈpɪs(k)ɪən
AM ˈpɪs(k)ɪən, pəˈsiən

Pisces
BR ˈpʌɪsiːz
AM ˈpaɪsiz

piscicultural
BR ˌpɪsɪˈkʌltʃ(ə)rəl, ˌpɪsɪˈkʌltʃ(ə)r|
AM ˈpɪsəˌkəltʃ(ə)rəl

pisciculture
BR ˈpɪsɪˌkʌltʃə(r)
AM ˈpɪsəˌkəltʃər

pisciculturist
BR ˌpɪsɪˈkʌltʃ(ə)rɪst, -s
AM ˈpɪsəˌkəltʃ(ə)rəst, -s

piscina
BR pɪˈsiːnə(r), -z
AM pəˈsnə, pəˈsaɪnə, -z

piscine¹
adjective
BR ˈpɪs(k)ʌɪn, ˈpɪs(k)iːn
AM ˈpɪsin, ˈpɪsaɪn

piscine²
noun
BR ˈpɪsiːn, pɪˈsiːn, -z
AM pəˈsin, ˈpɪsin, -z

piscivorous
BR pɪˈsɪv(ə)rəs
AM pəˈsɪv(ə)rəs

pisco
BR ˈpɪskəʊ
AM ˈpɪskoʊ

Pisgah
BR ˈpɪzgə(r)
AM ˈpɪzgə

pish
BR pɪʃ
AM pɪʃ

Pisidia
BR pʌɪˈsɪdɪə(r)
AM pəˈsɪdɪə, paɪˈsɪdɪə

Pisidian
BR pʌɪˈsɪdɪən, -z
AM pəˈsɪdɪən, paɪˈsɪdɪən, -z

pisiform
BR ˈpɪsɪfɔːm
AM ˈpaɪsəˌfɔ(ə)rm, ˈpaɪzəˌfɔ(ə)rm

pismire
BR ˈpɪsˌmʌɪə(r), -z
AM ˈpɪsˌmaɪ(ə)r, ˈpɪzˌmaɪ(ə)r, -z

piss
BR pɪs, -ɪz, -ɪŋ, -t
AM pɪs, -ɪz, -ɪŋ, -t

Pissarro
BR pɪˈsɑːrəʊ
AM pɪˈsɑˌroʊ

pissoir
BR ˈpɪswɑː(r), -z
AM pɪˈswɑr, -z

pisspot
BR ˈpɪspɒt, -s

AM 'pɪs,pɑt, -s

piss-taker
BR 'pɪs,teɪkə(r), -z
AM 'pɪs,teɪkər, -z

piss-taking
BR 'pɪs,teɪkɪŋ
AM 'pɪs,teɪkɪŋ

piss-up
BR 'pɪsʌp, -s
AM 'pɪsəp, -s

pistachio
BR pɪ'stɑː(t)ʃɪəʊ,
pɪ'sta(t)ʃɪəʊ, -z
AM pə'stæʃɪoʊ,
pə'staʃɪoʊ, -z

piste
BR piːst, -s
AM pist, -s

pisteur
BR piː'stə:(r), -z
AM pi'stər, -z

pistil
BR 'pɪst(ɪ)l, -z
AM 'pɪstl̩, -z

pistillary
BR 'pɪstɪl(ə)ri,
'pɪstl̩(ə)ri
AM 'pɪstə,lɛri

pistillate
BR 'pɪstɪlət, 'pɪstl̩ət,
'pɪstɪleɪt, 'pɪstl̩eɪt
AM 'pɪstə,leɪt, 'pɪstələt

pistilliferous
BR ,pɪstɪ'lɪf(ə)rəs
AM ,pɪstə'lɪf(ə)rəs

pistilline
BR 'pɪstɪlm, 'pɪstl̩m,
'pɪstɪliːn, 'pɪstl̩iːn
AM 'pɪstələn,
'pɪstə,laɪn

pistol
BR 'pɪstl̩, -z
AM 'pɪstl̩, -z

pistole
BR 'pɪstəʊl, pɪ'stəʊl, -z
AM pə'stoʊl, -z

pistoleer
BR ,pɪstə'lɪə(r), -z
AM ,pɪstə'lɪ(ə)r, -z

piston
BR 'pɪst(ə)n, -z
AM 'pɪstən, -z

pistou
BR 'piːstuː
AM pi'stu

pit
BR pɪt, -s, -ɪŋ, -ɪd
AM pɪ|t, -ts, -dɪŋ, -dɪd

pita
BR 'pɪtə(r), 'piːtə(r)
AM 'pidə

pit-a-pat
BR ,pɪtə'pat, 'pɪtəpat
AM 'pɪdə,pæt

Pitcairn
BR 'pɪtkɛːn
AM 'pɪt,kɛrn

pitch
BR pɪtʃ, -ɪz, -ɪŋ, -t
AM pɪtʃ, -ɪz, -ɪŋ, -t

pitchblack
BR ,pɪtʃ'blak
AM ,pɪtʃ'blæk

pitchblende
BR 'pɪtʃblɛnd
AM 'pɪtʃ,blɛnd

pitcher
BR 'pɪtʃə(r), -z
AM 'pɪtʃər, -z

pitcherful
BR 'pɪtʃəfʊl, -z
AM 'pɪtʃər,fʊl, -z

pitchfork
BR 'pɪtʃfɔːk, -s, -ɪŋ, -t
AM 'pɪtʃ,fɔ(ə)rk, -s, -ɪŋ,
-t

pitchman
BR 'pɪtʃmən
AM 'pɪtʃmən

pitchmen
BR 'pɪtʃmən
AM 'pɪtʃmən

pitchout
BR 'pɪtʃaʊt, -s
AM 'pɪtʃ,aʊt, -s

pitchpine
BR 'pɪtʃpʌɪn
AM 'pɪtʃ,paɪn

pitchpipe
BR 'pɪtʃpʌɪp, -s
AM 'pɪtʃ,paɪp, -s

pitchstone
BR 'pɪtʃstəʊn
AM 'pɪtʃ,stoʊn

pitchy
BR 'pɪtʃi
AM 'pɪtʃi

piteous
BR 'pɪtɪəs
AM 'pɪdiəs

piteously
BR 'pɪtɪəsli
AM 'pɪdiəsli

piteousness
BR 'pɪtɪəsnəs
AM 'pɪdiəsnəs

pitfall
BR 'pɪtfɔːl, -z
AM 'pɪt,fɔl, 'pɪt,fɑl, -z

pith
BR pɪθ
AM pɪθ

pithead
BR 'pɪthɛd, -z
AM 'pɪt,(h)ɛd, -z

Pithecanthropus
BR ,pɪθɪ'kanθrəpəs
AM ,pɪθə'kænθrəpəs,
,pɪθə,kæn'θroʊpəs

pithecoid
BR 'pɪθɪkɔɪd, -z
AM 'pɪθə,kɔɪd, -z

pithily
BR 'pɪθɪli

AM 'pɪθɪli

pithiness
BR 'pɪθɪnɪs
AM 'pɪθɪnɪs

pithless
BR 'pɪθləs
AM 'pɪθləs

pithoi
BR 'pɪθɔɪ, 'pʌɪθɔɪ
AM 'pɪ,θɔɪ, 'paɪ,θɔɪ

pithos
BR 'pɪθɒs, 'pʌɪθɒs
AM 'pɪ,θɒs, 'paɪ,θɒs,
'pɪ,θɑs, 'paɪ,θɑs

pithy
BR 'pɪθi
AM 'pɪθi

pitiable
BR 'pɪtɪəbl
AM 'pɪdiəbəl

pitiableness
BR 'pɪtɪəblnəs
AM 'pɪdiəbəlnəs

pitiably
BR 'pɪtɪəbli
AM 'pɪdiəbli

pitiful
BR 'pɪtɪf(ʊ)l
AM 'pɪdifəl

pitifully
BR 'pɪtɪfəli, 'pɪtɪfl̩i
AM 'pɪdifəli

pitifulness
BR 'pɪtɪf(ʊ)lnəs
AM 'pɪdifəlnəs

pitiless
BR 'pɪtɪlɪs
AM 'pɪdilɪs

pitilessly
BR 'pɪtɪlɪsli
AM 'pɪdilɪsli

pitilessness
BR 'pɪtɪlɪsnɪs
AM 'pɪdilɪsnɪs

Pitlochry
BR pɪt'lɒxri, pɪt'lɒkri
AM pɪt'lɑkri

pitman
BR 'pɪtmən
AM 'pɪtmən

pitmen
BR 'pɪtmən
AM 'pɪtmən

Pitney
BR 'pɪtni
AM 'pɪtni

piton
BR 'piːtɒn, 'piːtɒ̃, -z
AM 'pi,tɑn, -z

Pitot tube
BR 'piːtəʊ tjuːb, +
tʃuːb, -z
AM pi'toʊ ,t(j)ub,
'pidoʊ +, -z

pitpan
BR 'pɪtpan, -z
AM 'pɪt,pæn, -z

Pitsea
BR 'pɪtsi:
AM 'pɪtsi

Pitt
BR pɪt
AM pɪt

pitta
BR 'pɪtə(r)
AM 'pɪdə

pittance
BR 'pɪt(ə)ns, -ɪz
AM 'pɪtn̩s, -ɪz

Pittenweem
BR 'pɪtn̩'wiːm
AM ,pɪtn̩'wim

pitter-patter
BR 'pɪtə,patə(r),
,pɪtə'patə(r)
AM 'pɪdər,pædər

Pitti
BR 'pɪti
AM 'pɪdi

Pittman
BR 'pɪtmən
AM 'pɪtmən

pittosporum
BR pɪ'tɒsp(ə)rəm, -z
AM pə'tɑspərəm,
,pɪdə'spɔrəm, -z

Pitt-Rivers
BR ,pɪt'rɪvəz
AM ,pɪt'rɪvərz

Pitts
BR pɪts
AM pɪts

Pittsburgh
BR 'pɪtsbə:g
AM 'pɪts,bərg

pituitary
BR pɪ'tjuːɪt(ə)ri,
pɪ'tʃuːɪt(ə)ri
AM pə't(j)uə,tɛri

pituri
BR 'pɪtjʊəri, 'pɪtjʊri,
'pɪtʃ(ə)ri
AM 'pɪtʃəri

pity
BR 'pɪt|i, -ɪz, -ɪɪŋ, -ɪd
AM 'pɪdi, -z, -ɪŋ, -d

pityingly
BR 'pɪtɪɪŋli
AM 'pɪdiɪŋli

pityriasis
BR ,pɪtɪ'rʌɪəsɪs
AM ,pɪdə'raɪəsəs

più
BR pjuː
AM pju, pi'u

Pius
BR 'pʌɪəs
AM 'paɪəs

pivot
BR 'pɪvət, -s, -ɪŋ, -ɪd
AM 'pɪvə|t, -ts, -dɪŋ,
-dəd

pivotability
BR ,pɪvətə'bɪlɪti

AM ˌpɪvədəˈbɪlɪdi

pivotable
BR ˈpɪvətəbl
AM ˈpɪvədəbəl

pivotal
BR ˈpɪvətl
AM ˈpɪvədl

pix
BR pɪks
AM pɪks

pixel
BR ˈpɪksl, -z
AM ˈpɪksəl, -z

pixie
BR ˈpɪks|i, -ɪz
AM ˈpɪksi, -z

pixilated
BR ˈpɪksɪleɪtɪd
AM ˈpɪksəˌleɪdɪd

pixy
BR ˈpɪks|i, -ɪz
AM ˈpɪksi, -z

Pizarro
BR pɪˈzɑːrəʊ
AM pəˈzɑroʊ

pizazz
BR pɪˈzaz
AM pəˈzæz

pizza
BR ˈpiːtsə(r), -z
AM ˈpitsə, -z

pizzazz
BR pɪˈzaz
AM pəˈzæz

pizzeria
BR ˌpiːtsəˈriːə(r),
ˌpɪtsəˈriːə(r), -z
AM ˌpitsəˈriə, -z

Pizzey
BR ˈpɪtsi, ˈpɪzi
AM ˈpɪtsi, ˈpɪzi

pizzicato
BR ˌpɪtsɪˈkɑːtəʊ, -z
AM ˌpɪtsəˈkɑdoʊ, -z

pizzle
BR ˈpɪzl, -z
AM ˈpɪzl, -z

PJ's
BR ˌpiːˈdʒeɪz
AM ˈpiˌdʒeɪz

placability
BR ˌplakəˈbɪlɪti
AM ˌplækəˈbɪlɪdi

placable
BR ˈplakəbl
AM ˈplækəbəl

placableness
BR ˈplakəblnəs
AM ˈplækəbəlnəs

placably
BR ˈplakəbli
AM ˈplækəbli

placard
BR ˈplakɑːd, -z
AM ˈplækərd,
ˈplæˌkɑrd, -z

placate
BR pləˈkeɪt, -s, -ɪŋ, -ɪd
AM ˈpleɪˌkeɪ|t, -ts, -dɪŋ,
-dɪd

placatingly
BR pləˈkeɪtɪŋli
AM pləˈkeɪdɪŋli

placation
BR pləˈkeɪʃn
AM pləˈkeɪʃən

placatory
BR pləˈkeɪt(ə)ri,
ˈplakət(ə)ri
AM ˈpleɪkəˌtɔri,
ˈplækəˌtɔri

place
BR pleɪs, -ɪz, -ɪŋ, -t
AM pleɪs, -ɪz, -ɪŋ, -t

placebo
BR pləˈsiːbəʊ, -z
AM pləˈsiboʊ, -z

placeholder
BR ˈpleɪsˌhəʊldə(r), -z
AM ˈpleɪsˌ(h)oʊldər, -z

placeless
BR ˈpleɪslɪs
AM ˈpleɪslɪs

placement
BR ˈpleɪsm(ə)nt, -s
AM ˈpleɪsmənt, -s

placenta
BR pləˈsentə(r), -z
AM pləˈsen(t)ə, -z

placental
BR pləˈsentl, -z
AM pləˈsen(t)l, -z

placer
BR ˈpleɪsə(r), -z
AM ˈpleɪsər, -z

placet
BR ˈpleɪsɛt, ˈpleɪsɪt, -s
AM ˈpleɪsɪt, -s

placid
BR ˈplasɪd
AM ˈplæsəd

placidity
BR pləˈsɪdɪti
AM plæˈsɪdɪdi,
pləˈsɪdɪdi

placidly
BR ˈplasɪdli
AM ˈplæsədli

placidness
BR ˈplasɪdnɪs
AM ˈplæsədnəs

placing
BR ˈpleɪsɪŋ, -z
AM ˈpleɪsɪŋ, -z

placket
BR ˈplakɪt, -s
AM ˈplækət, -s

placoid
BR ˈplakɔɪd, -z
AM ˈplæˌkɔɪd, -z

plafond
BR plaˈfɒ̃, plaˈfɒnd, -z
AM pləˈfɑnd, -z

plagal
BR ˈpleɪgl
AM ˈpleɪgəl

plage
BR plɑːʒ, -ɪz
AM plɑʒ, -əz

plagiarise
BR ˈpleɪdʒ(i)ərʌɪz, -ɪz,
-ɪŋ, -d
AM ˈpleɪdʒəˌraɪz, -ɪz,
-ɪŋ, -d

plagiariser
BR ˈpleɪdʒ(i)ərʌɪzə(r),
-z
AM ˈpleɪdʒəˌraɪzər, -z

plagiarism
BR ˈpleɪdʒ(i)ərɪz(ə)m
AM ˈpleɪdʒəˌrɪzəm

plagiarist
BR ˈpleɪdʒ(i)ərɪst, -s
AM ˈpleɪdʒərəst, -s

plagiaristic
BR ˌpleɪdʒ(i)əˈrɪstɪk
AM ˌpleɪdʒəˈrɪstɪk

plagiarize
BR ˈpleɪdʒ(i)ərʌɪz, -ɪz,
-ɪŋ, -d
AM ˈpleɪdʒəˌraɪz, -ɪz,
-ɪŋ, -d

plagiarizer
BR ˈpleɪdʒ(i)ərʌɪzə(r),
-z
AM ˈpleɪdʒəˌraɪzər, -z

plagiocephalic
BR ˌpleɪdʒɪəʊsɪˈfalɪk,
ˌpleɪdʒɪəʊkɪˈfalɪk
AM ˌpleɪdʒiəsəˈfælɪk

plagioclase
BR ˈpleɪdʒɪəkleɪz,
ˈpleɪdʒɪəkleɪs, -ɪz
AM ˈpleɪdʒiəˌkleɪs,
ˈpleɪdʒiəˌkleɪz, -əz

plagioclastic
BR ˌpleɪdʒɪəˈklastɪk
AM ˌpleɪdʒiəˈklæstɪk

plagiostome
BR ˈpleɪdʒɪəstəʊm, -z
AM ˈpleɪdʒiəˌstoʊm, -z

plague
BR pleɪg, -z, -ɪŋ, -d
AM pleɪg, -z, -ɪŋ, -d

plagueily
BR ˈpleɪgɪli
AM ˈpleɪgɪli

plagueiness
BR ˈpleɪgɪnɪs
AM ˈpleɪgɪnɪs

plaguesome
BR ˈpleɪgs(ə)m
AM ˈpleɪgsəm

plaguey
BR ˈpleɪgi
AM ˈpleɪgi

plaguily
BR ˈpleɪgɪli
AM ˈpleɪgɪli

plaguiness
BR ˈpleɪgɪnɪs

AM ˈpleɪgɪnɪs

plaguy
BR ˈpleɪgi
AM ˈpleɪgi

plaice
BR pleɪs
AM pleɪs

plaid
BR plad, -z
AM plæd, -z

Plaid Cymru
BR ˌplʌɪd ˈkamri,
+ ˈkʌmri
AM ˌplaɪd ˈkʊmri

plaided
BR ˈpladɪd
AM ˈplædəd

plain
BR pleɪn, -z, -ə(r), -ɪst
AM pleɪn, -z, -ər, -ɪst

plainchant
BR ˈpleɪntʃɑːnt,
ˈpleɪntʃant, -s
AM ˈpleɪnˌtʃænt, -s

plainclothes
BR ˌpleɪnˈkləʊ(ð)z
AM ˌpleɪnˈkloʊ(ð)z

plainly
BR ˈpleɪnli
AM ˈpleɪnli

plainness
BR ˈpleɪnnɪs
AM ˈpleɪ(n)nɪs

plainsman
BR ˈpleɪnzmən
AM ˈpleɪnzmən

plainsmen
BR ˈpleɪnzmən
AM ˈpleɪnzmən

plainsong
BR ˈpleɪnsɒŋ
AM ˈpleɪnˌsɔŋ,
ˈpleɪnˌsɑŋ

plainspoken
BR ˌpleɪnˈspəʊk(ə)n
AM ˌpleɪnˈspoʊkən

plainswoman
BR ˈpleɪnzˌwʊmən
AM ˈpleɪnzˌwʊmən

plainswomen
BR ˈpleɪnzˌwɪmɪn
AM ˈpleɪnzˌwɪmɪn

plaint
BR pleɪnt, -s
AM pleɪnt, -s

plaintiff
BR ˈpleɪntɪf, -s
AM ˈpleɪn(t)ɪf, -s

plaintive
BR ˈpleɪntɪv
AM ˈpleɪn(t)ɪv

plaintively
BR ˈpleɪntɪvli
AM ˈpleɪn(t)ɪvli

plaintiveness
BR ˈpleɪntɪvnɪs
AM ˈpleɪn(t)ɪvnɪs

Plaistow¹
place in U.K.
BR ˈplɑːstəʊ, ˈplastəʊ
AM ˈplæstoʊ

Plaistow²
surname
BR ˈplɑːstəʊ, ˈplastəʊ, ˈpleɪstəʊ
AM ˈplæstoʊ, ˈpleɪstoʊ

plait
BR plat, -s, -ɪŋ, -ɪd
AM pleɪt, plæt, -ts, -dɪŋ, -dɪd\-dəd

plan
BR plan, -z, -ɪŋ, -d
AM plæn, -z, -ɪŋ, -d

planar
BR ˈpleɪnə(r)
AM ˈpleɪnər

planarian
BR pləˈnɛːrɪən, -z
AM pləˈnɛrɪən, -z

planchet
BR ˈplan(t)ʃɪt, -s
AM ˈplæn(t)ʃət, -s

planchette
BR plɑːnˈʃɛt, planˈʃɛt, plɒˈʃɛt, -s
AM plænˈʃɛt, -s

Planck
BR plaŋk
AM plæŋk

plane
BR pleɪn, -z, -ɪŋ, -d
AM pleɪn, -z, -ɪŋ, -d

planeload
BR ˈpleɪnləʊd, -z
AM ˈpleɪnˌloʊd, -z

planemaker
BR ˈpleɪnˌmeɪkə(r), -z
AM ˈpleɪnˌmeɪkər, -z

planemaking
BR ˈpleɪnˌmeɪkɪŋ
AM ˈpleɪnˌmeɪkɪŋ

planer
BR ˈpleɪnə(r), -z
AM ˈpleɪnər, -z

planet
BR ˈplanɪt, -s
AM ˈplænət, -s

planetaria
BR ˌplanɪˈtɛːrɪə(r)
AM ˌplænəˈtɛrɪə

planetarium
BR ˌplanɪˈtɛːrɪəm, -z
AM ˌplænəˈtɛriəm, -z

planetary
BR ˈplanɪt(ə)ri
AM ˈplænəˌtɛri

planetesimal
BR ˌplanɪˈtɛsɪml
AM ˌplænəˈtɛsəməl

planetoid
BR ˈplanɪtɔɪd, -z
AM ˈplænəˌtɔɪd, -z

planetologist
BR ˌplanɪˈtɒlədʒɪst, -s

BR ˌplænəˈtɑlədʒəst, -s

planetology
BR ˌplanɪˈtɒlədʒi
AM ˌplænəˈtɑlədʒi

plangency
BR ˈplan(d)ʒ(ə)nsi
AM ˈplændʒənsi

plangent
BR ˈplan(d)ʒ(ə)nt
AM ˈplændʒənt

plangently
BR ˈplan(d)ʒ(ə)ntli
AM ˈplændʒəntli

planimeter
BR plaˈnɪmɪtə(r), pləˈnɪmɪtə(r), -z
AM pləˈnɪmədər, -z

planimetric
BR ˌplanɪˈmɛtrɪk
AM ˌplanəˈmɛtrɪk

planimetrical
BR ˌplanɪˈmɛtrɪkl
AM ˌplanəˈmɛtrəkəl

planimetry
BR plaˈnɪmɪtri, pləˈnɪmɪtri
AM pləˈnɪmətri

planish
BR ˈplanɪʃ, -ɪʃɪz, -ɪʃɪŋ, -ɪʃt
AM ˈplænɪʃ, -ɪz, -ɪŋ, -t

planisher
BR ˈplanɪʃə(r), -z
AM ˈplænɪʃər, -z

planisphere
BR ˈplanɪsfɪə(r), -z
AM ˈplænəˌsfɪ(ə)r, -z

planispheric
BR ˌplanɪˈsfɛrɪk
AM ˌplænəˈsfɛrɪk

plank
BR plaŋk, -ks, -kɪŋ, -(k)t
AM plæŋk, -ks, -kɪŋ, -(k)t

plankton
BR ˈplaŋ(k)tən
AM ˈplæŋktən

planktonic
BR plaŋ(k)ˈtɒnɪk
AM plæŋkˈtɑnɪk

planner
BR ˈplanə(r), -z
AM ˈplænər, -z

planoconcave
BR ˌpleɪnəʊˈkɒnkeɪv, ˌpleɪnəʊˈkɒŋkeɪv
AM ˌpleɪnoʊˈkɑnˌkeɪv

planoconvex
BR ˌpleɪnəʊˈkɒnvɛks
AM ˌpleɪnoʊˈkɑnˈvɛks

planographic
BR ˌplanəˈɡrafɪk
AM ˌplænəˈɡræfɪk

planography
BR plaˈnɒɡrəfi, pləˈnɒɡrəfi
AM pləˈnɑɡrəfi

planometer
BR plaˈnɒmɪtə(r), pləˈnɒmɪtə(r), -z
AM pləˈnɑmədər, -z

plant
BR plɑːnt, plant, -s, -ɪŋ, -ɪd
AM plænt, -ts, -(t)ɪŋ, -(t)əd

plantable
BR ˈplɑːntəbl, ˈplantəbl
AM ˈplæn(t)əbəl

Plantagenet
BR planˈtadʒɪnɪt, planˈtadʒɪt, -s
AM plænˈtædʒənət, -s

plantain
BR ˈplantɪn, ˈplanteɪn, -z
AM ˈplænt(ə)n, -z

plantar
BR ˈplantə(r), ˈplantɑ(r)
AM ˈplæn(t)ər

plantation
BR plɑːnˈteɪʃn, planˈteɪʃn, -z
AM plænˈteɪʃən, -z

planter
BR ˈplɑːntə(r), ˈplantə(r), -z
AM ˈplæn(t)ər, -z

plantigrade
BR ˈplantɪɡreɪd, -z
AM ˈplæn(t)əˌɡreɪd, -z

Plantin
BR ˈplantɪn
AM ˈplæntn

planting
BR ˈplɑːntɪŋ, ˈplantɪŋ, -z
AM ˈplæn(t)ɪŋ, -z

plantlet
BR ˈplɑːntlɪt, ˈplantlɪt, -s
AM ˈplæn(t)lət, -s

plantlike
BR ˈplɑːntlʌɪk, ˈplantlʌɪk
AM ˈplæntˌlaɪk

plaque
BR plak, plɑːk
AM plæk

plaquette
BR plaˈkɛt, -s
AM plæˈkɛt, -s

plash
BR plaʃ, -ɪz, -ɪŋ, -t
AM plæʃ, -əz, -ɪŋ, -t

plashy
BR ˈplaʃi
AM ˈplæʃi

plasm
BR ˈplaz(ə)m
AM ˈplæzəm

plasma
BR ˈplazmə(r)
AM ˈplæzmə

plasmacyte
BR ˈplazməsʌɪt, -s
AM ˈplæzməˌsaɪt, -s

plasmagel
BR ˈplazmədʒɛl
AM ˈplæzməˌdʒɛl

plasmagene
BR ˈplazmədʒiːn, -z
AM ˈplæzməˌdʒin, -z

plasmapheresis
BR ˌplazməˈfɛrɪsɪs, ˌplazməfəˈriːsɪs
AM ˌplæzməfəˈrisɪs, ˌplæzməˈfɛrəsɪs

plasmasol
BR ˈplazməsɒl
AM ˈplæzməˌsɒl, ˈplæzməˌsɑl

plasmatic
BR plazˈmatɪk
AM plæzˈmædɪk

plasmic
BR ˈplazmɪk
AM ˈplæzmɪk

plasmid
BR ˈplazmɪd, -z
AM ˈplæzmɪd, -z

plasmodesma
BR ˌplazməˈdɛzmə(r)
AM ˌplæzməˈdɛzmə

plasmodesmata
BR ˌplazməˈdɛzmətə(r)
AM ˌplæzməˈdɛzmədə

plasmodia
BR plazˈməʊdɪə(r)
AM plæzˈmoʊdɪə

plasmodial
BR plazˈməʊdɪəl
AM plæzˈmoʊdɪəl

plasmodium
BR plazˈməʊdɪəm
AM plæzˈmoʊdɪəm

plasmolyse
BR ˈplazməlʌɪz, -ɪz, -ɪŋ, -t
AM ˈplæzməˌlaɪz, -ɪz, -ɪŋ, -t

plasmolysis
BR plazˈmɒlɪsɪs
AM plæzˈmɑləsəs

plasmolyze
BR ˈplazməlʌɪz, -ɪz, -ɪŋ, -d
AM ˈplæzməˌlaɪz, -ɪŋ, -d

Plassey
BR ˈplasi
AM ˈplæsi

plaster
BR ˈplɑːstə(r), ˈplastə(r), -əz, -(ə)rɪŋ, -əd

AM ˈplæst|ər, -ərz,
-(ə)rɪŋ, -ərd
plasterboard
BR ˈplɑːstəbɔːd,
ˈplɑstəbɔːd
AM ˈplæstərˌbɔː(ə)rd
plasterer
BR ˈplɑːst(ə)rə(r),
ˈplɑst(ə)rə(r), -z
AM ˈplæstərər, -z
plasterwork
BR ˈplɑːstəwəːk,
ˈplɑstəwəːk
AM ˈplæstərˌwərk
plastery
BR ˈplɑːst(ə)ri,
ˈplɑst(ə)ri
AM ˈplæst(ə)ri
plastic
BR ˈplæstɪk, -s
AM ˈplæstɪk, -s
plastically
BR ˈplæstɪkli
AM ˈplæstək(ə)li
Plasticine®
BR ˈplæstəsiːn,
ˈplɑːstəsiːn
AM ˈplæstəˌsin
plasticisation
BR ˌplæstɪsaɪˈzeɪʃn
AM ˌplæstəsəˈzeɪʃən,
ˌplæstəˌsaɪˈzeɪʃən
plasticise
BR ˈplæstɪsaɪz, -ɪz, -ɪŋ,
-d
AM ˈplæstəˌsaɪz, -ɪz, -ɪŋ,
-d
plasticiser
BR ˈplæstɪsaɪzə(r)
AM ˈplæstəˌsaɪzər
plasticity
BR plaˈstɪsɪti
AM plæˈstɪsɪdi
plasticization
BR ˌplæstɪsaɪˈzeɪʃn
AM ˌplæstəsəˈzeɪʃən,
ˌplæstəˌsaɪˈzeɪʃən
plasticize
BR ˈplæstɪsaɪz, -ɪz, -ɪŋ,
-d
AM ˈplæstəˌsaɪz, -ɪz, -ɪŋ,
-d
plasticizer
BR ˈplæstɪsaɪzə(r), -z
AM ˈplæstəˌsaɪzər, -z
plasticky
BR ˈplæstɪki
AM ˈplæstɪki
plastid
BR ˈplæstɪd, -z
AM ˈplæstəd, -z
plastral
BR ˈplæstr(ə)l
AM ˈplæstrəl
plastron
BR ˈplæstr(ə)n, -z
AM ˈplæstrən, -z

plat
BR plæt, -s
AM plæt, -s
Plataea
BR pləˈtiːə(r)
AM pləˈtiə
platan
BR ˈplæt(ə)n, -z
AM ˈplætn, -z
plat du jour
BR ˌplɑː də ˈʒʊə(r),
+ duː +
AM ˌplɑ də ˈʒʊ(ə)r
plate
BR pleɪt, -s, -ɪŋ, -ɪd
AM pleɪt, -ts, -dɪŋ, -dɪd
plateau
BR ˈplætəʊ, plaˈtəʊ,
pləˈtəʊ, -z
AM plæˈtoʊ, -z
plateaux
BR ˈplætəʊz, plaˈtəʊz,
pləˈtəʊz
AM plæˈtoʊ
plateful
BR ˈpleɪtfʊl, -z
AM ˈpleɪtˌfʊl, -z
platelayer
BR ˈpleɪtˌleɪə(r), -z
AM ˈpleɪtˌleɪər, -z
plateless
BR ˈpleɪtlɪs
AM ˈpleɪtlɪs
platelet
BR ˈpleɪtlɪt, -s
AM ˈpleɪtlɪt, -s
platen
BR ˈplæt(ə)n, -z
AM ˈplætn, -z
plater
BR ˈpleɪtə(r), -z
AM ˈpleɪdər, -z
plateresque
BR ˌplætərˈɛsk
AM ˌplædəˈrɛsk
platform
BR ˈplætfɔːm, -z
AM ˈplætˌfɔ(ə)rm, -z
Plath
BR plɑːθ
AM plæθ
plating
BR ˈpleɪtɪŋ, -z
AM ˈpleɪdɪŋ, -z
platinic
BR pləˈtɪnɪk
AM pləˈtɪnɪk
platinisation
BR ˌplætɪnaɪˈzeɪʃn,
ˌplætnaɪˈzeɪʃn
AM ˌplætnəˈzeɪʃən,
ˌplætnˌaɪˈzeɪʃən
platinise
BR ˈplætɪnaɪz,
ˈplætnaɪz, -ɪz, -ɪŋ, -d
AM ˈplætnˌaɪz, -ɪz, -ɪŋ, -d

platinization
BR ˌplætɪnaɪˈzeɪʃn,
ˌplætnaɪˈzeɪʃn
AM ˌplætnəˈzeɪʃən,
ˌplætnˌaɪˈzeɪʃən
platinize
BR ˈplætɪnaɪz,
ˈplætnaɪz, -ɪz, -ɪŋ, -d
AM ˈplætnˌaɪz, -ɪz, -ɪŋ, -d
platinoid
BR ˈplætɪnɔɪd,
ˈplætnɔɪd, -z
AM ˈplætnˌɔɪd, -z
platinotype
BR ˈplætɪnəʊtaɪp,
ˈplætnəʊtaɪp, -s
AM ˈplætnoʊˌtaɪp, -s
platinum
BR ˈplætɪnəm,
ˈplætnəm
AM ˈplædənəm,
ˈplætnəm, ˈplætnm
platitude
BR ˈplætɪtjuːd,
ˈplætɪtʃuːd, -z
AM ˈplædəˌt(j)ud, -z
platitudinarian
BR ˌplætɪˌtjuːdɪˈnɛːrɪən,
ˌplætɪˌtʃuːdɪˈnɛːrɪən,
-z
AM ˌplædəˌt(j)udnˈɛriən,
-z
platitudinise
BR ˌplætɪˈtjuːdɪnaɪz,
ˌplætɪˈtʃuːdɪnaɪz, -ɪz,
-ɪŋ, -d
AM ˌplædəˈt(j)udnˌaɪz,
-ɪz, -ɪŋ, -d
platitudinize
BR ˌplætɪˈtjuːdɪnaɪz,
ˌplætɪˈtʃuːdɪnaɪz, -ɪz,
-ɪŋ, -d
AM ˌplædəˈt(j)udnˌaɪz,
-ɪz, -ɪŋ, -d
platitudinous
BR ˌplætɪˈtjuːdɪnəs,
ˌplætɪˈtʃuːdɪnəs
AM ˌplædəˈt(j)udnəs
Plato
BR ˈpleɪtəʊ
AM ˈpleɪdoʊ
Platonic
BR pləˈtɒnɪk
AM pləˈtɑnɪk
platonical
BR pləˈtɒnɪkl
AM pləˈtɑnəkəl
Platonically
BR pləˈtɒnɪkli
AM pləˈtɑnək(ə)li
Platonism
BR ˈpleɪtənɪz(ə)m,
ˈpleɪtnɪz(ə)m
AM ˈpleɪtnˌɪzəm
Platonist
BR ˈpleɪtənɪst,
ˈpleɪtnɪst, -s
AM ˈpleɪtnəst, -s

platoon
BR pləˈtuːn, -z
AM pləˈtun, -z
plats du jour
BR ˌplɑː də ˈʒʊə(r),
+ duː +
AM ˌplɑ də ˈʒʊ(ə)r
Platt
BR plat
AM plæt
Plattdeutsch
BR ˈplatdɔɪtʃ
AM ˈplætˌdɔɪtʃ
platteland
BR ˈplatəland
AM ˈplædəˌlænd
plattelander
BR ˈplatˌlandə(r), -z
AM ˈplætˌlændər, -z
platter
BR ˈplatə(r), -z
AM ˈplædər, -z
platy
BR ˈpleɪti
AM ˈpleɪdi
platyhelminth
BR ˌplatɪˈhɛlmɪnθ, -s
AM ˌplædiˈhɛlmənθ, -s
platypus
BR ˈplatɪpəs, ˈplatɪpʊs,
-ɪz
AM ˈplædəpəs,
ˈplædəˌpʊs, -əz
platyrrhine
BR ˈplatɪrʌɪn, -z
AM ˈplædəˌraɪn,
ˈplædərən, -z
plaudit
BR ˈplɔːdɪt, -s
AM ˈplɒdət, ˈpladət, -s
plausibility
BR ˌplɔːzɪˈbɪlɪti
AM ˌplɒzəˈbɪlɪdi,
ˌplazəˈbɪlɪdi
plausible
BR ˈplɔːzɪbl
AM ˈplɒzəbəl, ˈplazəbəl
plausibly
BR ˈplɔːzɪbli
AM ˈplɒzəbli, ˈplazəbli
Plautus
BR ˈplɔːtəs
AM ˈplɒdəs, ˈpladəs
play
BR pleɪ, -z, -ɪŋ, -d
AM pleɪ, -z, -ɪŋ, -d
playa
BR ˈplʌɪə(r), -z
AM ˈplaɪə, -z
playability
BR ˌpleɪəˈbɪlɪti
AM ˌpleɪəˈbɪlɪdi
playable
BR ˈpleɪəbl
AM ˈpleɪəbəl
play-act
BR ˈpleɪakt, -s, -ɪŋ, -ɪd

AM 'pleɪˌæk|(t), -(t)s,
-tɪŋ, -təd

play-actor
BR 'pleɪˌaktə(r), -z
AM 'pleɪˌæktər, -z

playback
BR 'pleɪbak, -s
AM 'pleɪˌbæk, -s

playbill
BR 'pleɪbɪl, -z
AM 'pleɪˌbɪl, -z

playbook
BR 'pleɪbʊk, -s
AM 'pleɪˌbʊk, -s

playboy
BR 'pleɪbɔɪ, -z
AM 'pleɪˌbɔɪ, -z

player
BR 'pleɪə(r), -z
AM 'pleɪər, -z

player-piano
BR ˌpleɪəpɪ'anəʊ, -z
AM 'pleɪərpiˌænoʊ, -z

Playfair
BR 'pleɪfɛː(r)
AM 'pleɪˌfɛ(ə)r

playfellow
BR 'pleɪˌfɛləʊ, -z
AM 'pleɪˌfɛloʊ, -z

playful
BR 'pleɪf(ʊ)l
AM 'pleɪfəl

playfully
BR 'pleɪf(ʊ)li, 'pleɪʃli
AM 'pleɪfəli

playfulness
BR 'pleɪf(ʊ)lnəs
AM 'pleɪfəlnəs

playgirl
BR 'pleɪɡəːl, -z
AM 'pleɪˌɡərl, -z

playgoer
BR 'pleɪˌɡəʊə(r), -z
AM 'pleɪˌɡoʊər, -z

playground
BR 'pleɪɡraʊnd, -z
AM 'pleɪˌɡraʊnd, -z

playgroup
BR 'pleɪɡruːp, -s
AM 'pleɪˌɡrup, -s

playhouse
BR 'pleɪhaʊ|s, -zɪz
AM 'pleɪˌhaʊ|s, -zəz

playlet
BR 'pleɪlɪt, -s
AM 'pleɪlət, -s

playlist
BR 'pleɪlɪst, -s
AM 'pleɪˌlɪst, -s

playmaker
BR 'pleɪˌmeɪkə(r), -z
AM 'pleɪˌmeɪkər, -z

playmate
BR 'pleɪmeɪt, -s
AM 'pleɪˌmeɪt, -s

playoff
BR 'pleɪɒf

AM 'pleɪˌɔf, 'pleɪˌɑf

playpen
BR 'pleɪpɛn, -z
AM 'pleɪˌpɛn, -z

playroom
BR 'pleɪruːm,
'pleɪrʊm, -z
AM 'pleɪˌrum,
'pleɪˌrʊm, -z

playschool
BR 'pleɪskuːl, -z
AM 'pleɪˌskul, -z

playsuit
BR 'pleɪs(j)uːt, -s
AM 'pleɪˌsut, -s

Playtex®
BR 'pleɪtɛks
AM 'pleɪˌtɛks

plaything
BR 'pleɪθɪŋ, -z
AM 'pleɪˌθɪŋ, -z

playtime
BR 'pleɪtaɪm
AM 'pleɪˌtaɪm

playwear
BR 'pleɪwɛː(r)
AM 'pleɪˌwɛ(ə)r

playwright
BR 'pleɪrʌɪt, -s
AM 'pleɪˌraɪt, -s

playwriting
BR 'pleɪˌrʌɪtɪŋ
AM 'pleɪˌraɪdɪŋ

plaza
BR 'plɑːzə(r), -z
AM 'plɑzə, 'plæzə, -z

plc
BR ˌpiːɛl'siː, -z
AM ˌpiˌɛl'si, -z

plea
BR pliː, -z
AM pli, -z

pleach
BR pliːtʃ, -ɪz, -ɪŋ, -t
AM plitʃ, -ɪz, -ɪŋ, -t

plead
BR pliːd, -z, -ɪŋ, -ɪd
AM plid, -z, -ɪŋ, -ɪd

pleadable
BR 'pliːdəbl
AM 'plidəbəl

pleader
BR 'pliːdə(r), -z
AM 'plidər, -z

pleading
BR 'pliːdɪŋ, -z
AM 'plidɪŋ, -z

pleadingly
BR 'pliːdɪŋli
AM 'plidɪŋli

pleasance
BR 'plɛzns, -ɪz
AM 'plɛzns, -əz

pleasant
BR 'plɛznt
AM 'plɛznt

---

pleasantly
BR 'plɛzntli
AM 'plɛzn(t)li

pleasantness
BR 'plɛzntnəs
AM 'plɛzn(t)nəs

pleasantry
BR 'plɛzntr|i, -ɪz
AM 'plɛzntri, -z

pleasaunce
BR 'plɛzns
AM 'plɛzns

please
BR pliːz, -ɪz, -ɪŋ, -d
AM pliz, -ɪz, -ɪŋ, -d

pleasingly
BR 'pliːzɪŋli
AM 'plizɪŋli

pleasurable
BR 'plɛʒ(ə)rəbl
AM 'plɛʒ(ə)r(ə)bəl

pleasurableness
BR 'plɛʒ(ə)rəblnəs
AM 'plɛʒ(ə)rəbəlnəs,
'plɛʒərbəlnəs

pleasurably
BR 'plɛʒ(ə)rəbli
AM 'plɛʒ(ə)rəbli,
'plɛʒərbli

pleasure
BR 'plɛʒə(r), -z
AM 'plɛʒər, -z

pleat
BR pliːt, -s, -ɪŋ, -ɪd
AM pli|t, -ts, -dɪŋ, -dɪd

pleb
BR plɛb, -z
AM plɛb, -z

plebby
BR 'plɛbi
AM 'plɛbi

plebe
BR pliːb, -z
AM plib, -z

plebeian
BR plɪ'biːən, -z
AM plə'biən, -z

plebeianism
BR plɪ'biːɪnɪz(ə)m
AM plə'biəˌnɪzəm

plebiscitary
BR plɪ'bɪsɪt(ə)ri
AM plə'bɪsəˌtɛri

plebiscite
BR 'plɛbɪsɪt, 'plɛbɪsʌɪt,
-s
AM 'plɛbəˌsaɪt, -s

plectra
BR 'plɛktrə(r)
AM 'plɛktrə

plectron
BR 'plɛktr(ə)n
AM 'plɛktr(ə)n

plectrum
BR 'plɛktrəm, -z
AM 'plɛktrəm, -z

---

pled
BR plɛd
AM plɛd

pledge
BR plɛdʒ, -ɪz, -ɪŋ, -d
AM plɛdʒ, -əz, -ɪŋ, -d

pledgeable
BR 'plɛdʒəbl
AM 'plɛdʒəbəl

pledgee
BR plɛ'dʒiː, -z
AM plɛ'dʒi, -z

pledger
BR 'plɛdʒə(r), -z
AM 'plɛdʒər, -z

pledget
BR 'plɛdʒɪt, -s
AM 'plɛdʒət, -s

pledgor
BR 'plɛdʒə(r), -z
AM 'plɛdʒər, -z

pleiad
BR 'plʌɪəd, -z
AM 'pliəd, -z

Pleiades
BR 'plʌɪədiːz
AM 'pliədiz

plein-air
BR ˌpleɪn'ɛː(r)
AM ˌpleɪn'ɛ(ə)r

plein-airist
BR ˌpleɪn'ɛːrɪst, -s
AM ˌpleɪn'ɛrəst, -s

pleiotropic
BR ˌplʌɪə'trəʊpɪk,
ˌplʌɪə'trɒpɪk
AM ˌplaɪə'troʊpɪk,
ˌplaɪə'trɑpɪk

pleiotropism
BR ˌplʌɪə'trəʊpɪz(ə)m
AM ˌplaɪə'troʊpɪzm

pleiotropy
BR plʌɪ'ɒtrəpi
AM plaɪ'ɑtrəpi

Pleistocene
BR 'plʌɪstəsiːn
AM 'plaɪstəˌsin

plena
BR 'pliːnə(r)
AM 'plɛnə, 'plinə

plenarily
BR 'pliːn(ə)rɪli
AM 'plɛnər(ə)li,
plə'nɛrəli

plenary
BR 'pliːn(ə)r|i, -ɪz
AM 'plɛnəri, -z

plenipotentiary
BR ˌplɛnɪpə'tɛnʃ(ə)r|i,
-ɪz
AM 'plɛnəpə'tɛn(t)ʃəri,
-z

plenitude
BR 'plɛnɪtjuːd,
'plɛnɪtʃuːd
AM 'plɛnəˌt(j)ud

plenteous
BR ˈplɛntɪəs
AM ˈplen(t)iəs

plenteously
BR ˈplɛntɪəsli
AM ˈplen(t)iəsli

plenteousness
BR ˈplɛntɪəsnəs
AM ˈplen(t)iəsnəs

plentiful
BR ˈplɛntɪf(ʊ)l
AM ˈplen(t)əfəl

plentifully
BR ˈplɛntɪfʊli, ˈplɛntɪfli
AM ˈplen(t)əfəli

plentifulness
BR ˈplɛntɪf(ʊ)lnəs
AM ˈplen(t)əfəlnəs

plenty
BR ˈplɛnti
AM ˈplen(t)i

plenum
BR ˈpliːnəm, -z
AM ˈplɛnəm, ˈplinəm, -z

pleochroic
BR ˌpliːəˈkrəʊɪk
AM ˌpliːəˈkroʊɪk

pleochroism
BR ˌpliːəˈkrəʊɪz(ə)m
AM ˌpliːəˈkroʊˌɪzəm

pleomorphic
BR ˌpliːəˈmɔːfɪk
AM ˌpliːəˈmɔrfɪk

pleomorphism
BR ˌpliːəˈmɔːfɪz(ə)m
AM ˌpliːəˈmɔrˌfɪzəm

pleonasm
BR ˈpliːənaz(ə)m, -z
AM ˈpliːəˌnæzəm, -z

pleonastic
BR ˌpliːəˈnastɪk
AM ˌpliːəˈnæstɪk

pleonastically
BR ˌpliːəˈnastɪkli
AM ˌpliːəˈnæstək(ə)li

plesiosaur
BR ˈpliːzɪəsɔː(r), -z
AM ˈplisiəˌsɔ(ə)r, -z

plesiosauri
BR ˌpliːzɪəˈsɔːraɪ
AM ˌplisiəˈsɔˌraɪ

plesiosaurus
BR ˌpliːzɪəˈsɔːrəs, -ɪz
AM ˌplisiəˈsɔrəs, -əz

plessor
BR ˈplɛsə(r), -z
AM ˈplɛsər, -z

plethora
BR ˈplɛθ(ə)rə(r)
AM ˈplɛθərə

plethoric
BR ˈplɛθ(ə)rɪk, plɛˈθɒrɪk, plɪˈθɒrɪk
AM ˈplɛθərɪk, pləˈθɔrɪk

plethorically
BR plɛˈθɒrɪkli, plɪˈθɒrɪkli
AM pləˈθɔrək(ə)li

pleura
BR ˈplʊərə(r), ˈplɔːrə(r)
AM ˈplʊrə

pleural
BR ˈplʊərəl, ˈplʊərl, ˈplɔːrəl, ˈplɔːrl̩
AM ˈplʊrəl

pleurisy
BR ˈplʊərəsi, ˈplɔːrəsi
AM ˈplurəsi, ˈplʊrəsi

pleuritic
BR plʊəˈrɪtɪk, plʊˈrɪtɪk
AM plʊˈrɪdɪk, pləˈrɪdɪk

pleurodynia
BR ˌplʊərəˈdɪnɪə(r), ˌplɔːrəˈdɪnɪə(r)
AM ˌplʊrəˈdɪnɪə

pleuron
BR ˈplʊərɒn, ˈplɔːrɒn
AM ˈplʊˌrɑn

pleuropneumonia
BR ˌplʊərəʊnjuːˈməʊnɪə(r), ˌplɔːrəʊnjuːˈməʊnɪə(r)
AM ˌplurəˌn(j)uˈmoʊniə

Pleven
BR ˈplɛvn
AM ˈplɛvən

plew
BR pluː, -z
AM plu, -z

plexiform
BR ˈplɛksɪfɔːm
AM ˈplɛksəˌfɔ(ə)rm

Plexiglass®
BR ˈplɛksɪglɑːs, ˈplɛksɪglas
AM ˈplɛksəˌglæs

plexor
BR ˈplɛksə(r), -z
AM ˈplɛksər, -z

plexus
BR ˈplɛksəs, -ɪz
AM ˈplɛksəs, -ɪz

pliability
BR ˌplʌɪəˈbɪlɪti
AM ˌplaɪəˈbɪlɪdi

pliable
BR ˈplʌɪəbl
AM ˈplaɪəbəl

pliableness
BR ˈplʌɪəblnəs
AM ˈplaɪəbəlnəs

pliably
BR ˈplʌɪəbli
AM ˈplaɪəbli

pliancy
BR ˈplʌɪənsi
AM ˈplaɪənsi

pliant
BR ˈplʌɪənt
AM ˈplaɪənt

pliantly
BR ˈplʌɪəntli
AM ˈplaɪən(t)li

pliantness
BR ˈplʌɪəntnəs
AM ˈplaɪən(t)nəs

plicate
BR ˈplʌɪkət, ˈplʌɪkeɪt
AM ˈplaɪˌkeɪt, ˈplaɪkɪt

plicated
BR plɪˈkeɪtɪd, plʌɪˈkeɪtɪd
AM ˈplaɪˌkeɪdɪd, ˈplaɪkɪdɪd

plication
BR plɪˈkeɪʃn, plʌɪˈkeɪʃn, -z
AM plaɪˈkeɪʃən, -z

plié
BR ˈpliːeɪ, -z
AM pliˈeɪ, -z

pliers
BR ˈplʌɪəz
AM ˈplaɪərz

plight
BR plʌɪt, -s, -ɪŋ, -ɪd
AM plaɪ|t, -ts, -dɪŋ, -dɪd

plimsole
BR ˈplɪmsl, ˈplɪmsəʊl, -z
AM ˈplɪmsəl, ˈplɪmˌsɔl, ˈplɪmˌsɑl, -z

plimsoll
BR ˈplɪmsl, -z
AM ˈplɪmsəl, ˈplɪmˌsɔl, ˈplɪmˌsɑl, -z

pling
BR plɪŋ, -z
AM plɪŋ, -z

plink
BR plɪŋk, -s
AM plɪŋk, -s

Plinlimmon
BR plɪnˈlɪmən
AM plɪnˈlɪmən

plinth
BR plɪnθ, -s
AM plɪnθ, -s

Pliny
BR ˈplɪni
AM ˈplɪni, ˈplaɪni

Pliocene
BR ˈplʌɪə(ʊ)siːn
AM ˈplaɪəˌsin

plissé
BR ˈpliːseɪ
AM pliˈseɪ, pləˈseɪ

plod
BR plɒd, -z, -ɪŋ, -ɪd
AM plɑd, -z, -ɪŋ, -əd

plodder
BR ˈplɒdə(r), -z
AM ˈplɑdər, -z

ploddingly
BR ˈplɒdɪŋli
AM ˈplɑdɪŋli

ploidy
BR ˈplɔɪd|i, -ɪz
AM ˈplɔɪdi, -z

Plomer
BR ˈpluːmə(r), ˈpləʊmə(r)
AM ˈploʊmər

Plomley
BR ˈplʌmli
AM ˈpləmli

plonk
BR plɒŋ|k, -ks, -kɪŋ, -(k)t
AM plɑŋ|k, -ks, -kɪŋ, -(k)t

plonker
BR ˈplɒŋkə(r), -z
AM ˈplɑŋkər, -z

plonko
BR ˈplɒŋkəʊ, -z
AM ˈplɑŋˌkoʊ, -z

plop
BR plɒp, -s, -ɪŋ, -t
AM plɑp, -s, -ɪŋ, -t

plosion
BR ˈpləʊʒn, -z
AM ˈploʊʒən, -z

plosive
BR ˈpləʊsɪv, -z
AM ˈploʊzɪv, ˈploʊsɪv, -z

plot
BR plɒt, -s, -ɪŋ, -ɪd
AM plɑ|t, -ts, -ɪŋ, -dəd

Plotinus
BR plɒˈtʌɪnəs, pləˈtʌɪnəs
AM pləˈtaɪnəs, plɔˈtaɪnəs, plɑˈtaɪnəs

plotless
BR ˈplɒtləs
AM ˈplɑtləs

plotlessness
BR ˈplɒtləsnəs
AM ˈplɑtləsnəs

plotter
BR ˈplɒtə(r), -z
AM ˈplɑdər, -z

plough
BR plaʊ, -z, -ɪŋ, -d
AM plaʊ, -z, -ɪŋ, -d

ploughable
BR ˈplaʊəbl
AM ˈplaʊəbəl

ploughboy
BR ˈplaʊbɔɪ, -z
AM ˈplaʊˌbɔɪ, -z

plougher
BR ˈplaʊə(r), -z
AM ˈplaʊər, -z

ploughland
BR ˈplaʊland
AM ˈplaʊˌlænd

ploughman
BR ˈplaʊmən
AM ˈplaʊmən

ploughmen
BR ˈplaʊmən
AM ˈplaʊmən

ploughshare
BR ˈplaʊʃɛː(r), -z
AM ˈplaʊˌʃɛ(ə)r, -z

Plouviez
BR ˈpluːvɪeɪ
AM ˈpluviɪeɪ, ˌpluviˈeɪ

plover
BR ˈplʌvə(r), -z
AM ˈplʌvər, ˈplʊvər, -z

plow
BR plaʊ, -z, -ɪŋ, -d
AM plaʊ, -z, -ɪŋ, -d

plowable
BR ˈplaʊəbl
AM ˈplaʊəbəl

plowboy
BR ˈplaʊbɔɪ, -z
AM ˈplaʊˌbɔɪ, -z

Plowden
BR ˈplaʊdn
AM ˈplaʊdən

plower
BR ˈplaʊə(r)
AM ˈplaʊər

plowland
BR ˈplaʊland
AM ˈplaʊˌlænd

plowman
BR ˈplaʊmən
AM ˈplaʊmən

plowmen
BR ˈplaʊmən
AM ˈplaʊmən

Plowright
BR ˈplaʊrʌɪt
AM ˈplaʊˌraɪt

plowshare
BR ˈplaʊʃɛː(r), -z
AM ˈplaʊˌʃɛ(ə)r, -z

ploy
BR plɔɪ, -z
AM plɔɪ, -z

pluck
BR plʌk, -s, -ɪŋ, -t
AM plək, -s, -ɪŋ, -t

plucker
BR ˈplʌkə(r), -z
AM ˈpləkər, -z

pluckily
BR ˈplʌkɪli
AM ˈpləkəli

pluckiness
BR ˈplʌkɪnɪs
AM ˈpləkɪnɪs

pluckless
BR ˈplʌkləs
AM ˈpləkləs

plucky
BR ˈplʌk|i, -ɪə(r), -ɪɪst
AM ˈpləki, -ər, -ɪst

plug
BR plʌg, -z, -ɪŋ, -d
AM pləg, -z, -ɪŋ, -d

plugger
BR ˈplʌgə(r), -z
AM ˈpləgər, -z

plughole
BR ˈplʌghəʊl, -z
AM ˈpləg,(h)oʊl, -z

plugola
BR plʌˈgəʊlə(r)
AM pləˈgoʊlə

plug-ugly
BR ˈplʌgˈʌgli
AM ˈpləgˈəgli

plum
BR plʌm, -z
AM pləm, -z

plumage
BR ˈpluːm|ɪdʒ, -ɪdʒɪz, -ɪdʒd
AM ˈplumɪdʒ, -ɪz, -d

plumassier
BR ˌpluːməˈsɪə(r), -z
AM ˌpluməˈsɪ(ə)r, -z

plumb
BR plʌm, -z, -ɪŋ, -d
AM pləm, -z, -ɪŋ, -d

plumbaginous
BR plʌmˈbadʒɪnəs
AM ˌpləmˈbædʒənəs

plumbago
BR plʌmˈbeɪgəʊ
AM ˌpləmˈbeɪgoʊ

plumbate
BR ˈplʌmbeɪt, -s
AM ˈpləmˌbeɪt, -s

plumbeous
BR ˈplʌmbɪəs
AM ˈpləmbɪəs

plumber
BR ˈplʌmə(r), -z
AM ˈpləmər, -z

plumbic
BR ˈplʌmbɪk
AM ˈpləmbɪk

plumbiferous
BR plʌmˈbɪf(ə)rəs
AM ˌpləmˈbɪfərəs

plumbism
BR ˈplʌmbɪz(ə)m
AM ˈpləmˌbɪzəm

plumbless
BR ˈplʌmləs
AM ˈpləmləs

plumbline
BR ˈplʌmlʌɪn, -z
AM ˈpləmˌlaɪn, -z

plumbous
BR ˈplʌmbəs
AM ˈpləmbəs

plumbum
BR ˈplʌmbəm
AM ˈpləmbəm

plume
BR pluːm, -z
AM plum, -z

plumeless
BR ˈpluːmləs
AM ˈplumləs

plumelike
BR ˈpluːmlʌɪk
AM ˈplumˌlaɪk

plumery
BR ˈpluːm(ə)ri
AM ˈpluməri

Plummer
BR ˈplʌmə(r)
AM ˈpləmər

plummet
BR ˈplʌm|ɪt, -ɪts, -ɪtɪŋ, -ɪtɪd
AM ˈpləmə|t, -ts, -dɪŋ, -dəd

plummily
BR ˈplʌmɪli
AM ˈpləməli

plumminess
BR ˈplʌmɪnɪs
AM ˈpləmɪnɪs

plummy
BR ˈplʌm|i, -ɪə(r), -ɪɪst
AM ˈpləmi, -ər, -ɪst

plumose
BR ˈpluːməʊs, pluːˈməʊs
AM ˈpluˌmoʊs, ˈpluˌmoʊz

plump
BR plʌm|p, -(p)s, -pɪŋ, -(p)t, -pə(r), -pɪst
AM pləmp, -s, -ɪŋ, -t, -ər, -əst

plumpish
BR ˈplʌmpɪʃ
AM ˈpləmpɪʃ

plumply
BR ˈplʌmpli
AM ˈpləmpli

plumpness
BR ˈplʌmpnəs
AM ˈpləmpnəs

Plumpton
BR ˈplʌm(p)tən
AM ˈpləm(p)tən

Plumptre
BR ˈplʌm(p)triː
AM ˈpləm(p)tri

plumpy
BR ˈplʌmpi
AM ˈpləmpi

Plumstead
BR ˈplʌmstɪd, ˈplʌmstɛd
AM ˈpləmˌstɛd

Plumtre
BR ˈplʌmtriː
AM ˈpləmˌtri

plumulaceous
BR ˌpluːmjəˈleɪʃəs
AM ˌplumjəˈleɪʃəs

plumular
BR ˈpluːmjələ(r)
AM ˈplumjələr

plumule
BR ˈpluːmjuːl, -z
AM ˈplumˌjul, -z

plumy
BR ˈpluːm|i, -ɪə(r), -ɪɪst
AM ˈplumi, -ər, -ɪst

plunder
BR ˈplʌnd|ə(r), -əz, -(ə)rɪŋ, -əd
AM ˈpləndər, -ərz, -(ə)rɪŋ, -ərd

plunderer
BR ˈplʌnd(ə)rə(r), -z
AM ˈplənd(ə)rər, -z

plundering
BR ˈplʌnd(ə)rɪŋ, -z
AM ˈplənd(ə)rɪŋ, -z

plunderous
BR ˈplʌnd(ə)rəs
AM ˈplənd(ə)rəs

plunge
BR plʌn(d)ʒ, -ɪz, -ɪŋ, -d
AM pləndʒ, -əz, -ɪŋ, -d

plunger
BR ˈplʌn(d)ʒə(r), -z
AM ˈpləndʒər, -z

plunk
BR plʌŋk, -s
AM pləŋk, -s

Plunket
BR ˈplʌŋkɪt
AM ˈpləŋkət

Plunkett
BR ˈplʌŋkɪt
AM ˈpləŋkət

pluperfect
BR ˌpluːˈpəːfɪkt, -s
AM ˌpluˈpɜrfək(t), -(t)s

plural
BR ˈplʊərəl, ˈplʊərl̩, ˈplɔːrəl, ˈplɔːrl̩, -z
AM ˈplʊrəl, -z

pluralisation
BR ˌplʊərəlʌɪˈzeɪʃn, ˌplʊərl̩ʌɪˈzeɪʃn, ˌplɔːrəlʌɪˈzeɪʃn, ˌplɔːrl̩ʌɪˈzeɪʃn
AM ˌplʊrələˈzeɪʃən, ˌplʊrəˌlaɪˈzeɪʃən

pluralise
BR ˈplʊərəlʌɪz, ˈplʊərl̩ʌɪz, ˈplɔːrəlʌɪz, ˈplɔːrl̩ʌɪz, -ɪz, -ɪŋ, -d
AM ˈplʊrəˌlaɪz, -ɪz, -ɪŋ, -d

pluralism
BR ˈplʊərəlɪz(ə)m, ˈplʊərl̩ɪz(ə)m, ˈplɔːrəlɪz(ə)m, ˈplɔːrl̩ɪz(ə)m
AM ˈplʊrəˌlɪzəm

pluralist
BR ˈplʊərəlɪst, ˈplʊərl̩ɪst, ˈplɔːrəlɪst, ˈplɔːrl̩ɪst, -s
AM ˈplʊrələst, -s

pluralistic
BR ˌplʊərəˈlɪstɪk, ˌplʊərl̩ˈɪstɪk,

,plɔːrə'lɪstɪk,
,plɔːr]'ɪstɪk
AM ,plʊrə'lɪstɪk

pluralistically
BR ,plʊərə'lɪstɪkli,
,plʊər]'ɪstɪkli,
,plɔːrə'lɪstɪkli,
,plɔːr]'ɪstɪkli
AM ,plʊrə'lɪstək(ə)li

plurality
BR plʊə'ralɪti,
plɔː'ralɪti, plə'ralɪti
AM plʊ'rælədi,
plə'rælədi

pluralization
BR ,plʊərəlaɪ'zeɪʃn,
,plʊər]aɪ'zeɪʃn,
,plɔːrəlaɪ'zeɪʃn,
,plɔːr]aɪ'zeɪʃn
AM ,plʊrələ'zeɪʃən,
,plʊrə,laɪ'zeɪʃən

pluralize
BR 'plʊərəlaɪz,
'plʊər]aɪz,
'plɔːrəlaɪz, 'plɔːr]aɪz,
-ɪz, -ɪŋ, -d
AM 'plʊrə,laɪz, -ɪz, -ɪŋ,
-d

plurally
BR 'plʊərəli, 'plʊər]i,
'plɔːrəli, 'plɔːr]i
AM 'plʊrəli

pluripotential
BR ,plʊərɪpə'tenʃl,
,plɔːrɪpə'tenʃl
AM ,plʊrəpə'ten(t)ʃəl

pluripresence
BR ,plʊərɪ'prezns,
,plɔːrɪ'prezns
AM ,plʊrə'prezns

plurry
BR 'plʌri
AM 'pləri

plus
BR plʌs, -ɪz
AM pləs, -əz

plus ça change
BR ,plu: sa 'ʃɒʒ
AM ,plu sa 'ʃɒnʒ, ,plu
sa 'ʃanʒ

plus-fours
BR ,plʌs'fɔːz
AM ,pləs'fɔ(ə)rz

plush
BR plʌʃ, -ə(r), -ɪst
AM pləʃ, -ər, -əst

plushily
BR 'plʌʃɪli
AM 'pləʃəli

plushiness
BR 'plʌʃɪnɪs
AM 'pləʃɪnɪs

plushly
BR 'plʌʃli
AM 'pləʃli

plushness
BR 'plʌʃnəs
AM 'pləʃnəs

plushy
BR 'plʌʃ|i, -ɪə(r), -ɪɪst
AM 'pləʃi, -ər, -ɪst

Plutarch
BR 'pluːtɑːk
AM 'pluːtɑrk

plutarchy
BR 'pluːtɑːk|i, -ɪz
AM 'pluːtɑrki, -z

Pluto
BR 'pluːtəʊ
AM 'pludoʊ

plutocracy
BR plu:'tɒkrəs|i, -ɪz
AM plu'tɑkrəsi, -z

plutocrat
BR 'pluːtəkrat, -s
AM 'pludə,kræt, -s

plutocratic
BR ,pluːtə'kratɪk
AM ,pludə'krædɪk

plutocratically
BR ,pluːtə'kratɪkli
AM ,pludə'krædək(ə)li

plutolatry
BR plu:'tɒlətri
AM plu'tɑlətri

pluton
BR 'pluːtɒn, -z
AM 'pluːtɑn, -z

Plutonian
BR plu:'təʊnɪən
AM plu'toʊnɪən

Plutonic
BR plu:'tɒnɪk
AM plu'tɑnɪk

Plutonism
BR 'pluːtənɪz(ə)m,
'pluːtn,ɪz(ə)m
AM 'plutn,ɪzəm

plutonium
BR plu:'təʊnɪəm
AM plu'toʊnɪəm

pluvial
BR 'pluːvɪəl
AM 'pluvɪəl

pluviometer
BR ,pluːvɪ'ɒmɪtə(r), -z
AM ,pluvi'amədər, -z

pluviometric
BR ,pluːvɪə(ʊ)'metrɪk
AM ,pluvioʊ'metrɪk

pluviometrical
BR ,pluːvɪə(ʊ)'metrɪkl
AM ,pluvioʊ'metrəkəl

pluviometrically
BR ,pluːvɪə(ʊ)'metrɪkli
AM ,pluvioʊ'metrək(ə)li

pluvious
BR 'pluːvɪəs
AM 'pluvɪəs

ply
BR plaɪ, -z, -ɪŋ, -d
AM plai, -z, -ɪŋ, -d

Plymouth
BR 'plɪməθ
AM 'plɪməθ

Plynlimon
BR plɪn'lɪmən
AM plɪn'lɪmən

plywood
BR 'plaɪwʊd
AM 'plaɪ,wʊd

pneumatic
BR nju:'matɪk,
njʊ'matɪk, -s
AM n(j)u'mædɪk, -s

pneumatically
BR nju:'matɪkli,
njʊ'matɪkli
AM n(j)u'mædək(ə)li

pneumaticity
BR ,nju:mə'tɪsɪti
AM ,n(j)umə'tɪsɪdi

pneumatocyst
BR 'njuːmətəsɪst,
nju:'matəsɪst,
njʊ'matəsɪst, -s
AM n(j)u'mædə,sɪst,
-s

pneumatological
BR ,njuːmətə'lɒdʒɪkl
AM ,n(j)umədə'lɑdʒəkəl

pneumatology
BR ,njuːmə'tɒlədʒi
AM ,n(j)umə'talədʒi

pneumatophore
BR 'njuːmətəfɔː(r),
nju:'matəfɔː(r),
njʊ'matəfɔː(r), -z
AM n(j)u'mædə,fɔ(ə)r,
-z

pneumococcus
BR ,njuːmə(ʊ)'kɒkəs
AM ,n(j)umoʊ'kakəs

pneumoconiosis
BR ,njuːmə(ʊ),kəʊnɪ-
'əʊsɪs
AM ,n(j)umoʊ,koʊni-
'oʊsəs

pneumocystis
BR ,njuːmə(ʊ)'sɪstɪs
AM 'n(j)umoʊ,sɪstɪs

pneumogastric
BR ,njuːmə(ʊ)'gastrɪk
AM ,n(j)umoʊ'gæstrɪk

pneumonectomy
BR ,njuːmə(ʊ)'nektəm|i,
-ɪz
AM ,n(j)umoʊ'nektəmi,
-z

pneumonia
BR nju:'məʊnɪə(r),
njʊ'məʊnɪə(r)
AM nə'moʊnjə,
n(j)u'moʊnjə

pneumonic
BR nju:'mɒnɪk,
njʊ'mɒnɪk
AM n(j)u'manɪk

pneumonitis
BR ,njuːmə'naɪtɪs
AM ,n(j)umə'naɪdɪs

pneumothorax
BR ,njuːmə'θɔːraks

AM ,n(j)umoʊ'θɔræks

Pnyx
BR (p)nɪks
AM (p)niks

PO
BR ,pi:'əʊ, -z
AM ,pi'oʊ, -z

po
BR pəʊ
AM poʊ

poach
BR pəʊtʃ, -ɪz, -ɪŋ, -t
AM poʊtʃ, -ɪz, -ɪŋ, -t

poacher
BR 'pəʊtʃə(r), -z
AM 'poʊtʃər, -z

poblano
BR pɒ'blɑːnəʊ, -z
AM pə'blɑnoʊ, -z

Pocahontas
BR ,pɒkə'hɒntəs
AM ,poʊkə'han(t)əs

pochard
BR 'pɒtʃəd, 'pəʊtʃəd, -z
AM 'poʊtʃərd, -z

pochette
BR pɒ'ʃet, -s
AM poʊ'ʃet, -s

pock
BR pɒk, -s, -ɪŋ, -t
AM pak, -s, -ɪŋ, -t

pocket
BR 'pɒk|ɪt, -ɪts, -ɪtɪŋ,
-ɪtɪd
AM 'pakə|t, -ts, -dɪŋ,
-dəd

pocketable
BR 'pɒkɪtəbl
AM 'pakətəbəl

pocketbook
BR 'pɒkɪtbʊk, -s
AM 'pakə(t),bʊk, -s

pocketful
BR 'pɒkɪtfʊl, -z
AM 'pakət,fʊl, -z

pocketless
BR 'pɒkɪtlɪs
AM 'pakətləs

pockety
BR 'pɒkɪti
AM 'pakədi

Pocklington
BR 'pɒklɪŋt(ə)n
AM 'paklɪŋtən

pockmark
BR 'pɒkmɑːk, -s, -ɪŋ, -t
AM 'pak,mark, -s, -ɪŋ, -t

pocky
BR 'pɒki
AM 'paki

poco
BR 'pəʊkəʊ
AM 'poʊkoʊ

Pocock
BR 'pəʊkɒk
AM 'poʊ,kak

pococurante
BR ˌpəʊkəʊkjʊ'rant|i,
-iz
AM ˌpoʊkoʊkjə'ræn(t)i,
-z

pococuranteism
BR ˌpəʊkəʊkjʊ'rantɪ-
ɪz(ə)m
AM ˌpoʊkoʊkjə'ræn(t)i-
ˌɪzəm

pococurantism
BR ˌpəʊkəʊkjʊ'rant-
ɪz(ə)m
AM ˌpoʊkoʊkjə-
'ræn,tɪzəm

Pocono
BR 'pəʊkənəʊ, -z
AM 'poʊkəˌnoʊ, -z

pod
BR pɒd, -z
AM pɑd, -z

podagra
BR pɒ'dagrə(r),
pə'dagrə(r)
AM pə'dægrə,
'padəgrə

podagral
BR pɒ'dagr(ə)l,
pə'dagr(ə)l
AM pə'dægrə,
'padəgrəl

podagric
BR pɒ'dagrɪk,
pə'dagrɪk
AM pə'dægrɪk,
'padəgrɪk

podagrous
BR pɒ'dagrəs,
pə'dagrəs
AM pə'dægrəs,
'padəgrəs

poddy
BR pɒd|i, -iz
AM pɑdi, -z

podestà
BR ˌpəʊdə'stɑː(r)
AM ˌpoʊdə'stɑ

podgily
BR pɒdʒɪli
AM 'padʒəli

podginess
BR pɒdʒɪnɪs
AM padʒɪnɪs

podgy
BR pɒdʒ|i, -ɪə(r), -ɪɪst
AM padʒi, -ər, -ɪst

podia
BR 'pəʊdɪə(r)
AM 'poʊdɪə

podiatrist
BR pə(ʊ)'dʌɪətrɪst, -s
AM pə'daɪətrəst, -s

podiatry
BR pə(ʊ)'dʌɪətri
AM pə'daɪətri

podium
BR 'pəʊdɪəm, -z
AM 'poʊdɪəm, -z

podophyllin
BR ˌpɒdə'fɪlɪn
AM ˌpɑdə'fɪlɪn

podsol
BR 'pɒdsɒl, -z
AM 'pad,sɔl, 'pad,sal, -z

podunk
BR 'pəʊdʌŋk, -s
AM 'poʊ,dəŋk, -s

podzol
BR 'pɒdzɒl, -z
AM 'pad,sɔl, 'pad,sal, -z

podzolisation
BR ˌpɒdzəlʌɪ'zeɪʃn,
ˌpɒdzl̩ʌɪ'zeɪʃn
AM ˌpadzələ'zeɪʃən,
ˌpadzə,laɪ'zeɪʃən

podzolise
BR 'pɒdzəlʌɪz,
'pɒdzl̩ʌɪz, -ɪz, -ɪŋ, -d
AM 'padzə,laɪz, -ɪz, -ɪŋ,
-d

podzolization
BR ˌpɒdzəlʌɪ'zeɪʃn,
ˌpɒdzl̩ʌɪ'zeɪʃn
AM ˌpadzələ'zeɪʃən,
ˌpadzə,laɪ'zeɪʃən

podzolize
BR 'pɒdzəlʌɪz,
'pɒdzl̩ʌɪz, -ɪz, -ɪŋ, -d
AM 'padzə,laɪz, -ɪz, -ɪŋ,
-d

Poe
BR pəʊ
AM poʊ

poem
BR 'pəʊɪm, -z
AM 'poʊ(ə)m, -z

poesy
BR 'pəʊɪzi
AM 'poʊəzi, 'poʊəsi

poet
BR 'pəʊɪt, -s
AM 'poʊət, -s

poetaster
BR ˌpəʊɪ'tastə(r),
'pəʊɪtastə(r),
ˌpəʊɪ'teɪstə(r),
'pəʊɪteɪstə(r), -z
AM 'poʊə,tæstər, -z

poetess
BR 'pəʊɪtɪs, ˌpəʊɪ'tɛs,
-ɪz
AM 'poʊədəs, -əz

poetic
BR pəʊ'ɛtɪk, -s
AM poʊ'ɛdɪk, -s

poetical
BR pəʊ'ɛtɪkl
AM poʊ'ɛdəkəl

poetically
BR pəʊ'ɛtɪkli
AM poʊ'ɛdək(ə)li

poeticise
BR pəʊ'ɛtɪsʌɪz, -ɪz, -ɪŋ,
-d
AM poʊ'ɛdə,saɪz, -ɪz,
-ɪŋ, -d

poeticize
BR pəʊ'ɛtɪsʌɪz, -ɪz, -ɪŋ,
-d
AM poʊ'ɛdə,saɪz, -ɪz,
-ɪŋ, -d

poetise
BR 'pəʊɪtʌɪz, -ɪz, -ɪŋ, -d
AM 'poʊə,taɪz, -ɪz, -ɪŋ,
-d

poetize
BR 'pəʊɪtʌɪz, -ɪz, -ɪŋ, -d
AM 'poʊə,taɪz, -ɪz, -ɪŋ,
-d

Poet Laureate
BR ˌpəʊɪt 'lɔːrɪət,
+ 'lɒrɪət, -s
AM 'poʊət 'lɔriːt, -s

poetry
BR 'pəʊɪtri
AM 'poʊətri

po-faced
BR ˌpəʊ'feɪst
AM 'poʊ,feɪst

pogey
BR 'pəʊgi
AM 'poʊgi

pogo
BR 'pəʊgəʊ, -z, -ɪŋ, -d
AM 'poʊgoʊ, -z, -ɪŋ, -d

pogrom
BR 'pɒgrəm, 'pɒgrɒm,
-z
AM poʊ'grəm, -z

Pogue
BR pəʊg, -z
AM poʊg, -z

poi
BR pɔɪ
AM pɔɪ

poignance
BR 'pɔɪnjəns
AM 'pɔɪn(j)əns

poignancy
BR 'pɔɪnjənsi
AM 'pɔɪn(j)ənsi

poignant
BR 'pɔɪnjənt
AM 'pɔɪn(j)ənt

poignantly
BR 'pɔɪnjəntli
AM 'pɔɪn(j)ən(t)li

poikilotherm
BR 'pɔɪkɪlə,θəːm, -z
AM pɔɪ'kɪlə,θərm,
'pɔɪkəloʊ,θərm, -z

poikilothermal
BR ˌpɔɪkɪlə'θəːml
AM pɔɪ,kɪlə'θərml,
ˌpɔɪkəloʊ'θərml

poikilothermia
BR ˌpɔɪkɪlə'θəːmɪə(r)
AM pɔɪ,kɪlə'θərmɪə,
ˌpɔɪkəloʊ'θərmɪə

poikilothermic
BR ˌpɔɪkɪlə'θəːmɪk
AM pɔɪ,kɪlə'θərmɪk,
ˌpɔɪkəloʊ'θərmɪk

poikilothermy
BR 'pɔɪkɪlə,θəːmi
AM pɔɪ'kɪlə,θərmi,
'pɔɪkəloʊ,θərmi

poilu
BR 'pwɑːluː, ˌpwɑː'luː,
-z
AM pwɑ'lu, -z

poinciana
BR ˌpɔɪnsɪ'ɑːnə(r), -z
AM ˌpɔɪnsi'ɑnə, -z

poind
BR pɔɪnd, pɪnd, -z, -ɪŋ,
-ɪd
AM pɪnd, -z, -ɪŋ, -ɪd

Poindexter
BR 'pɔɪn,dɛkstə(r)
AM 'pɔɪn,dɛkstər

poinsettia
BR pɔɪn'sɛtɪə(r)
AM pɔɪn'sɛd(i)ə

point
BR pɔɪnt, -s, -ɪŋ, -ɪd
AM pɔɪn|t, -ts, -(t)ɪŋ,
-(t)ɪd

point-blank
BR ˌpɔɪnt'blaŋk
AM ˌpɔɪn(t)'blæŋk

point duty
BR 'pɔɪnt ˌdjuːti,
+ ˌdʒuːti
AM 'pɔɪnt ˌd(j)udi

pointe
BR pwãt
AM pwɑnt

pointedly
BR 'pɔɪntɪdli
AM 'pɔɪn(t)ɪdli

pointedness
BR 'pɔɪntɪdnɪs
AM 'pɔɪn(t)ɪdnɪs

pointer
BR 'pɔɪntə(r), -z
AM 'pɔɪn(t)ər, -z

pointes
BR pwãt
AM pwɑnt(s)

pointillism
BR 'pwãtjɪz(ə)m,
'pɔɪntɪlɪz(ə)m
AM 'pwɑn(t)lɪzəm

pointillist
BR 'pwãtjɪst,
'pɔɪntɪlɪst
AM 'pwɑn(t)ləst

pointillistic
BR ˌpwãtɪ'jɪstɪk,
ˌpɔɪntɪ'lɪstɪk
AM ˌpwɑn(t)l'ɪstɪk

pointless
BR 'pɔɪntlɪs
AM 'pɔɪn(t)lɪs

pointlessly
BR 'pɔɪntlɪsli
AM 'pɔɪn(t)lɪsli

pointlessness
BR 'pɔɪntlɪsnɪs
AM 'pɔɪn(t)lɪsnɪs

Pointon
BR ˈpɔɪntən
AM ˈpɔɪn(t)ən

pointsman
BR ˈpɔɪntsmən
AM ˈpɔɪn(t)smən

pointsmen
BR ˈpɔɪntsmən
AM ˈpɔɪn(t)smən

point-to-point
BR ˌpɔɪnt(t)əˈpɔɪnt, -s
AM ˌpɔɪn(t)təˈpɔɪnt, -s

pointy
BR ˈpɔɪnt|i, -ɪə(r), -ɪɪst
AM ˈpɔɪn(t)i, -ər, -ɪɪst

Poirot
BR ˈpwɑːrəʊ
AM pwɑˈroʊ

poise
BR pɔɪz, -ɪz, -ɪŋ, -d
AM pɔɪz, -ɪz, -ɪŋ, -d

poison
BR ˈpɔɪz|n, -nz, -n̩ɪŋ\-nɪŋ, -nd
AM ˈpɔɪzn̩, -z, -ɪŋ, -d

poisoner
BR ˈpɔɪznə(r), ˈpɔɪznə(r), -z
AM ˈpɔɪznʲər, -z

poisoning
BR ˈpɔɪznɪŋ, ˈpɔɪznɪŋ, -z
AM ˈpɔɪznɪŋ, -z

poisonous
BR ˈpɔɪznəs, ˈpɔɪznəs
AM ˈpɔɪznəs, ˈpɔɪznəs

poisonously
BR ˈpɔɪznəsli, ˈpɔɪznəsli
AM ˈpɔɪznəsli, ˈpɔɪznəsli

poisonousness
BR ˈpɔɪznəsnəs, ˈpɔɪznəsnəs
AM ˈpɔɪznəsnəs, ˈpɔɪznəsnəs

Poisson distribution
BR ˌpwɑːsɒn ˌdɪstrɪˈbjuːʃn, ˌpwasɒn +, ˌpwɑːsɒ̃ +, ˌpwasɒ̃ +, -z
AM ˌpwɑˈsɑn ˌdɪstrəˌbjuʃən, -z

Poitier
BR ˈpwɒtɪeɪ, ˈpwɑːtɪeɪ
AM ˌpwadiˈeɪ

Poitiers
BR ˈpwɒtɪeɪ
AM ˌpwadiˈeɪ

Poitou
BR ˌpwɒˈtuː
AM ˌpwɑˈtu

poke
BR pəʊk, -s, -ɪŋ, -t
AM poʊk, -s, -ɪŋ, -t

poker
BR ˈpəʊkə(r), -z
AM ˈpoʊkər, -z

pokerwork
BR ˈpəʊkəwəːk
AM ˈpoʊkərˌwɜrk

pokeweed
BR ˈpəʊkwiːd, -z
AM ˈpoʊkˌwid, -z

pokey
BR ˈpəʊk|i, -ɪə(r), -ɪɪst
AM ˈpoʊki, -ər, -ɪɪst

pokily
BR ˈpəʊkɪli
AM ˈpoʊkəli

pokiness
BR ˈpəʊkɪnɪs
AM ˈpoʊkinɪs

poky
BR ˈpəʊk|i, -ɪə(r), -ɪɪst
AM ˈpoʊki, -ər, -ɪɪst

pol
BR pɒl, -z
AM pɑl, -z

polacca
BR pə(ʊ)ˈlakə(r), -z
AM poʊˈlɑkə, -z

Polack
BR ˈpəʊlak, -s
AM ˈpoʊˌlɑk, -s

polacre
BR pə(ʊ)ˈlɑːkə(r), -z
AM poʊˈlækər, -z

Polak
BR ˈpəʊlak, -s
AM ˈpoʊˌlɑk, -s

Poland
BR ˈpəʊlənd
AM ˈpoʊlənd

Polanski
BR pəˈlanski
AM pəˈlænski

polar
BR ˈpəʊlə(r)
AM ˈpoʊlər

polarimeter
BR ˌpəʊləˈrɪmɪtə(r), -z
AM ˌpoʊləˈrɪmədər, -z

polarimetric
BR ˌpəʊlərɪˈmɛtrɪk
AM ˌpoʊlərəˈmɛtrɪk

polarimetry
BR ˌpəʊləˈrɪmɪtri
AM ˌpoʊləˈrɪmɛtri

Polaris
BR pəˈlɑːrɪs
AM pəˈlɛrəs

polarisable
BR ˈpəʊləraɪzəbl
AM ˈpoʊləˌraɪzəbəl

polarisation
BR ˌpəʊləraɪˈzeɪʃn
AM ˌpoʊləˈreɪʃən, ˌpoʊləˌraɪˈzeɪʃən

polariscope
BR pəˈlarɪskəʊp, -s
AM pəˈlɛrəˌskoʊp, poʊˈlɛrəˌskoʊp, -s

polariscopic
BR pəˌlarɪˈskɒpɪk

AM poʊˌlɛrəˈskɑpɪk

polarise
BR ˈpəʊləraɪz, -ɪz, -ɪŋ, -d
AM ˈpoʊləˌraɪz, -ɪz, -ɪŋ, -d

polariser
BR ˈpəʊləraɪzə(r), -z
AM ˈpoʊləˌraɪzər, -z

polarity
BR pə(ʊ)ˈlarɪti
AM pəˈlɛrədi, poʊˈlɛrədi

polarizable
BR ˈpəʊləraɪzəbl
AM ˈpoʊləˌraɪzəbəl

polarization
BR ˌpəʊləraɪˈzeɪʃn
AM ˌpoʊləˈzeɪʃən, ˌpoʊləˌraɪˈzeɪʃən

polarize
BR ˈpəʊləraɪz, -ɪz, -ɪŋ, -d
AM ˈpoʊləˌraɪz, -ɪz, -ɪŋ, -d

polarizer
BR ˈpəʊləraɪzə(r), -z
AM ˈpoʊləˌraɪzər, -z

polarly
BR ˈpəʊləli
AM ˈpoʊlərli

polarographic
BR ˌpəʊlərəˈgrafɪk
AM ˌpoʊlərəˈgræfɪk, poʊˌlɛrəˈgræfɪk

polarography
BR ˌpəʊləˈrɒgrəfi
AM ˌpoʊləˈrɑgrəfi

Polaroid®
BR ˈpəʊlərɔɪd, -z
AM ˈpoʊləˌrɔɪd, -z

polder
BR ˈpəʊldə(r), ˈpɒldə(r), -z
AM ˈpoʊldər, -z

pole
BR pəʊl, -z, -ɪŋ, -d
AM poʊl, -z, -ɪŋ, -d

poleax
BR ˈpəʊlaks, -ɪz, -ɪŋ, -t
AM ˈpoʊˌlæks, -ɪz, -ɪŋ, -t

pole-axe
BR ˈpəʊlaks, -ɪz, -ɪŋ, -t
AM ˈpoʊˌlæks, -ɪz, -ɪŋ, -t

polecat
BR ˈpəʊlkat, -s
AM ˈpoʊlˌkæt, -s

Polegate
BR ˈpəʊlgeɪt
AM ˈpoʊlˌgeɪt

polemic
BR pəˈlɛmɪk, -s
AM pəˈlɛmɪk, -s

polemical
BR pəˈlɛmɪkl
AM pəˈlɛməkəl

polemically
BR pəˈlɛmɪkli
AM pəˈlɛmək(ə)li

polemicise
BR pəˈlɛmɪsaɪz, -ɪz, -ɪŋ, -d
AM pəˈlɛməˌsaɪz, -ɪz, -ɪŋ, -d

polemicist
BR pəˈlɛmɪsɪst, -s
AM pəˈlɛməsəst, -s

polemicize
BR pəˈlɛmɪsaɪz, -ɪz, -ɪŋ, -d
AM pəˈlɛməˌsaɪz, -ɪz, -ɪŋ, -d

polenta
BR pəˈlɛntə(r)
AM poʊˈlɛn(t)ə

polestar
BR ˈpəʊlstɑː(r)
AM ˈpoʊlˌstar

polevault
BR ˈpəʊlvɔːlt, ˈpəʊlvɒlt, -s, -ɪŋ, -ɪd
AM ˈpoʊlˌvɔlt, ˈpoʊlˌvɑlt, -s, -ɪŋ, -əd

pole-vaulter
BR ˈpəʊlˌvɔːltə(r), ˈpəʊlˌvɒltə(r), -z
AM ˈpoʊlˌvɔltər, ˈpoʊlˌvɑltər, -z

poleward
BR ˈpəʊlwəd, -z
AM ˈpoʊlwərd, -z

police
BR pʊˈliːs, pliːs, -ɪz, -ɪŋ, -t
AM pəˈlis, -ɪz, -ɪŋ, -t

policeman
BR pʊˈliːsmən, ˈpliːsmən
AM pəˈlismən

policemen
BR pʊˈliːsmən, ˈpliːsmən
AM pəˈlismən

policewoman
BR pʊˈliːsˌwʊmən, ˈpliːsˌwʊmən
AM pəˈlisˌwʊmən

policewomen
BR pʊˈliːsˌwɪmɪn, ˈpliːsˌwɪmɪn
AM pəˈlisˌwɪmɪn

policlinic
BR ˈpɒlɪˈklɪnɪk, -s
AM ˈpɑləˈklɪnɪk, -s

policy
BR ˈpɒlɪs|i, -ɪz
AM ˈpɑləsi, -z

policyholder
BR ˈpɒlɪsiˌhəʊldə(r), -z
AM ˈpɑləsiˌhoʊldər, -z

polimorphism
BR ˌpɒlɪˈmɔːfɪz(ə)m
AM ˌpɑliˈmɔrˌfɪzəm

polio
 BR ˈpəʊliəʊ
 AM ˈpoʊlioʊ
poliomyelitis
 BR ˌpəʊliəʊˌmʌɪəˈlʌɪtɪs
 AM ˌpoʊlioʊˌmaɪəˈlaɪdɪs
polis
 police
 BR ˈpɒlɪs
 AM ˈpoʊləs, ˈpoʊlɪs
Polisario
 BR ˌpɒlɪˈsɑːriəʊ
 AM ˌpɒləˈsɑrioʊ,
 ˌpɑləˈsɑrioʊ
Polish
 adjective 'of Poland'
 BR ˈpəʊlɪʃ
 AM ˈpoʊlɪʃ
polish
 noun, verb
 BR ˈpɒl|ɪʃ, -ɪʃɪz, -ɪʃɪŋ,
 -ɪʃt
 AM ˈpɑlɪʃ, -ɪz, -ɪŋ, -t
polishable
 BR ˈpɒlɪʃəbl
 AM ˈpɑləʃəbəl
polisher
 BR ˈpɒlɪʃə(r), -z
 AM ˈpɑlɪʃər, -z
Politburo
 BR ˈpɒlɪtˌbjʊərəʊ,
 ˈpɒlɪtˌbjɔːrəʊ
 AM ˈpɑlətˌbjʊroʊ,
 ˈpoʊlətˌbjʊroʊ
 RUS pəlʲitbʲuˈro
polite
 BR pəˈlʌɪt
 AM pəˈlaɪt
politely
 BR pəˈlʌɪtli
 AM pəˈlaɪtli
politeness
 BR pəˈlʌɪtnɪs, -ɪz
 AM pəˈlaɪtnɪs, -ɪz
politesse
 BR ˌpɒlɪˈtɛs
 AM ˌpɑləˈtɛs
politic
 BR ˈpɒlɪtɪk, -s, -ɪŋ, -t
 AM ˈpɑlətɪk, -s, -ɪŋ, -t
political
 BR pəˈlɪtɪkl
 AM pəˈlɪdɪkəl
politically
 BR pəˈlɪtɪkli
 AM pəˈlɪdɪk(ə)li
politician
 BR ˌpɒlɪˈtɪʃn, -z
 AM ˌpɑləˈtɪʃən, -z
politicisation
 BR pəˌlɪtɪsʌɪˈzeɪʃn
 AM pəˌlɪdɪsɪˈzeɪʃən,
 pəˌlɪdɪˌsaɪˈzeɪʃən
politicise
 BR pəˈlɪtɪsʌɪz, -ɪz, -ɪŋ,
 -d
 AM pəˈlɪdɪˌsaɪz, -ɪz, -ɪŋ,
 -d

politicization
 BR pəˌlɪtɪsʌɪˈzeɪʃn
 AM pəˌlɪdɪsɪˈzeɪʃən,
 pəˌlɪdɪˌsaɪˈzeɪʃən
politicize
 BR pəˈlɪtɪsʌɪz, -ɪz, -ɪŋ,
 -d
 AM pəˈlɪdɪˌsaɪz, -ɪz, -ɪŋ,
 -d
politicking
 BR ˈpɒlɪtɪkɪŋ
 AM ˈpɑlətɪkɪŋ
politicly
 BR ˈpɒlɪtɪkli
 AM ˈpɑləˌtɪkli
politico
 BR pəˈlɪtɪkəʊ, -z
 AM pəˈlɪdɪkoʊ, -z
polity
 BR ˈpɒlɪt|i, -ɪz
 AM ˈpɑlədi, -z
polje
 BR ˈpɒljə(r), -z
 AM ˈpɑljə, -z
Polk
 BR pəʊk
 AM poʊk
polka
 BR ˈpɒlkə(r), -z
 AM ˈpoʊ(l)kə, -z
polkadot
 BR ˈpɒlkədɒt, -s
 AM ˈpoʊkəˌdɑt, -s
poll[1]
 vote
 BR pəʊl, -z, -ɪŋ, -d
 AM poʊl, -z, -ɪŋ, -d
poll[2]
 parrot
 BR pɒl
 AM pɑl
pollack
 BR ˈpɒlək, -s
 AM ˈpɑlək, -s
pollan
 BR ˈpɒlən, -z
 AM ˈpɑlən, -z
pollard
 BR ˈpɒləd, ˈpɒlɑːd, -z,
 -ɪŋ, -ɪd
 AM ˈpɑlərd, -z, -ɪŋ, -ɪd
pollee
 BR pəʊˈliː, -z
 AM poʊˈli, -z
pollen
 BR ˈpɒlən, -z
 AM ˈpɑlən, -z
pollenless
 BR ˈpɒlənləs
 AM ˈpɑlənləs
pollex
 BR ˈpɒlɛks, -ɪz
 AM ˈpɑˌlɛks, -əz
pollicitation
 BR ˌpɒlɪsɪˈteɪn
 AM pəˌlɪsəˈteɪʃən

pollie
 BR ˈpɒl|i, -ɪz
 AM ˈpɑli, -z
pollinate
 BR ˈpɒlɪneɪt, -s, -ɪŋ, -ɪd
 AM ˈpɑləˌneɪ|t, -ts, -dɪŋ,
 -dɪd
pollination
 BR ˌpɒlɪˈneɪʃn
 AM ˌpɑləˈneɪʃən
pollinator
 BR ˈpɒlɪneɪtə(r), -z
 AM ˈpɑləˌneɪdər, -z
pollinia
 BR pəˈlɪnɪə(r)
 AM pəˈlɪniə
pollinic
 BR pəˈlɪnɪk
 AM pəˈlɪnɪk
polliniferous
 BR ˌpɒlɪˈnɪf(ə)rəs
 AM ˌpɑləˈnɪf(ə)rəs
pollinium
 BR pəˈlɪnɪəm
 AM pəˈlɪniəm
Pollitt
 BR ˈpɒlɪt
 AM ˈpɑlət
polliwog
 BR ˈpɒlɪwɒg, -z
 AM ˈpɑliˌwɑg,
 ˈpɑliˌwag, -z
pollock
 BR ˈpɒlək, -s
 AM ˈpɑlək, -s
pollster
 BR ˈpəʊlstə(r), -z
 AM ˈpoʊlztər,
 ˈpoʊlstər, -z
pollutant
 BR pəˈl(j)uːtnt, -s
 AM pəˈlutnt, -s
pollute
 BR pəˈl(j)uːt, -s, -ɪŋ, -ɪd
 AM pəˈlu|t, -ts, -dɪŋ,
 -dəd
polluter
 BR pəˈl(j)uːtə(r), -z
 AM pəˈludər, -z
pollution
 BR pəˈl(j)uːʃn
 AM pəˈluʃən
Pollux
 BR ˈpɒləks
 AM ˈpɑləks
polly
 BR ˈpɒl|i, -ɪz
 AM ˈpɑli, -z
Pollyanna
 BR ˌpɒlɪˈanə(r), -z
 AM ˌpɑliˈænə, -z
Pollyannaish
 BR ˌpɒlɪˈanə(r)ɪʃ
 AM ˌpɑliˈænɪʃ
Pollyannaism
 BR ˌpɒlɪˈanə(r)ɪz(ə)m
 AM ˌpɑliˈænəˌɪzəm

pollywog
 BR ˈpɒlɪwɒg, -z
 AM ˈpɑliˌwɑg,
 ˈpɑliˌwag, -z
polo
 BR ˈpəʊləʊ
 AM ˈpoʊloʊ
polocrosse
 BR ˈpəʊləʊkrɒs
 AM ˈpoʊloʊˌkrɔs,
 ˈpoʊloʊˌkrɑs
polonaise
 BR ˌpɒləˈneɪz, -ɪz
 AM ˌpɑləˈneɪz,
 ˌpoʊləˈneɪz, -ɪz
polonium
 BR pəˈləʊnɪəm
 AM pəˈloʊniəm
Polonius
 BR pəˈləʊnɪəs
 AM pəˈloʊniəs
polony
 BR pəˈləʊn|i, -ɪz
 AM pəˈloʊni, -z
Polperro
 BR pɒlˈpɛrəʊ
 AM ˌpɒlˈpɛroʊ,
 ˌpɑlˈpɛroʊ
poltergeist
 BR ˈpɒltəgʌɪst, -s
 AM ˈpoʊltərˌgaɪst, -s
poltroon
 BR pɒlˈtruːn, -z
 AM pɑlˈtrun,
 poʊlˈtrun, -z
poltroonery
 BR pɒlˈtruːn(ə)ri
 AM pɑlˈtrunəri,
 poʊlˈtrunəri
poly
 BR ˈpɒl|i, -ɪz
 AM ˈpɑli, -z
polyadelphous
 BR ˌpɒlɪəˈdɛlfəs
 AM ˌpɑliəˈdɛlfəs
polyamide
 BR ˌpɒlɪˈamʌɪd, -z
 AM ˌpɑliˈæmaɪd, -z
polyandrous
 BR ˌpɒlɪˈandrəs
 AM ˌpɑliˈændrəs
polyandry
 BR ˈpɒlɪandri,
 ˌpɒlɪˈandri
 AM ˈpɑliˌændri
polyantha
 BR ˌpɒlɪˈanθə(r), -z
 AM ˌpɑliˈænθə, -z
polyanthus
 BR ˌpɒlɪˈanθəs, -ɪz
 AM ˌpɑliˈænθəs, -əz
polyatomic
 BR ˌpɒlɪəˈtɒmɪk
 AM ˌpɑliəˈtɑmɪk
polybag
 BR ˈpɒlɪbag, -z
 AM ˈpɑliˌbæg, -z

polybasic
BR ˌpɒlɪˈbeɪsɪk
AM ˌpɑliˈbeɪsɪk

Polybius
BR pəˈlɪbiəs, pɒˈlɪbiəs
AM pəˈlɪbiəs

polycarbonate
BR ˌpɒlɪˈkɑːbəneɪt,
ˌpɒlɪˈkɑːbənət, -s
AM ˌpɑliˈkɑːbənət, -s

Polycarp
BR ˈpɒlɪkɑːp
AM ˈpɑliˌkɑːrp

Polycell®
BR ˈpɒlɪsɛl
AM ˈpɑliˌsɛl

polychaetan
BR ˌpɒlɪˈkiːtn
AM ˌpɑliˈkiːtn

polychaete
BR ˈpɒlɪkiːt, -s
AM ˈpɑliˌkit, -s

polychaetous
BR ˌpɒlɪˈkiːtəs
AM ˌpɑliˈkidəs

polychlorinated
BR ˌpɒlɪˈklɔːrɪneɪtɪd,
ˌpɒlɪˈklɒrɪneɪtɪd
AM ˌpɑliˈklɔːrəˌneɪdɪd

polychromatic
BR ˌpɒlɪkrəˈmatɪk
AM ˌpɑlɪkrəˈmædɪk,
ˈpɑlɪkrəʊˈmædɪk

polychromatism
BR ˌpɒlɪˈkrəʊmətɪz(ə)m
AM ˌpɑliˈkrəʊməˌtɪzəm

polychrome
BR ˈpɒlɪkrəʊm
AM ˈpɑliˌkroʊm

polychromic
BR ˌpɒlɪˈkrəʊmɪk
AM ˌpɑliˈkroʊmɪk

polychromous
BR ˌpɒlɪˈkrəʊməs
AM ˌpɑliˈkroʊməs

polychromy
BR ˈpɒlɪˌkrəʊmi
AM ˈpɑliˌkroʊmi

polyclinic
BR ˌpɒlɪˈklɪnɪk, -s
AM ˌpɑliˈklɪnɪk, -s

Polyclitus
BR ˌpɒlɪˈklʌɪtəs
AM ˌpɑliˈklaɪdɪs

polycotton
BR ˈpɒlɪˈkɒtn
AM ˈpɑliˈkɑtn

Polycrates
BR pəˈlɪkrətiːz,
pɒˈlɪkrətiːz
AM pəˈlɪkrətiz

polycrystal
BR ˈpɒlɪˌkrɪstl, -z
AM ˈpɑliˌkrɪstəl, -z

polycrystalline
BR ˌpɒlɪˈkrɪstəlʌɪn,
ˌpɒlɪˈkrɪstlʌɪn

ˌpɑliˈkrɪstələn,
ˈpɑliˈkrɪstəˌlaɪn

polycyclic
BR ˌpɒlɪˈsaɪklɪk, -s
AM ˌpɑliˈsaɪklɪk,
ˌpɑliˈsaɪklɪk, -s

polycythaemia
BR ˌpɒlɪsʌɪˈθiːmɪə(r)
AM ˌpɑliˌsaɪˈθiːmiə

polycythemia
BR ˌpɒlɪsʌɪˈθiːmɪə(r)
AM ˌpɑliˌsaɪˈθiːmiə

polydactyl
BR ˌpɒlɪˈdakt(ɪ)l, -z
AM ˌpɑliˈdæktl, -z

polydaemonism
BR ˌpɒlɪˈdiːmənɪz(ə)m
AM ˌpɑliˈdiːməˌnɪzəm

polydipsia
BR ˌpɒlɪˈdɪpsɪə(r)
AM ˌpɑliˈdɪpsiə

polyester
BR ˌpɒlɪˈɛstə(r)
AM ˈpɑliˌɛstər

polyethene
BR ˈpɒlɪˌɛθiːn
AM ˈpɑliəˌθin

polyethylene
BR ˌpɒlɪˈɛθɪliːn,
ˌpɒlɪˈɛθɪliːn
AM ˌpɑliˈɛθəlin

Polyfilla®
BR ˈpɒlɪˌfɪlə(r)
AM ˈpɑliˌfɪlə

polygamic
BR ˌpɒlɪˈgamɪk
AM ˌpɑliˈgæmɪk

polygamist
BR pəˈlɪgəmɪst,
pɒˈlɪgəmɪst, -s
AM pəˈlɪgəməst, -s

polygamous
BR pəˈlɪgəməs,
pɒˈlɪgəməs
AM pəˈlɪgəməs

polygamously
BR pəˈlɪgəməsli,
pɒˈlɪgəməsli
AM pəˈlɪgəməsli

polygamy
BR pəˈlɪgəmi,
pɒˈlɪgəmi
AM pəˈlɪgəmi

polygene
BR ˈpɒlɪdʒiːn, -z
AM ˈpɑliˌdʒin, -z

polygenesis
BR ˌpɒlɪˈdʒɛnɪsɪs
AM ˌpɑliˈdʒɛnəsəs

polygenetic
BR ˌpɒlɪdʒɪˈnɛtɪk
AM ˈpɑlidʒəˈnɛdɪk

polygenic
BR ˌpɒlɪˈdʒɛnɪk
AM ˌpɑliˈdʒɛnɪk

polygenism
BR pəˈlɪdʒɪnɪz(ə)m,
pəˈlɪdʒɪz(ə)m,
pɒˈlɪdʒɪnɪz(ə)m,
pɒˈlɪdʒɪnɪz(ə)m
AM pəˈlɪdʒəˌnɪzəm

polygenist
BR pəˈlɪdʒɪnɪst,
pəˈlɪdʒɪnɪst,
pɒˈlɪdʒɪnɪst,
pɒˈlɪdʒɪnɪst, -s
ˌpəˈlɪdʒənəst, -s

polygeny
BR pəˈlɪdʒɪni,
pəˈlɪdʒɪni, pɒˈlɪdʒɪni,
pɒˈlɪdʒɪni
AM pəˈlɪdʒəni

polyglot
BR ˈpɒlɪglɒt, -s
AM ˈpɑliˌglɑt, -s

polyglottal
BR ˌpɒlɪˈglɒtl
AM ˌpɑliˈgladl

polyglottic
BR ˌpɒlɪˈglɒtɪk
AM ˌpɑliˈgladɪk

polyglottism
BR ˈpɒlɪglɒtɪz(ə)m
AM ˌpɑliˈglaˌtɪzəm

polygon
BR ˈpɒlɪg(ə)n,
ˈpɒlɪgɒn, -z
AM ˈpɑliˌgɑn, -z

polygonal
BR pəˈlɪgənl, pəˈlɪgn̩l,
pɒˈlɪgənl, pɒˈlɪgn̩l
AM pəˈlɪgənəl

polygonum
BR pəˈlɪgənəm,
pəˈlɪgn̩əm,
pɒˈlɪgənəm,
pɒˈlɪgn̩əm
AM pəˈlɪgənəm

polygraph
BR ˈpɒlɪgrɑːf,
ˈpɒlɪgraf, -s
AM ˈpɑliˌgræf, -s

polygynous
BR pəˈlɪdʒɪnəs,
pɒˈlɪdʒɪnəs
AM pəˈlɪdʒɪnəs

polygyny
BR pəˈlɪdʒɪni,
pɒˈlɪdʒɪni
AM pəˈlɪdʒɪni

polyhedra
BR ˌpɒlɪˈhiːdrə(r)
AM ˌpɑliˈhidrə

polyhedral
BR ˌpɒlɪˈhiːdr(ə)l
AM ˌpɑliˈhidrəl

polyhedric
BR ˌpɒlɪˈhiːdrɪk
AM ˌpɑliˈhidrɪk

polyhedron
BR ˌpɒlɪˈhiːdr(ə)n, -z
AM ˌpɑliˈhidrən, -z

polyhistor
BR ˌpɒlɪˈhɪstə(r), -z
AM ˈpɑliˌhɪstər, -z

Polyhymnia
BR ˌpɒlɪˈhɪmnɪə(r)
AM ˌpɑliˈhɪmniə

polymath
BR ˈpɒlɪmaθ, -s
AM ˈpɑliˌmæθ, -s

polymathic
BR ˌpɒlɪˈmaθɪk
AM ˌpɑliˈmæθɪk

polymathy
BR pəˈlɪməθi,
pɒˈlɪməθi
AM pəˈlɪməθi

polymer
BR ˈpɒlɪmə(r), -z
AM ˈpɑləmər, -z

polymerase
BR ˈpɒlɪməreɪz,
pəˈlɪməreɪz,
pɒˈlɪməreɪz, -ɪz
AM pəˈlɪməˌreɪz, -ɪz

polymeric
BR ˌpɒlɪˈmɛrɪk
AM ˌpɑliˈmɛrɪk

polymerisation
BR ˌpɒlɪmərʌɪˈzeɪʃn
AM pəˌlɪmərəˈzeɪʃən,
ˌpɑləmərəˈzeɪʃən,
ˌpɑləməˌraɪˈzeɪʃən

polymerise
BR ˈpɒlɪmərʌɪz, -ɪz, -ɪŋ,
-d
AM pəˈlɪməˌraɪz,
ˈpɑləməˌraɪz, -ɪz, -ɪŋ,
-d

polymerism
BR ˈpɒlɪmərɪz(ə)m
AM ˈpɑləməˌrɪzəm,
pəˈlɪməˌrɪzəm

polymerization
BR ˌpɒlɪmərʌɪˈzeɪʃn
AM pəˌlɪmərəˈzeɪʃən,
ˌpɑləmərəˈzeɪʃən,
ˌpɑləməˌraɪˈzeɪʃən

polymerize
BR ˈpɒlɪmərʌɪz, -ɪz, -ɪŋ,
-d
AM pəˈlɪməˌraɪz,
ˈpɑləməˌraɪz, -ɪz, -ɪŋ,
-d

polymerous
BR pəˈlɪm(ə)rəs,
pɒˈlɪm(ə)rəs
AM pəˈlɪmərəs

polymorph
BR ˈpɒlɪmɔːf, -s
AM ˈpɑliˌmɔ(ə)rf, -s

polymorphic
BR ˌpɒlɪˈmɔːfɪk
AM ˌpɑliˈmɔrfɪk

polymorphism
BR ˌpɒlɪˈmɔːfɪz(ə)m
AM ˌpɑliˈmɔrˌfɪzəm

polymorphous
BR ˌpɒlɪˈmɔːfəs

Polynesia
BR ˌpɒlɪˈniːzjə(r),
ˌpɒlɪˈniːʒə(r)
AM ˌpaləˈniʒə,
ˌpaləˈniʃə

Polynesian
BR ˌpɒlɪˈniːzj(ə)n,
ˌpɒlɪˈniːʒ(ə)n, -z
AM ˌpaləˈniʒən,
ˌpaləˈniʃən, -z

polyneuritic
BR ˌpɒlmjʊˈrɪtɪk,
ˌpɒlnjʊəˈrɪtɪk
AM ˌpalən(j)uˈrɪdɪk,
ˌpalən(j)əˈrɪdɪk

polyneuritis
BR ˌpɒlmjʊˈrʌɪtɪs,
ˌpɒlnjʊəˈrʌɪtɪs
AM ˌpalən(j)uˈraɪdɪs,
ˌpalən(j)əˈraɪdɪs

Polynices
BR ˌpɒlɪˈnʌɪsiːz
AM ˌpaliˈnaɪsiz

polynomial
BR ˌpɒlɪˈnəʊmɪəl, -z
AM ˌpaliˈnoʊmiəl,
ˌpaləˈnoʊmiəl, -z

polynya
BR pəˈ(ʊ)lɪnjə(r)
AM ˌpalənˈjɑ

polyopia
BR ˌpɒlɪˈəʊpɪə(r)
AM ˌpaliˈoʊpiə

polyp
BR ˈpɒlɪp, -s
AM ˈpaləp, -s

polypary
BR ˈpɒlɪp(ə)r|i, -ɪz
AM ˈpaləˌpɛri, -z

polypeptide
BR ˌpɒlɪˈpɛptʌɪd
AM ˌpaliˈpɛpˌtaɪd

polyphagous
BR pəˈlɪfəgəs
AM pəˈlɪfəgəs

polyphase
BR ˈpɒlɪfeɪz, -ɪz
AM ˈpaliˌfeɪz, -ɪz

polyphasic
BR ˌpɒlɪˈfeɪzɪk
AM ˌpaliˈfeɪzɪk

Polyphemus
BR ˌpɒlɪˈfiːməs
AM ˌpaliˈfiməs

polyphone
BR ˈpɒlɪfəʊn, -z
AM ˈpaliˌfoʊn, -z

polyphonic
BR ˌpɒlɪˈfɒnɪk
AM ˌpaliˈfɑnɪk,
ˌpaləˈfɑnɪk

polyphonically
BR ˌpɒlɪˈfɒnɪkli
AM ˌpaliˈfɑnək(ə)li,
ˌpaləˈfɑnək(ə)li

polyphonous
BR pəˈlɪfənəs,
pəˈlɪfnəs, pɒˈlɪfənəs,
pɒˈlɪfnəs
AM pəˈlɪfənəs

polyphony
BR pəˈlɪfəni, pəˈlɪfni,
pɒˈlɪfəni, pɒˈlɪfni
AM pəˈlɪfəni

polyphosphate
BR ˌpɒlɪˈfɒsfeɪt, -s
AM ˌpaliˈfɑsfeɪt, -s

polyphyletic
BR ˌpɒlɪfʌɪˈlɛtɪk
AM ˌpalifaɪˈlɛdɪk

polypi
BR ˈpɒlɪpʌɪ
AM ˈpaləˌpaɪ

polyploid
BR ˈpɒlɪplɔɪd, -z
AM ˈpaləˌplɔɪd, -z

polyploidy
BR ˈpɒlɪplɔɪdi
AM ˈpaləˌplɔɪdi

polypod
BR ˈpɒlɪpɒd
AM ˈpaləˌpad

polypody
BR ˈpɒlɪpəʊd|i, -ɪz
AM ˈpaliˌpoʊdi, -z

polypoid
BR ˈpɒlɪpɔɪd
AM ˈpaləˌpɔɪd

polyposis
BR ˌpɒlɪˈpəʊsɪs
AM ˌpaləˈpoʊsɪs

polypous
BR ˈpɒlɪpəs
AM ˈpaləpəs

polypropene
BR ˌpɒlɪˈprəʊpiːn, -z
AM ˌpaliˈproʊˌpin, -z

polypropylene
BR ˌpɒlɪˈprəʊpɪliːn
AM ˌpaləˈproʊpəˌlin

polyptych
BR ˈpɒlɪptɪk, -s
AM ˈpalɪpˌtɪk,
pəˈlɪptɪk, -s

polypus
BR ˈpɒlɪpəs
AM ˈpaləpəs

polyrhythm
BR ˈpɒlɪˌrɪð(ə)m, -z
AM ˈpaliˌrɪðəm, -z

polysaccharide
BR ˌpɒlɪˈsakərʌɪd, -z
AM ˌpaliˈsækəˌraɪd, -z

polysemic
BR ˌpɒlɪˈsiːmɪk
AM ˌpaliˈsimɪk

polysemous
BR ˌpɒlɪˈsiːməs
AM ˌpaliˈsiməs,
ˌpaləˈsiməs

polysemy
BR pəˈlɪsɪmi,
ˈpɒlɪˌsi:mi
AM pəˈlɪsɪmi

polystyrene
BR ˌpɒlɪˈstʌɪriːn
AM ˈpaliˈstaɪˌrin,
ˈpaləˈstaɪˌrin

polysyllabic
BR ˌpɒlɪsɪˈlabɪk
AM ˌpalisəˈlæbɪk,
ˈpaləsəˈlæbɪk

polysyllabically
BR ˌpɒlɪsɪˈlabɪkli
AM ˌpalisaˈlæbək(ə)li,
ˈpaləsəˈlæbək(ə)li

polysyllable
BR ˈpɒlɪˌsɪləbl, -z
AM ˈpaliˈsɪləbəl,
ˈpaləˈsɪləbəl, -z

polysynthetic
BR ˌpɒlɪsɪnˈθɛtɪk
AM ˌpaləsɪnˈθɛdɪk,
ˌpaliˌsɪnˈθɛdɪk

polytechnic
BR ˌpɒlɪˈtɛknɪk, -s
AM ˌpaləˈtɛknɪk, -s

**polytetrafluoro-
ethylene**
BR ˌpɒlɪˌtɛtrəˌfluərəʊ-
ˈɛθɪliːn,
ˌpɒlɪˌtɛtrəˌflɔːrəʊˈɛθɪ-
liːn
AM ˈpaliˌtɛtrəˌflʊrou-
ˈɛθəˌlin

polytheism
BR ˈpɒlɪθiːɪz(ə)m,
ˈpɒlɪˌθiːɪz(ə)m
AM ˈpaliθɪˌɪzəm,
ˈpaləθɪˌɪzəm,
ˈpaliˈθiːɪzəm

polytheist
BR ˈpɒlɪθiːɪst,
ˈpɒlɪˌθiːɪst, -s
AM ˈpaliˈθiːɪst, -s

polytheistic
BR ˌpɒlɪθiˈɪstɪk
AM ˌpaliˌθiˈɪstɪk,
ˌpaləθiˈɪstɪk

polythene
BR ˈpɒlɪθiːn
AM ˈpaləθin

polytonal
BR ˌpɒlɪˈtəʊnl
AM ˌpaliˈtoʊnəl

polytonality
BR ˌpɒlɪtə(ʊ)ˈnalɪti
AM ˌpaliˌtouˈnælədi

polyunsaturate
BR ˌpɒlɪʌnˈsatʃʊreɪt,
ˌpɒlɪʌnˈsatjʊreɪt, -ɪd
AM ˈpaliənˈsætʃəˌreɪt,
-dɪd

polyunsaturates
BR ˌpɒlɪʌnˈsatʃʊrəts,
ˌpɒlɪʌnˈsatjʊrəts
AM ˈpaliənˈsætʃ(ə)rəts

polyurethane
BR ˌpɒlɪˈjʊərɪθeɪn,
ˌpɒlɪˈjɔːrɪθeɪn
AM ˈpaliˈjurəˌθeɪn,
ˈpaləˈjurəˌθeɪn

polyvalence
BR ˌpɒlɪˈveɪləns,
ˌpɒlɪˈveɪlns
AM ˌpaliˈveɪləns,
ˈpaləˈveɪləns

polyvalent
BR ˌpɒlɪˈveɪlənt,
ˌpɒlɪˈveɪlnt
AM ˌpaliˈveɪlənt,
ˈpaləˈveɪlənt

polyvinyl
BR ˌpɒlɪˈvʌɪn(ɪ)l
AM ˈpaliˈvaɪnl,
ˈpaləˈvaɪnl

polyzoan
BR ˌpɒlɪˈzəʊən, -z
AM ˌpaliˈzouən, -z

Polzeath
BR pɒlˈzɛθ, pɒlˈziːθ
AM ˈpɔlziθ, ˈpɑlziθ

pom
BR pɒm, -z
AM pɑm, -z

pomace
BR ˈpʌmɪs, ˈpɒmɪs, -ɪz
AM ˈpəməs, -ɪz

pomade
BR pəˈmɑːd, -z
AM pəˈmeɪd, pouˈmeɪd,
-z

Pomagne®
BR pəˈ(ʊ)meɪn
AM pouˈmeɪn

pomander
BR ˈpɒmandə(r),
ˈpəʊmandə(r),
pəˈmandə(r), -z
AM pouˈmændər, -z

pomatum
BR pəˈ(ʊ)meɪtəm, -z,
-ɪŋ, -d
AM pəˈmadəm,
pəˈmeɪdəm,
pəˈmadəm, -z, -ɪŋ, -d

pombe
BR ˈpɒmbeɪ
AM ˈpamˌbeɪ

pome
BR pəʊm, -z
AM poʊm, -z

pomegranate
BR ˈpɒmɪgranɪt, -s
AM ˈpaməˌgrænət, -s

pomelo
BR ˈpɒmɪləʊ, ˈpʌmɪləʊ,
pəˈmɛləʊ, -z
AM ˈpaməloʊ, -z

Pomerania
BR ˌpɒməˈreɪnɪə(r)
AM ˌpaməˈreɪnɪə

Pomeranian
BR ˌpɒməˈreɪnɪən, -z
AM ˌpaməˈreɪnɪən, -z

Pomeroy
BR 'pɒmərɔɪ,
'pəʊmərɔɪ
AM 'pɑmə,rɔɪ

pomfret
BR 'pɒmfrɪt
AM 'pɑmfrət

pomiculture
BR 'pɒmɪˌkʌltʃə(r)
AM 'pɑməˌkəltʃər

pomiferous
BR pə'mɪf(ə)rəs
AM pə'mɪf(ə)rəs

pommel[1]
noun, part of saddle
BR 'pʌml, 'pɒml, -z
AM 'pɑməl, -z

pommel[2]
verb
BR 'pʌml|l, -lz,
-lɪŋ\-əlɪŋ, -ld
AM 'pɑml|əl, -əlz,
-(ə)lɪŋ, -əld

pommie
BR 'pɒm|i, -iz
AM 'pɑmi, -z

pommy
BR 'pɒm|i, -iz
AM 'pɑmi, -z

pomological
BR ˌpɒmə'lɒdʒɪkl
AM ˌpɑmə'lɑdʒəkəl

pomologist
BR pə(ʊ)'mɒlədʒɪst,
pɒ'mɒlədʒɪst, -s
AM pə'mɑlədʒəst, -s

pomology
BR pə(ʊ)'mɒlədʒi,
pɒ'mɒlədʒi
AM pə'mɑlədʒi

Pomona
BR pə'məʊnə(r)
AM pə'moʊnə

pomp
BR pɒmp
AM pɑmp

Pompadour
BR ˌpɒmpə'dʊə(r),
'pɒmpədɔː(r)
AM ˌpɑmpə'dɔ(ə)r,
ˌpɑmpə'dʊ(ə)r

pompano
BR 'pɒmpənəʊ, -z
AM 'pɑmpəˌnoʊ, -z

Pompeii
BR pɒm'peɪ(i)
AM pɑm'peɪ(i)

Pompey
BR 'pɒmpi
AM 'pɑmpi

Pompidou
BR 'pɒmpɪduː
AM 'pɑmpəˌdu,
'pɑmpiˌdu

pompom
BR 'pɒmpɒm, -z
AM 'pɑmˌpɑm, -z

pompon
BR 'pɒmpɒn, -z
AM 'pɑmˌpɑn, -z

pomposity
BR pɒm'pɒsɪti
AM pɑm'pɑsədi

pompous
BR 'pɒmpəs
AM 'pɑmpəs

pompously
BR 'pɒmpəsli
AM 'pɑmpəsli

pompousness
BR 'pɒmpəsnəs
AM 'pɑmpəsnəs

'pon
upon
BR pɒn, pən
AM pɑn, pən

ponce
BR pɒns, -ɪz, -ɪŋ, -t
AM pɑns, -əz, -ɪŋ, -t

ponceau
BR 'pɒnsəʊ, -z
AM pɑn'soʊ, -z

ponceaux
BR 'pɒnsəʊz
AM pɑn'soʊ

poncey
BR 'pɒns|i, -ɪə(r), -ɪɪst
AM 'pɑnsi, -ər, -ɪst

poncho
BR 'pɒn(t)ʃəʊ, -z
AM 'pɑn(t)ʃoʊ, -z

poncy
BR 'pɒns|i, -ɪə(r), -ɪɪst
AM 'pɑnsi, -ər, -ɪst

pond
BR pɒnd, -z
AM pɑnd, -z

pondage
BR 'pɒndɪdʒ
AM 'pɑndɪdʒ

ponder
BR 'pɒnd|ə(r), -əz,
-(ə)rɪŋ, -əd
AM 'pɑnd|ər, -ərz,
-(ə)rɪŋ, -ərd

ponderability
BR pɒnd(ə)rə'bɪlɪti
AM ˌpɑnd(ə)rə'bɪlɪdi

ponderable
BR 'pɒnd(ə)rəbl
AM 'pɑnd(ə)rəbəl

ponderation
BR ˌpɒndə'reɪʃn
AM ˌpɑndə'reɪʃən

pondering
BR 'pɒnd(ə)rɪŋ, -z
AM 'pɑnd(ə)rɪŋ, -z

ponderosa
BR ˌpɒndə'rəʊzə(r),
ˌpɒndə'rəʊsə(r), -z
AM ˌpɑndə'roʊsə, -z

ponderosity
BR ˌpɒndə'rɒsɪti
AM ˌpɑndə'rasədi

ponderous
BR 'pɒnd(ə)rəs
AM 'pɑnd(ə)rəs

ponderously
BR 'pɒnd(ə)rəsli
AM 'pɑnd(ə)rəsli

ponderousness
BR 'pɒnd(ə)rəsnəs
AM 'pɑnd(ə)rəsnəs

Pondicherry
BR ˌpɒndɪ'tʃeri
AM ˌpɑndə'tʃeri

pondweed
BR 'pɒndwiːd
AM 'pɑnd(d)ˌwid

pone
BR pəʊn
AM poʊn

pong
BR pɒŋ, -z, -ɪŋ, -d
AM pɔŋ, pɑŋ, -z, -ɪŋ, -d

ponga
BR 'pʌŋə(r), -z
AM 'pɑŋə, -z

pongal
BR 'pɒŋgl
AM 'pɔŋ(g)əl, 'pɑŋ(g)əl

pongee
BR pɒn'dʒiː, 'pɒndʒiː,
-z
AM pɑn'dʒi, pɑn'dʒi, -z

pongid
BR 'pɒn(d)ʒɪd, -z
AM 'pɑndʒəd, -z

pongo
BR 'pɒŋgəʊ, -z
AM 'pɔŋgoʊ, 'pɑŋgoʊ,
-z

pongy
BR 'pɒŋ|i, -ɪə(r), -ɪɪst
AM 'pɑŋi, -ər, -ɪst

poniard
BR 'pɒnjəd, 'pɒnjɑːd, -z
AM 'pɑnjərd, -z

pons
BR pɒnz, -ɪz
AM pɑnz, -əz

pons asinorum
BR ˌpɒnz ˌæsɪ'nɔːrəm
AM ˌpɑnz ˌæsn'ɔrəm

Ponsonby
BR 'pɒns(ə)nbi
AM 'pɑnsənbi

pons Varolii
BR ˌpɒnz və'rəʊliaɪ
AM ˌpɑnz və'roʊliˌaɪ

pont
BR pɒnt, -s
AM pɑnt, -s

Pontardawe
BR ˌpɒntə'daʊi
AM ˌpɑn(t)ər'daʊi
WE ˌpɒntar'dawe

Pontardulais
BR ˌpɒntə'dɪləs
AM ˌpɑn(t)ər'dɪləs
WE ˌpɒntar'dɪlaɪs

Pontefract
BR 'pɒntɪfrakt
AM 'pɑn(t)ə,fræk(t)

Ponteland
BR pɒn'tiːlənd
AM pɑn'tiland

pontes
BR 'pɒntiːz
AM 'pɑnˌtiz

pontes asinorum
BR ˌpɒntiːz
ˌasɪ'nɔːrəm
AM ˌpɑnˌtiz ˌæsn'ɔrəm

pontes Varolii
BR ˌpɒntiːz və'rəʊliaɪ
AM ˌpɑnˌtiz və'roʊliˌaɪ

Pontiac
BR 'pɒntiak, -s
AM 'pɑn(t)iˌæk, -s

Pontianak
BR ˌpɒntɪ'ɑːnak,
ˌpɒntɪ'anak
AM ˌpɑn(t)i'ɑnək

pontifex
BR 'pɒntɪfɛks
AM 'pɑn(t)əˌfɛks

pontiff
BR 'pɒntɪf, -s
AM 'pɑn(t)əf, -s

pontific
BR pɒn'tɪfɪk
AM pɑn'tɪfɪk

pontifical
BR pɒn'tɪfɪkl, -z
AM pɑn'tɪfɪkəl, -z

pontificalia
BR ˌpɒntɪfɪ'keɪliə(r)
AM pɑnˌtɪfə'keɪljə,
ˌpɑn(t)əfə'keɪljə,
pɑnˌtɪfə'keɪliə,
ˌpɑn(t)əfə'keɪliə

pontifically
BR pɒn'tɪfɪkli
AM pɑn'tɪfɪk(ə)li

pontificate[1]
noun
BR pɒn'tɪfɪkət, -s
AM pɑn'tɪfɪkət, -s

pontificate[2]
verb
BR pɒn'tɪfɪkeɪt, -s, -ɪŋ,
-ɪd
AM pɑn'tɪfɪˌkeɪt, -ts,
-dɪŋ, -dɪd

pontification
BR pɒnˌtɪfɪ'keɪʃn,
ˌpɒntɪfɪ'keɪʃn
AM ˌpɑnˌtɪfə'keɪʃən,
ˌpɑn(t)əfə'keɪʃən

pontifices
BR pɒn'tɪfɪsiːz
AM pɑn'tɪfəˌsiz

Pontin
BR 'pɒntɪn
AM 'pɑntn

Pontine Marshes
BR ˌpɒntaɪn 'mɑːʃɪz

AM ˈpɒn‚tɪn mɑːʃəz,
ˈpɒn‚taɪn +

Ponting
BR ˈpɒntɪŋ
AM ˈpɑːn(t)ɪŋ

Pontius
BR ˈpɒntəs, ˈpɒn(t)ʃəs
AM ˈpɑːn(t)ʃəs

pontoon
BR pɒnˈtuːn, -z
AM ‚pɑːnˈtun, -z

Pontormo
BR pɒnˈtɔːməʊ
AM pɑːnˈtɔːr‚moʊ,
pɑːnˈtɔːr‚moʊ

Pontus
BR ˈpɒntəs
AM ˈpɑːn(t)əs

Pontypool
BR ‚pɒntɪˈpuːl
AM ‚pɑːn(t)iˈpul

Pontypridd
BR ‚pɒntɪˈpriːð
AM ‚pɑːn(t)iˈprɪð
WE ‚pɒntʌˈprɪð

pony
BR ˈpəʊn|i, -ɪz
AM ˈpoʊni, -z

ponytail
BR ˈpəʊnɪteɪl, -z
AM ˈpoʊni‚teɪl, -z

Ponzi scheme
BR ˈpɒnzi skiːm, -z
AM ˈpɑːnzi ‚skiːm, -z

poo
BR puː, -z, -ɪŋ, -d
AM pu, -z, -ɪŋ, -d

pooch
BR puːtʃ, -ɪz
AM putʃ, -əz

poodle
BR ˈpuːdl, -z
AM ˈpudəl, -z

poof
BR pʊf, puːf, -s
AM puf, -s

poofter
BR ˈpʊftə(r), ˈpuːftə(r), -z
AM ˈpuftər, -z

poofy
BR ˈpuːf|i, -iə(r), -ɪɪst
AM ˈpufi, -ər, -ɪɪst

pooh
BR p(h)uː, -z, -ɪŋ, -d
AM pu, -z, -ɪŋ, -d

pooh-bah
BR ‚puːˈbɑː(r), -z
AM ˈpu‚bɑ, -z

pooh-pooh
BR ‚puːˈpuː, -z, -ɪŋ, -d
AM ˈpuˈpu, -z, -ɪŋ, -d

pooja
BR ˈpuːdʒə(r), -z
AM ˈpudʒə, -z

poojah
BR ˈpuːdʒə(r), -z

AM ˈpudʒə, -z

Pook
BR puːk
AM puk

pooka
BR ˈpuːkə(r), -z
AM ˈpukə, -z

pool
BR puːl, -z, -ɪŋ, -d
AM pul, -z, -ɪŋ, -d

Poole
BR puːl
AM pul

Pooley
BR ˈpuːli
AM ˈpuli

poolroom
BR ˈpuːlruːm, ˈpuːlrʊm, -z
AM ˈpul‚rum, ˈpul‚rʊm, -z

poolside
BR ˈpuːlsʌɪd
AM ˈpul‚saɪd

poon
BR puːn, -z
AM pun, -z

Poona
BR ˈpuːnə(r)
AM ˈpunə

poop
BR puːp, -s, -t
AM pup, -s, -t

pooper-scooper
BR ˈpuːpə‚skuːpə(r), -z
AM ˈpupər‚skupər, -z

poo-poo
BR ˈpuːpuː, -z
AM ˈpuˈpu, -z

poor
BR pɔː(r), pʊə(r), -ə(r), -ɪst
AM pʊ(ə)r, pɔ(ə)r, -ər, -əst

poorboy
BR ˈpɔːbɔɪ, -z
AM ˈpʊr‚bɔɪ, ˈpɔr‚bɔɪ, -z

poorhouse
BR ˈpɔːhaʊ|s,
ˈpʊəhaʊ|s, -zɪz
AM ˈpʊr‚(h)aʊ|s,
ˈpɔr‚(h)aʊ|s, -zəz

poorly
BR ˈpɔːli, ˈpʊəli
AM ˈpʊrli, ˈpɔrli

poorness
BR ˈpɔːnəs, ˈpʊənəs
AM ˈpʊrnəs, ˈpɔrnəs

Pooter
BR ˈpuːtə(r)
AM ˈpudər

Pooterish
BR ˈpuːt(ə)rɪʃ
AM ˈpudərɪʃ

pootle
BR ˈpuːt|l, -lz, -lɪŋ \-lɪŋ, -ld

AM ˈpudəl, -z, -ɪŋ, -d

poove
BR puːv, -z
AM puv, -z

pop
BR pɒp, -s, -ɪŋ, -t
AM pɑp, -s, -ɪŋ, -t

popadom
BR ˈpɒpədəm, -z
AM ˈpɑpədəm, -z

popadum
BR ˈpɒpədəm, -z
AM ˈpɑpədəm, -z

popcorn
BR ˈpɒpkɔːn
AM ˈpɑp‚kɔ(ə)rn

pope
BR pəʊp, -s
AM poʊp, -s

popedom
BR ˈpəʊpdəm
AM ˈpoʊpdəm

popeless
BR ˈpəʊpləs
AM ˈpoʊpləs

Popemobile
BR ˈpəʊpmə(ʊ)biːl, -z
AM ˈpoʊpmə‚bil, -z

popery
BR ˈpəʊp(ə)ri
AM ˈpoʊp(ə)ri

Popeye
BR ˈpɒpʌɪ
AM ˈpɑpaɪ

popeyed
BR ˈpɒpˈʌɪd
AM ˈpɑpaɪd

popgun
BR ˈpɒpgʌn, -z
AM ˈpɑp‚gən, -z

Popham
BR ˈpɒpəm
AM ˈpɑpəm

popinjay
BR ˈpɒpɪndʒeɪ, -z
AM ˈpɑpən‚dʒeɪ, -z

popish
BR ˈpəʊpɪʃ
AM ˈpoʊpɪʃ

popishly
BR ˈpəʊpɪʃli
AM ˈpoʊpɪʃli

popishness
BR ˈpəʊpɪʃnɪs
AM ˈpoʊpɪʃnɪs

poplar
BR ˈpɒplə(r), -z
AM ˈpɑplər, -z

poplin
BR ˈpɒplɪn
AM ˈpɑplən

popliteal
BR ‚pɒplɪˈtiːəl
AM ‚pɑpləˈtiəl

Popocatépetl
BR ‚pɒpəˌkatəˈpetl
AM ‚poʊpəˌkædəˈpɛdl

popover
BR ˈpɒp‚əʊvə(r), -z
AM ˈpɑp‚oʊvər, -z

poppa
BR ˈpɒpə(r), -z
AM ˈpɑpə, -z

poppadom
BR ˈpɒpədəm, -z
AM ˈpɑpədəm, -z

poppadum
BR ˈpɒpədəm, -z
AM ˈpɑpədəm, -z

popper
BR ˈpɒpə(r), -z
AM ˈpɑpər, -z

poppet
BR ˈpɒpɪt, -s
AM ˈpɑpət, -s

poppied
BR ˈpɒpɪd
AM ˈpɑpid

popple
BR ˈpɒp|l, -lz, -lɪŋ \-lɪŋ, -ld
AM ˈpɑpəl, -z, -ɪŋ, -d

Poppleton
BR ˈpɒplt(ə)n
AM ˈpɑpəltən

Popplewell
BR ˈpɒplwɛl
AM ˈpɑpl‚wɛl

popply
BR ˈpɒp|i, ˈpɒpli
AM ˈpɑp|i, ˈpɑpli

poppy
BR ˈpɒp|i, -ɪz
AM ˈpɑpi, -z

poppycock
BR ˈpɒpɪkɒk
AM ˈpɑpi‚kɑk

Popsicle®
BR ˈpɒpsɪkl, -z
AM ˈpɑpsəkəl,
ˈpɑp‚sɪkəl, -z

popsie
BR ˈpɒps|i, -ɪz
AM ˈpɑpsi, -z

popsy
BR ˈpɒps|i, -ɪz
AM ˈpɑpsi, -z

populace
BR ˈpɒpjələs
AM ˈpɑpjələs

popular
BR ˈpɒpjələ(r)
AM ˈpɑpjələr

popularisation
BR ‚pɒpjələrʌɪˈzeɪʃn, -z
AM ‚pɑpjələrəˈzeɪʃən,
‚pɑpjələ‚rarˈzeɪʃən, -z

popularise
BR ˈpɒpjələrʌɪz, -ɪz, -ɪŋ, -d
AM ˈpɑpjələ‚raɪz, -ɪz, -ɪŋ, -d

populariser
BR 'pɒpjʊlərʌɪzə(r), -z
AM 'pɑpjələˌraɪzər, -z

popularism
BR 'pɒpjʊlərɪz(ə)m
AM 'pɑpjələˌrɪzəm

popularity
BR ˌpɒpjʊ'larɪti
AM ˌpɑpjə'lɛrədi

popularization
BR ˌpɒpjʊlərʌɪ'zeɪʃn,
-z
AM ˌpɑpjələrə'zeɪʃən,
ˌpɑpjələˌraɪ'zeɪʃən, -z

popularize
BR 'pɒpjʊlərʌɪz, -ɪz,
-ɪŋ, -d
AM 'pɑpjələˌraɪz, -ɪz,
-ɪŋ, -d

popularizer
BR 'pɒpjʊlərʌɪzə(r), -z
AM 'pɑpjələˌraɪzər, -z

popularly
BR 'pɒpjʊləli
AM 'pɑpjələrli

populate
BR 'pɒpjʊleɪt, -s, -ɪŋ, -ɪd
AM 'pɑpjəˌleɪ|t, -ts,
-dɪŋ, -dɪd

population
BR ˌpɒpjʊ'leɪʃn, -z
AM ˌpɑpjə'leɪʃən, -z

populism
BR 'pɒpjʊlɪz(ə)m
AM 'pɑpjəˌlɪzəm

populist
BR 'pɒpjʊlɪst, -s
AM 'pɑpjələst, -s

populistic
BR ˌpɒpjʊ'lɪstɪk
AM ˌpɑpjə'lɪstɪk

populous
BR 'pɒpjʊləs
AM 'pɑpjələs

populously
BR 'pɒpjʊləsli
AM 'pɑpjələsli

populousness
BR 'pɒpjʊləsnəs
AM 'pɑpjələsnəs

porbeagle
BR 'pɔː.biːgl, -z
AM 'pɔrˌbigəl, -z

porcelain
BR 'pɔːslɪn, 'pɔːs(ə)lɪn,
'pɔːsleɪn, 'pɔːs(ə)leɪn
AM 'pɔrs(ə)lən

porcellaneous
BR ˌpɔːsɪ'leɪnɪəs
AM ˌpɔrsə'leɪnɪəs

porcellanous
BR pɔː'sɛlənəs
AM 'pɔrs(ə)lənəs

porch
BR pɔːtʃ, -ɪz, -t
AM pɔrtʃ, -əz, -t

Porchester
BR 'pɔːtʃɪstə(r)
AM 'pɔrtʃəstər

porchless
BR 'pɔːtʃləs
AM 'pɔrtʃləs

porcine
BR 'pɔːsʌɪn
AM 'pɔrˌsaɪn, 'pɔrˌsin,
'pɔrsn̩

porcini
BR pɔː'tʃiːni:
AM ˌpɔr'tʃini

porcupine
BR 'pɔːkjʊpʌɪn, -z
AM 'pɔrkjə.paɪn,
'pɔrki.paɪn, -z

porcupinish
BR 'pɔːkjʊpʌɪnɪʃ
AM 'pɔrkjə.paɪnɪʃ,
'pɔrki.paɪnɪʃ

porcupiny
BR 'pɔːkjʊpʌɪni
AM 'pɔrkjə.paɪni,
'pɔrki.paɪni

pore
BR pɔː(r), -z, -ɪŋ, -d
AM pɔ(ə)r, -z, -ɪŋ, -d

porgy
BR 'pɔːg|i, -ɪz
AM 'pɔrgi, -z

Pori
BR 'pɔːri
AM 'pɔri

porifer
BR 'pɔːrɪfə(r), -z
AM 'pɔrəfər, -z

poriferan
BR pə'rɪf(ə)rən,
pə'rɪf(ə)rŋ̩, -z
AM pə'rɪf(ə)rən, -z

porism
BR 'pɔːrɪz(ə)m,
'pɒrɪz(ə)m, -z
AM 'pɔˌrɪzəm, -z

porismatic
BR ˌpɔːrɪz'matɪk,
ˌpɒrɪz'matɪk
AM ˌpɔrəz'mædɪk

pork
BR pɔːk
AM pɔ(ə)rk

porker
BR 'pɔːkə(r), -z
AM 'pɔrkər, -z

porkling
BR 'pɔːklɪŋ, -z
AM 'pɔrklɪŋ, -z

porky
BR 'pɔːk|i, -ɪə(r), -ɪɪst
AM 'pɔrki, -ər, -ɪst

Porlock
BR 'pɔːlɒk
AM 'pɔrˌlɑk

porn
BR pɔːn
AM pɔ(ə)rn

porno
BR 'pɔːnəʊ
AM 'pɔrnoʊ

pornographer
BR pɔː'nɒgrəfə(r), -z
AM pɔr'nɑgrəfər, -z

pornographic
BR ˌpɔːnə'grafɪk
AM ˌpɔrnə'græfɪk

pornographically
BR ˌpɔːnə'grafɪkli
AM ˌpɔrnə'græfək(ə)li

pornography
BR pɔː'nɒgrəfi
AM pɔr'nɑgrəfi

poroplastic
BR ˌpɒrə'plastɪk
AM ˌpɔrə'plæstɪk

porosity
BR pɔː'rɒsɪti
AM pə'rɑsədi,
poʊ'rɑsədi

porous
BR 'pɔːrəs
AM 'pɔrəs

porously
BR 'pɔːrəsli
AM 'pɔrəsli

porousness
BR 'pɔːrəsnəs
AM 'pɔrəsnəs

porphyria
BR pɔː'fɪrɪə(r)
AM pɔr'fɪriə

porphyrin
BR 'pɔːf(ɪ)rɪn, -z
AM 'pɔrfərɪn, -z

porphyritic
BR ˌpɔːfɪ'rɪtɪk
AM ˌpɔrfə'rɪdɪk

porphyrogenite
BR ˌpɔːfɪ'rɒdʒɪnʌɪt, -s
AM ˌpɔrfə'rɑdʒəˌnaɪt,
ˌpɔrfərə'dʒɛˌnaɪt, -s

porphyry
BR 'pɔːf(ɪ)ri
AM 'pɔrfəri

porpoise
BR 'pɔːpəs, -ɪz
AM 'pɔrpəs, -əz

porrect
BR pə'rɛkt, -s, -ɪŋ, -ɪd
AM pə'rɛk|(t),
pɔ'rɛk|(t), -(t)s, -tɪŋ,
-tɪd

porridge
BR 'pɒrɪdʒ
AM 'pɔrɪdʒ

porridgy
BR 'pɒrɪdʒi
AM 'pɔrɪdʒi

porringer
BR 'pɒrɪn(d)ʒə(r), -z
AM 'pɔrənd̬ʒər, -z

Porsche®
BR pɔːʃ, 'pɔːʃə(r), -ɪz
AM 'pɔrʃ|(ə), -əz

Porsena
BR 'pɔːsɪnə(r),
'pɔːsnə(r)
AM 'pɔrsənə

Porson
BR 'pɔːsn
AM 'pɔrsən

port
BR pɔːt, -s, -ɪŋ, -ɪd
AM pɔ(ə)rt, -ts, 'pɔrdɪŋ,
'pɔrdəd

portability
BR ˌpɔːtə'bɪlɪti
AM ˌpɔrdə'bɪlɪdi

portable
BR 'pɔːtəbl
AM 'pɔrdəbəl

portableness
BR 'pɔːtəblnəs
AM 'pɔrdəbəlnəs

portably
BR 'pɔːtəbli
AM 'pɔrdəbli

portage
BR 'pɔːt|ɪdʒ, -ɪdʒɪz,
-ɪdʒɪŋ, -ɪdʒd
AM 'pɔrdɪdʒ, -ɪz, -ɪŋ, -d

Portakabin®
BR 'pɔːtəˌkabɪn, -z
AM 'pɔrdəˌkæbən, -z

portal
BR 'pɔːtl, -z
AM 'pɔrdl, -z

portamenti
BR ˌpɔːtə'mɛntiː
AM ˌpɔrdə'mɛn(t)i

portamento
BR ˌpɔːtə'mɛntəʊ, -z
AM ˌpɔrdə'mɛn(t)oʊ, -z

portative
BR 'pɔːtətɪv
AM 'pɔrdədɪv

Port-au-Prince
BR ˌpɔːtəʊ'prɪns
AM ˌpɔrdə'prɪns

portcullis
BR pɔːt'kʌlɪs, -ɪz, -t
AM ˌpɔrt'kələs, -ɪz, -t

Porte
BR pɔːt
AM pɔ(ə)rt

porte-cochère
BR ˌpɔːtkɒ'ʃɛː(r), -z
AM ˌpɔrtkoʊ'ʃɛ(ə)r, -z

portend
BR pɔː'tɛnd, -z, -ɪŋ, -ɪd
AM pɔr'tɛnd, -z, -ɪŋ, -əd

portent
BR 'pɔːtɛnt, 'pɔːt(ə)nt,
-s
AM 'pɔrˌtɛnt, -s

portentous
BR pɔː'tɛntəs
AM pɔr'tɛn(t)əs

portentously
BR pɔː'tɛntəsli
AM pɔr'tɛn(t)əsli

portentousness
BR pɔːˈtentəsnəs
AM pɔrˈten(t)əsnəs

Porteous
BR ˈpɔːtɪəs
AM ˈpɔrdiəs

porter
BR ˈpɔːtə(r), -z
AM ˈpɔrdər, -z

porterage
BR ˈpɔːt(ə)rɪdʒ
AM ˈpɔrdərədʒ

porterhouse
BR ˈpɔːtəhaʊs, -zɪz
AM ˈpɔrdər,(h)aʊs,
-zəz

Porteus
BR ˈpɔːtɪəs
AM ˈpɔrdiəs

portfire
BR ˈpɔːt,fʌɪə(r), -z
AM ˈpɔrt,faɪ(ə)r, -z

portfolio
BR pɔːtˈfəʊliəʊ, -z
AM pɔrtˈfoʊlioʊ, -z

Porth
BR pɔːθ
AM pɔ(ə)rθ

Port Harcourt
BR ,pɔːt ˈhɑːkɔːt
AM ,pɔrt ˈhɑr,kɔ(ə)rt

Porthcawl
BR ,pɔːθˈkɔːl
AM ,pɔrθˈkɔl, ,pɔrθˈkɑl

Port Hedland
BR ,pɔːt ˈhedlənd
AM ,pɔ(ə)rt ˈhedlənd

Porthmadog
BR pɔːθˈmadəg,
,pɔːθˈmadʊg
AM pɔrθˈmadəg

porthole
BR ˈpɔːthəʊl, -z
AM ˈpɔrt,(h)oʊl, -z

Portia
BR ˈpɔːʃə(r)
AM ˈpɔrʃə

portico
BR ˈpɔːtɪkəʊ, -z, -d
AM ˈpɔrdə,koʊ, -z, -d

portière
BR ,pɔːtɪˈɛː(r), -z
AM ,pɔrdiˈɛ(ə)r, -z

portion
BR ˈpɔːʃ|n, -nz,
-ŋɪŋ \-ənɪŋ, -nd
AM ˈpɔrʃ|ən, -ənz,
-(ə)nɪŋ, -ənd

portionless
BR ˈpɔːʃnləs,
ˈpɔːʃənləs
AM ˈpɔrʃənləs

Portishead
BR ˈpɔːtɪshed
AM ˈpɔrdəs,(h)ed

Portland
BR ˈpɔːtlənd

AM ˈpɔrtlən(d)

portliness
BR ˈpɔːtlɪnɪs
AM ˈpɔrtlinɪs

portly
BR ˈpɔːtl|i, -ɪə(r), -ɪɪst
AM ˈpɔrtli, -ər, -ɪst

Portmadoc
BR pɔːtˈmadək
AM ,pɔrtˈmædək

portmanteau
BR pɔːtˈmantəʊ, -z
AM ,pɔrtmænˈtoʊ,
pɔrtˈmæntoʊ, -z

portmanteaux
BR pɔːtˈmantəʊz
AM ,pɔrtmænˈtoʊ,
pɔrtˈmæntoʊ

Portmeirion
BR ,pɔːtˈmɛrɪən
AM ,pɔrtˈmɛrɪən
WE pɔrtˈmeɪrjɒn

Port Moresby
BR ,pɔːt ˈmɔːzbi
AM ,pɔrt ˈmɔrzbi

Portnoy
BR ˈpɔːtnɔɪ
AM ˈpɔrt,nɔɪ

Porto
BR ˈpɔːtəʊ
AM ˈpɔr,təʊ, ,pɔrdoʊ

Porto Alegre
BR ,pɔːtəʊ əˈlɛgrə(r)
AM ,pɔrdoʊ əˈlɛgrə

Portobello
BR ,pɔːtəˈbɛləʊ
AM ,pɔrdəˈbɛloʊ

Port-of-Spain
BR ,pɔːtəvˈspeɪn
AM ,pɔrtəv(v)ˈspeɪn

portolan
BR ˈpɔːtələn, ˈpɔːtʃlən,
-z
AM ˈpɔrdlən, -z

portolano
BR ,pɔːtəˈlɑːnəʊ,
,pɔːtʃˈɑːnəʊ, -z
AM ,pɔrdlˈɑnoʊ, -z

Porton
BR ˈpɔːtn
AM ˈpɔrtən

Porto Novo
BR ,pɔːtəʊ ˈnəʊvəʊ
AM ,pɔrdoʊ ˈnoʊ,voʊ

Porto Rican
BR ,pɔːtə ˈriːkən, -z
AM ,pɔrdə ˈrikən, -z

Porto Rico
BR ,pɔːtə ˈriːkəʊ
AM ,pɔrdə ˈrikoʊ

portrait
BR ˈpɔːtreɪt, ˈpɔːtrɪt, -s
AM ˈpɔrtrət, -s

portraitist
BR ˈpɔːtrɪtɪst,
ˈpɔːtreɪtɪst, -s
AM ˈpɔrtrədəst, -s

portraiture
BR ˈpɔːtrɪtʃə(r)
AM ˈpɔrtrətʃər,
ˈpɔrtrə,tʃʊ(ə)r,
ˈpɔrtrə,t(j)ʊ(ə)r

portray
BR pɔːˈtreɪ, -z, -ɪŋ, -d
AM pɔrˈtreɪ, -z, -ɪŋ, -d

portrayable
BR pɔːˈtreɪəbl
AM pɔrˈtreɪəbəl

portrayal
BR pɔːˈtreɪəl, -z
AM pɔrˈtreɪ(ə)l, -z

portrayer
BR pɔːˈtreɪə(r), -z
AM pɔrˈtreɪər, -z

Portreath
BR pɔːˈtriːθ
AM pɔrˈtriθ

Portree
BR pɔːˈtriː
AM pɔrˈtri

portreeve
BR ˈpɔːtriːv, -z
AM ˈpɔrt,riv, -z

Port Said
BR ,pɔːt ˈsʌɪd
AM ,pɔrt saɪˈid

Portsmouth
BR ˈpɔːtsməθ
AM ˈpɔrtsməθ

Port Stanley
BR ,pɔːt ˈstanli
AM ,pɔrt ˈstænli

Port Sudan
BR ,pɔːt sʊˈdɑːn,
+ sʊˈdan
AM ,pɔrt suˈdæn

Port Talbot
BR ,pɔː(t) ˈtɔːlbət,
+ ˈtalbət, + ˈtɒlbət
AM ,pɔrt ˈtælbət

Portugal
BR ˈpɔːtʃʊgl, ˈpɔːtjʊgl
AM ˈpɔrtʃəgəl

Portuguese
BR ,pɔːtʃʊˈgiːz,
,pɔːtjʊˈgiːz
AM ˈpɔrtʃə,giz

pose
BR pəʊz, -ɪz, -ɪŋ, -d
AM poʊz, -əz, -ɪŋ, -d

Poseidon
BR pəˈsʌɪdn, pɒˈsʌɪdn
AM pəˈsaɪdn,
poʊˈsaɪdn

poser
BR ˈpəʊzə(r), -z
AM ˈpoʊzər, -z

poseur
BR pəʊˈzəː(r), -z
AM poʊˈzər, -z

poseuse
BR pəʊˈzəːz
AM poʊˈzəz

poseuses
BR pəʊˈzəːz
AM poʊˈzʊz

posey
BR ˈpəʊzi
AM ˈpoʊzi

posh
BR pɒʃ, -ə(r), -ɪst
AM pɑʃ, -ər, -əst

poshly
BR ˈpɒʃli
AM ˈpɑʃli

poshness
BR ˈpɒʃnəs
AM ˈpɑʃnəs

posit
BR ˈpɒz|ɪt, -ɪts, -ɪtɪŋ,
-ɪtɪd
AM ˈpɑzə|t, -ts, -dɪŋ,
-dəd

position
BR pəˈzɪʃ|n, -nz,
-ŋɪŋ \-ənɪŋ, -nd
AM pəˈzɪʃ|ən, -ənz,
-(ə)nɪŋ, -ənd

positional
BR pəˈzɪʃ|ŋ(ə)l,
pəˈzɪʃən(ə)l
AM pəˈzɪʃ(ə)nəl

positionally
BR pəˈzɪʃŋəli,
pəˈzɪʃŋļi, pəˈzɪʃənļi,
pəˈzɪʃ(ə)nəli
AM pəˈzɪʃ(ə)nəli

positioner
BR pəˈzɪʃŋə(r),
pəˈzɪʃ(ə)nə(r), -z
AM pəˈzɪʃ(ə)nər, -z

positive
BR ˈpɒzɪtɪv, -z
AM ˈpɑzədɪv, ˈpɑztɪv, -z

positively
BR ˈpɒzɪtɪvli
AM ˈpɑzədɪvli,
ˈpɑztɪvli

positiveness
BR ˈpɒzɪtɪvnɪs
AM ˈpɑzədɪvnɪs,
ˈpɑztɪvnɪs

positivism
BR ˈpɒzɪtɪvɪz(ə)m
AM ˈpɑzədɪ,vɪzəm

positivist
BR ˈpɒzɪtɪvɪst, -s
AM ˈpɑzədɪ,vɪst, -s

positivistic
BR ,pɒzɪtɪˈvɪstɪk
AM ,pɑzədəˈvɪstɪk

positivistically
BR ,pɒzɪtɪˈvɪstɪkli
AM ,pɑzədəˈvɪstɪk(ə)li

positivity
BR ,pɒzɪˈtɪvɪti
AM ,pɑzəˈtɪvɪdi

positron
BR ˈpɒzɪtrɒn, -z
AM ˈpɑzə,trɑn, -z

positronic
BR ˌpɒzɪ'trɒnɪk
AM ˌpɑzə'trɑnɪk

positronium
BR ˌpɒzɪ'trəʊnɪəm, -z
AM ˌpɑzə'trooniəm, -z

posological
BR ˌpɒsə'lɒdʒɪkl
AM ˌpɑzə'lɑdʒəkəl

posology
BR pə(ʊ)'sɒlədʒi
AM pə'zɑlədʒi

poss.
BR pɒs
AM pɑs

posse
BR 'pɒs|i, -ɪz
AM 'pɑsi, -z

posse comitatus
BR ˌpɒsɪ ˌkɒmɪ'tɑːtəs, -ɪz
AM ˌpɑsi ˌkɑmə'tɑdəs, -əz

possess
BR pə'zes, -ɪz, -ɪŋ, -t
AM pə'zes, -əz, -ɪŋ, -t

possession
BR pə'zeʃn, -z
AM pə'zeʃən, -z

possessionless
BR pə'zeʃnləs
AM pə'zeʃənləs

possessive
BR pə'zesɪv
AM pə'zesɪv

possessively
BR pə'zesɪvli
AM pə'zesɪvli

possessiveness
BR pə'zesɪvnɪs
AM pə'zesɪvnɪs

possessor
BR pə'zesə(r), -z
AM pə'zesər, -z

possessory
BR pə'zes(ə)ri
AM pə'zesəri

posset
BR 'pɒs|ɪt, -ɪts, -ɪtɪŋ, -ɪtɪd
AM 'pɑsə|t, -ts, -dɪŋ, -dəd

possibility
BR ˌpɒsɪ'bɪlɪt|i, -ɪz
AM ˌpɑsə'bɪlɪdi, -z

possible
BR 'pɒsɪbl
AM 'pɑsəbəl

possibly
BR 'pɒsɪbli
AM 'pɑsəbli

possum
BR 'pɒsəm, -z
AM 'pɑsəm, -z

post
BR pəʊst, -s, -ɪŋ, -ɪd
AM poʊst, -s, -ɪŋ, -əd

postage
BR 'pəʊstɪdʒ
AM 'poʊstɪdʒ

postal
BR 'pəʊstl
AM 'poʊstəl

postally
BR 'pəʊstl̩i, 'pəʊstəli
AM 'poʊstəli

postbag
BR 'pəʊs(t)bag, -z
AM 'poʊs(t)bæg, -z

postbox
BR 'pəʊs(t)bɒks, -ɪz
AM 'poʊs(t)bɑks, -əz

postbus
BR 'pəʊs(t)bʌs, -ɪz
AM 'poʊs(t)bəs, -əz

postcard
BR 'pəʊs(t)kɑːd, -z
AM 'poʊs(t)kɑrd, -z

post-chaise
BR 'pəʊs(t)ʃeɪz, -ɪz
AM 'poʊs(t)ʃeɪz, -ɪz

postcode
BR 'pəʊs(t)kəʊd, -z
AM 'poʊs(t)koʊd, -z

postdate
BR ˌpəʊs(t)'deɪt, -s, -ɪŋ, -ɪd
AM ˌpoʊs(t)'deɪ|t, -ts, -dɪŋ, -dɪd

postdoc
BR 'pəʊs(t)dɒk, -s
AM 'poʊs(t)dɑk, -s

postdoctoral
BR ˌpəʊs(t)'dɒkt(ə)rəl, ˌpəʊs(t)'dɒkt(ə)r]
AM ˌpoʊs(t)'dɑkt(ə)rəl

poster
BR 'pəʊstə(r), -z
AM 'poʊstər, -z

poste restante
BR ˌpəʊst 'restɒnt
AM ˌpoʊs(t),rɛ'stɑnt

posterior
BR pɒ'stɪərɪə(r), -z
AM pɑ'stɪriər, poʊ'stɪriər, -z

posteriority
BR pɒˌstɪərɪ'ɒrɪti
AM pɑˌstɪri'ɔrədi

posteriorly
BR pɒ'stɪərɪəli
AM pɑ'stɪriərli, poʊ'stɪriərli

posterity
BR pɒ'sterɪti
AM pɑ'sterədi

postern
BR 'pɒst(ə)n, 'pəʊst(ə)n, -z
AM 'poʊstərn, 'pɑstərn, -z

postface
BR 'pəʊs(t)feɪs, -ɪz
AM 'poʊs(t),feɪs, -ɪz

postfix
BR ˌpəʊs(t)'fɪks, -ɪz, -ɪŋ, -t
AM ˌpoʊs(t)'fɪks, -ɪz, -ɪŋ, -t

Postgate
BR 'pəʊs(t)geɪt
AM 'poʊs(t),geɪt

postglacial
BR ˌpəʊs(t)'gleɪʃl, ˌpəʊs(t)'gleɪsɪəl
AM ˌpoʊs(t)'gleɪʃəl

postgrad
BR ˌpəʊs(t)'grad, -z
AM ˌpoʊs(t)'græd, -z

postgraduate
BR ˌpəʊs(t)'gradʒʊət, ˌpəʊs(t)'gradjʊət, -s
AM ˌpoʊs(t)'grædʒəwət, -s

posthaste
BR ˌpəʊst'heɪst
AM ˌpoʊs(t)'heɪst

post hoc
BR ˌpəʊst 'hɒk
AM ˌpoʊs(t) 'hɑk

posthole
BR 'pəʊsthəʊl, -z
AM 'poʊs(t),(h)oʊl, -z

posthorn
BR 'pəʊsthɔːn, -z
AM 'poʊs(t),(h)ɔ(ə)rn, -z

posthumous
BR 'pɒstʃʊməs, 'pɒstjʊməs
AM 'pɑstʃəməs, pɑ'st(j)uməs

posthumously
BR 'pɒstʃʊməsli, 'pɒstjʊməsli
AM 'pɑstʃəməsli, pɑ'st(j)uməsli

postiche
BR pɒ'stiːʃ, -ɪz
AM pɑ'stiʃ, 'pɑ,stiʃ, -ɪz

postie
BR 'pəʊst|i, -ɪz
AM 'poʊsti, -z

postil
BR 'pɒstɪl, -z
AM 'pɑstl, -z

postilion
BR pɒ'stɪlɪən, pə'stɪlɪən, -z
AM pɑ'stɪljən, poʊ'stɪljən, -z

postillion
BR pɒ'stɪlɪən, pə'stɪlɪən, -z
AM pɑ'stɪljən, poʊ'stɪljən, -z

posting
BR 'pəʊstɪŋ, -z
AM 'poʊstɪŋ, -z

Postlethwaite
BR 'pɒslθweɪt
AM 'pɑsəl,weɪt

postliminy
BR ˌpəʊs(t)'lɪmɪn|i, -ɪz
AM ˌpoʊs(t)'lɪmɪni, -z

postlude
BR 'pəʊs(t)luːd, -z
AM 'poʊs(t),lud, -z

postman
BR 'pəʊs(t)mən
AM 'poʊs(t)mən

postman's knock
BR ˌpəʊs(t)mənz 'nɒk
AM ˌpoʊs(t)mənz 'nak

postmark
BR 'pəʊs(t)mɑːk, -s, -ɪŋ, -t
AM 'poʊs(t),mark, -s, -ɪŋ, -t

postmaster
BR 'pəʊs(t)mɑːstə(r), 'pəʊs(t),mastə(r), -z
AM 'poʊs(t),mæstər, -z

postmen
BR 'pəʊs(t)mən
AM 'poʊs(t)mən

post meridian
BR ˌpəʊs(t) mɪ'rɪdɪən
AM ˌpoʊs(t) mə'rɪdiən

post meridiem
BR pəʊs(t) mɪ'rɪdɪəm
AM ˌpoʊs(t) mə'rɪdiəm

postmistress
BR 'pəʊs(t),mɪstrɪs, -ɪz
AM 'poʊs(t),mɪstrɪs, -ɪz

postmodern
BR ˌpəʊs(t)'mɒd(ə)n
AM ˌpoʊs(t)'madərn

postmodernism
BR ˌpəʊs(t)'mɒdnɪz(ə)m, ˌpəʊs(t)'mɒdənɪz(ə)m
AM ˌpoʊs(t)'madərn,ɪzəm

postmodernist
BR ˌpəʊs(t)'mɒdnɪst, ˌpəʊs(t)'mɒdənɪst, -s
AM ˌpoʊs(t)'madərnəst, -s

postmodernity
BR ˌpəʊs(t)məˈdəːnɪti, ˌpəʊs(t)mʊˈdəːnɪti
AM ˌpoʊs(t)məˈdərnədi, ˌpoʊs(t)moʊˈdərnədi, ˌpoʊs(t)mɑˈdɜrnədi, ˌpoʊs(t)məˈdɜrnədi

postmortem
BR ˌpəʊs(t)'mɔːtəm, -z
AM ˌpoʊs(t)'mɔrtəm, -z

postop
BR ˌpəʊst'ɒp
AM ˌpoʊs,tɑp

postoperative
BR ˌpəʊst'ɒp(ə)rətɪv
AM ˌpoʊs'tɑpərədɪv

postpaid
BR ˌpəʊs(t)'peɪd
AM ˌpoʊs(t)'peɪd

post-partum
BR ˌpəʊs(t)'pɑːtəm
AM ˌpoʊs(t)'pɑrdəm

postponable
BR pəˈspəʊnəbl,
ˌpəʊs(t)ˈpəʊnəbl
AM ˌpoʊs(t)ˈpoʊnəbəl,
pəˈspoʊnəbəl

postpone
BR pəˈspəʊn,
ˌpəʊs(t)ˈpəʊn, -z, -ɪŋ,
-d
AM ˌpoʊs(t)ˈpoʊn,
pəˈspoʊn, -z, -ɪŋ, -d

postponement
BR pəˈspəʊnm(ə)nt,
ˌpəʊs(t)ˈpəʊnm(ə)nt,
-s
AM ˌpoʊs(t)ˈpoʊnmənt,
pəˈspoʊnmənt, -s

postponer
BR pəˈspəʊnə(r),
ˌpəʊs(t)ˈpəʊnə(r), -z
AM ˌpoʊs(t)ˈpoʊnər,
pəˈspoʊnər, -z

postposition
BR ˌpəʊs(t)pəˈzɪʃn, -z
AM ˌpoʊs(t)pəˈzɪʃən, -z

postpositional
BR ˌpəʊs(t)pəˈzɪʃn(ə)l,
ˌpəʊs(t)pəˈzɪʃən(ə)l
AM ˌpoʊs(t)pəˈzɪʃ(ə)nəl

postpositive
BR ˌpəʊs(t)ˈpɒzɪtɪv
AM ˌpoʊs(t)ˈpɑzədɪv

postpositively
BR ˌpəʊs(t)ˈpɒzɪtɪvli
AM ˌpoʊs(t)ˈpɑzədɪvli

postprandial
BR ˌpəʊs(t)ˈprandɪəl
AM ˌpoʊs(t)ˈprændɪəl

post room
BR ˈpəʊst ruːm, + rʊm,
-z
AM ˈpoʊs(t) ˌrum,
+ ˌrʊm, -z

postscript
BR ˈpəʊs(t)skrɪpt, -s
AM ˈpoʊs(t)ˌskrɪpt, -s

postulant
BR ˈpɒstjʊlənt,
ˈpɒstjəlnt,
ˈpɒstʃʊlənt,
ˈpɒstʃʊlnt, -s
AM ˈpɑstʃələnt, -s

postulate[1]
noun
BR ˈpɒstjʊlət,
ˈpɒstʃʊlət, -s
AM ˈpɑstʃələt, -s

postulate[2]
verb
BR ˈpɒstjʊleɪt,
ˈpɒstʃʊleɪt, -s, -ɪŋ, -ɪd
AM ˈpɑstʃəˌleɪ|t, -ts,
-dɪŋ, -dɪd

postulation
BR ˌpɒstjʊˈleɪʃn,
ˌpɒstʃʊˈleɪʃn, -z
AM ˌpɑstʃəˈleɪʃən, -z

postulator
BR ˈpɒstjʊleɪtə(r),
ˈpɒstʃʊleɪtə(r), -z
AM ˈpɑstʃəˌleɪdər, -z

postural
BR ˈpɒstʃʊrəl,
ˈpɒstʃʊr|
AM ˈpɑstʃərəl

posture
BR ˈpɒstʃ|ə(r), -əz,
-(ə)rɪŋ, -əd
AM ˈpɑstʃər, -z, -ɪŋ, -d

posturer
BR ˈpɒstʃ(ə)rə(r), -z
AM ˈpɑstʃərər, -z

posturing
BR ˈpɒstʃ(ə)rɪŋ, -z
AM ˈpɑstʃərɪŋ, -z

postvocalic
BR ˌpəʊs(t)vəˈkalɪk
AM ˌpoʊs(t)voʊˈkælɪk

postwar
BR ˌpəʊs(t)ˈwɔː(r)
AM ˌpoʊs(t)ˈwɔ(ə)r

postwoman
BR ˈpəʊs(t)ˌwʊmən
AM ˈpoʊs(t)ˌwʊmən

postwomen
BR ˈpəʊs(t)ˌwɪmɪn
AM ˈpoʊs(t)ˌwɪmɪn

posy
BR ˈpəʊz|i, -ɪz
AM ˈpoʊzi, -z

pot
BR pɒt, -s, -ɪŋ, -ɪd
AM pɑ|t, -ts, -dɪŋ, -dəd

potability
BR ˌpəʊtəˈbɪlɪti
AM ˌpoʊdəˈbɪlɪdi

potable
BR ˈpəʊtəbl
AM ˈpoʊdəbəl

potableness
BR ˈpəʊtəblnəs
AM ˈpoʊdəbəlnəs

potage
BR pɒˈtɑːʒ, ˈpɒtɑːʒ, -ɪz
AM poʊˈtɑʒ, -əz

potager
BR ˈpɒtədʒə(r), -z
AM poʊˈtɑʒər, -z

potamic
BR pəˈtamɪk, pɒˈtamɪk
AM pəˈtæmɪk

potamology
BR ˌpɒtəˈmɒlədʒi
AM ˌpɑdəˈmɑlədʒi

potash
BR ˈpɒtaʃ
AM ˈpɑdˌæʃ

potassic
BR pəˈtasɪk
AM pəˈtæsɪk

potassium
BR pəˈtasɪəm
AM pəˈtæsiəm,
poʊˈtæsiəm

potation
BR pə(ʊ)ˈteɪʃn, -z
AM poʊˈteɪʃən, -z

potato
BR pəˈteɪtəʊ, -z
AM pəˈteɪdoʊ, -z

potatory
BR ˈpəʊtət(ə)ri
AM ˈpoʊdəˌtɔri

pot-au-feu
BR ˌpɒtɔːˈfə:(r), -z
AM ˌpɒdˌoʊˈfə, -z

potbelly
BR ˈpɒtˌbɛl|i, ˌpɒtˈbɛl|i,
-ɪz
AM ˈpɑtˌbɛli, -z

potboiler
BR ˈpɒtˌbɔɪlə(r), -z
AM ˈpɑtˌbɔɪlər, -z

potbound
BR ˈpɒtbaʊnd
AM ˈpɑtˌbaʊnd

potch
BR pɒtʃ, -ɪz
AM pɑtʃ, -əz

poteen
BR pɒˈt(ʃ)iːn,
pəˈt(ʃ)iːn
AM pɑˈtin, poʊˈtin

Potemkin
BR pəˈtɛmkɪn
AM pəˈtɛm(p)kən

potence
BR ˈpəʊtns
AM ˈpoʊtns

potency
BR ˈpəʊtnsi
AM ˈpoʊtnsi

potent
BR ˈpəʊtnt
AM ˈpoʊtnt

potentate
BR ˈpəʊtnteɪt, -s
AM ˈpoʊtnˌteɪt, -s

potential
BR pəˈtɛnʃl, -z
AM pəˈtɛn(t)ʃəl, -z

potentiality
BR pəˌtɛnʃɪˈalɪt|i, -ɪz
AM pəˌtɛn(t)ʃiˈælədi,
-z

potentially
BR pəˈtɛnʃli,
pəˈtɛnʃəli
AM pəˈtɛn(t)ʃəli

potentiate
BR pəˈtɛnʃieɪt, -s, -ɪŋ,
-ɪd
AM pəˈtɛn(t)ʃieɪ|t, -ts,
-dɪŋ, -dɪd

potentilla
BR ˌpəʊt(ə)nˈtɪlə(r), -z
AM ˌpoʊtnˈtɪlə, -z

potentiometer
BR pəˌtɛnʃɪˈɒmɪtə(r),
-z
AM pəˌtɛn(t)ʃiˈɑmədər,
-z

potentiometric
BR pəˌtɛnʃɪəˈmɛtrɪk
AM pəˌtɛn(t)ʃiəˈmɛtrɪk

potentiometry
BR pəˌtɛnʃɪˈɒmɪtri
AM pəˌtɛn(t)ʃiˈɑmətri

potentisation
BR ˌpəʊtntʌɪˈzeɪʃn
AM ˌpoʊtn(t)əˈzeɪʃən,
ˌpoʊtn,(t)aɪˈzeɪʃən

potentise
BR ˈpəʊtntʌɪz, -ɪz, -ɪŋ,
-d
AM ˈpoʊtnˌtaɪz, -ɪz, -ɪŋ,
-d

potentization
BR ˌpəʊtntʌɪˈzeɪʃn
AM ˌpoʊtn(t)əˈzeɪʃən,
ˌpoʊtn,(t)aɪˈzeɪʃən

potentize
BR ˈpəʊtntʌɪz, -ɪz, -ɪŋ,
-d
AM ˈpoʊtnˌtaɪz, -ɪz, -ɪŋ,
-d

potently
BR ˈpəʊtntli
AM ˈpoʊtn(t)li

potful
BR ˈpɒtfʊl, -z
AM ˈpɑtˌfʊl, -z

pothead
BR ˈpɒthɛd, -z
AM ˈpɑt,(h)ɛd, -z

potheen
BR pɒˈt(ʃ)iːn,
pəˈt(ʃ)iːn
AM pɑˈtin, poʊˈtin

pother
BR ˈpɒð|ə(r), -əz,
-(ə)rɪŋ, -əd
AM ˈpɑðər, -z, -ɪŋ, -d

potherb
BR ˈpɒthəːb, -z
AM ˈpɑt,(h)ərb, -z

pothole
BR ˈpɒthəʊl, -z, -ɪŋ, -d
AM ˈpɑt,(h)oʊl, -z, -ɪŋ,
-d

potholer
BR ˈpɒthəʊlə(r), -z
AM ˈpɑt,(h)oʊlər, -z

pothook
BR ˈpɒthʊk, -s
AM ˈpɑt,(h)ʊk, -s

pothouse
BR ˈpɒthaʊ|s, -zɪz
AM ˈpɑt,(h)aʊ|s, -zəz

potiche
BR pɒˈtiːʃ, pəˈtiːʃ, -ɪz
AM poʊˈtiʃ, -ɪz

potion
BR ˈpəʊʃn, -z
AM ˈpoʊʃən, -z

Potiphar
BR ˈpɒtɪfə(r),
ˈpɒtɪfɑː(r)
AM ˈpɑdəfər

potlatch
BR ˈpɒtlatʃ, -ɪz
AM ˈpɑtˌlætʃ, -əz

potlatching
BR ˈpɒtˌlatʃɪŋ
AM ˈpɑtˌlætʃɪŋ

Potomac
BR pəˈtəʊmak
AM pəˈtoʊmək

potoroo
BR ˌpəʊtəˈruː,
ˌpɒtəˈruː, -z
AM ˌpoʊdəˈru, -z

potpie
BR ˈpɒtpʌɪ
AM ˈpɑtˌpaɪ

potpourri
BR ˌpəʊˈpʊriː,
ˌpəʊpəˈriː, -z
AM ˌpoʊpəˈri, -z

potrero
BR pəˈtrɛːrəʊ, -z
AM pəˈtrɛˌroʊ, -z

Potsdam
BR ˈpɒtsdam
AM ˈpɑtsˌdæm

potsherd
BR ˈpɒt-ʃəːd, -z
AM ˈpɑtˌʃərd, -z

potshot
BR ˈpɒt-ʃɒt, -s
AM ˈpɑtˌʃɑt, -s

potstone
BR ˈpɒtstəʊn
AM ˈpɑtˌstoʊn

pottage
BR ˈpɒtɪdʒ
AM ˈpɑdɪdʒ

potter
BR ˈpɒt|ə(r), -əz,
-(ə)rɪŋ, -əd
AM ˈpɑdər, -z, -ɪŋ, -d

potterer
BR ˈpɒt(ə)rə(r), -z
AM ˈpɑdərər, -z

Potteries
BR ˈpɒt(ə)rɪz
AM ˈpɑdəriz

pottery
BR ˈpɒt(ə)r|i, -ɪz
AM ˈpɑdəri, -z

pottiness
BR ˈpɒtɪnɪs
AM ˈpɑdinɪs

pottle
BR ˈpɒtl, -z
AM ˈpɑdəl, -z

potto
BR ˈpɒtəʊ, -z
AM ˈpɑˌdoʊ, -z

Potts
BR pɒts
AM pɑts

potty
BR ˈpɒt|i, -ɪz, -ɪə(r), -ɪɪst
AM ˈpɑdi, -z, -ər, -ɪst

pouch
BR paʊtʃ, -ɪz, -ɪŋ, -t
AM paʊtʃ, -əz, -ɪŋ, -t

pouchy
BR ˈpaʊtʃ|i, -ɪə(r), -ɪɪst
AM ˈpaʊtʃi, -ər, -ɪst

pouf¹
homosexual
BR pʊf, puːf, -s
AM puf, -s

pouf²
seat, hair
BR puːf, -s
AM puf, -s

pouffe¹
homosexual
BR pʊf, puːf, -s
AM puf, -s

pouffe²
seat, hair
BR puːf, -s
AM puf, -s

Poughkeepsie
BR pəˈkɪpsi
AM pəˈkɪpsi

poulard
BR puːˈlɑːd, -z
AM puˈlɑrd, -z

Poulenc
BR ˈpuːlaŋk
AM puˈlɛŋk

Poulson
BR ˈpəʊls(ə)n
AM ˈpɒlsən, ˈpoʊlsən

poult¹
chicken
BR pəʊlt, -s
AM poʊlt, -s

poult²
fabric
BR puːlt, pʊlt
AM puːlt)

poult-de-soie
BR ˌpuːdəˈswɑː(r)
AM ˌpudəˈswɑ

Poulteney
BR ˈpəʊltni
AM ˈpoʊltni

Poulter
BR ˈpəʊltə(r)
AM ˈpoʊltər

poulterer
BR ˈpəʊlt(ə)rə(r), -z
AM ˈpoʊltərər, -z

poultice
BR ˈpəʊltɪs, -ɪz
AM ˈpoʊltəs, -ɪz

Poultney
BR ˈpəʊltni
AM ˈpoʊltni

Poulton
BR ˈpəʊlt(ə)n
AM ˈpoʊltən

poultry
BR ˈpəʊltri
AM ˈpoʊltri

poultryman
BR ˈpəʊltrɪmən
AM ˈpoʊltrimən

poultrymen
BR ˈpəʊltrɪmən
AM ˈpoʊltrimən

pounce
BR paʊns, -ɪz, -ɪŋ, -t
AM paʊns, -əz, -ɪŋ, -t

pouncer
BR ˈpaʊnsə(r), -z
AM ˈpaʊnsər, -z

pouncet-box
BR ˈpaʊnsɪtbɒks, -ɪz
AM ˈpaʊnsətˌbɑks, -əz

pound
BR paʊnd, -z, -ɪŋ, -ɪd
AM paʊnd, -z, -ɪŋ, -əd

poundage
BR ˈpaʊnd|ɪdʒ, -ɪdʒɪz
AM ˈpaʊndɪdʒ, -ɪz

poundal
BR ˈpaʊndl, -z
AM ˈpaʊndəl, -z

pounder
BR ˈpaʊndə(r), -z
AM ˈpaʊndər, -z

Pountney
BR ˈpaʊntni
AM ˈpoʊn(t)ni

pour
BR pɔː(r), -z, -ɪŋ, -d
AM pɔ(r)r, -z, -ɪŋ, -d

pourable
BR ˈpɔːrəbl
AM ˈpɔrəbəl

pourboire
BR ˈpʊəbwɑː(r),
ˈpɔːbwɑː(r), -z
AM pʊrˈbwɑr, -z

pourer
BR ˈpɔːrə(r), -z
AM ˈpɔrər, -z

pourparler
BR ˌpʊəˈpɑːleɪ,
ˌpɔːˈpɑːleɪ, -z
AM ˌpʊrˌpɑrˈleɪ, -z

pousada
BR pəˈ(ʊ)ˈsɑːdə(r), -z
AM poʊˈsɑdə, -z

poussette
BR puːˈset, -s, -ɪŋ, -ɪd
AM puˈse|t, -ts, -dɪŋ, -dɪd

Poussin
BR ˈpuːsan, ˈpuːsã
AM puˈsɛn

pout
BR paʊt, -s, -ɪŋ, -ɪd
AM paʊ|t, -ts, -dɪŋ, -dəd

pouter
BR ˈpaʊtə(r), -z
AM ˈpaʊdər, -z

poutingly
BR ˈpaʊtɪŋli
AM ˈpaʊdɪŋli

pouty
BR ˈpaʊt|i, -ɪə(r), -ɪɪst
AM ˈpaʊdi, -ər, -ɪst

poverty
BR ˈpɒvəti
AM ˈpɑvərdi

Povey
BR ˈpəʊvi
AM ˈpoʊvi

pow!
BR paʊ
AM paʊ

powan
BR ˈpəʊən, -z
AM ˈpoʊən, -z

powder
BR ˈpaʊd|ə(r), -əz,
-(ə)rɪŋ, -əd
AM ˈpaʊdər, -z, -ɪŋ, -d

powderiness
BR ˈpaʊd(ə)rɪnɪs
AM ˈpaʊdərinɪs

powderpuff
BR ˈpaʊdəpʌf, -s
AM ˈpaʊdərˌpəf, -s

powdery
BR ˈpaʊd(ə)ri
AM ˈpaʊdəri

Powell
BR ˈpaʊ(ə)l, ˈpəʊ(ə)l
AM ˈpaʊəl

power
BR ˈpaʊə(r), -z, -ɪŋ, -d
AM ˈpaʊ(ə)r, -z, -ɪŋ, -d

powerboat
BR ˈpaʊəbəʊt, -s
AM ˈpaʊ(ə)rˌboʊt, -s

powerful
BR ˈpaʊəf(ʊ)l
AM ˈpaʊ(ə)rfəl

powerfully
BR ˈpaʊəfʊli, ˈpaʊəfḷi
AM ˈpaʊ(ə)rfəli

powerfulness
BR ˈpaʊəf(ʊ)lnəs
AM ˈpaʊ(ə)rfəlnəs

powerhouse
BR ˈpaʊəhaʊ|s, -zɪz
AM ˈpaʊ(ə)rˌ(h)aʊ|s, -zəz

powerless
BR ˈpaʊələs
AM ˈpaʊ(ə)rləs

powerlessly
BR ˈpaʊələsli
AM ˈpaʊ(ə)rləsli

powerlessness
BR ˈpaʊələsnəs
AM ˈpaʊ(ə)rləsnəs

powerpack
BR ˈpaʊəpak, -s
AM ˈpaʊ(ə)rˌpæk, -s

powerpoint
BR ˈpaʊəpɔɪnt, -s
AM ˈpaʊ(ə)rˌpɔɪnt, -s

Powers
BR ˈpaʊəz

AM ˈpaʊərz
Powhatan
BR paʊˈhatn,
ˈpaʊəˌtan
AM paʊˈhætn
Powis
BR ˈpaʊɪs, ˈpaʊɪs
AM ˈpaʊɪs, ˈpoʊəs
powwow
BR ˈpaʊwaʊ, -z
AM ˈpaʊˌwaʊ, -z
Powys¹
surname
BR ˈpaʊɪs, ˈpaʊɪs
AM ˈpoʊəs
WE ˈpoʊɪs
Powys²
Welsh county
BR ˈpaʊɪs
AM ˈpaʊɪs
WE ˈpoʊɪs
pox
BR pɒks
AM pɑks
poxy
BR ˈpɒks|i, -ɪə(r), -ɪɪst
AM ˈpɑksi, -ər, -ɪst
Poznań
BR ˈpɒznan
AM ˈpɑznæn,
ˈpoʊznæn
POL ˈpɒznanʲ
pozzolana
BR ˌpɒtsəˈlɑːnə(r)
AM ˌpɑtʃəˈlɑnə
praam
BR pram, prɑːm, -z
AM præm, -z
practicability
BR ˌpraktɪkəˈbɪlɪti
AM ˌpræktəkəˈbɪlɪdi
practicable
BR ˈpraktɪkəbl
AM ˈpræktəkəbəl
practicableness
BR ˈpraktɪkəblnəs
AM ˈpræktəkəbəlnəs
practicably
BR ˈpraktɪkəbli
AM ˈpræktəkəbli
practical
BR ˈpraktɪkl
AM ˈpræktəkəl
practicality
BR ˌpraktɪˈkalɪt|i, -ɪz
AM ˌpræktəˈkælədi, -z
practically¹
almost
BR ˈpraktɪkli
AM ˈpræktək(ə)li
practically²
in a practical way
BR ˈpraktɪk(ə)li,
ˈpraktɪkl̩i
AM ˈpræktək(ə)li
practicalness
BR ˈpraktɪklnəs
AM ˈpræktəkəlnəs

practice
BR ˈprakt|ɪs, -ɪsɪz
AM ˈpræktəs, -əz
practicer
BR ˈpraktɪsə(r), -z
AM ˈpræktəsər, -z
practicum
BR ˈpraktɪkəm, -z
AM ˈpræktəkəm, -z
practise
BR ˈprakt|ɪs, -ɪsɪz,
-ɪsɪŋ, -ɪst
AM ˈpræktəs, -əz, -ɪŋ, -t
practiser
BR ˈpraktɪsə(r), -z
AM ˈpræktəsər, -z
practitioner
BR prakˈtɪʃnə(r),
prakˈtɪʃ(ə)nə(r), -z
AM prækˈtɪʃ(ə)nər, -z
prad
BR prad, -z
AM præd, -z
Prado
BR ˈprɑːdəʊ
AM ˈprɑˌdoʊ
praecipe
BR ˈpriːsɪp|i, -ɪz
AM ˈprisəpi, -z
praecocial
BR prɪˈkəʊʃl
AM priˈkoʊʃəl
praecox
BR ˈpriːkɒks
AM ˈpriˌkɑks
praedial
BR ˈpriːdɪəl
AM ˈpridiəl
praemunire
BR ˌpriːmjuːˈnɪəri,
ˌpriːmjəˈnɪəri
AM ˌprimjəˈnaɪri
praenomen
BR ˌpriːˈnəʊmɛn,
ˌpriːˈnəʊmən, -z
AM priˈnoʊmən, -z
praepostor
BR ˌpriːˈpɒstə(r), -z
AM priˈpɑstər, -z
praesidia
BR prɪˈsɪdɪə(r),
prɪˈzɪdɪə(r),
prʌɪˈsɪdɪə(r),
prʌɪˈzɪdɪə(r)
AM prəˈsɪdiə, prəˈzɪdiə
Praesidium
BR prɪˈsɪdɪəm,
prɪˈzɪdɪəm,
prʌɪˈsɪdɪəm,
prʌɪˈzɪdɪəm, -z
AM prəˈsɪdiəm,
prəˈzɪdiəm, -z
praetor
BR ˈpriːtə(r),
ˈpriːtɔː(r), -z
AM ˈpridər, -z

praetoria
BR prɪˈtɔːrɪə(r),
priːˈtɔːrɪə(r),
prʌɪˈtɔːrɪə(r)
AM prəˈtɔriə
praetorian
BR prɪˈtɔːrɪən,
priːˈtɔːrɪən,
prʌɪˈtɔːrɪən
AM prəˈtɔriən
praetorium
BR prɪˈtɔːrɪəm,
priːˈtɔːrɪəm,
prʌɪˈtɔːrɪəm, -z
AM prəˈtɔriəm, -z
praetorship
BR ˈpriːtəʃ|ɪp,
ˈpriːtɔːʃ|ɪp, -s
AM ˈpridərˌʃɪp, -s
pragmatic
BR praɡˈmatɪk, -s
AM præɡˈmædɪk, -s
pragmatical
BR praɡˈmatɪkl
AM præɡˈmædəkəl
pragmaticality
BR praɡˌmatɪˈkalɪti
AM præɡˌmædəˈkælədi
pragmatically
BR praɡˈmatɪkli
AM præɡˈmædək(ə)li
pragmatise
BR ˈpraɡmətʌɪz, -ɪz,
-ɪŋ, -d
AM ˈpræɡməˌtaɪz, -ɪz,
-ɪŋ, -d
pragmatism
BR ˈpraɡmətɪz(ə)m
AM ˈpræɡməˌtɪzəm
pragmatist
BR ˈpraɡmətɪst, -s
AM ˈpræɡmədəst, -s
pragmatistic
BR ˌpraɡməˈtɪstɪk
AM ˌpræɡməˈtɪstɪk
pragmatize
BR ˈpraɡmətʌɪz, -ɪz,
-ɪŋ, -d
AM ˈpræɡməˌtaɪz, -ɪz,
-ɪŋ, -d
Prague
BR prɑːɡ
AM prɑɡ
Praha
BR ˈprɑːhɑː(r)
AM ˈprɑˌhɑ
CZ ˈprʌhʌ
prahu
BR ˈprɑːhuː, -z
AM ˈprɑˌhu, -z
Praia
BR ˈprʌɪə(r)
AM ˈpraɪə
prairie
BR ˈprɛːr|i, -ɪz
AM ˈpreri, -z
praise
BR preɪz, -ɪz, -ɪŋ, -d

AM preɪz, -ɪz, -ɪŋ, -d
praiseful
BR ˈpreɪzf(ʊ)l
AM ˈpreɪzfəl
praiser
BR ˈpreɪzə(r), -z
AM ˈpreɪzər, -z
praiseworthily
BR ˈpreɪzˌwəːðɪli
AM ˈpreɪzˌwərðəli
praiseworthiness
BR ˈpreɪzˌwəːðɪnɪs
AM ˈpreɪzˌwərðɪnɪs
praiseworthy
BR ˈpreɪzˌwəːði
AM ˈpreɪzˌwərði
Prakrit
BR ˈprɑːkrɪt, -s
AM ˈprɑˌkrɪt, -s
praline
BR ˈprɑːliːn, ˈpreɪliːn,
-z
AM ˈpreɪˌlin, -z
pralltriller
BR ˈprɑːlˌtrɪlə(r), -z
AM ˈprɑlˌtrɪlər, -z
pram
BR pram, -z
AM præm, -z
prana
BR ˈprɑːnə(r)
AM ˈprɑnə
pranayama
BR ˌprɑːnʌˈjɑːmə(r),
ˌprɑːnəˈjɑːmə(r)
AM ˌprɑnəˈjɑmə
prance
BR prɑːns, prans, -ɪz,
-ɪŋ, -t
AM præns, -əz, -ɪŋ, -t
prancer
BR ˈprɑːnsə(r),
ˈpransə(r), -z
AM ˈprænsər, -z
prandial
BR ˈprandɪəl
AM ˈprændiəl
Prandtl
BR ˈprantl
AM ˈprændl
prang
BR praŋ, -z, -ɪŋ, -d
AM præŋ, -z, -ɪŋ, -d
prank
BR praŋk, -s
AM præŋk, -s
prankful
BR ˈpraŋkf(ʊ)l
AM ˈpræŋkfəl
prankish
BR ˈpraŋkɪʃ
AM ˈpræŋkɪʃ
pranksome
BR ˈpraŋks(ə)m
AM ˈpræŋksəm
prankster
BR ˈpraŋkstə(r), -z

prase
BR preɪz
AM preɪz

praseodymium
BR ˌpreɪzɪə(ʊ)'dɪmiəm
AM ˌpreɪziou'dɪmiəm

prat
BR prat, -s
AM præt, -s

prate
BR preɪt, -s, -ɪŋ, -ɪd
AM preɪ|t, -ts, -dɪŋ, -dɪd

prater
BR 'preɪtə(r), -z
AM 'preɪdər, -z

pratfall
BR 'pratfɔːl, -z
AM 'præt,fɔl, 'præt,fɑl, -z

pratie
BR 'preɪt|i, -ɪz
AM 'preɪdi, -z

pratincole
BR 'pratɪŋkəʊl, -z
AM 'prætn,koʊl, 'prædɪŋ,koʊl, -z

pratique
BR pra'tiːk, -s
AM præ'tik, prə'tik, -s

Pratt
BR prat
AM præt

prattle
BR 'prat|l, -lz, -|ɪŋ \-l-ɪŋ, -ld
AM 'prædəl, -z, -ɪŋ, -d

prattler
BR 'pratlə(r), 'pratlə(r), -z
AM 'prædlər, -z

prau
BR prɑːuː, -z
AM prɑʊ, -z

Pravda
BR 'prɑːvdə(r)
AM 'prɑvdə

prawn
BR prɔːn, -z
AM prɔn, prɑn, -z

praxes
BR 'praksiːz
AM 'præk,siz

praxis
BR 'praksɪs
AM 'præksəs

Praxiteles
BR prak'sɪtɪliːz, prak'sɪt|iːz
AM ˌpræk'sɪdə,liz

pray
BR preɪ, -z, -ɪŋ, -d
AM preɪ, -z, -ɪŋ, -d

prayer¹
person praying
BR 'preɪə(r), -z
AM 'preɪər, -z

prayer²
what is said to God
BR prɛː(r), -z
AM prɛ(ə)r, -z

prayerbook
BR 'prɛːbʊk, -s
AM 'prɛr,bʊk, -s

prayerful
BR 'prɛː f(ʊ)l
AM 'prɛrfəl

prayerfully
BR 'prɛːfəli, 'prɛːf|i
AM 'prɛrfəli

prayerfulness
BR 'prɛːf(ʊ)lnəs
AM 'prɛrfəlnəs

prayerless
BR 'prɛːləs
AM 'prɛrləs

preach
BR priːtʃ, -ɪz, -ɪŋ, -t
AM pritʃ, -ɪz, -ɪŋ, -t

preachable
BR 'priːtʃəbl
AM 'pritʃəbəl

preacher
BR 'priːtʃə(r), -z
AM 'pritʃər, -z

preachify
BR 'priːtʃɪfʌɪ, -z, -ɪŋ, -d
AM 'pritʃə,faɪ, -z, -ɪŋ, -d

preachiness
BR 'priːtʃɪnɪs
AM 'pritʃinɪs

preaching
BR 'priːtʃɪŋ, -z
AM 'pritʃɪŋ, -z

preachment
BR 'priːtʃm(ə)nt, -s
AM 'pritʃmənt, -s

preachy
BR 'priːtʃi
AM 'pritʃi

pre-adamite
BR ˌpriː'adəmʌɪt
AM ˌpri'ædə,maɪt

pre-adolescence
BR ˌpriːadə'lɛsns
AM ˌpri,ædə'lɛsəns

pre-adolescent
BR ˌpriːadə'lɛsnt, -s
AM ˌpri,ædə'lɛsənt, -s

preamble
BR 'priːambl, prɪ'ambl, -z
AM 'priː,æmbəl, -z

preambular
BR (ˌ)priː'ambjʊlə(r)
AM ˌpri'æmbjələr

preamp
BR 'priːamp, -s
AM 'pri,æmp, -s

preamplified
BR (ˌ)priː'amplɪfʌɪd
AM ˌpri'æmplə,faɪd

preamplifier
BR (ˌ)priː'amplɪfʌɪə(r), -z
AM ˌpri'æmplə,faɪər, -z

preamplify
BR (ˌ)priː'amplɪfʌɪ, -z, -ɪŋ, -d
AM ˌpri'æmplə,faɪ, -z, -ɪŋ, -d

prearrange
BR ˌpriːə'reɪn(d)ʒ, -ɪz, -ɪŋ, -d
AM ˌpriə'reɪndʒ, -ɪz, -ɪŋ, -d

prearrangement
BR ˌpriːə'reɪn(d)ʒm(ə)nt
AM ˌpriə'reɪndʒmənt

preatomic
BR ˌpriːə'tɒmɪk
AM ˌpriə'tɑmɪk

prebend
BR 'prɛb(ə)nd, -z
AM 'prɛbənd, -z

prebendal
BR 'prɛb(ə)ndl
AM 'prɛbəndəl

prebendary
BR 'prɛb(ə)nd(ə)r|i, -ɪz
AM 'prɛbən,dɛri, -z

prebendaryship
BR 'prɛb(ə)nd(ə)rɪʃɪp, -s
AM 'prɛbən,dɛri,ʃɪp, -s

pre-book
BR ˌpriː'bʊk, -s, -ɪŋ, -t
AM ˌpri'bʊk, -s, -ɪŋ, -t

pre-bookable
BR ˌpriː'bʊkəbl
AM ˌpri'bʊkəbəl

Precambrian
BR (ˌ)priː'kambrɪən
AM ˌpri'kæmbrɪən

precancerous
BR ˌpriː'kans(ə)rəs
AM ˌpri'kæns(ə)rəs

precancerously
BR ˌpriː'kans(ə)rəsli
AM ˌpri'kæns(ə)rəsli

precarious
BR prɪ'kɛːrɪəs
AM prə'kɛriəs

precariously
BR prɪ'kɛːrɪəsli
AM prə'kɛriəsli

precariousness
BR prɪ'kɛːrɪəsnəs
AM prə'kɛriəsnəs

precast
BR ˌpriː'kɑːst, ˌpriː'kast
AM ˌpri'kæst

precative
BR 'prɛkətɪv, -z
AM 'prɛkədɪv, -z

precatory
BR 'prɛkət(ə)ri
AM 'prɛkə,tori

precaution
BR prɪ'kɔːʃn, -z
AM pri'kɔʃən, prə'kɔʃən, pri'kɑʃən, prə'kɑʃən, -z

precautionary
BR prɪ'kɔːʃn(ə)ri
AM pri'kɔʃə,nɛri, prə'kɔʃə,nɛri, pri'kɑʃə,nɛri, prə'kɑʃə,nɛri

precede
BR ˌpriː'siːd, prɪ'siːd
AM pri'sid, prə'sid

precedence
BR 'prɛsɪd(ə)ns
AM 'prɛsədəns

precedency
BR 'prɛsɪd(ə)ns|i, -ɪz
AM 'prɛsədnsi, -z

precedent¹
adjective
BR prɪ'siːd(ə)nt
AM pri'sidnt, 'prɛsədənt

precedent²
noun
BR 'prɛsɪd(ə)nt, -s
AM 'prɛsədnt, -s

precedented
BR 'prɛsɪdəntɪd
AM 'prɛsə,dɛn(t)əd

precedently
BR 'prɛsɪd(ə)ntli
AM 'prɛsəd(ə)n(t)li

precent
BR prɪ'sɛnt, ˌpriː'sɛnt, -s, -ɪŋ, -ɪd
AM pri'sɛn|t, -ts, -(t)ɪŋ, -(t)əd

precentor
BR prɪ'sɛntə(r), ˌpri'sɛntə(r), -z
AM prə'sɛn(t)ər, -z

precentorship
BR prɪ'sɛntəʃɪp, ˌpri'sɛntəʃɪp, -s
AM prə'sɛn(t)ər,ʃɪp, -s

precentrices
BR prɪ'sɛntrɪsiːz, pri'sɛntrɪsiːz
AM pri'sɛntrə,siz

precentrix
BR prɪ'sɛntrɪks, ˌpri'sɛntrɪks, -ɪz
AM prə'sɛntrɪks, -ɪz

precept
BR 'priːsɛpt, -s
AM 'pri,sɛpt, -s

preceptive
BR prɪ'sɛptɪv
AM prə'sɛptɪv

preceptor
BR prɪ'sɛptə(r), -z
AM 'pri,sɛptər, -z

preceptorial
BR ˌpriːsɛp'tɔːrɪəl, pri,sɛp'tɔːrɪəl

AM priˌsɛpˈtɔːriəl
preceptorship
BR prɪˈsɛptəˌʃɪp, -s
AM ˈpriˌsɛptərˌʃɪp, -s
preceptress
BR prɪˈsɛptrɪs, -ɪz
AM priˈsɛptrəs, -əz
precession
BR prɪˈsɛʃn, -z
AM prəˈsɛʃən, -z
precessional
BR prɪˈsɛʃn(ə)l,
prɪˈsɛʃən(ə)l
AM prəˈsɛʃ(ə)nəl
precinct
BR ˈpriːsɪŋ(k)t, -s
AM ˈpriˌsɪŋ(k)t,
ˈpriˌsɪŋk(t), -(t)s
preciosity
BR ˌprɛʃɪˈɒsɪti,
ˌprɛsɪˈɒsɪti
AM ˌprɛʃiˈɑsədi
precious
BR ˈprɛʃəs
AM ˈprɛʃəs
preciously
BR ˈprɛʃəsli
AM ˈprɛʃəsli
preciousness
BR ˈprɛʃəsnəs
AM ˈprɛʃəsnəs
precipice
BR ˈprɛsɪpɪs, -ɪz
AM ˈprɛsəpəs, -əz
precipitability
BR prɪˌsɪpɪtəˈbɪlɪti
AM ˌprɛsəˌpɪdəˈbɪlɪdi
precipitable
BR prɪˈsɪpɪtəbl
AM prəˈsɪpədəbəl
precipitance
BR prɪˈsɪpɪt(ə)ns
AM prɪˈsɪpədəns,
prəˈsɪpədns
precipitancy
BR prɪˈsɪpɪt(ə)nsi
AM prɪˈsɪpədənsi,
prəˈsɪpədnsi
precipitant
BR prɪˈsɪpɪt(ə)nt
AM prɪˈsɪpədənt,
prəˈsɪpədnt
precipitantly
BR prɪˈsɪpɪt(ə)ntli
AM prɪˈsɪpədən(t)li,
prəˈsɪpədən(t)li
precipitate¹
adjective
BR prɪˈsɪpɪtət
AM prɪˈsɪpədət,
prəˈsɪpədət
precipitate²
verb
BR prɪˈsɪpɪteɪt, -s, -ɪŋ,
-ɪd
AM prɪˈsɪpəˌteɪt,
prəˈsɪpəˌteɪt, -ts, -dɪŋ,
-dɪd

precipitately
BR prɪˈsɪpɪtətli
AM prɪˈsɪpədətli,
prəˈsɪpədətli
precipitateness
BR prɪˈsɪpɪtətnəs
AM prɪˈsɪpədətnəs,
prəˈsɪpədətnəs
precipitation
BR prɪˌsɪpɪˈteɪʃn
AM priˌsɪpəˈteɪʃən,
prəˌsɪpəˈteɪʃən
precipitator
BR prɪˈsɪpɪteɪtə(r), -z
AM prɪˈsɪpəˌteɪdər,
prəˈsɪpəˌteɪdər, -z
precipitin
BR prɪˈsɪpɪtɪn
AM prɪˈsɪpɪdɪn
precipitous
BR prɪˈsɪpɪtəs
AM prɪˈsɪpədəs,
prəˈsɪpədəs
precipitously
BR prɪˈsɪpɪtəsli
AM prɪˈsɪpədəsli,
prəˈsɪpədəsli
precipitousness
BR prɪˈsɪpɪtəsnəs
AM prɪˈsɪpədəsnəs,
prəˈsɪpədəsnəs
precis
singular noun, verb
BR ˈpreɪsiː, -z, -ɪŋ, -d
AM ˈpreɪsi, -z, -ɪŋ, -d
precise
BR prɪˈsaɪs
AM prɪˈsaɪs, prəˈsaɪs
precisely
BR prɪˈsaɪsli
AM prɪˈsaɪsli,
prəˈsaɪsli
preciseness
BR prɪˈsaɪsnɪs
AM prɪˈsaɪsnɪs,
prəˈsaɪsnɪs
precisian
BR prɪˈsɪʒn, -z
AM prɪˈsɪʒən,
prəˈsɪʒən, -z
precisianism
BR prɪˈsɪʒnɪz(ə)m,
prɪˈsɪʒənɪz(ə)m
AM prɪˈsɪʒəˌnɪzəm,
prəˈsɪʒəˌnɪzəm
precision
BR prɪˈsɪʒn
AM prɪˈsɪʒən,
prəˈsɪʒən
precisionism
BR prɪˈsɪʒnɪz(ə)m,
prɪˈsɪʒənɪz(ə)m
AM prɪˈsɪʒəˌnɪzəm,
prəˈsɪʒəˌnɪzəm
precisionist
BR prɪˈsɪʒnɪst,
prɪˈsɪʒənɪst, -s

AM prɪˈsɪʒənəst,
prəˈsɪʒənəst, -s
preclassical
BR ˌpriːˈklasɪkl
AM prəˈklæsəkəl
preclinical
BR ˌpriːˈklɪnɪkl
AM prəˈklɪnɪkəl
preclude
BR prɪˈkluːd, -z, -ɪŋ, -ɪd
AM prəˈklud, prəˈklud,
-z, -ɪŋ, -əd
preclusion
BR prɪˈkluːʒn
AM prɪˈkluʒən,
prəˈkluʒən
preclusive
BR prɪˈkluːsɪv
AM prɪˈklusɪv,
prəˈklusɪv
precocial
BR prɪˈkəʊʃl, -z
AM prəˈkoʊʃəl, -z
precocious
BR prɪˈkəʊʃəs
AM prəˈkoʊʃəs
precociously
BR prɪˈkəʊʃəsli
AM prəˈkoʊʃəsli
precociousness
BR prɪˈkəʊʃəsnəs
AM prəˈkoʊʃəsnəs
precocity
BR prɪˈkɒsɪti
AM prəˈkɑsədi
precognition
BR ˌpriːkɒgˈnɪʃn,
ˌpriːkəgˈnɪʃn
AM ˌpriˌkɑgˈnɪʃən
precognitive
BR ˌpriːˈkɒgnɪtɪv
AM ˌpriːˈkɑgnədɪv
pre-coital
BR ˌpriːˈkəʊtl,
ˌpriːˈkɔɪ(ɪ)tl
AM ˌpriːˈkoʊədl
pre-coitally
BR ˌpriːˈkəʊtli,
ˌpriːˈkəʊtəli,
ˌpriːˈkɔɪ(ɪ)tli,
ˌpriːˈkɔɪ(ɪ)təli
AM ˌpriːˈkoʊədli
pre-Columbian
BR ˌpriːkəˈlʌmbɪən
AM ˌprikəˈləmbiən
precompensation
BR ˌpriːkɒmp(ə)nˈseɪʃn,
ˌpriːkɒmpɛnˈseɪʃn
AM ˌpriˌkɑmpənˈseɪʃən
preconceive
BR ˌpriːkənˈsiːv, -z, -ɪŋ,
-d
AM ˌprikənˈsiv, -z, -ɪŋ,
-d
preconception
BR ˌpriːkənˈsɛpʃn, -z
AM ˌprikənˈsɛpʃən, -z

preconcert
BR ˌpriːkənˈsəːt, -s, -ɪŋ,
-ɪd
AM ˌpriˈkɑnsər|t, -ts,
-dɪŋ, -dəd
precondition
BR ˌpriːkənˈdɪʃ|n, -nz,
-nɪŋ \-(ə)nɪŋ, -nd
AM ˈprikənˈdɪʃən, -z,
-ɪŋ, -d
preconisation
BR ˌpriːkənʌɪˈzeɪʃn
AM ˌprɛkənəˈzeɪʃən,
ˌprɛkəˌnaɪˈzeɪʃən
preconise
BR ˈpriːkənʌɪz, -ɪz, -ɪŋ,
-d
AM ˈprɛkəˌnaɪz, -ɪz, -ɪŋ,
-d
preconization
BR ˌpriːkənʌɪˈzeɪʃn
AM ˌprɛkənəˈzeɪʃən,
ˌprɛkəˌnaɪˈzeɪʃən
preconize
BR ˈpriːkənʌɪz, -ɪz, -ɪŋ,
-d
AM ˈprɛkəˌnaɪz, -ɪz, -ɪŋ,
-d
preconscious
BR ˌpriːˈkɒnʃəs
AM priˈkɑnʃəs
preconsciousness
BR ˌpriːˈkɒnʃəsnəs
AM priˈkɑnʃəsnəs
precook
BR ˌpriːˈkʊk, -s, -ɪŋ, -t
AM ˌpriˈkʊk, -s, -ɪŋ, -t
pre-cool
BR ˌpriːˈkuːl, -z, -ɪŋ, -d
AM ˌpriˈkul, -z, -ɪŋ, -d
precordial
BR ˌpriːˈkɔːdɪəl
AM priˈkɔrdiəl
precostal
BR ˌpriːˈkɒstl
AM priˈkoʊstəl
precursive
BR prɪˈkəːsɪv,
ˌpriːˈkəːsɪv
AM priˈkərsɪv,
prəˈkərsɪv
precursor
BR prɪˈkəːsə(r),
ˌpriːˈkəːsə(r), -z
AM ˈpriˌkərsər, -z
precursory
BR prɪˈkəːsri,
ˌpriːˈkəːs(ə)ri
AM priˈkərsəri,
prəˈkərsəri
pre-cut¹
adjective
BR ˌpriːˈkʌt
AM ˈpriˈkət
pre-cut²
verb
BR ˌpriːˈkʌt, -s, -ɪŋ
AM ˌpriˈkə|t, -ts, -dɪŋ

predacious
BR prɪˈdeɪʃəs
AM prəˈdeɪʃəs
predaciousness
BR prɪˈdeɪʃəsnəs
AM prəˈdeɪʃəsnəs
predacity
BR prɪˈdasɪti
AM prəˈdæsədi
predate
prey upon
BR prɪˈdeɪt, -s, -ɪŋ, -ɪd
AM ˈpreˈdeɪ|t, -ts, -dɪŋ, -dɪd
pre-date
give an earlier date
BR (ˌ)priːˈdeɪt, -s, -ɪŋ, -ɪd
AM ˈpriˈdeɪ|t, -ts, -dɪŋ, -dɪd
predation
BR prɪˈdeɪʃn
AM prəˈdeɪʃən
predator
BR ˈprɛdətə(r), -z
AM ˈprɛdədər, -z
predatorily
BR ˈprɛdət(ə)rɪli
AM ˈprɛdəˌtɔrəli
predatoriness
BR ˈprɛdət(ə)rɪnɪs
AM ˈprɛdəˌtɔrɪnɪs
predatory
BR ˈprɛdət(ə)ri
AM ˈprɛdəˌtɔri
predecease
BR ˌpriːdɪˈsiːs, -ɪz, -ɪŋ, -t
AM ˈpridəˈsis, -ɪz, -ɪŋ, -t
predecessor
BR ˈpriːdɪsɛsə(r), -z
AM ˈprɛdəˌsɛsər, ˈpridəˌsɛsər, -z
predella
BR prɪˈdɛlə(r), -z
AM prəˈdɛlə, -z
predestinarian
BR prɪːdɛstɪˈnɛːrɪən, -z
AM ˌpriˌdɛstəˈnɛrɪən, -z
predestinate
BR ˌpriːˈdɛstɪneɪt, prɪˈdɛstɪneɪt, -s, -ɪŋ, -ɪd
AM priˈdɛstəˌneɪ|t, -ts, -dɪŋ, -dɪd
predestination
BR priːˌdɛstɪˈneɪʃn, prɪˌdɛstɪˈneɪʃn, ˌpriːdɛstɪˈneɪʃn
AM priˌdɛstəˈneɪʃən
predestine
BR ˌpriːˈdɛst|(ɪ)n, prɪˈdɛst|(ɪ)n, -(ɪ)nz, -ŋɪŋ \-ɪnɪŋ, -(ɪ)nd
AM priˈdɛstən, -z, -ɪŋ, -d
predeterminable
BR ˌpriːdɪˈtəːmɪnəbl

AM ˌpridəˈtəːrmənəbəl
predeterminate
BR ˌpriːdɪˈtəːmɪnət
AM ˌpridəˈtəːrmənət
predetermination
BR ˌpriːdɪˌtəːmɪˈneɪʃn
AM ˌpridəˌtəːrməˈneɪʃən
predetermine
BR ˌpriːdɪˈtəːmɪn, -z, -ɪŋ, -d
AM ˈpridəˈtəːrmən, -z, -ɪŋ, -d
predial
BR ˌpriːˈdʌɪəl, -z
AM priˈdaɪəl, -z
predicability
BR ˌprɛdɪkəˈbɪlɪti
AM ˌprɛdɪkəˈbɪlɪdi
predicable
BR ˈprɛdɪkəbl
AM ˈprɛdəkəbəl
predicament
BR prɪˈdɪkəm(ə)nt, -s
AM prɪˈdɪkəmənt, prəˈdɪkəmənt, -s
predicant
BR ˈprɛdɪk(ə)nt, -s
AM ˈprɛdəkənt, -s
predicate¹
noun
BR ˈprɛdɪkət, -s
AM ˈprɛdəkət, -s
predicate²
verb
BR ˈprɛdɪkeɪt, -s, -ɪŋ, -ɪd
AM ˈprɛdəˌkeɪ|t, -ts, -dɪŋ, -dɪd
predication
BR ˌprɛdɪˈkeɪʃn, -z
AM ˌprɛdəˈkeɪʃən, -z
predicative
BR prɪˈdɪkətɪv, -z
AM ˈprɛdəˌkeɪdɪv, ˈprɛdəkədɪv, -z
predicatively
BR prɪˈdɪkətɪvli
AM ˈprɛdəˌkeɪdɪvli, ˈprɛdəkədɪvli
predicator
BR ˈprɛdɪkeɪtə(r), -z
AM ˈprɛdəˌkeɪdər, -z
predicatory
BR ˈprɛdɪkət(ə)ri
AM ˈprɛdəkəˌtori
predict
BR prɪˈdɪkt, -s, -ɪŋ, -ɪd
AM priˈdɪk|(t), prəˈdɪk|(t), -(t)s, -tɪŋ, -tɪd
predictability
BR prɪˌdɪktəˈbɪlɪti
AM priˌdɪktəˈbɪlɪdi, prəˌdɪktəˈbɪlɪdi
predictable
BR prɪˈdɪktəbl
AM priˈdɪktəbəl, prəˈdɪktəbəl

predictably
BR prɪˈdɪktəbli
AM priˈdɪktəbli, prəˈdɪktəbli
prediction
BR prɪˈdɪkʃn, -z
AM priˈdɪkʃən, prəˈdɪkʃən, -z
predictive
BR prɪˈdɪktɪv
AM priˈdɪktɪv, prəˈdɪktɪv
predictively
BR prɪˈdɪktɪvli
AM priˈdɪktɪvli, prəˈdɪktɪvli
predictor
BR prɪˈdɪktə(r), -z
AM priˈdɪktər, prəˈdɪktər, -z
predigest
BR ˌpriːdʌɪˈdʒɛst, -s, -ɪŋ
AM ˈpridaɪˈdʒɛst, ˌpridəˈdʒɛst, -s, -ɪŋ
predigested
BR ˌpriːdʌɪˈdʒɛstɪd
AM ˈpridaɪˈdʒɛstəd, ˌpridəˈdʒɛst
predigestion
BR ˌpriːdʌɪˈdʒɛstʃn
AM ˈpridaɪˈdʒɛstʃən, ˌpridaɪˈdʒɛtʃən, ˈpridəˈdʒɛʃtʃən, ˌpridəˈdʒɛstʃən
predikant
BR ˌprɛdɪˈkant, -s
AM ˈprɛdəkənt, -s
predilection
BR ˌpriːdɪˈlɛkʃn
AM ˈprɛdlˈɛkʃən, ˌprɛdəˈlɛkʃən, ˈpridlˈɛkʃən, ˌpridəˈlɛkʃən
predispose
BR ˌpriːdɪˈspəʊz, -ɪz, -ɪŋ, -d
AM ˈpridəˈspoʊz, -əz, -ɪŋ, -d
predisposition
BR ˌpriːdɪspəˈzɪʃn, -z
AM ˈpridɪspəˈzɪʃən, -z
prednisone
BR ˈprɛdnɪzəʊn
AM ˈprɛdnəˌzoʊn, ˈprɛdnəˌsoʊn
predominance
BR prɪˈdɒmɪnəns
AM priˈdɑmənəns, prəˈdamənəns
predominant
BR prɪˈdɒmɪnənt
AM priˈdamənənt, prəˈdamənənt
predominantly
BR prɪˈdɒmɪnəntli
AM priˈdamənən(t)li, prəˈdamənən(t)li

predominate
BR prɪˈdɒmɪneɪt, -s, -ɪŋ, -ɪd
AM priˈdaməˌneɪ|t, prəˈdaməˌneɪ|t, -ts, -dɪŋ, -dɪd
predominately
BR prɪˈdɒmɪnətli
AM priˈdamənətli, prəˈdamənətli
predomination
BR prɪˌdɒmɪˈneɪʃn
AM prəˌdaməˈneɪʃən, priˌdaməˈneɪʃən
predoom
BR ˌpriːˈduːm, -z, -ɪŋ, -d
AM priˈdum, -z, -ɪŋ, -d
predorsal
BR ˌpriːˈdɔːsl
AM priˈdɔrsəl
predynastic
BR ˌpriːdɪˈnastɪk
AM ˌpriˌdarˈnæstɪk, ˈpridəˈnæstɪk
Preece
BR priːs
AM pris
pre-echo
BR ˌpriːˈɛkəʊ, -z, -ɪŋ, -d
AM priˈɛkoʊ, -z, -ɪŋ, -d
pre-eclampsia
BR ˌpriːɪˈklam(p)sɪə(r)
AM ˈpriˌɪˈklæm(p)sɪə
pre-eclamptic
BR ˌpriːɪˈklam(p)tɪk
AM ˈpriˌɪˈklæm(p)tɪk
Preedy
BR ˈpriːdi
AM ˈpridi
pre-elect
BR ˌpriːɪˈlɛkt, -s, -ɪŋ, -d
AM ˈpriəˈlɛk|(t), ˌpriˌiˈlɛk|(t), -(t)s, -tɪŋ, -əd
pre-election
BR ˌpriːɪˈlɛkʃn, -z
AM ˈpriəˈlɛkʃən, ˌpriˌiˈlɛkʃən, -z
pre-embryonic
BR ˌpriːɛmbrɪˈɒnɪk
AM ˈpriˌɛmbriˈanɪk
preemie
BR ˈpriːm|i, -ɪz
AM ˈprimi, -z
preeminence
BR ˌpriːˈɛmɪnəns, prɪˈɛmɪnəns
AM priˈɛmənəns
preeminent
BR ˌpriːˈɛmɪnənt, prɪˈɛmɪnənt
AM priˈɛmənənt
preeminently
BR ˌpriːˈɛmɪnəntli, prɪˈɛmɪnəntli
AM priˈɛmənən(t)li

preempt
BR ˌpriːˈɛm(p)t,
prɪˈɛm(p)t, -s, -ɪŋ, -ɪd
AM priˈɛm(p)t, -s, -ɪŋ,
-əd

preemption
BR ˌpriːˈɛm(p)ʃn,
prɪˈɛm(p)ʃn
AM priˈɛm(p)ʃən

preemptive
BR ˌpriːˈɛm(p)tɪv,
prɪˈɛm(p)tɪv
AM priˈɛm(p)tɪv

preemptively
BR ˌpriːˈɛm(p)tɪvli,
prɪˈɛm(p)tɪvli
AM priˈɛm(p)tɪvli

preemptor
BR ˌpriːˈɛm(p)tə(r),
prɪˈɛm(p)tə(r), -z
AM priˈɛm(p)tər, -z

preemptory
BR ˌpriːˈɛm(p)t(ə)r|i,
prɪˈɛm(p)t(ə)r|i, -ɪz
AM priˈɛm(p)təri, -z

preen
BR priːn, -z, -ɪŋ, -d
AM prin, -z, -ɪŋ, -d

preener
BR ˈpriːnə(r), -z
AM ˈprinər, -z

pre-engage
BR ˌpriːɪnˈgeɪdʒ,
ˌpriːɛnˈgeɪdʒ,
ˌpriːɪŋˈgeɪdʒ,
ˌpriːɛŋˈgeɪdʒ, -ɪz, -ɪŋ,
-d
AM ˌpriːɪnˈgeɪdʒ, -ɪz, -ɪŋ,
-d

preengagement
BR ˌpriːɪnˈgeɪdʒm(ə)nt,
ˌpriːɛnˈgeɪdʒm(ə)nt,
ˌpriːɪŋˈgeɪdʒm(ə)nt,
ˌpriːɛŋˈgeɪdʒm(ə)nt,
-s
AM ˌpriːɪnˈgeɪdʒmənt,
-s

pre-establish
BR ˌpriːɪˈstablɪʃ, -ɪʃɪz,
-ɪʃɪŋ, -ɪʃt
AM ˌpriːɪˈstæblɪʃ, -ɪz,
-ɪŋ, -t

preexist
BR ˌpriːɪgˈzɪst,
ˌpriːɛgˈzɪst, -s, -ɪŋ, -ɪd
AM ˌpriːɪgˈzɪst, -s, -ɪŋ, -ɪd

preexistence
BR ˌpriːɪgˈzɪst(ə)ns,
ˌpriːɛgˈzɪst(ə)ns
AM ˌpriːɪgˈzɪstəns

preexistent
BR ˌpriːɪgˈzɪst(ə)nt,
ˌpriːɛgˈzɪst(ə)nt
AM ˌpriːɪgˈzɪstənt

prefab
BR ˈpriːfab, -z
AM priˈfæb, ˈpriːˌfæb, -z

prefabricate
BR ˌpriːˈfabrɪkeɪt, -s,
-ɪŋ, -ɪd
AM priˈfæbrəˌkeɪt, -s,
-dɪŋ, -dɪd

prefabrication
BR ˌpriːfabrɪˈkeɪʃn,
prɪˌfabrɪˈkeɪʃn
AM ˌpriˌfæbrəˈkeɪʃən

preface
BR ˈprɛfɪs, -ɪz, -ɪŋ, -t
AM ˈprɛfəs, -əz, -ɪŋ, -t

prefatorial
BR ˌprɛfəˈtɔːrɪəl
AM ˌprɛfəˈtɔriəl

prefatory
BR ˈprɛfət(ə)ri
AM ˈprɛfəˌtɔri

prefect
BR ˈpriːfɛkt, -s
AM ˈpriˌfɛk(t), -(t)s

prefectoral
BR priˈfɛkt(ə)rəl,
prɪˈfɛkt(ə)r|
AM priˈfɛkt(ə)rəl

prefectorial
BR ˌpriːfɛkˈtɔːrɪəl
AM ˌpriˌfɛkˈtɔriəl

prefectural
BR prɪˈfɛktʃ(ə)rəl,
prɪˈfɛktʃ(ə)r|
AM priˈfɛk(t)ʃ(ə)rəl

prefecture
BR ˈpriːfɛktʃ(ʊ)ə(r), -z
AM ˈpriˌfɛktʃər, -z

prefer
BR prɪˈfɜː(r), -z, -ɪŋ, -d
AM priˈfər, prəˈfər, -z,
-ɪŋ, -d

preferability
BR ˌprɛf(ə)rəˈbɪlɪti
AM ˌprɛf(ə)rəˈbɪlɪdi

preferable
BR ˈprɛf(ə)rəbl
AM ˈprɛf(ə)rəbəl

preferably
BR ˈprɛf(ə)rəbli
AM ˈprɛf(ə)rəbli,
ˈprɛfərbli

preference
BR ˈprɛf(ə)rəns,
ˈprɛf(ə)rn̩s, -ɪz
AM ˈprɛf(ə)rəns, -əz

preferential
BR ˌprɛfəˈrɛnʃl
AM ˌprɛfəˈrɛn(t)ʃəl

preferentially
BR ˌprɛfəˈrɛnʃli,
ˌprɛfəˈrɛnʃəli
AM ˌprɛfəˈrɛn(t)ʃəli

preferment
BR prɪˈfɜːm(ə)nt, -s
AM priˈfərmənt,
prəˈfərmənt, -s

prefiguration
BR ˌpriːfɪgəˈreɪʃn,
ˌpriːfɪgjʊˈreɪʃn,

pri:ˌfɪgəˈreɪʃn,
pri:ˌfɪgjʊˈreɪʃn
AM pri:ˌfɪgjəˈreɪʃən

prefigurative
BR (ˌ)priːˈfɪg(ə)rətɪv,
(ˌ)priːˈfɪgjʊrətɪv
AM priˈfɪgjərədɪv,
priˈfɪgjəˌreɪdɪv

prefigure
BR (ˌ)priːˈfɪglə(r), -əz,
-(ə)rɪŋ, -əd
AM priˈfɪgjər, -z, -ɪŋ, -d

prefigurement
BR (ˌ)priːˈfɪgəm(ə)nt
AM priˈfɪgjərmənt

prefix
BR ˈpriːfɪks, -ɪz, -ɪŋ, -t
AM ˈpriˌfɪks, -ɪz, -ɪŋ, -t

prefixation
BR ˌpriːfɪkˈseɪʃn
AM ˌprifɪkˈseɪʃən

prefixion
BR (ˌ)priːˈfɪkʃn
AM priˈfɪkʃən

prefixture
BR (ˌ)priːˈfɪkstʃə(r)
AM priˈfɪk(st)ʃər

preflight
BR ˌpriːˈflʌɪt, -s, -ɪŋ, -ɪd
AM ˈpriˌflaɪ|t, -ts, -dɪŋ,
-dɪd

preform
BR ˌpriːˈfɔːm, -z, -ɪŋ, -d
AM priˈfɔ(ə)rm, -z, -ɪŋ,
-d

preformation
BR ˌpriːfɔːˈmeɪʃn
AM ˌpriˌfɔrˈmeɪʃən

preformationist
BR ˌpriːfɔːˈmeɪʃn̩ɪst,
ˌpriːfɔːˈmeɪʃənɪst, -s
AM ˌpriˌfɔrˈmeɪʃənəst,
-s

preformative
BR ˌpriːˈfɔːmətɪv, -z
AM priˈfɔrmədɪv, -z

prefrontal
BR ˌpriːˈfrʌntl
AM priˈfrən(t)l

preglacial
BR ˌpriːˈgleɪʃl,
ˌpriːˈgleɪsɪəl
AM priˈgleɪʃəl

pregnable
BR ˈprɛgnəbl
AM ˈprɛgnəbəl

pregnancy
BR ˈprɛgnəns|i, -ɪz
AM ˈprɛgnənsi, -z

pregnant
BR ˈprɛgnənt
AM ˈprɛgnənt

pregnantly
BR ˈprɛgnəntli
AM ˈprɛgnən(t)li

preheat
BR ˌpriːˈhiːt, -s, -ɪŋ, -ɪd

AM priˈhi|t, -ts, -dɪŋ,
-dɪd

prehensile
BR ˌpriːˈhɛnsʌɪl,
prɪˈhɛnsʌɪl
AM priˈhɛnsəl,
prəˈhɛnsəl

prehensility
BR ˌpriːhɛnˈsɪlɪti
AM ˌpriˌhɛnˈsɪlɪdi

prehension
BR prɪˈhɛnʃn
AM priˈhɛn(t)ʃən

prehistorian
BR ˌpriːhɪˈstɔːrɪən, -z
AM ˌprihɪˈstɔriən, -z

prehistoric
BR ˌpriːhɪˈstɒrɪk
AM ˌprihɪˈstɔrɪk

prehistorically
BR ˌpriːhɪˈstɒrɪkli
AM ˌpri(h)ɪˈstɔrək(ə)li

prehistory
BR ˌpriːˈhɪst(ə)ri
AM priˈhɪstəri

prejudge
BR ˌpriːˈdʒʌdʒ, -ɪz, -ɪŋ,
-d
AM priˈdʒədʒ, -əz, -ɪŋ,
-d

prejudgement
BR ˌpriːˈdʒʌdʒm(ə)nt,
-s
AM priˈdʒədʒmənt, -s

prejudgment
BR ˌpriːˈdʒʌdʒm(ə)nt,
-s
AM priˈdʒədʒmənt, -s

prejudice
BR ˈprɛdʒʊd|ɪs, -ɪsɪz,
-ɪsɪŋ, -ɪst
AM ˈprɛdʒədəs, -əz, -ɪŋ,
-t

prejudicial
BR ˌprɛdʒʊˈdɪʃl
AM ˌprɛdʒəˈdɪʃəl

prejudicially
BR ˌprɛdʒʊˈdɪʃli,
ˌprɛdʒʊˈdɪʃəli
AM ˌprɛdʒəˈdɪʃəli

prelacy
BR ˈprɛləs|i, -ɪz
AM ˈprɛləsi, -z

prelapsarian
BR ˌpriːlapˈsɛːrɪən
AM ˌpriˌlæpˈsɛriən

prelate
BR ˈprɛlət, -s
AM ˈprɛlət, -s

prelatic
BR prɪˈlatɪk
AM prəˈlædɪk

prelatical
BR prɪˈlatɪkl
AM prəˈlædəkəl

prelature
BR ˈprɛlətʃə(r), -z

AM ˈprɛlətʃər,
ˈprɛlətʃʊ(ə)r, -z

prelect
BR prɪˈlɛkt, -s, -ɪŋ, -d
AM priˈlɛk|(t), -(t)s,
-tɪŋ, -əd

prelection
BR prɪˈlɛkʃn, -z
AM priˈlɛkʃən, -z

prelector
BR prɪˈlɛktə(r), -z
AM priˈlɛktər, -z

prelibation
BR ˌpriːˈlaɪˈbeɪʃn, -z
AM ˌpriˌlaɪˈbeɪʃən, -z

prelim
BR ˈpriːlɪm, prɪˈlɪm, -z
AM ˈpriˌlɪm, -z

preliminarily
BR prɪˈlɪmɪn(ə)rɪli
AM prəˌlɪməˈnɛrəli

preliminary
BR prɪˈlɪmɪn(ə)r|i, -ɪz
AM prəˈlɪməˌnɛri,
priˈlɪməˌnɛri, -z

preliterate
BR ˌpriːˈlɪt(ə)rət
AM priˈlɪdərət

prelude
BR ˈprɛljuːd, -z
AM ˈprɛlˌjud, ˈpreɪˌlud,
-z

preludial
BR prɪˈl(j)uːdiəl
AM prəˈl(j)udiəl

premarital
BR ˌpriːˈmarɪtl
AM priˈmɛrədl

premaritally
BR ˌpriːˈmarɪtl̩i,
ˌpriːˈmarɪtəli
AM priˈmɛrədl̩i

premature
BR ˈprɛmətʃə(r),
ˈprɛmətʃʊə(r),
ˈprɛmətjʊə(r),
ˈprɛmətʃɔː(r),
ˈprɛmətjɔː(r),
ˌprɛməˈtʃɔː(r),
ˌprɛməˈtjɔː(r)
AM ˌpriməˈtʃər,
ˈpriməˈtʃʊ(ə)r

prematurely
BR ˈprɛmətʃəli,
ˈprɛmətʃʊəli,
ˈprɛmətjʊəli,
ˈprɛmətʃɔːli,
ˌprɛməˈtʃɔːli,
ˌprɛməˈtjɔːli
AM ˌpriməˈtʃərli,
ˈpriməˈtʃʊrli

prematureness
BR ˈprɛmətʃənəs,
ˈprɛmətʃʊənəs,
ˈprɛmətjʊənəs,
ˈprɛmətʃɔːnəs,
ˈprɛmətjɔːnəs,

ˌprɛməˈtʃɔːnəs,
ˌprɛməˈtjɔːnəs
AM ˈpriməˈtʃərnəs,
ˈpriməˈtʃʊrnəs

prematurity
BR ˌprɛməˈtʃʊərɪti,
ˌprɛməˈtjʊərɪti,
ˌprɛməˈtʃɔːrɪti,
ˌprɛməˈtjɔːrɪti
AM ˌpriməˈtʃərədi,
ˌprɛməˈtʃʊrədi

premaxillary
BR ˌpriːˈmakˈsɪl(ə)ri
AM priˈmæksəˌlɛri

premed
BR ˌpriːˈmɛd, -z
AM ˈpriˈmɛd, -z

premedical
BR ˌpriːˈmɛdɪkl
AM priˈmɛdəkəl

premedication
BR ˌpriːmɛdɪˈkeɪn,
priˌmɛdɪˈkeɪn
AM ˈpriˌmɛdəˈkeɪʃən

premeditate
BR ˌpriːˈmɛdɪteɪt,
priˈmɛdɪteɪt, -s, -ɪŋ, -ɪd
AM priˈmɛdəˌteɪ|t, -ts,
-dɪŋ, -dɪd

premeditatedly
BR ˌpriːˈmɛdɪteɪtɪdli,
priˈmɛdɪteɪtɪdli
AM priˈmɛdəˌteɪdɪdli

premeditation
BR ˌpriːmɛdɪˈteɪʃn,
priˌmɛdɪˈteɪʃn
AM priˌmɛdəˈteɪʃən

premenstrual
BR ˌpriːˈmɛnstrʊəl,
ˌpriːˈmɛnstrʊl
AM priˈmɛnztr(əw)əl,
priˈmɛnstr(əw)əl

premenstrually
BR ˌpriːˈmɛnstrʊəli,
ˌpriːˈmɛnstrʊli
AM priˈmɛnztr(əw)əli,
priˈmɛnstr(əw)əli

premia
BR ˈpriːmɪə(r)
AM ˈprimiə

premie
BR ˈpriːm|i, -ɪz
AM ˈprimi, -z

premier
BR ˈprɛmɪə(r), -z
AM priˈmɪ(ə)r,
prəˈmɪ(ə)r, -z

première
BR ˈprɛmɪɛː(r), -z, -ɪŋ,
-d
AM priˈmɪ(ə)r,
prəˈmɪ(ə)r, -z, -ɪŋ, -d

premiership
BR ˈprɛmɪəˈʃɪp, -s
AM priˈmɪrˌʃɪp,
prəˈmɪrˌʃɪp, -s

premillennial
BR ˌpriːmɪˈlɛniəl

AM ˈpriməˈlɛniəl

premillennialism
BR ˌpriːmɪˈlɛniəlɪz(ə)m
AM ˈpriməˈleniəˌlɪzəm

premillennialist
BR ˌpriːmɪˈlɛniəlɪst, -s
AM ˈpriməˈlɛniələst, -s

premise¹
noun
BR ˈprɛm|ɪs, -ɪsɪz
AM ˈprɛmɪs, -əz

premise²
verb
BR ˈprɛm|ɪs, prɪˈmaɪz,
ˈprɛmɪsɪz \ prɪˈmaɪzɪz,
ˈprɛmɪsɪŋ \ prɪˈmaɪzɪŋ,
ˈprɛmɪst \ prɪˈmaɪzd
AM ˈprɛməs, -əz, -ɪŋ, -t

premises
plural noun
BR ˈprɛmɪsɪz
AM ˈprɛməsəz

premiss
BR ˈprɛm|ɪs, -ɪsɪz
AM ˈprɛməs, -əz

premium
BR ˈpriːmɪəm, -z
AM ˈprimiəm, -z

premolar
BR ˌpriːˈməʊlə(r), -z
AM priˈmoʊlər, -z

premonition
BR ˌprɛməˈnɪʃn,
ˌpriːməˈnɪʃn, -z
AM ˌpriməˈnɪʃən,
ˌprɛməˈnɪʃən, -z

premonitor
BR prɪˈmɒnɪtə(r), -z
AM priˈmanədər, -z

premonitorily
BR prɪˈmɒnɪt(ə)rɪli
AM priˈmanəˌtɔrəli

premonitory
BR prɪˈmɒnɪt(ə)ri
AM priˈmanəˌtɔri

**Premonstraten-
sian**
BR ˌpriːmɒnstrəˈten-
sɪən, -z
AM ˈprimɒnstrəˈten-
sɪən,
ˈprimɑnstrəˈtensiən,
-z

premorse
BR ˌpriːˈmɔːs
AM priˈmɔ(ə)rs

premotion
BR ˌpriːˈməʊʃn
AM priˈmoʊʃən

prenatal
BR ˌpriːˈneɪtl
AM priˈneɪdl

prenatally
BR ˌpriːˈneɪtl̩i
AM priˈneɪdl̩i

Prendergast
BR ˈprɛndəgɑːst,
ˈprɛndəgast

AM ˈprɛndərˌgæst

prentice
BR ˈprɛnt|ɪs, -ɪsɪz
AM ˈprɛn(t)əs, -əz

prenticeship
BR ˈprɛntɪsˌʃɪp, -s
AM ˈprɛn(t)əsˌʃɪp, -s

Prentiss
BR ˈprɛntɪs
AM ˈprɛn(t)əs

prenuptial
BR ˌpriːˈnʌpʃl
AM priˈnəpʃəl

preoccupation
BR priˌɒkjəˈpeɪʃn,
ˌpriːˈɒkjəˈpeɪʃn, -z
AM ˌpriˌɑkjəˈpeɪʃən, -z

preoccupy
BR priˈɒkjəpaɪ,
ˌpriːˈɒkjəpaɪ, -z, -ɪŋ, -d
AM priˈɑkjəˌpaɪ, -z, -ɪŋ,
-d

preocular
BR prɪˈɒkjələ(r),
ˌpriːˈɒkjələ(r)
AM priˈɑkjələr

preop
BR ˌpriːˈɒp, -s
AM ˈpriˌɑp, -s

preoperative
BR ˌpriːˈɒp(ə)rətɪv
AM priˈɑp(ə)rədɪv

preordain
BR ˌpriːɔːˈdeɪn, -z, -ɪŋ,
-d
AM ˈpriɔrˈdeɪn, -z, -ɪŋ,
-d

pre-owned
BR ˌpriːˈəʊnd
AM ˈpriˈoʊnd

prep
BR prɛp
AM prɛp

prepack
BR ˌpriːˈpak, -s, -ɪŋ, -t
AM priˈpæk, -s, -ɪŋ, -t

prepackage
BR ˌpriːˈpak|ɪdʒ, -ɪdʒɪz,
-ɪdʒɪŋ, -ɪdʒd
AM priˈpækɪdʒ, -ɪz, -ɪŋ,
-d

preparation
BR ˌprɛpəˈreɪʃn, -z
AM ˌprɛpəˈreɪʃən, -z

preparative
BR prɪˈparətɪv
AM prɪˈpɛrədɪv,
ˈprɛp(ə)rədɪv

preparatively
BR prɪˈparətɪvli
AM prɪˈpɛrədɪvli,
ˈprɛp(ə)rədɪvli

preparatorily
BR prɪˈparət(ə)rɪli
AM priˌpɛrəˈtɔrəli,
prəˌpɛrəˈtɔrəli

preparatory
BR prɪˈparət(ə)ri

AM prɪˈpɛrəˌtɔːri,
prəˈpɛrəˌtɔːri

prepare
BR prɪˈpɛː(r), -z, -ɪŋ, -d
AM prɪˈpɛ(ə)r,
prəˈpɛ(ə)r, -z, -ɪŋ, -d

preparedness
BR prɪˈpɛːrɪdnɪs
AM prəˈpɛr(ə)dnəs

preparer
BR prɪˈpɛːrə(r)
AM prɪˈpɛrər,
prəˈpɛrər

prepay
BR ˌpriːˈpeɪ, -z, -ɪŋ, -d
AM ˌpriːˈpeɪ, -z, -ɪŋ, -d

pre-payable
BR ˌpriːˈpeɪəbl
AM ˌpriːˈpeɪəbəl

prepayment
BR ˌpriːˈpeɪm(ə)nt, -s
AM prɪˈpeɪmənt, -s

prepense
BR prɪˈpɛns
AM prɪˈpɛns

prepensely
BR prɪˈpɛnsli
AM prɪˈpɛnsli

pre-plan
BR ˌpriːˈplan, -z, -ɪŋ, -d
AM prɪˈplæn, -z, -ɪŋ, -d

preponderance
BR prɪˈpɒnd(ə)rəns,
prɪˈpɒnd(ə)rn̩s
AM prəˈpɑnd(ə)rəns

preponderant
BR prɪˈpɒnd(ə)rənt,
prɪˈpɒnd(ə)rn̩t
AM prəˈpɑnd(ə)rənt

preponderantly
BR prɪˈpɒnd(ə)rəntli,
prɪˈpɒnd(ə)rn̩tli
AM prəˈpɑnd(ə)rən(t)li

preponderate
BR prɪˈpɒndəreɪt, -s,
-ɪŋ, -ɪd
AM prəˈpɑnd(ə)ˌreɪ|t,
-ts, -dɪŋ, -dɪd

prepose
BR ˌpriːˈpəʊz, -ɪz, -ɪŋ, -d
AM ˌpriːˈpoʊz, -əz, -ɪŋ, -d

preposition
BR ˌprɛpəˈzɪʃn, -z
AM ˌprɛpəˈzɪʃən, -z

pre-position
BR ˌpriːpəˈzɪʃ|n, -nz,
-nɪŋ\-nɪŋ, -nd
AM ˌpriːpəˈzɪʃən, -z, -ɪŋ,
-d

prepositional
BR ˌprɛpəˈzɪʃn(ə)l,
ˌprɛpəˈzɪʃən(ə)l
AM ˌprɛpəˈzɪʃ(ə)nəl

prepositionally
BR ˌprɛpəˈzɪʃnəli,
ˌprɛpəˈzɪʃn̩li,
ˌprɛpəˈzɪʃənli,
ˌprɛpəˈzɪʃ(ə)nəli

AM ˌprɛpəˈzɪʃ(ə)nəli

prepositive
BR (ˌ)priːˈpɒzɪtɪv
AM priːˈpɑzədɪv

prepossess
BR ˌpriːpəˈzɛs, -ɪz, -ɪŋ, -t
AM ˌpriːpəˈzɛs, -əz, -ɪŋ, -t

prepossession
BR ˌpriːpəˈzɛʃn, -z
AM ˌpriːpəˈzɛʃən, -z

preposterous
BR prɪˈpɒst(ə)rəs
AM prəˈpɑst(ə)rəs

preposterously
BR prɪˈpɒst(ə)rəsli
AM prəˈpɑst(ə)rəsli

preposterousness
BR prɪˈpɒst(ə)rəsnəs
AM prəˈpɑst(ə)rəsnəs

prepostor
BR prɪˈpɒstə(r), -z
AM prəˈpɑstər, -z

prepotence
BR ˌpriːˈpəʊtns
AM priːˈpoʊtns

prepotency
BR ˌpriːˈpəʊtnsi
AM priːˈpoʊtnsi

prepotent
BR ˌpriːˈpəʊtnt
AM ˌpriːˈpoʊtnt

preppie
BR ˈprɛp|i, -ɪz
AM ˈprɛpi, -z

preppy
BR ˈprɛp|i, -ɪz, -ɪə(r),
-ɪɪst
AM ˈprɛpi, -z, -ər, -ɪɪst

preprandial
BR ˌpriːˈprandɪəl
AM priːˈprændɪəl

pre-preference
BR ˌpriːˈprɛf(ə)rəns,
ˌpriːˈprɛf(ə)rn̩s
AM ˌpriːˈprɛf(ə)rəns

preprint¹
noun
BR ˈpriːprɪnt, -s
AM ˈpriːˌprɪnt, -s

preprint²
verb
BR ˌpriːˈprɪnt, -s, -ɪŋ,
-ɪd
AM priːˈprɪn|t, -ts,
-(t)ɪŋ, -(t)ɪd

preprocess
BR ˌpriːˈprəʊsɛs, -ɪz,
-ɪŋ, -t
AM priːˈprɑsəs, -əz, -ɪŋ,
-t

pre-processor
BR ˌpriːˈprəʊsɛsə(r), -z
AM priːˈprɑsəsər, -z

pre-production
BR ˌpriːprəˈdʌkʃn
AM ˌpriːprəˈdəkʃən

preprofessional
BR ˌpriːprəˈfɛʃn(ə)l,
ˌpriːprəˈfɛʃən(ə)l
AM ˌpriːprəˈfɛʃ(ə)nəl

pre-programme
BR ˌpriːˈprəʊgrəm, -z,
-ɪŋ, -d
AM priːˈproʊgrəm, -z,
-ɪŋ, -d

pre-pubertal
BR ˌpriːˈpjuːbətl
AM priːˈpjubərdl

pre-puberty
BR ˌpriːˈpjuːbəti
AM priːˈpjubərdi

prepubescence
BR ˌpriːpjuːˈbɛsns,
ˌpriːpjʊˈbɛsns
AM ˌpriːpjuˈbɛsəns

prepubescent
BR ˌpriːpjuːˈbɛsnt,
ˌpriːpjʊˈbɛsnt, -s
AM ˌpriːpjuˈbɛsənt, -s

pre-publication
BR ˌpriːˌpʌblɪˈkeɪʃn
AM priːˌpəbləˈkeɪʃən

prepuce
BR ˈpriːpjuːs, -ɪz
AM ˈpriːˌpjus, -əz

preputial
BR ˌpriːˈpjuːʃl
AM priːˈpjuʃəl

prequel
BR ˈpriːkw(ə)l, -z
AM ˈprikwəl, -z

Pre-Raphaelism
BR (ˌ)priːˈraf(ɪ)əlɪz(ə)m
AM ˈpriːˈrafiəˌlɪzəm,
priːˈræfiəˌlɪzəm

Pre-Raphaelite
BR (ˌ)priːˈraf(ɪ)əlʌɪt, -s
AM ˈpriːˈrafiəˌlaɪt,
priːˈræfiəˌlaɪt, -s

Pre-Raphaelitism
BR (ˌ)priːˈraf(ɪ)əlʌɪt-
ɪz(ə)m
AM ˈpriːrafiəˌlaɪˈtɪzəm,
priːˈrafiəˌlaɪdɪzəm,
priːˈræfiəˌlaɪˈtɪzəm,
priːˈræfiəˌlaɪdɪzəm

prerecord
BR ˌpriːrɪˈkɔːd, -z, -ɪŋ,
-ɪd
AM ˌprirəˈkɔ(ə)rd, -z,
-ɪŋ, -əd

preregister
BR ˌpriːˈrɛdʒɪst|ə(r),
-əz, -(ə)rɪŋ, -əd
AM ˌpriːˈrɛdʒəst|ər,
-ərz, -(ə)rɪŋ, -ərd

preregistration
BR ˌpriːˌrɛdʒɪˈstreɪʃn
AM ˌpriːˌrɛdʒəsˈtreɪʃən

prerequisite
BR (ˌ)priːˈrɛkwɪzɪt, -s
AM priːˈrɛkwəzət,
prəˈrɛkwəzət, -s

pre-revolutionary
BR ˌpriːˌrɛvəˈl(j)uːʃn̩-
(ə)ri
AM priːˌrɛvəˈluʃəˌnɛri

prerogative
BR prɪˈrɒgətɪv, -z
AM pəˈragədɪv,
prəˈragədɪv, -z

presage
BR ˈprɛs|ɪdʒ, -ɪdʒɪz,
-ɪdʒɪŋ, -ɪdʒd
AM prɪˈseɪdʒ, ˈprɛsɪdʒ,
-ɪz, -ɪŋ, -d

presager
BR ˈprɛsɪdʒə(r), -z
AM prɪˈseɪdʒər,
ˈprɛsɪdʒər, -z

presbyopia
BR ˌprɛzbɪˈəʊpɪə(r),
ˌprɛsbɪˈəʊpɪə(r)
AM ˌprɛzbiˈoʊpiə,
ˌprɛsbiˈoʊpiə

presbyopic
BR ˌprɛzbɪˈɒpɪk,
ˌprɛsbɪˈɒpɪk
AM ˌprɛzbiˈɑpɪk,
ˌprɛsbiˈɑpɪk

presbyter
BR ˈprɛzbɪtə(r),
ˈprɛsbɪtə(r), -z
AM ˈprɛzbədər,
ˈprɛsbədər, -z

presbyteral
BR prɛzˈbɪt(ə)rəl,
prɛzˈbɪt(ə)rl̩,
prɛsˈbɪt(ə)rəl,
prɛsˈbɪt(ə)rl̩
AM prɛsˈbɪtrəl,
prɛzˈbɪtrəl,
prɛsˈbɪdərəl,
prɛzˈbɪdərəl

presbyterate
BR prɛzˈbɪt(ə)rət,
prɛsˈbɪt(ə)rət, -s
AM prɛsˈbɪtrət,
prɛzˈbɪtrət,
prɛsˈbɪdərət,
prɛzˈbɪdərət,
prɛsˈbɪdəˌreɪt,
prɛzˈbɪdəˌreɪt, -s

presbyterial
BR ˌprɛzbɪˈtɪərɪəl,
ˌprɛsbɪˈtɪərɪəl
AM ˌprɛzbəˈtɪriəl,
ˌprɛsbəˈtɪriəl

Presbyterian
BR ˌprɛzbɪˈtɪərɪən,
ˌprɛsbɪˈtɪərɪən, -z
AM ˌprɛzbəˈtɪriən,
ˌprɛsbəˈtɪriən, -z

Presbyterianism
BR ˌprɛzbɪˈtɪərɪən-
ɪz(ə)m,
ˌprɛsbɪˈtɪərɪənɪz(ə)m
AM ˌprɛzbəˈtɪriəˌnɪzəm,
ˌprɛsbəˈtɪriəˌnɪzəm

presbytership
BR 'prɛzbɪtəʃɪp,
'prɛsbɪtəʃɪp, -s
AM 'prɛzbədər‚ʃɪp,
'prɛsbədər‚ʃɪp, -s

presbytery
BR 'prɛzbɪt(ə)r|i,
'prɛsbɪt(ə)r|i, -ɪz
AM 'prɛzbə‚tɛri,
'prɛsbə‚tɛri, -z

Prescely
BR prɪ'sɛli
AM prə'sɛli

preschool¹
adjective
BR ‚pri:'sku:l
AM ‚pri'skul

preschool²
noun
BR 'pri:sku:l, -z
AM 'pri‚skul, -z

pre-schooler
BR ‚pri:'sku:lə(r), -z
AM 'pri‚skulər, -z

prescience
BR 'prɛsɪəns
AM 'prɛʃ(i)əns

prescient
BR 'prɛsɪənt
AM 'prɛʃ(i)ənt

presciently
BR 'prɛsɪəntli
AM 'prɛʃ(i)ən(t)li

prescind
BR prɪ'sɪnd, ‚pri:'sɪnd,
-z, -ɪŋ, -ɪd
AM pri'sɪnd, -z, -ɪŋ, -ɪd

Prescot
BR 'prɛskət, 'prɛskɒt
AM 'prɛs‚kɑt, 'prɛskət

Prescott
BR 'prɛskət, 'prɛskɒt
AM 'prɛs‚kɑt, 'prɛskət

prescribe
BR prɪ'skrʌɪb, -z, -ɪŋ, -d
AM pri'skraɪb,
prə'skraɪb, -z, -ɪŋ, -d

prescriber
BR prɪ'skrʌɪbə(r), -z
AM pri'skraɪbər,
prə'skraɪbər, -z

prescript
BR 'pri:skrɪpt, -s
AM 'pri‚skrɪpt,
pri'skrɪpt, -s

prescription
BR prɪ'skrɪpʃn, -z
AM pri'skrɪpʃən,
prə'skrɪpʃən,
pər'skrɪpʃən, -z

prescriptive
BR prɪ'skrɪptɪv
AM pri'skrɪptɪv,
prə'skrɪptɪv

prescriptively
BR prɪ'skrɪptɪvli
AM pri'skrɪptɪvli,
prə'skrɪptɪvli

prescriptiveness
BR prɪ'skrɪptɪvnɪs
AM pri'skrɪptɪvnɪs,
prə'skrɪptɪvnɪs

prescriptivism
BR prɪ'skrɪptɪvɪz(ə)m
AM pri'skrɪptə‚vɪzəm,
prə'skrɪptə‚vɪzəm

prescriptivist
BR prɪ'skrɪptɪvɪst, -s
AM pri'skrɪptəvəst,
prə'skrɪptəvəst, -s

pre-season
BR ‚pri:'si:zn
AM ‚pri'sizn

Preseli
BR prɪ'sɛli
AM prə'sɛli
WE pre'seli

presence
BR 'prɛzns, -ɪz
AM 'prɛzns, -əz

present¹
military noun, verb
BR prɪ'zɛnt, -s, -ɪŋ, -ɪd
AM pri'zɛn|t, prə'zɛn|t,
-ts, -(t)ɪŋ, -(t)əd

present²
non-military noun,
adjective
BR 'prɛznt
AM 'prɛznt

presentability
BR prɪ‚zɛntə'bɪlɪti
AM prə‚zɛn(t)ə'bɪlɪdi,
pri‚zɛn(t)ə'bɪlɪdi

presentable
BR prɪ'zɛntəbl
AM prə'zɛn(t)əbəl,
pri'zɛn(t)əbəl

presentableness
BR prɪ'zɛntəblnəs
AM prə'zɛn(t)əbəlnəs,
pri'zɛn(t)əbəlnəs

presentably
BR prɪ'zɛntəbli
AM prə'zɛn(t)əbli,
pri'zɛn(t)əbli

presentation
BR ‚prɛzn'teɪʃn, -z
AM ‚prɛzn'teɪʃən,
‚pri‚zɛn'teɪʃən,
‚prizn'teɪʃən, -z

presentational
BR ‚prɛzn'teɪʃn(ə)l,
‚prɛzn'teɪʃən(ə)l
AM ‚prɛzn'teɪʃ(ə)nəl,
‚pri‚zɛn'teɪʃ(ə)nəl,
‚prizn'teɪʃ(ə)nəl

presentationally
BR ‚prɛzn'teɪʃnəli,
‚prɛzn'teɪʃn̩li,
‚prɛzn'teɪʃ(ə)nəli,
AM ‚prɛzn'teɪʃ(ə)nəli,
‚pri‚zɛn'teɪʃ(ə)nəli,
‚prizn'teɪʃ(ə)nəli

presentationism
BR ‚prɛzn'teɪʃnɪz(ə)m,
‚prɛzn'teɪʃənɪz(ə)m
AM ‚prɛzn'teɪʃə‚nɪzəm,
‚pri‚zɛn'teɪʃə‚nɪzəm,
‚prizn'teɪʃə‚nɪzəm

presentationist
BR ‚prɛzn'teɪʃnɪst,
‚prɛzn'teɪʃənɪst, -s
AM ‚prɛzn'teɪʃənəst,
‚pri‚zɛn'teɪʃənəst,
‚prizn'teɪʃənəst, -s

presentative
BR prɪ'zɛntətɪv
AM prə'zɛn(t)ədɪv,
pri'zɛn(t)ədɪv

present-day
BR ‚prɛznt'deɪ
AM ‚prɛzn(t)'deɪ

presentee
BR ‚prɛzn'ti:, -z
AM ‚prɛzn'ti, -z

presenter
BR prɪ'zɛntə(r), -z
AM prə'zɛn(t)ər,
pri'zɛn(t)ər, -z

presentient
BR prɪ'sɛnʃnt,
prɪ'sɛnʃiənt,
prɪ'sɛntiənt
AM pri'sen(t)ʃənt

presentiment
BR prɪ'zɛntɪm(ə)nt, -s
AM pri'zɛn(t)əmənt,
prə'zɛn(t)əmənt, -s

presently
BR 'prɛzntli
AM 'prɛzn(t)li

presentment
BR prɪ'zɛntm(ə)nt, -s
AM pri'zɛntmənt,
prə'zɛntmənt, -s

presentness
BR 'prɛzntnəs
AM 'prɛzn(t)nəs

preservable
BR prɪ'zə:vəbl
AM pri'zərvəbəl,
prə'zərvəbəl

preservation
BR ‚prɛzə'veɪʃn
AM ‚prɛzər'veɪʃən

preservationist
BR ‚prɛzə'veɪʃənɪst,
‚prɛzə'veɪʃnɪst, -s
AM ‚prɛzər'veɪʃənəst,
-s

preservative
BR prɪ'zə:vətɪv, -z
AM prə'zərvədɪv,
pri'zərvədɪv, -z

preserve
BR prɪ'zə:v, -z, -ɪŋ, -d
AM prə'zərv, pri'zərv,
-z, -ɪŋ, -d

preserver
BR prɪ'zə:və(r), -z

AM prə'zərvər,
pri'zərvər, -z

preset¹
noun
BR 'pri:sɛt, -s
AM 'pri‚sɛt, -s

preset²
verb
BR ‚pri:'sɛt, -s, -ɪŋ
AM pri'sɛ|t, -ts, -dɪŋ

preshrunk
BR ‚pri:'ʃrʌŋk
AM pri'ʃrəŋk

preside
BR prɪ'zaɪd, -z, -ɪŋ, -ɪd
AM prə'zaɪd, pri'zaɪd,
-z, -ɪŋ, -ɪd

presidency
BR 'prɛzɪd(ə)ns|i, -ɪz
AM 'prɛz(ə)dənsi,
'prɛzədnsi,
'prɛzə‚dɛnsi, -z

president
BR 'prɛzɪd(ə)nt, -s
AM 'prɛz(ə)dnt,
'prɛzə‚dɛnt, -s

president-elect
BR ‚prɛzɪd(ə)ntɪ'lɛkt
AM 'prɛz(ə)dən(t)ə-
'lɛk(t),
'prɛzədn(t)ə'lɛk(t),
'prɛzə‚dɛn(t)ə'lɛk(t)

presidential
BR ‚prɛzɪ'dɛnʃl
AM ‚prɛzə'dɛn(t)ʃəl

presidentially
BR ‚prɛzɪ'dɛnʃli,
‚prɛzɪ'dɛnʃəli
AM ‚prɛzə'dɛn(t)ʃəli

presidents-elect
BR ‚prɛzɪd(ə)ntsɪ'lɛkt
AM 'prɛz(ə)dən(t)sə-
'lɛk(t),
'prɛzədn(t)sə'lɛk(t),
'prɛzə‚dɛn(t)sə'lɛk(t)

presidentship
BR 'prɛzɪd(ə)ntʃɪp, -s
AM 'prɛz(ə)dənt‚ʃɪp,
'prɛzədnt‚ʃɪp,
'prɛzə‚dɛnt‚ʃɪp, -s

presidiary
BR prɪ'sɪdɪəri,
prɪ'zɪdɪəri
AM prə'sɪdi‚ɛri

presidio
BR prɪ'sɪdɪəʊ,
prɪ'zɪdɪəʊ
AM prə'sɪdioʊ

Presidium
BR prɪ'sɪdɪəm,
prɪ'zɪdɪəm, -z
AM prə'sɪdiəm, -z

Presley
BR 'prɛzli
AM 'prɛzli, 'prɛsli

presoak¹
noun
BR 'pri:səʊk, -s

AM ˈpriːˌsəʊk, -s

presoak²
verb
BR ˌpriːˈsəʊk, -s, -ɪŋ, -t
AM priːˈsəʊk, -s, -ɪŋ, -t

pre-Socratic
BR ˌpriːsəˈkrætɪk
AM ˌpriːsəˈkrædək

press
BR pres, -ɪz, -ɪŋ, -t
AM pres, -əz, -ɪŋ, -t

pressboard
BR ˈpresbɔːd
AM ˈpres,bɔ(ə)rd

Pressburg
BR ˈpresbəːg
AM ˈpres,bɜrg

pressgang
BR ˈpresgaŋ, -z, -ɪŋ, -d
AM ˈpres,gæŋ, -z, -ɪŋ, -d

pressie
BR ˈprez|i, -ɪz
AM ˈpresi, ˈprezi, -z

pressing
BR ˈpresɪŋ, -z
AM ˈpresɪŋ, -z

pressingly
BR ˈpresɪŋli
AM ˈpresɪŋli

pressman
BR ˈpresmən,
ˈpresman
AM ˈpres,mæn

pressmark
BR ˈpresmɑːk, -s
AM ˈpres,mɑrk, -s

pressmen
BR ˈpresmən,
ˈpresmen
AM ˈpresmən

pressroom
BR ˈpresruːm,
ˈpresrʊm, -z
AM ˈpres,rum,
ˈpres,rʊm, -z

pressrun
BR ˈpresrʌn, -z
AM ˈpres,rən, -z

press-up
BR ˈpresʌp, -s
AM ˈpresəp, -s

pressure
BR ˈpreʃ|ə(r), -əz,
-(ə)rɪŋ, -əd
AM ˈpreʃər, -z, -ɪŋ, -d

pressurisation
BR ˌpreʃ(ə)rʌɪˈzeɪʃn
AM ˌpreʃərəˈzeɪʃən,
ˌpreʃəˌraɪˈzeɪʃən

pressurise
BR ˈpreʃərʌɪz, -ɪz, -ɪŋ,
-d
AM ˈpreʃəˌraɪz, -ɪz, -ɪŋ,
-d

pressurization
BR ˌpreʃ(ə)rʌɪˈzeɪʃn
AM ˌpreʃərəˈzeɪʃən,
ˌpreʃəˌraɪˈzeɪʃən

pressurize
BR ˈpreʃərʌɪz, -ɪz, -ɪŋ,
-d
AM ˈpreʃəˌraɪz, -ɪz, -ɪŋ,
-d

Prestatyn
BR preˈstatɪn
AM preˈstæden

Prestcold
BR ˈpres(t)kəʊld
AM ˈpres(t),koʊld

Presteigne
BR preˈstiːn
AM preˈstin

Prestel®
BR ˈprestɛl
AM ˈpres,tɛl

Prester
BR ˈprestə(r)
AM ˈprestər

prestidigitation
BR ˌprestɪˌdɪdʒɪˈteɪʃn
AM ˌprestəˌdɪdʒəˈteɪʃən

prestidigitator
BR ˌprestɪˈdɪdʒɪteɪtə(r),
-z
AM ˌprestəˈdɪdʒəˌteɪdər,
-z

prestige
BR preˈstiː(d)ʒ
AM preˈstiː(d)ʒ

prestigeful
BR preˈstiː(d)ʒf(ʊ)l
AM preˈstiː(d)ʒ,fʊl

prestigious
BR preˈstɪdʒəs,
prɪˈstɪdʒəs
AM preˈstɪdʒ(i)əs

prestigiously
BR preˈstɪdʒəsli,
prɪˈstɪdʒəsli
AM preˈstɪdʒ(i)əsli

prestigiousness
BR preˈstɪdʒəsnəs,
prɪˈstɪdʒəsnəs
AM preˈstɪdʒ(i)əsnəs

prestissimo
BR preˈstɪsɪməʊ
AM preˈstɪsəˌmoʊ

presto
BR ˈprestəʊ, -z
AM ˈprestoʊ, -z

Preston
BR ˈprest(ə)n
AM ˈprestən

Prestonpans
BR ˌprest(ə)nˈpanz
AM ˌprestnˈpænz

prestressed
BR ˌpriːˈstrest
AM priːˈstres(t)

Prestwich
BR ˈprestwɪtʃ
AM ˈpres(t),wɪtʃ

Prestwick
BR ˈprestwɪk
AM ˈpres(t),wɪk

presumable
BR prɪˈzjuːməbl
AM priˈz(j)uməbəl,
prəˈz(j)uməbəl

presumably
BR prɪˈzjuːməbli
AM priˈz(j)uməbli,
prəˈz(j)uməbli

presume
BR prɪˈzjuːm, -z, -ɪŋ, -d
AM priˈz(j)um,
prəˈz(j)um, -z, -ɪŋ, -d

presumedly
BR prɪˈzjuːmɪdli
AM priˈz(j)um(ə)dli,
prəˈz(j)um(ə)dli

presumingly
BR prɪˈzjuːmɪŋli
AM priˈz(j)umɪŋli,
prəˈz(j)umɪŋli

presumingness
BR prɪˈzjuːmɪŋnɪs
AM priˈz(j)umɪŋnɪs,
prəˈz(j)umɪŋnɪs

presumption
BR prɪˈzʌm(p)ʃn, -z
AM priˈzəm(p)ʃən,
prəˈzəm(p)ʃən, -z

presumptive
BR prɪˈzʌm(p)tɪv
AM priˈzəm(p)tɪv,
prəˈzəm(p)tɪv

presumptively
BR prɪˈzʌm(p)tɪvli
AM priˈzəm(p)tɪvli,
prəˈzəm(p)tɪvli

presumptuous
BR prɪˈzʌm(p)tʃʊəs,
prɪˈzʌm(p)tjʊəs
AM priˈzəm(p)(t)ʃ(əw)-
əs,
prəˈzəm(p)(t)ʃ(əw)əs

presumptuously
BR prɪˈzʌm(p)tʃʊəsli,
prɪˈzʌm(p)tjʊəsli
AM priˈzəm(p)(t)ʃ(əw)-
əsli,
prəˈzəm(p)(t)ʃ(əw)əsli

**presumptuous-
ness**
BR prɪˈzʌm(p)tʃʊəsnəs,
prɪˈzʌm(p)tjʊəsnəs
AM priˈzəm(p)(t)ʃ(əw)-
əsnəs,
prəˈzəm(p)(t)ʃ(əw)-
əsnəs

presuppose
BR ˌpriːsəˈpəʊz, -ɪz, -ɪŋ,
-d
AM ˌpriːsəˈpoʊz, -əz, -ɪŋ,
-d

presupposition
BR ˌpriːsʌpəˈzɪʃn, -z
AM ˌpriːˌsəpəˈzɪʃən, -z

prêt-à-porter
BR ˌpretəˈpɔːteɪ
AM ˌpredəˈpɔrteɪ

pretax
BR ˌpriːˈtaks, -ɪz, -ɪŋ, -t
AM ˌpriːˈtæks, -əz, -ɪŋ, -t

preteen
BR ˌpriːˈtiːn, -z
AM ˌpriːˈtin, -z

pretence
BR prɪˈtens, -ɪz
AM priˈtens, prəˈtens,
ˈpriːˌtens, -əz

pretend
BR prɪˈtend, -z, -ɪŋ, -ɪd
AM priˈtend, prəˈtend,
-z, -ɪŋ, -əd

pretender
BR prɪˈtendə(r), -z
AM prəˈtendər,
priˈtendər, -z

pretense
BR prɪˈtens, -ɪz
AM priˈtens, prəˈtens,
ˈpriːˌtens, -əz

pretension
BR prɪˈtenʃn, -z
AM priˈten(t)ʃən,
prəˈten(t)ʃən, -z

pretentious
BR prɪˈtenʃəs
AM priˈten(t)ʃəs,
prəˈten(t)ʃəs

pretentiously
BR prɪˈtenʃəsli
AM priˈten(t)ʃəsli,
prəˈten(t)ʃəsli

pretentiousness
BR prɪˈtenʃəsnəs
AM priˈten(t)ʃəsnəs,
prəˈten(t)ʃəsnəs

preterhuman
BR ˌpriːtəˈhjuːmən
AM ˈpredər(ˈh)jumən,
ˈpridər(ˈh)jumən

preterit
BR ˈpret(ə)rɪt, -s
AM ˈpredərət, -s

preterite
BR ˈpret(ə)rɪt, -s
AM ˈpredərət, -s

preterition
BR ˌpriːtəˈrɪʃn, -z
AM ˌpredəˈrɪʃən, -z

pre-term
BR ˌpriːˈtəːm
AM priˈtɜrm

pretermission
BR ˌpriːtəˈmɪʃn
AM ˌpridərˈmɪʃən

pretermit
BR ˌpriːtəˈmɪt, -s, -ɪŋ,
-ɪd
AM priˈtərmə|t, -ts,
-dɪŋ, -dəd

preternatural
BR ˌpriːtəˈnatʃ(ə)rəl,
ˌpriːtəˈnatʃ(ə)rl
AM ˈpredərˈnætʃ(ə)rəl,
ˈpridərˈnætʃ(ə)rəl

preternaturalism
BR ˌpriːtəˈnatʃ(ə)rəl-
ɪz(ə)m,
ˌpriːtəˈnatʃ(ə)rˌlɪz(ə)m,
-z
AM ˌprɛdərˈnatʃ(ə)rə-
ˌlɪzəm,
ˈpridərˈnatʃ(ə)rəˌlɪzəm,
-z

preternaturally
BR ˌpriːtəˈnatʃ(ə)rəli,
ˌpriːtəˈnatʃ(ə)rˌli
AM ˌprɛdərˈnatʃ(ə)rəli,
ˈpridərˈnatʃ(ə)rəli

preternaturalness
BR ˌpriːtəˈnatʃ(ə)rəl-
nəs,
ˌpriːtəˈnatʃ(ə)rˌlnəs
AM ˌprɛdərˈnatʃ(ə)rəl-
nəs,
ˈpridərˈnatʃ(ə)rəlnəs

pretest
BR ˌpriːˈtɛst, -s, -ɪŋ, -ɪd
AM ˈpriːˌtɛs|t, -s, -ɪŋ, -əd

pretext
BR ˈpriːtɛkst, -s
AM ˈpriːˌtɛkst, -s

pretone
BR ˈpriːˈtəʊn, -z
AM priˈtoʊn, -z

pretonic
BR ˌpriːˈtɒnɪk, -s
AM priˈtɑnɪk, -s

pretor
BR ˈpriːtə(r),
ˈpriːtɔː(r), -z
AM ˈpridər, -z

Pretoria
BR prɪˈtɔːrɪə(r)
AM prəˈtɔriə

pretorian
BR prɪˈtɔːrɪən, -z
AM prəˈtɔriən, -z

pretorship
BR ˈpriːtəʃɪp,
ˈpriːtɔːʃɪp
AM ˈpridərˌʃɪp

pretreat
BR ˌpriːˈtriːt, -s, -ɪŋ, -ɪd
AM priˈtri|t, -ts, -dɪŋ,
-dɪd

pretreatment
BR ˌpriːˈtriːtm(ə)nt, -s
AM priˈtritmənt, -s

pretrial[1]
adjective
BR ˌpriːˈtrʌɪəl
AM ˈpriːˌtraɪəl

pretrial[2]
noun
BR ˈpriːtrʌɪəl, -z
AM ˈpriːˌtraɪəl, -z

prettification
BR ˌprɪtɪfɪˈkeɪʃn
AM ˌprɪdəfəˈkeɪʃən

prettifier
BR ˈprɪtɪfʌɪə(r), -z
AM ˈprɪdəˌfaɪər, -z

prettify
BR ˈprɪtɪfʌɪ, -z, -ɪŋ, -d
AM ˈprɪdəˌfaɪ, -z, -ɪŋ, -d

prettily
BR ˈprɪtɪli
AM ˈprɪdɪli

prettiness
BR ˈprɪtɪnɪs
AM ˈprɪdinɪs

pretty
BR ˈprɪt|i, -ɪə(r), -ɪɪst
AM ˈprɪdi, -ər, -ɪst

prettyish
BR ˈprɪtɪʃ
AM ˈprɪdɪʃ

prettyism
BR ˈprɪtɪɪz(ə)m
AM ˈprɪdiˌɪzəm

pretty-pretty
BR ˌprɪtɪˈprɪti
AM ˈprɪdiˈprɪdi

pretzel
BR ˈprɛtsl, -z
AM ˈprɛtsəl, -z

prevail
BR prɪˈveɪl, -z, -ɪŋ, -d
AM priˈveɪl, prəˈveɪl,
-z, -ɪŋ, -d

prevailingly
BR prɪˈveɪlɪŋli
AM priˈveɪlɪŋli,
prəˈveɪlɪŋli

prevalence
BR ˈprɛvələns,
ˈprɛvəlns, ˈprɛvl(ə)ns
AM ˈprɛv(ə)ləns

prevalent
BR ˈprɛvələnt,
ˈprɛvəlnt, ˈprɛvl(ə)nt
AM ˈprɛv(ə)lənt

prevalently
BR ˈprɛvələntli,
ˈprɛvəlntli,
ˈprɛvl(ə)ntli
AM ˈprɛv(ə)lən(t)li

prevaricate
BR prɪˈvarɪkeɪt, -s, -ɪŋ,
-ɪd
AM priˈvɛrəˌkeɪ|t,
prəˈvɛrəˌkeɪ|t, -ts, -dɪŋ,
-dɪd

prevarication
BR prɪˌvarɪˈkeɪʃn, -z
AM priˌvɛrəˈkeɪʃən,
prəˌvɛrəˈkeɪʃən, -z

prevaricator
BR prɪˈvarɪkeɪtə(r), -z
AM priˈvɛrəˌkeɪdər,
prəˈvɛrəˌkeɪdər, -z

prevenient
BR prɪˈviːnɪənt,
(ˌ)priːˈviːnɪənt
AM priˈviːnɪənt,
prəˈviniənt

preveniently
BR prɪˈviːnɪəntli,
(ˌ)priːˈviːnɪəntli

AM priˈviniən(t)li,
prəˈviniən(t)li

prevent
BR prɪˈvɛnt, -s, -ɪŋ, -ɪd
AM priˈvɛn|t,
prəˈvɛn|t, -ts, -(t)ɪŋ,
-(t)əd

preventability
BR prɪˌvɛntəˈbɪlɪti
AM priˌvɛn(t)əˈbɪlɪdi,
prəˌvɛn(t)əˈbɪlɪdi

preventable
BR prɪˈvɛntəbl
AM priˈvɛn(t)əbəl,
prəˈvɛn(t)əbəl

preventative
BR prɪˈvɛntətɪv, -z
AM priˈvɛn(t)ədɪv,
prəˈvɛn(t)ədɪv, -z

preventatively
BR prɪˈvɛntətɪvli
AM priˈvɛn(t)ədɪvli,
prəˈvɛn(t)ədɪvli

preventer
BR prɪˈvɛntə(r), -z
AM priˈvɛn(t)ər,
prəˈvɛn(t)ər, -z

prevention
BR prɪˈvɛnʃn
AM priˈvɛn(t)ʃən,
prəˈvɛn(t)ʃən

preventive
BR prɪˈvɛntɪv
AM priˈvɛn(t)ɪv,
prəˈvɛn(t)ɪv

preventively
BR prɪˈvɛntɪvli
AM priˈvɛn(t)ɪvli,
prəˈvɛn(t)ɪvli

preverbal
BR ˌpriːˈvəːbl
AM ˌpriːˈvərbəl

preverbally
BR ˌpriːˈvəːbli,
ˌpriːˈvəːbəli
AM ˌpriːˈvərbəli

preview
BR ˈpriːvjuː, -z, -ɪŋ, -d
AM ˈpriːˌvju, -z, -ɪŋ, -d

Previn
BR ˈprɛvɪn
AM ˈprɛvən

previous
BR ˈpriːvɪəs
AM ˈpriviəs

previously
BR ˈpriːvɪəsli
AM ˈpriviəsli

previousness
BR ˈpriːvɪəsnəs
AM ˈpriviəsnəs

previse
BR prɪˈvʌɪz, -ɪz, -ɪŋ, -d
AM priˈvaɪz, prəˈvaɪz,
-ɪz, -ɪŋ, -d

prevision
BR prɪˈvɪʒn

AM prɪˈvɪniən(t)li,
prəˈviniən(t)li

previsional
BR prɪˈvɪʒn(ə)l,
prɪˈvɪʒən(ə)l
AM priˈvɪʒ(ə)nəl,
prəˈvɪʒ(ə)nəl

prevocalic
BR ˌpriːvə(ʊ)ˈkalɪk
AM ˌprivoʊˈkælɪk

pre-vocational
BR ˌpriːvə(ʊ)ˈkeɪʃn(ə)l,
ˌpriːvə(ʊ)ˈkeɪʃən(ə)l
AM ˌpriˌvoʊˈkeɪʃ(ə)nəl

prevue
BR ˈpriːvjuː, -z
AM ˈpriˌvju, -z

prewar
BR ˌpriːˈwɔː(r)
AM priˈwɔ(ə)r

pre-wash
BR ˌpriːˈwɒʃ, -ɪz, -ɪŋ, -t
AM priˈwɒʃ, priˈwɑʃ,
-əz, -ɪŋ, -t

prex
BR prɛks, -ɪz
AM prɛks, -əz

prexy
BR ˈprɛks|i, -ɪz
AM ˈprɛksi, -z

prey
BR preɪ, -z, -ɪŋ, -d
AM preɪ, -z, -ɪŋ, -d

preyer
BR ˈpreɪə(r), -z
AM ˈpreɪər, -z

prezzie
BR ˈprɛz|i, -ɪz
AM ˈprɛzi, -z

Priam
BR ˈprʌɪam, ˈprʌɪəm
AM ˈpraɪəm

priapic
BR prʌɪˈapɪk
AM praɪˈæpɪk

priapism
BR ˈprʌɪəpɪz(ə)m
AM ˈpraɪəˌpɪzəm

Priapus
BR prʌɪˈeɪpəs
AM praɪˈeɪpəs

price
BR prʌɪs, -ɪz, -ɪŋ, -t
AM praɪs, -ɪz, -ɪŋ, -t

priceless
BR ˈprʌɪslɪs
AM ˈpraɪslɪs

pricelessly
BR ˈprʌɪslɪsli
AM ˈpraɪslɪsli

pricelessness
BR ˈprʌɪslɪsnɪs
AM ˈpraɪslɪsnɪs

pricer
BR ˈprʌɪsə(r), -z
AM ˈpraɪsər, -z

pricey
BR ˈpraɪs|i, -ɪə(r), -ɪɪst
AM ˈpraɪsi, -ər, -ɪst

priciness
BR ˈprɪsɪnɪs
AM ˈprɪsɪnɪs

prick
BR prɪk, -s, -ɪŋ, -t
AM prɪk, -s, -ɪŋ, -t

pricker
BR ˈprɪkə(r), -z
AM ˈprɪkər, -z

pricket
BR ˈprɪkɪt, -s
AM ˈprɪkɪt, -s

prickle
BR ˈprɪk|l, -lz, -lɪŋ \-lɪŋ, -ld
AM ˈprɪk|əl, -əlz, -(ə)lɪŋ, -əld

prickliness
BR ˈprɪklɪnɪs
AM ˈprɪk(ə)linɪs

prickly
BR ˈprɪkl|i, -ɪə(r), -ɪɪst
AM ˈprɪk(ə)li, -ər, -ɪst

pricy
BR ˈpraɪs|i, -ɪə(r), -ɪɪst
AM ˈpraɪsi, -ər, -ɪst

pride
BR praɪd, -z
AM praɪd, -z

prideful
BR ˈpraɪdf(ʊ)l
AM ˈpraɪdfəl

pridefully
BR ˈpraɪdfʊli, ˈpraɪdfli
AM ˈpraɪdfəli

prideless
BR ˈpraɪdlɪs
AM ˈpraɪdlɪs

prie-dieu
BR priːˈdjəː(r), -z
AM priːˈdjəː, -z

prie-dieux
BR priːˈdjəː(r), ˌpriːˈdjəːz
AM priːˈdjə

priest
BR priːst
AM prist

priestcraft
BR ˈpriːs(t)krɑːft, ˈpriːs(t)kraft
AM ˈpris(t)ˌkræft

priestess
BR ˈpriːˈstɛs, ˈpriːstɛs, ˈpriːstɪs, -ɪz
AM ˈpristɪs, -əz

priesthole
BR ˈpriːsthəʊl, -z
AM ˈprist,(h)oʊl, -z

priesthood
BR ˈpriːsthʊd
AM ˈprist,(h)ʊd

Priestland
BR ˈpriːs(t)lənd
AM ˈpris(t)ˌlænd

priestless
BR ˈpriːs(t)lɪs
AM ˈpris(t)lɪs

Priestley
BR ˈpriːs(t)li
AM ˈpris(t)li

priestlike
BR ˈpriːs(t)lʌɪk
AM ˈpris(t)ˌlaɪk

priestliness
BR ˈpriːs(t)lɪnɪs
AM ˈpris(t)linɪs

priestling
BR ˈpriːs(t)lɪŋ, -z
AM ˈpris(t)lɪŋ, -z

priestly
BR ˈpriːs(t)li
AM ˈpris(t)li

priests-in-charge
BR ˈpriːstsɪnˈtʃɑːdʒ
AM ˈpris(ts)ənˈtʃɑrdʒ

prig
BR prɪg, -z
AM prɪg, -z

priggery
BR ˈprɪg(ə)ri
AM ˈprɪgəri

priggish
BR ˈprɪgɪʃ
AM ˈprɪgɪʃ

priggishly
BR ˈprɪgɪʃli
AM ˈprɪgɪʃli

priggishness
BR ˈprɪgɪʃnɪs
AM ˈprɪgɪʃnɪs

priggism
BR ˈprɪgɪz(ə)m
AM ˈprɪˌgɪzəm

prim
BR prɪm
AM prɪm

prima ballerina
BR ˈpriːmə ˌbaləˈriːnə(r), -z
AM ˈpriːməˌbæləˈrinə, -z

primacy
BR ˈpraɪməsi
AM ˈpraɪməsi

prima donna
BR ˌpriːmə ˈdɒnə(r), -z
AM ˌpriːmə ˈdɑnə, ˈpriːmə +, -z

prima donna-ish
BR ˌpriːmə ˈdɒnə(r)ɪʃ
AM ˌpriːmə ˈdɑnəɪʃ, ˈpriːmə +

primaeval
BR prʌɪˈmiːvl
AM praɪˈmivəl

prima facie
BR ˌpraɪmə ˈfeɪʃ(ɪ)iː

AM ˌpriːmə ˈfeɪʃi(ˌi), + ˈfeɪʃə

prima inter pares
BR ˌpriːmə(r) ˌɪntəˈpɑːriːz, ˌpraɪmə(r) + ˈpeɪˌriz
AM ˌpriːmə ˌɪntər ˈpeɪˌriz

primal
BR ˈpraɪml
AM ˈpraɪməl

primally
BR ˈpraɪmli, ˈpraɪməli
AM ˈpraɪməli

primarily
BR ˈpraɪm(ə)rɪli, ˈpraɪm(ə)rli, praɪˈmɛrɪli
AM praɪˈmɛrəli, prəˈmɛrəli

primary
BR ˈpraɪm(ə)r|i, -ɪz
AM ˈpraɪˌmɛri, ˈpraɪm(ə)ri, -z

primate[1]
archbishop
BR ˈpraɪmət, ˈpraɪmeɪt, -s
AM ˈpraɪmɪt, ˈpraɪˌmeɪt, -s

primate[2]
higher mammal
BR ˈpraɪmeɪt, -s
AM ˈpraɪˌmeɪt, ˈpraɪmɪt, -s

primateship
BR ˈpraɪmət-ʃɪp, ˈpraɪmeɪt-ʃɪp, -s
AM ˈpraɪmɪtˌʃɪp, ˈpraɪˌmeɪtˌʃɪp, -s

primatial
BR ˈpraɪˈmeɪʃl
AM praɪˈmeɪʃəl

primatologist
BR ˌpraɪməˈtɒlədʒɪst, -s
AM ˌpraɪməˈtɑlədʒəst, -s

primatology
BR ˌpraɪməˈtɒlədʒi
AM ˌpraɪməˈtɑlədʒi

primavera
BR ˌpriːməˈvɛːrə(r), -z
AM ˌpriːməˈvɛrə, -z

prime
BR praɪm, -z, -ɪŋ, -d
AM praɪm, -z, -ɪŋ, -d

primeness
BR ˈpraɪmnɪs
AM ˈpraɪmnɪs

primer
BR ˈpraɪmə(r), -z
AM ˈpraɪmər, -z

primeval
BR prʌɪˈmiːvl
AM praɪˈmivəl

primevally
BR prʌɪˈmiːvl̩i, prʌɪˈmiːvəli

primigravida
BR ˌpraɪmɪˈgravɪdə(r), ˌpriːmɪˈgravɪdə(r), -z
AM ˌpraɪməˈgrævədə, -z

primigravidae
BR ˌpraɪmɪˈgravɪdiː, ˌpriːmɪˈgravɪdiː
AM ˌpraɪməˈgrævədi, ˈpraɪməˈgrævəˌdaɪ

primipara
BR praɪˈmɪp(ə)rə(r)
AM praɪˈmɪpərə

primiparae
BR praɪˈmɪp(ə)riː
AM praɪˈmɪpəri

primiparous
BR praɪˈmɪp(ə)rəs
AM praɪˈmɪpərəs

primitive
BR ˈprɪmɪtɪv, -z
AM ˈprɪmədɪv, -z

primitively
BR ˈprɪmɪtɪvli
AM ˈprɪmədɪvli

primitiveness
BR ˈprɪmɪtɪvnɪs
AM ˈprɪmədɪvnɪs

primitivism
BR ˈprɪmɪtɪvɪz(ə)m
AM ˈprɪmədəˌvɪzəm

primitivist
BR ˈprɪmɪtɪvɪst, -s
AM ˈprɪmədəvəst, -s

primly
BR ˈprɪmli
AM ˈprɪmli

primness
BR ˈprɪmnɪs
AM ˈprɪmnɪs

primo
BR ˈpriːməʊ, -z
AM ˈprimoʊ, -z

primogenital
BR ˌpraɪmə(ʊ)ˈdʒɛnɪtl
AM ˌpraɪmoʊˈdʒɛnədl

primogenitary
BR ˌpraɪmə(ʊ)ˈdʒɛnɪt-(ə)ri
AM ˌpraɪmoʊˈdʒɛnəˌtɛri

primogenitor
BR ˌpraɪmə(ʊ)ˈdʒɛnɪtə(r), -z
AM ˌpraɪmoʊˈdʒɛnədər, -z

primogeniture
BR ˌpraɪmə(ʊ)ˈdʒɛnɪtʃə(r)
AM ˌpraɪmoʊˈdʒɛnəˌtʃʊ(ə)r

primordia
BR prʌɪˈmɔːdɪə(r)
AM praɪˈmɔrdiə

primordial
BR prʌɪˈmɔːdɪəl, -z
AM praɪˈmɔrdiəl, -z

primordiality
BR prʌɪˌmɔːdrˈalɪti,
ˌprʌɪmɔːdrˈalɪti
AM ˈpraɪˌmɔrdiˈælədi

primordial
BR prʌɪˈmɔːdɪəli
AM praɪˈmɔrdiəli

primordium
BR prʌɪˈmɔːdɪəm
AM praɪˈmɔrdiəm

primp
BR prɪm|p, -ps, -pɪŋ,
-(p)t
AM prɪmp, -s, -ɪŋ, -t

primrose
BR ˈprɪmrəʊz, -ɪz
AM ˈprɪmˌroʊz, -əz

primula
BR ˈprɪmjʉlə(r), -z
AM ˈprɪmjələ, -z

primum mobile
BR ˌprʌɪməm
ˈməʊbɪl|i, ˌpriːməm +,
+ ˈməʊbl̩i, -ɪz
AM ˈpraɪməm
ˈmoʊbə,li, -z

primus
BR ˈprʌɪməs, -ɪz
AM ˈpraɪməs, -əz

**primus inter
pares**
BR ˌpriːməs ˌɪntə
ˈpɑːriːz, ˌprʌɪməs +
AM ˈpraɪməs ˌɪntər
ˈpeɪˌriz

prince
BR prɪns, -ɪz
AM prɪns, -ɪz

princedom
BR ˈprɪnsdəm, -z
AM ˈprɪnsdəm, -z

princelike
BR ˈprɪnslʌɪk
AM ˈprɪnsəˌlaɪk

princeliness
BR ˈprɪnslɪnɪs
AM ˈprɪnslinɪs

princeling
BR ˈprɪnslɪŋ, -z
AM ˈprɪnslɪŋ, -z

princely
BR ˈprɪnsl|i, -ɪə(r), -ɪɪst
AM ˈprɪnsli, -ər, -ɪst

princeship
BR ˈprɪnsˌʃɪp, -s
AM ˈprɪnsˌʃɪp, -s

princess
BR ˌprɪnˈsɛs, ˈprɪnsɪs,
ˈprɪnsɛs, -ɪz
AM ˈprɪnsɪs, ˈprɪnˌsɛs,
prɪnˈsɛs, -əz

Princeton
BR ˈprɪnstən
AM ˈprɪnstən

Princetown
BR ˈprɪnstaʊn
AM ˈprɪnsˌtoʊn

principal
BR ˈprɪnsɪpl, -z
AM ˈprɪnsəpəl, -z

principality
BR ˌprɪnsɪˈpalɪt|i, -ɪz
AM ˌprɪnsəˈpælədi, -z

principally
BR ˈprɪnsɪpl̩i,
ˈprɪnsɪp(ə)li
AM ˈprɪnsəp(ə)li

principalship
BR ˈprɪnsɪplˌʃɪp, -s
AM ˈprɪnsəpəlˌʃɪp, -s

principate
BR ˈprɪnsɪpət, -s
AM ˈprɪnsəˌpeɪt,
ˈprɪnsəpət, -s

Príncipe
BR ˈprɪnsɪpeɪ,
ˈprɪnsɪpi
AM ˈprɪn(t)səpi

Principia
BR prɪnˈsɪpɪə(r)
AM prɪnˈsɪpiə

principle
BR ˈprɪnsɪpl, -z, -d
AM ˈprɪnsəpəl, -z, -d

Pringle
BR ˈprɪŋgl
AM ˈprɪŋgəl

prink
BR prɪŋ|k, -ks, -kɪŋ,
-(k)t
AM prɪŋ|k, -ks, -kɪŋ,
-(k)t

Prinknash
BR ˈprɪnɪdʒ
AM ˈprɪnədʒ

print
BR prɪnt, -s, -ɪŋ, -ɪd
AM prɪn|t, -ts, -(t)ɪŋ,
-(t)ɪd

printability
BR ˌprɪntəˈbɪlɪti
AM ˌprɪn(t)əˈbɪlɪdi

printable
BR ˈprɪntəbl
AM ˈprɪn(t)əbəl

printer
BR ˈprɪntə(r), -z
AM ˈprɪn(t)ər, -z

printery
BR ˈprɪnt(ə)r|i, -ɪz
AM ˈprɪn(t)əri, -z

printhead
BR ˈprɪnthɛd, -z
AM ˈprɪnt,(h)ɛd, -z

printing
BR ˈprɪntɪŋ, -z
AM ˈprɪn(t)ɪŋ, -z

printless
BR ˈprɪntlɪs
AM ˈprɪn(t)lɪs

printmaker
BR ˈprɪntˌmeɪkə(r), -z
AM ˈprɪntˌmeɪkər, -z

printmaking
BR ˈprɪntˌmeɪkɪŋ
AM ˈprɪntˌmeɪkɪŋ

printout
BR ˈprɪntaʊt, -s
AM ˈprɪnˌtaʊt,
ˈprɪn(t)ˌaʊt, -s

printwheel
BR ˈprɪntwiːl, -z
AM ˈprɪnt,(h)wil, -z

printworks
BR ˈprɪntwəːks
AM ˈprɪntˌwərks

prion¹
bird
BR ˈprʌɪən, -z
AM ˈpraɪˌɑn, -z

prion²
infectious particle
BR ˈpriːɒn, -z
AM ˈpriˌɑn, -z

prior
BR ˈprʌɪə(r), -z
AM ˈpraɪ(ə)r, -z

priorate
BR ˈprʌɪərət, -s
AM ˈpraɪərət, -s

prioress
BR ˈprʌɪərɪs,
ˌprʌɪəˈrɛs, -ɪz
AM ˈpraɪ(ə)rəs, -əz

prioritisation
BR prʌɪˌɒrɪtʌɪˈzeɪʃn,
ˌprʌɪərɪtʌɪˈzeɪʃn
AM ˌpraɪˌɔrədəˈzeɪʃən,
ˌpraɪˌɔrəˌtaɪˈzeɪʃən

prioritise
BR prʌɪˈɒrɪtʌɪz,
ˈprʌɪərɪtʌɪz, -ɪz, -ɪŋ, -d
AM praɪˈɔrəˌtaɪz,
ˈpraɪərəˌtaɪz, -ɪz, -ɪŋ,
-d

prioritization
BR prʌɪˌɒrɪtʌɪˈzeɪʃn,
ˌprʌɪərɪtʌɪˈzeɪʃn
AM ˌpraɪˌɔrədəˈzeɪʃən,
ˌpraɪˌɔrəˌtaɪˈzeɪʃən

prioritize
BR prʌɪˈɒrɪtʌɪz,
ˈprʌɪərɪtʌɪz, -ɪz, -ɪŋ, -d
AM praɪˈɔrəˌtaɪz,
ˈpraɪərəˌtaɪz, -ɪz, -ɪŋ,
-d

priority
BR prʌɪˈɒrɪt|i, -ɪz
AM praɪˈɔrədi, -z

priorship
BR ˈprʌɪəʃɪp, -s
AM ˈpraɪərˌʃɪp, -s

priory
BR ˈprʌɪər|i, -ɪz
AM ˈpraɪ(ə)ri, -z

Priscian
BR ˈprɪʃɪən, ˈprɪʃn
AM ˈprɪʃən

Priscilla
BR prɪˈsɪlə(r)
AM prəˈsɪlə

prise
BR prʌɪz, -ɪz, -ɪŋ, -d
AM praɪz, -ɪz, -ɪŋ, -d

prism
BR ˈprɪz(ə)m, -z
AM ˈprɪzəm, -z

prismal
BR ˈprɪzml
AM ˈprɪzməl

prismatic
BR prɪzˈmatɪk
AM prɪzˈmædɪk

prismatically
BR prɪzˈmatɪkli
AM prɪzˈmædək(ə)li

prismoid
BR ˈprɪzmɔɪd, -z
AM ˈprɪzˌmɔɪd, -z

prismoidal
BR prɪzˈmɔɪdl
AM prɪzˈmɔɪdəl

prison
BR ˈprɪzn, -z
AM ˈprɪzn, -z

prisoner
BR ˈprɪznə(r),
ˈprɪzn̩ə(r), -z
AM ˈprɪznər, ˈprɪzn̩ər,
-z

prissily
BR ˈprɪsɪli
AM ˈprɪsɪli

prissiness
BR ˈprɪsɪnɪs
AM ˈprɪsɪnɪs

prissy
BR ˈprɪs|i, -ɪə(r), -ɪɪst
AM ˈprɪsi, -ər, -ɪst

Priština
BR ˈprɪʃtɪnə(r)
AM ˈprɪʃtɪnə

pristine
BR ˈprɪstiːn
AM ˈprɪˌstɪn, prɪˈstɪn

Pritchard
BR ˈprɪtʃəd, ˈprɪtʃɑːd
AM ˈprɪtʃərd

Pritchett
BR ˈprɪtʃɪt
AM ˈprɪtʃɪt

prithee
BR ˈprɪðiː
AM ˈprɪði

Pritt
BR prɪt
AM prɪt

privacy
BR ˈprɪvəsi, ˈprʌɪvəsi
AM ˈpraɪvəsi

private
BR ˈprʌɪvɪt, -s
AM ˈpraɪvɪt, -s

privateer
BR ˌprʌɪvɪˈtɪə(r), -z, -ɪŋ
AM ˌpraɪvəˈtɪ(ə)r, -z,
-ɪŋ

privateering
BR ˌpraɪvɪˈtɪərɪŋ
AM ˌpraɪvəˈtɪrɪŋ
privateersman
BR ˌpraɪvɪˈtɪəzmən
AM ˌpraɪvəˈtɪrzmən
privateersmen
BR ˌpraɪvɪˈtɪəzmən
AM ˌpraɪvəˈtɪrzmən
privately
BR ˈpraɪvɪtli
AM ˈpraɪvɪtli
privation
BR praɪˈveɪʃn, -z
AM praɪˈveɪʃən, -z
privatisation
BR ˌpraɪvɪtaɪˈzeɪʃn, -z
AM ˌpraɪvədəˈzeɪʃən,
ˌpraɪvəˌtaɪˈzeɪʃən, -z
privatise
BR ˈpraɪvɪtaɪz, -ɪz, -ɪŋ,
-d
AM ˈpraɪvəˌtaɪz, -ɪz, -ɪŋ,
-d
privatiser
BR ˈpraɪvɪtaɪzə(r), -z
AM ˈpraɪvəˌtaɪzər, -z
privative
BR ˈpraɪvɪtɪv
AM ˈpraɪvədɪv
privatively
BR ˈpraɪvɪtɪvli
AM ˈpraɪvədɪvli
privatization
BR ˌpraɪvɪtaɪˈzeɪʃn, -z
AM ˌpraɪvədəˈzeɪʃən,
ˌpraɪvəˌtaɪˈzeɪʃən, -z
privatize
BR ˈpraɪvɪtaɪz, -ɪz, -ɪŋ,
-d
AM ˈpraɪvəˌtaɪz, -ɪz, -ɪŋ,
-d
privatizer
BR ˈpraɪvɪtaɪzə(r), -z
AM ˈpraɪvəˌtaɪzər, -z
privet
BR ˈprɪvɪt, -s
AM ˈprɪvɪt, -s
privilege
BR ˈprɪv(ɪ)l|ɪdʒ,
ˈprɪv|lɪdʒ, -ɪdʒɪz
AM ˈprɪv(ə)lɪdʒ, -ɪz
privileged
BR ˈprɪv(ɪ)lɪdʒd,
ˈprɪv|ɪdʒd
AM ˈprɪv(ə)lɪdʒd
privily
BR ˈprɪvɪli
AM ˈprɪvɪli
privity
BR ˈprɪvɪt|i, -ɪz
AM ˈprɪvɪdi, -z
privy
BR ˈprɪv|i, -ɪz
AM ˈprɪvi, -z
prix¹
singular
BR priː

AM pri
prix²
plural
BR priː, priːz
AM pri, priz
prix fixe
BR ˌpriː ˈfiːks, + ˈfiːks
AM ˌpri ˈfiks
Prix Goncourt
BR ˌpriː gɒˈkʊə(r),
+ gɒˈkɔː(r)
AM ˌpri ˌgɒnˈkʊ(ə)r,
ˌpri ˌgɑnˈkʊ(ə)r
prize
BR prʌɪz, -ɪz, -ɪŋ, -d
AM praɪz, -ɪz, -ɪŋ, -d
prizefight
BR ˈprʌɪzfʌɪt, -s
AM ˈpraɪzˌfaɪt, -s
prizefighter
BR ˈprʌɪzˌfʌɪtə(r), -z
AM ˈpraɪzˌfaɪdər, -z
prizefighting
BR ˈprʌɪzˌfʌɪtɪŋ
AM ˈpraɪzˌfaɪdɪŋ
prizeman
BR ˈprʌɪzmən
AM ˈpraɪzmən
prizemen
BR ˈprʌɪzmən
AM ˈpraɪzmən
prizewinner
BR ˈprʌɪzˌwɪnə(r), -z
AM ˈpraɪzˌwɪnər, -z
prizewinning
BR ˈprʌɪzˌwɪnɪŋ
AM ˈpraɪzˌwɪnɪŋ
PRO
BR ˌpiːɑːrˈəʊ, -z
AM ˌpiˌɑrˈoʊ, -z
pro
BR prəʊ, -z
AM proʊ, -z
proa
BR ˈprəʊə(r), -z
AM ˈproʊə, -z
proaction
BR (ˌ)prəʊˈakʃn
AM proʊˈækʃən
proactive
BR (ˌ)prəʊˈaktɪv
AM proʊˈæktɪv
proactively
BR (ˌ)prəʊˈaktɪvli
AM proʊˈæktɪvli
proactivity
BR ˌprəʊakˈtɪvɪti
AM ˌproʊˌækˈtɪvɪdi
pro-am
BR ˌprəʊˈam, -z
AM ˌproʊˈæm, -z
probabilism
BR ˈprɒbəbɪlɪz(ə)m,
ˈprɒbəb|ɪz(ə)m
AM ˈprɑbəbəˌlɪzəm

probabilist
BR ˈprɒbəbɪlɪst,
ˈprɒbəb|ɪst, -s
AM ˈprɑbəbələst, -s
probabilistic
BR ˌprɒbəbɪˈlɪstɪk,
ˌprɒbəb|ˈɪstɪk
AM ˌprɑbəbəˈlɪstɪk
probability
BR ˌprɒbəˈbɪlɪt|i, -ɪz
AM ˌprɑbəˈbɪlɪdi, -z
probable
BR ˈprɒbəbl
AM ˈprɑbəbəl
probably
BR ˈprɒbəbli
AM ˈprɑbəbli
proband
BR ˈprəʊband,
ˈprəʊbənd, -z
AM ˈproʊˌbænd, -z
probang
BR ˈprəʊbaŋ, -z
AM ˈproʊˌbæŋ, -z
probate
BR ˈprəʊbeɪt, -s
AM ˈproʊˌbeɪt, -s
probation
BR prəˈbeɪʃn
AM proʊˈbeɪʃən
probational
BR prəˈbeɪʃn(ə)l,
prəˈbeɪʃən(ə)l
AM proʊˈbeɪʃ(ə)nəl
probationary
BR prəˈbeɪʃn(ə)ri
AM proʊˈbeɪʃəˌnɛri
probationer
BR prəˈbeɪʃnə(r),
prəˈbeɪʃ(ə)nə(r), -z
AM proʊˈbeɪʃ(ə)nər, -z
probationership
BR prəˈbeɪʃnəʃɪp,
prəˈbeɪʃ(ə)nəʃɪp, -s
AM proʊˈbeɪʃ(ə)nərˌʃɪp,
-s
probative
BR ˈprəʊbətɪv
AM ˈproʊbədɪv
probe
BR prəʊb, -z, -ɪŋ, -d
AM proʊb, -z, -ɪŋ, -d
probeable
BR ˈprəʊbəbl
AM ˈproʊbəbəl
prober
BR ˈprəʊbə(r), -z
AM ˈproʊbər, -z
probing
BR ˈprəʊbɪŋ, -z
AM ˈproʊbɪŋ, -z
probingly
BR ˈprəʊbɪŋli
AM ˈproʊbɪŋli
probit
BR ˈprɒbɪt, -s
AM ˈprɑbət, -s

probity
BR ˈprəʊbɪti
AM ˈproʊbədi
problem
BR ˈprɒbləm, -z
AM ˈprɑbləm, -z
problematic
BR ˌprɒbləˈmatɪk
AM ˌprɑbləˈmædɪk
problematical
BR ˌprɒbləˈmatɪkl
AM ˌprɑbləˈmædəkəl
problematically
BR ˌprɒbləˈmatɪkli
AM ˌprɑbləˈmædək(ə)li
problematisation
BR ˌprɒbləmətaɪˈzeɪʃn
AM ˌprɑbləmədəˈzeɪʃən,
ˌprɑbləməˌtaɪˈzeɪʃən
problematise
BR ˈprɒbləmətʌɪz, -ɪz,
-ɪŋ, -d
AM ˈprɑbləməˌtaɪz, -ɪz,
-ɪŋ, -d
problematization
BR ˌprɒbləmətaɪˈzeɪʃn
AM ˌprɑbləmədəˈzeɪʃən,
ˌprɑbləməˌtaɪˈzeɪʃən
problematize
BR ˈprɒbləmətʌɪz, -ɪz,
-ɪŋ, -d
AM ˈprɑbləməˌtaɪz, -ɪz,
-ɪŋ, -d
probosces
BR prəˈbɒsiːz
AM proʊˈbɑsiz
proboscidean
BR ˌprɒbəˈsɪdɪən, -z
AM ˌproʊbəˈsɪdiən,
proʊˌbɑsəˈdiən, -z
proboscidian
BR ˌprɒbəˈsɪdɪən, -z
AM ˌproʊbəˈsɪdiən,
proʊˌbɑsəˈdiən, -z
proboscidiferous
BR prəˌbɒsɪˈdɪf(ə)rəs
AM proʊˌbɑsəˈdɪf(ə)rəs
proboscidiform
BR ˌprɒbəˈsɪdɪfɔːm
AM ˌproʊbəˈsɪdəˌfɔ(ə)rm
proboscis
BR prəˈbɒs|ɪs, -ɪsɪz
AM proʊˈbɑs|əz,
proʊˈbɑs|kəs,
-ɪsɪz\-ɪsɪz
Probyn
BR ˈprəʊbɪn
AM ˈproʊbən
procain
BR ˈprəʊkeɪn
AM ˈproʊˌkeɪn
procaine
BR ˈprəʊkeɪn
AM ˈproʊˌkeɪn
procaryote
BR prəʊˈkarɪəʊt,
prəʊˈkarɪɒt, -s
AM proʊˈkɛriout, -s

procaryotic
BR prəʊˌkarɪˈɒtɪk,
ˌprəʊkarɪˈɒtɪk
AM prouˌkɛriˈɑdɪk
Procea
BR ˈprəʊsɪə(r)
AM ˈprousie
procedural
BR prəˈsiːdʒ(ə)rəl,
prəˈsiːdʒ(ə)r̩l
AM prəˈsidʒərəl,
prouˈsidʒərəl
procedurally
BR prəˈsiːdʒ(ə)rəli,
prəˈsiːdʒ(ə)r̩li
AM prəˈsidʒərəli,
prouˈsidʒərəli
procedure
BR prəˈsiːdʒə(r), -z
AM prəˈsidʒər,
prouˈsidʒər, -z
proceed
verb
BR prəˈsiːd, -z, -ɪŋ, -ɪd
AM prəˈsid, prouˈsid,
-z, -ɪŋ, -ɪd
proceedings
BR prəˈsiːdɪŋz
AM prəˈsidɪŋz,
prouˈsidɪŋz
proceeds
noun
BR ˈprəʊsiːdz
AM ˈprouˌsidz
process¹
*noun, verb, treat in a
process*
BR ˈprəʊsɛs, -ɪz, -ɪŋ, -t
AM ˈprɑˌsɛs, -əz, -ɪŋ, -t
process²
*verb, walk in
procession*
BR prəˈsɛs, -ɪz, -ɪŋ, -t
AM prəˈsɛs, -əz, -ɪŋ, -t
processable
BR ˈprəʊsəsəbl,
ˈprəʊsɛsəbl
AM ˈprɑsəsəbəl
procession
BR prəˈsɛʃn, -z
AM prəˈsɛʃən, -z
processional
BR prəˈsɛʃn(ə)l,
prəˈsɛʃən(ə)l, -z
AM prəˈsɛʃ(ə)nəl, -z
processionary
BR prəˈsɛʃn(ə)ri
AM prəˈsɛʃənri,
prəˈsɛʃnɛri
processionist
BR prəˈsɛʃnɪst,
prəˈsɛʃənɪst, -s
AM prəˈsɛʃ(ə)nəst, -s
processor
BR ˈprəʊsɛsə(r), -z
AM ˈprɑˌsɛsər, -z
procès-verbal
BR ˌprɒseɪvɛəˈbaːl, -z

AM ˌprouˌseɪˌvərˈbal, -z
procès-verbaux
BR ˌprɒseɪvɛəˈbəʊ
AM ˌprouˌseɪˌvərˈbou
pro-choice
BR ˌprəʊˈtʃɔɪs
AM ˌprouˈtʃɔɪs
prochronism
BR ˈprəʊkrənɪz(ə)m,
-z
AM ˈproukrəˌnɪzəm,
ˈprɑkrəˌnɪzəm, -z
proclaim
BR prəˈkleɪm, -z, -ɪŋ, -d
AM prəˈkleɪm,
prouˈkleɪm, -z, -ɪŋ, -d
proclaimer
BR prəˈkleɪmə(r), -z
AM prəˈkleɪmər, -z
proclamation
BR ˌprɒkləˈmeɪʃn, -z
AM ˌprɑkləˈmeɪʃən, -z
proclamatory
BR prəʊˈklamət(ə)ri
AM prəˈklæməˌtɔri
proclitic
BR prəʊˈklɪtɪk, -s
AM prouˈklɪdɪk, -s
proclitically
BR prəˈklɪtɪkli
AM prouˈklɪdɪk(ə)li
proclivity
BR prəˈklɪvɪt|i, -ɪz
AM prəˈklɪvɪdi,
prouˈklɪvɪdi, -z
Procne
BR ˈprɒkni
AM ˈprɑkni
proconsul
BR ˌprəʊˈkɒnsl
AM prouˈkɑnsəl
proconsular
BR ˌprəʊˈkɒnsjʊlə(r)
AM prouˈkɑns(j)(ə)lər
proconsulate
BR ˌprəʊˈkɒnsjʊlət, -s
AM prouˈkɑns(j)(ə)lət,
-s
proconsulship
BR ˌprəʊˈkɒnslˌʃɪp, -s
AM prouˈkɑnsəlˌʃɪp, -s
Procopius
BR prəʊˈkəʊpɪəs
AM prouˈkoupɪəs
procrastinate
BR prəˈkræstɪneɪt,
-s, -ɪŋ, -ɪd
AM prəˈkræstəˌneɪt,
prouˈkræstəˌneɪt, -ts,
-dɪŋ, -dɪd
procrastination
BR prəˈkræstɪˈneɪʃn
AM prəˌkræstəˈneɪʃən,
prouˈkræstəˈneɪʃən
procrastinative
BR prəʊˈkræstɪnətɪv
AM prəˈkræstəˌneɪdɪv,
prouˈkræstəˌneɪdɪv

procrastinator
BR prəˈ(ʊ)ˈkræstɪneɪt-
ə(r), -z
AM prəˈkræstəˌneɪdər,
prouˈkræstəˌneɪdər,
-z
procrastinatory
BR prəˈ(ʊ)ˈkræstɪnə-
t(ə)ri
AM prəˈkræstənəˌtɔri,
prouˈkræstənəˌtɔri
procreant
BR ˈprəʊkrɪənt
AM ˈproukrɪənt
procreate
BR ˈprəʊkrɪeɪt, -s, -ɪŋ,
-ɪd
AM ˈproukriˌeɪ|t, -ts,
-dɪŋ, -dɪd
procreation
BR ˌprəʊkrɪˈeɪʃn
AM ˌproukriˈeɪʃən
procreative
BR ˈprəʊkrɪeɪtɪv,
ˈprəʊkrɪətɪv
AM ˈproukriˌeɪdɪv
procreator
BR ˈprəʊkrɪeɪtə(r), -z
AM ˈproukriˌeɪdər, -z
Procrustean
BR prəˈ(ʊ)ˈkrʌstɪən
AM prouˈkrʌstiən
Procrustes
BR prəˈ(ʊ)ˈkrʌstiːz
AM prouˈkrʌstiz
Procter
BR ˈprɒktə(r)
AM ˈprɑktər
proctological
BR ˌprɒktəˈlɒdʒɪkl
AM ˌprɑktəˈlɑdʒəkəl
proctologist
BR prɒkˈtɒlədʒɪst, -s
AM prɑkˈtɑlədʒəst, -s
proctology
BR prɒkˈtɒlədʒi
AM prɑkˈtɑlədʒi
proctor
BR ˈprɒktə(r), -z
AM ˈprɑktər, -z
proctorial
BR prɒkˈtɔːrɪəl
AM prɑkˈtɔriəl
proctorship
BR ˈprɒktəˌʃɪp, -s
AM ˈprɑktərˌʃɪp, -s
proctoscope
BR ˈprɒktəskəʊp, -s
AM ˈprɑktəˌskoup, -s
procumbent
BR prəˈ(ʊ)ˈkʌmb(ə)nt
AM prouˈkəmbənt
procurable
BR prəˈkjʊərəbl,
prəˈkjɔːrəbl
AM prəˈkjʊrəbəl

procural
BR prəˈkjʊərəl,
prəˈkjʊərl̩,
prəˈkjɔːrəl, prəˈkjɔːrl̩
AM prəˈkjərəl
procurance
BR prəˈkjʊərəns,
prəˈkjʊərn̩s,
prəˈkjɔːrəns,
prəˈkjɔːrn̩s
AM prəˈkjʊrəns
procuration
BR ˌprɒkjəˈreɪʃn, -z
AM ˌprakjəˈreɪʃən, -z
procurator
BR ˈprɒkjʊreɪtə(r), -z
AM ˈprakjəˌreɪdər, -z
procurator fiscal
BR ˌprɒkjʊreɪtə ˈfɪskl
AM ˌprakjəˌreɪdər
ˈfɪskəl
procuratorial
BR ˌprɒkjʊərəˈtɔːrɪəl
AM ˌprakjərəˈtɔriəl
**procurators
fiscal**
BR ˌprɒkjʊreɪtəz ˈfɪskl
AM ˌprakjəˌreɪdərz
ˈfɪskəl
procuratorship
BR ˈprɒkjʊreɪtəˌʃɪp, -s
AM ˈprakjəreɪdərˌʃɪp,
-s
procuratory
BR ˈprɒkjʊrət(ə)ri
AM ˈprakjərəˌtɔri
procure
BR prəˈkjʊə(r),
prəˈkjɔː(r), -z, -ɪŋ, -d
AM prəˈkju(ə)r,
prouˈkjʊ(ə)r, -z, -ɪŋ, -d
procurement
BR prəˈkjʊəm(ə)nt,
prəˈkjɔːm(ə)nt, -s
AM prəˈkjurmənt,
prouˈkjurmənt, -s
procurer
BR prəˈkjʊərə(r),
prəˈkjɔːrə(r), -z
AM prəˈkjurər,
prouˈkjurər, -z
procuress
BR prəˈkjʊərɛs,
prəˈkjʊərɪs,
prəˈkjɔːrɛs,
prəˈkjɔːrɪs, -ɪz
AM prəˈkjurəs,
prouˈkjurəs, -əz
Procyon
BR ˈprəʊsɪən
AM ˈprousɪən
prod
BR prɒd, -z, -ɪŋ, -ɪd
AM prad; -z, -ɪŋ, -əd
prodder
BR ˈprɒdə(r), -z
AM ˈpradər, -z

prodigal
BR ˈprɒdɪgl, -z
AM ˈprɑdəgəl, -z

prodigalise
BR ˈprɒdɪglʌɪz
ˈprɒdɪgəlʌɪz, -ɪz, -ɪŋ, -d
AM ˈprɑdɪgəˌlaɪz, -ɪz, -ɪŋ, -d

prodigality
BR ˌprɒdɪˈgalɪti
AM ˌprɑdəˈgælədi

prodigalize
BR ˈprɒdɪglʌɪz
ˈprɒdɪgəlʌɪz, -ɪz, -ɪŋ, -d
AM ˈprɑdəgəˌlaɪz, -ɪz, -ɪŋ, -d

prodigally
BR ˈprɒdɪgli,
ˈprɒdɪgəli
AM ˈprɑdəgəli

prodigalness
BR ˈprɒdɪglnəs
AM ˈprɑdəgəlnəs

prodigious
BR prəˈdɪdʒəs
AM prəˈdɪdʒəs,
prouˈdɪdʒəs

prodigiously
BR prəˈdɪdʒəsli
AM prəˈdɪdʒəsli,
prouˈdɪdʒəsli

prodigiousness
BR prəˈdɪdʒəsnəs
AM prəˈdɪdʒəsnəs,
prouˈdɪdʒəsnəs

prodigy
BR ˈprɒdɪdʒ|i, -ɪz
AM ˈprɑdədʒi, -z

prodromal
BR ˈprɒdrəuml,
prə(ʊ)ˈdrəuml
AM prouˈdroumǝl

prodrome
BR ˈprəudrəum, -z
AM ˈprouˌdroum, -z

prodromic
BR prə(ʊ)ˈdrɒmɪk
AM prouˈdrɑmɪk

produce¹
noun
BR ˈprɒdjuːs,
ˈprɒdʒuːs
AM ˈprɑˌdus, ˈprouˌdus

produce²
verb
BR prəˈdjuːs,
prəˈdʒuːs, -ɪz, -ɪŋ, -t
AM prəˈd(j)us,
prouˈd(j)us, -əz, -ɪŋ, -t

producer
BR prəˈdjuːsə(r),
prəˈdʒuːsə(r), -z
AM prəˈd(j)usər,
prouˈd(j)usər, -z

producibility
BR prəˌdjuːsɪˈbɪlɪti,
prəˌdʒuːsɪˈbɪlɪti

AM prəˌd(j)usəˈbɪlɪdi,
prouˌd(j)usəˈbɪlɪdi

producible
BR prəˈdjuːsɪbl,
prəˈdʒuːsɪbl
AM prəˈd(j)usəbl,
prouˈd(j)usəbl

product
BR ˈprɒdʌkt, -s
AM ˈprɑdək(t), -(t)s

production
BR prəˈdʌkʃn, -z
AM prəˈdəkʃən,
prouˈdəkʃən, -z

productional
BR prəˈdʌkʃn(ə)l,
prəˈdʌkʃən(ə)l
AM prəˈdəkʃ(ə)nəl,
prouˈdəkʃ(ə)nəl

productive
BR prəˈdʌktɪv
AM prəˈdəktɪv,
prouˈdəktɪv

productively
BR prəˈdʌktɪvli
AM prəˈdəktɪvli,
prouˈdəktɪvli

productiveness
BR prəˈdʌktɪvnɪs
AM prəˈdəktɪvnɪs,
prouˈdəktɪvnɪs

productivity
BR ˌprɒdʌkˈtɪvɪti
AM prɑˌdəkˈtɪvɪdi,
ˌprouˌdəkˈtɪvɪdi

proem
BR ˈprəuɛm, -z
AM ˈprouˌɛm, -z

proemial
BR prəuˈɛmɪəl
AM prouˈɛmɪəl

Prof.
BR prɒf, -s
AM prɑf, prɑf, -s

profanation
BR ˌprɒfəˈneɪʃn, -z
AM ˌprɑfəˈneɪʃən, -z

profane
BR prəˈfeɪn, -ə(r), -ɪst
AM prəˈfeɪn, prouˈfeɪn,
-ər, -ɪst

profanely
BR prəˈfeɪnli
AM prəˈfeɪnli,
prouˈfeɪnli

profaneness
BR prəˈfeɪnnɪs
AM prəˈfeɪnnɪs,
prouˈfeɪnnɪs

profaner
BR prəˈfeɪnə(r), -z
AM prəˈfeɪnər,
prouˈfeɪnər, -z

profanity
BR prəˈfanɪt|i, -ɪz
AM prəˈfænədi,
prouˈfænədi, -z

profess
BR prəˈfɛs, -ɪz, -ɪŋ, -t
AM prəˈfɛs, prouˈfɛs,
-əz, -ɪŋ, -t

professedly
BR prəˈfɛsɪdli
AM prəˈfɛsədli,
prouˈfɛsədli

profession
BR prəˈfɛʃn, -z
AM prəˈfɛʃən,
prouˈfɛʃən, -z

professional
BR prəˈfɛʃn(ə)l,
prəˈfɛʃ(ə)n(ə)l, -z
AM prəˈfɛʃ(ə)nəl,
prouˈfɛʃ(ə)nəl, -z

**professionalisa-
tion**
BR prəˌfɛʃnəlʌɪˈzeɪʃn,
prəˌfɛʃn̩lʌɪˈzeɪʃn,
prəˌfɛʃənlʌɪˈzeɪʃn,
prəˌfɛʃ(ə)nəlʌɪˈzeɪʃn
AM prəˌfɛʃənləˈzeɪʃən,
prouˌfɛʃnələˈzeɪʃən,
prəˌfɛʃnələˈzeɪʃən,
prouˌfɛʃnələˈzeɪʃən,
prəˌfɛʃnəlˌaɪˈzeɪʃən,
prouˌfɛʃənlˌaɪˈzeɪʃən,
prəˌfɛʃnəˌlaɪˈzeɪʃən,
prouˌfɛʃnəˌlaɪˈzeɪʃən

professionalise
BR prəˈfɛʃnəlʌɪz,
prəˈfɛʃn̩lʌɪz,
prəˈfɛʃənlʌɪz,
prəˈfɛʃ(ə)nəlʌɪz, -ɪz,
-ɪŋ, -d
AM prəˈfɛʃənlˌaɪz,
prouˈfɛʃənlˌaɪz,
prəˈfɛʃnəˌlaɪz,
prouˈfɛʃnəˌlaɪz, -ɪz,
-ɪŋ, -d

professionalism
BR prəˈfɛʃnəlɪz(ə)m,
prəˈfɛʃn̩lɪz(ə)m,
prəˈfɛʃənlɪz(ə)m,
prəˈfɛʃ(ə)nəlɪz(ə)m
AM prəˈfɛʃənlˌɪzəm,
prouˈfɛʃənlˌɪzəm,
prəˈfɛʃnəˌlɪzəm,
prouˈfɛʃnəˌlɪzəm

**professionaliza-
tion**
BR prəˌfɛʃnəlʌɪˈzeɪʃn,
prəˌfɛʃn̩lʌɪˈzeɪʃn,
prəˌfɛʃənlʌɪˈzeɪʃn,
prəˌfɛʃ(ə)nəlʌɪˈzeɪʃn
AM prəˌfɛʃənləˈzeɪʃən,
prouˌfɛʃnələˈzeɪʃən,
prəˌfɛʃnələˈzeɪʃən,
prouˌfɛʃnələˈzeɪʃən,
prəˌfɛʃnəlˌaɪˈzeɪʃən,
prouˌfɛʃənlˌaɪˈzeɪʃən,
prəˌfɛʃnəˌlaɪˈzeɪʃən,
prouˌfɛʃnəˌlaɪˈzeɪʃən

professionalize
BR prəˈfɛʃnəlʌɪz,
prəˈfɛʃn̩lʌɪz,
prəˈfɛʃənlʌɪz,

professionally
BR prəˈfɛʃnəli,
prəˈfɛʃn̩li,
prəˈfɛʃənli,
prəˈfɛʃ(ə)nəli
AM prəˈfɛʃ(ə)nəli,
prouˈfɛʃ(ə)nəli

professionless
BR prəˈfɛʃnləs
AM prəˈfɛʃənləs,
prouˈfɛʃənləs

professor
BR prəˈfɛsə(r), -z
AM prəˈfɛsər,
prouˈfɛsər, -z

professorate
BR prəˈfɛs(ə)rət, -s
AM prəˈfɛsərət,
prouˈfɛsərət, -s

professorial
BR ˌprɒfɪˈsɔːrɪəl
AM ˌprɑfəˈsɔːrɪəl,
ˌproufəˈsɔːrɪəl

professorially
BR ˌprɒfɪˈsɔːrɪəli
AM ˌprɑfəˈsɔːrɪəli,
ˌproufəˈsɔːrɪəli

professoriate
BR ˌprɒfɪˈsɔːrɪət
AM ˌprɑfəˈsɔːrɪət,
ˌproufəˈsɔːrɪət

professorship
BR prəˈfɛsəˌʃɪp, -s
AM prəˈfɛsərˌʃɪp,
prouˈfɛsərˌʃɪp, -s

proffer
BR ˈprɒflə(r), -əz,
-(ə)rɪŋ, -əd
AM ˈprɑf|ər, -ərz,
-(ə)rɪŋ, -ərd

proficiency
BR prəˈfɪʃnsi
AM prəˈfɪʃənsi,
prouˈfɪʃənsi

proficient
BR prəˈfɪʃnt
AM prəˈfɪʃənt,
prouˈfɪʃənt

proficiently
BR prəˈfɪʃntli
AM prəˈfɪʃən(t)li,
prouˈfɪʃən(t)li

profile
BR ˈprəufʌɪl, -z, -ɪŋ, -d
AM ˈprouˌfaɪl, -z, -ɪŋ, -d

profiler
BR ˈprəufʌɪlə(r), -z
AM ˈprouˌfaɪlər, -z

profilist
BR ˈprəufʌɪlɪst, -s
AM ˈprouˌfaɪlɪst, -s

profit
BR 'prɒf|ɪt, -ɪts, -ɪtɪŋ,
-ɪtɪd
AM 'prɑfə|t, -ts, -dɪŋ,
-dəd
profitability
BR ˌprɒfɪtə'bɪlɪt|i, -ɪz
AM ˌprɑfədə'bɪlɪdi, -z
profitable
BR 'prɒfɪtəbl
AM 'prɑfədəbəl,
'prɑftəbəl
profitableness
BR 'prɒfɪtəblnəs
AM 'prɑfədəbəlnəs,
'prɑftəbəlnəs
profitably
BR 'prɒfɪtəbli
AM 'prɑfədəbli,
'prɑftəbli
profiteer
BR ˌprɒfɪ'tɪə(r), -z, -ɪŋ,
-d
AM ˌprɑfə'tɪ(ə)r, -z, -ɪŋ,
-d
profiterole
BR prə'fɪtərəʊl, -z
AM prə'fɪdəˌroʊl, -z
profitless
BR 'prɒfɪtlɪs
AM 'prɑfətləs
profligacy
BR 'prɒfləgəsi
AM 'prɑfləgəsi
profligate
BR 'prɒflɪgət, -s
AM 'prɑfləgət,
'prɑfləˌgeɪt, -s
profligately
BR 'prɒflɪgətli
AM 'prɑfləgətli
profligateness
BR 'prɒflɪgətnəs
AM 'prɑfləgətnəs
pro-forma
BR (ˌ)prəʊ'fɔːmə(r)
AM proʊ'fɔrmə
profound
BR prə'faʊnd, -ə(r), -ɪst
AM prə'faʊnd,
proʊ'faʊnd, -ər, -əst
profoundly
BR prə'faʊndli
AM prə'faʊn(d)li,
proʊ'faʊn(d)li
profoundness
BR prə'faʊn(d)nəs
AM prə'faʊn(d)nəs,
proʊ'faʊn(d)nəs
Profumo
BR prə'fjuːməʊ
AM prə'f(j)umoʊ
profundity
BR prə'fʌndɪt|i, -ɪz
AM prə'fəndədi,
proʊ'fəndədi, -z
profuse
BR prə'fjuːs, -ɪst

AM prə'fjus, proʊ'fjus,
-əst
profusely
BR prə'fjuːsli
AM prə'fjusli,
proʊ'fjusli
profuseness
BR prə'fjuːsnəs
AM prə'fjusnəs,
proʊ'fjusnəs
profusion
BR prə'fjuːʒn, -z
AM prə'fjuʒən,
proʊ'fjuʒən, -z
prog
BR prɒg, -z
AM prɑg, -z
progenitive
BR prə(ʊ)'dʒenɪtɪv
AM prə'dʒenədɪv,
proʊ'dʒenədɪv
progenitor
BR prə(ʊ)'dʒenɪtə(r),
-z
AM prə'dʒenədər,
proʊ'dʒenədər, -z
progenitorial
BR ˌprəʊdʒenɪ'tɔːrɪəl,
prə(ʊ)ˌdʒenɪ'tɔːrɪəl
AM prəˌdʒenə'tɔrɪəl,
proʊˌdʒenə'tɔrɪəl
progenitorship
BR prə(ʊ)'dʒenɪtəʃɪp,
-s
AM prə'dʒenədərˌʃɪp,
proʊ'dʒenədərˌʃɪp, -s
progenitress
BR prə(ʊ)'dʒenɪtres,
prə(ʊ)'dʒenɪtrɪs, -ɪz
AM prə'dʒenətrəs,
proʊ'dʒenətrəs, -əz
progenitrices
BR prə(ʊ)'dʒenɪtrɪsiːz
AM proʊ'dʒenɪtrɪsiz
progenitrix
BR prə(ʊ)'dʒenɪtrɪks,
-ɪz
AM prə'dʒenətrɪks,
proʊ'dʒenətrɪks, -ɪz
progeniture
BR prə(ʊ)'dʒenɪtʃə(r)
AM prə'dʒenətʃər,
proʊ'dʒenətʃər,
proʊ'dʒenətʃʊ(ə)r
progeny
BR 'prɒdʒɪn|i, -ɪz
AM 'prɑdʒəni, -z
progesterone
BR prə'dʒestərəʊn
AM proʊ'dʒestəˌroʊn
progestogen
BR prə'dʒestədʒ(ə)n,
-z
AM proʊ'dʒestədʒən,
-z
proglottid
BR prə(ʊ)'glɒtɪd, -z
AM ˌproʊ'glɑdɪd, -z

proglottis
BR prəʊ'glɒtɪs, -ɪz
AM proʊ'gladəs, -əz
prognathic
BR prɒg'naθɪk
AM prag'næθɪk
prognathism
BR 'prɒgnəθɪz(ə)m
AM 'prɑgnəˌθɪzəm
prognathous
BR prɒg'neɪθəs,
'prɒgnəθəs
AM 'pragnəθəs
prognoses
BR prɒg'nəʊsiːz
AM prag'noʊˌsiz
prognosis
BR prɒg'nəʊsɪs
AM prag'noʊsəs
prognostic
BR prɒg'nɒstɪk
AM prag'nastɪk
prognosticable
BR prɒg'nɒstɪkəbl
AM prag'nastəkəbəl
prognostically
BR prɒg'nɒstɪkli
AM prag'nastək(ə)li
prognosticate
BR prɒg'nɒstɪkeɪt, -s,
-ɪŋ, -ɪd
AM prag'nastəˌkeɪ|t,
-ts, -dɪŋ, -dɪd
prognostication
BR prɒgˌnɒstɪ'keɪʃn,
-z
AM pragˌnastə'keɪʃən,
-z
prognosticative
BR prɒg'nɒstɪkətɪv
AM prag'nastəˌkeɪdɪv,
prag'nastəkədɪv
prognosticator
BR prɒg'nɒstɪkeɪtə(r),
-z
AM prag'nastəˌkeɪdər,
-z
prognosticatory
BR prɒg'nɒstɪkət(ə)ri
AM prag'nastəkəˌtori
program
BR 'prəʊgram, -z, -ɪŋ,
-d
AM 'proʊˌgræm, -z, -ɪŋ,
-d
programable
BR 'prəʊgraməbl,
prə(ʊ)'graməbl
AM proʊ'græməbəl
programmability
BR ˌprəʊgramə'bɪlɪti,
prə(ʊ)ˌgramə'bɪlɪti
AM proʊˌgræmə'bɪlɪdi
programmable
BR 'prəʊgraməbl,
prə(ʊ)'graməbl
AM proʊ'græməbəl

programmatic
BR ˌprəʊgrə'matɪk
AM ˌproʊgrə'mædɪk
programmatically
BR ˌprəʊgrə'matɪkli
AM ˌproʊgrə'mædək-
(ə)li
programme
BR 'prəʊgram, -z, -ɪŋ,
-d
AM 'proʊˌgræm, -z, -ɪŋ,
-d
programmer
BR 'prəʊgramə(r), -z
AM 'proʊˌgræmər, -z
progress[1]
noun
BR 'prəʊgres, -ɪz
AM 'pragrəs, -əz
progress[2]
verb
BR prə(ʊ)'gres,
'prəʊgres, -ɪz, -ɪŋ, -d
AM prə'gres,
proʊ'gres, -əz, -ɪŋ, -d
progression
BR prə'greʃn, -z
AM prə'greʃən,
proʊ'greʃən, -z
progressional
BR prə'greʃn(ə)l,
prə'greʃən(ə)l
AM prə'greʃ(ə)nəl
proʊ'greʃ(ə)nəl
progressionist
BR prə'greʃnɪst,
prə'greʃənɪst, -s
AM prə'greʃənəst, -s
progressive
BR prə'gresɪv, -z
AM prə'gresɪv,
proʊ'gresɪv, -z
progressively
BR prə'gresɪvli
AM prə'gresɪvli,
proʊ'gresɪvli
progressiveness
BR prə'gresɪvnɪs
AM prə'gresɪvnɪs,
proʊ'gresɪvnɪs
progressivism
BR prə'gresɪvɪz(ə)m
AM prə'gresəˌvɪzəm,
proʊ'gresəˌvɪzəm
progressivist
BR prə'gresɪvɪst, -s
AM prə'gresəvəst,
proʊ'gresəvəst, -s
pro hac vice
BR ˌprəʊ hɑːk 'vʌɪsi,
+ hak +, + 'viːkeɪ
AM ˌproʊ ˌhæk 'vaɪsi
prohibit
BR prə(ʊ)'hɪb|ɪt, -ɪts,
-ɪtɪŋ, -ɪtɪd
AM prə'hɪbɪ|t,
proʊ'hɪbɪ|t, -ts, -dɪŋ,
-dɪd

prohibiter
BR prə(ʊ)'hɪbɪtə(r), -z
AM prə'hɪbɪdər,
proʊ'hɪbɪdər, -z

prohibition
BR ˌprəʊ(h)ɪ'bɪʃn, -z
AM ˌproʊ(h)ə'bɪʃən, -z

prohibitionary
BR ˌprəʊ(h)ɪ'bɪʃn(ə)ri
AM ˌproʊ(h)ə'bɪʃəˌneri

prohibitionism
BR ˌprəʊ(h)ɪ'bɪʃnɪz(ə)m,
ˌprəʊ(h)ɪ'bɪʃnɪz(ə)m
AM ˌproʊ(h)ə'bɪʃəˌnɪz-
əm

prohibitionist
BR ˌprəʊ(h)ɪ'bɪʃnɪst,
ˌprəʊ(h)ɪ'bɪʃənɪst, -s
AM ˌproʊ(h)ə'bɪʃ(ə)nəst,
-s

prohibitive
BR prə(ʊ)'hɪbɪtɪv
AM prə'hɪbədɪv,
proʊ'hɪbədɪv

prohibitively
BR prə(ʊ)'hɪbɪtɪvli
AM prə'hɪbədɪvli,
proʊ'hɪbədɪvli

prohibitiveness
BR prə(ʊ)'hɪbɪtɪvnɪs
AM prə'hɪbədɪvnɪs,
proʊ'hɪbədɪvnɪs

prohibitor
BR prə(ʊ)'hɪbɪtə(r), -z
AM prə'hɪbɪdər,
proʊ'hɪbɪdər, -z

prohibitory
BR prə(ʊ)'hɪbɪt(ə)ri
AM prə'hɪbɪˌtɔri,
proʊ'hɪbɪˌtɔri

project[1]
noun
BR 'prɒdʒekt, -s
AM 'prɑˌdʒek(t), -s

project[2]
verb
BR prə'dʒekt, -s, -ɪŋ, -ɪd
AM prə'dʒek|(t),
proʊ'dʒek|(t), -(t)s,
-tɪŋ, -təd

projectile
BR prə'dʒektʌɪl, -z
AM prə'dʒektl
prə'dʒekˌtaɪl,
proʊ'dʒektl,
proʊ'dʒekˌtaɪl, -z

projection
BR prə'dʒekʃn, -z
AM prə'dʒekʃən,
proʊ'dʒekʃən, -z

projectionist
BR prə'dʒekʃn̩ɪst,
prə'dʒekʃənɪst, -s
AM prə'dʒekʃənəst,
proʊ'dʒekʃənəst, -s

projective
BR prə'dʒektɪv

AM prə'dʒektɪv,
proʊ'dʒektɪv

projectively
BR prə'dʒektɪvli
AM prə'dʒektɪvli,
proʊ'dʒektɪvli

projector
BR prə'dʒektə(r), -z
AM prə'dʒektər,
proʊ'dʒektər, -z

prokaryote
BR prəʊ'karɪəʊt,
prəʊ'karɪɒt, -s
AM proʊ'kerioʊt, -s

prokaryotic
BR ˌprəʊˌkarɪ'ɒtɪk,
ˌprəʊkarɪ'ɒtɪk
AM proʊˌkeri'ɑdɪk

Prokofiev
BR prə'kɒfɪef
AM proʊ'kɒfiˌef,
proʊ'kɑfiˌef

prolactin
BR prəʊ'laktɪn
AM prəʊ'lækt(ə)n

prolapse
BR 'prəʊlaps, -ɪz, -ɪŋ, -t
AM proʊ'læps,
'proʊˌlæps, -əz, -ɪŋ, -t

prolapsus
BR prəʊ'lapsəs
AM proʊ'læpsəs,
'proʊˌlæpsəs

prolate
BR 'prəʊleɪt, prəʊ'leɪt
AM proʊ'leɪt, 'proʊˌleɪt

prolately
BR 'prəʊleɪtli,
prə(ʊ)'leɪtli
AM proʊ'leɪtli,
'proʊˌleɪtli

prolative
BR 'prəʊlətɪv,
prə(ʊ)'leɪtɪv
AM 'proʊlədɪv,
proʊ'leɪdɪv,
'proʊˌleɪdɪv

prole
BR prəʊl, -z
AM proʊl, -z

proleg
BR 'prəʊˌleg, -z
AM 'proʊˌleg, -z

prolegomena
BR ˌprəʊleˈgɒmɪnə(r),
ˌprəʊlɪ'gɒmɪnə(r)
AM ˌproʊlə'gɑmənə

prolegomenary
BR ˌprəʊle'gɒmɪn(ə)ri,
ˌprəʊlɪ'gɒmɪn(ə)ri
AM ˌproʊlə'gɑməˌneri

prolegomenon
BR ˌprəʊle'gɒmɪnən,
ˌprəʊlɪ'gɒmɪnən
AM ˌproʊlə'gɑməˌnɑn,
ˌproʊlə'gɑmənən

prolegomenous
BR ˌprəʊle'gɒmɪnəs,
ˌprəʊlɪ'gɒmɪnəs
AM ˌproʊlə'gɑmənəs

prolepses
BR prə(ʊ)'lepsi:z
AM proʊ'lepˌsiz

prolepsis
BR prə(ʊ)'lepsɪs
AM proʊ'lepsəs

proleptic
BR prə(ʊ)'leptɪk
AM proʊ'leptɪk

proletarian
BR ˌprəʊlɪ'tɛːrɪən, -z
AM ˌproʊlə'tɛriən, -z

proletarianisation
BR ˌprəʊlɪˌtɛːrɪənʌɪ-
'zeɪʃn
AM ˌproʊləˌteriənə-
'zeɪʃən,
ˌproʊləˌteriəˌnaɪ'zeɪʃən

proletarianise
BR ˌprəʊlɪ'tɛːrɪənʌɪz,
-ɪz, -ɪŋ, -d
AM ˌproʊlə'teriəˌnaɪz,
-ɪz, -ɪŋ, -d

proletarianism
BR ˌprəʊlɪ'tɛːrɪənɪz(ə)m
AM ˌproʊlə'teriəˌnɪzəm

proletarianization
BR ˌprəʊlɪˌtɛːrɪənʌɪ-
'zeɪʃn
AM ˌproʊləˌteriənə-
'zeɪʃən,
ˌproʊləˌteriəˌnaɪ'zeɪʃən

proletarianize
BR ˌprəʊlɪ'tɛːrɪənʌɪz,
-ɪz, -ɪŋ, -d
AM ˌproʊlə'teriəˌnaɪz,
-ɪz, -ɪŋ, -d

proletariat
BR ˌprəʊlɪ'tɛːrɪət
AM ˌproʊlə'teriət

pro-life
BR ˌprəʊ'lʌɪf
AM ˌproʊ'laɪf

proliferate
BR prə'lɪfəreɪt, -s, -ɪŋ,
-ɪd
AM prə'lɪfəˌreɪ|t,
proʊ'lɪfəˌreɪ|t, -ts, -dɪŋ,
-dɪd

proliferation
BR prəˌlɪfə'reɪʃn
AM prəˌlɪfə'reɪʃən,
proʊˌlɪfə'reɪʃən

proliferative
BR prə'lɪf(ə)rətɪv
AM prə'lɪfərədɪv,
proʊ'lɪfərədɪv,
prə'lɪfəˌreɪdɪv,
proʊ'lɪfəˌreɪdɪv

proliferator
BR prə'lɪfəreɪtə(r), -z
AM prə'lɪfəˌreɪdər,
proʊ'lɪfəˌreɪdər, -z

proliferous
BR prə'lɪf(ə)rəs
AM prə'lɪf(ə)rəs,
proʊ'lɪf(ə)rəs

prolific
BR prə'lɪfɪk
AM prə'lɪfɪk, proʊ'lɪfɪk

prolificacy
BR prə'lɪfɪkəsi
AM prə'lɪfɪkəsi,
proʊ'lɪfɪkəsi

prolifically
BR prə'lɪfɪkli
AM prə'lɪfɪk(ə)li,
proʊ'lɪfɪk(ə)li

prolificity
BR ˌprəʊlɪ'fɪsɪti
AM ˌproʊlə'fɪsɪdi

prolificness
BR prə'lɪfɪknɪs
AM prə'lɪfɪknɪs,
proʊ'lɪfɪknɪs

proline
BR 'prəʊli:n, -z
AM 'proʊˌlin, 'proʊlən,
-z

prolix
BR 'prəʊlɪks
AM proʊ'lɪks,
'proʊˌlɪks

prolixity
BR prə'lɪksɪti
AM proʊ'lɪksɪdi

prolixly
BR 'prəʊlɪksli
AM proʊ'lɪksli,
'proʊˌlɪksli

prolocutor
BR prəʊ'lɒkjʊtə(r), -z
AM proʊ'lɑkjədər, -z

prolocutorship
BR prəʊ'lɒkjʊtəʃɪp, -s
AM proʊ'lɑkjədərˌʃɪp,
-s

PROLOG
BR 'prəʊlɒg
AM 'proʊˌlɔg, 'proʊˌlɑg

prolog
BR 'prəʊlɒg, -z
AM 'proʊˌlɔg,
'proʊˌlɑg, -z

prologise
BR 'prəʊləgʌɪz, -ɪz, -ɪŋ,
-d
AM 'proʊləˌgaɪz, -ɪz,
-ɪŋ, -d

prologize
BR 'prəʊləgʌɪz, -ɪz, -ɪŋ,
-d
AM 'proʊləˌgaɪz, -ɪz,
-ɪŋ, -d

prologue
BR 'prəʊlɒg, -z
AM 'proʊˌlɔg,
'proʊˌlɑg, -z

prolong
BR prə'lɒŋ, -z, -ɪŋ, -d

AM prəˈlɒŋ, prooˈlɒŋ,
prəˈlaŋ, prooˈlaŋ, -z,
-ɪŋ, -d

prolongation
BR ˌprəʊlɒŋˈgeɪʃn,
ˌprʊlɒŋˈgeɪʃn
AM proʊˌlɒŋˈ(g)eɪʃən,
prəˌlɒŋˈ(g)eɪʃən,
prooˌlaŋˈ(g)eɪʃən,
prəˌlaŋˈ(g)eɪʃən

prolonger
BR prəˈlɒŋə(r), -z
AM prəˈlɒŋər,
prooˈlɒŋər, prəˈlaŋər,
prooˈlaŋər, -z

prolusion
BR prəˈl(j)uːʒn
AM prooˈl(j)uʒən

prolusory
BR prəˈl(j)uːz(ə)ri
AM prooˈl(j)uzəri

prom
BR prɒm, -z
AM pram, -z

promenade
BR ˌprɒməˈnɑːd,
ˈprɒmənɑːd, -z, -ɪŋ, -ɪd
AM ˈpraməˌneɪd,
ˈpraməˌnad, -z, -ɪŋ, -əd

promenader
BR ˌprɒməˈnɑːdə(r),
ˈprɒmənɑːdə(r), -z
AM ˈpraməˌneɪdər,
ˈpraməˌnadər, -z

promethazine
BR prə(ʊ)ˈmɛθəziːn
AM prooˈmɛθəˌzin,
prooˈmɛθəzən

Promethean
BR prəˈmiːθiən
AM prəˈmiθiən,
prooˈmiθiən

Prometheus
BR prəˈmiːθiəs
AM prəˈmiθiəs,
prooˈmiθiəs

promethium
BR prəˈmiːθiəm
AM prooˈmiθiəm

prominence
BR ˈprɒmɪnəns, -ɪz
AM ˈpramənəns, -əz

prominency
BR ˈprɒmɪnənsi
AM ˈpramənənsi

prominent
BR ˈprɒmɪnənt
AM ˈpramənənt

prominenti
BR ˌprɒmɪˈnɛnti(ː)
AM ˌpraməˈnɛn(t)i

prominently
BR ˈprɒmɪnəntli
AM ˈpramənən(t)li

promiscuity
BR ˌprɒmɪˈskjuːɪti
AM ˌpraməˈskjuədi,
ˌprooˌmɪˈskjuədi

promiscuous
BR prəˈmɪskjuəs
AM prəˈmɪskjəwəs

promiscuously
BR prəˈmɪskjuəsli
AM prəˈmɪskjəwəsli

promiscuousness
BR prəˈmɪskjuəsnəs
AM prəˈmɪskjəwəsnəs

promise
BR ˈprɒm|ɪs, -ɪsɪz, -ɪsɪŋ,
-ɪst
AM ˈpraməs, -əz, -ɪŋ, -t

promisee
BR ˌprɒmɪˈsiː, -z
AM ˌpraməˈsi, -z

promiser
BR ˈprɒmɪsə(r), -z
AM ˈpraməsər, -z

promisingly
BR ˈprɒmɪsɪŋli
AM ˈpraməsɪŋli

promisor
BR ˈprɒmɪsə(r), -z
AM ˈpraməsər, -z

promissory
BR ˈprɒmɪs(ə)ri
AM ˈpraməˌsori

prommer
BR ˈprɒmə(r), -z
AM ˈpramər, -z

promo
BR ˈprəʊməʊ, -z
AM ˈprooˌmoʊ, -z

promontory
BR ˈprɒm(ə)nt(ə)r|i,
-ɪz
AM ˈpramənˌtori, -z

promotability
BR prəˌməʊtəˈbɪlɪti
AM prəˌmoʊdəˈbɪlɪdi

promotable
BR prəˈməʊtəbl
AM prəˈmoʊdəbəl

promote
BR prəˈməʊt, -s, -ɪŋ, -ɪd
AM prəˈmoʊ|t, -ts, -dɪŋ,
-dəd

promoter
BR prəˈməʊtə(r), -z
AM prəˈmoʊdər, -z

promotion
BR prəˈməʊʃn, -z
AM prəˈmoʊʃən, -z

promotional
BR prəˈməʊʃn(ə)l,
prəˈməʊʃən(ə)l
AM prəˈmoʊʃ(ə)nəl

promotive
BR prəˈməʊtɪv
AM prəˈmoʊdɪv

prompt
BR prɒm(p)t, -s, -ɪŋ, -ɪd,
-ə(r), -ɪst
AM pram(p)t, -s, -ɪŋ,
-əd, -ər, -əst

prompter
BR ˈprɒm(p)tə(r), -z
AM ˈpram(p)tər, -z

prompting
BR ˈprɒm(p)tɪŋ, -z
AM ˈpram(p)tɪŋ, -z

promptitude
BR ˈprɒm(p)tɪtjuːd,
ˈprɒm(p)tɪtʃuːd
AM ˈpram(p)təˌtud

promptly
BR ˈprɒm(p)tli
AM ˈpram(p)tli,
ˈpramp(t)li

promptness
BR ˈprɒmp(t)nəs
AM ˈpramp(t)nəs

promulgate
BR ˈprɒmlgeɪt, -s, -ɪŋ,
-ɪd
AM ˈpraməlˌgeɪ|t, -ts,
-dɪŋ, -dɪd

promulgation
BR ˌprɒmlˈgeɪʃn, -z
AM ˌpraməlˈgeɪʃən,
ˌprooməlˈgeɪʃən, -z

promulgator
BR ˈprɒmlgeɪtə(r), -z
AM ˈpraməlˌgeɪdər, -z

promulge
BR prəˈmʌldʒ, -ɪz, -ɪŋ,
-d
AM prooˈməldʒ, -əz,
-ɪŋ, -d

pronaoi
BR prəʊˈneɪɔɪ
AM prooˈneɪˌɔɪ

pronaos
BR prəʊˈneɪɒs
AM prooˈneɪɑs

pronate
BR ˈprəʊneɪt, -s, -ɪŋ, -ɪd
AM ˈprooˌneɪ|t, -ts, -dɪŋ,
-dɪd

pronation
BR prəʊˈneɪʃn
AM prooˈneɪʃən

pronator
BR prəʊˈneɪtə(r), -z
AM ˈprooˌneɪdər, -z

prone
BR prəʊn, -ə(r), -ɪst
AM proon, -ər, -əst

pronely
BR ˈprəʊnli
AM ˈproonli

proneness
BR ˈprəʊnnəs
AM ˈproo(n)nəs

proneur
BR prəʊˈnɜː(r), -z
AM prooˈnər, -z

prong
BR prɒŋ, -z, -d
AM prɔŋ, praŋ, -z, -d

pronghorn
BR ˈprɒŋhɔːn, -z

pronominal
BR prə(ʊ)ˈnɒmɪnl
AM prəˈnamənəl,
prooˈnamənəl

pronominalise
BR prə(ʊ)ˈnɒmɪnlˌaɪz,
prə(ʊ)ˈnɒmɪnəlˌaɪz,
-ɪz, -ɪŋ, -d
AM prəˈnamənəˌlaɪz,
prooˈnamənəˌlaɪz,
-ɪz, -ɪŋ, -d

pronominalize
BR prə(ʊ)ˈnɒmɪnlˌaɪz,
prə(ʊ)ˈnɒmɪnəlˌaɪz,
-ɪz, -ɪŋ, -d
AM prəˈnamənəˌlaɪz,
prooˈnamənəˌlaɪz,
-ɪz, -ɪŋ, -d

pronominally
BR prə(ʊ)ˈnɒmɪnli,
prə(ʊ)ˈnɒmɪnəli
AM prəˈnamənəli,
prooˈnamənəli

pronoun
BR ˈprəʊnaʊn, -z
AM ˈprooˌnaʊn, -z

pronounce
BR prəˈnaʊns, -ɪz, -ɪŋ, -t
AM prəˈnaʊns, -əz, -ɪŋ,
-t

pronounceable
BR prəˈnaʊnsəbl
AM prəˈnaʊnsəbəl

pronouncedly
BR prəˈnaʊnsɪdli
AM prəˈnaʊnsədli

pronouncement
BR prəˈnaʊnsm(ə)nt,
-s
AM prəˈnaʊnsmənt, -s

pronouncer
BR prəˈnaʊnsə(r), -z
AM prəˈnaʊnsər, -z

pronto
BR ˈprɒntəʊ
AM ˈpran(t)oʊ

pronunciamento
BR prəˌnʌnsɪəˈmɛntəʊ,
prəˌnʌnʃ(i)əˈmɛntəʊ,
-z
AM prooˌnən(t)ʃ(i)ə-
ˈmɛn(t)oʊ, -z

pronunciation
BR prəˌnʌnsɪˈeɪʃn, -z
AM prəˌnənsiˈeɪʃən, -z

proof
BR pruːf, -s, -ɪŋ, -t
AM pruf, -s, -ɪŋ, -t

proofless
BR ˈpruːfləs
AM ˈprufləs

proofmark
BR ˈpruːfmɑːk, -s
AM ˈprufˌmark, -s

proof-plane
BR ˈpruːfpleɪn, -z

AM 'pruf,pleɪn, -z
proofread¹
present tense
BR 'pruːfriːd, -z, -ɪŋ
AM 'pruf,rid, -z, -ɪŋ
proofread²
past tense
BR 'pruːfrɛd
AM 'pruf,rɛd
proofreader
BR 'pruːf,riːdə(r), -z
AM 'pruf,ridər, -z
prop
BR prɒp, -s, -ɪŋ, -t
AM prap, -s, -ɪŋ, -t
propaedeutic
BR ,prəʊpiː'djuːtɪk,
,prəʊpiː'dʒuːtɪk, -s
AM ,proʊpi'd(j)udɪk, -s
propaedeutical
BR ,prəʊpiː'djuːtɪkl,
,prəʊpiː'dʒuːtɪkl
AM ,proʊpi'd(j)udəkəl
propaganda
BR ,prɒpə'gandə(r)
AM ,prapə'gændə
propagandise
BR ,prɒpə'gandʌɪz, -ɪz,
-ɪŋ, -d
AM ,prapə'gæn,daɪz,
-ɪz, -ɪŋ, -d
propagandism
BR ,prɒpə'gandɪz(ə)m
AM ,prapə'gæn,dɪzəm
propagandist
BR ,prɒpə'gandɪst, -s
AM ,prapə'gændəst, -s
propagandistic
BR ,prɒpəgan'dɪstɪk
AM ,prapə,gæn'dɪstɪk
propagandistically
BR ,prɒpəgan'dɪstɪkli
AM ,prapə,gæn'dɪstək-
(ə)li
propagandize
BR ,prɒpə'gandʌɪz, -ɪz,
-ɪŋ, -d
AM ,prapə'gæn,daɪz,
-ɪz, -ɪŋ, -d
propagate
BR 'prɒpəgeɪt, -s, -ɪŋ,
-ɪd
AM 'prapə,geɪ|t, -ts,
-dɪŋ, -dɪd
propagation
BR ,prɒpə'geɪʃn
AM ,prapə'geɪʃən
propagative
BR 'prɒpəgeɪtɪv
AM 'prapə,geɪdɪv
propagatively
BR 'prɒpəgeɪtɪvli
AM 'prapə,geɪdɪvli
propagator
BR 'prɒpəgeɪtə(r), -z
AM 'prapə,geɪdər, -z
propane
BR 'prəʊpeɪn

AM 'proʊ,peɪn
propanoic acid
BR ,prəʊpənɔɪk 'asɪd
AM ,proʊpə'nɔɪk
'æsəd
propanone
BR 'prəʊpənəʊn
AM 'proʊpə,noʊn
proparoxytone
BR ,prəʊpə'rɒksɪtəʊn,
-z
AM ,proʊpə'raksə,toʊn,
-z
propel
BR prə'pɛl, -z, -ɪŋ, -d
AM prə'pɛl, proʊ'pɛl,
-z, -ɪŋ, -d
propellant
BR prə'pɛlənt,
prə'pɛlnt, -s
AM prə'pɛlənt,
proʊ'pɛlənt, -s
propellent
BR prə'pɛlənt,
prə'pɛlnt
AM prə'pɛlənt,
proʊ'pɛlənt
propeller
BR prə'pɛlə(r), -z
AM prə'pɛlər,
proʊ'pɛlər, -z
propene
BR 'prəʊpiːn
AM 'proʊ,pin
propensity
BR prə'pɛnsɪt|i, -ɪz
AM prə'pɛnsədi,
proʊ'pɛnsədi, -z
proper
BR 'prɒpə(r)
AM 'prapər
properispomena
BR prə(ʊ),pɛrɪ'spɒm-
ɪnə(r)
AM proʊ,pɛri'spoʊmə-
nə,
proʊ,pɛri'spamənə
properispomenon
BR prə(ʊ),pɛrɪ'spɒmɪ-
nɒn
AM proʊ,pɛri'spoʊmə-
,nan,
proʊ,pɛri'spamə,nan,
proʊ,pɛri'spoʊmənən,
proʊ,pɛri'spamənən
properly
BR 'prɒp(ə)li
AM 'prapərli
properness
BR 'prɒpənəs
AM 'prapərnəs
propertied
BR 'prɒpətɪd
AM 'prapərdid
Propertius
BR prə(ʊ)'pɜː'ʃ(ɪ)əs
AM proʊ'pərʃ(i)əs

property
BR 'prɒpət|i, -ɪz
AM 'prapərdi, -z
prophase
BR 'prəʊfeɪz, -ɪz
AM 'proʊ,feɪz, -ɪz
prophecy
BR 'prɒfɪs|i, -ɪz
AM 'prafəsi, -z
prophesier
BR 'prɒfɪsʌɪə(r), -z
AM 'prafə,saɪ(ə)r, -z
prophesy
BR 'prɒfɪsʌɪ, -z, -ɪŋ, -d
AM 'prafə,saɪ, -z, -ɪŋ, -d
prophet
BR 'prɒfɪt, -s
AM 'prafət, -s
prophetess
BR ,prɒfɪ'tɛs, 'prɒfɪtɪs,
-ɪz
AM 'prafədəs, -əz
prophethood
BR 'prɒfɪthʊd
AM 'prafət,(h)ʊd
prophetic
BR prə'fɛtɪk
AM prə'fɛdɪk,
proʊ'fɛdɪk
prophetical
BR prə'fɛtɪkl
AM prə'fɛdəkəl,
proʊ'fɛdəkəl
prophetically
BR prə'fɛtɪkli
AM prə'fɛdək(ə)li,
proʊ'fɛdək(ə)li
propheticism
BR prə'fɛtɪsɪz(ə)m, -z
AM prə'fɛdə,sɪzəm,
proʊ'fɛdə,sɪzəm, -z
prophetism
BR 'prɒfɪtɪz(ə)m
AM 'prafə,tɪzəm
prophetship
BR 'prɒfɪtʃɪp
AM 'prafət,ʃɪp
prophylactic
BR ,prɒfɪ'laktɪk, -s
AM ,proʊfə'læktɪk, -s
prophylaxis
BR ,prɒfɪ'laksɪs
AM ,proʊfə'læksəs
propinquity
BR prə'pɪŋkwɪti
AM prə'pɪŋkwɪdi,
proʊ'pɪŋkwɪdi
propionate
BR 'prəʊpɪəneɪt, -s
AM 'proʊpiə,neɪt, -s
propionic acid
BR ,prəʊpɪanɪk 'asɪd
AM ,proʊpi'ænɪk
,æsəd
propitiate
BR prə'pɪʃɪeɪt, -s, -ɪŋ,
-ɪd

AM prə'pɪʃi,eɪ|t,
proʊ'pɪʃi,eɪ|t, -ts, -dɪŋ,
-dɪd
propitiation
BR prə,pɪʃɪ'eɪʃn, -z
AM prə,pɪʃi'eɪʃən,
proʊ,pɪʃi'eɪʃən, -z
propitiator
BR prə'pɪʃɪeɪtə(r), -z
AM prə'pɪʃi,eɪdər,
proʊ'pɪʃi,eɪdər, -z
propitiatorily
BR prə,pɪʃɪə'tɔːrɪli
AM prə,pɪʃiə'tɔːrəli,
proʊ,pɪʃiə'tɔːrəli
propitiatory
BR prə'pɪʃɪət(ə)ri
AM prə'pɪʃiə,tɔri,
proʊ'pɪʃiə,tɔri
propitious
BR prə'pɪʃəs
AM prə'pɪʃəs,
proʊ'pɪʃəs
propitiously
BR prə'pɪʃəsli
AM prə'pɪʃəsli,
proʊ'pɪʃəsli
propitiousness
BR prə'pɪʃəsnəs
AM prə'pɪʃəsnəs,
proʊ'pɪʃəsnəs
propjet
BR 'prɒpdʒɛt, -s
AM 'prap,dʒɛt, -s
propolis
BR 'prɒpəlɪs
AM 'prapələs
proponent
BR prə'pəʊnənt, -s
AM prə'poʊnənt,
proʊ'poʊnənt, -s
Propontis
BR prə(ʊ)'pɒntɪs
AM prə'pan(t)əs
proportion
BR prə'pɔː|ʃn, -nz,
-nɪŋ \-(ə)nɪŋ, -nd
AM prə'pɔrʃ|ən,
pər'pɔrʃ|ən, -ənz,
-(ə)nɪŋ, -ənd
proportionable
BR prə'pɔːʃnəbl,
prə'pɔːʃ(ə)nəbl
AM prə'pɔrʃənəbəl,
pər'pɔrʃənəbəl
proportionably
BR prə'pɔːʃnəbli,
prə'pɔːʃ(ə)nəbli
AM prə'pɔrʃənəbli,
pər'pɔrʃənəbli
proportional
BR prə'pɔːʃn̩(ə)l,
prə'pɔːʃən(ə)l
AM prə'pɔrʃ(ə)nəl,
pər'pɔrʃ(ə)nəl
proportionalist
BR prə'pɔːʃn̩lɪst,
prə'pɔːʃn̩lɪst,

prə'pɔː.ʃənl̩ɪst,
prə'pɔː.ʃ(ə)nəlɪst, -s
AM prə'pɔr.ʃənləst,
pər'pɔr.ʃənləst,
prə'pɔr.ʃnələst,
pər'pɔr.ʃnələst, -s
proportionality
BR prə,pɔː.ʃə'nælɪti
AM prə,pɔr.ʃə'næladi,
pər,pɔr.ʃə'næladi
proportionally
BR prə'pɔː.ʃnəli,
prə'pɔː.ʃn̩li,
prə'pɔː.ʃənli,
prə'pɔː.ʃ(ə)nəli
AM prə'pɔr.ʃ(ə)nəli,
pər'pɔr.ʃ(ə)nəli
proportionate
BR prə'pɔː.ʃənət,
prə'pɔː.ʃn̩ət
AM prə'pɔr.ʃ(ə)nət,
pər'pɔr.ʃ(ə)nət
proportionately
BR prə'pɔː.ʃənətli,
prə'pɔː.ʃn̩ətli
AM prə'pɔr.ʃ(ə)nətli,
pər'pɔr.ʃ(ə)nətli
proportionless
BR prə'pɔː.ʃnləs
AM prə'pɔr.ʃənləs,
pər'pɔr.ʃənləs
proportionment
BR prə'pɔː.ʃnm(ə)nt
AM prə'pɔr.ʃənmənt,
pər'pɔr.ʃənmənt
proposal
BR prə'pəʊzl, -z
AM prə'pouzəl, -z
propose
BR prə'pəʊz, -ɪz, -ɪŋ, -d
AM prə'pouz, -əz, -ɪŋ, -d
proposer
BR prə'pəʊzə(r), -z
AM prə'pouzər, -z
proposition
BR ,prɒpə'zɪʃ|n, -nz,
-ŋɪŋ \-nɪŋ, -nd
AM ,prɑpə'zɪʃən, -z, -ɪŋ,
-d
propositional
BR ,prɒpə'zɪʃn(ə)l,
,prɒpə'zɪʃən(ə)l
AM ,prɑpə'zɪʃ(ə)nəl
propositionally
BR ,prɒpə'zɪʃn̩əli,
,prɒpə'zɪʃn̩li,
,prɒpə'zɪʃənli,
,prɒpə'zɪʃ(ə)nəli
AM ,prɑpə'zɪʃ(ə)nəli
propound
BR prə'paʊnd, -z, -ɪŋ,
-ɪd
AM prə'paʊnd, -z, -ɪŋ,
-əd
propounder
BR prə'paʊndə(r), -z
AM prə'paʊndər, -z

propraetor
BR prəʊ'priːtə(r), -z
AM proʊ'pridər, -z
proprietary
BR prə'prʌɪət(ə)ri
AM p(r)ə'praɪə,teri
proprietor
BR prə'prʌɪətə(r), -z
AM p(r)ə'praɪədər, -z
proprietorial
BR prə,prʌɪə'tɔːriəl
AM p(r)ə,praɪə'tɔriəl
proprietorially
BR prə,prʌɪə'tɔːriəli
AM p(r)ə,praɪə'tɔriəli
proprietorship
BR prə'prʌɪətə,ʃɪp, -s
AM p(r)ə'praɪədər,ʃɪp,
-s
proprietress
BR prə'prʌɪətrɪs, -ɪz
AM p(r)ə'praɪətrəs, -əz
propriety
BR prə'prʌɪəti
AM p(r)ə'praɪədi
proprioception
BR ,prə(ʊ)prɪə'sɛpʃn
AM ,proʊpriə'sɛpʃən
proprioceptive
BR ,prə(ʊ)prɪə'sɛptɪv
AM ,proʊpriə'sɛptɪv
pro-proctor
BR prəʊ'prɒktə(r), -z
AM proʊ'prɑktər, -z
proptoses
BR prɒp'təʊsiːz
AM ,prɑp'toʊ,siz
proptosis
BR prɒp'təʊsɪs
AM ,prɑp'toʊsəs
propulsion
BR prə'pʌlʃn
AM prə'pəlʃən
propulsive
BR prə'pʌlsɪv
AM prə'pəlsɪv
propulsor
BR prə'pʌlsə(r), -z
AM prə'pəlsər, -z
propyl
BR 'prəʊp(ɪ)l
AM 'proʊpəl
propyla
BR 'prɒpɪlə(r),
'prəʊpɪlə(r), -z
AM 'prɑpələ, -z
propylaea
BR ,prɒpɪ'liːə(r),
,prəʊpɪ'liːə(r)
AM ,prɑpə'liə
propylaeum
BR ,prɒpɪ'liːəm,
,prəʊpɪ'liːəm
AM ,prɑpə'liəm
propylene
BR 'prəʊpɪli:n,
'prɒpɪli:n

AM 'proʊpə,lin
propylon
BR 'prɒpɪlɒn,
'prəʊpɪlɒn, -z
AM 'prɑpə,lɑn, -z
pro rata
BR (,)prəʊ 'rɑːtə(r)
AM proʊ 'reɪdə, proʊ
'rɑdə, proʊ 'rædə
prorate
BR ,prəʊ'reɪt, -s, -ɪŋ, -ɪd
AM ;proʊ;reɪ|t, -ts, -dɪŋ,
-dɪd
proration
BR prə(ʊ)'reɪʃn
AM proʊ'reɪʃən
prorogation
BR ,prəʊrə(ʊ)'geɪʃn, -z
AM ,proʊrə'geɪʃən, -z
prorogue
BR prə(ʊ)'rəʊg, -z, -ɪŋ,
-d
AM proʊ'roʊg,
prə'roʊg, -z, -ɪŋ, -d
pros
plural of pro
BR prəʊz
AM proʊz
prosaic
BR prə(ʊ)'zeɪɪk
AM prə'zeɪɪk,
proʊ'zeɪɪk
prosaically
BR prə(ʊ)'zeɪɪkli
AM prə'zeɪɪk(ə)li,
proʊ'zeɪɪk(ə)li
prosaicness
BR prə(ʊ)'zeɪɪknɪs
AM prə'zeɪɪknɪs,
proʊ'zeɪɪknɪs
prosaism
BR 'prəʊzeɪɪz(ə)m, -z
AM 'proʊzeɪ,ɪzəm, -z
prosaist
BR 'prəʊzeɪɪst, -s
AM 'proʊzeɪɪst, -s
proscenia
BR prə'siː.nɪə(r)
AM prə'siniə,
proʊ'siniə
proscenium
BR prə'siː.nɪəm, -z
AM prə'siniəm,
proʊ'siniəm, -z
prosciutto
BR prə'ʃuːtəʊ
AM prə'ʃudoʊ,
proʊ'ʃudoʊ
proscribe
BR prə(ʊ)'skrʌɪb, -z,
-ɪŋ, -d
AM proʊ'skraɪb, -z, -ɪŋ,
-d
proscription
BR prə(ʊ)ˌskrɪpʃn, -z
AM proʊ'skrɪpʃən, -z
proscriptive
BR prə(ʊ)'skrɪptɪv

AM proʊ'skrɪptɪv
prose
BR prəʊz
AM prouz
prosector
BR prə(ʊ)'sɛktə(r), -z
AM proʊ'sɛktər, -z
prosecutable
BR 'prɒsɪkjuːtəbl
AM 'prɑsə,kjudəbəl
prosecute
BR 'prɒsɪkjuːt, -s, -ɪŋ,
-ɪd
AM 'prɑsə,kju|t, -ts,
-dɪŋ, -dəd
prosecution
BR ,prɒsɪ'kjuːʃn, -z
AM ,prɑsə'kjuʃən, -z
prosecutor
BR 'prɒsɪkjuːtə(r), -z
AM 'prɑsə,kjudər, -z
prosecutorial
BR ,prɒsɪkjə'tɔːriəl
AM ,prɑsəkjə'tɔriəl
prosecutrices
BR ,prɒsɪ'kjuːtrɪsiːz
AM ,prɑsə'kjutrɪsiz
prosecutrix
BR 'prɒsɪkjuːtrɪks,
,prɒsɪ'kjuːtrɪks, -ɪz
AM 'prɑsəkjutrɪks, -ɪz
proselyte
BR 'prɒsɪlʌɪt, -s
AM 'prɑsə,laɪt, -s
proselytise
BR 'prɒsɪlɪtʌɪz,
'prɒsl̩tʌɪz, -ɪz, -ɪŋ, -d
AM 'prɑs(ə)lə,taɪz, -ɪz,
-ɪŋ, -d
proselytiser
BR 'prɒsɪlɪtʌɪzə(r),
'prɒsl̩tʌɪzə(r), -z
AM 'prɑs(ə)lə,taɪzər, -z
proselytism
BR 'prɒsɪlɪtɪz(ə)m,
'prɒsl̩tɪz(ə)m
AM 'prɑs(ə)lə,tɪzəm
proselytize
BR 'prɒsɪlɪtʌɪz,
'prɒsl̩tʌɪz, -ɪz, -ɪŋ, -d
AM 'prɑs(ə)lə,taɪz, -ɪz,
-ɪŋ, -d
proselytizer
BR 'prɒsɪlɪtʌɪzə(r),
'prɒsl̩tʌɪzə(r), -z
AM 'prɑs(ə)lə,taɪzər, -z
proseminar
BR ,prəʊ'sɛmɪnɑː(r), -z
AM 'proʊ'sɛmə,nɑr, -z
prosencephalon
BR ,prɒsɛn'sɛfəlɒn,
,prɒsɛn'sɛfl̩ɒn,
,prɒsɛn'kɛfəlɒn,
,prɒsɛn'kɛfl̩ɒn
AM ,prɑsn'sɛfə,lɑn
prosenchyma
BR prɒ'sɛŋkɪmə(r)
AM prɑ'sɛŋkəmə

prosenchymal
BR prɒˈsɛŋkɪml
AM prɑˈsɛŋkəməl

prosenchymata
BR ˌprɒsɛnˈkɪmətə(r)
AM ˌprɑsnˈkɪmədə

prosenchymatous
BR ˌprɒsɛnˈkɪmətəs
AM ˌprɑsnˈkɪmədəs

proser
BR ˈprəʊzə(r), -z
AM ˈproʊzər, -z

Proserpina
BR prəˈsɜːpɪnə(r)
AM proʊˈsɜrpənə

Proserpine
BR ˈprɒsəpʌɪn
AM proʊˈsɜrpəni,
ˈprɑsərˌpaɪn

prosify
BR ˈprəʊzɪfʌɪ, -z, -ɪŋ, -d
AM ˈproʊzəˌfaɪ, -z, -ɪŋ, -d

prosily
BR ˈprəʊzɪli
AM ˈproʊzəli

prosimian
BR prəʊˈsɪmɪən, -z
AM proʊˈsɪmɪən, -z

prosiness
BR ˈprəʊzɪnɪs
AM ˈproʊzɪnɪs

prosodic
BR prəˈ(ʊ)sɒdɪk,
prəˈ(ʊ)zɒdɪk
AM prəˈsɑdɪk,
proʊˈzɑdɪk

prosodically
BR prəˈ(ʊ)sɒdɪkli,
prəˈ(ʊ)zɒdɪkli
AM prəˈsɑdək(ə)li,
proʊˈzɑdək(ə)li

prosodist
BR ˈprɒsədɪst,
ˈprɒzədɪst,
ˈprəʊzədɪst, -s
AM ˈprɑsədəst, -s

prosody
BR ˈprɒsədi, ˈprɒzədi,
ˈprəʊzədi
AM ˈprɑsədi

prosopographer
BR ˌprɒsə(ʊ)ˈpɒɡrəfə(r), -z
AM ˌprɑsəˈpɑɡrəfər, -z

prosopographic
BR ˌprɒsə(ʊ)pəˈgrafɪk
AM ˌprɑsəpəˈgræfɪk

prosopographical
BR ˌprɒsə(ʊ)pəˈgrafɪkl
AM ˌprɑsəpəˈgræfəkəl

prosopography
BR ˌprɒsə(ʊ)ˈpɒgrəfi
AM ˌprɑsəˈpɑgrəfi

prosopopoeia
BR ˌprɒsə(ʊ)pəˈpiːə(r)
AM prəˌsoʊpəˈpiə,
ˌprɑsəpəˈpiə

prospect¹
noun
BR ˈprɒspɛkt, -s
AM ˈprɑˌspɛk(t), -s

prospect²
verb
BR prəˈspɛkt,
prɒˈspɛkt, ˈprɒspɛkt,
-s, -ɪŋ, -ɪd
AM ˈprɑˌspɛk|(t), -(t)s,
-tɪŋ, -təd

prospective
BR prəˈspɛktɪv
AM prəˈspɛktɪv,
prɑˈspɛktɪv

prospectively
BR prəˈspɛktɪvli
AM prəˈspɛktɪvli,
prɑˈspɛktɪvli

prospectiveness
BR prəˈspɛktɪvnɪs
AM prəˈspɛktɪvnɪs,
prɑˈspɛktɪvnɪs

prospectless
BR ˈprɒspɛk(t)ləs
AM ˈprɑˌspɛk(t)ləs

prospector
BR prəˈspɛktə(r),
prɒˈspɛktə(r),
ˈprɒspɛktə(r), -z
AM ˈprɑˌspɛktə(r), -z

prospectus
BR prəˈspɛktəs, -ɪz
AM prəˈspɛktəs, -əz

prosper
BR ˈprɒspə(r), -əz,
-(ə)rɪŋ, -əd
AM ˈprɑsp|ər, -ərz,
-(ə)rɪŋ, -ərd

prosperity
BR prɒˈspɛrɪti,
prəˈspɛrɪti
AM prɑˈspɛrədi

Prospero
BR ˈprɒsp(ə)rəʊ
AM ˈprɑspəroʊ

prosperous
BR ˈprɒsp(ə)rəs
AM ˈprɑsp(ə)rəs

prosperously
BR ˈprɒsp(ə)rəsli
AM ˈprɑsp(ə)rəsli

prosperousness
BR ˈprɒsp(ə)rəsnəs
AM ˈprɑsp(ə)rəsnəs

Prosser
BR ˈprɒsə(r)
AM ˈprɑsər, ˈprɑsər

Prost
BR prɒst
AM prɒst, prɑst

prostaglandin
BR ˌprɒstəˈglandɪn, -z
AM ˌprɑstəˈglændən, -z

prostate
BR ˈprɒsteɪt, -s
AM ˈprɑsˌteɪt, -s

prostatectomy
BR ˌprɒstəˈtɛktəm|i, -ɪz
AM ˌprɑstəˈtɛktəmi, -z

prostatic
BR prɒˈstatɪk
AM prɑˈstædɪk

prosthesis
BR (ˌ)prɒsˈθiːsɪs,
prəsˈθiːsɪs
AM prɑsˈθiːsɪs

prosthetic
BR (ˌ)prɒsˈθɛtɪk,
prəsˈθɛtɪk
AM prɑsˈθɛdɪk, -s

prosthetically
BR (ˌ)prɒsˈθɛtɪkli,
prəsˈθɛtɪkli
AM prɑsˈθɛdək(ə)li

prostitute
BR ˈprɒstɪtjuːt,
ˈprɒstɪtʃuːt, -s
AM ˈprɑstəˌt(j)ut, -s

prostitution
BR ˌprɒstɪˈtjuːʃn,
ˌprɒstɪˈtʃuːʃn
AM ˌprɑstəˈt(j)uʃən

prostitutional
BR ˌprɒstɪˈtjuːʃ(ə)l,
ˌprɒstɪˈtjuːʃən(ə)l,
ˌprɒstɪˈtʃuːʃ(ə)l,
ˌprɒstɪˈtʃuːʃən(ə)l
AM ˌprɑstəˈt(j)uʃ(ə)nəl

prostitutor
BR ˈprɒstɪtjuːtə(r),
ˈprɒstɪtʃuːtə(r), -z
AM ˈprɑstəˌt(j)udər, -z

prostrate¹
adjective
BR ˈprɒstreɪt
AM ˈprɑˌstreɪt

prostrate²
verb
BR prɒˈstreɪt,
prəˈstreɪt, -s, -ɪŋ, -ɪd
AM ˈprɑˌstreɪ|t, -ts,
-dɪŋ, -dɪd

prostration
BR prɒˈstreɪʃn,
prəˈstreɪʃn
AM prɑˈstreɪʃən

prostyle
BR ˈprəʊstʌɪl, -z
AM ˈproʊˌstaɪl, -z

prosy
BR ˈprəʊz|i, -ɪə(r), -ɪɪst
AM ˈproʊzi, -ər, -ɪst

protactinium
BR ˌprəʊtakˈtɪnɪəm
AM ˌproʊˌtækˈtɪnɪəm

protagonist
BR prə(ʊ)ˈtagənɪst,
prə(ʊ)ˈtagnɪst, -s
AM prəˈtæɡənəst,
proʊˈtæɡənəst, -s

Protagoras
BR prə(ʊ)ˈtagərəs,
prə(ʊ)ˈtag(ə)rəs

AM prəˈtæɡərəs,
proʊˈtæɡərəs

protamine
BR ˈprəʊtəmiːn, -z
AM ˈproʊdəˌmin,
ˈproʊdəmən, -z

protandrous
BR prə(ʊ)ˈtandrəs
AM ˌproʊˈtændrəs

protanope
BR ˈprəʊtənəʊp, -s
AM ˈproʊdəˌnoʊp, -s

protanopia
BR ˌprəʊtəˈnəʊpɪə(r)
AM ˌproʊdəˈnoʊpɪə

protases
BR ˈprɒtəsiːz
AM ˈprɑdəˌsiz

protasis
BR ˈprɒtəsɪs
AM ˈprɑdəsəs

protatic
BR prə(ʊ)ˈtatɪk
AM proʊˈtædɪk

protea
BR ˈprəʊtɪə(r), -z
AM ˈproʊdɪə, -z

protean
BR ˈprəʊtɪən,
prəʊˈtiːən
AM ˈproʊdɪən,
proʊˈtiən

protease
BR ˈprəʊtɪeɪz,
ˈprəʊtɪeɪs, -ɪz
AM ˈproʊdɪˌeɪz,
ˈproʊdiˌeɪs, -ɪz

protect
BR prəˈtɛkt, -s, -ɪŋ, -ɪd
AM prəˈtɛk|(t), -(t)s,
-tɪŋ, -təd

protectant
BR prəˈtɛkt(ə)nt, -s
AM prəˈtɛktnt, -s

protection
BR prəˈtɛkʃn
AM prəˈtɛkʃən

protectionism
BR prəˈtɛkʃnɪz(ə)m,
prəˈtɛkʃəniz(ə)m
AM prəˈtɛkʃəˌnɪzəm

protectionist
BR prəˈtɛkʃnɪst,
prəˈtɛkʃənɪst, -s
AM prəˈtɛkʃ(ə)nəst, -s

protective
BR prəˈtɛktɪv
AM prəˈtɛktɪv

protectively
BR prəˈtɛktɪvli
AM prəˈtɛktɪvli

protectiveness
BR prəˈtɛktɪvnɪs
AM prəˈtɛktɪvnɪs

protector
BR prəˈtɛktə(r), -z
AM prəˈtɛktər, -z

protectoral
BR prə'tɛkt(ə)rəl,
prə'tɛkt(ə)rl
AM prə'tɛkt(ə)rəl

protectorate
BR prə'tɛkt(ə)rət, -s
AM prə'tɛkt(ə)rət, -s

protectorship
BR prə'tɛktəʃɪp
AM prə'tɛktər‚ʃɪp

protectress
BR prə(ʊ)'tɛktrɛs,
prə(ʊ)'tɛktrɪs, -ɪz
AM 'prəʊtɛktrɛs, -əz

protégé
masculine
BR 'prɒtɪʒeɪ, -z
AM 'prəʊdə‚ʒeɪ, -z

protégée
feminine
BR 'prɒtɪʒeɪ, -z
AM 'prəʊdə‚ʒeɪ, -z

proteiform
BR 'prəʊtɪfɔːm
AM 'proʊdiə‚fɔ(ə)rm

protein
BR 'prəʊtiːn, -z
AM 'proʊ‚tin, -z

proteinaceous
BR ‚prəʊtɪ'neɪʃəs
AM ‚proʊ‚ti'neɪʃəs,
‚proʊdə'neɪʃəs

proteinic
BR prəʊ'tiːnɪk
AM proʊ'tinɪk

proteinous
BR prəʊ'tiːɪ(ɪ)nəs
AM proʊ'ti(ə)nəs

pro tem
BR (‚)prəʊ 'tɛm
AM 'proʊ 'tɛm

pro tempore
BR (‚)prəʊ 'tɛmp(ə)reɪ,
+ 'tɛmp(ə)ri
AM 'proʊ 'tɛmpə‚reɪ

proteolyses
BR ‚prəʊtɪ'ɒlɪsiːz
AM ‚proʊdi'ɑlə‚siz

proteolysis
BR ‚prəʊtɪ'ɒlɪsɪs
AM ‚proʊdi'ɑləsəs

proteolytic
BR ‚prəʊtɪə'lɪtɪk
AM ‚proʊdiə'lɪdɪk

Proterozoic
BR ‚prəʊt(ə)rə'zəʊɪk
AM ‚proʊtərə'zoʊɪk

protest[1]
noun
BR 'prəʊtɛst, -s
AM 'proʊ‚tɛst, -s

protest[2]
verb
BR prə'tɛst, -s, -ɪŋ, -ɪd
AM prə'tɛst, proʊ'tɛst,
-s, -ɪŋ, -əd

Protestant
BR 'prɒtɪst(ə)nt, -s

AM 'prɒdəstənt, -s

Protestantise
BR 'prɒtɪst(ə)ntʌɪz,
-ɪz, -ɪŋ, -d
AM 'prɒdəstən‚taɪz, -ɪz,
-ɪŋ, -d

Protestantism
BR 'prɒtɪst(ə)ntɪz(ə)m
AM 'prɒdəstən‚tɪzəm

Protestantize
BR 'prɒtɪst(ə)ntʌɪz,
-ɪz, -ɪŋ, -d
AM 'prɒdəstən‚taɪz, -ɪz,
-ɪŋ, -d

protestation
BR ‚prɒtɪ'steɪʃn, -z
AM ‚prɒdə'steɪʃən, -z

protester
BR prə'tɛstə(r), -z
AM 'proʊ‚tɛstər, -z

protestingly
BR prə'tɛstɪŋli
AM prə'tɛstɪŋli,
proʊ'tɛstɪŋli

protestor
BR prə'tɛstə(r), -z
AM 'proʊ‚tɛstər, -z

Proteus
BR 'prəʊtɪəs
AM 'proʊdiəs

prothalamia
BR ‚prəʊθə'leɪmɪə(r)
AM ‚proʊθə'leɪmɪə

prothalamion
BR ‚prəʊθə'leɪmɪən
AM ‚proʊθə'leɪmɪən

prothalamium
BR ‚prəʊθə'leɪmɪəm
AM ‚proʊθə'leɪmɪəm

prothalli
BR prəʊ'θalʌɪ,
prəʊ'θaliː
AM proʊ'θæ‚laɪ

prothallia
BR prəʊ'θaliə(r)
AM proʊ'θæljə,
proʊ'θæliə

prothallium
BR prəʊ'θaliəm
AM proʊ'θæliəm

prothallus
BR prəʊ'θaləs
AM proʊ'θæləs

Prothero
BR 'prɒðərəʊ
AM 'proʊ‚θ(ə)roʊ

Protheroe
BR 'prɒðərəʊ
AM 'proʊ‚θ(ə)roʊ

protheses
BR 'prɒθɪsiːz
AM 'prɑθə‚siz

prothesis
BR 'prɒθɪsɪs
AM 'prɑθəsəs

prothetic
BR prə(ʊ)'θɛtɪk

AM prə'θɛdɪk

prothetically
BR prə(ʊ)'θɛtɪkli
AM prə'θɛdək(ə)li

prothonotary
BR ‚prəʊθə'nəʊt(ə)r|i,
prə(ʊ)'θɒnət(ə)r|i, -ɪz
AM prə'θɒnə‚tɛri,
‚proʊθə'nɑdəri, -z

protist
BR 'prəʊtɪst, -s
AM 'proʊdəst, -s

protistology
BR ‚prəʊtɪs'tɒlədʒi
AM ‚proʊdə'stalədʒi

protium
BR 'prəʊtɪəm
AM 'proʊdiəm,
'proʊʃəm

protocol
BR 'prəʊtəkɒl, -z
AM 'proʊdə‚kɒl,
'proʊdə‚kal, -z

protogynous
BR prə(ʊ)'tɒdʒɪnəs
AM proʊ'tɑdʒənəs

protomartyr
BR ‚prəʊtəʊ'mɑːtə(r),
-z
AM 'proʊdoʊ'mɑrdər,
-z

proton
BR 'prəʊtɒn, -z
AM 'proʊ‚tan, -z

protonate
BR 'prəʊtəneɪt, -s, -ɪŋ,
-ɪd
AM 'proʊdə‚neɪt, -s, -ɪŋ,
-ɪd

protonic
BR prəʊ'tɒnɪk
AM proʊ'tanɪk

protonotary
BR ‚prəʊtə'nəʊt(ə)r|i,
prə(ʊ)'tɒnət(ə)r|i, -ɪz
AM ‚proʊdə'noʊdəri, -z

protopectin
BR ‚prəʊtə(ʊ)'pɛktɪn,
-z
AM ‚proʊdə'pɛktən, -z

protophyte
BR 'prəʊtəfʌɪt, -s
AM 'proʊdə‚faɪt, -s

protoplasm
BR 'prəʊtə(ʊ)plaz(ə)m
AM 'proʊdə‚plæzəm

protoplasmal
BR ‚prəʊtə(ʊ)'plazml
AM 'proʊdə‚plæzməl

protoplasmatic
BR ‚prəʊtə(ʊ)plaz'matɪk
AM 'proʊdə‚plæz'mædɪk

protoplasmic
BR ‚prəʊtə(ʊ)'plazmɪk
AM 'proʊdə‚plæzmɪk

protoplast
BR 'prəʊtə(ʊ)plast, -s
AM 'proʊdə‚plæst, -s

protoplastic
BR ‚prəʊtə(ʊ)'plastɪk
AM ‚proʊdə'plæstɪk

prototheria
BR ‚prəʊtə(ʊ)'θɪərɪə(r)
AM ‚proʊdə'θɪriə

prototherian
BR ‚prəʊtə(ʊ)'θɪərɪən,
-z
AM ‚proʊdə'θɪriən, -z

prototypal
BR 'prəʊtətʌɪpl,
‚prəʊtə(ʊ)'tʌɪpl
AM 'proʊdə‚taɪpəl

prototype
BR 'prəʊtətʌɪp, -s, -ɪŋ,
-t
AM 'proʊdə‚taɪp, -s, -ɪŋ,
-t

prototypic
BR ‚prəʊtə(ʊ)'tɪpɪk
AM ‚proʊdə'tɪpɪk

prototypical
BR ‚prəʊtə(ʊ)'tɪpɪkl
AM ‚proʊdə'tɪpəkəl

prototypically
BR ‚prəʊtə(ʊ)'tɪpɪkli
AM ‚proʊdə'tɪpɪk(ə)li

protozoa
BR ‚prəʊtə(ʊ)'zəʊə(r)
AM ‚proʊdə'zoʊə

protozoal
BR ‚prəʊtə(ʊ)'zəʊəl
AM ‚proʊdə'zoʊəl

protozoan
BR ‚prəʊtə(ʊ)'zəʊən
AM ‚proʊdə'zoʊən

protozoic
BR ‚prəʊtə(ʊ)'zəʊɪk
AM 'proʊdə'zoʊɪk

protozoology
BR ‚prəʊtə(ʊ)zuː'ɒlədʒi,
‚prəʊtə(ʊ)zəʊ'ɒlədʒi
AM 'proʊdoʊ‚zoʊ'wal-
ədʒi,
'proʊdoʊzə'walədʒi

protozoon
BR ‚prəʊtə(ʊ)'zəʊən,
‚prəʊtə(ʊ)'zəʊɒn
AM ‚proʊdə'zoʊən

protract
BR prə'trakt, -s, -ɪŋ, -ɪd
AM prə'træk|(t),
proʊ'træk|(t), -(t)s,
-tɪŋ, -təd

protracted
BR prə'traktɪd
AM prə'træktəd,
proʊ'træktəd

protractedly
BR prə'traktɪdli
AM prə'træktədli,
proʊ'træktədli

protractedness
BR prə'traktɪdnɪs
AM prə'træktədnəs,
proʊ'træktədnəs

protractile
BR prəˈtræktaɪl
AM prəˈtræktəl,
prouˈtræktəl,
prouˈtrækˌtaɪl,
prəˈtrækˌtaɪl

protraction
BR prəˈtrækʃn, -z
AM prəˈtrækʃən,
prouˈtrækʃən, -z

protractor
BR prəˈtræktə(r), -z
AM ˈprouˌtræktər, -z

protrude
BR prəˈtruːd, -z, -ɪŋ, -ɪd
AM prəˈtrud,
prouˈtrud, -z, -ɪŋ, -əd

protrudent
BR prəˈtruːdnt
AM prəˈtrudnt,
prouˈtrudnt

protrusible
BR prəˈtruːsɪbl
AM prəˈtrusəbəl,
prouˈtrusəbəl

protrusile
BR prəˈtruːsaɪl
AM prəˈtrusəl,
prouˈtrusəl,
prouˈtruˌsaɪl

protrusion
BR prəˈtruːʒn, -z
AM prəˈtruʒən,
prouˈtruʒən, -z

protrusive
BR prəˈtruːsɪv
AM prəˈtrusɪv,
prouˈtrusɪv

protrusively
BR prəˈtruːsɪvli
AM prəˈtrusɪvli,
prouˈtrusɪvli

protrusiveness
BR prəˈtruːsɪvnɪs
AM prəˈtrusɪvnɪs,
prouˈtrusɪvnɪs

protuberance
BR prəˈtjuːb(ə)rəns,
prəˈtjuːb(ə)rns,
prəˈtʃuːb(ə)rəns,
prəˈtʃuːb(ə)rns, -ɪz
AM prəˈt(j)ub(ə)rəns,
prouˈt(j)ub(ə)rəns,
-əz

protuberant
BR prəˈtjuːb(ə)rənt,
prəˈtjuːb(ə)rnt,
prəˈtʃuːb(ə)rənt,
prəˈtʃuːb(ə)rnt
AM prəˈt(j)ub(ə)rənt,
prouˈt(j)ub(ə)rənt

protuberantly
BR prəˈtjuːb(ə)rəntli,
prəˈtjuːb(ə)rntli,
prəˈtʃuːb(ə)rəntli,
prəˈtʃuːb(ə)rntli
AM prəˈt(j)ub(ə)rən(t)li,
prouˈt(j)ub(ə)rən(t)li

proud
BR praud, -ə(r), -ɪst
AM praud, -ər, -əst

Proudhon
BR ˈpruːdɒn
AM pruˈdɒn
FR pruˈdɔ̃

proudly
BR ˈpraudli
AM ˈpraudli

proudness
BR ˈpraudnəs
AM ˈpraudnəs

Proust
BR pruːst
AM prust

Prout
BR praut
AM praut

provability
BR ˌpruːvəˈbɪlɪti
AM ˌpruvəˈbɪlɪdi

provable
BR ˈpruːvəbl
AM ˈpruvəbəl

provableness
BR ˈpruːvəblnəs
AM ˈpruvəbəlnəs

provably
BR ˈpruːvəbli
AM ˈpruvəbli

prove
BR pruːv, -z, -ɪŋ, -d
AM pruv, -z, -ɪŋ, -d

proven
BR ˈpruːvn, ˈprəuvn
AM ˈpruvən

provenance
BR ˈprɒvɪnəns,
ˈprɒvnəns, -t
AM ˈpravənəns, -t

Provençal
BR ˌprɒvɒnˈsɑːl
AM ˌprouvənˈsal,
ˌpravənˈsal

Provence
BR prɒˈvɑːns, prɒˈvɒs
AM prouˈvans

provender
BR ˈprɒv(ɪ)ndə(r)
AM ˈpravəndər

provenience
BR prəˈviːnɪəns
AM prəˈvinjəns

proverb
BR ˈprɒvɜːb, -z
AM ˈpraˌvɜrb, -z

pro-verb
BR ˈprəuvɜːb, -z
AM ˈprouˌvɜrb, -z

proverbial
BR prəˈvɜːbɪəl
AM prəˈvɜrbɪəl

proverbiality
BR prəˌvɜːbɪˈalɪti
AM prəˌvɜrbiˈælədi

proverbially
BR prəˈvɜːbɪəli
AM prəˈvɜrbɪəli

Proverbs
BR ˈprɒvɜːbz
AM ˈpraˌvɜrbz

provide
BR prəˈvaɪd, -z, -ɪŋ, -d
AM prəˈvaid,
prouˈvaid, -z, -ɪŋ, -d

providence
BR ˈprɒvɪd(ə)ns
AM ˈpravəˌdɛns,
ˈpravədns

provident
BR ˈprɒvɪd(ə)nt
AM ˈpravədnt,
ˈpravəˌdɛnt

providential
BR ˌprɒvɪˈdɛnʃl
AM ˌpravəˈdɛn(t)ʃəl

providentially
BR ˌprɒvɪˈdɛnʃli,
ˌprɒvɪˈdɛnʃəli
AM ˌpravəˈdɛn(t)ʃəli

providently
BR ˈprɒvɪd(ə)ntli
AM ˈpravəˌdɛn(t)li,
ˈpravədn(t)li

provider
BR prəˈvaɪdə(r), -z
AM prəˈvaidər,
prouˈvaidər, -z

province
BR ˈprɒvɪns, -ɪnsɪz
AM ˈpravəns, -əz

provincial
BR prəˈvɪnʃl, -z
AM prəˈvɪn(t)ʃəl,
prouˈvɪn(t)ʃəl, -z

provincialise
BR prəˈvɪnʃaɪz,
prəˈvɪnʃəlaɪz, -ɪz, -ɪŋ,
-d
AM prəˈvɪn(t)ʃəˌlaɪz,
prouˈvɪn(t)ʃəˌlaɪz, -ɪz,
-ɪŋ, -d

provincialism
BR prəˈvɪnʃɪz(ə)m,
prəˈvɪnʃəlɪz(ə)m, -z
AM prəˈvɪn(t)ʃəˌlɪzəm,
prouˈvɪn(t)ʃəˌlɪzəm,
-z

provincialist
BR prəˈvɪnʃlɪst,
prəˈvɪnʃəlɪst, -s
AM prəˈvɪn(t)ʃələst,
prouˈvɪn(t)ʃələst, -s

provinciality
BR prəˌvɪnʃɪˈalɪti
AM prəˌvɪn(t)ʃiˈælədi,
prouˌvɪn(t)ʃiˈælədi

provincialize
BR prəˈvɪnʃaɪz,
prəˈvɪnʃəlaɪz, -ɪz, -ɪŋ,
-d

proverbially
BR prəˈvɜːbɪəli
AM prəˈvɜrbɪəli

proverbialise
prouˈvɪn(t)ʃəˌlaɪz, -ɪz,
-ɪŋ, -d

provincially
BR prəˈvɪnʃli,
prəˈvɪnʃəli
AM prəˈvɪn(t)ʃəli,
prouˈvɪn(t)ʃəli

provision
BR prəˈvɪʒ|n, -nz
-nɪŋ\-ənɪŋ, -nd
AM prəˈvɪʒən,
prouˈvɪʒən, -z, -ɪŋ, -d

provisional
BR prəˈvɪʒn(ə)l,
prəˈvɪʒən(ə)l, -z
AM prəˈvɪʒ(ə)nəl,
prouˈvɪʒ(ə)nəl, -z

provisionality
BR prəˌvɪʒəˈnalɪti
AM prəˌvɪʒəˈnælədi,
prouˌvɪʒəˈnælədi

provisionally
BR prəˈvɪʒnəli,
prəˈvɪʒnˌli,
prəˈvɪʒənli,
prəˈvɪʒ(ə)nəli
AM prəˈvɪʒ(ə)nəli,
prouˈvɪʒ(ə)nəli

provisionalness
BR prəˈvɪʒn(ə)lnəs,
prəˈvɪʒən(ə)lnəs
AM prəˈvɪʒnlnəs,
prouˈvɪʒnəlnəs,
prəˈvɪʒnəlnəs,
prouˈvɪʒnəlnəs

provisioner
BR prəˈvɪʒnə(r),
prəˈvɪʒənə(r), -z
AM prəˈvɪʒənər,
prouˈvɪʒənər, -z

provisionless
BR prəˈvɪʒnləs
AM prəˈvɪʒnləs,
prouˈvɪʒnləs

provisionment
BR prəˈvɪʒnm(ə)nt
AM prəˈvɪʒnmənt,
prouˈvɪʒnmənt

proviso
BR prəˈvaɪzəu, -z
AM prəˈvaizou,
prouˈvaizou, -z

provisor
BR prəˈvaɪzə(r), -z
AM prəˈvaizər,
prouˈvaizər, -z

provisorily
BR prəˈvaɪzərɪli
AM prəˈvaizərəli,
prouˈvaizərəli

provisory
BR prəˈvaɪz(ə)ri
AM prəˈvaizəri,
prouˈvaizəri

Provo
BR ˈprəuvəu, -z
AM ˈprouvou, -z

provocateur
BR prə͵vɒkə'təː(r)
AM prə͵vɑkə'tər
provocation
BR ͵prɒvə'keɪʃn, -z
AM ͵prɑvə'keɪʃən, -z
provocative
BR prə'vɒkətɪv
AM prə'vɑkədɪv,
proʊ'vɑkədɪv
provocatively
BR prə'vɒkətɪvli
AM prə'vɑkədɪvli,
proʊ'vɑkədɪvli
provocativeness
BR prə'vɒkətɪvnɪs
AM prə'vɑkədɪvnɪs,
proʊ'vɑkədɪvnɪs
provokable
BR prə'vəʊkəbl
AM prə'voʊkəbəl,
proʊ'voʊkəbəl
provoke
BR prə'vəʊk, -s, -ɪŋ, -t
AM prə'voʊk,
proʊ'voʊk, -s, -ɪŋ, -t
provoker
BR prə'vəʊkə(r), -z
AM prə'voʊkər,
proʊ'voʊkər, -z
provokingly
BR prə'vəʊkɪŋli
AM prə'voʊkɪŋli,
proʊ'voʊkɪŋli
provost
BR 'prɒvəst, 'prɒvɒst,
-s
AM 'proʊ͵voʊst,
'proʊvəst, -s
provost-marshall
BR prə͵vəʊ'mɑːʃl, -z
AM ͵proʊvoʊ'mɑrʃəl,
-z
provostship
BR 'prɒvəstʃɪp,
'prɒvɒstʃɪp
AM 'proʊ͵voʊst͵ʃɪp,
'proʊvəst͵ʃɪp
prow
BR praʊ, -z
AM praʊ, -z
prowess
BR 'praʊɪs, 'praʊɛs,
praʊ'ɛs
AM 'praʊ(w)əs
prowl
BR praʊl, -z, -ɪŋ, -d
AM 'praʊ(wə)l, -z, -ɪŋ,
-d
prowler
BR 'praʊlə(r), -z
AM 'praʊ(wə)lər, -z
Prowse
BR praʊz, praʊs
AM praʊz
prox.
BR prɒks

AM prɑks
proxemic
BR prɒk'siːmɪk, -s
AM prɑk'simɪk, -s
Proxima Centauri
BR ͵prɒksɪmə
sɛn'tɔːraɪ, + sɛn'tɔːriː
AM ͵praksəmə
͵sɛn'tɔ͵raɪ
proximal
BR 'prɒksɪml
AM 'praksəməl
proximally
BR 'prɒksɪmḷi,
'prɒksɪməli
AM 'praksəməli
proximate
BR 'prɒksɪmət
AM 'praksəmət
proximately
BR 'prɒksɪmətli
AM 'praksəmətli
proxime accessit
BR ͵prɒksɪmɪ ak'sɛsɪt,
͵prɒksɪmeɪ +
AM ͵praksəmə
æk'sɛsət
proximity
BR prɒk'sɪmɪti
AM prɑk'sɪmɪdi
proximo
BR 'prɒksɪməʊ
AM 'praksə͵moʊ
proxy
BR 'prɒks|i, -ɪz
AM 'prɑksi, -z
Prozac®
BR 'prəʊzak
AM 'proʊzæk
Pru
BR pruː
AM pru
prude
BR pruːd, -z
AM prud, -z
prudence
BR 'pruːdns
AM 'prudns
prudent
BR 'pruːdnt
AM 'prudnt
prudential
BR pruˈdɛnʃl
AM pruˈdɛn(t)ʃəl
prudentialism
BR pruˈdɛnʃlɪz(ə)m,
pruˈdɛnʃəlɪz(ə)m
AM pruˈdɛn(t)ʃə͵lɪzəm
prudentialist
BR pruˈdɛnʃlɪst,
pruˈdɛnʃəlɪst, -s
AM pruˈdɛn(t)ʃələst, -s
prudentially
BR pruˈdɛnʃli,
pruˈdɛnʃəli
AM pruˈdɛn(t)ʃəli

prudently
BR 'pruːdntli
AM 'prudn(t)li
prudery
BR 'pruːd(ə)ri
AM 'prudəri
Prudhoe
place in UK
BR 'prʌdəʊ
AM 'prədoʊ
Prudhoe Bay
BR ͵pruːdəʊ 'beɪ
AM ͵prud(h)oʊ 'beɪ
prudish
BR 'pruːdɪʃ
AM 'prudɪʃ
prudishly
BR 'pruːdɪʃli
AM 'prudɪʃli
prudishness
BR 'pruːdɪʃnɪs
AM 'prudɪʃnɪs
Prue
BR pruː
AM pru
Prufrock
BR 'pruːfrɒk
AM 'pruf͵rɑk
pruinose
BR 'pruːməʊs
AM 'pruə͵noʊs,
'pruə͵noʊz
Pruitt
BR 'pruːɪt
AM 'pruɪt
prune
BR pruːn, -z, -ɪŋ, -d
AM prun, -z, -ɪŋ, -d
prunella
BR pruˈnɛlə(r), -z
AM pruˈnɛlə, -z
pruner
BR 'pruːnə(r), -z
AM 'prunər, -z
prurience
BR 'prʊəriəns
AM 'prʊriəns,
'prʊriəns
pruriency
BR 'prʊəriənsi
AM 'prʊriənsi,
'prʊriənsi
prurient
BR 'prʊəriənt
AM 'prʊriənt,
'prʊriənt
pruriently
BR 'prʊəriəntli
AM 'prʊriən(t)li,
'prʊriən(t)li
pruriginous
BR prʊə'rɪdʒɪnəs
AM prʊ'rɪdʒənəs
prurigo
BR prʊə'rʌɪgəʊ
AM prʊ'raɪ͵goʊ

pruritic
BR prʊə'rɪtɪk
AM prʊ'rɪdɪk
pruritis
BR prʊə'rʌɪtɪs
AM prʊ'raɪdɪs
prusik
BR 'prʌs|ɪk, -ɪks, -ɪkɪŋ,
-ɪkt
AM 'prəsɪk, -s, -ɪŋ, -t
Prussia
BR 'prʌʃə(r)
AM 'prəʃə
Prussian
BR 'prʌʃn, -z
AM 'prəʃən, -z
prussic
BR 'prʌsɪk
AM 'prəsɪk
pry
BR prʌɪ, -z, -ɪŋ, -d
AM praɪ, -z, -ɪŋ, -d
Pryce
BR prʌɪs
AM praɪs
Pryde
BR prʌɪd
AM praɪd
pryingly
BR 'prʌɪɪŋli
AM 'praɪɪŋli
Prynne
BR prɪn
AM prɪn
prytany
BR 'prɪtən|i, -ɪz
AM 'prɪdəni, -z
Przewalski
BR ͵prəʒɪ'valski,
͵prəʒɪ'wɒlski
AM ͵prəʒə'wɒlski,
͵prəʒə'walski
RUS prʒɪ'valʲskʲij
psalm
BR sɑːm, -z
AM sɑ(l)m, -z
psalmbook
BR 'sɑːmbʊk, -s
AM 'sɑ(l)m͵bʊk, -s
psalmic
BR 'sɑːmɪk
AM 'sɑ(l)mɪk
psalmist
BR 'sɑːmɪst, -s
AM 'sɑ(l)məst, -s
psalmodic
BR sal'mɒdɪk
AM sɑ(l)'mɑdɪk
psalmodize
BR 'salmədʌɪz,
'sɑːmədaɪz, -ɪz, -ɪŋ, -d
AM 'sɑ(l)mə͵daɪz, -ɪz,
-ɪŋ, -d
psalmodist
BR 'sɑːmədɪst,
'salmədɪst, -s
AM 'sɑ(l)mədəst, -s

psalmodize
BR ˈsalmədʌɪz,
ˈsɑːmədʌɪz, -ɪz, -ɪŋ, -d
AM ˈsɑ(l)məˌdaɪz, -ɪz,
-ɪŋ, -d

psalmody
BR ˈsɑːmədi, ˈsalmədi
AM ˈsɑ(l)mədi

psalter
BR ˈsɔːltə(r), ˈsɒltə(r),
-z
AM ˈsɔltər, ˈsɑltər, -z

psalteria
BR sɔːlˈtɪəriə(r),
sɒlˈtɪərɪə(r)
AM sɔlˈtɪriə

psalterium
BR sɔːlˈtɪərɪəm,
sɒlˈtɪərɪəm, -z
AM sɔlˈtɪriəm,
ˌsɑlˈtɪriəm, -z

psaltery
BR ˈsɔːlt(ə)r|i,
ˈsɒlt(ə)r|i, -ɪz
AM ˈsɔltəri, ˈsɑltəri, -z

psephological
BR ˌsiːfəˈlɒdʒɪkl,
ˌsɛfəˈlɒdʒɪkl
AM ˌsifəˈlɑdʒəkəl

psephologically
BR ˌsiːfəˈlɒdʒɪkli,
ˌsɛfəˈlɒdʒɪkli
AM ˌsifəˈlɑdʒək(ə)li

psephologist
BR sɪˈfɒlədʒɪst,
siːˈfɒlədʒɪst,
sɛˈfɒlədʒɪst, -s
AM sɪˈfɑlədʒəst, -s

psephology
BR sɪˈfɒlədʒi,
siːˈfɒlədʒi, sɛˈfɒlədʒi
AM sɪˈfɑlədʒi

pseud
BR s(j)uːd, -z
AM sud, -z

pseudepigrapha
BR ˌs(j)uːdɪˈpɪgrəfə(r)
AM ˌsudəˈpɪgrəfə

pseudepigraphal
BR ˌs(j)uːdɪˈpɪgrəfl
AM ˌsudəˈpɪgrəfəl

pseudepigraphic
BR ˌs(j)uːdɪpɪˈgrafɪk
AM ˌsudˌɛpəˈgræfɪk

pseudepigraphical
BR ˌs(j)uːdɪpɪˈgrafɪkl
AM ˌsudˌɛpəˈgræfəkəl

pseudo
BR ˈs(j)uːdəʊ, -z
AM ˈsudoʊ, -z

pseudocarp
BR ˈs(j)uːdə(ʊ)kɑːp, -s
AM ˈsudoʊˌkɑrp, -s

pseudograph
BR ˈs(j)uːdə(ʊ)grɑːf,
ˈs(j)uːdə(ʊ)graf, -s
AM ˈsudoʊˌgræf, -s

pseudomorph
BR ˈs(j)uːdə(ʊ)mɔːf, -s
AM ˈsudoʊˌmɔ(ə)rf, -s

pseudomorphic
BR ˌs(j)uːdə(ʊ)ˈmɔːfɪk
AM ˌsudoʊˈmɔrfɪk

pseudomorphism
BR ˌs(j)uːdə(ʊ)ˈmɔːf-
ɪz(ə)m
AM ˌsudoʊˈmɔrˌfɪzəm

pseudomorphous
BR ˌs(j)uːdə(ʊ)ˈmɔːfəs
AM ˌsudoʊˈmɔrfəs

pseudonym
BR ˈs(j)uːdənɪm, -z
AM ˈsudnɪm, -z

pseudonymity
BR ˌs(j)uːdəˈnɪmɪti
AM ˌsudəˈnɪmɪdi

pseudonymous
BR ˌs(j)uːˈdɒnɪməs
AM suˈdɑnəməs

pseudonymously
BR ˌs(j)uːˈdɒnɪməsli
AM suˈdɑnəməsli

pseudopod
BR ˈs(j)uːdə(ʊ)pɒd, -z
AM ˈsudəˌpɑd, -z

pseudopodia
BR ˌs(j)uːdə(ʊ)ˈpəʊ-
dɪə(r)
AM ˌsudəˈpoʊdiə

pseudopodium
BR ˌs(j)uːdə(ʊ)ˈpəʊdɪəm
AM ˌsudəˈpoʊdiəm

pseudo-science
BR ˈs(j)uːdəʊˌsʌɪəns,
ˌs(j)uːdəʊˈsʌɪəns, -ɪz
AM ˈsudoʊˌsaɪəns, -əz

pseudo-scientific
BR ˌs(j)uːdəʊˌsʌɪənˈtɪfɪk
AM ˈsudoʊˌsaɪənˈtɪfɪk

pshaw
BR pɸ, (p)ʃɔː(r)
AM (p)ʃɔ

psi
BR (p)sʌɪ
AM (p)saɪ

p.s.i.
*pounds per square
inch*
BR ˌpiːɛsˈʌɪ
AM ˌpiˌɛsˈaɪ

psilanthropic
BR ˌsʌɪlanˈθrɒpɪk,
ˌsʌɪlənˈθrɒpɪk
AM ˌsaɪlənˈθrɑpɪk,
ˌsaɪˌlænˈθrɑpɪk

psilanthropism
BR sʌɪˈlanθrəpɪz(ə)m
AM saɪˈlænθrəˌpɪzəm

psilanthropist
BR sʌɪˈlanθrəpɪst, -s
AM saɪˈlænθrəpəst, -s

psilocybin
BR ˌsʌɪlə(ʊ)ˈsʌɪbɪn, -z
AM ˌsɪloʊˈsaɪbɪn,
ˌsaɪloʊˈsaɪbɪn, -z

psilosis
BR sʌɪˈləʊsɪs
AM saɪˈloʊsəs

Psion®
BR ˈsʌɪɒn
AM ˈsaɪˌɑn

psionic
BR sʌɪˈɒnɪk
AM saɪˈɑnɪk

psionically
BR sʌɪˈɒnɪkli
AM saɪˈɑnəkli

psittacine
BR ˈsɪtəsʌɪn
AM ˈsɪdəˌsaɪn

psittacosis
BR ˌsɪtəˈkəʊsɪs
AM ˌsɪdəˈkoʊsəs

psoae
BR ˈsəʊʌɪ
AM ˈsoʊˌaɪ

psoai
BR ˈsəʊiː
AM ˈsoʊˌi

psoas
BR ˈsəʊas, ˈsəʊəs, -ɪz
AM ˈsoʊəs, -əz

psoriasis
BR səˈrʌɪəsɪs
AM səˈraɪəsəs,
ˌsɔrˈaɪəsəs

psoriatic
BR ˌsɒrɪˈatɪk
AM ˌsɔriˈædɪk

psst
BR pst
AM pst

psych
BR sʌɪk, -s, -ɪŋ, -t
AM saɪk, -s, -ɪŋ, -t

psyche¹
noun
BR ˈsʌɪk|i, -ɪz
AM ˈsaɪki, -z

psyche²
verb
BR sʌɪk, -s, -ɪŋ, -t
AM saɪk, -s, -ɪŋ, -t

psychedelia
BR ˌsʌɪkɪˈdiːlɪə(r)
AM ˌsaɪkəˈdiljə,
ˌsaɪkəˈdiliə

psychedelic
BR ˌsʌɪkɪˈdɛlɪk
AM ˌsaɪkəˈdɛlɪk

psychedelically
BR ˌsʌɪkɪˈdɛlɪkli
AM ˌsaɪkəˈdɛlək(ə)li

psychiatric
BR ˌsʌɪkɪˈatrɪk
AM ˌsaɪkiˈætrɪk

psychiatrical
BR ˌsʌɪkɪˈatrɪkl
AM ˌsaɪkiˈætrəkəl

psychiatrically
BR ˌsʌɪkɪˈatrɪkli
AM ˌsaɪkiˈætrək(ə)li

psychiatrist
BR sʌɪˈkʌɪətrɪst,
səˈkʌɪətrɪst, -s
AM səˈkaɪətrəst,
saɪˈkaɪətrəst, -s

psychiatry
BR sʌɪˈkʌɪətri,
səˈkʌɪətri
AM səˈkaɪətri,
saɪˈkaɪətri

psychic
BR ˈsʌɪkɪk, -s
AM ˈsaɪkɪk, -s

psychical
BR ˈsʌɪkɪkl
AM ˈsaɪkɪkəl

psychically
BR ˈsʌɪkɪkli
AM ˈsaɪkɪk(ə)li

psychicism
BR ˈsʌɪkɪsɪz(ə)m
AM ˈsaɪkəˌsɪzəm

psychicist
BR ˈsʌɪkɪsɪst, -s
AM ˈsaɪkəsəst, -s

psycho
BR ˈsʌɪkəʊ, -z
AM ˈsaɪkoʊ, -z

psychoactive
BR ˌsʌɪkəʊˈaktɪv
AM ˌsaɪkoʊˈæktɪv

psychoanalyse
BR ˌsʌɪkəʊˈanəlʌɪz,
ˌsʌɪkəʊˈanl̩ʌɪz, -ɪz,
-ɪŋ, -d
AM ˌsaɪkoʊˈænəˌlaɪz,
-ɪz, -ɪŋ, -d

psychoanalysis
BR ˌsʌɪkəʊəˈnalɪsɪs
AM ˌsaɪkoʊəˈnæləsəs

psychoanalyst
BR ˌsʌɪkəʊˈanəlɪst,
ˌsʌɪkəʊˈanl̩ɪst, -s
AM ˌsaɪkoʊˈænələst, -s

psychoanalytic
BR ˌsʌɪkəʊˌanəˈlɪtɪk
AM ˌsaɪkoʊˌænəˈlɪdɪk

psychoanalytical
BR ˌsʌɪkəʊˌanəˈlɪtɪkl
AM ˌsaɪkoʊˌænəˈlɪdɪkəl

psychoanalytically
BR ˌsʌɪkəʊˌanəˈlɪtɪkli
AM ˌsaɪkoʊˌænəˈlɪdɪk-
(ə)li

psychoanalyze
BR ˌsʌɪkəʊˈanəlʌɪz,
ˌsʌɪkəʊˈanl̩ʌɪz, -ɪz,
-ɪŋ, -d
AM ˌsaɪkoʊˈænəˌlaɪz,
-ɪz, -ɪŋ, -d

psychobabble
BR ˈsʌɪkəʊˌbabl
AM ˈsaɪkoʊˌbæbəl

psychobiological
BR ˌsʌɪkəʊˌbʌɪəˈlɒdʒɪkl
AM ˈsaɪkoʊˌbaɪəˈlɑdʒ-
əkəl

psychobiologist 826 ptomain

psychobiologist
BR ˌsaɪkəʊbʌɪˈɒlədʒɪst,
-s
AM ˌsaɪkoʊˌbaɪˈɑlədʒəst,
-s

psychobiology
BR ˌsaɪkəʊbʌɪˈɒlədʒi
AM ˌsaɪkoʊˌbaɪˈɑlədʒi

psychodrama
BR ˈsʌɪkə(ʊ)ˌdrɑːmə(r),
-z
AM ˈsaɪkoʊˌdrɑmə, -z

psychodynamic
BR ˌsʌɪkə(ʊ)dʌɪˈnamɪk,
-s
AM ˌsaɪkoʊdaɪˈnæmɪk,
-s

psychodynamic-
ally
BR ˌsʌɪkə(ʊ)dʌɪˈnam-
ɪkli
AM ˌsaɪkoʊˌdaɪˈnæmə-
k(ə)li

psychogenesis
BR ˌsʌɪkəʊˈdʒɛnɪsɪs
AM ˌsaɪkoʊˈdʒɛnəsəs

psychogenic
BR ˌsʌɪkə(ʊ)ˈdʒɛnɪk
AM ˌsaɪkoʊˈdʒɛnɪk

psychograph
BR ˈsʌɪkə(ʊ)grɑːf,
ˈsʌɪkə(ʊ)graf, -s
AM ˈsaɪkəˌgræf, -s

psychokinesis
BR ˌsʌɪkəʊkɪˈniːsɪs,
ˌsʌɪkəʊkʌɪˈniːsɪs
AM ˌsaɪkoʊkəˈnisɪs,
ˈsaɪkoʊˌkaɪˈnisɪs

psychokinetic
BR ˌsʌɪkəʊkɪˈnɛtɪk,
ˌsʌɪkəʊkʌɪˈnɛtɪk
AM ˈsaɪkoʊkəˈnɛdɪk

psycholinguist
BR ˌsʌɪkəʊˈlɪŋgwɪst, -s
AM ˌsaɪkoʊˈlɪŋgwɪst, -s

psycholinguistic
BR ˌsʌɪkəʊlɪŋˈgwɪstɪk,
-s
AM ˌsaɪkoʊˌlɪŋˈgwɪstɪk,
-s

psychological
BR ˌsʌɪkəˈlɒdʒɪkl
AM ˌsaɪkəˈlɑdʒəkəl

psychologically
BR ˌsʌɪkəˈlɒdʒɪkli
AM ˌsaɪkəˈlɑdʒək(ə)li

psychologise
BR sʌɪˈkɒlədʒʌɪz, -ɪz,
-ɪŋ, -d
AM saɪˈkɑləˌdʒaɪz, -ɪz,
-ɪŋ, -d

psychologist
BR sʌɪˈkɒlədʒɪst, -s
AM saɪˈkɑlədʒəst, -s

psychologize
BR sʌɪˈkɒlədʒʌɪz, -ɪz,
-ɪŋ, -d

psychometric
BR ˌsʌɪkəˈmɛtrɪk, -s
AM ˌsaɪkəˈmɛtrɪk, -s

psychometrically
BR ˌsʌɪkəˈmɛtrɪkli
AM ˌsaɪkəˈmɛtrək(ə)li

psychometrist
BR sʌɪˈkɒmɪtrɪst, -s
AM saɪˈkɑmətrəst, -s

psychometry
BR sʌɪˈkɒmɪtri
AM saɪˈkɑmətri

psychomotor
BR ˌsʌɪkə(ʊ)ˈməʊtə(r)
AM ˌsaɪkoʊˈmoʊdər

psychoneuroses
BR ˌsʌɪkəʊnjʉˈrəʊsiːz,
ˌsʌɪkəʊnjʊəˈrəʊsiːz
AM ˈsaɪkoʊˌn(j)uˈroʊ-
ˌsiz,
ˈsaɪkoʊˌn(j)əˈroʊsiz

psychoneurosis
BR ˌsʌɪkəʊnjʉˈrəʊsɪs,
ˌsʌɪkəʊnjʊəˈrəʊsɪs
AM ˈsaɪkoʊˌn(j)uˈroʊ-
səs,
ˈsaɪkoʊˌn(j)əˈroʊsəs

psychoneurotic
BR ˌsʌɪkəʊnjʉˈrɒtɪk,
ˌsʌɪkəʊnjʊəˈrɒtɪk
AM ˈsaɪkoʊˌn(j)uˈrɑdɪk,
ˈsaɪkoʊˌn(j)əˈrɑdɪk

psychopath
BR ˈsʌɪkəpaθ, -s
AM ˈsaɪkəˌpæθ, -s

psychopathic
BR ˌsʌɪkəˈpaθɪk
AM ˌsaɪkəˈpæθɪk

psychopathically
BR ˌsʌɪkəˈpaθɪkli
AM ˌsaɪkəˈpæθək(ə)li

psychopatholog-
ical
BR ˌsʌɪkə(ʊ)ˌpaθəˈlɒdʒ-
ɪkl
AM ˈsaɪkəˌpæθəˈlɑdʒ-
əkəl

psychopathology
BR ˌsʌɪkəʊpəˈθɒlədʒi
AM ˌsaɪkoʊpəˈθɑlədʒi

psychopathy
BR sʌɪˈkɒpəθi
AM ˌsaɪˈkɑpəθi

psychopharma-
cology
BR ˌsʌɪkəʊˌfɑːmə-
ˈkɒlədʒi
AM ˌsaɪkoʊˌfɑrmə-
ˈkɑlədʒi

psychophysical
BR ˌsʌɪkəʊˈfɪzɪkl
AM ˌsaɪkəˈfɪzɪkəl

psychophysics
BR ˌsʌɪkəʊˈfɪzɪks
AM ˌsaɪkəˈfɪzɪks

psychophysiolog-
ical
BR ˌsʌɪkəʊˌfɪzɪəˈlɒdʒɪkl
AM ˈsaɪkəˌfɪzɪəˈladʒəkəl

psychophysiology
BR ˌsʌɪkəʊˌfɪzɪˈɒlədʒi
AM ˌsaɪkoʊˌfɪziˈɑlədʒi

psychoses
BR sʌɪˈkəʊsiːz
AM saɪˈkoʊˌsiz

psychosexual
BR ˌsʌɪkəʊˈsɛkʃʊəl,
ˌsʌɪkəʊˈsɛkʃ(ʉ)l,
ˌsʌɪkəʊˈsɛksjʊ(ə)l
AM ˌsaɪkoʊˈsɛkʃ(əw)əl

psychosexually
BR ˌsʌɪkəʊˈsɛkʃʊəli,
ˌsʌɪkəʊˈsɛkʃʉli,
ˌsʌɪkəʊˈsɛkʃli,
ˌsʌɪkəʊˈsɛksjʊ(ə)li
AM ˌsaɪkoʊˈsɛkʃ(əw)əli

psychosis
BR sʌɪˈkəʊsɪs
AM saɪˈkoʊsəs

psychosocial
BR ˌsʌɪkəʊˈsəʊʃl
AM ˌsaɪkoʊˈsoʊʃəl

psychosocially
BR ˌsʌɪkəʊˈsəʊʃli,
ˌsʌɪkəʊˈsəʊʃəli
AM ˌsaɪkoʊˈsoʊʃəli

psychosomatic
BR ˌsʌɪkə(ʊ)səˈmatɪk
AM ˌsaɪkoʊsəˈmædɪk

psychosomatic-
ally
BR ˌsʌɪkə(ʊ)səˈmatɪkli
AM ˌsaɪkoʊsəˈmædək-
(ə)li

psychosurgery
BR ˌsʌɪkəʊˈsəːdʒ(ə)ri
AM ˌsaɪkoʊˈsərdʒəri

psychosurgical
BR ˌsʌɪkəʊˈsəːdʒɪkl
AM ˌsaɪkəˈsərdʒəkəl

psychotherapeut-
ic
BR ˌsʌɪkəʊˌθɛrəˈpjuːtɪk
AM ˈsaɪkəˌθɛrəˈpjudɪk

psychotherapist
BR ˌsʌɪkə(ʊ)ˈθɛrəpɪst,
-s
AM ˈsaɪkoʊˈθɛrəpəst, -s

psychotherapy
BR ˌsʌɪkə(ʊ)ˈθɛrəpi
AM ˈsaɪkoʊˈθɛrəpi

psychotic
BR sʌɪˈkɒtɪk, -s
AM saɪˈkɑdɪk, -s

psychotically
BR sʌɪˈkɒtɪkli
AM saɪˈkɑdək(ə)li

psychotropic
BR ˌsʌɪkə(ʊ)ˈtrɒpɪk,
ˌsʌɪkə(ʊ)ˈtrəʊpɪk

AM ˌsaɪkəˈtrɑpɪk

psychrometer
BR sʌɪˈkrɒmɪtə(r), -z
AM saɪˈkrɑmədər, -z

psylla
BR ˈsɪlə(r)
AM ˈsɪlə

psyllid
BR ˈsɪlɪd
AM ˈsɪlɪd

psyllium
BR ˈsɪlɪəm
AM ˈsɪliəm

ptarmigan
BR ˈtɑːmɪg(ə)n, -z
AM ˈtarməgən, -z

pteranodon
BR təˈranədɒn,
təˈranədən, -z
AM təˈrænəˌdɑn, -z

pteridological
BR ˌtɛrɪdəˈlɒdʒɪkl
AM ˌtɛrədəˈladʒəkəl

pteridologist
BR ˌtɛrɪˈdɒlədʒɪst, -s
AM ˌtɛrəˈdalədʒəst, -s

pteridology
BR ˌtɛrɪˈdɒlədʒi
AM ˌtɛrəˈdalədʒi

pteridophyte
BR tɪˈrɪdəfʌɪt, -s
AM təˈrɪdəˌfaɪt,
ˈtɛrədəˌfaɪt, -s

pterodactyl
BR ˌtɛrəˈdakt(ɪ)l, -z
AM ˌtɛrəˈdæktəl, -z

pteropod
BR ˈtɛrəpɒd, -z
AM ˈtɛrəˌpɑd, -z

pterosaur
BR ˈtɛrəsɔː(r), -z
AM ˈtɛrəˌsɔ(ə)r, -z

pteroylglutamic
acid
BR ˌtɛrəʊɪlgluːˌtamɪk
ˈasɪd
AM ˌtɛrəwəlˌgluˈtæmɪk
ˈæsəd

pterygoid
process
BR ˈtɛrɪgɔɪd ˌprəʊsɛs,
-ɪz
AM ˈtɛrəˌgɔɪd ˌprɑˌsɛs,
+ ˌproʊˌsɛs, -əz

ptisan
BR tɪˈzan, -z
AM təˈzæn, ˈtɪzn, -z

Ptolemaic
BR ˌtɒləˈmeɪk
AM ˌtɑləˈmeɪk

Ptolemy
BR ˈtɒləmi
AM ˈtɑləmi

ptomain
BR ˈtəʊmeɪn,
tə(ʊ)ˈmeɪn
AM ˈtoʊˌmeɪn

ptomaine
BR ˈtəʊmeɪn,
təˈ(ʊ)meɪn
AM ˈtoʊˌmeɪn

ptosed
BR təʊzd
AM toʊzd

ptosis
BR ˈtəʊsɪs
AM ˈtoʊsəs

ptotic
BR ˈtəʊtɪk
AM ˈtoʊdɪk

ptyalin
BR ˈtʌɪəlɪn
AM ˈtaɪələn

pub
BR pʌb, -z
AM pəb, -z

pubcrawl
BR ˈpʌbkrɔːl, -z, -ɪŋ, -d
AM ˈpəbˌkrɔl,
ˈpəbˌkrɑl, -z, -ɪŋ, -d

pubertal
BR ˈpjuːbətl
AM ˈpjuːbərdəl

puberty
BR ˈpjuːbəti
AM ˈpjuːbərdi

pubes
BR ˈpjuːbiːz
AM ˈpjubiz

pubescence
BR pjuˈbɛsns
AM pjuˈbɛsəns

pubescent
BR pjuˈbɛsnt
AM pjuˈbɛsənt

pubic
BR ˈpjuːbɪk
AM ˈpjubɪk

pubis
BR ˈpjuːbɪs
AM ˈpjubəs

public
BR ˈpʌblɪk
AM ˈpəblɪk

publically
BR ˈpʌblɪkli
AM ˈpəblək(ə)li

publican
BR ˈpʌblɪk(ə)n, -z
AM ˈpəbləkən, -z

publication
BR ˌpʌblɪˈkeɪʃn, -z
AM ˌpəbləˈkeɪʃən, -z

publicise
BR ˈpʌblɪsʌɪz, -ɪz, -ɪŋ, -d
AM ˈpəbləˌsaɪz, -ɪz, -ɪŋ, -d

publicism
BR ˈpʌblɪsɪz(ə)m
AM ˈpəbləˌsɪzəm

publicist
BR ˈpʌblɪsɪst, -s
AM ˈpəbləsəst, -s

publicistic
BR ˌpʌblɪˈsɪstɪk
AM ˌpəbləˈsɪstɪk

publicity
BR pʌbˈlɪsɪti
AM pəˈblɪsɪdi

publicize
BR ˈpʌblɪsʌɪz, -ɪz, -ɪŋ, -d
AM ˈpəbləˌsaɪz, -ɪz, -ɪŋ, -d

publicly
BR ˈpʌblɪkli
AM ˈpəblɪk(ə)li

publish
BR ˈpʌblɪʃ, -ɪʃɪz, -ɪʃɪŋ, -ɪʃt
AM ˈpəblɪʃ, -ɪz, -ɪŋ, -t

publishable
BR ˈpʌblɪʃəbl
AM ˈpəblɪʃəbəl

publisher
BR ˈpʌblɪʃə(r), -z
AM ˈpəblɪʃər, -z

Publius
BR ˈpʌbliəs
AM ˈpəbliəs, ˈpubliəs

Puccini
BR pʊˈtʃiːni
AM pʊˈtʃini

puccoon
BR pəˈkuːn, pʌˈkuːn, -z
AM pəˈkun, -z

puce
BR pjuːs
AM pjus

puck
BR pʌk, -s
AM pək, -s

pucka
BR ˈpʌkə(r)
AM ˈpəkə

pucker
BR ˈpʌk|ə(r), -əz, -(ə)rɪŋ, -əd
AM ˈpəkər, -z, -ɪŋ, -d

puckery
BR ˈpʌk(ə)ri
AM ˈpəkəri

Puckett
BR ˈpʌkɪt
AM ˈpəkət

puckish
BR ˈpʌkɪʃ
AM ˈpəkɪʃ

puckishly
BR ˈpʌkɪʃli
AM ˈpəkɪʃli

puckishness
BR ˈpʌkɪʃnɪs
AM ˈpəkɪʃnɪs

pucklike
BR ˈpʌklʌɪk
AM ˈpəkˌlaɪk

pud
BR pʊd, -z
AM pəd, pʊd, -z

pudding
BR ˈpʊdɪŋ, -z
AM ˈpʊdɪŋ, -z

puddingy
BR ˈpʊdɪŋi
AM ˈpʊdɪŋ(g)i

puddle
BR ˈpʌd|l, -lz, -ˌlɪŋ \-lɪŋ, -ld
AM ˈpəd|əl, -əlz, -(ə)lɪŋ, -əld

puddler
BR ˈpʌdlə(r), ˈpʌdlə(r), -z
AM ˈpʌd(ə)lər, -z

puddly
BR ˈpʌdli, ˈpʌdli
AM ˈpədli

puddock
BR ˈpʌdək, -s
AM ˈpədək, -s

pudency
BR ˈpjuːdnsi
AM ˈpjudnsi

pudenda
BR pjuˈdɛndə(r)
AM pjuˈdɛndə

pudendal
BR pjuˈdɛndl
AM pjuˈdɛndəl

pudendum
BR pjuˈdɛndəm
AM pjuˈdɛndəm

pudeur
BR pjuːˈdɜː(r)
AM pjuˈdər

pudge
BR pʌdʒ, -ɪz
AM pədʒ, -əz

pudgily
BR ˈpʌdʒɪli
AM ˈpədʒəli

pudginess
BR ˈpʌdʒɪnɪs
AM ˈpədʒɪnɪs

pudgy
BR ˈpʌdʒ|i, -ɪə(r), -ɪɪst
AM ˈpədʒi, -ər, -ɪst

pudic
BR ˈpjuːdɪk
AM ˈpjudɪk

Pudsey
BR ˈpʌdzi, ˈpʌdsi
AM ˈpədzi, ˈpədsi

pudu
BR ˈpuːduː, -z
AM ˈpudu, -z

Puebla
BR ˈpwɛblə(r), ˈpweɪblə(r)
AM ˈpwɛblə

pueblo
BR ˈpwɛbləʊ, ˈpweɪbləʊ, -z
AM ˈpwɛbloʊ, -z

puerile
BR ˈpjʊərʌɪl, ˈpjɔːrʌɪl

AM ˈpjuːrəl, ˈpjuˌraɪl

puerilely
BR ˈpjʊərʌɪl(l)i, ˈpjɔːrʌɪl(l)i
AM ˈpjuːrəli, ˈpjuˌraɪli

puerility
BR pjuəˈrɪlɪt|i, pjɔːˈrɪlɪti, -ɪz
AM ˌpjuˈrɪlɪdi, -z

puerperal
BR pjuːˈɜːp(ə)rəl, pjuːˈɜːp(ə)r‖
AM pjuˈərp(ə)rəl

Puerto Rican
BR ˌpwɛːtə(ʊ)ˈriːk(ə)n, ˌpweːtə(ʊ) +, ˌpɔːtə(ʊ) +, -z
AM ˈpɔrdə ˈrɪkən, ˈpwɛrdə +, -z

Puerto Rico
BR ˌpwɛːtə(ʊ) ˈriːkəʊ, ˌpweːtə(ʊ) +, ˌpɔːtə(ʊ) +
AM ˈpɔrdə ˈrɪkoʊ, ˈpwɛrdə +

puff
BR pʌf, -s, -ɪŋ, -t
AM pəf, -s, -ɪŋ, -t

puffball
BR ˈpʌfbɔːl, -z
AM ˈpəfˌbɔl, ˈpəfˌbɑl, -z

puffer
BR ˈpʌfə(r), -z
AM ˈpəfər, -z

puffery
BR ˈpʌf(ə)ri
AM ˈpəfəri

puffily
BR ˈpʌfɪli
AM ˈpəfəli

puffin
BR ˈpʌfɪn, -z
AM ˈpəfən, -z

puffiness
BR ˈpʌfɪnɪs
AM ˈpəfɪnɪs

puff-puff
BR ˈpʌfpʌf, -s
AM ˈpəfˌpəf, -s

puffy
BR ˈpʌfl|i, -ɪə(r), -ɪɪst
AM ˈpəfi, -ər, -ɪst

pug
BR pʌg, -z
AM pəg, -z

pugaree
BR ˈpʌg(ə)r‖i, -ɪz
AM ˈpəg(ə)ri, -z

Puget Sound
BR ˌpjuːdʒɪt ˈsaʊnd
AM ˌpjudʒət ˈsaʊnd

puggaree
BR ˈpʌg(ə)r‖i, -ɪz
AM ˈpəg(ə)ri, -z

puggish
BR ˈpʌgɪʃ
AM ˈpəgɪʃ

puggy

828

pulverisator

puggy
BR ˈpʌgi
AM ˈpəgi

Pugh
BR pjuː
AM pju

Pughe
BR pjuː
AM pju

pugilism
BR ˈpjuːdʒɪlɪz(ə)m
AM ˈpjuːdʒəˌlɪzəm

pugilist
BR ˈpjuːdʒɪlɪst, -s
AM ˈpjuːdʒələst, -s

pugilistic
BR ˌpjuːdʒɪˈlɪstɪk
AM ˌpjuːdʒəˈlɪstɪk

Pugin
BR ˈpjuːdʒɪn
AM ˈpjuːdʒən

pugnacious
BR pʌgˈneɪʃəs
AM pəgˈneɪʃəs

pugnaciously
BR pʌgˈneɪʃəsli
AM pəgˈneɪʃəsli

pugnaciousness
BR pʌgˈneɪʃəsnəs
AM pəgˈneɪʃəsnəs

pugnacity
BR pʌgˈnasɪti
AM ˌpəgˈnæsədi

Pugwash
BR ˈpʌgwɒʃ
AM ˈpəgˌwɒʃ, ˈpəgˌwɑʃ

puisne
BR ˈpjuːni
AM ˈpjuni

puissance¹
general use
BR ˈpjuːɪsns, ˈpwɪsns
AM ˈpwɪsəns,
ˈpjuəsəns, pjuˈɪsəns

puissance²
show-jumping
BR ˈpwiːsns, ˈpwiːsɒs
AM ˈpwiːsəns,
ˈpwiˈsɑns

puissant
BR ˈpjuːɪsnt, ˈpwɪsnt
AM ˈpwɪsnt, ˈpjuəsnt,
pjuˈɪsnt

puissantly
BR ˈpjuːɪsntli,
ˈpwɪsntli
AM ˈpwɪsn(t)li,
ˈpjuəsn(t)li,
pjuˈɪsn(t)li

puja
BR ˈpuːdʒə(r), -z
AM ˈpudʒə, -z

puke
BR pjuːk, -s, -ɪŋ, -t
AM pjuk, -s, -ɪŋ, -t

pukeko
BR ˈpuːkɛkəʊ, -z
AM puˈkeɪˌkoʊ, -z

pukey
BR ˈpjuːki
AM ˈpjuki

pukka
BR ˈpʌkə(r)
AM ˈpəkə

pukkah
BR ˈpʌkə(r)
AM ˈpəkə

puku
BR ˈpuːkuː, -z
AM ˈpuˌku, -z

pul
BR puːl, -z
AM pul, -z

pula
BR ˈpʊlə(r), -z
AM ˈpʊlə, -z

pulao
BR pəˈlaʊ, -z
AM pəˈlaʊ, -z

Pulaski
BR pəˈlaski
AM pəˈlæski

Pulborough
BR ˈpʊlb(ə)rə(r)
AM ˈpʊlbərə

pulchritude
BR ˈpʌlkrɪtjuːd,
ˈpʌlkrɪtʃuːd
AM ˈpəlkrəˌt(j)ud

pulchritudinous
BR ˌpʌlkrɪˈtjuːdɪnəs,
ˌpʌlkrɪˈtʃuːdɪnəs
AM ˌpəlkrəˈt(j)udnəs

pule
BR pjuːl, -z, -ɪŋ, -d
AM pjul, -z, -ɪŋ, -d

puli
BR ˈpuːli
AM ˈpuli

Pulitzer
BR ˈpʊlɪtsə(r),
ˈpjuːlɪtsə(r)
AM ˈpʊlətsər,
ˈpjulətsər

pull
BR pʊl, -z, -ɪŋ, -d
AM pʊl, -z, -ɪŋ, -d

pullback
BR ˈpʊlbak, -s
AM ˈpʊlˌbæk, -s

pulldown
BR ˈpʊldaʊn
AM ˈpʊlˌdaʊn

Pullen
BR ˈpʊlɪn
AM ˈpʊlən

puller
BR ˈpʊlə(r), -z
AM ˈpʊlər, -z

pullet
BR ˈpʊlɪt, -s
AM ˈpʊlət, -s

pulley
BR ˈpʊli, -ɪz
AM ˈpʊli, -z

Pullman
BR ˈpʊlmən, -z
AM ˈpʊlmən, -z

pullout
BR ˈpʊlaʊt, -s
AM ˈpʊlˌaʊt, -s

pullover
BR ˈpʊlˌəʊvə(r), -z
AM ˈpʊlˌoʊvər, -z

pullthrough
BR ˈpʊlθruː, -z
AM ˈpʊlˌθru, -z

pullulant
BR ˈpʌljʊlənt,
ˈpʌljʊlnt
AM ˈpəljələnt

pullulate
BR ˈpʌljʊleɪt, -s, -ɪŋ, -ɪd
AM ˈpəljəˌleɪt, -ts, -dɪŋ,
-dɪd

pullulation
BR ˌpʌljʊˈleɪʃn, -z
AM ˌpəljəˈleɪʃən, -z

pull-up
BR ˈpʊlʌp, -s
AM ˈpʊləp, -s

Pulman
BR ˈpʊlmən
AM ˈpʊlmən

pulmonaria
BR ˌpʌlməˈnɛːrɪə(r)
AM ˌpəlməˈnɛrɪə

pulmonary
BR ˈpʌlmən(ə)ri,
ˈpʊlmən(ə)ri
AM ˈpəlməˌnɛri

pulmonate
BR ˈpʌlmənət,
ˈpʊlmənət
AM ˈpəlməˌneɪt,
ˈpəlmənət

pulmonic
BR pʌlˈmɒnɪk,
pʊlˈmɒnɪk
AM pəlˈmɑnɪk

pulmonically
BR pʌlˈmɒnɪkli,
pʊlˈmɒnɪkli
AM pəlˈmɑnək(ə)li

pulp
BR pʌlp, -s, -ɪŋ, -t
AM pəlp, -s, -ɪŋ, -t

pulper
BR ˈpʌlpə(r), -z
AM ˈpəlpər, -z

pulpiness
BR ˈpʌlpɪnɪs
AM ˈpəlpɪnɪs

pulpit
BR ˈpʊlpɪt, -s
AM ˈpəlpət, ˈpʊlpət, -s

pulpiteer
BR ˌpʊlpɪˈtɪə(r), -z, -ɪŋ,
-d
AM ˌpʊlpəˈtɪ(ə)r,
ˌpəlpəˈtɪ(ə)r, -z, -ɪŋ, -d

pulpless
BR ˈpʌlpləs

AM ˈpəlpləs

pulpous
BR ˈpʌlpəs
AM ˈpəlpəs

pulpwood
BR ˈpʌlpwʊd
AM ˈpəlpˌwʊd

pulpy
BR ˈpʌlpｌi, -ɪə(r), -ɪɪst
AM ˈpəlpi, -ər, -ɪst

pulque
BR ˈpʊlki, ˈpʊlkeɪ
AM ˈpʊlkeɪ, ˈpʊlki

pulsar
BR ˈpʌlsɑː(r), -z
AM ˈpəlˌsɑr, -z

pulsate
BR pʌlˈseɪt, -s, -ɪŋ, -ɪd
AM ˈpəlˌseɪ|t, -ts, -dɪŋ,
-dɪd

pulsatile
BR ˈpʌlsətʌɪl
AM ˈpəlsədl, ˈpəlsəˌtaɪl

pulsatilla
BR ˌpʌlsəˈtɪlə(r), -z
AM ˌpəlsəˈtɪlə, -z

pulsation
BR pʌlˈseɪʃn, -z
AM ˌpəlˈseɪʃən, -z

pulsative
BR ˈpʌlsətɪv
AM ˈpəlsədɪv

pulsator
BR pʌlˈseɪtə(r), -z
AM ˈpəlˌseɪdər, -z

pulsatory
BR pʌlˈseɪt(ə)ri
AM ˈpəlsəˌtori

pulse
BR pʌls, -ɪz
AM pəls, -əz

pulseless
BR ˈpʌlsləs
AM ˈpəlsləs

pulsimeter
BR pʌlˈsɪmɪtə(r), -z
AM ˌpəlˈsɪmədər, -z

Pulsometer
BR pʌlˈsʊmɪtə(r), -z
AM ˌpəlˈsɑmədər, -z

pultrude
BR pʊlˈtruːd, pʌlˈtruːd,
-z, -ɪŋ, -ɪd
AM pəlˈtrud, -z, -ɪŋ, -ɪd

pulverisable
BR ˈpʌlvərʌɪzəbl
AM ˈpəlvəˌraɪzəbəl

pulverisation
BR ˌpʌlv(ə)rʌɪˈzeɪʃn
AM ˌpəlvərəˈzeɪʃən,
ˌpəlvəˌraɪˈzeɪʃən

pulveriser
BR ˈpʌlv(ə)rʌɪzeɪtə(r),
-z
AM ˈpəlvərəˌzeɪdər,
ˈpəlvəˌraɪˌzeɪdər, -z

pulverise
BR ˈpʌlvəraɪz, -ɪz, -ɪŋ,
-d
AM ˈpəlvəˌraɪz, -ɪz, -ɪŋ,
-d

pulveriser
BR ˈpʌlvəraɪzə(r), -z
AM ˈpəlvəˌraɪzər, -z

pulverizable
BR ˈpʌlvəraɪzəbl
AM ˈpəlvəˌraɪzəbəl

pulverization
BR ˌpʌlvraɪˈzeɪʃn
AM ˌpəlvərəˈzeɪʃən,
ˌpəlvəˌraɪˈzeɪʃən

pulverizator
BR ˈpʌlv(ə)rʌɪzeɪtə(r),
-z
AM ˈpəlvərəˌzeɪdər,
ˈpəlvəˌraɪˌzeɪdər, -z

pulverize
BR ˈpʌlvəraɪz, -ɪz, -ɪŋ,
-d
AM ˈpəlvəˌraɪz, -ɪz, -ɪŋ,
-d

pulverizer
BR ˈpʌlvəraɪzə(r), -z
AM ˈpəlvəˌraɪzər, -z

pulverulent
BR pʌlˈverˌj(ʊ)lənt,
pʌlˈver(j)ʊln̩t
AM pəlˈverjələnt

pulvinate
BR ˈpʌlvɪneɪt, -s, -ɪŋ, -ɪd
AM ˈpəlvəˌneɪt, -ts,
-dɪŋ, -dɪd

puma
BR ˈpjuːmə(r), -z
AM ˈpjumə, -z

pumice
BR ˈpʌmɪs
AM ˈpəməs

pumiceous
BR pjuːˈmɪʃəs
AM pjuˈmɪʃəs

pummel
BR ˈpʌm|l, -lz,
-lɪŋ\-əlɪŋ, -ld
AM ˈpəm|əl, -əlz,
-(ə)lɪŋ, -əld

pump
BR pʌm|p, -ps, -pɪŋ,
-(p)t
AM pəmp, -s, -ɪŋ, -t

pumpernickel
BR ˈpʌmpəˌnɪkl,
ˈpʊmpəˌnɪkl
AM ˈpəmpərˌnɪkəl

Pumphrey
BR ˈpʌmfri
AM ˈpəmfri

pumpkin
BR ˈpʌm(p)kɪn, -z
AM ˈpəm(p)kən, -z

pumpkinseed
BR ˈpʌm(p)kɪnsiːd, -z
AM ˈpəm(p)kənˌsid, -z

pun
BR pʌn, -z, -ɪŋ, -d
AM pən, -z, -ɪŋ, -d

puna
BR ˈpuːnə(r), -z
AM ˈpunə, -z

punch
BR pʌn(t)ʃ, -ɪz, -ɪŋ, -t
AM pʌn(t)ʃ, -əz, -ɪŋ, -t

Punch and Judy
BR ˌpʌn(t)ʃ (ə)n(d)
ˈdʒuːdi
AM ˈpən(t)ʃ ən ˈdʒudi

punchbag
BR ˈpʌn(t)ʃbag, -z
AM ˈpən(t)ʃˌbæg, -z

punchball
BR ˈpʌn(t)ʃbɔːl, -z
AM ˈpənt ʃˌbɔl,
ˈpənt ʃˌbal, -z

punchbowl
BR ˈpʌn(t)ʃbəʊl, -z
AM ˈpən(t)ʃˌboʊl, -z

punchcard
BR ˈpʌn(t)ʃkɑːd, -z
AM ˈpən(t)ʃˌkard, -z

punchdrunk
BR ˈpʌn(t)ʃdrʌŋk,
ˌpʌn(t)ʃˈdrʌŋk
AM ˈpən(t)ʃˌdrəŋk

puncheon
BR ˈpʌn(t)ʃ(ə)n, -z
AM pən(t)ʃən, -z

puncher
BR ˈpʌn(t)ʃə(r), -z
AM ˈpən(t)ʃər, -z

punchily
BR ˈpʌn(t)ʃɪli
AM ˈpən(t)ʃəli

Punchinello
BR ˌpʌn(t)ʃɪˈnɛləʊ, -z
AM ˌpən(t)ʃəˈnɛloʊ, -z

punchiness
BR ˈpʌn(t)ʃɪnɪs
AM ˈpən(t)ʃinɪs

punchline
BR ˈpʌn(t)ʃlʌɪn, -z
AM ˈpən(t)ʃˌlaɪn, -z

punchup
BR ˈpʌn(t)ʃʌp, -s
AM ˈpən(t)ʃˌəp, -s

punchy
BR ˈpʌn(t)ʃ|i, -iə(r),
-ɪɪst
AM ˈpən(t)ʃi, -ər, -ɪst

puncta
BR ˈpʌn(k)tə(r)
AM ˈpən(k)tə

punctate
BR ˈpʌn(k)teɪt
AM ˈpən(k)ˌteɪt

punctation
BR ˌpʌn(k)ˈteɪʃn
AM ˌpən(k)ˈteɪʃən

punctilio
BR ˌpʌn(k)ˈtɪliəʊ
AM ˌpən(k)ˈtɪlioʊ

punctilious
BR ˌpʌn(k)ˈtɪliəs
AM ˌpən(k)ˈtɪliəs

punctiliously
BR ˌpʌn(k)ˈtɪliəsli
AM ˌpən(k)ˈtɪliəsli

punctiliousness
BR ˌpʌn(k)ˈtɪliəsnəs
AM ˌpən(k)ˈtɪliəsnəs

punctual
BR ˈpʌn(k)tʃʊəl,
ˈpʌn(k)tʃ(ʊ)l,
ˈpʌn(k)tjʊəl,
ˈpʌn(k)tjʊl
AM ˈpən(k)(t)ʃ(əw)əl

punctuality
BR ˌpʌn(k)tʃʊˈalɪti,
ˌpʌn(k)tjuˈalɪti
AM ˌpən(k)(t)ʃəˈwælədi

punctually
BR ˈpʌn(k)tʃʊəli,
ˈpʌn(k)tʃʊli,
ˈpʌn(k)tʃli,
ˈpʌn(k)tjʊəli,
ˈpʌn(k)tjʊli
AM ˈpən(k)(t)ʃ(əw)əli

punctuate
BR ˈpʌn(k)tʃʊeɪt,
ˈpʌn(k)tjʊeɪt, -s, -ɪŋ,
-ɪd
AM ˈpən(k)(t)ʃəˌweɪt,
-ts, -dɪŋ, -dɪd

punctuation
BR ˌpʌn(k)tʃʊˈeɪʃn,
ˌpʌn(k)tjʊˈeɪʃn
AM ˌpən(k)(t)ʃəˈweɪʃən

punctum
BR ˈpʌn(k)təm
AM ˈpən(k)təm

puncture
BR ˈpʌn(k)tʃə(r), -əz,
-(ə)rɪŋ, -əd
AM ˈpən(k)(t)ʃər, -z,
-ɪŋ, -d

pundit
BR ˈpʌndɪt, -s
AM ˈpəndət, -s

punditry
BR ˈpʌndɪtri
AM ˈpəndətri

pungency
BR ˈpʌn(d)ʒ(ə)nsi
AM ˈpəndʒənsi

pungent
BR ˈpʌn(d)ʒ(ə)nt
AM ˈpəndʒənt

pungently
BR ˈpʌn(d)ʒ(ə)ntli
AM ˈpəndʒən(t)li

Punic
BR ˈpjuːnɪk
AM ˈpjunɪk

punily
BR ˈpjuːnɪli
AM ˈpjunəli

puniness
BR ˈpjuːnɪnɪs
AM ˈpjuninɪs

punish
BR ˈpʌn|ɪʃ, -ɪʃɪz, -ɪʃɪŋ,
-ɪʃt
AM ˈpənɪʃ, -ɪz, -ɪŋ, -t

punishable
BR ˈpʌnɪʃəbl
AM ˈpənɪʃəbəl

punisher
BR ˈpʌnɪʃə(r), -z
AM ˈpənɪʃər, -z

punishingly
BR ˈpʌnɪʃɪŋli
AM ˈpənɪʃɪŋli

punishment
BR ˈpʌnɪʃm(ə)nt, -s
AM ˈpənɪʃmənt, -s

punitive
BR ˈpjuːnɪtɪv
AM ˈpjunədɪv

punitively
BR ˈpjuːnɪtɪvli
AM ˈpjunədɪvli

punitiveness
BR ˈpjuːnɪtɪvnɪs
AM ˈpjunədɪvnɪs

punitory
BR ˈpjuːnɪt(ə)ri
AM ˈpjunəˌtɔri

Punjab
BR pʌnˈdʒɑːb,
ˈpʌndʒɑːb, pʊnˈdʒɑːb,
ˈpʊndʒɑːb
AM ˈpənˌdʒɑb

Punjabi
BR pʌnˈdʒɑːbi,
pʊnˈdʒɑːbi
AM pənˈdʒɑbi

punk
BR pʌŋk, -s
AM pəŋk, -s

punka
BR ˈpʌŋkə(r), -z
AM ˈpəŋkə, -z

punkah
BR ˈpʌŋkə(r), -z
AM ˈpəŋkə, -z

punkah-wallah
BR ˈpʌŋkəˌwɒlə(r), -z
AM ˈpəŋkəˈwɑlə,
ˈpəŋkəˈwɑlə, -z

punkish
BR ˈpʌŋkɪʃ
AM ˈpəŋkɪʃ

punky
BR ˈpʌŋk|i, -iə(r), -ɪɪst
AM ˈpəŋki, -ər, -ɪst

punner
BR ˈpʌnə(r), -z
AM ˈpənər, -z

punnet
BR ˈpʌnɪt, -s
AM ˈpənət, -s

punningly
BR ˈpʌnɪŋli
AM ˈpənɪŋli

punster
BR ˈpʌnstə(r), -z

AM 'pənstər, -z

punt¹
gambling, kicking,
boating
BR pʌnt, -s, -ɪŋ, -ɪd
AM pən|t, -ts, -(t)ɪŋ,
-(t)əd

punt²
Irish pound
BR pʊnt, -s
AM pʊnt, -s

Punta Arenas
BR ˌpʊntə(r) əˈreɪnəs
AM ˈpʊn(tə) əˈreɪnəs

punter
BR ˈpʌntə(r), -z
AM ˈpən(t)ər, -z

puny
BR ˈpjuːn|i, -ɪə(r), -ɪɪst
AM ˈpjuni, -ər, -ɪst

pup
BR pʌp, -s
AM pəp, -s

pupa
BR ˈpjuːpə(r), -z
AM ˈpjupə, -z

pupae
BR ˈpjuːpiː
AM ˈpjupi, ˈpjuˌpaɪ,
ˈpjupeɪ

pupal
BR ˈpjuːpl
AM ˈpjupəl

pupate
BR pjuːˈpeɪt, -s, -ɪŋ, -ɪd
AM ˈpjuˌpeɪ|t, -ts, -dɪŋ,
-dɪd

pupation
BR pjuːˈpeɪʃn
AM ˌpjuˈpeɪʃən

pupil
BR ˈpjuːpl, -z
AM ˈpjupəl, -z

pupilage
BR ˈpjuːpɪl|ɪdʒ,
ˈpjuːpl|ɪdʒ, -ɪdʒɪz
AM ˈpjupəl|ɪdʒ, -ɪz

pupilar
BR ˈpjuːpɪlə(r),
ˈpjuːpl|ə(r)
AM ˈpjupələr

pupilarity
BR ˌpjuːpɪˈlarɪti
AM ˌpjuːpəˈlɛrədi

pupilary
BR ˈpjuːpɪl(ə)ri,
ˈpjuːpl(ə)ri
AM ˈpjupəˌlɛri

pupillage
BR ˈpjuːpɪlɪdʒ,
ˈpjuːplɪdʒ
AM ˈpjupəlɪdʒ

pupillar
BR ˈpjuːpɪlə(r),
ˈpjuːplə(r)
AM ˈpjupələr

pupillarity
BR ˌpjuːpɪˈlarɪti

AM ˌpjuːpəˈlɛrədi

pupillary
BR ˈpjuːpɪl(ə)ri,
ˈpjuːpl(ə)ri
AM ˈpjupəˌlɛri

pupiparous
BR pjuːˈpɪp(ə)rəs
AM pjuˈpɪpərəs

puppet
BR ˈpʌpɪt, -s
AM ˈpəpət, -s

puppeteer
BR ˌpʌpɪˈtɪə(r), -z
AM ˌpəpəˈtɪ(ə)r, -z

puppeteering
BR ˈpʌpɪtɪərɪŋ
AM ˈpəpəˌtɪrɪŋ

puppetry
BR ˈpʌpɪtri
AM ˈpəpətri

puppy
BR ˈpʌp|i, -ɪz
AM ˈpəpi, -z

puppyhood
BR ˈpʌpɪhʊd
AM ˈpəpiˌhʊd

puppyish
BR ˈpʌpiːʃ
AM ˈpəpiːʃ

Purana
BR pʊˈrɑːnə(r), -z
AM pʊˈrɑnə, -z

Puranic
BR pʊˈranɪk
AM pʊˈrɑnɪk

Purbeck
BR ˈpəːbek
AM ˈpərˌbek

purblind
BR ˈpəːblʌɪnd
AM ˈpərˌblaɪnd

purblindness
BR ˈpəːblʌɪn(d)nɪs
AM ˈpərˌblaɪn(d)nɪs

Purcell
BR ˈpəːsl, pəːˈsɛl
AM pərˈsɛl

purchasable
BR ˈpəːtʃɪsəbl
AM ˈpərtʃəsəbəl

purchase
BR ˈpəːtʃɪs, -ɪz, -ɪŋ, -t
AM ˈpərtʃəs, -əz, -ɪŋ, -t

purchaseable
BR ˈpəːtʃɪsəbl
AM ˈpərtʃəsəbəl

purchaser
BR ˈpəːtʃɪsə(r), -z
AM ˈpərtʃəsər, -z

purda
BR ˈpəːdɑː(r), ˈpəːdə(r)
AM ˈpərdə

purdah
BR ˈpəːdɑː(r), ˈpəːdə(r)
AM ˈpərdə

Purdie
BR ˈpəːdi

AM ˈpərdi

Purdon
BR ˈpəːdn
AM ˈpərdən

Purdue
BR ˈpəːdjuː
AM pərˈd(j)u

Purdy
BR ˈpəːdi
AM ˈpərdi

pure
BR pjʊə(r), pjɔː(r),
-ə(r), -ɪst
AM pjʊ(ə)r, -ər, -əst

pureblood
BR ˈpjʊəblʌd, ˈpjɔːblʌd
AM ˈpjʊrˌbləd

pureblooded
BR ˌpjʊəˈblʌdɪd,
ˌpjɔːˈblʌdɪd
AM ˈpjʊrˌblədəd

purebred¹
adjective
BR ˌpjʊəˈbrɛd,
ˌpjɔːˈbrɛd
AM ˈpjʊrˌbrɛd

purebred²
noun
BR ˈpjʊəbrɛd,
ˈpjɔːbrɛd, -z
AM ˈpjʊrˌbrɛd, -z

purée
BR ˈpjʊəreɪ, ˈpjɔːreɪ, -z
AM pjʊˈreɪ, pjəˈreɪ, -z

purely
BR ˈpjʊəli, ˈpjɔːli
AM ˈpjʊrli

pureness
BR ˈpjʊənəs, ˈpjɔːnəs
AM ˈpjʊrnəs

purfle
BR ˈpəːf]l, -lz, -lɪŋ \-lɪŋ,
-ld
AM ˈpərfəl, -z, -ɪŋ, -d

Purfleet
BR ˈpəːfliːt
AM ˈpərˌflit

purgation
BR pəːˈgeɪʃn
AM ˌpərˈgeɪʃən

purgative
BR ˈpəːgətɪv, -z
AM ˈpərgədɪv, -z

purgatorial
BR ˌpəːgəˈtɔːrɪəl
AM ˌpərgəˈtɔriəl

purgatory
BR ˈpəːgət(ə)ri
AM ˈpərgəˌtori

purge
BR pəːdʒ, -ɪz, -ɪŋ, -d
AM pərdʒ, -əz, -ɪŋ, -d

purger
BR ˈpəːdʒə(r), -z
AM ˈpərdʒər, -z

purification
BR ˌpjʊərɪfɪˈkeɪʃn,
ˌpjɔːrɪfɪˈkeɪʃn
AM ˌpjʊrəfəˈkeɪʃən

purificator
BR ˈpjʊərɪfɪkeɪtə(r),
ˈpjɔːrɪfɪkeɪtə(r), -z
AM ˈpjʊrəfəˌkeɪdər, -z

purificatory
BR ˌpjʊərɪfɪˈkeɪt(ə)ri,
ˌpjɔːrɪfɪˈkeɪt(ə)ri
AM pjuˈrɪfəkəˌtori

purifier
BR ˈpjʊərɪfʌɪə(r),
ˈpjɔːrɪfʌɪə(r), -z
AM ˈpjʊrəˌfaɪər, -z

purify
BR ˈpjʊərɪfʌɪ,
ˈpjɔːrɪfʌɪ, -z, -ɪŋ, -d
AM ˈpjʊrəˌfaɪ, -z, -ɪŋ, -d

Purim
BR ˈp(j)ʊərɪm, pʊˈriːm
AM ˈpʊrəm, ˈpʊrəm,
pʊˈrɪm

purine
BR ˈp(j)ʊəriːn,
ˈpjɔːriːn, -z
AM ˈpjʊˌrin, ˈpjʊrən, -z

purism
BR ˈpjʊərɪz(ə)m,
ˈpjɔːrɪz(ə)m
AM ˈpjʊˌrɪzəm

purist
BR ˈpjʊərɪst, ˈpjɔːrɪst,
-s
AM ˈpjʊrəst, -s

puristic
BR pjʊəˈrɪstɪk,
pjɔːˈrɪstɪk
AM pjʊˈrɪstɪk,
pjəˈrɪstɪk

puritan
BR ˈpjʊərɪt(ə)n,
ˈpjɔːrɪt(ə)n, -z
AM ˈpjʊrətn̩, ˈpjʊrədən,
-z

puritanic
BR ˌpjʊərɪˈtanɪk,
ˌpjɔːrɪˈtanɪk
AM ˌpjʊrəˈtænɪk

puritanical
BR ˌpjʊərɪˈtanɪkl,
ˌpjɔːrɪˈtanɪkl
AM ˌpjʊrəˈtænəkəl

puritanically
BR ˌpjʊərɪˈtanɪkli,
ˌpjɔːrɪˈtanɪkli
AM ˌpjʊrəˈtænək(ə)li

puritanism
BR ˈpjʊərɪtəˌnɪz(ə)m,
ˈpjʊərɪtɪz(ə)m,
ˈpjɔːrɪtəˌnɪz(ə)m,
ˈpjɔːrɪtnɪz(ə)m
AM ˈpjʊrətn̩ˌɪzəm,
ˈpjʊrətdəˌnɪzəm

purity
BR ˈpjʊərɪti, ˈpjɔːrɪti
AM ˈpjʊrədi

purl
BR pəːl, -z, -ɪŋ, -d
AM pərl, -z, -ɪŋ, -d

purler
BR 'pəːlə(r), -z
AM 'pərlər, -z

Purley
BR 'pəːli
AM 'pərli

purlieu
BR 'pəːljuː, -z
AM 'pərl(j)u, -z

purlieux
BR 'pəːljuːz
AM 'pərl(j)u

purlin
BR 'pəːlɪn, -z
AM 'pərlən, -z

purline
BR 'pəːlɪn, -z
AM 'pərlən, -z

purloin
BR pəːˈlɔɪn, -z, -ɪŋ, -d
AM pərˈlɔɪn, -z, -ɪŋ, -d

purloiner
BR pəːˈlɔɪnə(r), -z
AM pərˈlɔɪnər, -z

Purnell
BR pəːˈnɛl
AM pərˈnɛl

purple
BR 'pəːpl
AM 'pərpəl

purpleness
BR 'pəːplnəs
AM 'pərpəlnəs

purplish
BR 'pəːplɪʃ, 'pəːplɪʃ
AM 'pərp(ə)lɪʃ

purply
BR 'pəːpli, 'pəːpli
AM 'pərp(ə)li

purport¹
noun
BR 'pəːpɔːt, 'pəːpət
AM 'pərˌpɔ(ə)rt

purport²
verb
BR pəːˈpɔːt, -s, -ɪŋ, -ɪd
AM pərˈpɔ(ə)rt, -ts, -ˈpɔrdɪŋ, -ˈpɔrdəd

purportedly
BR pəːˈpɔːtɪdli
AM pərˈpɔrdədli

purpose
BR 'pəːpəs, -ɪz, -ɪŋ, -t
AM 'pərpəs, -əz, -ɪŋ, -t

purposeful
BR 'pəːpəsf(ʊ)l
AM 'pərpəsfəl

purposefully
BR 'pəːpəsfəli, 'pəːpəsfˌli
AM 'pərpəsfəli

purposefulness
BR 'pəːpəsf(ʊ)lnəs
AM 'pərpəsfəlnəs

purposeless
BR 'pəːpəsləs
AM 'pərpəsləs

purposelessly
BR 'pəːpəsləsli
AM 'pərpəsləsli

purposelessness
BR 'pəːpəsləsnəs
AM 'pərpəsləsnəs

purposely
BR 'pəːpəsli
AM 'pərpəsli

purposive
BR 'pəːpəsɪv
AM 'pərpəsɪv

purposively
BR 'pəːpəsɪvli
AM 'pərpəsɪvli

purposiveness
BR 'pəːpəsɪvnɪs
AM 'pərpəsɪvnɪs

purpura
BR 'pəːpjʊərə(r)
AM 'pərp(j)ərə

purpure
BR 'pəːpjʊə(r)
AM 'pərp(j)ər

purpuric
BR pəːˈpjʊərɪk, pəːˈpjɔːrɪk
AM pərˈp(j)ʊrɪk

purpurin
BR 'pəːpjʊrɪn
AM 'pərp(j)ərən

purr
BR pəː(r), -z, -ɪŋ, -d
AM pər, -z, -ɪŋ, -d

purse
BR pəːs, -ɪz, -ɪŋ, -t
AM pərs, -əz, -ɪŋ, -t

purseful
BR 'pəːsfʊl, -z
AM 'pərsfəl, -z

purser
BR 'pəːsə(r), -z
AM 'pərsər, -z

pursership
BR 'pəːsəʃɪp
AM 'pərsərˌʃɪp

purse-seine
BR 'pəːsseɪn, -z
AM 'pər(s)ˌseɪn, -z

purse-seiner
BR 'pəːsˌseɪnə(r), -z
AM 'pər(s)ˌseɪnər, -z

purse-strings
BR 'pəːsstrɪŋz
AM 'pər(s)ˌstrɪŋz

pursiness
BR 'pəːsɪnɪs
AM 'pərsɪnɪs

purslane
BR 'pəːslɪn, 'pəːsleɪn
AM 'pərslən, 'pərˌsleɪn

pursuable
BR pəˈsjuːəbl
AM pərˈs(j)uəbəl

pursuance
BR pəˈsjuːəns
AM pərˈs(j)uəns

pursuant
BR pəˈsjuːənt
AM pərˈs(j)uənt

pursuantly
BR pəˈsjuːəntli
AM pərˈs(j)uən(t)li

pursue
BR pəˈsjuː, -z, -ɪŋ, -d
AM pərˈs(j)u, -z, -ɪŋ, -d

pursuer
BR pəˈsjuːə(r), -z
AM pərˈs(j)uər, -z

pursuit
BR pəˈsjuːt, -s
AM pərˈs(j)ut, -s

pursuivant
BR 'pəːs(w)ɪv(ə)nt, -s
AM 'pərs(w)əvənt, 'pərs(w)ivənt, -s

pursy
BR 'pəːsi
AM 'pərsi

purulence
BR 'pjʊər(j)ələns, 'pjʊər(j)əlns
AM 'pjur(j)ələns

purulency
BR 'pjʊər(j)ələnsi, 'pjʊər(j)əlnsi
AM 'pjur(j)ələnsi

purulent
BR 'pjʊər(j)ələnt, 'pjʊər(j)əlnt
AM 'pjur(j)ələnt

purulently
BR 'pjʊər(j)ələntli, 'pjʊər(j)əlntli
AM 'pjur(j)ələntli

Purves
BR 'pəːvɪs
AM 'pərvəs

purvey
BR pəːˈveɪ, -z, -ɪŋ, -d
AM pərˈveɪ, -z, -ɪŋ, -d

purveyance
BR pəːˈveɪəns
AM pərˈveɪəns

purveyor
BR pəːˈveɪə(r), -z
AM pərˈveɪər, -z

purview
BR 'pəːvjuː, -z
AM 'pərˌvju, -z

Purvis
BR 'pəːvɪs
AM 'pərvəs

pus
BR pʌs
AM pʌs

Pusan
BR ˌpuːˈsan
AM puˈsæn

Pusey
BR 'pjuːzi

AM 'pjuzi

push
BR pʊʃ, -ɪz, -ɪŋ, -t
AM pʊʃ, -əz, -ɪŋ, -t

pushbike
BR 'pʊʃbaɪk, -s
AM 'pʊʃˌbaɪk, -s

pushbroom
BR 'pʊʃbruːm, 'pʊʃbrʊm, -z
AM 'pʊʃˌbrum, 'pʊʃˌbrum, -z

pushbutton
BR 'pʊʃˌbʌtn, -z
AM 'pʊʃˌbətn, -z

pushcart
BR 'pʊʃkɑːt, -s
AM 'pʊʃˌkɑrt, -s

push-chain
BR 'pʊʃtʃeɪn, -z
AM 'pʊʃˌtʃeɪn, -z

pushchair
BR 'pʊʃtʃɛː(r), -z
AM 'pʊʃˌtʃɛ(ə)r, -z

pushdown
BR 'pʊʃdaʊn, -z
AM 'pʊʃˌdaʊn, -z

pusher
BR 'pʊʃə(r), -z
AM 'pʊʃər, -z

pushful
BR 'pʊʃf(ʊ)l
AM 'pʊʃfəl

pushfully
BR 'pʊʃfəli, 'pʊʃfˌli
AM 'pʊʃfəli

pushfulnes
BR 'pʊʃf(ʊ)lnəs
AM 'pʊʃfəlnəs

pushily
BR 'pʊʃɪli
AM 'pʊʃəli

pushiness
BR 'pʊʃɪnɪs
AM 'pʊʃɪnɪs

pushingly
BR 'pʊʃɪŋli
AM 'pʊʃɪŋli

Pushkin
BR 'pʊʃkɪn
AM 'pʊʃkɪn
RUS 'pusˈkʲin

pushover
BR 'pʊʃˌəʊvə(r), -z
AM 'pʊʃˌoʊvər, -z

pushpin
BR 'pʊʃpɪn, -z
AM 'pʊʃˌpɪn, -z

push-pull
BR ˌpʊʃˈpʊl
AM ˌpʊʃˈpʊl

pushrod
BR 'pʊʃrɒd, -z
AM 'pʊʃˌrɑd, -z

pushstart
BR 'pʊʃstɑːt, -s, -ɪŋ, -ɪd

AM 'pʊʃ,stɑːr|t, -ts, -dɪŋ, -dəd

Pushto
BR 'pʌʃtəʊ
AM 'pəʃtoʊ

Pushtu
BR 'pʌʃtuː
AM 'pəʃtu

pushy
BR 'pʊʃ|i, -ɪə(r), -ɪɪst
AM 'pʊʃi, -ər, -ɪɪst

pusillanimity
BR ,pju:sɪlə'nɪmɪti, ,pju:slə'nɪmɪti, ,pju:zɪlə'nɪmɪti, ,pju:zlə'nɪmɪti
AM ,pjusələ'nɪmɪdi

pusillanimous
BR ,pju:sɪ'lanɪməs, ,pju:zɪ'lanɪməs
AM ,pjusə'lænəməs

pusillanimously
BR ,pju:sɪ'lanɪməsli, ,pju:zɪ'lanɪməsli
AM ,pjusə'lænəməsli

pusillanimousness
BR ,pju:sɪ'lanɪməsnəs, ,pju:zɪ'lanɪməsnəs
AM ,pjusə'lænəməsnəs

puss
BR pʊs, -ɪz
AM pʊs, -əz

pussy
BR 'pʊs|i, -ɪz
AM 'pʊsi, -z

pussycat
BR 'pʊsɪkat, -s
AM 'pʊsi,kæt, -s

pussyfoot
BR 'pʊsɪfʊt, -s, -ɪŋ, -ɪd
AM 'pʊsi,fʊ|t, -ts, -dɪŋ, -dəd

pussyfooter
BR 'pʊsɪ,fʊtə(r), -z
AM 'pʊsi,fʊdər, -z

pustulant
BR 'pʌstjʊlənt, 'pʌstjʊlnt, 'pʌstʃʊlənt, 'pʌstʃʊlnt
AM 'pəstʃələnt, 'pəstjələnt

pustular
BR 'pʌstjʊlə(r), 'pʌstʃʊlə(r)
AM 'pʌstʃələr, pə'stjələr

pustulate
BR 'pʌstjʊleɪt, 'pʌstʃʊleɪt, -s, -ɪŋ, -d
AM 'pəstʃə,leɪt, 'pəstjə,leɪ|t, -ts, -dɪŋ, -dɪd

pustulation
BR ,pʌsjʊ'leɪʃn, 'pʌstʃʊ'leɪʃn
AM ,pəstʃə'leɪʃən, ,pəstjə'leɪʃən

pustule
BR 'pʌstju:l, 'pʌstʃu:l, -z
AM 'pəstʃəl, pə'stjul, -z

pustulous
BR 'pʌstjʊləs, 'pʌstʃʊləs
AM 'pəstʃələs, pə'stjələs

put
BR pʊt, -s, -ɪŋ
AM pʊ|t, -ts, -dɪŋ

putative
BR 'pju:tətɪv
AM 'pjudədɪv

putatively
BR 'pju:tətɪvli
AM 'pjudədɪvli

putdown
BR 'pʊtdaʊn, -z
AM 'pʊt,daʊn, -z

putlock
BR 'pʊtlɒk, -s
AM 'pʊt,lak, -s

putlog
BR 'pʊtlɒg, -z
AM 'pʊt,lag, -z

Putnam
BR 'pʌtnəm
AM 'pətnəm

Putney
BR 'pʌtni
AM 'pətni

put-put
BR ,pʌt'pʌt, -s, -ɪŋ, -ɪd
AM 'pət'pə|t, -ts, -dɪŋ, -dəd

putrefacient
BR ,pju:trɪ'feɪʃnt
AM ,pjutrə'feɪʃənt

putrefaction
BR ,pju:trɪ'fakʃn
AM ,pjutrə'fækʃən

putrefactive
BR ,pju:trɪ'faktɪv
AM ,pjutrə'fæktɪv

putrefy
BR 'pju:trɪfʌɪ, -z, -ɪŋ, -d
AM 'pjutrə,faɪ, -z, -ɪŋ, -d

putrescence
BR pju:'trɛsns
AM pju'trɛsəns

putrescent
BR pju:'trɛsnt
AM pju'trɛsənt

putrescible
BR pju:'trɛsɪbl
AM pju:'trɛsəbəl

putrid
BR 'pju:trɪd
AM 'pjutrɪd

putridity
BR pju:'trɪdɪti
AM pju'trɪdɪdi

putridly
BR 'pju:trɪdli
AM 'pjutrɪdli

putridness
BR 'pju:trɪdnɪs
AM 'pjutrɪdnɪs

putsch
BR pʊtʃ, -ɪz
AM pʊtʃ, -əz

putt
BR pʌt, -s, -ɪŋ, -ɪd
AM pə|t, -ts, -dɪŋ, -dəd

puttee
BR 'pʌtiː, pʌ'tiː, -z
AM ,pə'ti, -z

Puttenham
BR 'pʌtnəm
AM 'pətnəm

putter¹
noun, someone who puts
BR 'pʊtə(r), -z
AM 'pʊdər, -z

putter²
noun, someone who putts
BR 'pʌtə(r), -z
AM 'pədər, -z

putter³
verb
BR 'pʌt|ə(r), -əz, -(ə)rɪŋ, -əd
AM 'pədər, -z, -ɪŋ, -d

putti
BR 'pʊti:
AM 'pudi

putting-green
BR 'pʌtɪŋgriːn, -z
AM 'pədɪŋ,grin, -z

Puttnam
BR 'pʌtnəm
AM 'pətnəm

putto
BR 'pʊtəʊ
AM 'pudoʊ

putt-putt
BR ,pʌt'pʌt, -s, -ɪŋ, -ɪd
AM 'pət'pə|t, -ts, -dɪŋ, -dəd

putty
BR 'pʌt|i, -ɪz, -ɪɪŋ, -ɪd
AM 'pədi, -z, -ɪŋ, -d

putz
BR pʊts, pʌts, -ɪz
AM pəts, -əz

puy
BR pwiː, -z
AM pwi, -z

puzzle
BR 'pʌz|l, -lz, -|ɪŋ \-lɪŋ, -ld
AM 'pəz|əl, -əlz, -(ə)lɪŋ, -əld

puzzlement
BR 'pʌzlm(ə)nt, -s
AM 'pəzlmənt, -s

puzzler
BR 'pʌzlə(r), 'pʌzlə(r), -z
AM 'pəz(ə)lər, -z

puzzling
BR 'pʌzlɪŋ, 'pʌzlɪŋ
AM 'pəz(ə)lɪŋ

puzzlingly
BR 'pʌzlɪŋli, 'pʌzlɪŋli
AM 'pəz(ə)lɪŋli

puzzolana
BR ,pʊtsə'lɑ:nə(r)
AM ,pʊtsə'lɑnə

Pwllheli
BR pʊ'ɬɛli, pʊ'θɛli
AM pʊ'θɛli
WE pʊ'ɬeli

pya
BR pjɑ:(r), -z
AM pi'ɑ, pjɑ, -z

pyaemia
BR pʌɪ'i:mɪə(r)
AM paɪ'imiə

pyaemic
BR pʌɪ'i:mɪk
AM paɪ'imɪk

pycnic
BR 'pɪknɪk, -s
AM 'pɪk,nɪk, -s

Pye
BR pʌɪ
AM paɪ

pye-dog
BR 'pʌɪdɒg, -z
AM 'paɪ,dɔg, 'paɪ,dag, -z

pyelitis
BR ,pʌɪə'lʌɪtɪs
AM ,paɪə'laɪdɪs

pyelogram
BR 'pʌɪələ(ʊ)gram, -z
AM 'paɪəloʊ,græm, 'paɪɛlə,græm, -z

pyelonephritis
BR ,pʌɪələʊnɪ'frʌɪtɪs
AM ,paɪloʊnə'fraɪdəs

pyemia
BR pʌɪ'i:mɪə(r)
AM paɪ'imiə

pyemic
BR pʌɪ'i:mɪk
AM paɪ'imɪk

pygmaean
BR pɪg'miːən
AM 'pɪgmiən, pɪg'miən

Pygmalion
BR pɪg'meɪlɪən
AM pɪg'meɪliən

pygmean
BR pɪg'miːən
AM 'pɪgmiən, pɪg'miən

pygmy
BR 'pɪgm|i, -ɪz
AM 'pɪgmi, -z

pyjama
BR pə'dʒɑ:mə(r), -z
AM pə'dʒɑmə, -z

pyknic
BR 'pɪknɪk, -s
AM 'pɪk,nɪk, -s

Pyle
BR pʌɪl

AM paɪl

pylon
BR ˈpʌɪlən, ˈpʌɪlɒn, -z
AM ˈpaɪˌlɑn, -z

pylori
BR pʌɪˈlɔːrʌɪ
AM paɪˈlɔˌraɪ

pyloric
BR pʌɪˈlɒrɪk
AM paɪˈlɔrɪk

pylorus
BR pʌɪˈlɔːrəs
AM paɪˈlɔrəs

Pylos
BR ˈpʌɪlɒs
AM ˈpaɪlɔs, ˈpaɪlɑs

Pym
BR pɪm
AM pɪm

Pymm
BR pɪm
AM pɪm

pyoid
BR ˈpʌɪɔɪd
AM ˈpaɪˌɔɪd

Pyongyang
BR ˌpjɒŋˈjaŋ
AM ˈpjɔŋˈjæŋ, ˈpjaŋˈjæŋ

pyorrhea
BR ˌpʌɪəˈriːə(r)
AM ˌpaɪəˈriə

pyorrhoea
BR ˌpʌɪəˈriːə(r)
AM ˌpaɪəˈriə

pyosis
BR pʌɪˈəʊsɪs
AM paɪˈousəs

pyracantha
BR ˌpʌɪrəˈkanθə(r), -z
AM ˌpaɪrəˈkænθə, -z

Pyrah
BR ˈpʌɪrə(r)
AM ˈpaɪrə

pyralid
BR pʌɪˈralɪd, pʌɪˈreɪlɪd, -z
AM ˈpɪrəˌlɪd, -z

pyramid
BR ˈpɪrəmɪd, -z
AM ˈpɪrəˌmɪd, -z

pyramidal
BR pɪˈramɪdl
AM pəˈræmədəl, ˌpɪrəˈmɪdəl

pyramidally
BR pɪˈramɪdl̩i, pɪˈramɪdəli
AM ˌpɪrəˈmɪdl̩i, pəˈræmədli

pyramidic
BR ˌpɪrəˈmɪdɪk
AM ˌpɪrəˈmɪdɪk

pyramidically
BR ˌpɪrəˈmɪdɪkli
AM ˌpɪrəˈmɪdɪk(ə)li

Pyramus
BR ˈpɪrəməs
AM ˈpɪrəməs

pyre
BR ˈpʌɪə(r), -z
AM ˈpaɪ(ə)r, -z

Pyrenean
BR ˌpɪrəˈniːən, -z
AM ˈpɪrəˈniən, -z

Pyrenees
BR ˌpɪrəˈniːz
AM ˈpɪrəˌniz

pyrethrin
BR pʌɪˈriːθrɪn
AM paɪˈriˌθrən, paɪˈrɛθrən

pyrethroid
BR pʌɪˈriːθrɔɪd, -z
AM paɪˈriˌθrɔɪd, -z

pyrethrum
BR pʌɪˈriːθrəm
AM paɪˈriˌθrəm, paɪˈrɛθrəm

pyretic
BR pʌɪˈrɛtɪk, pɪˈrɛtɪk
AM paɪˈrɛdɪk

Pyrex®
BR ˈpʌɪrɛks
AM ˈpaɪˌrɛks

pyrexia
BR pʌɪˈrɛksɪə(r)
AM paɪˈrɛksɪə

pyrexial
BR pʌɪˈrɛksɪəl
AM paɪˈrɛksɪəl

pyrexic
BR pʌɪˈrɛksɪk
AM paɪˈrɛksɪk

pyrexical
BR pʌɪˈrɛksɪkl
AM paɪˈrɛksəkəl

pyrheliometer
BR pəˌhiːlɪˈɒmɪtə(r), -z
AM ˈpaɪ(ə)rˌ(h)iliˈɑmədər, -z

pyridine
BR ˈpɪrɪdiːn
AM ˈpɪrəˌdin, ˈpɪrədn

pyridoxal
BR pɪrɪˈdɒksl
AM ˌpɪrɪˈdɑksəl

pyridoxine
BR pɪrɪˈdɒksiːn, ˌpɪrɪˈdɒksɪn
AM ˌpɪrəˈdaksin, ˌpɪrəˈdaksən

pyrimidine
BR pʌɪˈrɪmɪdiːn, pɪˈrɪmɪdiːn, -z
AM pəˈrɪməˌdin, paɪˈrɪməˌdin, paɪˈrɪmədn, -z

pyrite
BR ˈpʌɪrʌɪt
AM ˈpaɪˌraɪt

pyrites
BR pʌɪˈrʌɪtiːz, pɪˈrʌɪtiːz
AM pəˈraɪdiz, paɪˈraɪdiz

pyritic
BR pʌɪˈrɪtɪk
AM paɪˈrɪdɪk, pəˈrɪdɪk

pyritiferous
BR ˌpʌɪrʌɪˈtɪf(ə)rəs, ˌpʌɪrɪˈtɪf(ə)rəs
AM ˈpaɪˌraɪdˈɪf(ə)rəs

pyritise
BR ˈpʌɪrʌɪtʌɪz, ˈpʌɪrɪtʌɪz, -ɪz, -ɪŋ, -d
AM ˈpaɪˌraɪdˌaɪz, -ɪz, -ɪŋ, -d

pyritize
BR ˈpʌɪrʌɪtʌɪz, ˈpʌɪrɪtʌɪz, -ɪz, -ɪŋ, -d
AM ˈpaɪˌraɪdˌaɪz, -ɪz, -ɪŋ, -d

pyritous
BR ˈpʌɪrɪtəs, pʌɪˈrʌɪtəs
AM pəˈraɪdəs, paɪˈraɪdəs

pyro
BR ˈpʌɪrəʊ
AM ˈpaɪˌrou

pyroclast
BR ˈpʌɪrə(ʊ)klɑːst, ˈpʌɪrə(ʊ)klast, -s
AM ˈpaɪrouˌklæst, -s

pyroclastic
BR ˌpʌɪrə(ʊ)ˈklastɪk, -s
AM ˌpaɪrouˈklæstɪk, -s

pyroelectric
BR ˌpʌɪrəʊɪˈlɛktrɪk
AM ˈpaɪrouəˈlɛktrɪk, ˈpaɪrouiˈlektrɪk

pyroelectricity
BR ˌpʌɪrəʊɪˌlɛkˈtrɪsɪti, ˌpʌɪrəʊˌɛlɛkˈtrɪsɪti, ˌpʌɪrəʊˌɛlɪkˈtrɪsɪti, ˌpʌɪrəʊˌɪlɛkˈtrɪsɪti, ˌpʌɪrəʊˌiːlɛkˈtrɪsɪti
AM ˈpaɪrouəˌlɛkˈtrɪsɪdi, ˈpaɪrouiˌlɛkˈtrɪsɪdi

pyrogallic acid
BR ˌpʌɪrə(ʊ)galɪk ˈasɪd
AM ˈpaɪrouˈgælɪk ˈæsəd

pyrogallol
BR ˌpʌɪrə(ʊ)ˈgalɒl
AM ˌpaɪrouˈgæˌlɔl, ˌpaɪrouˈgæˌlɑl

pyrogenic
BR ˌpʌɪrə(ʊ)ˈdʒɛnɪk
AM ˌpaɪrouˈdʒɛnɪk

pyrogenous
BR pʌɪˈrɒdʒɪnəs
AM paɪˈradʒənəs

pyrography
BR pʌɪˈrɒgrəfi
AM paɪˈragrəfi

pyrolatry
BR pʌɪˈrɒlətri
AM paɪˈrɑlətri

pyroligneous
BR ˌpʌɪrəˈlɪgnɪəs
AM ˌpaɪrəˈlɪgnɪəs

pyrolyse
BR ˈpʌɪrəlʌɪz, -ɪz, -ɪŋ, -t
AM ˈpaɪrəˌlaɪz, -ɪz, -ɪŋ, -t

pyrolysis
BR pʌɪˈrɒlɪsɪs
AM paɪˈrɑləsəs

pyrolytic
BR ˌpʌɪrəˈlɪtɪk
AM ˌpaɪrəˈlɪdɪk

pyrolyze
BR ˈpʌɪrəlʌɪz, -ɪz, -ɪŋ, -d
AM ˈpaɪrəˌlaɪz, -ɪz, -ɪŋ, -d

pyromancy
BR ˈpʌɪrə(ʊ)ˌmansi
AM ˈpaɪrouˌmænsi

pyromania
BR ˌpʌɪrə(ʊ)ˈmeɪnɪə(r)
AM ˌpaɪrouˈmeɪnɪə

pyromaniac
BR ˌpʌɪrə(ʊ)ˈmeɪnɪak, -s
AM ˌpaɪrouˈmeɪniˌæk, -s

pyrometer
BR pʌɪˈrɒmɪtə(r), -z
AM paɪˈrɑmədər, -z

pyrometric
BR ˌpʌɪrə(ʊ)ˈmɛtrɪk
AM ˌpaɪrouˈmɛtrɪk

pyrometrically
BR ˌpʌɪrə(ʊ)ˈmɛtrɪkli
AM ˌpaɪrouˈmɛtrək(ə)li

pyrometry
BR pʌɪˈrɒmɪtri
AM paɪˈramətri

pyrope
BR ˈpʌɪrəʊp, -s
AM ˈpaɪˌroup, -s

pyrophoric
BR ˌpʌɪrə(ʊ)ˈfɒrɪk
AM ˌpaɪrouˈfɔrɪk

pyrosis
BR pʌɪˈrəʊsɪs
AM paɪˈrousəs

pyrotechnic
BR ˌpʌɪrə(ʊ)ˈtɛknɪk, -s
AM ˌpaɪrouˈtɛknɪk, -s

pyrotechnical
BR ˌpʌɪrə(ʊ)ˈtɛknɪkl
AM ˌpaɪrouˈtɛknəkəl

pyrotechnically
BR ˌpʌɪrə(ʊ)ˈtɛknɪkli
AM ˌpaɪrouˈtɛknək(ə)li

pyrotechnist
BR ˌpʌɪrə(ʊ)ˈtɛknɪst, -s
AM ˌpaɪrouˈtɛknəst, -s

pyrotechny
BR ˈpʌɪrə(ʊ)ˌtɛkni
AM ˈpaɪrouˌtɛkni

pyroxene
BR paɪˈrɒksiːn, -z
AM paɪˈrɑːkˌsin,
pəˈrɑːkˌsin, -z

pyroxylin
BR paɪˈrɒksɪlɪn,
pʌɪˈrɒksl̩ɪn
AM paɪˈrɑːksələn,
pəˈrɑːksələn

Pyrrha
BR ˈpɪrə(r)
AM ˈpɪrə

Pyrrhic
BR ˈpɪrɪk, -s
AM ˈpɪrɪk, -s

Pyrrho
BR ˈpɪrəʊ
AM ˈpɪroʊ

Pyrrhonian
BR pɪˈrəʊnɪən
AM pəˈroʊnɪən

Pyrrhonic
BR pɪˈrɒnɪk
AM pəˈrɑnɪk

Pyrrhonism
BR ˈpɪrənɪz(ə)m
AM ˈpɪrənɪzəm

Pyrrhonist
BR ˈpɪrənɪst, -s
AM ˈpɪrənəst, -s

Pyrrhus
BR ˈpɪrəs
AM ˈpɪrəs

pyruvate
BR pʌɪˈruːveɪt
AM paɪˈruˌveɪt,
pəˈruˌveɪt

pyruvic acid
BR pʌɪˌruːvɪk ˈasɪd
AM paɪˈruːvɪk ˈæsəd,
pəˈruvɪk +

Pythagoras
BR pʌɪˈθag(ə)rəs
AM paɪˈθægərəs,
pəˈθægərəs

Pythagorean
BR ˌpʌɪθagəˈriːən,
pʌɪˌθagəˈriːən

AM pəˌθæɡəˈriən,
paɪˌθæɡəˈriən

Pythia
BR ˈpɪθɪə(r)
AM ˈpɪθɪə

Pythian
BR ˈpɪθɪən
AM ˈpɪθɪən

Pythias
BR ˈpɪθɪəs
AM ˈpɪθɪəs

python
BR ˈpʌɪθn, -z
AM ˈpaɪˌθɑn, ˈpaɪθən, -z

Pythonesque
BR ˌpʌɪθəˈnɛsk
AM ˌpaɪθəˈnɛsk

pythonic
BR pʌɪˈθɒnɪk
AM paɪˈθɑnɪk

pyuria
BR pʌɪˈjʊərɪə(r)

AM paɪˈjʊriə

pyx
BR pɪks, -ɪz
AM pɪks, -ɪz

pyxides
BR ˈpɪksɪdiːz
AM ˈpɪksɪˌdiz

pyxidia
BR pɪkˈsɪdɪə(r)
AM pɪkˈsɪdɪə

pyxidium
BR pɪkˈsɪdɪəm
AM pɪkˈsɪdɪəm

pyxie
BR ˈpɪksʲi, -ɪz
AM ˈpɪksi, -z

pyxis
BR ˈpɪksɪs
AM ˈpɪksɪs

pzazz
BR pəˈzaz
AM pəˈzæz

Qq

q
BR kjuː, -z
AM kju, -z

Qantas®
BR 'kwɒntəs
AM 'kwan(t)əs

Qatar
BR 'katɑː(r), 'gɑtɑː(r),
'kʌtɑː(r), 'gʌtɑː(r),
kə'tɑː(r)
AM 'kɑˌtar, kə'tar

Qatari
BR ka'tɑːr|i, ga'tɑːr|i,
kʌ'tɑːr|i, gʌ'tɑːr|i,
kə'tɑːr|i, -ɪz
AM kɑ'tari, kə'tari, -z

Qattara
BR ka'tɑːrə(r),
kʌ'tɑːrə(r),
kə'tɑːrə(r)
AM kə'tɑrə, kə'tɑrə

Q-boat
BR 'kjuːbəʊt, -s
AM 'kjuˌboʊt, -s

Q.C.
BR ˌkjuː'siː, -z
AM ˌkju'si, -z

QED
BR ˌkjuːiː'diː
AM ˌkjuˌi'di

Q fever
BR 'kjuː ˌfiːvə(r)
AM 'kjuˌfivər

qibla
BR 'kɪblə(r)
AM 'kɪblə

Qinghai
BR ˌtʃɪŋ'hʌɪ
AM 'tʃɪŋ'hai

Q-ship
BR 'kjuːˌʃɪp, -s
AM 'kjuˌʃɪp, -s

q.t.
BR ˌkjuː'tiː
AM ˌkju'ti

qua
BR kweɪ, kwɑː(r)
AM kwɑ, kweɪ

Quaalude®
BR 'kweɪluːd, -z
AM 'kweɪˌlud, -z

quack
BR kwak, -s, -ɪŋ, -t
AM kwæk, -s, -ɪŋ, -t

quackery
BR 'kwak(ə)ri
AM 'kwækəri

quackish
BR 'kwakɪʃ
AM 'kwækɪʃ

quad
BR kwɒd, -z
AM kwɑd, -z

quadragenarian
BR ˌkwɒdrədʒɪ'nɛːriən,
-z
AM ˌkwɑdrədʒə'nɛriən,
-z

Quadragesima
BR ˌkwɒdrə'dʒɛsɪmə(r)
AM ˌkwɑdrə'dʒɛsəmə

quadragesimal
BR ˌkwɒdrə'dʒɛsɪml
AM ˌkwɑdrə'dʒɛsəməl

quadrangle
BR 'kwɒdraŋgl, -z
AM 'kwɑˌdræŋgəl, -z

quadrangular
BR kwɒ'draŋgjʊlə(r),
kwə'draŋgjʊlə(r)
AM kwɑ'dræŋgjələr

quadrant
BR 'kwɒdr(ə)nt, -s
AM 'kwɑdrənt, -s

quadrantal
BR kwɒ'drantl
AM kwɒ'dræn(t)l

quadraphonic
BR ˌkwɒdrə'fɒnɪk, -s
AM ˌkwɑdrə'fɑnɪk, -s

quadraphonically
BR ˌkwɒdrə'fɒnɪkli
AM ˌkwɑdrə'fɑnɪk(ə)li

quadraphony
BR kwɒ'drɒfəni,
kwɒ'drɒfni,
'kwɒdrəˌfɒni
AM kwɑ'drɑfəni

quadrat
BR 'kwɒdrət,
'kwɒdrat, -s
AM 'kwɑdræt,
'kwɑdrət, -s

quadrate¹
noun, adjective
BR 'kwɒdreɪt,
'kwɒdrət, -s
AM 'kwɑdreɪt,
'kwɑdrət, -s

quadrate²
verb
BR kwɒ'dreɪt
kwɒ'dreɪt, -s, -ɪŋ, -ɪd
AM 'kwɑdˌreɪt, -ts, -ts,
-dɪŋ, -dɪd

quadratic
BR kwɒ'dratɪk,
kwə'dratɪk, -s
AM kwɑ'drædɪk, -s

quadrature
BR 'kwɒdrətʃə(r)
AM 'kwɑdrətʃər,
'kwɑdrətʃʊ(ə)r

quadrennia
BR kwɒ'drɛnɪə(r),
kwə'drɛnɪə(r)
AM kwɑ'drɛnɪə

quadrennial
BR kwɒ'drɛnɪəl,
kwə'drɛnɪəl
AM kwɑ'drɛnɪəl

quadrennially
BR kwɒ'drɛnɪəli,
kwə'drɛnɪəli
AM kwɑ'drɛnɪəli

quadrennium
BR kwɒ'drɛnɪəm,
kwə'drɛnɪəm
AM kwɑ'drɛnɪəm

quadric
BR 'kwɒdrɪk
AM 'kwɑdrɪk

quadriceps
BR 'kwɒdrɪsɛps
AM 'kwɑdrəˌsɛps

quadrifid
BR 'kwɒdrɪfɪd
AM 'kwɑdrəˌfɪd

quadriga
BR kwɒ'driːgə(r),
kwə'driːgə(r),
kwɒ'drʌɪgə(r),
kwə'drʌɪgə(r), -z
AM kwɑ'draɪgə, -z

quadrilateral
BR ˌkwɒdrɪ'lat(ə)rəl,
ˌkwɒdrɪ'lat(ə)r|, -z
AM ˌkwɑdrə'lædərəl,
ˌkwɑdrə'lætrəl, -z

quadrilingual
BR ˌkwɒdrɪ'lɪŋgw(ə)l
AM ˌkwɑdrə'lɪŋgwəl

quadrille
BR kwɒ'drɪl, kwə'drɪl,
-z
AM kwɑ'drɪl,
k(w)ə'drɪl, -z

quadrillion
BR kwɒ'drɪljən,
kwə'drɪljən, -z
AM kwɑ'drɪljən, -z

quadrinomial
BR ˌkwɒdrɪ'nəʊmɪəl,
-z
AM ˌkwɑdrə'noʊmiəl,
-z

quadripartite
BR ˌkwɒdrɪ'pɑːtʌɪt
AM ˌkwɑdrə'partait

quadriplegia
BR ˌkwɒdrɪ'pliːdʒ(ɪ)ə(r)
AM ˌkwɑdrə'pli(d)ʒə

quadriplegic
BR ˌkwɒdrɪ'pliːdʒɪk, -s
AM ˌkwɑdrə'plidʒɪk, -s

quadrireme
BR 'kwɒdrɪriːm, -z
AM 'kwɑdrəˌrim, -z

quadrisyllabic
BR ˌkwɒdrɪsɪ'labɪk
AM ˌkwɑdrəsə'læbɪk

quadrisyllable
BR 'kwɒdrɪˌsɪləbl, -z
AM ˌkwɑdrə'sɪləbəl, -z

quadrivalent
BR ˌkwɒdrɪ'veɪlənt,
ˌkwɒdrɪ'veɪlnt
AM ˌkwɑdrə'veɪlənt

quadrivia
BR kwɒ'drɪvɪə(r),
kwə'drɪvɪə(r)
AM kwɑ'drɪvɪə

quadrivium
BR kwɒ'drɪvɪəm,
kwə'drɪvɪəm
AM kwɑ'drɪvɪəm

quadroon
BR kwɒ'druːn,
kwə'druːn, -z
AM kwɑ'drun, -z

quadrophonic
BR ˌkwɒdrə'fɒnɪk, -s
AM ˌkwɑdrə'fɑnɪk, -s

quadrophonically
BR ˌkwɒdrə'fɒnɪkli
AM ˌkwɑdrə'fɑnək(ə)li

quadrophony
BR kwɒ'drɒfəni,
kwɒ'drɒfni,
kwə'drɒfəni,
kwə'drɒfni
AM kwɑ'drɑfəni

quadrumanous
BR kwɒ'druːmənəs,
kwə'druːmənəs
AM kwɑ'drumənəs

quadruped
BR 'kwɒdrʊpɛd, -z
AM 'kwɑdrəˌpɛd, -z

quadrupedal
BR kwɒ'druːpɪdl,
kwə'druːpɪdl,
ˌkwɒdrʊ'piːdl,
ˌkwɒdrʊ'pɛdl
AM ˌkwɑdrə'pɛdəl,
kwɑ'drupədəl

quadruple
BR 'kwɒdrʊp|l,
kwɒ'druːp|l,
kwə'druːp|l, -lz,
-lɪŋ \-lɪŋ, -ld
AM kwɑ'drup[əl,
kwɑ'drup|əl,
kwɑ'drəp|əl,
kwɑ'drəp|əl, -əlz,
-(ə)lɪŋ, -əld

quadruplet
BR 'kwɒdrʊp|lɪt,
kwɒ'druːp|lɪt,
kwə'druːp|lɪt, -s
AM kwɑ'drəp|lət,
kwə'drəp|lət,
kwɑ'drup|lət,
kwə'drup|lət, -s

quadruplicate¹
noun, adjective
BR kwɒ'druːp|lɪkət,
kwə'druː|plɪkət, -s
AM kwɑ'drup|ləkət,
kwə'drup|ləkət, -s

quadruplicate²
verb
BR kwɒˈdruːplɪkeɪt,
kwəˈdruːplɪkeɪt, -s,
-ɪŋ, -ɪd
AM kwɑˈdruːpləˌkeɪ|t,
kwəˈdruːpləˌkeɪ|t, -ts,
-dɪŋ, -dɪd

quadruplication
BR kwɒˌdruːplɪˈkeɪʃn,
kwəˌdruːplɪˈkeɪʃn, -z
AM kwɑˌdruːpləˈkeɪʃən,
kwəˌdruːpləˈkeɪʃən, -z

quadruplicity
BR ˌkwɒdrəˈplɪsɪti
AM ˌkwɑdrəˈplɪsɪdi

quadruply
BR ˈkwɒdrəpli,
kwɒˈdruːpli,
kwəˈdruːpli
AM kwɑˈdrup(ə)li,
kwəˈdrup(ə)li,
kwɑˈdrəp(ə)li

quadrupole
BR ˈkwɒdrəpəʊl, -z
AM ˈkwɑdrəˌpoʊl, -z

quaere
BR ˈkwɪər|i, -ɪz, -ɪŋ, -ɪd
AM ˈkwɪri, -z, -ɪŋ, -d

quaestor
BR ˈkwiːstə(r),
ˈkwiːstɔː(r),
ˈkwʌɪstə(r),
ˈkwʌɪstɔː(r), -z
AM ˈkwɛstər, -z

quaestorial
BR kwiːˈstɔːrɪəl,
kwʌɪˈstɔːrɪəl
AM kwɛˈstɔːrɪəl

quaestorship
BR ˈkwiːstəʃɪp,
ˈkwʌɪstəʃɪp, -s
AM ˈkwɛstərʃɪp, -s

quaff
BR kwɒf, -s, -ɪŋ, -t
AM kwɑf, -s, -ɪŋ, -t

quaffable
BR ˈkwɒfəbl
AM ˈkwɑfəbəl

quaffer
BR ˈkwɒfə(r), -z
AM ˈkwɑfər, -z

quag
BR kwag, kwɒg, -z
AM kwæg, kwɑg, -z

quagga
BR ˈkwagə(r), -z
AM ˈkwægə, -z

quaggy
BR ˈkwag|i, ˈkwɒg|i,
-ɪə(r), -ɪɪst
AM ˈkwægi, -ər, -ɪst

Quaglino's®
BR kwagˈliːnəʊz
AM kwagˈliːnoʊz

quagmare
BR ˈkwagmʌɪə(r),
ˈkwɒgmʌɪə(r), -z

AM ˈkwægˌmaɪ(ə)r, -z

quahaug
BR ˈkwɔːhɒg,
ˈkwɑːhɒg, k(w)əˈhɔːg,
-z
AM ˈkwɔːˌhɒg,
ˈkwɑˌhag, -z

quahog
BR ˈkwɔːhɒg,
ˈkwɑːhɒg, k(w)əˈhɔːg,
-z
AM ˈkwɔːhɒg,
ˈkwɑˌhag, -z

quaich
BR kweɪx, kweɪk, -ɪz
AM kweɪk, -ɪz

Quaid
BR kweɪd
AM kweɪd

Quai d'Orsay
BR ˌkeɪ dɔːˈseɪ
AM ˈki dɔːˈseɪ

quail
BR kweɪl, -z, -ɪŋ, -d
AM kweɪl, -z, -ɪŋ, -d

quailery
BR ˈkweɪl(ə)r|i, -ɪz
AM ˈkweɪləri, -z

quaint
BR kweɪnt, -ə(r), -ɪst
AM kweɪn|t, -(t)ər,
-(t)ɪst

quaintly
BR ˈkweɪntli
AM ˈkweɪn(t)li

quaintness
BR ˈkweɪntnɪs
AM ˈkweɪn(t)nɪs

quake
BR kweɪk, -s, -ɪŋ, -t
AM kweɪk, -s, -ɪŋ, -t

Quaker
BR ˈkweɪkə(r), -z
AM ˈkweɪkər, -z

Quakerish
BR ˈkweɪk(ə)rɪʃ
AM ˈkweɪkərɪʃ

Quakerism
BR ˈkweɪk(ə)rɪz(ə)m,
-z
AM ˈkweɪkəˌrɪzəm, -z

Quakerly
BR ˈkweɪkəli
AM ˈkweɪkərli

quakily
BR ˈkweɪkɪli
AM ˈkweɪkɪli

quakiness
BR ˈkweɪkɪnɪs
AM ˈkweɪkɪnɪs

quaky
BR ˈkweɪk|i, -ɪə(r), -ɪɪst
AM ˈkweɪki, -ər, -ɪst

Qualcast®
BR ˈkwɒlkɑːst,
ˈkwɒlkast,
AM ˈkwɑlˌkæst,
ˈkwɔlˌkæst

qualifiable
BR ˈkwɒlɪfʌɪəbl
AM ˌkwaləˈfaɪəbəl,
ˌkwɒləˈfaɪəbəl

qualification
BR ˌkwɒlɪfɪˈkeɪʃn, -z
AM ˌkwaləfəˈkeɪʃən,
ˌkwɒləfəˈkeɪʃən, -z

qualificatory
BR ˈkwɒlɪfɪkət(ə)ri,
ˌkwɒlɪfɪˈkeɪt(ə)ri
AM ˈkwaləfəkəˌtɔri,
ˈkwɒləfəkəˌtɔri

qualifier
BR ˈkwɒlɪfʌɪə(r), -z
AM ˈkwaləˌfaɪər, -z,
ˈkwɒləˌfaɪər

qualify
BR ˈkwɒlɪfʌɪ, -z, -ɪŋ, -d
AM ˈkwaləˌfaɪ,
ˈkwɒləˌfaɪ, -z, -ɪŋ, -d

qualitative
BR ˈkwɒlɪtətɪv,
ˈkwɒlɪteɪtɪv
AM ˈkwaləˌteɪdɪv,
ˈkwɒləˈteɪdɪv

qualitatively
BR ˈkwɒlɪtətɪvli,
ˈkwɒlɪteɪtɪvli
AM ˈkwaləˌteɪdɪvli,
ˈkwɒləˈteɪdɪvli

quality
BR ˈkwɒlɪt|i, -ɪz
AM ˈkwɒlədi, ˈkwalədi,
-z

qualm
BR kwɑːm, -z
AM kwɑ(l)m, -z,
kwɔ(l)m

qualmish
BR ˈkwɑːmɪʃ
AM ˈkwɑ(l)mɪʃ,
ˈkwɔ(l)mɪʃ

quamash
BR kwəˈmaʃ,
ˈkwɒməʃ, -ɪz
AM kwəˈmæʃ,
ˈkwɔˌmæʃ, ˈkwaˌmæʃ

quandary
BR ˈkwɒnd(ə)r|i, -ɪz
AM ˈkwɑnd(ə)ri, -z

quango
BR ˈkwaŋgəʊ, -z
AM ˈkwæŋgoʊ, -z

quant
BR kwɒnt, -s, -ɪŋ, -ɪd
AM kwɑn|t, -ts, -ɪd)ɪŋ,
-(d)əd

quanta
BR ˈkwɒntə(r)
AM ˈkwan(t)ə

quantal
BR ˈkwɒntl
AM ˈkwan(t)əl

quantally
BR ˈkwɒntli,
ˈkwɒntəli
AM ˈkwan(t)li

Quantel
BR ˌkwɒnˈtɛl, ˈkwɒntɛl
AM ˌkwanˈtɛl,
ˈkwanˌtɛl

quantic
BR ˈkwɒntɪk
AM ˈkwan(t)ɪk

quantifiability
BR ˌkwɒntɪˌfaɪəˈbɪlɪti
AM ˌkwan(t)əˌfaɪəˈbɪlɪdi

quantifiable
BR ˈkwɒntɪfʌɪəbl
AM ˈkwan(t)əˌfaɪəbəl

quantification
BR ˌkwɒntɪfɪˈkeɪʃn
AM ˌkwan(t)əfəˈkeɪʃən

quantifier
BR ˈkwɒntɪfʌɪə(r), -z
AM ˈkwan(t)əˌfaɪər, -z

quantify
BR ˈkwɒntɪfʌɪ, -z, -ɪŋ, -d
AM ˈkwan(t)əˌfaɪ, -z,
-ɪŋ, -d

quantisation
BR ˌkwɒntʌɪˈzeɪʃn, -z
AM ˌkwan(t)əˈzeɪʃən,
ˌkwanˌtaɪˈzeɪʃən, -z

quantise
BR ˈkwɒntʌɪz, -ɪz, -ɪŋ,
-d
AM ˈkwanˌtaɪz, -ɪz, -ɪŋ,
-d

quantitative
BR ˈkwɒntɪtətɪv,
ˈkwɒntɪteɪtɪv
AM ˈkwan(t)əˌteɪdɪv

quantitatively
BR ˈkwɒntɪtətɪvli,
ˈkwɒntɪteɪtɪvli
AM ˈkwan(t)əˌteɪdɪvli

quantitive
BR ˈkwɒntɪtɪv
AM ˈkwan(t)ədɪv

quantitively
BR ˈkwɒntɪtɪvli
AM ˈkwan(t)ədɪvli

quantity
BR ˈkwɒntɪt|i, -ɪz
AM ˈkwan(t)ədi, -z

quantization
BR ˌkwɒntʌɪˈzeɪʃn, -z
AM ˌkwan(t)əˈzeɪʃən,
ˌkwanˌtaɪˈzeɪʃən, -z

quantize
BR ˈkwɒntʌɪz, -ɪz, -ɪŋ,
-d
AM ˈkwanˌtaɪz, -ɪz, -ɪŋ,
-d

Quantock
BR ˈkwɒntək,
ˈkwɒntɒk, -s
AM ˈkwan(t)ək, -s

quantum
BR ˈkwɒntəm
AM ˈkwan(t)əm

quaquaversal
BR ˌkweɪkwəˈvɜːsl
AM ˈkweɪkwəˈvɜːrsəl

quarantine
BR ˈkwɒrəntiːn,
ˈkwɒrn̩tiːn, -z, -ɪŋ, -d
AM ˈkwɔrənˌtin, -z, -ɪŋ,
-d

quark¹
subatomic particle
BR kwɑːk, -s
AM kwɑrk, -s

quark²
soft cheese
BR kwɑːk
AM kwɑrk

Quarndon
BR ˈk(w)ɔːndən
AM ˈkwɔrndən

quarrel
BR ˈkwɒrəl, ˈkwɒrl̩, -z,
-ɪŋ, -d
AM ˈkwɔrəl, -z, -ɪŋ, -d

quarreler
BR ˈkwɒrələ(r),
ˈkwɒrl̩ə(r), -z
AM ˈkwɔr(ə)lər, -z

quarreller
BR ˈkwɒrələ(r),
ˈkwɒrl̩ə(r), -z
AM ˈkwɔr(ə)lər, -z

quarrelsome
BR ˈkwɒrəls(ə)m,
ˈkwɒrl̩s(ə)m
AM ˈkwɔr(ə)lsəm

quarrelsomely
BR ˈkwɒrəls(ə)mli,
ˈkwɒrl̩s(ə)mli
AM ˈkwɔr(ə)lsəmli

quarrelsomeness
BR ˈkwɒrəls(ə)mnəs,
ˈkwɒrl̩s(ə)mnəs
AM ˈkwɔr(ə)lsəmnəs

quarrian
BR ˈkwɒriən, -z
AM ˈkwɔriən, -z

quarry
BR ˈkwɒr|i, -iz, -ɪɪŋ, -ɪd
AM ˈkwɔri, -z, -ɪn, -d

quarryman
BR ˈkwɒrɪmən
AM ˈkwɔrɪmən

quarrymen
BR ˈkwɒrɪmən
AM ˈkwɔrɪmən

quart
BR kwɔːt, -s
AM kwɔ(ə)rt, -s

quartan
BR ˈkwɔːtn
AM ˈkwɔrtn

quartation
BR kwɔːˈteɪʃn, -z
AM kwɔrˈteɪʃən, -z

quarte
BR kɑːt
AM kɑrt

quarter
BR ˈkwɔːt|ə(r), -əz,
-(ə)rɪŋ, -əd
AM ˈkwɔrdər, -z, -ɪŋ, -d

quarterage
BR ˈkwɔːt(ə)r|ɪdʒ,
-ɪdʒɪz
AM ˈkwɔrdərɪdʒ, -ɪz

quarterback
BR ˈkwɔːtəbak, -s
AM ˈkwɔrdərˌbæk, -s

quarterdeck
BR ˈkwɔːtədɛk, -s
AM ˈkwɔrdərˌdɛk, -s

quarterfinal
BR ˈkwɔːtəˌfʌɪnl,
ˌkwɔːtəˈfʌɪnl, -z
AM ˈkwɔrdərˈfaɪnəl, -z

quarter-hour
BR ˌkwɔːtərˈaʊə(r), -z
AM ˈkwɔrdərˈaʊər, -z

quartering
BR ˈkwɔːt(ə)rɪŋ, -z
AM ˈkwɔrdərɪŋ, -z

quarterlight
BR ˈkwɔːtəlʌɪt, -s
AM ˈkwɔrdərˌlaɪt, -s

quarter-line
BR ˈkwɔːtəlʌɪn, -z
AM ˈkwɔrdərˌlaɪn, -z

quarterly
BR ˈkwɔːtəli
AM ˈkwɔrdərli

Quartermaine
BR ˈkwɔːtəmeɪn
AM ˈkwɔrdərˌmeɪn

Quarterman
BR ˈkwɔːtəmən
AM ˈkwɔrdərmən

quartermaster
BR ˈkwɔːtəˌmɑːstə(r),
ˈkwɔːtəˌmɑstə(r), -z
AM ˈkwɔrdərˌmæstər,
-z

**Quartermaster
General**
BR ˌkwɔːtəmɑːstə
ˈdʒɛn(ə)rəl,
ˌkwɔːtəmɑstə +,
+ ˈdʒɛn(ə)rl̩, -z
AM ˌkwɔrdərˌmæstər
ˈdʒɛn(ə)rəl, -z

quartern
BR ˈkwɔːt(ə)n, -z
AM ˈkwɔrdərn, -z

quarterstaff
BR ˈkwɔːtəstɑːf,
ˈkwɔːtəstaf, -s
AM ˈkwɔrdərˌstæf, -s

quartet
BR kwɔːˈtɛt, -s
AM kwɔrˈtɛt, -s

quartette
BR kwɔːˈtɛt, -s
AM kwɔrˈtɛt, -s

quartic
BR ˈkwɔːtɪk, -s
AM ˈkwɔrdɪk, -s

quartile
BR ˈkwɔːtʌɪl, -z
AM ˈkwɔrˌtaɪl, ˈkwɔrdl̩,
-z

4to
quarto
BR ˈkwɔːtəʊ
AM ˈkwɔrdoʊ

quarto
BR ˈkwɔːtəʊ, -z
AM ˈkwɔrdoʊ, -z

quartz
BR kwɔːts
AM kwɔrts

quartzite
BR ˈkwɔːtsʌɪt
AM ˈkwɔrtˌsaɪt

quasar
BR ˈkweɪzɑː(r), -z
AM ˈkweɪˌzɑr, -z

quash
BR kwɒʃ, -ɪz, -ɪŋ, -t
AM kwɒʃ, kwɑʃ, -əz, -ɪŋ,
-t

quasi
BR ˈkweɪzʌɪ, ˈkwɑːzi
AM ˈkwɑzi, ˈkweɪˌzaɪ

Quasimodo
BR ˌkwɒzɪˈməʊdəʊ,
ˌkwɑːziˈməʊdəʊ,
ˌkwɑziˈməʊdəʊ
AM ˌkwɑziˈmoʊˌdoʊ

quassia
BR ˈkwɒʃ(ɪ)ə(r),
ˈkwɑʃ(ɪ)ə(r),
ˈkwɑsɪə(r), -z
AM ˈkwɑʃ(i)ə, ˈkwɑsɪə,
-z

quatercentenary
BR ˌkwatəsɛnˈtiːn(ə)r|i,
ˌkwatəsənˈtɛn(ə)r|i,
ˌkwɒtəsənˈtiːn(ə)r|i,
ˌkwɒtəsənˈtɛn(ə)r|i,
ˌkwatəˈsɛntnər|i,
ˌkwɒtəˈsɛntnər|i, -iz
AM ˈkwadərsɛnˈtɛnəri,
ˈkwadərˈsɛntnˌɛri, -z

Quatermass
BR ˈkweɪtəmas
AM ˈkweɪtərˌmæs

quaternary
BR kwəˈtəːn(ə)r|i, -iz
AM ˈkwadərˌnɛri, -z

quaternion
BR kwəˈtəːnɪən, -z
AM kwəˈtɜrnɪən,
kwəˈtɜrniən, -z

quaternity
BR kwəˈtəːnɪt|i, -iz
AM kwəˈtɜrnədi, -z

quatorzain
BR ˈkatəzeɪn, -z
AM kəˈtɔrˌzeɪm,
ˈkædərˌzeɪn,
kəˈtɔrzən, -z

quatorze
BR kəˈtɔːz, -ɪz
AM kəˈtɔ(ə)rz, -əz

quatrain
BR ˈkwɒtreɪn, -z
AM ˈkwɑˌtreɪn, -z

quatrefoil
BR ˈkatrəfɔɪl, -z
AM ˈkædərˌfɔɪl,
ˈkætrəˌfɔɪl, -z

quatrillion
BR kwɒˈtrɪljən,
kwəˈtrɪljən, -z
AM kwɑˈtrɪljən, -z

Quattro
BR ˈkwɒtrəʊ,
ˈkwatrəʊ, -z
AM ˈkwɑtroʊ, -z

quattrocentist
BR ˌkwatrə(ʊ)ˈtʃɛntɪst,
ˌkwɒtrə(ʊ)ˈtʃɛntɪst,
-s
AM ˌkwɑˌtroʊˈ(t)ʃɛn(t)əst,
-s

quattrocento
BR ˌkwatrə(ʊ)ˈtʃɛntəʊ,
ˌkwɒtrə(ʊ)ˈtʃɛntəʊ
AM ˌkwɑˌtroʊˈ(t)ʃɛntoʊ

quaver
BR ˈkweɪv|ə(r), -əz,
-(ə)rɪŋ, -əd
AM ˈkweɪv|ər, -ərz,
-(ə)rɪŋ, -ərd

quaveriness
BR ˈkweɪv(ə)rɪnɪs
AM ˈkweɪv(ə)rinɪs

quaveringly
BR ˈkweɪv(ə)rɪŋli
AM ˈkweɪv(ə)rɪŋli

quavery
BR ˈkweɪv(ə)ri
AM ˈkweɪv(ə)ri

quay
BR kiː, -z
AM ki, -z

quayage
BR ˈkiː|ɪdʒ, -ɪdʒɪz
AM ˈkiɪdʒ, -ɪz

Quayle
BR kweɪl
AM kweɪl

quayside
BR ˈkiːsʌɪd
AM ˈkiˌsaɪd

quean
BR kwiːn, -z
AM kwin, -z

queasily
BR ˈkwiːzɪli
AM ˈkwizɪli

queasiness
BR ˈkwiːzɪnɪs
AM ˈkwizɪnɪs

queasy
BR ˈkwiːzi
AM ˈkwizi

Québec
BR kwɪˈbɛk
AM k(w)əˈbɛk, keɪˈbɛk
FR kebɛk

Quebecer
BR kwɪˈbɛkə(r), -z
AM k(w)əˈbɛkər,
keɪˈbɛkər, -z

Quebecker
BR kwɪ'bɛkə(r), -z
AM k(w)ə'bɛkər,
keɪ'bɛkər, -z

Québecois
BR ˌkeɪbɛ'kwɑː(r)
AM ˌkeɪbɛ'kwɑ
FR kebekwa

quebracho
BR keɪ'brɑːtʃəʊ,
kɪ'brɑːtʃəʊ, -z
AM keɪ'brɑtʃoʊ,
kə'brɑtʃoʊ, -z

Quechua
BR 'kɛtʃwə(r)
AM 'kɛtʃwə

Quechuan
BR 'kɛtʃwən, -z
AM 'kɛtʃwən, -z

queen
BR kwiːn, -z, -ɪŋ, -d
AM kwin, -z, -ɪŋ, -d

Queenborough
BR 'kwiːnb(ə)rə(r)
AM 'kwinˌbərə

queendom
BR 'kwiːndəm, -z
AM 'kwindəm, -z

queenhood
BR 'kwiːnhʊd, -z
AM 'kwinˌ(h)ʊd, -z

queenie
BR 'kwiːnˌli, -ɪz
AM 'kwini, -z

queenless
BR 'kwiːnlɪs
AM 'kwinləs

queenlike
BR 'kwiːnlʌɪk
AM 'kwinˌlaɪk

queenliness
BR 'kwiːnlɪnɪs
AM 'kwinlinɪs

queenly
BR 'kwiːnlˌi, -ɪə(r),
-ɪɪst
AM 'kwinli, -ər, -ɪst

Queens
BR kwiːnz
AM kwinz

Queensberry
BR 'kwiːnzb(ə)ri
AM 'kwinzbəri

Queensferry
BR 'kwiːnzˌfɛri
AM 'kwinzˌfɛri

queenship
BR 'kwiːnʃɪp
AM 'kwinˌʃɪp

queen-size
BR 'kwiːnsʌɪz
AM 'kwinˌsaɪz

Queensland
BR 'kwiːnzlənd,
'kwiːnzland
AM 'kwinzlənd,
'kwinzˌlænd

Queenslander
BR 'kwiːnzləndə(r),
'kwiːnslandə(r), -z
AM 'kwinzləndər,
'kwinzˌlændər, -z

Queenstown
BR 'kwiːnztaʊn
AM 'kwinzˌtaʊn

Queensway
BR 'kwiːnzweɪ
AM 'kwinzˌweɪ

queer
BR kwɪə(r), -z, -ɪŋ, -d,
-ə(r), -ɪst
AM kwɪ(ə)r, -z, -ɪŋ, -d,
-ər, -ɪst

queerish
BR 'kwɪərɪʃ
AM 'kwɪrɪʃ

queerly
BR 'kwɪəli
AM 'kwɪrli

queerness
BR 'kwɪənəs
AM 'kwɪrnəs

quelia
BR 'kwiːliə(r), -z
AM 'kwiliə, -z

quell
BR kwɛl, -z, -ɪŋ, -d
AM kwɛl, -z, -ɪŋ, -d

queller
BR 'kwɛlə(r), -z
AM 'kwɛlər, -z

Quemoy
BR kɪ'mɔɪ
AM ki'mɔɪ

quench
BR kwɛn(t)ʃ, -ɪz, -ɪŋ, -t
AM kwɛn(t)ʃ, -ɪz, -ɪŋ, -t

quenchable
BR 'kwɛn(t)ʃəbl
AM 'kwɛn(t)ʃəbəl

quencher
BR 'kwɛn(t)ʃə(r), -z
AM 'kwɛn(t)ʃər, -z

quenchless
BR 'kwɛn(t)ʃləs
AM 'kwɛn(t)ʃləs

quenelle
BR kə'nɛl, -z
AM kə'nɛl, -z

Quentin
BR 'kwɛntɪn
AM 'kwɛntn

Quercia
BR 'kwəːʃə(r)
AM 'kwərʃə

querist
BR 'kwɪərɪst, -s
AM 'kwɪrəst, 'kwɛrəst,
-s

quern
BR kwəːn, -z
AM kwərn, -z

querulous
BR 'kwɛr(j)ʊləs

AM 'kwɛr(j)ələs

querulously
BR 'kwɛr(j)ʊləsli
AM 'kwɛrələsli

querulousness
BR 'kwɛr(j)ʊləsnəs
AM 'kwɛrələsnəs

query
BR 'kwɪərˌi, -ɪz, -ɪŋ, -ɪd
AM 'kwɪri, 'kwɛri, -z,
-ɪŋ, -d

quest
BR kwɛst, -s, -ɪŋ, -ɪd
AM kwɛst, -s, -ɪŋ, -ɪd

Quested
BR 'kwɛstɪd
AM 'kwɛstəd

quester
BR 'kwɛstə(r), -z
AM 'kwɛstər, -z

questingly
BR 'kwɛstɪŋli
AM 'kwɛstɪŋli

question
BR 'kwɛstʃ|(ə)n,
-(ə)nz, -ənɪŋ\-ɳɪŋ,
-(ə)nd
AM 'kwɛstʃ|ən,
'kwɛʃtʃ|ən, -ənz,
-(ə)nɪŋ, -ənd

questionability
BR ˌkwɛstʃənə'bɪlɪti,
ˌkwɛstʃnə'bɪlɪti
AM ˌkwɛstʃənə'bɪlɪdi,
ˌkwɛʃtʃənə'bɪlɪdi

questionable
BR 'kwɛstʃənəbl,
'kwɛstʃnəbl
AM 'kwɛstʃənəbəl,
'kwɛʃtʃənəbəl

questionableness
BR 'kwɛstʃənəblnəs,
'kwɛstʃnəblnəs
AM 'kwɛstʃənəbəlnəs

questionably
BR 'kwɛstʃənəbli,
'kwɛstʃnəbli
AM 'kwɛstʃənəbli

questionary
BR 'kwɛstʃən(ə)r|i,
'kwɛstʃn(ə)r|i, -ɪz
AM 'kwɛstʃənɛri, -z

questioner
BR 'kwɛstʃənə(r),
'kwɛstʃnə(r), -z
AM 'kwɛstʃənər, -z

questioningly
BR 'kwɛstʃənɪŋli,
'kwɛstʃnɪŋ
AM 'kwɛstʃənɪŋli

questionless
BR 'kwɛstʃ(ə)nləs
AM 'kwɛstʃənl,
'kwɛstʃənləs

questionnaire
BR ˌk(w)ɛstʃə'nɛː(r), -z
AM ˌkwɛstʃə'nɛ(ə)r,
ˌkwɛʃtʃə'nɛ(ə)r, -z

questor
BR 'kwɛstə(r),
'kwɛstɔː(r),
'kwiːstə(r), -z
AM 'kwɛstər, -z

Quetta
BR 'kwɛtə(r)
AM 'kwɛdə

quetzal
BR 'k(w)ɛtsl, kɛt'sal, -z
AM kɛt'sal, -z

Quetzalcóatl
BR 'kɛtslkəʊ'atl
AM ˌkɛtzəlkoʊ'atl

queue
BR kjuː, -z, -ɪŋ, -d
AM kju, -z, -ɪŋ, -d

Quezon
BR 'keɪzɒn, 'keɪsɒn
AM 'keɪzɑn

quibble
BR 'kwɪb|l, -lz,
-lɪŋ\-lɪŋ, -ld
AM 'kwɪbəl, -əlz,
-(ə)lɪŋ, -əld

quibbler
BR 'kwɪblə(r),
'kwɪblə(r), -z
AM 'kwɪb(ə)lər, -z

quibblingly
BR 'kwɪblɪŋli,
'kwɪblɪŋli
AM 'kwɪb(ə)lɪŋli

quiche
BR kiːʃ, -ɪz
AM kiʃ, -ɪz

Quichua
BR 'kɪtʃwə(r)
AM 'kɪtʃwə

quick
BR kwɪk, -ə(r), -ɪst
AM kwɪk, -ər, -ɪst

quicken
BR 'kwɪk|(ə)n, -(ə)nz,
-ɳɪŋ\-(ə)nɪŋ, -(ə)nd
AM 'kwɪk|ən, -ənz,
-(ə)nɪŋ, -ənd

quickie
BR 'kwɪk|i, -ɪz
AM 'kwɪki, -z

quicklime
BR 'kwɪklʌɪm
AM 'kwɪkˌlaɪm

quickly
BR 'kwɪkli
AM 'kwɪkli

quickness
BR 'kwɪknɪs
AM 'kwɪknəs

quicksand
BR 'kwɪksand, -z
AM 'kwɪkˌsænd, -z

quickset
BR ˌkwɪk'sɛt
AM 'kwɪkˌsɛt

quicksilver
BR 'kwɪkˌsɪlvə(r)
AM 'kwɪkˌsɪlvər

quickstep
BR ˈkwɪkstep, -s
AM ˈkwɪkˌstɛp, -s

quickthorn
BR ˈkwɪkθɔːn, -z
AM ˈkwɪkˌθɔ(ə)rn, -z

quick-witted
BR ˌkwɪkˈwɪtɪd
AM ˌkwɪkˈwɪdɪd

quick-wittedness
BR ˌkwɪkˈwɪtɪdnɪs
AM ˌkwɪkˈwɪdɪdnɪs

quid
BR kwɪd, -z
AM kwɪd, -z

quiddity
BR ˈkwɪdɪt|i, -ɪz
AM ˈkwɪdɪdi, -z

quidnunc
BR ˈkwɪdnʌŋk, -s
AM ˈkwɪdˈnəŋk, -s

quid pro quo
BR ˌkwɪd prəʊ ˈkwəʊ, -z
AM ˌkwɪd ˌproʊ ˈkwoʊ, -z

quiescence
BR kwiˈɛsns, kwʌiˈɛsns
AM kwaiˈɛsəns, kwiˈɛsəns

quiescency
BR kwiˈɛsnsi, kwʌiˈɛsnsi
AM ˌkwaiˈɛsənsi, kwiˈɛsənsi

quiescent
BR kwiˈɛsnt, kwʌiˈɛsnt
AM kwaiˈɛsənt, kwiˈɛsənt

quiescently
BR kwiˈɛsntli, kwʌiˈɛsntli
AM ˌkwaiˈɛsn(t)li, kwiˈɛsn(t)li

quiet
BR ˈkwʌiət, -s, -ɪŋ, -ɪd, -ə(r), -ɪst
AM ˈkwaiə|t, -ts, -dɪŋ, -dəd, -dər, -dəst

quieten
BR ˈkwʌiət|n, -nz, -ŋɪŋ \-nɪŋ, -nd
AM ˈkwaiətn, -z, -ɪŋ, -d

quietism
BR ˈkwʌɪtɪz(ə)m
AM ˈkwaiəˌtɪzəm

quietist
BR ˈkwʌɪtɪst, -s
AM ˈkwaiədəst, -s

quietistic
BR ˌkwʌɪˈtɪstɪk
AM ˌkwaiəˈtɪstɪk

quietly
BR ˈkwʌiətli
AM ˈkwaiətli

quietness
BR ˈkwʌiətnəs
AM ˈkwaiətnəs

quietude
BR ˈkwʌiɪtjuːd, ˈkwʌiɪtʃuːd
AM ˈkwaiəˌt(j)ud

quietus
BR kwʌiˈiːtəs, kwʌiˈeɪtəs, kwiˈeɪtəs
AM ˈkwaiədəs

quiff
BR kwɪf, -s
AM kwɪf, -s

Quigley
BR ˈkwɪgli
AM ˈkwɪgli

quill
BR kwɪl, -z
AM kwɪl, -z

quill-coverts
BR ˈkwɪlˌkʌvəts
AM ˈkwɪlˌkəvərts

Quiller-Couch
BR ˌkwɪləːˈkuːtʃ
AM ˌkwɪlərˈkaʊtʃ

quilling
BR ˈkwɪlɪŋ
AM ˈkwɪlɪŋ

Quilp
BR kwɪlp
AM kwɪlp

quilt
BR kwɪlt, -s, -ɪŋ, -ɪd
AM kwɪlt, -s, -ɪŋ, -ɪd

quilter
BR ˈkwɪltə(r), -z
AM ˈkwɪltər, -z

quim
BR kwɪm, -z
AM kwɪm, -z

quin
BR kwɪn, -z
AM kwɪn, -z

quinacrine
BR ˈkwɪnəkriːn, ˈkwɪnəkrɪn
AM ˈkwɪnəˌkrɪn

quinary
BR ˈkwʌɪn(ə)ri
AM ˈkwaiˌneri

quinate
BR ˈkwʌɪneɪt
AM ˈkwaiˌneɪt

quince
BR kwɪns, -ɪz
AM kwɪns, -ɪz

quincentenary
BR ˌkwɪnsɛnˈtiːn(ə)r|i, ˌkwɪnsɛnˈten(ə)r|i, -ɪz
AM ˌkwɪnˌsɛnˈtɛnəri, -z

quincentennial
BR ˌkwɪnsɛnˈtɛniəl
AM ˌkwɪnˌsɛnˈtɛniəl

Quincey
BR ˈkwɪnsi

AM ˈkwɪnsi

quincuncial
BR kwɪnˈkʌnʃl, kwɪŋˈkʌnʃl
AM ˌkwɪnˈkənʃl

quincuncially
BR kwɪnˈkʌnʃ|li, kwɪnˈkʌnʃəli, kwɪŋˈkʌnʃ|li, kwɪŋˈkʌnʃəli
AM ˌkwɪnˈkənʃəli

quincunx
BR ˈkwɪnkʌnks, ˈkwɪŋkʌnks, -ɪz
AM ˈkwɪnˌkən(k)s, -ɪz

quinella
BR kwɪˈnɛlə(r), -z
AM kwɪˈnɛlə, -z

quingentenary
BR ˌkwɪn(d)ʒ(ə)nˈtiːn(ə)r|i, ˌkwɪn(d)ʒ(ə)nˈtɛn(ə)r|i, -ɪz
AM ˌkwɪnˌgɛnˈtɛnəri, -z

quinine
BR ˈkwɪniːn, kwɪˈniːn
AM ˈkwaiˌnain

Quink®
BR kwɪŋk
AM kwɪŋk

Quinlan
BR ˈkwɪnlən
AM ˈkwɪnlən

Quinn
BR kwɪn
AM kwɪn

quinol
BR ˈkwɪnɒl
AM ˈkwɪnɔl, ˈkwɪnɑl

quinoline
BR ˈkwɪnəliːn, ˈkwɪnˌliːn, ˈkwɪnəlɪn, ˈkwɪnˌlɪn, -z
AM ˈkwɪnəlɪn, -z

quinone
BR ˈkwɪnəʊn, -z
AM ˈkwɪnoʊn, -z

quinquagenarian
BR ˌkwɪŋkwədʒɪˈneːriən, -z
AM ˌkwɪŋkwəˌdʒəˈneriən, -z

quinquagenary
BR kwɪŋˈkwadʒɪn(ə)r|i, kwɪnˈkwadʒɪn(ə)r|i, -ɪz
AM ˌkwɪŋˈkwædʒəneri, -z

Quinquagesima
BR ˌkwɪŋkwəˈdʒɛsɪmə(r)
AM ˌkwɪŋkwəˈdʒɛsəmə

quinquelateral
BR ˌkwɪŋkwɪˈlat(ə)rəl, ˌkwɪŋkwɪˈlat(ə)rl
AM ˌkwɪŋkwəˈlædərəl

quinquennia
BR kwɪŋˈkwɛniə(r), kwɪnˈkwɛniə(r)
AM kwɪŋˈkwɛniə

quinquennial
BR kwɪŋˈkwɛniəl, kwɪnˈkwɛniəl
AM kwɪŋˈkwɛniəl

quinquennially
BR kwɪŋˈkwɛniəli, kwɪnˈkwɛniəli
AM ˈkwɪŋkwɛniəli

quinquennium
BR kwɪŋˈkwɛniəm, kwɪnˈkwɛniəm, -z
AM kwɪŋˈkwɛniəm, -z

quinquereme
BR ˈkwɪŋkwɪriːm, -z
AM ˈkwɪŋkwəˌrim, -z

quinquevalent
BR ˌkwɪŋkwɪˈveɪlənt, ˌkwɪŋkwɪˈveɪlnt
AM ˌkwɪŋkwəˈveɪlənt

quinsied
BR ˈkwɪnzid
AM ˈkwɪnzid

quinsy
BR ˈkwɪnzi
AM ˈkwɪnzi

quint
BR k(w)ɪnt, -s
AM kwɪnt, -s

quinta
BR ˈk(w)ɪntə(r), -z
AM ˈkwɪn(t)ə, -z

quintain
BR ˈkwɪntɪn, -z
AM ˈkwɪntn, -z

quintal
BR ˈkwɪntl, -z
AM ˈkwɪn(t)l, -z

quintan
BR ˈkwɪntən, -z
AM ˈkwɪntn, -z

quinte
BR kãt
AM kwɪnt

quintessence
BR kwɪnˈtɛsns
AM kwɪnˈtɛsəns

quintessential
BR ˌkwɪntɪˈsɛnʃl
AM ˈkwɪn(t)əˈsɛn(t)ʃəl

quintessentially
BR ˌkwɪntɪˈsɛnʃ|li, ˌkwɪntɪˈsɛnʃəli
AM kwɪn(t)əˈsɛn(t)ʃəli

quintet
BR kwɪnˈtɛt, -s
AM kwɪnˈtɛt, -s

quintile
BR ˈkwɪnt(ɪ)l, ˈkwɪntʌɪl
AM :kwɪnˌtail, ˈkwɪntl, -z

Quintilian
BR kwɪnˈtɪliən

AM kwɪn'tɪljən,
kwɪn'tɪliən

quintillion
BR kwɪn'tɪljən
AM kwɪn'tɪljən

quintillionth
BR kwɪn'tɪljənθ
AM kwɪn'tɪljənθ

Quintin
BR 'kwɪntɪn
AM 'kwɪntn

Quinton
BR 'kwɪntən
AM 'kwɪn(t)ən

quintuple
BR 'kwɪntjʊp|l,
'kwɪntʃʊp|l,
kwɪn'tju:p|l,
kwɪn'tʃu:p|l, -lz,
-lɪŋ\-əlɪŋ, -ld
AM kwɪn't(j)up|əl,
kwɪn'təp|əl, -əlz,
-(ə)lɪŋ, -əld

quintuplet
BR 'kwɪntjʊp|ɪt,
'kwɪntʃʊp|ɪt,
kwɪn'tju:p|ɪt,
kwɪn'tʃu:p|ɪt, -s
AM kwɪn'təp|ət,
kwɪn't(j)upl|ət, -s

quintuplicate
BR kwɪn'tju:plɪkeɪt,
kwɪn'tʃu:plɪkeɪt, -s,
-ɪŋ, -ɪd
AM kwɪn'təplə,keɪ|t,
kwɪn't(j)uplə,keɪ|t,
-ts, -dɪŋ, -dɪd

quintuplication
BR kwɪn,tju:plɪ'keɪʃn,
kwɪn,tʃu:plɪ'keɪʃn, -z
AM kwɪn,təplə'keɪʃən,
kwɪn,t(j)uplə'keɪʃən,
-z

quintuply
BR 'kwɪntjʊpli,
'kwɪntʃʊpli
AM kwɪn't(j)up(ə)li

Quintus
BR 'kwɪntəs
AM 'kwɪn(t)əs

quip
BR kwɪp, -s, -ɪŋ, -t
AM kwɪp, -s, -ɪŋ, -t

quipster
BR 'kwɪpstə(r), -z
AM 'kwɪpstər, -z

quipu
BR 'ki:pu:, 'kwɪpu:, -z
AM 'kipu, 'kwɪpu, -z

quire
BR 'kwʌɪə(r), -z
AM 'kwaɪ(ə)r, -z

Quirinus
BR kwɪ'raɪnəs
AM kwə'raɪnəs

quirk
BR kwə:k, -s
AM kwərk, -s

Quirke
BR kwə:k
AM kwərk

quirkily
BR 'kwə:kɪli
AM 'kwərkəli

quirkiness
BR 'kwə:kɪnɪs
AM 'kwərkɪnɪs

quirkish
BR 'kwə:kɪʃ
AM 'kwərkɪʃ

quirky
BR 'kwə:k|i, -ɪə(r), -ɪɪst
AM 'kwərki, -ər, -ɪst

quirt
BR kwə:t, -s
AM kwərt, -s

quisling
BR 'kwɪzlɪŋ, -z
AM 'kwɪzlɪŋ, -z

quislingite
BR 'kwɪzlɪŋʌɪt, -s
AM 'kwɪzlɪŋ,aɪt, -s

quit
BR kwɪt, -s, -ɪŋ, -ɪd
AM kwɪ|t, -ts, -dɪŋ, -dɪd

quitch
BR kwɪtʃ
AM kwɪtʃ

quitclaim
BR 'kwɪtkleɪm, -z, -ɪŋ,
-d
AM 'kwɪt,kleɪm, -z, -ɪŋ,
-d

quite
BR kwʌɪt
AM kwaɪt

Quito
BR 'ki:təʊ
AM 'kidoʊ

quitrent
BR 'kwɪtrɛnt, -s
AM 'kwɪt,rɛnt, -s

quittance
BR 'kwɪt(ə)ns, -ɪz
AM 'kwɪtns, -ɪz

quitter
BR 'kwɪtə(r), -z
AM 'kwɪdər, -z

quiver
BR 'kwɪv|ə(r), -əz,
-(ə)rɪŋ, -əd
AM 'kwɪv|ər, -ərz,
-(ə)rɪŋ, -ərd

quiverful
BR 'kwɪvəfʊl, -z
AM 'kwɪvər,fʊl, -z

quivering
BR 'kwɪv(ə)rɪŋ, -z
AM 'kwɪvərɪŋ, -z

quiveringly
BR 'kwɪv(ə)rɪŋli
AM 'kwɪvərɪŋli

quivery
BR 'kwɪv(ə)ri
AM 'kwɪv(ə)ri

qui vive
BR ,ki: 'vi:v
AM ,ki 'viv

Quixote
BR 'kwɪksət,
'kwɪksəʊt, kɪ'həʊti
AM ki'(h)oʊdi,
ki'hoʊ,teɪ

quixotic
BR kwɪk'sɒtɪk
AM kwɪk'sadɪk

quixotically
BR kwɪk'sɒtɪkli
AM kwɪk'sadək(ə)li

quixotise
BR 'kwɪksətʌɪz, -ɪz, -ɪŋ,
-d
AM 'kwɪksə,taɪz, -ɪz,
-ɪŋ, -d

quixotism
BR 'kwɪksətɪz(ə)m
AM 'kwɪksə,tɪzəm

quixotize
BR 'kwɪksətʌɪz, -ɪz, -ɪŋ,
-d
AM 'kwɪksə,taɪz, -ɪz,
-ɪŋ, -d

quixotry
BR 'kwɪksɒtri
AM 'kwɪksətri

quiz
BR kwɪz, -ɪz, -ɪŋ, -d
AM kwɪz, -ɪz, -ɪŋ, -d

quizmaster
BR 'kwɪz,mɑ:stə(r),
'kwɪz,mɑstə(r), -z
AM 'kwɪz,mæstər, -z

quizshow
BR 'kwɪzʃəʊ, -z
AM 'kwɪz,ʃoʊ, -z

quizzer
BR 'kwɪzə(r), -z
AM 'kwɪzər, -z

quizzical
BR 'kwɪzɪkl
AM 'kwɪzəkəl

quizzicality
BR ,kwɪzɪ'kalɪti
AM ,kwɪzɪ'kælədi

quizzically
BR 'kwɪzɪkli
AM 'kwɪzək(ə)li

quizzicalness
BR 'kwɪzɪklnəs
AM 'kwɪzɪkəlnəs

Qum
BR kʊm
AM kʊm

Qumran
BR kʊm'rɑ:n
AM kʊm'ræn

quod
BR kwɒd, -z, -ɪŋ, -ɪd
AM kwad, -z, -ɪŋ, -ɪd

quodlibet
BR 'kwɒdlɪbɛt, -s

AM 'kwɑdlə,bɛt, -s

quodlibetarian
BR ,kwɒdlɪbɪ'tɛ:rɪən,
-z
AM ,kwɑdləbə'terɪən,
-z

quodlibetical
BR ,kwɒdlɪ'bɛtɪkl
AM ,kwɑdlə'bɛdəkəl

quodlibetically
BR ,kwɒdlɪ'bɛtɪkli
AM ,kwɑdlə'bɛdək(ə)li

quoin
BR k(w)ɔɪn, -z, -ɪŋ, -d
AM k(w)ɔɪn, -z, -ɪŋ, -d

quoit
BR k(w)ɔɪt, -s
AM k(w)ɔɪt, kweɪt, -s

quokka
BR 'kwɒkə(r), -z
AM 'kwakə, -z

quondam
BR 'kwɒndam,
'kwɒndəm
AM 'kwandəm,
'kwan,dæm,
'kwan,dam

Quonset®
BR 'kwɒnsɪt, -s
AM 'kwɒnsət,
'kwɑnsət, -s

quorate
BR 'kwɔ:reɪt
AM 'kwɔ,reɪt, 'kwɑ,reɪt

Quorn®
BR 'kwɔ:n
AM kwɔ(ə)rn

quorum
BR 'kwɔ:rəm, -z
AM 'kwɔrəm, -z

Quosh
BR kwɒʃ
AM kwɔʃ, kwɑʃ

quota
BR 'kwəʊtə(r), -z
AM 'kwoʊdə, -z

quotability
BR ,kwəʊtə'bɪlɪti
AM ,kwoʊdə'bɪlɪdi

quotable
BR 'kwəʊtəbl
AM 'kwoʊdəbəl

quotation
BR kwə(ʊ)'teɪʃn, -z
AM 'kwoʊ'teɪʃən, -z

quotative
BR 'kwəʊtətɪv
AM 'kwoʊdədɪv

quote
BR kwəʊt, -s, -ɪŋ, -ɪd
AM kwoʊ|t, -ts, -dɪŋ,
-dəd

quoth
BR kwəʊθ
AM kwoʊθ

quotha
BR ˈkwəʊθə(r)
AM ˈkwoʊθə
quotidian
BR kwəˈtɪdɪən,
kwɒˈtɪdɪən
AM kwoʊˈtɪdiən

quotient
BR ˈkwəʊʃnt, -s
AM ˈkwoʊʃənt, -s
Quran
BR kɔːˈrɑːn,
kəˈrɑːn
AM kɔˈræn, kəˈræn

Quranic
BR kɔːˈranɪk, kəˈranɪk
AM kɔˈrænɪk,
kəˈrænɪk
q.v.
BR ˌkjuːˈviː
AM ˌkjuˈvi

Qwaqwa
BR ˈkwɑːkwə(r)
AM ˈkwɑkwə

QWERTY
BR ˈkwɜːti
AM ˈkwɚdi

Rr

r
BR ɑː(r), -z
AM ɑr, -z

Raasey
BR 'rɑːseɪ
AM 'rɑseɪ

Rabat
BR rə'bæt, rə'bɑːt
AM rə'bɑt

Rabaul
BR rə'baʊl
AM rɑ'baʊl

rabbet
BR 'ræb|ɪt, -ɪts, -ɪtɪŋ,
-ɪtɪd
AM 'ræbə|t, -ts, -dɪŋ,
-dəd

rabbi
BR 'ræbʌɪ, -z
AM 'ræˌbaɪ, -z

Rabbie
BR 'ræbi
AM 'rɑbi

rabbin
BR 'ræbɪn, -z
AM 'ræbən, -z

rabbinate
BR 'ræbɪnət, 'ræbɪneɪt,
-s
AM 'ræbəˌneɪt,
'ræbənət, -s

rabbinic
BR rə'bɪnɪk
AM rə'bɪnɪk

rabbinical
BR rə'bɪnɪkl
AM rə'bɪnəkəl

rabbinically
BR rə'bɪnɪkli
AM rə'bɪnək(ə)li

rabbinism
BR 'ræbɪnɪz(ə)m
AM 'ræbəˌnɪzəm

rabbinist
BR 'ræbɪnɪst, -s
AM 'ræbənəst, -s

rabbit
BR 'ræb|ɪt, -ɪts, -ɪtɪŋ,
-ɪtɪd
AM 'ræbə|t, -ts, -dɪŋ,
-dəd

rabbity
BR 'ræbɪti
AM 'ræbədi

rabble
BR 'ræbl, -z
AM 'ræbəl, -z

rabble-rouser
BR 'ræblˌraʊzə(r), -z
AM 'ræbəlˌraʊzər, -z

Rabelais
BR 'ræbəleɪ
AM 'ræbəˌleɪ, ˌræbə'leɪ

Rabelaisian
BR ˌræbə'leɪzɪən,
ˌræbə'leɪʒn
AM ˌræbə'leɪzɪən,
ˌræbə'leɪʒən

rabi
BR 'rɑbiː, 'rʌbiː
AM 'rɑbi

rabid
BR 'ræbɪd, 'reɪbɪd
AM 'ræbəd

rabidity
BR rə'bɪdɪti
AM rə'bɪdɪdi

rabidly
BR 'ræbɪdli, 'reɪbɪdli
AM 'ræbədli

rabidness
BR 'ræbɪdnɪs,
'reɪbɪdnɪs
AM 'ræbədnəs

rabies
BR 'reɪbiːz, 'reɪbɪz
AM 'reɪbiz

Rabin
BR rɑ'biːn
AM rɑ'bin

Rabindranath
BR rə'bɪndrənɑːθ
AM rə'bɪndrənəθ

Rabinowitz
BR rə'bɪnəwɪts,
rə'bɪnəvɪts
AM rə'bɪnəˌwɪts

raccoon
BR rə'kuːn, rɑ'kuːn, -z
AM ræ'kun, rə'kun, -z

race
BR reɪs, -ɪz, -ɪŋ, -t
AM reɪs, -ɪz, -ɪŋ, -t

racecard
BR 'reɪskɑːd, -z
AM 'reɪsˌkɑrd, -z

racecourse
BR 'reɪskɔːs, -ɪz
AM 'reɪsˌkɔ(ə)rs, -əz

racegoer
BR 'reɪsˌgəʊə(r), -z
AM 'reɪsˌgoʊər, -z

racegoing
BR 'reɪsˌgəʊɪŋ
AM 'reɪsˌgoʊɪŋ

racehorse
BR 'reɪshɔːs, -ɪz
AM 'reɪsˌ(h)ɔ(ə)rs, -əz

racemate
BR 'reɪsmeɪt, -s
AM 'reɪsˌmeɪt, -s

raceme
BR rasiːm, rə'siːm,
rɑ'siːm, -z
AM reɪ'sim, rə'sim, -z

racemic
BR rə'siːmɪk,
ra'siːmɪk
AM reɪ'simɪk, rə'simɪk

racemise
BR 'ræsɪmʌɪz, -ɪz, -ɪŋ, -d
AM 'ræsəˌmaɪz,
reɪ'siˌmaɪz,
rə'siˌmaɪz, -ɪz, -ɪŋ, -d

racemize
BR 'ræsɪmʌɪz, -ɪz, -ɪŋ, -d
AM 'ræsəˌmaɪz,
reɪ'siˌmaɪz,
rə'siˌmaɪz, -ɪz, -ɪŋ, -d

racemose
BR 'rasɪməʊs
AM 'ræsəˌmoʊs,
'ræsəˌmoʊz

racer
BR 'reɪsə(r), -z
AM 'reɪsər, -z

racetrack
BR 'reɪstrak, -s
AM 'reɪsˌtræk, -s

raceway
BR 'reɪsweɪ, -z
AM 'reɪsˌweɪ, -z

Rachael
BR 'reɪtʃl
AM 'reɪtʃəl

Rachel
BR 'reɪtʃl
AM 'reɪtʃəl

rachel
BR rə'ʃɛl
AM rə'ʃɛl

rachidial
BR rə'kɪdɪəl
AM rə'kɪdɪəl

rachis
BR 'reɪkɪs
AM 'reɪkɪs

rachitic
BR rə'kɪtɪk, ra'kɪtɪk
AM rə'kɪdɪk

rachitis
BR rə'kʌɪtɪs, ra'kʌɪtɪs
AM rə'kaɪdɪs

Rachmaninov
BR rak'manɪnɒf
AM rak'manənɒf,
rak'manənɑf

Rachmanism
BR 'rakmənɪz(ə)m
AM 'rakməˌnɪzəm

racial
BR 'reɪʃl
AM 'reɪʃəl

racialism
BR 'reɪʃəlɪz(ə)m,
'reɪʃlɪz(ə)m
AM 'reɪʃəˌlɪzəm

racialist
BR 'reɪʃəlɪst, 'reɪʃlɪst,
-s
AM 'reɪʃələst, -s

racially
BR 'reɪʃli, 'reɪʃəli

racemic
AM 'reɪʃəli

racily
BR 'reɪsɪli
AM 'reɪsɪli

Racine
BR rɑ'siːn
AM rə'sin

raciness
BR 'reɪsɪnɪs
AM 'reɪsɪnɪs

racism
BR 'reɪsɪz(ə)m
AM 'reɪˌsɪzəm

racist
BR 'reɪsɪst, -s
AM 'reɪsɪst, -s

rack
BR rak, -s, -ɪŋ, -t
AM ræk, -s, -ɪŋ, -t

rack-and-pinion
BR ˌrak(ə)n(d)'pɪnjən
AM ˌrækən'pɪnɪən

racket
BR 'rak|ɪt, -ɪts, -ɪtɪŋ,
-ɪtɪd
AM 'rækə|t, -ts, -dɪŋ,
-dəd

racketball
BR 'rakɪtbɔːl
AM 'rækətˌbɒl,
'rækətˌbal

racketeer
BR ˌrakɪ'tɪə(r), -z, -ɪŋ
AM ˌrækə'tɪ(ə)r, -z, -ɪŋ

rackety
BR 'rakɪti
AM 'rækədi

Rackham
BR 'rakəm
AM 'rækəm

raclette
BR rɑ'klɛt, -s
AM rə'klɛt, -s

racon
BR 'reɪkɒn, -z
AM 'reɪˌkɑn, 'reɪkən, -z

raconteur
BR ˌrakɒn'tə(r), -z
AM ˌrɑˌkɑn'tər, -z

raconteuse
BR ˌrakɒn'təz
AM ˌrɑˌkɑn'təz

racoon
BR rə'kuːn, -z
AM ræ'kun, rə'kun, -z

racquet
BR 'rakɪt, -s
AM 'rækət, -s

racquetball
BR 'rakɪtbɔːl
AM 'rækətˌbɒl,
'rækətˌbal

racy
BR 'reɪs|i, -ɪə(r), -ɪɪst
AM 'reɪsi, -ər, -ɪst

rad
BR rad, -z

AM ræd, -z
RADA
BR 'rɑːdə(r)
AM 'rɑdə
radar
BR 'reɪdɑː(r)
AM 'reɪˌdɑr
Radcliff
BR 'rædklɪf
AM 'rædˌklɪf
Radcliffe
BR 'rædklɪf
AM 'rædˌklɪf
Radclyffe
BR 'rædklɪf
AM 'rædˌklɪf
raddle
BR 'rædl̩, -lz, -lɪŋ \-lɪŋ, -ld
AM 'rædl̩əl, -əlz, -(ə)lɪŋ, -əld
Radetsky
BR rə'dɛtski
AM rə'dɛtski
Radford
BR 'rædfəd
AM 'rædfərd
radial
BR 'reɪdɪəl
AM 'reɪdɪəl
radially
BR 'reɪdɪəli
AM 'reɪdɪəli
radian
BR 'reɪdɪən, -z
AM 'reɪdɪən, -z
radiance
BR 'reɪdɪəns
AM 'reɪdɪəns
radiancy
BR 'reɪdɪəns|i, -ɪz
AM 'reɪdɪənsi, -z
radiant
BR 'reɪdɪənt
AM 'reɪdɪənt
radiantly
BR 'reɪdɪəntli
AM 'reɪdɪən(t)li
radiate
BR 'reɪdɪeɪt, -s, -ɪŋ, -ɪd
AM 'reɪdiˌeɪt, -ts, -dɪŋ, -dɪd
radiately
BR 'reɪdɪeɪ(t)li
AM 'reɪdiɪ(t)li
radiation
BR 'reɪdi'eɪʃn, -z
AM 'reɪdi'eɪʃən, -z
radiational
BR ˌreɪdi'eɪʃn(ə)l, ˌreɪdɪ'eɪʃən(ə)l
AM ˌreɪdi'eɪʃ(ə)nəl
radiationally
BR ˌreɪdi'eɪʃnəli, ˌreɪdɪ'eɪʃn̩li, ˌreɪdɪ'eɪʃən̩li, ˌreɪdɪʃ(ə)nəli

AM ˌreɪdi'eɪʃ(ə)nəli
radiative
BR 'reɪdɪətɪv
AM 'reɪdiədɪv, 'reɪdiˌeɪdɪv
radiator
BR 'reɪdieɪtə(r), -z
AM 'reɪdiˌeɪdər, -z
radical
BR 'rædɪkl, -z
AM 'rædəkəl, -z
radicalisation
BR ˌrædɪkəlaɪ'zeɪʃn, ˌrædɪklʌɪ'zeɪʃn
AM ˌrædəkələ'zeɪʃən, ˌrædəkəˌlaɪ'zeɪʃən
radicalise
BR 'rædɪkəlʌɪz, 'rædɪklʌɪz, -ɪz, -ɪŋ, -d
AM 'rædəkəˌlaɪz, 'rædəklˌaɪz, -ɪz, -ɪŋ, -d
radicalism
BR 'rædɪkəlɪz(ə)m, 'rædɪklɪz(ə)m
AM 'rædəkəˌlɪzəm
radicalization
BR ˌrædɪkəlaɪ'zeɪʃn, ˌrædɪklʌɪ'zeɪʃn
AM ˌrædəkələ'zeɪʃən, ˌrædəkəˌlaɪ'zeɪʃən
radicalize
BR 'rædɪkəlʌɪz, 'rædɪklʌɪz, -ɪz, -ɪŋ, -d
AM 'rædəkəˌlaɪz, 'rædəklˌaɪz, -ɪz, -ɪŋ, -d
radically
BR 'rædɪkli
AM 'rædək(ə)li
radicalness
BR 'rædɪklnəs
AM 'rædəkəlnəs
radicchio
BR ra'diːkɪəʊ
AM ræ'dɪkioʊ, rə'dɪkioʊ
Radice
BR rə'diːtʃi
AM rə'dɪtʃi
radices
BR 'radɪsiːz, 'reɪdɪsiːz
AM 'rædəˌsiz, 'reɪdəˌsiz
radicle
BR 'rædɪkl, -z
AM 'rædəkəl, -z
radicular
BR ra'dɪkjələ(r), rə'dɪkjələ(r)
AM rə'dɪkjələr
radii
BR 'reɪdɪʌɪ
AM 'reɪdiˌaɪ
radio
BR 'reɪdiəʊ, -z, -ɪŋ, -d
AM 'reɪdioʊ, -z, -ɪŋ, -d
radioactive
BR ˌreɪdiəʊ'aktɪv
AM ˌreɪdiou'æktɪv

radioactively
BR ˌreɪdiəʊ'aktɪvli
AM ˌreɪdiou'æktɪvli
radioactivity
BR ˌreɪdiəʊak'tɪvɪti
AM ˌreɪdiouæk'tɪvɪdi
radio-assay
BR ˌreɪdiəʊə'seɪ, ˌreɪdiəʊ'aseɪ, -z, -ɪŋ, -d
AM 'reɪdiouˌæˌseɪ, -z, -ɪŋ, -d
radiobiological
BR ˌreɪdiəʊˌbʌɪə'lɒdʒɪkl
AM 'reɪdiouˌbaɪə'ladʒəkəl
radiobiologically
BR ˌreɪdiəʊˌbʌɪə'lɒdʒ-ɪkli
AM 'reɪdiouˌbaɪə'ladʒ-ək(ə)li
radiobiologist
BR ˌreɪdiəʊbʌɪ'ɒlədʒɪst, -s
AM 'reɪdiouˌbaɪ'ɑlədʒəst, -s
radiobiology
BR ˌreɪdiəʊbʌɪ'ɒlədʒi
AM 'reɪdiouˌbaɪ'ɑlədʒi
radiocarbon
BR ˌreɪdiəʊ'kɑːb(ə)n
AM 'reɪdiou'karbən
radiochemical
BR ˌreɪdiəʊ'kɛmɪkl
AM ˌreɪdiou'kɛməkəl
radiochemist
BR ˌreɪdiəʊ'kɛmɪst, -s
AM 'reɪdiou'kɛməst, -s
radiochemistry
BR ˌreɪdiəʊ'kɛmɪstri
AM ˌreɪdiou'kɛmɪstri
radiogenic
BR ˌreɪdiəʊ'dʒɛnɪk
AM ˌreɪdiou'dʒɛnɪk
radiogenically
BR ˌreɪdiəʊ'dʒɛnɪkli
AM ˌreɪdiou'dʒɛnək(ə)li
radio-goniometer
BR ˌreɪdiəʊˌgəʊni'ɒmɪtə(r), -z
AM 'reɪdiouˌgouni'amədər, -z
radiogram
BR 'reɪdiə(ʊ)gram, -z
AM 'reɪdiəˌgræm, 'reɪdiouˌgræm, -z
radiograph
BR 'reɪdiə(ʊ)grɑːf, 'reɪdiə(ʊ)graf, -s
AM 'reɪdiəˌgræf, 'reɪdiouˌgræf, -s
radiographer
BR 'reɪdi'ɒgrəfə(r), -z
AM ˌreɪdi'agrəfər, -z
radiographic
BR ˌreɪdiə'grafɪk
AM ˌreɪdiə'græfɪk, 'reɪdiou'græfɪk

radiographically
BR ˌreɪdiə'grafɪkli
AM 'reɪdiə'græfək(ə)li, 'reɪdiou'græfək(ə)li
radiography
BR 'reɪdi'ɒgrəfi
AM ˌreɪdi'agrəfi
radioimmunology
BR ˌreɪdiəʊˌɪmjə'nɒlədʒi
AM 'reɪdiouˌɪmjə'nalədʒi
radioisotope
BR ˌreɪdiəʊ'ʌɪsətəʊp, -s
AM 'reɪdiou'aɪsəˌtoup, -s
radioisotopic
BR ˌreɪdiəʊˌʌɪsə'tɒpɪk
AM 'reɪdiouˌaɪsə'tapɪk
radioisotopically
BR ˌreɪdiəʊˌʌɪsə'tɒpɪkli
AM 'reɪdiouˌaɪsə'tapək(ə)li
radiolaria
BR ˌreɪdiə(ʊ)'lɛːrɪə(r)
AM ˌreɪdiə'lɛrɪə
radiolarian
BR ˌreɪdiə(ʊ)'lɛːrɪən, -z
AM ˌreɪdiə'lɛrɪən, 'reɪdiou'lɛrɪən, -z
radiolocation
BR ˌreɪdiəʊlə(ʊ)'keɪʃn
AM ˌreɪdiouˌlou'keɪʃən
radiologic
BR ˌreɪdiə'lɒdʒɪk
AM 'reɪdiə'ladʒɪk
radiological
BR ˌreɪdiə'lɒdʒɪkl
AM 'reɪdiə'ladʒəkəl
radiologist
BR ˌreɪdi'ɒlədʒɪst, -s
AM ˌreɪdi'alədʒəst, -s
radiology
BR ˌreɪdi'ɒlədʒi
AM ˌreɪdi'alədʒi
radiometer
BR ˌreɪdi'ɒmɪtə(r), -z
AM ˌreɪdi'amədər, -z
radiometric
BR ˌreɪdiə'mɛtrɪk
AM ˌreɪdiə'mɛtrɪk
radiometry
BR ˌreɪdi'ɒmɪtri
AM ˌreɪdi'amətri
radionics
BR ˌreɪdi'ɒnɪks
AM ˌreɪdi'anɪks
radionuclide
BR ˌreɪdiəʊ'njuːklʌɪd, -z
AM 'reɪdiou'n(j)uˌklaɪd, -z
radio-opaque
BR ˌreɪdiəʊə(ʊ)'peɪk
AM ˌreɪdiouˌoʊ'peɪk
radiopacity
BR ˌreɪdiəʊ(ʊ)'pasɪti
AM 'reɪdiouˌoʊ'pæsədi

radiopaging	AM ˈrædnər	**raffishly**
BR ˈreɪdɪəʊˌpeɪdʒɪŋ	**Radnor**	BR ˈræfɪʃli
AM ˌreɪdioʊˈpeɪdʒɪŋ	BR ˈrædnə(r)	AM ˈræfɪʃli
radiopaque	AM ˈrædnər	**raffishness**
BR ˌreɪdɪə(ʊ)ˈpeɪk	**Radnorshire**	BR ˈræfɪʃnɪs
AM ˌreɪdioʊˈpeɪk	BR ˈrædnəʃ(ɪ)ə(r)	AM ˈræfɪʃnɪs
radiophonic	AM ˈrædnərʃɪ(ə)r	**raffle**
BR ˌreɪdɪə(ʊ)ˈfɒnɪk	**radome**	BR ˈræfl̩, -lz, -ǀɪŋ\-lɪŋ,
AM ˌreɪdiəˈfɑnɪk	BR ˈreɪdəʊm, -z	-ld
radioscopic	AM ˈreɪˌdoʊm, -z	AM ˈræfləl, -əlz, -(ə)lɪŋ,
BR ˌreɪdɪə(ʊ)ˈskɒpɪk	**radon**	-əld
AM ˌreɪdiəˈskɑpɪk	BR ˈreɪdɒn	**Raffles**
radioscopy	AM ˈreɪˌdɑn	BR ˈraflz
BR ˌreɪdɪˈɒskəpi	**Radox®**	AM ˈræfəlz
AM ˌreɪdiˈɑskəpi	BR ˈreɪdɒks	**rafflesia**
radiosonde	AM ˈreɪˌdɑks	BR rəˈfliːʒɪə(r),
BR ˈreɪdɪə(ʊ)sɒnd, -z	**radula**	rəˈfliːzɪə(r)
AM ˈreɪdioʊˌsɑnd, -z	BR ˈradjʊlə(r),	AM rəˈfliːʒ(i)ə, rəˈflizɪə
radiotelegraphy	ˈradʒʊlə(r)	**Rafsanjani**
BR ˌreɪdɪəʊtɪˈlɛɡrəfi	AM ˈrædʒələ	BR ˌrafsanˈdʒɑːni
AM ˌreɪdioʊtəˈlɛɡrəfi	**radulae**	AM ˌrɑfsɑnˈdʒɑni
radiotelephone	BR ˈradjʊliː, ˈradʒʊliː	**raft**
BR ˌreɪdɪəʊˈtɛlɪfəʊn, -z	AM ˈrædʒəli,	BR rɑːft, raft, -s, -ɪŋ, -ɪd
AM ˌreɪdioʊˈtɛləˌfoʊn,	ˈrædʒəˌlaɪ	AM ræft, -s, -ɪŋ, -əd
-z	**radular**	**rafter**
radio-telephonic	BR ˈradjʊlə(r),	BR ˈrɑːftə(r), ˈraftə(r),
BR ˌreɪdɪəʊˌtɛlɪˈfɒnɪk	ˈradʒʊlə(r)	-z, -d
AM ˌreɪdioʊˌtɛləˈfɑnɪk	AM ˈrædʒələr	AM ˈræftər, -z, -d
radio-telephony	**Rae**	**raftsman**
BR ˌreɪdɪəʊtɪˈlɛfəni,	BR reɪ	BR ˈrɑːf(t)smən,
ˌreɪdɪəʊtəˈlefn̩i	AM reɪ	ˈraf(t)smən
AM ˌreɪdioʊtəˈlɛfəni	**Raeburn**	AM ˈræf(t)smən
radiotelex	BR ˈreɪbəːn	**raftsmen**
BR ˌreɪdɪəʊˈtɛlɛks, -ɪz	AM ˈreɪˌbərn	BR ˈrɑːf(t)smən,
AM ˌreɪdioʊˈtɛˌlɛks, -əz	**Rael-Brook**	ˈraf(t)smən
radiotherapeutic	BR ˈreɪlbrʊk,	AM ˈræf(t)smən
BR ˌreɪdɪəʊˌθɛrəˈpjuːtɪk	ˌreɪlˈbrʊk	**rag**
AM ˌreɪdioʊˌθɛrəˈpjudɪk	AM ˈreɪlˌbrʊk	BR rag, -z, -ɪŋ, -d
radiotherapist	**Raelene**	AM ræg, -z, -ɪŋ, -d
BR ˌreɪdɪəʊˈθɛrəpɪst, -s	BR ˈreɪliːn	**raga**
AM ˌreɪdioʊˈθɛrəpəst,	AM ˈreɪlin, rerˈlin	BR ˈrɑːɡə(r), -z
-s	**RAF**	AM ˈrɑɡə, -z
radiotherapy	BR ˌɑːreɪˈɛf, raf	**ragamuffin**
BR ˌreɪdɪəʊˈθɛrəpi	AM ˌɑˌreɪˈɛf	BR ˈraɡəˌmʌfɪn, -z
AM ˌreɪdioʊˈθɛrəpi	**Rafe**	AM ˈræɡəˌməfən, -z
radish	BR reɪf	**rag-and-bone**
BR ˈrad|ɪʃ, -ɪʃɪz	AM reɪf	BR ˌraɡ(ə)n(d)ˈbəʊn
AM ˈrædɪʃ, -ɪz	**Rafferty**	AM ˌræɡənˈboʊn
radium	BR ˈrafəti	**ragbag**
BR ˈreɪdɪəm	AM ˈræfərdi	BR ˈraɡbaɡ, -z
AM ˈreɪdiəm	**Raffi**	AM ˈræɡˌbæɡ, -z
radius	BR ˈrafi	**Ragdoll**
BR ˈreɪdɪəs, -t	AM ˈræfi	BR ˈraɡdɒl, -z
AM ˈreɪdiəs, -t	**raffia**	AM ˈræɡˌdɑl, -z
radix	BR ˈrafɪə(r)	**rag doll**
BR ˈrad|ɪks, ˈreɪd|ɪks,	AM ˈræfɪə	BR ˌraɡ ˈdɒl, -z
-ɪksɪz	**raffinate**	AM ˈræɡ ˌdɑl, -z
AM ˈrædɪks, ˈreɪdɪks,	BR ˈrafɪneɪt, -s	**rage**
-ɪz	AM ˈræfəˌneɪt, -s	BR reɪdʒ, -ɪz, -ɪŋ, -d
Radlett	**raffinose**	AM reɪdʒ, -ɪz, -ɪŋ, -d
BR ˈradlɪt	BR ˈrafɪnəʊz, ˈrafɪnəʊs	**ragee**
AM ˈrædlət	AM ˈræfəˌnoʊs,	BR ˈrɑːɡiː
Radley	ˈræfəˌnoʊz	AM ˈræɡi
BR ˈradli	**raffish**	**ragged**
AM ˈrædli	BR ˈrafɪʃ	BR ˈraɡɪd, -ɪst
Radner	AM ˈræfɪʃ	AM ˈræɡəd, -əst
BR ˈradnə(r)		

raggedly	
BR ˈraɡɪdli	
AM ˈræɡədli	
raggedness	
BR ˈraɡɪdnɪs	
AM ˈræɡədnəs	
raggedy	
BR ˈraɡɪdi	
AM ˈræɡədi	
raggee	
BR ˈrɑːɡiː	
AM ˈræɡi	
raggle	
BR ˈraɡl, -z	
AM ˈræɡəl, -z	
raggle-taggle	
BR ˌraɡlˈtaɡl, ˈraɡlˌtaɡl	
AM ˈræɡlˌtæɡəl	
raglan	
BR ˈraɡlən	
AM ˈræɡlən	
ragman	
BR ˈraɡman, ˈraɡmən	
AM ˈræɡˌmæn,	
ˈræɡmən	
ragmen	
BR ˈraɡmɛn, ˈraɡmən	
AM ˈræɡˌmɛn,	
ˈræɡmən	
Ragnarök	
BR ˈraɡnərɒk,	
ˈraɡnərəːk	
AM ˈrɑɡnəˌrɔk,	
ˈrɑɡnəˌrɑk	
ragout	
BR ˈraɡuː, raˈɡuː, -z	
AM ræˈɡu, -z	
ragstone	
BR ˈraɡstəʊn	
AM ˈræɡˌstoʊn	
rags-to-riches	
BR ˌraɡztəˈrɪtʃɪz	
AM ˈræɡztəˈrɪtʃɪz	
ragtag	
BR ˈraɡtaɡ	
AM ˈræɡˌtæɡ	
ragtime	
BR ˈraɡtʌɪm	
AM ˈræɡˌtaɪm	
ragtop	
BR ˈraɡtɒp, -s	
AM ˈræɡˌtɑp, -s	
raguly	
BR ˈraɡjʊli	
AM ˈræɡjəli	
ragweed	
BR ˈraɡwiːd, -z	
AM ˈræɡˌwid, -z	
ragworm	
BR ˈraɡwəːm, -z	
AM ˈræɡˌwərm, -z	
ragwort	
BR ˈraɡwəːt, -s	
AM ˈræɡˌwərt,	
ˈræɡˌwɔ(ə)rt, -s	
rah	
BR rɑː(r), -z	

AM rɑ, -z
Rahman
BR 'rɑːmən
AM 'rɑmən
rah-rah
BR 'rɑːrɑː(r), -z
AM 'rɑ'rɑ, -z
rai
BR rʌɪ
AM rɑɪ
raid
BR reɪd, -z, -ɪŋ, -ɪd
AM reɪd, -z, -ɪŋ, -ɪd
raider
BR 'reɪdə(r), -z
AM 'reɪdər, -z
Raikes
BR reɪks
AM reɪks
rail
BR reɪl, -z, -ɪŋ, -d
AM reɪl, -z, -ɪŋ, -d
railage
BR 'reɪlɪdʒ
AM 'reɪlɪdʒ
railcar
BR 'reɪlkɑː(r), -z
AM 'reɪl,kɑr, -z
railcard
BR 'reɪlkɑːd, -z
AM 'reɪl,kɑrd, -z
railer
BR 'reɪlə(r), -z
AM 'reɪlər, -z
rail fence
BR 'reɪl fɛns, ,reɪl 'fɛns, -ɪz
AM 'reɪl ,fɛns, -əz
railhead
BR 'reɪlhɛd, -z
AM 'reɪl,(h)ɛd, -z
railing
BR 'reɪlɪŋ, -z
AM 'reɪlɪŋ, -z
raillery
BR 'reɪlər|i, -ɪz
AM 'reɪlər|i, -z
railless
BR 'reɪ(l)lɪs
AM 'reɪ(l)lɪs
railman
BR 'reɪlmən
AM 'reɪlmən
railmen
BR 'reɪlmən
AM 'reɪlmən
railroad
BR 'reɪlrəʊd, -z, -ɪŋ, -ɪd
AM 'reɪl,roʊd, -z, -ɪŋ, -əd
railway
BR 'reɪlweɪ, -z
AM 'reɪl,weɪ, -z
railwayman
BR 'reɪlweɪmən, 'reɪlwəmən
AM 'reɪl,weɪmən

railwaymen
BR 'reɪlweɪmən, 'reɪlwəmən
AM 'reɪl,weɪmən
raiment
BR 'reɪm(ə)nt
AM 'reɪmənt
rain
BR reɪn, -z, -ɪŋ, -d
AM reɪn, -z, -ɪŋ, -d
Raina
BR rʌɪ'iːnə(r), 'reɪnə(r)
AM 'reɪnə
rainbird
BR 'reɪnbɜːd, -z
AM 'reɪn,bɜrd, -z
rainbow
BR 'reɪnbəʊ, -z
AM 'reɪn,boʊ, -z
raincoat
BR 'reɪnkəʊt, -s
AM 'reɪn,koʊt, -s
raindrop
BR 'reɪndrɒp, -s
AM 'reɪn,drɑp, -s
Raine
BR reɪn
AM reɪn
rainfall
BR 'reɪnfɔːl
AM 'reɪn,fɔl, 'reɪn,fɑl
Rainford
BR 'reɪnfəd
AM 'reɪnfərd
rainforest
BR 'reɪn,fɒrɪst, -s
AM 'reɪn,fɔrəst, -s
raingauge
BR 'reɪngeɪdʒ, -ɪz
AM 'reɪn,geɪdʒ, -ɪz
Rainhill
BR ,reɪn'hɪl
AM ,reɪn'hɪl
Rainier[1]
mountain
BR 'reɪnɪə(r), rə'nɪə(r)
AM 'reɪnɪər, rə'nɪ(ə)r
Rainier[2]
prince of Monaco
BR 'reɪnɪeɪ
AM 'reɪnɪər
rainily
BR 'reɪnɪli
AM 'reɪnɪli
raininess
BR 'reɪnɪnɪs
AM 'reɪnɪnɪs
rainless
BR 'reɪnlɪs
AM 'reɪnlɪs
rainmaker
BR 'reɪn,meɪkə(r), -z
AM 'reɪn,meɪkər, -z
rainmaking
BR 'reɪn,meɪkɪŋ
AM 'reɪn,meɪkɪŋ

rainproof
BR 'reɪnpruːf, -s, -ɪŋ, -t
AM 'reɪn,pruf, -s, -ɪŋ, -t
rainstorm
BR 'reɪnstɔːm, -z
AM 'reɪn,stɔ(ə)rm, -z
rainswept
BR 'reɪnswɛpt
AM 'reɪn,swɛpt
rainwater
BR 'reɪn,wɔːtə(r)
AM 'reɪn,wɔdər, 'reɪn,wɑdər
rainwear
BR 'reɪnwɛː(r)
AM 'reɪn,wɛ(ə)r
rainy
BR 'reɪn|i, -ɪə(r), -ɪɪst
AM 'reɪni, -ər, -ɪst
Raisa
BR rʌɪ'iːsə(r), rɑː'iːsə(r)
AM rɑ'isə
raisable
BR 'reɪzəbl
AM 'reɪzəbəl
raise
BR reɪz, -ɪz, -ɪŋ, -d
AM reɪz, -ɪz, -ɪŋ, -d
raisin
BR 'reɪzn, -z
AM 'reɪzn, -z
raisiny
BR 'reɪzn̩i, 'reɪzɪni
AM 'reɪzn̩i
Raison
BR 'reɪzn
AM 'reɪzn
raison d'être
BR ,reɪzɒ̃ 'dɛtr(ər), ,reɪz(ɒ)n +
AM ,reɪ,zɔn 'dɛtrə
raisons d'être
BR ,reɪzɒ̃ 'dɛtr(ər), ,reɪz(ɒ)n +
AM ,reɪ,zɔn(z) 'dɛtrə
Raistrick
BR 'reɪstrɪk
AM 'reɪstrɪk
raj
BR rɑː(d)ʒ
AM rɑdʒ
raja
BR 'rɑːdʒə(r), -z
AM 'rɑ(d)ʒə, -z
rajah
BR 'rɑːdʒə(r), -z
AM 'rɑ(d)ʒə, -z
rajaship
BR 'rɑːdʒəʃɪp, -s
AM 'rɑ(d)ʒə,ʃɪp, -s
Rajasthan
BR ,rɑːdʒə'stɑːn
AM ,rɑdʒə'stɑn
Rajasthani
BR ,rɑːdʒə'stɑːn|i, -ɪz
AM ,rɑdʒə'stɑni, -z

Rajneesh
BR ,rɑːdʒ'niːʃ
AM ,rɑdʒ'niʃ
Rajpoot
BR 'rɑːdʒpʊt
AM 'rɑdʒ,pʊt
Rajput
BR 'rɑːdʒpʊt
AM 'rɑdʒ,pʊt
Rajputana
BR ,rɑːdʒpʊ'tɑːnə(r)
AM ,rɑdʒpə'tɑnə
Rajshahi
BR ,rɑːdʒ'ʃɑːhi
AM ,rɑdʒ'ʃɑ,(h)i
rake
BR reɪk, -s, -ɪŋ, -t
AM reɪk, -s, -ɪŋ, -t
raker
BR 'reɪkə(r), -z
AM 'reɪkər, -z
raki
BR 'rɑːki, 'raki, rə'kiː
AM 'reɪki, 'rɑki
rakish
BR 'reɪkɪʃ
AM 'reɪkɪʃ
rakishly
BR 'reɪkɪʃli
AM 'reɪkɪʃli
rakishness
BR 'reɪkɪʃnɪs
AM 'reɪkɪʃnɪs
raku
BR 'rɑːkuː
AM 'rɑ,ku
rale
BR rɑːl, ral, -z
AM rɑl, ræl, -z
Ralegh
BR 'rali, 'rɑːli, 'rɔːli
AM 'rɑli
Raleigh
BR 'rali, 'rɑːli, 'rɔːli
AM 'rɑli
Ralf
BR ralf, reɪf
AM rælf
rallentando
BR ,ralən'tandəʊ, ,raln̩'tandəʊ, -z
AM ,rɑlən'tandoʊ, ,rælən'tændoʊ, -z
rallier
BR 'ralɪə(r), -z
AM 'rælɪər, -z
ralline
BR 'ralʌɪn
AM 'ræ,laɪn
rally
BR 'ral|i, -ɪz, -ɪɪŋ, -ɪd
AM 'ræli, -z, -ɪŋ, -d
rallycross
BR 'ralɪkrɒs
AM 'ræli,krɔs, 'ræli,krɑs

Ralph
BR ralf, reɪf
AM rælf

ram
BR ram, -z, -ɪŋ, -d
AM ræm, -z, -ɪŋ, -d

Rama
BR 'rɑːmə(r)
AM 'rɑmə

Ramadan
BR 'ramədan,
ˌramə'dan,
ˌramə'dɑːn
AM ˌrɑmə'dɑn

Ramadhan
BR 'ramədan,
ˌramə'dan,
ˌramə'dɑːn
AM ˌrɑmə'dɑn

Ramakrishna
BR ˌrɑːmə'krɪʃnə(r)
AM ˌrɑmə'krɪʃnə

ramal
BR 'reɪml
AM 'reɪməl

Raman effect
BR 'rɑːmən ɪˌfɛkt
AM 'rɑmən əˌfɛk(t),
+ iˌfɛk(t)

Ramayana
BR rə'mɑːjənə(r)
AM ˌrɑmə'jɑnə

Rambert
BR 'rɒmbɛː(r),
'rɒbɛː(r)
AM 'rɑmˌbɛ(ə)r

ramble
BR 'rambl|l, -lz,
-lɪŋ\-l̩ŋ, -ld
AM 'ræmbəl, -əlz,
-(ə)lɪŋ, -əld

rambler
BR 'ramblə(r),
'ramblə̩(r), -z
AM 'ræmb(ə)lər, -z

rambling
BR 'ramblɪŋ,
'ramblɪ̩ŋ, -z
AM 'ræmb(ə)lɪŋ, -z

ramblingly
BR 'ramblɪŋli,
'ramblɪ̩ŋli
AM 'ræmb(ə)lɪŋli

Rambo
BR 'rambəʊ
AM 'ræmboʊ

rambunctious
BR ram'bʌŋ(k)ʃəs
AM ræm'bəŋ(k)ʃəs

rambunctiously
BR ram'bʌŋ(k)ʃəsli
AM ræm'bəŋ(k)ʃəsli

rambunctiousness
BR ram'bʌŋ(k)ʃəsnəs
AM ræm'bəŋ(k)ʃəsnəs

rambutan
BR ram'buːtn, -z
AM ræm'butn, -z

Rameau
BR 'rɑːməʊ, 'raməʊ
AM 'rɑ'moʊ

ramee
BR 'ram|i, -iz
AM 'ræmi, 'reɪmi, -z

ramekin
BR 'ram(ɪ)kɪn, -z
AM 'ræməkən, -z

ramen
BR 'rɑːmɛn
AM 'rɑˌmɛn

Rameses
BR 'ram(ɪ)siːz
AM 'ræm(ə)ˌsiz

rami
BR 'reɪmʌɪ, 'reɪmiː
AM 'reɪˌmaɪ

ramie
BR 'ram|i, -iz
AM 'rami, 'reɪmi, -z

ramification
BR ˌramɪfɪ'keɪʃn, -z
AM ˌræməfə'keɪʃən, -z

ramify
BR 'ramɪfʌɪ, -z, -ɪŋ, -d
AM 'ræməˌfaɪ, -z, -ɪŋ, -d

Ramillies
BR 'ramɪliːz, 'ramˌliːz
AM 'ræməˌliz

ramin
BR ra'miːn, -z
AM ræ'min, -z

Ramírez
BR rə'mɪərɛz,
ra'mɪərɛz
AM rə'mɪ(ə)rɛz

ramjet
BR 'ramdʒɛt, -s
AM 'ræmˌdʒɛt, -s

rammer
BR 'ramə(r), -z
AM 'ræmər, -z

rammy
BR 'ram|i, -iz
AM 'ræmi, -z

Ramón
BR rə'mɒn, ra'mɒn
AM rə'moʊn

Ramona
BR rə'məʊnə(r)
AM rə'moʊnə

Ramos
BR 'ramɒs
AM 'rɑmoʊs

ramose
BR 'raməʊs, 'reɪməʊs
AM 'ræˌmoʊs,
'ræˌmoʊz

ramp
BR ram|p, -ps, -pɪŋ,
-(p)t
AM ræmp, -s, -ɪŋ, -t

rampage[1]
noun
BR 'rampeɪdʒ, -ɪz
AM 'ræmˌpeɪdʒ, -ɪz

rampage[2]
verb
BR ram'peɪdʒ,
'rampeɪdʒ, -ɪz, -ɪŋ, -d
AM ˌræm'peɪdʒ, -ɪz, -ɪŋ,
-d

rampageous
BR ram'peɪdʒəs
AM ˌræm'peɪdʒəs

rampageously
BR ram'peɪdʒəsli
AM ˌræm'peɪdʒəsli

rampageousness
BR ram'peɪdʒəsnəs
AM ˌræm'peɪdʒəsnəs

rampager
BR ram'peɪdʒə(r),
'ramˌpeɪdʒə(r), -z
AM 'ræmˌpeɪdʒər, -z

rampancy
BR 'ramp(ə)nsi
AM 'ræmpənsi

rampant
BR 'ramp(ə)nt
AM 'ræmpənt

rampantly
BR 'ramp(ə)ntli
AM 'ræmpən(t)li

rampart
BR 'rampɑːt, -s
AM 'ræmˌpɑrt, -s

rampion
BR 'rampɪən, -z
AM 'ræmpɪən, -z

Rampton
BR 'ram(p)tən
AM 'ræm(p)tən

Rampur
BR 'rampʊə(r)
AM 'ræmˌpʊ(ə)r

ram-raid
BR 'ramreɪd, -z, -ɪŋ, -ɪd
AM 'ræmˌreɪd, -z, -ɪŋ,
-ɪd

ramrod
BR 'ramrɒd, -z
AM 'ræmˌrɑd, -z

Ramsaran
BR 'rɑːms(ə)rən,
'rɑːms(ə)rn̩
AM 'ræmsərən

Ramsay
BR 'ramzi
AM 'ræmzi

Ramsbotham
BR 'ramzˌbɒtəm,
'ramzˌbɒθəm
AM 'ræmzˌbadəm

Ramsbottom
BR 'ramzˌbɒtəm
AM 'ræmzˌbadəm

Ramsden
BR 'ramzdən
AM 'ræmzdən

Ramsey
BR 'ramzi
AM 'ræmzi

Ramsgate
BR 'ramzgeɪt
AM 'ræmzˌgeɪt

ramshackle
BR 'ramˌʃakl
AM 'ræmˌʃækəl

ramson
BR 'ramz(ə)n,
'rams(ə)n, -z
AM 'ræmzn,
'ræm(p)sən, -z

ramus
BR 'reɪməs
AM 'reɪməs

ran
BR ran
AM ræn

rance
BR rans
AM ræns

ranch
BR rɑːn(t)ʃ, ran(t)ʃ,
-ɪz, -ɪŋ, -t
AM ræn(t)ʃ, -əz, -ɪŋ, -t

rancher
BR 'rɑːn(t)ʃə(r),
'ran(t)ʃə(r), -z
AM 'ræn(t)ʃər, -z

ranchero
BR rɑːn'tʃɛːrəʊ,
ran'tʃɛːrəʊ, -z
AM ræn'tʃɛroʊ, -z

Ranchi
BR 'rɑːn(t)ʃi, 'ran(t)ʃi
AM 'ræn(t)ʃi

rancho
BR 'rɑːn(t)ʃəʊ,
'ran(t)ʃəʊ, -z
AM 'ræn(t)ʃoʊ, -z

rancid
BR 'ransɪd
AM 'rænsəd

rancidity
BR ran'sɪdɪti
AM ræn'sɪdɪdi

rancidness
BR 'ransɪdnɪs
AM 'rænsədnəs

rancor
BR 'raŋkə(r)
AM 'ræŋkər

rancorous
BR 'raŋk(ə)rəs
AM 'ræŋk(ə)rəs

rancorously
BR 'raŋk(ə)rəsli
AM 'ræŋk(ə)rəsli

rancour
BR 'raŋkə(r)
AM 'ræŋkər

rand
BR ran|d, rɑːn|t, ran|t,
rɒn|t, -dz\-ts
AM rænd, -s

Randal
BR 'randl
AM 'rændəl

Randall
BR ˈrandl
AM ˈrændl

randan
BR ˌranˈdan, -z
AM ˈrænˌdæn, rænˈdæn, -z

R and B
BR ˌɑːr ən(d) ˈbiː, + ŋ(d) +
AM ˌɑːr ən ˈbi

R and D
BR ˌɑːr ən(d) ˈdiː, + ŋ(d) +
AM ˌɑːr ən ˈdi

Randers
BR ˈrandəz
AM ˈrændərz

randily
BR ˈrandɪli
AM ˈrændɪli

randiness
BR ˈrandɪnɪs
AM ˈrændɪnɪs

Randolf
BR ˈrandɒlf
AM ˈrænˌdɒlf, ˈrænˌdɑlf

Randolph
BR ˈrandɒlf
AM ˈrænˌdɒlf, ˈrænˌdɑlf

random
BR ˈrandəm
AM ˈrændəm

randomisation
BR ˌrandəmʌɪˈzeɪʃn
AM ˌrændəməˈzeɪʃən, ˌrændəˌmaɪˈzeɪʃən

randomise
BR ˈrandəmʌɪz, -ɪz, -ɪŋ, -d
AM ˈrændəˌmaɪz, -ɪz, -ɪŋ, -d

randomization
BR ˌrandəmʌɪˈzeɪʃn
AM ˌrændəməˈzeɪʃən, ˌrændəˌmaɪˈzeɪʃən

randomize
BR ˈrandəmʌɪz, -ɪz, -ɪŋ, -d
AM ˈrændəˌmaɪz, -ɪz, -ɪŋ, -d

randomly
BR ˈrandəmli
AM ˈrændəmli

randomness
BR ˈrandəmnəs
AM ˈrændəmnəs

Randstad
BR ˈrandstat
AM ˈrænˌd(ə)stæt

randy
BR ˈrandi, -ɪə(r), -ɪɪst
AM ˈrændi, -ər, -ɪst

ranee
BR ˈrɑːniː, ˌrɑːˈniː, -z
AM ˈrɑni, rɑˈni, -z

Ranelagh
BR ˈranɪlə(r), ˈranlə(r)
AM ˈrænələ

rang
BR raŋ
AM ræŋ

rangatira
BR ˌraŋgəˈtɪərə(r), -z
AM ˌræŋgəˈtɪ(ə)rə, -z

range
BR reɪn(d)ʒ, -ɪz, -ɪŋ, -d
AM reɪndʒ, -ɪz, -ɪŋ, -d

rangé
BR rɒ̃ˈʒeɪ
AM rɑnˈʒeɪ

rangefinder
BR ˈreɪn(d)ʒˌfʌɪndə(r), -z
AM ˈreɪndʒˌfaɪndər, -z

rangeland
BR ˈreɪn(d)ʒland, -z
AM ˈreɪndʒˌlænd, -z

ranger
BR ˈreɪn(d)ʒə(r), -z
AM ˈreɪndʒər, -z

rangership
BR ˈreɪn(d)ʒəˌʃɪp, -s
AM ˈreɪndʒərˌʃɪp, -s

ranginess
BR ˈreɪn(d)ʒɪnɪs
AM ˈreɪndʒɪnɪs

Rangoon
BR raŋˈguːn
AM ræŋˈgun

rangy
BR ˈreɪn(d)ʒi, -ɪə(r), -ɪɪst
AM ˈreɪndʒi, -ər, -ɪst

rani
BR ˈrɑːniː, ˌrɑːˈniː, -z
AM ˈrɑni, rɑˈni, -z

Ranjit Singh
BR ˌran(d)ʒɪt ˈsɪŋ
AM ˌrændʒət ˈsɪŋ

Ranjitsinhji
BR ˌran(d)ʒɪtˈsɪn(d)ʒi
AM ˌrændʒətˌsɪndʒi

rank
BR raŋ|k, -ks, -kɪŋ, -(k)t, -kə(r), -kɪst
AM ræŋ|k, -ks, -kɪŋ, -(k)t, -kər, -kəst

rank-and-file
BR ˌraŋk(ə)n(d)ˈfʌɪl
AM ˌræŋkənˈfaɪl

ranker
BR ˈraŋkə(r), -z
AM ˈræŋkər, -z

Rankin
BR ˈraŋkɪn
AM ˈræŋkən

ranking
BR ˈraŋkɪŋ, -z
AM ˈræŋkɪŋ, -z

rankle
BR ˈraŋk|l, -lz, -lɪŋ \-lɪŋ, -ld
AM ˈræŋk|əl, -əlz, -(ə)lɪŋ, -əld

rankly
BR ˈraŋkli
AM ˈræŋkli

rankness
BR ˈraŋknəs
AM ˈræŋknəs

Rannoch
BR ˈranəx, ˈranək
AM ˈrænək

ransack
BR ˈransak, -s, -ɪŋ, -t
AM ˈrænˌsæk, -s, -ɪŋ, -t

ransacker
BR ˈransakə(r), -z
AM ˈrænˌsækər, -z

ransom
BR ˈrans|(ə)m, -(ə)mz, -əmɪŋ \-mɪŋ, -(ə)md
AM ˈrænsəm, -z, -ɪŋ, -d

Ransome
BR ˈrans(ə)m
AM ˈrænsəm

ransomer
BR ˈransəmə(r), ˈransmə(r), -z
AM ˈrænsəmər, -z

rant
BR rant, -s, -ɪŋ, -ɪd
AM ræn|t, -ts, -(t)ɪŋ, -(t)əd

ranter
BR ˈrantə(r), -z
AM ˈræn(t)ər, -z

ranting
BR ˈrantɪŋ, -z
AM ˈræn(t)ɪŋ, -z

rantingly
BR ˈrantɪŋli
AM ˈræn(t)ɪŋli

rantipole
BR ˈrantɪpəʊl, -z, -ɪŋ, -d
AM ˈræn(t)iˌpoʊl, -z, -ɪŋ, -d

Ranulf
BR ˈranəlf, ˈranʌlf
AM ˈrænəlf

Ranulph
BR ˈranəlf, ˈranʌlf
AM ˈrænəlf

ranunculaceous
BR rəˌnʌnkjəˈleɪʃəs
AM rəˌnənkjəˈleɪʃəs

ranunculi
BR rəˈnʌnkjʊlʌɪ, rəˈnʌnkjʊliː
AM rəˈnənkjəˌlaɪ

ranunculus
BR rəˈnʌnkjʊləs, -ɪz
AM rəˈnənkjələs, -əz

Raoul
BR raʊˈuːl, rɑːˈuːl
AM rɑˈul

rap
BR rap, -s, -ɪŋ, -t
AM ræp, -s, -ɪŋ, -t

rapacious
BR rəˈpeɪʃəs
AM rəˈpeɪʃəs

rapaciously
BR rəˈpeɪʃəsli
AM rəˈpeɪʃəsli

rapaciousness
BR rəˈpeɪʃəsnəs
AM rəˈpeɪʃəsnəs

rapacity
BR rəˈpasɪti
AM rəˈpæsədi

rape
BR reɪp, -s, -ɪŋ, -t
AM reɪp, -s, -ɪŋ, -t

raper
BR ˈreɪpə(r), -z
AM ˈreɪpər, -z

rapeseed
BR ˈreɪpsiːd
AM ˈreɪpˌsid

Raphael[1]
Italian artist
BR ˈrafeɪ(ə)l, ˈrafʌɪɛl
AM ˈrɑfaɪˌɛl

Raphael[2]
BR ˈrafeɪ(ə)l
AM ˈræfiəl, ˈreɪfiəl, ˌræfiˈɛl, ˌræfaɪˈɛl

raphia
BR ˈrafiə(r), -z
AM ˈreɪfiə, ˈræfiə, -z

raphide
BR ˈreɪfʌɪd, -z
AM ˈreɪfɪd, ˈreɪˌfɪd, -z

rapid
BR ˈrap|ɪd, -ɪdz, -ɪdɪst
AM ˈræpəd, -z, -ɪst

rapid-fire
BR ˌrapɪdˈfʌɪə(r)
AM ˈræpədˌfaɪ(ə)r

rapidity
BR rəˈpɪdɪti
AM rəˈpɪdɪdi, ræˈpɪdɪdi

rapidly
BR ˈrapɪdli
AM ˈræpədli

rapidness
BR ˈrapɪdnɪs
AM ˈræpədnəs

rapier
BR ˈreɪpɪə(r), -z
AM ˈreɪpɪər, -z

rapine
BR ˈrapʌɪn, ˈrapɪn
AM ˈræpən, ˈræpˌpaɪn, ˈreɪˌpaɪn

rapist
BR ˈreɪpɪst, -s
AM ˈreɪpɪst, -s

Rappahannock
BR ˌrapəˈhanək
AM ˌræpəˈhænək

rapparee
BR ˌrapəˈriː, -z
AM ˌræpəˈriː, -z

rappee
BR raˈpiː
AM ræˈpi

rappel
BR raˈpɛl, rəˈpɛl, -z, -ɪŋ, -d
AM rəˈpɛl, -z, -ɪŋ, -d

rapper
BR ˈrapə(r), -z
AM ˈræpər, -z

rapport
BR raˈpɔː(r), rəˈpɔː(r)
AM ræˈpɔː(ə)r, rəˈpɔː(ə)r

rapporteur
BR ˌrapɔːˈtɜː(r), -z
AM ˌræˌpɔrˈtər, -z

rapprochement
BR rəˈprɒʃmɒ̃, raˈprɒʃmɒ̃, -z
AM ˌræˌprɒʃˈmɑnt, ˌrɑˌprɒʃˈmɑnt, -z

rapscallion
BR rapˈskaliən, -z
AM ræpˈskæljən, ræpˈskælien, -z

rapt
BR rapt
AM ræp(t)

raptly
BR ˈraptli
AM ˈræp(t)li

raptness
BR ˈrap(t)nəs
AM ˈræp(t)nəs

raptor
BR ˈraptə(r), -z
AM ˈræptər, -z

raptorial
BR rapˈtɔːriəl
AM ræpˈtoriəl

rapture
BR ˈraptʃə(r), -z, -d
AM ˈræp(t)ʃər, -z, -d

rapturous
BR ˈraptʃ(ə)rəs
AM ˈræp(t)ʃərəs

rapturously
BR ˈraptʃ(ə)rəsli
AM ˈræp(t)ʃərəsli

rapturousness
BR ˈraptʃ(ə)rəsnəs
AM ˈræp(t)ʃərəsnəs

Rapunzel
BR rəˈpʌnzl
AM rəˈpənzəl

Raquel
BR raˈkɛl, rəˈkɛl
AM rəˈkɛl, ˌræˈkɛl

rara avis
BR ˌrɑːrə ˈeɪvɪs, ˌrɛːrə +, + ˈɑːvɪs, + ˈavɪs
AM ˌrɑrə ˈeɪvɪs

rare
BR rɛː(r), -ə(r), -ɪst
AM rɛ(ə)r, -ər, -əst

rarebit
BR ˈrɛːbɪt, ˈrabɪt, -s
AM ˈrɛrbət, -s

raree-show
BR ˈrɛːrɪʃəʊ, -z
AM ˈrɛriˌʃoʊ, -z

rarefaction
BR ˌrɛːrɪˈfakʃn
AM ˌrɛrəˈfækʃən

rarefactive
BR ˌrɛːrɪˈfaktɪv
AM ˌrɛrəˈfæktɪv

rarefication
BR ˌrɛːrɪfɪˈkeɪʃn
AM ˌrɛrəfəˈkeɪʃən

rarefy
BR ˈrɛːrɪfʌɪ, -z, -ɪŋ, -d
AM ˈrɛrəˌfaɪ, -z, -ɪŋ, -d

rarely
BR ˈrɛːli
AM ˈrɛrli

rareness
BR ˈrɛːnəs
AM ˈrɛrnəs

rarify
BR ˈrɛːrɪfʌɪ, -z, -ɪŋ, -d
AM ˈrɛrəˌfaɪ, -z, -ɪŋ, -d

raring
BR ˈrɛːrɪŋ
AM ˈrɛrɪŋ

rarity
BR ˈrɛːrɪt|i, -ɪz
AM ˈrɛrədi, -z

Rarotonga
BR ˌrɛːrəˈtɒŋgə(r), ˌrarəˈtɒŋgə(r)
AM ˌrɛrəˈtɒngə, ˌrɛrəˈtɑŋgə

Rarotongan
BR ˌrɛːrəˈtɒŋg(ə)n, ˌrarəˈtɒŋg(ə)n, -z
AM ˌrɛrəˈtɒŋgən, ˌrɛrəˈtɑŋgən, -z

rascal
BR ˈrɑːskl, ˈraskl, -z
AM ˈræskəl, -z

rascaldom
BR ˈrɑːskldəm, ˈraskldəm
AM ˈræskəldəm

rascalism
BR ˈrɑːsklɪz(ə)m, ˈrɑːskəlɪz(ə)m, ˈrasklɪz(ə)m, ˈraskəlɪz(ə)m
AM ˈræskəˌlɪzəm

rascality
BR rasˈkalɪt|i, -ɪz
AM ræsˈkælədi, -z

rascally
BR ˈrɑːskl̩i, ˈrɑːskəli, ˈraskl̩i, ˈraskəli
AM ˈræsk(ə)li

raschel
BR ˈraʃl, -z

AM rɑːˈʃɛl, -z

rase
BR reɪz, -ɪz, -ɪŋ, -d
AM reɪz, -ɪz, -ɪŋ, -d

rash
BR raʃ, -ə(r), -ɪst
AM ræʃ, -ə(r), -ɪst

rasher
BR ˈraʃə(r), -z
AM ˈræʃər, -z

Rashid
BR raˈʃiːd
AM rəˈʃid

rashly
BR ˈraʃli
AM ˈræʃli

rashness
BR ˈraʃnəs
AM ˈræʃnəs

Rasmussen
BR ˈrazmʊsn, ˈrasmʊsn
AM ˈræs,mʊsən, ˈræsməsən

rasp
BR rɑːsp, rasp, -s, -ɪŋ, -t
AM ræsp, -s, -ɪŋ, -t

raspatory
BR ˈrɑːspət(ə)ri, ˈraspət(ə)r|i, -ɪz
AM ˈræspəˌtɔri, -z

raspberry
BR ˈrɑːzb(ə)r|i, ˈrazb(ə)r|i, -ɪz
AM ˈræz,bɛri, -z

rasper
BR ˈrɑːspə(r), ˈraspə(r), -z
AM ˈræspər, -z

raspingly
BR ˈrɑːspɪŋli, ˈraspɪŋli
AM ˈræspɪŋli

Rasputin
BR raˈspjuːtɪn
AM ræˈspjutn

raspy
BR ˈrɑːspi, ˈraspi
AM ˈræspi

Rasta
BR ˈrastə(r), -z
AM ˈræstə, -z

Rastafari
BR ˌrastəˈfɑːr|i, -ɪz
AM ˌræstəˈfɛri, -z

Rastafarian
BR ˌrastəˈfɛːrɪən, ˌrastəˈfɑːrɪən, -z
AM ˌræstəˈfɛriən, -z

Rastafarianism
BR ˌrastəˈfɛːrɪənɪz(ə)m, ˌrastəˈfɑːrɪənɪz(ə)m
AM ˌræstəˈfɛriə,nɪzəm

raster
BR ˈrastə(r), -z
AM ˈræstər, -z

rasterisation
BR ˌrast(ə)rʌɪˈzeɪʃn

AM ˌræstərəˈzeɪʃən, ˌræstəˌraɪˈzeɪʃən

rasterise
BR ˈrast(ə)rʌɪz, -ɪz, -ɪŋ, -d
AM ˈræstəˌraɪz, -ɪz, -ɪŋ, -d

rasteriser
BR ˈrast(ə)rʌɪzə(r), -z
AM ˈræstəˌraɪzər, -z

rasterization
BR ˌrast(ə)rʌɪˈzeɪʃn
AM ˌræstərəˈzeɪʃən, ˌræstəˌraɪˈzeɪʃən

rasterize
BR ˈrast(ə)rʌɪz, -ɪz, -ɪŋ, -d
AM ˈræstəˌraɪz, -ɪz, -ɪŋ, -d

rasterizer
BR ˈrast(ə)rʌɪzə(r), -z
AM ˈræstəˌraɪzər, -z

Rastrick
BR ˈrastrɪk
AM ˈræstrɪk

Rastus
BR ˈrastəs
AM ˈræstəs

rat
BR rat, -s, -ɪŋ, -ɪd
AM ræ|t, -ts, -dɪŋ, -dəd

rata[1]
in pro rata
BR ˈrɑːtə(r)
AM ˈrædə, ˈrɑdə

rata[2]
tree
BR ˈrɑːtə(r), -z
AM ˈrɑdə, -z

ratability
BR ˌreɪtəˈbɪlɪti
AM ˌreɪdəˈbɪlɪdi

ratable
BR ˈreɪtəbl
AM ˈreɪdəbəl

ratably
BR ˈreɪtəbli
AM ˈreɪdəbli

ratafia
BR ˌratəˈfɪə(r), ˌratəˈfiːə(r), -z
AM ˌrædəˈfiə, -z

ratan
BR rəˈtan, raˈtan, -z
AM ræˈtæn, rəˈtæn, -z

rataplan
BR ˌratəˈplan, -z, -ɪŋ, -d
AM ˈrɑdəˌplæn, -z, -ɪŋ, -d

rat-arsed
BR ˌratˈɑːst, ˈratɑːst
AM ˈrædˌɑrst

rat-a-tat
BR ˌratəˈtat, -s
AM ˈrædəˈtæt, -s

rat-a-tat-tat
BR ˌratətatˈtat
AM ˈrædəˌtæ(t)ˈtæt

ratatouille
BR ˌratəˈtwiː, -z
AM ˌrædəˈtui, -z

ratbag
BR ˈratbag, -z
AM ˈrætˌbæg, -z

ratcatcher
BR ˈratˌkatʃə(r), -z
AM ˈrætˌkætʃər, -z

ratch
BR ratʃ, -ɪz
AM rætʃ, -əz

ratchet
BR ˈratʃɪt, -s
AM ˈrætʃət, -s

Ratcliff
BR ˈratklɪf
AM ˈrætˌklɪf

Ratcliffe
BR ˈratklɪf
AM ˈrætˌklɪf

rate
BR reɪt, -s, -ɪŋ, -ɪd
AM reɪ|t, -ts, -dɪŋ, -dɪd

rateability
BR ˌreɪtəˈbɪlɪti
AM ˌreɪdəˈbɪlɪdi

rateable
BR ˈreɪtəbl
AM ˈreɪdəbəl

rateably
BR ˈreɪtəbli
AM ˈreɪdɪbli

ratecap
BR ˈreɪtkap, -s, -ɪŋ, -t
AM ˈreɪtˌkæp, -s, -ɪŋ, -t

ratel
BR ˈreɪtl, ˈrɑːtl, -z
AM ˈreɪdl, ˈrɑdl, -z

ratepayer
BR ˈreɪtˌpeɪə(r), -z
AM ˈreɪtˌpeɪər, -z

ratfink
BR ˈratfɪŋk, -s
AM ˈrætˌfɪŋk, -s

Rathbone
BR ˈraθbəʊn
AM ˈræθˌboʊn

rathe
BR reɪð
AM reɪð, ræθ

rather
BR ˈrɑːðə(r)
AM ˈræðər

rathe-ripe
BR ˈreɪðˌraɪp, -s
AM ˈreɪðˌraɪp, -s

Rathlin
BR ˈraθlɪn
AM ˈræθlən

rathole
BR ˈrathəʊl, -z
AM ˈrætˌ(h)oʊl, -z

rathskeller
BR ˈrɑːtˌskɛlə(r), -z
AM ˈrɑtˌskɛlər,
ˈrætˌskɛlər, -z

ratifiable
BR ˈratɪfʌɪəbl
AM ˈrædəˌfaɪəbəl

ratification
BR ˌratɪfɪˈkeɪʃn, -z
AM ˌrædəfəˈkeɪʃən, -z

ratifier
BR ˈratɪfʌɪə(r), -z
AM ˈrædəˌfaɪər, -z

ratify
BR ˈratɪfʌɪ, -z, -ɪŋ, -d
AM ˈrædəˌfaɪ, -z, -ɪŋ, -d

rating
BR ˈreɪtɪŋ, -z
AM ˈreɪdɪŋ, -z

ratio
BR ˈreɪʃɪəʊ, -z
AM ˈreɪʃ(i)oʊ, -z

ratiocinate
BR ˌratɪˈɒsɪneɪt,
ˌraʃɪˈɒsɪneɪt, -s, -ɪŋ, -ɪd
AM ˌreɪdiˈoʊsnˌeɪ|t,
ˌræʃiˈoʊsnˌeɪ|t, -ts,
-dɪŋ, -dɪd

ratiocination
BR ˌratɪˌɒsɪˈneɪʃn,
ˌraʃɪˌɒsɪˈneɪʃn, -z
AM ˌræʃiˌoʊsnˈeɪʃən,
-z

ratiocinative
BR ˌratɪˈɒsɪnətɪv,
ˌraʃɪˈɒsɪnətɪv
AM ˌræʃiˈoʊsəˌneɪdɪv

ratiocinator
BR ˌratɪˈɒsɪneɪtə(r),
ˌraʃɪˈɒsɪneɪtə(r), -z
AM ˌræʃiˈoʊsəˌneɪdər,
-z

ration
BR ˈraʃ|n, -nz,
-nɪŋ \-(ə)nɪŋ, -nd
AM ˈræʃ|ən, ˈreɪʃ|ən,
-ənz, -(ə)nɪŋ, -ənd

rational
BR ˈraʃn(ə)l, ˈraʃən(ə)l
AM ˈræʃ(ə)nəl

rationale
BR ˌraʃəˈnɑːl,
ˌraʃəˈnal, -z
AM ˌræʃəˈnæl, -z

rationalisation
BR ˌraʃnəlʌɪˈzeɪʃn,
ˌraʃnlʌɪˈzeɪʃn,
ˌraʃənlʌɪˈzeɪʃn,
ˌraʃ(ə)nəlʌɪˈzeɪʃn
AM ˌræʃənləˈzeɪʃən,
ˌræʃnələˈzeɪʃən,
ˌræʃənlˌaɪˈzeɪʃən,
ˌræʃnəˌlarˈzeɪʃən

rationalise
BR ˈraʃnəlʌɪz,
ˈraʃnlʌɪz, ˈraʃənlʌɪz,
ˈraʃ(ə)nəlʌɪz, -ɪz, -ɪŋ,
-d
AM ˈræʃənlˌaɪz,
ˈræʃnəˌlaɪz, -ɪz, -ɪŋ, -d

rationaliser
BR ˈraʃnəlʌɪzə(r),
ˈraʃnlʌɪzə(r),
ˈraʃənlʌɪzə(r),
ˈraʃ(ə)nəlʌɪzə(r), -z
AM ˈræʃənlˌaɪzər,
ˈræʃnəˌlaɪzər, -z

rationalism
BR ˈraʃnəlɪz(ə)m,
ˈraʃnlɪz(ə)m,
ˈraʃənlɪz(ə)m,
ˈraʃ(ə)nəlɪz(ə)m
AM ˈræʃənlˌɪzəm,
ˈræʃnəˌlɪzəm

rationalist
BR ˈraʃnəlɪst,
ˈraʃnlɪst, ˈraʃənlɪst,
ˈraʃ(ə)nəlɪst, -s
AM ˈræʃənləst,
ˈræʃnələst, -s

rationalistic
BR ˌraʃnəˈlɪstɪk,
ˌraʃnlˈɪstɪk,
ˌraʃənlˈɪstɪk,
ˌraʃ(ə)nəˈlɪstɪk
AM ˌræʃənlˈɪstɪk,
ˌræʃnəˈlɪstɪk

rationalistically
BR ˌraʃnəˈlɪstɪkli,
ˌraʃnlˈɪstɪkli,
ˌraʃənlˈɪstɪkli,
ˌraʃ(ə)nəˈlɪstɪkli
AM ˌræʃənlˈɪstək(ə)li,
ˈræʃnəˈlɪstək(ə)li

rationality
BR ˌraʃəˈnalɪti
AM ˌræʃəˈnælədi

rationalization
BR ˌraʃnəlʌɪˈzeɪʃn,
ˌraʃnlʌɪˈzeɪʃn,
ˌraʃ(ə)nəlʌɪˈzeɪʃn
AM ˌræʃənləˈzeɪʃən,
ˌræʃnələˈzeɪʃən,
ˌræʃənlˌaɪˈzeɪʃən,
ˌræʃnəˌlarˈzeɪʃən

rationalize
BR ˈraʃnəlʌɪz,
ˈraʃnlʌɪz, ˈraʃənlʌɪz,
ˈraʃ(ə)nəlʌɪz, -ɪz, -ɪŋ,
-d
AM ˈræʃənlˌaɪz,
ˈræʃnəˌlaɪz, -ɪz, -ɪŋ, -d

rationalizer
BR ˈraʃnəlʌɪzə(r),
ˈraʃnlʌɪzə(r),
ˈraʃənlʌɪzə(r),
ˈraʃ(ə)nəlʌɪzə(r), -z
AM ˈræʃənlˌaɪzər,
ˈræʃnəˌlaɪzər, -z

rationally
BR ˈraʃnəli, ˈraʃnli,
ˈraʃənli, ˈraʃ(ə)nəli
AM ˈræʃ(ə)nəli

ratite
BR ˈratʌɪt, -s
AM ˈræˌtaɪt, -s

ratlin
BR ˈratlɪn, -z

rationaliser AM ˈrætlən, -z

ratline
BR ˈratlɪn, -z
AM ˈrætlən, -z

Ratner
BR ˈratnə(r)
AM ˈrætnər

ratoon
BR rəˈtuːn, raˈtuːn, -z,
-ɪŋ, -d
AM rəˈtun, -z, -ɪŋ, -d

ratrace
BR ˈratreɪs
AM ˈrætˌreɪs

ratsbane
BR ˈratsbeɪn, -z
AM ˈrætsˌbeɪn, -z

Ratskeller
BR ˈratˌskɛlə(r), -z
AM ˈrɑtˌskɛlər,
ˈrætˌskɛlər, -z

rat's-tail
BR ˈratsteɪl
AM ˈrætsˌteɪl

rattan
BR rəˈtan, raˈtan, -z
AM ræˈtæn, rəˈtæn, -z

rat-tat
BR ˌratˈtat
AM ˌrætˈtæt

Rattenbury
BR ˈratnb(ə)ri
AM ˈrætnˌbɛri

ratter
BR ˈratə(r), -z
AM ˈrædər, -z

Rattigan
BR ˈratɪɡ(ə)n
AM ˈrædəɡən

rattily
BR ˈratɪli
AM ˈrædəli

rattiness
BR ˈratnɪs
AM ˈrædnɪs

rattle
BR ˈrat|l, -lz, -lɪŋ \-lɪŋ,
-ld
AM ˈrædəl, -z, -ɪŋ, -d

rattlebox
BR ˈratlbɒks, -ɪz
AM ˈrædlˌbɑks, -əz

rattler
BR ˈratlə(r), ˈratlə(r),
-z
AM ˈrædlər, ˈrætlər, -z

rattlesnake
BR ˈratlsneɪk, -s
AM ˈrædlˌsneɪk, -s

rattletrap
BR ˈratltrap, -s
AM ˈrædlˌtræp, -s

rattling
BR ˈratlɪŋ, ˈratlɪŋ, -z
AM ˈrædlɪŋ, -z

rattly
BR ˈratli, ˈratli

AM 'rædli

Rattray
BR 'ratrɪ, 'ratreɪ
AM 'rætreɪ

ratty
BR 'ratǀi, -ɪə(r), -ɪɪst
AM 'rædi, -ər, -ɪst

raucous
BR 'rɔːkəs
AM 'rɔkəs, 'rɑkəs

raucously
BR 'rɔːkəsli
AM 'rɔkəsli, 'rɑkəsli

raucousness
BR 'rɔːkəsnəs
AM 'rɔkəsnəs,
'rɑkəsnəs

raunch
BR rɔːn(t)ʃ
AM rɔn(t)ʃ, rɑn(t)ʃ

raunchily
BR 'rɔːn(t)ʃɪli
AM 'rɔn(t)ʃəli,
'rɑn(t)ʃəli

raunchiness
BR 'rɔːn(t)ʃɪnɪs
AM 'rɔn(t)ʃɪnɪs,
'rɑn(t)ʃɪnɪs

raunchy
BR 'rɔːn(t)ʃǀi, -ɪə(r),
-ɪɪst
AM 'rɔn(t)ʃi, 'rɑn(t)ʃi,
-ər, -ɪst

ravage
BR 'ravǀɪdʒ, -ɪdʒɪz,
-ɪdʒɪŋ, -ɪdʒd
AM 'rævɪdʒ, -ɪz, -ɪŋ, -d

ravager
BR 'ravɪdʒə(r), -z
AM 'rævɪdʒər, -z

rave
BR reɪv, -z, -ɪŋ, -d
AM reɪv, -z, -ɪŋ, -d

Ravel
BR rə'vɛl
AM rə'vɛl

ravel
BR 'ravǀl, -lz,
-lɪŋ \-(ə)lɪŋ, -ld
AM 'rævǀəl, -əlz, -(ə)lɪŋ,
-əld

ravelin
BR 'ravǀlɪn, 'rav(ə)lɪn,
-z
AM 'rævlən, -z

raven¹
noun, adjective
BR 'reɪvn, -z
AM 'reɪvən, -z

raven²
verb
BR 'ravǀn, -nz,
-nɪŋ \-(ə)nɪŋ, -nd
AM 'rævǀən, -ənz,
-(ə)nɪŋ, -ənd

Ravenglass
BR 'reɪvnglɑːs,
'reɪvŋglɑːs,
'reɪvnglas, 'reɪvŋglas
AM 'reɪvən,glæs

Ravenna
BR rə'vɛnə(r)
AM rə'vɛnə

ravenous
BR 'ravnəs, 'ravənəs
AM 'ræv(ə)nəs

ravenously
BR 'ravnəsli,
'ravənəsli
AM 'ræv(ə)nəsli

ravenousness
BR 'ravnəsnəs,
'ravənəsnəs
AM 'ræv(ə)nəsnəs

raver
BR 'reɪvə(r), -z
AM 'reɪvər, -z

rave-up
BR 'reɪvʌp, -s
AM 'reɪv,əp, -s

ravin
BR 'ravɪn, -z
AM 'rævən, -z

ravine¹
plunder
BR 'ravɪn, -z
AM 'rævən, -z

ravine²
valley
BR rə'viːn, -z, -d
AM rə'vin, -z, -d

raving
BR 'reɪvɪŋ, -z
AM 'reɪvɪŋ, -z

ravingly
BR 'reɪvɪŋli
AM 'reɪvɪŋli

ravioli
BR ˌravɪ'əʊli
AM ˌrævi'oʊli

ravish
BR 'ravǀɪʃ, -ɪʃɪz, -ɪʃɪŋ,
-ɪʃt
AM 'rævɪʃ, -ɪz, -ɪŋ, -t

ravisher
BR 'ravɪʃə(r), -z
AM 'rævɪʃər, -z

ravishing
BR 'ravɪʃɪŋ
AM 'rævɪʃɪŋ

ravishingly
BR 'ravɪʃɪŋli
AM 'rævɪʃɪŋli

ravishment
BR 'ravɪʃm(ə)nt
AM 'rævɪʃmənt

raw
BR rɔː(r), -ə(r), -ɪst
AM rɔ, rɑ, -ər, -əst

Rawalpindi
BR ˌrɔːl'pɪndi,
ˌrɔːw(ə)l'pɪndi,
ˌrɑːw(ə)l'pɪndi

AM ˌrɔw(ə)l'pɪndi

Rawdon
BR 'rɔːdn
AM 'rɔdən, 'rɑdən

rawhide
BR 'rɔːhʌɪd, -z
AM 'rɔ,(h)aɪd,
'rɑ,(h)aɪd, -z

Rawle
BR rɔːl
AM rɔl, rɑl

Rawlings
BR 'rɔːlɪŋz
AM 'rɔlɪŋz, 'rɑlɪŋz

Rawlins
BR 'rɔːlɪnz
AM 'rɔlɪnz, 'rɑlɪnz

Rawlinson
BR 'rɔːlɪns(ə)n
AM 'rɔlɪnsən,
'rɑlɪnsən

Rawlplug®
BR 'rɔːlplʌg, -z
AM 'rɔl,pləg, 'rɑl,pləg,
-z

Rawls
BR rɔːlz
AM rɔlz, rɑlz

rawly
BR 'rɔːli
AM 'rɔli, 'rɑli

rawness
BR 'rɔːnəs
AM 'rɔnəs, 'rɑnəs

Rawson
BR 'rɔːsn
AM 'rɔsən, 'rɑsən

Rawtenstall
BR 'rɒtnstɔːl,
'rɔːtnstɔːl
AM 'rɔtn,stɔl,
'rɑtn,stɑl

ray
BR reɪ, -z
AM reɪ, -z

rayah
BR 'rʌɪə(r), -z
AM 'raɪə, -z

Rayburn
BR 'reɪbəːn
AM 'reɪ,bərn

Rayleen
BR 'reɪliːn
AM 'reɪlin

Rayleigh
BR 'reɪli
AM 'reɪli

rayless
BR 'reɪlɪs
AM 'reɪləs

raylet
BR 'reɪlɪt, -s
AM 'reɪlət, -s

Raymond
BR 'reɪmənd
AM 'reɪmən(d)

Rayner
BR 'reɪnə(r)
AM 'reɪnər

Raynes
BR reɪnz
AM reɪnz

rayon
BR 'reɪɒn, 'reɪən
AM 'reɪ,ɑn

raze
BR reɪz, -ɪz, -ɪŋ, -d
AM reɪz, -ɪz, -ɪŋ, -d

razoo
BR rɑː'zʊ, rə'zuː, 'rɑːzʊ,
-z
AM rə'zu, -z

razor
BR 'reɪzǀə(r), -əz,
-(ə)rɪŋ, -əd
AM 'reɪzər, -z, -ɪŋ, -d

razorback
BR 'reɪzəbak, -s
AM 'reɪzər,bæk, -s

razorbill
BR 'reɪzəbɪl, -z
AM 'reɪzər,bɪl, -z

razorblade
BR 'reɪzəbleɪd, -z
AM 'reɪzər,bleɪd, -z

razorshell
BR 'reɪzəʃɛl, -z
AM 'reɪzər,ʃɛl, -z

razz
BR raz, -ɪz, -ɪŋ, -d
AM ræz, -ɪz, -ɪŋ, -d

razzamatazz
BR 'raz(ə)mətaz,
ˌraz(ə)mə'taz
AM 'ræz(ə)mə,tæz

razzamattazz
BR 'raz(ə)mətaz,
ˌraz(ə)mə'taz
AM 'ræz(ə)mə,tæz

razzia
BR 'razɪə(r), -z
AM 'ræzɪə, -z

razzle
BR 'razl
AM 'ræzəl

razzle-dazzle
BR 'razl,dazl,
ˌrazl'dazl
AM 'ræzəl'dæzəl

razzmatazz
BR 'razmətaz,
ˌrazmə'taz
AM 'ræz(ə)mə,tæz

razzmattazz
BR 'razmətaz,
ˌrazmə'taz
AM 'ræzmə,tæz

re¹
preposition
BR reɪ, riː
AM reɪ, ri

re²
Tonic Sol-fa
BR reɪ

AM reɪ

Rea
BR reɪ, riː, 'riːə(r)
AM 'riːə)

reabsorb
BR ˌriːəb'zɔːb,
ˌriːəb'sɔːb, -z, -ɪŋ, -d
AM ˌriəb'sɔ(ə)rb,
ˌriəb'zɔ(ə)rb, -z, -ɪŋ, -d

reabsorption
BR ˌriːəb'sɔːpʃn,
ˌriːəb'zɔːpʃn, -z
AM ˌriəb'sɔrpʃən,
ˌriəb'zɔrpʃən, -z

reaccept
BR ˌriːək'sept, -s, -ɪŋ, -d
AM ˌriək'sept, -s, -ɪŋ, -d

reacceptance
BR ˌriːək'sept(ə)ns, -ɪz
AM ˌriək'septns, -əz

reaccustom
BR ˌriːə'kʌstəm, -z, -ɪŋ, -d
AM ˌriə'kəstəm, -z, -ɪŋ, -d

reach
BR riːtʃ, -ɪz, -ɪŋ, -t
AM riːtʃ, -ɪz, -ɪŋ, -t

reachable
BR 'riːtʃəbl
AM 'ritʃəbəl

reacher
BR 'riːtʃə(r), -z
AM 'ritʃər, -z

reacquaint
BR ˌriːə'kweɪnt, -s, -ɪŋ, -ɪd
AM ˌriə'kweɪn|t, -ts, -(t)ɪŋ, -(t)ɪd

reacquaintance
BR ˌriːə'kweɪnt(ə)ns, -ɪz
AM ˌriə'kweɪn(t)ns, -əz

reacquire
BR ˌriːə'kwʌɪə(r), -z, -ɪŋ, -d
AM ˌriə'kwaɪ(ə)r, -z, -ɪŋ, -d

reacquisition
BR ˌriːəkwɪ'zɪʃn, -z
AM riˌækwə'zɪʃən, -z

react
BR rɪ'ækt, -s, -ɪŋ, -ɪd
AM ri'æk|(t), -(t)s, -tɪŋ, -təd

reactance
BR rɪ'akt(ə)ns, -ɪz
AM ri'æktns, -əz

reactant
BR rɪ'akt(ə)nt, -s
AM ri'æktnt, -s

reaction
BR rɪ'akʃn, -z
AM ri'ækʃən, -z

reactionary
BR rɪ'akʃn(ə)r|i, -ɪz
AM ri'ækʃəˌnɛri, -z

reactionist
BR rɪ'akʃnɪst,
rɪ'akʃənɪst, -s
AM ri'ækʃənəst, -s

reactivate
BR rɪ'aktɪveɪt, -s, -ɪŋ, -ɪd
AM ri'æktəˌveɪ|t, -ts, -dɪŋ, -dɪd

reactivation
BR rɪˌaktɪ'veɪʃn
AM ri,æktə'veɪʃən

reactive
BR rɪ'aktɪv
AM ri'æktɪv

reactively
BR rɪ'aktɪvli
AM ri'æktɪvli

reactivity
BR ˌriːak'tɪvɪt|i, -ɪz
AM ˌri,æk'tɪvɪdi, -z

reactor
BR rɪ'aktə(r), -z
AM ri'æktər, -z

Read
BR riːd
AM rid

read¹
present tense
BR riːd, -z, -ɪŋ
AM rid, -z, -ɪŋ

read²
past tense
BR red
AM red

readability
BR ˌriːdə'bɪlɪti
AM ˌridə'bɪlɪdi

readable
BR 'riːdəbl
AM 'ridəbəl

readableness
BR 'riːdəblnəs
AM 'ridəbəlnəs

readably
BR 'riːdəbli
AM 'ridəbli

readapt
BR ˌriːə'dapt, -s, -ɪŋ, -d
AM ˌriː'ə'dæpt, -s, -ɪŋ, -d

readaptation
BR ˌriːədap'teɪʃn,
ˌriːadap'teɪʃn, -z
AM ri,ædəp'teɪʃən, -z

readdress
BR ˌriːə'dres, -ɪz, -ɪŋ, -t
AM ˌriə'dres, -ɪz, -ɪŋ, -t

Reade
BR riːd
AM rid

reader
BR 'riːdə(r), -z
AM 'ridər, -z

readership
BR 'riːdəʃɪp, -s
AM 'ridərˌʃɪp, -s

readily
BR 'rɛdɪli
AM 'rɛdəli

read-in
BR 'riːdɪn, -z
AM 'rid,ɪn, -z

readiness
BR 'rɛdɪnɪs
AM 'rɛdinɪs

Reading
UK town
BR 'rɛdɪŋ
AM 'rɛdɪŋ

reading
BR 'riːdɪŋ, -z
AM 'ridɪŋ, -z

readjust
BR ˌriːə'dʒʌst, -s, -ɪŋ, -ɪd
AM ˌriə'dʒəst, -s, -ɪŋ, -ɪd

readjustment
BR ˌriːə'dʒʌs(t)m(ə)nt, -s
AM ˌriə'dʒəs(t)mənt, -s

Readman
BR 'rɛdmən
AM 'rɛdmən

readmission
BR ˌriːəd'mɪʃn, -z
AM ˌriəd'mɪʃən, -z

readmit
BR ˌriːəd'mɪt, -s, -ɪŋ, -ɪd
AM ˌriəd'mɪ|t, -ts, -dɪŋ, -dɪd

readmittance
BR ˌriːəd'mɪtns
AM ˌriəd'mɪtns

read-only memory
BR ˌriːdəʊnlɪ 'mem(ə)r|i, -ɪz
AM 'rid,ounli 'mem(ə)ri, -z

readopt
BR ˌriːə'dɒpt, -s, -ɪŋ, -d
AM ˌriə'dɑpt, -s, -ɪŋ, -d

readoption
BR ˌriːə'dɒpʃn, -z
AM ˌriə'dɑpʃən, -z

readout
BR 'riːdaʊt, -s
AM 'ri,daʊt, -s

readthrough
BR 'riːdθruː, -z
AM 'rid,θru, -z

re-advertise
BR rɪ'advətʌɪz, -ɪz, -ɪŋ, -d
AM ri'ædvərˌtaɪz, -ɪz, -ɪŋ, -d

re-advertisement
BR ˌriːəd'vəːtɪsm(ə)nt,
ˌriːəd'vəːtɪzm(ə)nt, -s
AM ri'ædvərˌtaɪzmənt, -s

read-write
BR ˌriːd'rʌɪt

AM 'rid'raɪt

ready
BR 'rɛd|i, -ɪə(r), -ɪɪst
AM 'rɛdi, -ər, -ɪst

ready-to-serve
BR ˌrɛdɪtə'səːv
AM ˌrɛdidə'sərv

ready-to-wear
BR ˌrɛdɪtə'wɛː(r)
AM ˌrɛdidə'wɛ(ə)r

reaffirm
BR ˌriːə'fəːm, -z, -ɪŋ, -d
AM ˌriː'ə'fərm, -z, -ɪŋ, -d

reaffirmation
BR ˌriːafə'meɪʃn,
rɪ,afə'meɪʃn, -z
AM ˌriː,æfər'meɪʃən, -z

reafforest
BR ˌriːə'fɒrɪst, -s, -ɪŋ, -ɪd
AM ˌriə'fɔrəst, -s, -ɪŋ, -əd

reafforestation
BR ˌriːəˌfɒrɪ'steɪʃn
AM ˌriəˌfɔrəs'teɪʃən

Reagan
BR 'reɪg(ə)n
AM 'reɪgən

reagency
BR rɪ'eɪdʒ(ə)ns|i, -ɪz
AM ri'eɪdʒənsi, -z

reagent
BR rɪ'eɪdʒ(ə)nt, -s
AM ri'eɪdʒənt, -s

real¹
adjective
BR rɪəl
AM 'ri(ə)l

real²
money
BR reɪ'ɑːl, -z
AM reɪ'al, ri'al, -z

realgar
BR rɪ'algə(r),
rɪ'algɑ(r), -z
AM ri'ælgər, ri'ælˌgɑr, -z

realign
BR ˌriːə'lʌɪn, -z, -ɪŋ, -d
AM ˌriə'laɪn, -z, -ɪŋ, -d

realignment
BR ˌriːə'lʌɪnm(ə)nt, -s
AM ˌriə'laɪnmənt, -s

realisability
BR ˌriːələʌɪzə'bɪlɪt|i, -ɪz
AM ˌriələaɪzə'bɪlɪdi, -z

realisable
BR 'rɪələʌɪzəbl
AM ˌriə'laɪzəbəl

realisation
BR ˌrɪələʌɪ'zeɪʃn,
ˌrɪəlɪ'zeɪʃn, -z
AM ˌri(ə)lə'zeɪʃən, -z

realise
BR 'rɪələʌɪz, -ɪz, -ɪŋ, -d
AM 'ri(ə)ˌlaɪz, -ɪz, -ɪŋ, -d

realiser
BR ˈrɪəlʌɪzə(r), -z
AM ˈriə,laɪzər, -z

realism
BR ˈrɪəlɪz(ə)m
AM ˈriə,lɪzəm

realist
BR ˈrɪəlɪst, -s
AM ˈriələst, -s

realistic
BR ,rɪəˈlɪstɪk
AM ,riəˈlɪstɪk

realistically
BR ,rɪəˈlɪstɪkli
AM ,riəˈlɪstɪk(ə)li

reality
BR rɪˈalɪt|i, -ɪz
AM riˈælədi, -z

realizability
BR ,rɪəlʌɪzəˈbɪlɪt|i, -ɪz
AM ,riəlaɪzəˈbɪlɪdi, -z

realizable
BR ˈrɪəlʌɪzəbl
AM ˈriəˈlaɪzəbəl

realization
BR ,rɪəlʌɪˈzeɪʃn,
,rɪəlɪˈzeɪʃn, -z
AM ,ri(ə)ləˈzeɪʃən, -z

realize
BR ˈrɪəlʌɪz, -ɪz, -ɪŋ, -d
AM ˈri(ə),laɪz, -ɪz, -ɪŋ, -d

realizer
BR ˈrɪəlʌɪzə(r), -z
AM ˈri(ə),laɪzər, -z

reallocate
BR ,riːˈaləkeɪt, -s, -ɪŋ, -ɪd
AM riˈælə,keɪt, -ts, -dɪŋ, -dəd

reallocation
BR ,riːaləˈkeɪʃn, rɪ,aləˈkeɪʃn
AM ,ri,ælə'keɪʃən

reallot
BR ,riːəˈlɒt, -s, -ɪŋ, -ɪd
AM ˈriə'la|t, -ts, -dɪŋ, -dəd

reallotment
BR ,riːəˈlɒtm(ə)nt, -s
AM ˈriə'latmənt, -s

really
BR ˈrɪəli, ˈriːli
AM ˈri(ə)li

realm
BR rɛlm, -z
AM rɛlm, -z

realness
BR ˈrɪəlnəs
AM ˈri(ə)lnəs

Realpolitik
BR reɪˈɑːlpɒlɪ,tiːk
AM reɪˈɑl,pɒlɪ,tik, reɪˈɑl,pɑlɪ,tik

realtor
BR ˈrɪəltə(r), ˈrɪəltɔː(r), -z
AM ˈri(ə)ltər, ˈri(ə)l,tɔ(ə)r, -z

realty
BR ˈrɪəlti
AM ˈri(ə)lti

ream
BR riːm, -z
AM rim, -z

reamer
BR ˈriːmə(r), -z
AM ˈrimər, -z

reanalyse
BR (,)riːˈanlʌɪz, (,)riːˈanəlʌɪz, -ɪz, -ɪŋ, -d
AM riˈænl,aɪz, riˈænə,laɪz, -ɪz, -ɪŋ, -d

reanalyses
BR ,riːəˈnalɪsiːz
AM ˈriə'næləsiz

reanalysis
BR ,riːəˈnalɪsɪs
AM ˈriə'næləsɪs

reanalyze
BR (,)riːˈanlʌɪz, (,)riːˈanəlʌɪz, -ɪz, -ɪŋ, -d
AM riˈænl,aɪz, riˈænə,laɪz, -ɪz, -ɪŋ, -d

reanimate
BR (,)riːˈanɪmeɪt, -s, -ɪŋ, -ɪd
AM riˈænə,meɪ|t, -ts, -dɪŋ, -dɪd

reanimation
BR ,riːanɪˈmeɪʃn, ri,anɪˈmeɪʃn
AM ,ri,ænəˈmeɪʃən

reap
BR riːp, -s, -ɪŋ, -t
AM rip, -s, -ɪŋ, -t

reaper
BR ˈriːpə(r), -z
AM ˈripər, -z

reappear
BR ,riːəˈpɪə(r), -z, -ɪŋ, -d
AM ˈriə'pɪ(ə)r, -z, -ɪŋ, -d

reappearance
BR ,riːəˈpɪərəns, ,riːəˈpɪərəns, -ɪz
AM ˈriə'pɪrəns, -əz

reapplication
BR ,riːaplɪˈkeɪʃn, -z
AM ,ri,æplə'keɪʃən, -z

reapply
BR ,riːəˈplʌɪ, -z, -ɪŋ, -d
AM ˈriə'plaɪ, -z, -ɪŋ, -d

reappoint
BR ,riːəˈpɔɪnt, -s, -ɪŋ, -ɪd
AM ˈriə'pɔɪn|t, -ts, -(t)ɪŋ, -(t)ɪd

reappointment
BR ,riːəˈpɔɪntm(ə)nt, -s
AM ˈriə'pɔɪntmənt, -s

reapportion
BR ,riːəˈpɔːʃn, -z, -ɪŋ, -d
AM ˈriə'pɔrʃən, -z, -ɪŋ, -d

reapportionment
BR ,riːəˈpɔːʃnm(ə)nt, -s

realty (column 3)

AM ˈriə'pɔrʃənmənt, -s

reappraisal
BR ,riːəˈpreɪzl, -z
AM ˈriə'preɪzəl, -z

reappraise
BR ,riːəˈpreɪz, -ɪz, -ɪŋ, -d
AM ˈriə'preɪz, -ɪz, -ɪŋ, -d

rear
BR rɪə(r), -z, -ɪŋ, -d
AM rɪ(ə)r, -z, -ɪŋ, -d

Reardon
BR ˈrɪəd(ə)n
AM ˈrɪrdən

rearer
BR ˈrɪərə(r), -z
AM ˈrɪrər, -z

rearm
BR riːˈɑːm, rɪˈɑːm, -z, -ɪŋ, -d
AM riˈarm, -z, -ɪŋ, -d

rearmament
BR ,riːˈɑːməm(ə)nt, rɪˈɑːməm(ə)nt
AM riˈarməmənt

rearmost
BR ˈrɪəməʊst
AM ˈrɪr,moʊst

rearrange
BR ,riːəˈreɪn(d)ʒ, -ɪz, -ɪŋ, -d
AM ˈriə'reɪndʒ, -ɪz, -ɪŋ, -d

rearrangement
BR ,riːəˈreɪn(d)ʒm(ə)nt, -s
AM ˈriə'reɪndʒmənt, -s

rearrest
BR ,riːəˈrɛst, -s, -ɪŋ, -ɪd
AM ˈriə'rɛst, -s, -ɪŋ, -əd

rearview
BR ˈrɪə'vjuː
AM ˈrɪr'vju

rearward
BR ˈrɪəwəd
AM ˈrɪrwərd

rear-wheel drive
BR ,rɪəwiːl ˈdrʌɪv
AM ˈrɪr,(h)wil ˈdraɪv

reascend
BR ,riːəˈsɛnd, -z, -ɪŋ, -ɪd
AM ˈriə'sɛnd, -z, -ɪŋ, -əd

reascension
BR ,riːəˈsɛnʃn, -z
AM ˈriə'sɛn(t)ʃən, -z

reason
BR ˈriːz|n, -nz, -nɪŋ \-(ə)nɪŋ, -nd
AM ˈrizn, -z, -ɪŋ, -d

reasonable
BR ˈriːznəbl, ˈriːz(ə)nəbl
AM ˈriznəbəl, ˈriznəbəl

reasonableness
BR ˈriːznəblnəs, ˈriːz(ə)nəblnəs
AM ˈriznəbəlnəs, ˈriznəbəlnəs

reasonably
BR ˈriːznəbli, ˈriːz(ə)nəbli
AM ˈriznəbli, ˈriznəbli

reasoner
BR ˈriːznə(r), ˈriːz(ə)nə(r), -z
AM ˈriznər, ˈriznər, -z

reasoning
BR ˈriːznɪŋ, ˈriːz(ə)nɪŋ, -z
AM ˈriznɪŋ, ˈriznɪŋ, -z

reasonless
BR ˈriːznləs
AM ˈriznləs

reassemble
BR ,riːəˈsɛmb|l, -lz, -lɪŋ \-lɪŋ, -ld
AM ˈriə'sɛmbəl, -z, -ɪŋ, -d

reassembly
BR ,riːəˈsɛmbl|i, -ɪz
AM ˈriə'sɛmbli, -z

reassert
BR ,riːəˈsəːt, -s, -ɪŋ, -ɪd
AM ˈriə'sər|t, -ts, -dɪŋ, -dəd

reassertion
BR ,riːəˈsəːʃn
AM ˈriə'sərʃən

reassess
BR ,riːəˈsɛs, -ɪz, -ɪŋ, -t
AM ˈriə'sɛs, -əz, -ɪŋ, -t

reassessment
BR ,riːəˈsɛs(ə)nt, -s
AM ˈriə'sɛsmənt, -s

reassign
BR ,riːəˈsʌɪn, -z, -ɪŋ, -d
AM ˈriə'saɪn, -z, -ɪŋ, -d

reassignment
BR ,riːəˈsʌɪnm(ə)nt, -s
AM ˈriə'saɪnmənt, -s

reassume
BR ,riːəˈsjuːm, -z, -ɪŋ, -d
AM ˈriə's(j)um, -z, -ɪŋ, -d

reassumption
BR ,riːəˈsʌm(p)ʃn, -z
AM ˈriə'səm(p)ʃən, -z

reassurance
BR ,riːəˈʃʊərəns, ,riːəˈʃʊərns, ,riːəˈʃɔːrəns, ,riːəˈʃɔːrns
AM ˈriə'ʃʊrəns

reassure
BR ,riːəˈʃʊə(r), ,riːəˈʃɔː(r), -z, -ɪŋ, -d
AM ˈriə'ʃʊ(ə)r, -z, -ɪŋ, -d

reassurer
BR ,riːəˈʃʊərə(r), ,riːəˈʃɔːrə(r), -z
AM ˈriə'ʃʊrər, -z

reassuring
BR ,riːəˈʃʊərɪŋ, ,riːəˈʃɔːrɪŋ
AM ˈriə'ʃʊrɪŋ

reassuringly
BR ˌriːəˈʃʊərɪŋli,
ˌriːəˈʃɔːrɪŋli
AM ˌriəˈʃʊrɪŋli

reattach
BR ˌriːəˈtatʃ, -ɪz, -ɪŋ, -t
AM ˌriəˈtætʃ, -əz, -ɪŋ, -t

reattachment
BR ˌriːəˈtatʃm(ə)nt, -s
AM ˌriəˈtætʃmənt, -s

reattain
BR ˌriːəˈteɪn, -z, -ɪŋ, -d
AM ˌriəˈteɪn, -z, -ɪŋ, -d

reattainment
BR ˌriːəˈteɪnm(ə)nt, -s
AM ˌriəˈteɪnmənt, -s

reattempt
BR ˌriːəˈtɛm(p)t, -s, -ɪŋ, -ɪd
AM ˌriəˈtɛm(p)t, -s, -ɪŋ, -əd

reave
BR riːv, -z, -ɪŋ, -d
AM riv, -z, -ɪŋ, -d

reawaken
BR ˌriːəˈweɪk|(ə)n, -(ə)nz, -(ə)nɪŋ \-n̩ɪŋ, -(ə)nd
AM ˌriəˈweɪk|ən, -ənz, -(ə)nɪŋ, -ənd

Reay
BR reɪ
AM reɪ

reb
BR rɛb, -z
AM rɛb, -z

rebadge
BR ˌriːˈbadʒ, -ɪz, -ɪŋ, -d
AM ˌriˈbædʒ, -ɪz, -ɪŋ, -d

rebalance
BR ˌriːˈbaləns, ˌriːˈbal̩s, -ɪz, -ɪŋ, -t
AM rəˈbæləns, riˈbæləns, -əz, -ɪŋ, -t

rebaptise
BR ˌriːbapˈtʌɪz, -ɪz, -ɪŋ, -d
AM rəˈbæp.taɪz, ˌriˈbæp.taɪz, -ɪz, -ɪŋ, -d

rebaptize
BR ˌriːbapˈtʌɪz, -ɪz, -ɪŋ, -d
AM rəˈbæp.taɪz, ˌriˈbæp.taɪz, -ɪz, -ɪŋ, -d

rebar
noun
BR ˈriːbɑː(r)
AM ˈribar

rebarbative
BR rɪˈbɑːbətɪv
AM rəˈbarbədɪv

rebase
BR ˌriːˈbeɪs, -ɪz, -ɪŋ, -t
AM ˌriˈbeɪs, riˈbeɪs, -ɪz, -ɪŋ, -t

rebatable
BR ˈriːbeɪtəbl
AM ˈriˌbeɪdəbəl

rebate¹
finance
BR ˈriːbeɪt, -s
AM ˈriˌbeɪt, -s

rebate²
joint
BR ˈriːbeɪt, ˈrabɪt, -s, -ɪŋ, -ɪd
AM ˈræbɪt, ˈriˌbeɪ|t, -ts, -dɪŋ, -dɪd

rebater
BR ˈriːbeɪtə(r), -z
AM ˈriˌbeɪdər, -z

rebbe
BR ˈrɛbə(r), -z
AM ˈrɛbə, -z

rebbetzin
BR ˈrɛbɪtsɪn, -z
AM ˈrɛbətsɪn, -z

rebec
BR ˈriːbɛk, -s
AM ˈrɛbək, ˈriˌbɛk, -s

Rebecca
BR rɪˈbɛkə(r)
AM rəˈbɛkə

rebeck
BR ˈriːbɛk, -s
AM ˈrɛbək, ˈriˌbɛk, -s

rebel¹
noun
BR ˈrɛbl, -z
AM ˈrɛbəl, -z

rebel²
verb
BR rɪˈbɛl, -z, -ɪŋ, -d
AM rəˈbɛl, -z, -ɪŋ, -d

rebellion
BR rɪˈbɛljən, -z
AM rəˈbɛljən, riˈbɛljən, -z

rebellious
BR rɪˈbɛljəs
AM rəˈbɛljəs, riˈbɛljəs

rebelliously
BR rɪˈbɛljəsli
AM rəˈbɛljəsli, riˈbɛljəsli

rebelliousness
BR rɪˈbɛljəsnəs
AM rəˈbɛljəsnəs, riˈbɛljəsnəs

rebid¹
noun
BR ˈriːbɪd, -z
AM ˈriˌbɪd, -z

rebid²
verb
BR ˌriːˈbɪd, -z, -ɪŋ
AM ˌriˈbɪd, -z, -ɪŋ

rebind
BR ˌriːˈbʌɪnd, -z, -ɪŋ
AM ˌriˈbaɪnd, -z, -ɪŋ

rebirth
BR ˌriːˈbəːθ, ˈriːbəːθ, -s
AM riˈbərθ, -s

rebirther
BR ˌriːˈbəːθə(r), ˈriːbəːθə(r), -z

rebirthing
BR ˌriːˈbəːθɪŋ, ˈriːbəːθɪŋ, -z
AM riˈbərθɪŋ, -z

reboot
BR ˌriːˈbuːt, -s, -ɪŋ, -ɪd
AM ˌriˈbu|t, -ts, -dɪŋ, -dəd

rebore
BR ˌriːˈbɔː(r), -z, -ɪŋ, -d
AM ˌriˈbɔ(ə)r, -z, -ɪŋ, -d

reborn
BR ˌriːˈbɔːn
AM riˈbɔ(ə)rn

rebound¹
adjective
BR ˌriːˈbaʊnd
AM ˌriˌbaʊnd

rebound²
noun
BR ˈriːbaʊnd
AM ˈriˌbaʊnd

rebound³
past tense of rebind
BR ˌriːˈbaʊnd
AM ˌriˌbaʊnd

rebound⁴
verb, of basketball
BR rɪˈbaʊnd, -z, -ɪŋ, -ɪd
AM ˌriˌbaʊnd, -z, -ɪŋ, -əd

rebounder
BR rɪˈbaʊndə(r), -z
AM ˌriˌbaʊndər, -z

rebozo
BR rɪˈbəʊzəʊ, -z
AM rəˈbouzou, -z

rebroadcast
BR ˌriːˈbrɔːdkɑːst, ˌriːˈbrɔːdkast, -s, -ɪŋ
AM ˌriˈbrɔdˌkæst, ˈriˈbrɑdˌkæst, -s, -ɪŋ

rebuff
BR rɪˈbʌf, -s, -ɪŋ, -t
AM rəˈbəf, riˈbəf, -s, -ɪŋ, -t

rebuild¹
noun
BR ˈriːbɪld, -z
AM ˈriˌbɪld, -z

rebuild²
verb
BR (ˌ)riːˈbɪld, -z, -ɪŋ
AM riˈbɪld, -z, -ɪŋ

rebuilder
BR (ˌ)riːˈbɪldə(r), -z
AM riˈbɪldər, -z

rebuilding
BR (ˌ)riːˈbɪldɪŋ, -z
AM riˈbɪldɪŋ, -z

rebuilt
BR (ˌ)riːˈbɪlt
AM riˈbɪlt, ˈriˈbɪlt

rebuke
BR rɪˈbjuːk, -s, -ɪŋ, -t
AM rəˈbjuk, riˈbjuk, -s, -ɪŋ, -t

rebuker
BR rɪˈbjuːkə(r), -z
AM rəˈbjukər, riˈbjukər, -z

rebukingly
BR rɪˈbjuːkɪŋli
AM rəˈbjukɪŋli, riˈbjukɪŋli

reburial
BR ˌriːˈbɛriəl, -z
AM riˈbɛriəl, -z

rebury
BR ˌriːˈbɛr|i, -ɪz, -ɪɪŋ, -ɪd
AM riˈbɛri, -z, -ɪŋ, -d

rebus
BR ˈriːbəs, -ɪz
AM ˈribəs, -əz

rebut
BR rɪˈbʌt, -s, -ɪŋ, -ɪd
AM rəˈbə|t, riˈbə|t, -ts, -dɪŋ, -dəd

rebutment
BR rɪˈbʌtm(ə)nt, -s
AM rəˈbətmənt, riˈbətmənt, -s

rebuttable
BR rɪˈbʌtəbl
AM rəˈbədəbəl, riˈbədəbəl

rebuttal
BR rɪˈbʌtl, -z
AM rəˈbədl, riˈbədl, -z

rebutter
BR rɪˈbʌtə(r), -z
AM rəˈbədər, riˈbədər, -z

rec
BR rɛk
AM rɛk

recalcitrance
BR rɪˈkalsɪtr(ə)ns
AM rəˈkælsətrəns, riˈkælsətrəns

recalcitrant
BR rɪˈkalsɪtr(ə)nt, -s
AM rəˈkælsətrənt, riˈkælsətrənt, -s

recalcitrantly
BR rɪˈkalsɪtr(ə)ntli
AM rəˈkælsətrən(t)li, riˈkælsətrən(t)li

recalculate
BR ˌriːˈkalkjʊleɪt, -s, -ɪŋ, -ɪd
AM rəˈkælkjəˌleɪ|t, riˈkælkjəˌleɪ|t, -ts, -dɪŋ, -dɪd

recalculation
BR ˌriːkalkjʊˈleɪʃn, -z
AM rəˌkælkjəˈleɪʃən, riˌkælkjəˈleɪʃən, -z

recalesce
BR ˌriːkəˈlɛs, -ɪz, -ɪŋ, -t
AM ˌrikəˈlɛs, -əz, -ɪŋ, -t

recalescence
BR ˌriːkəˈlɛsns
AM ˌrikəˈlɛsns

recall[1]
noun, something
called back for
correction
BR rɪˈkɔːl, -z
AM ˈriˌkɔl, ˈriˌkal, -z

recall[2]
noun, something
remembered
BR rɪˈkɔːl, ˈriːkɔːl
AM ˈriˌkɔl, rəˈkɔl,
riˈkɔl, ˈriˌkal, rəˈkal,
riˈkal

recall[3]
verb
BR rɪˈkɔːl, -z, -ɪŋ, -d
AM rəˈkɔl, riˈkɔl,
rəˈkal, riˈkal, -z, -ɪŋ, -d

recallable
BR rɪˈkɔːləbl
AM rəˈkɔləbəl,
riˈkɔləbəl, rəˈkaləbəl,
riˈkaləbəl

recant
BR rɪˈkant, -s, -ɪŋ, -ɪd
AM rəˈkæn|t, riˈkæn|t,
-ts, -(t)ɪŋ, -(t)əd

recantation
BR ˌriːkanˈteɪʃn, -z
AM ˌriːkænˈteɪʃən, -z

recanter
BR rɪˈkantə(r), -z
AM rəˈkæn(t)ər,
riˈkæn(t)ər, -z

recap[1]
noun
BR ˈriːkap, -s
AM ˈriːˌkæp, -s

recap[2]
verb
BR riːˈkap, ˈriːkap, -s,
-ɪŋ, -t
AM riˈkæp, -s, -ɪŋ, -t

recapitalisation
BR (ˌ)riːˌkapɪtlʌɪˈzeɪʃn
AM rəˌkæpədləˈzeɪʃən,
riˌkæpədləˈzeɪʃən,
rəˌkæpədlˌaɪˈzeɪʃən,
riˌkæpədlˌaɪˈzeɪʃən,
rəˌkæpədələˈzeɪʃən,
riˌkæpədələˈzeɪʃən,
rəˌkæpədəˌlaɪˈzeɪʃən,
riˌkæpədəˌlaɪˈzeɪʃən

recapitalise
BR (ˌ)riːˈkapɪtlʌɪz, -ɪz,
-ɪŋ, -d
AM rəˈkæpədlˌaɪz,
riˈkæpədlˌaɪz,
rəˈkæpədəˌlaɪz,
riˈkæpədəˌlaɪz, -ɪz, -ɪŋ,
-d

recapitalization
BR (ˌ)riːˌkapɪtlʌɪˈzeɪʃn
AM rəˌkæpədləˈzeɪʃən,
riˌkæpədləˈzeɪʃən,
rəˌkæpədlˌaɪˈzeɪʃən,
riˌkæpədlˌaɪˈzeɪʃən,
rəˌkæpədələˈzeɪʃən,
riˌkæpədələˈzeɪʃən,

rəˌkæpədəˌlaɪˈzeɪʃən,
riˌkæpədəˌlaɪˈzeɪʃən

recapitalize
BR (ˌ)riːˈkapɪtlʌɪz, -ɪz,
-ɪŋ, -d
AM rəˈkæpədlˌaɪz,
riˈkæpədlˌaɪz,
rəˈkæpədəˌlaɪz,
riˈkæpədəˌlaɪz, -ɪz, -ɪŋ,
-d

recapitulate
BR ˌriːkəˈpɪtʃʊleɪt,
ˌriːkəˈpɪtjʊleɪt, -s, -ɪŋ,
-ɪd
AM ˌriːkəˈpɪtʃəˌleɪ|t, -ts,
-dɪŋ, -dɪd

recapitulation
BR ˌriːkəˌpɪtʃʊˈleɪʃn,
ˌriːkəˌpɪtjʊˈleɪʃn, -z
AM ˌriːkəˌpɪtʃəˈleɪʃən,
-z

recapitulative
BR ˌriːkəˈpɪtʃʊlətɪv,
ˌriːkəˈpɪtjʊlətɪv
AM ˌriːkəˈpɪtʃʊlədɪv,
ˌriːkəˈpɪtʃəˌleɪdɪv

recapitulatory
BR ˌriːkəˈpɪtʃʊlət(ə)ri,
ˌriːkəˈpɪtjʊlət(ə)ri
AM ˌriːkəˈpɪtʃələˌtɔri

recapture
BR (ˌ)riːˈkaptʃ|ə(r),
-əz, -(ə)rɪŋ, -əd
AM riˈkæptʃ|ər, -ərz,
-(ə)rɪŋ, -ərd

recast
BR ˌriːˈkɑːst, riːˈkast,
-s, -ɪŋ
AM riˈkæst, -s, -ɪŋ

recce
BR ˈrɛk|i, -ɪz, -ɪɪŋ, -ɪd
AM ˈrɛki, -z, -ɪŋ, -d

recede
BR rɪˈsiːd, -z, -ɪŋ, -ɪd
AM rəˈsid, riˈsid, -z, -ɪŋ,
-ɪd

re-cede
BR ˌriːˈsiːd, -z, -ɪŋ, -ɪd
AM ˌriˈsid, -z, -ɪŋ, -ɪd

receipt
BR rɪˈsiːt, -s, -ɪŋ, -ɪd
AM rəˈsi|t, riˈsi|t, -ts,
-dɪŋ, -dɪd

receivable
BR rɪˈsiːvəbl
AM rəˈsivəbəl,
riˈsivəbəl

receive
BR rɪˈsiːv, -z, -ɪŋ, -d
AM rəˈsiv, riˈsiv, -z, -ɪŋ,
-d

receiver
BR rɪˈsiːvə(r), -z
AM rəˈsivər, riˈsivər, -z

receivership
BR rɪˈsiːvəʃɪp, -s
AM rəˈsivərˌʃɪp,
riˈsivərˌʃɪp, -s

recency
BR ˈriːsnsi
AM ˈrisənsi

recension
BR rɪˈsɛnʃn, -z
AM rəˈsɛnʃən,
riˈsɛnʃən, -z

recent
BR ˈriːsnt
AM ˈrisənt

recently
BR ˈriːsntli
AM ˈrisn(t)li

recentness
BR ˈriːsntnəs
AM ˈrisn(t)nɪs

recep
BR ˈriːsɛp, -s
AM ˈriˌsɛp, -s

receptacle
BR rɪˈsɛptəkl, -z
AM rəˈsɛptəkəl,
riˈsɛptəkəl, -z

reception
BR rɪˈsɛpʃn, -z
AM rəˈsɛpʃən,
riˈsɛpʃən, -z

receptionist
BR rɪˈsɛpʃnɪst,
rɪˈsɛpʃənɪst, -s
AM rəˈsɛpʃənəst,
riˈsɛpʃənəst, -s

receptive
BR rɪˈsɛptɪv
AM rəˈsɛptɪv, riˈsɛptɪv

receptively
BR rɪˈsɛptɪvli
AM rəˈsɛptɪvli,
riˈsɛptɪvli

receptiveness
BR rɪˈsɛptɪvnɪs
AM rəˈsɛptɪvnɪs,
riˈsɛptɪvnɪs

receptivity
BR ˌriːsɛpˈtɪvɪti
AM ˌriˌsɛpˈtɪvɪdi

receptor
BR rɪˈsɛptə(r), -z
AM riˈsɛptər, -z

recess[1]
noun
BR rɪˈsɛs, ˈriːsɛs, -ɪz
AM ˈriˌsɛs, rəˈsɛs,
riˈsɛs, -əz

recess[2]
verb
BR rɪˈsɛs, -ɪz, -ɪŋ, -t
AM ˈriˌsɛs, rəˈsɛs,
riˈsɛs, -əz, -ɪŋ, -t

recession
BR rɪˈsɛʃn, -z
AM rəˈsɛʃən, riˈsɛʃən,
-z

recessional
BR rɪˈsɛʃŋ(ə)l,
rɪˈsɛʃən(ə)l, -z
AM rəˈsɛʃ(ə)nəl,
riˈsɛʃ(ə)nəl, -z

recessionary
BR rɪˈsɛʃŋ(ə)ri
AM rəˈsɛʃəˌnɛri,
riˈsɛʃəˌnɛri

recessive
BR rɪˈsɛsɪv
AM rəˈsɛsɪv, riˈsɛsɪv

recessively
BR rɪˈsɛsɪvli
AM rəˈsɛsɪvli,
riˈsɛsɪvli

recessiveness
BR rɪˈsɛsɪvnɪs
AM rəˈsɛsɪvnɪs,
riˈsɛsɪvnɪs

Rechabite
BR ˈrɛkəbʌɪt, -s
AM ˈrɛkəˌbaɪt, -s

recharge
BR ˌriːˈtʃɑːdʒ, -ɪz, -ɪŋ, -d
AM riˈtʃɑrdʒ, -əz, -ɪŋ, -d

rechargeable
BR ˌriːˈtʃɑːdʒəbl
AM riˈtʃɑrdʒəbəl

recharger
BR ˌriːˈtʃɑːdʒə(r), -z
AM riˈtʃɑrdʒər, -z

réchauffé
BR reɪˈʃəʊfeɪ, -z
AM ˌreɪˌʃoʊˈfeɪ, -z

recheck
BR ˌriːˈtʃɛk, -s, -ɪŋ, -t
AM riˈtʃɛk, -s, -ɪŋ, -t

recherché
BR rəˈʃɛːʃeɪ
AM rəˌʃɛrˈʃeɪ

rechristen
BR ˌkrɪs|n, -nz,
-ɳɪŋ \-(ə)nɪŋ, -nd
AM riˈkrɪsn, -z, -ɪŋ, -d

recidivism
BR rɪˈsɪdɪvɪz(ə)m
AM rəˈsɪdəˌvɪzəm,
riˈsɪdəˌvɪzəm

recidivist
BR rɪˈsɪdɪvɪst, -s
AM rəˈsɪdəvəst,
riˈsɪdəvəst, -s

recidivistic
BR rɪˌsɪdɪˈvɪstɪk
AM rəˌsɪdəˈvɪstɪk,
riˌsɪdəˈvɪstɪk

Recife
BR rɛˈsiːfeɪ
AM rɛˈsifeɪ
B PORT xeˈsifi
L PORT Rəˈsifə

recipe
BR ˈrɛsɪp|i, -ɪz
AM ˈrɛsəˌpi, -z

recipiency
BR rɪˈsɪpiənsi
AM rəˈsɪpiənsi,
riˈsɪpiənsi

recipient
BR rɪˈsɪpiənt, -s

AM rəˈsɪpɪənt,
riˈsɪpiənt, -s

reciprocal
BR rɪˈsɪprəkl, -z
AM rəˈsɪprəkəl,
riˈsɪprəkəl, -z

reciprocality
BR rɪˌsɪprəˈkalɪt|i, -ɪz
AM rə,sɪprəˈkælədi,
ri,sɪprəˈkælədi, -z

reciprocally
BR rɪˈsɪprəkļi,
rɪˈsɪprəkəli
AM rəˈsɪprək(ə)li,
riˈsɪprək(ə)li

reciprocalness
BR rɪˈsɪprəklnəs
AM rəˈsɪprəkəlnəs,
riˈsɪprəkəlnəs

reciprocate
BR rɪˈsɪprəkeɪt, -s, -ɪŋ,
-ɪd
AM rəˈsɪprə,keɪ|t,
riˈsɪprə,keɪ|t, -ts, -dɪŋ,
-dɪd

reciprocation
BR rɪˌsɪprəˈkeɪʃn
AM rə,sɪprəˈkeɪʃən,
ri,sɪprəˈkeɪʃən

reciprocator
BR rɪˈsɪprəkeɪtə(r), -z
AM rəˈsɪprə,keɪdər,
riˈsɪprə,keɪdər, -z

reciprocity
BR ,rɛsɪˈprɒsɪti
AM ,rɛsəˈprɑsədi

recirculate
BR ,riːˈsɜːkjʊleɪt, -s,
-ɪŋ, -ɪd
AM rəˈsɜːkjə,leɪ|t,
riˈsɜːkjə,leɪ|t, -ts,
-dɪŋ, -dɪd

recirculation
BR riː,səːkjʊˈleɪʃn, -z
AM rə,sɜːkjəˈleɪʃən,
ri,sɜːkjəˈleɪʃən, -z

recision
BR rɪˈsɪʒn, -z
AM riˈsɪʒən, rəˈsɪʒən, -z

recital
BR rɪˈsaɪtl, -z
AM rəˈsaɪdl, riˈsaɪdl, -z

recitalist
BR rɪˈsaɪtlɪst, -s
AM rəˈsaɪdļəst,
riˈsaɪdļəst, -s

recitation
BR ,rɛsɪˈteɪʃn, -z
AM ,rɛsəˈteɪʃən, -z

recitative
BR ,rɛsɪtəˈtiːv, -z
AM ,rɛsədəˈtiv, -z

recite
BR rɪˈsaɪt, -s, -ɪŋ, -ɪd
AM rəˈsaɪ|t, riˈsaɪ|t, -ts,
-dɪŋ, -dɪd

reciter
BR rɪˈsaɪtə(r), -z

AM rəˈsaɪdər,
riˈsaɪdər, -z

reck
BR rɛk, -s, -ɪŋ, -t
AM rɛk, -s, -ɪŋ, -t

reckless
BR ˈrɛkləs
AM ˈrɛkləs

recklessly
BR ˈrɛkləsli
AM ˈrɛkləsli

recklessness
BR ˈrɛkləsnəs
AM ˈrɛkləsnəs

reckon
BR ˈrɛk|(ə)n, -(ə)nz,
-(ə)nɪŋ \-ɪŋ, -(ə)nd
AM ˈrɛk|ən, -ənz,
-(ə)nɪŋ, -ənd

reckoner
BR ˈrɛk(ə)nə(r),
ˈrɛknə(r), -z
AM ˈrɛk(ə)nər, -z

reckoning
BR ˈrɛk(ə)nɪŋ, ˈrɛknɪŋ,
-z
AM ˈrɛk(ə)nɪŋ, -z

reclaim
BR rɪˈkleɪm, ,riːˈkleɪm,
-z, -ɪŋ, -d
AM rəˈkleɪm, riˈkleɪm,
-z, -ɪŋ, -d

reclaimable
BR rɪˈkleɪməbl,
,riːˈkleɪməbl
AM rəˈkleɪməbəl,
riˈkleɪməbəl

reclaimer
BR rɪˈkleɪmə(r),
,riːˈkleɪmə(r), -z
AM rəˈkleɪmər,
riˈkleɪmər, -z

reclamation
BR ,rɛkləˈmeɪʃn
AM ,rɛkləˈmeɪʃən

reclassification
BR riː,klasɪfɪˈkeɪʃn, -z
AM rə,klæsəfəˈkeɪʃən,
ri,klæsəfəˈkeɪʃən, -z

reclassify
BR ,riːˈklasɪfʌɪ, -z, -ɪŋ,
-d
AM rəˈklæsə,faɪ,
riˈklæsə,faɪ, -z, -ɪŋ, -d

reclinable
BR rɪˈklʌɪnəbl
AM rəˈklaɪnəbəl,
riˈklaɪnəbəl

reclinate
BR ˈrɛklɪneɪt
AM ˈrɛklə,neɪt,
ˈrɛklənət

recline
BR rɪˈklʌɪn, -z, -ɪŋ, -d
AM rəˈklaɪn, riˈklaɪn,
-z, -ɪŋ, -d

recliner
BR rɪˈklʌɪnə(r), -z

AM rəˈklaɪnər,
riˈklaɪnər, -z

reclosable
BR ,riːˈkləʊzəbl
AM riˈkloʊzəbəl

reclothe
BR ,riːˈkləʊð, -z, -ɪŋ, -d
AM ,riˈkloʊ|ð, -(ð)z,
-ðɪŋ, -ðd

recluse
BR rɪˈkluːs, -ɪz
AM ˈrɛ,klus, rəˈklus,
riˈklus, ˈrɛ,kluz,
rəˈkluz, riˈkluz, -əz

reclusion
BR rɪˈkluːʒn
AM rəˈkluʒən,
riˈkluʒən

reclusive
BR rɪˈkluːsɪv
AM rəˈklusɪv,
rəˈkluzɪv

reclusiveness
BR rɪˈkluːsɪvnɪs
AM rəˈklusɪvnɪs,
rəˈkluzɪvnɪs

recode
BR ,riːˈkəʊd, -z, -ɪŋ, -ɪd
AM ,riˈkoʊd, -z, -ɪŋ, -əd

recognisability
BR ,rɛkəg,nʌɪzəˈbɪlɪti
AM ,rɛkə(g),naɪzəˈbɪlɪdi

recognisable
BR ˈrɛkəgnʌɪzəbl,
,rɛkəgˈnʌɪzəbl
AM ,rɛkə(g)ˈnaɪzəbəl

recognisably
BR ˈrɛkəgnʌɪzəbli,
,rɛkəgˈnʌɪzəbli
AM ,rɛkə(g)ˈnaɪzəbli

recognisance
BR rɪˈkɒgnɪz(ə)ns, -ɪz
AM rəˈkɑgnəzəns,
riˈkɑgnəzəns, -əz

recognisant
BR rɪˈkɒgnɪz(ə)nt
AM rəˈkɑgnəznt,
riˈkɑgnəznt

recognise
BR ˈrɛkəgnʌɪz, -ɪz, -ɪŋ,
-d
AM ˈrɛkə(g),naɪz, -ɪz,
-ɪŋ, -d

recogniser
BR ˈrɛkəgnʌɪzə(r), -z
AM ˈrɛkə(g),naɪzər, -z

recognition
BR ,rɛkəgˈnɪʃn
AM ,rɛkəgˈnɪʃən

recognitory
BR rɪˈkɒgnɪt(ə)ri
AM rəˈkɑgnə,tori,
riˈkɑgnə,tori

recognizability
BR ,rɛkəg,nʌɪzəˈbɪlɪti
AM ,rɛkə(g),naɪzəˈbɪlɪdi

recognizable
BR ˈrɛkəgnʌɪzəbl,
,rɛkəgˈnʌɪzəbl
AM ,rɛkə(g)ˈnaɪzəbəl

recognizably
BR ˈrɛkəgnʌɪzəbli,
,rɛkəgˈnʌɪzəbli
AM ,rɛkə(g)ˈnaɪzəbli

recognizance
BR rɪˈkɒgnɪz(ə)ns, -ɪz
AM rəˈkɑgnəzəns,
riˈkɑgnəzns, -əz

recognizant
BR rɪˈkɒgnɪz(ə)nt
AM rəˈkɑgnəznt,
riˈkɑgnəznt

recognize
BR ˈrɛkəgnʌɪz, -ɪz, -ɪŋ,
-d
AM ˈrɛkə(g),naɪz, -ɪz,
-ɪŋ, -d

recognizer
BR ˈrɛkəgnʌɪzə(r), -z
AM ˈrɛkə(g),naɪzər, -z

recoil¹
noun
BR ˈriːkɔɪl, -z
AM ˈri,kɔɪl, -z

recoil²
verb
BR rɪˈkɔɪl, -z, -ɪŋ, -d
AM rəˈkɔɪl, riˈkɔɪl, -z,
-ɪŋ, -d

recoilless
BR ˈkɔɪlɪs, ˈriːkɔɪlɪs
AM rəˈkɔɪlɪs, riˈkɔɪlɪs

recoin
BR ,riːˈkɔɪn, -z, -ɪŋ, -d
AM ,riˈkɔɪn, -z, -ɪŋ, -d

recollect¹
collect again
BR ,riːkəˈlɛkt, -s, -ɪŋ, -ɪd
AM ˈrikəˈlɛk|(t), -(t)s,
-tɪŋ, -təd

recollect²
remember
BR ,rɛkəˈlɛkt, -s, -ɪŋ, -ɪd
AM ,rɛkəˈlɛk|(t), -(t)s,
-tɪŋ, -təd

recollection
BR ,rɛkəˈlɛkʃn, -z
AM ,rɛkəˈlɛkʃən, -z

recollective
BR ,rɛkəˈlɛktɪv
AM ,rɛkəˈlɛktɪv

recolonisation
BR (,)riːˌkɒlənʌɪˈzeɪʃn,
-z
AM ri,kɑlənəˈzeɪʃən,
ri,kɑlə,naɪˈzeɪʃən, -z

recolonise
BR (,)riːˈkɒlənʌɪz, -ɪz,
-ɪŋ, -d
AM ˈriˈkɑlə,naɪz, -ɪz,
-ɪŋ, -d

recolonization
BR (,)riːˌkɒlənʌɪˈzeɪʃn,
-z

AM ri,kɑlənə'zeɪʃən, ri,kɑlə,naɪ'zeɪʃən, -z

recolonize
BR (,)ri:'kɒlənʌɪz, -ɪz, -ɪŋ, -d
AM 'ri:'kɑlə,naɪz, -ɪz, -ɪŋ, -d

recolor
BR ri:'kʌlə(r), -z, -ɪŋ, -d
AM 'ri:'kələr, -z, -ɪŋ, -d

recolour
BR ,ri:'kʌlə(r), -z, -ɪŋ, -d
AM 'ri:'kələr, -z, -ɪŋ, -d

recombinant
BR (,)ri:'kɒmbɪnənt, rɪ'kɒmbɪnənt, -s
AM ri'kɑmbənənt, -s

recombination
BR ,ri:kɒmbɪ'neɪʃn, -z
AM ,ri,kəmbə'neɪʃən, -z

recombine
BR ,ri:kəm'bʌɪn, -z, -ɪŋ, -d
AM ,rikəm'baɪn, -z, -ɪŋ, -d

recommence
BR ,ri:kə'mens, ,rekə'mens, -ɪz, -ɪŋ, -t
AM ,rikə'mens, -əz, -ɪŋ, -t

recommencement
BR ,ri:kə'mensm(ə)nt, ,rekə'mensm(ə)nt, -s
AM ,rikə'mensmənt, -s

recommend
BR ,rekə'mend, -z, -ɪŋ, -ɪd
AM ,rekə'mend, -z, -ɪŋ, -əd

recommendable
BR ,rekə'mendəbl
AM ,rekə'mendəbəl

recommendation
BR ,rekəmen'deɪʃn, ,rekə(m)n'deɪʃn, -z
AM ,rekəmən'deɪʃən, ,rekə,men'deɪʃən, -z

recommendatory
BR ,rekə'mendət(ə)ri
AM ,rekə'mendə,tori

recommender
BR ,rekə'mendə(r), -z
AM ,rekə'mendər, -z

recommission
BR ,ri:kə'mɪʃ|n, -nz, -nɪŋ \-nɪŋ, -nd
AM 'rikə'mɪʃən, -z, -ɪŋ, -d

recommit
BR ,ri:kə'mɪt, -s, -ɪŋ, -ɪd
AM 'rikə'mɪ|t, -ts, -dɪŋ, -dɪd

recommitment
BR ,ri:kə'mɪtm(ə)nt, -s
AM 'rikə'mɪtmənt, -s

recommittal
BR ,ri:kə'mɪtl, -z

recompense
BR 'rekəmpens, -ɪz, -ɪŋ, -t
AM 'rɛkəm,pɛns, -əz, -ɪŋ, -t

recompose
BR ,ri:kəm'pəʊz, -ɪz, -ɪŋ, -d
AM 'rikəm'poʊz, -əz, -ɪŋ, -d

reconcilability
BR ,rek(ə)n,sʌɪlə'bɪlɪti
AM ,rɛkən,saɪlə'bɪlɪdi

reconcilable
BR 'rek(ə)nsʌɪləbl, ,rɛk(ə)n'sʌɪləbl
AM 'rɛkən'saɪləbəl

reconcilably
BR 'rek(ə)nsʌɪləbli, ,rɛk(ə)n'sʌɪləbli
AM 'rɛkən'saɪləbli

reconcile
BR 'rek(ə)nsʌɪl, -z, -ɪŋ, -d
AM 'rɛkən,saɪl, -z, -ɪŋ, -d

reconcilement
BR 'rek(ə)nsʌɪlm(ə)nt, -s
AM 'rɛkən,saɪlmənt, -s

reconciler
BR 'rek(ə)nsʌɪlə(r), -z
AM 'rɛkən,saɪlər, -z

reconciliation
BR ,rek(ə)nsɪlɪ'eɪʃn, -z
AM ,rɛkən,sɪli'eɪʃən, -z

reconciliatory
BR ,rek(ə)n'sɪliət(ə)ri
AM ,rɛkən'sɪliə,tori

recondite
BR 'rek(ə)ndʌɪt, rɪ'kɒndʌɪt
AM 'rɛkən,daɪt, rə'kan,daɪt, rɪ'kan,daɪt

reconditely
BR 'rek(ə)ndʌɪtli, rɪ'kɒndʌɪtli
AM 'rɛkən,daɪtli, rə'kan,daɪtli, rɪ'kan,daɪtli

reconditeness
BR 'rek(ə)ndʌɪtnɪs, rɪ'kɒndʌɪtnɪs
AM 'rɛkən,daɪtnɪs, rə'kan,daɪtnɪs, rɪ'kan,daɪtnɪs

recondition
BR ,ri:kən'dɪʃ|n, -nz, -nɪŋ \-nɪŋ, -nd
AM 'rikən'dɪʃ|ən, -ənz, -(ə)nɪŋ, -ənd

reconditioner
BR ,ri:kən'dɪʃ ə(r), ,ri:kən'dɪʃ(ə)nə(r), -z
AM 'rikən'dɪʃ(ə)nər, -z

reconduct
BR ,ri:kən'dʌkt, -s, -ɪŋ, -ɪd
AM 'rikən'dək|(t), -(t)s, -tɪŋ, -təd

reconfiguration
BR ,ri:kən,fɪgə'reɪʃn, ,ri:kən,fɪgjʊ'reɪʃn, -z
AM 'rikən,fɪg(j)ə'reɪʃən, -z

reconfigure
BR ,ri:kən'fɪgə(r), -z, -ɪŋ, -d
AM 'rikən'fɪgjər, -z, -ɪŋ, -d

reconfirm
BR ,ri:kən'fə:m, -z, -ɪŋ, -d
AM ,rikən'fərm, -z, -ɪŋ, -d

reconfirmation
BR ,ri:kɒnfə'meɪʃn, -z
AM ,ri,kanfər'meɪʃən, -z

reconnaissance
BR rɪ'kɒnɪs(ə)ns, -ɪz
AM rɪ'kanəsəns, rə'kanəsəns, -ɪz

reconnect
BR ,ri:kə'nekt, -s, -ɪŋ, -ɪd
AM 'rikə'nek|(t), -(t)s, -tɪŋ, -təd

reconnection
BR ,ri:kə'nekʃn, -z
AM 'rikə'nekʃən, -z

reconnoiter
BR ,rekə'nɔɪt|ə(r), -əz, -(ə)rɪŋ, -əd
AM ,rekə'nɔɪ|dər, ,rikə'nɔɪ|dər, -dərz, -dərɪŋ \-trɪŋ, -dərd

reconnoitre
BR ,ri:kə'nɔɪt|ə(r), -əz, -(ə)rɪŋ, -əd
AM ,rekə'nɔɪ|dər, ,rikə'nɔɪ|dər, -dərz, -dərɪŋ \-trɪŋ, -dərd

reconquer
BR ,ri:'kɒŋk|ə(r), -əz, -(ə)rɪŋ, -əd
AM rɪ'kaŋk|ər, -ərz, -(ə)rɪŋ, -ərd

reconquest
BR ,ri:'kɒŋkwest, -s
AM rɪ'kaŋkwest, -s

reconsecrate
BR ,ri:'kɒnsɪkreɪt, -s, -ɪŋ, -ɪd
AM ,rɪ'kansɛ,kreɪ|t, -ts, -dɪŋ, -dɪd

reconsecration
BR ,ri:kɒnsɪ'kreɪʃn
AM ,ri,kansə'kreɪʃən

reconsider
BR ,ri:kən'sɪd|ə(r), -əz, -(ə)rɪŋ, -əd

AM 'rikən'sɪdər, -z, -ɪŋ, -d

reconsideration
BR ,ri:kən,sɪdə'reɪʃn
AM 'rikən,sɪdə'reɪʃən

reconsign
BR ,ri:kən'sʌɪn, -z, -ɪŋ, -d
AM 'rikən'saɪn, -z, -ɪŋ, -d

reconsignment
BR ,ri:kən'sʌɪnm(ə)nt, -s
AM 'rikən'saɪnmənt, -s

reconsolidate
BR ,ri:kən'sɒlɪdeɪt, -s, -ɪŋ, -ɪd
AM 'rikən'salə,deɪ|t, -ts, -dɪŋ, -dɪd

reconsolidation
BR ,ri:kən,sɒlɪ'deɪʃn, -z
AM 'rikən,salə'deɪʃən, -z

reconstitute
BR ,ri:'kɒnstɪtjuːt, ,ri:'kɒnstɪtʃuːt, -s, -ɪŋ, -ɪd
AM rɪ'kanstə,t(j)u|t, -ts, -dɪŋ, -dəd

reconstitution
BR ,ri:kɒnstɪ'tjuːʃn, ,ri:kɒnstɪ'tʃuːʃn
AM ,ri,kanstə't(j)uʃən

reconstruct
BR ,ri:kən'strʌkt, -s, -ɪŋ, -ɪd
AM 'rikən'strək|(t), -(t)s, -tɪŋ, -təd

reconstructable
BR ,ri:kən'strʌktəbl
AM 'rikən'strʌktəbəl

reconstruction
BR ,ri:kən'strʌkʃn, -z
AM 'rikən'strʌkʃən, -z

reconstructive
BR ,ri:kən'strʌktɪv
AM 'rikən'strʌktɪv

reconstructor
BR ,ri:kən'strʌktə(r), -z
AM 'rikən'strʌktər, -z

reconvene
BR ,ri:kən'viːn, -z, -ɪŋ, -d
AM 'rikən'vin, -z, -ɪŋ, -d

reconversion
BR ,ri:kən'vəːʃn, -z
AM 'rikən'vərʒən, -z

reconvert
BR ,ri:kən'vəːt, -s, -ɪŋ, -ɪd
AM 'rikən'vər|t, -ts, -dɪŋ, -dəd

record¹
noun
BR 'rekɔːd, -z
AM 'rɛkərd, -z

record²
verb
BR rɪˈkɔːd, -z, -ɪŋ, -ɪd
AM rəˈkɔː(ə)rd,
riˈkɔ(ə)rd, -z, -ɪŋ, -əd

recordable
BR rɪˈkɔːdəbl
AM rəˈkɔrdəbəl,
riˈkɔrdəbəl

recorder
BR rɪˈkɔːdə(r), -z
AM rəˈkɔrdər,
riˈkɔrdər, -z

recordership
BR rɪˈkɔːdəʃɪp, -s
AM rəˈkɔrdərˌʃɪp,
riˈkɔrdərˌʃɪp, -s

recording
BR rɪˈkɔːdɪŋ, -z
AM rəˈkɔrdɪŋ,
riˈkɔrdɪŋ, -z

recordist
BR rɪˈkɔːdɪst, -s
AM rəˈkɔrdəst,
riˈkɔrdəst, -s

record-player
BR ˈrɛkɔːdˌpleɪə(r), -z
AM ˈrɛkərdˌpleɪər, -z

recount¹
noun
BR ˈriːkaʊnt, -s
AM ˈriːkaʊnt, -s

recount²
verb, count again
BR ˌriːˈkaʊnt, -s, -ɪŋ, -ɪd
AM ˌriːˈkaʊnt,
rəˈkaʊnt, -ts, -(t)ɪŋ,
-(t)əd

recount³
verb, tell
BR rɪˈkaʊnt, -s, -ɪŋ, -ɪd
AM rɪˈkaʊnt,
rəˈkaʊnt, -ts, -(t)ɪŋ,
-(t)əd

recoup
BR rɪˈkuːp, -s, -ɪŋ, -t
AM rɪˈkup, rəˈkup, -s,
-ɪŋ, -t

recoupable
BR rɪˈkuːpəbl
AM rɪˈkupəbəl,
rəˈkupəbəl

recoupment
BR rɪˈkuːpm(ə)nt, -s
AM rɪˈkupmənt,
rəˈkupmənt, -s

recourse
BR rɪˈkɔːs
AM ˈriˌkɔ(ə)rs,
riˈkɔ(ə)rs

recover¹
cover again
BR ˌriːˈkʌvə(r), -əz,
-(ə)rɪŋ, -əd
AM riˈkəvər, -ərz,
-(ə)rɪŋ, -ərd

recover²
regain
BR rɪˈkʌvə(r), -əz,
-(ə)rɪŋ, -əd
AM rəˈkəvər,
riˈkəvər, -ərz, -(ə)rɪŋ,
-ərd

recoverability
BR rɪˌkʌv(ə)rəˈbɪltɪ|i,
-ɪz
AM ˌriˌkəv(ə)rəˈbɪlɪdi,
-z

recoverable
BR rɪˈkʌv(ə)rəbl
AM rəˈkəv(ə)rəbəl,
riˈkəv(ə)rəbəl

recoverer
BR rɪˈkʌv(ə)rə(r), -z
AM rəˈkəv(ə)rər,
riˈkəv(ə)rər, -z

recovery
BR rɪˈkʌv(ə)r|i, -ɪz
AM rəˈkəv(ə)ri,
riˈkəv(ə)ri, -z

recreancy
BR ˈrɛkrɪənsi
AM ˈrɛkrɪənsi

recreant
BR ˈrɛkrɪənt, -s
AM ˈrɛkrɪənt, -s

recreantly
BR ˈrɛkrɪəntli
AM ˈrɛkriən(t)li

recreate¹
create again
BR ˌriːkrɪˈeɪt, -s, -ɪŋ, -ɪd
AM ˌrikriˈeɪ|t, -ts, -dɪŋ,
-dɪd

recreate²
refresh, enliven
BR ˈrɛkrɪeɪt, -s, -ɪŋ, -ɪd
AM ˈrɛkriˌeɪ|t, -ts, -dɪŋ,
-dɪd

recreation¹
creating again
BR ˌriːkrɪˈeɪʃn, -z
AM ˌrikriˈeɪʃən, -z

recreation²
exercise, refreshment
BR ˌrɛkrɪˈeɪʃn, -z
AM ˌrɛkriˈeɪʃən, -z

recreational
BR ˌrɛkrɪˈeɪʃn(ə)l,
ˌrɛkrɪˈeɪʃən(ə)l
AM ˌrɛkriˈeɪʃ(ə)nəl

recreationally
BR ˌrɛkrɪˈeɪʃn̩li,
ˌrɛkrɪˈeɪʃn̩li,
ˌrɛkrɪˈeɪʃənli,
ˌrɛkrɪˈeɪʃ(ə)nəli
AM ˌrɛkriˈeɪʃ(ə)nəli

recreative
BR ˈrɛkrɪeɪtɪv,
ˈrɛkrɪətɪv
AM ˈrɛkriˈeɪdɪv

recriminate
BR rɪˈkrɪmɪneɪt, -s, -ɪŋ,
-ɪd

AM rəˈkrɪmə̩neɪ|t,
riˈkrɪmə̩neɪ|t, -ts,
-dɪŋ, -dɪd

recrimination
BR rɪˌkrɪmɪˈneɪʃn, -z
AM rəˌkrɪmɪˈneɪʃən,
riˌkrɪmɪˈneɪʃən, -z

recriminative
BR rɪˈkrɪmɪnətɪv
AM rɪˈkrɪmənədɪv,
riˈkrɪmənədɪv,
rəˈkrɪmə̩neɪdɪv,
riˈkrɪmə̩neɪdɪv

recriminatory
BR rɪˈkrɪmɪnət(ə)ri
AM rəˈkrɪmənəˌtɔri,
riˈkrɪmənəˌtɔri

recross
BR ˌriːˈkrɒs, -ɪz, -ɪŋ, -t
AM ˌriˈkrɔs, ˌriˈkrɑs,
-əz, -ɪŋ, -t

recrudesce
BR ˌriːkruːˈdɛs,
ˌrɛkruːˈdɛs, -ɪz, -ɪŋ, -t
AM ˌrikruˈdɛs, -ɪz, -ɪŋ, -t

recrudescence
BR ˌriːkruːˈdɛsns,
ˌrɛkruːˈdɛsns
AM ˌrikruˈdɛsəns

recrudescent
BR ˌriːkruːˈdɛsnt,
ˌrɛkruːˈdɛsnt
AM ˌrikruˈdɛsənt

recruit
BR rɪˈkruːt, -s, -ɪŋ, -ɪd
AM rəˈkru|t, riˈkru|t,
-ts, -dɪŋ, -dəd

recruitable
BR rɪˈkruːtəbl
AM rəˈkrudəbəl,
riˈkrudəbəl

recruital
BR rɪˈkruːtl, -z
AM rəˈkrudl, riˈkrudl,
-z

recruiter
BR rɪˈkruːtə(r), -z
AM rəˈkrudər,
riˈkrudər, -z

recruitment
BR rɪˈkruːtm(ə)nt
AM rəˈkrutmənt,
riˈkrutmənt

recrystallisation
BR ˌriːˌkrɪstl̩ʌɪˈzeɪʃn,
ˌriːˌkrɪstəlʌɪˈzeɪʃn
AM ˌriˌkrɪstələˈzeɪʃən,
ˌriˌkrɪstə̩laɪˈzeɪʃən

recrystallise
BR ˌriːˈkrɪstl̩ʌɪz,
ˌriːˈkrɪstəlʌɪz, -ɪz, -ɪŋ,
-d
AM ˌriˈkrɪstə̩laɪz, -ɪz,
-ɪŋ, -d

recrystallization
BR ˌriːˌkrɪstl̩ʌɪˈzeɪʃn,
ˌriːˌkrɪstəlʌɪˈzeɪʃn, -z

recrystallisation
AM rəˈkrɪmə̩neɪ|t,
riˈkrɪmə̩neɪ|t, -ts,
-dɪŋ, -dɪd

recrystallization
BR ˌriːˌkrɪstələˈzeɪʃən,
ˌriˌkrɪstə̩laɪˈzeɪʃən,
-z

recrystallize
BR ˌriːˈkrɪstl̩ʌɪz,
ˌriːˈkrɪstəlʌɪz, -ɪz, -ɪŋ,
-d
AM ˌriˈkrɪstə̩laɪz, -ɪz,
-ɪŋ, -d

recta
BR ˈrɛktə(r)
AM ˈrɛktə

rectal
BR ˈrɛktl
AM ˈrɛkt(ə)l

rectally
BR ˈrɛktli, ˈrɛktəli
AM ˈrɛkt(ə)li

rectangle
BR ˈrɛktaŋgl
AM ˈrɛkˌtæŋgəl

rectangular
BR rɛkˈtaŋgjələ(r)
AM rɛkˈtæŋgjələr

rectangularity
BR rɛkˌtaŋgjʊˈlarɪti
AM rɛkˌtæŋgjəˈlɛrədi

rectangularly
BR rɛkˈtaŋgjʊləli
AM rɛkˈtæŋgjələrli

recti
BR ˈrɛktʌɪ
AM ˈrɛkˌtaɪ

rectifiable
BR ˈrɛktɪfʌɪəbl
AM ˈrɛktəˌfaɪəbəl

rectification
BR ˌrɛktɪfɪˈkeɪʃn, -z
AM ˌrɛktəfəˈkeɪʃən, -z

rectifier
BR ˈrɛktɪfʌɪə(r), -z
AM ˈrɛktəˌfaɪər, -z

rectify
BR ˈrɛktɪfʌɪ, -z, -ɪŋ, -d
AM ˈrɛktəˌfaɪ, -z, -ɪŋ, -d

rectilineal
BR ˌrɛktɪˈlɪnɪəl
AM ˌrɛktəˈlɪniəl

rectilinear
BR ˌrɛktɪˈlɪnɪə(r)
AM ˌrɛktəˈlɪniər

rectilinearity
BR ˌrɛktɪˌlɪnɪˈarɪti
AM ˌrɛktəˌlɪniˈɛrədi

rectilinearly
BR ˌrɛktɪˈlɪnɪəli
AM ˌrɛktəˈlɪniərli

rectitude
BR ˈrɛktɪtjuːd,
ˈrɛktɪtʃuːd
AM ˈrɛktəˌt(j)ud

recto
BR ˈrɛktəʊ
AM ˈrɛktoʊ

rector
BR ˈrɛktə(r), -z
AM ˈrɛktər, -z

rectoral
BR ˈrɛkt(ə)rəl,
ˈrɛkt(ə)rl
AM ˈrɛkt(ə)rəl

rectorate
BR ˈrɛkt(ə)rət, -s
AM ˈrɛkt(ə)rət, -s

rectorial
BR rɛkˈtɔːrɪəl
AM rɛkˈtorɪəl

rectorship
BR ˈrɛktəʃɪp, -s
AM ˈrɛktər‚ʃɪp, -s

rectory
BR ˈrɛkt(ə)r|i, -ɪz
AM ˈrɛkt(ə)ri, -z

rectrices
BR ˈrɛktrɪsiːz
AM ˈrɛk‚trə‚siz

rectrix
BR ˈrɛktrɪks, -ɪz
AM ˈrɛk‚trɪks, -ɪz

rectum
BR ˈrɛktəm, -z
AM ˈrɛktəm, -z

rectus
BR ˈrɛktəs
AM ˈrɛktəs

recumbence
BR rɪˈkʌmb(ə)ns
AM rəˈkʌmbəns,
rɪˈkʌmbəns

recumbency
BR rɪˈkʌmb(ə)nsi
AM rəˈkʌmbənsi,
rɪˈkʌmbənsi

recumbent
BR rɪˈkʌmb(ə)nt
AM rəˈkʌmbənt,
rɪˈkʌmbənt

recumbently
BR rɪˈkʌmb(ə)ntli
AM rəˈkʌmbən(t)li,
rɪˈkʌmbən(t)li

recuperable
BR rɪˈk(j)uːp(ə)rəbl
AM rəˈkupərəbəl,
rɪˈkupərəbəl

recuperate
BR rɪˈk(j)uːpəreɪt, -s,
-ɪŋ, -ɪd
AM rəˈkupə‚reɪt,
rɪˈkupə‚reɪt, -ts, -dɪŋ,
-dɪd

recuperation
BR rɪˌk(j)uːpəˈreɪʃn
AM rəˌkupəˈreɪʃən,
rɪˌkupəˈreɪʃən

recuperative
BR rɪˈk(j)uːp(ə)rətɪv
AM rəˈkupə‚reɪdɪv,
rɪˈkupə‚reɪdɪv,
rəˈkup(ə)rədɪv,
rɪˈkup(ə)rədɪv

recuperator
BR rɪˈk(j)uːpəreɪtə(r),
-z

recur
BR rɪˈkəː(r), -z, -ɪŋ, -d
AM rəˈkər, rɪˈkər, -z,
-ɪŋ, -d

recurrence
BR rɪˈkʌrəns, rɪˈkʌrn̩s,
-ɪz
AM rəˈkərəns,
rɪˈkərəns, -əz

recurrent
BR rɪˈkʌrənt, rɪˈkʌrn̩t
AM rəˈkərənt,
rɪˈkərənt

recurrently
BR rɪˈkʌrəntli,
rɪˈkʌrn̩tli
AM rəˈkərən(t)li,
rɪˈkərən(t)li

recursion
BR rɪˈkəːʃn, rɪˈkəːʒn, -z
AM rəˈkərʒən, -z

recursive
BR rɪˈkəːsɪv, -z
AM rəˈkərsɪv,
rɪˈkərsɪv, -z

recursively
BR rɪˈkəːsɪvli
AM rəˈkərsɪvli,
rɪˈkərsɪvli

recurvate
BR rɪˈkəːveɪt
AM rəˈkər‚veɪt,
rɪˈkər‚veɪt, rəˈkərvət,
rɪˈkərvət

recurvature
BR rɪˈkəːvətʃə(r), -z
AM rɪˈkərvətʃər,
rɪˈkərvətʃʊ(ə)r, -z

recurve
BR ‚riːˈkəːv, -z, -ɪŋ, -d
AM rəˈkərv, rɪˈkərv, -z,
-ɪŋ, -d

recusance
BR ˈrɛkjʊz(ə)ns
AM rəˈkjuzns

recusancy
BR ˈrɛkjʊz(ə)nsi
AM rəˈkjuznsi

recusant
BR ˈrɛkjʊz(ə)nt, -s
AM rəˈkjuznt, -s

recyclable
BR ‚riːˈsaɪkləbl
AM riˈsaɪkləbəl

recycle
BR ‚riːˈsʌɪk|l, -lz, -lɪŋ,
-ld
AM riˈsaɪk|əl, -əlz,
-(ə)lɪŋ, -əld

recycler
BR ‚riːˈsʌɪklə(r), -z
AM riˈsaɪklər, -z

red
BR rɛd, -z, -ə(r), -ɪst
AM rɛd, -z, -ər, -əst

redact
BR rɪˈdakt, -s, -ɪŋ, -ɪd
AM rəˈdækl(t),
rɪˈdækl(t), -(t)s, -tɪŋ,
-təd

redaction
BR rɪˈdakʃn, -z
AM rəˈdækʃən,
rɪˈdækʃən, -z

redactional
BR rɪˈdakʃn(ə)l,
rɪˈdakʃən(ə)l
AM rəˈdækʃ(ə)nəl,
rɪˈdækʃ(ə)nəl

redactor
BR rɪˈdaktə(r), -z
AM rəˈdæktər,
rɪˈdæktər, -z

redan
BR rɪˈdan, -z
AM rəˈdæn, -z

redback
BR ˈrɛdbak, -s
AM ˈrɛd‚bæk, -s

red bark
BR ‚rɛd ˈbɑːk
AM ‚rɛd ˈbark

red-blooded
BR ‚rɛd ˈblʌdɪd
AM ˈrɛd‚blədəd

red-bloodedness
BR ‚rɛd ˈblʌdɪdnɪs
AM ˈrɛd‚blədədnəs

redbreast
BR ˈrɛdbrɛst, -s
AM ˈrɛd‚brɛst, -s

redbrick
adjective
BR ˈrɛdbrɪk, ‚rɛdˈbrɪk
AM ˈrɛd‚brɪk

Redbridge
BR ˈrɛdbrɪdʒ
AM ˈrɛd‚brɪdʒ

redbud
BR ˈrɛdbʌd, -z
AM ˈrɛd‚bəd, -z

redcap
BR ˈrɛdkap, -s
AM ˈrɛd‚kæp, -s

Redcar
BR ˈrɛdkə(r),
ˈrɛdkɑː(r)
AM ˈrɛdkər, ˈrɛd‚kɑr

redcoat
BR ˈrɛdkəʊt, -s
AM ˈrɛd‚koʊt, -s

redcurrant
BR ‚rɛd ˈkʌrənt,
‚rɛdˈkʌrn̩t, -s
AM ˈrɛd‚kərənt, -s

redd
BR rɛd, -z, -ɪŋ, -ɪd
AM rɛd, -z, -ɪŋ, -əd

Reddaway
BR ˈrɛdəweɪ
AM ˈrɛdə‚weɪ

redden
BR ˈrɛd|n, -nz,
-nɪŋ\-nɪŋ, -nd
AM rɛdən, -z, -ɪŋ, -d

reddish
BR ˈrɛdɪʃ
AM ˈrɛdɪʃ

reddishness
BR ˈrɛdɪʃnɪs
AM ˈrɛdɪʃnɪs

Redditch
BR ˈrɛdɪtʃ
AM ˈrɛdɪtʃ

reddle
BR ˈrɛdl
AM ˈrɛdəl

red-dog
BR ˈrɛddɒg
AM ˈrɛd‚dɔg, ˈrɛd‚dɑg

reddy
BR ˈrɛdi
AM ˈrɛdi

rede
BR riːd, -z, -ɪŋ, -ɪd
AM rid, -z, -ɪŋ, -ɪd

redecorate
BR (‚)riːˈdɛkəreɪt, -s,
-ɪŋ, -ɪd
AM riˈdɛkə‚reɪ|t, -ts,
-dɪŋ, -dɪd

redecoration
BR ‚riːdɛkəˈreɪʃn,
riːˌdɛkəˈreɪʃn
AM ‚ridɛkəˈreɪʃən

rededicate
BR (‚)riːˈdɛdɪkeɪt, -s,
-ɪŋ, -ɪd
AM ‚riˈdɛdə‚keɪ|t, -ts,
-dɪŋ, -dɪd

rededication
BR ‚riːdɛdɪˈkeɪʃn,
riːˌdɛdɪˈkeɪʃn
AM ‚ridɛdəˈkeɪʃən

redeem
BR rɪˈdiːm, -z, -ɪŋ, -d
AM rəˈdim, rɪˈdim, -z,
-ɪŋ, -d

redeemable
BR rɪˈdiːməbl
AM rəˈdiməbəl,
rɪˈdiməbəl

redeemer
BR rɪˈdiːmə(r), -z
AM rəˈdimər, rɪˈdimər,
-z

redefine
BR ‚riːdɪˈfʌɪn, -z, -ɪŋ, -d
AM ‚ridəˈfaɪn, -z, -ɪŋ, -d

redefinition
BR ‚riːdɛfɪˈnɪʃn, -z
AM ‚ridɛfəˈnɪʃən, -z

redemption
BR rɪˈdɛm(p)ʃn, -z
AM rəˈdɛm(p)ʃən,
rɪˈdɛm(p)ʃən, -z

redemptive
BR rɪˈdɛm(p)tɪv

Redemptorist (continued)
AM rəˈdɛm(p)tɪv,
riˈdɛm(p)tɪv
Redemptorist
BR rɪˈdɛm(p)t(ə)rɪst,
-s
AM rəˈdɛm(p)tərəst,
riˈdɛm(p)tərəst, -s
redeploy
BR ˌriːdɪˈplɔɪ, -z, -ɪŋ, -d
AM ˌridəˈplɔɪ, -z, -ɪŋ, -d
redeployment
BR ˌriːdɪˈplɔɪm(ə)nt, -s
AM ˌridəˈplɔɪmənt, -s
redescend
BR ˌriːdɪˈsɛnd, -z, -ɪŋ,
-ɪd
AM ˌridəˈsɛnd, -z, -ɪŋ,
-əd
Redesdale
BR ˈriːdzdeɪl
AM ˈridzˌdeɪl
redesign
BR ˌriːdɪˈzaɪn, -z, -ɪŋ, -d
AM ˌridəˈzaɪn, -z, -ɪŋ, -d
redesignate
BR ˌriːˈdɛzɪgneɪt, -s, -ɪŋ,
-ɪd
AM ˌriˈdɛzəgˌneɪt, -ts,
-dɪŋ, -dɪd
redesignation
BR ˌriːˌdɛzɪgˈneɪʃn
AM ˌriˌdɛzəgˈneɪʃən
redetermination
BR ˌriːdɪˌtəːmɪˈneɪʃn,
-z
AM ˌridəˌtərməˈneɪʃən,
-z
redetermine
BR ˌriːdɪˈtəːmɪn, -z, -ɪŋ,
-d
AM ˌridəˈtərmən, -z,
-ɪŋ, -d
redevelop
BR ˌriːdɪˈvɛləp, -s, -ɪŋ, -t
AM ˌridəˈvɛləp, -s, -ɪŋ, -t
redeveloper
BR ˌriːdɪˈvɛləpə(r), -z
AM ˌridəˈvɛləpər, -z
redevelopment
BR ˌriːdɪˈvɛləpm(ə)nt,
-s
AM ˌridəˈvɛləpmənt, -s
red-eye
BR ˈrɛdaɪ
AM ˈrɛdˌaɪ
red-faced
BR ˌrɛdˈfeɪst
AM ˈrɛdˈfeɪst
Redfearn
BR ˈrɛdfəːn
AM ˈrɛdˌfərn
Redfern
BR ˈrɛdfəːn
AM ˈrɛdˌfərn
redfish
BR ˈrɛdfɪʃ, -ɪz
AM ˈrɛdˌfɪʃ, -ɪz

Redford
BR ˈrɛdfəd
AM ˈrɛdfərd
Redgrave
BR ˈrɛdgreɪv
AM ˈrɛdˌgreɪv
redhanded
BR ˌrɛdˈhandɪd
AM ˈrɛdˈhændəd
redhead
BR ˈrɛdhɛd, -z
AM ˈrɛdˌ(h)ɛd, -z
Redhill
BR ˈrɛdhɪl
AM ˈrɛdˌ(h)ɪl
redial
BR ˌriːˈdaɪ(ə)l, -z, -ɪŋ, -d
AM ˈriˌdaɪəl, -z, -ɪŋ, -d
redid
BR ˌriːˈdɪd
AM riˈdɪd
rediffuse
BR ˌriːdɪˈfjuːz, -ɪz, -ɪŋ,
-d
AM ˌridəˈfjuz, -əz, -ɪŋ, -d
rediffusion
BR ˌriːdɪˈfjuːʒn
AM ˌridəˈfjuʒən
redingote
BR ˈrɛdɪŋgəʊt, -s
AM ˈrɛdɪŋˌgoʊt, -s
redintegrate
BR rɪˈdɪntɪgreɪt, -s, -ɪŋ,
-ɪd
AM rəˈdɪn(t)əˌgreɪt,
riˈdɪn(t)əˌgreɪt, -ts,
-dɪŋ, -dɪd
redintegration
BR rɪˌdɪntɪˈgreɪʃn, -z
AM rəˌdɪn(t)əˈgreɪʃən,
riˌdɪn(t)əˈgreɪʃən, -z
redintegrative
BR rɪˈdɪntɪˌgreɪtɪv
AM rəˈdɪn(t)əˌgreɪdɪv,
riˈdɪn(t)əˌgreɪdɪv
redirect
BR ˌriːdɪˈrɛkt,
ˌriːdaɪˈrɛkt, -s, -ɪŋ, -ɪd
AM ˌridəˈrɛk|(t),
ˈriˌdaɪˈrɛk|(t), -(t)s,
-tɪŋ, -təd
redirection
BR ˌriːdɪˈrɛkʃn,
ˌriːdaɪˈrɛkʃn
AM ˌridəˈrɛkʃən,
ˈriˌdaɪˈrɛkʃən
rediscover
BR ˌriːdɪˈskʌvlə(r), -əz,
-(ə)rɪŋ, -əd
AM ˌridəˈskəvlər, -ərz,
-(ə)rɪŋ, -ərd
rediscoverer
BR ˌriːdɪˈskʌv(ə)rə(r),
-z
AM ˌridəˈskʌv(ə)rər, -z
rediscovery
BR ˌriːdɪˈskʌv(ə)ri
AM ˌridəˈskʌv(ə)ri

redissolution
BR ˌriːdɪsəˈl(j)uːʃn, -z
AM ˌriˌdɪsəˈluʃən, -z
redissolve
BR ˌriːdɪˈzɒlv, -z, -ɪŋ, -d
AM ˌridəˈzɒlv,
ˌridəˈzɑlv, -z, -ɪŋ, -d
redistribute
BR ˌriːdɪˈstrɪbjuːt,
riːˈdɪstrɪbjuːt, -s, -ɪŋ,
-ɪd
AM ˌridəˈstrɪˌbjult, -ts,
-dɪŋ, -dəd
redistribution
BR ˌriːdɪstrɪˈbjuːʃn
AM ˌridəstrəˈbjuʃən
redistributive
BR ˌriːdɪˈstrɪbjuːtɪv,
riːˈdɪstrɪbjuːtɪv
AM ˌridəˈstrɪˌbjudɪv
redivide
BR ˌriːdɪˈvʌɪd, -z, -ɪŋ,
-ɪd
AM ˌridəˈvaɪd, -z, -ɪŋ,
-ɪd
redivision
BR ˌriːdɪˈvɪʒn, -z
AM ˌridəˈvɪʒən, -z
redivivus
BR ˌrɛdɪˈvaɪvəs,
ˌrɛdɪˈviːvəs
AM ˌrɛdəˈvaɪvəs,
ˌrɛdəˈvivəs
redleg
BR ˈrɛdlɛg, -z
AM ˈrɛdˌlɛg, -z
redline
BR ˈrɛdlʌɪn, -z
AM ˈrɛdˌlaɪn, -z
redly
BR ˈrɛdli
AM ˈrɛdli
Redmond
BR ˈrɛdmənd
AM ˈrɛdmən(d)
redneck
BR ˈrɛdnɛk, -s
AM ˈrɛdˌnɛk, -s
redness
BR ˈrɛdnəs
AM ˈrɛdnəs
redo
BR ˌriːˈduː, -ɪŋ
AM riˈdu, -ɪŋ
redoes
BR ˌriːˈdʌz
AM riˈdəz
redolence
BR ˈrɛdələns, ˈrɛdəlns,
ˈrɛdl̩(ə)ns
AM ˈrɛdələns
redolent
BR ˈrɛdələnt, ˈrɛdəlnt,
ˈrɛdl̩(ə)nt
AM ˈrɛdələnt
redolently
BR ˈrɛdələntli,
ˈrɛdəlntli, ˈrɛdl̩(ə)ntli

AM ˈrɛdlən(t)li
redone
BR ˌriːˈdʌn
AM riˈdən
redouble
BR ˌriːˈdʌb|l, rɪˈdʌb|l,
-lz, -lɪŋ\-lɪŋ, -ld
AM riˈdəbəl, -əlz,
-(ə)lɪŋ, -əld
redoubt
BR rɪˈdaʊt, -s
AM rəˈdaʊt, riˈdaʊt, -s
redoubtable
BR rɪˈdaʊtəbl
AM rəˈdaʊdəbəl,
riˈdaʊdəbəl
redoubtably
BR rɪˈdaʊtəbli
AM rəˈdaʊdəbli,
riˈdaʊdəbli
redound
BR rɪˈdaʊnd, -z, -ɪŋ, -ɪd
AM rəˈdaʊnd,
riˈdaʊnd, -z, -ɪŋ, -ɪd
redox
BR ˈriːdɒks
AM ˈriˌdɑks
redpoll
BR ˈrɛdpəʊl, ˈrɛdpɒl, -z
AM ˈrɛdˌpoʊl, -z
redraft
BR ˌriːˈdrɑːft, ˌriːˈdraft,
-s, -ɪŋ, -ɪd
AM riˈdræft, -s, -ɪŋ, -ɪd
redraw
BR ˌriːˈdrɔː(r), -z, -ɪŋ
AM riˈdrɔ, rəˈdrɑ, -z, -ɪŋ
redrawn
BR ˌriːˈdrɔːn
AM riˈdrɔn, riˈdrɑn
redress[1]
correct, amend
BR rɪˈdrɛs, -ɪz, -ɪŋ, -t
AM rəˈdrɛs, riˈdrɛs, -əz,
-ɪŋ, -t
redress[2]
dress again
BR ˌriːˈdrɛs, -ɪz, -ɪŋ, -t
AM riˈdrɛs, -əz, -ɪŋ, -t
redressable
BR rɪˈdrɛsəbl
AM rəˈdrɛsəbəl,
riˈdrɛsəbəl
redressal
BR rɪˈdrɛsl, -z
AM rəˈdrɛsəl, riˈdrɛsəl,
-z
redresser
BR rɪˈdrɛsə(r), -z
AM rəˈdrɛsər,
riˈdrɛsər, -z
redressment
BR rɪˈdrɛsm(ə)nt, -s
AM rəˈdrɛsmənt,
riˈdrɛsmənt, -s
redrew
BR ˌriːˈdruː
AM rəˈdru, riˈdru

Redruth
BR ˌredˈruːθ, ˈredruːθ
AM ˌredˈruːθ

redshank
BR ˈredʃaŋk, -s
AM ˈredˌʃæŋk, -s

redshirt
BR ˈredʃəːt, -s
AM ˈredˌʃərt, -s

redskin
BR ˈredskɪn, -z
AM ˈredˌskɪn, -z

redstart
BR ˈredstɑːt, -s
AM ˈredˌstɑrt, -s

reduce
BR rɪˈdjuːs, rɪˈdʒuːs, -ɪz, -ɪŋ, -t
AM rəˈd(j)us, rɪˈd(j)us, -əz, -ɪŋ, -t

reducer
BR rɪˈdjuːsə(r), rɪˈdʒuːsə(r), -z
AM rəˈd(j)usər, rɪˈd(j)usər, -z

reducibility
BR rɪˌdjuːsɪˈbɪlɪti, rɪˌdʒuːsɪˈbɪlɪti
AM rəˌd(j)usəˈbɪlɪdi, rɪˌd(j)usəˈbɪlɪdi

reducible
BR rɪˈdjuːsɪbl, rɪˈdʒuːsɪbl
AM rəˈd(j)usəbəl, rɪˈd(j)usəbəl

reductio ad absurdum
BR rɪˌdʌktɪəʊ ad əbˈsəːdəm, + abˈsəːdəm
AM rəˈdəkʃioʊ æd əbˈsərdəm, rɪˈdəkʃioʊ +, rəˈdəktioʊ +, rɪˈdəktioʊ +

reduction
BR rɪˈdʌkʃn, -z
AM rəˈdəkʃən, rɪˈdəkʃən, -z

reductionism
BR rɪˈdʌkʃnɪz(ə)m, rɪˈdʌkʃənɪz(ə)m
AM rəˈdəkʃəˌnɪzəm, rɪˈdəkʃəˌnɪzəm

reductionist
BR rɪˈdʌkʃnɪst, rɪˈdʌkʃənɪst, -s
AM rəˈdəkʃənəst, rɪˈdəkʃənəst, -s

reductionistic
BR rɪˌdʌkʃəˈnɪstɪk
AM rəˌdəkʃəˈnɪstɪk, rɪˌdəkʃəˈnɪstɪk

reductive
BR rɪˈdʌktɪv
AM rəˈdəktɪv, rɪˈdəktɪv

redundance
BR rɪˈdʌnd(ə)ns

AM rəˈdənd(ə)ns, rɪˈdənd(ə)ns

redundancy
BR rɪˈdʌnd(ə)ns|i, -ɪz
AM rəˈdənd(ə)nsi, rɪˈdənd(ə)nsi, -z

redundant
BR rɪˈdʌnd(ə)nt
AM rəˈdənd(ə)nt, rɪˈdənd(ə)nt

redundantly
BR rɪˈdʌnd(ə)ntli
AM rəˈdənd(ə)n(t)li, rɪˈdənd(ə)n(t)li

reduplicate
BR rɪˈdjuːplɪkeɪt, ˌriːˈdjuːplɪkeɪt, rɪˈdʒuːplɪkeɪt, ˌriːˈdʒuːplɪkeɪt, -s, -ɪŋ, -ɪd
AM riˈd(j)upləˌkeɪt, rəˈd(j)upləˌkeɪt, -ts, -dɪŋ, -dɪd

reduplication
BR rɪˌdjuːplɪˈkeɪʃn, rɪˌdʒuːplɪˈkeɪʃn
AM riˌd(j)upləˈkeɪʃən, rəˌd(j)upləˈkeɪʃən

reduplicative
BR rɪˈdjuːplɪkətɪv, rɪˈdʒuːplɪkətɪv
AM riˈd(j)upləˌkeɪdɪv, rəˈd(j)upləˌkeɪdɪv

redux
BR ˈriːdʌks
AM ˈriːdəks

Redvers
BR ˈredvəz
AM ˈredvərz

redwing
BR ˈredwɪŋ, -z
AM ˈredˌwɪŋ, -z

redwood
BR ˈredwʊd, -z
AM ˈredˌwʊd, -z

redye
BR ˌriːˈdʌɪ, -z, -ɪŋ, -d
AM riˈdaɪ, -z, -ɪŋ, -d

reebok
BR ˈriːbɒk, -s
AM ˈriːbak, -s

Reece
BR riːs
AM ris

re-echo
BR ˌriːˈekəʊ, rɪˈekəʊ, -z, -ɪŋ, -d
AM riˈekoʊ, -z, -ɪŋ, -d

reed
BR riːd, -z
AM rid, -z

reed-bed
BR ˈriːdbed, -z
AM ˈridˌbed, -z

reedbuck
BR ˈriːdbʌk, -s
AM ˈridˌbək, -s

reeded
BR ˈriːdɪd
AM ˈridɪd

reedification
BR rɪˌedɪfɪˈkeɪʃn
AM riˌedəfəˈkeɪʃən

reedify
BR ˌriːˈedɪfʌɪ, -z, -ɪŋ, -d
AM riˈedəˌfaɪ, -z, -ɪŋ, -d

reedily
BR ˈriːdɪli
AM ˈridɪli

reediness
BR ˈriːdɪnɪs
AM ˈridɪnɪs

reeding
BR ˈriːdɪŋ, -z
AM ˈridɪŋ, -z

re-edit
BR ˌriːˈedɪt, rɪˈedɪt, -ɪts, -ɪtɪŋ, -ɪtɪd
AM riˈedəɪt, -ts, -dɪŋ, -dəd

re-edition
BR ˌriːˈedɪʃn, -z
AM riˌeˈdɪʃən, -z

reedling
BR ˈriːdlɪŋ, -z
AM ˈridlɪŋ, -z

re-educate
BR ˌriːˈedjʊkeɪt, rɪˈedjʊkeɪt, ˌriːˈedʒʊkeɪt, rɪˈedʒʊkeɪt, -s, -ɪŋ, -ɪd
AM riˈedʒəˌkeɪt, -ts, -dɪŋ, -dɪd

re-education
BR ˌriːˈedjʊˈkeɪʃn, rɪˌedjʊˈkeɪʃn, ˌriːˈedʒʊˈkeɪʃn, rɪˌedʒʊˈkeɪʃn
AM riˌedʒəˈkeɪʃən

reed-warbler
BR ˈriːdˌwɔːblə(r), -z
AM ˈridˌwɔrblər, -z

reedy
BR ˈriːd|i, -ɪə(r), -ɪɪst
AM ˈridi, -ər, -ɪst

reef
BR riːf, -s, -ɪŋ, -t
AM rif, -s, -ɪŋ, -t

reefer
BR ˈriːfə(r), -z
AM ˈrifər, -z

reefpoint
BR ˈriːfpɔɪnt, -s
AM ˈrifˌpɔɪnt, -s

reek
BR riːk, -s, -ɪŋ, -t
AM rik, -s, -ɪŋ, -t

reeky
BR ˈriːk|i, -ɪə(r), -ɪɪst
AM ˈriki, -ər, -ɪst

reel
BR riːl, -z, -ɪŋ, -d
AM ril, -z, -ɪŋ, -d

re-elect
BR ˌriːɪˈlekt, -s, -ɪŋ, -ɪd

AM ˌriəˈlek|(t), -(t)s, -tɪŋ, -təd

re-election
BR ˌriːɪˈlekʃn, -z
AM ˈriəˈlekʃən, -z

reeler
BR ˈriːlə(r), -z
AM ˈrilər, -z

re-eligible
BR rɪˈelɪdʒɪbl
AM riˈelədʒəbəl

re-embark
BR ˌriːɪmˈbɑːk, -s, -ɪŋ, -t
AM ˈriəmˈbɑrk, ˌriˌemˈbɑrk, -s, -ɪŋ, -t

re-embarkation
BR ˌriːembɑːˈkeɪʃn, -z
AM ˌriˌembɑrˈkeɪʃən, -z

re-emerge
BR ˌriːɪˈməːdʒ, -ɪz, -ɪŋ, -d
AM ˈriəˈmərdʒ, ˌriˌiˈmərdʒ, -əz, -ɪŋ, -d

re-emergence
BR ˌriːɪˈməːdʒ(ə)ns, -ɪz
AM ˈriəˈmərdʒəns, ˌriˌiˈmərdʒəns, -əz

re-emergent
BR ˌriːɪˈməːdʒ(ə)nt
AM ˈriəˈmərdʒənt, ˌriˌiˈmərdʒənt

re-emphases
BR (ˌ)riːˈemfəsiːz
AM riˈemfəsiz

re-emphasis
BR (ˌ)riːˈemfəsɪs
AM riˈemfəsəs

re-emphasise
BR (ˌ)riːˈemfəsʌɪz, -ɪz, -ɪŋ, -d
AM riˈemfəˌsaɪz, -ɪz, -ɪŋ, -d

re-emphasize
BR (ˌ)riːˈemfəsʌɪz, -ɪz, -ɪŋ, -d
AM riˈemfəˌsaɪz, -ɪz, -ɪŋ, -d

re-employ
BR ˌriːɪmˈplɔɪ, ˌriːemˈplɔɪ, -z, -ɪŋ, -d
AM ˈriəmˈplɔɪ, ˌriˌemˈplɔɪ, -z, -ɪŋ, -d

re-employment
BR ˌriːɪmˈplɔɪm(ə)nt, ˌriːemˈplɔɪm(ə)nt, -s
AM ˈriəmˈplɔɪmənt, ˌriˌemˈplɔɪmənt, -s

re-enact
BR ˌriːɪˈnakt, -s, -ɪŋ, -ɪd
AM ˈriəˈnæk|(t), -(t)s, -tɪŋ, -təd

re-enactment
BR ˌriːɪˈnak(t)m(ə)nt, -s
AM ˈriəˈnæk(t)mənt, -s

re-enforce
BR ˌriːɪnˈfɔːs, -ɪz, -ɪŋ, -t

AM ˌriənˈfɔ(ə)rs, -əz,
-ɪŋ, -t

re-enforcement
BR ˌriːɪnˈfɔːsm(ə)nt
AM ˌriənˈforsmənt

re-engage
BR ˌriːɪnˈɡeɪdʒ,
ˌriːɛnˈɡeɪdʒ,
ˌriːɪŋˈɡeɪdʒ,
ˌriːɛŋˈɡeɪdʒ, -ɪz, -ɪŋ, -d
AM ˌriənˈɡeɪdʒ, -ɪz, -ɪŋ,
-d

re-engagement
BR ˌriːɪnˈɡeɪdʒm(ə)nt,
ˌriːɛnˈɡeɪdʒm(ə)nt,
ˌriːɪŋˈɡeɪdʒm(ə)nt,
ˌriːɛŋˈɡeɪdʒm(ə)nt, -s
AM ˌriənˈɡeɪdʒmənt, -s

re-engineer
BR ˌriːɛn(d)ʒɪˈnɪə(r),
-z, -ɪŋ, -d
AM riˌɛndʒəˈnɪ(ə)r, -z,
-ɪŋ, -d

re-enlist
BR ˌriːɪnˈlɪst, -s, -ɪŋ, -ɪd
AM ˌriənˈlɪst, -s, -ɪŋ, -ɪd

re-enlister
BR ˌriːɪnˈlɪstə(r), -z
AM ˌriənˈlɪstər, -z

re-enlistment
BR ˌriːɪnˈlɪs(t)m(ə)nt,
-s
AM ˌriənˈlɪs(t)mənt, -s

re-enter
BR ˌriːˈɛntə(r),
rɪˈɛntə(r), -əz, -(ə)rɪŋ,
-əd
AM riˈɛn(t)ər, -ərz,
-(ə)rɪŋ, -ərd

re-entrance
BR ˌriːˈɛntr(ə)ns,
rɪˈɛntr(ə)ns, -ɪz
AM riˈɛntrəns, -əz

re-entrant
BR ˌriːˈɛntr(ə)nt,
rɪˈɛntr(ə)nt, -s
AM riˈɛntrənt, -s

re-entry
BR ˌriːˈɛntr|i, rɪˈɛntr|i,
-ɪz
AM riˈɛntri, -z

re-equip
BR ˌriːˈiˈkwɪp, -s, -ɪŋ, -t
AM ˌriəˈkwɪp, -s, -ɪŋ, -t

re-erect
BR ˌriːɪˈrɛkt, -s, -ɪŋ, -d
AM ˌriəˈrɛk|(t), -(t)s,
-tɪŋ, -təd

re-erection
BR ˌriːɪˈrɛkʃn
AM ˌriəˈrɛkʃən

Rees
BR riːs
AM ris

Reese
BR riːs
AM ris

re-establish
BR ˌriːˈstablɪʃ, -ɪʃɪz,
-ɪʃɪŋ, -ɪʃt
AM ˌriəsˈtæblɪʃ,
ˌriɛsˈtæblɪʃ, -ɪz, -ɪŋ, -t

re-establishment
BR ˌriːˈstablɪʃm(ə)nt,
-s
AM ˌriəsˈtæblɪʃmənt,
ˌriɛsˈtæblɪʃmənt, -s

re-evaluate
BR ˌriːɪˈvaljʊeɪt, -s, -ɪŋ,
-ɪd
AM ˌriəˈvæljəˌweɪ|t, -ts,
-dɪŋ, -dɪd

re-evaluation
BR ˌriːɪˌvaljʊˈeɪʃn, -z
AM ˌriəˌvæljəˈweɪʃən,
-z

reeve
BR riːv, -z
AM riv, -z

Reeves
BR riːvz
AM rivz

re-examination
BR ˌriːɪɡˌzamɪˈneɪʃn, -z
AM ˌriːɡˌzæməˈneɪʃən,
ˌriɛɡˌzæməˈneɪʃən, -z

re-examine
BR ˌriːɪɡˈzam|ɪn, -ɪnz,
-ɪnɪŋ, -ɪnd
AM ˌriːɡˈzæmən,
ˌriɛɡˈzæmən, -z, -ɪŋ, -d

re-export
BR ˌriːˈɛkspɔːt,
rɪˈɛkspɔːt, -s, -ɪŋ, -ɪd
AM ˌriˈɛkspɔ(ə)rt, -ts,
-pɔrdɪŋ, -pɔrdəd

re-exportation
BR ˌriːɛkspɔːˈteɪʃn, -z
AM ˌriˌɛkspɔrˈteɪʃən,
-z

re-exporter
BR ˌriːˈɛkspɔːtə(r),
rɪˈɛkspɔːtə(r), -z
AM ˌriˈɛkspɔrdər, -z

ref
BR rɛf, -s
AM rɛf, -s

reface
BR (ˌ)riːˈfeɪs, -ɪz, -ɪŋ, -t
AM riˈfeɪs, -ɪz, -ɪŋ, -t

refashion
BR (ˌ)riːˈfaʃ|n, -nz,
-ənɪŋ\-ŋɪŋ, -nd
AM riˈfæʃ|ən, -ənz,
-(ə)nɪŋ, -ənd

refection
BR rɪˈfɛkʃn
AM rəˈfɛkʃən,
riˈfɛkʃən

refectory
BR rɪˈfɛkt(ə)r|i, -ɪz
AM rəˈfɛkt(ə)ri,
riˈfɛkt(ə)ri, -z

refer
BR rɪˈfɜː(r), -z, -ɪŋ, -d

AM rəˈfɜr, riˈfɜr, -z, -ɪŋ,
-d

referable
BR rɪˈfɜːrəbl,
ˈrɛf(ə)rəbl
AM rəˈfɜːrəbəl,
riˈfɜːrəbəl,
ˈrɛf(ə)rəbəl

referee
BR ˌrɛfəˈriː, -z
AM ˌrɛfəˈri, -z

reference
BR ˈrɛf(ə)rəns,
ˈrɛf(ə)rn̩s, -ɪz
AM ˈrɛf(ə)rəns, -əz

referenda
BR ˌrɛfəˈrɛndə(r)
AM ˌrɛfəˈrɛndə

referendum
BR ˌrɛfəˈrɛndəm, -z
AM ˌrɛfəˈrɛndəm, -z

referent
BR ˈrɛf(ə)rənt,
ˈrɛf(ə)rn̩t, -s
AM ˈrɛf(ə)rənt, -s

referential
BR ˌrɛfəˈrɛnʃl
AM ˌrɛfəˈrɛn(t)ʃəl

referentiality
BR ˌrɛfəˌrɛnʃɪˈalɪti
AM ˌrɛfəˌrɛn(t)ʃiˈælədi

referentially
BR ˌrɛfəˈrɛnʃli,
ˌrɛfəˈrɛnʃəli
AM ˌrɛfəˈrɛn(t)ʃəli

referral
BR rɪˈfɜːrəl, rɪˈfɜːr|l, -z
AM rəˈfɜːrəl, riˈfɜːrəl, -z

referrer
BR rɪˈfɜːrə(r), -z
AM rəˈfɜːrər, riˈfɜːrər, -z

refill¹
noun
BR ˈriːfɪl, -z
AM ˈriːfɪl, -z

refill²
verb
BR ˌriːˈfɪl, -z, -ɪŋ, -d
AM riˈfɪl, -z, -ɪŋ, -d

refillable
BR ˌriːˈfɪləbl
AM riˈfɪləbəl

refinable
BR rɪˈfʌɪnəbl
AM rəˈfʌɪnəbəl,
riˈfʌɪnəbəl

refinance
BR ˌriːfʌɪˈnans,
ˌriːˈfʌɪnans,
ˌriːˈfʌɪnans, -ɪz, -ɪŋ, -d
AM ˌriːfəˈnæns,
riˈfʌɪˌnæns, -əz, -ɪŋ, -d

refine
BR rɪˈfʌɪn, -z, -ɪŋ, -d
AM rəˈfʌɪn, riˈfʌɪn, -z,
-ɪŋ, -d

refinement
BR rɪˈfʌɪnm(ə)nt, -s

AM rəˈfʌɪnmənt,
riˈfʌɪnmənt, -s

refiner
BR rɪˈfʌɪnə(r), -z
AM rəˈfʌɪnər, riˈfʌɪnər,
-z

refinery
BR rɪˈfʌɪn(ə)r|i, -ɪz
AM rəˈfʌɪn(ə)ri,
riˈfʌɪn(ə)ri, -z

refinish
BR ˌriːˈfɪn|ɪʃ, -ɪʃɪz,
-ɪʃɪŋ, -ɪʃt
AM rəˈfɪnɪʃ, riˈfɪnɪʃ, -ɪz,
-ɪŋ, -t

refit¹
noun
BR ˈriːfɪt, -s
AM ˈriˌfɪt, -s

refit²
verb
BR ˌriːˈfɪt, -s, -ɪŋ, -ɪd
AM riˈfɪ|t, -ts, -dɪŋ, -dɪd

refitment
BR ˌriːˈfɪtm(ə)nt, -s
AM riˈfɪtmənt, -s

reflag
BR ˌriːˈflag, -z, -ɪŋ, -d
AM riˈflæg, -z, -ɪŋ, -d

reflate
BR ˌriːˈfleɪt, rɪˈfleɪt, -s,
-ɪŋ, -ɪd
AM rəˈfleɪ|t, riˈfleɪ|t, -ts,
-dɪŋ, -dɪd

reflation
BR ˌriːˈfleɪʃn, rɪˈfleɪʃn
AM rəˈfleɪʃən,
riˈfleɪʃən

reflationary
BR ˌriːˈfleɪʃn̩(ə)ri,
rɪˈfleɪʃn̩(ə)ri
AM rəˈfleɪʃəˌnɛri,
riˈfleɪʃəˌnɛri

reflect
BR rɪˈflɛkt, -s, -ɪŋ, -ɪd
AM rəˈflɛk|(t),
riˈflɛk|(t), -(t)s, -tɪŋ,
-təd

reflectance
BR rɪˈflɛkt(ə)ns, -ɪz
AM rəˈflɛkt(ə)ns,
riˈflɛkt(ə)ns, -əz

reflection
BR rɪˈflɛkʃn, -z
AM rəˈflɛkʃən,
riˈflɛkʃən, -z

reflectional
BR rɪˈflɛkʃn̩(ə)l,
rɪˈflɛkʃən(ə)l
AM rəˈflɛkʃ(ə)nəl,
riˈflɛkʃ(ə)nəl

reflective
BR rɪˈflɛktɪv
AM rəˈflɛktɪv,
riˈflɛktɪv

reflectively
BR rɪˈflɛktɪvli

AM rə'flɛktɪvli,
ri'flɛktɪvli
reflectiveness
BR rɪ'flɛktɪvnɪs
AM rə'flɛktɪvnɪs,
ri'flɛktɪvnɪs
reflectivity
BR ˌriːflɛk'tɪvɪti,
rɪˌflɛk'tɪvɪt|i, -ɪz
AM rə'flɛk'tɪvɪdi,
riˌflɛk'tɪvɪdi, -z
reflector
BR rɪ'flɛktə(r), -z
AM rə'flɛktər,
ri'flɛktər, -z
reflet
BR rɪ'fleɪ
AM rə'fleɪ, ri'fleɪ-z
reflex
BR 'riːflɛks, -ɪz, -t
AM 'riˌflɛks, -əz, -t
reflexibility
BR ˌrɪˈflɛksɪ'bɪlɪti,
rɪˌflɛksɪ'bɪlɪti
AM ˌriflɛksə'bɪlɪdi
reflexible
BR rɪ'flɛksɪbl
AM rə'flɛksəbəl,
ri'flɛksəbəl
reflexion
BR rɪ'flɛkʃn, -z
AM rə'flɛkʃən,
ri'flɛkʃən, -z
reflexive
BR rɪ'flɛksɪv, -z
AM rə'flɛksɪv,
ri'flɛksɪv, -z
reflexively
BR rɪ'flɛksɪvli
AM rə'flɛksɪvli,
ri'flɛksɪvli
reflexiveness
BR rɪ'flɛksɪvnɪs
AM rə'flɛksɪvnɪs,
ri'flɛksɪvnɪs
reflexivity
BR ˌriːflɛk'sɪvɪti
AM ˌriflɛk'sɪvɪdi
reflexologist
BR ˌriːflɛk'sɒlədʒɪst, -s
AM ˌriflɛk'sɑːlədʒəst, -s
reflexology
BR ˌriːflɛk'sɒlədʒi
AM ˌriflɛk'sɑːlədʒi
refloat
BR ˌriːˈfləʊt, -s, -ɪŋ, -ɪd
AM ri'floʊ|t, -ts, -ɪŋ,
-dəd
refluence
BR 'rɛflʊəns, -ɪz
AM 'rɛˌfluəns, -əz
refluent
BR 'rɛflʊənt
AM 'rɛˌfluənt
reflux
BR 'riːflʌks, -ɪz
AM 'riˌflʌks, -əz

refocus
BR ˌriːˈfəʊkəs, -ɪz, -ɪŋ, -t
AM ri'foʊkəs, -əz, -ɪŋ, -t
refold
BR ˌriːˈfəʊld, -z, -ɪŋ, -ɪd
AM ri'foʊld, -z, -ɪŋ, -əd
reforest
BR (ˌ)riːˈfɒrɪst, -s, -ɪŋ, -ɪd
AM ri'fɔːrəst, -s, -ɪŋ, -ɪd
reforestation
BR ˌriːfɒrɪ'steɪʃn,
riːˌfɒrɪ'steɪʃn
AM ˌriˌfɔrə'steɪʃən
reforge
BR ˌriːˈfɔːdʒ, -ɪz, -ɪŋ, -d
AM ri'fɔrdʒ, -əz, -ɪŋ, -d
reform¹
correct, make better
BR rɪ'fɔːm, -z, -ɪŋ, -d
AM rə'fɔ(ə)rm,
ri'fɔ(ə)rm, -z, -ɪŋ, -d
reform²
form again
BR ˌriːˈfɔːm, -z, -ɪŋ, -d
AM ri'fɔ(ə)rm, -z, -ɪŋ, -d
reformable
BR rɪ'fɔːməbl
AM rə'fɔrməbəl,
ri'fɔrməbəl
reformat
BR ˌriːˈfɔːmat, -s, -ɪŋ, -ɪd
AM ri'for,mæ|t, -ts,
-dɪŋ, -dəd
reformation
BR ˌrɛfə'meɪʃn, -z
AM ˌrɛfər'meɪʃən, -z
re-formation
BR ˌriːfɔː'meɪʃn, -z
AM ˌriˌfɔr'meɪʃən, -z
reformational
BR ˌrɛfə'meɪʃn(ə)l,
ˌrɛfə'meɪʃən(ə)l
AM ˌrɛfər'meɪʃ(ə)nəl
reformative
BR rɪ'fɔːmətɪv
AM rə'fɔrmədɪv,
ri'fɔrmədɪv
reformatory
BR rɪ'fɔːmət(ə)r|i, -ɪz
AM rə'fɔrmə,tɔri,
ri'fɔrmə,tɔri, -z
reformer
BR rɪ'fɔːmə(r), -z
AM rə'fɔrmər,
ri'fɔrmər, -z
reformism
BR rɪ'fɔːmɪz(ə)m
AM rə'fɔr,mɪzəm,
ri'fɔr,mɪzəm
reformist
BR rɪ'fɔːmɪst
AM rə'fɔrməst,
ri'fɔrməst
reformulate
BR ˌriːˈfɔːmjʊleɪt, -s,
-ɪŋ, -ɪd

AM rə'fɔrmjəˌleɪ|t,
ri'fɔrmjəˌleɪ|t, -ts,
-dɪŋ, -dɪd
reformulation
BR ˌriːˈfɔːmjə'leɪʃn, -z
AM rəˌfɔrmjə'leɪʃən,
riˌfɔrmjə'leɪʃən, -z
refract
BR rɪ'frakt, -s, -ɪŋ, -ɪd
AM rə'fræk|(t),
ri'fræk|(t), -(t)s, -tɪŋ,
-təd
refraction
BR rɪ'frakʃn
AM rə'frækʃən,
ri'frækʃən
refractive
BR rɪ'fraktɪv
AM rə'fræktɪv,
ri'fræktɪv
refractometer
BR ˌriːfrak'tɒmɪtə(r),
rɪˌfrak'tɒmɪtə(r), -z
AM rəˌfræk'tɑmədər,
riˌfræk'tɑmədər, -z
refractometric
BR rɪˌfraktə'mɛtrɪk
AM rəˌfræktə'mɛtrɪk,
riˌfræktə'mɛtrɪk
refractometry
BR ˌriːfrak'tɒmɪtri,
rɪˌfrak'tɒmɪtri
AM rəˌfræk'tɑmətri,
riˌfræk'tɑmətri
refractor
BR rɪ'fraktə(r), -z
AM rə'fræktər,
ri'fræktər, -z
refractorily
BR rɪ'frakt(ə)r|i
AM rə'fræk,tɔrəli,
ri'fræk,tɔrəli
refractoriness
BR rɪ'frakt(ə)rmɪs
AM rə'fræk,tɔrinɪs,
ri'fræk,tɔrinəs
refractory
BR rɪ'frakt(ə)ri
AM rə'fræk,tɔri,
ri'fræk,tɔri
refrain
BR rɪ'freɪn, -z, -ɪŋ, -d
AM rə'freɪn, ri'freɪn, -z,
-ɪŋ, -d
refrainment
BR rɪ'freɪnm(ə)nt, -s
AM rə'freɪnmənt,
ri'freɪnmənt, -s
refrangibility
BR rɪˌfran(d)ʒɪ'bɪlɪti
AM rəˌfrænd͡ʒə'bɪlɪdi,
riˌfrænd͡ʒə'bɪlɪdi
refrangible
BR rɪ'fran(d)ʒɪbl
AM rə'frand͡ʒəbəl,
ri'frand͡ʒəbəl
refreeze
BR ˌriːˈfriːz, -ɪz, -ɪŋ

AM rə'friz, ri'friz, -ɪz,
-ɪŋ
refresh
BR rɪ'frɛʃ, -ɪz, -ɪŋ, -d
AM rə'frɛʃ, ri'frɛʃ, -əz,
-ɪŋ, -t
refresher
BR rɪ'frɛʃə(r), -z
AM rə'frɛʃər, ri'frɛʃər,
-z
refreshingly
BR rɪ'frɛʃɪŋli
AM rə'frɛʃɪŋli,
ri'frɛʃɪŋli
refreshment
BR rɪ'frɛʃm(ə)nt, -s
AM rə'frɛʃmənt,
ri'frɛʃmənt, -s
refried
BR ˌriːˈfraɪd
AM ˌriˈfraɪd
refrigerant
BR rɪ'frɪdʒ(ə)rənt,
rɪ'frɪdʒ(ə)rnt, -s
AM rə'frɪdʒ(ə)rənt,
ri'frɪdʒ(ə)rənt, -s
refrigerate
BR rɪ'frɪdʒəreɪt, -s, -ɪŋ,
-ɪd
AM rə'frɪdʒəˌreɪ|t,
ri'frɪdʒəˌreɪ|t, -ts, -dɪŋ,
-dɪd
refrigeration
BR rɪˌfrɪdʒə'reɪʃn
AM rəˌfrɪdʒə'reɪʃən,
riˌfrɪdʒə'reɪʃən
refrigerative
BR rɪ'frɪdʒ(ə)rətɪv
AM rə'frɪdʒərədɪv,
ri'frɪdʒərədɪv
refrigerator
BR rɪ'frɪdʒəreɪtə(r), -z
AM rə'frɪdʒəˌreɪdər,
ri'frɪdʒəˌreɪdər, -z
refrigeratory
BR rɪ'frɪdʒ(ə)rət(ə)ri
AM rə'frɪdʒ(ə)rəˌtɔri,
ri'frɪdʒ(ə)rəˌtɔri
refringent
BR rɪ'frɪn(d)ʒ(ə)nt
AM rə'frɪndʒənt,
ri'frɪndʒənt
refroze
BR ˌriːˈfrəʊz
AM rə'froʊz, ri'froʊz
refrozen
BR ˌriːˈfrəʊzn
AM rə'froʊzən,
ˌriˈfroʊzən
reft
BR rɛft
AM rɛft
refuel
BR rɪ'fjuːəl, -z, -ɪŋ, -d
AM ri'fju(ə)l, -z, -ɪŋ, -d
refuge
BR 'rɛfjuːdʒ, -ɪz
AM 'rɛfjudʒ, -ɪz

refugee
BR ˌrɛfjʊˈdʒiː,
ˌrɛfjʊˈdʒiː, -z
AM ˈrɛfjəˌdʒi, -z

refulgence
BR rɪˈfʌldʒ(ə)ns
AM rəˈfʌldʒəns,
ri·fəldʒəns

refulgent
BR rɪˈfʌldʒ(ə)nt
AM rəˈfʌldʒənt,
ri·fəldʒənt

refulgently
BR rɪˈfʌldʒ(ə)ntli
AM rəˈfʌldʒən(t)li,
ri·fəldʒən(t)li

refund¹
noun
BR ˈriːfʌnd, -z
AM ˈriˌfənd, -z

refund²
verb
BR (ˌ)riːˈfʌnd, rɪˈfʌnd,
ˈriːfʌnd, -z, -ɪŋ, -ɪd
AM rəˈfənd, riˈfənd, -z,
-ɪŋ, -əd

re-fund
BR ˌriːˈfʌnd, ˈriːfʌnd,
-z, -ɪŋ, -ɪd
AM riˈfənd, -z, -ɪŋ, -əd

refundable
BR (ˌ)riːˈfʌndəbl,
rɪˈfʌndəbl,
ˈriːfʌndəbl
AM rəˈfəndəbəl,
riˈfəndəbəl

refunder
BR (ˌ)riːˈfʌndə(r),
rɪˈfʌndə(r),
ˈriːfʌndə(r), -z
AM ˈriˌfəndər

refundment
BR (ˌ)riːˈfʌndm(ə)nt,
rɪˈfʌndm(ə)nt,
ˈriːfʌndm(ə)nt, -s
AM rəˈfən(d)mənt,
riˈfən(d)mənt, -s

refurbish
BR (ˌ)riːˈfəːbɪʃ, -ɪʃɪz,
-ɪʃɪŋ, -ɪʃt
AM riˈfərbɪʃ, -ɪz, -ɪŋ, -t

refurbishment
BR (ˌ)riːˈfəːbɪʃm(ə)nt,
-s
AM riˈfərbɪʃmənt, -s

refurnish
BR (ˌ)riːˈfəːnɪʃ, -ɪʃɪz,
-ɪʃɪŋ, -ɪʃt
AM riˈfərnɪʃ, -ɪz, -ɪŋ, -t

refusable
BR rɪˈfjuːzəbl
AM rəˈfjuzəbəl,
riˈfjuzəbəl

refusal
BR rɪˈfjuːzl, -z
AM rəˈfjuzəl, riˈfjuzəl,
-z

refuse¹
noun
BR ˈrɛfjuːs
AM ˈrɛˌfjuz

refuse²
verb
BR rɪˈfjuːz, -ɪz, -ɪŋ, -d
AM rəˈfjuz, riˈfjuz, -əz,
-ɪŋ, -d

refusenik
BR rɪˈfjuːznɪk, -s
AM rəˈfjuznɪk,
riˈfjuznɪk, -s

refuser
BR rɪˈfjuːzə(r), -z
AM rəˈfjuzər, riˈfjuzər,
-z

refutability
BR rɪˌfjuːtəˈbɪlɪti,
ˌrɛfjʊtəˈbɪlɪti
AM rəˌfjudəˈbɪlɪdi,
riˌfjudəˈbɪlɪdi,
ˌrɛfjədəˈbɪlɪdi

refutable
BR rɪˈfjuːtəbl,
ˈrɛfjʊtəbl
AM rəˈfjudəbəl,
riˈfjudəbəl,
ˈrɛfjədəbəl

refutal
BR rɪˈfjuːtl, -z
AM rəˈfjudl, riˈfjudl, -z

refutation
BR ˌrɛfjʊˈteɪʃn, -z
AM ˌrɛfjəˈteɪʃən, -z

refute
BR rɪˈfjuːt, -s, -ɪŋ, -ɪd
AM rəˈfju|t, riˈfju|t, -ts,
-dɪŋ, -dəd

refuter
BR rɪˈfjuːtə(r), -z
AM rəˈfjudər, riˈfjudər,
-z

reg
BR rɛdʒ
AM rɛdʒ

regain
BR rɪˈgeɪn, ˌriːˈgeɪn, -z,
-ɪŋ, -d
AM riˈgeɪn, rəˈgeɪn, -z,
-ɪŋ, -d

regal
BR ˈriːgl
AM ˈrigəl

regale
BR rɪˈgeɪl, -z, -ɪŋ, -d
AM rəˈgeɪl, riˈgeɪl, -z,
-ɪŋ, -d

regalement
BR rɪˈgeɪlm(ə)nt, -s
AM rəˈgeɪlmənt,
riˈgeɪlmənt, -s

regalia
BR rɪˈgeɪlɪə(r)
AM rəˈgeɪljə, rəˈgeɪliə

regalism
BR ˈriːglɪz(ə)m,
ˈriːgəlɪz(ə)m

regality
BR riːˈgalɪti, -ɪz
AM riˈgælədi, -z

regally
BR ˈriːgli, ˈriːgəli
AM ˈrigəli

Regan
BR ˈriːg(ə)n
AM ˈrigən, ˈreɪgən

regard
BR rɪˈgɑːd, -z, -ɪŋ, -ɪd
AM rəˈgɑrd, riˈgɑrd, -z,
-ɪŋ, -əd

regardant
BR rɪˈgɑːdnt
AM rəˈgɑrdnt,
riˈgɑrdnt

regardful
BR rɪˈgɑːdf(ʊ)l
AM rəˈgɑrdfəl,
riˈgɑrdfəl

regardfully
BR rɪˈgɑːdfʊli,
rɪˈgɑːdfli
AM rəˈgɑrdfəli,
riˈgɑrdfəli

regardfulness
BR rɪˈgɑːdf(ʊ)lnəs
AM rəˈgɑrdfəlnəs,
riˈgɑrdfəlnəs

regardless
BR rɪˈgɑːdləs
AM rəˈgɑrdləs,
riˈgɑrdləs

regardlessly
BR rɪˈgɑːdləsli
AM rəˈgɑrdləsli,
riˈgɑrdləsli

regardlessness
BR rɪˈgɑːdləsnəs
AM rəˈgɑrdləsnəs,
riˈgɑrdləsnəs

regather
BR ˌriːˈgaðə(r), -əz,
-(ə)rɪŋ, -əd
AM riˈgæð|ər, -ərz,
-(ə)rɪŋ, -ərd

regatta
BR rɪˈgatə(r), -z
AM rəˈgædə, rəˈgadə, -z

regelate
BR ˌriːdʒɪˈleɪt, -s, -ɪŋ, -ɪd
AM ˌriˈdʒəˌleɪ|t, -ts,
-dɪŋ, -dɪd

regelation
BR ˌriːdʒɪˈleɪʃn, -z
AM ˌridʒəˈleɪʃən, -z

regency
BR ˈriːdʒ(ə)ns|i, -ɪz
AM ˈridʒənsi, -z

regenerate¹
adjective
BR rɪˈdʒɛn(ə)rət
AM riˈdʒɛn(ə)rət,
rəˈdʒɛn(ə)rət

regenerate²
verb
BR rɪˈdʒɛnəreɪt,
ˌriːˈdʒɛnəreɪt, -s, -ɪŋ,
-ɪd
AM riˈdʒɛnəˌreɪ|t,
rəˈdʒɛnəˌreɪ|t, -ts, -dɪŋ,
-dɪd

regeneration
BR rɪˌdʒɛnəˈreɪʃn,
ˌriːdʒɛnəˈreɪʃn
AM riˌdʒɛnəˈreɪʃən,
rəˌdʒɛnəˈreɪʃən

regenerative
BR rɪˈdʒɛn(ə)rətɪv
AM riˈdʒɛnərədɪv,
rəˈdʒɛnərədɪv

regeneratively
BR rɪˈdʒɛn(ə)rətɪvli
AM riˈdʒɛnərədɪvli,
rəˈdʒɛnərədɪvli

regenerator
BR rɪˈdʒɛnəreɪtə(r),
ˌriːˈdʒɛnəreɪtə(r), -z
AM riˈdʒɛnəˌreɪdər,
rəˈdʒɛnəˌreɪdər, -z

regeneses
BR ˌriːˈdʒɛnɪsiːz
AM riˈdʒɛnəˌsiz

regenesis
BR ˌriːˈdʒɛnɪsɪs
AM riˈdʒɛnəsəs

regent
BR ˈriːdʒ(ə)nt, -s
AM ˈridʒənt, -s

regentship
BR ˈriːdʒ(ə)ntʃɪp, -s
AM ˈridʒəntˌʃɪp, -s

regerminate
BR ˌriːˈdʒəːmɪneɪt, -s,
-ɪŋ, -ɪd
AM riˈdʒərməˌneɪ|t, -ts,
-dɪŋ, -dɪd

regermination
BR ˌriːdʒəˈmɪˈneɪʃn, -z
AM ˌriˌdʒərməˈneɪʃən,
-z

reggae
BR ˈrɛgeɪ
AM ˈrɛgeɪ

regicidal
BR ˌrɛdʒɪˈsʌɪdl
AM ˌrɛdʒəˈsaɪdəl

regicide
BR ˈrɛdʒɪsʌɪd, -z
AM ˈrɛdʒəˌsaɪd, -z

regild
BR ˌriːˈgɪld, -z, -ɪŋ, -ɪd
AM riˈgɪld, -z, -ɪŋ, -ɪd

regilt
BR ˌriːˈgɪlt
AM riˈgɪlt

régime
BR reɪˈʒiːm, rɛˈʒiːm,
rəˈʒiːm, -z
AM reɪˈʒim, rəˈʒim, -z

regimen
BR ˈredʒɪmən,
ˈreʒɪmen, -z
AM ˈredʒəmən,
ˈredʒə,men, -z
regiment[1]
noun
BR ˈredʒɪm(ə)nt, -s
AM ˈredʒəmənt, -s
regiment[2]
verb
BR ˈredʒɪment, -s, -ɪŋ,
-ɪd
AM ˈredʒə,men|t, -ts,
-(t)ɪŋ, -(t)əd
regimental
BR ˌredʒɪˈmentl, -z
AM ˌredʒɪˈmen(t)l, -z
regimentally
BR ˌredʒɪˈmentli
AM ˈredʒɪmen(t)li
regimentation
BR ˌredʒɪmenˈteɪʃn,
ˌredʒɪm(ə)nˈteɪʃn
AM ˌredʒəmənˈteɪʃən,
ˌredʒə,menˈteɪʃən
Regina
BR rɪˈdʒaɪnə(r)
AM rəˈdʒinə
Reginald
BR ˈredʒɪnld
AM ˈredʒənld
region
BR ˈriːdʒ(ə)n, -z
AM ˈriːdʒən, -z
regional
BR ˈriːdʒn(ə)l,
ˈriːdʒən(ə)l
AM ˈriːdʒ(ə)nəl
regionalisation
BR ˌriːdʒnəlaɪˈzeɪʃn,
ˌriːdʒn̩laɪˈzeɪʃn,
ˌriːdʒ(ə)nəlaɪˈzeɪʃn
AM ˌriːdʒnələˈzeɪʃən,
ˌriːdʒnələˈzeɪʃən,
ˌriːdʒnl̩,aɪˈzeɪʃən,
ˌriːdʒnə,laɪˈzeɪʃən
regionalise
BR ˈriːdʒnəlaɪz,
ˈriːdʒn̩laɪz,
ˈriːdʒn̩laɪz,
ˈriːdʒ(ə)nəlaɪz, -ɪz, -ɪŋ,
-d
AM ˈriːdʒnl̩,aɪz,
ˈriːdʒnə,laɪz, -ɪz, -ɪŋ, -d
regionalism
BR ˈriːdʒnəlɪz(ə)m,
ˈriːdʒn̩lɪz(ə)m,
ˈriːdʒn̩lɪz(ə)m,
ˈriːdʒ(ə)nəlɪz(ə)m
AM ˈriːdʒnl̩,ɪsəm,
ˈriːdʒnə,lɪsəm
regionalist
BR ˈriːdʒnəlɪst,
ˈriːdʒn̩lɪst,
ˈriːdʒn̩lɪst,
ˈriːdʒ(ə)nəlɪst, -s

AM ˈriːdʒənləst,
ˈriːdʒnələst, -s
regionalization
BR ˌriːdʒnəlaɪˈzeɪʃn,
ˌriːdʒn̩laɪˈzeɪʃn,
ˌriːdʒn̩laɪˈzeɪʃn,
ˌriːdʒ(ə)nəlaɪˈzeɪʃn
AM ˌriːdʒnələˈzeɪʃən,
ˌriːdʒnələˈzeɪʃən,
ˌriːdʒnl̩,aɪˈzeɪʃən,
ˌriːdʒnə,laɪˈzeɪʃən
regionalize
BR ˈriːdʒnəlaɪz,
ˈriːdʒn̩laɪz,
ˈriːdʒn̩laɪz,
ˈriːdʒ(ə)nəlaɪz, -ɪz, -ɪŋ,
-d
AM ˈriːdʒnl̩,aɪz,
ˈriːdʒnə,laɪz, -ɪz, -ɪŋ, -d
regionally
BR ˈriːdʒn̩ali, ˈriːdʒn̩li,
ˈriːdʒən̩li,
ˈriːdʒ(ə)nəli
AM ˈriːdʒ(ə)nəli
Regis
BR ˈriːdʒɪs
AM ˈriːdʒɪs
régisseur
BR ˌreɪʒɪˈsəː(r), -z
AM ˌreɪdʒɪˈsər, -z
register
BR ˈredʒɪst|ə(r), -əz,
-(ə)rɪŋ, -əd
AM ˈredʒəst|ər, -ərz,
-(ə)rɪŋ, -ərd
registrable
BR ˈredʒɪstrəbl
AM ˈredʒəstrəbəl
registrant
BR ˈredʒɪstr(ə)nt, -s
AM ˈredʒəstrənt, -s
registrar
BR ˌredʒɪˈstrɑː(r),
ˈredʒɪstrɑː(r), -z
AM ˈredʒə,strɑr, -z
**Registrar
General**
BR ˌredʒɪstrɑː
ˈdʒen(ə)rəl,
+ ˈdʒen(ə)r̩, -z
AM ˈredʒə,strɑr
ˈdʒen(ə)rəl, -z
registrarship
BR ˌredʒɪˈstrɑːʃɪp,
ˈredʒɪstrɑːʃɪp, -s
AM ˈredʒə,strɑrʃɪp, -s
registrary
BR ˈredʒɪstrər|i, -ɪz
AM ˈredʒə,streri, -z
registration
BR ˌredʒɪˈstreɪʃn, -z
AM ˌredʒəˈstreɪʃən, -z
registry
BR ˈredʒɪstr|i, -ɪz
AM ˈredʒəstri, -z
Regius
BR ˈriːdʒ(ɪ)əs
AM ˈriːdʒ(i)əs

reglaze
BR ˌriːˈgleɪz, -ɪz, -ɪŋ, -d
AM ˌriːˈgleɪz, -ɪz, -ɪŋ, -d
reglet
BR ˈreglɪt, -s
AM ˈreglət, -s
regnal
BR ˈregnl
AM ˈregnəl
regnant
BR ˈregnənt
AM ˈregnənt
regolith
BR ˈregəlɪθ, -s
AM ˈregə,lɪθ, -s
regorge
BR ˌriːˈgɔːdʒ, -ɪz, -ɪŋ, -d
AM ˌriːˈgɔrdʒ, -əz, -ɪŋ, -d
regrade
BR ˌriːˈgreɪd, -z, -ɪŋ, -ɪd
AM riːˈgreɪd, -z, -ɪŋ, -ɪd
regrate
BR ˌriːˈgreɪt, -s, -ɪŋ, -ɪd
AM riːˈgreɪ|t, -ts, -dɪŋ,
-dɪd
regreen
BR ˌriːˈgriːn, -z, -ɪŋ, -d
AM riːˈgrin, -z, -ɪŋ, -d
regress[1]
noun
BR ˈriːgres
AM ˈri,gres
regress[2]
verb
BR rɪˈgres, ˌriːˈgres, -ɪz,
-ɪŋ, -t
AM rəˈgres, riˈgres, -əz,
-ɪŋ, -t
regression
BR rɪˈgreʃn, ˌriːˈgreʃn,
-z
AM rəˈgreʃən,
riˈgreʃən, -z
regressive
BR rɪˈgresɪv,
ˌriːˈgresɪv
AM riˈgresɪv, riˈgresɪv
regressively
BR rɪˈgresɪvli,
ˌriːˈgresɪvli
AM riˈgresɪvli,
riˈgresɪvli
regressiveness
BR rɪˈgresɪvnɪs,
ˌriːˈgresɪvnɪs
AM riˈgresɪvnɪs,
riˈgresɪvnɪs
regret
BR rɪˈgret, -s, -ɪŋ, -ɪd
AM rəˈgre|t, riˈgre|t, -ts,
-dɪŋ, -dəd
regretful
BR rɪˈgretf(ʊ)l
AM rəˈgretfəl,
riˈgretfəl
regretfully
BR rɪˈgretfʊli,
rɪˈgretfl̩i

AM rəˈgretfəli,
riˈgretfəli
regretfulness
BR rɪˈgretf(ʊ)lnəs
AM rəˈgretfəlnəs,
riˈgretfəlnəs
regrettable
BR rɪˈgretəbl
AM rəˈgredəbəl,
riˈgredəbəl
regrettably
BR rɪˈgretəbli
AM rəˈgredəbli,
riˈgredəbli
regrew
BR ˌriːˈgruː
AM riˈgru
regroup
BR ˌriːˈgruːp, -s, -ɪŋ, -t
AM riˈgrup, -s, -ɪŋ, -t
regroupment
BR ˌriːˈgruːpm(ə)nt, -s
AM riˈgrupmənt, -s
regrow
BR ˌriːˈgrəʊ, -z, -ɪŋ
AM riˈgroʊ, -z, -ɪŋ
regrown
BR ˌriːˈgrəʊn
AM riˈgroʊn
regrowth
BR ˌriːˈgrəʊθ, -s
AM riˈgroʊθ, -s
regulable
BR ˈregjʊləbl
AM ˈregjələbəl
regular
BR ˈregjʊlə(r), -z
AM ˈreg(jə)lər, -z
regularisation
BR ˌregjʊləraɪˈzeɪʃn
AM ˌregjələrəˈzeɪʃən,
ˌregjələ,raɪˈzeɪʃən
regularise
BR ˈregjʊləraɪz, -ɪz, -ɪŋ,
-d
AM ˈregjələ,raɪz, -ɪz,
-ɪŋ, -d
regularity
BR ˌregjʊˈlarɪti
AM ˌregjəˈlerədi
regularization
BR ˌregjʊləraɪˈzeɪʃn
AM ˌregjələrəˈzeɪʃən,
ˌregjələ,raɪˈzeɪʃən
regularize
BR ˈregjʊləraɪz, -ɪz, -ɪŋ,
-d
AM ˈregjələ,raɪz, -ɪz,
-ɪŋ, -d
regularly
BR ˈregjʊləli
AM ˈreg(jə)lərli
regulate
BR ˈregjʊleɪt, -s, -ɪŋ, -ɪd
AM ˈregjə,leɪ|t, -ts, -dɪŋ,
-dɪd
regulation
BR ˌregjʊˈleɪʃn, -z

AM ˌrɛg(j)əˈleɪʃən, -z

regulative
BR ˈrɛgjʊlətɪv
AM ˈrɛgjələdɪv,
ˈrɛgjəˌleɪdɪv

regulator
BR ˈrɛgjʊleɪtə(r), -z
AM ˈrɛgjəˌleɪdər, -z

regulatory
BR ˈrɛgjʊlət(ə)ri,
ˌrɛgjʊˈleɪt(ə)ri
AM ˈrɛgjələˌtɔri

reguli
BR ˈrɛgjʊlʌɪ, ˈrɛgjʊli:
AM ˈrɛgjəˌlʌɪ

reguline
BR ˈrɛgjʊlʌɪn
AM ˈrɛgjələn,
ˈrɛgjəˌlʌɪn

regulo
BR ˈrɛgjʊləʊ, -z
AM ˈrɛgjəlou, -z

regulus
BR ˈrɛgjʊləs, -ɪz
AM ˈrɛgjələs, -əz

regurgitate
BR rɪˈgɜːdʒɪteɪt,
ˌriːˈgɜːdʒɪteɪt, -s, -ɪŋ,
-ɪd
AM rəˈgɜrdʒəˌteɪt,
riˈgɜrdʒəˌteɪt, -ts,
-dɪŋ, -dɪd

regurgitation
BR rɪˌgɜːdʒɪˈteɪʃn,
ˌriːgɜːdʒɪˈteɪʃn
AM rəˌgɜrdʒəˈteɪʃən,
riˌgɜrdʒəˈteɪʃən

rehab
BR ˈriːhab
AM ˈriˌhæb

rehabilitate
BR ˌriː(h)əˈbɪlɪteɪt, -s,
-ɪŋ, -ɪd
AM ˌri(h)əˈbɪləˌteɪt,
-ts, -dɪŋ, -dɪd

rehabilitation
BR ˌriː(h)əˌbɪlɪˈteɪʃn
AM ˌri(h)əˌbɪliˈteɪʃən

rehabilitative
BR ˌriː(h)əˈbɪlɪtətɪv
AM ˌri(h)əˈbɪləˌteɪdɪv

rehandle
BR ˌriːˈhand|l, -lz,
-lɪŋ \-lɪŋ, -ld
AM riˈhæn(d)əl, -z, -ɪŋ,
-d

rehang
BR (ˌ)riːˈhaŋ, -z, -ɪŋ
AM riˈhæŋ, -z, -ɪŋ

rehash[1]
noun
BR ˈriːhaʃ, -ɪz
AM ˈriˌhæʃ, -ɪz

rehash[2]
verb
BR (ˌ)riːˈhaʃ, -ɪz, -ɪŋ, -t
AM riˈhæʃ, -ɪz, -ɪŋ, -d

rehear
BR ˌriːˈhɪə(r), -z, -ɪŋ
AM riˈhɪ(ə)r, -z, -ɪŋ

reheard
BR ˌriːˈhɜːd
AM riˈhɜrd

rehearsal
BR rɪˈhɜːs|l, -z
AM rəˈhɜrsəl,
riˈhɜrsəl, -z

rehearse
BR rɪˈhɜːs, -ɪz, -ɪŋ, -t
AM rəˈhɜrs, riˈhɜrs, -əz,
-ɪŋ, -t

rehearser
BR rɪˈhɜːsə(r), -z
AM rəˈhɜrsər,
ˈriˈhɜrsər, -z

reheat
BR ˌriːˈhiːt, -s, -ɪŋ, -ɪd
AM riˈhiˌlt, -ts, -dɪŋ, -dɪd

reheater
BR ˌriːˈhiːtə(r), -z
AM riˈhidər, -z

reheel
BR ˌriːˈhiːl, -z, -ɪŋ, -d
AM riˈhil, -z, -ɪŋ, -d

Rehnquist
BR ˈrɛnkwɪst
AM ˈrɛnˌkwɪst
SW reːnˈkvɪst

Rehoboam
BR ˌriː(h)əˈbəʊəm, -z
AM ˌri(h)əˈbouəm, -z

rehome
BR ˌriːˈhəʊm, -z, -ɪŋ, -d
AM riˈhoum, -z, -ɪŋ, -d

rehouse
BR ˌriːˈhaʊz, -ɪz, -ɪŋ, -d
AM riˈhaʊz, -əz, -ɪŋ, -d

rehung
BR (ˌ)riːˈhʌŋ
AM riˈhəŋ

rehydratable
BR riˈhʌɪˈdreɪtəbl
AM riˈhaɪˌdreɪdəbəl

rehydrate
BR ˌriːhʌɪˈdreɪt, -s, -ɪŋ,
-ɪd
AM riˈhaɪˌdreɪ|t, -ts,
-dɪŋ, -dɪd

rehydration
BR ˌriːhʌɪˈdreɪʃn
AM ˌriˈhaɪˈdreɪʃən

Reich
BR rʌɪx, rʌɪk
AM raɪk

Reichstag
BR ˈrʌɪxstɑːg,
ˈrʌɪʃstɑːg, ˈrʌɪkstɑːg
AM ˈraɪkˌstæg

Reid
BR riːd
AM rid

reification
BR ˌreɪɪfɪˈkeɪʃn,
ˌriːɪfɪˈkeɪʃn

AM ˌriəfəˈkeɪʃən,
ˌreɪəfəˈkeɪʃən

reificatory
BR ˌreɪɪfɪˈkeɪt(ə)ri,
ˌriːɪfɪˈkeɪt(ə)ri
AM reɪˈɪfəkəˌtɔri,
riˈɪfəkəˌtɔri

reify
BR ˈreɪfʌɪ, ˈriːɪfʌɪ, -z,
-ɪŋ, -d
AM ˈriəˌfaɪ, -z, -ɪŋ, -d

Reigate
BR ˈrʌɪgeɪt, ˈrʌɪgət
AM ˈraɪˌgeɪt

reign
BR reɪn, -z, -ɪŋ, -d
AM reɪn, -z, -ɪŋ, -d

reignite
BR ˌriːɪgˈnʌɪt, -s, -ɪŋ, -ɪd
AM ˌriɪgˈnaɪ|t, -ts, -dɪŋ,
-dɪd

Reilly
BR ˈrʌɪli
AM ˈraɪli

reimbursable
BR ˌriːɪmˈbɜːsəbl
AM ˈriɪmˈbɜrsəbəl

reimburse
BR ˌriːɪmˈbɜːs, -ɪz, -ɪŋ, -t
AM ˈriɪmˈbɜrs, -əz, -ɪŋ,
-t

reimbursement
BR ˌriːɪmˈbɜːsm(ə)nt,
-s
AM ˈriɪmˈbɜrsmənt, -s

reimburser
BR ˌriːɪmˈbɜːsə(r), -z
AM ˈriɪmˈbɜrsər, -z

reimport
BR ˌriːɪmˈpɔːt, -s, -ɪŋ,
-ɪd
AM riˈɪmˌpɔ(ə)rt,
riˌɪmˈpɔ(ə)rt, -ts,
-pɔrdɪŋ, -pɔrdəd

reimportation
BR ˌriːɪmpɔːˈteɪʃn
AM ˌriˌɪmpɔrˈteɪʃən

reimpose
BR ˌriːɪmˈpəʊz, -ɪz, -ɪŋ,
-d
AM ˈriɪmˈpouz, -əz, -ɪŋ,
-d

reimposition
BR ˌriːɪmpəˈzɪʃn
AM ˌriˌɪmpəˈzɪʃən

Reims
BR riːmz
AM rimz
FR RɛS

rein
BR reɪn, -z, -ɪŋ, -d
AM reɪn, -z, -ɪŋ, -d

reincarnate[1]
adjective
BR ˌriːɪnˈkɑːnət,
ˌriːɪŋˈkɑːnət
AM ˈriɪnˈkɑrnət,
ˈriɪŋˈkɑrˌnət

reincarnate[2]
verb
BR ˌriːɪnˈkɑːneɪt,
ˌriːɪŋˈkɑːneɪt, -s, -ɪŋ,
-ɪd
AM ˈriɪnˈkɑrˌneɪt,
ˈriɪŋˈkɑrˌneɪ|t, -ts,
-dɪŋ, -dɪd

reincarnation
BR ˌriːɪnkɑːˈneɪʃn,
ˌriːɪŋkɑːˈneɪʃn, -z
AM ˈriɪnˌkɑrˈneɪʃən,
ˈriɪŋˌkɑrˈneɪʃən, -z

reincorporate
BR ˌriːɪnˈkɔːpəreɪt,
ˌriːɪŋˈkɔːpəreɪt, -s, -ɪŋ,
-ɪd
AM ˈriɪnˈkɔrpəˌreɪt,
ˈriɪŋˈkɔrpəreɪ|t, -ts,
-dɪŋ, -dɪd

reincorporation
BR ˌriːɪnˌkɔːpəˈreɪʃn,
ˌriːɪŋˌkɔːpəˈreɪʃn
AM ˈriɪnˌkɔrpəˈreɪʃən,
ˈriɪŋˌkɔrpəˈreɪʃən

reindeer
BR ˈreɪndɪə(r), -z
AM ˈreɪnˌdɪ(ə)r, -z

reinfect
BR ˌriːɪnˈfɛkt, -s, -ɪŋ, -ɪd
AM ˈriɪnˈfɛk|(t), -(t)s,
-tɪŋ, -təd

reinfection
BR ˌriːɪnˈfɛkʃn, -z
AM ˈriɪnˈfɛkʃən, -z

reinforce
BR ˌriːɪnˈfɔːs, -ɪz, -ɪŋ, -t
AM ˈriɪnˈfɔ(ə)rs, -əz,
-ɪŋ, -t

reinforcement
BR ˌriːɪnˈfɔːsm(ə)nt, -s
AM ˈriɪnˈfɔrsmənt, -s

reinforcer
BR ˌriːɪnˈfɔːsə(r), -z
AM ˈriɪnˈfɔrsər, -z

Reinhardt
BR ˈrʌɪnhɑːt
AM ˈraɪnˌ(h)ɑrt

reinject
BR ˌriːɪnˈdʒɛkt, -s, -ɪŋ,
-ɪd
AM ˈriɪnˈdʒɛk|(t), -(t)s,
-tɪŋ, -təd

reinless
BR ˈreɪnlɪs
AM ˈreɪnlɪs

reinsert
BR ˌriːɪnˈsɜːt, -s, -ɪŋ, -ɪd
AM ˈriɪnˈsɜr|t, -ts, -dɪŋ,
-dəd

reinsertion
BR ˌriːɪnˈsɜːʃn, -z
AM ˈriɪnˈsɜrʃən, -z

reinspect
BR ˌriːɪnˈspɛkt, -s, -ɪŋ,
-ɪd

reinstal
BR ˌriːmzˈpɛk|(t),
ˌriːmˈspɛk|(t), -(t)s,
-tɪŋ, -təd

reinstal
BR ˌriːɪnˈstɔːl, -z, -ɪŋ, -d
AM ˌriːɪnˈstɔl, ˈriːɪnˌstɔl,
ˈriːnzˈtɔl, ˈriːmˈstɑl, -z,
-ɪŋ, -d

reinstall
BR ˌriːɪnˈstɔːl, -z, -ɪŋ, -d
AM ˌriːnzˈtɔl, ˈriːmˈstɔl,
ˈriːnzˈtɑl, ˈriːmˈstɑl, -z,
-ɪŋ, -d

reinstate
BR ˌriːɪnˈsteɪt, -s, -ɪŋ,
-ɪd
AM ˈriːmˈsteɪ|t, -ts, -dɪŋ,
-dɪd

reinstatement
BR ˌriːɪnˈsteɪtm(ə)nt,
-s
AM ˈriːmˈsteɪtmənt, -s

reinstitute
BR ˌriːˈɪnstɪtjuːt,
ˌriːˈɪnstɪtʃuːt, -s, -ɪŋ, -d
AM ˈriˈɪnstəˌt(j)u|t, -ts,
-dɪŋ, -dɪd

reinstitution
BR ˌriːɪnstɪˈtjuːʃn,
ˌriːmstɪˈtʃuːʃn
AM ˌriˌɪnstəˈt(j)uʃən

reinsurance
BR ˌriːmˈʃʊərəns,
ˌriːmˈʃʊərŋs,
ˌriːmˈʃɔːrəns,
ˌriːmˈʃɔːrŋs
AM ˈriːmʃʊrəns

reinsure
BR ˌriːmˈʃʊə(r),
ˌriːmˈʃɔː(r), -z, -ɪŋ, -d
AM ˈriːmˈʃʊ(ə)r, -z, -ɪŋ,
-d

reinsurer
BR ˌriːmˈʃʊərə(r),
ˌriːmˈʃɔːrə(r), -z
AM ˈriːmˈʃʊrər, -z

reintegrate
BR ˌriːˈɪntɪgreɪt, -s, -ɪŋ,
-ɪd
AM ˈriˈɪn(t)əˌgreɪ|t, -ts,
-dɪŋ, -dɪd

reintegration
BR ˌriːɪntɪˈgreɪʃn
AM ˌriˌɪn(t)əˈgreɪʃən

reinter
BR ˌriːɪnˈtəː(r), -z, -ɪŋ,
-d
AM ˈriːmˈtər, -z, -ɪŋ, -d

reinterment
BR ˌriːɪnˈtəːm(ə)nt, -s
AM ˈriːmˈtərmənt, -s

reinterpret
BR ˌriːɪnˈtəːprɪt, -s, -ɪŋ,
-ɪd
AM ˈriːmˈtərprə|t, -ts,
-dɪŋ, -dəd

reinterpretation
BR ˌriːɪnˌtəːprɪˈteɪʃn,
-z
AM ˈriːmˌtərprəˈteɪʃən,
-z

reintroduce
BR ˌriːɪntrəˈdjuːs,
ˌriːɪntrəˈdʒuːs, -ɪz, -ɪŋ,
-t
AM ˈriːmtrəˈd(j)us, -ɪz,
-ɪŋ, -t

reintroduction
BR ˌriːɪntrəˈdʌkʃn
AM ˈriːmtrəˈdəkʃən

reinvent
BR ˌriːɪnˈvɛnt, -s, -ɪŋ,
-ɪd
AM ˈriːmˈven|t, -ts,
-(t)ɪŋ, -(t)əd

reinvention
BR ˌriːɪnˈvɛnʃn
AM ˈriːmˈvɛnʃən

reinvest
BR ˌriːɪnˈvɛst, -s, -ɪŋ, -ɪd
AM ˈriːmˈvest, -s, -ɪŋ, -ɪd

reinvestigate
BR ˌriːɪnˈvɛstɪgeɪt, -s,
-ɪŋ, -d
AM ˈriːmˈvestəˌgeɪ|t, -ts,
-dɪŋ, -dɪd

reinvestigation
BR ˌriːɪnˌvɛstɪˈgeɪʃn, -z
AM ˈriːmˌvestəˈgeɪʃən,
-z

reinvestment
BR ˌriːɪnˈvɛs(t)m(ə)nt,
-s
AM ˈriːmˈvestmənt, -s

reinvigorate
BR ˌriːɪnˈvɪgəreɪt, -s,
-ɪŋ, -ɪd
AM ˈriːmˈvɪgəˌreɪ|t, -ts,
-dɪŋ, -dɪd

reinvigoration
BR ˌriːɪnˌvɪgəˈreɪʃn
AM ˈriːmˌvɪgəˈreɪʃən

reissue
BR ˌriːˈɪʃ(j)uː, ˌriːˈɪsjuː,
-z, -ɪŋ, -d
AM riˈɪʃu, -z, -ɪŋ, -d

reiterate
BR riːˈɪtəreɪt,
ˌriːˈɪtəreɪt, -s, -ɪŋ, -ɪd
AM riˈɪdəˌreɪ|t, -ts, -dɪŋ,
-dɪd

reiteration
BR riːˌɪtəˈreɪʃn,
ˌriːˌɪtəˈreɪʃn
AM riˌɪdəˈreɪʃən

reiterative
BR riːˈɪt(ə)rətɪv,
ˌriːˈɪt(ə)rətɪv
AM riˈɪdəˌreɪdɪv,
riˈɪdərədɪv

Reith
BR riːθ
AM riθ

reive
BR riːv, -z, -ɪŋ, -d
AM riv, -z, -ɪŋ, -d

reiver
BR ˈriːvə(r), -z
AM ˈrivər, -z

reject¹
noun
BR ˈriːdʒɛkt, -s
AM ˈriˌdʒɛk(t), -s

reject²
verb
BR rɪˈdʒɛkt, -s, -ɪŋ, -ɪd
AM rəˈdʒɛk|(t),
riˈdʒɛk|(t), -(t)s, -tɪŋ,
-təd

rejectable
BR rɪˈdʒɛktəbl
AM rəˈdʒɛktəbəl,
riˈdʒɛktəbəl

rejectamenta
BR rɪˌdʒɛktəˈmɛntə(r)
AM rəˌdʒɛktəˈmɛn(t)ə,
riˌdʒɛktəˈmɛn(t)ə

rejecter
BR rɪˈdʒɛktə(r), -z
AM rəˈdʒɛktər,
riˈdʒɛktər, -z

rejection
BR rɪˈdʒɛkʃn, -z
AM rəˈdʒɛkʃən,
riˈdʒɛkʃən, -z

rejectionist
BR rɪˈdʒɛkʃnɪst,
rɪˈdʒɛkʃənɪst, -s
AM rəˈdʒɛkʃənəst,
rəˈdʒɛkʃnəst,
riˈdʒɛkʃənəst,
riˈdʒɛkʃnəst, -s

rejective
BR rɪˈdʒɛktɪv
AM rəˈdʒɛktɪv,
riˈdʒɛktɪv

rejector
BR rɪˈdʒɛktə(r), -z
AM rəˈdʒɛktər,
riˈdʒɛktər, -z

rejig
BR ˌriːˈdʒɪg, -z, -ɪŋ, -d
AM riˈdʒɪg, -z, -ɪŋ, -d

rejoice
BR rɪˈdʒɔɪs, -ɪz, -ɪŋ, -t
AM rəˈdʒɔɪs, riˈdʒɔɪs,
-ɪz, -ɪŋ, -t

rejoicer
BR rɪˈdʒɔɪsə(r), -z
AM rəˈdʒɔɪsər,
riˈdʒɔɪsər, -z

rejoicing
BR rɪˈdʒɔɪsɪŋ, -z
AM rəˈdʒɔɪsɪŋ,
riˈdʒɔɪsɪŋ, -z

rejoicingly
BR rɪˈdʒɔɪsɪŋli
AM rəˈdʒɔɪsɪŋli,
riˈdʒɔɪsɪŋli

rejoin¹
answer
BR rɪˈdʒɔɪn, -z, -ɪŋ, -d
AM rəˈdʒɔɪn, riˈdʒɔɪn,
-z, -ɪŋ, -d

rejoin²
join again
BR ˌriːˈdʒɔɪn, -z, -ɪŋ, -d
AM riˈdʒɔɪn, -z, -ɪŋ, -d

rejoinder
BR rɪˈdʒɔɪndə(r), -z
AM rəˈdʒɔɪndər,
riˈdʒɔɪndər, -z

rejuvenate
BR rɪˈdʒuːvɪneɪt, -s, -ɪŋ,
-ɪd
AM rəˈdʒuvəˌneɪ|t,
riˈdʒuvəˌneɪ|t, -ts, -dɪŋ,
-dɪd

rejuvenation
BR rɪˌdʒuːvɪˈneɪʃn
AM rəˌdʒuvəˈneɪʃən,
riˌdʒuvəˈneɪʃən

rejuvenator
BR rɪˈdʒuːvɪneɪtə(r), -z
AM rəˈdʒuvəˌneɪdər,
riˈdʒuvəˌneɪdər, -z

rejuvenesce
BR ˌriːdʒuːvɪˈnɛs,
rɪˌdʒuːvɪˈnɛs, -ɪz, -ɪŋ, -d
AM rəˌdʒuvəˈnɛs,
riˌdʒuvəˈnɛs, -əz, -ɪŋ,
-t

rejuvenescence
BR ˌriːdʒuːvɪˈnɛsns,
rɪˌdʒuːvɪˈnɛsns
AM rəˌdʒuvəˈnɛsəns,
riˌdʒuvəˈnɛsəns

rejuvenescent
BR ˌriːdʒuːvɪˈnɛsnt,
rɪˌdʒuːvɪˈnɛsnt
AM rəˌdʒuvəˈnɛsənt,
riˌdʒuvəˈnɛsənt

rekindle
BR (ˌ)riːˈkɪnd|l, -lz,
-lɪŋ \-lŋ, -ld
AM riˈkɪn|dəl, -dəlz,
-(d)(ə)lɪŋ, -dəld

relabel
BR (ˌ)riːˈleɪb|l, -lz,
-lɪŋ \-lŋ, -ld
AM riˈleɪbəl, -z, -ɪŋ, -d

relapse¹
noun
BR ˈriːlaps, ˈriːlaps, -ɪz
AM ˈriˌlæps, -əz

relapse²
verb
BR rɪˈlaps, -ɪz, -ɪŋ, -t
AM rəˈlæps, riˈlæps,
ˈriˌlæps, -əz, -ɪŋ, -t

relapser
BR rɪˈlapsə(r), -z
AM rəˈlæpsər,
riˈlæpsər, ˈriˌlæpsər,
-z

relatable
BR rɪˈleɪtəbl

relate
AM rəˈleɪdəbəl,
riˈleɪdəbəl
relate
BR rɪˈleɪt, -s, -ɪŋ, -ɪd
AM rəˈleɪt, riˈleɪt, -ts,
-dɪŋ, -dɪd
relatedness
BR rɪˈleɪtɪdnɪs
AM rəˈleɪdɪdnɪs,
riˈleɪdɪdnɪs
relater
BR rɪˈleɪtə(r), -z
AM rəˈleɪdər, riˈleɪdər,
-z
relation
BR rɪˈleɪʃn, -z
AM rəˈleɪʃən, riˈleɪʃən,
-z
relational
BR rɪˈleɪʃn(ə)l,
rɪˈleɪʃən(ə)l
AM rəˈleɪʃ(ə)nəl,
riˈleɪʃ(ə)nəl
relationally
BR rɪˈleɪʃnəli,
rɪˈleɪʃn̩li, rɪˈleɪʃənl̩i,
rɪˈleɪʃ(ə)nəli
AM rəˈleɪʃ(ə)nəli,
riˈleɪʃ(ə)nəli
relationism
BR rɪˈleɪʃnɪz(ə)m,
rɪˈleɪʃənɪz(ə)m
AM rəˈleɪʃə,nɪzəm,
riˈleɪʃə,nɪzəm
relationist
BR rɪˈleɪʃnɪst,
rɪˈleɪʃənɪst, -s
AM rəˈleɪʃənəst,
riˈleɪʃənəst, -s
relationship
BR rɪˈleɪʃnʃɪp, -s
AM rəˈleɪʃən,ʃɪp,
riˈleɪʃən,ʃɪp, -s
relatival
BR ˌrɛləˈtʌɪvl
AM ˌrɛləˈtaɪvəl
relative
BR ˈrɛlətɪv, -z
AM ˈrɛlədɪv, -z
relatively
BR ˈrɛlətɪvli
AM ˈrɛlədɪvli
relativeness
BR ˈrɛlətɪvnɪs
AM ˈrɛlədɪvnɪs
relativisation
BR ˌrɛlətɪvʌɪˈzeɪʃn
AM ˌrɛlədəvəˈzeɪʃən,
ˌrɛlədə,vaɪˈzeɪʃən
relativise
BR ˈrɛlətɪvʌɪz, -ɪz, -ɪŋ,
-d
AM ˈrɛlədə,vaɪz, -ɪz, -ɪŋ,
-d
relativism
BR ˈrɛlətɪvɪz(ə)m
AM ˈrɛlədə,vɪzəm

relativist
BR ˈrɛlətɪvɪst, -s
AM ˈrɛlədəvəst, -s
relativistic
BR ˌrɛlətɪˈvɪstɪk
AM ˌrɛlədəˈvɪstɪk
relativistically
BR ˌrɛlətɪˈvɪstɪkli
AM ˌrɛlədəˈvɪstək(ə)li
relativity
BR ˌrɛləˈtɪvɪti
AM ˌrɛləˈtɪvɪdi
relativization
BR ˌrɛlətɪvʌɪˈzeɪʃn
AM ˌrɛlədəvəˈzeɪʃən,
ˌrɛlədə,vaɪˈzeɪʃən
relativize
BR ˈrɛlətɪvʌɪz, -ɪz, -ɪŋ,
-d
AM ˈrɛlədə,vaɪz, -ɪz, -ɪŋ,
-d
relator
BR rɪˈleɪtə(r), -z
AM rəˈleɪdər, riˈleɪdər,
-z
relaunch¹
noun
BR ˈriːlɔːn(t)ʃ, -ɪz
AM riˈlɔn(t)ʃ,
riˈlɑn(t)ʃ, -əz
relaunch²
verb
BR ˌriːˈlɔːn(t)ʃ, -ɪz, -ɪŋ,
-t
AM riˈlɔn(t)ʃ,
riˈlɑn(t)ʃ, -əz, -ɪŋ, -t
relax
BR rɪˈlaks, -ɪz, -ɪŋ, -t
AM rəˈlæks, riˈlæks,
-əz, -ɪŋ, -t
relaxant
BR rɪˈlaksnt, -s
AM rəˈlæksənt, -s
relaxation
BR ˌriːlakˈseɪʃn, -z
AM rəˌlækˈseɪʃən,
riˌlækˈseɪʃən, -z
relaxedly
BR rɪˈlaksɪdli
AM rəˈlæksədli,
riˈlæksədli
relaxedness
BR rɪˈlaksɪdnɪs
AM rəˈlæksədnəs,
riˈlæksədnəs
relaxer
BR rɪˈlaksə(r), -z
AM rəˈlæksər,
riˈlæksər, -z
relay¹
noun
BR ˈriːleɪ, -z
AM ˈri,leɪ, -z
relay²
verb, broadcast
BR ˈriːleɪ, -z, -ɪŋ, -d
AM riˈleɪ, rəˈleɪ, ˈri,leɪ,
-z, -ɪŋ, -d

relay³
verb, lay again
BR ˌriˈleɪ, -z, -ɪŋ, -d
AM riˈleɪ, -z, -ɪŋ, -d
relearn
BR ˌriˈlɜːn, -z, -ɪŋ, -d
AM riˈlɚn, -z, -ɪŋ, -d
releasable
BR rɪˈliːsəbl
AM rəˈlisəbəl,
riˈlisəbəl
release¹
noun new lease
BR ˌriːˈliːs, -ɪz
AM riˈlis, -z
release²
noun, verb,
freedom/free
BR rɪˈliːs, -ɪz, -ɪŋ, -t
AM rəˈlis, riˈlis, -ɪz, -ɪŋ,
-t
releasee
BR rɪˌliːˈsiː, -z
AM rəˌliˈsi, riˌliˈsi, -z
releaser
BR rɪˈliːsə(r), -z
AM rəˈlisər, riˈlisər, -z
releasor
BR rɪˈliːsə(r), -z
AM rəˈlisər, riˈlisər, -z
relegable
BR ˈrɛlɪɡəbl
AM ˈrɛləɡəbəl
relegate
BR ˈrɛlɪɡeɪt, -s, -ɪŋ, -ɪd
AM ˈrɛlə,ɡeɪt, -ts, -dɪŋ,
-dɪd
relegation
BR ˌrɛlɪˈɡeɪʃn
AM ˌrɛləˈɡeɪʃən
relent
BR rɪˈlɛnt, -s, -ɪŋ, -ɪd
AM rəˈlɛnt, riˈlɛnt, -ts,
-(t)ɪŋ, -(t)əd
relentless
BR rɪˈlɛntləs
AM rəˈlɛn(t)ləs,
riˈlɛn(t)ləs
relentlessly
BR rɪˈlɛntləsli
AM rəˈlɛn(t)ləsli,
riˈlɛn(t)ləsli
relentlessness
BR rɪˈlɛntləsnəs
AM rəˈlɛn(t)ləsnəs,
riˈlɛn(t)ləsnəs
relet
BR ˌriːˈlɛt, -s, -ɪŋ
AM riˈlɛ|t, -ts, -dɪŋ
relevance
BR ˈrɛlɪv(ə)ns
AM ˈrɛləvəns
relevancy
BR ˈrɛlɪv(ə)nsi
AM ˈrɛləvənsi
relevant
BR ˈrɛlɪv(ə)nt
AM ˈrɛləvənt

relevantly
BR ˈrɛlɪv(ə)ntli
AM ˈrɛləvən(t)li
relevé
BR ˌrələˈveɪ, -z
AM ˌrələˈveɪ, -z
reliability
BR rɪˌlʌɪəˈbɪlɪti
AM rəˌlaɪəˈbɪlɪdi,
riˌlaɪəˈbɪlɪdi
reliable
BR rɪˈlʌɪəbl
AM rəˈlaɪəbəl,
riˈlaɪəbəl
reliableness
BR rɪˈlʌɪəblnəs
AM rəˈlaɪəbəlnəs,
riˈlaɪəbəlnəs
reliably
BR rɪˈlʌɪəbli
AM rəˈlaɪəbli,
riˈlaɪəbli
reliance
BR rɪˈlʌɪəns
AM rəˈlaɪəns, riˈlaɪəns
reliant
BR rɪˈlʌɪənt
AM rəˈlaɪənt, riˈlaɪənt
relic
BR ˈrɛlɪk, -s
AM ˈrɛlɪk, -s
relict
BR ˈrɛlɪkt, -s
AM ˈrɛlɪk|(t), -(t)s
relief
BR rɪˈliːf, -s
AM rəˈlif, riˈlif, -s
relievable
BR rɪˈliːvəbl
AM rəˈlivəbəl,
riˈlivəbəl
relieve
BR rɪˈliːv, -z, -ɪŋ, -d
AM rəˈliv, riˈliv, -z, -ɪŋ,
-d
reliever
BR rɪˈliːvə(r), -z
AM rəˈlivər, riˈlivər, -z
relievo
BR rɪˈliːvəʊ,
ˌrɛlɪˈeɪvəʊ, -z
AM riˈlivoʊ, -z
relight
BR ˌriːˈlʌɪt, -s, -ɪŋ, -ɪd
AM riˈlaɪ|t, -ts, -dɪŋ,
-dɪd
religion
BR rɪˈlɪdʒ(ə)n, -z
AM rəˈlɪdʒən, riˈlɪdʒən,
-z
religioner
BR rɪˈlɪdʒ(ə)nə(r),
rɪˈlɪdʒn̩ə(r), -z
AM rəˈlɪdʒənər,
riˈlɪdʒənər, -z
religionism
BR rɪˈlɪdʒn̩ɪz(ə)m,
rɪˈlɪdʒənɪz(ə)m

religionist
AM rə'lɪdʒəˌnɪzəm,
ri'lɪdʒəˌnɪzəm
religionist
BR rɪ'lɪdʒənɪst,
rɪ'lɪdʒnɪst, -s
AM rə'lɪdʒənəst,
ri'lɪdʒənəst, -s
religionless
BR rɪ'lɪdʒənləs,
rɪ'lɪdʒnləs
AM rə'lɪdʒənləs,
ri'lɪdʒənləs
religiose
BR rɪ'lɪdʒɪəʊs
AM rə'lɪdʒiˌoʊs
religiosity
BR rɪˌlɪdʒɪ'ɒsɪti
AM rəˌlɪdʒi'ɑsədi
religious
BR rɪ'lɪdʒəs
AM rə'lɪdʒəs, ri'lɪdʒəs
religiously
BR rɪ'lɪdʒəsli
AM rə'lɪdʒəsli,
ri'lɪdʒəsli
religiousness
BR rɪ'lɪdʒəsnəs
AM rə'lɪdʒəsnəs,
ri'lɪdʒəsnəs
reline
BR ˌriː'lʌɪn, -z, -ɪŋ, -d
AM ri'laɪn, -z, -ɪŋ, -d
relinquish
BR rɪ'lɪŋkw|ɪʃ, -ɪʃɪz,
-ɪʃɪŋ, -ɪʃt
AM rə'lɪŋkwɪʃ,
ri'lɪŋkwɪʃ, -ɪz, -ɪŋ, -t
relinquishment
BR rɪ'lɪŋkwɪʃm(ə)nt,
-s
AM rə'lɪŋkwɪʃmənt,
ri'lɪŋkwɪʃmənt, -s
reliquary
BR 'relɪkwər|i, -ɪz
AM 'reləˌkwɛri, -z
reliquiae
BR rɪ'lɪkwiː
AM rə'lɪkwiˌi,
rə'lɪkwiˌaɪ
relish
BR 'rel|ɪʃ, -ɪʃɪz, -ɪʃɪŋ,
-ɪʃt
AM 'relɪʃ, -ɪz, -ɪŋ, -t
relishable
BR 'relɪʃəbl
AM 'reləʃəbəl
relit
BR ˌriː'lɪt
AM ri'lɪt
relive
BR ˌriː'lɪv, -z, -ɪŋ, -d
AM ri'lɪv, -z, -ɪŋ, -d
reload
BR ˌri'ləʊd, -z, -ɪŋ, -ɪd
AM ri'loʊd, -z, -ɪŋ, -əd
relocate
BR ˌriːlə(ʊ)'keɪt, -s, -ɪŋ,
-ɪd

AM ri'loʊˌkeɪ|t,
ˌriloʊ'keɪ|t, -ts, -dɪŋ,
-dɪd
relocation
BR ˌriːlə(ʊ)'keɪʃn
AM ˌriloʊ'keɪʃən
relucent
BR ˌriː'luːs(ə)nt
AM ri'lusənt
reluctance
BR rɪ'lʌkt(ə)ns
AM rə'ləkt(ə)ns,
ri'lək(ə)ns
reluctant
BR rɪ'lʌkt(ə)nt
AM rə'ləktnt, ri'ləktnt
reluctantly
BR rɪ'lʌkt(ə)ntli
AM rə'ləktən(t)li,
ri'ləktən(t)li
rely
BR rɪ'lʌɪ, -z, -ɪŋ, -d
AM rə'laɪ, ri'laɪ, -z, -ɪŋ,
-d
REM
BR ˌɑːriː'ɛm
AM ˌɑr'i'ɛm
rem
BR rɛm, -z
AM rɛm, -z
remade
BR ˌriː'meɪd
AM ri'meɪd
remain
BR rɪ'meɪn, -z, -ɪŋ, -d
AM rə'meɪn, ri'meɪn,
-z, -ɪŋ, -d
remainder
BR rɪ'meɪnd|ə(r), -əz,
-(ə)rɪŋ, -əd
AM rə'meɪnd|ər,
ri'meɪnd|ər, -ərz,
-(ə)rɪŋ, -ərd
remake¹
noun
BR 'riːmeɪk, -s
AM 'riˌmeɪk, -s
remake²
verb
BR ˌriː'meɪk, -s, -ɪŋ
AM ri'meɪk, -s, -ɪŋ
reman
BR ˌriː'man, -z, -ɪŋ, -d
AM ri'mæn, -z, -ɪŋ, -d
remand
BR rɪ'mɑːnd, rɪ'mand,
-z, -ɪŋ, -ɪd
AM rə'mænd,
ri'mænd, -z, -ɪŋ, -əd
remanence
BR 'rɛmənəns, -ɪz
AM 'rɛmənəns, -əz
remanent
BR 'rɛmənənt
AM 'rɛmənənt
remark¹
comment, notice
BR rɪ'mɑːk, -s, -ɪŋ, -t

AM rə'mɑrk, ri'mɑrk,
-s, -ɪŋ, -t
remark²
mark again
BR ˌriː'mɑːk, -s, -ɪŋ, -t
AM ri'mɑrk, -s, -ɪŋ, -t
remarkable
BR rɪ'mɑːkəbl
AM rə'mɑrkəbəl,
ri'mɑrkəbəl
remarkableness
BR rɪ'mɑːkəblnəs
AM rə'mɑrkəbəlnəs,
ri'mɑrkəbəlnəs
remarkably
BR rɪ'mɑːkəbli
AM rə'mɑrkəbli,
ri'mɑrkəbli
remarriage
BR ˌriː'mar|ɪdʒ, -ɪdʒɪz
AM ri'mɛrɪdʒ, -ɪz
remarry
BR ˌriː'mar|i, -ɪz, -ɪɪŋ,
-ɪd
AM ri'mɛri, -z, -ɪŋ, -d
remaster
BR ˌriː'mɑːst|ə(r),
ˌriː'mast|ə(r), -əz,
-(ə)rɪŋ, -əd
AM ri'mæstər, -z, -ɪŋ, -d
rematch¹
noun
BR 'riːmatʃ, -ɪz
AM 'riˌmætʃ, -əz
rematch²
verb
BR ˌriː'matʃ, -ɪz, -ɪŋ, -t
AM ri'mætʃ, -əz, -ɪŋ, -t
Rembrandt
BR 'rɛmbrant, -s
AM 'rɛmˌbrænt, -s
REME
BR 'riːmi
AM 'rimi
remeasure
BR ˌriː'mɛʒ|ə(r), -əz,
-(ə)rɪŋ, -əd
AM ri'mɛʒər, -z, -ɪŋ, -d
remeasurement
BR ˌriː'mɛʒəm(ə)nt, -s
AM ri'mɛʒərmənt, -s
remediable
BR rɪ'miːdɪəbl
AM rə'midiəbəl,
ri'midiəbəl
remedial
BR rɪ'miːdɪəl
AM rə'midiəl,
ri'midiəl
remedially
BR rɪ'miːdɪəli
AM rə'midiəli,
ri'midiəli
remediless
BR 'rɛmɪdɪlɪs
AM 'rɛmədɪlɪs
remedy
BR 'rɛmɪd|i, -ɪz, -ɪɪŋ, -ɪd

remake²

AM rə'mɑrk, ri'mɑrk,
-s, -ɪŋ, -t
remember
BR rɪ'mɛmb|ə(r), -əz,
-(ə)rɪŋ, -əd
AM rə'mɛmb|ər,
ri'mɛmb|ər, -ərz,
-(ə)rɪŋ, -ərd
rememberable
BR rɪ'mɛmb(ə)rəbl
AM rə'mɛmb(ə)rəbəl,
ri'mɛmb(ə)rəbəl
rememberer
BR rɪ'mɛmb(ə)rə(r), -z
AM rə'mɛmb(ə)rər,
ri'mɛmb(ə)rər, -z
remembrance
BR rɪ'mɛmbr(ə)ns, -ɪz
AM rə'mɛmbrəns,
ri'mɛmbrəns, -əz
remembrancer
BR rɪ'mɛmbr(ə)nsə(r),
-z
AM rə'mɛmbrənsər,
ri'mɛmbrənsər, -z
remex
BR 'riːmɛks, -ɪz
AM 'riˌmɛks, -əz
remind
BR rɪ'mʌɪnd, -z, -ɪŋ, -ɪd
AM rə'maɪnd,
ri'maɪnd, -z, -ɪŋ, -ɪd
reminder
BR rɪ'mʌɪndə(r), -z
AM rə'maɪndər,
ri'maɪndər, -z
remindful
BR rɪ'mʌɪn(d)f(ʊ)l
AM rə'maɪn(d)fəl,
ri'maɪn(d)fəl
Remington®
BR 'rɛmɪŋt(ə)n
AM 'rɛmɪŋtən
reminisce
BR ˌrɛmɪ'nɪs, -ɪz, -ɪŋ, -t
AM ˌrɛmə'nɪs, -ɪz, -ɪŋ, -t
reminiscence
BR ˌrɛmɪ'nɪsns, -ɪz
AM ˌrɛmə'nɪsəns, -ɪz
reminiscent
BR ˌrɛmɪ'nɪsnt
AM ˌrɛmə'nɪsənt
reminiscential
BR ˌrɛmɪnɪ'sɛnʃl
AM ˌrɛmənə'sɛn(t)ʃəl
reminiscently
BR ˌrɛmɪ'nɪsntli
AM ˌrɛmə'nɪsn(t)li
reminiscer
BR ˌrɛmɪ'nɪsə(r), -z
AM ˌrɛmə'nɪsər, -z
remint
BR ˌriː'mɪnt, -s, -ɪŋ, -ɪd
AM ri'mɪn|t, -ts, -(t)ɪŋ,
-(t)ɪd
remise
BR rɪ'mʌɪz, -ɪz, -ɪŋ, -d
AM rə'maɪz, ri'maɪz,
-ɪz, -ɪŋ, -d

remiss
BR rɪˈmɪs
AM rəˈmɪs, rɪˈmɪs

remissible
BR rɪˈmɪsɪbl
AM rəˈmɪsɪbəl,
rɪˈmɪsɪbəl

remission
BR rɪˈmɪʃn, -z
AM rəˈmɪʃən,
rɪˈmɪʃən, -z

remissive
BR rɪˈmɪsɪv
AM rəˈmɪsɪv, rɪˈmɪsɪv

remissly
BR rɪˈmɪsli
AM rəˈmɪsli, rɪˈmɪsli

remissness
BR rɪˈmɪsnɪs
AM rəˈmɪsnɪs,
rɪˈmɪsnɪs

remit[1]
noun
BR ˈriːmɪt, -s
AM rəˈmɪt, rɪˈmɪt,
ˈriːmɪt, -s

remit[2]
verb
BR rɪˈmɪt, -s, -ɪŋ, -ɪd
AM rəˈmɪt, rɪˈmɪt, -ts,
-dɪŋ, -dɪd

remittable
BR rɪˈmɪtəbl
AM rɪˈmɪdəbəl,
rɪˈmɪdəbəl

remittal
BR rɪˈmɪtl, -z
AM rɪˈmɪdl, rɪˈmɪdl, -z

remittance
BR rɪˈmɪt(ə)ns, -ɪz
AM rəˈmɪtns, rɪˈmɪtns,
-ɪz

remittee
BR rɪˌmɪˈtiː, -z
AM rəˌmɪˈti, rɪˌmɪˈti, -z

remittent
BR rɪˈmɪt(ə)nt
AM rəˈmɪtnt, rɪˈmɪtnt

remitter
BR rɪˈmɪtə(r), -z
AM rəˈmɪdər, rɪˈmɪdər,
-z

remix
BR ˌriːˈmɪks, -ɪz, -ɪŋ, -t
AM rɪˈmɪks, -əz, -ɪŋ, -t

remixer
BR ˌriːˈmɪksə(r), -z
AM rɪˈmɪksər, -z

remnant
BR ˈremnənt, -s
AM ˈremnənt, -s

remodel
BR (ˌ)riːˈmɒdl̩, -lz,
-l̩ɪŋ\-lɪŋ, -ld
AM riˈmɑdəl, -əlz,
-(ə)lɪŋ, -əld

remodification
BR ˌriːmɒdɪfɪˈkeɪʃn, -z

AM ˌriːˌmɑdəfəˈkeɪʃən,
-z

remodify
BR ˌriːˈmɒdɪfaɪ, -z, -ɪŋ,
-d
AM riˈmɑdəˌfaɪ, -z, -ɪŋ,
-d

remold[1]
noun
BR ˈriːməʊld, -z
AM ˈriˌmoʊld, -z

remold[2]
verb
BR ˌriːˈməʊld, -z, -ɪŋ, -ɪd
AM riˈmoʊld, -z, -ɪŋ, -əd

remonetisation
BR ˌriːmʌnɪtaɪˈzeɪʃn
AM riˌmɑnədəˈzeɪʃən,
riˌmɑnəˌtaɪˈzeɪʃən

remonetise
BR ˌriːˈmʌnɪtaɪz, -ɪz,
-ɪŋ, -d
AM riˈmɑnəˌtaɪz, -ɪz,
-ɪŋ, -d

remonetization
BR ˌriːmʌnɪtaɪˈzeɪʃn
AM riˌmɑnədəˈzeɪʃən,
riˌmɑnəˌtaɪˈzeɪʃən

remonetize
BR ˌriːˈmʌnɪtaɪz, -ɪz,
-ɪŋ, -d
AM riˈmɑnəˌtaɪz, -ɪz,
-ɪŋ, -d

remonstrance
BR rɪˈmɒnstr(ə)ns, -ɪz
AM rəˈmɑnstrəns,
rɪˈmɑnstrəns, -əz

remonstrant
BR rɪˈmɒnstr(ə)nt
AM rəˈmɑnstrənt,
rɪˈmɑnstrənt

remonstrantly
BR rɪˈmɒnstr(ə)ntli
AM rəˈmɑnstrən(t)li,
rɪˈmɑnstrən(t)li

remonstrate
BR ˈremənstreɪt, -s, -ɪŋ,
-ɪd
AM rɪˈmɑnˌstreɪt,
rɪˈmɑnˌstreɪt,
ˈremənˌstreɪt, -ts,
-dɪŋ, -dɪd

remonstration
BR ˌremənˈstreɪʃn, -z
AM rəˌmɑnˈstreɪʃən,
rɪˌmɑnˈstreɪʃən,
ˌremənˈstreɪʃən, -z

remonstrative
BR rɪˈmɒnstrətɪv
AM rəˈmɑnstrədɪv,
rɪˈmɑnstrədɪv,
ˈremənˌstreɪdɪv

remonstrator
BR ˈremənstreɪtə(r), -z
AM rəˈmɑnˌstreɪdər,
rɪˈmɑnˌstreɪdər,
ˈremənˌstreɪdər, -z

remontant
BR rɪˈmɒnt(ə)nt, -s
AM rəˈmɑntnt,
rɪˈmɑntnt, -s

remora
BR ˈrem(ə)rə(r),
rɪˈmɔːrə(r), -z
AM ˈremərə, -z

remorse
BR rɪˈmɔːs
AM rəˈmɔ(ə)rs,
rɪˈmɔ(ə)rs

remorseful
BR rɪˈmɔːsf(ʊ)l
AM rəˈmɔrsfəl,
rɪˈmɔrsfəl

remorsefully
BR rɪˈmɔːsfʊli,
rɪˈmɔːsfli
AM rəˈmɔrsfəli,
rɪˈmɔrsfəli

remorsefulness
BR rɪˈmɔːsf(ʊ)lnəs
AM rəˈmɔrsfəlnəs,
rɪˈmɔrsfəlnəs

remorseless
BR rɪˈmɔːsləs
AM rəˈmɔrsləs,
rɪˈmɔrsləs

remorselessly
BR rɪˈmɔːsləsli
AM rəˈmɔrsləsli,
rɪˈmɔrsləsli

remorselessness
BR rɪˈmɔːsləsnəs
AM rəˈmɔrsləsnəs,
rɪˈmɔrsləsnəs

remortgage
BR ˌriːˈmɔːgɪdʒ, -ɪdʒɪz,
-ɪdʒɪŋ, -ɪdʒd
AM riˈmɔrgɪdʒ, -ɪz, -ɪŋ,
-d

remote
BR rɪˈməʊt, -ə(r), -ɪst
AM rəˈmoʊt, rɪˈmoʊt,
-dər, -dəst

remotely
BR rɪˈməʊtli
AM rəˈmoʊtli,
rɪˈmoʊtli

remoteness
BR rɪˈməʊtnəs
AM rəˈmoʊtnəs,
rɪˈmoʊtnəs

remould[1]
noun
BR ˈriːməʊld, -z
AM ˈriˌmoʊld, -z

remould[2]
verb
BR ˌriːˈməʊld, -z, -ɪŋ, -ɪd
AM rəˈmoʊld,
rɪˈmoʊld, -z, -ɪŋ, -əd

remount[1]
noun
BR ˈriːmaʊnt, -s
AM ˈriˌmaʊnt, -s

remount[2]
verb
BR ˌriːˈmaʊnt, -s, -ɪŋ,
-ɪd
AM rəˈmaʊnt,
rɪˈmaʊnt, -ts, -(t)ɪŋ,
-(t)əd

removability
BR rɪˌmuːvəˈbɪlɪti
AM rəˌmuvəˈbɪlɪdi,
rɪˌmuvəˈbɪlɪdi

removable
BR rɪˈmuːvəbl
AM rəˈmuvəbəl,
rɪˈmuvəbəl

removal
BR rɪˈmuːvl̩, -z
AM rəˈmuvəl,
rɪˈmuvəl, -z

remove
BR rɪˈmuːv, -z, -ɪŋ, -d
AM rəˈmuv, rɪˈmuv, -z,
-ɪŋ, -d

removeable
BR rɪˈmuːvəbl
AM rəˈmuvəbəl,
rɪˈmuvəbəl

remover
BR rɪˈmuːvə(r), -z
AM rəˈmuvər,
rɪˈmuvər, -z

Remploy®
BR ˈremplɔɪ
AM ˈremplɔɪ

remunerate
BR rɪˈmjuːnəreɪt, -s,
-ɪŋ, -ɪd
AM rəˈmjunəˌreɪt,
rɪˈmjunəˌreɪt, -ts,
-dɪŋ, -dɪd

remuneration
BR rɪˌmjuːnəˈreɪʃn
AM rəˌmjunəˈreɪʃən,
rɪˌmjunəˈreɪʃən

remunerative
BR rɪˈmjuːn(ə)rətɪv
AM rəˈmjun(ə)rədɪv,
rɪˈmjun(ə)rədɪv,
rəˈmjunəˌreɪdɪv,
rɪˈmjunəˌreɪdɪv

remuneratory
BR rɪˈmjuːn(ə)rət(ə)ri
AM rəˈmjun(ə)rəˌtɔri,
rɪˈmjun(ə)rəˌtɔri

Remus
BR ˈriːməs
AM ˈriməs

Renaissance
BR rɪˈneɪs(ə)ns,
rɪˈneɪsɑːns, -ɪz
AM ˌrenəˈsɑns, -əz

renal
BR ˈriːnl
AM ˈrinəl

rename
BR (ˌ)riːˈneɪm, -z, -ɪŋ, -d
AM riˈneɪm, -z, -ɪŋ, -d

renascence
BR rɪˈnasns, rɪˈneɪsns, -ɪz
AM rəˈneɪsəns, rɪˈneɪsəns ˌrəˈnæsəns, rɪˈnæsns, -əz

renascent
BR rɪˈnasnt, rɪˈneɪsnt
AM rəˈneɪsənt, rɪˈneɪsənt, rəˈnæsənt, rɪˈnæsənt

Renata
BR rɪˈnɑːtə(r)
AM rəˈnɑːdə

renationalisation
BR ˌriːnaʃn̩əlaɪˈzeɪʃn̩, ˌriːnaʃn̩laɪˈzeɪʃn̩, ˌriːnaʃənlaɪˈzeɪʃn̩, ˌriːnaʃ(ə)nəlaɪˈzeɪʃn̩
AM ˌriːˌnæʃənləˈzeɪʃən, ˌriːˌnæʃnələˈzeɪʃən, ˌriːˌnæʃənlˌɑːˈzeɪʃən, ˌriːˌnæʃnəlˌɑːˈzeɪʃən

renationalise
BR ˌriːˈnaʃn̩əlaɪz, ˌriːˈnaʃn̩laɪz, ˌriːˈnaʃənlaɪz, ˌriːˈnaʃ(ə)nəlaɪz, -ɪz, -ɪŋ, -d
AM ˌriːˈnæʃənlˌaɪz, ˌriːˈnæʃnəlˌaɪz, -ɪz, -ɪŋ, -d

renationalization
BR ˌriːnaʃn̩əlaɪˈzeɪʃn̩, ˌriːnaʃn̩laɪˈzeɪʃn̩, ˌriːnaʃənlaɪˈzeɪʃn̩, ˌriːnaʃ(ə)nəlaɪˈzeɪʃn̩
AM ˌriːˌnæʃənləˈzeɪʃən, ˌriːˌnæʃnələˈzeɪʃən, ˌriːˌnæʃənlˌɑːˈzeɪʃən, ˌriːˌnæʃnəlˌɑːˈzeɪʃən

renationalize
BR ˌriːˈnaʃn̩əlaɪz, ˌriːˈnaʃn̩laɪz, ˌriːˈnaʃənlaɪz, ˌriːˈnaʃ(ə)nəlaɪz, -ɪz, -ɪŋ, -d
AM ˌriːˈnæʃənlˌaɪz, ˌriːˈnæʃnəlˌaɪz, -ɪz, -ɪŋ, -d

Renault®
BR ˈrɛnəʊ, -z
AM rəˈnoʊ, rəˈnɔːlt, rəˈnɑlt, -z\-ts

rencontre
BR rɛnˈkɒntə(r), -z
AM rɛnˈkɑn(t)ər, -z

rencounter
BR rɛnˈkaʊntə(r), -əz, -(ə)rɪŋ, -əd
AM rɛnˈkaʊn(t)ər, -z, -ɪŋ, -d

rend
BR rɛnd, -z, -ɪŋ
AM rɛnd, -z, -ɪŋ

Rendall
BR ˈrɛndl
AM ˈrɛndəl

Rendell
BR ˈrɛndl
AM ˈrɛndəl

render
BR ˈrɛndlə(r), -əz, -(ə)rɪŋ, -əd
AM ˈrɛndlər, -ərz, -(ə)rɪŋ, -ərd

renderer
BR ˈrɛnd(ə)rə(r), -z
AM ˈrɛndərər, -z

rendering
BR ˈrɛnd(ə)rɪŋ, -z
AM ˈrɛnd(ə)rɪŋ, -z

render-set
BR ˈrɛndəsɛt, -s, -ɪŋ
AM ˈrɛndərˌsɛlt, -ts, -dɪŋ

rendezvous
BR ˈrɒndɪvuː, ˈrɒndeɪvuː, -z, -ɪŋ, -d
AM ˈrɑndəˌvu, ˈrɑndeɪˌvu, -z, -ɪŋ, -d

rendition
BR rɛnˈdɪʃn, -z
AM rɛnˈdɪʃən, -z

rendzina
BR rɛn(d)ˈziːnə(r)
AM rɛn(d)ˈzinə

René
BR ˈrɛneɪ, ˈrəneɪ, rəˈneɪ
AM rəˈneɪ

Renée
BR ˈrɛneɪ, ˈrəneɪ, rəˈneɪ, ˈriːni
AM rəˈneɪ

renegade
BR ˈrɛnɪɡeɪd, -z
AM ˈrɛnəˌɡeɪd, -z

renegado
BR ˌrɛnɪˈɡɑːdəʊ, -z
AM ˌrɛnəˈɡɑˌdoʊ, -z

renege
BR rɪˈniːɡ, rɪˈneɪɡ, -z, -ɪŋ, -d
AM rəˈnɛɡ, rɪˈnɛɡ, -z, -ɪŋ, -d

reneger
BR rɪˈniːɡə(r), rɪˈneɪɡə(r), -z
AM rəˈnɛɡər, rɪˈnɛɡər, -z

renegotiable
BR ˌriːnɪˈɡəʊʃ(i)əbl
AM ˌrinəˈɡoʊʃ(i)əbəl

renegotiate
BR ˌriːnɪˈɡəʊʃieɪt, ˌriːnɪˈɡəʊsieɪt, -s, -ɪŋ, -ɪd
AM ˌrinəˈɡoʊʃiˌeɪlt, -ts, -dɪŋ, -dɪd

renegotiation
BR ˌriːnɪˌɡəʊʃiˈeɪʃn, ˌriːnɪˌɡəʊsiˈeɪʃn, -z
AM ˌrinəˌɡoʊʃiˈeɪʃən, ˌrinəˌɡoʊsiˈeɪʃən, -z

renegue
BR rɪˈniːɡ, rɪˈneɪɡ, -z, -ɪŋ, -d
AM rəˈnɛɡ, rɪˈnɛɡ, -z, -ɪŋ, -d

reneguer
BR rɪˈniːɡə(r), rɪˈneɪɡə(r), -z
AM rəˈnɛɡər, rɪˈnɛɡər, -z

renew
BR rɪˈnjuː, -z, -ɪŋ, -d
AM rəˈn(j)u, rɪˈn(j)u, -z, -ɪŋ, -d

renewability
BR rɪˌnjuːəˈbɪlɪti
AM rəˌn(j)uəˈbɪlɪdi, rɪˌn(j)uəˈbɪlɪdi

renewable
BR rɪˈnjuːəbl
AM rəˈn(j)uəbəl, rɪˈn(j)uəbəl

renewal
BR rɪˈnjuːəl, -z
AM rəˈn(j)uəl, rɪˈn(j)uəl, -z

renewer
BR rɪˈnjuːə(r), -z
AM rəˈn(j)uər, rɪˈn(j)uər, -z

Renfrew
BR ˈrɛnfruː
AM ˈrɛnfru

reniform
BR ˈrɛnɪfɔːm
AM ˈrɛnəˌfɔ(ə)rm, ˈreɪnəˌfɔ(ə)rm

renitence
BR ˈrɛnɪtns
AM ˈrɛnətns

renitency
BR ˈrɛnɪtnsi
AM ˈrɛnətnsi

renitent
BR ˈrɛnɪtnt
AM ˈrɛnətnt

renminbi
BR ˈrɛnmɪnbi
AM ˈrɛnmɪnbi

Rennes
BR rɛn
AM rɛn(s)

rennet
BR ˈrɛnɪt
AM ˈrɛnət

Rennie
BR ˈrɛni
AM ˈrɛni

rennin
BR ˈrɛnɪn
AM ˈrɛnən

Reno
BR ˈriːnəʊ
AM ˈrinoʊ

Renoir
BR ˈrɛnwɑː(r), rəˈnwɑː(r), -z

AM ˈrɛnˌwɑr, rəˈnwɑr, -z

renominate
BR ˌriːˈnɒmɪneɪt, -s, -ɪŋ, -ɪd
AM riˈnɑməˌneɪlt, -ts, -dɪŋ, -dɪd

renomination
BR ˌriːnɒmɪˈneɪʃn, -z
AM ˌriˌnɑməˈneɪʃən, -z

renounce
BR rɪˈnaʊns, -ɪz, -ɪŋ, -t
AM rəˈnaʊns, rɪˈnaʊns, -əz, -ɪŋ, -t

renounceable
BR rɪˈnaʊnsəbl
AM rəˈnaʊnsəbəl, rɪˈnaʊnsəbəl

renouncement
BR rɪˈnaʊnsm(ə)nt, -s
AM rəˈnaʊnsmənt, rɪˈnaʊnsmənt, -s

renouncer
BR rɪˈnaʊnsə(r), -z
AM rəˈnaʊnsər, rɪˈnaʊnsər, -z

renovate
BR ˈrɛnəveɪt, -s, -ɪŋ, -ɪd
AM ˈrɛnəˌveɪlt, -ts, -dɪŋ, -dɪd

renovation
BR ˌrɛnəˈveɪʃn, -z
AM ˌrɛnəˈveɪʃən, -z

renovative
BR ˈrɛnəveɪtɪv
AM ˈrɛnəˌveɪdɪv

renovator
BR ˈrɛnəveɪtə(r), -z
AM ˈrɛnəˌveɪdər, -z

renown
BR rɪˈnaʊn, -d
AM rəˈnaʊn, rɪˈnaʊn, -d

Renshaw
BR ˈrɛnʃɔː(r)
AM ˈrɛnˌʃɔ

rent
BR rɛnt, -s, -ɪŋ, -ɪd
AM rɛnlt, -ts, -(t)ɪŋ, -(t)əd

rentability
BR ˈrɛntəˈbɪlɪti
AM ˌrɛn(t)əˈbɪlɪdi

rentable
BR ˈrɛntəbl
AM ˈrɛn(t)əbəl

rent-a-car
BR ˈrɛntəkɑː(r)
AM ˈrɛn(t)əˌkɑr

rental
BR ˈrɛntl, -z
AM ˈrɛn(t)l, -z

rentboy
BR ˈrɛntbɔɪ, -z
AM ˈrɛntˌbɔɪ, -z

renter
BR ˈrɛntə(r), -z
AM ˈrɛn(t)ər, -z

rentier
BR ˈrɒntɪeɪ, -z
AM ˌrɑːnˈtjeɪ, -z

Rentokil®
BR ˈrentə(ʊ)kɪl
AM ˈren(t)əˌkɪl

Renton
BR ˈrentən
AM ˈren(t)ən

renumber
BR ˌriːˈnʌmbˌə(r), -əz, -(ə)rɪŋ, -əd
AM riːˈnʌmbər, -z, -ɪŋ, -d

renunciant
BR rɪˈnʌnsɪənt, -s
AM rəˈnʌnsiənt, riˈnʌnsiənt, -s

renunciation
BR rɪˌnʌnsɪˈeɪʃn, -z
AM rəˌnʌnsiˈeɪʃən, riˌnʌnsiˈeɪʃən, -z

renunciative
BR rɪˈnʌnsɪətɪv
AM rəˈnʌnsiədɪv, riˈnʌnsiədɪv, rəˈnʌnsiˌeɪdɪv, riˈnʌnsiˌeɪdɪv

renunciatory
BR rɪˈnʌnsɪət(ə)ri
AM rəˈnʌnsiəˌtɔːri, riˈnʌnsiəˌtɔːri

renvoi
BR ˈrɒnvwɑː(r), -z
AM ˈrenˌvɔːɪ, -z

Renwick
BR ˈren(w)ɪk
AM ˈrenwɪk

reoccupation
BR ˌriːˌɒkjəˈpeɪʃn, riˌɒkjəˈpeɪʃn, -z
AM ˌriːˌɑkjəˈpeɪʃən, -z

reoccupy
BR ˌriːˈɒkjəpʌɪ, rɪˈɒkjəpʌɪ, -z, -ɪŋ, -d
AM riˈɑkjəˌpaɪ, -z, -ɪŋ, -d

reoccur
BR ˌriːəˈkəː(r), -z, -ɪŋ, -d
AM ˌriəˈkər, -z, -ɪŋ, -d

reoccurrence
BR ˌriːəˈkʌrəns, ˌriːəˈkʌrn̩s, -ɪz
AM ˌriəˈkərəns, -əz

reoffend
BR ˌriːəˈfend, -z, -ɪŋ, -ɪd
AM ˌriəˈfend, -z, -ɪŋ, -əd

reopen
BR ˌriːˈəʊp|(ə)n, rɪˈəʊp|(ə)n, -(ə)nz, -(ə)nɪŋ\-n̩ɪŋ, -nd
AM riˈoʊp|ən, -ənz, -(ə)nɪŋ, -(ə)nd

reopening
BR ˌriːˈəʊp(ə)nɪŋ, rɪˈəʊp(ə)nɪŋ, ˌriːˈəʊpn̩ɪŋ, rɪˈəʊpn̩ɪŋ, -z
AM riˈoʊp(ə)nɪŋ, -z

reorder
BR ˌriːˈɔːd|ə(r), rɪˈɔːdə(r), -əz, -(ə)rɪŋ, -əd
AM riˈɔrdər, -z, -ɪŋ, -d

reorganisation
BR rɪˌɔːgənʌɪˈzeɪʃn, rɪˌɔːgʌɪˈzeɪʃn, ˌriːˌɔːgənʌɪˈzeɪʃn, ˌriːˌɔːgʌɪˈzeɪʃn
AM ˌriˌɔrgənəˈzeɪʃən, ˌriˌɔrgəˌnaɪˈzeɪʃən

reorganise
BR rɪˈɔːgənʌɪz, rɪˈɔːgʌɪz, ˌriːˈɔːgənʌɪz, ˌriːˈɔːgʌɪz, -ɪz, -ɪŋ, -d
AM riˈɔrgəˌnaɪz, -ɪz, -ɪŋ, -d

reorganiser
BR rɪˈɔːgənʌɪzə(r), rɪˈɔːgʌɪzə(r), ˌriːˈɔːgənʌɪzə(r), ˌriːˈɔːgʌɪzə(r), -z
AM riˈɔrgəˌnaɪzər, -z

reorganization
BR rɪˌɔːgənʌɪˈzeɪʃn, rɪˌɔːgʌɪˈzeɪʃn, ˌriːˌɔːgənʌɪˈzeɪʃn, ˌriːˌɔːgʌɪˈzeɪʃn
AM ˌriˌɔrgənəˈzeɪʃən, ˌriˌɔrgəˌnaɪˈzeɪʃən

reorganize
BR rɪˈɔːgənʌɪz, rɪˈɔːgʌɪz, ˌriːˈɔːgənʌɪz, ˌriːˈɔːgʌɪz, -ɪz, -ɪŋ, -d
AM riˈɔrgəˌnaɪz, -ɪz, -ɪŋ, -d

reorganizer
BR rɪˈɔːgənʌɪzə(r), rɪˈɔːgʌɪzə(r), ˌriːˈɔːgənʌɪzə(r), ˌriːˈɔːgʌɪzə(r), -z
AM riˈɔrgəˌnaɪzər, -z

reorient
BR rɪˈɔːrɪent, rɪˈɒrɪent, ˌriːˈɔːrɪent, ˌriːˈɒrɪent, -s, -ɪŋ, -ɪd
AM riˈɔriən|t, -ts, -(t)ɪŋ, -(t)əd

reorientate
BR rɪˈɔːrɪənteɪt, ˌriːˈɔːrɪənteɪt, rɪˈɒrɪənteɪt, ˌriːˈɒrɪənteɪt, -s, -ɪŋ, -ɪd
AM riˈɔriənˌteɪ|t, -ts, -dɪŋ, -dɪd

reorientation
BR rɪˌɔːrɪənˈteɪʃn, ˌriːˌɔːrɪənˈteɪʃn, rɪˌɒrɪənˈteɪʃn, ˌriːˌɒrɪənˈteɪʃn
AM ˌriˌɔriənˈteɪʃən

rep
BR rep, -s
AM rep, -s

repack
BR ˌriːˈpak, -s, -ɪŋ, -t
AM riˈpæk, -s, -ɪŋ, -t

repackage
BR ˌriːˈpak|ɪdʒ, -ɪdʒɪz, -ɪdʒɪŋ, -ɪdʒd
AM riˈpækɪdʒ, -ɪz, -ɪŋ, -d

repaginate
BR ˌriːˈpadʒɪneɪt, -s, -ɪŋ, -ɪd
AM riˈpædʒəˌneɪ|t, -ts, -dɪŋ, -dɪd

repagination
BR ˌriːpadʒɪˈneɪʃn, riˌpadʒɪˈneɪʃn, -z
AM riˌpædʒəˈneɪʃən, -z

repaid¹
paid again
BR ˌriːˈpeɪd
AM riˈpeɪd

repaid²
paid back
BR rɪˈpeɪd, (ˌ)riːˈpeɪd
AM rəˈpeɪd, riˈpeɪd

repaint
BR ˌriːˈpeɪnt, -s, -ɪŋ, -ɪd
AM riˈpeɪn|t, -ts, -(t)ɪŋ, -(t)ɪd

repair
BR rɪˈpɛː(r), -z, -ɪŋ, -d
AM rəˈpɛ(ə)r, riˈpɛ(ə)r, -z, -ɪŋ, -d

repairable
BR rɪˈpɛːrəbl
AM rəˈpɛrəbəl, riˈpɛrəbəl

repairer
BR rɪˈpɛːrə(r), -z
AM rəˈpɛrər, riˈpɛrər, -z

repairman
BR rɪˈpɛːˌman
AM rəˈpɛrˌmæn, riˈpɛrˌmæn

repairmen
BR rɪˈpɛːˌmen
AM rəˈpɛrˌmen, riˈpɛrˌmen

repand
BR rɪˈpand
AM rəˈpænd, riˈpænd

repaper
BR ˌriːˈpeɪp|ə(r), -əz, -(ə)rɪŋ, -əd
AM riˈpeɪpər, -z, -ɪŋ, -d

reparability
BR ˌrep(ə)rəˈbɪlɪti
AM ˌrep(ə)rəˈbɪlɪdi

reparable
BR ˈrep(ə)rəbl
AM ˈrep(ə)rəbəl

reparably
BR ˈrep(ə)rəbli
AM ˈrep(ə)rəbli

reparation
BR ˌrepəˈreɪʃn, -z
AM ˌrepəˈreɪʃən, -z

reparative
BR rɪˈparətɪv, ˈrep(ə)rətɪv
AM rəˈpɛrədɪv, riˈpɛrədɪv

repartee
BR ˌrepɑːˈtiː
AM ˈrɛˌpɑrˈti, ˌrɛpərˈti

repartition
BR ˌriːpɑːˈtɪʃn, -nz, -nɪŋ\-ənɪŋ, -nd
AM ˌriˌpɑrˈtɪʃən, -z, -ɪŋ, -d

repass
BR ˌriːˈpɑːs, ˌriːˈpas, -ɪz, -ɪŋ, -t
AM riˈpæs, -əz, -ɪŋ, -t

repast
BR rɪˈpɑːst, rɪˈpast, -s
AM rəˈpæst, riˈpæst, -s

repat
noun, repatriate
BR ˈriːpat, -s
AM ˈriˌpæt, -s

repatriate
BR ˌriːˈpatrɪeɪt, rɪˈpatrɪeɪt, -s, -ɪŋ, -ɪd
AM riˈpeɪtriˌeɪ|t, riˈpætriˌeɪ|t, -ts, -dɪŋ, -dɪd

repatriation
BR ˌriːpatrɪˈeɪʃn, rɪˌpatrɪˈeɪʃn, -z
AM riˌpeɪtriˈeɪʃən, riˌpætriˈeɪʃən, -z

repay¹
pay again
BR ˌriːˈpeɪ, -z, -ɪŋ, -d
AM riˈpeɪ, -z, -ɪŋ, -d

repay²
pay back
BR rɪˈpeɪ, (ˌ)riːˈpeɪ, -z, -ɪŋ, -d
AM riˈpeɪ, rəˈpeɪ, -z, -ɪŋ, -d

repayable
BR rɪˈpeɪəbl, (ˌ)riːˈpeɪəbl
AM riˈpeɪəbəl, rəˈpeɪəbəl

repayment
BR rɪˈpeɪm(ə)nt, (ˌ)riːˈpeɪm(ə)nt, -s
AM riˈpeɪmənt, rəˈpeɪmənt, -s

repeal
BR rɪˈpiːl, -z, -ɪŋ, -d
AM riˈpil, riˈpil, -z, -ɪŋ, -d

repealable
BR rɪˈpiːləbl
AM rəˈpiləbəl, riˈpiləbəl

repeat
BR rɪˈpiːt, -s, -ɪŋ, -ɪd
AM rəˈpi|t, riˈpi|t, -ts, -dɪŋ, -dɪd

repeatability
BR rɪˌpiːtəˈbɪlɪti
AM rəˌpidəˈbɪlɪdi,
riˌpidəˈbɪlɪdi

repeatable
BR rɪˈpiːtəbl
AM rəˈpidəbəl,
riˈpidəbəl

repeatedly
BR rɪˈpiːtɪdli
AM rəˈpidɪdli,
riˈpidɪdli

repeater
BR rɪˈpiːtə(r), -z
AM rəˈpidər, riˈpidər,
-z

repêchage
BR ˈrepɪʃɑːʒ, ˌrepɪˈʃɑːʒ,
-ɪz
AM ˌrepəˈʃɑʒ, -əz

repel
BR rɪˈpɛl, -z, -ɪŋ, -d
AM rəˈpɛl, riˈpɛl, -z, -ɪŋ,
-d

repellence
BR rɪˈpɛləns, rɪˈpɛl̩ns
AM rəˈpɛləns,
riˈpɛləns

repellency
BR rɪˈpɛlənsi, rɪˈpɛl̩nsi
AM rəˈpɛlənsi,
riˈpɛlənsi

repellent
BR rɪˈpɛlənt, rɪˈpɛl̩nt
AM rəˈpɛlənt, riˈpɛlənt

repellently
BR rɪˈpɛləntli,
rɪˈpɛl̩ntli
AM rəˈpɛlən(t)li,
riˈpɛlən(t)li

repeller
BR rɪˈpɛlə(r), -z
AM rəˈpɛlər, riˈpɛlər, -z

repent
BR rɪˈpɛnt, -s, -ɪŋ, -ɪd
AM rəˈpɛn|t, riˈpɛn|t,
-ts, -(t)ɪŋ, -(t)əd

repentance
BR rɪˈpɛnt(ə)ns, -ɪz
AM rəˈpɛntns,
riˈpɛntns, -əz

repentant
BR rɪˈpɛnt(ə)nt
AM rəˈpɛn(t)nt,
riˈpɛn(t)nt

repentantly
BR rɪˈpɛnt(ə)ntli
AM rəˈpɛntn(t)li,
riˈpɛntn(t)li

repenter
BR rɪˈpɛntə(r), -z
AM rəˈpɛn(t)ər,
riˈpɛn(t)ər, -z

repeople
BR ˌriːˈpiːp|l, -lz,
-lɪŋ\-lɪŋ, -ld
AM riˈpip|əl, -əlz,
-(ə)lɪŋ, -əld

repercussion
BR ˌriːpəˈkʌʃn, -z
AM ˌripərˈkəʃən,
ˌrɛpərˈkəʃən, -z

repercussive
BR ˌriːpəˈkʌsɪv
AM ˌripərˈkəsɪv,
ˌrɛpərˈkəsɪv

repertoire
BR ˈrepətwɑː(r), -z
AM ˈrɛpə(r)ˌtwɑr, -z

repertory
BR ˈrepət(ə)r|i, -ɪz
AM ˈrɛpə(r)ˌtɔri, -z

repetend
BR ˈrepɪtend,
ˌrepɪˈtend, -z
AM ˈrɛpəˌtend, -z

répétiteur
BR rɪˌpetɪˈtɜː(r), -z
AM rəˌpediˈtər, -z

repetition
BR ˌrepɪˈtɪʃn, -z
AM ˌrɛpəˈtɪʃən, -z

repetitional
BR ˌrepɪˈtɪʃn̩(ə)l,
ˌrepɪˈtɪʃən(ə)l
AM ˌrɛpəˈtɪʃ(ə)nəl

repetitionary
BR ˌrepəˈtɪʃn̩(ə)ri
AM ˌrɛpəˈtɪʃəˌnɛri

repetitious
BR ˌrepɪˈtɪʃəs
AM ˌrɛpəˈtɪʃəs

repetitiously
BR ˌrepɪˈtɪʃəsli
AM ˌrɛpəˈtɪʃəsli

repetitiousness
BR ˌrepɪˈtɪʃəsnəs
AM ˌrɛpəˈtɪʃəsnəs

repetitive
BR rɪˈpetɪtɪv
AM rəˈpedədɪv,
riˈpedədɪv

repetitively
BR rɪˈpetɪtɪvli
AM rəˈpedədɪvli,
riˈpedədɪvli

repetitiveness
BR rɪˈpetɪtɪvnɪs
AM rəˈpedədɪvnɪs,
riˈpedədɪvnɪs

rephrase
BR ˌriːˈfreɪz, -ɪz, -ɪŋ, -d
AM riˈfreɪz, -ɪz, -ɪŋ, -d

repine
BR rɪˈpaɪn, -z, -ɪŋ, -d
AM rəˈpaɪn, riˈpaɪn, -z,
-ɪŋ, -d

repique
BR rɪˈpiːk, -s, -ɪŋ, -t
AM rɪˈpik, rəˈpik, -s, -ɪŋ,
-t

replace
BR rɪˈpleɪs, (ˌ)riːˈpleɪs,
-ɪz, -ɪŋ, -t

replaceable
BR rɪˈpleɪsəbl,
(ˌ)riːˈpleɪsəbl
AM rəˈpleɪsəbəl,
riˈpleɪsəbəl

replacement
BR rɪˈpleɪsm(ə)nt,
(ˌ)riːˈpleɪsm(ə)nt, -s
AM rəˈpleɪsmənt,
riˈpleɪsmənt, -s

replacer
BR rɪˈpleɪsə(r),
(ˌ)riːˈpleɪsə(r), -z
AM rəˈpleɪsər,
riˈpleɪsər, -z

replan
BR ˌriːˈplaːnt, -z, -ɪŋ, -d
AM riˈplæn, -z, -ɪŋ, -d

replant
BR ˌriːˈplaːnt,
ˌriːˈplant, -s, -ɪŋ, -ɪd
AM riˈplæn|t, -ts, -(t)ɪŋ,
-(t)əd

replay¹
noun
BR ˈriːpleɪ, -z
AM ˈriˌpleɪ, -z

replay²
verb
BR ˌriːˈpleɪ, -z, -ɪŋ, -d
AM riˈpleɪ, -z, -ɪŋ, -d

replenish
BR rɪˈplɛnɪʃ, -ɪʃɪz,
-ɪʃɪŋ, -ɪʃt
AM rəˈplɛnɪʃ, riˈplɛnɪʃ,
-ɪz, -ɪŋ, -t

replenisher
BR rɪˈplɛnɪʃə(r), -z
AM rəˈplɛnɪʃər,
riˈplɛnɪʃər, -z

replenishment
BR rɪˈplɛnɪʃm(ə)nt, -s
AM rəˈplɛnɪʃmənt,
riˈplɛnɪʃmənt, -s

replete
BR rɪˈpliːt
AM rəˈplit, riˈplit

repleteness
BR rɪˈpliːtnɪs
AM rəˈplitnɪs,
riˈplitnɪs

repletion
BR rɪˈpliːʃn
AM rəˈpliʃən, riˈpliʃən

replevin
BR rɪˈplɛvɪn
AM rəˈplɛvən,
riˈplɛvən

replevy
BR rɪˈplɛv|i, -ɪz, -ɪɪŋ, -ɪd
AM rəˈplɛvi, riˈplɛvi, -z,
-ɪŋ, -d

replica
BR ˈreplɪkə(r), -z
AM ˈrɛpləkə, -z

replaceable
AM rəˈpleɪs, riˈpleɪs,
-ɪz, -ɪŋ, -t

replaceable
BR rɪˈpleɪsəbl,
(ˌ)riːˈpleɪsəbl
AM rəˈpleɪsəbəl,
riˈpleɪsəbəl

replicability
BR ˌreplɪkəˈbɪlɪti
AM ˌrɛpləkəˈbɪlɪdi

replicable
BR ˈreplɪkəbl
AM ˈrɛpləkəbəl

replicate
BR ˈreplɪkeɪt, -s, -ɪŋ, -ɪd
AM ˈreplə,keɪ|t, -ts,
-dɪŋ, -dɪd

replication
BR ˌreplɪˈkeɪʃn
AM ˌreplə,keɪʃən

replicative
BR ˈreplɪkətɪv
AM ˈreplə,keɪdɪv,
ˈrɛpləkədɪv

replicator
BR ˈreplɪkeɪtə(r), -z
AM ˈrɛplə,keɪdər, -z

replier
BR rɪˈplaɪə(r), -z
AM rəˈplaɪər, riˈplaɪər,
-z

reply
BR rɪˈplaɪ, -z, -ɪŋ, -d
AM rəˈplaɪ, riˈplaɪ, -z,
-ɪŋ, -d

reply-paid
BR rɪˌplaɪˈpeɪd
AM rəˈplaɪˈpeɪd,
riˈplaɪˈpeɪd

repo
BR ˈriːpəʊ, -z
AM ˈriˌpoʊ, -z

repoint
BR ˌriːˈpoɪnt, -s, -ɪŋ, -ɪd
AM riˈpoɪn|t, -ts, -(t)ɪŋ,
-(t)ɪd

repolish
BR ˌriːˈpɒlɪʃ, -ɪʃɪz,
-ɪʃɪŋ, -ɪʃt
AM riˈpalɪʃ, -ɪz, -ɪŋ, -t

repopulate
BR ˌriːˈpɒpjʊleɪt, -s,
-ɪŋ, -ɪd
AM riˈpapjəˌleɪ|t, -ts,
-dɪŋ, -dɪd

repopulation
BR ˌriːˌpɒpjʊˈleɪʃn,
riːˌpɒpjʊˈleɪʃn
AM ˌriˌpapjəˈleɪʃən

report
BR rɪˈpɔːt, -s, -ɪŋ, -ɪd
AM rəˈpɔ(ə)rt,
riˈpɔ(ə)rt, -ts,
-ˈpɔrdɪŋ, -ˈpɔrdəd

reportable
BR rɪˈpɔːtəbl
AM rəˈpɔrdəbəl,
riˈpɔrdəbəl

reportage
BR ˌrepɔːˈtɑː(d)ʒ,
rɪˈpɔːtɪdʒ
AM rəˈpɔrdɪdʒ,
riˈpɔrdɪdʒ

reportedly
BR rɪˈpɔːtɪdli

AM rəˈpɔːdədli,
riˈpɔːdədli

reporter
BR rɪˈpɔːtə(r), -z
AM rəˈpɔːrdər,
riˈpɔːrdər, -z

reportorial
BR ˌrɛpɔːˈtɔːriəl,
ˌriːpɔːˈtɔːriəl
AM ˌrɛpərˈtɔːriəl

reportorially
BR ˌrɛpɔːˈtɔːriəli,
ˌriːpɔːˈtɔːriəli
AM ˌrɛpərˈtɔːriəli

reposal
BR rɪˈpəʊzəl, -z
AM rəˈpoʊzəl,
riˈpoʊzəl, -z

repose
BR rɪˈpəʊz, -ɪz, -ɪŋ, -d
AM rəˈpoʊz, riˈpoʊz,
-əz, -ɪŋ, -d

reposeful
BR rɪˈpəʊzf(ʊ)l
AM rəˈpoʊzfəl,
riˈpoʊzfəl

reposefully
BR rɪˈpəʊzfʊli,
rɪˈpəʊzfli
AM rəˈpoʊzfəli,
riˈpoʊzfəli

reposefulness
BR rɪˈpəʊzf(ʊ)lnəs
AM rəˈpoʊzfəlnəs,
riˈpoʊzfəlnəs

reposition
BR ˌriːpəˈzɪʃ|n, -nz,
-nɪŋ\-nɪŋ, -nd
AM ˌriːpəˈzɪʃ|ən, -ənz,
-(ə)nɪŋ, -ənd

repository
BR rɪˈpɒzɪt(ə)r|i, -ɪz
AM rəˈpɑːzəˌtɔːri,
riˈpɑːzəˌtɔːri, -z

repossess
BR ˌriːpəˈzɛs, -ɪz, -ɪŋ, -t
AM ˌriːpəˈzɛs, -ɪz, -ɪŋ, -t

repossession
BR ˌriːpəˈzɛʃn, -z
AM ˌriːpəˈzɛʃən, -z

repossessor
BR ˌriːpəˈzɛsə(r), -z
AM ˌriːpəˈzɛsər, -z

repot
BR ˌriːˈpɒt, -s, -ɪŋ, -ɪd
AM riˈpɑːlt, -ts, -dɪŋ,
-dəd

repoussé
BR rɪˈpuːseɪ
AM rəˌpuːseɪ

repp
BR rɛp, -s, -t
AM rɛp, -s, -t

reprehend
BR ˌrɛprɪˈhend, -z, -ɪŋ,
-ɪd
AM ˌrɛprəˈhend, -z, -ɪŋ,
-ed

reprehensibility
BR ˌrɛprɪˌhensɪˈbɪlɪti
AM ˌrɛprəˌhensəˈbɪlɪdi

reprehensible
BR ˌrɛprɪˈhensɪbl
AM ˌrɛprəˈhensəbəl

reprehensibly
BR ˌrɛprɪˈhensɪbli
AM ˌrɛprəˈhensəbli

reprehension
BR ˌrɛprɪˈhenʃn
AM ˌrɛprəˈhenʃən

represent
BR ˌrɛprɪˈzent, -s, -ɪŋ,
-ɪd
AM ˌrɛprəˈzen|t, -ts,
-(t)ɪŋ, -(t)əd

re-present
BR ˌriːprɪˈzent, -s, -ɪŋ,
-ɪd
AM ˌriprəˈzen|t, -ts,
-(t)ɪŋ, -(t)ɪd

representability
BR ˌrɛprɪˌzentəˈbɪlɪti
AM ˌrɛprəˌzen(t)əˈbɪːdi

representable
BR ˌrɛprɪˈzentəbl
AM ˌrɛprəˈzen(t)əbəl

representation
BR ˌrɛprɪz(ɛ)nˈteɪʃn, -z
AM ˌrɛprəˌzenˈteɪʃən,
ˌrɛprəzənˈteɪʃən, -z

re-presentation
BR ˌriːˌprez(ə)nˈteɪʃn
AM ˌriˌpreznˈteɪʃən,
ˌriˌpriˌzenˈteɪʃən

representational
BR ˌrɛprɪz(ɛ)nˈteɪʃn(ə)l,
ˌrɛprɪz(ɛ)nˈteɪʃən(ə)l
AM ˌrɛprəˌzenˈteɪʃ(ə)nəl,
ˌrɛprəzənˈteɪʃ(ə)nəl

**representational-
ism**
BR ˌrɛprɪz(ɛ)nˈteɪʃnəl-
ɪz(ə)m,
ˌrɛprɪz(ɛ)nˈteɪʃnʲ-
ɪz(ə)m,
ˌrɛprɪz(ɛ)nˈteɪʃnʲ-
ɪz(ə)m,
ˌrɛprɪz(ɛ)nˈteɪʃ(ə)nəl-
ɪz(ə)m
AM ˌrɛprəˌzenˈteɪʃnəl-
ˌɪzəm,
ˌrɛprəzənˈteɪʃnəlˌɪzəm,
ˌrɛprəˌzenˈteɪʃnəˌlɪzəm,
ˌrɛprəzənˈteɪʃnəˌlɪzəm

**representational-
ist**
BR ˌrɛprɪz(ɛ)nˈteɪʃnəl-
ɪst,
ˌrɛprɪz(ɛ)nˈteɪʃnʲɪst,
ˌrɛprɪz(ɛ)nˈteɪʃnəl-
ist,
ˌrɛprɪz(ɛ)nˈteɪʃ(ə)nəl-
ɪst, -s
AM ˌrɛprəˌzenˈteɪʃnəl-
əst,
ˌrɛprəzənˈteɪʃnələst,

ˌrɛprəˌzenˈteɪʃnələst,
ˌrɛprəzənˈteɪʃnələst,
-s

representationism
BR ˌrɛprɪz(ɛ)nˈteɪʃn̩-
ɪz(ə)m,
ˌrɛprɪz(ɛ)nˈteɪʃən-
ɪz(ə)m
AM ˌrɛprəˌzenˈteɪʃə-
ˌnɪzəm,
ˌrɛprəzənˈteɪʃəˌnɪzəm

representationist
BR ˌrɛprɪz(ɛ)nˈteɪʃn̩ɪst,
ˌrɛprɪz(ɛ)nˈteɪʃənɪst,
-s
AM ˌrɛprəˌzenˈteɪʃənəst,
ˌrɛprəzənˈteɪʃənəst,
-s

representative
BR ˌrɛprɪˈzentətɪv, -z
AM ˌrɛprəˈzen(t)ədɪv,
-z

representatively
BR ˌrɛprɪˈzentətɪvli
AM ˌrɛprəˈzen(t)ədɪvli

**representative-
ness**
BR ˌrɛprɪˈzentətɪvnɪs
AM ˌrɛprəˈzen(t)ədɪvnɪs

repress
BR rɪˈprɛs, -ɪz, -ɪŋ, -t
AM rəˈprɛs, riˈprɛs, -əz,
-ɪŋ, -t

represser
BR rɪˈprɛsə(r), -z
AM rəˈprɛsər,
riˈprɛsər, -z

repressible
BR rɪˈprɛsɪbl
AM rəˈprɛsəbəl,
riˈprɛsəbəl

repression
BR rɪˈprɛʃn, -z
AM rəˈprɛʃən,
riˈprɛʃən, -z

repressive
BR rɪˈprɛsɪv
AM rəˈprɛsɪv, riˈprɛsɪv

repressively
BR rɪˈprɛsɪvli
AM rəˈprɛsɪvli,
riˈprɛsɪvli

repressiveness
BR rɪˈprɛsɪvnɪs
AM rəˈprɛsɪvnɪs,
riˈprɛsɪvnɪs

repressor
BR rɪˈprɛsə(r), -z
AM rəˈprɛsər,
riˈprɛsər, -z

repressurisation
BR ˌriːˌprɛʃ(ə)raɪˈzeɪʃn
AM ˌriˌprɛʃərəˈzeɪʃən,
ˌriˌprɛʃəˌraɪˈzeɪʃən

repressurise
BR ˌriːˈprɛʃəraɪz, -ɪz,
-ɪŋ, -d
AM riˈprɛʃəˌraɪz, -ɪz,
-ɪŋ, -d

repressurization
BR ˌriːˌprɛʃ(ə)raɪˈzeɪʃn
AM ˌriˌprɛʃərəˈzeɪʃən,
ˌriˌprɛʃəˌraɪˈzeɪʃən

repressurize
BR ˌriːˈprɛʃəraɪz, -ɪz,
-ɪŋ, -d
AM riˈprɛʃəˌraɪz, -ɪz,
-ɪŋ, -d

reprice
BR riˈpraɪs, -ɪz, -ɪŋ, -t
AM riˈpraɪs, -ɪz, -ɪŋ, -t

reprieve
BR rɪˈpriːv, -z, -ɪŋ, -d
AM rəˈpriv, riˈpriv, -z,
-ɪŋ, -d

reprimand
BR ˈrɛprɪmɑːnd,
ˈrɛprɪmand, -z, -ɪŋ, -ɪd
AM ˈrɛprəˌmænd, -z,
-ɪŋ, -əd

reprint[1]
noun
BR ˈriːprɪnt, -s
AM ˈriˌprɪnt, -s

reprint[2]
verb
BR ˌriːˈprɪnt, -s, -ɪŋ, -ɪd
AM riˈprɪn|t, -ts, -(t)ɪŋ,
-(t)ɪd

reprinter
BR ˌriːˈprɪntə(r), -z
AM riˈprɪn(t)ər, -z

reprinting
BR ˌriːˈprɪntɪŋ, -z
AM riˈprɪn(t)ɪŋ, -z

reprisal
BR rɪˈpraɪzl, -z
AM rəˈpraɪzəl,
riˈpraɪzəl, -z

reprise
BR rɪˈpriːz, -ɪz
AM rəˈpraɪz, riˈpraɪz,
-ɪz

repro
BR ˈriːprəʊ, -z
AM ˈriˌproʊ, -z

reproach
BR rɪˈprəʊtʃ, -ɪz, -ɪŋ, -t
AM rəˈproʊtʃ,
riˈproʊtʃ, -əz, -ɪŋ, -t

reproachable
BR rɪˈprəʊtʃəbl
AM rəˈproʊtʃəbəl,
riˈproʊtʃəbəl

reproacher
BR rɪˈprəʊtʃə(r), -z
AM rəˈproʊtʃər,
riˈproʊtʃər, -z

reproachful
BR rɪˈprəʊtʃf(ʊ)l
AM rəˈproʊtʃfəl,
riˈproʊtʃfəl

reproachfully
BR rɪˈprəʊtʃfʊli,
rɪˈpəʊtʃfli

reproachfulness
BR rɪ'prəʊtʃf(ʊ)lnəs,
rɪ'prəʊtʃfəlnəs

reproachingly
BR rɪ'prəʊtʃɪŋli
AM rə'prəʊtʃɪŋli,
rɪ'prəʊtʃɪŋli

reprobate
BR 'reprəbeɪt, -s, -ɪŋ,
-ɪd
AM 'reprə‚beɪt, -ts,
-dɪŋ, -dɪd

reprobation
BR ‚reprə'beɪʃn
AM ‚reprə'beɪʃən

reprocess
BR ‚riː'prəʊses, -ɪz, -ɪŋ,
-t
AM ri'prɑ‚ses, -əz, -ɪŋ, -t

reproduce
BR ‚riː·prə'djuːs,
‚ri·prə'dʒuːs, -ɪz, -ɪŋ, -t
AM ‚riprə'd(j)us,
‚riprə'dʒus, -əz, -ɪŋ, -t

reproducer
BR ‚riː·prə'djuːsə(r),
‚ri·prə'dʒuːsə(r), -z
AM ‚riprə'd(j)usər,
'riprə'dʒusər, -z

reproducibility
BR ‚riː·prə‚dju·sɪ'bɪlɪti,
‚ri·prə‚dʒu·sɪ'bɪlɪti
AM ‚riprə‚d(j)usə'bɪlɪdi,
'riprə‚dʒusə'bɪlɪdi

reproducible
BR ‚riː·prə'dju·sɪbl,
‚ri·prə'dʒu·sɪbl
AM ‚riprə'd(j)usəbəl,
'riprə'dʒusəbəl

reproducibly
BR ‚riː·prə'dju·sɪbli,
‚ri·prə'dʒu·sɪbli
AM ‚riprə'd(j)usəbli,
'riprə'dʒusəbli

reproduction
BR ‚riː·prə'dʌkʃn, -z
AM ‚riprə'dəkʃən, -z

reproductive
BR ‚riː·prə'dʌktɪv
AM ‚riprə'dəktɪv

reproductively
BR ‚riː·prə'dʌktɪvli
AM ‚riprə'dəktɪvli

reproductiveness
BR ‚riː·prə'dʌktɪvnɪs
AM ‚riprə'dəktɪvnɪs

reprogram
BR ‚riː·'prəʊgram, -z,
-ɪŋ, -d
AM ri'prəʊ‚græm, -z,
-ɪŋ, -d

reprogrammable
BR ‚riː·'prəʊgraməbl
AM ri‚prəʊ'græməbəl,
ri'prəʊgraməbəl

reprographer
BR rɪ'prɒgrəfə(r), -z
AM rə'prɑgrəfər,
rɪ'prɑgrəfər, -z

reprographic
BR ‚riː·prə'grafɪk,
‚reprə'grafɪk, -s
AM 'reprə'græfɪk,
'riprə'græfɪk, -s

reprographically
BR ‚riː·prə'grafɪkli,
‚reprə'grafɪkli
AM 'reprə'græfək(ə)li,
'riprə'græfək(ə)li

reprography
BR rɪ'prɒgrəfi
AM rə'prɑgrəfi,
rɪ'prɑgrəfi

reproof¹
noun
BR rɪ'pruː.f, -s
AM rə'pruf, rɪ'pruf, -s

reproof²
verb
BR ‚riː·'pruː.f, -s, -ɪŋ, -t
AM ri'pruf, -s, -ɪŋ, -t

reprovable
BR rɪ'pruː·vəbl
AM rə'pruvəbəl,
rɪ'pruvəbəl

reproval
BR rɪ'pruː·vl, -z
AM rə'pruvəl,
rɪ'pruvəl, -z

reprove
BR rɪ'pruː·v, -z, -ɪŋ, -d
AM rə'pruv, rɪ'pruv, -z,
-ɪŋ, -d

reprover
BR rɪ'pruː·və(r), -z
AM rə'pruvər,
rɪ'pruvər, -z

reproving
BR rɪ'pruː·vɪŋ
AM rə'pruvɪŋ,
rɪ'pruvɪŋ

reprovingly
BR rɪ'pruː·vɪŋli
AM rə'pruvɪŋli,
rɪ'pruvɪŋli

reptant
BR 'reptənt
AM 'reptnt

reptile
BR 'reptʌɪl, -z
AM 'reptl, 'rep‚taɪl, -z

reptilian
BR rep'tɪlɪən, -z
AM rep'tɪljən,
rep'tɪlɪən, -z

Repton
BR 'rept(ə)n
AM 'reptən

republic
BR rɪ'pʌblɪk, -s
AM rə'pəblɪk,
rɪ'pəblɪk, -s

republican
BR rɪ'pʌblɪk(ə)n, -z
AM rə'pəbləkən,
rɪ'pəbləkən, -z

republicanism
BR rɪ'pʌblɪkənɪz(ə)m,
rɪ'pʌblɪknɪz(ə)m
AM rə'pəbləkə‚nɪzəm,
rɪ'pəbləkə‚nɪzəm

republication
BR ‚riː·pʌblɪ'keɪʃn, -z
AM ri‚pəblə'keɪʃən,
rə‚pəblə'keɪʃən, -z

republish
BR ‚riː·'pʌblɪʃ, -ɪʃɪz,
-ɪʃɪŋ, -ɪʃt
AM ri'pəblɪʃ, rə'pəblɪʃ,
-ɪz, -ɪŋ, -t

repudiable
BR rɪ'pjuː·dɪəbl
AM rə'pjudiəbəl,
rɪ'pjudiəbəl

repudiate
BR rɪ'pjuː·dɪeɪt, -s, -ɪŋ,
-ɪd
AM rə'pjudi‚eɪt,
rɪ'pjudi‚eɪt, -ts, -dɪŋ,
-dɪd

repudiation
BR rɪ‚pjuː·dɪ'eɪʃn
AM rə‚pjudi'eɪʃən,
rɪ‚pjudi'eɪʃən

repudiator
BR rɪ'pjuː·dɪeɪtə(r), -z
AM rə'pjudi‚eɪdər,
rɪ'pjudi‚eɪdər, -z

repugnance
BR rɪ'pʌgnəns
AM rə'pəgnəns,
rɪ'pəgnəns

repugnant
BR rɪ'pʌgnənt
AM rə'pəgnənt,
rɪ'pəgnənt

repugnantly
BR rɪ'pʌgnəntli
AM rə'pəgnən(t)li,
rɪ'pəgnən(t)li

repulse
BR rɪ'pʌls, -ɪz, -ɪŋ, -t
AM rə'pəls, rɪ'pəls, -əz,
-ɪŋ, -t

repulsion
BR rɪ'pʌlʃn
AM rə'pəlʃən,
rɪ'pəlʃən

repulsive
BR rɪ'pʌlsɪv
AM rə'pəlsɪv, rɪ'pəlsɪv

repulsively
BR rɪ'pʌlsɪvli
AM rə'pəlsɪvli,
rɪ'pəlsɪvli

repulsiveness
BR rɪ'pʌlsɪvnɪs
AM rə'pəlsɪvnɪs,
rɪ'pəlsɪvnɪs

repurchase
BR ‚riː·'pəːtʃɪs, -ɪz, -ɪŋ, -t
AM ri'pərtʃəs, -əz, -ɪŋ,
-t

repurification
BR ‚riː·pjʊərɪfɪ'keɪʃn,
‚riː·pjɔːrɪfɪ'keɪʃn, -z
AM rə‚pjʊrəfə'keɪʃən,
rɪ‚pjʊrəfə'keɪʃən, -z

repurify
BR ‚riː·'pjʊərɪfʌɪ,
‚riː·'pjɔːrɪfʌɪ, -z, -ɪŋ, -d
AM ri'pjʊrə‚faɪ, -z, -ɪŋ,
-d

reputability
BR ‚repjʊtə'bɪlɪti
AM ‚repjədə'bɪlɪdi

reputable
BR 'repjʊtəbl
AM 'repjədəbəl

reputably
BR 'repjʊtəbli
AM 'repjədəbli

reputation
BR ‚repjʊ'teɪʃn, -z
AM ‚repjə'teɪʃən, -z

repute
BR rɪ'pjuːt
AM rə'pjut, rɪ'pjut

reputed
BR rɪ'pjuːtɪd
AM rə'pjudəd,
rɪ'pjudəd

reputedly
BR rɪ'pjuːtɪdli
AM rə'pjudədli,
rɪ'pjudədli

request
BR rɪ'kwest, -s, -ɪŋ, -ɪd
AM rə'kwest, rɪ'kwest,
-s, -ɪŋ, -əd

requester
BR rɪ'kwestə(r), -z
AM rə'kwestər,
rɪ'kwestər, -z

requicken
BR ‚riː·'kwɪk|(ə)n,
-(ə)nz, -n̩ɪŋ \-(ə)nɪŋ,
-(ə)nd
AM ri'kwɪk|ən, -ənz,
-(ə)nɪŋ, -ənd

requiem
BR 'rekwɪəm,
'rekwɪem, -z
AM 'rekwiəm,
'reɪkwiəm, -z

requiescat
BR ‚rekwɪ'eskat, -s
AM ‚rekwi'es‚kat, -s

require
BR rɪ'kwʌɪə(r), -z, -ɪŋ,
-d
AM rə'kwaɪ(ə)r,
rɪ'kwaɪ(ə)r, -z, -ɪŋ, -d

requirement
BR rɪ'kwʌɪəm(ə)nt, -s
AM rə'kwaɪ(ə)rmənt,
rɪ'kwaɪ(ə)rmənt, -s

requirer
BR rɪˈkwʌɪərə(r), -z
AM rəˈkwaɪ(ə)rər,
rɪˈkwaɪ(ə)rər, -z

requisite
BR ˈrɛkwɪzɪt, -s
AM ˈrɛkwəzət, -s

requisitely
BR ˈrɛkwɪzɪtli
AM ˈrɛkwəzətli

requisiteness
BR ˈrɛkwɪzɪtnɪs
AM ˈrɛkwəzətnəs

requisition
BR ˌrɛkwɪˈzɪʃn, -nz,
-n̩ɪŋ, -nd
AM ˌrɛkwəˈzɪʃ|ən, -ənz,
-(ə)nɪŋ, -ənd

requisitioner
BR ˌrɛkwɪˈzɪʃnə(r), -z
AM ˌrɛkwəˈzɪʃ(ə)nər,
-z

requisitionist
BR ˌrɛkwɪˈzɪʃn̩ɪst, -s
AM ˌrɛkwəˈzɪʃ(ə)nəst,
-s

requital
BR rɪˈkwʌɪtl
AM rəˈkwaɪdl,
rɪˈkwaɪdl

requite
BR rɪˈkwʌɪt, -s, -ɪŋ, -ɪd
AM rəˈkwaɪ|t,
rɪˈkwaɪ|t, -ts, -dɪŋ, -dɪd

reran
BR (ˌ)riːˈran
AM riˈræn

rerate
BR ˌriːˈreɪt, -s, -ɪŋ, -ɪd
AM riˈreɪ|t, -ts, -dɪŋ,
-dɪd

re-read¹
present tense
BR (ˌ)riːˈriːd, -z, -ɪŋ
AM riˈrid, -z, -ɪŋ

re-read²
past tense
BR (ˌ)riːˈrɛd
AM riˈrɛd

re-readable
BR (ˌ)riːˈriːdəbl
AM riˈridəbl

re-record
BR ˌriːrɪˈkɔːd, -z, -ɪŋ, -ɪd
AM ˈrirəˈkɔ(ə)rd, -z, -ɪŋ,
-əd

reredos
BR ˈrɪədɒs, -ɪz
AM ˈrɛrəˌdɑs, ˈrɪrəˌdɑs,
-əz

re-release
BR ˌriːrɪˈliːs, -ɪz, -ɪŋ, -t
AM ˈrirəˈlis, -ɪz, -ɪŋ, -t

re-roof
BR ˌriːˈruːf, riːˈrʊf, -s,
-ɪŋ, -t
AM riˈruf, riˈrʊf, -s, -ɪŋ,
-t

re-route
BR ˌriːˈruːt, -s, -ɪŋ, -ɪd
AM riˈraʊ|t, riˈru|t, -ts,
-dɪŋ, -dəd

rerun
noun
BR ˈriːrʌn, -z
AM ˈriˌrən, -z

re-run
verb
BR (ˌ)riːˈrʌn, -z, -ɪŋ
AM riˈrən, -z, -ɪŋ

res
BR reɪz, riːz
AM reɪs

resalable
BR ˌriːˈseɪləbl
AM riˈseɪləbl

resale
BR ˈriːseɪl, -z
AM ˈriˌseɪl, -z

resaleable
BR ˌriːˈseɪləbl
AM riˈseɪləbl

resat
BR ˌriːˈsat
AM riˈsæt

reschedule
BR ˌriːˈʃɛdjəl,
ˌriːˈʃɛdjuːl,
ˌriːˈʃɛdʒəl,
ˌriːˈskɛdjəl,
ˌriːˈskɛdjuːl, -z, -ɪŋ, -d
AM riˈskɛdʒəl, -z, -ɪŋ, -d

rescind
BR rɪˈsɪnd, -z, -ɪŋ, -ɪd
AM rəˈsɪnd, riˈsɪnd, -z,
-ɪŋ, -ɪd

rescindable
BR rɪˈsɪndəbl
AM rəˈsɪndəbl,
riˈsɪndəbl

rescindment
BR rɪˈsɪn(d)m(ə)nt, -s
AM rəˈsɪn(d)mənt,
riˈsɪn(d)mənt, -s

rescission
BR rɪˈsɪʒn
AM rəˈsɪʒən, riˈsɪʒən

rescript
BR ˈriːskrɪpt, -s
AM ˈriˌskrɪpt, -s

rescuable
BR ˈrɛskjʊəbl
AM ˈrɛskjuəbəl,
ˈrɛskjəwəbəl

rescue
BR ˈrɛskjuː, -z, -ɪŋ, -d
AM ˈrɛskju, -uz,
-uɪŋ \-əwɪŋ, -ud

rescuer
BR ˈrɛskjuːə(r), -z
AM ˈrɛskjuər,
ˈrɛskjəwər, -z

reseal
BR ˌriːˈsiːl, -z, -ɪŋ, -d
AM riˈsil, -z, -ɪŋ, -d

resealable
BR ˌriːˈsiːləbl
AM riˈsiləbl

research¹
noun
BR rɪˈsəːtʃ, ˈriːsəːtʃ, -ɪz
AM ˈriˌsərtʃ, rəˈsərtʃ,
riˈsərtʃ, -əz

research²
verb
BR rɪˈsəːtʃ, -ɪz, -ɪŋ, -t
AM rəˈsərtʃ, riˈsərtʃ,
ˈriˌsərtʃ, -əz, -ɪŋ, -t

researchable
BR rɪˈsəːtʃəbl
AM rəˈsərtʃəbəl,
riˈsərtʃəbəl,
ˈriˌsərtʃəbəl

researcher
BR rɪˈsəːtʃə(r),
ˈriːsəːtʃə(r), -z
AM rəˈsərtʃər,
riˈsərtʃər, ˈriˌsərtʃər,
-z

reseat
BR ˌriːˈsiːt, -s, -ɪŋ, -ɪd
AM rəˈsi|t, riˈsi|t, -ts,
-dɪŋ, -dɪd

resect
BR rɪˈsɛkt, -s, -ɪŋ, -ɪd
AM rəˈsɛk|(t),
riˈsɛk|(t), -(t)s, -tɪŋ,
-təd

resection
BR rɪˈsɛkʃn, -z
AM rəˈsɛkʃən,
riˈsɛkʃən, -z

resectional
BR rɪˈsɛkʃn(ə)l,
rɪˈsɛkʃən(ə)l
AM rəˈsɛkʃ(ə)nəl,
riˈsɛkʃ(ə)nəl

resectionist
BR rɪˈsɛkʃn̩ɪst,
rɪˈsɛkʃənɪst, -s
AM rəˈsɛkʃənəst,
riˈsɛkʃənəst, -s

reseda
BR ˈrɛsɪdə(r),
rɪˈsiːdə(r), -z
AM rəˈsidə, -z

reseed
BR ˌriːˈsiːd, -z, -ɪŋ, -ɪd
AM riˈsid, -z, -ɪŋ, -ɪd

reselect
BR ˌriːsɪˈlɛkt, -s, -ɪŋ, -ɪd
AM ˈrisəˈlɛk|(t), -(t)s,
-tɪŋ, -təd

reselection
BR ˌriːsɪˈlɛkʃn, -z
AM ˈrisəˈlɛkʃən, -z

resell
BR ˌriːˈsɛl, -z, -ɪŋ
AM riˈsɛl, -z, -ɪŋ

reseller
BR ˌriːˈsɛlə(r), -z
AM riˈsɛlər, -z

resealable
BR ˌriːˈsiːləbl
AM riˈsiləbl

research¹
noun
BR rɪˈsəːtʃ, ˈriːsəːtʃ, -ɪz
AM ˈriˌsərtʃ, rəˈsərtʃ,
riˈsərtʃ, -əz

resemblance
BR rɪˈzɛmbl(ə)ns, -ɪz
AM rəˈzɛmbləns,
rɪˈzɛmbləns, -əz

resemblant
BR rɪˈzɛmbl(ə)nt
AM rəˈzɛmblənt,
rɪˈzɛmblənt

resemble
BR rɪˈzɛmb|l, -lz,
-|ɪŋ \-lɪŋ, -ld
AM rəˈzɛmbəl,
rɪˈzɛmbəl, -əlz, -(ə)lɪŋ,
-əld

resembler
BR rɪˈzɛmblə(r), -z
AM rəˈzɛmblər,
rɪˈzɛmblər, -z

resent
BR rɪˈzɛnt, -s, -ɪŋ, -ɪd
AM rəˈzen|t, rɪˈzen|t,
-ts, -(t)ɪŋ, -(t)əd

resentful
BR rɪˈzɛntf(ʊ)l
AM rəˈzɛntfəl,
rɪˈzɛntfəl

resentfully
BR rɪˈzɛntfʊli,
rɪˈzɛntfli
AM rəˈzɛntfəli,
rɪˈzɛntfəli

resentfulness
BR rɪˈzɛntf(ʊ)lnəs
AM rəˈzɛntfəlnəs,
rɪˈzɛntfəlnəs

resentment
BR rɪˈzɛntm(ə)nt, -s
AM rəˈzɛntmənt,
rɪˈzɛntmənt, -s

reserpine
BR ˈrɛsəpiːn, ˈrɛsəpɪn,
rɪˈsəːpiːn
AM rəˈsərpən,
rɪˈsərpən, rəˈsərˌpin,
rɪˈsərˌpin, ˈrɛsərˌpin,
ˈrɛsərpən

reservable
BR rɪˈzəːvəbl
AM rəˈzərvəbəl,
rɪˈzərvəbəl

reservation
BR ˌrɛzəˈveɪʃn, -z
AM ˌrɛzərˈveɪʃən, -z

reserve
BR rɪˈzəːv, -z, -ɪŋ, -d
AM rəˈzərv, rɪˈzərv, -z,
-ɪŋ, -d

re-serve
BR ˌriːˈsəːv, -z, -ɪŋ, -d
AM riˈsərv, -z, -ɪŋ, -d

reservedly
BR rɪˈzəːvɪdli
AM rəˈzərvədli,
rɪˈzərvədli

reservedness
BR rɪˈzəːvɪdnɪs
AM rəˈzərvədnəs,
rɪˈzərvədnəs

reserver
BR rɪˈzɜːvə(r), -z
AM rəˈzɜrvər,
riˈzɜrvər, -z

reservist
BR rɪˈzɜːvɪst, -s
AM rəˈzɜrvəst,
riˈzɜrvəst, -s

reservoir
BR ˈrezəvwɑː(r), -z
AM ˈrezə(r)ˌvwɑr, -z

reset
BR ˌriːˈset, -s, -ɪŋ
AM riˈse|t, -ts, -dɪŋ

resettability
BR ˌriːsetəˈbɪlɪti,
rɪˌsetəˈbɪlɪti
AM ˌriˌsedəˈbɪlɪdi

resettable
BR ˌriːˈsetəbl
AM riˈsedəbəl

resettle
BR (ˌ)riːˈset|l, -lz,
-lɪŋ\-lŋ, -ld
AM riˈsedəl, -z, -ɪŋ, -d

resettlement
BR (ˌ)riːˈsetlm(ə)nt
AM riˈsedlmənt

reshape
BR ˌriːˈʃeɪp, -s, -ɪŋ, -t
AM riˈʃeɪp, -s, -ɪŋ, -t

reship
BR ˌriːˈʃɪp, -s, -ɪŋ, -t
AM riˈʃɪp, -s, -ɪŋ, -t

reshuffle[1]
noun
BR ˈriːʃʌfl, -z
AM riˈʃəfəl, -z

reshuffle[2]
verb
BR ˌriːˈʃʌf|l, -lz,
-lɪŋ\-lŋ, -ld
AM riˈʃəf|əl, -əlz,
-(ə)lŋ, -əld

reside
BR rɪˈzʌɪd, -z, -ɪŋ, -ɪd
AM rəˈzaɪd, riˈzaɪd, -z,
-ɪŋ, -ɪd

residence
BR ˈrezɪd(ə)ns, -ɪz
AM ˈrez(ə)d(ə)ns, -əz

residency
BR ˈrezɪd(ə)ns|i, -ɪz
AM ˈrez(ə)d(ə)nsi, -z

resident
BR ˈrezɪd(ə)nt, -s
AM ˈrez(ə)d(ə)nt, -s

residential
BR ˌrezɪˈdenʃl
AM ˌrezəˈden(t)ʃəl

residentially
BR ˌrezɪˈdenʃli,
ˌrezɪˈdenʃəli
AM ˌrezəˈden(t)ʃəli

residentiary
BR ˌrezɪˈdenʃ(ə)r|i, -ɪz

reserʼden(t)ʃi,εri
AM ˌrezɪˈden(t)ʃiˌεri,
ˌrezɪˈden(t)ʃiˌεri,
ˌrezɪˈden(t)ʃəri, -z

residentship
BR ˈrezɪd(ə)ntʃɪp, -s
AM ˈrez(ə)dəntˌʃɪp,
ˈrezədntˌʃɪp, -s

residua
BR rɪˈzɪdjʊə(r)
rɪˈzɪdʒʊə(r)
AM rəˈsɪdʒ(ə)wə,
riˈsɪdʒ(ə)wə

residual
BR rɪˈzɪdjʊl, rɪˈzɪdjʊəl,
rɪˈzɪdʒ(ʊ)l, rɪˈzɪdʒʊəl,
-z
AM rəˈsɪdʒ(ə)wəl,
riˈsɪdʒ(ə)wəl,
rəˈsɪdʒəl, riˈsɪdʒəl, -z

residually
BR rɪˈzɪdjʊli,
rɪˈzɪdjʊəli, rɪˈzɪdʒʊli,
rɪˈzɪdʒ|li, rɪˈzɪdʒʊəli
AM rəˈsɪdʒ(ə)wəli,
riˈsɪdʒ(ə)wəli,
rəˈsɪdʒəli, riˈsɪdʒəli

residuary
BR rɪˈzɪdjʊri,
rɪˈzɪdjʊəri,
rɪˈzɪdʒ(ʊ)ri,
rɪˈzɪdʒʊəri
AM rəˈsɪdʒəˌwεri,
riˈsɪdʒəˌwεri

residue
BR ˈrezɪdjuː, ˈrezɪdʒuː,
-z
AM ˈrezəˌd(j)u, -z

residuum
BR rɪˈzɪdjʊəm,
rɪˈzɪdʒʊəm
AM rəˈsɪdʒ(ə)wəm,
riˈsɪdʒ(ə)wəm

resign[1]
give up
BR rɪˈzʌɪn, -z, -ɪŋ, -d
AM rəˈzaɪn, riˈzaɪn, -z,
-ɪŋ, -d

resign[2]
sign again
BR ˌriːˈsaɪn, -z, -ɪŋ, -d
AM riˈsaɪn, -z, -ɪŋ, -d

resignal
BR ˌriːˈsɪgnl, -z, -ɪŋ, -d
AM riˈsɪgnəl, -z, -ɪŋ, -d

resignation
BR ˌrezɪgˈneɪʃn, -z
AM ˌrezəgˈneɪʃən, -z

resigned
BR rɪˈzʌɪnd
AM rəˈzaɪnd, riˈzaɪnd

resignedly
BR rɪˈzʌɪnɪdli
AM rəˈzaɪnədli,
riˈzaɪnədli

resignedness
BR rɪˈzʌɪnɪdnɪs
AM rəˈzaɪnədnəs,
riˈzaɪnədnəs

resigner
BR rɪˈzʌɪnə(r), -z
AM rəˈzaɪnər,
riˈzaɪnər, -z

resile
BR rɪˈzʌɪl, -z, -ɪŋ, -d
AM rəˈzaɪl, riˈzaɪl, -z,
-ɪŋ, -d

resilience
BR rɪˈzɪlɪəns
AM rəˈzɪlɪəns,
rəˈzɪljəns

resiliency
BR rɪˈzɪlɪənsi
AM rəˈzɪlɪənsi,
rəˈzɪljənsi

resilient
BR rɪˈzɪlɪənt
AM rəˈzɪliənt,
rəˈzɪljənt

resiliently
BR rɪˈzɪlɪəntli
AM rəˈzɪliən(t)li,
rəˈzɪljən(t)li

re-silver
BR ˌriːˈsɪlv|ə(r), -əz,
-(ə)rɪŋ, -əd
AM riˈsɪlvər, -z, -ɪŋ, -d

resin
BR ˈrezɪn, -z
AM ˈrezən, -z

resinate
BR ˈrezɪneɪt, ˈrezɪneɪt,
-s, -ɪŋ, -ɪd
AM ˈrezəˌneɪ|t, -ts, -dɪŋ,
-dɪd

resiniferous
BR ˌrezɪˈnɪf(ə)rəs,
ˌrezɪˈɪf(ə)rəs
AM ˌrezəˈnɪf(ə)rəs

resinification
BR ˌrezɪnɪfɪˈkeɪʃn,
ˌrezɪnɪfɪˈkeɪʃn
AM ˌrezənəfəˈkeɪʃən

resiniform
BR ˈrezɪnɪfɔːm,
ˈrezɪnɪfɔːm
AM ˈrezənəˌfɔ(ə)rm

resinify
BR ˈrezɪnɪfʌɪ, ˈrezɪnɪfʌɪ,
-z, -ɪŋ, -d
AM ˈrezənəˌfaɪ, -z, -ɪŋ,
-d

resinoid
BR ˈrezɪnɔɪd, ˈrezɪnɔɪd,
-z
AM ˈrezəˌnɔɪd, -z

resinous
BR ˈrezɪnəs, ˈrezɪnəs
AM ˈrezənəs

resist
BR rɪˈzɪst, -s, -ɪŋ, -ɪd
AM rəˈzɪst, riˈzɪst, -s,
-ɪŋ, -ɪd

resistance
BR rɪˈzɪst(ə)ns, -ɪz
AM rəˈzɪstəns,
riˈzɪstəns, -əz

resistant
BR rɪˈzɪst(ə)nt
AM rəˈzɪstənt,
riˈzɪstənt

resister
BR rɪˈzɪstə(r), -z
AM rəˈzɪstər, riˈzɪstər,
-z

resistibility
BR rɪˌzɪstɪˈbɪlɪti
AM rəˌzɪstəˈbɪlɪdi,
riˌzɪstəˈbɪlɪdi

resistible
BR rɪˈzɪstɪbl
AM rəˈzɪstəbəl,
riˈzɪstəbəl

resistibly
BR rɪˈzɪstɪbli
AM rəˈzɪstəbli,
riˈzɪstəbli

resistive
BR rɪˈzɪstɪv
AM rəˈzɪstɪv, riˈzɪstɪv

resistivity
BR ˌrizːɪˈstɪvɪti,
ˌrezɪˈstɪvɪti,
rɪˌzɪsˈtɪvɪti
AM rəˌzɪsˈtɪvɪdi,
riˌzɪsˈtɪvɪdi

resistless
BR rɪˈzɪs(t)lɪs
AM rəˈzɪs(t)lɪs,
riˈzɪs(t)lɪs

resistlessly
BR rɪˈzɪs(t)lɪsli
AM rəˈzɪs(t)lɪsli,
riˈzɪs(t)lɪsli

resistor
BR rɪˈzɪstə(r), -z
AM rəˈzɪstər, riˈzɪstər,
-z

resit[1]
noun
BR ˈriːsɪt, -s
AM ˈriˌsɪt, -s

resit[2]
verb
BR ˌriːˈsɪt, -s, -ɪŋ
AM riˈsɪ|t, -ts, -dɪŋ

resite
BR ˌriːˈsʌɪt, -s, -ɪŋ, -ɪd
AM riˈsaɪ|t, -ts, -dɪŋ,
-dɪd

resize
BR ˌriːˈsʌɪz, -ɪz, -ɪŋ, -d
AM riˈsaɪz, -ɪz, -ɪŋ, -d

resold
BR ˌriːˈsəʊld
AM riˈsoʊld

resole
BR ˌriːˈsəʊl, -z, -ɪŋ, -d
AM riˈsoʊl, -z, -ɪŋ, -d

resoluble
BR ˌriːˈsɒljʊbl
AM rəˈzɑljəbəl,
riˈzɑljəbəl

resolute
BR ˈrezəl(j)uːt

AM ˈrezə‚l(j)ut
resolutely
  BR ˈrezəl(j)uːtli
  AM ˈrezə‚l(j)utli
resoluteness
  BR ˈrezəl(j)uːtnəs
  AM ˈrezə‚l(j)uːtnəs
resolution
  BR ‚rezəˈl(j)uːʃn, -z
  AM ‚rezəˈluʃən, -z
resolutive
  BR ˈrezəl(j)uːtɪv
  AM rəˈzaljədɪv,
  ˈrezə‚ludɪv
resolvability
  BR rɪ‚zɒlvəˈbɪlɪti
  AM rə‚zɒlvəˈbɪlɪdi,
  ri‚zɒlvəˈbɪlɪdi,
  rə‚zalvəˈbɪlɪdi,
  ri‚zalvəˈbɪlɪdi
resolvable
  BR rɪˈzɒlvəbl
  AM rəˈzɒlvəbəl,
  ri‚zɒlvəbəl,
  rəˈzalvəbəl,
  ri‚zalvəbəl
resolve
  BR rɪˈzɒlv, -z, -ɪŋ, -d
  AM rəˈzɒlv, riˈzɒlv,
  rəˈzalv, riˈzalv, -z, -ɪŋ,
  -d
resolvedly
  BR rɪˈzɒlvɪdli
  AM rəˈzɒlvədli,
  riˈzɒlvədli,
  rəˈzalvədli,
  riˈzalvədli
resolvedness
  BR rɪˈzɒlvɪdnɪs
  AM rəˈzɒlvədnəs,
  riˈzɒlvədnəs,
  rəˈzalvədnəs,
  riˈzalvədnəs
Resolven
  BR rɪˈzɒlv(ə)n
  AM rəˈzɒlvən,
  rəˈzalvən
resolvent
  BR rɪˈzɒlv(ə)nt, -s
  AM rəˈzɒlvənt,
  riˈzɒlvənt, rəˈzalvənt,
  riˈzalvənt, -s
resolver
  BR rɪˈzɒlvə(r), -z
  AM rəˈzɒlvər, riˈzɒlvər,
  rəˈzalvər, riˈzalvər, -z
resonance
  BR ˈrezənəns, ˈrezn̩əns,
  -ɪz
  AM ˈrezənəns,
  ˈrezn̩əns, -əz
resonant
  BR ˈrezənənt, ˈrezn̩ənt
  AM ˈrezənənt, ˈrezn̩ənt
resonantly
  BR ˈrezənəntli,
  ˈrezn̩əntli

AM ˈrezənən(t)li,
ˈrezn̩ən(t)li
resonate
  BR ˈrezəneɪt, ˈrezn̩eɪt,
  -s, -ɪŋ, -ɪd
  AM ˈrezn̩‚eɪt, -ts, -dɪŋ,
  -dɪd
resonator
  BR ˈrezəneɪtə(r),
  ˈrezn̩eɪtə(r), -z
  AM ˈrezn̩‚eɪdər, -z
resorb
  BR rɪˈsɔːb, rɪˈzɔːb, -z,
  -ɪŋ, -d
  AM rəˈsɔ(ə)rb,
  riˈsɔ(ə)rb, rəˈzɔ(ə)rb,
  riˈzɔ(ə)rb, -z, -ɪŋ, -d
resorbence
  BR rɪˈsɔːb(ə)ns
  rɪˈzɔːb(ə)ns
  AM rəˈsɔrbəns,
  riˈsɔrbəns,
  rəˈzɔrbəns,
  riˈzɔrbəns
resorbent
  BR rɪˈsɔːb(ə)nt
  rɪˈzɔːb(ə)nt
  AM rəˈsɔrbənt,
  riˈsɔrbənt,
  rəˈzɔrbənt, riˈzɔrbənt
resorcin
  BR rɪˈzɔːsɪn
  AM rəˈzɔrsən,
  riˈzɔrsən
resorcinol
  BR rɪˈzɔːsɪnɒl
  AM rəˈzɔrsə‚nɑl,
  riˈzɔrsə‚nɑl
resorption
  BR rɪˈsɔːpʃn, rɪˈzɔːpʃn
  AM rəˈsɔrpʃən,
  rəˈzɔrpʃən,
  riˈsɔrpʃən, riˈzɔrpʃən
resorptive
  BR rɪˈsɔːptɪv, rɪˈzɔːptɪv
  AM rəˈsɔrptɪv,
  rəˈzɔrptɪv, riˈsɔrptɪv,
  riˈzɔrptɪv
resort[1]
  noun, verb, make use
  of, visit
  BR rɪˈzɔːt, -s, -ɪŋ, -ɪd
  AM rəˈzɔ(ə)rt,
  riˈzɔ(ə)rt, -ts, -ˈzɔrdɪŋ,
  -ˈzɔrdəd
resort[2]
  verb, sort again
  BR ‚riːˈsɔːt, -s, -ɪŋ, -ɪd
  AM riˈsɔ(ə)rt, -ts,
  -ˈsɔrdɪŋ, -ˈsɔrdəd
resorter
  BR rɪˈzɔːtə(r), -z
  AM rəˈzɔrdər,
  riˈzɔrdər, -z
resound
  BR rɪˈzaʊnd, -z, -ɪŋ, -ɪd
  AM rəˈzaʊnd, riˈzaʊnd,
  -z, -ɪŋ, -əd

resoundingly
  BR rɪˈzaʊndɪŋli
  AM rəˈzaʊndɪŋli,
  riˈzaʊndɪŋli
resource
  BR rɪˈzɔːs, rɪˈsɔːs, -ɪz
  AM ˈriː‚sɔ(ə)rs,
  rəˈsɔ(ə)rs, riˈsɔ(ə)rs,
  -əz
resourceful
  BR rɪˈzɔːsf(ʊ)l,
  rɪˈsɔːsf(ʊ)l
  AM rəˈsɔrsfəl,
  riˈsɔrsfəl
resourcefully
  BR rɪˈzɔːsfʊli,
  rɪˈzɔːsfli, rɪˈsɔːsfʊli,
  rɪˈsɔːsfli
  AM rəˈsɔrsfəli,
  riˈsɔrsfəli
resourcefulness
  BR rɪˈzɔːsf(ʊ)lnəs,
  rɪˈsɔːsf(ʊ)lnəs
  AM rəˈsɔrsfəlnəs,
  riˈsɔrsfəlsnəs
resourceless
  BR rɪˈzɔːsləs, rɪˈsɔːsləs
  AM ˈriː‚sɔrsləs,
  rəˈsɔrsləs, riˈsɔrsləs
resourcelessness
  BR rɪˈzɔːsləsnəs,
  rɪˈsɔːsləsnəs
  AM ˈriː‚sɔrsləsnəs,
  rəˈsɔrsləsnəs,
  riˈsɔrsləsnəs
respect
  BR rɪˈspekt, -s, -ɪŋ, -ɪd
  AM rəˈspek|(t),
  riˈspek|(t), -(t)s, -tɪŋ,
  -təd
respectability
  BR rɪ‚spektəˈbɪlɪti
  AM rə‚spektəˈbɪlɪdi,
  ri‚spektəˈbɪlɪdi
respectable
  BR rɪˈspektəbl
  AM rəˈspektəbəl,
  riˈspektəbəl
respectableness
  BR rɪˈspektəblnəs
  AM rəˈspektəbəlnəs,
  riˈspektəbəlnəs
respectably
  BR rɪˈspektəbli
  AM rəˈspektəbli,
  riˈspektəbli
respecter
  BR rɪˈspektə(r), -z
  AM rəˈspektər,
  riˈspektər, -z
respectful
  BR rɪˈspekt(t)f(ʊ)l
  AM rəˈspek(t)fəl,
  riˈspek(t)fəl
respectfully
  BR rɪˈspek(t)fəli,
  rɪˈspek(t)fli

AM rəˈspek(t)fəli,
riˈspek(t)fəli
respectfulness
  BR rɪˈspek(t)f(ʊ)lnəs
  AM rəˈspek(t)fəlnəs,
  riˈspek(t)fəlnəs
respective
  BR rɪˈspektɪv
  AM rəˈspektɪv,
  riˈspektɪv
respectively
  BR rɪˈspektɪvli
  AM rəˈspektɪvli,
  riˈspektɪvli
respell
  BR ‚riːˈspel, -z, -ɪŋ, -d
  AM rɪˈspel, -z, -ɪŋ, -d
Respighi
  BR rɪˈspiːgi, reˈspiːgi
  AM rəˈspɪgi
respirable
  BR ˈresp(ɪ)rəbl
  AM ˈrespərəbəl
respirate
  BR ˈrespɪreɪt, -s, -ɪŋ, -ɪd
  AM ˈrespə‚reɪ|t, -ts,
  -dɪŋ, -dɪd
respiration
  BR ‚respɪˈreɪʃn
  AM ‚respəˈreɪʃən
respirator
  BR ˈrespɪreɪtə(r), -z
  AM ‚respəˈreɪdər, -z
respiratory
  BR ˈrespɪrət(ə)ri,
  rɪˈspɪrət(ə)ri,
  rɪˈspʌɪ(ə)rət(ə)ri
  AM ˈrespə)rə‚tɔri,
  rəˈspaɪrə‚tɔri
respire
  BR rɪˈspʌɪə(r), -z, -ɪŋ, -d
  AM rəˈspaɪ(ə)r,
  riˈspaɪ(ə)r, -z, -ɪŋ, -d
respite
  BR ˈrespʌɪt, ˈrespɪt, -s,
  -ɪŋ, -ɪd
  AM ˈrespə|t, -ts, -dɪŋ,
  -dəd
resplendence
  BR rɪˈsplend(ə)ns
  AM rəˈsplend(ə)ns,
  riˈsplend(ə)ns
resplendency
  BR rɪˈsplend(ə)nsi
  AM rəˈsplend(ə)nsi,
  riˈsplend(ə)nsi
resplendent
  BR rɪˈsplend(ə)nt
  AM rəˈsplendənt,
  riˈsplendənt
resplendently
  BR rɪˈsplend(ə)ntli
  AM rəˈsplendən(t)li,
  riˈsplendən(t)li
respond
  BR rɪˈspɒnd, -z, -ɪŋ, -ɪd
  AM rəˈspand, riˈspand,
  -z, -ɪŋ, -əd

respondence
BR rɪˈspɒnd(ə)ns, -ɪz
AM rəˈspænd(ə)ns,
rɪˈspænd(ə)ns, -əz

respondency
BR rɪˈspɒnd(ə)nsi
AM rəˈspænd(ə)nsi,
rɪˈspænd(ə)nsi

respondent
BR rɪˈspɒnd(ə)nt, -s
AM rəˈspændənt,
rɪˈspændənt, -s

responder
BR rɪˈspɒndə(r), -z
AM rəˈspændər,
rɪˈspændər, -z

response
BR rɪˈspɒns, -ɪz
AM rəˈspæns, rɪˈspæns,
-əz

responsibility
BR rɪˌspɒnsɪˈbɪlɪt|i, -ɪz
AM rəˌspænsəˈbɪlɪdi,
rɪˌspænsəˈbɪlɪdi, -z

responsible
BR rɪˈspɒnsɪbl
AM rəˈspænsəbəl,
rɪˈspænsəbəl

responsibleness
BR rɪˈspɒnsɪblnəs
AM rəˈspænsəbəlnəs,
rɪˈspænsəbəlnəs

responsibly
BR rɪˈspɒnsɪbli
AM rəˈspænsəbli,
rɪˈspænsəbli

responsive
BR rɪˈspɒnsɪv
AM rəˈspænsɪv,
rɪˈspænsɪv

responsively
BR rɪˈspɒnsɪvli
AM rəˈspænsɪvli,
rɪˈspænsɪvli

responsiveness
BR rɪˈspɒnsɪvnɪs
AM rəˈspænsɪvnɪs,
rɪˈspænsɪvnɪs

responsory
BR rɪˈspɒns(ə)r|i, -ɪz
AM rəˈspænsəri,
rɪˈspænsəri, -z

respray¹
noun
BR ˈriːspreɪ, -z
AM ˈriːspreɪ, -z

respray²
verb
BR ˌriːˈspreɪ, -z, -ɪŋ, -d
AM riˈspreɪ, -z, -ɪŋ, -d

res publica
BR (ˌ)reɪz ˈpʊblɪkə(r),
+ ˈpʌblɪkə(r)
AM ˈreɪs ˈpʊbləkə

rest
BR rest, -s, -ɪŋ, -ɪd
AM rest, -s, -ɪŋ, -əd

restage
BR ˌriːˈsteɪdʒ, -ɪz, -ɪŋ, -d
AM riˈsteɪdʒ, -ɪz, -ɪŋ, -d

restart¹
noun
BR ˈriːstɑːt, -s
AM ˈriˌstɑrt, -s

restart²
verb
BR ˌriːˈstɑːt, -s, -ɪŋ, -ɪd
AM riˈstɑr|t, -ts, -dɪŋ,
-dəd

restate
BR ˌriːˈsteɪt, -s, -ɪŋ, -ɪd
AM riˈsteɪ|t, -ts, -dɪŋ,
-dɪd

restatement
BR ˌriːˈsteɪtm(ə)nt, -s
AM riˈsteɪtmənt, -s

restaurant
BR ˈrest(ʃ)(ə)rɑːnt,
ˈrest(ʃ)(ə)rɒnt,
ˈrest(ʃ)(ə)rənt,
ˈrest(ʃ)(ə)rn̩t,
ˈrest(ʃ)(ə)rɒ̃, -s
AM ˈrest(ə)rənt,
ˈrestəˌrɑnt, ˈreˌstrɑnt,
-s

restauranteur
BR ˌrestərɑːnˈtɜː(r),
ˌrest(ʃ)ərɒnˈtɜː(r),
ˌrest(ʃ)(ə)rənˈtɜː(r),
ˌrest(ʃ)(ə)rn̩ˈtɜː(r),
ˌrest(ʃ)ərɒ̃ˈtɜː(r), -z
AM ˈrestərənˈtɜr,
ˈrestəˌrɑnˈtɜr, -z

restaurateur
BR ˌrest(ə)rəˈtɜː(r), -z
AM ˈrestərəˈtɜr,
ˈrestəˌrɑˈtɜr, -z

restful
BR ˈres(t)f(ʊ)l
AM ˈres(t)fəl

restfully
BR ˈres(t)fʊli,
ˈres(t)fli
AM ˈres(t)fəli

restfulness
BR ˈres(t)f(ʊ)lnəs
AM ˈres(t)fəlnəs

resthouse
BR ˈresthaʊs, -zɪz
AM ˈrest(h)aʊ|s, -zəz

resting-place
BR ˈrestɪŋpleɪs, -ɪz
AM ˈrestɪŋpleɪs, -ɪz

restitution
BR ˌrestɪˈtjuːʃn,
ˌrestɪˈtʃuːʃn
AM ˌrestəˈt(j)uʃən

restitutive
BR ˈrestɪtjuːtɪv,
ˈrestɪtʃuːtɪv
AM ˈrestəˌt(j)utɪv

restive
BR ˈrestɪv
AM ˈrestɪv

restively
BR ˈrestɪvli
AM ˈrestɪvli

restiveness
BR ˈrestɪvnəs
AM ˈrestɪvnɪs

restless
BR ˈres(t)ləs
AM ˈres(t)ləs

restlessly
BR ˈres(t)ləsli
AM ˈres(t)ləsli

restlessness
BR ˈres(t)ləsnəs
AM ˈres(t)ləsnəs

restock
BR ˌriːˈstɒk, -s, -ɪŋ, -t
AM riˈstɑk, -s, -ɪŋ, -t

restorable
BR rɪˈstɔːrəbl
AM rəˈstɔrəbəl,
rɪˈstɔrəbəl

restoration
BR ˌrestəˈreɪʃn, -z
AM ˌrestəˈreɪʃən, -z

restorationism
BR ˌrestəˈreɪʃnɪz(ə)m,
ˌrestəˈreɪʃənɪz(ə)m
AM ˌrestəˈreɪʃəˌnɪzəm

restorationist
BR ˌrestəˈreɪʃnɪst,
ˌrestəˈreɪʃənɪst, -s
AM ˌrestəˈreɪʃənəst, -s

restorative
BR rɪˈstɒrətɪv,
rɪˈstɔːrətɪv, -z
AM rəˈstɔrədɪv, -z

restoratively
BR rɪˈstɒrətɪvli,
rɪˈstɔːrətɪvli
AM rəˈstɔrədɪvli

restore
BR rɪˈstɔː(r), -z, -ɪŋ, -d
AM rəˈstɔ(ə)r,
rɪˈstɔ(ə)r, -z, -ɪŋ, -d

restorer
BR rɪˈstɔːrə(r), -z
AM rəˈstɔrər, rɪˈstɔrər,
-z

restrain¹
hold back
BR rɪˈstreɪn, -z, -ɪŋ, -d
AM rəˈstreɪn, rɪˈstreɪn,
-z, -ɪŋ, -d

restrain²
strain again
BR ˌriːˈstreɪn, -z, -ɪŋ, -d
AM riˈstreɪn, -z, -ɪŋ, -d

restrainable
BR rɪˈstreɪnəbl
AM rəˈstreɪnəbəl,
rɪˈstreɪnəbəl

restrainedly
BR rɪˈstreɪnɪdli
AM rəˈstreɪnɪdli,
rɪˈstreɪnɪdli

restrainer
BR rɪˈstreɪnə(r), -z

restrainer (cont.)
AM rəˈstreɪnər,
rɪˈstreɪnər, -z

restraint
BR rɪˈstreɪnt, -s
AM rəˈstreɪnt,
rɪˈstreɪnt, -s

restrict
BR rɪˈstrɪkt, -s, -ɪŋ, -ɪd
AM rəˈstrɪk|(t),
rɪˈstrɪk|(t), -(t)s, -tɪŋ,
-tɪd

restrictedly
BR rɪˈstrɪktɪdli
AM rəˈstrɪktɪdli,
rɪˈstrɪktɪdli

restrictedness
BR rɪˈstrɪktɪdnɪs
AM rəˈstrɪktɪdnɪs,
rɪˈstrɪktɪdnɪs

restriction
BR rɪˈstrɪkʃn, -z
AM rəˈstrɪkʃən,
rɪˈstrɪkʃən, -z

restrictionist
BR rɪˈstrɪkʃnɪst,
rɪˈstrɪkʃənɪst, -s
AM rəˈstrɪkʃənəst,
rɪˈstrɪkʃənəst, -s

restrictive
BR rɪˈstrɪktɪv
AM rəˈstrɪktɪv,
rɪˈstrɪktɪv

restrictively
BR rɪˈstrɪktɪvli
AM rəˈstrɪktɪvli,
rɪˈstrɪktɪvli

restrictiveness
BR rɪˈstrɪktɪvnɪs
AM rəˈstrɪktɪvnɪs,
rɪˈstrɪktɪvnɪs

restring
BR ˌriːˈstrɪŋ, -z, -ɪŋ
AM riˈstrɪŋ, -z, -ɪŋ

restroom
BR ˈrestruːm,
ˈrestrʊm, -z
AM ˈres(t)ˌrum,
ˈres(t)ˌrʊm, -z

restructure
BR ˌriːˈstrʌktʃ|ə(r),
-əz, -(ə)rɪŋ, -əd
AM riˈstrək(t)ʃər, -z,
-ɪŋ, -d

restructuring
BR ˌriːˈstrʌktʃ(ə)rɪŋ,
-z
AM riˈstrək(t)ʃərɪŋ, -z

restrung
BR ˌriːˈstrʌŋ
AM riˈstrʌŋ

restudy
BR ˌriːˈstʌd|i, -ɪz, -ɪɪŋ,
-ɪd
AM riˈstʌdi, -z, -ɪŋ, -d

restyle
BR ˌriːˈstaɪl, -z, -ɪŋ, -d
AM riˈstaɪl, -z, -ɪŋ, -d

resubmit
BR ˌriːsəbˈmɪt, -s, -ɪŋ,
-ɪd
AM ˈriːsəbˈmɪ|t, -ts, -dɪŋ,
-dɪd

result
BR rɪˈzʌlt, -s, -ɪŋ, -ɪd
AM rəˈzəlt, riˈzəlt, -s,
-ɪŋ, -əd

resultant
BR rɪˈzʌlt(ə)nt
AM rəˈzəltnt, riˈzəltnt

resultful
BR rɪˈzʌltf(ʊ)l
AM rəˈzəltfəl, riˈzəltfəl

resultless
BR rɪˈzʌltləs
AM rəˈzəltləs,
riˈzəltləs

resumable
BR rɪˈzjuːməbl
AM rəˈz(j)uməbəl,
riˈz(j)uməbəl

resume[1]
noun
BR ˈrezjʊmeɪ,
ˈreɪzjʊmeɪ,
rɪˈzjuːmeɪ, -z
AM ˈrezəˌmeɪ, -z

resume[2]
verb
BR rɪˈzjuːm, -z, -ɪŋ, -d
AM rəˈz(j)um,
riˈz(j)um, -z, -ɪŋ, -d

résumé
BR ˈrezjʊmeɪ,
ˈreɪzjʊmeɪ,
rɪˈzjuːmeɪ, -z
AM ˈrezəˌmeɪ, -z

resumption
BR rɪˈzʌm(p)ʃn, -z
AM rəˈzəm(p)ʃən,
riˈzəm(p)ʃən, -z

resumptive
BR rɪˈzʌm(p)tɪv
AM rəˈzəm(p)tɪv,
riˈzəm(p)tɪv

resupinate
BR ˌriːˈsjuːpɪnət
AM riˈs(j)upəˌneɪt,
riˈs(j)upənət

resupply
BR ˌriːsəˈplʌɪ, -z, -ɪŋ, -d
AM ˌrisəˈplaɪ, -z, -ɪŋ, -d

resurface
BR ˌriːˈsəːfɪs, -z, -ɪŋ, -t
AM riˈsərfəs, -əz, -ɪŋ, -t

resurgence
BR rɪˈsəːdʒ(ə)ns
AM rəˈsərdʒəns,
riˈsərdʒəns

resurgent
BR rɪˈsəːdʒ(ə)nt
AM rəˈsərdʒənt,
riˈsərdʒənt

resurrect
BR ˌrezəˈrekt, -s, -ɪŋ, -ɪd

AM ˌrezəˈrek|(t),
ˌrezəˈrek|(t), -(t)s, -tɪŋ,
-təd

resurrection
BR ˌrezəˈrekʃn, -z
AM ˌrezəˈrekʃən,
ˌrezəˈrekʃən, -z

resurrectional
BR ˌrezəˈrekʃn(ə)l,
ˌrezəˈrekʃən(ə)l
AM ˌrezəˈrekʃ(ə)nəl

resurvey
BR ˌriːˈsəːveɪ,
ˌriːˈsəːveɪ, -z, -ɪŋ, -d
AM riˈsərˌveɪ,
riˌsərˈveɪ, -z, -ɪŋ, -d

resuscitate
BR rɪˈsʌsɪteɪt, -s, -ɪŋ, -ɪd
AM rəˈsəsəˌteɪ|t,
riˈsəsəˌteɪ|t, -ts, -dɪŋ,
-dɪd

resuscitation
BR rɪˌsʌsɪˈteɪʃn
AM rəˌsəsəˈteɪʃən,
riˌsəsəˈteɪʃən

resuscitative
BR rɪˈsʌsɪtətɪv
AM rəˈsəsəˌteɪdɪv,
riˈsəsəˌteɪdɪv

resuscitator
BR rɪˈsʌsɪteɪtə(r), -z
AM rəˈsəsəˌteɪdər,
riˈsəsəˌteɪdər, -z

ret
BR ret, -s, -ɪŋ, -ɪd
AM re|t, -ts, -dɪŋ, -dəd

retable
BR rɪˈteɪbl, -z
AM rəˈteɪbəl, riˈteɪbəl,
-z

retail[1]
selling
BR ˈriːteɪl, -z, -ɪŋ, -d
AM ˈriːˌteɪl, -z, -ɪŋ, -d

retail[2]
tell
BR rɪˈteɪl, -z, -ɪŋ, -d
AM rəˈteɪl, riˈteɪl, -z, -ɪŋ,
-d

retailer[1]
seller
BR ˈriːteɪlə(r), -z
AM ˈriːˌteɪlər, -z

retailer[2]
teller
BR rɪˈteɪlə(r), -z
AM rəˈteɪlər, riˈteɪlər,
-z

retain
BR rɪˈteɪn, -z, -ɪŋ, -d
AM rəˈteɪn, riˈteɪn, -z,
-ɪŋ, -d

retainability
BR rɪˌteɪnəˈbɪlɪti
AM rəˌteɪnəˈbɪlɪdi,
riˌteɪnəˈbɪlɪdi

retainable
BR rɪˈteɪnəbl

AM rəˈteɪnəbəl,
riˈteɪnəbəl

retainer
BR rɪˈteɪnə(r), -z
AM rəˈteɪnər, riˈteɪnər,
-z

retainment
BR rɪˈteɪnm(ə)nt, -s
AM rəˈteɪnmənt,
riˈteɪnmənt, -s

retake[1]
noun
BR ˈriːteɪk, -s
AM ˈriːˌteɪk, -s

retake[2]
verb
BR (ˌ)riːˈteɪk, -s, -ɪŋ
AM riˈteɪk, riˈteɪk, -s,
-ɪŋ

retaken
BR (ˌ)riːˈteɪk(ə)n
AM rəˈteɪkən,
riˈteɪkən

retaliate
BR rɪˈtalɪeɪt, -s, -ɪŋ, -ɪd
AM rəˈtæliˌeɪ|t,
riˈtæliˌeɪ|t, -ts, -dɪŋ,
-dɪd

retaliation
BR rɪˌtalɪˈeɪʃn
AM rəˌtæliˈeɪʃən,
riˌtæliˈeɪʃən

retaliative
BR rɪˈtalɪətɪv
AM rəˈtæliədɪv,
riˈtæliədɪv

retaliator
BR rɪˈtalɪeɪtə(r), -z
AM rəˈtæliˌeɪdər,
riˈtæliˌeɪdər, -z

retaliatory
BR rɪˈtalɪət(ə)ri
AM rəˈtæliəˌtori,
riˈtæliəˌtori,
rəˈtæljəˌtori,
riˈtæljəˌtori

retard[1]
*noun, retarded
person*
BR ˈriːtɑːd, -z
AM ˈritɑrd, -z

retard[2]
*verb, noun,
slowdown*
BR rɪˈtɑːd, -z, -ɪŋ, -ɪd
AM rəˈtɑrd, riˈtɑrd, -z,
-ɪŋ, -əd

retardant
BR rɪˈtɑːd(ə)nt, -s
AM rəˈtɑrdənt,
riˈtɑrdənt, -s

retardate
BR rɪˈtɑːdeɪt, -s
AM rəˈtɑrˌdeɪt,
riˈtɑrˌdeɪt, -s

retardation
BR ˌriːtɑːˈdeɪʃn
AM ˌriːtɑrˈdeɪʃən

retardative
BR rɪˈtɑːdətɪv
AM rəˈtɑrdədɪv,
riˈtɑrdədɪv

retardatory
BR rɪˈtɑːdət(ə)ri
AM rəˈtɑrdəˌtori,
riˈtɑrdəˌtori

retarded
BR rɪˈtɑːdɪd
AM rəˈtɑrdəd,
riˈtɑrdəd

retarder
BR rɪˈtɑːdə(r), -z
AM rəˈtɑrdər,
riˈtɑrdər, -z

retardment
BR rɪˈtɑːdm(ə)nt, -s
AM rəˈtɑrdmənt,
riˈtɑrdmənt, -s

retaught
BR ˌriːˈtɔːt
AM riˈtɔt, riˈtɑt

retch
BR retʃ, -ɪz, -ɪŋ, -t
AM retʃ, -əz, -ɪŋ, -t

rete
BR ˈriːti
AM ˈridi

reteach
BR ˌriːˈtiːtʃ, -ɪz, -ɪŋ
AM riˈtitʃ, -ɪz, -ɪŋ

retell
BR ˌriːˈtel, -z, -ɪŋ
AM riˈtel, -z, -ɪŋ

retention
BR rɪˈtenʃn
AM rəˈtenʃən,
riˈtenʃən

retentive
BR rɪˈtentɪv
AM rəˈten(t)ɪv,
riˈten(t)ɪv

retentively
BR rɪˈtentɪvli
AM rəˈten(t)ɪvli,
riˈten(t)ɪvli

retentiveness
BR rɪˈtentɪvnɪs
AM rəˈten(t)ɪvnɪs,
riˈten(t)ɪvnɪs

retest[1]
noun
BR ˈriːtest, -s
AM ˈriːˌtest, -s

retest[2]
verb
BR ˌriːˈtest, -s, -ɪŋ, -ɪd
AM riˈtest, -s, -ɪŋ, -əd

retexture
BR ˌriːˈtekstʃʃə(r), -əz,
-(ə)rɪŋ, -əd
AM riˈtek(st)ʃər, -z, -ɪŋ,
-d

Retford
BR ˈretfəd
AM ˈretfərd

rethink¹
noun
BR 'ri:θɪŋk, -s
AM 'ri:ˌθɪŋk, -s

rethink²
verb
BR ˌri:'θɪŋk, -s, -ɪŋ
AM ri'θɪŋk, -s, -ɪŋ

rethought
BR ˌri:'θɔːt
AM ri'θɑt, ri'θɑt

retia
BR 'ri:ʃ(ɪ)ə(r),
'ri:tɪə(r)
AM 'ri:ʃ(i)ə, 'ridiə

retiarii
BR ˌretɪ'ɑːriː,
ˌretɪ'ɑːrɪɑɪ, ˌretɪ'ɛːriː,
ˌretɪ'ɛːrɪɑɪ
AM ˌriʃi'ɛriɑɪ

retiarius
BR ˌretɪ'ɑːriəs,
ˌretɪ'ɛːriəs
AM ˌriʃi'ɛriəs

retiary
BR 'ri:ʃɪər|i, -ɪz
AM 'riʃi,ɛri, -z

reticence
BR 'retɪs(ə)ns
AM 'redəsəns

reticent
BR 'retɪs(ə)nt
AM 'redəsənt

reticently
BR 'retɪs(ə)ntli
AM 'redəsən(t)li

reticle
BR 'retɪkl, -z
AM 'redəkəl, -z

reticula
BR rɪ'tɪkjʊlə(r)
AM rə'tɪkjələ

reticular
BR rɪ'tɪkjʊlə(r)
AM rə'tɪkjələr

reticulate¹
adjective
BR rɪ'tɪkjʊlət
AM rə'tɪkjələt,
ri'tɪkjələt,
rə'tɪkjəˌleɪt,
ri'tɪkjəˌleɪt

reticulate²
verb
BR rɪ'tɪkjʊleɪt, -s, -ɪŋ,
-ɪd
AM rə'tɪkjəˌleɪ|t,
ri'tɪkjə'leɪ|t, -ts, -dɪŋ,
-dɪd

reticulately
BR rɪ'tɪkjʊlətli
AM rə'tɪkjələtli,
ri'tɪkjələtli,
rə'tɪkjəˌleɪtli,
ri'tɪkjəˌleɪtli

reticulation
BR rɪˌtɪkjʊ'leɪʃn

AM rəˌtɪkjə'leɪʃən,
riˌtɪkjə'leɪʃən

reticule
BR 'retɪkjuːl, -z
AM 'redəˌkjul, -z

reticulocyte
BR rɪ'tɪkjʊləsʌɪt, -s
AM rə'tɪkjələˌsaɪt, -s

reticulose
BR rɪ'tɪkjʊləʊs
AM rə'tɪkjəˌloʊs,
rə'tɪkjəˌloʊz

reticulum
BR rɪ'tɪkjʊləm
AM rə'tɪkjələm

retie
BR ˌri:'tʌɪ, -z, -ɪŋ, -d
AM ri'taɪ, -z, -ɪŋ, -d

retiform
BR 'retɪfɔːm
AM 'redəˌfɔ(ə)rm

retina
BR 'retɪnə(r), -z
AM 'retnə, -z

retinae
BR 'retniː
AM 'retn̩i, 'retn̩aɪ

retinal
BR 'retɪnl
AM 'retn̩l

retinitis
BR ˌretɪ'nʌɪtɪs
AM ˌretn'aɪdɪs

**retinitis
pigmentosa**
BR ˌretɪˌnʌɪtɪs
ˌpɪgmen'təʊzə(r)
AM ˌretn'aɪdɪs
ˌpɪgmən'toʊzə

retinoid
BR 'retɪnɔɪd, -z
AM 'retn̩ˌɔɪd, -z

retinol
BR 'retɪnɒl
AM 'retn̩ɑl

retinopathy
BR ˌretɪ'nɒpəθi
AM ˌretn'ɑpəθi

retinue
BR 'retɪnjuː, -z
AM 'retn̩(j)u, -z

retiracy
BR rɪ'tʌɪərəsi
AM rə'taɪ(ə)rəsi

retiral
BR rɪ'tʌɪərəl, rɪ'tʌɪərl̩,
-z
AM rə'taɪrəl, -z

retire
BR rɪ'tʌɪə(r), -z, -ɪŋ, -d
AM rə'taɪ(ə)r,
ri'taɪ(ə)r, -z, -ɪŋ, -d

retiredness
BR rɪ'tʌɪədnəs
AM rə'taɪrdnəs,
ri'taɪrdnəs

retiree
BR ˌriːtʌɪə'riː, -z
AM ri,taɪ'ri, rə'taɪˌri, -z

retirement
BR rɪ'tʌɪəm(ə)nt, -s
AM rə'taɪrmənt,
ri'taɪrmənt, -s

retirer
BR rɪ'tʌɪərə(r), -z
AM rə'taɪrər, ri'taɪrər,
-z

retiring
BR rɪ'tʌɪərɪŋ
AM rə'taɪrɪŋ, ri'taɪrɪŋ

retiringly
BR rɪ'tʌɪərɪŋli
AM rə'taɪrɪŋli,
ri'taɪrɪŋli

retitle
BR ˌriː'tʌɪt|l, -lz,
-lɪŋ\-lɪŋ, -ld
AM ri'taɪdəl, -z, -ɪŋ, -d

retold
BR ˌriː'təʊld
AM ri'toʊld

retook
BR (ˌ)riː'tʊk
AM ri'tʊk

retool
BR ˌriː'tuːl, -z, -ɪŋ, -d
AM ri'tul, -z, -ɪŋ, -d

retort
BR rɪ'tɔːt, -s, -ɪŋ, -ɪd
AM rə'tɔ(ə)rt,
ri'tɔ(ə)rt, -ts, -'tɔrdɪŋ,
-'tɔrdəd

retortion
BR rɪ'tɔːʃn, -z
AM rə'tɔrʃən,
ri'tɔrʃən, -z

retouch
BR ˌriː'tʌtʃ, -ɪz, -ɪŋ, -t
AM ri'tətʃ, -əz, -ɪŋ, -t

retoucher
BR ˌriː'tʌtʃə(r), -z
AM ri'tətʃər, -z

retrace
BR ˌriː'treɪs, rɪ'treɪs,
-ɪz, -ɪŋ, -t
AM ri'treɪs, -ɪz, -ɪŋ, -t

retract
BR rɪ'trakt, -s, -ɪŋ, -ɪd
AM rə'træk|(t),
ri'træk|(t), -(t)s, -ɪŋ,
-təd

retractable
BR rɪ'traktəbl
AM rə'træktəbəl,
ri'træktəbəl

retraction
BR ˌriː'trak'teɪʃn
AM ˌriˌtræk'teɪʃən

retractible
BR rɪ'traktəbl
AM rə'træktəbəl,
ri'træktəbəl

retractile
BR rɪ'traktʌɪl

AM rə'træktl̩

retractility
BR rɪˌtrak'tɪlɪti
AM rəˌtræk'tɪlɪdi,
riˌtræk'tɪlɪdi

retraction
BR rɪ'trakʃn, -z
AM rə'trækʃən,
ri'trækʃən, -z

retractive
BR rɪ'traktɪv
AM rə'træktɪv,
ri'træktɪv

retractor
BR rɪ'traktə(r), -z
AM rə'træktər,
ri'træktər, -z

retrain
BR ˌriː'treɪn, -z, -ɪŋ, -d
AM ri'treɪn, -z, -ɪŋ, -d

retral
BR ˌriː'tr(ə)l
AM 'ritrəl

retranslate
BR ˌriː'trans'leɪt,
ˌriː'trɑːns'leɪt,
ˌriː'tranz'leɪt,
ˌriː'trɑːnz'leɪt, -s, -ɪŋ,
-ɪd
AM ˌri'trænz'leɪ|t,
ˌriˌtrænz'leɪ|t, -ts,
-dɪŋ, -dɪd

retranslation
BR ˌriː'trans'leɪʃn,
ˌriː'trɑːns'leɪʃn,
ˌriː'tranz'leɪʃn,
ˌriː'trɑːnz'leɪʃn, -z
AM ˌriˌtrænz'leɪʃən, -z

retransmission
BR ˌriː'tranz'mɪʃn,
ˌriː'trɑːnz'mɪʃn,
ˌriː'trans'mɪʃn,
ˌriː'trɑːns'mɪʃn, -z
AM ˌriˌtræn'smɪʃən, -z

retransmit
BR ˌriː'tranz'mɪt,
ˌriː'trɑːnz'mɪt,
ˌriː'trans'mɪt,
ˌriː'trɑːns'mɪt, -s, -ɪŋ,
-ɪd
AM ˌriˌtræn'smɪ|t, -ts,
-dɪŋ, -dɪd

retread¹
noun
BR 'riː'tred, -z
AM 'riˌtred, -z

retread²
verb
BR ˌriː'tred, -z, -ɪŋ
AM ri'tred, -z, -ɪŋ

retreat
BR rɪ'triːt, -s, -ɪŋ, -ɪd
AM rə'tri|t, ri'tri|t, -ts,
-dɪŋ, -dɪd

retrench
BR rɪ'tren(t)ʃ, -ɪz, -ɪŋ, -t
AM rɪ'tren(t)ʃ,
ri'tren(t)ʃ, -əz, -ɪŋ, -t

retrenchment
BR rɪˈtrɛn(t)ʃm(ə)nt,
-s
AM rəˈtrɛn(t)ʃmənt,
ri'trɛn(t)ʃmənt, -z

retrial
BR ˌriːˈtrʌɪəl, ˈriːtrʌɪəl,
-z
AM ˈriːtraɪəl, -z

retribution
BR ˌrɛtrɪˈbjuːʃn
AM ˌrɛtrəˈbjuʃən

retributive
BR rɪˈtrɪbjʊtɪv
AM rəˈtrɪbjədɪv,
ri'trɪbjədɪv

retributively
BR rɪˈtrɪbjʊtɪvli
AM rəˈtrɪbjədɪvli,
ri'trɪbjədɪvli

retributory
BR rɪˈtrɪbjʊt(ə)ri
AM rəˈtrɪbjəˌtɔri,
ri'trɪbjəˌtɔri

retrievable
BR rɪˈtriːvəbl
AM rəˈtrivəbəl,
ri'trivəbəl

retrievableness
BR rɪˈtriːvəblnəs
AM rəˈtrivəbəlnəs,
ri'trivəbəlnəs

retrievably
BR rɪˈtriːvəbli
AM rəˈtrivəbli,
ri'trivəbli

retrieval
BR rɪˈtriːvl
AM rəˈtrivəl, ri'trivəl

retrieve
BR rɪˈtriːv, -z, -ɪŋ, -d
AM rəˈtriv, ri'triv, -z,
-ɪŋ, -d

retriever
BR rɪˈtriːvə(r), -z
AM rəˈtrivər, ri'trivər,
-z

retrim
BR ˌriːˈtrɪm, -z, -ɪŋ, -d
AM ri'trɪm, -z, -ɪŋ, -d

retro
BR ˈrɛtrəʊ, -z
AM ˈrɛtroʊ, -z

retroact
BR ˌrɛtrəʊˈakt, -s, -ɪŋ,
-ɪd
AM ˌrɛtroʊˈæk|(t),
-(t)s, -tɪŋ, -təd

retroaction
BR ˌrɛtrəʊˈakʃn, -z
AM ˌrɛtroʊˈækʃən, -z

retroactive
BR ˌrɛtrəʊˈaktɪv
AM ˌrɛtroʊˈæktɪv

retroactively
BR ˌrɛtrəʊˈaktɪvli
AM ˌrɛtroʊˈæktɪvli

retroactivity
BR ˌrɛtrəʊakˈtɪvɪti
AM ˈrɛtroʊˌækˈtɪvɪdi

retrocede
BR ˌrɛtrə(ʊ)ˈsiːd, -z, -ɪŋ,
-ɪd
AM ˌrɛtrəˈsid, -z, -ɪŋ, -ɪd

retrocedence
BR ˌrɛtrə(ʊ)ˈsiːdns
AM ˌrɛtroʊˈsidns

retrocedent
BR ˌrɛtrə(ʊ)ˈsiːdnt
AM ˌrɛtroʊˈsidnt

retrocession
BR ˌrɛtrə(ʊ)ˈsɛʃn, -z
AM ˌrɛtrəˈsɛʃən, -z

retrocessive
BR ˌrɛtrə(ʊ)ˈsɛsɪv
AM ˌrɛtroʊˈsɛsɪv

retrochoir
BR ˈrɛtrəʊˌkwʌɪə(r), -z
AM ˈrɛtroʊˌkwaɪ(ə)r, -z

retrod
BR ˌriːˈtrɒd
AM ri'trɑd

retrodden
BR ˌriːˈtrɒdn
AM ri'trɑdən

retrofit
BR ˈrɛtrəʊˈfɪt, -s, -ɪŋ, -ɪd
AM ˈrɛtroʊˈfɪ|t, -ts, -dɪŋ,
-dɪd

retroflection
BR ˌrɛtrə(ʊ)ˈflɛkʃn
AM ˌrɛtrəˈflɛkʃən

retroflex
BR ˈrɛtrə(ʊ)flɛks, -t
AM ˈrɛtrəˌflɛks, -t

retroflexion
BR ˌrɛtrə(ʊ)ˈflɛkʃn
AM ˌrɛtrəˈflɛkʃən

retrogradation
BR ˌrɛtrəʊgrəˈdeɪʃn, -z
AM ˌrɛtroʊgreɪˈdeɪʃən,
-z

retrograde
BR ˈrɛtrə(ʊ)greɪd
AM ˈrɛtrəˌgreɪd

retrogradely
BR ˈrɛtrə(ʊ)greɪdli
AM ˈrɛtrəˌgreɪdli

retrogress
BR ˌrɛtrə(ʊ)ˈgrɛs, -ɪz,
-ɪŋ, -t
AM ˌrɛtrəˈgrɛs, -əz, -ɪŋ,
-t

retrogression
BR ˌrɛtrə(ʊ)ˈgrɛʃn, -z
AM ˌrɛtrəˈgrɛʃən

retrogressive
BR ˌrɛtrə(ʊ)ˈgrɛsɪv
AM ˌrɛtrəˈgrɛsɪv

retrogressively
BR ˌrɛtrə(ʊ)ˈgrɛsɪvli
AM ˌrɛtrəˈgrɛsɪvli

retroject
BR ˈrɛtrə(ʊ)dʒɛkt, -s,
-ɪŋ, -ɪd
AM ˈrɛtrəˌdʒɛk|(t),
-(t)s, -tɪŋ, -təd

retro-rocket
BR ˈrɛtrəʊˌrɒkɪt, -s
AM ˈrɛtroʊˌrɑkət, -s

retrorse
BR rɪˈtrɔːs
AM rəˈtrɔ(ə)rs

retrorsely
BR rɪˈtrɔːsli
AM rəˈtrɔrsli

retrospect
BR ˈrɛtrəspɛkt, -s
AM ˈrɛtrəˌspɛk(t), -s

retrospection
BR ˌrɛtrə(ʊ)ˈspɛkʃn
AM ˌrɛtrəˈspɛkʃən

retrospective
BR ˌrɛtrə(ʊ)ˈspɛktɪv
AM ˌrɛtrəˈspɛktɪv

retrospectively
BR ˌrɛtrə(ʊ)ˈspɛktɪvli
AM ˌrɛtrəˈspɛktɪvli

retrosternal
BR ˌrɛtrəʊˈstəːnl
AM ˈrɛtroʊˈstərnəl

retroussé
BR rɪˈtruːseɪ
AM ˌrɛtroʊˈseɪ

retroversion
BR ˌrɛtrə(ʊ)ˈvəːʃn
AM ˌrɛtrəˈvərʒən

retrovert[1]
noun
BR ˈrɛtrəvəːt, -s
AM ˈrɛtrəˌvərt, -s

retrovert[2]
verb
BR ˌrɛtrə(ʊ)ˈvəːt, -s, -ɪŋ,
-ɪd
AM ˌrɛtrəˈvər|t, -ts,
-dɪŋ, -dəd

Retrovir
BR ˈrɛtrə(ʊ)vɪə(r)
AM ˈrɛtroʊˌvɪ(ə)r

retrovirus
BR ˈrɛtrəʊˌvʌɪrəs, -ɪz
AM ˈrɛtroʊˌvaɪrəs, -ɪz

retry
BR ˌriːˈtrʌɪ, -z, -ɪŋ, -d
AM ri'traɪ, -z, -ɪŋ, -d

retsina
BR rɛtˈsiːnə(r),
ˈrɛtsɪnə(r)
AM ˈrɛtsənə

Rett
BR rɛt
AM rɛt

rettery
BR ˈrɛt(ə)r|i, -ɪz
AM ˈrɛdəri, -z

retune
BR ˌriːˈtjuːn, ˌriːˈtʃuːn,
-z, -ɪŋ, -d
AM ri't(j)un, -z, -ɪŋ, -d

returf
BR ˌriːˈtəːf, -s, -ɪŋ, -t
AM ri'tərf, -s, -ɪŋ, -t

return
BR rɪˈtəːn, -z, -ɪŋ, -d
AM rəˈtərn, ri'tərn, -z,
-ɪŋ, -d

returnable
BR rɪˈtəːnəbl
AM rəˈtərnəbəl,
ri'tərnəbəl

returnee
BR rɪˌtəːˈniː, ˌriːtəːˈniː,
-z
AM rəˌtərˈni, ri,tərˈni,
-z

returner
BR rɪˈtəːnə(r), -z
AM rəˈtərnər,
ri'tərnər, -z

returning officer
BR rɪˈtəːnɪŋ ˌɒfɪsə(r)
-z
AM rəˈtərnɪŋ ˌɔfəsər,
+ ˌɑfəsər, -z

returnless
BR rɪˈtəːnləs
AM rəˈtərnləs,
ri'tərnləs

retuse
BR rɪˈtjuːs, rɪˈtʃuːs
AM ˌrəˈt(j)uz

retying
BR ˌriːˈtʌɪɪŋ
AM ri'taɪɪŋ

retype
BR ˌriːˈtʌɪp, -s, -ɪŋ, -t
AM ri'taɪp, -s, -ɪŋ, -t

Reuben
BR ˈruːb(ɪ)n
AM ˈrubən

reunification
BR ˌriːjuːnɪfɪˈkeɪʃn,
rɪˌjuːnɪfɪˈkeɪʃn
AM ˌriˌjunəfəˈkeɪʃən

reunify
BR (ˌ)riːˈjuːnɪfʌɪ, -z, -ɪŋ,
-d
AM ri'junəˌfaɪ, -z, -ɪŋ, -d

Réunion
BR ri'juːnɪən
AM ri'junjən
FR ʀeynjõ

reunion
BR (ˌ)riːˈjuːnɪən, -z
AM ri'junjən, -z

reunite
BR ˌriːjəˈnʌɪt,
ˌriːjuˈnaɪt, -s, -ɪŋ, -ɪd
AM ˈrijuˈnaɪ|t, -ts, -dɪŋ,
-dɪd

reupholster
BR ˌriːˌʌpˈhəʊlst|ə(r),
-əz, -(ə)rɪŋ, -əd
AM ˌriˌəp'(h)oʊlstər, -z,
-ɪŋ, -d

reupholstery
BR ˌriːˌʌpˈhəʊlst(ə)ri

AM ˌriːəpˈ(h)oʊlstəri

reurge
BR ˌriːˈɜːdʒ, -ɪz, -ɪŋ, -d
AM riˈɜrdʒ, -əz, -ɪŋ, -d

reusable
BR ˌriːˈjuːzəbl
AM riˈjuzəbəl

re-use¹
noun
BR ˌriːˈjuːs
AM riˈjus

re-use²
verb
BR ˌriːˈjuːz, -ɪz, -ɪŋ, -d
AM riˈjuz, -əz, -ɪŋ, -d

reuseable
BR ˌriːˈjuːzəbl
AM riˈjuzəbəl

Reuter
BR ˈrɔɪtə(r), -z
AM ˈrɔɪdər, -z

reutilisation
BR ˌriːjuːtɪlaɪˈzeɪʃn, ˌriːjuːtˌlaɪˈzeɪʃn, rɪˌjuːtɪlaɪˈzeɪʃn, rɪˌjuːtˌlaɪˈzeɪʃn
AM ˌriˌjudləˈzeɪʃən, ˈriˌjudlaɪˈzeɪʃən

reutilise
BR ˌriːˈjuːtɪlaɪz, ˌriːˈjuːtˌlaɪz, rɪˈjuːtɪlaɪz, rɪˈjuːtˌlaɪz, -ɪz, -ɪŋ, -d
AM riˈjudlˌaɪz, -ɪz, -ɪŋ, -d

reutilization
BR ˌriːjuːtɪlaɪˈzeɪʃn, ˌriːjuːtˌlaɪˈzeɪʃn, rɪˌjuːtɪlaɪˈzeɪʃn, rɪˌjuːtˌlaɪˈzeɪʃn
AM ˌriˌjudləˈzeɪʃən, ˈriˌjudlaɪˈzeɪʃən

reutilize
BR ˌriːˈjuːtɪlaɪz, rɪˈjuːtɪlaɪz, rɪˈjuːtˌlaɪz, rɪˈjuːtˌlaɪz, -ɪz, -ɪŋ, -d
AM riˈjudlˌaɪz, -ɪz, -ɪŋ, -d

Rev.
BR rɛv, ˈrɛv(ə)rənd, ˈrɛv(ə)rnd
AM ˈrɛvərnd, ˈrɛv(ə)rənd

rev
BR rɛv, -z, -ɪŋ, -d
AM rɛv, -z, -ɪŋ, -d

revaccinate
BR ˌriːˈvæksɪneɪt, -s, -ɪŋ, -ɪd
AM riˈvæksəˌneɪt, -ts, -dɪŋ, -dɪd

revaccination
BR ˌriːˌvæksɪˈneɪʃn, -z
AM riˌvæksəˈneɪʃən, -z

revalorisation
BR ˌriːˌvæləraɪˈzeɪʃn, -z

AM ˌriˌvælərəˈzeɪʃən, ˈriˌvæləˌraɪˈzeɪʃən, -z

revalorise
BR ˌriːˈvæləraɪz, -ɪz, -ɪŋ, -d
AM riˈvæləˌraɪz, -ɪz, -ɪŋ, -d

revalorization
BR ˌriːˌvæləraɪˈzeɪʃn, -z
AM ˌriˌvælərəˈzeɪʃən, ˈriˌvæləˌraɪˈzeɪʃən, -z

revalorize
BR ˌriːˈvæləraɪz, -ɪz, -ɪŋ, -d
AM riˈvæləˌraɪz, -ɪz, -ɪŋ, -d

revaluation
BR ˌriːˈvæljʊˈeɪʃn, -z
AM ˌriˌvæljəˈweɪʃən, -z

revalue
BR ˌriːˈvæljuː, -uːz, -ʊɪŋ, -uːd
AM riˈvæljˌu, -uz, -əwɪŋ, -ud

revamp
BR (ˌ)riːˈvæmp, -ps, -pɪŋ, -(p)t
AM riˈvæmp, -s, -ɪŋ, -t

revanchism
BR ˈrævɑːn(t)ʃɪz(ə)m
AM rəˈvɑn(t)ʃˌɪzəm

revanchist
BR rɪˈvɑːn(t)ʃɪst, -s
AM rəˈvɑn(t)ʃəst, -s

revarnish
BR ˌriːˈvɑːnɪʃ, -ɪʃɪz, -ɪʃɪŋ, -ɪʃt
AM riˈvɑrnɪʃ, -ɪz, -ɪŋ, -t

revcounter
BR ˈrɛvˌkaʊntə(r), -z
AM ˈrɛvˌkaʊn(t)ər, -z

reveal
BR rɪˈviːl, -z, -ɪŋ, -d
AM rəˈvil, riˈvil, -z, -ɪŋ, -d

revealable
BR rɪˈviːləbl
AM rəˈviləbəl, riˈviləbəl

revealer
BR rɪˈviːlə(r), -z
AM rəˈvilər, riˈvilər, -z

revealing
BR rɪˈviːlɪŋ
AM rəˈvilɪŋ, riˈvilɪŋ

revealingly
BR rɪˈviːlɪŋli
AM rəˈvilɪŋli, riˈvilɪŋli

reveille
BR rɪˈvæli, -ɪz
AM ˈrɛvəli, -z

revel
BR ˈrɛvl, -lz, -ɪŋ\-lɪŋ, -ld
AM ˈrɛvəl, -əlz, -(ə)lɪŋ, -əld

revelation
BR ˌrɛvəˈleɪʃn, -z

AM ˌrɛvəˈleɪʃən, -z

revelational
BR ˌrɛvəˈleɪʃn(ə)l, ˌrɛvəˈleɪʃən(ə)l
AM ˌrɛvəˈleɪʃ(ə)nəl

revelationist
BR ˌrɛvəˈleɪʃnɪst, ˌrɛvəˈleɪʃənɪst, -s
AM ˌrɛvəˈleɪʃənəst, -z

revelatory
BR ˌrɛvəˈleɪt(ə)ri, ˈrɛvələt(ə)ri, ˈrɛvlət(ə)ri
AM rəˈvɛləˌtɔri

reveler
BR ˈrɛvlə(r), ˈrɛvlə(r), -z
AM ˈrɛv(ə)lər, -z

reveller
BR ˈrɛvlə(r), ˈrɛvlə(r), -z
AM ˈrɛv(ə)lər, -z

revelry
BR ˈrɛvlri, -ɪz
AM ˈrɛvəlri, -z

revenant
BR ˈrɛvɪnənt, -s
AM ˈrɛvənənt, ˈrɛvəˌnɑnt, -z

revendication
BR rɪˌvɛndɪˈkeɪʃn, -z
AM rəˌvɛndəˈkeɪʃən, -z

revenge
BR rɪˈvɛn(d)ʒ, -ɪz, -ɪŋ, -d
AM rəˈvɛndʒ, riˈvɛndʒ, -əz, -ɪŋ, -d

revengeful
BR rɪˈvɛn(d)ʒf(ʊ)l
AM rəˈvɛndʒfəl, riˈvɛndʒfəl

revengefully
BR rɪˈvɛn(d)ʒfəli, rɪˈvɛn(d)ʒfli
AM rəˈvɛndʒfəli, riˈvɛndʒfəli

revengefulness
BR rɪˈvɛn(d)ʒf(ʊ)lnəs
AM rəˈvɛndʒfəlnəs, riˈvɛndʒfəlnəs

revenger
BR rɪˈvɛn(d)ʒə(r), -z
AM rəˈvɛndʒər, riˈvɛndʒər, -z

revenue
BR ˈrɛvɪnjuː, -z
AM ˈrɛvəˌn(j)u, -z

reverb
reverberation
BR rɪˈvɜːb, -z
AM rəˈvɜrb, -z

reverberant
BR rɪˈvɜːb(ə)rənt, rɪˈvɜːb(ə)rnt
AM rəˈvɜrb(ə)rənt, riˈvɜrb(ə)rənt

---

reverberantly
BR rɪˈvɜːb(ə)rəntli, rɪˈvɜːb(ə)rntli
AM rəˈvɜrb(ə)rən(t)li, riˈvɜrb(ə)rən(t)li

reverberate
BR rɪˈvɜːbəreɪt, -s, -ɪŋ, -ɪd
AM rəˈvɜrbəˌreɪt, riˈvɜrbəˌreɪt, -ts, -dɪŋ, -dɪd

reverberation
BR rɪˌvɜːbəˈreɪʃn, -z
AM rəˌvɜrbəˈreɪʃən, riˌvɜrbəˈreɪʃən, -z

reverberative
BR rɪˈvɜːb(ə)rətɪv
AM rəˈvɜrbərədɪv, riˈvɜrbərədɪv, rəˈvɜrbəˌreɪdɪv, riˈvɜrbəˌreɪdɪv

reverberator
BR rɪˈvɜːbəreɪtə(r), -z
AM rəˈvɜrbəˌreɪdər, riˈvɜrbəˌreɪdər, -z

reverberatory
BR rɪˈvɜːb(ə)rət(ə)ri, rɪˈvɜːbəreɪt(ə)ri
AM rəˈvɜrb(ə)rəˌtɔri, riˈvɜrb(ə)rəˌtɔri

revere
BR rɪˈvɪə(r), -z, -ɪŋ, -d
AM rəˈvɪ(ə)r, riˈvɪ(ə)r, -z, -ɪŋ, -d

reverence
BR ˈrɛv(ə)rəns, ˈrɛv(ə)rns, -ɪz, -ɪŋ, -t
AM ˈrɛvərns, ˈrɛv(ə)rəns, -əz, -ɪŋ, -t

reverend
BR ˈrɛv(ə)rənd, ˈrɛv(ə)rnd, -z
AM ˈrɛvərnd, ˈrɛv(ə)rənd

reverent
BR ˈrɛv(ə)rənt, ˈrɛv(ə)rnt
AM ˈrɛv(ə)rənt

reverential
BR ˌrɛvəˈrɛnʃl
AM ˌrɛvəˈrɛn(t)ʃəl

reverentially
BR ˌrɛvəˈrɛnʃli, ˌrɛvəˈrɛnʃəli
AM ˌrɛvəˈrɛn(t)ʃəli

reverently
BR ˈrɛv(ə)rəntli, ˈrɛvərntli
AM ˈrɛvərŋ(t)li, ˈrɛv(ə)rən(t)li

reverie
BR ˈrɛv(ə)r|i, -ɪz
AM ˈrɛvəri, -z

revers¹
singular
BR rɪˈvɪə(r)
AM rəˈvɪ(ə)r, rɪˈvɪ(ə)r, rəˈvɛ(ə)r, rɪˈvɛ(ə)r

revers[2]
plural
BR rɪˈvɪəz
AM rəˈvɪ(ə)rz,
rɪˈvɪ(ə)rz, rəˈvɛ(ə)rz,
rɪˈvɛ(ə)rz
reversal
BR rɪˈvəːsl, -z
AM rəˈvərsəl,
rɪˈvərsəl, -z
reverse[1]
noun
BR rɪˈvəːs
AM rəˈvərs, ˈrɪvərs
reverse[2]
*noun, contrasted
with obverse*
BR ˈriːvəːs
AM rəˈvərs, rɪˈvərs
reverse[3]
verb, adjective
BR rɪˈvəːs, -ɪz, -ɪŋ, -t
AM rəˈvərs, rɪˈvərs, -əz,
-ɪŋ, -t
reversely
BR rɪˈvəːsli
AM rəˈvərsli, rɪˈvərsli
reverser
BR rɪˈvəːsə(r), -z
AM rəˈvərsər,
rɪˈvərsər, -z
reversibility
BR rɪˌvəːsəˈbɪlɪti
AM rəˌvərsəˈbɪlɪdi,
rɪˌvərsəˈbɪlɪdi
reversible
BR rɪˈvəːsɪbl
AM rəˈvərsəbəl,
rɪˈvərsəbəl
reversibleness
BR rɪˈvəːsɪblnəs
AM rəˈvərsəbəlnəs,
rɪˈvərsəbəlnəs
reversibly
BR rɪˈvəːsɪbli
AM rəˈvərsəbli,
rɪˈvərsəbli
reversion
BR rɪˈvəːʃn, -z
AM rəˈvərʒən,
rɪˈvərʒən, rəˈvərʃən,
rɪˈvərʃən, -z
reversional
BR rɪˈvəːʃn(ə)l,
rɪˈvəːʃən(ə)l
AM rəˈvərʒ(ə)nəl,
rɪˈvərʒ(ə)nəl,
rəˈvərʃ(ə)nəl,
rɪˈvərʃ(ə)nəl
reversionary
BR rɪˈvəːʃn(ə)ri
AM rəˈvərʒəˌneri,
rɪˈvərʒəˌneri,
rəˈvərʃəˌneri,
rɪˈvərʃəˌneri
reversioner
BR rɪˈvəːʃnə(r), -z

AM rəˈvərʒənər,
rɪˈvərʒənər,
rəˈvərʃənər,
rɪˈvərʃənər, -z
revert
BR rɪˈvəːt, -s, -ɪŋ, -ɪd
AM rəˈvər|t, rɪˈvər|t,
-ts, -dɪŋ, -dəd
reverter
BR rɪˈvəːtə(r), -z
AM rəˈvərdər,
rɪˈvərdər, -z
revertible
BR rɪˈvəːtɪbl
AM rəˈvərdəbəl,
rɪˈvərdəbəl
revet
BR rɪˈvɛt, -s, -ɪŋ, -ɪd
AM rəˈvɛ|t, rɪˈvɛ|t, -ts,
-dɪŋ, -dəd
revetment
BR rɪˈvɛtm(ə)nt, -s
AM rəˈvɛtmənt,
rɪˈvɛtmənt, -s
revictual
BR ˌriːˈvɪt|l, -lz,
-lɪŋ \-lɪŋ, -ld
AM riˈvɪdl, -z, -ɪŋ, -d
Revie
BR ˈriːvi
AM ˈrivi
review
BR rɪˈvjuː, -z, -ɪŋ, -d
AM rəˈvju, rɪˈvju, -z, -ɪŋ,
-d
reviewable
BR rɪˈvjuːbl
AM rəˈvjuəbəl,
rɪˈvjuəbəl
reviewal
BR rɪˈvjuːəl, -z
AM rəˈvjuəl, rɪˈvjuəl, -z
reviewer
BR rɪˈvjuːə(r), -z
AM rəˈvjuər, rɪˈvjuər,
-z
revile
BR rɪˈvaɪl, -z, -ɪŋ, -d
AM rəˈvaɪl, rɪˈvaɪl, -z,
-ɪŋ, -d
revilement
BR rɪˈvaɪlm(ə)nt, -s
AM rəˈvaɪlmənt,
rɪˈvaɪlmənt, -z
reviler
BR rɪˈvaɪlə(r), -z
AM rəˈvaɪlər, rɪˈvaɪlər,
-z
reviling
BR rɪˈvaɪlɪŋ, -z
AM rəˈvaɪlɪŋ, rɪˈvaɪlɪŋ,
-z
revisable
BR rɪˈvaɪzəbl
AM rəˈvaɪzəbəl,
rɪˈvaɪzəbəl
revisal
BR rɪˈvaɪzl, -z

AM rəˈvaɪzəl, rɪˈvaɪzəl,
-z
revise
BR rɪˈvaɪz, -ɪz, -ɪŋ, -d
AM rəˈvaɪz, rɪˈvaɪz, -ɪz,
-ɪŋ, -d
**Revised
Standard
Version**
BR rɪˌvaɪzd ˈstandəd
ˌvəːʃn, + ˌvəːʒn
AM rəˈvaɪzd
ˈstændərd ˌvərʒən,
rɪˈvaɪzd +
reviser
BR rɪˈvaɪzə(r), -z
AM rəˈvaɪzər,
rɪˈvaɪzər, -z
revision
BR rɪˈvɪʒn, -z
AM rəˈvɪʒən, rɪˈvɪʒən,
-z
revisionary
BR rɪˈvɪʒn(ə)ri
AM rəˈvɪʒəˌneri,
rɪˈvɪʒəˌneri
revisionism
BR rɪˈvɪʒnɪz(ə)m
AM rəˈvɪʒəˌnɪzəm,
rɪˈvɪʒəˌnɪzəm
revisionist
BR rɪˈvɪʒnɪst, -s
AM rəˈvɪʒ(ə)nəst,
rɪˈvɪʒ(ə)nəst, -s
revisit
BR ˌriːˈvɪz|ɪt, -ɪts, -ɪtɪŋ,
-ɪtɪd
AM riˈvɪsɪ|t, -s, -ɪŋ, -ɪd
revisory
BR rɪˈvaɪz(ə)ri
AM rəˈvaɪzəri,
rɪˈvaɪzəri
revitalisation
BR ˌriːvaɪtl̩aɪˈzeɪʃn,
ˌriːvaɪtəlaɪˈzeɪʃn,
riːˌvaɪtl̩aɪˈzeɪʃn,
riːˌvaɪtəlaɪˈzeɪʃn
AM riˌvaɪdl̩əˈzeɪʃən,
riˌvaɪdl̩aɪˈzeɪʃən
revitalise
BR (ˌ)riːˈvaɪtl̩aɪz,
(ˌ)riːˈvaɪtəlaɪz, -ɪz, -ɪŋ,
-d
AM riˈvaɪdəˌlaɪz, -ɪz,
-ɪŋ, -d
revitalization
BR ˌriːvaɪtl̩aɪˈzeɪʃn,
ˌriːvaɪtəlaɪˈzeɪʃn,
riːˌvaɪtl̩aɪˈzeɪʃn,
riːˌvaɪtəlaɪˈzeɪʃn
AM riˌvaɪdl̩əˈzeɪʃən,
riˌvaɪdl̩aɪˈzeɪʃən
revitalize
BR (ˌ)riːˈvaɪtl̩aɪz,
(ˌ)riːˈvaɪtəlaɪz, -ɪz, -ɪŋ,
-d
AM riˈvaɪdəˌlaɪz, -ɪz,
-ɪŋ, -d

revivable
BR rɪˈvaɪvəbl
AM rəˈvaɪvəbəl,
rɪˈvaɪvəbəl
revival
BR rɪˈvaɪvl, -z
AM rəˈvaɪvəl,
rɪˈvaɪvəl, -z
revivalism
BR rɪˈvaɪvl̩ɪz(ə)m,
rɪˈvaɪvəlɪz(ə)m
AM rəˈvaɪvəˌlɪzəm,
rɪˈvaɪvəˌlɪzəm
revivalist
BR rɪˈvaɪvl̩ɪst,
rɪˈvaɪvəlɪst, -s
AM rəˈvaɪv(ə)ləst,
rɪˈvaɪv(ə)ləst, -s
revivalistic
BR rɪˌvaɪvl̩ˈɪstɪk,
rɪˌvaɪvəˈlɪstɪk
AM ˌrəˌvaɪvəˈlɪstɪk,
ˌrɪˌvaɪvəˈlɪstɪk
revive
BR rɪˈvaɪv, -z, -ɪŋ, -d
AM rəˈvaɪv, rɪˈvaɪv, -z,
-ɪŋ, -d
reviver
BR rɪˈvaɪvə(r), -z
AM rəˈvaɪvər,
rɪˈvaɪvər, -z
revivification
BR ˌriːvɪvɪfɪˈkeɪʃn,
riːˌvɪvɪfɪˈkeɪʃn
AM ˌriˌvɪvəfəˈkeɪʃən
revivify
BR (ˌ)riːˈvɪvɪfaɪ, -z, -ɪŋ,
-d
AM riˈvɪvəˌfaɪ, -z, -ɪŋ, -d
reviviscence
BR ˌrevɪˈvɪsns
AM ˌrevəˈvɪsəns
reviviscent
BR ˌrevɪˈvɪsnt
AM ˌrevəˈvɪsənt
Revlon®
BR ˈrevlɒn
AM ˈrev,lɑn
revocability
BR ˌrevəkəˈbɪlɪti
AM ˌrevəkəˈbɪlɪdi,
rəˌvoʊkəˈbɪlɪdi,
rɪˌvoʊkəˈbɪlɪdi
revocable
BR ˈrevəkəbl
AM ˈrevəkəbəl,
rəˈvoʊkəbəl,
rɪˈvoʊkəbəl
revocation
BR ˌrevəˈkeɪʃn, -z
AM ˌrevəˈkeɪʃən,
riˌvoʊˈkeɪʃən, -z
revocatory
BR ˈrevəkət(ə)ri
AM ˈrevəkəˌtori,
rəˈvoʊkəˌtori,
rɪˈvoʊkəˌtori

revoke
BR rɪˈvəʊk, -s, -ɪŋ, -t
AM rəˈvoʊk, riˈvoʊk, -s, -ɪŋ, -t

revoker
BR rɪˈvəʊkə(r), -z
AM rəˈvoʊkər, riˈvoʊkər, -z

revolt
BR rɪˈvəʊlt, -s, -ɪŋ, -ɪd
AM rəˈvoʊlt, riˈvoʊlt, -s, -ɪŋ, -əd

revolting
BR rɪˈvəʊltɪŋ
AM rəˈvoʊltɪŋ, riˈvoʊltɪŋ

revoltingly
BR rɪˈvəʊltɪŋli
AM rəˈvoʊltɪŋli, riˈvoʊltɪŋli

revolute
adjective
BR ˈrevəl(j)uːt
AM ˈrevəˌl(j)ut

revolution
BR ˌrevəˈl(j)uːʃn, -z
AM ˌrevəˈluʃən, -z

revolutionary
BR ˌrevəˈl(j)uːʃn̩(ə)r|i, -iz
AM ˌrevəˈluʃəˌnɛri, -z

revolutionise
BR ˌrevəˈl(j)uːʃn̩ʌɪz, ˌrevəˈl(j)uːʃənʌɪz, -ɪz, -ɪŋ, -d
AM ˌrevəˈluʃəˌnaɪz, -ɪz, -ɪŋ, -d

revolutionism
BR ˌrevəˈl(j)uːʃnɪz(ə)m, ˌrevəˈl(j)uːʃənɪz(ə)m
AM ˌrevəˈluʃəˌnɪzəm

revolutionist
BR ˌrevəˈl(j)uːʃnɪst, ˌrevəˈl(j)uːʃənɪst, -s
AM ˌrevəˈluʃənəst, -s

revolutionize
BR ˌrevəˈl(j)uːʃn̩ʌɪz, ˌrevəˈl(j)uːʃənʌɪz, -ɪz, -ɪŋ, -d
AM ˌrevəˈluʃəˌnaɪz, -ɪz, -ɪŋ, -d

revolvable
BR rɪˈvɒlvəbl
AM rəˈvolvəbəl, riˈvolvəbəl, rəˈvalvəbəl, riˈvalvəbəl

revolve
BR rɪˈvɒlv, -z, -ɪŋ, -d
AM rəˈvolv, riˈvolv, rəˈvalv, riˈvalv, -z, -ɪŋ, -d

revolver
BR rɪˈvɒlvə(r), -z
AM rəˈvolvər, riˈvolvər, rəˈvalvər, riˈvalvər, -z

revue
BR rɪˈvjuː, -z
AM rəˈvju, riˈvju, -z

revulsion
BR rɪˈvʌlʃn
AM rəˈvəlʃən, riˈvəlʃən

revulsive
BR rɪˈvʌlsɪv
AM rəˈvəlsɪv, riˈvəlsɪv

reward
BR rɪˈwɔːd, -z, -ɪŋ, -ɪd
AM rəˈwɔ(ə)rd, riˈwɔ(ə)rd, -z, -ɪŋ, -əd

rewardingly
BR rɪˈwɔːdɪŋli
AM rəˈwɔrdɪŋli, riˈwɔrdɪŋli

rewardless
BR rɪˈwɔːdləs
AM rəˈwɔrdləs, riˈwɔrdləs

rewarewa
BR ˌreɪwəˈreɪwə(r), -z
AM ˈreɪwəˈreɪwə, -z

rewash
BR ˌriːˈwɒʃ, -ɪz, -ɪŋ, -t
AM riˈwɒʃ, riˈwaʃ, -əz, -ɪŋ, -t

reweigh
BR ˌriːˈweɪ, -z, -ɪŋ, -d
AM riˈweɪ, -z, -ɪŋ, -d

rewind¹
noun
BR ˈriːwʌɪnd, -z
AM ˈriˌwaɪnd, -z

rewind²
verb
BR (ˌ)riːˈwʌɪnd, -z, -ɪŋ
AM riˈwaɪnd, -z, -ɪŋ

rewinder
BR (ˌ)riːˈwʌɪndə(r), -z
AM riˈwaɪndər, -z

rewirable
BR ˌriːˈwʌɪərəbl
AM riˈwaɪrəbəl

rewire
BR ˌriːˈwʌɪə(r), -z, -ɪŋ, -d
AM riˈwaɪ(ə)r, -z, -ɪŋ, -d

reword
BR ˌriːˈwəːd, -z, -ɪŋ, -ɪd
AM riˈwɔ(ə)rd, -z, -ɪŋ, -əd

rework
BR ˌriːˈwəːk, -s, -ɪŋ, -t
AM riˈwərk, -s, -ɪŋ, -t

reworking
BR ˌriːˈwəːkɪŋ, -z
AM riˈwərkɪŋ, -z

rewound
BR (ˌ)riːˈwaʊnd
AM riˈwaʊnd

rewrap
BR ˌriːˈrap, -s, -ɪŋ, -t
AM riˈræp, -s, -ɪŋ, -t

rewrite
BR ˌriːˈrʌɪt, -s, -ɪŋ

AM riˈraɪ|t, -ts, -dɪŋ

rewritten
BR ˌriːˈrɪtn
AM riˈrɪtn

rewrote
BR ˌriːˈrəʊt
AM riˈroʊt

Rex
BR rɛks
AM rɛks

Rexine®
BR ˈrɛksiːn
AM ˈrɛkˌsin, ˈrɛksən

Rey
BR reɪ
AM reɪ

Reyes
BR rʌɪz, reɪz
AM ˈreɪəs

Reykjavik
BR ˈrɛkjəvɪk, ˈreɪkjəvɪk
AM ˈreɪkjəˌvɪk

reynard
BR ˈreɪnɑːd, ˈrɛnəd, -z
AM reɪˈnard, ˈrɛˌnard, ˈreɪnard, ˈrɛnərd, -z

Reynolds
BR ˈrɛnldz
AM ˈrɛnəl(d)z

Rh
BR ˌɑːrˈeɪtʃ
AM ˌɑrˈeɪtʃ

rhabdomancy
BR ˈrabdəˌmansi
AM ˈræbdəˌmænsi

Rhadamanthine
BR ˌradəˈmanθʌɪn
AM ˈrædəˈmænˌθin, ˈrædəˈmænˌθaɪn

Rhadamanthus
BR ˌradəˈmanθəs
AM ˈrædəˈmænθəs

Rhaetian
BR ˈriːʃn, ˈriːʃɪən, -z
AM ˈreɪʃ(i)ən, -z

Rhaetic
BR ˈriːtɪk, -s
AM ˈreɪdɪk, -z

Rhaeto-Romance
BR ˌriːtəʊrə(ʊ)ˈmans, -ɪz
AM ˈrɪdoʊˌroʊˈmæns, -əz

Rhaeto-Romanic
BR ˌriːtəʊrə(ʊ)ˈmanɪk, -s
AM ˈrɪdoʊˌroʊˈmænɪk, -z

rhapsode
BR ˈrapsəʊd, -z
AM ˈræpˌsoʊd, -z

rhapsodic
BR rapˈsɒdɪk
AM (h)ræpˈsɑdɪk

rhapsodical
BR rapˈsɒdɪkl

AM (h)ræpˈsɑdəkəl

rhapsodically
BR rapˈsɒdɪkli
AM (h)ræpˈsɑdək(ə)li

rhapsodise
BR ˈrapsədʌɪz, -ɪz, -ɪŋ, -d
AM ˈ(h)ræpsəˌdaɪz, -ɪz, -ɪŋ, -d

rhapsodist
BR ˈrapsədɪst, -s
AM ˈ(h)ræpsədəst, -z

rhapsodize
BR ˈrapsədʌɪz, -ɪz, -ɪŋ, -d
AM ˈ(h)ræpsəˌdaɪz, -ɪz, -ɪŋ, -d

rhapsody
BR ˈrapsəd|i, -ɪz
AM ˈ(h)ræpsədi, -z

rhatany
BR ˈratəni, ˈratn̩i, -ɪz
AM ˈrætni

Rhayader
BR ˈrʌɪədə(r)
AM ˈraɪədər

rhea
BR rɪə(r), ˈriːə(r), -z
AM ˈriə, -z

rhebok
BR ˈriːbɒk, -s
AM ˈriˌbak, -s

Rheims
BR riːmz
AM rimz
FR Rɛ̃s

Rhein
BR rʌɪn
AM raɪn

rheme
BR riːm, -z
AM rim, -z

Rhemish
BR ˈriːmɪʃ
AM ˈrimɪʃ

Rhenish
BR ˈrɛnɪʃ
AM ˈrɛnɪʃ

rhenium
BR ˈriːnɪəm
AM ˈriniəm

rheological
BR ˌrɪəˈlɒdʒɪkl
AM ˌriəˈladʒəkəl

rheologist
BR riˈɒlədʒɪst, -s
AM riˈalədʒəst, -z

rheology
BR riˈɒlədʒi
AM riˈalədʒi

rheostat
BR ˈriːəstat, -s
AM ˈriəˌstæt, -s

rheostatic
BR ˌriːə(ʊ)ˈstatɪk
AM ˌriəˈstædɪk

rheotropic
BR ˌriːə(ʊ)'trɒpɪk,
ˌriːə(ʊ)'trəʊpɪk
AM ˌriə'trɑpɪk

rheotropism
BR ˌriːə(ʊ)'trəʊpɪz(ə)m
AM ˌriə'trɑˌpɪzəm

rhesus
BR 'riːsəs, -ɪz
AM 'risəs, -əz

rhesus-negative
BR ˌriːsəs'nɛgətɪv
AM ˌrisəs'nɛgədɪv

rhesus-positive
BR ˌriːsəs'pɒzɪtɪv
AM ˌrisəs'pɑzədɪv

rhetor
BR 'riːtə(r)
AM 'rɛdər

rhetoric
BR 'rɛtərɪk
AM 'rɛdərɪk

rhetorical
BR rɪ'tɒrɪkl
AM rə'tɔrəkəl

rhetorically
BR rɪ'tɒrɪkli
AM rə'tɔrək(ə)li

rhetorician
BR ˌrɛtə'rɪʃn, -z
AM ˌrɛdə'rɪʃən, -z

Rhett
BR rɛt
AM rɛt

rheum
BR ruːm
AM (h)rum

rheumatic
BR ruː'matɪk, -s
AM ru'mædɪk, -s

rheumatically
BR ruː'matɪkli
AM ru'mædək(ə)li

rheumatic fever
BR ruːˌmatɪk 'fiːvə(r)
AM ruːˌmædɪk 'fivər

rheumaticky
BR ruː'matɪki
AM ru'mædəki,
rə'mædəki

rheumatism
BR 'ruːmətɪz(ə)m
AM 'ruməˌtɪzəm

rheumatoid
BR 'ruːmətɔɪd
AM 'ruməˌtɔɪd

rheumatological
BR ˌruːmətə'lɒdʒɪkl
AM ˌrumədə'lɑdʒəkəl

rheumatologist
BR ˌruːmə'tɒlədʒɪst, -s
AM ˌrumə'tɑlədʒəst, -s

rheumatology
BR ˌruːmə'tɒlədʒi
AM ˌrumə'tɑlədʒi

rheumy
BR 'ruːmi

AM 'rumi

Rhiannon
BR rɪ'anən, rɪ'anɒn
AM ri'ænən

rhinal
BR 'rʌɪnl
AM 'raɪnəl

Rhine
BR rʌɪn
AM raɪn

Rhineland
BR 'rʌɪnland
AM 'raɪnˌlænd

Rhineland-Palatinate
BR ˌrʌɪnlandpə'latɪnət
AM 'raɪnˌlændpə'lætnət,
'raɪnˌlændpə'lætneɪt

rhinestone
BR 'rʌɪnstəʊn, -z
AM 'raɪnˌstoʊn, -z

rhinitis
BR rʌɪ'nʌɪtɪs
AM raɪ'naɪdɪs

rhino
BR 'rʌɪnəʊ, -z
AM 'raɪnoʊ, -z

rhinoceros
BR rʌɪ'nɒs(ə)rəs, -ɪz
AM raɪ'nɑs(ə)rəs, -ɪz

rhinocerotic
BR rʌɪˌnɒsə'rɒtɪk
AM raɪˌnɑsə'rɑdɪk,
ˌraɪnəsə'rɑdɪk

rhinopharyngeal
BR ˌrʌɪnəʊfə'rɪn(d)ʒ-
(ɪ)əl,
ˌrʌɪnəʊfə'rɪn(d)ʒl
AM ˌraɪnoʊfə'rɪn(d)ʒ-
(i)əl

rhinoplastic
BR ˌrʌɪnə(ʊ)'plastɪk
AM ˌraɪnoʊ'plæstɪk

rhinoplasty
BR 'rʌɪnə(ʊ)ˌplasti
AM 'raɪnoʊˌplæsti

rhinoscope
BR 'rʌɪnəskəʊp, -s
AM 'raɪnəˌskoʊp, -z

rhizocarp
BR 'rʌɪzəʊkɑːp, -s
AM 'raɪzoʊˌkɑrp, -z

rhizoid
BR 'rʌɪzɔɪd
AM 'raɪˌzɔɪd

rhizome
BR 'rʌɪzəʊm, -z
AM 'raɪˌzoʊm, -z

rhizopod
BR 'rʌɪzə(ʊ)pɒd, -z
AM 'raɪzəˌpɑd, -z

rho
BR rəʊ
AM roʊ

Rhoda
BR 'rəʊdə(r)
AM 'roʊdə

rhodamine
BR 'rəʊdəmiːn, -z
AM 'roʊdəˌmin,
'roʊdəmən, -z

Rhode Island
BR ˌrəʊd 'ʌɪlənd
AM roʊ'daɪlənd

Rhodes
BR rəʊdz
AM roʊdz

Rhodesia
BR rə(ʊ)'diːʃə(r),
rə(ʊ)'diːʒə(r)
AM roʊ'diːʒə

Rhodesian
BR rə(ʊ)'diːʃn,
rə(ʊ)'diːʒn, -z
AM roʊ'diːʒən, -z

Rhodian
BR 'rəʊdɪən, -z
AM 'roʊdiən, -z

rhodium
BR 'rəʊdɪəm
AM 'roʊdiəm

rhodochrosite
BR ˌrəʊdə'krəʊsʌɪt
AM ˌroʊdə'kroʊˌsaɪt,
roʊ'dɑkrəˌsaɪt

rhododendron
BR ˌrəʊdə'dɛndr(ə)n,
-z
AM ˌroʊdə'dɛndrən, -z

Rhodope
BR 'rɒdəpi, rɒ'dəʊpi
AM 'rɑdəpi

Rhodophyta
BR ˌrəʊdə(ʊ)'fʌɪtə(r)
AM ˌroʊdoʊ'faɪtə

rhodopsin
BR rə(ʊ)'dɒpsɪn
AM roʊ'dɑpsən

rhodora
BR rə(ʊ)'dɔːrə(r), -z
AM rə'dɔrə, -z

Rhodri
BR 'rɒdri
AM 'rɑdri

rhomb
BR rɒm(b), -z
AM rɑm(b), -z

rhombi
BR 'rɒmbʌɪ
AM 'rɑmˌbaɪ

rhombic
BR 'rɒmbɪk
AM 'rɑmbɪk

rhombohedra
BR ˌrɒmbə'hiːdrə(r)
AM ˌrɑmboʊ'hidrə

rhombohedral
BR ˌrɒmbə'hiːdr(ə)l
AM ˌrɑmboʊ'hidrəl

rhombohedron
BR ˌrɒmbə'hiːdrən, -z
AM ˌrɑmboʊ'hidrən,
ˌrɑmboʊ'hiˌdran, -z

rhomboid
BR 'rɒmbɔɪd, -z
AM 'rɑmˌbɔɪd, -z

rhomboidal
BR rɒm'bɔɪdl
AM rɑm'bɔɪdəl

rhomboidally
BR rɒm'bɔɪdli
AM rɑm'bɔɪd(ə)li

rhomboidei
BR rɒm'bɔɪdɪʌɪ
AM rɑm'bɔɪdiˌi

rhomboideus
BR rɒm'bɔɪdɪəs
AM rɑm'bɔɪdiəs

rhombus
BR 'rɒmbəs, -ɪz
AM 'rɑmbəs, -əz

rhona
BR 'rəʊnə(r)
AM 'roʊnə

Rhondda
BR 'rɒnðə(r),
'rɒndə(r)
AM 'rɑndə
WE 'rɒnðə

Rhône
BR rəʊn
AM roʊn

Rhoose
BR ruːs
AM rus

Rhos
BR rəʊs
AM roʊs
WE ros

Rhossili
BR rɒ'sɪli
AM rə'sɪli

rhotic
BR 'rəʊtɪk, -s
AM 'roʊdɪk, -s

rhoticity
BR rə(ʊ)'tɪsɪti
AM roʊ'tɪsɪdi

rhubarb
BR 'ruːbɑːb
AM 'ruˌbɑrb

Rhuddlan
BR 'rɪðlən, 'rʌðlən
AM 'rɪðlən
WE 'rɪðlan

Rhum
BR rʌm
AM rʊm

rhumb
BR rʌm, -z
AM rəm, -z

rhumba
BR 'rʌmbə(r), -z, -ɪŋ, -d
AM 'rəmbə, -z, -ɪŋ, -d

rhumb-line
BR 'rʌmlʌɪn, -z
AM 'rəmˌlaɪn, -z

Rhydderch
BR 'rʌðəx, 'rʌðək
AM 'rəðək

WE 'rʌðerx

Rhydding
BR 'rɪdɪŋ
AM 'rɪdɪŋ

Rhyl
BR rɪl
AM rɪl

rhyme
BR raɪm, -z, -ɪŋ, -d
AM raɪm, -z, -ɪŋ, -d

rhymeless
BR 'raɪmlɪs
AM 'raɪmlɪs

rhymer
BR 'raɪmə(r), -z
AM 'raɪmər, -z

rhymester
BR 'raɪmstə(r), -z
AM 'raɪmstər, -z

rhymist
BR 'raɪmɪst, -s
AM 'raɪmɪst, -z

Rhymney
BR 'rʌmni
AM 'rʊmni

rhyolite
BR 'raɪəlaɪt, -s
AM 'raɪəˌlaɪt, -s

Rhys
BR ri:s
AM rɪs

rhythm
BR 'rɪð(ə)m, -z
AM 'rɪðəm, -z

rhythm-and-blues
BR ˌrɪðm̩(ə)n(d)'blu:z, ˌrɪðəm(ə)n(d)'blu:z
AM 'rɪðəmənˌbluz

rhythmic
BR 'rɪðmɪk
AM 'rɪðmɪk

rhythmical
BR 'rɪðmɪkl
AM 'rɪðmɪkəl

rhythmically
BR 'rɪðmɪkli
AM 'rɪðmɪk(ə)li

rhythmicity
BR ˌrɪð'mɪsɪti
AM ˌrɪð'mɪsɪdi

rhythmist
BR 'rɪðmɪst, -s
AM 'rɪðmɪst, -z

rhythmless
BR 'rɪð(ə)mləs
AM 'rɪðəmləs

ria
BR 'ri:ə(r), -z
AM 'riə, -z

rial
BR rɪ'ɑ:l, 'ri:ɑ:l, -z
AM ri'(j)ɑl, -z

rialto
BR rɪ'altəʊ, -z
AM ri'æl,təʊ, -z

rib
BR rɪb, -z, -ɪŋ, -d
AM rɪb, -z, -ɪŋ, -d

ribald
BR 'rɪbld, 'rɪbɔːld
AM 'rɪbəld, 'rɪˌbɔld, 'raɪˌbɔld, 'rɪˌbald, 'raɪˌbald

ribaldry
BR 'rɪbldri
AM 'rɪbəldri, 'rɪˌbɔldri, 'raɪˌbɔldri, 'rɪˌbaldri, 'raɪˌbaldri

riband
BR 'rɪb(ə)nd, -z
AM 'rɪbən(d), -z

Ribbentrop
BR 'rɪbntrɒp
AM 'rɪb(ə)n,trɑp

ribber
BR 'rɪbə(r), -z
AM 'rɪbər, -z

ribbing
BR 'rɪbɪŋ, -z
AM 'rɪbɪŋ, -z

Ribble
BR 'rɪbl
AM 'rɪbəl

ribbon
BR 'rɪb(ə)n, -z, -d
AM 'rɪbən, -z, -d

ribbonfish
BR 'rɪb(ə)nfɪʃ
AM 'rɪbən,fɪʃ

ribcage
BR 'rɪbkeɪdʒ, -ɪz
AM 'rɪb,keɪdʒ, -ɪz

Ribena®
BR raɪ'bi:nə(r)
AM raɪ'binə

ribless
BR 'rɪblɪs
AM 'rɪblɪs

riboflavin
BR ˌraɪbə(ʊ)'fleɪvɪn
AM ˌraɪbə'fleɪvɪn

riboflavine
BR ˌraɪbə(ʊ)'fleɪvi:n
AM ˌraɪbə'fleɪvin

ribonucleic
BR ˌraɪbə(ʊ)nju:'kleɪɪk
AM ˌraɪboʊn(j)u'kliɪk

ribose
BR 'raɪbəʊz, 'raɪbəʊs, -ɪz
AM 'raɪ,boʊz, 'raɪ,boʊs, -əz

ribosomal
BR ˌraɪbə(ʊ)'səʊml
AM raɪ'basəməl

ribosome
BR 'raɪbəsəʊm, -z
AM 'raɪbə,soʊm, -z

ribwort
BR 'rɪbwɜːt, -s
AM 'rɪbwərt, 'rɪb,wɔ(ə)rt, -z

Ricardo
BR rɪ'kɑ:dəʊ
AM rə'kɑrdoʊ

rice
BR rʌɪs
AM raɪs

ricer
BR 'rʌɪsə(r), -z
AM 'raɪsər, -z

ricercar
BR ˌri:tʃə'kɑ:(r), ˌri:tʃəkɑ:(r), -z
AM ˌritʃər'kɑr, -z

ricercare
BR ˌri:tʃə'kɑ:reɪ, ˌri:tʃə'kɑ:r|i, ˌri:tʃəkɑ:reɪ, 'ri:tʃəkɑ:r|i, -ɪz
AM ˌritʃər'kɑ,reɪ, -z

rich
BR rɪtʃ, -ɪz, -ə(r), -ɪst
AM rɪtʃ, -ɪz, -ə(r), -ɪst

Richard
BR 'rɪtʃəd
AM 'rɪtʃərd

Richards
BR 'rɪtʃədz
AM 'rɪtʃərdz

Richardson
BR 'rɪtʃəds(ə)n
AM 'rɪtʃərdsən

Richelieu
BR 'ri:ʃ(ə)ljə:(r), 'rɪʃ(ə)ljə:(r)
AM 'rɪʃəl(j)u, rɪʃəl'ju

richen
BR 'rɪtʃ|n, -nz, -ŋɪŋ-\-(ə)nɪŋ, -d
AM 'rɪtʃən, -z, -ɪŋ, -d

Richie
BR 'rɪtʃi
AM 'rɪtʃi

richly
BR 'rɪtʃli
AM 'rɪtʃli

Richmal
BR 'rɪtʃml
AM 'rɪtʃməl

Richmond
BR 'rɪtʃm(ə)nd
AM 'rɪtʃmən(d)

richness
BR 'rɪtʃnɪs
AM 'rɪtʃnɪs

Richter
BR 'rɪktə(r)
AM 'rɪktər

ricin
BR 'rʌɪsɪn, 'rɪsɪn
AM 'raɪsən, 'rɪsən

rick
BR rɪk, -s
AM rɪk, -s

Rickard
BR 'rɪkɑːd
AM 'rɪkərd

Rickards
BR 'rɪkɑːdz
AM 'rɪkərdz

Rickenbacker
BR 'rɪk(ə)nbakə(r)
AM 'rɪkən,bækər

ricketily
BR 'rɪkɪtɪli
AM 'rɪkɪdɪli

ricketiness
BR 'rɪkɪtɪnɪs
AM 'rɪkɪdɪnɪs

rickets
BR 'rɪkɪts
AM 'rɪkɪts

Rickett
BR 'rɪkɪt
AM 'rɪkɪt

Ricketts
BR 'rɪkɪts
AM 'rɪkɪts

rickettsia
BR rɪ'kɛtsɪə(r), -z
AM rə'kɛtsɪə, -z

rickettsiae
BR rɪ'kɛtsi:
AM rə'kɛtsi,i, rə'kɛtsi,aɪ

rickettsial
BR rɪ'kɛtsɪəl
AM rə'kɛtsɪəl

rickety
BR 'rɪkɪt|i, -ɪə(r), -ɪɪst
AM 'rɪkɪdi, -ər, -ɪst

rickey
BR 'rɪk|i, -ɪz
AM 'rɪki, -z

Rickmansworth
BR 'rɪkmənzwə:θ
AM 'rɪkmənz,wərθ

Rickover
BR 'rɪkəʊvə(r)
AM 'rɪk,oʊvər

rickrack
BR 'rɪkrak
AM 'rɪk,ræk

Ricks
BR rɪks
AM rɪks

ricksha
BR 'rɪkʃɔ:(r), -z
AM 'rɪk,ʃɔ, 'rɪk,ʃɑ, -z

rickshaw
BR 'rɪkʃɔ:(r), -z
AM 'rɪk,ʃɔ, 'rɪk,ʃɑ, -z

Ricky
BR 'rɪki
AM 'rɪki

ricochet
BR 'rɪkəʃ|eɪ, 'rɪkəʃ|ɛt, -eɪz\-ɛts, -eɪɪŋ\-ɛtɪŋ, -eɪd\-ɛtd
AM 'rɪkə,ʃeɪ, -z, -ɪŋ, -d

Ricoh
BR 'ri:kəʊ
AM 'rikoʊ

ricotta
BR rɪˈkɒtə(r)
AM rəˈkɑdə

ricrac
BR ˈrɪkrak, -s
AM ˈrɪkˌræk, -z

rictal
BR ˈrɪktl
AM ˈrɪktl

rictus
BR ˈrɪktəs
AM ˈrɪktəs

rid
BR rɪd, -z, -ɪŋ
AM rɪd, -z, -ɪŋ

ridable
BR ˈrʌɪdəbl
AM ˈraɪdəbəl

riddance
BR ˈrɪd(ə)ns
AM ˈrɪdns

Riddell
BR rɪˈdɛl, ˈrɪdl
AM ˈrɪdəl, rəˈdɛl

ridden
BR ˈrɪdn
AM ˈrɪdən

Ridding
BR ˈrɪdɪŋ
AM ˈrɪdɪŋ

riddle
BR ˈrɪd|l, -lz, -ḷɪŋ\-lɪŋ, -ld
AM ˈrɪd|əl, -əlz, -(ə)lɪŋ, -əld

riddler
BR ˈrɪdlə(r), ˈrɪdlə(r), -z
AM ˈrɪd(ə)lər, -z

riddlingly
BR ˈrɪdl̩ɪŋli, ˈrɪdlɪŋli
AM ˈrɪd(ə)lɪŋli

ride
BR rʌɪd, -z, -ɪŋ
AM raɪd, -z, -ɪŋ

rideable
BR ˈrʌɪdəbl
AM ˈraɪdəbəl

Rideout
BR ˈrʌɪdaʊt
AM ˈraɪˌdaʊt

rider
BR ˈrʌɪdə(r), -z
AM ˈraɪdər, -z

riderless
BR ˈrʌɪdələs
AM ˈraɪdərləs

ridge
BR rɪdʒ, -ɪz, -ɪŋ, -d
AM rɪdʒ, -ɪz, -ɪŋ, -d

ridgel
BR ˈrɪdʒl, -z
AM ˈrɪdʒəl, -z

ridgepole
BR ˈrɪdʒpəʊl, -z
AM ˈrɪdʒˌpoʊl, -z

ridgeway
BR ˈrɪdʒweɪ, -z
AM ˈrɪdʒˌweɪ, -z

Ridgway
BR ˈrɪdʒweɪ
AM ˈrɪdʒˌweɪ

ridgy
BR ˈrɪdʒ|i, -ɪə(r), -ɪɪst
AM ˈrɪdʒi, -ər, -ɪst

ridicule
BR ˈrɪdɪkjuːl, -z, -ɪŋ, -d
AM ˈrɪdɪˌkjul, -z, -ɪŋ, -d

ridiculous
BR rɪˈdɪkjʉləs
AM rəˈdɪkjələs

ridiculously
BR rɪˈdɪkjʉləsli
AM rəˈdɪkjələsli

ridiculousness
BR rɪˈdɪkjʉləsnəs
AM rəˈdɪkjələsnəs

riding
BR ˈrʌɪdɪŋ, -z
AM ˈraɪdɪŋ, -z

Ridley
BR ˈrɪdli
AM ˈrɪdli

Riemann
BR ˈriːmən
AM ˈrimən

Riesling
BR ˈriːzlɪŋ, ˈriːslɪŋ
AM ˈrizlɪŋ, ˈrisˌlɪŋ

Rievaulx
BR ˈriːvəʊ, ˈrɪvəz
AM riˈvoʊ, ˈrivoʊ

Rif
BR rɪf
AM rɪf

rifampicin
BR rɪˈfampɪsɪn
AM rəˈfæmpəsɪn

rifampin
BR rɪˈfampɪn
AM rəˈfæmpɪn

rife
BR rʌɪf
AM raɪf

rifeness
BR ˈrʌɪfnɪs
AM ˈraɪfnɪs

riff
BR rɪf, -s
AM rɪf, -s

riffle
BR ˈrɪf|l, -lz, -ḷɪŋ\-lɪŋ, -ld
AM ˈrɪf|əl, -əlz, -(ə)lɪŋ, -əld

riffraff
BR ˈrɪfraf
AM ˈrɪˌfræf

Rifkind
BR ˈrɪfkɪnd
AM ˈrɪfkɪnd

rifle
BR ˈrʌɪf|l, -lz, -ḷɪŋ\-lɪŋ, -ld
AM ˈraɪf|əl, -əlz, -(ə)lɪŋ, -əld

rifleman
BR ˈrʌɪflmən
AM ˈraɪfəlmən

riflemen
BR ˈrʌɪflmən
AM ˈraɪfəlmən

riflescope
BR ˈrʌɪflskəʊp, -s
AM ˈraɪflˌskoʊp, -z

rifling
BR ˈrʌɪflɪŋ, ˈrʌɪflɪŋ, -z
AM ˈraɪf(ə)lɪŋ, -z

rift
BR rɪft, -s
AM rɪft, -s

riftless
BR ˈrɪftlɪs
AM ˈrɪf(t)lɪs

rifty
BR ˈrɪft|i, -ɪə(r), -ɪɪst
AM ˈrɪfti, -ər, -ɪst

rig
BR rɪg, -z, -ɪŋ, -d
AM rɪg, -z, -ɪŋ, -d

Riga
BR ˈriːgə(r)
AM ˈrigə

rigadoon
BR ˌrɪgəˈduːn, -z
AM ˌrɪgəˈdun, -z

rigamarole
BR ˈrɪg(ə)mərəʊl, -z
AM ˈrɪg(ə)məˌroʊl, -z

rigatoni
BR ˌrɪgəˈtəʊni
AM ˌrɪgəˈtoʊni

Rigby
BR ˈrɪgbi
AM ˈrɪgbi

Rigel
BR ˈrʌɪgl, ˈrʌɪdʒl
AM ˈraɪdʒəl

Rigg
BR rɪg
AM rɪg

Riggs
BR rɪgz
AM rɪgz

rigger
BR ˈrɪgə(r), -z
AM ˈrɪgər, -z

rigging
BR ˈrɪgɪŋ, -z
AM ˈrɪgɪŋ, -z

right
BR rʌɪt, -s, -ɪŋ, -ɪd
AM raɪ|t, -ts, -dɪŋ, -dɪd

rightable
BR ˈrʌɪtəbl
AM ˈraɪdəbəl

rightabout
BR ˈrʌɪtəˈbaʊt
AM ˈraɪdəˌbaʊt

rightangle
BR ˈrʌɪtˌaŋgl, -z, -d
AM ˈraɪtˌæŋgəl, -z, -d

right-back
BR ˈrʌɪtbak, ˌrʌɪtˈbak, -s
AM ˈraɪtˌbæk, -z

righten
BR ˈrʌɪt|n, -nz, -ṇɪŋ\-nɪŋ, -nd
AM ˈraɪtn, -z, -ɪŋ, -d

righteous
BR ˈrʌɪtʃəs
AM ˈraɪtʃəs

righteously
BR ˈrʌɪtʃəsli
AM ˈraɪtʃəsli

righteousness
BR ˈrʌɪtʃəsnəs
AM ˈraɪtʃəsnəs

righter
BR ˈrʌɪtə(r), -z
AM ˈraɪdər, -z

rightful
BR ˈrʌɪtf(ʉ)l
AM ˈraɪtfəl

rightfully
BR ˈrʌɪtfʉli, ˈrʌɪtfli
AM ˈraɪtfəli

rightfulness
BR ˈrʌɪtf(ʉ)lnəs
AM ˈraɪtfəlnəs

righthand
BR ˌrʌɪtˈhand
AM ˌraɪtˈhænd, ˈraɪdænd

right-handed
BR ˌrʌɪtˈhandɪd
AM ˌraɪtˈhæn(d)əd, ˈraɪdæn(d)əd

right-handedly
BR ˌrʌɪtˈhandɪdli
AM ˌraɪtˈhæn(d)ədli, ˈraɪdæn(d)ədli

right-handedness
BR ˌrʌɪtˈhandɪdnɪs
AM ˌraɪtˈhæn(d)ədnəs, ˈraɪdæn(d)ədnəs

right-hander
BR ˌrʌɪtˈhandə(r)
AM ˌraɪtˈhændər, ˈraɪdændər

rightho
BR ˌrʌɪtˈ(h)əʊ
AM ˌraɪtˈ(h)oʊ

rightish
BR ˈrʌɪtɪʃ
AM ˈraɪdɪʃ

rightism
BR ˈrʌɪtɪz(ə)m
AM ˈraɪˌtɪzəm

rightist
BR ˈrʌɪtɪst, -s
AM ˈraɪdɪst, -s

rightless
BR ˈraɪtlɪs
AM ˈraɪtlɪs

rightlessness
BR ˈraɪtlɪsnɪs
AM ˈraɪtlɪsnɪs

rightly
BR ˈraɪtli
AM ˈraɪtli

rightmost
BR ˈraɪtməʊst
AM ˈraɪtˌmoʊst

rightness
BR ˈraɪtnɪs
AM ˈraɪtnəs

righto
BR ˌraɪtˈəʊ
AM ˌraɪˈdoʊ

rightward
BR ˈraɪtwəd, -z
AM ˈraɪtwərd, -z

rigid
BR ˈrɪdʒɪd
AM ˈrɪdʒɪd

rigidify
BR rɪˈdʒɪdɪfaɪ, -z, -ɪŋ, -d
AM rəˈdʒɪdəˌfaɪ, -z, -ɪŋ, -d

rigidity
BR rɪˈdʒɪdɪti
AM rəˈdʒɪdɪdi

rigidly
BR ˈrɪdʒɪdli
AM ˈrɪdʒɪdli

rigidness
BR ˈrɪdʒɪdnɪs
AM ˈrɪdʒɪdnɪs

rigmarole
BR ˈrɪgmərəʊl, -z
AM ˈrɪg(ə)məˌroʊl, -z

rigor¹
shivering
BR ˈraɪgɔː(r), ˈrɪgə(r)
AM ˈrɪgər

rigor²
BR ˈrɪgə(r), -z
AM ˈrɪgər, -z

rigorism
BR ˈrɪg(ə)rɪz(ə)m
AM ˈrɪgəˌrɪzəm

rigor mortis
BR ˌrɪgə ˈmɔːtɪs
AM ˌrɪgər ˈmɔrdəs

rigorous
BR ˈrɪg(ə)rəs
AM ˈrɪg(ə)rəs

rigorously
BR ˈrɪg(ə)rəsli
AM ˈrɪg(ə)rəsli

rigorousness
BR ˈrɪg(ə)rəsnəs
AM ˈrɪg(ə)rəsnəs

rigour
BR ˈrɪgə(r), -z
AM ˈrɪgər, -z

Rigsby
BR ˈrɪgzbi

AM ˈrɪgzbi

Rigveda
BR ˌrɪgˈveɪdə(r)
AM ˌrɪgˈveɪdə

Rijeka
BR rɪˈjekə(r)
AM rɪˈjekə

Rijksmuseum
BR ˈraɪksmjuːˌziːəm
AM ˈraɪksˌmuziəm
DU ˈreɪksmyzeəm

Rikki
BR ˈrɪki
AM ˈrɪki

Rikki-Tiki-Tavi
BR ˌrɪkɪˌtɪkɪˈtɑːvi, ˌrɪkɪˌtɪkɪˈteɪvi
AM ˌrɪkiˌtɪkiˈtævi

rile
BR raɪl, -z, -ɪŋ, -d
AM raɪl, -z, -ɪŋ, -d

Riley
BR ˈraɪli
AM ˈraɪli

rilievo
BR rɪˈljeɪvəʊ, -z
AM riˈli(eɪ)voʊ, -z

Rilke
BR ˈrɪlkə(r)
AM ˈrɪlkə

rill
BR rɪl, -z
AM rɪl, -z

rille
BR rɪl, -z
AM ˈrɪlə, -z

rillettes
BR riːˈjet
AM riˈjet(s)

rim
BR rɪm, -z, -d
AM rɪm, -z, -d

Rimbaud
BR ˈrambəʊ
AM ræmˈboʊ

rime
BR raɪm
AM raɪm

rimester
BR ˈraɪmstə(r), -z
AM ˈraɪmstər, -z

rimfire
BR ˈrɪmfaɪə(r)
AM ˈrɪmˌfaɪ(ə)r

Rimini
BR ˈrɪmɪni
AM ˈrɪmɪni

rimless
BR ˈrɪmlɪs
AM ˈrɪmlɪs

Rimmer
BR ˈrɪmə(r)
AM ˈrɪmər

Rimmon
BR ˈrɪmən
AM ˈrɪmən

rimose
BR raɪˈməʊs
AM raɪˈmoʊs, raɪˈmoʊz

rimous
BR ˈraɪməs
AM ˈraɪməs

rimrock
BR ˈrɪmrɒk, -s
AM ˈrɪmˌrɑk, -s

Rimsky-Korsakov
BR ˌrɪmskɪˈkɔːsəkɒf
AM ˈrɪmskiˈkɔrsəˌkɔf, ˈrɪmskiˈkɔrsəˌkaf

rimu
BR ˈriːmuː, -z
AM ˈrɪmu, -z

rimy
BR ˈraɪm‖i, -ɪə(r), -ɪɪst
AM ˈraɪmi, -ər, -ɪst

rind
BR raɪnd, -z
AM raɪnd, -z

rinderpest
BR ˈrɪndəpest
AM ˈrɪndərˌpest

rindless
BR ˈraɪndlɪs
AM ˈraɪn(d)lɪs

ring
BR rɪŋ, -z, -ɪŋ, -d
AM rɪŋ, -z, -ɪŋ, -d

ringbark
BR ˈrɪŋbɑːk, -s, -ɪŋ, -t
AM ˈrɪŋˌbɑrk, -s, -ɪŋ, -t

ringbinder
BR ˌrɪŋˈbaɪndə(r), ˈrɪŋˌbaɪndə(r), -z
AM ˈrɪŋˌbaɪndər, -z

ringbolt
BR ˈrɪŋbəʊlt, -s
AM ˈrɪŋˌboʊlt, -z

ring-dove
BR ˈrɪŋdʌv, -z
AM ˈrɪŋˌdəv, -z

ringent
BR ˈrɪn(d)ʒ(ə)nt
AM ˈrɪndʒənt

ringer
BR ˈrɪŋə(r), -z
AM ˈrɪŋər, -z

ring-fence
BR ˈrɪŋfens, ˌrɪŋˈfens, -ɪz, -ɪŋ, -t
AM ˈrɪŋˌfens, -əz, -ɪŋ, -t

ringhals
BR ˈrɪŋhals, -ɪz
AM ˈrɪŋ(h)ælz, -əz

ringingly
BR ˈrɪŋɪŋli
AM ˈrɪŋɪŋli

ringleader
BR ˈrɪŋˌliːdə(r), -z
AM ˈrɪŋˌlidər, -z

ringless
BR ˈrɪŋlɪs
AM ˈrɪŋlɪs

ringlet
BR ˈrɪŋlɪt, -s
AM ˈrɪŋlɪt, -s

ringleted
BR ˈrɪŋlɪtɪd
AM ˈrɪŋlɪdɪd

ringletted
BR ˈrɪŋlɪtɪd
AM ˈrɪŋlɪdɪd

ringlety
BR ˈrɪŋlɪti
AM ˈrɪŋlɪdi

ringmaster
BR ˈrɪŋˌmɑːstə(r), ˈrɪŋˌmɑstə(r), -z
AM ˈrɪŋˌmæstər, -z

ringpull
BR ˈrɪŋpʊl, -z
AM ˈrɪŋˌpʊl, -z

ringside
BR ˈrɪŋsaɪd
AM ˈrɪŋˌsaɪd

ringsider
BR ˈrɪŋsaɪdə(r), -z
AM ˈrɪŋˌsaɪdər, -z

ringster
BR ˈrɪŋstə(r), -z
AM ˈrɪŋstər, -z

ringtail
BR ˈrɪŋteɪl, -z
AM ˈrɪŋˌteɪl, -z

Ringwood
BR ˈrɪŋwʊd
AM ˈrɪŋˌwʊd

ringworm
BR ˈrɪŋwəːm
AM ˈrɪŋˌwərm

rink
BR rɪŋk, -s
AM rɪŋk, -s

rinkhals
BR ˈrɪŋ(k)hals, -ɪz
AM ˈrɪŋ(k)ˌ(h)ælz, -əz

rinky-dink
BR ˈrɪŋkɪdɪŋk
AM ˈrɪŋkiˈdɪŋk

rinse
BR rɪns, -ɪz, -ɪŋ, -t
AM rɪns, -əz, -ɪŋ, -t

rinser
BR ˈrɪnsə(r), -z
AM ˈrɪnsər, -z

Rintoul
BR rɪnˈtuːl, ˈrɪntuːl
AM rɪnˈtul, ˈrɪnˌtul

Rio
BR ˈriːəʊ
AM ˈrioʊ

Rio de Janeiro
BR ˌriːəʊ də (d)ʒəˈnɪərəʊ
AM ˈrioʊ ˌdeɪ (d)ʒəˈnɛroʊ, ˈrioʊ ˌdi (d)ʒəˈnɛroʊ
B PORT ˌxiu de ʒaˈnejru
L PORT ˌʁiu də ʒɐˈnajru

Río de la Plata
BR ˌriːəʊ də lə
ˈplɑːtə(r), + ˈplætə(r)
AM ˈriːoʊ ˌdeɪ lə ˈplɑdə

Río de Oro
BR ˌriːəʊ dɪ ˈɔːrəʊ
AM ˈriːoʊ di ˈɔ‚roʊ

Río Grande
BR ˌriːəʊ ˈgrænd(i)
AM ˈriːoʊ ˈgrænd

Rioja
BR rɪˈəʊkə(r),
rɪˈɒkə(r), rɪˈəʊxə(r),
rɪˈɒxə(r)
AM riˈoʊhɑ

Río Muni
BR ˌriːəʊ ˈm(j)uːni
AM ˈriːoʊ ˈm(j)uni

Riordan
BR ˈrɪəd(ə)n
AM ˈrɪ(ə)rdən

Ríos
BR ˈriːəʊs
AM ˈrioʊs

riot
BR ˈrʌɪət, -s, -ɪŋ, -ɪd
AM ˈraɪə|t, -ts, -dɪŋ,
-dəd

rioter
BR ˈrʌɪətə(r), -z
AM ˈraɪədər, -z

riotless
BR ˈrɪətləs
AM ˈraɪətləs

riotous
BR ˈrʌɪətəs
AM ˈraɪədəs

riotously
BR ˈrʌɪətəsli
AM ˈraɪədəsli

riotousness
BR ˈrʌɪətəsnəs
AM ˈraɪədəsnəs

RIP
BR ˌɑːrʌɪˈpiː
AM ˌɑrˌaɪˈpi

rip
BR rɪp, -s, -ɪŋ, -t
AM rɪp, -s, -ɪŋ, -t

riparian
BR rʌɪˈpɛːrɪən,
rɪˈpɛːrɪən
AM rəˈpɛrɪən,
raɪˈpɛrɪən

ripcord
BR ˈrɪpkɔːd, -z
AM ˈrɪpˌkɔ(ə)rd, -z

ripe
BR rʌɪp, -ə(r), -ɪst
AM raɪp, -ər, -ɪst

ripely
BR ˈrʌɪpli
AM ˈraɪpli

ripen
BR ˈrʌɪp|(ə)n, -(ə)nz,
-(ə)nɪŋ \-ŋɪŋ, -nd
AM ˈraɪp|ən, -ənz,
-(ə)nɪŋ, -ənd

ripeness
BR ˈrʌɪpnɪs
AM ˈraɪpnɪs

ripieno
BR ˈrɪpɪˈeɪnəʊ, -z
AM rəpˈjeɪnoʊ, -z

Ripley
BR ˈrɪpli
AM ˈrɪpli

rip-off
BR ˈrɪpɒf, -s
AM ˈrɪpˌɔf, ˈrɪpˌɑf, -s

Ripon
BR ˈrɪp(ə)n
AM ˈrɪpən

ripost
BR rɪˈpɒst, -s, -ɪŋ, -ɪd
AM rəˈpoʊst, riˈpoʊst,
-s, -ɪŋ, -əd

riposte
BR rɪˈpɒst, -s, -ɪŋ, -ɪd
AM rəˈpoʊst, riˈpoʊst,
-s, -ɪŋ, -əd

ripper
BR ˈrɪpə(r), -z
AM ˈrɪpər, -z

ripple
BR ˈrɪp|l, -lz, -lɪŋ \-lɪŋ,
-ld
AM ˈrɪp|əl, -əlz, -(ə)lɪŋ,
-əld

ripplet
BR ˈrɪplɪt, -s
AM ˈrɪplɪt, -z

ripply
BR ˈrɪpli, ˈrɪpli
AM ˈrɪp(ə)li

Rippon
BR ˈrɪp(ə)n
AM ˈrɪpən

riprap
BR ˈrɪprap, -s, -ɪŋ, -t
AM ˈrɪpˌræp, -s, -ɪŋ, -t

riproaring
BR ˈrɪpˈrɔːrɪŋ
AM ˈrɪpˈrɔrɪŋ

riproaringly
BR ˈrɪpˈrɔːrɪŋli
AM ˈrɪpˈrɔrɪŋli

ripsaw
BR ˈrɪpsɔː(r), -z
AM ˈrɪpˌsɔ, ˈrɪpˌsɑ, -z

ripsnorter
BR ˈrɪpˌsnɔːtə(r), -z
AM ˈrɪpˈsnɔrdər, -z

ripsnorting
BR ˈrɪpˌsnɔːtɪŋ
AM ˈrɪpˈsnɔrdɪŋ

ripsnortingly
BR ˈrɪpˌsnɔːtɪŋli
AM ˈrɪpˈsnɔrdɪŋli

ripstop
BR ˈrɪpstɒp, -s
AM ˈrɪpˌstɑp, -s

riptide
BR ˈrɪptʌɪd, -z
AM ˈrɪpˌtaɪd, -z

Ripuarian
BR ˈrɪpjʊˈɛːrɪən, -z
AM ˈrɪp(j)əˈwɛrɪən, -z

Rip van Winkle
BR ˌrɪp van ˈwɪŋkl
AM ˌrɪp ˌvæn ˈwɪŋkəl

Risborough
BR ˈrɪzb(ə)rə(r)
AM ˈrɪzˌbərə

RISC
BR rɪsk
AM rɪsk

Risca
BR ˈrɪskə(r)
AM ˈrɪskə

rise
BR rʌɪz, -ɪz, -ɪŋ
AM raɪz, -ɪz, -ɪŋ

risen
BR ˈrɪzn
AM ˈrɪzn

riser
BR ˈrʌɪzə(r), -z
AM ˈraɪzər, -z

rishi
BR ˈrɪʃ|i, -ɪz
AM ˈrɪʃi, -z

risibility
BR ˈrɪzɪˈbɪlɪti,
ˈrʌɪzɪˈbɪlɪti
AM ˈrɪzəˈbɪlɪdi

risible
BR ˈrɪzɪbl, ˈrʌɪzɪbl
AM ˈrɪzəbəl

risibly
BR ˈrɪzɪbli, ˈrʌɪzɪbli
AM ˈrɪzəbli

rising
BR ˈrʌɪzɪŋ, -z
AM ˈraɪzɪŋ, -z

risk
BR rɪsk, -s, -ɪŋ, -t
AM rɪsk, -s, -ɪŋ, -t

riskily
BR ˈrɪskɪli
AM ˈrɪskɪli

riskiness
BR ˈrɪskɪnɪs
AM ˈrɪskɪnɪs

risky
BR ˈrɪsk|i, -ɪə(r), -ɪɪst
AM ˈrɪski, -ər, -ɪst

Risorgimento
BR rɪˌsɔːdʒɪˈmɛntəʊ
AM riˌsɔrdʒəˈmɛnˌ(t)oʊ

risotto
BR rɪˈzɒtəʊ, -z
AM rəˈzɒtoʊ, rəˈsɒdoʊ,
rəˈzɑdoʊ, rəˈsɑdoʊ, -z

risqué
BR ˈrɪskeɪ, rɪˈskeɪ
AM rɪˈskeɪ, rɪˈskeɪ

rissole
BR ˈrɪsəʊl, -z
AM rəˈsoʊl, ˈrɪˌsoʊl, -z

rit.
BR rɪt

AM rɪt

Rita
BR ˈriːtə(r)
AM ˈridə

Ritalin®
BR ˈrɪtəlɪn
AM ˈrɪdəlɪn

ritardando
BR ˌrɪtɑːˈdandəʊ, -z
AM ˌriˌtɑrˈdɑnˌdoʊ, -z

Ritchie
BR ˈrɪtʃi
AM ˈrɪtʃi

rite
BR rʌɪt, -s
AM raɪt, -s

riteless
BR ˈrʌɪtlɪs
AM ˈraɪtlɪs

ritenuti
BR ˌrɪtəˈn(j)uːti
AM ˌridəˈnudi

ritenuto
BR ˌrɪtəˈn(j)uːtəʊ, -z
AM ˌridəˈnudoʊ, -z

ritornelli
BR ˌrɪtəˈnɛli:,
ˌritɔːˈnɛli:
AM ˌridərˈnɛli

ritornello
BR ˌrɪtəˈnɛləʊ,
ˌritɔːˈnɛləʊ, -z
AM ˌridərˈnɛloʊ, -z

Ritson
BR ˈrɪts(ə)n
AM ˈrɪtsən

Ritter
BR ˈrɪtə(r)
AM ˈrɪdər

ritual
BR ˈrɪtʃʊəl, ˈrɪtʃ(ʊ)l,
ˈrɪtjʊəl, ˈrɪtjʊl, -z
AM ˈrɪtʃ(əw)əl, -z

ritualisation
BR ˌrɪtʃʊəlʌɪˈzeɪʃn,
ˌrɪtʃʊlʌɪˈzeɪʃn,
ˌrɪtʃlʌɪˈzeɪʃn,
ˌrɪtjʊəlʌɪˈzeɪʃn,
ˌrɪtjʊlʌɪˈzeɪʃn
AM ˌrɪtʃ(əw)ələˈzeɪʃən,
ˌrɪtʃ(əw)əˌlaɪˈzeɪʃən

ritualise
BR ˈrɪtʃʊəlʌɪz,
ˈrɪtʃʊlʌɪz, ˈrɪtʃlʌɪz,
ˈrɪtjʊəlʌɪz, ˈrɪtjʊlʌɪz,
-ɪz, -ɪŋ, -d
AM ˈrɪtʃ(əw)əˌlaɪz, -ɪz,
-ɪŋ, -d

ritualism
BR ˈrɪtʃʊəlɪz(ə)m,
ˈrɪtʃʊlɪz(ə)m,
ˈrɪtʃlɪz(ə)m,
ˈrɪtjʊəlɪz(ə)m,
ˈrɪtjʊlɪz(ə)m
AM ˈrɪtʃ(əw)əˌlɪzəm

ritualistic
BR ˌrɪtʃʊəˈlɪstɪk,
ˌrɪtʃˈəˈlɪstɪk,

ritualistically
,rɪtʃ'ɪstɪk,
,rɪtjʊə'lɪstɪk,
,rɪtjʊ'lɪstɪk
AM ,rɪtʃ(əw)ə'lɪstɪk

ritualistically
BR rɪtʃʊə'lɪstɪkli,
,rɪtʃ'ə'lɪstɪkli,
,rɪtjʊə'lɪstɪk,
,rɪtjʊ'lɪstɪkli
AM ,rɪtʃ(əw)ə'lɪstək(ə)li

ritualization
BR ,rɪtʃʊəlaɪ'zeɪʃn,
,rɪtʃəlaɪ'zeɪʃn,
,rɪtʃʌɪ'zeɪʃn,
,rɪtjʊəlaɪ'zeɪʃn,
,rɪtjəlaɪ'zeɪʃn
AM ,rɪtʃ(əw)ələ'zeɪʃən,
,rɪtʃ(əw)ə,laɪ'zeɪʃən

ritualize
BR 'rɪtʃʊəlaɪz,
'rɪtʃəlaɪz, 'rɪtʃʃlaɪz,
'rɪtjʊəlaɪz, 'rɪtjəlaɪz,
-ɪz, -ɪŋ, -d
AM 'rɪtʃ(əw)ə,laɪz, -ɪz,
-ɪŋ, -d

ritually
BR 'rɪtʃʊəli, 'rɪtʃʊli,
'rɪtʃli, 'rɪtjʊəli,
'rɪtjəli
AM 'rɪtʃ(əw)əli

Ritz
BR rɪts
AM rɪts

ritzily
BR 'rɪtsɪli
AM 'rɪtsɪli

ritziness
BR 'rɪtsɪnɪs
AM 'rɪtsɪnɪs

ritzy
BR 'rɪts|i, -ɪə(r), -ɪɪst
AM 'rɪtsi, -ər, -ɪst

rival
BR 'rAɪv|l, -lz,
-|ɪŋ\-əlɪŋ, -ld
AM 'raɪv|əl, -əlz, -(ə)lɪŋ,
-əld

rivalry
BR 'rAɪvlr|i, -ɪz
AM 'raɪvəlri, -z

rive
BR rAɪv, -z, -ɪŋ, -d
AM raɪv, -z, -ɪŋ, -d

Rivelin
BR 'rɪv|lɪn, 'rɪvlɪn
AM 'rɪvələn

riven
BR 'rɪvn
AM 'rɪvən

river[1]
one who rives
BR 'rAɪvə(r), -z
AM 'raɪvər, -z

river[2]
water
BR 'rɪvə(r), -z, -d
AM 'rɪvər, -z, -d

Rivera
BR rɪ'vɛːrə(r)
AM rə'verə

riverain
BR 'rɪvəreɪn, -z
AM 'rɪvə,reɪn, -z

riverbank
BR 'rɪvəbaŋk, -s
AM 'rɪvər,bæŋk, -s

riverbed
BR 'rɪvəbed, -z
AM 'rɪvər,bed, -z

riverboat
BR 'rɪvəbəʊt, -s
AM 'rɪvər,bəʊt, -s

riverfront
BR 'rɪvəfrʌnt, -s
AM 'rɪvər,frʌnt, -s

Riverina
BR ,rɪvə'riːnə(r)
AM ,rɪvə'rinə

riverine
BR 'rɪvərʌɪn
AM 'rɪvə,raɪn, 'rɪvərən

riverless
BR 'rɪvələs
AM 'rɪvərləs

Rivers
BR 'rɪvəz
AM 'rɪvərz

riverside
BR 'rɪvəsʌɪd
AM 'rɪvər,saɪd

rivet
BR 'rɪv|ɪt, -ɪts, -ɪtɪŋ,
-ɪtɪd
AM 'rɪvɪ|t, -ts, -dɪŋ, -dɪd

riveter
BR 'rɪvɪtə(r), -z
AM 'rɪvɪdər, -z

Riviera
BR ,rɪvɪ'ɛːrə(r)
AM ,rɪvɪ'ɛrə, rɪ'vjərə

rivière
BR ,rɪvɪ'ɛː(r), -ɪz
AM ,rɪvɪ'ɛ(ə)r, rɪ'vjeɪ,
-z

rivulet
BR 'rɪvjʊlɪt, 'rɪvjʊlet,
-s
AM 'rɪv(j)ələt, -s

Rix
BR rɪks
AM rɪks

Riyadh
BR rɪ'jad, 'riːad, rɪ'jɑːd
AM ri'jad

riyal
BR rɪ'ɑːl, rɪ'al, 'riːɑːl,
'riːal, -z
AM ri'(j)ɔl, ri'(j)ɑl, -z

Rizla®
BR 'rɪzlə(r)
AM 'rɪzlər

roach
BR rəʊtʃ, -ɪz
AM rəʊtʃ, -əz

road
BR rəʊd, -z
AM roʊd, -z

roadability
BR ,rəʊdə'bɪlɪti
AM ,roʊdə'bɪlɪdi

roadbed
BR 'rəʊdbed, -z
AM 'roʊd,bed, -z

roadblock
BR 'rəʊdblɒk, -s
AM 'roʊd,blɑk, -s

roadhog
BR 'rəʊdhɒg, -z
AM 'roʊd,(h)ɔg,
'roʊd,(h)ɑg, -z

roadholding
BR 'rəʊd,həʊldɪŋ
AM 'roʊd,(h)oʊldɪŋ

roadhouse
BR 'rəʊdhaʊ|s, -zɪz
AM 'roʊd,(h)aʊ|s, -zəz

roadie
BR 'rəʊd|i, -ɪz
AM 'roʊdi, -z

roadless
BR 'rəʊdləs
AM 'roʊdləs

roadliner
BR 'rəʊd,lʌɪnə(r), -z
AM 'roʊd,laɪnər, -z

roadman
BR 'rəʊdman,
'rəʊdmən
AM 'roʊd,mæn,
'roʊdmən

roadmen
BR 'rəʊdmen,
'rəʊdmən
AM 'roʊd,men,
'roʊdmən

roadroller
BR 'rəʊd,rəʊlə(r), -z
AM 'roʊd,roʊlər, -z

roadrunner
BR 'rəʊd,rʌnə(r), -z
AM 'roʊd,rənər, -z

roadshow
BR 'rəʊdʃəʊ, -z
AM 'roʊd,ʃoʊ, -z

roadside
BR 'rəʊdsʌɪd
AM 'roʊd,saɪd

roadstead
BR 'rəʊdsted, -z
AM 'roʊd,sted, -z

roadster
BR 'rəʊdstə(r), -z
AM 'roʊdstər, -z

roadtest
BR 'rəʊdtest, -s, -ɪŋ, -ɪd
AM 'roʊd,test, -s, -ɪŋ,
-əd

roadway
BR 'rəʊdweɪ, -z
AM 'roʊd,weɪ, -z

roadwork
BR 'rəʊdwəːk, -s
AM 'roʊd,wərk, -s

roadworthiness
BR 'rəʊd,wəːðɪnɪs
AM 'roʊd,wərðɪnɪs

roadworthy
BR 'rəʊd,wəːði
AM 'roʊd,wərði

Roald
BR 'rəʊəld
AM 'roʊəld
NO 'ruːal

roam
BR rəʊm, -z, -ɪŋ, -d
AM roʊm, -z, -ɪŋ, -d

roamer
BR 'rəʊmə(r), -z
AM 'roʊmər, -z

roan
BR rəʊn, -z
AM roʊn, -z

Roanoke
BR 'rəʊənəʊk
AM 'roʊə,noʊk

roar
BR rɔː(r), -z, -ɪŋ, -d
AM rɔ(ə)r, -z, -ɪŋ, -d

roarer
BR 'rɔːrə(r), -z
AM 'rɔrər, -z

roaring
BR 'rɔːrɪŋ, -z
AM 'rɔrɪŋ, -z

roaringly
BR 'rɔːrɪŋli
AM 'rɔrɪŋli

roast
BR rəʊst, -s, -ɪŋ, -ɪd
AM roʊst, -s, -ɪŋ, -əd

roaster
BR 'rəʊstə(r), -z
AM 'roʊstər, -z

roasting
BR 'rəʊstɪŋ, -z
AM 'roʊstɪŋ, -z

Roath
BR rəʊθ
AM roʊθ

rob
BR rɒb, -z, -ɪŋ, -d
AM rɑb, -z, -ɪŋ, -d

Robb
BR rɒb
AM rɑb

Robben Island
BR ,rɒb(ɪ)n 'ʌɪlənd
AM ,rɑbən 'aɪlənd

robber
BR 'rɒbə(r), -z
AM 'rɑbər, -z

robbery
BR 'rɒb(ə)r|i, -ɪz
AM 'rɑb(ə)ri, -z

Robbia
della Robbia
BR 'rɒbɪə(r)

Robbie
BR 'rɒbi
AM 'rɑbi

Robbins
BR 'rɒbɪnz
AM 'rɑbənz

robe
BR rəʊb, -z, -ɪŋ, -d
AM roʊb, -z, -ɪŋ, -d

Robens
BR 'rəʊb(ɪ)nz
AM 'roʊbənz

Roberson
BR 'rəʊbəs(ə)n
AM 'roʊbərsən

Robert
BR 'rɒbət
AM 'rɑbərt

Roberta
BR rə(ʊ)'bəːtə(r),
rɒ'bəːtə(r)
AM rə'bərdə

Roberts
BR 'rɒbəts
AM 'rɑbərts

Robertson
BR 'rɒbəts(ə)n
AM 'rɑbərtsən

Robeson
BR 'rəʊbs(ə)n
AM 'roʊb(ə)sən

Robespierre
BR 'rəʊbzpɪɛː(r),
'rəʊbzpɪə(r)
AM 'roʊbz'spjeɪ

Robey
BR 'rəʊbi
AM 'roʊbi

robin
BR 'rɒbɪn, -z
AM 'rɑbən, -z

Robina
BR rə(ʊ)'biːnə(r),
rɒ'biːnə(r)
AM rə'binə

Robin Goodfellow
BR ,rɒbɪn 'gʊd,fɛləʊ
AM ,rɑbən 'gʊd,fɛloʊ

Robin Hood
BR ,rɒbɪn 'hʊd
AM 'rɑbən ,(h)ʊd

robinia
BR rə(ʊ)'bɪnɪə(r),
rɒ'bɪnɪə(r), -z
AM roʊ'bɪniə, -z

Robins
BR 'rɒbɪnz, 'rəʊbɪnz
AM 'rɑbənz

Robinson
BR 'rɒbɪns(ə)n
AM 'rɑbənsən

Robinson Crusoe
BR ,rɒbɪns(ə)n 'kruːsəʊ
AM ,rɑbənsən 'kru,soʊ

roborant
BR 'rəʊb(ə)rənt,
'rəʊb(ə)rn̩t,
'rɒb(ə)rənt,
'rɒb(ə)rn̩t, -s
AM 'rɑbərənt,
'roʊbərənt, -z

robot
BR 'rəʊbɒt, -s
AM 'roʊ,bɑt, 'roʊbət, -s

robotic
BR rə(ʊ)'bɒtɪk, -s
AM roʊ'bɑdɪk, -s

robotically
BR rə(ʊ)'bɒtɪkli
AM roʊ'bɑdək(ə)li

robotisation
BR ,rəʊbətʌɪ'zeɪʃn̩
AM ,roʊbədə'zeɪʃən,
,roʊbə,tɑɪ'zeɪʃən

robotise
BR 'rəʊbətʌɪz, -ɪz, -ɪŋ,
-d
AM 'roʊbə,tɑɪz, -ɪz, -ɪŋ,
-d

robotization
BR ,rəʊbətʌɪ'zeɪʃn̩
AM ,roʊbədə'zeɪʃən,
,roʊbə,tɑɪ'zeɪʃən

robotize
BR 'rəʊbətʌɪz, -ɪz, -ɪŋ,
-d
AM 'roʊbə,tɑɪz, -ɪz, -ɪŋ,
-d

Rob Roy
BR ,rɒb 'rɔɪ
AM ,rɑb 'rɔɪ

Robsart
BR 'rɒbsɑːt
AM 'rɑb,sɑrt

Robson
BR 'rɒbs(ə)n
AM 'rɑbsən

robust
BR rə(ʊ)'bʌst,
'rəʊbʌst
AM roʊ'bəst, 'roʊ,bəst

robustious
BR rə(ʊ)'bʌstɪəs,
rə(ʊ)'bʌstʃəs
AM roʊ'bəstʃəs,
rə'bəstʃəs

robustly
BR rə(ʊ)'bʌstli,
'rəʊbʌstli
AM roʊ'bəs(t)li,
'roʊ,bəs(t)li

robustness
BR rə(ʊ)'bʌs(t)nəs,
'rəʊbʌs(t)nəs
AM roʊ'bəs(t)nəs,
'roʊ,bəs(t)nəs

Roby
BR 'rəʊbi
AM 'roʊbi

roc
BR rɒk, -s
AM rɑk, -s

rocaille
BR rə(ʊ)'kʌɪ
AM roʊ'kaɪ

rocambole
BR 'rɒk(ə)mbəʊl, -z
AM 'rɑkəm,boʊl, -z

Rocco
BR 'rɒkəʊ
AM 'rɑkoʊ

Rochdale
BR 'rɒtʃdeɪl
AM 'rɑtʃ,deɪl

Roche
BR rəʊ(t)ʃ, rɒʃ
AM roʊʃ

Rochelle
BR rɒ'ʃɛl, rə'ʃɛl
AM rə'ʃɛl

roche moutonnée
BR rɒʃ muː'tɒneɪ, -z
AM ,rɒʃ ,mutn'eɪ, -z

Rochester
BR 'rɒtʃɪstə(r)
AM 'rɑtʃ,əstər

rochet
BR 'rɒtʃɪt, -s
AM 'rɑtʃət, -s

Rochford
BR 'rɒtʃfəd
AM 'rɑtʃfə(r)d

rock
BR rɒk, -s, -ɪŋ, -t
AM rɑk, -s, -ɪŋ, -t

rockabilly
BR 'rɒkə,bɪli
AM 'rɑkə,bɪli

Rockall
BR 'rɒkɔːl
AM 'rɑk,ɔl, 'rɑk,ɑl

rock and roll
BR ,rɒk (ə)n(d) 'rəʊl
AM ,rɑk ən 'roʊl

rock and roller
BR ,rɒk (ə)n(d)
'rəʊlə(r), -z
AM ,rɑk ən 'roʊlər, -z

rock-bed
BR 'rɒkbɛd, -z
AM 'rɑk,bɛd, -z

rock-bottom
BR rɒk'bɒtəm
AM 'rɑk'badəm

rockbound
BR 'rɒkbaʊnd
AM 'rɑk,baʊnd

rockburst
BR 'rɒkbəːst, -s
AM 'rɑk,bərst, -z

rock-cake
BR 'rɒkkeɪk, -s
AM 'rɑ(k),keɪk, -z

rock-candy
BR 'rɒk'kandi
AM 'rɑ(k)'kændi

Rockefeller
BR 'rɒkə,fɛlə(r)

AM 'rɑkə,fɛlər

rocker
BR 'rɒkə(r), -z
AM 'rɑkər, -z

rockery
BR 'rɒk(ə)r|i, -ɪz
AM 'rɑkəri, -z

rocket
BR 'rɒk|ɪt, -ɪts, -ɪtɪŋ,
-ɪtɪd
AM 'rɑkə|t, -ts, -dɪŋ,
-dəd

rocketeer
BR ,rɒkɪ'tɪə(r), -z
AM ,rɑkə'tɪ(ə)r, -z

rocketry
BR 'rɒkɪtri
AM 'rɑkətri

rocketship
BR 'rɒkɪtʃɪp, -s
AM 'rɑkət,ʃɪp, -s

rockfall
BR 'rɒkfɔːl, -z
AM 'rɑk,fɔl, 'rɑk,fɑl, -z

rockfish
BR 'rɒkfɪʃ
AM 'rɑk,fɪʃ

Rockhampton
BR rɒk'ham(p)tən
AM rɑk'hæm(p)tən

rockhopper
BR 'rɒk,hɒpə(r), -z
AM 'rɑk,(h)ɑpər, -z

Rockies
BR 'rɒkɪz
AM 'rɑkiz

rockily
BR 'rɒkɪli
AM 'rɑkəli

rockiness
BR 'rɒkɪnɪs
AM 'rɑkinɪs

rockless
BR 'rɒkləs
AM 'rɑkləs

rocklet
BR 'rɒklɪt, -s
AM 'rɑklət, -z

rocklike
BR 'rɒklʌɪk
AM 'rɑk,laɪk

rockling
BR 'rɒklɪŋ, -z
AM 'rɑklɪŋ, -z

Rockne
BR 'rɒkni
AM 'rɑkni

rock 'n roll
BR ,rɒk (ə)n 'rəʊl
AM 'rɑk ən 'roʊl

rock 'n roller
BR ,rɒk (ə)n 'rəʊlə(r)
AM 'rɑk ən 'roʊlər

Rockwell
BR 'rɒkw(ɛ)l
AM 'rɑk,wɛl

rock-wool
BR 'rɒkwʊl
AM 'rɑk,wʊl

rocky
BR 'rɒk|i, -ɪə(r), -ɪɪst
AM 'rɑki, -ər, -ɪst

Rocky Mountains
BR ,rɒkɪ 'maʊntɪnz
AM ,rɑki 'maʊn(tə)nz

rococo
BR rə'kəʊkəʊ
AM rə'koʊkoʊ,
rou'koʊkoʊ,
'roukə,koʊ

rod
BR rɒd, -z
AM rɑd, -z

Roddenberry
BR 'rɒdnb(ə)ri
AM 'rɑdn,bɛri

Roddick
BR 'rɒdɪk
AM 'rɑdək

Roddy
BR 'rɒdi
AM 'rɑdi

rode
BR rəʊd
AM roʊd

rodent
BR 'rəʊdnt, -s
AM 'roʊdnt, -s

rodential
BR rə(ʊ)'dɛnʃl
AM roʊ'dɛn(t)ʃəl

rodenticide
BR rə(ʊ)'dɛntɪsʌɪd, -z
AM roʊ'dɛn(t)ə,saɪd, -z

rodeo
BR 'rəʊdɪəʊ,
rə(ʊ)'deɪəʊ, -z
AM 'roʊdi,oʊ,
roʊ'deɪoʊ, -z

Roderick
BR 'rɒd(ə)rɪk
AM 'rɑd(ə)rɪk

Rodger
BR 'rɒdʒə(r)
AM 'rɑdʒər

Rodgers
BR 'rɒdʒəz
AM 'rɑdʒərz

rodham
BR 'rɒdəm, -z
AM 'rɑdəm, -z

Rodin
BR 'rəʊdan, 'rəʊdã
AM roʊ'dæn

rodless
BR 'rɒdləs
AM 'rɑdləs

rodlet
BR 'rɒdlɪt, -s
AM 'rɑdlət, -z

rodlike
BR 'rɒdlʌɪk
AM 'rɑd,laɪk

Rodney
BR 'rɒdni
AM 'rɑdni

rodomontade
BR ,rɒdəmɒn'tɑːd,
,rɒdəmɒn'teɪd, -z
AM ,rɑdəmən'teɪd,
,rɑdə,man'teɪd,
'rɑdəmən'tɑd,
,rɑdə,man'tɑd, -z

Rodrigues
BR rɒ'driːgez
AM ,rɑd'rigəs,
,rɑd'ri,gɛz

Rodriguez
BR rɒ'driːgez
AM ,rɑd'rigəs,
,rɑd'ri,gɛz

Rodriquez
BR rɒ'driːkez
AM ,rɑd'rik(w)əs,
,rɑd'ri,k(w)ɛz

roe
BR rəʊ, -z, -d
AM roʊ, -z, -d

roebuck
BR 'rəʊbʌk, -s
AM 'roʊ,bək, -s

Roedean
BR 'rəʊdiːn
AM 'roʊ,din

roe-deer
BR 'rəʊdɪə(r)
AM 'roʊ,dɪ(ə)r

Roehampton
BR rəʊ'ham(p)tən,
'rəʊham(p)tən
AM ,roʊ'hæm(p)tən,
'rou,(h)æm(p)tən

roentgen
BR 'rʌntjən, 'rɜːntjən,
'rɒntjən, 'rʌntgən,
'rɜːntgən, 'rɒntgən
AM 'rɛntgən,
'rɛntdʒən

roentgenography
BR ,rʌntjə'nɒgrəfi,
,rɜːntjə'nɒgrəfi,
,rɒntjə'nɒgrəfi,
,rʌntgə'nɒgrəfi,
,rɜːntgə'nɒgrəfi,
,rɒntgə'nɒgrəfi
AM ,rɛntgə'nagrəfi,
,rɛntdʒə'nagrəfi

roentgenology
BR ,rʌntjə'nɒlədʒi,
,rɜːntjə'nɒlədʒi,
,rɒntjə'nɒlədʒi,
,rʌntgə'nɒlədʒi,
,rɜːntgə'nɒlədʒi,
,rɒntgə'nɒlədʒi
AM ,rɛntgə'nalədʒi,
,rɛntdʒə'nalədʒi

Roffey
BR 'rɒfi
AM 'rɔfi, 'rɑfi

rogation
BR rə(ʊ)'geɪʃn, -z

AM roʊ'geɪʃən, -z

rogational
BR rə(ʊ)'geɪʃn̩(ə)l,
rə(ʊ)'geɪʃən(ə)l
AM roʊ'geɪʃ(ə)nəl

Rogationtide
BR rə(ʊ)'geɪʃntʌɪd
AM roʊ'geɪʃən,taɪd

roger
BR 'rɒdʒ|ə(r), -əz,
-(ə)rɪŋ, -əd
AM 'rɑdʒər, -z, -ɪŋ, -d

Rogers
BR 'rɒdʒəz
AM 'rɑdʒərz

Roget
BR 'rɒʒeɪ
AM ,roʊ'ʒeɪ

rogue
BR rəʊg, -z
AM roʊg, -z

roguery
BR 'rəʊg(ə)r|i, -ɪz
AM 'roʊgəri, -z

roguish
BR 'rəʊgɪʃ
AM 'roʊgɪʃ

roguishly
BR 'rəʊgɪʃli
AM 'roʊgɪʃli

roguishness
BR 'rəʊgɪʃnɪs
AM 'roʊgɪʃnɪs

Rohan
BR 'rəʊən
AM 'roʊ,hæn, 'roʊən

roil
BR rɔɪl, -z, -ɪŋ, -d
AM rɔɪl, -z, -ɪŋ, -d

roister
BR 'rɔɪst|ə(r), -əz,
-(ə)rɪŋ, -əd
AM 'rɔɪst|ər, -ərz,
-(ə)rɪŋ, -ərd

roisterer
BR 'rɔɪst(ə)rə(r), -z
AM 'rɔɪst(ə)rər, -z

roistering
BR 'rɔɪst(ə)rɪŋ, -z
AM 'rɔɪst(ə)rɪŋ, -z

roisterous
BR 'rɔɪst(ə)rəs
AM 'rɔɪst(ə)rəs

Rojas
BR 'rəʊhas
AM 'roʊ,has

Rokeby
BR 'rəʊkbi
AM 'roʊkbi

Roker
BR 'rəʊkə(r)
AM 'roʊkər

Roland
BR 'rəʊlənd
AM 'roʊlən(d)

rôle
BR rəʊl, -z

AM roʊl, -z

role-play
BR 'rəʊlpleɪ, -z
AM 'roʊl,pleɪ, -z

Rolex®
BR 'rəʊlɛks
AM 'roʊ,lɛks

Rolf
BR rɒlf
AM rɔlf, rɑlf

Rolfe
BR rɒlf
AM rɔlf, rɑlf

roll
BR rəʊl, -z, -ɪŋ, -d
AM roʊl, -z, -ɪŋ, -d

rollable
BR 'rəʊləbl
AM 'roʊləbəl

rollaway
BR 'rəʊləweɪ, -z
AM 'roʊlə,weɪ, -z

rollback
BR 'rəʊlbak, -s
AM 'roʊl,bæk, -s

rollbar
BR 'rəʊlbɑː(r), -z
AM 'roʊl,bar, -z

rollcall
BR 'rəʊlkɔːl, -z
AM 'roʊl,kɔl, 'roʊl,kɑl,
-z

Rollei
BR 'rəʊlʌɪ
AM 'roʊlaɪ

roller
BR 'rəʊlə(r), -z
AM 'roʊlər, -z

rollerball
BR 'rəʊləbɔːl, -z
AM 'roʊlər,bɔl,
'roʊlər,bal, -z

rollerblade
BR 'rəʊləbleɪd, -z, -ɪŋ,
-ɪd
AM 'roʊlər,bleɪd, -z,
-ɪŋ, -ɪd

rollerblader
BR 'rəʊlə,bleɪdə(r), -z
AM 'roʊlər,bleɪdər, -z

rollick
BR 'rɒl|ɪk, -ɪks, -ɪkɪŋ,
-ɪkt
AM 'ralɪk, -s, -ɪŋ, -t

rollickingly
BR 'rɒlɪkɪŋli
AM 'ralɪkɪŋli

Rollins
BR 'rɒlɪnz
AM 'ralənz

rollmop
BR 'rəʊlmɒp, -s
AM 'roʊl,map, -s

Rollo
BR 'rɒləʊ
AM 'ralou

roll-on
BR ˈrəʊlɒn, -z
AM ˈroʊlˌɑn, -z

roll-on roll-off
BR ˌrəʊlɒnˈrəʊlˈɒf
AM ˌroʊlˌɑnˈroʊlˈɑf

Rolls
BR rəʊlz
AM roʊlz

Rolls-Royce®
BR ˌrəʊlzˈrɔɪs, -ɪz
AM ˌroʊlzˈrɔɪs, -ɪz

rolltop
BR ˌrəʊlˈtɒp
AM ˈroʊlˌtɑp, -s

Rolo®
BR ˈrəʊləʊ, -z
AM ˈroʊloʊ, -z

roly-poly
BR ˌrəʊlɪˈpəʊl|i, -ɪz
AM ˈroʊliˈpoʊli, -z

ROM
BR rɒm
AM rɑm

Rom
BR rɒm, rəʊm, -z
AM roʊm, -z

Roma
BR ˈrəʊmə(r)
AM ˈroʊmə

Romaic
BR rə(ʊ)ˈmeɪɪk
AM roʊˈmeɪɪk

romaine
BR rə(ʊ)ˈmeɪn
AM roʊˈmeɪn

romaji
BR ˈrəʊmədʒi
AM ˈroʊmədʒi

Roman
BR ˈrəʊmən, -z
AM ˈroʊmən, -z

roman-à-clef
BR ˌrəʊmɑːnɑːˈkleɪ,
rə(ʊ)ˌmɑːnɑːˈkleɪ, -z
AM ˌroʊˌmɑnəˈkleɪ, -z

Roman Catholic
BR ˌrəʊmən ˈkaθ(ə)lɪk,
ˌrəʊmən ˈkaθlɪk, -s
AM ˌroʊmən
ˈkæθ(ə)lɪk, -s

**Roman
Catholicism**
BR ˌrəʊmən
kəˈθɒlɪsɪz(ə)m
AM ˈroʊmən
kəˈθɑlə,sɪzəm

Romance
noun, language
BR rə(ʊ)ˈmans,
AM roʊˈmæns,
ˈroʊˌmæns

romance¹
noun, love, fantasy
BR rə(ʊ)ˈmans,
ˈrəʊmans, -ɪz
AM roʊˈmæns,
ˈroʊˌmæns, -əz

romance²
verb
BR rə(ʊ)ˈmans,
ˈrəʊmans, -ɪz, -ɪŋ, -t
AM roʊˈmæns,
ˈroʊˌmæns, -əz, -ɪŋ, -t

romancer
BR rə(ʊ)ˈmansə(r),
ˈrəʊmansə(r), -z
AM roʊˈmænsər,
ˈroʊˌmænsər, -z

Romanesque
BR ˌrəʊməˈnɛsk
AM ˌroʊməˈnɛsk

roman-fleuve
BR ˌrəʊmɑːnˈflɜːv,
rə(ʊ)ˌmɑːnˈflɜːv, -z
AM ˌroʊˌmɑnˈflɜv, -z

Romania
BR ruːˈmeɪnɪə(r),
rʊˈmeɪnɪə(r),
rə(ʊ)ˈmeɪnɪə(r)
AM roʊˈmeɪnɪə,
ruˈmeɪnɪə

Romanian
BR ruːˈmeɪnɪən,
rʊˈmeɪnɪən,
rə(ʊ)ˈmeɪnɪən, -z
AM roʊˈmeɪnɪən,
ruˈmeɪnɪən, -z

Romanic
BR rə(ʊ)ˈmanɪk
AM roʊˈmænɪk

romanisation
BR ˌrəʊmənʌɪˈzeɪʃn
AM ˌroʊmənəˈzeɪʃən,
ˌroʊmənaɪˈzeɪʃən

romanise
BR ˈrəʊmənʌɪz, -ɪz, -ɪŋ,
-d
AM ˈroʊməˌnaɪz, -ɪz,
-ɪŋ, -d

Romanish
BR ˈrəʊmənɪʃ
AM ˈroʊmənɪʃ

Romanism
BR ˈrəʊmənɪz(ə)m
AM ˈroʊməˌnɪzəm

Romanist
BR ˈrəʊmənɪst, -s
AM ˈroʊmənəst, -s

romanization
BR ˌrəʊmənʌɪˈzeɪʃn
AM ˌroʊmənəˈzeɪʃən,
ˌroʊmənaɪˈzeɪʃən

romanize
BR ˈrəʊmənʌɪz, -ɪz, -ɪŋ,
-d
AM ˈroʊməˌnaɪz, -ɪz,
-ɪŋ, -d

Romano
BR rə(ʊ)ˈmɑːnəʊ,
ˈrəʊmənəʊ, -z
AM roʊˈmɑnoʊ, -z

Romano-
BR rə(ʊ)ˈmɑːnəʊ,
ˈrəʊmənəʊ
AM roʊˈmɑnoʊ

Romano-British
BR rə(ʊ),mɑːnəʊˈbrɪtɪʃ,
ˌrəʊmənəʊˈbrɪtɪʃ
AM roʊˌmɑnoʊˈbrɪdɪʃ

Romanov
BR ˈrəʊmənɒf,
ˈrəʊmənɒv
AM ˈroʊməˌnɒv,
ˈroʊməˌnɒf,
ˈroʊməˌnɒv,
ˈroʊməˌnɒf
RUS rɑˈmanəf

romans-à-clef
BR ˌrəʊmɑːnɑːˈkleɪ,
rə(ʊ)ˌmɑːnɑːˈkleɪ
AM ˌroʊˌmɑnəˈkleɪ

Romansh
BR rə(ʊ)ˈmanʃ
AM roʊˈmɑn(t)ʃ,
roʊˈmæn(t)ʃ

romantic
BR rə(ʊ)ˈmantɪk, -s
AM roʊˈmæn(t)ɪk, -s

romantical
BR rə(ʊ)ˈmantɪkl
AM roʊˈmæn(t)əkəl

romantically
BR rə(ʊ)ˈmantɪkli
AM roʊˈmæn(t)ək(ə)li

romanticisation
BR rə(ʊ),mantɪsʌɪˈzeɪʃn
AM roʊˌmæn(t)əsəˈzeɪ-
ʃən,
roʊˌmæn(t)ə,saɪˈzeɪʃən

romanticise
BR rə(ʊ)ˈmantɪsʌɪz,
-ɪz, -ɪŋ, -d
AM roʊˈmæn(t)əˌsaɪz,
-ɪz, -ɪŋ, -d

romanticism
BR ˈrə(ʊ)ˈmantɪsɪz(ə)m
AM roʊˈmæn(t)ə,sɪzəm

romanticist
BR rə(ʊ)ˈmantɪsɪst, -s
AM roʊˈmæn(t)əsəst,
-s

romanticization
BR rə(ʊ),mantɪsʌɪˈzeɪʃn
AM roʊˌmæn(t)əsəˈzeɪ-
ʃən,
roʊˌmæn(t)ə,saɪˈzeɪʃən

romanticize
BR rə(ʊ)ˈmantɪsʌɪz,
-ɪz, -ɪŋ, -d
AM roʊˈmæn(t)əˌsaɪz,
-ɪz, -ɪŋ, -d

Romany
BR ˈrəʊmən|i, -ɪz
AM ˈroʊməni, ˈrɑməni,
-z

Romberg
BR ˈrɒmbɜːg
AM ˈrɑm,bɜrg

Rome
BR rəʊm
AM roʊm

Romeo
BR ˈrəʊmɪəʊ, -z

AM ˈroʊmɪoʊ, -z

romer
BR ˈrəʊmə(r), -z
AM ˈroʊmər, -z

Romero
BR rɒˈmɛːrəʊ,
rəˈmɛːrəʊ
AM rəˈmɛroʊ,
roʊˈmɛroʊ

Romish
BR ˈrəʊmɪʃ
AM ˈroʊmɪʃ

Rommel
BR ˈrɒml
AM ˈrɑməl

Romney
BR ˈrɒmni
AM ˈrɑmni

romneya
BR ˈrɒmnɪə(r), -z
AM ˈrɑmnɪə, -z

romp
BR rɒm|p, -ps, -pɪŋ,
-(p)t
AM rɑmp, -s, -ɪŋ, -t

romper
BR ˈrɒmpə(r), -z
AM ˈrɑmpər, -z

rompingly
BR ˈrɒmpɪŋli
AM ˈrɑmpɪŋli

rompy
BR ˈrɒmp|i, -ɪə(r), -ɪɪst
AM ˈrɑmpi, -ər, -ɪɪst

Romsey
BR ˈrɒmzi
AM ˈrɑmzi

Romulus
BR ˈrɒmjʊləs
AM ˈrɑmjələs

Ron
BR rɒn
AM rɑn

rona
BR ˈrəʊnə(r)
AM ˈroʊnə

Ronald
BR ˈrɒnld
AM ˈrɑnəl(d)

Ronaldsay
BR ˈrɒnl(d)seɪ
AM ˈrɑnəl(d)ˌseɪ

Ronaldsway
BR ˈrɒnl(d)zweɪ
AM ˈrɑnəl(d)ˌzweɪ

Ronan
BR ˈrəʊnən
AM ˈroʊnən

Roncesvalles
BR ˈrɒsəvɑːl, ˈrɒsəval
AM ˌrɒnsəˈval(z),
ˌrɑnsəˈval(z)

rondavel
BR rɒnˈdɑːvl, -z
AM ˈrɑndəˌvɛl, -z

ronde
BR rɒnd, -z

rondeau
AM rɑnd, -z
rondeau
BR 'rɒndəʊ, -z
AM 'rɑnˌdoʊ, -z
rondeaux
BR 'rɒndəʊ(z)
AM 'rɑnˌdoʊ
rondel
BR 'rɒndl, -z
AM 'rɑndəl, ˌrɑn'dɛl, -z
rondo
BR 'rɒndəʊ, -z
AM 'rɑnˌdoʊ, -z
Rondônia
BR rɒn'dəʊniə(r)
AM rɑn'doʊniə,
ˌrɑn'doʊniə
rone
BR rəʊn, -z
AM roʊn, -z
roneo
BR 'rəʊniəʊ, -z, -ɪŋ, -d
AM 'roʊnioʊ, -z, -ɪŋ, -d
ronggeng
BR 'rɒŋgeŋ, -z
AM 'rɔŋgeŋ, 'rɑŋgeŋ, -z
ronin
BR 'rəʊnɪn, -z
AM 'roʊnən, -z
Ronnie
BR 'rɒni
AM 'rɑni
Ronsard
BR rɒn'sɑː(r)
AM rɒn'sɑr, rɑn'sɑr
Ronson®
BR 'rɒns(ə)n
AM 'rɑnsən
röntgen
BR 'rʌntjən, 'rɜːntjən,
'rɒntjən, 'rʌntgən,
'rɜːntgən, 'rɒntgən
AM 'rɛntgən,
'rɛntdʒən
röntgenography
BR ˌrʌntjə'nɒgrəfi,
ˌrɜːntjə'nɒgrəfi,
ˌrɒntjə'nɒgrəfi,
ˌrʌntgə'nɒgrəfi,
ˌrɜːntgə'nɒgrəfi,
ˌrɒntgə'nɒgrəfi
AM ˌrɛntgə'nɑgrəfi,
ˌrɛntdʒə'nɑgrəfi
röntgenology
BR ˌrʌntjə'nɒlədʒi,
ˌrɜːntjə'nɒlədʒi,
ˌrɒntjə'nɒlədʒi,
ˌrʌntgə'nɒlədʒi,
ˌrɜːntgə'nɒlədʒi,
ˌrɒntgə'nɒlədʒi
AM ˌrɛntgə'nɑlədʒi,
ˌrɛntdʒə'nɑlədʒi
roo
BR ruː, -z
AM ru, -z
rood
BR ruːd, -z
AM rud, -z

roodscreen
BR 'ruːdskriːn, -z
AM 'rudˌskrin, -z
roof
BR ruːf, rʊf,
ruːfs\ruːvz\rʊfs,
'ruːfɪŋ\rʊˈvɪŋ\'rʊfɪŋ,
ruːft\rʊˈvd\rʊft
AM ruf, rʊf, -s, -ɪŋ, -t
roofage
BR 'ruːfˌɪdʒ, -ɪdʒɪz
AM 'rufɪdʒ, 'rʊfɪdʒ, -ɪz
roofer
BR 'ruːfə(r), 'rʊfə(r), -z
AM 'rufər, 'rʊfər, -z
roofing
BR 'ruːfɪŋ, 'ruːvɪŋ,
'rʊfɪŋ
AM 'rufɪŋ, 'rʊfɪŋ
roofless
BR 'ruːfləs, 'rʊfləs
AM 'rufləs, 'rʊfləs
roofline
BR 'ruːfˌlʌɪn, 'rʊfˌlʌɪn,
-z
AM 'rufˌlaɪn, 'rʊfˌlaɪn,
-z
roofscape
BR 'ruːfskeɪp,
'rʊfskeɪp, -s
AM 'rufˌskeɪp,
'rʊfˌskeɪp, -z
rooftop
BR 'ruːftɒp, 'rʊftɒp, -s
AM 'rufˌtɑp, 'rʊfˌtɑp, -s
rooftree
BR 'ruːftriː, 'rʊftriː, -z
AM 'rufˌtri, 'rʊfˌtri, -z
rooibos
BR 'rɔɪbɒs, -ɪz
AM 'rɔɪbɑs, -əz
rooinek
BR 'rɔɪnɛk, -s
AM 'rɔɪnɛk, -s
rook
BR rʊk, -s, -ɪŋ, -t
AM rʊk, -s, -ɪŋ, -t
Rooke
BR rʊk
AM rʊk
rookery
BR 'rʊk(ə)r|i, -ɪz
AM 'rʊkəri, -z
rookie
BR 'rʊk|i, -ɪz
AM 'rʊki, -z
rooklet
BR 'rʊklɪt, -s
AM 'rʊklət, -s
rookling
BR 'rʊklɪŋ, -z
AM 'rʊklɪŋ, -z
rooky
BR 'rʊk|i, -ɪz
AM 'rʊki, -z
room
BR ruːm, rʊm, -z
AM rum, rʊm, -z

Roome
BR ruːm
AM rum, rʊm
roomer
BR 'ruːmə(r),
'rʊmə(r), -z
AM 'rumər, 'rʊmər, -z
roomette
BR ruːˈmɛt, rʊˈmɛt, -s
AM ruˈmɛt, rʊˈmɛt, -s
roomful
BR 'ruːmfʊl, 'rʊmfʊl, -z
AM 'rumˌfʊl, 'rʊmˌfʊl,
-z
roomie
BR 'ruːm|i, 'rʊm|i, -ɪz
AM 'rumi, 'rʊmi, -z
roomily
BR 'ruːmɪli, 'rʊmɪli
AM 'ruməli, 'rʊməli
roominess
BR 'ruːmɪnɪs, 'rʊmɪnɪs
AM 'rumɪnɪs, 'rʊmɪnɪs
roommate
BR 'ruːmmeɪt,
'rʊmmeɪt, -s
AM 'ru(m)ˌmeɪt,
'rʊ(m)ˌmeɪt, -s
roomy
BR 'ruːm|i, 'rʊm|i,
-ɪə(r), -ɪɪst
AM 'rumi, 'rʊmi, -ər,
-ɪst
Rooney
BR 'ruːni
AM 'runi
Roosevelt
BR 'rəʊzəvɛlt,
'ruːzəvɛlt
AM 'roʊzəˌvɛlt
roost
BR ruːst, -s, -ɪŋ, -ɪd
AM rust, -s, -ɪŋ, -əd
rooster
BR 'ruːstə(r), -z
AM 'rustər, -z
root
BR ruːt, -s, -ɪŋ, -ɪd
AM ru|t, rʊ|t, -ts, -dɪŋ,
-dəd
rootage
BR 'ruːtˌɪdʒ, -ɪdʒɪz
AM 'rudɪdʒ, 'rʊdɪdʒ, -ɪz
rootbeer
BR 'ruːtbɪə(r)
AM 'rutˌbɪ(ə)r,
'rʊtˌbɪ(ə)r
rootedness
BR 'ruːtɪdnɪs
AM 'rudədnəs,
'rʊdədnəs
rooter
BR 'ruːtə(r), -z
AM 'rudər, 'rʊdər, -z
Rootes
BR ruːts
AM ruts, rʊts

rootle
BR 'ruːt|l, -lz, -lɪŋ\-lɪŋ,
-ld
AM 'rudəl, 'rʊdəl, -z,
-ɪŋ, -d
rootless
BR 'ruːtləs
AM 'rutləs, 'rʊtləs
rootlessness
BR 'ruːtləsnəs
AM 'rutləsnəs,
'rʊtləsnəs
rootlet
BR 'ruːtlɪt, -s
AM 'rutlət, 'rʊtlət, -z
rootlike
BR 'ruːtlʌɪk
AM 'rutˌlaɪk, 'rʊtˌlaɪk
root-mean-square
BR ˌruːtˌmiːn'skwɛː(r),
-z
AM 'rutˌminˈskwɛ(ə)r,
'rʊtˌminˈskwɛ(ə)r, -z
rootstock
BR 'ruːtstɒk, -s
AM 'rutˌstak, 'rʊtˌstak,
-s
rootsy
BR 'ruːts|i, -ɪə(r), -ɪɪst
AM 'rutsi, 'rʊtsi, -ər,
-ɪst
rooty
BR 'ruːt|i, -ɪə(r), -ɪɪst
AM 'rudi, 'rʊdi, -ər, -ɪst
rooves
BR ruːvz
AM ruvz
rope
BR rəʊp, -s, -ɪŋ, -t
AM roʊp, -s, -ɪŋ, -t
ropeable
BR 'rəʊpəbl
AM 'roʊpəbəl
ropedancer
BR 'rəʊpˌdɑːnsə(r),
'rəʊpˌdansə(r), -z
AM 'roʊpˌdænsər, -z
ropemanship
BR 'rəʊpmənʃɪp
AM 'roʊpmənˌʃɪp
Roper
BR 'rəʊpə(r)
AM 'roʊpər
ropewalk
BR 'rəʊpwɔːk, -s
AM 'roʊpˌwɔk,
'roʊpˌwak, -s
ropeway
BR 'rəʊpweɪ, -z
AM 'roʊpˌweɪ, -z
ropey
BR 'rəʊp|i, -ɪə(r), -ɪɪst
AM 'roʊpi, -ər, -ɪst
ropily
BR 'rəʊpɪli
AM 'roʊpəli

ropiness
BR ˈrəʊpɪnɪs
AM ˈroʊpɪnɪs

roping
BR ˈrəʊpɪŋ, -z
AM ˈroʊpɪŋ, -z

ropy
BR ˈrəʊp|i, -iə(r), -ɪɪst
AM ˈroʊpi, -ər, -ɪɪst

roque
BR rəʊk
AM roʊk

Roquefort®
BR ˈrɒkfɔ:(r), -z
AM ˈroʊkfərt, -s

roquelaure
BR ˈrɒk(ə)lɔ:(r), -z
AM ˈrɒkə͵lɔ(ə)r,
ˈroʊkə͵lɔ(ə)r, -z

roquet
BR ˈrəʊk|i, ˈrəʊk|eɪ,
-ɪz \-eɪz, -ɪɪŋ \-eɪɪŋ,
-ɪd \-eɪd
AM roʊˈkeɪ, -z, -ɪŋ, -d

Roraima
BR rɒˈrʌɪmə(r)
AM rɔˈraɪmə

Rorke
BR rɔ:k
AM rɔ(ə)rk

ro-ro
BR ˈrəʊrəʊ, -z
AM ˈroʊ͵roʊ, -z

rorqual
BR ˈrɔ:kw(ə)l, -z
AM ˈrɔrkwəl, -z

Rorschach test
BR ˈrɔ:ʃɑ:k test,
ˈrɔ:ʃak +, -s
AM ˈrɔr͵ʃak ͵test,
ˈrɔr͵ʒak +, -s

rort
BR rɔ:t, -s
AM rɔ(ə)rt, -s

rorty
BR ˈrɔ:t|i, -iə(r), -ɪɪst
AM ˈrɔrdi, -ər, -ɪɪst

Rory
BR ˈrɔ:ri
AM ˈrɔri

Ros
BR rɒz
AM raz

Rosa
BR ˈrəʊzə(r)
AM ˈroʊzə

rosace
BR ˈrəʊzeɪs, -ɪz
AM ˈroʊzeɪs, ˈroʊzəs,
-əs

rosaceous
BR rə(ʊ)ˈzeɪʃəs
AM roʊˈzeɪʃəs

Rosaleen
BR ˈrɒzəli:n, ˈrəʊzəli:n
AM ˈroʊzə͵lin

Rosalie
BR ˈrəʊzəli
AM ˈroʊzəli

Rosalind
BR ˈrɒzəlɪnd
AM ˈroʊz(ə)lən(d),
ˈraz(ə)lən(d)

rosaline
BR ˈrəʊzəli:n, -z
AM ˈroʊzə͵lin,
ˈroʊz(ə)lən, -z

Rosalyn
BR ˈrɒzəlɪn
AM ˈroʊz(ə)lən,
ˈraz(ə)lən

Rosamond
BR ˈrɒzəmʌnd
AM ˈroʊzəmən(d)

Rosamund
BR ˈrɒzəmʌnd
AM ˈroʊzəmən(d)

rosaniline
BR rə(ʊ)ˈzanɪli:n,
rə(ʊ)ˈzanļi:n,
rə(ʊ)ˈzanɪlʌɪn,
rə(ʊ)ˈzanļʌɪn,
rə(ʊ)ˈzanɪlɪn,
rə(ʊ)ˈzanļɪn
AM roʊˈzænə͵laɪn,
roʊˈzænələn

Rosanna
BR rə(ʊ)ˈzanə(r)
AM roʊˈzænə

Rosanne
BR rə(ʊ)ˈzan
AM roʊˈzæn

rosaria
BR rə(ʊ)ˈzeːrɪə(r)
AM roʊˈzeriə

rosarian
BR rə(ʊ)ˈzeːrɪən, -z
AM roʊˈzeriən, -z

Rosario
BR rə(ʊ)ˈzɑːrɪəʊ
AM roʊˈsɑrioʊ

rosarium
BR rə(ʊ)ˈzeːrɪəm
AM roʊˈzeriəm

rosary
BR ˈrəʊz(ə)r|i, -ɪz
AM ˈroʊz(ə)ri, -z

Roscian
BR ˈrɒsɪən, ˈrɒʃɪən,
ˈrɒʃ(ə)n
AM ˈraʃ(i)ən

Roscius
BR ˈrɒsɪəs, ˈrɒʃɪəs
AM ˈrɑsiəs, ˈrɑʃiəs

roscoe
BR ˈrɒskəʊ, -z
AM ˈraskoʊ, -z

Roscommon
BR rɒsˈkɒmən
AM rɑsˈkɑmən

rose
BR rəʊz, -ɪz
AM roʊz, -əz

rosé
BR ˈrəʊzeɪ
AM roʊˈzeɪ

Roseanne
BR rə(ʊ)ˈzan
AM roʊˈzæn

roseate
BR ˈrəʊzɪət, ˈrəʊzɪeɪt
AM ˈroʊziɪt, ˈroʊzi͵eɪt

rosebay
BR ˈrəʊzbeɪ
AM ˈroʊz͵beɪ

Rosebery
BR ˈrəʊzb(ə)ri
AM ˈroʊz͵beri

rosebowl
BR ˈrəʊzbəʊl, -z
AM ˈroʊz͵boʊl, -z

rosebud
BR ˈrəʊzbʌd, -z
AM ˈroʊz͵bəd, -z

rosebush
BR ˈrəʊzbʊʃ, -ɪz
AM ˈroʊz͵bʊʃ, -əz

rose-chafer
BR ˈrəʊz͵tʃeɪfə(r), -z
AM ˈroʊz͵tʃeɪfər, -z

rosehip
BR ˈrəʊzhɪp, -s
AM ˈroʊz͵(h)ɪp, -s

roseless
BR ˈrəʊzləs
AM ˈroʊzləs

roselike
BR ˈrəʊzlʌɪk
AM ˈroʊz͵laɪk

rosella
BR rə(ʊ)ˈzelə(r)
AM roʊˈzelə

rosemaling
BR ˈrəʊzə͵mɑːlɪŋ,
ˈrəʊzə͵mɔːlɪŋ,
ˈrəʊsə͵mɑːlɪŋ,
ˈrəʊsə͵mɔːlɪŋ
AM ˈroʊzə͵malɪŋ

rosemary
BR ˈrəʊzm(ə)r|i, -ɪz
AM ˈroʊz͵meri, -z

Rosen
BR ˈrəʊzn
AM ˈroʊzn

Rosenberg
BR ˈrəʊznbə:g
AM ˈroʊzən͵bərg

Rosencrantz
BR ˈrəʊznkran(t)s
AM ˈroʊzən͵kræn(t)s

Rosenthal
BR ˈrəʊzntɑːl,
ˈrəʊznθɔːl
AM ˈroʊzən͵θɔl,
ˈroʊzən͵θɑl

Rosenwald
BR ˈrəʊznwɔːld
AM ˈroʊzən͵wald

roseola
BR rə(ʊ)ˈzi:ələ(r),
͵rəʊzɪˈəʊlə(r), -z
AM ͵roʊziˈoʊlə,
roʊˈziələ, -z

roseolar
BR rə(ʊ)ˈzi:ələ(r),
͵rəʊzɪˈəʊlə(r)
AM ͵roʊziˈoʊlər,
roʊˈziələr

roseolous
BR rə(ʊ)ˈzi:ələs,
͵rəʊzɪˈəʊləs
AM ͵roʊziˈoʊləs,
roʊˈziələs

rosery
BR ˈrəʊz(ə)r|i, -ɪz
AM ˈroʊzəri, -z

Rosetta Stone
BR rə(ʊ)ˈzetə stəʊn
AM roʊˈzedə ͵stoʊn

rosette
BR rə(ʊ)ˈzet, -s
AM roʊˈzet, -s

rosetted
BR rə(ʊ)ˈzetɪd
AM roʊˈzedəd

Rosewall
BR ˈrəʊzwɔ:l
AM ˈroʊz͵wɔl,
ˈroʊz͵wal

rosewater
BR ˈrəʊz͵wɔːtə(r)
AM ˈroʊz͵wɔdər,
ˈroʊz͵wadər

rosewood
BR ˈrəʊzwʊd
AM ˈroʊz͵wʊd

Rosh Hashana
BR ͵rɒʃ həˈʃɑːnə(r)
AM ͵rɒʃ(hə)ˈʃɑnə,
͵raʃ(hə)ˈʃɑnə

Rosh Hashanah
BR ͵rɒʃ həˈʃɑːnə(r)
AM ͵rɒʃ(hə)ˈʃɑnə,
͵raʃ(hə)ˈʃɑnə

Rosicrucian
BR ͵rəʊzɪˈkru:ʃn, -z
AM ͵roʊzəˈkruʃən,
͵razəˈkruʃən, -z

Rosicrucianism
BR ͵rəʊzɪˈkru:ʃnɪz(ə)m,
͵rəʊzɪˈkru:ʃənɪz(ə)m
AM ͵roʊzəˈkruʃə͵nɪzəm,
͵razəˈkruʃə͵nɪzəm

Rosie
BR ˈrəʊzi
AM ˈroʊzi

rosily
BR ˈrəʊzɪli
AM ˈroʊzəli

rosin
BR ˈrɒzɪn
AM ˈrazn

rosiness
BR ˈrəʊzɪnɪs
AM ˈroʊzɪnɪs

rosiny
BR 'rɒzɪni, 'rɒzn̩i
AM 'razn̩i

Roskilde
BR 'rɒskɪld
AM 'rɑs,kɪld(ə)
DAN 'RAS,kilə

Roslea
BR (,)rɒs'leɪ
AM rɔs'leɪ, rɑs'leɪ

rosoglio
BR rə(ʊ)'zəʊlɪəʊ,
rɒ'zəʊlɪəʊ, -z
AM roʊ'zoʊlioʊ,
rɔ'zoʊlioʊ, -z

rosolio
BR rə(ʊ)'zəʊlɪəʊ,
rɒ'zəʊlɪəʊ, -z
AM roʊ'zoʊlioʊ,
rɔ'zoʊlioʊ, -z

ROSPA, RoSPA
BR 'rɒspə(r)
AM 'raspə

Ross
BR rɒs
AM rɔs, rɑs

Rossellini
BR ,rɒsə'liːni
AM ,rɔsə'lini,
,rɑsə'lini

Rossendale
BR 'rɒsndeɪl
AM 'rɔsən,deɪl,
'rɑsən,deɪl

Rosser
BR 'rɒsə(r)
AM 'rɔsər, 'rasər

Rossetti
BR rə'zɛti, rɒ'zɛti
AM rə'zɛdi, ,roʊ'zɛdi

Rossi
BR 'rɒsi
AM 'rɔsi, 'rasi

Rossini
BR rɒ'siːni, rə'siːni
AM rə'sini

Rossiter
BR 'rɒsɪtə(r)
AM 'rɔsədər, 'rasədər

Rosslare
BR ,rɒs'lɛː(r)
AM ,rɑs'lɛ(ə)r

Rosslyn
BR 'rɒslɪn
AM 'rɔslən, 'raslən

Ross-on-Wye
BR ,rɒsɒn'wʌɪ
AM ,rɔs,ɑn'waɪ,
,rɑs,ɑn'waɪ

roster
BR 'rɒst|ə(r), -əz,
-(ə)rɪŋ, -əd
AM 'rɔst|ər, 'rast|ər,
-ərz, -(ə)rɪŋ, -ərd

Rostock
BR 'rɒstɒk
AM 'rastɑk

rostra
BR 'rɒstrə(r)
AM 'rɔstrə, 'rastrə

rostral
BR 'rɒstr(ə)l
AM 'rɔstrəl, 'rastrəl

rostrally
BR 'rɒstrəli, 'rɒstr|i
AM 'rɔstrəli, 'rastrəli

rostrate
BR 'rɒstrət, 'rɒstreɪt
AM 'rɔs,treɪt, 'ras,treɪt

rostrated
BR rɒ'streɪtɪd
AM 'rɔs,treɪdɪd,
'ras,treɪdɪd

Rostrevor
BR (,)rɒs'trɛvə(r)
AM rɔs'trɛvər,
ras'trɛvər

rostriferous
BR rɒ'strɪf(ə)rəs
AM rɔs'trɪf(ə)rəs,
ras'trɪf(ə)rəs

rostriform
BR 'rɒstrɪfɔːm
AM 'rastrə,fɔ(ə)rm,
'rɔstrə,fɔ(ə)rm

Rostropovich
BR ,rɒstrə'pəʊvɪtʃ
AM ,rɔstrə'poʊvɪtʃ,
,rastrə'poʊvɪtʃ

rostrum
BR 'rɒstrəm, -z
AM 'rɔstrəm, 'rastrəm,
-z

Roswell
BR 'rɒzwɛl
AM 'raz,wɛl

rosy
BR 'rəʊz|i, -ɪə(r), -ɪɪst
AM 'roʊzi, -ər, -ɪst

Rosyth
BR rɒ'sʌɪθ, rə'sʌɪθ
AM rə'saɪθ

rot
BR rɒt, -s, -ɪŋ, -ɪd
AM rɑ|t, -ts, -dɪŋ, -dəd

rota
BR 'rəʊtə(r), -z, -d
AM 'roʊdə, -z, -d

Rotarian
BR rə(ʊ)'tɛːrɪən, -z
AM roʊ'tɛriən, -z

rotary
BR 'rəʊt(ə)r|i, -ɪz
AM 'roʊdəri, -z

rotatable
BR rə(ʊ)'teɪtəbl
AM 'roʊ,teɪdəbəl,
roʊ'teɪdəbəl

rotate
BR rə(ʊ)'teɪt, -s, -ɪŋ, -ɪd
AM 'roʊ,teɪ|t, -ts, -dɪŋ,
-dɪd

rotation
BR rə(ʊ)'teɪʃn, -z
AM roʊ'teɪʃən, -z

rotational
BR rə(ʊ)'teɪʃn̩(ə)l,
rə(ʊ)'teɪʃən(ə)l
AM roʊ'teɪʃ(ə)nəl

rotationally
BR rə(ʊ)'teɪʃn̩əli,
rə(ʊ)'teɪʃn̩|i,
rə(ʊ)'teɪʃən|i,
rə(ʊ)'teɪʃ(ə)nəli
AM roʊ'teɪʃ(ə)nəli

rotative
BR rə(ʊ)'teɪtɪv,
'rəʊtətɪv
AM 'roʊdədɪv,
roʊ'teɪdɪv

rotatively
BR rə(ʊ)'teɪtɪvli,
'rəʊtətɪvli
AM 'roʊdədɪvli,
roʊ'teɪdɪvli

rotator
BR rə(ʊ)'teɪtə(r), -z
AM 'roʊ,teɪdər, -z

rotatory
BR rə(ʊ)'teɪt(ə)ri,
'rəʊtət(ə)ri
AM 'roʊdə,tɔri

rotavate
BR 'rəʊtəveɪt, -s, -ɪŋ, -ɪd
AM 'roʊdə,veɪ|t, -ts,
-dɪŋ, -dɪd

Rotavator®
BR 'rəʊtəveɪtə(r), -z
AM 'roʊdə,veɪdər, -z

rotavirus
BR 'rəʊtə,vʌɪrəs, -ɪz
AM 'roʊdə,vaɪrəs, -əz

rote
BR rəʊt
AM roʊt

rotenone
BR 'rəʊtɪnəʊn
AM 'roʊtn̩,oʊn

rotgut
BR 'rɒtgʌt
AM 'rat,gət

Roth
BR rɒθ, rəʊθ
AM rɔθ, rɑθ

Rothamsted
BR 'rɒθ(ə)mstɛd
AM 'raθəm,stɛd

Rother
BR 'rɒðə(r)
AM 'raðər

Rotherham
BR 'rɒð(ə)rəm
AM 'raðərəm

Rotherhithe
BR 'rɒðəhʌɪð
AM 'raðər,(h)aɪð

Rothermere
BR 'rɒðəmɪə(r)
AM 'raðər,mɪ(ə)r

Rothesay
BR 'rɒθsi, 'rɒθseɪ
AM 'raθsi

Rothko
BR 'rɒθkəʊ
AM 'raθkoʊ, 'rɑθkoʊ

Rothman
BR 'rɒθmən
AM 'raθmən

Rothschild
BR 'rɒθ(s)tʃʌɪld
AM 'rɔθ,tʃaɪld,
'raθ,tʃaɪld

Rothwell
BR 'rɒθw(ɛ)l
AM 'raθ,wɛl

roti
BR 'rəʊt|i, -ɪz
AM 'roʊdi, -z

rotifer
BR 'rəʊtɪfə(r), -z
AM 'roʊdəfər, -z

Rotifera
BR rəʊ'tɪf(ə)rə(r)
AM roʊ'tɪfərə

rotisserie
BR rə(ʊ)'tɪs(ə)r|i, -ɪz
AM roʊ'tɪsəri, -z

rotogravure
BR ,rəʊtə(ʊ)grə'vjʊə(r)
AM 'roʊdəgrə'vjʊ(ə)r

rotor
BR 'rəʊtə(r), -z
AM 'roʊdər, -z

rotorscope
BR 'rəʊtəskəʊp, -s, -ɪŋ,
-t
AM 'roʊdər,skoʊp, -s,
-ɪŋ, -t

Rotorua
BR ,rəʊtə'ruː.ə(r)
AM ,roʊdə'ruə

rotovate
BR 'rəʊtəveɪt, -s, -ɪŋ, -ɪd
AM 'roʊdə,veɪ|t, -ts,
-dɪŋ, -dəd

Rotovator
BR 'rəʊtəveɪtə(r), -z
AM 'roʊdə,veɪdər, -z

rot-proof
BR 'rɒtpruːf
AM 'rat'pruf

rotten
BR 'rɒtn̩, -ɪst
AM 'ratn̩, -ɪst

rottenly
BR 'rɒtn̩li
AM 'ratn̩li

rottenness
BR 'rɒtnnəs
AM 'rat(n)nəs

rotter
BR 'rɒtə(r), -z
AM 'radər, -z

Rotterdam
BR 'rɒtədam
AM 'radər,dæm

Rottingdean
BR 'rɒtɪŋdiːn,
,rɒtɪŋ'diːn

AM ˈrɑdɪŋˌdin
Rottweiler
BR ˈrɒtˌwʌɪlə(r), -z
AM ˈrɑtˌwaɪlər, -z
rotund
BR rə(ʊ)ˈtʌnd
AM roʊˈtənd
rotunda
BR rə(ʊ)ˈtʌndə(r), -z
AM roʊˈtəndə, -z
rotundity
BR rə(ʊ)ˈtʌndɪti
AM roʊˈtəndədi
rotundly
BR rə(ʊ)ˈtʌndli
AM roʊˈtən(d)li
rotundness
BR rə(ʊ)ˈtʌn(d)nəs
AM roʊˈtən(d)nəs
Rouault
BR ˌruːˈəʊ
AM ruˈoʊ
rouble
BR ˈruːbl, -z
AM ˈrubəl, -z
roucou
BR ˌruːˈkuː, -z
AM ˈruˌku, -z
roué
BR ˈruːeɪ, -z
AM ruˈeɪ, -z
Rouen
BR ˈruːɒ̃
AM ˈrwɑn
rouge
BR ruːʒ, -ɪz, -ɪŋ, -d
AM ruʒ, -əz, -ɪŋ, -d
rouge-et-noir
BR ˌruːʒerˈnwɑː(r)
AM ˌruʒerˈnwɑr
rough
BR rʌf, -s, -ɪŋ, -t, -ə(r), -ɪst
AM rəf, -s, -ɪŋ, -t, -ər, -əst
roughage
BR ˈrʌfɪdʒ
AM ˈrəfɪdʒ
rough-and-ready
BR ˌrʌf(ə)n(d)ˈrɛdi
AM ˌrəfən(d)ˈrɛdi
rough-and-tumble
BR ˌrʌf(ə)n(d)ˈtʌmbl
AM ˌrəfən(d)ˈtəmbəl
roughcast
BR ˈrʌfkɑːst, ˈrʌfkast
AM ˈrəfˌkæst
roughen
BR ˈrʌfn̩, -nz, -nɪŋ \ -nɪŋ, -nd
AM ˈrəfən, -z, -ɪŋ, -d
roughhouse
BR ˈrʌfhaʊs, -zɪz, -sɪŋ \ -zɪŋ, -st \ -zd
AM ˈrəf(h)aʊs, -zəz, -zɪŋ, -zd

roughie
BR ˈrʌfli, -ɪz
AM ˈrəfi, -z
roughish
BR ˈrʌfɪʃ
AM ˈrəfɪʃ
roughly
BR ˈrʌfli
AM ˈrəfli
roughneck
BR ˈrʌknɛk, -s
AM ˈrəfˌnɛk, -s
roughness
BR ˈrʌfnəs
AM ˈrəfnəs
roughrider
BR ˈrʌfˌrʌɪdə(r), -z
AM ˈrəfˌraɪdər, -z
roughshod
BR ˈrʌfʃɒd
AM ˈrəfˌʃɑd
Rough Tor
BR ˌraʊ ˈtɔː(r)
AM ˌraʊ ˈtɔ(ə)r
roughy
BR ˈrʌfli, -ɪz
AM ˈrəfi, -z
rouille
BR ˈruːi
AM ˈrui
roulade
BR rʊˈlɑːd, -z
AM ˌruˈlɑd, -z
rouleau
BR ˈruːləʊ, rʊˈləʊ, -z
AM ruˈloʊ, -z
rouleaux
BR ˈruːləʊz, rʊˈləʊz
AM ruˈloʊ
roulement
BR ˈruːlmɒ̃
AM ˈrulmən(t)
roulette
BR ruːˈlɛt, rʊˈlɛt
AM ruˈlɛt
Roumania
BR ruːˈmeɪnɪə(r), rʊˈmeɪnɪə(r)
AM roʊˈmeɪniə, ruˈmeɪniə
Roumanian
BR ruːˈmeɪniən, rʊˈmeɪniən, -z
AM roʊˈmeɪniən, ruˈmeɪniən, -z
Roumelia
BR ruːˈmiːlɪə(r), rʊˈmiːlɪə(r)
AM ruˈmiljə, ruˈmiliə
round
BR raʊnd, -z, -ɪŋ, -ɪd, -ə(r), -ɪst
AM raʊnd, -z, -ɪŋ, -əd, -ər, -əst
roundabout
BR ˈraʊndəbaʊt, -s
AM ˈraʊndəˌbaʊt, -s

round-arm
BR ˈraʊndɑːm
AM ˈraʊnˌdɑrm
roundel
BR ˈraʊndl̩, -z
AM ˈraʊndəl, roʊnˈdɛl, -z
roundelay
BR ˈraʊndɪleɪ, -z
AM ˈraʊndəˌleɪ, ˈrɑndəˌleɪ, -z
rounder
BR ˈraʊndə(r), -z
AM ˈraʊndər, -z
Roundhay
BR ˈraʊnd(h)eɪ
AM ˈraʊnd(h)eɪ
Roundhead
BR ˈraʊndhɛd, -z
AM ˈraʊnd,(h)ɛd, -z
roundhouse
BR ˈraʊndhaʊs, -zɪz
AM ˈraʊnd,(h)aʊs, -zəz
roundish
BR ˈraʊndɪʃ
AM ˈraʊndɪʃ
roundly
BR ˈraʊndli
AM ˈraʊn(d)li
roundness
BR ˈraʊn(d)nəs
AM ˈraʊn(d)nəs
round robin
BR ˌraʊnd ˈrɒbɪn, -z
AM ˈraʊn(d) ˌrɑbən, -z
round-shouldered
BR ˌraʊn(d)ˈʃəʊldəd
AM ˈraʊn(d)ˌʃoʊldərd
roundsman
BR ˈraʊn(d)zmən
AM ˈraʊn(d)zmən
roundsmen
BR ˈraʊn(d)zmən
AM ˈraʊn(d)zmən
roundup
BR ˈraʊndʌp, -s
AM ˈraʊndˌəp, -s
roundworm
BR ˈraʊn(d)wəːm, -z
AM ˈraʊn(d)ˌwɜrm, -z
Rountree
BR ˈraʊntriː
AM ˈraʊnˌtri
roup
BR ruːp
AM rup
roupy
BR ˈruːpi
AM ˈrupi
Rourke
BR rɔːk
AM rɔ(ə)rk
Rous
BR raʊs
AM raʊs, raʊz

rousable
BR ˈraʊzəbl
AM ˈraʊzəbəl
Rouse
BR raʊs
AM raʊs, raʊz
rouse
BR raʊz, -ɪz, -ɪŋ, -d
AM raʊz, -əz, -ɪŋ, -d
rouseabout
BR ˈraʊzəbaʊt, -s
AM ˈraʊzəˌbaʊt, -z
rouser
BR ˈraʊzə(r), -z
AM ˈraʊzər, -z
rousingly
BR ˈraʊzɪŋli
AM ˈraʊzɪŋli
Rousse
BR ruːs
AM rus
Rousseau
BR ˈruːsəʊ
AM ruˈsoʊ
Roussillon
BR ˈruːsɪjɒ̃
AM ˌrusiˈjon
roust
BR raʊst, -s
AM raʊst, -s
roustabout
BR ˈraʊstəbaʊt, -s
AM ˈraʊstəˌbaʊt, -s
rout
BR raʊt, -s, -ɪŋ, -ɪd
AM raʊt, -ts, -dɪŋ, -dəd
route
BR ruːt, -s, -ɪŋ, -ɪd
AM rut, raʊt, -ts, -dɪŋ, -dəd
router
BR ˈruːtə(r), -z
AM ˈraʊdər, -z
Routh
BR raʊθ
AM raʊθ
routine
BR ruːˈtiːn, rʊˈtiːn, -z
AM ruˈtin, -z
routinely
BR ruːˈtiːnli, rʊˈtiːnli
AM ruˈtinli
routinisation
BR ruːˌtiːnʌɪˈzeɪʃn, rʊˌtiːnʌɪˈzeɪʃn
AM ˌrutnəˈzeɪʃən, ˌrutn̩ˈzeɪʃən
routinise
BR ˈruːtiːnʌɪz, rʊˈtiːnʌɪz, -ɪz, -ɪŋ, -d
AM ˈrutn̩ˌaɪz, -ɪz, -ɪŋ, -d
routinism
BR ruːˈtiːnɪz(ə)m, rʊˈtiːnɪz(ə)m
AM ˈrutn̩ˌɪzəm

routinist
BR ruː'tiːnɪst,
rʊ'tiːnɪst, -s
AM 'rutnəst, -s

routinization
BR ruːˌtiːnaɪ'zeɪʃn,
rʊˌtiːnaɪ'zeɪʃn
AM ˌrutnə'zeɪʃən,
ˌrutnˌaɪ'zeɪʃən

routinize
BR ruː'tiːnaɪz,
rʊ'tiːnaɪz, -ɪz, -ɪŋ, -d
AM 'rutnˌaɪz, -ɪz, -ɪŋ, -d

Routledge
BR 'raʊtlɪdʒ, 'rʌtlɪdʒ
AM 'raʊtlɪdʒ

roux¹
singular
BR ruː
AM ru

roux²
plural
BR ruːz
AM ru(z)

rove
BR rəʊv, -z, -ɪŋ, -d
AM roʊv, -z, -ɪŋ, -d

rover
BR 'rəʊvə(r), -z
AM 'roʊvər, -z

row¹
noise, argument
BR raʊ, -z, -ɪŋ, -d
AM raʊ, -z, -ɪŋ, -d

row²
noun, things in a line;
verb propel a boat
with oars
BR rəʊ, -z, -ɪŋ, -d
AM roʊ, -z, -ɪŋ, -d

Rowallan
BR rəʊ'alən
AM roʊ'ælən

rowan
BR 'rəʊən, 'raʊən, -z
AM 'raʊən, 'roʊən, -z

rowboat
BR 'rəʊbəʊt, -s
AM 'roʊˌboʊt, -s

Rowbotham
BR 'rəʊˌbɒtəm
AM 'roʊˌbɑdəm

Rowbottom
BR 'rəʊˌbɒtəm
AM 'roʊˌbɑdəm

rowdily
BR 'raʊdɪli
AM 'raʊdəli

rowdiness
BR 'raʊdɪnɪs
AM 'raʊdɪnɪs

rowdy
BR 'raʊd|i, -ɪə(r), -ɪɪst
AM 'raʊdi, -ər, -ɪst

rowdyism
BR 'raʊdɪɪz(ə)m
AM 'raʊdiˌɪzəm

Rowe
BR rəʊ
AM roʊ

rowel
BR 'raʊ(ə)l, -z
AM 'raʊ(ə)l, -z

rowen
BR 'raʊən
AM 'raʊən, 'roʊən

Rowena
BR rəʊ'iːnə(r)
AM roʊ'inə

Rowenta®
BR rəʊ'entə(r)
AM roʊ'en(t)ə

rower
BR 'rəʊə(r), -z
AM 'roʊər, -z

rowhouse
BR 'rəʊhaʊ|s, -zɪz
AM 'roʊˌhaʊ|s, -zəz

Rowland
BR 'rəʊlənd
AM 'roʊlən(d)

Rowlands
BR 'rəʊlən(d)z
AM 'roʊlən(d)s

Rowlandson
BR 'rəʊlən(d)s(ə)n
AM 'roʊlən(d)sən

Rowley
BR 'raʊli
AM 'roʊli

rowlock
BR 'rɒlək, 'rəʊlɒk, -s
AM 'roʊˌlɑk, -s

Rowntree
BR 'raʊntriː
AM 'raʊnˌtri

Rowse
BR raʊs
AM raʊz

Rowton
BR 'raʊtn
AM 'raʊtn

Roxana
BR rɒk'sɑːnə(r)
AM rɑk'sænə

Roxanna
BR rɒk'sanə(r)
AM rɑk'sænə

Roxanne
BR rɒk'san
AM rɑk'sæn

Roxburgh
BR 'rɒksb(ə)rə(r)
AM 'rɑk,bərə

Roxy
BR 'rɒksi
AM 'rɑksi

Roy
BR rɔɪ
AM rɔɪ

royal
BR 'rɔɪəl, -z
AM 'rɔɪ(ə)l, -z

royalism
BR 'rɔɪəlɪz(ə)m
AM 'rɔɪəlɪzəm

royalist
BR 'rɔɪəlɪst, -s
AM 'rɔɪələst, -s

royalistic
BR ˌrɔɪə'lɪstɪk
AM ˌrɔɪə'lɪstɪk

royally
BR 'rɔɪəli
AM 'rɔɪəli

royalty
BR 'rɔɪəlt|i, -ɪz
AM 'rɔɪ(ə)lti, -z

Royce
BR rɔɪs
AM rɔɪs

Royle
BR rɔɪl
AM rɔɪl

Royston
BR 'rɔɪst(ə)n
AM 'rɔɪstən

Roz
BR rɒz
AM rɑz

rozzer
BR 'rɒzə(r), -z
AM 'rɑzər, -z

Ruabon
BR rʊ'ab(ə)n
AM ru'abəb
WE rʊ'abɒn

Ruanda
BR rʊ'andə(r)
AM ru'andə

Ruandan
BR rʊ'andən, -z
AM ru'andən, -z

Ruaridh
BR 'rʊəri, 'rɔːri
AM 'rʊəri
IR 'rʊəriː

rub
BR rʌb, -z, -ɪŋ, -d
AM rəb, -z, -ɪŋ, -d

rub-a-dub
BR 'rʌbəˌdʌb,
ˌrʌbə'dʌb, -z, -ɪŋ, -d
AM 'rəbə'dəb, -z, -ɪŋ, -d

rub-a-dub-dub
BR ˌrʌbədʌb'dʌb
AM 'rəbə'dəb'dəb

Rubáiyát
BR 'ruːbʌɪ(j)at,
ruː'bʌɪ(j)at
AM 'rubi,(j)at,
'ru,baɪ,(j)at

rubato
BR rəˈbaːtəʊ, -z
AM ru'badoʊ, -z

rubber
BR 'rʌbə(r), -z
AM 'rəbər, -z

rubberiness
BR 'rʌb(ə)rɪnɪs

rubberise
BR 'rʌbərʌɪz, -ɪz, -ɪŋ, -d
AM 'rəbəˌraɪz, -ɪz, -ɪŋ, -d

rubberize
BR 'rʌbərʌɪz, -ɪz, -ɪŋ, -d
AM 'rəbəˌraɪz, -ɪz, -ɪŋ, -d

rubberneck
BR 'rʌbənɛk, -s, -ɪŋ, -t
AM 'rəbərˌnɛk, -s, -ɪŋ, -t

rubbery
BR 'rʌb(ə)ri
AM 'rəbəri

rubbing
BR 'rʌbɪŋ, -z
AM 'rəbɪŋ, -z

rubbish
BR 'rʌb|ɪʃ, -ɪʃɪz, -ɪʃɪŋ,
-ɪʃt
AM 'rəbɪ.ʃ, -ɪʃɪz, -ɪʃɪŋ,
-ɪʃt

rubbishy
BR 'rʌbɪʃi
AM 'rəbəʃi

rubbity
BR ˌrʌbɪt|i, -ɪz
AM 'rəbədi, -z

rubble
BR 'rʌbl
AM 'rəbəl

rubblework
BR 'rʌblwəːk
AM 'rəbəlˌwərk

rubbly
BR 'rʌb|i
AM 'rəb(ə)li

Rubbra
BR 'rʌbrə(r)
AM 'rəbrə

rubdown
BR 'rʌbdaʊn, -z
AM 'rəbˌdaʊn, -z

rube
BR ruːb, -z
AM rub, -z

rubefacient
BR ˌruːbɪ'feɪʃnt, -s
AM ˌrubə'feɪʃənt, -s

rubefaction
BR ˌruːbɪ'fækʃən
AM ˌrubə'fækʃən

rubefy
BR 'ruːbɪfʌɪ, -z, -ɪŋ, -d
AM 'rubəˌfaɪ, -z, -ɪŋ, -d

rubella
BR ruː'bɛlə(r),
rə'bɛlə(r)
AM ru'bɛlə

rubellite
BR 'ruːbɪlʌɪt, -s
AM 'rubəˌlaɪt, -s

Ruben
BR 'ruːb(ɪ)n
AM 'rubən

rubenesque
BR ˌruːbɪ'nɛsk
AM ˌrubə'nɛsk

Rubens
BR ˈruːb(ɪ)nz
AM ˈrubɛnz

rubeola
BR rʊˈbiːələ(r),
ˌruːbɪˈəʊlə(r)
AM ˌrubiˈoʊlə

Rubery
BR ˈruːb(ə)ri
AM ˈrubəri

Rubicon
BR ˈruːbɪk(ə)n,
ˈruːbɪkɒn
AM ˈrubəˌkɑn

rubicund
BR ˈruːbɪk(ə)nd,
ˈruːbɪkʌnd
AM ˈrubəkənd

rubicundity
BR ˌruːbɪˈkʌndɪti
AM ˌrubəˈkəndədi

rubidium
BR ruːˈbɪdɪəm,
rʊˈbɪdɪəm
AM ruˈbɪdiəm

rubify
BR ˈruːbɪfʌɪ, -z, -ɪŋ, -d
AM ˈrubəˌfaɪ, -z, -ɪŋ, -d

rubiginous
BR ruːˈbɪdʒɪnəs,
rʊˈbɪdʒɪnəs
AM ˌruˈbɪdʒɪnɪs

Rubik
BR ˈruːbɪk
AM ˈrubɪk

Rubin
BR ˈruːbɪn
AM ˈrubən

Rubinstein
BR ˈruːb(ɪ)nstʌɪn
AM ˈrubənˌstin,
ˈrubənˌstain

ruble
BR ˈruːbl, -z
AM ˈrubəl, -z

rubric
BR ˈruːbrɪk, -s
AM ˈruˌbrɪk, -s

rubrical
BR ˈruːbrɪkl
AM ˈrubrəkəl

rubricate
BR ˈruːbrɪkeɪt, -s, -ɪŋ, -ɪd
AM ˈrubrəˌkeɪlt, -ts, -dɪŋ, -dɪd

rubrication
BR ˌruːbrɪˈkeɪʃn
AM ˌrubrəˈkeɪʃən

rubricator
BR ˈrʌbrɪkeɪtə(r), -z
AM ˈrubrəˌkeɪdər, -z

rubrician
BR ruːˈbrɪʃn, -z
AM ruˈbrɪʃən, -z

rubricism
BR ˈruːbrɪsɪz(ə)m
AM ˈrubrəˌsɪzəm

rubricist
BR ˈruːbrɪsɪst, -s
AM ˈrubrəsəst, -s

ruby
BR ˈruːbli, -ɪz
AM ˈrubi, -z

ruche
BR ruːʃ, -ɪz, -ɪŋ, -t
AM ruʃ, -ɪz, -ɪŋ, -t

ruck
BR rʌk, -s, -ɪŋ, -t
AM rək, -s, -ɪŋ, -t

ruckle
BR ˈrʌkl, -z, -ɪŋ, -d
AM ˈrəkəl, -z, -ɪŋ, -d

rucksack
BR ˈrʌksak, -s
AM ˈrəkˌsæk, ˈrʊkˌsæk, -s

ruckus
BR ˈrʌkəs, -ɪz
AM ˈrəkəs, -ɪz

rucola
BR ˈruːkələ(r)
AM ˈrukələ

ruction
BR ˈrʌkʃn, -z
AM ˈrəkʃən, -z

rudaceous
BR rʊˈdeɪʃəs
AM ˈrudeɪʃəs

rudbeckia
BR rʌdˈbɛkɪə(r),
ˌruːdˈbɛkɪə(r), -z
AM ˌrudˈbɛkiə, -z

rudd
BR rʌd, -z
AM rəd, -z

rudder
BR ˈrʌdə(r), -z
AM ˈrədər, -z

rudderless
BR ˈrʌdələs
AM ˈrədərləs

Ruddigore
BR ˈrʌdɪɡɔː(r)
AM ˈrʊdəˌɡɔ(ə)r

ruddily
BR ˈrʌdɪli
AM ˈrədəli

ruddiness
BR ˈrʌdɪnɪs
AM ˈrədinɪs

ruddle
BR ˈrʌd|l, -lz, -lɪŋ\-lɪŋ, -ld
AM ˈrəd|əl, -əlz, -(ə)lɪŋ, -əld

ruddock
BR ˈrʌdək, -s
AM ˈrədək, -s

ruddy
BR ˈrʌd|i, -ɪə(r), -ɪɪst
AM ˈrʊdi, -ər, -ɪst

rude
BR ruːd, -ə(r), -ɪst
AM rud, -ər, -əst

rudely
BR ˈruːdli
AM ˈrudli

rudeness
BR ˈruːdnəs
AM ˈrudnəs

ruderal
BR ˈruːd(ə)rəl,
ˈruːd(ə)r|, -z
AM ˈrudərəl, -z

rudery
BR ˈruːdər|i, -ɪz
AM ˈruderi, -z

Rudge
BR rʌdʒ
AM rədʒ

Rudi
BR ˈruːdi
AM ˈrudi

rudiment
BR ˈruːdɪm(ə)nt, -s
AM ˈrudəmənt, -s

rudimental
BR ˌruːdɪˈmentl
AM ˌrudəˈmen(t)l

rudimentarily
BR ˈruːdɪˈment(ə)rɪli
AM ˌrudəmənˈtɛrəli

rudimentariness
BR ˌruːdɪˈment(ə)rɪnɪs
AM ˌrudəˈmen(t)ərinɪs

rudimentary
BR ˌruːdɪˈment(ə)ri
AM ˌrudəˈmen(t)əri

rudish
BR ˈruːdɪʃ
AM ˈrudɪʃ

Rudolf
BR ˈruːdɒlf
AM ˈrudɔlf, ˈrudalf

Rudolph
BR ˈruːdɒlf
AM ˈrudɔlf, ˈrudalf

Rudy
BR ˈruːdi
AM ˈrudi

Rudyard
BR ˈrʌdjəd, ˈrʌdʒəd, ˈrʌdjɑːd
AM ˈrədjərd

rue
BR ruː, -z, -ɪŋ, -d
AM ru, -z, -ɪŋ, -d

rueful
BR ˈruːf(ʊ)l
AM ˈrufəl

ruefully
BR ˈruːfʊli, ˈruːfli
AM ˈrufəli

ruefulness
BR ˈruːf(ʊ)lnəs
AM ˈrufəlnəs

rufescence
BR ruːˈfɛsns
AM ruːˈfɛsəns

rufescent
BR ruːˈfɛsnt

AM ruːˈfɛsənt

ruff
BR rʌf, -s, -ɪŋ, -t
AM rəf, -s, -ɪŋ, -t

ruffian
BR ˈrʌfɪən, -z
AM ˈrəfiən, -z

ruffianism
BR ˈrʌfɪənɪz(ə)m
AM ˈrəfiənɪzəm

ruffianly
BR ˈrʌfɪənli
AM ˈrəfiənli

ruffle
BR ˈrʌf|l, -lz, -lɪŋ\-lɪŋ, -ld
AM ˈrəf|əl, -əlz, -(ə)lɪŋ, -əld

rufflike
BR ˈrʌflʌɪk
AM ˈrəfˌlaɪk

Rufford
BR ˈrʌfəd
AM ˈrəfərd

rufous
BR ˈruːfəs
AM ˈrufəs

Rufus
BR ˈruːfəs
AM ˈrufəs

rug
BR rʌɡ, -z
AM rəɡ, -z

Rugbeian
BR rʌɡˈbiːən, -z
AM ˈrəɡbiən, -z

rugby
BR ˈrʌɡbi
AM ˈrəɡbi

Rugeley
BR ˈruːdʒli
AM ˈrudʒli

Rügen
BR ˈruːdʒ(ə)n
AM ˈrudʒɛn
GER ˈrʏɡn

rugged
BR ˈrʌɡɪd
AM ˈrəɡəd

ruggedly
BR ˈrʌɡɪdli
AM ˈrəɡədli

ruggedness
BR ˈrʌɡɪdnɪs
AM ˈrəɡədnəs

rugger
BR ˈrʌɡə(r)
AM ˈrəɡər

rugola
BR ˈruːɡələ(r)
AM ˈruɡələ

rugosa
BR ruːˈɡəʊzə(r), -z
AM ruˈɡoʊzə, -z

rugose
BR ˈruːɡəʊs, ˈruːɡəʊz, rʊˈɡəʊs

AM 'ruːgoʊz, 'rugoʊs

rugosely
BR 'ruːgəʊsli,
'ruːgəʊzli, rʊ'gəʊsli
AM ru'goʊzli,
ru'goʊsli

rugosity
BR ru:'gɒsɪti, rʊ'gɒsɪti
AM ru'gasədi

Ruhr
BR 'rʊə(r)
AM 'rʊ(ə)r

ruin
BR 'ruːɪn, -ɪnz, -nɪŋ,
-ɪnd
AM 'ruən, 'ruˌɪn, -z, -ɪŋ,
-d

ruination
BR ˌruːɪ'neɪʃn
AM ˌruə'neɪʃən

ruinous
BR 'ruːɪnəs
AM 'ruənəs

ruinously
BR 'ruːɪnəsli
AM 'ruənəsli

ruinousness
BR 'ruːɪnəsnəs
AM 'ruənəsnəs

Ruislip
BR 'raɪslɪp
AM 'raɪsləp

Ruiz
BR 'ruːɪz
AM ru'iz
SP 'rrwiθ, 'rrwis

rule
BR ruːl, -z, -ɪŋ, -d
AM rul, -z, -ɪŋ, -d

rulebook
BR 'ruːlbʊk, -s
AM 'rulˌbʊk, -s

ruleless
BR 'ruːl(l)əs
AM 'ru(l)ləs

ruler
BR 'ruːlə(r), -z
AM 'rulər, -z

rulership
BR 'ruːləʃɪp, -s
AM 'rulərˌʃɪp, -s

ruling
BR 'ruːlɪŋ, -z
AM 'rulɪŋ, -z

rum
BR rʌm, -ə(r), -ɪst
AM rəm, -ər, -əst

Rumania
BR ru:'meɪnɪə(r),
rʊ'meɪnɪə(r)
AM roʊ'meɪnɪə,
ru'meɪnɪə

Rumanian
BR ru:'meɪnɪən,
rʊ'meɪnɪən
AM roʊ'meɪnɪən,
ru'meɪnɪən

Rumansh
BR rʊ'manʃ, rʊ'mɑːnʃ
AM ro'manʃ, ru'manʃ

rumba
BR 'rʌmbə(r), -z
AM 'rəmbə, -z

rum baba
BR ˌrʌm 'bɑːbə(r), -z
AM ˌrəm 'babə, -z

Rumbelow
BR 'rʌmbɪləʊ
AM 'rəmbəˌloʊ

rumble
BR 'rʌmb|l, -lz,
-lɪŋ \ -lɪŋ, -ld
AM 'rəmbəl, -əlz,
-(ə)lɪŋ, -əld

rumbler
BR 'rʌmblə(r),
'rʌmblə(r), -z
AM 'rəmb(ə)lər, -z

rumbling
BR 'rʌmblɪŋ,
'rʌmblɪŋ, -z
AM 'rəmb(ə)lɪŋ, -z

Rumbold
BR 'rʌmbəʊld
AM 'rəmˌboʊld

rumbustious
BR rʌm'bʌstʃəs,
rʌm'bʌstɪəs
AM 'rəm'bəstʃəs

rumbustiously
BR rʌm'bʌstʃəsli,
rʌm'bʌstɪəsli
AM rəm'bəstʃəsli,
rəm'bəsdɪəsli

rumbustiousness
BR rʌm'bʌstʃəsnəs,
rʌm'bʌstɪəsnəs
AM rəm'bəstʃəsnəs,
rəm'bəsdɪəsnəs

Rumelia
BR rʊ'miːlɪə(r)
AM ru'miljə, ru'miliə

rumen
BR 'ruːmɛn, 'ruːmɪn, -z
AM 'rumən, -z

Rumi
BR 'ruːmi
AM 'rumi

rumina
BR 'ruːmɪnə(r)
AM 'rumənə

ruminant
BR 'ruːmɪnənt, -s
AM 'rumənənt, -s

ruminate
BR 'ruːmɪneɪt, -s, -ɪŋ,
-ɪd
AM 'ruməˌneɪt, -ts,
-dɪŋ, -dəd

rumination
BR ˌruːmɪ'neɪʃn, -z
AM ˌruːmə'neɪʃən, -z

ruminative
BR 'ruːmɪnətɪv

AM 'ruməˌneɪdɪv,
'rumənədɪv

ruminatively
BR 'ruːmɪnətɪvli
AM 'ruməˌneɪdɪvli,
'rumənəˌdɪvli

ruminator
BR 'ruːmɪneɪtə(r), -z
AM 'ruməˌneɪdər, -z

rumly
BR 'rʌmli
AM 'rəmli

rummage
BR 'rʌm|ɪdʒ, -ɪdʒɪz,
-ɪdʒɪŋ, -ɪdʒd
AM 'rəmədʒ, -əz, -ɪŋ, -d

rummager
BR 'rʌmɪdʒə(r), -z
AM 'rəmədʒər, -z

rummer
BR 'rʌmə(r), -z
AM 'rəmər, -z

rummily
BR 'rʌmɪli
AM 'rəməli

rumminess
BR 'rʌmɪnɪs
AM 'rəmɪnɪs

rummy
BR 'rʌm|i, -ɪə(r), -ɪɪst
AM 'rəmi, -ər, -ɪst

rumness
BR 'rʌmnəs
AM 'rəmnəs

rumor
BR 'ruːmə(r), -z, -d
AM 'rumər, -z, -d

rumour
BR 'ruːmə(r), -z, -d
AM 'rumər, -z, -d

rump
BR rʌmp, -s
AM rəmp, -s

Rumpelstiltskin
BR ˌrʌmpl'stɪltskɪn
AM ˌrəmpl'stɪl(t)skɪn

rumple
BR 'rʌmp|l, -lz,
-lɪŋ \ -lɪŋ, -ld
AM 'rəmpəl, -əlz,
-(ə)lɪŋ, -əld

rumpless
BR 'rʌmpləs
AM 'rəmpləs

rumply
BR 'rʌmpļi
AM 'rəmp(ə)li

Rumpole
BR 'rʌmpəʊl
AM 'rəmˌpoʊl

rumpus
BR 'rʌmpəs, -ɪz
AM 'rəmpəs, -ɪz

rumpy
BR 'rʌmp|i, -ɪz
AM 'rəmpi, -z

rumpy-pumpy
BR ˌrʌmpɪ'pʌmpi
AM ˌrəmpi'pəmpi

rumrunner
BR 'rʌmˌrʌnə(r), -z
AM 'rəmˌrənər, -z

run
BR rʌn, -z, -ɪŋ
AM rən, -z, -ɪŋ

runabout
BR 'rʌnəbaʊt, -s
AM 'rənəˌbaʊt, -s

runagate
BR 'rʌnəgeɪt, -s
AM 'rənəˌgeɪt, -s

runaround
BR 'rʌnəraʊnd
AM 'rənəˌraʊnd

runaway
BR 'rʌnəweɪ, -z
AM 'rənəˌweɪ, -z

runback
BR 'rʌnbak, -s
AM 'rənˌbæk, -s

runcible
BR 'rʌnsɪbl
AM 'rənsəbəl

Runcie
BR 'rʌnsi
AM 'rənsi

Runciman
BR 'rʌnsɪmən
AM 'rənsəmən

runcinate
BR 'rʌnsɪnət
AM 'rənsəˌneɪt

Runcorn
BR 'rʌnkɔːn, 'rʌŋkɔːn
AM 'rənˌkɔ(ə)rn

rundale
BR 'rʌndeɪl, -z
AM 'rənˌdeɪl, -z

Rundle
BR 'rʌndl
AM 'rənd(ə)l

rundown
noun
BR 'rʌndaʊn, -z
AM 'rənˌdaʊn, -z

run-down
adjective
BR ˌrʌn'daʊn
AM ˌrən'daʊn

rune
BR ruːn, -z
AM run, -z

rung
BR rʌŋ, -z, -d
AM rəŋ, -z, -d

rungless
BR 'rʌŋləs
AM 'rəŋləs

runic
BR 'ruːnɪk
AM 'runɪk

run-in
BR 'rʌnɪn, -z

AM 'rən,ın, -z

runlet
BR 'rʌnlɪt, -s
AM 'rənlət, -s

runnable
BR 'rʌnəbl
AM 'rənəbəl

runnel
BR 'rʌnl, -z
AM 'rənəl, -z

runner
BR 'rʌnə(r), -z
AM 'rənər, -z

runniness
BR 'rʌnɪnɪs
AM 'rənɪnɪs

runningboard
BR 'rʌnɪŋbɔːd, -z
AM 'rənɪŋ,bɔ(ə)rd, -z

runny
BR 'rʌn|i, -iə(r), -ɪst
AM 'rəni, -ər, -ɪst

Runnymede
BR 'rʌnɪmiːd
AM 'rəni,mid

runt
BR rʌnt, -s
AM rənt, -s

runthrough
BR 'rʌnθruː, -z
AM 'rən,θru, -z

runty
BR 'rʌnti
AM 'rən(t)i

runup
BR 'rʌnʌp, -s
AM 'rən,əp, -s

runway
BR 'rʌnweɪ, -z
AM 'rən,weɪ, -z

Runyon
BR 'rʌnjən
AM 'rənjən

rupee
BR 'ruːˈpiː, ruˈpiː, -z
AM ruˈpi, 'rupi, -z

Rupert
BR 'ruːpət
AM 'rupərt

rupiah
BR ruˈpiːə(r), -z
AM ruˈpiə, -z

rupturable
BR 'rʌptʃ(ə)rəbl
AM 'rəp(t)ʃərəbəl

rupture
BR 'rʌptʃ|ə(r), -əz,
-(ə)rɪŋ, -əd
AM 'rəp(t)ʃ|ər, -ərz,
-(ə)rɪŋ, -ərd

rural
BR 'ruərəl, 'ruərl̩
AM 'rurəl

ruralisation
BR ,ruərələ\ʌ'zeɪʃn,
,ruərl̩ʌɪ'zeɪʃn

AM ,ruərələ'zeɪʃən,
,ruərə,laɪ'zeɪʃən

ruralise
BR 'ruərəlʌɪz,
'ruərl̩ʌɪz, -ɪz, -ɪŋ, -d
AM 'rurə,laɪz, -ɪz, -ɪŋ, -d

ruralism
BR 'ruərəlɪz(ə)m,
'ruərl̩ɪz(ə)m
AM 'rurə,lɪzəm

ruralist
BR 'ruərəlɪst,
'ruərl̩ɪst, -s
AM 'rurələst, -s

rurality
BR ruˈralɪt|i, -ɪz
AM ,ruˈrælədi, -z

ruralization
BR ,ruərələʌɪ'zeɪʃn,
,ruərl̩ʌɪ'zeɪʃn
AM ,ruərələ'zeɪʃən,
,ruərə,laɪ'zeɪʃən

ruralize
BR 'ruərəlʌɪz,
'ruərl̩ʌɪz, -ɪz, -ɪŋ, -d
AM 'rurə,laɪz, -ɪz, -ɪŋ, -d

rurally
BR 'ruərəli, 'ruərl̩i
AM 'rurəli

ruridecanal
BR ,ruərɪdɪ'keɪnl,
,ruərɪ'dɛkənl,
,ruərɪ'dɛknl̩
AM ,rurə'dɛkənəl

Rurik
BR 'ruərɪk
AM 'rurɪk
RUS 'rʲurʲik

Ruritania
BR ,ruərɪ'teɪnɪə(r)
AM ,rurə'teɪnɪə

Ruritanian
BR ,ruərɪ'teɪnɪən, -z
AM ,rurə'teɪnɪən, -z

rusa
BR 'ruːsə(r), -z
AM 'rusə, -z

ruse
BR ruːz, -ɪz
AM ruz, rus, -ɪz

rush
BR rʌʃ, -ɪz, -ɪŋ, -t
AM rəʃ, -ɪz, -ɪŋ, -t

Rushdie
BR 'ruʃdi, 'rʌʃdi
AM 'rəʃdi

rushee
BR rʌˈʃiː, -z
AM rəˈʃi, -z

rusher
BR 'rʌʃə(r), -z
AM 'rəʃər, -z

rush-hour
BR 'rʌʃauə(r), -z
AM 'rəʃ,au(ə)r, -z

rushingly
BR 'rʌʃɪŋli
AM 'rəʃɪŋli

---

rushlight
BR 'rʌʃlaɪt, -s
AM 'rəʃ,laɪt, -s

rushlike
BR 'rʌʃlaɪk
AM 'rəʃ,laɪk

Rushmore
BR 'rʌʃmɔː(r)
AM 'rəʃmɔ(ə)r

Rusholme
BR 'rʌʃhəʊm
AM 'rəʃ,(h)oʊm

Rushton
BR 'rʌʃt(ə)n
AM 'rəʃtən

Rushworth
BR 'rʌʃwəːθ, 'rʌʃwəθ
AM 'rəʃ,wərθ

rushy
BR 'rʌʃ|i, -iə(r), -ɪɪst
AM 'rəʃi, -ər, -ɪst

rusk
BR rʌsk, -s
AM rəsk, -s

Ruski
BR 'rʌsk|i, -ɪz
AM 'rəski, 'ruski, -z

Ruskin
BR 'rʌskɪn
AM 'rəskən

Rusky
BR 'rʌsk|i, -ɪz
AM 'rəski, 'ruski, -z

Russ
BR rʌs
AM rəs

russe
BR ruːs
AM rus

Russell
BR 'rʌsl
AM 'rəsɛl

russet
BR 'rʌsɪt, -s
AM 'rəsət, -s

russety
BR 'rʌsɪti
AM 'rəsədi

Russia
BR 'rʌʃə(r)
AM 'rəʃə

Russian
BR 'rʌʃn, -z
AM 'rəʃən, -z

Russianisation
BR ,rʌʃʌɪ'zeɪʃn,
,rʌʃənʌɪ'zeɪʃn
AM ,rəʃənə'zeɪʃən,
,rəʃə,naɪ'zeɪʃən

Russianise
BR 'rʌʃnʌɪz, 'rʌʃənʌɪz,
-ɪz, -ɪŋ, -d
AM 'rəʃə,naɪz, -ɪz, -ɪŋ,
-d

Russianization
BR ,rʌʃnʌɪ'zeɪʃn,
,rʌʃənʌɪ'zeɪʃn

AM ,rəʃənə'zeɪʃən,
,rəʃə,naɪ'zeɪʃən

Russianize
BR 'rʌʃnʌɪz, 'rʌʃənʌɪz,
-ɪz, -ɪŋ, -d
AM 'rəʃə,naɪz, -ɪz, -ɪŋ,
-d

Russianness
BR 'rʌʃ(ə)nnəs
AM 'rəʃə(n)nəs

Russification
BR ,rʌsɪfɪ'keɪʃn
AM ,rəsəfə'keɪʃən

Russify
BR 'rʌsɪfʌɪ, -z, -ɪŋ, -d
AM 'rəsə,faɪ, -z, -ɪŋ, -d

Russki
BR 'rʌsk|i, -ɪz
AM 'rəski, 'ruski, -z

Russky
BR 'rʌsk|i, -ɪz
AM 'rəski, 'ruski, -z

Russo
BR 'rʌsəʊ
AM 'rəsou, 'rusou

Russo-
BR 'rʌsəʊ
AM 'rəsou

Russophile
BR 'rʌsə(ʊ)fʌɪl, -z
AM 'rəsə,faɪl, -z

Russophobe
BR 'rʌsə(ʊ)fəʊb, -z
AM 'rəsə,foʊb, -z

Russophobia
BR ,rʌsəʊ'fəʊbɪə(r)
AM ,rəsə'foʊbɪə

rust
BR rʌst, -s, -ɪŋ, -ɪd
AM rəst, -s, -ɪŋ, -ɪd

rust-belt
BR 'rʌs(t)bɛlt
AM 'rəs(t),bɛlt

rustbucket
BR 'rʌs(t),bʌkɪt, -s
AM 'rəs(t),bəkət, -s

rustic
BR 'rʌstɪk, -s
AM 'rəstɪk, -s

rustically
BR 'rʌstɪkli
AM 'rəstək(ə)li

rusticate
BR 'rʌstɪkeɪt, -s, -ɪŋ, -ɪd
AM 'rəstə,keɪ|t, -ts,
-dɪŋ, -dɪd

rustication
BR ,rʌstɪ'keɪʃn
AM ,rəstə'keɪʃən

rusticity
BR rʌ'stɪsɪti
AM rə'stɪsɪdi

rustily
BR 'rʌstɪli
AM 'rəstəli

rustiness
BR 'rʌstɪnɪs

rustle
BR 'rʌstɪɪs

rustle
BR 'rʌs|l, -lz, -lɪŋ \ -lɪŋ,
-ld
AM 'rəs|əl, -əlz, -(ə)lɪŋ,
-əld

rustler
BR 'rʌslə(r), -z
AM 'rəslər, -z

rustless
BR 'rʌstləs
AM 'rəs(t)ləs

rustling
BR 'rʌslɪŋ, 'rʌslɪŋ, -z
AM 'rəs(t)lɪŋ, -z

rustproof
BR 'rʌs(t)pruːf, -s, -ɪŋ,
-t
AM 'rəs(t)ˌpruf, -s, -ɪŋ,
-t

rustre
BR 'rʌstə(r), -z
AM 'rəstər, -z

rusty
BR 'rʌst|i, -ɪə(r), -ɪɪst
AM 'rʌsti, -ər, -ɪst

rut
BR rʌt, -s, -ɪŋ, -ɪd
AM rət|t, -ts, -dɪŋ, -dəd

rutabaga
BR ˌruːtəˈbeɪɡə(r),
'ruːtəˌbeɪɡə(r), -z
AM 'rudəˌbeɪɡə, -z

Rutgers
BR 'rʌtɡəz
AM 'rətɡərz

ruth
BR ruːθ
AM ruθ

Ruthenia
BR rʊ'θiːnɪə(r)

ruthenium
BR rʊ'θiːnɪəm
AM ru'θiniəm

Rutherford
BR 'rʌðəfəd
AM 'rəðərfərd

rutherfordium
BR ˌrʌðəˈfɔːdɪəm
AM ˌrəðərˈfɔrdiəm

ruthful
BR 'ruːθf(ʊ)l
AM 'ruθfəl

ruthfully
BR 'ruːθfʊli, 'ruːθfli
AM 'ruθfəli

ruthfulness
BR 'ruːθ(ʊ)lnəs
AM 'ruθfəlnəs

ruthless
BR 'ruːθləs
AM 'ruθləs

ruthlessly
BR 'ruːθləsli
AM 'ruθləsli

ruthlessness
BR 'ruːθləsnəs
AM 'ruθləsnəs

Ruthven
BR 'rɪvn, 'rʌθv(ə)n,
'ruːθv(ə)n
AM 'ruθvən

rutile
BR 'ruːtʌɪl, -z
AM 'ruˌtil, 'ruˌtaɪl, -z

rutin
BR 'ruːtɪn
AM 'rudɪn

Rutland
BR 'rʌtlənd
AM 'rətlənd

Rutledge
BR 'rʌtlɪdʒ

AM 'rətlədʒ

ruttish
BR 'rʌtɪʃ
AM 'rədɪʃ

rutty
BR 'rʌti
AM 'rədi

Ruwenzori
BR ˌruːənˈzɔːri
AM ˌruwənˈzɔri

R-value
BR 'ɑːˌvalju
AM 'ɑrˌvælju

Rwanda
BR rʊ'andə(r)
AM rʊ'andə, rə'wandə

Rwandan
BR rʊ'andən, -z
AM ru'andən,
rə'wandən, -z

Rwandese
BR rʊˌan'diːz
AM ruˌan'diz,
rəˌwan'diz

Rx
BR ˌɑːr'ɛks
AM ˌɑr'ɛks

Ryan
BR 'rʌɪən
AM 'raɪən

Rycroft
BR 'rʌɪkrɒft
AM 'raɪˌkrɔft,
'raɪˌkraft

Rydal
BR 'rʌɪdl
AM 'raɪd(ə)l

Ryde
BR rʌɪd
AM raɪd

Ryder
BR 'rʌɪdə(r)
AM 'raɪdər

rye
BR rʌɪ
AM raɪ

ryegrass
BR 'rʌɪɡrɑːs, 'rʌɪɡras
AM 'raɪˌɡræs

Ryland
BR 'rʌɪlənd
AM 'raɪlən(d)

Rylands
BR 'rʌɪlən(d)z
AM 'raɪlən(d)z

Ryle
BR 'rʌɪl
AM 'raɪl

Ryles
BR 'rʌɪlz
AM 'raɪlz

Ryman
BR 'rʌɪmən
AM 'raɪmən

ryokan
BR rɪ'əʊkən, rɪ'əʊkan,
-z
AM ri'oʊkən, -z

ryot
BR 'rʌɪət, -s
AM 'raɪət, -s

Ryton
BR 'rʌɪtn
AM 'raɪtn

ryu
BR rɪ'uː, -z
AM ri'u, -z

Ryvita®
BR (ˌ)rʌɪ'viːtə(r)
AM raɪ'vidə

Ss

s
BR ɛs, -ɪz
AM ɛs, -əz

Saab®
BR sɑːb, -z
AM sɑb, -z

Saadi
BR 'sɑːdi
AM 'sɑdi

Saar
BR sɑː(r)
AM sɑr

Saarbrücken
BR 'sɑːˌbrʊk(ə)n
AM 'sɑrˌbrʊkən
GER ˌzaːˈɐ'brʏkn

Saarinen
BR 'sɑːrɪnən
AM 'sɑrənən

Saarland
BR 'sɑːland
AM 'sɑrˌlænd

Saba
BR 'sɑːbə(r)
AM 'sɑbə

sabadilla
BR ˌsabə'dɪlə(r)
AM ˌsæbə'dɪlə

Sabaean
BR sə'biːən, -z
AM sə'biən, 'sɑbiən, -z

Sabah
BR 'sɑːbə(r)
AM 'sɑbə

Sabaism
BR 'sɑːbə(r)ɪz(ə)m
AM 'sɑbəˌɪzəm

Sabaoth
BR 'sabeɪɒθ, sə'beɪɒθ
AM 'sæbeɪˌɑθ

Sabatier
BR sə'batɪeɪ
AM sə̩badi'eɪ

sabayon
BR 'sabʌɪjɒ̃
AM sæbaɪ'ɒn

sabbatarian
BR ˌsabə'tɛːrɪən, -z
AM ˌsæbə'tɛriən, -z

sabbatarianism
BR ˌsabə'tɛːrɪənɪz(ə)m
AM ˌsæbə'tɛriəˌnɪzəm

sabbath
BR 'sabəθ, -s
AM 'sæbəθ, -s

sabbatic
BR sə'batɪk, -s
AM sə'bædɪk, -s

sabbatical
BR sə'batɪkl, -z
AM sə'bædəkəl, -z

sabbatically
BR sə'batɪkli
AM sə'bædək(ə)li

sabbatisation
BR ˌsabətʌɪ'zeɪʃn
AM ˌsæbədə'zeɪʃən,
ˌsæbəˌtaɪ'zeɪʃən

sabbatise
BR 'sabətʌɪz, -ɪz, -ɪŋ, -d
AM 'sæbəˌtaɪz, -ɪz, -ɪŋ, -d

sabbatization
BR ˌsabətʌɪ'zeɪʃn
AM ˌsæbədə'zeɪʃən,
ˌsæbəˌtaɪ'zeɪʃən

sabbatize
BR 'sabətʌɪz, -ɪz, -ɪŋ, -d
AM 'sæbəˌtaɪz, -ɪz, -ɪŋ, -d

Sabellian
BR sə'bɛlɪən, -z
AM sə'bɛljən,
sə'bɛliən, -z

saber
BR 'seɪb|ə(r), -əz,
-(ə)rɪŋ, -əd
AM 'seɪb|ər, -ərz,
-(ə)rɪŋ, -ərd

sabertooth
BR 'seɪbətuːθ
AM 'seɪbərˌtuθ

Sabian
BR 'seɪbɪən, -z
AM 'seɪbiən, -z

sabicu
BR ˌsabɪ'kuː, -z
AM 'sæbəˌku, -z

Sabin
BR 'seɪbɪn, 'sabɪn
AM 'seɪbən

Sabina
BR sə'biːnə(r)
AM sə'biːnə

Sabine[1]
people
BR 'sabʌɪn, -z
AM 'seɪˌbaɪn, 'seɪˌbin, -z

Sabine[2]
surname
BR 'sabʌɪn, 'seɪbʌɪn, 'seɪbɪn
AM 'seɪbən, 'seɪˌbin

Sabine[3]
U.S. river and lake
BR sə'biːn
AM sə'bin

sabir
BR sə'bɪə(r)
AM sə'bɪ(ə)r

sable
BR 'seɪbl, -z, -d
AM 'seɪbəl, -z, -d

sably
BR 'seɪbli
AM 'seɪb(ə)li

sabot
BR 'sabəʊ, -z, -d

AM ˌsæ'bəʊ, -z, -d

sabotage
BR 'sabətɑː(d)ʒ, -ɪz, -ɪŋ, -d
AM ˌsæbəˌtɑʒ, -əz, -ɪŋ, -d

saboteur
BR ˌsabə'təː(r), -z
AM ˌsæbə'tər, -z

sabra
BR 'sɑːbrə(r), 'sabrə(r), -z
AM 'sɑbrə, -z

sabre
BR 'seɪb|ə(r), -əz, -(ə)rɪŋ, -əd
AM 'seɪb|ər, -ərz, -(ə)rɪŋ, -ərd

sabretache
BR 'seɪbətaʃ, -ɪz
AM 'seɪbərˌtæʃ, -əz

sabretooth
BR 'seɪbətuːθ
AM 'seɪbərˌtuθ

sabreur
BR sə'brə:(r), -z
AM 'sæˌbrər, sɑ'brər, -z

Sabrina
BR sə'briːnə(r)
AM sə'brinə

sac
BR sak, -s
AM sæk, -s

saccade
BR sə'kɑːd, sa'kɑːd, -z
AM sə'kad, sæ'kad, -z

saccadic
BR sə'kadɪk
AM sə'kædɪk, sæ'kædɪk

saccate
BR 'sakeɪt
AM 'sæˌkeɪt

saccharide
BR 'sakərʌɪd, -z
AM 'sækəˌraɪd, -z

saccharimeter
BR ˌsakə'rɪmɪtə(r), -z
AM ˌsækə'rɪmədər, -z

saccharimetry
BR ˌsakə'rɪmɪtri
AM ˌsækə'rɪmətri

saccharin
BR 'sak(ə)rɪn, 'sakəriːn, -z
AM 'sæk(ə)rən, -z

saccharine
BR 'sak(ə)rɪn, 'sakəriːn, -z
AM 'sæk(ə)rən, -z

saccharogenic
BR ˌsak(ə)rə(ʊ)'dʒɛnɪk
AM ˌsækəroʊ'dʒɛnɪk

saccharometer
BR ˌsakə'rɒmɪtə(r), -z
AM ˌsækə'rɑmədər, -z

saccharometry
BR ˌsakə'rɒmɪtri
AM ˌsækə'rɑmətri

saccharose
BR 'sakərəʊz, 'sakərəʊs
AM 'sækəˌroʊs, 'sækəˌroʊz

sacciform
BR 'saksɪfɔːm
AM 'sæk(s)əˌfɔ(ə)rm

saccular
BR 'sakjʊlə(r)
AM 'sækjələr

sacculate
BR 'sakjʊleɪt, -ɪd
AM 'sækjəˌleɪ|t, -dɪd

sacculation
BR ˌsakjʊ'leɪʃn, -z
AM ˌsækjə'leɪʃən, -z

saccule
BR 'sakjuːl, -z
AM 'sæˌkjul, -z

sacerdotage
BR ˌsakə'dəʊtɪdʒ
AM ˌsæsər'doʊdɪdʒ, ˌsækər'doʊdɪdʒ

sacerdotal
BR ˌsakə'dəʊtl
AM ˌsæsər'doʊdl, ˌsækər'doʊdl

sacerdotalism
BR ˌsakə'dəʊtlɪz(ə)m
AM ˌsæsər'doʊdlˌɪzəm, ˌsækər'doʊdlˌɪzəm

sacerdotalist
BR ˌsakə'dəʊtlɪst, -s
AM ˌsæsər'doʊdləst, ˌsækər'doʊdləst, -s

sacerdotally
BR ˌsakə'dəʊtli, ˌsakə'dəʊtəli
AM ˌsæsər'doʊdli, ˌsækər'doʊdli

Sacha
BR 'saʃə(r)
AM 'sɑʃə, 'sætʃə

sachem
BR 'seɪtʃəm, -z
AM 'seɪtʃəm, -z

Sachertorte
BR 'zakəˌtɔːtə(r)
AM 'sɑkərˌtɔ(ə)rt, 'sækərˌtɔ(ə)rt

Sachertorten
BR 'zakəˌtɔːt(ə)n
AM 'sɑkərˌtɔ(ə)rtn, 'sækərˌtɔ(ə)rtn

sachet
BR 'saʃeɪ, -z
AM sæ'ʃeɪ, -z

Sacheverell
BR sə'ʃɛvr(ə)l
AM sə̩ʃɛvə'rɛl

Sachs
BR saks
AM sæks

Sachsen
BR 'saks(ə)n
AM 'sæksən

sack
BR sak, -s, -ıŋ, -t
AM sæk, -s, -ıŋ, -t

sackable
BR 'sakəbl
AM 'sækəbəl

sackbut
BR 'sakbʌt, -s
AM 'sæk‚bət, -s

sackcloth
BR 'sakklɒθ
AM 'sæk‚clɔθ, 'sæk‚claθ

sacker
BR 'sakə(r), -z
AM 'sækər, -z

sackful
BR 'sakfʊl, -z
AM 'sæk‚fʊl, -z

sacking
BR 'sakıŋ, -z
AM 'sækıŋ, -z

sackless
BR 'sakləs
AM 'sækləs

sacklike
BR 'saklʌık
AM 'sæk‚laık

Sackville
BR 'sakvıl
AM 'sæk‚vıl

sacra
BR 'seıkrə(r), 'sakrə(r)
AM 'sækrə, 'seıkrə

sacral
BR 'seıkr(ə)l, 'sakr(ə)l
AM 'sækrəl, 'seıkrəl

sacrament
BR 'sakrəm(ə)nt, -s
AM 'sækrəmənt, -s

sacramental
BR ‚sakrə'mentl
AM ‚sækrə'men(t)l

sacramentalism
BR ‚sakrə'mentlız(ə)m
AM ‚sækrə'men(t)l‚ızəm

sacramentalist
BR ‚sakrə'mentlıst, -s
AM ‚sækrə'men(t)ləst, -s

sacramentality
BR ‚sakrəmən'talıti, ‚sakrəmen'talıti
AM ‚sækrəmən'tælədi, ‚sækrə‚men'tælədi

sacramentally
BR ‚sakrə'mentli, ‚sakrə'mentəli
AM ‚sækrə'men(t)li

sacramentarian
BR ‚sakrəmən'tɛːrıən, ‚sakrəmen'tɛːrıən, -z
AM ‚sækrəmən'terıən, 'sækrə‚men'terıən, -z

Sacramento
BR ‚sakrə'mentəʊ
AM ‚sækrə'men(t)oʊ

sacraria
BR sə'krɛːrıə(r)
AM sə'krɛrıə

sacrarium
BR sə'krɛːrıəm
AM sə'krɛrıəm

sacred
BR 'seıkrıd
AM 'seıkrıd

sacredly
BR 'seıkrıdli
AM 'seıkrıdli

sacredness
BR 'seıkrıdnıs
AM 'seıkrıdnıs

sacrementality
BR ‚sakrəm(ə)n'talıti, ‚sakrəmen'talıti
AM 'sækrəmən'tælədi, 'sækrə‚men'tælədi

sacrifice
BR 'sakrıfʌıs, -ız, -ıŋ, -t
AM 'sækrə‚faıs, -ız, -ıŋ, -t

sacrificial
BR ‚sakrı'fıʃl
AM ‚sækrə'fıʃəl

sacrificially
BR ‚sakrı'fıʃli, ‚sakrı'fıʃəli
AM ‚sækrə'fıʃəli

sacrilege
BR 'sakrılıdʒ
AM 'sækrəlıdʒ

sacrilegious
BR ‚sakrı'lıdʒəs
AM ‚sækrə'lıdʒəs

sacrilegiously
BR ‚sakrı'lıdʒəsli
AM ‚sækrə'lıdʒəsli

sacriligious
BR ‚sakrı'lıdʒəs
AM ‚sækrə'lıdʒəs

sacriligiously
BR ‚sakrı'lıdʒəsli
AM ‚sækrə'lıdʒəsli

sacring
BR 'seıkrıŋ
AM 'seıkrıŋ

sacrist
BR 'seıkrıst, 'sakrıst, -s
AM 'seıkrəst, 'sækrəst, -s

sacristan
BR 'sakrıst(ə)n, -z
AM 'sækrəstən, -z

sacristy
BR 'sakrıst‚i, -ız
AM 'sækrəsti, -z

sacroiliac
BR ‚sakrəʊ'ılıak, ‚seıkrəʊ'ılıak
AM ‚sækroʊ'ıli‚æk

sacrosanct
BR 'sakrə(ʊ)san(k)t
AM 'sækroʊ‚sæŋ(k)t, 'sækrə‚sæŋ(k)t, 'sækroʊ‚sæŋk(t), 'sækrə‚sæŋk(t)

sacrosanctity
BR ‚sakrə'san(k)tıti
AM ‚sækroʊ'sæŋ(k)tədi

sacrum
BR 'seıkrəm, 'sakrəm, -z
AM 'sækrəm, 'seıkrəm, -z

sad
BR sad, -ə(r), -ıst
AM sæd, -ər, -əst

Sadat
BR sə'dat
AM sə'dɑt

sadden
BR 'sadn, -z, -ıŋ, -d
AM 'sædən, -z, -ıŋ, -d

saddish
BR 'sadıʃ
AM 'sædıʃ

saddle
BR 'sad|l, -lz, -lıŋ \-lıŋ, -ld
AM 'sæd|əl, -əlz, -(ə)lıŋ, -əld

saddleback
BR 'sadlbak, -s, -t
AM 'sædl‚bæk, -s, -t

saddlebag
BR 'sadlbag, -z
AM 'sædl‚bæg, -z

saddle bow
BR 'sadəl bəʊ, -z
AM 'sædəl ‚boʊ, -z

saddlecloth
BR 'sadlklɒ|θ, -θs \-ðz
AM 'sædl‚klɒ|θ, 'sædl‚klɑ|θ, -θs \-ðz

saddleless
BR 'sadlləs
AM 'sædlləs

saddler
BR 'sadlə(r), -z
AM 'sæd(ə)lər, -z

saddlery
BR 'sadləri
AM 'sædlri, 'sædləri

Sadducean
BR ‚sadjʊ'siːən, ‚sadjʊ'siːən
AM ‚sædʒə'sıən, ‚sædjə'sıən

Sadducee
BR 'sadjʊsiː, 'sadʒʊsiː, -z
AM 'sædʒə‚si, 'sædjə‚si, -z

Sadduceeism
BR ‚sadjʊsiːız(ə)m, 'sadʒʊsiːız(ə)m
AM 'sædʒə‚si‚ızəm, 'sædjə‚si‚ızəm

Sade
writer
BR sɑːd
AM sɑd

sadhu
BR 'sɑːduː, -z
AM 'sɑ‚du, -z

Sadie
BR 'seıdi
AM 'seıdi

sad-iron
BR 'sad‚ʌıən, -z
AM 'sæd‚aı(ə)rn, -z

sadism
BR 'seıdız(ə)m
AM 'seı‚dızəm

sadist
BR 'seıdıst, -s
AM 'seıdıst, -s

sadistic
BR sə'dıstık
AM sə'dıstık

sadistically
BR sə'dıstıkli
AM sə'dıstək(ə)li

Sadler
BR 'sadlə(r)
AM 'sæd(ə)lər

sadly
BR 'sadli
AM 'sædli

sadness
BR 'sadnəs, -ız
AM 'sædnəs, -əz

sadomasochism
BR ‚seıdəʊ'masəkız(ə)m
AM ‚sædoʊ'mæsə‚kızəm, 'seıdoʊ'mæsə‚kızəm

sadomasochist
BR ‚seıdəʊ'masəkıst, -s
AM ‚sædoʊ'mæsəkəst, 'seıdoʊ'mæsəkəst, -s

sadomasochistic
BR ‚seıdəʊ‚masə'kıstık
AM ‚sædoʊ‚mæsə'kıstık, 'seıdoʊ‚mæsə'kıstık

s.a.e.
BR ‚eseı'iː, -z
AM ‚ɛs‚eı'i, -z

saeter
BR 'seıtə(r), 'sɛtə(r), -z
AM 'sɛdər, 'seıdər, -z

safari
BR sə'fɑːr‚i, -ız
AM sə'fɑri, -z

safe
BR seıf, -ə(r), -ıst
AM seıf, -ər, -ıst

safebreaker
BR 'seıf‚breıkə(r), -z
AM 'seıf‚breıkər, -z

safe-conduct
BR ‚seıf'kɒndʌkt, -s
AM 'seıf'kɑndək|(t), -(t)s

safecracker
BR 'seɪf,krækə(r), -z
AM 'seɪf,krækər, -z

safeguard
BR 'seɪfgɑːd, -z, -ɪŋ, -ɪd
AM 'seɪf,gɑrd, -z, -ɪŋ, -əd

safekeeping
BR ,seɪf'kiːpɪŋ
AM 'seɪf,kipɪŋ

safely
BR 'seɪfli
AM 'seɪfli

safeness
BR 'seɪfnɪs
AM 'seɪfnɪs

safety
BR 'seɪfti
AM 'seɪfti

safety-first
BR ,seɪftɪ'fɜːst
AM ,seɪfti'fərst

safetyman
BR 'seɪftɪman
AM 'seɪfti,mæn

safetymen
BR 'seɪftɪmɛn
AM 'seɪfti,mɛn

Safeway
BR 'seɪfweɪ
AM 'seɪf,weɪ

safflower
BR 'saflaʊə(r), -z
AM 'sæf,laʊər, -z

saffron
BR 'safrən
AM 'sæfrən

saffrony
BR 'safrəni
AM 'sæfrəni

safranin
BR 'safrənɪn,
'safrəniːn, -z
AM 'sæfrə,nin,
'sæfrənən, -z

safranine
BR 'safrəniːn, -z
AM 'sæfrə,nin,
'sæfrənən, -z

sag
BR sag, -z, -ɪŋ, -d
AM sæg, -z, -ɪŋ, -d

saga
BR 'sɑːgə(r), -z
AM 'sɑgə, -z

sagacious
BR sə'geɪʃəs
AM sə'geɪʃəs

sagaciously
BR sə'geɪʃəsli
AM sə'geɪʃəsli

sagaciousness
BR sə'geɪʃəsnəs
AM sə'geɪʃəsnəs

sagacity
BR sə'gasɪti
AM sə'gæsədi

sagamore
BR 'sagəmɔː(r), -z
AM 'sægə,mɔ(ə)r, -z

Sagan
BR sa'gan
AM 'seɪgən

Sagar
BR 'seɪgə(r)
AM 'seɪgər

sage
BR seɪdʒ, -ɪz
AM seɪdʒ, -ɪz

sagebrush
BR 'seɪdʒbrʌʃ
AM 'seɪdʒ,brʌʃ

sagely
BR 'seɪdʒli
AM 'seɪdʒli

sageness
BR 'seɪdʒnɪs
AM 'seɪdʒnɪs

Sager
BR 'seɪgə(r)
AM 'seɪgər

sageship
BR 'seɪdʒʃɪp, -s
AM 'seɪdʒ,ʃɪp, -s

saggar
BR 'sagə(r), -z
AM 'sægər, -z

saggy
BR 'sag|i, -ɪə(r), -ɪɪst
AM 'sægi, -ər, -ɪst

Saginaw
BR 'sagɪnɔː(r)
AM 'sægə,nɔ, 'sægə,nɑ

sagitta
BR sə'dʒɪtə(r),
sə'gɪtə(r), 'sadʒɪtə(r),
-z
AM sə'dʒɪdə, 'sædʒədə,
-z

sagittal
BR 'sadʒɪtl
AM 'sædʒədl

Sagittarian
BR ,sadʒɪ'tɛːrɪən, -z
AM ,sædʒə'tɛrɪən, -z

Sagittarius
BR ,sadʒɪ'tɛːrɪəs
AM ,sædʒə'tɛrɪəs

sagittate
BR 'sadʒɪteɪt
AM 'sædʒə,teɪt

sago
BR 'seɪgəʊ
AM 'seɪgoʊ

saguaro
BR sə'gwɑːrəʊ, -z
AM sə'(g)wɑroʊ, -z

sagy
BR 'seɪdʒi
AM 'seɪdʒi

Sahara
BR sə'hɑːrə(r)
AM sə'hɛrə, sə'hɑrə

Saharan
BR sə'hɑːrən, -z
AM sə'hɛrən, sə'hɑrən,
-z

Sahel
BR sə'hɛl, sɑː'hɛl
AM sə'hɛl

Sahelian
BR sə'hiːlɪən,
sɑː'hiːlɪən
AM sə'hilɪən

sahib
BR sɑːb, 'sɑː(h)ɪb, -z
AM ,sɑ(h)ɪb, -z

sahuaro
BR sə'wɑːrəʊ, -z
AM sə'(h)wɑroʊ, -z

Said
BR sʌɪd
AM sɑid

said
BR sɛd
AM sɛd

Saida
BR 'sʌɪdə(r)
AM 'saɪdə

saiga
BR 'sʌɪgə(r), 'seɪgə(r),
-z
AM 'saɪgə, -z

Saigon
BR sʌɪ'gɒn
AM saɪ'gɑn

sail
BR seɪl, -z, -ɪŋ, -d
AM seɪl, -z, -ɪŋ, -d

sailable
BR 'seɪləbl
AM 'seɪləbəl

sailbag
BR 'seɪlbag, -z
AM 'seɪl,bæg, -z

sailboard
BR 'seɪlbɔːd, -z
AM 'seɪl,bɔ(ə)rd, -z

sailboarder
BR 'seɪlbɔːdə(r), -z
AM 'seɪl,bɔrdər, -z

sailboarding
BR 'seɪlbɔːdɪŋ
AM 'seɪl,bɔrdɪŋ

sailboat
BR 'seɪlbəʊt, -s
AM 'seɪl,boʊt, -s

sailcloth
BR 'seɪlklɒθ
AM 'seɪl,klɔθ, 'seɪl,klɑθ

sailer
BR 'seɪlə(r), -z
AM 'seɪlər, -z

sailfish
BR 'seɪlfɪʃ
AM 'seɪl,fɪʃ

sail-fluke
BR 'seɪlfluːk, -s
AM 'seɪl,fluk, -s

sailing
BR 'seɪlɪŋ, -z
AM 'seɪlɪŋ, -z

sailless
BR 'seɪllɪs
AM 'seɪ(l)lɪs

sailmaker
BR 'seɪl,meɪkə(r), -z
AM 'seɪl,meɪkər, -z

sailor
BR 'seɪlə(r), -z
AM 'seɪlər, -z

sailoring
BR 'seɪlərɪŋ
AM 'seɪlərɪŋ

sailorless
BR 'seɪlələs
AM 'seɪlərləs

sailorly
BR 'seɪləli
AM 'seɪlərli

sailplane
BR 'seɪlpleɪn, -z
AM 'seɪl,pleɪn, -z

sainfoin
BR 'sanfɔɪn, 'seɪnfɔɪn
AM 'seɪn,fɔɪn

Sainsbury
BR 'seɪnzb(ə)ri
AM 'seɪnz,bɛri

saint
BR seɪnt, -s
AM seɪnt, -s

saintdom
BR 'seɪntdəm, -z
AM 'seɪntdəm, -z

sainted
BR 'seɪntɪd
AM 'seɪn(t)ɪd

Saint Elmo's fire
BR snt ,ɛlməʊz 'fʌɪə(r)
AM ,seɪn(t) 'ɛlmoʊz
'faɪ(ə)r

Saint-Étienne
BR ,sãtɛ'tjɛn
AM sɛn(t),eɪ'tjɛn

sainthood
BR 'seɪnthʊd
AM 'seɪn(t),(h)ʊd

saintlike
BR 'seɪntlʌɪk
AM 'seɪnt,laɪk

saintliness
BR 'seɪntlɪnɪs
AM 'seɪntlinɪs

saintling
BR 'seɪntlɪŋ, -z
AM 'seɪntlɪŋ, -z

saintly
BR 'seɪntl|i, -ɪə(r), -ɪɪst
AM 'seɪn(t)li, -ər, -ɪst

Saint-Malo
BR s(ə)nt 'mɑːləʊ
AM ,sɑn mə'loʊ

Saint-Moritz
BR ,san mə'rɪts, s(ə)nt
'mɒrɪts

AM seɪn(t) məˈrɪts

saintpaulia
BR ˌseɪnt'pɔːlɪə(r), -z
AM ˌseɪnt'pɔljə,
ˌseɪnt'pɑljə,
ˌseɪnt'pɒlɪə,
ˌseɪnt'pɑlɪə, -z

Saint-Saëns
BR ˌsãˈsɒ̃(s), ˌsãˈsɒ̃z
AM ˌsæn'sɑnz

saintship
BR 'seɪntʃɪp, -s
AM 'seɪntˌʃɪp, -s

Saint-Tropez
BR ˌsã trɒ'peɪ
AM ˌsɑn trə'peɪ

Saipan
BR ˌsaɪ'pan
AM ˌsaɪ'pæn

Saisho
BR 'seɪʃəʊ
AM 'seɪˌʃoʊ

saith
BR sɛθ
AM sɛθ, 'seɪɪθ

saithe
BR seɪθ, seɪð
AM seɪð

Sajama
BR sə'hɑːmə(r)
AM sə'hɑmə

Sakai
BR 'sɑːkʌɪ
AM 'sɑkˌaɪ

sake
BR seɪk, -s
AM seɪk, -s

saké
BR 'sɑːki, 'sakeɪ
AM 'sɑki

saker
BR 'seɪkə(r), -z
AM 'seɪkər, -z

sakeret
BR 'seɪkərɪt, -s
AM 'seɪkərət, -s

Sakhalin
BR 'sakəliːn, 'sakəlɪn,
ˌsakə'liːn, ˌsakə'lɪn
AM 'sækəˌlin

Sakharov
BR 'sakərɒf, 'sakərɒv
AM 'sækəˌrɔv,
'sækəˌraf, 'sækəˌrɑv

saki
BR 'sɑːk|i, -ɪz
AM 'sɑki, -z

Sakta
BR 'ʃɑːktə(r), -z
AM 'ʃɑktə, -z

Sakti
BR 'ʃakti
AM 'ʃɑkti

Saktism
BR 'ʃɑːktɪz(ə)m
AM 'ʃɑkˌtɪzəm

sal
BR sal
AM sæl

salaam
BR sə'lɑːm, -z, -ɪŋ, -d
AM sə'lɑm, -z, -ɪŋ, -d

salability
BR ˌseɪlə'bɪlɪti
AM ˌseɪlə'bɪlɪdi

salable
BR 'seɪləbl
AM 'seɪləbəl

salacious
BR sə'leɪʃəs
AM sə'leɪʃəs

salaciously
BR sə'leɪʃəsli
AM sə'leɪʃəsli

salaciousness
BR sə'leɪʃəsnəs
AM sə'leɪʃəsnəs

salacity
BR sə'lasɪti
AM sə'læsədi

salad
BR 'saləd, -z
AM 'sæləd, -z

salade
BR sə'lɑːd, -z
AM sə'lad, -z

Saladin
BR 'salədɪn
AM 'sælədn

Salamanca
BR ˌsalə'maŋkə(r)
AM ˌsælə'mæŋkə

salamander
BR 'saləmandə(r), -z
AM 'sæləˌmændər, -z

salamandrian
BR ˌsalə'mandrɪən
AM ˌsælə'mændrɪən

salamandrine
BR ˌsalə'mandrʌɪn,
ˌsalə'mandrɪn
AM ˌsælə'mændrən

salamandroid
BR ˌsalə'mandrɔɪd, -z
AM ˌsælə'mænˌdrɔɪd,
-z

salami
BR sə'lɑːmi
AM sə'lɑmi

Salamis
BR 'saləmɪs
AM 'saləməs

sal ammoniac
BR ˌsal ə'məʊnɪak
AM ˌsæl ə'moʊniˌæk

Salang
BR sa'laŋ
AM sɑ'laŋ

salangane
BR 'salaŋgeɪn, -z
AM 'sælənˌgæn,
'sælənˌgeɪn, -z

salariat
BR sə'lɛːrɪət
AM sə'lɛrɪət, sə'lɛriˌæt

salary
BR 'sal(ə)r|i, -ɪz, -ɪd
AM 'sæl(ə)ri, -z, -d

salaryman
BR 'sal(ə)rɪmən
AM 'sæl(ə)rimən

salarymen
BR 'sal(ə)rɪmən
AM 'sæl(ə)rimən

salat
BR sa'lɑːt
AM sa'lat

Salazar
BR ˌsalə'zɑː(r)
AM 'sæləˌzɑr

salbutamol
BR sal'bjuːtəmɒl
AM sæl'bjutəmɔl,
sæl'bjutəmɑl

salchow
BR 'salkəʊ, -z
AM 'sɑlkoʊ, -z

Salcombe
BR 'sɔːlkəm, 'sɒlkəm
AM 'sɔlkəm, 'sɑlkəm

sale
BR seɪl, -z
AM seɪl, -z

saleability
BR ˌseɪlə'bɪlɪti
AM ˌseɪlə'bɪlɪdi

saleable
BR 'seɪləbl
AM 'seɪləbəl

Salem
BR 'seɪləm
AM 'seɪləm

salep
BR 'saləp, 'saləp
AM 'sæləp, sə'lɛp

saleratus
BR ˌsalə'reɪtəs
AM ˌsælə'reɪdəs

Salerno
BR sə'lə:nəʊ
AM sə'lərnoʊ,
sə'lɛrnoʊ

saleroom
BR 'seɪlruːm, 'seɪlrʊm,
-z
AM 'seɪlˌrum,
'seɪlˌrʊm, -z

salesclerk
BR 'seɪlzklɑːk, -s
AM 'seɪlzˌklɜrk, -s

salesgirl
BR 'seɪlzgəːl, -z
AM 'seɪlzˌgərl, -z

Salesian
BR sə'liːzɪən, sə'liːʒn,
-z
AM sə'liʒən, -z

saleslady
BR 'seɪlzˌleɪd|i, -ɪz

salariat
AM 'seɪlzˌleɪdi, -z

salesman
BR 'seɪlzmən
AM 'seɪlzmən

salesmanship
BR 'seɪlzmənʃɪp
AM 'seɪlzmənˌʃɪp

salesmen
BR 'seɪlzmən
AM 'seɪlzmən

salesperson
BR 'seɪlzˌpəːsn
AM 'seɪlzˌpərsən

salesroom
BR 'seɪlzruːm,
'seɪlzrʊm,
AM 'seɪlzˌrum,
'seɪlzˌrʊm, -z

saleswoman
BR 'seɪlzˌwʊmən
AM 'seɪlzˌwʊmən

saleswomen
BR 'seɪlzˌwɪmɪn
AM 'seɪlzˌwɪmɪn

Salford
BR 'sɔːlfəd, 'sɒlfəd
AM 'sɔlfərd, 'sælfərd,
'sɑlfərd

Salian
BR 'seɪlɪən, -z
AM 'seɪljən, 'seɪlɪən, -z

Salic
BR 'salɪk, 'seɪlɪk
AM 'seɪlɪk, 'sælɪk

salicet
BR 'salɪsɛt, -s
AM 'sæləˌsɛt, -s

salicin
BR 'salɪsɪn
AM 'sæləsən

salicine
BR 'salɪsiːn, 'salɪsɪn
AM 'sæləˌsin, 'sæləsən

salicional
BR sə'lɪʃn(ə)l,
sə'lɪʃən(ə)l, -z
AM sə'lɪʃ(ə)nəl, -z

salicylate
BR sə'lɪsɪleɪt, -s
AM sə'lɪsəˌleɪt,
sə'lɪsələt, -s

salicylic
BR ˌsalɪ'sɪlɪk
AM ˌsæləˈsɪlɪk

salicylic acid
BR ˌsalɪsɪlɪk 'asɪd
AM ˌsælə'sɪlɪk 'æsəd

salience
BR 'seɪlɪəns
AM 'seɪljəns, 'seɪlɪəns

saliency
BR 'seɪlɪənsi
AM 'seɪljənsi,
'seɪlɪənsi

salient
BR 'seɪlɪənt, -s

salientian
AM ˈseɪljənt, ˈseɪliənt,
-s

salientian
BR ˌseɪliˈɛnʃn, -z
AM ˌseɪliˌɛn(t)ʃən, -z

saliently
BR ˈseɪliəntli
AM ˈseɪljən(t)li,
ˈseɪliən(t)li

Salieri
BR ˌsæliˈɛːri
AM ˌsɑliˈɛri

saliferous
BR səˈlɪf(ə)rəs
AM səˈlɪf(ə)rəs

salify
BR ˈsælɪfʌɪ, -z, -ɪŋ, -d
AM ˈsæləˌfaɪ, -z, -ɪŋ, -d

Salina
BR səˈlʌɪmə(r)
AM səˈlinə

salina
BR səˈlʌɪmə(r), -z
AM səˈlinə, səˈlaɪnə, -z

Salinas
BR səˈliːnəs
AM səˈlinəs

saline
BR ˈseɪlʌɪn
AM ˈseɪˌlin

Salinger
BR ˈsælɪn(d)ʒə(r)
AM ˈsæləndʒər

salinisation
BR ˌsælɪnʌɪˈzeɪʃn
AM ˌsælənəˈzeɪʃən,
ˌsæləˌnaɪˈzeɪʃən

salinity
BR səˈlɪnɪti
AM seɪˈlɪnɪdi, səˈlɪnɪdi

salinization
BR ˌsælɪnʌɪˈzeɪʃn
AM ˌsælənəˈzeɪʃən,
ˌsæləˌnaɪˈzeɪʃən

salinometer
BR ˌsælɪˈnɒmɪtə(r), -z
AM ˌsæləˈnɑmədər, -z

Salisbury
BR ˈsɔːlzb(ə)ri,
ˈsɒlzb(ə)ri
AM ˈsɔlz,bɛri,
ˈsɔlzb(ə)ri, ˈsalz,bɛri,
ˈsalzb(ə)ri

Salish
BR ˈseɪlɪʃ
AM ˈseɪlɪʃ

saliva
BR səˈlʌɪvə(r)
AM səˈlaɪvə

salivary
BR səˈlʌɪv(ə)ri
AM ˈsæləˌvɛri

salivate
BR ˈsælɪveɪt, -s, -ɪŋ, -ɪd
AM ˈsæləˌveɪt, -ts, -dɪŋ,
-dɪd

salivation
BR ˌsalɪˈveɪʃn
AM ˌsæləˈveɪʃən

Salkeld
BR ˈsɔːlkɛld, ˈsɒlkɛld
AM ˈsɔl,kɛld, ˈsal,kɛld

Salk vaccine
BR ˈsɔːlk ˌvaksiːn
AM ˈsɔk vækˈsin, ˈsak
vækˈsin

sallee
BR ˈsalˌji, -ɪz
AM ˈsæli, -z

sallenders
BR ˈsalɪndəz
AM ˈsæləndərz

sallet
BR ˈsalɪt, -s
AM ˈsælət, -s

Sallis
BR ˈsalɪs
AM ˈsæləs

sallow
BR ˈsaləʊ, -z, -d
AM ˈsæloʊ, -z, -d

sallowish
BR ˈsaləʊɪʃ
AM ˈsæləwɪʃ

sallowness
BR ˈsaləʊnəs
AM ˈsæloʊnəs

sallowy
BR ˈsaləʊi
AM ˈsæləwi

Sallust
BR ˈsaləst
AM ˈsæləst

sally
BR ˈsalˌji, -ɪz, -ɪŋ, -ɪd
AM ˈsæli, -z, -ɪŋ, -d

Sally Lunn
BR ˌsalɪ ˈlʌn, -z
AM ˌsæli ˈlən, -z

sallyport
BR ˈsalɪpɔːt, -s
AM ˈsæli,pɔ(ə)rt, -s

salmagundi
BR ˌsalmaˈɡʌndˌji, -ɪz
AM ˌsælməˈɡəndi, -z

salmanazar
BR ˌsalmaˈneɪzə(r), -z
AM ˌsælməˈnæzər,
ˌsælməˈnazər, -z

salmis
BR ˈsalmˌji, -ɪz
AM ˈsælmi, -z

salmon
BR ˈsamən
AM ˈsæ(l)mən

salmonella
BR ˌsalməˈnɛlə(r)
AM ˌsælməˈnɛlə

salmonellosis
BR ˌsalmənɛˈləʊsɪs
AM ˌsælməˌnɛˈlousəs

salmonid
BR ˈsamənɪd, -z

salivation
AM ˈsæ(l)mənəd,
ˈsæ(l)məˌnɪd, -z

salmonoid
BR ˈsamənɔɪd, -z
AM ˈsæ(l)məˌnɔɪd, -z

salmony
BR ˈsaməni
AM ˈsæ(l)məni

Salome
BR səˈləʊmi
AM ˌsaləˈmeɪ, səˈloʊmi

salon
BR ˈsalɒ̃, ˈsalɒn, -z
AM səˈlɑn, -z

Salonica
BR səˈlɒnɪkə(r)
AM səˈlɑnəkə,
səˈlanəkə

saloon
BR səˈluːn, -z
AM səˈlun, -z

Salop
BR ˈsaləp
AM ˈsæləp

salopette
BR ˌsaləˈpɛt, ˈsaləpɛt, -s
AM ˌsæləˈpɛt, -s

Salopian
BR səˈləʊpɪən, -z
AM səˈloʊpiən, -z

salpiglossis
BR ˌsalpɪˈɡlɒsɪs
AM ˌsælpəˈɡlasəs,
ˌsælpəˈɡlosəs

salpingectomy
BR ˌsalpɪnˈdʒɛktəmˌji,
-ɪz
AM ˌsælpənˈdʒɛktəmi,
-z

salpingitis
BR ˌsalpɪnˈdʒʌɪtɪs
AM ˌsælpənˈdʒaɪdɪs

salsa
BR ˈsalsə(r)
AM ˈsalsə

salsify
BR ˈsalsɪfi
AM ˈsælsəfi, ˈsælsəˌfaɪ

salt
BR ˈsɔːlt, sɒlt, -s, -ɪŋ, -ɪd
AM sɔlt, salt, -s, -ɪŋ, -əd

Saltaire
BR ˌsɔːlˈtɛː(r), sɒlˈtɛː(r)
AM sɔlˈtɛ(ə)r,
salˈtɛ(ə)r

salt-and-pepper
BR ˌsɔːlt(ə)n(d)ˈpɛpə(r)
AM ˈsɔltnˌpɛpər,
ˈsaltnˌpɛpər

saltarelli
BR ˌsaltəˈrɛliː,
ˌsɔːltəˈrɛliː,
ˌsɒltəˈrɛli:
AM ˌsɔltəˈrɛli,
ˌsaltəˈrɛli, ˌsæltəˈrɛli

saltarello
BR ˌsaltəˈrɛləʊ,
ˌsɔːltəˈrɛləʊ,
ˌsɒltəˈrɛləʊ, -z
AM ˌsɔltəˈrɛˌloʊ,
ˌsaltəˈrɛˌloʊ,
ˌsæltəˈrɛˌloʊ, -z

Saltash
BR ˈsɔːltaʃ, ˈsɒltaʃ
AM ˈsɔl,tæʃ, ˈsal,tæʃ

saltation
BR salˈteɪʃn, sɔːlˈteɪʃn,
sɒlˈteɪʃn, -z
AM ˌsɔlˈteɪʃən,
ˌsalˈteɪʃən, -z

saltatorial
BR ˌsaltəˈtɔːrɪəl,
ˌsɔːltəˈtɔːrɪəl,
ˌsɒltəˈtɔːrɪəl
AM ˌsɔltəˈtɔriəl,
ˌsaltəˈtɔriəl,
ˈsæltəˈtɔriəl

saltatory
BR ˈsaltət(ə)ri,
ˈsɔːltət(ə)ri,
ˈsɒltət(ə)ri
AM ˈsɔltəˌtɔri,
ˈsaltəˌtɔri, ˈsæltəˌtɔri

saltbox
BR ˈsɔːltbɒks,
ˈsɒltbɒks, -ɪz
AM ˈsɔlt,baks,
ˈsalt,baks, -əz

Saltburn
BR ˈsɔːltbəːn, ˈsɒltbəːn
AM ˈsɔlt,bərn,
ˈsalt,bərn

saltbush
BR ˈsɔːltbʊʃ, ˈsɒltbʊʃ,
-ɪz
AM ˈsɔlt,bʊʃ, ˈsalt,bʊʃ,
-əz

saltcellar
BR ˈsɔːlt,sɛlə(r),
ˈsɒlt,sɛlə(r), -z
AM ˈsɔlt,sɛlər,
ˈsalt,sɛlər, -z

salter
BR ˈsɔːltə(r), ˈsɒltə(r),
-z
AM ˈsɔltər, ˈsaltər, -z

saltern
BR ˈsɔːltən, ˈsɒltən, -z
AM ˈsɔltərn, ˈsaltərn, -z

Salterton
BR ˈsɔːltət(ə)n,
ˈsɒltət(ə)n
AM ˈsɔltərtən,
ˈsaltərtən

Salthouse
BR ˈsɔːlthaʊs,
ˈsɒlthaʊs
AM ˈsɔlt,(h)aʊs,
ˈsalt,(h)aʊs

saltigrade
BR ˈsaltɪɡreɪd,
ˈsɔːltɪɡreɪd,
ˈsɒltɪɡreɪd, -z

saltimbocca
AM 'sɒltə,greɪd,
'sɑːltə,greɪd, -z
saltimbocca
BR ,saltɪm'bɒkə(r)
AM ,sɑːltəm'boʊkə,
,sɔːltəm'boʊkə
saltine
BR sɔːl'tiːn, sɒl'tiːn, -z
AM sɔl'tin, sɑl'tin, -z
saltiness
BR 'sɔːltɪnɪs, 'sɒltɪnɪs
AM 'sɔltɪnɪs, 'sɑltɪnɪs
salting
BR 'sɔːltɪŋ, 'sɒltɪŋ, -z
AM 'sɔltɪŋ, 'sɑltɪŋ, -z
saltire
BR 'sɔːltaɪə(r),
'sɒltʌɪə(r), -z
AM 'sɔl,taɪ(ə)r
'sɑl,taɪ(ə)r,
'sæl,taɪ(ə)r, -z
saltirewise
BR 'sɔːltaɪəwaɪz,
'sɒltʌɪəwʌɪz
AM 'sɔl,taɪ(ə)r,waɪz,
'sɑl,taɪ(ə)r,waɪz,
'sæl,taɪ(ə)r,waɪz
saltish
BR 'sɔːltɪʃ, 'sɒltɪʃ
AM 'sɔltɪʃ, 'sɑltɪʃ
Salt Lake City
BR ,sɔːlt leɪk 'sɪti,
,sɒlt +
AM ,sɔl(t) ,leɪk 'sɪdi,
,sɑl(t) ,leɪk 'sɪdi
saltless
BR 'sɔːltləs, 'sɒltləs
AM 'sɔltləs, 'sɑltləs
Saltley
BR 'sɔːltli, 'sɒltli
AM 'sɔltli, 'sɑltli
saltlick
BR 'sɔːltlɪk, 'sɒltlɪk, -s
AM 'sɔlt,lɪk, 'sɑlt,lɪk, -s
saltly
BR 'sɔːltli, 'sɒltli
AM 'sɔltli, 'sɑltli
Saltmarsh
BR 'sɔːltmɑːʃ,
'sɒltmɑːʃ
AM 'sɔlt,mɑrʃ,
'sɑlt,mɑrʃ
saltness
BR 'sɔːltnəs, 'sɒltnəs
AM 'sɔltnəs, 'sɑltnəs
saltpan
BR 'sɔːltpan, 'sɒltpan,
-z
AM 'sɔlt,pæn,
'sɑlt,pæn, -z
saltpeter
BR 'sɔːltpiːtə(r),
'sɒlt'piːtə(r)
AM 'sɔlt'pidər,
'sɑlt'pidər
saltpetre
BR 'sɔːlt'piːtə(r),
'sɒlt'piːtə(r)

AM ,sɒlt'pidər,
,sɑlt'pidər
saltshaker
BR 'sɔːlt,ʃeɪkə(r),
'sɒlt,ʃeɪkə(r), -z
AM 'sɔlt,ʃeɪkər,
'sɑlt,ʃeɪkər, -z
saltus
BR 'saltəs, -ɪz
AM 'sæltəs, 'sɔltəs,
'sɑltəs, -əz
saltwater
BR 'sɔːlt,wɔːtə(r),
'sɒlt,wɔːtə(r)
AM 'sɔlt,wɔdər,
'sɑlt,wɑdər
saltwort
BR 'sɔːltwɜːt, 'sɒltwɜːt,
-s
AM 'sɔltwərt,
'sɔltwɔ(ə)rt,
'saltwərt,
'saltwɔ(ə)rt, -s
salty
BR 'sɔːlt|i, 'sɒlt|i, -ɪə(r),
-ɪɪst
AM 'sɔlti, 'sɑlti, -ər, -ɪst
salubrious
BR sə'l(j)uːbrɪəs
AM sə'lubrɪəs
salubriously
BR sə'l(j)uːbrɪəsli
AM sə'lubrɪəsli
salubriousness
BR sə'l(j)uːbrɪəsnəs
AM sə'lubrɪəsnəs
salubrity
BR sə'l(j)uːbrɪti
AM sə'lubrədi
saluki
BR sə'luː|k|i, -ɪz
AM sə'luki, -z
salutarily
BR 'saljʉtrɪli
AM ,sæljə'terəli
salutary
BR 'saljʉt(ə)ri
AM 'sæljə,teri
salutation
BR ,saljʉ'teɪʃn, -z
AM ,sæljə'teɪʃən, -z
salutational
BR ,saljʉ'teɪʃn(ə)l,
,saljʉ'teɪʃən(ə)l
AM ,sæljə'teɪʃ(ə)nəl
salutatorian
BR sə,l(j)uːtə'tɔːrɪən,
-z
AM sə,ludə'tɔrɪən,
,sælədə'tɔrɪən, -z
salutatory
BR sə'l(j)uːtət(ə)ri
AM sə'ludə,tɔri
salute
BR sə'l(j)uːt, -s, -ɪŋ, -ɪd
AM sə'lu|t, -ts, -dɪŋ,
-dəd

saluter
BR sə'l(j)uːtə(r), -z
AM sə'ludər, -z
salvable
BR 'salvəbl
AM 'sælvəbəl
Salvador
BR 'salvadɔː(r),
,salvə'dɔː(r)
AM 'sælvə,dɔ(ə)r
Salvadoran
BR ,salva'dɔːrən, -z
AM ,sælvə'dɔrən, -z
Salvadorean
BR ,salva'dɔːrɪən, -z
AM ,sælvə'dorɪən, -z
Salvadorian
BR ,salva'dɔːrɪən, -z
AM ,sælvə'dorɪən, -z
salvage
BR 'salv|ɪdʒ, -ɪdʒɪz,
-ɪdʒɪŋ, -ɪdʒd
AM 'sælvɪdʒ, -ɪz, -ɪŋ, -d
salvageable
BR 'salvɪdʒəbl
AM 'sælvədʒəbəl
salvager
BR 'salvɪdʒə(r), -z
AM 'sælvədʒər, -z
Salvarsan
BR 'salvəsan
AM 'sælvər,sæn
salvation
BR sal'veɪʃn, -z
AM sæl'veɪʃən, -z
Salvation Army
BR sal,veɪʃn 'ɑːmi
AM sal'veɪʃən 'ɑrmi
salvationism
BR sal'veɪʃŋɪz(ə)m,
sal'veɪʃənɪz(ə)m
AM sæl'veɪʃ(ə),nɪzəm
salvationist
BR sal'veɪʃŋɪst,
sal'veɪʃənɪst, -s
AM sæl'veɪʃ(ə)nəst, -s
salve
BR salv, -z, -ɪŋ, -d
AM sæ(l)v, -z, -ɪŋ, -d
salver
BR 'salvə(r), -z
AM 'sælvər, -z
Salvesen
BR 'salvɪs(ə)n
AM 'sælvəsən
Salveson
BR 'salvɪs(ə)n
AM 'sælvəsən
salvia
BR 'salvɪə(r), -z
AM 'sælvɪə, -z
salvo
BR 'salvəʊ, -z
AM 'sæl,voʊ, -z
sal volatile
BR sal və'latəli,
+ və'latl|i

saltuer
AM ,sæl və'ladl|i
salvor
BR 'salvə(r), -z
AM 'sælvər, -z
Salyut
BR sal'juːt, -s
AM 'sæl,jut, -s
Salzburg
BR 'saltsbɜːg,
'sɔːltsbɜːg, 'sɒltsbɜːg
AM 'sɔlz,bɜrg,
'sɑlz,bɜrg, 'sɔlts,bɜrg,
'sɑlts,bɜrg
Sam
BR sam
AM sæm
samadhi
BR sə'mɑːdi
AM sə'mɑdi
Samantha
BR sə'manθə(r)
AM sə'mænθə
Samar
BR 'sɑːmə(r)
AM sə'mɑr, 'sɑ,mɑr
Samara
BR sə'mɑːrə(r)
AM sə'mɑrə
samara
BR sə'mɑːrə(r), -z
AM 'sæmərə, sə'mɛrə,
-z
Samaria
BR sə'mɛːrɪə(r)
AM sə'mɛrɪə
Samaritan
BR sə'marɪt(ə)n, -z
AM sə'mɛrətn,
sə'mɛrədən, -z
Samaritanism
BR sə'marɪtənɪz(ə)m,
sə'marɪtnɪz(ə)m
AM sə'mɛrətn,ɪzəm,
sə'mɛrədə,nɪzəm
samarium
BR sə'mɛːrɪəm, -z
AM sə'mɛrɪəm, -z
Samarkand
BR ,samaː'kand,
'saməkand
AM 'sæmər,kænd,
,sæmar'kænd
Samarra
BR sə'mɑːrə(r)
AM sə'mɑrə
Sama-Veda
BR ,sɑːmə'veɪdə(r)
AM 'sɑmə'veɪdə
samba
BR 'sambə(r), -z
AM 'sɑmbə, -z
sambar
BR 'sɑːmbə(r),
'sambə(r), -z
AM 'sɑmbər, 'sæmbər,
-z

sambhar
BR 'sɑːmbə(r),
'sambə(r), -z
AM 'sɑːmbər, 'sæmbər,
-z

sambo
BR 'sambəʊ, -z
AM 'sæmboʊ, -z

sambur
BR 'sɑːmbə(r),
'sambə(r), -z
AM 'sɑːmbər, 'sæmbər,
-z

same
BR seɪm
AM seɪm

same-day
BR ˌseɪm'deɪ
AM ˌseɪm'deɪ

samel
BR 'sam(ə)l
AM 'sæməl

sameness
BR 'seɪmnɪs
AM 'seɪmnɪs

same-sex
BR ˌseɪm'sɛks
AM ˌseɪm'sɛks

samey
BR 'seɪmi
AM 'seɪmi

sameyness
BR 'seɪmɪnɪs
AM 'seɪmɪnɪs

samfu
BR 'samfuː, -z
AM 'sæmˌfu, -z

Samhain
BR 'saʊɪn, 'sawɪn, -z
AM 'saʊən, -z
IR 'səʊnʲ

Samian
BR 'seɪmɪən, -z
AM 'seɪmɪən, -z

samisen
BR 'samɪsɛn, -z
AM 'sæməˌsɛn, -z

samite
BR 'samʌɪt, 'seɪmʌɪt, -s
AM 'sæˌmaɪt, 'seɪˌmaɪt,
-s

samizdat
BR 'samɪzdat,
ˌsamɪz'dat
AM 'sɑːmɪz'dæt

Samlesbury
BR 'samzb(ə)ri,
'sɑːmzb(ə)ri
AM 'sæmzˌbɛri

samlet
BR 'samlɪt, -s
AM 'sæmlət, -s

Sammy
BR 'sami
AM 'sæmi

Samnite
BR 'samnʌɪt, -s
AM 'sæmˌnaɪt, -s

Samoa
BR sə'məʊə(r)
AM sə'moʊə

Samoan
BR sə'məʊən, -z
AM sə'moʊən, -z

Sámos
BR 'seɪmɒs, 'samɒs
AM 'seɪˌmɒs, 'seɪˌmɑs

samosa
BR sə'məʊsə(r),
sə'muːsə(r), -z
AM sə'moʊsə, -z

Samothrace
BR 'samə(ʊ)θreɪs
AM 'sæməˌθreɪs

samovar
BR 'saməvɑː(r),
ˌsamə'vɑː(r), -z
AM 'sæməˌvɑr, -z

samoyed
BR ˌsamɔɪ'ɛd,
sə'bɔɪɛd, -z
AM 'sæməˌjɛd,
'sæmɔɪˌjɛd, -z

Samoyedic
BR ˌsamɔɪ'ɛdɪk,
ˌsamə'jedɪk
AM ˌsæmə'jedɪk

samp
BR samp
AM sæmp

sampan
BR 'sampan, -z
AM 'sæmˌpæn, -z

samphire
BR 'samfʌɪə(r)
AM 'sæmˌfaɪ(ə)r

sample
BR 'sɑːmp|l, 'samp|l,
-lz, -lɪŋ \-lɪŋ, -ld
AM 'sæmp|əl, -əlz,
-(ə)lɪŋ, -əld

sampler
BR 'sɑːmplə(r),
'samplə(r), -z
AM 'sæmp(ə)lər, -z

sampling
BR 'sɑːmplɪŋ,
'sɑːmp|lɪŋ, 'samplɪŋ,
'samp|lɪŋ, -z
AM 'sæmp(ə)lɪŋ, -z

Sampson
BR 'sam(p)s(ə)n
AM 'sæm(p)sən

samsara
BR səm'sɑːrə(r)
AM səm'sɑrə

samsaric
BR sam'sarɪk
AM sæm'sɛrɪk

samskara
BR səm'skɑːrə(r), -z
AM sæm'skɑrə, -z

Samson
BR 'sams(ə)n
AM 'sæmsən

Samsung
BR 'samsʌŋ, 'samsʊŋ
AM 'sæmˌsəŋ

Samuel
BR 'samjʊəl, 'samjʊl
AM 'sæmjə(wə)l

Samuels
BR 'samjʊəlz,
'samjʊlz
AM 'sæmj(u)əlz

samurai
BR 'sam(j)ʊrʌɪ, -z
AM 'sæməˌraɪ, -z

san
sanatorium
BR san, -z
AM sæn, -z

Sana'a
BR sɑː'nɑː(r)
AM sɑ'nɑ

San Andreas
BR ˌsan anˌdreɪəs
AM ˌsæn ænˈdreɪəz

San Antonio
BR ˌsan an'təʊnɪəʊ
AM ˌsæn ˌən'toʊnɪoʊ,
ˌsæn ˌæn'toʊnɪoʊ

sanataria
BR ˌsanə'tɛːrɪə(r)
AM ˌsænə'tɛrɪə

sanatarium
BR ˌsanə'tɛːrɪəm, -z
AM ˌsænə'tɛrɪəm, -z

sanative
BR 'sanətɪv
AM 'sænədɪv

Sanatogen®
BR sə'natədʒ(ə)n,
sə'natədʒɛn
AM sə'nædədʒən

sanatoria
BR ˌsanə'tɔːrɪə(r)
AM ˌsænə'tɔrɪə

sanatorium
BR ˌsanə'tɔːrɪəm, -z
AM ˌsænə'tɔrɪəm, -z

sanatory
BR 'sanət(ə)ri
AM 'sænəˌtori

sanbenito
BR ˌsanbə'niːtəʊ, -z
AM ˌsænbə'nidoʊ, -z

San Bernardino
BR ˌsan ˌbəːnə'diːnəʊ
AM ˌsæn bərnə'dinoʊ

Sánchez
BR 'santʃez
AM 'sæn(t)ʃɛz

Sancho
BR 'san(t)ʃəʊ
AM 'sɑn(t)ʃoʊ

San Clemente
BR ˌsan klɪ'mɛnti
AM ˌsæn klə'mɛn(t)i

sancta
BR 'saŋ(k)tə(r)
AM 'sæŋ(k)tə

sancta
sanctorum
BR ˌsaŋ(k)tə
saŋ(k)'tɔːrəm
AM ˌsæŋ(k)tə
ˌsæŋ(k)'tɔrəm

sanctification
BR ˌsaŋ(k)tɪfɪ'keɪʃn
AM ˌsæŋ(k)təfə'keɪʃən

sanctifier
BR 'saŋ(k)tɪfʌɪə(r), -z
AM 'sæŋ(k)təˌfaɪər, -z

sanctify
BR 'saŋ(k)tɪfʌɪ, -z, -ɪŋ,
-d
AM 'sæŋ(k)təˌfaɪ, -z,
-ɪŋ, -d

sanctimonious
BR ˌsaŋ(k)tɪ'məʊnɪəs
AM ˌsæŋ(k)tə'moʊnɪəs

sanctimoniously
BR ˌsaŋ(k)tɪ'məʊnɪəsli
AM ˌsæŋ(k)tə'moʊnɪəsli

sanctimoniousness
BR ˌsaŋ(k)tɪ'məʊnɪəsnəs
AM ˌsæŋ(k)tə'moʊnɪəsnəs

sanctimony
BR 'saŋ(k)tɪməni,
'saŋ(k)tɪməʊni
AM 'sæŋ(k)təˌmoʊni

sanction
BR 'saŋ(k)ʃ|n, -nz,
-nɪŋ \-ənɪŋ, -nd
AM 'sæŋ(k)ʃ|ən, -ənz,
-(ə)nɪŋ, -ənd

sanctionable
BR 'saŋ(k)ʃnəbl,
'saŋ(k)ʃənəbl
AM 'sæŋ(k)ʃənəbəl

sanctitude
BR 'saŋ(k)tɪtjuːd,
'saŋ(k)tɪtʃuːd
AM 'sæŋ(k)təˌt(j)ud

sanctity
BR 'saŋ(k)tɪt|i, -ɪz
AM 'sæŋ(k)tədi, -z

sanctuary
BR 'saŋ(k)tʃʊər|i,
'saŋ(k)tʃʊr|i,
'saŋ(k)tjʊər|i,
'saŋ(k)tjʊr|i, -ɪz
AM 'sæŋk(t)ʃəˌwɛri,
-ɪz

sanctum
BR 'saŋ(k)təm, -z
AM 'sæŋ(k)təm, -z

sanctum
sanctorum
BR ˌsaŋ(k)təm
saŋ(k)'tɔːrəm, -z
AM ˌsæŋ(k)təm
ˌsæŋ(k)'tɔrəm, -z

Sanctus
BR 'saŋ(k)təs, -ɪz
AM 'sæŋ(k)təs, -əz

Sand
George, French
writer
BR sɒ̃
AM sɑn

sand
BR sand, -z, -ɪŋ, -ɪd
AM sænd, -z, -ɪŋ, -əd

sandal
BR 'sandl, -z
AM 'sændəl, -z

sandalwood
BR 'sandlwʊd
AM 'sændl,wʊd

sandarac
BR 'sandərak, -s
AM 'sændə,ræk, -s

sandarach
BR 'sandərak, -s
AM 'sændə,ræk, -s

Sandbach
BR 'san(d)batʃ
AM 'sæn(d),bɑk

sandbag
BR 'san(d)bag, -z, -ɪŋ,
-d
AM 'sæn(d),bæg, -z, -ɪŋ,
-d

sandbagger
BR 'san(d)bagə(r), -z
AM 'sæn(d)bægər, -z

sandbank
BR 'san(d)baŋk, -s
AM 'sæn(d),bæŋk, -s

sandbar
BR 'san(d)bɑː(r), -z
AM 'sæn(d),bɑr, -z

sand-bath
BR 'san(d)|bɑːθ,
'san(d)|baθ,
-bɑːðz \-bɑːθs \-baθs
AM 'sæn(d),bæθ, -s, -ðz

sandblast
BR 'san(d)blɑːst,
'san(d)blast, -s, -ɪŋ, -ɪd
AM 'sæn(d),blæst, -s,
-ɪŋ, -əd

sandblaster
BR 'san(d),blɑːstə(r),
'san(d),blastə(r), -z
AM 'sæn(d),blæstər, -z

sandbox
BR 'san(d)bɒks, -ɪz
AM 'sæn(d),bɑks, -əz

sandboy
BR 'san(d)bɔɪ, -z
AM 'sæn(d),bɔɪ, -z

Sandburg
BR 'san(d)bəg
AM 'sæn(d),bərg

sandcastle
BR 'san(d),kɑːsl,
'san(d),kasl, -z
AM 'sæn(d),kæsəl, -z

sander
BR 'sandə(r), -z
AM 'sændər, -z

sanderling
BR 'sandəlɪŋ, -z
AM 'sændərlɪŋ, -z

sanders
BR 'sandəz, -ɪz
AM 'sændərz, -əz

Sanderson
BR 'sɑːndəs(ə)n,
'sandəs(ə)n
AM 'sændərsən

Sanderstead
BR 'sɑːndəstɛd,
'sɑːndəstɪd,
'sɑːndəstɛd,
'sandəstɛd
AM 'sændər,stɛd

Sandes
BR 'sandz
AM 'sæn(d)z

sandfly
BR 'san(d)flʌɪ, -z
AM 'sæn(d),flaɪ, -z

Sandford
BR 'san(d)fəd
AM 'sæn(d)fərd

Sandgate
BR 'san(d)geɪt
AM 'sæn(d),geɪt

sandglass
BR 'san(d)glɑːs,
'san(d)glas, -ɪz
AM 'sæn(d),glæs, -əz

sandgrouse
BR 'san(d)graʊs
AM 'sæn(d),graʊs

sandhi
BR 'sandi, 'sandhiː
AM 'sændi, 'sandi

sandhog
BR 'sandhɒg, -z
AM 'sæn(d),(h)ɔg,
'sæn(d),(h)ɑg, -z

Sandhurst
BR 'sandhəst
AM 'sæn(d),(h)ərst

San Diego
BR ,san dɪ'eɪgəʊ
AM ,sæn dɪ'eɪgoʊ

sandiness
BR 'sandɪnɪs
AM 'sændɪnɪs

Sandinista
BR ,sandɪ'nɪstə(r), -z
AM ,sændə'nɪstə, -z

sandiver
BR 'sandɪvə(r)
AM 'sændəvər

sandlike
BR 'sandlʌɪk
AM 'sæn(d),laɪk

sandlot
BR 'sandlɒt, -s
AM 'sæn(d),lɑt, -s

sandman
BR 'san(d)man
AM 'sæn(d),mæn

Sandoval
BR 'sandəval
AM 'sændə,vɑl

Sandown
BR 'sandaʊn
AM 'sæn,daʊn

Sandoz
BR 'sandɒz
AM 'sændoʊz

sandpaper
BR 'san(d),peɪpə(r),
-əz, -(ə)rɪŋ, -əd
AM 'sæn(d),peɪpər,
-ərz, -(ə)rɪŋ, -ərd

sandpiper
BR 'san(d),pʌɪpə(r), -z
AM 'sæn(d),paɪpər, -z

sandpit
BR 'san(d),pɪt, -s
AM 'sæn(d),pɪt, -s

Sandra
BR 'sandrə(r),
'sɑːndrə(r)
AM 'sændrə

Sandringham
BR 'sandrɪŋəm
AM 'sændrɪŋəm

Sands
BR sandz
AM sæn(d)z

sandshoe
BR 'san(d),ʃuː, -z
AM 'sæn(d),ʃu, -z

sandsoap
BR 'san(d),səʊp, -s
AM 'sæn(d),soʊp, -s

sandstock
BR 'san(d),stɒk, -s
AM 'sæn(d),stɑk, -s

sandstone
BR 'san(d),stəʊn
AM 'sæn(d),stoʊn

sandstorm
BR 'san(d),stɔːm, -z
AM 'sæn(d),stɔ(ə)rm,
-z

Sandwich
town
BR 'san(d)wɪtʃ,
'san(d)wɪdʒ
AM 'sæn,(d)wɪtʃ

sandwich
BR 'sanwɪdʒ,
'samwɪdʒ, 'sanwɪtʃ,
'samwɪtʃ, -ɪz, -ɪŋ, -t
AM 'sæn,(d)wɪ|tʃ,
-tʃɪz \-dʒɪz
-tʃɪŋ \-dʒɪŋ, -tʃt

sandwich-board
BR 'sanwɪdʒ bɔːd,
'samwɪdʒ bɔːd,
'sanwɪtʃ bɔːd,
'samwɪtʃ bɔːd, -z
AM 'sæn,(d)wɪtʃ,
bɔ(ə)rd, -z

sandwich-man
BR 'sanwɪdʒman,
'samwɪdʒman,

sandwich-men
'sanwɪtʃman,
'samwɪtʃman
AM 'sæn,(d)wɪdʒ,mæn

sandwich-men
BR 'sanwɪdʒmɛn,
'samwɪdʒmɛn,
'sanwɪtʃmɛn,
'samwɪtʃmɛn
AM 'sæn,(d)wɪdʒ,mɛn

sandwort
BR 'san(d)wəːt, -s
AM 'sæn(d)wərt,
'sæn(d),wɔ(ə)rt, -s

sandy
BR 'sand|i, -ɪə(r), -ɪɪst
AM 'sændi, -ər, -ɪst

sandyish
BR 'sandɪɪʃ
AM 'sændɪɪʃ

Sandys
BR sandz
AM sæn(d)z

sane
BR seɪn, -ə(r), -ɪst
AM seɪn, -ər, -ɪst

sanely
BR 'seɪnli
AM 'seɪnli

saneness
BR 'seɪnnɪs
AM 'seɪ(n)nɪs

San Fernando
BR ,san fə'nandəʊ
AM ,sæn fər'nændoʊ

Sanford
BR 'sanfəd
AM 'sænfərd

sanforise
BR 'sanfərʌɪz, -ɪz, -ɪŋ,
-d
AM 'sænfə,raɪz, -ɪz, -ɪŋ,
-d

sanforize
BR 'sanfərʌɪz, -ɪz, -ɪŋ,
-d
AM 'sænfə,raɪz, -ɪz, -ɪŋ,
-d

San Francisco
BR ,san fr(ə)n'sɪskəʊ
AM ,sæn frən'sɪskoʊ,
,sæn ,fræn'sɪskoʊ

sang
BR saŋ
AM sæŋ

sanga
BR 'saŋgə(r), -z
AM 'sæŋgə, -z

sangar
BR 'saŋgə(r), -z
AM 'sæŋgər, -z

sangaree
BR ,saŋgə'riː
AM ,sæŋgə'ri

sang-de-bœuf
BR ,saŋdə'bəːf
AM 'sæŋdə'bəf

Sanger
BR 'saŋə(r)

AM 'sæŋ(g)ər
sang-froid
 BR ˌsɒŋ'frwɑ:(r),
 ˌsɑːŋ'frwɑ:(r),
 ˌsɑŋ'frwɑ:(r)
 AM sæŋ'f(r)wɑ,
 sɑŋ'f(r)wɑ
sangha
 BR 'sʌŋgə(r),
 'saŋgə(r), -z
 AM 'sɑŋ(g)ə, -z
Sango
 BR 'saŋgəʊ, 'sɑːŋgəʊ
 AM 'sɑŋˌgoʊ
sangrail
 BR saŋ'greɪl
 AM sæŋ'greɪl
sangría
 BR san'gri:ə(r),
 'saŋgrɪə(r)
 AM sæŋ'griə
Sangster
 BR 'saŋstə(r)
 AM 'sæŋstər
sanguification
 BR ˌsaŋwɪfɪ'keɪʃn
 AM ˌsæŋgwəfə'keɪʃən
sanguinarily
 BR 'saŋgwɪn(ə)rɪli
 AM 'sæŋgwəˌnɛrəli
sanguinariness
 BR 'saŋgwɪn(ə)rɪnɪs
 AM 'sæŋgwəˌnɛrɪnɪs
sanguinary
 BR 'saŋgwɪn(ə)ri
 AM 'sæŋgwəˌnɛri
sanguine
 BR 'saŋgwɪn
 AM 'sæŋgwən
sanguinely
 BR 'saŋgwɪnli
 AM 'sæŋgwənli
sanguineness
 BR 'saŋgwɪnnɪs
 AM 'sæŋgwə(n)nɪs
sanguineous
 BR saŋ'gwɪnɪəs
 AM sæŋ'gwɪnɪəs
sanguinity
 BR saŋ'gwɪnɪti
 AM sæŋ'gwɪnɪdi
Sanhedrim
 BR san'hɛdrɪm,
 san'hi:drɪm,
 'sanɪdrɪm
 AM sæn'hidrɪm,
 san'hidrɪm,
 sæn'hɛdrəm,
 san'hɛdrəm
Sanhedrin
 BR san'hɛdrɪn,
 san'hi:drɪn,
 'sanɪdrɪn
 AM sæn'hidrɪn,
 san'hidrɪn,
 sæn'hɛdrən,
 san'hɛdrən

sanicle
 BR 'sanɪkl, -z
 AM 'sænəkl, -z
sanidine
 BR 'sanɪdi:n
 AM 'sænəˌdin
sanies
 BR 'seɪnɪi:z
 AM 'seɪniˌiz
sanify
 BR 'sanɪfaɪ, -z, -ɪŋ, -d
 AM 'sænəˌfaɪ, -z, -ɪŋ, -d
sanious
 BR 'seɪnɪəs
 AM 'seɪnɪəs
sanitaria
 BR ˌsanɪ'tɛːrɪə(r)
 AM ˌsænə'tɛriə
sanitarian
 BR ˌsanɪ'tɛːrɪən, -z
 AM ˌsænə'tɛriən, -z
sanitarily
 BR 'sanɪtrɪli
 AM ˌsænəˌtɛrəli
sanitariness
 BR 'sanɪtrɪnɪs
 AM ˌsænəˌterɪnɪs
sanitarium
 BR ˌsanɪ'tɛːrɪəm, -z
 AM ˌsænə'tɛriəm, -z
sanitary
 BR 'sanɪt(ə)ri
 AM 'sænəˌteri
sanitate
 BR 'sanɪteɪt, -s, -ɪŋ, -ɪd
 AM 'sænəˌteɪ|t, -ts, -dɪŋ, -dɪd
sanitation
 BR ˌsanɪ'teɪʃn
 AM ˌsænə'teɪʃən
sanitationist
 BR ˌsanɪ'teɪʃnɪst, ˌsanɪ'teɪʃənɪst, -s
 AM ˌsænə'teɪʃənəst, -s
sanitisation
 BR ˌsanɪtaɪ'zeɪʃn
 AM ˌsænədə'zeɪʃən, ˌsænəˌtaɪ'zeɪʃən
sanitise
 BR 'sanɪtaɪz, -ɪz, -ɪŋ, -d
 AM 'sænəˌtaɪz, -ɪz, -ɪŋ, -d
sanitiser
 BR 'sanɪtaɪzə(r), -z
 AM 'sænəˌtaɪzər, -z
sanitization
 BR ˌsanɪtaɪ'zeɪʃn
 AM ˌsænədə'zeɪʃən, ˌsænəˌtaɪ'zeɪʃən
sanitize
 BR 'sanɪtaɪz, -ɪz, -ɪŋ, -d
 AM 'sænəˌtaɪz, -ɪz, -ɪŋ, -d
sanitizer
 BR 'sanɪtaɪzə(r), -z
 AM 'sænəˌtaɪzər, -z

sanitoria
 BR ˌsanɪ'tɔːrɪə(r)
 AM ˌsænə'tɔriə
sanitorium
 BR ˌsanɪ'tɔːrɪəm, -z
 AM ˌsænə'tɔriəm, -z
sanity
 BR 'sanɪti
 AM 'sænədi
San Jacinto
 BR ˌsan dʒə'sɪntəʊ
 AM ˌsæn dʒə'sɪn(t)oʊ
San José
 BR ˌsan həʊ'zeɪ
 AM ˌsæn (h)oʊ'zeɪ
San Juan
 BR san 'hwɑːn
 AM san '(h)wɑn
sank
 BR saŋk
 AM sæŋk
Sankey
 BR 'saŋki
 AM 'sæŋki
San Marino
 BR ˌsan mə'ri:nəʊ
 AM ˌsæn mə'rinoʊ
sannyasi
 BR sən'jɑ:si
 AM sən'jɑsi
sanpro
 sanitary protection
 BR 'sanprəʊ
 AM 'sænˌproʊ
San Quentin
 BR san 'kwɛntɪn
 AM ˌsæn 'kwɛntn
sans
 BR sanz
 AM sænz
San Salvador
 BR san 'salvədɔ:(r)
 AM ˌsæn 'sælvəˌdɔ(ə)r
 SP san ˌsalβa'ðor
sans-culotte
 BR ˌsan(z)kjə'lɒt, -s
 AM ˌsæn(z)kjə'lɑt, -s
sans-culottism
 BR ˌsan(z)kjə'lɒtɪz(ə)m
 AM ˌsæn(z)kjə'lɑˌtɪzəm
sanserif
 BR ˌsan(z)'sɛrɪf
 AM ˌsæn'sɛrəf
Sanskrit
 BR 'sanskrɪt
 AM 'sænˌskrɪt
Sanskritic
 BR san'skrɪtɪk
 AM sæn'skrɪdɪk
Sanskritist
 BR 'sanskrɪtɪst, -s
 AM 'sænskrətəst, -s
Sansom
 BR 'sans(ə)m
 AM 'sænsəm
Sanson
 BR 'sansn

AM 'sænsən
Sansovino
 BR ˌsansə'vi:nəʊ
 AM ˌsænsə'vinoʊ
sans serif
 BR ˌsan(z) 'sɛrɪf
 AM ˌsæn(z) 'sɛrəf
Santa
 BR 'santə(r), -z
 AM 'sæn(t)ə, -z
Santa Ana
 BR ˌsantə(r) 'anə(r)
 AM ˌsæn(t)ə 'ænə
Santa Catarina
 BR ˌsantə ˌkatə'ri:nə(r)
 AM ˌsæn(t)ə ˌkædə'rinə
Santa Claus
 BR ˌsantə 'klɔ:z, 'santə klɔ:z, -ɪz
 AM ˌsæn(t)ə ˌklɔz, 'sæn(t)ə ˌklɑz, -əz
Santa Cruz
 BR ˌsantə 'kru:z
 AM ˌsæn(t)ə 'kruz
Santa Fé
 BR ˌsantə 'feɪ
 AM ˌsæn(t)ə 'feɪ
Santander
 BR ˌsantan'dɛː(r), ˌsantən'dɛː(r), san'tandə(r)
 AM ˌsanˌtan'dɛ(ə)r
Santayana
 BR ˌsantə'jɑ:nə(r)
 AM ˌsantə'jɑnɑ
Santiago
 BR ˌsanti'ɑ:gəʊ
 AM ˌsæn(t)i'ɑgoʊ
Santiago de Compostela
 BR ˌsanti'ɑ:gəʊ də ˌkɒmpə'stɛlə(r)
 AM ˌsæn(t)i'ɑgoʊ də ˌkɑmpə'stɛlə
Santo Domingo
 BR ˌsantəʊ də'mɪŋgəʊ
 AM ˌsæn(t)oʊ də'mɪŋgoʊ
santolina
 BR ˌsantə'li:nə(r), -z
 AM ˌsæn(t)ə'linə, -z
santonica
 BR san'tɒnɪkə(r), -z
 AM sæn'tɑnəkə, -z
santonin
 BR 'santənɪn
 AM 'sæntnən
Santoríni
 BR ˌsantə'ri:ni
 AM ˌsæn(t)ə'rini
Santos
 BR 'santɒs
 AM 'sæntoʊs
sanyasi
 BR sən'jɑ:si
 AM sən'jɑ:si

Sanyo®
BR 'sanjəʊ
AM 'sænjoʊ

São Paulo
BR saʊ(m) 'paʊləʊ
AM ˌsaʊ(m) 'paʊloʊ

São Tomé
BR ˌsaʊ(n) təʊ'meɪ
AM ˌsaʊ toʊ'meɪ

sap
BR sap, -s, -ɪŋ, -t
AM sæp, -s, -ɪŋ, -t

sapajou
BR 'sapədʒuː, -z
AM 'sæpə,(d)ʒu,
ˌsæpə'(d)ʒu, -z

sapan
BR 'sapan
AM sə'pæn, 'sæ,pæn

sapanwood
BR 'sapanwʊd
AM sə'pæn,wʊd,
'sæ,pæn,wʊd

sapele
BR sə'piːli
AM sə'pili

sapful
BR 'sapf(ʊ)l
AM 'sæpfəl

saphenous
BR sə'fiːnəs
AM sə'finəs

sapid
BR 'sapɪd
AM 'sæpəd

sapidity
BR sə'pɪdɪti
AM sə'pɪdɪdi

sapience
BR 'seɪpɪəns
AM 'seɪpɪəns, 'sæpɪəns

sapiens
BR 'sapɪɛnz
AM 'seɪpɪəns, 'sæpɪəns

sapient
BR 'seɪpɪənt
AM 'seɪpɪənt,
'sæpɪəntli

sapiential
BR ˌseɪpɪ'ɛnʃl
AM ˌseɪpi'ɛn(t)ʃəl,
ˌsæpi'ɛn(t)ʃəl

sapiently
BR 'seɪpɪəntli
AM 'seɪpɪən(t)li,
'sæpɪən(t)li

Sapir
BR sə'pɪə(r), 'seɪpɪə(r)
AM sə'pɪ(ə)r

sapless
BR 'saplǝs
AM 'sæpləs

sapling
BR 'saplɪŋ, -z
AM 'sæplɪŋ, -z

sapodilla
BR ˌsapə'dɪlə(r), -z

AM ˌsæpə'dɪlə, -z

saponaceous
BR ˌsapə'neɪʃəs
AM ˌsæpə'neɪʃəs

saponifiable
BR sə'pɒnɪfʌɪəbl
AM sə'pɑnəˌfaɪəbəl

saponification
BR sə,pɒnɪfɪ'keɪʃn
AM sə,pɑnəfə'keɪʃən

saponify
BR sə'pɒnɪfʌɪ, -z, -ɪŋ, -d
AM sə'pɑnə,faɪ, -z, -ɪŋ,
-d

saponin
BR 'sapənɪn, -z
AM 'sæpənən, -z

sapor
BR 'seɪpɔː(r), 'seɪpə(r),
-z
AM 'seɪpər, -z

sappanwood
BR 'sapənwʊd
AM sə'pæn,wʊd,
'sæ,pæn,wʊd

sapper
BR 'sapə(r), -z
AM 'sæpər, -z

Sapphic
BR 'safɪk, -s
AM 'sæfɪk, -s

sapphire
BR 'safʌɪə(r), -z
AM 'sæ,faɪ(ə)r, -z

sapphirine
BR 'safɪrʌɪn, 'safɪrɪn,
-z
AM 'sæfərən,
'sæfəˌrin, 'sæfəˌraɪn,
-z

Sapphism
BR 'safɪz(ə)m
AM 'sæˌfɪzəm

Sappho
BR 'safəʊ
AM 'sæfoʊ

sappily
BR 'sapɪli
AM 'sæpɪli

sappiness
BR 'sapɪnɪs
AM 'sæpɪnɪs

Sapporo
BR sə'pɔːrəʊ
AM sə'pɔroʊ

sappy
BR 'sapi
AM 'sæpi

saprogenic
BR ˌsaprə(ʊ)'dʒɛnɪk
AM ˌsæproʊ'dʒɛnɪk

saprophagous
BR sə'prɒfəgəs
AM sə'prɑfəgəs

saprophile
BR 'saprə(ʊ)fʌɪl, -z
AM 'sæprə,faɪl, -z

---

saprophilous
BR sə'prɒfɪləs
AM sə'prɑfələs

saprophyte
BR 'saprə(ʊ)fʌɪt, -s
AM 'sæprəˌfaɪt, -s

saprophytic
BR ˌsaprə'fɪtɪk
AM ˌsæprə'fɪdɪk

sapsucker
BR 'sap,sʌkə(r), -z
AM 'sæp,sʌkər, -z

sapwood
BR 'sapwʊd
AM 'sæp,wʊd

Sara
BR 'sɛːrə(r), 'saːrə(r)
AM 'sɛrə

saraband
BR 'sarəband, -z
AM 'sɛrə,bænd, -z

sarabande
BR 'sarəband, -z
AM 'sɛrə,bænd, -z

Saracen
BR 'sarəsn, -z
AM 'sɛrəsən, -z

Saracenic
BR ˌsarə'sɛnɪk
AM ˌsɛrə'sɛnɪk

Saragossa
BR ˌsarə'gɒsə(r)
AM ˌsɛrə'gɒsə,
ˌsɛrə'gɑsə

Sarah
BR 'sɛːrə(r)
AM 'sɛrə

Sarajevo
BR ˌsarə'jeɪvəʊ
AM ˌsarə'jeɪvoʊ

saran
BR sə'ran
AM sə'ræn

sarangi
BR saː'rʌŋɡˌli,
sə'raŋgli, -ɪz
AM sə'raŋgi, sə'ræŋgi,
-z

Saransk
BR sə'ransk
AM sə'rɑnsk

Saranwrap
BR sə'ranrap
AM sə'ræn,ræp

sarape
BR sɛ'rɑːp|eɪ, sə'rɑːp|i,
-eɪz \-ɪz
AM sə'rɑpi, sə'rɑpeɪ, -z

Saratoga
BR ˌsarə'təʊɡə(r)
AM ˌsɛrə'toʊɡə

Sarawak
BR sə'rɑːwak
AM sə'rɑwæk

sarcasm
BR 'saːkaz(ə)m
AM 'sɑr,kæzəm

---

sarcastic
BR saː'kastɪk
AM sɑr'kæstɪk

sarcastically
BR saː'kastɪkli
AM sɑr'kæstək(ə)li

sarcelle
BR saː'sɛl, -z
AM sɑr'sɛl, -z

sarcenet
BR 'saːsnɪt
AM 'sɑrsnət

sarcoma
BR saː'kəʊmə(r), -z
AM sɑr'koʊmə, -z

sarcomata
BR saː'kəʊmətə(r)
AM sɑr'koʊmədə

sarcomatosis
BR saːˌkəʊmə'təʊsɪs
AM sɑrˌkoʊmə'toʊsəs

sarcomatous
BR saː'kəʊmətəs
AM sɑr'koʊmədəs

sarcophagi
BR saː'kɒfəgʌɪ,
saː'kɒfədʒʌɪ
AM sɑr'kafə,gaɪ,
sɑr'kafəˌdʒaɪ

sarcophagus
BR saː'kɒfəgəs, -ɪz
AM sɑr'kɑfəgəs, -əz

sarcoplasm
BR 'saːkəplaz(ə)m
AM 'sɑrkəˌplæzəm

sarcoptic
BR saː'kɒptɪk
AM sɑr'kɑptɪk

sarcous
BR 'saːkəs
AM 'sɑrkəs

sard
BR saːd, -z
AM sɑrd, -z

Sardanapalian
BR ˌsaː'dənə'peɪlɪən,
ˌsaː'dnə'peɪlɪən
AM 'sɑrdnə,peɪlɪən,
'sɑrdnə,peɪljən,
'sɑrdnə,pɑlɪən,
'sɑrdnə,pɑljən

Sardanapalus
BR ˌsaːdə'napələs,
ˌsaːdn'apələs,
ˌsaːdə'naplǝs
AM sɑrdn'apələs

Sardegna
BR saː'dɛnjə(r)
AM sɑr'dɛnjə

sardelle
BR saː'dɛl, -z
AM sɑr'dɛl(ə), -z

sardine[1]
fish
BR saː'diːn, -z
AM sɑr'din, -z

sardine²
stone
BR ˈsɑːdʌɪn
AM ˈsɑrˌdʌɪn, ˈsɑrdn

Sardinia
BR sɑːˈdɪnɪə(r)
AM sɑrˈdɪnɪə

Sardinian
BR sɑːˈdɪnɪən, -z
AM sɑrˈdɪnɪən, -z

Sardis
BR ˈsɑːdɪs
AM ˈsɑrdəs

sardius
BR ˈsɑːdɪəs, -ɪz
AM ˈsɑrdɪəs, -əz

sardonic
BR sɑːˈdɒnɪk
AM sɑrˈdɑnɪk

sardonically
BR sɑːˈdɒnɪkli
AM sɑrˈdɑnək(ə)li

sardonicism
BR sɑːˈdɒnɪsɪz(ə)m, -z
AM sɑrˈdɑnəˌsɪzəm, -z

sardonyx
BR ˈsɑːdənɪks,
sɑːˈdɒnɪks, -ɪz
AM sɑrˈdɑnɪks, -ɪz

saree
BR ˈsɑːrˌli, -ɪz
AM ˈsɑri, -z

Sargant
BR ˈsɑːdʒ(ə)nt
AM ˈsɑrdʒənt

Sargasso
BR sɑːˈgasəʊ
AM sɑrˈgæsoʊ

sarge
BR sɑːdʒ
AM sɑrdʒ

Sargent
BR ˈsɑːdʒnt
AM ˈsɑrdʒənt

Sargodha
BR sɑːˈɡəʊdə(r)
AM sɑrˈɡoʊdə

Sargon
BR ˈsɑːgɒn
AM ˈsɑrˌɡɒn, ˈsɑrˌɡɑn

sari
BR ˈsɑːrˌli, -ɪz
AM ˈsɑri, -z

sarin
BR sɑːˈriːn, ˈsɑrɪn
AM sɑˈrin

sark
BR sɑːk, -s
AM sɑrk, -s

sarkily
BR ˈsɑːkɪli
AM ˈsɑrkəli

sarkiness
BR ˈsɑːkɪnɪs
AM ˈsɑrkɪnɪs

sarking
BR ˈsɑːkɪŋ

sarky
BR ˈsɑːkˌli, -ɪə(r), -ɪɪst
AM ˈsɑrki, -ər, -ɪst

Sarmatia
BR sɑːˈmeɪʃ(ɪ)ə(r)
AM sɑrˈmeɪʃ(i)ə

Sarmatian
BR sɑːˈmeɪʃn, -z
AM sɑrˈmeɪʃən, -z

sarmentose
BR sɑːmˈ(ə)ntəʊs,
ˌsɑːmˈ(ə)nˈtəʊs,
ˈsɑːmˈ(ə)ntəʊz,
ˌsɑːmˈ(ə)nˈtəʊz
AM sɑrˈmɛnˌtoʊz,
ˈsɑrmənˌtoʊz,
sɑrˈmɛnˌtoʊs,
ˈsɑrmənˌtoʊs

sarmentous
BR sɑːˈmɛntəs
AM sɑrˈmɛn(t)əs

sarnie
sandwich
BR ˈsɑːnˌli, -ɪz
AM ˈsɑrni, -z

sarod
BR səˈrəʊd, -z
AM səˈroʊd, -z

sarong
BR səˈrɒŋ, -z
AM səˈrɔŋ, səˈrɑŋ, -z

Saronic
BR səˈrɒnɪk
AM səˈrɑnɪk

Saros
BR ˈsɛːrɒs
AM ˈsɛrɔs, ˈsɛrɑs

Saroyan
BR səˈrɔɪən
AM səˈrɔɪən

sarracenia
BR ˌsarəˈsiːnɪə(r)
AM ˌsɛrəˈsiniə

Sarre
BR sɑː(r)
AM sɑr

sarrusophone
BR səˈruːzəfəʊn, -z
AM səˈruzəˌfoʊn,
səˈrəsəˌfoʊn, -z

sarsaparilla
BR ˌsɑːsˈ(ə)pəˈrɪlə(r),
ˌsas(ə)pəˈrɪlə(r), -z
AM ˌsɑrs(ə)pəˈrɪlə,
ˌsæspəˈrɪlə, -z

sarsen
BR ˈsɑːsn, -z
AM ˈsɑrsən, -z

sarsenet
BR ˈsɑːs(ə)nɪt, ˈsɑːsnɪt
AM ˈsɑrsnət

Sarson
BR ˈsɑːsn
AM ˈsɑrsən

Sarto
BR ˈsɑːtəʊ
AM ˈsɑrˌtoʊ

sartorial
BR sɑːˈtɔːrɪəl
AM sɑrˈtorɪəl

sartorially
BR sɑːˈtɔːrɪəli
AM sɑrˈtorɪəli

sartorii
BR sɑːˈtɔːrɪʌɪ
AM sɑrˈtɔriˌʌɪ

sartorius
BR sɑːˈtɔːrɪəs
AM sɑrˈtɔriəs

Sartre
BR ˈsɑːtrə(r)
AM ˈsɑrtr(ə)

Sartrean
BR ˈsɑːtrɪən, -z
AM ˈsɑrtriən, -z

Sarum
BR ˈsɛːrəm
AM ˈsɛrəm

SAS¹
computer program
BR sas
AM sæs

SAS²
military unit, airline
BR ˌɛsˈeɪˈɛs
AM ˌɛsˌeɪˈɛs

sash
BR saʃ, -ɪz, -t
AM sæʃ, -əz, -t

Sasha
BR ˈsaʃə(r)
AM ˈsɑʃə

sashay
BR ˈsaʃeɪ, -z, -ɪŋ, -d
AM sæˈʃeɪ, -z, -ɪŋ, -d

sashimi
BR ˈsaʃimi
AM sɑˈʃimi

sasin
BR ˈsasɪn, -z
AM ˈseɪsɪn, ˈsæsn, -z

sasine
BR ˈseɪsɪn, -z
AM ˈseɪsn, -z

Saskatchewan
BR səˈskatʃʊən
AM səˈskætʃəwən,
sæˈskætʃəwən

Saskatoon
BR ˌsaskəˈtuːn
AM ˌsæskəˈtun

Saskia
BR ˈsaskɪə(r)
AM ˈsæskiə

sasquatch
BR ˈsaskwatʃ,
ˈsaskwɒtʃ
AM ˈsæsˌkwætʃ,
ˈsæsˌkwɑtʃ

sass
BR sas, -ɪz, -ɪŋ, -t
AM sæs, -əz, -ɪŋ, -t

sassaby
BR ˈsasəbˌli, -ɪz

sassafras
BR ˈsasəfras, -ɪz
AM ˈsæs(ə)ˌfræs, -əz

Sassanian
BR saˈseɪnɪən, -z
AM səˈsænɪən,
səˈseɪnɪən, -z

Sassanid
BR ˈsasənɪd, -z
AM ˈsæsənəd,
səˈsænəd, -z

Sassenach
BR ˈsasənax, ˈsasənak,
-s
AM ˈsæsəˌnæk, -s

sassily
BR ˈsasɪli
AM ˈsæsəli

sassiness
BR ˈsasɪnɪs
AM ˈsæsɪnɪs

Sassoon
BR səˈsuːn
AM səˈsun, ˌsæˈsun

sassy
BR ˈsasˌli, -ɪə(r), -ɪɪst
AM ˈsæsi, -ər, -ɪst

sastrugi
BR səˈstruːgi
sɑˈstruːgi
AM səˈstrugi,
sæˈstrugi, ˈzæstrəgi,
ˈsæstrəgi

SAT®
BR ˌɛsˈeɪˈtiː
AM ˌɛsˌeɪˈti

sat
BR sat
AM sæt

Satan
BR ˈseɪtn
AM ˈseɪtn

satang
BR saˈtaŋ, -z
AM saˈtaŋ, -z

satanic
BR səˈtanɪk
AM səˈtænɪk,
seɪˈtænɪk

satanically
BR səˈtanɪkli
AM səˈtænək(ə)li,
seɪˈtænək(ə)li

satanise
BR ˈseɪtnˌʌɪz, -ɪz, -ɪŋ, -d
AM ˈseɪtnˌaɪz, -ɪz, -ɪŋ, -d

satanism
BR ˈseɪtnˌɪz(ə)m
AM ˈseɪtnˌɪzəm

satanist
BR ˈseɪtnˌɪst, -s
AM ˈseɪtnˌəst, -s

satanize
BR ˈseɪtnˌʌɪz, -ɪz, -ɪŋ, -d
AM ˈseɪtnˌaɪz, -ɪz, -ɪŋ, -d

satanology
BR ˌseɪtn̩ˈɒlədʒi
AM ˌseɪtn̩ˈɑːlədʒi

satay
BR ˈsateɪ, -z
AM ˈsæˌteɪ, -z

satchel
BR ˈsatʃl, -z
AM ˈsætʃəl, -z

satcom
BR ˈsatkɒm
AM ˈsætkɑm

sate
BR seɪt, -s, -ɪŋ, -ɪd
AM seɪt, -ts, -dɪŋ, -dɪd

saté
BR ˈsateɪ, -z
AM ˈsæˌteɪ, -z

sateen
BR saˈtiːn, səˈtiːn, -z
AM sæˈtin, səˈtin, -z

sateless
BR ˈseɪtlɪs
AM ˈseɪtlɪs

satellite
BR ˈsatəlʌɪt, ˈsatl̩ʌɪt, -s
AM ˈsædl̩ˌaɪt, -s

satellitic
BR ˌsatəˈlɪtɪk, ˌsatl̩ˈɪtɪk
AM ˌsædl̩ˈɪdɪk

satellitism
BR ˈsatəlʌɪtɪz(ə)m,
ˈsatl̩ʌɪtɪz(ə)m
AM ˈsædl̩ˌaɪˌtɪzəm

satem
BR ˈsɑːtəm, ˈsatəm,
ˈseɪtəm
AM ˈsɑdəm

sati
BR sʌˈtiː, ˈsʌti, -z
AM ˌsəˈti, ˈsəˌti, -z

satiable
BR ˈseɪʃəbl
AM ˈseɪʃəbəl

satiate¹
adjective
BR ˈseɪʃɪət
AM ˈseɪʃɪət

satiate²
verb
BR ˈseɪʃɪeɪt, -s, -ɪŋ, -ɪd
AM ˈseɪʃiˌeɪlt, -ts, -dɪŋ,
-dɪd

satiation
BR ˌseɪʃɪˈeɪʃn
AM ˌseɪʃiˈeɪʃən

Satie
BR ˈsati
AM ˈsɑti

satiety
BR səˈtʌɪti
AM səˈtaɪədi

satin
BR ˈsatɪn, -z
AM ˈsætn, -z

satinet
BR ˌsatɪˈnɛt, -s

AM ˈsætnˈɛt, -s

satinette
BR ˌsatɪˈnɛt
AM ˌsætnˈɛt

satinflower
BR ˈsatɪnˌflaʊə(r)
AM ˈsætnˌflaʊ(ə)r

satinised
BR ˈsatɪnʌɪzd
AM ˈsætnˌaɪzd

satinized
BR ˈsatɪnʌɪzd
AM ˈsætnˌaɪzd

satinwood
BR ˈsatɪnwʊd
AM ˈsætnˌwʊd

satiny
BR ˈsatɪni
AM ˈsætn̩i

satire
BR ˈsatʌɪə(r), -z
AM ˈsæˌtaɪ(ə)r, -z

satiric
BR səˈtɪrɪk
AM səˈtɪrɪk

satirical
BR səˈtɪrɪkl
AM səˈtɪrəkəl

satirically
BR səˈtɪrɪkli
AM səˈtɪrək(ə)li

satirisation
BR ˌsatɪrʌɪˈzeɪʃn
AM ˌsædərəˈzeɪʃən,
ˌsædəˌraɪˈzeɪʃən

satirise
BR ˈsatɪrʌɪz, -ɪz, -ɪŋ, -d
AM ˈsædəˌraɪz, -ɪz, -ɪŋ,
-d

satirist
BR ˈsatɪrɪst, -s
AM ˈsædərəst, -s

satirization
BR ˌsatɪrʌɪˈzeɪʃn
AM ˌsædərəˈzeɪʃən,
ˌsædəˌraɪˈzeɪʃən

satirize
BR ˈsatɪrʌɪz, -ɪz, -ɪŋ, -d
AM ˈsædəˌraɪz, -ɪz, -ɪŋ,
-d

satisfaction
BR ˌsatɪsˈfakʃn
AM ˌsædəˈsfækʃən

satisfactorily
BR ˌsatɪsˈfakt(ə)rɪli
AM ˌsædəˈsfæktərəli

satisfactoriness
BR ˌsatɪsˈfakt(ə)rɪnɪs
AM ˌsædəˈsfæktərɪnɪs

satisfactory
BR ˌsatɪsˈfakt(ə)ri
AM ˌsædəˈsfæktəri

satisfiability
BR ˌsatɪsfʌɪəˈbɪlɪti
AM ˌsædəˌsfaɪəˈbɪlɪdi

satisfiable
BR ˈsatɪsfʌɪəbl

AM ˈsædəˌsfaɪəbəl

satisfiedly
BR ˈsatɪsfʌɪdli
AM ˈsædəˌsfaɪ(ə)dli

satisfy
BR ˈsatɪsfʌɪ, -z, -ɪŋ, -d
AM ˈsædəˌsfaɪ, -z, -ɪŋ, -d

satisfyingly
BR ˈsatɪsfʌɪɪŋli
AM ˈsædəˌsfaɪɪŋli

satnav
satellite navigation
BR ˈsatnav
AM ˈsætˌnæv

satori
BR səˈtɔːri
AM səˈtɔri

satranji
BR ʃəˈtran(d)ʒi, -ɪz
AM səˈtrɑndʒi, -z

satrap
BR ˈsatrəp, ˈsatrap, -s
AM ˈseɪˌtræp, ˈsæˌtræp,
-s

satrapy
BR ˈsatrəp|i, -ɪz
AM ˈseɪtrəpi, ˈsætrəpi,
-z

satsuma
BR satˈsuːmə(r), -z
AM sætˈsumə,
ˈsætsəmə, -z

Satterfield
BR ˈsatəfiːld
AM ˈsædərˌfild

Satterthwaite
BR ˈsatəθweɪt
AM ˈsædərˌθweɪt

saturable
BR ˈsatʃ(ə)rəbl,
ˈsatjərəbl
AM ˈsætʃər(ə)bəl

saturant
BR ˈsatʃ(ə)rənt,
ˈsatʃ(ə)rn̩t,
ˈsatjʊrənt, ˈsatjɜrn̩t,
-s
AM ˈsætʃərənt, -s

saturate
BR ˈsatʃəreɪt,
ˈsatjʊreɪt, -s, -ɪŋ, -ɪd
AM ˈsætʃəˌreɪlt, -ts,
-dɪŋ, -dɪd

saturation
BR ˌsatʃəˈreɪʃn,
ˌsatjʊˈreɪʃn
AM ˌsætʃəˈreɪʃən

Saturday
BR ˈsatəd|eɪ, ˈsatəd|i,
-eɪz\-ɪz
AM ˈsædərˌdeɪ,
ˈsædərdi, -z

Saturn
BR ˈsat(ə)n
AM ˈsædərn

saturnalia
BR ˌsatəˈneɪlɪə(r)

AM ˌsædərˈneɪljə,
ˌsædərˈneɪliə

saturnalian
BR ˌsatəˈneɪlɪən
AM ˌsædərˈneɪljən,
ˌsædərˈneɪliən

Saturnian
BR səˈtɜːnɪən
AM səˈtɜrnɪən

saturnic
BR səˈtɜːnɪk
AM səˈtɜrnɪk

saturniid
BR səˈtɜːnɪɪd, -z
AM səˈtɜrnɪɪd, -z

saturnine
BR ˈsatənʌɪn
AM ˈsædərˌnaɪn,
ˈsædərˌnin

saturnism
BR ˈsatənɪz(ə)m
AM ˈsædərˌnɪzəm

satyagraha
BR sʌˈtjɑːgrəhɑː(r)
AM səˈtjɑgrəhə,
ˈsətjəˌgrɑ(h)ə

satyr
BR ˈsatə(r), -z
AM ˈsædər, ˈseɪdər, -z

satyriasis
BR ˌsatɪˈrʌɪəsɪs
AM ˌsædəˈraɪəsəs,
ˌseɪdəˈraɪəsəs

satyric
BR səˈtɪrɪk
AM səˈtɪrɪk, seɪˈtɪrɪk

satyrid
BR ˈsatɪrɪd, -z
AM ˈsædərəd,
ˈseɪdərəd, -z

sauce
BR sɔːs, -ɪz
AM sɔs, sɑs, -əz

sauceboat
BR ˈsɔːsbəʊt, -s
AM ˈsɔsˌbout, ˈsɑsˌbout,
-s

saucebox
BR ˈsɔːsbɒks, -ɪz
AM ˈsɔsˌbɑks,
ˈsɑsˌbɑks, -əz

sauceless
BR ˈsɔːsləs
AM ˈsɔsləs, ˈsɑsləs

saucepan
BR ˈsɔːspən, -z
AM ˈsɔsˌpæn, ˈsɑsˌpæn,
-z

saucepanful
BR ˈsɔːspənfʊl, -z
AM ˈsɔsˌpænˌfʊl,
ˈsɑsˌpænˌfʊl, -z

saucepot
BR ˈsɔːspɒt, -s
AM ˈsɔsˌpɑt, ˈsɑsˌpɑt, -s

saucer
BR ˈsɔːsə(r), -z
AM ˈsɔsər, ˈsɑsər, -z

saucerful
BR ˈsɔːsəfʊl, -z
AM ˈsɔsər͵fʊl, ˈsasər͵fʊl, -z

saucerless
BR ˈsɔːsələs
AM ˈsɔsərləs, ˈsasərləs

Sauchiehall
BR ͵sɒxiˈhɔːl, ͵sɒxiˈhɒl
AM ͵sɒkiˈhɔl, ͵sakiˈhal

saucily
BR ˈsɔːsɪli
AM ˈsɔsəli, ˈsasəli

sauciness
BR ˈsɔːsɪnɪs
AM ˈsɔsɪnɪs, ˈsasɪnɪs

saucy
BR ˈsɔːs|i, -ɪə(r), -ɪɪst
AM ˈsɔsi, ˈsasi, -ər, -ɪst

Saud
BR saʊd
AM saʊd

Saudi
BR ˈsaʊd|i, -ɪz
AM ˈsaʊdi, ˈsɒdi, ˈsadi, -z

Saudi Arabia
BR ͵saʊdɪ əˈreɪbiə(r)
AM ˈsaʊdi əˈreɪbiə, ˈsɒdi +, ˈsadi +

Saudi Arabian
BR ͵saʊdɪ əˈreɪbiən, -z
AM ˈsaʊdi əˈreɪbiən, ˈsɒdi +, ˈsadi +, -z

sauerbraten
BR ˈsaʊə͵brɑːtn
AM ˈsaʊ(ə)r͵brɑtn

sauerkraut
BR ˈsaʊəkraʊt
AM ˈsaʊ(ə)r͵kraʊt

sauger
BR ˈsɔːgə(r), -z
AM ˈsɔgər, ˈsagər, -z

Saul
BR sɔːl
AM sɔl, sal

sault¹
a leap
BR saʊ
AM saʊ

sault²
fast water, waterfall
BR saʊ, suː, -z
AM su, -z

Saumur
BR ˈsəʊmjʊə(r), -z
AM ˈsomər, ˈsamər, -z

sauna
BR ˈsɔːnə(r), ˈsaʊnə(r), -z
AM ˈsɔnə, ˈsanə, ˈsaʊnə, -z

Saunders
BR ˈsɔːndəz
AM ˈsɔndərz

Saundersfoot
BR ˈsɔːndəzfʊt

AM ˈsɒndərz͵fʊt, ˈsandərz͵fʊt

saunter
BR ˈsɔːnt|ə(r), -əz, -(ə)rɪŋ, -əd
AM ˈsɒn|t(ər, ˈsan|t(ər, -t(ərz, -t(ərɪŋ \ -trɪŋ, -t(ərd

saunterer
BR ˈsɔːnt(ə)rə(r), -z
AM ˈsɒn(t)ərər, ˈsɒntrər, ˈsan(t)ərər, ˈsantrər, -z

saurian
BR ˈsɔːrɪən, -z
AM ˈsɔrɪən, -z

saurischian
BR sɔːˈrɪskɪən, -z
AM sɔˈrɪskɪən, -z

sauropod
BR ˈsɔːrəpɒd, -z
AM ˈsɔrə͵pɑd, -z

saury
BR ˈsɔːr|i, -ɪz
AM ˈsɔri, -z

sausage
BR ˈsɒs|ɪdʒ, -ɪdʒɪz
AM ˈsɔsɪdʒ, ˈsasɪdʒ, -ɪz

Saussure
BR sə(ʊ)ˈs(j)ʊə(r)
AM soʊˈsʊ(ə)r, soʊˈʃʊ(ə)r

sauté
BR ˈsəʊteɪ, -z, -ɪŋ, -d
AM sɔˈteɪ, soʊˈteɪ, -z, -ɪŋ, -d

Sauterne
BR səʊˈtɜːn, -z
AM soʊˈtɜrn, sɔˈtɜrn, -z

Sauternes
BR səʊˈtɜːn, -z
AM soʊˈtɜrn, sɔˈtɜrn, -z

sauve qui peut
BR ͵səʊv kiː ˈpə(r)
AM ͵soʊv ͵ki ˈpə

Sauveterrian
BR ͵səʊvəˈtɛːrɪən, -z
AM ͵soʊvəˈtɛrɪən, -z

Sauvignon
BR ˈsəʊviːnjɒn, ˈsəʊvɪnjɒn, ˈsəʊviːnjɒ̃, ˈsəʊvɪnjɒ̃, -z
AM ͵soʊvəˈnjɒn, ͵soʊvəˈnjan, -z

savable
BR ˈseɪvəbl
AM ˈseɪvəbəl

savage
BR ˈsav|ɪdʒ, -ɪdʒɪz, -ɪdʒɪŋ, -ɪdʒd
AM ˈsævɪdʒ, -ɪz, -ɪŋ, -d

savagedom
BR ˈsavɪdʒdəm
AM ˈsævɪdʒdəm

savagely
BR ˈsavɪdʒli
AM ˈsævɪdʒli

savageness
BR ˈsavɪdʒnɪs
AM ˈsævɪdʒnɪs

savagery
BR ˈsavɪdʒ(ə)ri
AM ˈsævədʒ(ə)ri

savanna
BR səˈvanə(r), -z
AM səˈvænə, -z

savannah
BR səˈvanə(r), -z
AM səˈvænə, -z

savant
BR ˈsavnt, -s
AM sæˈvan(t), saˈvant, səˈvant, -s

savante
BR ˈsavnt, -s
AM sæˈvan(t), saˈvant, səˈvant, -s

savarin
BR ˈsavərɪn, -z
AM ˈsævərən, -z

savate
BR səˈvaːt
AM səˈvæt

save
BR seɪv, -z, -ɪŋ, -d
AM seɪv, -z, -ɪŋ, -d

saveloy
BR ˈsavəlɔɪ, -z
AM ˈsævə͵lɔɪ, -z

saver
BR ˈseɪvə(r), -z
AM ˈseɪvər, -z

Savernake
BR ˈsavənak
AM ˈsævər͵næk

Savery
BR ˈseɪv(ə)ri
AM ˈseɪv(ə)ri

Savile
BR ˈsav(ɪ)l
AM səˈvɪl, ˈsævəl

savin
BR ˈsavɪn, -z
AM ˈsævɪn, -z

savine
BR ˈsavɪn, -z
AM ˈsævɪn, -z

saving
BR ˈseɪvɪŋ, -z
AM ˈseɪvɪŋ, -z

savior
BR ˈseɪvjə(r), -z
AM ˈseɪvjər, -z

saviour
BR ˈseɪvjə(r), -z
AM ˈseɪvjər, -z

Savlon®
BR ˈsavlɒn
AM ˈsæv(ə)lɑn

savoir faire
BR ͵savwɑː ˈfɛː(r)
AM ͵sæv͵wɑr ˈfɛ(ə)r

savoir vivre
BR ͵savwɑː ˈviːvrə(r)

AM ͵sæv͵wɑr ˈvivrə

Savonarola
BR ͵savənəˈrəʊlə(r), ͵savnəˈrəʊlə(r)
AM ͵sævənəˈrɒlə, ͵sævənəˈroʊlə

Savonlinna
BR ͵sav(ə)nˈlɪnə(r)
AM ͵sævənˈlɪnə

Savonnerie
BR ˈsavɒnri, -ɪz
AM ˈsævənri, -z

savor
BR ˈseɪv|ə(r), -əz, -(ə)rɪŋ, -əd
AM ˈseɪv|ər, -ərz, -(ə)rɪŋ, -ərd

savorily
BR ˈseɪv(ə)rɪli
AM ˈseɪv(ə)rəli

savoriness
BR ˈseɪv(ə)rɪnɪs
AM ˈseɪv(ə)rinɪs

savorless
BR ˈseɪvələs
AM ˈseɪvərləs

savory
BR ˈseɪv(ə)r|i, -ɪz
AM ˈseɪv(ə)ri, -z

savour
BR ˈseɪv|ə(r), -əz, -(ə)rɪŋ, -əd
AM ˈseɪv|ər, -ərz, -(ə)rɪŋ, -ərd

savourily
BR ˈseɪv(ə)rɪli
AM ˈseɪv(ə)rəli

savouriness
BR ˈseɪv(ə)rɪnɪs
AM ˈseɪv(ə)rinɪs

savourless
BR ˈseɪvələs
AM ˈseɪvərləs

savoury
BR ˈseɪv(ə)r|i, -ɪz
AM ˈseɪv(ə)ri, -z

savoy
BR səˈvɔɪ
AM ˈsæ͵vɔɪ, səˈvɔɪ

Savoyard
BR səˈvɔɪɑːd, ͵savɔɪˈɑːd, -z
AM səˈvɔɪərd, ˈsæ͵vɔɪ(j)ɑrd, -z

savvy
BR ˈsavi
AM ˈsævi

saw
BR sɔː(r), -z, -ɪŋ, -d
AM sɔ, sɑ, -z, -ɪŋ, -d

sawbench
BR ˈsɔːben(t)ʃ, -ɪz
AM ˈsɔ͵ben(t)ʃ, ˈsɑ͵ben(t)ʃ, -əz

sawbill
BR ˈsɔːbɪl, -z
AM ˈsɔ͵bɪl, ˈsɑ͵bɪl, -z

sawbones
BR 'sɔːbəʊnz
AM 'sɔːˌbəʊnz,
'saˌbəʊnz

Sawbridgeworth
BR 'sɔːbrɪdʒwəːθ,
'sɔːbrɪdʒwəθ
AM 'sɔːbrɪdʒˌwəθ,
'sɑbrɪdʒˌwəθ

sawbuck
BR 'sɔːbʌk, -s
AM 'sɔːˌbək, 'sɑˌbək, -s

sawcut
BR 'sɔːkʌt, -s
AM 'sɔːˌkət, 'sɑˌkət, -s

sawdust
BR 'sɔːdʌst
AM 'sɔːˌdəst, 'sɑˌdəst

sawfish
BR 'sɔːfɪʃ
AM 'sɔːˌfɪʃ, 'sɑˌfɪʃ

sawfly
BR 'sɔːflaɪ, -z
AM 'sɔːˌflaɪ, 'sɑˌflaɪ, -z

sawgrass
BR 'sɔːgrɑːs, 'sɔːgras,
-ɪz
AM 'sɔːgræs, 'sɑˌgræs,
-əz

sawhorse
BR 'sɔːhɔːs, -ɪz
AM 'sɔːˌhɔː(ə)rs,
'sɑˌhɔː(ə)rs, -əz

sawlike
BR 'sɔːlaɪk
AM 'sɔːˌlaɪk, 'sɑˌlaɪk

sawmill
BR 'sɔːmɪl, -z
AM 'sɔːˌmɪl, 'sɑˌmɪl, -z

sawn
BR sɔːn
AM sɔn, sɑn

sawpit
BR 'sɔːpɪt, -s
AM 'sɔːˌpɪt, 'sɑˌpɪt, -s

sawtooth
BR 'sɔːtuːθ, 'sɔːtʊθ
AM 'sɔːˌtuːθ, 'sɑˌtʊθ

sawtoothed
BR ˌsɔːˈtuːθt, ˌsɔːˈtʊθt
AM 'sɔːˌtuːθt, 'sɑˌtʊθt

sawyer
BR 'sɔːjə(r), 'sɔɪə(r), -z
AM 'sɔjər, 'sɔɪər, -z

sax
BR saks, -ɪz
AM sæks, -əz

Saxa
BR 'saksə(r)
AM 'sæksə

saxatile
BR 'saksətʌɪl,
'saksətɪl
AM 'sæksəˌtaɪl,
'sæksədl

saxboard
BR 'saksbɔːd, -z
AM 'sæksˌbɔː(ə)rd, -z

Saxby
BR 'saksbi
AM 'sæksbi

saxe
BR saks, -ɪz
AM sæks, -əz

Saxe-Coburg-Gotha
BR saks,kəʊbəːg-
'gəʊtə(r)
AM 'sæksˈkoʊbərg-
'goʊθə

saxhorn
BR 'sakshɔːn, -z
AM 'sæks,(h)ɔː(ə)rn, -z

saxicoline
BR sak'sɪkəlʌɪn,
sak'sɪkˌlʌɪn
AM sæk'sɪkəˌlaɪn,
sæk'sɪkələn

saxicolous
BR sak'sɪkələs,
sak'sɪkˌləs
AM sæk'sɪkələs

saxifrage
BR 'saksɪfreɪ(d)ʒ, -ɪz
AM 'sæksəˌfreɪ(d)ʒ, -ɪz

saxist
BR 'saksɪst, -s
AM 'sæksəst, -s

Saxmundham
BR saks'mʌndəm
AM sæks'mʌndəm

Saxo
BR 'saksəʊ
AM 'sæksoʊ

Saxon
BR 'saksn, -z
AM 'sæksən, -z

Saxondom
BR 'saksndəm
AM 'sæksəndəm

Saxone
BR ˌsak'səʊn, 'saksəʊn
AM ˌsæk'soʊn,
'sækˌsoʊn

Saxonise
BR 'saksnʌɪz, -ɪz, -ɪŋ, -d
AM 'sæksəˌnaɪz, -ɪz, -ɪŋ,
-d

Saxonism
BR 'saksnɪz(ə)m
AM 'sæksəˌnɪzəm

Saxonist
BR 'saksnɪst, -s
AM 'sæksənəst, -s

Saxonize
BR 'saksnʌɪz, -ɪz, -ɪŋ, -d
AM 'sæksəˌnaɪz, -ɪz, -ɪŋ,
-d

saxony
BR 'saksən|i, 'saksn|i,
-ɪz
AM 'sæksəni, -z

saxophone
BR 'saksəfəʊn, -z
AM 'sæksəˌfoʊn, -z

saxophonic
BR ˌsaksə'fɒnɪk
AM ˌsæksə'fɑnɪk

saxophonist
BR sak'sɒfənɪst,
sak'sɒfˌnɪst, -s
AM 'sæksəˌfoʊnəst, -s

Saxton
BR 'sakst(ə)n
AM 'sækstən

say
BR seɪ, -ɪŋ
AM seɪ, -ɪŋ

sayable
BR 'seɪəbl
AM 'seɪəbəl

Sayce
BR seɪs
AM seɪs

sayer
BR 'seɪə(r), -z
AM 'seɪər, -z

Sayers
BR 'seɪəz
AM 'seɪərz

saying
BR 'seɪɪŋ, -z
AM 'seɪɪŋ, -z

says
BR sɛz
AM sɛz

say-so
BR 'seɪsəʊ
AM 'seɪˌsoʊ

S-bend
BR 'ɛsbɛnd, -z
AM 'ɛsˌbɛnd, -z

scab
BR skab, -z, -ɪŋ, -d
AM skæb, -z, -ɪŋ, -d

scabbard
BR 'skabəd, -z
AM 'skæbərd, -z

scabbard-fish
BR 'skabədfɪʃ, -ɪz
AM 'skæbərdˌfɪʃ, -ɪz

scabbiness
BR 'skabɪnɪs
AM 'skæbinɪs

scabby
BR 'skabi
AM 'skæbi

scabies
BR 'skeɪbɪz, 'skeɪbiːz
AM 'skeɪbiz

scabious
BR 'skeɪbɪəs, -ɪz
AM 'skeɪbɪəs, -əz

scablike
BR 'skablʌɪk
AM 'skæbˌlaɪk

scabrous
BR 'skeɪbrəs, 'skabrəs
AM 'skæbrəs

scabrously
BR 'skeɪbrəsli,
'skabrəsli

scabrousli
AM 'skæbrəsli

scabrousness
BR 'skeɪbrəsnəs,
'skabrəsnəs
AM 'skæbrəsnəs

scad
BR skad, -z
AM skæd, -z

Scafell
BR skɔː'fɛl
AM 'skæfəl, skɔː'fɛl,
skɑ'fɛl

scaffold
BR 'skafəʊld, 'skafld,
-z
AM 'skæfəld,
'skæˌfoʊld, -z

scaffolder
BR 'skafldə(r), -z
AM 'skæfəldər,
'skæˌfoʊldər, -z

scaffolding
BR 'skafldɪŋ,
AM 'skæfəldɪŋ,
'skæˌfoʊldɪŋ, -z

scagliola
BR skal'jəʊlə(r)
AM skæl'joʊlə

scalability
BR ˌskeɪlə'bɪlɪti
AM ˌskeɪlə'bɪlɪdi

scalable
BR 'skeɪləbl
AM 'skeɪləbəl

scalar
BR 'skeɪlə(r), -z
AM 'skeɪlər, -z

scalariform
BR skə'larɪfɔːm
AM skə'lɛrəˌfɔ(ə)rm

scalawag
BR 'skalɪwag, -z
AM 'skælə,wæg,
'skæliˌwæg, -z

scald
BR skɔːld, -z, -ɪŋ, -d
AM skold, skɑld, -z, -ɪŋ,
-əd

scalder
BR 'skɔːldə(r), -z
AM 'skoldər, 'skɑldər,
-z

scale
BR skeɪl, -z, -ɪŋ, -d
AM skeɪl, -z, -ɪŋ, -d

scaleless
BR 'skeɪllɪs
AM 'skeɪl(l)lɪs

scalelike
BR 'skeɪllʌɪk
AM 'skeɪlˌlaɪk

scale-moss
BR 'skeɪlmɒs, -ɪz
AM 'skeɪlˌmɒs,
'skeɪlˌmɑs, -əz

scalene
BR 'skeɪliːn
AM ˌskeɪˌlin

scaleni
BR skeɪˈliːnaɪ
AM skeɪˈliːˌnaɪ

scalenus
BR skeɪˈliːnəs
AM skeɪˈliːnəs

scaler
BR ˈskeɪlə(r), -z
AM ˈskeɪlər, -z

Scalextric
BR skəˈlɛkstrɪk
AM skəˈlɛkstrɪk

Scaliger
BR ˈskalɪdʒə(r)
AM ˈskælədʒər

scaliness
BR ˈskeɪlɪnɪs
AM ˈskeɪlɪnɪs

scallawag
BR ˈskalɪwag, -z
AM ˈskælə,wæg,
ˈskæli,wæg, -z

scallion
BR ˈskalɪən, -z
AM ˈskæljən, ˈskælɪən,
-z

scallop
BR ˈskɒləp, ˈskaləp, -s,
-ɪŋ, -t
AM ˈskɑləp, ˈskæləp, -s,
-ɪŋ, -t

scalloper
BR ˈskɒləpə(r),
ˈskaləpə(r), -z
AM ˈskɑləpər,
ˈskæləpər, -z

scallywag
BR ˈskalɪwag, -z
AM ˈskælə,wæg,
ˈskæli,wæg, -z

scaloppine
BR ˌskalə(ʊ)ˈpiːnʲi, -ɪz
AM ˌskælæˈpini, -z

scalp
BR skalp, -s, -ɪŋ, -t
AM skælp, -s, -ɪŋ, -t

scalpel
BR ˈskalpl, -z
AM ˈskælpəl, -z

scalper
BR ˈskalpə(r), -z
AM ˈskælpər, -z

scalpless
BR ˈskalpləs
AM ˈskælpləs

scalpriform
BR ˈskalprɪfɔːm
AM ˈskælprəˌfɔ(ə)rm

scaly
BR ˈskeɪlʲi, -ɪə(r), -ɪɪst
AM ˈskeɪli, -ər, -ɪst

scam
BR skam, -z, -ɪŋ, -d
AM skæm, -z, -ɪŋ, -d

Scammell
BR ˈskaml
AM ˈskæməl

scammony
BR ˈskamənʲi, -ɪz
AM ˈskæməni, -z

scamp
BR skamp, -s
AM skæmp, -s

scamper
BR ˈskampʲə(r), -əz,
-(ə)rɪŋ, -əd
AM ˈskæmpʲər, -ərz,
-(ə)rɪŋ, -ərd

scampi
BR ˈskampi
AM ˈskæmpi

scampish
BR ˈskampɪʃ
AM ˈskæmpɪʃ

scan
BR skan, -z, -ɪŋ, -d
AM skæn, -z, -ɪŋ, -d

scandal
BR ˈskandl, -z
AM ˈskændəl, -z

scandalise
BR ˈskandəlaɪz,
ˈskandlˌaɪz, -ɪz, -ɪŋ, -d
AM ˈskændlˌaɪz, -ɪz, -ɪŋ,
-d

scandalize
BR ˈskandəlaɪz,
ˈskandlˌaɪz, -ɪz, -ɪŋ, -d
AM ˈskændlˌaɪz, -ɪz, -ɪŋ,
-d

scandalmonger
BR ˈskandlˌmʌŋgə(r),
-z
AM ˈskændlˌmɑŋgər,
ˈskændlˌməŋgər, -z

scandalous
BR ˈskandələs,
ˈskandləs
AM ˈskændləs

scandalously
BR ˈskandələsli,
ˈskandləsli
AM ˈskændləsli

scandalousness
BR ˈskandələsnəs,
ˈskandləsnəs
AM ˈskændləsnəs

scandent
BR ˈskandənt
AM ˈskændnt

Scanderbeg
BR ˈskandəbeg
AM ˈskændəˌbɛrg

Scandia
BR ˈskandɪə(r)
AM ˈskændɪə

Scandinavia
BR ˌskandɪˈneɪvɪə(r)
AM ˌskændəˈneɪvɪə

Scandinavian
BR ˌskandɪˈneɪvɪən, -z
AM ˌskændəˈneɪvɪən,
-z

scandium
BR ˈskandɪəm

scammony
AM ˈskændɪəm

Scanlon
BR ˈskanlən
AM ˈskænlən

scannable
BR ˈskanəbl
AM ˈskænəbəl

scanner
BR ˈskanə(r), -z
AM ˈskænər, -z

scansion
BR ˈskanʃn
AM ˈskænʃən

scansorial
BR skanˈsɔːrɪəl
AM skænˈsɔrɪəl

scant
BR skant
AM skænt

scanties
BR ˈskantɪz
AM ˈskæn(t)iz

scantily
BR ˈskantɪli
AM ˈskæn(t)əli

scantiness
BR ˈskantɪnɪs
AM ˈskæn(t)inɪs

scantling
BR ˈskantlɪŋ, -z
AM ˈskæn(t)lɪŋ, -z

scantly
BR ˈskantli
AM ˈskæn(t)li

scantness
BR ˈskantnəs
AM ˈskæn(t)nəs

scanty
BR ˈskantʲi, -ɪz, -ɪə(r),
-ɪɪst
AM ˈskæn(t)i, -z, -ər,
-ɪst

Scapa Flow
BR ˌskɑːpə ˈfləʊ,
ˌskapə +
AM ˌskæpə ˈfloʊ

scape
BR skeɪp, -s
AM skeɪp, -s

scapegoat
BR ˈskeɪpgəʊt, -s
AM ˈskeɪp,goʊt, -s

scapegoater
BR ˈskeɪpgəʊtə(r), -z
AM ˈskeɪp,goʊdər, -z

scapegrace
BR ˈskeɪpgreɪs, -ɪz
AM ˈskeɪp,greɪs, -ɪz

scaphoid
BR ˈskafɔɪd, -z
AM ˈskæˌfɔɪd, -z

scapula
BR ˈskapjʊlə(r), -z
AM ˈskæpjələ, -z

scapulae
BR ˈskapjʊliː

scapuli
AM ˈskæpjəˌli,
ˈskæpjəˌlaɪ

scapular
BR ˈskapjʊlə(r)
AM ˈskæpjələr

scapulary
BR ˈskapjʊlərʲi, -ɪz
AM ˈskæpjəˌlɛri, -z

scar
BR skɑː(r), -z, -ɪŋ, -d
AM skɑr, -z, -ɪŋ, -d

scarab
BR ˈskarəb, -z
AM ˈskɛrəb, -z

scarabaei
BR ˌskarəˈbiːaɪ
AM ˌskɛrəˈbiˌaɪ

scarabaeid
BR ˌskarəˈbiːɪd, -z
AM ˌskɛrəˈbiɪd, -z

scarabaeus
BR ˌskarəˈbiːəs
AM ˌskɛrəˈbiəs

scaramouch
BR ˈskarəmuːʃ, -ɪz
AM ˈskɛrəˌmu(t)ʃ, -əz

scaramouche
BR ˈskarəmuːʃ, -ɪz
AM ˈskɛrəˌmu(t)ʃ, -əz

Scarborough
BR ˈskɑːb(ə)rə(r)
AM ˈskɑrb(ə)rə

scarce
BR skɛːs, -ə(r), -ɪst
AM skɛ(ə)rs, -ər, -əst

scarcely
BR ˈskɛːsli
AM ˈskɛrsli

scarceness
BR ˈskɛːsnəs
AM ˈskɛrsnəs

scarcity
BR ˈskɛːsɪtʲi, -ɪz
AM ˈskɛrsədi, -z

scare
BR skɛː(r), -z, -ɪŋ, -d
AM skɛ(ə)r, -z, -ɪŋ, -d

scarecrow
BR ˈskɛːkrəʊ, -z
AM ˈskɛrˌkrɑʊ, -z

scaredy-cat
BR ˈskɛːdɪkat, -s
AM ˈskɛrdiˌkæt, -s

scaremonger
BR ˈskɛːˌmʌŋgə(r), -z
AM ˈskɛrˌmɑŋgər,
ˈskɛrˌməŋgər, -z

scaremongering
BR ˈskɛːˌmʌŋg(ə)rɪŋ,
-z
AM ˈskɛrˌmɑŋg(ə)rɪŋ,
ˈskɛrˌməŋg(ə)rɪŋ, -z

scarer
BR ˈskɛːrə(r), -z
AM ˈskɛrər, -z

scarf
BR skɑːf, -t

AM skɑrf, -t

Scarfe
BR skɑːf
AM skɑrf

Scargill
BR 'skɑːgɪl
AM 'skɑr,gɪl

scarification
BR ,skærɪfɪ'keɪʃn,
,skeːrɪfɪ'keɪʃn
AM ,skerəfə'keɪʃən

scarificator
BR 'skærɪfɪkeɪtə(r),
'skeːrɪfɪkeɪtə(r), -z
AM 'skerəfə,keɪdər, -z

scarifier
BR 'skærɪfʌɪə(r),
'skeːrɪfʌɪə(r), -z
AM 'skerə,faɪər, -z

scarify¹
cut
BR 'skærɪfʌɪ, 'skeːrɪfʌɪ,
-z, -ɪŋ, -d
AM 'skerə,faɪ, -z, -ɪŋ, -d

scarify²
frighten
BR 'skeːrɪfʌɪ, -z, -ɪŋ, -d
AM 'skerəfaɪ, -z, -ɪŋ, -d

scarily
BR 'skeːrɪli
AM 'skerəli

scariness
BR 'skeːrɪnɪs
AM 'skerinɪs

scarious
BR 'skeːrɪəs
AM 'skeriəs

Scarisbrick
BR 'skeːzbrɪk
AM 'skerz,brɪk

scarlatina
BR ,skɑːlə'tiːnə(r)
AM ,skɑrlə'tinə

Scarlatti
BR skɑː'lati
AM skɑr'lɑdi

scarless
BR 'skɑːləs
AM 'skɑrləs

scarlet
BR 'skɑːlɪt
AM 'skɑrlət

Scarlett
BR 'skɑːlɪt
AM 'skɑrlət

Scarman
BR 'skɑːmən
AM 'skɑrmən

scaroid
BR 'skarɔɪd, 'skeːrɔɪd,
-z
AM 'skeː,rɔɪd, -z

scarp
BR skɑːp, -s
AM skɑrp, -s

scarper
BR 'skɑːp|ə(r), -əz,
-(ə)rɪŋ, -əd
AM 'skɑrpər, -z, -ɪŋ, -d

Scart
BR skɑːt
AM skɑrt

scarus
BR 'skeːrəs, -ɪz
AM 'skeːrəs, -əz

scarves
BR skɑːvz
AM skɑrvz

scary
BR 'skeːr|i, -ɪə(r), -ɪɪst
AM 'skeri, -ər, -ɪst

Scase
BR skeɪs
AM skeɪs

scat
BR skat, -s, -ɪŋ, -ɪd
AM skæt, -ts, -dɪŋ, -dəd

scathe
BR skeɪð, -z, -ɪŋ, -d
AM skeɪð, -z, -ɪŋ, -d

scatheless
BR 'skeɪðlɪs
AM 'skeɪðlɪs

scathing
BR 'skeɪðɪŋ
AM 'skeɪðɪŋ

scathingly
BR 'skeɪðɪŋli
AM 'skeɪðɪŋli

scatological
BR ,skatə'lɒdʒɪkl
AM ,skædl'ɑdʒəkəl

scatologist
BR ska'tɒlədʒɪst,
skə'tɒlədʒɪst, -s
AM skæ'tɑlədʒəst,
skæ'tɑlədʒəst, -s

scatology
BR ska'tɒlədʒi,
skə'tɒlədʒi
AM skæ'tɑlədʒi,
skæ'tɑlədʒi

scatophagous
BR ska'tɒfəgəs,
skə'tɒfəgəs
AM skæ'tɑfəgəs,
skæ'tafəgəs

scatter
BR 'skat|ə(r), -əz,
-(ə)rɪŋ, -əd
AM 'skædjər, -ərz,
-(ə)rɪŋ, -ərd

scatterbrain
BR 'skatəbreɪn, -z, -d
AM 'skædər,breɪn, -z,
-d

scatterer
BR 'skat(ə)rə(r), -z
AM 'skædərər, -z

scattergram
BR 'skatəgram, -z
AM 'skædər,græm, -z

scattergun
BR 'skatəgʌn, -z
AM 'skædər,gən, -z

scatterplot
BR 'skatəplɒt, -s
AM 'skædər,plɑt, -s

scattershot
BR 'skatəʃɒt, -s
AM 'skædər,ʃɑt, -s

scattily
BR 'skatɪli
AM 'skædəli

scattiness
BR 'skatɪnɪs
AM 'skædinɪs

scatty
BR 'skat|i, -ɪə(r), -ɪɪst
AM 'skædi, -ər, -ɪst

scaup
BR skɔːp, -s
AM skɒp, skɑp, -s

scauper
BR 'skɔːpə(r), -z
AM 'skɒpər, 'skɑpər, -z

scaur
BR skɔː(r)
AM skɑr

scavenge
BR 'skav(ɪ)n(d)ʒ, -ɪz,
-ɪŋ, -d
AM 'skævəndʒ, -əz, -ɪŋ,
-d

scavenger
BR 'skav(ɪ)n(d)ʒə(r),
-z
AM 'skævəndʒər, -z

scavengery
BR 'skav(ɪ)n(d)ʒ(ə)ri
AM 'skævəndʒ(ə)ri

scazon
BR 'skeɪzn, 'skazn, -z
AM 'skeɪzən, -z

scean dhu
BR ,skiː'ən 'duː, -z
AM ,skiən 'du, -z

scena
BR 'ʃeɪnə(r), -z
AM 'ʃeɪnə, -z

scenario
BR sɪ'nɑːrɪəʊ,
sɪ'neːrɪəʊ, -z
AM sə'nerioʊ, -z

scenarist
BR sɪ'nɑːrɪst,
'siːn(ə)rɪst, -s
AM sə'nerəst, -s

scend
BR send, -z, -ɪŋ, -ɪd
AM send, -z, -ɪŋ, -əd

scene
BR siːn, -z
AM sin, -z

scenery
BR 'siːn(ə)ri
AM 'sin(ə)ri

sceneshifter
BR 'siːn,ʃɪftə(r), -z
AM 'sin,ʃɪftər, -z

scenester
BR 'siːnstə(r), -z
AM 'sinstər, -z

scenic
BR 'siːnɪk
AM 'sinɪk

scenically
BR 'siːnɪkli
AM 'sinɪk(ə)li

scent
BR sent, -s, -ɪŋ, -ɪd
AM sent, -ts, -(t)ɪŋ,
-(t)əd

scentless
BR 'sentləs
AM 'sen(t)ləs

scepsis
BR 'skepsɪs
AM 'skepsəs

scepter
BR 'septə(r), -z, -d
AM 'septər, -z, -d

sceptic
BR 'skeptɪk, -s
AM 'skeptɪk, -s

sceptical
BR 'skeptɪkl
AM 'skeptəkəl

sceptically
BR 'skeptɪkli
AM 'skeptək(ə)li

scepticism
BR 'skeptɪsɪz(ə)m
AM 'skeptə,sɪzəm

sceptre
BR 'septə(r), -z, -d
AM 'septər, -z, -d

Schadenfreude
BR 'ʃɑːdn,frɔɪdə(r)
AM 'ʃɑdən,frɔɪdə

Schaefer
BR 'ʃefə(r)
AM 'ʃeɪfər

Schaeffer
BR 'ʃeɪfə(r)
AM 'ʃeɪfər

Schafer
BR 'ʃeɪfə(r)
AM 'ʃeɪfər

Schapiro
BR ʃə'pɪərəʊ
AM ʃə'pɪroʊ

schappe
BR ʃap, 'ʃapə(r), -s
AM 'ʃapə, -s

schedule
BR 'ʃedjʊl, 'ʃedjuːl,
'ʃedʒʊl, 'skedʒʊl,
'skedjuːl, 'skedʒʊl, -z,
-ɪŋ, -d
AM 'skedʒəl, -z, -ɪŋ, -d

scheduler
BR 'ʃedjʊlə(r),
'ʃedjuːlə(r),

'ʃɛdʒələ(r),
'skɛdjələ(r),
'skɛdju:lə(r),
'skɛdʒələ(r), -z
AM 'skɛdʒələr, -z
Scheele
BR 'ʃeɪlə(r)
AM 'ʃeɪlə
scheelite
BR 'ʃi:laɪt, -s
AM 'ʃeɪˌlaɪt, -s
Scheherazade
BR ʃəˌhɛrə'zɑːdə(r)
AM ʃəˌhɛrə'zɑːd
Schelde
BR 'ʃɛldə, skɛld
AM 'ʃɛldə, skɛld
Scheldt
BR ʃɛlt, skɛlt
AM ʃɛlt, skɛlt
Schelling
BR 'ʃelɪŋ
AM 'ʃelɪŋ
schema
BR 'ski:mə(r), -z
AM 'skiːmə, -z
schemata
BR 'ski:mətə(r)
AM 'skiːmədə
schematic
BR ski:'mætɪk,
skɪ'mætɪk
AM skə'mædɪk,
ski'mædɪk
schematically
BR ski:'mætɪkli,
skɪ'mætɪkli
AM skə'mædək(ə)li,
ski'mædək(ə)li
schematisation
BR ˌski:mətʌɪ'zeɪʃn, -z
AM ˌskiːmədə'zeɪʃən,
ˌskiːməˌtaɪ'zeɪʃən, -z
schematise
BR 'ski:mətʌɪz, -ɪz, -ɪŋ,
-d
AM 'skiːməˌtaɪz, -ɪz, -ɪŋ,
-d
schematism
BR 'ski:mətɪz(ə)m, -z
AM 'skiːməˌtɪzəm, -z
schematization
BR ˌski:mətʌɪ'zeɪʃn, -z
AM ˌskiːmədə'zeɪʃən,
ˌskiːməˌtaɪ'zeɪʃən, -z
schematize
BR 'ski:mətʌɪz, -ɪz, -ɪŋ,
-d
AM 'skiːməˌtaɪz, -ɪz, -ɪŋ,
-d
scheme
BR ski:m, -z, -ɪŋ, -d
AM skim, -z, -ɪŋ, -d
schemer
BR 'ski:mə(r), -z
AM 'skiːmər, -z
scheming
BR 'ski:mɪŋ, -z

AM 'skimɪŋ, -z
schemingly
BR 'ski:mɪŋli
AM 'skimɪŋli
schemozzle
BR ʃɪ'mɒzl, -z
AM ʃə'mɑzl, -z
Schenectady
BR skɪ'nɛktədi
AM skə'nɛktədi
scherzando
BR skɛːt'sandəʊ,
skɛːt'sandəʊ, -z
AM skɛrt'sandoʊ, -z
scherzo
BR 'skɛːtsəʊ, 'skəːtsəʊ,
-z
AM 'skɛrtsoʊ, -z
Schiaparelli
BR ˌʃapə'rɛli
AM ˌʃapə'rɛli
IT skjapa'rɛlli
Schick
BR ʃɪk
AM ʃɪk
Schiedam
BR skɪ'dam
AM ski'dæm
DU 'sxi:dam
Schiele
BR 'ʃi:lə(r)
AM 'ʃilə
Schiller
BR 'ʃɪlə(r)
AM 'ʃɪlər
Schilling
BR 'ʃɪlɪŋ, -z
AM 'ʃɪlɪŋ, -z
schipperke
BR 'skɪpəkǀi, 'ʃɪpəkǀi,
-ɪz
AM 'skɪpərki, -z
schism
BR 's(k)ɪz(ə)m, -z
AM 's(k)ɪzəm, 'ʃɪzəm,
-z
schismatic
BR s(k)ɪz'matɪk, -s
AM s(k)ɪz'mædɪk, -s
schismatical
BR s(k)ɪz'matɪkl
AM s(k)ɪz'mædəkəl
schismatically
BR s(k)ɪz'matɪkli
AM s(k)ɪz'mædək(ə)li
schismatise
BR 's(k)ɪzmətʌɪz, -ɪz,
-ɪŋ, -d
AM 's(k)ɪzməˌtaɪz, -ɪz,
-ɪŋ, -d
schismatize
BR 's(k)ɪzmətʌɪz, -ɪz,
-ɪŋ, -d
schist
BR ʃɪst, -s
AM ʃɪst, -s

schistose
BR 'ʃɪstəʊs
AM 'ʃɪstoʊs, 'ʃɪstoʊz
schistosome
BR 'ʃɪstəsəʊm, -z
AM 'ʃɪstəˌsoʊm, -z
schistosomiases
BR ˌʃɪstə(ʊ)sə'mʌɪəsi:z
AM 'ʃɪstoʊsə'maɪə,siz
schistosomiasis
BR ˌʃɪstə(ʊ)sə'mʌɪəsɪs
AM 'ʃɪstoʊsə'maɪəsəs
schizanthus
BR skɪ'zanθəs, -ɪz
AM skə'zænθəs, -əz
schizo
BR 'skɪtsəʊ, -z
AM 'skɪtsoʊ, -z
schizocarp
BR 'skɪtsə(ʊ)kɑːp,
'skʌɪzə(ʊ)kɑːp, -s
AM 'skɪtsoʊˌkarp, -s
schizocarpic
BR ˌskɪtsə(ʊ)'kɑːpɪk,
ˌskʌɪzə(ʊ)'kɑːpɪk
AM 'skɪtsə'karpɪk
schizocarpous
BR ˌskɪtsə(ʊ)'kɑːpəs,
ˌskʌɪzə(ʊ)'kɑːpəs
AM 'skɪtsə'karpəs
schizogenous
BR skɪt'sɒdʒɪnəs,
ʃʌɪ'zɒdʒɪnəs
AM skɪt'sadʒənəs
schizogeny
BR skɪt'sɒdʒɪni,
ʃʌɪ'zɒdʒɪni
AM skɪt'sadʒəni
schizoid
BR 'skɪtsɔɪd
AM 'skɪtˌsɔɪd
schizomycete
BR ˌskɪtsə(ʊ)'mʌɪsiːt,
ˌskɪtsə(ʊ)'mʌɪsiːt, -s
AM 'skɪtsoʊ'maɪˌsit, -s
schizont
BR 'skɪzɒnt, 'ʃʌɪzɒnt,
-s
AM 'skɪzɑnt, -s
schizophrenia
BR ˌskɪtsə'fri:nɪə(r)
AM ˌskɪtsə'freniə,
ˌskɪtsə'friniə
schizophrenic
BR ˌskɪtsə'frenɪk, -s
AM ˌskɪtsə'frenɪk,
ˌskɪtsə'frinɪk, -s
schizostylis
BR ˌskɪtsə(ʊ)'stʌɪlɪs,
ʃʌɪzə(ʊ)'stʌɪlɪs
AM ˌskɪtsoʊ'staɪlɪs
schizothymia
BR ˌskɪtsə(ʊ)'θʌɪmɪə(r)
AM 'skɪtsoʊ'θaɪmiə
schizothymic
BR ˌskɪtsə(ʊ)'θʌɪmɪk
AM 'skɪtsoʊ'θaɪmɪk

schizotype
BR 'skɪtsə(ʊ)tʌɪp, -s
AM 'skɪtsəˌtaɪp, -s
Schlegel
BR 'ʃleɪgl
AM 'ʃleɪgəl
Schleicher
BR 'ʃlʌɪkə(r),
'ʃlʌɪxə(r)
AM 'ʃlaɪkər
schlemiel
BR ʃlə'mi:l, -z
AM ʃlə'mi(ə)l, -z
schlepp
BR ʃlep, -s, -ɪŋ, -t
AM ʃlep, -s, -ɪŋ, -t
Schlesinger
BR 'ʃlesɪn(d)ʒə(r)
AM 'ʃlesɪndʒər,
'ʃlesɪŋər
Schleswig
BR 'ʃlezvɪg, 'ʃlesvɪg,
'ʃlezwɪg
AM 'ʃlezwɪg
Schliemann
BR 'ʃli:mən
AM 'ʃliman
schlieren
BR 'ʃlɪərən, 'ʃlɪərn̩, -z
AM 'ʃlɪrən, -z
schlock
BR ʃlɒk, -s
AM ʃlɑk, -s
schlocky
BR 'ʃlɒki
AM 'ʃlɑki
schmaltz
BR ʃmɔːlts
AM ʃmolts, ʃmalts
schmaltzy
BR 'ʃmɔːtlsi, -ɪə(r),
-ɪɪst
AM 'ʃmoltsi, 'ʃmaltsi,
-ər, -ɪst
schmalz
BR ʃmɔːlts
AM ʃmolts, ʃmalts
schmalzy
BR 'ʃmɔːtlsi, -ɪə(r),
-ɪɪst
AM 'ʃmoltsi, 'ʃmaltsi,
-ər, -ɪst
Schmidt
BR ʃmɪt
AM ʃmɪt
Schmitt
BR ʃmɪt
AM ʃmɪt
schmo
BR ʃməʊ, -z
AM ʃmoʊ, -z
schmoe
BR ʃməʊ, -z
AM ʃmoʊ, -z
schmooze
BR ʃmu:z, -ɪz, -ɪŋ, -d
AM ʃmuz, -əz, -ɪŋ, -d

schmuck
BR ʃmʌk, -s
AM ʃmək, -s

schnapps
BR ʃnaps
AM ʃnɑps

schnauzer
BR ʃnaʊtsə(r), ʃnaʊzə(r), -z
AM ʃnaʊzər, -z

Schneider
BR ʃnaɪdə(r)
AM snaɪdər, ʃnaɪdər

schnitzel
BR ʃnɪtsl, -z
AM ʃnɪtsəl, -z

schnook
BR ʃnʊk, -s
AM ʃnʊk, -s

schnorkel
BR ʃnɔːk|l, snɔːk|l, -lz, -lɪŋ \-lɪŋ, -ld
AM ʃnɔrk|əl, snɔrk|əl, -əlz, -(ə)lɪŋ, -əld

schnorrer
BR ʃnɒrə(r), ʃnɔːrə(r), -z
AM ʃnɔrər, -z

schnozz
BR ʃnɒz, -ɪz
AM ʃnɑz, -əz

schnozzle
BR ʃnɒzl, -z
AM ʃnɑzəl, -z

Schoenberg
BR ʃəːnbəːg
AM ʃənbərg, ʃoʊnbərg

Schofield
BR ʃəʊfiːld
AM ʃoʊˌfild

scholar
BR ʃkɒlə(r), -z
AM ʃkɑlər, -z

scholarliness
BR ʃkɒləlɪnɪs
AM ʃkɑlərlɪnɪs

scholarly
BR ʃkɒləli
AM ʃkɑlərli

scholarship
BR ʃkɒləʃɪp, -s
AM ʃkɑlər,ʃɪp, -s

scholastic
BR skəˈlastɪk
AM skəˈlæstɪk

scholastically
BR skəˈlastɪkli
AM skəˈlæstək(ə)li

scholasticism
BR skəˈlastɪsɪz(ə)m
AM skəˈlæstəˌsɪzəm

Scholefield
BR ˈskəʊlfiːld
AM ˈskoʊ(l)ˌfild

Scholes
BR skəʊlz

AM skəʊlz

Scholfield
BR ˈskəʊ(l)fiːld
AM ˈskoʊ(l)ˌfild

scholia
BR ˈskəʊliə(r)
AM ˈskoʊljə, ˈskoʊliə

scholiast
BR ˈskəʊliast, -s
AM ˈskoʊliˌæst, -s

scholiastic
BR ˌskəʊliˈastɪk
AM ˌskoʊliˈæstɪk

scholium
BR ˈskəʊliəm, -z
AM ˈskoʊliəm, -z

Scholl
BR ʃɒl, ʃəʊl
AM ʃoʊl, ʃɔl, ʃɑl

Schönberg
BR ˈʃəːnbəːg
AM ˈʃənbərg, ˈʃoʊnbərg

Schonfield
BR ˈskɒnfiːld
AM ˈskɑnˌfild

school
BR skuːl, -z, -ɪŋ, -d
AM skuːl, -z, -ɪŋ, -d

schoolable
BR ˈskuːləbl
AM ˈskuːləbəl

school-age
BR ˈskuːleɪdʒ
AM ˌskuːlˈeɪdʒ

schoolbook
BR ˈskuːlbʊk, -s
AM ˈskuːlˌbʊk, -s

schoolboy
BR ˈskuːlbɔɪ, -z
AM ˈskuːlˌbɔɪ, -z

schoolbus
BR ˌskuːlˈbʌs
AM ˈskuːlbʌs, -ɪz

schoolchild
BR ˈskuːltʃʌɪld
AM ˈskuːlˌtʃaɪld

schoolchildren
BR ˈskuːltʃɪldr(ə)n
AM ˈskuːlˌtʃɪldrən

schooldays
BR ˈskuːldeɪz
AM ˈskuːlˌdeɪz

schoolfellow
BR ˈskuːlfɛləʊ, -z
AM ˈskuːlˌfeloʊ, -z

schoolgirl
BR ˈskuːlɡəːl, -z
AM ˈskuːlˌɡərl, -z

schoolhouse
BR ˈskuːlhaʊ|s, -zɪz
AM ˈskuːlˌ(h)aʊ|s, -zəz

schoolie
BR ˈskuːl|i, -ɪz
AM ˈskuːli, -z

schooling
BR ˈskuːlɪŋ
AM ˈskuːlɪŋ

schoolkid
BR ˈskuːlkɪd, -z
AM ˈskuːlˌkɪd, -z

schoolman
BR ˈskuːlman, ˈskuːlmən
AM ˈskuːlmən, ˈskuːlˌmæn

schoolmarm
BR ˈskuːlmɑːm, -z
AM ˈskuːlˌmɑ(r)m, -z

schoolmarmish
BR ˈskuːlmɑːmɪʃ
AM ˈskuːlˌmɑ(r)mɪʃ

schoolmaster
BR ˈskuːlmɑːstə(r), ˈskuːlˌmɑstə(r), -z
AM ˈskuːlˌmæstər, -z

schoolmastering
BR ˈskuːlˌmɑːst(ə)rɪŋ, ˈskuːlˌmɑst(ə)rɪŋ
AM ˈskuːlˌmæst(ə)rɪŋ

schoolmasterly
BR ˈskuːlˌmɑːstəli, ˈskuːlˌmɑstəli
AM ˈskuːlˌmæstərli

schoolmate
BR ˈskuːlmeɪt, -s
AM ˈskuːlˌmeɪt, -s

schoolmen
BR ˈskuːlmɛn, ˈskuːlmən
AM ˈskuːlmən, ˈskuːlˌmɛn

schoolmistress
BR ˈskuːlˌmɪstrɪs, -ɪz
AM ˈskuːlˌmɪstrɪs, -ɪz

schoolmistressy
BR ˈskuːlˌmɪstrɪsi
AM ˈskuːlˌmɪstrɪsi

schoolroom
BR ˈskuːlruːm, ˈskuːlrʊm, -z
AM ˈskuːlˌrum, ˈskuːlˌrʊm, -z

schoolteacher
BR ˈskuːlˌtiːtʃə(r), -z
AM ˈskuːlˌtitʃər, -z

schoolteaching
BR ˈskuːlˌtiːtʃɪŋ
AM ˈskuːlˌtitʃɪŋ

schooltime
BR ˈskuːltʌɪm
AM ˈskuːlˌtaɪm

schoolwork
BR ˈskuːlwəːk
AM ˈskuːlˌwərk

schoolyard
BR ˈskuːljɑːd, -z
AM ˈskuːlˌjɑrd, -z

schooner
BR ˈskuːnə(r), -z
AM ˈskunər, -z

Schopenhauer
BR ˈʃəʊp(ə)nhaʊə(r), ˈʃɒp(ə)nhaʊə(r)
AM ˈʃoʊpən,(h)aʊər

schorl
BR ʃɔːl
AM ʃɔrl

schottische
BR ʃɒˈtiːʃ, ʃəˈtiːʃ, -ɪz
AM ˈʃɑdɪʃ, -ɪʃɪz

Schreiber
BR ˈʃrʌɪbə(r)
AM ˈʃraɪbər

Schroder
BR ˈʃrəʊdə(r)
AM ˈʃroʊdər

Schrödinger
BR ˈʃrəːdɪŋə(r), ˈʃrəʊdɪŋə(r)
AM ˈʃreɪdɪŋ(ɡ)ər, ˈʃroʊdɪŋ(ɡ)ər

Schroeder
BR ˈʃrəʊdə(r), ˈʃrəːdə(r)
AM ˈʃroʊdər, ˈʃreɪdər

schtick
BR ʃtɪk
AM ʃtɪk

schtuck
BR ʃtʊk
AM ʃtʊk

Schubert
BR ˈʃuːbət
AM ˈʃubərt

Schubertian
BR ʃuːˈbəːtɪən, -z
AM ʃuˈbərdiən, -z

Schultz
BR ʃults
AM ʃults

Schulz
BR ʃults
AM ʃults

Schumacher
BR ˈʃuːmakə(r)
AM ˈʃuˌmɑkər

Schumann
BR ˈʃuːmən
AM ˈʃumən, ˈʃuˌmɑn

schuss
BR ʃus, ʃuːs, -ɪz, -ɪŋ, -t
AM ʃus, ʃʊs, -əz, -ɪŋ, -t

Schütz
BR ʃuːts
AM ʃʊts

Schuyler
BR ˈskʌɪlə(r)
AM ˈskaɪlər

schwa
BR ʃwɑː(r), ʃvɑː(r), -z
AM ʃwɑ, -z

Schwann
BR ʃwɒn, ʃvan
AM ʃwɑn

Schwartz
BR ʃwɔːts
AM ʃwɔ(ə)rts

Schwarz
BR ʃwɔːts
AM ʃwɔ(ə)rts

Schwarzkopf
BR ʃvɑːtskɒ(p)f,
'ʃwɑːtskɒ(p)f,
'ʃwɔːtskɒ(p)f
AM ʃwɔ(ə)rts‚kɔ(p)f

Schwarzwald
BR ʃvɑːtsvald
AM ʃwɔ(ə)rts‚wɑld

Schweitzer
BR ʃwaɪtsə(r),
'ʃvaɪtsə(r)
AM ʃwaɪtsər

Schweppes®
BR ʃweps
AM ʃweps

Schyler
BR 'skʌɪlə(r)
AM 'skaɪlər

sciagram
BR 'sʌɪəgram, -z
AM 'saɪə‚græm, -z

sciagraph
BR 'sʌɪəgrɑːf,
'sʌɪəgraf, -s, -ɪŋ, -t
AM 'saɪə‚græf, -s, -ɪŋ, -t

sciagraphic
BR 'sʌɪə'grafɪk
AM 'saɪə'græfɪk

sciagraphy
BR sʌɪ'agrəfi
AM saɪ'ægrəfi

sciamachy
BR sʌɪ'aməki
AM saɪ'æməki

sciatic
BR sʌɪ'atɪk
AM saɪ'ædɪk

sciatica
BR sʌɪ'atɪkə(r)
AM saɪ'ædəkə

sciatically
BR sʌɪ'atɪkli
AM saɪ'ædək(ə)li

science
BR 'sʌɪəns, -ɪz
AM 'saɪəns, -əz

scienter
adverb
BR sʌɪ'ɛntə(r)
AM saɪ'ɛn(t)ər

sciential
BR sʌɪ'ɛnʃl, -z
AM saɪ'ɛn(t)ʃəl, -z

scientific
BR ‚sʌɪən'tɪfɪk
AM ‚saɪən'tɪfɪk

scientifically
BR ‚sʌɪən'tɪfɪkli
AM ‚saɪən'tɪfɪk(ə)li

scientism
BR 'sʌɪəntɪz(ə)m
AM 'saɪən‚tɪzəm

scientist
BR 'sʌɪəntɪst, -s

AM 'saɪən(t)əst, -s

scientistic
BR ‚sʌɪən'tɪstɪk
AM ‚saɪən'tɪstɪk

Scientologist
BR ‚sʌɪən'tɒlədʒɪst, -s
AM ‚saɪən'tɑlədʒəst, -s

Scientology®
BR ‚sʌɪən'tɒlədʒi
AM ‚saɪən'tɑlədʒi

sci-fi
BR 'sʌɪfʌɪ
AM 'saɪ'faɪ

scilicet
BR 'sɪlɪsɛt, 'sʌɪlɪsɛt,
'skiːlɪkɛt
AM 'sɪlə‚sɛt, 'skilə‚kɛt

scilla
BR 'sɪlə(r), -z
AM 'sɪlə, -z

Scillies
BR 'sɪlɪz
AM 'sɪliz

Scillonian
BR sɪ'ləʊnɪən, -z
AM sə'loʊnɪən, -z

Scilly
BR 'sɪli
AM 'sɪli

scimitar
BR 'sɪmɪtə(r), -z
AM 'sɪmədər,
'sɪmə‚tɑr, -z

scintigram
BR 'sɪntɪgram, -z
AM 'sɪn(t)ə‚græm, -z

scintigraphy
BR sɪn'tɪgrəfi
AM sɪn'tɪgrəfi

scintilla
BR s(ɪ)n'tɪlə(r), -z
AM sɪn'tɪlə, -z

scintillant
adjective
BR 'sɪntɪlənt, 'sɪntɪln̩t
AM 'sɪn(t)lənt

scintillate
BR 'sɪntɪleɪt, -s, -ɪŋ, -ɪd
AM 'sɪn(t)l‚eɪt, -ts,
-dɪŋ, -dɪd

scintillatingly
BR 'sɪntɪleɪtɪŋli
AM 'sɪn(t)l‚eɪdɪŋli

scintillation
BR ‚sɪntɪ'leɪʃn
AM ‚sɪn(t)l'eɪʃən

scintiscan
BR 'sɪntɪskan, -z
AM 'sɪn(t)ə‚skæn, -z

sciolism
BR 'sʌɪəlɪz(ə)m
AM 'saɪə‚lɪzəm

sciolist
BR 'sʌɪəlɪst, -s
AM 'saɪələst, -s

sciolistic
BR ‚sʌɪə'lɪstɪk

AM ‚saɪə'lɪstɪk

scion
BR 'sʌɪən, -z
AM 'saɪən, -z

Scipio
BR 'skɪpɪəʊ, 'sɪpɪəʊ
AM 's(k)ɪpioʊ

scire facias
BR ‚sʌɪrɪ 'feɪʃɪas,
+ 'feɪʃɪəs
AM ‚saɪrɪ 'feɪʃ(i)əs

scirocco
BR sɪ'rɒkəʊ, -z
AM sə'rɑkoʊ, ʃə'rɑkoʊ,
-z

scirrhi
BR 'sɪrʌɪ
AM 's(k)ɪ‚raɪ, 'skɪ‚ri

scirrhoid
BR 'sɪrɔɪd
AM 's(k)ɪ‚rɔɪd

scirrhosity
BR sɪ'rɒsɪti
AM s(k)ɪ'rɑsədi

scirrhous
BR 'sɪrəs
AM 's(k)ɪrəs

scirrhus
BR 'sɪrəs
AM 's(k)ɪrəs

scissel
BR 'skɪsl
AM 'sɪsəl, 'sɪzəl

scissile
BR 'sɪsʌɪl, 'sɪs(ɪ)l
AM 'sɪsəl, 'sɪ‚saɪl

scission
BR 'sɪʒn, 'sɪʃn, -z
AM 'sɪʒən, 'sɪʃən, -z

scissor
BR 'sɪz|ə(r), -əz, -(ə)rɪŋ,
-əd
AM 'sɪz|ər, -ərz, -(ə)rɪŋ,
-ərd

scissorwise
BR 'sɪzəwʌɪz
AM 'sɪzər‚waɪz

sciurine
BR 'sʌɪjʊrʌɪn,
'saɪjərɪn
AM 'saɪ(j)ə‚rin,
'saɪ(j)ərən

sciuroid
BR 'sʌɪjʊrɔɪd
AM 'saɪ(j)ə‚rɔɪd

sclera
BR 'sklɪərə(r)
AM 'sklɛrə

scleral
BR 'sklɪərəl, 'sklɪərl̩
AM 'sklɛrəl

sclerenchyma
BR sklɪə'rɛŋkɪmə(r),
sklɪ'rɛŋkɪmə(r), -z
AM sklə'rɛŋkəmə, -z

sclerenchymata
BR sklɪə'rɛŋkɪmətə(r),
sklɪ'rɛŋkɪmətə(r)
AM sklə‚rɛŋkə'mɑdə

sclerite
BR 'sklɪərʌɪt, 'sklɛrʌɪt
AM 'skli‚raɪt, 'sklɛ‚raɪt

scleritis
BR sklɪə'rʌɪtɪs,
sklɪ'rʌɪtɪs
AM sklə'raɪdɪs

scleroderma
BR ‚sklɪərə(ʊ)'dəːmə(r),
‚sklɛrə'dəːmə(r)
AM ‚sklɛrə'dərmə

scleroid
BR 'sklɪərɔɪd,
'sklɛrɔɪd
AM 'sklɛ‚rɔɪd

scleroma
BR sklɪ'rəʊmə(r)
AM sklə'roʊmə

scleromata
BR sklɪ'rəʊmətə(r)
AM sklə'roʊmədə

sclerometer
BR sklɪ'rɒmɪtə(r), -z
AM sklə'rɑmədər, -z

sclerophyll
BR 'sklɪərə(ʊ)fɪl,
'sklɛrə(ʊ)fɪl, -z
AM 'sklɛrə‚fɪl, -z

sclerophyllous
BR sklɪ'rɒfɪləs
AM sklə'rɑfələs

scleroprotein
BR ‚sklɪərə(ʊ)'prəʊtiːn,
‚sklɛrə(ʊ)'prəʊtiːn, -z
AM ‚sklɛroʊ'proʊ‚tin,
-z

sclerosed
BR 'sklɪərəʊzd,
'sklɛrəʊzd
AM 'sklɛ‚roʊzd

scleroses
BR sklɪ'rəʊsiːz
AM sklə'roʊ‚siz

sclerosis
BR sklɪ'rəʊsɪs
AM sklə'roʊsəz

sclerotherapy
BR ‚sklɪərə(ʊ)'θɛrəpi,
‚sklɛrə(ʊ)'θɛrəpi
AM ‚sklɛrə'θɛrəpi

sclerotic
BR sklɪ'rɒtɪk
AM sklə'rɑdɪk

sclerotin
BR 'sklɪərətɪn,
'sklɛrətɪn
AM 'sklɛrətɪn

sclerotised
BR 'sklɪərətʌɪzd,
'sklɛrətʌɪzd
AM 'sklɛrə‚taɪzd

sclerotitis
BR ‚sklɪərə(ʊ)'tʌɪtɪs,
‚sklɛrə(ʊ)'tʌɪtɪs

sclerotium
AM ˌsklɛrəˈtaɪdɪs

sclerotium
BR sklɪˈrəʊtiəm
AM skləˈrəʊtiəm

sclerotized
BR ˈsklɪərətaɪzd,
ˈsklɛrətaɪzd
AM ˈsklɛrəˌtaɪzd

sclerotomy
BR sklɪˈrɒtəm|i, -ɪz
AM skləˈrɑdəmi, -z

sclerous
BR ˈsklɪərəs, ˈsklɛrəs
AM ˈsklɛrəs

Scobie
BR ˈskəʊbi
AM ˈskoʊbi

Scoby
BR ˈskəʊbi
AM ˈskoʊbi

scoff
BR skɒf, -s, -ɪŋ, -t
AM skɔf, skaf, -s, -ɪŋ, -t

scoffer
BR ˈskɒfə(r), -z
AM ˈskɔfər, ˈskafər, -z

scoffingly
BR ˈskɒfɪŋli
AM ˈskɔfɪŋli, ˈskafɪŋli

Scofield
BR ˈskəʊfiːld
AM ˈskoʊˌfild

scold
BR skəʊld, -z, -ɪŋ, -ɪd
AM skoʊld, -z, -ɪŋ, -əd

scolder
BR ˈskəʊldə(r), -z
AM ˈskoʊldər, -z

scolding
BR ˈskəʊldɪŋ, -z
AM ˈskoʊldɪŋ, -z

scolex
BR ˈskəʊlɛks, -ɪz
AM ˈskoʊˌlɛks, -əz

scolices
BR ˈskəʊlɪsiːz
AM ˈskoʊləsiz

scoliosis
BR ˌskɒlɪˈəʊsɪs
AM ˌskoʊliˈoʊsəs

scoliotic
BR ˌskɒlɪˈɒtɪk
AM ˌskoʊliˈɑdɪk

scollop
BR ˈskɒləp, -s, -ɪŋ, -t
AM ˈskaləp, ˈskæləp, -s, -ɪŋ, -t

scolopendria
BR ˌskɒləˈpɛndrɪə(r)
AM ˌskaləˈpɛndriə

scolopendrium
BR ˌskɒləˈpɛndrɪəm
AM ˌskaləˈpɛndriəm

scomber
BR ˈskɒmbə(r), -z
AM ˈskambər, -z

scombrid
BR ˈskɒmbrɪd, -z
AM ˈskambrəd, -z

scombroid
BR ˈskɒmbrɔɪd, -z
AM ˈskamˌbrɔɪd, -z

sconce
BR skɒns, -ɪz
AM skans, -əz

Scone
place in Scotland
BR skuːn
AM skun, skoʊn

scone
BR skɒn, skəʊn, -z
AM skoʊn, -z

scoop
BR skuːp, -s, -ɪŋ, -t
AM skup, -s, -ɪŋ, -t

scooper
BR ˈskuːpə(r), -z
AM ˈskupər, -z

scoopful
BR ˈskuːpfʊl, -z
AM ˈskupˌfʊl, -z

scoot
BR skuːt, -s, -ɪŋ, -ɪd
AM sku|t, -ts, -ɪŋ, -dəd

scooter
BR ˈskuːt|ə(r), -əz, -(ə)rɪŋ, -əd
AM ˈskudər, -z, -ɪŋ, -d

scooterist
BR ˈskuːt(ə)rɪst, -s
AM ˈskudərəst, -s

scopa
BR ˈskəʊpə(r)
AM ˈskoʊpə

scopae
BR ˈskəʊpiː
AM ˈskoʊpi

scope
BR skəʊp, -s
AM skoʊp, -s

scopolamine
BR skəˈpɒləmiːn, skəˈpɒləmɪn
AM skəˈpɑləˌmin

scopula
BR ˈskɒpjələ(r)
AM ˈskɑpjələ

scopulae
BR ˈskɒpjəliː
AM ˈskɑpjəli, ˈskɑpjəˌlaɪ

Scopus
BR ˈskəʊpəs
AM ˈskoʊpəs

scorbutic
BR skɔːˈbjuːtɪk
AM skɔrˈbjudɪk

scorbutically
BR skɔːˈbjuːtɪkli
AM skɔrˈbjudək(ə)li

scorch
BR skɔːtʃ, -ɪz, -ɪŋ, -t
AM skɔrtʃ, -əz, -ɪŋ, -t

scorcher
BR ˈskɔːtʃə(r), -z
AM ˈskɔrtʃər, -z

scorchingly
BR ˈskɔːtʃɪŋli
AM ˈskɔrtʃɪŋli

scordatura
BR ˌskɔːdəˈtjʊərə(r), ˌskɔːdəˈtʃʊərə(r)
AM ˌskɔrdəˈt(j)ʊrə

score
BR skɔː(r), -z, -ɪŋ, -d
AM skɔ(ə)r, -z, -ɪŋ, -d

scoreboard
BR ˈskɔːbɔːd, -z
AM ˈskɔrˌbɔ(ə)rd, -z

scorebook
BR ˈskɔːbʊk, -s
AM ˈskɔrˌbʊk, -s

scorecard
BR ˈskɔːkɑːd, -z
AM ˈskɔrˌkard, -z

scoreine
BR ˈskɔːriːn, -z
AM ˈskɔrin, -z

scorekeeper
BR ˈskɔːˌkiːpə(r), -z
AM ˈskɔrˌkipər, -z

scoreless
BR ˈskɔːləs
AM ˈskɔrləs

scorer
BR ˈskɔːrə(r), -z
AM ˈskɔrər, -z

score sheet
BR ˈskɔːˌʃiːt, -s
AM ˈskɔrˌʃit, -s

scoria
BR ˈskɔːrɪə(r)
AM ˈskɔriə

scoriaceous
BR ˌskɔːrɪˈeɪʃəs
AM ˌskɔriˈeɪʃəs

scoriae
BR ˈskɔːriː
AM ˈskɔriaɪ, ˈskɔrii

scorification
BR ˌskɔːrɪfɪˈkeɪʃn
AM ˌskɔrəfəˈkeɪʃən

scorifier
BR ˈskɔːrɪfaɪə(r)
AM ˈskɔrəˌfaɪər

scorify
BR ˈskɔːrɪfaɪ, -z, -ɪŋ, -d
AM ˈskɔrəˌfaɪ, -z, -ɪŋ, -d

scoring
BR ˈskɔːrɪŋ
AM ˈskɔrɪŋ

scorn
BR skɔːn, -z, -ɪŋ, -d
AM skɔ(ə)rn, -z, -ɪŋ, -d

scorner
BR ˈskɔːnə(r), -z
AM ˈskɔrnər, -z

scornful
BR ˈskɔːnf(ʊ)l
AM ˈskɔrnfəl

scornfully
BR ˈskɔːnfəli, ˈskɔːnfli
AM ˈskɔrnfəli

scornfulness
BR ˈskɔːnf(ʊ)lnəs
AM ˈskɔrnfəlnəs

scorp
BR skɔːp, -s
AM skɔ(ə)rp, -s

scorper
BR ˈskɔːpə(r), -z
AM ˈskɔrpər, -z

Scorpian
BR ˈskɔːpɪən, -z
AM ˈskɔrpiən, -z

Scorpio
BR ˈskɔːpɪəʊ, -z
AM ˈskɔrpioʊ, -z

scorpioid
BR ˈskɔːpɪɔɪd, -z
AM ˈskɔrpiˌɔɪd, -z

scorpion
BR ˈskɔːpɪən, -z
AM ˈskɔrpiən, -z

Scorpius
BR ˈskɔːpɪəs
AM ˈskɔrpiəs

scorzonera
BR ˌskɔːtsəˈnɪərə(r)
AM ˌskɔrzəˈnɪrə

Scot
BR skɒt, -s
AM skat, -s

scotch
BR skɒtʃ, -ɪz, -ɪŋ, -t
AM skatʃ, -əz, -ɪŋ, -t

Scotchman
BR ˈskɒtʃmən
AM ˈskatʃmən

Scotchmen
BR ˈskɒtʃmən
AM ˈskatʃmən

Scotchwoman
BR ˈskɒtʃˌwʊmən
AM ˈskatʃˌwʊmən

Scotchwomen
BR ˈskɒtʃˌwɪmɪn
AM ˈskatʃˌwɪmɪn

scoter
BR ˈskəʊtə(r), -z
AM ˈskoʊdər, -z

scot-free
BR ˌskɒtˈfriː
AM ˌskatˈfri

Scotia
BR ˈskəʊʃə(r)
AM ˈskoʊʃə

Scoticise
BR ˈskɒtɪsaɪz, -ɪz, -ɪŋ, -d
AM ˈskadəˌsaɪz, -ɪz, -ɪŋ, -d

Scoticism
BR ˈskɒtɪsɪz(ə)m, -z
AM ˈskadəˌsɪzəm, -z

Scoticize
BR ˈskɒtɪsaɪz, -ɪz, -ɪŋ, -d

AM 'skɑdə͵saɪz, -ɪz, -ɪŋ,
-d

Scotism
BR 'skɒtɪz(ə)m, -z
AM 'skɑ͵tɪzəm, -z

Scotist
BR 'skɒtɪst, -s
AM 'skɑdəst, -s

Scotland
BR 'skɒtlənd
AM 'skɑtlən(d)

scotoma
BR skə'təʊmə(r), -z
AM skə'toʊmə, -z

scotomata
BR skə'təʊmətə(r)
AM skə'toʊmədə

Scots
BR skɒts
AM skɑts

Scotsman
BR 'skɒtsmən
AM 'skɑtsmən

Scotsmen
BR 'skɒtsmən
AM 'skɑtsmən

Scotswoman
BR 'skɒts͵wʊmən
AM 'skɑts͵wʊmən

Scotswomen
BR 'skɒts͵wɪmɪn
AM 'skɑts͵wɪmɪn

Scott
BR skɒt
AM skɑt

Scotticise
BR 'skɒtɪsʌɪz, -ɪz, -ɪŋ, -d
AM 'skɑdə͵saɪz, -ɪz, -ɪŋ,
-d

Scotticism
BR 'skɒtɪsɪz(ə)m, -z
AM 'skɑdə͵sɪzəm, -z

Scotticize
BR 'skɒtɪsʌɪz, -ɪz, -ɪŋ, -d
AM 'skɑdə͵saɪz, -ɪz, -ɪŋ,
-d

Scottie
BR 'skɒt|i, -iz
AM 'skɑdi, -z

Scottish
BR 'skɒtɪʃ
AM 'skɑdɪʃ

Scottishness
BR 'skɒtɪʃnɪs
AM 'skɑdɪʃnɪs

Scotty
BR 'skɒt|i, -iz
AM 'skɑdi, -z

scoundrel
BR 'skaʊndr(ə)l, -z
AM 'skaʊndrəl, -z

scoundreldom
BR 'skaʊndr(ə)ld(ə)m
AM 'skaʊndreldəm

scoundrelism
BR 'skaʊndrəlɪz(ə)m,
'skaʊndr͵lɪz(ə)m

AM 'skaʊndrə͵lɪzəm

scoundrelly
BR 'skaʊndrəli,
'skaʊndr͵li
AM 'skaʊndrəli

scour
BR 'skaʊə(r), -z, -ɪŋ, -d
AM 'skaʊ(ə)r, -z, -ɪŋ, -d

scourer
BR 'skaʊərə(r), -z
AM 'skaʊ(ə)rər, -z

Scourfield
BR 'skaʊəfiːld
AM 'skaʊ(ə)r͵fild

scourge
BR skɜːdʒ, -ɪz, -ɪŋ, -d
AM skɜrdʒ, -əz, -ɪŋ, -d

scourger
BR 'skɜːdʒə(r), -z
AM 'skɜrdʒər, -z

scourings
BR 'skaʊərɪŋz
AM 'skaʊ(ə)rɪŋz

Scouser
BR 'skaʊsə(r), -z
AM 'skaʊsər, -z

Scout
BR skaʊt, -s
AM skaʊt, -s

scout
BR skaʊt, -s, -ɪŋ, -ɪd
AM skaʊ|t, -ts, -dɪŋ,
-dəd

scouter
BR 'skaʊtə(r), -z
AM 'skaʊdər, -z

Scoutmaster
BR 'skaʊt͵mɑːstə(r),
'skaʊt͵mɑstə(r), -z
AM 'skaʊt͵mæstər, -z

scow
BR skaʊ, -z
AM skaʊ, -z

scowl
BR skaʊl, -z, -ɪŋ, -d
AM skaʊl, -z, -ɪŋ, -d

scowler
BR 'skaʊlə(r), -z
AM 'skaʊlər, -z

scrabble
BR 'skrab|l, -lz,
-lɪŋ \ -lɪŋ, -ld
AM 'skræbəl, -əlz,
-(ə)lɪŋ, -əld

scrag
BR skrag, -z, -ɪŋ, -d
AM skræg, -z, -ɪŋ, -d

scrag-end
BR ͵skrag'end, -z
AM ͵skræg'end, -z

scraggily
BR 'skragɪli
AM 'skrægəli

scragginess
BR 'skragɪnɪs
AM 'skrægɪnɪs

scraggly
BR 'skragli, 'skragḷi
AM 'skræg(ə)li

scraggy
BR 'skragli, -ɪə(r), -ɪɪst
AM 'skrægi, -ər, -ɪst

scram
BR skram, -z, -ɪŋ, -d
AM skræm, -z, -ɪŋ, -d

scramble
BR 'skramb|l, -lz,
-lɪŋ \ -lɪŋ, -ld
AM 'skræmbəl, -əlz,
-(ə)lɪŋ, -əld

scrambler
BR 'skramblə(r), -z
AM 'skræmb(ə)lər, -z

scramjet
BR 'skramdʒet, -s
AM 'skræmdʒet, -s

scran
BR skran
AM skræn

Scranton
BR 'skrantən
AM 'skræn(t)ən

scrap
BR skrap, -s, -ɪŋ, -t
AM skræp, -s, -ɪŋ, -t

scrapbook
BR 'skrapbʊk, -s
AM 'skræp͵bʊk, -s

scrape
BR skreɪp, -s, -ɪŋ, -t
AM skreɪp, -s, -ɪŋ, -t

scraper
BR 'skreɪpə(r), -z
AM 'skreɪpər, -z

scraperboard
BR 'skreɪpəbɔːd, -z
AM 'screɪpər͵bɔ(ə)rd,
-z

scrapheap
BR 'skraphiːp, -s
AM 'skræp͵(h)ip, -s

scrapie
BR 'skreɪpi
AM 'skreɪpi

scraping
BR 'skreɪpɪŋ, -z
AM 'skreɪpɪŋ, -z

scrapper
BR 'skrapə(r), -z
AM 'skræpər, -z

scrappily
BR 'skrapɪli
AM 'skræpəli

scrappiness
BR 'skrapɪnɪs
AM 'skræpɪnɪs

scrapple
BR 'skrapl
AM 'skræpəl

scrappy
BR 'skrapli, -ɪə(r), -ɪɪst
AM 'skræpi, -ər, -ɪst

scrapyard
BR 'skrapjɑːd, -z
AM 'skræp͵jɑrd, -z

scratch
BR skratʃ, -ɪz, -ɪŋ, -t
AM skrætʃ, -əz, -ɪŋ, -t

scratchboard
BR 'skratʃbɔːd, -z
AM 'skrætʃ͵bɔ(ə)rd, -z

scratcher
BR 'skratʃə(r), -z
AM 'skrætʃər, -z

scratchily
BR 'skratʃɪli
AM 'skrætʃəli

scratchiness
BR 'skratʃɪnɪs
AM 'skrætʃɪnɪs

scratchings
BR 'skratʃɪŋz
AM 'skrætʃɪŋz

scratchpad
BR 'skratʃpad, -z
AM 'skrætʃ͵pæd, -z

Scratchwood
BR 'skratʃwʊd
AM 'skrætʃ͵wʊd

scratchy
BR 'skratʃ|i, -ɪə(r), -ɪɪst
AM 'skrætʃi, -ər, -ɪst

scrawl
BR skrɔːl, -z, -ɪŋ, -d
AM skrɔl, skral, -z, -ɪŋ,
-d

scrawly
BR 'skrɔːli
AM 'skrɔli, 'skrali

scrawniness
BR 'skrɔːnɪnɪs
AM 'skrɔnɪnɪs,
'skranɪnɪs

scrawny
BR 'skrɔːn|i, -ɪə(r), -ɪɪst
AM 'skrɔni, 'skrani,
-ər, -ɪst

scream
BR skriːm, -z, -ɪŋ, -d
AM skrim, -z, -ɪŋ, -d

screamer
BR 'skriːmə(r), -z
AM 'skrimər, -z

screamingly
BR 'skriːmɪŋli
AM 'skrimɪŋli

scree
BR skriː, -z
AM skri, -z

screech
BR skriːtʃ, -ɪz, -ɪŋ, -t
AM skritʃ, -ɪz, -ɪŋ, -t

screecher
BR 'skriːtʃə(r), -z
AM 'skritʃər, -z

screechy
BR 'skriːtʃ|i, -ɪə(r),
-ɪɪst
AM 'skritʃi, -ər, -ɪst

screed
BR skriːd, -z
AM skrid, -z

screen
BR skriːn, -z, -ɪŋ, -d
AM skrin, -z, -ɪŋ, -d

screenable
BR 'skriːnəbl
AM 'skrinəbəl

screener
BR 'skriːnə(r), -z
AM 'skrinər, -z

screening
BR 'skriːnɪŋ, -z
AM 'skrinɪŋ, -z

screenplay
BR 'skriːnpleɪ, -z
AM 'skrin,pleɪ, -z

screen-print
BR 'skriːnprɪnt, -s, -ɪŋ, -ɪd
AM 'skrin,prɪn|t, -ts, -(t)ɪŋ, -(t)ɪd

screenwriter
BR 'skriːn,rʌɪtə(r), -z
AM 'skrin,raɪdər, -z

screenwriting
BR 'skriːn,rʌɪtɪŋ
AM 'skrin,raɪdɪŋ

screw
BR skruː, -z, -ɪŋ, -d
AM skru, -z, -ɪŋ, -d

screwable
BR 'skruːəbl
AM 'skruəbəl

screwball
BR 'skruːbɔːl, -z
AM 'skru,bɔl, 'skru,bɑl, -z

screwdriver
BR 'skruː,drʌɪvə(r), -z
AM 'skru,draɪvər, -z

screwer
BR 'skruːə(r), -z
AM 'skru(ə)r, -z

screwiness
BR 'skruːɪnɪs
AM 'skruinɪs

screwtop
noun
BR 'skruːtɒp, ,skruː'tɒp, -s
AM 'skru,tɑp, -s

screw-top
adjective
BR ,skruː'tɒp
AM 'skru,tɑp

screwup
BR 'skruːʌp, -s
AM 'skru,əp, -s

screwworm
BR 'skruːwɜːm, -z
AM 'skru,wɜrm, -z

screwy
BR 'skruː|i, -ɪə(r), -ɪɪst
AM 'skrui, -ər, -ɪst

Scriabin
BR skrɪ'abɪn, skrɪ'ɑːbɪn
AM skri'ɑbən
RUS 'skr'ab'in

scribal
BR 'skrʌɪbl
AM 'skraɪbəl

scribble
BR 'skrɪb|l, -lz, -lɪŋ\-lɪŋ, -ld
AM 'skrɪbəl, -əlz, -(ə)lɪŋ, -əld

scribbler
BR 'skrɪblə(r), 'skrɪblə(r), -z
AM 'skrɪb(ə)lər, -z

scribbling
BR 'skrɪb|lɪŋ, 'skrɪblɪŋ, -z
AM 'skrɪb(ə)lɪŋ, -z

scribbling-pad
BR 'skrɪb|lɪŋpad, 'skrɪblɪŋpad, -z
AM 'skrɪblɪŋ,pæd, -z

scribbly
BR 'skrɪb|li, 'skrɪbli
AM 'skrɪbli

scribe
BR skrʌɪb, -z, -ɪŋ, -d
AM skraɪb, -z, -ɪŋ, -d

scriber
BR 'skrʌɪbə(r), -z
AM 'skraɪbər, -z

scrim
BR skrɪm, -z
AM skrɪm, -z

Scrimgeour
BR 'skrɪmdʒə(r)
AM 'skrɪmdʒər

Scrimger
BR 'skrɪmdʒə(r)
AM 'skrɪmdʒər

scrimmage
BR 'skrɪm|ɪdʒ, -ɪdʒɪz
AM 'skrɪmɪdʒ, -ɪz

scrimmager
BR 'skrɪmɪdʒə(r), -z
AM 'skrɪmədʒər, -z

scrimp
BR skrɪm|p, -ps, -pɪŋ, -(p)t
AM skrɪm|p, -ps, -pɪŋ, -(p)t

scrimpy
BR 'skrɪmp|i, -ɪə(r), -ɪɪst
AM 'skrɪmpi, -ər, -ɪst

scrimshank
BR 'skrɪmʃaŋ|k, -ks, -kɪŋ, -(k)t
AM 'skrɪmˌʃæŋ|k, -ks, -kɪŋ, -(k)t

scrimshanker
BR 'skrɪmʃaŋkə(r), -z
AM 'skrɪmˌʃæŋkər, -z

---

scrimshaw
BR 'skrɪmˌʃɔː(r), -z, -ɪŋ, -d
AM 'skrɪmˌʃɔ, 'skrɪmˌʃɑ, -z, -ɪŋ, -d

scrip
BR skrɪp, -s
AM skrɪp, -s

scripsit
BR 'skrɪpsɪt
AM 'skrɪpsɪt

script
BR skrɪp|t, -(t)s, -tɪŋ, -tɪd
AM skrɪp|(t), -(t)s, -tɪŋ, -tɪd

scriptoria
BR skrɪp'tɔːrɪə(r)
AM ,skrɪp'tɔriə

scriptorial
BR skrɪp'tɔːrɪəl
AM ,skrɪp'tɔriəl

scriptorium
BR skrɪp'tɔːrɪəm, -z
AM ,skrɪp'tɔriəm, -z

scriptory
BR 'skrɪpt(ə)r|i, -ɪz
AM 'skrɪptəri, -z

scriptural
BR 'skrɪptʃ(ə)rəl, 'skrɪptʃ(ə)rl
AM 'skrɪp(t)ʃ(ə)rəl

scripturalism
BR 'skrɪptʃ(ə)rəlɪz(ə)m, 'skrɪptʃ(ə)rlɪz(ə)m
AM 'skrɪp(t)ʃ(ə)rəˌlɪz-əm

scripturalist
BR 'skrɪptʃ(ə)rəlɪst, 'skrɪptʃ(ə)rlɪst, -s
AM 'skrɪp(t)ʃ(ə)rələst, -s

scripturally
BR 'skrɪptʃ(ə)rəli, 'skrɪptʃ(ə)rli
AM 'skrɪp(t)ʃ(ə)rəli

scripture
BR 'skrɪptʃə(r), -z
AM 'skrɪp(t)ʃər, -z

Scriptures
BR 'skrɪptʃəz
AM 'skrɪp(t)ʃərz

scriptwriter
BR 'skrɪp(t),rʌɪtə(r), -z
AM 'skrɪp(t),raɪdər, -z

scriptwriting
BR 'skrɪp(t),rʌɪtɪŋ
AM 'skrɪp(t),raɪdɪŋ

scrivener
BR 'skrɪv(ə)nə(r), 'skrɪvnə(r), -z
AM 'skrɪv(ə)nər, -z

scrobiculate
BR skrə(ʊ)'bɪkjʉlət, skrə(ʊ)'bɪkjʉleɪt, AM skroʊ'bɪkjəˌleɪt, skroʊ'bɪkjələt

---

scrod
BR skrɒd, -z
AM skrɑd, -z

scrofula
BR 'skrɒfjʉlə(r)
AM 'skrɒfjələ, 'skrɑfjələ

scrofulous
BR 'skrɒfjʉləs
AM 'skrɒfjələs, 'skrɑfjələs

scrofulously
BR 'skrɒfjʉləsli
AM 'skrɒfjələsli, 'skrɑfjələsli

scrofulousness
BR 'skrɒfjʉləsnəs
AM 'skrɒfjələsnəs, 'skrɑfjələsnəs

scroll
BR skrəʊl, -z, -ɪŋ, -d
AM skroʊl, -z, -ɪŋ, -d

scroller
BR 'skrəʊlə(r), -z
AM 'skroʊlər, -z

scrollwork
BR 'skrəʊlwɜːk
AM 'skroʊl,wɜrk

scrooge
BR skruːdʒ, -ɪz
AM skrudʒ, -əz

scrota
BR 'skrəʊtə(r)
AM 'skroʊdə

scrotal
BR 'skrəʊtl
AM 'skroʊdl

scrotitis
BR skrəʊ'tʌɪtɪs
AM skroʊ,taɪdɪs

scrotocele
BR 'skrəʊtəsiːl, -z
AM 'skroʊdə,sil, -z

scrotum
BR 'skrəʊtəm, -z
AM 'skroʊdəm, -z

scrounge
BR skraʊn(d)ʒ, -ɪz, -ɪŋ, -d
AM skraʊndʒ, -əz, -ɪŋ, -d

scrounger
BR 'skraʊn(d)ʒə(r), -z
AM 'skraʊndʒər, -z

scrub
BR skrʌb, -z, -ɪŋ, -d
AM skrəb, -z, -ɪŋ, -d

scrubber
BR 'skrʌbə(r), -z
AM 'skrəbər, -z

scrubbily
BR 'skrʌbɪli
AM 'skrəbəli

scrubby
BR 'skrʌb|i, -ɪə(r), -ɪɪst
AM 'skrəbi, -ər, -ɪst

scrubland
BR 'skrʌbland, -z
AM 'skrəb‚lænd, -z

scrubwoman
BR 'skrʌb‚wʊmən
AM 'skrəb‚wʊmən

scrubwomen
BR 'skrʌb‚wɪmɪn
AM 'skrʌb‚wɪmɪn

scruff
BR skrʌf, -s
AM skrəf, -s

scruffily
BR 'skrʌfɪli
AM 'skrəfəli

scruffiness
BR 'skrʌfɪnɪs
AM 'skrəfɪnɪs

scruffy
BR 'skrʌfli, -ɪə(r), -ɪɪst
AM 'skrəfi, -ər, -ɪst

scrum
BR skrʌm, -z, -ɪŋ, -d
AM skrəm, -z, -ɪŋ, -d

scrum-half
BR ‚skrʌm'hɑːf, -s
AM 'skrəm‚(h)æf, -s

scrummage
BR 'skrʌm|ɪdʒ, -ɪdʒɪz,
-ɪdʒɪŋ, -ɪdʒd
AM 'skrəmɪdʒ, -ɪz, -ɪŋ,
-d

scrummager
BR 'skrʌmɪdʒə(r), -z
AM 'skrəmədʒər, -z

scrummy
BR 'skrʌm|i, -ɪə(r),
-ɪɪst
AM 'skrəmi, -ər, -ɪst

scrump
BR skrʌm|p, -ps, -pɪŋ,
-(p)t
AM skrəm|p, -(p)s, -pɪŋ,
-(p)t

scrumple
BR 'skrʌmp|l, -lz,
-lɪŋ\-l̩ŋ, -ld
AM 'skrəmpəl, -z, -ɪŋ, -d

scrumptious
BR 'skrʌm(p)ʃəs
AM 'skrəm(p)ʃəs

scrumptiously
BR 'skrʌm(p)ʃəsli
AM 'skrəm(p)ʃəsli

scrumptiousness
BR 'skrʌm(p)ʃəsnəs
AM 'skrəm(p)ʃəsnəs

scrumpy
BR skrʌmpi
AM 'skrəmpi

scrunch
BR skrʌn(t)ʃ, -ɪz, -ɪŋ, -t
AM skrən(t)ʃ, -əz, -ɪŋ, -t

scruple
BR 'skruː:p|l, -lz,
-lɪŋ\-lŋ, -ld
AM 'skrupəl, -əlz,
-(ə)lɪŋ, -əld

scrupulosity
BR ‚skruː:pjʊ'lɒsɪti
AM ‚skrupjə'lɑsədi

scrupulous
BR 'skruː:pjʊləs
AM 'skrupjələs

scrupulously
BR 'skruː:pjʊləsli
AM 'skrupjələsli

scrupulousness
BR 'skruː:pjʊləsnəs
AM 'skrupjələsnəs

scrutable
BR 'skruː:təbl
AM 'skrudəbəl

scrutator
BR skruː'teɪtə(r), -z
AM 'skru‚teɪdər, -z

scrutineer
BR ‚skruː:tɪ'nɪə(r),
‚skru:tŋ'ɪə(r), -z
AM 'skrutn̩'ɪ(ə)r, -z

scrutinisation
BR ‚skruː:tɪnaɪ'zeɪʃn,
‚skruː:tŋaɪ'zeɪʃən
AM ‚skrutŋə'zeɪʃən,
‚skrutn̩‚aɪ'zeɪʃən

scrutinise
BR 'skruː:tɪnaɪz,
'skruː:tŋaɪz, -ɪz, -ɪŋ, -d
AM 'skrutn̩‚aɪz, -ɪz, -ɪŋ,
-d

scrutiniser
BR 'skruː:tɪnaɪzə(r),
'skruː:tŋaɪzə(r), -z
AM 'skrutn̩‚aɪzər, -z

scrutinization
BR ‚skruː:tɪnaɪ'zeɪʃn,
‚skruː:tŋaɪ'zeɪʃn
AM ‚skrutŋə'zeɪʃən,
‚skrutn̩‚aɪ'zeɪʃən

scrutinize
BR 'skruː:tɪnaɪz,
'skruː:tŋaɪz, -ɪz, -ɪŋ, -d
AM 'skrutn̩‚aɪz, -ɪz, -ɪŋ,
-d

scrutinizer
BR 'skruː:tɪnaɪzə(r),
'skruː:tŋaɪzə(r), -z
AM 'skrutn̩‚aɪzər, -z

scrutiny
BR 'skruː:tɪn|i,
'skruː:tŋ|i, -ɪz
AM 'skrutn̩i, -z

Scruton
BR 'skruː:tn̩
AM 'skrutn̩

scry
BR skrʌɪ, -z, -ɪŋ, -d
AM skraɪ, -z, -ɪŋ, -d

scryer
BR 'skrʌɪə(r), -z
AM 'skraɪər, -z

SCSI
BR 'skʌzi
AM 'skəzi

scuba
BR 'sk(j)uːbə(r), -z

AM 'skubə, -z

scuba-dive
BR 'sk(j)uːbədʌɪv, -z,
-ɪŋ, -d
AM 'skubə‚daɪv, -z, -ɪŋ,
-d

scud
BR skʌd, -z, -ɪŋ, -ɪd
AM skəd, -z, -ɪŋ, -əd

Scudamore
BR 'sk(j)uːdəmɔː(r)
AM 'sk(j)udə‚mɔ(ə)r

scuff
BR skʌf, -s, -ɪŋ, -t
AM skəf, -s, -ɪŋ, -t

scuffle
BR 'skʌf|l, -lz, -lɪŋ\-lŋ,
-ld
AM 'skəf|əl, -əlz, -(ə)lɪŋ,
-əld

scuffmark
BR 'skʌfmɑːk, -s
AM 'skəf‚mɑrk, -s

sculduggery
BR skʌl'dʌg(ə)ri
AM skəl'dəgəri

scull
BR skʌl, -z, -ɪŋ, -d
AM skəl, -z, -ɪŋ, -d

sculler
BR 'skʌlə(r), -z
AM 'skələr, -z

scullery
BR 'skʌl(ə)r|i, -ɪz
AM 'skəl(ə)ri, -z

scullerymaid
BR 'skʌl(ə)rɪmeɪd, -z
AM 'skəl(ə)ri‚meɪd, -z

Sculley
BR 'skʌli
AM 'skəli

scullion
BR 'skʌlɪən, -z
AM 'skəljən, 'skɔliən,
-z

Scully
BR 'skʌli
AM 'skəli

sculp
BR skʌlp, -s, -ɪŋ, -t
AM skəlp, -s, -ɪŋ, -t

sculpin
BR 'skʌlpɪn, -z
AM 'skəlpən, -z

sculpt
BR skʌlpt, -s, -ɪŋ, -ɪd
AM skəlpt, -s, -ɪŋ, -əd

sculptor
BR 'skʌlptə(r), -z
AM 'skəlptər, -z

sculptress
BR 'skʌlptrɪs, -ɪz
AM 'skəlptrəs, -əz

sculptural
BR 'skʌlptptʃ(ə)rəl,
'skʌlptʃ(ə)r|
AM 'skəlp(t)ʃ(ə)rəl

sculpturally
BR 'skʌltptʃ(ə)rəli,
'skʌlptʃ(ə)r]i
AM 'skəlp(t)ʃ(ə)rəli

sculpture
BR 'skʌlptʃə(r), -z, -ɪŋ,
-d
AM 'skəlp(t)ʃər, -z, -ɪŋ,
-d

sculpturesque
BR ‚skʌlptʃə'resk
AM ‚skəlp(t)ʃə'resk

scum
BR skʌm, -z, -ɪŋ, -d
AM skəm, -z, -ɪŋ, -d

scumbag
BR 'skʌmbag, -z
AM 'skəm‚bæg, -z

scumble
BR 'skʌmb|l, -z, -ɪŋ, -d
AM 'skəmbəl, -z, -ɪŋ, -d

scummy
BR 'skʌmi
AM 'skəmi

scuncheon
BR 'skʌn(t)ʃ(ə)n, -z
AM 'skən(t)ʃən, -z

scunge
BR skʌn(d)ʒ, -ɪz
AM skəndʒ, -əz

scungy
BR 'skʌn(d)ʒ|i, -ɪə(r),
-ɪɪst
AM 'skəndʒi, -ər, -ɪst

scunner
BR 'skʌn|ə(r), -əz,
-(ə)rɪŋ, -əd
AM 'skənər, -z, -ɪŋ, -d

Scunthorpe
BR 'skʌnθɔːp
AM 'skən‚θɔ(ə)rp

scup
BR skʌp
AM skəp

scupper
BR 'skʌp|ə(r), -əz,
-(ə)rɪŋ, -əd
AM 'skəpər, -z, -ɪŋ, -d

scurf
BR skə:f
AM skərf

scurfiness
BR 'skə:fɪnɪs
AM 'skərfɪnɪs

scurfy
BR 'skə:fi
AM 'skərfi

scurrility
BR skə'rɪlɪti, skʌ'rɪlɪti
AM skə'rɪlɪdi

scurrilous
BR 'skʌrɪləs
AM 'skərələs

scurrilously
BR 'skʌrɪləsli
AM 'skərələsli

scurrilousness
BR 'skʌrɪləsnəs
AM 'skərələsnəs

scurry
BR 'skʌr|i, -ɪz, -ɪɪŋ, -ɪd
AM 'skəri, -z, -ɪŋ, -d

scurvied
BR 'skə:vɪd
AM 'skərvid

scurvily
BR 'skə:vɪli
AM 'skərvəli

scurviness
BR 'skə:vɪnɪs
AM 'skərvinɪs

scurvy
BR 'skə:v|i, -ɪə(r), -ɪɪst
AM 'skərvi, -ər, -ɪst

'scuse
BR skju:z
AM skjuz

scut
BR skʌt, -s
AM skət, -s

scuta
BR 'skju:tə(r)
AM 'sk(j)udə

scutage
BR 'skju:t|ɪdʒ, -ɪdʒɪz
AM 'sk(j)udɪdʒ, -ɪz

scutal
BR 'skju:tl
AM 'sk(j)udl

Scutari
BR skʊ'tɑ:ri,
'sku:t(ə)ri
AM sku'tari

scutate
BR 'skju:teɪt
AM 'sk(j)u,teɪt

scutch
BR skʌtʃ, -ɪz, -ɪɪŋ, -t
AM skətʃ, -əz, -ɪɪŋ, -t

scutcheon
BR 'skʌtʃ(ə)n, -z
AM 'skətʃən, -z

scutcher
BR 'skʌtʃə(r), -z
AM 'skətʃər, -z

scute
BR skju:t, -s
AM sk(j)ut, -s

scutella
BR skju:'telə(r)
AM sk(j)u'telə

scutellate
BR 'skju:tɪleɪt,
'sku:tɪlət
AM sk(j)u'telət,
'sk(j)udl,eɪt

scutellation
BR ,skju:tɪ'leɪʃn, -z
AM ,sk(j)udl'eɪʃən, -z

scutellum
BR skju:'teləm
AM sk(j)u'teləm

scutiform
BR 'skju:tɪfɔ:m
AM 'sk(j)udə,fɔ(ə)rm

scutter
BR 'skʌt|ə(r), -əz,
-(ə)rɪŋ, -əd
AM 'skədər, -z, -ɪɪŋ, -d

scuttle
BR 'skʌt|l, -lz, -lɪŋ\-lɪŋ,
-ld
AM 'skədəl, -z, -ɪɪŋ, -d

scuttlebutt
BR 'skʌtlbʌt, -s
AM 'skədl,bət, -s

scutum
BR 'skju:təm, -z
AM 'sk(j)udəm, -z

scuzzy
BR 'skʌz|i, -ɪə(r), -ɪɪst
AM 'skəzi, -ər, -ɪst

Scylla and Charybdis
BR ,sɪlə(r) ən(d)
kə'rɪbdɪs, + ŋ(d) +
AM ,sɪl(ə) ən kə'rɪbdɪs,
+ tʃə'rɪbdɪs

scyphi
BR 'sʌɪfʌɪ
AM 'saɪ,faɪ

scyphiform
BR 'sʌɪfɪfɔ:m
AM 'saɪfə,fɔ(ə)rm

scyphose
BR 'sʌɪfəʊs
AM 'saɪ,foʊs, 'saɪ,foʊz

scyphozoan
BR ,sʌɪfə'zəʊən, -z
AM ,saɪfə'zoʊən, -z

scyphus
BR 'sʌɪfəs
AM 'saɪfəs

scythe
BR sʌɪð, -z, -ɪɪŋ, -d
AM saɪð, -z, -ɪɪŋ, -d

Scythia
BR 'sɪðɪə(r)
AM 'sɪθɪə

Scythian
BR 'sɪðɪən
AM 'sɪθɪən

'sdeath
BR zdɛθ
AM zdɛθ

sea
BR si:, -z
AM si, -z

seabag
BR 'si:bag, -z
AM 'si,bæg, -z

seabed
BR 'si:bed
AM 'si,bed

seabird
BR 'si:bə:d, -z
AM 'si,bərd, -z

seaboard
BR 'si:bɔ:d

scutiform (col 3)

AM 'si,bɔ(ə)rd

sea-boat
BR 'si:bəʊt, -s
AM 'si,boʊt, -s

seaboot
BR 'si:bu:t, -s
AM 'si,but, -s

seaborne
BR 'si:bɔ:n
AM 'si,bɔ(ə)rn

seacoast
BR 'si:kəʊst, -s
AM 'si,koust, -s

seacock
BR 'si:kɒk, -s
AM 'si,kak, -s

seadog
BR 'si:dɒg, -z
AM 'si,dɔg, 'si,dag, -z

Sea Dyak
BR 'si: ,daɪak
AM 'si ,daɪ,æk

seafarer
BR 'si:,fɛ:rə(r), -z
AM 'si,fɛrər, -z

seafaring
BR 'si:,fɛ:rɪɪŋ
AM 'si,fɛrɪɪŋ

sea floor
BR 'si: flɔ:(r), ,si:
'flɔ:(r), -z
AM 'si ,flɔ(ə)r, -z

seafood
BR 'si:fu:d
AM 'si,fud

Seaford
BR 'si:fəd
AM 'sifərd

Seaforth
BR 'si:fɔ:θ
AM 'si,fɔ(ə)rθ

seafront
BR 'si:frʌnt, -s
AM 'si,frənt, -s

Seaga
BR sɪ'ɑ:gə(r)
AM si'ɑgə

seagoing
BR 'si:,gəʊɪɪŋ
AM 'si,goʊɪɪŋ

seagull
BR 'si:gʌl, -z
AM 'si,gəl, -z

seahorse
BR 'si:hɔ:s, -ɪz
AM 'si,hɔ(ə)rs, -əz

seakale
BR 'si:keɪl
AM 'si,keɪl

seal
BR si:l, -z, -ɪɪŋ, -d
AM si(ə)l, -z, -ɪɪŋ, -d

sealable
BR 'si:ləbl
AM 'siləbəl

sealant
BR 'si:lənt, 'si:lŋt, -s

AM 'silənt, -s

Seale
BR si:l
AM si(ə)l

sealed-beam
BR ,si:ld'bi:m
AM 'sil(d),bim

sealer
BR 'si:lə(r), -z
AM 'silər, -z

sealery
BR 'si:l(ə)r|i, -ɪz
AM 'siləri, -z

Sealey
BR 'si:li
AM 'sili

Sealink
BR 'si:lɪŋk
AM 'si,lɪŋk

sealpoint
BR 'si:lpɔɪnt, -s
AM 'si(ə)l,pɔɪnt, -s

sealskin
BR 'si:lskɪn, -z
AM 'si(ə)l,skɪn, -z

sealstone
BR 'si:lstəʊn, -z
AM 'si(ə)l,stoʊn, -z

Sealyham
BR 'si:lɪəm, -z
AM 'silɪəm, -z

seam
BR si:m, -z, -ɪɪŋ, -d
AM sim, -z, -ɪɪŋ, -d

seaman
BR 'si:mən
AM 'simən

seamanlike
BR 'si:mənlʌɪk
AM 'simən,laɪk

seamanly
BR 'si:mənli
AM 'simənli

seamanship
BR 'si:mənʃɪp
AM 'simən,ʃɪp

seamark
BR 'si:mɑ:k, -s
AM 'si,mɑrk, -s

Seamas
BR 'ʃeɪməs
AM 'ʃeɪməs

seamen
BR 'si:mən
AM 'simən

seamer
BR 'si:mə(r), -z
AM 'simər, -z

seamew
BR 'si:mju:, -z
AM 'si,mju, -z

seaminess
BR 'si:mɪnɪs
AM 'simɪnɪs

seamless
BR 'si:mlɪs
AM 'simlɪs

seamlessly
BR ˈsiːmlɪsli
AM ˈsimlɪsli

seamlessness
BR ˈsiːmlɪsnɪs
AM ˈsimlɪsnɪs

seamstress
BR ˈsiːmstrɪs, -ɪz
AM ˈsimstrɪs, -əz

Seamus
BR ˈʃeɪməs
AM ˈʃeɪməs

seamy
BR ˈsiːm|i, -ɪə(r), -ɪɪst
AM ˈsimi, -ər, -ɪst

Sean
BR ʃɔːn
AM ʃɒn, ʃɑn

Seanad
BR ˈʃanəd
AM ˈʃænəd

séance
BR ˈseɪɒ̃s, ˈseɪɑːns, -ɪz
AM ˈseɪˌɑns, -əz

seaplane
BR ˈsiːpleɪn, -z
AM ˈsiˌpleɪn, -z

seaport
BR ˈsiːpɔːt, -s
AM ˈsiˌpɔ(ə)rt, -s

seaquake
BR ˈsiːkweɪk, -s
AM ˈsiˌkweɪk, -s

sear
BR sɪə(r), -z, -ɪŋ, -d
AM sɪ(ə)r, -z, -ɪŋ, -d

search
BR səːtʃ, -ɪz, -ɪŋ, -t
AM sərtʃ, -əz, -ɪŋ, -t

searchable
BR ˈsəːtʃəbl
AM ˈsərtʃəbəl

searcher
BR ˈsəːtʃə(r), -z
AM ˈsərtʃər, -z

searchingly
BR ˈsəːtʃɪŋli
AM ˈsərtʃɪŋli

searchless
BR ˈsəːtʃləs
AM ˈsərtʃləs

searchlight
BR ˈsəːtʃlaɪt, -s
AM ˈsərtʃˌlaɪt, -s

searingly
BR ˈsɪərɪŋli
AM ˈsɪrɪŋli

Searle
BR səːl
AM sərl

Sears
BR sɪəz
AM sɪ(ə)rz

Seascale
BR ˈsiːskeɪl
AM ˈsiˌskeɪl

seascape
BR ˈsiːskeɪp, -s
AM ˈsiˌskeɪp, -s

seashell
BR ˈsiːʃel, -z
AM ˈsiˌʃel, -z

seashore
BR ˈsiːʃɔː(r)
AM ˈsiˌʃɔ(ə)r

seasick
BR ˈsiːsɪk
AM ˈsiˌsɪk

seasickness
BR ˈsiːsɪknɪs
AM ˈsiˌsɪknɪs

seaside
BR ˈsiːsaɪd
AM ˈsiˌsaɪd

season
BR ˈsiːz|n, -nz,
-nɪŋ \-(ə)nɪŋ, -nd
AM ˈsizn, -z, -ɪŋ, -d

seasonable
BR ˈsiːznəbl,
ˈsiːz(ə)nəbl
AM ˈsiznəbəl, ˈsiznəbəl

seasonableness
BR ˈsiːznəblnəs,
ˈsiːz(ə)nəblnəs
AM ˈsiznəbəlnəs,
ˈsiznəbəlnəs

seasonably
BR ˈsiːznəbli,
ˈsiːz(ə)nəbli
AM ˈsiznəbli, ˈsiznəbli

seasonal
BR ˈsiːzn(ə)l,
ˈsiːz(ə)n(ə)l
AM ˈsiznəl

seasonality
BR ˌsiːzəˈnalɪti
AM ˌsizəˈnælədi

seasonally
BR ˈsiːzn̩li, ˈsiːzn̩əli,
ˈsiːz(ə)nəli
AM ˈsiz(ə)nəli

seasoner
BR ˈsiːznə(r),
ˈsiːz(ə)nə(r), -z
AM ˈsiznər, -z

seasoning
BR ˈsiːznɪŋ, ˈsiːz(ə)nɪŋ,
-z
AM ˈsiznɪŋ, ˈsiznɪŋ, -z

seasonless
BR ˈsiːznləs
AM ˈsiznlɪs

seat
BR siːt, -s, -ɪŋ, -ɪd
AM si|t, -ts, -dɪŋ, -dɪd

seatbelt
BR ˈsiːtbelt, -s
AM ˈsiˌtbelt, -s

seatless
BR ˈsiːtlɪs
AM ˈsiːtlɪs

seatmate
BR ˈsiːtmeɪt, -s

AM ˈsɪtˌmeɪt, -s

SEATO
BR ˈsiːtəʊ
AM ˈsidoʊ

Seaton
BR ˈsiːtn
AM ˈsitn

seatrein
BR ˈsiːtreɪn, -z
AM ˈsiˌtreɪn, -z

Seattle
BR sɪˈatl
AM siˈædəl

seawall
BR ˌsiːˈwɔːl, ˈsiːwɔːl, -z
AM ˈsiˌwɔl, ˈsiˌwɑl, -z

seaward
BR ˈsiːwəd, -z
AM ˈsiwərd, -z

seawater
BR ˈsiːˌwɔːtə(r)
AM ˈsiˌwɔdər,
ˈsiˌwɑdər

seaway
BR ˈsiːweɪ, -z
AM ˈsiˌweɪ, -z

seaweed
BR ˈsiːwiːd
AM ˈsiˌwid

seaworthiness
BR ˈsiːˌwəːðɪnɪs
AM ˈsiˌwərðinɪs

seaworthy
BR ˈsiːˌwəːði
AM ˈsiˌwərði

Seb
BR seb
AM seb

sebaceous
BR sɪˈbeɪʃəs
AM səˈbeɪʃəs

Sebastian
BR sɪˈbastɪən
AM səˈbæstʃən

Sebastopol
BR sɪˈbastəp(ɒ)l
AM səˈbæstəˌpoʊl

Sebat
BR sɪˈbat, ˈsiːbat
AM səˈbæt

sebesten
BR sɪˈbestn, -z
AM səˈbestən, -z

seborrhea
BR ˌsebəˈriːə(r)
AM ˌsebəˈriə

seborrheic
BR ˌsebəˈriːɪk
AM ˌsebəˈriɪk

seborrhoea
BR ˌsebəˈriːə(r)
AM ˌsebəˈriə

seborrhoeic
BR ˌsebəˈriːɪk
AM ˌsebəˈriik

Sebring
BR ˈsiːbrɪŋ

AM ˈsibrɪŋ

sebum
BR ˈsiːbəm
AM ˈsibəm

sec
BR sek, -s
AM sek, -s

secant
BR ˈsiːk(ə)nt, -s
AM ˈsiˌkænt, ˈsikənt, -s

secateurs
BR ˌsekəˈtəːz, ˈsekətəːz
AM ˈsekəˌtərz

secco
BR ˈsekəʊ
AM ˈsekoʊ

secede
BR sɪˈsiːd, -z, -ɪŋ, -ɪd
AM səˈsid, siˈsid, -z, -ɪŋ,
-ɪd

seceder
BR sɪˈsiːdə(r), -z
AM səˈsidər, siˈsidər, -z

secession
BR sɪˈseʃn, -z
AM səˈseʃən, -z

secessional
BR sɪˈseʃn(ə)l,
sɪˈseʃən)l
AM səˈseʃ(ə)nəl

secessionism
BR sɪˈseʃnɪz(ə)m,
sɪˈseʃnɪz(ə)m
AM səˈseʃəˌnɪzəm

secessionist
BR sɪˈseʃnɪst,
sɪˈseʃnɪst, -s
AM səˈseʃənəst, -s

Secker
BR ˈsekə(r)
AM ˈsekər

seclude
BR sɪˈkluːd, -z, -ɪŋ, -ɪd
AM səˈklud, -z, -ɪŋ, -əd

seclusion
BR sɪˈkluːʒn
AM səˈkluʒən

seclusionist
BR sɪˈkluːʒnɪst, -s
AM səˈkluʒənəst, -s

seclusive
BR sɪˈkluːsɪv
AM səˈklusɪv

Secombe
BR ˈsiːkəm
AM ˈsikəm

second[1]
number, time,
support
BR ˈsek(ə)nd, -z, -ɪŋ, -ɪd
AM ˈsekənd, -z, -ɪŋ, -əd

second[2]
verb, move to special
duties
BR sɪˈkɒnd, -z, -ɪŋ, -ɪd
AM səˈkɑnd, ˈsekənd,
-z, -ɪŋ, -əd

secondarily
BR ˈsɛk(ə)nd(ə)rɪli
AM ˌsɛkənˈdɛrəli

secondariness
BR ˈsɛk(ə)nd(ə)rɪnɪs
AM ˈsɛkənˌdɛrɪnɪs

secondary
BR ˈsɛk(ə)nd(ə)r|i, -ɪz
AM ˈsɛkənˌdɛri, -z

seconde
BR səˈkɒd, -z
AM səˈkɑnd, -z

secondee
BR ˌsɛk(ə)nˈdiː, -z
AM ˌsɛkənˈdi, -z

seconder
BR ˈsɛk(ə)ndə(r), -z
AM ˈsɛkəndər, -z

second hand[1]
clock dial
BR ˈsɛk(ə)nd hand
AM ˈsɛkən(d) ˌ(h)ænd

second hand[2]
used
BR ˌsɛk(ə)nd ˈhand
AM ˌsɛkən(d) ˈhænd

secondi
BR seˈkɒndiː, seˈkɒndi:
AM səˈkɑndi

secondly
BR ˈsɛk(ə)ndli
AM ˈsɛkən(d)li

secondment
BR sɪˈkɒn(d)m(ə)nt, -s
AM səˈkɑn(d)mənt, ˈsɛkən(d)mənt, -s

secondo
BR sɪˈkɒndəʊ, seˈkɒndəʊ
AM səˈkɑndou, səˈkɑndou

secrecy
BR ˈsiːkrɪsi
AM ˈsikrəsi

secret
BR ˈsiːkrɪt, -s
AM ˈsikrɪt, -s

secretaire
BR ˌsɛkrɪˈtɛː(r), -z
AM ˌsɛkrəˈtɛ(ə)r, -z

secretarial
BR ˌsɛkrɪˈtɛːrɪəl
AM ˌsɛkrəˈtɛriəl

secretariat
BR ˌsɛkrɪˈtɛːrɪət, ˌsɛkrɪˈtɛːrɪat, -s
AM ˌsɛkrəˈtɛriət, -s

secretary
BR ˈsɛkrɪt(ə)r|i, ˈsɛkrɪtɛr|i, -ɪz
AM ˈsɛkrəˌtɛri, -z

secretary-general
BR ˌsɛkrɪt(ə)rɪˈdʒɛn(ə)rəl, ˌsɛkrɪt(ə)rɪˈdʒɛn(ə)rl, ˌsɛkrɪtɛrɪˈdʒɛn(ə)rəl, ˌsɛkrɪtɛrɪˈdʒɛn(ə)rl, -z
AM ˌsɛkrəˌtɛriˈdʒɛn(ə)rəl, -z

secretaryship
BR ˈsɛkrɪt(ə)rɪʃɪp, -s
AM ˈsɛkrəˌtɛriˌʃɪp, -s

secrete
BR sɪˈkriːt, -s, -ɪŋ, -ɪd
AM səˈkri|t, sɪˈkri|t, -ts, -dɪŋ, -dɪd

secretion
BR sɪˈkriːʃn, -z
AM səˈkriʃən, sɪˈkriʃən, -z

secretive
BR ˈsiːkrɪtɪv
AM ˈsikrɪdɪv

secretively
BR ˈsiːkrɪtɪvli
AM ˈsikrɪdɪvli

secretiveness
BR ˈsiːkrɪtɪvnɪs
AM ˈsikrɪdɪvnɪs

secretly
BR ˈsiːkrɪtli
AM ˈsikrɪtli

secretor
BR sɪˈkriːtə(r), -z
AM səˈkridər, sɪˈkridər, -z

secretory
BR sɪˈkriːt(ə)ri
AM səˈkridəri, ˈsikrəˌtɔri

sect
BR sɛkt, -s
AM sɛk(t), -(t)s

sectarian
BR sɛkˈtɛːrɪən, -z
AM sɛkˈtɛriən, -z

sectarianise
BR sɛkˈtɛːrɪənʌɪz, -ɪz, -ɪŋ, -d
AM sɛkˈtɛriəˌnaɪz, -ɪz, -ɪŋ, -d

sectarianism
BR sɛkˈtɛːrɪənɪz(ə)m
AM sɛkˈtɛriəˌnɪzəm

sectarianize
BR sɛkˈtɛːrɪənʌɪz, -ɪz, -ɪŋ, -d
AM sɛkˈtɛriəˌnaɪz, -ɪz, -ɪŋ, -d

sectary
BR ˈsɛkt(ə)r|i, -ɪz
AM ˈsɛktəri, -z

section
BR ˈsɛkʃn, -z
AM ˈsɛkʃən, -z

sectional
BR ˈsɛkʃn(ə)l, ˈsɛkʃən(ə)l
AM ˈsɛkʃ(ə)nəl

sectionalise
BR ˈsɛkʃnəlʌɪz, ˈsɛkʃnlʌɪz, ˈsɛkʃənlʌɪz, ˈsɛkʃ(ə)nəlʌɪz, -ɪz, -ɪŋ, -d
AM ˈsɛkʃənlˌaɪz, ˈsɛkʃnəˌlaɪz, -ɪz, -ɪŋ, -d

sectionalism
BR ˈsɛkʃnəlɪz(ə)m, ˈsɛkʃnlɪz(ə)m, ˈsɛkʃənlɪz(ə)m, ˈsɛkʃ(ə)nəlɪz(ə)m
AM ˈsɛkʃənlˌɪzəm, ˈsɛkʃnəˌlɪzəm

sectionalist
BR ˈsɛkʃnəlɪst, ˈsɛkʃnlɪst, ˈsɛkʃənlɪst, ˈsɛkʃ(ə)nəlɪst, -s
AM ˈsɛkʃənləst, ˈsɛkʃnələst, -s

sectionalize
BR ˈsɛkʃnəlʌɪz, ˈsɛkʃnlʌɪz, ˈsɛkʃənlʌɪz, ˈsɛkʃ(ə)nəlʌɪz, -ɪz, -ɪŋ, -d
AM ˈsɛkʃənlˌaɪz, ˈsɛkʃnəˌlaɪz, -ɪz, -ɪŋ, -d

sectionally
BR ˈsɛkʃnəli, ˈsɛkʃnli, ˈsɛkʃənli, ˈsɛkʃ(ə)nəli
AM ˈsɛkʃ(ə)nəli

sector
BR ˈsɛktə(r), -z
AM ˈsɛktər, -z

sectoral
BR ˈsɛkt(ə)rəl, ˈsɛkt(ə)rl
AM ˈsɛktərəl

sectorial
BR sɛkˈtɔːrɪəl
AM sɛkˈtɔriəl

secular
BR ˈsɛkjələ(r)
AM ˈsɛkjələr

secularisation
BR ˌsɛkjʊlərʌɪˈzeɪʃn
AM ˌsɛkjələrəˈzeɪʃən, ˌsɛkjələˌraɪˈzeɪʃən

secularise
BR ˈsɛkjʊlərʌɪz, -ɪz, -ɪŋ, -d
AM ˈsɛkjələˌraɪz, -ɪz, -ɪŋ, -d

secularism
BR ˈsɛkjʊlərɪz(ə)m
AM ˈsɛkjələˌrɪzəm

secularist
BR ˈsɛkjʊlərɪst, -s
AM ˈsɛkjələrəst, -s

secularity
BR ˌsɛkjʊˈlarɪti
AM ˌsɛkjəˈlɛrədi

secularization
BR ˌsɛkjʊlərʌɪˈzeɪʃn
AM ˌsɛkjələrəˈzeɪʃən, ˌsɛkjələˌraɪˈzeɪʃən

secularize
BR ˈsɛkjʊlərʌɪz, -ɪz, -ɪŋ, -d
AM ˈsɛkjələˌraɪz, -ɪz, -ɪŋ, -d

secularly
BR ˈsɛkjʊləli
AM ˈsɛkjələrli

secund
BR sɪˈkʌnd
AM ˈsi,kənd, səˈkənd

Secunderabad
BR sɪˈkʌnd(ə)rəbad, sɪˈkʌnd(ə)rəbɑ:d
AM səˈkɛnd(ə)rəˌbad, səˈkɛnd(ə)rəˌbæd

secundly
BR sɪˈkʌn(d)li
AM ˈsi,kən(d)li, səˈkən(d)li

securable
BR sɪˈkjʊərəbl, sɪˈkjɔːrəbl
AM səˈkjʊrəbəl

secure
BR sɪˈkjʊə(r), sɪˈkjɔː(r), -z, -ɪŋ, -d, -ə(r), -ɪst
AM səˈkjʊ(ə)r, -z, -ɪŋ, -d, -ər, -əst

securely
BR sɪˈkjʊəli, sɪˈkjɔːli
AM səˈkjʊrli

securement
BR sɪˈkjʊəm(ə)nt, sɪˈkjɔːm(ə)nt, -s
AM səˈkjʊrmənt, -s

Securicor®
BR sɪˈkjʊərɪkɔː(r), sɪˈkjɔːrɪkɔː(r)
AM səˈk(j)ʊrəˌkɔ(ə)r

securitisation
BR sɪˌkjʊərɪtʌɪˈzeɪʃn, sɪˌkjɔːrɪtʌɪˈzeɪʃn
AM səˌkjʊrədəˈzeɪʃən, səˌkjʊrəˌtaɪˈzeɪʃən

securitise
BR sɪˈkjʊərɪtʌɪz, sɪˈkjɔːrɪtʌɪz, -ɪz, -ɪŋ, -d
AM səˈkjʊrəˌtaɪz, -ɪz, -ɪŋ, -d

securitization
BR sɪˌkjʊərɪtʌɪˈzeɪʃn, sɪˌkjɔːrɪtʌɪˈzeɪʃn
AM səˌkjʊrədəˈzeɪʃən, səˌkjʊrəˌtaɪˈzeɪʃən

securitize
BR sɪˈkjʊərɪtʌɪz, sɪˈkjɔːrɪtʌɪz, -ɪz, -ɪŋ, -d
AM səˈkjʊrəˌtaɪz, -ɪz, -ɪŋ, -d

security
BR sɪˈkjʊərɪti, sɪˈkjɔːrɪt|i, -ɪz
AM səˈkjʊrədi, -z

sedan
BR sɪˈdan, -z
AM səˈdæn, -z

sedate
BR sɪ'deɪt, -s, -ɪŋ, -ɪd
AM sə'deɪ|t, -ts, -dɪŋ, -dɪd

sedately
BR sɪ'deɪtli
AM sə'deɪtli

sedateness
BR sɪ'deɪtnɪs
AM sə'deɪtnɪs

sedation
BR sɪ'deɪʃn
AM sə'deɪʃən

sedative
BR 'sɛdətɪv, -z
AM 'sɛdədɪv, -z

Sedburgh
BR 'sɛdb(ə)rə(r), 'sɛdbə(r), 'sɛdbə:g
AM 'sɛd,bərə, 'sɛd,bərg

Seddon
BR 'sɛdn
AM 'sɛdən

sedentarily
BR 'sɛd(ə)nt(ə)rɪli
AM 'sɛdn,tɛrəli

sedentariness
BR 'sɛd(ə)ntrɪnɪs
AM 'sɛdn,tɛrɪnɪs

sedentary
BR 'sɛd(ə)nt(ə)ri
AM 'sɛdn,tɛri

Seder
BR 'seɪdə(r)
AM 'seɪdər

sederunt
BR sɪ'dɪərənt, sɪ'dɛ:rənt, -s
AM sə'dɪrənt, -s

sedge
BR sɛdʒ, -ɪz
AM sɛdʒ, -əz

Sedgefield
BR 'sɛdʒfi:ld
AM 'sɛdʒ,fild

Sedgemoor
BR 'sɛdʒmɔ:(r)
AM 'sɛdʒ,mɔ(ə)r

Sedgewick
BR 'sɛdʒwɪk
AM 'sɛdʒ,wɪk

Sedgwick
BR 'sɛdʒwɪk
AM 'sɛdʒ,wɪk

sedgy
BR 'sɛdʒi
AM 'sɛdʒi

sedile
BR sɪ'dʌɪli
AM sə'daɪli

sedilia
BR sɪ'dɪlɪə(r), sɪ'di:lɪə(r), sɪ'dʌɪlɪə(r)
AM sə'dɪljə, sə'dɪliə

sediment
BR 'sɛdɪm(ə)nt, -s

AM 'sɛdəmənt, -s

sedimentary
BR ,sɛdɪ'mɛnt(ə)ri
AM ,sɛdə'mɛn(t)əri

sedimentation
BR ,sɛdɪm(ə)n'teɪʃn, -z
AM ,sɛdəmən'teɪʃən, -z

sedition
BR sɪ'dɪʃn
AM sə'dɪʃən

seditionary
BR sɪ'dɪʃ(ə)r|i, -ɪz
AM sə'dɪʃə,nɛri, -z

seditionist
BR sɪ'dɪʃnɪst, sɪ'dɪʃənɪst, -s
AM sə'dɪʃənəst, -s

seditious
BR sɪ'dɪʃəs
AM sə'dɪʃəs

seditiously
BR sɪ'dɪʃəsli
AM sə'dɪʃəsli

seditiousness
BR sɪ'dɪʃəsnəs
AM sə'dɪʃəsnəs

seduce
BR sɪ'dju:s, sɪ'dʒu:s, -ɪz, -ɪŋ, -t
AM sə'd(j)us, -z, -ɪŋ, -t

seducer
BR sɪ'dju:sə(r), sɪ'dʒu:sə(r), -z
AM sə'd(j)usər, -z

seducible
BR sɪ'dju:sɪbl, sɪ'dʒu:sɪbl
AM sə'd(j)usəbəl

seduction
BR sɪ'dʌkʃn, -z
AM sə'dəkʃən, -z

seductive
BR sɪ'dʌktɪv
AM sə'dəktɪv

seductively
BR sɪ'dʌktɪvli
AM sə'dəktɪvli

seductiveness
BR sɪ'dʌktɪvnɪs
AM sə'dəktɪvnɪs

seductress
BR sɪ'dʌktrɪs, -ɪz
AM sə'dəktrəs, -əz

sedulity
BR sɪ'dju:lɪti, sɪ'dʒu:lɪti
AM sə'dʒulədi

sedulous
BR 'sɛdjʊləs, 'sɛdʒʊləs
AM 'sɛdʒələs

sedulously
BR 'sɛdjʊləsli, 'sɛdʒʊləsli
AM 'sɛdʒələsli

sedulousness
BR 'sɛdjʊləsnəs, 'sɛdʒʊləsnəs

sedum
BR 'si:dəm, -z
AM 'sidəm, -z

see
BR si:, -z, -ɪŋ
AM si, -z, -ɪŋ

seeable
BR 'si:əbl
AM 'siəbəl

seed
BR si:d, -z, -ɪŋ, -ɪd
AM sid, -z, -ɪŋ, -ɪd

seedbed
BR 'si:dbɛd, -z
AM 'sid,bɛd, -z

seedcake
BR 'si:dkeɪk, -s
AM 'sid,keɪk, -s

seedcorn
BR 'si:dkɔ:n
AM 'sid,kɔ(ə)rn

seeder
BR 'si:də(r), -z
AM 'sidər, -z

seedily
BR 'si:dɪli
AM 'sidɪli

seediness
BR 'si:dɪnɪs
AM 'sidɪnɪs

seedless
BR 'si:dlɪs
AM 'sidlɪs

seedling
BR 'si:dlɪŋ, -z
AM 'sidlɪŋ, -z

seedsman
BR 'si:dzmən
AM 'sidzmən

seedsmen
BR 'si:dzmən
AM 'sidzmən

seedy
BR 'si:d|i, -ɪə(r), -ɪɪst
AM 'sidi, -ər, -ɪst

Seeger
BR 'si:gə(r)
AM 'sigər

seeing-eye dog
BR ,si:ɪŋ'ʌɪ dɒg, -z
AM ,siɪŋ'aɪ ,dɒg, ,siɪŋ'aɪ ,dɑg, -z

seek
BR si:k, -s, -ɪŋ
AM sik, -s, -ɪŋ

seeker
BR 'si:kə(r), -z
AM 'sikər, -z

seel
BR si:l, -z, -ɪŋ, -d
AM si(ə)l, -z, -ɪŋ, -d

Seeley
BR 'si:li
AM 'sili

Seely
BR 'si:li

AM 'sili

seem
BR si:m, -z, -ɪŋ, -d
AM sim, -z, -ɪŋ, -d

seemingly
BR si:mɪŋli
AM 'simɪŋli

seemliness
BR 'si:mlɪnɪs
AM 'simlɪnɪs

seemly
BR 'si:ml|i, -ɪə(r), -ɪɪst
AM 'simli, -ər, -ɪst

seen
BR si:n
AM sin

seep
BR si:p, -s, -ɪŋ, -t
AM sip, -s, -ɪŋ, -t

seepage
BR 'si:p|ɪdʒ, -ɪdʒɪz
AM 'sipɪdʒ, -ɪz

seer[1]
prophet
BR sɪə(r), 'si:ə(r), -z
AM sɪ(ə)r, -z

seer[2]
someone who sees
BR 'si:ə(r), sɪə(r), -z
AM 'siər, sɪ(ə)r, -z

seersucker
BR 'sɪə,sʌkə(r)
AM 'sɪr,səkər

seesaw
BR 'si:sɔː(r), -z, -ɪŋ, -d
AM 'si,sɔ, 'si,sɑ, -z, -ɪŋ, -d

seethe
BR si:ð, -z, -ɪŋ, -d
AM sið, -z, -ɪŋ, -d

seethingly
BR 'si:ðɪŋli
AM 'siðɪŋli

see-through
BR 'si:θru:
AM 'si,θru

Seféris
BR 'sɛf(ə)rɪs
AM 'sɛf(ə)rəs
GR se'feri:s

Segal
BR 'si:gl
AM 'sigəl

segment[1]
noun
BR 'sɛgm(ə)nt, -s
AM 'sɛgmənt, -s

segment[2]
verb
BR sɛg'mɛnt, -s, -ɪŋ, -ɪd
AM 'sɛg,mɛn|t, ,sɛg'mɛn|t, -ts, -(t)ɪŋ, -(t)əd

segmental
BR sɛg'mɛntl
AM sɛg'mɛn(t)l

segmentalisation
BR sɛg,mɛntlʌɪˈzeɪʃn
AM seg,men(t)ləˈzeɪʃən,
seg,men(t)l,aɪˈzeɪʃən

segmentalise
BR ˈzeɪmzʊkt,
ˈzeɪmzʊxt
AM seg'men(t)l,aɪz, -ɪz,
-ɪŋ, -d
AM seg'men(t)l,aɪz, -ɪz,
-ɪŋ, -d

segmentalization
BR seg,mɛntlʌɪˈzeɪʃn
AM seg,men(t)lə'zeɪʃən,
seg,men(t)l,aɪˈzeɪʃən

segmentalize
BR seg'mɛntlʌɪz, -ɪz,
-ɪŋ, -d
AM seg'men(t)l,aɪz, -ɪz,
-ɪŋ, -d

segmentally
BR seg'mɛntli,
seg'mɛntəli
AM sɛg'mɛn(t)li

segmentary
BR ˈsɛgmənt(ə)ri
AM ˈsegmən,teri

segmentation
BR ,segmən'teɪʃn,
,sɛgmɛn'teɪʃn
AM ,segmən'teɪʃən,
,sɛg,mɛn'teɪʃən

sego
BR ˈsiːgəʊ, -z
AM ˈsiɡoʊ, -z

Segovia
BR sɪˈɡəʊvɪə(r)
AM səˈɡoʊviə
SP seˈvoβia

Segrave
BR ˈsiːgreɪv
AM ˈsiˌgreɪv

segregable
BR ˈsɛgrɪgəbl
AM ˈsɛgrəgəbəl

segregate
BR ˈsɛgrɪgeɪt, -s, -ɪŋ, -ɪd
AM ˈsegrə,geɪt, -ts,
-dɪŋ, -dɪd

segregation
BR ,sɛgrɪˈgeɪʃn
AM ,segrə'geɪʃən

segregational
BR ,sɛgrɪˈgeɪʃn(ə)l,
,sɛgrɪˈgeɪʃən(ə)l
AM ,segrə'geɪʃ(ə)nəl

segregationist
BR ,sɛgrɪˈgeɪʃnɪst,
,sɛgrɪˈgeɪʃənɪst, -s
AM ,segrə'geɪʃənəst, -s

segregative
BR ˈsɛgrɪgeɪtɪv
AM ˈsegrəˌgeɪdɪv

segue
BR ˈsɛgweɪ, ˈseɪgweɪ,
ˈsɛgwi, ˈseɪgwi,
-eɪz\-ɪz, -eɪɪŋ \-ɪɪŋ,
-eɪd\-ɪd
AM ˈsɛ,gweɪ, ˈseɪ,gweɪ,
-z, -ɪŋ, -d

seguidilla
BR ,segɪˈdiː(l)jə(r), -z
AM ,segɪˈdi(j)ə, -z

Sehnsucht
BR ˈzeɪnzʊkt,
ˈzeɪnzʊxt
AM ˈseɪn,zʊkt

sei
BR seɪ
AM seɪ

seicentist
BR seɪ'tʃɛntɪst, -s
AM seɪˈ(t)ʃɛn(t)əst, -s

seicento
BR seɪ'tʃɛntəʊ
AM seɪ'(t)ʃɛn,(t)oʊ

seicentoist
BR seɪ'tʃɛntəʊɪst, -s
AM seɪˈ(t)ʃɛn(t)əwəst,
-s

seiche
BR seɪʃ, -ɪz
AM seɪ(t)ʃ, -ɪz

seif
BR siːf, seɪf, -s
AM seɪf, sif, -s

Seifert
BR ˈsiːfət
AM ˈsifərt, ˈsaɪfərt
GER ˈzaɪfɐt

Seigel
BR ˈsiːgl
AM ˈsigəl

seigneur
BR sɛˈnjəː(r),
seɪˈnjəː(r), ˈseɪnjə(r),
-z
AM seɪnˈjər, sɛnˈjər, -z

seigneurial
BR sɛˈnjʊərɪəl,
seɪˈnjʊərɪəl,
sɛˈnjəːrɪəl,
seɪˈnjəːrɪəl
AM seɪnˈjʊriəl,
sɛnˈjəriəl, sɛnˈjəriəl,
sɛnˈjəriəl

seigneury
BR ˈseɪnjəːˌji, -ɪz
AM ˈseɪnjəri, -z

seignior
BR ˈseɪnjə(r), -z
AM seɪnˈjər, -z

seigniorage
BR ˈseɪnjərɪdʒ, -ɪdʒɪz
AM ˈseɪnjərɪdʒ, -ɪz

seigniorial
BR sɛˈnjɔːrɪəl,
seɪˈnjɔːrɪəl,
seɪnˈjəriəl

seigniory
BR ˈseɪnjəːˌji, -ɪz
AM ˈseɪnjəri, -z

seignorage
BR ˈseɪnjərɪdʒ, -ɪdʒɪz
AM seɪnˈjərɪdʒ, -ɪz

Seine
BR seɪn

seine
BR sɛn, seɪn

seine
BR seɪn, -z
AM seɪn, -z

seiner
BR ˈseɪnə(r), -z
AM ˈseɪnər, -z

seise
BR siːz, -d
AM siz, -d

seisin
BR ˈsiːzɪn, -z
AM ˈsizn, -z

seismal
BR ˈsaɪzml
AM ˈsaɪzməl

seismic
BR ˈsaɪzmɪk
AM ˈsaɪzmɪk

seismical
BR ˈsaɪzmɪkl
AM ˈsaɪzməkəl

seismically
BR ˈsaɪzmɪkli
AM ˈsaɪzmək(ə)li

seismicity
BR saɪzˈmɪsɪti
AM saɪzˈmɪsɪdi

seismogram
BR ˈsaɪzməgram, -z
AM ˈsaɪzmə,græm, -z

seismograph
BR ˈsaɪzməgrɑːf,
ˈsaɪzməgraf, -s
AM ˈsaɪzmə,græf, -s

seismographer
BR saɪzˈmɒgrəfə(r), -z
AM saɪzˈmɑgrəfər, -z

seismographic
BR ,saɪzməˈgrafɪk
AM ,saɪzməˈgræfɪk

seismographical
BR ,saɪzməˈgrafɪkl
AM ,saɪzməˈgræfəkəl

seismographically
BR ,saɪzməˈgrafɪkli
AM ,saɪzməˈgræfək(ə)li

seismography
BR saɪzˈmɒgrəfi
AM saɪzˈmɑgrəfi

seismological
BR ,saɪzməˈlɒdʒɪkl
AM ,saɪzməˈlɑdʒəkəl

seismologically
BR ,saɪzməˈlɒdʒɪkli
AM ,saɪzməˈlɑdʒək(ə)li

seismologist
BR saɪzˈmɒlədʒɪst, -s
AM saɪzˈmɑlədʒəst, -s

seismology
BR saɪzˈmɒlədʒi
AM saɪzˈmɑlədʒi

seismometer
BR saɪzˈmɒmɪtə(r), -z
AM saɪzˈmɑmədər, -z

seismometric
BR ,saɪzməˈmɛtrɪk
AM ,saɪzməˈmɛtrɪk

seismometrical
BR ,saɪzmaˈmɛtrɪkl
AM ,saɪzməˈmɛtrəkəl

seismometry
BR saɪzˈmɒmɪtri
AM saɪzˈmɑmətri

seismoscope
BR ˈsaɪzməskəʊp, -s
AM ˈsaɪzmə,skoʊp, -s

seismoscopic
BR ,saɪzməˈskɒpɪk
AM ,saɪzməˈskɑpɪk

seizable
BR ˈsiːzəbl
AM ˈsizəbəl

seize
BR siːz, -ɪz, -ɪŋ, -d
AM siz, -ɪz, -ɪŋ, -d

seizer
BR ˈsiːzə(r), -z
AM ˈsizər, -z

seizin
BR ˈsiːzɪn, -z
AM ˈsizn, -z

seizure
BR ˈsiːʒə(r), -z
AM ˈsiʒər, -z

sejant
BR ˈsiːdʒ(ə)nt
AM ˈsidʒənt

Sejanus
BR sɪˈdʒeɪnəs
AM səˈdʒeɪnəs

selachian
BR sɪˈleɪkɪən, -z
AM səˈleɪkiən, -z

seladang
BR sɪˈlɑːdaŋ, -z
AM səˈlɑˌdɑŋ, -z

Selborne
BR ˈsɛlbɔːn
AM ˈsɛl,bɔ(ə)rn

Selbourne
BR ˈsɛlbɔːn
AM ˈsɛl,bɔ(ə)rn

Selby
BR ˈsɛlbi
AM ˈsɛlbi

seldom
BR ˈsɛldəm
AM ˈsɛldəm

select
BR sɪˈlɛkt, -s, -ɪŋ, -ɪd
AM səˈlɛk|(t), -(t)s, -tɪŋ,
-təd

selectable
BR sɪˈlɛktəbl
AM səˈlɛktəbəl

selectee
BR sə,lɛkˈtiː, -z
AM sə,lɛkˈti, -z

selection
BR sɪˈlɛkʃn, -z
AM səˈlɛkʃən, -z

selectional
BR sɪˈlɛkʃn̩(ə)l,
sɪˈlɛkʃən(ə)l
AM səˈlɛkʃ(ə)nəl

selectionally
BR sɪˈlɛkʃn̩əli,
sɪˈlɛkʃn̩li,
sɪˈlɛkʃən̩li,
sɪˈlɛkʃ(ə)nəli
AM səˈlɛkʃ(ə)nəli

selective
BR sɪˈlɛktɪv
AM səˈlɛktɪv

selectively
BR sɪˈlɛktɪvli
AM səˈlɛktɪvli

selectiveness
BR sɪˈlɛktɪvnɪs
AM səˈlɛktɪvnɪs

selectivity
BR sɪˌlɛkˈtɪvɪti,
ˌsɪlɛkˈtɪvɪti,
ˌsiːlɛkˈtɪvɪti,
ˌsɛlɛkˈtɪvɪti
AM səˌlɛkˈtɪvɪdi

selectman
BR sɪˈlɛk(t)mən,
sɪˈlɛk(t)man
AM səˈlɛk(t)mən

selectmen
BR sɪˈlɛk(t)mən,
sɪˈlɛk(t)mɛn
AM səˈlɛk(t)mən

selectness
BR sɪˈlɛk(t)nəs
AM səˈlɛk(t)nəs

selector
BR sɪˈlɛktə(r), -z
AM səˈlɛktər, -z

Selena
BR sɪˈliːnə(r)
AM səˈlinə

selenate
BR ˈsɛlɪneɪt, -s
AM ˈsɛləˌneɪt, -s

Selene
BR sɪˈliːni
AM səˈlini

selenic
BR sɪˈliːnɪk, sɪˈlɛnɪk
AM səˈlɛnɪk, səˈlinɪk

selenide
BR ˈsɛlɪnaɪd, -z
AM ˈsɛləˌnaɪd,
ˈsɛlənəd, -z

selenious
BR sɪˈliːnɪəs
AM səˈlinɪəs

selenite
BR ˈsɛlɪnaɪt
AM ˈsɛləˌnaɪt

selenitic
BR ˌsɛlɪˈnɪtɪk
AM ˌsɛləˈnɪdɪk

selenium
BR sɪˈliːnɪəm
AM səˈliniəm

selenocentric
BR sɪˌliːnə(ʊ)ˈsɛntrɪk
AM səˌlinouˈsɛntrɪk

selenodont
BR sɪˈliːnə(ʊ)dɒnt, -s
AM səˈlinəˌdɑnt,
səˈlinədənt, -s

selenographer
BR ˌsɛlɪˈnɒɡrəfə(r), -z
AM ˌsɛləˈnɑɡrəfər, -z

selenographic
BR ˌsɛlɪnəˈɡrafɪk
AM ˌsɛlənəˈɡræfɪk

selenography
BR ˌsɛlɪˈnɒɡrəfi
AM ˌsɛləˈnɑɡrəfi

selenologist
BR ˌsɛlɪˈnɒlədʒɪst, -s
AM ˌsɛləˈnɑlədʒəst, -s

selenology
BR ˌsɛlɪˈnɒlədʒi
AM ˌsɛləˈnɑlədʒi

Seleucid
BR sɪˈl(j)uːsɪd, -z
AM səˈl(j)usəd, -z

self
BR sɛlf
AM sɛlf

self-abandon
BR ˌsɛlfəˈbænd(ə)n, -d
AM ˌsɛlfəˈbændən, -d

self-abandonment
BR ˌsɛlfəˈbænd(ə)n-
m(ə)nt
AM ˌsɛlfəˈbændənmənt

self-abasement
BR ˌsɛlfəˈbeɪsm(ə)nt
AM ˌsɛlfəˈbeɪsmənt

self-abhorrence
BR ˌsɛlfəbˈhɒrəns,
ˌsɛlfəbˈhɔrn̩s
AM ˌsɛlfəbˈhɔrəns

self-abnegation
BR ˌsɛlfæbnɪˈɡeɪʃn
AM ˌsɛlfˈæbnəˈɡeɪʃən

self-absorbed
BR ˌsɛlfəbˈzɔːbd
AM ˌsɛlfəbˈzɔ(ə)rbd

self-absorption
BR ˌsɛlfəbˈzɔːpʃn
AM ˌsɛlfəbˈzɔrpʃən

self-abuse
BR ˌsɛlfəˈbjuːs
AM ˌsɛlfəˈbjus

self-accusation
BR ˌsɛlfakjʊˈzeɪʃn
AM ˌsɛlfˈækjəˈzeɪʃən

self-accusatory
BR ˌsɛlfəˈkjuːzət(ə)ri
AM ˌsɛlfəˈkjuzəˌtori

self-acting
BR ˌsɛlfˈaktɪŋ
AM ˈsɛlfˈæktɪŋ

self-action
BR ˌsɛlfˈakʃn
AM ˈsɛlfˈækʃən

self-activity
BR ˌsɛlfakˈtɪvɪti,
ˌsɛlfəkˈtɪvɪti
AM ˈsɛlfəkˈtɪvɪdi

self-addressed
BR ˌsɛlfəˈdrɛst
AM ˈsɛlfəˈdrɛst

self-adhesive
BR ˌsɛlfədˈhiːsɪv,
ˌsɛlfədˈhiːzɪv
AM ˈsɛlfədˈhiziv,
ˈsɛlfədˈhisɪv

self-adjusting
BR ˌsɛlfəˈdʒʌstɪŋ
AM ˈsɛlfəˈdʒəstɪŋ

self-adjustment
BR ˌsɛlfəˈdʒʌs(t)m(ə)nt
AM ˈsɛlfəˈdʒəs(t)mənt

self-admiration
BR ˌsɛlfadmɪˈreɪʃn
AM ˈsɛlfˈædməˈreɪʃən

self-advancement
BR ˌsɛlfədˈvɑːnsm(ə)nt,
ˌsɛlfədˈvansm(ə)nt
AM ˈsɛlfədˈvænsmənt

self-advertisement
BR ˌsɛlfədˈvəːtɪsm(ə)nt,
ˌsɛlfədˈvəːtɪzm(ə)nt
AM ˈsɛlfˈædvərˌtaɪz-
mənt

self-advertiser
BR ˌsɛlfˈadvətaɪzə(r),
-z
AM ˈsɛlfˈædvərˌtaɪzər,
-z

self-affirmation
BR ˌsɛlfafəˈmeɪʃn
AM ˈsɛlfˌæfərˈmeɪʃən

self-aggrandisement
BR ˌsɛlfəˈɡrandɪzm(ə)nt
AM ˈsɛlfəˈɡrænˌdaɪz-
mənt

self-aggrandising
BR ˌsɛlfəˈɡrandʌɪzɪŋ
AM ˈsɛlfəˈɡrænˌdaɪzɪŋ

self-aggrandizement
BR ˌsɛlfəˈɡrandɪzm(ə)nt
AM ˈsɛlfəˈɡrænˌdaɪz-
mənt

self-aggrandizing
BR ˌsɛlfəˈɡrandʌɪzɪŋ
AM ˈsɛlfəˈɡrænˌdaɪzɪŋ

self-analysing
BR ˌsɛlfˈanəlʌɪzɪŋ,
ˌsɛlfanlʌɪzɪŋ
AM ˈsɛlfˈænəˌlaɪzɪŋ

self-analysis
BR ˌsɛlfəˈnalɪsɪs
AM ˈsɛlfəˈnæləsəs

self-appointed
BR ˌsɛlfəˈpɔɪntɪd
AM ˈsɛlfəˈpɔɪn(t)ɪd

self-appreciation
BR ˌsɛlfəˌpriːʃɪˈeɪʃn,
ˌsɛlfəˌpriːsɪˈeɪʃn
AM ˈsɛlfəˌpriʃiˈeɪʃən,
ˈsɛlfəˌprisiˈeɪʃən

self-approbation
BR ˌsɛlfaprəˈbeɪʃn
AM ˈsɛlfˌæprəˈbeɪʃən

self-approval
BR ˌsɛlfəˈpruːvl
AM ˈsɛlfəˈpruvəl

self-assembly
BR ˌsɛlfəˈsɛmbli
AM ˈsɛlfəˈsɛmbli

self-asserting
BR ˌsɛlfəˈsəːtɪŋ
AM ˈsɛlfəˈsərdɪŋ

self-assertion
BR ˌsɛlfəˈsəːʃn
AM ˈsɛlfəˈsərʃən

self-assertive
BR ˌsɛlfəˈsəːtɪv
AM ˈsɛlfəˈsərdɪv

self-assertiveness
BR ˌsɛlfəˈsəːtɪvnɪs
AM ˈsɛlfəˈsərdɪvnɪs

self-assurance
BR ˌsɛlfəˈʃʊərəns,
ˌsɛlfəˈʃʊərn̩s,
ˌsɛlfəˈʃɔːrəns,
ˌsɛlfəˈʃɔːrn̩s
AM ˈsɛlfəˈʃʊrəns

self-assured
BR ˌsɛlfəˈʃʊəd,
ˌsɛlfəˈʃɔːd
AM ˈsɛlfəˈʃʊ(ə)rd

self-assuredly
BR ˌsɛlfəˈʃʊədli,
ˌsɛlfəˈʃɔːdli
AM ˈsɛlfəˈʃʊr(ə)dli

self-aware
BR ˌsɛlfəˈwɛː(r)
AM ˈsɛlfəˈwɛ(ə)r

self-awareness
BR ˌsɛlfəˈwɛːnəs
AM ˈsɛlfəˈwɛrnəs

self-begotten
BR ˌsɛlfbɪˈɡɒtn
AM ˈsɛlfbəˈɡɑtn

self-betrayal
BR ˌsɛlfbɪˈtreɪəl
AM ˈsɛlfbəˈtreɪəl

self-binder
BR ˌsɛlfˈbaɪndə(r), -z
AM ˈsɛlfbaɪndər, -z

self-born
BR ˌsɛlfˈbɔːn
AM ˈsɛlfbɔ(ə)rn

self-catering
BR ˌsɛlfˈkeɪt(ə)rɪŋ
AM ˈsɛlfˈkeɪdərɪŋ,
ˈsɛlfkeɪtrɪŋ

self-censorship
BR ˌsɛlfˈsɛnsəʃɪp
AM ˈsɛlfˈsɛnsərˌʃɪp

self-centered
BR ˌsɛlfˈsɛntəd

AM ˈsɛlfˈsen(t)ərd

self-centeredly
BR ˌsɛlfˈsɛntədli
AM ˌsɛlfˈsɛn(t)ərdli

self-centeredness
BR ˌsɛlfˈsɛntədnəs
AM ˌsɛlfˈsɛn(t)ərdnəs

self-centred
BR ˌsɛlfˈsɛntəd
AM ˌsɛlfˈsɛn(t)ərd

self-centredly
BR ˌsɛlfˈsɛntədli
AM ˌsɛlfˈsɛn(t)ərdli

self-centredness
BR ˌsɛlfˈsɛntədnəs
AM ˌsɛlfˈsɛn(t)ərdnəs

self-certification
BR ˌsɛlfˌsə:tɪfɪˈkeɪʃn
AM ˌsɛlfˌsərdəfəˈkeɪʃən

self-certify
BR ˌsɛlfˈsə:tɪfʌɪ, -z, -ɪŋ, -d
AM ˌsɛlfˈsərdəˌfaɪ, -z, -ɪŋ, -d

self-cleaning
BR ˌsɛlfˈkli:nɪŋ
AM ˌsɛlfˈkli:nɪŋ

self-closing
BR ˌsɛlfˈkləʊzɪŋ
AM ˌsɛlfˈkloʊzɪŋ

self-cocking
BR ˌsɛlfˈkɒkɪŋ
AM ˌsɛlfˈkɑkɪŋ

self-collected
BR ˌsɛlfkəˈlɛktɪd
AM ˌsɛlfkəˈlɛktəd

self-colored
BR ˌsɛlfˈkʌləd
AM ˌsɛlfˈkələrd

self-coloured
BR ˌsɛlfˈkʌləd
AM ˌsɛlfˈkələrd

self-command
BR ˌsɛlfkəˈmɑ:nd
AM ˌsɛlfkəˈmænd

self-communion
BR ˌsɛlfkəˈmju:nɪən
AM ˌsɛlfkəˈmjuniən

self-conceit
BR ˌsɛlfkənˈsi:t, -ɪd
AM ˌsɛlfkənˈsit, -ɪd

self-condemnation
BR ˌsɛlfˌkɒndɛmˈneɪʃn
AM ˌsɛlfˌkɑnˌdɛmˈneɪʃən

self-condemned
BR ˌsɛlfkənˈdɛmd
AM ˌsɛlfkənˈdɛmd

self-confessed
BR ˌsɛlfkənˈfɛst
AM ˌsɛlfkənˈfɛst

self-confidence
BR ˌsɛlfˈkɒnfɪd(ə)ns
AM ˌsɛlfˈkɑnfədns

self-confident
BR ˌsɛlfˈkɒnfɪd(ə)nt

AM ˌsɛlfˈkɑnfədnt

self-confidently
BR ˌsɛlfˈkɒnfɪd(ə)ntli
AM ˌsɛlfˈkɑnfəd(ə)n(t)li

self-congratulation
BR ˌsɛlfkənˌgratʃʊ-ˈleɪʃn, ˌsɛlfkən̩gratʃəˈleɪʃn, ˌsɛlfkən̩gratjʊˈleɪʃn, ˌsɛlfkən̩gratjʊ̈ˈleɪʃn
AM ˌsɛlfkən̩grætʃə-ˈleɪʃən

self-congratulatory
BR ˌsɛlfkən̩gratʃʊ̈ˈleɪt(ə)ri, ˌsɛlfkən̩gratʃəˈleɪt(ə)ri, ˌsɛlfkən̩gratjʊˈleɪt(ə)ri, ˌsɛlfkən̩gratjʊ̈ˈleɪt(ə)ri, ˌsɛlfkən̩gratʃʊ̈lət(ə)ri, ˌsɛlfkən̩gratʃʊ̈lət(ə)ri, ˌsɛlfkən̩gratjʊlət(ə)ri, ˌsɛlfkən̩gratjʊ̈lət(ə)ri
AM ˌsɛlfkən̩grætʃ(ə)lə-̩tɔri

self-conquest
BR ˌsɛlfˈkɒŋkwɛst
AM ˌsɛlfˈkɑŋkwəst

self-conscious
BR ˌsɛlfˈkɒnʃəs
AM ˌsɛlfˈkɑnʃəs

self-consciously
BR ˌsɛlfˈkɒnʃəsli
AM ˌsɛlfˈkɑnʃəsli

self-consciousness
BR ˌsɛlfˈkɒnʃəsnəs
AM ˌsɛlfˈkɑnʃəsnəs

self-consistency
BR ˌsɛlfkənˈsɪst(ə)nsi
AM ˌsɛlfkənˈsɪstənsi

self-consistent
BR ˌsɛlfkənˈsɪst(ə)nt
AM ˌsɛlfkənˈsɪstənt

self-constituted
BR ˌsɛlfˈkɒnstɪtju:tɪd, ˌsɛlfkɒnstɪtˈʃu:tɪd
AM ˌsɛlfˈkɑnstə̩t(j)udəd

self-contained
BR ˌsɛlfkənˈteɪnd
AM ˌsɛlfkənˈteɪnd

self-containment
BR ˌsɛlfkənˈtɛmm(ə)nt
AM ˌsɛlfkənˈteɪmmənt

self-contempt
BR ˌsɛlfkənˈtɛm(p)t
AM ˌsɛlfkənˈtɛm(p)t

self-contemptuous
BR ˌsɛlfkənˈtɛm(p)tjʊəs, ˌsɛlfkənˈtɛm(p)tʃʊəs
AM ˌsɛlfkənˈtɛm(pt)-ʃ(əw)əs

self-content
BR ˌsɛlfkənˈtɛnt
AM ˌsɛlfkənˈtɛnt

self-contented
BR ˌsɛlfkənˈtɛntɪd
AM ˌsɛlfkənˈtɛn(t)əd

self-contradiction
BR ˌsɛlfkɒntrəˈdɪkʃn, -z
AM ˌsɛlfˌkɑntrəˈdɪkʃən, -z

self-contradictory
BR ˌsɛlfkɒntrəˈdɪkt-(ə)ri
AM ˌsɛlfˌkɑntrəˈdɪkt-(ə)ri

self-control
BR ˌsɛlfkənˈtrəʊl
AM ˌsɛlfkənˈtroʊl

self-controlled
BR ˌsɛlfkənˈtrəʊld
AM ˌsɛlfkənˈtroʊld

self-convicted
BR ˌsɛlfkənˈvɪktɪd
AM ˌsɛlfkənˈvɪktɪd

self-correcting
BR ˌsɛlfkəˈrɛktɪŋ
AM ˌsɛlfkəˈrɛktɪŋ

self-created
BR ˌsɛlfkrɪˈeɪtɪd
AM ˌsɛlfkriˈeɪdɪd

self-creation
BR ˌsɛlfkrɪˈeɪʃn
AM ˌsɛlfkriˈeɪʃən

self-critical
BR ˌsɛlfˈkrɪtɪkl
AM ˌsɛlfˈkrɪdəkəl

self-criticism
BR ˌsɛlfˈkrɪtɪsɪz(ə)m
AM ˌsɛlfˈkrɪdə̩sɪzəm

self-deceit
BR ˌsɛlfdɪˈsi:t
AM ˌsɛlfdəˈsit

self-deceiver
BR ˌsɛlfdɪˈsi:və(r), -z
AM ˌsɛlfdəˈsivər, -z

self-deceiving
BR ˌsɛlfdɪˈsi:vɪŋ
AM ˌsɛlfdəˈsivɪŋ

self-deception
BR ˌsɛlfdɪˈsɛpʃn
AM ˌsɛlfdəˈsɛpʃən

self-deceptive
BR ˌsɛlfdɪˈsɛptɪv
AM ˌsɛlfdəˈsɛptɪv

self-defeating
BR ˌsɛlfdɪˈfi:tɪŋ
AM ˌsɛlfdəˈfidɪŋ

self-defence
BR ˌsɛlfdɪˈfɛns
AM ˌsɛlfdəˈfɛns, ˈsɛlfdiˈfɛns

self-defense
BR ˌsɛlfdɪˈfɛns
AM ˌsɛlfdəˈfɛns, ˈsɛlfdiˈfɛns

self-defensive
BR ˌsɛlfdɪˈfɛnsɪv
AM ˌsɛlfdəˈfɛnsɪv, ˈsɛlfdiˈfɛnsɪv

self-delight
BR ˌsɛlfdɪˈlʌɪt
AM ˌsɛlfdəˈlaɪt, ˈsɛlfdiˈlaɪt

self-delusion
BR ˌsɛlfdɪˈl(j)u:ʒn, -z
AM ˌsɛlfdəˈluʒən, -z

self-denial
BR ˌsɛlfdɪˈnʌɪəl
AM ˌsɛlfdəˈnaɪəl, ˈsɛlfdiˈnaɪəl

self-denying
BR ˌsɛlfdɪˈnʌɪɪŋ
AM ˌsɛlfdəˈnaɪɪŋ, ˈsɛlfdiˈnaɪɪŋ

self-dependence
BR ˌsɛlfdɪˈpɛnd(ə)ns
AM ˌsɛlfdəˈpɛndns, ˈsɛlfdiˈpɛndns

self-dependent
BR ˌsɛlfdɪˈpɛnd(ə)nt
AM ˌsɛlfdəˈpɛndnt, ˈsɛlfdiˈpɛndnt

self-deprecating
BR ˌsɛlfdɛprɪkeɪtɪŋ
AM ˌsɛlfdɛprəˌkeɪdɪŋ

self-deprecatingly
BR ˌsɛlfdɛprɪkeɪtɪŋli
AM ˌsɛlfdɛprəˌkeɪdɪŋli

self-deprecation
BR ˌsɛlfdɛprɪˈkeɪʃn
AM ˌsɛlfˌdɛprəˈkeɪʃən

self-despair
BR ˌsɛlfdɪˈspɛ:(r)
AM ˌsɛlfdəˈspɛ(ə)r, ˈsɛlfdiˈspɛ(ə)r

self-destroying
BR ˌsɛlfdɪˈstrɔɪɪŋ
AM ˌsɛlfdəˈstrɔɪɪŋ, ˈsɛlfdiˈstrɔɪɪŋ

self-destruct
BR ˌsɛlfdɪˈstrʌkt, -s, -ɪŋ, -ɪd
AM ˌsɛlfdəˈstrək|(t), ˈsɛlfdiˈstrək|(t), -(t)s, -tɪŋ, -təd

self-destruction
BR ˌsɛlfdɪˈstrʌkʃn
AM ˌsɛlfdəˈstrəkʃən, ˈsɛlfdiˈstrəkʃən

self-destructive
BR ˌsɛlfdɪˈstrʌktɪv
AM ˌsɛlfdəˈstrʌktɪv, ˈsɛlfdiˈstrəktɪv

self-destructively
BR ˌsɛlfdɪˈstrʌktɪvli
AM ˌsɛlfdəˈstrəktɪvli, ˈsɛlfdiˈstrəktɪvli

self-determination
BR ˌsɛlfdɪˌtə:mɪˈneɪʃn

AM ˌsɛlfdəˌtɜrməˈneɪʃən, ˈsɛlfdiˌtɜrməˈneɪʃən

self-determined
BR ˌsɛlfdɪˈtɜːmɪnd
AM ˌsɛlfdəˈtɜrmənd, ˈsɛlfdiˈtɜrmənd

self-determining
BR ˌsɛlfdɪˈtɜːmɪnɪŋ
AM ˌsɛlfdəˈtɜrmənɪŋ, ˈsɛlfdiˈtɜrmənɪŋ

self-development
BR ˌsɛlfdɪˈvɛləpm(ə)nt
AM ˌsɛlfdəˈvɛləpmənt, ˈsɛlfdiˈvɛləpmənt

self-devotion
BR ˌsɛlfdɪˈvəʊʃn
AM ˌsɛlfdəˈvoʊʃən, ˈsɛlfdiˈvoʊʃən

self-discipline
BR ˈsɛlfˈdɪsɪplɪn, -d
AM ˌsɛlfˈdɪsəplən, -d

self-discovery
BR ˌsɛlfdɪˈskʌv(ə)ri
AM ˌsɛlfdəˈskʌv(ə)ri

self-disgust
BR ˌsɛlfdɪsˈgʌst, ˌsɛlfdɪzˈgʌst
AM ˌsɛlfdɪsˈgəst, ˈsɛlfdəˈzgəst

self-doubt
BR ˌsɛlfˈdaʊt
AM ˌsɛlfˈdaʊt

self-drive
BR ˌsɛlfˈdrʌɪv
AM ˌsɛlfˈdraɪv

self-educated
BR ˌsɛlfˈɛdjʊkeɪtɪd, ˌsɛlfˈɛdʒʊkeɪtɪd
AM ˌsɛlfˈɛdʒəˌkeɪdɪd

self-education
BR ˌsɛlfɛdjʊˈkeɪʃn, ˌsɛlfɛdʒʊˈkeɪʃn
AM ˌsɛlfˈɛdʒəˈkeɪʃən

self-effacement
BR ˌsɛlfɪˈfeɪsm(ə)nt
AM ˌsɛlfəˈfeɪsmənt

self-effacing
BR ˌsɛlfɪˈfeɪsɪŋ
AM ˌsɛlfəˈfeɪsɪŋ

self-effacingly
BR ˌsɛlfɪˈfeɪsɪŋli
AM ˌsɛlfəˈfeɪsɪŋli

self-elective
BR ˌsɛlfɪˈlɛktɪv
AM ˌsɛlfəˈlɛktɪv

self-employed
BR ˌsɛlfɪmˈplɔɪd, ˌsɛlfɛmˈplɔɪd
AM ˌsɛlfəmˈplɔɪd

self-employment
BR ˌsɛlfɪmˈplɔɪm(ə)nt, ˌsɛlfɛmˈplɔɪm(ə)nt
AM ˌsɛlfəmˈplɔɪmənt

self-esteem
BR ˌsɛlfɪˈstiːm
AM ˌsɛlfəˈstim

self-evidence
BR ˌsɛlfˈɛvɪd(ə)ns

AM ˌsɛlfˈɛvədns

self-evident
BR ˌsɛlfˈɛvɪd(ə)nt
AM ˌsɛlfˈɛvədnt

self-evidently
BR ˌsɛlfˈɛvɪd(ə)ntli
AM ˌsɛlfˈɛvədən(t)li

self-examination
BR ˌsɛlfɪgˌzamɪˈneɪʃn, ˌsɛlfɛgˌzamɪˈneɪʃn
AM ˌsɛlfɪgˌzæməˈneɪ-ʃən, ˌsɛlfɛgˌzæməˈneɪʃən

self-executing
BR ˌsɛlfɪgˈzɪst(ə)nt, ˌsɛlfɛgˈzɪst(ə)nt
AM ˌsɛlfɪgˈzɪstənt, ˌsɛlfɛgˈzɪstənt

self-existent
BR ˌsɛlfɪgˈzɪst(ə)nt, ˌsɛlfɛgˈzɪst(ə)nt
AM ˌsɛlfɪgˈzɪstənt, ˌsɛlfɛgˈzɪstənt

self-explanatory
BR ˌsɛlfɪkˈsplanət(ə)ri, ˌsɛlfɛkˈsplanət(ə)ri
AM ˌsɛlfɪkˈsplænəˌtɔri, ˌsɛlfɛkˈsplænəˌtɔri

self-expression
BR ˌsɛlfɪkˈsprɛʃn, ˌsɛlfɛkˈsprɛʃn
AM ˌsɛlfɛkˈsprɛʃn, ˌsɛlfəkˈsprɛʃən

self-expressive
BR ˌsɛlfɪkˈsprɛsɪv, ˌsɛlfɛkˈsprɛsɪv
AM ˌsɛlfɛkˈsprɛsɪv, ˌsɛlfəkˈsprɛsɪv

self-faced
BR ˌsɛlfˈfeɪst
AM ˌsɛlfˈfeɪst

self-feeder
BR ˌsɛlfˈfiːdə(r), -z
AM ˌsɛlfˈfidər, -z

self-feeding
BR ˌsɛlfˈfiːdɪŋ
AM ˌsɛlfˈfidɪŋ

self-fertile
BR ˌsɛlfˈfɜːtʌɪl
AM ˌsɛlfˈfɜrdl

self-fertilisation
BR ˌsɛl(f)fəˌtɪlʌɪˈzeɪʃn, ˌsɛl(f)fəːtʃʌɪˈzeɪʃn
AM ˌsɛl(f)ˌfɜrdləˈzeɪʃən, ˌsɛl(f)ˌfɜrdlˌaɪˈzeɪʃən

self-fertilised
BR ˌsɛlfˈfɜːtɪlʌɪzd, ˌsɛlfˈfəːtʃʌɪzd
AM ˌsɛl(f)ˈfɜrdlˌaɪzd

self-fertilising
BR ˌsɛlfˈfɜːtɪlʌɪzɪŋ, ˌsɛlfˈfəːtʃʌɪzɪŋ
AM ˌsɛl(f)ˈfɜrdlˌaɪzɪŋ

self-fertility
BR ˌsɛl(f)fəːˈtɪlɪti, ˌsɛl(f)fəˈtɪlɪti
AM ˌsɛl(f)fərˈtɪlɪdi

self-fertilization
BR ˌsɛl(f)fəːtɪlʌɪˈzeɪʃn, ˌsɛl(f)fəːtʃʌɪˈzeɪʃn

AM ˌsɛl(f)ˌfɜrdləˈzeɪʃən, ˌsɛl(f)ˌfɜrdlˌaɪˈzeɪʃən

self-fertilized
BR ˌsɛlffəːˈtɪlʌɪzd, ˌsɛlffəːtʃʌɪzd
AM ˌsɛl(f)ˈfɜrdlˌaɪzd

self-fertilizing
BR ˌsɛlffəːˈtɪlʌɪzɪŋ, ˌsɛlffəːtʃʌɪzɪŋ
AM ˌsɛl(f)ˈfɜrdlˌaɪzɪŋ

self-finance
BR ˌsɛlfˈfʌɪnans, ˌsɛl(f)fʌɪˈnans, ˌsɛl(f)fɪˈnans, -ɪz-, -ɪŋ, -t
AM ˌsɛl(f)ˈfaɪˌnæns, ˌsɛl(f)fɪˈnæns, -əz-, -ɪŋ, -t

self-flattering
BR ˌsɛlfˈflat(ə)rɪŋ
AM ˌsɛl(f)ˈflædərɪŋ

self-flattery
BR ˌsɛlfˈflat(ə)ri
AM ˌsɛl(f)ˈflædəri

self-forgetful
BR ˌsɛl(f)fəˈgɛtf(ʊ)l
AM ˌsɛl(f)fərˈgɛtfəl

self-forgetfulness
BR ˌsɛl(f)fəˈgɛtf(ʊ)lnəs
AM ˌsɛl(f)fərˈgɛtfəlnəs

self-fulfilling
BR ˌsɛl(f)fʊlˈfɪlɪŋ
AM ˌsɛl(f)fə(l)ˈfɪlɪŋ

self-fulfillment
BR ˌsɛl(f)fʊlˈfɪlm(ə)nt
AM ˌsɛl(f)fə(l)ˈfɪlmənt

self-fulfilment
BR ˌsɛl(f)fʊlˈfɪlm(ə)nt
AM ˌsɛl(f)fə(l)ˈfɪlmənt

self-generating
BR ˌsɛlfˈdʒɛnəreɪtɪŋ
AM ˌsɛlfˈdʒɛnəˌreɪdɪŋ

self-glorification
BR ˌsɛl(f)ˌglɔːrɪfɪˈkeɪʃn
AM ˌsɛl(f)ˌglɔrəfəˈkeɪʃən

self-governed
BR ˌsɛlfˈgʌvənd
AM ˌsɛlfˈgəvərnd

self-governing
BR ˌsɛlfˈgʌvənɪŋ, ˌsɛlfˈgʌvnɪŋ
AM ˌsɛlfˈgəvərnɪŋ

self-government
BR ˌsɛlfˈgʌvnm(ə)nt, ˌsɛlfˈgʌvəm(ə)nt
AM ˌsɛlfˈgəvər(n)mənt, + ˈgəvə(r)mənt

self-gratification
BR ˌsɛlfˌgratɪfɪˈkeɪʃn
AM ˌsɛlfˌgrædəfəˈkeɪʃən

self-gratifying
BR ˌsɛlfˈgratɪfʌɪɪŋ
AM ˌsɛlfˈgrædəˌfaɪɪŋ

self-hate
BR ˌsɛlfˈheɪt
AM ˌsɛlfˈheɪt

self-hatred
BR ˌsɛlfˈheɪtrɪd
AM ˌsɛlfˈheɪtrəd

self-heal
BR ˌsɛlfˈhiːl, -z
AM ˌsɛlfˈhil, -z

self-help
BR ˌsɛlfˈhɛlp
AM ˌsɛlfˈhɛlp

selfhood
BR ˈsɛlfhʊd
AM ˈsɛlf,(h)ʊd

self-image
BR ˌsɛlfˈɪmɪdʒ, -ɪdʒɪz
AM ˌsɛlfˈɪmɪdʒ, -ɪz

self-immolating
BR ˌsɛlfˈɪməleɪtɪŋ
AM ˌsɛlfˈɪməˌleɪdɪŋ

self-immolation
BR ˌsɛlfɪməˈleɪʃn
AM ˌsɛlfˌɪməˈleɪʃən

self-importance
BR ˌsɛlfɪmˈpɔːt(ə)ns
AM ˌsɛlfəmˈpɔrtns

self-important
BR ˌsɛlfɪmˈpɔːt(ə)nt
AM ˌsɛlfəmˈpɔrtnt

self-importantly
BR ˌsɛlfɪmˈpɔːt(ə)ntli
AM ˌsɛlfəmˈpɔrtn(t)li

self-imposed
BR ˌsɛlfɪmˈpəʊzd
AM ˌsɛlfəmˈpoʊzd

self-improvement
BR ˌsɛlfɪmˈpruːvm(ə)nt
AM ˌsɛlfəmˈpruvmənt

self-induced
BR ˌsɛlfɪnˈdjuːst, ˌsɛlfɪnˈdʒuːst
AM ˌsɛlfənˈd(j)ust

self-inductance
BR ˌsɛlfɪnˈdʌkt(ə)ns
AM ˌsɛlfənˈdəktns

self-induction
BR ˌsɛlfɪnˈdʌkʃn
AM ˌsɛlfənˈdəkʃən

self-inductive
BR ˌsɛlfɪnˈdʌktɪv
AM ˌsɛlfənˈdəktɪv

self-indulgence
BR ˌsɛlfɪnˈdʌldʒ(ə)ns
AM ˌsɛlfənˈdəldʒəns

self-indulgent
BR ˌsɛlfɪnˈdʌldʒ(ə)nt
AM ˌsɛlfənˈdəldʒənt

self-indulgently
BR ˌsɛlfɪnˈdʌldʒ(ə)ntli
AM ˌsɛlfənˈdəldʒən(t)li

self-inflicted
BR ˌsɛlfɪnˈflɪktɪd
AM ˌsɛlfənˈflɪktɪd

self-insurance
BR ˌsɛlfɪnˈʃʊərəns, ˌsɛlfɪnˈʃʊərns, ˌsɛlfɪnˈʃɔːrəns, ˌsɛlfɪnˈʃɔːrns

AM ˌselfənˈʃʊrəns

self-insured
BR ˌselfɪnˈʃʊəd,
ˌselfɪnˈʃɔːd
AM ˌselfənˈʃʊ(ə)rd

self-interest
BR ˌselfˈmtrɪst,
ˌselfɪnt(ə)rest
AM selfˈɪn(t)rəst,
selfˈɪntrəst

self-interested
BR ˌselfˈmtrɪstɪd,
ˌselfɪnt(ə)restɪd
AM selfˈɪn(t)ərestəd,
selfˈɪntrəstəd

self-involvement
BR ˌselfɪnˈvɒlvm(ə)nt
AM ˌselfənˈvɒlvmənt,
ˌselfənˈvalvmənt

selfish
BR ˈselfɪʃ
AM ˈselfɪʃ

selfishly
BR ˈselfɪʃli
AM ˈselfɪʃli

selfishness
BR ˈselfɪʃnɪs
AM ˈselfɪʃnɪs

self-justification
BR ˌselfˌdʒʌstɪfɪˈkeɪʃn
AM ˌselfˌdʒəstəfəˈkeɪʃən

self-justifying
BR ˌselfˈdʒʌstɪfaɪɪŋ
AM ˌselfˈdʒəstəˌfaɪɪŋ

self-knowledge
BR ˌselfˈnɒlɪdʒ
AM ˌselfˈnalɪdʒ

selfless
BR ˈselfləs
AM ˈselfləs

selflessly
BR ˈselfləsli
AM ˈselfləsli

selflessness
BR ˈselfləsnəs
AM ˈselfləsnəs

self-loader
BR ˌselfˈləʊdə(r), -z
AM ˌselfˈloʊdər, -z

self-loading
BR ˌselfˈləʊdɪŋ
AM ˌselfˈloʊdɪŋ

self-locking
BR ˌselfˈlɒkɪŋ
AM ˌselfˈlakɪŋ

self-love
BR ˌselfˈlʌv
AM ˌselfˈləv

self-made
BR ˌselfˈmeɪd
AM ˌselfˈmeɪd

self-mastery
BR ˌselfˈmɑːst(ə)ri,
ˌselfˈmast(ə)ri
AM ˌselfˈmæst(ə)ri

selfmate
BR ˈselfmeɪt, -s

AM ˈselfmeɪt, -s

self-mocking
BR ˌselfˈmɒkɪŋ
AM ˌselfˈmakɪŋ

self-motion
BR ˌselfˈməʊʃn
AM ˌselfˈmoʊʃən

self-motivated
BR ˌselfˈməʊtɪveɪtɪd
AM ˌselfˈmoʊdəˌveɪdɪd

self-motivation
BR ˌselfˌməʊtɪˈveɪʃn
AM ˌselfˌmoʊdəˈveɪʃən

self-moving
BR ˌselfˈmuːvɪŋ
AM ˌselfˈmuvɪŋ

self-murder
BR ˌselfˈmɜːdə(r)
AM ˌselfˈmɜrdər

self-murderer
BR ˌselfˈmɜːd(ə)rə(r),
-z
AM ˌselfˈmɜrd(ə)rər, -z

self-mutilation
BR ˌselfmjuːtɪˈleɪʃn, -z
AM ˌselfˌmjudəˈleɪʃən,
-z

self-neglect
BR ˌselfnɪˈglekt
AM ˈselfnəˈglek(t)

selfness
BR ˈselfnəs
AM ˈselfnəs

self-obsessed
BR ˌselfəbˈsest
AM ˈselfəbˈsest

self-opinion
BR ˌselfəˈpɪnjən
AM ˌselfəˈpɪnjən

self-opinionated
BR ˌselfəˈpɪnjəneɪtɪd
AM ˌselfəˈpɪnjəˌneɪdɪd

self-parody
BR ˌselfˈparədi
AM ˈselfˈperədi

**self-
perpetuating**
BR ˌselfpəˈpetʃueɪtɪŋ,
ˌselfpəˈpetjueɪtɪŋ
AM ˈselfpərˈpetʃəˌweɪdɪŋ

**self-
perpetuation**
BR ˌselfpəˌpetʃʊˈeɪʃn,
ˌselfpəˌpetjʊˈeɪʃn
AM ˈselfpərˌpetʃəˈweɪ-
ʃən

self-pity
BR ˌselfˈpɪti
AM ˌselfˈpɪdi

self-pitying
BR ˌselfˈpɪtɪɪŋ
AM ˌselfˈpɪdiɪŋ

self-pityingly
BR ˌselfˈpɪtɪɪŋli
AM ˌselfˈpɪdiɪŋli

self-pollinated
BR ˌselfˈpɒlɪneɪtɪd

AM ˌselfˈpɑləˌneɪdɪd

self-pollinating
BR ˌselfˈpɒlɪneɪtɪŋ
AM ˌselfˈpɑləˌneɪdɪŋ

self-pollination
BR ˌselfpɒlɪˈneɪʃn
AM ˌselfˌpɑləˈneɪʃən

self-pollinator
BR ˌselfˈpɒlɪneɪtə(r), -z
AM ˌselfˈpɑləˌneɪdər, -z

self-portrait
BR ˌselfˈpɔːtreɪt,
ˌselfˈpɔːtrɪt, -s
AM ˌselfˈpɔrtrət, -s

self-possessed
BR ˌselfpəˈzest
AM ˌselfpəˈzest

self-possession
BR ˌselfpəˈzeʃn
AM ˌselfpəˈzeʃən

self-praise
BR ˌselfˈpreɪz
AM ˌselfˈpreɪz

self-preservation
BR ˌselfprezəˈveɪʃn
AM ˌselfˌprezərˈveɪʃən

self-proclaimed
BR ˌselfprəˈkleɪmd
AM ˌselfprəˈkleɪmd

self-propagating
BR ˌselfˈprɒpəgeɪtɪŋ
AM ˌselfˈprɑpəˌgeɪdɪŋ

self-propelled
BR ˌselfprəˈpeld
AM ˌselfprəˈpeld

self-propelling
BR ˌselfprəˈpelɪŋ
AM ˌselfprəˈpelɪŋ

self-protection
BR ˌselfprəˈtekʃn
AM ˌselfprəˈtekʃən

self-protective
BR ˌselfprəˈtektɪv
AM ˌselfprəˈtektɪv

self-raising
BR ˌselfˈreɪzɪŋ
AM ˌselfˈreɪzɪŋ

self-realisation
BR ˌselfˌrɪəlaɪˈzeɪʃn
AM ˌselfˌri(ə)ləˈzeɪʃən,
ˌselfˌriəˌlaɪˈzeɪʃən

self-realization
BR ˌselfˌrɪəlaɪˈzeɪʃn
AM ˌselfˌri(ə)ləˈzeɪʃən,
ˌselfˌriəˌlaɪˈzeɪʃən

self-recording
BR ˌselfrɪˈkɔːdɪŋ
AM ˌselfrɪˈkɔrdɪŋ

self-regard
BR ˌselfrɪˈgɑːd
AM ˌselfrəˈgard

self-regarding
BR ˌselfrɪˈgɑːdɪŋ
AM ˌselfrəˈgardɪŋ

self-registering
BR ˌselfˈredʒɪst(ə)rɪŋ
AM ˌselfˈredʒəst(ə)rɪŋ

self-regulating
BR ˌselfˈregjʊleɪtɪŋ
AM ˌselfˈregjəˌleɪdɪŋ

self-regulation
BR ˌselfˈregjʊˈleɪʃn
AM ˌselfˈregjəˈleɪʃən

self-regulatory
BR ˌselfˈregjʊlət(ə)ri
AM ˌselfˈregjələˌtɔri

self-reliance
BR ˌselfrɪˈlaɪəns
AM ˌselfrəˈlaɪəns,
ˌselfriˈlaɪəns

self-reliant
BR ˌselfrɪˈlaɪənt
AM ˌselfrəˈlaɪənt,
ˌselfriˈlaɪənt

self-reliantly
BR ˌselfrɪˈlaɪəntli
AM ˌselfrəˈlaɪən(t)li,
ˌselfriˈlaɪən(t)li

self-renewal
BR ˌselfrɪˈnjuəl
AM ˌselfrəˈnjuəl,
ˌselfriˈnjuəl

self-renunciation
BR ˌselfrɪˌnʌnsiˈeɪʃn
AM ˌselfrəˌnʌnsiˈeɪʃən,
ˌselfriˌnʌnsiˈeɪʃən

self-reproach
BR ˌselfrɪˈprəʊtʃ
AM ˌselfrəˈproʊtʃ,
ˌselfriˈproʊtʃ

self-reproachful
BR ˌselfrɪˈprəʊtʃf(ə)l
AM ˌselfrəˈproʊtʃfəl,
ˌselfriˈproʊtʃfəl

self-respect
BR ˌselfrɪˈspekt
AM ˌselfrəˈspek(t),
ˌselfriˈspek(t)

self-respecting
BR ˌselfrɪˈspektɪŋ
AM ˌselfrəˈspektɪŋ,
ˌselfriˈspektɪŋ

self-restrained
BR ˌselfrɪˈstreɪnd
AM ˌselfrəˈstreɪnd,
ˌselfriˈstreɪnd

self-restraint
BR ˌselfrɪˈstreɪnt
AM ˌselfrəˈstreɪnt,
ˌselfriˈstreɪnt

self-revealing
BR ˌselfrɪˈviːlɪŋ
AM ˌselfrəˈvilɪŋ

self-revelation
BR ˌselfrevəˈleɪʃn
AM ˌselfˌrevəˈleɪʃən

Selfridge
BR ˈselfrɪdʒ
AM ˈselfrɪdʒ

self-righteous
BR ˌselfˈraɪtʃəs
AM ˌselfˈraɪtʃəs

self-righteously
BR ˌselfˈraɪtʃəsli
AM ˌselfˈraɪtʃəsli

self-righteousness
BR ˌselfˈrʌɪtʃəsnəs
AM ˌselfˈrʌɪtʃəsnəs

self-righting
BR ˌselfˈrʌɪtɪŋ
AM ˌselfˌraɪdɪŋ

self-rising
BR ˌselfˈrʌɪzɪŋ
AM ˌselfˈraɪzɪŋ

self-rule
BR ˌselfˈruːl
AM ˌselfˈrul

self-sacrifice
BR ˌselfˈsakrɪfʌɪs
AM ˌselfˈsækrəˌfaɪs

self-sacrificing
BR ˌselfˈsakrɪfʌɪsɪŋ
AM ˌselfˈsækrəˌfaɪsɪŋ

selfsame
BR ˈselfseɪm,
ˌselfˈseɪm
AM ˈselfseɪm

self-satisfaction
BR ˌselfsatɪsˈfakʃn
AM ˌselfˌsædəsˈfækʃən

self-satisfied
BR ˌselfˈsatɪsfʌɪd
AM ˌselfˈsædəˌsfaɪd

self-satisfiedly
BR ˌselfˈsatɪsfʌɪdli
AM ˌselfˈsædəˌsfaɪ(ə)dli

self-sealing
BR ˌselfˈsiːlɪŋ
AM ˌselfˈsilɪŋ

self-seed
BR ˌselfˈsiːd, -z, -ɪŋ, -ɪd
AM ˌselfˈsid, -z, -ɪŋ, -ɪd

self-seeker
BR ˌselfˈsiːkə(r), -z
AM ˌselfˈsikər, -z

self-seeking
BR ˌselfˈsiːkɪŋ
AM ˌselfˈsikɪŋ

self-selecting
BR ˌselfsɪˈlɛktɪŋ
AM ˌselfsəˈlɛktɪŋ

self-selection
BR ˌselfsɪˈlɛkʃn
AM ˌselfsəˈlɛkʃən

self-service
BR ˌselfˈsəːvɪs
AM ˌselfˈsərvəs

self-serving
BR ˌselfˈsəːvɪŋ
AM ˌselfˈsərvɪŋ

self-slaughter
BR ˌselfˈslɔːtə(r)
AM ˌselfˈslɔdər,
ˌselfˈsladər

self-sown
BR ˌselfˈsəʊn
AM ˌselfˈsoʊn

self-starter
BR ˌselfˈstɑːtə(r), -z
AM ˌselfˈstɑrdər, -z

self-sterile
BR ˌselfˈstɛrʌɪl
AM ˌselfˈstɛrəl

self-sterility
BR ˌselfstəˈrɪlɪti
AM ˌselfstəˈrɪlɪdi

self-styled
BR ˌselfˈstʌɪld
AM ˌselfˈstaɪld

self-sufficiency
BR ˌselfsəˈfɪʃnsi
AM ˌselfsəˈfɪʃənsi

self-sufficient
BR ˌselfsəˈfɪʃnt
AM ˌselfsəˈfɪʃənt

self-sufficiently
BR ˌselfsəˈfɪʃntli
AM ˌselfsəˈfɪʃən(t)li

self-sufficing
BR ˌselfsəˈfʌɪsɪŋ
AM ˌselfsəˈfaɪsɪŋ

self-suggestion
BR ˌselfsəˈdʒɛstʃn
AM ˌselfsəˈdʒɛstʃən,
ˌselfsəˈdʒɛstʃən

self-support
BR ˌselfsəˈpɔːt
AM ˌselfsəˈpɔ(ə)rt

self-supporting
BR ˌselfsəˈpɔːtɪŋ
AM ˌselfsəˈpɔrdɪŋ

self-surrender
BR ˌselfsəˈrɛndə(r)
AM ˌselfˌsərendər

self-sustained
BR ˌselfsəˈsteɪnd
AM ˌselfsəsˈteɪnd

self-sustaining
BR ˌselfsəˈsteɪnɪŋ
AM ˌselfsəsˈteɪnɪŋ

self-tapping
BR ˌselfˈtapɪŋ
AM ˌselfˈtæpɪŋ

self-taught
BR ˌselfˈtɔːt
AM ˌselfˈtɔt, ˈselfˈtat

self-torture
BR ˌselfˈtɔːtʃə(r)
AM ˌselfˈtɔrtʃər

self-understanding
BR ˌselfʌndəˈstandɪŋ
AM ˌselfˌəndərˈstændɪŋ

self-will
BR ˌselfˈwɪl
AM ˌselfˈwɪl

self-willed
BR ˌselfˈwɪld
AM ˌselfˈwɪld

self-winding
BR ˌselfˈwʌɪndɪŋ
AM ˌselfˈwaɪndɪŋ

self-worth
BR ˌselfˈwəːθ
AM ˌselfˈwərθ

Seligman
BR ˈsɛlɪgmən

AM ˈsɛlɪgmən,
ˈsɪlɪgmən

Seligmann
BR ˈsɛlɪgmən
AM ˈsɛlɪgmən,
ˈsɪlɪgmən
GER ˈzeːlɪçman

Selima
BR sɪˈliːmə(r)
AM səˈlimə

Selina
BR sɪˈliːnə(r)
AM səˈlinə

Seljuk
BR sɛlˈdʒuːk,
ˈsɛldʒuːk, -s
AM sɛlˈdʒuk, ˈsɛlˌdʒuk,
-s

Seljukian
BR sɛlˈdʒuːkɪən, -z
AM sɛlˈdʒukiən, -z

Selkirk
BR ˈsɛlkəːk
AM ˈsɛlˌkərk

sell
BR sɛl, -z, -ɪŋ
AM sɛl, -z, -ɪŋ

sellable
BR ˈsɛləbl
AM ˈsɛləbəl

Sellafield
BR ˈsɛləfiːld
AM ˈsɛləˌfild

Sellar
BR ˈsɛlə(r)
AM ˈsɛlər

Sellars
BR ˈsɛləz
AM ˈsɛlərz

sell-by date
BR ˈsɛlbʌɪ deɪt, -s
AM ˈsɛlˌbaɪ ˌdeɪt, -s

seller
BR ˈsɛlə(r), -z
AM ˈsɛlər, -z

Sellers
BR ˈsɛləz
AM ˈsɛlərz

Sellick
BR ˈsɛlɪk
AM ˈsɛlək

sellotape®
BR ˈsɛlə(ʊ)teɪp, -s, -ɪŋ, -t
AM ˈsɛləˌteɪp, -s, -ɪŋ, -t

sellout
BR ˈsɛlaʊt, -s
AM ˈsɛlˌaʊt, -s

Selma
BR ˈsɛlmə(r)
AM ˈsɛlmə

Selous
BR səˈluː
AM səˈlu

Selsey
BR ˈsɛlsi
AM ˈsɛlsi

seltzer
BR ˈsɛltsə(r)
AM ˈsɛltsər

selvage
BR ˈsɛlv|ɪdʒ, -ɪdʒɪz
AM ˈsɛlvɪdʒ, -ɪz

Selvas
BR ˈsɛlvəs
AM ˈsɛlvəs

selvedge
BR ˈsɛlv|ɪdʒ, -ɪdʒɪz
AM ˈsɛlvɪdʒ, -ɪz

selves
BR sɛlvz
AM sɛlvz

Selwyn
BR ˈsɛlwɪn
AM ˈsɛlwən

Selznick
BR ˈsɛlznɪk
AM ˈsɛlznɪk

SEM
BR sɛm
AM sɛm

semanteme
BR sɪˈmantiːm, -z
AM səˈmænˌtim, -z

semantic
BR sɪˈmantɪk, -s
AM səˈmæn(t)ɪk, -s

semantically
BR sɪˈmantɪkli
AM səˈmæn(t)ək(ə)li

semantician
BR sɪˌmanˈtɪʃn, -z
AM səˌmænˈtɪʃn, -z

semanticise
BR sɪˈmantɪsʌɪz, -ɪz, -ɪŋ, -d
AM səˈmæn(t)əˌsaɪz, -ɪz, -ɪŋ, -d

semanticism
BR sɪˈmantɪsɪz(ə)m
AM səˈmæn(t)əˌsɪzəm

semanticist
BR sɪˈmantɪsɪst, -s
AM səˈmæn(t)əsəst, -s

semanticize
BR sɪˈmantɪsʌɪz, -ɪz, -ɪŋ, -d
AM səˈmæn(t)əˌsaɪz, -ɪz, -ɪŋ, -d

semaphore
BR ˈsɛməfɔː(r), -z, -ɪŋ, -d
AM ˈsɛməˌfɔ(ə)r, -z, -ɪŋ, -d

semaphoric
BR ˌsɛməˈfɒrɪk
AM ˌsɛməˈfɔrɪk

semaphorically
BR ˌsɛməˈfɒrɪkli
AM ˌsɛməˈfɔrək(ə)li

Semarang
BR sɪˈmɑːraŋ
AM səˈmɑˌraŋ

semasiological
BR sɪˌmeɪziəˈlɒdʒɪkl,
sɪˌmeɪsɪəˈlɒdʒɪkl
AM səˌmeɪsiəˈlɑdʒəkəl,
səˌmeɪziəˈlɑdʒəkəl

semasiology
BR sɪˌmeɪzɪˈɒlədʒi,
sɪˌmeɪsɪˈɒlədʒi
AM səˌmeɪsiˈɑlədʒi,
səˌmeɪziˈɑlədʒi

sematic
BR sɪˈmatɪk
AM səˈmædɪk

semblable
BR ˈsɛmbləbl, -z
AM ˈsɛmbləbəl, -z

semblance
BR ˈsɛmbl(ə)ns, -ɪz
AM ˈsɛmbləns, -əz

semé
masculine
BR ˈsemi, ˈsemeɪ
AM səˈmeɪ, ˈsɛˌmeɪ

semée
feminine
BR ˈsemi, ˈsemeɪ
AM səˈmeɪ, ˈsɛˌmeɪ

semeiology
BR ˌsemiˈɒlədʒi,
siːmɪˈɒlədʒi
AM ˌsiˌmiˈɑlədʒi,
ˌsɛˌmiˈɑlədʒi

semeiotics
BR ˈsemiˈɒtɪks,
siːmɪˈɒtɪks
AM ˌsɛˌmiˈɑdɪks,
ˌsiˌmiˈɑdɪks

Semele
BR ˈsɛmɪli, ˈsemˌli
AM ˈsɛməli

sememe
BR ˈsiːmiːm, -z
AM ˈseˌmim, -z

semen
BR ˈsiːmən
AM ˈsimən

Semer Water
BR ˈsemə ˌwɔːtə(r)
AM ˈsemər ˌwɔdər,
+ ˌwɑdər

semester
BR sɪˈmɛstə(r), -z
AM səˈmɛstər, -z

semi
BR ˈsemˌli, -ɪz
AM ˈseˌmaɪ, ˈsemi, -z

semiaquatic
BR ˌsemiəˈkwatɪk
AM ˌseˌmaɪəˈkwadɪk,
ˈsemiəˈkwadɪk

semiautomatic
BR ˌsemɪˌɔːtəˈmatɪk, -s
AM ˌseˌmaɪˌodəˈmædɪk,
ˈsemiˌodəˈmædɪk,
ˌsɛˌmaɪˌodəˈmædɪk,
ˈsemiˌodəˈmædɪk, -s

semibreve
BR ˈsemɪbriːv, -z

semicircle
BR ˈsemiˌsəːkl, -z
AM ˈsɛˌmaɪˌsərkəl,
ˈsemiˌsərkəl, -z

semicircular
BR ˌsemiˈsəːkjʊlə(r)
AM ˈsemiˈsərkjələr,
ˈsɛˌmaɪˈsərkjələr

semicolon
BR ˌsemiˈkəʊlən,
ˌsemiˈkəʊlɒn,
ˈsemiˌkəʊlən,
ˈsemiˌkəʊlɒn, -z
AM ˌsemiˈkoʊlən,
ˈsemaɪˌkoʊlən, -z

semiconducting
BR ˌsemɪkənˈdʌktɪŋ
AM ˈsemɪkənˌdəktɪŋ,
ˈsɛˌmaɪkənˌdəktɪŋ

semiconductor
BR ˌsemɪkənˈdʌktə(r),
-z
AM ˌsemɪkənˌdəktər,
ˈsɛˌmaɪkənˌdəktər, -z

semi-conscious
BR ˌsemiˈkɒnʃəs
AM ˌsɛˌmaɪˈkɑnʃəs,
ˈsemiˈkɑnʃəs

semicylinder
BR ˌsemiˌsɪlɪndə(r), -z
AM ˈsemiˌsɪləndər,
ˈsɛˌmaɪˌsɪləndər, -z

semicylindrical
BR ˌsemɪsɪˈlɪndrɪkl
AM ˈsemisəˈlɪndrɪkəl,
ˈsɛˌmaɪsəˈlɪndrɪkəl

**semidemisemi-
quaver**
BR ˌsemiˌdemiˈsemi-
ˌkweɪvə(r), -z
AM ˈsemiˌdemiˈsemaɪ-
ˌkweɪvər,
ˈsemiˌdemiˈsemi-
ˌkweɪvər, -z

semidetached
BR ˌsemɪdɪˈtatʃt
AM ˈsemidəˈtætʃt,
ˈsemidiˈtætʃt,
ˌsɛˌmaɪdəˈtætʃt,
ˌsɛˌmaɪdiˈtætʃt

semidiameter
BR ˌsemɪdaɪˈamɪtə(r),
-z
AM ˌsemiˌdaɪˈæmədər,
ˈsemaɪˌdaɪˈæmədər,
-z

semifinal
BR ˌsemɪˈfaɪnl,
ˈsemɪfaɪnl, -z
AM ˌsɛˌmaɪˈfaɪnəl,
ˈsemiˈfaɪnəl, -z

semifinalist
BR ˌsemɪˈfaɪnlɪst,
ˈsemɪˈfaɪnəlɪst, -s
AM ˌsɛˌmaɪˈfaɪnləst,
ˈsemiˈfaɪnləst, -s

semigloss
BR ˈsemɪglɒs, -ɪz
AM ˈsemiˌglɒs,
ˈsɛˌmaɪˌglɒs,
ˈsemiˌglɑs,
ˈsɛˌmaɪˌglɑs, -əz

Semillon
BR ˈsemɪjɒ̃, ˈsemɪlɒn,
-z
AM ˈsemilˌjɑn, -z

seminal
BR ˈsemɪnl
AM ˈsemənəl

seminally
BR ˈsemɪnli, ˈsemɪnəli
AM ˈsem(ə)nəli

seminar
BR ˈsemɪnɑː(r), -z
AM ˈsemənˌɑr, -z

seminarian
BR ˌsemɪˈnɛːrɪən, -z
AM ˌsemənˈɛrɪən, -z

seminarist
BR ˈsemɪn(ə)rɪst, -s
AM ˈsemənˌɛrəst,
ˈsemənərəst, -s

seminary
BR ˈsemɪn(ə)r|i, -ɪz
AM ˈsemənˌɛri, -z

seminiferous
BR ˌsemɪˈnɪf(ə)rəs
AM ˌsemənˈnɪf(ə)rəs

Seminole
BR ˈsemɪnəʊl, -z
AM ˈsemənˌnoʊl, -z

semiological
BR ˌsemiəˈlɒdʒɪkl,
siːmɪəˈlɒdʒɪkl
AM ˌsiˌmiˈɑlədʒəkəl,
ˌsɛˌmiəˈlɑdʒəkəl

semiologist
BR ˌsemiˈɒlədʒɪst,
siːmɪˈɒlədʒɪst, -s
AM ˌsiˌmiˈɑlədʒəst,
ˌsɛˌmiˈɑlədʒəst, -s

semiology
BR ˌsemiˈɒlədʒi,
siːmɪˈɒlədʒ
AM ˌsiˌmiˈɑlədʒi,
ˌsemiˈɑlədʒi

semiotic
BR ˈsemiˈɒtɪk,
siːmɪˈɒtɪk, -s
AM ˌsemiˈɑdɪk,
ˈsimiˈɑdɪk, -s

semiotical
BR ˌsemiˈɒtɪkl,
siːmɪˈɒtɪkl
AM ˈsemiˈɑdəkəl,
ˈsimiˈɑdəkəl

semiotically
BR ˌsemiˈɒtɪkli,
siːmɪˈɒtɪkli
AM ˈsemiˈɑdək(ə)li,
ˈsimiˈɑdəkəli

semiotician
BR ˌsemiəˈtɪʃn,
siːmɪəˈtɪʃn, -z

semigloss (AM)
AM ˈsemiəˈtɪʃən,
ˈsimiəˈtɪʃən, -z

semipalmated
BR ˌsemiˈpalmeɪtɪd
AM ˈsɛˌmaɪˈpælˌmeɪdɪd,
ˌsɛˌmaɪˈpɑ(l)ˌmeɪdɪd,
ˈsemiˈpælˌmeɪdɪd,
ˈsemiˈpɑ(l)ˌmeɪdɪd

semipermeable
BR ˌsemiˈpəːmɪəbl
AM ˈsemiˈpərmiəbəl,
ˈsɛˌmaɪˈpərmiəbəl

semiprecious
BR ˌsemiˈpreʃəs
AM ˈsɛˌmaɪˈpreʃəs,
ˈsemiˈpreʃəs

semiprivate
BR ˌsemiˈprʌɪvɪt
AM ˈsemiˈpraɪvət,
ˈsɛˌmaɪˈpraɪvət

**semi-
professional**
BR ˌsemiprəˈfeʃn(ə)l,
ˌsemiprəˈfeʃən(ə)l, -z
AM ˈsɛˌmaɪprəˈfeʃ(ə)nəl,
ˈsemiprəˈfeʃ(ə)nəl, -z

semiquaver
BR ˈsemiˌkweɪvə(r), -z
AM ˈsɛˌmaɪˈkweɪvər,
ˈsemiˈkweɪvər, -z

Semiramis
BR səˈmɪrəmɪs,
sɪˈmɪrəmɪs
AM səˈmɪrəməs,
səˈmɪrəməs

semiretired
BR ˌsemiriˈtʌɪəd
AM ˈsemirəˈtaɪ(ə)rd,
ˈsɛˌmaɪrəˈtaɪ(ə)rd

semisoft
BR ˌsemiˈsɒft
AM ˈsemiˈsɒft,
ˈsɛˌmaɪˈsɒft,
ˈsemiˈsɑft,
ˈsɛˌmaɪˈsɑft

semisweet
BR ˌsemiˈswiːt
AM ˈsemiˈswit,
ˈsɛˌmaɪˈswit

Semite
BR ˈsiːmʌɪt, ˈsemʌɪt, -s
AM ˈsɛˌmaɪt, -s

Semitic
BR sɪˈmɪtɪk
AM səˈmɪdɪk

Semitisation
BR ˌsemɪtʌɪˈzeɪʃn
AM ˈsemədəˈzeɪʃən,
ˌseməˌtɑrˈzeɪʃən

Semitise
BR ˈsemɪtʌɪz, -ɪz, -ɪŋ, -d
AM ˈseməˌtaɪz, -ɪz, -ɪŋ,
-d

Semitism
BR ˈsemɪtɪz(ə)m
AM ˈseməˌtɪzəm

Semitist
BR ˈsemɪtɪst, -s

AM 'sɛmədəst, -s
Semitization
BR ˌsɛmɪtʌɪ'zeɪʃn
AM ˌsɛmədə'zeɪʃən,
ˌsɛməˌtaɪ'zeɪʃən
Semitize
BR 'sɛmɪtʌɪz, -ɪz, -ɪŋ, -d
AM 'sɛməˌtaɪz, -ɪz, -ɪŋ, -d
semitone
BR 'sɛmɪtəʊn, -z
AM 'sɛmiˌtoʊn, 'sɛˌmaɪˌtoʊn. -z
semitrailer
BR 'sɛmɪˌtreɪlə(r), -z
AM ˌsɛˌmaɪ'treɪlər, ˌsɛmi'treɪlər, -z
semitropical
BR ˌsɛmɪ'trɒpɪkl
AM ˌsɛmi'trɑpəkəl, ˌsɛˌmaɪ'trɑpəkəl
semi-tropics
BR ˌsɛmi'trɒpɪks
AM ˌsɛmi'trɑpɪks, ˌsɛˌmaɪ'trɑpɪks
semivowel
BR 'sɛmɪˌvaʊəl, 'sɛmɪvaʊl, -z
AM ˌsɛmi'vaʊ(ə)l, ˌsɛˌmaɪ'vaʊ(ə)l, -z
semmit
BR 'sɛmɪt, -s
AM 'sɛmət, -s
semolina
BR ˌsɛmə'liːnə(r)
AM ˌsɛmə'linə
Semper
BR 'sɛmpə(r)
AM 'sɛmpər
sempervivum
BR ˌsɛmpə'vʌɪvəm
AM ˌsɛmpər'vaɪvəm
sempiternal
BR ˌsɛmpɪ'təːnl
AM ˌsɛmpə'tərnəl
sempiternally
BR ˌsɛmpɪ'təːnəli, ˌsɛmpɪ'təːnli
AM ˌsɛmpə'tərnəli
sempiternity
BR ˌsɛmpɪ'təːnɪti
AM ˌsɛmpə'tərnədi
Semple
BR 'sɛmpl
AM 'sɛmpəl
semplice
BR 'sɛmplɪtʃi, 'sɛmplɪtʃeɪ
AM 'sɛmpləˌtʃeɪ
sempre
BR 'sɛmpreɪ
AM 'sɛmˌpreɪ
sempstress
BR 'sɛm(p)strɪs, -ɪz
AM 'sɛm(p)strəs, -əz
Semtex®
BR 'sɛmtɛks
AM 'sɛmˌtɛks

senarii
BR sɪ'nɛːrɪʌɪ
AM sə'nɛri,aɪ, si'nɛri,aɪ
senarius
BR sɪ'nɛːrɪəs
AM sə'nɛriəs, si'nɛriəs
senary
BR 'siːn(ə)ri, 'sɛn(ə)ri
AM 'sinəri, 'sɛnəri
senate
BR 'sɛnɪt, -s
AM 'sɛnət, -s
senator
BR 'sɛnɪtə(r), -z
AM 'sɛnədər, -z
senatorial
BR ˌsɛnɪ'tɔːrɪəl
AM ˌsɛnə'toriəl
senatorially
BR ˌsɛnɪ'tɔːrɪəli
AM ˌsɛnə'toriəli
senatorship
BR 'sɛnɪtəʃɪp, -s
AM 'sɛnədərˌʃɪp, -s
send
BR sɛnd, -z, -ɪŋ
AM sɛnd, -z, -ɪŋ
sendable
BR 'sɛndəbl
AM 'sɛndəbəl
Sendai
BR 'sɛndʌɪ
AM 'sɛnˌdaɪ
sendal
BR 'sɛndl, -z
AM 'sɛndəl, -z
sender
BR 'sɛndə(r), -z
AM 'sɛndər, -z
sending-off
BR ˌsɛndɪŋ'ɒf, -s
ˌsɛndɪŋ'ɑf, -s
Seneca
BR 'sɛnɪkə(r)
AM 'sɛnəkə
senecio
BR sɪ'niːsɪəʊ, sɪ'niːʃɪəʊ, -z
AM si'nisioʊ, si'niʃioʊ, -z
Senegal
BR ˌsɛnɪ'gɔːl
AM ˌsɛnə'gɔl, ˌsɛnə'gɑl
Senegalese
BR ˌsɛnɪgə'liːz
AM ˌsɛnəgə'liz
senesce
BR sɪ'nɛs, -ɪz, -ɪŋ, -t
AM sə'nɛs, -əz, -ɪŋ, -t
senescence
BR sɪ'nɛsns
AM sə'nɛsəns
senescent
BR sɪ'nɛsnt
AM sə'nɛsənt

seneschal
BR 'sɛnɪʃl, -z
AM 'sɛnəʃəl, 'sɛnəˌʃɑl, -z
Senghenydd
BR sɛŋ'hɛnɪð
AM sɛŋ'hɛnɪð
Senhor
BR sɛ'njɔː(r), sə'njɔː(r), -z
AM seɪn'jɔ(ə)r, sɪn'jɔ(ə)r, -z
Senhora
BR sɛ'njɔːrə(r), sə'njɔːrə(r), -z
AM seɪn'jɔrə, sɪn'jɔrə, -z
Senhores
BR sɛ'njɔːreɪz, sə'njɔːreɪz
AM seɪn'jɔreɪs, sɪn'jɔreɪs
Senhorita
BR ˌsɛnjə'riːtə(r), ˌsɛnjɔː'riːtə(r), -z
AM ˌseɪnjə'ridə, ˌsɛnjə'ridə, -z
senile
BR 'siːnʌɪl
AM 'siˌnaɪl
senility
BR sɪ'nɪlɪti
AM sə'nɪlɪdi, sɛ'nɪlɪdi
senior
BR 'siːnɪə(r), -z
AM 'sinjər, 'siniər, -z
seniority
BR ˌsiːnɪ'ɒrɪti
AM sin'jɔrədi
seniti
BR 'sɛnti
AM sə'nɪdi
Senlac
BR 'sɛnlak
AM 'sɛnlæk
senna
BR 'sɛnə(r)
AM 'sɛnə
Sennacherib
BR sɪ'nakərɪb, sɛ'nakərɪb
AM sə'nækəˌrɪb
sennet
BR 'sɛnɪt
AM 'sɛnət
Sennett
BR 'sɛnɪt
AM 'sɛnət
sennight
BR 'sɛnʌɪt, -s
AM 'sɛnaɪt, -s
sennit
BR 'sɛnɪt
AM 'sɛnət
señor
BR sɛ'njɔː(r), sə'njɔː(r), -z

AM seɪn'jɔ(ə)r, sɪn'jɔ(ə)r, -z
señora
BR sɛ'njɔːrə(r), sə'njɔːrə(r), -z
AM seɪn'jɔrə, sɪn'jɔrə, -z
señores
BR sɛ'njɔːreɪz, sə'njɔːreɪz
AM seɪn'jɔreɪs, sɪn'jɔreɪs
señorita
BR ˌsɛnjə'riːtə(r), ˌsɛnjɔː'riːtə(r), -z
AM ˌseɪnjə'ridə, ˌsɛnjə'ridə, -z
sensa
BR 'sɛnsə(r)
AM 'sɛnsə
sensate
BR 'sɛnseɪt
AM 'sɛnˌseɪt
sensation
BR s(ɛ)n'seɪʃn, -z
AM sɛn'seɪʃən, sən'seɪʃən, -z
sensational
BR s(ɛ)n'seɪʃn(ə)l, s(ɛ)n'seɪʃən(ə)l
AM sɛn'seɪʃ(ə)nəl, sən'seɪʃ(ə)nəl
sensationalise
BR s(ɛ)n'seɪʃnəlʌɪz, s(ɛ)n'seɪʃnlʌɪz, s(ɛ)n'seɪʃənlʌɪz, s(ɛ)n'seɪʃ(ə)nəlʌɪz, -ɪz, -ɪŋ, -d
AM sɛn'seɪʃənlˌaɪz, sən'seɪʃənlˌaɪz, sɛn'seɪʃnəˌlaɪz, sən'seɪʃnəˌlaɪz, -ɪz, -ɪŋ, -d
sensationalism
BR s(ɛ)n'seɪʃnəlɪz(ə)m, s(ɛ)n'seɪʃnlɪz(ə)m, s(ɛ)n'seɪʃənlɪz(ə)m, s(ɛ)n'seɪʃ(ə)nəlɪz(ə)m
AM sɛn'seɪʃənlˌɪzəm, sən'seɪʃənlˌɪzəm, sɛn'seɪʃnəˌlɪzəm, sən'seɪʃnəˌlɪzəm
sensationalist
BR s(ɛ)n'seɪʃnəlɪst, s(ɛ)n'seɪʃnlɪst, s(ɛ)n'seɪʃənlɪst, s(ɛ)n'seɪʃ(ə)nəlɪst, -s
AM sɛn'seɪʃənləst, sən'seɪʃənləst, sɛn'seɪʃnələst, sən'seɪʃnələst, -s
sensationalistic
BR s(ɛ)nˌseɪʃnə'lɪstɪk, s(ɛ)nˌseɪʃnl'ɪstɪk, s(ɛ)nˌseɪʃənl'ɪstɪk, s(ɛ)nˌseɪʃ(ə)nə'lɪstɪk
AM sɛnˌseɪʃənl'ɪstɪk, sənˌseɪʃənl'ɪstɪk,

sɛn,seɪʃnə'lɪstɪk
sən,seɪʃnə'lɪstɪk
sensationalize
BR s(ɛ)n'seɪʃnəlʌɪz,
s(ɛ)n'seɪʃnḷʌɪz,
s(ɛ)n'seɪʃənḷʌɪz,
s(ɛ)n'seɪʃ(ə)nəlʌɪz,
-ɪz, -ɪŋ, -d
AM sɛn'seɪʃnḷaɪz,
sɛn'seɪʃnḷ,aɪz,
sɛn'seɪʃnə,laɪz,
sən'seɪʃnə,laɪz, -ɪz,
-ɪŋ, -d
sensationally
BR s(ɛ)n'seɪʃnəli,
s(ɛ)n'seɪʃnḷi,
s(ɛ)n'seɪʃənḷi,
s(ɛ)n'seɪʃ(ə)nəli
AM sɛn'seɪʃ(ə)nəli,
sən'seɪʃ(ə)nəli
sense
BR sɛns, -ɪz, -ɪŋ, -t
AM sɛns, -əz, -ɪŋ, -t
senseless
BR 'sɛnsləs
AM 'sɛnsləs
senselessly
BR 'sɛnsləsli
AM 'sɛnsləsli
senselessness
BR 'sɛnsləsnəs
AM 'sɛnsləsnəs
sense-organ
BR 'sɛns,ɔːg(ə)n, -z
AM 'sɛns,ɔrgən, -z
sensibility
BR ,sɛnsɪ'bɪlɪt|i, -iz
AM ,sɛnsə'bɪlɪdi, -z
sensible
BR 'sɛnsɪbl
AM 'sɛnsəbəl
sensibleness
BR 'sɛnsɪblnəs
AM 'sɛnsəbəlnəs
sensibly
BR 'sɛnsɪbli
AM 'sɛnsəbli
sensitisation
BR ,sɛnsɪtʌɪ'zeɪʃn
AM ,sɛnsədə'zeɪʃən,
,sɛnsə,taɪ'zeɪʃən
sensitise
BR 'sɛnsɪtʌɪz, -ɪz, -ɪŋ, -d
AM 'sɛnsə,taɪz, -ɪz, -ɪŋ,
-d
sensitiser
BR 'sɛnsɪtʌɪzə(r), -z
AM 'sɛnsə,taɪzər, -z
sensitive
BR 'sɛnsɪtɪv
AM 'sɛnsədɪv
sensitively
BR 'sɛnsɪtɪvli
AM 'sɛnsədɪvli
sensitiveness
BR 'sɛnsɪtɪvnɪs
AM 'sɛnsədɪvnɪs

sensitivity
BR ,sɛnsɪ'tɪvɪti
AM ,sɛnsə'tɪvɪdi
sensitization
BR ,sɛnsɪtʌɪ'zeɪʃn
AM ,sɛnsədə'zeɪʃən,
,sɛnsə,taɪ'zeɪʃən
sensitize
BR 'sɛnsɪtʌɪz, -ɪz, -ɪŋ, -d
AM 'sɛnsə,taɪz, -ɪz, -ɪŋ,
-d
sensitizer
BR 'sɛnsɪtʌɪzə(r), -z
AM 'sɛnsə,taɪzər, -z
sensitometer
BR ,sɛnsɪ'tɒmɪtə(r), -z
AM ,sɛnsə'tɑmədər, -z
Sensodyne®
BR 'sɛnsə(ʊ)dʌɪn
AM 'sɛnsə,dam
sensor
BR 'sɛnsə(r), -z
AM 'sɛnsər, -z
sensoria
BR sɛn'sɔːrɪə(r)
AM sɛn'sɔriə
sensorial
BR sɛn'sɔːriəl
AM sɛn'sɔriəl
sensorially
BR sɛn'sɔːriəli
AM sɛn'sɔriəli
sensorily
BR 'sɛns(ə)rɪli
AM 'sɛnsərəli,
sɛn'sɔrəli
sensorium
BR sɛn'sɔːrɪəm, -z
AM sɛn'sɔriəm, -z
sensory
BR 'sɛns(ə)ri
AM 'sɛnsəri
sensual
BR 'sɛnsjʊəl, 'sɛnsjʊl,
'sɛnʃʊəl, 'sɛnʃ(ʊ)l
AM 'sɛn(t)ʃ(əw)əl
sensualise
BR 'sɛnsjʊəlʌɪz,
'sɛnsjʊlʌɪz,
'sɛnʃʊəlʌɪz,
'sɛnʃʊlʌɪz, 'sɛnʃlʌɪz,
-ɪz, -ɪŋ, -d
AM 'sɛn(t)ʃ(əw)ə,laɪz,
-ɪz, -ɪŋ, -d
sensualism
BR 'sɛnsjʊəlɪz(ə)m,
'sɛnsjʊlɪz(ə)m,
'sɛnʃʊəlɪz(ə)m,
'sɛnʃʊlɪz(ə)m,
'sɛnʃlɪz(ə)m
AM 'sɛn(t)ʃ(əw)ə,lɪzəm
sensualist
BR 'sɛnsjʊəlɪst,
'sɛnsjʊlɪst,
'sɛnʃʊəlɪst,
'sɛnʃʊlɪst, 'sɛnʃlɪst,
-s

AM 'sɛn(t)ʃ(əw)ələst,
-s
sensuality
BR ,sɛnsjʊ'alɪti,
,sɛnʃʊ'alɪti
AM ,sɛn(t)ʃə'wælədi
sensualize
BR 'sɛnsjʊəlʌɪz,
'sɛnsjəlʌɪz,
'sɛnʃʊəlʌɪz,
'sɛnʃʊlʌɪz, 'sɛnʃlʌɪz,
-ɪz, -ɪŋ, -d
AM 'sɛn(t)ʃ(əw)ə,laɪz,
-ɪz, -ɪŋ, -d
sensually
BR 'sɛnsjʊəli,
'sɛnsjəli, 'sɛnʃʊəli,
'sɛnʃʊli, 'sɛnʃli
AM 'sɛn(t)ʃ(əw)əli
sensualness
BR 'sɛnsjʊəlnəs,
'sɛnsjʊlnəs,
'sɛnʃʊəlnəs,
'sɛnʃ(ʊ)lnəs
AM 'sɛn(t)ʃ(əw)əlnəs
sensum
BR 'sɛnsəm
AM 'sɛnsəm
sensuous
BR 'sɛnsjʊəs, 'sɛnʃʊəs
AM 'sɛn(t)ʃəwəs
sensuously
BR 'sɛnsjʊəs,
'sɛnʃʊəsli
AM 'sɛn(t)ʃəwəsli
sensuousness
BR 'sɛnsjʊəsnəs,
'sɛnʃʊəsnəs
AM 'sɛn(t)ʃəwəsnəs
sensu stricto
BR ,sɛnsuː 'strɪktəʊ
AM ,sɛnsu 'strɪktoʊ
sent
BR sɛnt
AM sɛnt
sente
BR 'sɛnt|i, -ɪz
AM 'sɛn,ti, -z
sentence
BR 'sɛnt(ə)ns, -ɪz, -ɪŋ, -t
AM 'sɛntns, 'sɛn(t)əns,
-əz, -ɪŋ, -t
sentential
BR sɛn'tɛnʃl
AM sɛn'tɛn(t)ʃəl
sententious
BR sɛn'tɛnʃəs
AM sɛn'tɛn(t)ʃəs
sententiously
BR sɛn'tɛnʃəsli
AM sɛn'tɛn(t)ʃəsli
sententiousness
BR sɛn'tɛnʃəsnəs
AM sɛn'tɛn(t)ʃəsnəs
sentience
BR 'sɛnʃns, 'sɛnʃɪəns,
'sɛntɪəns
AM 'sɛn(t)ʃ(i)əns

sentiency
BR 'sɛnʃnsi,
'sɛnʃɪənsi, 'sɛntɪənsi
AM 'sɛn(t)ʃ(i)ənsi
sentient
BR 'sɛnʃnt, 'sɛnʃɪənt,
'sɛntɪənt
AM 'sɛn(t)ʃ(i)ənt
sentiently
BR 'sɛnʃntli,
'sɛnʃɪəntli,
'sɛntɪəntli
AM 'sɛn(t)ʃ(i)ən(t)li
sentiment
BR 'sɛntɪm(ə)nt, -s
AM 'sɛn(t)əmənt, -s
sentimental
BR ,sɛntɪ'mɛntl
AM ,sɛn(t)ə'mɛn(t)l
sentimentalisation
BR ,sɛntɪmɛntḷʌɪ'zeɪʃn,
,sɛntɪmɛntəlʌɪ'zeɪʃn,
sɛntɪ,mɛntḷʌɪ'zeɪʃn,
sɛntɪ,mɛntəlʌɪ'zeɪʃn
AM ,sɛn(t)ə,mɛn(t)ḷə'zeɪʃən,
,sɛn(t)ə,mɛn(t)ḷ,aɪ'zeɪʃən
sentimentalise
BR ,sɛntɪ'mɛntḷʌɪz,
,sɛntɪ'mɛntəlʌɪz, -ɪz,
-ɪŋ, -d
AM ,sɛn(t)ə'mɛn(t)ḷ,aɪz,
-ɪz, -ɪŋ, -d
sentimentalism
BR ,sɛntɪ'mɛntḷɪz(ə)m,
,sɛntɪ'mɛntəlɪz(ə)m
AM ,sɛn(t)ə'mɛn(t)ḷ-
,ɪzəm
sentimentalist
BR ,sɛntɪ'mɛntḷɪst,
,sɛntɪ'mɛntəlɪst, -s
AM ,sɛn(t)ə'mɛn(t)ləst,
-s
sentimentality
BR ,sɛntɪmɛn'talɪti,
,sɛntɪm(ə)n'talɪti
AM ,sɛn(t)ə,mɛn'tælədi,
,sɛn(t)əmən'tælədi
sentimentalization
BR ,sɛntɪmɛntḷʌɪ'zeɪʃn,
,sɛntɪmɛntəlʌɪ'zeɪʃn,
sɛntɪ,mɛntḷʌɪ'zeɪʃn,
sɛntɪ,mɛntəlʌɪ'zeɪʃn
AM ,sɛn(t)ə,mɛn(t)ḷə-
'zeɪʃən,
,sɛn(t)ə,mɛn(t)ḷ,aɪ'zeɪ-
ʃən
sentimentalize
BR ,sɛntɪ'mɛntḷʌɪz,
,sɛntɪ'mɛntəlʌɪz, -ɪz,
-ɪŋ, -d
AM ,sɛn(t)ə'mɛn(t)ḷ,aɪz,
-ɪz, -ɪŋ, -d
sentimentally
BR ,sɛntɪ'mɛntḷi,
,sɛntɪ'mɛntəli
AM ,sɛn(t)ə'mɛn(t)li
sentinel
BR 'sɛntɪnl, -z

sentry
BR ˈsentr|i, -ɪz
AM ˈsentri, -z

Senussi
BR sɛˈnuːsi, sɪˈnuːsi
AM səˈnusi

Seonaid
BR ʃəˈneɪd
AM ʃəˈneɪd

Seoul
BR səʊl
AM soʊl

sepal
BR ˈsep(ə)l, ˈsiːp(ə)l, -z
AM ˈsipəl, ˈsepəl, -z

separability
BR ˌsep(ə)rəˈbɪlɪti
AM ˌsep(ə)rəˈbɪlɪdi

separable
BR ˈsep(ə)rəbl
AM ˈsep(ə)rəbəl

separableness
BR ˈsep(ə)rəblnəs
AM ˈsep(ə)rəbəlnəs

separably
BR ˈsep(ə)rəbli
AM ˈsep(ə)rəbli

separate¹
adjective
BR ˈsep(ə)rət
AM ˈsep(ə)rət

separate²
verb
BR ˈsepəreɪt, -s, -ɪŋ, -ɪd-
AM ˈsepəˌreɪ|t, -ts, -dɪŋ, -dɪd

separately
BR ˈsep(ə)rətli
AM ˈsep(ə)rətli

separateness
BR ˈsep(ə)rətnəs
AM ˈsep(ə)rətnəs

separation
BR ˌsepəˈreɪʃn, -z
AM ˌsepəˈreɪʃən, -z

separatism
BR ˈsep(ə)rətɪz(ə)m
AM ˈsep(ə)rəˌtɪzəm

separatist
BR ˈsep(ə)rətɪst, -s
AM ˈsep(ə)rədəst, -s

separative
BR ˈsep(ə)rətɪv
AM ˈsep(ə)rədɪv

separator
BR ˈsepəreɪtə(r), -z
AM ˈsepəˌreɪdər, -z

separatory
BR ˈsep(ə)rət(ə)ri
AM ˈsep(ə)rəˌtɔri

Sephardi
BR sɪˈfɑːdi, seˈfɑːdi
AM səˈfardi

Sephardic
BR sɪˈfɑːdɪk, seˈfɑːdɪk
AM səˈfardɪk

Sephardim
BR səˈfɑːdɪm,
seˈfɑːdɪm
AM səˈfardəm,
sə,fɑrˈdim

sepia
BR ˈsiːpiə(r)
AM ˈsipiə

sepoy
BR ˈsiːpɔɪ, -z
AM ˈsiˌpɔɪ, -z

seppuku
BR seˈpuːkuː
AM ˈsepuˌku, səˈpuˌku

sepses
BR ˈsepsiːz
AM ˈsepˌsiz

sepsis
BR ˈsepsɪs
AM ˈsepsəs

sept
BR sept, -s
AM sept, -s

septa
BR ˈseptə(r)
AM ˈseptə

septal
BR ˈseptl
AM ˈseptl

septate
BR ˈsepteɪt
AM ˈsepˌteɪt

septation
BR sepˈteɪʃn
AM sepˈteɪʃən

septcentenary
BR ˌsep(t)senˈtiːn(ə)r|i,
ˌsep(t)senˈten(ə)r|i,
sepˈtsentɪn(ə)r|i, -ɪz
AM ˌsep(t)senˈtenəri,
ˈsep(t)ˈsentnˌeri, -z

September
BR sepˈtembə(r),
səpˈtembə(r), -z
AM sepˈtembər,
səpˈtembər, -z

septenarii
BR ˌseptɪˈnɛːrɪʌɪ
AM ˌseptəˈnɛriˌaɪ

septenarius
BR ˌseptɪˈnɛːrɪəs
AM ˌseptəˈnɛriəs

septenary
BR sepˈtiːn(ə)r|i,
sepˈten(ə)r|i,
ˈseptɪn(ə)r|i, -ɪz
AM sepˈten(ə)ri,
ˈseptəˌneri, -z

septenate
BR ˈsepteneɪt,
sepˈtiːneɪt
AM sepˈtɛˌneɪt,
ˈseptəˌneɪt

septennia
BR sepˈtenɪə(r)
AM sepˈtenɪə, sepˈtenjə

septennial
BR sepˈtenɪəl

Sephardim
AM sepˈtenjəl,
sepˈtenɪəl

septennium
BR sepˈtenɪəm
AM sepˈtenɪəm,
sepˈtenjəm

septet
BR sepˈtɛt, -s
AM sepˈtɛt, -s

septfoil
BR ˈsep(t)fɔɪl, -z
AM ˈsep(t)ˌfɔɪl, -z

septic
BR ˈseptɪk
AM ˈseptɪk

septicaemia
BR ˌseptɪˈsiːmɪə(r)
AM ˌseptəˈsimiə

septicaemic
BR ˌseptɪˈsiːmɪk
AM ˌseptəˈsimɪk

septically
BR ˈseptɪkli
AM ˈseptək(ə)li

septicemia
BR ˌseptɪˈsiːmɪə(r)
AM ˌseptəˈsimiə

septicemic
BR ˌseptɪˈsiːmɪk
AM ˌseptəˈsimɪk

septicity
BR sepˈtɪsɪti
AM sepˈtɪsɪdi

septilateral
BR ˌseptɪˈlat(ə)rəl,
ˌseptɪˈlat(ə)rl
AM ˌseptəˈlædərəl,
ˌseptəˈlætrəl

septillion
BR sepˈtɪljən
AM sepˈtɪljən

septimal
BR ˈseptɪml
AM ˈseptəməl

septime
BR ˈseptiːm, -s
AM ˈseptəm, ˈsepˌtim,
-z

Septimus
BR ˈseptɪməs
AM ˈseptɪməs

septivalent
BR ˌseptɪˈveɪlənt,
ˌseptɪˈveɪlɪt
AM ˌseptəˈveɪlənt

septuagenarian
BR ˌseptjʊədʒɪˈnɛːrɪən,
ˌseptʃ(ʊ)ədʒɪˈnɛːrɪən,
-z
AM ˌseptʃə(wə)dʒəˈnɛr-
iən,
ˈseptʃəˌwædʒəˈnɛriən,
-z

septuagenary
BR ˌseptjʊəˈdʒiːn(ə)ri,
ˌseptjʊəˈdʒen(ə)ri,
ˌseptʃʊəˈdʒiːn(ə)ri,

ˌseptʃʊəˈdʒen(ə)r|i,
-ɪz
AM ˌseptʃə(wə)ˈdʒenəri,
ˈseptʃə(wə)dʒəˌneri,
-z

Septuagesima
BR ˌseptjʊəˈdʒesɪmə(r),
ˌseptʃʊəˈdʒesɪmə(r)
AM ˌsep(t)ʃəwəˈdʒesəmə

Septuagint
BR ˈseptjʊədʒɪnt,
ˈseptʃʊədʒɪnt
AM ˈsep(t)ʃəwəˌdʒɪnt

septum
BR ˈseptəm, -z
AM ˈseptəm, -z

septuple
BR ˈseptjʊpl,
ˈseptʃʊpl, sepˈtjuːpl,
sepˈtʃuːpl
AM ˈseptəpəl,
sepˈt(j)upəl

septuplet
BR ˈseptjʊplɪt,
ˈseptʃʊplɪt,
sepˈtjuːplɪt,
sepˈtʃuːplɪt, -s
AM sepˈtəplət,
sepˈt(j)uplət, -s

sepulcher
BR ˈseplkə(r), -z
AM ˈsepəlkər, -z

sepulchral
BR sɪˈpʌlkr(ə)l
AM səˈpəlkrəl,
seˈpəlkrəl

sepulchrally
BR sɪˈpʌlkrəli
AM səˈpəlkrəli,
seˈpəlkrəli

sepulchre
BR ˈseplkə(r), -z
AM ˈsepəlkər, -z

sepulture
BR ˈsepltʃə(r),
ˈsepltjʊə(r), -z
AM ˈsepəltʃər,
ˈsepəltʃʊ(ə)r, -z

Sepulveda
BR sɪˈpʌlvɪdə(r),
sɪˈpʊlvɪdə(r)
AM səˈpəlvədə

sequacious
BR sɪˈkweɪʃəs
AM səˈkweɪʃəs,
siˈkweɪʃəs

sequaciously
BR sɪˈkweɪʃəsli
AM səˈkweɪʃəsli,
siˈkweɪʃəsli

sequacity
BR sɪˈkwasɪti
AM səˈkwæsədi,
siˈkwæsədi

sequel
BR ˈsiːkw(ə)l, -z
AM ˈsikwəl, -z

sequela
BR sɪˈkwiːlə(r),
sɪˈkwɛlə(r)
AM sɪˈkwɛlə

sequelae
BR sɪˈkwiːliː, sɪˈkwɛli:
AM sɪˈkwɛli, sɪˈkwɛˌlaɪ

sequence
BR ˈsiːkw(ə)ns, -ɪz
AM ˈsikwəns,
ˈsiˌkwɛns, -əz

sequencer
BR ˈsiːkw(ə)nsə(r), -z
AM ˈsikwənsər,
ˈsiˌkwɛnsər, -z

sequent
BR ˈsiːkw(ə)nt
AM ˈsikwənt, ˈsiˌkwɛnt

sequential
BR sɪˈkwɛnʃl
AM səˈkwɛn(t)ʃəl,
sɪˈkwɛn(t)ʃəl

sequentiality
BR sɪˌkwɛnʃɪˈalɪti
AM səˌkwɛn(t)ʃiˈælədi,
sɪˌkwɛn(t)ʃiˈælədi

sequentially
BR sɪˈkwɛnʃli,
sɪˈkwɛnʃəli
AM səˈkwɛn(t)ʃəli,
sɪˈkwɛn(t)ʃəli

sequently
BR ˈsiːkw(ə)ntli
AM ˈsikwən(t)li,
ˈsiˌkwɛn(t)li

sequester
BR sɪˈkwɛst|ə(r), -əz,
-(ə)rɪŋ, -əd
AM səˈkwɛstər,
sɪˈkwɛstər, -z, -ɪŋ, -d

sequestra
BR sɪˈkwɛstrə(r)
AM səˈkwɛstrə,
sɪˈkwɛstrə

sequestrable
BR sɪˈkwɛstrəbl
AM səˈkwɛstrəbəl,
sɪˈkwɛstrəbəl

sequestral
BR sɪˈkwɛstr(ə)l
AM səˈkwɛstrəl,
sɪˈkwɛstrəl

sequestrate
BR ˈsiːkwəstreɪt,
ˈsiːkwɛstreɪt, -s, -ɪŋ,
-ɪd
AM ˈsikwəˌstreɪ|t,
ˈsɛkwəˌstreɪt,
səˈkwɛsˌtreɪt, -ts,
-dɪŋ, -dɪd

sequestration
BR ˌsiːkwəˈstreɪʃn,
ˌsiːkwɛˈstreɪʃn, -z
AM ˌsikwəˈstreɪʃən,
ˌsɛkwəˈstreɪʃən, -z

sequestrator
BR ˈsiːkwəstreɪtə(r),
ˈsiːkwɛstreɪtə(r), -z

AM ˈsikwəˌstreɪdər,
ˈsɛkwəˌstreɪdər,
səˈkwɛsˌtreɪdər, -z

sequestrotomy
BR ˌsiːkwəˈstrɒtəm|i,
ˌsiːkwɛˈstrɒtəm|i, -ɪz
AM ˌsikwəˈstrɑdəmi,
ˌsɛkwəˈstrɑdəmi, -z

sequestrum
BR sɪˈkwɛstrəm
AM səˈkwɛstrəm,
sɪˈkwɛstrəm

sequin
BR ˈsiːkwɪn, -z, -d
AM ˈsikwɪn, -z, -d

sequitur
BR ˈsɛkwɪtə(r)
AM ˈsɛkwədər

sequoia
BR sɪˈkwɔɪə(r), -z
AM səˈkɔɪə, -z

sera
BR ˈsɪərə(r)
AM ˈsirə

serac
BR ˈsɛrak, -s
AM səˈræk, -s

seraglio
BR səˈrɑːliəʊ, -z
AM səˈrɑljoʊ, -z

serai
BR sɪˈrʌɪ, -z
AM səˈrɑɪ, -z

serang
BR səˈraŋ, -z
AM səˈræŋ, -z

serape
BR sɪˈrɑːp|i, -ɪz
AM səˈrɑpi, -z

seraph
BR ˈsɛrəf, -s
AM ˈsɛrəf, -s

seraphic
BR sɪˈrafɪk
AM səˈræfɪk

seraphical
BR sɪˈrafɪkl
AM səˈræfəkəl

seraphically
BR sɪˈrafɪkli
AM səˈræfək(ə)li

seraphim
BR ˈsɛrəfɪm
AM ˈsɛrəˌfɪm

Seraphina
BR ˌsɛrəˈfiːnə(r)
AM ˌsɛrəˈfinə

Serapis
BR ˈsɛrəpɪs, sɪˈreɪpɪs
AM səˈreɪpɪs

Serb
BR səːb, -z
AM sərb, -z

Serbia
BR ˈsəːbɪə(r)
AM ˈsərbiə

Serbian
BR ˈsəːbɪən, -z
AM ˈsərbiən, -z

Serbo-Croat
BR ˌsəːbəʊˈkrəʊat, -s
AM ˈsərboʊˌkroʊat, -s

Serbo-Croatian
BR ˌsəːbəʊkrəʊˈeɪʃn
AM ˈsərbouˌkroʊˈeɪʃən

Serbonian
BR səːˈbəʊnɪən
AM sərˈbounɪən

SERC
*Science and
Engineering
Research Council*
BR ˌɛsiːɑːˈsiː
AM ˌɛsiˌɑrˈsi

sere
BR sɪə(r)
AM sɪ(ə)r

serein
BR səˈran, səˈrɑ̃
AM səˈrɛn

Seremban
BR ˈsɛrəmban
AM ˈsɛrəmˌbæn

Serena
BR sɪˈriːnə(r)
AM səˈrinə

serenade
BR ˌsɛrəˈneɪd, -z, -ɪŋ, -ɪd
AM ˌsɛrəˈneɪd, -z, -ɪŋ,
-ɪd

serenader
BR ˌsɛrəˈneɪdə(r), -z
AM ˌsɛrəˈneɪdər, -z

serenata
BR ˌsɛrəˈnɑːtə(r), -z
AM ˌsɛrəˈnɑdə, -z

serendipitous
BR ˌsɛrənˈdɪpɪtəs,
ˌsɛrn̩ˈdɪpɪtəs
AM ˌsɛrənˈdɪpədəs

serendipitously
BR ˌsɛrənˈdɪpɪtəsli,
ˌsɛrn̩ˈdɪpɪtəsli
AM ˌsɛrənˈdɪpədəsli

serendipity
BR ˌsɛrənˈdɪpɪti,
ˌsɛrn̩ˈdɪpɪti
AM ˌsɛrənˈdɪpɪdi

serene
BR sɪˈriːn
AM səˈrin

serenely
BR sɪˈriːnli
AM səˈrinli

sereneness
BR sɪˈriːnnɪs
AM səˈri(n)nɪs

Serengeti
BR ˌsɛrənˈgɛti,
ˌsɛrn̩ˈgɛti
AM ˌsɛrənˈgɛdi

serenity
BR sɪˈrɛnɪti
AM səˈrɛnədi

serf
BR səːf, -s
AM sərf, -s

serfage
BR ˈsəːfɪdʒ
AM ˈsərfɪdʒ

serfdom
BR ˈsəːfdəm
AM ˈsərfdəm

serfhood
BR ˈsəːfhʊd
AM ˈsərfˌ(h)ʊd

serge
BR səːdʒ, -ɪz
AM sərdʒ, -əz

sergeancy
BR ˈsɑːdʒ(ə)ns|i, -ɪz
AM ˈsardʒənsi, -z

sergeant
BR ˈsɑːdʒ(ə)nt, -s
AM ˈsardʒənt, -s

sergeant-major
BR ˌsɑːdʒ(ə)ntˈmeɪdʒə(r),
-z
AM ˈsardʒəntˈmeɪdʒər,
-z

sergeantship
BR ˈsɑːdʒ(ə)ntʃɪp, -s
AM ˈsardʒəntˌʃɪp, -s

Sergei
BR ˈsəːgeɪ, səːˈgeɪ
AM ˈsərˌgeɪ, sərˈgeɪ

Sergio
BR ˈsəːdʒɪəʊ
AM ˈsərdʒioʊ

Sergius
BR ˈsəːdʒɪəs
AM ˈsərdʒiəs

serial
BR ˈsɪərɪəl, -z
AM ˈsiriəl, -z

serialisation
BR ˌsɪərɪəlʌɪˈzeɪʃn, -z
AM ˌsɪriələˈzeɪʃən,
ˌsɪriəˌlaɪˈzeɪʃən, -z

serialise
BR ˈsɪərɪəlʌɪz, -ɪz, -ɪŋ,
-d
AM ˈsɪriəˌlaɪz, -ɪz, -ɪŋ, -d

serialism
BR ˈsɪərɪəlɪz(ə)m
AM ˈsɪriəˌlɪzəm

serialist
BR ˈsɪərɪəlɪst, -s
AM ˈsɪriələst, -s

seriality
BR ˌsɪərɪˈalɪti
AM ˌsɪriˈælədi

serialization
BR ˌsɪərɪəlʌɪˈzeɪʃn, -z
AM ˌsɪriələˈzeɪʃən,
ˌsɪriəˌlaɪˈzeɪʃən, -z

serialize
BR ˈsɪərɪəlʌɪz, -ɪz, -ɪŋ,
-d
AM ˈsɪriəˌlaɪz, -ɪz, -ɪŋ, -d

serially
BR ˈsɪərɪəli
AM ˈsɪriəli

seriate¹
adjective
BR ˈsɪərɪət
AM ˈsɪriət

seriate²
verb
BR ˈsɪərɪeɪt, -s, -ɪŋ, -ɪd
AM ˈsɪriˌeɪt, -ts, -dɪŋ, -dɪd

seriatim
BR ˌsɪərɪˈeɪtɪm, ˌserɪˈeɪtɪm, ˌsɪərɪˈɑːtɪm, ˌserɪˈɑːtɪm
AM ˌsɪriˈeɪdɪm, ˌsɪriˈædəm

seriation
BR ˌsɪərɪˈeɪʃn, -z
AM ˌsɪriˈeɪʃən, -z

Seric
BR ˈserɪk
AM ˈsɪrɪk, ˈserɪk

sericeous
BR sɪˈrɪʃəs
AM səˈrɪʃəs

sericultural
BR ˌsɪərɪˈkʌltʃ(ə)rəl, ˌsɪərɪˈkʌltʃ(ə)rl̩, ˌserɪˈkʌltʃ(ə)rəl, ˌserɪˈkʌltʃ(ə)rl̩
AM ˌserəˈkəltʃ(ə)rəl

sericulture
BR ˈsɪərɪˌkʌltʃə(r), ˈserɪˌkʌltʃə(r)
AM ˈserəˌkəltʃər

sericulturist
BR ˌsɪərɪˈkʌltʃ(ə)rɪst, ˌserɪˈkʌltʃ(ə)rɪst, -s
AM ˌserəˈkəltʃ(ə)rəst, -s

seriema
BR ˌserɪˈiːmə(r), -z
AM ˌseriˈemə, ˌseriˈeɪmə, -z

series
BR ˈsɪərɪz
AM ˈsɪriz

serif
BR ˈserɪf, -s, -t
AM ˈserəf, -s, -t

serigraph
BR ˈserɪgrɑːf, ˈserɪgraf, -s
AM ˈserəˌgræf, -s

serigrapher
BR sɪˈrɪgrəfə(r), -z
AM səˈrɪgrəfər, -z

serigraphy
BR sɪˈrɪgrəfi
AM səˈrɪgrəfi

serin
BR ˈserɪn, -z
AM ˈserən, -z

serine
BR ˈsɪəriːn, ˈserɪn, ˈseriːn, ˈserɪn
AM ˈseˌrin, ˈserən

serinette
BR ˌserɪˈnet, -s
AM ˌserəˈnet, -s

seringa
BR sɪˈrɪŋgə(r), -z
AM səˈrɪŋgə, -z

Seringapatam
BR sɪˌrɪŋgəpəˈtɑːm, sɪˌrɪŋgəpəˈtam
AM səˌrɪŋgəpəˈtam

serio-comic
BR ˌsɪərɪəʊˈkɒmɪk
AM ˌsɪriouˈkamɪk

serio-comically
BR ˌsɪərɪəʊˈkɒmɪkli
AM ˌsɪriouˈkamək(ə)li

serious
BR ˈsɪərɪəs
AM ˈsɪriəs

seriously
BR ˈsɪərɪəsli
AM ˈsɪriəsli

seriousness
BR ˈsɪərɪəsnəs
AM ˈsɪriəsnəs

serjeant
BR ˈsɑːdʒ(ə)nt, -s
AM ˈsardʒənt, -s

serjeantship
BR ˈsɑːdʒ(ə)ntʃɪp, -s
AM ˈsardʒəntˌʃɪp, -s

Serkin
BR ˈsɜːkɪn
AM ˈsɜrkən

Serle
BR sɜːl
AM sɜrl

sermon
BR ˈsɜːmən, -z
AM ˈsɜrmən, -z

sermonette
BR ˌsɜːməˈnet, -s
AM ˌsɜrməˈnet, -s

sermonise
BR ˈsɜːmənʌɪz, -ɪz, -ɪŋ, -d
AM ˈsɜrməˌnʌɪz, -ɪz, -ɪŋ, -d

sermoniser
BR ˈsɜːmənʌɪzə(r), -z
AM ˈsɜrməˌnʌɪzər, -z

sermonize
BR ˈsɜːmənʌɪz, -ɪz, -ɪŋ, -d
AM ˈsɜrməˌnʌɪz, -ɪz, -ɪŋ, -d

sermonizer
BR ˈsɜːmənʌɪzə(r), -z
AM ˈsɜrməˌnʌɪzər, -z

seroconvert
BR ˌsɪərəʊkənˈvɜːt, -s, -ɪŋ, -ɪd
AM ˌsɪrəkənˈvɜrt, -ts, -dɪŋ, -dəd

serological
BR ˌsɪərəˈlɒdʒɪkl
AM ˌsɪrəˈladʒəkəl, ˌserəˈladʒəkəl

serologist
BR sɪəˈrɒlədʒɪst, sɪˈrɒlədʒɪst, -s
AM sɪˈralədʒəst, -s

serology
BR sɪəˈrɒlədʒi, sɪˈrɒlədʒi
AM sɪˈralədʒi

seronegative
BR ˌsɪərəʊˈnegətɪv
AM ˌsɪrouˈnegədɪv, ˌserouˈnegədɪv

seropositive
BR ˌsɪərəʊˈpɒzɪtɪv
AM ˌsɪrouˈpazədɪv, ˌserouˈpazədɪv

serosa
BR sɪˈrəʊsə(r)
AM səˈrousə, səˈrouzə

serosity
BR sɪəˈrɒsɪti
AM səˈrasədi

Serota
BR sɪˈrəʊtə(r)
AM səˈroudə

serotine
BR ˈserə(ʊ)tʌɪn, -z
AM ˈserətn, ˈserəˌtʌɪn, ˈserəˌtin, -z

serotonin
BR ˌserə(ʊ)ˈtəʊnɪn, -z
AM ˌserəˈtounən, ˌsɪrəˈtounən, -z

serotype
BR ˈsɪərə(ʊ)tʌɪp, ˈserə(ʊ)tʌɪp, -s
AM ˈsɪrəˌtʌɪp, ˈserəˌtʌɪp, -s

serous
BR ˈsɪərəs
AM ˈsɪrəs

serow
BR ˈserəʊ, -z
AM ˈserou, -z

Serpell
BR ˈsɜːpl
AM ˈsɜrpəl

Serpens
BR ˈsɜːpenz, ˈsɜːp(ə)nz
AM ˈsɜrpəns

serpent
BR ˈsɜːp(ə)nt, -s
AM ˈsɜrpənt, -s

serpentiform
BR sɜːˈpentɪfɔːm
AM sɜrˈpen(t)əˌfɔ(ə)rm

serpentine
BR ˈsɜːp(ə)ntʌɪn
AM ˈsɜrpənˌtin, ˈsɜrpənˌtʌɪn

serpiginous
BR sɜːˈpɪdʒɪnəs
AM sɜrˈpɪdʒənəs

SERPS
BR sɜːps
AM sɜrps

serpula
BR ˈsɜːpjʊlə(r)
AM ˈsɜrpjələ

serpulae
BR ˈsɜːpjʊliː
AM ˈsɜrpjəli, ˈsɜrpjəˌlaɪ

serra
BR ˈserə(r)
AM ˈserə

serradella
BR ˌserəˈdelə(r), -z
AM ˌserəˈdelə, -z

serradilla
BR ˌserəˈdɪlə(r), -z
AM ˌserəˈdɪlə, -z

serrae
BR ˈseriː
AM ˈseri, ˈseˌraɪ

serran
BR ˈserən, -z
AM ˈserən, -z

serranid
BR ˈserənɪd, -z
AM ˈserənəd, -z

serrate¹
adjective
BR ˈsereɪt
AM ˈseˌreɪt, ˈserət

serrate²
verb
BR sɪˈreɪt, -s, -ɪŋ, -ɪd
AM ˈseˌreɪt, səˈreɪt, -ts, -dɪŋ, -dɪd

serration
BR sɪˈreɪʃn, -z
AM sɛˈreɪʃən, -z

serried
BR ˈserɪd
AM ˈserɪd

serrulate
BR ˈserjʊleɪt, ˈserjʊlət
AM ˈser(j)ələt, ˈser(j)əleɪt

serrulation
BR ˌserjʊˈleɪʃn, -z
AM ˌser(j)əˈleɪʃən, -z

serum
BR ˈsɪərəm, -z
AM ˈsɪrəm, -z

serval
BR ˈsɜːvl, -z
AM ˈsɜrvəl, sɜrˈvæl, -z

servant
BR ˈsɜːv(ə)nt, -s
AM ˈsɜrvənt, -s

serve
BR sɜːv, -z, -ɪŋ, -d
AM sɜrv, -z, -ɪŋ, -d

server
BR ˈsɜːvə(r), -z
AM ˈsɜrvər, -z

servery
BR ˈsɜːv(ə)r|i, -ɪz

AM 'sɜːvəri, -z
Servian
BR 'sɜːvɪən
AM 'sɜrviən

service
BR 'sɜːv|ɪs, -ɪsɪz, -ɪsɪŋ, -ɪst
AM 'sɜrvəs, -əz, -ɪŋ, -t

serviceability
BR ˌsɜːvɪsə'bɪlɪti
AM ˌsɜrvəsə'bɪlɪdi

serviceable
BR 'sɜːvɪsəbl
AM 'sɜrvəsəbl

serviceableness
BR 'sɜːvɪsəblnəs
AM 'sɜrvəsəbəlnəs

serviceably
BR 'sɜːvɪsəbli
AM 'sɜrvəsəbli

serviceberry
BR 'sɜːvɪsˌber|i, -ɪz
AM 'sɜrvəsˌberi, -z

serviceman
BR 'sɜːvɪsmən
AM 'sɜrvəsˌmæn, 'sɜrvəsmən

servicemen
BR 'sɜːvɪsmən
AM 'sɜrvəsˌmɛn, 'sɜrvəsmən

servicewoman
BR 'sɜːvɪsˌwʊmən
AM 'sɜrvəsˌwʊmən

servicewomen
BR 'sɜːvɪsˌwɪmɪn
AM 'sɜrvəsˌwɪmɪn

serviette
BR ˌsɜːvɪ'ɛt, -s
AM ˌsɜrvi'ɛt, -s

servile
BR 'sɜːvaɪl
AM 'sɜrvəl, 'sɜrˌvaɪl

servilely
BR 'sɜːvaɪlli
AM 'sɜrvəli, 'sɜrˌvaɪli

servility
BR sə'vɪlɪti
AM sər'vɪlɪdi

serving
BR 'sɜːvɪŋ, -z
AM 'sɜrvɪŋ, -z

Servis
BR 'sɜːvɪs
AM 'sɜrvəs

Servite
BR 'sɜːvaɪt, -s
AM 'sɜrˌvaɪt, -s

servitor
BR 'sɜːvɪtə(r), -z
AM 'sɜrvədər, 'sɜrvəˌtɔ(ə)r, -z

servitorship
BR 'sɜːvɪtəʃɪp, -s
AM 'sɜrvədərˌʃɪp, 'sɜrvəˌtɔrˌʃɪp, -s

servitude
BR 'sɜːvɪtjuːd, 'sɜːvɪtʃuːd
AM 'sɜrvəˌt(j)ud

servo
BR 'sɜːvəʊ, -z
AM 'sɜrvoʊ, -z

sesame
BR 'sɛsəmi
AM 'sɛsəmi

sesamoid
BR 'sɛsəmɔɪd
AM 'sɛsəˌmɔɪd

sesamum
BR 'sɛsəməm
AM 'sɛsəməm

Sesotho
BR sɪ'səʊtəʊ, sɛ'səʊtəʊ
AM sə'soʊtʊ, sə'sɑdoʊ

sesquicentenary
BR ˌsɛskwɪsɛn'tiːn(ə)r|i, ˌsɛskwɪsɛn'tɛn(ə)r|i, -ɪz
AM ˌsɛskwəsɛn'tɛnəri, -z

sesquicentennial
BR ˌsɛskwɪsɛn'tɛnɪəl
AM ˌsɛskwɪsɛn'tɛnɪəl, ˌsɛskwəsən'tɛnɪəl

sesquipedalian
BR ˌsɛskwɪpɪ'deɪlɪən
AM ˌsɛskwəpə'deɪljən, 'sɛskwəpə'deɪlɪən

sesquiplicate
BR 'sɛskwɪplɪkeɪt, 'sɛskwɪplɪkət
AM 'sɛskwəˌplɪkeɪt, 'sɛskwəˌplɪkɪt

sess
BR sɛs
AM sɛs

sessile
BR 'sɛsaɪl
AM 'sɛsəl, 'sɛˌsaɪl

session
BR 'sɛʃn, -z
AM 'sɛʃən, -z

sessional
BR 'sɛʃ(ə)l, 'sɛʃən(ə)l, -z
AM 'sɛʃ(ə)nəl, -z

sesterce
BR 'sɛstə:s, -ə:sɪz\-əsɪz\-əsi:z
AM 'sɛstərs, -əz

sestertia
BR sɛ'stə:tɪə(r), sɛ'stə:ʃ(ɪ)ə(r)
AM sɛ'stərˌʃ(i)ə, sə'stərˌʃ(i)ə

sestertii
BR sɛ'stə:tɪaɪ, sɛ'stə:ʃɪaɪ
AM sɛ'stərˌʃi,aɪ, sə'stərˌʃi,aɪ

sestertium
BR sɛ'stə:tɪəm, sɛ'stə:ʃ(ɪ)əm

AM sɛ'stərˌʃ(i)əm, sə'stərˌʃ(i)əm

sestertius
BR sɛ'stə:tɪəs, sɛ'stə:ʃ(ɪ)əs
AM sɛ'stərˌʃ(i)əs, sə'stərˌʃ(i)əs

sestet
BR sɛs'tɛt, -s
AM sɛs'tɛt, -s

sestina
BR sɛ'stiːnə(r), -z
AM sɛ'stiːnə, 'sɛstənə, -z

set
BR sɛt, -s, -ɪŋ
AM sɛ|t, -ts, -dɪŋ

seta
BR 'siːtə(r)
AM 'sidə

setaceous
BR sɪ'teɪʃəs
AM sə'teɪʃəs

setae
BR 'siːtiː
AM 'sidi, 'si,taɪ

setaside
BR 'sɛtəsaɪd, -z
AM 'sɛdəˌsaɪd, -z

setback
BR 'sɛtbak, -s
AM 'sɛtˌbæk, -s

Seth
BR sɛθ
AM sɛθ

SETI
BR 'sɛti
AM 'sɛdi

setiferous
BR sɪ'tɪf(ə)rəs
AM sə'tɪf(ə)rəs

setigerous
BR sɪ'tɪdʒ(ə)rəs
AM sə'tɪdʒ(ə)rəs

seton
BR 'siːtn, -z
AM 'sitn, -z

setose
BR 'siːtəʊs, 'siːtəʊz
AM 'si,toʊs, 'si,toʊz

set-piece
BR 'sɛt'piːs
AM 'sɛt,pis

setscrew
BR 'sɛtskruː, -z
AM 'sɛt,skru, -z

setsquare
BR 'sɛtskwɛː(r), -z
AM 'sɛt,skwɛ(ə)r, -z

Setswana
BR sɛt'swaːnə(r)
AM sɛt'swɑnə

sett
BR sɛt, -s
AM sɛt, -s

settee
BR sɛ'tiː, -z

AM sɛ'stərʃ(i)əm, sə'stərʃ(i)əm

setter
BR 'sɛtə(r), -z
AM 'sɛdər, -z

setterwort
BR 'sɛtəwəːt
AM 'sɛdərwərt, 'sɛdərˌwɔ(ə)rt

setting
BR 'sɛtɪŋ, -z
AM 'sɛdɪŋ, -z

settle
BR 'sɛt|l, -lz, -lɪŋ\-lɪŋ, -ld
AM 'sɛ|dəl, -dlz, -dlɪŋ\-tlɪŋ, -dld

settleable
BR 'sɛtləbl, 'sɛtlbl
AM 'sɛdləbəl, 'sɛtləbl

settlement
BR 'sɛtlm(ə)nt, -s
AM 'sɛdlmənt, -s

settler
BR 'sɛtlə(r), 'sɛtlə(r), -z
AM 'sɛdlər, 'sɛtlər, -z

settlor
BR 'sɛtlə(r), 'sɛtlə(r), -z
AM 'sɛdlər, 'sɛtlər, -z

set-to
BR ˌsɛt'tuː, 'sɛttuː, -z
AM 'sɛt,tu, -z

setup
BR 'sɛtʌp, -s
AM 'sɛd,əp, -s

setwall
BR 'sɛtw(ə)l, -z
AM 'sɛt,wɔl, 'sɛt,wɑl, -z

Seurat
BR 'sɜːrɑː(r)
AM sɜ'rɑː

Sevastopol
BR sɛ'vastəpɒl, sə'vastəpɒl
AM sɛ'vɑstəˌpɒl, sə'vɑstəˌpɒl, sɛ'vɑstəˌpoʊl, sə'vɑstəˌpoʊl
RUS sʲiva'stopəlʲ

seven
BR 'sɛvn, -z
AM 'sɛvən, -z

sevenfold
BR 'sɛvnfəʊld
AM 'sɛvən,foʊld

Sevenoaks
BR 'sɛvnəʊks
AM 'sɛvən,oʊks

seventeen
BR ˌsɛvn'tiːn
AM ˌsɛvən'tin

seventeenth
BR ˌsɛvn'tiːnθ
AM ˌsɛvən'tinθ

seventh
BR 'sɛvnθ, -s
AM 'sɛvənθ, -s

seventhly
BR ˈsɛvnθli
AM ˈsɛvənθli

seventieth
BR ˈsɛvntɪɪθ, -s
AM ˈsɛvən(t)ɪəθ, -s

seventy
BR ˈsɛvnt|i, -iz
AM ˈsɛvən(t)i, -z

seventyfold
BR ˈsɛvntɪfəʊld
AM ˈsɛvən(t)iˌfoʊld

Seven Up®
BR ˌsɛvn ˈʌp, -s
AM ˌsɛvən ˈəp, -s

sever
BR ˈsɛv|ə(r), -əz,
-(ə)rɪŋ, -əd
AM ˈsɛv|ər, -ərz, -(ə)rɪŋ,
-ərd

severable
BR ˈsɛv(ə)rəbl
AM ˈsɛv(ə)rəbəl

several
BR ˈsɛv(ə)rəl, ˈsɛv(ə)r|
AM ˈsɛv(ə)rəl

severally
BR ˈsɛv(ə)rəli,
ˈsɛv(ə)r|i
AM ˈsɛv(ə)rəli

severalty
BR ˈsɛv(ə)rəlti,
ˈsɛv(ə)r|ti, -iz
AM ˈsɛv(ə)rəlti, -z

severance
BR ˈsɛv(ə)rəns,
ˈsɛv(ə)rns
AM ˈsɛv(ə)rəns,
ˈsɛvərəns

severe
BR sɪˈvɪə(r), -ə(r), -ɪst
AM səˈvɪ(ə)r, -ər, -est

severely
BR sɪˈvɪəli
AM səˈvɪrli

severity
BR sɪˈvɛrɪt|i, -iz
AM səˈvɛrədi, -z

Severn
BR ˈsɛvn
AM ˈsɛvərn

Severus
BR sɪˈvɪərəs
AM səˈvɪrəs

severy
BR ˈsɛv(ə)r|i, -iz
AM ˈsɛv(ə)ri, -z

seviche
BR sɛˈviːtʃeɪ
AM səˈvitʃeɪ

Seville
BR sɪˈvɪl, ˈsɛv(ɪ)l
AM səˈvɪl

Sèvres
BR ˈsɛvr(ər), ˈseɪvr(ər)
AM ˈsɛvrə

sew
BR səʊ, -z, -ɪŋ, -d
AM soʊ, -z, -ɪŋ, -d

sewage
BR ˈs(j)uːɪdʒ
AM ˈsuɪdʒ

Sewall
BR ˈs(j)uːəl
AM ˈsuəl

Seward
BR ˈsiːwəd, ˈsjuːəd
AM ˈsuərd

Sewell
BR ˈs(j)uːəl
AM ˈsuəl

sewellel
BR sɪˈwɛləl, -z
AM səˈwɛləl, -z

sewen
BR ˈsjuːn, -z
AM ˈsuən, -z

sewer¹
person who sews
BR ˈsəʊə(r), -z
AM ˈsoʊər, -z

sewer²
*pipe for sewage,
servant*
BR ˈs(j)uːə(r), -z
AM ˈsuər, ˈsʊ(ə)r, -z

sewerage
BR ˈs(j)uːərɪdʒ
AM ˈsuərɪdʒ

sewin
BR ˈsjuːɪn, -z
AM ˈsuən, -z

sewn
BR səʊn
AM soʊn

sex
BR sɛks, -ɪz, -ɪŋ, -t
AM sɛks, -əz, -ɪŋ, -t

sexagenarian
BR ˌsɛksədʒɪˈnɛːrɪən,
-z
AM ˌsɛksədʒəˈnɛrɪən,
-z

sexagenary
BR sɛkˈsadʒɪn(ə)r|i,
sɛkˈsadʒɪn(ə)r|i, -iz
AM sɛkˈsædʒəˌnɛri, -z

Sexagesima
BR ˌsɛksəˈdʒɛsɪmə(r)
AM ˌsɛksəˈdʒɛsəmə

sexagesimal
BR ˌsɛksəˈdʒɛsɪml, -z
AM ˌsɛksəˈdʒɛsəməl, -z

sexagesimally
BR ˌsɛksəˈdʒɛsɪml̩i,
ˌsɛksəˈdʒɛsɪməli
AM ˌsɛksəˈdʒɛsəməli

sexangular
BR sɛkˈsaŋgjələ(r)
AM sɛkˈsæŋgjələr

sexcentenary
BR ˌsɛksɛnˈtiːn(ə)r|i,
ˌsɛksɛnˈtɛn(ə)r|i, -iz

sexenarie
AM ˌsɛksɛnˈtɛnəri,
ˌsɛk(s)ˈsɛntnˌɛri, -z

sexennial
BR sɛkˈsɛnɪəl
AM sɛˈksɛnɪəl

sexer
BR ˈsɛksə(r), -z
AM ˈsɛksər, -z

sexfoil
BR ˈsɛksfɔɪl, -z
AM ˈsɛksˌfɔɪl, -z

sexily
BR ˈsɛksɪli
AM ˈsɛksəli

sexiness
BR ˈsɛksɪnɪs
AM ˈsɛksɪnɪs

sexism
BR ˈsɛksɪz(ə)m
AM ˈsɛkˌsɪzəm

sexist
BR ˈsɛksɪst, -s
AM ˈsɛksəst, -s

sexisyllabic
BR ˌsɛksɪsɪˈlabɪk
AM ˌsɛksəsəˈlæbɪk

sexisyllable
BR ˈsɛksɪˌsɪləbl,
ˌsɛksɪˈsɪləbl, -z
AM ˌsɛksəˈsɪləbəl, -z

sexivalent
BR ˌsɛksɪˈveɪlənt,
ˌsɛksɪˈveɪlnt
AM ˈsɛksəˌveɪlənt

sexless
BR ˈsɛksləs
AM ˈsɛksləs

sexlessly
BR ˈsɛksləsli
AM ˈsɛksləsli

sexlessness
BR ˈsɛksləsnəs
AM ˈsɛksləsnəs

sexological
BR ˌsɛksəˈlɒdʒɪkl
AM ˌsɛksəˈlɑdʒəkəl

sexologist
BR sɛkˈsɒlədʒɪst, -s
AM sɛkˈsɑlədʒəst, -s

sexology
BR sɛkˈsɒlədʒi
AM sɛkˈsɑlədʒi

sexpartite
BR sɛksˈpɑːtaɪt
AM sɛksˈpɑrˌtaɪt

sexploitation
BR ˌsɛksplɔɪˈteɪʃn
AM ˌsɛksplɔɪˈteɪʃən

sexpot
BR ˈsɛkspɒt, -s
AM ˈsɛksˌpɑt, -s

sexstarved
BR ˈsɛk(s)stɑːvd
AM ˈsɛk(s)ˌstɑrvd

sext
BR sɛkst
AM sɛkst

sextain
BR ˈsɛksteɪn, -z
AM ˈsɛkˌsteɪn, -z

Sextans
BR ˈsɛkst(ə)nz
AM ˈsɛkstənz

sextant
BR ˈsɛkst(ə)nt, -s
AM ˈsɛkstənt, -s

sextet
BR (ˌ)sɛkˈstɛt,
(ˌ)sɛksˈtɛt, -s
AM sɛkˈstɛt, -s

sextile
BR ˈsɛkstʌɪl
AM ˈsɛkˌstaɪl

sextillion
BR sɛkˈstɪljən, -z
AM sɛkˈstɪljən, -z

sextillionth
BR sɛkˈstɪljənθ, -s
AM sɛkˈstɪljənθ, -s

sexto
BR ˈsɛkstəʊ, -z
AM ˈsɛkˌstoʊ, -z

sextodecimo
BR ˌsɛkstəʊˈdɛsɪməʊ,
-z
AM ˌsɛkstəˈdɛsəˌmoʊ,
-z

sexton
BR ˈsɛkst(ə)n, -z
AM ˈsɛkstən, -z

sextuple
BR ˈsɛkstjʊpl,
ˈsɛkstʃʊpl
AM sɛkˈst(j)upəl,
ˌsɛksˈtəpəl

sextuplet
BR sɛksˈtjuːplɪt,
sɛksˈtʃuːplɪt,
ˈsɛkstjʊplɪt,
ˈsɛkstʃʊplɪt, -s
AM sɛkˈstʊplət, -s

sextuply
BR ˈsɛkstjʊpli,
ˈsɛkstʃʊpli
AM sɛkˈst(j)upli,
ˌsɛksˈtəpli

sexual
BR ˈsɛkʃʊəl, ˈsɛkʃ(ʊ)l,
ˈsɛksjʊ(ə)l
AM ˈsɛkʃ(əw)əl

sexualise
BR ˈsɛkʃʊəlʌɪz,
ˈsɛkʃʊ̩lʌɪz, ˈsɛkʃlʌɪz,
ˈsɛksjʊ(ə)lʌɪz, -ɪz, -ɪŋ,
-d
AM ˈsɛkʃ(əw)əˌlaɪz, -ɪz,
-ɪŋ, -d

sexualist
BR ˈsɛkʃʊəlɪst,
ˈsɛkʃʊ̩lɪst, ˈsɛkʃlɪst,
ˈsɛksjʊ(ə)lɪst, -s
AM ˈsɛkʃ(əw)ələst, -s

sexuality
BR ˌsɛkʃʊˈalɪti,
ˌsɛksjʊˈalɪti

AM ˌsɛkʃəˈwælədi

sexualize
BR ˈsɛkʃʊəlaɪz, ˈsɛkʃʉlaɪz, ˈsɛkʃlaɪz, ˈsɛksjʊ(ə)laɪz, -ɪz, -ɪŋ, -d
AM ˈsɛkʃ(əw)əˌlaɪz, -ɪz, -ɪŋ, -d

sexually
BR ˈsɛkʃʊəli, ˈsɛkʃʉli, ˈsɛkʃli, ˈsɛksjʊ(ə)li
AM ˈsɛkʃ(əw)əli

sexvalent
BR (ˌ)sɛksˈveɪlənt, (ˌ)sɛksˈveɪln̩t
AM ˌsɛksˈveɪlənt

sexy
BR ˈsɛksˌi, -ɪə(r), -ɪɪst
AM ˈsɛksi, -ər, -ɪst

Seychelles
BR seɪˈʃɛlz
AM seɪˈʃɛlz

Seychellois
BR ˌseɪʃɛlˈwɑː(r)
AM ˌseɪʃɛlˈwɑ

Seychelloise
BR ˌseɪʃɛlˈwɑːz
AM ˌseɪʃɛlˈwɑ(z)

Seyfert
BR ˈsiːfət, ˈsʌɪfət
AM ˈsifərt, ˈsaɪfərt

Seymour
BR ˈsiːmɔː(r)
AM ˈsiˌmɔ(ə)r

sez
BR sɛz
AM sɛz

Sfax
BR sfaks
AM sfæks

sforzandi
BR sfɔːtˈsandiː
AM sfɔrtˈsandi

sforzando
BR sfɔːtˈsandəʊ, -z
AM sfɔrtˈsandoʊ, -z

sforzato
BR sfɔːtˈsatəʊ
AM sfɔrtˈsadoʊ, sfɔrtˈsadou

sfumati
BR sfuːˈmɑːtiː
AM sfuˈmɑdi

sfumato
BR sfuːˈmɑːtəʊ
AM sfuˈmɑdou

sgraffiti
BR zgrɑˈfiːtiː, skrɑˈfiːti
AM zgrɑˈfidi, skrɑˈfidi

sgraffito
BR zgrɑˈfiːtəʊ, sgrɑˈfiːtəʊ
AM zgrɑˈfidou, skrɑˈfidou

Sgurr
BR ˈskʊə(r)
AM ˈsgʊ(ə)r

sh!
BR ʃ
AM ʃ

Shaba
BR ˈʃɑːbə(r)
AM ˈʃabə

shabbat
BR ʃəˈbat, -s
AM ʃəˈbat, -s

shabbily
BR ˈʃabɪli
AM ˈʃæbəli

shabbiness
BR ˈʃabɪnɪs
AM ˈʃæbinɪs

shabbos
BR ˈʃabəs, -ɪz
AM ˈʃabəs, -əz

shabby
BR ˈʃabˌi, -ɪə(r), -ɪɪst
AM ˈʃæbi, -ər, -ɪst

shabbyish
BR ˈʃabɪɪʃ
AM ˈʃæbiɪʃ

shabrack
BR ˈʃabrak, -s
AM ˈʃæˌbræk, -s

shack
BR ʃak, -s, -ɪŋ, -t
AM ʃæk, -s, -ɪŋ, -t

shackle
BR ˈʃakl̩, -lz, -lɪŋ \-lɪŋ, -ld
AM ˈʃækl̩əl, -əlz, -(ə)lɪŋ, -əld

Shackleton
BR ˈʃaklt(ə)n
AM ˈʃækəltən

shad
BR ʃad
AM ʃæd

Shadbolt
BR ˈʃadbəʊlt
AM ˈʃædˌboʊlt

shadbush
BR ˈʃadbʊʃ, -ɪz
AM ˈʃædˌbʊʃ, -əz

shaddock
BR ˈʃadək, -s
AM ˈʃædək, -s

shade
BR ʃeɪd, -z, -ɪŋ, -ɪd
AM ʃeɪd, -z, -ɪŋ, -ɪd

shadeless
BR ˈʃeɪdlɪs
AM ˈʃeɪdlɪs

shadily
BR ˈʃeɪdɪli
AM ˈʃeɪdɪli

shadiness
BR ˈʃeɪdɪnɪs
AM ˈʃeɪdɪnɪs

shading
BR ˈʃeɪdɪŋ, -z
AM ˈʃeɪdɪŋ, -z

shadoof
BR ʃəˈduːf, ʃɑˈduːf, -s

AM ʃəˈduf, ʃɑˈduf, ʃæˈduf, -s

shadow
BR ˈʃadəʊ, -z, -ɪŋ, -d
AM ˈʃædˌoʊ, -oʊz, -əwɪŋ, -oʊd

shadowbox
BR ˈʃadə(ʊ)bɒks, -ɪz, -ɪŋ, -t
AM ˈʃædəˌbaks, ˈʃædoʊˌbaks, -əz, -ɪŋ, -t

shadower
BR ˈʃadəʊə(r), -z
AM ˈʃædəwər, -z

shadowgraph
BR ˈʃadəʊɡrɑːf, ˈʃadəʊɡraf, -s
AM ˈʃædoʊˌɡræf, -s

shadowiness
BR ˈʃadəʊɪnɪs
AM ˈʃædəwɪnɪs

shadowless
BR ˈʃadəʊləs
AM ˈʃædoʊləs

shadowy
BR ˈʃadəʊi
AM ˈʃædəwi

Shadrach
BR ˈʃadrak, ˈʃeɪdrak
AM ˈʃædˌræk

Shadwell
BR ˈʃadw(ɛ)l
AM ˈʃædˌwɛl

shady
BR ˈʃeɪdˌi, -ɪə(r), -ɪɪst
AM ˈʃeɪdi, -ər, -ɪst

SHAEF
BR ʃeɪf
AM ʃeɪf

Shaeffer
BR ˈʃeɪfə(r)
AM ˈʃeɪfər

Shafer
BR ˈʃeɪfə(r)
AM ˈʃeɪfər

Shaffer
BR ˈʃafə(r)
AM ˈʃæfər

shaft
BR ʃɑːft, ʃaft, -s, -ɪŋ, -ɪd
AM ʃæft, -s, -ɪŋ, -əd

Shaftesbury
BR ˈʃɑːf(t)sb(ə)ri, ˈʃaf(t)sb(ə)ri
AM ˈʃæf(t)s,bɛri, ˈʃæf(t)sb(ə)ri

Shafto
BR ˈʃɑːftəʊ, ˈʃaftəʊ
AM ˈʃæfˌtou

Shaftoe
BR ˈʃɑːftəʊ, ˈʃaftəʊ
AM ˈʃæfˌtou

shag
BR ʃag, -z, -ɪŋ, -d
AM ʃæg, -z, -ɪŋ, -d

shagbark
BR ˈʃagbɑːk, -s
AM ˈʃæɡˌbark, -s

shagger
BR ˈʃagə(r), -z
AM ˈʃægər, -z

shaggily
BR ˈʃagɪli
AM ˈʃægəli

shagginess
BR ˈʃagɪnɪs
AM ˈʃæginɪs

shaggy
BR ˈʃagˌi, -ɪə(r), -ɪst
AM ˈʃægi, -ər, -ɪst

shaggy-dog
BR ˌʃagiˈdɒg
AM ˌʃægiˈdag

shagreen
BR ʃəˈgriːn, ʃaˈgriːn
AM ʃæˈgrin, ʃəˈgrin

shah
BR ʃɑː(r), -z
AM ʃɑ, -z

shahdom
BR ˈʃɑːdəm, -z
AM ˈʃadəm, -z

shaikh
BR ʃeɪk, ʃiːk, -s
AM ʃik, ʃeɪk, -s

Shaka
BR ˈʃɑːkə(r)
AM ˈʃakə, ˈʃækə

shake
BR ʃeɪk, -s, -ɪŋ
AM ʃeɪk, -s, -ɪŋ

shakeable
BR ˈʃeɪkəbl
AM ˈʃeɪkəbəl

shakedown
BR ˈʃeɪkdaʊn, -z
AM ˈʃeɪkˌdaʊn, -z

shaken
BR ˈʃeɪk(ə)n
AM ˈʃeɪkən

shaker
BR ˈʃeɪkə(r), -z
AM ˈʃeɪkər, -z

Shakeress
BR ˈʃeɪkərɛs, ˈʃeɪk(ə)rɪs, ˌʃeɪkərˈɛs, -ɪz
AM ˈʃeɪk(ə)rəs, -əz

Shakerism
BR ˈʃeɪk(ə)rɪz(ə)m
AM ˈʃeɪk(ə)ˌrɪzəm

Shakeshaft
BR ˈʃeɪkˌʃɑːft, ˈʃeɪkˌʃaft
AM ˈʃeɪkˌʃæft

Shakespeare
BR ˈʃeɪkspɪə(r)
AM ˈʃeɪkˌspɪ(ə)r

Shakespearean
BR ʃeɪkˈspɪərɪən, -z
AM ʃeɪkˈspɪriən, -z

Shakespeareana
BR ʃeɪkˌspɪərɪˈɑːnə(r),
ˌʃeɪkspɪərɪˈɑːnə(r)
AM ʃeɪkˌspɪrɪˈɑːnə

Shakespearian
BR ʃeɪkˈspɪərɪən, -z
AM ʃeɪkˈspɪrɪən, -z

Shakespeariana
BR ʃeɪkˌspɪərɪˈɑːnə(r),
ˌʃeɪkspɪərɪˈɑːnə(r)
AM ʃeɪkˌspɪrɪˈɑːnə

shakeup
BR ˈʃeɪkʌp, -s
AM ˈʃeɪkˌəp, -s

shakily
BR ˈʃeɪkɪli
AM ˈʃeɪkɪli

shakiness
BR ˈʃeɪkɪnɪs
AM ˈʃeɪkɪnɪs

shako
BR ˈʃeɪkəʊ, ˈʃakəʊ, -z
AM ˈʃækoʊ, ˈʃeɪkoʊ, -z

shakuhachi
BR ˌʃakuˈhaːtʃi,
ˌʃakʊˈhatʃi, -ɪz
AM ˌʃakuˈhatʃi, -z

shaky
BR ˈʃeɪki, -ɪə(r), -ɪɪst
AM ˈʃeɪki, -ər, -ɪst

Shaldon
BR ˈʃɔːld(ə)n,
ˈʃɒld(ə)n, ˈʃald(ə)n
AM ˈʃɔldən, ˈʃældən,
ˈʃaldən

shale
BR ʃeɪl
AM ʃeɪl

shaley
BR ˈʃeɪli
AM ˈʃeɪli

shaliness
BR ˈʃeɪlɪnɪs
AM ˈʃeɪlɪnɪs

shall¹
strong form
BR ʃal
AM ʃæl

shall²
weak form
BR ʃ(ə)l
AM ʃəl

shalloon
BR ʃəˈluːn, -z
AM ʃəˈlun, -z

shallop
BR ˈʃaləp, -s
AM ˈʃæləp, -s

shallot
BR ʃəˈlɒt, -s
AM ʃəˈlɑt, ˈʃælət, -s

shallow
BR ˈʃaləʊ, -z, -ə(r), -ɪst
AM ˈʃæl|oʊ, -oʊz, -əwər,
-əwəst

shallowly
BR ˈʃaləʊli
AM ˈʃæloʊli

shallowness
BR ˈʃaləʊnəs
AM ˈʃæloʊnəs

Shalmaneser
BR ˌʃalməˈniːzə(r)
AM ˌʃælməˈnizər

shalom
BR ʃəˈlɒm, ʃaˈlɒm,
ʃəˈləʊm, ʃaˈləʊm
AM ʃɑˈloʊm, ʃɑˈloʊm

shalt¹
strong form
BR ʃalt
AM ʃælt

shalt²
weak form
BR ʃ(ə)lt
AM ʃalt

shalwar
BR ˈʃʌlvaː(r), -z
AM ˈʃʌlˌwɑr, -z

shaly
BR ˈʃeɪl|i, -ɪə(r), -ɪɪst
AM ˈʃeɪli, -ər, -ɪst

sham
BR ʃam, -z, -ɪŋ, -d
AM ʃæm, -z, -ɪŋ, -d

shaman
BR ˈʃɑːmən, ˈʃamən,
ˈʃeɪmən, -z
AM ˈʃɑmən, ˈʃeɪmən, -z

shamanic
BR ʃəˈmanɪk,
ʃeɪˈmanɪk
AM ʃəˈmænɪk,
ʃeɪˈmænɪk

shamanism
BR ˈʃɑːmənɪz(ə)m,
ˈʃamənɪz(ə)m,
ˈʃeɪmənɪz(ə)m
AM ˈʃɑməˌnɪzəm,
ˈʃeɪməˌnɪzəm

shamanist
BR ˈʃɑːmənɪst,
ˈʃamənɪst,
ˈʃeɪmənɪst, -s
AM ˈʃɑmənəst,
ˈʃeɪmənəst, -s

shamanistic
BR ˌʃɑːməˈnɪstɪk,
ˌʃaməˈnɪstɪk,
ˌʃeɪməˈnɪstɪk
AM ˌʃɑməˈnɪstɪk,
ˌʃeɪməˈnɪstɪk

shamateur
BR ˈʃamət(ʃ)ə(r),
ˌʃaməˈtəː(r), -z
AM ˈʃæmədər,
ˈʃæməˌtər, ˌʃæməˈtər,
ˌʃæməˈt(j)ʊ(ə)r, -z

shamateurish
BR ˈʃamət(ə)rɪʃ,
ˌʃaməˈtəːrɪʃ,
AM ˌʃæməˈtərɪʃ,
ˈʃæməˈt(j)ʊrɪʃ,
ˈʃæməˈtʃʊrɪʃ

shamateurishly
AM ˈʃeɪmɪŋli

shamateurishly
AM ʃamət(ə)rɪʃli,
ˈʃamətʃ(ə)rɪʃli,
ˌʃaməˈtəːrɪʃli
AM ˈʃæməˈtərɪʃli,
ˈʃæməˈt(j)ʊrɪʃli,
ˌʃæməˈtʃʊrɪʃli

shamateurishness
BR ˈʃamət(ə)rɪʃnɪs,
ˈʃamətʃ(ə)rɪʃnɪs,
ˌʃaməˈtəːrɪʃnɪs
AM ˈʃæməˈtərɪʃnɪs,
ˈʃæməˈt(j)ʊrɪʃnɪs,
ˈʃæməˈtʃʊrɪʃnɪs

shamateurism
BR ˈʃamət(ə)rɪz(ə)m,
ˈʃamətʃ(ə)rɪz(ə)m,
ˌʃaməˈtəːrɪz(ə)m
AM ˈʃæmədəˌrɪzəm,
ˈʃæməˌt(j)ʊˌrɪzəm,
ˈʃæməˌtʃʊˌrɪzəm

shamble
BR ˈʃamb|l, -lz,
-lɪŋ\-lɪŋ, -ld
AM ˈʃæmbəl, -əlz,
-(ə)lɪŋ, -əld

shambolic
BR ʃamˈbɒlɪk
AM ʃæmˈbɑlɪk

shambolically
BR ʃamˈbɒlɪkli
AM ˌʃæmˈbɑlək(ə)li

shame
BR ʃeɪm, -z, -ɪŋ, -d
AM ʃeɪm, -z, -ɪŋ, -d

shamefaced
BR ˌʃeɪmˈfeɪst
AM ˈʃeɪmˈfeɪst

shamefacedly
BR ˌʃeɪmˈfeɪstli,
ˌʃeɪmˈfeɪsɪdli
AM ˈʃeɪmˈfeɪsɪdli,
ˈʃeɪmˈfeɪstli

shamefacedness
BR ˌʃeɪmˈfeɪstnɪs,
ˌʃeɪmˈfeɪsɪdnɪs
AM ˈʃeɪmˈfeɪsɪdnɪs,
ˈʃeɪmˈfeɪstnɪs

shameful
BR ˈʃeɪmf(ʊ)l
AM ˈʃeɪmfəl

shamefully
BR ˈʃeɪmfʊli, ˈʃeɪmfˌli
AM ˈʃeɪmfəli

shamefulness
BR ˈʃeɪmf(ʊ)lnəs
AM ˈʃeɪmfəlnəs

shameless
BR ˈʃeɪmlɪs
AM ˈʃeɪmlɪs

shamelessly
BR ˈʃeɪmlɪsli
AM ˈʃeɪmlɪsli

shamelessness
BR ˈʃeɪmlɪsnɪs
AM ˈʃeɪmlɪsnɪs

shamingly
BR ˈʃeɪmɪŋli

shamateurishly
AM ˈʃeɪmɪŋli

Shamir
BR ʃəˈmɪə(r)
AM ʃəˈmɪ(ə)r

shammer
BR ˈʃamə(r), -z
AM ˈʃæmər, -z

shammy
BR ˈʃam|i, -ɪz
AM ˈʃæmi, -ɪz

shampoo
BR ʃamˈpuː, -z, -ɪŋ, -d
AM ʃæmˈpu, -z, -ɪŋ, -d

shamrock
BR ˈʃamrɒk, -s
AM ˈʃæmˌrɑk, -s

Shamu
BR ʃaˈmuː
AM ʃæˈmu, ʃɑˈmu

shamus
BR ˈʃeɪməs, -ɪz
AM ˈʃeɪməs, -əz

Shan¹
forename
BR ʃaːn
AM ʃæn

Shan²
people, language
BR ʃaːn, ʃan
AM ʃæn

Shandean
BR ˈʃandɪən, -z
AM ˈʃændɪən, -z

shandrydan
BR ˈʃandrɪdan, -z
AM ˈʃændriˌdæn, -z

shandy
BR ˈʃand|i, -ɪz
AM ˈʃændi, -ɪz

shandygaff
BR ˈʃandɪgaf, -s
AM ˈʃændiˌgæf, -s

Shane
BR ʃeɪn
AM ʃeɪn

Shang
BR ʃaŋ
AM ʃæŋ

shanghai
BR ˌʃaŋˈhʌɪ, -z, -ɪŋ, -d
AM ˌʃæŋˈhaɪ, -z, -ɪŋ, -d

Shangri-La
BR ˌʃaŋgrɪˈlaː(r), -z
AM ˌʃæŋgrɪˈlɑ, -z

shank
BR ʃaŋ|k, -ks, -(k)t
AM ʃæŋ|k, -ks, -kɪŋ,
-(k)t

Shankar
BR ˈʃaŋkaː(r)
AM ˈʃæŋˌkɑr

Shankill
BR ˈʃaŋkɪl
AM ˈʃæŋkəl

Shanklin
BR ˈʃaŋklɪn
AM ˈʃæŋklən

Shankly
BR ˈʃaŋkli
AM ˈʃæŋkli

Shanks
BR ʃaŋks
AM ʃæŋks

Shannon
BR ˈʃanən
AM ˈʃænən

shanny
BR ˈʃan|i, -ɪz
AM ˈʃæni, -z

Shansi
BR ʃanˈsiː
AM ˈʃænˈʃi

shan't
BR ʃɑːnt
AM ʃænt

shantung
BR ʃanˈtʌŋ
AM ʃænˈtəŋ

shanty
BR ˈʃant|i, -ɪz
AM ˈʃæn(t)i, -z

shantyman
BR ˈʃantɪmən
AM ˈʃæn(t)i,mæn

shantymen
BR ˈʃantɪmɛn
AM ˈʃæn(t)i,mɛn

shantytown
BR ˈʃantɪtaʊn, -z
AM ˈʃæn(t)i,taʊn, -z

Shanxi
BR ʃanˈsiː
AM ˈʃænˈʃi

shap
BR ʃap
AM ʃæp

shapable
BR ˈʃeɪpəbl
AM ˈʃeɪpəbəl

SHAPE
BR ʃeɪp
AM ʃeɪp

shape
BR ʃeɪp, -s, -ɪŋ, -t
AM ʃeɪp, -s, -ɪŋ, -t

shapeable
BR ˈʃeɪpəbl
AM ˈʃeɪpəbəl

shapechanger
BR ˈʃeɪp,tʃeɪn(d)ʒə(r), -z
AM ˈʃeɪp,tʃeɪndʒər, -z

shapechanging
BR ˈʃeɪp,tʃeɪn(d)ʒɪŋ
AM ˈʃeɪp,tʃeɪndʒɪŋ

shapeless
BR ˈʃeɪplɪs
AM ˈʃeɪplɪs

shapelessly
BR ˈʃeɪplɪsli
AM ˈʃeɪplɪsli

shapelessness
BR ˈʃeɪplɪsnɪs
AM ˈʃeɪplɪsnɪs

shapeliness
BR ˈʃeɪplɪnɪs
AM ˈʃeɪplɪnɪs

shapely
BR ˈʃeɪpl|i, -ɪə(r), -ɪɪst
AM ˈʃeɪpli, -ər, -ɪst

shaper
BR ˈʃeɪpə(r), -z
AM ˈʃeɪpər, -z

shaping
BR ˈʃeɪpɪŋ, -z
AM ˈʃeɪpɪŋ, -z

Shapiro
BR ʃəˈpɪərəʊ
AM ʃəˈpɪroʊ

shard
BR ʃɑːd, -z
AM ʃɑrd, -z

share
BR ʃɛː(r), -z, -ɪŋ, -d
AM ʃɛ(ə)r, -z, -ɪŋ, -d

shareable
BR ˈʃɛːrəbl
AM ˈʃɛrəbl

sharecrop
BR ˈʃɛːkrɒp, -s, -ɪŋ, -t
AM ˈʃɛrˌkrɑp, -s, -ɪŋ, -t

sharecropper
BR ˈʃɛːˌkrɒpə(r), -z
AM ˈʃɛrˌkrɑpər, -z

share-farmer
BR ˈʃɛːˌfɑːmə(r), -z
AM ˈʃɛrˌfɑrmər, -z

shareholder
BR ˈʃɛːˌhəʊldə(r), -z
AM ˈʃɛr,(h)oʊldər, -z

shareholding
BR ˈʃɛːˌhəʊldɪŋ, -z
AM ˈʃɛr,(h)oʊldɪŋ, -z

share-out
BR ˈʃɛːraʊt, -s
AM ˈʃɛr,aʊt, -s

sharer
BR ˈʃɛːrə(r), -z
AM ˈʃɛrər, -z

shareware
BR ˈʃɛːˌwɛː(r)
AM ˈʃɛr,wɛ(ə)r

sharia
BR ʃəˈriːə(r),
ʃɑːˈriːə(r)
AM ʃəˈriːə

shariah
BR ʃəˈriːə(r),
ʃɑːˈriːə(r)
AM ʃəˈriːə

Sharif
BR ʃəˈriːf, ʃaˈriːf
AM ʃəˈrif

Sharjah
BR ˈʃɑː(d)ʒɑː(r),
ˈʃɑː(d)ʒə(r)
AM ˈʃɑr(d)ʒə

shark
BR ʃɑːk, -s
AM ʃɑrk, -s

sharkskin
BR ˈʃɑːkskɪn
AM ˈʃɑrkˌskɪn

Sharman
BR ˈʃɑːmən
AM ˈʃɑrmən

Sharon¹
personal name
BR ˈʃarən, ˌʃarn
AM ˈʃɛrən

Sharon²
placename
BR ˈʃɛːrən, ˈʃɛːrn,
ˈʃɑːrən, ˈʃɑːrn, ˈʃarən,
ˈʃarn
AM ˈʃɛrən

sharon fruit
BR ˈʃɛːrən fruːt,
ˈʃɛːrn +, ˈʃɑːrən +,
ˈʃɑːrn +, ˈʃarən +,
ˈʃarn +, -s
AM ˈʃɛrən ˌfrut, -s

sharp
BR ʃɑːp, -s, -ə(r), -ɪst
AM ʃɑrp, -s, -ər, -əst

Sharpe
BR ʃɑːp
AM ʃɑrp

shar-pei
BR ˌʃɑːˈpeɪ, -z
AM ˈʃɑrˈpeɪ, -z

sharpen
BR ˈʃɑːp|(ə)n, -(ə)nz,
-(ə)nɪŋ-\-nɪŋ, -(ə)nd
AM ˈʃɑrp|ən, -ənz,
-(ə)nɪŋ, -ənd

sharpener
BR ˈʃɑːp(ə)nə(r),
ˈʃɑːpnə(r), -z
AM ˈʃɑrp(ə)nər, -z

sharpening
BR ˈʃɑːp(ə)nɪŋ,
ˈʃɑːpnɪŋ, -z
AM ˈʃɑrp(ə)nɪŋ, -z

sharper
BR ˈʃɑːpə(r), -z
AM ˈʃɑrpər, -z

Sharpeville
BR ˈʃɑːpvɪl
AM ˈʃɑrpvəl, ˈʃɑrp,vɪl

sharpie
BR ˈʃɑːp|i, -ɪz
AM ˈʃɑrpi, -z

sharpish
BR ˈʃɑːpɪʃ
AM ˈʃɑrpɪʃ

Sharples
BR ˈʃɑːplz
AM ˈʃɑrpəlz

sharply
BR ˈʃɑːpli
AM ˈʃɑrpli

sharpness
BR ˈʃɑːpnəs
AM ˈʃɑrpnəs

sharpshooter
BR ˈʃɑːpˌʃuːtə(r), -z
AM ˈʃɑrpˌʃudər, -z

sharpshooting
BR ˈʃɑːpˌʃuːtɪŋ
AM ˈʃɑrpˌʃudɪŋ

sharpy
BR ˈʃɑːp|i, -ɪz
AM ˈʃɑrpi, -z

Sharron
BR ˈʃarən, ˌʃarn
AM ˈʃɛrən

Sharwood
BR ˈʃɑːwʊd
AM ˈʃɑrˌwʊd

shashlik
BR ˈʃaʃlɪk, ˈʃɑːʃlɪk, -s
AM ˈʃaʃˌlɪk, ˈʃɑʃˈlɪk, -s

Shasta
BR ˈʃastə(r), -z
AM ˈʃæstə, -z

Shastra
BR ˈʃɑːstrə(r),
ˈʃastrə(r)
AM ˈʃɑstrə

shat
BR ʃat
AM ʃæt

Shatner
BR ˈʃatnə(r)
AM ˈʃætnər

Shatt al-Arab
BR ˌʃat alˈarəb
AM ˌʃæd ˌælˈɛrəb, ˈʃɑd
ˌalˈɛrəb

shatter
BR ˈʃat|ə(r), -əz,
-(ə)rɪŋ, -əd
AM ˈʃædər, -z, -ɪŋ, -d

shatterer
BR ˈʃat(ə)rə(r), -z
AM ˈʃædərər, -z

shatteringly
BR ˈʃat(ə)rɪŋli
AM ˈʃædərɪŋli

shatterproof
BR ˈʃatəpruːf
AM ˈʃædərˌpruf

Shaughnessy
BR ˈʃɔːnəsi
AM ˈʃɔnəsi, ˈʃanəsi

Shaun
BR ʃɔːn
AM ʃɔn, ʃɑn

shave
BR ʃeɪv, -z, -ɪŋ, -d
AM ʃeɪv, -z, -ɪŋ, -d

shaveling
BR ˈʃeɪvlɪŋ, -z
AM ˈʃeɪvlɪŋ, -z

shaven
BR ˈʃeɪvn
AM ˈʃeɪvən

shaver
BR ˈʃeɪvə(r), -z
AM ˈʃeɪvər, -z

shavetail
BR ˈʃeɪvteɪl, -z
AM ˈʃeɪvˌteɪl, -z

Shavian
BR ˈʃeɪvɪən
AM ˈʃeɪvɪən, ˈʃeɪvjən

shaving
BR ˈʃeɪvɪŋ, -z
AM ˈʃeɪvɪŋ, -z

Shavuot
BR ʃəˈvuːəs, ˌʃɑːvuˈɒt
AM ʃəˈvuˌoʊt,
ʃəˈvuˌoʊθ

Shavuoth
BR ʃəˈvuːəs, ˌʃɑːvuˈɒt
AM ʃəˈvuˌoʊt,
ʃəˈvuˌoʊθ

shaw
BR ʃɔː(r), -z
AM ʃɔ, ʃɑ, -z

Shawcross
BR ˈʃɔːkrɒs
AM ˈʃɔˌkrɔs, ˈʃɑˌkrɑs

shawl
BR ʃɔːl, -z, -d
AM ʃɔl, ʃɑl, -z, -d

shawm
BR ʃɔːm, -z
AM ʃɔm, ʃɑm, -z

Shawnee
BR ʃɔːˈniː, -z
AM ʃɔˈni, ʃɑˈni, -z

shay
BR ʃeɪ, -z
AM ʃeɪ, -z

shchi
BR ˈʃtʃiː
AM ˈʃtʃi

she¹
strong form
BR ʃiː
AM ʃi

she²
weak form
BR ʃɪ
AM ʃɪ

shea
BR ʃiː, -z
AM ʃi, ʃeɪ, -z

sheading
BR ˈʃiːdɪŋ, -z
AM ˈʃidɪŋ, -z

sheaf
BR ʃiːf
AM ʃif

shealing
BR ˈʃiːlɪŋ, -z
AM ˈʃilɪŋ, -z

shear
BR ʃɪə(r), -z, -ɪŋ, -d
AM ʃɪ(ə)r, -z, -ɪŋ, -d

shearbill
BR ˈʃɪəbɪl, -z
AM ˈʃɪrˌbɪl, -z

Sheard
BR ʃɪəd, ʃəːd, ʃɛːd
AM ʃɪ(ə)rd

shearer
BR ˈʃɪərə(r), -z
AM ˈʃɪrər, -z

shearing
BR ˈʃɪərɪŋ, -z
AM ˈʃɪrɪŋ, -z

shearling
BR ˈʃɪəlɪŋ, -z
AM ˈʃɪrlɪŋ, -z

Shearman
BR ˈʃɪəmən
AM ˈʃɪrmən

shearpin
BR ˈʃɪəpɪn, -z
AM ˈʃɪrˌpɪn, -z

sheartail
BR ˈʃɪəteɪl, -z
AM ˈʃɪrˌteɪl, -z

shearwater
BR ˈʃɪəˌwɔːtə(r), -z
AM ˈʃɪrˌwɔdər,
ˈʃɪrˌwɑdər, -z

sheatfish
BR ˈʃiːtfɪʃ, -ɪz
AM ˈʃitˌfɪʃ, -ɪz

sheath
BR ʃiːθ, -ðz\-θs
AM ʃiθ, -ðz\-θs

sheathe
BR ʃiːð, -z, -ɪŋ, -d
AM ʃið, -z, -ɪŋ, -d

sheathing
BR ˈʃiːðɪŋ, -z
AM ˈʃiðɪŋ, -z

sheathless
BR ˈʃiːθlɪs
AM ˈʃiθlɪs

sheave
BR ʃiːv, -z, -ɪŋ, -d
AM ʃiv, -z, -ɪŋ, -d

Sheba
BR ˈʃiːbə(r)
AM ˈʃibə

shebang
BR ʃɪˈbaŋ
AM ʃəˈbæŋ

Shebat
BR ˈʃiːbat
AM ʃəˈbat

shebeen
BR ʃɪˈbiːn, -z
AM ʃəˈbin, -z

she-cat
BR ˈʃiːkat, -s
AM ˈʃiˌkæt, -s

Shechinah
BR ʃɛˈkaɪnə(r),
ʃɪˈkaɪnə(r)
AM ʃɛˈkaɪnə, ʃəˈkaɪnə

shed
BR ʃɛd, -z, -ɪŋ
AM ʃɛd, -z, -ɪŋ

she'd
BR ʃiːd, ʃɪd
AM ʃid, ʃɪd

shedder
BR ˈʃɛdə(r), -z
AM ˈʃɛdər, -z

she-devil
BR ˈʃiːˌdɛvl, -z

shedhand
BR ˈʃɛdhand, -z
AM ˈʃɛd(h)ænd, -z

Sheehan
BR ˈʃiːhən
AM ˈʃiən

Sheehy
BR ˈʃiː(h)i
AM ˈʃi(h)i

Sheelagh
BR ˈʃiːlə(r)
AM ˈʃilə

sheela-na-gig
BR ˈʃiːlənəˌgɪg, -z
AM ˈʃilənəˌgɪg, -z

sheen
BR ʃiːn
AM ʃin

Sheena
BR ˈʃiːnə(r)
AM ˈʃinə

Sheene
BR ʃiːn
AM ʃin

sheeny
BR ˈʃiːn|i, -ɪə(r), -ɪɪst
AM ˈʃini, -ər, -ɪst

sheep
BR ʃiːp
AM ʃip

sheepdip
BR ˈʃiːpdɪp
AM ˈʃipˌdɪp

sheepdog
BR ˈʃiːpdɒg, -z
AM ˈʃipˌdɔg, ˈʃipˌdɑg, -z

sheepfold
BR ˈʃiːpfəʊld, -z
AM ˈʃipˌfoʊld, -z

sheepish
BR ˈʃiːpɪʃ
AM ˈʃipɪʃ

sheepishly
BR ˈʃiːpɪʃli
AM ˈʃipɪʃli

sheepishness
BR ˈʃiːpɪʃnɪs
AM ˈʃipɪʃnɪs

sheeplike
BR ˈʃiːplaɪk
AM ˈʃipˌlaɪk

sheepmeat
BR ˈʃiːpmiːt
AM ˈʃipˌmit

sheeprun
BR ˈʃiːprʌn, -z
AM ˈʃipˌrʌn, -z

sheep's-bit
BR ˈʃiːpsbɪt, -s
AM ˈʃipsˌbɪt, -s

sheepshank
BR ˈʃiːpʃaŋk, -s
AM ˈʃipˌʃæŋk, -s

sheepskin
BR ˈʃiːpskɪn, -z
AM ˈʃipˌskɪn, -z

sheepwalk
BR ˈʃiːpwɔːk, -s
AM ˈʃipˌwɔk, ˈʃipˌwɑk, -s

sheer
BR ʃɪə(r), -z, -ɪŋ, -d
AM ʃɪ(ə)r, -z, -ɪŋ, -d

sheerlegs
BR ˈʃɪəlɛgz
AM ˈʃɪrˌlɛgz

sheerly
BR ˈʃɪəli
AM ˈʃɪrli

sheerness
BR ˈʃɪənəs
AM ˈʃɪrnəs

sheet
BR ʃiːt, -s, -ɪŋ, -ɪd
AM ʃi|t, -ts, -dɪŋ, -dɪd

sheetfed
BR ˌʃiːtˈfɛd
AM ˈʃitˌfɛd

sheetfeeder
BR ˈʃiːtˌfiːdə(r), -z
AM ˈʃitˌfidər, -z

Sheetrock®
BR ˈʃiːtˌrɒk
AM ˈʃitˌrɑk

Sheffield
BR ˈʃɛfiːld
AM ˈʃɛfild

sheik
BR ʃeɪk, ʃiːk, -s
AM ʃik, ʃeɪk, -s

sheikdom
BR ˈʃeɪkdəm, ˈʃiːkdəm, -z
AM ˈʃikdəm, ˈʃeɪkdəm, -z

sheikh
BR ʃeɪk, ʃiːk, -s
AM ʃik, ʃeɪk, -s

sheikhdom
BR ˈʃeɪkdəm, ˈʃiːkdəm, -z
AM ˈʃikdəm, ˈʃeɪkdəm, -z

sheila
BR ˈʃiːlə(r), -z
AM ˈʃilə, -z

shekel
BR ˈʃɛkl, -z
AM ˈʃɛkəl, -z

Shekinah
BR ʃɛˈkaɪnə(r),
ʃɪˈkaɪnə(r)
AM ʃɛˈkaɪnə, ʃəˈkaɪnə

Shelagh
BR ˈʃiːlə(r)
AM ˈʃilə

Shelburne
BR ˈʃɛlbəːn, ˈʃɛlb(ə)n
AM ˈʃɛlbərn

Sheldon
BR ˈʃɛld(ə)n
AM ˈʃɛldən

Sheldonian
BR ʃɛlˈdəʊnɪən
AM ʃɛlˈdoʊnɪən
sheldrake
BR ˈʃɛldreɪk, -s
AM ˈʃɛlˌdreɪk, -s
shelduck
BR ˈʃɛldʌk, -s
AM ˈʃɛlˌdək, -s
shelf
BR ʃɛlf
AM ʃɛlf
shelfful
BR ˈʃɛlfʊl, -z
AM ˈʃɛl(f)ˌfʊl, -z
shelf-life
BR ˈʃɛlflaɪf
AM ˈʃɛlfˌlaɪf
shell
BR ʃɛl, -z, -ɪŋ, -d
AM ʃɛl, -z, -ɪŋ, -d
she'll¹
strong form
BR ʃiːl
AM ʃil
she'll²
weak form
BR ʃɪl
AM ʃɪl
shellac
BR ʃəˈlak, ˈʃɛlak, -s, -ɪŋ,
-t
AM ʃəˈlæk, -s, -ɪŋ, -t
shellback
BR ˈʃɛlbak, -s
AM ˈʃɛlˌbæk, -s
shell-bit
BR ˈʃɛlbɪt, -s
AM ˈʃɛlˌbɪt, -s
Shelley
BR ˈʃɛli
AM ˈʃɛli
shellfire
BR ˈʃɛlˌfʌɪə(r)
AM ˈʃɛlˌfaɪ(ə)r
shellfish
BR ˈʃɛlfɪʃ
AM ˈʃɛlˌfɪʃ
shell-less
BR ˈʃɛlləs
AM ˈʃɛ(l)ləs
Shell-Mex
BR ˌʃɛlˈmɛks
AM ˌʃɛlˈmɛks
shellproof
BR ˈʃɛlpruːf
AM ˈʃɛlˌpruf
shellshock
BR ˈʃɛlʃɒk
AM ˈʃɛlˌʃak
shelly
BR ˈʃɛli
AM ˈʃɛli
Shelta
BR ˈʃɛltə(r)
AM ˈʃɛltə

shelter
BR ˈʃɛlt|ə(r), -əz,
-(ə)rɪŋ, -əd
AM ˈʃɛlt|ər, -ərz,
-(ə)rɪŋ, -ərd
shelterer
BR ˈʃɛlt(ə)rə(r), -z
AM ˈʃɛltərər, -z
shelterless
BR ˈʃɛltələs
AM ˈʃɛltərləs
sheltie
BR ˈʃɛlt|i, -ɪz
AM ˈʃɛlti, -z
Shelton
BR ˈʃɛlt(ə)n
AM ˈʃɛltən
shelty
BR ˈʃɛlt|i, -ɪz
AM ˈʃɛlti, -z
shelve
BR ʃɛlv, -z, -ɪŋ, -d
AM ʃɛlv, -z, -ɪŋ, -d
shelver
BR ˈʃɛlvə(r), -z
AM ˈʃɛlvər, -z
shelves
BR ʃɛlvz
AM ʃɛlvz
Shem
BR ʃɛm
AM ʃɛm
Shema
BR ˈʃeɪmə(r),
ʃɛˈmɑː(r), -z
AM ʃəˈmɑ, -z
shemozzle
BR ʃɪˈmɒzl, -z
AM ʃəˈmazəl, -z
Shena
BR ˈʃiːnə(r)
AM ˈʃinə, ˈʃeɪnə
Shenandoah
BR ˌʃɛnənˈdəʊə(r)
AM ˌʃɛnənˈdoʊə
shenanigan
BR ʃɪˈnanɪg(ə)n, -z
AM ʃəˈnænəgən, -z
Shenfield
BR ˈʃɛnfiːld
AM ˈʃɛnˌfild
Shensi
BR ˈʃɛnˈsiː
AM ˈʃɛnˈʃi
Shenyang
BR ˈʃɛnˈjaŋ
AM ˈʃɛnˈjæŋ
Shenzhen
BR ˈʃɛnˈʒɛn
AM ˈʃɛnˈʒɛn
Sheol
BR ˈʃiːəʊl, ˈʃiːɒl
AM ˈʃiˌɒl, ˈʃiˌoʊl, ˈʃiˌɑl
Shepard
BR ˈʃɛpəd
AM ˈʃɛpərd

shepherd
BR ˈʃɛpəd, -z, -ɪŋ, -ɪd-
AM ˈʃɛpərd, -z, -ɪŋ, -əd-
shepherdess
BR ˈʃɛpədɛs, ˈʃɛpədɪs,
ˌʃɛpəˈdɛs, -ɪz
AM ˈʃɛpərdəs, -əz
Sheppard
BR ˈʃɛpəd
AM ˈʃɛpərd
Sheppey
BR ˈʃɛpi
AM ˈʃɛpi
Shepshed
BR ˈʃɛpʃɛd
AM ˈʃɛpstən
Shepton
BR ˈʃɛpt(ə)n
AM ˈʃɛptn
Shepton Mallet
BR ˌʃɛpt(ə)n ˈmalɪt
AM ˌʃɛptn ˈmælət
Sher
BR ʃəː(r), ʃɛː(r)
AM ʃər
sherardise
BR ˈʃɛrədʌɪz, -ɪz, -ɪŋ, -d
AM ʃəˈrɑrˌdaɪz,
ˈʃɛrərˌdaɪz, -ɪz, -ɪŋ, -d
sherardize
BR ˈʃɛrədʌɪz, -ɪz, -ɪŋ, -d
AM ʃəˈrɑrˌdaɪz,
ˈʃɛrərˌdaɪz, -ɪz, -ɪŋ, -d
Sheraton
BR ˈʃɛrət(ə)n
AM ˈʃɛrətn
sherbet
BR ˈʃəːbət
AM ˈʃərbə(r)t
Sherborne
BR ˈʃəːb(ə)n, ˈʃəːbɔːn
AM ˈʃərˌbɔ(ə)rn
Sherbourne
BR ˈʃəːb(ə)n, ˈʃəːbɔːn
AM ˈʃərˌbɔ(ə)rn
Sherbrooke
BR ˈʃəːbrʊk
AM ˈʃərˌbrʊk
sherd
BR ʃəːd, -z
AM ʃərd, -z
Shere
BR ʃɪə(r)
AM ʃɪ(ə)r
shereef
BR ʃəˈriːf, -s
AM ʃəˈrif, -s
sheria
BR ʃəˈriːə(r)
AM ʃəˈriə
Sheridan
BR ˈʃɛrɪdn
AM ˈʃɛrədən
sherif
BR ʃəˈriːf, -s
AM ʃəˈrif, -s

sheriff
BR ˈʃɛrɪf, -s
AM ˈʃɛrəf, -s
sheriffalty
BR ˈʃɛrɪflt|i, -ɪz
AM ˈʃɛrəfəlti, -z
sheriffdom
BR ˈʃɛrɪfdəm, -z
AM ˈʃɛrəfdəm, -z
sheriffhood
BR ˈʃɛrɪfhʊd, -z
AM ˈʃɛrəf,(h)ʊd, -z
sheriffship
BR ˈʃɛrɪfʃɪp, -s
AM ˈʃɛrəfˌʃɪp, -s
Sheringham
BR ˈʃɛrɪŋəm
AM ˈʃɛrɪŋəm
sherlock
BR ˈʃəːlɒk, -s
AM ˈʃərˌlɑk, -s
Sherman
BR ˈʃəːmən
AM ˈʃərmən
sherpa
BR ˈʃəːpə(r), -z
AM ˈʃərpə, -z
Sherrin
BR ˈʃɛrɪn
AM ˈʃɛrən
Sherrington
BR ˈʃɛrɪŋt(ə)n
AM ˈʃɛrɪŋtən
sherry
BR ˈʃɛr|i, -ɪz
AM ˈʃɛri, -z
Sherwood
BR ˈʃəːwʊd
AM ˈʃərˌwʊd
Sheryl
BR ˈʃɛrɪl, ˈʃɛrl̩
AM ˈʃɛrəl
she's¹
strong form
BR ʃiːz
AM ʃiz
she's²
weak form
BR ʃɪz
AM ʃɪz
Shetland
BR ˈʃɛtlənd, -z
AM ˈʃɛtlənd, -z
Shetlander
BR ˈʃɛtləndə(r), -z
AM ˈʃɛtləndər, -z
sheva
BR ʃəˈvɑː(r), -z
AM ʃəˈvɑ, -z
Shevardnadze
BR ˌʃɛvədˈnɑːdzə(r)
AM ˌʃɛvərdˈnɑdzə
RUS ʃɪvardˈnadzʲi
Shevat
BR ˈʃiːvat
AM ʃəˈvat

shew
BR ʃəʊ, -z, -ɪŋ, -d
AM ʃoʊ, -z, -ɪŋ, -d

shewbread
BR ˈʃəʊbrɛd
AM ˈʃoʊˌbrɛd

shewn
BR ʃəʊn
AM ʃoʊn

she-wolf
BR ˌʃiːwʊlf
AM ˌʃiˌwʊlf

she-wolves
BR ˌʃiːwʊlvz
AM ˌʃiˌwʊlvz

Shia
BR ˈʃiːə(r), -z
AM ˈʃiɑ, -z

Shi'a
BR ˈʃiːə(r), -z
AM ˈʃiɑ, -z

Shiah
BR ˈʃiːə(r), -z
AM ˈʃiɑ, -z

shiatsu
BR ʃɪˈɑːtsuː, ʃɪˈatsuː
AM ˈʃiˌɑtˌsu

shibboleth
BR ˈʃɪbəlɛθ, ˈʃɪbələθ, -s
AM ˈʃɪbələθ, -s

shicer
BR ˈʃʌɪsə(r), -z
AM ˈʃaɪsər, -z

shicker
BR ˈʃɪkˌlə(r), -əz,
-(ə)rɪŋ, -əd
AM ˈʃɪkər, -z, -ɪŋ, -d

shicksa
BR ˈʃɪksə(r), -z
AM ˈʃɪksə, -z

shied
BR ʃʌɪd
AM ʃaɪd

shield
BR ʃiːld, -z, -ɪŋ, -ɪd
AM ʃild, -z, -ɪŋ, -ɪd

shieldbug
BR ˈʃiːldbʌg
AM ˈʃil(d)ˌbəg

shieldless
BR ˈʃiːldlɪs
AM ˈʃi(ld)lɪs

Shields
BR ʃiːldz
AM ʃi(ə)l(d)z

shieling
BR ˈʃiːlɪŋ, -z
AM ˈʃilɪŋ, -z

shift
BR ʃɪft, -s, -ɪŋ, -ɪd
AM ʃɪft, -s, -ɪŋ, -ɪd

shiftable
BR ˈʃɪftəbl
AM ˈʃɪftəbəl

shifter
BR ˈʃɪftə(r), -z
AM ˈʃɪftər, -z

shiftily
BR ˈʃɪftɪli
AM ˈʃɪftɪli

shiftiness
BR ˈʃɪftɪnɪs
AM ˈʃɪftɪnɪs

shiftless
BR ˈʃɪftlɪs
AM ˈʃɪf(t)lɪs

shiftlessly
BR ˈʃɪftlɪsli
AM ˈʃɪf(t)lɪsli

shiftlessness
BR ˈʃɪftlɪsnɪs
AM ˈʃɪf(t)lɪsnɪs

shifty
BR ˈʃɪftˌli, -ɪə(r), -ɪɪst
AM ˈʃɪftˌli, -ər, -ɪst

shigella
BR ʃɪˈgɛlə(r), -z
AM ʃəˈgɛlə, -z

shiglet
BR ˈʃɪglɪt
AM ˈʃɪglɪt

shih-tzu
BR ˌʃiːˈtsuː, -z
AM ˈʃiˌtsu, -z

Shiism
BR ˈʃiːɪz(ə)m
AM ˈʃiɪzəm

Shi'ism
BR ˈʃiːɪz(ə)m
AM ˈʃiɪzəm

Shiite
BR ˈʃiːʌɪt, -s
AM ˈʃiˌaɪt, -s

Shi'ite
BR ˈʃiːʌɪt, -s
AM ˈʃiˌaɪt, -s

shikar
BR ʃɪˈkɑː(r), -z, -ɪŋ, -d
AM ʃəˈkɑr, -z, -ɪŋ, -d

shikara
BR sɪˈkɑːrə(r), -z
AM ʃəˈkɑrə, -z

shikari
BR ʃɪˈkɑːrˌli, -ɪz
AM ʃəˈkɑri, -z

Shikoku
BR ˌʃiːˈkəʊkuː
AM ʃəˈkoʊˌku,
ʃəˈkɑˌku

shiksa
BR ˈʃɪksə(r), -z
AM ˈʃɪksə, -z

shill
BR ʃɪl, -z
AM ʃɪl, -z

shillelagh
BR ʃɪˈleɪlˌlə(r), ʃɪˈleɪlˌli,
-ɪz
AM ʃəˈleɪli, -z

shilling
BR ˈʃɪlɪŋ, -z
AM ˈʃɪlɪŋ, -z

shillingsworth
BR ˈʃɪlɪŋzwəːθ, -s

AM ˈʃɪlɪŋzˌwərθ, -s

Shillong
BR ʃɪˈlɒŋ
AM ʃəˈlɔŋ, ʃəˈlɑŋ

Shilluk
BR ʃɪˈlʊk
AM ʃəˈlʊk

shilly-shallier
BR ˈʃɪliˌʃalɪə(r), -z
AM ˈʃɪliˌʃæliər, -z

shilly-shally
BR ˈʃɪliˌʃalˌli, -ɪz, -ɪɪŋ,
-ɪd
AM ˈʃɪliˌʃæli, -z, -ɪŋ, -d

shilly-shallyer
BR ˈʃɪliˌʃalɪə(r), -z
AM ˈʃɪliˌʃæliər, -z

Shiloh
BR ˈʃʌɪləʊ
AM ˈʃaɪloʊ

Shilton
BR ˈʃɪlt(ə)n
AM ˈʃɪltən

shim
BR ʃɪm, -z
AM ʃɪm, -z

shimmer
BR ˈʃɪmˌlə(r), -əz,
-(ə)rɪŋ, -əd
AM ˈʃɪmˌlər, -ərz,
-(ə)rɪŋ, -ərd

shimmeringly
BR ˈʃɪm(ə)rɪŋli
AM ˈʃɪm(ə)rɪŋli

shimmery
BR ˈʃɪm(ə)ri
AM ˈʃɪm(ə)ri

shimmy
BR ˈʃɪmˌli, -ɪz, -ɪɪŋ, -ɪd
AM ˈʃɪmi, -z, -ɪŋ, -d

shin
BR ʃɪn, -z, -ɪŋ, -d
AM ʃɪn, -z, -ɪŋ, -d

shinbone
BR ˈʃɪnbəʊn, -z
AM ˈʃɪnˌboʊn, -z

shindig
BR ˈʃɪndɪg, -z
AM ˈʃɪnˌdɪg, -z

shindy
BR ˈʃɪndˌli, -ɪz
AM ˈʃɪndi, -z

shine
BR ʃʌɪn, -z, -ɪŋ, -d
AM ʃaɪn, -z, -ɪŋ, -d

shiner
BR ˈʃʌɪnə(r), -z
AM ˈʃaɪnər, -z

shingle
BR ˈʃɪŋgl, -z
AM ˈʃɪŋgəl, -z

shingly
BR ˈʃɪŋgli
AM ˈʃɪŋg(ə)li

shinily
BR ˈʃʌɪnɪli
AM ˈʃaɪnɪli

AM ˈʃɪlɪŋzˌwərθ, -s

shininess
BR ˈʃʌɪnɪnɪs
AM ˈʃaɪnɪnɪs

shiningly
BR ˈʃʌɪnɪŋli
AM ˈʃaɪnɪŋli

shinny
BR ˈʃɪnˌli, -ɪz, -ɪŋ, -ɪd
AM ˈʃɪni, -z, -ɪŋ, -d

shinsplints
BR ˈʃɪnsplɪnts
AM ˈʃɪnˌsplɪnts

Shinto
BR ˈʃɪntəʊ
AM ˈʃɪn(t)oʊ

Shintoism
BR ˈʃɪntəʊɪz(ə)m
AM ˈʃɪn(t)oʊˌ(w)ɪzəm

Shintoist
BR ˈʃɪntəʊɪst, -s
AM ˈʃɪn(t)oʊ(w)əst, -s

shinty
BR ˈʃɪntˌli
AM ˈʃɪn(t)i

Shinwell
BR ˈʃɪnwˌ(ɛ)l
AM ˈʃɪnˌwel

shiny
BR ˈʃʌɪnˌli, -ɪə(r), -ɪɪst
AM ˈʃaɪni, -ər, -ɪst

ship
BR ʃɪp, -s, -ɪŋ, -t
AM ʃɪp, -s, -ɪŋ, -t

shipboard
BR ˈʃɪpbɔːd
AM ˈʃɪpˌbɔ(ə)rd

shipbroker
BR ˈʃɪpˌbrəʊkə(r), -z
AM ˈʃɪpˌbroʊkər, -z

shipbuilder
BR ˈʃɪpˌbɪldə(r), -z
AM ˈʃɪpˌbɪldər, -z

shipbuilding
BR ˈʃɪpˌbɪldɪŋ
AM ˈʃɪpˌbɪldɪŋ

shiplap
BR ˈʃɪplap, -s, -ɪŋ, -t
AM ˈʃɪpˌlæp, -s, -ɪŋ, -t

shipless
BR ˈʃɪplɪs
AM ˈʃɪplɪs

Shipley
BR ˈʃɪpli
AM ˈʃɪpli

shipload
BR ˈʃɪpləʊd, -z
AM ˈʃɪpˌloʊd, -z

Shipman
BR ˈʃɪpmən
AM ˈʃɪpmən

shipmaster
BR ˈʃɪpˌmɑːstə(r),
ˈʃɪpˌmastə(r), -z
AM ˈʃɪpˌmæstər, -z

shipmate
BR ˈʃɪpmeɪt, -s
AM ˈʃɪpˌmeɪt, -s

shipment
BR ˈʃɪpm(ə)nt, -s
AM ˈʃɪpmənt, -s
shipowner
BR ˈʃɪp͵əʊnə(r), -z
AM ˈʃɪp͵oʊnər, -z
shippable
BR ˈʃɪpəbl
AM ˈʃɪpəbəl
Shippam
BR ˈʃɪpəm
AM ˈʃɪpəm
shipper
BR ˈʃɪpə(r), -z
AM ˈʃɪpər, -z
ship-rigged
BR ˈʃɪpˈrɪgd
AM ˈʃɪp͵rɪgd
shipshape
BR ˈʃɪpʃeɪp, ͵ʃɪpˈʃeɪp
AM ˈʃɪp͵ʃeɪp
Shipston
BR ˈʃɪpst(ə)n
AM ˈʃɪpstən
Shipton
BR ˈʃɪpt(ə)n
AM ˈʃɪptən
ship-to-shore
BR ͵ʃɪptəˈʃɔː(r)
AM ͵ʃɪptəˈʃɔ(ə)r
shipway
BR ˈʃɪpweɪ, -z
AM ˈʃɪp͵weɪ, -z
shipworm
BR ˈʃɪpwɜːm, -z
AM ˈʃɪp͵wɜrm, -z
shipwreck
BR ˈʃɪprɛk, -s, -ɪŋ, -t
AM ˈʃɪp͵rɛk, -s, -ɪŋ, -t
shipwright
BR ˈʃɪpraɪt, -s
AM ˈʃɪp͵raɪt, -s
shipyard
BR ˈʃɪpjɑːd, -z
AM ˈʃɪp͵jɑrd, -z
shiralee
BR ˈʃɪrəliː, -z
AM ˈʃɪrəli, -z
Shiraz
BR ˈʃɪəraz, ʃɪˈraz, -ɪz
AM ʃ(ɪ)əˈrɑz, -əz
shire
BR ˈʃʌɪə(r), -z
AM ˈʃaɪ(ə)r, -z
-shire
county suffix
BR ʃ(ɪ)ə(r)
AM ʃɪ(ə)r, ʃər, ͵ʃaɪ(ə)r
shire-horse
BR ˈʃʌɪəhɔːs, -ɪz
AM ˈʃaɪ(ə)r͵(h)ɔ(ə)rs,
-əz
shirk
BR ʃɜːk, -s, -ɪŋ, -t
AM ʃɜrk, -s, -ɪŋ, -t
shirker
BR ˈʃɜːkə(r), -z

AM ˈʃɜrkər, -z
Shirley
BR ˈʃɜːli
AM ˈʃɜrli
shirr
BR ʃɜː(r), -z, -ɪŋ, -d
AM ʃɜr, -z, -ɪŋ, -d
shirt
BR ʃɜːt, -s, -ɪd
AM ʃɜr|t, -ts, -dəd
shirtdress
BR ˈʃɜːtdrɛs, -ɪz
AM ˈʃɜrt͵drɛs, -əz
shirtfront
BR ˈʃɜːtfrʌnt, -s
AM ˈʃɜrt͵frʌnt, -s
shirtily
BR ˈʃɜːtɪli
AM ˈʃɜrdəli
shirtiness
BR ˈʃɜːtɪnɪs
AM ˈʃɜrdɪnɪs
shirting
BR ˈʃɜːtɪŋ, -z
AM ˈʃɜrdɪŋ, -z
shirtless
BR ˈʃɜːtləs
AM ˈʃɜrtləs
shirtsleeve
BR ˈʃɜːtsliːv, -z, -d
AM ˈʃɜrt͵sliv, -z, -d
shirttail
BR ˈʃɜːtteɪl, -z
AM ˈʃɜr(t)͵teɪl, -z
shirtwaist
BR ˈʃɜːt͵weɪst, -s
AM ˈʃɜrt͵weɪst, -s
shirtwaister
BR ˈʃɜːt͵weɪstə(r),
͵ʃɜːtˈweɪstə(r), -z
AM ˈʃɜrt͵weɪstər, -z
shirty
BR ˈʃɜːt|i, -ɪə(r), -ɪɪst
AM ˈʃɜrdi, -ər, -ɪst
shish kebab
BR ˈʃɪʃ kɪ͵bab, ͵ʃɪʃ
kɪˈbab, -z
AM ˈʃɪʃ kə͵bab, -z
shit
BR ʃɪt, -s, -ɪŋ, -ɪd
AM ʃɪ|t, -ts, -dɪŋ, -dəd
shitbag
BR ˈʃɪtbag, -z
AM ˈʃɪt͵bæg, -z
shit creek
BR ͵ʃɪt ˈkriːk
AM ͵ʃɪt ˈkrik
shite
BR ʃʌɪt
AM ʃaɪt
shithouse
BR ˈʃɪthaʊ|s, -zɪz
AM ˈʃɪt͵(h)aʊ|s, -zəz
shitless
BR ˈʃɪtlɪs
AM ˈʃɪtlɪs

shit-scared
BR ͵ʃɪtˈskɛːd
AM ͵ʃɪtˈskɛ(ə)rd
shittim
BR ˈʃɪtɪm
AM ˈʃɪdəm
shitty
BR ˈʃɪt|i, -ɪə(r), -ɪɪst
AM ˈʃɪdi, -ər, -ɪst
shiv
BR ʃɪv, -z
AM ʃɪv, -z
Shiva
BR ˈʃiːvə(r)
AM ˈʃivə
shivaree
BR ͵ʃɪvəˈriː, -z
AM ͵ʃɪvəˈri, -z
shiver
BR ˈʃɪv|ə(r), -əz,
-(ə)rɪŋ, -əd
AM ˈʃɪv|ər, -ərz, -(ə)rɪŋ,
-ərd
shiverer
BR ˈʃɪv(ə)rə(r), -z
AM ˈʃɪv(ə)rər, -z
shiveringly
BR ˈʃɪv(ə)rɪŋli
AM ˈʃɪv(ə)rɪŋli
shivery
BR ˈʃɪv(ə)ri
AM ˈʃɪv(ə)ri
shivoo
BR ʃɪˈvuː, -z
AM ʃəˈvu, -z
shlemiel
BR ʃlɪˈmɪəl, -z
AM ʃləˈmi(ə)l, -z
shlep
BR ʃlɛp
AM ʃlɛp
Shloer®
BR ʃləː(r)
AM ʃlər, ʃlɔ(ə)r
shmear
BR ʃmɪə(r)
AM ʃmɪ(ə)r
shmuck
BR ʃmək
AM ʃmək
shoal
BR ʃəʊl, -z, -ɪŋ, -d
AM ʃoʊl, -z, -ɪŋ, -d
shoaly
BR ˈʃəʊli
AM ˈʃoʊli
shoat
BR ʃəʊt, -s
AM ʃoʊt, -s
shochet
BR ˈʃɒket, ˈʃɒxet, -s
AM ˈʃɑkət, -s
shock
BR ʃɒk, -s, -ɪŋ, -t
AM ʃɑk, -s, -ɪŋ, -t
shockability
BR ͵ʃɒkəˈbɪlɪti

AM ͵ʃɑkəˈbɪlɪdi
shockable
BR ˈʃɒkəbl
AM ˈʃɑkəbəl
shocker
BR ˈʃɒkə(r), -z
AM ˈʃɑkər, -z
shocking
BR ˈʃɒkɪŋ
AM ˈʃɑkɪŋ
shockingly
BR ˈʃɒkɪŋli
AM ˈʃɑkɪŋli
shockingness
BR ˈʃɒkɪŋnɪs
AM ˈʃɑkɪŋnɪs
shockproof
BR ˈʃɒkpruːf
AM ˈʃɑk͵pruf
shod
BR ʃɒd
AM ʃɑd
shoddily
BR ˈʃɒdɪli
AM ˈʃɑdəli
shoddiness
BR ˈʃɒdɪnɪs
AM ˈʃɑdɪnɪs
shoddy
BR ˈʃɒd|i, -ɪə(r), -ɪɪst
AM ˈʃɑdi, -ər, -ɪst
shoe
BR ʃuː, -z, -ɪŋ, -d
AM ʃu, -z, -ɪŋ, -d
shoebill
BR ˈʃuːbɪl, -z
AM ˈʃu͵bɪl, -z
shoeblack
BR ˈʃuːblak, -s
AM ˈʃu͵blæk, -s
shoebox
BR ˈʃuːbɒks, -ɪz
AM ˈʃu͵bɑks, -əz
Shoeburyness
BR ͵ʃuːb(ə)rɪˈnɛs
AM ͵ʃubəriˈnɛs
shoehorn
BR ˈʃuːhɔːn, -z, -ɪŋ, -d
AM ˈʃu͵hɔ(ə)rn, -z, -ɪŋ,
-d
shoelace
BR ˈʃuːleɪs, -ɪz
AM ˈʃu͵leɪs, -ɪz
shoeleather
BR ˈʃuː͵lɛðə(r)
AM ˈʃu͵lɛðər
shoeless
BR ˈʃuːləs
AM ˈʃuləs
shoemaker
BR ˈʃuː͵meɪkə(r), -z
AM ˈʃu͵meɪkər, -z
shoemaking
BR ˈʃuː͵meɪkɪŋ
AM ˈʃu͵meɪkɪŋ
shoepolish
BR ˈʃuː͵pɒlɪʃ

AM 'ʃuːpɑlɪʃ

shoeshine
BR 'ʃuːʃaɪn
AM 'ʃuːʃaɪn

shoestring
BR 'ʃuːstrɪŋ
AM 'ʃuːstrɪŋ

shoetree
BR 'ʃuːtriː, -z
AM 'ʃuːtriː, -z

shofar
BR 'ʃəʊfə(r)
AM 'ʃoʊfɑr

shofroth
BR 'ʃəʊfrəʊt
AM 'ʃoʊˈfrɔθ, 'ʃoʊˈfrɑθ

shogun
BR 'ʃəʊɡʌn, 'ʃəʊɡ(ə)n, -z
AM 'ʃoʊɡən, -z

shogunate
BR 'ʃəʊɡəneɪt, 'ʃəʊɡneɪt, 'ʃəʊɡənət, 'ʃəʊɡnət, -s
AM 'ʃoʊɡənət, 'ʃoʊɡə,neɪt, -s

Sholokhov
BR 'ʃɒləkɒf
AM 'ʃɒlə,kɒv, 'ʃɒlə,kɔf, 'ʃɑlə,kʌv, 'ʃɑlə,kɑf

Sholto
BR 'ʃɒltəʊ
AM 'ʃɒltoʊ, 'ʃɑltoʊ

Shona[1]
African people and language
BR 'ʃɒnə(r), 'ʃəʊnə(r)
AM 'ʃoʊnə

Shona[2]
forename
BR 'ʃəʊnə(r)
AM 'ʃoʊnə, 'ʃɒnə, 'ʃɑnə

shone
BR 'ʃɒn
AM 'ʃoʊn

shonky
BR 'ʃɒŋk|i, -ɪə(r), -ɪɪst
AM 'ʃɒŋki, 'ʃɑŋki, -ər, -ɪst

shoo
BR 'ʃuː, -z, -ɪŋ, -d
AM 'ʃu, -z, -ɪŋ, -d

shoofly
BR 'ʃuːflʌɪ, -z
AM 'ʃuːflaɪ, -z

shoo-in
BR 'ʃuːɪn, -z
AM 'ʃuˌɪn, -z

shook
BR ʃʊk
AM ʃʊk

shoot
BR 'ʃuːt, -s, -ɪŋ
AM ʃuːt, -ts, -dɪŋ

shootable
BR 'ʃuːtəbl
AM 'ʃudəbəl

shoot'em up
BR 'ʃuːtəm ʌp, -s
AM 'ʃudə,m əp, -s

shooter
BR 'ʃuːtə(r), -z
AM 'ʃudər, -z

shooting
BR 'ʃuːtɪŋ, -z
AM 'ʃudɪŋ, -z

shoot-out
BR 'ʃuːtaʊt, -s
AM 'ʃuˌdaʊt, -s

shoot-up
BR 'ʃuːtʌp, -s
AM 'ʃudəp, -s

shop
BR 'ʃɒp, -s, -ɪŋ, -t
AM 'ʃɑp, -s, -ɪŋ, -t

shopaholic
BR ˌʃɒpə'hɒlɪk, -s
AM ˌʃɑpə'hɑlɪk, -s

shop-bought
BR 'ʃɒp'bɔːt
AM 'ʃɑp'bɔt, 'ʃɑp'bɑt

shopfitter
BR 'ʃɒp,fɪtə(r), -z
AM 'ʃɑp,fɪdər, -z

shopfitting
BR 'ʃɒp,fɪtɪŋ
AM 'ʃɑp,fɪdɪŋ

shop-floor
BR ,ʃɒp'flɔː(r), ,ʃɒpflɔː(r), -z
AM ,ʃɑp,flɔ(ə)r, -z

shopfront
BR 'ʃɒpfrʌnt, -s
AM 'ʃɑp,frʌnt, -s

shopgirl
BR 'ʃɒpɡəːl, -z
AM 'ʃɑp,ɡərl, -z

shopkeeper
BR 'ʃɒp,kiːpə(r), -z
AM 'ʃɑp,kipər, -z

shopkeeping
BR 'ʃɒp,kiːpɪŋ
AM 'ʃɑp,kipɪŋ

shopless
BR 'ʃɒpləs
AM 'ʃɑpləs

shoplift
BR 'ʃɒplɪft, -s, -ɪŋ, -ɪd
AM 'ʃɑp,lɪft, -s, -ɪŋ, -ɪd

shoplifter
BR 'ʃɒp,lɪftə(r), -z
AM 'ʃɑp,lɪftər, -z

shopman
BR 'ʃɒpmən
AM 'ʃɑpmən

shopmen
BR 'ʃɒpmən
AM 'ʃɑpmən

shopper
BR 'ʃɒpə(r), -z
AM 'ʃɑpər, -z

shoppy
BR 'ʃɒpi
AM 'ʃɑpi

shopsoiled
BR 'ʃɒpsɔɪld, ,ʃɒp'sɔɪld
AM 'ʃɑp,sɔɪld

shoptalk
BR 'ʃɒptɔːk, -s
AM 'ʃɑp,tɔk, 'ʃɑp,tak, -s

shopwalker
BR 'ʃɒp,wɔːkə(r), -z
AM 'ʃɑp,wɔkər, 'ʃɑp,wakər, -z

shopworker
BR 'ʃɒp,wɜːkə(r), -z
AM 'ʃɑp,wərkər, -z

shopworn
BR 'ʃɒpwɔːn
AM 'ʃɑp,wɔ(ə)rn

shoran
BR 'ʃɔːran, 'ʃɒran
AM 'ʃɔ,ræn

shore
BR ʃɔː(r), -z, -ɪŋ, -d
AM ʃɔ(ə)r, -z, -ɪŋ, -d

shore-based
BR ʃɔː'beɪst, 'ʃɔːbeɪst
AM 'ʃɔr,beɪst

shorebird
BR 'ʃɔːbəːd, -z
AM 'ʃɔr,bərd, -z

Shoreditch
BR 'ʃɔːdɪtʃ
AM 'ʃɔr,dɪtʃ

shorefront
BR 'ʃɔːfrʌnt, -s
AM 'ʃɔr,frʌnt, -s

Shoreham
BR 'ʃɔːrəm
AM 'ʃɔrəm

shoreless
BR 'ʃɔːləs
AM 'ʃɔrləs

shoreline
BR 'ʃɔːlʌɪn, -z
AM 'ʃɔr,laɪn, -z

shoreward
BR 'ʃɔːwəd, -z
AM 'ʃɔrwərd, -z

shoreweed
BR 'ʃɔːwiːd, -z
AM 'ʃɔr,wid, -z

shoring
BR 'ʃɔːrɪŋ
AM 'ʃɔrɪŋ

shorn
BR ʃɔːn
AM ʃɔ(ə)rn

short
BR ʃɔːt, -s, -ɪŋ, -ɪd, -ə(r), -ɪst
AM ʃɔ(ə)rt, -ts, 'ʃɔrdɪŋ, 'ʃɔrdəd, 'ʃɔrdər, 'ʃɔrdəst

shortage
BR 'ʃɔːt|ɪdʒ, -ɪdʒɪz
AM 'ʃɔrdɪdʒ, -ɪz

short-arm
BR 'ʃɔːtɑːm, ,ʃɔːt'ɑːm
AM 'ʃɔrd,ɑrm

shortbread
BR 'ʃɔːtbrɛd
AM 'ʃɔrt,brɛd

shortcake
BR 'ʃɔːtkeɪk
AM 'ʃɔrt,keɪk

short-change
BR ʃɔːt'tʃeɪn(d)ʒ, -ɪz, -ɪŋ, -d
AM 'ʃɔrt'tʃeɪndʒ, -ɪz, -ɪŋ, -d

short-circuit
BR ʃɔːt'səːk|ɪt, -ɪts, -ɪtɪŋ, -ɪtɪd
AM 'ʃɔrt'sərkə|t, -ts, -dɪŋ, -dəd

shortcoming
BR 'ʃɔːt,kʌmɪŋ, ,ʃɔːt'kʌmɪŋ, -z
AM 'ʃɔrt'kəmɪŋ, -z

shortcrust
BR 'ʃɔːtkrʌst
AM 'ʃɔrt,krəst

shortcut
BR ,ʃɔːt'kʌt, 'ʃɔːtkʌt, -s
AM 'ʃɔrt,kət, -s

short-dated
BR ,ʃɔːt'deɪtɪd
AM 'ʃɔrt'deɪdɪd

short-eared owl
BR ,ʃɔːtɪəd 'aʊl, -z
AM 'ʃɔr,dɪ(ə)rd 'aʊl, -z

shorten
BR 'ʃɔːt|n, -nz, -nɪŋ\-nɪŋ, -nd
AM 'ʃɔrtən, -z, -ɪŋ, -d

Shorter
BR 'ʃɔːtə(r)
AM 'ʃɔrdər

shortfall
BR 'ʃɔːtfɔːl, -z
AM 'ʃɔrt,fɔl, 'ʃɔrt,fal, -z

shorthair
BR 'ʃɔːthɛː(r), -z
AM 'ʃɔrt,(h)ɛ(ə)r, -z

short-haired
BR ʃɔːt'hɛːd
AM 'ʃɔrt'hɛ(ə)rd

shorthand
BR 'ʃɔːthand
AM 'ʃɔrt,(h)ænd

shorthanded
BR ,ʃɔːt'handɪd
AM 'ʃɔrt'hændəd

shorthaul
BR 'ʃɔːthɔːl, ,ʃɔːt'hɔːl
AM 'ʃɔrt,(h)ɔl, 'ʃɔrt,(h)al

short-head
BR ,ʃɔːt'hɛd, -z, -ɪŋ, -ɪd
AM 'ʃɔrt,(h)ɛd, -z, -ɪŋ, -əd

shorthold
BR 'ʃɔːthəʊld
AM 'ʃɔrt,(h)oʊld

shorthorn
BR ˈʃɔːthɔːn, -z
AM ˈʃɔrt,(h)ɔ(ə)rn, -z

shortie
BR ˈʃɔːt|i, -ɪz
AM ˈʃɔrdi, -z

shortish
BR ˈʃɔːtɪʃ
AM ˈʃɔrdɪʃ

shortlist
BR ˈʃɔːtlɪst, -s, -ɪŋ, -ɪd
AM ˈʃɔrt,lɪst, -s, -ɪŋ, -ɪd

shortly
BR ˈʃɔːtli
AM ˈʃɔrtli

shortness
BR ˈʃɔːtnəs
AM ˈʃɔrtnəs

short-order
BR ˌʃɔːtˈɔːdə(r)
AM ˈʃɔrˌdɔrdər

shortsighted
BR ˌʃɔːtˈsʌɪtɪd
AM ˈʃɔrtˈsaɪdɪd

shortsightedly
BR ˌʃɔːtˈsʌɪtɪdli
AM ˈʃɔrtˈsaɪdɪdli

shortsightedness
BR ˌʃɔːtˈsʌɪtɪdnɪs
AM ˈʃɔrtˈsaɪdɪdnɪs

shortstay
BR ˌʃɔːtˈsteɪ
AM ˈʃɔrtˈsteɪ

shortstop
BR ˈʃɔːtstɒp, -s
AM ˈʃɔrtˌstɑp, -s

shortwave
BR ˌʃɔːtˈweɪv, ˈʃɔːtweɪv
AM ˈʃɔrtˈweɪv

shortweight
BR ˌʃɔːtˈweɪt
AM ˈʃɔrtˌweɪt

shorty
BR ˈʃɔːt|i, -ɪz
AM ˈʃɔrdi, -z

Shoshone
BR ʃə(ʊ)ˈʃəʊn|i, -ɪz
AM ʃoʊˈʃoʊni, ʃəˈʃoʊni, -z

Shoshonean
BR ʃə(ʊ)ˈʃəʊnɪən
AM ʃoʊˈʃoʊnɪən, ʃəˈʃoʊnɪən

Shostakovich
BR ˌʃɒstəˈkəʊvɪtʃ
AM ˌʃɒstəˈkoʊvɪtʃ, ˌʃɑstəˈkoʊvɪtʃ

shot
BR ˈʃɒt, -s
AM ˈʃɑt, -s

shotgun
BR ˈʃɒtɡʌn, -z
AM ˈʃɑt,ɡən, -z

shotproof
BR ˈʃɒtpruːf
AM ˈʃɑt,pruf

shotten
BR ˈʃɒtn
AM ˈʃɑtn

should¹
strong form
BR ʃʊd
AM ʃʊd

should²
weak form
BR ʃəd
AM ʃəd

shoulder
BR ˈʃəʊld|ə(r), -əz, -(ə)rɪŋ, -əd
AM ˈʃoʊldər, -z, -ɪŋ, -d

shouldn't
BR ˈʃʊdnt
AM ˈʃʊdnt

shout
BR ˈʃaʊt, -s, -ɪŋ, -ɪd
AM ˈʃaʊ|t, -ts, -dɪŋ, -dəd

shouter
BR ˈʃaʊtə(r), -z
AM ˈʃaʊdər, -z

shove
BR ˈʃʌv, -z, -ɪŋ, -d
AM ˈʃəv, -z, -ɪŋ, -d

shove-halfpenny
BR ˌʃʌvˈheɪpni
AM ˈʃəvˈheɪp(ə)ni

shove-ha'penny
BR ˌʃʌvˈheɪpni
AM ˈʃəvˈheɪp(ə)ni

shovel
BR ˈʃʌv|l, -lz, -lɪŋ\-lɪŋ, -ld
AM ˈʃəv|əl, -əlz, -(ə)lɪŋ, -əldz

shovelboard
BR ˈʃʌvlbɔːd
AM ˈʃəvəl,bɔ(ə)rd

shoveler
BR ˈʃʌvlə(r), ˈʃʌvlə(r), -z
AM ˈʃəv(ə)lər, -z

shovelful
BR ˈʃʌvlfʊl, -z
AM ˈʃəvəl,fʊl, -z

shovelhead
BR ˈʃʌvlhɛd, -z
AM ˈʃəvl,(h)ɛd, -z

shoveller
BR ˈʃʌvlə(r), ˈʃʌvlə(r), -z
AM ˈʃəv(ə)lər, -z

show
BR ˈʃəʊ, -z, -ɪŋ, -d
AM ˈʃoʊ, -z, -ɪŋ, -d

show-and-tell
BR ˌʃəʊ ən(d) ˈtɛl, + ŋ(d) +
AM ˈʃoʊ ən ˈtɛl

showband
BR ˈʃəʊband, -z
AM ˈʃoʊ,bænd, -z

showbiz
BR ˈʃəʊbɪz
AM ˈʃoʊ,bɪz

showboat
BR ˈʃəʊbəʊt, -s
AM ˈʃoʊ,bout, -s

showcard
BR ˈʃəʊkɑːd, -z
AM ˈʃoʊ,kɑrd, -z

showcase
BR ˈʃəʊkeɪs, -ɪz
AM ˈʃoʊ,keɪs, -ɪz

showdown
BR ˈʃəʊdaʊn, -z
AM ˈʃoʊ,daʊn, -z

shower¹
person who shows
BR ˈʃəʊə(r), -z
AM ˈʃoʊ(ə)r, -z

shower²
rain
BR ˈʃaʊə(r), -z, -ɪŋ, -d
AM ˈʃaʊ(ə)r, -z, -ɪŋ, -d

showerproof
BR ˈʃaʊəpruːf, -t
AM ˈʃaʊ(ə)r,pruf, -t

showery
BR ˈʃaʊ(ə)ri
AM ˈʃaʊ(ə)ri

showgirl
BR ˈʃəʊɡəːl, -z
AM ˈʃoʊ,ɡərl, -z

showground
BR ˈʃəʊɡraʊnd, -z
AM ˈʃoʊ,ɡraʊnd, -z

showily
BR ˈʃəʊɪli
AM ˈʃoʊəli

showiness
BR ˈʃəʊɪnɪs
AM ˈʃoʊɪnɪs

showing
BR ˈʃəʊɪŋ, -z
AM ˈʃoʊɪŋ, -z

showjump
BR ˈʃəʊdʒʌm|p, -ps, -pɪŋ, -(p)t
AM ˈʃoʊ,dʒəmp, -s, -ɪŋ, -t

showjumper
BR ˈʃəʊ,dʒʌmpə(r), -z
AM ˈʃoʊ,dʒəmpər, -z

showjumping
BR ˈʃəʊ,dʒʌmpɪŋ
AM ˈʃoʊ,dʒəmpɪŋ

showman
BR ˈʃəʊmən
AM ˈʃoʊmən

showmanship
BR ˈʃəʊmənʃɪp
AM ˈʃoʊmən,ʃɪp

showmen
BR ˈʃəʊmən
AM ˈʃoʊmən

shown
BR ˈʃəʊn
AM ˈʃoʊn

show-off
BR ˈʃəʊɒf, -s
AM ˈʃoʊ,ɔf, ˈʃoʊ,ɑf, -s

showpiece
BR ˈʃəʊpiːs, -ɪz
AM ˈʃoʊ,pis, -ɪz

showplace
BR ˈʃəʊpleɪs, -ɪz
AM ˈʃoʊ,pleɪs, -ɪz

showroom
BR ˈʃəʊruːm, ˈʃəʊrʊm, -z
AM ˈʃoʊ,rum, ˈʃoʊ,rʊm, -z

showstopper
BR ˈʃəʊ,stɒpə(r), -z
AM ˈʃoʊ,stɑpər, -z

showstopping
BR ˈʃəʊ,stɒpɪŋ
AM ˈʃoʊ,stɑpɪŋ

showtime
BR ˈʃəʊtʌɪm
AM ˈʃoʊ,taɪm

showy
BR ˈʃəʊ|i, -ɪə(r), -ɪɪst
AM ˈʃoʊi, -ər, -ɪst

shoyu
BR ˈʃəʊjuː
AM ˈʃoʊju

shrank
BR ˈʃraŋk
AM ˈʃræŋk

shrapnel
BR ˈʃrapnl
AM ˈʃræpnəl

shred
BR ˈʃrɛd, -z, -ɪŋ, -ɪd
AM ˈʃrɛd, -z, -ɪŋ, -əd

shredder
BR ˈʃrɛdə(r), -z
AM ˈʃrɛdər, -z

Shreveport
BR ˈʃriːvpɔːt
AM ˈʃriv,pɔ(ə)rt

shrew
BR ˈʃruː, -z
AM ˈʃru, -z

shrewd
BR ˈʃruːd, -ə(r), -ɪst
AM ˈʃrud, -ər, -əst

shrewdly
BR ˈʃruːdli
AM ˈʃrudli

shrewdness
BR ˈʃruːdnəs
AM ˈʃrudnəs

shrewish
BR ˈʃruːɪʃ
AM ˈʃruɪʃ

shrewishly
BR ˈʃruːɪʃli
AM ˈʃruɪʃli

shrewishness
BR ˈʃruːɪʃnɪs
AM ˈʃruɪʃnɪs

Shrewsbury
BR ˈʃrəʊzb(ə)ri, ˈʃruːzb(ə)ri
AM ˈʃruz,bɛri, ˈʃruzb(ə)ri

shriek
BR ʃriːk, -s, -ɪŋ, -t
AM ʃrik, -s, -ɪŋ, -t
shrieker
BR ʃriːkə(r), -z
AM ʃrikər, -z
shrieval
BR ʃriːvl
AM ʃrivəl
shrievalty
BR ʃriːvlti, -ɪz
AM ʃrivəlti, -z
shrift
BR ʃrɪft
AM ʃrɪft
shrike
BR ʃrʌɪk, -s
AM ʃraik, -s
shrill
BR ʃrɪl, -z, -ɪŋ, -d, -ə(r),
-ɪst
AM ʃrɪl, -z, -ɪŋ, -d, -ər,
-ɪst
shrillness
BR ʃrɪlnɪs
AM ʃrɪlnɪs
shrilly
BR ʃrɪ(l)li
AM ʃrɪ(l)li
shrimp
BR ʃrɪmp, -s, -ɪŋ
AM ʃrɪmp, -s, -ɪŋ
shrimper
BR ʃrɪmpə(r), -z
AM ʃrɪmpər, -z
Shrimpton
BR ʃrɪm(p)t(ə)n
AM ʃrɪm(p)tən
shrine
BR ʃrʌɪn, -z
AM ʃrain, -z
Shriner
BR ʃrʌɪnə(r)
AM ʃrainər
shrink
BR ʃrɪŋk, -s, -ɪŋ
AM ʃrɪŋk, -s, -ɪŋ
shrinkable
BR ʃrɪŋkəbl
AM ʃrɪŋkəbəl
shrinkage
BR ʃrɪŋkɪdʒ
AM ʃrɪŋkɪdʒ
shrinker
BR ʃrɪŋkə(r), -z
AM ʃrɪŋkər, -z
shrinking
BR ʃrɪŋkɪŋ
AM ʃrɪŋkɪŋ
shrinkingly
BR ʃrɪŋkɪŋli
AM ʃrɪŋkɪŋli
shrinkpack
BR ʃrɪŋkpak
AM ʃrɪŋkˌpæk
shrinkproof
BR ʃrɪŋkpruːf

AM ʃrɪŋkˌpruf
shrive
BR ʃrʌɪv, -z, -ɪŋ
AM ʃraiv, -z, -ɪŋ
shrivel
BR ʃrɪv|l, -lz, -l̩ɪŋ\-lɪŋ,
-ld
AM ʃrɪv|əl, -əlz, -(ə)lɪŋ,
-əld
shriven
BR ʃrɪvn
AM ʃrɪvən
Shrivenham
BR ʃrɪvnəm
AM ʃrɪvənəm
Shropshire
BR ʃrɒpʃ(ɪ)ə(r)
AM ʃrapˌʃɪ(ə)r
shroud
BR ʃraʊd, -z, -ɪŋ, -d-
AM ʃraʊd, -z, -ɪŋ, -əd
shroudless
BR ʃraʊdləs
AM ʃrədləs
shrove
BR ʃrəʊv
AM ʃrouv
Shrovetide
BR ʃrəʊvtʌɪd
AM ʃrouvˌtaid
shrub
BR ʃrʌb, -z
AM ʃrəb, -z
shrubbery
BR ʃrʌb(ə)r|i, -ɪz
AM ʃrəb(ə)ri, -z
shrubbiness
BR ʃrʌbinɪs
AM ʃrəbinɪs
shrubby
BR ʃrʌb|i, -ɪə(r), -ɪɪst
AM ʃrəbi, -ər, -ɪst
shrug
BR ʃrʌg, -z, -ɪŋ, -d
AM ʃrəg, -z, -ɪŋ, -d
shrunk
BR ʃrʌŋk
AM ʃrəŋk
shrunken
BR ʃrʌŋk(ə)n
AM ʃrəŋkən
shtick
BR ʃtɪk, -s
AM ʃtɪk, -s
shtuck
BR ʃtʊk
AM ʃtʊk
shuck
BR ʃʌk, -s, -ɪŋ, -t
AM ʃək, -s, -ɪŋ, -t
Shuckburgh
BR ʃʌkb(ə)rə(r)
AM ʃəkˌbərə
shucker
BR ʃʌkə(r), -z
AM ʃəkər, -z

shudder
BR ʃʌd|ə(r), -əz,
-(ə)rɪŋ, -əd
AM ʃədər, -z, -ɪŋ, -d
shudderingly
BR ʃʌd(ə)rɪŋli
AM ʃəd(ə)rɪŋli
shuddery
BR ʃʌd(ə)ri
AM ʃəd(ə)ri
shuffle
BR ʃʌf|l, -lz, -l̩ɪŋ\-lɪŋ,
-ld
AM ʃəf|əl, -əlz, -(ə)lɪŋ,
-əld
shuffleboard
BR ʃʌflbɔːd, -z
AM ʃəfəlˌbɔ(ə)rd, -z
Shufflebottom
BR ʃʌflˌbʊtəm
AM ʃəfəlˌbadəm
shuffler
BR ʃʌflə(r), ʃʌflə(r),
-z
AM ʃəf(ə)lər, -z
Shufflewick
BR ʃʌflwɪk
AM ʃəfəlˌwɪk
shuffling
BR ʃʌflɪŋ, ʃʌflɪŋ, -z
AM ʃəf(ə)lɪŋ, -z
shufti
BR ʃʊft|i, -ɪz
AM ʃʊfti, -z
shufty
BR ʃʊft|i, -ɪz
AM ʃʊfti, -z
shul
BR ʃuːl, ʃʊl, -z
AM ʃul, ʃʊl, -z
Shula
BR ʃuːlə(r)
AM ʃulə
shuln
BR ʃuːln, ʃʊln
AM ʃuln, ʃʊln
Shumen
BR ʃuːmɛn
AM ʃumɛn
shun
BR ʃʌn, -z, -ɪŋ, -d
AM ʃən, -z, -ɪŋ, -d
shunt
BR ʃʌnt, -s, -ɪŋ, -ɪd
AM ʃən|t, -ts, -(t)ɪŋ,
-(t)əd
shunter
BR ʃʌntə(r), -z
AM ʃən(t)ər, -z
shush
BR ʃʌʃ, ʃʊʃ
AM ʃʊʃ, ʃəʃ
Shuster
BR ʃʊstə(r), ʃuːstə(r)
AM ʃustər
shut
BR ʃʌt, -s, -ɪŋ

AM ʃə|t, -ts, -dɪŋ
shutdown
BR ʃʌtdaʊn, -z
AM ʃətˌdaʊn, -z
Shute
BR ʃuːt
AM ʃut
Shuter
BR ʃuːtə(r)
AM ʃudər
shut-eye
BR ʃʌtʌɪ
AM ʃədˌaɪ
shut-in
BR ʃʌtɪn, -z
AM ʃədˌɪn, -z
shut-off
BR ʃʌtɒf, -s
AM ʃədˌɔf, ʃədˌɑf, -s
shut-out
BR ʃʌtaʊt, -s
AM ʃədˌaʊt, -s
shutter
BR ʃʌt|ə(r), -əz,
-(ə)rɪŋ, -əd-
AM ʃə|dər, -dərz,
-dərɪŋ\-trɪŋ, -dərd
shutterbug
BR ʃʌtəbʌg, -z
AM ʃədərˌbəg, -z
shutterless
BR ʃʌtələs
AM ʃədərləs
shuttle
BR ʃʌt|l, -z, -ɪŋ, -d
AM ʃəd|əl, -z, -ɪŋ, -d
shuttlecock
BR ʃʌtlkɒk, -s
AM ʃədl̩ˌkak, -s
Shuttleworth
BR ʃʌtlwəːθ, ʃʌtlwəθ
AM ʃədəlˌwərθ
Shuy
BR ʃʌɪ
AM ʃai
shwa
BR ʃwɑː(r), ʃvɑː(r), -z
AM ʃwɑ, ʃvɑ, -z
shy
BR ʃʌɪ, -z, -ɪŋ, -d, -ə(r),
-ɪst
AM ʃai, -z, -ɪŋ, -d, -ər, -ɪst
shyer
BR ʃʌɪə(r), -z
AM ʃaiər, -z
Shylock
BR ʃʌɪlɒk
AM ʃaiˌlak
shyly
BR ʃʌɪli
AM ʃaili
shyness
BR ʃʌɪnɪs
AM ʃainɪs
shyster
BR ʃʌɪstə(r), -z
AM ʃaistər, -z

si
BR siː
AM si

sial
BR 'saɪəl
AM 'saɪəl

sialagogue
BR saɪ'æləgɒg, -z
AM saɪ'ælə,gɑg, -z

sialogogue
BR saɪ'æləgɒg, -z
AM saɪ'ælə,gɑg, -z

Siam
BR saɪ'æm
AM saɪ'æm

siamang
BR 'siːəmaŋ, 'saɪəmaŋ, -z
AM 'siə,maŋ, -z

Siamese
BR ,saɪə'miːz
AM 'saɪə'miz

Siân
BR ʃɑːn
AM ʃɑn

sib
BR sɪb, -z
AM sɪb, -z

Sibelius
BR sɪ'beɪliəs
AM sə'beɪliəs

Siberia
BR saɪ'bɪərɪə(r)
AM saɪ'bɪriə

Siberian
BR saɪ'bɪərɪən, -z
AM saɪ'bɪriən, -z

sibilance
BR 'sɪbɪləns, 'sɪbɪln̩s, 'sɪbl̩(ə)ns
AM 'sɪbələns

sibilancy
BR 'sɪbɪlənsi, 'sɪbɪln̩si, 'sɪbl̩(ə)nsi
AM 'sɪbələnsi

sibilant
BR 'sɪbɪlənt, 'sɪbɪln̩t, 'sɪbl̩(ə)nt, -s
AM 'sɪbələnt, -s

sibilate
BR 'sɪbɪleɪt, -s, -ɪŋ, -ɪd-
AM 'sɪbə,leɪt, -ts, -dɪŋ, -dɪd

sibilation
BR ,sɪbɪ'leɪʃn̩, -z
AM ,sɪbə'leɪʃən, -z

Sibley
BR 'sɪbli
AM 'sɪbli

sibling
BR 'sɪblɪŋ, -z
AM 'sɪblɪŋ, -z

sibship
BR 'sɪbʃɪp, -s
AM 'sɪb,ʃɪp, -s

sibyl
BR 'sɪb(ɪ)l, -z

sibyl
BR 'sɪbɪl, -z

sibylline
BR 'sɪbɪlʌɪn
AM 'sɪbə,laɪn, 'sɪbə,lin

sic
BR sɪk
AM sɪk

siccative
BR 'sɪkətɪv, -z
AM 'sɪkədɪv, -z

sice
BR saɪs, -ɪz
AM saɪs, saɪz, -ɪz

Sichuan
BR ,sɪtʃ'waːn
AM 'sɪ'tʃwɑn

Sicilia
BR sɪ'sɪlɪə(r)
AM sə'sɪljə, sə'sɪliə

Sicilian
BR sɪ'sɪliən, -z
AM sə'sɪljən, sə'sɪliən, -z

siciliana
BR sɪ,sɪlɪ'ɑːnə(r), -z
AM sə,sɪli'ɑnə, -z

siciliano
BR sɪ,sɪlɪ'ɑːnəʊ, -z
AM sə,sɪli'ɑ,noʊ, -z

Sicily
BR 'sɪsɪli, 'sɪsl̩i
AM 'sɪsl̩i

sick
BR sɪk, -ə(r), -ɪst
AM sɪk, -ər, -ɪst

sickbay
BR 'sɪkbeɪ, -z
AM 'sɪk,beɪ, -z

sickbed
BR 'sɪkbɛd, -z
AM 'sɪk,bɛd, -z

sicken
BR 'sɪkl̩(ə)n, -nz, -nɪŋ\-(ə)nɪŋ, -nd
AM 'sɪkl̩ən, -ənz, -(ə)nɪŋ, -ənd

sickener
BR 'sɪknə(r), 'sɪk(ə)nə(r), -z
AM 'sɪk(ə)nər, -z

sickeningly
BR 'sɪknɪŋli, 'sɪk(ə)nɪŋli
AM 'sɪk(ə)nɪŋli

Sickert
BR 'sɪkət
AM 'sɪkərt

sickie
BR 'sɪk|i, -ɪz
AM 'sɪki, -z

sickish
BR 'sɪkɪʃ
AM 'sɪkɪʃ

sickle
BR 'sɪkl̩, -z
AM 'sɪkəl, -z

sickliness
BR 'sɪklɪnɪs
AM 'sɪklinɪs

sicklist
BR 'sɪklɪst, -s
AM 'sɪk,lɪst, -s

sickly
BR 'sɪkl|i, -ɪə(r), -ɪɪst
AM 'sɪkli, -ər, -ɪst

sickness
BR 'sɪknɪs
AM 'sɪknɪs

sicko
BR 'sɪkəʊ, -z
AM 'sɪkoʊ, -z

sickroom
BR 'sɪkruːm, 'sɪkrʊm, -z
AM 'sɪk,rum, 'sɪk,rʊm, -z

Sid
BR sɪd
AM sɪd

sidalcea
BR sɪ'dalsɪə(r), -z
AM saɪ'dælʃiə, sə'dælʃiə, -z

Sidcup
BR 'sɪdkʌp, 'sɪdkəp
AM 'sɪd,kəp

Siddall
BR 'sɪdɔːl
AM 'sɪdɔl, 'sɪdal

Siddeley
BR 'sɪdl̩i
AM 'sɪd(ə)li

Siddons
BR 'sɪdnz
AM 'sɪdnz

side
BR saɪd, -z, -ɪŋ, -ɪd-
AM saɪd, -z, -ɪŋ, -ɪd-

sidearm
BR 'saɪdɑːm, -z
AM 'saɪd,ɑrm, -z

sideband
BR 'saɪdband, -z
AM 'saɪd,bænd, -z

sidebar
BR 'saɪdbɑː(r), -z
AM 'saɪd,bɑr, -z

sideboard
BR 'saɪdbɔːd, -z
AM 'saɪd,bɔ(ə)rd, -z

Sidebotham
BR 'saɪd,bɒtəm, 'saɪd,bəʊθ(ə)m, ,sɪdɪbə'tɑːm
AM 'saɪd,bɑdəm

Sidebottom
BR 'saɪd,bɒtəm, ,sɪdɪbə'tɑːm
AM 'saɪd,bɑdəm

sideburn
BR 'saɪdbəːn, -z
AM 'saɪd,bərn, -z

sidecar
BR 'saɪdkɑː(r), -z
AM 'saɪd,kɑr, -z

sidedish
BR 'saɪddɪʃ, -ɪz
AM 'saɪ(d),dɪʃ, -ɪz

sidedness
BR 'saɪdɪdnɪs
AM 'saɪdɪdnɪs

sidehill
BR 'saɪdhɪl, -z
AM 'saɪd,(h)ɪl, -z

sidekick
BR 'saɪdkɪk, -s
AM 'saɪd,kɪk, -s

sidelamp
BR 'saɪdlamp, -s
AM 'saɪd,læmp, -s

sideless
BR 'saɪdlɪs
AM 'saɪdlɪs

sidelight
BR 'saɪdlaɪt, -s
AM 'saɪd,laɪt, -s

sideline
BR 'saɪdlʌɪn, -z
AM 'saɪd,laɪn, -z

sidelong
BR 'saɪdlɒŋ
AM 'saɪd,lɒŋ, 'saɪd,lɑŋ

sideman
BR 'saɪdman
AM 'saɪd,mæn

sidemen
BR 'saɪdmɛn
AM 'saɪd,mɛn

side-on
BR ,saɪd'ɒn
AM ,saɪd'ɑn

sidepiece
BR 'saɪdpiːs, -ɪz
AM 'saɪd,pis, -ɪz

sidereal
BR saɪ'dɪərɪəl
AM saɪ'dɪriəl

siderite
BR 'saɪdərʌɪt
AM 'saɪdə,raɪt

siderostat
BR 'sɪd(ə)rə(ʊ)stat, -s
AM 'sɪdərə,stæt, -s

sidesaddle
BR 'saɪd,sadl̩, -z
AM 'saɪd,sædəl, -z

sideshow
BR 'saɪdʃəʊ, -z
AM 'saɪd,ʃoʊ, -z

sideslip
BR 'saɪdslɪp, -s, -ɪŋ, -t
AM 'saɪd,slɪp, -s, -ɪŋ, -t

sidesman
BR 'saɪdzmən
AM 'saɪdzmən

sidesmen
BR 'saɪdzmən
AM 'saɪdzmən

sidesplitting
BR ˈsʌɪdˌsplɪtɪŋ
AM ˈsaɪdˌsplɪdɪŋ

sidestep
BR ˈsʌɪdstɛp, -s, -ɪŋ, -t
AM ˈsaɪdˌstɛp, -s, -ɪŋ, -t

sidestepper
BR ˈsʌɪdˌstɛpə(r), -z
AM ˈsaɪdˌstɛpər, -z

sidestroke
BR ˈsʌɪdstrəʊk
AM ˈsaɪdˌstroʊk

sideswipe
BR ˈsʌɪdswʌɪp, -s, -ɪŋ, -t
AM ˈsaɪdˌswaɪp, -s, -ɪŋ, -t

sidetrack
BR ˈsʌɪdtrak, -s, -ɪŋ, -t
AM ˈsaɪ(d)ˌtræk, -s, -ɪŋ, -t

sidewalk
BR ˈsʌɪdwɔːk, -s
AM ˈsaɪdˌwɔk, ˈsaɪdˌwɑk, -s

sideward
BR ˈsʌɪdwəd, -z
AM ˈsaɪdwərd, -z

sideways
BR ˈsʌɪdweɪz
AM ˈsaɪdˌweɪz

sidewinder
BR ˈsʌɪdˌwʌɪndə(r), -z
AM ˈsaɪdˌwaɪndər, -z

sidewise
BR ˈsʌɪdwʌɪz
AM ˈsaɪdˌwaɪz

Sidgewick
BR ˈsɪdʒwɪk
AM ˈsɪdʒˌwɪk

siding
BR ˈsʌɪdɪŋ, -z
AM ˈsaɪdɪŋ, -z

sidle
BR ˈsʌɪd|l, -lz, -l̩ɪŋ \ -lɪŋ, -ld
AM ˈsaɪd|əl, -əlz, -(ə)lɪŋ, -əld

Sidmouth
BR ˈsɪdməθ
AM ˈsɪdməθ

Sidney
BR ˈsɪdni
AM ˈsɪdni

Sidon
BR ˈsʌɪdn
AM ˈsaɪdn

Sidra
BR ˈsɪdrə(r)
AM ˈsɪdrə

SIDS
BR sɪdz
AM sɪdz

siege
BR siː(d)ʒ, -ɪz
AM siː(d)ʒ, -ɪz

Siegel
BR ˈsiːgl

AM ˈsiːgəl

Siegfried
BR ˈsiːgfriːd
AM ˈsiːgˌfrid

Sieg Heil
BR ˌsiːg ˈhʌɪl, ˌziːg +
AM ˌsig ˈhaɪl, ˌzig +

Siemens
BR ˈsiːmənz
AM ˈsimənz

Siena
BR sɪˈɛnə(r)
AM siˈɛnə

Sienese
BR ˌsiːəˈniːz
AM ˌsiəˈniz

sienna
BR sɪˈɛnə(r), -z
AM siˈɛnə, -z

sierra
BR sɪˈɛrə(r), -z
AM siˈɛrə, -z

Sierra Leone
BR sɪˌɛrə lɪˈəʊn(i)
AM siˌɛrəliˈoʊn

Sierra Leonian
BR sɪˌɛrə lɪˈəʊnɪən, -z
AM siˌɛrə liˈoʊniən, -z

Sierra Madre
BR sɪˌɛrə ˈmadreɪ
AM siˌɛrə ˈmɑˌdreɪ

Sierra Nevada
BR sɪˌɛrə nɪˈvaːdə(r)
AM siˌɛrə nəˈvɑdə, + nəˈvædə

siesta
BR sɪˈɛstə(r), -z
AM siˈɛstə, -z

sieve
BR sɪv, -z, -ɪŋ, -d
AM sɪv, siv, -z, -ɪŋ, -d

sievelike
BR ˈsɪvlʌɪk
AM ˈsɪvˌlaɪk, ˈsivˌlaɪk

sievert
BR ˈsiːvət, -s
AM ˈsɪvərt, ˈsivərt, -s

sifaka
BR sɪˈfakə(r), -z
AM səˈfækə, -z

siffleur
BR siːˈfləː(r), -z
AM siˈflər, -z

siffleuse
BR siːˈfləːz, -ɪz
AM siˈfləz, -əz

sift
BR sɪft, -s, -ɪŋ, -ɪd
AM sɪft, -s, -ɪŋ, -ɪd

Sifta
BR ˈsɪftə(r)
AM ˈsɪftə

sifter
BR ˈsɪftə(r), -z
AM ˈsɪftər, -z

Sigal
BR ˈsiːgl

AM ˈsiːgəl

sigh
BR sʌɪ, -z, -ɪŋ, -d
AM saɪ, -z, -ɪŋ, -d

sight
BR sʌɪt, -s, -ɪŋ, -ɪd
AM saɪ|t, -ts, -dɪŋ, -dɪd

sighter
BR ˈsʌɪtə(r), -z
AM ˈsaɪdər, -z

sighting
BR ˈsʌɪtɪŋ, -z
AM ˈsaɪdɪŋ, -z

sightless
BR ˈsʌɪtlɪs
AM ˈsaɪtlɪs

sightlessly
BR ˈsʌɪtlɪsli
AM ˈsaɪtlɪsli

sightlessness
BR ˈsʌɪtlɪsnɪs
AM ˈsaɪtlɪsnɪs

sightline
BR ˈsʌɪtlʌɪn, -z
AM ˈsaɪtˌlaɪn, -z

sightliness
BR ˈsʌɪtlɪnɪs
AM ˈsaɪtlinɪs

sightly
BR ˈsʌɪtli
AM ˈsaɪtli

sight-read¹
present tense
BR ˈsʌɪtriːd, -z, -ɪŋ
AM ˈsaɪtˌrid, -z, -ɪŋ

sight-read²
past tense
BR ˈsʌɪtrɛd
AM ˈsaɪtˌrɛd

sight-reader
BR ˈsʌɪtˌriːdə(r), -z
AM ˈsaɪtˌridər, -z

sight-sang
BR ˈsʌɪtsaŋ
AM ˈsaɪtˌsæŋ

sightsaw
BR ˈsʌɪtsɔː(r)
AM ˈsaɪtˌsɔ

sightscreen
BR ˈsʌɪtskriːn, -z
AM ˈsaɪtˌskrin, -z

sightsee
BR ˈsʌɪtsiː, -z, -ɪŋ
AM ˈsaɪtˌsi, -z, -ɪŋ

sightseeing
BR ˈsʌɪtˌsiːɪŋ
AM ˈsaɪtˌsiɪŋ

sightseer
BR ˈsʌɪtˌsiːə(r), -z
AM ˈsaɪtˌsi(ə)r, -z

sight-sing
BR ˈsʌɪtsɪŋ, -z
AM ˈsaɪtˌsɪŋ, -z

sight-singing
BR ˈsʌɪtˌsɪŋɪŋ
AM ˈsaɪtˌsɪŋɪŋ

AM ˈsiːgəl

sigh

AM ˈsiːgəl

sightworthy
BR ˈsʌɪtˌwəːði
AM ˈsaɪtˌwərði

sigil
BR ˈsɪdʒ(ɪ)l, -z
AM ˈsɪdʒɪl, -z

sigillate
BR ˈsɪdʒɪleɪt
AM ˈsɪdʒəˌleɪt

Sigismond
BR ˈsɪgɪzmənd, ˈsɪgɪsmənd
AM ˈsɪgɪsmənd

Sigismund
BR ˈsɪgɪzmənd, ˈsɪgɪsmənd
AM ˈsɪgɪsmənd

sigla
BR ˈsɪglə(r)
AM ˈsɪglə

siglum
BR ˈsɪgləm
AM ˈsɪgləm

sigma
BR ˈsɪgmə(r), -z
AM ˈsɪgmə, -z

sigmate
BR ˈsɪgmeɪt
AM ˈsɪgˌmeɪt

sigmatic
BR sɪgˈmatɪk
AM sɪgˈmædɪk

sigmoid
BR ˈsɪgmɔɪd
AM ˈsɪgˌmɔɪd

sigmoidoscope
BR sɪgˈmɔɪdəskəʊp
AM sɪgˈmɔɪdəˌskoʊp

sigmoidoscopic
BR sɪgˌmɔɪdəˈskɒpɪk
AM sɪgˌmɔɪdəˈskɑpɪk

sigmoidoscopy
BR ˌsɪgmɔɪˈdɒskəpi
AM ˌsɪgmɔɪˈdɑskəpi

Sigmund
BR ˈsɪgmənd
AM ˈsɪgmənd

sign
BR sʌɪn, -z, -ɪŋ, -d
AM saɪn, -z, -ɪŋ, -d

signable
BR ˈsʌɪnəbl
AM ˈsaɪnəbəl

signal
BR ˈsɪgn|l, -lz, -l̩ɪŋ \ -əlɪŋ, -ld
AM ˈsɪgnəl, -z, -ɪŋ, -d

signalise
BR ˈsɪgnəlʌɪz, ˈsɪgnl̩ʌɪz, -ɪz, -ɪŋ, -d
AM ˈsɪgnəˌlaɪz, -ɪz, -ɪŋ, -d

signalize
BR ˈsɪgnəlʌɪz, ˈsɪgnl̩ʌɪz, -ɪz, -ɪŋ, -d
AM ˈsɪgnəˌlaɪz, -ɪz, -ɪŋ, -d

signaller
BR ˈsɪɡnələ(r),
ˈsɪɡnlə(r), -z
AM ˈsɪɡnələr, -z

signally
BR ˈsɪɡnəli, ˈsɪɡnl̩i
AM ˈsɪɡnəli

signalman
BR ˈsɪɡnlmən
AM ˈsɪɡnəlmən

signalmen
BR ˈsɪɡnlmən
AM ˈsɪɡnəlmən

signary
BR ˈsɪɡnər|i, -ɪz
AM ˈsɪɡnəri, -z

signatory
BR ˈsɪɡnət(ə)r|i, -ɪz
AM ˈsɪɡnəˌtɔri, -z

signature
BR ˈsɪɡnətʃə(r), -z
AM ˈsɪɡnətʃər,
ˈsɪɡnətʃʊ(ə)r|| -z

signboard
BR ˈsɑɪnbɔːd, -z
AM ˈsɑɪnˌbɔ(ə)rd, -z

signer
BR ˈsɑɪnə(r), -z
AM ˈsɑɪnər, -z

signet
BR ˈsɪɡnɪt, -s
AM ˈsɪɡnɪt, -s

significance
BR sɪɡˈnɪfɪk(ə)ns
AM sɪɡˈnɪfɪkəns

significancy
BR sɪɡˈnɪfɪk(ə)ns|i, -ɪz
AM sɪɡˈnɪfɪkənsi, -z

significant
BR sɪɡˈnɪfɪk(ə)nt
AM sɪɡˈnɪfɪkənt

significantly
BR sɪɡˈnɪfɪk(ə)ntli
AM sɪɡˈnɪfɪkən(t)li

signification
BR ˌsɪɡnɪfɪˈkeɪʃn
AM ˌsɪɡnəfəˈkeɪʃən

significative
BR sɪɡˈnɪfɪkətɪv
AM sɪɡˈnɪfɪkədɪv

signified
BR ˈsɪɡnɪfɑɪd, -z
AM ˈsɪɡnəˌfɑɪd, -z

signifier
BR ˈsɪɡnɪfɑɪə(r), -z
AM ˈsɪɡnəˌfɑɪ(ə)r, -z

signify
BR ˈsɪɡnɪfɑɪ, -z, -ɪŋ, -d
AM ˈsɪɡnəˌfɑɪ, -z, -ɪŋ, -d

signing
BR ˈsɑɪnɪŋ, -z
AM ˈsɑɪnɪŋ, -z

signor
BR siːnˈjɔː(r),
ˈsiːnjɔː(r), -z
AM sinˈjɔ(ə)r, -z

signora
BR siːnˈjɔːrə(r), -z
AM sinˈjɔrə, -z

signorina
BR ˌsiːnjɔːˈriːnə(r),
ˌsiːnjəˈriːnə(r), -z
AM ˌsinjəˈrinə, -z

signory
BR ˈsiːnjəri
AM ˈsinjeri

signpost
BR ˈsɑɪnpəʊst, -s, -ɪd
AM ˈsɑɪnˌpoʊst, -s, -əd

signwriter
BR ˈsɑɪnˌrɑɪtə(r), -z
AM ˈsɑɪnˌrɑɪdər, -z

signwriting
BR ˈsɑɪnˌrɑɪtɪŋ
AM ˈsɑɪnˌrɑɪdɪŋ

Sigurd
BR ˈsɪɡɜːd
AM ˈsɪɡərd

Sihanouk
BR ˈsɪənʊk
AM ˈsɪənʊk

Sihanoukville
BR ˈsɪənʊkvɪl
AM ˈsɪənʊkˌvɪl

sika
BR ˈsiːkə(r), -z
AM ˈsiːkə, -z

Sikh
BR siːk, -s
AM sik, -s

Sikhism
BR ˈsiːkɪz(ə)m
AM ˈsiˌkɪzəm

Sikkim
BR ˈsɪkɪm
AM ˈsɪkɪm

Sikkimese
BR ˌsɪkɪˈmiːz
AM ˌsɪkɪˈmiz

Sikorsky
BR sɪˈkɔːski
AM səˈkɔrski

silage
BR ˈsɑɪlɪdʒ
AM ˈsɑɪlɪdʒ

silane
BR ˈsɑɪleɪn
AM ˈsɑɪleɪn

Silas
BR ˈsɑɪləs
AM ˈsɑɪləs

Silchester
BR ˈsɪltʃɪstə(r),
ˈsɪltʃestə(r)
AM ˈsɪlˌtʃestər

Silcox
BR ˈsɪlkɒks
AM ˈsɪlˌkɑks

sild
BR sɪld, -z
AM sɪld, -z

silence
BR ˈsɑɪləns, ˈsɑɪlns, -ɪz,
-ɪŋ, -t
AM ˈsɑɪləns, -əz, -ɪŋ, -t

silencer
BR ˈsɑɪlənsə(r),
ˈsɑɪlnsə(r), -z
AM ˈsɑɪlənsər, -z

sileni
BR sɑɪˈliːnɑɪ
AM sɑɪˈliˌnɑɪ

silent
BR ˈsɑɪlənt, ˈsɑɪlnt
AM ˈsɑɪlənt

silently
BR ˈsɑɪləntli, ˈsɑɪlntli
AM ˈsɑɪlən(t)li

silenus
BR sɑɪˈliːnəs
AM sɑɪˈlinəs

Silesia
BR sɑɪˈliːzɪə(r),
sɑɪˈliːʒə(r),
sɑɪˈliːʃə(r)
AM sɑɪˈliʒə, sɑɪˈliʃə,
səˈliʒə, səˈliʃə

Silesian
BR sɑɪˈliːzɪən,
sɑɪˈliːʒn, sɑɪˈliːʃn, -z
AM sɑɪˈliʒən, sɑɪˈliʃən,
səˈliʒən, səˈliʃən, -z

silex
BR ˈsɑɪleks
AM ˈsɑɪˌleks

silhouette
BR ˌsɪluˈet, -s, -ɪŋ, -ɪd
AM ˌsɪləˈwet, -ts, -dɪŋ,
-dəd

silica
BR ˈsɪlɪkə(r)
AM ˈsɪlɪkə

silicate
BR ˈsɪlɪkət, ˈsɪlɪkeɪt, -s
AM ˈsɪləˌkeɪt, ˈsɪlɪkɪt, -s

siliceous
BR sɪˈlɪʃəs
AM səˈlɪʃəs

silicic
BR sɪˈlɪsɪk
AM səˈlɪsɪk

silicide
BR ˈsɪlɪsɑɪd
AM ˈsɪlɪsaɪd

siliciferous
BR ˌsɪlɪˈsɪf(ə)rəs
AM ˌsɪləˈsɪf(ə)rəs

silicification
BR sɪˌlɪsɪfɪˈkeɪʃn
AM sɪˌləsəfəˈkeɪʃən

silicify
BR sɪˈlɪsɪfɑɪ, -z, -ɪŋ, -d
AM səˈlɪsəˌfɑɪ, -z, -ɪŋ, -d

silicon
BR ˈsɪlɪk(ə)n
AM ˈsɪləˌkɑn, ˈsɪlɪkən

silicone
BR ˈsɪlɪkəʊn
AM ˈsɪləˌkoʊn

Silicon Valley
BR ˌsɪlɪk(ə)n ˈvæli
AM ˈsɪləˌkɑn ˈvæli,
ˌsɪlɪkən +

silicosis
BR ˌsɪlɪˈkəʊsɪs
AM ˌsɪləˈkoʊsəs

silicotic
BR ˌsɪlɪˈkɒtɪk
AM ˌsɪləˈkɑdɪk

siliqua
BR ˈsɪlɪkwə(r)
AM ˈsɪləkwə

siliquae
BR ˈsɪlɪkwiː, ˈsɪlɪkwʌɪ
AM ˈsɪləkwi, ˈsɪləˌkwaɪ

silique
BR sɪˈliːk, -s
AM səˈlik, ˈsɪlɪk, -s

siliquose
BR ˈsɪlɪkwəʊs
AM ˈsɪləˌkwoʊs,
ˈsɪləˌkwoʊz

siliquous
BR ˈsɪlɪkwəs
AM ˈsɪləkwəs

silk
BR sɪlk, -s
AM sɪlk, -s

silken
BR ˈsɪlk(ə)n
AM ˈsɪlkən

silkily
BR ˈsɪlkɪli
AM ˈsɪlkɪli

Silkin
BR ˈsɪlkɪn
AM ˈsɪlkən

silkiness
BR ˈsɪlkɪnɪs
AM ˈsɪlkɪnɪs

silklike
BR ˈsɪlklʌɪk
AM ˈsɪlkˌlaɪk

silkscreen
BR ˈsɪlkskriːn, -z, -ɪŋ, -d
AM ˈsɪlkˌskrin, -z, -ɪŋ,
-d

silkworm
BR ˈsɪlkwəːm, -z
AM ˈsɪlkˌwərm, -z

silky
BR ˈsɪlk|i, -ɪə(r), -ɪɪst
AM ˈsɪlki, -ər, -ɪst

sill
BR sɪl, -z
AM sɪl, -z

sillabub
BR ˈsɪləbʌb, -z
AM ˈsɪləˌbəb, -z

Sillars
BR ˈsɪləz
AM ˈsɪlərz

siller
BR ˈsɪlə(r)
AM ˈsɪlər

sillily
BR 'sɪlɪli
AM 'sɪlɪli

sillimanite
BR 'sɪlɪmənʌɪt, -s
AM 'sɪləmə,naɪt, -s

silliness
BR 'sɪlinɪs
AM 'sɪlinɪs

Sillitoe
BR 'sɪlɪtəʊ
AM 'sɪli,toʊ

Silloth
BR 'sɪləθ
AM 'sɪləθ

Sills
BR sɪlz
AM sɪlz

silly
BR 'sɪl|i, -iə(r), -iɪst
AM 'sɪli, -ər, -ɪst

silo
BR 'sʌɪləʊ, -z
AM 'saɪloʊ, -z

Siloam
BR sʌɪ'ləʊəm, sɪ'ləʊəm
AM ,sʌɪ'loʊəm, 'saɪləm

Silsoe
BR 'sɪlsəʊ
AM 'sɪl,soʊ

silt
BR sɪlt, -s, -ɪŋ, -ɪd
AM sɪlt, -s, -ɪŋ, -ɪd

siltation
BR sɪl'teɪʃn
AM sɪl'teɪʃən

siltstone
BR 'sɪltstəʊn, -z
AM 'sɪlt,stoʊn, -z

silty
BR 'sɪlti
AM 'sɪlti

Silures
BR sʌɪ'l(j)ʊəri:z, sʌɪ'ljɔːri:z
AM saɪ'lʊriz

Silurian
BR sʌɪ'l(j)ʊəriən, sʌɪ'ljɔːriən
AM sə'lʊriən, saɪ'lʊriən

Silva
BR 'sɪlvə(r), -z
AM 'sɪlvə, -z

silvan
BR 'sɪlv(ə)n
AM 'sɪlvən

Silvanus
BR sɪl'veɪnəs
AM sɪl'veɪnəs

silver
BR 'sɪlv|ə(r), -əz, -(ə)rɪŋ, -əd
AM 'sɪlv|ər, -ərz, -(ə)rɪŋ, -ərd

silver birch
BR ,sɪlvə 'bɜːtʃ, -ɪz
AM ,sɪlvər 'bɜrtʃ, -əz

silverfish
BR 'sɪlvəfɪʃ, -ɪz
AM 'sɪlvər,fɪʃ, -ɪz

silveriness
BR 'sɪlv(ə)rɪnɪs
AM 'sɪlv(ə)rɪnɪs

Silverman
BR 'sɪlvəmən
AM 'sɪlvərmən

silvern
BR 'sɪlv(ə)n
AM 'sɪlvərn

silver-plate
BR ,sɪlvə'pleɪt, -s, -ɪŋ, -ɪd
AM ,sɪlvər'pleɪ|t, -ts, -dɪŋ, -dɪd

silverside
BR 'sɪlvəsʌɪd, -z
AM 'sɪlvər,saɪd, -z

silversmith
BR 'sɪlvəsmɪθ, -s
AM 'sɪlvər,smɪθ, -s

silversmithing
BR 'sɪlvə,smɪθɪŋ
AM 'sɪlvər,smɪðɪŋ

Silverstone
BR 'sɪlvəstəʊn, 'sɪlvəstən
AM 'sɪlvər,stoʊn

silverware
BR 'sɪlvəwɛː(r)
AM 'sɪlvər,wɛ(ə)r

silverweed
BR 'sɪlvəwiːd, -z
AM 'sɪlvər,wid, -z

silvery
BR 'sɪlv(ə)ri
AM 'sɪlv(ə)ri

Silvester
BR 'sɪlvɛstə(r), 'sɪlvɪstə(r), s(ɪ)l'vɛstə(r)
AM sɪl'vɛstər

silvicultural
BR ,sɪlvɪ'kʌltʃ(ə)rəl, ,sɪlvɪ'kʌltʃ(ə)rl
AM ,sɪlvə'kəltʃ(ə)rəl

silviculture
BR 'sɪlvɪ,kʌltʃə(r)
AM 'sɪlvə,kəltʃər

silviculturist
BR ,sɪlvɪ'kʌltʃ(ə)rɪst, -s
AM ,sɪlvə'kəltʃ(ə)rəst, -s

Silvie
BR 'sɪlvi
AM 'sɪlvi

Silvikrin®
BR 'sɪlvɪkrɪn
AM 'sɪlvɪ,krɪn

Sim
BR sɪm
AM sɪm

sima
BR 'sʌɪmə(r)
AM 'saɪmə

simazine
BR 'sʌɪməzi:n
AM 'saɪmə,zin

Simca®
BR 'sɪmkə(r), -z
AM 'sɪmkə, -z

simcha
BR 'sɪmtʃə(r), 'sɪmxə(r), -z
AM 'sɪmkə, -z

Simcox
BR 'sɪmkɒks
AM 'sɪm,kɑks

Simenon
BR 'si:mənɒ, 'si:mənɒn
AM ,si:mə'nɔn, ,si:mə'nɑn

Simeon
BR 'sɪmiən
AM 'sɪmiən

Simes
BR sʌɪmz
AM saɪmz

simian
BR 'sɪmiən, -z
AM 'sɪmiən, -z

similar
BR 'sɪm(ɪ)lə(r)
AM 'sɪm(ə)lər

similarity
BR ,sɪmɪ'larɪt|i, -ɪz
AM ,sɪmə'lɛrədi, -z

similarly
BR 'sɪm(ɪ)ləli
AM 'sɪm(ə)lərli

simile
BR 'sɪmɪl|i, -ɪz
AM 'sɪmɪli, -z

similitude
BR sɪ'mɪlɪtjuːd, sɪ'mɪlɪtʃuːd, -z
AM sɪ'mɪlə,t(j)ud, -z

Simla
BR 'sɪmlə(r)
AM 'sɪmlə

Simm
BR sɪm
AM sɪm

simmer
BR 'sɪm|ə(r), -əz, -(ə)rɪŋ, -əd
AM 'sɪm|ər, -ərz, -(ə)rɪŋ, -ərd

Simmonds
BR 'sɪmən(d)z
AM 'sɪmənz

Simmons
BR 'sɪmənz
AM 'sɪmənz

Simms
BR sɪmz
AM sɪmz

simnel
BR 'sɪmnl
AM 'sɪmnəl

simoleon
BR sɪ'məʊliən
AM sə'moʊliən

Simon
BR 'saɪmən
AM 'saɪmən

Simonds
BR 'sɪmən(d)z, ,sʌɪmən(d)z
AM 'sɪmənz, 'saɪmənz

Simone
BR sɪ'məʊn
AM sə'moʊn, sɪ'moʊn

simoniac
BR sɪ'məʊniak, -s
AM sə'moʊni,æk, -s

simoniacal
BR ,sɪmə'nʌɪəkl
AM ,saɪmə'naɪəkəl

simoniacally
BR ,sɪmə'nʌɪəkli
AM ,saɪmə'naɪək(ə)li

Simonides
BR sʌɪ'mɒnɪdi:z
AM saɪ'mɑnə,diz

simonize
BR 'sʌɪmənʌɪz, -ɪz, -ɪŋ, -d
AM 'saɪmə,naɪz, -ɪz, -ɪŋ, -d

simon-pure
BR ,sʌɪmən'pjʊə(r), ,sʌɪmən'pjɔː(r)
AM 'saɪmən,pjʊ(ə)r

Simons
BR 'sʌɪmənz
AM 'saɪmənz

simony
BR 'sɪməni, 'sɪmənɪ
AM 'saɪməni, 'sɪməni

simoom
BR sɪ'mu:m, -z
AM sə'mum, -z

simoon
BR sɪ'mu:n, -z
AM sə'mun, -z

simp
BR sɪmp, -s
AM sɪmp, -s

simpatico
BR sɪm'patɪkəʊ, -z
AM sɪm'pædə,koʊ, -z

simper
BR 'sɪmp|ə(r), -əz, -(ə)rɪŋ, -əd
AM 'sɪmp|ər, -ərz, -(ə)rɪŋ, -ərd

simperingly
BR 'sɪmp(ə)rɪŋli
AM 'sɪmp(ə)rɪŋli

Simpkin
BR 'sɪm(p)kɪn
AM 'sɪmkɪn

Simpkins
BR ˈsɪm(p)kɪnz
AM ˈsɪmkɪnz

Simpkinson
BR ˈsɪm(p)kɪns(ə)n
AM ˈsɪmkɪnsən

simple
BR ˈsɪmpl, -z, -ə(r), -ɪst
AM ˈsɪmpəl, -əlz,
-(ə)lər, -(ə)ləst

simple-hearted
BR ˌsɪmplˈhɑːtɪd
AM ˈsɪmpəlˌhɑrdəd

simple-minded
BR ˌsɪmplˈmaɪndɪd
AM ˈsɪmpəlˌmaɪndɪd

simple-mindedly
BR ˌsɪmplˈmaɪndɪdli
AM ˈsɪmpəlˌmaɪndɪdli

simple-mindedness
BR ˌsɪmplˈmaɪndɪdnɪs
AM ˈsɪmpəlˌmaɪndɪdnɪs

simpleness
BR ˈsɪmplnəs
AM ˈsɪmpəlnəs

simpleton
BR ˈsɪmplt(ə)n, -z
AM ˈsɪmpəltən, -z

simplex
BR ˈsɪmplɛks
AM ˈsɪmpleks

simplicity
BR sɪmˈplɪsɪti
AM sɪmˈplɪsɪdi

simplification
BR ˌsɪmplɪfɪˈkeɪʃn, -z
AM ˌsɪmpləfəˈkeɪʃən, -z

simplify
BR ˈsɪmplɪfaɪ, -z, -ɪŋ, -d
AM ˈsɪmpləˌfaɪ, -z, -ɪŋ, -d

simplism
BR ˈsɪmplɪz(ə)m
AM ˈsɪmˌplɪzəm

simplistic
BR sɪmˈplɪstɪk
AM sɪmˈplɪstɪk

simplistically
BR sɪmˈplɪstɪkli
AM sɪmˈplɪstək(ə)li

Simplon
BR ˈsɪmplɒn
AM ˈsɪmˌplɒn,
ˈsɪmˌplɑn

Simplot
BR ˈsɪmplɒt
AM ˈsɪmˌplɑt

simply
BR ˈsɪmpli
AM ˈsɪmpli

Simpson
BR ˈsɪm(p)sn
AM ˈsɪm(p)sən

Sims
BR sɪmz

AM sɪmz
Simson
BR ˈsɪmsn
AM ˈsɪmsən

simulacra
BR ˌsɪmjʊˈleɪkrə(r)
AM ˌsɪmjəˈleɪkrə,
ˌsɪmjʊˈlækrə

simulacrum
BR ˌsɪmjʊˈleɪkrəm
AM ˌsɪmjəˈleɪkrəm,
ˌsɪmjʊˈlækrəm

simulate
BR ˈsɪmjʊleɪt, -s, -ɪŋ, -ɪd
AM ˈsɪmjəˌleɪt, -ts,
-ɪŋ, -ɪd

simulation
BR ˌsɪmjʊˈleɪʃn, -z
AM ˌsɪmjəˈleɪʃən, -z

simulative
BR ˈsɪmjʊlətɪv
AM ˈsɪmjələdɪv,
ˈsɪmjəˌleɪdɪv

simulator
BR ˈsɪmjʊleɪtə(r), -z
AM ˈsɪmjəˌleɪdər, -z

simulcast
BR ˈsɪmlkɑːst,
ˈsɪmlkast, -s
AM ˈsaɪməlˌkæst, -s

simultaneity
BR ˌsɪmltəˈneɪɪti,
ˌsɪmltəˈniːɪti
AM ˌsaɪməltəˈniːɪdi

simultaneous
BR ˌsɪmlˈteɪnɪəs
AM ˌsaɪməlˈteɪnɪəs

simultaneously
BR ˌsɪmlˈteɪnɪəsli
AM ˌsaɪməlˈteɪnɪəsli

simultaneousness
BR ˌsɪmlˈteɪnɪəsnəs
AM ˌsaɪməlˈteɪnɪəsnəs

simurg
BR sɪˈmɜːg, -z
AM siˈmɜrg, -z

sin
BR sɪn, -z, -ɪŋ, -d
AM sɪn, -z, -ɪŋ, -d

Sinai
BR ˈsaɪn(i)aɪ
AM ˈsaɪˌnaɪ

Sinaitic
BR ˌsaɪneɪˈɪtɪk,
ˌsaɪnɪˈɪtɪk
AM ˌsɪnəˈɪdɪk

Sinanthropus
BR sɪˈnænθrəpəs
AM sɪnˈænθrəpəs,
səˈnænθrəpəs

sinapism
BR ˈsɪnəpɪz(ə)m, -z
AM ˈsɪnəˌpɪzəm, -z

Sinatra
BR sɪˈnɑːtrə(r)
AM səˈnɑtrə

Sinbad
BR ˈsɪnbad
AM ˈsɪnˌbæd

sin-bin
BR ˈsɪnbɪn, -z
AM ˈsɪnˌbɪn, -z

since
BR sɪns
AM sɪns

sincere
BR s(ɪ)nˈsɪə(r), -ə(r),
-ɪst
AM sɪnˈsɪ(ə)r, -ər, -ɪst

sincerely
BR s(ɪ)nˈsɪəli
AM sɪnˈsɪrli

sincereness
BR s(ɪ)nˈsɪənəs
AM sɪnˈsɪrnəs

sincerity
BR s(ɪ)nˈsɛrɪti
AM sɪnˈsɛrədi

sincipital
BR s(ɪ)nˈsɪpɪtl
AM sɪnˈsɪpɪdl

sinciput
BR ˈsɪnsɪpʌt, -s
AM ˈsɪnsəpət, -s

Sinclair
BR ˈsɪŋklɛː(r),
ˈsɪŋkleː(r), sɪŋˈklɛː(r),
sɪnˈklɛː(r)
AM sɪnˈklɛ(ə)r,
sɪŋˈklɛ(ə)r

Sind
BR sɪnd
AM sɪnd

Sindebele
BR ˌsɪndəˈbiːli,
ˌsɪndəˈbeɪli
AM ˌsɪndəˈbili

Sindh
BR sɪnd
AM sɪnd

Sindhi
BR ˈsɪndʲi, -ɪz
AM ˈsɪndi, -z

Sindi
BR ˈsɪndʲi, -ɪz
AM ˈsɪndi, -z

sindonology
BR ˌsɪndəˈnɒlədʒi
AM ˌsɪndəˈnɑlədʒi

Sindy
BR ˈsɪndi
AM ˈsɪndi

sine
trigonometry
BR saɪn, -z
AM saɪn, -z

Sinéad
BR ʃɪˈneɪd
AM ʃəˈneɪd

sinecure
BR ˈsɪnɪkjʊə(r),
ˈsaɪnɪkjʊə(r),
ˈsɪnɪkjɔː(r),
ˈsaɪnɪkjɔː(r), -z

Sinbad
AM ˈsɪnəˌkjʊ(ə)r, -z

sinecurism
BR ˈsɪnɪkjʊərɪz(ə)m,
ˈsaɪnɪkjʊərɪz(ə)m,
ˈsɪnɪkjɔːrɪz(ə)m,
ˈsaɪnɪkjɔːrɪz(ə)m
AM ˈsɪnəˌkjʊˌrɪzəm

sinecurist
BR ˈsɪnɪkjʊərɪst,
ˈsaɪnɪkjʊərɪst,
ˈsɪnɪkjɔːrɪst,
ˈsaɪnɪkjɔːrɪst, -s
AM ˈsɪnəˌkjʊrəst, -s

sine die
BR ˌsaɪni ˈdaɪiː, ˌsɪni +,
+ diːeɪ
AM ˌsɪnə ˈdiə

sine qua non
BR ˌsɪni kwɑː ˈnɒn,
ˌsaɪni +, + kweɪ +,
+ ˈnəʊn
AM ˌsɪnə ˌkwɑ ˈnoʊn,
+ ˈnɑn

sinew
BR ˈsɪnjuː, -z
AM ˈsɪnju, -z

sinewless
BR ˈsɪnjuːləs
AM ˈsɪnjuləs

sinewy
BR ˈsɪnjuːi
AM ˈsɪn(j)əwi

sinfonia
BR sɪnˈfəʊnɪə(r),
ˌsɪnfəˈniːə(r), -z
AM ˌsɪnfəˈniə,
ˌsɪnˈfoʊniə, -z

sinfonietta
BR ˌsɪnfəʊnɪˈɛtə(r),
ˌsɪnfɒnɪˈɛtə(r), -z
AM ˌsɪnfənˈjɛdə,
ˌsɪnfoʊnˈjɛdə, -z

sinful
BR ˈsɪnf(ʊ)l
AM ˈsɪnfəl

sinfully
BR ˈsɪnfʊli, ˈsɪnfl̩i
AM ˈsɪnfəli

sinfulness
BR ˈsɪnf(ʊ)lnəs
AM ˈsɪnfəlnəs

sing
BR sɪŋ, -z, -ɪŋ
AM sɪŋ, -z, -ɪŋ

singable
BR ˈsɪŋəbl
AM ˈsɪŋəbəl

singalong
BR ˈsɪŋəlɒŋ
AM ˈsɪŋəˌlɔŋ, ˈsɪŋəˌlɑŋ

Singapore
BR ˌsɪŋ(g)əˈpɔː(r)
AM ˈsɪŋəˌpɔ(ə)r

Singaporean
BR ˌsɪŋ(g)əˈpɔːrɪən, -z
AM ˌsɪŋəˈpɔriən, -z

singe
BR sɪn(d)ʒ, -ɪz, -ɪŋ, -d

AM sɪndʒ, -ɪz, -ɪŋ, -d

singer
BR ˈsɪŋə(r), -z
AM ˈsɪŋɚ, -z

singer-songwriter
BR ˌsɪŋəˈsəʊrʌɪtə(r), -z
AM ˈsɪŋɚˈsɒŋˌraɪdɚ, ˈsɪŋɚˈsɑŋˌraɪdɚ, -z

Singh
BR sɪŋ
AM sɪŋ

Singhalese
BR ˌsɪŋɡəˈliːz, ˌsɪŋ(h)əˈliːz
AM ˈsɪŋɡəˈliːz, ˈsɪŋ(h)əˈliːz

singingly
BR ˈsɪŋɪŋli
AM ˈsɪŋɪŋli

single
BR ˈsɪŋɡ|l, -lz, -lɪŋ \ -lɪŋ, -ld
AM ˈsɪŋɡ|əl, -əlz, -(ə)lɪŋ, -əld

single-lens reflex
BR ˌsɪŋɡllenz ˈriːfleks, -ɪz
AM ˈsɪŋɡə(l)ˌlenz ˈriːˌfleks, -əz

single-minded
BR ˌsɪŋɡlˈmʌɪndɪd
AM ˈsɪŋɡəlˈmaɪndɪd

single-mindedly
BR ˌsɪŋɡlˈmʌɪndɪdli
AM ˈsɪŋɡəlˈmaɪndɪdli

single-mindedness
BR ˌsɪŋɡlˈmʌɪndɪdnɪs
AM ˈsɪŋɡəlˈmaɪndɪdnɪs

singleness
BR ˈsɪŋɡlnəs
AM ˈsɪŋɡəlnəs

singlestick
BR ˈsɪŋɡlstɪk, -s
AM ˈsɪŋɡəlˌstɪk, -s

singlet
BR ˈsɪŋɡlɪt, -s
AM ˈsɪŋɡlɪt, -s

singleton¹
BR ˈsɪŋɡlt(ə)n, -z
AM ˈsɪŋɡəlt(ə)n, -z

singleton²
BR ˈsɪŋɡlt(ə)n, -z
AM ˈsɪŋɡəltən, -z

singletree
BR ˈsɪŋɡltriː, -z
AM ˈsɪŋɡəlˌtri, -z

singly
BR ˈsɪŋɡli
AM ˈsɪŋɡli

singsong
BR ˈsɪŋsɒŋ, -z
AM ˈsɪŋˌsɔŋ, ˈsɪŋˌsɑŋ, -z

singular
BR ˈsɪŋɡjələ(r), -z
AM ˈsɪŋɡjələr, -z

singularisation
BR ˌsɪŋɡjələrʌɪˈzeɪʃn
AM ˌsɪŋɡjələrəˈzeɪʃən, ˌsɪŋɡjələˌraɪˈzeɪʃən, ˌsɪŋɡjəˌlerəˈzeɪʃən

singularise
BR ˈsɪŋɡjələrʌɪz, -ɪz, -ɪŋ, -d
AM ˈsɪŋɡjələˌraɪz, -ɪz, -ɪŋ, -d

singularity
BR ˌsɪŋɡjəˈlarɪt|i, -ɪz
AM ˌsɪŋɡjəˈleradi, -z

singularization
BR ˌsɪŋɡjələrʌɪˈzeɪʃn
AM ˌsɪŋɡjələrəˈzeɪʃən, ˌsɪŋɡjələˌraɪˈzeɪʃən, ˌsɪŋɡjəˌlerəˈzeɪʃən

singularize
BR ˈsɪŋɡjələrʌɪz, -ɪz, -ɪŋ, -d
AM ˈsɪŋɡjələˌraɪz, -ɪz, -ɪŋ, -d

singularly
BR ˈsɪŋɡjələli
AM ˈsɪŋɡjələrli

sinh
hyperbolic sine
BR ʃʌɪn, sɪn(t)ʃ, ˌsʌɪnˈeɪtʃ
AM saɪn, ˌsaɪnˈeɪtʃ

Sinhala
BR sɪnˈhɑːlə(r)
AM sɪnˈhɑlə

Sinhalese
BR ˌsɪn(h)əˈliːz, ˌsɪŋɡəˈliːz, ˌsɪŋ(h)əˈliːz
AM ˈsɪŋɡəˈliːz, ˈsɪŋ(h)əˈliːz

sinister
BR ˈsɪnɪstə(r)
AM ˈsɪnɪstər

sinisterly
BR ˈsɪnɪstəli
AM ˈsɪnɪstərli

sinisterness
BR ˈsɪnɪstənəs
AM ˈsɪnɪstərnəs

sinistral
BR ˈsɪnɪstr(ə)l
AM ˈsɪnɪstrəl, səˈnɪstrəl

sinistrality
BR ˌsɪnɪˈstralɪti
AM ˌsɪnəˈstrælədi

sinistrally
BR ˈsɪnɪstrəli, ˈsɪnɪstr̩li
AM ˈsɪnɪstrəli, səˈnɪstrəli

sinistrorse
BR ˈsɪnɪstrɔːs
AM ˈsɪnəˌstrɔ(ə)rs

sinistrorsely
BR ˈsɪnɪstrɔːsli
AM ˈsɪnəˌstrɔrsli

Sinitic
BR sʌɪˈnɪtɪk, sɪˈnɪtɪk
AM səˈnɪdɪk

sink
BR sɪŋk, -s, -ɪŋ
AM sɪŋk, -s, -ɪŋ

sinkable
BR ˈsɪŋkəbl
AM ˈsɪŋkəbəl

sinkage
BR ˈsɪŋkɪdʒ, -ɪdʒɪz
AM ˈsɪŋkɪdʒ, -ɪz

sinker
BR ˈsɪŋkə(r), -z
AM ˈsɪŋkər, -z

sinkhole
BR ˈsɪŋkhəʊl, -z
AM ˈsɪŋk(h)oʊl, -z

Sinkiang
BR ˌsɪnˈkjaŋ
AM ˌsɪnˈkjæŋ

sinking
BR ˈsɪŋkɪŋ, -z
AM ˈsɪŋkɪŋ, -z

sinless
BR ˈsɪnlɪs
AM ˈsɪnlɪs

sinlessly
BR ˈsɪnlɪsli
AM ˈsɪnlɪsli

sinlessness
BR ˈsɪnlɪsnɪs
AM ˈsɪnlɪsnɪs

sinner
BR ˈsɪnə(r), -z
AM ˈsɪnər, -z

sinnet
BR ˈsɪnɪt, -s
AM ˈsɪnɪt, -s

Sinn Fein
BR ʃɪn ˈfeɪn
AM ˌʃɪn ˈfeɪn
IR ˌsʲinʲ ˈfʲeːnʲ

Sinn Feiner
BR ʃɪn ˈfeɪnə(r), -z
AM ˌʃɪn ˈfeɪnər, -z

Sinnott
BR ˈsɪnət
AM ˈsɪnət

Sino-
BR ˈsʌɪnəʊ
AM ˈsaɪnoʊ

Sino-British
BR ˌsʌɪnəʊˈbrɪtɪʃ
AM ˌsaɪnoʊˈbrɪdɪʃ

Sino-Japanese
BR ˌsʌɪnəʊˌdʒapəˈniːz
AM ˌsaɪnoʊˌdʒæpəˈniz

sinological
BR ˌsʌɪnəˈlɒdʒɪkl, ˌsɪnəˈlɒdʒɪkl
AM ˌsaɪnəˈlɑdʒəkəl, ˌsɪnəˈlɑdʒəkəl

Sinologist
BR sʌɪˈnɒlədʒɪst, sɪˈnɒlədʒɪst, -s
AM saɪˈnɑlədʒəst, -s

Sinologue
BR ˈsʌɪnəlɒɡ, ˈsɪnəlɒɡ, -z
AM ˈsaɪnəˌlɔɡ, ˈsaɪnəˌlɑɡ, -z

Sinology
BR sʌɪˈnɒlədʒi, sɪˈnɒlədʒi
AM saɪˈnɑlədʒi

Sinomania
BR ˌsʌɪnə(ʊ)ˈmeɪniə(r)
AM ˌsaɪnoʊˈmeɪniə

Sinophile
BR ˈsʌɪnəfʌɪl, -z
AM ˈsaɪnəˌfaɪl, -z

Sinophobe
BR ˈsʌɪnəfəʊb, -z
AM ˈsaɪnəˌfoʊb, -z

Sinophobia
BR ˌsʌɪnə(ʊ)ˈfəʊbɪə(r)
AM ˌsaɪnoʊˈfoʊbiə

sinopia
BR sɪˈnəʊpiə(r)
AM səˈnoʊpiə

Sino-Soviet
BR ˌsʌɪnəʊˈsəʊviət
AM ˌsaɪnoʊˈsoʊviət

Sino-Tibetan
BR ˌsʌɪnəʊtɪˈbetn, -z
AM ˌsaɪnoʊˌtəˈbetn, -z

sinter
BR ˈsɪntə(r), -z
AM ˈsɪn(t)ər, -z

Sintra
BR ˈsɪntrə(r)
AM ˈsɪntrə

sinuate
BR ˈsɪnjʊeɪt
AM ˈsɪnjəweɪt

sinuosity
BR ˌsɪnjʊˈɒsɪt|i, -ɪz
AM ˌsɪnjəˈwɑsədi, -z

sinuous
BR ˈsɪnjʊəs
AM ˈsɪnjəwəs

sinuously
BR ˈsɪnjʊəsli
AM ˈsɪnjəwəsli

sinuousness
BR ˈsɪnjʊəsnəs
AM ˈsɪnjəwəsnəs

sinus
BR ˈsʌɪnəs, -ɪz
AM ˈsaɪnəs, -əz

sinusitis
BR ˌsʌɪnəˈsʌɪtɪs
AM ˌsaɪnəˈsaɪdɪs

sinusoid
BR ˈsʌɪnəsɔɪd, -z
AM ˈsaɪnəˌsɔɪd, -z

sinusoidal
BR ˌsʌɪnəˈsɔɪdl
AM ˌsaɪnəˈsɔɪdəl

sinusoidally
BR ˌsʌɪnəˈsɔɪdļi
AM ˌsaɪnəˈsɔɪd(ə)li

Siobhan
BR ʃɪˈvɔːn
AM ʃəˈvɑːn

Sion
BR ˈsaɪən
AM ˈsaɪən

Sioned
BR ˈʃɒnɪd
AM ˈʃɑnəd

Siouan
BR ˈsuːən
AM ˈsuən

Sioux
BR suː
AM suː

sip
BR sɪp, -s, -ɪŋ, -t
AM sɪp, -s, -ɪŋ, -t

sipe
BR saɪp, -s, -ɪŋ, -t
AM saɪp, -s, -ɪŋ, -t

siphon
BR ˈsaɪfn̩, -nz,
-ŋɪŋ \-ənɪŋ, -nd
AM ˈsaɪfən, -ənz,
-(ə)nɪŋ, -ənd

siphonage
BR ˈsaɪfənɪdʒ,
ˈsaɪfn̩ɪdʒ
AM ˈsaɪfənɪdʒ

siphonal
BR ˈsaɪfənl̩, ˈsaɪfn̩l̩
AM ˈsaɪfənəl

siphonic
BR saɪˈfɒnɪk
AM saɪˈfɑnɪk

siphonophore
BR saɪˈfɒnə(ʊ)fɔ:(r), -z
AM saɪˈfɑnəfɔ(ə)r, -z

siphuncle
BR ˈsaɪˌfʌŋkl̩, -z
AM ˈsaɪˌfʌŋkəl, -z

sipper
BR ˈsɪpə(r), -z
AM ˈsɪpər, -z

sippet
BR ˈsɪpɪt, -s
AM ˈsɪpɪt, -s

sir[1]
strong form
BR sɜː(r), -z
AM sɜr, -z

sir[2]
weak form
BR sə(r)
AM sər

sircar
BR ˈsəːkɑː(r), -z
AM ˈsərˌkɑr, -z

sirdar
BR ˈsəːdɑː(r), -z
AM ˈsərˌdɑr, -z

sire
BR ˈsaɪə(r), -z, -ɪŋ, -d
AM ˈsaɪ(ə)r, -z, -ɪŋ, -d

siren
BR ˈsaɪrən, ˈsaɪrn̩, -z

AM ˈsaɪrən, -z

sirenian
BR saɪˈriːniən, -z
AM saɪˈriniən, -z

sirgang
BR ˈsəːgaŋ, -z
AM ˈsərˌgæŋ, -z

Sirhowy
BR səːˈhaʊi
AM sərˈhaʊi

Sirius
BR ˈsɪriəs
AM ˈsɪriəs

sirloin
BR ˈsəːlɔɪn, -z
AM ˈsərˌlɔɪn, -z

sirocco
BR sɪˈrɒkəʊ, -z
AM səˈrɑkoʊ, -z

sirrah
BR ˈsɪrə(r)
AM ˈsɪrə

sirree
BR səˈriː
AM səˈri

Sirte
BR ˈsəːti
AM ˈsərdi

sirup
BR ˈsɪrəp
AM ˈsɪrəp, ˈsərəp

sis
BR sɪs
AM sɪs

sisal
BR ˈsaɪsl̩, ˈsaɪzl̩
AM ˈsaɪsəl, ˈsaɪzəl

siskin
BR ˈsɪskɪn, -z
AM ˈsɪskɪn, -z

Sisley
BR ˈsɪzli
AM ˈsɪsli

Sissie
BR ˈsɪsi
AM ˈsɪsi

sissified
BR ˈsɪsɪfʌɪd
AM ˈsɪsəˌfaɪd

sissiness
BR ˈsɪsɪnɪs
AM ˈsɪsɪnɪs

Sissons
BR ˈsɪsnz
AM ˈsɪsənz

sissoo
BR ˈsɪsuː, -z
AM ˈsɪˌsu, -z

sissy
BR ˈsɪs|i, -iz
AM ˈsɪsi, -z

sissyish
BR ˈsɪsɪɪʃ
AM ˈsɪsɪɪʃ

sister
BR ˈsɪstə(r), -z
AM ˈsɪstər, -z

sisterhood
BR ˈsɪstəhʊd, -z
AM ˈsɪstər,(h)ʊd, -z

sister-in-law
BR ˈsɪst(ə)rɪnˌlɔː(r), -z
AM ˈsɪstərənˌlɔ,
ˈsɪstərənˌlɑ, -z

sisterless
BR ˈsɪstələs
AM ˈsɪstərləs

sisterliness
BR ˈsɪstəlɪnɪs
AM ˈsɪstərlɪnɪs

sisterly
BR ˈsɪstəli
AM ˈsɪstərli

sisters-in-law
BR ˈsɪstəzɪnˌlɔː(r)
AM ˈsɪstərzənˌlɔ,
ˈsɪstərzənˌlɑ

Sistine
BR ˈsɪstiːn
AM ˈsɪˌstin

sistra
BR ˈsɪstrə(r)
AM ˈsɪstrə

sistroid
BR ˈsɪstrɔɪd
AM ˈsɪstrɔɪd

sistrum
BR ˈsɪstrəm, -z
AM ˈsɪstrəm, -z

Sisyphean
BR ˌsɪsɪˈfiːən
AM ˌsɪsəˈfiən

Sisyphian
BR ˌsɪsɪˈfiːən
AM ˌsɪsəˈfiən

Sisyphus
BR ˈsɪsɪfəs
AM ˈsɪsɪfəs

sit
BR sɪt, -s, -ɪŋ
AM sɪt, -ts, -dɪŋ

Sita
BR ˈsiːtə(r)
AM ˈsidə

sitar
BR ˈsɪtɑː(r), sɪˈtɑː(r), -z
AM səˈtɑr, ˈsɪˌtɑr, -z

sitarist
BR ˈsɪtɑːrɪst, sɪˈtɑːrɪst,
-s
AM ˈsɪˌtɑrəst, səˈtɑrəst,
-s

sitatunga
BR ˌsɪtəˈtʊŋgə(r)
AM ˌsɪdəˈtʊŋgə

sitcom
BR ˈsɪtkɒm, -z
AM ˈsɪtˌkɑm, -z

sitdown
BR ˈsɪtdaʊn, ˌsɪtˈdaʊn,
-z
AM ˈsɪtˌdaʊn, -z

site
BR saɪt, -s, -ɪŋ, -ɪd

AM saɪt, -ts, -dɪŋ, -dɪd

sit-fast
BR ˈsɪtfɑːst, ˈsɪtfast, -s
AM ˈsɪtˌfæst, -s

sit-in
BR ˈsɪtɪn, -z
AM ˈsɪdˌɪn, -z

Sitka
BR ˈsɪtkə(r), -z
AM ˈsɪtkə, -z

sitophobia
BR ˌsaɪtəˈfəʊbiə(r)
AM ˌsaɪdəˈfoʊbiə,
ˌsaɪˌtoʊˈfoʊbiə

sitrep
BR ˈsɪtrɛp, -s
AM ˈsɪtˌrɛp, -s

sitringee
BR sɪˈtrɪn(d)ʒiː, -z
AM səˈtrɪngi, -z

sits vac
BR ˌsɪts ˈvak
AM ˌsɪts ˈvæk

Sittang
BR ˈsɪtaŋ
AM ˈsɪˌtæŋ

sitter
BR ˈsɪtə(r), -z
AM ˈsɪdər, -z

sitter-in
BR ˌsɪtərˈɪn
AM ˌsɪdərˈɪn

sitters-in
BR ˌsɪtəzˈɪn
AM ˌsɪdərzˈɪn

sitting
BR ˈsɪtɪŋ, -z
AM ˈsɪdɪŋ, -z

Sittingbourne
BR ˈsɪtɪŋbɔːn
AM ˈsɪdɪŋˌbɔ(ə)rn

Sitting Bull
BR ˌsɪtɪŋ ˈbʊl
AM ˌsɪdɪŋ ˈbʊl

situ
BR ˈsɪtjuː, ˈsɪtʃuː
AM ˈsɪˌt(j)u

situate[1]
adjective
BR ˈsɪtjʊət, ˈsɪtjʊeɪt,
ˈsɪtʃʊət, ˈsɪtʃʊeɪt
AM ˈsɪtʃəˌweɪt,
ˈsɪtʃəwət

situate[2]
verb
BR ˈsɪtjʊeɪt, ˈsɪtʃʊeɪt,
-s, -ɪŋ, -ɪd
AM ˈsɪtʃəˌweɪt, -ts,
-dɪŋ, -dɪd

situation
BR ˌsɪtjʊˈeɪʃn̩,
ˌsɪtʃʊˈeɪʃn̩, -z
AM ˌsɪtʃəˈweɪʃən, -z

situational
BR ˌsɪtjʊˈeɪʃn̩(ə)l,
ˌsɪtjʊˈeɪʃən(ə)l,
ˌsɪtʃʊˈeɪʃn̩(ə)l,
ˌsɪtʃʊˈeɪʃən(ə)l

situationally
AM ˌsɪtʃəˈweɪʃ(ə)nəl

situationally
BR ˌsɪtjʊˈeɪʃnəli,
ˌsɪtjʊˈeɪʃ(ə)nəli,
ˌsɪtʃʊˈeɪʃnəli,
ˌsɪtʃʊˈeɪʃ(ə)nəli
AM ˌsɪtʃəˈweɪʃ(ə)nəli

situationism
BR ˌsɪtjʊˈeɪʃnɪz(ə)m,
ˌsɪtjʊˈeɪʃənɪz(ə)m,
ˌsɪtʃʊˈeɪʃnɪz(ə)m,
ˌsɪtʃʊˈeɪʃənɪz(ə)m
AM ˌsɪtʃəˈweɪʃəˌnɪzəm

situationist
BR ˌsɪtjʊˈeɪʃnɪst,
ˌsɪtjʊˈeɪʃənɪst,
ˌsɪtʃʊˈeɪʃnɪst,
ˌsɪtʃʊˈeɪʃənɪst, -s
AM ˌsɪtʃəˈweɪʃənəst, -s

sit-up
BR ˈsɪtʌp, -s
AM ˈsɪdəp, -s

sit-upon
BR ˈsɪtəpɒn, -z
AM ˈsɪdəpɑn, -z

Sitwell
BR ˈsɪtw(ɛ)l
AM ˈsɪtˌwɛl

sitz
BR sɪts
AM sɪts

sitz-bath
BR ˈsɪtsˌbɑːθ, ˈsɪtsˌbæθ,
-bɑːðz \ -bɑːθs \ -baðs
AM ˈsɪtsˌbæθ, -s, -ðz

Sitzkrieg
BR ˈsɪtskriːg, -z
AM ˈsɪtsˌkrig, -z

sitzmark
BR ˈsɪtsmɑːk, -s
AM ˈsɪtsˌmɑrk, -s

Siva
BR ˈʃiːvə(r), ˈsiːvə(r)
AM ˈsivə, ˈʃivə

Sivaism
BR ˈʃiːvə(r)ɪz(ə)m,
ˈsiːvə(r)ɪz(ə)m
AM ˈsivəˌɪzəm,
ˈʃivəˌɪzəm

Sivaite
BR ˈʃiːvə(r)ʌɪt,
ˈsiːvə(r)ʌɪt, -s
AM ˈsivəˌaɪt, ˈʃivəˌaɪt,
-s

Sivan
BR ˈʃiːvn, ˈsiːvn
AM ˈsivən, ˈʃivən

Siwash
BR ˈsʌɪwɒʃ
AM ˈsaɪˌwɒʃ, ˈsaɪˌwɑʃ

six
BR sɪks, -ɪz
AM sɪks, -ɪz

sixain
BR ˈsɪkseɪn, -z
AM ˈsɪkˌseɪn, -z

sixer
BR ˈsɪksə(r), -z

sixfold
AM ˈsɪksər, -z

sixfold
BR ˈsɪksfəʊld
AM ˈsɪksˌfoʊld

six-footer
BR ˈsɪksˈfʊtə(r), -z
AM ˈsɪksˈfʊdər, -z

sixgun
BR ˈsɪksɡʌn, -z
AM ˈsɪksˌɡən, -z

sixpence
BR ˈsɪkspəns
AM ˈsɪksˌpens,
ˈsɪkspəns

sixpenny
BR ˈsɪkspəni
AM ˈsɪksˌpeni,
ˈsɪkspəni

six-shooter
BR ˈsɪkˌʃuːtə(r), -z
AM ˈsɪk(s)ˌʃudər, -z

sixte
BR sɪkst, -s
AM sɪkst, -s

sixteen
BR ˌsɪksˈtiːn
AM ˌsɪkˈstin

sixteenmo
BR ˌsɪksˈtiːnməʊ
AM ˌsɪksˈtinˌmoʊ

sixteenth
BR ˌsɪksˈtiːnθ, -s
AM ˌsɪkˈstinθ, -s

sixth
BR sɪksθ, -s
AM sɪksθ, -s

sixth-former
BR ˈsɪksθˌfɔːmə(r), -z
AM ˈsɪksθˌfɔrmər, -z

sixthly
BR ˈsɪksθli
AM ˈsɪksθli

sixtieth
BR ˈsɪkstɪɪθ, -s
AM ˈsɪkstiɪθ, -s

Sixtine
BR ˈsɪkstiːn, ˈsɪkstʌɪn
AM ˈsɪksˌtin

Sixtus
BR ˈsɪkstəs
AM ˈsɪkstəs

sixty
BR ˈsɪkst‖i, -ɪz
AM ˈsɪksti, -z

sixtyfold
BR ˈsɪkstɪfəʊld
AM ˈsɪkstiˌfoʊld

sixty-fourmo
BR ˌsɪkstiˈfɔːməʊ, -z
AM ˌsɪkstiˈfɔrˌmoʊ, -z

sizable
BR ˈsʌɪzəbl
AM ˈsaɪzəbəl

sizar
BR ˈsʌɪzə(r), -z
AM ˈsaɪzər, -z

sizarship
BR ˈsʌɪzəˌʃɪp, -s
AM ˈsaɪzərˌʃɪp, -s

size
BR sʌɪz, -ɪz, -ɪŋ, -d
AM saɪz, -ɪz, -ɪŋ, -d

sizeable
BR ˈsʌɪzəbl
AM ˈsaɪzəbəl

sizeably
BR ˈsʌɪzəbli
AM ˈsaɪzəbli

sizer
BR ˈsʌɪzə(r), -z
AM ˈsaɪzər, -z

Sizewell
BR ˈsʌɪzw(ɛ)l
AM ˈsaɪzˌwɛl

sizy
BR ˈsʌɪzi
AM ˈsaɪzi

sizzle
BR ˈsɪz‖l, -lz, -ˌlɪŋ \ -lɪŋ,
-ld
AM ˈsɪz‖əl, -əlz, -(ə)lɪŋ,
-əld

sizzler
BR ˈsɪzlə(r), ˈsɪzlə(r),
-z
AM ˈsɪz(ə)lər, -z

sjambok
BR ˈʃambɒk, -s, -ɪŋ, -t
AM ʃæmˈbɑk,
ˈʃæmˌbɑk, ˈʃæmbək,
-s, -ɪŋ, -t

ska
BR skɑː(r)
AM skɑ

Skagerrak
BR ˈskagərak
AM ˈskægəˌræk

Skagway
BR ˈskagweɪ
AM ˈskægˌweɪ

skald
BR skɔːld, skald, -z
AM skɔld, skɑld, -z

skaldic
BR ˈskɔːldɪk, ˈskaldɪk
AM ˈskɔldɪk, ˈskɑldɪk

Skanda
BR ˈskandə(r)
AM ˈskændə

Skara Brae
BR ˌskarəˈbreɪ
AM ˌskɛrəˈbreɪ

skarn
BR skɑːn
AM skɑrn

skat
BR skat
AM skæt

skate
BR skeɪt, -s, -ɪŋ, -ɪd
AM skeɪ‖t, -ts, -dɪŋ, -dɪd

skateboard
BR ˈskeɪtbɔːd, -z, -ɪŋ

skateboarder
AM ˈskeɪtˌbɔ(ə)rd, -z,
-ɪŋ

skateboarder
BR ˈskeɪtˌbɔːdə(r), -z
AM ˈskeɪtˌbɔrdər, -z

skatepark
BR ˈskeɪtpɑːk, -s
AM ˈskeɪtˌpɑrk, -s

skater
BR ˈskeɪtə(r), -z
AM ˈskeɪdər, -z

skating-rink
BR ˈskeɪtɪŋrɪŋk, -s
AM ˈskeɪdɪŋˌrɪŋk, -s

skean
BR ˈskiːən, skiːn, -z
AM ˈski(ə)n, -z

skean dhu
BR ˌskiː(ə)n ˈduː, -z
AM ˌski(ə)n ˈðu, -z

Skeat
BR skiːt
AM skit

sked
BR skɛd, -z, -ɪŋ, -ɪd
AM skɛd, -z, -ɪŋ, -əd

skedaddle
BR skɪˈdad‖l, -lz,
-ˌlɪŋ \ -lɪŋ, -ld
AM skəˈdædˌdəl, -əlz,
-(ə)lɪŋ, -əld

skeet
BR skiːt
AM skit

skeeter
BR ˈskiːtə(r), -z, -ɪŋ, -d
AM ˈskidər, -z, -ɪŋ, -d

Skeffington
BR ˈskɛfɪŋt(ə)n
AM ˈskɛfɪŋtən

skeg
BR skɛg, -z
AM skɛg, -z

Skegness
BR ˌskɛgˈnɛs
AM ˌskɛgˈnɛs

skein
BR skeɪn, -z
AM skeɪn, -z

skeletal
BR ˈskɛlɪtl, skɪˈliːtl
AM ˈskɛlədl

skeletally
BR ˈskɛlɪt‖li, ˈskɛlɪtəli,
skɪˈliːt‖li, skɪˈliːtəli
AM ˈskɛləd‖li

skeleton
BR ˈskɛlɪtn, -z
AM ˈskɛlətn, -z

skeletonise
BR ˈskɛlɪtnʌɪz,
ˈskɛlɪtənʌɪz, -ɪz, -ɪŋ, -d
AM ˈskɛlətnˌaɪz, -ɪz, -ɪŋ,
-d

skeletonize
BR ˈskɛlɪtnʌɪz,
ˈskɛlɪtənʌɪz, -ɪz, -ɪŋ, -d

AM 'skɛlətn̩ˌaɪz, -ɪz, -ɪŋ, -d

Skelmersdale
BR 'skɛlməzdeɪl
AM 'skɛlmərzˌdeɪl

Skelton
BR 'skɛlt(ə)n
AM 'skɛlt(ə)n

skep
BR skɛp, -s
AM skɛp, -s

skepsis
BR 'skɛpsɪs
AM 'skɛpsəs

skeptic
BR 'skɛptɪk
AM 'skɛptɪk

skeptical
BR 'skɛptɪkl
AM 'skɛptəkəl

skeptically
BR 'skɛptɪkli
AM 'skɛptək(ə)li

skepticism
BR 'skɛptɪsɪz(ə)m
AM 'skɛptəˌsɪzəm

skerrick
BR 'skɛrɪk, -s
AM 'skɛrɪk, -s

skerry
BR 'skɛr|i, -ɪz
AM 'skɛri, -z

sketch
BR skɛtʃ, -ɪz, -ɪŋ, -t
AM skɛtʃ, -əz, -ɪŋ, -t

sketchbook
BR 'skɛtʃbʊk, -s
AM 'skɛtʃˌbʊk, -s

sketcher
BR 'skɛtʃə(r), -z
AM 'skɛtʃər, -z

sketchily
BR 'skɛtʃɪli
AM 'skɛtʃəli

sketchiness
BR 'skɛtʃɪnɪs
AM 'skɛtʃɪnɪs

Sketchley
BR 'skɛtʃli
AM 'skɛtʃli

sketchpad
BR 'skɛtʃpad, -z
AM 'skɛtʃˌpæd, -z

sketchy
BR 'skɛtʃ|i, -ɪə(r), -ɪɪst
AM 'skɛtʃi, -ər, -ɪst

skeuomorph
BR 'skju:ə(ʊ)mɔːf, -s
AM 'skjuəˌmɔ(ə)rf, -s

skeuomorphic
BR ˌskju:ə'mɔːfɪk
AM ˌskjuə'mɔrfɪk

skew
BR skju:, -z, -ɪŋ, -d
AM skju:, -z, -ɪŋ, -d

skewback
BR 'skju:bak, -s

AM 'skju,bæk, -s

skewbald
BR 'skju:bɔːld, -z
AM 'sju,bold, 'sju,bald, -z

Skewen
BR 'skju:ɪn
AM 'skjuən

skewer
BR 'skju:ə(r), -z, -ɪŋ, -d
AM 'skju(w)ər, 'skjʊ(ə)r, -z, -ɪŋ, -d

skewness
BR 'skju:nəs
AM 'skjunəs

skew-whiff
BR ˌskju:'wɪf
AM ˌskju,wɪf

ski
BR ski:, -z, -ɪŋ, -d
AM ski, -z, -ɪŋ, -d

skiable
BR 'ski:əbl
AM 'skiəbəl

skiagram
BR 'skʌɪəgram, -z
AM 'skaɪəˌgræm, -z

skiagraph
BR 'skʌɪəgrɑːf, 'skʌɪəgraf, -s
AM 'skaɪəˌgræf, -s

skiagraphy
BR skʌɪ'agrəfi
AM skaɪ'agrəfi

skiamachy
BR skʌɪ'aməki
AM skaɪ'æməki

skibob
BR 'ski:bɒb, -z
AM 'ski,bab, -z

ski-bobber
BR 'ski:ˌbɒbə(r), -z
AM 'ski,babər, -z

skiboot
BR 'ski:bu:t, -s
AM 'ski,but, -s

skid
BR skɪd, -z, -ɪŋ, -ɪd
AM skɪd, -z, -ɪŋ, -ɪd

Skiddaw
BR 'skɪdɔː(r)
AM 'skɪdɔ, skə'dɔ, 'skɪdɑ, skə'dɑ

skiddoo
BR skɪ'du:, -z
AM skə'du, -z

skidlid
BR 'skɪdlɪd, -z
AM 'skɪd,lɪd, -z

skidmark
BR 'skɪdmɑːk, -s
AM 'skɪd,mɑrk, -s

skidoo
BR skɪ'du:, -z
AM skə'du, -z

skidpan
BR 'skɪdpan, -z

AM 'skɪd,pæn, -z

skidproof
BR 'skɪdpru:f
AM 'skɪd,pruf

skid row
BR ˌskɪd 'rəʊ
AM ˌskɪd ˌroʊ

skier
BR 'ski:ə(r), -z
AM 'skiər, -z

skiff
BR skɪf, -s
AM skɪf, -s

skiffle
BR 'skɪfl
AM 'skɪfəl

ski-jorer
BR 'ski:dʒɔːrə(r), ˌski:'dʒɔːrə(r), -z
AM 'ski,dʒɔrər, ˌski'dʒɔrər, -z

ski-joring
BR 'ski:dʒɔːrɪŋ, ˌski:'dʒɔːrɪŋ
AM 'ski,dʒɔrɪŋ, ˌski'dʒɔrɪŋ

ski-jump
BR 'ski:dʒʌmp, -s
AM 'ski,dʒəmp, -s

skilful
BR 'skɪlf(ʊ)l
AM 'skɪlfəl

skilfully
BR 'skɪlfʊli, 'skɪlfʃi
AM 'skɪlf(ə)li

skilfulness
BR 'skɪlf(ʊ)lnəs
AM 'skɪlfəlnəs

skilift
BR 'ski:lɪft, -s
AM 'ski,lɪft, -s

skill
BR skɪl, -z, -d
AM skɪl, -z, -d

skillet
BR 'skɪlɪt, -s
AM 'skɪlɪt, -s

skillful
BR 'skɪlf(ʊ)l
AM 'skɪlfəl

skillfully
BR 'skɪlfʊli, 'skɪlfʃi
AM 'skɪlfəli

skillfulness
BR 'skɪlf(ʊ)lnəs
AM 'skɪlfəlnəs

skill-less
BR 'skɪlls
AM 'skɪl(l)əs

skilly
BR 'skɪl|i, -ɪz
AM 'skɪli, -z

skim
BR skɪm, -z, -ɪŋ, -d
AM skɪm, -z, -ɪŋ, -d

skimmer
BR 'skɪmə(r), -z

AM 'skɪmər, -z

skimmia
BR 'skɪmɪə(r), -z
AM 'skɪmiə, -z

skimp
BR skɪm|p, -ps, -pɪŋ, -(p)t
AM skɪmp, -s, -ɪŋ, -t

skimpily
BR 'skɪmpɪli
AM 'skɪmpɪli

skimpiness
BR 'skɪmpɪnɪs
AM 'skɪmpɪnɪs

skimpy
BR 'skɪmp|i, -ɪə(r), -ɪɪst
AM 'skɪmpi, -ər, -ɪst

skin
BR skɪn, -z, -ɪŋ, -d
AM skɪn, -z, -ɪŋ, -d

skincare
BR 'skɪnkɛ:(r)
AM 'skɪn,kɛ(ə)r

skin-deep
BR ˌskɪn'di:p
AM ˌskɪn'dip

skin-dive
BR 'skɪndʌɪv, -z, -ɪŋ
AM 'skɪn,daɪv, -z, -ɪŋ

skinflick
BR 'skɪnflɪk, -s
AM 'skɪn,flɪk, -s

skinflint
BR 'skɪnflɪnt, -s
AM 'skɪn,flɪnt, -s

skinful
BR 'skɪnfʊl, -z
AM 'skɪn,fʊl, -z

skinhead
BR 'skɪnhɛd, -z
AM 'skɪn,(h)ɛd, -z

skink
BR skɪŋk, -s
AM skɪŋk, -s

skinless
BR 'skɪnlɪs
AM 'skɪnlɪs

skinlike
BR 'skɪnlʌɪk
AM 'skɪn,laɪk

skinner
BR 'skɪnə(r), -z
AM 'skɪnər, -z

Skinnerian
BR skɪ'nɪərɪən
AM skɪ'nɪrɪən

Skinnerism
BR 'skɪnərɪz(ə)m
AM 'skɪnə,rɪzəm

skinniness
BR 'skɪnɪnɪs
AM 'skɪnɪnɪs

skinny
BR 'skɪn|i, -ɪə(r), -ɪɪst
AM 'skɪni, -ər, -ɪst

skinny-dip
BR 'skɪnidɪp, -s, -ɪŋ, -t

skint
AM 'skɪnɪˌdɪp, -s, -ɪŋ, -t

skint
BR skɪnt
AM skɪnt

skintight
BR ˌskɪn'tʌɪt
AM ˌskɪn'taɪt

skip
BR skɪp, -s, -ɪŋ, -t
AM skɪp, -s, -ɪŋ, -t

skipjack
BR 'skɪpdʒak, -s
AM 'skɪpˌdʒæk, -s

ski-plane
BR 'skiːpleɪn, -z
AM 'skiˌpleɪn, -z

skipper
BR 'skɪp|ə(r), -əz,
-(ə)rɪŋ, -əd
AM 'skɪpər, -z, -ɪŋ, -d

skippet
BR 'skɪpɪt, -s
AM 'skɪpɪt, -s

skipping-rope
BR 'skɪpɪŋrəʊp, -s
AM 'skɪpɪŋˌroʊp, -s

Skipton
BR 'skɪpt(ə)n
AM 'skɪptən

skirl
BR skəːl, -z, -ɪŋ, -d
AM skɜrl, -z, -ɪŋ, -d

skirmish
BR 'skəːm|ɪʃ, -ɪʃɪz,
-ɪʃɪŋ, -ɪʃt
AM 'skɜrmɪʃ, -ɪz, -ɪŋ, -t

skirmisher
BR 'skəːmɪʃə(r), -z
AM 'skɜrmɪʃər, -z

skirr
BR skəː(r), -z, -ɪŋ, -d
AM skɜr, -z, -ɪŋ, -d

skirret
BR 'skɪrɪt, -s
AM 'skɜrət, -s

skirt
BR skəːt, -s, -ɪŋ, -ɪd
AM skɜr|t, -ts, -dɪŋ, -dəd

skirting
BR 'skəːtɪŋ, -z
AM 'skɜrdɪŋ, -z

skirtless
BR 'skəːtləs
AM 'skɜrtləs

skit
BR skɪt, -s
AM skɪt, -s

skite
BR skʌɪt, -s, -ɪŋ, -ɪd
AM skaɪ|t, -ts, -dɪŋ, -dɪd

skitter
BR 'skɪt|ə(r), -əz,
-(ə)rɪŋ, -əd
AM 'skɪdər, -z, -ɪŋ, -d

skittery
BR 'skɪt(ə)ri
AM 'skɪdəri

skittish
BR 'skɪtɪʃ
AM 'skɪdɪʃ

skittishly
BR 'skɪtɪʃli
AM 'skɪdɪʃli

skittishness
BR 'skɪtɪʃnɪs
AM 'skɪdɪʃnɪs

skittle
BR 'skɪt|l, -lz, -lɪŋ\-lɪŋ,
-ld
AM 'skɪdəl, -z, -ɪŋ, -d

skive
BR skʌɪv, -z, -ɪŋ, -d
AM skaɪv, -z, -ɪŋ, -d

skiver
BR 'skʌɪvə(r), -z
AM 'skaɪvər, -z

Skivvies
BR 'skɪvɪz
AM 'skɪviz

skivvy
BR 'skɪv|i, -ɪz, -ɪɪŋ, -ɪd
AM 'skɪvi, -z, -ɪŋ, -d

skiwear
BR 'skiːwɛː(r)
AM 'skiˌwɛ(ə)r

skoal
BR skəʊl
AM skoʊ(ə)l

Skoda®
BR 'skəʊdə(r), -z
AM 'skoʊdə, -z

Skokholm
BR 'skɒkhəʊm,
'skəʊkəm
AM 'skɑk,(h)oʊm,
'skoʊkəm

skol
BR skɒl, skəʊl
AM skoʊl

skookum
BR 'skuːkəm
AM 'skukəm

Skryabin
BR skrɪ'abɪn,
skrɪ'ɑːbɪn
AM skri'ɑbən
RUS 'skrʲab'in

skua
BR 'skjuːə(r), -z
AM 'skjuə, -z

Skues
BR skjuːz
AM skjuz

skulduggery
BR skʌl'dʌɡ(ə)ri
AM ˌskəl'dəɡ(ə)ri

skulk
BR skʌlk, -s, -ɪŋ, -t
AM skəlk, -s, -ɪŋ, -t

skulker
BR 'skʌlkə(r), -z
AM 'skəlkər, -z

skull
BR skʌl, -z

AM skəl, -z

skullcap
BR 'skʌlkap, -s
AM 'skəlˌkæp, -s

skullduggery
BR skʌl'dʌɡ(ə)ri
AM ˌskəl'dəɡ(ə)ri

skunk
BR skʌŋk, -s
AM skəŋk, -s

sky
BR skʌɪ, -z, -ɪŋ, -d
AM skaɪ, -z, -ɪŋ, -d

skycap
BR 'skʌɪkap, -s
AM 'skaɪˌkæp, -s

skydive
BR 'skʌɪdʌɪv
AM 'skaɪˌdaɪv

skydiver
BR 'skʌɪˌdʌɪvə(r), -z
AM 'skaɪˌdaɪvər, -z

skydiving
BR 'skʌɪˌdʌɪvɪŋ
AM 'skaɪˌdaɪvɪŋ

Skye
BR skʌɪ
AM skaɪ

skyer
BR 'skʌɪə(r), -z
AM 'skaɪər, -z

skyey
BR 'skʌɪi
AM 'skaɪi

sky-high
BR ˌskʌɪ'hʌɪ
AM ˌskaɪ'haɪ

skyhook
BR 'skʌɪhʊk, -s
AM 'skaɪˌhʊk, -s

skyjack
BR 'skʌɪdʒak, -s, -ɪŋ, -t
AM 'skaɪˌdʒæk, -s, -ɪŋ, -t

skyjacker
BR 'skʌɪdʒakə(r), -z
AM 'skaɪˌdʒækər, -z

Skylab
BR 'skʌɪlab
AM 'skaɪˌlæb

skylark
BR 'skʌɪlɑːk, -s, -ɪŋ, -t
AM 'skaɪˌlɑrk, -s, -ɪŋ, -t

skyless
BR 'skʌɪlɪs
AM 'skaɪləs

skylight
BR 'skʌɪlʌɪt, -s
AM 'skaɪˌlaɪt, -s

skyline
BR 'skʌɪlʌɪn, -z
AM 'skaɪˌlaɪn, -z

skyrocket
BR 'skʌɪˌrɒk|ɪt, -ɪts,
-ɪtɪŋ, -ɪtɪd
AM 'skaɪˌrɑkə|t, -ts,
-dɪŋ, -dɪd

skysail
BR 'skʌɪseɪl, -z
AM 'skaɪˌseɪl, -z

skyscape
BR 'skʌɪskeɪp, -s
AM 'skaɪˌskeɪp, -s

skyscraper
BR 'skʌɪˌskreɪpə(r), -z
AM 'skaɪˌskreɪpər, -z

skywalk
BR 'skʌɪwɔːk, -s, -ɪŋ, -t
AM 'skaɪˌwɔk,
'skaɪˌwɑk, -s, -ɪŋ, -t

skyward
BR 'skʌɪwəd, -z
AM 'skaɪwərd, -z

skywatch
BR 'skʌɪwɒtʃ, -ɪz
AM 'skaɪˌwɑtʃ, -əz

skyway
BR 'skʌɪweɪ, -z
AM 'skaɪˌweɪ, -z

skywriting
BR 'skʌɪˌrʌɪtɪŋ
AM 'skaɪˌraɪdɪŋ

slab
BR slab, -z
AM slæb, -z

slab-sided
BR ˌslab'sʌɪdɪd
AM 'slæb'saɪdɪd

slack
BR slak, -s, -ɪŋ, -t, -ɪst
AM slæk, -s, -ɪŋ, -t

slacken
BR 'slak|(ə)n, -(ə)nz,
-nɪŋ\-(ə)nɪŋ, -(ə)nd
AM 'slæk|ən, -ənz,
-(ə)nɪŋ, -ənd

slacker
BR 'slakə(r), -z
AM 'slækər, -z

slackly
BR 'slakli
AM 'slækli

slackness
BR 'slaknəs
AM 'slæknəs

Slade
BR sleɪd
AM sleɪd

slag
BR slag, -z
AM slæg, -z

slaggy
BR 'slag|i, -ɪə(r), -ɪɪst
AM 'slægi, -ər, -ɪst

slagheap
BR 'slaghiːp, -s
AM 'slæg,(h)ip, -s

slain
BR sleɪn
AM sleɪn

slàinte
BR 'slɑːn(d)ʒə(r),
'slɑːntʃə(r)
AM 'slɑn(d)ʒə

IR 'slɑːnˈtʲə

Slaithwaite
BR 'slaθweɪt, 'slaʊɪt
AM 'slæθˌweɪt

slake
BR sleɪk, -s, -ɪŋ, -t
AM sleɪk, -s, -ɪŋ, -t

slalom
BR 'slɑːləm, -z
AM 'slɑləm, -z

slam
BR slam, -z, -ɪŋ, -d
AM slæm, -z, -ɪŋ, -d

slambang
BR ˌslam'baŋ
AM 'slæm'bæŋg

slammer
BR 'slamə(r), -z
AM 'slæmər, -z

slander
BR 'slɑːndə(r),
'slandə(r), -əz,
-(ə)rɪŋ, -əd
AM 'slænd|ər, -ərz,
-(ə)rɪŋ, -ərd

slanderer
BR 'slɑːnd(ə)rə(r),
'sland(ə)rə(r), -z
AM 'slænd(ə)rər, -z

slanderous
BR 'slɑːnd(ə)rəs,
'sland(ə)rəs
AM 'slænd(ə)rəs

slanderously
BR 'slɑːnd(ə)rəsli,
'sland(ə)rəsli
AM 'slænd(ə)rəsli

slanderousness
BR 'slɑːnd(ə)rəsnəs,
'sland(ə)rəsnəs
AM 'slænd(ə)rəsnəs

slang
BR slaŋ, -z, -ɪŋ, -d
AM slæŋ, -z, -ɪŋ, -d

slangily
BR 'slaŋɪli
AM 'slæŋɡəli

slanginess
BR 'slaŋɪnɪs
AM 'slæŋɡinɪs

slangy
BR 'slaŋ|i, -ɪə(r), -ɪɪst
AM 'slæŋɡi, -ər, -ɪst

slant
BR slɑːnt, slant, -s, -ɪŋ, -ɪd
AM slæn|t, -ts, -(t)ɪŋ, -(t)əd

slantways
BR 'slɑːntweɪz, 'slantweɪz
AM 'slæntˌweɪz

slantwise
BR 'slɑːntwʌɪz, 'slantwʌɪz
AM 'slæntˌwaɪz

slap
BR slap, -s, -ɪŋ, -t

AM slæp, -s, -ɪŋ, -t

slap-bang
BR ˌslap'baŋ, 'slapbaŋ
AM 'slæpˌbæŋ

slapdash
BR 'slapdaʃ
AM 'slæpˌdæʃ

slaphappy
BR ˌslap'hapi
AM 'slæpˌ(h)æpi

slapjack
BR 'slapdʒak, -s
AM 'slæpˌdʒæk, -s

slapshot
BR 'slapʃɒt, -s
AM 'slæpˌʃɑt, -s

slapstick
BR 'slapstɪk
AM 'slæpˌstɪk

slap-up
BR ˌslapʌp, ˌslap'ʌp
AM 'slæpəp

slash
BR slaʃ, -ɪz, -ɪŋ, -t
AM slæʃ, -əz, -ɪŋ, -t

slash-and-burn
BR ˌslaʃ(ə)n(d)'bəːn
AM 'slæʃˌən'bərn

slasher
BR 'slaʃə(r), -z
AM 'slæʃər, -z

slat
BR slat, -s
AM slæt, -s

slate
BR sleɪt, -s, -ɪŋ, -ɪd
AM sleɪ|t, -ts, -dɪŋ, -dɪd

slater
BR 'sleɪtə(r), -z
AM 'sleɪdər, -z

slather
BR 'slaðə(r), -əz, -(ə)rɪŋ, -əd
AM 'slæð|ər, -ərz, -(ə)rɪŋ, -ərd

slating
BR 'sleɪtɪŋ, -z
AM 'sleɪdɪŋ, -z

slattern
BR 'slatn, 'slatəːn, -z
AM 'slædərn, -z

slatternliness
BR 'slatnlɪnɪs
AM 'slædərnlɪnɪs

slatternly
BR 'slatnli
AM 'slædərnli

Slattery
BR 'slat(ə)ri
AM 'slædəri

slaty
BR 'sleɪti
AM 'sleɪdi

slaughter
BR 'slɔːt|ə(r), -əz, -(ə)rɪŋ, -əd

AM 'slɔ|dər, 'slɑ|dər, -dərz, -ərɪŋ \ -trɪŋ, -dərd

slaughterer
BR 'slɔːt(ə)rə(r), -z
AM 'slɔdərər, 'slɑdərər, -z

slaughterhouse
BR 'slɔːtəhaʊ|s, -zɪz
AM 'slɔdər,(h)aʊ|s, 'slɑdər,(h)aʊ|s, -zəz

slaughterous
BR 'slɔːt(ə)rəs
AM 'slɔtərəs, 'slɑtərəs

Slav
BR slɑːv, -z
AM slɑv, -z

slave
BR sleɪv, -z, -ɪŋ, -d
AM sleɪv, -z, -ɪŋ, -d

slave-driver
BR 'sleɪvˌdrʌɪvə(r), -z
AM 'sleɪvˌdraɪvər, -z

slaveholder
BR 'sleɪvˌhəʊldə(r), -z
AM 'sleɪvˌ(h)oʊldər, -z

slaver[1]
noun, slave-trader
BR 'sleɪvə(r), -z
AM 'sleɪvər, -z

slaver[2]
verb, drool
BR 'slav|ə(r), 'sleɪv|ə(r), -əz, -(ə)rɪŋ, -əd
AM 'slæv|ər, 'sleɪvər, -ərz, -(ə)rɪŋ, -ərd

slavery
BR 'sleɪv(ə)ri
AM 'sleɪv(ə)ri

slavey
BR 'sleɪvi
AM 'sleɪvi

Slavic
BR 'slɑːvɪk
AM 'slavɪk

slavish
BR 'sleɪvɪʃ
AM 'sleɪvɪʃ

slavishly
BR 'sleɪvɪʃli
AM 'sleɪvɪʃli

slavishness
BR 'sleɪvɪʃnɪs
AM 'sleɪvɪʃnɪs

Slavism
BR 'slɑːvɪz(ə)m
AM 'slɑvɪzəm

Slavonia
BR slə'vəʊnɪə(r)
AM slə'voʊnɪə

Slavonian
BR slə'vəʊnɪən, -z
AM slə'voʊnɪən, -z

Slavonic
BR slə'vɒnɪk
AM slə'vɑnɪk

Slavophile
BR 'slɑːvəʊfʌɪl, -z
AM 'slavəˌfaɪl, -z

Slavophobe
BR 'slɑːvəʊfəʊb, -z
AM 'slavəˌfoʊb, -z

slaw
BR slɔː(r)
AM slɔ

slay
BR sleɪ, -z, -ɪŋ, -d
AM sleɪ, -z, -ɪŋ, -d

slayer
BR 'sleɪə(r), -z
AM 'sleɪər, -z

slaying
BR 'sleɪɪŋ, -z
AM 'sleɪɪŋ, -z

Slazenger
BR 'slaz(ɪ)n(d)ʒə(r)
AM 'sleɪzɪndʒər, 'sleɪzɪŋər

Sleaford
BR 'sliːfəd
AM 'slifərd

sleaze
BR sliːz
AM sliz

sleazily
BR 'sliːzɪli
AM 'slizɪli

sleaziness
BR 'sliːzɪnɪs
AM 'slizɪnɪs

sleazoid
BR 'sliːzɔɪd, -z
AM 'slizɔɪd, -z

sleazy
BR 'sliːz|i, -ɪə(r), -ɪɪst
AM 'slizi, -ər, -ɪst

sled
BR slɛd, -z, -ɪŋ, -ɪd
AM slɛd, -z, -ɪŋ, -ɪd

sledge
BR slɛdʒ, -ɪz, -ɪŋ, -d
AM slɛdʒ, -ɪz, -ɪŋ, -d

sledgehammer
BR 'slɛdʒˌhamə(r), -z
AM 'slɛdʒˌ(h)æmər, -z

sleek
BR sliːk, -ə(r), -ɪst
AM slik, -ər, -ɪst

sleekly
BR 'sliːkli
AM 'slikli

sleekness
BR 'sliːknɪs
AM 'sliknəs

sleeky
BR 'sliːki
AM 'sliki

sleep
BR sliːp, -s, -ɪŋ
AM slip, -s, -ɪŋ

Sleepeezee
BR ˌsliːp'iːzi, 'sliːpˌiːzi
AM 'slipˌizi

sleeper
BR ˈsliːpə(r), -z
AM ˈslipər, -z

sleepily
BR ˈsliːpɪli
AM ˈslipɪli

sleepiness
BR ˈsliːpɪnɪs
AM ˈslipɪnɪs

sleepless
BR ˈsliːplɪs
AM ˈsliplɪs

sleeplessly
BR ˈsliːplɪsli
AM ˈsliplɪsli

sleeplessness
BR ˈsliːplɪsnɪs
AM ˈsliplɪsnɪs

sleepwalk
BR ˈsliːpwɔːk, -s, -ɪŋ, -t
AM ˈslipˌwɔk,
ˈslipˌwɑk, -s, -ɪŋ, -t

sleepwalker
BR ˈsliːpˌwɔːkə(r), -z
AM ˈslipˌwɔkər,
ˈslipˌwɑkər, -z

sleepwalking
BR ˈsliːpˌwɔːkɪŋ
AM ˈslipˌwɔkɪŋ,
ˈslipˌwɑkɪŋ

sleepwear
BR ˈsliːpwɛː(r)
AM ˈslipˌwɛ(ə)r

sleepy
BR ˈsliːp|i, -iə(r), -ɪɪst
AM ˈslipi, -ər, -ɪst

sleepyhead
BR ˈsliːpɪhɛd, -z
AM ˈslipiˌhɛd, -z

sleet
BR sliːt, -s, -ɪŋ, -ɪd
AM slijt, -ts, -dɪŋ, -dɪd

sleetiness
BR ˈsliːtɪnɪs
AM ˈslidɪnɪs

sleety
BR ˈsliːti
AM ˈslidi

sleeve
BR sliːv, -z, -d
AM sliv, -z, -d

sleeveless
BR ˈsliːvlɪs
AM ˈslivlɪs

sleeving
BR ˈsliːvɪŋ, -z
AM ˈslivɪŋ, -z

sleigh
BR sleɪ, -z, -ɪŋ, -d
AM sleɪ, -z, -ɪŋ, -d

sleight
BR slaɪt
AM slaɪt

slender
BR ˈslɛnd|ə(r),
-(ə)rə(r), -(ə)rɪst
AM ˈslɛndər, -ər, -əst

slenderise
BR ˈslɛndərʌɪz, -ɪz, -ɪŋ,
-d
AM ˈslɛndəˌraɪz, -ɪz, -ɪŋ,
-d

slenderize
BR ˈslɛndərʌɪz, -ɪz, -ɪŋ,
-d
AM ˈslɛndəˌraɪz, -ɪz, -ɪŋ,
-d

slenderly
BR ˈslɛndəli
AM ˈslɛndərli

slenderness
BR ˈslɛndənəs
AM ˈslɛndərnəs

slept
BR slɛpt
AM slɛpt

Slessor
BR ˈslɛsə(r)
AM ˈslɛsər

sleuth
BR sl(j)uːθ, -s, -ɪŋ, -t
AM sluθ, -s, -ɪŋ, -t

sleuthhound
BR sl(j)uːθhaʊnd, -z
AM sluθ,(h)aʊnd, -z

slew
BR sluː, -z, -ɪŋ, -d
AM slu, -z, -ɪŋ, -d

sley
BR sleɪ, -z
AM sleɪ, -z

slice
BR slʌɪs, -ɪz, -ɪŋ, -t
AM slaɪs, -ɪz, -ɪŋ, -t

sliceable
BR ˈslʌɪsəbl
AM ˈslaɪsəbəl

slicer
BR ˈslʌɪsə(r), -z
AM ˈslaɪsər, -z

slick
BR slɪk, -s, -ɪŋ, -t, -ə(r),
-ɪst
AM slɪk, -s, -ɪŋ, -t, -ər,
-ɪst

slicker
BR ˈslɪkə(r), -z
AM ˈslɪkər, -z

slickly
BR ˈslɪkli
AM ˈslɪkli

slickness
BR ˈslɪknɪs
AM ˈslɪknəs

slid
BR slɪd
AM slɪd

slidable
BR ˈslʌɪdəbl
AM ˈslɪdəbəl

slidably
BR ˈslʌɪdəbli
AM ˈslɪdəbli

slide
BR slʌɪd, -z, -ɪŋ
AM slaɪd, -z, -ɪŋ

slider
BR ˈslʌɪdə(r), -z
AM ˈslaɪdər, -z

slideway
BR ˈslʌɪdweɪ, -z
AM ˈslaɪdˌweɪ, -z

slight
BR slʌɪt, -s, -ɪŋ, -ɪd,
-ə(r), -ɪst
AM slaɪ|t, -ts, -dɪŋ, -dɪd,
-dər, -dɪst, -tli, -tnɪs

slightingly
BR ˈslʌɪtɪŋli
AM ˈslaɪdɪŋli

slightish
BR ˈslʌɪtɪʃ
AM ˈslaɪdɪʃ

slightly
BR ˈslʌɪtli
AM ˈslaɪtli

slightness
BR ˈslʌɪtnɪs
AM ˈslaɪtnəs

Sligo
BR ˈslʌɪɡəʊ
AM ˈslaɪɡoʊ

slily
BR ˈslʌɪli
AM ˈslaɪli

slim
BR slɪm, -z, -ɪŋ, -d
AM slɪm, -z, -ɪŋ, -d

slime
BR slʌɪm
AM slaɪm

slimily
BR ˈslʌɪmɪli
AM ˈslaɪmɪli

sliminess
BR ˈslʌɪmɪnɪs
AM ˈslaɪmɪnɪs

slim-jim
BR ˌslɪmˈdʒɪm, -z
AM ˈslɪmˌdʒɪm, -z

slimline
BR ˈslɪmlʌɪn
AM ˈslɪmˌlaɪn

slimly
BR ˈslɪmli
AM ˈslɪmli

slimmer
BR ˈslɪmə(r), -z
AM ˈslɪmər, -z

slimmish
BR ˈslɪmɪʃ
AM ˈslɪmɪʃ

slimness
BR ˈslɪmnɪs
AM ˈslɪmnəs

slimy
BR ˈslʌɪm|i, -iə(r), -ɪɪst
AM ˈslaɪmi, -ər, -ɪst

sling
BR slɪŋ, -z, -ɪŋ

AM slɪŋ, -z, -ɪŋ

slingback
BR ˈslɪŋbak, -s
AM ˈslɪŋˌbæk, -s

slinger
BR ˈslɪŋə(r), -z
AM ˈslɪŋər, -z

slingshot
BR ˈslɪŋʃɒt, -s
AM ˈslɪŋˌʃɑt, -s

slink
BR slɪŋk, -s, -ɪŋ
AM slɪŋk, -s, -ɪŋ

slinkily
BR ˈslɪŋkɪli
AM ˈslɪŋkɪli

slinkiness
BR ˈslɪŋkɪnɪs
AM ˈslɪŋkɪnɪs

slinkweed
BR ˈslɪŋkwiːd
AM ˈslɪŋkˌwid

slinky
BR ˈslɪŋk|i, -iə(r), -ɪɪst
AM ˈslɪŋki, -ər, -ɪst

slip
BR slɪp, -s, -ɪŋ, -t
AM slɪp, -s, -ɪŋ, -t

slipcase
BR ˈslɪpkeɪs, -ɪz
AM ˈslɪpˌkeɪs, -ɪz

slipcover
BR ˈslɪpˌkʌvə(r), -z
AM ˈslɪpˌkəvər, -z

slipknot
BR ˈslɪpnɒt, -s
AM ˈslɪpˌnɑt, -s

slipover
BR ˈslɪpˌəʊvə(r), -z
AM ˈslɪpˌoʊvər, -z

slippage
BR ˈslɪp|ɪdʒ, -ɪdʒɪz
AM ˈslɪpɪdʒ, -ɪz

slipper
BR ˈslɪpə(r), -z
AM ˈslɪpər, -z

slipperily
BR ˈslɪp(ə)rɪli
AM ˈslɪp(ə)rəli

slipperiness
BR ˈslɪp(ə)rɪnɪs
AM ˈslɪp(ə)rɪnɪs

slipperwort
BR ˈslɪpəwəːt, -s
AM ˈslɪpərwərt,
ˈslɪpərwɔ(ə)rt, -s

slippery
BR ˈslɪp(ə)r|i, -iə(r),
-ɪɪst
AM ˈslɪp(ə)ri, -ər, -ɪst

slippiness
BR ˈslɪpɪnɪs
AM ˈslɪpɪnɪs

slippy
BR ˈslɪp|i, -iə(r), -ɪɪst
AM ˈslɪpi, -ər, -ɪst

slipshod
BR ˈslɪpʃɒd
AM ˈslɪpˌʃɑd

slipstitch
BR ˈslɪpstɪtʃ, -ɪz, -ɪŋ, -t
AM ˈslɪpˌstɪtʃ, -ɪz, -ɪŋ, -t

slipstream
BR ˈslɪpstriːm, -z, -ɪŋ, -d
AM ˈslɪpˌstrim, -z, -ɪŋ, -d

slip-ware
BR ˈslɪpwɛː(r), -z
AM ˈslɪpˌwɛ(ə)r, -z

slipway
BR ˈslɪpweɪ, -z
AM ˈslɪpˌweɪ, -z

slit
BR slɪt, -s, -ɪŋ, -ɪd
AM slɪ|t, -ts, -ɪŋ, -t

slither
BR ˈslɪð|ə(r), -əz, -(ə)rɪŋ, -əd
AM ˈslɪð|ər, -ərz, -(ə)rɪŋ, -ərd

slithery
BR ˈslɪð(ə)ri
AM ˈslɪð(ə)ri

slitter
BR ˈslɪtə(r), -z
AM ˈslɪdər, -z

slitty
BR ˈslɪt|i, -ɪə(r), -ɪɪst
AM ˈslɪdi, -ər, -ɪst

sliver
BR ˈslɪv|ə(r), ˈslʌɪv|ə(r), -əz, -(ə)rɪŋ, -əd
AM ˈslɪvər, ˈslaɪvər, -z, -ɪŋ, -d

slivovitz
BR ˈslɪvəvɪts
AM ˈslɪvəˌvɪts

Sloan
BR sləʊn
AM sloʊn

Sloane
BR sləʊn, -z
AM sloʊn, -z

Sloaney
BR ˈsləʊni
AM ˈsloʊni

slob
BR slɒb, -z
AM slɑb, -z

slobber
BR ˈslɒb|ə(r), -əz, -(ə)rɪŋ, -əd
AM ˈslɑbər, -ərz, -(ə)rɪŋ, -ərd

slobberiness
BR ˈslɒb(ə)rɪnɪs
AM ˈslɑb(ə)rɪnɪs

slobbery
BR ˈslɒb(ə)ri
AM ˈslɑb(ə)ri

slobbish
BR ˈslɒbɪʃ
AM ˈslɑbɪʃ

Slocombe
BR ˈsləʊkəm
AM ˈsloʊkəm

Slocum
BR ˈsləʊkəm
AM ˈsloʊkəm

sloe
BR sləʊ, -z
AM sloʊ, -z

sloe-eyed
BR ˌsləʊˈʌɪd
AM ˈsloʊˌaɪd

slog
BR slɒg, -z, -ɪŋ, -d
AM slɑg, -z, -ɪŋ, -d

slogan
BR ˈsləʊg(ə)n, -z
AM ˈsloʊgən, -z

slogger
BR ˈslɒgə(r), -z
AM ˈslɑgər, -z

sloid
BR slɔɪd, -z
AM slɔɪd, -z

Sloman
BR ˈsləʊmən
AM ˈsloʊmən

slo-mo
BR ˈsləʊməʊ
AM ˈsloʊˈmoʊ

sloop
BR sluːp, -s
AM slup, -s

sloosh
BR sluːʃ, -ɪz, -ɪŋ, -t
AM sluʃ, -əz, -ɪŋ, -t

sloot
BR sluːt, -s
AM slut, -s

slop
BR slɒp, -s, -ɪŋ, -t
AM slɑp, -s, -ɪŋ, -t

slope
BR sləʊp, -s, -ɪŋ, -t
AM sloʊp, -s, -ɪŋ, -t

slopewise
BR ˈsləʊpwʌɪz
AM ˈsloʊpˌwaɪz

sloppily
BR ˈslɒpɪli
AM ˈslɑpəli

sloppiness
BR ˈslɒpɪnɪs
AM ˈslɑpɪnɪs

sloppy
BR ˈslɒp|i, -ɪə(r), -ɪɪst
AM ˈslɑpi, -ər, -ɪst

slosh
BR slɒʃ, -ɪz, -ɪŋ, -t
AM slɑʃ, -ɪz, -ɪŋ, -t

sloshy
BR ˈslɒʃ|i, -ɪə(r), -ɪɪst
AM ˈslɑʃi, -ər, -ɪst

slot
BR slɒt, -s, -ɪŋ, -ɪd
AM slɑ|t, -ts, -dɪŋ, -dəd

slotback
BR ˈslɒtbak, -s
AM ˈslɑtˌbæk, -s

slot car
BR ˈslɒt kɑː(r), -z
AM ˈslɑt ˌkɑr, -z

sloth
BR sləʊθ, -s
AM slɔθ, slouθ, slɑθ, -s

slothful
BR ˈsləʊθf(ʊ)l
AM ˈslɔθfəl, ˈslouθfəl, ˈslɑθfəl

slothfully
BR ˈsləʊθfʊli, ˈsləʊθfʃi
AM ˈslɔθfəli, ˈslɑθfəl, ˈslouθfəl

slothfulness
BR ˈslɒθf(ʊ)lnəs
AM ˈslɔθfəlnəs, ˈslɑθfəlnəs, ˈslouθfəlnəs

slouch
BR slaʊtʃ, -ɪz, -ɪŋ, -t
AM slaʊtʃ, -ɪz, -ɪŋ, -t

slouchy
BR ˈslaʊtʃ|i, -ɪə(r), -ɪɪst
AM ˈslaʊtʃi, -ər, -ɪst

Slough
BR slaʊ
AM slaʊ

slough¹
noun, wet place
BR slaʊ, -z
AM slu, slaʊ, -z

slough²
verb, shed skin of snake etc
BR slʌf, -s, -ɪŋ, -t
AM sləf, -s, -ɪŋ, -t

sloughy
BR ˈslʌf|i, -ɪə(r), -ɪɪst
AM ˈsləfi, -ər, -ɪst

Slovak
BR ˈsləʊvak, -s
AM ˈsloʊˌvak, ˈsloʊˌvæk, -s

Slovakia
BR slə(ʊ)ˈvakɪə(r), slə(ʊ)ˈvɑːkɪə(r)
AM sloʊˈvakɪə

sloven
BR ˈslʌvn, -z
AM ˈsləvən, -z

Slovene
BR ˈsləʊviːn, -z
AM ˈsloʊˌvin, -z

Slovenia
BR slə(ʊ)ˈviːnɪə(r)
AM sloʊˈvinɪə

Slovenian
BR slə(ʊ)ˈviːnɪən, -z
AM sloʊˈvinɪən, -z

slovenliness
BR ˈslʌvnlɪnɪs
AM ˈsləvənlɪnɪs, ˈslavənlɪnɪs

slovenly
BR ˈslʌvnli
AM ˈsləvənli, ˈslavənli

slovenry
BR ˈslʌvnri
AM ˈsləvənri, ˈslavənri

slow
BR sləʊ, -z, -ɪŋ, -d, -ə(r), -ɪst
AM sloʊ, -z, -ɪŋ, -d, -ər, -əst

slowcoach
BR ˈsləʊkəʊtʃ, -ɪz
AM ˈsloʊˌkoʊtʃ, -ɪz

slowdown
BR ˈsləʊdaʊn, -z
AM ˈsloʊˌdaʊn, -z

slowish
BR ˈsləʊɪʃ
AM ˈsloʊɪʃ

slowly
BR ˈsləʊli
AM ˈsloʊli

slowness
BR ˈsləʊnəs
AM ˈsloʊnəs

slowpoke
BR ˈsləʊpəʊk, -s
AM ˈsloʊˌpoʊk, -s

slowworm
BR ˈsləʊwəːm, -z
AM ˈsloʊˌwɜrm, -z

slub
BR slʌb, -z, -ɪŋ, -d
AM sləb, -z, -ɪŋ, -d

sludge
BR slʌdʒ
AM slədʒ

sludgy
BR ˈslʌdʒi
AM ˈslədʒi

slue
BR sluː, -z, -ɪŋ, -d
AM slu, -z, -ɪŋ, -d

sluff
BR slʌf, -s, -ɪŋ, -t
AM sləf, -s, -ɪŋ, -t

slug
BR slʌg, -z, -ɪŋ, -d
AM sləg, -z, -ɪŋ, -d

slugabed
BR ˈslʌgəbɛd, -z
AM ˈsləgəˌbɛd, -z

slugfest
BR ˈslʌgfɛst, -s
AM ˈsləgˌfɛst, -s

sluggard
BR ˈslʌgəd, -z
AM ˈsləgərd, -z

sluggardliness
BR ˈslʌgədlɪnɪs
AM ˈsləgərdlɪnɪs

sluggardly
BR ˈslʌgədli
AM ˈsləgərdli

slugger
BR 'slʌɡə(r), -z
AM 'slʌɡər, -z

sluggish
BR 'slʌɡɪʃ
AM 'slʌɡɪʃ

sluggishly
BR 'slʌɡɪʃli
AM 'slʌɡɪʃli

sluggishness
BR 'slʌɡɪʃnɪs
AM 'slʌɡɪʃnɪs

sluice
BR sluːs, -ɪz, -ɪŋ, -t
AM slus, -ɪz, -ɪŋ, -t

sluicegate
BR 'sluːsɡeɪt, -s
AM 'slusɡeɪt, -s

sluiceway
BR 'sluːsweɪ, -z
AM 'slusweɪ, -z

sluit
BR 'sluːɪt, -s
AM 'sluɪt, -s

slum
BR slʌm, -z, -ɪŋ, -d
AM sləm, -z, -ɪŋ, -d

slumber
BR 'slʌmblə(r), -əz,
-(ə)rɪŋ, -əd
AM 'sləmblər, -ərz,
-(ə)rɪŋ, -ərd

slumberer
BR 'slʌmb(ə)rə(r), -z
AM 'sləmbərər, -z

slumberous
BR 'slʌmb(ə)rəs
AM 'sləmbərəs

slumbrous
BR 'slʌmbrəs
AM 'sləmbrəs

slumgullion
BR slʌm'ɡʌljən
AM 'sləm'ɡəliən,
'sləm'ɡəljən

slumlord
BR 'slʌmlɔːd, -z
AM 'sləm'lɔ(ə)rd, -z

slumminess
BR 'slʌmɪnɪs
AM 'sləmɪnɪs

slummock
BR 'slʌmək, -s
AM 'sləmək, -s

slummy
BR 'slʌm|i, -ɪə(r), -ɪɪst
AM 'sləmi, -ər, -ɪst

slump
BR slʌm|p, -ps, -pɪŋ,
-(p)t
AM sləmp, -s, -ɪŋ, -t

slung
BR slʌŋ
AM sləŋ

slunk
BR slʌŋk
AM sləŋk

slur
BR slə:(r), -z, -ɪŋ, -d
AM slər, -z, -ɪŋ, -d

slurp
BR slə:p, -s, -ɪŋ, -t
AM slərp, -s, -ɪŋ, -t

slurry
BR 'slʌri
AM 'sləri

slush
BR slʌʃ
AM sləʃ

slushiness
BR 'slʌʃɪnɪs
AM 'sləʃɪnɪs

slushy
BR 'slʌʃ|i, -ɪə(r), -ɪɪst
AM 'sləʃi, -ər, -ɪst

slut
BR slʌt, -s
AM slət, -s

sluttish
BR 'slʌtɪʃ
AM 'slətɪʃ

sluttishly
BR 'slʌtɪʃli
AM 'slətɪʃli

sluttishness
BR 'slʌtɪʃnɪs
AM 'slətɪʃnɪs

sly
BR slaɪ, -ə(r), -ɪst
AM slaɪ, -ər, -ɪst

slyboots
BR 'slaɪbuːts
AM 'slaɪ,buts

slyly
BR 'slaɪli
AM 'slaɪli

slyness
BR 'slaɪnɪs
AM 'slaɪnɪs

slype
BR slaɪp, -s
AM slaɪp, -s

smack
BR smak, -s, -ɪŋ, -t
AM smæk, -s, -ɪŋ, -t

smacker
BR 'smakə(r), -z
AM 'smækər, -z

smackeroo
BR ,smakə'ru:, -z
AM ,smækə'ru, -z

Smail
BR smeɪl
AM smeɪl

Smails
BR smeɪlz
AM smeɪlz

Smale
BR smeɪl
AM smeɪl

Smales
BR smeɪlz
AM smeɪlz

small[1]
BR smɔːl, -z, -ə(r), -ɪst
AM smɔl, smal, -z, -ər,
-əst

small[2]
BR smɔːl, -z, -ə(r), -ɪst
AM smɔl, -z, -ər, -əst

smallage
BR 'smɔːlɪdʒ
AM 'smɔlɪdʒ, 'smalɪdʒ

Smalley
BR 'smɔːli
AM 'smɔli, 'smali

smallgoods
BR 'smɔːlɡʊdz
AM 'smɔl,ɡʊdz,
'smal,ɡʊdz

smallholder
BR 'smɔːl,həʊldə(r), -z
AM 'smɔl,(h)oʊldər,
'smal,(h)oʊldər, -z

smallholding
BR 'smɔːl,həʊldɪŋ, -z
AM 'smɔl,(h)oʊldɪŋ,
'smal,(h)oʊldɪŋ, -z

smallish
BR 'smɔːlɪʃ
AM 'smɔlɪʃ, 'smalɪʃ

small-minded
BR ,smɔːl'maɪndɪd
AM 'smɔl'maɪn(d)ɪd,
'smal'maɪn(d)ɪd

small-mindedly
BR ,smɔːl'maɪndɪdli
AM 'smɔl'maɪn(d)ɪdli,
'smal'maɪn(d)ɪdli

small-mindedness
BR ,smɔːl'maɪndɪdnɪs
AM 'smɔl
'maɪn(d)ɪdnɪs,
'smal +

smallness
BR 'smɔːlnəs
AM 'smɔlnəs, 'smalnəs

Smallpiece
BR 'smɔːlpiːs
AM 'smɔl,pis, 'smal,pis

smallpox
BR 'smɔːlpɒks
AM 'smɔl,paks,
'smal,paks

smalltalk
BR 'smɔːltɔːk
AM 'smɔl,tɔk,
'smal,tak

smallwares
BR 'smɔːlweːz
AM 'smɔl,wɛ(ə)rz,
'smal,wɛ(ə)rz

Smallwood
BR 'smɔːlwʊd
AM 'smɔl,wʊd,
'smal,wʊd

smalt
BR smɔːlt, smɒlt
AM smɔlt, smalt

smarm
BR smɑːm, -z, -ɪŋ, -d
AM smɑrm, -z, -ɪŋ, -d

smarmily
BR 'smɑːmɪli
AM 'smɑrməli

smarminess
BR 'smɑːmɪnɪs
AM 'smɑrmɪnɪs

smarmy
BR 'smɑːm|i, -ɪə(r),
-ɪɪst
AM 'smɑrmi, -ər, -ɪst

smart
BR smɑːt, -s, -ɪŋ, -ɪd,
-ə(r), -ɪst
AM smɑr|t, -ts, -dɪŋ,
-dəd, -dər, -dəst, -tli,
-tnəs

smart alec
BR 'smɑːt ,alɪk, -s
AM 'smɑrd ,ælək, -s

smart aleck
BR 'smɑːt ,alɪk, -s
AM 'smɑrd ,ælək, -s

smart-alecky
BR 'smɑːt ,alɪki
AM 'smɑrd,æləki

smart alick
BR 'smɑːt ,alɪk, -s
AM 'smɑrd ,ælək, -s

smart-arse
BR 'smɑːtɑːs, -ɪz
AM 'smɑrd,æs,
'smɑrd,ɑrs, -ɪz

smart-ass
BR 'smɑːtɑːs, -ɪz
AM 'smɑrd,æs, -ɪz

smarten
BR 'smɑːt|n, -nz,
-nɪŋ \-nɪŋ, -nd
AM 'smɑrtən, -z, -ɪŋ, -d

Smartie
BR 'smɑːt|i, -ɪz
AM 'smɑrdi, -z

smartingly
BR 'smɑːtɪŋli
AM 'smɑrdɪŋli

smartish
BR 'smɑːtɪʃ
AM 'smɑrdɪʃ

smartly
BR 'smɑːtli
AM 'smɑrtli

smartness
BR 'smɑːtnəs
AM 'smɑrtnəs

smartweed
BR 'smɑːtwiːd
AM 'smɑrt,wid

smarty
BR 'smɑːt|i, -ɪz
AM 'smɑrdi, -z

smarty-boots
BR 'smɑːtibuːts
AM 'smɑrdi,buts

smarty-pants
BR 'smɑːtɪpants
AM 'smɑrdiˌpæn(t)s

smash
BR smaʃ, -ɪz, -ɪŋ, -t
AM smæʃ, -əz, -ɪŋ, -t

smash-and-grab
BR ˌsmaʃ(ə)n(d)'grab
AM ˌsmæʃən'græb

smasher
BR 'smaʃə(r), -z
AM 'smæʃər, -z

smashingly
BR 'smaʃɪŋli
AM 'smæʃɪŋli

smatter
BR 'smatə(r), -z
AM 'smædər, -z

smatterer
BR 'smat(ə)rə(r), -z
AM 'smædərər, -z

smattering
BR 'smat(ə)rɪŋ, -z
AM 'smædərɪŋ, -z

smear
BR smɪə(r), -z, -ɪŋ, -d
AM smɪ(ə)r, -z, -ɪŋ, -d

smearer
BR 'smɪərə(r), -z
AM 'smɪrər, -z

smeariness
BR 'smɪərɪnɪs
AM 'smɪrɪnɪs

smeary
BR 'smɪəri
AM 'smɪri

smectic
BR 'smɛktɪk, -s
AM 'smɛktɪk, -s

Smedley
BR 'smɛdli
AM 'smɛdli

smegma
BR 'smɛgmə(r)
AM 'smɛgmə

smegmatic
BR smɛg'matɪk
AM ˌsmɛg'mædɪk

smell
BR smɛl, -z, -ɪŋ
AM smɛl, -z, -ɪŋ

smellable
BR 'smɛləbl
AM 'smɛləbəl

smeller
BR 'smɛlə(r), -z
AM 'smɛlər, -z

smelliness
BR 'smɛlnɪs
AM 'smɛlnɪs

smell-less
BR 'smɛlləs
AM 'smɛl(l)ləs

smelly
BR 'smɛl|i, -ɪə(r), -ɪɪst
AM 'smɛli, -ər, -ɪst

smelt
BR smɛlt, -s, -ɪŋ, -ɪd
AM smɛlt, -s, -ɪŋ, -əd

smelter
BR 'smɛltə(r), -z
AM 'smɛltər, -z

smeltery
BR 'smɛlt(ə)r|i, -ɪz
AM 'smɛlt(ə)ri, -z

Smersh
BR sməːʃ
AM smərʃ

Smetana
BR 'smɛtənə(r),
  'smɛtnə(r)
AM 'smɛtnə

Smethurst
BR 'smɛθ(h)əːst
AM 'smɛθ,(h)ərst

Smethwick
BR 'smɛðɪk
AM 'smɛðɪk

smew
BR smjuː, -z
AM smju, -z

smidgen
BR 'smɪdʒ(ɪ)n, -z
AM 'smɪdʒɪn, -z

smidgeon
BR 'smɪdʒ(ɪ)n, -z
AM 'smɪdʒɪn, -z

smidgin
BR 'smɪdʒ(ɪ)n, -z
AM 'smɪdʒɪn, -z

Smike
BR smaɪk
AM smaɪk

smilax
BR 'smaɪlaks
AM 'smaɪˌlæks

smile
BR smaɪl, -z, -ɪŋ, -d
AM smaɪl, -z, -ɪŋ, -d

smileless
BR 'smaɪllɪs
AM 'smaɪ(l)ləs

smiler
BR 'smaɪlə(r), -z
AM 'smaɪlər, -z

Smiles
BR smaɪlz
AM smaɪlz

smiley
BR 'smaɪli
AM 'smaɪli

smilingly
BR 'smaɪlɪŋli
AM 'smaɪlɪŋli

Smily
BR 'smaɪli
AM 'smaɪli

smirch
BR sməːtʃ, -ɪz, -ɪŋ, -t
AM smərtʃ, -ɪz, -ɪŋ, -t

smirk
BR sməːk, -s, -ɪŋ, -t
AM smərk, -s, -ɪŋ, -t

smirker
BR 'sməːkə(r), -z
AM 'smərkər, -z

smirkily
BR 'sməːkɪli
AM 'smərkəli

smirkingly
BR 'sməːkɪŋli
AM 'smərkɪŋli

smirky
BR 'sməːki
AM 'smərki

smit
BR smɪt
AM smɪt

smite
BR smaɪt, -s, -ɪŋ
AM smaɪ|t, -ts, -dɪŋ

smiter
BR 'smaɪtə(r), -z
AM 'smaɪdər, -z

smith
BR smɪθ, -s
AM smɪθ, -s

smithereens
BR ˌsmɪðə'riːnz
AM ˌsmɪðə'rinz

Smithers
BR 'smɪðəz
AM 'smɪðərz

smithery
BR 'smɪθ(ə)r|i, -ɪz
AM 'smɪð(ə)ri, -z

Smithfield
BR 'smɪθfiːld
AM 'smɪθˌfild

Smithson
BR 'smɪθs(ə)n
AM 'smɪθsən

Smithsonian
BR smɪθ'səʊnɪən
AM ˌsmɪθ'soʊnɪən,
  ˌsmɪθ'soʊnɪən

smithy
BR 'smɪð|i, 'smɪθ|i, -ɪz
AM 'smɪθi, -z

smitten
BR 'smɪtn
AM 'smɪtn

smock
BR smɒk, -s, -ɪŋ, -t
AM smɑk, -s, -ɪŋ, -t

smog
BR smɒg
AM smɔg, smɑg

smoggy
BR 'smɒg|i, -ɪə(r), -ɪɪst
AM 'smɔgi, 'smɑgi, -ər,
  -ɪst

smokable
BR 'sməʊkəbl
AM 'smoʊkəbəl

smoke
BR sməʊk, -s, -ɪŋ, -t
AM smoʊk, -s, -ɪŋ, -t

smoke-free
BR ˌsməʊk'friː

smoke-ho
BR 'sməʊkhəʊ, -z
AM 'smoʊkˌ(h)oʊ, -z

smokehouse
BR 'sməʊkhaʊ|s, -zɪz
AM 'smoʊkˌ(h)aʊ|s,
  -zəz

smokeless
BR 'sməʊkləs
AM 'smoʊkləs

smoker
BR 'sməʊkə(r), -z
AM 'smoʊkər, -z

smokescreen
BR 'sməʊkskriːn, -z
AM 'smoʊkˌskrin, -z

smokestack
BR 'sməʊkstak, -s
AM 'smoʊkˌstæk, -s

smokily
BR 'sməʊkɪli
AM 'smoʊkəli

smokiness
BR 'sməʊkɪnɪs
AM 'smoʊkɪnɪs

smoko
BR 'sməʊkəʊ, -z
AM 'smoʊkoʊ, -z

smoky
BR 'sməʊk|i, -ɪə(r),
  -ɪɪst
AM 'smoʊki, -ər, -ɪst

smolder
BR 'sməʊldə(r), -əz,
  -(ə)rɪŋ, -əd
AM 'smoʊldər, -z, -ɪŋ, -d

smolderingly
BR 'sməʊld(ə)rɪŋli
AM 'smoʊld(ə)rɪŋli

smoleable
BR 'sməʊləbl
AM 'smoʊləbəl

Smolensk
BR smə(ʊ)'lɛnsk
AM smoʊ'lɛnsk

Smollett
BR 'smɒlɪt
AM 'smɑlət

smolt
BR sməʊlt, -s
AM smoʊlt, -s

smooch
BR smuːtʃ, -ɪz, -ɪŋ, -t
AM smutʃ, -ɪz, -ɪŋ, -t

smoocher
BR 'smuːtʃə(r), -z
AM 'smutʃər, -z

smoochy
BR 'smuːtʃi
AM 'smutʃi

smoodge
BR smuːdʒ, -ɪz, -ɪŋ, -d
AM smuːdʒ, -əz, -ɪŋ, -d

smooth
BR smuːð, -z, -ɪŋ, -d,
  -ə(r), -ɪst

AM smuð, -z, -ıŋ, -d, -ər, -əst

smoothable
BR 'smu:ðəbl
AM 'smuðəbəl

smooth-bore
BR 'smu:ð'bɔː(r), -z
AM 'smuð,bɔ(ə)r, -z

smoothe
BR smu:ð, -z, -ıŋ, -d
AM smuð, -z, -ıŋ, -d

smoother
BR 'smu:ðə(r), -z
AM 'smuðər, -z

smooth-faced
BR ,smu:ð'feıst
AM 'smuð,feıst

smoothie
BR 'smu:ð|i, -ız
AM 'smuði, -z

smoothish
BR 'smu:ðıʃ
AM 'smuðıʃ

smoothly
BR 'smu:ðli
AM 'smuðli

smoothness
BR 'smu:ðnəs
AM 'smuðnəs

smooth-talk
BR 'smu:ðtɔ:k, -s, -ıŋ, -t
AM 'smuð,tɔk, 'smuð,tak, -s, -ıŋ, -t

smooth-tongued
BR ,smu:ð'tʌŋd
AM 'smuð,təŋgd

smoothy
BR 'smu:ð|i, -ız
AM 'smuði, -z

smorgasbord
BR 'smɔ:gəsbɔːd, 'smɔːgəzbɔːd, -z
AM 'smɔrgəs,bɔ(ə)rd, -z

smorzando
BR smɔː'tsandəʊ, -z
AM smɔr'tsɑndoʊ, -z

smote
BR sməʊt
AM smoʊt

smother
BR 'smʌð|ə(r), -əz, -(ə)rıŋ, -əd
AM 'smʌð|ər, -ərz, -(ə)rıŋ, -ərd

smothery
BR 'smʌð(ə)ri
AM 'smʌðəri

smoulder
BR 'sməʊld|ə(r), -əz, -(ə)rıŋ, -əd
AM 'smoʊldər, -z, -ıŋ, -d

smoulderingly
BR 'sməʊld(ə)rıŋli
AM 'smoʊld(ə)rıŋli

smriti
BR 'smrıti

AM 'smrıdi

smudge
BR smʌdʒ, -ız, -ıŋ, -d
AM smədʒ, -ız, -ıŋ, -d

smudgeless
BR 'smʌdʒləs
AM 'smədʒləs

smudgepot
BR 'smʌdʒppt, -s
AM 'smədʒ,pɑt, -s

smudgily
BR 'smʌdʒıli
AM 'smədʒəli

smudginess
BR 'smʌdʒınıs
AM 'smədʒınıs

smudgy
BR 'smʌdʒ|i, -ıə(r), -ııst
AM 'smədʒi, -ər, -ııst

smug
BR smʌg
AM sməg

smuggle
BR 'smʌg|l, -lz, -lıŋ \ -lıŋ, -ld
AM 'sməg|əl, -əlz, -(ə)lıŋ, -əld

smuggler
BR 'smʌglə(r), 'smʌglə(r), -z
AM 'sməg(ə)lər, -z

smugly
BR smʌgli
AM sməgli

smugness
BR 'smʌgnəs
AM 'sməgnəs

smurf
BR smə:f, -s
AM smərf, -s

smut
BR smʌt, -s
AM smət, -s

Smuts
BR smʌts
AM sməts

smuttily
BR 'smʌtıli
AM 'smədəli

smuttiness
BR 'smʌtınıs
AM 'smədınıs

smutty
BR 'smʌt|i, -ıə(r), -ııst
AM 'smədi, -ər, -ııst

Smyrna
BR smə:nə(r)
AM 'smırnə

Smyth
BR smıθ, smʌıθ, smʌıð
AM smıθ

Smythe
BR smʌıð, smʌıθ
AM smaıθ, smaıð

snack
BR snak, -s, -ıŋ, -t

AM snæk, -s, -ıŋ, -t

Snaefell
BR ,sneı'fεl
AM 'sneı,fεl

snaffle
BR 'snafl, -lz, -lıŋ \ -lıŋ, -ld
AM 'snæf|əl, -əlz, -(ə)lıŋ, -əld

snafu
BR sna'fu:, -z, -ıŋ, -d
AM snæ'fu, -z, -ıŋ, -d

snag
BR snag, -z, -ıŋ, -d
AM snæg, -z, -ıŋ, -d

Snagge
BR snag
AM snæg

snaggletooth
BR 'snagltu:θ
AM 'snægəl,tuθ

snaggle-toothed
BR ,snagl'tu:θt
AM 'snægəl,tuθt

snaggy
BR 'snagi
AM 'snægi

snail
BR sneıl, -z
AM sneıl, -z

Snaith
BR sneıθ
AM sneıθ

snake
BR sneık, -s, -ıŋ, -t
AM sneık, -s, -ıŋ, -t

snakebite
BR 'sneıkbʌıt, -s
AM 'sneık,baıt, -s

snake-charmer
BR 'sneık,tʃɑ:mə(r), -z
AM 'sneık,tʃɑrmər, -z

snakelike
BR 'sneıklʌık
AM 'sneık,laık

snakeroot
BR 'sneıkru:t, -s
AM 'snæk,rut, -s

snakeskin
BR 'sneıkskın
AM 'sneık,skın

snakily
BR 'sneıkıli
AM 'sneıkıli

snakiness
BR 'sneıkınıs
AM 'sneıkınıs

snaky
BR 'sneıki
AM 'sneıki

snap
BR snap, -s, -ıŋ, -t
AM snæp, -s, -ıŋ, -t

snapdragon
BR 'snap,drag(ə)n, -z
AM 'snæp,drægən, -z

Snape
BR sneıp
AM sneıp

snappable
BR 'snapəbl
AM 'snæpəbəl

snapper
BR 'snapə(r), -z
AM 'snæpər, -z

snappily
BR 'snapıli
AM 'snæpəli

snappiness
BR 'snapınıs
AM 'snæpınıs

snappingly
BR 'snapıŋli
AM 'snæpıŋli

snappish
BR 'snapıʃ
AM 'snæpıʃ

snappishly
BR 'snapıʃli
AM 'snæpıʃli

snappishness
BR 'snapıʃnıs
AM 'snæpıʃnıs

snappy
BR 'snap|i, -ıə(r), -ııst
AM 'snæpi, -ər, -ııst

snapshot
BR 'snapʃpt, -s
AM 'snæp,ʃɑt, -s

snare
BR snεə(r), -z, -ıŋ, -d
AM snε(ə)r, -z, -ıŋ, -d

snarer
BR 'snεːrə(r), -z
AM 'snεrər, -z

snark
BR snɑ:k, -s
AM snɑrk, -s

snarl
BR snɑ:l, -z, -ıŋ, -d
AM snɑrl, -z, -ıŋ, -d

snarler
BR 'snɑ:lə(r), -z
AM 'snɑrlər, -z

snarlingly
BR 'snɑ:lıŋli
AM 'snɑrlıŋli

snarl-up
BR 'snɑ:lʌp, -s
AM 'snɑrl,əp, -s

snarly
BR 'snɑ:l|i, -ıə(r), -ııst
AM 'snɑrli, -ər, -ııst

snatch
BR snatʃ, -ız, -ıŋ, -t
AM snætʃ, -əz, -ıŋ, -t

snatcher
BR 'snatʃə(r), -z
AM 'snætʃər, -z

snatchily
BR 'snatʃıli
AM 'snætʃəli

snatchy
BR ˈsnætʃ|i, -ɪə(r), -ɪɪst
AM ˈsnætʃi, -ər, -ɪst

snavel
BR ˈsnav|l, -lz,
-|ɪŋ\-|ɪŋ, -ld
AM ˈsnævəl, -z, -ɪŋ, -d

snazzily
BR ˈsnazɪli
AM ˈsnæzəli

snazziness
BR ˈsnazɪnɪs
AM ˈsnæzinɪs

snazzy
BR ˈsnaz|i, -ɪə(r), -ɪɪst
AM ˈsnæzi, -ər, -ɪst

sneak
BR sniːk, -s, -ɪŋ, -t
AM snik, -s, -ɪŋ, -t

sneaker
BR ˈsniːkə(r), -z
AM ˈsnikər, -z

sneakily
BR ˈsniːkɪli
AM ˈsnikəli

sneakiness
BR ˈsniːkɪnɪs
AM ˈsnikinɪs

sneakingly
BR ˈsniːkɪŋli
AM ˈsnikɪŋli

sneak-thief
BR ˈsniːkθiːf
AM ˈsnikˌθif

sneak-thieves
BR ˈsniːkθiːvz
AM ˈsnikˌθivz

sneaky
BR ˈsniːk|i, -ɪə(r), -ɪɪst
AM ˈsniki, -ər, -ɪst

sneck
BR snɛk, -s, -ɪŋ, -t
AM snɛk, -s, -ɪŋ, -t

Sneddon
BR ˈsnɛdn
AM ˈsnɛdn

Sneek
BR sniːk
AM snik

sneer
BR snɪə(r), -z, -ɪŋ, -d
AM snɪ(ə)r, -z, -ɪŋ, -d

sneerer
BR ˈsnɪərə(r), -z
AM ˈsnɪrər, -z

sneeringly
BR ˈsnɪərɪŋli
AM ˈsnɪrɪŋli

sneeze
BR sniːz, -ɪz, -ɪŋ, -d
AM sniz, -ɪz, -ɪŋ, -d

sneezer
BR ˈsniːzə(r), -z
AM ˈsnizər, -z

sneezeweed
BR ˈsniːzwiːd, -z
AM ˈsnizˌwid, -z

sneezewort
BR ˈsniːzwɜːt
AM ˈsnizwɜrt,
ˈsnizcwə(r)t

sneezy
BR ˈsniːzi
AM ˈsnizi

Snelgrove
BR ˈsnɛlgrəuv
AM ˈsnɛlˌgrouv

Snell
BR snɛl
AM snɛl

Snellgrove
BR ˈsnɛlgrəuv
AM ˈsnɛlˌgrouv

snib
BR snɪb, -z, -ɪŋ, -d
AM snɪb, -z, -ɪŋ, -d

snick
BR snɪk, -s, -ɪŋ, -t
AM snɪk, -s, -ɪŋ, -t

snicker
BR ˈsnɪk|ə(r), -əz,
-(ə)rɪŋ, -əd
AM ˈsnɪk|ər, -ərz,
-(ə)rɪŋ, -ərd

snickeringly
BR ˈsnɪk(ə)rɪŋli
AM ˈsnɪk(ə)rɪŋli

Snickers®
BR ˈsnɪkəz
AM ˈsnɪkərz

snicket
BR ˈsnɪkɪt, -s
AM ˈsnɪkɪt, -s

snide
BR snʌɪd
AM snaɪd

snidely
BR snʌɪdli
AM snaɪdli

snideness
BR snʌɪdnɪs
AM snaɪdnɪs

Snider
BR ˈsnʌɪdə(r)
AM ˈsnaɪdər

sniff
BR snɪf, -s, -ɪŋ, -t
AM snɪf, -s, -ɪŋ, -t

sniffable
BR ˈsnɪfəbl
AM ˈsnɪfəbəl

sniffer
BR ˈsnɪfə(r), -z
AM ˈsnɪfər, -z

sniffily
BR ˈsnɪfɪli
AM ˈsnɪfəli

sniffiness
BR ˈsnɪfɪnɪs
AM ˈsnɪfinɪs

sniffingly
BR ˈsnɪfɪŋli
AM ˈsnɪfɪŋli

sniffle
BR ˈsnɪf|l, -lz, -ˌlɪŋ\-ˌlɪŋ,
-ld
AM ˈsnɪf|əl, -əlz, -(ə)lɪŋ,
-əld

sniffler
BR ˈsnɪflə(r),
ˈsnɪfl|ə(r), -z
AM ˈsnɪf(ə)lər, -z

sniffly
BR ˈsnɪfli, ˈsnɪfl̩i
AM ˈsnɪf(ə)li

sniffy
BR ˈsnɪf|i, -ɪə(r), -ɪɪst
AM ˈsnɪfi, -ər, -ɪst

snifter
BR ˈsnɪftə(r), -z
AM ˈsnɪftər, -z

snig
BR snɪg, -z, -ɪŋ, -d
AM snɪg, -z, -ɪŋ, -d

snigger
BR ˈsnɪg|ə(r), -əz,
-(ə)rɪŋ, -əd
AM ˈsnɪg|ər, -ərz,
-(ə)rɪŋ, -ərd

sniggerer
BR ˈsnɪg(ə)rə(r), -z
AM ˈsnɪg(ə)rər, -z

sniggeringly
BR ˈsnɪg(ə)rɪŋli
AM ˈsnɪg(ə)rɪŋli

sniggle
BR ˈsnɪg|l, -lz, -ˌlɪŋ\-ˌlɪŋ,
-ld
AM ˈsnɪg|əl, -əlz,
-(ə)lɪŋ, -əld

snip
BR snɪp, -s, -ɪŋ, -t
AM snɪp, -s, -ɪŋ, -t

snipe
BR snʌɪp, -s, -ɪŋ, -t
AM snaɪp, -s, -ɪŋ, -t

sniper
BR ˈsnʌɪpə(r), -z
AM ˈsnaɪpər, -z

snipper
BR ˈsnɪpə(r), -z
AM ˈsnɪpər, -z

snippet
BR ˈsnɪpɪt, -s
AM ˈsnɪpɪt, -s

snippety
BR ˈsnɪpɪti
AM ˈsnɪpɪdi

snippily
BR ˈsnɪpɪli
AM ˈsnɪpəli

snippiness
BR ˈsnɪpɪnɪs
AM ˈsnɪpɪnɪs

snipping
BR ˈsnɪpɪŋ, -z
AM ˈsnɪpɪŋ, -z

snippy
BR ˈsnɪp|i, -ɪə(r), -ɪɪst
AM ˈsnɪpi, -ər, -ɪst

snit
BR snɪt, -s
AM snɪt, -s

snitch
BR snɪtʃ, -ɪz, -ɪŋ, -t
AM snɪtʃ, -ɪz, -ɪŋ, -t

snitcher
BR ˈsnɪtʃə(r), -z
AM ˈsnɪtʃər, -z

snivel
BR ˈsnɪv|l, -lz,
-ˌlɪŋ\-(ə)lɪŋ, -ld
AM ˈsnɪv|əl, -əlz,
-(ə)lɪŋ, -əld

sniveller
BR ˈsnɪvlə(r),
ˈsnɪv(ə)lə(r), -z
AM ˈsnɪv(ə)lər, -z

snivellingly
BR ˈsnɪvlɪŋli,
ˈsnɪv(ə)lɪŋli
AM ˈsnɪv(ə)lɪŋli

snob
BR snɒb, -z
AM snɑb, -z

snobbery
BR ˈsnɒb(ə)ri
AM ˈsnɑb(ə)ri

snobbish
BR ˈsnɒbɪʃ
AM ˈsnɑbɪʃ

snobbishly
BR ˈsnɒbɪʃli
AM ˈsnɑbɪʃli

snobbishness
BR ˈsnɒbɪʃnɪs
AM ˈsnɑbɪʃnɪs

snobby
BR ˈsnɒb|i, -ɪə(r), -ɪɪst
AM ˈsnɑbi, -ər, -ɪst

SNOBOL
BR ˈsnəubɒl
AM ˈsnouˌbɑl,
ˈsnouˌbɑl

Sno-Cat®
BR ˈsnəukat, -s
AM ˈsnouˌkæt, -s

Snodgrass
BR ˈsnɒdgrɑːs,
ˈsnɒdgras
AM ˈsnɑdˌgræs

snoek
BR snuːk
AM snuk

snog
BR snɒg, -z, -ɪŋ, -d
AM snɑg, -z, -ɪŋ, -d

snood
BR snuːd, -z
AM snud, -z

snook
BR snuːk, -s
AM snuk, snʊk, -s

snooker
BR ˈsnuːk|ə(r), -əz,
-(ə)rɪŋ, -əd
AM ˈsnʊkər, -z, -ɪŋ, -d

snoop
BR snu:p, -s, -ɪŋ, -t
AM snup, -s, -ɪŋ, -t

snooper
BR 'snu:pə(r), -z
AM 'snupər, -z

snooperscope
BR 'snu:pəskəʊp, -s
AM 'snupər,skoʊp, -s

snoopy
BR 'snu:pi
AM 'snupi

snoot
BR snu:t, -s
AM snut, -s

snootily
BR 'snu:tɪli
AM 'snudəli

snootiness
BR 'snu:tɪnɪs
AM 'snudɪnɪs

snooty
BR 'snu:t|i, -ɪə(r), -ɪɪst
AM 'snudi, -ər, -ɪst

snooze
BR snu:z, -ɪz, -ɪŋ, -d
AM snuz, -ɪz, -ɪŋ, -d

snoozer
BR 'snu:zə(r), -z
AM 'snuzər, -z

snoozy
BR 'snu:z|i, -ɪə(r), -ɪɪst
AM 'snuzi, -ər, -ɪst

snore
BR snɔ:(r), -z, -ɪŋ, -d
AM snɔ:(ə)r, -z, -ɪŋ, -d

snorer
BR 'snɔ:rə(r), -z
AM 'snɔrər, -z

snoringly
BR 'snɔ:rɪŋli
AM 'snɔrɪŋli

snorkel
BR 'snɔ:k|l, -lz,
-l|ŋ\-lŋ, -ld
AM 'snɔrk|əl, -əlz,
-(ə)lŋ, -əld

snorkeler
BR 'snɔ:klə(r),
'snɔ:klə(r), -z
AM 'snɔrk(ə)lər, -z

snorkeller
BR 'snɔ:klə(r),
'snɔ:klə(r), -z
AM 'snɔrk(ə)lər, -z

Snorri
BR 'snɒri
AM 'snɔri

snort
BR snɔ:t, -s, -ɪŋ, -ɪd
AM snɔ:(ə)rt, -ts,
'snɔrdɪŋ, 'snɔrdəd

snorter
BR 'snɔ:tə(r), -z
AM 'snɔrdər, -z

snot
BR snɒt

AM snɑt

snottily
BR 'snɒtɪli
AM 'snɑdəli

snottiness
BR 'snɒtɪnɪs
AM 'snɑdɪnɪs

snotty
BR 'snɒt|i, -ɪə(r), -ɪɪst
AM 'snɑdi, -ər, -ɪst

snotty-nosed
BR ,snɒtɪ'nəʊzd
AM 'snɑdɪ'noʊzd

snout
BR snaʊt, -s, -ɪd
AM snaʊ|t, -ts, -dəd

snoutlike
BR 'snaʊtlaɪk
AM 'snaʊt,laɪk

snouty
BR 'snaʊti
AM 'snaʊdi

snow
BR snəʊ, -z, -ɪŋ, -d
AM snoʊ, -z, -ɪŋ, -d

snowball
BR 'snəʊbɔ:l, -z, -ɪŋ, -d
AM 'snoʊ,bɔl,
'snoʊ,bal, -z, -ɪŋ, -d

snowbank
BR 'snəʊbaŋk, -s
AM 'snoʊ,baŋk, -s

snowbelt
BR 'snəʊbelt
AM 'snoʊ,belt

snowberry
BR 'snəʊb(ə)r|i,
'snəʊ,ber|i, -ɪz
AM 'snoʊ,beri, -z

snowbird
BR 'snəʊbɜ:d, -z
AM 'snoʊ,bɜrd, -z

snowblind
BR 'snəʊblaɪnd
AM 'snoʊ,blaɪnd

snow-blindness
BR 'snəʊ,blaɪn(d)nɪs
AM 'snoʊ,blaɪn(d)nɪs

snowblower
BR 'snəʊ,bləʊə(r), -z
AM 'snoʊ,bloʊər, -z

snowboard
BR 'snəʊbɔ:d, -z
AM 'snoʊ,bɔ(ə)rd, -z

snowboarder
BR 'snəʊbɔ:də(r), -z
AM 'snoʊ,bɔrdər, -z

snowboarding
BR 'snəʊbɔ:dɪŋ
AM 'snoʊ,bɔrdɪŋ

snowboot
BR 'snəʊbu:t, -s
AM 'snoʊ,but, -s

snowbound
BR 'snəʊbaʊnd
AM 'snoʊ,baʊnd

snow-broth
BR 'snəʊbrɒθ
AM 'snoʊ,brɔθ,
'snoʊ,brɑθ

snowcap
BR 'snəʊkap, -s
AM 'snoʊ,kæp, -s

snow-capped
BR 'snəʊkapt
AM 'snoʊ,kæpt

Snowcem®
BR 'snəʊsem
AM 'snoʊsəm

snowclad
BR 'snəʊklad
AM 'snoʊ,klæd

snowcone
BR 'snəʊkəʊn, -z
AM 'snoʊ,koʊn, -z

Snowden
BR 'snəʊdn
AM 'snoʊdn

Snowdon
BR 'snəʊdn
AM 'snoʊdn

Snowdonia
BR snə(ʊ)'dəʊnɪə(r)
AM snoʊ'doʊnɪə,
snoʊ'doʊnjə

snowdrift
BR 'snəʊdrɪft, -s
AM 'snoʊ,drɪft, -s

snowdrop
BR 'snəʊdrɒp, -s
AM 'snoʊ,drɑp, -s

snowfall
BR 'snəʊfɔ:l, -z
AM 'snoʊ,fɔl, 'snoʊ,fal,
-z

snowfield
BR 'snəʊfi:ld, -z
AM 'snoʊ,fild, -z

snowflake
BR 'snəʊfleɪk, -s
AM 'snoʊ,fleɪk, -s

snowily
BR 'snəʊɪli
AM 'snoʊəli

snowiness
BR 'snəʊɪnɪs
AM 'snoʊɪnɪs

snowless
BR 'snəʊləs
AM 'snoʊləs

snowlike
BR 'snəʊlaɪk
AM 'snoʊ,laɪk

snowline
BR 'snəʊlaɪn, -z
AM 'snoʊ,laɪn, -z

snowmaking
BR 'snəʊ,meɪkɪŋ
AM 'snoʊ,meɪkɪŋ

snowman
BR 'snəʊman
AM 'snoʊ,mæn

snowmen
BR 'snəʊmen
AM 'snoʊ,men

snowmobile
BR 'snəʊmə(ʊ)bi:l, -z
AM 'snoʊmə,bil,
'snoʊmoʊ,bil, -z

snowplough
BR 'snəʊplaʊ, -z
AM 'snoʊ,plaʊ, -z

snowplow
BR 'snəʊplaʊ, -z
AM 'snoʊ,plaʊ, -z

snowscape
BR 'snəʊskeɪp, -s
AM 'snoʊ,skeɪp, -s

snowshoe
BR 'snəʊʃu:, -z
AM 'snoʊ,ʃu, -z

snowshoer
BR 'snəʊ,ʃu:ə(r), -z
AM 'snoʊ,ʃuər, -z

snowstorm
BR 'snəʊstɔ:m, -z
AM 'snoʊ,stɔ(ə)rm, -z

snowsuit
BR 'snəʊs(j)u:t, -s
AM 'snoʊ,s(j)ut, -s

Snow-white
BR ,snəʊ'wʌɪt
AM ,snoʊ'(h)waɪt

snowy
BR 'snəʊi
AM 'snoʊi

snub
BR snʌb, -z, -ɪŋ, -d
AM snəb, -z, -ɪŋ, -d

snubber
BR 'snʌbə(r), -z
AM 'snəbər, -z

snubbingly
BR 'snʌbɪŋli
AM 'snəbɪŋli

snub-nosed
BR ,snʌb'nəʊzd
AM ,snəb'noʊzd

snuck
BR snʌk
AM snək

snuff
BR snʌf, -s, -ɪŋ, -t
AM snəf, -s, -ɪŋ, -t

snuffbox
BR 'snʌfbɒks, -ɪz
AM 'snəf,baks, -əz

snuffer
BR 'snʌfə(r), -z
AM 'snəfər, -z

snuffle
BR 'snʌf|l, -lz, -lɪŋ\-lɪŋ,
-ld
AM 'snəf|əl, -əlz, -(ə)lɪŋ,
-əld

snuffler
BR 'snʌflə(r),
'snʌflə(r), -z
AM 'snəf(ə)lər, -z

snuffly
BR ˈsnʌfli, ˈsnʌfli
AM ˈsnəf(ə)li

snuffy
BR ˈsnʌfi
AM ˈsnəfi

snug
BR snʌg, -z, -ə(r), -ɪst
AM snəg, -z, -ər, -əst

snuggery
BR ˈsnʌg(ə)r|i, -iz
AM ˈsnəg(ə)ri, -z

snuggle
BR ˈsnʌg|l̩, -lz
-lɪŋ\-lɪŋ, -ld
AM ˈsnəg|əl, -əlz,
-(ə)lɪŋ, -əld

snuggly
BR ˈsnʌgli, ˈsnʌgli
AM ˈsnəgli

snugly
BR ˈsnʌgli
AM ˈsnəgli

snugness
BR ˈsnʌgnəs
AM ˈsnəgnəs

Snyder
BR ˈsnʌɪdə(r)
AM ˈsnaɪdər

so
BR səʊ
AM soʊ

soak
BR səʊk, -s, -ɪŋ, -t
AM soʊk, -s, -ɪŋ, -t

soakage
BR ˈsəʊkɪdʒ
AM ˈsoʊkɪdʒ

soakaway
BR ˈsəʊkəweɪ, -z
AM ˈsoʊkəˌweɪ, -z

soaker
BR ˈsəʊkə(r), -z
AM ˈsoʊkər, -z

soaking
BR ˈsəʊkɪŋ, -z
AM ˈsoʊkɪŋ, -z

Soames
BR səʊmz
AM soʊmz

so-and-so
BR ˈsəʊənsəʊ, -z
AM ˈsoʊənˌsoʊ, -z

Soane
BR səʊn
AM soʊn

soap
BR səʊp, -s, -ɪŋ, -t
AM soʊp, -s, -ɪŋ, -t

soapbark
BR ˈsəʊpbɑːk, -s
AM ˈsoʊpˌbɑrk, -s

soapberry
BR ˈsəʊpˌbɛr|i, -iz
AM ˈsoʊpˌbɛri, -z

soapbox
BR ˈsəʊpbɒks, -ɪz

AM ˈsoʊpˌbɑks, -əz

soapily
BR ˈsəʊpɪli
AM ˈsoʊpəli

soapiness
BR ˈsəʊpɪnɪs
AM ˈsoʊpɪnɪs

soapless
BR ˈsəʊpləs
AM ˈsoʊpləs

soaplike
BR ˈsəʊplʌɪk
AM ˈsoʊpˌlaɪk

soapstone
BR ˈsəʊpstəʊn, -z
AM ˈsoʊpˌstoʊn, -z

soapsuds
BR ˈsəʊpsʌdz
AM ˈsoʊpˌsədz

soapwort
BR ˈsəʊpwɜːt, -s
AM ˈsoʊpwərt,
ˈsoʊpˌwɔ(ə)rt, -s

soapy
BR ˈsəʊp|i, -ɪə(r), -ɪɪst
AM ˈsoʊpi, -ər, -ɪst

soar
BR sɔː(r), -z, -ɪŋ, -d
AM sɔ(ə)r, -z, -ɪŋ, -d

soarer
BR ˈsɔːrə(r), -z
AM ˈsɔrər, -z

soaringly
BR ˈsɔːrɪŋli
AM ˈsɔrɪŋli

SOAS
BR ˈsəʊas, ˈsəʊaz
AM ˈsoʊæs

Soay
BR ˈsəʊeɪ
AM ˈsoʊeɪ

SOB
BR ˌɛsəʊˈbiː, -z
AM ˌɛˈsoʊˈbi, -z

sob
BR sɒb, -z, -ɪŋ, -d
AM sɑb, -z, -ɪŋ, -d

sobber
BR ˈsɒbə(r), -z
AM ˈsɑbər, -z

sobbingly
BR ˈsɒbɪŋli
AM ˈsɑbɪŋli

Sobell
BR ˈsəʊbɛl
AM ˈsoʊbəl

sober
BR ˈsəʊb|ə(r), -əz,
-(ə)rɪŋ, -əd, -(ə)rə(r),
-(ə)rɪst
AM ˈsoʊb|ər, -ərz,
-(ə)rɪŋ, -ərd, -ərər,
-ərəst

soberingly
BR ˈsəʊb(ə)rɪŋli
AM ˈsoʊb(ə)rɪŋli

soberly
BR ˈsəʊbəli
AM ˈsoʊbərli

Sobers
BR ˈsəʊbəz
AM ˈsoʊbərz

Sobranie®
BR sə(ʊ)ˈbrɑːni
AM soʊˈbrɑni

sobriety
BR sə(ʊ)ˈbrʌɪti
AM səˈbraɪədi,
soʊˈbraɪədi

sobriquet
BR ˈsəʊbrɪkeɪ, -z
AM ˈsoʊbrəˌkeɪ,
ˈsoʊbrəˌket,
-ˈkeɪz\-ˈkɛts

soca
BR ˈsəʊkə(r)
AM ˈsoʊkə

socage
BR ˈsɒkɪdʒ
AM ˈsɑkɪdʒ

so-called
BR ˌsəʊˈkɔːld
AM ˌsoʊˈkɔld, ˈsoʊˌkald

soccage
BR ˈsɒkɪdʒ
AM ˈsɑkɪdʒ

soccer
BR ˈsɒkə(r)
AM ˈsakər

sociability
BR ˌsəʊʃəˈbɪlɪti
AM ˌsoʊʃəˈbɪlɪdi

sociable
BR ˈsəʊʃəbl̩
AM ˈsoʊʃəbəl

sociableness
BR ˈsəʊʃəblnəs
AM ˈsoʊʃəbəlnəs

sociably
BR ˈsəʊʃəbli
AM ˈsoʊʃəbli

social
BR ˈsəʊʃl̩
AM ˈsoʊʃəl

socialisation
BR ˌsəʊʃəlʌɪˈzeɪʃn,
ˌsəʊʃlʌɪˈzeɪʃn
AM ˌsoʊʃələˈzeɪʃən,
ˌsoʊʃəˌlaɪˈzeɪʃən

socialise
BR ˈsəʊʃəlʌɪz,
ˈsəʊʃlʌɪz, -ɪz, -ɪŋ, -d
AM ˈsoʊʃəˌlaɪz, -ɪz, -ɪŋ,
-d

socialism
BR ˈsəʊʃəlɪz(ə)m,
ˈsəʊʃlɪz(ə)m
AM ˈsoʊʃəˌlɪzəm

socialist
BR ˈsəʊʃəlɪst,
ˈsəʊʃlɪst, -s
AM ˈsoʊʃələst, -s

socialistic
BR ˌsəʊʃəˈlɪstɪk,
ˌsəʊʃlˈɪstɪk
AM ˌsoʊʃəˈlɪstɪk

socialistically
BR ˌsəʊʃəˈlɪstɪkli,
ˌsəʊʃlˈɪstɪkli
AM ˌsoʊʃəˈlɪstək(ə)li

socialite
BR ˈsəʊʃəlʌɪt,
ˈsəʊʃlʌɪt, -s
AM ˈsoʊʃəˌlaɪt, -s

sociality
BR ˌsəʊʃɪˈalɪti
AM ˌsoʊʃiˈælədi

socialization
BR ˌsəʊʃəlʌɪˈzeɪʃn,
ˌsəʊʃlʌɪˈzeɪʃn
AM ˌsoʊʃələˈzeɪʃən,
ˌsoʊʃəˌlaɪˈzeɪʃən

socialize
BR ˈsəʊʃəlʌɪz,
ˈsəʊʃlʌɪz, -ɪz, -ɪŋ, -d
AM ˈsoʊʃəˌlaɪz, -ɪz, -ɪŋ,
-d

socially
BR ˈsəʊʃli, ˈsəʊʃəli
AM ˈsoʊʃəli

social science
BR ˈsəʊʃl̩ ˈsʌɪəns, -ɪz
AM ˈsoʊʃəl ˈsaɪəns, -ɪz

social security
BR ˌsəʊʃl̩ sɪˈkjʊərɪti,
+ sɪˈkjɔːrɪti
AM ˌsoʊʃəl səˈkjʊrədi

social service
BR ˌsəʊʃl̩ ˈsɜːvɪs, -ɪsɪz
AM ˌsoʊʃəl ˈsərvəs, -ɪz

social studies
BR ˌsəʊʃl̩ ˈstʌdiz
AM ˌsoʊʃəl ˌstədiz

social work
BR ˌsəʊʃl̩ wɜːk
AM ˌsoʊʃəl ˌwərk

societal
BR səˈsʌɪətl̩
AM səˈsaɪədl

societally
BR səˈsʌɪətl̩i,
səˈsʌɪətəli
AM səˈsaɪədl̩i

society
BR səˈsʌɪət|i, -ɪz
AM səˈsaɪədi, -z

Socinian
BR sə(ʊ)ˈsɪnɪən, -z
AM soʊˈsɪnɪən, -z

Socinus
BR sə(ʊ)ˈsʌɪnəs
AM soʊˈsaɪnəs

sociobiological
BR ˌsəʊʃ(ɪ)əʊˌbʌɪəˈlɒdʒ-
ɪkl,
ˌsəʊsɪəʊˌbʌɪəˈlɒdʒɪkl
AM ˈsoʊsɪoʊˌbaɪəˈlɑdʒə-
kəl,
ˈsoʊʃ(i)oʊˌbaɪəˈlɑdʒə-
kəl

sociobiologically
BR ˌsəʊʃ(i)əʊˌbaɪəˈlɒdʒ-
ɪkli,
ˌsəʊsiəʊˌbaɪəˈlɒdʒɪkli
AM ˈsoʊsiouˌbaɪəˈlɑdʒ-
ək(ə)li,
ˈsoʊʃ(i)ouˌbaɪəˈlɑdʒ-
ək(ə)li

sociobiologist
BR ˌsəʊʃ(i)əʊbʌɪˈplə-
dʒɪst,
ˌsəʊsiəʊbʌɪˈblədʒɪst,
-s
AM ˈsoʊsiouˌbaɪˈalə-
dʒəst,
ˈsoʊʃ(i)ouˌbaɪˈalə-
dʒəst, -s

sociobiology
BR ˌsəʊʃ(i)əʊbʌɪˈplədʒi,
ˌsəʊsiəʊbʌɪˈblədʒi
AM ˈsoʊsiouˌbaɪˈalədʒi,
ˈsoʊʃ(i)ouˌbaɪˈalədʒi

socio-cultural
BR ˌsəʊʃ(i)əʊˈkʌltʃ(ə)-
rəl,
ˌsəʊʃ(i)əʊˈkʌltʃ(ə)r‖,
ˌsəʊsiəʊˈkʌltʃ(ə)rəl,
ˌsəʊsiəʊˈkʌltʃ(ə)r‖
AM ˈsoʊsiouˈkəltʃ(ə)rəl,
ˈsoʊʃ(i)ouˈkəltʃ(ə)rəl

socioculturally
BR ˌsəʊʃ(i)əʊˈkʌltʃ(ə)-
rəli,
ˌsəʊʃ(i)əʊˈkʌltʃ(ə)r‖i,
ˌsəʊsiəʊˈkʌltʃ(ə)rəli,
ˌsəʊsiəʊˈkʌltʃ(ə)r‖i
AM ˈsoʊsiouˈkəltʃ(ə)-
rəli,
ˈsoʊʃ(i)ouˈkəltʃ(ə)rəli

socio-economic
BR ˌsəʊʃ(i)əʊˌi:kəˈnɒm-
ɪk,
ˌsəʊsiəʊˌi:kəˈnɒmɪk,
ˌsəʊʃ(i)əʊˌɛkəˈnɒmɪk,
ˌsəʊsiəʊˌɛkəˈnɒmɪk,
-s
AM ˈsoʊsiouˌikəˈnamɪk,
ˈsoʊʃ(i)ouˌikəˈnamɪk,
ˈsoʊsiouˌɛkəˈnamɪk,
ˈsoʊʃ(i)ouˌɛkəˈnamɪk,
-s

**socio-
economically**
BR ˌsəʊʃ(i)əʊˌi:kəˈnɒm-
ɪkli,
ˌsəʊsiəʊˌi:kəˈnɒmɪkli,
ˌsəʊʃ(i)əʊˌɛkəˈnɒmɪkli,
ˌsəʊsiəʊˌɛkəˈnɒmɪkli
AM ˈsoʊsiouˌikəˈnam-
ək(ə)li,
ˈsoʊʃ(i)ouˌikəˈnamək-
(ə)li,
ˈsoʊsiouˌɛkəˈnamək-
(ə)li,
ˈsoʊʃ(i)ouˌɛkəˈnamək-
(ə)li

sociolinguist
BR ˌsəʊʃ(i)əʊˈlɪŋgwɪst,
ˌsəʊsiəʊˈlɪŋgwɪst, -s

AM ˈsoʊsiouˈlɪŋgwɪst,
ˈsoʊʃ(i)ouˈlɪŋgwɪst, -s

sociolinguistic
BR ˌsəʊʃ(i)əʊlɪŋˈgwɪst-
ɪk,
ˌsəʊsiəʊlɪŋˈgwɪstɪk,
-s
AM ˈsoʊsiouˌlɪŋˈgwɪstɪk,
ˈsoʊʃ(i)ouˌlɪŋˈgwɪstɪk,
-s

sociolinguistically
BR ˌsəʊʃ(i)əʊlɪŋˈgwɪst-
ɪkli,
ˌsəʊsiəʊlɪŋˈgwɪstɪkli
AM ˈsoʊsiouˌlɪŋˈgwɪst-
ək(ə)li,
ˈsoʊʃ(i)ouˌlɪŋˈgwɪst-
ək(ə)li

sociological
BR ˌsəʊʃ(i)əˈlɒdʒɪkl,
səʊsiəˈlɒdʒɪkl
AM ˈsoʊsiəˈladʒəkəl,
ˈsoʊʃ(i)əˈladʒəkəl

sociologically
BR ˌsəʊʃ(i)əˈlɒdʒɪkli,
səʊsiəˈlɒdʒɪkli
AM ˈsoʊsiəˈladʒəkəli,
ˈsoʊʃ(i)əˈladʒəkəli

sociologist
BR ˌsəʊʃiˈɒlədʒɪst,
ˌsəʊsiˈɒlədʒɪst, -s
AM ˈsoʊsiˈalədʒəst,
ˈsoʊʃ(i)ˈalədʒəst, -s

sociology
BR ˌsəʊʃiˈɒlədʒi,
ˌsəʊsiˈɒlədʒi
AM ˈsoʊsiˈalədʒi,
ˈsoʊʃ(i)ˈalədʒi

sociometric
BR ˌsəʊʃ(i)ə(ʊ)ˈmɛtrɪk,
ˌsəʊsiə(ʊ)ˈmɛtrɪk
AM ˈsoʊsiouˈmɛtrɪk,
ˈsoʊʃ(i)ouˈmɛtrɪk

sociometrically
BR ˌsəʊʃ(i)ə(ʊ)ˈmɛtrɪk-
li, ˌsəʊsiə(ʊ)ˈmɛtrɪkli
AM ˈsoʊsiouˈmɛtrə-
k(ə)li,
ˈsoʊʃ(i)ouˈmɛtrək(ə)li

sociometrist
BR ˌsəʊʃiˈɒmɪtrɪst,
ˌsəʊsiˈɒmɪtrɪst, -s
AM ˈsoʊsiˈamətrəst,
ˈsoʊʃiˈamətrəst, -s

sociometry
BR ˌsəʊʃiˈɒmɪtri,
ˌsəʊsiˈɒmɪtri
AM ˈsoʊsiˈamətri,
ˈsoʊʃiˈamətri

sociopath
BR ˈsəʊʃ(i)ə(ʊ)paθ,
ˈsəʊsi(ʊ)paθ, -s
AM ˈsoʊsiəˌpæθ,
ˈsoʊʃ(i)əˌpæθ, -s

sociopathic
BR ˌsəʊʃ(i)ə(ʊ)ˈpaθɪk,
ˌsəʊsiə(ʊ)ˈpaθɪk

AM ˈsoʊsiəˈpæθɪk,
ˈsoʊʃ(i)əˈpæθɪk

sociopathology
BR ˌsəʊʃ(i)əʊpəˈθɒlədʒi,
ˌsəʊsiəʊpəˈθɒlədʒi
AM ˈsoʊsioupəˈθalədʒi,
ˈsoʊʃ(i)oupəˈθalədʒi

socio-political
BR ˌsəʊʃ(i)əʊpəˈlɪtɪkl,
ˌsəʊsiəʊpəˈlɪtɪkl
AM ˈsoʊsioupəˈlɪdəkəl,
ˈsoʊʃ(i)oupəˈlɪdəkəl

sock
BR sɒk, -s, -ɪŋ, -t
AM sak, -s, -ɪŋ, -t

socket
BR ˈsɒkɪt, -s
AM ˈsakət, -s

sockeye
BR ˈsɒkʌɪ, -z
AM ˈsakˌaɪ, -z

sockless
BR ˈsɒkləs
AM ˈsakləs

socko
BR ˈsɒkəʊ, -z
AM ˈsakoʊ, -z

socle
BR ˈsəʊkl, ˈsɒkl, -z
AM ˈsakəl, -z

Socotra
BR səˈkəʊtrə(r)
AM səˈkoʊtrə

Socrates
BR ˈsɒkrəti:z
AM ˈsakrəˌtiz

Socratic
BR səˈkratɪk
AM səˈkrædɪk

Socratically
BR səˈkratɪkli
AM səˈkrædək(ə)li

sod
BR sɒd, -z, -ɪŋ
AM sad, -z, -ɪŋ

soda
BR ˈsəʊdə(r), -z
AM ˈsoʊdə, -z

sodalite
BR ˈsəʊdəlʌɪt
AM ˈsoʊdəlaɪt

sodality
BR sə(ʊ)ˈdalɪtˌli, -ɪz
AM soʊˈdælədi, -z

sodbuster
BR ˈsɒdˌbʌstə(r), -z
AM ˈsadˌbəstər, -z

sodden
BR ˈsɒdn
AM ˈsadən

soddenly
BR ˈsɒdnli
AM ˈsadnli

soddenness
BR ˈsɒdnnəs
AM ˈsad(n)nəs

Soddy
BR ˈsɒdi
AM ˈsadi

sodic
BR ˈsəʊdɪk
AM ˈsadɪk

sodium
BR ˈsəʊdiəm
AM ˈsoʊdiəm

sodium bicarb
BR ˈsəʊdiəm ˈbaɪkɑ:b
AM ˈsoʊdiəm ˈbaɪˌkɑrb

**sodium
bicarbonate**
BR ˈsəʊdiəm
ˌbaɪˈkɑ:bənət,
+ˌbaɪˈkɑ:bnət
AM ˈsoʊdiəm
ˌbaɪˈkɑrbəˌneɪt,
+ˌbaɪˈkɑrbənət

**sodium
carbonate**
BR ˈsəʊdiəm
ˈkɑ:bənət, + ˈkɑ:bənət
AM ˈsoʊdiəm
ˈkɑrbəˌneɪt

sodium chloride
BR ˈsəʊdiəm ˈklɔ:rʌɪd
AM ˈsoʊdiəm ˈklɔˌraɪd

**sodium
hydroxide**
BR ˈsəʊdiəm
hʌɪˈdrɒksʌɪd
AM ˈsoʊdiəm
haɪˈdrakˌsaɪd

sodium nitrate
BR ˈsəʊdiəm ˈnʌɪtreɪt
AM ˈsoʊdiəm ˈnaɪˌtreɪt

Sodom
BR ˈsɒdəm
AM ˈsadəm

sodomise
BR ˈsɒdəmʌɪz, -ɪz, -ɪŋ,
-d
AM ˈsadəˌmaɪz, -ɪz, -ɪŋ,
-d

sodomite
BR ˈsɒdəmʌɪt, -s
AM ˈsadəˌmaɪt, -s

sodomize
BR ˈsɒdəmʌɪz, -ɪz, -ɪŋ,
-d
AM ˈsadəˌmaɪz, -ɪz, -ɪŋ,
-d

sodomy
BR ˈsɒdəmi
AM ˈsadəmi

Sodor
BR ˈsəʊdɔ:(r)
AM ˈsoʊˌdɔ(ə)r

soever
BR səʊˈɛvə(r)
AM səˈwɛvər, soʊˈɛvər

sofa
BR ˈsəʊfə(r), -z
AM ˈsoʊfə, -z

sofabed
BR ˈsəʊfəbɛd, -z

AM 'soʊfəˌbæd, -z

Sofar
BR 'səʊfɑː(r)
AM 'soʊˌfɑr

soffit
BR 'sɒfɪt, -s
AM 'sɑfət, -s

Sofia
BR 'səʊfiə(r),
sə(ʊ)'fiːə(r)
AM soʊ'fiə, 'soʊfiə

soft
BR sɒft, -ə(r), -ɪst
AM sɑft, sɑft, -ər, -əst

softa
BR 'sɒftə(r), -z
AM 'sɑftə, 'sɑftə, -z

softback
BR 'sɒf(t)bak, -s
AM 'sɔf(t)ˌbæk,
'saf(t)ˌbæk, -s

softball
BR 'sɒf(t)bɔːl
AM 'sɔf(t)ˌbɔl,
'saf(t)ˌbal

softbound
BR 'sɒf(t)baʊnd
AM 'sɔf(t)ˌbaʊnd,
'saf(t)ˌbaʊnd

softcore
BR 'sɒf(t)kɔː(r)
AM 'sɔf(t)ˌkɔ(ə)r,
'saf(t)ˌkɔ(ə)r

softcover
BR 'sɒf(t)kʌvə(r)
AM 'sɔf(t)ˌkʌvər,
'saf(t)ˌkʌvər

soft-drink
BR 'sɒf(t)drɪŋk, -s
AM 'sɔf(t)ˌdrɪŋk,
'saf(t)ˌdrɪŋk, -s

soften
BR 'sɒfln, -nz,
-nɪŋ \ -ŋɪn, -nd
AM 'sɔflən, 'saflən,
-ənz, -(ə)nɪŋ, -ənd

softener
BR 'sɔːfnə(r),
'sɔːfŋə(r), -z
AM 'sɔf(ə)nər,
'saf(ə)nər, -z

softie
BR 'sɒftli, -ɪz
AM 'sɔfti, 'safti, -z

softish
BR 'sɒftɪʃ
AM 'sɔftɪʃ, 'saftɪʃ

softly
BR 'sɒftli
AM 'sɔf(t)li, 'saf(t)li

softly-softly
adjective
BR 'sɒftlɪˈsɒftli
AM 'sɔf(t)liˈsɒf(t)li,
'saf(t)liˈsaf(t)li

softness
BR 'sɒf(t)nəs

AM 'sɒf(t)nəs,
'saf(t)nəs

software
BR 'sɒf(t)weə(r)
AM 'sɔf(t)ˌwe(ə)r,
'saf(t)ˌwe(ə)r

softwood
BR 'sɒf(t)wʊd
AM 'sɔf(t)ˌwʊd,
'saf(t)ˌwʊd

softy
BR 'sɒftli, -ɪz
AM 'sɔfti, 'safti, -z

SOGAT
BR 'səʊgat
AM 'soʊˌgæt

soggily
BR 'sɒɡɪli
AM 'saɡəli

sogginess
BR 'sɒɡɪnɪs
AM 'saɡɪnɪs

soggy
BR 'sɒɡli, -ɪə(r), -ɪɪst
AM 'saɡi, -ər, -ɪst

soh
BR səʊ, -z
AM soʊ, -z

Soho
BR 'səʊhəʊ, ˌsəʊ'həʊ
AM 'soʊ,hoʊ

soi-disant
BR ˌswɑː'diːzɒ̃,
ˌswɑː'diː'zɒ̃
AM ˈswadi'zan(t)

soigné
BR 'swɑːnjeɪ
AM swɑn'jeɪ

soignée
BR 'swɑːnjeɪ
AM swɑn'jeɪ

soil
BR sɔɪl, -z, -ɪŋ, -d
AM sɔɪl, -z, -ɪŋ, -d

soil-less
BR 'sɔɪllɪs
AM 'sɔɪ(l)lɪs

soilpipe
BR 'sɔɪlpʌɪp, -s
AM 'sɔɪlˌpaɪp, -s

soily
BR 'sɔɪli
AM 'sɔɪli

soirée
BR 'swɑːreɪ, -z
AM swɑ'reɪ, -z

soixante-neuf
BR ˌswasɒ̃'nɜːf
AM ˌswaˌsan'nəf

sojourn
BR 'sɒdʒl(ə)n,
'sʌdʒl(ə)n, 'sɒdʒɜːn,
'sʌdʒɜːn, -(ə)nz,
-nɪŋ \ -ənɪŋ, -(ə)nd
AM 'soʊˌdʒɜrn, -z, -ɪŋ, -d

sojourner
BR 'sɒdʒnə(r),
'sɒdʒənə(r),
'sʌdʒnə(r),
'sʌdʒənə(r), -z
AM 'soʊˌdʒɜrnər, -z

soke
BR səʊk, -s
AM soʊk, -s

sol
BR sɒl, -z
AM sɔl, sal, -z

sola
BR 'səʊlə(r)
AM 'soʊlə

solace
BR 'sɒlɪs, -ɪz, -ɪŋ, -t
AM 'saləs, -əz, -ɪŋ, -t

solan
BR 'səʊlən, -z
AM 'soʊlən, -z

solanaceous
BR ˌsɒlə'neɪʃəs
AM ˌsalə'neɪʃəs

solander
BR sə'landə(r), -z
AM sə'lændər, -z

solar
BR 'səʊlə(r)
AM 'soʊlər

solaria
BR sə'lɛːrɪə(r)
AM sə'lɛrɪə, soʊ'lɛrɪə

solarisation
BR ˌsəʊlərʌɪ'zeɪʃn
AM ˌsoʊlərə'zeɪʃən,
ˌsoʊlə,raɪ'zeɪʃən

solarise
BR 'səʊlərʌɪz, -ɪz, -ɪŋ, -d
AM 'soʊlə,raɪz, -ɪz, -ɪŋ,
-d

solarism
BR 'səʊlərɪz(ə)m
AM 'soʊlə,rɪzəm

solarist
BR 'səʊlərɪst, -s
AM 'soʊlərəst, -s

solarium
BR sə'lɛːrɪəm, -z
AM sə'lɛrɪəm,
soʊ'lɛrɪəm, -z

solarization
BR ˌsəʊlərʌɪ'zeɪʃn
AM ˌsoʊlərə'zeɪʃən,
ˌsoʊlə,raɪ'zeɪʃən

solarize
BR 'səʊlərʌɪz, -ɪz, -ɪŋ, -d
AM 'soʊlə,raɪz, -ɪz, -ɪŋ,
-d

solar plexus
BR ˌsəʊlə 'plɛksəs, -ɪz
AM ˌsoʊlər 'plɛksəs, -əz

solar system
BR 'səʊlə ˌsɪstɪm, -z
AM 'soʊlər ˌsɪstəm, -z

SOLAS
BR 'səʊləs
AM 'soʊləs

sojourner
BR 'sɒdʒnə(r),
'sɒdʒənə(r),

solatia
BR sə(ʊ)'leɪʃl(ɪ)ə(r)
AM sə'leɪʃiə

solatium
BR sə(ʊ)'leɪʃl(ɪ)əm, -z
AM sə'leɪʃl(i)əm, -z

sold
BR səʊld
AM soʊld

soldanella
BR ˌsɒldə'nɛlə(r), -z
AM ˌsaldə'nɛlə,
ˌsoʊldə'nɛlə, -z

solder
BR 'sɒldl(ə)r,
'səʊldl(ə)r, -əz,
-(ə)rɪŋ, -əd
AM 'sadər, -z, -ɪŋ, -d

solderable
BR 'sɒld(ə)rəbl,
'səʊld(ə)rəbl
AM 'sadərəbəl

solderer
BR 'sɒld(ə)rə(r),
'səʊld(ə)rə(r), -z
AM 'sad(ə)rər, -z

soldier
BR 'səʊldʒl(ə)r, -əz,
-(ə)rɪŋ, -əd
AM 'soʊldʒl(ə)r, -ərz,
-(ə)rɪŋ, -ərd

soldierly
BR 'səʊldʒəli
AM 'soʊldʒərli

soldiership
BR 'səʊldʒəʃɪp
AM 'soʊldʒərˌʃɪp

soldiery
BR 'səʊldʒ(ə)ri
AM 'soʊldʒ(ə)ri

sole
BR səʊl, -z, -ɪŋ, -d
AM soʊl, -z, -ɪŋ, -d

solecism
BR 'sɒlɪsɪz(ə)m
AM 'salə,sɪzəm,
'soʊlə,sɪzəm

solecist
BR 'sɒlɪsɪst, -s
AM 'saləsəst,
'soʊləsəst, -s

solecistic
BR ˌsɒlɪ'sɪstɪk
AM ˌsalə'sɪstɪk,
ˌsoʊlə'sɪstɪk

Soledad
BR 'sɒlɪdad
AM 'soʊləˌdæd
SP sole'ðað

solely
BR 'səʊ(l)li
AM 'soʊ(l)li

solemn
BR 'sɒləm
AM 'saləm

solemnisation
BR ˌsɒləmnʌɪ'zeɪʃn, -z

AM ˌsɑləmnə'zeɪʃən, ˌsɑləmˌnaɪ'zeɪʃən, -z

solemnise
BR 'sɒləmnʌɪz, -ɪz, -ɪŋ, -d
AM 'sɑləmˌnaɪz, -ɪz, -ɪŋ, -d

solemnity
BR sə'lemnɪti
AM sə'lemnədi, -z

solemnization
BR ˌsɒləmnʌɪ'zeɪʃn, -z
AM ˌsɑləmnə'zeɪʃən, ˌsɑləmˌnaɪ'zeɪʃən, -z

solemnize
BR 'sɒləmnʌɪz, -ɪz, -ɪŋ, -d
AM 'sɑləmˌnaɪz, -ɪz, -ɪŋ, -d

solemnly
BR 'sɒləmli
AM 'sɑləmli

solemnness
BR 'sɒləmnəs
AM 'sɑləmnəs

solen
BR 'səʊlən, -z
AM 'soʊlən, 'soʊˌlen, -z

solenodon
BR sə'lenədən, sə'li:nədən, -z
AM soʊ'li:nəˌdɑn, soʊ'lenəˌdɑn, -z

solenoid
BR 'səʊlənɔɪnd, -z
AM 'sɑləˌnɔɪd, -z

solenoidal
BR ˌsəʊlə'nɔɪdl
AM ˌsɑlə'nɔɪdəl

Solent
BR 'səʊlənt, 'səʊlnt
AM 'soʊlənt

soleplate
BR 'səʊlpleɪt, -s
AM 'soʊlˌpleɪt, -s

sol-fa
BR ˌsɒl'fɑ:(r)
AM ˌsoʊl'fɑ

solfatara
BR ˌsɒlfə'tɑ:rə(r), -z
AM ˌsɑlfə'tɛrə, ˌsoʊlfə'tɛrə, -z

solfeggi
BR sɒl'fedʒi:
AM sɑl'fedʒi

solfeggio
BR sɒl'fedʒɪəʊ, -z
AM sɑl'fedʒioʊ, -z

soli
BR 'səʊli
AM 'soʊli

solicit
BR sə'lɪs|ɪt, -ɪts, -ɪtɪŋ, -ɪtɪd
AM sə'lɪsɪ|t, -ts, -dɪŋ, -dɪd

solicitation
BR səˌlɪsɪ'teɪʃn

AM səˌlɪsə'teɪʃən

solicitor
BR sə'lɪsɪtə(r), -z
AM sə'lɪsədər, -z

Solicitor-General
BR səˌlɪsɪtə'dʒen(ə)rəl, səˌlɪsɪtə'dʒen(ə)r|
AM səˌlɪsɪdər'dʒen(ə)- rəl

Solicitors-General
BR səˌlɪsɪtəz'dʒen(ə)rəl, səˌlɪsɪtəz'dʒen(ə)r|
AM səˌlɪsɪdərz'dʒen(ə)- rəl

solicitous
BR sə'lɪsɪtəs
AM sə'lɪsədəs

solicitously
BR sə'lɪsɪtəsli
AM sə'lɪsədəsli

solicitousness
BR sə'lɪsɪtəsnəs
AM sə'lɪsədəsnəs

solicitude
BR sə'lɪsɪtju:d, sə'lɪsɪtʃu:d
AM sə'lɪsəˌt(j)ud

solid
BR 'sɒlɪd, -z
AM 'sɑləd, -z

solidago
BR ˌsɒlɪ'deɪgəʊ
AM ˌsɑlə'deɪgoʊ

solidarity
BR ˌsɒlɪ'darɪti
AM ˌsɑlə'dɛrədi

solidi
BR 'sɒlɪdʌɪ, 'sɒlɪdi:
AM 'sɑləˌdaɪ

solidifiable
BR sə'lɪdɪfʌɪəbl
AM sə'lɪdə'faɪəbəl

solidification
BR səˌlɪdɪfɪ'keɪʃn
AM səˌlɪdəfə'keɪʃən

solidifier
BR sə'lɪdɪfʌɪə(r), -z
AM sə'lɪdəˌfaɪər, -z

solidify
BR sə'lɪdɪfʌɪ, -z, -ɪŋ, -d
AM sə'lɪdəˌfaɪ, -z, -ɪŋ, -d

solidity
BR sə'lɪdɪti
AM sə'lɪdɪdi

solidly
BR 'sɒlɪdli
AM 'sɑlədli

solidness
BR 'sɒlɪdnɪs
AM 'sɑlədnɪs

solidungulate
BR ˌsɒlɪ'dʌŋgjʊlət, -s
AM ˌsɑlə'dəŋgjələt, ˌsɑlə'dəŋgjəˌleɪt, -s

solidus
BR 'sɒlɪdəs

AM 'sɑlədəs

solifidian
BR ˌsɒlɪ'fɪdiən, -z
AM ˌsɑlə'fɪdiən, -z

solifluction
BR ˌsɒlɪ'flʌkʃn
AM ˌsɑlə'fləkʃən

Solihull
BR ˌsəʊlɪ'hʌl, ˌsɒlɪ'hʌl
AM ˌsɑlə'həl, ˌsoʊlə'həl

soliloquise
BR sə'lɪləkwʌɪz, -ɪz, -ɪŋ, -d
AM sə'lɪləˌkwaɪz, -ɪz, -ɪŋ, -d

soliloquist
BR sə'lɪləkwɪst, -s
AM sə'lɪləkwəst, -s

soliloquize
BR sə'lɪləkwʌɪz, -ɪz, -ɪŋ, -d
AM sə'lɪləˌkwaɪz, -ɪz, -ɪŋ, -d

soliloquy
BR sə'lɪləkw|i, -ɪz
AM sə'lɪləkwi, -z

soliped
BR 'sɒlɪpɛd, -z
AM 'sɑləˌpɛd, -z

solipsism
BR 'sɒlɪpsɪz(ə)m, -z
AM 'soʊləpˌsɪzəm, 'sɑləpˌsɪzəm, sə'lɪpˌsɪzəm, -z

solipsist
BR 'sɒlɪpsɪst, -s
AM 'soʊləpsəst, 'sɑləpsəst, sə'lɪpsɪst, -s

solipsistic
BR ˌsɒlɪp'sɪstɪk
AM ˌsoʊləp'sɪstɪk, ˌsɑləp'sɪstɪk

solipsistically
BR ˌsɒlɪp'sɪstɪkli
AM ˌsoʊləp'sɪstək(ə)li, ˌsɑləp'sɪstək(ə)li

solitaire
BR ˌsɒlɪ'tɛ:(r), 'sɒlɪtɛ:(r)
AM ˌsɑlə'tɛ(ə)r

solitarily
BR 'sɒlɪt(ə)rɪli
AM 'sɑləˌtɛrəli

solitariness
BR 'sɒlɪt(ə)rɪnɪs
AM 'sɑləˌterɪnɪs

solitary
BR 'sɒlɪt(ə)r|i, -ɪz
AM 'sɑləˌteri, -z

solitude
BR 'sɒlɪtju:d, 'sɒlɪtʃu:d
AM 'sɑləˌt(j)ud

solleret
BR ˌsɒlə'rɛt, -s
AM ˌsɑlə'rɛt, -s

solmizate
BR 'sɒlmɪzeɪt, -s, -ɪŋ, -ɪd
AM 'sɑlməˌzeɪ|t, -ts, -dɪŋ, -dɪd

solmization
BR ˌsɒlmɪ'zeɪʃn
AM ˌsɑlmə'zeɪʃən

solo
BR 'səʊləʊ, -z, -ɪŋ, -d
AM 'soʊˌl|oʊ, -oʊz, -əwɪŋ \-oʊɪŋ, -oʊ-

soloist
BR 'səʊləʊɪst, -s
AM 'soʊləwəst

Solomon
BR 'sɒləmən
AM 'sɑləmən

Solomonic
BR ˌsɒlə'mɒnɪk
AM ˌsɑlə'mɑnɪk

Solon
BR 'səʊlɒn, 'səʊlən
AM 'soʊlən

solstice
BR 'sɒlstɪs, -ɪz
AM 'soʊlstəs, 'sɑlstəs, -əz

solstitial
BR sɒl'stɪʃl
AM sɑl'stɪʃəl, soʊl'stɪʃəl

Solti
BR 'ʃɒlti
AM 'ʃoʊlti

solubilisation
BR ˌsɒljʊbɪlʌɪ'zeɪʃn, ˌsɒljʊbɪlʌɪ'zeɪʃn
AM ˌsɑljəbələ'zeɪʃən, ˌsɑljəbəˌlaɪ'zeɪʃən

solubilise
BR 'sɒljʊbɪlʌɪz, 'sɒljʊbʊlʌɪz, -ɪz, -ɪŋ, -d
AM 'sɑljəbəˌlaɪz, -ɪz, -ɪŋ, -d

solubility
BR ˌsɒljə'bɪlɪti
AM ˌsɑljə'bɪlɪdi

solubilization
BR ˌsɒljʊbɪlʌɪ'zeɪʃn, ˌsɒljʊbɪlʌɪ'zeɪʃn
AM ˌsɑljəbələ'zeɪʃən, ˌsɑljəbəˌlaɪ'zeɪʃən

solubilize
BR 'sɒljʊbɪlʌɪz, 'sɒljʊbʊlʌɪz, -ɪz, -ɪŋ, -d
AM 'sɑljəbəˌlaɪz, -ɪz, -ɪŋ, -d

soluble
BR 'sɒljʊbl
AM 'sɑljəbəl

solus
BR 'səʊləs
AM 'soʊləs

solute
BR 'sɒlju:t, -s
AM 'sɑlˌjut, -s

solution
BR sə'l(j)uːʃn, -z
AM sə'luʃən, -z

Solutrean
BR sə'l(j)uːtriən, -z
AM sə'lutriən, -z

solvability
BR ˌsɒlvə'bɪlɪti
AM ˌsɑlvə'bɪlɪdi

solvable
BR 'sɒlvəbl
AM 'sɑlvəbəl

solvate
BR 'sɒlveɪt, -s, -ɪŋ, -ɪd-
AM 'sɑlˌveɪt, -ts, -dɪŋ, -dɪd

solvation
BR sɒl'veɪʃn, -z
AM sɑl'veɪʃən, -z

Solvay
BR 'sɒlveɪ
AM 'sɒlveɪ, 'sɑlveɪ

solve
BR sɒlv, -z, -ɪŋ, -d
AM sɑlv, -z, -ɪŋ, -d

solvency
BR 'sɒlv(ə)nsi
AM 'sɑlvənsi

solvent
BR 'sɒlv(ə)nt, -s
AM 'sɑlvənt, -s

solver
BR 'sɒlvə(r), -z
AM 'sɑlvər, -z

Solway Firth
BR ˌsɒlweɪ 'fɜːθ
AM ˌsɔlweɪ 'fɝθ, ˌsɑlweɪ 'fɝθ

Solzhenitsyn
BR ˌsɒlʒɪ'nɪtsɪn
AM ˌsoʊlʒə'nɪtsən

soma
BR 'səʊmə(r)
AM 'soʊmə

Somali
BR sə'mɑːlli, -ɪz
AM sə'mali, soʊ'mali, -z

Somalia
BR sə'mɑːliə(r)
AM sə'mɑljə, soʊ'mɑljə, sə'mɑliə, soʊ'mɑliə

Somalian
BR sə'mɑːliən, -z
AM sə'mɑljən, soʊ'mɑljən, sə'mɑliən, soʊ'mɑliən, -z

Somaliland
BR sə'mɑːliland
AM sə'maliˌlænd, soʊ'maliˌlænd

somatic
BR sə'mætɪk
AM sə'mædɪk

somatically
BR sə'mætɪkli

somatogenic
BR ˌsəʊmətə(ʊ)'dʒɛnɪk, sə‚matə'dʒɛnɪk
AM sə‚mædə'dʒɛnɪk

somatology
BR ˌsəʊmə'tɒlədʒi
AM ˌsoʊmə'tɑlədʒi

somatotonic
BR ˌsəʊmətə(ʊ)'tɒnɪk, sə‚matə'tɒnɪk
AM sə‚mædə'tɑnɪk

somatotrophin
BR ˌsəʊmətə(ʊ)'trə(ʊ)fɪn, sə‚matə'trəʊfɪn, -z
AM sə‚mædə'troʊfən, -z

somatotropin
BR ˌsəʊmətə(ʊ)'trə(ʊ)pɪn, sə‚matə'trəʊpɪn, -z
AM sə‚mædə'troʊpən, -z

somatotype
BR 'səʊmətə(ʊ)tʌɪp, sə‚matətʌɪp, -s
AM 'sə‚mædəˌtaɪp, -s

somber
BR 'sɒmbə(r)
AM 'sambər

somberly
BR 'sɒmbəli
AM 'sambərli

somberness
BR 'sɒmbənəs
AM 'sambərnəs

sombre
BR 'sɒmbə(r)
AM 'sambər

sombrely
BR 'sɒmbəli
AM 'sambərli

sombreness
BR 'sɒmbənəs
AM 'sambərnəs

sombrero
BR sɒm'brɛːrəʊ, -z
AM səm'brɛroʊ, sam'brɛroʊ, -z

sombrous
BR 'sɒmbrəs
AM 'sambrəs

some[1]
strong form
BR sʌm
AM səm

some[2]
weak form
BR s(ə)m
AM s(ə)m

somebody
BR 'sʌmbədˌi, 'sʌmˌbɒdˌi, -ɪz
AM 'sam badi, 'səmbədi, -z

someday
BR 'sʌmdeɪ
AM 'səmˌdeɪ

somehow
BR 'sʌmhaʊ
AM 'səmˌ(h)aʊ

someone
BR 'sʌmwʌn
AM 'səmˌwən

someplace
BR 'sʌmpleɪs
AM 'səmˌpleɪs

Somerfield
BR 'sʌməfiːld
AM 'səmərˌfild

Somers
BR 'sʌməz
AM 'səmərz

somersault
BR 'sʌməsɔːlt, 'sʌməsɒlt, -s, -ɪŋ, -ɪd
AM 'səmərˌsɔlt, 'səmərˌsalt, -s, -ɪŋ, -ɪd

Somerset
BR 'sʌməsət
AM 'səmərˌsɛt

Somerville
BR 'sʌməvɪl
AM 'səmərˌvɪl

something
BR 'sʌmθɪŋ
AM 'səmˌθɪŋ

sometime
BR 'sʌmtʌɪm, -z
AM 'səmˌtaɪm, -z

someway
BR 'sʌmweɪ
AM 'səmˌweɪ

somewhat
BR 'sʌmwɒt
AM 'səmˌ(h)wat

somewhen
BR 'sʌmwɛn
AM 'səmˌ(h)wɛn

somewhere
BR 'sʌmwɛː(r)
AM 'səmˌ(h)wɛ(ə)r

somite
BR 'səʊmʌɪt, -s
AM 'soʊˌmaɪt, -s

somitic
BR sə(ʊ)'mɪtɪk
AM soʊ'mɪdɪk

Somme
BR sɒm
AM sɔm, sam

sommelier
BR sɒ'mɛliə(r), sɒ'mɛlieɪ, sʌ'mɛliə(r), sʌ'mɛlieɪ, ˌsʌml'jeɪ, -z
AM ˌsəməl'jeɪ, -z

somnambulant
BR sɒm'nambjʊlənt, sɒm'nambjʊlnt, -s
AM sam'næmbjələnt, -s

somnambulantly
BR sɒm'nambjʊləntli, sɒm'nambjʊlntli
AM sam'næmbjələn(t)li

somnambulism
BR sɒm'nambjʊlɪz(ə)m
AM sam'næmbjəˌlɪzəm

somnambulist
BR sɒm'nambjʊlɪst, -s
AM sam'nambjələst, -s

somnambulistic
BR sɒmˌnambjʊ'lɪstɪk
AM sam‚næmbjə'lɪstɪk

somnambulistically
BR sɒmˌnambjʊ'lɪstɪkli
AM sam‚næmbjə'lɪstɪk(ə)li

somniferous
BR sɒm'nɪf(ə)rəs
AM sam'nɪf(ə)rəs

somnolence
BR 'sɒmnələns, 'sɒmnəlns
AM 'samnələns

somnolency
BR 'sɒmnələnsi, 'sɒmnəlnsi
AM 'samnələnsi

somnolent
BR 'sɒmnələnt, 'sɒmnəlnt
AM 'samnələnt

somnolently
BR 'sɒmnələntli, 'sɒmnəlntli
AM 'samnələn(t)li

Somoza
BR sə'məʊzə(r)
AM sə'moʊzə

son
BR sʌn, -z
AM sən, -z

sonagram
BR 'səʊnəgram, 'sɒnəgram, -z
AM 'soʊnəˌgræm, 'sanəˌgræm, -z

sonagraph
BR 'səʊnəgrɑːf, 'sɒnəgrɑːf, 'səʊnəgraf, 'sɒnəgraf, -s
AM 'soʊnəˌgræf, 'sanəˌgræf, -s

sonancy
BR 'səʊnənsi
AM 'soʊnənsi

sonant
BR 'səʊnənt, -s
AM 'soʊnənt, -s

sonar
BR 'səʊnɑː(r), -z
AM 'soʊˌnar, -z

sonata
BR sə'nɑːtə(r), snˈɑːtə(r), -z
AM sə'nɑdə, -z

sonatina
BR ˌsɒnə'tiːnə(r), -z
AM ˌsanə'tinə, -z

sonde
BR sɒnd, -z
AM sand, -z

Sondheim
BR 'sɒndhʌɪm
AM 'sɑnd,(h)aɪm

sone
BR səʊn, -z
AM soʊn, -z

son et lumière
BR ,sɒn eɪ 'luːmɪɛː(r),
-z
AM ,sɔn eɪ ,lum'jɛ(ə)r,
-z

song
BR sɒŋ, -z
AM sɔŋ, sɑŋ, -z

songbird
BR 'sɒŋbɜːd, -z
AM 'sɔŋ,bɜrd,
'sɑŋ,bɜrd, -z

songbook
BR 'sɒŋbʊk, -s
AM 'sɔŋ,bʊk, 'sɑŋ,bʊk,
-s

songfest
BR 'sɒŋfɛst, -s
AM 'sɔŋ,fɛst, 'sɑŋ,fɛst,
-s

songful
BR 'sɒŋf(ʊ)l
AM 'sɔŋfəl, 'sɑŋfəl

songfully
BR 'sɒŋfʊli, 'sɒŋfli
AM 'sɔŋfəli, 'sɑŋfəli

songless
BR 'sɒŋləs
AM 'sɔŋləs, 'sɑŋləs

songsmith
BR 'sɒŋsmɪθ
AM 'sɔŋ,smɪθ,
'sɑŋ,smɪθ

songster
BR 'sɒŋstə(r), -z
AM 'sɔŋstər, 'sɑŋstər,
-z

songstress
BR 'sɒŋstrɪs, -ɪz
AM 'sɔŋstrəs,
'sɑŋstrəs, -əz

songthrush
BR 'sɒŋθrʌʃ, -ɪz
AM 'sɔŋ,θrʌʃ,
'sɑŋ,θrʌʃ, -əz

songwriter
BR 'sɒŋ,rʌɪtə(r), -z
AM 'sɔŋ,raɪdər,
'sɑŋ,raɪdər, -z

songwriting
BR 'sɒŋ,rʌɪtɪŋ
AM 'sɔŋ,raɪdɪŋ,
'sɑŋ,raɪdɪŋ

Sonia
BR 'sɒnɪə(r), 'sɒnjə(r)
AM 'sɑnjə, 'soʊnjə

sonic
BR 'sɒnɪk
AM 'sɑnɪk

sonically
BR 'sɒnɪkli
AM 'sɑnək(ə)li

son-in-law
BR 'sʌnɪnlɔː(r), -z
AM 'sənən,lɔ,
'sənən,lɑ, -z

Sonja
BR 'sɒnɪə(r), 'sɒnjə(r)
AM 'sɑnjə, 'sɑndʒə

sonless
BR 'sʌnləs
AM 'sənləs

sonnet
BR 'sɒnɪt, -s
AM 'sɑnət, -s

sonneteer
BR ,sɒnɪ'tɪə(r), -z
AM ,sɑnə'tɪ(ə)r, -z

Sonning
BR 'sʌnɪŋ, 'sɒnɪŋ
AM 'sɑnɪŋ

sonny
BR 'sʌn|i, -ɪz
AM 'səni, -z

sonobuoy
BR 'səʊnəbɔɪ,
'sɒnəbɔɪ, -z
AM 'soʊnə,bui,
'soʊnə,bɔi, 'sɑnə,bui,
'sɑnə,bɔi, -z

son-of-a-bitch
BR ,sʌnəvə'bɪtʃ
AM ,sənəvə'bɪtʃ

son-of-a-gun
BR ,sʌnəvə'gʌn
AM ,sənəvə'gən

sonogram
BR 'səʊnəgram,
'sɒnəgram, -z
AM 'soʊnə,græm,
'sɑnə,græm, -z

sonograph
BR 'səʊnəgrɑːf,
'sɒnəgrɑːf,
'səʊnəgraf, 'sɒnəgraf,
-s
AM 'soʊnə,græf,
'sɑnə,græf, -s

sonometer
BR sə'nɒmɪtə(r), -z
AM sə'nɑmədər, -z

Sonora
BR sə'nɔːrə(r)
AM sə'nɔrə

sonorant
BR 'sɒn(ə)rənt,
'sɒn(ə)rn̩t
AM 'sɑnərənt,
sə'nɔrənt

sonority
BR sə'nɒrɪti
AM sə'nɔrədi

sonorous
BR 'sɒn(ə)rəs
AM 'sɑnərəs

sonorously
BR 'sɒn(ə)rəsli
AM 'sɑnərəsli

sonorousness
BR 'sɒn(ə)rəsnəs

AM 'sɑnərəsnəs

sonship
BR 'sʌnʃɪp
AM 'sən,ʃɪp

sonsie
BR 'sɒns|i, -ɪə(r), -ɪıst
AM 'sənzi, -ər, -ɪst

sons-in-law
BR 'sʌnzɪnlɔː(r)
AM 'sənzən,lɔ,
'sənzən,lɑ

sons-of-bitches
BR ,sʌnzəv'bɪtʃɪz
AM ,sənzə(v)'bɪtʃɪz

sons-of-guns
BR ,sʌnzəv'gʌnz
AM ,sənzə(v)'gənz

sonsy
BR 'sɒns|i, -ɪə(r), -ɪıst
AM 'sənzi, -ər, -ɪst

Sontag
BR 'sɒntag
AM 'sɑn,tæg

Sonya
BR 'sɒnɪə(r), 'sɒnjə(r)
AM 'sɑnjə, 'soʊnjə

sool
BR suːl, -z, -ɪŋ, -d
AM sul, -z, -ɪŋ, -d

sooler
BR 'suːlə(r), -z
AM 'sulər, -z

soon
BR suːn, -ə(r), -ɪst
AM sun, -ər, -əst

soonish
BR 'suːnɪʃ
AM 'sunɪʃ

soot
BR sʊt
AM sʊt

sooterkin
BR 'suːtəkɪn, -z
AM 'sʊdərkən, -z

sooth
BR suːθ
AM suθ

soothe
BR suːð, -z, -ɪŋ, -d
AM sʊð, -z, -ɪŋ, -d

soother
BR 'suːðə(r), -z
AM 'sʊðər, -z

soothingly
BR 'suːðɪŋli
AM 'suðɪŋli

soothsaid
BR 'suːθsɛd
AM 'suθ,sɛd

soothsay
BR 'suːθseɪ, -z, -ɪŋ
AM 'suθ,seɪ, -z, -ɪŋ

soothsayer
BR 'suːθ,seɪə(r), -z
AM 'suθ,seɪər, -z

sootily
BR 'sʊtɪli

AM 'sʊdəli

sootiness
BR 'sʊtɪnɪs
AM 'sʊdɪnɪs

sooty
BR 'sʊt|i, -ɪə(r), -ɪıst
AM 'sʊdi, -ər, -ɪst

sop
BR sɒp, -s, -ɪŋ, -t
AM sɑp, -s, -ɪŋ, -t

Soper
BR 'səʊpə(r)
AM 'soʊpər

Sophia
BR sə(ʊ)'fʌɪə(r),
sə(ʊ)'fiːə(r)
AM soʊ'fiə, 'soʊfiə

Sophie
BR 'səʊfi
AM 'soʊfi

sophism
BR 'sɒfɪz(ə)m
AM 'sɑ,fɪzəm,
'soʊ,fɪzəm

sophist
BR 'sɒfɪst, -s
AM 'sɑfəst, 'soʊfəst, -s

sophister
BR 'sɒfɪstə(r), -z
AM 'sɑfəstər, -z

sophistic
BR sə'fɪstɪk
AM sə'fɪstɪk

sophistical
BR sə'fɪstɪkl
AM sə'fɪstəkəl

sophistically
BR sə'fɪstɪkli
AM sə'fɪstək(ə)li

sophisticate¹
noun
BR sə'fɪstɪkeɪt,
sə'fɪstɪkət, -s
AM sə'fɪstə,keɪt,
sə'fɪstəkət, -s

sophisticate²
verb
BR sə'fɪstɪkeɪt, -s, -ɪŋ,
-ɪd
AM sə'fɪstə,keɪt, -ts,
-dɪŋ, -dɪd

sophisticatedly
BR sə'fɪstɪkeɪtɪdli
AM sə'fɪstə,keɪdɪdli

sophistication
BR sə,fɪstɪ'keɪʃn
AM sə,fɪstə'keɪʃən

sophistry
BR 'sɒfɪstri
AM 'sɑfəstri, 'soʊfəstri

Sophoclean
BR ,sɒfə'kliːən
AM ,sɑfə'klien

Sophocles
BR 'sɒfəkliːz
AM 'sɑfə,kliz

sophomore
BR ˈsɒfəmɔː(r), -z
AM ˈsɒf(ə),mɔ(ə)r,
ˈsaf(ə),mɔ(ə)r, -z

sophomoric
BR ,sɒfəˈmɒrɪk
AM ,sɒf(ə)ˈmɔrɪk,
,saf(ə)ˈmɔrɪk

Sophy
BR ˈsəʊʃ]i, -ɪz
AM ˈsoʊfi, -z

soporiferous
BR ,sɒpəˈrɪf(ə)rəs
AM ,sapəˈrɪf(ə)rəs

soporific
BR ,sɒpəˈrɪfɪk
AM ,sapəˈrɪfɪk

soporifically
BR ,sɒpəˈrɪfɪkli
AM ,sapəˈrɪfək(ə)li

soppily
BR ˈsɒpɪli
AM ˈsapəli

soppiness
BR ˈsɒpɪnɪs
AM ˈsapinɪs

sopping
BR ˈsɒpɪŋ
AM ˈsapɪŋ

soppy
BR ˈsɒp]i, -ɪə(r), -ɪɪst
AM ˈsapi, -ər, -ɪst

sopranino
BR ,sɒprəˈniːnəʊ, -z
AM ,saprəˈniːnoʊ, -z

sopranist
BR səˈprɑːnɪst, -s
AM səˈprænəst,
səˈprɑnəst, -s

soprano
BR səˈprɑːnəʊ, -z
AM səˈprænoʊ,
səˈprɑnoʊ, -z

Sopwith
BR ˈsɒpwɪθ
AM ˈsap,wɪθ

sora
BR ˈsɔːrə(r), ˈsəʊrə(r), -z
AM ˈsɔrə, -z

Soraya
BR səˈrʌɪə(r)
AM səˈraɪə

sorb[1]
BR sɔːb, -z
AM sɔ(ə)rb, -z

sorb[2]
BR sɔːb, -z
AM sɔ(ə)rb, -z

sorbefacient
BR ,sɔːbɪˈfeɪʃ(ə)nt, -s
AM ,sɔːbəˈfeɪʃənt, -s

sorbet
BR ˈsɔːbeɪ, ˈsɔːbɪt, -s
AM ˈsɔrbət, -s

Sorbian
BR ˈsɔːbɪən, -z

AM ˈsɔrbɪən, -z

sorbic
BR ˈsɔːbɪk
AM ˈsɔrbɪk

sorbitol
BR ˈsɔːbɪtɒl
AM ˈsɔrbə,tɔl, ˈsɔrbə,tal

sorbo
BR ˈsɔːbəʊ
AM ˈsɔr,boʊ

Sorbonne
BR sɔːˈbɒn
AM sɔrˈbɑn

sorbose
BR ˈsɔːbəʊz, ˈsɔːbəʊs
AM ˈsɔr,boʊs

sorcerer
BR ˈsɔːs(ə)rə(r), -z
AM ˈsɔrs(ə)rər, -z

sorceress
BR ˈsɔːs(ə)rɪs, ˈsɔːs(ə)rɛs, -ɪz
AM ˈsɔrs(ə)rəs, -əz

sorcerous
BR ˈsɔːs(ə)rəs
AM ˈsɔrs(ə)rəs

sorcery
BR ˈsɔːs(ə)ri
AM ˈsɔrs(ə)ri

sordid
BR ˈsɔːdɪd
AM ˈsɔrdəd

sordidly
BR ˈsɔːdɪdli
AM ˈsɔrdədli

sordidness
BR ˈsɔːdɪdnɪs
AM ˈsɔrdədnɪs

sordini
BR sɔːˈdiːni:
AM sɔrˈdini

sordino
BR sɔːˈdiːnəʊ
AM sɔrˈdinoʊ

sordor
BR ˈsɔːdə(r), -z
AM ˈsɔrdər, ˈsɔr,dɔ(ə)r, -z

sore
BR sɔː(r), -z, -ə(r), -ɪst
AM sɔ(ə)r, -z, -ər, -əst

sorehead
BR ˈsɔːhɛd, -z
AM ˈsɔr,(h)ɛd, -z

sorel
BR ˈsɒrəl, ˈsɒrl̩, -z
AM ˈsɔrəl, -z

sorely
BR ˈsɔːli
AM ˈsɔrli

soreness
BR ˈsɔːnəs
AM ˈsɔrnəs

Sørensen
BR ˈsɒrəns(ə)n, ˈsɒrn̩s(ə)n

AM ˈsɔrənsən
DAN ˈsœʌˈsən
NO ˈsəːrensen

sorghum
BR ˈsɔːgəm
AM ˈsɔrgəm

sori
BR ˈsɔːrʌɪ
AM ˈsɔ,raɪ

sorites
BR səˈrʌɪtiːz
AM səˈraɪdiz

soritical
BR səˈrɪtɪkl
AM səˈrɪdɪkl

Soroptimist
BR səˈrɒptɪmɪst, -s
AM səˈrɑptəməst, -s

sororicidal
BR sə,rɒrɪˈsʌɪdl
AM sə,rɔrəˈsaɪdəl

sororicide
BR səˈrɒrɪsʌɪd, -z
AM səˈrɔrə,saɪd, -z

sorority
BR səˈrɒrɪt]i, -ɪz
AM səˈrɔrədi, -z

soroses
BR səˈrəʊsiːz
AM səˈroʊ,siz

sorosis
BR səˈrəʊsɪs
AM səˈroʊsəs

sorption
BR ˈsɔːpʃn
AM ˈsɔrpʃən

sorrel
BR ˈsɒrəl, ˈsɒrl̩, -z
AM ˈsɔrəl, -z

Sorrell
BR ˈsɒrəl, ˈsɒrl̩
AM ˈsɔrəl

Sorrento
BR səˈrɛntəʊ
AM səˈrɛn(t)oʊ

sorrily
BR ˈsɒrɪli
AM ˈsɔrəli, ˈsarəli

sorriness
BR ˈsɒrɪnɪs
AM ˈsɔrinɪs, ˈsarinɪs

sorrow
BR ˈsɒrəʊ, -z, -ɪŋ, -d
AM ˈsɔroʊ, ˈsaroʊ, -z, -ɪŋ, -d

sorrower
BR ˈsɒrəʊə(r), -z
AM ˈsɔroʊər, ˈsaroʊər, -z

sorrowful
BR ˈsɒrə(ʊ)f(ʊ)l
AM ˈsɔrəfəl, ˈsarəfəl

sorrowfully
BR ˈsɒrə(ʊ)fʊli, ˈsɒrə(ʊ)f]li
AM ˈsɔrəf(ə)li, ˈsarəf(ə)li

sorrowfulness
BR ˈsɒrə(ʊ)f(ʊ)lnɪs
AM ˈsɔrəfəlnəs, ˈsarəfəlnəs

sorry
BR ˈsɒr]i, -ɪə(r), -ɪɪst
AM ˈsɔri, ˈsari, -ər, -ɪst

sort
BR sɔːt, -s, -ɪŋ, -ɪd
AM sɔ(ə)rt, -ts, ˈsɔrdɪŋ, ˈsɔrdəd

sorta
BR ˈsɔːtə(r)
AM ˈsɔrdə

sortable
BR ˈsɔːtəbl
AM ˈsɔrdəbəl

sortal
BR ˈsɔːtl, -z
AM ˈsɔrdl, -z

sorter
BR ˈsɔːtə(r), -z
AM ˈsɔrdər, -z

sortie
BR ˈsɔːt]i, -ɪz
AM ˈsɔrdi, ˈsɔrˈti, -z

sortilege
BR ˈsɔːtɪlɪdʒ
AM ˈsɔrdlɪdʒ

sortition
BR sɔːˈtɪʃn, -z
AM sɔrˈtɪʃən, -z

sorus
BR ˈsɔːrəs
AM ˈsɔrəs

SOS
BR ,ɛsəʊˈɛs, -ɪz
AM ,ɛs,oʊˈɛs, -əz

so-so
BR ˈsəʊsəʊ, ˌsəʊˈsəʊ
AM ˈsoʊˈsoʊ

sostenuto
BR ,sɒstɪˈn(j)uːtəʊ
AM ˈsɒstəˈnudoʊ, ˈsɑstəˈnudoʊ

sot
BR sɒt, -s
AM sɑt, -s

soteriological
BR sə(ʊ),tɪərɪəˈlɒdʒɪkl
AM soʊ,tɪrɪəˈladʒəkəl

soteriology
BR sə(ʊ),tɪərɪˈɒlədʒi
AM soʊ,tɪriˈɑlədʒi

Sotheby
BR ˈsʌðəb]i, -ɪz
AM ˈsəðəbi, -z

Sothic
BR ˈsəʊθɪk, ˈsɒθɪk
AM ˈsoʊθɪk, ˈsɑθɪk

Sotho
BR ˈsuːtuː, ˈsəʊtəʊ, -z
AM ˈsoʊdoʊ, ˈsoʊθoʊ, -z

Soto
BR ˈsəʊtəʊ
AM ˈsoʊdoʊ

sottish
BR 'sɒtɪʃ
AM 'sɑdɪʃ

sottishly
BR 'sɒtɪʃli
AM 'sɑdɪʃli

sottishness
BR 'sɒtɪʃnɪs
AM 'sɑdɪʃnɪs

sotto voce
BR ˌsɒtəʊ 'vəʊtʃi
AM ˌsɑdoʊ 'voʊtʃi,
ˌsoʊdoʊ +

sou
BR suː, -z
AM suː, -z

soubrette
BR suː'brɛt, sʊ'brɛt, -s
AM suˈbrɛt, -s

soubriquet
BR 'suːbrɪkeɪ, -z
AM ˌsuːbrəˈkeɪ,
ˈsuːbrəˌkeɪ,
-ˈkeɪz\-ˈkɛts

souchong
BR ˌsuːʼ(t)ʃɒŋ, -z
AM ˌsuːʼtʃɒŋ, ˈsuːʼtʃɑŋ, -z

souffle
sound
BR 'suːfl, -z
AM 'sufəl, -z

soufflé
food
BR 'suːfleɪ, -z
AM suˈfleɪ, -z

Soufrière
BR ˌsuːfriˈɛː(r)
AM ˌsufriˈ(j)ɛ(ə)r

sough
BR saʊ, sʌf, saʊz\sʌfs,
saʊɪŋ\sʌfɪŋ,
saʊd\sʌft
AM səf, saʊ, səfs\saʊz,
səfɪŋ\saʊɪŋ,
səft\saʊd

sought
BR sɔːt
AM sɔt, sɑt

sought-after
BR 'sɔːt,ɑːftə(r),
'sɔːt,ɑftə(r)
AM 'sɔd,æftər,
'sɑd,æftər

souk
BR suːk, -s
AM suk, -s

soukous
BR 'suːkəs, 'suːkuːs
AM 'sukəs

soul
BR səʊl, -z
AM soʊl, -z

Soulbury
BR 'səʊlb(ə)ri
AM 'soʊl,bɛri

soulful
BR 'səʊlf(ʊ)l
AM 'soʊlfəl

soulfully
BR 'səʊlfʊli, 'səʊlfʃi
AM 'soʊlfəli

soulfulness
BR 'səʊlf(ʊ)lnəs
AM 'soʊlfəlnəs

soulless
BR 'səʊlləs
AM 'soʊ(l)ləs

soullessly
BR 'səʊlləsli
AM 'soʊ(l)ləsli

soullessness
BR 'səʊlləsnəs
AM 'soʊ(l)ləsnəs

soulmate
BR 'səʊlmeɪt, -s
AM 'soʊl,meɪt, -s

soulster
BR 'səʊlstə(r), -z
AM 'soʊlstər, -z

sound
BR saʊnd, -z, -ɪŋ, -ɪd-
-ə(r), -ɪst
AM saʊnd, -z, -ɪŋ, -əd-
-ər, -əst

soundalike
BR 'saʊndəlʌɪk, -s
AM 'saʊndə,laɪk, -s

soundbite
BR 'saʊn(d)bʌɪt, -s
AM 'saʊn(d),baɪt, -s

soundboard
BR 'saʊn(d)bɔːd, -z
AM 'saʊn(d),bɔ(ə)rd, -z

soundbox
BR 'saʊn(d)bɒks, -ɪz
AM 'saʊn(d),bɑks, -əz

soundcheck
BR 'saʊn(d)tʃɛk, -s
AM 'saʊn(d),tʃɛk, -s

sounder
BR 'saʊndə(r), -z
AM 'saʊndər, -z

soundhole
BR 'saʊndhəʊl, -z
AM 'saʊn(d),(h)oʊl, -z

sounding
BR 'saʊndɪŋ, -z
AM 'saʊndɪŋ, -z

soundless
BR 'saʊndləs
AM 'saʊn(d)ləs

soundlessly
BR 'saʊndləsli
AM 'saʊn(d)ləsli

soundlessness
BR 'saʊndləsnəs
AM 'saʊn(d)ləsnəs

soundly
BR 'saʊndli
AM 'saʊn(d)li

soundness
BR 'saʊn(d)nəs
AM 'saʊn(d)nəs

soundproof
BR 'saʊn(d)pruːf, -s,
-ɪŋ, -t
AM 'saʊn(d),pruf, -s,
-ɪŋ, -t

soundstage
BR 'saʊn(d)steɪdʒ, -ɪz
AM 'saʊn(d),steɪdʒ, -ɪz

soundtrack
BR 'saʊn(d)trak, -s
AM 'saʊn(d),træk, -s

Souness
BR 'suːnɪs
AM 'suːnəs

soup
BR suːp, -s, -ɪŋ, -t
AM sup, -s, -ɪŋ, -t

soupcon
BR 'suːpsɒ̃, 'suːpsɒn, -z
AM sup'sɒn, sup'sɑn, -z

soupçon
BR 'suːpsɒ̃, 'suːpsɒn, -z
AM sup'sɒn, sup'sɑn, -z

souped-up
BR ˌsuːpt'ʌp
AM ˌsup'təp

soupily
BR 'suːpɪli
AM 'supəli

soupiness
BR 'suːpɪnɪs
AM 'supɪnɪs

soupspoon
BR 'suːpspuːn, -z
AM 'sup,spun, -z

soupy
BR 'suːpˌi, -ɪə(r), -ɪɪst
AM 'supi, -ər, -ɪɪst

sour
BR 'saʊə(r), -z, -ɪŋ, -d,
-ə(r), -ɪst
AM 'saʊər, -z, -ɪŋ, -d, -ər,
-əst

source
BR sɔːs, -ɪz
AM sɔ(ə)rs, -əz

sourcebook
BR 'sɔːsbʊk, -s
AM 'sɔrs,bʊk, -s

sourdough
BR 'saʊədəʊ
AM 'saʊər,doʊ

sour grapes
BR ˌsaʊə 'greɪps
AM ˌsaʊər 'greɪps

sourish
BR 'saʊərɪʃ
AM 'saʊərɪʃ

sourly
BR 'saʊəli
AM 'saʊərli

sourness
BR 'saʊənəs
AM 'saʊərnəs

sourpuss
BR 'saʊəpʊs, -ɪz
AM 'saʊər,pʊs, -əz

soursop
BR 'saʊəsɒp, -s
AM 'saʊər,sɑp, -s

Sousa
BR 'suːzə(r)
AM 'suzə

sousaphone
BR 'suːzəfəʊn, -z
AM 'suzə,foʊn, -z

sousaphonist
BR 'suːzəfəʊnɪst, -s
AM 'suzə,foʊnəst, -s

souse
BR saʊs, -ɪz, -ɪŋ, -t
AM saʊs, -əz, -ɪŋ, -t

souslik
BR 'suːslɪk, -s
AM 'suslɪk, -s

Sousse
BR suːs
AM sus

sous vide
BR suː 'viːd
AM su 'vid

soutache
BR suːˈtaʃ, -ɪz
AM suˈtaʃ, -əz

soutane
BR suːˈtɑːn, suːˈtan, -z
AM suˈtan, -z

souteneur
BR ˌsuːtəˈnɜː(r), -z
AM ˌsudəˈnər, ˌsutn'ər,
-z

souter
BR 'suːtə(r), -z
AM 'sudər, -z

souterrain
BR 'suːtəreɪn, -z
AM ˌsutəˈreɪn, -z

south
BR saʊθ
AM saʊθ

South Africa
BR ˌsaʊθ 'afrɪkə(r)
AM ˌsaʊθ 'æfrəkə

South African
BR ˌsaʊθ 'afrɪk(ə)n, -z
AM ˌsaʊθ 'æfrəkən, -z

Southall¹
place in UK
BR 'saʊθɔːl
AM 'saʊθɔl, 'saʊθal

Southall²
surname
BR 'sʌðl, 'sʌðɔːl
AM 'səθəl

Southam
BR 'saʊð(ə)m
AM 'saʊθəm

South America
BR ˌsaʊθ əˈmɛrɪkə(r)
AM ˌsaʊθ əˈmɛrəkə

South American
BR ˌsaʊθ əˈmɛrɪk(ə)n,
-z
AM ˌsaʊθ əˈmɛrəkən, -z

Southampton
BR ˌsaʊθˈham(p)tən,
saʊˈθam(p)tən
AM ˌsaʊθˈ(h)æm(p)tən

southbound
BR ˈsaʊθbaʊnd
AM ˈsaʊθˌbaʊnd

South Carolina
BR ˌsaʊθ
ˌkarəˈlaɪnə(r)
AM ˌsaʊθˌkɛrəˈlaɪnə

South China Sea
BR ˌsaʊθ ˌtʃʌɪnə ˈsiː
AM ˌsaʊθ ˌtʃaɪnə ˈsi

South Dakota
BR ˌsaʊθ dəˈkəʊtə(r)
AM ˌsaʊθdəˈkoʊdə

Southdown
BR ˈsaʊθdaʊn, -z
AM ˈsaʊθˌdaʊn, -z

southeast
BR ˌsaʊθˈiːst
AM ˌsaʊθˈist

southeaster
BR ˌsaʊθˈiːstə(r), -z
AM ˌsaʊθˈistər, -z

southeasterly
BR ˌsaʊθˈiːstəlｊi, -ɪz
AM ˌsaʊθˈistərli, -z

southeastern
BR ˌsaʊθˈiːst(ə)n
AM ˌsaʊθˈistərn

south-easterner
BR ˌsaʊθˈiːstənə(r),
ˌsaʊθˈiːstnə(r), -z
AM ˌsaʊθˈistərnər, -z

southeastward
BR ˌsaʊθˈiːstwəd, -z
AM ˌsaʊθˈis(t)wərd, -z

Southend
BR ˌsaʊθˈɛnd
AM ˌsaʊθˈɛnd

souther
BR ˈsaʊðə(r), -z
AM ˈsaʊðər, -z

southerliness
BR ˈsʌðəlɪnɪs
AM ˈsəðərlɪnɪs

southerly
BR ˈsʌðəli
AM ˈsəðərli

southern
BR ˈsʌðn
AM ˈsəðərn

Southerndown
BR ˈsʌðndaʊn
AM ˈsəðərnˌdaʊn

southerner
BR ˈsaʊðənə(r),
ˈsaʊðnə(r), -z
AM ˈsəðərnər, -z

southernmost
BR ˈsʌðnməʊst
AM ˈsəðərnˌmoʊst

southernwood
BR ˈsʌðnwʊd, -z
AM ˈsəðərnˌwʊd, -z

Southey
BR ˈsaʊði, ˈsʌði
AM ˈsaʊði, ˈsəði

southing
BR ˈsaʊðɪŋ, ˈsaʊθɪŋ, -z
AM ˈsaʊðɪŋ, -z

southland
BR ˈsaʊθland
AM ˈsaʊθˌlænd

southpaw
BR ˈsaʊθpɔː(r), -z
AM ˈsaʊθˌpɔ, ˈsaʊθˌpɑ, -z

south-southeast[1]
BR ˌsaʊθsaʊθˈiːst
AM ˌsaʊθˌsaʊθˈist

south-southeast[2]
nautical use
BR ˌsaʊsaʊˈiːst
AM ˌsaʊˌsaʊˈist

south-southwest[1]
BR ˌsaʊθsaʊθˈwɛst
AM ˌsaʊθˌsaʊθˈwɛst

south-southwest[2]
nautical use
BR ˌsaʊsaʊˈwɛst
AM ˌsaʊˌsaʊˈwɛst

South Utsire
BR ˌsaʊθ ʊtˈsɪərə(r)
AM ˌsaʊθ ʊtˈsɪ(ə)r

southward
BR ˈsaʊθwəd, -z
AM ˈsaʊθwərd, -z

southwardly
BR ˈsaʊθwədli
AM ˈsaʊθwərdli

Southwark
BR ˈsʌðək
AM ˈsəðərk,
ˈsaʊθˌwərk

Southwell
BR ˈsʌðl, ˈsaʊθw(ɛ)l
AM ˈsaʊθˌwɛl

southwest
BR ˌsaʊθˈwɛst
AM ˌsaʊθˈwɛst

southwester[1]
BR ˌsaʊθˈwɛstə(r), -z
AM ˌsaʊθˈwɛstər, -z

southwester[2]
nautical use
BR ˌsaʊˈwɛstə(r), -z
AM ˌsaʊˈwɛstər, -z

southwesterly[1]
BR ˌsaʊθˈwɛstəlｊi, -ɪz
AM ˌsaʊθˈwɛstərli, -z

southwesterly[2]
nautical use
BR ˌsaʊˈwɛstəlｊi, -ɪz
AM ˌsaʊˈwɛstərli, -z

southwestern
BR ˌsaʊθˈwɛst(ə)n
AM ˌsaʊθˈwɛstərn

southwesterner
BR ˌsaʊθˈwɛstənə(r),
ˌsaʊθˈwɛstnə(r), -z

southwestward, -z
BR ˌsaʊθˈwɛstwəd, -z
AM ˌsaʊθˈwɛs(t)wərd,
-z

Southwold
BR ˈsaʊθwəʊld
AM ˈsaʊθˌwoʊld

Souttar
BR ˈsuːtə(r)
AM ˈsudər

Soutter
BR ˈsuːtə(r)
AM ˈsudər

souvenir
BR ˌsuːvəˈnɪə(r), -z
AM ˌsuvəˈnɪ(ə)r, -z

souvlaki
BR suːˈvlɑːki
AM suˈvlɑki

souvlakia
BR suːˈvlɑːkɪə(r)
AM suˈvlɑkiə

sou'wester
BR ˌsaʊˈwɛstə(r), -z
AM ˌsaʊˈwɛstər, -z

sovereign
BR ˈsɒvr(ɪ)n, -z
AM ˈsɑv(ə)rən,
ˈsɑvərn, -z

sovereignly
BR ˈsɒvr(ɪ)nli
AM ˈsɑv(ə)rənli,
ˈsɑvərnli

sovereignty
BR ˈsɒvr(ɪ)nti
AM ˈsɑv(ə)rən(t)i,
ˈsɑvərn(t)i

soviet
BR ˈsəʊvɪət, ˈsɒvɪət, -s
AM ˈsoʊviət, ˈsoʊviˌɛt,
-s

Sovietisation
BR ˌsəʊvɪətʌɪˈzeɪʃn,
ˌsɒvɪətʌɪˈzeɪʃn
AM ˌsoʊviədəˈzeɪʃən,
ˌsoʊviəˌtaɪˈzeɪʃən

Sovietise
BR ˌsəʊvɪətʌɪz,
ˈsɒvɪətʌɪz, -ɪz, -ɪŋ, -d
AM ˌsoʊviəˌtaɪz, -ɪz, -ɪŋ,
-d

Sovietization
BR ˌsəʊvɪətʌɪˈzeɪʃn,
ˌsɒvɪətʌɪˈzeɪʃn
AM ˌsoʊviədəˈzeɪʃən,
ˌsoʊviəˌtaɪˈzeɪʃən

Sovietize
BR ˈsəʊvɪətʌɪz,
ˈsɒvɪətʌɪz, -ɪz, -ɪŋ, -d
AM ˈsoʊviəˌtaɪz, -ɪz, -ɪŋ,
-d

sovietologist
BR ˌsəʊvɪəˈtɒlədʒɪst,
ˌsɒvɪəˈtɒlədʒɪst, -s
AM ˌsoʊviəˈtɑlədʒəst,
-s

Soviet Union
BR ˌsəʊvɪət ˈjuːnɪən,
ˌsɒvɪət +
AM ˌsoʊviət ˈjunjən,
ˌsoʊviet ˈjunjən

sow[1]
noun
BR saʊ, -z
AM saʊ, -z

sow[2]
verb
BR səʊ, -z, -ɪŋ, -d
AM soʊ, -z, -ɪŋ, -d

sowback
BR ˈsaʊbak, -s
AM ˈsaʊˌbæk, -s

sowbelly
BR ˈsaʊˌbɛlｊi, -ɪz
AM ˈsaʊˌbɛli, -z

sowbread
BR ˈsaʊbrɛd, -z
AM ˈsaʊˌbrɛd, -z

sower
BR ˈsəʊə(r), -z
AM ˈsoʊər, -z

Sowerby
BR ˈsaʊəbi
AM ˈsaʊərbi

Sowetan
BR səˈwɛtən, -z
AM səˈwɛtn, -z

Soweto
BR səˈwɛtəʊ
AM səˈwɛdoʊ

sowing
BR ˈsəʊɪŋ, -z
AM ˈsoʊɪŋ, -z

sown
BR səʊn
AM soʊn

sowthistle
BR ˈsaʊˌθɪsl, -z
AM ˈsaʊˌθɪsəl, -z

sox
BR sɒks
AM sɑks

soy
BR sɔɪ
AM sɔɪ

soya
BR ˈsɔɪə(r)
AM ˈsɔɪ(ə)

soybean
BR ˈsɔɪbiːn, -z
AM ˈsɔɪˌbin, -z

Soyinka
BR ʃɔɪˈɪŋkə(r)
AM sɔɪˈɪŋkə

Soyuz
AM ˈsɑˌjuz, ˈsɔɪˌjuz
RUS saˈjus

sozzled
BR ˈsɒzld
AM ˈsɑzəld

spa
BR spɑː(r), -z

AM spɑ, -z

space
BR speis, -iz, -iŋ, -t
AM speis, -iz, -iŋ, -t

space-age
BR 'speiseidʒ
AM 'speis,eidʒ

spacecraft
BR 'speiskrɑːft, 'speiskraft
AM 'speis,kræf(t)

spaced-out
BR ,speist'aut
AM 'speis'taut

spaceflight
BR 'speisflʌit, -s
AM 'speis,flait, -s

spacelab
BR 'speislab, -z
AM 'speis,læb, -z

spaceman
BR 'speisman, 'speisman
AM 'speis,mæn, 'speisman

spacemen
BR 'speismɛn, 'speisman
AM 'speis,mɛn, 'speisman

spacer
BR 'speisə(r), -z
AM 'speisər, -z

spaceship
BR 'speisʃip, -s
AM 'spei(s),ʃip, -s

spaceshot
BR 'speisʃɒt, -s
AM 'spei(s),ʃɑt, -s

spacesuit
BR 'speiss(j)uːt, -s
AM 'spei(s),sut, -s

spacewalk
BR 'speiswɔːk, -s
AM 'speis,wɔk, 'speis,wɑk, -s

spaceward
BR 'speiswəd
AM 'speiswərd

spacewoman
BR 'speis,wuman
AM 'speis,wuman

spacewomen
BR 'speis,wimin
AM 'speis,wimin

spacey
BR 'speis|i, -iə(r), -ɪɪst
AM 'speisi, -ər, -ɪst

spacial
BR 'speiʃl
AM 'speiʃəl

spacing
BR 'speisiŋ, -z
AM 'speisiŋ, -z

spacious
BR 'speiʃəs
AM 'speiʃəs

spaciously
BR 'speiʃəsli
AM 'speiʃəsli

spaciousness
BR 'speiʃəsnəs
AM 'speiʃəsnəs

spacy
BR 'speis|i, -iə(r), -ɪɪst
AM 'speisi, -ər, -ɪst

spade
BR speid, -z, -iŋ, -id
AM speid, -z, -iŋ, -id

spadeful
BR 'speidful, -z
AM 'speid,ful, -z

spadework
BR 'speidwəːk
AM 'speid,wərk

spadiceous
BR sper'diʃəs, spə'deiʃəs
AM sper'diʃəs, spə'diʃəs

spadicose
BR 'speidikəus
AM 'speidə,kous, 'speidə,kouz

spadille
BR spə'dɪl, -z
AM spə'dɪl, -z

spadix
BR 'speidiks, -iz
AM 'speidiks, -iz

spado
BR 'spadəu, -z
AM 'spædou, -z

spae
BR spei, -z, -iŋ, -d
AM spei, -z, -iŋ, -d

spaewife
BR 'speiwʌif
AM 'spei,waif

spaewives
BR 'speiwʌivz
AM 'spei,waivz

spaghetti
BR spə'gɛti
AM spə'gɛdi

spaghettini
BR ,spagɛ'tiːni, ,spagə'tiːni
AM ,spægə'tini

spahi
BR 'spɑːhiː, -z
AM 'spɑ(h)i, -z

Spain
BR spein
AM spein

spake
BR speik
AM speik

Spalding
BR 'spɔːldiŋ
AM 'spɔldiŋ, 'spaldiŋ

spall
BR spɔːl, -z, -iŋ, -d
AM spɔl, spal, -z, -iŋ, -d

spallation
BR spɔː'leiʃn, -z
AM spɔ'leiʃən, spɑ'leiʃən, -z

spalpeen
BR 'spalpiːn, -z
AM 'spɔl,pin, 'spal,pin, -z

Spam®
BR spam
AM spæm

span
BR span, -z, -iŋ, -d
AM spæn, -z, -iŋ, -d

spanakopita
BR ,spanə'kɒpitə(r)
AM ,spænə'kəpədə, ,spænə'kapədə

Spandau
BR 'spandau, 'ʃpandau
AM 'spændau

spandrel
BR 'spandr(ə)l, -z
AM 'spændrəl, -z

spang
BR spaŋ
AM spæŋ

spangle
BR 'spaŋg|l, -lz, -lɪŋ \-l-ɪŋ, -ld
AM 'spæŋg|əl, -əlz, -(ə)lɪŋ, -əld

Spanglish
BR 'spaŋglɪʃ
AM 'spæŋglɪʃ

spangly
BR 'spaŋgl|i, 'spaŋgl|i, -iə(r), -ɪɪst
AM 'spæŋ(ə)li, -ər, -ɪst

Spaniard
BR 'spanjəd, -z
AM 'spænjərd, -z

spaniel
BR 'spanjəl, -z
AM 'spænjəl, -z

Spanier
BR 'spanjə(r), 'spanjei
AM 'spænjər

Spanish
BR 'spanɪʃ
AM 'spænɪʃ

Spanish-American
BR ,spanɪʃə'mɛrɪk(ə)n
AM ,spænɪʃə'mɛrəkən

Spanishness
BR 'spanɪʃnɪs
AM 'spænɪʃnɪs

spank
BR spaŋ|k, -ks, -kɪŋ, -(k)t
AM spæŋ|k, -ks, -kɪŋ, -(k)t

spanker
BR 'spaŋkə(r), -z
AM 'spæŋkər, -z

spanking
BR 'spaŋkɪŋ, -z

AM 'spæŋkɪŋ, -z

spanner
BR 'spanə(r), -z
AM 'spænər, -z

Spansule®
BR 'spansjuːl, -z
AM 'spæn,s(j)ul, -z

spar
BR spɑː(r), -z, -iŋ, -d
AM spɑr, -z, -iŋ, -d

sparable
BR 'sparəbl, -z
AM 'sparəbəl, -z

sparaxes
BR spə'raksiːz
AM spə'ræksiz

sparaxis
BR spə'raksis
AM spə'ræksəs

spare
BR spɛː(r), -z, -iŋ, -d, -ə(r), -ɪst
AM spɛ(ə)r, -z, -iŋ, -d, -ər, -əst

sparely
BR 'spɛːli
AM 'spɛrli

spareness
BR 'spɛːnəs
AM 'spɛrnəs

spare part
BR ,spɛː 'pɑːt, -s
AM ,spɛr 'pɑrt, -s

sparer
BR 'spɛːrə(r), -z
AM 'spɛrər, -z

sparerib
BR 'spɛːrɪb, -z
AM 'spɛr,rɪb, -z

spare-time
BR ,spɛː'tʌim
AM ,spɛr'taim

sparge
BR spɑːdʒ, -iz, -iŋ, -d
AM spɑrdʒ, -əz, -iŋ, -d

sparger
BR 'spɑːdʒə(r), -z
AM 'spɑrdʒər, -z

sparid
BR 'sparɪd, 'speirɪd, -z
AM 'spɛrəd, -z

sparing
BR 'spɛːriŋ
AM 'spɛriŋ

sparingly
BR 'spɛːriŋli
AM 'spɛriŋli

sparingness
BR 'spɛːriŋnɪs
AM 'spɛriŋnɪs

spark
BR spɑːk, -s, -iŋ, -t
AM spɑrk, -s, -iŋ, -t

Sparke
BR spɑːk
AM spɑrk

sparkish
BR 'spɑːkɪʃ
AM 'spɑrkɪʃ

sparkle
BR 'spɑːk|l, -lz,
-lɪŋ\-lɪŋ, -d
AM 'spɑrk|əl, -əlz,
-(ə)lɪŋ, -əld

sparkler
BR 'spɑːklə(r), -z
AM 'spɑrk(ə)lər, -z

sparkless
BR 'spɑːkləs
AM 'spɑrkləs

sparklet
BR 'spɑːklɪt, -s
AM 'spɑrklət, -s

sparklingly
BR 'spɑːklɪŋli
AM 'spɑrk(ə)lɪŋli

sparkly
BR 'spɑːkli
AM 'spɑrk(ə)li

Sparks
BR spɑːks
AM spɑrks

sparky
BR 'spɑːk|i, -iz
AM 'spɑrki, -z

sparling
BR 'spɑːlɪŋ
AM 'spɑrlɪŋ

sparoid
BR 'spærɔɪd, -z
AM 'spɛˌrɔɪd, -z

sparrow
BR 'spærəʊ, -z
AM 'spɛroʊ, -z

sparrowhawk
BR 'spærə(ʊ)hɔːk, -s
AM 'spɛroʊˌhɔk,
'spɛroʊˌhɑk, -s

sparry
BR 'spɑːri
AM 'spɑri

sparse
BR spɑːs
AM spɑrs

sparsely
BR spɑːsli
AM spɑrsli

sparseness
BR spɑːsnəs
AM spɑrsnəs

sparsity
BR 'spɑːsɪti
AM 'spɑrsədi

Sparta
BR 'spɑːtə(r)
AM 'spɑrdə

Spartacist
BR 'spɑːtəsɪst, -s
AM 'spɑrdəsəst, -s

Spartacus
BR 'spɑːtəkəs
AM 'spɑrdəkəs

spartan
BR 'spɑːtn, -z
AM 'spɑrtn, -z

spasm
BR 'spaz(ə)m, -z
AM 'spæzəm, -z

spasmodic
BR spaz'mɒdɪk
AM spæz'mɑdɪk

spasmodically
BR spaz'mɒdɪkli
AM spæz'mɑdək(ə)li

spastic
BR 'spastɪk, -s
AM 'spæstɪk, -s

spastically
BR 'spastɪkli
AM 'spæstək(ə)li

spasticity
BR spa'stɪsɪti
AM spæ'stɪsɪdi

spat
BR spat, -s
AM spæt, -s

spatchcock
BR 'spatʃkɒk, -s, -ɪŋ, -t
AM 'spætʃˌkɑk, -s, -ɪŋ, -t

spate
BR speɪt, -s
AM speɪt, -s

spathaceous
BR spə'θeɪʃəs
AM spə'θeɪʃəs

spathe
BR speɪð, -z
AM speɪð, -z

spathic
BR 'spaθɪk
AM 'speɪθɪk

spathose
BR 'spaθəʊs
AM 'speɪˌθoʊs,
'speɪˌθoʊz

spatial
BR 'speɪʃl
AM 'speɪʃəl

spatialise
BR 'speɪʃəlʌɪz,
'speɪʃlʌɪz, -ɪz, -ɪŋ, -d
AM 'speɪʃəˌlaɪz, -ɪz, -ɪŋ, -d

spatiality
BR ˌspeɪʃɪ'alɪti
AM ˌspeɪʃi'ælədi

spatialize
BR 'speɪʃəlʌɪz,
'speɪʃlʌɪz, -ɪz, -ɪŋ, -d
AM 'speɪʃəˌlaɪz, -ɪz, -ɪŋ, -d

spatially
BR 'speɪʃli, 'speɪʃəli
AM 'speɪʃəli

spatio-temporal
BR ˌspeɪʃ(ɪ)əʊ'tɛmp-
(ə)rəl,
ˌspeɪʃ(ɪ)əʊ'tɛmp(ə)rl
AM ˌspeɪʃ(i)oʊ'tɛmp-
(ə)rəl

spatio-temporally
BR ˌspeɪʃ(ɪ)əʊ'tɛmp-
(ə)rəli,
ˌspeɪʃ(ɪ)əʊ'tɛmp(ə)rli
AM ˌspeɪʃ(i)oʊ'tɛmp-
(ə)rəli

Spätlese
BR 'ʃpɛtˌleɪzə(r), -z
AM 'ʃpeɪtˌleɪzə, -z

Spätlesen
BR 'ʃpɛtˌleɪzn
AM 'ʃpɛtˌleɪzn

spatter
BR 'spat|ə(r), -əz,
-(ə)rɪŋ, -əd
AM 'spæd|ər, -ərz,
-(ə)rɪŋ, -ərd

spatterdash
BR 'spatədaʃ, -ɪz
AM 'spædər,dæʃ, -əz

spatula
BR 'spatjʊlə(r),
'spatʃʊlə(r), -z
AM 'spætʃələ, -z

spatulae
BR 'spatjʊliː,
'spatʃʊliː
AM 'spætʃəli,
'spætʃəˌlaɪ

spatulate
BR 'spatjʊlət,
'spatʃʊlət
AM 'spætʃələt

Spätzle
BR 'ʃpɛtslə(r), 'ʃpɛtsl
AM 'ʃpɛtsl

spavin
BR 'spav(ɪ)n, -d
AM 'spævən, -d

spawn
BR spɔːn, -z, -ɪŋ, -d
AM spɔn, spɑn, -z, -ɪŋ, -d

spawner
BR 'spɔːnə(r), -z
AM 'spɔnər, 'spɑnər, -z

spawning
BR 'spɔːnɪŋ, -z
AM 'spɔnɪŋ, 'spɑnɪŋ, -z

spay
BR speɪ, -z, -ɪŋ, -d
AM speɪ, -z, -ɪŋ, -d

Speaight
BR speɪt
AM speɪt

speak
BR spiːk, -s, -ɪŋ
AM spik, -s, -ɪŋ

speakable
BR 'spiːkəbl
AM 'spikəbəl

speakeasy
BR 'spiːkˌiːz|i, -ɪz
AM 'spikˌizi, -z

speaker
BR 'spiːkə(r), -z
AM 'spikər, -z

speakerphone
BR 'spiːkəfəʊn
AM 'spikərˌfoʊn

speakership
BR 'spiːkəʃɪp, -s
AM 'spikərˌʃɪp, -s

speaking clock
BR ˌspiːkɪŋ 'klɒk, -s
AM ˌspikɪŋ 'klɑk, -s

spear
BR spɪə(r), -z, -ɪŋ, -d
AM spɪ(ə)r, -z, -ɪŋ, -d

spearfish
BR 'spɪəfɪʃ, -ɪz
AM 'spɪrˌfɪʃ, -ɪz

speargun
BR 'spɪəɡʌn, -z
AM 'spɪrˌɡən, -z

spearhead
BR 'spɪəhɛd, -z, -ɪŋ, -ɪd
AM 'spɪr,(h)ɛd, -z, -ɪŋ, -əd

spearman
BR 'spɪəmən
AM 'spɪrmən

spearmen
BR 'spɪəmən
AM 'spɪrmən

spearmint
BR 'spɪəmɪnt
AM 'spɪrˌmɪnt

Spears
BR spɪəz
AM spɪ(ə)rz

spearwort
BR 'spɪəwəːt, -s
AM 'spɪrwərt,
'spɪrˌwɔ(ə)rt, -s

spec
BR spɛk, -s
AM spɛk, -s

special
BR 'spɛʃl, -z
AM 'spɛʃəl, -z

specialisation
BR ˌspɛʃəlʌɪ'zeɪʃn,
ˌspɛʃlʌɪ'zeɪʃn, -z
AM ˌspɛʃələ'zeɪʃən,
ˌspɛʃəˌlaɪ'zeɪʃən, -z

specialise
BR 'spɛʃəlʌɪz,
'spɛʃlʌɪz, -ɪz, -ɪŋ, -d
AM 'spɛʃəˌlaɪz, -ɪz, -ɪŋ, -d

specialism
BR 'spɛʃəlɪz(ə)m,
'spɛʃlɪz(ə)m
AM 'spɛʃəˌlɪzəm

specialist
BR 'spɛʃəlɪst,
'spɛʃlɪst, -s
AM 'spɛʃ(ə)ləst, -s

specialistic
BR ˌspɛʃə'lɪstɪk
AM ˌspɛʃə'lɪstɪk

speciality
BR ˌspɛʃɪ'alɪt|i, -ɪz
AM ˌspɛʃi'ælədi, -z

specialization
BR ˌspeʃəlaɪˈzeɪʃn,
ˌspeʃʃʌɪˈzeɪʃn, -z
AM ˈspeʃələˈzeɪʃən,
ˈspeʃəˌlaɪˈzeɪʃən, -z

specialize
BR ˈspeʃəlʌɪz,
ˈspeʃʃʌɪz, -ɪz, -ɪŋ, -d
AM ˈspeʃəˌlaɪz, -ɪz, -ɪŋ,
-d

specially
BR ˈspeʃ(ə)li, ˈspeʃʃi
AM ˈspeʃəli

specialness
BR ˈspeʃlnəs
AM ˈspeʃəlnəs

specialty
BR ˈspeʃlt|i, -ɪz
AM ˈspeʃəlti, -z

speciation
BR ˌspi:ʃɪˈeɪʃn, -z
AM ˌspiʃiˈeɪʃən,
ˌspisiˈeɪʃən, -z

specie
BR ˈspi:ʃi:, ˈspi:ʃi
AM ˈspiʃi, ˈspisi

species
BR ˈspi:ʃɪz, ˈspi:ʃi:z,
ˈspi:sɪz, ˈspi:si:z
AM ˈspiʃiz, ˈspisiz

speciesism
BR ˈspi:ʃɪzɪz(ə)m,
ˈspi:sɪzɪz(ə)m
AM ˈspiʃiˌzɪzəm,
ˈspisiˌzɪzəm

speciesist
BR ˈspi:ʃɪzɪst,
ˈspi:sɪzɪst, -s
AM ˈspiʃizɪst,
ˈspisizɪst, -s

specifiable
BR ˈspesɪfʌɪəbl
AM ˈspesəˈfaɪəbl

specific
BR spɪˈsɪfɪk, -s
AM spəˈsɪfɪk, -s

specifically
BR spɪˈsɪfɪkli
AM spəˈsɪfək(ə)li

specification
BR ˌspesɪfɪˈkeɪʃn, -z
AM ˌspesəfəˈkeɪʃən, -z

specificity
BR ˌspesɪˈfɪsɪti
AM ˌspesəˈfɪsɪdi

specificness
BR ˈspɪˈsɪfɪknɪs
AM spəˈsɪfɪknɪs

specifier
BR ˈspesɪfʌɪə(r), -z
AM ˈspesəˌfaɪər, -z

specify
BR ˈspesɪfʌɪ, -z, -ɪŋ, -d
AM ˈspesəˌfaɪ, -z, -ɪŋ, -d

specimen
BR ˈspesɪmɪn, -z
AM ˈspesəmən, -z

speciological
BR ˌspi:ʃɪəˈlɒdʒɪkl,
ˌspi:sɪəˈlɒdʒɪkl
AM ˌspiʃiəˈladʒəkəl,
ˌspisiəˈladʒəkəl

speciology
BR ˌspi:ʃɪˈɒlədʒi,
ˌspi:sɪˈɒlədʒi
AM ˌspiʃiˈalədʒi,
ˌspisiəˈalədʒi

speciosity
BR ˌspi:ʃiˈɒsɪti,
ˌspi:sɪˈɒsɪti
AM ˌspiʃiˈasədi,
ˌspisiəˈasədi

specious
BR ˈspi:ʃəs
AM ˈspiʃəs

speciously
BR ˈspi:ʃəsli
AM ˈspiʃəsli

speciousness
BR ˈspi:ʃəsnəs
AM ˈspiʃəsnəs

speck
BR spɛk, -s
AM spɛk, -s

speckle
BR ˈspɛk|l, -lz,
-lɪŋ \-lɪŋ, -d
AM ˈspɛkəl, -z, -ɪŋ, -d

speckless
BR ˈspɛkləs
AM ˈspɛkləs

specs
BR ˈspɛks
AM ˈspɛks

spectacle
BR ˈspɛktəkl, -z, -ld
AM ˈspɛktəkəl, -z, -ld

spectacular
BR spɛkˈtakjʉlə(r), -z
AM spɛkˈtækjələr, -z

spectacularly
BR spɛkˈtakjʉləli
AM spɛkˈtækjələrli

spectate
BR spɛkˈteɪt, -s, -ɪŋ, -ɪd
AM ˈspɛkˈteɪ|t, -ts, -dɪŋ,
-dɪd

spectator
BR spɛkˈteɪtə(r), -z
AM ˈspɛkˌteɪdər, -z

spectatorial
BR ˌspɛktəˈtɔːrɪəl
AM ˌspɛktəˈtɔriəl

specter
BR ˈspɛktə(r), -z
AM ˈspɛktər, -z

Spector
BR ˈspɛktə(r)
AM ˈspɛktər

spectra
BR ˈspɛktrə(r)
AM ˈspɛktrə

spectral
BR ˈspɛktr(ə)l
AM ˈspɛktrəl

spectrally
BR ˈspɛktrəli,
ˈspɛktrʃi
AM ˈspɛktrəli

spectre
BR ˈspɛktə(r), -z
AM ˈspɛktər, -z

spectrochemistry
BR ˌspɛktrə(ʊ)ˈkɛmɪstri
AM ˌspɛktroʊˈkɛmestri

spectrogram
BR ˈspɛktrə(ʊ)gram, -z
AM ˈspɛktrəˌgræm, -z

spectrograph
BR ˈspɛktrə(ʊ)grɑːf,
ˈspɛktrə(ʊ)graf, -s
AM ˈspɛktrəˌgræf, -s

spectrographic
BR ˌspɛktrəˈgrafɪk
AM ˌspɛktrəˈgræfɪk

**spectrographic-
ally**
BR ˌspɛktrəˈgrafɪkli
AM ˌspɛktrəˈgræfək-
(ə)li

spectrography
BR spɛkˈtrɒgrəfi
AM spɛkˈtragrəfi

spectroheliograph
BR ˌspɛktrəʊˈhiːlɪəgrɑːf,
ˌspɛktrəʊˈhiːlɪəgraf,
-s
AM ˌspɛktroʊˈhiliəˌgræf,
-s

spectrohelioscope
BR ˌspɛktrəʊˈhiːlɪə-
skəʊp, -s
AM ˌspɛktroʊˈhiliə-
ˌskoʊp, -s

spectrometer
BR spɛkˈtrɒmɪtə(r), -z
AM spɛkˈtramədər, -z

spectrometric
BR ˌspɛktrəˈmɛtrɪk
AM ˌspɛktrəˈmɛtrɪk

spectrometry
BR spɛkˈtrɒmɪtri
AM spɛkˈtramətri

**spectrophoto-
meter**
BR ˌspɛktrə(ʊ)fəˈtɒ-
mɪtə(r), -z
AM ˌspɛktroʊfəˈtɑ-
mədər, -z

**spectrophoto-
metric**
BR ˌspɛktrə(ʊ)ˌfəʊtə-
ˈmɛtrɪk
AM ˌspɛktrəˌfoʊdə-
ˈmɛtrɪk

**spectrophoto-
metry**
BR ˌspɛktrə(ʊ)fəˈtɒ-
mɪtri
AM ˌspɛktroʊfəˈtɑ-
mətri

spectroscope
BR ˈspɛktrəskəʊp, -s

AM ˈspɛktrəˌskoʊp, -s

spectroscopic
BR ˌspɛktrəˈskɒpɪk
AM ˌspɛktrəˈskɑpɪk

spectroscopical
BR ˌspɛktrəˈskɒpɪkl
AM ˌspɛktrəˈskɑpəkəl

spectroscopist
BR spɛkˈtrɒskəpɪst, -s
AM spɛkˈtraskəpəst, -s

spectroscopy
BR spɛkˈtrɒskəpi
AM spɛkˈtraskəpi

spectrum
BR ˈspɛktrəm, -z
AM ˈspɛktrəm, -z

specula
BR ˈspɛkjʉlə(r)
AM ˈspəkjələ

specular
BR ˈspɛkjʉlə(r)
AM ˈspɛkjələr

speculate
BR ˈspɛkjʉleɪt, -s, -ɪŋ,
-ɪd
AM ˈspɛk(j)əˌleɪ|t, -ts,
-dɪŋ, -dɪd

speculation
BR ˌspɛkjʉˈleɪʃn, -z
AM ˌspɛkjʉˈleɪʃən, -z

speculative
BR ˈspɛkjʉlətɪv
AM ˈspɛkjələdɪv,
ˈspɛkjəˌleɪdɪv

speculatively
BR ˈspɛkjʉlətɪvli
AM ˈspɛkjəˌleɪdɪvli,
ˈspɛkjələdɪvli

speculativeness
BR ˈspɛkjʉlətɪvnɪs
AM ˈspɛkjəˌleɪdɪvnɪs,
ˈspɛkjələdɪvnɪs

speculator
BR ˈspɛkjʉleɪtə(r), -z
AM ˈspɛkjəˌleɪdər, -z

speculum
BR ˈspɛkjʉləm
AM ˈspəkjələm

sped
BR spɛd
AM spɛd

speech
BR spiːtʃ, -ɪz
AM spitʃ, -ɪz

speechful
BR ˈspiːtʃf(ʉ)l
AM ˈspitʃˌfʉl

speechification
BR ˌspiːtʃɪfɪˈkeɪʃn, -z
AM ˌspitʃəfəˈkeɪʃən, -z

speechifier
BR ˈspiːtʃɪfʌɪə(r), -z
AM ˈspitʃəˌfaɪər, -z

speechify
BR ˈspiːtʃɪfʌɪ, -z, -ɪŋ, -d
AM ˈspitʃəˌfaɪ, -z, -ɪŋ, -d

speechless
BR 'spiːtʃlɪs
AM 'spiːtʃlɪs

speechlessly
BR 'spiːtʃlɪsli
AM 'spiːtʃlɪsli

speechlessness
BR 'spiːtʃlɪsnɪs
AM 'spiːtʃlɪsnɪs

speed
BR spiːd, -z, -ɪŋ, -ɪd
AM spiːd, -z, -ɪŋ, -ɪd

speedball
BR 'spiːdbɔːl
AM 'spiːdbɔːl, 'spiːdbɑːl

speedboat
BR 'spiːdbəʊt, -s
AM 'spiːdboʊt, -s

speeder
BR 'spiːdə(r), -z
AM 'spiːdər, -z

speedily
BR 'spiːdɪli
AM 'spiːdɪli

speediness
BR 'spiːdɪnɪs
AM 'spiːdɪnɪs

speedo
BR 'spiːdəʊ, -z
AM 'spiːdoʊ, -z

speedometer
BR spiː'dɒmɪtə(r),
spɪ'dɒmɪtə(r), -z
AM spə'dɑmədər, -z

speedster
BR 'spiːdstə(r), -z
AM 'spiːdstər, -z

speedway
BR 'spiːdweɪ, -z
AM 'spiːdweɪ, -z

speedwell
BR 'spiːdwɛl
AM 'spiːdwɛl

speedy
BR 'spiːdʲi, -ɪə(r), -ɪɪst
AM 'spiːdi, -ər, -ɪst

Speight
BR speɪt
AM speɪt

Speir
BR spɪə(r)
AM spɪ(ə)r

speiss
BR spʌɪs
AM spaɪs

Speke
BR spiːk
AM spik

speleological
BR ,spiːliə'lɒdʒɪkl
AM ,spiːliə'lɑdʒəkəl

speleologist
BR ,spiːli'ɒlədʒɪst, -s
AM ,spiːli'ɑlədʒəst, -s

speleology
BR ,spiːlɪ'ɒlədʒi
AM ,spiːli'ɑlədʒi

spell
BR spɛl, -z, -ɪŋ, -d
AM spɛl, -z, -ɪŋ, -d

spellable
BR 'spɛləbl
AM 'spɛləbəl

spellbind
BR 'spɛlbʌɪnd, -z, -ɪŋ
AM 'spɛl,baɪnd, -z, -ɪŋ

spellbinder
BR 'spɛl,bʌɪndə(r), -z
AM 'spɛl,baɪndər, -z

spellbindingly
BR 'spɛl,bʌɪndɪŋli
AM 'spɛl,baɪndɪŋli

spellbound
BR 'spɛlbaʊnd
AM 'spɛl,baʊnd

speller
BR 'spɛlə(r), -z
AM 'spɛlər, -z

spellican
BR 'spɛlɪk(ə)n, -z
AM 'spɛləkən, -z

spelling
BR 'spɛlɪŋ, -z
AM 'spɛlɪŋ, -z

Spellman
BR 'spɛlmən
AM 'spɛlmən

spelt
BR spɛlt
AM spɛlt

spelter
BR 'spɛltə(r)
AM 'spɛltər

spelunker
BR spɪ'lʌŋkə(r), -z
AM spə'ləŋkər,
spi'ləŋkər, -z

spelunking
BR spɪ'lʌŋkɪŋ
AM spə'ləŋkɪŋ,
spi'ləŋkɪŋ

Spen
BR spɛn
AM spɛn

Spenborough
BR 'spɛnb(ə)rə(r)
AM 'spɛn,bərə

spence
BR spɛns, -ɪz
AM spɛns, -əz

spencer
BR 'spɛnsə(r), -z
AM 'spɛnsər, -z

spend
BR spɛnd, -z, -ɪŋ
AM spɛnd, -z, -ɪŋ

spendable
BR 'spɛndəbl
AM 'spɛndəbəl

spender
BR 'spɛndə(r), -z
AM 'spɛndər, -z

spendthrift
BR 'spɛn(d)θrɪft, -s

AM 'spɛn(d),θrɪft, -s

Spens
BR spɛnz
AM spɛnz

Spenser
BR 'spɛnsə(r)
AM 'spɛnsər

Spenserian
BR spɛn'sɪərɪən
AM spɛn'sɪriən,
spɛn'sɛriən

spent
BR spɛnt
AM spɛnt

sperm
BR spɜːm, -z
AM spɜrm, -z

spermaceti
BR ,spɜː'məsɛti,
,spɜː'məsiːti
AM ,spɜrmə'sɛdi

spermacetic
BR ,spɜː'məsɛtɪk,
,spɜː'məsiːtɪk
AM ,spɜrmə'sɛdɪk

spermary
BR 'spɜː'm(ə)r|i, -ɪz
AM 'spɜrməri, -z

spermatheca
BR ,spɜː'mə'θiːkə(r)
AM ,spɜrmə'θikə

spermathecae
BR ,spɜː'mə'θiːkiː
AM ,spɜrmə'θiki,
,spɜrmə'θiːkaɪ

spermatic
BR spɜː'matɪk
AM spɜr'mædɪk

spermatid
BR 'spɜː'mətɪd, -z
AM 'spɜrmə,tɪd, -z

spermatidal
BR ,spɜː'mə'tʌɪdl
AM ,spɜrmə'taɪdəl

spermatoblast
BR 'spɜː'mətə(ʊ)blɑːst,
spɜː'matə(ʊ)blɑːst,
'spɜː'mətə(ʊ)blast,
spɜː'matə(ʊ)blast, -s
AM spɜr'mædə,blæst,
-s

spermatocyte
BR 'spɜː'mətə(ʊ)sʌɪt,
spɜː'matə(ʊ)sʌɪt, -s
AM spɜr'mædə,saɪt, -s

spermatogenesis
BR ,spɜː'mətə(ʊ)'dʒɛnɪ-
sɪs
AM ,spɜrmædə'dʒɛnəsəs

spermatogenetic
BR ,spɜː'mətəʊdʒɪ'nɛtɪk
AM ,spɜrmədədʒə'nɛdɪk

spermatogonia
BR ,spɜː'mətə'gəʊnɪə(r)
AM ,spɜr,mædə'goʊnɪə

spermatogonium
BR ,spɜː'mətə'gəʊnɪəm
AM ,spɜr,mædə'goʊnɪəm

spermatophore
BR 'spɜː'mətə(ʊ)fɔː(r),
spɜː'matəfɔː(r), -z
AM spɜr'mædə,fɔ(ə)r,
-z

spermatophoric
BR ,spɜː'mətə'fɒrɪk
AM ,spɜrmədə'fɔrɪk

spermatophyte
BR 'spɜː'mətə(ʊ)fʌɪt,
spɜː'matəfʌɪt, -s
AM spɜr'mædə,faɪt, -s

spermatozoa
BR ,spɜː'mətə'zəʊə(r)
AM ,spɜrmədə'zoʊə,
spɜr,mædə'zoʊə

spermatozoal
BR ,spɜː'mətə'zəʊəl
AM ,spɜrmədə'zoʊəl,
spɜr,mædə'zoʊəl

spermatozoan
BR ,spɜː'mətə'zəʊən
AM ,spɜrmædə'zoʊən,
spɜr,mædə'zoʊən

spermatozoic
BR ,spɜː'mətə'zəʊɪk
AM ,spɜrmædə'zoʊɪk,
spɜr,mædə'zoʊɪk

spermatozoid
BR ,spɜː'mətə'zəʊɪd, -z
AM ,spɜrmædə'zoʊəd,
spɜr,mædə'zoʊəd, -z

spermatozoon
BR ,spɜː'mətə'zəʊən,
,spɜː'mətə'zəʊɒn
AM ,spɜrmædə'zoʊən,
spɜr,mædə'zoʊən

spermicidal
BR ,spɜː'mɪ'sʌɪdl
AM ,spɜrmə'saɪdəl

spermicide
BR 'spɜː'mɪsʌɪd, -z
AM 'spɜrmə,saɪd, -z

spermidine
BR 'spɜː'mɪdiːn
AM 'spɜrmə,din

spermine
BR 'spɜː'miːn
AM 'spɜrmin

spermoblast
BR 'spɜː'məblɑːst,
'spɜː'məblast, -s
AM 'spɜrmə,blæst, -s

spermocyte
BR 'spɜː'məsʌɪt, -s
AM 'spɜrmə,saɪt, -s

spermogenesis
BR ,spɜː'mə'dʒɛnɪsɪs
AM ,spɜrmə'dʒɛnəsəs

spermogonia
BR ,spɜː'mə'gəʊnɪə(r)
AM ,spɜrmə'goʊnɪə

spermogonium
BR ,spɜː'mə'gəʊnɪəm
AM ,spɜrmə'goʊnɪəm

spermophore
BR 'spɜː'məfɔː(r), -z
AM 'spɜrmə,fɔ(ə)r, -z

spermophyte
BR ˈspəːməfʌɪt, -s
AM ˈspɜːrməˌfaɪt, -s

spermozoa
BR ˌspəːməˈzəʊə(r)
AM ˌspɜːrməˈzoʊə

spermozoid
BR ˈspəːməzɔɪd, -z
AM ˈspɜːrməˌzɔɪd, -z

spermozoon
BR ˌspəːməˈzəʊən,
ˌspəːməˈzəʊɒn
AM ˌspɜːrməˈzoʊən

sperm whale
BR ˈspəːm weɪl, -z
AM ˈspɜːrm ˌweɪl, -z

spessartine
BR ˈspɛsətiːn
AM ˈspɛsərˌtin

spew
BR spjuː, -z, -ɪŋ, -d
AM spju, -z, -ɪŋ, -d

spewer
BR ˈspjuːə(r), -z
AM ˈspjuər, -z

Spey
BR speɪ
AM speɪ

sphagnum
BR ˈsfagnəm,
ˈspagnəm
AM ˈsfægnəm

sphalerite
BR ˈsfalərʌɪt, -s
AM ˈsfæləˌraɪt, -s

sphene
BR sfiːn
AM sfin

sphenoid
BR ˈsfiːnɔɪd, -z
AM ˈsfiːnɔɪd, -z

sphenoidal
BR sfiːˈnɔɪdl
AM sfiːˈnɔɪdəl

spheral
BR ˈsfɪərl
AM ˈsfɪrəl

sphere
BR sfɪə(r), -z
AM sfɪ(ə)r, -z

spheric
BR ˈsfɛrɪk, ˈsfɪərɪk, -s
AM ˈsfɪrɪk, ˈsfɛrɪk, -s

spherical
BR ˈsfɛrɪkl
AM ˈsfɪrəkəl, ˈsfɛrəkəl

spherically
BR ˈsfɛrɪkli
AM ˈsfɪrək(ə)li,
ˈsfɛrək(ə)li

sphericity
BR sfɪˈrɪsɪti, sfɛˈrɪsɪti
AM sfəˈrɪsɪdi

spheroid
BR ˈsfɪərɔɪd, ˈsfɛrɔɪd, -z
AM ˈsfɪˌrɔɪd, ˈsfɛˌrɔɪd, -z

spheroidal
BR sfɪˈrɔɪdl
AM sfɪˈrɔɪdəl,
sfəˈrɔɪdəl

spheroidicity
BR ˌsfɪərɔɪˈdɪsɪti,
ˌsfɛrɔɪˈdɪsɪti
AM ˌsfɪrɔɪˈdɪsɪdi,
ˌsfɛrɔɪˈdɪsɪdi

spherometer
BR ˌsfɪəˈrɒmɪtə(r), -z
AM sfəˈramədər, -z

spherular
BR ˈsfɛr(j)ələ(r)
AM ˈsfɪr(j)ulər,
ˈsfɛr(j)ulər

spherule
BR ˈsfɛr(j)uːl, -z
AM ˈsfɪrul, ˈsfɛrul, -z

spherulite
BR ˈsfɛr(j)ʊlʌɪt, -s
AM ˈsfɪr(j)əˌlaɪt,
ˈsfɛr(j)əˌlaɪt, -s

spherulitic
BR ˌsfɛr(j)ʊˈlɪtɪk
AM ˌsfɪr(j)əˈlɪdɪk,
ˌsfɛr(j)əˈlɪdɪk

sphincter
BR ˈsfɪŋ(k)tə(r), -z, -d
AM ˈsfɪŋ(k)tər, -z, -d

sphincteral
BR ˈsfɪŋ(k)t(ə)rəl,
ˈsfɪŋ(k)t(ə)rl
AM ˈsfɪŋ(k)t(ə)rəl

sphincterial
BR ˌsfɪŋ(k)ˈtɪərɪəl
AM ˌsfɪŋ(k)ˈtɪrɪəl

sphincteric
BR ˌsfɪŋ(k)ˈtɛrɪk
AM ˌsfɪŋ(k)ˈtɛrɪk

sphingid
BR ˈsfɪŋ(d)ʒɪd,
ˈsfɪŋɡɪd, -z
AM ˈsfɪndʒɪd, ˈsfɪŋɡɪd,
-z

sphingomyelin
BR ˌsfɪŋɡə(ʊ)ˈmʌɪəlɪn
AM ˌsfɪŋɡoʊˈmaɪəlɪn

sphingosine
BR ˈsfɪŋɡə(ʊ)sʌɪn
AM ˈsfɪŋɡoʊˌsin,
ˈsfɪŋɡoʊˌsain

sphinx
BR sfɪŋks, -ɪz
AM sfɪŋks, -ɪz

sphragistics
BR sfrəˈdʒɪstɪks
AM sfrəˈdʒɪstɪks

sphygmogram
BR ˈsfɪɡməɡram, -z
AM ˈsfɪɡməˌɡræm, -z

sphygmograph
BR ˈsfɪɡməɡrɑːf,
ˈsfɪɡməɡraf, -s
AM ˈsfɪɡməˌɡræf, -s

sphygmographic
BR ˌsfɪɡməˈɡrafɪk
AM ˌsfɪɡməˈɡræfɪk

sphygmographic-ally
BR ˌsfɪɡməˈɡrafɪkli
AM ˌsfɪɡməˈɡræfək(ə)li

sphygmography
BR sfɪɡˈmɒɡrəfi
AM sfɪɡˈmaɡrəfi

sphygmological
BR ˌsfɪɡməˈlɒdʒɪkl
AM ˌsfɪɡməˈladʒəkəl

sphygmology
BR sfɪɡˈmɒlədʒi
AM sfɪɡˈmalədʒi

sphygmomano-meter
BR ˌsfɪɡməʊməˈnɒm-
ɪtə(r), -z
AM ˌsfɪɡmoʊməˈnɑm-
ədər, -z

sphygmomano-metric
BR ˌsfɪɡməʊˌmanə-
ˈmɛtrɪk
AM ˌsfɪɡmoʊˌmɑnə-
ˈmɛtrɪk

spic
BR spɪk, -s
AM spɪk, -s

spica
BR ˈspʌɪkə(r), -z
AM ˈspaɪkə, -z

spicate
BR ˈspʌɪkeɪt, ˈspʌɪkət
AM ˈspaɪˌkeɪt

spicated
BR spɪˈkeɪtɪd,
spʌɪˈkeɪtɪd
AM ˈspaɪˌkeɪdɪd

spiccato
BR spɪˈkɑːtəʊ, -z
AM spəˈkɑdou, -z

spice
BR spʌɪs, -ɪz, -ɪŋ, -t
AM spaɪs, -ɪz, -ɪŋ, -t

spiceberry
BR ˈspʌɪsˌbɛr|i, -ɪz
AM ˈspaɪsˌbɛri, -z

spicebush
BR ˈspʌɪsbʊʃ, -ɪz
AM ˈspaɪsˌbʊʃ, -əz

spicery
BR ˈspʌɪs(ə)r|i, -ɪz
AM ˈspaɪs(ə)ri, -z

spicey
BR ˈspʌɪsi
AM ˈspaɪsi

spicily
BR ˈspʌɪsɪli
AM ˈspaɪsɪli

spiciness
BR ˈspʌɪsɪnɪs
AM ˈspaɪsɪnɪs

spick
BR spɪk, -s
AM spɪk, -s

spick-and-span
BR ˌspɪk(ə)n(d)ˈspan
AM ˌspɪkənˈspæn

spicknel
BR ˈspɪknl, -z
AM ˈspɪknəl, -z

spicular
BR ˈspɪkjələ(r)
AM ˈspɪkjələr

spiculate
BR ˈspɪkjələt
AM ˈspɪkjələt,
ˈspɪkjəˌleɪt

spicule
BR ˈspɪkjuːl
ˈspʌɪkjuːl, -z
AM ˈspɪˌkjul, -z

spicy
BR ˈspʌɪs|i, -ɪə(r), -ɪɪst
AM ˈspaɪsi, -ər, -ɪst

spider
BR ˈspʌɪdə(r), -z
AM ˈspaɪdər, -z

spiderish
BR ˈspʌɪd(ə)rɪʃ
AM ˈspaɪdərɪʃ

spiderman
BR ˈspʌɪdəman
AM ˈspaɪdərˌmæn

spidermen
BR ˈspʌɪdəmɛn
AM ˈspaɪdərˌmɛn

spiderwort
BR ˈspʌɪdəwəːt, -s
AM ˈspaɪdərwərt,
ˈspaɪdərwɔ(ə)rt, -s

spidery
BR ˈspʌɪd(ə)ri
AM ˈspaɪdəri

Spiegal
BR ˈspiːɡl, ˈʃpiːɡl
AM ˈspiɡəl

spiegeleisen
BR ˈspiːɡlˌʌɪzn
AM ˈspiɡəˌlaɪsən

Spiegl
BR ˈspiːɡl, ˈʃpiːɡl
AM ˈspiɡəl

spiel
BR ʃpiːl, spiːl, -z
AM spi(ə)l, ʃpi(ə)l, -z

Spielberg
BR ˈspiːlbəːɡ
AM ˈspilˌbɜrɡ

spieler
BR ˈʃpiːlə(r), ˈspiːlə(r),
-z
AM ˈspi(ə)lər,
ˈʃpi(ə)lər, -z

spiffily
BR ˈspɪfɪli
AM ˈspɪfɪli

spiffiness
BR ˈspɪfnɪs
AM ˈspɪfinɪs

spiffing
BR ˈspɪfɪŋ
AM ˈspɪfɪŋ

spifflicate
BR ˈspɪflɪkeɪt, -s, -ɪŋ, -ɪd

AM 'spɪf(ə)lə̩keɪt, -ts, -dɪŋ, -dɪd

spifflication
BR ˌspɪflɪ'keɪʃn
AM ˌspɪf(ə)lə'keɪʃən

spiffy
BR 'spɪf|i, -ɪə(r), -ɪɪst
AM 'spɪfi, -ər, -ɪst

spiflicate
BR 'spɪflɪkeɪt, -s, -ɪŋ, -ɪd
AM 'spɪf(ə)lə̩keɪt, -ts, -dɪŋ, -dɪd

spiflication
BR ˌspɪflɪ'keɪʃn
AM ˌspɪf(ə)lə'keɪʃən

spignel
BR 'spɪgnl, -z
AM 'spɪgnəl, -z

spigot
BR 'spɪgət, -s
AM 'spɪgət, -s

spik
BR spɪk, -s
AM spɪk, -s

spike
BR spaɪk, -s, -ɪŋ, -t
AM spaɪk, -s, -ɪŋ, -t

spikelet
BR 'spaɪklɪt, -s
AM 'spaɪklɪt, -s

spikenard
BR 'spaɪknɑːd
AM 'spaɪk̩nɑrd

spikily
BR 'spaɪkɪli
AM 'spaɪkɪli

spikiness
BR 'spaɪkɪnɪs
AM 'spaɪkɪnɪs

spiky
BR 'spaɪk|i, -ɪə(r), -ɪɪst
AM 'spaɪki, -ər, -ɪst

spile
BR spaɪl, -z, -ɪŋ, -d
AM spaɪl, -z, -ɪŋ, -d

spill
BR spɪl, -z, -ɪŋ, -d
AM spɪl, -z, -ɪŋ, -d

spillage
BR 'spɪl|ɪdʒ, -ɪdʒɪz
AM 'spɪlɪdʒ, -ɪz

Spillane
BR spɪ'leɪn
AM spə'leɪn

spiller
BR 'spɪlə(r), -z
AM 'spɪlər, -z

spillikin
BR 'spɪlɪkɪn, -z
AM 'spɪləkɪn, -z

spillover
BR 'spɪlˌəʊvə(r), -z
AM 'spɪlˌoʊvər, -z

spillway
BR 'spɪlweɪ, -z
AM 'spɪlˌweɪ, -z

Spilsbury
BR 'spɪlzb(ə)ri
AM 'spɪlzˌbɛri

spilt
BR spɪlt
AM spɪlt

spilth
BR spɪlθ, -s
AM spɪlθ, -s

spin
BR spɪn, -z, -ɪŋ
AM spɪn, -z, -ɪŋ

spina bifida
BR ˌspaɪnə 'bɪfɪdə(r)
AM ˌspaɪnə 'bɪfədə

spinaceous
BR spɪ'neɪʃəs
AM spə'neɪʃəs, spɪ'neɪʃəs

spinach
BR 'spɪnɪdʒ, 'spɪnɪtʃ
AM 'spɪnɪtʃ

spinachy
BR 'spɪnɪdʒi, 'spɪnɪtʃi
AM 'spɪnɪtʃi

spinal
BR 'spaɪnl
AM 'spaɪnəl

spinally
BR 'spaɪnl̩i
AM 'spaɪnəli

spindle
BR 'spɪndl, -z
AM 'spɪndəl, -z

spindleshanks
BR 'spɪndlʃæŋks
AM 'spɪndl̩ˌʃæŋks

spindly
BR 'spɪndli
AM 'spɪn(d)li

spin-drier
BR ˌspɪn'draɪə(r), 'spɪnˌdraɪə(r), -z
AM 'spɪnˌdraɪər, -z

spindrift
BR 'spɪndrɪft
AM 'spɪnˌdrɪft

spin-dry
BR ˌspɪn'draɪ, -z, -ɪŋ, -d
AM 'spɪnˌdraɪ, -z, -ɪŋ, -d

spine
BR spaɪn, -z, -d
AM spaɪn, -z, -d

spinel
BR spɪ'nɛl, -z
AM spə'nɛl, -z

spineless
BR 'spaɪnlɪs
AM 'spaɪnlɪs

spinelessly
BR 'spaɪnlɪsli
AM 'spaɪnlɪsli

spinelessness
BR 'spaɪnlɪsnɪs
AM 'spaɪnlɪsnɪs

spinet
BR spɪ'nɛt, 'spɪnɪt, -s

AM 'spɪnɪt, -s

spinifex
BR 'spɪnɪfɛks
AM 'spɪnəˌfɛks

spininess
BR 'spaɪnɪnɪs
AM 'spaɪnɪnɪs

Spink
BR spɪŋk
AM spɪŋk

Spinks
BR spɪŋks
AM spɪŋks

spinnaker
BR 'spɪnəkə(r), -z
AM 'spɪnəkər, -z

spinner
BR 'spɪnə(r), -z
AM 'spɪnər, -z

spinneret
BR ˌspɪnə'rɛt, -s
AM ˌspɪnə'rɛt, -s

spinney
BR 'spɪn|i, -ɪz
AM 'spɪni, -z

spin-off
BR 'spɪnɒf, -s
AM 'spɪnˌɔf, 'spɪnˌɑf, -s

spinose
BR 'spaɪnəʊs
AM 'spaɪˌnoʊs, 'spaɪˌnoʊz

spinous
BR 'spaɪnəs
AM 'spaɪnəs

spin-out
BR 'spɪnaʊt, -s
AM 'spɪnˌaʊt, -s

Spinoza
BR spɪ'nəʊzə(r)
AM spə'noʊzə

Spinozism
BR spɪ'nəʊzɪz(ə)m
AM spə'noʊˌzɪzəm

Spinozist
BR spɪ'nəʊzɪst, -s
AM spə'noʊzəst, -s

Spinozistic
BR ˌspɪnə'zɪstɪk
AM ˌspɪnə'zɪstɪk

spinster
BR 'spɪnstə(r), -z
AM 'spɪnstər, -z

spinsterhood
BR 'spɪnstəhʊd
AM 'spɪnstərˌ(h)ʊd

spinsterish
BR 'spɪnst(ə)rɪʃ
AM 'spɪnst(ə)rɪʃ

spinsterishness
BR 'spɪnst(ə)rɪʃnɪs
AM 'spɪnst(ə)rɪʃnɪs

spinthariscope
BR spɪn'θarɪskəʊp, -s
AM spɪn'θɛrəˌskoʊp, -s

spinule
BR 'spɪnjuːl, -z

AM 'spɪnɪt, -s

spinulose
BR 'spɪnjʊləʊs
AM 'spaɪnjəˌloʊs, 'spɪnjəˌloʊs 'spaɪnjəˌloʊz, 'spɪnjəˌloʊz

spinulous
BR 'spɪnjʊləs
AM 'spaɪnjələs, 'spɪnjələs

spiny
BR 'spaɪni
AM 'spaɪni

Spion Kop
BR ˌspaɪən 'kɒp
AM ˌspaɪən 'kɑp

spiracle
BR 'spaɪrəkl, -z
AM 'spaɪrəkəl, 'spɪrəkəl, -z

spiracula
BR spaɪ'rakjʊlə(r)
AM spə'rækjələ, spaɪ'rækjələ

spiracular
BR spaɪ'rakjʊlə(r)
AM spə'rækjələr, spaɪ'rækjələr

spiraculum
BR spaɪ'rakjʊləm
AM spə'rækjələm, spaɪ'rækjələm

spiraea
BR spaɪ'riːə(r), -z
AM spaɪ'riə, -z

spiral
BR 'spaɪrəl, 'spaɪrl̩, -z, -ɪŋ, -d
AM 'spaɪrəl, -z, -ɪŋ, -d

spirality
BR spaɪ'ralɪti
AM ˌspaɪ'rælədi

spirally
BR 'spaɪrəli, 'spaɪrl̩i
AM 'spaɪrəli

spirant
BR 'spaɪrənt, 'spaɪrn̩t, -s
AM 'spaɪrənt, -s

spire
BR 'spaɪə(r), -z, -d
AM 'spaɪ(ə)r, -z, -d

spirea
BR spaɪ'riːə(r)
AM spaɪ'riə

spirilla
BR spaɪ'rɪlə(r)
AM spaɪ'rɪlə

spirillum
BR spaɪ'rɪləm
AM spaɪ'rɪləm

spirit
BR 'spɪr|ɪt, -ɪts, -ɪtɪŋ, -ɪtɪd
AM 'spɪrɪ|t, -ts, -dɪŋ, -dɪd

spiritedly
BR 'spɪrɪtɪdli
AM 'spɪrɪdɪdli

spiritedness
BR 'spɪrɪtɪdnɪs
AM 'spɪrɪdɪdnɪs

spiritism
BR 'spɪrɪtɪz(ə)m
AM 'spɪrəˌtɪzəm

spiritist
BR 'spɪrɪtɪst, -s
AM 'spɪrədəst, -s

spiritless
BR 'spɪrɪtlɪs
AM 'spɪrɪtlɪs

spiritlessly
BR 'spɪrɪtlɪsli
AM 'spɪrɪtlɪsli

spiritlessness
BR 'spɪrɪtlɪsnɪs
AM 'spɪrɪtlɪsnɪs

spiritous
BR 'spɪrɪtəs
AM 'spɪrɪdəs

spiritual
BR 'spɪrɪtʃʊəl,
'spɪrɪtʃ(ʊ)l,
'spɪrɪtjʊəl, 'spɪrɪtjʊl
AM 'spɪrɪtʃ(əw)əl

spiritualisation
BR ˌspɪrɪtʃʊlaɪ'zeɪʃn,
ˌspɪrɪtʃlʌɪ'zeɪʃn,
ˌspɪrɪtjʊlʌɪ'zeɪʃn
AM ˌspɪrɪtʃ(əw)ələ'zeɪ-
ʃən,
ˌspɪrɪtʃ(əw)əˌlaɪ'zeɪʃən

spiritualise
BR 'spɪrɪtʃʊlʌɪz,
'spɪrɪtʃlʌɪz,
'spɪrɪtjʊlʌɪz, -ɪz, -ɪŋ, -d
AM 'spɪrɪtʃ(əw)əˌlaɪz,
-ɪz, -ɪŋ, -d

spiritualism
BR 'spɪrɪtʃʊlɪz(ə)m,
'spɪrɪtʃlɪz(ə)m,
'spɪrɪtjʊlɪz(ə)m
AM 'spɪrɪtʃ(əw)əˌlɪzəm

spiritualist
BR 'spɪrɪtʃʊlɪst,
'spɪrɪtʃlɪst,
'spɪrɪtjʊlɪst, -s
AM 'spɪrɪtʃ(əw)ələst,
-s

spiritualistic
BR ˌspɪrɪtʃʊ'lɪstɪk,
ˌspɪrɪtʃl'ɪstɪk,
ˌspɪrɪtjʊ'lɪstɪk
AM ˌspɪrɪtʃ(əw)ə'lɪstɪk

spirituality
BR ˌspɪrɪtʃʊ'alɪti,
ˌspɪrɪtjʊ'alɪti
AM ˌspɪrɪtʃ(əw)ə'wælədi

spiritualization
BR ˌspɪrɪtʃʊlʌɪ'zeɪʃn,
ˌspɪrɪtʃlʌɪ'zeɪʃn,
ˌspɪrɪtjʊlʌɪ'zeɪʃn
AM ˌspɪrɪtʃ(əw)ələ'zeɪ-
ʃən,

ˌspɪrɪtʃ(əw)əˌlaɪ'zeɪʃən

spiritualize
BR 'spɪrɪtʃʊlʌɪz,
'spɪrɪtʃlʌɪz,
'spɪrɪtjʊlʌɪz, -ɪz, -ɪŋ, -d
AM 'spɪrɪtʃ(əw)əˌlaɪz,
-ɪz, -ɪŋ, -d

spiritually
BR 'spɪrɪtʃʊəli,
'spɪrɪtʃʊli, 'spɪrɪtʃli,
'spɪrɪtjʊəli, 'spɪrɪtjʊli
AM 'spɪrɪtʃ(əw)əli

spiritualness
BR 'spɪrɪtʃʊəlnəs,
'spɪrɪtʃ(ʊ)lnəs,
'spɪrɪtjʊəlnəs,
'spɪrɪtjʊlnəs
AM 'spɪrɪtʃ(əw)əlnəs

spirituel
BR ˌspɪrɪtʃʊ'ɛl,
ˌspɪrɪtjʊ'ɛl
AM ˌspɪrətʃə'wɛl

spirituelle
BR ˌspɪrɪtʃʊ'ɛl,
ˌspɪrɪtjʊ'ɛl
AM ˌspɪrətʃə'wɛl

spirituous
BR 'spɪrɪtʃʊəs,
'spɪrɪtjʊəs
AM 'spɪrɪtʃ(əw)əs

spirituousness
BR 'spɪrɪtʃʊəsnəs,
'spɪrɪtjʊəsnəs
AM 'spɪrɪtʃ(əw)əsnəs

spirketing
BR 'spəːkɪtɪŋ
AM 'spərkədɪŋ

spirochaete
BR 'spʌɪrəkiːt, -s
AM 'spaɪrəˌkit, -s

spirochete
BR 'spʌɪrəkiːt, -s
AM 'spaɪrəˌkit, -s

spirograph
BR 'spʌɪrəgrɑːf,
'spʌɪrəgraf, -s
AM 'spaɪrəˌgræf, -s

spirographic
BR ˌspʌɪrə'grafɪk
AM ˌspaɪrə'græfɪk

spirographically
BR ˌspʌɪrə'grafɪkli
AM ˌspaɪrə'græfək(ə)li

spirogyra
BR ˌspʌɪrə'dʒʌɪrə(r)
AM ˌspaɪrə'dʒaɪrə

spirometer
BR spʌɪ'rɒmɪtə(r), -z
AM spaɪ'rɑmədər, -z

spirt
BR spəːt, -s, -ɪŋ, -ɪd
AM spərt, -ts, -dɪŋ, -dəd

spiry
BR 'spʌɪr(ə)ri
AM 'spaɪri

spit
BR spɪt, -s, -ɪŋ, -ɪd
AM spɪt|t, -ts, -dɪŋ, -dɪd

Spitalfields
BR 'spɪtlfiːldz
AM 'spɪdəlˌfildz

spit-and-polish
BR ˌspɪt(ə)n(d)'pɒlɪʃ
AM ˌspɪdən'pɑlɪʃ

spitball
BR 'spɪtbɔːl, -z
AM 'spɪtˌbɒl, 'spɪtˌbɑl,
-z

spitballer
BR 'spɪtˌbɔːlə(r), -z
AM 'spɪtˌbɒlər,
'spɪtˌbɑlər, -z

spitchcock
BR 'spɪtʃkɒk, -s, -ɪŋ, -t
AM 'spɪtʃˌkɑk, -s, -ɪŋ, -t

spite
BR spʌɪt, -s, -ɪŋ, -ɪd
AM spaɪt, -ts, -dɪŋ, -dɪd

spiteful
BR 'spʌɪtf(ʊ)l
AM 'spaɪtfəl

spitefully
BR 'spʌɪtfʊli, 'spʌɪtfli
AM 'spaɪtf(ə)li

spitefulness
BR 'spʌɪtf(ʊ)lnəs
AM 'spaɪtfəlnəs

spitfire
BR 'spɪtˌfʌɪə(r), -z
AM 'spɪtˌfaɪ(ə)r, -z

Spithead
BR spɪt'hɛd
AM spɪt'hɛd

Spitsbergen
BR 'spɪtsˌbəːg(ə)n
AM 'spɪtsˌbərgən

spitter
BR 'spɪtə(r), -z
AM 'spɪdər, -z

spittle
BR 'spɪtl
AM 'spɪdəl

spittly
BR 'spɪtli
AM 'spɪdli

spittoon
BR spɪ'tuːn, -z
AM spɪ'tun, -z

spitty
BR 'spɪti
AM 'spɪdi

spitz
BR spɪts, -ɪz
AM spɪts, -ɪz

spiv
BR spɪv, -z
AM spɪv, -z

spivish
BR 'spɪvɪʃ
AM 'spɪvɪʃ

spivvery
BR 'spɪv(ə)ri
AM 'spɪv(ə)ri

spivvish
BR 'spɪvɪʃ

spivish
AM 'spɪvɪʃ

spivvy
BR 'spɪvi
AM 'spɪvi

splake
BR spleɪk, -s
AM spleɪk, -s

splanchnic
BR 'splaŋknɪk
AM 'splæŋknɪk

splanchnology
BR ˌsplaŋk'nɒlədʒi
AM ˌsplæŋk'nɑlədʒi

splanchnotomy
BR ˌsplaŋk'nɒtəm|i, -ɪz
AM ˌsplæŋk'nɑdəmi, -z

splash
BR splaʃ, -ɪz, -ɪŋ, -t
AM splæʃ, -əz, -ɪŋ, -t

splashback
BR 'splaʃbak, -s
AM 'splæʃˌbæk, -s

splashboard
BR 'splaʃbɔːd, -z
AM 'splæʃˌbɔ(ə)rd, -z

splashdown
BR 'splaʃdaʊn, -z
AM 'splæʃˌdaʊn, -z

splashily
BR 'splaʃɪli
AM 'splæʃəli

splashiness
BR 'splaʃɪnɪs
AM 'splæʃɪnɪs

splashy
BR 'splaʃi
AM 'splæʃi

splat
BR splat, -s
AM splæt, -s

splatter
BR 'splatə(r), -əz,
-(ə)rɪŋ, -əd
AM 'splædər, -z, -ɪŋ, -d

splay
BR spleɪ, -z, -ɪŋ, -d
AM spleɪ, -z, -ɪŋ, -d

splay-feet
BR ˌspleɪ'fiːt
AM 'spleɪˌfit

splay-foot
BR ˌspleɪ'fʊt
AM 'spleɪˌfʊt

splay-footed
BR ˌspleɪ'fʊtɪd
AM 'spleɪˌfʊdəd

spleen
BR spliːn, -z
AM splin, -z

spleenful
BR 'spliːnf(ʊ)l
AM 'splinfəl

spleenwort
BR 'spliːnwəːt, -s
AM 'splinwərt,
'splinˌwɔ(ə)rt, -s

spleeny
BR 'spliːn|i, -ɪə(r), -ɪɪst
AM 'splini, -ər, -ɪst

splendent
BR 'splend(ə)nt
AM 'splɛndənt

splendid
BR 'splendɪd
AM 'splɛndəd

splendidly
BR 'splendɪdli
AM 'splɛndədli

splendidness
BR 'splendɪdnɪs
AM 'splɛndədnəs

splendiferous
BR splɛn'dɪf(ə)rəs
AM splɛn'dɪf(ə)rəs

splendiferously
BR splɛn'dɪf(ə)rəsli
AM splɛn'dɪf(ə)rəsli

splendiferousness
BR splɛn'dɪf(ə)rəsnəs
AM splɛn'dɪf(ə)rəsnəs

splendor
BR 'splendə(r), -z
AM 'splɛndər, -z

splendour
BR 'splendə(r), -z
AM 'splɛndər, -z

splenectomy
BR spliː'nɛktəm|i,
splɪ'nɛktəm|i, -ɪz
AM splə'nɛktəmi, -z

splenetic
BR splɪ'nɛtɪk
AM splə'nɛdɪk

splenetically
BR splɪ'nɛtɪkli
AM splə'nɛdək(ə)li

splenial
BR 'spliːnɪəl
AM 'splinɪəl

splenic
BR 'spliːnɪk, 'splɛnɪk
AM 'splinɪk, 'splɛnɪk

splenii
BR 'spliːnɪʌɪ
AM 'splini,aɪ

splenitis
BR spliː'nʌɪtɪs,
splɪ'nʌɪtɪs
AM spli'naɪdɪs

splenius
BR 'spliːnɪəs
AM 'splinɪəs

splenoid
BR 'spliːnɔɪd,
'splɛnɔɪd
AM 'spli,nɔɪd,
'splɛ,nɔɪd

splenology
BR spliː'nɒlədʒi,
splɪ'nɒlədʒi
splə'nɒlədʒi

splenomegaly
BR ,spliːnə(ʊ)'mɛɡəl|i,
,splɪːnə(ʊ)'mɛɡl|i, -ɪz
AM ,splinə'mɛɡəli,
,splɛnə'mɛɡəli, -z

splenotomy
BR spliː'nɒtəm|i,
splɪ'nɒtəm|i, -ɪz
AM spli'nɑdəmi,
splə'nɑdəmi, -z

splice
BR splʌɪs, -ɪz, -ɪŋ, -t
AM splaɪs, -ɪz, -ɪŋ, -t

splicer
BR 'splʌɪsə(r), -z
AM 'splaɪsər, -z

splif
BR splɪf, -s
AM splɪf, -s

spliff
BR splɪf, -s
AM splɪf, -s

spline
BR splʌɪn, -z
AM splaɪn, -z

splint
BR splɪnt, -s, -ɪŋ, -ɪd
AM splɪn|t, -ts, -(t)ɪŋ, -(t)əd

splint-bone
BR 'splɪntbəʊn, -z
AM 'splɪnt,boʊn, -z

splint-coal
BR 'splɪntkəʊl, -z
AM 'splɪnt,koʊl, -z

splinter
BR 'splɪnt|ə(r), -əz, -(ə)rɪŋ, -əd
AM 'splɪn(t)ər, -z, -ɪŋ, -d

splintery
BR 'splɪnt(ə)ri
AM 'splɪn(t)əri

split
BR splɪt, -s, -ɪŋ, -ɪd
AM splɪ|t, -ts, -dɪŋ, -dɪd

split-level
BR ,splɪt'lɛvl
AM 'splɪt,lɛvəl

split-second
BR ,splɪt'sɛknd
AM 'splɪt,sɛkənd

splitter
BR 'splɪtə(r), -z
AM 'splɪt(d)ər, -z

split-up
BR 'splɪtʌp, -s
AM 'splɪd,əp, -s

splodge
BR splɒdʒ, -ɪz
AM splɑdʒ, -əz

splodginess
BR 'splɒdʒɪnɪs
AM 'splɑdʒɪnɪs

splodgy
BR 'splɒdʒ|i, -ɪə(r), -ɪɪst
AM 'splɑdʒi, -ər, -ɪst

sploosh
BR spluːʃ, -ɪz, -ɪŋ, -t
AM spluʃ, -əz, -ɪŋ, -t

splosh
BR splɒʃ, -ɪz, -ɪŋ, -t
AM splɑʃ, -əz, -ɪŋ, -t

splotch
BR splɒtʃ, -ɪz
AM splɑtʃ, -əz

splotchiness
BR 'splɒtʃɪnɪs
AM 'splɑtʃɪnɪs

splotchy
BR 'splɒtʃ|i, -ɪə(r), -ɪɪst
AM 'splɑtʃi, -ər, -ɪst

Splott
BR splɒt
AM splɑt

splurge
BR splɜːdʒ, -ɪz, -ɪŋ, -d
AM splɜrdʒ, -əz, -ɪŋ, -d

splutter
BR 'splʌt|ə(r), -əz, -(ə)rɪŋ, -əd
AM 'spləd|ər, -z, -ɪŋ, -d

splutterer
BR 'splʌt(ə)rə(r), -z
AM 'splədərər, -z

splutteringly
BR 'splʌt(ə)rɪŋli
AM 'splədərɪŋli

spluttery
BR 'splʌt(ə)ri
AM 'splədəri

Spock
BR spɒk
AM spak

Spode®
BR spəʊd
AM spoʊd

spodosol
BR 'spɒdəsɒl
AM 'spɑdə,sɔl, 'spɑdə,sɑl

spodumene
BR 'spɒdjʊmiːn
AM 'spɑdjə,min

Spofforth
BR 'spɒfəθ
AM 'spafərθ

spoil
BR spɔɪl, -z, -ɪŋ, -d
AM spɔɪl, -z, -ɪŋ, -d

spoilage
BR 'spɔɪlɪdʒ
AM 'spɔɪlɪdʒ

spoiler
BR 'spɔɪlə(r), -z
AM 'spɔɪlər, -z

spoilsman
BR 'spɔɪlzmən
AM 'spɔɪlzmən

spoilsmen
BR 'spɔɪlzmən
AM 'spɔɪlzmən

spoilsport
BR 'spɔɪlspɔːt, -s

AM 'spɔɪl,spɔ(ə)rt, -s

spoilt
BR spɔɪlt
AM spɔɪlt

Spokane
BR spəʊ'kan
AM spoʊ'kæn

spoke
BR spəʊk, -s
AM spoʊk, -s

spoke-bone
BR 'spəʊkbəʊn, -z
AM 'spoʊk,boʊn, -z

spoken
BR 'spəʊk(ə)n
AM 'spoʊkən

spokeshave
BR 'spəʊkʃeɪv, -z
AM 'spoʊk,ʃeɪv, -z

spokesman
BR 'spəʊksmən
AM 'spoʊksmən

spokesmen
BR 'spəʊksmən
AM 'spoʊksmən

spokesperson
BR 'spəʊks,pɜːsn, -z
AM 'spoʊks,pɜrsən, -z

spokeswoman
BR 'spəʊks,wʊmən
AM 'spoʊks,wʊmən

spokeswomen
BR 'spəʊks,wɪmɪn
AM 'spoʊks,wɪmɪn

spokewise
BR 'spəʊkwʌɪz
AM 'spoʊk,waɪz

spoliation
BR ,spəʊlɪ'eɪʃn
AM ,spoʊli'eɪʃən

spoliator
BR 'spəʊlɪeɪtə(r), -z
AM 'spoʊli,eɪdər, -z

spoliatory
BR 'spəʊlɪət(ə)ri
AM 'spoʊliə,tɔri

spondaic
BR spɒn'deɪɪk
AM span'deɪɪk

spondee
BR 'spɒndiː, -z
AM 'spandi, -z

Spondon
BR 'spɒndən
AM 'spandən

spondulicks
BR spɒn'd(j)uːlɪks
AM span'd(j)ulɪks

spondylitis
BR ,spɒndɪ'lʌɪtɪs
AM ,spɑndə'laɪdɪs

Spong
BR spɒŋ
AM spɑŋ

sponge
BR spʌn(d)ʒ, -ɪz, -ɪŋ, -d
AM spəndʒ, -əz, -ɪŋ, -d

spongeable
BR 'spʌn(d)ʒəbl
AM 'spʌnd(d)ʒəbəl

spongelike
BR 'spʌn(d)ʒlaɪk
AM 'spʌnd(d)ʒlaɪk

sponger
BR 'spʌn(d)ʒə(r), -z
AM 'spʌnd(d)ʒər, -z

spongiform
BR 'spʌn(d)ʒɪfɔːm
AM 'spʌnd(d)ʒəˌfɔː(ə)rm

spongily
BR 'spʌn(d)ʒɪli
AM 'spʌnd(d)ʒəli

sponginess
BR 'spʌn(d)ʒɪnɪs
AM 'spʌnd(d)ʒɪnɪs

spongy
BR 'spʌn(d)ʒi, -ɪə(r),
-ɪɪst
AM 'spʌnd(d)ʒi, -ər, -ɪɪst

sponsion
BR 'spɒnʃn
AM 'spʌnʃən

sponson
BR 'spɒnsn, -z
AM 'spʌnsən, -z

sponsor
BR 'spɒns|ə(r), -əz,
-(ə)rɪŋ, -əd
AM 'spɑːn(t)sər, -z, -ɪŋ,
-d

sponsorial
BR spɒn'sɔːriəl
AM spɑːn'sɔːriəl

sponsorship
BR 'spɒnsəʃɪp
AM 'spɑːn(t)sərˌʃɪp

spontaneity
BR ˌspɒntə'neɪɪti,
ˌspɒntə'niːɪti
AM ˌspɑːn(t)ə'niːɪdi

spontaneous
BR spɒn'teɪniəs
AM spɑːn'teɪniəs

spontaneously
BR spɒn'teɪniəsli
AM spɑːn'teɪniəsli

spontaneousness
BR spɒn'teɪniəsnəs
AM spɑːn'teɪniəsnəs

spontoon
BR spɒn'tuːn, -z
AM ˌspɑːn'tuːn, -z

spoof
BR spuːf, -s, -ɪŋ, -t
AM spuːf, -s, -ɪŋ, -t

spoofer
BR 'spuːfə(r), -z
AM 'spuːfər, -z

spoofery
BR 'spuːf(ə)ri
AM 'spuːfəri

spook
BR spuːk, -s, -ɪŋ, -t
AM spuːk, -s, -ɪŋ, -t

spookily
BR 'spuːkɪli
AM 'spʊkəli

spookiness
BR 'spuːkɪnɪs
AM 'spʊkɪnɪs

spooky
BR 'spuːk|i, -ɪə(r), -ɪɪst
AM 'spʊki, -ər, -ɪst

spool
BR spuːl, -z, -ɪŋ, -d
AM spuːl, -z, -ɪŋ, -d

spoon
BR spuːn, -z, -ɪŋ, -d
AM spuːn, -z, -ɪŋ, -d

spoonbeak
BR 'spuːnbiːk, -s
AM 'spuːnˌbik, -s

spoonbill
BR 'spuːnbɪl, -z
AM 'spuːnˌbɪl, -z

spoon-bread
BR 'spuːnbrɛd, -z
AM 'spuːnˌbrɛd, -z

spooner
BR 'spuːnə(r), -z
AM 'spuːnər, -z

spoonerism
BR 'spuːnərɪz(ə)m, -z
AM 'spuːnəˌrɪzəm, -z

spoonfed
BR 'spuːnfɛd
AM 'spuːnˌfɛd

spoonfeed
BR 'spuːnfiːd, -z, -ɪŋ
AM 'spuːnˌfid, -z, -ɪŋ

spoonful
BR 'spuːnfʊl, -z
AM 'spuːnˌfʊl, -z

spoonily
BR 'spuːnɪli
AM 'spuːnəli

spooniness
BR 'spuːnɪnɪs
AM 'spuːnɪnɪs

spoonsful
BR 'spuːnzfʊl
AM 'spuːnzˌfʊl

spoony
BR 'spuːn|i, -ɪə(r), -ɪɪst
AM 'spuːni, -ər, -ɪst

spoor
BR spʊə(r), spɔː(r), -z
AM spʊ(ə)r, spɔ(ə)r, -z

spoorer
BR 'spʊərə(r),
'spɔːrə(r), -z
AM 'spʊrər, 'spɔrər, -z

Sporades
BR 'spɒrədiːz,
spə'rɑːdiːz
AM 'spɔrəˌdiz

sporadic
BR spə'radɪk
AM spə'rædɪk

sporadically
BR spə'radɪkli

AM spə'rædək(ə)li

sporangia
BR spə'ran(d)ʒɪə(r)
AM spə'rænd(d)ʒɪə,
spoʊ'rændʒɪə

sporangial
BR spə'ran(d)ʒɪəl
AM spə'rændʒɪəl,
spoʊ'rændʒɪəl

sporangium
BR spə'ran(d)ʒɪəm
AM spə'rændʒɪəm,
spoʊ'rændʒɪəm

spore
BR spɔː(r), -z
AM spɔ(ə)r, -z

sporogenesis
BR ˌspɒrə(ʊ)'dʒɛnɪsɪs
AM ˌspɒroʊ'dʒɛnəsəs

sporogenous
BR spə'rɒdʒɪnəs
AM spə'rɑːdʒənəs,
spoʊ'rɑːdʒənəs

sporophore
BR 'spɒrəfɔː(r),
'spɔːrəfɔː, -z
AM 'spɔrəˌfɔ(ə)r, -z

sporophyte
BR 'spɒrə(ʊ)faɪt,
'spɔːrə(ʊ)faɪt, -s
AM 'spɔrəˌfaɪt, -s

sporophytic
BR ˌspɒrə(ʊ)'fɪtɪk,
ˌspɔːrə(ʊ)'fɪtɪk
AM ˌspɔrə'fɪdɪk

sporophytically
BR ˌspɒrə(ʊ)'fɪtɪkli,
ˌspɔːrə(ʊ)'fɪtɪkli
AM ˌspɔrə'fɪdɪk(ə)li

sporozoite
BR ˌspɒrə(ʊ)'zəʊʌɪt,
ˌspɔːrə(ʊ)'zəʊʌɪt, -s
AM ˌspɔrə'zoʊˌaɪt, -s

sporran
BR 'spɒrən, 'spɒrn̩, -z
AM 'spɑrən, -z

sport
BR spɔːt, -s, -ɪŋ, -ɪd
AM spɔ(ə)rt, -ts,
'spɔrdɪŋ, 'spɔrdəd

sporter
BR 'spɔːtə(r), -z
AM 'spɔrdər, -z

sportif
BR spɔː'tiːf
AM spɔr'tif

sportily
BR 'spɔːtɪli
AM 'spɔrdəli

sportiness
BR 'spɔːtɪnɪs
AM 'spɔrdɪnɪs

sportingly
BR 'spɔːtɪŋli
AM 'spɔrdɪŋli

sportive
BR 'spɔːtɪv
AM 'spɔrdɪv

sportively
BR 'spɔːtɪvli
AM 'spɔrdɪvli

sportiveness
BR 'spɔːtɪvnɪs
AM 'spɔrdɪvnɪs

sportscast
BR 'spɔːtskɑːst,
'spɔːtskast, -s, -ɪŋ
AM 'spɔrtsˌkæst, -s, -ɪŋ

sportscaster
BR 'spɔːtsˌkɑːstə(r),
'spɔːtsˌkastə(r),
AM 'spɔrtsˌkæstər, -z

sportshirt
BR 'spɔːtʃɜːt, -s
AM 'spɔrtˌʃɜrt, -s

sportsman
BR 'spɔːtsmən
AM 'spɔrtsmən

sportsmanlike
BR 'spɔːtsmənlaɪk
AM 'spɔrtsmənˌlaɪk

sportsmanly
BR 'spɔːtsmənli
AM 'spɔrtsmənli

sportsmanship
BR 'spɔːtsmənʃɪp
AM 'spɔrtsmənˌʃɪp

sportsmen
BR 'spɔːtsmən
AM 'spɔrtsmən

sportspeople
BR 'spɔːtsˌpiːpl
AM 'spɔrtsˌpipəl

sportsperson
BR 'spɔːtsˌpɜːsn, -z
AM 'spɔrtsˌpɜrsən, -z

sportswear
BR 'spɔːtsweː(r)
AM 'spɔrtsˌwɛ(ə)r

sportswoman
BR 'spɔːtsˌwʊmən
AM 'spɔrtsˌwʊmən

sportswomen
BR 'spɔːtsˌwɪmɪn
AM 'spɔrtsˌwɪmɪn

sportswriter
BR 'spɔːtsˌraɪtə(r), -z
AM 'spɔrtsˌraɪdər, -z

sporty
BR 'spɔːti
AM 'spɔrdi

sporular
BR 'spɒrjʊlə(r)
AM 'spɔrjələr

sporule
BR 'spɒr(j)uːl, -z
AM 'spɔrˌjul, -z

spot
BR spɒt, -s, -ɪŋ, -ɪd
AM spɑ|t, -ts, -dɪŋ, -dəd

spot-check
BR ˌspɒt'tʃɛk, -s, -ɪŋ, -t
AM 'spɑtˌtʃɛk, -s, -ɪŋ, -t

spotlamp
BR 'spɒtlamp, -s

AM 'spɒt,læmp, -s

spotless
BR 'spɒtləs
AM 'spɑtləs

spotlessly
BR 'spɒtləsli
AM 'spɑtləsli

spotlessness
BR 'spɒtləsnəs
AM 'spɑtləsnəs

spotlight
BR 'spɒtlʌɪt, -s, -ɪŋ, -ɪd
AM 'spɑt,laɪt, -ts, -dɪŋ, -dɪd

spot-on
BR ,spɒt'ɒn
AM ,spɑd'ɑn

spottedness
BR 'spɒtɪdnɪs
AM 'spɑdədnəs

spotter
BR 'spɒtə(r), -z
AM 'spɑdər, -z

spottily
BR 'spɒtɪli
AM 'spɑdəli

spottiness
BR 'spɒtɪnɪs
AM 'spɑdɪnɪs

Spottiswoode
BR 'spɒt(ɪ)swʊd, 'spɒtɪzwʊd
AM 'spɑts,wʊd, 'spɑdəs,wʊd

spotty
BR 'spɒt|i, -ɪə(r), -ɪɪst
AM 'spɑdi, -ər, -ɪst

spotweld
BR 'spɒtwɛld, -z, -ɪŋ, -ɪd
AM 'spɑt,wɛld, -z, -ɪŋ, -əd

spotwelder
BR 'spɒt,wɛldə(r), -z
AM 'spɑt,wɛldər, -z

spousal
BR 'spaʊzl, -z
AM 'spaʊzəl, -z

spouse
BR spaʊs, spaʊz, -ɪz
AM spaʊs, -əz

spout
BR spaʊt, -s, -ɪŋ, -ɪd
AM spaʊ|t, -ts, -dɪŋ, -dəd

spouter
BR 'spaʊtə(r), -z
AM 'spaʊdər, -z

spoutless
BR 'spaʊtləs
AM 'spaʊtləs

Sprachgefühl
BR 'ʃprɑːxɡəfuːl, 'ʃpraxɡefuːl
AM 'ʃprakɡə,f(j)ul

sprag
BR sprag, -z
AM spræg, -z

Spragge
BR sprag
AM spræg

Sprague
BR spreɪɡ
AM spreɪɡ

sprain
BR spreɪn, -z, -ɪŋ, -d
AM spreɪn, -z, -ɪŋ, -d

spraing
BR spreɪŋ
AM spreɪŋ

spraint
BR spreɪnt, -s
AM spreɪnt, -s

sprang
BR spraŋ
AM spræŋ

sprat
BR sprat, -s, -ɪŋ
AM spræ|t, -ts, -dɪŋ

Spratly Islands
BR 'spratlɪ ,ʌɪlən(d)z
AM 'sprætli ,aɪlən(d)z

Spratt
BR sprat
AM spræt

spratter
BR 'spratə(r), -z
AM 'sprædər, -z

sprauncy
BR 'sprɔːns|i, -ɪə(r), -ɪɪst
AM 'sprɒnsi, 'spransi, -ər, -ɪst

sprawl
BR sprɔːl, -z, -ɪŋ, -d
AM sprɔl, spral, -z, -ɪŋ, -d

sprawler
BR 'sprɔːlə(r), -z
AM 'sprɔlər, 'spralər, -z

sprawlingly
BR 'sprɔːlɪŋli
AM 'sprɔlɪŋli, 'spralɪŋli

spray
BR spreɪ, -z, -ɪŋ, -d
AM spreɪ, -z, -ɪŋ, -d

sprayable
BR 'spreɪəbl
AM 'spreɪəbəl

spray-dry
BR 'spreɪdrʌɪ, -z, -ɪŋ, -d
AM 'spreɪ,draɪ, -z, -ɪŋ, -d

sprayer
BR 'spreɪə(r), -z
AM 'spreɪər, -z

sprayey
BR 'spreɪi
AM 'spreɪi

spray-paint
BR 'spreɪpeɪnt, -s, -ɪŋ, -ɪd
AM 'spreɪ,peɪn|t, -ts, -(t)ɪŋ, -(t)ɪd

spread
BR sprɛd, -z, -ɪŋ
AM sprɛd, -z, -ɪŋ

spreadable
BR 'sprɛdəbl
AM 'sprɛdəbəl

spread-eagle
BR ,sprɛd'iːɡḷ, 'spredi:ɡḷ, -lz, -ḷɪŋ \-lɪŋ, -ld
AM 'sprɛd'iɡḷəl, -əlz, -(ə)lɪŋ, -əld

spreader
BR 'sprɛdə(r), -z
AM 'sprɛdər, -z

spreadsheet
BR 'sprɛdʃiːt, -s
AM 'sprɛd,ʃit, -s

spree
BR spriː, -z
AM spri, -z

sprig
BR sprɪɡ, -z
AM sprɪɡ, -z

spriggy
BR 'sprɪɡ|i, -ɪə(r), -ɪɪst
AM 'sprɪɡi, -ər, -ɪst

sprightliness
BR 'sprʌɪtlɪnɪs
AM 'spraɪtlinɪs

sprightly
BR 'sprʌɪtl|i, -ɪə(r), -ɪɪst
AM 'spraɪtli, -ər, -ɪst

sprigtail
BR 'sprɪɡteɪl, -z
AM 'sprɪɡ,teɪl, -z

spring
BR sprɪŋ, -z, -ɪŋ
AM sprɪŋ, -z, -ɪŋ

spring balance
BR ,sprɪŋ 'baləns, + 'balns, -ɪz
AM 'sprɪŋ ,bæləns, -əz

springboard
BR 'sprɪŋbɔːd, -z
AM 'sprɪŋ,bɔ(ə)rd, -z

springbok
BR 'sprɪŋbɒk, -s
AM 'sprɪŋbak, -s

spring-clean¹
noun
BR 'sprɪŋkliːn, -z
AM 'sprɪŋ,klin, -z

spring-clean²
verb
BR ,sprɪŋ'kliːn, 'sprɪŋkliːn, -z, -ɪŋ, -d
AM 'sprɪŋ'klin, -z, -ɪŋ, -d

spring-cleaning
BR ,sprɪŋ'kliːnɪŋ, 'sprɪŋkliːnɪŋ
AM 'sprɪŋ'klinɪŋ

springe
BR sprɪn(d)ʒ, -ɪz
AM sprɪndʒ, -ɪz

springer
BR 'sprɪŋə(r), -z
AM 'sprɪŋər, -z

Springfield
BR 'sprɪŋfiːld
AM 'sprɪŋ,fild

springform
BR 'sprɪŋfɔːm, -z
AM 'sprɪŋ,fɔ(ə)rm, -z

springhouse
BR 'sprɪŋhaʊ|s, -zɪz
AM 'sprɪŋ,(h)aʊ|s, -zəz

springily
BR 'sprɪŋɪli
AM 'sprɪŋɪli

springiness
BR 'sprɪŋɪnɪs
AM 'sprɪŋɪnɪs

springless
BR 'sprɪŋlɪs
AM 'sprɪŋlɪs

springlet
BR 'sprɪŋlɪt, -s
AM 'sprɪŋlɪt, -s

springlike
BR 'sprɪŋlʌɪk
AM 'sprɪŋ,laɪk

spring-loaded
BR ,sprɪŋ'ləʊdɪd
AM 'sprɪŋ,loʊdəd

Springs
BR sprɪŋz
AM sprɪŋz

Springsteen
BR 'sprɪŋstiːn
AM 'sprɪŋ,stin

springtail
BR 'sprɪŋteɪl, -z
AM 'sprɪŋ,teɪl, -z

springtide
season of Spring
BR 'sprɪŋtʌɪd, -z
AM 'sprɪŋ,taɪd, -z

springtime
BR 'sprɪŋtʌɪm
AM 'sprɪŋ,taɪm

springwater
BR 'sprɪŋ,wɔːtə(r)
AM 'sprɪŋ,wɔdər, 'sprɪŋ,wadər

springy
BR 'sprɪŋ|i, -ɪə(r), -ɪɪst
AM 'sprɪŋi, -ər, -ɪst

sprinkle
BR 'sprɪŋk|ḷ, -lz, -ḷɪŋ \-lɪŋ, -ld
AM 'sprɪŋkəl, -əlz, -(ə)lɪŋ, -əld

sprinkler
BR 'sprɪŋklə(r), 'sprɪŋkḷə(r), -z
AM 'sprɪŋk(ə)lər, -z

sprinkling
BR 'sprɪŋklɪŋ, 'sprɪŋkḷɪŋ, -z
AM 'sprɪŋk(ə)lɪŋ, -z

sprint
BR sprɪnt, -s, -ɪŋ, -ɪd
AM sprɪn|t, -ts, -(t)ɪŋ,
-(t)ɪd

sprinter
BR 'sprɪntə(r), -z
AM 'sprɪn(t)ər, -z

sprit
BR sprɪt, -s
AM sprɪt, -s

sprite
BR sprʌɪt, -s
AM sprʌɪt, -s

spritely
BR 'sprʌɪtli
AM 'sprʌɪtli

spritsail
BR 'sprɪtsl, 'sprɪtseɪl,
-z
AM 'sprɪtsəl,
'sprɪt,seɪl, -z

spritz
BR sprɪts, -ɪz, -ɪŋ, -t
AM sprɪts, -ɪz, -ɪŋ, -d

spritzer
BR 'sprɪtsə(r), -z
AM 'sprɪtsər, -z

sprocket
BR 'sprɒkɪt, -s
AM 'sprakət, -s

sprog
BR sprɒg, -z
AM sprag, -z

Sproughton
BR 'sprɔːtn
AM 'sprɔtn, 'sprɑtn

Sproule
BR sprəʊl, spruːl
AM sprul

sprout
BR spraʊt, -s, -ɪŋ, -ɪd
AM spraʊ|t, -ts, -dɪŋ,
-dəd

spruce
BR spruːs, -ɪz, -ə(r), -ɪst
AM sprus, -əz, -ər, -əst

sprucely
BR 'spruːsli
AM 'sprusli

spruceness
BR 'spruːsnəs
AM 'sprusnəs

sprucer
BR 'spruːsə(r), -z
AM 'sprusər, -z

sprue
BR spruː, -z
AM spru, -z

spruik
BR spruːk, -s, -ɪŋ, -t
AM spruk, -s, -ɪŋ, -t

spruiker
BR 'spruːkə(r), -z
AM 'sprukər, -z

spruit
BR spreɪt, -s
AM sprʌt, spreɪt, -s

AFK sprœɪt

sprung
BR sprʌŋ
AM sprəŋ

spry
BR sprʌɪ, -ə(r), -ɪst
AM sprai, -ər, -ɪst

spryly
BR 'sprʌɪli
AM 'sprʌɪli

spryness
BR 'sprʌɪnɪs
AM 'sprʌɪnɪs

spud
BR spʌd, -z
AM spəd, -z

spue
BR spjuː, -z, -ɪŋ, -d
AM spju, -z, -ɪŋ, -d

spumante
BR sp(j)ʊ'mant|i, -ɪz
AM sp(j)u'man(t)i,
sp(j)ə'man(t)i, -z

spume
BR spjuːm
AM spjum

spumoni
BR sp(j)ʊ'məʊni
AM spu'məʊni,
spə'məʊni

spumous
BR 'spjuːməs
AM 'spjuməs

spumy
BR 'spjuːm|i, -ɪə(r),
-ɪɪst
AM 'spjumi, -ər, -ɪst

spun
BR spʌn
AM spən

spunk
BR spʌŋk
AM spəŋk

spunkily
BR 'spʌŋkɪli
AM 'spəŋkəli

spunkiness
BR 'spʌŋkɪnɪs
AM 'spəŋkɪnɪs

spunky
BR 'spʌŋk|i, -ɪə(r), -ɪɪst
AM 'spəŋki, -ər, -ɪst

spur
BR spəː(r), -z, -ɪŋ, -d
AM spər, -z, -ɪŋ, -d

spurge
BR 'spəːdʒ, -ɪz
AM 'spərdʒ, -əz

Spurgeon
BR 'spəːdʒ(ə)n
AM 'spərdʒən

spurious
BR 'spjʊərɪəs,
'spjɔːrɪəs
AM 'sp(j)ʊrɪəs,
'spjurɪəs

spuriously
BR 'spjʊərɪəsli,
'spjɔːrɪəsli
AM 'sp(j)ʊrɪəsli,
'spjurɪəsli

spuriousness
BR 'spjʊərɪəsnəs,
'spjɔːrɪəsnəs
AM 'sp(j)ʊrɪəsnəs,
'spjurɪəsnəs

spurless
BR 'spəːləs
AM 'spərləs

Spurling
BR 'spəːlɪŋ
AM 'spərlɪŋ

spurn
BR spəːn, -z, -ɪŋ, -d
AM spərn, -z, -ɪŋ, -d

spurner
BR 'spəːnə(r), -z
AM 'spərnər, -z

**spur-of-the-
moment**
BR ˌspəːrə(v)ðə'məʊ-
m(ə)nt
AM ˌspərə(v)ðə'moʊ-
mənt

Spurrell
BR 'spʌrəl, 'spʌrl̩
AM 'spərəl

spurrey
BR 'spʌr|i, -ɪz
AM 'spəri, -z

spurrier
BR 'spʌrɪə(r),
'spəːrɪə(r), -z
AM 'spəriər, -z

spurry
BR 'spəːr|i, -ɪz
AM 'spəri, -z

spurt
BR spəːt, -s, -ɪŋ, -ɪd
AM spər|t, -ts, -dɪŋ, -dəd

spurwort
BR 'spəːwəːt, -s
AM 'spərwərt,
'spərwɔ(ə)rt, -s

sputa
BR spjuːtə(r)
AM 'spjudə

sputnik
BR 'spʊtnɪk, 'spʌtnɪk,
-s
AM 'spʊtnɪk, 'spətnɪk,
-s

sputter
BR 'spʌtə(r), -əz,
-(ə)rɪŋ, -əd
AM 'spə|dər, -dərz,
-dərɪŋ\-trɪŋ, -dərd

sputterer
BR 'spʌt(ə)rə(r), -z
AM 'spədərər, -z

sputum
BR 'spjuːtəm
AM 'spjudəm

spy
BR spʌɪ, -z, -ɪŋ, -d
AM spai, -z, -ɪŋ, -d

spycatcher
BR 'spʌɪˌkatʃə(r), -z
AM 'spaɪˌkætʃər, -z

spyglass
BR 'spʌɪglɑːs,
'spʌɪglas, -ɪz
AM 'spaɪˌglæs, -əz

spyhole
BR 'spʌɪhəʊl, -z
AM 'spaɪˌhoʊl, -z

spymaster
BR 'spʌɪˌmɑːstə(r),
'spʌɪˌmastə(r), -z
AM 'spaɪˌmæstər, -z

Sqezy
BR 'skwiːzi
AM 'skwizi

squab
BR skwɒb, -z
AM skwɑb, -z

squabble
BR 'skwɒb|l̩, -lz,
-lɪŋ\-lɪŋ, -ld
AM 'skwɑbəl, -əlz,
-(ə)lɪŋ, -əld

squabbler
BR 'skwɒblə(r),
'skwɒblə(r), -z
AM 'skwɑb(ə)lər, -z

squabby
BR 'skwɒbi
AM 'skwɑbi

squab-chick
BR 'skwɒbtʃɪk, -s
AM 'skwɑbˌtʃɪk, -s

squacco
BR 'skwakəʊ, -z
AM 'skwakoʊ, -z

squad
BR skwɒd, -z
AM skwɑd, -z

squaddie
BR 'skwɒd|i, -ɪz
AM 'skwɑdi, -z

squaddy
BR 'skwɒd|i, -ɪz
AM 'skwɑdi, -z

squadron
BR 'skwɒdr(ə)n, -z
AM 'skwɑdrən, -z

squail
BR skweɪl, -z
AM skweɪl, -z

squalid
BR 'skwɒlɪd
AM 'skwɒlɪd, 'skwɑlɪd

squalidity
BR skwɒ'lɪdɪti
AM ˌskwɒ'lɪdɪdi,
ˌskwɑ'lɪdɪdi

squalidly
BR 'skwɒlɪdli
AM 'skwɒlɪdli,
'skwɑlɪdli

squalidness
BR 'skwɒlɪdnɪs
AM 'skwɒlɪdnɪs,
'skwɑlɪdnɪs

squall
BR skwɔːl, -z, -ɪŋ, -d
AM skwɔl, skwɑl, -z,
-ɪŋ, -d

squally
BR 'skwɔːli
AM 'skwɔli, 'skwɑli

squaloid
BR 'skweɪlɔɪd, -z
AM 'skweɪˌlɔɪd, -z

squalor
BR 'skwɒlə(r)
AM 'skwɒlər, 'skwɑlər

squama
BR 'skweɪmə(r)
AM 'skweɪmə

squamae
BR 'skweɪmiː
AM 'skweɪmi,
'skweɪˌmaɪ

squamate
BR 'skweɪmət
AM 'skweɪˌmeɪt

Squamish
BR 'skwɑːmɪʃ, -ɪʃɪz
AM 'skwɑmɪʃ, -əz

squamose
BR 'skweɪməʊs
AM 'skweɪˌmoʊs,
'skweɪˌmoʊz

squamous
BR 'skweɪməs
AM 'skweɪməs

squamously
BR 'skweɪməsli
AM 'skweɪməsli

squamousness
BR 'skweɪməsnəs
AM 'skweɪməsnəs

squamule
BR 'skwæmjuːl,
'skweɪmjuːl, -z
AM 'skwæˌmjul,
'skwɑˌmjul,
'skweɪˌmjul, -z

squander
BR 'skwɒndə(r), -əz,
-(ə)rɪŋ, -əd
AM 'skwɑndər, -ərz,
-(ə)rɪŋ, -ərd

squanderer
BR 'skwɒnd(ə)rə(r), -z
AM 'skwɑnd(ə)rər, -z

square
BR skweː(r), -z, -ɪŋ, -d,
-ə(r), -ɪst
AM skweɪ(ε)r, -z, -ɪŋ, -d,
-ər, -əst

square-bashing
BR 'skweːˌbaʃɪŋ
AM 'skweɪr, bæʃɪŋ

square-built
BR ˌskweː'bɪlt
AM ˌskweɪr'bɪlt

squaredance
BR 'skweːdɑːns,
'skweːdans, -ɪz, -ɪŋ
AM 'skweɪrˌdæns, -əz,
-ɪŋ

square deal
BR ˌskweː 'diːl, -z
AM ˌskweɪr 'dil, -z

square-eyed
BR ˌskweːr'ʌɪd
AM ˌskweɪr'aɪd

squarely
BR 'skweːli
AM 'skweːrli

squareness
BR 'skweːnəs
AM 'skweɪrnəs

squarer
BR 'skweːrə(r), -z
AM 'skweɪrər, -z

square-rigged
BR ˌskweː'rɪgd
AM ˌskweɪr'rɪgd

square-rigger
BR ˌskweː'rɪgə(r), -z
AM ˌskweɪr'rɪgər, -z

square root
BR ˌskweː 'ruːt, -s
AM ˌskweɪr 'rut, -s

Squarial
BR 'skweːrɪəl, -z
AM 'skweɪrɪəl, -z

squarish
BR 'skweːrɪʃ
AM 'skweɪrɪʃ

squarrose
BR 'skwɒrəʊs,
skwɒ'rəʊs,
'skwarəʊs, skwa'rəʊs
AM 'skwɑˌroʊs,
'skwɑˌroʊz

squash
BR skwɒʃ, -ɪz, -ɪŋ, -t
AM skwɔʃ, skwɑʃ, -əz,
-ɪŋ, -t

squashily
BR 'skwɒʃɪli
AM 'skwɔʃəli,
'skwɑʃəli

squashiness
BR 'skwɒʃɪnɪs
AM 'skwɔʃɪnɪs,
'skwɑʃɪnɪs

squashy
BR 'skwɒʃ|i, -ɪə(r), -ɪɪst
AM 'skwɔʃi, 'skwɑʃi,
-ər, -ɪst

squat
BR skwɒt, -s, -ɪŋ, -ɪd
AM skwɑ|t, -ts, -dɪŋ,
-dəd

squatly
BR 'skwɒtli
AM 'skwɑtli

squatness
BR 'skwɒtnəs
AM 'skwɑtnəs

squatter
BR 'skwɒtə(r), -z
AM 'skwɑdər, -z

squaw
BR skwɔː(r), -z
AM skwɔ, skwɑ, -z

squawk
BR skwɔːk, -s, -ɪŋ, -t
AM skwɔk, skwɑk, -s,
-ɪŋ, -t

squawker
BR 'skwɔːkə(r), -z
AM 'skwɔkər,
'skwɑkər, -z

squeak
BR skwiːk, -s, -ɪŋ, -t
AM skwik, -s, -ɪŋ, -t

squeaker
BR 'skwiːkə(r), -z
AM 'skwikər, -z

squeakily
BR 'skwiːkɪli
AM 'skwikɪli

squeakiness
BR 'skwiːkɪnɪs
AM 'skwikɪnɪs

squeaky
BR 'skwiːk|i, -ɪə(r),
-ɪɪst
AM 'skwiki, -ər, -ɪst

squeal
BR skwiːl, -z, -ɪŋ, -d
AM skwil, -z, -ɪŋ, -d

squealer
BR 'skwiːlə(r), -z
AM 'skwilər, -z

squeamish
BR 'skwiːmɪʃ
AM 'skwimɪʃ

squeamishly
BR 'skwiːmɪʃli
AM 'skwimɪʃli

squeamishness
BR 'skwiːmɪʃnɪs
AM 'skwimɪʃnɪs

squeegee
BR 'skwiːdʒiː, -z, -ɪŋ, -d
AM 'skwiˌdʒi, -z, -ɪŋ, -d

Squeers
BR skwɪəz
AM skwɪ(ə)rz

squeezable
BR 'skwiːzəbl
AM 'skwizəbəl

squeeze
BR skwiːz, -ɪz, -ɪŋ, -d
AM skwiz, -əz, -ɪŋ, -d

squeezebox
BR 'skwiːzbɒks, -ɪz
AM 'skwizˌbɑks, -əz

squeezer
BR 'skwiːzə(r), -z
AM 'skwizər, -z

squelch
BR skwɛltʃ, -ɪz, -ɪŋ, -t
AM skwɛltʃ, -əz, -ɪŋ, -t

squelcher
BR 'skwɛltʃə(r), -z
AM 'skwɛltʃər, -z

squelchiness
BR 'skwɛltʃɪnɪs
AM 'skwɛltʃɪnɪs

squelchy
BR 'skwɛltʃ|i, -ɪə(r),
-ɪɪst
AM 'skwɛltʃi, -ər, -ɪst

squib
BR skwɪb, -z
AM skwɪb, -z

squid
BR skwɪd, -z
AM skwɪd, -z

squidginess
BR 'skwɪdʒɪnɪs
AM 'skwɪdʒɪnɪs

squidgy
BR 'skwɪdʒ|i, -ɪə(r),
-ɪɪst
AM 'skwɪdʒi, -ər, -ɪst

squiffed
BR 'skwɪft
AM 'skwɪft

squiffy
BR 'skwɪf|i, -ɪə(r), -ɪɪst
AM 'skwɪfi, -ər, -ɪst

squiggle
BR 'skwɪg|l, -lz,
-lɪŋ\-lɪŋ, -ld
AM 'skwɪg|əl, -əlz,
-(ə)lɪŋ, -əld

squiggly
BR 'skwɪg|li, 'skwɪgli
AM 'skwɪg(ə)li

squill
BR skwɪl, -z
AM skwɪl, -z

squillion
BR 'skwɪljən, -z
AM 'skwɪljən,
'skwɪliən, -z

squinancywort
BR 'skwɪnənsɪˌwəːt
AM 'skwɪnɪnsi,wərt,
'skwɪnɪnsi,w(ə)rt

squinch
BR skwɪn(t)ʃ, -ɪz
AM skwɪn(t)ʃ, -ɪz

squint
BR skwɪnt, -s, -ɪŋ, -ɪd
AM skwɪn|t, -ts, -(t)ɪŋ,
-(t)ɪd

squinter
BR 'skwɪntə(r), -z
AM 'skwɪn(t)ər, -z

squinty
BR 'skwɪnti
AM 'skwɪn(t)i

squirarchy
BR 'skwʌɪərɑːk|i, -ɪz
AM 'skwaɪ(ə)ˌrɑrki, -z

squire
BR skwʌɪə(r), -z, -ɪŋ, -d
AM skwaɪ(ə)r, -z, -ɪŋ, -d

squirearch
BR ˈskwʌɪərɑːk, -ɪz
AM ˈskwaɪ(ə)ˌrɑrk, -əz
squirearchical
BR ˌskwʌɪəˈrɑːkɪkl
AM ˌskwaɪ(ə)ˈrɑrkəkəl
squirearchy
BR ˈskwʌɪərɑːki, -ɪz
AM ˈskwaɪ(ə)ˌrɑrki, -z
squiredom
BR ˈskwʌɪədəm, -z
AM ˈskwaɪ(ə)dəm, -z
squireen
BR ˌskwʌɪəˈriːn, -z
AM skwaɪˈrin, -z
squirehood
BR ˈskwʌɪəhʊd, -z
AM ˈskwaɪ(ə)r,(h)ʊd, -z
squirelet
BR ˈskwʌɪəlɪt, -s
AM ˈskwaɪ(ə)rlət, -s
squireling
BR ˈskwʌɪəlɪŋ, -z
AM ˈskwaɪ(ə)rlɪŋ, -z
squirely
BR ˈskwʌɪəli
AM ˈskwaɪ(ə)rli
squireship
BR ˈskwʌɪəʃɪp, -s
AM ˈskwaɪ(ə)r,ʃɪp, -s
squirl
BR skwəːl, -z
AM skwərl, -z
squirm
BR skwəːm, -z, -ɪŋ, -d
AM skwərm, -z, -ɪŋ, -d
squirmer
BR ˈskwəːmə(r), -z
AM ˈskwərmər, -z
squirmy
BR ˈskwəːmi
AM ˈskwərmi
squirrel
BR ˈskwɪrəl, ˈskwɜrl, -z
AM ˈskwərəl, -z
squirrelly
BR ˈskwɪrəli, ˈskwɪrˌli
AM ˈskwər(ə)li
squirt
BR skwəːt, -s, -ɪŋ, -ɪd
AM skwər|t, -ts, -dɪŋ, -dəd
squirter
BR ˈskwəːtə(r), -z
AM ˈskwərdər, -z
squish
BR skwɪʃ, -ɪz, -ɪŋ, -t
AM skwɪʃ, -ɪz, -ɪŋ, -t
squishiness
BR ˈskwɪʃɪnɪs
AM ˈskwɪʃɪnɪs
squishy
BR ˈskwɪʃ|i, -ɪə(r), -ɪɪst
AM ˈskwɪʃi, -ər, -ɪst
squit
BR skwɪt, -s

AM skwɪt, -s
squitch
BR skwɪtʃ, -ɪz
AM skwɪtʃ, -ɪz
squitters
BR ˈskwɪtəz
AM ˈskwɪdərz
squiz
BR skwɪz
AM skwɪz
squoze
BR skwəʊz, -d
AM skwoʊz, -d
Sri Lanka
BR ˌsriː ˈlaŋkə(r), ˌsriː +, ˌʃriː +, ˌʃriː +
AM ˈsriː ˈlæŋkə
Sri Lankan
BR ˌsriː ˈlaŋkən, sriː +, ʃrɪ +, ʃriː +, -z
AM ˈsriː ˈlæŋkən, -z
Srinagar
BR srɪˈnʌɡə(r), sriːˈnʌɡə(r), ʃrɪˈnʌɡə(r), ʃriːˈnʌɡə(r)
AM srɪˈnɑɡər, srɪˈnəɡər
srubbiness
BR ˈskrʌbɪnɪs
AM ˈskrəbɪnɪs
ssh
BR ʃ
AM ʃ
St
saint
BR s(ə)nt, seɪnt
AM seɪn(t), s(ə)n(t)
St.
street
BR striːt
AM strit
stab
BR stab, -z, -ɪŋ, -d
AM stæb, -z, -ɪŋ, -d
stabber
BR ˈstabə(r), -z
AM ˈstæbər, -z
stabbing
BR ˈstabɪŋ, -z
AM ˈstæbɪŋ, -z
stabile
BR ˈsteɪbʌɪl, -z
AM ˈsteɪˌbɪl, -z
stabilisation
BR ˌsteɪbɪlʌɪˈzeɪʃn, ˌsteɪblʌɪˈzeɪʃn
AM ˌsteɪbələˈzeɪʃən, ˌsteɪbəˌlaɪˈzeɪʃən
stabilise
BR ˈsteɪbɪlʌɪz, ˈsteɪblʌɪz, -ɪz, -ɪŋ, -d
AM ˈsteɪbəˌlaɪz, -ɪz, -ɪŋ, -d
stabiliser
BR ˈsteɪbɪlʌɪzə(r), ˈsteɪblʌɪzə(r), -z
AM ˈsteɪbəˌlaɪzər, -z

stability
BR stəˈbɪlɪti
AM stəˈbɪlɪdi
stabilization
BR ˌsteɪbɪlʌɪˈzeɪʃn, ˌsteɪblʌɪˈzeɪʃn
AM ˌsteɪbələˈzeɪʃən, ˌsteɪbəˌlaɪˈzeɪʃən
stabilize
BR ˈsteɪbɪlʌɪz, ˈsteɪblʌɪz, -ɪz, -ɪŋ, -d
AM ˈsteɪbəˌlaɪz, -ɪz, -ɪŋ, -d
stabilizer
BR ˈsteɪbɪlʌɪzə(r), ˈsteɪblʌɪzə(r), -z
AM ˈsteɪbəˌlaɪzər, -z
stable
BR steɪb|l, -lz, -lɪŋ \ -lɪŋ, -ld, -lə(r)\ -lə(r), -lɪst\ -lɪst
AM ˈsteɪbəl, -əlz, -(ə)lɪŋ, -əld, -(ə)lər, -(ə)ləst
stableful
BR ˈsteɪblfʊl, -z
AM ˈsteɪbəl,fʊl, -z
stableman
BR ˈsteɪblmən
AM ˈsteɪbəl,mæn
stablemate
BR ˈsteɪblmeɪt, -s
AM ˈsteɪbəl,meɪt, -s
stablemen
BR ˈsteɪblmən
AM ˈsteɪbəl,mæn
stableness
BR ˈsteɪblnəs
AM ˈsteɪbəlnəs
stablish
BR ˈstabl|ɪʃ, -ɪʃɪz, -ɪʃɪŋ, -ɪʃt
AM ˈstæblɪʃ, -ɪz, -ɪŋ, -t
stably
BR ˈsteɪbli, ˈsteɪbl̩i
AM ˈsteɪb(ə)li
staccato
BR stəˈkɑːtəʊ
AM stəˈkɑdoʊ
Stacey
BR ˈsteɪsi
AM ˈsteɪsi
stack
BR stak, -s, -ɪŋ, -t
AM stæk, -s, -ɪŋ, -t
stackable
BR ˈstakəbl
AM ˈstækəbəl
stacker
BR ˈstakə(r), -z
AM ˈstækər, -z
Stackhouse
BR ˈstakhaʊs
AM ˈstæk,(h)aʊs
stacte
BR ˈstaktiː, -z
AM ˈstækti, -z

Stacy
BR ˈsteɪsi
AM ˈsteɪsi
staddle
BR ˈstadl, -z
AM ˈstædəl, -z
stadia
BR ˈsteɪdɪə(r)
AM ˈsteɪdɪə
stadium
BR ˈsteɪdɪəm, -z
AM ˈsteɪdɪəm, -z
stadtholder
BR ˈstad,həʊldə(r), -z
AM ˈstæd,(h)oʊldər, -z
stadtholdership
BR ˈstad,həʊldəʃɪp, -s
AM ˈstæd,(h)oʊldər,ʃɪp, -s
staff
BR stɑːf, staf, -s, -ɪŋ, -t
AM stæf, -s, -ɪŋ, -t
Staffa
BR ˈstafə(r)
AM ˈstæfə
staffage
BR ˈstɑːfɪdʒ, ˈstafɪdʒ
AM ˈstæfɪdʒ
staffer
BR ˈstɑːfə(r), ˈstafə(r), -z
AM ˈstæfər, -z
Stafford
BR ˈstafəd
AM ˈstæfərd
Staffordshire
BR ˈstafədʃ(ɪ)ə(r)
AM ˈstæfərd,ʃɪ(ə)r
staffroom
BR ˈstɑːfruːm, ˈstɑːfrʊm, ˈstafruːm, -z
AM ˈstæf,rum, ˈstæf,rʊm, -z
Staffs.
Staffordshire
BR stafs
AM stæfs
stag
BR stag, -z
AM stæg, -z
stage
BR steɪdʒ, -ɪz, -ɪŋ, -d
AM steɪdʒ, -ɪz, -ɪŋ, -d
stageability
BR ˌsteɪdʒəˈbɪlɪti
AM ˌsteɪdʒəˈbɪlɪdi
stageable
BR ˈsteɪdʒəbl
AM ˈsteɪdʒəbəl
stagecoach
BR ˈsteɪdʒkəʊtʃ, -ɪz
AM ˈsteɪdʒ,koʊtʃ, -əz
stagecraft
BR ˈsteɪdʒkrɑːft, ˈsteɪdʒkraft
AM ˈsteɪdʒ,kræft

stagehand
BR ˈsteɪdʒhand, -z
AM ˈsteɪdʒˌ(h)ænd, -z

stage-manage
BR ˌsteɪdʒˈmanˌɪdʒ,
ˈsteɪdʒˌmanˌɪdʒ,
-ɪdʒɪz, -ɪdʒɪŋ, -ɪdʒd
AM ˈsteɪdʒˌmænɪdʒ,
-ɪz, -ɪŋ, -d

stager
BR ˈsteɪdʒə(r), -z
AM ˈsteɪdʒər, -z

stagestruck
BR ˈsteɪdʒstrʌk
AM ˈsteɪdʒˌstrʌk

stage whisper
BR ˌsteɪdʒ ˈwɪspə(r), -z
AM ˈsteɪdʒ ˌ(h)wɪspər,
-z

stagey
BR ˈsteɪdʒi
AM ˈsteɪdʒi

stagflation
BR ˌstagˈfleɪʃn
AM ˌstægˈfleɪʃən

Stagg
BR stag
AM stæg

stagger
BR ˈstaglə(r), -əz,
-(ə)rɪŋ, -əd
AM ˈstæglər, -ərz,
-(ə)rɪŋ, -ərd

staggerer
BR ˈstag(ə)rə(r), -z
AM ˈstæg(ə)rər, -z

staggeringly
BR ˈstag(ə)rɪŋli
AM ˈstæg(ə)rɪŋli

staghound
BR ˈstaghaʊnd, -z
AM ˈstægˌ(h)aʊnd, -z

stagily
BR ˈsteɪdʒɪli
AM ˈsteɪdʒɪli

staginess
BR ˈsteɪdʒɪnɪs
AM ˈsteɪdʒɪnɪs

staging
BR ˈsteɪdʒɪŋ
AM ˈsteɪdʒɪŋ

stagnancy
BR ˈstagnənsi
AM ˈstægnənsi

stagnant
BR ˈstagnənt
AM ˈstægnənt

stagnantly
BR ˈstagnən(t)li
AM ˈstægnən(t)li

stagnate
BR stagˈneɪt, -s, -ɪŋ, -ɪd
AM ˈstægˌneɪt, -ts, -dɪŋ, -dɪd

stagnation
BR stagˈneɪʃn
AM stægˈneɪʃən

stagnicolous
BR stagˈnɪkələs,
stagˈnɪkləs
AM stægˈnɪkələs

stagy
BR ˈsteɪdʒi, -ɪə(r), -ɪɪst
AM ˈsteɪdʒi, -ər, -ɪst

staid
BR steɪd
AM steɪd

staidly
BR ˈsteɪdli
AM ˈsteɪdli

staidness
BR ˈsteɪdnɪs
AM ˈsteɪdnɪs

stain
BR steɪn, -z, -ɪŋ, -d
AM steɪn, -z, -ɪŋ, -d

stainable
BR ˈsteɪnəbl
AM ˈsteɪnəbəl

stained-glass
BR ˌsteɪndˈglɑːs,
ˌsteɪndˈglas
AM ˈsteɪn(d)ˌglæs

stainer
BR ˈsteɪnə(r), -z
AM ˈsteɪnər, -z

Staines
BR steɪnz
AM steɪnz

Stainforth
BR ˈsteɪnfəθ, ˈsteɪnfɔːθ
AM ˈsteɪnˌfɔ(ə)rθ

stainless
BR ˈsteɪnlɪs
AM ˈsteɪnlɪs

stainlessly
BR ˈsteɪnlɪsli
AM ˈsteɪnlɪsli

stainlessness
BR ˈsteɪnlɪsnɪs
AM ˈsteɪnlɪsnɪs

Stainton
BR ˈsteɪntən
AM ˈsteɪn(tə)n

stair
BR stɛː(r), -z
AM stɛ(ə)r, -z

staircase
BR ˈstɛːkeɪs, -ɪz
AM ˈstɛrˌkeɪs, -ɪz

stairhead
BR ˈstɛːhɛd, -z
AM ˈstɛrˌ(h)ɛd, -z

stairlift
BR ˈstɛːlɪft, -s
AM ˈstɛrˌlɪft, -s

stairway
BR ˈstɛːweɪ, -z
AM ˈstɛrˌweɪ, -z

stairwell
BR ˈstɛːwɛl, -z
AM ˈstɛrˌwɛl, -z

staithe
BR steɪð, -z
AM steɪð, -z

stake
BR steɪk, -s, -ɪŋ, -t
AM steɪk, -s, -ɪŋ, -t

stakeboat
BR ˈsteɪkbəʊt, -s
AM ˈsteɪkˌboʊt, -s

stakebuilding
BR ˈsteɪkˌbɪldɪŋ
AM ˈsteɪkˌbɪldɪŋ

stakeholder
BR ˈsteɪkˌhəʊldə(r), -z
AM ˈsteɪkˌ(h)oʊldər, -z

stakeout
BR ˈsteɪkaʊt, -s
AM ˈsteɪkˌaʊt, -s

staker
BR ˈsteɪkə(r), -z
AM ˈsteɪkər, -z

Stakhanovism
BR stəˈkanəvɪz(ə)m,
staˈkanəvɪz(ə)m
AM stəˈkanəˌvɪzəm

Stakhanovist
BR stəˈkanəvɪst,
staˈkanəvɪst, -s
AM stəˈkanəvəst, -s

Stakhanovite
BR stəˈkanəvʌɪt,
staˈkanəvʌɪt, -s
AM stəˈkanəˌvaɪt, -s

stalactic
BR stəˈlaktɪk
AM stəˈlæktɪk

stalactiform
BR stəˈlaktɪfɔːm
AM stəˈlæktəˌfɔ(ə)rm

stalactite
BR ˈstaləktʌɪt, -s
AM stəˈlækˌtaɪt, -s

stalactitic
BR ˌstaləkˈtɪtɪk
AM ˌstæləkˈtɪdɪk

Stalag
BR ˈstalag, -z
AM ˈstɑˌlag, -z

stalagmite
BR ˈstaləgmʌɪt, -s
AM stəˈlægˌmaɪt, -s

stalagmitic
BR ˌstalagˈmɪtɪk
AM ˌstæləgˈmɪdɪk

St Albans
BR s(ə)nt ˈɔːlb(ə)nz,
+ ˈɒlb(ə)nz
AM seɪn(t) ˈɔlbənz,
seɪn(t) ˈɑlbənz

stale
BR steɪl, -ə(r), -ɪst
AM steɪl, -ər, -ɪst

stalely
BR ˈsteɪ(l)li
AM ˈsteɪ(l)li

stalemate
BR ˈsteɪlmeɪt, -s, -ɪŋ, -ɪd
AM ˈsteɪlˌmeɪt, -ts, -dɪŋ, -dɪd

staleness
BR ˈsteɪlnɪs
AM ˈsteɪlnɪs

Stalin
BR ˈstɑːlɪn
AM ˈstɑlən

Stalingrad
BR ˈstɑːlɪngrad
AM ˈstɑlənˌgræd,
ˈstɑlənˌgrad
RUS stəlʲinˈgrat

Stalinism
BR ˈstɑːlɪnɪz(ə)m
AM ˈstɑləˌnɪzəm

Stalinist
BR ˈstɑːlɪnɪst, -s
AM ˈstɑlənəst, -s

stalk
BR stɔːk, -s, -ɪŋ, -t
AM stɔk, stɑk, -s, -ɪŋ, -t

stalker
BR ˈstɔːkə(r), -z
AM ˈstɔkər, ˈstɑkər, -z

stalk-eyed
BR ˌstɔːkˈʌɪd
AM ˈstɔkˌaɪd, ˈstɑkˌaɪd

stalkless
BR ˈstɔːkləs
AM ˈstɔkləs, ˈstɑkləs

stalklet
BR ˈstɔːklɪt, -s
AM ˈstɔklət, ˈstɑklət, -s

stalklike
BR ˈstɔːklʌɪk
AM ˈstɔkˌlaɪk,
ˈstɑkˌlaɪk

stalky
BR ˈstɔːki
AM ˈstɔki, ˈstɑki

stall
BR stɔːl, -z, -ɪŋ, -d
AM stɔl, stɑl, -z, -ɪŋ, -d

stallage
BR ˈstɔːljɪdʒ, -ɪdʒɪz
AM ˈstɔlɪdʒ, ˈstɑlɪdʒ, -ɪz

stallholder
BR ˈstɔːlˌhəʊldə(r), -z
AM ˈstɔlˌ(h)oʊldər,
ˈstɑlˌ(h)oʊldər, -z

stallion
BR ˈstaljən, -z
AM ˈstæljən, -z

Stallybrass
BR ˈstalɪbrɑːs,
ˈstalɪbras
AM ˈstæliˌbræs

stalwart
BR ˈstɔːlwət, ˈstɒlwət,
-s
AM ˈstɔlwərt,
ˈstɑlwərt, -s

stalwartly
BR ˈstɔːlwətli,
ˈstɒlwətli
AM ˈstɔlwərtli,
ˈstɑlwərtli

stalwartness
BR ˈstɔːlwətnəs,
ˈstɒlwətnəs
AM ˈstɔːlwɚtnəs,
ˈstɑlwɚtnəs

Stalybridge
BR ˈsteɪlɪbrɪdʒ
AM ˈsteɪliˌbrɪdʒ

Stamboul
BR stamˈbuːl
AM stæmˈbul

stamen
BR ˈsteɪmən, ˈsteɪmɛn,
-z
AM ˈsteɪmɪn, -z

stamina
BR ˈstamɪnə(r)
AM ˈstæmənə

staminal
BR ˈstamɪnl
AM ˈstæmənəl

staminate
BR ˈstamɪnət
AM ˈstæməˌneɪt

staminiferous
BR ˌstamɪˈnɪf(ə)rəs
AM ˌstæməˈnɪf(ə)rəs

stammer
BR ˈstam|ə(r), -əz,
-(ə)rɪŋ, -əd
AM ˈstæm|ɚ, -ɚz,
-(ə)rɪŋ, -ɚd

stammerer
BR ˈstam(ə)rə(r), -z
AM ˈstæm(ə)rɚr, -z

stammeringly
BR ˈstam(ə)rɪŋli
AM ˈstæm(ə)rɪŋli

stamp
BR stam|p, -ps, -pɪŋ,
-(p)t
AM stæmp, -s, -ɪŋ, -t

stampede
BR stamˈpiːd, -z, -ɪŋ, -ɪd
AM stæmˈpid, -z, -ɪŋ, -ɪd

stampeder
BR stamˈpiːdə(r), -z
AM stæmˈpidɚr, -z

stamper
BR ˈstampə(r), -z
AM ˈstæmpɚr, -z

Stanbury
BR ˈstanb(ə)ri
AM ˈstænˌbɛri

stance
BR stɑːns, stans, -ɪz
AM stæns, -əz

stanch
BR stɑːn(t)ʃ, stan(t)ʃ,
-ɪz, -ɪŋ, -t
AM stɔn(t)ʃ, stan(t)ʃ,
-əz, -ɪŋ, -t

stanchion
BR ˈstanʃn, -z
AM ˈstæn(t)ʃən, -z

stand
BR stand, -z, -ɪŋ
AM stænd, -z, -ɪŋ

stand-alone
BR ˈstandələʊn
AM ˈstændəˌloʊn

standard
BR ˈstandəd, -z
AM ˈstændɚd, -z

Standardbred
BR ˈstandədbrɛd, -z
AM ˈstændɚdˌbrɛd, -z

standardisable
BR ˈstandədʌɪzəbl
AM ˈstændɚrˌdaɪzəbəl

standardisation
BR ˌstandədʌɪˈzeɪʃn
AM ˌstændɚrdəˈzeɪʃən,
ˌstændɚrˌdaɪˈzeɪʃən

standardise
BR ˈstandədʌɪz, -ɪz, -ɪŋ,
-d
AM ˈstændɚrˌdaɪz, -ɪz,
-ɪŋ, -d

standardiser
BR ˈstandədʌɪzə(r), -z
AM ˈstændɚrˌdaɪzɚr, -z

standardizable
BR ˈstandədʌɪzəbl
AM ˈstændɚrˌdaɪzəbəl

standardization
BR ˌstandədʌɪˈzeɪʃn
AM ˌstændɚrdəˈzeɪʃən,
ˌstændɚrˌdaɪˈzeɪʃən

standardize
BR ˈstandədʌɪz, -ɪz, -ɪŋ,
-d
AM ˈstændɚrˌdaɪz, -ɪz,
-ɪŋ, -d

standardizer
BR ˈstandədʌɪzə(r), -z
AM ˈstændɚrˌdaɪzɚr, -z

standby
BR ˈstan(d)bʌɪ, -z
AM ˈstæn(d)ˌbaɪ, -z

standee
BR stanˈdiː, -z
AM stænˈdi, -z

stander
BR ˈstandə(r), -z
AM ˈstændɚr, -z

stand-in
BR ˈstandɪn, -z
AM ˈstændˌɪn, -z

standing
BR ˈstandɪŋ, -z
AM ˈstændɪŋ, -z

Standish
BR ˈstandɪʃ
AM ˈstændɪʃ

stand-off
BR ˈstandɒf, -s
AM ˈstændˌɔf,
ˈstændˌɑf, -s

standoffish
BR ˌstandˈɒfɪʃ
AM ˌstændˈɔfɪʃ,
ˌstændˈɑfɪʃ

standoffishly
BR ˌstandˈɒfɪʃli

standoffishli
AM ˌstændˈɔfɪʃli,
ˌstændˈɑfɪʃli

standoffishness
BR ˌstandˈɒfɪʃnɪs
AM ˌstændˈɔfɪʃnɪs,
ˌstændˈɑfɪʃnɪs

standout
BR ˈstandaʊt, -s
AM ˈstændˌaʊt, -s

standpipe
BR ˈstan(d)pʌɪp, -s
AM ˈstæn(d)ˌpaɪp, -s

standpoint
BR ˈstan(d)pɔɪnt, -s
AM ˈstæn(d)ˌpɔɪnt, -s

St Andrews
BR s(ə)nt ˈandruː
AM seɪn(t) ˈændruz

standstill
BR ˈstan(d)stɪl, -z
AM ˈstæn(d)ˌstɪl, -z

stand-to
BR ˈstan(d)tuː,
ˌstan(d)ˈtuː
AM ˈstæn(d)ˈtu

Stanford
BR ˈstanfəd
AM ˈstænfɚd

Stanhope
BR ˈstanəp, ˈstanhəʊp
AM ˈstæn(h)oʊp,
ˈstænəp

Stanislas
BR ˈstanɪslas,
ˈstanɪsləs, ˈstanɪslɑːs
AM ˈstænəˌslas

Stanislaus
BR ˈstanɪslaʊs,
ˈstanɪslɔːs
AM ˈstænəˌslas

Stanislavsky
BR ˌstanɪˈslavski
AM ˌstænəˈslɑfski

stank
BR staŋk
AM stæŋk

Stanley
BR ˈstanli
AM ˈstænli

Stanleyville
BR ˈstanlɪvɪl
AM ˈstænliˌvɪl

Stanmore
BR ˈstanmɔː(r)
AM ˈstænˌmɔ(ə)r

Stannard
BR ˈstanəd
AM ˈstænɚrd

stannary
BR ˈstan(ə)r|i, -ɪz
AM ˈstænəri, -z

stannate
BR ˈstaneɪt
AM ˈstæˌneɪt

stannic
BR ˈstanɪk
AM ˈstænɪk

stannite
BR ˈstanʌɪt, -s
AM ˈstæˌnaɪt, -s

stannous
BR ˈstanəs
AM ˈstænəs

Stansfield
BR ˈstanzfiːld,
ˈstansfiːld
AM ˈstænzˌfild

Stansgate
BR ˈstanzgeɪt
AM ˈstænzˌgeɪt

Stansted
BR ˈstanstɛd, ˈstanstɪd
AM ˈstænstəd,
ˈstænˌstɛd

Stanton
BR ˈstantən
AM ˈstæn(t)ən

Stanway
BR ˈstanweɪ
AM ˈstænˌweɪ

Stanwell
BR ˈstanw(ɛ)l
AM ˈstænˌwɛl

Stanwick
BR ˈstan(w)ɪk
AM ˈstænˌwɪk

stanza
BR ˈstanzə(r), -z, -d
AM ˈstænzə, -z, -d

stanzaic
BR stanˈzeɪɪk
AM stænˈzeɪɪk

stapedes
BR stəˈpiːdiːz
AM stəˈpiˌdiz

stapelia
BR stəˈpiːlɪə(r), -z
AM stəˈpiljə, stəˈpiliə,
-z

stapes
BR ˈsteɪpiːz
AM ˈsteɪˌpiz

staphylococcal
BR ˌstaf(ə)ləˈkɒkl,
ˌstafləˈkɒkl
AM ˌstæf(ə)ləˈkɑkəl

staphylococcus
BR ˌstaf(ə)ləˈkɒkəs,
ˌstafləˈkɒkəs
AM ˌstæf(ə)ləˈkɑkəs

staple
BR ˈsteɪp|l, -lz,
-lɪŋ \-lɪŋ, -ld
AM ˈsteɪp|əl, -əlz,
-(ə)lɪŋ, -əld

Stapleford¹
place in UK
BR ˈstaplfəd
AM ˈstæpəlfɚrd

Stapleford²
surname
BR ˈsteɪplfəd
AM ˈsteɪpəlfɚrd

Staplehurst
BR ˈsteɪplhəːst

AM 'steɪpəl‚(h)ərst

stapler
BR 'steɪplə(r),
'steɪplə(r), -z
AM 'steɪp(ə)lər, -z

Stapleton
BR 'steɪplt(ə)n
AM 'steɪpəltən

star
BR stɑː(r), -z, -ɪŋ, -d
AM stɑr, -z, -ɪŋ, -d

Stara Zagora
BR ‚stɑːrə zə'gɔːrə(r)
AM ‚stɑrə zə'gɔrə

starboard
BR 'stɑːbəd, 'stɑːbɔːd
AM 'stɑrbərd,
'stɑr‚bɔ(ə)rd

starburst
BR 'stɑːbɜːst, -s
AM 'stɑr‚bɜrst, -s

starch
BR stɑːtʃ, -ɪz, -ɪŋ, -t
AM stɑrtʃ, -əz, -ɪŋ, -t

starcher
BR 'stɑːtʃə(r), -z
AM 'stɑrtʃər, -z

starchily
BR 'stɑːtʃɪli
AM 'stɑrtʃəli

starchiness
BR 'stɑːtʃɪnɪs
AM 'stɑrtʃɪnɪs

starch-reduced
BR ‚stɑːtʃrɪ'djuːst,
‚stɑːtʃrɪ'dʒuːst
AM 'stɑrtʃrə‚d(j)ust,
'stɑrtʃri‚d(j)ust

starchy
BR 'stɑːtʃi, -ɪə(r), -ɪɪst
AM 'stɑrtʃi, -ər, -ɪst

star-crossed
BR 'stɑːkrɒst,
‚stɑː'krɒst
AM 'stɑr‚krɔst,
'stɑr‚krɑst

stardom
BR 'stɑːdəm
AM 'stɑrdəm

stardust
BR 'stɑːdʌst
AM 'stɑr‚dəst

stare
BR stɛː(r), -z, -ɪŋ, -d
AM stɛ(ə)r, -z, -ɪŋ, -d

starer
BR 'stɛːrə(r), -z
AM 'stɛrər, -z

starfish
BR 'stɑːfɪʃ, -ɪz
AM 'stɑr‚fɪʃ, -ɪz

stargaze
BR 'stɑːgeɪz, -ɪz, -ɪŋ, -d
AM 'stɑr‚geɪz, -ɪz, -ɪŋ, -d

stargazer
BR 'stɑː‚geɪzə(r), -z
AM 'stɑr‚geɪzər, -z

stargazing
BR 'stɑː‚geɪzɪŋ
AM 'stɑr‚geɪzɪŋ

stark
BR stɑːk, -ə(r), -ɪst
AM stɑrk, -ər, -əst

starkers
BR 'stɑːkəz
AM 'stɑrkərz

Starkey
BR 'stɑːki
AM 'stɑrki

Starkie
BR 'stɑːki
AM 'stɑrki

starkly
BR 'stɑːkli
AM 'stɑrkli

starkness
BR 'stɑːknəs
AM 'stɑrknəs

starless
BR 'stɑːləs
AM 'stɑrləs

starlet
BR 'stɑːlɪt, -s
AM 'stɑrlət, -s

starlight
BR 'stɑːlaɪt
AM 'stɑr‚laɪt

starlike
BR 'stɑːlaɪk
AM 'stɑr‚laɪk

starling
BR 'stɑːlɪŋ, -z
AM 'stɑrlɪŋ, -z

starlit
BR 'stɑːlɪt
AM 'stɑr‚lɪt

Starr
BR stɑː(r)
AM stɑr

starrily
BR 'stɑːrɪli
AM 'stɑrəli

starriness
BR 'stɑːrɪnɪs
AM 'stɑrɪnɪs

starry
BR 'stɑːri
AM 'stɑri

starry-eyed
BR ‚stɑːrɪ'aɪd
AM 'stɑri‚aɪd

Stars and Bars
BR ‚stɑːz (ə)n(d) 'bɑːz
AM 'stɑrz ən 'bɑrz

Stars and Stripes
BR ‚stɑːz (ə)n(d)
'straɪps
AM 'stɑrz ən 'straɪps

starship
BR 'stɑː‚ʃɪp, -s
AM 'stɑr‚ʃɪp, -s

START
BR stɑːt
AM start

start
BR stɑːt, -s, -ɪŋ, -ɪd
AM stɑrt, -ts, -dɪŋ, -dəd

starter
BR 'stɑːtə(r), -z
AM 'stɑrdər, -z

startle
BR 'stɑːtl, -lz, -lɪŋ \-lɪŋ,
-ld
AM 'stɑrdəl, -z, -ɪŋ, -d

startler
BR 'stɑːtlə(r),
'stɑːtlə(r), -z
AM 'stɑrdlər, -z

startlingly
BR 'stɑːtlɪŋli
'stɑːtlɪŋli
AM 'stɑrdlɪŋli

start-up
BR 'stɑːtʌp, -s
AM 'stɑrdəp, -s

star turn
BR ‚stɑː 'tɜːn, -z
AM 'stɑr ‚tɜrn, -z

starvation
BR stɑː'veɪʃn
AM stɑr'veɪʃən

starve
BR stɑːv, -z, -ɪŋ, -d
AM stɑrv, -z, -ɪŋ, -d

starveling
BR 'stɑːvlɪŋ, -z
AM 'stɑrvlɪŋ, -z

starwort
BR 'stɑːwɜːt, -s
AM 'stɑrwərt,
'stɑr‚wɔ(ə)rt, -s

stases
BR 'steɪsiːz
AM 'steɪt‚siz

stash
BR staʃ, -ɪz, -ɪŋ, -t
AM stæʃ, -əz, -ɪŋ, -t

Stasi
BR 'stɑːzi
AM 'stɑzi

stasis
BR 'steɪsɪs
AM 'steɪsɪs

stat
BR stat, -s
AM stæt, -s

statable
BR 'steɪtəbl
AM 'steɪdəbəl

statal
BR 'steɪtl
AM 'steɪdl

state
BR steɪt, -s, -ɪŋ, -ɪd
AM steɪt, -ts, -dɪŋ, -dɪd

statecraft
BR 'steɪtkrɑːft,
'steɪtkraft
AM 'steɪt‚kræft

statedly
BR 'steɪtɪdli

AM 'steɪtɪdli

statehood
BR 'steɪthʊd
AM 'steɪt‚(h)ʊd

statehouse
BR 'steɪthaʊ|s, -zɪz
AM 'steɪt‚(h)aʊ|s, -zəz

stateless
BR 'steɪtlɪs
AM 'steɪtlɪs

statelessness
BR 'steɪtlɪsnɪs
AM 'steɪtlɪsnɪs

statelet
BR 'steɪtlɪt, -s
AM 'steɪtlɪt, -s

stateliness
BR 'steɪtlɪnɪs
AM 'steɪtlɪnɪs

stately
BR 'steɪtl|i, -ɪə(r), -ɪɪst
AM 'steɪtli, -ər, -ɪst

statement
BR 'steɪtm(ə)nt, -s
AM 'steɪtmənt, -s

Staten Island
BR ‚statn 'aɪlənd
AM ‚stætn 'aɪlənd

state-of-the-art
BR ‚steɪtə(v)ðɪ'ɑːt
AM 'steɪdə(v)ðɪ'ɑrt,
'steɪdə(v)ðə'ɑrt

stater
BR 'steɪtə(r), -z
AM 'steɪdər, -z

stateroom
BR 'steɪtruːm,
'steɪtrʊm, -z
AM 'steɪt‚rum,
'steɪt‚rʊm, -z

stateside
BR 'steɪtsaɪd
AM 'steɪt‚saɪd

statesman
BR 'steɪtsmən
AM 'steɪtsmən

statesmanlike
BR 'steɪtsmənlaɪk
AM 'steɪtsmən‚laɪk

statesmanly
BR 'steɪtsmənli
AM 'steɪtsmənli

statesmanship
BR 'steɪtsmənʃɪp
AM 'steɪtsmən‚ʃɪp

statesmen
BR 'steɪtsmən
AM 'steɪtsmən

statesperson
BR 'steɪtspɜːsn, -z
AM 'steɪts‚pərsən, -z

stateswoman
BR 'steɪts‚wʊmən
AM 'steɪts‚wʊmən

stateswomen
BR 'steɪts‚wɪmɪn
AM 'steɪts‚wɪmɪn

statewide
 BR ˌsteɪt'wʌɪd
 AM ˈsteɪtˌwaɪd

Statham
 BR 'steɪθ(ə)m,
 'steɪð(ə)m
 AM 'steɪdəm, 'stæðəm

static
 BR 'statɪk, -s
 AM 'stædɪk, -s

statical
 BR 'statɪkl
 AM 'stædəkəl

statically
 BR 'statɪkli
 AM 'stædək(ə)li

statice
 BR 'statɪs|i, -ɪz
 AM 'stædəsi, -z

station
 BR 'steɪʃ|n, -nz,
 -nɪŋ\-(ə)nɪŋ, -n̩d
 AM 'steɪʃən, -z, -ɪŋ, -d

stationariness
 BR 'steɪʃn̩rɪnɪs,
 'steɪʃən(ə)rɪnɪs
 AM 'steɪʃəˌnɛrinɪs

stationary
 BR 'steɪʃn̩(ə)ri,
 'steɪʃən(ə)ri
 AM 'steɪʃəˌnɛri

stationer
 BR 'steɪʃn̩ə(r),
 'steɪʃənə(r), -z
 AM 'steɪʃ(ə)nər, -z

stationery
 BR 'steɪʃn̩(ə)ri,
 'steɪʃən(ə)ri
 AM 'steɪʃəˌnɛri

station-keeping
 BR 'steɪʃn̩ˌkiːpɪŋ
 AM 'steɪʃənˌkipɪŋ

statism
 BR 'steɪtɪz(ə)m
 AM 'steɪdɪzəm

statist
 BR 'steɪtɪst, -s
 AM 'steɪdɪst, -s

statistic
 BR stə'tɪstɪk, -s
 AM stə'tɪstɪk, -s

statistical
 BR stə'tɪstɪkl
 AM stə'tɪstəkəl

statistically
 BR stə'tɪstɪkli
 AM stə'tɪstək(ə)li

statistician
 BR ˌstatɪ'stɪʃn, -z
 AM ˌstædə'stɪʃən, -z

Statius
 BR 'steɪʃ(ɪ)əs, 'steɪtɪəs
 AM 'steɪʃ(i)əs

stative
 BR 'steɪtɪv
 AM 'steɪdɪv

stator
 BR 'steɪtə(r), -z
 AM 'steɪdər, -z

statoscope
 BR 'statəskəʊp, -s
 AM 'stædəˌskoʊp, -s

stats
 BR stats
 AM stæts

statuary
 BR 'statʃʊəri,
 'statʃʊri, 'statjʊəri,
 'statjʊri
 AM 'stætʃəˌwɛri

statue
 BR 'statʃuː, 'statjuː, -z,
 -d
 AM 'stætʃu, -z, -d

statuesque
 BR ˌstatʃʊ'ɛsk,
 ˌstatjʊ'ɛsk
 AM ˌstætʃə'wɛsk

statuesquely
 BR ˌstatʃʊ'ɛskli,
 ˌstatjʊ'ɛskli
 AM ˌstætʃə'wɛskli

statuesqueness
 BR ˌstatʃʊ'ɛsknəs,
 ˌstatjʊ'ɛsknəs
 AM ˌstætʃə'wɛsknəs

statuette
 BR ˌstatʃʊ'ɛt, ˌstatjʊ'ɛt,
 -s
 AM ˌstætʃə'wɛt, -s

stature
 BR 'statʃə(r),
 'statjə(r), -d
 AM 'stætʃər, -d

status
 BR 'steɪtəs, -ɪz
 AM 'steɪdəs, 'stædəs,
 -əz

status quo
 BR ˌsteɪtəs 'kwəʊ
 AM ˌsteɪdəs 'kwoʊ,
 ˌstædəs +

statutable
 BR 'statʃuːtəbl,
 'statjuːtəbl
 AM 'stætʃudəbəl,
 'stætʃədəbəl

statutably
 BR 'statʃuːtəbli,
 'statjuːtəbli
 AM 'stætʃudəbli,
 'stætʃədəbli

statute
 BR 'statʃuːt, 'statjuːt,
 -s
 AM 'stætʃut, -s

statute-barred
 BR ˌstatʃuːt'bɑːd,
 ˌstatjuːt'bɑːd
 AM 'stætʃutˌbard

statutorily
 BR 'statʃʊtrɪli,
 'statjʊtrɪli
 AM ˌstætʃə'tɔrəli

statutory
 BR statʃʊt(ə)ri,
 statjʊt(ə)ri
 AM 'stætʃəˌtɔri

staunch
 BR stɔːn(t)ʃ, -ɪz, -ɪŋ, -t,
 -ə(r), -ɪst
 AM stɔn(t)ʃ, stɑn(t)ʃ,
 -əz, -ɪŋ, -t, -ər, -əst

staunchly
 BR 'stɔːn(t)ʃli
 AM 'stɔn(t)ʃli,
 'stɑn(t)ʃli

staunchness
 BR 'stɔːn(t)ʃnəs
 AM 'stɔn(t)ʃnəs,
 'stɑn(t)ʃnəs

Staunton¹
 place in UK
 BR 'stɔːnt(ə)n
 AM 'stɔn(t)ən,
 'stɑn(t)ən

Staunton²
 place in USA
 BR 'stant(ə)n
 AM 'stæn(t)ən

staurolite
 BR 'stɔːrəlʌɪt
 AM 'stɔrəˌlaɪt

stauroscope
 BR 'stɔːrəskəʊp, -s
 AM 'stɔrəˌskoʊp, -s

stauroscopic
 BR ˌstɔːrə'skɒpɪk
 AM ˌstɔrə'skɑpɪk

stauroscopically
 BR ˌstɔːrə'skɒpɪkli
 AM ˌstɔrə'skɑpək(ə)li

Stavanger
 BR stə'vaŋə(r)
 AM stə'væŋər

stave
 BR steɪv, -z, -ɪŋ, -d
 AM steɪv, -z, -ɪŋ, -d

stavesacre
 BR 'steɪvzˌeɪkə(r), -z
 AM 'steɪvzˌeɪkər, -z

stay
 BR steɪ, -z, -ɪŋ, -d
 AM steɪ, -z, -ɪŋ, -d

stay-at-home
 BR 'steɪəthəʊm, -z
 AM 'steɪətˌ(h)oʊm, -z

stayer
 BR 'steɪə(r), -z
 AM 'steɪər, -z

staysail
 BR 'steɪsl, 'steɪseɪl, -z
 AM 'steɪsəl, 'steɪˌseɪl, -z

St Bernard
 BR s(ə)nt 'bəːnəd, -z
 AM seɪn(t) bər'nard, -z

stead
 BR stɛd
 AM stɛd

steadfast
 BR 'stɛdfɑːst, 'stɛdfast,
 'stɛdfəst

 AM 'stɛdˌfæst

steadfastly
 BR 'stɛdfɑːstli,
 'stɛdfastli, 'stɛdfəstli
 AM 'stɛdˌfæs(t)li

steadfastness
 BR 'stɛdfɑːs(t)nəs,
 'stɛdfas(t)nəs,
 'stɛdfəs(t)nəs
 AM 'stɛdˌfæs(t)nəs

steadier
 BR 'stɛdɪə(r), -z
 AM 'stɛdiər, -z

steadily
 BR 'stɛdɪli
 AM 'stɛdəli

steadiness
 BR 'stɛdɪnɪs
 AM 'stɛdinɪs

steading
 BR 'stɛdɪŋ, -z
 AM 'stɛdɪŋ, -z

Steadman
 BR 'stɛdmən
 AM 'stɛdmən

steady
 BR 'stɛd|i, -ɪz, -ɪŋ, -ɪd,
 -ɪə(r), -ɪɪst
 AM 'stɛdi, -z, -ɪŋ, -d, -ər,
 -ɪst

steak
 BR steɪk, -s, -ɪŋ
 AM steɪk, -s, -ɪŋ

steakhouse
 BR 'steɪkhaʊ|s, -zɪz
 AM 'steɪkˌ(h)aʊ|s, -zəz

steal
 BR stiːl, -z, -ɪŋ
 AM stil, -z, -ɪŋ

stealer
 BR 'stiːlə(r), -z
 AM 'stilər, -z

stealth
 BR stɛlθ
 AM stɛlθ

stealthily
 BR 'stɛlθɪli
 AM 'stɛlθəli

stealthiness
 BR 'stɛlθɪnɪs
 AM 'stɛlθinɪs

stealthy
 BR 'stɛlθ|i, -ɪə(r), -ɪɪst
 AM 'stɛlθi, -ər, -ɪst

steam
 BR stiːm, -z, -ɪŋ, -d
 AM stim, -z, -ɪŋ, -d

steamboat
 BR 'stiːmbəʊt, -s
 AM 'stimˌboʊt, -s

steamer
 BR 'stiːmə(r), -z
 AM 'stimər, -z

steamfitter
 BR 'stiːmˌfɪtə(r), -z
 AM 'stimˌfɪdər, -z

steamily
BR 'sti:mɪli
AM 'stimɪli

steaminess
BR 'sti:mɪnɪs
AM 'stimɪnɪs

steaming
BR 'sti:mɪŋ, -z
AM 'stimɪŋ, -z

steamroller
BR 'sti:m‚rəʊlə(r), -z, -ɪŋ, -d
AM 'stim‚roʊlər, -z, -ɪŋ, -d

steamship
BR 'sti:m‚ʃɪp, -s
AM 'stim‚ʃɪp, -s

steamshovel
BR 'sti:m‚ʃʌvl
AM 'stim‚ʃəvəl

steamy
BR 'sti:m|i, -ɪə(r), -ɪɪst
AM 'stimi, -ər, -ɪst

stearate
BR 'stɪəreɪt, -s
AM 'stɪ(ə)‚reɪt, -s

stearic
BR stɪ'ærɪk
AM stɪ'ɛrɪk

stearin
BR 'stɪərɪn
AM 'stɪrɪn

Stearn
BR stə:n
AM stɜrn

Stearne
BR stə:n
AM stɜrn

steatite
BR 'stɪətʌɪt, -s
AM 'stɪə‚taɪt, -s

steatitic
BR ‚stɪə'tɪtɪk
AM ‚stɪə'tɪdɪk

steatopygia
BR ‚stɪətə(ʊ)'pɪdʒɪə(r), ‚stɪətə(ʊ)'pʌɪdʒɪə(r)
AM ‚stiədə'pɪdʒiə, ‚stiədə'paɪdʒiə, ‚stiədə'pɪgiə, ‚stiədə'paɪgiə

steatopygous
BR ‚stɪətə(ʊ)'pʌɪgəs, ‚stɪə'tɒpɪgəs
AM ‚stiədə'paɪgəs, ‚stiə'tɑpəgəs

steatorrhoea
BR ‚stɪ:ətə'ri:ə(r)
AM ‚stiədə'riə

steatosis
BR ‚stɪə'təʊsɪs
AM ‚stiə'toʊsɪs

Stechford
BR 'stɛtʃfəd
AM 'stɛtʃfərd

stedfast
BR 'stɛdfɑːst, 'stɛdfast, 'stɛdfəst

AM 'stɛd‚fæst

stedfastly
BR 'stɛdfɑːstli, 'stɛdfastli, 'stɛdfəstli
AM 'stɛd‚fæs(t)li

stedfastness
BR 'stɛdfɑːs(t)nəs, 'stɛdfas(t)nəs, 'stɛdfəs(t)nəs
AM 'stɛd‚fæs(t)nəs

Stedman
BR 'stɛdmən
AM 'stɛdmən

steed
BR 'sti:d, -z
AM stid, -z

steel
BR sti:l, -z, -ɪŋ, -d
AM stil, -z, -ɪŋ, -d

Steele
BR sti:l
AM stil

steelhead
BR 'sti:lhɛd, -z
AM 'stil(h)ɛd, -z

steeliness
BR 'sti:lnɪs
AM 'stilnɪs

steelwork
BR 'sti:lwə:k, -s
AM 'stil‚wərk, -s

steelworker
BR 'sti:l‚wə:kə(r), -z
AM 'stil‚wərkər, -z

steelworks
BR 'sti:lwə:ks
AM 'stil‚wərks

steely
BR 'sti:l|i, -ɪə(r), -ɪɪst
AM 'stili, -ər, -ɪst

steelyard
BR 'stɪljəd, 'sti:ljɑːd, -z
AM 'stil‚jɑrd, -z

Steen
BR sti:n
AM stin, stem

steenbok
BR 'sti:nbɒk, -s
AM 'stin‚bak, -s

steenkirk
BR 'sti:nkə:k, -s
AM 'stin‚kərk, -s

steep
BR sti:p, -s, -ɪŋ, -t, -ə(r), -ɪst
AM stip, -s, -ɪŋ, -t, -ər, -ɪst

steepen
BR 'sti:p|(ə)n, -(ə)nz, -(ə)nɪŋ\-‚nɪŋ, -(ə)nd
AM 'stipən, -ənz, -(ə)nɪŋ, -ənd

steepish
BR 'sti:pɪʃ
AM 'stipɪʃ

steeple
BR 'sti:pl, -z, -d

AM 'stipəl, -z, -d

steeplechase
BR 'sti:pltʃeɪs, -ɪz
AM 'stipəl‚tʃeɪs, -ɪz

steeplechaser
BR 'sti:pl‚tʃeɪsə(r), -z
AM 'stipəl‚tʃeɪsər, -z

steeplechasing
BR 'sti:pl‚tʃeɪsɪŋ
AM 'stipəl‚tʃeɪsɪŋ

steeplejack
BR 'sti:pldʒak, -s
AM 'stipəl‚dʒæk, -s

steeply
BR 'sti:pli
AM 'stipli

steepness
BR 'sti:pnɪs
AM 'stipnɪs

steer
BR stɪə(r), -z, -ɪŋ, -d
AM stɪ(ə)r, -z, -ɪŋ, -d

steerable
BR 'stɪərəbl
AM 'stɪrəbəl

steerage
BR 'stɪərɪdʒ
AM 'stɪrɪdʒ

steerageway
BR 'stɪərɪdʒweɪ
AM 'stɪrɪdʒ‚weɪ

steerer
BR 'stɪərə(r), -z
AM 'stɪrər, -z

steersman
BR 'stɪəzmən
AM 'stɪrzmən

steersmen
BR 'stɪəzmən
AM 'stɪrzmən

steeve
BR sti:v, -z, -ɪŋ, -d
AM stiv, -z, -ɪŋ, -d

Stefanie
BR 'stɛfəni, 'stɛfni
AM 'stɛfəni

stegosaur
BR 'stɛgəsɔː(r), -z
AM 'stɛgə‚sɔ(ə)r, -z

stegosaurus
BR ‚stɛgə'sɔːrəs, -ɪz
AM ‚stɛgə'sorəs, -əz

Steichen
BR 'staɪk(ə)n
AM 'staɪkən
GER 'ʃtaɪçn

Steiermark
BR 'ʃtaɪəmɑːk
AM 'ʃtaɪər‚mɑrk

Steiger
BR 'staɪgə(r)
AM 'staɪgər

stein
BR staɪn, -z
AM staɪn, -z

Steinbeck
BR 'staɪnbɛk

AM 'staɪn‚bɛk

Steinberg
BR 'staɪnbə:g
AM 'staɪn‚bərg

steinbock
BR 'staɪnbɒk, -s
AM 'staɪn‚bak, -s

steinbok
BR 'staɪnbɒk, -s
AM 'staɪn‚bak, -s

Steiner
BR 'staɪnə(r)
AM 'staɪnər

Steinway®
BR 'staɪnweɪ, -z
AM 'staɪn‚weɪ, -z

stela
BR 'sti:lə(r)
AM 'stilə

stelae
BR 'sti:li:
AM 'stili, 'sti‚laɪ

stelar
BR 'sti:lə(r)
AM 'stilər

stele
BR sti:l, 'sti:li
AM stil, 'stili

Stella
BR 'stɛlə(r)
AM 'stɛlə

stellar
BR 'stɛlə(r)
AM 'stɛlər

stellate
BR 'stɛleɪt, 'stɛlət
AM 'stɛlət, 'stɛ‚leɪt

stellated
BR 'stɛleɪtɪd, 'stɛlətɪd
AM 'stɛlədəd, 'stɛ‚leɪtɪd

stelliform
BR 'stɛlɪfɔ:m
AM 'stɛlə‚fɔ(ə)rm

stellini
BR stɛ'li:ni:, stɪ'li:ni:
AM stə'lini, stɛ'lini

stellular
BR 'stɛljʊlə(r)
AM 'stɛljələr

stem
BR stɛm, -z, -ɪŋ, -d
AM stɛm, -z, -ɪŋ, -d

stemless
BR 'stɛmləs
AM 'stɛmləs

stemlet
BR 'stɛmlɪt, -s
AM 'stɛmlət, -s

stemlike
BR 'stɛmlʌɪk
AM 'stɛm‚laɪk

stemma
BR 'stɛmə(r), -z
AM 'stɛmə, -z

stemple
BR 'stɛmpl, -z

AM 'stɛmpəl, -z

stemware
BR 'stɛmwɛ:(r)
AM 'stɛm,wɛ(ə)r

stench
BR stɛn(t)ʃ, -ɪz, -ɪŋ, -t
AM stɛn(t)ʃ, -əz, -ɪŋ, -t

stencil
BR 'stɛns|l, -lz,
-|ɪŋ\-lɪŋ, -ld
AM 'stɛns|əl, -əlz,
-(ə)lɪŋ, -əld

Stendhal
BR 'stɒndɑːl, stɛn'dɑːl
AM stɛn'dɑl

Sten gun
BR 'stɛn gʌn, -z
AM 'stɛn ,gən, -z

steno
stenographer
BR 'stɛnəʊ, -z
AM 'stɛnoʊ, -z

stenograph
BR 'stɛnəgrɑ:f,
'stɛnəgraf, -s
AM 'stɛnə,græf, -s

stenographer
BR stɪ'nɒgrəfə(r),
stɛ'nɒgrəfə(r), -z
AM stə'nɑgrəfər, -z

stenographic
BR ,stɛnə'grafɪk
AM ,stɛnə'græfɪk

stenography
BR stɪ'nɒgrəfi,
stɛ'nɒgrəfi
AM stə'nɑgrəfi

stenoses
BR stɪ'nəʊsiːz,
stɛ'nəʊsiːz
AM stə'noʊsiz

stenosis
BR stɪ'nəʊsɪs,
stɛ'nəʊsɪs
AM stə'noʊsəs

stenotic
BR stɪ'nɒtɪk, stɛ'nɒtɪk
AM stə'nɑdɪk

stenotype
BR 'stɛnətʌɪp, -s
AM 'stɛnə,taɪp, -s

stenotypist
BR 'stɛnə,tʌɪpɪst, -s
AM 'stɛnə,taɪpɪst, -s

stent
BR stɛnt
AM stɛnt

stentor
BR 'stɛntɔ:(r),
'stɛntə(r), -z
AM 'stɛn,tɔ(ə)r,
'stɛn(t)ər, -z

stentorian
BR stɛn'tɔ:rɪən
AM stɛn'tɔrɪən

step
BR stɛp, -s, -ɪŋ, -t
AM stɛp, -s, -ɪŋ, -t

stepbrother
BR 'stɛp,brʌðə(r), -z
AM 'stɛp,brəðər, -z

step-by-step
BR ,stɛpbaɪ'stɛp
AM 'stɛpbaɪ'stɛp

stepchild
BR 'stɛptʃʌɪld
AM 'stɛp,tʃaɪld

stepchildren
BR 'stɛp,tʃɪldr(ə)n
AM 'stɛp,tʃɪldrən

stepdad
BR 'stɛpdad, -z
AM 'stɛp,dæd, -z

stepdaughter
BR 'stɛp,dɔ:tə(r), -z
AM 'stɛp,dɔdər,
'stɛp,dɑdər, -z

step-down
BR 'stɛpdaʊn, -z
AM 'stɛp,daʊn, -z

stepfamily
BR 'stɛp,fam(ɪ)l|i,
'stɛp,fam|l|i, -ɪz
AM 'stɛp,fæm(ə)li, -z

stepfather
BR 'stɛp,fɑ:ðə(r), -z
AM 'stɛp,faðər, -z

Stephanie
BR 'stɛfəni, 'stɛfni
AM 'stɛfəni

stephanotis
BR ,stɛfə'nəʊtɪs
AM ,stɛfə'noʊdəs

Stephen
BR 'sti:vn
AM 'stivən, 'stɛfən

Stephens
BR 'sti:vnz
AM 'stivənz

Stephenson
BR 'sti:vns(ə)n
AM 'stivənsən

stepladder
BR 'stɛp,ladə(r), -z
AM 'stɛp,lædər, -z

steplike
BR 'stɛplʌɪk
AM 'stɛp,laɪk

stepmother
BR 'stɛp,mʌðə(r), -z
AM 'stɛp,məðər, -z

Stepney
BR 'stɛpni
AM 'stɛpni

step-parent
BR 'stɛp,pɛːrənt,
'stɛp,pɛːrnt, -s
AM 'stɛp,pɛrənt, -s

steppe
BR stɛp, -s
AM stɛp, -s

stepping-stone
BR 'stɛpɪŋstəʊn, -z
AM 'stɛpɪŋ,stoʊn, -z

stepsister
BR 'stɛp,sɪstə(r), -z
AM 'stɛp,sɪstər, -z

stepson
BR 'stɛpsʌn, -z
AM 'stɛp,sən, -z

stepstool
BR 'stɛpstu:l, -z
AM 'stɛp,stul, -z

Steptoe
BR 'stɛptəʊ
AM 'stɛp,toʊ

stepwise
BR 'stɛpwʌɪz
AM 'stɛp,waɪz

Steradent
BR 'stɛrədɛnt
AM 'stɛrədnt

steradian
BR stə'reɪdɪən, -z
AM stə'reɪdɪən, -z

stercoraceous
BR ,stə:kə'reɪʃəs
AM ,stərkə'reɪʃəs

stercoral
BR stə'kɔ:rəl, stə'kɔːrl̩
AM stər'kɔrəl

stere
BR stɪə(r), -z
AM stɪ(ə)r, -z

stereo
BR 'stɛrɪəʊ, -z
AM 'stɛrioʊ, -z

stereobate
BR 'stɛrɪə(ʊ)beɪt, -s
AM 'stɛrɪə,beɪt, -s

stereochemistry
BR ,stɛrɪəʊ'kɛmɪstri
AM ,stɛrɪə'kɛməstri

stereograph
BR 'stɛrɪə(ʊ)grɑ:f,
'stɛrɪə(ʊ)graf, -s
AM 'stɛrɪə,græf, -s

stereography
BR ,stɛrɪ'ɒgrəfi
AM ,stɛri'ɑgrəfi

stereoisomer
BR ,stɛrɪəʊ'ʌɪsəmə(r),
-z
AM ,stɛrioʊ'aɪsəmər,
-z

stereometry
BR ,stɛrɪ'ɒmɪtri
AM ,stɛri'ɑmətri

stereophonic
BR ,stɛrɪə(ʊ)'fɒnɪk
AM ,stɛrɪə'fɑnɪk

stereophonically
BR ,stɛrɪə'fɒnɪkli
AM ,stɛrɪə'fɑnək(ə)li

stereophony
BR ,stɛrɪ'ɒfəni,
,stɛrɪ'ɑfəni
AM ,stɛri'ɑfəni

stereopsis
BR ,stɛrɪ'ɒpsɪs
AM ,stɛri'ɑpsəs

stereoptic
BR ,stɛrɪ'ɒptɪk, -s
AM ,stɛri'ɑptɪk, -s

stereopticon
BR ,stɛrɪ'ɒptɪkɒn, -z
AM ,stɛri'ɑptə,kɑn, -z

stereoscope
BR 'stɛrɪəskəʊp, -s
AM 'stɛrɪə,skoʊp, -s

stereoscopic
BR ,stɛrɪə'skɒpɪk
AM ,stɛrɪə'skɑpɪk

stereoscopically
BR ,stɛrɪə'skɒpɪkli
AM ,stɛrɪə'skɑpək(ə)li

stereoscopy
BR ,stɛrɪ'ɒskəpi
AM ,stɛri'ɑskəpi

stereospecific
BR ,stɛrɪəʊspɪ'sɪfɪk
AM ,stɛrɪəspə'sɪfɪk

stereospecifically
BR ,stɛrɪəʊspɪ'sɪfɪkli
AM ,stɛrɪəspə'sɪfɪk(ə)li

stereospecificity
BR ,stɛrɪəʊ,spɛsɪ'fɪsɪti
AM ,stɛrɪə,spɛsə'fɪsɪdi

stereotactic
BR ,stɛrɪə(ʊ)'taktɪk
AM ,stɛrɪə'tæktɪk

stereotaxic
BR ,stɛrɪə(ʊ)'taksɪk
AM ,stɛrɪə'tæksɪk

stereotaxis
BR ,stɛrɪə(ʊ)'taksɪs
AM ,stɛrɪə'tæksəs

stereotaxy
BR 'stɛrɪə,taksi
AM 'stɛrɪə'tæksi

stereotype
BR 'stɛrɪətʌɪp, -s, -ɪŋ, -t
AM 'stɛrɪə,taɪp, -s, -ɪŋ, -t

stereotypic
BR ,stɛrɪə(ʊ)'tɪpɪk
AM ,stɛrɪə'tɪpɪk

stereotypical
BR ,stɛrɪə(ʊ)'tɪpɪkl
AM ,stɛrɪə'tɪpɪkəl

stereotypically
BR ,stɛrɪə(ʊ)'tɪpɪkli
AM ,stɛrɪə'tɪpɪk(ə)li

stereotypy
BR 'stɛrɪə,tʌɪpi
AM 'stɛrɪə,taɪpi

Stergene
BR stə:'dʒi:n
AM stər,dʒin

steric
BR 'stɛrɪk, 'stɪərɪk
AM 'stɪrɪk

sterile
BR 'stɛrʌɪl
AM 'stɛrəl

sterilely
BR 'stɛrʌɪlli
AM 'stɛrə(l)li

sterilisable
BR ˈsterɪlʌɪzəbl
AM ˈsterəˌlaɪzəbəl

sterilisation
BR ˌsterɪlʌɪˈzeɪʃn,
ˌsterˌlʌɪˈzeɪʃn
AM ˌsterələˈzeɪʃən,
ˌsterəˌlaɪˈzeɪʃən

sterilise
BR ˈsterɪlʌɪz, -ɪz, -ɪŋ, -d
AM ˈsterəˌlaɪz, -ɪz, -ɪŋ, -d

steriliser
BR ˈsterɪlʌɪzə(r), -z
AM ˈsterəˌlaɪzər, -z

sterility
BR stəˈrɪlɪti
AM stəˈrɪlɪdi, stɛˈrɪlɪdi

sterilizable
BR ˈsterɪlʌɪzəbl
AM ˈsterəˌlaɪzəbəl

sterilization
BR ˌsterɪlʌɪˈzeɪʃn,
ˌsterˌlʌɪˈzeɪʃn, -z
AM ˌsterələˈzeɪʃən,
ˌsterəˌlaɪˈzeɪʃən, -z

sterilize
BR ˈsterɪlʌɪz, -ɪz, -ɪŋ, -d
AM ˈsterəˌlaɪz, -ɪz, -ɪŋ, -d

sterilizer
BR ˈsterɪlʌɪzə(r), -z
AM ˈsterəˌlaɪzər, -z

sterlet
BR ˈstəːlɪt, -s
AM ˈstərlət, -s

sterling
BR ˈstəːlɪŋ
AM ˈstərlɪŋ

sterlingness
BR ˈstəːlɪŋnɪs
AM ˈstərlɪŋnɪs

stern
BR stəːn, -z, -ə(r), -ɪst
AM stərn, -z, -ər, -əst

sterna
BR ˈstəːnə(r)
AM ˈstərnə

sternal
BR ˈstəːnl
AM ˈstərnəl

Sterne
BR stəːn
AM stərn

sternly
BR ˈstəːnli
AM ˈstərnli

sternmost
BR ˈstəːnməʊst
AM ˈstərnˌmoʊst

sternness
BR ˈstəːnnəs
AM ˈstər(n)nəs

Sterno®
BR ˈstəːnəʊ
AM ˈstərnoʊ

sternpost
BR ˈstəːnpəʊst, -s
AM ˈstərnˌpoʊst, -s

sternum
BR ˈstəːnəm, -z
AM ˈstərnəm, -z

sternutation
BR ˌstəːnjʊˈteɪʃn, -z
AM ˌstərnjəˈteɪʃən, -z

sternutator
BR ˈstəːnjʊteɪtə(r), -z
AM ˈstərnjəˌteɪdər, -z

sternutatory
BR stəːˈnjuːtət(ə)ri,
ˌstəːnjʊˈteɪt(ə)ri
AM stərˈnjudəˌtɔri

sternward
BR ˈstəːnwəd, -z
AM ˈstərnwərd, -z

sternway
BR ˈstəːnweɪ
AM ˈstərnˌweɪ

stern-wheeler
BR ˌstəːnˈwiːlə(r),
ˈstəːnˌwiːlə(r), -z
AM ˈstərnˌ(h)wilər, -z

steroid
BR ˈsterɔɪd, ˈstɪərɔɪd, -z
AM ˈstɛˌrɔɪd, ˈstɪˌrɔɪd, -z

steroidal
BR ˈsterɔɪdl, ˈstɪərɔɪdl
AM stɛˈrɔɪdəl, stɪˈrɔɪdəl

stertor
BR ˈstəːtə(r)
AM ˈstərdər

stertorous
BR ˈstəːt(ə)rəs
AM ˈstərdərəs

stertorously
BR ˈstəːt(ə)rəsli
AM ˈstərdərəsli

stertorousness
BR ˈstəːt(ə)rəsnəs
AM ˈstərdərəsnəs

stet
BR stɛt
AM stɛt

stethoscope
BR ˈsteθəskəʊp, -s
AM ˈstɛθəˌskoʊp, -s

stethoscopic
BR ˌsteθəˈskɒpɪk
AM ˌstɛθəˈskɑpɪk

stethoscopical
BR ˌsteθəˈskɒpɪkl
AM ˌstɛθəˈskɑpəkəl

stethoscopically
BR ˌsteθəˈskɒpɪkli
AM ˌstɛθəˈskɑpək(ə)li

stethoscopist
BR stɛˈθɒskəpɪst, -s
AM stɛˈθɑskəpəst,
ˈstɛθəˌskoʊpəst, -s

stethoscopy
BR stɛˈθɒskəpi
AM stɛˈθɑskəpi,
ˈstɛθəˌskoʊpi

Stetson®
BR ˈstɛtsn, -z
AM ˈstɛtsən, -z

Steuart
BR ˈstjuːət, ˈstʃuːət
AM ˈst(j)uərt

Steuben
BR ˈst(j)uːb(ə)n
AM ˈst(j)ubən

Stevas
BR ˈstiːvəs
AM ˈstivəs

Steve
BR stiːv
AM stiv

stevedore
BR ˈstiːvɪdɔː(r), -z, -ɪŋ
AM ˈstivəˌdɔ(ə)r, -z, -ɪŋ

Steven
BR ˈstiːvn
AM ˈstivən

Stevenage
BR ˈstiːv(ə)nɪdʒ,
ˈstiːvnɪdʒ
AM ˈstivənɪdʒ

stevengraph
BR ˈstiːvngrɑːf,
ˈstiːvngraf, -s
AM ˈstivənˌgræf, -s

Stevens
BR ˈstiːvnz
AM ˈstivənz

Stevenson
BR ˈstiːvns(ə)n
AM ˈstivənsən

stew
BR stjuː, stʃuː, -z, -ɪŋ, -d
AM st(j)u, -z, -ɪŋ, -d

steward
BR ˈstjuːəd, ˈstʃuːəd, -z, -ɪŋ, -ɪd
AM ˈst(j)uərd, -z, -ɪŋ, -əd

stewardess
BR ˈstjuːədɪs,
ˌstjuːəˈdes, ˈstʃuːədɪs,
ˌstʃuːəˈdes, -ɪz
AM ˈst(j)uərdəs, -əz

stewardship
BR ˈstjuːədʃɪp,
ˈstʃuːədʃɪp, -s
AM ˈst(j)uərdˌʃɪp, -s

Stewart
BR ˈstjuːət, ˈstʃuːət
AM ˈst(j)uərt

stewpan
BR ˈstjuːpan,
ˈstʃuːpan, -z
AM ˈst(j)uˌpæn, -z

stewpot
BR ˈstjuːpɒt, ˈstʃuːpɒt, -s
AM ˈst(j)uˌpɑt, -s

Steyning
BR ˈstenɪŋ
AM ˈstenɪŋ

stg.
BR ˈstəːlɪŋ
AM ˈstərlɪŋ

St George
BR s(ə)nt ˈdʒɔːdʒ
AM seɪn(t) ˈdʒɔrdʒ

St Gotthard
BR s(ə)n(t) ˈgɒtəd,
+ ˈgɒtɑːd
AM seɪn(t) ˈgɑdərd,
seɪn(t) ˈgɑdɑrd

St Helena
island
BR ˌsent ɪˈliːnə(r),
ˌs(ə)nt həˈliːnə(r)
AM seɪn(t) həˈlinə

St Helens
BR s(ə)nt ˈhɛlənz
AM seɪn(t) ˈhɛlənz

St Helier
BR s(ə)nt ˈhɛliə(r)
AM seɪn(t) ˈhɛliər

sthenia
BR ˈsθeniə(r)
AM ˈsθeniə

sthenic
BR ˈsθenɪk
AM ˈsθenɪk

stichomythia
BR ˌstɪkəˈmɪθiə(r), -z
AM ˌstɪkəˈmɪθiə, -z

stick
BR stɪk, -s, -ɪŋ
AM stɪk, -s, -ɪŋ

stickability
BR ˌstɪkəˈbɪlɪti
AM ˌstɪkəˈbɪlɪdi

stickball
BR ˈstɪkbɔːl
AM ˈstɪkˌbɔl, ˈstɪkˌbɑl

sticker
BR ˈstɪkə(r), -z
AM ˈstɪkər, -z

stickily
BR ˈstɪkɪli
AM ˈstɪkɪli

stickiness
BR ˈstɪkɪnɪs
AM ˈstɪkɪnɪs

stick-in-the-mud
BR ˈstɪkɪnðəˌmʌd, -z
AM ˈstɪkɪnðəˌməd, -z

stickjaw
BR ˈstɪkdʒɔː(r), -z
AM ˈstɪkˌdʒɔ, ˈstɪkˌdʒɑ, -z

stickleback
BR ˈstɪklbak, -s
AM ˈstɪkəlˌbæk, -s

stickler
BR ˈstɪklə(r), -z
AM ˈstɪk(ə)lər, -z

stickless
BR ˈstɪklɪs

AM 'stɪklɪs

sticklike
BR 'stɪklʌɪk
AM 'stɪk,laɪk

stickpin
BR 'stɪkpɪn, -z
AM 'stɪk,pɪn, -z

stickshift
BR 'stɪkʃɪft, -s
AM 'stɪk,ʃɪft, -s

stick-to-it-ive
BR ,stɪk'tuːɪtɪv
AM ,stɪk'tuədɪv

stick-to-it-iveness
BR ,stɪk'tuːɪtɪvnɪs
AM ,stɪk'tuədɪvnɪs

stickum
BR 'stɪkəm, -z
AM 'stɪkəm, -z

stick-up
BR 'stɪkʌp, -z
AM 'stɪkəp, -s

stickweed
BR 'stɪkwiːd, -z
AM 'stɪk,wid, -z

sticky
BR 'stɪk|i, -ɪə(r), -ɪɪst
AM 'stɪki, -ər, -ɪst

stickybeak
BR 'stɪkɪbiːk, -s, -ɪŋ, -t
AM 'stɪki,bik, -s, -ɪŋ, -t

Stieglitz
BR 'stiːglɪts
AM 'stiglɪts

stifado
BR stɪ'fɑːdəʊ
AM stə'fadoʊ

stiff
BR stɪf, -s, -ə(r), -ɪst
AM stɪf, -s, -ər, -əst

stiffen
BR 'stɪf|n, -nz, -nɪŋ\-nɪŋ, -nd
AM 'stɪfən, -ənz, -(ə)nɪŋ, -ənd

stiffener
BR 'stɪfnə(r), 'stɪfnə(r), -z
AM 'stɪf(ə)nər, -z

stiffening
BR 'stɪfnɪŋ, 'stɪfnɪŋ, -z
AM 'stɪf(ə)nɪŋ, -z

stiffish
BR 'stɪfɪʃ
AM 'stɪfɪʃ

Stiffkey
BR 'stɪfkiː, 'st(j)uːki
AM 'stɪfki

stiffly
BR 'stɪfli
AM 'stɪfli

stiffness
BR 'stɪfnɪs
AM 'stɪfnɪs

stiffy
BR 'stɪf|i, -ɪz

AM 'stɪfi, -z

stifle
BR 'stʌɪf|l, -lz, -lɪŋ\-lɪŋ, -ld
AM 'staɪf|əl, -əlz, -(ə)lɪŋ, -əld

stifler
BR 'stʌɪflə(r), 'stʌɪflə(r), -z
AM 'staɪf(ə)lər, -z

stiflingly
BR 'stʌɪflɪŋli, 'stʌɪflɪŋli
AM 'staɪf(ə)lɪŋli

stigma
BR 'stɪgmə(r)
AM 'stɪgmə

stigmata
BR 'stɪgmətə(r), stɪg'mɑːtə(r)
AM stɪg'mɑdə, 'stɪgmədə

stigmatic
BR stɪg'matɪk, -s
AM stɪg'mædɪk, -s

stigmatically
BR stɪg'matɪkli
AM stɪg'mædək(ə)li

stigmatisation
BR ,stɪgmətʌɪ'zeɪʃn
AM ,stɪgmədə'zeɪʃən, ,stɪgmə,taɪ'zeɪʃən

stigmatise
BR 'stɪgmətʌɪz, -ɪz, -ɪŋ, -d
AM 'stɪgmə,taɪz, -ɪz, -ɪŋ, -d

stigmatist
BR 'stɪgmətɪst, -s
AM 'stɪgmədəst, -s

stigmatization
BR ,stɪgmətʌɪ'zeɪʃn
AM ,stɪgmədə'zeɪʃən, ,stɪgmə,taɪ'zeɪʃən

stigmatize
BR 'stɪgmətʌɪz, -ɪz, -ɪŋ, -d
AM 'stɪgmə,taɪz, -ɪz, -ɪŋ, -d

stilb
BR stɪlb, -z
AM stɪlb, -z

stilbene
BR 'stɪlbiːn
AM 'stɪl,bin

stilbestrol
BR stɪl'biːstrɒl, stɪl'bestrɒl, stɪl'biːstr(ə)l, stɪl'bestr(ə)l
AM stɪl'bes,trɒl, stɪl'bes,trɑl

stilbite
BR 'stɪlbʌɪt
AM 'stɪl,baɪt

stilboestrol
BR stɪl'biːstrɒl, stɪl'bestrɒl,

stɪl'biːstr(ə)l, stɪl'bestr(ə)l
AM stɪl'bes,trɒl, stɪl'bes,trɑl

stile
BR stʌɪl, -z
AM staɪl, -z

Stiles
BR stʌɪlz
AM staɪlz

stiletto
BR stɪ'lɛtəʊ, -z
AM stə'ledoʊ, -z

Stilgoe
BR 'stɪlgəʊ
AM 'stɪlgoʊ

stili
BR 'stʌɪlʌɪ
AM 'staɪ,laɪ

Stilicho
BR 'stɪlɪkəʊ
AM 'stɪlɪkoʊ

still
BR stɪl, -z, -ɪŋ, -d, -ə(r), -ɪst
AM stɪl, -z, -ɪŋ, -d, -ər, -ɪst

stillage
BR 'stɪl|ɪdʒ, -ɪdʒɪz
AM 'stɪlɪdʒ, -ɪz

stillbirth
BR 'stɪlbɜːθ, stɪl'bɜːθ, -s
AM 'stɪl,bərθ, -s

stillborn
BR 'stɪlbɔːn, ,stɪl'bɔːn
AM 'stɪl,bɔ(ə)rn

stillicide
BR 'stɪlɪsʌɪd, -z
AM 'stɪli,saɪd, -z

still-life
BR ,stɪl'lʌɪf
AM 'stɪl,laɪf

stillness
BR 'stɪlnɪs, -ɪz
AM 'stɪlnɪs, -ɪz

stillroom
BR 'stɪlruːm, 'stɪlrʊm, -z
AM 'stɪl,rum, 'stɪl,rʊm, -z

Stillson
BR 'stɪls(ə)n, -z
AM 'stɪlsən, -z

stilly[1]
adjective
BR 'stɪli
AM 'stɪli

stilly[2]
adverb
BR 'stɪlli
AM 'stɪlli

stilt
BR stɪlt, -s
AM stɪlt, -s

stilted
BR 'stɪltɪd
AM 'stɪltɪd

stiltedly
BR 'stɪltɪdli
AM 'stɪltɪdli

stiltedness
BR 'stɪltɪdnɪs
AM 'stɪltɪdnɪs

stiltless
BR 'stɪltlɪs
AM 'stɪltlɪs

Stilton®
BR 'stɪlt(ə)n
AM 'stɪlt(ə)n

stilus
BR 'stʌɪləs, -ɪz
AM 'staɪləs, -əz

Stimson
BR 'stɪms(ə)n
AM 'stɪmsən

stimulant
BR 'stɪmjʊlənt, 'stɪmjələnt, -s
AM 'stɪmjələnt, -s

stimulate
BR 'stɪmjʊleɪt, -s, -ɪŋ, -ɪd
AM 'stɪmjə,leɪ|t, -ts, -dɪŋ, -dɪd

stimulatingly
BR 'stɪmjʊleɪtɪŋli
AM 'stɪmjə,leɪdɪŋli

stimulation
BR ,stɪmjʊ'leɪʃn, -z
AM ,stɪmjə'leɪʃən, -z

stimulative
BR 'stɪmjʊlətɪv, -z
AM 'stɪmjə,leɪdɪv, 'stɪmjələdɪv, -z

stimulator
BR 'stɪmjʊleɪtə(r), -z
AM 'stɪmjə,leɪdər, -z

stimulatory
BR 'stɪmjʊlət(ə)ri
AM 'stɪmjələ,tɔri

stimuli
BR 'stɪmjʊlʌɪ, 'stɪmjʊliː
AM 'stɪmjə,laɪ

stimulus
BR 'stɪmjʊləs
AM 'stɪmjələs

stimy
BR 'stʌɪm|i, -ɪz, -ɪɪŋ, -ɪd
AM 'staɪmi, -z, -ɪŋ, -d

sting
BR stɪŋ, -z, -ɪŋ
AM stɪŋ, -z, -ɪŋ

stingaree
BR ,stɪŋgə'riː, 'stɪŋgəri:, -z
AM 'stɪŋə,ri, -z

stinger
BR 'stɪŋə(r), -z
AM 'stɪŋər, -z

stingily
BR 'stɪn(d)ʒɪli
AM 'stɪndʒɪli

stinginess
BR 'stɪn(d)ʒɪnɪs
AM 'stɪndʒɪnɪs

stingingly
BR 'stɪŋɪŋli
AM 'stɪŋɪŋli

stingless
BR 'stɪŋlɪs
AM 'stɪŋlɪs

stinglike
BR 'stɪŋlʌɪk
AM 'stɪŋlaɪk

stingray
BR 'stɪŋreɪ, -z
AM 'stɪŋˌreɪ, -z

stingy¹
miserly
BR 'stɪn(d)ʒ|i, -ɪə(r),
-ɪɪst
AM 'stɪndʒi, -ər, -ɪst

stingy²
with a sting
BR 'stɪŋi
AM 'stɪŋi

stink
BR stɪŋk, -s, -ɪŋ
AM stɪŋk, -s, -ɪŋ

stinkard
BR 'stɪŋkəd, -z
AM 'stɪŋkərd, -z

stinkbomb
BR 'stɪŋkbɒm, -z
AM 'stɪŋkˌbɑm, -z

stinker
BR 'stɪŋkə(r), -z
AM 'stɪŋkər, -z

stinkhorn
BR 'stɪŋkhɔːn, -z
AM 'stɪŋk,(h)ɔ(ə)rn, -z

stinkingly
BR 'stɪŋkɪŋli
AM 'stɪŋkɪŋli

stinko
BR 'stɪŋkəʊ
AM 'stɪŋkoʊ

stinkpot
BR 'stɪŋkpɒt, -s
AM 'stɪŋkˌpɑt, -s

stinkweed
BR 'stɪŋkwiːd, -z
AM 'stɪŋk,wid, -z

stinkwood
BR 'stɪŋkwʊd, -z
AM 'stɪŋk,wʊd, -z

stinky
BR 'stɪŋk|i, -ɪə(r), -ɪɪst
AM 'stɪŋki, -ər, -ɪst

stint
BR stɪnt, -s, -ɪŋ, -ɪd
AM stɪn|t, -ts, -(t)ɪŋ,
-(t)ɪd

stinter
BR 'stɪntə(r), -z
AM 'stɪn(t)ər, -z

stintless
BR 'stɪntlɪs
AM 'stɪn(t)lɪs

stipe
BR stʌɪp, -s
AM staɪp, -s

stipel
BR 'stʌɪpl, -z
AM 'staɪpəl, -z

stipellate
BR stɪ'pɛlət, -s
AM 'staɪ'pɛlət,
stə'pɛlət, 'staɪpə,leɪt,
-s

stipend
BR 'stʌɪpɛnd, -z
AM 'staɪˌpɛnd,
'staɪpənd, -z

stipendiary
BR stʌɪ'pɛndjər|i, -ɪz
AM staɪ'pɛndi,ɛri, -z

stipes
BR 'stʌɪpiːz
AM 'staɪˌpiz

stipiform
BR 'stʌɪpɪfɔːm
AM 'staɪpə,fɔ(ə)rm

stipitate
BR 'stɪpɪtət
AM 'stɪpə,teɪt

stipitiform
BR 'stɪpɪtɪfɔːm
AM 'stɪpədə,fɔ(ə)rm

stipple
BR 'stɪp|l, -lz, -lɪŋ \-lɪŋ,
-ld
AM 'stɪp|əl, -əlz, -(ə)lɪŋ,
-əld

stippler
BR 'stɪplə(r),
'stɪplə(r), -z
AM 'stɪp(ə)lər, -z

stipular
BR 'stɪpjʊlə(r)
AM 'stɪpjələr

stipulate
BR 'stɪpjʊleɪt, -s, -ɪŋ,
-ɪd
AM 'stɪpjə,leɪ|t, -ts,
-dɪŋ, -dɪd

stipulation
BR ˌstɪpjʊ'leɪʃn, -z
AM ˌstɪpjə'leɪʃən, -z

stipulator
BR 'stɪpjʊleɪtə(r), -z
AM 'stɪpjə,leɪdər, -z

stipulatory
BR 'stɪpjʊlət(ə)ri,
ˌstɪpjʊ'leɪt(ə)ri
AM 'stɪpjələ,tɔri

stipule
BR 'stɪpjuːl, -z
AM 'stɪpjul, -z

stir
BR stɜː(r), -z, -ɪŋ, -d
AM stər, -z, -ɪŋ, -d

stir-crazy
BR 'stɜːˌkreɪzi,
ˌstɜː'kreɪzi
AM 'stər,kreɪzi

stir-fry
BR 'stə:frʌɪ, ˌstə:'frʌɪ,
-z, -ɪŋ, -d
AM 'stər,fraɪ, -z, -ɪŋ, -d

stirk
BR stɜːk, -s
AM stərk, -s

stirless
BR 'stɜːləs
AM 'stərləs

Stirling
BR 'stɜːlɪŋ
AM 'stərlɪŋ

stirpes
BR 'stɜːpiːz
AM 'stər,piz

stirpiculture
BR 'stɜːpɪ,kʌltʃə(r)
AM 'stərpə,kəltʃər

stirps
BR stɜːps
AM stərps

stirrer
BR 'stɜːrə(r), -z
AM 'stərər, -z

stirring
BR 'stɜːrɪŋ, -z
AM 'stərɪŋ, -z

stirringly
BR 'stɜːrɪŋli
AM 'stərɪŋli

stirrup
BR 'stɪrəp, -s
AM 'stɪrəp, -s

stishovite
BR 'stɪʃəvʌɪt
AM 'stɪʃə,vaɪt

stitch
BR stɪtʃ, -ɪz, -ɪŋ, -t
AM stɪtʃ, -ɪz, -ɪŋ, -t

stitcher
BR 'stɪtʃə(r), -z
AM 'stɪtʃər, -z

stitchery
BR 'stɪtʃ(ə)ri
AM 'stɪtʃəri

stitchless
BR 'stɪtʃlɪs
AM 'stɪtʃlɪs

stitchwork
BR 'stɪtʃwɜːk
AM 'stɪtʃˌwərk

stitchwort
BR 'stɪtʃwɜːt, -s
AM 'stɪtʃwərt,
'stɪtʃˌwɔ(ə)rt, -s

stiver
BR 'stʌɪvə(r), -z
AM 'staɪvər, -z

Stivichall
BR 'stʌɪtʃl, 'staɪtʃɔːl
AM 'staɪtʃəl

St John
BR s(ə)nt 'dʒɒn
AM seɪn(t) 'dʒɑn

St John's
BR s(ə)nt 'dʒɒnz

AM seɪn(t) 'dʒɑnz

St Kilda
BR s(ə)nt 'kɪldə(r)
AM seɪn(t) 'kɪldə

St Kitts
BR s(ə)nt 'kɪts
AM seɪn(t) 'kɪts

St Kitts-Nevis
BR s(ə)nt ˌkɪts'niːvɪs
AM seɪn(t) 'kɪts'nivɪs

St Lawrence
BR s(ə)nt 'lɒrəns,
+ 'lɒrns
AM seɪn(t) 'lɔrəns

St Leger
BR s(ə)nt 'lɛdʒə(r)
AM seɪn(t) 'lɛdʒər

St Louis¹
BR s(ə)nt 'luːi
AM seɪn(t) 'lui(s)

St Louis²
US city
BR s(ə)nt 'luːɪs
AM ˌseɪn(t)'luəs

St Lucia
BR s(ə)nt 'luːʃ(ɪ)ə(r),
+ 'luːsɪə(r)
AM ˌseɪnt'luʃə,
ˌseɪnt,lu'siə,
ˌsən(t)'luʃə,
ˌsən(t),lu'siə

stoa
BR 'stəʊə(r)
AM 'stoʊə

stoat
BR stəʊt, -s
AM stoʊt, -s

stob
BR stɒb, -z
AM stɑb, -z

stochastic
BR stə'kastɪk,
stɒ'kastɪk
AM stə'kæstɪk

stochastically
BR stə'kastɪkli,
stɒ'kastɪkli
AM stə'kæstək(ə)li

stock
BR stɒk, -s, -ɪŋ, -t
AM stɑk, -s, -ɪŋ, -t

stockade
BR stɒ'keɪd, -z, -ɪŋ, -ɪd
AM stɑ'keɪd, -z, -ɪŋ, -ɪd

stockbreeder
BR 'stɒkˌbriːdə(r), -z
AM 'stɑkˌbridər, -z

stockbreeding
BR 'stɒkˌbriːdɪŋ
AM 'stɑkˌbridɪŋ

Stockbridge
BR 'stɒkbrɪdʒ
AM 'stɑkˌbrɪdʒ

stockbroker
BR 'stɒkˌbrəʊkə(r), -z
AM 'stɑkˌbroʊkər, -z

stockbrokerage
BR 'stɒk,brəʊk(ə)rɪdʒ
AM 'stak,brook(ə)rɪdʒ

stockbroking
BR 'stɒk,brəʊkɪŋ
AM 'stak,brookɪŋ

stockcar
BR 'stɒkkɑː(r), -z
AM 'sta(k),kar, -z

Stockdale
BR 'stɒkdeɪl
AM 'stak,deɪl

stocker
BR 'stɒkə(r), -z
AM 'stakər, -z

stock exchange
BR 'stɒk ɪks,tʃeɪn(d)ʒ,
-ɪz
AM 'stak əks,tʃeɪndʒ,
-ɪz

stockfish
BR 'stɒkfɪʃ
AM 'stak,fɪʃ

Stockhausen
BR 'stɒk,haʊzn,
'ʃtɒk,haʊzn
AM 'stak,(h)aʊzn

stockholder
BR 'stɒk,həʊldə(r), -z
AM 'stak,(h)oʊldər, -z

stockholding
BR 'stɒk,həʊldɪŋ, -z
AM 'stak,(h)oʊldɪŋ, -z

Stockholm
BR 'stɒkhəʊm
AM 'stak,(h)oʊ(l)m

stockily
BR 'stɒkɪli
AM 'stakəli

stockiness
BR 'stɒkɪnɪs
AM 'stakɪnɪs

stockinet
BR ,stɒkɪ'nɛt
AM ,stakə'nɛt

stockinette
BR ,stɒkɪ'nɛt
AM ,stakə'nɛt

stocking
BR 'stɒkɪŋ, -z, -d
AM 'stakɪŋ, -z, -d

stockingless
BR 'stɒkɪŋlɪs
AM 'stakɪŋlɪs

stock-in-trade
BR ,stɒkɪn'treɪd
AM ,stakən'treɪd

stockist
BR 'stɒkɪst, -s
AM 'stakəst, -s

stockjobber
BR 'stɒk,dʒɒbə(r), -z
AM 'stak,dʒɑbər, -z

stockjobbing
BR 'stɒk,dʒɒbɪŋ
AM 'stak,dʒɑbɪŋ

stockless
BR 'stɒkləs
AM 'stakləs

stocklist
BR 'stɒklɪst, -s
AM 'stak,lɪst, -s

stockman
BR 'stɒkmən
AM 'stakmən,
'stak,mæn

stockmen
BR 'stɒkmən
AM 'stakmən,
'stak,mɛn

stockout
BR 'stɒkaʊt, -s
AM 'stak,aʊt, -s

stockpile
BR 'stɒkpʌɪl, -z, -ɪŋ, -d
AM 'stak,paɪl, -z, -ɪŋ, -d

stockpiler
BR 'stɒk,pʌɪlə(r), -z
AM 'stak,paɪlər, -z

Stockport
BR 'stɒkpɔːt
AM 'stak,pɔ(ə)rt

stockpot
BR 'stɒkpɒt, -s
AM 'stak,pat, -s

stockroom
BR 'stɒkruːm,
'stɒkrʊm, -z
AM 'stak,rum,
'stak,rʊm, -z

Stocks
BR 'stɒks
AM 'staks

Stocksbridge
BR 'stɒksbrɪdʒ
AM 'staks,brɪdʒ

stock-still
BR ,stɒk'stɪl
AM 'stak'stɪl

stocktake
BR 'stɒkteɪk, -s
AM 'stak,teɪk, -s

stocktaking
BR 'stɒk,teɪkɪŋ
AM 'stak,teɪkɪŋ

Stockton
BR 'stɒktən
AM 'staktən

Stockton-on-Tees
BR ,stɒktənɒn'tiːz
AM 'staktənən'tiz

Stockwell
BR 'stɒkw(ɛ)l
AM 'stak,wɛl

Stockwood
BR 'stɒkwʊd
AM 'stak,wʊd

stocky
BR 'stɒk|i, -ɪə(r), -ɪɪst
AM 'staki, -ər, -ɪst

stockyard
BR 'stɒkjɑːd, -z

AM 'stak,jard, -z

Stoddard
BR 'stɒdəd, 'stɒdɑːd
AM 'stadərd

Stoddart
BR 'stɒdət, 'stɒdɑːt
AM 'stadərt

stodge
BR stɒdʒ
AM stadʒ

stodgily
BR 'stɒdʒɪli
AM 'stadʒəli

stodginess
BR 'stɒdʒɪnɪs
AM 'stadʒɪnɪs

stodgy
BR 'stɒdʒ|i, -ɪə(r), -ɪɪst
AM 'stadʒi, -ər, -ɪst

stoep
BR stuːp, -s
AM stup, -s

stogey
BR 'stəʊg|i, -ɪz
AM 'stoʊgi, -z

stogie
BR 'stəʊg|i, -ɪz
AM 'stoʊgi, -z

Stogumber
BR stə(ʊ)'gʌmbə(r),
'stɒgəmbə(r)
AM stə'gəmbər

Stogursey
BR stə(ʊ)'gəːzi
AM stə'gərzi

stogy
BR 'stəʊg|i, -ɪz
AM 'stoʊgi, -z

Stoic
BR 'stəʊɪk, -s
AM 'stoʊɪk, -s

stoical
BR 'stəʊɪkl
AM 'stoʊəkəl

stoically
BR 'stəʊɪkli
AM 'stoʊək(ə)li

stoichiometric
BR ,stɔɪkɪə'mɛtrɪk
AM ,stɔɪkioʊ'mɛtrɪk

stoichiometrical
BR ,stɔɪkɪə'mɛtrɪkl
AM ,stɔɪkioʊ'mɛtrəkəl

stoichiometrically
BR ,stɔɪkɪə'mɛtrɪkli
AM ,stɔɪkioʊ'mɛtrək-
(ə)li

stoichiometry
BR ,stɔɪkɪ'ɒmɪtri
AM ,stɔɪkɪ'amətri

Stoicism
BR 'stəʊɪsɪz(ə)m
AM 'stoʊə,sɪzəm

stoke
BR stəʊk, -s, -ɪŋ, -t
AM stoʊk, -s, -ɪŋ, -t

stokehold
BR 'stəʊkhəʊld, -z
AM 'stoʊk,(h)oʊld, -z

stokehole
BR 'stəʊkhəʊl, -z
AM 'stoʊk,(h)oʊl, -z

Stoke-on-Trent
BR ,stəʊkɒn'trɛnt
AM 'stoʊkən'trɛnt

Stoker
BR 'stəʊkə(r)
AM 'stoʊkər

stoker
BR 'stəʊkə(r), -z
AM 'stoʊkər, -z

stokes
BR stəʊks
AM stoʊks

Stokowski
BR stə'kɒfski
AM stə'kaʊski

STOL
BR stɒl, 'ɛstɒl
AM stɔl, stal

stola
BR 'stəʊlə(r), -z
AM 'stoʊlə, -z

stolae
BR 'stəʊliː
AM 'stoʊli, 'stoʊ,laɪ

stole
BR stəʊl, -z
AM stoʊl, -z

stolen
BR 'stəʊlən
AM 'stoʊlən

stolid
BR 'stɒlɪd
AM 'staləd

stolidity
BR stə'lɪdɪti, stɒ'lɪdɪti
AM stə'lɪdɪdi

stolidly
BR 'stɒlɪdli
AM 'stalədli

stolidness
BR 'stɒlɪdnɪs
AM 'stalədnəs

Stollen
BR 'stɒlən, 'ʃtɒlən, -z
AM 'ʃtələn, 'stələn, -z

stolon
BR 'stəʊlɒn, 'stəʊlən,
-z
AM 'stoʊlən, -z

stolonate
BR 'stəʊləneɪt
AM 'stoʊlənət,
'stoʊlə,neɪt

stoloniferous
BR ,stəʊlə'nɪf(ə)rəs
AM ,stoʊlə'nɪf(ə)rəs

stoma
BR 'stəʊmə(r), -z
AM 'stoʊmə, -z

stomach
BR ˈstʌmək, -s, -ɪŋ, -t
AM ˈstəmək, -s, -ɪŋ, -t

stomachache
BR ˈstʌmək,eɪk, -s
AM ˈstəmək,eɪk, -s

stomacher
BR ˈstʌməkə(r), -z
AM ˈstəməkər, -z

stomachful
BR ˈstʌməkfʊl, -z
AM ˈstəmək,fʊl, -z

stomachic
BR stəˈmakɪk
AM stəˈmækɪk

stomachless
BR ˈstʌmətkləs
AM ˈstəməkləs

stomal
BR ˈstəʊml
AM ˈstoʊməl

stomata
BR ˈstəʊmətə(r),
stəˈmɑːtə(r)
AM ˈstoʊmədə,
ˌstoʊˈmɑdə

stomatal
BR ˈstəʊmətl, ˈstɒmətl
AM ˈstoʊmədl,
ˈstɑmədl

stomatitis
BR ˌstəʊməˈtʌɪtɪs
AM ˌstoʊməˈtaɪdɪs

stomatological
BR ˌstəʊmətəˈlɒdʒɪkl
AM ˌstoʊmədəˈladʒəkəl

stomatologist
BR ˌstəʊməˈtɒlədʒɪst,
-s
AM ˌstoʊməˈtalədʒəst,
-s

stomatology
BR ˌstəʊməˈtɒlədʒi
AM ˌstoʊməˈtalədʒi

stomp
BR stɒm|p, -ps, -pɪŋ,
-(p)t
AM stɒmp, stamp, -s,
-ɪŋ, -t

stomper
BR ˈstɒmpə(r), -z
AM ˈstɒmpər,
ˈstampər, -z

stone
BR stəʊn, -z, -ɪŋ, -d
AM stoʊn, -z, -ɪŋ, -d

Stonebridge
BR ˈstəʊnbrɪdʒ
AM ˈstoʊn,brɪdʒ

stonechat
BR ˈstəʊntʃat, -s
AM ˈstoʊn,tʃæt, -s

stonecrop
BR ˈstəʊnkrɒp, -s
AM ˈstoʊnə,krap, -s

stonecutter
BR ˈstəʊn,kʌtə(r), -z
AM ˈstoʊn,kədər, -z

stonefish
BR ˈstəʊnfɪʃ, -ɪz
AM ˈstoʊn,fɪʃ, -ɪz

stonefly
BR ˈstəʊnflaɪ, -z
AM ˈstoʊn,flaɪ, -z

stoneground
BR ˌstəʊnˈgraʊnd
AM ˌstoʊnˈgraʊn(d)

stonehatch
BR ˈstəʊnhatʃ, -ɪz
AM ˈstoʊn,(h)ætʃ, -əz

Stonehaven
BR ˌstəʊnˈheɪvn
AM ˌstoʊn,(h)eɪvən

Stonehenge
BR ˌstəʊnˈhɛn(d)ʒ
AM ˌstoʊn,(h)ɛndʒ

Stonehouse
BR ˈstəʊnhaʊs
AM ˈstoʊn,(h)aʊs

Stoneleigh
BR ˈstəʊnli
AM ˈstoʊnli

stoneless
BR ˈstəʊnləs
AM ˈstoʊnləs

stonemason
BR ˈstəʊn,meɪsn, -z
AM ˈstoʊn,meɪsən, -z

stonemasonry
BR ˈstəʊn,meɪsnri
AM ˈstoʊn,meɪsnri

stone-pit
BR ˈstəʊnpɪt, -s
AM ˈstoʊn,pɪt, -s

stoner
BR ˈstəʊnə(r), -z
AM ˈstoʊnər, -z

stonewall
BR ˈstəʊnˈwɔːl,
ˈstəʊnwɔːl, -z, -ɪŋ, -d
AM ˈstoʊn,wɔl,
ˈstoʊn,wal, -z, -ɪŋ, -d

stonewaller
BR ˌstəʊnˈwɔːlə(r),
ˈstəʊn,wɔːlə(r), -z
AM ˈstoʊn,wɔlər,
ˈstoʊn,walər, -z

stoneware
BR ˈstəʊnwɛː(r)
AM ˈstoʊn,wɛ(ə)r

stonewashed
BR ˈstəʊnwɒʃt
AM ˈstoʊn,wɔʃt,
ˈstoʊn,waʃt

stoneweed
BR ˈstəʊnwiːd, -z
AM ˈstoʊn,wid, -z

stonework
BR ˈstəʊnwəːk
AM ˈstoʊn,wərk

stoneworker
BR ˈstəʊn,wəːkə(r), -z
AM ˈstoʊn,wərkər, -z

stonewort
BR ˈstəʊnwəːt, -s
AM ˈstoʊnwərt,
ˈstoʊn,wɔ(ə)rt, -s

stonily
BR ˈstəʊnɪli
AM ˈstoʊnəli

stoniness
BR ˈstəʊnɪnɪs
AM ˈstoʊnɪnɪs

stonker
BR ˈstɒŋklə(r), -əz,
-(ə)rɪŋ, -əd
AM ˈstɒŋkər, ˈstaŋkər,
-z, -ɪŋ, -d

stonking
BR ˈstɒŋkɪŋ
AM ˈstɒŋkɪŋ, ˈstaŋkɪŋ

Stonor
BR ˈstəʊnə(r)
AM ˈstoʊnər

stony
BR ˈstəʊn|i, -ɪə(r), -ɪɪst
AM ˈstoʊni, -ər, -ɪst

stony-broke
BR ˌstəʊnɪˈbrəʊk
AM ˌstoʊniˈbroʊk

stony-hearted
BR ˌstəʊnɪˈhɑːtɪd
AM ˈstoʊniˈhɑrdəd

stood
BR stʊd
AM stʊd

stooge
BR stuːdʒ, -ɪz, -ɪŋ, -d
AM studʒ, -əz, -ɪŋ, -d

stook
BR stuːk, stʊk, -s, -ɪŋ, -t
AM stʊk, stuk, -s, -ɪŋ, -t

stool
BR stuːl, -z
AM stul, -z

stoolball
BR ˈstuːlbɔːl
AM ˈstul,bɔl, ˈstul,bal

stoolie
BR ˈstuːl|i, -ɪz
AM ˈstuli, -z

stoolpigeon
BR ˈstuːl,pɪdʒɪn, -z
AM ˈstul,pɪdʒɪn, -z

stoop
BR stuːp, -s, -ɪŋ, -t
AM stup, -s, -ɪŋ, -t

stop
BR stɒp, -s, -ɪŋ, -t
AM stap, -s, -ɪŋ, -t

stop-and-go
BR ˌstɒp(ə)n(d)ˈgəʊ
AM ˌstapənˈgoʊ

stopbank
BR ˈstɒpbaŋk, -s
AM ˈstap,bæŋk, -s

stopcock
BR ˈstɒpkɒk, -s
AM ˈstap,kak, -s

stope
BR stəʊp, -s
AM stoʊp, -s

Stopes
BR stəʊps
AM stoʊps

stopgap
BR ˈstɒpgap, -s
AM ˈstap,gæp, -s

stop-go
BR ˌstɒpˈgəʊ
AM ˌstapˈgoʊ

stopless
BR ˈstɒpləs
AM ˈstapləs

stoplight
BR ˈstɒplaɪt, -s
AM ˈstap,laɪt, -s

stopoff
BR ˈstɒpɒf, -s
AM ˈstap,ɔf, ˈstap,af, -s

stopover
BR ˈstɒp,əʊvə(r), -z
AM ˈstap,oʊvər, -z

stoppable
BR ˈstɒpəbl
AM ˈstapəbəl

stoppage
BR ˈstɒp|ɪdʒ, -ɪdʒɪz
AM ˈstapɪdʒ, -ɪz

Stoppard
BR ˈstɒpɑːd
AM ˈstapərd, ˈsta,pard

stopper
BR ˈstɒplə(r), -əz,
-(ə)rɪŋ, -əd
AM ˈstapər, -z, -ɪŋ, -d

stopping
BR ˈstɒpɪŋ, -z
AM ˈstapɪŋ, -z

stopple
BR ˈstɒp|l, -lz, -l̩ɪŋ \-lɪŋ,
-ld
AM ˈstapəl, -əlz,
-(ə)lɪŋ, -əld

stop press
BR ˌstɒp ˈprɛs
AM ˌstap ˈprɛs

stop-start
BR ˌstɒpˈstɑːt
AM ˈstapˈstart

stopwatch
BR ˈstɒpwɒtʃ, -ɪz
AM ˈstap,watʃ, -əz

storable
BR ˈstɔːrəbl
AM ˈstɔrəbəl

storage
BR ˈstɔːrɪdʒ
AM ˈstɔrɪdʒ

storax
BR ˈstɔːraks, -ɪz
AM ˈstɔ,ræks, -əz

store
BR stɔː(r), -z, -ɪŋ, -d
AM stɔ(ə)r, -z, -ɪŋ, -d

storefront
BR 'stɔːfrʌnt, -s
AM 'stɔrˌfrənt, -s

storehouse
BR 'stɔːhaʊ|s, -zɪz
AM 'stɔrˌ(h)aʊ|s, -zəz

storekeeper
BR 'stɔːˌkiːpə(r), -z
AM 'stɔrˌkipər, -z

storeman
BR 'stɔːmən
AM 'stɔrmən

storemen
BR 'stɔːmən
AM 'stɔrmən

storer
BR 'stɔːrə(r), -z
AM 'stɔrər, -z

storeroom
BR 'stɔːruːm, 'stɔːrʊm, -z
AM 'stɔrˌrum, 'stɔrˌrʊm, -z

storey
BR 'stɔːr|i, -iz, -ɪd
AM 'stɔri, -z, -d

storiated
BR 'stɔːrɪeɪtɪd
AM 'stɔriˌeɪdɪd

storiation
BR ˌstɔːrɪ'eɪʃn, -z
AM ˌstɔriˈeɪʃən, -z

storied
BR 'stɔːrɪd
AM 'stɔrid

stork
BR stɔːk, -s
AM stɔ(ə)rk, -s

storksbill
BR 'stɔːksbɪl, -z
AM 'stɔrksˌbɪl, -z

storm
BR stɔːm, -z, -ɪŋ, -d
AM stɔ(ə)rm, -z, -ɪŋ, -d

stormbound
BR 'stɔːmbaʊnd
AM 'stɔrmˌbaʊnd

stormdoor
BR 'stɔːmdɔː(r), -z
AM 'stɔrmˌdɔ(ə)r, -z

stormer
BR 'stɔːmə(r), -z
AM 'stɔrmər, -z

stormily
BR 'stɔːmɪli
AM 'stɔrməli

storminess
BR 'stɔːmɪnɪs
AM 'stɔrmɪnɪs

stormless
BR 'stɔːmləs
AM 'stɔrmləs

Stormont
BR 'stɔːmɒnt, 'stɔːm(ə)nt
AM 'stɔrˌmant

stormproof
BR 'stɔːmpruːf
AM 'stɔrmˌpruf

storm-tossed
BR 'stɔːmtɒst
AM 'stɔrmˌtɔst, 'stɔrmˌtɑst

stormy
BR 'stɔːm|i, -ɪə(r), -ɪɪst
AM 'stɔrmi, -ər, -ɪst

stormy petrel
BR ˌstɔːmɪ 'petr(ə)l, -z
AM 'stɔrmi 'petrəl, -z

Stornoway
BR 'stɔːnəweɪ
AM 'stɔrnəˌweɪ

Storr
BR stɔː(r)
AM stɔ(ə)r

Storrs
BR stɔːz
AM stɔrz

Stortford
BR 'stɔː(t)fəd
AM 'stɔr(t)fərd

story
BR 'stɔːr|i, -iz
AM 'stɔri, -z

storyboard
BR 'stɔːrɪbɔːd, -z
AM 'stɔriˌbɔ(ə)rd, -z

storybook
BR 'stɔːrɪbʊk, -s
AM 'stɔriˌbʊk, -s

storyline
BR 'stɔːrɪlʌɪm, -z
AM 'stɔriˌlaɪm, -z

storyteller
BR 'stɔːrɪˌtelə(r), -z
AM 'stɔriˌtelər, -z

storytelling
BR 'stɔːrɪˌtelɪŋ
AM 'stɔriˌtelɪŋ

stot
BR stɒt, -s, -ɪŋ, -ɪd
AM stɑ|t, -ts, -dɪŋ, -dəd

stotinka
BR stɒ'tɪŋkə(r), stə'tɪŋkə(r)
AM stə'tɪŋkə, stɑ'tɪŋkə

stotinki
BR stɒ'tɪŋki, stə'tɪŋki
AM stə'tɪŋki, stɑ'tɪŋki

stotious
BR 'stəʊʃəs
AM 'stoʊʃəs

Stott
BR stɒt
AM stɑt

Stoughton
BR 'stəʊtn, 'staʊtn, 'stɔːtn
AM 'stoʊtn, 'stɑtn

stoup
BR stuːp, -s
AM stup, -s

Stour¹
East Anglia UK
BR stʊə(r)
AM stʊ(ə)r

Stour²
Warwickshire UK
BR 'staʊə(r)
AM 'staʊ(ə)r

Stour³
BR staʊə(r)
AM stɔʊr, 'staʊ(ə)r

Stourbridge
BR 'staʊəbrɪdʒ
AM 'staʊrˌbrɪdʒ

Stourport
BR 'staʊəpɔːt
AM 'staʊrˌpɔ(ə)rt

Stourton
BR 'stəːtn
AM 'staʊrtən

stoush
BR staʊʃ, -ɪz, -ɪŋ, -t
AM staʊʃ, -əz, -ɪŋ, -t

stout
BR staʊt, -s, -ə(r), -ɪst
AM staʊ|t, -ts, -dər, -dəst

stoutish
BR 'staʊtɪʃ
AM 'staʊdɪʃ

stoutly
BR 'staʊtli
AM 'staʊtli

stoutness
BR 'staʊtnəs
AM 'staʊtnəs

stove
BR stəʊv, -z
AM stoʊv, -z

stovepipe
BR 'stəʊvpʌɪp, -s
AM 'stoʊvˌpaɪp, -s

stove-pipe hat
BR ˌstəʊvpʌɪp 'hat, -s
AM ˌstoʊvˌpaɪp 'hæt, -s

stow
BR stəʊ, -z, -ɪŋ, -d
AM stoʊ, -z, -ɪŋ, -d

stowage
BR 'stəʊɪdʒ
AM 'stoʊɪdʒ

stowaway
BR 'stəʊəweɪ, -z
AM 'stoʊəˌweɪ, -z

Stowe
BR stəʊ
AM stoʊ

Stowmarket
BR 'stəʊˌmaːkɪt
AM 'stoʊˌmɑrkət

Stow-on-the-Wold
BR ˌstəʊɒnðə'wəʊld
AM ˌstoʊɑnðə'woʊld

St Peter Port
BR s(ə)nt 'piːtə pɔːt
AM seɪn(t) 'pidər ˌpɔ(ə)rt

St Petersburg
BR s(ə)nt 'piːtəzbəːg
AM seɪn(t) 'pidərzˌbərg

Strabane
BR strə'ban
AM ˌstrə'bæn

strabismal
BR strə'bɪzml
AM strə'bɪzməl

strabismic
BR strə'bɪzmɪk
AM strə'bɪzmɪk

strabismus
BR strə'bɪzməs
AM strə'bɪzməs

Strabo
BR 'streɪbəʊ
AM 'streɪboʊ

Strachan¹
traditionally
BR strɔːn
AM strɔn, strɑn

Strachan²
BR 'strak(ə)n, 'strax(ə)n
AM 'streɪkən, 'strækən

Strachey
BR 'streɪtʃi
AM 'streɪtʃi

Strad
BR strad, -z
AM stræd, -z

Stradbroke
BR 'stradbrʊk
AM 'stræd,brʊk

straddle
BR 'stradl|l, -lz, -lɪŋ\-lɪŋ, -ld
AM 'stræd|əl, -əlz, -(ə)lɪŋ, -əld

straddler
BR 'stradlə(r), 'stradlə(r), -z
AM 'stræd(ə)lər, -z

Stradivari
BR ˌstradɪ'vaːri
AM ˌstrædɪ'vari

Stradivarius
BR ˌstradɪ've:rɪəs, ˌstradɪ'va:rɪəs, -ɪz
AM ˌstrædə'veriəs, -əz

Stradling
BR 'stradlɪŋ
AM 'strædlɪŋ

strafe
BR stra:f, streɪf, -s, -ɪŋ, -t
AM streɪf, -s, -ɪŋ, -t

Strafford
BR 'strafəd
AM 'stræfərd

strafing
BR 'stra:fɪŋ, 'streɪfɪŋ, -z

AM 'streɪfɪŋ, -z

straggle
BR 'stragl̩, -lz,
-lɪŋ\-lm̩, -ld
AM 'strægləl, -əlz,
-(ə)lɪŋ, -əld

straggler
BR 'stragləy(r),
'straglə(r), -z
AM 'stræg(ə)lər, -z

straggly
BR 'stragl̩i, 'straglli,
-ɪə(r), -ɪɪst
AM 'stræg(ə)li, -ər, -ɪst

straight
BR streɪt, -s, -ə(r), -ɪst
AM streɪ|t, -ts, -dər,
-dəst

straightaway¹
adverb
BR ˌstreɪtə'weɪ
AM ˌstreɪdə'weɪ

straightaway²
noun
BR 'streɪtəweɪ, -z
AM 'streɪdə,weɪ, -z

straightedge
BR 'streɪtɛdʒ, -ɪz
AM 'streɪd,ɛdʒ, -ɪz

straight-eight
BR 'streɪt'eɪt, -s
AM ˌstreɪd'eɪt, -s

straighten
BR 'streɪt|n̩, -nz,
-nɪŋ\-n̩ɪŋ, -nd
AM 'streɪt|n̩, -nz, -n̩ɪŋ,
-nd

straightener
BR 'streɪtnə(r),
ˌstreɪtnə(r), -z
AM 'streɪtnər, -z

straightforward
BR 'streɪt'fɔːwəd
AM 'streɪt'fɔrwərd

straightforwardly
BR 'streɪt'fɔːwədli
AM 'streɪt'fɔrwərdli

**straightforward-
ness**
BR 'streɪt'fɔːwədnəs
AM 'streɪt'fɔrwərdnəs

straightish
BR 'streɪtɪʃ
AM 'streɪdɪʃ

straightjacket
BR 'streɪt,dʒak|ɪt, -s,
-ɪtɪŋ, -ɪtɪd
AM 'streɪt,dʒækə|t, -ts,
-dɪŋ, -dəd

straightlaced
BR ˌstreɪt'leɪst
AM 'streɪt,leɪst

straightly
BR 'streɪtli
AM 'streɪtli

straightness
BR 'streɪtnɪs
AM 'streɪtnɪs

straight-out
BR ˌstreɪt'aʊt
AM ˌstreɪd'aʊt

straight-up
BR 'streɪt'ʌp
AM ˌstreɪd'əp

straightway
BR 'streɪt'weɪ
AM 'streɪt,weɪ

strain
BR streɪn, -z, -ɪŋ, -d
AM streɪn, -z, -ɪŋ, -d

strainable
BR 'streɪnəbl
AM 'streɪnəbəl

strainer
BR 'streɪnə(r), -z
AM 'streɪnər, -z

strait
BR streɪt, -s
AM streɪt, -s

straiten
BR 'streɪt|n̩, -nz,
-nɪŋ\-n̩ɪŋ, -nd
AM 'streɪt|n̩, -nz, -n̩ɪŋ,
-nd

straitjacket
BR 'streɪt,dʒak|ɪt, -ɪts,
-ɪtɪŋ, -ɪtɪd
AM 'streɪt,dʒækə|t, -ts,
-dɪŋ, -dəd

straitlaced
BR ˌstreɪt'leɪst
AM 'streɪt,leɪst

straitly
BR 'streɪtli
AM 'streɪtli

straitness
BR 'streɪtnɪs
AM 'streɪtnɪs

strake
BR streɪk, -s
AM streɪk, -s

stramonium
BR strə'məʊnɪəm
AM strə'moʊnɪəm

strand
BR strand, -z, -ɪŋ, -ɪd
AM strænd, -z, -ɪŋ, -əd

stranding
BR 'strandɪŋ, -z
AM 'strændɪŋ, -z

Strang
BR straŋ
AM stræŋ

strange
BR streɪn(d)ʒ, -ə(r),
-ɪst
AM streɪndʒ, -ər, -ɪst

strangely
BR 'streɪn(d)ʒli
AM 'streɪndʒli

strangeness
BR 'streɪn(d)ʒnɪs
AM 'streɪndʒnɪs

stranger
BR 'streɪn(d)ʒə(r), -z

AM 'streɪndʒər, -z

Strangeways
BR 'streɪn(d)ʒweɪz
AM 'streɪndʒ,weɪz

Strangford
BR 'straŋfəd
AM 'stræŋfərd

strangle
BR 'straŋg|l, -lz,
-lɪŋ\-lm̩, -ld
AM 'stræŋg|əl, -əlz,
-(ə)lɪŋ, -əlɪŋ-blə

stranglehold
BR 'straŋglhəʊld, -z
AM 'stræŋgəl,(h)oʊld,
-z

strangler
BR 'straŋglə(r), -z
AM 'stræŋg(ə)lər, -z

strangling
BR 'straŋglɪŋ,
'straŋglɪŋ, -z
AM 'stræŋg(ə)lɪŋ, -z

strangulate
BR 'straŋgjʊleɪt, -s, -ɪŋ,
-ɪd
AM 'stræŋgjə,leɪ|t, -ts,
-dɪŋ, -dɪd

strangulation
BR ˌstraŋgjʊ'leɪʃn, -z
AM ˌstræŋgjə'leɪʃən, -z

strangurious
BR ˌstraŋ'gjʊərɪəs,
ˌstraŋ'gjɔːrɪəs
AM ˌstræŋ'gjʊrɪəs

strangury
BR 'straŋgjʊr|i, -ɪz
AM 'stræŋgjəri, -z

Stranraer
BR stran'rɑː(r)
AM stræn'rɑr

strap
BR strap, -s, -ɪŋ, -t
AM stræp, -s, -ɪŋ, -t

strap-hang
BR 'straphaŋ, -z, -ɪŋ
AM 'stræp,(h)æŋ, -z,
-ɪŋ

straphanger
BR 'strap,haŋə(r), -z
AM 'stræp,(h)æŋər, -z

straphanging
BR 'strap,haŋɪŋ
AM 'stræp,(h)æŋɪŋ

strap-hung
BR 'straphʌŋ
AM 'stræp,(h)ʌŋ

strapless
BR 'strapləs
AM 'stræpləs

strapline
BR 'straplʌɪn, -z
AM 'stræp,laɪn, -z

strappado
BR strə'pɑːdəʊ,
strə'peɪdəʊ, -z
AM strə'peɪdoʊ,
strə'pɑ,doʊ, -z

strapper
BR 'strapə(r), -z
AM 'stræpər, -z

strappy
BR 'strapi
AM 'stræpi

Strasberg
BR 'strasbɜːg
AM 'stras,bɜrg,
'stras,bɜrg

Strasbourg
BR 'strazbɜːg
AM 'stras,bɜrg,
'straz,bɜrg

strass
BR stras
AM stræs

strata
BR 'strɑːtə(r)
AM 'streɪdə, 'strɑdə,
'strædə

stratagem
BR 'stratədʒəm,
'stratədʒɛm, -z
AM 'strædə,dʒəm, -z

stratal
BR 'strɑːtl, 'streɪtl
AM 'streɪdl, 'strɑdl,
'strædl

strategic
BR strə'tiːdʒɪk, -s
AM strə'tidʒɪk, -s

strategical
BR strə'tiːdʒɪkl
AM strə'tidʒɪkəl

strategically
BR strə'tiːdʒɪkli
AM strə'tidʒɪk(ə)li

strategist
BR 'stratɪdʒɪst, -s
AM 'strædədʒəst, -s

strategy
BR 'stratɪdʒ|i, -ɪz
AM 'strædədʒi, -z

**Stratford-on-
Avon**
BR ˌstratfədɒn'eɪvn
AM ˌstrætfərd,ɑn'eɪvan

**Stratford-upon-
Avon**
BR ˌstratfədəpɒn'eɪvn
AM ˌstrætfərdə,pʌn-
'eɪvn

strath
BR straθ, -s
AM stræθ, -s

Strathclyde
BR straθ'klʌɪd
AM stræθ'klaɪd

Strathleven
BR straθ'liːvn
AM stræθ'livən

Strathmore
BR straθ'mɔː(r)
AM stræθ'mɔ(ə)r

strathspey
BR straθ'speɪ, -z
AM stræθ'speɪ, -z

strati
BR 'streɪtʌɪ
AM 'streɪd‚aɪ

straticulate
BR strə'tɪkjʊlət
AM strə'tɪkjələt,
strə'tɪkjə‚leɪt

stratification
BR ‚stratɪfɪ'keɪʃn, -z
AM ‚strædəfə'keɪʃən, -z

stratificational
BR ‚stratɪfɪ'keɪʃn(ə)l,
‚sratɪfɪ'keɪʃən(ə)l
AM ‚strædəfə'keɪʃ(ə)nəl

stratify
BR 'stratɪfʌɪ, -z, -ɪŋ, -d
AM 'strædə‚faɪ, -z, -ɪŋ, -d

stratigraphic
BR ‚stratɪ'grafɪk
AM ‚strædə'græfɪk

stratigraphical
BR ‚stratɪ'grafɪkl
AM ‚strædə'græfəkəl

stratigraphy
BR strə'tɪgrəfi
AM strə'tɪgrəfi

stratocirrus
BR ‚stratə(ʊ)'sɪrəs, ‚streɪtə(ʊ)'sɪrəs, -ɪz
AM ‚strædoʊ'sɪrəs, ‚streɪdoʊ'sɪrəs, -əz

stratocracy
BR strə'tɒkrəs|i, -ɪz
AM strə'takrəsi, -z

stratocumuli
BR ‚stratə(ʊ)'kju:mjʊ‚lʌɪ, ‚streɪtə(ʊ)'kju:mjʊlʌɪ
AM ‚strædoʊ'kjumjə‚laɪ, ‚streɪdoʊ'kjumjə‚laɪ

stratocumulus
BR ‚stratə(ʊ)'kju:mjʊ‚ləs, ‚streɪtə(ʊ)'kju:mjʊləs
AM ‚strædoʊ'kjumjələs, ‚streɪdoʊ'kjumjələs

stratopause
BR 'stratə(ʊ)pɔːz
AM 'strædə‚pɔz, 'strædə‚paz

stratosphere
BR 'stratəsfɪə(r)
AM 'strædə‚sfɪ(ə)r

stratospheric
BR ‚stratə'sfɛrɪk
AM ‚strædə'sfɪrɪk

stratum
BR 'stra:təm, 'streɪtəm
AM 'streɪdəm, 'stradəm, 'strædəm

stratus
BR 'stra:təs, 'streɪtəs
AM 'streɪdəs, 'stradəs, 'strædəs

Strauss
BR straʊs
AM straʊs

Stravinsky
BR strə'vɪnski
AM strə'vɪnski

straw
BR strɔː(r), -z
AM stra, strɔ, -z

strawberry
BR 'strɔː'b(ə)r|i, -ɪz
AM 'strɔ‚beri, 'strɒbəri, 'stra‚beri, 'strabəri, -z

strawboard
BR 'strɔːbɔːd
AM 'strɔ‚bɔ(ə)rd, 'stra‚bɔ(ə)rd

strawboss
BR 'strɔːbɒs, -ɪz
AM 'strɔ‚bɒs, 'stra‚bas, -əz

strawman
BR 'strɔːman
AM 'strɔ‚mæn, 'stra‚mæn

strawmen
BR 'strɔːmen
AM 'strɔ‚men, 'stra‚men

strawy
BR 'strɔː(r)i
AM 'strɔi, 'strɑi

stray
BR streɪ, -z, -ɪŋ, -d
AM streɪ, -z, -ɪŋ, -d

strayer
BR 'streɪə(r), -z
AM 'streɪər, -z

streak
BR stri:k, -s, -ɪŋ, -t
AM strik, -s, -ɪŋ, -t

streaker
BR 'stri:kə(r), -z
AM 'strikər, -z

streakily
BR 'stri:kɪli
AM 'strikɪli

streakiness
BR 'stri:kɪnɪs
AM 'strikɪnɪs

streaky
BR 'stri:k|i, -ɪə(r), -ɪɪst
AM 'striki, -ər, -ɪst

stream
BR stri:m, -z, -ɪŋ, -d
AM strim, -z, -ɪŋ, -d

streambed
BR 'stri:mbɛd, -z
AM 'strim‚bɛd, -z

streamer
BR 'stri:mə(r), -z
AM 'strimər, -z

streamless
BR 'stri:mlɪs

streamlet
BR 'stri:mlɪt, -s
AM 'strimlət, -s

streamline
BR 'stri:mlʌɪn, -z, -ɪŋ, -d
AM 'strim‚laɪn, -z, -ɪŋ, -d

Streatfield
BR 'stretfi:ld
AM 'strɛt‚fild

Streatham
BR 'strɛtəm
AM 'strɛdəm

Streatley
BR 'stri:tli
AM 'stritli

Streep
BR stri:p
AM strip

street
BR stri:t, -s, -ɪd
AM stri|t, -ts, -dɪd

streetcar
BR 'stri:tka:(r), -z
AM 'strit‚kar, -z

street-cred
BR 'stri:t'krɛd, 'stri:tkrɛd
AM 'strit‚krɛd

Streeter
BR 'stri:tə(r)
AM 'stridər

streetlight
BR 'stri:tlʌɪt, -s
AM 'strit‚laɪt, -s

streetwalker
BR 'stri:t‚wɔːkə(r), -z
AM 'strit‚wɔkər, 'strit‚wakər, -z

streetwalking
BR 'stri:t‚wɔːkɪŋ
AM 'strit‚wɔkɪŋ, 'strit‚wakɪŋ

streetward
BR 'stri:twəd
AM 'stritwərd

streetwise
BR 'stri:twʌɪz
AM 'strit‚waɪz

Streisand
BR 'strʌɪsand, 'strʌɪsənd
AM 'straɪ‚sæn(d)

strelitzia
BR strə'lɪtsɪə(r), -z
AM strə'lɪtsɪə, -z

strength
BR strɛŋ(k)θ, -s
AM strɛŋ(k)θ, strɛnθ, -s

strengthen
BR 'strɛŋ(k)θ|n, -nz, -(ə)nɪŋ \-‚nɪŋ, -nd
AM 'strɛŋ(k)θ|ən, -ənz, -(ə)nɪŋ, -ənd

strengthener
BR 'strɛŋ(k)θ(ə)nə(r), 'strɛŋ(k)θnə(r), -z
AM 'strɛŋ(k)θ(ə)nər, -z

strengthless
BR 'strɛŋ(k)θləs
AM 'strɛŋ(k)θləs, 'strɛnθləs

strenuous
BR 'strɛnjʊəs
AM 'strɛnjəwəs

strenuously
BR 'strɛnjʊəsli
AM 'strɛnjəwəsli

strenuousness
BR 'strɛnjʊəsnəs
AM 'strɛnjəwəsnəs

strep
BR strɛp
AM strɛp

streptocarpi
BR ‚strɛptə(ʊ)'ka:pʌɪ
AM ‚strɛptə'kar‚paɪ

streptocarpus
BR ‚strɛptə(ʊ)'ka:pəs
AM ‚strɛptə'karpəs

streptococcal
BR ‚strɛptə'kɒkl
AM ‚strɛptə'kakəl

streptococci
BR ‚strɛptə'kɒkʌɪ
AM ‚strɛptə'ka‚kaɪ

streptococcus
BR ‚strɛptə'kɒkəs
AM ‚strɛptə'kakəs

streptomycin
BR ‚strɛptə'mʌɪsɪn
AM ‚strɛptə'maɪ(ə)sn

stress
BR strɛs, -ɪz, -ɪŋ, -t
AM strɛs, -əz, -ɪŋ, -t

stressful
BR 'strɛsf(ʊ)l
AM 'strɛsfəl

stressfully
BR 'strɛsfʊli, 'strɛsfli
AM 'strɛsfəli

stressfulness
BR 'strɛsf(ʊ)lnəs
AM 'strɛsfəlnəs

stressless
BR 'strɛsləs
AM 'strɛsləs

stretch
BR strɛtʃ, -ɪz, -ɪŋ, -t
AM strɛtʃ, -əz, -ɪŋ, -t

stretchability
BR ‚strɛtʃə'bɪlɪti
AM ‚strɛtʃə'bɪlɪdi

stretchable
BR 'strɛtʃəbl
AM 'strɛtʃəbəl

stretcher
BR 'strɛtʃə(r), -z
AM 'strɛtʃər, -z

stretchiness
BR 'strɛtʃɪnɪs

AM 'stretʃinɪs

stretchy
BR 'stretʃ|i, -ɪə(r), -ɪɪst
AM 'stretʃi, -ər, -ɪst

Stretford
BR 'stretfəd
AM 'stretfərd

stretto
BR 'stretəʊ
AM 'stredoʊ

Stretton
BR 'stretn
AM 'stretn

streusel
BR 'strɔɪzl, 'struːzl, -z
AM 'strusəl, 'struzəl, -z

Strevens
BR 'strevnz
AM 'strevənz

strew
BR struː, -z, -ɪŋ, -d, -n
AM stru, -z, -ɪŋ, -d, -n

strewer
BR 'struːə(r), -z
AM 'struər, -z

strewth
BR struːθ
AM struθ

stria
BR 'straɪə(r)
AM 'straɪə

striae
BR 'straɪiː
AM 'straɪ‚i, 'straɪ‚aɪ

striate
BR 'straɪeɪt, -s, -ɪŋ, -d
AM 'straɪ‚eɪ|t, -ts, -dɪŋ, -dɪd

striated
adjective
BR straɪ'eɪtɪd
AM 'straɪ‚eɪdɪd

striation
BR straɪ'eɪʃn, -z
AM straɪ'eɪʃən, -z

striature
BR 'straɪətʃə(r)
AM 'straɪətʃʊ(ə)r, 'straɪətʃər

strick
BR strɪk
AM strɪk

stricken
BR 'strɪk(ə)n
AM 'strɪkən

Strickland
BR 'strɪklənd
AM 'strɪklənd

strickle
BR 'strɪk|l, -lz,
-lɪŋ\-lɪŋ, -ld
AM 'strɪk|əl, -əlz,
-(ə)lɪŋ, -əld

strict
BR strɪkt, -ə(r), -ɪst
AM strɪk|(t), -ər, -ɪst

strictly
BR 'strɪk(t)li
AM 'strɪk(t)li

strictness
BR 'strɪk(t)nəs
AM 'strɪk(t)nəs

stricture
BR 'strɪktʃə(r), -z
AM 'strɪk(t)ʃər, -z

strictured
BR 'strɪktʃəd
AM 'strɪk(t)ʃərd

stridden
BR 'strɪdn
AM 'strɪdən

stride
BR straɪd, -z, -ɪŋ
AM straɪd, -z, -ɪŋ

stridence
BR 'straɪdns
AM 'straɪdns

stridency
BR 'straɪdnsi
AM 'straɪdnsi

strident
BR 'straɪdnt
AM 'straɪdnt

stridently
BR 'straɪdntli
AM 'straɪdn(t)li

strider
BR 'straɪdə(r), -z
AM 'straɪdər, -z

stridor
BR 'straɪdə(r), -z
AM 'straɪdər, -z

stridulant
BR 'strɪdjʊlənt,
'strɪdjəlnt,
'strɪdʒələnt,
'strɪdʒəlnt
AM 'strɪdʒələnt

stridulate
BR 'strɪdjʊleɪt,
'strɪdʒəleɪt, -s, -ɪŋ, -ɪd
AM 'strɪdʒə‚leɪ|t, -ts,
-dɪŋ, -dɪd

stridulation
BR ‚strɪdjʊ'leɪʃn,
‚strɪdʒʊ'leɪʃn, -z
AM ‚strɪdʒə'leɪʃən, -z

strife
BR straɪf
AM straɪf

strigil
BR 'strɪdʒ(ɪ)l, -z
AM 'strɪdʒəl, -z

strigose
BR 'straɪgəʊs
AM 'straɪ‚goʊs,
'straɪ‚goʊz

strikable
BR 'straɪkəbl
AM 'straɪkəbəl

strike
BR straɪk, -s, -ɪŋ
AM straɪk, -s, -ɪŋ

strikebound
BR 'straɪkbaʊnd
AM 'straɪk‚baʊnd

strikebreaker
BR 'straɪk‚breɪkə(r), -z
AM 'straɪk‚breɪkər, -z

strikebreaking
BR 'straɪk‚breɪkɪŋ
AM 'straɪk‚breɪkɪŋ

strikeout
BR straɪkaʊt, -s
AM 'straɪk‚aʊt, -s

strikeover
BR 'straɪk‚əʊvə(r), -z
AM 'straɪk‚oʊvər, -z

striker
BR 'straɪkə(r), -z
AM 'straɪkər, -z

strike-slip fault
BR 'straɪkslɪp ‚fɔːlt,
+ ‚fɒlt, -s
AM 'straɪk‚slɪp ‚fɔlt,
'straɪk‚slɪp ‚fɑlt, -s

strikingly
BR 'straɪkɪŋli
AM 'straɪkɪŋli

strikingness
BR 'straɪkɪŋnɪs
AM 'straɪkɪŋnɪs

strimmer®
BR 'strɪmə(r), -z
AM 'strɪmər, -z

Strindberg
BR 'strɪn(d)bəːg
AM 'strɪn(d)‚bɜrg
sw strɪnd'bɛrj

Strine
BR straɪn
AM straɪn

string
BR strɪŋ, -z, -ɪŋ
AM strɪŋ, -z, -ɪŋ

stringboard
BR 'strɪŋbɔːd, -z
AM 'strɪŋ‚bɔ(ə)rd, -z

stringency
BR 'strɪn(d)ʒ(ə)nsi
AM 'strɪndʒənsi

stringendo
BR strɪn'dʒendəʊ, -z
AM strɪn'dʒendoʊ, -z

stringent
BR 'strɪn(d)ʒ(ə)nt
AM 'strɪndʒənt

stringently
BR 'strɪn(d)ʒ(ə)ntli
AM 'strɪndʒən(t)li

stringer
BR 'strɪŋə(r), -z
AM 'strɪŋər, -z

stringhalt
BR 'strɪŋhɔːlt,
'strɪŋhɒlt, -s
AM 'strɪŋ‚(h)ɔlt,
'strɪŋ‚(h)ɑlt, -s

stringily
BR 'strɪŋɪli

AM 'strɪŋɪli

stringiness
BR 'strɪŋɪnɪs
AM 'strɪŋɪnɪs

stringless
BR 'strɪŋlɪs
AM 'strɪŋlɪs

stringlike
BR 'strɪŋlaɪk
AM 'strɪŋ‚laɪk

stringy
BR 'strɪŋ|i, -ɪə(r), -ɪɪst
AM 'strɪŋi, -ər, -ɪst

stringy-bark
BR 'strɪŋɪbɑːk, -s
AM 'strɪŋi‚bark, -s

strip
BR strɪp, -s, -ɪŋ, -t
AM strɪp, -s, -ɪŋ, -t

stripe
BR straɪp, -s, -ɪŋ, -t
AM straɪp, -s, -ɪŋ, -t

stripling
BR 'strɪplɪŋ, -z
AM 'strɪplɪŋ, -z

stripper
BR 'strɪpə(r), -z
AM 'strɪpər, -z

stripperama
BR ‚strɪpə'rɑːmə(r)
AM ‚strɪpə'ramə

striptease
BR 'strɪptiːz, ‚strɪp'tiːz
AM 'strɪp'tiz

stripteaser
BR 'strɪp‚tiːzə(r),
‚strɪp'tiːzə(r), -z
AM 'strɪp'tizər, -z

stripy
BR 'straɪp|i, -ɪə(r), -ɪɪst
AM 'straɪpi, -ər, -ɪst

strive
BR straɪv, -z, -ɪŋ, -d
AM straɪv, -z, -ɪŋ, -d

striver
BR 'straɪvə(r), -z
AM 'straɪvər, -z

strobe
BR strəʊb, -z
AM stroʊb, -z

strobila
BR strə'baɪlə(r)
AM strə'baɪlə

strobilae
BR strə'baɪlaɪ,
strə'baɪliː
AM strə'baɪli,
strə'baɪ‚laɪ

strobile
BR 'strəʊbaɪl, -z
AM 'stroʊbəl, -z

strobili
BR 'strəʊbɪlaɪ
AM 'stroʊbə‚laɪ

strobilus
BR 'strəʊbɪləs
AM 'stroʊbələs

stroboscope
BR 'strəʊbəskəʊp, -s
AM 'stroʊbə,skoʊp, -s

stroboscopic
BR ,strəʊbə'skɒpɪk
AM ,stroʊbə'skɑpɪk

stroboscopical
BR ,strəʊbə'skɒpɪkl
AM ,stroʊbə'skɑpəkəl

stroboscopically
BR ,strəʊbə'skɒpɪkli
AM ,stroʊbə'skɑpək(ə)li

strode
BR strəʊd
AM stroʊd

Stroganoff
BR 'strɒɡənɒf, -s
AM 'stroʊɡə,nɔf, -s

stroke
BR strəʊk, -s, -ɪŋ, -t
AM stroʊk, -s, -ɪŋ, -t

strokeplay
BR 'strəʊkpleɪ
AM 'stroʊk,pleɪ

stroll
BR strəʊl, -z, -ɪŋ, -d
AM stroʊl, -z, -ɪŋ, -d

stroller
BR 'strəʊlə(r), -z
AM 'stroʊlər, -z

stroma
BR 'strəʊmə(r)
AM 'stroʊmə

stromata
BR 'strəʊmətə(r)
AM 'stroʊmədə

stromatic
BR strə(ʊ)'mætɪk
AM stroʊ'mædɪk

stromatolite
BR strə(ʊ)'mætəlaɪt, -s
AM stroʊ'mædə,laɪt, -s

Stromboli
BR 'strɒmbəli, 'strɒmbl̩i
AM 'strɑmbəli

Stromness
BR 'strɒmnɛs, 'strʌmnɛs
AM 'strɑm,nɛs

strong
BR strɒŋ, -ɡə(r), -ɡɪst
AM strɔŋ, strɑŋ, -ɡər, -ɡəst

strongbox
BR 'strɒŋbɒks, -ɪz
AM 'strɔŋ,bɑks, 'strɑŋ,bɑks, -əz

stronghold
BR 'strɒŋhəʊld, -z
AM 'strɔŋ,(h)oʊld, 'strɑŋ,(h)oʊld, -z

strongish
BR 'strɒŋɪʃ
AM 'strɔŋɪʃ, 'strɑŋɪʃ

strongly
BR 'strɒŋli

AM 'strɔŋli, 'strɑŋli

strongman
BR 'strɒŋman
AM 'strɔŋ,mæn, 'strɑŋ,mæn

strongmen
BR 'strɒŋmɛn
AM 'strɔŋ,mɛn, 'strɑŋ,mɛn

strongpoint
BR 'strɒŋpɔɪnt, -s
AM 'strɔŋ,pɔɪnt, 'strɑŋ,pɔɪnt, -s

strongroom
BR 'strɒŋruːm, 'strɒŋrʊm, -z
AM 'strɔŋ,rum, 'strɔŋ,rʊm, 'strɑŋ,rum, 'strɑŋ,rʊm, -z

strongyle
BR 'strɒndʒ(ɪ)l, -z
AM 'strɒndʒəl, -z

strontia
BR 'strɒntɪə(r), 'strɒnʃ(ɪ)ə(r)
AM 'stranʃiə, 'strantiə

strontium
BR 'strɒntɪəm, 'strɒnʃ(ɪ)əm
AM 'stran(t)ʃiəm, 'strantiəm

Strood
BR struːd
AM strud

strop
BR strɒp, -s, -ɪŋ, -t
AM strɑp, -s, -ɪŋ, -t

strophanthin
BR strə(ʊ)'fanθɪn, strʊ'fanθɪn
AM stroʊ'fænθən

strophe
BR 'strəʊfli, 'strɒfli, -ɪz
AM 'stroʊfi, -z

strophic
BR 'strɒfɪk, 'strəʊfɪk
AM 'stroʊfɪk, 'strafɪk

stroppily
BR 'strɒpɪli
AM 'strapəli

stroppiness
BR 'strɒpɪnɪs
AM 'strapɪnɪs

stroppy
BR 'strɒp|i, -ɪə(r), -ɪɪst
AM 'strapi, -ər, -ɪst

Stroud
BR straʊd
AM straʊd

strove
BR strəʊv
AM stroʊv

strow
BR strəʊ, -z, -ɪŋ, -d
AM stroʊ, -z, -ɪŋ, -d

strown
BR strəʊn

AM stroʊn

struck
BR strʌk
AM strək

structural
BR 'strʌktʃ(ə)rəl, 'strʌktʃ(ə)rl
AM 'strək(t)ʃ(ə)rəl

structuralism
BR 'strʌktʃ(ə)rəlɪz(ə)m, 'strʌktʃ(ə)rlɪz(ə)m
AM 'strək(t)ʃ(ə)rə,lɪzəm

structuralist
BR 'strʌktʃ(ə)rəlɪst, 'strʌktʃ(ə)rlɪst, -s
AM 'strək(t)ʃ(ə)rələst, -s

structurally
BR 'strʌktʃ(ə)rəli, 'strʌktʃ(ə)rl̩i
AM 'strək(t)ʃ(ə)rəli

structure
BR 'strʌktʃ|ə(r), -əz, -(ə)rɪŋ, -əd
AM 'strək(t)ʃər, -z, -ɪŋ, -d

structureless
BR 'strʌktʃ(ə)ləs
AM 'strək(t)ʃərləs

strudel
BR 'struːdl, -z
AM 'strudəl, -z

struggle
BR 'strʌɡ|l, -lz, -l̩ɪŋ \-lɪŋ, -ld
AM 'strəɡ|əl, -əlz, -(ə)lɪŋ, -əld

struggler
BR 'strʌɡlə(r), 'strʌɡlə(r), -z
AM 'strəɡ(ə)lər, -z

strum
BR strʌm, -z, -ɪŋ, -d
AM strəm, -z, -ɪŋ, -d

struma
BR 'struːmə(r)
AM 'strumə

strumae
BR 'struːmiː
AM 'strumi, 'stru,maɪ

Strumble
BR 'strʌmbl
AM 'strəmbəl

strummer
BR 'strʌmə(r), -z
AM 'strəmər, -z

strumose
BR 'struːməs, 'struːməʊs
AM 'stru,moʊs, 'stru,moʊz

strumous
BR 'struːməs
AM 'struməs

strumpet
BR 'strʌmpɪt, -s
AM 'strəmpət, -s

strung
BR strʌŋ
AM strəŋ

strut
BR strʌt, -s, -ɪŋ, -ɪd
AM strə|t, -ts, -dɪŋ, -dəd

'struth
BR struːθ
AM struθ

struthious
BR 'struːθɪəs
AM 'struθiəs, 'struðiəs

Strutt
BR strʌt
AM strət

strutter
BR 'strʌtə(r), -z
AM 'strədər, -z

struttingly
BR 'strʌtɪŋli
AM 'strədɪŋli

Struwwelpeter
BR ,struːəl'piːtə(r), 'struːəl,piːtə(r)
AM 'struəl,pidər

strychnic
BR 'strɪknɪk
AM 'strɪknɪk

strychnine
BR 'strɪkniːn
AM 'strɪk,naɪn, 'strɪk,nin

strychninism
BR 'strɪknɪnɪz(ə)m
AM 'strɪknə,nɪzəm

strychnism
BR 'strɪknɪz(ə)m
AM 'strɪk,nɪzəm

St Thomas
BR s(ə)nt 'tɒməs
AM seɪn(t) 'taməs

Stuart
BR 'stjuːət, 'stʃuːət, -s
AM 'st(j)uərt, -s

stub
BR stʌb, -z, -ɪŋ, -d
AM stəb, -z, -ɪŋ, -d

stubbily
BR 'stʌbɪli
AM 'stəbəli

stubbiness
BR 'stʌbɪnɪs
AM 'stəbinɪs

stubble
BR 'stʌbl, -d
AM 'stəbəl, -d

stubbly
BR 'stʌbli
AM 'stəb(ə)li

stubborn
BR 'stʌbən, 'stʌbn̩, -ə(r), -ɪst
AM 'stəbərn, -ər, -əst

stubbornly
BR 'stʌb(ə)nli
AM 'stəbərnli

stubbornness
BR ˈstʌb(ə)nnəs
AM ˈstəbər(n)nəs

Stubbs
BR stʌbz
AM stəbz

stubby
BR ˈstʌb|i, -ɪə(r), -ɪɪst
AM ˈstəbi, -ər, -ɪst

stucco
BR ˈstʌkəʊ
AM ˈstəkoʊ

stuccowork
BR ˈstʌkəʊwɜːk
AM ˈstəkoʊˌwərk

stuck
BR stʌk
AM stək

stuck-up
BR ˌstʌkˈʌp
AM ˈstəkˈəp

stud
BR stʌd, -z, -ɪŋ, -ɪd
AM stəd, -z, -ɪŋ, -əd

studbook
BR ˈstʌdbʊk, -s
AM ˈstədˌbʊk, -s

studding-sail¹
BR ˈstʌdɪŋseɪl, -z
AM ˈstədɪŋˌseɪl, -z

studding-sail²
nautical use
BR ˈstʌnsl, -z
AM ˈstənsəl, -z

Studebaker
BR ˈst(j)uːdəˌbeɪkə(r)
AM ˈstudəˌbeɪkər

student
BR ˈstjuːdnt, ˈstʃuːdnt, -s
AM ˈst(j)udnt, -s

studentship
BR ˈstjuːdntʃɪp, ˈstʃuːdntʃɪp, -s
AM ˈst(j)udntˌʃɪp, -s

studiedly
BR ˈstʌdɪdli
AM ˈstədidli

studiedness
BR ˈstʌdɪdnɪs
AM ˈstədidnɪs

studio
BR ˈstjuːdɪəʊ, ˈstʃuːdɪəʊ
AM ˈst(j)udioʊ, -z

studious
BR ˈstjuːdɪəs, ˈstʃuːdɪəs
AM ˈst(j)udiəs

studiously
BR ˈstjuːdɪəs, ˈstʃuːdɪəsli
AM ˈst(j)udiəsli

studiousness
BR ˈstjuːdɪəsnəs, ˈstʃuːdɪəsnəs
AM ˈst(j)udiəsnəs

Studland
BR ˈstʌdlənd
AM ˈstədlənd

Studley
BR ˈstʌdli
AM ˈstədli

study
BR ˈstʌd|i, -ɪz, -ɪɪŋ, -ɪd
AM ˈstədi, -z, -ɪŋ, -d

stuff
BR stʌf, -s, -ɪŋ, -t
AM stəf, -s, -ɪŋ, -t

stuffer
BR ˈstʌfə(r), -z
AM ˈstəfər, -z

stuffily
BR ˈstʌfɪli
AM ˈstəfəli

stuffiness
BR ˈstʌfɪnɪs
AM ˈstəfinɪs

stuffing
BR ˈstʌfɪŋ, -z
AM ˈstəfɪŋ, -z

stuffy
BR ˈstʌf|i, -ɪə(r), -ɪɪst
AM ˈstəfi, -ər, -ɪst

Stuka
BR ˈstuːkə(r), ˈʃtuːkə(r), -z
AM ˈstukə, ˈʃtukə, -z

stultification
BR ˌstʌltɪfɪˈkeɪʃn
AM ˌstəltəfəˈkeɪʃən

stultifier
BR ˈstʌltɪfʌɪə(r), -z
AM ˈstəltəˌfaɪər, -z

stultify
BR ˈstʌltɪfʌɪ, -z, -ɪŋ, -d
AM ˈstəltəˌfaɪ, -z, -ɪŋ, -d

stum¹
silent
BR ʃtʊm
AM ʃtʊm

stum²
BR stʌm, -z, -ɪŋ, -d
AM stəm, -z, -ɪŋ, -d

stumble
BR ˈstʌmb|l, -lz, -lɪŋ\-lɪŋ, -ld
AM ˈstəmbəl, -əlz, -(ə)lɪŋ, -əld

stumblebum
BR ˈstʌmblbʌm, -z
AM ˈstəmbəlˌbəm, -z

stumbler
BR ˈstʌmblə(r), -z
AM ˈstəmb(ə)lər, -z

stumblingly
BR ˈstʌmblɪŋli
AM ˈstəmb(ə)lɪŋli

stumer
BR ˈstjuːmə(r), ˈstʃuːmə(r), -z
AM ˈst(j)umər, -z

stumm
silent
BR ʃtʊm
AM ʃtʊm

stump
BR stʌm|p, -ps, -pɪŋ, -(p)t
AM stəm|p, -ps, -pɪŋ, -(p)t

stumper
BR ˈstʌmpə(r), -z
AM ˈstəmpər, -z

stumpily
BR ˈstʌmpɪli
AM ˈstəmpəli

stumpiness
BR ˈstʌmpɪnɪs
AM ˈstəmpinɪs

stumpy
BR ˈstʌmp|i, -ɪə(r), -ɪɪst
AM ˈstəmpi, -ər, -ɪst

stun
BR stʌn, -z, -ɪŋ, -d
AM stən, -z, -ɪŋ, -d

stung
BR stʌŋ
AM stəŋ

stunk
BR stʌŋk
AM stəŋk

stunner
BR ˈstʌnə(r), -z
AM ˈstənər, -z

stunningly
BR ˈstʌnɪŋli
AM ˈstənɪŋli

stunsail
BR ˈstʌnsl, -z
AM ˈstənsəl, -z

stunt
BR stʌnt, -s, -ɪŋ, -ɪd
AM stən|t, -ts, -(t)ɪŋ, -(t)əd

stuntedness
BR ˈstʌntɪdnɪs
AM ˈstən(t)ədnəs

stunter
BR ˈstʌntə(r), -z
AM ˈstən(t)ər, -z

stuntman
BR ˈstʌntman
AM ˈstəntˌmæn

stuntmen
BR ˈstʌntmɛn
AM ˈstəntˌmɛn

stupa
BR ˈstuːpə(r), -z
AM ˈst(j)upə, -z

stupe
BR stjuːp, -s, -ɪŋ, -t
AM st(j)up, -s, -ɪŋ, -t

stupefacient
BR ˌstjuːpɪˈfeɪʃnt, ˌstʃuːpɪˈfeɪʃnt, -s
AM ˌst(j)upəˈfeɪʃənt, -s

stupefaction
BR ˌstjuːpɪˈfakʃn, ˌstʃuːpɪˈfakʃn
AM ˌst(j)upəˈfækʃən

stupefactive
BR ˌstjuːpɪˈfaktɪv, ˌstʃuːpɪˈfaktɪv
AM ˌst(j)upəˈfæktɪv

stupefier
BR ˈstjuːpɪfʌɪə(r), ˈstʃuːpɪfʌɪə(r), -z
AM ˈst(j)upəˌfaɪər, -z

stupefy
BR ˈstjuːpɪfʌɪ, ˈstʃuːpɪfʌɪ, -z, -ɪŋ, -d
AM ˈst(j)upəˌfaɪ, -z, -ɪŋ, -d

stupefyingly
BR ˈstjuːpɪfʌɪɪŋli, ˈstʃuːpɪfʌɪɪŋli
AM ˈst(j)upəˌfaɪɪŋli

stupendous
BR stjuːˈpɛndəs, stʃuːˈpɛndəs, stjəˈpɛndəs, stʃəˈpɛndəs
AM st(j)uˈpɛndəs

stupendously
BR stjuːˈpɛndəsli, stʃuːˈpɛndəsli, stjəˈpɛndəsli, stʃəˈpɛndəsli
AM st(j)uˈpɛndəsli

stupendousness
BR stjuːˈpɛndəsnəs, stʃuːˈpɛndəsnəs, stjəˈpɛndəsnəs, stʃəˈpɛndəsnəs
AM st(j)uˈpɛndəsnəs

stupid
BR ˈstjuːpɪd, ˈstʃuːpɪd
AM ˈst(j)upəd

stupidity
BR stjuːˈpɪdɪti, stʃuːˈpɪdɪti, stjəˈpɪdɪt|i, stʃəˈpɪdɪti, -ɪz
AM st(j)uˈpɪdɪdi, -z

stupidly
BR ˈstjuːpɪdli, ˈstʃuːpɪdli
AM ˈst(j)upədli

stupor
BR ˈstjuːpə(r), ˈstʃuːpə(r), -z
AM ˈst(j)upər, -z

stuporous
BR ˈstjuːp(ə)rəs, ˈstʃuːp(ə)rəs
AM ˈst(j)upərəs

sturdied
BR ˈstɜːdɪd
AM ˈstərdid

sturdily
BR ˈstɜːdɪli
AM ˈstərdəli

sturdiness
BR ˈstɜːdɪnɪs

AM 'stɜrdɪnɪs

sturdy
BR 'stɜːd|i, -ɪə(r), -ɪɪst
AM 'stɜrdi, -ər, -ɪst

sturgeon
BR 'stɜːdʒ(ə)n, -z
AM 'stɜrdʒən, -z

Sturmabteilung
BR ʃtʊəmab,tʌɪlʊŋ
AM 'ʃtʊrməb,taɪlʊŋ

Sturminster
BR 'stɜːˌmɪnstə(r)
AM 'stɜrˌmɪnstər

Sturm und Drang
BR ˌʃtʊəm ʊnt 'draŋ
AM 'ʃtʊrm ʊn(d) 'dræŋ

Sturt
BR stɜːt
AM stɜrt

Sturtevant
BR 'stɜːtɪv(ə)nt
AM 'stɜrdəvənt

Sturtivant
BR 'stɜːtɪv(ə)nt
AM 'stɜrdəvənt

Stuttaford
BR 'stʌtəfəd
AM 'stədəfərd

stutter
BR 'stʌt|ə(r), -əz,
-(ə)rɪŋ, -əd
AM 'stədər, -z, -ɪŋ, -d

stutterer
BR 'stʌt(ə)rə(r), -z
AM 'stədərər, -z

stutteringly
BR 'stʌt(ə)rɪŋli
AM 'stədərɪŋli

Stuttgart
BR 'stʊtgaːt, 'ʃtʊtgaːt
AM 'stʊt,gart, 'ʃtʊt,gart,
'stət,gart, 'ʃtʊt,gart,
'ʃtət,gart

Stuyvesant
BR 'stʌɪvɪs(ə)nt
AM 'staɪvəsənt,
'stɔɪvəsənt

St Valentine
BR s(ə)nt 'valəntʌɪn,
+ 'valntʌɪn
AM ˌseɪn(t)
'vælən,taɪn

St Vincent
BR s(ə)nt 'vɪns(ə)nt
AM ˌseɪn(t) 'vɪnsənt

St Vitus
BR s(ə)nt 'vʌɪtəs, -ɪz
AM ˌseɪnt 'vaɪdəs,
ˌsən(t) +, -əz

sty
BR stʌɪ, -z
AM staɪ, -z

stye
BR stʌɪ, -z
AM staɪ, -z

Stygian
BR 'stɪdʒɪən
AM 'stɪdʒ(i)ən

style
BR stʌɪl, -z, -ɪŋ, -d
AM staɪl, -z, -ɪŋ, -d

stylebook
BR 'stʌɪlbʊk, -s
AM 'staɪl,bʊk, -s

styleless
BR 'stʌɪllɪs
AM 'staɪ(l)lɪs

stylelessness
BR 'stʌɪllɪsnɪs
AM 'staɪ(l)lɪsnɪs

styler
BR 'stʌɪlə(r), -z
AM 'staɪlər, -z

Styles
BR stʌɪlz
AM staɪlz

stylet
BR 'stʌɪlɪt, -s
AM staɪˈlet, 'staɪlət, -s

styli
BR 'stʌɪlʌɪ
AM 'staɪˌlaɪ

stylisation
BR ˌstʌɪlʌɪ'zeɪʃn
AM ˌstaɪlə'zeɪʃən,
ˌstaɪ,laɪ'zeɪʃən

stylise
BR 'stʌɪlʌɪz, -ɪz, -ɪŋ, -d
AM 'staɪ,laɪz, -ɪz, -ɪŋ, -d

stylish
BR 'stʌɪlɪʃ
AM 'staɪlɪʃ

stylishly
BR 'stʌɪlɪʃli
AM 'staɪlɪʃli

stylishness
BR 'stʌɪlɪʃnɪs
AM 'staɪlɪʃnɪs

stylist
BR 'stʌɪlɪst, -s
AM 'staɪlɪst, -s

stylistic
BR stʌɪ'lɪstɪk,
stə'lɪstɪk, -s
AM staɪ'lɪstɪk, -s

stylistically
BR stʌɪ'lɪstɪkli
AM staɪ'lɪstɪk(ə)li

stylite
BR 'stʌɪlʌɪt, -s
AM 'staɪ,laɪt, -s

Stylites
BR stʌɪ'lʌɪtiːz
AM staɪ'laɪdiz

stylization
BR ˌstʌɪlʌɪ'zeɪʃn
AM ˌstaɪlə'zeɪʃən,
ˌstaɪ,laɪ'zeɪʃən

stylize
BR 'stʌɪlʌɪz, -ɪz, -ɪŋ, -d
AM 'staɪ,laɪz, -ɪz, -ɪŋ, -d

stylo
BR 'stʌɪləʊ, -z
AM 'staɪloʊ, -z

stylobate
BR 'stʌɪləbeɪt, -s
AM 'staɪlə,beɪt, -s

stylograph
BR 'stʌɪləgraːf,
'stʌɪləgraf, -s
AM 'staɪlə,græf, -s

stylographic
BR ˌstʌɪlə'grafɪk
AM ˌstaɪlə'græfɪk

styloid
BR 'stʌɪlɔɪd, -z
AM 'staɪ,lɔɪd, -z

stylus
BR 'stʌɪləs, -ɪz
AM 'staɪləs, -əz

stymie
BR 'stʌɪm|i, -ɪz, -ɪŋ, -id
AM 'staɪmi, -z, -ɪŋ, -d

stymy
BR 'stʌɪm|i, -ɪz, -ɪŋ, -id
AM 'staɪmi, -z, -ɪŋ, -d

styptic
BR 'stɪptɪk
AM 'stɪptɪk

styrax
BR 'stʌɪraks
AM 'staɪ,ræks

styrene
BR 'stʌɪriːn
AM 'staɪ,rin

Styria
BR 'stɪrɪə(r)
AM 'stɪriə

Styrofoam®
BR 'stʌɪrə(ʊ)fəʊm
AM 'staɪrə,foʊm

Styron
BR 'stʌɪrɒn
AM 'staɪrən

Styx
BR stɪks
AM stɪks

Su
BR suː
AM suː

suability
BR ˌs(j)uːə'bɪlɪti
AM ˌsuə'bɪlɪdi

suable
BR 's(j)uːəbl
AM 'suəbəl

suasion
BR 'sweɪʒn
AM 'sweɪʒən

suasive
BR 'sweɪsɪv, 'sweɪzɪv
AM 'sweɪzɪv

suave
BR swɑːv, -ə(r), -ɪst
AM swɑv, -ər, -əst

suavely
BR 'swɑːvli
AM 'suɑvli

suaveness
BR 'swɑːvnəs
AM 'suɑvnəs

suavity
BR 'swɑːvɪti
AM 'swɑvədi

sub
BR sʌb, -z, -ɪŋ, -d
AM səb, -z, -ɪŋ, -d

subabdominal
BR ˌsʌbəb'dɒmɪnl
AM ˌsəbəb'damənəl

subacid
BR ˌsʌb'asɪd
AM ˌsəb'æsəd

subacidity
BR ˌsʌbə'sɪdɪti
AM ˌsəbə'sɪdɪdi

subacute
BR ˌsʌbə'kjuːt
AM ˌsəbə'kjut

subacutely
BR ˌsʌbə'kjuːtli
AM ˌsəbə'kjutli

subagency
BR ˌsʌb'eɪdʒ(ə)ns|i, -ɪz
AM ˌsəb'eɪdʒənsi, -z

subagent
BR ˌsʌb'eɪdʒ(ə)nt, -s
AM ˌsəb'eɪdʒənt, -s

subahdar
BR ˌsʌbə'dɑː(r),
ˌsuːbə'dɑː(r), -z
AM ˌsəbə'dɑr, -z

subalpine
BR ˌsʌb'alpʌɪn
AM ˌsəb'æl,paɪn

subaltern
BR 'sʌblt(ə)n, -z
AM sə'bɑltərn,
sə'bɑltərn, -z

subantarctic
BR ˌsʌban'tɑːktɪk
AM ˌsubən'tɑrktɪk

subaqua
BR ˌsʌb'akwə(r)
AM ˌsəb'akwə

subaquatic
BR ˌsʌbə'kwatɪk
AM ˌsəbə'kwɑdɪk

subaqueous
BR ˌsʌb'eɪkwɪəs,
ˌsʌb'akwɪəs
AM ˌsəb'eɪkwɪəs,
ˌsəb'ækwɪəs

subarctic
BR ˌsʌb'ɑːktɪk
AM ˌsəb'ɑr(k)tɪk

Subaru®
BR 'suːbəruː,
sə'bɑːruː, -z
AM 'subə,ru, -z

subastral
BR ˌsʌb'astr(ə)l
AM ˌsəb'æstrəl

subatomic
BR ˌsʌbə'tɒmɪk

AM ˌsəbəˈtɑmɪk

subaudition
BR ˌsʌbɔːˈdɪʃn
AM ˌsəbɔːˈdɪʃən, ˌsəbəˈdɪʃən

subaxillary
BR ˌsʌbakˈsɪl(ə)ri
AM ˌsəbˈæksəˌlɛri

sub-basement
BR ˌsʌbˈbeɪsm(ə)nt, -s
AM ˈsəbˈbeɪsmənt, -s

sub-branch
BR ˈsʌbbrɑːn(t)ʃ, ˈsʌbbran(t)ʃ, -ɪz
AM ˈsəbˌbræn(t)ʃ, -əz, -ɪŋ, -t

sub-breed
BR ˈsʌbbriːd, -z
AM ˈsəbˌbrid, -z

Subbuteo®
BR səˈb(j)uːtɪəʊ
AM səˈb(j)udioʊ

subcategorisation
BR ˌsʌbkatɪgərʌɪˈzeɪʃn, -z
AM ˈsəbˌkædəg(ə)rəˈzeɪʃən, ˈsəbˌkædəgəˌraɪˈzeɪʃən, -z

subcategorise
BR ˈsʌbˈkatɪgərʌɪz, -ɪz, -ɪŋ, -d
AM ˈsəbˈkædəgəˌraɪz, ˈsəbˈkædəgəˌraɪz, -ɪz, -ɪŋ, -d

subcategorization
BR ˌsʌbkatɪgərʌɪˈzeɪʃn, -z
AM ˈsəbˌkædəg(ə)rəˈzeɪʃən, ˈsəbˌkædəgəˌraɪˈzeɪʃən, -z

subcategorize
BR ˈsʌbˈkatɪgərʌɪz, -ɪz, -ɪŋ, -d
AM ˈsəbˈkædəgəˌraɪz, ˈsəbˈkædəgəˌraɪz, -ɪz, -ɪŋ, -d

subcategory
BR ˈsʌbˌkatɪg(ə)r|i, -ɪz
AM ˈsʌbˌkædəˌgɔri, -z

subcaudal
BR ˈsʌbˈkɔːdl
AM ˈsəbˈkɔdəl, ˈsəbˈkɑdəl

subclass
BR ˈsʌbklɑːs, ˈsʌbklas, -ɪz
AM ˈsəbˌklæs, -əz

subclassification
BR ˌsʌbklasɪfɪˈkeɪʃn
AM ˈsəbˌklæsəfəˈkeɪʃən

sub-clause
BR ˈsʌbklɔːz, -ɪz
AM ˈsəbˌklɔz, ˈsəbˌklɑz, -əz

subclavian
BR ˌsʌbˈkleɪvɪən

subclinical
BR ˌsʌbˈklɪnɪkl
AM ˈsəbˈklɪnɪkəl

subcommissioner
BR ˌsʌbkəˈmɪʃnə(r), ˌsʌbkəˈmɪʃ(ə)nə(r), -z
AM ˌsəbkəˈmɪʃ(ə)nər, -z

subcommittee
BR ˈsʌbkəˌmɪt|i, -ɪz
AM ˈsəbkəˌmɪdi, -z

subcompact
BR ˈsʌbˈkɒmpakt, -s
AM ˈsəbˈkɑmˌpæk(t), -(t)s

subconical
BR ˌsʌbˈkɒnɪkl
AM ˈsəbˈkɑnəkəl

subconscious
BR ˌsʌbˈkɒnʃəs, səbˈkɒnʃəs
AM ˌsəbˈkɑnʃəs

subconsciously
BR ˌsʌbˈkɒnʃəsli, səbˈkɒnʃəsli
AM ˌsəbˈkɑnʃəsli

subconsciousness
BR ˌsʌbˈkɒnʃəsnəs, səbˈkɒnʃəsnəs
AM ˌsəbˈkɑnʃəsnəs

subcontinent
BR ˌsʌbˈkɒntɪnənt, ˈsʌbˌkɒntɪnənt, -s
AM ˈsəbˈkɑntɪnənt, -s

subcontinental
BR ˌsʌbkɒntɪˈnɛntl
AM ˌsəbˌkɑn(t)əˈnɛn(t)l

subcontract
BR ˌsʌbkənˈtrakt, ˈsʌbkəntrakt, -s, -ɪŋ, -ɪd
AM ˈsəbˈkɑnˌtræk|(t), -(t)s, -ɪŋ, -təd

subcontractor
BR ˈsʌbkənˌtraktə(r), -z
AM ˈsəbˈkɑnˌtræktər, -z

subcontrary
BR ˌsʌbˈkɒntrər|i, -ɪz
AM ˌsəbˈkɑntrəri, -z

subcordate
BR ˌsʌbˈkɔːdeɪt
AM ˈsəbˈkɔrdeɪt

subcortical
BR ˌsʌbˈkɔːtɪkl
AM ˈsəbˈkɔrdəkəl

subcostal
BR ˌsʌbˈkɒstl
AM ˈsəbˈkɒstl, ˈsəbˈkɑstl

subcranial
BR ˌsʌbˈkreɪnɪəl
AM ˈsəbˈkreɪnɪəl

subcritical
BR ˌsʌbˈkrɪtɪkl
AM ˈsəbˈkrɪdɪkəl

subcultural
BR ˌsʌbˈkʌltʃ(ə)rəl, ˌsʌbˈkʌltʃ(ə)r|
AM ˈsəbˈkəltʃ(ə)rəl

subculture
BR ˈsʌbˌkʌltʃə(r), -z
AM ˈsəbˌkəltʃər, -z

subcutaneous
BR ˌsʌbkjʉˈteɪnɪəs
AM ˌsəbkjuˈteɪnɪəs

subcutaneously
BR ˌsʌbkjʉˈteɪnɪəsli
AM ˌsəbkjuˈteɪnɪəsli

subcuticular
BR ˌsʌbkjʉˈtɪkjələ(r)
AM ˌsəbkjʉˈtɪkjələr

subdeacon
BR ˌsʌbˈdiːk(ə)n, ˈsʌbdiːk(ə)n, -z
AM ˈsəbˈdikən, -z

subdean
BR ˌsʌbˈdiːn, ˈsʌbdiːn, -z
AM ˈsəbˈdin, -z

subdeanery
BR ˌsʌbˈdiːn(ə)r|i, ˈsʌbˌdiːn(ə)r|i, -ɪz
AM ˌsəbˈdinəri, -z

subdecanal
BR ˌsʌbˈdɛkənl
AM ˈsəbˈdɛkənəl

subdeliria
BR ˌsʌbdɪˈlɪrɪə(r), ˌsʌbdɪˈlɪərɪə(r)
AM ˌsəbdəˈlɪriə, ˌsəbdiˈlɪriə

subdelirious
BR ˌsʌbdɪˈlɪrɪəs, ˌsʌbdɪˈlɪərɪəs
AM ˌsəbdəˈlɪriəs, ˌsəbdiˈlɪriəs

subdelirium
BR ˌsʌbdɪˈlɪrɪəm, ˌsʌbdɪˈlɪərɪəm
AM ˌsəbdəˈlɪriəm, ˌsəbdiˈlɪriəm

subdiaconate
BR ˌsʌbdʌɪˈakəneɪt, ˌsʌbdʌɪˈakənət, ˌsʌbdʌɪˈaknət, -s
AM ˌsəbdaɪˈækənət, ˌsəbdiˈækənət, -s

subdivide
BR ˌsʌbdɪˈvʌɪd, ˈsʌbdɪvʌɪd, -z, -ɪŋ, -ɪd
AM ˈsəbdəˈvaɪd, -z, -ɪŋ, -ɪd

subdivision
BR ˈsʌbdɪˌvɪʒn, ˌsʌbdɪˈvɪʒn, -z
AM ˈsəbdəˌvɪʒən, -z

subdominant
BR ˌsʌbˈdɒmɪnənt, -s
AM ˈsəbˈdɑmənənt, -s

subduable
BR səbˈdjuːəbl, səbˈdʒuːəbl
AM səbˈd(j)uəbəl

subdual
BR səbˈdjuːəl, səbˈdʒuːəl, -z
AM səbˈd(j)uəl, -z

subduct
BR səbˈdʌkt, ˌsʌbˈdʌkt, -s, -ɪŋ, -d
AM səbˈdək|(t), -(t)s, -tɪŋ, -təd

subduction
BR səbˈdʌkʃn, ˌsʌbˈdʌkʃn
AM səbˈdəkʃən

subdue
BR səbˈdjuː, səbˈdʒuː, -z, -ɪŋ, -d
AM səbˈd(j)u, -z, -ɪŋ, -d

subdural
BR ˌsʌbˈdjʊərl, ˌsʌbˈdjɔːrl, ˌsʌbˈdʒʊərl, ˌsʌbˈdʒɔːrl
AM ˌsəbˈd(j)ʊrəl

subedit
BR ˌsʌbˈɛd|ɪt, ˈsʌbˌɛd|ɪt, -s, -ɪtɪŋ, -ɪtɪd
AM ˈsəbˈɛdə|t, -ts, -dɪŋ, -dəd

subeditor
BR ˌsʌbˈɛdɪtə(r), ˈsʌbˌɛdɪtə(r), -z
AM ˈsəbˈɛdədər, -z

sub-editorial
BR ˌsʌbɛdɪˈtɔːrɪəl
AM ˌsəbˌɛdəˈtɔriəl

subeditorship
BR ˈsʌbˈɛdɪtəˌʃɪp, -s
AM ˈsəbˈɛdədərˌʃɪp, -s

suberect
BR ˌsʌbɪˈrɛkt
AM ˌsəbəˈrɛk(t)

subereous
BR s(j)uːˈbɪərɪəs
AM suˈbɪriəs

suberic
BR s(j)uːˈbɛrɪk
AM suˈbɛrɪk

suberose
BR ˈs(j)uːb(ə)rəʊs
AM ˈsəbəˌroʊs, ˈsəbəˌroʊz

subfamily
BR ˈsʌbˌfam(ɪ)l|i, ˈsʌbˌfaml|i, -ɪz
AM ˈsəbˈfæm(ə)li, -z

subfloor
BR ˈsʌbflɔː(r), -z
AM ˈsəbˌflɔ(ə)r, -z

subform
BR ˈsʌbfɔːm, -z
AM ˈsəbˌfɔ(ə)rm, -z

sub-frame
BR ˈsʌbfreɪm, -z
AM ˈsəbˌfreɪm, -z

subfusc
BR ˈsʌbfʌsk
AM ˈsəbˈfəsk

subgenera
BR 'sʌb,dʒɛn(ə)rə(r)
AM 'səb,dʒɛnərə

subgeneric
BR ,sʌbdʒɪ'nɛrɪk
AM ,səbdʒə'nɛrɪk

subgenus
BR 'sʌb,dʒiːnəs
AM 'səb,dʒinəs

subglacial
BR ,sʌb'gleɪʃl
AM ,səb'gleɪʃəl

subgroup
BR 'sʌbgruːp, -s
AM 'səb,grup, -s

subhead
BR 'sʌbhɛd, -z
AM 'səb,(h)ɛd, -z

subheading
BR 'sʌb,hɛdɪŋ, -z
AM 'səb,(h)ɛdɪŋ, -z

subhuman
BR ,sʌb'hjuːmən, -z
AM ,səb'(h)jumən, -z

subjacent
BR ,sʌb'dʒeɪs(ə)nt,
səb'dʒeɪs(ə)nt
AM ,səb'dʒeɪsnt

subject¹
noun
BR 'sʌbdʒɪkt,
'sʌbdʒɛkt, -s
AM 'səbdʒək(t), -s

subject²
verb
BR səb'dʒɛkt, -s, -ɪŋ, -ɪd
AM səb'dʒɛk|(t), -(t)s,
-tɪŋ, -təd

subjection
BR səb'dʒɛkʃn
AM səb'dʒɛkʃən

subjective
BR səb'dʒɛktɪv,
,sʌb'dʒɛktɪv
AM səb'dʒɛktɪv

subjectively
BR səb'dʒɛktɪvli,
,sʌb'dʒɛktɪvli
AM səb'dʒɛktɪvli

subjectiveness
BR səb'dʒɛktɪvnɪs,
,sʌb'dʒɛktɪvnɪs
AM səb'dʒɛktɪvnɪs

subjectivism
BR səb'dʒɛktɪvɪz(ə)m,
,sʌb'dʒɛktɪvɪz(ə)m
AM səb'dʒɛktə,vɪzəm

subjectivist
BR səb'dʒɛktɪvɪst,
,sʌb'dʒɛktɪvɪst, -s
AM səb'dʒɛktəvəst, -s

subjectivity
BR ,sʌbdʒɛk'tɪvɪti,
,sʌbdʒɪk'tɪvɪti
AM ,səb,dʒɛk'tɪvɪdi

subjectless
BR ,sʌbdʒɪk(t)ləs,
'sʌbdʒɛk(t)ləs
AM ,səb'dʒak(t)ləs

subjoin
BR ,sʌb'dʒɔɪn,
səb'dʒɔɪn, -z, -ɪŋ, -d
AM ,səb'dʒɔɪn, -z, -ɪŋ, -d

subjoint
BR ,sʌbdʒɔɪnt, -s
AM 'səb,dʒɔɪnt, -s

sub judice
BR ,sʌb 'dʒuːdɪsiː,
səb +
AM ,səb 'judə,keɪ,
+ 'dʒudə,si

subjugable
BR 'sʌbdʒʊgəbl
AM 'səbdʒəgəbəl

subjugate
BR 'sʌbdʒʊgeɪt, -s, -ɪŋ,
-ɪd
AM 'səbdʒə,geɪ|t, -ts,
-dɪŋ, -dɪd

subjugation
BR ,sʌbdʒʊ'geɪʃn
AM ,səbdʒə'geɪʃən

subjugator
BR 'sʌbdʒʊgeɪtə(r), -z
AM 'səbdʒə,geɪdər, -z

subjunctive
BR səb'dʒʌŋ(k)tɪv, -z
AM səb'dʒəŋ(k)tɪv, -z

subjunctively
BR səb'dʒʌŋ(k)tɪvli
AM səb'dʒəŋ(k)tɪvli

subkingdom
BR 'sʌb,kɪŋdəm, -z
AM 'səb,kɪŋdəm, -z

sublapsarian
BR ,sʌblap'sɛːrɪən, -z
AM ,səblæp'sɛrɪən, -z

sublease¹
noun
BR 'sʌbliːs, -ɪz
AM 'səb,lis, -ɪz

sublease²
verb
BR ,sʌb'liːs, -ɪz, -ɪŋ, -t
AM səb'lis, -ɪz, -ɪŋ, -t

sub-lessee
BR ,sʌblɛ'siː, -z
AM 'səb,lɛ'si, -z

sub-lessor
BR 'sʌb,lɛsə(r),
,sʌb'lɛsə(r), -z
AM 'səb'lɛsər, -z

sublet
BR ,sʌb'lɛt, -s, -ɪŋ
AM 'səb'lɛ|t, -ts, -dɪŋ

sub-librarian
BR ,sʌblaɪ'brɛːrɪən, -z
AM ,səb,laɪ'brɛrɪən, -z

sub-licence
BR 'sʌb,lʌɪsns, -ɪz
AM 'səb,laɪsəns, -əz

sub-license
BR ,sʌb'lʌɪsns, -ɪz, -ɪŋ,
-t
AM ,səb'laɪsns, -əz, -ɪŋ,
-t

sub-licensee
BR ,sʌblʌɪsn'siː, -z
AM ,səb,laɪsn'si, -z

sub-licensor
BR ,sʌb'lʌɪsnsə(r), -z
AM ,səb'laɪsnsər, -z

sublieutenant
BR ,sʌblɛf'tɛnənt, -s
AM ,səb,lu'tɛnənt, -s

sublimate
BR 'sʌblɪmeɪt, -s, -ɪŋ,
-ɪd
AM 'səblə,meɪ|t, -ts,
-dɪŋ, -dɪd

sublimation
BR ,sʌblɪ'meɪʃn
AM ,səblə'meɪʃən

sublime
BR sə'blʌɪm, -ə(r), -ɪst
AM sə'blaɪm, -ər, -ɪst

sublimely
BR sə'blʌɪmli
AM sə'blaɪmli

Sublime Porte
BR sə,blʌɪm 'pɔːt
AM sə,blaɪm 'pɔ(ə)rt

subliminal
BR ,sʌb'lɪmɪnl,
sə'blɪmɪnl
AM sə'blɪmənəl

subliminally
BR ,sʌb'lɪmɪnli,
,sʌb'lɪmɪnəli,
sə'blɪmɪnli,
sə'blɪmɪnəli
AM sə'blɪmənəli

sublimity
BR sə'blɪmɪti
AM sə'blɪmɪdi

sublingual
BR ,sʌb'lɪŋgw(ə)l
AM ,səb'lɪŋgwəl

sublittoral
BR ,sʌb'lɪt(ə)rəl,
,sʌb'lɪt(ə)r|
AM ,səb'lɪdərəl

sublunary
BR ,sʌb'luːn(ə)ri
AM ,səb'lunəri

subluxation
BR ,sʌblʌk'seɪʃn, -z
AM ,səb,lək'seɪʃən, -z

submachine gun
BR ,sʌbmə'ʃiːn gʌn, -z
AM ,səbmə'ʃin ,gən, -z

subman
BR 'sʌbman
AM 'səb,mæn

submarginal
BR ,sʌb'maːdʒɪnl
AM ,səb'mardʒənəl

submarine
BR ,sʌbmə'riːn,
'sʌbməriːn, -z
AM 'səbmə,rin, -z

submariner
BR ,sʌb'marɪnə(r), -z
AM səb'mɛrənər, -z

submaster
BR 'sʌb,maːstə(r),
'sʌb,mastə(r), -z
AM 'səb,mæstər, -z

submaxillary
BR ,sʌb'maksɪl(ə)ri,
,sʌbmak'sɪl(ə)ri
AM ,səb'mæksə,lɛri

submediant
BR ,sʌb'miːdɪənt, -s
AM ,səb'midiənt, -s

submen
BR 'sʌbmɛn
AM 'səb,mɛn

submental
BR ,sʌb'mɛntl
AM ,səb'mɛn(t)l

submerge
BR səb'məːdʒ, -ɪz, -ɪŋ,
-d
AM səb'mərdʒ, -əz, -ɪŋ,
-d

submergence
BR səb'məːdʒ(ə)ns
AM səb'mərdʒəns

submergible
BR səb'məːdʒɪbl
AM səb'mərdʒəbəl

submerse
BR səb'məːs, -ɪz, -ɪŋ, -t
AM səb'mərs, -əz, -ɪŋ, -t

submersible
BR səb'məːsɪbl, -z
AM səb'mərsəbəl, -z

submersion
BR səb'məːʃn,
səb'məːʒn, -z
AM səb'mərʒən,
səb'mərʃən, -z

submicroscopic
BR ,sʌbmʌɪkrə'skɒpɪk
AM 'səb,maɪkrə'skɑpɪk

subminiature
BR ,sʌb'mɪnɪtʃə(r)
AM ,səb'mɪn(i)ə,tʃʊ(ə)r,
,səb'mɪn(i)ətʃər

submission
BR səb'mɪʃn, -z
AM səb'mɪʃən, -z

submissive
BR səb'mɪsɪv
AM səb'mɪsɪv

submissively
BR səb'mɪsɪvli
AM səb'mɪsɪvli

submissiveness
BR səb'mɪsɪvnɪs
AM səb'mɪsɪvnɪs

submit
BR səb'mɪt, -s, -ɪŋ, -ɪd

AM səb'mɪlt, -ts, -dɪŋ, -dɪd

submittal
BR səb'mɪtl, -z
AM səb'mɪdl, -z

submitter
BR sʌb'mɪtə(r), -z
AM səb'mɪdər, -z

submultiple
BR sʌb'mʌltɪpl, -z
AM səb'məltəpəl, -z

subnormal
BR sʌb'nɔːml
AM səb'nɔːrməl

subnormality
BR sʌbnɔːˈmælɪti
AM səbˌnɔːrˈmælədi

sub-nuclear
BR sʌb'njuːkliə(r)
AM səb'n(j)ukliər

subocular
BR sʌb'ɒkjʊlə(r)
AM səb'ɑkjələr

suborbital
BR sʌb'ɔːbɪtl
AM səb'ɔːrbədl

suborder
BR sʌb'ɔːdə(r), -z
AM səb'ɔːrdər, -z

subordinal
BR sʌb'ɔːdɪnl
AM səb'ɔːrdənəl

subordinary
BR sʌb'ɔːdɪn(ə)r|i,
ˌsʌb'ɔːdn(ə)r|i, -ɪz
AM səb'ɔːrdn̩ˌɛri, -z

subordinate[1]
noun, adjective
BR sə'bɔːdɪnət,
sə'bɔːdnət, -s
AM sə'bɔːrdn̩ət, -s

subordinate[2]
verb
BR sə'bɔːdɪneɪt, -s, -ɪŋ,
-ɪd
AM sə'bɔːrdn̩ˌeɪlt, -ts,
-dɪŋ, -dɪd

subordinately
BR sə'bɔːdɪnətli,
sə'bɔːdnətli
AM sə'bɔːrdn̩ətli

subordination
BR səˌbɔːdɪˈneɪʃn
AM səˌbɔːrdn̩ˈeɪʃən

subordinative
BR sə'bɔːdɪnətɪv,
sə'bɔːdnətɪv
AM sə'bɔːrdn̩ədɪv

suborn
BR sə'bɔːn, -z, -ɪŋ, -d
AM sə'bɔː(ə)rn, -z, -ɪŋ, -d

subornation
BR sʌbɔːˈneɪʃn
AM ˌsəbɔrˈneɪʃən

suborner
BR sə'bɔːnə(r), -z
AM sə'bɔːrnər, -z

suboxide
BR sʌb'ɒksaɪd, -z
AM ˌsəb'ɑkˌsaɪd, -z

sub-paragraph
BR sʌb'pærəgrɑːf,
ˌsʌb'pærəgrɑːf,
'sʌb,pærəgraf,
ˌsʌb'pærəgraf, -s
AM ˌsəb'perəˌgræf, -s

subphyla
BR 'sʌb,fʌɪlə(r)
AM 'səb,faɪlə

subphylum
BR 'sʌb,fʌɪləm
AM 'səb,faɪləm

subplot
BR 'sʌbplɒt, -s
AM 'səb,plɑt, -s

subpoena
BR sə(b)'piːnə(r), -z,
-ɪŋ, -d
AM sə'pinə, -z, -ɪŋ, -d

subprior
BR 'sʌb,prʌɪə(r), -z
AM 'səb,praɪər, -z

subprocess
BR 'sʌb,prəʊses, -ɪz
AM 'səb,prɑsəs, -əz

subprogram
BR 'sʌb,prəʊgræm,
'sʌb,prəʊgrəm, -z
AM 'səb,proʊgrəm, -z

subregion
BR 'sʌb,riːdʒ(ə)n, -z
AM 'səb,ridʒən, -z

subregional
BR ˌsʌb'riːdʒn(ə)l,
ˌsʌb'riːdʒən(ə)l
AM 'səb'ridʒ(ə)nəl

subreption
BR sə'brepʃn, -z
AM sə'brepʃən, -z

subrogate
BR 'sʌbrəgeɪt, -s, -ɪŋ,
-ɪd
AM 'səbrə,geɪlt, -ts,
-dɪŋ, -dɪd

subrogation
BR ˌsʌbrə'geɪʃn
AM ˌsəbrə'geɪʃən

sub rosa
BR ˌsʌb 'rəʊzə(r)
AM ˌsəb 'rouzə

subroutine
BR 'sʌbruːtiːn,
'sʌbruːtiːn, -z
AM 'səbruˌtin, -z

sub-Saharan
BR ˌsʌbsə'hɑːrən,
ˌsʌbsə'hɑːrŋ
AM ˌsəbsə'hɛrən

subscribe
BR səb'skrʌɪb, -z, -ɪŋ, -d
AM səb'skraɪb, -z, -ɪŋ,
-d

subscriber
BR səb'skrʌɪbə(r), -z
AM səb'skraɪbər, -z

subscript
BR 'sʌbskrɪpt, -s
AM 'səb,skrɪpt, -s

subscription
BR səb'skrɪpʃn, -z
AM səb'skrɪpʃən, -z

subsection
BR 'sʌb,sekʃn, -z
AM 'səb,sekʃən, -z

sub-sector
BR 'sʌb,sektə(r), -z
AM 'səb,sektər, -z

subsellia
BR səb'selɪə(r)
AM 'səb'sel]ə,
ˌsəb'selɪə

subsellium
BR səb'selɪəm
AM ˌsəb'selɪəm

subsequence
BR 'sʌbsɪkw(ə)ns
AM 'səbsəkwəns

sub-sequence
BR 'sʌb,siːkw(ə)ns, -ɪz
AM 'səb,sikwəns, -əz

subsequent
BR 'sʌbsɪkw(ə)nt
AM 'səbsəkwənt

subsequently
BR 'sʌbsɪkw(ə)ntli
AM 'səbsəkwən(t)li

subserve
BR səb'səːv, -z, -ɪŋ, -d
AM səb'sərv, -z, -ɪŋ, -d

subservience
BR səb'səːvɪəns
AM səb'sərvɪəns

subserviency
BR səb'səːvɪənsi
AM səb'sərvɪənsi

subservient
BR səb'səːvɪənt
AM səb'sərvɪənt

subserviently
BR səb'səːvɪəntli
AM səb'sərvɪən(t)li

subset
BR 'sʌbset, -s
AM 'səb,set, -s

subshrub
BR 'sʌbʃrʌb, -z
AM 'səb,ʃrəb, -z

subside
BR səb'sʌɪd, -z, -ɪŋ, -ɪd
AM səb'saɪd, -z, -ɪŋ, -ɪd

subsidence
BR səb'sʌɪdns,
'sʌbsɪdns, -ɪz
AM səb'saɪdns,
'səbsədns, -ɪz

subsidiarily
BR səb'sɪdɪərɪli
AM səb'sɪdi'erəli

subsidiariness
BR səb'sɪdɪərɪnɪs
AM səb'sɪdi,erɪnɪs

subsidiarity
BR səb,sɪdɪ'arɪti
AM səb,sɪdi'ɛrədi

subsidiary
BR səb'sɪdɪər|i, -ɪz
AM səb'sɪdi,ɛri, -z

subsidisation
BR ˌsʌbsɪdʌɪ'zeɪʃn
AM ˌsəbsədə'zeɪʃən,
ˌsəbsə,daɪ'zeɪʃən

subsidise
BR 'sʌbsɪdʌɪz, -ɪz, -ɪŋ,
-d
AM 'səbsə,daɪz, -ɪz, -ɪŋ,
-d

subsidiser
BR 'sʌbsɪdʌɪzə(r)
AM 'səbsə,daɪzər

subsidization
BR ˌsʌbsɪdʌɪ'zeɪʃn
AM ˌsəbsədə'zeɪʃən,
ˌsəbsə,daɪ'zeɪʃən

subsidize
BR 'sʌbsɪdʌɪz, -ɪz, -ɪŋ,
-d
AM 'səbsə,daɪz, -ɪz, -ɪŋ,
-d

subsidizer
BR 'sʌbsɪdʌɪzə(r), -z
AM 'səbsə,daɪzər, -z

subsidy
BR 'sʌbsɪd|i, -ɪz
AM 'səbsədi, -z

subsist
BR səb'sɪst, -s, -ɪŋ, -ɪd
AM səb'sɪst, -s, -ɪŋ, -ɪd

subsistence
BR səb'sɪst(ə)ns
AM səb'sɪstəns

subsistent
BR səb'sɪst(ə)nt
AM səb'sɪstənt

subsoil
BR 'sʌbsɔɪl, -z
AM 'səb,sɔɪl, -z

subsonic
BR ˌsʌb'sɒnɪk
AM 'səb'sɑnɪk

subsonically
BR ˌsʌb'sɒnɪkli
AM ˌsəb'sɑnək(ə)li

subspecies
BR 'sʌb,spi·ʃɪz,
'sʌb,spi·ʃi·z,
'sʌb,spi·sɪz,
'sʌb,spi·si·z
AM 'səb,spiʃiz,
'səb,spisiz

subspecific
BR ˌsʌbspɪ'sɪfɪk
AM ˌsəbspə'sɪfɪk

substance
BR 'sʌbst(ə)ns, -ɪz
AM 'səbstəns, -əz

substandard
BR ˌsʌb'standəd
AM 'səb'stændərd

substantial
BR səb'stanʃl,
səb'stɑːnʃl
AM ,səb'stæn(t)ʃəl

substantialise
BR səb'stanʃəlʌɪz,
səb'stanʃlʌɪz,
səb'stɑːnʃəlʌɪz,
səb'stɑːnʃlʌɪz, -ɪz, -ɪŋ,
-d
AM ,səb'stæn(t)ʃəˌlʌɪz,
-ɪz, -ɪŋ, -d

substantialism
BR səb'stanʃəlɪz(ə)m,
səb'stanʃlɪz(ə)m,
səb'stɑːnʃəlɪz(ə)m,
səb'stɑːnʃlɪz(ə)m
AM ,səb'stæn(t)ʃəˌlɪzəm

substantialist
BR ,sʌb'stanʃəlɪst,
,sʌb'stanʃlɪst,
,sʌb'stɑːnʃəlɪst,
,sʌb'stɑːnʃlɪst, -s
AM ,səb'stæn(t)ʃələst,
-s

substantiality
BR səb,stanʃɪ'alɪti,
səb,stɑːnʃɪ'alɪti
AM səb,stæn(t)ʃi'ælədi

substantialize
BR səb'stanʃəlʌɪz,
səb'stanʃlʌɪz,
səb'stɑːnʃəlʌɪz,
səb'stɑːnʃlʌɪz, -ɪz, -ɪŋ,
-d
AM ,səb'stæn(t)ʃəˌlʌɪz,
-ɪz, -ɪŋ, -d

substantially
BR səb'stanʃəli,
səb'stanʃli,
səb'stɑːnʃəli,
səb'stɑːnʃli
AM ,səb'stæn(t)ʃəli

substantialness
BR səb'stanʃlnəs,
səb'stɑːnʃlnəs
AM ,səb'stæn(t)ʃəlnəs

substantiate
BR səb'stanʃɪeɪt,
səb'stansɪeɪt,
səb'stɑːnʃɪeɪt,
səb'stɑːnsɪeɪt, -s, -ɪŋ,
-ɪd
AM səb'stæn(t)ʃiˌeɪlt,
-ts, -dɪŋ, -dɪd

substantiation
BR səb,stanʃɪ'eɪʃn,
səb,stansɪ'eɪʃn,
səb,stɑːnʃɪ'eɪʃn,
səb,stɑːnsɪ'eɪʃn,
AM səb,stæn(t)ʃi'eɪʃən

substantival
BR ,sʌbst(ə)n'tʌɪvl
AM ,səbstən'taɪvəl

substantive¹
noun
BR ,sʌbst(ə)ntɪv,
səb'stantɪv, -z
AM ,səbstən(t)ɪv, -z

substantive²
adjective
BR səb'stantɪv,
'sʌbst(ə)ntɪv
AM ,səbstən(t)ɪv,
səb'stæn(t)ɪv

substantively
BR səb'stantɪvli,
'sʌbst(ə)ntɪvli
AM ,səbstən(t)ɪvli,
səb'stæn(t)ɪvli

substantiveness
BR səb'stantɪvnɪs,
'sʌbst(ə)ntɪvnɪs
AM ,səbstən(t)ɪvnɪs,
səb'stæn(t)ɪvnɪs

substation
BR 'sʌb,steɪʃn, -z
AM ,səb,steɪʃən, -z

substituent
BR səb'stɪtjʊənt,
səb'stɪtʃʊənt, -s
AM ,səb'stɪtʃ(əw)ənt,
-s

substitutability
BR ,sʌbstɪtju:tə'bɪlɪti,
,sʌbstɪtʃu:tə'bɪlɪti
AM ,səbstə,t(j)udə'bɪlɪdi

substitutable
BR 'sʌbstɪtju:təbl,
'sʌbstɪtʃu:təbl
AM 'səbstə,t(j)udəbəl

substitute
BR 'sʌbstɪtju:t,
'sʌbstɪtʃu:t, -s, -ɪŋ, -ɪd
AM 'səbstə,t(j)u|t, -ts,
-dɪŋ, -dəd

substitution
BR ,sʌbstɪ'tju:ʃn,
,sʌbstɪ'tʃu:ʃn, -z
AM ,səbstə't(j)uʃən, -z

substitutional
BR ,sʌbstɪ'tju:ʃn(ə)l,
,sʌbstɪ'tju:ʃən(ə)l,
,sʌbstɪ'tʃu:ʃn(ə)l,
,sʌbstɪ'tʃu:ʃən(ə)l
AM ,səbstə't(j)uʃ(ə)nəl

substitutionary
BR ,sʌbstɪ'tju:ʃn(ə)ri,
,sʌbstɪ'tʃu:ʃn(ə)ri
AM ,səbstə't(j)uʃə,neri

substitutive
BR 'sʌbstɪtju:tɪv,
'sʌbstɪtʃu:tɪv
AM 'səbstə,t(j)udɪv

substrata
BR ,sʌb,strɑː'tɑː(r),
'sʌb,streɪtə(r),
,sʌb'strɑː'tə(r),
,sʌb'streɪtə(r)
AM 'səb,streɪdə,
'səb,strɑːdə,
'səb,strædə

substrate
BR 'sʌbstreɪt, -s
AM 'səb,streɪt, -s

substratum
BR 'sʌb,strɑː:təm,
'sʌb,streɪtəm,
,sʌb'strɑː:təm,
,sʌb'streɪtəm
AM 'səb,streɪdəm,
'səb,strɑːdəm,
'səb,strædəm

substructural
BR ,sʌb'strʌktʃ(ə)rəl,
,sʌb'strʌktʃ(ə)rl
AM ,səb'strək(t)ʃ(ə)rəl

substructure
BR 'sʌb,strʌktʃə(r), -z
AM ,səb'strək(t)ʃər, -z

subsumable
BR səb'sju:məbl
AM səb's(j)uməbəl

subsume
BR səb'sju:m, -z, -ɪŋ, -d
AM səb's(j)um, -z, -ɪŋ,
-d

subsumption
BR səb'sʌm(p)ʃn, -z
AM səb'səmpʃən, -z

subsurface
BR 'sʌb,sə:fɪs, -ɪz
AM 'səb,sərfəs, -əz

subsystem
BR 'sʌb,sɪstɪm, -z
AM 'səb,sɪstəm, -z

subtenancy
BR ,sʌb'tɛnəns|i,
'sʌb,tɛnəns|i, -ɪz
AM ,səb'tɛnənsi, -z

subtenant
BR ,sʌb'tɛnənt,
'sʌb,tɛnənt, -s
AM ,səb'tɛnənt, -s

subtend
BR səb'tɛnd, -z, -ɪŋ, -ɪd
AM səb'tɛnd, -z, -ɪŋ, -əd

subterfuge
BR 'sʌbtəfju:(d)ʒ, -ɪz
AM 'səbtər,fjudʒ, -əz

subterminal
BR ,sʌb'tə:mɪnl
AM ,səb'tərmənəl

subterranean
BR ,sʌbtə'reɪnɪən
AM ,səbtə'reɪnɪən

subterraneously
BR ,sʌbtə'reɪnɪəsli
AM ,səbtə'reɪnɪəsli

subtext
BR 'sʌbtɛkst, -s
AM 'səb,tɛkst, -s

subtilisation
BR ,sʌtɪlʌɪ'zeɪʃn
AM ,sədlə'zeɪʃən,
,sədlˌaɪ'zeɪʃən

subtilise
BR 'sʌtɪlʌɪz, -ɪz, -ɪŋ, -d
AM 'sədlˌaɪz, -ɪz, -ɪŋ, -d

subtilization
BR ,sʌtɪlʌɪ'zeɪʃn

subtilize
BR 'sʌtɪlʌɪz, -ɪz, -ɪŋ, -d
AM 'sədlˌaɪz, -ɪz, -ɪŋ, -d

subtitle
BR 'sʌb,tʌɪtl, -z, -d
AM 'səb,taɪdəl, -z, -d

subtle
BR 'sʌt|l, -lə(r)\-lə(r),
-lɪst\-lɪst
AM 'sədəl, -ər, -əst

subtleness
BR 'sʌtlnəs
AM 'sədlnəs

subtlety
BR 'sʌtlt|i, -ɪz
AM 'sədldi, 'sədlti, -z

subtly
BR 'sʌt|li, 'sʌtli
AM 'sədli

subtonic
BR ,sʌb'tɒnɪk, -s
AM ,səb'tɑnɪk, -s

subtopia
BR ,sʌb'təʊpɪə(r), -z
AM ,səb'toʊpɪə, -z

subtopian
BR ,sʌb'təʊpɪən
AM ,səb'toʊpɪən

subtotal
BR 'sʌb,təʊtl,
,sʌb'təʊtl, -z
AM 'sub'toʊdl, -z

subtract
BR səb'trakt, -s, -ɪŋ, -ɪd
AM səb'træk(t), -(t)s,
-tɪŋ, -təd

subtracter
BR səb'traktə(r), -z
AM səb'træktər, -z

subtraction
BR səb'trakʃn, -z
AM səb'trækʃən, -z

subtractive
BR səb'traktɪv
AM səb'træktɪv

subtractor
BR səb'traktə(r), -z
AM səb'træktər, -z

subtrahend
BR 'sʌbtrəhend, -z
AM 'səbtrə,hend, -z

subtropical
BR ,sʌb'trɒpɪkl
AM səb'trapəkəl

subtropics
BR 'sʌb,trɒpɪks,
,sʌb'trɒpɪks
AM ,səb'trapɪks, -z

subtype
BR 'sʌbtʌɪp, -s
AM ,səb,taɪp, -s

subulate
BR 'sʌbjəleɪt
AM 'səbjə,leɪt,
'səbjələt

sub-unit
BR 'sʌb juːnɪt, -s
AM 'səb junət, -s

suburb
BR 'sʌbəːb, -z
AM 'səbɜːrb, -z

suburban
BR sə'bəːb(ə)n
AM sə'bɜːrbən

suburbanisation
BR sə,bəːbənʌɪ'zeɪʃn,
sə,bəː'bnʌɪ'zeɪʃn
AM sə,bɜːrbənə'zeɪʃən,
sə,bɜːrbə,naɪ'zeɪʃən

suburbanise
BR sə'bəːbənʌɪz,
sə'bəː'bnʌɪz, -ɪz, -ɪŋ, -d
AM sə'bɜːrbə,naɪz, -ɪz,
-ɪŋ, -d

suburbanite
BR sə'bəːbənʌɪt,
sə'bəː'bnʌɪt, -s
AM sə'bɜːrbə,naɪt, -s

suburbanization
BR sə,bəːbənʌɪ'zeɪʃn,
sə,bəː'bnʌɪ'zeɪʃn
AM sə,bɜːrbənə'zeɪʃən,
sə,bɜːrbə,naɪ'zeɪʃən

suburbanize
BR sə'bəːbənʌɪz,
sə'bəː'bnʌɪz, -ɪz, -ɪŋ, -d
AM sə'bɜːrbə,naɪz, -ɪz,
-ɪŋ, -d

suburbia
BR sə'bəːbɪə(r)
AM sə'bɜːrbɪə

subvariety
BR 'sʌbvə,rʌɪɪt|i, -ɪz
AM 'səbvə,raɪədi, -z

subvention
BR səb'vɛnʃn, -z
AM səb'vɛn(t)ʃən, -z

subversion
BR səb'vəːʃn, -z
AM səb'vɜːrʒən,
səb'vɜːrʃən, -z

subversive
BR səb'vəːsɪv, -z
AM səb'vɜːrsɪv, -z

subversively
BR səb'vəːsɪvli
AM səb'vɜːrsɪvli

subversiveness
BR səb'vəːsɪvnɪs
AM səb'vɜːrsɪvnɪs

subvert
BR səb'vəːt, -s, -ɪŋ, -ɪd
AM səb'vɜːr|t, -ts, -dɪŋ,
-dəd

subverter
BR səb'vəːtə(r), -z
AM səb'vɜːrdər, -z

subway
BR 'sʌbweɪ, -z
AM 'səb,weɪ, -z

sub-zero
BR 'sʌb'zɪərəʊ

AM 'səb'zɪroʊ,
'səb'zɪroʊ

succedanea
BR ,sʌksɪ'deɪnɪə(r)
AM ,səksə'deɪnɪə

succedaneous
BR ,sʌksɪ'deɪnɪəs
AM ,səksə'deɪnɪəs

succedaneum
BR ,sʌksɪ'deɪnɪəm
AM ,səksə'deɪnɪəm

succeed
BR sək'siːd, -z, -ɪŋ, -ɪd
AM sək'sid, -z, -ɪŋ, -ɪd

succeeder
BR sək'siːdə(r), -z
AM sək'sidər, -z

succentor
BR sək'sɛntə(r), -z
AM sək'sɛn(t)ər, -z

succentorship
BR sək'sɛntəʃɪp, -s
AM sək'sɛn(t)ər,ʃɪp, -s

**succès de
scandale**
BR sək,seɪ də ,skɒ'dɑːl
AM sək,seɪ də
,skɑn'dal

success
BR sək'sɛs, -ɪz
AM sək'sɛs, -əz

successful
BR sək'sɛsf(ʊ)l
AM sək'sɛsfəl

successfully
BR sək'sɛsfʊli,
sək'sɛsfli
AM sək'sɛsfəli

successfulness
BR sək'sɛsf(ʊ)lnəs
AM sək'sɛsfəlnəs

succession
BR sək'sɛʃn, -z
AM sək'sɛʃən, -z

successional
BR sək'sɛʃn(ə)l,
sək'sɛʃən(ə)l
AM sək'sɛʃ(ə)nəl

successive
BR sək'sɛsɪv
AM sək'sɛsɪv

successively
BR sək'sɛsɪvli
AM sək'sɛsɪvli

successiveness
BR sək'sɛsɪvnɪs
AM sək'sɛsɪvnɪs

successor
BR sək'sɛsə(r), -z
AM sək'sɛsər, -z

succinate
BR 'sʌksɪneɪt
AM 'səksə,neɪt

succinct
BR sək'sɪŋ(k)t
AM sə(k)'sɪŋ(k)t,
sə(k)'sɪŋk(t)

succinctly
BR sək'sɪŋ(k)tli,
sək'sɪŋk(t)li
AM sə(k)'sɪŋ(k)tli,
sə(k)'sɪŋk(t)li

succinctness
BR sək'sɪŋ(k)tnɪs,
sək'sɪŋk(t)nɪs
AM sə(k)'sɪŋ(k)tnɪs,
sə(k)'sɪŋk(t)nɪs

succinic
BR sʌk'sɪnɪk,
sək'sɪnɪk
AM sək'sɪnɪk

succor
BR 'sʌk|ə(r), -əz,
-(ə)rɪŋ, -əd
AM 'səkər, -z, -ɪŋ, -d

succorless
BR 'sʌkələs
AM 'səkərləs

succory
BR 'sʌk(ə)r|i, -ɪz
AM 'səkəri, -z

succotash
BR 'sʌkətaʃ
AM 'səkə,tæʃ

Succoth
BR sʊ'kaʊt, 'sʌkəθ
AM 'suːˌkoʊt

succour
BR 'sʌk|ə(r), -əz,
-(ə)rɪŋ, -əd
AM 'səkər, -z, -ɪŋ, -d

succourless
BR 'sʌkələs
AM 'səkərləs

succuba
BR 'sʌkjʊbə(r)
AM 'səkjəbə

succubae
BR 'sʌkjʊbiː,
'sʌkjʊbʌɪ
AM 'səkjəbi, 'səkjəˌbaɪ

succubi
BR 'sʌkjʊbʌɪ
AM 'səkjəˌbaɪ

succubus
BR 'sʌkjʊbəs
AM 'səkjəbəs

succulence
BR 'sʌkjʊləns,
'sʌkjʊlns
AM 'səkjələns

succulent
BR 'sʌkjʊlənt,
'sʌkjʊlnt
AM 'səkjələnt

succulently
BR 'sʌkjʊləntli,
'sʌkjʊlntli
AM 'səkjələn(t)li

succumb
BR sə'kʌm, -z, -ɪŋ, -d
AM sə'kəm, -z, -ɪŋ, -d

succursal
BR sə'kəːsl
AM sə'kɜːrsəl

succuss
BR 'sʌkəs, -ɪz, -ɪŋ, -t
AM 'səkəs, -əz, -ɪŋ, -t

succussion
BR sə'kʌʃn, -z
AM sə'kəʃən, -z

such¹
strong form
BR sʌtʃ
AM sətʃ

such²
weak form
BR sətʃ
AM sətʃ

such-and-such
BR 'sʌtʃ(ə)n(d)sʌtʃ
AM 'sətʃən'sətʃ

Suchard
BR 'suːˌʃɑː(d)
AM suː'ʃard

Suchet
BR 'suːˌʃeɪ
AM suː'ʃeɪ

suchlike
BR 'sʌtʃlʌɪk
AM 'sətʃ,laɪk

suck
BR sʌk, -s, -ɪŋ, -t
AM sək, -s, -ɪŋ, -t

sucker
BR 'sʌkə(r), -z, -d
AM 'səkər, -z, -d

suckle
BR 'sʌk|l, -lz, -|ɪŋ \-lɪŋ,
-ld
AM 'sək|əl, -əlz, -(ə)lɪŋ,
-əld

suckler
BR 'sʌklə(r), -z
AM 'sək(ə)lər, -z

Suckling
BR 'sʌklɪŋ
AM 'səklɪŋ

suckling
noun
BR 'sʌklɪŋ, -z
AM 'sək(ə)lɪŋ, -z

sucre
BR 'suːkreɪ, -z
AM 'suˌkreɪ, -z

sucrose
BR 's(j)uːkrəʊz,
's(j)uːkrəʊs
AM 'suˌkroʊs,
'suˌkroʊz

suction
BR 'sʌkʃn
AM 'səkʃən

suctorial
BR sʌk'tɔːrɪəl,
sək'tɔːrɪəl
AM sək'tɔːriəl

suctorian
BR sʌk'tɔːrɪən,
sək'tɔːrɪən, -z
AM sək'tɔːriən, -z

Sudan
BR sʊ'dɑːn, sʊ'dan

AM suˈdæn

Sudanese
BR ˌsuːdəˈniːz
AM ˌsudəˈniz

sudaria
BR s(j)uːˈdɛːrɪə(r)
AM suˈdɛrɪə

sudarium
BR s(j)uːˈdɛːrɪəm
AM suˈdɛrɪəm

sudatoria
BR ˌs(j)uːdəˈtɔːrɪə(r)
AM ˌsudəˈtɔrɪə

sudatorium
BR ˌs(j)uːdəˈtɔːrɪəm
AM ˌsudəˈtɔriəm

sudatory
BR ˈs(j)uːdət(ə)r|i, -ɪz
AM ˈsudəˌtɔri, -z

Sudbury
BR ˈsʌdb(ə)ri
AM ˈsədˌbɛri, ˈsədbəri

sudd
BR sʌd, -z
AM səd, -z

Suddaby
BR ˈsʌdəbi
AM ˈsədəbi

sudden
BR ˈsʌdn
AM ˈsədən

suddenly
BR ˈsʌdnli
AM ˈsədnli

suddenness
BR ˈsʌdnnəs
AM ˈsəd(n)nəs

Sudetenland
BR səˈdeɪtnland
AM suˈdeɪtnˌlænd

sudoriferous
BR ˌs(j)uːdəˈrɪf(ə)rəs
AM ˌsudəˈrɪf(ə)rəs

sudorific
BR ˌs(j)uːdəˈrɪfɪk, -s
AM ˌsudəˈrɪfɪk, -s

Sudra
BR ˈsuːdrə(r), -z
AM ˈsudrə, -z

suds
BR sʌdz
AM sədz

sudsy
BR ˈsʌdzi
AM ˈsədzi

sue
BR s(j)uː, -z, -ɪŋ, -d
AM su, -z, -ɪŋ, -d

suède
BR sweɪd
AM sweɪd

suer
BR ˈs(j)uːə(r), -z
AM ˈsuər, -z

suet
BR ˈs(j)uːɪt
AM ˈsuət

Suetonius
BR s(j)uːˈtəʊnɪəs
AM suəˈtoʊnɪəs

suety
BR ˈs(j)uːɪti
AM ˈsuədi

Suez
BR ˈs(j)uːɪz
AM suˈɛz, ˈsuˌɛz

suffer
BR ˈsʌf|ə(r), -əz,
-(ə)rɪŋ, -əd
AM ˈsʌf|ər, -ərz, -(ə)rɪŋ,
-ərd

sufferable
BR ˈsʌf(ə)rəbl
AM ˈsəf(ə)rəbəl

sufferance
BR ˈsʌf(ə)rəns,
ˈsʌf(ə)rns
AM ˈsəf(ə)rəns

sufferer
BR ˈsʌf(ə)rə(r), -z
AM ˈsəf(ə)rər, -z

suffering
BR ˈsʌf(ə)rɪŋ, -z
AM ˈsəf(ə)rɪŋ, -z

suffice
BR səˈfʌɪs, -ɪz, -ɪŋ, -t
AM səˈfaɪs, -ɪz, -ɪŋ, -t

sufficiency
BR səˈfɪʃnsi
AM səˈfɪʃənsi

sufficient
BR səˈfɪʃnt
AM səˈfɪʃənt

sufficiently
BR səˈfɪʃntli
AM səˈfɪʃən(t)li

suffix¹
noun
BR ˈsʌfɪks, -ɪksɪz,
-ɪksɪŋ, -ɪkst
AM ˈsəfɪks, -ɪz, -ɪŋ, -t

suffix²
verb
BR ˈsʌfɪks, səˈfɪks,
ˈsʌfɪksɪz, səˈfɪksɪz,
ˈsʌfɪksɪŋ, səˈfɪksɪŋ,
ˈsʌfɪkst, səˈfɪkst
AM ˈsəfɪks, səˈfɪks, -ɪz,
-ɪŋ, -d

suffixation
BR ˌsʌfɪkˈseɪʃn
AM ˌsəfək'seɪʃən

suffocate
BR ˈsʌfəkeɪt, -s, -ɪŋ, -ɪd
AM ˈsəfəˌkeɪ|t, -ts, -dɪŋ,
-dɪd

suffocating
BR ˈsʌfəkeɪtɪŋ
AM ˈsəfəˌkeɪdɪŋ

suffocatingly
BR ˈsʌfəkeɪtɪŋli
AM ˈsəfəˌkeɪdɪŋli

suffocation
BR ˌsʌfəˈkeɪʃn
AM ˌsəfəˈkeɪʃən

Suffolk
BR ˈsʌfək
AM ˈsəfək

suffragan
BR ˈsʌfrəg(ə)n, -z
AM ˈsəfrəgən, -z

suffraganship
BR ˈsʌfrəg(ə)nˌʃɪp, -s
AM ˈsəfrəgənˌʃɪp, -s

suffrage
BR ˈsʌfr|ɪdʒ, -ɪdʒɪz
AM ˈsəfrɪdʒ, -ɪz

suffragette
BR ˌsʌfrəˈdʒɛt, -s
AM ˌsəfrəˈdʒɛt, -s

suffragism
BR ˈsʌfrədʒɪz(ə)m
AM ˈsəfrəˌdʒɪzəm

suffragist
BR ˈsʌfrədʒɪst, -s
AM ˈsəfrədʒəst, -s

suffuse
BR səˈfjuːz, -ɪz, -ɪŋ, -d
AM səˈfjuz, -əz, -ɪŋ, -d

suffusion
BR səˈfjuːʒn, -z
AM səˈfjuʒən, -z

Sufi
BR ˈsuːfli, -ɪz
AM ˈsufi, -z

Sufic
BR ˈsuːfɪk
AM ˈsufɪk

Sufism
BR ˈsuːfɪz(ə)m
AM ˈsuˌfɪzəm

sugar
BR ˈʃʊg|ə(r), -əz,
-(ə)rɪŋ, -əd
AM ˈʃʊgər, -z, -ɪŋ, -d

sugarbeet
BR ˈʃʊgəbiːt
AM ˈʃʊgərˌbit

sugarbush
BR ˈʃʊgəbʊʃ, -ɪz
AM ˈʃʊgərˌbʊʃ, -əz

sugarcane
BR ˈʃʊgəkeɪn
AM ˈʃʊgərˌkeɪn

sugarcoated
BR ˌʃʊgəˈkəʊtɪd
AM ˈʃʊgərˌkoʊdəd

sugarhouse
BR ˈʃʊgəhaʊs, -ɪz
AM ˈʃʊgərˌ(h)aʊs, -əz

sugariness
BR ˈʃʊg(ə)rɪnɪs
AM ˈsʊgərɪnɪs

sugarless
BR ˈʃʊgələs
AM ˈsugərləs

sugarloaf
BR ˈʃʊgələʊf
AM ˈʃʊgərˌloʊf

sugarloaves
BR ˈʃʊgələʊvz
AM ˈʃʊgərˌloʊvz

sugarplum
BR ˈʃʊgəplʌm, -z
AM ˈʃʊgərˌpləm, -z

sugary
BR ˈʃʊg(ə)ri
AM ˈʃʊgəri

suggest
BR səˈdʒɛst, -s, -ɪŋ, -ɪd
AM sə(g)ˈdʒɛst, -s, -ɪŋ,
-əd

suggester
BR səˈdʒɛstə(r), -z
AM sə(g)ˈdʒɛstər, -z

suggestibility
BR səˌdʒɛstɪˈbɪlɪti
AM sə(g)ˌdʒɛstəˈbɪlɪdi

suggestible
BR səˈdʒɛstɪbl
AM sə(g)ˈdʒɛstəbəl

suggestion
BR səˈdʒɛstʃ(ə)n, -z
AM sə(g)ˈdʒɛstʃən,
sə(g)ˈdʒɛˌtʃən, -z

suggestive
BR səˈdʒɛstɪv
AM sə(g)ˈdʒɛstɪv

suggestively
BR səˈdʒɛstɪvli
AM sə(g)ˈdʒɛstɪvli

suggestiveness
BR səˈdʒɛstɪvnɪs
AM sə(g)ˈdʒɛstɪvnɪs

Sui
BR sweɪ
AM sweɪ

suicidal
BR ˌs(j)uːɪˈsʌɪdl
AM ˌsuəˈsaɪdəl

suicidally
BR ˌs(j)uːɪˈsʌɪdli
AM ˌsuəˈsaɪdli

suicide
BR ˈs(j)uːɪsʌɪd, -z
AM ˈsuəˌsaɪd, -z

sui generis
BR ˌs(j)uːˈʌɪ
ˈdʒɛn(ə)rɪs, ˌs(j)uːˈiː +,
+ ˈgɛn(ə)rɪs
AM ˌsui ˈdʒɛnərəs,
ˌsuˌaɪ +

sui juris
BR ˌs(j)uːˈʌɪ ˈdʒʊərɪs,
ˌs(j)uːˈiː +, + ˈjʊərɪs
AM ˌsui ˈdʒʊrəs, ˌsui
ˈjurəs

suint
BR swɪnt, ˈs(j)uːɪnt
AM ˈsuənt, swɪnt

suit
BR s(j)uːt, -s, -ɪŋ, -ɪd
AM suː|t, -ts, -dɪŋ, -dəd

suitability
BR ˌs(j)uːtəˈbɪlɪti
AM ˌsudəˈbɪlɪdi

suitable
BR ˈs(j)uːtəbl
AM ˈsudəbəl

suitableness
BR 'sjuːtəblnəs
AM 'suːdəbəlnəs

suitably
BR 'sjuːtəbli
AM 'suːdəbli

suitcase
BR 'sjuːtkeɪs, -ɪz
AM 'suːtˌkeɪs, -ɪz

suitcaseful
BR 'sjuːtkeɪsfʊl, -z
AM 'suːtˌkeɪsˌfʊl, -z

suite
BR swiːt, -s
AM swiːt, -s

suiting
BR 'sjuːtɪŋ, -z
AM 'suːdɪŋ, -z

suitor
BR 'sjuːtə(r), -z
AM 'suːdər, -z

suk
BR suːk, -s
AM suːk, -s

Sukarno
BR suːˈkɑːnəʊ
AM suˈkɑrnoʊ

Sukey
BR 'suːki
AM 'suːki

Sukhotai
BR ˌsʊkəˈtʌɪ
AM ˌsʊkəˈtaɪ

Sukie
BR 'suːki
AM 'suːki

sukiyaki
BR ˌsuːkɪˈjɑːki, ˌsʊkɪˈjɑːki, suːkɪˈjɑːki, sʊkɪˈjɑːki
AM sʊkiˈjɑki

Sukkur
BR 'sʊkə(r)
AM 'sʊkər

Sulawesi
BR ˌsuːləˈweɪsi
AM ˌsuːləˈweɪsi

sulcate
BR 'sʌlkeɪt
AM 'sʌlˌkeɪt

sulci
BR 'sʌlsʌɪ, 'sʌlkʌɪ, 'sʌlsiː, 'sʌlkiː
AM 'sʌlˌsaɪ

sulcus
BR 'sʌlkəs
AM 'sʌlkəs

Suleiman
BR sʊˈleɪmən
AM sʊˈleɪmən, 'suleɪˌmɑn

sulfa
BR 'sʌlfə(r)
AM 'sʌlfə

sulfadimidine
BR ˌsʌlfəˈdʌɪmɪdiːn
AM ˌsʌlfəˈdaɪməˌdin

sulfa drug
BR 'sʌlfə drʌg, -z
AM 'sʌlfə ˌdrʌg, -z

sulfamate
BR 'sʌlfəmeɪt
AM 'sʌlfəˌmeɪt

sulfanilamide
BR ˌsʌlfəˈnɪləmʌɪd, -z
AM ˌsʌlfəˈnɪləˌmaɪd, -z

sulfate
BR 'sʌlfeɪt, -s
AM 'sʌlˌfeɪt, -s

sulfide
BR 'sʌlfʌɪd, -z
AM 'sʌlˌfaɪd, -z

sulfite
BR 'sʌlfʌɪt, -s
AM 'sʌlˌfaɪt, -s

sulfonamide
BR sʌlˈfɒnəmʌɪd, -z
AM sʌlˈfɑnəˌmaɪd, -z

sulfonate
BR 'sʌlfəneɪt
AM 'sʌlfəˌneɪt

sulfonation
BR ˌsʌlfəˈneɪʃn
AM ˌsʌlfəˈneɪʃən

sulfone
BR 'sʌlfəʊn, -z
AM 'sʌlˌfoʊn, -z

sulfonic
BR sʌlˈfɒnɪk
AM sʌlˈfɑnɪk

sulfur
BR 'sʌlfə(r)
AM 'sʌlfər

sulfurate
BR 'sʌlfjʊreɪt
AM 'sʌlf(j)əˌreɪt

sulfuration
BR ˌsʌlfjʊˈreɪʃn
AM ˌsʌlf(j)əˈreɪʃən

sulfurator
BR 'sʌlfjʊreɪtə(r)
AM 'sʌlf(j)əˌreɪdər

sulfureous
BR sʌlˈfjʊərɪəs, sʌlˈfjɔːrɪəs
AM səlˈf(j)ərɪəs

sulfuretted
BR ˌsʌlfjʊˈretɪd, 'sʌlfjʊretɪd
AM 'sʌlf(j)əˈredəd

sulfuric
BR sʌlˈfjʊərɪk, sʌlˈfjɔːrɪk
AM 'sʌlˈfjʊrɪk

sulfurisation
BR ˌsʌlfjʊrʌɪˈzeɪʃn
AM ˌsʌlf(j)ərəˈzeɪʃən, ˌsʌlf(j)əˌraɪˈzeɪʃən

sulfurise
BR 'sʌlfjʊrʌɪz
AM 'sʌlf(j)əˌraɪz

sulfurization
BR ˌsʌlfjʊrʌɪˈzeɪʃn

AM ˌsʌlf(j)ərəˈzeɪʃən, ˌsʌlf(j)əˌraɪˈzeɪʃən

sulfurize
BR 'sʌlfjʊrʌɪz
AM 'sʌlf(j)əˌraɪz

sulfurous
BR 'sʌlf(ə)rəs, 'sʌlfjʊrəs
AM 'sʌlfərəs

sulfury
BR 'sʌlf(ə)ri, 'sʌlfjʊri
AM 'sʌlfəri

Sulgrave
BR 'sʌlgreɪv
AM 'sʌlˌgreɪv

sulk
BR sʌlk, -s, -ɪŋ, -t
AM sʌlk, -s, -ɪŋ, -t

sulker
BR 'sʌlkə(r), -z
AM 'sʌlkər, -z

sulkily
BR 'sʌlkɪli
AM 'sʌlkəli

sulkiness
BR 'sʌlkɪnɪs
AM 'sʌlkɪnɪs

sulky
BR 'sʌlk|i, -ɪə(r), -ɪɪst
AM 'sʌlki, -ər, -ɪst

Sulla
BR 'sʌlə(r), 'sʊlə(r)
AM 'sʊlə

sullage
BR 'sʌlɪdʒ
AM 'sʌlɪdʒ

sullen
BR 'sʌlən, -ɪst
AM 'sʌlən, -ɪst

sullenly
BR 'sʌlənli
AM 'sʌlənli

sullenness
BR 'sʌlənnəs
AM 'sʌlə(n)nəs

Sullivan
BR 'sʌlɪvn
AM 'sʌləvən

Sullom Voe
BR ˌsʌləm 'vəʊ, ˌsuːləm +
AM ˌsʌləm 'voʊ

sully
BR 'sʌl|i, -ɪz, -ɪɪŋ, -ɪd-
AM 'səli, -z, -ɪŋ, -d

sulpha
BR 'sʌlfə(r)
AM 'sʌlfə

sulphadimidine
BR ˌsʌlfəˈdʌɪmɪdiːn
AM ˌsʌlfəˈdaɪməˌdin

sulphamate
BR 'sʌlfəmeɪt
AM 'sʌlfəˌmeɪt

sulphanilamide
BR ˌsʌlfəˈnɪləmʌɪd, -z
AM ˌsʌlfəˈnɪləˌmaɪd, -z

sulphate
BR 'sʌlfeɪt, -s
AM 'sʌlˌfeɪt, -s

sulphide
BR 'sʌlfʌɪd, -z
AM 'sʌlˌfaɪd, -z

sulphite
BR 'sʌlfʌɪt, -s
AM 'sʌlˌfaɪt, -s

sulphonamide
BR sʌlˈfɒnəmʌɪd, -z
AM səlˈfɑnəˌmaɪd, -z

sulphonate
BR 'sʌlfəneɪt
AM 'sʌlfəˌneɪt

sulphonation
BR ˌsʌlfəˈneɪʃn
AM ˌsʌlfəˈneɪʃən

sulphone
BR 'sʌlfəʊn, -z
AM 'sʌlˌfoʊn, -z

sulphonic
BR sʌlˈfɒnɪk
AM səlˈfɑnɪk

sulphur
BR 'sʌlfə(r)
AM 'sʌlfər

sulphurate
BR 'sʌlfjʊreɪt
AM 'sʌlf(j)əˌreɪt

sulphuration
BR ˌsʌlfjʊˈreɪʃn
AM ˌsʌlf(j)əˈreɪʃən

sulphurator
BR 'sʌlfjʊreɪtə(r)
AM 'sʌlf(j)əˌreɪdər

sulphureous
BR sʌlˈfjʊərɪəs, sʌlˈfjɔːrɪəs
AM əlˈf(j)ərɪəs

sulphuretted
BR ˌsʌlfjʊˈretɪd, 'sʌlfjʊretɪd
AM 'sʌlf(j)əˈredəd

sulphuric
BR sʌlˈfjʊərɪk, sʌlˈfjɔːrɪk
AM 'sʌlˈfjurɪk

sulphurisation
BR ˌsʌlfjʊrʌɪˈzeɪʃn
AM ˌsʌlf(j)ərəˈzeɪʃən, ˌsʌlf(j)əˌraɪˈzeɪʃən

sulphurise
BR 'sʌlfjʊrʌɪz, -ɪz, -ɪŋ, -d
AM 'sʌlf(j)əˌraɪz, -ɪz, -ɪŋ, -d

sulphurization
BR ˌsʌlfjʊrʌɪˈzeɪʃn
AM ˌsʌlf(j)ərəˈzeɪʃən, ˌsʌlf(j)əˌraɪˈzeɪʃən

sulphurize
BR 'sʌlfjʊrʌɪz, -ɪz, -ɪŋ, -d
AM 'sʌlf(j)əˌraɪz, -ɪz, -ɪŋ, -d

sulphurous
BR ˈsʌlf(ə)rəs,
ˈsʌlfjʊərəs
AM ˈsəlfərəs

sulphury
BR ˈsʌlf(ə)ri, ˈsʌlfjʊəri
AM ˈsəlfəri

sultan
BR ˈsʌlt(ə)n, -z
AM ˈsəltn̩, -z

sultana
BR s(ə)lˈtɑːnə(r),
ˌsʌlˈtɑːnə(r), -z
AM ˌsəlˈtænə, səlˈtɑːnə,
-z

sultanate
BR ˈsʌltənət, ˈsʌltnət,
ˈsʌltəneɪt, ˈsʌltn̩eɪt, -s
AM ˈsəltn̩ət, ˈsəltn̩eɪt,
-s

sultrily
BR ˈsʌltrɪli
AM ˈsəltrəli

sultriness
BR ˈsʌltrɪnɪs
AM ˈsəltrɪnɪs

sultry
BR ˈsʌltr|i, -ɪə(r), -ɪɪst
AM ˈsəltri, -ər, -ɪɪst

sulu
BR ˈsuːluː, -z
AM ˈsuːlu, -z

sum
BR sʌm, -z, -ɪŋ, -d
AM səm, -z, -ɪŋ, -d

sumac
BR ˈs(j)uːmak,
ˈʃuːmak, -s
AM ˈsuˌmæk, ˈʃuˌmæk,
-s

sumach
BR ˈs(j)uːmak,
ˈʃuːmak, -s
AM ˈsuˌmæk, ˈʃuˌmæk,
-s

Sumatra
BR sʊˈmɑːtrə(r)
AM səˈmɑtrə

Sumatran
BR sʊˈmɑːtr(ə)n, -z
AM səˈmɑtrən, -z

Sumburgh
BR ˈsʌmb(ə)rə(r)
AM ˈsəmˌbərə

Sumer
BR ˈsuːmə(r)
AM ˈsumər

Sumerian
BR ˈs(j)ʊˈmɪərɪən,
s(j)ʊˈmɛːrɪən, -z
AM səˈmɛrɪən,
suˈmɛrɪən, -z

Sumitomo
BR ˌsuːmɪˈtəʊməʊ
AM ˌsuməˈtoʊmoʊ

summa
BR ˈsʌmə(r), ˈsʊmə(r)

summa cum laude
BR ˌsʌmə kʌm ˈlaʊdeɪ,
ˌsʊmə kʊm +
AM ˌsʊmə ˌkʊm ˈlaʊdə,
ˈsʊmə ˌkʊm +,
+ ˈlaʊdi

summarily
BR ˈsʌm(ə)rɪli
AM səˈmɛrəli,
ˈsəmərəli

summariness
BR ˈsʌm(ə)rɪnɪs
AM səˈmɛrɪnɪs,
ˈsəmərɪnɪs

summarisable
BR ˈsʌmərʌɪzəbl
AM ˈsəməˌraɪzəbəl

summarisation
BR ˌsʌmərʌɪˈzeɪʃn
AM ˌsəmərəˈzeɪʃən,
ˌsəməˌraɪˈzeɪʃən

summarise
BR ˈsʌmərʌɪz, -ɪz, -ɪŋ,
-d
AM ˈsəməˌraɪz, -ɪz, -ɪŋ,
-d

summariser
BR ˈsʌmərʌɪzə(r), -z
AM ˈsəməˌraɪzər, -z

summarist
BR ˈsʌmərɪst, -s
AM ˈsəmərəst, -s

summarizable
BR ˈsʌmərʌɪzəbl
AM ˈsəməˌraɪzəbəl

summarization
BR ˌsʌmərʌɪˈzeɪʃn
AM ˌsəmərəˈzeɪʃən,
ˌsəməˌraɪˈzeɪʃən

summarize
BR ˈsʌmərʌɪz, -ɪz, -ɪŋ,
-d
AM ˈsəməˌraɪz, -ɪz, -ɪŋ,
-d

summarizer
BR ˈsʌmərʌɪzə(r), -z
AM ˈsəməˌraɪzər, -z

summary
BR ˈsʌm(ə)r|i, -ɪz
AM ˈsəməri, -z

summation
BR sʌˈmeɪʃn,
səˈmeɪʃn, -z
AM səˈmeɪʃən, -z

summational
BR səˈmeɪʃn̩(ə)l,
səˈmeɪʃən(ə)l
AM səˈmeɪʃ(ə)nəl

summer
BR ˈsʌmə(r), -z
AM ˈsəmər, -z

Summerfield
BR ˈsʌməfiːld
AM ˈsəmərˌfild

Summerhayes
BR ˈsʌməheɪz
AM ˈsəmərˌ(h)eɪz

Summerhill
BR ˈsʌməhɪl
AM ˈsəmərˌ(h)ɪl

summerhouse
BR ˈsʌməhaʊ|s, -zɪz
AM ˈsəmərˌ(h)aʊ|s,
-zəz

summerise
BR ˈsʌmərʌɪz, -ɪz, -ɪŋ,
-d
AM ˈsəməˌraɪz, -ɪz, -ɪŋ,
-d

summerize
BR ˈsʌmərʌɪz, -ɪz, -ɪŋ,
-d
AM ˈsəməˌraɪz, -ɪz, -ɪŋ,
-d

summerless
BR ˈsʌmələs
AM ˈsəmərləs

summerly
BR ˈsʌməli
AM ˈsəmərli

Summers
BR ˈsʌməz
AM ˈsəmərz

summersault
BR ˈsʌməsɔːlt,
ˈsʌməsɒlt, -s, -ɪŋ, -ɪd
AM ˈsəmərˌsɔlt,
ˈsəmərˌsɑlt, -ts, -dɪŋ,
-dəd

summertime
BR ˈsʌmətʌɪm
AM ˈsəmərˌtaɪm

summer-weight
BR ˈsʌməweɪt
AM ˈsəmərˌweɪt

summery
BR ˈsʌm(ə)ri
AM ˈsəməri

summings-up
BR ˌsʌmɪŋzˈʌp
AM ˌsəmɪŋzˈəp

summing-up
BR ˌsʌmɪŋˈʌp
AM ˌsəmɪŋˈəp

summit
BR ˈsʌmɪt, -s
AM ˈsəmət, -s

summiteer
BR ˌsʌmɪˈtɪə(r), -z
AM ˌsəməˌtɪ(ə)r, -z

summitless
BR ˈsʌmɪtlɪs
AM ˈsəmətləs

summitry
BR ˈsʌmɪtri
AM ˈsəmətri

summon
BR ˈsʌmən, -z, -ɪŋ, -d
AM ˈsəmən, -z, -ɪŋ, -d

summonable
BR ˈsʌmənəbl
AM ˈsəmənəbəl

summoner
BR ˈsʌmənə(r), -z
AM ˈsəmənər, -z

summons
BR ˈsʌmənz, -ɪz, -ɪŋ, -d
AM ˈsəmənz, -ɪz, -ɪŋ, -d

summum bonum
BR ˌsʌmem ˈbəʊnəm,
ˌsʊməm +, + ˈbɒnəm
AM ˈsʊməm ˈboʊnəm,
ˈsʊməm +

Sumner
BR ˈsʌmnə(r)
AM ˈsəmnər

sumo
BR ˈsuːməʊ
AM ˈsumoʊ

sump
BR sʌmp, -s
AM səmp, -s

sumpter
BR ˈsʌm(p)tə(r), -z
AM ˈsəm(p)tər, -z

sumptuary
BR ˈsʌm(p)tʃʊəri,
ˈsʌmtʃʊri,
ˈsʌm(p)tjʊəri,
ˈsʌm(p)tjʊri
AM ˈsəm(p)(t)ʃəˌwɛri

sumptuosity
BR ˌsʌm(p)tʃʊˈɒsɪti,
ˌsʌm(p)tjʊˈɒsɪti
AM ˌsəm(p)(t)ʃəˈwɑsədi

sumptuous
BR ˈsʌm(p)tʃʊəs,
ˈsʌm(p)tjʊəs
AM ˈsəm(p)(t)ʃ(əw)əs

sumptuously
BR ˈsʌm(p)tʃʊəsli,
ˈsʌm(p)tjʊəsli
AM ˈsəm(p)(t)ʃ(əw)əsli

sumptuousness
BR ˈsʌm(p)tʃʊəsnəs,
ˈsʌm(p)tjʊəsnəs
AM ˈsəm(p)(t)ʃ(əw)əsnəs

Sumter
BR ˈsʌmtə(r)
AM ˈsəmtər

sun
BR sʌn, -z, -ɪŋ, -d
AM sən, -z, -ɪŋ, -d

sun-baked
BR ˈsʌnbeɪkt
AM ˈsənˌbeɪkt

sunbathe
BR ˈsʌnbeɪð, -z, -ɪŋ, -d
AM ˈsənˌbeɪð, -z, -ɪŋ, -d

sunbather
BR ˈsʌnbeɪðə(r), -z
AM ˈsənˌbeɪðər, -z

sunbeam
BR ˈsʌnbiːm, -z
AM ˈsənˌbim, -z

sunbed
BR ˈsʌnbɛd, -z
AM ˈsənˌbɛd, -z

Sunbelt
BR ˈsʌnbɛlt

sunbird
BR ˈsʌnbɜːd, -z
AM ˈsʌnˌbɝd, -z

sunblind
BR ˈsʌnblʌɪnd, -z
AM ˈsʌnˌblaɪnd, -z

sunblock
BR ˈsʌnblɒk, -s
AM ˈsʌnˌblɑk, -s

sunbonnet
BR ˈsʌnˌbɒnɪt, -s
AM ˈsʌnˌbɑnət, -s

sunbow
BR ˈsʌnbəʊ, -z
AM ˈsʌnˌboʊ, -z

sunburn
BR ˈsʌnbɜːn, -d
AM ˈsʌnˌbɝn, -d

sunburnt
BR ˈsʌnbɜːnt
AM ˈsʌnˌbɝnt

sunburst
BR ˈsʌnbɜːst, -s
AM ˈsʌnˌbɝst, -s

Sunbury
BR ˈsʌnb(ə)ri
AM ˈsʌnˌbɛri, ˈsʌnbəri

Sun City
BR ˌsʌn ˈsɪti
AM ˌsʌn ˈsɪdi

Sunda
BR ˈsʌndə(r),
ˈsʊndə(r)
AM ˈsʌndə

sundae
BR ˈsʌnd|eɪ, ˈsʌnd|i,
-eɪz\-ɪz
AM ˈsʌnˌdeɪ, -z

Sundanese
BR ˌsʌndəˈniːz
AM ˌsʌndəˈniz

Sunday
BR ˈsʌnd|eɪ, ˈsʌnd|i,
-eɪz\-ɪz
AM ˈsʌnˌdeɪ, ˈsʌndi, -z

Sunday best
BR ˌsʌndeɪ ˈbɛst,
ˌsʌndi +
AM ˈsʌnˌdeɪ ˈbɛst,
ˈsʌndi +

Sunday school
BR ˈsʌndeɪ ˌskuːl,
ˈsʌndi +, -z
AM ˈsʌnˌdeɪ ˌskul,
ˈsʌndi +, -z

sundeck
BR ˈsʌndɛk, -s
AM ˈsʌnˌdɛk, -s

sunder
BR ˈsʌnd|ə(r), -əz,
-(ə)rɪŋ, -əd
AM ˈsʌnd|ər, -ərz,
-(ə)rɪŋ, -ərd

Sunderland
BR ˈsʌndələnd
AM ˈsʌndərlənd

sundew
BR ˈsʌndjuː, -z
AM ˈsʌnˌd(j)u, -z

sundial
BR ˈsʌnˌdʌɪəl, -z
AM ˈsʌnˌdaɪəl, -z

sundown
BR ˈsʌndaʊn
AM ˈsʌnˌdaʊn

sundowner
BR ˈsʌnˌdaʊnə(r), -z
AM ˈsʌnˌdaʊnər, -z

sundrenched
BR ˈsʌndrɛn(t)ʃt
AM ˈsʌnˌdrɛn(t)ʃt

sundress
BR ˈsʌndrɛs, -ɪz
AM ˈsʌnˌdrɛs, -əz

sun-dried
BR ˈsʌndrʌɪd,
ˌsʌnˈdrʌɪd
AM ˈsʌnˌdraɪd

sundriesman
BR ˈsʌndrɪzmən
AM ˈsʌndriz̩ˌmæn

sundriesmen
BR ˈsʌndrɪzmən
AM ˈsʌndriz̩ˌmɛn

sundry
noun, adjective
'various'
BR ˈsʌndr|i, -ɪz
AM ˈsʌndri, -z

sunfast
BR ˈsʌnfɑːst, ˈsʌnfast
AM ˈsʌnˌfæst

sunfish
BR ˈsʌnfɪʃ, -ɪz
AM ˈsʌnˌfɪʃ, -ɪz

sunflower
BR ˈsʌnˌflaʊə(r), -z
AM ˈsʌnˌflaʊər, -z

sung
BR ˈsʌŋ
AM ˈsʌŋ

sunglasses
BR ˈsʌnˌglɑːsɪz,
ˈsʌnˌglasɪz
AM ˈsʌnˌglæsəz

sun-god
BR ˈsʌnɡɒd, -z
AM ˈsʌnˌɡɑd, -z

sunhat
BR ˈsʌnhat, -s
AM ˈsʌnˌ(h)æt, -s

sunk
BR ˈsʌŋk
AM ˈsʌŋk

sunken
BR ˈsʌŋk(ə)n
AM ˈsʌŋkən

Sunkist
BR ˈsʌnkɪst
AM ˈsʌnˌkɪst

sunlamp
BR ˈsʌnlamp, -s
AM ˈsʌnˌlæmp, -s

sunless
BR ˈsʌnləs
AM ˈsʌnləs

sunlessness
BR ˈsʌnləsnəs
AM ˈsʌnələsnəs

sunlight
BR ˈsʌnlʌɪt
AM ˈsʌnˌlaɪt

sunlike
BR ˈsʌnlʌɪk
AM ˈsʌnˌlaɪk

sunlit
BR ˈsʌnlɪt
AM ˈsʌnˌlɪt

sunlounger
BR ˈsʌnˌlaʊn(d)ʒə(r),
-z
AM ˈsʌnˌlaʊndʒər, -z

sun-lover
BR ˈsʌnˌlʌvə(r), -z
AM ˈsʌnˌləvər, -z

sunn
BR ˈsʌn
AM ˈsʌn

Sunna
BR ˈsʊnə(r), ˈsʌnə(r)
AM ˈsʌnə, ˈsʊnə

Sunni
BR ˈsʊn|i, ˈsʌn|i, -ɪz
AM ˈsʊni, -z

sunnily
BR ˈsʌnɪli
AM ˈsʌnəli

sunniness
BR ˈsʌnɪnɪs
AM ˈsʌnɪnɪs

Sunningdale
BR ˈsʌnɪŋdeɪl
AM ˈsʌnɪŋˌdeɪl

Sunnite
BR ˈsʊnʌɪt, ˈsʌnʌɪt, -s
AM ˈsəˌnaɪt, -s

sunny
BR ˈsʌn|i, -ɪə(r), -ɪɪst
AM ˈsʌni, -ər, -ɪst

sunproof
BR ˈsʌnpruːf
AM ˈsʌnˌpruf

sunray
BR ˈsʌnreɪ, -z
AM ˈsʌnˌreɪ, -z

sunrise
BR ˈsʌnrʌɪz, -ɪz
AM ˈsʌnˌraɪz, -ɪz

sunroof
BR ˈsʌnruːf, ˈsʌnrʊf, -s
AM ˈsʌnˌruf, -s

sunroom
BR ˈsʌnruːm, ˈsʌnrʊm,
-z
AM ˈsʌnˌrum,
ˈsʌnˌrʊm, -z

sunscreen
BR ˈsʌnskriːn
AM ˈsʌnˌskrin

sunset
BR ˈsʌnsɛt, -s
AM ˈsʌnˌsɛt, -s

sunshade
BR ˈsʌnʃeɪd, -z
AM ˈsʌnˌʃeɪd, -z

sunshine
BR ˈsʌnʃʌɪn
AM ˈsʌnˌʃaɪn

sunshiny
BR ˈsʌnʃʌɪni
AM ˈsʌnˌʃaɪni

sunspot
BR ˈsʌnspɒt, -s
AM ˈsʌnˌspɑt, -s

sunstar
BR ˈsʌnstɑː(r), -z
AM ˈsʌnˌstɑr, -z

sunstone
BR ˈsʌnstəʊn, -z
AM ˈsʌnˌstoʊn, -z

sunstroke
BR ˈsʌnstrəʊk
AM ˈsʌnˌstroʊk

sunstruck
BR ˈsʌnstrʌk
AM ˈsʌnˌstrʌk

sunsuit
BR ˈsʌns(j)uːt, -s
AM ˈsʌnˌsut, -s

suntan
BR ˈsʌntan, -z, -d
AM ˈsʌnˌtæn, -z, -d

Suntory®
BR sʌnˈtɔːri, ˈsʌntɔːri
AM sʌnˈtɔri

suntrap
BR ˈsʌntrap, -s
AM ˈsʌnˌtræp, -s

sunup
BR ˈsʌnʌp, -s
AM ˈsʌnˌəp, -s

sunward
BR ˈsʌnwəd, -z
AM ˈsʌnwərd, -z

Sun Yat-sen
BR ˌsʊn jatˈsɛn
AM ˌsʊn ˌjætˈsɛn

sup
BR ˈsʌp, -s, -ɪŋ, -t
AM ˈsəp, -s, -ɪŋ, -t

super
BR ˈs(j)uːpə(r)
AM ˈsupər

superable
BR ˈs(j)uːp(ə)rəbl
AM ˈsup(ə)rəbəl

superableness
BR ˈs(j)uːp(ə)rəblnəs
AM ˈsup(ə)rəblnəs

superabound
BR ˌs(j)uːp(ə)rəˈbaʊnd,
-z, -ɪŋ, -ɪd
AM ˌsupərəˈbaʊnd, -z,
-ɪŋ, -əd

superabundance
BR ˌs(j)uːp(ə)rəˈbʌn-
dəns
AM ˈsupərəˈbʌndns

superabundant
BR ˌs(j)uːp(ə)rəˈbʌn-
dənt
AM ˈsupərəˈbʌndnt

superabundantly
BR ˌs(j)uːp(ə)rəˈbʌn-
dəntli
AM ˈsupərəˈbʌndən(t)-
li

superadd
BR ˌs(j)uːpərˈad, -z, -ɪŋ,
-ɪd
AM ˈsupərˈæd, -z, -ɪŋ,
-əd

superaddition
BR ˌs(j)uːpərəˈdɪʃn, -z
AM ˈsupərəˈdɪʃən, -z

superaltar
BR ˈs(j)uːpərˌɔːltə(r),
ˈs(j)uːpərˌɒltə(r), -z
AM ˈsupərˈɔltər,
ˈsupərˈɑltər, -z

superannuable
BR ˌs(j)uːpərˈanjʊəbl
AM ˈsupərˈænjəwəbəl

superannuate
BR ˌs(j)uːpərˈanjʊeɪt,
-s, -ɪŋ, -ɪd
AM ˈsupərˈænjəˌweɪt,
-ts, -dɪŋ, -dɪd

superannuation
BR ˌs(j)uːpərˌanjʊˈeɪʃn
AM ˈsupərˌænjəˈweɪʃən

superaqueous
BR ˌs(j)uːpərˈakwɪəs,
ˌs(j)uːpərˈeɪkwɪəs
AM ˈsupərˈɑkwɪəs,
ˌsupərˈækwɪəs,
ˌsupərˈeɪkwɪəs

superb
BR s(j)uːˈpɜːb,
s(j)ʊˈpɜːb
AM suˈpərb, səˈpərb

superbly
BR s(j)uːˈpɜːbli,
s(j)ʊˈpɜːbli
AM suˈpərbli, səˈpərbli

superbness
BR s(j)uːˈpɜːbnəs,
s(j)ʊˈpɜːbnəs
AM suˈpərbnəs,
səˈpərbnəs

Super Bowl
BR ˈs(j)uːpə bəʊl, -z
AM ˈsupər ˌboʊl, -z

supercalender
BR ˌs(j)uːpəˈkalɪnd|ə(r),
-əz, -(ə)rɪŋ, -əd
AM ˈsupərˈkæləndər,
-z, -ɪŋ, -d

supercargo
BR ˈs(j)uːpəˌkaːgəʊ, -z
AM ˈsupərˌkargoʊ, -z

supercelestial
BR ˌs(j)uːpəsrˈlestɪəl
AM ˈsupərsəˈlestʃəl,
ˌsupərsəˈlesdiəl

supercharge
BR ˈs(j)uːpətʃaːdʒ, -ɪz,
-ɪŋ, -d
AM ˈsupərˌtʃardʒ, -əz,
-ɪŋ, -d

supercharger
BR ˈs(j)uːpəˌtʃaːdʒə(r),
-z
AM ˈsupərˌtʃardʒər, -z

superciliary
BR ˌs(j)uːpəˈsɪlɪəri
AM ˈsupərˈsɪliəri

supercilious
BR ˌs(j)uːpəˈsɪlɪəs
AM ˈsupərˈsɪliəs

superciliously
BR ˌs(j)uːpəˈsɪlɪəsli
AM ˈsupərˈsɪliəsli

superciliousness
BR ˌs(j)uːpəˈsɪlɪəsnəs
AM ˈsupərˈsɪliəsnəs

superclass
BR ˈs(j)uːpəˌklaːs,
ˈs(j)uːpəˈklas, -ɪz
AM ˈsupərˌklæs, -əz

supercolumnar
BR ˌs(j)uːpəkəˈlʌmnə(r)
AM ˈsupərkəˈləmnər

supercolumniation
BR ˌs(j)uːpəkəˌlʌmni-
ˈeɪʃn
AM ˈsupərkəˌləmniˈeɪ-
ʃən

supercomputer
BR ˈs(j)uːpəkəmˌpjuː-
tə(r), -z
AM ˈsupərkəmˌpjudər,
-z

supercomputing
BR ˈs(j)uːpəkəmˌpjuːtɪŋ
AM ˈsupərkəmˌpjudɪŋ

superconducting
BR ˌs(j)uːpəkənˈdʌktɪŋ
AM ˈsupərkənˈdəktɪŋ

superconductive
BR ˌs(j)uːpəkənˈdʌktɪv
AM ˈsupərkənˈdəktɪv

superconductivity
BR ˌs(j)uːpəˌkɒndʌkˈtɪv-
ɪti
AM ˈsupərˌkɑndəkˈtɪv-
ɪdi

superconductor
BR ˈs(j)uːpəkənˌdʌk-
tə(r), -z
AM ˈsupərkənˌdəktər,
-z

superconscious
BR ˌs(j)uːpəˈkɒnʃəs
AM ˈsupərˈkɑnʃəs

superconsciously
BR ˌs(j)uːpəˈkɒnʃəsli
AM ˈsupərˈkɑnʃəsli

**superconscious-
ness**
BR ˌs(j)uːpəˈkɒnʃəsnəs
AM ˈsupərˈkɑnʃəsnəs

supercontinent
BR ˈs(j)uːpəˌkɒntɪnənt,
-s
AM ˈsupərˌkɑntnənt, -s

supercool
BR ˌs(j)uːpəˈkuːl,
ˈs(j)uːpəkuːl, -z, -ɪŋ, -d
AM ˈsupərˈkul, -z, -ɪŋ, -d

supercritical
BR ˌs(j)uːpəˈkrɪtɪkl
AM ˈsupərˈkrɪdɪkəl

superduper
BR ˌs(j)uːpəˈduːpə(r)
AM ˈsupərˈdupər

superego
BR ˌs(j)uːpərˌiːgəʊ, -z
AM ˈsupərˈigoʊ, -z

superelevation
BR ˌs(j)uːpərˌelɪˈveɪʃn,
-z
AM ˈsupərˌeləˈveɪʃən,
-z

supereminence
BR ˌs(j)uːpərˈemɪnəns,
-ɪz
AM ˈsupərˈemənəns,
-əz

supereminent
BR ˌs(j)uːpərˈemɪnənt
AM ˈsupərˈemənənt

supereminently
BR ˌs(j)uːpərˈemɪnəntli
AM ˈsupərˈemənən(t)li

supererogation
BR ˌs(j)uːpərˌerəˈgeɪʃn
AM ˈsupərˌerəˈgeɪʃən

supererogatory
BR ˌs(j)uːpərɪˈrɒgət(ə)ri
AM ˈsupərəˈragəˌtori

superexcellence
BR ˌs(j)uːpərˈeksələns,
ˌs(j)uːpərˈeksəlns,
ˌs(j)uːpərˈeksl(ə)ns
AM ˈsupərˈeksələns

superexcellent
BR ˌs(j)uːpərˈeksələnt,
ˌs(j)uːpərˈeksəlnt,
ˌs(j)uːpərˈeksl(ə)nt
AM ˈsupərˈeks(ə)lənt

superexcellently
BR ˌs(j)uːpərˈeksələntli,
ˌs(j)uːpərˈeksəlntli,
ˌs(j)uːpərˈeksl(ə)ntli
AM ˈsupərˈeks(ə)lən(t)li

superfamily
BR ˌs(j)uːpəˈfam(ɪ)l|i,
ˈs(j)uːpəˌfam]|i, -ɪz
AM ˈsupərˈfæm(ə)li, -z

superfatted
BR ˌs(j)uːpəˈfatɪd
AM ˈsupərˈfædəd

superfecta
BR ˌs(j)uːpəˈfektə(r)
AM ˈsupərˈfektə

superfecundation
BR ˌs(j)uːpəˌfɛk(ə)n-
ˈdeɪʃn,
ˌs(j)uːpəˌfɛkənˈdeɪʃn,
ˌs(j)uːpəˌfiːk(ə)nˈdeɪʃn,
ˌs(j)uːpəˌfiːkʌnˈdeɪʃn,
-z
AM ˈsupərˌfɛkənˈdeɪʃən,
-z

superfetation
BR ˌs(j)uːpəfiːˈteɪʃn, -z
AM ˈsupərˌfiˈteɪʃən, -z

superficial
BR ˌs(j)uːpəˈfɪʃl
AM ˈsupərˈfɪʃəl

superficiality
BR ˌs(j)uːpəˌfɪʃɪˈalɪt|i,
-ɪz
AM ˈsupərˌfɪʃiˈælədi, -z

superficially
BR ˌs(j)uːpəˈfɪʃ|li,
ˌs(j)uːpəˈfɪʃəli
AM ˈsupərˈfɪʃəli

superficialness
BR ˌs(j)uːpəˈfɪʃlnəs
AM ˈsupərˈfɪʃəlnəs

superficies
BR ˌs(j)uːpəˈfɪʃ(ɪ)iːz
AM ˈsupərˈfɪʃiz

superfine
BR ˈs(j)uːpəfʌɪn,
ˌs(j)uːpəˈfʌɪn
AM ˈsupərˈfaɪn

superfluid
BR ˈs(j)uːpəˌfluːɪd, -z
AM ˈsupərˌflu(w)əd, -z

superfluidity
BR ˌs(j)uːpəflu:ˈɪdɪti
AM ˈsupərˌfluˈɪdɪdi

superfluity
BR ˌs(j)uːpəˈfluːɪt|i, -ɪz
AM ˈsupərˈfluədi, -z

superfluous
BR s(j)uːˈpɜːfluəs,
s(j)ʊˈpɜːfluəs
AM suˈpərfləwəs

superfluously
BR s(j)uːˈpɜːfluəsli,
s(j)ʊˈpɜːfluəsli
AM suˈpərfləwəsli

superfluousness
BR s(j)uːˈpɜːfluəsnəs,
s(j)ʊˈpɜːfluəsnəs
AM suˈpərfləwəsnəs

supergiant
BR ˈs(j)uːpəˌdʒʌɪənt, -s
AM ˈsupərˌdʒaɪənt, -s

superglue
BR ˈs(j)uːpəgluː, -z, -ɪŋ,
-d
AM ˈsupərˌglu, -z, -ɪŋ, -d

supergrass
BR ˈs(j)uːpəgraːs,
ˈs(j)uːpəgras, -ɪz
AM ˈsupərˌgræs, -əz

supergun
BR ˈs(j)uːpəgʌn, -z
AM ˈsupərˌgən, -z

superheat
BR ˌs(j)uːpəˈhiːt, -s, -ɪŋ, -ɪd
AM ˌsupərˈhiːt, -ts, -dɪŋ, -dɪd

superheater
BR ˈs(j)uːpəˌhiːtə(r), -z
AM ˈsupərˌhidər, -z

superhero
BR ˈs(j)uːpəˌhɪərəʊ, -z
AM ˈsupərˌ(h)ɪroʊ, -z

superhet
BR ˈs(j)uːpəhɛt, -s
AM ˈsupərˌ(h)ɛt, -s

superheterodyne
BR ˌs(j)uːpəˈhɛt(ə)rəˌdaɪn, -z
AM ˌsupərˈhɛdərəˌdaɪn, -z

superhighway
BR ˈs(j)uːpəˌhaɪweɪ, -z
AM ˈsupərˌhaɪˌweɪ, -z

superhuman
BR ˌs(j)uːpəˈhjuːmən
AM ˌsupərˈ(h)jumən

superhumanly
BR ˌs(j)uːpəˈhjuːmənli
AM ˌsupərˈ(h)jumənli

superhumeral
BR ˌs(j)uːpəˈhjuːm(ə)rəl, ˌs(j)uːpəˈhjuːm(ə)rl̩, -z
AM ˌsupərˈ(h)jumərəl, -z

superimpose
BR ˌs(j)uːp(ə)rɪmˈpəʊz, -ɪz, -ɪŋ, -d
AM ˌsup(ə)rəmˈpoʊz, -əz, -ɪŋ, -d

superimposition
BR ˌs(j)uːpərˌɪmpəˈzɪʃn, -z
AM ˌsup(ə)rəmpəˈzɪʃən, -z

superincumbent
BR ˌs(j)uːp(ə)rɪnˈkʌmb(ə)nt
AM ˌsup(ə)rɪnˈkəmbənt, ˌsup(ə)rɪŋˈkəmbənt

superinduce
BR ˌs(j)uːp(ə)rɪnˈdjuːs, ˌs(j)uːp(ə)rɪnˈdʒuːs, -ɪz, -ɪŋ, -t
AM ˌsup(ə)rɪnˈd(j)us, -əz, -ɪŋ, -t

superintend
BR ˌs(j)uːp(ə)rɪnˈtɛnd, -z, -ɪŋ, -ɪd
AM ˌsup(ə)r(ə)nˈtɛnd, -z, -ɪŋ, -əd

superintendence
BR ˌs(j)uːp(ə)rɪnˈtɛnd(ə)ns
AM ˌsup(ə)r(ə)nˈtɛndəns

superintendency
BR ˌs(j)uːp(ə)rɪnˈtɛnd(ə)nsi
AM ˌsup(ə)r(ə)nˈtɛndnsi

superintendent
BR ˌs(j)uːp(ə)rɪnˈtɛnd(ə)nt, -s
AM ˌsup(ə)rɪnˈtɛndənt, -s

superior
BR ˌs(j)uːˈpɪərɪə(r), ˌs(j)ʊˈpɪərɪə(r), -z
AM səˈpɪriər, -z

superioress
BR ˌs(j)uːˈpɪərɪərɪs, ˌs(j)ʊˈpɪərɪərɪs, -ɪz
AM səˈpɪriəˌrɛs, -əz

superiority
BR ˌs(j)uːˌpɪərɪˈɒrɪti, ˌs(j)ʊˌpɪərɪˈɒrɪti
AM səˌpɪriˈɔrədi

superiorly
BR ˌs(j)uːˈpɪərɪəli, ˌs(j)ʊˈpɪərɪəli
AM səˈpɪriərli

superjacent
BR ˌs(j)uːpəˈdʒeɪs(ə)nt
AM ˌsupərˈdʒeɪsənt

superlative
BR ˌs(j)uːˈpɜːlətɪv, ˌs(j)ʊˈpɜːlətɪv, -z
AM səˈpərlədɪv, -z

superlatively
BR ˌs(j)uːˈpɜːlətɪvli, ˌs(j)ʊˈpɜːlətɪvli
AM səˈpərlədɪvli

superlativeness
BR ˌs(j)uːˈpɜːlətɪvnɪs, ˌs(j)ʊˈpɜːlətɪvnɪs
AM səˈpərlədɪvnɪs

superluminal
BR ˌs(j)uːpəˈl(j)uːmɪnl̩
AM ˌsupərˈlumənəl

superlunary
BR ˌs(j)uːpəˈluːn(ə)ri
AM ˌsupərˈlunəri

Superman
BR ˈs(j)uːpəmæn
AM ˈsupərˌmæn

supermarket
BR ˈs(j)uːpəˌmɑːkɪt, -s
AM ˈsupərˌmɑrkət, -s

supermen
BR ˈs(j)uːpəmɛn
AM ˈsupərˌmɛn

supermini
BR ˈs(j)uːpəˌmɪnˌl̩i, -ɪz
AM ˈsupərˌmɪni, -z

supermodel
BR ˈs(j)uːpəˌmɒdl̩, -z
AM ˈsupərˌmɑdəl, -z

supermundane
BR ˌs(j)uːpəmʌnˈdeɪn
AM ˌsupərˌmənˈdeɪn

supernacular
BR ˌs(j)uːpəˈnakjələ(r)
AM ˌsupərˈnækjələr

supernaculum
BR ˌs(j)uːpəˈnakjələm
AM ˌsupərˈnækjələm

supernal
BR ˌs(j)uːˈpɜːnl̩, ˌs(j)ʊˈpɜːnl̩
AM səˈpərnəl

supernally
BR ˌs(j)uːˈpɜːnl̩i, ˌs(j)uːˈpɜːnəli, ˌs(j)ʊˈpɜːnl̩i, ˌs(j)ʊˈpɜːnəli
AM səˈpərnəli

supernatant
BR ˌs(j)uːpəˈneɪt(ə)nt, -s
AM ˌsupərˈneɪtnt, -s

supernatural
BR ˌs(j)uːpəˈnatʃ(ə)rəl, ˌs(j)uːpəˈnatʃ(ə)rl̩
AM ˌsupərˈnætʃ(ə)rəl

supernaturalise
BR ˌs(j)uːpəˈnatʃ(ə)rəlˌʌɪz, ˌs(j)uːpəˈnatʃ(ə)rl̩ˌʌɪz, -ɪz, -ɪŋ, -d
AM ˌsupərˈnætʃ(ə)rəˌlaɪz, -ɪz, -ɪŋ, -d

supernaturalism
BR ˌs(j)uːpəˈnatʃ(ə)rəlˌɪz(ə)m, ˌs(j)uːpəˈnatʃ(ə)rl̩ˌɪz(ə)m
AM ˌsupərˈnætʃ(ə)rəˌlɪzəm

supernaturalist
BR ˌs(j)uːpəˈnatʃ(ə)rəlˌɪst, ˌs(j)uːpəˈnatʃ(ə)rl̩ɪst, -s
AM ˌsupərˈnætʃ(ə)rəlˌəst, -s

supernaturalize
BR ˌs(j)uːpəˈnatʃ(ə)rəlˌʌɪz, ˌs(j)uːpəˈnatʃ(ə)rl̩ˌʌɪz, -ɪz, -ɪŋ, -d
AM ˌsupərˈnætʃ(ə)rəˌlaɪz, -ɪz, -ɪŋ, -d

supernaturally
BR ˌs(j)uːpəˈnatʃ(ə)rəli, ˌs(j)uːpəˈnatʃ(ə)rl̩i
AM ˌsupərˈnætʃ(ə)rəli

supernaturalness
BR ˌs(j)uːpəˈnatʃ(ə)rəlˌnəs, ˌs(j)uːpəˈnatʃ(ə)rl̩nəs
AM ˌsupərˈnætʃ(ə)rəlˌnəs

supernormal
BR ˌs(j)uːpəˈnɔːml̩
AM ˌsupərˈnɔrml̩

supernormality
BR ˌs(j)uːpənɔːˈmalɪti
AM ˌsupərˌnɔrˈmælədi

supernova
BR ˈs(j)uːpəˌnəʊvə(r), ˌs(j)uːpəˈnəʊvə(r), -z
AM ˌsupərˈnoʊvə, -z

supernovae
BR ˈs(j)uːpəˌnəʊviː, ˌs(j)uːpəˈnəʊviː
AM ˌsupərˈnoʊˌvi

supernumerary
BR ˌs(j)uːpəˈnjuːmər(ər)ˌli, -ɪz
AM ˌsupərˈn(j)uməˌrɛri, -z

superorder
BR ˌs(j)uːpərˌɔːdə(r), -z
AM ˌsupərˌɔrdər, -z

superordinal
BR ˌs(j)uːpərˈɔːdɪnl̩, ˌs(j)uːpərˈɔːdnl̩
AM ˌsupərˈɔrdnl̩

superordinate
BR ˌs(j)uːpərˈɔːdɪnət, ˌs(j)uːpərˈɔːdnət, -s
AM ˌsupərˈɔrd(ə)nət, -s

superphosphate
BR ˈs(j)uːpəˌfɒsfeɪt, -s
AM ˈsupərˌfɑsˌfeɪt, -s

superphysical
BR ˌs(j)uːpəˈfɪzɪkl̩
AM ˌsupərˈfɪzɪkəl

superpose
BR ˌs(j)uːpəˈpəʊz, -ɪz, -ɪŋ, -d
AM ˌsupərˈpoʊz, -əz, -ɪŋ, -d

superposition
BR ˌs(j)uːpəpəˈzɪʃn, -z
AM ˌsuərpəˈzɪʃən, -z

superpower
BR ˈs(j)uːpəˌpaʊə(r), -z
AM ˈsupərˌpaʊər, -z

supersaturate
BR ˌs(j)uːpəˈsatʃ˞eɪt, ˌs(j)uːpəˈsatʃ˞eɪt, -s, -ɪŋ, -ɪd
AM ˌsupərˈsætʃəˌreɪt, -ts, -dɪŋ, -dɪd

supersaturation
BR ˌs(j)uːpəˈsatʃ˞eɪʃn, ˌs(j)uːpəˌsatʃəˈreɪʃn
AM ˌsupərˌsætʃəˈreɪʃən

superscribe
BR ˌs(j)uːpəˈskrʌɪb, ˈs(j)uːpəskrʌɪb, -z, -ɪŋ, -d
AM ˌsupərˈskraɪb, -z, -ɪŋ, -d

superscript
BR ˈs(j)uːpəskrɪpt, -s
AM ˈsupərˌskrɪpt, -s

superscription
BR ˌs(j)uːpəˈskrɪpʃn, -z
AM ˌsupərˈskrɪpʃən, -z

supersede
BR ˌs(j)uːpəˈsiːd, -z, -ɪŋ, -ɪd
AM ˌsupərˈsid, -z, -ɪŋ, -ɪd

supersedence
BR ˌs(j)uːpəˈsiːdns

AM ˌsupərˈsidns

supersedure
BR ˌs(j)uːpəˈsiːdʒə(r)
AM ˌsupərˈsidʒər

supersession
BR ˌs(j)uːpəˈsɛʃn
AM ˌsupərˈsɛʃən

supersonic
BR ˌs(j)uːpəˈsɒnɪk, -s
AM ˌsupərˈsɑnɪk, -s

supersonically
BR ˌs(j)uːpəˈsɒnɪkli
AM ˌsupərˈsɑnək(ə)li

superstar
BR ˈs(j)uːpəstɑː(r), -z
AM ˈsupərˌstɑr, -z

superstardom
BR ˈs(j)uːpəstɑːdəm
AM ˈsupərˌstɑrdəm

superstate
BR ˈs(j)uːpəsteɪt, -s
AM ˈsupərˌsteɪt, -s

superstition
BR ˌs(j)uːpəˈstɪʃn, -z
AM ˌsupərˈstɪʃən, -z

superstitious
BR ˌs(j)uːpəˈstɪʃəs
AM ˌsupərˈstɪʃəs

superstitiously
BR ˌs(j)uːpəˈstɪʃəsli
AM ˌsupərˈstɪʃəsli

superstitiousness
BR ˌs(j)uːpəˈstɪʃəsnəs
AM ˌsupərˈstɪʃəsnəs

superstore
BR ˈs(j)uːpəstɔː(r), -z
AM ˈsupərˌstɔ(ə)r, -z

superstrata
BR ˈs(j)uːpəˌstrɑːtə(r),
ˈs(j)uːpəˌstreɪtə(r)
AM ˈsupərˌstreɪdə,
ˈsupərˌstrɑːdə,
ˈsupərˌstrɑːdə

superstrate
BR ˈs(j)uːpəstreɪt, -s
AM ˈsupərˌstreɪt, -s

superstratum
BR ˈs(j)uːpəˌstrɑːtəm,
ˈs(j)uːpəˌstreɪtəm
AM ˈsupərˌstreɪdəm,
ˈsupərˌstrædəm,
ˈsupərˌstrɑːdəm

superstructural
BR ˌs(j)uːpəˈstrʌktʃ(ə)-
rəl,
ˌs(j)uːpəˈstrʌktʃ(ə)r̩l
AM ˌsupərˈstrək(t)ʃ(ə)-
rəl

superstructure
BR ˈs(j)uːpəˌstrʌktʃə(r),
-z
AM ˈsupərˌstrək(t)ʃər,
-z

supersubtle
BR ˌs(j)uːpəˈsʌtl
AM ˌsupərˈsədəl

supersubtlety
BR ˌs(j)uːpəˈsʌtlt̩i, -ɪz

supertanker
BR ˈs(j)uːpəˌtaŋkə(r),
-z
AM ˈsupərˌtæŋkər, -z

supertax
BR ˈs(j)uːpətaks, -ɪz
AM ˈsupərˌtæks, -əz

supertemporal
BR ˌs(j)uːpəˈtɛmp(ə)rəl,
ˌs(j)uːpəˈtɛmp(ə)r̩l
AM ˌsupərˈtɛmp(ə)rəl

superterrene
BR ˌs(j)uːpəˈtɛriːn,
ˌs(j)uːpətəˈriːn
AM ˌsupərtəˈrin

superterrestrial
BR ˌs(j)uːpətɪˈrɛstriəl
AM ˌsupərtəˈrɛstriəl

supertitle
BR ˈs(j)uːpəˌtʌɪtl, -z
AM ˈsupərˌtaɪdəl, -z

supertonic
BR ˈs(j)uːpəˌtɒnɪk, -s
AM ˈsupərˌtɑnɪk, -s

supervene
BR ˌs(j)uːpəˈviːn, -z,
-ɪŋ, -d
AM ˌsupərˈvin, -z, -ɪŋ, -d

supervenient
BR ˌs(j)uːpəˈviːnɪənt
AM ˌsupərˈvinɪənt,
ˌsupərˈvinjənt

supervention
BR ˌs(j)uːpəˈvɛnʃn
AM ˌsupərˈvɛn(t)ʃən

supervise
BR ˈs(j)uːpəvʌɪz, -ɪz,
-ɪŋ, -d
AM ˈsupərˌvaɪz, -ɪz, -ɪŋ,
-d

supervision
BR ˌs(j)uːpəˈvɪʒn
AM ˌsupərˈvɪʒən

supervisor
BR ˈsuːpəvʌɪzə(r), -z
AM ˈsupərˌvaɪzər, -z

supervisory
BR ˌs(j)uːpəˈvʌɪz(ə)ri,
ˈs(j)uːpəvʌɪz(ə)ri
AM ˈsupərˌvaɪzəri

superwoman
BR ˈs(j)uːpəˌwʊmən
AM ˈsupərˌwʊmən

superwomen
BR ˈs(j)uːpəˌwɪmm
AM ˈsupərˌwɪmɪn

supinate
BR ˈs(j)uːpɪneɪt, -s, -ɪŋ,
-ɪd
AM ˈsupəˌneɪt, -ts, -dɪŋ,
-dɪd

supination
BR ˌs(j)uːpɪˈneɪʃn, -z
AM ˌsupəˈneɪʃən, -z

supinator
BR ˈs(j)uːpɪneɪtə(r), -z
AM ˈsupəˌneɪdər, -z

supine
BR ˈs(j)uːpʌɪn
AM ˈsuˌpaɪn

supinely
BR ˈs(j)uːpʌɪnli
AM ˈsuˌpaɪnli

supineness
BR ˈs(j)uːpʌɪnnɪs
AM ˈsuˌpaɪ(n)nɪs

supper
BR ˈsʌpə(r), -z
AM ˈsəpər, -z

supperless
BR ˈsʌpələs
AM ˈsəpərləs

suppertime
BR ˈsʌpətʌɪm, -z
AM ˈsəpərˌtaɪm, -z

supplant
BR səˈplɑːnt, səˈplant,
-s, -ɪŋ, -ɪd
AM səˈplæn|t, -ts, -(t)ɪŋ,
-(t)əd

supplanter
BR səˈplɑːntə(r),
səˈplantə(r), -z
AM səˈplæn(t)ər, -z

supple
BR ˈsʌpl
AM ˈsəpəl

supplejack
BR ˈsʌpldʒak, -s
AM ˈsəpəlˌdʒæk, -s

supplely
BR ˈsʌpl(l)i, ˈsʌpli
AM ˈsəp(ə)li

supplement¹
noun
BR ˈsʌplɪm(ə)nt, -s
AM ˈsəpləmənt, -s

supplement²
verb
BR ˈsʌplɪment, -s, -ɪŋ,
-ɪd
AM ˈsəpləˌmen|t,
ˈsəpləmən|t, -ts, -(t)ɪŋ,
-(t)əd

supplemental
BR ˌsʌplɪˈmentl
AM ˌsəpləˈmen(t)l

supplementally
BR ˌsʌplɪˈmentl̩i,
ˌsʌplɪˈmentəli
AM ˌsəpləˈmen(t)li

supplementarily
BR ˌsʌplɪˈment(ə)rɪli,
ˌsʌplɪˈment(ə)rɪli
AM ˌsəpləˌmenˈtɛrəli

supplementary
BR ˌsʌplɪˈment(ə)r|i,
-ɪz
AM ˌsəpləˈmen(t)əri, -z

supplementation
BR ˌsʌplɪmənˈteɪʃn,
ˌsʌplɪm(ə)nˈteɪʃn
AM ˌsəpləˌmenˈteɪʃən

suppleness
BR ˈsʌplnəs

AM ˈsəpəlnəs

suppletion
BR səˈpliːʃn
AM səˈpliʃən

suppletive
BR səˈpliːtɪv, ˈsʌplɪtɪv,
-z
AM səˈplidɪv, ˈsəplədɪv,
-z

suppliant
BR ˈsʌplɪənt, -s
AM ˈsəplɪənt, -s

suppliantly
BR ˈsʌplɪəntli
AM ˈsəplɪənt(l)li

supplicant
BR ˈsʌplɪk(ə)nt, -s
AM ˈsəpləkənt, -s

supplicate
BR ˈsʌplɪkeɪt, -s, -ɪŋ, -ɪd
AM ˈsəpləˌkeɪt, -ts, -ts,
-dɪŋ, -dɪd

supplication
BR ˌsʌplɪˈkeɪʃn, -z
AM ˌsəpləˈkeɪʃən, -z

supplicatory
BR ˈsʌplɪkət(ə)ri,
ˌsʌplɪˈkeɪt(ə)ri
AM ˈsəpləkəˌtɔri

supplier
BR səˈplʌɪə(r), -z
AM səˈplaɪər, -z

supply
BR səˈplʌɪ, -z, -ɪŋ, -d
AM səˈplaɪ, -z, -ɪŋ, -d

support
BR səˈpɔːt, -s, -ɪŋ, -ɪd
AM səˈpɔ(ə)rt, -ts,
-ˈpɔrdɪŋ, -ˈpɔrdəd

supportability
BR səˌpɔːtəˈbɪlɪti
AM səˌpɔrdəˈbɪlɪdi

supportable
BR səˈpɔːtəbl
AM səˈpɔrdəbəl

supportably
BR səˈpɔːtəbli
AM səˈpɔrdəbli

supporter
BR səˈpɔːtə(r), -z
AM səˈpɔrdər, -z

supportingly
BR səˈpɔːtɪŋli
AM səˈpɔrdɪŋli

supportive
BR səˈpɔːtɪv
AM səˈpɔrdɪv

supportively
BR səˈpɔːtɪvli
AM səˈpɔrdɪvli

supportiveness
BR səˈpɔːtɪvnɪs
AM səˈpɔrdɪvnɪs

supportless
BR səˈpɔːtləs
AM səˈpɔrtləs

supposable
BR sə'pəʊzəbl
AM sə'poʊzəbəl

suppose
BR sə'pəʊz, -ɪz, -ɪŋ, -d
AM sə'poʊz, -əz, -ɪŋ, -d

supposedly
BR sə'pəʊzɪdli
AM sə'poʊzədli

supposition
BR ˌsʌpə'zɪʃn, -z
AM ˌsəpə'zɪʃən, -z

suppositional
BR ˌsʌpə'zɪʃn(ə)l,
ˌsʌpə'zɪʃən(ə)l
AM ˌsəpə'zɪʃ(ə)nəl

suppositionally
BR ˌsʌpə'zɪʃnəli,
ˌsʌpə'zɪʃn̩li,
ˌsʌpə'zɪʃənl̩i,
ˌsʌpə'zɪʃ(ə)nəli
AM ˌsəpə'zɪʃ(ə)nəli

suppositious
BR ˌsʌpə'zɪʃəs
AM ˌsəpə'zɪʃəs

suppositiously
BR ˌsʌpə'zɪʃəsli
AM ˌsəpə'zɪʃəsli

**suppositious-
ness**
BR ˌsʌpə'zɪʃəsnəs
AM ˌsəpə'zɪʃəsnəs

supposititious
BR sə,pɒzɪ'tɪʃəs
AM sə,pɑzə'tɪʃəs

supposititiously
BR sə,pɒzɪ'tɪʃəsli
AM sə,pɑzə'tɪʃəsli

**supposititious-
ness**
BR sə,pɒzɪ'tɪʃəsnəs
AM sə,pɑzə'tɪʃəsnəs

suppository
BR sə'pɒzɪt(ə)r|i, -ɪz
AM sə'pɑzə,tɔri, -z

suppress
BR sə'prɛs, -ɪz, -ɪŋ, -t
AM sə'prɛs, -əz, -ɪŋ, -t

suppressant
BR sə'prɛs(ə)nt, -s
AM sə'prɛsənt, -s

suppressible
BR sə'prɛsɪbl
AM sə'prɛsəbəl

suppression
BR sə'prɛʃn
AM sə'prɛʃən

suppressive
BR sə'prɛsɪv
AM sə'prɛsɪv

suppressor
BR sə'prɛsə(r), -z
AM sə'prɛsər, -z

suppurate
BR 'sʌpjʊreɪt, -s, -ɪŋ,
-ɪd
AM 'səpjə,reɪ|t, -ts,
-dɪŋ, -dɪd

suppuration
BR ˌsʌpjʊ'reɪʃn
AM ˌsəpjə'reɪʃən

suppurative
BR 'sʌpjʊərətɪv
AM 'səpjə,reɪdɪv,
'səp(jə)rədɪv

supra
BR 's(j)uːprə(r)
AM 'suprə

supralapsarian
BR ˌs(j)uːprəlap'sɛːriən,
-z
AM ˌsuprə,læp'sɛriən,
-z

supramaxillary
BR ˌs(j)uːprəmak'sɪl-
(ə)ri
AM ˌsuprə'mæksə,lɛri

supramundane
BR ˌs(j)uːprə'mʌndeɪn
AM ˌsuprə,mən'deɪn

supranational
BR ˌs(j)uːprə'naʃn̩(ə)l,
ˌs(j)uːprə'naʃən(ə)l
AM ˌsuprə'næʃ(ə)nəl

supranationalism
BR ˌs(j)uːprə'naʃn̩əl-
ɪz(ə)m,
ˌs(j)uːprə'naʃn̩ɪz(ə)m,
ˌs(j)uːprə'naʃənlɪz(ə)m,
ˌs(j)uːprə'naʃ(ə)nəl-
ɪz(ə)m
AM ˌsuprə'næʃənl,ɪzəm,
ˌsuprə'næʃnəl,ɪzəm

supranationality
BR ˌs(j)uːprə,naʃ(ə)-
'nalɪti
AM ˌsuprə,næʃə'nælədi

supraorbital
BR ˌs(j)uːprə(r)'ɔːbɪtl
AM ˌsuprə'ɔrbədl

suprarenal
BR ˌs(j)uːprə'riːnl
AM ˌsuprə'rinəl

suprasegmental
BR ˌs(j)uːprəsɛg'mɛntl
AM ˌsuprə,sɛg'mɛn(t)l

supremacism
BR s(j)ʊ'prɛməsɪz(ə)m,
s(j)uː'prɛməsɪz(ə)m
AM sə'prɛmə,sɪzəm,
su'prɛmə,sɪzəm

supremacist
BR s(j)ʊ'prɛməsɪst,
s(j)uː'prɛməsɪst, -s
AM sə'prɛməsəst,
su'prɛməsəst, -s

supremacy
BR s(j)ʊ'prɛməsi,
s(j)uː'prɛməsi
AM sə'prɛməsi,
su'prɛməsi

suprematism
BR s(j)ʊ'prɛmətɪz(ə)m,
s(j)uː'prɛmətɪz(ə)m
AM sə'prɛmə,tɪzəm,
su'prɛmə,tɪzəm

supreme
BR s(j)ʊ'priːm,
s(j)uː'priːm
AM sə'prim, su'prim

suprême
BR s(j)uː'prɛm, -z
AM sʊ'prɛm, -z

supremely
BR s(j)ʊ'priːmli,
s(j)uː'priːmli
AM sə'primli,
su'primli

supremeness
BR s(j)ʊ'priːmnɪs,
s(j)uː'priːmnɪs
AM sə'primnɪs,
su'primnɪs

supremo
BR s(j)ʊ'priːməʊ,
s(j)uː'priːməʊ, -z
AM sə'primoʊ,
su'primoʊ, -z

sura
BR 'sʊərə(r), -z
AM 'surə, -z

Surabaya
BR ˌsʊərə'bʌɪə(r)
AM ˌsurə'baɪə

surah
BR 'sʊərə(r), -z
AM 'surə, -z

surahi
BR sʊ'rɑːh|i, -ɪz
AM sə'rɑhi, -z

sural
BR 's(j)ʊərəl, 's(j)ʊərl̩
AM 'surəl

Surat
BR sʊ'rat, 's(j)ʊərat
AM 'su,ræt

Surbiton
BR 'səːbɪt(ə)n
AM 'sərbətn

surcease
BR səː'siːs, -ɪz, -ɪŋ, -t
AM 'sər,siz, -ɪz, -ɪŋ, -t

surcharge
BR 'səːtʃɑːdʒ, -ɪz, -ɪŋ, -d
AM 'sər,tʃɑrdʒ, -əz, -ɪŋ,
-d

surcingle
BR 'səː,sɪŋgl, -z
AM 'sər,sɪŋgəl, -z

surcoat
BR 'səːkəʊt, -s
AM 'sər,koʊt, -s

surculose
BR 'səːkjʊləʊs
AM 'sərkjə,loʊs,
'sərkjə,loʊz

surd
BR səːd, -z
AM sərd, -z

surdity
BR 'səːdɪti
AM 'sərdədi

sure
BR ʃʊə(r), ʃɔː(r), -ə(r),
-ɪst
AM ʃʊ(ə)r, -ər, -əst

sure-enough
BR ˌʃʊərɪ'nʌf,
ˌʃɔːrɪ'nʌf
AM ˌʃʊr(ə)'nəf

surefire
BR 'ʃʊə,fʌɪə(r),
'ʃɔː,fʌɪə(r)
AM 'ʃʊr'faɪ(ə)r

surefooted
BR ˌʃʊə'fʊtɪd, ˌʃɔː'fʊtɪd
AM 'ʃʊr'fʊdəd

surefootedly
BR ˌʃʊə'fʊtɪdli,
ˌʃɔː'fʊtɪdli
AM 'ʃʊr'fʊdədli

surefootedness
BR ˌʃɔː'fʊtɪdnɪs,
ˌʃʊə'fʊtɪdnɪs
AM 'ʃʊr'fʊdədnəs

surehanded
BR ˌʃʊə'handɪd,
ˌʃɔː'handɪd
AM 'ʃʊr'hæn(d)əd

surehandedly
BR ˌʃʊə'handɪdli,
ˌʃɔː'handɪdli
AM 'ʃʊr'hæn(d)ədli

surehandedness
BR ˌʃʊə'handɪdnɪs,
ˌʃɔː'handɪdnɪs
AM 'ʃʊr'hæn(d)ədnəs

surely
BR 'ʃʊəli, 'ʃɔːli
AM 'ʃʊrli

sureness
BR 'ʃʊənəs, 'ʃɔːnəs
AM 'ʃʊrnəs

surety
BR 'ʃʊərɪt|i, 'ʃɔːrɪti, -ɪz
AM 'ʃʊrədi, -z

suretyship
BR 'ʃʊərɪti,ʃɪp,
'ʃɔːrɪti,ʃɪp
AM 'ʃʊrədi,ʃɪp

surf
BR səːf, -s, -ɪŋ, -t
AM sərf, -s, -ɪŋ, -t

surface
BR 'səːfɪs, -ɪz, -ɪŋ, -t
AM 'sərfəs, -əz, -ɪŋ, -t

surfacer
BR 'səːfɪsə(r), -z
AM 'sərfəsər, -z

surface-to-air
BR ,səːfɪstʊ'ɛː(r)
AM ,sərfəstə'ɛ(ə)r

**surface-to-
surface**
BR ,səːfɪstə'səːfɪs
AM ,sərfəstə'sərfəs

surfactant
BR səː'fakt(ə)nt
AM sər'fæktənt

surfbird
BR ˈsəːfbɜːd, -z
AM ˈsərfˌbɜrd, -z

surfboard
BR ˈsəːfbɜːd, -z
AM ˈsərfˌbɔ(ə)rd, -z

surfboat
BR ˈsəːfbəʊt, -s
AM ˈsərfˌboʊt, -s

surfeit
BR ˈsəːfɪt, -s, -ɪŋ, -ɪd
AM ˈsərfə|t, -ts, -dɪŋ, -dəd

surfer
BR ˈsəːfə(r), -z
AM ˈsərfər, -z

surficial
BR səːˈfɪʃl
AM sərˈfɪʃəl

surficially
BR səːˈfɪʃli, səːˈfɪʃəli
AM sərˈfɪʃəli

surfy
BR ˈsəːfˌli, -ɪə(r), -ɪɪst
AM ˈsərfi, -ər, -ɪst

surge
BR səːdʒ, -ɪz, -ɪŋ, -d
AM sərdʒ, -əz, -ɪŋ, -d

surgeon
BR ˈsəːdʒ(ə)n, -z
AM ˈsərdʒən, -z

surgery
BR ˈsəːdʒ(ə)r|i, -ɪz
AM ˈsərdʒ(ə)ri, -z

surgical
BR ˈsəːdʒɪkl
AM ˈsərdʒəkəl

surgically
BR ˈsəːdʒɪkli
AM ˈsərdʒək(ə)li

suricate
BR ˈs(j)ʊərɪkeɪt, -s
AM ˈʃʊrəˌkeɪt, -s

Surinam
BR ˈs(j)ʊərɪnam
AM ˈsʊrəˌnæm, ˈsʊrəˌnɑm

Suriname
BR ˈs(j)ʊərɪnam
AM ˈsʊrəˌnæm, ˈsʊrəˌnɑm

Surinamer
BR ˌs(j)ʊərɪˈnɑːmə(r), -z
AM ˈsʊrəˌnæmər, ˈsʊrəˌnɑmər, -z

Surinamese
BR ˌs(j)ʊərɪnəˈmiːz
AM ˌsʊrənəˈmiz

surlily
BR ˈsəːlɪli
AM ˈsərləli

surliness
BR ˈsəːlmɪs
AM ˈsərlinɪs

surly
BR ˈsəːl|i, -ɪə(r), -ɪɪst
AM ˈsərli, -ər, -ɪst

surmise[1]
noun
BR səˈmaɪz, ˈsəːmaɪz, -ɪz
AM sərˈmaɪz, ˈsərˌmaɪz, -ɪz

surmise[2]
verb
BR səˈmaɪz, -ɪz, -ɪŋ, -d
AM sərˈmaɪz, -ɪz, -ɪŋ, -d

surmount
BR səˈmaʊnt, -s, -ɪŋ, -ɪd
AM sərˈmaʊn|t, -ts, -(t)ɪŋ, -(t)əd

surmountable
BR səˈmaʊntəbl
AM sərˈmaʊn(t)əbəl

surmullet
BR səːˈmʌlɪt
AM sərˈmələt

surname
BR ˈsəːneɪm, -z, -d
AM ˈsərˌneɪm, -z, -d

surpass
BR səˈpɑːs, səˈpas, -ɪz, -ɪŋ, -t
AM sərˈpæs, -əz, -ɪŋ, -t

surpassable
BR səˈpɑːsəbl, səˈpasəbl
AM sərˈpæsəbəl

surpassing
BR səˈpɑːsɪŋ, səˈpasɪŋ
AM sərˈpæsɪŋ

surpassingly
BR səˈpɑːsɪŋli, səˈpasɪŋli
AM sərˈpæsɪŋli

surplice
BR ˈsəːplɪs, -ɪz, -t
AM ˈsərpləs, -əz, -t

surplus
BR ˈsəːpləs, -ɪz
AM ˈsərpləs, -əz

surplusage
BR ˈsəːpləsɪdʒ
AM ˈsərpləsɪdʒ

surprise
BR səˈpraɪz, -ɪz, -ɪŋ, -d
AM sə(r)ˈpraɪz, -ɪz, -ɪŋ, -d

surprisedly
BR səˈpraɪz(ɪ)dli
AM sə(r)ˈpraɪz(ɪ)dli

surprising
BR səˈpraɪzɪŋ
AM sə(r)ˈpraɪzɪŋ

surprisingly
BR səˈpraɪzɪŋli
AM sə(r)ˈpraɪzɪŋli

surprisingness
BR səˈpraɪzɪŋnɪs
AM sə(r)ˈpraɪzɪŋnɪs

surra
BR ˈsʊərə(r), ˈsʌrə(r)
AM ˈsʊrə, ˈsərə

surreal
BR səˈrɪəl
AM səˈriəl

surrealism
BR səˈrɪəlɪz(ə)m
AM səˈriəˌlɪzəm

surrealist
BR səˈrɪəlɪst, -s
AM səˈriəlɪst, -s

surrealistic
BR səˌrɪəˈlɪstɪk
AM səˌriəˈlɪstɪk, ˌsəriəˈlɪstɪk

surrealistically
BR səˌrɪəˈlɪstɪkli
AM səˌriəˈlɪstɪk(ə)li

surreality
BR ˌsʌrɪˈalɪti
AM ˌsəriˈælədi

surreally
BR səˈrɪəli
AM səˈriəli

surrebuttal
BR ˌsʌrɪˈbʌtl, -z
AM ˌsərəˈbətl, -z

surrebutter
BR ˌsʌrɪˈbʌtə(r), -z
AM ˌsərəˈbədər, -z

surrejoinder
BR ˌsʌrɪˈdʒɔɪndə(r), -z
AM ˌsərəˈdʒɔɪndər, -z

surrender
BR səˈrend|ə(r), -əz, -(ə)rɪŋ, -əd
AM səˈrend|ər, -ərz, -(ə)rɪŋ, -ərd

surreptitious
BR ˌsʌrɪpˈtɪʃəs
AM ˌsərəpˈtɪʃəs

surreptitiously
BR ˌsʌrɪpˈtɪʃəsli
AM ˌsərəpˈtɪʃəsli

surreptitiousness
BR ˌsʌrɪpˈtɪʃəsnəs
AM ˌsərəˈptɪʃəsnəs

surrey
BR ˈsʌr|i, -ɪz
AM ˈsəri, -z

Surridge
BR ˈsʌrɪdʒ
AM ˈsərɪdʒ

surrogacy
BR ˈsʌrəgəs|i, -ɪz
AM ˈsərəgəsi, -z

surrogate
BR ˈsʌrəgət, ˈsʌrəgeɪt, -s
AM ˈsərəgət, ˈsərəˌgeɪt, -s

surrogateship
BR ˈsʌrəgətˌʃɪp, ˈsʌrəgeɪtˌʃɪp, -s
AM ˈsərəgətˌʃɪp, ˈsərəˌgeɪtˌʃɪp, -s

surround
BR səˈraʊnd, -z, -ɪŋ, -ɪd

surround
AM səˈraʊnd, -z, -ɪŋ, -əd

surrounding
BR səˈraʊndɪŋ, -z
AM səˈraʊndɪŋ, -z

surtax
BR ˈsəːtaks, -ɪz
AM ˈsərˌtæks, -əz

Surtees
BR ˈsəːtiːz
AM ˈsərtiz

surtitle
BR ˈsəːˌtʌɪtl, -z
AM ˈsərˈtaɪdəl, -z

surtout
BR ˈsəːtuː, -z
AM ˌsərˈtu(t), -z

Surtsey
BR ˈsəːtsi
AM ˈsərtsi

surveillance
BR səˈveɪləns, səˈveɪlɲs, səːˈveɪləns, səːˈveɪlɲs
AM sərˈveɪləns

survey[1]
noun
BR ˈsəːveɪ, -z
AM ˈsərˌveɪ, -z

survey[2]
verb
BR səˈveɪ, ˈsəːveɪ, -z, -ɪŋ, -d
AM sərˈveɪ, -z, -ɪŋ, -d

surveyor
BR səˈveɪə(r), -z
AM sərˈveɪər, -z

surveyorship
BR səˈveɪəˌʃɪp, -s
AM sərˈveɪərˌʃɪp, -s

survivability
BR səˌvaɪvəˈbɪlɪti
AM sərˌvaɪvəˈbɪlɪdi

survivable
BR səˈvaɪvəbl
AM sərˈvaɪvəbəl

survival
BR səˈvaɪvl, -z
AM sərˈvaɪvəl, -z

survivalism
BR səˈvaɪvˌlɪz(ə)m
AM sərˈvaɪvəˌlɪzəm

survivalist
BR səˈvaɪvlɪst, -s
AM sərˈvaɪvələst, -s

survive
BR səˈvaɪv, -z, -ɪŋ, -d
AM sərˈvaɪv, -z, -ɪŋ, -d

survivor
BR səˈvaɪvə(r), -z
AM sərˈvaɪvər, -z

survivorship
BR səˈvaɪvəˌʃɪp
AM sərˈvaɪvərˌʃɪp

Surya
BR ˈsʊərɪə(r)
AM ˈsʊriə

sus
BR sʌs, -ɪz, -ɪŋ, -t
AM səs, -əz, -ɪŋ, -t

Susa
BR 'suːzə(r), 'suːsə(r)
AM 'suːzə, 'susə

Susan
BR 'suːzn
AM 'suzn

Susanna
BR sʊ'zænə(r)
AM su'zænə

Susannah
BR sʊ'zænə(r)
AM su'zænə

Susanne
BR sʊ'zan
AM su'zæn

susceptibility
BR sə,septɪ'bɪlɪti
AM sə,septə'bɪlɪdi

susceptible
BR sə'septɪbl
AM sə'septəbəl

susceptibly
BR sə'septɪbli
AM sə'septəbli

susceptive
BR sə'septɪv
AM sə'septɪv

sushi
BR 'suːʃi
AM 'suʃi

Susie
BR 'suːzi
AM 'suzi

suslik
BR 'sʊslɪk, 'sʌslɪk, -s
AM 'səs,lɪk, -s

suspect[1]
noun
BR 'sʌspekt, -s
AM 'səs,pek(t), -s

suspect[2]
verb
BR sə'spekt, -s, -ɪŋ, -ɪd
AM sə'spek(t), -(t)s,
-ɪŋ, -təd

suspend
BR sə'spend, -z, -ɪŋ, -ɪd
AM sə'spend, -z, -ɪŋ, -əd

suspender
BR sə'spendə(r), -z
AM sə'spendər, -z

suspense
BR sə'spens
AM sə'spens

suspenseful
BR sə'spensf(ʊ)l
AM sə'spensfəl

suspensible
BR sə'spensɪbl
AM sə'spensəbəl

suspension
BR sə'spenʃn, -z
AM sə'spen(t)ʃən, -z

suspensive
BR sə'spensɪv
AM sə'spensɪv

suspensively
BR sə'spensɪvli
AM sə'spensɪvli

suspensiveness
BR sə'spensɪvnɪs
AM sə'spensɪvnɪs

suspensory
BR sə'spens(ə)ri
AM sə'spensəri

suspicion
BR sə'spɪʃn, -z
AM sə'spɪʃən, -z

suspicious
BR sə'spɪʃəs
AM sə'spɪʃəs

suspiciously
BR sə'spɪʃəsli
AM sə'spɪʃəsli

suspiciousness
BR sə'spɪʃəsnəs
AM sə'spɪʃəsnəs

suspiration
BR ,sʌspɪ'reɪʃn, -z
AM ,səspə'reɪʃən, -z

suspire
BR sə'spʌɪə(r), -z, -ɪŋ,
-d
AM sə'spaɪ(ə)r, -z, -ɪŋ,
-d

Susquehanna
BR ,sʌskwɪ'hanə(r)
AM ,səskwə'hænə

suss
BR sʌs, -ɪz, -ɪŋ, -t
AM səs, -əz, -ɪŋ, -t

Sussex
BR 'sʌsɪks
AM 'səsəks

sustain
BR sə'steɪn, -z, -ɪŋ, -d
AM sə'steɪn, -z, -ɪŋ, -d

sustainability
BR sə,steɪnə'bɪlɪti
AM sə,steɪnə'bɪlɪdi

sustainable
BR sə'steɪnəbl
AM sə'steɪnəbəl

sustainably
BR sə'steɪnəbli
AM sə'steɪnəbli

sustainedly
BR sə'steɪnɪdli
AM sə'steɪnɪdli

sustainer
BR sə'steɪnə(r), -z
AM sə'steɪnər, -z

sustainment
BR sə'steɪnm(ə)nt
AM sə'steɪnmənt

sustenance
BR 'sʌstɪnəns
AM 'səstənəns

sustentation
BR ,sʌsten'teɪʃn,
,sʌst(ə)n'teɪʃn
AM ,səst(ə)n'teɪʃən

susurration
BR ,s(j)uːsʌ'reɪʃn, -z
AM ,susə'reɪʃən, -z

susurrus
BR s(j)uː'sʌrəs
AM sʊ'sərəs

Sutch
BR sʌtʃ
AM sətʃ

Sutcliff
BR 'sʌtklɪf
AM 'sət,klɪf

Sutcliffe
BR 'sʌtklɪf
AM 'sət,klɪf

Sutherland
BR 'sʌðələnd
AM 'səðərlən(d)

Sutlej
BR 'sʌtlɪdʒ
AM 'sətlɪdʒ

sutler
BR 'sʌtlə(r), -z
AM 'sətlər, -z

sutra
BR 'suːtrə(r), -z
AM 'sutrə, -z

Sutro
BR 'suːtrəʊ
AM 'sutroʊ

suttee
BR sʌ'tiː, 'sʌtiː, -z
AM sə'ti, 'su,ti, -z

Sutter
BR 'sʌtə(r)
AM 'sədər

Sutton
BR 'sʌtn
AM 'sətn

Sutton Coldfield
BR ,sʌtn 'kəʊl(d)fiːld
AM ,sətn 'koʊl(d),fild

Sutton Hoo
BR ,sʌtn 'huː
AM ,sətn 'hu

sutural
BR 'suːtʃ(ə)rəl,
'suːtʃ(ə)rl
AM 'sutʃərəl

suture
BR 'suːtʃə(r), -z
AM 'sutʃər, -z

Suva
BR 'suːvə(r)
AM 'suvə

Suwannee
BR sʊ'wɒni, 'swɒni
AM 'swani, sə'wani

Suzanna
BR sʊ'zanə(r)
AM su'zænə

Suzanne
BR sʊ'zan

sustentation
AM su'zæn

suzerain
BR 'suːzəreɪn,
'suːz(ə)rən,
'suːz(ə)rn, -z
AM 'suzərən,
'suzə,reɪn

suzerainty
BR 'suːzəreɪnt|i,
'suːz(ə)rənt|i,
'suːz(ə)rn̩ti, -ɪz
AM 'suzərənti,
'suzə,reɪnti, -z

Suzette
BR sʊ'zet
AM su'zet, sə'zet

Suzie
BR 'suːzi
AM 'suzi

Suzuki®
BR sʊ'zuːk|i, -ɪz
AM sə'zuki, -z

Suzy
BR 'suːzi
AM 'suzi

Svalbard
BR 'svalbɑː
AM 'sval,bɑrd

svarabhakti
BR ,svarə'bakti:,
,svɑːrə'bakti:,
,svʌrə'bʌkti-
AM ,sfɑrə'bakti

svelte
BR svelt
AM svelt, sfelt

Svengali
BR sven'gɑːl|i,
sfen'gɑːl|i, -ɪz
AM sven'gali,
sfen'gali, -z

Sverdlovsk
BR ,sveː'd'lɒfsk,
,sveː'd'lɒvsk
AM ,svərd'lɒfsk,
,svərd'lafsk

swab
BR swɒb, -z, -ɪŋ, -d
AM swɑb, -z, -ɪŋ, -d

swabbie
BR 'swɒb|i, -ɪz
AM 'swabi, -z

swabby
BR 'swɒb|i, -ɪz
AM 'swabi, -z

Swabia
BR 'sweɪbɪə(r)
AM 'sweɪbiə

Swabian
BR 'sweɪbɪən, -z
AM 'sweɪbiən, -z

swaddie
BR 'swɒd|i, -ɪz
AM 'swadi, -z

swaddle
BR 'swɒd|l, -lz,
-lɪŋ\-lɪŋ, -ld

swaddy
AM ˈswɒd|əl, -əlz,
-(ə)lɪŋ, -əld

swaddy
BR ˈswɒd|i, -ɪz
AM ˈswɑdi, -z

Swadeshi
BR swəˈdeɪʃi
AM swəˈdeɪʃi

Swadlincote
BR ˈswɒdlɪnkəʊt
AM ˈswɑdlɪŋˌkoʊt

Swaffer
BR ˈswɒfə(r)
AM ˈswɑfər

Swaffham
BR ˈswɒf(ə)m
AM ˈswɑfəm

swag
BR swæg
AM swæg

swage
BR sweɪdʒ, -ɪz
AM sw|eɪdʒ, sw|ɛdʒ,
-eɪdʒɪz\-ɛdʒəz

Swaggart
BR ˈswagət
AM ˈswægərt

swagger
BR ˈswag|ə(r), -əz,
-(ə)rɪŋ, -əd
AM ˈswæg|ər, -ərz,
-(ə)rɪŋ, -ərd

swaggerer
BR ˈswag(ə)rə(r), -z
AM ˈswæg(ə)rər, -z

swaggeringly
BR ˈswag(ə)rɪŋli
AM ˈswæg(ə)rɪŋli

swaggie
BR ˈswag|i, -ɪz
AM ˈswægi, -z

swagman
BR ˈswagman
AM ˈswægˌmæn

swagmen
BR ˈswagmɛn
AM ˈswægˌmɛn

Swahili
BR swɑˈhiːli, swəˈhiːli
AM swɑˈhili

swain
BR sweɪn, -z
AM sweɪn, -z

Swainson
BR sweɪns(ə)n
AM ˈsweɪnsən

swale
BR sweɪl, -z
AM sweɪl, -z

Swaledale
BR ˈsweɪldeɪl
AM ˈsweɪlˌdeɪl

Swales
BR sweɪlz
AM sweɪlz

swallow
BR ˈswɒləʊ, -z, -ɪŋ, -d

swallow
AM ˈswɒl|oʊ, -oʊz,
-əwɪŋ \-oʊɪŋ, -oʊd

swallowable
BR ˈswɒləʊəbl
AM ˈswɑləwəbəl

swallow-dive
BR ˈswɒlə(ʊ)daɪv, -z,
-ɪŋ, -d
AM ˈswɑloʊˌdaɪv, -z,
-ɪŋ, -d

swallower
BR ˈswɒləʊə(r), -z
AM ˈswɑləwər, -z

swallow-hole
BR ˈswɒləʊhəʊl, -z
AM ˈswɑloʊˌhoʊl, -z

swallowtail
BR ˈswɒlə(ʊ)teɪl, -z, -d
AM ˈswɑloʊˌteɪl, -z, -d

swam
BR swam
AM swæm

swami
BR ˈswɑːm|i, -ɪz
AM ˈswɑmi, -z

swamp
BR ˈswɒm|p, -ps, -pɪŋ,
-(p)t
AM swɑmp, -s, -ɪŋ, -t

swampiness
BR ˈswɒmpɪnɪs
AM ˈswɑmpinɪs

swampland
BR ˈswɒmpland, -z
AM ˈswɑmpˌlænd, -z

swampy
BR ˈswɒmp|i, -ɪə(r),
-ɪɪst
AM ˈswɑmpi, -ər, -ɪst

swan
BR swɒn, -z, -ɪŋ, -d
AM swɑn, -z, -ɪŋ, -d

Swanage
BR ˈswɒnɪdʒ
AM ˈswɑnɪdʒ

swandive
BR ˈswɒndɑɪv, -z
AM ˈswɑnˌdaɪv, -z

Swanee
BR ˈswɒni
AM ˈswɑni

swank
BR swaŋ|k, -ks, -kɪŋ,
-(k)t
AM swæŋ|k, -ks, -kɪŋ,
-(k)t

swankily
BR ˈswaŋkɪli
AM ˈswæŋkəli

swankiness
BR ˈswaŋkɪnɪs
AM ˈswæŋkinɪs

swankpot
BR ˈswaŋkpɒt, -s
AM ˈswæŋkˌpɑt, -s

swanky
BR ˈswaŋk|i, -ɪə(r),
-ɪɪst
AM ˈswæŋki, -ər, -ɪst

Swanley
BR ˈswɒnli
AM ˈswɑnli

swanlike
BR ˈswɒnlaɪk
AM ˈswɑnˌlaɪk

Swann
BR swɒn
AM swɑn

swan-neck
BR ˈswɒnnɛk, -s
AM ˈswɑ(n)ˌnɛk, -s

swannery
BR ˈswɒn(ə)r|i, -ɪz
AM ˈswɑnəri, -z

Swanscombe
BR ˈswɒnzkəm
AM ˈswɑnzkəm

swansdown
BR ˈswɒnzdaʊn
AM ˈswɑnzˌdaʊn

Swansea
BR ˈswɒnzi
AM ˈswɑnzi, ˈswɑnzi

Swanson
BR ˈswɒnsn
AM ˈswɑnsən

swansong
BR ˈswɒnsɒŋ, -z
AM ˈswɑnˌsɒŋ,
ˈswɑnˌsɑŋ, -z

Swanton
BR ˈswɒntən
AM ˈswɑn(t)ən

swan-upping
BR ˌswɒnˈʌpɪŋ,
ˈswɒnˌʌpɪŋ
AM ˈswɑnˌəpɪŋ

swap
BR swɒp, -s, -ɪŋ, -t
AM swɑp, -s, -ɪŋ, -t

SWAPO
BR ˈswɑːpəʊ
AM ˈswɑˌpoʊ

swapper
BR ˈswɒpə(r), -z
AM ˈswɑpər, -z

Swaraj
BR swəˈrɑːdʒ
AM swəˈrɑdʒ

Swarajist
BR swəˈrɑːdʒɪst, -s
AM swəˈrɑdʒəst, -s

Swarbrick
BR ˈswɔːbrɪk
AM ˈswɑrˌbrɪk

sward
BR swɔːd, -z, -ɪd
AM swɔ(ə)rd, -z, -əd

sware
BR swɛː(r)
AM swɛ(ə)r

swarf
BR swɔːf
AM swɔ(ə)rf

Swarfega®
BR swɔːˈfiːgə(r)
AM swɑrˈfigə

swarm
BR swɔːm, -z, -ɪŋ, -d
AM swɔ(ə)rm, -z, -ɪŋ, -d

swart
BR swɔːt
AM swɔ(ə)rt

swarthily
BR ˈswɔːðɪli
AM ˈswɔrðəli

swarthiness
BR ˈswɔːðmɪs
AM ˈswɔrðinɪs

swarthy
BR ˈswɔːð|i, -ɪə(r), -ɪɪst
AM ˈswɔrði, -ər, -ɪst

Swartz
BR swɔːts
AM swɔ(ə)rts

swash
BR swɒʃ, -ɪz, -ɪŋ, -t
AM swɔʃ, swɑʃ, -əz, -ɪŋ,
-t

swashbuckler
BR ˈswɒʃˌbʌklə(r), -z
AM ˈswɔʃˌbək(ə)lər,
ˈswɑʃˌbək(ə)lər, -z

swashbuckling
BR ˈswɒʃˌbʌklɪŋ
AM ˈswɔʃˌbək(ə)lɪŋ,
ˈswɑʃˌbək(ə)lɪŋ

swastika
BR ˈswɒstɪkə(r), -z
AM ˈswɑstəkə, -z

swat
BR swɒt, -s, -ɪŋ, -ɪd
AM swɑ|t, -ts, -dɪŋ, -dəd

swatch
BR swɒtʃ, -ɪz
AM swɑtʃ, -əz

swath
BR swɒθ, swɔːθ, -s
AM swɑθ, -s

swathe
BR sweɪð, -z, -ɪŋ, -d
AM sweɪð, -z, -ɪŋ, -d

SWAT team
BR ˈswɒt tiːm, -z
AM ˈswɑ(t) ˌtim, -z

swatter
BR ˈswɒtə(r), -z
AM ˈswɑdər, -z

sway
BR sweɪ, -z, -ɪŋ, -d
AM sweɪ, -z, -ɪŋ, -d

Swazi
BR ˈswɑːz|i, -ɪz
AM ˈswɑzi, -z

Swaziland
BR ˈswɑːzɪland
AM ˈswɑzɪˌlænd

swear
BR swɛː(r), -z, -ɪŋ
AM swɛ(ə)r, -z, -ɪŋ

swearer
BR 'swɛːrə(r), -z
AM 'swɛrər, -z

swearword
BR 'swɛːwəːd, -z
AM 'swɛr,wərd, -z

sweat
BR swɛt, -s, -ɪŋ, -ɪd
AM swɛt, -ts, -ɪŋ, -ɪd

sweatband
BR 'swɛtband, -z
AM 'swɛt,bænd, -z

sweatbox
BR 'swɛtbɒks, -ɪz
AM 'swɛt,bɑks, -əz

sweater
BR 'swɛtə(r), -z
AM 'swɛdər, -z

sweatily
BR 'swɛtɪli
AM 'swɛdəli

sweatiness
BR 'swɛtɪnɪs
AM 'swɛdɪnɪs

sweatpants
BR 'swɛtpants
AM 'swɛt,pæn(t)s

sweatshirt
BR 'swɛtʃəːt, -s
AM 'swɛt,ʃərt, -s

sweatshop
BR 'swɛtʃɒp, -s
AM 'swɛt,sɑp, -s

sweatsuit
BR 'swɛtsuːt, -s
AM 'swɛt,sut, -s

sweaty
BR 'swɛt|i, -ɪə(r), -ɪɪst
AM 'swɛdi, -ər, -ɪst

Swede
BR swiːd, -z
AM swid, -z

Sweden
BR 'swiːdn
AM 'swidən

Swedenborg
BR 'swiːdnbɔːg
AM 'swidn,bɔrg
SW 'sveːdɛnbʊrj

Swedenborgian
BR ,swiːdn'bɔːgiən, ,swiːdn'bɔːdʒiən
AM ,swidən'bɔrgiən

Swedish
BR 'swiːdɪʃ
AM 'swidɪʃ

Sweeney
BR 'swiːni
AM 'swini

sweep
BR swiːp, -s, -ɪŋ
AM swip, -z, -ɪŋ

sweepback
BR 'swiːpbak, -s

AM 'swip,bæk, -s

sweeper
BR 'swiːpə(r), -z
AM 'swipər, -z

sweeping
BR 'swiːpɪŋ, -z
AM 'swipɪŋ, -z

sweepingly
BR 'swiːpɪŋli
AM 'swipɪŋli

sweepingness
BR 'swiːpɪŋnɪs
AM 'swipɪŋnɪs

sweepstake
BR 'swiːpsteɪk, -s
AM 'swip,steɪk, -s

sweet
BR swiːt, -s, -ə(r), -ɪst
AM swi|t, -ts, -dər, -dɪst

sweet-and-sour
BR ,swiːt(ə)n(d)'sauə(r)
AM ,swidən'sau(ə)r

sweetbread
BR 'swiːtbrɛd, -z
AM 'swit,brɛd, -z

sweetbriar
BR 'swiːt,brʌɪə(r), -z
AM 'swit,braɪər, -z

sweetbrier
BR 'swiːt,brʌɪə(r), -z
AM 'swit,braɪər, -z

sweetcorn
BR 'swiːtkɔːn
AM 'swit,kɔ(ə)rn

sweeten
BR 'swiːt|n, -nz, -nɪŋ\-n̩ɪŋ, -nd
AM 'switn, -z, -ɪŋ, -d

sweetener
BR 'swiːtnə(r), 'swiːtn̩ə(r), -z
AM 'switn̩ər, 'switnər, -z

sweetening
BR 'swiːtnɪŋ, 'swiːtn̩ɪŋ, -z
AM 'switn̩ɪŋ, 'switnɪŋ, -z

Sweetex®
BR 'swiːtɛks
AM 'swi,tɛks

sweetheart
BR 'swiːthɑːt, -s
AM 'swit,(h)ɑrt, -s

sweetie
BR 'swiːt|i, -ɪz
AM 'swidi, -z

sweetie-pie
BR 'swiːtɪpʌɪ, -z
AM 'swidi,paɪ, -z

sweeting
BR 'swiːtɪŋ, -z
AM 'swidɪŋ, -z

sweetish
BR 'swiːtɪʃ
AM 'swidɪʃ

sweetly
BR 'swiːtli
AM 'switli

sweetmeal
BR 'swiːtmiːl
AM 'swit,mil

sweetmeat
BR 'swiːtmiːt, -s
AM 'swit,mit, -s

sweetness
BR 'swiːtnɪs
AM 'switnɪs

sweetshop
BR 'swiːtʃɒp, -s
AM 'swit,ʃɑp, -s

sweetsop
BR 'swiːtsɒp, -s
AM 'swit,sɑp, -s

sweet-talk
BR 'swiːttɔːk, -s, -ɪŋ, -t
AM 'swi(t),tɔk, -s, -ɪŋ, -t

sweety
BR 'swiːt|i, -ɪz
AM 'swidi, -z

swell
BR swɛl, -z, -ɪŋ, -d
AM swɛl, -z, -ɪŋ, -d

swelling
BR 'swɛlɪŋ, -z
AM 'swɛlɪŋ, -z

swellish
BR 'swɛlɪʃ
AM 'swɛlɪʃ

swelter
BR 'swɛlt|ə(r), -əz, -(ə)rɪŋ, -əd
AM 'swɛltər, -ərz, -(ə)rɪŋ, -ərd

swelteringly
BR 'swɛlt(ə)rɪŋli
AM 'swɛlt(ə)rɪŋli

Swenson
BR 'swɛns(ə)n
AM 'swɛnsən

swept
BR swɛpt
AM swɛpt

swerve
BR swəːv, -z, -ɪŋ, -d
AM swərv, -z, -ɪŋ, -d

swerveless
BR 'swəːvləs
AM 'swərvləs

swerver
BR 'swəːvə(r), -z
AM 'swərvər, -z

swift
BR swɪft, -s, -ə(r), -ɪst
AM swɪft, -s, -ər, -ɪst

swiftie
BR 'swɪft|i, -ɪz
AM 'swɪfti, -z

swiftlet
BR 'swɪftlɪt, -s
AM 'swɪf(t)lət, -s

swiftly
BR 'swɪftli
AM 'swɪf(t)li

swiftness
BR 'swɪf(t)nɪs
AM 'swɪf(t)nɪs

swig
BR swɪg, -z, -ɪŋ, -d
AM swɪg, -z, -ɪŋ, -d

swigger
BR 'swɪgə(r), -z
AM 'swɪgər, -z

swill
BR swɪl, -z, -ɪŋ, -d
AM swɪl, -z, -ɪŋ, -d

swiller
BR 'swɪlə(r), -z
AM 'swɪlər, -z

swim
BR swɪm, -z, -ɪŋ
AM swɪm, -z, -ɪŋ

swimmable
BR 'swɪməbl
AM 'swɪməbəl

swimmer
BR 'swɪmə(r), -z
AM 'swɪmər, -z

swimmeret
BR ,swɪmə'rɛt, -s
AM ,swɪmə'rɛt, -s

swimmingly
BR 'swɪmɪŋli
AM 'swɪmɪŋgli

swimsuit
BR 'swɪms(j)uːt, -s, -ɪd
AM 'swɪm,sut, -ts, -dəd

swimwear
BR 'swɪmwɛː(r)
AM 'swɪm,wɛ(ə)r

Swinburne
BR 'swɪnbəːn
AM 'swɪn,bərn

swindle
BR 'swɪnd|l, -lz, -lɪŋ\-lɪŋ, -ld
AM 'swɪn|dəl, -dəlz, -(d)(ə)lɪŋ, -dəld

swindler
BR 'swɪndlə(r), -z
AM 'swɪn(də)lər, -z

Swindon
BR 'swɪndən
AM 'swɪndən

swine
BR swʌɪn
AM swaɪn

swineherd
BR 'swʌɪnhəːd, -z
AM 'swaɪn,(h)ərd, -z

swinery
BR 'swʌɪn(ə)r|i, -ɪz
AM 'swaɪnəri, -z

swing
BR swɪŋ, -z, -ɪŋ
AM swɪŋ, -z, -ɪŋ

swingbin
BR 'swɪŋbɪn, -z

AM 'swɪŋ,bɪn, -z

swingboat
BR 'swɪŋbəʊt, -s
AM 'swɪŋ,boʊt, -s

swinge
BR swɪn(d)ʒ, -ɪz, -ɪŋ, -d
AM swɪndʒ, -ɪz, -ɪŋ, -d

swingeingly
BR 'swɪn(d)ʒɪŋli
AM 'swɪndʒɪŋli

swinger
BR 'swɪŋə(r), -z
AM 'swɪŋər, -z

swingingly
BR 'swɪŋɪŋli
AM 'swɪŋɪŋli

swingle
BR 'swɪŋg‖l, -lz,
-lɪŋ\-lɪŋ, -ld
AM 'swɪŋgəl, -əlz,
-(ə)lɪŋ, -əld

Swingler
BR 'swɪŋglə(r)
AM 'swɪŋ(g)lər

swingletree
BR 'swɪŋgltriː, -z
AM 'swɪŋgl,tri, -z

swingometer
BR swɪŋ'ɒmɪtə(r), -z
AM swɪŋ'(g)amədər, -z

swingy
BR 'swɪŋ‖i, -ɪə(r), -ɪɪst
AM 'swɪŋi, -ər, -ɪst

swinish
BR 'swʌɪnɪʃ
AM 'swamɪʃ

swinishly
BR 'swʌɪnɪʃli
AM 'swamɪʃli

swinishness
BR 'swʌɪnɪʃnɪs
AM 'swamɪʃnɪs

Swinnerton
BR 'swɪnət(ə)n
AM 'swɪnərt(ə)n

Swinton
BR 'swɪntən
AM 'swɪn(t)ən

swipe
BR swʌɪp, -s, -ɪŋ, -t
AM swaɪp, -s, -ɪŋ, -t

swiper
BR 'swʌɪpə(r), -z
AM 'swaɪpər, -z

swipple
BR 'swɪpl, -z
AM 'swɪpəl, -z

swirl
BR swəːl, -z, -ɪŋ, -d
AM swərl, -z, -ɪŋ, -d

swirly
BR 'swəːl‖i, -ɪə(r), -ɪɪst
AM 'swərli, -ər, -ɪst

swish
BR swɪʃ, -ɪz, -ɪŋ, -t, -ə(r),
-ɪst

AM swɪʃ, -ɪz, -ɪŋ, -t, -ər,
-ɪst

swishily
BR 'swɪʃɪli
AM 'swɪʃɪli

swishiness
BR 'swɪʃɪnɪs
AM 'swɪʃɪnɪs

swishy
BR 'swɪʃ‖i, -ɪə(r), -ɪɪst
AM 'swɪʃi, -ər, -ɪst

Swiss
BR swɪs
AM swɪs

Swissair®
BR 'swɪsɜː(r)
AM 'swɪs'ɛ(ə)r

switch
BR swɪtʃ, -ɪz, -ɪŋ, -t
AM swɪtʃ, -ɪz, -ɪŋ, -t

switchable
BR 'swɪtʃəbl
AM 'swɪtʃəbəl

switchback
BR 'swɪtʃbak, -s
AM 'swɪtʃ,bæk, -s

switchblade
BR 'swɪtʃbleɪd, -z
AM 'swɪtʃ,bleɪd, -z

switchboard
BR 'swɪtʃbɔːd, -z
AM 'swɪtʃ,bɔ(ə)rd, -z

switcher
BR 'swɪtʃə(r), -z
AM 'swɪtʃər, -z

switcheroo
BR ,swɪtʃə'ruː, -z
AM ,swɪtʃə'ru, -z

switchgear
BR 'swɪtʃgɪə(r)
AM 'swɪtʃ,gɪ(ə)r

switchman
BR 'swɪtʃmən
AM 'swɪtʃmən

switchmen
BR 'swɪtʃmən
AM 'swɪtʃmən

switch-over
BR 'swɪtʃ,əʊvə(r), -z
AM 'swɪtʃ,oʊvər, -z

switchyard
BR 'swɪtʃjɑːd, -z
AM 'swɪtʃ,jɑrd, -z

swither
BR 'swɪðə(r), -əz,
-(ə)rɪŋ, -əd
AM 'swɪðər, -z, -ɪŋ, -d

Swithin
BR 'swɪð(ɪ)n
AM 'swɪðɪn

Swithun
BR 'swɪðən
AM 'swɪðɪn

Switzerland
BR 'swɪtsələnd,
'swɪtsländ
AM 'swɪtsərlənd

swive
BR swʌɪv, -z, -ɪŋ, -d
AM swaɪv, -z, -ɪŋ, -d

swivel
BR 'swɪv‖l, -lz,
-lɪŋ\-lɪŋ, -ld
AM 'swɪvəl, -əlz,
-(ə)lɪŋ, -əld

swiz
BR swɪz, -ɪz
AM swɪz, -ɪz

swizz
BR swɪz, -ɪz
AM swɪz, -ɪz

swizzle
BR 'swɪz‖l, -lz, -lɪŋ\-lɪŋ,
-ld
AM 'swɪzəl, -əlz,
-(ə)lɪŋ, -əld

swob
BR swɒb, -z, -ɪŋ, -d
AM swɑb, -z, -ɪŋ, -d

swollen
BR 'swəʊlən
AM 'swoʊlən

swoon
BR swuːn, -z, -ɪŋ, -d
AM swun, -z, -ɪŋ, -d

swoop
BR swuːp, -s, -ɪŋ, -t
AM swup, -s, -ɪŋ, -t

swoosh
BR swuːʃ, swʊʃ, -ɪz, -ɪŋ,
-t
AM swuʃ, -əz, -ɪŋ, -t

swop
BR swɒp, -s, -ɪŋ, -t
AM swɑp, -s, -ɪŋ, -t

sword
BR sɔːd, -z
AM sɔ(ə)rd, -z

swordbearer
BR 'sɔːd,bɛːrə(r), -z
AM 'sɔrd,bɛrər, -z

swordbelt
BR 'sɔːdbelt, -s
AM 'sɔrd,bɛlt, -s

swordbill
BR 'sɔːdbɪl, -z
AM 'sɔrd,bɪl, -z

swordfish
BR 'sɔːdfɪʃ, -ɪz
AM 'sɔrd,fɪʃ, -ɪz

swordlike
BR 'sɔːdlʌɪk
AM 'sɔrd,laɪk

swordplay
BR 'sɔːdpleɪ
AM 'sɔrd,pleɪ

swordsman
BR 'sɔːdzmən
AM 'sɔrdzmən

swordsmanship
BR 'sɔːdzmənʃɪp
AM 'sɔrdzmən,ʃɪp

swordsmen
BR 'sɔːdzmən

AM 'sɔrdzmən

swordstick
BR 'sɔːdstɪk, -s
AM 'sɔrd,stɪk, -s

swordtail
BR 'sɔːdteɪl, -z
AM 'sɔrd,teɪl, -z

swore
BR swɔː(r)
AM swɔ(ə)r

sworn
BR swɔːn
AM swɔ(ə)rn

swot
BR swɒt, -s, -ɪŋ, -ɪd-
AM swɑt, -ts, -dɪŋ, -dəd

swotter
BR 'swɒtə(r), -z
AM 'swɑdər, -z

swum
BR swʌm
AM swəm

swung
BR swʌŋ
AM swəŋ

swy
BR swʌɪ, -z
AM swaɪ, -z

sybarite
BR 'sɪbərʌɪt, -s
AM 'sɪbə,raɪt, -s

sybaritic
BR ,sɪbə'rɪtɪk
AM ,sɪbə'rɪdɪk

sybaritical
BR ,sɪbə'rɪtɪkl
AM ,sɪbə'rɪdəkəl

sybaritically
BR ,sɪbə'rɪtɪkli
AM ,sɪbə'rɪdək(ə)li

sybaritism
BR 'sɪbərʌɪtɪz(ə)m
AM 'sɪbə,raɪ,tɪzəm

sybil
BR 'sɪb(ɪ)l, -z
AM 'sɪbɪl, -z

sycamine
BR 'sɪkəmɪn,
'sɪkəmʌɪn, -z
AM 'sɪkəmən,
'sɪkə,maɪn, -z

syce
BR sʌɪs, -ɪz
AM saɪs, -ɪz

sycomore
BR 'sɪkəmɔː(r), -z
AM 'sɪkə,mɔ(ə)r, -z

syconia
BR sʌɪ'kəʊnɪə(r)
AM saɪ'koʊnɪə

syconium
BR sʌɪ'kəʊnɪəm
AM saɪ'koʊnɪəm

sycophancy
BR 'sɪkəf(ə)ns‖i, -ɪz
AM 'sɪkəfənsi,
'sɪkə,fænsi, -z

sycophant
BR ˈsɪkəf(ə)nt,
ˈsɪkəfant, -s
AM ˈsɪkəfənt,
ˈsɪkəˌfænt, -s

sycophantic
BR ˌsɪkəˈfantɪk
AM ˌsɪkəˈfæn(t)ɪk

sycophantically
BR ˌsɪkəˈfantɪkli
AM ˌsɪkəˈfæn(t)ək(ə)li

sycoses
BR saɪˈkəʊsiːz
AM saɪˈkoʊˌsiz

sycosis
BR saɪˈkəʊsɪs
AM saɪˈkoʊsəs

Sydney
BR ˈsɪdni
AM ˈsɪdni

Sydneysider
BR ˈsɪdnɪˌsʌɪdə(r), -z
AM ˈsɪdniˌsaɪdər, -z

syenite
BR ˈsʌɪənʌɪt, -s
AM ˈsaɪəˌnaɪt, -s

syenitic
BR ˌsʌɪəˈnɪtɪk
AM ˌsaɪəˈnɪdɪk

Sykes
BR saɪks
AM saɪks

syllabary
BR ˈsɪləb(ə)r|i, -ɪz
AM ˈsɪləˌbɛri, -z

syllabi
BR ˈsɪləbʌɪ
AM ˈsɪləˌbaɪ

syllabic
BR sɪˈlabɪk
AM səˈlæbɪk

syllabically
BR sɪˈlabɪkli
AM səˈlæbək(ə)li

syllabication
BR sɪˌlabɪˈkeɪʃn
AM səˌlæbəˈkeɪʃən

syllabicity
BR ˌsɪləˈbɪsɪti
AM ˌsɪləˈbɪsɪdi

syllabification
BR sɪˌlabɪfɪˈkeɪʃn
AM səˌlæbəfəˈkeɪʃən

syllabify
BR sɪˈlabɪfʌɪ, -z, -ɪŋ, -d
AM səˈlæbəˌfaɪ, -z, -ɪŋ,
-d

syllabise
BR ˈsɪləbʌɪz, -ɪz, -ɪŋ, -d
AM ˈsɪləˌbaɪz, -ɪz, -ɪŋ, -d

syllabize
BR ˈsɪləbʌɪz, -ɪz, -ɪŋ, -d
AM ˈsɪləˌbaɪz, -ɪz, -ɪŋ, -d

syllable
BR ˈsɪləbl, -z
AM ˈsɪləbəl, -z

syllabub
BR ˈsɪləbʌb, -z
AM ˈsɪləˌbəb, -z

syllabus
BR ˈsɪləbəs, -ɪz
AM ˈsɪləbəs, -əz

syllepses
BR sɪˈlɛpsiːz
AM səˈlɛpsiz

syllepsis
BR sɪˈlɛpsɪs
AM səˈlɛpsəs

sylleptic
BR sɪˈlɛptɪk
AM səˈlɛptɪk

sylleptically
BR sɪˈlɛptɪkli
AM səˈlɛptək(ə)li

syllogise
BR ˈsɪlədʒʌɪz, -ɪz, -ɪŋ, -d
AM ˈsɪləˌdʒaɪz, -ɪz, -ɪŋ,
-d

syllogism
BR ˈsɪləˌdʒɪz(ə)m, -z
AM ˈsɪləˌdʒɪzəm, -z

syllogistic
BR ˌsɪləˈdʒɪstɪk
AM ˌsɪləˈdʒɪstɪk

syllogistically
BR ˌsɪləˈdʒɪstɪkli
AM ˌsɪləˈdʒɪstək(ə)li

syllogize
BR ˈsɪlədʒʌɪz, -ɪz, -ɪŋ, -d
AM ˈsɪləˌdʒaɪz, -ɪz, -ɪŋ,
-d

sylph
BR sɪlf, -s
AM sɪlf, -s

Sylphides
BR sɪlˈfiːd
AM sɪlˈfid

sylphlike
BR ˈsɪlflʌɪk
AM ˈsɪlfˌlaɪk

sylva
BR ˈsɪlvə(r), -z
AM ˈsɪlvə, -z

sylvae
BR ˈsɪlviː
AM ˈsɪlvi, ˈsɪlˌvaɪ

sylvan
BR ˈsɪlv(ə)n
AM ˈsɪlvən

sylvatic
BR s(ɪ)lˈvatɪk
AM sɪlˈvædɪk

Sylvester
BR ˈsɪlvɛstə(r),
ˈsɪlvɪstə(r),
s(ɪ)lˈvɛstə(r)
AM sɪlˈvɛstər

Sylvia
BR ˈsɪlvɪə(r)
AM ˈsɪlviə

sylviculture
BR ˈsɪlvɪˌkʌltʃə(r)
AM ˈsɪlvəˌkəltʃər

Sylvie
BR ˈsɪlvi
AM ˈsɪlvi

sylvine
BR ˈsɪlviːn
AM ˈsɪlvin

sylvite
BR ˈsɪlvʌɪt
AM ˈsɪlvait

symbiont
BR ˈsɪmbʌɪɒnt,
ˈsɪmbɪɒnt, -s
AM ˈsɪmbaɪˌant,
ˈsɪmbiˌant, -s

symbioses
BR ˌsɪmbʌɪˈəʊsiːz,
ˌsɪmbɪˈəʊsiːz
AM ˌsɪmbaɪˈoʊˌsis,
ˌsɪmbiˈoʊˌsis

symbiosis
BR ˌsɪmbʌɪˈəʊsɪs,
ˌsɪmbɪˈəʊsɪs
AM ˌsɪmbaɪˈoʊsəs,
ˌsɪmbiˈoʊsəs

symbiotic
BR ˌsɪmbʌɪˈɒtɪk,
ˌsɪmbɪˈɒtɪk
AM ˌsɪmbaɪˈadɪk,
ˌsɪmbiˈadɪk

symbiotically
BR ˌsɪmbʌɪˈɒtɪkli,
ˌsɪmbɪˈɒtɪkli
AM ˌsɪmbaɪˈadək(ə)li,
ˌsɪmbiˈadək(ə)li

symbol
BR ˈsɪmbl, -z
AM ˈsɪmbəl, -z

symbolic
BR sɪmˈbɒlɪk, -s
AM sɪmˈbalɪk, -s

symbolical
BR sɪmˈbɒlɪkl
AM sɪmˈbaləkəl

symbolically
BR sɪmˈbɒlɪkli
AM sɪmˈbalək(ə)li

symbolisation
BR ˌsɪmbəlʌɪˈzeɪʃn,
ˌsɪmblʌɪˈzeɪʃn
AM ˌsɪmbələˈzeɪʃən,
ˌsɪmbəˌlaɪˈzeɪʃən

symbolise
BR ˈsɪmbəlʌɪz,
ˈsɪmblʌɪz, -ɪz, -ɪŋ, -d
AM ˈsɪmbəˌlaɪz, -ɪz, -ɪŋ,
-d

symbolism
BR ˈsɪmbəlɪz(ə)m,
ˈsɪmblɪz(ə)m
AM ˈsɪmbəˌlɪzəm

symbolist
BR ˈsɪmbəlɪst,
ˈsɪmblɪst, -s
AM ˈsɪmbələst, -s

symbolistic
BR ˌsɪmbəˈlɪstɪk,
ˌsɪmblˈɪstɪk
AM ˌsɪmbəˈlɪstɪk

symbolization
BR ˌsɪmbəlʌɪˈzeɪʃn,
ˌsɪmblʌɪˈzeɪʃn
AM ˌsɪmbələˈzeɪʃən,
ˌsɪmbəˌlaɪˈzeɪʃən

symbolize
BR ˈsɪmbəlʌɪz,
ˈsɪmblʌɪz, -ɪz, IN, -d
AM ˈsɪmbəˌlaɪz, -ɪz, -ɪŋ,
-d

symbology
BR sɪmˈbɒlədʒi
AM sɪmˈbalədʒi

symbolology
BR ˌsɪmbəˈlɒlədʒi,
ˌsɪmblˈɒlədʒi
AM ˌsɪmbəˈlaləðʒi

Symes
BR sʌɪmz
AM saɪmz

Symington
BR ˈsɪmɪŋt(ə)n,
ˈsʌɪmɪŋt(ə)n
AM ˈsaɪmɪŋtən

symmetric
BR sɪˈmɛtrɪk
AM səˈmɛtrɪk

symmetrical
BR sɪˈmɛtrɪkl
AM səˈmɛtrəkəl

symmetrically
BR sɪˈmɛtrɪkli
AM səˈmɛtrək(ə)li

symmetricalness
BR sɪˈmɛtrɪklnəs
AM səˈmɛtrəkəlnəs

symmetrise
BR ˈsɪmətrʌɪz, -ɪz, -ɪŋ,
-d
AM ˈsɪməˌtraɪz, -ɪz, -ɪŋ,
-d

symmetrize
BR ˈsɪmətrʌɪz, -ɪz, -ɪŋ,
-d
AM ˈsɪməˌtraɪz, -ɪz, -ɪŋ,
-d

symmetrophobia
BR ˌsɪmətrəˈfəʊbɪə(r)
AM ˌsɪmətrəˈfoʊbiə

symmetry
BR ˈsɪmɪtri
AM ˈsɪmɪtri

Symon
BR ˈsʌɪmən
AM ˈsaɪmən

Symonds
BR ˈsɪm(ə)n(d)z,
ˈsʌɪmən(d)z
AM ˈsaɪmənz

Symonds Yat
BR ˈsɪm(ə)n(d)z ˈjat
AM ˈsaɪmənz ˈjæt

Symons
BR ˈsɪm(ə)nz,
ˈsʌɪm(ə)nz
AM ˈsaɪmənz

sympathectomy
BR ˌsɪmpə'θɛktəm|i, -ɪz
AM ˌsɪmpə'θɛktəmi, -z

sympathetic
BR ˌsɪmpə'θɛtɪk
AM ˌsɪmpə'θɛdɪk

sympathetically
BR ˌsɪmpə'θɛtɪkli
AM ˌsɪmpə'θɛdək(ə)li

sympathise
BR 'sɪmpəθʌɪz, -ɪz, -ɪŋ, -d
AM 'sɪmpə,θaɪz, -ɪz, -ɪŋ, -d

sympathiser
BR 'sɪmpəθʌɪzə(r), -z
AM 'sɪmpə,θaɪzər, -z

sympathize
BR 'sɪmpəθʌɪz, -ɪz, -ɪŋ, -d
AM 'sɪmpə,θaɪz, -ɪz, -ɪŋ, -d

sympathizer
BR 'sɪmpəθʌɪzə(r), -z
AM 'sɪmpə,θaɪzər, -z

sympathy
BR 'sɪmpəθ|i, -ɪz
AM 'sɪmpəθi, -z

sympatric
BR sɪm'patrɪk
AM sɪm'pætrɪk

sympetalous
BR sɪm'pɛtləs
AM sɪm'pɛdləs

symphonic
BR sɪm'fɒnɪk
AM sɪm'fɑnɪk

symphonically
BR sɪm'fɒnɪkli
AM sɪm'fɑnək(ə)li

symphonious
BR sɪm'fəʊnɪəs
AM sɪm'foʊnɪəs

symphonist
BR 'sɪmfənɪst, -s
AM 'sɪmfənəst, -s

symphony
BR 'sɪmfən|i, -ɪz
AM 'sɪmfəni, -z

symphyllous
BR sɪm'fɪləs
AM sɪm(p)'fɪləs

symphyseal
BR sɪm'fɪzɪəl
AM sɪm'fɪzɪəl

symphyses
BR 'sɪmfɪsiːz
AM 'sɪmfə,siz

symphysial
BR sɪm'fɪzɪəl
AM sɪm'fɪzɪəl

symphysis
BR 'sɪmfɪsɪs
AM 'sɪm(p)fəsəs

symplasm
BR 'sɪmplaz(ə)m

AM 'sɪm,plæzm

symplast
BR 'sɪmplast, -s
AM 'sɪm,plæst, -s

sympodia
BR sɪm'pəʊdɪə(r)
AM sɪm'poʊdɪə

sympodial
BR sɪm'pəʊdɪəl
AM sɪm'poʊdɪəl

sympodially
BR sɪm'pəʊdɪəli
AM sɪm'poʊdɪəli

sympodium
BR sɪm'pəʊdɪəm
AM sɪm'poʊdɪəm

symposia
BR sɪm'pəʊzɪə(r)
AM sɪm'poʊzɪə

symposiac
BR sɪm'pəʊzɪak, -s
AM sɪm'poʊzɪ,æk, -s

symposial
BR sɪm'pəʊzɪəl
AM sɪm'poʊzɪəl

symposiarch
BR sɪm'pəʊzɪɑːk, -s
AM sɪm'poʊzɪ,ɑrk, -s

symposiast
BR sɪm'pəʊzɪast, -s
AM sɪm'poʊzɪast, -s

symposium
BR sɪm'pəʊzɪəm, -z
AM sɪm'poʊzɪəm, -z

symptom
BR 'sɪm(p)təm, -z
AM 'sɪm(p)təm, -z

symptomatic
BR ˌsɪm(p)tə'matɪk
AM ˌsɪm(p)tə'mædɪk

symptomatically
BR ˌsɪm(p)tə'matɪkli
AM ˌsɪm(p)tə'mædək(ə)li

symptomatology
BR ˌsɪm(p)təmə'tɒlədʒi
AM ˌsɪm(p)təmə'talədʒi

symptomless
BR 'sɪm(p)təmləs
AM 'sɪm(p)təmləs

synaereses
BR sɪ'nɪərəsiːz
AM sə'nɛrə,siz, sɪ'nɪrə,siz

synaeresis
BR sɪ'nɪərəsɪs
AM sə'nɛrəsəs, sə'nɪrəsəs

synaesthesia
BR ˌsɪnɪs'θiːzɪə(r), ˌsɪnɪs'θiːʒə(r)
AM ˌsɪnɪs'θiʒ(i)ə, ˌsɪnɪs'θiziə

synaesthetic
BR ˌsɪnɪs'θɛtɪk
AM ˌsɪnɪs'θɛdɪk

synagogal
BR ˌsɪnə'gɒgl
AM ˌsɪnə'gɑgəl

synagogical
BR ˌsɪnə'gɒdʒɪkl, ˌsɪnə'gɒgɪkl
AM ˌsɪnə'gɑdʒəkəl

synagogue
BR 'sɪnəgɒg, -z
AM 'sɪnə,gɑg, -z

synallagmatic
BR ˌsɪnəlag'matɪk
AM ˌsɪnəlæg'mædɪk

synantherous
BR sɪ'nanθ(ə)rəs
AM sə'nænθərəs

synanthous
BR sɪ'nanθəs
AM sə'nænθəs

synapse
BR 'sʌɪnaps, 'sɪnaps, -ɪz
AM 'sɪn,æps, -əz

synapses
BR sɪ'napsiːz
AM sə'næp,siz

synapsis
BR sɪ'napsɪs
AM sə'næpsəs

synaptic
BR sɪ'naptɪk
AM sə'næptɪk

synaptically
BR sɪ'naptɪkli
AM sə'næptək(ə)li

synarchy
BR 'sɪnɑːki
AM 'sɪnərki

synarthroses
BR ˌsɪnɑː'θrəʊsiːz
AM ˌsɪ,nɑr'θroʊ,siz

synarthrosis
BR ˌsɪnɑː'θrəʊsɪs
AM ˌsɪ,nɑr'θroʊsəs

sync
BR sɪŋ|k, -ks, -kɪŋ, -(k)t
AM sɪŋk, -s, -ɪŋ, -t

syncarp
BR 'sɪŋkɑːp, -s
AM 'sɪn,kɑrp, -s

syncarpous
BR sɪn'kɑːpəs
AM sɪn'kɑrpəs

synch
BR sɪŋ|k, -ks, -kɪŋ, -(k)t
AM sɪŋk, -s, -ɪŋ, -t

synchondroses
BR ˌsɪŋkɒn'drəʊsiːz
AM ˌsɪŋkən'droʊ,siz

synchondrosis
BR ˌsɪŋkɒn'drəʊsɪs
AM ˌsɪŋkən'droʊsəs

synchro
BR 'sɪŋkrəʊ
AM 'sɪŋkroʊ, 'sɪnkroʊ

synchrocyclotron
BR ˌsɪŋkrəʊ'sʌɪklətrɒn, -z
AM 'sɪŋkrə'saɪklə,trɑn, 'sɪkrə'saɪklə,trɑn, -z

synchroflash
BR 'sɪŋkrəflaʃ, -ɪz
AM 'sɪŋkroʊ,flæʃ, 'sɪnkroʊ,flæʃ, -əz

synchromesh
BR 'sɪŋkrəmɛʃ
AM 'sɪŋkroʊ,mɛʃ, 'sɪnkroʊ,mɛʃ

synchronic
BR sɪn'krɒnɪk, sɪŋ'krɒnɪk
AM sɪŋ'krɑnɪk, sɪn'krɑnɪk

synchronically
BR sɪn'krɒnɪkli, sɪŋ'krɒnɪkli
AM sɪŋ'krɑnək(ə)li, sɪn'krɑnək(ə)li

synchronicity
BR ˌsɪŋkrə'nɪsɪti
AM ˌsɪŋkrə'nɪsɪdi, ˌsɪnkrə'nɪsɪdi

synchronisation
BR ˌsɪŋkrənʌɪ'zeɪʃn
AM ˌsɪŋkrənə'zeɪʃən, ˌsɪŋkrə,naɪ'zeɪʃən, ˌsɪnkrənə'zeɪʃən, ˌsɪnkrə,naɪ'zeɪʃən

synchronise
BR 'sɪŋkrənʌɪz, -ɪz, -ɪŋ, -d
AM 'sɪŋkrə,naɪz, 'sɪnkrə,naɪz, -ɪz, -ɪŋ, -d

synchroniser
BR 'sɪŋkrənʌɪzə(r)
AM 'sɪŋkrə,naɪzər, 'sɪnkrə,naɪzər

synchronism
BR 'sɪŋkrənɪz(ə)m
AM 'sɪŋkrə,nɪzəm, 'sɪnkrə,nɪzəm

synchronistic
BR ˌsɪŋkrə'nɪstɪk
AM ˌsɪŋkrə'nɪstɪk, ˌsɪnkrə'nɪstɪk

synchronistically
BR ˌsɪŋkrə'nɪstɪkli
AM ˌsɪŋkrə'nɪstɪk(ə)li, ˌsɪnkrə'nɪstɪk(ə)li

synchronization
BR ˌsɪŋkrənʌɪ'zeɪʃn
AM ˌsɪŋkrənə'zeɪʃən, ˌsɪŋkrə,naɪ'zeɪʃən, ˌsɪnkrənə'zeɪʃən, ˌsɪnkrə,naɪ'zeɪʃən

synchronize
BR 'sɪŋkrənʌɪz, -ɪz, -ɪŋ, -d
AM 'sɪŋkrə,naɪz, 'sɪnkrə,naɪz, -ɪz, -ɪŋ, -d

synchronizer
BR 'sɪŋkrənʌɪzə(r), -z

synchronous
AM ˈsɪŋkrəˌnaɪzər,
ˈsɪnkrəˌnaɪzər, -z
synchronous
BR ˈsɪŋkrənəs
AM ˈsɪŋkrənəs,
ˈsɪnkrənəs
synchronously
BR ˈsɪŋkrənəsli
AM ˈsɪŋkrənəsli,
ˈsɪnkrənəsli
synchronousness
BR ˈsɪŋkrənəsnəs
AM ˈsɪŋkrənəsnəs,
ˈsɪnkrənəsnəs
synchrony
BR ˈsɪŋkrəni
AM ˈsɪŋkrəni,
ˈsɪnkrəni
synchrotron
BR ˈsɪŋkrətrɒn, -z
AM ˈsɪŋkrəˌtrɑn,
ˈsɪnkrəˌtrɑn, -z
synclinal
BR sɪnˈklaɪnl,
sɪŋˈklaɪnl
AM sɪŋˈklaɪnəl
syncline
BR ˈsɪŋklaɪn, -z
AM ˈsɪŋˌklaɪn, -z
syncopal
BR ˈsɪŋkəpl
AM ˈsɪŋkəpəl
syncopate
BR ˈsɪŋkəpeɪt, -s, -ɪŋ,
-ɪd
AM ˈsɪŋkəˌpeɪt, -ts,
-dɪŋ, -dɪd
syncopation
BR ˌsɪŋkəˈpeɪʃn
AM ˌsɪŋkəˈpeɪʃən
syncopator
BR ˈsɪŋkəpeɪtə(r), -z
AM ˈsɪŋkəˌpeɪdər, -z
syncope
BR ˈsɪŋkəpi
AM ˈsɪŋkəpi
syncretic
BR sɪnˈkrɛtɪk,
sɪŋˈkrɛtɪk
AM sɪŋˈkrɛdɪk,
sɪnˈkrɛdɪk
syncretise
BR ˈsɪŋkrɪtʌɪz, -ɪz, -ɪŋ,
-d
AM ˈsɪŋkrəˌtaɪz,
ˈsɪnkrəˌtaɪz, -ɪz, -ɪŋ, -d
syncretism
BR ˈsɪŋkrɪtɪz(ə)m
AM ˈsɪŋkrəˌtɪzəm,
ˈsɪnkrəˌtɪzəm
syncretist
BR ˈsɪŋkrɪtɪst, -s
AM ˈsɪŋkrədəst,
ˈsɪnkrədəst, -s
syncretistic
BR ˌsɪŋkrɪˈtɪstɪk
AM ˌsɪŋkrəˈtɪstɪk,
ˌsɪnkrəˈtɪstɪk

syncretize
BR ˈsɪŋkrɪtʌɪz, -ɪz, -ɪŋ,
-d
AM ˈsɪŋkrəˌtaɪz,
ˈsɪnkrəˌtaɪz, -ɪz, -ɪŋ, -d
syncytia
BR sɪnˈsɪtɪə(r)
AM sɪnˈsɪʃə
syncytial
BR sɪnˈsɪʃl
AM sɪnˈsɪʃəl
syncytium
BR sɪnˈsɪtɪəm
AM sɪnˈsɪʃəm
syndactyl
BR sɪnˈdakt(ɪ)l
AM sɪnˈdæktl
syndactylism
BR sɪnˈdaktɪlɪz(ə)m,
sɪnˈdaktlɪz(ə)m
AM sɪnˈdæktlˌɪzəm
syndactylous
BR sɪnˈdaktɪləs,
sɪnˈdaktləs
AM sɪnˈdæktələs
syndactyly
BR sɪnˈdaktɪli,
sɪnˈdaktli
AM sɪnˈdæktəli
syndeses
BR ˈsɪndɪsiːz
AM ˈsɪndəˌsiz
syndesis
BR ˈsɪndɪsɪs
AM ˈsɪndəsəs
syndesmoses
BR ˌsɪndɛzˈməʊsiːz
AM ˌsɪnˌdɛzˈmoʊˌsiz
syndesmosis
BR ˌsɪndɛzˈməʊsɪs
AM ˌsɪnˌdɛzˈmoʊsəs
syndetic
BR sɪnˈdɛtɪk
AM sɪnˈdɛdɪk
syndic
BR ˈsɪndɪk, -s
AM ˈsɪndɪk, -s
syndical
BR ˈsɪndɪkl
AM ˈsɪndɪkəl
syndicalism
BR ˈsɪndɪkəlɪz(ə)m,
ˈsɪndɪklˌɪz(ə)m
AM ˈsɪndəkəˌlɪzəm
syndicalist
BR ˈsɪndɪkəlɪst,
ˈsɪndɪklˌɪst, -s
AM ˈsɪndəkələst, -s
syndicate[1]
noun
BR ˈsɪndɪkət, -s
AM ˈsɪndɪkɪt, -s
syndicate[2]
verb
BR ˈsɪndɪkeɪt, -s, -ɪŋ, -ɪd
AM ˈsɪndəˌkeɪt, -ts,
-dɪŋ, -dɪd

syndication
BR ˌsɪndɪˈkeɪʃn
AM ˌsɪndəˈkeɪʃən
syndrome
BR ˈsɪndrəʊm, -z
AM ˈsɪnˌdroʊm, -z
syndromic
BR sɪnˈdrɒmɪk
AM sɪnˈdrɑmɪk
syne
BR sʌɪn
AM saɪn
synecdoche
BR sɪˈnɛkdəki
AM səˈnɛkdəki
synecdochic
BR sɪˈnɛkdəkɪk
AM səˈnɛkdəkɪk
synecious
BR sɪˈniːʃəs
AM səˈniːʃəs
synecological
BR ˌsiːnɪkəˈlɒdʒɪkl,
ˌsɪnɛkəˈlɒdʒɪkl
AM ˌsɪnˌɛkəˈlɑdʒəkəl,
ˌsɪnˌikəˈlɑdʒəkəl
synecologist
BR ˌsɪnɪˈkɒlədʒɪst, -s
AM ˌsiːniˈkɑlədʒəst,
ˌsɪnəˈkɑlədʒəst, -s
synecology
BR ˌsɪnɪˈkɒlədʒi
AM ˌsɪnˌiˈkɑlədʒi,
ˌsɪnˌɛkəlɑdʒi
synereses
BR sɪˈnɪərəsiːz
AM səˈnɛrəˌsiz,
sɪˈnɪrəˌsiz
syneresis
BR sɪˈnɪərəsɪs
AM səˈnɛrəsəs,
səˈnɪrəsəs
synergetic
BR ˌsɪnəˈdʒɛtɪk
AM ˌsɪnərˈdʒɛdɪk
synergic
BR sɪˈnɜːdʒɪk
AM səˈnɜrdʒɪk
synergism
BR ˈsɪnədʒɪz(ə)m
AM ˈsɪnərˌdʒɪzəm
synergist
BR ˈsɪnədʒɪst, -s
AM ˈsɪnərdʒəst, -s
synergistic
BR ˌsɪnəˈdʒɪstɪk
AM ˌsɪnərˈdʒɪstɪk
synergistically
BR ˌsɪnəˈdʒɪstɪkli
AM ˌsɪnərˈdʒɪstək(ə)li
synergy
BR ˈsɪnədʒi
AM ˈsɪnərdʒi
synesis
BR ˈsɪnɪsɪs
AM ˈsɪnəsəs

synesthesia
BR ˌsɪnɪsˈθiːzɪə(r),
ˌsɪnɪsˈθiːʒə(r)
AM ˌsɪnɪsˈθiːʒ(i)ə,
ˌsɪnɪsˈθiːziə
syngamous
BR ˈsɪŋgəməs
AM ˈsɪŋgəməs
syngamy
BR ˈsɪŋgəmi
AM ˈsɪŋgəmi
Synge
BR sɪŋ
AM sɪŋ
syngenesis
BR sɪnˈdʒɛnɪsɪs
AM sɪnˈdʒɛnəsəs
syngnathous
BR ˈsɪŋnəθəs
AM ˈsɪŋnəθəs
synizeses
BR ˌsɪnɪˈziːsiːz
AM ˌsɪnəˈziˌsiz
synizesis
BR ˌsɪnɪˈziːsɪs
AM ˌsɪnəˈzisɪs
synod
BR ˈsɪnəd, ˈsɪnɒd, -z
AM ˈsɪnəd, -z
synodal
BR ˈsɪnədl
AM ˈsɪnədəl
synodic
BR sɪˈnɒdɪk
AM səˈnɑdɪk
synodical
BR sɪˈnɒdɪkl
AM səˈnɑdəkəl
synodically
BR sɪˈnɒdɪkli
AM səˈnɑdək(ə)li
synoecious
BR sɪˈniːʃəs
AM səˈniːʃəs
synonym
BR ˈsɪnənɪm, -z
AM ˈsɪnəˌnɪm, -z
synonymic
BR ˌsɪnəˈnɪmɪk
AM ˌsɪnəˈnɪmɪk
synonymity
BR ˌsɪnəˈnɪmɪti
AM ˌsɪnəˈnɪmɪdi
synonymous
BR sɪˈnɒnɪməs
AM səˈnɑnəməs
synonymously
BR sɪˈnɒnɪməsli
AM səˈnɑnəməsli
synonymousness
BR sɪˈnɒnɪməsnəs
AM səˈnɑnəməsnəs
synonymy
BR sɪˈnɒnɪmi
AM səˈnɑnəmi
synopses
BR sɪˈnɒpsiːz

synopsis
AM sə'nɑp͵siz
BR sɪ'nɒpsɪs
AM sə'nɑpsəs

synopsise
BR sɪ'nɒpsʌɪz, -ɪz, -ɪŋ, -d
AM sə'nɑp͵saɪz, -ɪz, -ɪŋ, -d

synopsize
BR sɪ'nɒpsʌɪz, -ɪz, -ɪŋ, -d
AM sə'nɑp͵saɪz, -ɪz, -ɪŋ, -d

synoptic
BR sɪ'nɒptɪk, -s
AM sə'nɑptɪk, -s

synoptical
BR sɪ'nɒptɪkl
AM sə'nɑptəkəl

synoptically
BR sɪ'nɒptɪkli
AM sə'nɑptək(ə)li

synoptist
BR sɪ'nɒptɪst, -s
AM sə'nɑptəst, -s

synostoses
BR ͵sɪnɒ'stəʊsiːz
AM ͵sɪnɑ'stoʊsiz

synostosis
BR ͵sɪnɒ'stəʊsɪs
AM ͵sɪ͵nɑ'stoʊsəs

synovia
BR sʌɪ'nəʊviə(r), sɪ'nəʊviə(r)
AM sə'noʊviə

synovial
BR sʌɪ'nəʊviəl, sɪ'nəʊviəl
AM sə'noʊviəl

synovitis
BR ͵sʌɪnə(ʊ)'vʌɪtɪs, ͵sɪnə'vʌɪtɪs
AM ͵sɪnə'vaɪdɪs

syntactic
BR sɪn'taktɪk
AM sɪn'tæktɪk

syntactical
BR sɪn'taktɪkl
AM sɪn'tæktəkəl

syntactically
BR sɪn'taktɪkli
AM sɪn'tæktək(ə)li

syntagm
BR 'sɪntam, -z
AM 'sɪn͵tæm, -z

syntagma
BR sɪn'tagmə(r)
AM sɪn'tægmə

syntagmata
BR sɪn'tagmətə(r)
AM sɪn'tægmədə

syntagmatic
BR ͵sɪntag'matɪk
AM ͵sɪn͵tæg'mædɪk

syntagmatically
BR ͵sɪntag'matɪkli

AM ͵sɪn͵tæg'mædək(ə)li

syntagmic
BR sɪn'tagmɪk
AM ͵sɪn'tægmɪk

syntax
BR 'sɪntaks
AM 'sɪn͵tæks

syntheses
BR 'sɪnθɪsiːz
AM 'sɪnθə͵siz

synthesis
BR 'sɪnθɪsɪs
AM 'sɪnθəsəs

synthesise
BR 'sɪnθɪsʌɪz, -ɪz, -ɪŋ, -d
AM 'sɪnθə͵saɪz, -ɪz, -ɪŋ, -d

synthesiser
BR 'sɪnθɪsʌɪzə(r), -z
AM 'sɪnθə͵saɪzər, -z

synthesist
BR 'sɪnθɪsɪst, -s
AM 'sɪnθəsəst, -s

synthesize
BR 'sɪnθɪsʌɪz, -ɪz, -ɪŋ, -d
AM 'sɪnθə͵saɪz, -ɪz, -ɪŋ, -d

synthesizer
BR 'sɪnθɪsʌɪzə(r), -z
AM 'sɪnθə͵saɪzər, -z

synthetic
BR sɪn'θɛtɪk, -s
AM sɪn'θɛdɪk, -s

synthetical
BR sɪn'θɛtɪkl
AM sɪn'θɛdəkəl

synthetically
BR sɪn'θɛtɪkli
AM sɪn'θɛdək(ə)li

synthetise
BR 'sɪnθɪtʌɪz, -ɪz, -ɪŋ, -d
AM 'sɪnθə͵taɪz, -ɪz, -ɪŋ, -d

synthetize
BR 'sɪnθɪtʌɪz, -ɪz, -ɪŋ, -d
AM 'sɪnθə͵taɪz, -ɪz, -ɪŋ, -d

syntype
BR 'sɪntʌɪp, -s
AM 'sɪn͵taɪp, -s

Syon
BR 'sʌɪən
AM 'saɪən

syphilis
BR 'sɪfɪlɪs, 'sɪfl̩ɪs
AM 'sɪf(ə)lɪs, 'sɪfələs

syphilise
BR 'sɪfɪlʌɪz, 'sɪfl̩ʌɪz, -ɪz, -ɪŋ, -d
AM 'sɪf(ə)͵laɪz, -ɪz, -ɪŋ, -d

syphilitic
BR ͵sɪfɪ'lɪtɪk
AM ͵sɪf(ə)'lɪdɪk

syphilize
BR 'sɪfɪlʌɪz, 'sɪfl̩ʌɪz, -ɪz, -ɪŋ, -d

AM ͵sɪn͵tæg'mædək(ə)li
-d

syphiloid
BR 'sɪfɪlɔɪd, 'sɪfl̩ɔɪd
AM 'sɪf(ə)͵lɔɪd

syphon
BR 'sʌɪfl̩n, -nz, -nɪŋ \-(ə)nɪŋ, -nd
AM 'saɪfl̩ən, -ənz, -(ə)nɪŋ, -ənd

Syracuse¹
New York
BR 'sɪrəkjuːs, 'sɪrəkjuːz
AM 'sɪrə͵kjuz

Syracuse²
Sicily
BR 'sʌɪrəkjuːz, 'sʌɪrəkjuːs
AM 'sɪrə͵kjus, 'sɪrə͵kjuz

syren
BR 'sʌɪrən, -z
AM 'saɪrən, -z

syrette®
BR sɪ'rɛt, -s
AM sə'rɛt, -s

Syria
BR 'sɪrɪə(r)
AM 'sɪriə

Syriac
BR 'sɪrɪak
AM 'sɪri͵æk

Syrian
BR 'sɪrɪən, -z
AM 'sɪriən, -z

syringa
BR sɪ'rɪŋgə(r), -z
AM sə'rɪŋgə, -z

syringe
BR sɪ'rɪn(d)ʒ, -ɪz, -ɪŋ, -d
AM sə'rɪndʒ, 'sɪrɪndʒ, -ɪz, -ɪŋ, -d

syringeal
BR sɪ'rɪn(d)ʒɪəl
AM sə'rɪndʒiəl

syrinx
BR 'sɪrɪŋks, -ɪz
AM 'sɪrɪŋks, -ɪz

Syro-Phoenician
BR ͵sʌɪrəʊfɪ'nɪʃn, ͵sʌɪrəʊfɪ'niːʃn, -z
AM 'saɪroʊfə'nɪʃən, 'sɪroʊfə'nɪʃən, -z

syrphid
BR 'səːfɪd, -z
AM 'sərfəd, -z

syrup
BR 'sɪrəp, -s
AM 'sɪrəp, -s

syrupy
BR 'sɪrəpi
AM 'sɪrəpi

syssarcoses
BR ͵sɪsɑ:'kəʊsiːz
AM ͵sɪsɑr'koʊ͵siz

syssarcosis
BR ͵sɪsɑː'kəʊsɪs

AM ͵sɪsɑr'koʊsəs

systaltic
BR sɪ'staltɪk
AM sə'stɔltɪk, sə'stæltɪk, sə'staltɪk

system
BR 'sɪstɪm, -z
AM 'sɪstɪm, -z

systematic
BR ͵sɪstɪ'matɪk, -s
AM ͵sɪstə'mædɪk, -s

systematically
BR ͵sɪstɪ'matɪkli
AM ͵sɪstə'mædək(ə)li

systematisation
BR ͵sɪstɪmətʌɪ'zeɪʃn
AM ͵sɪstəmədə'zeɪʃən, ͵sɪstəmə͵taɪ'zeɪʃən

systematise
BR 'sɪstɪmətʌɪz, -ɪz, -ɪŋ, -d
AM 'sɪstəmə͵taɪz, -ɪz, -ɪŋ, -d

systematiser
BR 'sɪstɪmətʌɪzə(r)
AM 'sɪstəmə͵taɪzər

systematism
BR 'sɪstɪmətɪz(ə)m
AM 'sɪstəmə͵tɪzəm

systematist
BR 'sɪstɪmətɪst, -s
AM 'sɪstəmədəst, -s

systematization
BR ͵sɪstɪmətʌɪ'zeɪʃn
AM ͵sɪstəmədə'zeɪʃən, ͵sɪstəmə͵taɪ'zeɪʃən

systematize
BR 'sɪstɪmətʌɪz, -ɪz, -ɪŋ, -d
AM 'sɪstəmə͵taɪz, -ɪz, -ɪŋ, -d

systematizer
BR 'sɪstɪmətʌɪzə(r), -z
AM 'sɪstəmə͵taɪzər, -z

systemic
BR sɪ'stiːmɪk, sɪ'stɛmɪk, -s
AM sə'stɛmɪk, -s

systemically
BR sɪ'stiːmɪkli, sɪ'stɛmɪkli
AM sə'stɛmək(ə)li

systemisation
BR ͵sɪstɪmʌɪ'zeɪʃn
AM ͵sɪstəmə'zeɪʃən, ͵sɪstə͵maɪ'zeɪʃən

systemise
BR 'sɪstɪmʌɪz, -ɪz, -ɪŋ, -d
AM 'sɪstə͵maɪz, -ɪz, -ɪŋ, -d

systemiser
BR 'sɪstɪmʌɪzə(r), -z
AM 'sɪstə͵maɪzər, -z

systemization
BR ͵sɪstɪmʌɪ'zeɪʃn
AM ͵sɪstəmə'zeɪʃən, ͵sɪstə͵maɪ'zeɪʃən

systemize
BR 'sɪstɪmʌɪz, -ɪz, -ɪŋ,
-d
AM 'sɪstəˌmaɪz, -ɪz, -ɪŋ,
-d

systemizer
BR 'sɪstɪmʌɪzə(r), -z
AM 'sɪstəˌmaɪzər, -z

systemless
BR 'sɪstɪmlɪs
AM 'sɪstɪmlɪs

systole
BR 'sɪstəli
AM 'sɪstəli

systolic
BR sɪ'stɒlɪk
AM sə'stɑlɪk

Syston
BR 'sʌɪst(ə)n
AM 'saɪstən

syzygy
BR 'sɪzɪdʒi, zɪ-
AM 'sɪzɪdʒɪ, -z

Szechuan
BR ˌsɛ(t)ʃ'wɑːn

AM ˌsɛ(t)ʃ'wɑn

Szechwan
BR ˌsɛ(t)ʃ'wɑːn
AM ˌsɛ(t)ʃ'wɑn

Szeged
BR 'sɛgɛd
AM 'sɛgˌɛd

Tt

t
BR tiː, -z
AM tiː, -z

't
it
BR t
AM t

TA
BR ˌtiːˈeɪ, -z
AM ˌtiːˈeɪ, -z

ta
BR tɑː(r)
AM tɑ

Taal
BR tɑːl
AM tɑl

tab
BR tab, -z
AM tæb, -z

tabard
BR ˈtabəd, ˈtabɑːd, -z
AM ˈtæbərd, -z

tabaret
BR ˈtabərɪt, -s
AM ˈtæbərət, -s

Tabasco
BR təˈbaskəʊ
AM təˈbæskoʊ

tabby
BR ˈtabɪi, -ɪz
AM ˈtæbi, -z

tabernacle
BR ˈtabənakl, -z, -d
AM ˈtæbərˌnækəl, -z, -d

tabes
BR ˈteɪbiːz
AM ˈteɪˌbiz

tabetic
BR təˈbɛtɪk
AM təˈbɛdɪk

tabinet
BR ˈtabɪnɪt, -s
AM ˈtæbəˌnɛt, -s

Tabitha
BR ˈtabɪθə(r)
AM ˈtæbəθə

tabla
BR ˈtablə(r), -z
AM ˈtæblə, -z

tablature
BR ˈtablətʃə(r), -z
AM ˈtæblətʃər, ˈtæblətʃʊ(ə)r, -z

table
BR ˈteɪb|l, -lz, -lɪŋ \-lɪŋ, -ld
AM ˈteɪbəl, -əlz, -(ə)lɪŋ, -əld

tableau
BR ˈtabləʊ
AM ˌtæˈbloʊ, ˌtɑˈbloʊ

tableau vivant
BR ˌtabləʊ ˈviːvɒ̃, -z
AM ˌtɑˈbloʊ vɪˈvɑnt, -s

tableaux
BR ˈtabləʊz
AM ˌtæˈbloʊz, ˌtɑˈbloʊz

tableaux vivants
BR ˌtabləʊ ˈviːvɒ̃(z)
AM ˌtɑˈbloʊ vɪˈvɑnts

tablecloth
BR ˈteɪblklɒ|θ, -ðs
AM ˈteɪbəlˌklɔ|θ, ˈteɪbəlˌklɑ|θ, -ðs

table d'hôte
BR ˌtɑːbl ˈdəʊt
AM ˌtabəl ˈdoʊt

tableful
BR ˈteɪblfʊl, -z
AM ˈteɪbəlˌfʊl, -z

table lamp
BR ˈteɪbl lamp, -s
AM ˈteɪbəl ˌ(l)æmp, -s

tableland
BR ˈteɪblland
AM ˈteɪbəlˌ(l)ænd

Table Mountain
BR ˌteɪbl ˈmaʊntɪn
AM ˈteɪbəl ˈmaʊntɪn

tables d'hôte
BR ˌtɑːbl ˈdəʊt
AM ˌtabəl(z) ˈdoʊt

tablespoon
BR ˈteɪblspuːn, -z
AM ˈteɪbəlˌspun, -z

tablespoonful
BR ˈteɪblˌspuːnfʊl, -z
AM ˈteɪbəlˌspunˌfʊl, -z

tablespoonsful
BR ˈteɪblˌspuːnzfʊl
AM ˈteɪbəlˌspunzˌfʊl

tablet
BR ˈtablɪt, -s
AM ˈtæblət, -s

tabletop
BR ˈteɪblˌtɒp, -s
AM ˈteɪbəlˌtɑp, -s

tableware
BR ˈteɪblwɛː(r)
AM ˈteɪbəlˌwɛ(ə)r

tablier
BR ˈtablɪeɪ, -z
AM ˈtæbliˈeɪ, -z

tabloid
BR ˈtablɔɪd, -z
AM ˈtæbˌlɔɪd, -z

taboo
BR təˈbuː, -z, -ɪŋ, -d
AM təˈbu, -z, -ɪŋ, -d

tabor
BR ˈteɪbə(r), ˈteɪbɔː(r), -z
AM ˈteɪbər, -z

taboret
BR ˈtabərɪt, ˈtabəreɪ, -s
AM ˌtæbəˈrɛt, ˈtæbərət, -s

tabouret
BR ˈtabərɪt, ˈtabəreɪ, -s
AM ˌtæbəˈrɛt, ˈtæbərət, -s

Tabriz
BR təˈbriːz
AM təˈbriz

tabu
BR təˈbuː, -z
AM təˈbu, -z

tabula
BR ˈtabjələ(r)
AM ˈtæbjələ

tabulae
BR ˈtabjəliː
AM ˈtæbjəli, ˈtæbjəˌlaɪ

tabular
BR ˈtabjələ(r)
AM ˈtæbjələr

tabula rasa
BR ˌtabjələ ˈrɑːzə(r)
AM ˌtab(j)ʊlə ˈrɑzə

tabularly
BR ˈtabjələli
AM ˈtæbjələrli

tabulate
BR ˈtabjəleɪt, -s, -ɪŋ, -ɪd
AM ˈtæbjəˌleɪt, -ts, -dɪŋ, -dɪd

tabulation
BR ˌtabjəˈleɪʃn, -z
AM ˌtæbjəˈleɪʃən, -z

tabulator
BR ˈtabjəleɪtə(r), -z
AM ˈtæbjəˌleɪdər, -z

tabun
BR ˈtɑːbʊn
AM ˈtɑbʊn

tacamahac
BR ˈtak(ə)məhak, -s
AM ˈtæk(ə)məˌhæk, -s

tacet
BR ˈtasɪt, ˈteɪsɪt, -s
AM ˈteɪsət, ˈtɑˌkɛt, -s

tach
BR tak, -s
AM tæk, -s

tachism
BR ˈtaʃɪz(ə)m
AM ˈtæˌʃɪzəm

tachistoscope
BR təˈkɪstəskəʊp, təˈkɪstəskəʊp, -s
AM təˈkɪstəˌskoʊp, -s

tachistoscopic
BR təˌkɪstəˈskɒpɪk, təˌkɪstəˈskɒpɪk
AM təˌkɪstəˈskɑpɪk

tacho
tachometer
BR ˈtakəʊ, -z
AM ˈtækoʊ, -z

tachograph
BR ˈtakəgrɑːf, ˈtakəgraf, -s
AM ˈtækəˌgræf, -s

tachometer
BR təˈkɒmɪtə(r), təˈkɒmɪtə(r), -z
AM tæˈkɑmədər, təˈkɑmədər, -z

tachycardia
BR ˌtakɪˈkɑːdɪə(r)
AM ˌtækəˈkɑrdiə

tachygrapher
BR təˈkɪgrəfə(r), təˈkɪgrəfə(r), -z
AM tæˈkɪgrəfər, təˈkɪgrəfər, -z

tachygraphic
BR ˌtakɪˈgrafɪk
AM ˌtækəˈgræfɪk

tachygraphical
BR ˌtakɪˈgrafɪkl
AM ˌtækəˈgræfəkəl

tachygraphy
BR təˈkɪgrəfi, təˈkɪgrəfi
AM tæˈkɪgrəfi, təˈkɪgrəfi

tachymeter
BR təˈkɪmɪtə(r), təˈkɪmɪtə(r), -z
AM tæˈkɪmədər, təˈkɪmədər, -z

tachymetry
BR təˈkɪmɪtri
AM təˈkɪmɪtri
AM tæˈkɪmətri, təˈkɪmətri

tachyon
BR ˈtakɪɒn
AM ˈtækiˌɑn

tacit
BR ˈtasɪt
AM ˈtæsət

Tacitean
BR ˌtasɪˈtiːən, təˈsɪtɪən
AM ˌtæsəˈtiən, təˈsɪdiən

tacitly
BR ˈtasɪtli
AM ˈtæsətli

tacitness
BR ˈtasɪtnɪs
AM ˈtæsətnɪs

taciturn
BR ˈtasɪtəːn
AM ˈtæsəˌtərn

taciturnity
BR ˌtasɪˈtəːnɪti
AM ˌtæsəˈtərnədi

taciturnly
BR ˈtasɪtəːnli
AM ˈtæsəˌtərnli

Tacitus
BR ˈtasɪtəs
AM ˈtæsədəs

tack
BR tak, -s, -ɪŋ, -t
AM tæk, -s, -ɪŋ, -t

tackboard
BR ˈtakbɔːd, -z
AM ˈtækˌbɔ(ə)rd, -z

tacker
BR ˈtakə(r), -z
AM ˈtækər, -z

tackily
BR ˈtakɪli
AM ˈtækəli

tackiness
BR ˈtakɪnɪs
AM ˈtækɪnɪs

tackle
BR ˈtak|l, -lz, -l̩ɪŋ \-l̩ɪŋ, -ld
AM ˈtæk|əl, -əlz, -(ə)lɪŋ, -əld

tackler
BR ˈtak|ə(r) ˈtaklə(r), -z
AM ˈtæk(ə)lər, -z

tacky
BR ˈtak|i, -ɪə(r), -ɪɪst
AM ˈtæki, -ər, -ɪɪst

taco
BR ˈtakəʊ, ˈtɑːkəʊ, -z
AM ˈtɑːkoʊ, -z

Tacoma
BR təˈkəʊmə(r)
AM təˈkoʊmə

taconite
BR ˈtakənʌɪt, -s
AM ˈtækəˌnaɪt, -s

tact
BR takt
AM tæk(t)

tactful
BR ˈtaktf(ʊ)l
AM ˈtæk(t)fəl

tactfully
BR ˈtaktfʊli, ˈtaktfl̩i
AM ˈtæk(t)fəli

tactfulness
BR ˈtaktf(ʊ)lnəs
AM ˈtæk(t)fəlnəs

tactic
BR ˈtaktɪk, -s
AM ˈtæktɪk, -s

tactical
BR ˈtaktɪkl
AM ˈtæktəkəl

tactically
BR ˈtaktɪkli
AM ˈtæktək(ə)li

tactician
BR takˈtɪʃn, -z
AM tækˈtɪʃən, -z

tactile
BR ˈtaktʌɪl
AM ˈtæktl, ˈtækˌtaɪl

tactility
BR takˈtɪlɪti
AM tækˈtɪlɪdi

tactless
BR ˈtaktləs
AM ˈtæk(t)ləs

tactlessly
BR ˈtaktləsli
AM ˈtæk(t)ləsli

tactlessness
BR ˈtaktləsnəs
AM ˈtæk(t)ləsnəs

tactual
BR ˈtaktʃʊəl, ˈtaktʃ(ʊ)l, ˈtaktjʊəl, ˈtaktjʊl
AM ˈtæk(t)ʃ(əw)əl

tactually
BR ˈtaktʃʊəli, ˈtaktʃʊli, ˈtaktʃl̩i, ˈtaktjʊəli, ˈtaktjʊli
AM ˈtæk(t)ʃ(əw)əli

tad
BR tad, -z
AM tæd, -z

Tadcaster
BR ˈtadˌkastə(r), ˈtadkəstə(r), ˈtadˌkɑːstə(r)
AM ˈtædˌkæstər

Tadema
BR ˈtadɪmə(r)
AM ˈtadəmə

Tadjik
BR ˈtɑːdʒɪk, tɑːˈdʒiːk, -s
AM tɑˈdʒɪk, -s

Tadjikistan
BR təˌdʒiːkɪˈstɑːn, təˌdʒiːkɪˈstan
AM təˈdʒikəˌstæn

tadpole
BR ˈtadpəʊl, -z
AM ˈtædˌpoʊl, -z

Tadzhik
BR ˈtɑːdʒɪk, tɑːˈdʒiːk, -s
AM tɑˈdʒɪk, -s

Tadzhikistan
BR təˌdʒiːkɪˈstɑːn, təˌdʒiːkɪˈstan
AM təˈdʒikəˌstæn

tae kwon do
BR ˌtʌɪ ˌkwɒn ˈdəʊ
AM ˌtaɪ ˌkwɑn ˈdoʊ

ta'en
BR teɪn
AM teɪn

taenia
BR ˈtiːnɪə(r)
AM ˈtiniə

taeniae
BR ˈtiːnɪː
AM ˈtiniˌi, ˈtiniˌaɪ

taenioid
BR ˈtiːnɪɔɪd
AM ˈtiniˌɔɪd

Taff
BR taf, -s
AM tæf, -s

taffeta
BR ˈtafɪtə(r)
AM ˈtæfədə

taffrail
BR ˈtafreɪl, ˈtafr(ɪ)l, -z
AM ˈtæfrəl, ˈtæˌfreɪl, -z

taffy
BR ˈtaf|i, -ɪz
AM ˈtæfi, -z

tafia
BR ˈtafɪə(r), -z
AM ˈtæfiə, -z

Taft
BR taft
AM tæft

tag
BR tag, -z, -ɪŋ, -d
AM tæg, -z, -ɪŋ, -d

Tagalog
BR təˈgɑːlɒg, təˈgɑːləg, təˈgalɒg, təˈgaləg
AM təˈgaləg, ˈtægəˌlɔg, ˈtægəˌlag

tagalong
BR ˈtagəlɒŋ, -z
AM ˈtægəˌlɔŋ, ˈtægəˌlaŋ, -z

Taganrog
BR ˈtagənrɒg
AM ˈtægənˌrɔg, ˈtægənˌrag

tag end
BR ˈtag ɛnd, -z
AM ˈtæg ˌɛnd, -z

tagetes
BR ˈtadʒɪtiːz, təˈdʒiːtiːz
AM ˈtædʒəˌtiz, təˈdʒɛdiz

Taggart
BR ˈtagət
AM ˈtægərt

tagliatelle
BR ˌtaljəˈtɛli
AM ˌtæljəˈtɛl

tagmeme
BR ˈtagmiːm, -z
AM ˈtægˌmim, -z

tagmemics
BR tagˈmiːmɪks
AM tægˈmimɪks

Tagore
BR təˈgɔː(r)
AM təˈgɔ(ə)r

Tagus
BR ˈteɪgəs
AM ˈteɪgəs

Tahiti
BR tɑːˈhiːti, təˈhiːti
AM təˈhidi, tɑˈhidi

Tahitian
BR tɑːˈhiːʃn, təˈhiːʃn, -z
AM təˈhiʃən, tɑˈhiʃən, -z

Tahoe
BR ˈtɑːhəʊ
AM ˈtɑˌhoʊ

tahr
BR tɑː(r), -z
AM tɑr, -z

tahsil
BR tɑːˈsiːl, -z
AM tɑˈsi(ə)l, -z

tahsildar
BR ˌtɑːsiːlˈdɑː(r), -z
AM ˌtɑsilˈdɑr, -z

Tai
BR tʌɪ
AM taɪ

Tai'an
BR ˌtʌɪˈɑːn
AM ˈtaɪˈɑn

tai chi
BR ˌtʌɪ ˈtʃiː
AM ˌtaɪ ˈtʃi

t'ai chi
BR ˌtʌɪ ˈtʃiː
AM ˌtaɪ ˈtʃi

t'ai chi ch'uan
BR ˌtʌɪ ˌtʃiː ˈtʃwɑːn
AM ˌtaɪ ˌtʃi ˈtʃwɑn

Taichung
BR ˌtʌɪˈtʃʊŋ
AM ˈtaɪˈtʃʊŋ

taig
BR teɪg, -z
AM teɪg, -z

taiga
BR ˈtʌɪgə(r), ˈtʌɪgɑː(r), -z
AM ˈtaɪgə, taɪˈgɑ, -z

tail
BR teɪl, -z, -ɪŋ, -d
AM teɪl, -z, -ɪŋ, -d

tailback
BR ˈteɪlbak, -s
AM ˈtaɪlˌbæk, -s

tailboard
BR ˈteɪlbɔːd, -z
AM ˈteɪlˌbɔ(ə)rd, -z

tailbone
BR ˈteɪlbəʊn, -z
AM ˈtaɪlˌboʊn, -z

tailcoat
BR ˈteɪlkəʊt, ˌteɪlˈkəʊt, -s
AM ˈteɪlˌkoʊt, -s

tail-end
BR ˌteɪl ˈɛnd, -z
AM ˌteɪl ˈɛnd, -z

tail-ender
BR ˌteɪlˈɛndə(r), -z
AM ˌteɪlˈɛndər, -z

tailgate
BR ˈteɪlgeɪt, -s, -ɪŋ, -ɪd
AM ˈteɪlˌgeɪt, -ts, -dɪŋ, -dɪd

tailgater
BR ˈteɪlgeɪtə(r), -z
AM ˈteɪlˌgeɪdər, -z

tailie
BR ˈteɪl|i, -ɪz
AM ˈteɪli, -z

tailing
BR ˈteɪlɪŋ, -z
AM ˈteɪlɪŋ, -z

tail lamp
BR ˈteɪl lamp, -s
AM ˈteɪl ˌ(l)æmp, -s

Tailleferre
BR ˌtʌɪˈfɛː(r), ˈtʌɪfɛː(r)
AM ˌtaɪəˈfɛ(ə)r

tailless
BR ˈteɪlɪs
AM ˈteɪ(l)ləs

taillight
BR ˈteɪlˌlaɪt, -s
AM ˈteɪlˌ(l)aɪt, -s

tailor
BR ˈteɪlə(r), -z
AM ˈteɪlər, -z

tailoress
BR ˈteɪləˈres, -ɪz
AM ˈteɪlərəs, -əz

tailor-made
BR ˈteɪləˈmeɪd
AM ˈteɪlərˈmeɪd

tailpiece
BR ˈteɪlpiːs, -ɪz
AM ˈteɪlˌpis, -ɪz

tailpipe
BR ˈteɪlpʌɪp, -s
AM ˈteɪlˌpaɪp, -s

tailplane
BR ˈteɪlpleɪn, -z
AM ˈteɪlˌpleɪn, -z

tailspin
BR ˈteɪlspɪn, -z
AM ˈteɪlˌspɪn, -z

tailstock
BR ˈteɪlstɒk, -s
AM ˈteɪlˌstak, -s

tailwheel
BR ˈteɪlwiːl, -z
AM ˈteɪlˌ(h)wil, -z

tailwind
BR ˈteɪlwɪnd, -z
AM ˈteɪlˌwɪnd, -z

Taimyr
BR ˌtaɪˈmɪə(r)
AM taɪˈmɪ(ə)r

Tainan
BR ˌtaɪˈnan
AM ˌtaɪˈnæn

taint
BR teɪnt, -s, -ɪŋ, -ɪd
AM teɪn|t, -ts, -(t)ɪŋ, -(t)ɪd

taintless
BR ˈteɪntlɪs
AM ˈteɪn(t)lɪs

taipan
BR ˈtʌɪpan, -z
AM ˈtaɪˌpæn, -z

Taipei
BR ˌtʌɪˈpeɪ
AM ˌtaɪˈpeɪ

Taiping
BR ˌtʌɪˈpɪŋ
AM ˌtaɪˈpɪŋ

Tait
BR teɪt
AM teɪt

Taiwan
BR ˌtʌɪˈwaːn, ˌtʌɪˈwɒn
AM ˌtaɪˈwan

Taiwanese
BR ˌtʌɪwəˈniːz
AM ˌtaɪˌwɑˈniz

taj
BR taː(d)ʒ, -ɪz
AM ta(d)ʒ, -əz

Tajik
BR ˈtaːdʒɪk, taːˈdʒiːk, -s
AM taˈdʒɪk, -s

Tajikistan
BR təˌdʒiːkɪˈstaːn, təˌdʒiːkɪˈstan
AM təˈdʒikəˌstæn

Taj Mahal
BR ˌtaː(d)ʒ məˈhaːl
AM ˌta(d)ʒ məˈhal

Tajo
BR ˈtaːhəʊ
AM ˈtahoʊ

taka
BR ˈtaːkaː(r)
AM ˈtakə

takable
BR ˈteɪkəbl
AM ˈteɪkəbəl

takahe
BR ˈtaːkəh|i, -ɪz
AM təˈkaɪ, -z

take
BR teɪk, -s, -ɪŋ
AM teɪk, -s, -ɪŋ

takeaway
BR ˈteɪkəweɪ, -z
AM ˈteɪkəˌweɪ, -z

takedown
BR ˈteɪkdaʊn, -z
AM ˈteɪkˌdaʊn, -z

take-home
BR ˈteɪkhəʊm, -z
AM ˈteɪkˌ(h)oʊm, -z

take-in
BR ˈteɪkɪn, -z
AM ˈteɪkˌɪn, -z

taken
BR ˈteɪk(ə)n
AM ˈteɪkən

takeoff
BR ˈteɪkɒf, -s
AM ˈteɪkˌɒf, ˈteɪkˌaf, -s

takeout
BR ˈteɪkaʊt, -s
AM ˈteɪkˌaʊt, -s

takeover
BR ˈteɪkˌəʊvə(r), -z
AM ˈteɪkˌoʊvər, -z

taker
BR ˈteɪkə(r), -z
AM ˈteɪkər, -z

takeup
BR ˈteɪkʌp, -s
AM ˈteɪkˌəp, -s

taking
BR ˈteɪkɪŋ, -z
AM ˈteɪkɪŋ, -z

takingly
BR ˈteɪkɪŋli
AM ˈteɪkɪŋli

takingness
BR ˈteɪkɪŋnɪs
AM ˈteɪkɪŋnɪs

Taklimakan
BR ˌtaklɪməˈkaːn
AM ˌtakləməˈkan

tala
BR ˈtaːlə(r), -z
AM ˈtaːlə, -z

talapoin
BR ˈtaləpɔɪn, -z
AM ˈtælə,pɔɪn, ˈtælə,pwɑn, -z

talaria
BR təˈlɛːrɪə(r)
AM təˈlɛriə

talbot
BR ˈtɔːlbət, ˈtɒlbət, -s
AM ˈtælbət, ˈtɒlbət, ˈtalbət, -s

talbot²
BR ˈtɔːlbət, ˈtɒlbət, -s
AM ˈtælbət, ˈtɒlbət, ˈtalbət, -s

talc
BR talk
AM tælk

talcose
BR ˈtalkəʊs, ˈtalkəʊz
AM ˈtæl,koʊs, ˈtæl,koʊz

talcous
BR ˈtalkəs
AM ˈtælkəs

talcum
BR ˈtalkəm
AM ˈtælkəm

talcy
BR ˈtalki
AM ˈtælki

tale
BR teɪl
AM teɪl

talebearer
BR ˈteɪlˌbɛːrə(r), -z
AM ˈteɪlˌbɛrər, -z

talebearing
BR ˈteɪlˌbɛːrɪŋ
AM ˈteɪlˌbɛrɪŋ

talent
BR ˈtalənt, ˈtalnt, -s, -ɪd
AM ˈtælənt, -s, -əd

talentless
BR ˈtaləntləs, ˈtalntləs
AM ˈtælən(t)ləs

tales¹
people chosen for a jury
BR ˈteɪliːz
AM ˈteɪˌliz

tales²
plural of tale
BR teɪlz
AM teɪlz

talesman
BR ˈteɪlzmən
AM ˈteɪlzmən

talesmen
BR ˈteɪlzmən
AM ˈteɪlzmən

taleteller
BR ˈteɪlˌtelə(r), -z
AM ˈteɪlˌtelər, -z

Talgarth
BR ˈtalgaːθ
AM ˈtælˌgarθ

tali
BR ˈteɪlʌɪ
AM ˈteɪˌlaɪ

talion
BR ˈtalɪən, -z
AM ˈtælɪən, -z

talipes
BR ˈtalɪpiːz
AM ˈtæləˌpiz

talipot
BR ˈtalɪpɒt, -s
AM ˈtæləˌpat, -s

talisman
BR ˈtalɪzmən, ˈtalɪsmən, -z
AM ˈtæləsmən, ˈtæləzmən, -z

talismanic
BR ˌtalɪzˈmanɪk
AM ˌtæləzˈmænɪk

talk
BR tɔːk, -s, -ɪŋ, -t
AM tɔk, tak, -s, -ɪŋ, -t

talkathon
BR ˈtɔːkəθɒn, -z
AM ˈtɔkəˌθan, ˈtakəˌθan, -z

talkative
BR ˈtɔːkətɪv
AM ˈtɔkədɪv, ˈtakədɪv

talkatively
BR ˈtɔːkətɪvli
AM ˈtɔkədɪvli, ˈtakədɪvli

talkativeness
BR ˈtɔːkətɪvnɪs
AM ˈtɔkədɪvnɪs, ˈtakədɪvnɪs

talkback
BR ˈtɔːkbak, -s
AM ˈtɔkˌbæk, ˈtakˌbæk, -s

talker
BR ˈtɔːkə(r), -z
AM ˈtɔkər, ˈtakər, -z

talkfest
BR ˈtɔːkfest, -s
AM ˈtɔkˌfɛst, ˈtakˌfɛst, -s

talkie
BR ˈtɔːk|i, -ɪz
AM ˈtɔki, ˈtaki, -z

tall
BR tɔːl, -ə(r), -ɪst
AM tɔl, tal, -ər, -əst

tallage
BR ˈtal|ɪdʒ, -ɪdʒɪz
AM ˈtæləˌdʒ, -ɪz

Tallahassee
BR ˌtaləˈhasi
AM ˌtæləˈhæsi

tallboy
BR 'tɔːlbɔɪ, -z
AM 'tɔl,bɔɪ, 'tɑl,bɔɪ, -z

Talley
BR 'tali
AM 'tæli

Talleyrand
BR 'talɪrand
AM 'tæli,rænd

Tallin
BR 'talɪn, ta'liːn
AM 'tælən

Tallinn
BR 'talɪn, ta'liːn
AM 'tælən

Tallis
BR 'talɪs
AM 'tæləs

tallish
BR 'tɔːlɪʃ
AM 'tɔlɪʃ, 'talɪʃ

tallith
BR 'talɪθ, 'taːlɪθ, 'talɪs, 'taːlɪs
AM 'taləs, 'taləθ

tallness
BR 'tɔːlnəs
AM 'tɔlnəs, 'talnəs

tallow
BR 'taləʊ
AM 'tæloʊ

tallowish
BR 'taləʊʃ
AM 'tæləwɪʃ

tallowy
BR 'taləʊi
AM 'tæləwi

Tallulah
BR tə'luːlə(r)
AM tə'lulə

tally
BR 'tal|i, -ɪz, -ɪŋ, -ɪd
AM 'tæli, -z, -ɪŋ, -d

tally-ho
BR talɪ'həʊ, -z
AM ,tæli'hoʊ, -z

tallyman
BR 'talɪmən, 'talɪman
AM 'tæli,mæn

tallymen
BR 'talɪmən, 'talɪmen
AM 'tæli,men

Talmud
BR 'talmʊd, 'talmʌd
AM 'tal,mʊd, 'tælməd

Talmudic
BR tal'mʊdɪk, tal'mʌdɪk
AM tæl'm(j)udɪk, tæl'mʊdɪk, tal'm(j)udɪk, tal'mʊdɪk

Talmudical
BR tal'mʊdɪkl, tal'mʌdɪkl
AM tæl'm(j)udəkəl, tæl'mʊdəkəl,

tal'm(j)udəkəl, tal'mʊdəkəl

Talmudist
BR 'talmʊdɪst, 'talmʌdɪst, -s
AM 'tal,mʊdəst, 'tælmədəst, -s

talon
BR 'talən, -z, -d
AM 'tælən, -z, -d

talus
BR 'teɪləs
AM 'teɪləs

Talybont
BR talɪ'bɒnt
AM ,tæli'bɑnt

Tal-y-bont
BR talɪ'bɒnt
AM ,tæli'bɑnt
WE ,talʌ'bɒnt

Tal-y-llyn
BR ,talɪ'ɬɪn, talɪ'lɪn
AM ,tæli'lɪn
WE ,talʌ'ɬɪn

TAM
BR tam
AM tæm

tam
BR tam, -z
AM tæm, -z

tamable
BR 'teɪməbl
AM 'teɪməbəl

tamale
BR tə'mɑːl|i, -ɪz
AM tə'mɑli, -z

tamandua
BR tə'mand(j)ʊə(r), tə'mandʒʊə(r), ,taman'd(j)uːə(r), -z
AM tə'mændəwə, tə'mændʒəwə, -z

tamanoir
BR 'tamənwɑː(r), -z
AM 'tæmən'wɑr, -z

Tamar
BR 'teɪmɑː(r)
AM 'teɪmɑr

Tamara
BR tə'mɑːrə(r), 'tam(ə)rə(r)
AM tə'mɛrə, 'tæmərə

tamarack
BR 'tamərak, -s
AM 'tæm(ə),ræk, -s

tamari
BR tə'mɑːri
AM tə'mɑri

tamarillo
BR ,tamə'rɪləʊ, -z
AM ,tæmə'rɪloʊ, -z

tamarin
BR 'tam(ə)rɪn, -z
AM 'tæm(ə)rən, 'tæmə,rɪn, -z

tamarind
BR 'tam(ə)rɪnd, -z

AM 'tæm(ə)rənd, 'tæmə,rɪnd, -z

tamarisk
BR 'tam(ə)rɪsk, -s
AM 'tæm(ə)rəsk, 'tæmə,rɪsk, -s

tambala
BR tam'bɑːlə(r), -z
AM tɑm'bɑlə, -z

tamber
BR 'tambə(r), -z
AM 'tæmbər, -z

Tambo
BR 'tambəʊ
AM 'tæmboʊ

tambour
BR 'tambʊə(r), 'tambɔː(r), -z
AM 'tæm,bʊ(ə)r, -z

tamboura
BR tam'bʊərə(r), tam'bɔːrə(r), -z
AM 'tæm'bʊrə, -z

tambourin
BR 'tambərɪn, -z
AM 'tæmbə'rɪn, -z

tambourine
BR ,tambə'riːn, -z
AM ,tæmbə'rɪn, -z

tambourinist
BR ,tambə'riːnɪst, -s
AM ,tæmbə'rɪnɪst, -s

Tamburlaine
BR 'tambə:leɪn
AM 'tæmbər,leɪn

tame
BR teɪm, -z, -ɪŋ, -d
AM teɪm, -z, -ɪŋ, -d

tameability
BR ,teɪmə'bɪlɪti
AM ,teɪmə'bɪlɪdi

tameable
BR 'teɪməbl
AM 'teɪməbəl

tameableness
BR 'teɪməblnəs
AM 'teɪməbəlnəs

tamely
BR 'teɪmli
AM 'teɪmli

tameness
BR 'teɪmnɪs
AM 'teɪmnəs

tamer
BR 'teɪmə(r), -z
AM 'teɪmər, -z

Tamerlane
BR 'taməleɪn
AM 'tæmər,leɪn

Tamil
BR 'tam(ɪ)l, -z
AM 'tæməl, -z

Tamilian
BR tə'mɪliən
AM tə'mɪljən, tə'mɪliən

Tamil Nadu
BR ,tam(ɪ)l 'nɑːduː
AM 'tæməl nɑ'du

Tamla Motown
BR ,tamlə 'məʊtaʊn
AM ,tæmlə 'moʊ,taʊn

Tammany
BR 'taməni
AM 'tæməni

Tammie
BR 'tami
AM 'tæmi

tammy
BR 'tam|i, -ɪz
AM 'tæmi, -z

tam-o'-shanter
BR ,tamə'ʃantə(r), -z
AM 'tæmə,ʃæn(t)ər, -z

tamp
BR tam|p, -ps, -pɪŋ, -(p)t
AM tæm|p, -ps, -pɪŋ, -(p)t

Tampa
BR 'tampə(r)
AM 'tæmpə

tampan
BR 'tampan, -z
AM 'tæm,pæn, -z

tamper
BR 'tamp|ə(r), -əz, -(ə)rɪŋ, -əd
AM 'tæmp|ər, -ərz, -(ə)rɪŋ, -ərd

Tampere
BR 'tampərə(r)
AM 'tæmpərə

tamperer
BR 'tamp(ə)rə(r), -z
AM 'tæmp(ə)rər, -z

tampering
BR 'tamp(ə)rɪŋ, -z
AM 'tæmp(ə)rɪŋ, -z

tamper-proof
BR 'tampəpruːf
AM 'tæmpər,pruf

Tampico
BR tam'piːkəʊ
AM tæm'pi,koʊ

tampion
BR 'tampiən, -z
AM 'tæmpiən, -z

tampon
BR 'tampɒn, 'tampən, -z
AM 'tæm,pɑn, -z

tamponade
BR 'tampə,neɪd, -z
AM ,tæmpə'neɪd, -z

tamponage
BR 'tampənɪdʒ
AM 'tæmpənɪdʒ

tam-tam
BR 'tamtam, -z
AM 'tæm,tæm, -z

Tamworth
BR 'tamwəθ, -s

AM 'tæm,wərθ, -s

tan
BR tan, -z, -ɪŋ, -d
AM tæn, -z, -ɪŋ, -d

tanager
BR 'tanədʒə(r), -z
AM 'tænədʒər, -z

Tanagra
BR 'tanəɡrə(r), -z
AM 'tænəɡrə, -z

Tánaiste
BR 'tɔːnɪʃt(ʃ)ə(r),
'tɑːnɪʃt(ʃ)ə(r)
AM 'tɑnɪʃt(ʃ)ə
IR 'tɑːnəʃt'ə

Tananarive
BR ,tananə'riːv
AM ,tænənə'riv

tanbark
BR 'tanbɑːk, -s
AM 'tæn,bɑrk, -s

Tancred
BR 'taŋkrɪd, 'taŋkrɛd
AM 'tæŋkrəd

tandem
BR 'tandəm, -z
AM 'tændəm, -z

tandoor
BR 'tanduə(r),
tan'duə(r), 'tandɔː(r),
tan'dɔː(r), -z
AM tæn'dʊ(ə)r, -z

tandoori
BR tan'dʊər|i,
tan'dɔːr|i, -iz
AM tæn'dʊri, -z

Tandy
BR 'tandi
AM 'tændi

tang
BR taŋ, -z
AM tæŋ, -z

tanga
BR 'taŋɡə(r), -z
AM 'tæŋɡə, -z

Tanganyika
BR ,taŋɡən'jiːkə(r)
AM ,tæŋɡə'nikə

Tanganyikan
BR ,taŋɡən'jiːkən, -z
AM ,tæŋɡə'nikən, -z

tangelo
BR 'tan(d)ʒələʊ, -z
AM 'tændʒə,loʊ, -z

tangency
BR 'tan(d)ʒ(ə)ns|i, -iz
AM 'tændʒənsi, -z

tangent
BR 'tan(d)ʒ(ə)nt, -s
AM 'tændʒənt, -s

tangential
BR tan'dʒɛn(t)ʃl
AM tæn'dʒɛn(t)ʃəl

tangentially
BR tan'dʒɛn(t)ʃli,
tan'dʒɛnʃəli
AM tæn'dʒɛn(t)ʃəli

tangerine
BR ,tan(d)ʒə'riːn, -z
AM ,tændʒə'rin, -z

tanghin
BR 'taŋɡɪn, -z
AM 'tæŋɡən, -z

tangibility
BR ,tandʒɪ'bɪlɪti
AM ,tændʒə'bilɪdi

tangible
BR 'tandʒɪbl
AM 'tændʒəbəl

tangibleness
BR 'tandʒɪblnəs
AM 'tændʒəbəlnəs

tangibly
BR 'tan(d)ʒɪbli
AM 'tændʒəbli

Tangier
BR tan'dʒɪə(r)
AM tæn'dʒɪ(ə)r

Tangiers
BR tan'dʒɪəz
AM tæn'dʒɪ(ə)rz

tanginess
BR 'taŋɪnɪs
AM 'tæŋɪnɪs

tangle
BR 'taŋɡl|, -lz, -lɪŋ \-lɪŋ, -ld
AM 'tæŋɡ|əl, -əlz, -(ə)lɪŋ, -əld

Tanglewood
BR 'taŋlwʊd
AM 'tæŋɡəl,wʊd

tangly
BR 'taŋl|i, -iə(r), -ɪɪst
AM 'tæŋli, 'tæŋ(ə)li, -ər, -ɪst

Tangmere
BR 'taŋmɪə(r)
AM 'tæŋ,mɪ(ə)r

tango
BR 'taŋɡəʊ, -z, -ɪŋ, -d
AM 'tæŋɡoʊ, -z, -ɪŋ, -d

tangram
BR 'tangram, -z
AM 'tæŋ,græm, 'tæn,græm, -z

tangy
BR 'taŋ|i, -iə(r), -ɪɪst
AM 'tæŋi, -ər, -ɪst

tanh
BR θan, tanʃ, tan'eɪtʃ
AM θæn, 'tænʃ, ,tæn'eɪtʃ

Tania
BR 'tɑːnɪə(r), 'tanɪə(r)
AM 'tæniə, 'tɑniə

tanist
BR 'tanɪst, -s
AM 'tænəst, 'θɒnəst, 'θɑnəst, -s

tanistry
BR 'tanɪstri
AM 'tænəstri, 'θɒnəstri, 'θɑnəstri

tank
BR taŋ|k, -ks, -ɪŋ, -(k)t
AM tæŋ|k, -ks, -ɪŋ, -(k)t

tanka
BR 'taŋkə(r), 'tɑːŋkə(r), -z
AM 'tɑŋkə, -z

tankage
BR 'taŋk|ɪdʒ, -ɪdʒɪz
AM 'tæŋkɪdʒ, -ɪz

tankard
BR 'taŋkəd, -z
AM 'tæŋkərd, -z

tanker
BR 'taŋk|ə(r), -əz, -(ə)rɪŋ, -əd
AM 'tæŋkər, -z, -ɪŋ, -d

tankful
BR 'taŋkfʊl, -z
AM 'tæŋk,fʊl, -z

tankless
BR 'taŋkləs
AM 'tæŋkləs

tanksuit
BR 'taŋks(j)uːt, -s
AM 'tæŋk,sut, -s

tanktop
BR 'taŋktɒp, -s
AM 'tæŋk,tɑp, -s

tannable
BR 'tanəbl
AM 'tænəbəl

tannage
BR 'tan|ɪdʒ, -ɪdʒɪz
AM 'tænɪdʒ, -ɪz

tannate
BR 'taneɪt, -s
AM 'tæ,neɪt, -s

tanner
BR 'tanə(r), -z
AM 'tænər, -z

tannery
BR 'tan(ə)r|i, -iz
AM 'tænəri, -z

Tannhäuser
BR 'tan,hɔɪzə(r)
AM 'tæn,hɔɪzər

tannic
BR 'tanɪk
AM 'tænɪk

tannic acid
BR ,tanɪk 'asɪd
AM ,tænɪk 'æsəd

tannin
BR 'tanɪn
AM 'tænən

tannish
BR 'tanɪʃ
AM 'tænɪʃ

tannoy®
BR 'tanɔɪ, -z
AM 'tæ,nɔɪ, -z

Tanqueray
BR 'taŋkəreɪ, 'taŋk(ə)ri
AM 'tæŋkə,reɪ

tanrec
BR 'tanrɛk, -s
AM 'tænrɛk, -s

Tansey
BR 'tanzi
AM 'tænzi

tansy
BR 'tanz|i, -ɪz
AM 'tænzi, -z

tantalic
BR tan'talɪk
AM tæn'tælɪk

tantalisation
BR ,tantəlʌɪ'zeɪʃn, ,tantʃʌɪ'zeɪʃn
AM ,tæn(t)lə' zeɪʃən, ,tæn(t)lʌɪ'zeɪʃən

tantalise
BR 'tantəlʌɪz, 'tantʃʌɪz, -ɪz, -ɪŋ, -d
AM 'tæn(t)l,ʌɪz, -ɪz, -ɪŋ, -d

tantaliser
BR 'tantəlʌɪzə(r), 'tantʃʌɪzə(r), -z
AM 'tæn(t)l,ʌɪzər, -z

tantalisingly
BR 'tantəlʌɪzɪŋli, 'tantʃʌɪzɪŋli
AM 'tæn(t)l,ʌɪzɪŋli

tantalite
BR 'tantəlʌɪt, 'tantʃʌɪt
AM 'tæn(t)l,ʌɪt

tantalization
BR ,tantəlʌɪ'zeɪʃn, ,tantʃʌɪ'zeɪʃn
AM ,tæn(t)lə'zeɪʃən, ,tæn(t)lʌɪ'zeɪʃən

tantalize
BR 'tantəlʌɪz, 'tantʃʌɪz, -ɪz, -ɪŋ, -d
AM 'tæn(t)l,ʌɪz, -ɪz, -ɪŋ, -d

tantalizer
BR 'tantəlʌɪzə(r), 'tantʃʌɪzə(r), -z
AM 'tæn(t)l,ʌɪzər, -z

tantalizingly
BR 'tantəlʌɪzɪŋli, 'tantʃʌɪzɪŋli
AM 'tæn(t)l,ʌɪzɪŋli

tantalous
BR 'tantələs, 'tantʃləs
AM 'tæn(t)ləs

tantalum
BR 'tantələm, 'tantʃləm
AM 'tæn(t)ləm

tantalus
BR 'tantələs, 'tantʃləs, -ɪz
AM 'tæn(t)ləs, -əz

tantamount
BR 'tantəmaʊnt
AM 'tæn(t)ə,maʊnt

tantivy
BR tan'tɪv|i, -ɪz
AM tæn'tɪvi, -z

tant mieux
BR ˌtɒ̃ ˈmjuː(r)
AM ˌtɑn ˈmjɜ

tant pis
BR ˌtɒ̃ ˈpiː
AM ˌtɑn ˈpi

tantra
BR ˈtantrə(r), -z
AM ˈtɑntrə, -z

tantric
BR ˈtantrɪk
AM ˈtɑntrɪk

tantrism
BR ˈtantrɪz(ə)m
AM ˈtɑn.trɪzəm

tantrist
BR ˈtantrɪst, -s
AM ˈtɑntrəst, -s

tantrum
BR ˈtantrəm, -z
AM ˈtɑntrəm, -z

Tanya
BR ˈtɑːniə(r), ˈtaniə(r)
AM ˈtɑnjə, ˈtænjə

Tanzania
BR ˌtanzəˈniːə(r)
AM ˌtænzəˈniə

Tanzanian
BR ˌtanzəˈniːən, -z
AM ˌtænzəˈniən, -z

Tao
BR tau, ˈtɑːəu, -z
AM tau, -z

Taoiseach
BR ˈtiːʃək, ˈtiːʃəx
AM ˈtiʃək

Taoism
BR ˈtauɪz(ə)m,
ˈtɑːəuɪz(ə)m
AM ˈtau.ɪzəm

Taoist
BR ˈtauɪst, ˈtɑːəuɪst, -s
AM ˈtauəst, -s

Taoistic
BR tauˈɪstɪk,
ˌtɑːəuˈɪstɪk
AM tauˈɪstɪk

Taormina
BR ˌtauəˈmiːnə(r)
AM ˌtauˈrminə

Taos
BR taus
AM ˈtɑ.ous

tap
BR tap, -s, -ɪŋ, -t
AM tæp, -s, -ɪŋ, -t

tapa
BR ˈtapə(r), ˈtɑːpə(r), -z
AM ˈtɑpə, -z

tap-dance
BR ˈtapdɑːns,
ˈtapdans, -ɪz, -ɪŋ,
AM ˈtæpˌdæns, -əz, -ɪŋ,
-t

tap-dancer
BR ˈtapˌdɑːnsə(r),
ˈtapˌdansə(r), -z

AM ˈtæpˌdænsər, -z

tape
BR teɪp, -s, -ɪŋ, -t
AM teɪp, -s, -ɪŋ, -t

tapeable
BR ˈteɪpəbl
AM ˈteɪpəbəl

tapeless
BR ˈteɪplɪs
AM ˈteɪplɪs

tapelike
BR ˈteɪplʌɪk
AM ˈteɪpˌlaɪk

taper
BR ˈteɪp|ə(r), -əz,
-(ə)rɪŋ, -əd
AM ˈteɪp|ər, -ərz,
-(ə)rɪŋ, -ərd

taperecord
BR ˈteɪprɪˌkɔːd, -z, -ɪŋ,
-ɪ-
AM ˈteɪprəˌkɔ(ə)rd, -z,
-ɪŋ, -əd

tapestry
BR ˈtapɪstr|i, -ɪz, -ɪd
AM ˈtæpəstri, -z, -d

tapeta
BR təˈpiːtə(r)
AM təˈpidə

tapetum
BR təˈpiːtəm, -z
AM təˈpidəm, -z

tapeworm
BR ˈteɪpwəːm, -z
AM ˈteɪpˌwɜrm, -z

tapioca
BR ˌtapɪˈəukə(r)
AM ˌtæpiˈoukə

tapir
BR ˈteɪp(ɪ)ə(r), -z
AM ˈteɪpər, -z

tapiroid
BR ˈteɪp(ɪ)ərɔɪd, -z
AM ˈteɪpəˌrɔɪd, -z

tapis
BR ˈtapi, ˈtapiː
AM ˈtɑpi, tɑˈpi

tapless
BR ˈtapləs
AM ˈtæpləs

Taplin
BR ˈtaplɪn
AM ˈtæplən

Taplow
BR ˈtapləu
AM ˈtæpˌlou

tapotement
BR təˈpəutm(ə)nt
AM təˈpoutmənt

Tapp
BR tap
AM tæp

tappable
BR ˈtapəbl
AM ˈtæpəbəl

tapper
BR ˈtapə(r), -z

AM ˈtæpər, -z

tappet
BR ˈtapɪt, -s
AM ˈtæpət, -s

tapping
BR ˈtapɪŋ, -z
AM ˈtæpɪŋ, -z

taproom
BR ˈtapruːm, ˈtaprʊm,
-z
AM ˈtæpˌrum,
ˈtæpˌrʊm, -z

taproot
BR ˈtapruːt, -s
AM ˈtæpˌrut, -s

Tapsell
BR ˈtapsl
AM ˈtæpsəl

tapster
BR ˈtapstə(r), -z
AM ˈtæpstər, -z

tap-tap
BR ˌtapˈtap, -s
AM ˌtæpˈtæp, -s

tapu
taboo
BR ˈtɑːpuː, -z, -ɪŋ, -d
AM ˈtɑˌpu, -z, -ɪŋ, -d

tap water
BR ˈtap ˌwɔːtə(r)
AM ˈtæp ˌwadər, +
ˌwodər

taqueria
BR ˌtɑːkəˈriːə(r), -z
AM ˌtɑkəˈriə, -z

tar
BR tɑː(r), -z, -ɪŋ, -d
AM tɑr, -z, -ɪŋ, -d

Tara[1]
house in US
BR ˈtarə(r)
AM ˈtɛrə

Tara[2]
Ireland
BR ˈtɑːrə(r)
AM ˈtɑrə

taradiddle
BR ˈtarəˌdɪdl,
ˌtarəˈdɪdl, -z
AM ˈtɛrəˈdɪdəl, -z

tarakihi
BR ˌtarəˈkiːhi,
ˌtarəˈkiː,
ˌtarəˈkiːhɪz\ˌtarəˈkiːz
AM ˌtɛrəˈkiːhi, -z

taramasalata
BR ˌtarəməsəˈlɑːtə(r),
təˌraməsəˈlɑːtə(r)
AM ˌtɛrəməsəˈlɑdə

taramosalata
BR ˌtarəməsəˈlɑːtə(r),
təˌraməsəˈlɑːtə(r)
AM ˌtɛrəməsəˈlɑdə

Taranaki
BR ˌtarəˈnaki,
ˌtarəˈnɑːki
AM ˌtɛrəˈnaki

AM ˈtæpər, -z

tarantass
BR ˌtarənˈtas, ˌtarṇˈtas,
-ɪz
AM ˌtarənˈtɑs, -əz

tarantella
BR ˌtarənˈtɛlə(r),
ˌtarṇˈtɛlə(r), -z
AM ˌtɛrənˈtɛlə, -z

tarantism
BR ˈtarəntɪz(ə)m,
ˈtarṇtɪz(ə)m
AM ˈtɛrənˌtɪzəm

tarantula
BR təˈrantjələ(r),
təˈrantʃələ(r),
təˈrantʃlə(r), -z
AM təˈræn(t)ʃələ, -z

taraxacum
BR təˈraksəkəm, -z
AM təˈræksəkəm, -z

Tarbert
BR ˈtɑːbət
AM ˈtarbərt

Tarbet
BR ˈtɑːbɪt
AM ˈtarbət

tarboosh
BR tɑːˈbuːʃ, -ɪz
AM tarˈbuʃ, tarˈbuʃ, -əz

tarbrush
BR ˈtɑːbrʌʃ, -ɪz
AM ˈtarˌbrəʃ, -əz

Tarbuck
BR ˈtɑːbʌk
AM ˈtarˌbək

Tardenoisian
BR ˌtɑːdɪˈnɔɪzɪən
AM ˌtardəˈnɔɪzɪən

tardigrade
BR ˈtɑːdɪgreɪd, -z
AM ˈtardəˌgreɪd, -z

tardily
BR ˈtɑːdɪli
AM ˈtardəli

tardiness
BR ˈtɑːdɪnɪs
AM ˈtardɪnɪs

Tardis
BR ˈtɑːdɪs
AM ˈtardəs

tardive
dyskinesia
BR ˌtɑːdɪv
ˌdɪskɪˈniːzɪə(r)
AM ˌtardɪv
ˌdɪskɪˈniziə,
ˌdɪskɪˈniʒə

tardy
BR ˈtɑːd|i, -ɪə(r), -ɪɪst
AM ˈtardi, -ər, -ɪst

tare
BR tɛː(r), -z
AM tɛ(ə)r, -z

target
BR ˈtɑːg|ɪt, -ɪts, -ɪtɪŋ,
-ɪtɪd
AM ˈtargə|t, -ts, -dɪŋ,
-dəd

targetable
BR ˈtɑːɡɪtəbl
AM ˈtɑrɡədəbəl

Targum
BR ˈtɑːɡəm, tɑːˈɡuːm, -z
AM ˈtɑrˌɡʊm, ˈtɑrˌɡum, -z

Targumist
BR ˈtɑːɡəmɪst, -s
AM ˈtɑrˌɡʊməst, ˈtɑrˌɡuməst, -s

Tarheel
BR ˈtɑːhiːl, -z
AM ˈtɑrˌ(h)il, -z

tariff
BR ˈtærɪf, -s
AM ˈtɛrəf, -s

Tariq
BR ˈtɑːrɪk
AM ˈtɑrək

Tarka
BR ˈtɑːkə(r)
AM ˈtɑrkə

tarlatan
BR ˈtɑːlətn, -z
AM ˈtɑrlətn, -z

Tarleton
BR ˈtɑːlt(ə)n
AM ˈtɑrltən, ˈtɑrletn

Tarmac®
BR ˈtɑːmak
AM ˈtɑrˌmæk

tarmacadam
BR ˈtɑːməˌkadəm
AM ˈtɑrməˈkædəm

tarn
BR tɑːn, -z
AM tɑrn, -z

tarnation
interjection
BR tɑːˈneɪʃn
AM tɑrˈneɪʃən

tarnish
BR ˈtɑːnɪʃ, -ɪʃɪz, -ɪʃɪŋ, -ɪʃt
AM ˈtɑrnɪʃ, -ɪz, -ɪŋ, -t

tarnishable
BR ˈtɑːnɪʃəbl
AM ˈtɑrnəʃəbəl

taro
BR ˈtɑːrəʊ, -z
AM ˈtɛroʊ, -z

tarot
BR ˈtɑːrəʊ
AM ˈtɛroʊ

tarp
BR tɑːp, -s
AM tɑrp, -s

tarpan
BR ˈtɑːpan, -z
AM ˈtɑrˌpæn, -z

tarpaulin
BR tɑːˈpɔːlɪn, -z
AM tɑrˈpɔlən, ˈtɑrpələn, tɑrˈpɑlən, -z

Tarpeia
BR tɑːˈpiːə(r)

Tarpeian
BR tɑːˈpiːən
AM tɑrˈpeɪən

tarpon
BR ˈtɑːp(ə)n, -z
AM ˈtɑrpən, -z

Tarporley
BR ˈtɑːpəli, ˈtɑːpļi
AM ˈtɑrpərli

Tarquin
BR ˈtɑːkwɪn
AM ˈtɑrkwən

tarradiddle
BR ˈtarəˌdɪdl, ˌtarəˈdɪdl, -z
AM ˈtɛrəˌdɪdəl, -z

tarragon
BR ˈtarəɡ(ə)n
AM ˈtɛrəˌɡɑn, ˈtɛrəɡən

Tarragona
BR ˌtarəˈɡɒnə(r)
AM ˌtarəˈɡoʊnə

Tarrasa
BR təˈrɑːsə(r)
AM təˈrɑsə

tarrier
BR ˈtariə(r), -z
AM ˈtariər, -z

tarriness
BR ˈtarɪnɪs
AM ˈtarinɪs

tarry¹
covered with tar
BR ˈtɑːr|i, -ɪə(r), -ɪɪst
AM ˈtɑri, -ər, -ɪst

tarry²
wait
BR ˈtar|i, -ɪz, -ɪŋ, -ɪd
AM ˈtɛri, -z, -ɪŋ, -d

tarsal
BR ˈtɑːsl, -z
AM ˈtɑrsəl, -z

Tarshish
BR ˈtɑːʃɪʃ
AM ˈtɑrʃɪʃ

tarsi
BR ˈtɑːsʌɪ
AM ˈtɑrˌsɑɪ

tarsia
BR ˈtɑːsɪə(r)
AM ˈtɑrsɪə

tarsier
BR ˈtɑːsɪə(r), -z
AM ˈtɑrsɪər, -z

Tarski
BR ˈtɑːski
AM ˈtɑrski

tarsus
BR ˈtɑːsəs
AM ˈtɑrsəs

tart
BR tɑːt, -s, -ɪŋ, -ɪd
AM tɑr|t, -ts, -dɪŋ, -dəd

tartan
BR ˈtɑːt(ə)n, -z
AM ˈtɑrtn, -z

tartar¹
deposit on teeth etc
BR ˈtɑːtə(r), ˈtɑːtɑː(r)
AM ˈtɑrdər

tartar²
person
BR ˈtɑːtə(r), -z
AM ˈtɑrdər, -z

tartare
BR tɑːˈtɑː(r)
AM tɑ(r)ˈtɑr

tartaric
BR tɑːˈtarɪk
AM tɑrˈtɛrɪk

tartaric acid
BR tɑːˌtarɪk ˈasɪd
AM tɑrˌtɛrɪk ˈæsəd

tartarise
BR ˈtɑːtərʌɪz, -ɪz, -ɪŋ, -d
AM ˈtɑrdəˌrɑɪz, -ɪz, -ɪŋ, -d

tartarize
BR ˈtɑːtərʌɪz, -ɪz, -ɪŋ, -d
AM ˈtɑrdəˌrɑɪz, -ɪz, -ɪŋ, -d

tartar sauce
BR ˌtɑːtə ˈsɔːs, ˌtɑːtɑː +
AM ˈtɑrdər ˌsɔs, ˈtɑrdər ˌsɑs

Tartarus
BR ˈtɑːt(ə)rəs
AM ˈtɑrdərəs

Tartary
BR ˈtɑːt(ə)ri
AM ˈtɑrdəri

tartily
BR ˈtɑːtɪli
AM ˈtɑrdəli

tartiness
BR ˈtɑːtɪnɪs
AM ˈtɑrdinɪs

tartlet
BR ˈtɑːtlɪt, -s
AM ˈtɑrtlət, -s

tartly
BR ˈtɑːtli
AM ˈtɑrtli

tartness
BR ˈtɑːtnəs
AM ˈtɑrtnəs

tartrate
BR ˈtɑːtreɪt, -s
AM ˈtɑrˌtreɪt, -s

tartrazine
BR ˈtɑːtrəziːn
AM ˈtɑrtrəˌzin, ˈtɑrtrəzən

Tartuffe
BR (ˌ)tɑːˈtuːf
AM ˌtɑrˈtuf

tarty
BR ˈtɑːt|i, -ɪə(r), -ɪɪst
AM ˈtɑrdi, -ər, -ɪst

Tarzan
BR ˈtɑːzn
AM ˈtɑrˌzæn, ˈtɑrzən

Tashkent
BR ˌtaʃˈkɛnt
AM ˌtæʃˈkɛnt

task
BR tɑːsk, task, -s, -ɪŋ, -t
AM tæsk, -s, -ɪŋ, -t

Tasker
BR ˈtɑːskə(r), ˈtɑskə(r)
AM ˈtæskər

taskmaster
BR ˈtɑːsk,mɑːstə(r), ˈtask,mastə(r), -z
AM ˈtæsk,mæstər, -z

taskmistress
BR ˈtɑːsk,mɪstrɪs, ˈtask,mɪstrɪs, -ɪz
AM ˈtæsk,mɪstrɪs, -ɪz

Tasman
BR ˈtazmən
AM ˈtæzmən

Tasmania
BR taz'meɪnɪə(r)
AM ˌtæzˈmeɪnjə, tæzˈmeɪnɪə

Tasmanian
BR taz'meɪnɪən, -z
AM tæzˈmeɪnjən, tæzˈmeɪnɪən, -z

tass
BR tas, -ɪz
AM tæs, -əz

tassa
BR ˈtasə(r)
AM ˈtasə

tassel
BR ˈtasl, -z, -d
AM ˈtæsəl, -z, -d

tassie
BR ˈtas|i, -ɪz
AM ˈtæsi, -z

Tasso
BR ˈtasəʊ
AM ˈtæsoʊ

taste
BR teɪst, -s, -ɪŋ, -ɪd
AM teɪst, -s, -ɪŋ, -ɪd

tasteable
BR ˈteɪstəbl
AM ˈteɪstəbəl

taste bud
BR ˈteɪs(t) bʌd, -z
AM ˈteɪs(t) ˌbəd, -z

tasteful
BR ˈteɪs(t)f(ʊ)l
AM ˈteɪs(t)fəl

tastefully
BR ˈteɪs(t)fʊli, ˈteɪs(t)fli
AM ˈteɪs(t)fəli

tastefulness
BR ˈteɪs(t)f(ʊ)lnəs
AM ˈteɪs(t)fəlnəs

tasteless
BR ˈteɪs(t)lɪs
AM ˈteɪs(t)lɪs

tastelessly
BR ˈteɪs(t)lɪsli

AM 'teɪs(t)lɪsli

tastelessness
BR 'teɪs(t)lɪsnɪs
AM 'teɪs(t)lɪsnɪs

taster
BR 'teɪstə(r), -z
AM 'teɪstər, -z

tastily
BR 'teɪstɪli
AM 'teɪstɪli

tastiness
BR 'teɪstɪnɪs
AM 'teɪstɪnɪs

tasting
BR 'teɪstɪŋ, -z
AM 'teɪstɪŋ, -z

tasty
BR 'teɪst|i, -ɪə(r), -ɪɪst
AM 'teɪsti, -ər, -ɪst

tat
BR tat, -s, -ɪŋ, -ɪd
AM tæt, -ts, -dɪŋ, -dəd

tata
BR tɑ'tɑ:(r), tə'tɑ:(r)
AM tɑ'tɑ

tatami
BR tə'tɑ:m|i, tɑ'tɑ:m|i, tɑ:'tɑ:m|i, -ɪz
AM tə'tɑmi, -z

Tatar
BR 'tɑ:tə(r), -z
AM 'tɑdər, -z

Tatarstan
BR ˌtɑ:tə'stɑ:n, ˌtɑ:tə'stan
AM 'tɑdərˌstæn

Tatchell
BR 'tatʃl
AM 'tætʃəl

Tate
BR teɪt
AM teɪt

tater
potato
BR 'teɪtə(r), -z
AM 'teɪdər, -z

Tatham
BR 'teɪθ(ə)m, 'teɪð(ə)m, 'tatəm
AM 'tædəm

Tati
BR 'tati
AM tɑ'ti

Tatiana
BR ˌtatɪ'ɑ:nə(r)
AM ˌtɑdi'ɑnə

tatler
BR 'tatlə(r), -z
AM 'tædlər, 'tætlər, -z

tatou
BR 'tatu:, -z
AM tə'tu, -z

Tatra
BR 'tɑ:trə(r), 'tatrə(r)
AM 'tætrə

Tatras
BR 'tɑ:trəs, 'tatrəs

AM 'tætrəz

tatter
BR 'tatə(r), -z, -d
AM 'tædər, -z, -d

tatterdemalion
BR ˌtatədɪ'meɪlɪən, -z
AM ˌtædərdə'meɪljən, ˌtædərdi'meɪljən, -z

tattersall¹
BR 'tatəs(ɔ:)l, -z
AM 'tædərˌsɔl, 'tædərˌsal, -z

tattersall²
BR 'tatəs(ɔ:)l, -z
AM 'tædərˌsɔl, 'tædərˌsal, -z

tattery
BR 'tat(ə)ri
AM 'tædəri

tattie
potato
BR 'tat|i, -ɪz
AM 'tædi, -z

tattily
BR 'tatɪli
AM 'tædəli

tattiness
BR 'tatɪnɪs
AM 'tædɪnɪs

tattle
BR 'tat|l, -lz, -l̩ɪŋ\-lɪŋ, -ld
AM 'tædəl, -z, -ɪŋ, -d

tattler
BR 'tatlə(r), 'tatlə(r), -z
AM 'tædlər, 'tætlər, -z

tattletale
BR 'tatlteɪl, -z
AM 'tædl̩ˌteɪl, -z

Tatton
BR 'tatn
AM 'tætn

tattoo
BR tə'tu:, tɑ'tu:, -z, -ɪŋ, -d
AM tæ'tu, -z, -ɪŋ, -d

tattooer
BR tə'tu:ə(r), tɑ'tu:ə(r), -z
AM tæ'tuər, -z

tattooist
BR tə'tu:ɪst, tɑ'tu:ɪst, -s
AM tæ'tuəst, -s

tatty
BR 'tat|i, -ɪə(r), -ɪɪst
AM 'tædi, -ər, -ɪst

Tatum
BR 'teɪtəm
AM 'teɪdəm

tau
BR tɔ:(r), taʊ
AM taʊ, tɔ

taught
BR tɔ:t
AM tɔt, tɑt

taunt
BR tɔ:nt, -s, -ɪŋ, -ɪd-
AM tɔn|t, tɑn|t, -ts, -(t)ɪŋ, -(t)əd

taunter
BR 'tɔ:ntə(r), -z
AM 'tɔn(t)ər, 'tɑn(t)ər, -z

tauntingly
BR 'tɔ:ntɪŋli
AM 'tɔn(t)ɪŋli, 'tɑn(t)ɪŋli

Taunton
BR 'tɔ:ntən
AM 'tɔn(t)ən, 'tɑn(t)ən

Taunus
BR 'tɔ:nəs, 'taʊnəs
AM 'tɔnəs, 'taʊnəs

taupe
BR təʊp
AM toʊp

Taupo
BR 'taʊpəʊ
AM 'taʊpoʊ

taupy
BR 'təʊpi
AM 'toʊpi

Tauranga
BR taʊ'raŋgə(r)
AM taʊ'raŋgə

Taurean
BR 'tɔ:rɪən, tɔ:'ri:ən, -z
AM 'tɔrɪən, tɔ'riən, -z

taurine¹
amido-ethyl-sulphonic acid
BR 'tɔ:ri:n
AM 'tɔˌrin

taurine²
bovine
BR 'tɔ:rʌɪn
AM 'tɔˌraɪn

tauromachy
BR tɔ:'rɒmək|i, -ɪz
AM tɔ'raməki, -z

Taurus
BR 'tɔ:rəs
AM 'tɔrəs

taut
BR tɔ:t, -ə(r), -ɪst
AM tɔ|t, tɑ|t, -dər, -dəst

tauten
BR 'tɔ:t|n, -nz, -n̩ɪŋ\-nɪŋ, -nd
AM 'tɔtn, 'tɑtn, -z, -ɪŋ, -d

tautly
BR 'tɔ:tli
AM 'tɔtli, 'tɑtli

tautness
BR 'tɔ:tnəs
AM 'tɔtnəs, 'tɑtnəs

tautochrone
BR 'tɔ:təkrəʊn, -z
AM 'tɔdəˌkroʊn, 'tɑdəˌkroʊn, -z

tautog
BR tɔ:'tɒg, -z
AM tɔ'tɔg, tɑ'tag, -z

tautologic
BR ˌtɔ:tə'lɒdʒɪk
AM ˌtɔdl'adʒɪk, ˌtɑdl'adʒɪk

tautological
BR ˌtɔ:tə'lɒdʒɪkl
AM ˌtɔdl'adʒəkəl, ˌtɑdl'adʒəkəl

tautologically
BR ˌtɔ:tə'lɒdʒɪk(ə)li
AM ˌtɔdl'adʒək(ə)li, ˌtɑdl'adʒək(ə)li

tautologise
BR tɔ:'tɒlədʒʌɪz, -ɪz, -ɪŋ, -d
AM tɑ'tɑləˌdʒaɪz, tɑ'tɑləˌdʒaɪz, -ɪz, -ɪŋ, -d

tautologist
BR tɔ:'tɒlədʒɪst, -s
AM tɑ'tɑlədʒəst, tɑ'tɑlədʒəst, -s

tautologize
BR tɔ:'tɒlədʒʌɪz, -ɪz, -ɪŋ, -d
AM tɑ'tɑləˌdʒaɪz, tɑ'tɑləˌdʒaɪz, -ɪz, -ɪŋ, -d

tautologous
BR tɔ:'tɒləgəs
AM tɑ'tɑləgəs, tɑ'tɑləgəs

tautology
BR tɔ:'tɒlədʒ|i, -ɪz
AM tɑ'tɑlədʒi, tɑ'tɑlədʒi, -z

tautomer
BR 'tɔ:təmə(r), -z
AM 'tɔdəmər, 'tɑdəmər, -z

tautomeric
BR ˌtɔ:tə'merɪk
AM ˌtɔdə'merɪk, ˌtɑdə'merɪk

tautomerism
BR tɔ:'tɒməriz(ə)m
AM tɔ'tɑməˌrizəm, tɑ'tɑməˌrizəm

tautophony
BR tɔ:'tɒfən|i, tɔ:'tɒfn̩i, -ɪz
AM tɔ'tafəni, tɑ'tafəni, -z

Tavare
BR 'tavəreɪ
AM ˌtævə'reɪ, 'tævəˌreɪ

Tavaré
BR 'tavəreɪ
AM ˌtævə'reɪ, 'tævəˌreɪ

tavern
BR 'tavn, -z
AM 'tævərn, -z

taverna
BR tə'və:nə(r), -z
AM tə'vərnə, -z

Taverner
BR 'tavnə(r),
'tavənə(r)
AM 'tævərnər

Taverners
BR 'tavnəz
AM 'tævərnərz

Tavistock
BR 'tavıstɒk
AM 'tævə,stɑk

taw
BR tɔː(r), -z, -ıŋ, -d
AM tɔ, tɑ, -z, -ıŋ, -d

tawa
BR 'tɑːwə(r)
AM 'tɑwə

tawdrily
BR 'tɔːdrıli
AM 'tɔdrəli, 'tɑdrəli

tawdriness
BR 'tɔːdrınıs
AM 'tɔdrinıs, 'tɑdrinıs

tawdry
BR 'tɔːdr|i, -ıə(r), -ıst
AM 'tɔdri, 'tɑdri, -ər,
-ıst

Tawe
river
BR 'taʊi
AM 'taʊi

tawer
BR 'tɔːə(r), -z
AM tɔ(ə)r, -z

tawniness
BR 'tɔːnınıs
AM 'tɔnınıs, 'tɑnınıs

tawny
BR 'tɔːn|i, -ıə(r), -ıst
AM 'tɔni, 'tɑni, -ər, -ıst

taws
BR tɔːz, -ız
AM tɔz, tɑz, -ız

tawse
BR tɔːz, -ız
AM tɔz, tɑz, -ız

tax
BR taks, -ız, -ıŋ, -t
AM tæks, -əz, -ıŋ, -t

taxa
BR 'taksə(r)
AM 'tæksə

taxability
BR ,taksə'bılıti
AM ,tæksə'bılıdi

taxable
BR 'taksəbl
AM 'tæksəbəl

taxation
BR tak'seıʃn
AM tæk'seıʃən

tax-deductible
BR ,taksdı'dʌktıbl
AM ,tæksdə'dəktəbəl

tax-efficient
BR ,taksı'fıʃnt
AM ,tæksə'fıʃənt

taxer
BR 'taksə(r), -z
AM 'tæksər, -z

taxes
plural of taxis
BR 'taksiːz
AM 'tæk,siz

taxi
BR 'taks|i, -ız, -ıŋ, -ıd
AM 'tæksi, -z, -ıŋ, -d

taxicab
BR 'taksıkab, -z
AM 'tæksi,kæb, -z

taxidermal
BR ,taksı'də:ml
AM ,tæksə'dərml

taxidermic
BR ,taksı'də:mık
AM ,tæksə'dərmık

taxidermist
BR 'taksıdə:mıst,
tak'sıdəmıst, -s
AM 'tæksə,dərməst, -s

taxidermy
BR 'taksıdə:mi,
tak'sıdəmi
AM 'tæksə,dərmi

taximeter
BR 'taksı,miːtə(r), -z
AM 'tæksi,midər, -z

taxingly
BR 'taksıŋli
AM 'tæksıŋli

taxis
reflex
BR 'taksıs
AM 'tæksəs

taxiway
BR 'taksıweı, -z
AM 'tæksi,weı, -z

taxless
BR 'taksləs
AM 'tæksləs

taxman
BR 'taksman
AM 'tæks,mæn

taxmen
BR 'taksmen
AM 'tæks,men

taxol®
BR 'taksɒl
AM 'tæksɔl, 'tæksɑl

taxon
BR 'taksɒn
AM 'tæk,sɑn

taxonomic
BR ,taksə'nɒmık
AM ,tæksə'nɑmık

taxonomical
BR ,taksə'nɒmıkl
AM ,tæksə'nɑməkəl

taxonomically
BR ,taksə'nɒmıkli
AM ,tæksə'nɑmək(ə)li

taxonomist
BR tak'sɒnəmıst, -s
AM tæk'sɑnəməst, -s

taxonomy
BR tak'sɒnəm|i, -ız
AM tæk'sɑnəmi, -z

taxpayer
BR 'taks,peıə(r), -z
AM 'tæks,peıər, -z

taxpaying
BR 'taks,peııŋ
AM 'tæks,peııŋ

Tay
BR teı
AM teı

tayberry
BR 'teıb(ə)r|i, -ız
AM 'teı,beri, 'teıbəri, -z

Tayler
BR 'teılə(r)
AM 'teılər

Taylor
BR 'teılə(r)
AM 'teılər

tayra
BR 'tʌırə(r), -z
AM 'tʌırə, -z

Tay-Sachs
BR teı'saks
AM teı'sæks

Tayside
BR 'teısʌıd
AM 'teı,saıd

tazza
BR 'tɑːtsə(r), -z
AM 'tɑtsə, -z

Tbilisi
BR tbı'liːsi
AM ,təbə'lisi

Tblisi
BR tbı'liːsi
AM ,təbə'lisi

Tchad
BR tʃad
AM tʃæd

Tchadian
BR tʃadıən, -z
AM tʃædıən, -z

Tchaikovsky
BR tʃʌı'kɒfski,
tʃʌı'kɒvzki
AM tʃaı'kɔfski,
tʃaı'kafski,
tʃaı'kaʊski

TD
BR ,tiː'diː, -z
AM 'ti'di, -z

te
BR tiː
AM ti

tea
BR tiː, -z
AM ti, -z

teabag
BR 'tiːbag, -z
AM 'ti,bæg, -z

teaball
BR 'tiːbɔːl, -z
AM 'ti,bɔl, 'ti,bɑl, -z

teabread
BR 'tiːbred
AM 'ti,bred

teacake
BR 'tiːkeık, -s
AM 'ti,keık, -s

teach
BR tiːtʃ, -ız, -ıŋ
AM titʃ, -əz, -ıŋ

teachability
BR ,tiːtʃə'bılıti
AM ,titʃə'bılıdi

teachable
BR 'tiːtʃəbl
AM 'titʃəbəl

teachableness
BR 'tiːtʃəblnəs
AM 'titʃəbəlnəs

teacher
BR 'tiːtʃə(r), -z
AM 'titʃər, -z

teacherly
BR 'tiːtʃəli
AM 'titʃərli

teach-in
BR 'tiːtʃın, -z
AM 'titʃ,ın, -z

teaching
BR 'tiːtʃıŋ, -z
AM 'titʃıŋ, -z

teacup
BR 'tiːkʌp, -s
AM 'ti,kəp, -s

teacupful
BR 'tiːkʌpfʊl, -z
AM 'ti,kəp,fʊl, -z

teacupsful
BR 'tiːkʌpsfʊl
AM 'ti,kəps,fʊl

teagarden
BR 'tiː,gɑːdn, -z
AM 'ti,gɑrdən, -z

teahouse
BR 'tiː,haʊ|s, -zız
AM 'ti,haʊ|s, -zəz

teak
BR tiːk
AM tik

teakettle
BR 'tiː,ketl, -z
AM 'ti,kedəl, -z

teal
BR tiːl
AM til

tealeaf
BR 'tiːliːf
AM 'ti,lif

tealeaves
BR 'tiːliːvz
AM 'ti,livz

team
BR tiːm, -z, -ıŋ, -d
AM tim, -z, -ıŋ, -d

teammate
BR 'tiːmmeıt, -s
AM 'ti(m),meıt, -s

teamster
BR 'tiːmstə(r), -z
AM 'tiːmstər, -z

team-teaching
BR 'tiːm,tiːtʃɪŋ,
,tiːm'tiːtʃɪŋ
AM 'tiːm,titʃɪŋ

teamwork
BR 'tiːmwɜːk
AM 'tiːm,wɜrk

teapot
BR 'tiːpɒt, -s
AM 'tiː,pɑt, -s

teapoy
BR 'tiːpɔɪ, -z
AM 'tiː,pɔɪ, -z

tear¹
crying
BR tɪə(r), -z
AM tɪ(ə)r, -z

tear²
rip
BR tɛː(r), -z, -ɪŋ
AM tɛ(ə)r, -z, -ɪŋ

tearable
BR 'tɛːrəbl
AM 'tɛrəbəl

tearaway
BR 'tɛːrəweɪ, -z
AM 'tɛrə,weɪ, -z

teardrop
BR 'tɪədrɒp, -s
AM 'tɪr,drɑp, -s

tearer
BR 'tɛːrə(r), -z
AM 'tɛrər, -z

tearful
BR 'tɪəf(ʊ)l
AM 'tɪrfəl

tearfully
BR 'tɪəfʊli, 'tɪəfʃi
AM 'tɪrfəli

tearfulness
BR 'tɪəf(ʊ)lnəs
AM 'tɪrfəlnəs

teargas
BR 'tɪəgas, -ɪz, -ɪŋ, -d
AM 'tɪr,gæs, -əz, -ɪŋ, -d

tearjerker
BR 'tɪə,dʒɜːkə(r), -z
AM 'tɪr,dʒɜrkər, -z

tear-jerking
BR 'tɪə,dʒɜːkɪŋ
AM 'tɪr,dʒɜrkɪŋ

tearless
BR 'tɪələs
AM 'tɪrləs

tearlessly
BR 'tɪələsli
AM 'tɪrləsli

tearlessness
BR 'tɪələsnəs
AM 'tɪrləsnəs

tearlike
BR 'tɪəlʌɪk
AM 'tɪr,laɪk

tear-off
BR 'tɛːrɒf
AM 'tɛr,ɔf, 'tɛr,ɑf

tearoom
BR 'tiːruːm, 'tiːrʊm, -z
AM 'tiː,rum, 'tiː,rʊm, -z

tearstained
BR 'trəsteɪnd
AM 'tɪr,steɪnd

teary
BR 'tɪəri
AM 'tɪri

Teasdale
BR 'tiːzdeɪl
AM 'tiz,deɪl

tease
BR tiːz, -ɪz, -ɪŋ, -d
AM tiz, -ɪz, -ɪŋ, -d

teasel
BR 'tiːz|l, -lz, -lɪŋ \-lɪŋ,
-ld
AM 'tiz|əl, -əlz, -(ə)lɪŋ,
-əld

teaseler
BR 'tiːzlə(r), 'tiːzlə(r),
-z
AM 'tiz(ə)lər, -z

teaser
BR 'tiːzə(r), -z
AM 'tizər, -z

teaset
BR 'tiːsɛt, -s
AM 'tiː,sɛt, -s

teashop
BR 'tiːʃɒp, -s
AM 'tiː,ʃɑp, -s

teasingly
BR 'tiːzɪŋli
AM 'tizɪŋli

Teasmade®
BR 'tiːzmeɪd
AM 'tiz,meɪd

teaspoon
BR 'tiːspuːn, -z
AM 'tiː,spun, -z

teaspoonful
BR 'tiːspuːnfʊl, -z
AM 'tiː,spunfʊl, -z

teaspoonsful
BR 'tiːspuːnzfʊl
AM 'tiː,spunzfʊl

teat
BR tiːt, -s
AM tit, -s

tea table
BR 'tiː,teɪbl, -z
AM 'ti,teɪbəl, -z

teatime
BR 'tiːtʌɪm
AM 'tiː,taɪm

teazel
BR 'tiːz|l, -lz, -lɪŋ \-lɪŋ,
-ld
AM 'tiz|əl, -əlz, -(ə)lɪŋ,
-əld

teazle
BR 'tiːz|l, -lz, -lɪŋ \-lɪŋ,
-ld
AM 'tiz|əl, -əlz, -(ə)lɪŋ,
-əld

Tebay
BR 'tiːbeɪ
AM 'tibeɪ

Tebbit
BR 'tɛbɪt
AM 'tɛbət

Tebbitt
BR 'tɛbɪt
AM 'tɛbət

tec
BR tɛk, -s
AM tɛk, -s

tech
BR tɛk
AM tɛk

techie
BR 'tɛk|i, -ɪz
AM 'tɛki, -z

techily
BR 'tɛtʃɪli
AM 'tɛtʃəli

techiness
BR 'tɛtʃɪnɪs
AM 'tɛtʃɪnɪs, 'tɛkɪnɪs

technetium
BR tɛk'niːʃ(ɪ)əm
AM tɛk'nɪʃ(i)əm

technic
BR 'tɛknɪk, -s
AM 'tɛknɪk, -s

technical
BR 'tɛknɪkl, -z
AM 'tɛknəkəl, -z

technicality
BR ,tɛknɪ'kalɪt|i, -ɪz
AM ,tɛknə'kælədi, -z

technically
BR 'tɛknɪkli
AM 'tɛknək(ə)li

technicalness
BR 'tɛknɪklnəs
AM 'tɛknəkəlnəs

technician
BR tɛk'nɪʃn, -z
AM tɛk'nɪʃən, -z

technicist
BR 'tɛknɪsɪst, -s
AM 'tɛknəsəst, -s

technicolor
BR 'tɛknɪ,kʌlə(r), -d
AM 'tɛknə,kələr, -d

technicolour
BR 'tɛknɪ,kʌlə(r)
AM 'tɛknə,kələr

technique
BR tɛk'niːk, -s
AM tɛk'nik, -s

techno
BR 'tɛknəʊ
AM 'tɛknoʊ

technobabble
BR 'tɛknə(ʊ),babl

teazle
AM 'tɛknəʊ,bæbəl

technocracy
BR tɛk'nɒkrəs|i, -ɪz
AM tɛk'nɑkrəsi, -z

technocrat
BR 'tɛknəkrat, -s
AM 'tɛknə,kræt, -s

technocratic
BR ,tɛknə'kratɪk
AM ,tɛknə'krætɪk

technocratically
BR ,tɛknə'kratɪkli
AM ,tɛknə'krædək(ə)li

technological
BR ,tɛknə'lɒdʒɪkl
AM ,tɛknə'lɑdʒəkəl

technologically
BR ,tɛknə'lɒdʒɪkli
AM ,tɛknə'lɑdʒək(ə)li

technologist
BR tɛk'nɒlədʒɪst, -s
AM tɛk'nɑlədʒəst, -s

technology
BR tɛk'nɒlədʒ|i, -ɪz
AM tɛk'nɑlədʒi, -z

technophile
BR 'tɛknə(ʊ)fʌɪl, -z
AM 'tɛknə,faɪl, -z

technophobe
BR 'tɛknə(ʊ)fəʊb, -z
AM 'tɛknə,foʊb, -z

technophobia
BR ,tɛknə(ʊ)'fəʊbɪə(r)
AM ,tɛknə'foʊbiə

technophobic
BR ,tɛknə(ʊ)'fəʊbɪk
AM ,tɛknə'foʊbɪk

technospeak
BR 'tɛknə(ʊ)spiːk
AM 'tɛknə,spik

techy
BR 'tɛtʃ|i, -ɪə(r), -ɪɪst
AM 'tɛtʃi, 'tɛki, -ər, -ɪst

Teck
BR tɛk
AM tɛk

tectonic
BR tɛk'tɒnɪk, -s
AM tɛk'tɑnɪk, -s

tectonically
BR tɛk'tɒnɪkli
AM tɛk'tɑnək(ə)li

tectorial
BR tɛk'tɔːrɪəl
AM tɛk'tɔriəl

tectrices
BR 'tɛktrɪsiːz
AM 'tɛktrə,siz

tectrix
BR 'tɛktrɪks, -ɪz
AM 'tɛk,trɪks, -ɪz

Tecumseh
BR tɪ'kʌmsə(r)
AM tə'kəmsə

Tecwyn
BR 'tɛkwɪn
AM 'tɛkwən

ted
BR tɛd, -z, -ɪŋ, -ɪd
AM tɛd, -z, -ɪŋ, -əd

tedder
BR 'tɛdə(r), -z
AM 'tɛdər, -z

Teddington
BR 'tɛdɪŋt(ə)n
AM 'tɛdɪŋtən

teddy
BR 'tɛd|i, -ɪz
AM 'tɛdi, -z

Te Deum
BR ˌti: 'di:əm, ˌteɪ
'deɪəm, -z
AM teɪ 'deɪəm, ti +, -z

tedious
BR 'ti:dɪəs
AM 'tidiəs

tediously
BR 'ti:dɪəsli
AM 'tidiəsli

tediousness
BR 'ti:dɪəsnəs
AM 'tidiəsnəs

tedium
BR 'ti:dɪəm
AM 'tidiəm

tee
BR ti:, -z, -ɪŋ, -d
AM tim, -z, -ɪŋ, -d

tee-hee
BR ˌti:'hi:, -z, -ɪŋ, -d
AM ˌti'hi, -z, -ɪŋ, -d

teem
BR ti:m, -z, -ɪŋ, -d
AM tim, -z, -ɪŋ, -d

teen
BR ti:n, -z
AM tin, -z

teenage
BR 'ti:neɪdʒ, -d
AM 'ti,neɪdʒ, -d

teenager
BR 'ti:n,eɪdʒə(r), -z
AM 'ti,neɪdʒər, -z

teensy
BR 'ti:nz|i, -ɪɪst
AM 'tinsi, -ɪst

teensy-weensy
BR ˌti:nzɪ'wi:nzi
AM 'tinsi'winsi

teeny
BR 'ti:n|i, -ɪɪst
AM 'tini, -ɪst

teenybopper
BR 'ti:nɪˌbɒpə(r), -z
AM 'tini,bɑpər, -z

teeny-weeny
BR ˌti:nɪ'wi:ni
AM 'tini'wini

teepee
BR 'ti:pi:, -z
AM 'ti,pi, -z

Tees
BR ti:z
AM tiz

Teesdale
BR 'ti:zdeɪl
AM 'tiz,deɪl

teeshirt
BR 'ti:ʃɜːt, -s
AM 'ti,ʃɜrt, -s

tee-square
BR 'ti:skwɛː(r), -z
AM 'ti,skwɛ(ə)r, -z

Teesside
BR 'ti:(z)saɪd
AM 'ti(z),saɪd

teeter
BR 'ti:t|ə(r), -əz,
-(ə)rɪŋ, -əd
AM 'tidər, -z, -ɪŋ, -d

teeterboard
BR 'ti:təbɔːd, -z
AM 'tidər,bɔ(ə)rd, -z

teeter-tatter
BR 'ti:tə,tatə(r), -z
AM 'tidər,tadər, -z

teeter-totter
BR 'ti:tə,tɒtə(r), -z
AM 'tidər,tadər, -z

teeth
BR ti:θ
AM tiθ

teethe
BR ti:ð, -z, -ɪŋ, -d
AM tið, -z, -ɪŋ, -d

teething ring
BR 'ti:ðɪŋ rɪŋ, -z
AM 'tiðɪŋ ,rɪŋ, -z

teetotal
BR ˌti:'təʊtl
AM ˌti,toʊtl

teetotaler
BR ˌti:'təʊtlə(r),
ˌti:'təʊtlə(r), -z
AM ˌti,toʊdlər, -z

teetotalism
BR ˌti:'təʊtlɪz(ə)m
AM ˌti'toʊdl,ɪzəm

teetotaller
BR ˌti:'təʊtlə(r),
ˌti:'təʊtlə(r), -z
AM ˌti,toʊdlər, -z

teetotally
BR ˌti:'təʊtl|i,
ˌti:'təʊtəli
AM ˌti,toʊdli

teetotum
BR ti:'təʊtəm, -z
AM ti'toʊdəm, -z

teff
BR tɛf, -s
AM tɛf, -s

TEFL
BR 'tɛfl
AM 'tɛfəl

Teflon®
BR 'tɛflɒn
AM 'tɛf,lɑn

teg
BR tɛg, -z
AM tɛg, -z

Tegucigalpa
BR ˌtɛgʊsɪ'galpə(r),
tɪˌguːsɪ'galpə(r)
AM tə,gusə'gælpə

tegular
BR 'tɛgjʊlə(r)
AM 'tɛgjələr

tegularly
BR 'tɛgjʊləli
AM 'tɛgjələrli

tegument
BR 'tɛgjʊm(ə)nt, -s
AM 'tɛgjəmənt, -s

tegumental
BR ˌtɛgjʊ'mɛntl
AM ˌtɛgjə'mɛn(t)l

tegumentary
BR ˌtɛgjʊ'mɛnt(ə)ri
AM ˌtɛgjə'mɛn(t)əri

Teheran
BR ˌteɪ(ə)'raːn,
ˌtɛ(ə)'raːn, ˌteɪ(ə)'ran,
ˌtɛ(ə)'ran
AM ˌteə'ræn, ˌteə'ran

Tehran
BR ˌteɪ(ə)'raːn,
ˌtɛ(ə)'raːn, ˌteɪ(ə)'ran,
ˌtɛ(ə)'ran
AM ˌteə'ræn, ˌteə'ran

Teign
BR ti:n, tɪn
AM tin

Teignmouth
BR 'tɪnməθ, 'ti:nməθ
AM 'tinməθ

**Teilhard de
Chardin**
BR ˌteɪɑ: də 'ʃɑːdã,
+ 'ʃɑːdan
AM tɛˌjɑrd də ʃɑr'dɛn

Te Kanawa
BR ˌteɪ 'kɑːnəwə(r)
AM ˌteɪ 'kɑnəwə

teknonymous
BR tɛk'nɒnɪməs
AM tɛk'nɑnəməs

teknonymy
BR tɛk'nɒnɪmi
AM tɛk'nɑnəmi

tektite
BR 'tɛktʌɪt, -s
AM 'tɛk,taɪt, -s

telaesthesia
BR ˌtɛlɪs'θi:zɪə(r),
ˌtɛlɪs'θi:ʒə(r)
AM ˌtɛləsθiʒ(i)ə,
ˌtɛləsθiziə

telaesthetic
BR ˌtɛləs'θɛtɪk
AM ˌtɛləs'θɛdɪk

telamon
BR 'tɛləmən, 'tɛləmɒn,
-z
AM 'tɛlə,mɑn, -z

Tel Aviv
BR ˌtɛl ə'vi:v
AM ˌtɛl ə'viv

tele
BR 'tɛl|i, -ɪz
AM 'tɛli, -z

tele-ad
BR 'tɛlɪad, -z
AM 'tɛli,æd, -z

telebanking
BR 'tɛlɪˌbaŋkɪŋ
AM 'tɛlə,bæŋkɪŋ

telecamera
BR 'tɛlɪˌkam(ə)rə(r), -z
AM 'tɛlə,kæm(ə)rə, -z

telecast
BR 'tɛlɪkɑːst, 'tɛlɪkast,
-s, -ɪŋ, -ɪd
AM 'tɛlə,kæst, -s, -ɪŋ,
-əd

telecaster
BR 'tɛlɪˌkɑːstə(r),
'tɛlɪˌkastə(r), -z
AM 'tɛlə,kæstər, -z

telecine
BR 'tɛlɪˌsɪni
AM 'tɛlə'sɪni

Telecom®
BR 'tɛlɪkɒm
AM 'tɛlə,kɑm

telecomms
BR 'tɛlɪkɒmz
AM 'tɛlə,kɑmz

telecommunication
BR ˌtɛlɪkə,mjuːnɪ'keɪʃn,
-z
AM ˌtɛləkə,mjunə'keɪʃən,
-z

telecommute
BR ˌtɛlɪkə'mjuːt, -s, -ɪŋ,
-ɪd
AM 'tɛləkə'mju|t, -ts,
-dɪŋ, -dɪd

telecommuter
BR 'tɛlɪkə,mjuːtə(r), -z
AM 'tɛləkə'mjudər, -z

telecoms
BR 'tɛlɪkɒmz
AM 'tɛlə,kɑmz

teleconference
BR ˌtɛlɪ'kɒnf(ə)rəns,
'tɛlɪ'kɒnf(ə)rəns,
'tɛlɪˌkɒnf(ə)rəns,
'tɛlɪˌkɒnf(ə)rəns, -ɪz
AM 'tɛlə,kanf(ə)rəns,
-əz

teleconferencing
BR ˌtɛlɪ'kɒnf(ə)rənsɪŋ,
ˌtɛlɪ'kɒnf(ə)rɪŋsɪŋ,
'tɛlɪˌkɒnf(ə)rɪŋsɪŋ,
'tɛlɪˌkɒnf(ə)rɪŋsɪŋ
AM 'tɛlə,kanf(ə)rənsɪŋ

telecottage
BR 'tɛlɪˌkɒt|ɪdʒ, -ɪdʒɪz,
-ɪdʒɪŋ, -ɪdʒd
AM 'tɛlə,kadɪdʒ, -ɪz, -ɪŋ

telecourse
BR 'tɛlɪkɔːs, -ɪz
AM 'tɛlə,kɔ(ə)rs, -əz

teledu¹
stinking badger
BR ˈtelɪduː, -z
AM ˈtelədu, -z

teledu²
Welsh, television
BR tɪˈlɛdi
AM təˈlɛdi
WE teˈledi

tele-evangelism
BR ˌtelɪˈvan(d)ʒəl-
ɪz(ə)m,
ˌtelɪˈvan(d)ʒlɪz(ə)m
AM ˌteliˈvændʒə‚lɪzəm

tele-evangelist
BR ˌtelɪˈvan(d)ʒəlɪst,
ˌtelɪˈvan(d)ʒlɪst, -s
AM ˌteliˈvændʒələst, -s

telefacsimile
BR ˌtelɪfakˈsɪmɪl|i,
ˌtelɪfakˈsɪml|i, -ɪz
AM ˌteləˌfækˈsɪməli, -z

Telefax®
BR ˈtelɪfaks, -ɪz, -ɪŋ, -t
AM ˈteləˌfæks, -əz, -ɪŋ, -t

telefilm
BR ˈtelɪfɪlm, -z
AM ˈteləˌfɪlm, -z

telegenic
BR ˌtelɪˈdʒenɪk
AM ˌteləˈdʒenɪk

telegonic
BR ˌtelɪˈɡɒnɪk
AM ˌteləˈɡɑnɪk

telegony
BR tɪˈlɛɡəni, tɪˈlɛɡ̃ni
AM təˈlɛɡəni

telegram
BR ˈtelɪɡram, -z, -ɪŋ, -d
AM ˈteləˌɡræm, -z, -ɪŋ, -d

telegraph
BR ˈtelɪɡrɑːf, ˈtelɪɡraf,
-s, -ɪŋ, -t
AM ˈteləˌɡræf, -s, -ɪŋ, -t

telegrapher
BR tɪˈlɛɡrəfə(r), -z
AM təˈlɛɡrəfər,
ˈteləˌɡræfər, -z

telegraphese
BR ˌtelɪɡrəˈfiːz
AM ˈtelǝɡræˈfiz

telegraphic
BR ˌtelɪˈɡrafɪk
AM ˌteləˈɡræfɪk

telegraphically
BR ˌtelɪˈɡrafɪkli
AM ˌteləˈɡræfək(ə)li

telegraphist
BR tɪˈlɛɡrəfɪst, -s
AM təˈlɛɡrəfəst,
ˈteləˌɡræfəst, -s

telegraphy
BR tɪˈlɛɡrəfi
AM təˈlɛɡrəfi

Telegu
BR ˈtelɪɡuː, -z
AM ˈteləˌɡu, -z

telekinesis
BR ˌtelɪkʌɪˈniːsɪs,
ˌtelɪkɪˈniːsɪs
AM ˌteləˈkɪnəsəs,
ˌteləkəˈnisɪs

telekinetic
BR ˌtelɪkʌɪˈnetɪk,
ˌtelɪkɪˈnetɪk
AM ˌteləkəˈnedɪk

Telemachus
BR tɪˈlɛməkəs
AM təˈlɛməkəs

Telemann
BR ˈteɪləman,
ˈteləman
AM ˈteləˌman

telemark
BR ˈtelɪmɑːk, -s
AM ˈteləˌmɑrk, -s

telemarketer
BR ˈtelɪˌmɑːkɪtə(r), -z
AM ˈteləˌmɑrkədər, -z

telemarketing
BR ˈtelɪˌmɑːkɪtɪŋ
AM ˈteləˌmɑrkədɪŋ

telemessage
BR ˈtelɪˌmes|ɪdʒ, -ɪdʒɪz
AM ˈteləˌmesɪdʒ, -ɪz

telemeter
BR tɪˈlɛmɪt|ə(r),
ˈtelɪˌmiːt|ə(r), -əz,
-(ə)rɪŋ, -əd
AM ˈteləˌmidər, -z, -ɪŋ,
-d

telemetric
BR ˌtelɪˈmetrɪk
AM ˌteləˈmetrɪk

telemetry
BR tɪˈlɛmɪtri
AM təˈlɛmətri

teleologic
BR ˌtiːlɪəˈlɒdʒɪk,
ˌtelɪəˈlɒdʒɪk
AM ˌtiliəˈlɑdʒɪk ˈtiliə-
ˈlɑdʒɪk

teleological
BR ˌtiːlɪəˈlɒdʒɪkl,
ˌtelɪəˈlɒdʒɪkl
AM ˌtiliəˈlɑdʒəkəl,
ˈtiliəˈlɑdʒəkəl

teleologically
BR ˌtiːlɪəˈlɒdʒɪkli,
ˌtelɪəˈlɒdʒɪkli
AM ˌtiliəˈlɑdʒək(ə)li,
ˈtiliəˈlɑdʒək(ə)li

teleologism
BR ˌtiːlɪˈɒlədʒɪz(ə)m,
ˌtelɪˈɒlədʒɪz(ə)m
AM ˌtiliˈɑləˌdʒɪzəm,
ˈteliˈɑləˌdʒɪzəm

teleologist
BR ˌtiːlɪˈɒlədʒɪst,
ˌtelɪˈɒlədʒɪst, -s
AM ˌtiliˈɑlədʒəst,
ˈteliˈɑlədʒəst, -s

teleology
BR ˌtiːlɪˈɒlədʒi,
ˌtelɪˈɒlədʒi

telekinesis
AM ˌtili|ˈa-lədʒi,
ˌteliə|ˈalədʒi

teleost
BR ˈtiːlɪɒst, ˈtelɪɒst, -s
AM ˈtiliˌɑst, ˈteliˌɑst, -s

telepath
BR ˈtelɪpaθ, -s
AM ˈteləpæθ, -ðz\-θs

telepathic
BR ˌtelɪˈpaθɪk
AM ˌteləˈpæθɪk

telepathically
BR ˌtelɪˈpaθɪkli
AM ˌteləˈpæθək(ə)li

telepathise
BR tɪˈlɛpəθʌɪz, -ɪz, -ɪŋ,
-d
AM təˈlɛpəˌθaɪz, -ɪz, -ɪŋ,
-d

telepathist
BR tɪˈlɛpəθɪst, -s
AM təˈlɛpəθəst, -s

telepathize
BR tɪˈlɛpəˌθʌɪz, -ɪz, -ɪŋ,
-d
AM təˈlɛpəˌθaɪz, -ɪz, -ɪŋ,
-d

telepathy
BR tɪˈlɛpəθi
AM təˈlɛpəθi

téléphérique
BR ˌtelɪfəˈriːk, -s
AM ˌteləfəˈrik, -s

telephone
BR ˈtelɪfəʊn, -z, -ɪŋ, -d
AM ˈteləˌfoʊn, -z, -ɪŋ, -d

telephonic
BR ˌtelɪˈfɒnɪk
AM ˌteləˈfɑnɪk

telephonically
BR ˌtelɪˈfɒnɪkli
AM ˌteləˈfɑnək(ə)li

telephonist
BR tɪˈlɛfənɪst,
tɪˈlɛfn̩ɪst, -s
AM təˈlɛfənəst,
ˈteləˈfɑnəst, -s

telephony
BR tɪˈlɛfəni, tɪˈlɛfn̩i
AM təˈlɛfəni,
ˈteləˌfoʊni

telephoto
BR ˌtelɪˈfəʊtəʊ
AM ˌteləˈfoʊdoʊ

telephotograph
BR ˌtelɪˈfəʊtəɡrɑːf,
ˌtelɪˈfəʊtəɡraf, -s
AM ˌteləˈfoʊdəˌɡræf, -s

telephotographic
BR ˌtelɪˌfəʊtəˈɡrafɪk
AM ˌteləˌfoʊdəˈɡræfɪk

**telephotographic-
ally**
BR ˌtelɪˌfəʊtəˈɡrafɪkli
AM ˌteləˌfoʊdəˈɡræfək-
(ə)li

telephotography
BR ˌtelɪfəˈtɒɡrəfi

AM ˌteləfəˈtɑɡrəfi

teleplay
BR ˈtelɪpleɪ, -z
AM ˈteləˌpleɪ, -z

telepoint
BR ˈtelɪpɔɪnt, -s
AM ˈteləˌpɔɪnt, -s

teleport
BR ˈtelɪpɔːt, -s, -ɪŋ, -ɪd
AM ˈteləˌpɔ(ə)rt, -ts,
-ˌpɔrdɪŋ, -ˌpɔrdəd

teleportation
BR ˌtelɪpɔːˈteɪʃn, -z
AM ˌteləˌpɔrˈteɪʃən, -z

teleprinter
BR ˈtelɪˌprɪntə(r), -z
AM ˈteləˌprɪn(t)ər, -z

teleprompt
BR ˈtelɪprɒm(p)t, -s
AM ˈteləˌprɑm(p)t, -s

teleprompter
BR ˈtelɪˌprɒm(p)tə(r),
-z
AM ˈteləˌprɑm(p)tər, -z

telerecord¹
noun
BR ˈtelɪˌrɛkɔːd, -z
AM ˈteləˌrɛkərd, -z

telerecord²
verb
BR ˈtelɪrɪˌkɔːd,
ˌtelɪrɪˈkɔːd, -z, -ɪŋ, -ɪd
AM ˈtelərəˈkɔ(ə)rd, -z,
-ɪŋ, -ɪd

telerecording
noun
BR ˈtelɪrɪˌkɔːdɪŋ, -z
AM ˈtelərəˈkɔrdɪŋ, -z

telergy
BR ˈteləˌdʒi
AM ˈtelərˌdʒi

telesales
BR ˈtelɪseɪlz
AM ˈteləˌseɪlz

telescope
BR ˈtelɪskəʊp, -s
AM ˈteləˌskoʊp, -s

telescopic
BR ˌtelɪˈskɒpɪk
AM ˌteləˈskɑpɪk

telescopically
BR ˌtelɪˈskɒpɪkli
AM ˌteləˈskɑpək(ə)li

teleshopping
BR ˈtelɪˌʃɒpɪŋ
AM ˈteləˌʃɑpɪŋ

telesoftware
BR ˈtelɪˌsɒftwɛː(r)
AM ˈteləˈsɒf(t)ˌwɛ(ə)r,
ˌteləˈsɑf(t)ˌwɛ(ə)r

telesthesia
BR ˌtelɪsˈθiːzɪə(r),
ˌtelɪsˈθiːʒə(r)
AM ˌtelɪsˈθiʒ(i)ə,
ˌteləsˈθiziə

telesthetic
BR ˌtelɪsˈθɛtɪk
AM ˌteləsˈθɛdɪk

Teletex®
BR 'telɪteks
AM 'telə̩teks

teletext
BR 'telɪtekst
AM 'telə̩tekst

telethon
BR 'telɪθɒn, -z
AM 'telə̩θɑn, -z

teletype
BR 'telɪtʌɪp, -s, -ɪŋ, -t
AM 'telə̩tʌɪp, -s, -ɪŋ, -t

teletypewriter
BR ̩telɪ'tʌɪprʌɪtə(r), -z
AM ̩telə'tʌɪp̩rʌɪdər, -z

televangelism
BR telɪ'van(d)ʒəlɪz(ə)m, ̩telɪ'van(d)ʒlɪz(ə)m
AM ̩telə'vændʒə̩lɪzəm

televangelist
BR telɪ'van(d)ʒəlɪst, ̩telɪ'van(d)ʒlɪst, -s
AM ̩telə'vændʒələst, -s

teleview
BR 'telɪvjuː, -z, -ɪŋ, -d
AM 'telə̩vju, -z, -ɪŋ, -d

televiewer
BR 'telɪ̩vjuːə(r), -z
AM 'telə̩vjuər, -z

televisable
BR 'telɪvʌɪzəbl
AM 'telə̩vaɪzəbəl

televise
BR 'telɪvʌɪz, -ɪz, -ɪŋ, -d
AM 'telə̩vaɪz, -ɪz, -ɪŋ, -d

television
BR 'telɪ̩vɪʒn, ̩telɪ'vɪʒn, -z
AM 'telə̩vɪʒən, -z

televisor
BR 'telɪvʌɪzə(r), -z
AM 'telə̩vaɪzər, -z

televisual
BR ̩telɪ'vɪʒʊ(ə)l, ̩telɪ'vɪʒjʊ(ə)l, ̩telɪ'vɪʒ(ʉ)l, ̩telɪ'vɪʒj(ʉ)l
AM ̩telə'vɪʒ(əw)əl

televisually
BR ̩telɪ'vɪʒ(j)ʊəli, ̩telɪ'vɪʒ(j)əli, ̩telɪ'vɪʒʊəli, ̩telɪ'vɪʒjʊəli
AM ̩telə'vɪʒ(əw)əli

telework
BR 'telɪwəːk, -s, -ɪŋ, -t
AM 'telə̩wərk, -s, -ɪŋ, -t

teleworker
BR 'telɪ̩wəːkə(r), -z
AM 'telə̩wərkər, -z

Telex
BR 'teleks, -ɪz, -ɪŋ, -t
AM 'teleks, -əz, -ɪŋ, -t

telfer
BR 'telfə(r), -z
AM 'telfər, -z

Telford
BR 'telfəd

AM 'telfərd

tell
BR tel, -z, -ɪŋ
AM tel, -z, -ɪŋ

tellable
BR 'teləbl
AM 'teləbəl

teller
BR 'telə(r), -z
AM 'telər, -z

tellership
BR 'teləʃɪp, -s
AM 'telər̩ʃɪp, -s

telling
BR 'telɪŋ, -z
AM 'telɪŋ, -z

tellingly
BR 'telɪŋli
AM 'telɪŋli

telling-off
BR ̩telɪŋ'ɒf
AM ̩telɪŋ'ɔf, ̩telɪŋ'ɑf

tellings-off
BR ̩telɪŋz'ɒf
AM ̩telɪŋz'ɔf, ̩telɪŋz'ɑf

telltale
BR 'telteɪl, -z
AM 'tel̩teɪl, -z

tellurate
BR 'teljʊreɪt, -s
AM 'teljə̩reɪt, -s

tellurian
BR te'ljʊərɪən, tɪ'ljʊərɪən, te'ljɔːrɪən, tɪ'ljɔːrɪən, -z
AM tə'l(j)ʊrɪən, -z

telluric
BR te'ljʊərɪk, tɪ'ljʊərɪk, te'ljɔːrɪk, tɪ'ljɔːrɪk
AM tə'l(j)ʊrɪk

telluride
BR 'teljʊrʌɪd
AM 'teljə̩raɪd

tellurite
BR 'teljʊrʌɪt, -s
AM 'teljə̩raɪt, -s

tellurium
BR te'ljʊərɪəm, tɪ'ljʊərɪəm, te'ljɔːrɪəm, tɪ'ljɔːrɪəm
AM tə'l(j)ʊrɪəm

tellurous
BR 'teljʊərəs
AM 'teljərəs

telly
BR 'telji, -ɪz
AM 'teli, -z

telnet
BR 'telnet, -s, -ɪŋ, -ɪd
AM 'telnet, -ts, -dɪŋ, -dɪd

teloi
BR 'telɔɪ
AM 'telɔɪ

telomere
BR 'tiːləmɪə(r), 'teləmɪə(r)
AM 'teləmɪ(ə)r, 'tiləmɪ(ə)r

telos
BR 'telɒs
AM 'telɒs, 'teləs

telpher
BR 'telfə(r), -z
AM 'telfər, -z

telpherage
BR 'telf(ə)rɪdʒ
AM 'telfərɪdʒ

telson
BR 'telsn, -z
AM 'telsən, -z

Telstar®
BR 'telstɑː(r)
AM 'tel̩stɑr

Telugu
BR 'telʊguː, -z
AM 'telə̩gu, -z

temblor
BR tem'blɔː(r), -z
AM 'temblər, 'tem̩blɔ(ə)r, -z

temerarious
BR ̩teməˈreːrɪəs
AM ̩temə'reːrɪəs

temerity
BR tɪ'merɪti
AM tə'merədi

Temne
BR 'temnjiː, 'tɪmnjiː, -ɪz
AM 'temni, 'tɪmni, -z

temp
BR temp, -ps, -pɪŋ, -(p)t
AM temp, -ps, -ps, -pɪŋ, -(p)t

temper
BR 'templə(r), -əz, -(ə)rɪŋ, -əd
AM 'templər, -ərz, -(ə)rɪŋ, -ərd

tempera
BR 'temp(ə)rə(r)
AM 'tempərə

temperable
BR 'temp(ə)rəbl
AM 'temp(ə)rəbəl

temperament
BR 'temprəm(ə)nt, -s
AM 'temp(ə)rəmənt, -s

temperamental
BR ̩temprə'mentl
AM ̩temp(ə)rə'men(t)l

temperamentally
BR ̩temprə'mentli, ̩temprə'mentəli
AM ̩temp(ə)rə'men(t)li

temperance
BR temp(ə)rəns, 'temp(ə)rns
AM 'temp(ə)rəns

temperate
BR 'temp(ə)rət
AM 'temp(ə)rət

temperately
BR 'temp(ə)rətli
AM 'temp(ə)rətli

temperateness
BR 'temp(ə)rətnəs
AM 'temp(ə)rətnəs

temperative
BR 'temp(ə)rətɪv
AM 'temp(ə)rədɪv

temperature
BR 'temprɪtʃə(r), -z
AM 'tempə(rə)tʃər, 'tempə̩rə̩tʃʊ(ə)r, -z

temperedly
BR 'tempədli
AM 'tempərdli

temperer
BR 'temp(ə)rə(r), -z
AM 'temp(ə)rər, -z

Temperley
BR 'tempəli
AM 'tempərli

tempersome
BR 'tempəs(ə)m
AM 'tempərsəm

Temperton
BR 'tempət(ə)n
AM 'tempərtən

tempest
BR 'tempɪst, -s
AM 'tempəst, -s

tempestuous
BR tem'pestʃʊəs, tem'pestjʊəs
AM tem'pestʃ(əw)əs

tempestuously
BR tem'pestʃʊəsli, tem'pestjʊəsli
AM tem'pestʃ(əw)əsli

tempestuousness
BR tem'pestʃʊəsnəs, tem'pestjʊəsnəs
AM tem'pestʃ(əw)əsnəs

tempi
BR 'tempiː
AM 'tempi

Templar
BR 'templə(r), -z
AM 'templər, -z

template
BR 'templeɪt, 'templɪt, -s
AM 'tem̩pleɪt, 'templət, -s

temple
BR 'templ, -z
AM 'tempəl, -z

templet
BR 'templɪt, -s
AM 'templət, -s

Templeton
BR 'templt(ə)n
AM 'tempəltən

tempo
BR 'tempəʊ, -z
AM 'tempoʊ, -z

tempora
BR 'temp(ə)rə(r)
AM 'tempərə

temporal
BR 'temp(ə)rəl,
'temp(ə)rl̩
AM 'temp(ə)rəl

temporality
BR ˌtempə'ralɪti
AM ˌtempə'rælədi

temporally
BR 'temp(ə)rəli,
'temp(ə)rl̩i
AM 'temp(ə)rəli

temporarily
BR 'temp(ə)r(ər)ɪli
AM ˌtempə'rerəli

temporariness
BR 'temp(ə)r(ər)ɪnɪs
AM ˌtempə'rerinɪs

temporary
BR 'temp(ə)r(ər)|i, -ɪz
AM 'tempə'reri, -z

temporisation
BR ˌtemp(ə)rʌɪ'zeɪʃ|n
AM ˌtempərə'zeɪʃən,
ˌtempə,raɪ'zeɪʃən

temporise
BR 'tempərʌɪz, -ɪz, -ɪŋ,
-d
AM 'tempə,raɪz, -ɪz, -ɪŋ,
-d

temporiser
BR 'tempərʌɪzə(r), -z
AM 'tempə,raɪzər, -z

temporization
BR ˌtemp(ə)rʌɪ'zeɪʃn
AM ˌtempərə'zeɪʃən,
ˌtempə,raɪ'zeɪʃən

temporize
BR 'tempərʌɪz, -ɪz, -ɪŋ,
-d
AM 'tempə,raɪz, -ɪz, -ɪŋ,
-d

temporizer
BR 'tempərʌɪzə(r), -z
AM 'tempə,raɪzər, -z

tempt
BR tem(p)t, -s, -ɪŋ, -ɪd
AM tem(p)t, -s, -ɪŋ, -əd

temptability
BR ˌtem(p)tə'bɪlɪti
AM ˌtem(p)tə'bɪlɪdi

temptable
BR 'tem(p)təbl
AM 'tem(p)təbəl

temptation
BR ˌtem(p)'teɪʃn, -z
AM ˌtem(p)'teɪʃən, -z

tempter
BR 'tem(p)tə(r), -z
AM 'tem(p)tər, -z

tempting
BR 'tem(p)tɪŋ
AM 'tem(p)tɪŋ

temptingly
BR 'tem(p)tɪŋli
AM 'tem(p)tɪŋli

temptress
BR 'tem(p)trɪs, -ɪz
AM 'tem(p)trəs, -əz

tempura
BR tem'pʊərə(r),
'temp(ə)rə(r)
AM tem'pʊrə, 'tempərə

ten
BR ten, -z
AM ten, -z

tenability
BR ˌtenə'bɪlɪti
AM ˌtenə'bɪlɪdi

tenable
BR 'tenəbl
AM 'tenəbəl

tenableness
BR 'tenəblnəs
AM 'tenəbəlnəs

tenace
BR 'teneɪs, 'tenɪs,
tɛ'neɪs, -ɪz
AM 'tɛˌn|eɪs, 'ten|əs,
-eɪsɪz\-əsəz

tenacious
BR tɪ'neɪʃəs
AM tə'neɪʃəs

tenaciously
BR tɪ'neɪʃəsli
AM tə'neɪʃəsli

tenaciousness
BR tɪ'neɪʃəsnəs
AM tə'neɪʃəsnəs

tenacity
BR tɪ'nasɪti
AM tə'næsədi

tenacula
BR tɪ'nakjʊlə(r)
AM tə'nækjələ

tenaculum
BR tɪ'nakjʊləm
AM tə'nækjələm

tenancy
BR 'tenəns|i, -ɪz
AM 'tenənsi, -z

tenant
BR 'tenənt, -s
AM 'tenənt, -s

tenantable
BR 'tenəntəbl
AM 'tenən(t)əbəl

tenantless
BR 'tenəntləs
AM 'tenən(t)ləs

tenantry
BR 'tenəntri
AM 'tenəntri

Tenbury
BR 'tenb(ə)ri
AM 'ten,bɛri

Tenby
BR 'tenbi
AM 'tenbi

tench
BR ten(t)ʃ, -ɪz
AM ten(t)ʃ, -əz

tend
BR tend, -z, -ɪŋ, -ɪd
AM tend, -z, -ɪŋ, -əd

tendance
BR 'tendəns
AM 'tendəns

tendencious
BR ten'denʃəs
AM ten'denʃəs

tendenciously
BR ten'denʃəsli
AM ten'denʃəsli

tendenciousness
BR ten'denʃəsnəs
AM ten'denʃəsnəs

tendency
BR 'tendəns|i, -ɪz
AM 'tendnsi, -z

tendentious
BR ten'denʃəs
AM ten'denʃəs

tendentiously
BR ten'denʃəsli
AM ten'denʃəsli

tendentiousness
BR ten'denʃəsnəs
AM ten'denʃəsnəs

tender
BR 'tend|ə(r), -əz,
-(ə)rɪŋ, -əd, -(ə)rə(r),
-(ə)rɪst
AM 'tend|ər, -ərz,
-(ə)rɪŋ, -ərd, -ər-, -əst

tenderer
BR 'tend(ə)rə(r), -z
AM 'tend(ə)rər, -z

tender-eyed
BR ˌtendər'ʌɪd
AM 'tendər,aɪd

tenderfoot
BR 'tendəfʊt, -s
AM 'tendər,fʊt, -s

tenderhearted
BR ˌtendə'hɑːtɪd
AM 'tendər,hɑrdəd

tenderheartedly
BR ˌtendə'hɑːtɪdli
AM 'tendər,hɑrdədli

**tenderhearted-
ness**
BR ˌtendə'hɑːtɪdnɪs
AM 'tendər,hɑrdədnəs

tenderise
BR 'tendərʌɪz, -ɪz, -ɪŋ,
-d
AM 'tendə,raɪz, -ɪz, -ɪŋ,
-d

tenderiser
BR 'tendərʌɪzə(r)
AM 'tendə,raɪzər

tenderize
BR 'tendərʌɪz, -ɪz, -ɪŋ,
-d
AM 'tendə,raɪz, -ɪz, -ɪŋ,
-d

tenderizer
BR 'tendərʌɪzə(r), -z
AM 'tendə,raɪzər, -z

tenderloin
BR 'tendəlɔɪn, -z
AM 'tendər,lɔɪn, -z

tenderly
BR 'tendəli
AM 'tendərli

tenderness
BR 'tendənəs
AM 'tendərnəs

tendinitis
BR ˌtendə'nʌɪtɪs
AM ˌtendə'naɪdɪs

tendinous
BR 'tendɪnəs
AM 'tendənəs

tendon
BR 'tendən, -z
AM 'tendən, -z

tendonitis
BR ˌtendə'nʌɪtɪs
AM ˌtendə'naɪdɪs

tendresse
BR tɒ'dres
AM ten'dres

tendril
BR 'tendr(ɪ)l, -z
AM 'tendrəl, -z

tenebrae
BR 'tenɪbriː, 'tenɪbreɪ
AM 'tenə,breɪ, 'tenəbri,
'tenə,braɪ

tenebrous
BR 'tenɪbrəs
AM 'tenəbrəs

Tenedos
BR 'tenɪdɒs
AM 'tenədɒs, 'tenədas

tenement
BR 'tenɪm(ə)nt, -s
AM 'tenəmənt, -s

tenemental
BR ˌtenɪ'mentl̩
AM ˌtenə'men(t)l̩

tenementary
BR ˌtenɪ'ment(ə)ri
AM ˌtenə'men(t)əri

Tenerife
BR ˌtenə'riːf
AM ˌtenə'rɪf
SP tene'rife

tenesmus
BR tɪ'nezməs
AM tə'nezməs,
tə'nɛzməs

tenet
BR 'tenɪt, -s
AM 'tenət, -s

tenfold
BR 'tenfəʊld
AM 'ten,foʊld

ten-gallon hat
BR ˌten,galən 'hat, -s
AM 'ten'gælən 'hæt, -s

Teng Hsiao-p'ing
BR ˌteŋ siaʊ'pɪŋ,
+ ʃaʊ'pɪŋ
AM 'tɛŋ ˌsiaʊ'pɪŋ

tenia
BR ˈtiːniə(r)
AM ˈtiniə

Teniers
BR ˈtɛnɪəz
AM ˈtɛnɪɚz

tenioid
BR ˈtiːnɪɔɪd
AM ˈtini.ɔɪd

Tenison
BR ˈtɛnɪs(ə)n
AM ˈtɛnəsən

Tenko
BR ˈtɛŋkəʊ
AM ˈtɛŋkoʊ

Tennant
BR ˈtɛnənt
AM ˈtɛnənt

tenné
BR ˈtɛni, -z
AM ˈtɛni, -z

tenner
BR ˈtɛnə(r), -z
AM ˈtɛnɚ, -z

Tennessean
BR ˌtɛnɪˈsiːən, -z
AM ˌtɛnəˈsiən, -z

Tennessee
BR ˌtɛnɪˈsiː
AM ˌtɛnəˈsi

Tennesseean
BR ˌtɛnɪˈsiːən, -z
AM ˌtɛnəˈsiən, -z

Tenniel
BR ˈtɛnɪəl
AM ˈtɛniəl

tennis
BR ˈtɛnɪs
AM ˈtɛnəs

Tennison
BR ˈtɛnɪs(ə)n
AM ˈtɛnəsən

tenno
BR ˈtɛnəʊ, -z
AM ˈtɛnoʊ, -z

tenny
BR ˈtɛni, -ɪz
AM ˈtɛni, -z

Tennyson
BR ˈtɛnɪs(ə)n
AM ˈtɛnəsən

Tennysonian
BR ˌtɛnɪˈsəʊnɪən
AM ˌtɛnəˈsoʊniən

Tenochtitlán
BR ˌtɛnɒtʃtɪˈtlɑːn
AM təˌnɑtʃtəˈtlɑn

tenon
BR ˈtɛnən, -z
AM ˈtɛnən, -z

tenoner
BR ˈtɛnənə(r), -z
AM ˈtɛnənɚ, -z

tenon-saw
BR ˈtɛnənsɔː(r), -z
AM ˈtɛnən.sɔ, ˈtɛnən.sɑ, -z

tenor
BR ˈtɛnə(r), -z
AM ˈtɛnɚ, -z

tenorist
BR ˈtɛnərɪst, -s
AM ˈtɛnərəst, -s

tenosynovitis
BR ˌtɛnəʊˌsʌɪnəˈvʌɪtɪs
AM ˌtɛnoʊˌsaɪnəˈvaɪdɪs

tenotomy
BR tɪˈnɒtəm|i, -ɪz
AM təˈnɑdəmi, -z

tenour
BR ˈtɛnə(r)
AM ˈtɛnɚ

tenpence
BR ˈtɛnpəns, -ɪz
AM ˈtɛnpəns, -əz

tenpenny
BR ˈtɛnpən|i, -ɪz
AM ˈtɛn.pɛni, -z

tenpin
BR ˈtɛnpɪn, -z
AM ˈtɛn.pɪn, -z

tenpin bowling
BR ˌtɛnpɪn ˈbəʊlɪŋ
AM ˌtɛn.pɪn ˈboʊlɪŋ

tenrec
BR ˈtɛnrɛk, -s
AM ˈtɛn.rɛk, -s

tense
BR tɛns, -ɪz, -ə(r), -ɪst
AM tɛns, -əz, -ɚ, -əst

tenseless
BR ˈtɛnsləs
AM ˈtɛnsləs

tensely
BR ˈtɛnsli
AM ˈtɛnsli

tenseness
BR ˈtɛnsnəs
AM ˈtɛnsnəs

tensile
BR ˈtɛnsʌɪl
AM ˈtɛnsəl, ˈtɛnˌsaɪl

tensility
BR tɛnˈsɪlɪti
AM tɛnˈsɪlɪdi

tensimeter
BR tɛnˈsɪmɪtə(r), -z
AM tɛnˈsɪmɪdɚ, -z

tension
BR ˈtɛnʃn, -z
AM ˈtɛnʃən, -z

tensional
BR ˈtɛnʃn(ə)l, ˈtɛnʃən(ə)l
AM ˈtɛnʃ(ə)nəl

tensionally
BR ˈtɛnʃnəli, ˈtɛnʃnʃi, ˈtɛnʃənʃi, ˈtɛnʃ(ə)nəli
AM ˈtɛnʃ(ə)nəli

tensioner
BR ˈtɛnʃnə(r), ˈtɛnʃənə(r), -z
AM ˈtɛnʃənɚ, -z

tensionless
BR ˈtɛnʃ(ə)nləs
AM ˈtɛnʃənləs

tensity
BR ˈtɛnsɪti
AM ˈtɛnsədi

tenson
BR ˈtɛnsn, -z
AM ˈtɛnsən, -z

tensor
BR ˈtɛnsə(r), -z
AM ˈtɛnsɚ, ˈtɛnˌsɔ(ə)r, -z

tensorial
BR tɛnˈsɔːrɪəl
AM tɛnˈsoriəl

tent
BR tɛnt, -s, -ɪŋ, -ɪd
AM tɛn|t, -ts, -(t)ŋ, -(t)əd

tentacle
BR ˈtɛntəkl, -z, -d
AM ˈtɛn(t)əkəl, -z, -d

tentacular
BR tɛnˈtakjʊlə(r)
AM tɛnˈtækjəlɚ

tentaculate
BR tɛnˈtakjʊlət
AM tɛnˈtækjələt

tentage
BR ˈtɛntɪdʒ
AM ˈtɛn(t)ɪdʒ

tentative
BR ˈtɛntətɪv, -z
AM ˈtɛn(t)ədɪv, -z

tentatively
BR ˈtɛntətɪvli
AM ˈtɛn(t)ədɪvli

tentativeness
BR ˈtɛntətɪvnɪs
AM ˈtɛn(t)ədɪvnɪs

tenter
BR ˈtɛntə(r), -z
AM ˈtɛn(t)ɚ, -z

Tenterden
BR ˈtɛntəd(ə)n
AM ˈtɛn(t)ɚdən

tenterhook
BR ˈtɛntəhʊk, -s
AM ˈtɛn(t)ɚ,(h)ʊk, -s

tenth
BR tɛnθ, -s
AM tɛnθ, -s

tenthly
BR ˈtɛnθli
AM ˈtɛnθli

tenth-rate
BR ˌtɛnθˈreɪt
AM ˌtɛnθˈreɪt

tenuis
BR ˈtɛnjʊɪs, -ɪz
AM ˈtɛnjəwəs, -əz

tenuity
BR tɪˈnjuːɪti, tɛˈnjuːɪti
AM tɛˈn(j)uədi, təˈn(j)uədi

tenuous
BR ˈtɛnjʊəs
AM ˈtɛnjəwəs

tenuously
BR ˈtɛnjʊəsli
AM ˈtɛnjəwəsli

tenuousness
BR ˈtɛnjʊəsnəs
AM ˈtɛnjəwəsnəs

tenure
BR ˈtɛnjə(r), -d
AM ˈtɛnjɚ, -d

tenurial
BR tɛˈnjʊərɪəl, tɪˈnjʊərɪəl, tɛˈnjɔːrɪəl, tɪˈnjɔːrɪəl
AM tɛˈnjʊriəl

tenurially
BR tɛˈnjʊərɪəli, tɪˈnjʊərɪəli, tɛˈnjɔːrɪəli, tɪˈnjɔːrɪəli
AM tɛˈnjʊriəli, təˈnjʊriəli

tenuto
BR tɛˈnjuːtəʊ, tɪˈnjuːtəʊ
AM tɛˈnudoʊ, -z

Tenzing Norgay
BR ˌtɛnzɪŋ ˈnɔːɡeɪ
AM ˌtɛnzɪŋ ˈnɔrˌɡeɪ

tenzon
BR ˈtɛnzn, -z
AM ˈtɛnzən, -z

teocalli
BR ˌtiːə(ʊ)ˈkalli, -ɪz
AM ˌtioʊˈkɑli, -z

tepee
BR ˈtiːpiː, -z
AM ˈtiˌpi, -z

tephra
BR ˈtɛfrə(r), -z
AM ˈtɛfrə, -z

tepid
BR ˈtɛpɪd
AM ˈtɛpəd

tepidaria
BR ˌtɛpɪˈdɛːrɪə(r)
AM ˌtɛpəˈdɛriə

tepidarium
BR ˌtɛpɪˈdɛːrɪəm
AM ˌtɛpəˈdɛriəm

tepidity
BR tɛˈpɪdɪti, tɪˈpɪdɪti
AM təˈpɪdɪdi

tepidly
BR ˈtɛpɪdli
AM ˈtɛpədli

tepidness
BR ˈtɛpɪdnɪs
AM ˈtɛpədnəs

tequila
BR tɪˈkiːlə(r)
AM təˈkilə

terabyte
BR ˈtɛrəbʌɪt, -s
AM ˈtɛrəˌbaɪt, -s

teraflop
BR ˈterəflɒp, -s
AM ˈterəˌflɑp, -s

terai
BR təˈrʌɪ, -z
AM təˈraɪ, -z

terameter
BR ˈterəˌmiːtə(r), -z
AM ˈterəˌmiːdər, -z

terametre
BR ˈterəˌmiːtə(r), -z
AM ˈterəˌmiːdər, -z

teraph
BR ˈterəf, -s
AM ˈterəf, -s

teraphim
BR ˈterəfɪm
AM ˈterəfɪm

teratogen
BR tɛˈratədʒ(ə)n,
tɪˈratədʒ(ə)n,
ˈterətədʒ(ə)n, -z
AM tɛˈrædədʒən,
ˈterədədʒən, -z

teratogenic
BR tɛˌratə(ʊ)ˈdʒɛnɪk,
tɪˌratə(ʊ)ˈdʒɛnɪk,
ˌterətə(ʊ)ˈdʒɛnɪk
AM ˌterədəˈdʒɛnɪk,
ˈterəˌtoʊˈdʒɛnɪk

teratogeny
BR ˌterəˈtɒdʒɪni
AM ˌterəˈtɑdʒeni

teratological
BR ˌterəˈtɒdʒɪkl
AM ˌterədəˈlɑdʒəkəl

teratologist
BR ˌterəˈtɒlədʒɪst, -s
AM ˌterəˈtɑlədʒəst, -s

teratology
BR ˌterəˈtɒlədʒi
AM ˌterəˈtɑlədʒi

teratoma
BR ˌterəˈtəʊmə(r), -z
AM ˌterəˈtoʊmə, -z

teratomata
BR ˌterəˈtəʊmətə(r)
AM ˌterəˈtoʊmədə

terawatt
BR ˈterəwɒt, -s
AM ˈterəˌwɑt, -s

terbium
BR ˈtəːbɪəm
AM ˈtərbiəm

terce
BR təːs, -ɪz
AM tərs, -əz

tercel
BR ˈtəːsl, -z
AM ˈtərsəl, -z

tercentenary
BR ˌtəːsɛnˈtiːn(ə)r|i,
ˌtəːs(ə)nˈtiːn(ə)r|i,
ˌtəːsɛnˈten(ə)r|i,
ˌtəːs(ə)nˈten(ə)r|i, -iz
AM ˈtərsənˈtenəri,
ˌtərˈsɛntnˌɛri, -z

tercentennial
BR ˌtəːsɛnˈteniəl,
ˌtəːs(ə)nˈteniəl, -z
AM ˌtɛrsənˈteniəl,
ˈtɛrˌsɛnˈteniəl, -z

tercet
BR ˈtəːsɪt, -s
AM ˈtərsət, -s

terebinth
BR ˈterɪbɪnθ, -s
AM ˈterəˌbinθ, -s

terebinthine
BR ˌterɪˈbɪnθʌɪn
AM ˌterəˈbɪnθən

terebra
BR ˈterɪbrə(r),
tɪˈriːbrə(r)
AM ˈterəbrə, təˈribrə

terebrae
BR ˈterɪbriː, tɪˈriːbriː,
ˈterɪbreɪ, tɪˈriːbreɪ
AM ˈterɪbri, təˈribri,
təˈriˌbraɪ, ˈterəˌbraɪ

terebrant
BR ˈterɪbr(ə)nt,
tɪˈriːbr(ə)nt, -s
AM ˈterəˌbrænt,
təˈribrənt, -s

teredo
BR tɪˈriːdəʊ, tɛˈriːdəʊ,
-z
AM tɛˈridoʊ, təˈridoʊ,
-z

Terence
BR ˈterəns, ˈterns
AM ˈterəns

Teresa
BR tɪˈriːzə(r),
tɪˈreɪzə(r), tɪˈriːsə(r),
tɪˈreɪsə(r)
AM təˈrisə, təˈreɪsə,
təˈrizə, təˈreɪzə

Terese
BR tɪˈriːz, tɪˈriːs, tɪˈreɪz,
tɛˈreɪz
AM təˈrisə, təˈreɪsə,
təˈrizə, təˈreɪzə

Teresina
BR ˌterɪˈziːnə(r),
ˌterɪˈsiːnə(r)
AM ˌterəˈsinə,
ˌterəˈzinə

terete
BR təˈriːt
AM ˈtɛˌrit

tergal
BR ˈtəːgl
AM ˈtərgəl

tergiversate
BR ˈtəːdʒɪvəseɪt,
ˈtəːdʒɪˌvəːseɪt, -s, -ɪŋ,
-ɪd
AM ˈtərdʒəvərˌseɪt,
ˌtərdʒəˈvərˌseɪt, -ts,
-dɪŋ, -dɪd

tergiversation
BR ˌtəːdʒɪvəˈseɪʃn
AM ˌtərdʒəvərˈseɪʃən

tergiversator
BR ˈtəːdʒɪvəˌseɪtə(r), -z
AM ˈtərdʒəvərˌseɪdər,
ˌtərdʒəˈvərˌseɪdər, -z

teriyaki
BR ˌterɪˈjaːki, ˌterɪˈjaki
AM ˌteriˈjaki

term
BR təːm, -z, -ɪŋ, -d
AM tərm, -z, -ɪŋ, -d

termagant
BR ˈtəːməg(ə)nt, -s
AM ˈtərməgənt, -s

terminable
BR ˈtəːmɪnəbl
AM ˈtərmənəbəl

terminableness
BR ˈtəːmɪnəblnəs
AM ˈtərmənəbəlnəs

terminal
BR ˈtəːmɪnl, -z
AM ˈtərmənəl, -z

terminally
BR ˈtəːmɪnli,
ˈtəːmɪnəli
AM ˈtərmənəli

terminate
BR ˈtəːmɪneɪt, -s, -ɪŋ, -d
AM ˈtərməˌneɪ|t, -ts,
-dɪŋ, -dɪd

termination
BR ˌtəːmɪˈneɪʃn, -z
AM ˌtərməˈneɪʃən, -z

terminational
BR ˌtəːmɪˈneɪʃn(ə)l,
ˌtəːmɪˈneɪʃən(ə)l
AM ˌtərməˈneɪʃ(ə)nəl

terminator
BR ˈtəːmɪneɪtə(r), -z
AM ˈtərməˌneɪdər, -z

termini
BR ˈtəːmɪnʌɪ
AM ˈtərməˌnaɪ,
ˈtərməni

terminism
BR ˈtəːmɪnɪz(ə)m
AM ˈtərməˌnɪzəm

terminist
BR ˈtəːmɪnɪst, -s
AM ˈtərmənəst, -s

terminological
BR ˌtəːmɪnəˈlɒdʒɪkl
AM ˌtərmənəˈlɑdʒəkəl

terminologically
BR ˌtəːmɪnəˈlɒdʒɪkli
AM ˌtərmənəˈlɑdʒək-
(ə)li

terminologist
BR ˌtəːmɪˈnɒlədʒɪst, -s
AM ˌtərməˈnɑlədʒəst,
-s

terminology
BR ˌtəːmɪˈnɒlədʒ|i, -iz
AM ˌtərməˈnɑlədʒi, -z

terminus
BR ˈtəːmɪnəs, -ɪz
AM ˈtərmənəs, -əz

termitaria
BR ˌtəːmɪˈtɛːrɪə(r)
AM ˌtərməˈteriə

termitarium
BR ˌtəːmɪˈtɛːrɪəm
AM ˌtərməˈteriəm

termitary
BR ˈtəːmɪt(ə)r|i, -iz
AM ˈtərməˌteri, -z

termite
BR ˈtəːmʌɪt, -s
AM ˈtərˌmaɪt, -s

termless
BR ˈtəːmləs
AM ˈtərmləs

termly
BR ˈtəːmli
AM ˈtərmli

termor
BR ˈtəːmə(r), -z
AM ˈtərmər, -z

tern
BR təːn, -z
AM tərn, -z

ternary
BR ˈtəːn(ə)r|i, -iz
AM ˈtərnəri, -z

ternate
BR ˈtəːnət, ˈtəːneɪt
AM ˈtərneɪt, ˈtərnət

ternately
BR ˈtəːnətli, ˈtəːneɪtli
AM ˈtərneɪtli, ˈtərnətli

terne
BR təːn
AM tərn

terne-plate
BR ˈtəːnpleɪt
AM ˈtərnˌpleɪt

terpene
BR ˈtəːpiːn, -z
AM ˈtərˌpin, -z

Terpsichore
BR ˌtəːpˈsɪk(ə)ri
AM ˌtərpˈsɪkəri

Terpsichorean
BR ˌtəːpsɪkəˈriːən,
ˌtəːpsɪˈkɔːrɪən
AM ˌtərpsɪˌkɔˈriən,
ˌtərpsəkəˈriən

terra
BR ˈterə(r)
AM ˈterə

terra alba
BR ˌterə(r) ˈalbə(r)
AM ˌterə ˈælbə

terrace
BR ˈterɪs, -ɪz, -ɪŋ, -t
AM ˈterəs, -əz, -ɪŋ, -t

terracotta
BR ˌterəˈkɒtə(r)
AM ˌterəˈkɑdə

Terra del Fuego
BR ˌterə dɛl fʊˈeɪgəʊ
AM ˌterə dɛl fʊˈeɪgoʊ

terra firma
BR ˌterə ˈfəːmə(r)

AM ˈterə ˈfɜːmə
terrain
 BR tɪˈreɪn, teˈreɪn, -z
 AM təˈreɪn, teˈreɪn, -z
terra incognita
 BR ˌterə(r)
 ˌɪŋkɒgˈniːtə(r),
 ɪŋˈkɒgnɪtə(r)
 AM ˈterə ˌɪnˌkagˈnidə,
 + ənˈkagnədə
terramara
 BR ˌterəˈmɑːrə(r)
 AM ˌterəˈmɑrə
terramare
 BR ˌterəˈmɑːˈrˌji, -ɪz
 AM ˌterəˈmɑri, -z
Terramycin®
 BR ˌterəˈmʌɪsɪn
 AM ˌterəˈmaɪsɪn
terrane
 BR teˈreɪn, -z
 AM təˈreɪn, -z
terrapin
 BR ˈterəpɪn, -z
 AM ˈterəˌpɪn, -z
terraria
 BR teˈreːrɪə(r),
 tɪˈreːrɪə(r)
 AM təˈreriə
terrarium
 BR teˈreːrɪəm,
 tɪˈreːrɪəm
 AM təˈreriəm
terra sigillata
 BR ˌterə ˌsɪdʒɪˈleɪtə(r)
 AM ˌterə ˌsɪdʒəˈladə
terrazzo
 BR teˈratsəʊ, tɪˈratsəʊ
 AM təˈrɑzoʊ, toˈratsoʊ
Terre Haute
 BR ˌterə ˈhəʊt
 AM ˌterə ˈhot
Terrell
 BR ˈterḷ
 AM ˈterəl, təˈrel
terrene
 BR teˈriːn, teˈriːn
 AM təˈrin, ˈteˌrin
terreplein
 BR ˈteːpleɪn, -z
 AM ˈterəˌpleɪn, -z
terrestrial
 BR tɪˈrestrɪəl,
 teˈrestrɪəl, -z
 AM təˈrestrɪəl, -z
terrestrially
 BR tɪˈrestrɪəli,
 teˈrestrɪəli
 AM təˈrestrɪəli
terret
 BR ˈterɪt, -s
 AM ˈterət, -s
terre-verte
 BR ˌteːˈveːt
 AM terˈvert
terrible
 BR ˈterɪbl

AM ˈterəbəl
terribleness
 BR ˈterɪblnəs
 AM ˈterəbəlnəs
terribly
 BR ˈterɪbli
 AM ˈterəbli
terricolous
 BR teˈrɪkələs, teˈrɪkḷəs
 AM teˈrɪkələs,
 təˈrɪkələs
terrier
 BR ˈterɪə(r), -z
 AM ˈteriər, -z
terrific
 BR təˈrɪfɪk
 AM təˈrɪfɪk
terrifically
 BR təˈrɪfɪkli
 AM təˈrɪfɪk(ə)li
terrifier
 BR ˈterɪfʌɪə(r), -z
 AM ˈterəˌfaɪər, -z
terrify
 BR ˈterɪfʌɪ, -z, -ɪŋ, -d
 AM ˈterəˌfaɪ, -z, -ɪŋ, -d
terrifyingly
 BR ˈterɪfʌɪɪŋli
 AM ˈterəˌfaɪɪŋli
terrigenous
 BR teˈrɪdʒɪnəs
 AM teˈrɪdʒənəs,
 təˈrɪdʒənəs
terrine
 BR teˈriːn, təˈriːn,
 ˈteriːn, -z
 AM təˈrin, teˈrin, -z
territ
 BR ˈterɪt, -s
 AM ˈterət, -s
territorial
 BR ˌterɪˈtɔːrɪəl, -z
 AM ˌterəˈtorɪəl, -z
territorialisation
 BR ˌterɪˌtɔːrɪəlʌɪˈzeɪʃn
 AM ˌterəˌtorɪələˈzeɪʃən,
 ˌterəˌtorɪəˌlaɪˈzeɪʃən
territorialise
 BR ˌterɪˈtɔːrɪəlʌɪz, -ɪz,
 -ɪŋ, -d
 AM ˌterəˈtorɪəˌlaɪz, -ɪz,
 -ɪŋ, -d
territorialism
 BR ˌterɪˈtɔːrɪəlɪz(ə)m
 AM ˌterəˈtorɪəˌlɪzəm
territoriality
 BR ˌterɪˌtɔːrɪˈalɪti
 AM ˌterəˌtoriˈælədi
territorialization
 BR ˌterɪˌtɔːrɪəlʌɪˈzeɪʃn
 AM ˌterəˌtorɪələˈzeɪʃən,
 ˌterəˌtorɪəˌlaɪˈzeɪʃən
territorialize
 BR ˌterɪˈtɔːrɪəlʌɪz, -ɪz,
 -ɪŋ, -d
 AM ˌterəˈtorɪəˌlaɪz, -ɪz,
 -ɪŋ, -d

territorially
 BR ˌterɪˈtɔːrɪəli
 AM ˌterəˈtorɪəli
territory
 BR ˈterɪt(ə)r|i, -ɪz
 AM ˈterəˌtori, -z
terror
 BR ˈterə(r), -z
 AM ˈterər, -z
terrorisation
 BR ˌterərʌɪˈzeɪʃn
 AM ˌterərəˈzeɪʃən,
 ˌterəˌraɪˈzeɪʃən
terrorise
 BR ˈterərʌɪz, -ɪz, -ɪŋ, -d
 AM ˈterəˌraɪz, -ɪz, -ɪŋ, -d
terroriser
 BR ˈterərʌɪzə(r), -z
 AM ˈterəˌraɪzər, -z
terrorism
 BR ˈterərɪz(ə)m
 AM ˈterəˌrɪzəm
terrorist
 BR ˈterərɪst, -s
 AM ˈterərəst, -s
terroristic
 BR ˌterəˈrɪstɪk
 AM ˌterəˈrɪstɪk
terroristically
 BR ˌterəˈrɪstɪkli
 AM ˌterəˈrɪstɪk(ə)li
terrorization
 BR ˌterərʌɪˈzeɪʃn
 AM ˌterərəˈzeɪʃən,
 ˌterəˌraɪˈzeɪʃən
terrorize
 BR ˈterərʌɪz, -ɪz, -ɪŋ, -d
 AM ˈterəˌraɪz, -ɪz, -ɪŋ, -d
terrorizer
 BR ˈterərʌɪzə(r), -z
 AM ˈterəˌraɪzər, -z
terry
 BR ˈteri
 AM ˈteri
terse
 BR təːs, -ə(r), -ɪst
 AM tərs, -ər, -əst
tersely
 BR ˈtəːsli
 AM ˈtərsli
terseness
 BR ˈtəːsnəs
 AM ˈtərsnəs
tertian
 BR ˈtəːʃn
 AM ˈtərʃən
tertiary
 BR ˈtəːʃ(ə)ri
 AM ˈtərʃiˌeri, ˈtərʃəri
tertium quid
 BR ˌtəːʃɪəm ˈkwɪd,
 ˌtəːtɪəm +
 AM ˈtərʃ(i)əm ˈkwɪd,
 ˈtərdiəm +
Tertius
 BR ˈtəːʃ(ɪ)əs
 AM ˈtərʃ(i)əs

Tertullian
 BR təˈtʌlɪən
 AM tərˈtəljən,
 tərˈtəlion
tervalent
 BR (ˌ)təːˈveɪlənt,
 (ˌ)təːˈveɪln̩t
 AM tərˈveɪlənt
terylene®
 BR ˈterɪliːn
 AM ˈterəˌlin
terza rima
 BR ˌtəːtsə ˈriːmə(r),
 ˌteːtsə +
 AM ˌtərtsə ˈrimə
terzetti
 BR teːtˈseti, təːtˈseti
 AM tərˈtsedi
terzetto
 BR teːtˈsetəʊ,
 təːtˈsetəʊ, -z
 AM tərˈtsedoʊ, -z
Tesco
 BR ˈteskəʊ
 AM ˈteskoʊ
TESL
 BR ˈtesl
 AM ˈtesəl
tesla
 BR ˈteslə(r), -z
 AM ˈteslə, -z
TESOL
 BR ˈtesɒl
 AM ˈteˌsɒl, ˈtiˌsɒl,
 ˈteˌsɑl, ˈtiˌsɑl
Tess
 BR tes
 AM tes
TESSA
 BR ˈtesə(r)
 AM ˈtesə
tessellate
 BR ˈtesɪleɪt, -s, -ɪŋ, -ɪd
 AM ˈtesəˌleɪt, -ts, -dɪŋ,
 -dɪd
tessellation
 BR ˌtesɪˈleɪʃn, -z
 AM ˌtesəˈleɪʃən, -z
tessera
 BR ˈtes(ə)rə(r)
 AM ˈtesərə
tesserae
 BR ˈtes(ə)riː
 AM ˈtesəˌraɪ, ˈtesəri
tesseral
 BR ˈtes(ə)rəl, ˈtes(ə)rḷ
 AM ˈtesərəl
tessitura
 BR ˌtesɪˈt(j)ʊərə(r), -z
 AM ˌtesəˈtʊrə, -z
test
 BR test, -s, -ɪŋ, -ɪd
 AM test, -s, -ɪŋ, -əd
testa
 BR ˈtestə(r)
 AM ˈtestə

testability
BR ˌtestəˈbɪlɪti
AM ˌtestəˈbɪlɪdi

testable
BR ˈtestəbl
AM ˈtestəbəl

testaceous
BR tɛˈsteɪʃəs
AM tɛˈsteɪʃəs

testacy
BR ˈtestəs|i, -ɪz
AM ˈtestəsi, -z

testae
BR ˈtesti:
AM ˈtesti, ˈtɛsˌtaɪ

testament
BR ˈtestəm(ə)nt, -s
AM ˈtestəmənt, -s

testamental
BR ˌtestəˈmentl
AM ˌtestəˈmen(t)l

testamentarily
BR ˌtestəˈment(ə)rɪli
AM ˌtestəˈmen(t)ərəli

testamentary
BR ˌtestəˈment(ə)ri
AM ˌtestəˈmen(t)əri

testamur
BR tɛˈsteɪmə(r), -z
AM tɛˈsteɪmər, -z

testate
BR ˈtesteɪt, ˈtestət
AM ˈtɛˌsteɪt, ˈtestət

testation
BR tɛˈsteɪʃn, -z
AM tɛˈsteɪʃən, -z

testator
BR tɛˈsteɪtə(r), -z
AM ˈtɛˌsteɪdər, -z

testatrices
BR tɛˈsteɪtrɪsi:z
AM tɛˈsteɪtrəˌsiz,
ˌtestəˈtraɪˌsiz

testatrix
BR tɛˈsteɪtrɪks, -ɪz
AM ˈtɛˌsteɪˌtrɪks,
tɛˈsteɪˌtrɪks, -ɪz

Test-Ban Treaty
BR ˈtes(t)ban ˌtri:ti
AM ˌtes(t)ˌbæn ˌtridi

testee
BR tesˈti:, -z
AM tɛsˈti, -z

testentry
BR ˈtestntr|i, -ɪz
AM ˈtestəntri, -z

tester
BR ˈtestə(r), -z
AM ˈtestər, -z

testes
BR ˈtesti:z
AM ˈtɛsˌtiz

testicle
BR ˈtestɪkl, -z
AM ˈtestəkəl, -z

testicular
BR tɛˈstɪkjʊlə(r)

testiculate
BR tɛˈstɪkjələt
AM tɛˈstɪkjələt,
tɛˈstɪkjəˌleɪt

testification
BR ˌtestɪfɪˈkeɪʃn, -z
AM ˌtestəfəˈkeɪʃən, -z

testifier
BR ˈtestɪfʌɪə(r), -z
AM ˈtestəˌfaɪər, -z

testify
BR ˈtestɪfʌɪ, -z, -ɪŋ, -d
AM ˈtestəˌfaɪ, -z, -ɪŋ, -d

testily
BR ˈtestɪli
AM ˈtestəli

testimonial
BR ˌtestɪˈməʊniəl, -z
AM ˌtestəˈmoʊniəl, -z

testimony
BR ˈtestɪmən|i, -ɪz
AM ˈtestəˌmoʊni, -z

testiness
BR ˈtestɪnɪs
AM ˈtestɪnɪs

testis
BR ˈtestɪs
AM ˈtestəs

testosterone
BR tɛˈstɒstərəʊn
AM tɛˈstɑstəˌroʊn

testudinal
BR tɛˈst(j)u:dɪnl,
tɛˈstʃu:dɪnl
AM tɛˈst(j)udn̩l

testudines
BR tɛˈst(j)u:dɪni:z,
tɛˈstʃu:dɪni:z
AM tɛˈst(j)udn̩ˌiz

testudo
BR tɛˈst(j)u:dəʊ,
tɛˈstʃu:dəʊ, -z
AM tɛˈstudoʊ, -z

testy
BR ˈtest|i, -ɪə(r), -ɪɪst
AM ˈtesti, -ɪər, -ɪɪst

tetanic
BR tɪˈtanɪk, tɛˈtanɪk
AM tɛˈtænɪk

tetanically
BR tɪˈtanɪkli,
tɛˈtanɪkli
AM tɛˈtænək(ə)li

tetanise
BR ˈtetənʌɪz, ˈtetn̩ʌɪz,
-ɪz, -ɪŋ, -d
AM ˈtetn̩ˌaɪz, -ɪz, -ɪŋ, -d

tetanize
BR ˈtetənʌɪz, ˈtetn̩ʌɪz,
-ɪz, -ɪŋ, -d
AM ˈtetn̩ˌaɪz, -ɪz, -ɪŋ, -d

tetanoid
BR ˈtetənɔɪd, ˈtetn̩ɔɪd
AM ˈtetn̩ˌɔɪd

tetanus
BR ˈtetənəs, ˈtetn̩əs

testican
AM ˈtetnəs, ˈtetn̩əs

tetany
BR ˈtetəni, ˈtetn̩i
AM ˈtetn̩i, ˈtetni

Tetbury
BR ˈtetb(ə)ri
AM ˈtetˌbɛri

tetchily
BR ˈtetʃɪli
AM ˈtetʃəli

tetchiness
BR ˈtetʃɪnɪs
AM ˈtetʃɪnɪs

tetchy
BR ˈtetʃ|i, -ɪə(r), -ɪɪst
AM ˈtetʃi, -ər, -ɪst

tête-à-tête
BR ˌteɪtɑːˈteɪt,
ˌteɪtəˈteɪt, -s
AM ˌtɛdəˈtɛt, -s

tête-bêche
BR ˌtetˈbeʃ, ˌteɪtˈbeʃ
AM ˌtetˈbeʃ

tether
BR ˈteðə|ə(r), -əz,
-(ə)rɪŋ, -əd
AM ˈteð|ər, -ərz, -(ə)rɪŋ,
-ərd

Tethys
BR ˈti:θɪs, ˈtɛθɪs
AM ˈteθəs

Tetley
BR ˈtetli
AM ˈtetli

Teton
BR ˈti:tɒn, -z
AM ˈti:tɑn, -z

tetra
BR ˈtetrə(r)
AM ˈtetrə

tetrachloride
BR ˌtetrəˈklɒːrʌɪd
AM ˌtetrəˈklɔˌraɪd

**tetrachloroethyl-
ene**
BR ˌtetrəˌklɒːrəʊˈeθɪliːn,
ˌtetrəˌklɒːrəʊˈeθliːn
AM ˌtetrəˌklɔroʊˈeθəˌlin

tetrachord
BR ˈtetrəkɔːd, -z
AM ˈtetrəˌkɔ(ə)rd, -z

tetracyclic
BR ˌtetrəˈsʌɪklɪk
AM ˌtetrəˈsaɪklɪk

tetracycline
BR ˌtetrəˈsʌɪkliːn,
ˌtetrəˈsʌɪklɪn, -z
AM ˌtetrəˈsaɪˌklin, -z

tetrad
BR ˈtetrad, -z
AM ˈtɛˌtræd, -z

tetradactyl
BR ˌtetrəˈdakt(ɪ)l, -z
AM ˌtetrəˈdæktl, -z

tetradactylous
BR ˌtetrəˈdaktɪləs
AM ˌtetrəˈdæktələs

tetraethyl
BR ˌtetrə(r)ˈeθ(ɪ)l,
ˌtetrə(r)ˈeθʌɪl,
ˌtetrə(r)ˈiːθʌɪl
AM ˌtetrəˈeθəl

tetragon
BR ˈtetrəg(ə)n,
ˈtetrəgɒn, -z
AM ˈtetrəˌgɑn, -z

tetragonal
BR tɛˈtrag(ə)nl,
tɪˈtrag(ə)nl
AM tɛˈtrægənəl

tetragonally
BR tɛˈtragənl|i,
tɛˈtragənəli,
tɪˈtragənl|i,
tɪˈtragənəli
AM tɛˈtrægənəli

tetragram
BR ˈtetrəgram, -z
AM ˈtetrəˌgræm, -z

tetragrammaton
BR ˌtetrəˈgramət(ə)n,
ˌtetrəˈgramətɒn
AM ˌtetrəˈgræmə,tɑn

tetragynous
BR tɛˈtradʒɪnəs,
tɪˈtradʒɪnəs
AM tɛˈtrædʒənəs

tetrahedra
BR ˌtetrəˈhiːdrə(r)
AM ˌtetrəˈhidrə

tetrahedral
BR ˌtetrəˈhiːdr(ə)l
AM ˌtetrəˈhidrəl

tetrahedron
BR ˌtetrəˈhiːdr(ə)n, -z
AM ˌtetrəˈhidrən, -z

tetralogy
BR tɛˈtraləˌdʒ|i,
tɪˈtraləˌdʒ|i, -ɪz
AM tɛˈtraləˌdʒi, -z

tetramerous
BR tɛˈtram(ə)rəs,
tɪˈtram(ə)rəs
AM tɛˈtræmərəs

tetrameter
BR tɛˈtramɪtə(r),
tɪˈtramɪtə(r), -z
AM tɛˈtræmədər, -z

tetramorph
BR ˈtetrəmɔːf, -s
AM ˈtetrəˌmɔ(ə)rf, -s

tetrandrous
BR tɛˈtrandrəs,
tɪˈtrandrəs
AM tɛˈtrændrəs

tetraplegia
BR ˌtetrəˈpliːdʒ(ɪ)ə(r)
AM ˌtetrəˈpli(d)ʒ(ɪ)ə

tetraplegic
BR ˌtetrəˈpliːdʒɪk, -s
AM ˌtetrəˈplidʒɪk, -s

tetraploid
BR ˈtetrəplɔɪd, -z
AM ˈtetrəˌplɔɪd, -z

tetrapod
BR ˈtɛtrəpɒd, -z
AM ˈtɛtrə.pad, -z

tetrapodous
BR tɛˈtrapədəs,
tɪˈtrapədəs
AM tɛˈtræpədəs

tetrapterous
BR tɛˈtrapt(ə)rəs,
tɪˈtrapt(ə)rəs
AM tɛˈtræptərəs

tetrarch
BR ˈtɛtrɑːk, -s
AM ˈtɛ.trɑrk, -s

tetrarchate
BR ˈtɛtrɑːkeɪt, -s
AM ˈtɛ.trɑr.keɪt, -s

tetrarchical
BR tɛˈtrɑːkɪkl,
tɪˈtrɑːkɪkl
AM təˈtrɑrkəkəl,
tɛˈtrɑrkəkəl

tetrarchy
BR ˈtɛtrɑːk|i, -ɪz
AM ˈtɛ.trɑrki, -z

tetrastich
BR ˈtɛtrəstɪk, -s
AM ˈtɛtrə.stɪk, -s

tetrastyle
BR ˈtɛtrəstʌɪl, -z
AM ˈtɛtrə.staɪl, -z

tetrasyllabic
BR ˌtɛtrəsɪˈlabɪk
AM ˌtɛtrəsəˈlæbɪk

tetrasyllable
BR ˈtɛtrə.sɪləbl,
ˌtɛtrəˈsɪləbl, -z
AM ˌtɛtrəˈsɪləbəl, -z

tetrathlon
BR tɛˈtraθlən,
tɪˈtraθlən, tɛˈtraθlɒn,
tɪˈtraθlɒn, -z
AM təˈtræθ.lɑn,
tɛˈtræθ.lɑn, -z

tetratomic
BR ˌtɛtrəˈtɒmɪk
AM ˌtɛtrəˈtɑmɪk

tetravalent
BR ˌtɛtrəˈveɪlənt,
ˌtɛtrəˈveɪlnt
AM ˌtɛtrəˈveɪlənt

Tetrazzini
BR ˌtɛtrəˈziːni
AM ˌtɛtrəˈzini

tetrode
BR ˈtɛtrəʊd, -z
AM ˈtɛ.troʊd, -z

tetrodotoxin
BR ˌtɛtrə(ʊ)də(ʊ)ˈtɒksɪn
AM ˌtɛtroʊdoʊˈtɑksɪn

tetroxide
BR tɛˈtrɒksʌɪd,
tɪˈtrɒksʌɪd
AM tɛˈtrɑk.saɪd

tetter
BR ˈtɛtə(r)
AM ˈtɛdər

Teuton
BR ˈtjuːt(ə)n,
tʃuːt(ə)n, -z
AM ˈt(j)utn, ˈt(j)u.tɑn ,
-z

Teutonic
BR ˌtjuːˈtɒnɪk,
tʃuːˈtɒnɪk
AM ˌt(j)uˈtɑnɪk

Teutonicism
BR tjuːˈtɒnɪsɪz(ə)m,
tʃuːˈtɒnɪsɪz(ə)m
AM ˌt(j)uˈtɑnə.sɪzəm

Tevet
BR ˈtɛvɛt
AM teɪˈvɛt, ˈteɪ.vɛθ

Teviot
BR ˈtiːvɪət, ˈtɛvɪət
AM ˈtɛviət

Tewkesbury
BR ˈtjuːksb(ə)ri,
ˈtʃuːksb(ə)ri
AM ˈt(j)uks.bɛri

Tex
BR tɛks
AM tɛks

Texan
BR ˈtɛksn, -z
AM ˈtɛksən, -z

Texas
BR ˈtɛksəs
AM ˈtɛksəs

Texel
BR ˈtɛksl
AM ˈtɛksəl

Tex-Mex
BR ˌtɛksˈmɛks
AM ˌtɛksˈmɛks

text
BR tɛkst, -s
AM tɛkst, -s

textbook
BR ˈtɛks(t)bʊk, -s
AM ˈtɛks(t).bʊk, -s

textbookish
BR ˈtɛks(t)bʊkɪʃ
AM ˈtɛks(t).bʊkɪʃ

textile
BR ˈtɛkstʌɪl, -z
AM ˈtɛks.staɪl, -z

textless
BR ˈtɛks(t)ləs
AM ˈtɛks(t)ləs

textual
BR ˈtɛkstʃʊəl,
ˈtɛkstʃ(ʉ)l, ˈtɛkstjʊəl,
ˈtɛkstjʊl
AM ˈtɛk(st)ʃ(əw)əl

textualism
BR ˈtɛkstʃʊəlɪz(ə)m,
ˈtɛkstʃʉlɪz(ə)m,
ˈtɛkstʃʃlɪz(ə)m,
ˌtɛkstjʊəlɪz(ə)m,
ˈtɛkstjʉlɪz(ə)m
AM ˈtɛk(st)ʃ(əw)ə.lɪzəm

textualist
BR ˈtɛkstʃʊəlɪst,
ˈtɛkstʃʉlɪst,

ˈtɛkstʃʃlɪst,
ˈtɛkstjʊəlɪst,
ˈtɛkstjʉlɪst
AM ˈtɛk(st)ʃ(əw)ələst

textuality
BR ˌtɛkstʃʊˈalɪti,
ˌtɛkstjʊˈalɪti
AM ˌtɛk(st)ʃəˈwælədi

textually
BR ˈtɛkstʃʊəli,
ˈtɛkstʃʉli, ˈtɛkstʃʃli,
ˈtɛkstjʊəli, ˈtɛkstjʉli
AM ˈtɛk(st)ʃ(əw)əli

textural
BR ˈtɛkstʃ(ə)rəl,
ˈtɛkstʃ(ə)rl
AM ˈtɛk(st)ʃərəl

texturally
BR ˈtɛkstʃ(ə)rəli,
ˈtɛkstʃ(ə)rli
AM ˈtɛk(st)ʃərəli

texture
BR ˈtɛkstʃə(r), -z, -d
AM ˈtɛk(st)ʃər, -z, -d

textureless
BR ˈtɛkstʃələs
AM ˈtɛk(st)ʃərləs

texturise
BR ˈtɛkstʃərʌɪz, -ɪz, -ɪŋ,
-d
AM ˈtɛk(st)ʃə,raɪz, -ɪz,
-ɪŋ, -d

texturize
BR ˈtɛkstʃərʌɪz, -ɪz, -ɪŋ,
-d
AM ˈtɛk(st)ʃə,raɪz, -ɪz,
-ɪŋ, -d

TGIF
BR ˌtiːdʒiːʌɪˈɛf
AM ˌtiˌdʒiˌaɪˈɛf

Thackeray
BR ˈθak(ə)ri,
ˈθak(ə)reɪ
AM ˈθæk(ə)ri

Thaddeus
BR ˈθadɪəs
AM ˈθædiəs

Thai
BR tʌɪ, -z
AM taɪ, -z

Thailand
BR ˈtʌɪland, ˈtʌɪlənd
AM ˈtaɪ.lænd

Thailander
BR ˈtʌɪlandə(r),
ˈtʌɪləndə(r), -z
AM ˈtaɪ.lændər,
ˈtaɪləndər, -z

thalamic
BR θəˈlamɪk
AM θəˈlæmɪk

thalamus
BR ˈθaləməs
AM ˈθæləməs

thalassaemia
BR ˌθaləˈsiːmɪə(r)
AM ˌθælə.ˈsimiə

thalassemia
BR ˌθaləˈsiːmɪə(r)
AM ˌθælə.ˈsimiə

thalassic
BR θəˈlasɪk
AM θəˈlæsɪk

thalassotherapy
BR θə.lasəʊˈθɛrəpi
AM ˈθælə.soʊˈθɛrəpi

thaler
BR ˈtɑːlə(r), -z
AM ˈtɑlər, -z

Thales
BR ˈθeɪliːz
AM ˈθeɪ.liz

Thalia
BR ˈθeɪlɪə(r), θəˈlʌɪə(r)
AM ˈθeɪljə, ˈθeɪliə

thalidomide
BR θəˈlɪdəmʌɪd
AM θəˈlɪdə.maɪd

thalli
BR ˈθalʌɪ, ˈθali:
AM ˈθæli

thallic
BR ˈθalɪk
AM ˈθælɪk

thallium
BR ˈθalɪəm
AM ˈθæliəm

thalloid
BR ˈθalɔɪd
AM ˈθæ.lɔɪd

thallophyte
BR ˈθaləfʌɪt, -s
AM ˈθælə.faɪt, -s

thallous
BR ˈθaləs
AM ˈθæləs

thallus
BR ˈθaləs
AM ˈθæləs

thalweg
BR ˈtɑːlvɛg, ˈθɑːlvɛg, -z
AM ˈtæl.vɛg, -z

Thame
BR teɪm
AM teɪm, θeɪm

Thames¹
in Connecticut
BR teɪmz, θeɪmz
AM teɪmz, θeɪmz

Thames²
in England, Canada,
New Zealand
BR tɛmz
AM tɛmz

Thammuz
BR ˈtamʊz
AM ˈtamʊz

than¹
strong form
BR ðan
AM ðæn

than²
weak form
BR ð(ə)n

AM ðən

thanage
BR 'θeɪnɪdʒ
AM 'θeɪnɪdʒ

thanatology
BR ˌθænə'tɒlədʒi
AM ˌθænə'tɑlədʒi

thane
BR θeɪn, -z
AM θeɪn, -z

thanedom
BR 'θeɪndəm, -z
AM 'θeɪndəm, -z

thaneship
BR 'θeɪnʃɪp, -s
AM 'θeɪnˌʃɪp, -s

Thanet
BR 'θænɪt
AM 'θænət

thank
BR θæŋk, -ks, -kɪŋ,
-(k)t
AM θæŋk, -ks, -kɪŋ,
-(k)t

thankful
BR 'θæŋkf(ʊ)l
AM 'θæŋkfəl

thankfully
BR 'θæŋkfʊli, 'θæŋkfl̩i
AM 'θæŋkfəli

thankfulness
BR 'θæŋkf(ʊ)nəs
AM 'θæŋkfəlnəs

thankless
BR 'θæŋkləs
AM 'θæŋkləs

thanklessly
BR 'θæŋkləsli
AM 'θæŋkləsli

thanklessness
BR 'θæŋkləsnəs
AM 'θæŋkləsnəs

thank-offering
BR 'θæŋkˌɒf(ə)rɪŋ, -z
AM 'θæŋkˌɒfərɪŋ,
'θæŋkˌɑfərɪŋ, -z

thanksgiving
BR ˌθæŋks'gɪvɪŋ,
'θæŋksˌgɪvɪŋ, -z
AM ˌθæŋks'gɪvɪŋ, -z

thank you
BR 'θæŋk ju:
AM 'θæŋk ˌju

thar
BR tɑ:(r), -z
AM tɑr, -z

that¹
*demonstrative
pronoun, adverb,
determiner*
BR ðæt
AM ðæt

that²
*relative pronoun,
conjunction–strong
form*
BR ðæt
AM ðæt

that³
*relative pronoun,
conjunction–weak
form*
BR ðət
AM ðət

thatch
BR θætʃ, -ɪz, -ɪŋ, -t
AM θætʃ, -əz, -ɪŋ, -t

thatcher
BR 'θætʃə(r), -z
AM 'θætʃər, -z

Thatcherism
BR 'θætʃ(ə)rɪz(ə)m
AM 'θætʃəˌrɪzm

Thatcherite
BR 'θætʃərʌɪt, -s
AM 'θætʃəˌrɑɪt, -s

thaumatology
BR θɔ:mə'tɒlədʒi
AM ˌθɔmə'tɑlədʒi,
ˌθɑmə'tɑlədʒi

thaumatrope
BR 'θɔ:mətrəʊp, -s
AM 'θɔməˌtroʊp,
'θɑməˌtroʊp, -s

thaumaturge
BR 'θɔ:mətɜ:dʒ, -ɪz
AM 'θɔməˌtɜrdʒ,
'θɑməˌtɜrdʒ, -z

thaumaturgic
BR ˌθɔ:mə'tɜ:dʒɪk
AM ˌθɔmə'tɜrdʒɪk,
ˌθɑmə'tɜrdʒɪk

thaumaturgical
BR ˌθɔ:mə'tɜ:dʒɪkl
AM ˌθɔmə'tɜrdʒəkəl,
ˌθɑmə'tɜrdʒəkəl

thaumaturgist
BR 'θɔ:mətɜ:dʒɪst, -s
AM 'θɔməˌtɜrdʒəst,
'θɑməˌtɜrdʒəst, -s

thaumaturgy
BR 'θɔ:mətɜ:dʒi
AM 'θɔməˌtɜrdʒi,
'θɑməˌtɜrdʒi

thaw
BR θɔ:(r), -z, -ɪŋ, -d
AM θɔ, θɑ, -z, -ɪŋ, -d

thawless
BR 'θɔ:ləs
AM 'θɔləs, 'θɑləs

THC
BR ˌti:eɪtʃ'si:
AM ˌti:eɪtʃ'si

the¹
strong form
BR ði:
AM ði

the²
*weak form before
consonants*
BR ðə
AM ð(ə)

the³
*weak form before
vowels*
BR ðɪ, ði:

AM ði

Thea
BR 'θi:ə(r)
AM 'θiə

theandric
BR θi:'ændrɪk
AM θi'ændrɪk

theanthropic
BR ˌθi:ən'θrɒpɪk
AM ˌθiən'θrɑpɪk

thearchy
BR 'θi:ɑːk|i, -ɪz
AM 'θiˌɑrki, -z

theater
BR 'θɪətə(r), -z
AM 'θiədər, -z

theatergoer
BR 'θɪətəˌgəʊə(r), -z
AM 'θiədərˌgoʊər, -z

theatergoing
BR 'θɪətəˌgəʊɪŋ
AM 'θiədərˌgoʊɪŋ

**theater-in-the-
round**
BR ˌθɪət(ə)rɪnðə'raʊnd
AM ˌθiədərənðə'raʊnd

theatre
BR 'θɪətə(r), -z
AM 'θiədər, -z

theatregoer
BR 'θɪətəˌgəʊə(r), -z
AM 'θiədərˌgoʊər, -z

theatregoing
BR 'θɪətəˌgəʊɪŋ
AM 'θiədərˌgoʊɪŋ

**theatre-in-the-
round**
BR ˌθɪət(ə)rɪnðə'raʊnd
AM ˌθiədərənðə'raʊnd

theatric
BR θɪ'ætrɪk, -s
AM θi'ætrɪk, -s

theatrical
BR θɪ'ætrɪkl, -z
AM θi'ætrəkəl, -z

theatricalisation
BR θɪˌatrɪkl̩ʌɪ'zeɪʃn,
θɪˌatrɪkəlʌɪ'zeɪʃn
AM θiˌætrəkələ'zeɪʃən,
θiˌætrəkəˌlaɪ'zeɪʃən

theatricalise
BR θɪ'atrɪkl̩ʌɪz,
θɪ'atrɪkəlʌɪz, -ɪz, -ɪŋ,
-d
AM θi'ætrəkəˌlaɪz, -ɪz,
-ɪŋ, -d

theatricalism
BR θɪ'atrɪkl̩ɪz(ə)m,
θɪ'atrɪkəlɪz(ə)m
AM θi'ætrəkəˌlɪzəm

theatricality
BR θɪˌatrɪ'kalɪti
AM θiˌætrə'kælədi

theatricalization
BR θɪˌatrɪkl̩ʌɪ'zeɪʃn,
θɪˌatrɪkəlʌɪ'zeɪʃn
AM θiˌætrəkələ'zeɪʃən,
θiˌætrəkəˌlaɪ'zeɪʃən

theatricalize
BR θɪ'atrɪkl̩ʌɪz,
θɪ'atrɪkəlʌɪz, -ɪz, -ɪŋ,
-d
AM θi'ætrəkəˌlaɪz, -ɪz,
-ɪŋ, -d

theatrically
BR θɪ'atrɪkli
AM θi'ætrək(ə)li

Theban
BR 'θi:bn, -z
AM 'θibən, -z

thebe
BR 'θeɪbeɪ
AM 'tɛbɛ

Thebes
BR θi:bz
AM θibz

theca
BR 'θi:kə(r)
AM 'θikə

thecae
BR 'θi:si:, 'θi:ki:
AM 'θi,si, 'θiki, 'θi,saɪ,
'θi,kaɪ

thecate
BR 'θi:keɪt, 'θi:kət
AM 'θi,keɪt

thé dansant
BR ˌteɪ ˌdɒ'sɒ̃, -z
AM ˌteɪ ˌdɑn'sɑn, -z

thee
BR ði:
AM ði

theft
BR θɛft, -s
AM θɛft, -s

thegn
BR θeɪn, -z
AM θeɪn, -z

theine
BR 'θi:i:n, 'θi:ɪn
AM 'θi,in, 'θiin

their¹
strong form
BR ðɛ:(r)
AM ðɛ(ə)r

their²
weak form
BR ðə(r)
AM ðər

theirs
BR ðɛːz
AM ðɛ(ə)rz

theirselves
BR ðɛ:'sɛlvz
AM ðɛr'sɛlvz

theism
BR 'θi:ɪz(ə)m
AM 'θi,ɪzəm

theist
BR 'θi:ɪst, -s
AM 'θiɪst, -s

theistic
BR θi:'ɪstɪk
AM θi'ɪstɪk

theistical
BR θiːˈɪstɪkl
AM θiˈɪstɪkəl

theistically
BR θiːˈɪstɪkli
AM θiˈɪstək(ə)li

Thelma
BR ˈθɛlmə(r)
AM ˈθɛlmə

Thelwall
BR ˈθɛlwɔːl
AM ˈθɛl,wɔl, ˈθɛl,wɑl

Thelwell
BR ˈθɛlw(ɛ)l
AM ˈθɛl,wɛl

them¹
strong form
BR ðɛm
AM ðɛm

them²
weak form
BR ð(ə)m
AM ðəm

thematic
BR θiːˈmatɪk, θɪˈmatɪk, -s
AM θəˈmædɪk, -s

thematically
BR θiːˈmatɪkli, θɪˈmatɪkli
AM θəˈmædək(ə)li

theme
BR θiːm, -z
AM θim, -z

Themistocles
BR θɪˈmɪstəkliːz, θɛˈmɪstəkliːz
AM θəˈmɪstə,kliz

themself
BR ð(ə)mˈsɛlf
AM ðəmˈsɛlf, ðɛmˈsɛlf

themselves
BR ð(ə)mˈsɛlvz
AM ðəmˈsɛlvz, ðɛmˈsɛlvz

then
BR ðɛn
AM ðɛn

thenar
BR ˈθiːnə(r), ˈθiːnɑː(r), -z
AM ˈθi,nɑr, -z

thence
BR ðɛns
AM ðɛns

thenceforth
BR ˌðɛnsˈfɔːθ
AM ˌðɛnsˌfɔ(ə)rθ

thenceforward
BR ˌðɛnsˈfɔːwəd
AM ˌðɛnsˈfɔrwərd

Theo
BR ˈθiːəʊ
AM ˈθioʊ

Theobald
BR ˈθiːəbɔːld
AM ˈθiəˈbɔld, ˌθiəˈbald

theobromine
BR ˌθiə(ʊ)ˈbrəʊmiːn, ˌθiə(ʊ)ˈbrəʊmɪn
AM ˌθiəˈbroʊ,min, ˌθiəˈbroʊmən

theocentric
BR ˌθiːə(ʊ)ˈsɛntrɪk
AM ˌθioʊˈsɛntrɪk

theocentrism
BR ˌθiːə(ʊ)ˈsɛntrɪz(ə)m
AM ˌθioʊˈsɛn,trɪzəm

theocracy
BR θiˈɒkrəsˌ|i, -ɪz
AM θiˈakrəsi, -z

theocrasy
BR ˈθiːəˌkreɪsi, θiˈɒkrəsi
AM θiˈakrəsi

theocrat
BR ˈθiəkrat, -s
AM ˈθiəˌkræt, -s

theocratic
BR ˌθiəˈkratɪk
AM ˌθiəˈkrædɪk

theocratically
BR ˌθiəˈkratɪkli
AM ˌθiəˈkrædək(ə)li

Theocritus
BR θiˈɒkrɪtəs
AM θiˈakrədəs

theodicean
BR θɪˌɒdɪˈsiːən
AM θi,ədəˈsiən

theodicy
BR θɪˈɒdɪsi
AM θiˈadəsi

theodolite
BR θɪˈɒdəlʌɪt, θɪˈɒdˌlʌɪt, -s
AM θiˈadə,laɪt, -s

theodolitic
BR θɪˌɒdəˈlɪtɪk, θɪˌɒdˈlɪtɪk
AM θi,ədəˈlɪdɪk

Theodora
BR ˌθiːəˈdɔːrə(r)
AM ˌθiəˈdɔrə

Theodorákis
BR ˌθiːədəˈrɑːkɪs, ˌθiːədəˈrakɪs
AM ˌθiədəˈrɑkəs

Theodore
BR ˈθiːədɔː(r)
AM ˈθiəˌdɔ(ə)r

Theodoric
BR θɪˈɒd(ə)rɪk
AM ˌθiˈadərɪk

Theodosius
BR ˌθiːəˈdəʊsɪəs
AM ˌθiəˈdoʊʃ(i)əs

theogonist
BR θɪˈɒɡənɪst, θɪˈɒɡnɪst, -s
AM θiˈaɡənəst, -s

theogony
BR θɪˈɒɡənˌ|i, θɪˈɒɡni, -ɪz
AM θiˈaɡəni, -z

theologian
BR ˌθiːɪəˈləʊdʒ(ə)n, ˌθiːəˈləʊdʒɪən, -z
AM ˌθiəˈloʊdʒən, -z

theological
BR ˌθiːəˈlɒdʒɪkl
AM ˌθiəˈladʒəkəl

theologically
BR ˌθiːəˈlɒdʒɪkli
AM ˌθiəˈladʒək(ə)li

theologise
BR θɪˈɒlədʒʌɪz, -ɪz, -ɪŋ, -d
AM θiˈalə,dʒaɪz, -ɪz, -ɪŋ, -d

theologist
BR θɪˈɒlədʒɪst, -s
AM θiˈalədʒəst, -s

theologize
BR θɪˈɒlədʒʌɪz, -ɪz, -ɪŋ, -d
AM θiˈalə,dʒaɪz, -ɪz, -ɪŋ, -d

theology
BR θɪˈɒlədʒi
AM θiˈalədʒi

theomachy
BR θɪˈɒməkˌ|i, -ɪz
AM θiˈaməki, -z

theomania
BR ˌθiə(ʊ)ˌmeɪnɪə(r)
AM ˌθiəˈmeɪniə

theophany
BR θɪˈɒfənˌ|i, θɪˈɒfˌn|i, -ɪz
AM θiˈafəni, -z

Theophilus
BR θɪˈɒfɪləs, θɪˈɒfˌləs
AM θiˈafələs

theophoric
BR ˌθiːəˈfɒrɪk
AM ˌθiəˈfɔrɪk

Theophrastus
BR ˌθiːəˈfrastəs
AM ˌθiəˈfræstəs

theophylline
BR ˌθiːəˈfiːliːn, ˌθiːəˈfɪliːn
AM θiˈafələn, ˌθiəˈfɪlin

theorbist
BR θɪˈɔːbɪst, -s
AM θiˈɔrbəst, -s

theorbo
BR θɪˈɔːbəʊ, -z
AM θiˈɔrboʊ, -z

theorem
BR ˈθiərəm, -z
AM ˈθiərəm, ˈθɪrəm, -z

theorematic
BR ˌθiərəˈmatɪk
AM ˌθiərəˈmædɪk, ˌθɪrəˈmædɪk

theoretic
BR θiəˈrɛtɪk
AM ˌθiəˈrɛdɪk

theoretical
BR ˌθiəˈrɛtɪkl
AM ˌθiəˈrɛdəkəl

theoretically
BR ˌθiəˈrɛtɪkli
AM ˌθiəˈrɛdək(ə)li

theoretician
BR ˈθiərəˈtɪʃn, -z
AM ˌθiərəˈtɪʃən, ˌθɪrəˈtɪʃən, -z

theorisation
BR θiərʌɪˈzeɪʃn
AM ˌθiərəˈzeɪʃən, ˌθiə,raɪˈzeɪʃən, ˌθɪrəˈzeɪʃən, ˌθɪ,raɪˈzeɪʃən

theorise
BR ˈθiərʌɪz, -ɪz, -ɪŋ, -d
AM ˈθiə,raɪz, ˈθɪ,raɪz, -ɪz, -ɪŋ, -d

theoriser
BR ˈθiərʌɪzə(r)
AM ˈθiə,raɪzər, ˈθɪ,raɪzər

theorist
BR ˈθiərɪst, -s
AM ˈθiərɪst, ˈθɪrɪst, -s

theorization
BR θiərʌɪˈzeɪʃn
AM ˌθiərəˈzeɪʃən, ˌθiə,raɪˈzeɪʃən, ˌθɪrəˈzeɪʃən, ˌθɪ,raɪˈzeɪʃən

theorize
BR ˈθiərʌɪz, -ɪz, -ɪŋ, -d
AM ˈθiə,raɪz, ˈθɪ,raɪz, -ɪz, -ɪŋ, -d

theorizer
BR ˈθiərʌɪzə(r), -z
AM ˈθiə,raɪzər, ˈθɪ,raɪzər, -z

theory
BR ˈθiərˌ|i, -ɪz
AM ˈθiəri, ˈθɪri, -z

theosoph
BR ˈθiəsɒf, -s
AM ˈθiə,saf, -s

theosopher
BR θɪˈɒsəfə(r), -z
AM θiˈasəfər, -z

theosophic
BR ˌθiəˈsɒfɪk
AM ˌθiəˈsafɪk

theosophical
BR ˌθiəˈsɒfɪkl
AM ˌθiəˈsafəkəl

theosophically
BR ˌθiəˈsɒfɪkli
AM ˌθiəˈsafək(ə)li

theosophise
BR θɪˈɒsəfʌɪz, -ɪz, -ɪŋ, -d
AM θiˈasə,faɪz, -ɪz, -ɪŋ, -d

theosophism
BR θɪˈɒsəfɪz(ə)m
AM θiˈasə,fɪzəm

theosophist
BR θɪˈɒsəfɪst, -s
AM θiˈasəfəst, -s

theosophize
BR θɪˈɒsəfʌɪz, -ɪz, -ɪŋ, -d

theosophy
AM θiˈəsəˌfaɪz, -ɪz, -ɪŋ, -d

theosophy
BR θɪˈɒsəfi
AM θiˈɒsəfi

Thera
BR ˈθɪərə(r)
AM ˈθɪrə

therabouts
BR ˌðɛrəˈbaʊts, ˈðɛrəbaʊts
AM ˈðɛrəˌbaʊts, ˌðɛrəˈbaʊts

Theran
BR ˈθɪərən
AM ˈθɪrən

therapeutic
BR ˌθɛrəˈpjuːtɪk, -s
AM ˌθɛrəˈpjuːdɪk, -s

therapeutical
BR ˌθɛrəˈpjuːtɪkl
AM ˌθɛrəˈpjudəkəl

therapeutically
BR ˌθɛrəˈpjuːtɪkli
AM ˌθɛrəˈpjudək(ə)li

therapeutist
BR ˌθɛrəˈpjuːtɪst, -s
AM ˌθɛrəˈpjudəst, -s

therapist
BR ˈθɛrəpɪst, -s
AM ˈθɛrəpəst, -s

therapsid
BR θɛˈrapsɪd, θɪˈrapsɪd, -z
AM θəˈræpsɪd, -z

therapy
BR ˈθɛrəp|i, -iz
AM ˈθɛrəpi, -z

Theravada
BR ˌθɛrəˈvɑːdə(r)
AM ˌθɛrəˈvɑdə

there¹
strong form
BR ðɛː(r)
AM ðɛ(ə)r

there²
weak form
BR ðə(r)
AM ðər

thereabout
BR ˌðɛːrəˈbaʊt, ˈðɛːrəbaʊt, -s
AM ˈðɛrəˌbaʊt, ˌðɛrəˈbaʊt, -s

thereafter
BR ˌðɛːrˈɑːftə(r), ˌðɛːrˈaftə(r)
AM ˌðɛrˈæftər

thereanent
BR ˌðɛːrəˈnɛnt
AM ˌðɛrəˈnɛnt

thereat
BR ˌðɛːrˈat
AM ˌðɛrˈæt

thereby
BR ˌðɛːˈbʌɪ, ˈðɛːbʌɪ
AM ˌðɛrˈbaɪ

therefor
for that
BR ˌðɛːˈfɔː(r)
AM ˌðɛrˈfɔ(ə)r

therefore
BR ˈðɛːfɔː(r)
AM ˈðɛrˌfɔ(ə)r

therefrom
BR ˌðɛːˈfrɒm
AM ˌðɛrˈfrɑm

therein
BR ˌðɛːrˈɪn
AM ˌðɛrˈɪn

thereinafter
BR ˌðɛːrɪnˈɑːftə(r), ˌðɛːrɪnˈaftə(r)
AM ˌðɛrənˈæftər

thereinbefore
BR ˌðɛːrɪnbɪˈfɔː(r)
AM ˌðɛrənbəˈfɔ(ə)r

thereinto
BR ˌðɛːrˈɪntu:
AM ˌðɛrˈɪnˌtu

theremin
BR ˈθɛrəmɪn, -z
AM ˈθɛrəmən, -z

thereof
BR ˌðɛːrˈɒv
AM ðɛrˈɑv

thereon
BR ˌðɛːrˈɒn
AM ðɛrˈɑn

thereout
BR ˌðɛːrˈaʊt
AM ðɛrˈaʊt

Theresa
BR təˈriːzə(r), təˈriːsə(r)
AM təˈrisə, təˈreɪsə, təˈrizə, təˈreɪzə

therethrough
BR ˌðɛːˈθru:
AM ðɛrˈθru

thereto
BR ˌðɛːˈtu:
AM ðɛrˈtu

theretofore
BR ˌðɛːtʊˈfɔː(r)
AM ˌðɛrdəˈfɔ(ə)r

thereunder
BR ˌðɛːrˈʌndə(r)
AM ðɛrˈəndər

thereunto
BR ˌðɛːrˈʌntu:, ˌðɛːrʌnˈtu:
AM ˌðɛˌrənˈtu

thereupon
BR ˌðɛːrəˈpɒn, ˈðɛːrəpɒn
AM ˈðɛrəˌpɑn

therewith
BR ˌðɛːˈwɪð
AM ðɛrˈwɪð

therewithal
BR ˌðɛːwɪðˈɔːl, ˌðɛːwɪðˈɔːl

therefor
BR ˌðɛrwəˌθɒl, ˈðɛrwəˌðɒl, ˈðɛrwəˌθɑl, ˈðɛrwəˌðɑl

theriac
BR ˈθɪərɪak, -s
AM ˈθɪriˌæk, -s

therianthropic
BR ˌθɪərɪanˈθrɒpɪk, ˌθɪərɪənˈθrɒpɪk
AM ˌθɪriənˈθrɑpɪk, ˌθɪriˌænˈθrɑpɪk

theriomorphic
BR ˌθɪərɪə(ʊ)ˈmɔːfɪk
AM ˌθɪriəˈmɔrfɪk

therm
BR θəːm, -z
AM θərm, -z

thermae
BR ˈθəːmi:
AM ˈðərmi, ˈðərˌmaɪ

thermal
BR ˈθəːml, -z
AM ˈθərməl, -z

thermalisation
BR ˌθəːm|lʌɪˈzeɪʃn, ˌθəːməlʌɪˈzeɪʃn
AM ˌθərmələˈzeɪʃən, ˌθərməˌlaɪˈzeɪʃən

thermalise
BR ˈθəːm|lʌɪz, ˈθəːməlʌɪz, -ɪz, -ɪŋ, -d
AM ˈθərməˌlaɪz, -ɪz, -ɪŋ, -d

thermalization
BR ˌθəːm|lʌɪˈzeɪʃn, ˌθəːməlʌɪˈzeɪʃn
AM ˌθərmələˈzeɪʃən, ˌθərməˌlaɪˈzeɪʃən

thermalize
BR ˈθəːm|lʌɪz, ˈθəːməlʌɪz, -ɪz, -ɪŋ, -d
AM ˈθərməˌlaɪz, -ɪz, -ɪŋ, -d

thermally
BR ˈθəːm|li, ˈθəːməli
AM ˈθərməli

thermic
BR ˈθəːmɪk
AM ˈθərmɪk

thermically
BR ˈθəːmɪkli
AM ˈθərmək(ə)li

thermidor
BR ˈθəːmɪdɔː(r)
AM ˈðərməˌdɔ(ə)r

thermion
BR ˈθəːmɪən, ˈθəːmɪɒn, -z
AM ˈθərmˌaɪən, -z

thermionic
BR ˌθəːmɪˈɒnɪk, -s
AM ˌθərmiˈɑnɪk, -s

thermistor
BR θəːˈmɪstə(r), ˈθəːmɪstə(r)
AM ˈθərˌmɪstər, ˌθərˈmɪstər

thermit
BR ˈθəːmɪt
AM ˈθərmət

thermite
BR ˈθəːmʌɪt, -s
AM ˈθərˌmaɪt, -s

thermochemical
BR ˌθəːməʊˈkɛmɪkl
AM ˌθərmoʊˈkɛməkəl

thermochemistry
BR ˌθəːməʊˈkɛmɪstri
AM ˌθərmoʊˈkɛməstri

thermocline
BR ˈθəːmə(ʊ)klʌɪn
AM ˈθərməˌklaɪn

thermocouple
BR ˈθəːmə(ʊ)ˌkʌpl
AM ˈθərməˌkəpəl

thermodynamic
BR ˌθəːmə(ʊ)dʌɪˈnamɪk, -s
AM ˌθərmoʊˌdaɪˈnæmɪk, -s

thermodynamical
BR ˌθəːmə(ʊ)dʌɪˈnamɪkl
AM ˌθərmoʊˌdaɪˈnæməkəl

thermodynamically
BR ˌθəːmə(ʊ)dʌɪˈnamɪkli
AM ˌθərmoʊˌdaɪˈnæmək(ə)li

thermodynamicist
BR ˌθəːmə(ʊ)dʌɪˈnamɪsɪst, -s
AM ˌθərmoʊˌdaɪˈnæməsəst, -s

thermoelectric
BR ˌθəːməʊˈlɛktrɪk
AM ˌθərmoʊəˈlɛktrɪk, ˌθərmoʊ͜ɪˈlɛktrɪk

thermoelectrically
BR ˌθəːməʊˈlɛktrɪkli
AM ˌθərmoʊəˈlɛktrək(ə)li, ˌθərmoʊ͜ɪˈlɛktrək(ə)li

thermoelectricity
BR ˌθəːməʊ͜ɪˌlɛkˈtrɪsɪti, ˌθəːməʊˌɛlɛkˈtrɪsɪti, ˌθəːməʊ͜ɛlɪkˈtrɪsɪti, ˌθəːməʊ͜ɪˌlɛkˈtrɪsɪti, ˌθəːməʊˌiːlɛkˈtrɪsɪti
AM ˌθərmoʊəˌlekˈtrɪsɪdi, ˌθərmoʊ͜ɪˌlekˈtrɪsɪdi

thermogenesis
BR ˌθəːmə(ʊ)ˈdʒɛnɪsɪs
AM ˌθərməˈdʒɛnəsəs

thermogram
BR ˈθəːməgram, -z
AM ˈθərməˌgræm, -z

thermograph
BR ˈθəːməgrɑːf, ˈθəːməgraf, -s
AM ˈθərməˌgræf, -s

thermographic
BR ˌθəːmə(ʊ)ˈgrafɪk
AM ˌθərməˈgræfɪk

thermography
BR θəːˈmɒgrəfi
AM θərˈmɑgrəfi

thermohaline
BR ˌθɜːməˈ(ʊ)ˈheɪlʌɪn,
ˌθɜːmə(ʊ)ˈheɪliːn
AM ˌθɜrməˈheɪlɪn,
ˌθɜrməˈheɪlaɪn

thermokarst
BR ˈθɜːmə(ʊ)kɑːst
AM ˈθɜrməˌkɑrst

thermolabile
BR ˌθɜːməʊˈleɪbʌɪl
AM ˌθɜrməˈleɪˌbaɪl,
ˌθɜrməˈleɪbəl

**thermolumines-
cence**
BR ˌθɜːməʊˌluːmɪˈnɛsns
AM ˈθɜrmoʊˌlumɪˈnɛs-
əns

**thermolumines-
cent**
BR ˌθɜːməʊˌluːmɪˈnɛsnt
AM ˈθɜrmoʊˌlumɪˈnɛ-
sənt

thermolysis
BR θɜːˈmɒlɪsɪs
AM θɜrˈmɑləsəs

thermolytic
BR ˌθɜːməˈlɪtɪk
AM ˌθɜrməˈlɪdɪk

thermometer
BR θəˈmɒmɪtə(r), -z
AM θərˈmɑmədər, -z

thermometric
BR ˌθɜːməˈmɛtrɪk
AM ˌθɜrməˈmɛtrɪk

thermometrical
BR ˌθɜːməˈmɛtrɪkl
AM ˌθɜrməˈmɛtrəkəl

thermometrically
BR ˌθɜːməˈmɛtrɪkli
AM ˌθɜrməˈmɛtrək(ə)li

thermometry
BR θəˈmɒmɪtri
AM θərˈmɑmətri

thermonuclear
BR ˌθɜːməʊˈnjuːklɪə(r)
AM ˌθɜrmoʊˈn(j)uklɪ(ə)r

thermophile
BR ˈθɜːməfʌɪl, -z
AM ˈθɜrməˌfaɪl, -z

thermophilic
BR ˌθɜːməˈfɪlɪk
AM ˌθɜrməˈfɪlɪk

thermopile
BR ˈθɜːməpʌɪl, -z
AM ˈθɜrməˌpaɪl, -z

thermoplastic
BR ˌθɜːməʊˈplastɪk, -s
AM ˌθɜrmoʊˈplæstɪk,
-s

Thermopylae
BR θəˈmɒpɪliː,
θəˈmɒpɪli,
θəˈmɒpɪliː,
θəːˈmɒpli
AM θərˈmɑpəˌli

Thermos®
BR ˈθɜːməs, -ɪz
AM ˈθɜrməs, -əz

thermoset
BR ˈθɜːmə(ʊ)sɛt
AM ˈθɜrmoʊˌsɛt

thermosetting
BR ˈθɜːməʊˌsɛtɪŋ
AM ˈθɜrmoʊˌsɛdɪŋ

thermosphere
BR ˈθɜːməsfɪə(r)
AM ˈθɜrməˌsfɪ(ə)r

thermostable
BR ˈθɜːməʊˈsteɪbl
AM ˈðɜrmoʊˌsteɪbəl

thermostat
BR ˈθɜːməstat, -s
AM ˈθɜrməˌstæt, -s

thermostatic
BR ˌθɜːmə(ʊ)ˈstatɪk
AM ˌθɜrməˈstædɪk

thermostatically
BR ˌθɜːmə(ʊ)ˈstatɪkli
AM ˌθɜrməˈstædək(ə)li

thermotactic
BR ˌθɜːmə(ʊ)ˈtaktɪk
AM ˌθɜrməˈtæktɪk

thermotaxic
BR ˌθɜːmə(ʊ)ˈtaksɪk
AM ˌθɜrməˈtæksɪk

thermotaxis
BR ˌθɜːmə(ʊ)ˈtaksɪs
AM ˌθɜrməˈtæksəs

thermotropic
BR ˌθɜːməˈtrɒpɪk,
ˌθɜːməˈtrəʊpɪk
AM ˌθɜrməˈtrɑpɪk

thermotropism
BR ˌθɜːmə(ʊ)ˈtrəʊp-
ɪz(ə)m
AM ˌθɜrməˈtrɑˌpɪzəm

theropod
BR ˈθɪərəpɒd, -z
AM ˈθɪrəˌpɑd, -z

Theroux
BR θəˈruː
AM θəˈru

thesauri
BR θɪˈsɔːrʌɪ
AM θəˈsɔˌraɪ

thesaurus
BR θɪˈsɔːrəs, -ɪz
AM θəˈsɔrəs, -əz

these
BR ðiːz
AM ðiz

theses
BR ˈθiːsiːz
AM ˈθiˌsiz

Theseus
BR ˈθiːsɪəs, ˈθiːsjuːs
AM ˈθisɪəs

thesis[1]
dissertation
BR ˈθiːsɪs
AM ˈθisɪs

thesis[2]
rhythm
BR ˈθɛsɪs
AM ˈθisɪs, ˈθɛsəs

thesp
BR θɛsp, -s
AM θɛsp, -s

thespian
BR ˈθɛspɪən, -z
AM ˈθɛspiən, -z

Thespis
BR ˈθɛspɪs
AM ˈθɛspəs

Thessalian
BR θɛˈseɪlɪən,
θɪˈseɪlɪən, -z
AM θɛˈseɪlɪən,
θɛˈseɪliən, -z

Thessalonian
BR ˌθɛsəˈləʊnɪən, -z
AM ˌθɛsəˈloʊnɪən, -z

Thessalonica
BR ˌθɛsəˈlɒnɪkə(r)
AM ˌθɛsəˈlɑnəkə

Thessaloníki
BR ˌθɛsələˈniːki
AM ˌθɛsələˈniki

Thessaly
BR ˈθɛsəli
AM ˈθɛsəli

theta
BR ˈθiːtə(r), -z
AM ˈθeɪdə, ˈθidə, -z

thetic
BR ˈθɛtɪk
AM ˈθɛdɪk

Thetis
BR ˈθɛtɪs, ˈθiːtɪs
AM ˈθidəs, ˈθɛdəs

theurgic
BR θɪˈəːdʒɪk
AM θiˈɜrdʒɪk

theurgical
BR θɪˈəːdʒɪkl
AM θiˈɜrdʒəkəl

theurgist
BR ˈθiːədʒɪst, -s
AM ˈθiərdʒəst, -s

theurgy
BR ˈθiːəːdʒi
AM ˈθiərdʒi

thew
BR θjuː, -z
AM θ(j)u, -z

they[1]
strong form
BR ðeɪ
AM ðeɪ

they[2]
weak form
BR ðeɪ
AM ðeɪ, ðɛ

they'd
BR ðeɪd
AM ðeɪd

they'll
BR ðeɪl
AM ðeɪl

they're
BR ðɛː(r)
AM ˈðeɪ(ə)r, ðɛ(ə)r

they've
BR ðeɪv
AM ðeɪv

thiamin
BR ˈθʌɪəmɪn
AM ˈθaɪəmən,
ˈθaɪəˌmin

thiamine
BR ˈθʌɪəmiːn,
ˈθʌɪəmɪn
AM ˈθaɪəmən,
ˈθaɪəˌmin

thiazide
BR ˈθʌɪəzʌɪd, -z
AM ˈθaɪəˌzaɪd, -z

thiazole
BR ˈθʌɪˈeɪzəʊl
AM ˈθaɪəˌzoʊl

thick
BR θɪk, -ə(r), -ɪst
AM θɪk, -ər, -ɪst

thick and thin
BR ˌθɪk (ə)n(d) ˈθɪn
AM ˌθɪk ən ˈθɪn

thicken
BR ˈθɪk|(ə)n, -(ə)nz,
-nɪŋ \-(ə)nɪŋ, -(ə)nd
AM ˈθɪk|ən, -ənz,
-(ə)nɪŋ, -ənd

thickener
BR ˈθɪk(ə)nə(r),
ˈθɪknə(r), -z
AM ˈθɪk(ə)nər, -z

thickening
BR ˈθɪk(ə)nɪŋ, ˈθɪkn̩ɪŋ,
-z
AM ˈθɪk(ə)nɪŋ, -z

thicket
BR ˈθɪkɪt, -s
AM ˈθɪkɪt, -s

thickhead
BR ˈθɪkhɛd, -z
AM ˈθɪk,(h)ɛd, -z

thickheaded
BR ˌθɪkˈhɛdɪd
AM ˌθɪkˈhɛdəd

thickheadedness
BR ˌθɪkˈhɛdɪdnɪs
AM ˌθɪkˈhɛdədnəs

thickie
BR ˈθɪk|i, -ɪz
AM ˈθɪki, -z

thickish
BR ˈθɪkɪʃ
AM ˈθɪkɪʃ

thickly
BR ˈθɪkli
AM ˈθɪkli

thicknee
BR ˈθɪkniː, -z
AM ˈθɪk,ni, -z

thickness
BR ˈθɪknɪs, -ɪz, -ɪŋ, -t
AM ˈθɪknɪs, -ɪz, -ɪŋ, -t

thicknesser
BR ˈθɪknɪsə(r), -z
AM ˈθɪknɪsər, -z

thicko
BR ˈθɪkəʊ, -z
AM ˈθɪkoʊ, -z

thickset
BR ˌθɪkˈsɛt
AM ˈθɪk‚sɛt

thick-skinned
BR ˌθɪkˈskɪnd
AM ˈθɪkˈskɪnd

thick-skulled
BR ˌθɪkˈskʌld
AM ˈθɪkˈskəld

thick-witted
BR ˌθɪkˈwɪtɪd
AM ˈθɪkˈwɪdɪd

thief
BR θiːf
AM θif

thieve
BR θiːv, -z, -ɪŋ, -d
AM θiv, -z, -ɪŋ, -d

thievery
BR ˈθiːv(ə)ri
AM ˈθiv(ə)ri

thieves
BR θiːvz
AM θivz

thievish
BR ˈθiːvɪʃ
AM ˈθivɪʃ

thievishly
BR ˈθiːvɪʃli
AM ˈθivɪʃli

thievishness
BR ˈθiːvɪʃnɪs
AM ˈθivɪʃnɪs

thigh
BR θaɪ, -z
AM θaɪ, -z

thighbone
BR ˈθaɪbəʊn, -z
AM ˈθaɪ‚boʊn, -z

thill
BR θɪl, -z
AM θɪl, -z

thiller
BR ˈθɪlə(r), -z
AM ˈθɪlər, -z

thimble
BR ˈθɪmbl, -z
AM ˈθɪmbəl, -z

thimbleful
BR ˈθɪmblfʊl, -z
AM ˈθɪmbəl‚fʊl, -z

thimblerig
BR ˈθɪmblrɪg, -z, -ɪŋ, -d
AM ˈθɪmbəl‚rɪg, -z, -ɪŋ, -d

thimblerigger
BR ˈθɪmbl‚rɪgə(r), -z
AM ˈθɪmbəl‚rɪgər, -z

thimerosal
BR θaɪˈmɛrəsal
AM θaɪˈmɛrə‚sæl

thin
BR θɪn, -z, -ɪŋ, -d, -ə(r), -ɪst

AM θɪn, -z, -ɪŋ, -d, -ər, -ɪst

thine
BR ðaɪn
AM ðaɪn

thing
BR θɪŋ, -z
AM θɪŋ, -z

thingamabob
BR ˈθɪŋəmɪbɒb, -z
AM ˈθɪŋəm(ə)‚bɑb, -z

thingamajig
BR ˈθɪŋəmɪdʒɪg, -z
AM ˈθɪŋəmə‚dʒɪg, -z

thingambob
BR ˈθɪŋəmbɒb, -z
AM ˈθɪŋəm‚bɑb, -z

thingamy
BR ˈθɪŋəmli, -ɪz
AM ˈθɪŋəmi, -z

thingum
BR ˈθɪŋəm, -z
AM ˈθɪŋəm, -z

thingumabob
BR ˈθɪŋəmɪbɒb, -z
AM ˈθɪŋəmə‚bɑb, -z

thingumajig
BR ˈθɪŋəmɪdʒɪg, -z
AM ˈθɪŋəmə‚dʒɪg, -z

thingummy
BR ˈθɪŋəmli, -ɪz
AM ˈθɪŋəmi, -z

thingy
BR ˈθɪŋli, -ɪz
AM ˈθɪŋi, -z

think
BR θɪŋk, -s, -ɪŋ
AM θɪŋk, -s, -ɪŋ

thinkable
BR ˈθɪŋkəbl
AM ˈθɪŋkəbəl

thinker
BR ˈθɪŋkə(r), -z
AM ˈθɪŋkər, -z

think-tank
BR ˈθɪŋktæŋk, -s
AM ˈθɪŋk‚tæŋk, -s

thinly
BR ˈθɪnli
AM ˈθɪnli

thinner
BR ˈθɪnə(r), -z
AM ˈθɪnər, -z

thinness
BR ˈθɪnnɪs
AM ˈθɪ(n)nɪs

thinning
BR ˈθɪnɪŋ, -z
AM ˈθɪnɪŋ, -z

thinnish
BR ˈθɪnɪʃ
AM ˈθɪnɪʃ

thin-skinned
BR ˌθɪnˈskɪnd
AM ˈθɪnˈskɪnd

thio
BR ˈθaɪəʊ

AM ˈθaɪoʊ

thiocyanate
BR ˌθaɪəʊˈsaɪəneɪt, -s
AM ˌθaɪəˈsaɪəneɪt, -s

thiol
BR ˈθaɪɒl
AM ˈθaɪ‚ɔl, ˈθaɪ‚ɑl

thionate
BR ˈθaɪəneɪt
AM ˈθaɪə‚neɪt

thionyl
BR ˈθaɪənɪl
AM ˈθaɪənɪl

thiopentone
BR ˌθaɪə(ʊ)ˈpɛntəʊn
AM ˌθaɪəˈpɛntoʊn

thiosulphate
BR ˌθaɪə(ʊ)ˈsʌlfeɪt
AM ˌθaɪəˈsəl‚feɪt

thiourea
BR ˌθaɪəʊjəˈriːə(r)
AM ˈθaɪoʊjəˈriə

Thira
BR ˈθɪərə(r)
AM ˈθɪrə

third
BR θəːd, -z
AM θərd, -z

thirdhand
BR ˌθəːˈdˈhand
AM ˈθərdˈhænd

thirdly
BR ˈθəːdli
AM ˈθərdli

Thirlmere
BR ˈθəːlmɪə(r)
AM ˈθərlˌmɪ(ə)r

Thirsk
BR θəːsk
AM θərsk

thirst
BR θəːst, -s, -ɪŋ, -ɪd
AM θərst, -s, -ɪŋ, -əd

thirstily
BR ˈθəːstɪli
AM ˈθərstəli

thirstiness
BR ˈθəːstɪnɪs
AM ˈθərstɪnɪs

thirstless
BR ˈθəːstləs
AM ˈθərs(t)ləs

thirsty
BR ˈθəːstli, -ɪə(r), -ɪɪst
AM ˈθərsti, -ər, -ɪst

thirteen
BR ˌθəːˈtiːn
AM ˌθərˈtin

thirteenth
BR ˌθəːˈtiːnθ, -s
AM ˌθərˈtinθ, -s

thirtieth
BR ˈθəːtɪɪθ, -s
AM ˈθərdiɪθ, -s

thirty
BR ˈθəːtli, -ɪz
AM ˈθərdi, -z

thirtyfold
BR ˈθəːtɪfəʊld
AM ˈθərdiˌfoʊld

thirtysomething
BR ˌθəːtiˈsʌmθɪŋ, -z
AM ˈθərdiˌsəmθɪŋ, -z

thirty-twomo
BR ˌθəːtɪˈtuːməʊ
AM ˌθərdiˈtuˌmoʊ

this¹
strong form
BR ðɪs
AM ðɪs

this²
weak form
BR ðɪs
AM ðəs

Thisbe
BR ˈθɪzbi
AM ˈθɪzbi

thistle
BR ˈθɪsl, -z
AM ˈθɪsəl, -z

thistledown
BR ˈθɪsldaʊn
AM ˈθɪsəlˌdaʊn

thistly
BR ˈθɪsli, ˈθɪsli
AM ˈθɪs(ə)li

thither
BR ˈðɪðə(r)
AM ˈðɪðər

thitherto
BR ˌðɪðəˈtuː
AM ˈðɪðərˈtu

thitherward
BR ˈðɪðəwəd, -z
AM ˈðɪðərwərd, -z

thixotropic
BR ˌθɪksəˈtrɒpɪk,
ˌθɪksəˈtrəʊpɪk
AM ˌθɪksəˈtrɑpɪk

thixotropy
BR θɪkˈsɒtrəpi
AM θɪkˈsɑtrəpi

tho'
BR ðəʊ
AM ðoʊ

thole
BR θəʊl, -z
AM θoʊl, -z

tholepin
BR ˈθəʊlpɪn, -z
AM ˈθoʊlˌpɪn, -z

tholi
BR ˈθəʊlaɪ
AM ˈθoʊˌlai

tholoi
BR ˈθəʊlɔɪ
AM ˈθoʊˌlɔi

tholos
BR ˈθəʊlɒs, ˈθɒlɒs
AM ˈθoʊˌlɔs, ˈθoʊˌlɑs

tholus
BR ˈθəʊləs
AM ˈθoʊləs

Thom
BR tɒm
AM tɑm

Thomas
BR 'tɒməs
AM 'tɑməs

Thomasina
BR ˌtɒmə'siːnə(r)
AM ˌtɑmə'sinə

Thomism
BR 'təʊmɪz(ə)m
AM 'toʊ mɪzəm

Thomist
BR 'təʊmɪst, -s
AM 'toʊməst, -s

Thomistic
BR tə'mɪstɪk
AM tə'mɪstɪk

Thomistical
BR tə'mɪstɪkl
AM tə'mɪstəkəl

Thompson
BR 'tɒm(p)sn
AM 'tɑm(p)sən

Thomson
BR 'tɒmsn
AM 'tɑmsən

thong
BR θɒŋ, -z
AM θɒŋ, θɑŋ, -z

Thor
BR θɔː(r)
AM θɔ(ə)r

Thora
BR 'θɔːrə(r)
AM 'θɔrə

thoracal
BR 'θɔːrəkl
AM 'θɔrəkəl

thoraces
BR 'θɔːrəsiːz,
θɔː'reɪsiːz
AM 'θɔrəˌsiz

thoracic
BR θɔː'ræsɪk, θə'ræsɪk
AM θə'ræsɪk, θɔ'ræsɪk

thorax
BR 'θɔːræks, -ɪz
AM 'θɔˌræks, -ɪz

Thorazine®
BR 'θɔːrəziːn
AM 'θɔrəˌzin

Thorburn
BR 'θɔːbɜːn
AM 'θɔrˌbɜrn

Thoreau
BR 'θɔːrəʊ, θɔː'rəʊ,
θə'rəʊ
AM θə'roʊ, θɔː'roʊ

thoria
BR 'θɔːrɪə(r)
AM 'θɔrɪə

thorite
BR 'θɔːraɪt
AM 'θɔˌraɪt

thorium
BR 'θɔːrɪəm

AM 'θɔrɪəm

thorn
BR θɔːn, -z
AM θɔ(ə)rn, -z

Thornaby
BR 'θɔːnəbi
AM 'θɔrnəbi

thornback
BR 'θɔːnbak, -s
AM 'θɔrnˌbæk, -s

thornbill
BR 'θɔːnbɪl, -z
AM 'θɔrnˌbɪl, -z

Thorndike
BR 'θɔːndʌɪk
AM 'θɔrnˌdaɪk

Thorne
BR θɔːn
AM θɔ(ə)rn

Thorner
BR 'θɔːnə(r)
AM 'θɔrnər

Thorneycroft
BR 'θɔːnɪkrɒft
AM 'θɔrniˌkrɔft

Thornhill
BR 'θɔːnhɪl
AM 'θɔrnˌ(h)ɪl

thornily
BR 'θɔːnɪli
AM 'θɔrnəli

thorniness
BR 'θɔːnɪnɪs
AM 'θɔrnɪnɪs

thornless
BR 'θɔːnləs
AM 'θɔrnləs

Thornley
BR 'θɔːnli
AM 'θɔrnli

thornproof
BR 'θɔːnpruːf
AM 'θɔrnˌpruf

thorntail
BR 'θɔːnteɪl, -z
AM 'θɔrnˌteɪl, -z

Thornton
BR 'θɔːntən
AM 'θɔrn(t)n

thorny
BR 'θɔːn|i, -ɪə(r), -ɪɪst
AM 'θɔrni, -ər, -ɪst

Thorogood
BR 'θʌrəgʊd
AM 'θərəˌgʊd

thorough
BR 'θʌrə(r)
AM 'θərə, 'θəroʊ

thoroughbred
BR 'θʌrəbrɛd, -z
AM 'θərəˌbrɛd, -z

thoroughfare
BR 'θʌrəfɛː(r), -z
AM 'θərəˌfɛ(ə)r, -z

thoroughgoing
BR ˌθʌrə'gəʊɪŋ
AM 'θərəˌgoʊɪŋ

thoroughly
BR 'θʌrəli
AM 'θərəli, 'θəroʊli

thoroughness
BR 'θʌrənəs
AM 'θərənəs,
'θəroʊnəs

thorough-wax
BR 'θʌrəwaks
AM 'θərəˌwæks

thorow-wax
BR 'θʌrəwaks
AM 'θərəˌwæks

Thorp
BR θɔːp
AM θɔ(ə)rp

Thorpe
BR θɔːp
AM θɔ(ə)rp

those
BR ðəʊz
AM ðoʊz

Thoth
BR θəʊθ, təʊt, θɒθ
AM θoθ, toʊt, θɑθ

thou
BR ðaʊ
AM ðaʊ

though
BR ðəʊ
AM ðoʊ

thought
BR θɔːt, -s
AM θɔt, θɑt, -s

thoughtful
BR 'θɔːtf(ʊ)l
AM 'θɔtfəl, 'θɑtfəl

thoughtfully
BR 'θɔːtfʊli, 'θɔːtfli
AM 'θɔtfəli, 'θɑtfəli

thoughtfulness
BR 'θɔːtf(ʊ)lnəs
AM 'θɔtfəlnəs,
'θɑtfəlnəs

thoughtless
BR 'θɔːtləs
AM 'θɔtləs, 'θɑtləs

thoughtlessly
BR 'θɔːtləsli
AM 'θɔtləsli, 'θɑtləsli

thoughtlessness
BR 'θɔːtləsnəs
AM 'θɔtləsnəs,
'θɑtləsnəs

thought-provoking
BR 'θɔːtprəˌvəʊkɪŋ
AM 'θɔtprəˌvoʊkɪŋ,
'θɑtprəˌvoʊkɪŋ

thousand
BR 'θaʊzn|d, -(d)z
AM 'θaʊzn(d), -z

thousandfold
BR 'θaʊzn(d)fəʊld
AM 'θaʊzn(d)ˌfoʊld

thousandth
BR 'θaʊzn(t)θ, -s

thoroughly
BR 'θʌrəli
AM 'θɑʊzn(t)θ, -s

Thrace
BR θreɪs
AM θreɪs

Thracian
BR 'θreɪʃn, -z
AM 'θreɪʃən, -z

thraldom
BR 'θrɔːldəm
AM 'θrɔldəm, 'θrɑldəm

thrall
BR θrɔːl
AM θrɔl, θrɑl

thralldom
BR 'θrɔːldəm
AM 'θrɔldəm, 'θrɑldəm

thrang
BR θraŋ
AM θræŋ

thrash
BR θraʃ, -ɪz, -ɪŋ, -t
AM θræʃ, -əz, -ɪŋ, -t

thrasher
BR 'θraʃə(r), -z
AM 'θræʃər, -z

thrashing
BR 'θraʃɪŋ, -z
AM 'θræʃɪŋ, -z

thrasonical
BR θrə'sɒnɪkl
AM θreɪ'sɑnəkl

thrasonically
BR θrə'sɒnɪkli
AM θreɪ'sɑnək(ə)li

thrawn
BR θrɔːn
AM θrɔn, θrɑn

thread
BR θrɛd, -z, -ɪŋ, -ɪd
AM θrɛd, -z, -ɪŋ, -əd

threadbare
BR 'θrɛdbɛː(r)
AM 'θrɛdˌbɛ(ə)r

threader
BR 'θrɛdə(r), -z
AM 'θrɛdər, -z

threadfin
BR 'θrɛdfɪn, -z
AM 'θrɛdˌfɪn, -z

threadfish
BR 'θrɛdfɪʃ, -ɪz
AM 'θrɛdˌfɪʃ, -ɪz

threadlike
BR 'θrɛdlaɪk
AM 'θrɛdˌlaɪk

Threadneedle
BR ˌθrɛd'niːdl,
'θrɛdˌniːdl
AM 'θrɛdˌnidəl

threadworm
BR 'θrɛdwəːm, -z
AM 'θrɛdˌwərm, -z

thready
BR 'θrɛd|i, -ɪə(r), -ɪɪst
AM 'θrɛdi, -ər, -ɪst

threat
BR θrɛt, -s

threaten
AM θrεtn, -s

threaten
BR 'θrεt|n, -nz,
-nɪŋ\-nɪŋ, -nd
AM 'θrεt|n, -nz, -nɪŋ, -nd

threatener
BR 'θrεtnə(r),
'θrεtnə(r), -z
AM 'θrεtnər, 'θrεtnər, -z

threateningly
BR 'θrεtnɪŋli,
'θrεtnɪŋli
AM 'θrεtnɪŋli,
'θrεtnɪŋli

three
BR θriː, -z
AM θriː, -z

three-bagger
BR ˌθriː'bagə(r), -z
AM ˌθriː'bægər, -z

three-base hit
BR ˌθriːbeɪs 'hɪt, -s
AM ˌθriːbeɪs 'hɪt, -s

three-card trick
BR ˌθriːkɑːd 'trɪk, -s
AM ˌθriːˌkɑrd 'trɪk, -s

three-cornered
BR ˌθriː'kɔːnəd
AM ˌθriː'kɔrnərd

three-D
BR ˌθriː'diː
AM ˌθriː'di

three-decker
BR ˌθriːˌdεkə(r), -z
AM ˌθriːˌdεkər, -z

three-dimensional
BR ˌθriːdaɪ'mεnʃn(ə)l,
ˌθriːdaɪ'mεnʃən(ə)l,
ˌθriːdɪ'mεnʃn(ə)l,
ˌθriːdɪ'mεnʃən(ə)l
AM ˌθriːdə'men(t)ʃ(ə)nəl,
ˌθriːˌdaɪ'men(t)ʃ(ə)nəl

threefold
BR 'θriːfəʊld,
ˌθriː'fəʊld
AM 'θriːfoʊld

three-handed
BR ˌθriː'handɪd
AM ˌθriːˈhændəd

three-legged
BR ˌθriː'lεgɪd
AM ˌθriːˈlεgəd

threeness
BR 'θriːnɪs
AM 'θriːnɪs

threepence
BR 'θrεp(ə)ns, -ɪz
AM 'θrεpəns, 'θriːˌpεns,
-əz

threepenny
BR 'θrεp(ə)ni, 'θrεpni
AM 'θriːˌpεni

three-ply¹
adjective
BR ˌθriː'plʌɪ, 'θriːplʌɪ
AM ˌθriːˈplaɪ

three-ply²
noun
BR 'θriːplʌɪ
AM 'θriːplaɪ

three-point
BR ˌθriː'pɔɪnt
AM ˌθriː'pɔɪnt

three-pointer
BR ˌθriː'pɔɪntə(r), -z
AM ˌθriː'pɔɪn(t)ər, -z

three-point landing
BR ˌθriːpɔɪnt 'landɪŋ, -z
AM ˌθriːpɔɪnt 'lændɪŋ, -z

three-point turn
BR ˌθriːpɔɪnt(t) 'təːn, -z
AM ˌθriːpɔɪnt(t) 'tərn, -z

three-quarter
BR ˌθriː'kwɔːtə(r), -z
AM ˌθriː'kwɔ(r)dər, -z

three R's
BR ˌθriː 'ɑːz
AM ˌθriː 'ɑrz

threescore
BR ˌθriː'skɔː(r), -z
AM ˌθriː'skɔ(ə)r, -z

threesome
BR 'θriːs(ə)m, -z
AM 'θriːsəm, -z

three-way
BR ˌθriː'weɪ
AM 'θriːˌweɪ

three-wheeler
BR ˌθriː'wiːlə(r), -z
AM ˌθriː'(h)wilər, -z

Threlfall
BR 'θrεlfɔːl
AM 'θrεlˌfɔl, 'θrεlˌfal

Threlkeld
BR 'θrεlkεld
AM 'θrεlˌkεl(d)

thremmatology
BR ˌθrεmə'tɒlədʒi
AM ˌθrεmə'tɑlədʒi

threnode
BR 'θrεnəʊd, 'θriːnəʊd, -z
AM 'θriːˌnoʊd, 'θrεˌnoʊd, -z

threnodial
BR θrɪ'nəʊdiəl
AM θrə'noʊdiəl

threnodic
BR θrɪ'nɒdɪk
AM θrə'nɑdɪk

threnodist
BR 'θrεnədɪst,
'θriːnədɪst, -s
AM 'θrεnədəst, -s

threnody
BR 'θrεnəd|i,
'θriːnəd|i, -ɪz
AM 'θrεnədi, -z

threonine
BR 'θriəniːn
AM 'θriəˌnin, 'θriənən

thresh
BR θrεʃ, -ɪz, -ɪŋ, -t
AM θrεʃ, -əz, -ɪŋ, -t

thresher
BR 'θrεʃə(r), -z
AM 'θrεʃər, -z

threshold
BR 'θrεʃ(h)əʊld, -z
AM 'θrεʃ,(h)oʊld, -z

threw
BR θruː
AM θru

thrice
BR θrʌɪs
AM θraɪs

thrift
BR θrɪft, -s
AM θrɪft, -s

thriftily
BR 'θrɪftɪli
AM 'θrɪftɪli

thriftiness
BR 'θrɪftɪnɪs
AM 'θrɪftɪnɪs

thriftless
BR 'θrɪftlɪs
AM 'θrɪf(t)lɪs

thriftlessly
BR 'θrɪf(t)lɪsli
AM 'θrɪf(t)lɪsli

thriftlessness
BR 'θrɪftlɪsnɪs
AM 'θrɪf(t)lɪsnɪs

thrifty
BR 'θrɪft|i, -ɪə(r), -ɪɪst
AM 'θrɪfti, -ər, -ɪst

thrill
BR θrɪl, -z, -ɪŋ, -d
AM θrɪl, -z, -ɪŋ, -d

thriller
BR 'θrɪlə(r), -z
AM 'θrɪlər, -z

thrillingly
BR 'θrɪlɪŋli
AM 'θrɪlɪŋli

thrips
BR θrɪps
AM θrɪps

thrive
BR θrʌɪv, -z, -ɪŋ, -d
AM θraɪv, -z, -ɪŋ, -d

thriven
BR 'θrɪvn
AM 'θrɪvən

thro
BR θruː
AM θru

thro'
BR θruː
AM θru

throat
BR θrəʊt, -s
AM θroʊt, -s

throatily
BR 'θrəʊtɪli
AM 'θroʊdəli

throatiness
BR 'θrəʊtɪnɪs
AM 'θroʊdɪnɪs

throaty
BR 'θrəʊt|i, -ɪə(r), -ɪɪst
AM 'θroʊdi, -ər, -ɪst

throb
BR θrɒb, -z, -ɪŋ, -d
AM θrɑb, -z, -ɪŋ, -d

throe
BR θrəʊ, -z
AM θroʊ, -z

Throgmorton
BR 'θrɒgmɔːtn, θrɒgˈmɔːtn
AM 'θrɑgˌmɔrtn

thrombi
BR 'θrɒmbʌɪ
AM 'θrɑmˌbaɪ

thrombin
BR 'θrɒmbɪn, -z
AM 'θrɑmbən, -z

thrombocyte
BR 'θrɒmbəsʌɪt, -s
AM 'θrɑmbəˌsaɪt, -s

thrombolysis
BR θrɒm'bɒlɪsɪs
AM ˌθrɑmbə'laɪsɪs

thrombose
BR 'θrɒmbəʊz, 'θrɒmbəʊs, θrɒmˈbəʊz,
θrɒm'bəʊs, -ɪz, -ɪŋ, -d
AM 'θrɑmˌboʊs, 'θrɑmˌboʊz, -əz, -ɪŋ, -d

thromboses
BR θrɒm'bəʊsiːz
AM θrɑm'boʊˌsiz

thrombosis
BR θrɒm'bəʊsɪs
AM θrɑm'boʊsəs

thrombotic
BR θrɒm'bɒtɪk
AM ˌθrɑm'bɑdɪk

thrombus
BR 'θrɒmbəs
AM 'θrɑmbəs

throne
BR θrəʊn, -z, -ɪŋ, -d
AM θroʊn, -z, -ɪŋ, -d

throneless
BR 'θrəʊnləs
AM 'θroʊnləs

throng
BR θrɒŋ, -z, -ɪŋ, -d
AM θrɔŋ, θrɑŋ, -z, -ɪŋ, -d

throstle
BR 'θrɒsl, -z
AM 'θrɔsəl, 'θrɑsəl, -z

throttle
BR 'θrɒt|l, -lz, -lɪŋ\-lɪŋ, -ld
AM 'θrɑdəl, -z, -ɪŋ, -d

throttlehold
BR 'θrɒtlhəʊld
AM 'θrɑdl,(h)oʊld

throttler
BR ˈθrɒtlə(r),
ˈθrɒtlə(r), -z
AM ˈθrɑdlər, ˈθrɑtlər, -z

through
BR θruː
AM θru

throughout
BR θruːˈaʊt, θrʊˈaʊt
AM θruˈaʊt

throughput
BR ˈθruːpʊt
AM ˈθruˌpʊt

throughway
BR ˈθruːweɪ, -z
AM ˈθruˌweɪ, -z

throve
BR θrəʊv
AM θroʊv

throw
BR θrəʊ, -z, -ɪŋ
AM θroʊ, -z, -ɪŋ

throwable
BR ˈθrəʊəbl
AM ˈθroʊəbəl

throwaway
BR ˈθrəʊəweɪ
AM ˈθroʊəˌweɪ

throwback
BR ˈθrəʊbak, -s
AM ˈθroʊˌbæk, -s

thrower
BR ˈθrəʊə(r), -z
AM ˈθroʊər, -z

throw-in
BR ˈθrəʊɪn, -z
AM ˈθroʊˌɪn, -z

thrown
BR θrəʊn
AM θroʊn

throw-off
BR ˈθrəʊɒf, -s
AM ˈθroʊˌɔf, ˈθroʊˌɑf, -s

throw-out
BR ˈθrəʊaʊt, -s
AM ˈθroʊˌaʊt, -s

throwster
BR ˈθrəʊstə(r), -z
AM ˈθroʊstər, -z

thru
BR θruː
AM θru

thrum
BR θrʌm, -z, -ɪŋ, -d
AM θrəm, -z, -ɪŋ, -d

thrummer
BR ˈθrʌmə(r), -z
AM ˈθrəmər, -z

thrummy
BR ˈθrʌm|i, -ɪə(r), -ɪɪst
AM ˈθrəmi, -ər, -ɪst

thrush
BR θrʌʃ, -ɪz
AM θrəʃ, -əz

thrust
BR θrʌst, -s, -ɪŋ
AM θrəst, -s, -ɪŋ

thruster
BR ˈθrʌstə(r), -z
AM ˈθrəstər, -z

thrutch
BR θrʌtʃ, -ɪz
AM θrətʃ, -əz

thruway
BR ˈθruːweɪ, -z
AM ˈθruˌweɪ, -z

Thucydides
BR θjuːˈsɪdɪdiːz
AM θuˈsɪdiˌdiz

thud
BR θʌd, -z, -ɪŋ, -ɪd
AM θəd, -z, -ɪŋ, -əd

thuddingly
BR ˈθʌdɪŋli
AM ˈθədɪŋli

thug
BR θʌg, -z
AM θəg, -z

thuggee
BR θʌˈgiː, ˈθʌgi
AM ˈθəgi

thuggery
BR ˈθʌg(ə)ri
AM ˈθəgəri

thuggish
BR ˈθʌgɪʃ
AM ˈθəgɪʃ

thuggishly
BR ˈθʌgɪʃli
AM ˈθəgɪʃli

thuggishness
BR ˈθʌgɪʃnɪs
AM ˈθəgɪʃnɪs

thuggism
BR ˈθʌgɪz(ə)m
AM ˈθəˌgɪzəm

thuja
BR ˈθ(j)uːjə(r),
ˈθ(j)uːdʒə(r), -z
AM ˈθujə, -z

Thule[1]
in classical geography
BR θjuːl, ˈθ(j)uːli
AM ˈtul(ə), θul

Thule[2]
in Greenland
BR ˈtuːli, ˈtuːlə(r)
AM ˈtuˌli

thulium
BR ˈθjuːlɪəm
AM ˈθ(j)ulɪəm

thumb
BR θʌm, -z, -ɪŋ, -d
AM θəm, -z, -ɪŋ, -d

thumbless
BR ˈθʌmləs
AM ˈθəmləs

thumbnail
BR ˈθʌmneɪl
AM ˈθəmˌneɪl

thumbprint
BR ˈθʌmprɪnt, -s
AM ˈθəmˌprɪnt, -s

thumbscrew
BR ˈθʌmskruː, -z
AM ˈθəmˌskru, -z

thumbs-down
BR ˌθʌmzˈdaʊn
AM ˌθəmzˈdaʊn

thumbstall
BR ˈθʌmstɔːl, -z
AM ˈθəmˌstɔl,
ˈθəmˌstɑl, -z

thumbs-up
BR ˌθʌmzˈʌp
AM ˌθəmzˈəp

thumbtack
BR ˈθʌmtak, -s
AM ˈθəmˌtæk, -s

thump
BR θʌm|p, -ps, -pɪŋ, -(p)t
AM θəm|p, -ps, -pɪŋ, -(p)t

thumper
BR ˈθʌmpə(r), -z
AM ˈθəmpər, -z

thunder
BR ˈθʌnd|ə(r), -əz, -(ə)rɪŋ, -əd
AM ˈθʌnd|ər, -ərz, -(ə)rɪŋ, -ərd

thunderball
BR ˈθʌndəbɔːl, -z
AM ˈθʌndərˌbɔl, ˈθəndərˌbɑl, -z

Thunder Bay
BR ˌθʌndəˈbeɪ
AM ˌθəndərˈbeɪ

thunderbird
BR ˈθʌndəbɜːd, -z
AM ˈθəndərˌbɜrd, -z

thunderbolt
BR ˈθʌndəbəʊlt, -s
AM ˈθəndərˌboʊlt, -s

thunderbox
BR ˈθʌndəbɒks, -ɪz
AM ˈθəndərˌbɑks, -əz

thunderbug
BR ˈθʌndəbʌg, -z
AM ˈθəndərˌbəg, -z

thunderclap
BR ˈθʌndəklap, -s
AM ˈθəndərˌklæp, -s

thundercloud
BR ˈθʌndəklaʊd, -z
AM ˈθəndərˌklaʊd, -z

thunderer
BR ˈθʌnd(ə)rə(r), -z
AM ˈθʌnd(ə)rər, -z

thunderflash
BR ˈθʌndəflaʃ, -ɪz
AM ˈθəndərˌflæʃ, -əz

thunderfly
BR ˈθʌndəflʌɪ, -z
AM ˈθəndərˌflaɪ, -z

thunderhead
BR ˈθʌndəhɛd, -z
AM ˈθəndərˌ(h)ɛd, -z

thunderiness
BR ˈθʌnd(ə)rɪnɪs
AM ˈθənd(ə)rɪnɪs

thundering
BR ˈθʌnd(ə)rɪŋ, -z
AM ˈθənd(ə)rɪŋ, -z

thunderingly
BR ˈθʌnd(ə)rɪŋli
AM ˈθənd(ə)rɪŋli

thunderless
BR ˈθʌndələs
AM ˈθəndərləs

thunderous
BR ˈθʌnd(ə)rəs
AM ˈθənd(ə)rəs

thunderously
BR ˈθʌnd(ə)rəsli
AM ˈθənd(ə)rəsli

thunderousness
BR ˈθʌnd(ə)rəsnəs
AM ˈθənd(ə)rəsnəs

thundershower
BR ˈθʌndəˌʃaʊə(r), -z
AM ˈθəndərˌʃaʊər, -z

thunderstorm
BR ˈθʌndəstɔːm, -z
AM ˈθəndərˌstɔ(ə)rm, -z

thunderstruck
BR ˈθʌndəstrʌk
AM ˈθəndərˌstrək

thundery
BR ˈθʌnd(ə)ri
AM ˈθənd(ə)ri

thunk
BR θʌŋ|k, -ks, -kɪŋ, -(k)t
AM θəŋk, -s, -ɪŋ, -t

Thurber
BR ˈθɜːbə(r)
AM ˈθɜrbər

Thurgau
BR ˈtʊəgaʊ
AM ˈtʊrˌgaʊ

thurible
BR ˈθjʊərɪbl, ˈθjɔːrɪbl, -z
AM ˈθ(j)ʊrəbəl, ˈθɜrəbəl, -z

thurifer
BR ˈθjʊərɪfə(r), ˈθjɔːrɪfə(r), -z
AM ˈθ(j)ʊrəfər, ˈθɜrəfər, -z

thuriferous
BR θjəˈrɪf(ə)rəs
AM θ(j)ʊˈrɪf(ə)rəs, θəˈrɪf(ə)rəs

thurification
BR ˌθjʊərɪfɪˈkeɪʃn, ˌθjɔːrɪfɪˈkeɪʃn
AM ˌθ(j)ʊrəfəˈkeɪʃən

Thuringia
BR θ(j)ʊˈrɪn(d)ʒɪə(r)
AM θʊˈrɪndʒ(i)ə

Thuringian
BR θ(j)ʊˈrɪn(d)ʒɪən, -z
AM θ(j)ʊˈrɪndʒ(i)ən, -z

Thurrock
BR 'θʌrək
AM 'θərək

Thursday
BR 'θəːzd|eɪ, 'θəːzd|i,
-eɪz\-ɪz
AM 'θərz,deɪ, 'θərzdi, -z

Thurso
BR 'θəːsəʊ
AM 'θərsoʊ

Thurston
BR 'θəːst(ə)n
AM 'θərstən

thus
BR ðʌs
AM ðəs

thusly
BR 'ðʌsli
AM 'ðəsli

thuya
BR 'θuːjə(r), -z
AM 'θujə, -z

thwack
BR θwak, -s, -ɪŋ, -t
AM θwæk, -s, -ɪŋ, -t

Thwaite
BR θweɪt
AM θweɪt

thwart
BR θwɔːt, -s, -ɪŋ, -ɪd
AM θwɔ(ə)r|t, -ts, -dɪŋ,
-dəd

thy
BR ðʌɪ
AM ðaɪ

Thyestean
BR θʌɪˈɛstɪən
AM θaɪˈɛstɪən

Thyestes
BR θʌɪˈɛstiːz
AM θaɪˈɛstiz

thylacine
BR 'θʌɪləsʌɪn,
'θʌɪləsiːn, ,θʌɪləsɪn, -z
AM 'θaɪlə,saɪn,
'θaɪləsən, -z

thyme
BR tʌɪm
AM taɪm

thymi
BR 'θʌɪmʌɪ
AM 'θaɪ,maɪ

thymine
BR 'θʌɪmiːn
AM 'θaɪ,min, 'θaɪəmən

thymol
BR 'θʌɪmɒl
AM 'θaɪ,mɔl, 'θaɪ,mɑl

thymus
BR 'θʌɪməs, -ɪz
AM 'θaɪməs, -ɪz

thymy
BR 'θʌɪmi
AM 'taɪmi

thyratron
BR 'θʌɪrətrɒn, -z
AM 'θaɪrə,trɑn, -z

thyristor
BR θʌɪˈrɪstə(r), -z
AM θaɪˈrɪstər, -z

thyroid
BR 'θʌɪrɔɪd, -z
AM 'θaɪ,rɔɪd, -z

thyrotoxicosis
BR ,θʌɪrəʊ,tɒksɪˈkəʊsɪs
AM ,θaɪrə,taksəˈkoʊsəs

thyrotropin
BR ,θʌɪrə(ʊ)ˈtrəʊpɪn
AM ,θaɪrə'troʊpɪn

thyroxine
BR θʌɪˈrɒksiːn
AM θaɪˈraksən,
θaɪ'rak,sin

thyrsi
BR 'θəːsʌɪ
AM 'θər,saɪ

thyrsus
BR 'θəːsəs
AM 'θərsəs

Thysanoptera
BR ,θʌɪsəˈnɒpt(ə)rə(r)
AM ,θaɪsə'naptərə

thysanopteran
BR ,θʌɪsəˈnɒpt(ə)rən,
,θʌɪsə'nɒpt(ə)rn, -z
AM ,θaɪsə'naptərən, -z

thysanopterous
BR ,θʌɪsəˈnɒpt(ə)rəs
AM ,θaɪsə'naptərəs

Thysanura
BR ,θʌɪsəˈn(j)ʊərə(r)
AM ,θaɪsə'n(j)ʊrə

thysanuran
BR ,θʌɪsəˈn(j)ʊərən, -z
AM ,θaɪsə'n(j)ʊrən, -z

thysanurous
BR ,θʌɪsəˈn(j)ʊərəs
AM ,θaɪsə'n(j)ʊrəs

thyself
BR ðʌɪˈsɛlf
AM ðaɪ'sɛlf

Thyssen
BR 'tiːsn
AM 'tisən

ti
BR tiː
AM ti

Tia Maria®
BR ,tiːə məˈriːə(r), -z
AM ,tiə mə'riə, -z

**Tiananmen
Square**
BR tɪ,anənmən
'skwɛː(r)
AM tiˈɛnə(n),mɛn
'skwɛ(ə)r

tiara
BR tɪˈɑːrə(r), -z, -d
AM tiˈɛrə, tiˈɑrə, -z, -d

Tibbett
BR 'tɪbɪt
AM 'tɪbət

Tibbitts
BR 'tɪbɪts

AM 'tɪbəts

Tibbs
BR tɪbz
AM tɪbs

Tiber
BR 'tʌɪbə(r)
AM 'taɪbər

Tiberias
BR tʌɪˈbɪərɪas,
tʌɪ'bɪərɪəs
AM taɪ'bɪərɪəs

Tiberius
BR tʌɪˈbɪərɪəs
AM taɪ'birɪəs

Tibesti
BR tɪˈbɛsti
AM tə'bɛsti

Tibet
BR tɪˈbɛt
AM tə'bɛt

Tibetan
BR tɪˈbɛtn, -z
AM tə'bɛtn, -z

tibia
BR 'tɪbɪə(r), -z
AM 'tɪbɪə, -z

tibiae
BR 'tɪbiː
AM 'tɪbi,i, 'tɪbi,aɪ

tibial
BR 'tɪbɪəl
AM 'tɪbɪəl

tibiotarsi
BR ,tɪbɪəʊˈtɑːsʌɪ
AM ,tɪbioʊ'tɑr,saɪ

tibiotarsus
BR ,tɪbɪəʊˈtɑːsəs
AM ,tɪbioʊ'tarsəs

Tibullus
BR tɪ'bʊləs
AM tɪ'bʊləs

tic
BR tɪk, -s
AM tɪk, -s

tice
BR tʌɪs, -ɪz, -ɪŋ, -t
AM taɪs, -ɪz, -ɪŋ, -t

Tichborne
BR 'tɪtʃbɔːn
AM 'tɪtʃ,bɔ(ə)rn

Ticino
BR tɪ'tʃiːnəʊ
AM tɪ'tʃi,noʊ

tick
BR tɪk, -s, -ɪŋ, -t
AM tɪk, -s, -ɪŋ, -t

tick-bird
BR 'tɪkbəːd, -z
AM 'tɪk,bərd, -z

ticker
BR 'tɪkə(r), -z
AM 'tɪkər, -z

tickertape
BR 'tɪkəteɪp, -s
AM 'tɪkər,teɪp, -s

ticket
BR 'tɪk|ɪt, -ɪts, -ɪtɪŋ,
-ɪtɪd
AM 'tɪkɪ|t, -ts, -dɪŋ, -dɪd

ticketless
BR 'tɪkɪtlɪs
AM 'tɪkɪtlɪs

**ticket-of-leave
man**
BR ,tɪkɪtəv'liːv man
AM ,tɪkɪdə(v)'liv ,mæn

**ticket-of-leave
men**
BR ,tɪkɪtəv'liːv mɛn
AM ,tɪkɪdə(v)'liv ,mɛn

tickety-boo
BR ,tɪkɪtɪ'buː
AM ,tɪkɪdi'bu

ticking
BR 'tɪkɪŋ, -z
AM 'tɪkɪŋ, -z

tickle
BR 'tɪk|l, -lz, -lɪŋ \-lɪŋ,
-ld
AM 'tɪk|əl, -əlz, -(ə)lɪŋ,
-əld

tickler
BR 'tɪklə(r), 'tɪklə(r),
-z
AM 'tɪk(ə)lər, -z

tickless
BR 'tɪklɪs
AM 'tɪklɪs

ticklish
BR 'tɪkl|ɪʃ, 'tɪklɪʃ
AM 'tɪk(ə)lɪʃ

ticklishly
BR 'tɪklɪʃli, 'tɪklɪʃli
AM 'tɪk(ə)lɪʃli

ticklishness
BR 'tɪklɪʃnɪs,
'tɪklɪʃnɪs
AM 'tɪk(ə)lɪʃnɪs

tickly
BR 'tɪkl|i, 'tɪkli
AM 'tɪk(ə)li

tickover
BR 'tɪkəʊvə(r)
AM 'tɪk,oʊvər

tick-tack
BR 'tɪktak, -s
AM 'tɪk,tæk, -s

tick-tack-toe
BR ,tɪktak'təʊ
AM 'tɪk,tæk'toʊ

tick-tock
BR 'tɪktɒk, ,tɪk'tɒk, -s
AM 'tɪk,tak, -s

ticky-tacky
BR 'tɪkɪ,taki
AM 'tɪki,tæki

Ticonderoga
BR ,tʌɪkɒndəˈrəʊgə(r),
tʌɪ,kɒndə'rəʊgə(r)
AM ,taɪ,kandə'roʊgə

tic-tac
BR 'tɪktak
AM 'tɪk,tæk

tic-tac-toe
BR ˌtɪktak'təʊ
AM ˈtɪkˌtæk'toʊ

tidal
BR 'taɪdl
AM 'taɪdəl

tidally
BR 'taɪdl̩i
AM 'taɪdli

tidbit
BR 'tɪdbɪt, -s
AM 'tɪdˌbɪt, -s

tiddledywink
BR 'tɪdldɪˌwɪŋk, -s
AM 'tɪdl(d)iˌwɪŋk, -s

tiddler
BR 'tɪdlə(r), 'tɪdlə(r), -z
AM 'tɪd(ə)lər, -z

Tiddles
BR 'tɪdlz
AM 'tɪdəlz

tiddlewink
BR 'tɪdlɪwɪŋk, 'tɪdl̩wɪŋk, -s
AM 'tɪdliˌwɪŋk, 'tɪdl̩iˌwɪŋk, -s

tiddly
BR 'tɪdl̩i, 'tɪdl̩i, -ɪə(r), -ɪɪst
AM 'tɪdli, 'tɪdl̩i, -ər, -ɪɪst

tiddlywink
BR 'tɪdlɪwɪŋk, 'tɪdl̩wɪŋk, -s
AM 'tɪdliˌwɪŋk, 'tɪdl̩iˌwɪŋk, -s

tide
BR tʌɪd, -z, -ɪŋ, -ɪd
AM taɪd, -z, -ɪŋ, -ɪd

tideland
BR 'tʌɪdland, -z
AM 'taɪdˌlænd, -z

tideless
BR 'tʌɪdlɪs
AM 'taɪdlɪs

tideline
BR 'tʌɪdlʌɪn, -z
AM 'taɪdˌlaɪn, -z

tidemark
BR 'tʌɪdmɑːk, -s
AM 'taɪdˌmɑrk, -s

Tidenham
BR 'tɪdn̩əm
AM 'tɪd(ə)nəm

Tideswell
BR 'tʌɪdzwɛl
AM 'taɪdzˌwɛl

tidewaiter
BR 'tʌɪdˌweɪtə(r), -z
AM 'taɪdˌweɪdər, -z

tidewater
BR 'tʌɪdˌwɔːtə(r)
AM 'taɪdˌwɒdər, 'taɪdˌwɑdər

tidewave
BR 'tʌɪdweɪv, -z
AM 'taɪdˌweɪv, -z

tideway
BR 'tʌɪdweɪ, -z
AM 'taɪdˌweɪ, -z

tidily
BR 'tʌɪdɪli
AM 'taɪdɪli

tidiness
BR 'tʌɪdinɪs
AM 'taɪdinɪs

tidings
BR 'tʌɪdɪŋz
AM 'taɪdɪŋz

Tidmarsh
BR 'tɪdmɑːʃ
AM 'tɪdˌmɑrʃ

tidy
BR 'tʌɪdli, -ɪz, -ɪɪŋ, -ɪd, -ɪə(r), -ɪɪst
AM 'taɪdi, -z, -ɪŋ, -d, -ər, -ɪst

tie
BR tʌɪ, -z, -ɪŋ, -d
AM taɪ, -z, -ɪŋ, -d

tieback
BR 'tʌɪbak, -s
AM 'taɪˌbæk, -s

tiebreak
BR 'tʌɪbreɪk, -s
AM 'taɪˌbreɪk, -s

tie-breaker
BR 'tʌɪˌbreɪkə(r), -z
AM 'taɪˌbreɪkər, -z

tie-breaking
BR 'tʌɪˌbreɪkɪŋ
AM 'taɪˌbreɪkɪŋ

tie-dye
BR 'tʌɪdʌɪ, -z, -ɪŋ, -d
AM 'taɪˌdaɪ, -z, -ɪŋ, -d

tieless
BR 'tʌɪlɪs
AM 'taɪlɪs

Tientsin
BR ˌtjɛn'(t)sɪn
AM tiˈɛn(t)sɪn

tiepin
BR 'tʌɪpɪn, -z
AM 'taɪˌpɪn, -z

Tiepolo
BR tɪ'ɛpələʊ, tɪ'ɛpləʊ
AM ti'ɛpəˌloʊ

tier¹
a person who ties
BR 'tʌɪə(r), -z
AM 'taɪər, -z

tier²
layer, level
BR tɪə(r), -z, -d
AM tɪ(ə)r, -z, -d

tierce
BR tɪəs, -t
AM tɪ(ə)rs, -t

tiercel
BR 'tɪəsl, 'təːsl, -z
AM 'tɪ(ə)rsəl, -z

tiercet
BR 'tɪəsɪt, 'təːsɪt, -s
AM 'tɪrsət, -s

Tierney
BR 'tɪəni
AM 'tɪrni

Tierra del Fuego
BR tɪˌɛrə dɛl 'fweɪɡəʊ, + f(j)ʊ'eɪɡəʊ
AM 'tiərə dɛl fʊ'eɪɡoʊ

tiff
BR tɪf, -s
AM tɪf, -s

tiffany
BR 'tɪfəni, 'tɪfn̩i
AM 'tɪfəni

tiffin
BR 'tɪfɪn
AM 'tɪfɪn

Tiflis
BR 'tɪflɪs
AM 'tɪflɪs, tə'flis

tig
BR tɪg, -z, -ɪŋ, -d
AM tɪg, -z, -ɪŋ, -d

tiger
BR 'tʌɪɡə(r), -z
AM 'taɪɡər, -z

tigerish
BR 'tʌɪɡ(ə)rɪʃ
AM 'taɪɡ(ə)rɪʃ

tigerishly
BR 'tʌɪɡ(ə)rɪʃli
AM 'taɪɡ(ə)rɪʃli

tiger moth
BR 'tʌɪɡə mɒθ, ˌtʌɪɡə 'mɒθ, -s
AM 'taɪɡər ˌmɒθ, + ˌmɑθ, -s

Tigers
BR 'tʌɪɡəz
AM 'taɪɡərz

tiger's-eye
BR 'tʌɪɡəzʌɪ
AM 'taɪɡərzˌaɪ

tigerskin
BR 'tʌɪɡəskɪn, -z
AM 'taɪɡərˌskɪn, -z

Tighe
BR tʌɪ
AM taɪ

tight
BR tʌɪt, -s, -ə(r), -ɪst
AM taɪt, -ts, -dər, -dɪst

tighten
BR 'tʌɪt|n, -nz, -n̩ɪŋ \ -nɪŋ, -nd
AM 'taɪtn, -z, -ɪŋ, -d

tightener
BR 'tʌɪtnə(r), 'tʌɪtnə(r), -z
AM ˌtaɪtnər, ˌtaɪtnər, -z

tight-fisted
BR ˌtʌɪt'fɪstɪd
AM ˌtaɪt'fɪstɪd

tight-fistedly
BR ˌtʌɪt'fɪstɪdli
AM ˌtaɪt'fɪstɪdli

tight-fistedness
BR ˌtʌɪt'fɪstɪdnɪs

AM ˌtaɪt'fɪstɪdnɪs

tightly
BR 'tʌɪtli
AM 'taɪtli

tightness
BR 'tʌɪtnɪs
AM 'taɪtnɪs

tightrope
BR 'tʌɪtrəʊp, -s
AM 'taɪtˌroʊp, -s

tightwad
BR 'tʌɪtwɒd, -z
AM 'taɪtˌwɑd, -z

Tiglath-pileser
BR ˌtɪɡlaθpʌɪ'liːzə(r), ˌtɪɡlaθpɪ'liːzə(r)
AM ˌtɪɡlæθpə'lizər

tiglic
BR 'tɪɡlɪk
AM 'tɪɡlɪk

tigon
BR 'tʌɪɡ(ə)n, 'tʌɪɡɒn, -z
AM 'taɪɡən, -z

Tigray
BR 'tɪɡreɪ
AM tə'ɡreɪ

Tigrayan
BR tɪ'ɡreɪən, -z
AM tə'ɡreɪən, -z

Tigre
BR 'tɪɡreɪ
AM 'tiɡreɪ

Tigrean
BR tɪ'ɡreɪən, -z
AM tə'ɡreɪən, -z

tigress
BR 'tʌɪɡrɪs, 'tʌɪɡrɛs, -ɪz
AM 'taɪɡrɪs, -ɪz

Tigrinya
BR tɪ'ɡrɪnjə(r), tɪ'ɡriːnjə(r)
AM tə'ɡrɪnjə

Tigris
BR 'tʌɪɡrɪs
AM 'taɪɡrɪs

Tijuana
BR ˌtiə'wɑːnə(r), tɪ'wɑːnə(r)
AM ˌtiə'wɑnə
SP ti'xwana

tike
BR tʌɪk, -s
AM taɪk, -s

tiki
BR 'tiːk|i, -ɪz
AM 'tiki, -z

tikka
BR 'tiːkə(r), 'tɪkə(r)
AM 'tɪkə

til
BR tɪl
AM tɪl

'til
BR tɪl
AM tɪl

tilapia
BR tɪˈlapɪə(r),
tɪˈleɪpɪə(r), -z
AM təˈlɑpiə, -z

Tilburg
BR ˈtɪlbə:g
AM ˈtɪl,bɜrg

tilbury
BR ˈtɪlb(ə)r|i, -ɪz
AM ˈtɪl,bɛri, -z

Tilda
BR ˈtɪldə(r)
AM ˈtɪldə

tilde
BR ˈtɪld|ə(r), ˈtɪld|i, -ɪz
AM ˈtɪldə, -z

Tilden
BR ˈtɪld(ə)n
AM ˈtɪldən

tile
BR taɪl, -z, -ɪŋ, -d
AM taɪl, -z, -ɪŋ, -d

Tilehurst
BR ˈtaɪlhə:st
AM ˈtaɪl,(h)ərst

tiler
BR ˈtaɪlə(r), -z
AM ˈtaɪlər, -z

tiling
BR ˈtaɪlɪŋ, -z
AM ˈtaɪlɪŋ, -z

till
BR tɪl, -z, -ɪŋ, -d
AM tɪl, -z, -ɪŋ, -d

tillable
BR ˈtɪləbl
AM ˈtɪləbəl

tillage
BR ˈtɪlɪdʒ
AM ˈtɪlɪdʒ

tiller
BR ˈtɪlə(r), -z, -ɪŋ, -d
AM ˈtɪlər, -z, -ɪŋ, -d

Tilley
BR ˈtɪli
AM ˈtɪli

Tilley lamp®
BR ˈtɪlɪ lamp, -s
AM ˈtɪlɪ ˌlæmp, -s

Tillich
BR ˈtɪlɪk
AM ˈtɪlɪk

Tilly
BR ˈtɪli
AM ˈtɪli

Tilsit
BR ˈtɪlsɪt, ˈtɪlzɪt
AM ˈtɪlsɪt, ˈtɪlzɪt

tilt
BR tɪlt, -s, -ɪŋ, -ɪd
AM tɪlt, -s, -ɪŋ, -ɪd

tilter
BR ˈtɪltə(r), -z
AM ˈtɪltər, -z

tilth
BR tɪlθ
AM tɪlθ

tilt-hammer
BR ˈtɪlt,hamə(r), -z
AM ˈtɪlt,(h)æmər, -z

tiltyard
BR ˈtɪltjɑ:d, -z
AM ˈtɪlt,jɑrd, -z

Tim
BR tɪm
AM tɪm

Timaru
BR ˈtɪmɑru:
AM ˈtɪmə,ru

timbal
BR ˈtɪmbl, -z
AM ˈtɪmbəl, -z

timbale
BR tam'bɑ:l, ˈtɪmbl, -z
AM ˈtɪmbəl, ˌtɪm'bɑl, -z

timber
BR ˈtɪmb|ə(r), -əz,
-(ə)rɪŋ, -əd
AM ˈtɪmb|ər, -ərz,
-(ə)rɪŋ, -ərd

timberjack
BR ˈtɪmbəjak, -s
AM ˈtɪmbər,jæk, -s

Timberlake
BR ˈtɪmbəleɪk
AM ˈtɪmbər,eɪk

timberland
BR ˈtɪmbəland, -z
AM ˈtɪmbər,lænd, -z

timberline
BR ˈtɪmbəlaɪn
AM ˈtɪmbər,laɪn

timberwork
BR ˈtɪmbəwək
AM ˈtɪmbər,wərk

timbre
BR ˈtambə(r),
ˈtɪmbə(r)
AM ˈtæmbər

timbrel
BR ˈtɪmbr(ə)l, -z
AM ˈtɪmbrəl, -z

Timbuctoo
BR ˌtɪmbʌk'tu:
AM ˈtɪmbək'tu

Timbuktu
BR ˌtɪmbʌk'tu:
AM ˈtɪmbək'tu

time
BR taɪm, -z, -ɪŋ, -d
AM taɪm, -z, -ɪŋ, -d

time-expired
BR ˌtaɪmɪk'spaɪəd,
ˌtaɪmɛk'spaɪəd,
ˈtaɪmɪk,spaɪəd,
ˈtaɪmɛk,spaɪəd
AM ˈtaɪmək,spaɪ(ə)rd

timekeeper
BR ˈtaɪm,ki:pə(r), -z
AM ˈtaɪm,kipər, -z

timekeeping
BR ˈtaɪm,ki:pɪŋ
AM ˈtaɪm,kipɪŋ

timeless
BR ˈtaɪmlɪs
AM ˈtaɪmlɪs

timelessly
BR ˈtaɪmlɪsli
AM ˈtaɪmlɪsli

timelessness
BR ˈtaɪmlɪsnɪs
AM ˈtaɪmlɪsnɪs

timeliness
BR ˈtaɪmlinɪs
AM ˈtaɪmlinɪs

timely
BR ˈtaɪml|i, -ɪə(r), -ɪɪst
AM ˈtaɪmli, -ər, -ɪst

timeous
BR ˈtaɪməs
AM ˈtaɪməs

timeously
BR ˈtaɪməsli
AM ˈtaɪməsli

time-out
BR ˌtaɪm'aʊt, -s
AM ˌtaɪm'aʊt, -s

timepiece
BR ˈtaɪmpi:s, -ɪz
AM ˈtaɪm,pis, -ɪz

timer
BR ˈtaɪmə(r), -z
AM ˈtaɪmər, -z

Times
BR taɪmz
AM taɪmz

timesaving
BR ˈtaɪm,seɪvɪŋ
AM ˈtaɪm,seɪvɪŋ

timescale
BR ˈtaɪmskeɪl, -z
AM ˈtaɪm,skeɪl, -z

timeserver
BR ˈtaɪm,sə:və(r), -z
AM ˈtaɪm,sərvər, -z

timeserving
BR ˈtaɪm,sə:vɪŋ
AM ˈtaɪm,sərvɪŋ

timeshare
BR ˈtaɪmʃɛ:(r), -z
AM ˈtaɪm,ʃɛ(ə)r, -z

time-sharing
BR ˈtaɪmʃɛ:rɪŋ
AM ˈtaɪm,ʃɛrɪŋ

timesheet
BR ˈtaɪmʃiːt, -s
AM ˈtaɪm,ʃit, -s

timetable
BR ˈtaɪm,teɪb|l, -lz,
-lɪŋ \-lɪŋ, -ld
AM ˈtaɪm,teɪbəl, -əlz,
-(ə)lɪŋ, -əld

timework
BR ˈtaɪmwə:k
AM ˈtaɪm,wərk

timeworker
BR ˈtaɪm,wə:kə(r), -z
AM ˈtaɪm,wərkər, -z

timeworn
BR ˈtaɪmwɔ:n

timeworn
AM ˈtaɪm,wɔ(ə)rn

Timex®
BR ˈtaɪmɛks
AM ˈtaɪ,mɛks

timid
BR ˈtɪmɪd
AM ˈtɪmɪd

timidity
BR tɪˈmɪdɪti
AM təˈmɪdɪdi

timidly
BR ˈtɪmɪdli
AM ˈtɪmɪdli

timidness
BR ˈtɪmɪdnɪs
AM ˈtɪmɪdnɪs

timing
BR ˈtaɪmɪŋ, -z
AM ˈtaɪmɪŋ, -z

Timişoara
BR ˌtɪmɪˈʃwɑ:rə(r)
AM ˌtɪmɪˈʃwɑrə

Timms
BR tɪmz
AM tɪmz

Timmy
BR ˈtɪmi
AM ˈtɪmi

timocracy
BR tɪˈmɒkrəs|i, -ɪz
AM təˈmɑkrəsi, -z

timocratic
BR ˌtɪmə'kratɪk
AM ˌtɪmə'krædɪk

Timon
BR ˈtaɪmən, ˈtaɪmɒn
AM ˈtaɪmən

Timor
BR ˈtiːmɔː(r)
AM ˈti,mɔ(ə)r

Timorese
BR ˌtɪmə'ri:z,
ˌti:mər'i:z
AM ˌtɪmə'riz

timorous
BR ˈtɪm(ə)rəs
AM ˈtɪm(ə)rəs

timorously
BR ˈtɪm(ə)rəsli
AM ˈtɪm(ə)rəsli

timorousness
BR ˈtɪm(ə)rəsnəs
AM ˈtɪm(ə)rəsnəs

Timotei®
BR ˈtɪməteɪ
AM ˈtɪmə,teɪ

timothy
BR ˈtɪməθi
AM ˈtɪməθi

timpani
BR ˈtɪmpəni
AM ˈtɪmpəni

timpanist
BR ˈtɪmpənɪst, -s
AM ˈtɪmpənəst, -s

Timpson
BR ˈtɪm(p)sn

tin
AM 'tɪm(p)sən

tin
BR tɪn, -z, -ɪŋ, -d
AM tɪn, -z, -ɪŋ, -d

tinamou
BR 'tɪnəmuː, -z
AM 'tɪnə‚mu, -z

tinctorial
BR tɪŋ(k)'tɔːriəl
AM tɪŋ(k)'tɔriəl

tincture
BR 'tɪŋ(k)tʃ|ə(r), -əz,
-(ə)rɪŋ, -əd
AM 'tɪŋ(k)|(t)ʃər,
-(t)ʃərz,
-tʃərɪŋ \-ʃ(ə)rɪŋ,
-(t)ʃərd

tindal
BR 'tɪndl, -z
AM 'tɪndəl, -z

Tindale
BR 'tɪnd(eɪ)l
AM 'tɪn‚deɪl

Tindall
BR 'tɪnd(ɔː)l
AM 'tɪndəl

Tindell
BR 'tɪnd(ɛ)l
AM 'tɪndəl

tinder
BR 'tɪndə(r)
AM 'tɪndər

tinderbox
BR 'tɪndəbɒks, -ɪz
AM 'tɪndər‚baks, -əz

tindery
BR 'tɪnd(ə)ri
AM 'tɪndəri

tine
BR tʌɪn, -z, -d
AM taɪn, -z, -d

tinea
BR 'tɪnɪə(r)
AM 'tɪnɪə

tinfoil
BR 'tɪnfɔɪl
AM 'tɪn‚fɔɪl

ting
BR tɪŋ, -z, -ɪŋ, -d
AM tɪŋ, -z, -ɪŋ, -d

tinge
BR tɪn(d)ʒ, -ɪz, -ɪŋ, -d
AM tɪndʒ, -ɪz, -ɪŋ, -d

tingle
BR 'tɪŋg|l, -lz, -l̩ɪŋ \-lɪŋ,
-ld
AM 'tɪŋg|əl, -əlz, -(ə)lɪŋ,
-əld

tingly
BR 'tɪŋl|i, 'tɪŋgl|i,
-ɪə(r), -ɪɪst
AM 'tɪŋg(ə)li, -ər, -ɪɪst

Tingwall
BR 'tɪŋw(ə)l, 'tɪŋwɔːl
AM 'tɪŋ‚wɒl, 'tɪŋ‚wɑl

tinhorn
BR 'tɪnhɔːn, -z

tin
AM 'tɪn‚(h)ɔ(ə)rn, -z

tinily
BR 'tʌɪnɪli
AM 'taɪnɪli

tininess
BR 'tʌɪnɪnɪs
AM 'taɪnɪnɪs

tinker
BR 'tɪŋk|ə(r), -əz,
-(ə)rɪŋ, -əd
AM 'tɪŋk|ər, -ərz,
-(ə)rɪŋ, -ərd

tinkerer
BR 'tɪŋk(ə)rə(r), -z
AM 'tɪŋk(ə)rər, -z

tinkering
BR 'tɪŋk(ə)rɪŋ, -z
AM 'tɪŋk(ə)rɪŋ, -z

tinkle
BR 'tɪŋk|l, -lz, -l̩ɪŋ \-lɪŋ,
-ld
AM 'tɪŋk|əl, -əlz, -(ə)lɪŋ,
-əld

tinkling
BR 'tɪŋklɪŋ, 'tɪŋkl̩ɪŋ, -z
AM 'tɪŋk(ə)lɪŋ, -z

tinkly
BR 'tɪŋkli, 'tɪŋkl̩i
AM 'tɪŋk(ə)li

tinner
BR 'tɪnə(r), -z
AM 'tɪnər, -z

tinnily
BR 'tɪnɪli
AM 'tɪnɪli

tinniness
BR 'tɪnɪnɪs
AM 'tɪnɪnɪs

tinnitus
BR 'tɪnɪtəs, tɪ'nʌɪtəs
AM 'tɪnədəs

tinny
BR 'tɪn|i, -ɪə(r), -ɪɪst
AM 'tɪni, -ər, -ɪɪst

Tin Pan Alley
BR ‚tɪn pan 'ali
AM ‚tɪn ‚pæn 'æli

tinpot
BR 'tɪnpɒt
AM 'tɪn‚pɑt

tinsel
BR 'tɪnsl, -d
AM 'tɪnsəl, -d

tinselly
BR 'tɪnsl̩i
AM 'tɪnsəli

Tinseltown
BR 'tɪnsltaʊn
AM 'tɪnsəl‚taʊn

Tinsley
BR 'tɪnzli
AM 'tɪnzli

tinsmith
BR 'tɪnsmɪθ, -s
AM 'tɪn‚smɪθ, -s

tinsnips
BR 'tɪnsnɪps

tin
AM 'tɪn‚snɪps

tinstone
BR 'tɪnstəʊn
AM 'tɪn‚stoʊn

tint
AM tɪnt, -s, -ɪŋ, -ɪd
AM tɪn|t, -ts, -(t)ɪŋ,
-(t)əd

tintack
BR 'tɪntak, -s
AM 'tɪn‚tæk, -s

Tintagel
BR tɪn'tadʒl
AM tɪn'tædʒəl

tinter
BR 'tɪntə(r), -z
AM 'tɪn(t)ər, -z

Tintern
BR 'tɪntən
AM 'tɪn(t)ərn

tintinnabula
BR ‚tɪntɪ'nabjʉlə(r)
AM ‚tɪn(t)ə'næbjələ

tintinnabular
BR ‚tɪntɪ'nabjʉlə(r)
AM ‚tɪn(t)ə'næbjələr

tintinnabulary
BR ‚tɪntɪ'nabjʉləri
AM ‚tɪn(t)ə'næbjə‚lɛri

tintinnabulation
BR ‚tɪntɪ‚nabjʉ'leɪʃn,
-z
AM ‚tɪn(t)ə‚næbjə'leɪ-
ʃən, -z

tintinnabulous
BR ‚tɪntɪ'nabjʉləs
AM ‚tɪn(t)ə'næbjələs

tintinnabulum
BR ‚tɪntɪ'nabjʉləm
AM ‚tɪn(t)ə'næbjələm

Tintoretto
BR ‚tɪntə'rɛtəʊ, -z
AM ‚tɪn(t)ə'rɛdoʊ, -z

tintype
BR 'tɪntʌɪp
AM 'tɪn‚taɪp

tinware
BR 'tɪnwɛː(r), -z
AM 'tɪn‚wɛ(ə)r, -z

tiny
BR 'tʌɪn|i, -ɪə(r), -ɪɪst
AM 'taɪni, -ər, -ɪɪst

Tío Pepe®
BR ‚tiːəʊ 'pɛpi, + 'pɛpeɪ
AM ‚tioʊ 'pɛpɛ

tip
BR tɪp, -s, -ɪŋ, -t
AM tɪp, -s, -ɪŋ, -t

tip-and-run
BR ‚tɪp(ə)n(d)'rʌn
AM ‚tɪpən'rən

tip-cart
BR 'tɪpkɑːt, -s
AM 'tɪp‚kɑrt, -s

tipcat
BR 'tɪpkat
AM 'tɪp‚kæt

tipless
BR 'tɪplɪs
AM 'tɪplɪs

tipper
BR 'tɪpə(r), -z
AM 'tɪpər, -z

Tipperary
BR ‚tɪpə'rɛːri
AM ‚tɪpə'rɛri

tippet
BR 'tɪpɪt, -s
AM 'tɪpɪt, -s

Tippett
BR 'tɪpɪt
AM 'tɪpɪt

Tipp-Ex®
BR 'tɪpɛks, -ɪz, -ɪŋ, -t
AM 'tɪ‚pɛks, -əz, -ɪŋ, -t

tipple
BR 'tɪp|l, -lz, -l̩ɪŋ \-lɪŋ,
-ld
AM 'tɪp|əl, -əlz, -(ə)lɪŋ,
-əld

tippler
BR 'tɪpl̩ə(r), 'tɪplə(r),
-z
AM 'tɪp(ə)lər, -z

tippy
BR 'tɪp|i, -ɪə(r), -ɪɪst
AM 'tɪpi, -ər, -ɪɪst

tipsily
BR 'tɪpsɪli
AM 'tɪpsɪli

tipsiness
BR 'tɪpsɪnɪs
AM 'tɪpsɪnɪs

tipstaff
BR 'tɪpstɑːf, 'tɪpstaf, -s
AM 'tɪp‚stæf, -s

tipstaves
BR 'tɪpsteɪvz
AM 'tɪp‚steɪvz

tipster
BR 'tɪpstə(r), -z
AM 'tɪpstər, -z

tipsy
BR 'tɪps|i, -ɪə(r), -ɪɪst
AM 'tɪpsi, -ər, -ɪɪst

tipsy-cake
BR 'tɪpsɪkeɪk, -s
AM 'tɪpsi‚keɪk, -s

tiptoe
BR 'tɪptəʊ, -z, -ɪŋ, -d
AM 'tɪp‚toʊ, -z, -ɪŋ, -d

tiptop
BR 'tɪp'tɒp
AM 'tɪp'tɑp

tirade
BR tʌɪ'reɪd, tɪ'reɪd, -z
AM 'taɪ‚reɪd, ‚taɪ'reɪd,
-z

tirailleur
BR ‚tɪrʌɪ'əː(r), -z
AM ‚tɪraɪ'(j)ər, -z

tiramisu
BR ‚tɪrəmɪ'suː
AM ‚tɪrəmə'su

Tirana
BR tɪ'rɑːnə(r)
AM tɪ'rɑnə

Tiranë
BR tɪ'rɑːnə(r)
AM tɪ'rɑnə

tire
BR 'tʌɪə(r), -z, -ɪŋ, -d
AM 'taɪ(ə)r, -z, -ɪŋ, -d

tiredly
BR 'tʌɪədli
AM 'taɪ(ə)rdli

tiredness
BR 'tʌɪədnəs
AM 'taɪ(ə)rdnəs

Tiree
BR tʌɪ'riː
AM taɪ'ri

tire gauge
BR 'tʌɪə geɪdʒ
AM 'taɪ(ə)r ˌgeɪdʒ

tireless
BR 'tʌɪələs
AM 'taɪ(ə)rləs

tirelessly
BR 'tʌɪələsli
AM 'taɪ(ə)rləsli

tirelessness
BR 'tʌɪələsnəs
AM 'taɪ(ə)rləsnəs

Tiresias
BR tʌɪ'riːsɪəs,
tʌɪ'riːsɪas
AM tɪ'risiəs

tiresome
BR 'tʌɪəs(ə)m
AM 'taɪ(ə)rsəm

tiresomely
BR 'tʌɪəs(ə)mli
AM 'taɪ(ə)rsəmli

tiresomeness
BR 'tʌɪəs(ə)mnəs
AM 'taɪ(ə)rsəmnəs

tiro
BR 'tʌɪrəʊ, -z
AM 'taɪroʊ, -z

Tirol
BR tɪ'rəʊl, 'tɪrəl, 'tɪrl
AM tə'roʊl, 'tɪˌroʊl

Tirpitz
BR 'təːpɪts
AM 'tərpɪts

'tis
BR tɪz
AM tɪz

tisane
BR tɪ'zan, ti:'zan, -z
AM tə'zæn, -z

Tishri
BR 'tɪʃriː
AM 'tɪʃri

Tisiphone
BR tɪ'sɪfəni, tɪ'sɪfn̩i,
tʌɪ'sɪfəni, tʌɪ'sɪfn̩i
AM tɪ'sɪfəni

Tissot
BR 'ti:səʊ

AM təˈsoʊ

tissue
BR 'tɪʃuː, 'tɪsjuː, -z
AM 'tɪʃu, -z

tit
BR tɪt, -s
AM tɪt, -s

titan
BR 'tʌɪtn̩, -z
AM 'taɪtn̩, -z

titanate
BR 'tʌɪtəneɪt, 'tʌɪtn̩eɪt
AM 'taɪtn̩ˌeɪt

Titaness
BR 'tʌɪtn̩ɪs, ˌtʌɪtn̩'ɛs, -ɪz
AM 'taɪtn̩ɪs, -ɪz

Titania
BR tɪ'tɑːnɪə(r),
tɪ'teɪnɪə(r)
AM taɪ'teɪniə, tə'taniə

titanic
BR tʌɪ'tanɪk
AM taɪ'tænɪk

titanically
BR tʌɪ'tanɪkli
AM taɪ'tænək(ə)li

titanium
BR tʌɪ'teɪnɪəm,
tɪ'teɪnɪəm
AM taɪ'teɪniəm,
tə'teɪniəm

titbit
BR 'tɪtbɪt, -s
AM 'tɪtˌbɪt, -s

titch
BR tɪtʃ, -ɪz
AM tɪtʃ, -ɪz

titchiness
BR 'tɪtʃɪnɪs
AM 'tɪtʃɪnɪs

titchy
BR 'tɪtʃʃi, -ɪə(r), -ɪɪst
AM 'tɪtʃi, -ər, -ɪst

titer
BR 'tʌɪtə(r), -z
AM 'taɪdər, -z

titfer
BR 'tɪtfə(r), -z
AM 'tɪtfər, -z

tit-for-tat
BR 'tɪtfə'tat
AM 'tɪtfər'tæt

tithable
BR 'tʌɪðəbl
AM 'taɪðəbəl

tithe
BR tʌɪð, -z, -ɪŋ, -d
AM taɪð, -z, -ɪŋ, -d

tithing
BR 'tʌɪðɪŋ, -z
AM 'taɪðɪŋ, -z

Tithonus
BR tɪ'θəʊnəs,
tʌɪ'θəʊnəs
AM taɪ'θoʊnəs

titi[1]
bird
BR 'ti:ti:, -z
AM 'ti,ti, -z

titi[2]
monkey
BR 'ti:ti:, tɪ'ti:, -z
AM 'ti,ti, tə'ti, -z

titi[3]
tree
BR 'ti:ti:, 'tʌɪtʌɪ, -z
AM 'ti,ti, 'taɪ,taɪ, -z

Titian
BR 'tɪʃn̩, -z
AM 'tɪʃən, -z

Titicaca
BR ˌtɪtɪ'kɑːkɑː(r),
ˌtɪtɪ'kɑːkə(r)
AM ˌtɪdi'kɑkə

titillate
BR 'tɪtɪleɪt, -s, -ɪŋ, -ɪd
AM 'tɪdəˌleɪt, -ts, -dɪŋ,
-dɪd

titillatingly
BR 'tɪtɪleɪtɪŋli
AM 'tɪdəˌleɪdɪŋli

titillation
BR ˌtɪtɪ'leɪʃn̩, -z
AM ˌtɪdə'leɪʃən, -z

titivate
BR 'tɪtɪveɪt, -s, -ɪŋ, -ɪd
AM 'tɪdəˌveɪt, -ts, -dɪŋ,
-dɪd

titivation
BR ˌtɪtɪ'veɪʃn̩, -z
AM ˌtɪdə'veɪʃən, -z

titlark
BR 'tɪtlɑːk, -s
AM 'tɪtˌlɑrk, -s

title
BR 'tʌɪtl̩, -z, -d
AM 'taɪd(ə)l, -z, -d

titleholder
BR 'tʌɪtl̩ˌhəʊldə(r), -z
AM 'taɪdl̩ˌ(h)oʊldər, -z

titling
BR 'tʌɪtlɪŋ, -z
AM 'taɪdlɪŋ, -z

Titmarsh
BR 'tɪtmɑːʃ
AM 'tɪtˌmɑrʃ

titmice
BR 'tɪtmʌɪs
AM 'tɪtˌmaɪs

titmouse
BR 'tɪtmaʊs
AM 'tɪtˌmaʊs

Titmus
BR 'tɪtməs
AM 'tɪtməs

Tito
BR 'ti:təʊ
AM 'tidoʊ

Titograd
BR 'ti:tə(ʊ)grad
AM 'tidoʊˌgræd

Titoism
BR 'ti:təʊɪz(ə)m
AM 'tidoʊˌɪzəm,
'tidəˌwɪzəm

Titoist
BR 'ti:təʊɪst, -s
AM 'tidoʊəst,
'tidəwəst, -s

titrant
BR 'tʌɪtr(ə)nt, -s
AM 'taɪtrənt, -s

titratable
BR tʌɪ'treɪtəbl,
'tʌɪtreɪtəbl,
'tʌɪtrətəbl
AM 'taɪˌtreɪdəbl

titrate
BR tʌɪ'treɪt, 'tʌɪtreɪt,
-s, -ɪŋ, -ɪd
AM 'taɪˌtreɪt, -ts, -dɪŋ,
-dɪd

titration
BR tʌɪ'treɪʃn̩, -z
AM ˌtaɪ'treɪʃən, -z

titre
BR 'tʌɪtə(r), -z
AM 'taɪdər, -z

titter
BR 'tɪt|ə(r), -əz, -(ə)rɪŋ,
-əd
AM 'tɪdər, -z, -ɪŋ, -d

titterer
BR 'tɪt(ə)rə(r), -z
AM 'tɪdərər, -z

titteringly
BR ˌtɪt(ə)rɪŋli
AM 'tɪdərɪŋli

tittivate
BR 'tɪtɪveɪt, -s, -ɪŋ, -ɪd
AM 'tɪdəˌveɪt, -ts, -dɪŋ,
-dɪd

tittle
BR 'tɪtl̩, -z
AM 'tɪdəl, -z

tittlebat
BR 'tɪtlbat, -s
AM 'tɪdl̩ˌbæt, -s

tittle-tattle
BR 'tɪtl̩ˌtatl
AM 'tɪdəlˌtædəl

tittup
BR 'tɪtəp, -s, -ɪŋ, -t
AM 'tɪdəp, -s, -ɪŋ, -t

tittuppy
BR 'tɪtəpi
AM 'tɪdəpi

titty
BR 'tɪt|i, -ɪz
AM 'tɪdi, -z

titubation
BR ˌtɪtjʊ'beɪʃn̩,
ˌtɪtʃʊ'beɪʃn̩
AM ˌtɪtʃə'beɪʃən

titular
BR 'tɪtʃʊ̆lə(r),
'tɪtjʊ̆lə(r)
AM 'tɪtʃələr

titularly
BR ˈtɪtʃʊləli, ˈtɪtjʊləli
AM ˈtɪtʃələrli

Titus
BR ˈtaɪtəs
AM ˈtaɪdəs

Tiverton
BR ˈtɪvət(ə)n
AM ˈtɪvərt(ə)n

Tivoli
BR ˈtɪvəli
AM ˈtɪvəli

tiz
BR tɪz
AM tɪz

Tizard
BR ˈtɪzɑːd, ˈtɪzəd
AM ˈtɪzərd

Tizer®
BR ˈtaɪzə(r)
AM ˈtaɪzər

tizz
BR tɪz
AM tɪz

tizzy
BR ˈtɪz|i, -ɪz
AM ˈtɪzi, -z

T-joint
BR ˈtiːdʒɔɪnt, -s
AM ˈtiˌdʒɔɪnt, -s

T-junction
BR ˈtiːˌdʒʌŋ(k)ʃn, -z
AM ˈtiˌdʒəŋ(k)ʃən, -z

TKO
BR ˌtiːˈkeɪˈəʊ
AM ˌtiˈkeɪˈoʊ

Tlaxcala
BR tlɑːsˈkɑːlə(r)
AM tlɑˈskɑlə

Tlemcen
BR tlɛmˈsɛn
AM tlɛmˈsɛn

Tlingit
BR ˈtlɪŋgɪt, ˈtlɪŋkɪt, ˈklɪŋkɪt, -s
AM ˈtlɪn(g)ɪt, -s

tmesis
BR ˈtmiːsɪs, təˈmiːsɪs
AM təˈmisɪs

TNT
BR ˌtiːɛnˈtiː
AM ˌtiˌɛnˈti

to[1]
adverb
BR tuː
AM tu

to[2]
preposition, strong form
BR tuː
AM tu

to[3]
preposition, weak form
BR tʊ
AM tə

toad
BR təʊd, -z
AM toʊd, -z

toadfish
BR ˈtəʊdfɪʃ, -ɪz
AM ˈtoʊdˌfɪʃ, -ɪz

toadflax
BR ˈtəʊdflaks
AM ˈtoʊdˌflæks

toad-in-the-hole
BR ˌtəʊdɪnðəˈhəʊl
AM ˌtoʊdənðəˈhoʊl

toadish
BR ˈtəʊdɪʃ
AM ˈtoʊdɪʃ

toadlet
BR ˈtəʊdlɪt, -s
AM ˈtoʊdlət, -s

toadlike
BR ˈtəʊdlʌɪk
AM ˈtoʊdˌlaɪk

toadstone
BR ˈtəʊdstəʊn, -z
AM ˈtoʊdˌstoʊn, -z

toadstool
BR ˈtəʊdstuːl, -z
AM ˈtoʊdˌstul, -z

toady
BR ˈtəʊd|i, -ɪz, -ɪŋ, -ɪd
AM ˈtoʊdi, -z, -ɪŋ, -d

toadyish
BR ˈtəʊdɪɪʃ
AM ˈtoʊdiɪʃ

toadyism
BR ˈtəʊdɪɪz(ə)m
AM ˈtoʊdiˌɪzəm

to-and-fro
BR ˌtuːən(d)ˈfrəʊ, ˌtuːŋ(d)ˈfrəʊ
AM ˌtuənˈfroʊ

toast
BR təʊst, -s, -ɪŋ, -ɪd
AM toʊst, -s, -ɪŋ, -əd

toaster
BR ˈtəʊstə(r), -z
AM ˈtoʊstər, -z

toastie
BR ˈtəʊst|i, -ɪz
AM ˈtoʊsti, -z

toastmaster
BR ˈtəʊs(t)ˌmɑːstə(r), ˈtəʊs(t)ˌmɑstə(r), -z
AM ˈtoʊs(t)ˌmæstər, -z

toastmistress
BR ˈtəʊs(t)ˌmɪstrɪs, -ɪz
AM ˈtoʊs(t)ˌmɪstrɪs, -ɪz

toastrack
BR ˈtəʊstrak, -s
AM ˈtoʊs(t)ˌræk, -s

toasty
BR ˈtəʊsti
AM ˈtoʊsti

tobacco
BR təˈbakəʊ, -z
AM təˈbækoʊ, -z

tobacconist
BR təˈbakənɪst, təˈbaknɪst, -s
AM təˈbækənəst, -s

Tobagan
BR təˈbeɪg(ə)n, -z
AM təˈbeɪgən, -z

Tobago
BR təˈbeɪgəʊ
AM təˈbeɪgoʊ

Tobagonian
BR ˌtəʊbəˈgəʊnɪən, -z
AM ˌtoʊbəˈgounɪən, -z

Tobermory
BR ˌtəʊbəʊˈmɔːri
AM ˌtoʊbəˈmɔri

Tobias
BR təˈbʌɪəs
AM təˈbaɪəs

Tobin
BR ˈtəʊbɪn
AM ˈtoʊbən

Tobit
BR ˈtəʊbɪt
AM ˈtoʊbət

Toblerone®
BR ˈtəʊbləʊˈrəʊn, ˈtəʊblərəʊn
AM ˈtoʊbləˈroʊn

toboggan
BR təˈbɒg|(ə)n, -(ə)nz, -ənɪŋ\-ŋɪŋ, -(ə)nd
AM təˈbagən, -z, -ɪŋ, -d

tobogganer
BR təˈbɒgənə(r), təˈbɒgnə(r), -z
AM təˈbagənər, -z

tobogganist
BR təˈbɒgənɪst, təˈbɒgnɪst, -s
AM təˈbagənəst, -s

Tobruk
BR təˈbrʊk
AM təˈbrʊk

toby
BR ˈtəʊb|i, -ɪz
AM ˈtoʊbi, -z

toccata
BR təˈkɑːtə(r), -z
AM təˈkɑdə, -z

Toc H
BR ˌtɒk ˈeɪtʃ
AM ˌtɑk ˈeɪtʃ

Tocharian
BR təˈkɛːrɪən, tɒˈkɛːrɪən, təˈkɑːrɪən, tɒˈkɑːrɪən, -z
AM toʊˈkɛrɪən, -z

tocher
BR ˈtɒxə(r), ˈtɒkə(r), -z
AM ˈtɑkər, -z

tocopherol
BR tɒˈkɒfərɒl, təˈkɒfərɒl, -z
AM təˈkɑfəˌrɔl, təˈkɑfəˌroʊl, -z

Tocqueville
BR ˈtɒkvɪl, ˈtəʊkvɪl

AM ˈtoʊkˌvɪl

tocsin
BR ˈtɒksɪn, -z
AM ˈtɑksən, -z

tod
BR tɒd
AM tɑd

today
BR təˈdeɪ
AM təˈdeɪ

Todd
BR tɒd
AM tɑd

toddle
BR ˈtɒd|l, -lz, -lɪŋ\-lɪŋ, -ld
AM ˈtɑd|əl, -əlz, -(ə)lɪŋ, -əld

toddler
BR ˈtɒdlə(r), ˈtɒdlə(r), -z
AM ˈtɑd(ə)lər, ˈtɑdlər, -z

toddlerhood
BR ˈtɒdləhʊd, ˈtɒdləhʊd
AM ˈtɑdlər,(h)ʊd

toddy
BR ˈtɒdi
AM ˈtɑdi

todger
BR ˈtɒdʒə(r), -z
AM ˈtɑdʒər, -z

Todhunter
BR ˈtɒdˌhʌntə(r)
AM ˈtɑd,(h)ən(t)ər

Todmorden
BR ˈtɒdməd(ə)n
AM ˈtɑd,mɔrdən

to-do
BR təˈduː
AM təˈdu

tody
BR ˈtəʊd|i, -ɪz
AM ˈtoʊdi, -z

toe
BR təʊ, -z, -ɪŋ, -d
AM toʊ, -z, -ɪŋ, -d

toea
BR ˈtɔɪə(r), -z
AM ˈtɔɪə, -z

toecap
BR ˈtəʊkap, -s
AM ˈtoʊˌkæp, -s

toehold
BR ˈtəʊhəʊld, -z
AM ˈtoʊˌhoʊld, -z

toeless
BR ˈtəʊləs
AM ˈtoʊləs

toenail
BR ˈtəʊneɪl, -z
AM ˈtoʊˌneɪl, -z

toey
BR ˈtəʊi
AM ˈtoʊi

toff
BR tɒf, -s
AM tɑf, -s

toffee
BR 'tɒf/i, -ɪz
AM 'tɔfi, 'tɑfi, -z

toffeeish
BR 'tɒfiɪʃ
AM 'tɔfiɪʃ, 'tɑfiɪʃ

toffee-nosed
BR 'tɒfɪnəʊzd, ˌtɒf'nəʊzd
AM 'tɔfiˌnoʊzd, 'tɑfiˌnoʊzd

toft
BR tɒft, -s
AM tɔft, tɑft, -s

tofu
BR 'təʊfuː
AM ˌtoʊ'fu

tog
BR tɒg, -z, -ɪŋ, -d
AM tɑg, -z, -ɪŋ, -d

toga
BR 'təʊgə(r), -z, -d
AM 'toʊgə, -z, -d

together
BR tə'gɛðə(r)
AM tə'gɛðər

togetherness
BR tə'gɛðənəs
AM tə'gɛðərnəs

toggery
BR 'tɒg(ə)ri
AM 'tagəri

toggle
BR 'tɒgl, -z
AM 'tagəl, -z

Togo
BR 'təʊgəʊ
AM 'toʊgoʊ

Togolese
BR ˌtəʊgə'liːz
AM ˌtoʊgoʊ'liz, ˌtoʊgə'liz

toil
BR tɔɪl, -z, -ɪŋ, -d
AM tɔɪl, -z, -ɪŋ, -d

toile
BR twɑːl
AM twɑl

toiler
BR 'tɔɪlə(r), -z
AM 'tɔɪlər, -z

toilet
BR 'tɔɪlɪt, -s
AM 'tɔɪlɪt, -s

toiletry
BR 'tɔɪlɪtr/i, -ɪz
AM 'tɔɪlətri, -z

toilette
BR twɑː'lɛt, -s
AM twɑ'lɛt, -s

toilsome
BR 'tɔɪls(ə)m
AM 'tɔɪlsəm

toilsomely
BR 'tɔɪls(ə)mli
AM 'tɔɪlsəmli

toilsomeness
BR 'tɔɪls(ə)mnəs
AM 'tɔɪlsəmnəs

toilworn
BR 'tɔɪlwɔːn
AM 'tɔɪlˌwɔ(ə)rn

toing and froing
BR ˌtuːɪŋ (ə)n(d) 'frəʊɪŋ, -z
AM ˌtuɪŋ ən 'froʊɪŋ, -z

toings and froings
BR ˌtuːɪŋz (ə)n(d) 'frəʊɪŋz
AM ˌtuɪŋz ən 'froʊɪŋz

Tojo
BR 'təʊdʒəʊ
AM 'toʊˌdʒoʊ

tokamak
BR 'təʊkəmak, -s
AM 'toʊkəˌmæk, -s

tokay
BR tə(ʊ)'keɪ, 'təʊkeɪ, tɒ'keɪ, 'tɒkeɪ, -z
AM toʊ'keɪ, -z

toke
BR təʊk
AM toʊk

Tokelau
BR 'təʊkəlaʊ, 'tɒkəlaʊ
AM 'toʊkəˌlaʊ

token
BR 'təʊk(ə)n, -z
AM 'toʊkən, -z

tokenism
BR 'təʊkənɪz(ə)m, 'təʊkɪnɪz(ə)m
AM 'toʊkəˌnɪzəm

tokenist
BR 'təʊkənɪst, 'təʊkɪnɪst
AM 'toʊkənəst

tokenistic
BR ˌtəʊkə'nɪstɪk, ˌtəʊkn'ɪstɪk
AM ˌtoʊkə'nɪstɪk

Tokharian
BR tə'kɑːrɪən, tʊ'kɑːrɪən, tə'kɛːrɪən, tʊ'kɛːrɪən
AM toʊ'kɛrɪən

Toklas
BR 'təʊkləs
AM 'toʊkləs

Tok Pisin
BR ˌtɒk 'pɪsɪn
AM ˌtak 'pɪsɪn

Tokugawa
BR ˌtəʊkʊ'gɑːwə(r)
AM ˌtoʊku'gɑwə

Tokyo
BR 'təʊkɪəʊ
AM 'toʊkiˌoʊ

tola
BR 'təʊlə(r), -z

AM 'təʊlə, -z

tolbooth
BR 'təʊlbuː|ð, 'tɒlbuː|ð, 'təʊlbuː|θ, 'tɒlbuː|θ, -ðz\-θs
AM 'toʊl,bu|θ, -θs\-ðz

tolbutamide
BR tɒl'bjuːtəmʌɪd
AM tal'bjudəˌmaɪd

told
BR təʊld
AM toʊld

Toledo¹
place in Spain
BR tə'leɪdəʊ
AM tə'leɪdoʊ

Toledo²
place in US
BR tə'liːdəʊ
AM tə'lidoʊ

tolerability
BR ˌtɒl(ə)rə'bɪlɪti
AM ˌtal(ə)rə'bɪlɪdi

tolerable
BR 'tɒl(ə)rəbl
AM 'tal(ə)rəbəl, 'talərbəl

tolerableness
BR 'tɒl(ə)rəblnəs
AM 'tal(ə)rəbəlnəs, 'talərbəlnəs

tolerably
BR 'tɒl(ə)rəbli
AM 'tal(ə)rəbli, 'talərbli

tolerance
BR 'tɒl(ə)rəns, 'tɒl(ə)rṇs
AM 'tal(ə)rəns

tolerant
BR 'tɒl(ə)rənt, 'tɒl(ə)rṇt
AM 'tal(ə)rənt

tolerantly
BR 'tɒl(ə)rəntli, 'tɒl(ə)rṇtli
AM 'tal(ə)rən(t)li

tolerate
BR 'tɒləreɪt, -s, -ɪŋ, -ɪd
AM 'taləˌreɪ|t, -ts, -dɪŋ, -dɪd

toleration
BR ˌtɒlə'reɪʃn
AM ˌtalə'reɪʃən

tolerator
BR 'tɒləreɪtə(r), -z
AM 'taləˌreɪdər, -z

Tolima
BR tɒ'liːmə(r)
AM tə'limə

Tolkien
BR 'tɒlkiːn
AM 'toʊlˌkin

toll
BR təʊl, -z, -ɪŋ, -d
AM toʊl, -z, -ɪŋ, -d

tollbooth
BR 'təʊlbuː|ð, 'tɒlbuː|ð, 'təʊlbuː|θ, 'tɒlbuː|θ, -ðz\-θs
AM 'toʊl,bu|θ, -θs\-ðz

tollbridge
BR 'təʊlbrɪdʒ, -ɪz
AM 'toʊl,brɪdʒ, -ɪz

Tolley
BR 'tɒli
AM 'tali

tollgate
BR 'təʊlgeɪt, -s
AM 'toʊl,geɪt, -s

tollhouse
BR 'təʊlhaʊ|s, -zɪz
AM 'toʊl,(h)aʊ|s, -zəz

tollroad
BR 'təʊlrəʊd, -z
AM 'toʊl,roʊd, -z

Tollund
BR 'tɒlənd
AM 'talənd

tollway
BR 'təʊlweɪ, -z
AM 'toʊl,weɪ, -z

Tolpuddle
BR 'tɒl,pʌdl
AM 'tal,pədəl

Tolstoy
BR 'tɒlstɔɪ
AM 'toʊlz,tɔɪ

Toltec
BR 'tɒltɛk, -s
AM 'tɒl,tɛk, 'tal,tɛk, -s

Toltecan
BR tɒl'tɛk(ə)n, -z
AM tɒl'tɛkən, tal'tɛkən, -z

tolu
BR tɒ'luː, 'təʊluː
AM tə'lu, toʊ'lu

toluene
BR 'tɒljʊiːn
AM 'talju,in

toluic
BR tɒ'ljuːɪk, tə'ljuːɪk
AM tə'luɪk, 'taljəwɪk

toluol
BR 'tɒljʊɒl
AM 'taljəwɔl, 'taljəwal

tom
BR tɒm, -z
AM tam, -z

tomahawk
BR 'tɒməhɔːk, -s
AM 'tamə,hɔk, 'tamə,hak, -s

tomalley
BR 'tɒmal/i, -ɪz
AM 'tam,æli, -z

tomatillo
BR ˌtɒmə'tɪl(j)əʊ, -z
AM ˌtoʊmə'ti(j)oʊ, -z

tomato
BR tə'mɑːtəʊ, -z
AM tə'meɪdoʊ, -z

tomatoey
BR təˈmɑːtəʊi
AM təˈmeɪdoʊi

tomb
BR tuːm, -z
AM tum, -z

tombac
BR ˈtɒmbak
AM ˈtɑmˌbæk

tombak
BR ˈtɒmbak
AM ˈtɑmˌbæk

Tombaugh
BR ˈtɒmbɔː(r)
AM ˈtɑmbɔ, ˈtɑmbɑ

tombola
BR tɒmˈbəʊlə(r)
AM ˈtɑmbələ

tombolo
BR tɒmˈbəʊləʊ, -z
AM ˈtɑmboʊloʊ, -z

Tombouctou
BR ˌtɒmbʌkˈtuː
AM ˌtɑmbəkˈtu

tomboy
BR ˈtɒmbɔɪ, -z
AM ˈtɑmˌbɔɪ, -z

tomboyish
BR ˈtɒmbɔɪʃ
AM ˈtɑmˌbɔɪʃ

tomboyishness
BR ˈtɒmbɔɪʃnɪs
AM ˈtɑmbɔɪʃnɪs

Tombs
BR tuːmz
AM tumz

tombstone
BR ˈtuːmstəʊn, -z
AM ˈtumˌstoʊn, -z

tomcat
BR ˈtɒmkat, -s
AM ˈtɑmˌkæt, -s

tome
BR təʊm, -z
AM toʊm, -z

tomenta
BR tə(ʊ)ˈmɛntə(r)
AM toʊˈmɛn(t)ə

tomentose
BR təˈmɛntəʊs, ˈtəʊm(ə)ntəʊs
AM toʊˈmɛntoʊs, ˈtoʊmənˌtoʊs

tomentous
BR təˈmɛntəs, ˈtəʊm(ə)ntəs
AM toʊˈmɛn(t)əs, ˈtoʊmən(t)əs

tomentum
BR tə(ʊ)ˈmɛntəm
AM toʊˈmɛn(t)əm

tomfool
BR ˌtɒmˈfuːl, -z
AM ˈtɑmˈful, -z

tomfoolery
BR (ˌ)tɒmˈfuːl(ə)ri
AM tɑmˈful(ə)ri

Tomintoul
BR ˌtɒmɪnˈtuːl, ˌtɒmɪnˈtaʊl
AM ˌtɑmənˈtaʊl, ˌtɑmənˈtul

Tomlin
BR ˈtɒmlɪn
AM ˈtɑmlən

Tomlinson
BR ˈtɒmlɪns(ə)n
AM ˈtɑmlənsən

tommy
BR ˈtɒmli, -ɪz
AM ˈtɑmi, -z

tommyrot
BR ˈtɒmɪrɒt, ˌtɒmɪˈrɒt
AM ˈtɑmiˌrɑt

tomogram
BR ˈtəʊməgram, ˈtɒməgram, -z
AM ˈtoʊməˌgræm, -z

tomograph
BR ˈtəʊməgrɑːf, ˈtəʊməgraf, ˈtɒməgrɑːf, ˈtɒməgraf, -s
AM ˈtoʊməˌgræf, -s

tomographic
BR ˌtəʊməˈgrafɪk, ˌtɒməˈgrafɪk
AM ˌtoʊməˈgræfɪk

tomography
BR tə(ʊ)ˈmɒgrəfi
AM toʊˈmɑgrəfi

Tomor
BR ˈtəʊmə(r)
AM ˈtoʊmər

tomorrow
BR təˈmɒrəʊ
AM təˈmɑroʊ, təˈmɔroʊ

tompion
BR ˈtɒmpɪən, -z
AM ˈtɑmpɪən, -z

Tompkins
BR ˈtɒm(p)kɪnz
AM ˈtɑm(p)kənz

Tompkinson
BR ˈtɒm(p)kɪns(ə)n
AM ˈtɑm(p)kənsən

tompot
BR ˈtɒmpɒt, -s
AM ˈtɑmˌpɑt, -s

Toms
BR tɒmz
AM tɑmz

Tomsk
BR tɒmsk
AM tɑmsk

tomtit
BR ˈtɒmtɪt, ˌtɒmˈtɪt, -s
AM ˈtɑmˈtɪt, -s

tomtom
BR ˈtɒmtɒm, -z
AM ˈtɑmˌtɑm, -z

ton¹
fashion
BR tɔ̃, -z

ton²
weight
BR tʌn, -z
AM tən, -z

tonal
BR ˈtəʊnl
AM ˈtoʊnəl

tonality
BR tə(ʊ)ˈnalɪt|i, -ɪz
AM toʊˈnælədi, təˈnælədi, -z

tonally
BR ˈtəʊnli, ˈtəʊnəli
AM ˈtoʊnəli

Tonbridge
BR ˈtʌnbrɪdʒ
AM ˈtɑnˌbrɪdʒ

tondi
BR ˈtɒndi
AM ˈtɑndi

tondo
BR ˈtɒndəʊ
AM ˈtɑndoʊ

tone
BR təʊn, -z, -ɪŋ, -d
AM toʊn, -z, -ɪŋ, -d

tonearm
BR ˈtəʊnɑːm, -z
AM ˈtoʊnˌɑrm, -z

toneburst
BR ˈtəʊnbɜːst, -s
AM ˈtoʊnˌbɜrst, -s

tone-deaf
BR ˌtəʊnˈdɛf
AM ˈtoʊnˌdɛf

toneless
BR ˈtəʊnləs
AM ˈtoʊnləs

tonelessly
BR ˈtəʊnləsli
AM ˈtoʊnləsli

tonelessness
BR ˈtəʊnləsnəs
AM ˈtoʊnləsnəs

toneme
BR ˈtəʊniːm, -z
AM ˈtoʊˌnim, -z

tonemic
BR tə(ʊ)ˈniːmɪk, -s
AM toʊˈnimɪk, -s

tonemically
BR tə(ʊ)ˈniːmɪkli
AM toʊˈnimək(ə)li

tonepad
BR ˈtəʊnpad, -z
AM ˈtoʊnˌpæd, -z

toner
BR ˈtəʊnə(r), -z
AM ˈtoʊnər, -z

tone-row
BR ˈtəʊnrəʊ, -z
AM ˈtoʊnˌroʊ, -z

tonetic
BR tə(ʊ)ˈnɛtɪk, -s
AM toʊˈnɛdɪk, -s

tonetically
BR tə(ʊ)ˈnɛtɪkli
AM toʊˈnɛdək(ə)li

tong
BR tɒŋ, -z
AM tɔŋ, tɑŋ, -z

tonga
BR ˈtɒŋ(g)ə(r), -z
AM ˈtɑŋgə, -z

Tongan
BR ˈtɒŋ(g)ən, -z
AM ˈtɑŋgən, -z

Tongariro
BR ˌtɒŋ(g)əˈriːrəʊ
AM ˌtɑŋgəˈrɪroʊ

Tonge¹
placename
BR tɒŋ
AM tɔŋ, tɑŋ

Tonge²
surname
BR tɒŋ, tʌn, tɒn(d)ʒ
AM tən, tɔŋ, tɑŋ

tongkang
BR tɒŋˈkaŋ, -z
AM ˌtɔŋˈkæŋ, ˌtɑŋˈkæŋ, -z

tongue
BR tʌŋ, -z, -ɪŋ, -d
AM tən, -z, -ɪŋ, -d

tongue-and-groove
BR ˌtʌŋ(ə)n(d)ˈgruːv
AM ˈtəŋənˈgruv

tongue-in-cheek
BR ˌtʌŋɪnˈtʃiːk
AM ˌtəŋənˈtʃik

tongue-lashing
BR ˈtʌŋˌlaʃɪŋ, -z
AM ˈtəŋˌlæʃɪŋ, -z

tongueless
BR ˈtʌŋləs
AM ˈtəŋləs

tongue-tie
BR ˈtʌŋtaɪ, -z, -d
AM ˈtəŋˌtaɪ, -z, -d

tonguing
BR ˈtʌŋɪŋ
AM ˈtəŋɪŋ

Toni
BR ˈtəʊni
AM ˈtoʊni

Tonia
BR ˈtəʊnɪə(r)
AM ˈtɑnjə

tonic
BR ˈtɒnɪk, -s
AM ˈtɑnɪk, -s

tonically
BR ˈtɒnɪkli
AM ˈtɑnək(ə)li

tonicity
BR tə(ʊ)ˈnɪsɪt|i, -ɪz
AM toʊˈnɪsɪdi, -z

tonic sol-fa
BR ˌtɒnɪk ˌsɒlˈfɑː(r), + ˈsɒlfɑː(r)

AM ˌtænɪk ˌsɒ(l)ˈfɑ

tonify
BR ˈtəʊnɪfaɪ, -z, -ɪŋ, -d
AM ˈtoʊnəfaɪ, -z, -ɪŋ, -d

tonight
BR təˈnaɪt
AM təˈnaɪt

tonish
BR ˈtəʊnɪʃ
AM ˈtoʊnɪʃ

Tonkin[1]
surname
BR ˈtɒŋkɪn
AM ˈtɒŋkən

Tonkin[2]
Vietnam
BR ˌtɒnˈkɪn, ˌtɒŋˈkɪn
AM ˌtɑnˈkɪn, ˌtɑŋˈkɪn

Tonks
BR tɒŋks
AM tɒŋks, tɑŋks

ton-mile
BR tʌnmaɪl,
ˌtʌnˈmaɪl, -z
AM ˈtʌnˌmaɪl, -z

tonnage
BR ˈtʌnˌɪdʒ, -ɪdʒɪz
AM ˈtʌnɪdʒ, -ɪz

tonne
BR tʌn, -z
AM tʌn, -z

tonneau
BR ˈtɒnəʊ, -z
AM təˈnoʊ, ˈtɑnoʊ, -z

tonneaux
BR ˈtɒnəʊ(z)
AM təˈnoʊ, ˈtɑnoʊ

tonometer
BR tə(ʊ)ˈnɒmɪtə(r), -z
AM toʊˈnɑmədər, -z

tonsil
BR ˈtɒnsl, -z
AM ˈtɑnsəl, -z

tonsilitis
BR ˌtɒnsɪˈlaɪtɪs,
ˌtɒnslˈaɪtɪs
AM ˌtɑnsəˈlaɪdɪs

tonsillar
BR ˈtɒnsɪlə(r),
ˈtɒnslə(r)
AM ˈtɑnsələr

tonsillectomy
BR ˌtɒnsɪˈlɛktəmi,
ˌtɒnslˈɛktəmi, -ɪz
AM ˌtɑnsəˈlɛktəmi, -z

tonsillitis
BR ˌtɒnsɪˈlaɪtɪs,
ˌtɒnslˈaɪtɪs
AM ˌtɑnsəˈlaɪdɪs

tonsorial
BR tɒnˈsɔːrɪəl
AM tɑnˈsɔriəl

tonsure
BR ˈtɒnʃə(r),
ˈtɒnsj(ʊ)ə(r), -d
AM ˈtɑn(t)ʃər, -z, -d

tontine
BR ˈtɒntiːn, ˈtɒntʌɪn,
tɒnˈtiːn
AM ˈtɑnˌtin

Tonto
BR ˈtɒntəʊ
AM ˈtɒn(t)oʊ, ˈtɑn(t)oʊ

Tonton Macoute
BR ˌtɒntɒn məˈkuːt, -s
AM ˌtɒnˌtɒn məˈkut,
ˌtɑnˌtɑn məˈkut, -s

ton-up
BR ˈtʌnʌp, -s
AM ˈtənəp, -s

tonus
BR ˈtəʊnəs
AM ˈtoʊnəs

tony
BR ˈtəʊn|i, -ɪz
AM ˈtoʊni, -ɪz

Tonypandy
BR ˌtɒnɪˈpandi
AM ˌtɒniˈpændi,
ˌtɑniˈpændi

Tonyrefail
BR ˌtɒnɪˈrɛvʌɪl
AM ˌtɒniˈrɛvaɪl,
ˌtɑniˈrevaɪl
WE ˌtɒnʌˈrevaɪl

too
BR tuː
AM tu

toodle-oo
BR ˌtuːdlˈuː
AM ˌtudəlˈu

toodle-pip
BR ˌtuːdlˈpɪp
AM ˌtudəlˈpɪp

Toogood
BR ˈtuːgʊd
AM ˈtuˌgʊd

took
BR tʊk
AM tʊk

tool
BR tuːl, -z, -ɪŋ, -d
AM tul, -z, -ɪŋ, -d

toolbox
BR ˈtuːlbɒks, -ɪz
AM ˈtulˌbɑks, -əz

toolchest
BR ˈtuːltʃɛst, -s
AM ˈtulˌtʃɛst, -s

tooler
BR ˈtuːlə(r), -z
AM ˈtulər, -z

toolkit
BR ˈtuːlkɪt, -s
AM ˈtulˌkɪt, -s

toolmaker
BR ˈtuːlˌmeɪkə(r), -z
AM ˈtulˌmeɪkər, -z

toolmaking
BR ˈtuːlˌmeɪkɪŋ
AM ˈtulˌmeɪkɪŋ

toolroom
BR ˈtuːlruːm, ˈtuːlrʊm,
-z
AM ˈtulˌrum, ˈtulˌrʊm,
-z

toolshed
BR ˈtuːlʃɛd, -z
AM ˈtulˌʃɛd, -z

Toombs
BR tuːmz
AM tumz

toot
BR tuːt, -s, -ɪŋ, -ɪd
AM tuːt, -ts, -dɪŋ, -dəd

Tootal
BR ˈtuːtl
AM ˈtudl

tooter
BR ˈtuːtə(r), -z
AM ˈtudər, -z

tooth
BR tuːθ, -s, -ɪŋ, -t
AM tuθ, -s, -ɪŋ, -t

toothache
BR ˈtuːθeɪk, -s
AM ˈtuθˌeɪk, -s

tooth-billed
BR ˌtuːθˈbɪld
AM ˈtuθˌbɪld

toothbrush
BR ˈtuːθbrʌʃ, -ɪz
AM ˈtuθˌbrəʃ, -əz

toothcomb
BR ˈtuːθkəʊm, -z
AM ˈtuθˌkoʊm, -z

tooth-glass
BR ˈtuːθglɑːs, ˈtuːθglas,
-ɪz
AM ˈtuθˌglæs, -əz

toothily
BR ˈtuːθɪli
AM ˈtuθəli

toothiness
BR ˈtuːθɪnɪs
AM ˈtuθinɪs

toothless
BR ˈtuːθləs
AM ˈtuθləs

toothlike
BR ˈtuːθlʌɪk
AM ˈtuθˌlaɪk

toothpaste
BR ˈtuːθpeɪst
AM ˈtuθˌpeɪst

toothpick
BR ˈtuːθpɪk, -s
AM ˈtuθˌpɪk, -s

toothsome
BR ˈtuːθs(ə)m
AM ˈtuθsəm

toothsomely
BR ˈtuːθs(ə)mli
AM ˈtuθsəmli

toothsomeness
BR ˈtuːθs(ə)mnəs
AM ˈtuθsəmnəs

toothwort
BR tuːˈθəwɜːt, -s
AM ˈtuθwərt,
ˈtuθwɔ(ə)rt, -s

toothy
BR ˈtuːθ|i, -ɪə(r), -ɪɪst
AM ˈtuθi, -ər, -ɪst

Tooting
BR ˈtuːtɪŋ
AM ˈtudɪŋ

tootle
BR ˈtuːt|l, -lz, -lɪŋ\-lɪŋ,
-ld
AM ˈtudəl, -z, -ɪŋ, -d

tootler
BR ˈtuːtlə(r), ˈtuːtlə(r),
-z
AM ˈtudlər, -z

too-too
BR ˈtuːtuː, ˌtuːˈtuː
AM ˈtuˌtu

tootsie
BR ˈtʊts|i, -ɪz
AM ˈtʊtsi, -z

tootsy
BR ˈtʊts|i, -ɪz
AM ˈtʊtsi, -z

Toowoomba
BR tə'wʊmbə(r)
AM təˈwʊmbə

top
BR tɒp, -s, -ɪŋ, -t
AM tɑp, -s, -ɪŋ, -t

topaz
BR ˈtəʊpaz, -ɪz
AM ˈtoʊˌpæz, -əz

topazolite
BR təˈpazəlʌɪt
AM toʊˈpæzəˌlaɪt

topboot
BR ˈtɒpbuːt, -s
AM ˈtɑpˌbut, -s

topcoat
BR ˈtɒpkəʊt, -s
AM ˈtɑpˌkoʊt, -s

top-dress
verb
BR ˌtɒpˈdrɛs, -ɪz, -ɪŋ, -t
AM ˈtɑpˌdrɛs, -əz, -ɪŋ, -t

tope
BR təʊp, -s
AM toʊp, -s

topee
BR ˈtəʊpiː, -z
AM ˈtoʊpi, -z

Topeka
BR təˈpiːkə(r)
AM təˈpikə

toper
BR ˈtəʊpə(r), -z
AM ˈtoʊpər, -z

topgallant
BR ˈtɒpˌgalənt,
ˈtɒpˌgalnt, təˈgalənt,
təˈgalnt, -s
AM təpˈgælənt,
ˈtɑpˌgælənt,
təˈgælənt, -s

Topham
BR 'tɒp(ə)m
AM 'tɑpəm

top-hamper
BR 'tɒp,hampə(r)
AM 'tɑp,(h)æmpər

top-hatted
BR 'tɒp,hatɪd
AM 'tɑp,'hædəd

top-heavily
BR 'tɒp,hɛvɪli
AM 'tɑp,(h)ɛvəli

top-heaviness
BR 'tɒp,hɛvɪnɪs
AM 'tɑp,(h)ɛvɪnɪs

top-heavy
BR 'tɒp,hɛvi
AM 'tɑp,(h)ɛvi

Tophet
BR 'təʊfɪt
AM 'toʊfət

tophi
BR 'təʊfaɪ
AM 'toʊ,faɪ

tophus
BR 'təʊfəs
AM 'toʊfəs

topi
BR 'təʊpiː, -z
AM 'toʊpi, -z

topiarian
BR ,təʊpɪˈɛːrɪən, -z
AM ,toʊpiˈɛrɪən, -z

topiarist
BR 'təʊpɪərɪst, -s
AM 'toʊpiərəst, -s

topiary
BR 'təʊpɪəri
AM 'toʊpiˌɛri

topic
BR 'tɒpɪk
AM 'tɑpɪk

topical
BR 'tɒpɪkl
AM 'tɑpəkəl

topicality
BR ,tɒpɪˈkalɪti
AM ,tɑpəˈkælədi

topicalization
BR ,tɒpɪklaɪˈzeɪʃn,
,tɒpɪkələˈzeɪʃn
AM ,tɑpəkələˈzeɪʃən,
,tɑpəkəˌlaɪˈzeɪʃən

topicalize
BR 'tɒpɪklaɪz,
'tɒpɪkəlaɪz, -ɪz, -ɪŋ, -d
AM 'tɑpəkəˌlaɪz, -ɪz, -ɪŋ, -d

topically
BR 'tɒpɪkli, 'tɒpɪk(ə)li
AM 'tɑpək(ə)li

topknot
BR 'tɒpnɒt, -s
AM 'tɑp,nɑt, -s

Toplady
BR 'tɒp,leɪdi
AM 'tɑp,leɪdi

topless
BR 'tɒpləs
AM 'tɑpləs

toplessness
BR 'tɒpləsnəs
AM 'tɑpləsnəs

toplofty
BR 'tɒp'lɒfti
AM 'tɑp,lɒfti, 'tɑp,lɑfti

topman
BR 'tɒpman
AM 'tɑp,mæn

topmast
BR 'tɒpmɑːst, 'tɒpmast, -s
AM 'tɑp,mæst, -s

topmen
BR 'tɒpmen
AM 'tɑp,men

topmost
BR 'tɒpməʊst
AM 'tɑp,moʊst

topnotch
BR ,tɒp'nɒtʃ
AM 'tɑp'nɑtʃ

top-notcher
BR ,tɒp'nɒtʃə(r), -z
AM 'tɑp'nɑtʃər, -z

topo
BR 'tɒpəʊ, -z
AM 'tɑpoʊ, -z

topographer
BR tə'pɒgrəfə(r), tɒ'pɒgrəfə(r), -z
AM tə'pɑgrəfər, -z

topographic
BR ,tɒpə'grafɪk
AM ,tɑpə'græfɪk

topographical
BR ,tɒpə'grafɪkl
AM ,tɑpə'græfəkəl

topographically
BR ,tɒpə'grafɪk(ə)li
AM ,tɑpə'græfək(ə)li

topography
BR tə'pɒgrəfi, tɒ'pɒgrəfi
AM tə'pɑgrəfi

topoi
BR 'tɒpɔɪ
AM 'toʊ,pɔɪ

topological
BR ,tɒpə'lɒdʒɪkl
AM ,tɑpə'lɑdʒəkəl

topologically
BR ,tɒpə'lɒdʒɪkli
AM ,tɑpə'lɑdʒək(ə)li

topologist
BR tə'pɒlədʒɪst, tɒ'pɒlədʒɪst, -s
AM tə'pɑlədʒəst, -s

topology
BR tə'pɒlədʒi, tɒ'pɒlədʒi
AM tə'pɑlədʒi

Topolsky
BR tə'pɒlski

AM tə'pɒlski, tə'pɑlski

toponym
BR 'tɒpənɪm, -z
AM 'tɑpə,nɪm, -z

toponymic
BR ,tɒpə'nɪmɪk
AM ,tɑpə'nɪmɪk

toponymy
BR tə'pɒnəmi, tɒ'pɒnəmi
AM tə'pɑnəmi

topos
BR 'tɒpɒs
AM 'toʊ,pɒus

topper
BR 'tɒpə(r), -z
AM 'tɑpər, -z

topping
BR 'tɒpɪŋ, -z
AM 'tɑpɪŋ, -z

topple
BR 'tɒpl|, -lz, -lɪŋ \-lɪŋ, -ld
AM 'tɑplə|l, -əlz, -(ə)lɪŋ, -əld

topsail
BR 'tɒpseɪl, 'tɒpsl, -z
AM 'tɑpsəl, 'tɑp,seɪl, -z

topside
BR 'tɒpsaɪd
AM 'tɑp,saɪd

topslice
BR 'tɒpslaɪs
AM 'tɑp,slaɪs

top-slicing
BR 'tɒp,slaɪsɪŋ
AM 'tɑp,slaɪsɪŋ

topsoil
BR 'tɒpsɔɪl
AM 'tɑp,sɔɪl

topspin
BR 'tɒpspɪn
AM 'tɑp,spin

topstitch
BR 'tɒpstɪtʃ, -ɪz, -ɪŋ, -t
AM 'tɑp,stɪtʃ, -ɪz, -ɪŋ, -t

Topsy
BR 'tɒpsi
AM 'tɑpsi

topsy-turvily
BR ,tɒpsi'tɜːvili
AM ,tɑpsi'tərvəli

topsy-turviness
BR ,tɒpsi'tɜːvɪnɪs
AM ,tɑpsi'tərvɪnɪs

topsy-turvy
BR ,tɒpsi'tɜːvi
AM ,tɑpsi'tərvi

top-up
BR 'tɒpʌp, -s
AM 'tɑpəp, -s

toque
BR təʊk, -s
AM toʊk, -s

toquilla
BR tə(ʊ)'kiː(j)ə(r), -z
AM toʊ'kiː(j)ə, -z

tor
BR tɔː(r), -z
AM tɔ(ə)r, -z

Torah
BR 'tɔːrə(r), 'təʊrə(r), ,tɔː'rɑː(r)
AM 'toʊrə, 'tɔrə

Torbay
BR ,tɔː'beɪ
AM ,tɔr'beɪ

torc
BR tɔːk, -s
AM tɔ(ə)rk, -s

torch
BR tɔːtʃ, -ɪz, -ɪŋ, -t
AM tɔrtʃ, -əz, -ɪŋ, -t

torch-bearer
BR 'tɔːtʃ,bɛːrə(r), -z
AM 'tɔrtʃ,bɛrər, -z

torchère
BR tɔː'ʃɛː(r), -z
AM tɔr'ʃɛ(ə)r, -z

torchlight
BR 'tɔːtʃlaɪt
AM 'tɔrtʃ,laɪt

torchlit
BR 'tɔːtʃlɪt
AM 'tɔrtʃlɪt

torchon
BR 'tɔːʃɒn, 'tɔːʃ(ə)n, -z
AM 'tɔrʃɑn, -z

Tordoff
BR 'tɔːdɒf
AM 'tɔrˌdɒf, 'tɔrˌdɑf

tore
BR tɔː(r)
AM tɔ(ə)r

toreador
BR 'tɒrɪədɔː(r), -z
AM 'tɔriəˌdɔ(ə)r, -z

torero
BR tə'rɛːrəʊ, -z
AM tə'rɛroʊ, -z

toreutic
BR tə'ruːtɪk, -s
AM tə'rudɪk, -s

Torfaen
BR tɔː'vʌɪn
AM ,tɔr'vaɪn

torgoch
BR 'tɔːgɒx, 'tɔːgɒk, -s
AM 'tɔrˌgɑk, 'tɔrˌgoʊk, -s
WE tɒr'gɒx

tori
BR 'tɔːraɪ
AM 'tɔ,raɪ, 'toʊ,raɪ

toric
BR 'tɒrɪk, 'tɔːrɪk
AM 'tɔrɪk

torii
BR 'tɔːriː
AM 'tɔri,i

Torino
BR tə'riːnəʊ, tɒ'riːnəʊ
AM tə'rinoʊ

torment¹
noun
BR 'tɔːmɛnt,
'tɔːm(ə)nt, -s
AM 'tɔːr,mɛnt, -s

torment²
verb
BR tɔː'mɛnt, -s, -ɪŋ, -ɪd
AM tɔːr'mɛn|t, -ts, -(t)ɪŋ,
-(t)əd

tormentedly
BR tɔː'mɛntɪdli
AM tɔr'mɛn(t)ədli

tormentil
BR 'tɔːm(ə)ntɪl, -z
AM 'tɔːrmən,tɪl, -z

tormentingly
BR tɔː'mɛntɪŋli
AM tɔr'mɛn(t)ɪŋli

tormentor
BR tɔː'mɛntə(r), -z
AM tɔr'mɛn(t)ər, -z

torn
BR tɔːn
AM tɔ(ə)rn

tornadic
BR tɔː'nadɪk
AM tɔr'neɪdɪk,
tɔr'nædɪk

tornado
BR tɔː'neɪdəʊ, -z
AM tɔr'neɪdoʊ, -z

Tornio
BR 'tɔːnɪəʊ
AM 'tɔːrnioʊ

toroid
BR 'tɔːrɔɪd, -z
AM 'tɔr,ɔɪr, -z

toroidal
BR tɔː'rɔɪdl
AM 'tɔr'ɔɪdəl

toroidally
BR tɔː'rɔɪdli,
tɔː'rɔɪdəli
AM 'tɔr'tɔr,tɔr(d(ə)li

Toronto
BR tə'rɒntəʊ
AM tə'ran(t)oʊ,
tə'rɒn(t)oʊ

torose
BR 'tɔːrəʊs, 'tɔːrəʊs
AM 'tɔr,oʊs, 'tɔr,oʊz

torpedo
BR tɔː'piːdəʊ, -z, -ɪŋ, -d
AM tɔr'pidoʊ, -z, -ɪŋ, -d

torpefy
BR 'tɔːpɪfʌɪ, -z, -ɪŋ, -d
AM 'tɔːrpə,faɪ, -z, -ɪŋ, -d

torpid
BR 'tɔːpɪd
AM 'tɔːrpəd

torpidity
BR tɔː'pɪdɪti
AM tɔr'pɪdɪdi

torpidly
BR 'tɔːpɪdli
AM 'tɔːrpədli

torpidness
BR 'tɔːpɪdnɪs
AM 'tɔːrpədnəs

torpor
BR 'tɔːpə(r)
AM 'tɔːrpər

torporific
BR ,tɔːpə'rɪfɪk
AM ,tɔːrpə'rɪfɪk

torquate
BR 'tɔːkweɪt
AM 'tɔr,kweɪt

Torquay
BR ,tɔː'kiː
AM tɔr'ki

torque
BR tɔːk, -s, -ɪŋ, -t
AM tɔ(ə)rk, -s, -ɪŋ, -t

Torquemada
BR ,tɔːkwɪ'mɑːdə(r)
AM ,tɔrkə'madə

torr
BR tɔː(r), -z
AM tɔ(ə)r, -z

Torrance
BR 'tɒrəns, 'tɒrn̩s
AM 'tɔrəns

torrefaction
BR ,tɒrɪ'fakʃn
AM ,tɔrə'fækʃən

torrefy
BR 'tɒrɪfʌɪ, -z, -ɪŋ, -d
AM 'tɔrə,faɪ, -z, -ɪŋ, -d

Torremolinos
BR ,tɒrɪmə'liːnɒs
AM ,tɔrəmə'linəs

torrent
BR 'tɒrənt, 'tɒrn̩t, -s
AM 'tɔrənt, -s

torrential
BR tə'rɛnʃl
AM tɔ'rɛn(t)ʃəl,
tə'rɛn(t)ʃəl

torrentially
BR tə'rɛnʃli,
tə'rɛnʃəli
AM tɔ'rɛn(t)ʃəli,
tə'rɛn(t)ʃəli

Torres
BR 'tɒrɪs, 'tɒrɪz, 'tɔːrɪs,
'tɔːrɪz
AM 'tɔrəs, 'tɔr,ɛz

Torrez
BR 'tɒrɪs, 'tɒrɪz, 'tɔːrɪs,
'tɔːrɪz
AM 'tɔr,ɛz, 'tɔrəs

Torricelli
BR ,tɒrɪ'tʃɛli
AM ,tɔrə'tʃɛli

torrid
BR 'tɒrɪd
AM 'tɔrəd

torridity
BR tə'rɪdɪti
AM tə'rɪdɪdi

torridly
BR 'tɒrɪdli

AM 'tɒrədli

torridness
BR 'tɒrɪdnɪs
AM 'tɔrɪdnɪs

torse
BR tɔːs, -ɪz
AM tɔ(ə)rs, -əz

torsel
BR 'tɔːsl, -z
AM 'tɔːrsəl, -z

Tórshavn
BR 'tɔːz,hɑːvn
AM 'tɔrs,hæv(ə)n
DAN 'tɔʌˈs,haw'n

torsion
BR 'tɔːʃn
AM 'tɔrʃən

torsional
BR 'tɔːʃn(ə)l,
'tɔːʃən(ə)l
AM 'tɔrʃ(ə)nəl

torsionally
BR 'tɔːʃn̩əli, 'tɔːʃn̩li,
'tɔːʃən̩li, 'tɔːʃ(ə)nəli
AM 'tɔrʃ(ə)nəli

torsionless
BR 'tɔːʃnləs
AM 'tɔːrʃənləs

torsk
BR tɔːsk, -s
AM tɔ(ə)rsk, -s

torso
BR 'tɔːsəʊ, -z
AM 'tɔrsoʊ, -z

tort
BR tɔːt, -s
AM tɔ(ə)rt, -s

torte
BR tɔːtə(r), tɔːt,
'tɔːtəz\tɔːts
AM tɔ(ə)rt, -s

Tortelier
BR tɔː'tɛlɪeɪ
AM tɔr,tɛli'eɪ
FR tɔrtəlje

tortellini
BR ,tɔːtɪ'liːni, ,tɔːtl'iːni
AM ,tɔrdl'ini

tortelloni
BR ,tɔːtɪ'ləʊni,
,tɔːtl'əʊni
AM ,tɔrdl'oʊni

torten
BR 'tɔːtn
AM 'tɔrtən

tortfeasor
BR 'tɔːtfiːzə(r),
,tɔːt'fiːzə(r), -z
AM 'tɔrt'fizər,
'tɔrt,fi,zɔ(ə)r, -z

torticollis
BR ,tɔːtɪ'kɒlɪs
AM ,tɔrdə'kaləs

tortilla
BR tɔː'tiːjə(r), -z
AM tɔr'ti(j)ə, -z

tortious
BR 'tɔːʃəs
AM 'tɔrʃəs

tortiously
BR 'tɔːʃəsli
AM 'tɔrʃəsli

tortoise
BR 'tɔːtəs, 'tɔːtɔɪs,
'tɔːtɔɪz, -ɪz
AM 'tɔrdəs, -əz

tortoise-like
BR 'tɔːtəslʌɪk,
'tɔːtɔɪslʌɪk,
'tɔːtɔɪzlʌɪk
AM 'tɔrdəs,laɪk

tortoiseshell
BR 'tɔːtəʃɛl
AM 'tɔrdə(s),ʃɛl

Tortola
BR tɔː'təʊlə(r)
AM 'tɔr'toʊlə

tortrices
BR 'tɔːtrɪsiːz
AM 'tɔrtrə,siz

tortrix
BR 'tɔːtrɪks, -ɪz
AM 'tɔrtrɪks, -ɪz

tortuosity
BR ,tɔːtʃʊ'ɒsɪti,
,tɔːtjʊ'ɒsɪti
AM ,tɔrtʃə'wasədi

tortuous
BR 'tɔːtʃʊəs, 'tɔːtjʊəs
AM 'tɔrtʃ(əw)əs

tortuously
BR 'tɔːtʃʊəsli,
'tɔːtjʊəsli
AM 'tɔrtʃ(əw)əsli

tortuousness
BR 'tɔːtʃʊəsnəs,
'tɔːtjʊəsnəs
AM 'tɔrtʃ(əw)əsnəs

torturable
BR 'tɔːtʃ(ə)rəbl
AM 'tɔrtʃ(ə)rəbəl

torture
BR 'tɔːtʃ|ə(r), -əz,
-(ə)rɪŋ, -əd
AM 'tɔrtʃ|ər, -ərz,
-(ə)rɪŋ, -ərd

torturer
BR 'tɔːtʃ(ə)rə(r), -z
AM 'tɔrtʃ(ə)rər, -z

torturous
BR 'tɔːtʃ(ə)rəs
AM 'tɔrtʃ(ə)rəs

torturously
BR 'tɔːtʃ(ə)rəsli
AM 'tɔrtʃ(ə)rəsli

torula
BR 'tɒruːlə(r),
'tɒrjʊlə(r)
AM 'tɔr(j)ələ

torulae
BR 'tɒruːliː, 'tɒrjʊliː
AM 'tɔr(j)əli,
'tɔr(j)ə,laɪ

torus
BR ˈtɔːrəs, -ɪz
AM ˈtɔrəs, -əz

Torvill
BR ˈtɔːvɪl
AM ˈtɔrˌvɪl

Tory
BR ˈtɔːr|i, -ɪz
AM ˈtɔri, -z

Toryism
BR ˈtɔːrɪɪz(ə)m
AM ˈtɔriˌɪzəm

Toscana
BR tɒˈskaːnə(r)
AM tɔˈskanə, taˈskanə

Toscanini
BR ˌtɒskəˈniːni
AM ˌtɔskəˈnini, ˌtaskəˈnini

tosh
BR tɒʃ
AM taʃ

Toshack
BR ˈtɒʃak
AM ˈtɔˌʃæk, ˈtaˌʃæk

Tosk
BR tɒsk, -s
AM task, -s

toss
BR tɒs, -ɪz, -ɪŋ, -t
AM tas, tɔs, -ɪz, -ɪŋ, -t

tosser
BR ˈtɒsə(r), -z
AM ˈtɔsər, ˈtasər, -z

tosspot
BR ˈtɒspɒt, -s
AM ˈtɔsˌpat, ˈtasˌpat, -s

toss-up
BR ˈtɒsʌp, -s
AM ˈtɔsəp, ˈtasəp, -s

tostada
BR tɒˈstaːdə(r), -z
AM təˈstadə, toʊˈstadə, -z

tostado
BR tɒˈstaːdəʊ, -z
AM təˈstadoʊ, toʊˈstadoʊ, -z

tostone
BR tɒˈstəʊnaɪ, -z
AM ˌtoʊˈstoʊneɪ, -z

tot
BR tɒt, -s, -ɪŋ, -ɪd
AM ta|t, -ts, -dɪŋ, -dəd

total
BR ˈtəʊt|l, -lz, -lɪŋ \-lɪŋ, -ld
AM ˈtoʊdl, -z, -ɪŋ, -d

totalisation
BR ˌtəʊtlaɪˈzeɪʃn, ˌtəʊtələɪˈzeɪʃn
AM ˌtoʊdləˈzeɪʃən, ˌtoʊdlˌaɪˈzeɪʃən

totalisator
BR ˈtəʊtlˌaɪˌzeɪtə(r), ˈtəʊtələɪˌzeɪtə(r), -z
AM ˈtoʊdləˌzeɪdər, -z

totalise
BR ˈtəʊtlˌaɪz, ˈtəʊtələɪz, -ɪz, -ɪŋ, -d
AM ˈtoʊdlˌaɪz, -ɪz, -ɪŋ, -d

totaliser
BR ˈtəʊtlˌaɪzə(r), ˈtəʊtələɪzə(r), -z
AM ˈtoʊdlˌaɪzər, -z

totalitarian
BR ˌtəʊtalɪˈtɛːrɪən, tə(ʊ)ˌtalɪˈtɛːrɪən
AM toʊˌtæləˈtɛrɪən

totalitarianism
BR ˌtəʊtalɪˈtɛːrɪənɪz-(ə)m, tə(ʊ)ˌtalɪˈtɛːrɪənɪz(ə)m
AM toʊˌtæləˈtɛriəˌnɪzəm

totality
BR tə(ʊ)ˈtalɪti
AM toʊˈtælədi

totalization
BR ˌtəʊtlaɪˈzeɪʃn, ˌtəʊtələɪˈzeɪʃn
AM ˌtoʊdləˈzeɪʃən, ˌtoʊdlˌaɪˈzeɪʃən

totalizator
BR ˈtəʊtlˌaɪˌzeɪtə(r), ˈtəʊtələɪˌzeɪtə(r), -z
AM ˈtoʊdləˌzeɪdər, -z

totalize
BR ˈtəʊtlˌaɪz, ˈtəʊtələɪz, -ɪz, -ɪŋ, -d
AM ˈtoʊdlˌaɪz, -ɪz, -ɪŋ, -d

totalizer
BR ˈtəʊtlˌaɪzə(r), ˈtəʊtələɪzə(r), -z
AM ˈtoʊdlˌaɪzər, -z

totally
BR ˈtəʊtli, ˈtəʊtali
AM ˈtoʊdli, ˈtoʊdli

totaquine
BR ˈtəʊtəkwiːn
AM ˈtoʊdəˌkwin

tote
BR təʊt, -s, -ɪŋ, -ɪd
AM toʊ|t, -ts, -dɪŋ, -dəd

totem
BR ˈtəʊtəm, -z
AM ˈtoʊdəm, -z

totemic
BR tə(ʊ)ˈtɛmɪk
AM toʊˈtɛmɪk

totemism
BR ˈtəʊtəmɪz(ə)m
AM ˈtoʊdəˌmɪzəm

totemist
BR ˈtəʊtəmɪst, -s
AM ˈtoʊdəməst, -s

totemistic
BR ˌtəʊtəˈmɪstɪk
AM ˌtoʊdəˈmɪstɪk

toter
BR ˈtəʊtə(r), -z
AM ˈtoʊdər, -z

t'other
BR ˈtʌðə(r)
AM ˈtəðər

totipotent
BR təʊˈtɪpət(ə)nt
AM ˌtoʊdəˈpoʊtnt

Totnes
BR ˈtɒtnɪs
AM ˈtɒtnəs, ˈtatnəs

toto
BR ˈtəʊtəʊ
AM ˈtoʊdoʊ, ˈtoʊˌtoʊ

Tottenham
BR ˈtɒtnəm, ˈtɒtnəm
AM ˈtatnəm, ˈtatnəm

totter
BR ˈtɒt|ə(r), -əz, -(ə)rɪŋ, -əd
AM ˈtadər, -z, -ɪŋ, -d

totterer
BR ˈtɒt(ə)rə(r), -z
AM ˈtadərər, -z

tottery
BR ˈtɒt(ə)ri
AM ˈtadəri

tottings-up
BR ˌtɒtɪŋzˈʌp
AM ˌtadɪŋzˈəp

totting-up
BR ˌtɒtɪŋˈʌp
AM ˌtadɪŋˈəp

totty
BR ˈtɒti
AM ˈtadi

toucan
BR ˈtuːkən, ˈtuːkan, -z
AM ˈtuˌkæn, ˈtuˌkan, -z

touch
BR tʌtʃ, -ɪz, -ɪŋ, -t
AM tətʃ, -ɪz, -ɪŋ, -t

touchable
BR ˈtʌtʃəbl
AM ˈtətʃəbəl

touch-and-go
BR ˌtʌtʃ(ə)n(d)ˈgəʊ
AM ˈtətʃənˈgoʊ

touchback
BR ˈtʌtʃbak, -s
AM ˈtətʃˌbæk, -s

touchdown
BR ˈtʌtʃdaʊn, -z
AM ˈtətʃˌdaʊn, -z

touché
BR ˈtuːʃeɪ, tuːˈʃeɪ
AM tuˈʃeɪ

toucher
BR ˈtʌtʃə(r), -z
AM ˈtətʃər, -z

touchily
BR ˈtʌtʃɪli
AM ˈtətʃəli

touchiness
BR ˈtʌtʃɪnɪs
AM ˈtətʃinɪs

touchingly
BR ˈtʌtʃɪŋli
AM ˈtətʃɪŋli

touchingness
BR ˈtʌtʃɪŋnɪs
AM ˈtətʃɪŋnɪs

touch-in-goal
BR ˈtʌtʃɪngəʊl, -z
AM ˈtʌtʃənˌgoʊl, -z

touchline
BR ˈtʌtʃlaɪn, -z
AM ˈtətʃˌlaɪn, -z

touch-me-not
BR ˈtʌtʃmɪmɒt, -s
AM ˈtətʃˌmiˈnat, -s

touchpad
BR ˈtʌtʃpad, -z
AM ˈtətʃˌpæd, -z

touchpaper
BR ˈtʌtʃˌpeɪpə(r)
AM ˈtətʃˌpeɪpər

touchstone
BR ˈtʌtʃstəʊn, -z
AM ˈtətʃˌstoʊn, -z

touchwood
BR ˈtʌtʃwʊd
AM ˈtətʃˌwʊd

touchy
BR ˈtʌtʃ|i, -ɪə(r), -ɪɪst
AM ˈtətʃi, -ər, -ɪst

Tough[1]
Scottish place and surname
BR tuːx
AM tuk

Tough[2]
surname, except Scottish
BR tʌf
AM təf

tough
BR tʌf, -s, -ɪŋ, -t, -ə(r), -ɪst
AM tʌf, -s, -ɪŋ, -t, -ər, -əst

toughen
BR ˈtʌf|n, -nz, -nɪŋ \-nɪŋ, -nd
AM ˈtəf|ən, -ənz, -(ə)nɪŋ, -ənd

toughener
BR ˈtʌfnə(r), ˈtʌfnə(r), -z
AM ˈtəf(ə)nər, -z

toughie
BR ˈtʌf|i, -ɪz
AM ˈtəfi, -z

toughish
BR ˈtʌfɪʃ
AM ˈtəfɪʃ

toughly
BR ˈtʌfli
AM ˈtəfli

tough-minded
BR ˈtʌfˈmaɪndɪd
AM ˈtəfˈmaɪndɪd

tough-mindedness
BR ˈtʌfˈmaɪndɪdnɪs
AM ˈtəfˈmaɪn(d)ɪdnɪs

toughness
BR ˈtʌfnəs
AM ˈtəfnəs

Toulon
BR tuːˈlɒ̃

AM tuˈlɒn, tuˈlɑn

Toulouse
BR tuːˈluːz, təˈluːz
AM tuːˈluz

**Toulouse-
Lautrec**
BR təˌluːzlə(ʊ)ˈtrɛk,
ˌtuːluːzlə(ʊ)ˈtrɛk
AM tʊˌlusˌləˈtrɛk

toupée
BR ˈtuːpeɪ, -z
AM tuˈpeɪ, -z

tour
BR tʊə(r), tɔː(r), -z, -ɪŋ,
-d
AM tʊ(ə)r, -z, -ɪŋ, -d

touraco
BR ˈtʊərəkəʊ, -z
AM ˈtʊrəˌkoʊ, -z

tour de force
BR ˌtʊə də ˈfɔːs, ˌtɔː +
AM ˌtʊr də ˈfɔ(ə)rs

tourer
BR ˈtʊərə(r), ˈtɔːrə(r),
-z
AM ˈtʊrər, -z

touring car
BR ˈtʊərɪŋ kɑː(r),
ˈtɔːrɪŋ +, -z
AM ˈtɜrɪŋ ˌkɑr, -z

tourism
BR ˈtʊərɪz(ə)m,
ˈtɔːrɪz(ə)m
AM ˈtɜrɪzəm

tourist
BR ˈtʊərɪst, ˈtɔːrɪst, -s,
-ɪd
AM ˈtɜrəst, -s, -əd

touristic
BR tʊəˈrɪstɪk, tɔːˈrɪstɪk
AM təˈrɪstɪk

touristically
BR tʊəˈrɪstɪkli,
tɔːˈrɪstɪkli
AM təˈrɪstɪk(ə)li

touristy
BR ˈtʊərɪsti, ˈtɔːrɪsti
AM ˈtɜrəsti

tourmaline
BR ˈtɔːməliːn,
ˈtʊəməliːn, -z
AM ˈtʊrmələn,
ˈtʊrməˌlin, -z

Tournai
BR tʊəˈneɪ
AM tʊrˈneɪ

tournament
BR ˈtʊənəm(ə)nt,
ˈtɔːnəm(ə)nt,
ˈtɜːnəm(ə)nt, -s
AM ˈtɜrnəmənt, -s

tournedos
BR ˈtʊənədəʊ,
ˈtɔːnədəʊ, ˈtɜːnədəʊ, -z
AM ˌtʊrnəˈdoʊ, -z

tourney
BR ˈtʊən|i, ˈtɔːn|i,
ˈtɜːn|i, -iz

AM ˈtɜːni, -z

tourniquet
BR ˈtʊənɪkeɪ, ˈtɔːnɪkeɪ,
ˈtɜːnɪkeɪ, -z
AM ˈtɜrnəkət, -s

Tours
BR tʊə(r), tʊəz
AM tʊ(ə)r(z)

tours de force
BR ˌtʊə(z) də ˈfɔːs,
ˌtɔː(z) +
AM ˌtʊrz də ˈfɔ(ə)rs

tousle
BR ˈtaʊz|l, -lz, -lɪŋ, -ld
AM ˈtaʊz|əl, -əlz, -(ə)lɪŋ,
-əld

tousle-haired
BR ˈtaʊzlˈhɛːd
AM ˈtaʊzəlˌhɛ(ə)rd

tous-les-mois
BR ˌtuːleɪˈmwɑː(r), -z
AM ˌtuləˈmwɑ, -z

tout
BR taʊt, -s, -ɪŋ, -ɪd
AM taʊ|t, -ts, -dɪŋ, -dəd

tout court
BR ˌtuː ˈkɔː(r)
AM ˌtu ˈkɔ(ə)r

tout de suite
BR ˌtuː də ˈswiːt, ˌtuːt
ˈswiːt
AM ˌtut ˈswit

tout ensemble
BR ˌtuːt ɒnˈsɒmbl,
+ ðˈsɒbl
AM ˌtut ɑnˈsɑmbəl

touter
BR ˈtaʊtə(r), -z
AM ˈtaʊdər, -z

tovarich
BR təˈvɑːrɪʃ, tʊˈvɑːrɪʃ,
-ɪz
AM təˈvɑrɪ(t)ʃ, -ɪz

tovarish
BR təˈvɑːrɪʃ, tʊˈvɑːrɪʃ,
-ɪz
AM təˈvɑrɪʃ, -ɪz

Tovey
BR ˈtəʊvi, ˈtʌvi
AM ˈtoʊvi

tow
BR təʊ, -z, -ɪŋ, -d
AM toʊ, -z, -ɪŋ, -d

towable
BR ˈtəʊəbl
AM ˈtoʊəbəl

towage
BR ˈtəʊɪdʒ
AM ˈtoʊɪdʒ

toward
BR təˈwɔːd, -z
AM ˈtɔ(ə)rd,
t(ə)ˈwɔ(ə)rd,
twɔ(ə)rd, -z

towardness
BR təˈwɔːdnəs
AM ˈtɔrdnəs,
ˈt(ə)wɔrdnəs

AM ˈtɜːni, -z

towbar
BR ˈtəʊbɑː(r), -z
AM ˈtoʊˌbɑr, -z

towboat
BR ˈtəʊbəʊt, -s
AM ˈtoʊˌboʊt, -s

Towcester
BR ˈtəʊstə(r)
AM ˈtoʊstər

towel
BR ˈtaʊ(ə)l, -z, -ɪŋ, -d
AM ˈtaʊ(ə)l, -z, -ɪŋ, -d

toweling
BR ˈtaʊ(ə)lɪŋ, -z
AM ˈtaʊ(ə)lɪŋ, -z

towelling
BR ˈtaʊ(ə)lɪŋ, -z
AM ˈtaʊ(ə)lɪŋ, -z

tower¹
*noun 'something that
tows'*
BR ˈtəʊə(r), -z
AM ˈtoʊər, -z

tower²
*noun 'type of
building', verb*
BR ˈtaʊə(r), -z, -ɪŋ, -d
AM ˈtaʊ(ə)r, -z, -ɪŋ, -d

Towers
BR ˈtaʊəz
AM ˈtaʊərs

towery
BR ˈtaʊəri
AM ˈtaʊəri

towhead
BR ˈtəʊhɛd, -z
AM ˈtoʊˌhɛd, -z

tow-headed
BR ˌtəʊˈhɛdɪd
AM ˈtoʊˌ(h)ɛdəd

towhee
BR ˈtəʊhiː
AM ˈtoʊˌhi

towline
BR ˈtəʊlaɪn, -z
AM ˈtoʊˌlaɪn, -z

town
BR taʊn, -z
AM taʊn, -z

town clerk
BR ˌtaʊn ˈklɑːk, -s
AM ˌtaʊn ˈklɜrk, -s

town crier
BR ˌtaʊn ˈkraɪə(r), -z
AM ˌtaʊn ˈkraɪər, -z

Towne
BR taʊn
AM taʊn

townee
BR ˈtaʊn|i, -iz
AM ˈtaʊˈni, -z

Townes
BR taʊnz
AM taʊnz

town hall
BR ˌtaʊn ˈhɔːl, -z

AM ˈtaʊn ˈhɔl, ˈtaʊn
ˈhɑl, -z

townhouse
BR ˈtaʊnhaʊ|s, -zɪz
AM ˈtaʊnˌ(h)aʊ|s, -zəz

townie
BR ˈtaʊn|i, -iz
AM ˈtaʊni, -z

townish
BR ˈtaʊnɪʃ
AM ˈtaʊnɪʃ

townless
BR ˈtaʊnləs
AM ˈtaʊnləs

townlet
BR ˈtaʊnlɪt, -s
AM ˈtaʊnlət, -s

Townley
BR ˈtaʊnli
AM ˈtaʊnli

town-major
BR ˌtaʊnˌmeɪdʒə(r), -z
AM ˈtaʊnˌmeɪdʒər, -z

townscape
BR ˈtaʊnskeɪp, -s
AM ˈtaʊnˌskeɪp, -s

Townsend
BR ˈtaʊnzend
AM ˈtaʊnzˌend

townsfolk
BR ˈtaʊnzfəʊk
AM ˈtaʊnzˌfoʊk

Townshend
BR ˈtaʊnzend
AM ˈtaʊnzˌend

township
BR ˈtaʊnʃɪp, -s
AM ˈtaʊnˌʃɪp, -s

townsman
BR ˈtaʊnzmən
AM ˈtaʊnzmən

townsmen
BR ˈtaʊnzmən
AM ˈtaʊnzmən

townspeople
BR ˈtaʊnzˌpiːpl
AM ˈtaʊnzˌpipəl

Townsville
BR ˈtaʊnzvɪl
AM ˈtaʊnzˌvɪl

townswoman
BR ˈtaʊnzˌwʊmən
AM ˈtaʊnzˌwʊmən

townswomen
BR ˈtaʊnzˌwɪmɪn
AM ˈtaʊnzˌwɪmɪn

**Townswomen's
Guild**
BR ˌtaʊnzwɪmɪnz ˈɡɪld
AM ˈtaʊnzˌwɪmɪnz
ˌɡɪld

townward
BR ˈtaʊnwəd, -z
AM ˈtaʊnwərd, -z

towny
BR ˈtaʊn|i, -iz
AM ˈtaʊni, -z

towpath
BR ˈtəʊpɑːθ, ˈtəʊpaθ,
ˈtəʊpɑːðz ˈtəʊpadz
ˈtəʊpaθs
AM ˈtoʊˌpæ|θ, -ðz\-θs

towplane
BR ˈtəʊpleɪn, -z
AM ˈtoʊˌpleɪn, -z

towrope
BR ˈtəʊrəʊp, -s
AM ˈtoʊˌroʊp, -s

Towy
BR ˈtaʊi
AM ˈtaʊi

towy
BR ˈtaʊi
AM ˈtoʊi

Towyn
BR ˈtaʊɪn
AM ˈtaʊən

toxaemia
BR tɒkˈsiːmɪə(r)
AM tɑkˈsimiə

toxaemic
BR tɒkˈsiːmɪk
AM tɑkˈsimɪk

toxaphene
BR ˈtɒksəfiːn
AM ˈtɑksəˌfin

toxemia
BR tɒkˈsiːmɪə(r)
AM tɑkˈsimiə

toxemic
BR tɒkˈsiːmɪk
AM tɑkˈsimɪk

toxic
BR ˈtɒksɪk
AM ˈtɑksɪk

toxically
BR ˈtɒksɪkli
AM ˈtɑksɪk(ə)li

toxicant
BR ˈtɒksɪk(ə)nt, -s
AM ˈtɑksəkənt, -s

toxicity
BR tɒkˈsɪsɪti
AM tɑkˈsɪsədi

toxicological
BR ˌtɒksɪkəˈlɒdʒɪkl
AM ˌtɑksəkəˈlɑdʒəkəl

toxicologist
BR ˌtɒksɪˈkɒlədʒɪst, -s
AM ˌtɑksəˈkɑlədʒəst, -s

toxicology
BR ˌtɒksɪˈkɒlədʒi
AM ˌtɑksəˈkɑlədʒi

toxicomania
BR ˌtɒksɪkəˈmeɪnɪə(r)
AM ˌtɑksəkoʊˈmeɪniə

toxigenic
BR ˌtɒksɪˈdʒɛnɪk
AM ˌtɑksəˈdʒɛnɪk

toxigenicity
BR ˌtɒksɪdʒəˈnɪsɪti
AM ˌtɑksədʒəˈnɪsɪdi

toxin
BR ˈtɒksɪn, -z

AM ˈtɑksən, -z

toxocara
BR ˌtɒksəˈkɑːrə(r), -z
AM ˌtɑksəˈkɛrə, -z

toxocariasis
BR ˌtɒksəkəˈraɪəsɪs
AM ˈtɑksəkəˈraɪəsəs

toxophilite
BR tɒkˈsɒfəlʌɪt,
tɒkˈsɒfˌlaɪt, -s
AM tɑkˈsɑfəˌlaɪt, -s

toxophily
BR tɒkˈsɒfɪli, tɒkˈsɒfˌli
AM tɑkˈsɑfəli

toxoplasmosis
BR ˌtɒksəʊplazˈməʊsɪs
AM ˌtɑksəˌplæzˈmoʊsɪs

Toxteth
BR ˈtɒkstɛθ, ˈtɒkstɪθ
AM ˈtɑkstəθ

toy
BR tɔɪ, -z, -ɪŋ, -d
AM tɔɪ, -z, -ɪŋ, -d

Toyah
BR ˈtɔɪə(r)
AM ˈtɔɪə

toyboy
BR ˈtɔɪbɔɪ, -z
AM ˈtɔɪˌbɔɪ, -z

toylike
BR ˈtɔɪlʌɪk
AM ˈtɔɪˌlaɪk

toymaker
BR ˈtɔɪˌmeɪkə(r), -z
AM ˈtɔɪˌmeɪkər, -z

Toynbee
BR ˈtɔɪnbi
AM ˈtɔɪnbi

Toyota®
BR tɔɪˈəʊtə(r), -z
AM tɔɪˈoʊdə, -z

toyshop
BR ˈtɔɪʃɒp, -s
AM ˈtɔɪˌʃɑp, -s

toystore
BR ˈtɔɪstɔː(r), -z
AM ˈtɔɪˌstɔ(ə)r, -z

toytown
BR ˈtɔɪtaʊn
AM ˈtɔɪˌtaʊn

Tozer
BR ˈtəʊzə(r)
AM ˈtoʊzər

T-piece
BR ˈtiːpiːs, -ɪz
AM ˈtiˌpis, -ɪz

trabeate
BR ˈtreɪbeɪt
AM ˈtreɪbiˌeɪt, ˈtreɪbiɪt

trabeation
BR ˌtreɪbiˈeɪʃn
AM ˌtreɪbiˈeɪʃən

trabecula
BR trəˈbɛkjələ(r), -z
AM trəˈbɛkjələ, -z

trabeculae
BR trəˈbɛkjəliː

AM trəˈbɛkjəli,
trəˈbɛkjəˌlaɪ

trabecular
BR trəˈbɛkjələ(r)
AM trəˈbɛkjələr

trabeculate
BR trəˈbɛkjʊlət
AM trəˈbɛkjələt

tracasserie
BR trəˈkas(ə)rˌi, -ɪz
AM trəˈkasəˌri, -z

trace
BR treɪs, -ɪz, -ɪŋ, -t
AM treɪs, -z, -ɪŋ, -t

traceability
BR ˈtreɪsəˈbɪlɪti
AM ˌtreɪsəˈbɪlɪdi

traceable
BR ˈtreɪsəbl
AM ˈtreɪsəbəl

traceableness
BR ˈtreɪsəblnəs
AM ˈtreɪsəbəlnəs

trace-horse
BR ˈtreɪshɔːs, -ɪz
AM treɪs,(h)ɔ(ə)rs, -əz

traceless
BR ˈtreɪslɪs
AM ˈtreɪslɪs

tracer
BR ˈtreɪsə(r), -z
AM ˈtreɪsər, -z

traceried
BR ˈtreɪs(ə)rɪd
AM ˈtreɪs(ə)rɪd

tracery
BR ˈtreɪs(ə)rˌi, -ɪz
AM ˈtreɪs(ə)ri, -z

Tracey
BR ˈtreɪsi
AM ˈtreɪsi

trachea
BR trəˈkiːə(r),
ˈtreɪkɪə(r), -z
AM ˈtreɪkiə, -z

tracheae
BR trəˈkiːiː, ˈtreɪkiː
AM ˈtreɪkiˌi, ˈtreɪkiˌaɪ

tracheal
BR ˈtreɪkɪəl, trəˈkiːəl
AM trəˈkiəl

tracheate
BR ˈtreɪkɪeɪt, trəˈkiːeɪt
AM ˈtreɪkiˌeɪt, ˈtreɪkiˌeɪt

tracheostomy
BR ˌtrakɪˈɒstəmˌli, -ɪz
AM ˌtreɪkiˈɑstəmi, -z

tracheotomy
BR ˌtrakɪˈɒtəmˌli, -ɪz
AM ˌtreɪkiˈɑdəmi, -z

trachoma
BR trəˈkəʊmə(r)
AM trəˈkoʊmə

trachomatous
BR trəˈkəʊmətəs
AM trəˈkoʊmədəs

trachyte
BR ˈtreɪkʌɪt, ˈtrakʌɪt, -s
AM ˈtreɪˌkaɪt, ˈtræˌkaɪt, -s

trachytic
BR trəˈkɪtɪk
AM trəˈkɪdɪk

tracing
BR ˈtreɪsɪŋ, -z
AM ˈtreɪsɪŋ, -z

track
BR trak, -s, -ɪŋ, -t
AM træk, -s, -ɪŋ, -t

trackage
BR ˈtrakɪdʒ
AM ˈtrækɪdʒ

track-and-field
BR ˌtrak(ə)n(d)ˈfiːld
AM ˌtrækənˈfild

trackbed
BR ˈtrakbɛd, -z
AM ˈtrækˌbɛd, -z

tracker
BR ˈtrakə(r), -z
AM ˈtrækər, -z

tracking
BR ˈtrakɪŋ, -z
AM ˈtrækɪŋ, -z

tracklayer
BR ˈtrakˌleɪə(r), -z
AM ˈtrækˌleɪər, -z

tracklaying
BR ˈtrakˌleɪɪŋ
AM ˈtrækˌleɪɪŋ

tracklement
BR ˈtraklm(ə)nt, -s
AM ˈtrækəlmənt, -s

trackless
BR ˈtrakləs
AM ˈtrækləs

tracklessness
BR ˈtrakləsnəs
AM ˈtrækləsnəs

trackman
BR ˈtrakmən, ˈtrakman
AM ˈtrækmən, ˈtrækˌmæn

trackmen
BR ˈtrakmən, ˈtrakmɛn
AM ˈtrækmən, ˈtrækˌmɛn

trackside
BR ˈtraksʌɪd
AM ˈtrækˌsaɪd

tracksuit
BR ˈtraks(j)uːt, -s, -ɪd
AM ˈtrækˌsu|t, -ts, -dəd

trackway
BR ˈtrakweɪ, -z
AM ˈtrækˌweɪ, -z

tract
BR trakt, -s
AM træk|(t), -(t)s

tractability
BR ˌtraktəˈbɪlɪti
AM ˌtræktəˈbɪlɪdi

tractable
BR ˈtraktəbl
AM ˈtræktəbəl

tractableness
BR ˈtraktəblnəs
AM ˈtræktəbəlnəs

tractably
BR ˈtraktəbli
AM ˈtræktəbli

Tractarian
BR trakˈtɛːrɪən, -z
AM trækˈtɛrɪən, -z

tractarian
BR trakˈtɛːrɪən, -z
AM trækˈtɛrɪən, -z

Tractarianism
BR trakˈtɛːrɪənɪz(ə)m
AM trækˈtɛrɪəˌnɪzəm

tractate
BR ˈtrakteɪt, -s
AM ˈtrækˌteɪt, -s

traction
BR ˈtrakʃn
AM ˈtrækʃən

tractional
BR ˈtrakʃn(ə)l,
ˈtrakʃən(ə)l
AM ˈtrækʃ(ə)nəl

tractive
BR ˈtraktɪv
AM ˈtræktɪv

tractor
BR ˈtraktə(r), -z
AM ˈtræktər, -z

tractorfeed
BR ˈtraktəfiːd
AM ˈtræktərˌfid

Tracy
BR ˈtreɪsi
AM ˈtreɪsi

trad
BR trad
AM træd

tradable
BR ˈtreɪdəbl
AM ˈtreɪdəbəl

trade
BR treɪd, -z, -ɪŋ, -ɪd
AM treɪd, -z, -ɪŋ, -ɪd

tradeable
BR ˈtreɪdəbl
AM ˈtreɪdəbəl

trademark
BR ˈtreɪdmɑːk, -s
AM ˈtreɪdˌmɑrk, -s

trader
BR ˈtreɪdə(r), -z
AM ˈtreɪdər, -z

tradescantia
BR ˌtradɪˈskantɪə(r)
AM ˌtrædəˈskæn(t)ʃ(i)ə,
ˌtrædəˈskæn(t)ɪə

tradesman
BR ˈtreɪdzmən

AM ˈtreɪdzmən

tradesmen
BR ˈtreɪdzmən
AM ˈtreɪdzmən

tradespeople
BR ˈtreɪdzˌpiːpl
AM ˈtreɪdzˌpipəl

trades union
BR ˌtreɪdz ˈjuːnɪən, -z
AM ˌtreɪdz ˈjunjən, -z

trades unionism
BR ˌtreɪdz
ˈjuːnɪənɪz(ə)m
AM ˌtreɪdz
ˈjunjəˌnɪzəm

trades unionist
BR ˌtreɪdz ˈjuːnɪənɪst,
-s
AM ˌtreɪdz ˈjunjənəst,
-s

trade union
BR ˌtreɪd ˈjuːnɪən, -z
AM ˌtreɪd ˌjunjən, -z

trade unionism
BR ˌtreɪd
ˈjuːnɪənɪz(ə)m
AM ˌtreɪd ˈjunjəˌnɪzəm

trade unionist
BR ˌtreɪd ˈjuːnɪənɪst, -s
AM ˌtreɪdˈjunjənəst, -s

trade-weighted
BR ˈtreɪdˌweɪtɪd
AM ˈtreɪdˌweɪdɪd

tradewind
BR ˈtreɪdwɪnd, -z
AM ˈtreɪdˌwɪnd, -z

tradition
BR trəˈdɪʃn, -z
AM trəˈdɪʃən, -z

traditional
BR trəˈdɪʃn(ə)l,
trəˈdɪʃən(ə)l
AM trəˈdɪʃ(ə)nəl

traditionalism
BR trəˈdɪʃnəlɪz(ə)m,
trəˈdɪʃnlɪz(ə)m,
trəˈdɪʃənlɪz(ə)m,
trəˈdɪʃ(ə)nəlɪz(ə)m
AM trəˈdɪʃənlˌɪzəm,
trəˈdɪʃnəˌlɪzəm

traditionalist
BR trəˈdɪʃnəlɪst,
trəˈdɪʃnlɪst,
trəˈdɪʃənlɪst,
trəˈdɪʃ(ə)nəlɪst, -s
AM trəˈdɪʃənləst,
trəˈdɪʃnələst, -s

traditionalistic
BR trəˌdɪʃnəˈlɪstɪk,
trəˌdɪʃnlˈɪstɪk,
trəˌdɪʃənlˈɪstɪk,
trəˌdɪʃ(ə)nlˈɪstɪk,
trəˌdɪʃənlˈɪstɪk,
trəˌdɪʃnəˈlɪstɪk
AM trəˌdɪʃnəˈlɪstɪk,
trəˌdɪʃnəˈlɪstɪk

traditionally
BR trəˈdɪʃnəli,
trəˈdɪʃnli,

trəˈdɪʃənli,
trəˈdɪʃ(ə)nəli
AM trəˈdɪʃ(ə)nəli

traditionary
BR trəˈdɪʃn(ə)ri
AM trəˈdɪʃəˌnɛri

traditionist
BR trəˈdɪʃnɪst,
trəˈdɪʃənɪst, -s
AM trəˈdɪʃənəst, -s

traditionless
BR trəˈdɪʃnləs
AM trəˈdɪʃənləs

traditor
BR ˈtradɪtə(r), -z
AM ˈtrædədər, -z

traditores
BR ˌtradɪˈtɔːriːz
AM ˌtrædəˈtɔˌriz

traduce
BR trəˈdjuːs, trəˈdʒuːs,
-ɪz, -ɪŋ, -t
AM trəˈd(j)us, -əz, -ɪŋ, -t

traducement
BR trəˈdjuːsm(ə)nt,
trəˈdʒuːsm(ə)nt
AM trəˈd(j)usmənt

traducer
BR trəˈdjuːsə(r),
trəˈdʒuːsə(r), -z
AM trəˈd(j)usər, -z

traducian
BR trəˈdjuːsɪən,
trəˈdʒuːsɪən,
trəˈdʒuːʃn, -z
AM trəˈd(j)uʃən, -z

traducianism
BR trəˈdjuːsɪənɪz(ə)m,
trəˈdjuːʃnɪz(ə)m,
trəˈdʒuːsɪənɪz(ə)m,
trəˈdʒuːʃnɪz(ə)m
AM trəˈd(j)uʃəˌnɪzəm

traducianist
BR trəˈdjuːsɪənɪst,
trəˈdjuːʃnɪst,
trəˈdʒuːsɪənɪst,
trəˈdʒuːʃnɪst, -s
AM trəˈd(j)uʃənəst, -s

Trafalgar
BR trəˈfalgə(r),
ˌtraflˈgɑː(r)
AM trəˈfælgər,
trəˈfɔlgər, trəˈfalgər

traffic
BR ˈtraflɪk, -ɪks, -ɪkɪŋ,
-ɪkt
AM ˈtræfɪk, -s, -ɪŋ, -t

trafficator
BR ˈtrafɪkeɪtə(r), -z
AM ˈtræfəˌkeɪdər, -z

trafficker
BR ˈtrafɪkə(r), -z
AM ˈtræfɪkər, -z

trafficless
BR ˈtrafɪklɪs
AM ˈtræfɪkləs

Trafford
BR ˈtrafəd
AM ˈtræfərd

tragacanth
BR ˈtragəkanθ
AM ˈtrægəˌkænθ

tragedian
BR trəˈdʒiːdɪən, -z
AM trəˈdʒidiən, -z

tragedienne
BR trəˌdʒiːdɪˈɛn, -z
AM trəˌdʒidiˈɛn, -z

tragedy
BR ˈtradʒɪdi, -ɪz
AM ˈtrædʒədi, -ɪz

tragi
BR ˈtreɪgaɪ, ˈtreɪdʒaɪ
AM ˈtreɪgaɪ, ˈtreɪdʒaɪ

tragic
BR ˈtradʒɪk
AM ˈtrædʒɪk

tragical
BR ˈtradʒɪkl
AM ˈtrædʒəkəl

tragically
BR ˈtradʒɪkli
AM ˈtrædʒək(ə)li

tragicomedy
BR ˌtradʒɪˈkɒmɪdi, -ɪz
AM ˌtrædʒəˈkamədi, -z

tragicomic
BR ˌtradʒɪˈkɒmɪk
AM ˌtrædʒəˈkamɪk

tragicomical
BR ˌtradʒɪˈkɒmɪkl
AM ˌtrædʒəˈkaməkəl

tragicomically
BR ˌtradʒɪˈkɒmɪkli
AM ˌtrædʒəˈkamək(ə)li

tragopan
BR ˈtragəpan, -z
AM ˈtrægəˌpæn, -z

tragus
BR ˈtreɪgəs
AM ˈtreɪgəs

Traherne
BR trəˈhəːn
AM trəˈhərn

**trahison des
clercs**
BR ˌtrɑːˌɪzð deɪ ˈklɛː(r)
AM treɪˌzan deɪ ˈklɛrk

trail
BR treɪl, -z, -ɪŋ, -d
AM treɪl, -z, -ɪŋ, -d

trailblazer
BR ˈtreɪlˌbleɪzə(r), -z
AM ˈtreɪlˌbleɪzər, -z

trailblazing
BR ˈtreɪlˌbleɪzɪŋ
AM ˈtreɪlˌbleɪzɪŋ

trailer
BR ˈtreɪlə(r), -z, -ɪŋ, -d
AM ˈtreɪlər, -z, -ɪŋ, -d

train
BR treɪn, -z, -ɪŋ, -d
AM treɪn, -z, -ɪŋ, -d

trainability
BR ˌtreɪnə'bɪlɪti
AM ˌtreɪnə'bɪlɪdi

trainable
BR 'treɪnəbl
AM 'treɪnəbəl

trainband
BR 'treɪnband, -z
AM 'treɪnˌbænd, -z

trainee
BR ˌtreɪ'niː, -z
AM ˌtreɪ'ni, -z

traineeship
BR ˌtreɪ'niːˌʃɪp, -s
AM ˌtreɪ'niˌʃɪp, -s

trainer
BR 'treɪnə(r), -z
AM 'treɪnər, -z

trainless
BR 'treɪnlɪs
AM 'treɪnlɪs

trainload
BR 'treɪnləʊd, -z
AM 'treɪnˌloʊd, -z

trainman
BR 'treɪnman
AM 'treɪnˌmæn

trainmen
BR 'treɪnmɛn
AM 'treɪnˌmɛn

train-mile
BR 'treɪnmaɪl, -z
AM 'treɪnˌmaɪl, -z

trainsick
BR 'treɪnsɪk
AM 'treɪnˌsɪk

trainsickness
BR 'treɪnsɪknɪs
AM 'treɪnˌsɪknɪs

traipse
BR treɪps, -ɪz, -ɪŋ, -t
AM treɪps, -ɪz, -ɪŋ, -t

trait
BR treɪ|(t), -z \ -ts
AM treɪt, -s

traitor
BR 'treɪtə(r), -z
AM 'treɪdər, -z

traitorous
BR 'treɪt(ə)rəs
AM 'treɪdərəs, 'treɪtrəs

traitorously
BR 'treɪt(ə)rəsli
AM 'treɪdərəsli, 'treɪtrəsli

traitorousness
BR 'treɪt(ə)rəsnəs
AM 'treɪdərəsnəs, 'treɪtrəsnəs

traitress
BR 'treɪtrɪs, -ɪz
AM 'treɪdərəs, 'treɪtrɪs, -ɪz

Trajan
BR 'treɪdʒ(ə)n
AM 'treɪdʒən

trajectory
BR trə'dʒɛkt(ə)r|i, -ɪz
AM trə'dʒɛkt(ə)ri, -z

tra-la
BR trɑː'lɑː(r), trə'lɑː(r)
AM trə'lɑ, 'trɑ'lɑ

Tralee
BR trə'liː
AM trə'li

tram
BR tram, -z
AM træm, -z

tramcar
BR 'tramkɑː(r), -z
AM 'træmˌkɑr, -z

Traminer
BR trə'miːnə(r)
AM trə'minər

tramline
BR 'tramlaɪn, -z
AM 'træmˌlaɪn, -z

trammel
BR 'tram|l, -lz, -lɪŋ \ -əlɪŋ, -ld
AM 'træm|əl, -əlz, -(ə)lɪŋ, -əld

trammie
BR 'tram|i, -ɪz
AM 'træmi, -z

tramontana
BR ˌtramɒn'tɑːnə(r), -z
AM ˌtramən'tanə, -z

tramontane
BR trə'mɒnteɪn, -z
AM trə'manˌteɪn, -z

tramp
BR tram|p, -ps, -pɪŋ, -(p)t
AM træmp, -s, -ɪŋ, -t

tramper
BR 'trampə(r), -z
AM 'træmpər, -z

trampish
BR 'trampɪʃ
AM 'træmpɪʃ

trample
BR 'tramp|l, -lz, -lɪŋ \ -lɪŋ, -ld
AM 'træmp|əl, -əlz, -(ə)lɪŋ, -əld

trampler
BR 'tramplə(r), 'trampl̩ə(r), -z
AM 'træmp(ə)lər, -z

trampoline
BR 'trampəliːn, ˌtrampə'liːn, -z, -ɪŋ
AM ˌtræmpə'lin, -z, -ɪŋ

trampolinist
BR 'trampəliːnɪst, ˌtrampə'liːnɪst, -s
AM ˌtræmpə'linɪst, -s

tramway
BR 'tramweɪ, -z
AM 'træmˌweɪ, -z

trance
BR trɑːns, trans, -ɪz
AM træns, -əz

tranche
BR trɑːn(t)ʃ, tran(t)ʃ, -ɪz
AM træn(t)ʃ, -əz

Tranmere
BR 'tranmɪə(r)
AM 'trænˌmɪ(ə)r

tranny
BR 'tran|i, -ɪz
AM 'træni, -z

tranquil
BR 'traŋkw(ɪ)l
AM 'træŋkwəl, 'trænkwəl

tranquilisation
BR ˌtraŋkwɪlaɪ'zeɪʃn
AM ˌtræŋkwələ'zeɪʃən, ˌtrænkwələ'zeɪʃən, ˌtræŋkwə'laɪ'zeɪʃən, ˌtrænkwə'laɪ'zeɪʃən

tranquilise
BR 'traŋkwɪlaɪz, -ɪz, -ɪŋ, -d
AM 'træŋkwə'laɪz, 'trænkwə'laɪz, -ɪz, -ɪŋ, -d

tranquiliser
BR 'traŋkwɪlaɪzə(r), -z
AM 'træŋkwə'laɪzər, 'trænkwə'laɪzər, -z

tranquility
BR traŋ'kwɪlɪti
AM træŋ'kwɪlɪdi, træn'kwɪlɪdi

tranquilization
BR ˌtraŋkwɪlaɪ'zeɪʃn
AM ˌtræŋkwələ'zeɪʃən, ˌtrænkwələ'zeɪʃən, ˌtræŋkwə'laɪ'zeɪʃən, ˌtrænkwə'laɪ'zeɪʃən

tranquilize
BR 'traŋkwɪlaɪz, -ɪz, -ɪŋ, -d
AM 'træŋkwə'laɪz, 'trænkwə'laɪz, -ɪz, -ɪŋ, -d

tranquilizer
BR 'traŋkwɪlaɪzə(r), -z
AM 'træŋkwə'laɪzər, 'trænkwə'laɪzər, -z

tranquillisation
BR ˌtraŋkwɪlaɪ'zeɪʃn
AM ˌtræŋkwələ'zeɪʃən, ˌtrænkwələ'zeɪʃən, ˌtræŋkwə'laɪ'zeɪʃən, ˌtrænkwə'laɪ'zeɪʃən

tranquillise
BR 'traŋkwɪlaɪz, -ɪz, -ɪŋ, -d
AM 'træŋkwə'laɪz, 'trænkwə'laɪz, -ɪz, -ɪŋ, -d

tranquilliser
BR 'traŋkwɪlaɪzə(r), -z
AM 'træŋkwə'laɪzər, 'trænkwə'laɪzər, -z

tranquillity
BR traŋ'kwɪlɪti

tranquillization
BR ˌtraŋkwɪlaɪ'zeɪʃn
AM ˌtræŋkwələ'zeɪʃən, ˌtræŋkwələ'zeɪʃən, ˌtræŋkwə'laɪ'zeɪʃən, ˌtrænkwə'laɪ'zeɪʃən

tranquillize
BR 'traŋkwɪlaɪz, -ɪz, -ɪŋ, -d
AM 'træŋkwə'laɪz, 'træŋkwə'laɪz, -ɪz, -ɪŋ, -d

tranquillizer
BR 'traŋkwɪlaɪzə(r), -z
AM 'træŋkwə'laɪzər, 'træŋkwə'laɪzər, -z

tranquilly
BR 'traŋkwɪli, 'traŋkwl̩i
AM 'træŋkwəli, 'trænkwəli

transact
BR tran'zakt, trɑːn'zakt, tran'sakt, trɑːn'sakt, -s, -ɪŋ, -ɪd
AM træn'zæk|(t), træn(t)'sæk|(t), -(t)s, -tɪŋ, -təd

transaction
BR tran'zakʃn, trɑːn'zakʃn, tran'sakʃn, trɑːn'sakʃn, -z
AM træn'zækʃən, træn(t)'sækʃən, -z

transactional
BR tran'zakʃn(ə)l, trɑːn'zakʃn(ə)l, tran'sakʃn(ə)l, trɑːn'sakʃn(ə)l
AM træn'zækʃ(ə)nəl, træn(t)'sækʃ(ə)nəl

transactionally
BR tran'zakʃnəli, tran'zakʃ(ə)nəli, trɑːn'zakʃnəli, trɑːn'zakʃ(ə)nəli, tran'sakʃnəli, tran'sakʃ(ə)nəli, trɑːn'sakʃnəli, trɑːn'sakʃ(ə)nəli
AM træn'zækʃ(ə)nəli, træn(t)'sækʃ(ə)nəli

transactor
BR tran'zaktə(r), trɑːn'zaktə(r), tran'saktə(r), trɑːn'saktə(r), -z
AM træn'zæktər, træn(t)'sæktər, -z

transalpine
BR (ˌ)tranz'alpaɪn, (ˌ)trɑːnz'alpaɪn, (ˌ)trans'alpaɪn, (ˌ)trɑːns'alpaɪn
AM ˌtræn'zælpaɪn, ˌtræn(t)'sælpaɪn

transatlantic
BR ˌtranzət'lantɪk,
ˌtraːnzət'lantɪk,
ˌtransət'lantɪk,
ˌtraːnsət'lantɪk
AM ˌtrænzət'læn(t)ɪk,
ˌtræn(t)sət'læn(t)ɪk

transaxle
BR 'tranzˌaksl,
'traːnzˌaksl,
'transˌaksl,
'traːnsˌaksl, -z

Transcaucasia
BR ˌtranzkɔː'keɪzɪə(r),
ˌtranzkɔː'keɪʒə(r),
ˌtraːnzkɔː'keɪzɪə(r),
ˌtraːnzkɔː'keɪʒə(r),
ˌtranskɔː'keɪzɪə(r),
ˌtranskɔː'keɪʒə(r),
ˌtraːnskɔː'keɪzɪə(r),
ˌtraːnskɔː'keɪʒə(r)
AM ˌtrænzˌkɔ'keɪʒə,
ˌtræn(t)sˌkɔ'keɪʒə,
ˌtrænzˌkɑ'keɪʒə,
ˌtræn(t)sˌkɑ'keɪʒə

Transcaucasian
BR ˌtranzkɔː'keɪzɪən,
ˌtranzkɔː'keɪʒ(ə)n,
ˌtraːnzkɔː'keɪzɪən,
ˌtraːnzkɔː'keɪʒ(ə)n,
ˌtranskɔː'keɪzɪən,
ˌtranskɔː'keɪʒ(ə)n,
ˌtraːnskɔː'keɪzɪən,
ˌtraːnskɔː'keɪʒ(ə)n
AM ˌtrænzˌkɔ'keɪʒən,
ˌtræn(t)sˌkɔ'keɪʒən,
ˌtrænzˌkɑ'keɪʒən,
ˌtræn(t)sˌkɑ'keɪʒən

transceiver
BR tran'siːvə(r),
traːn'siːvə(r), -z
AM trænz'sivər,
træn(t)'sivər, -z

transcend
BR tran'sɛnd,
traːn'sɛnd, -z, -ɪŋ, -ɪd
AM træn(t)'sɛnd, -z,
-ɪŋ, -ɪd

transcendence
BR tran'sɛnd(ə)ns,
traːn'sɛnd(ə)ns
AM træn(t)'sɛndəns

transcendency
BR tran'sɛnd(ə)nsi,
traːn'sɛnd(ə)nsi
AM træn(t)'sɛndnsi

transcendent
BR tran'sɛnd(ə)nt,
traːn'sɛnd(ə)nt
AM træn(t)'sɛndənt

transcendental
BR ˌtrans(ɛ)n'dɛntl,
ˌtraːns(ɛ)n'dɛntl,
AM ˌtræn‿(t)sɛn'dɛn(t)l,
ˌtræn(t)sn'dɛn(t)l

transcendentalise
BR ˌtrans(ɛ)n'dɛntlʌɪz,
ˌtraːns(ɛ)n'dɛntlʌɪz,
-ɪz, -ɪŋ, -d
AM ˌtræn‿(t)sɛn'dɛn(t)lˌʌɪz,
ˌtræn(t)sn'dɛn(t)lˌʌɪz,
-ɪz, -ɪŋ, -d

**transcendental-
ism¹**
BR ˌtrans(ɛ)n'dɛntlɪz-
(ə)m,
ˌtraːns(ɛ)n'dɛntlɪz(ə)m
AM ˌtræn(t)sɛn'dɛn(t)l-
ˌɪzəm,
ˌtræn(t)sn'dɛn(t)lˌɪzəm

**transcendental-
ism²**
BR ˌtrans(ɛ)n'dɛntlɪz-
(ə)m,
ˌtraːns(ɛ)n'dɛntlɪz(ə)m
AM ˌtræn(t)sɛn'dɛn(t)l-
ˌɪzəm,
ˌtræn(t)sn'dɛn(t)lˌɪzəm

transcendentalist
BR ˌtrans(ɛ)n'dɛntlɪst,
ˌtraːns(ɛ)n'dɛntlɪst, -s
AM ˌtræn(t)sɛn'dɛn(t)l-
əst,
'træn(t)sn'dɛn(t)ləst,
-s

transcendentalize
BR ˌtrans(ɛ)n'dɛntlʌɪz,
ˌtraːns(ɛ)n'dɛntlʌɪz,
-ɪz, -ɪŋ, -d
AM ˌtræn‿(t)sɛn'dɛn(t)l-
ˌʌɪz,
ˌtræn(t)sn'dɛn(t)lˌʌɪz,
-ɪz, -ɪŋ, -d

transcendentally
BR ˌtrans(ɛ)n'dɛntlˌi,
ˌtraːns(ɛ)n'dɛntlˌi
AM ˌtræn‿(t)sɛn'dɛn(t)li,
ˌtræn(t)sn'dɛn(t)li

transcendently
BR tran'sɛnd(ə)ntli,
traːn'sɛnd(ə)ntli
AM træn(t)'sɛndən(t)li

transcode
BR ˌtranz'kəʊd,
ˌtraːnz'kəʊd,
ˌtrans'kəʊd,
ˌtraːns'kəʊd, -z, -ɪŋ, -ɪd
AM ˌtrænz'koʊd,
ˌtræn(t)s'koʊd, -z, -ɪŋ,
-əd

transcontinental
BR ˌtranzkɒntɪ'nɛntl,
ˌtraːnzkɒntɪ'nɛntl,
ˌtranskɒntɪ'nɛntl,
ˌtraːnskɒntɪ'nɛntl
AM ˌtrænz'kɑntn'ɛn(t)l,
'træn(t),skɑntn'ɛn(t)l

transcontinentally
BR ˌtranzkɒntɪ'nɛntlˌi,
ˌtraːnzkɒntɪ'nɛntlˌi,
ˌtranskɒntɪ'nɛntlˌi,
ˌtraːnskɒntɪ'nɛntlˌi

AM ˌtrænzˌkantn'ɛn(t)li,
'træn(t)ˌskantn'ɛn(t)li

transcribe
BR tran'skrʌɪb,
traːn'skrʌɪb, -z, -ɪŋ, -d
AM træn(t)'skraɪb, -z,
-ɪŋ, -d

transcriber
BR tran'skrʌɪbə(r),
traːn'skrʌɪbə(r), -z
AM træn(t)'skraɪbər,
-z

transcript
BR 'transkrɪpt,
'traːnskrɪpt, -s
AM 'trænz‿krɪpt,
'træn(t)ˌskrɪpt, -s

transcription
BR tran'skrɪpʃn,
traːn'skrɪpʃn, -z
AM træn(t)'skrɪpʃən,
-z

transcriptional
BR tran'skrɪpʃn(ə)l,
traːn'skrɪpʃn(ə)l
AM træn(t)'skrɪpʃ(ə)nəl

transcriptive
BR tran'skrɪptɪv,
traːn'skrɪptɪv
AM 'trænz‿krɪptɪv,
'træn(t)ˌskrɪptɪv

transcutaneous
BR ˌtranzkjʉ'teɪnɪəs,
ˌtraːnzkjʉ'teɪnɪəs,
ˌtranskjʉ'teɪnɪəs,
ˌtraːnskjʉ'teɪnɪəs
AM ˌtræn(t)skju'teɪnɪəs,
ˌtrænzkju'teɪnɪəs

transduce
BR tranz'djuːs,
tranz'dʒuːs,
traːnz'djuːs,
traːnz'dʒuːs,
trans'djuːs,
trans'dʒuːs,
traːns'djuːs,
traːns'dʒuːs, -ɪz, -ɪŋ, -t
AM trænz'd(j)us,
træn(t)s'd(j)us, -əz,
-ɪŋ, -t

transducer
BR tranz'djuːsə(r),
tranz'dʒuːsə(r),
traːnz'djuːsə(r),
traːnz'dʒuːsə(r),
trans'djuːsə(r),
trans'dʒuːsə(r),
traːns'djuːsə(r),
traːns'dʒuːsə(r), -z
AM trænz'd(j)usər,
træn(t)s'd(j)usər, -z

transduction
BR ˌtranz'dʌkʃn,
ˌtraːnz'dʌkʃn,
ˌtrans'dʌkʃn,
ˌtraːns'dʌkʃn
AM ˌtrænz'dəkʃən,
ˌtræn(t)s'dəkʃən

transect
BR tran'sɛkt,
traːn'sɛkt, -s, -ɪŋ, -ɪd
AM træn(t)'sɛk|(t),
-(t)s, -tɪŋ, -təd

transection
BR tran'sɛkʃn,
traːn'sɛkʃn, -z
AM træn(t)'sɛkʃən, -z

transept
BR 'transɛpt,
'traːnsɛpt, -s
AM 'træn(t)ˌsɛpt, -s

transeptal
BR tran'sɛptl,
traːn'sɛptl
AM 'træn(t)sɛptl

transexual
BR tran(s)'sɛkʃʊəl,
tran(s)'sɛkʃ(ʉ)l,
tran(s)'sɛksjʊ(ə)l,
traːn(s)'sɛkʃʊəl,
traːn(s)'sɛkʃ(ʉ)l,
traːn(s)'sɛksjʊ(ə)l,
tranz'sɛkʃʊəl,
tranz'sɛkʃ(ʉ)l,
tranz'sɛksjʊ(ə)l,
traːnz'sɛkʃʊəl,
traːnz'sɛkʃ(ʉ)l,
traːnz'sɛksjʊ(ə)l, -z
AM ˌtræn(t)'sɛkʃ(əw)əl,
-z

transexualism
BR ˌtran(z)'sɛkʃʊəl-
ˌɪz(ə)m,
ˌtran(z)'sɛkʃʉlɪz(ə)m,
tran(z)'sɛkʃ|ɪz(ə)m,
ˌtran(z)'sɛksjʊ(ə)l-
ˌɪz(ə)m,
ˌtraːn(z)'sɛkʃʊəlɪz(ə)m,
ˌtraːn(z)'sɛkʃʉlɪz(ə)m,
traːn(z)'sɛkʃ|ɪz(ə)m,
ˌtraːn(z)'sɛksjʊ(ə)lɪz-
(ə)m
AM ˌtræn(t)'sɛkʃ(əw)ə-
ˌlɪzəm

transfer¹
noun
BR 'transfəː(r),
'traːnsfəː(r),
'tranzfəː(r),
'traːnzfəː(r), -z
AM 'træn(t)sfər, -z

transfer²
verb
BR trans'fəː(r),
traːns'fəː(r),
'transfəː(r),
'traːnsfəː(r),
tranz'fəː(r),
traːnz'fəː(r),
'tranzfəː(r), -z, -ɪŋ, -d
AM træn(t)s'fər,
'træn(t)sfər, -z, -ɪŋ, -d

transferability
BR trans‿fəːrə'bɪlti,
ˌtransf(ə)rə'bɪlti,
traːns‿fəːrə'bɪlti,

transferable
ˌtrɑːnsfˈərəˈbɪlɪti,
ˌtranzˌfəˈrəˈbɪlɪti,
ˌtranzfˈ(ə)rəˈbɪlɪti,
ˌtrɑːnzˌfəˈrəˈbɪlɪti,
AM ˌtræn(t)sfərəˈbɪlɪdi

transferable
BR transˈfəːrəbl,
ˌtrɑːnsˈfəːrəbl,
ˈtransfˈ(ə)rəbl,
ˈtrɑːnsf(ə)rəbl,
tranzˈfəːrəbl,
ˌtrɑːnzˈfəːrəbl,
ˈtranzf(ə)rəbl,
ˈtrɑːnzf(ə)rəbl
AM træn(t)sˈfərəbəl,
ˈtræn(t)sfərəbəl

transfer-book
BR ˈtransfəːbʊk,
ˈtrɑːnsfəːbʊk,
ˈtranzfəːbʊk,
ˈtrɑːnzfəːbʊk, -s
AM ˈtræn(t)sfərˌbʊk, -s

transferee
BR ˌtransfəˈriː,
ˌtrɑːnsfəˈriː,
ˌtranzfəˈriː,
ˌtrɑːnzfəˈriː, -z
AM ˌtræn(t)sfəˈriː, -z

transference
BR ˈtransf(ə)rəns,
ˈtransf(ə)rn̩s,
ˈtrɑːnsf(ə)rəns,
ˈtrɑːnsf(ə)rn̩s,
ˈtranzf(ə)rəns,
ˈtranzf(ə)rn̩s,
ˈtrɑːnzf(ə)rəns,
ˈtrɑːnzf(ə)rn̩s, -ɪz
AM ˈtræn(t)sfərəns,
ˈtræn(t)sfərəns,
ˈtræn(t)sfrəns, -ɪz

transferor
BR transˈfəːrə(r),
ˌtrɑːnsˈfəːrə(r),
ˈtransfəˈrə(r),
ˈtrɑːnsfəˈrə(r),
tranzˈfəːrə(r),
ˌtrɑːnzˈfəːrə(r),
ˈtranzfəˈrə(r),
ˈtrɑːnzfəˈrə(r), -z
AM træn(t)sˈfərər,
ˈtræn(t)sfərər, -z

transfer-paper
BR ˈtransfəːˌpeɪpə(r),
ˈtrɑːnsfəːˌpeɪpə(r),
ˈtranzfəːˌpeɪpə(r),
ˈtrɑːnzfəːˌpeɪpə(r), -z
AM ˈtræn(t)sfərˌpeɪpər,
-z

transferral
BR transˈfəːrəl,
ˌtrɑːnsˈfəːrəl,
ˈtransˈfərl̩,
ˌtrɑːnsˈfəːrl̩,
tranzˈfəːrəl,
ˌtrɑːnzˈfəːrəl,
ˈtranzˈfərl̩,
ˌtrɑːnzˈfəːrl̩, -z

transferrer
BR transˈfəːrə(r),
ˌtrɑːnsˈfəːrə(r),
ˈtransfəˈrə(r),
ˈtrɑːnsfəˈrə(r),
tranzˈfəːrə(r),
ˌtrɑːnzˈfəːrə(r),
ˈtranzfəˈrə(r),
ˈtrɑːnzfəˈrə(r), -z
AM træn(t)sˈfərər,
ˈtræn(t)sfərər, -z

transferrin
BR tranzˈfɛrɪn,
ˈtransˈfɛrɪn,
ˈtrɑːnzˈfɛrɪn,
ˈtrɑːnsˈfɛrɪn
AM træn(t)sˈfɛrən

transfer RNA
BR ˈtransfəːr ˌɑːrɛnˈeɪ,
ˌtrɑːnsfəːr +,
ˈtranzfəː(r) +,
ˈtrɑːnzfəː(r) +
AM ˌtræn(t)sfər
ˌɑːrˌɛnˈeɪ

transfiguration
BR ˌtransfɪgəˈreɪʃn,
ˌtrɑːnsfɪgəˈreɪʃn,
transˌfɪgəˈreɪʃn,
trɑːnsˌfɪgəˈreɪʃn,
ˌtranzfɪgəˈreɪʃn,
tranzˌfɪgəˈreɪʃn,
trɑːnzˌfɪgəˈreɪʃn, -z
AM træn(t)sˌfɪgjəˈreɪ-
ʃən, -z

transfigure
BR transˈfɪgə(r),
trɑːnsˈfɪgə(r),
tranzˈfɪgə(r),
trɑːnzˈfɪgə(r), -z, -ɪŋ,
-d
AM træn(t)sˈfɪgər, -z,
-ɪŋ, -d

transfinite
BR tranzˈfʌɪnʌɪt,
trɑːnzˈfʌɪnʌɪt,
transˈfʌɪnʌɪt,
trɑːnsˈfʌɪnʌɪt
AM træn(t)sˈfaɪˌnaɪt

transfix
BR transˈfɪks,
trɑːnsˈfɪks,
tranzˈfɪks, trɑːnzˈfɪks,
-ɪz, -ɪŋ, -t
AM træn(t)sˈfɪks, -ɪz,
-ɪŋ, -t

transfixion
BR transˈfɪkʃn,
trɑːnsˈfɪkʃn,
tranzˈfɪkʃn,
trɑːnzˈfɪkʃn
AM træn(t)sˈfɪkʃən

transform
BR transˈfɔːm,
trɑːnsˈfɔːm,
tranzˈfɔːm,
trɑːnzˈfɔːm, -z, -ɪŋ, -d

transformable
BR transˈfɔːməbl,
trɑːnsˈfɔːməbl,
tranzˈfɔːməbl,
trɑːnzˈfɔːməbl
AM træn(t)sˈfɔːrməbəl

transformation
BR ˌtransfəˈmeɪʃn,
ˌtrɑːnsfəˈmeɪʃn,
ˌtranzfəˈmeɪʃn,
ˌtrɑːnzfəˈmeɪʃn, -z
AM ˌtræn(t)sfərˈmeɪʃən,
-z

transformational
BR ˌtransfəˈmeɪʃn(ə)l,
ˌtrɑːnsfəˈmeɪʃn(ə)l,
ˌtranzfəˈmeɪʃn(ə)l,
ˌtrɑːnzfəˈmeɪʃn(ə)l
AM ˌtræn(t)sfərˈmeɪ-
ʃ(ə)nəl

transformationally
BR ˌtransfəˈmeɪʃnəli,
ˌtransfəˈmeɪʃ(ə)nəli,
ˌtrɑːnsfəˈmeɪʃnəli,
ˌtrɑːnsfəˈmeɪʃ(ə)nəli,
ˌtranzfəˈmeɪʃnəli,
ˌtranzfəˈmeɪʃ(ə)nəli,
ˌtrɑːnzfəˈmeɪʃnəli,
ˌtrɑːnzfəˈmeɪʃ(ə)nəli
AM ˌtræn(t)sfərˈmeɪ-
ʃ(ə)nəli

transformative
BR transˈfɔːmətɪv,
trɑːnsˈfɔːmətɪv,
tranzˈfɔːmətɪv,
trɑːnzˈfɔːmɪtɪv
AM træn(t)sˈfɔːrmədɪv

transformer
BR transˈfɔːmə(r),
trɑːnsˈfɔːmə(r),
tranzˈfɔːmə(r),
trɑːnzˈfɔːmə(r), -z
AM træn(t)sˈfɔːrmər, -z

transfuse
BR transˈfjuːz,
trɑːnsˈfjuːz,
tranzˈfjuːz,
trɑːnzˈfjuːz, -ɪz, -ɪŋ, -d
AM træn(t)sˈfjuz, -ɪz,
-ɪŋ, -d

transfusion
BR transˈfjuːʒn,
trɑːnsˈfjuːʃn,
tranzˈfjuːʒn,
trɑːnzˈfjuːʒn, -z
AM træn(t)sˈfjuʒən, -z

transgenic
BR tranzˈdʒɛnɪk,
trɑːnzˈdʒɛnɪk,
transˈdʒɛnɪk,
trɑːnsˈdʒɛnɪk
AM træn(t)sˈdʒɛnɪk,
træn(t)sˈdʒɛnɪk

transgress
BR tranzˈgrɛs,
trɑːnzˈgrɛs,

AM træn(t)sˈfɔ(ə)rm,
-z, -ɪŋ, -d

transˈgrɛs,
trɑːnsˈgrɛs, -ɪz, -ɪŋ, -t
AM trænzˈgrɛs,
træn(t)sˈgrɛs, -əz, -ɪŋ,
-t

transgression
BR tranzˈgrɛʃn,
trɑːnzˈgrɛʃn,
transˈgrɛʃn,
trɑːnsˈgrɛʃn, -z
AM trænzˈgrɛʃən,
træn(t)sˈgrɛʃən, -z

transgressional
BR tranzˈgrɛʃn(ə)l,
trɑːnzˈgrɛʃn(ə)l,
trɑːnzˈgrɛʃən(ə)l,
trɑːnsˈgrɛʃn(ə)l
AM trænzˈgrɛʃ(ə)nəl,
træn(t)sˈgrɛʃ(ə)nəl

transgressive
BR tranzˈgrɛsɪv,
trɑːnzˈgrɛsɪv,
transˈgrɛsɪv,
trɑːnsˈgrɛsɪv
AM trænzˈgrɛsɪv,
træn(t)sˈgrɛsɪv

transgressor
BR tranzˈgrɛsə(r),
trɑːnzˈgrɛsə(r),
transˈgrɛsə(r),
trɑːnsˈgrɛsə(r), -z
AM trænzˈgrɛsər,
træn(t)sˈgrɛsər, -z

tranship
BR transˈʃɪp,
trɑːnsˈʃɪp, tranzˈʃɪp,
trɑːnzˈʃɪp, -s, -ɪŋ,
AM ˌtræn(s)ˈʃɪp, -s, -ɪŋ,
-t

transhipment
BR transˈʃɪpm(ə)nt,
trɑːnsˈʃɪpm(ə)nt,
tranzˈʃɪpm(ə)nt,
trɑːnzˈʃɪpm(ə)nt, -s
AM ˌtræn(s)ˈʃɪpmənt,
-s

transhumance
BR tranzˈhjuːməns,
trɑːnzˈhjuːməns,
transˈhjuːməns,
trɑːnsˈhjuːməns
AM trænzˈ(h)jumæns,
træn(t)sˈ(h)jumæns

transience
BR ˈtranzɪəns,
ˈtrɑːnzɪəns,
ˈtransɪəns,
ˈtrɑːnsɪəns
AM ˈtræn(t)ʃəns,
ˈtrænʒəns

transiency
BR ˈtranzɪənsi,
ˈtrɑːnzɪənsi,
ˈtransɪənsi,
ˈtrɑːnsɪənsi
AM ˈtræn(t)ʃənsi,
ˈtrænʒənsi

transient
BR 'tranzɪənt,
'trɑːnzɪənt,
'transɪənt,
'trɑːnsɪənt, -s
AM 'træn(t)ʃənt,
'trænʒənt, -s

transiently
BR 'tranzɪəntli,
'trɑːnzɪəntli,
'transɪəntli,
'trɑːnsɪəntli
AM 'træn(t)ʃən(t)li,
'trænʒən(t)li

transientness
BR 'tranzɪəntnəs,
'trɑːnzɪəntnəs,
'transɪəntnəs,
'trɑːnsɪəntnəs
AM 'træn(t)ʃən(t)nəs,
'trænʒən(t)nəs

transilluminate
BR ˌtranzɪ'l(j)uːmɪneɪt,
ˌtrɑːnzɪ'l(j)uːmɪneɪt,
ˌtransɪ'l(j)uːmɪneɪt,
ˌtrɑːnsɪ'l(j)uːmɪneɪt,
-s, -ɪŋ, -ɪd
AM ˌtrænzə'lumə,neɪt,
ˌtræn(t)sə'lumə,neɪt,
-ts, -dɪŋ, -dɪd

transillumination
BR ˌtranzɪˌl(j)uːmɪ-
'neɪʃn,
ˌtrɑːnzɪˌl(j)uːmɪ'neɪʃn,
ˌtransɪˌl(j)uːmɪ'neɪʃn,
ˌtrɑːnsɪˌl(j)uːmɪ'neɪʃn
AM ˌtrænzəˌlumə'neɪ-
ʃən,
'træn(t)səˌlumə'neɪʃən

transire
BR tran'zʌɪə(r),
trɑːn'zʌɪə(r),
tran'sʌɪə(r),
trɑːn'sʌɪə(r),
tran'zʌɪri, trɑːn'zʌɪri,
tran'sʌɪri, trɑːn'sʌɪri
AM træn'zɑɪri

transires
BR tran'zʌɪəz,
trɑːn'zʌɪəz,
tran'sʌɪəz,
trɑːn'sʌɪəz,
tran'zʌɪrɪz,
trɑːn'zʌɪrɪz,
tran'sʌɪrɪz,
trɑːn'sʌɪrɪz
AM træn'zɑɪrɪz

transistor
BR tran'zɪstə(r),
trɑːn'zɪstə(r),
tran'sɪstə(r),
trɑːn'sɪstə(r), -z
AM træn'zɪstər, -z

transistorisation
BR tranˌzɪstərʌɪ'zeɪʃn,
trɑːnˌzɪstərʌɪ'zeɪʃn,
tranˌsɪstərʌɪ'zeɪʃn,
trɑːnˌsɪstərʌɪ'zeɪʃn

AM trænˌzɪstərə'zeɪʃən,
trænˌzɪstəˌraɪ'zeɪʃən

transistorise
BR tran'zɪstərʌɪz,
trɑːn'zɪstərʌɪz,
tran'sɪstərʌɪz,
trɑːn'sɪstərʌɪz, -ɪz, -ɪŋ,
-d
AM træn'zɪstə,raɪz, -ɪz,
-ɪŋ, -d

transistorization
BR tranˌzɪstərʌɪ'zeɪʃn,
trɑːnˌzɪstərʌɪ'zeɪʃn,
tranˌsɪstərʌɪ'zeɪʃn,
trɑːnˌsɪstərʌɪ'zeɪʃn
AM trænˌzɪstərə'zeɪʃən,
trænˌzɪstəˌraɪ'zeɪʃən

transistorize
BR tran'zɪstərʌɪz,
trɑːn'zɪstərʌɪz,
tran'sɪstərʌɪz,
trɑːn'sɪstərʌɪz, -ɪz, -ɪŋ,
-d
AM træn'zɪstə,raɪz, -ɪz,
-ɪŋ, -d

transit
BR 'transɪt, 'trɑːnsɪt,
'tranzɪt, 'trɑːnzɪt, -s
AM 'trænzət, -s

transition
BR tran'zɪʃn,
trɑːn'zɪʃn, tran'sɪʃn,
trɑːn'sɪʃn, -z
AM træn'zɪʃən, -z

transitional
BR tran'zɪʃn(ə)l,
trɑːn'zɪʃn(ə)l,
tran'sɪʃn(ə)l,
trɑːn'sɪʃn(ə)l
AM træn'zɪʃ(ə)nəl

transitionally
BR tran'zɪʃnəli,
tran'zɪʃ(ə)nəli,
trɑːn'zɪʃnəli,
trɑːn'zɪʃ(ə)nəli,
tran'sɪʃnəli,
tran'sɪʃ(ə)nəli,
trɑːn'sɪʃnəli,
trɑːn'sɪʃ(ə)nəli
AM træn'zɪʃ(ə)nəli

transitionary
BR tran'zɪʃn(ə)ri,
trɑːn'zɪʃn(ə)ri,
tran'sɪʃn(ə)ri,
trɑːn'sɪʃn(ə)ri
AM træn'zɪʃəˌneri

transitive
BR 'tranzɪtɪv,
'trɑːnzɪtɪv, 'transɪtɪv,
'trɑːnsɪtɪv
AM 'trænzədɪv,
'træn(t)sədɪv

transitively
BR 'tranzɪtɪvli,
'trɑːnzɪtɪvli,
'transɪtɪvli,
'trɑːnsɪtɪvli
AM 'trænzədɪvli,
'træn(t)sədɪvli

transitiveness
BR 'tranzɪtɪvnɪs,
'trɑːnzɪtɪvnɪs,
'transɪtɪvnɪs,
'trɑːnsɪtɪvnɪs
AM 'trænzədɪvnɪs,
'træn(t)sədɪvnɪs

transitivity
BR ˌtranzɪ'tɪvɪti,
ˌtrɑːnzɪ'tɪvɪti,
ˌtransɪ'tɪvɪti,
ˌtrɑːnsɪ'tɪvɪti
AM ˌtrænzə'tɪvɪdi,
ˌtræn(t)sə'tɪvɪdi

transitorily
BR 'tranzɪt(ə)rɪli,
'trɑːnzɪt(ə)rɪli,
'transɪt(ə)rɪli,
'trɑːnsɪt(ə)rɪli
AM 'trænzəˌtɔrəli,
'træn(t)səˌtɔrəli

transitoriness
BR 'tranzɪt(ə)rɪnɪs,
'trɑːnzɪt(ə)rɪnɪs,
'transɪt(ə)rɪnɪs,
'trɑːnsɪt(ə)rɪnɪs
AM 'trænzəˌtɔrɪnɪs,
'træn(t)səˌtɔrɪnɪs

transitory
BR 'tranzɪt(ə)ri,
'trɑːnzɪt(ə)ri,
'transɪt(ə)ri,
'trɑːnsɪt(ə)ri
AM 'trænzəˌtɔri,
'træn(t)səˌtɔri

Transjordan
BR (ˌ)tranz'dʒɔːdn,
(ˌ)trɑːnz'dʒɔːdn,
(ˌ)trans'dʒɔːdn,
(ˌ)trɑːns'dʒɔːdn
AM trænz'dʒɔrdən

Transjordanian
BR ˌtranzdʒɔː'deɪnɪən,
ˌtrɑːnzdʒɔː'deɪnɪən,
ˌtransdʒɔː'deɪnɪən,
ˌtrɑːnsdʒɔː'deɪnɪən, -z
AM ˌtrænzˌdʒɔr'deɪnɪən,
-z

Transkei
BR (ˌ)trans'kʌɪ,
(ˌ)trɑːns'kʌɪ,
(ˌ)tranz'kʌɪ,
(ˌ)trɑːnz'kʌɪ
AM træn(t)'skaɪ

translatability
BR transˌleɪtə'bɪlɪti,
trɑːnsˌleɪtə'bɪlɪti,
tranzˌleɪtə'bɪlɪti,
trɑːnzˌleɪtə'bɪlɪti
AM trænzˌleɪdə'bɪlɪdi,
ˌtræn(t)sˌleɪdə'bɪlɪdi

translatable
BR trans'leɪtəbl,
trɑːns'leɪtəbl,
tranz'leɪtəbl,
trɑːnz'leɪtəbl
AM trænz'leɪdəbəl,
træn(t)s'leɪdəbəl

translate
BR trans'leɪt,
trɑːns'leɪt, tranz'leɪt,
trɑːnz'leɪt, -s, -ɪŋ, -ɪd
AM trænz'leɪt,
træn(t)s'leɪt, -ts, -dɪŋ,
-dɪd

translation
BR trans'leɪʃn,
trɑːns'leɪʃn,
tranz'leɪʃn,
trɑːnz'leɪʃn, -z
AM trænz'leɪʃən,
træn(t)s'leɪʃən, -z

translational
BR trans'leɪʃn(ə)l,
trɑːns'leɪʃn(ə)l,
tranz'leɪʃn(ə)l,
trɑːnz'leɪʃn(ə)l
AM trænz'leɪʃ(ə)nəl,
træn(t)s'leɪʃ(ə)nəl

translationally
BR trans'leɪʃnəli,
trans'leɪʃ(ə)nəli,
trɑːns'leɪʃnəli,
trɑːns'leɪʃ(ə)nəli,
tranz'leɪʃnəli,
tranz'leɪʃ(ə)nəli,
trɑːnz'leɪʃnəli,
trɑːnz'leɪʃ(ə)nəli
AM trænz'leɪʃ(ə)nəli,
træn(t)s'leɪʃ(ə)nəli

translator
BR trans'leɪtə(r),
trɑːns'leɪtə(r),
tranz'leɪtə(r),
trɑːnz'leɪtə(r), -z
AM 'trænzˌleɪdər,
'træn(t)sˌleɪdər, -z

transliterate
BR trans'lɪtəreɪt,
trɑːns'lɪtəreɪt,
tranz'lɪtəreɪt,
trɑːnz'lɪtəreɪt, -s, -ɪŋ,
-ɪd
AM trænz'lɪdə,reɪt,
træn(t)s'lɪdə,reɪt, -ts,
-dɪŋ, -dɪd

transliteration
BR transˌlɪtə'reɪʃn,
ˌtranslɪtə'reɪʃn,
trɑːnsˌlɪtə'reɪʃn,
ˌtrɑːnslɪtə'reɪʃn,
tranzˌlɪtə'reɪʃn,
ˌtranzlɪtə'reɪʃn,
trɑːnzˌlɪtə'reɪʃn,
ˌtrɑːnzlɪtə'reɪʃn, -z
AM trænzˌlɪdə'reɪʃən,
træn(t)sˌlɪdə'reɪʃən,
-z

transliterator
BR trans'lɪtəreɪtə(r),
trɑːns'lɪtəreɪtə(r),
tranz'lɪtəreɪtə(r),
trɑːnz'lɪtəreɪtə(r), -z
AM trænz'lɪdəˌreɪdər,
træn(t)s'lɪdəˌreɪdər,
-z

translocate
BR ˌtrænslə(ʊ)ˈkeɪt,
ˌtrɑːnslə(ʊ)ˈkeɪt,
ˌtrænzlə(ʊ)ˈkeɪt,
ˌtrɑːnzlə(ʊ)ˈkeɪt, -s,
-ɪŋ, -ɪd
AM trænzˈloʊˌkeɪ|t,
træn(t)sˈloʊˌkeɪ|t, -ts,
-dɪŋ, -dɪd

translocation
BR ˌtrænslə(ʊ)ˈkeɪʃn,
ˌtrɑːnslə(ʊ)ˈkeɪʃn,
ˌtrænzlə(ʊ)ˈkeɪʃn,
ˌtrɑːnzlə(ʊ)ˈkeɪʃn, -z
AM trænzˌloʊˈkeɪʃən,
træn(t)sˌloʊˈkeɪʃən,
-z

translucence
BR transˈluːsns,
trɑːnsˈluːsns,
tranzˈluːsns,
trɑːnzˈluːsns
AM trænzˈluːsəns,
træn(t)sˈluːsəns

translucency
BR transˈluːsnsi,
trɑːnsˈluːsnsi,
tranzˈluːsnsi,
trɑːnzˈluːsnsi
AM trænzˈluːsənsi,
træn(t)sˈluːsənsi

translucent
BR transˈluːsnt,
trɑːnsˈluːsnt,
tranzˈluːsnt,
trɑːnzˈluːsnt
AM trænzˈluːsənt,
træn(t)sˈluːsənt

translucently
BR transˈluːsntli,
trɑːnsˈluːsntli,
tranzˈluːsntli,
trɑːnzˈluːsntli
AM trænzˈlusn(t)li,
træn(t)sˈlusn(t)li

translunar
BR transˈluːnə(r),
trɑːnsˈluːnə(r),
tranzˈluːnə(r),
trɑːnzˈluːnə(r)
AM ˌtrænzˈlunər,
ˌtræn(t)sˈlunər

translunary
BR transˈluːn(ə)ri,
trɑːnsˈluːn(ə)ri,
tranzˈluːn(ə)ri,
trɑːnzˈluːn(ə)ri
AM trænzˈlunəri,
træn(t)sˈlunəri

transmarine
BR ˌtrænzməˈriːn,
ˌtrɑːnzməˈriːn,
ˌtransməˈriːn,
ˌtrɑːnsməˈriːn,
AM ˌtrænzməˈrin,
ˌtræn(t)sməˈrin

transmigrant
BR trænzˈmaɪgr(ə)nt,
trɑːnzˈmaɪgr(ə)nt,

transˈmaɪgr(ə)nt,
trɑːnsˈmaɪgr(ə)nt, -s
AM trænzˈmaɪgrənt,
træn(t)sˈmaɪgrənt, -s

transmigrate
BR ˌtrænzmaɪˈgreɪt,
ˌtrɑːnzmaɪˈgreɪt,
ˌtransmaɪˈgreɪt,
ˌtrɑːnsmaɪˈgreɪt, -s,
-ɪŋ, -ɪd
AM trænzˈmaɪˌgreɪ|t,
træn(t)sˈmaɪˌgreɪ|t,
-ts, -dɪŋ, -dɪd

transmigration
BR ˌtrænzmaɪˈgreɪʃn,
ˌtrɑːnzmaɪˈgreɪʃn,
ˌtransmaɪˈgreɪʃn,
ˌtrɑːnsmaɪˈgreɪʃn, -z
AM ˌtrænzˌmaɪˈgreɪʃən,
ˌtræn(t)sˌmaɪˈgreɪʃən,
-z

transmigrator
BR ˌtrænzmaɪˈgreɪtə(r),
ˌtrɑːnzmaɪˈgreɪtə(r),
ˌtransmaɪˈgreɪtə(r),
ˌtrɑːnsmaɪˈgreɪtə(r),
-z
AM trænzˈmaɪˌgreɪdər,
træn(t)sˈmaɪˌgreɪdər,
-z

transmigratory
BR tranzˈmaɪgrət(ə)ri,
ˌtranzmaɪˈgreɪt(ə)ri,
trɑːnzˈmaɪgrət(ə)ri,
ˌtrɑːnzmaɪˈgreɪt(ə)ri,
transˈmaɪgrət(ə)ri,
ˌtransmaɪˈgreɪt(ə)ri,
trɑːnsˈmaɪgrət(ə)ri,
ˌtrɑːnsmaɪˈgreɪt(ə)ri
AM trænzˈmaɪgrəˌtɔri,
træn(t)sˈmaɪgrəˌtɔri

transmissibility
BR tranzˌmɪsɪˈbɪləti,
ˌtranzmɪsɪˈbɪləti,
trɑːnzˌmɪsɪˈbɪləti,
ˌtrɑːnzmɪsɪˈbɪləti,
transˌmɪsɪˈbɪləti,
ˌtransmɪsɪˈbɪləti,
trɑːnsˌmɪsɪˈbɪləti,
ˌtrɑːnsmɪsɪˈbɪləti
AM trænzˌmɪsəˈbɪləti,
træn(t)sˌmɪsəˈbɪlɪdi

transmissible
BR tranzˈmɪsɪbl,
trɑːnzˈmɪsɪbl,
transˈmɪsɪbl,
trɑːnsˈmɪsɪbl
AM trænzˈmɪsəbəl,
træn(t)sˈmɪsəbəl

transmission
BR tranzˈmɪʃn,
trɑːnzˈmɪʃn,
transˈmɪʃn,
trɑːnsˈmɪʃn, -z
AM trænzˈmɪʃən,
træn(t)sˈmɪʃən, -z

transmissive
BR tranzˈmɪsɪv,
trɑːnzˈmɪsɪv,

transˈmɪsɪv,
trɑːnsˈmɪsɪv
AM trænzˈmɪsɪv,
træn(t)sˈmɪsɪv

transmit
BR tranzˈmɪt,
trɑːnzˈmɪt, transˈmɪt,
trɑːnsˈmɪt, -s, -ɪŋ, -ɪd
AM trænzˈmɪ|t,
træn(t)sˈmɪ|t, -ts,
-dɪŋ, -dɪd

transmittable
BR tranzˈmɪtəbl,
trɑːnzˈmɪtəbl,
transˈmɪtəbl,
trɑːnsˈmɪtəbl
AM trænzˈmɪdəbəl,
træn(t)sˈmɪdəbəl

transmittal
BR tranzˈmɪtl,
trɑːnzˈmɪtl,
transˈmɪtl,
trɑːnsˈmɪtl, -z
AM trænzˈmɪdl,
træn(t)sˈmɪdl, -z

transmitter
BR tranzˈmɪtə(r),
trɑːnzˈmɪtə(r),
transˈmɪtə(r),
trɑːnsˈmɪtə(r), -z
AM trænzˈmɪdər,
træn(t)sˈmɪdər, -z

transmogrification
BR tranzˌmɒgrɪfɪˈkeɪʃn,
ˌtranzmɒgrɪfɪˈkeɪʃn,
trɑːnzˌmɒgrɪfɪˈkeɪʃn,
ˌtrɑːnzmɒgrɪfɪˈkeɪʃn,
transˌmɒgrɪfɪˈkeɪʃn,
ˌtransmɒgrɪfɪˈkeɪʃn,
trɑːnsˌmɒgrɪfɪˈkeɪʃn,
ˌtrɑːnsmɒgrɪfɪˈkeɪʃn
AM trænzˌmɑgrəfəˈkeɪ-
ʃən,
træn(t)sˌmɑgrəfəˈkeɪ-
ʃən

transmogrify
BR tranzˈmɒgrɪfaɪ,
trɑːnzˈmɒgrɪfaɪ,
transˈmɒgrɪfaɪ,
trɑːnsˈmɒgrɪfaɪ, -z,
-ɪŋ, -d
AM trænzˈmɑgrəˌfaɪ,
træn(t)sˈmɑgrəˌfaɪ,
-z, -ɪŋ, -d

transmontane
BR tranzˈmɒnteɪn,
trɑːnzˈmɒnteɪn,
transˈmɒnteɪn,
trɑːnsˈmɒnteɪn
AM trænzˈmɑnˌteɪn,
træn(t)sˈmɑnˌteɪn

transmutability
BR tranzˌmjuːtəˈbɪləti,
ˌtranzmjuːtəˈbɪləti,
trɑːnzˌmjuːtəˈbɪləti,
ˌtrɑːnzmjuːtəˈbɪləti,
transˌmjuːtəˈbɪləti,
ˌtransmjuːtəˈbɪləti,

transmutable
BR trɑːnsˌmjuːtəˈbɪləti,
ˌtrɑːnsmjuːtəˈbɪlɪti:
AM trænzˌmjudəˈbɪlɪdi,
træn(t)sˌmjudəˈbɪlɪdi

transmutable
BR tranzˈmjuːtəbl,
trɑːnzˈmjuːtəbl,
transˈmjuːtəbl,
trɑːnsˈmjuːtəbl
AM trænzˈmjudəbəl,
træn(t)sˈmjudəbəl

transmutation
BR ˌtranzmjuːˈteɪʃn,
ˌtranzmjəˈteɪʃn,
ˌtrɑːnzmjuːˈteɪʃn,
ˌtrɑːnzmjəˈteɪʃn,
ˌtransmjuːˈteɪʃn,
ˌtransmjəˈteɪʃn,
ˌtrɑːnsmjuːˈteɪʃn,
ˌtrɑːnsmjəˈteɪʃn, -z
AM ˌtrænzmjuːˈteɪʃən,
ˌtræn(t)smjuːˈteɪʃən,
-z

transmutational
BR ˌtranzmjuːˈteɪʃn̩(ə)l,
ˌtranzmjəˈteɪʃn̩(ə)l,
ˌtrɑːnzmjuːˈteɪʃn̩(ə)l,
ˌtrɑːnzmjəˈteɪʃn̩(ə)l,
ˌtransmjuːˈteɪʃn̩(ə)l,
ˌtransmjəˈteɪʃn̩(ə)l,
ˌtrɑːnsmjuːˈteɪʃn̩(ə)l,
ˌtrɑːnsmjəˈteɪʃn̩(ə)l
AM ˌtrænzmjuːˈteɪʃ(ə)nəl,
ˌtræn(t)smjuːˈteɪʃ(ə)nəl

transmutationist
BR ˌtranzmjuːˈteɪʃn̩ɪst,
ˌtranzmjəˈteɪʃn̩ɪst,
ˌtrɑːnzmjuːˈteɪʃn̩ɪst,
ˌtrɑːnzmjəˈteɪʃn̩ɪst,
ˌtransmjuːˈteɪʃn̩ɪst,
ˌtransmjəˈteɪʃn̩ɪst,
ˌtrɑːnsmjuːˈteɪʃn̩ɪst,
ˌtrɑːnsmjəˈteɪʃn̩ɪst, -s
AM ˌtrænzmjuːˈteɪʃənəst,
ˌtræn(t)smjuːˈteɪʃənəst,
-s

transmutative
BR tranzˈmjuːtətɪv,
trɑːnzˈmjuːtətɪv,
transˈmjuːtətɪv,
trɑːnsˈmjuːtətɪv
AM trænzˈmjudədɪv,
træn(t)sˈmjudədɪv

transmute
BR tranzˈmjuːt,
trɑːnzˈmjuːt,
transˈmjuːt,
trɑːnsˈmjuːt, -s, -ɪŋ, -ɪd
AM trænzˈmjuːt,
træn(t)sˈmjuː|t, -ts,
-dɪŋ, -dəd

transmuter
BR tranzˈmjuːtə(r),
trɑːnzˈmjuːtə(r),
transˈmjuːtə(r),
trɑːnsˈmjuːtə(r), -z
AM trænzˈmjudər,
træn(t)sˈmjudər, -z

transnational
BR tranz'næʃn(ə)l,
traːnz'næʃn(ə)l,
trans'næʃn(ə)l,
traːns'næʃn(ə)l, -z
AM trænz'næʃ(ə)nəl,
træn(t)s'næʃ(ə)nəl,
-z

transoceanic
BR ˌtranzəʊʃi'anık,
ˌtraːnzəʊʃi'anık,
ˌtranzəʊsı'anık,
ˌtraːnzəʊsı'anık,
ˌtransəʊʃi'anık,
ˌtraːnsəʊʃi'anık,
ˌtransəʊsı'anık,
ˌtraːnsəʊsı'anık
AM ˌtrænzoʊʃi'ænık

transom
BR trans(ə)m, -z, -d
AM 'træn(t)səm, -z, -d

transonic
BR tran'sɒnık,
traːn'sɒnık
AM træn(t)'sanık

transpacific
BR ˌtranspə'sıfık,
ˌtraːnspə'sıfık,
ˌtranzpə'sıfık,
ˌtraːnzpə'sıfık
AM ˌtræn(t)spə'sıfık

transpadane
BR 'transpədem,
'traːnspədem,
'tranzpədem,
'traːnzpədem
AM 'træn(t)spəˌdem,
træn(t)s'peıˌdem

transparence
BR tran'sparəns,
tran'sparns,
traːn'sparəns,
traːn'sparns,
tran'spɛːrəns,
tran'spɛːrns,
traːn'spɛːrəns,
traːn'spɛːrns
AM træn(t)'spɛrəns

transparency
BR tran'sparns|i,
traːn'sparns|i,
tran'spɛːrəns|i,
traːn'spɛːrəns|i, -ız
AM træn(t)'spɛrənsi,
-z

transparent
BR tran'sparnt,
traːn'sparnt,
tran'spɛːrnt,
traːn'spɛːrnt
AM træn(t)'spɛrənt

transparently
BR tran'sparntli,
traːn'sparntli,
tran'spɛːrntli,
traːn'spɛːrntli
AM træn(t)'spɛrən(t)li

transparentness
BR tran'sparntnəs,
traːn'sparntnəs,
tran'spɛːrntnəs,
traːn'spɛːrntnəs
AM træn(t)'spɛrən(t)nəs

trans-Pennine
BR trans'pɛnʌın,
traːns'pɛnʌın,
tranz'pɛnʌın,
traːnz'pɛnʌın
AM træn(t)s'pɛˌnaın

transpersonal
BR trans'pəːsn̩l,
trans'pəː(s)(ə)nl,
traːns'pəːsn̩l,
traːns'pəː(s)(ə)nl,
tranz'pəːsn̩l,
tranz'pəː(s)(ə)nl,
traːnz'pəːsn̩l,
traːnz'pəː(s)(ə)nl
AM træn(t)s'pərs(ə)nəl

transpierce
BR trans'pıəs,
traːns'pıəs,
tranz'pıəs,
traːnz'pıəs, -ız, -ıŋ, -t
AM træn(t)s'pı(ə)rs,
-əz, -ıŋ, -t

transpirable
BR tran'spʌıərəbl,
traːn'spʌıərəbl
AM træn(t)'spaı(ə)rə-
bəl, træn(t)'spaıərbəl

transpiration
BR ˌtranspı'reıʃn,
ˌtraːnspı'reıʃn
AM ˌtræn(t)spə'reıʃən

transpiratory
BR tran'spʌırət(ə)ri,
traːn'spʌırət(ə)ri
AM træn(t)'spaırəˌtɔri

transpire
BR tran'spʌıə(r),
traːn'spʌıə(r), -z, -ıŋ,
-d
AM træn(t)'spaı(ə)r,
-z, -ıŋ, -d

transplant[1]
noun
BR 'transplaːnt,
'traːnsplaːnt,
'transplant, -s
AM 'træn(t)sˌplænt, -s

transplant[2]
verb
BR trans'plaːnt,
traːns'plaːnt,
trans'plant, -s, -ıŋ, -ıd
AM træn(t)s'plænt,
-ts, -(t)ıŋ, -(t)əd

transplantable
BR trans'plaːntəbl,
traːns'plaːntəbl,
trans'plantəbl
AM træn(t)s'plæn(t)ə-
bəl

transplantation
BR ˌtransplaːn'teıʃn,
ˌtraːnsplaːn'teıʃn,
ˌtransplan'teıʃn, -z
AM ˌtræn(t)sˌplæn'teı-
ʃən, -z

transplanter
BR trans'plaːntə(r),
traːns'plaːntə(r),
trans'plantə(r), -z
AM træn(t)s'plæn(t)ər,
-z

transponder
BR tran'spɒndə(r),
traːn'spɒndə(r), -z
AM træn(t)'spandər, -z

transpontine
BR trans'pɒntʌın,
traːns'pɒntʌın,
tranz'pɒntʌın,
traːnz'pɒntʌın
AM træn(t)'spanˌtaın

transport[1]
noun
BR 'transpɔːt,
'traːnspɔːt, -s
AM 'træn(t)sˌpɔ(ə)rt,
-s

transport[2]
verb
BR tran'spɔːt,
traːn'spɔːt, -s, -ıŋ, -ıd
AM træn(t)s'pɔ(ə)rt,
-ts, -'pɔrdıŋ, -'pɔrdəd

transportability
BR tranˌspɔːtə'bılıti,
ˌtranspɔːtə'bılıti,
traːnˌspɔːtə'bılıti,
ˌtraːnspɔːtə'bılıti
AM ˌtræn(t)sˌpɔrdə'bıl-
ıdi

transportable
BR tran'spɔːtəbl,
traːn'spɔːtəbl
AM træn(t)s'pɔrdəbəl

transportation
BR ˌtranspə'teıʃn,
ˌtraːnspɔː'teıʃn,
ˌtraːnspə'teıʃn,
ˌtraːnspɔː'teıʃn
AM ˌtræn(t)spər'teıʃən

transporter
BR tran'spɔːtə(r),
traːn'spɔːtə(r), -z
AM træn(t)s'pɔrdər, -z

transposable
BR tran'spəʊzəbl,
traːn'spəʊzəbl
AM træn(t)s'poʊzəbəl

transposal
BR tran'spəʊzl,
traːn'spəʊzl
AM træn(t)s'poʊzəl

transpose
BR tran'spəʊz,
traːn'spəʊz, -ız, -ıŋ, -d
AM træn(t)s'poʊz, -ız,
-ıŋ, -d

transposer
BR tran'spəʊzə(r),
traːn'spəʊzə(r), -z
AM træn(t)s'poʊzər, -z

transposition
BR ˌtranspə'zıʃn,
ˌtraːnspə'zıʃn,
ˌtranzpə'zıʃn,
ˌtraːnzpə'zıʃn, -z
AM ˌtræn(t)spə'zıʃən,
-z

transpositional
BR ˌtranspə'zıʃn(ə)l,
ˌtraːnspə'zıʃn(ə)l,
ˌtranzpə'zıʃn(ə)l,
ˌtraːnzpə'zıʃn(ə)l
AM ˌtræn(t)spə'zıʃ(ə)nəl

transpositive
BR trans'pɒzıtıv,
traːns'pɒzıtıv,
tranz'spɒzıtıv,
traːnz'pɒzıtıv
AM træn(t)s'pazədıv

transputer
BR tran'spjuːtə(r),
traːn'spjuːtə(r), -z
AM træn(t)s'spjudər, -z

transsexual
BR tran(s)'sɛkʃʊəl,
tran(s)'sɛkʃ(ɵ)l,
tran(s)'sɛksju(ə)l,
traːn(s)'sɛkʃʊəl,
traːn(s)'sɛkʃ(ɵ)l,
traːn(s)'sɛksju(ə)l,
tranz'sɛkʃʊəl,
tranz'sɛkʃ(ɵ)l,
tranz'sɛksju(ə)l,
traːnz'sɛkʃʊəl,
traːnz'sɛkʃ(ɵ)l,
traːnz'sɛksju(ə)l, -z
AM træn(t)(s)'sɛkʃ(əw)əl,
-z

transsexualism
BR tran(z)'sɛkʃʊəlız(ə)m,
tran(z)'sɛkʃɵlız(ə)m,
tran(z)'sɛkʃʃlız(ə)m,
tran(z)'sɛksju(ə)lız(ə)m,
traːn(z)'sɛkʃʊəlız(ə)m,
traːn(z)'sɛkʃɵlız(ə)m,
traːn(z)'sɛkʃʃlız(ə)m,
traːn(z)'sɛksju(ə)lız(ə)m
AM træn(t)(s)'sɛkʃ(əw)əˌlız

transship
BR tran(s)'ʃıp,
traːn(s)'ʃıp,
tranz'ʃıp, traːnz'ʃıp,
-s, -ıŋ, -t
AM træn(t)(s)'ʃıp, -s,
-ıŋ, -t

transshipment
BR tran(s)'ʃıpm(ə)nt,
traːn(s)'ʃıpm(ə)nt,
tranz'ʃıpm(ə)nt,
traːnz'ʃıpm(ə)nt, -s
AM træn(t)(s)'ʃıpmənt,
-s

trans-Siberian
BR ˌtran(s)sʌı'bıərıən,
ˌtraːn(s)sʌı'bıərıən,

,tranzsʌɪ'bɪərɪən,
,trɑːnzsʌɪ'bɪərɪən
AM ,træn(t)s,saɪ'bɪr-
ɪən

trans-sonic
BR tran(s)'sɒnɪk,
trɑːn(s)'sɒnɪk,
tranz'sɒnɪk,
trɑːnz'sɒnɪk
AM træn(t)s,sɒnɪk

transubstantiate
BR ,transəb'stanʃɪeɪt,
,trɑːnsəb'stanʃɪeɪt,
,transəb'stansɪeɪt,
,trɑːnsəb'stansɪeɪt, -s,
-ɪŋ, -d
AM ,træn(t)səb'stæn-
(t)ʃi,eɪ|t, -ts, -dɪŋ, -dɪd

transubstantiation
BR ,transəb,stanʃɪ'eɪʃn,
,trɑːnsəb,stanʃɪ'eɪʃn,
,transəb,stansɪ'eɪʃn,
,trɑːnsəb,stansɪ'eɪʃn
AM ,træn(t)səb,stæn-
(t)ʃi'eɪʃən

transudation
BR ,transjʊ'deɪʃn,
,trɑːnsjʊ'deɪʃn,
,tranzjʊ'deɪʃn,
,trɑːnzjʊ'deɪʃn
AM ,træn(t)sə'deɪʃən

transudatory
BR tran(s)'sjuːdət(ə)ri,
trɑːn(s)'sjuːdət(ə)ri,
tran'zjuːdət(ə)ri,
trɑːn'zjuːdət(ə)ri
AM træn(t)s'sudə,tɔri

transude
BR tran'sjuːd,
trɑːn'sjuːd,
tran'zjuːd,
trɑːn'zjuːd, -z, -ɪŋ, -ɪd
AM træn(t)'s(j)ud, -z,
-ɪŋ, -əd

transuranic
BR ,transjʊ'ranɪk,
,trɑːnsjʊ'ranɪk,
,tranzjʊ'ranɪk,
,trɑːnzjʊ'ranɪk
AM ,træn(t)sjə'rænɪk

Transvaal
BR 'tranzvɑːl,
'trɑːnzvɑːl,
(,)tranz'vɑːl,
(,)trɑːnz'vɑːl,
'transvɑːl, 'trɑːnsvɑːl,
(,)trans'vɑːl,
(,)trɑːns'vɑːl
AM trænz'vɑl

Transvaaler
BR 'tranzvɑːlə(r),
'trɑːnzvɑːlə(r),
(,)tranz'vɑːlə(r),
(,)trɑːnz'vɑːlə(r),
'transvɑːlə(r),
'trɑːnsvɑːlə(r),
(,)trans'vɑːlə(r),
(,)trɑːns'vɑːlə(r), -z
AM trænz'vɑlər, -z

transversal
BR tranz'vɜːsl,
trɑːnz'vɜːsl,
trans'vɜːsl,
trɑːns'vɜːsl, -z
AM trænz'vɜrsəl,
træn(t)s'vɜrsəl, -z

transversality
BR ,tranzvɜː'salɪti,
,trɑːnzvɜː'salɪti,
,transvɜː'salɪti,
,trɑːnsvɜː'salɪti
AM ,trænzvɜr'sælədi,
,træn(t)svɜr'sælədi

transversally
BR (,)tranz'vɜːsli,
(,)trɑːnz'vɜːsli,
(,)trans'vɜːsli,
(,)trɑːns'vɜːsli
AM trænz'vɜrsəli,
træn(t)s'vɜrsəli

transverse
BR (,)tranz'vɜːs,
(,)trɑːnz'vɜːs,
(,)trans'vɜːs,
(,)trɑːns'vɜːs
AM trænz'vɜrs,
træn(t)s'vɜrs

transversely
BR (,)tranz'vɜːsli,
(,)trɑːnz'vɜːsli,
(,)trans'vɜːsli,
(,)trɑːns'vɜːsli
AM trænz'vɜrsli,
træn(t)s'vɜrsli

transvest
BR tranz'vest,
trɑːnz'vest,
trans'vest,
trɑːns'vest, -s, -ɪŋ, -ɪd
AM trænz'vest,
træn(t)s'vest, -s, -ɪŋ,
-əd

transvestism
BR tranz'vestɪz(ə)m,
trɑːnz'vestɪz(ə)m,
trans'vestɪz(ə)m,
trɑːns'vestɪz(ə)m
AM trænz'ves,tɪzəm,
træn(t)s'ves,tɪzəm

transvestist
BR tranz'vestɪst,
trɑːnz'vestɪst,
trans'vestɪst,
trɑːns'vestɪst, -s
AM trænz'vestəst,
træn(t)s'vestəst, -s

transvestite
BR tranz'vestʌɪt,
trɑːnz'vestʌɪt,
trans'vestʌɪt,
trɑːns'vestʌɪt, -s
AM trænz'ves,taɪt,
træn(t)s'ves,taɪt, -s

Transworld
BR ,tranz'wɜːld,
,trɑːnz'wɜːld,
,trans'wɜːld,
,trɑːns'wɜːld

AM ,trænz'wɜːld,
'træn(t)s'wɜːld

Transylvania
BR ,trans(ɪ)l'veɪnɪə(r),
,trɑːns(ɪ)l'veɪnɪə(r)
AM ,træn(t)səl'veɪnɪə,
,træn(t)səl'veɪnjə

Transylvanian
BR ,trans(ɪ)l'veɪnɪən,
,trɑːns(ɪ)l'veɪnɪən, -z
AM ,træn(t)səl'veɪnɪən,
,træn(t)səl'veɪnjən,
-z

tranter
BR 'trantə(r), -z
AM 'træn(t)ər, -z

trap
BR trap, -s, -ɪŋ, -t
AM træp, -s, -ɪŋ, -t

trap-ball
BR 'trapbɔːl
AM 'træp,bɔl,
'træp,bɑl

trapdoor
BR ,trap'dɔː(r),
'trapdɔː(r), -z
AM 'træp,dɔ(ə)r, -z

trapes
BR treɪps, -ɪz, -ɪŋ, -t
AM treɪps, -ɪz, -ɪŋ, -t

trapeze
BR trə'piːz, -ɪz
AM trə'piz, træ'piz, -ɪz

trapezia
BR trə'piːzɪə(r)
AM trə'pizɪə

trapezium
BR trə'piːzɪəm, -z
AM trə'pizɪəm, -z

trapezoid
BR trə'piːzɔɪd, -z
AM 'træpə,zɔɪd, -z

trapezoidal
BR ,trapɪ'zɔɪdl
AM ,træpə'zɔɪdəl

traplike
BR 'traplʌɪk
AM 'træp,laɪk

trappean
BR 'trapɪən
AM 'træpɪən

trapper
BR 'trapə(r), -z
AM 'træpər, -z

trappings
BR 'trapɪŋz
AM 'træpɪŋz

Trappist
BR 'trapɪst, -s
AM 'træpəst, -s

Trappistine
BR 'trapɪstiːn
AM 'træpə,stin

trapse
BR treɪps, -ɪz, -ɪŋ, -t
AM treɪps, -ɪz, -ɪŋ, -t

trapshooter
BR 'trap,ʃuːtə(r), -z
AM 'træp,ʃudər, -z

trapshooting
BR 'trap,ʃuːtɪŋ
AM 'træp,ʃudɪŋ

trash
BR traʃ, -ɪz, -ɪŋ, -t
AM træʃ, -əz, -ɪŋ, -t

trashcan
BR 'traʃkan, -z
AM 'træʃ,kæn, -z

trashery
BR 'traʃ(ə)r|i, -ɪz
AM 'træʃəri, -z

trashily
BR 'traʃɪli
AM 'træʃəli

trashiness
BR 'traʃɪnɪs
AM 'træʃinɪs

trashman
BR 'traʃman
AM 'træʃ,mæn

trashmen
BR 'traʃmen
AM 'træʃ,men

trashy
BR 'traʃ|i, -ɪə(r), -ɪɪst
AM 'træʃ|i, -ər, -ɪst

Trás-os-Montes
BR ,trɑː'səz'mɒnteɪz
AM 'trasəz'mɑn,teɪz
B PORT ,trasos'montʃis
L PORT ,trazuʒ'môtəʃ

trass
BR tras
AM træs

trattoria
BR ,tratə'riːə(r), -z
AM ,trɑdə'riə, -z

trauma
BR 'trɔːmə(r),
'traʊmə(r), -z
AM 'trɔmə, 'traʊmə, -z

traumata
BR 'trɔːmətə(r),
'traʊmətə(r)
AM 'trɔmədə,
'traʊmədə

traumatic
BR trɔː'matɪk,
traʊ'matɪk
AM trə'mædɪk,
trə'mædɪk,
trɑ'mædɪk

traumatically
BR trɔː'matɪkli,
traʊ'matɪkli
AM trɔ'mædək(ə)li,
trɑ'mædək(ə)li

traumatisation
BR ,trɔːmətʌɪ'zeɪʃn,
,traʊmətʌɪ'zeɪʃn
AM ,trɔmədə'zeɪʃən,
,trɔmə,taɪ'zeɪʃən,
,traʊmədə'zeɪʃən,
,trɑmə,taɪ'zeɪʃən

traumatise
BR ˈtrɔːmətʌɪz,
ˈtraʊmətʌɪz, -ɪz, -ɪŋ, -d
AM ˈtrɔːmə,taɪz,
ˈtraʊmə,taɪz, -ɪz, -ɪŋ, -d

traumatism
BR ˈtrɔːmətɪz(ə)m,
ˈtraʊmətɪz(ə)m
AM ˈtrɔːmə,tɪzəm,
ˈtraʊmə,tɪzəm

traumatization
BR ,trɔːmətʌɪˈzeɪʃn,
,traʊmətʌɪˈzeɪʃn
AM ,trɔːmədəˈzeɪʃən,
,trɔːmə,taɪˈzeɪʃən,
,traʊmədəˈzeɪʃən,
,traʊmə,taɪˈzeɪʃən

traumatize
BR ˈtrɔːmətʌɪz,
ˈtraʊmətʌɪz, -ɪz, -ɪŋ, -d
AM ˈtrɔːmə,taɪz,
ˈtraʊmə,taɪz, -ɪz, -ɪŋ, -d

travail
BR ˈtraveɪl, -z, -ɪŋ, -d
AM trəˈveɪ(ə)l,
ˈtræ,veɪl, -z, -ɪŋ, -d

travel
BR ˈtrav|l, -lz, -|ɪŋ\-lɪŋ,
-ld
AM ˈtræv|əl, -əlz,
-(ə)lɪŋ, -əld

traveler
BR ˈtravlə(r),
ˈtravlə(r), -z
AM ˈtræv(ə)lər, -z

traveller
BR ˈtravlə(r),
ˈtravlə(r), -z
AM ˈtræv(ə)lər, -z

Travelodge®
BR ˈtravəlɒdʒ
AM ˈtrævə,lɑdʒ

travelog
BR ˈtravəlɒg, -z
AM ˈtrævə,lɒg,
ˈtrævə,lag, -z

travelogue
BR ˈtravəlɒg, -z
AM ˈtrævə,lɒg,
ˈtrævə,lag, -z

Travers
BR ˈtravəz
AM ˈtrævərs

traversable
BR ˈtravəsəbl,
trəˈvəːsəbl
AM trəˈvərsəbəl

traversal
BR trəˈvəːsl
AM trəˈvərsəl

traverse
BR ˈtravəs, trəˈvəːs, -ɪz,
-ɪŋ, -t
AM trəˈvərs, -əz, -ɪŋ, -t

traverser
BR ˈtravəsə(r),
trəˈvəːsə(r), -z
AM trəˈvərsər, -z

travertine
BR ˈtravətiːn, -z
AM ˈtrævər,tin, -z

travesty
BR ˈtravɪst|i, -ɪz, -ɪɪŋ,
-ɪd
AM ˈtrævəsti, -z, -ɪŋ, -d

Traviata
BR ˌtravɪˈɑːtə(r)
AM ˌtravɪˈɑdə

Travis
BR ˈtravɪs
AM ˈtrævəs

travois¹
singular
BR trəˈvɔɪ, ˈtravɔɪ
AM ˈtræ,vɔɪ, trəˈvɔɪ,
trəvˈwɑ

travois²
plural
BR trəˈvɔɪz, ˈtravɔɪz
AM ˈtræ,vɔɪ(z),
trəˈvɔɪ(z), trəvˈwɑ(z)

trawl
BR trɔːl, -z, -ɪŋ, -d
AM trɔl, tral, -z, -ɪŋ, -d

trawler
BR ˈtrɔːlə(r), -z
AM ˈtrɔlər, ˈtralər, -z

trawlerman
BR ˈtrɔːləmən
AM ˈtrɔlərmən,
ˈtralərmən

trawlermen
BR ˈtrɔːləmən
AM ˈtrɔlərmən,
ˈtralərmən

Trawsfynydd
BR ˌtraʊsˈvʌnɪð,
ˌtraʊzˈvʌnɪð
AM ˌtraʊsˈvənəθ

tray
BR treɪ, -z
AM treɪ, -z

trayful
BR ˈtreɪfʊl, -z
AM ˈtreɪ,fʊl, -z

treacherous
BR ˈtretʃ(ə)rəs
AM ˈtretʃ(ə)rəs

treacherously
BR ˈtretʃ(ə)rəsli
AM ˈtretʃ(ə)rəsli

treacherousness
BR ˈtretʃ(ə)rəsnəs
AM ˈtretʃ(ə)rəsnəs

treachery
BR ˈtretʃ(ə)r|i, -ɪz
AM ˈtretʃ(ə)ri, -z

treacle
BR ˈtriːkl
AM ˈtrikəl

treacliness
BR ˈtriːkl|ɪnɪs,
ˈtriːklɪnɪs
AM ˈtrik(ə)linɪs

treacly
BR ˈtriːkl̩i, ˈtriːkli

AM ˈtrik(ə)li

Treacy
BR ˈtriːsi
AM ˈtrisi

tread
BR tred, -z, -ɪŋ, -ɪd
AM tred, -z, -ɪŋ, -əd

treader
BR ˈtredə(r), -z
AM ˈtredər, -z

treadle
BR ˈtredl, -z
AM ˈtredəl, -z

treadmill
BR ˈtredmɪl, -z
AM ˈtred,mɪl, -z

treadwheel
BR ˈtredwiːl, -z
AM ˈtred,(h)wil, -z

treason
BR ˈtriːzn, -z
AM ˈtrizn, -z

treasonable
BR ˈtriːznəbl,
ˈtriːz(ə)nəbl
AM ˈtriznəbəl

treasonableness
BR ˈtriːznəblnəs,
ˈtriːz(ə)nəblnəs
AM ˈtriznəbəlnəs

treasonably
BR ˈtriːznəbli,
ˈtriːz(ə)nəbli
AM ˈtriz(ə)nəbli

treasonous
BR ˈtriːznəs,
ˈtriːz(ə)nəs
AM ˈtriznəs

treasure
BR ˈtreʒ|ə(r), -əz,
-(ə)rɪŋ, -əd
AM ˈtreʒ|ər, -ərz,
-(ə)rɪŋ, -ərd

treasurehouse
BR ˈtreʒəhaʊ|s, -zɪz
AM ˈtreʒər,(h)aʊ|s, -zəz

treasurer
BR ˈtreʒ(ə)rə(r), -z
AM ˈtreʒ(ə)rər, -z

treasurership
BR ˈtreʒ(ə)rəʃɪp, -s
AM ˈtreʒ(ə)rər,ʃɪp, -s

treasury
BR ˈtreʒ(ə)r|i, -ɪz
AM ˈtreʒ(ə)ri, -z

treat
BR triːt, -s, -ɪŋ, -ɪd
AM trilt, -ts, -dɪŋ, -dɪd

treatable
BR ˈtriːtəbl
AM ˈtridəbəl

treater
BR ˈtriːtə(r), -z
AM ˈtridər, -z

treatise
BR ˈtriːtɪz, ˈtriːtɪs, -ɪz
AM ˈtridɪs, -ɪz

treatment
BR ˈtriːtm(ə)nt, -s
AM ˈtritmənt, -s

treaty
BR ˈtriːt|i, -ɪz
AM ˈtridi, -z

Trebizond
BR ˈtrebɪzɒnd
AM ˈtrebɪ,zand

treble
BR ˈtreb|l, -lz, -|ɪŋ\-lɪŋ,
-ld
AM ˈtrebəl, -əlz, -(ə)lɪŋ,
-əld

treble chance
BR ˌtrebl ˈtʃɑːns,
+ ˈtʃans
AM ˌtrebəl ˈtʃæns

treble clef
BR ˌtrebl ˈklef, -s
AM ˌtrebəl ˌklef, -s

Treblinka
BR trɪˈblɪŋkə(r),
trəˈblɪŋkə(r)
AM trəˈblɪŋkə,
treˈblɪŋkə

trebly
BR ˈtrebli
AM ˈtrebli

Trebor
BR ˈtriːbɔː(r)
AM ˈtribə(r)

trebuchet
BR ˈtreb(j)ʊʃet, -s
AM ˌtreb(j)əˈʃet, -s

trecentist
BR treɪˈtʃentɪst, -s
AM treɪˈ(t)ʃen(t)əst, -s

trecento
BR treɪˈtʃentəʊ
AM treɪˈ(t)ʃen(t)oʊ
IT treˈtʃento

Tredegar
BR trɪˈdiːgə(r)
AM trəˈdigər

tree
BR triː, -z, -ɪŋ, -d
AM tri, -z, -ɪŋ, -d

treecreeper
BR ˈtriː,kriːpə(r), -z
AM ˈtri,kripər, -z

treehouse
BR ˈtriːhaʊ|s, -zɪz
AM ˈtri,haʊ|s, -zəz

treeless
BR ˈtriːlɪs
AM ˈtrilɪs

treelessness
BR ˈtriːlɪsnɪs
AM ˈtrilɪsnɪs

treeline
BR ˈtriːlʌɪn
AM ˈtri,lain

treen
BR triːn
AM trin

treenail
BR ˈtriːneɪl, ˈtrɛnl, -z
AM ˈtriˌneɪl, ˈtrɛnl, -z

treetop
BR ˈtriːtɒp, -s
AM ˈtriˌtɑp, -s

trefa
BR ˈtreɪfə(r)
AM ˈtreɪfə

Trefgarne
BR ˈtrɛvɡɑːn, ˈtrɛfɡɑːn
AM ˈtrɛfˌɡɑrn

trefoil
BR ˈtrɛfɔɪl, ˈtriːfɔɪl,
trɪˈfɔɪl, -z, -d
AM ˈtriˌfɔɪl, ˈtrɛˌfɔɪl, -z,
-d

Trefusis
BR trɪˈfjuːsɪs
AM trəˈfjusəs

Tregaron
BR trɪˈɡarən, trɪˈɡarn̩
AM trəˈɡɛrən

trehalose
BR ˈtriːhələʊs,
trɪˈhɑːləʊs,
AM ˈtri(h)əˌloʊs

trek
BR trɛk, -s, -ɪŋ, -t
AM trɛk, -s, -ɪŋ, -t

trekker
BR ˈtrɛkə(r), -z
AM ˈtrɛkər, -z

Trelawney
BR trɪˈlɔːni
AM trəˈlɔni, trəˈlɑni

trellis
BR ˈtrɛlɪs, -ɪz, -t
AM ˈtrɛləs, -əz, -t

trellis-work
BR ˈtrɛlɪswəːk, -s
AM ˈtrɛləsˌwərk, -s

Tremain
BR trɪˈmeɪn
AM trəˈmeɪn

trematode
BR ˈtrɛmətəʊd,
ˈtriːmətəʊd, -z
AM ˈtrɛməˌtoʊd,
ˈtriməˌtoʊd, -z

tremble
BR ˈtrɛmbl̩, -z, -ɪŋ, -d
AM ˈtrɛmbəl, -əlz,
-(ə)lɪŋ, -əld

trembler
BR ˈtrɛmblə(r), -z
AM ˈtrɛmb(ə)lər, -z

trembling
BR ˈtrɛmblɪŋ, -z
AM ˈtrɛmb(ə)lɪŋ, -z

tremblingly
BR ˈtrɛmblɪŋli
AM ˈtrɛmb(ə)lɪŋli

trembly
BR ˈtrɛmbli
AM ˈtrɛmb(ə)li

tremendous
BR trɪˈmɛndəs
AM trəˈmɛndəs,
triˈmɛndəs

tremendously
BR trɪˈmɛndəsli
AM trəˈmɛndəsli,
triˈmɛndəsli

tremendousness
BR trɪˈmɛndəsnəs
AM trəˈmɛndəsnəs,
triˈmɛndəsnəs

Tremlett
BR ˈtrɛmlɪt
AM ˈtrɛmlət

tremolo
BR ˈtrɛmələʊ,
ˈtrɛmləʊ, -z
AM ˈtrɛməˌloʊ, -z

tremor
BR ˈtrɛmə(r), -z
AM ˈtrɛmər, -z

tremulant
BR ˈtrɛmjʊlənt,
ˈtrɛmjʊln̩t
AM ˈtrɛmjələnt

tremulous
BR ˈtrɛmjʊləs
AM ˈtrɛmjələs

tremulously
BR ˈtrɛmjʊləsli
AM ˈtrɛmjələsli

tremulousness
BR ˈtrɛmjʊləsnəs
AM ˈtrɛmjələsnəs

trenail
BR ˈtriːneɪl, ˈtrɛnl, -z
AM ˈtriˌneɪl, ˈtrɛnl, -z

trench
BR trɛn(t)ʃ, -ɪz
AM trɛn(t)ʃ, -əz

trenchancy
BR ˈtrɛn(t)ʃ(ə)nsi
AM ˈtrɛn(t)ʃənsi

trenchant
BR ˈtrɛn(t)ʃ(ə)nt
AM ˈtrɛn(t)ʃənt

trenchantly
BR ˈtrɛn(t)ʃ(ə)n(t)li
AM ˈtrɛn(t)ʃəntli

Trenchard
BR ˈtrɛn(t)ʃɑːd,
ˈtrɛn(t)ʃəd
AM ˈtrɛn(t)ʃərd

trencher
BR ˈtrɛn(t)ʃə(r), -z
AM ˈtrɛn(t)ʃər, -z

trencherman
BR ˈtrɛn(t)ʃəmən
AM ˈtrɛn(t)ʃərmən

trenchermen
BR ˈtrɛn(t)ʃəmən
AM ˈtrɛn(t)ʃərmən

trend
BR trɛnd, -z, -ɪŋ, -ɪd
AM trɛnd, -z, -ɪŋ, -əd

trendily
BR ˈtrɛndɪli
AM ˈtrɛndəli

trendiness
BR ˈtrɛndɪnɪs
AM ˈtrɛndɪnɪs

trendsetter
BR ˈtrɛndˌsɛtə(r), -z
AM ˈtrɛn(d)ˌsɛdər, -z

trendsetting
BR ˈtrɛndˌsɛtɪŋ
AM ˈtrɛn(d)ˌsɛdɪŋ

trendy
BR ˈtrɛnd|i, -ɪz, -ɪə(r),
-ɪɪst
AM ˈtrɛndi, -z, -ər, -ɪst

Trent
BR trɛnt
AM trɛnt

trental
BR ˈtrɛntl̩, -z
AM ˈtrɛn(t)l, -z

trente-et-quarante
BR ˌtrɒteɪkaˈrɒt
AM ˌtrɑn(t)əkəˈrɑnt

Trentham
BR ˈtrɛntəm
AM ˈtrɛn(t)əm

Trentino-Alto
BR trɛnˌtiːnəʊˈaltəʊ
AM trɛnˌtinoʊˈaltoʊ

Trento
BR ˈtrɛntəʊ
AM ˈtrɛn(t)oʊ

Trenton
BR ˈtrɛnt(ə)n
AM ˈtrɛnt(ə)n

Treorchy
BR trɪˈɔːki
AM triˈɔrki

trepan
BR trɪˈpan, -z, -ɪŋ, -d
AM trəˈpæn, triˈpæn,
-z, -ɪŋ, -d

trepanation
BR ˌtrɛpəˈneɪʃn, -z
AM ˌtrɛpəˈneɪʃən, -z

trepang
BR trɪˈpaŋ, -z
AM trəˈpæŋ, triˈpæŋ, -z

trephination
BR ˌtrɛfɪˈneɪʃn
AM ˌtrɛfəˈneɪʃən

trephine
BR trɪˈfiːn, trɪˈfʌɪn, -z,
-ɪŋ, -d
AM ˈtriˌfaɪn, -z, -ɪŋ, -d

trepidation
BR ˌtrɛpɪˈdeɪʃn
AM ˌtrɛpəˈdeɪʃən

treponemata
BR ˌtrɛpəˈniːmətə(r)
AM ˌtrɛpəˈnimədə

treponeme
BR ˈtriːpəniːm, -z
AM ˈtrɛpənim, -z

treponima
BR ˌtrɛpəˈniːmə(r)
AM ˌtrɛpəˈnimə

Tresillian
BR trɪˈsɪliən
AM trəˈsɪljən,
trəˈsɪliən

trespass
BR ˈtrɛspəs, -ɪz, -ɪŋ, -t
AM ˈtrɛspəs, ˈtrɛˌspæs,
-əz, -ɪŋ, -t

trespasser
BR ˈtrɛspəsə(r), -z
AM ˈtrɛˌspæsər,
ˈtrɛspəsər, -z

tress
BR trɛs, -ɪz
AM trɛs, -əz

tressure
BR ˈtrɛʃə(r),
ˈtrɛs(j)ʊə(r), -z
AM ˈtrɛʃər, -z

tressy
BR ˈtrɛsi
AM ˈtrɛsi

trestle
BR ˈtrɛsl̩, -z
AM ˈtrɛsəl, -z

tret
BR trɛt, -s
AM trɛt, -s

Tretchikoff
BR ˈtrɛtʃɪkɒf
AM ˈtrɛtʃəˌkɔf,
ˈtrɛtʃəˌkɑf

Trethowan
BR trɪˈθaʊən, trɪˈθaʊən
AM trəˈθoʊən,
trəˈθaʊən

Tretyakov
BR ˈtrɛtjəkɒv
AM ˈtrɛtjəˌkɒv,
ˈtrɛtjəˌkɑv
RUS trʲitʲjɪˈkof

trevally
BR trɪˈval|i, -ɪz
AM trəˈvæli, -z

Trevelyan
BR trɪˈvɛliən,
trɪˈvɪliən
AM trəˈvɛljən,
trəˈvɛliən

Trevethick
BR trɪˈvɛθɪk
AM trəˈvɛθɪk

Trevino
BR trɪˈviːnəʊ
AM trəˈvinoʊ

Trevithick
BR trɪˈvɪθɪk
AM ˈtrəˈvɪθɪk

Trevor
BR ˈtrɛvə(r)
AM ˈtrɛvər

trews
BR truːz
AM truz

trey
BR treɪ, -z
AM treɪ, -z

triable
BR 'traɪəbl
AM 'traɪəbəl

triacetate
BR traɪ'æsɪteɪt, -s
AM traɪ'æsə‚teɪt, -s

triacid
BR traɪ'æsɪd, -z
AM traɪ'æsəd, -z

triad
BR 'traɪad, -z
AM 'traɪˌæd, -z

triadelphous
BR ‚traɪə'dɛlfəs
AM ‚traɪə'dɛlfəs

triadic
BR traɪ'adɪk
AM traɪ'ædɪk

triadically
BR traɪ'adɪkli
AM traɪ'ædək(ə)li

triage
BR 'triːɑːʒ, 'traɪɑːʒ,
'triːɪdʒ, 'traɪɪdʒ
AM 'triɑʒ

trial
BR 'traɪəl, -z, -ɪŋ, -d
AM 'traɪ(ə)l, -z, -ɪŋ, -d

trial and error
BR ‚traɪ(ə)l ən(d)
'ɛrə(r), + n̩(d) +
AM ‚traɪ(ə)l ən 'ɛrər

trialist
BR 'traɪəlɪst, -s
AM 'traɪələst, -s

triallist
BR 'traɪəlɪst, -s
AM 'traɪələst, -s

trial marriage
BR ‚traɪəl 'marˌɪdʒ,
-ɪdʒɪz
AM 'træɪ(ə)l 'mɛrɪdʒ,
-ɪz

trial run
BR ‚traɪəl 'rʌn, -z
AM 'traɪ(ə)l 'rən, -z

triandrous
BR traɪ'andrəs
AM traɪ'ændrəs

triangle
BR 'traɪaŋgl, 'traɪəŋgl,
-z
AM 'traɪˌæŋgəl, -z

triangular
BR traɪ'aŋgjʊlə(r)
AM traɪ'æŋgjələr

triangularity
BR traɪˌaŋgjʊ'larɪti
AM traɪˌæŋgjə'lɛrədi

triangularly
BR traɪ'aŋgjʊləli
AM traɪ'æŋgjələrli

triangulate¹
adjective
BR traɪ'aŋgjʊlət
AM traɪ'æŋgjələt

triangulate²
verb
BR traɪ'aŋgjʊleɪt, -s,
-ɪŋ, -ɪd
AM traɪ'æŋgjə‚leɪt, -ts,
-dɪŋ, -dɪd

triangulately
BR traɪ'aŋgjʊlətli
AM traɪ'æŋgjələtli

triangulation
BR traɪˌaŋgjʊ'leɪʃn,
‚traɪaŋgjʊ'leɪʃn
AM traɪˌæŋgjə'leɪʃən

Trianon
BR 'triːənɒn
AM 'triəˌnɑn

triantelope
BR traɪ'antɪləʊp, -s
AM traɪ'æn(t)ə‚loʊp, -s

Trias
BR 'traɪas
AM 'traɪəs

Triassic
BR traɪ'asɪk
AM traɪ'æsɪk

triathlete
BR traɪ'aθliːt, -s
AM traɪ'æθ(ə)‚lit, -s

triathlon
BR traɪ'aθlən,
traɪ'aθlɒn, -z
AM traɪ'æθ(ə)lən,
traɪ'æθ(ə)‚lɑn, -z

triatomic
BR ‚traɪə'tɒmɪk
AM ‚traɪə'tɑmɪk

triaxial
BR traɪ'aksɪəl
AM traɪ'æksɪəl

tribade
BR 'trɪbəd, -z
AM 'traɪbəd, trə'bad, -z

tribadism
BR 'trɪbədɪz(ə)m
AM 'trɪbə‚dɪzəm

tribal
BR 'traɪbl
AM 'traɪbəl

tribalism
BR 'traɪbəlɪz(ə)m,
'traɪblɪz(ə)m
AM 'traɪbə‚lɪzəm

tribalist
BR 'traɪbəlɪst,
'traɪblɪst, -s
AM 'traɪbələst, -s

tribalistic
BR ‚traɪbə'lɪstɪk,
‚traɪbl'ɪstɪk
AM ‚traɪbə'lɪstɪk

tribally
BR 'traɪbəli, 'traɪblˌi
AM 'trɪbəli

tribasic
BR traɪ'beɪsɪk
AM traɪ'beɪsɪk

tribe
BR traɪb, -z
AM traɪb, -z

tribesman
BR 'traɪbzmən
AM 'traɪbzmən

tribesmen
BR 'traɪbzmən
AM 'traɪbzmən

tribespeople
BR 'traɪbz‚piːpl
AM 'traɪbz‚pipəl

tribeswoman
BR 'traɪbz‚wʊmən
AM 'traɪbz‚wʊmən

tribeswomen
BR 'traɪbz‚wimin
AM 'traɪbz‚wimɪn

triblet
BR 'trɪblɪt, -s
AM 'trɪblɪt, -s

triboelectricity
BR ‚traɪbəʊɪ‚lɛk'trɪsɪti,
‚traɪbəʊˌɛlɛk'trɪsɪti,
‚traɪbəʊ‚ɛlɪk'trɪsɪti,
‚traɪbəʊˌɪlɛk'trɪsɪti,
‚traɪbəʊˌiːlɛk'trɪsɪti
AM ‚traɪboʊələk'trɪsɪdi,
‚traɪboʊˌɪlək'trɪsɪdi

tribologist
BR traɪ'bɒlədʒɪst, -s
AM traɪ'balədʒəst, -s

tribology
BR traɪ'bɒlədʒi
AM traɪ'balədʒi

triboluminescence
BR ‚traɪbəʊˌl(j)uːmɪ-
'nɛsns
AM ‚traɪboʊˌlumə'nɛs-
əns

triboluminescent
BR ‚traɪbəʊˌl(j)uːmɪ-
'nɛsnt
AM ‚traɪboʊˌlumə'nɛs-
ənt

tribometer
BR traɪ'bɒmɪtə(r), -z
AM traɪ'bamədər, -z

tribrach
BR 'traɪbrak, 'trɪbrak,
-s
AM 'traɪˌbræk, -s

tribrachic
BR traɪ'brakɪk,
trɪ'brakɪk
AM traɪ'brækɪk

tribulation
BR ‚trɪbjʊ'leɪʃn
AM ‚trɪbjə'leɪʃən

tribunal
BR traɪ'bjuːnl, -z
AM traɪ'bjunəl,
trə'bjunəl, -z

tribunate
BR 'trɪbjʊnət,
'trɪbjʊneɪt, -s
AM 'trɪbjənət,
'trɪbjə‚neɪt, -s

tribune
BR 'trɪbjuːn, -z
AM 'trɪbjun, -z

tribuneship
BR 'trɪbjuːnˌʃɪp, -s
AM 'trɪbjunˌʃɪp, -s

tribunicial
BR ‚trɪbjʊ'nɪʃl
AM ‚trɪbjə'nɪʃəl

tribunician
BR ‚trɪbjʊ'nɪʃn, -z
AM ‚trɪbjə'nɪʃən, -z

tribunitial
BR ‚trɪbjʊ'nɪʃl
AM ‚trɪbjə'nɪʃəl

tributarily
BR 'trɪbjʊt(ə)rɪli
AM 'trɪbjə'tɛrəli

tributariness
BR 'trɪbjʊt(ə)rɪnɪs
AM 'trɪbjə‚tɛrɪnɪs

tributary
BR 'trɪbjʊt(ə)r|i, -ɪz
AM 'trɪbjə‚tɛri, -z

tribute
BR 'trɪbjuːt, -s
AM 'trɪbjut, -s

tricameral
BR (‚)traɪ'kam(ə)rəl
(‚)traɪ'kam(ə)r|
AM ‚traɪ'kæm(ə)rəl

tricar
BR 'traɪkɑː(r), -z
AM 'traɪˌkar, -z

trice
BR traɪs
AM traɪs

Tricel®
BR 'traɪsɛl
AM 'traɪˌsɛl

tricentenary
BR ‚traɪsɛn'tiːn(ə)r|i,
‚traɪsɛn'tɛn(ə)r|,
traɪ'sɛntɪn(ə)r|i, -ɪz
AM traɪ'sɛn(t)ə‚nɛri,
traɪ‚sɛn'tɛnəri, -z

triceps
BR 'traɪsɛps, -ɪz
AM 'traɪˌsɛps, -ɪz

triceratops
BR traɪ'sɛrətɒps
AM traɪ'sɛrə‚taps

trichiasis
BR trɪ'kʌɪəsɪs,
‚trɪkɪ'eɪsɪs
AM trə'kaɪəsəs

trichina
BR trɪ'kʌɪnə(r),
trɪ'kiːnə(r), -z
AM trə'kaɪnə, trə'kinə,
-z

trichinae
BR trɪ'kʌɪniː; trɪ'kiːniː:

AM trəˈkaɪni, trəˈkini

Trichinopoly
BR ˌtritʃɪˈnɒpəli,
ˌtritʃɪˈnɒpl̩i
AM ˌtrɪkəˈnɑpəli

trichinosis
BR ˌtrɪkɪˈnəʊsɪs
AM ˌtrɪkəˈnoʊsəs

trichinous
BR ˈtrɪkɪnəs
AM ˈtrɪkənəs

trichloride
BR traɪˈklɔːraɪd, -z
AM traɪˈklɔˌraɪd, -z

trichloroethane
BR ˌtraɪklɔːrəʊˈiːθeɪn,
traɪˌklɔːrəʊˈiːθeɪn
AM ˌtraɪˌklɔːroʊˈɛˌθeɪn

trichogenous
BR trɪˈkɒdʒɪnəs
AM trəˈkɑdʒənəs

trichological
BR ˌtrɪkəˈlɒdʒɪkl
AM ˌtrɪkəˈlɑdʒəkəl

trichologist
BR trɪˈkɒlədʒɪst, -s
AM trəˈkɑlədʒəst, -s

trichology
BR trɪˈkɒlədʒi
AM trəˈkɑlədʒi

trichome
BR ˈtrɪkəʊm,
ˈtrɪkəʊm, -z
AM ˈtraɪˌkoʊm,
ˈtrɪˌkoʊm, -z

trichomonad
BR ˌtrɪkə(ʊ)ˈmɒnad, -z
AM ˌtrɪkəˈmɑˌnæd,
ˌtrɪkəˈmoʊˌnæd, -z

trichomoniasis
BR ˌtrɪkə(ʊ)mə(ʊ)ˈnaɪ-
əsɪs
AM ˌtrɪkəmə-naɪəsəs

trichopathic
BR ˌtrɪkə(ʊ)ˈpaθɪk
AM ˌtrɪkəˈpæθɪk

trichopathy
BR trɪˈkɒpəθi
AM trəˈkɑpəθi

Trichoptera
BR traɪˈkɒpt(ə)rə(r)
AM traɪˈkɑptərə

trichopteran
BR traɪˈkɒpt(ə)rən,
traɪˈkɒpt(ə)rn, -z
AM trəˈkɑptərən, -z

trichopterous
BR traɪˈkɒpt(ə)rəs
AM trəˈkɑpt(ə)rəs

trichord
BR ˈtraɪkɔːd, -z
AM ˈtraɪˌkɔ(ə)rd, -z

trichotomic
BR ˌtraɪkəˈtɒmɪk,
ˌtrɪkəˈtɒmɪk
AM ˌtrɪkəˈtɑmɪk

trichotomise
BR traɪˈkɒtəmʌɪz,
trɪˈkɒtəmʌɪz, -ɪz, -ɪŋ,
-d
AM trəˈkɑdəˌmaɪz,
ˌtraɪˈkɑdəˌmaɪz, -ɪz,
-ɪŋ, -d

trichotomize
BR traɪˈkɒtəmʌɪz,
trɪˈkɒtəmʌɪz, -ɪz, -ɪŋ,
-d
AM trəˈkɑdəˌmaɪz,
ˌtraɪˈkɑdəˌmaɪz, -ɪz,
-ɪŋ, -d

trichotomous
BR traɪˈkɒtəməs,
trɪˈkɒtəməs
AM trəˈkɑdəməs,
ˌtraɪˈkɑdəməs

trichotomy
BR traɪˈkɒtəmi,
trɪˈkɒtəmi
AM traɪˈkɑdəmi

trichroic
BR traɪˈkrəʊɪk
AM traɪˈkroʊɪk

trichroism
BR ˈtraɪkrəʊɪz(ə)m
AM ˈtraɪkrəʊˌwɪzəm

trichromatic
BR ˌtraɪkrə(ʊ)ˈmatɪk
AM ˌtraɪˌkroʊˈmædɪk

trichromatism
BR traɪˈkrəʊmətɪz(ə)m
AM ˌtraɪˈkroʊməˌtɪzəm

Tricia
BR ˈtrɪʃə(r)
AM ˈtrɪʃə

Tricity®
BR ˈtrɪsɪti
AM ˈtraɪˌsɪdi

tri-city
BR ˌtraɪˈsɪti, ˈtraɪˌsɪti
AM ˈtraɪˈsɪdi

trick
BR trɪk, -s, -ɪŋ, -t
AM trɪk, -s, -ɪŋ, -t

tricker
BR ˈtrɪkə(r), -z
AM ˈtrɪkər, -z

trickery
BR ˈtrɪk(ə)ri
AM ˈtrɪk(ə)ri

trickily
BR ˈtrɪkɪli
AM ˈtrɪkəli

trickiness
BR ˈtrɪkɪnɪs
AM ˈtrɪkɪnɪs

trickish
BR ˈtrɪkɪʃ
AM ˈtrɪkɪʃ

trickle
BR ˈtrɪk|l, -lz, -lɪŋ \-lɪŋ,
-ld
AM ˈtrɪk|əl, -əlz, -(ə)lɪŋ,
-əld

trickler
BR ˈtrɪklə(r),
ˈtrɪklə(r), -z
AM ˈtrɪk(ə)lər, -z

trickless
BR ˈtrɪklɪs
AM ˈtrɪklɪs

trickly
BR ˈtrɪkli, ˈtrɪkli
AM ˈtrɪk(ə)li

trick-or-treat
BR ˌtrɪkɔːˈtriːt
AM ˌtrɪkərˈtrit

tricksily
BR ˈtrɪksɪli
AM ˈtrɪksəli

tricksiness
BR ˈtrɪksɪnɪs
AM ˈtrɪksɪnɪs

trickster
BR ˈtrɪkstə(r), -z
AM ˈtrɪkstər, -z

tricksy
BR ˈtrɪks|i, -ɪə(r), -ɪɪst
AM ˈtrɪksi, -ər, -ɪst

tricky
BR ˈtrɪk|i, -ɪə(r), -ɪɪst
AM ˈtrɪki, -ər, -ɪst

triclinia
BR traɪˈklɪnɪə(r),
trɪˈklɪnɪə(r)
AM traɪˈklɪnɪə

triclinic
BR traɪˈklɪnɪk
AM traɪˈklɪnɪk

triclinium
BR traɪˈklɪnɪəm,
trɪˈklɪnɪəm
AM traɪˈklɪnɪəm

tricolor
BR ˈtrɪkələ(r),
ˈtrɪklə(r),
ˈtraɪˌkʌlə(r), -z
AM ˈtraɪˌkələr, -z

tricolored
BR ˈtraɪˌkʌləd,
ˌtraɪˈkʌləd
AM ˈtraɪˌkələrd

tricolour
BR ˈtrɪkələ(r),
ˈtrɪklə(r),
ˈtraɪˌkʌlə(r), -z
AM ˈtraɪˌkələr, -z

tricoloured
BR ˈtraɪˌkʌləd,
ˌtraɪˈkʌləd
AM ˈtraɪˌkələrd

tricorn
BR ˈtraɪkɔːn, -z
AM ˈtraɪˌkɔ(ə)rn, -z

tricorne
BR ˈtraɪkɔːn, -z
AM ˈtraɪˌkɔ(ə)rn, -z

tricot
BR ˈtrɪkəʊ, ˈtriːkəʊ, -z
AM ˈtrɪkoʊ, -z

tricotyledonous
BR ˌtraɪkɒtɪˈliːdŋəs,
ˌtraɪkɒtl̩ˈiːdŋəs
AM ˌtraɪˌkɑdəˈlidŋəs

tricrotic
BR traɪˈkrɒtɪk
AM traɪˈkrɑdɪk

tricuspid
BR traɪˈkʌspɪd
AM traɪˈkəspəd

tricycle
BR ˈtraɪsɪkl, -z
AM ˈtraɪsɪkəl,
ˈtraɪˌsɪkəl, -z

tricyclic
BR traɪˈsaɪklɪk,
ˌtraɪˈsɪklɪk
AM ˌtraɪˈsaɪklɪk,
ˌtraɪˈsɪklɪk

tricyclist
BR ˈtraɪsɪklɪst, -s
AM ˈtraɪsɪklɪst,
ˈtraɪˌsɪklɪst, -s

tridactyl
BR traɪˈdakt(ɪ)l
AM traɪˈdæktl

tridactylous
BR traɪˈdaktɪləs,
traɪˈdaktləs
AM traɪˈdæktələs

trident
BR ˈtraɪd(ə)nt, -s
AM ˈtraɪdnt, -s

tridentate
BR traɪˈdenteɪt
AM ˌtraɪˈdenˌteɪt

Tridentine
BR traɪˈdentʌɪn,
trɪˈdentʌɪn
AM traɪˈdenˌtin,
traɪˈdenˌtaɪn

tridigitate
BR traɪˈdɪdʒɪteɪt
AM traɪˈdɪdʒəˌteɪt

tridimensional
BR ˌtraɪdɪˈmenʃn̩(ə)l,
ˌtraɪdɪˈmenʃən(ə)l,
ˌtraɪdaɪˈmenʃn̩(ə)l,
ˌtraɪdaɪˈmenʃən(ə)l
AM ˌtraɪdəˈmen(t)ʃ(ə)nəl

triduum
BR ˈtrɪdjʊəm,
ˈtraɪdjʊəm
AM ˈtrɪdjəwəm,
ˈtrɪdʒəwəm

tridymite
BR ˈtrɪdɪmʌɪt, -s
AM ˈtrɪdəˌmaɪt, -s

tried
BR traɪd
AM traɪd

triene
BR ˈtraɪiːn, -z
AM ˈtraɪin, -z

triennia
BR traɪˈɛnɪə(r)
AM traɪˈɛnɪə

triennial
BR trɑɪˈenɪəl
AM traɪˈenɪəl

triennially
BR trɑɪˈenɪəli
AM traɪˈenɪəli

triennium
BR trɑɪˈenɪəm, -z
AM traɪˈenɪəm, -z

Trier
BR ˈtrɪə(r)
AM ˈtri(ə)r

trier
BR ˈtrɑɪə(r), -z
AM ˈtraɪər, -z

trierarchy
BR ˈtrɑɪərɑːk|i, -ɪz
AM ˈtraɪəˌrɑrki, -z

Trieste
BR triˈest
AM triˈest
IT triˈeste

trifacial
BR trɑɪˈfeɪʃl
AM traɪˈfeɪʃəl

trifecta
BR trɑɪˈfektə(r)
AM traɪˈfektə

triffid
BR ˈtrɪfɪd, -z
AM ˈtrɪfɪd, -z

trifid
BR ˈtrɑɪfɪd
AM ˈtrɪfɪd

trifle
BR ˈtrɑɪf|l, -lz, -lɪŋ \ -lɪŋ, -ld
AM ˈtraɪf|əl, -əlz, -(ə)lɪŋ, -əld

trifler
BR ˈtrɑɪflə(r), ˈtrɑɪfl̩ə(r), -z
AM ˈtraɪf(ə)lər, -z

triflingly
BR ˈtrɑɪflɪŋli, ˈtrɑɪfl̩ɪŋli
AM ˈtraɪf(ə)lɪŋli

triflingness
BR ˈtrɑɪflɪŋnɪs, ˈtrɑɪfl̩ŋnɪs
AM ˈtraɪf(ə)lɪŋnɪs

trifocal
BR trɑɪˈfəʊkl, -z
AM ˈtraɪˌfoʊkəl, -z

trifoliate
BR trɑɪˈfəʊlɪət
AM traɪˈfoʊliət, traɪˈfoʊliˌeɪt

triforia
BR trɑɪˈfɔːrɪə(r)
AM traɪˈfɔriə

triforium
BR trɑɪˈfɔːrɪəm, -z
AM traɪˈfɔriəm, -z

triform
BR ˈtrɑɪfɔːm
AM ˈtraɪˌfɔ(ə)rm

trifurcate
BR ˈtrɑɪfəkeɪt, -s, -ɪŋ, -ɪd
AM ˈtraɪfərˌkeɪ|t, -ts, -dɪŋ, -dɪd

trig
BR trɪg, -z
AM trɪg, -z

trigamist
BR ˈtrɪgəmɪst, -s
AM ˈtrɪgəməst, -s

trigamous
BR ˈtrɪgəməs
AM ˈtrɪgəməs

trigamy
BR ˈtrɪgəmi
AM ˈtrɪgəmi

trigeminal
BR trɑɪˈdʒemɪnl
AM traɪˈdʒemənəl

trigemini
BR trɑɪˈdʒemɪnɑɪ
AM traɪˈdʒeməˌnaɪ

trigeminus
BR trɑɪˈdʒemɪnəs
AM traɪˈdʒemənəs

trigger
BR ˈtrɪg|ə(r), -əz, -(ə)rɪŋ, -əd
AM ˈtrɪgər, -z, -ɪŋ, -d

triggerfish
BR ˈtrɪgəfɪʃ
AM ˈtrɪgərˌfɪʃ

triglyceride
BR trɑɪˈglɪsərɑɪd, -z
AM traɪˈglɪsəˌraɪd, -z

triglyph
BR ˈtrɑɪglɪf, -s
AM ˈtraɪˌglɪf, -s

triglyphic
BR trɑɪˈglɪfɪk
AM traɪˈglɪfɪk

triglyphical
BR trɑɪˈglɪfɪkl
AM traɪˈglɪfɪkəl

trigon
BR ˈtrɑɪg(ə)n, ˈtrɑɪgɒn, -z
AM ˈtraɪˌgɑn, -z

trigonal
BR ˈtrɪgənl
AM ˈtrɪgənəl

trigonally
BR ˈtrɪgən|li, ˈtrɪgənəli
AM ˈtrɪgənəli

trigoneutic
BR ˌtrɑɪgəˈnjuːtɪk
AM ˌtraɪgəˈn(j)udɪk

trigonometric
BR ˌtrɪgənəˈmetrɪk, ˌtrɪgnəˈmetrɪk
AM ˌtrɪgənəˈmetrɪk

trigonometrical
BR ˌtrɪgənəˈmetrɪkl, ˌtrɪgnəˈmetrɪkl
AM ˌtrɪgənəˈmetrəkəl

trigonometrically
BR ˌtrɪgənəˈmetrɪkli, ˌtrɪgnəˈmetrɪkli
AM ˌtrɪgənəˈmetrək(ə)li

trigonometry
BR ˌtrɪgəˈnɒmɪtri
AM ˌtrɪgəˈnɑmətri

trigram
BR ˈtrɑɪgram, -z
AM ˈtraɪˌgræm, -z

trigraph
BR ˈtrɑɪgrɑːf, ˈtrɑɪgraf, -s
AM ˈtraɪˌgræf, -s

trigynous
BR ˈtrɪdʒɪnəs
AM ˈtrɪdʒɪnəs

trihedra
BR trɑɪˈhiːdrə(r), trɑɪˈhedrə(r)
AM traɪˈhidrə

trihedral
BR trɑɪˈhiːdr(ə)l, trɑɪˈhedr(ə)l
AM traɪˈhidrəl

trihedron
BR trɑɪˈhiːdrən, trɑɪˈhedrən, -z
AM traɪˈhidrən, -z

trihydric
BR trɑɪˈhɑɪdrɪk
AM traɪˈhaɪdrɪk

trijet
BR ˈtrɑɪdʒet, -s
AM ˈtraɪˌdʒet, -s

trike
BR trɑɪk, -s
AM traɪk, -s

trilabiate
BR trɑɪˈleɪbɪət
AM traɪˈleɪbiˌeɪt

trilaminar
BR trɑɪˈlamɪnə(r)
AM traɪˈlæmənər

trilateral
BR trɑɪˈlat(ə)rəl, trɑɪˈlat(ə)r|l
AM traɪˈlædərəl, traɪˈlætrəl

trilaterally
BR trɑɪˈlat(ə)rəli, trɑɪˈlat(ə)r|li
AM traɪˈlædərəli, traɪˈlætrəli

trilateralness
BR trɑɪˈlat(ə)rəlnəs, trɑɪˈlat(ə)r|nəs
AM traɪˈlædərəlnəs, traɪˈlætrəlnəs

trilby
BR ˈtrɪlb|i, -ɪz, -d
AM ˈtrɪlbi, -z, -d

trilemma
BR trɑɪˈlemə(r), -z
AM traɪˈlemə, -z

trilinear
BR trɑɪˈlɪnɪə(r)
AM traɪˈlɪni(ə)r

trilingual
BR trɑɪˈlɪŋgw(ə)l
AM traɪˈlɪŋgwəl

trilingualism
BR trɑɪˈlɪŋgwəlɪz(ə)m, traɪˈlɪŋgwlɪz(ə)m
AM traɪˈlɪŋgwəˌlɪzəm

triliteral
BR trɑɪˈlɪt(ə)rəl, traɪˈlɪt(ə)r|l
AM traɪˈlɪdərəl, traɪˈlɪtrəl

trilith
BR ˈtrɑɪlɪθ, -s
AM ˈtraɪˌlɪθ, -s

trilithic
BR trɑɪˈlɪθɪk
AM traɪˈlɪθɪk

trilithon
BR ˈtrɪlɪθɒn, -z
AM ˈtrɪləˌθɑn, -z

trill
BR trɪl, -z, -ɪŋ, -d
AM trɪl, -z, -ɪŋ, -d

Trilling
BR ˈtrɪlɪŋ
AM ˈtrɪlɪŋ

trillion
BR ˈtrɪljən, -z
AM ˈtrɪljən, -z

trillionth
BR ˈtrɪljənθ
AM ˈtrɪljənθ

trillium
BR ˈtrɪlɪəm
AM ˈtrɪliəm

trilobate
BR trɑɪˈləʊbeɪt
AM ˈtraɪləˌbeɪt

trilobite
BR ˈtrɑɪlə(ʊ)bɑɪt, ˈtrɪlə(ʊ)bɑɪt, -s
AM ˈtraɪləˌbaɪt, ˈtrɪləˌbaɪt, -s

trilocular
BR trɑɪˈlɒkjələ(r)
AM traɪˈlɑkjələr

trilogy
BR ˈtrɪləd͡ʒ|i, -ɪz
AM ˈtrɪlədʒi, -z

trim
BR trɪm, -z, -ɪŋ, -d
AM trɪm, -z, -ɪŋ, -d

trimaran
BR ˈtrɑɪməran, -z
AM ˈtraɪməˌræn, -z

Trimble
BR ˈtrɪmbl
AM ˈtrɪmbəl

trimer
BR ˈtrɑɪmə(r), -z
AM ˈtraɪmər, -z

trimeric
BR trɑɪˈmerɪk
AM traɪˈmerɪk

trimerous
BR ˈtrɪm(ə)rəs

trimester
triquetra

AM 'trɪmərəs

trimester
BR traɪ'mɛstə(r),
'traɪmɛstə(r), -z
AM 'traɪ,mɛstər, -z

trimestral
BR traɪ'mɛstr(ə)l
AM traɪ'mɛstrəl

trimeter
BR 'trɪmɪtə(r),
'traɪ,mi:tə(r), -z
AM 'trɪmədər, -z

trimetric
BR traɪ'mɛtrɪk
AM traɪ'mɛtrɪk

trimetrical
BR traɪ'mɛtrɪkl
AM traɪ'mɛtrəkəl

trimly
BR 'trɪmli
AM 'trɪmli

trimmer
BR 'trɪmə(r), -z
AM 'trɪmər, -z

trimming
BR 'trɪmɪŋ, -z
AM 'trɪmɪŋ, -z

trimness
BR 'trɪmnɪs
AM 'trɪmnɪs

trimorphic
BR traɪ'mɔ:fɪk
AM traɪ'mɔrfɪk

trimorphism
BR traɪ'mɔ:fɪz(ə)m
AM traɪ'mɔr,fɪzəm

trimorphous
BR traɪ'mɔ:fəs
AM traɪ'mɔrfəs

Trimurti
BR trɪ'mʊəti
AM tri'mʊrdi

trinal
BR 'traɪnl
AM 'traɪnəl

Trincomalee
BR ,trɪŋkəmə'li:
AM ,trɪŋkəmə'li

trine
BR traɪn, -z
AM traɪn, -z

Tring
BR trɪŋ
AM trɪŋ

Trini
BR 'tri:n|i, -iz
AM 'trini, -z

Trinian's
BR 'trɪnɪənz
AM 'trɪnɪənz

Trinidad
BR 'trɪnɪdad
AM 'trɪnə,dæd

Trinidad and Tobago
BR 'trɪnɪdad (ə)n(d) tə'beɪgəʊ

AM 'trɪnədæd ən tə'beɪgoʊ

Trinidadian
BR ,trɪnɪ'dadɪən, -z
AM ,trɪnə'dædɪən, ,trɪnə'deɪdɪən, -z

Trinitarian
BR ,trɪnɪ'tɛ:rɪən, -z
AM ,trɪnə'tɛrɪən, -z

Trinitarianism
BR ,trɪnɪ'tɛ:rɪənɪz(ə)m
AM ,trɪnə'tɛrɪə,nɪzəm

trinitrotoluene
BR ,traɪ,naɪtrəʊ'tɒljʊ-i:n
AM trai,naɪtroʊ'taljə-,win

trinitrotoluol
BR ,traɪ,naɪtrəʊ'tɒljʊɒl
AM traɪ'naɪtroʊ'taljə-,wɒl, traɪ,naɪtroʊ'taljə,wal

trinity
BR 'trɪnɪt|i, -iz
AM 'trɪnɪdi, -z

trinket
BR 'trɪŋkɪt, -s
AM 'trɪŋkɪt, -s

trinketry
BR 'trɪŋkɪtri
AM 'trɪŋkɪtri

trinomial
BR traɪ'nəʊmɪəl
AM traɪ'noʊmɪəl

trinomialism
BR traɪ'nəʊmɪəlɪz(ə)m
AM traɪ'noʊmɪə,lɪzəm

trio
BR 'tri:əʊ, -z
AM 'trioʊ, -z

triode
BR 'traɪəʊd, -z
AM 'traɪoʊd, -z

trioecious
BR traɪ'i:ʃəs
AM traɪ'iʃəs

triolet
BR 'tri:ə(ʊ)lɛt, 'traɪə(ʊ)lɛt, 'tri:ə(ʊ)lɪt, 'traɪə(ʊ)lɪt, -s
AM 'triələt, -s

trioxide
BR traɪ'ɒksaɪd, -z
AM traɪ'ak,saɪd, -z

trip
BR trɪp, -s, -ɪŋ, -t
AM trɪp, -s, -ɪŋ, -t

tripartite
BR traɪ'pɑ:taɪt
AM traɪ'pɑr,taɪt

tripartitely
BR traɪ'pɑ:taɪtli
AM traɪ'pɑr,taɪtli

tripartition
BR ,traɪpɑ:'tɪʃn
AM ,traɪpɑr'tɪʃən

tripe
BR traɪp
AM traɪp

tripetalous
BR traɪ'pɛtl̩əs, traɪ'pɛtələs
AM traɪ'pɛdləs

triphibious
BR traɪ'fɪbɪəs
AM traɪ'fɪbɪəs

triphosphate
BR traɪ'fɒsfeɪt, -s
AM traɪ'fas,feɪt, -s

triphthong
BR 'trɪfθɒŋ, 'trɪpθɒŋ, -z
AM 'trɪf,θɒŋ, 'trɪp,θɒŋ, 'trɪf,θɑŋ, 'trɪp,θɑŋ, -z

triphthongal
BR 'trɪfθɒŋgl, ,trɪp'θɒŋgl
AM trɪf'θɒŋ(g)əl, trɪp'θɒŋ(g)əl, trɪf'θɑŋ(g)əl, trɪp'θɑŋ(g)əl

triphyllous
BR traɪ'fɪləs
AM traɪ'fɪləs

tripinnate
BR traɪ'pɪneɪt, traɪ'pɪnɪt
AM traɪ'pɪ,neɪt, traɪ'pɪnɪt

Tripitaka
BR traɪ'pɪtəkə(r), ,trɪpɪ'tɑ:kə(r)
AM ,trɪpi'takə

triplane
BR 'traɪpleɪn, -z
AM 'traɪ,pleɪn, -z

triple
BR 'trɪp|l, -lz, -lɪŋ \-lɪŋ, -ld
AM 'trɪp|əl, -əlz, -(ə)lɪŋ, -əld

triple crown
BR ,trɪpl 'kraʊn, -z
AM ,trɪpəl 'kraʊn, -z

triple-header
BR ,trɪpl'hɛdə(r), -z
AM ,trɪpəl'hɛdər, -z

triplet
BR 'trɪplɪt, -s
AM 'trɪplɪt, -s

triplex
BR 'trɪplɛks
AM 'trɪ,plɛks

triplicate¹
noun, adjective
BR 'trɪplɪkət
AM 'trɪpləkət

triplicate²
verb
BR 'trɪplɪkeɪt, -s, -ɪŋ, -ɪd
AM 'trɪplə,keɪ|t, -ts, -dɪŋ, -dɪd

triplication
BR ,trɪplɪ'keɪʃn, -z
AM ,trɪplə'keɪʃən, -z

triplicity
BR trɪ'plɪsɪt|i, -iz
AM trɪ'plɪsɪdi, -z

triploid
BR 'trɪplɔɪd, -z
AM 'trɪplɔɪd, -z

triploidy
BR 'trɪplɔɪdi
AM 'trɪ,plɔɪdi

triply
BR 'trɪpli
AM 'trɪp(ə)li

tripmeter
BR 'trɪp,mi:tə(r), -z
AM 'trɪp,midər, -z

tripod
BR 'traɪpɒd, -z
AM 'traɪ,pad, -z

tripodal
BR 'trɪpədl
AM 'traɪ'poʊdəl

tripoli
BR 'trɪpəl|i, 'trɪpl̩|i, -iz
AM 'trɪpəli, -z

Tripolis
BR 'trɪpəlɪs, 'trɪplɪs
AM 'trɪp(ə)ləs

Tripolitania
BR ,trɪpəlɪ'teɪmɪə(r), ,trɪplɪ'teɪnɪə(r), trɪ,pɒlɪ'teɪnɪə(r)
AM ,trɪpələ'teɪnɪə

Tripolitanian
BR ,trɪpəlɪ'teɪnɪən, ,trɪplɪ'teɪnɪən, trɪ,pɒlɪ'teɪnɪən
AM ,trɪpələ'teɪnɪən, -z

tripos
BR 'trɪpɒs, -ɪz
AM 'traɪ,pas, -əz

Tripp
BR trɪp
AM trɪp

tripper
BR 'trɪpə(r), -z
AM 'trɪpər, -z

trippingly
BR 'trɪpɪŋli
AM 'trɪpɪŋli

trippy
BR 'trɪpi
AM 'trɪpi

triptych
BR 'trɪptɪk, -s
AM 'trɪptɪk, -s

triptyque
BR trɪp'ti:k, -s
AM trɪp'tik, 'trɪptɪk, -s

Tripura
BR 'trɪp(ə)rə(r)
AM 'trɪpʊrə

tripwire
BR 'trɪp,waɪə(r), -z
AM 'trɪp,waɪ(ə)r, -z

triquetra
BR traɪ'kwi:trə(r), traɪ'kwɛtrə(r), -z

triquetrae
- AM traˈkwitrə,
  traˈkwɛtrə, -z

triquetrae
- BR traɪˈkwiːtriː,
  trʌɪˈkwɛtriː
- AM traɪˈkwitri,
  traˈkwɛtri,
  traˈkwɪˌtraɪ,
  traˈkwɛˌtraɪ

triquetral
- BR trʌɪˈkwiːtr(ə)l,
  trʌɪˈkwɛtr(ə)l
- AM traˈkwitrəl,
  traˈkwɛtrəl

triquetrous
- BR trʌɪˈkwiːtrəs,
  trʌɪˈkwɛtrəs
- AM traˈkwitrəs,
  traˈkwɛtrəs

trireme
- BR ˈtrʌɪriːm, -z
- AM ˈtraɪˌrim, -z

trisaccharide
- BR trʌɪˈsakərʌɪd, -z
- AM traɪˈsækəˌraɪd, -z

Trisagion
- BR trɪˈsagɪən,
  trɪˈseɪgɪən, -z
- AM triˈsægɪən, -z

trisect
- BR trʌɪˈsɛkt, -s, -ɪŋ, -ɪd
- AM traɪˈsɛk|(t), -(t)s,
  -ɪŋ, -təd

trisection
- BR trʌɪˈsɛkʃn, -z
- AM traɪˈsɛkʃən, -z

trisector
- BR trʌɪˈsɛktə(r), -z
- AM traɪˈsɛktər, -z

Trish
- BR trɪʃ
- AM trɪʃ

Trisha
- BR ˈtrɪʃə(r)
- AM ˈtrɪʃə

trishaw
- BR ˈtrʌɪʃɔː(r), -z
- AM ˈtraɪˌʃɔ, ˈtraɪˌʃɑ, -z

triskelion
- BR trɪˈskɛlɪən,
  trʌɪˈskɛlɪən, -z
- AM traɪˈskɛlɪən,
  trəˈskɛlɪən,
  traɪˈskɛliˌɑn,
  trəˈskɛliˌɑn, -z

trismus
- BR ˈtrɪzməs, -ɪz
- AM ˈtrɪzməs, -ɪz

trisomy
- BR ˈtrɪsəmi
- AM ˈtrɪsɪmi

Tristan
- BR ˈtrɪst(ə)n
- AM ˈtrɪsˌtan, ˈtrɪstən

Tristan da Cunha
- BR ˈtrɪst(ə)n də
  ˈkuːn(j)ə(r)
- AM ˈtrɪstən də ˈkun(j)ə

Tri-Star
- BR ˈtrʌɪstɑː(r)
- AM ˈtraɪˌstɑr

triste
- BR triːst
- AM trist

tristesse
- BR triːˈstɛs
- AM triˈstɛs

tristichous
- BR ˈtrɪstɪkəs
- AM ˈtrɪstəkəs

tristigmatic
- BR ˌtrʌɪstɪɡˈmatɪk
- AM ˌtrɪstɪɡˈmædɪk

Tristram
- BR ˈtrɪstrəm
- AM ˈtrɪstrəm

tristylous
- BR trʌɪˈstʌɪləs
- AM traɪˈstaɪləs

trisulcate
- BR trʌɪˈsʌlkeɪt
- AM traɪˈsəlˌkeɪt

trisyllabic
- BR ˌtrʌɪsɪˈlabɪk
- AM ˌtraɪsəˈlæbɪk

trisyllabically
- BR ˌtrʌɪsɪˈlabɪkli
- AM ˌtraɪsəˈlæbək(ə)li

trisyllable
- BR trʌɪˈsɪləbl,
  ˈtrʌɪˌsɪləbl, -z
- AM traɪˈsɪləbəl, -z

tritagonist
- BR trʌɪˈtaɡənɪst,
  trʌɪˈtaɡnɪst, -s
- AM traɪˈtæɡənəst, -s

tritanope
- BR ˈtrɪtənəʊp, -s
- AM ˈtrɪtnˌoʊp, -s

tritanopia
- BR ˌtrɪtəˈnəʊpɪə(r)
- AM ˌtrɪtnˈoʊpiə

trite
- BR trʌɪt, -ə(r), -ɪst
- AM traɪ|t, -dər, -dəst

tritely
- BR ˈtrʌɪtli
- AM ˈtraɪtli

triteness
- BR ˈtrʌɪtnɪs
- AM ˈtraɪtnəs

triternate
- BR trʌɪˈtəːnət,
  trʌɪˈtəːneɪt
- AM traɪˈtərneɪt,
  traɪˈtərnət

tritheism
- BR ˈtrʌɪθiːɪz(ə)m,
  trʌɪˈθiːɪz(ə)m
- AM traɪˈθiˌɪzəm

tritheist
- BR ˈtrʌɪθiːɪst,
  trʌɪˈθiːɪst, -s
- AM traɪˈθiːɪst, -s

tritiate
- BR ˈtrɪtɪeɪt, -s, -ɪŋ, -ɪd
- AM ˈtrɪdiˌeɪ|t, ˈtrɪʃiˌeɪ|t,
  -ts, -dɪŋ, -dɪd

tritiation
- BR ˌtrɪtɪˈeɪʃn
- AM ˌtrɪʃiˈeɪʃən

triticale
- BR ˌtrɪtɪˈkeɪli
- AM ˌtrɪdɪˈkeɪli

tritium
- BR ˈtrɪtɪəm
- AM ˈtrɪdiəm

triton
- BR ˈtrʌɪt(ə)n, -z
- AM ˈtraɪtn, -z

tritone
- BR ˈtrʌɪtəʊn, -z
- AM ˈtraɪˌtoʊn, -z

triturable
- BR ˈtrɪtjʊrəbl,
  ˈtrɪtʃ(ʊ)rəbl
- AM ˈtrɪtʃərəbəl

triturate
- BR ˈtrɪtjʊreɪt,
  ˈtrɪtʃʊreɪt, -s, -ɪŋ, -ɪd
- AM ˈtrɪtʃəˌreɪ|t, -ts,
  -dɪŋ, -dɪd

trituration
- BR ˌtrɪtjʊˈreɪʃn,
  ˌtrɪtʃʊˈreɪʃn
- AM ˌtrɪtʃəˈreɪʃən

triturator
- BR ˈtrɪtjʊreɪtə(r),
  ˈtrɪtʃʊreɪtə(r), -z
- AM ˈtrɪtʃəˌreɪdər, -z

triumph
- BR ˈtrʌɪəmf, ˈtrʌɪʌmf,
  -s, -ɪŋ, -t
- AM ˈtraɪəmf, -s, -ɪŋ, -t

triumphal
- BR trʌɪˈʌmfl
- AM traɪˈəmfəl

triumphalism
- BR trʌɪˈʌmf|ɪz(ə)m,
  trʌɪˈʌmfəlɪz(ə)m
- AM traɪˈəmfəˌlɪzəm

triumphalist
- BR trʌɪˈʌmf|ɪst,
  trʌɪˈʌmfəlɪst
- AM traɪˈəmfələst

triumphally
- BR trʌɪˈʌmfli,
  trʌɪˈʌmfəli
- AM traɪˈəmfəli

triumphant
- BR trʌɪˈʌmf(ə)nt
- AM traɪˈəmfənt

triumphantly
- BR trʌɪˈʌmf(ə)ntli
- AM traɪˈəmfən(t)li

triumvir
- BR trʌɪˈʌmvə(r),
  ˈtrʌɪəmvə(r), -z
- AM traɪˈəmvər, -z

triumviral
- BR trʌɪˈʌmvɪrəl,
  trʌɪˈʌmvɪrl̩

triumviral
- AM traɪˈəmvərəl

triumvirate
- BR trʌɪˈʌmvɪrət, -s
- AM traɪˈəmvərət,
  traɪˈəmvəˌreɪt, -s

triune
- BR ˈtrʌɪjuːn
- AM ˈtraɪ(j)un

triunity
- BR trʌɪˈjuːnɪt|i, -ɪz
- AM traɪˈjunədi, -z

trivalency
- BR (ˌ)trʌɪˈveɪləns|i,
  (ˌ)trʌɪˈveɪlns|i, -ɪz
- AM traɪˈveɪlənsi, -z

trivalent
- BR (ˌ)trʌɪˈveɪlənt,
  (ˌ)trʌɪˈveɪlnt
- AM trʌɪˈveɪlənt

trivet
- BR ˈtrɪvɪt, -s
- AM ˈtrɪvɪt, -s

trivia
- BR ˈtrɪvɪə(r)
- AM ˈtrɪviə

trivial
- BR ˈtrɪvɪəl
- AM ˈtrɪviəl

trivialisation
- BR ˌtrɪvɪəlʌɪˈzeɪʃn
- AM ˌtrɪviələˈzeɪʃən,
  ˌtrɪviəˌlaɪˈzeɪʃən

trivialise
- BR ˈtrɪvɪəlʌɪz, -ɪz, -ɪŋ,
  -d
- AM ˈtrɪviəˌlaɪz, -ɪz, -ɪŋ,
  -d

triviality
- BR ˌtrɪvɪˈalɪt|i, -ɪz
- AM ˌtrɪviˈælədi, -z

trivialization
- BR ˌtrɪvɪəlʌɪˈzeɪʃn
- AM ˌtrɪviələˈzeɪʃən,
  ˌtrɪviəˌlaɪˈzeɪʃən

trivialize
- BR ˈtrɪvɪəlʌɪz, -ɪz, -ɪŋ,
  -d
- AM ˈtrɪviəˌlaɪz, -ɪz, -ɪŋ,
  -d

trivially
- BR ˈtrɪvɪəli
- AM ˈtrɪviəli

trivialness
- BR ˈtrɪvɪəlnəs
- AM ˈtrɪviəlnəs

trivium
- BR ˈtrɪvɪəm
- AM ˈtrɪviəm

tri-weekly
- BR (ˌ)trʌɪˈwiːkli
- AM traɪˈwikli

Trixie
- BR ˈtrɪksi
- AM ˈtrɪksi

Troad
- BR trəʊd
- AM troʊd

Troas
BR 'trəʊas
AM 'trəʊəs

Trobriand
BR 'trəʊbriənd,
'trəʊbriand
AM 'troʊˌbriand

Trocadero
BR ˌtrɒkə'dɪərəʊ,
ˌtrɒkə'dɛːrəʊ
AM ˌtrɑkə'dɛroʊ

trocar
BR 'trəʊkɑː(r), -z
AM 'troʊˌkɑr, -z

trochaic
BR trə(ʊ)'keɪk
AM troʊ'keɪk

trochal
BR 'trəʊkl
AM 'troʊkəl

trochanter
BR trə(ʊ)'kantə(r), -z
AM troʊ'kæn(t)ər, -z

troche
BR trəʊʃ, -z
AM 'troʊˌki, -z

trochee
BR 'trəʊkiː, -z
AM 'troʊˌki, -z

trochi
BR 'trəʊkʌɪ, 'trɒkʌɪ
AM 'troʊˌkaɪ

trochlea
BR 'trɒkliə(r)
AM 'trɑkliə

trochleae
BR 'trɒkliː
AM 'trɑkliˌi, 'trɑkliˌaɪ

trochlear
BR 'trɒkliə(r)
AM 'trɑkliər

trochoid
BR 'trəʊkɔɪd, -z
AM 'troʊˌkɔɪd, -z

trochoidal
BR trə(ʊ)'kɔɪdl
AM troʊ'kɔɪdəl

trochus
BR 'trəʊkəs, 'trɒkəs,
-ɪz
AM 'troʊkəs, -əz

troctolite
BR 'trɒktəlʌɪt
AM 'trɑktəˌlaɪt

trod
BR trɒd
AM trɑd

trodden
BR 'trɒdn
AM 'trɑdən

trog
BR trɒg, -z
AM trɑg, -z

troglodyte
cave-dweller
BR 'trɒglədʌɪt, -s
AM 'trɑgləˌdaɪt, -s

troglodytes
wren
BR ˌtrɒglə'dʌɪtiːz
AM ˌtrɑglə'daɪˌtiz

troglodytic
BR ˌtrɒglə'dɪtɪk
AM ˌtrɑglə'dɪdɪk

troglodytical
BR ˌtrɒglə'dɪtɪkl
AM ˌtrɑglə'dɪdɪkəl

troglodytism
BR 'trɒglədʌɪtɪz(ə)m
AM 'trɑgləˌdaɪˌtɪzəm,
'trɑgləˌdaɪˌtɪzəm

trogon
BR 'trəʊgɒn, -z
AM 'troʊˌgɑn, -z

troika
BR 'trɔɪkə(r), -z
AM 'trɔɪkə, -z

troilism
BR 'trɔɪlɪz(ə)m
AM 'trɔɪˌlɪzəm

Troilus
BR 'trɔɪləs
AM 'trɔɪləs

Trojan
BR 'trəʊdʒ(ə)n, -z
AM 'troʊdʒən, -z

Trojan horse
BR ˌtrəʊdʒ(ə)n 'hɔːs,
-ɪz
AM ˌtroʊdʒən 'hɔ(ə)rs,
-əz

troll¹
noun
BR trɒl, trəʊl, -z
AM troʊl, -z

troll²
verb
BR trəʊl, trɒl, -z, -ɪŋ, -d
AM troʊl, -z, -ɪŋ, -d

troller
BR 'trəʊlə(r), 'trɒlə(r),
-z
AM 'troʊlər, -z

trolley
BR 'trɒlˌi, -ɪz
AM 'trɑli, -z

trolleybus
BR 'trɒlibʌs, -ɪz
AM 'trɑliˌbəs, -əz

trollop
BR 'trɒləp, -s
AM 'trɑləp, -s

Trollope
BR 'trɒləp
AM 'trɑləp

trollopish
BR 'trɒləpɪʃ
AM 'trɑləpɪʃ

trollopy
BR 'trɒləpi
AM 'trɑləpi

Tromans
BR 'trəʊmənz
AM 'troʊmənz

trombone
BR trɒm'bəʊn, -z
AM tram'boʊn,
trəm'boʊn, -z

trombonist
BR trɒm'bəʊnɪst, -s
AM tram'boʊnəst,
trəm'boʊnəst, -s

trommel
BR 'trɒml, -z
AM 'trɑməl, -z

tromometer
BR trə'mɒmɪtə(r), -z
AM trə'mɑmədər, -z

tromometric
BR ˌtrɒmə'mɛtrɪk
AM ˌtrɑmə'mɛtrɪk

tromp
BR trɒm|p, -ps, -pɪŋ,
-(p)t
AM tramp, -s, -ɪŋ, -t

trompe
BR trɒmp, -s
AM tramp, -s

trompe l'œil
BR ˌtrɔ̃'plɔɪ, ˌtrɒm'plɔɪ
AM ˌtrɔm'plɔɪ

trona
BR 'trəʊnə(r)
AM 'troʊnə

tronc
BR trɒŋk, -s
AM trɑŋk, -s

Trondheim
BR 'trɒn(d)hʌɪm
AM 'trɑn(d),(h)aɪm
NO 'trunheim,
'tronheim

Troon
BR truːn
AM trun

troop
BR truːp, -s, -ɪŋ, -t
AM trup, -s, -ɪŋ, -t

trooper
BR 'truːpə(r), -z
AM 'trupər, -z

troopship
BR 'truːpʃɪp, -s
AM 'trupˌʃɪp, -s

tropaeola
BR trə(ʊ)'piːələ(r)
AM troʊ'piələ

tropaeolum
BR trə(ʊ)'piːələm, -z
AM troʊ'piələm, -z

trope
BR trəʊp, -s
AM troʊp, -s

trophic
BR 'trɒfɪk, 'trəʊfɪk
AM 'troʊfɪk

trophied
BR 'trəʊfid
AM 'troʊfid

trophoblast
BR 'trɒfə(ʊ)blɑːst,
'trɒfə(ʊ)blast, -s
AM 'trɑfəˌblæst, -s

trophoneuroses
BR ˌtrɒfəʊnjə'rəʊsiːz,
ˌtrɒfəʊnjʊə'rəʊsiːz
AM ˌtrɑfəˌn(j)u'roʊsiz,
'trɑfən(j)ə'roʊsiz

trophoneurosis
BR ˌtrɒfəʊnjə'rəʊsɪs,
ˌtrɒfəʊnjʊə'rəʊsɪs
AM ˌtrɑfəˌn(j)u'roʊsəs,
'trɑfən(j)ə'roʊsəz

trophy
BR 'trəʊfˌi, -z
AM 'troʊfi, -z

tropic
BR 'trɒpɪk, -s
AM 'trɑpɪk, -s

tropical
BR 'trɒpɪkl, -z
AM 'trɑpəkəl, -z

tropically
BR 'trɒpɪkli
AM 'trɑpək(ə)li

tropism
BR 'trəʊpɪz(ə)m
AM 'troʊˌpɪzəm

tropological
BR ˌtrɒpə'lɒdʒɪkl
AM ˌtrɑpə'lɑdʒəkəl

tropology
BR trə'pɒlədʒi
AM trə'pɑlədʒi

tropopause
BR 'trɒpəpɔːz
AM 'trɑpəˌpɔz,
'trɑpəˌpaz

troposphere
BR 'trɒpəsfɪə(r)
AM 'trɑpəˌsfɪ(ə)r

tropospheric
BR ˌtrɒpə'sfɛrɪk
AM ˌtrɑpə'sfɛrɪk

troppo
BR 'trɒpəʊ
AM 'trɑpoʊ

Trossachs
BR 'trɒsəks
AM 'trɑsəks

trot
BR trɒt, -s, -ɪŋ, -ɪd
AM trɑ|t, -ts, -dɪŋ, -dəd

troth
BR trəʊθ, trɒθ
AM trɔθ, troʊθ, trɑθ

Trotsky
BR 'trɒtski
AM 'trɑtski

Trotskyism
BR 'trɒtskɪɪz(ə)m
AM 'trɑtskiˌɪzəm

Trotskyist
BR 'trɒtskɪɪst, -s
AM 'trɑtskiˌɪst, -s

Trotskyite
BR 'trɒtskɪaɪt, -s
AM 'trɑtski,aɪt, -s

trotter
BR 'trɒtə(r), -z
AM 'trɑdər, -z

trotting race
BR 'trɒtɪŋ reɪs, -ɪz
AM 'trɑdɪŋ ,reɪs, -ɪz

trottoir
BR 'trɒtwɑː(r)
AM trɑ'twɑr, -z

trotyl
BR 'trəʊtɪl, 'trəʊtʌɪl
AM 'troʊdl

troubadour
BR 'truːbədɔː(r),
'truː,bədʊə(r), -z
AM 'truːbə,dɔ(ə)r,
'truːbə,dʊ(ə)r, -z

trouble
BR 'trʌb|l, -lz, -lɪŋ \-lɪŋ,
-ld
AM 'trəbəl, -əlz, -(ə)lɪŋ,
-əld

troublemaker
BR 'trʌbl,meɪkə(r), -z
AM 'trəbəl,meɪkər, -z

trouble-making
BR 'trʌbl,meɪkɪŋ
AM 'trəbəl,meɪkɪŋ

troubler
BR 'trʌblə(r), -z
AM 'trəb(ə)lər, -z

troubleshoot
BR 'trʌblʃuːt, -s, -ɪŋ
AM 'trəbəl,ʃu|t, -ts, -dɪŋ

troubleshooter
BR 'trʌbl,ʃuːtə(r), -z
AM 'trəbəl,ʃudər, -z

troubleshot
BR 'trʌblʃɒt
AM 'trəbəl,ʃɑt

troublesome
BR 'trʌbls(ə)m
AM 'trəbəlsəm

troublesomely
BR 'trʌbls(ə)mli
AM 'trəbəlsəmli

troublesomeness
BR 'trʌbls(ə)mnəs
AM 'trəbəlsəmnəs

troublous
BR 'trʌbləs
AM 'trəbləs

trough
BR trɒf, -s
AM trɒf, trɑf, -s

trounce
BR traʊns, -ɪz, -ɪŋ, -t
AM traʊns, -əz, -ɪŋ, -t

trouncer
BR 'traʊnsə(r), -z
AM 'traʊnsər, -z

troupe
BR truːp, -s
AM trup, -s

trouper
BR 'truːpə(r), -z
AM 'trupər, -z

trouser
BR 'traʊzə(r), -z, -d
AM 'traʊzər, -z, -d

trouserless
BR 'traʊzələs
AM 'traʊzərləs

trousseau
BR 'truːsəʊ, -z
AM 'tru,soʊ, 'truː'soʊ, -z

trousseaux
BR 'truːsəʊ(z)
AM 'tru,soʊ, 'truː'soʊ

trout
BR traʊt
AM traʊt

troutlet
BR 'traʊtlɪt, -s
AM 'traʊtlət, -s

troutling
BR 'traʊtlɪŋ, -z
AM 'traʊtlɪŋ, -z

trouty
BR 'traʊti
AM 'traʊdi

trouvaille
BR truː'vʌɪ\truː'vʌɪz
AM tru'vaɪ, -z

trouvère
BR truː'vɛ(r)\truː'vɛːz
AM tru'vɛ(ə)r, -z

trove
BR trəʊv
AM troʊv

trover
BR 'trəʊvə(r), -z
AM 'troʊvər, -z

trow
BR trəʊ, traʊ
AM troʊ

Trowbridge
BR 'trəʊbrɪdʒ
AM 'troʊ,brɪdʒ

trowel
BR 'traʊ(ə)l, -z, -ɪŋ, -d
AM 'traʊ(ə)l, -z, -ɪŋ, -d

Trowell
BR 'traʊ(ə)l, 'trəʊ(ə)l
AM 'traʊəl, 'troʊəl

troy
BR trɔɪ
AM trɔɪ

truancy
BR 'truːənsi
AM 'truənsi

truant
BR 'truːənt, -s, -ɪŋ, -d
AM 'truənt, -s, -ɪŋ, -əd

Trubetskoy
BR tru'betskɔɪ,
,truː'bet'skɔɪ
AM trə'bet,skɔɪ

Trubshaw
BR 'trʌbʃɔː(r)
AM 'trəb,ʃɔ

truce
BR truːs, -ɪz
AM trus, -əz

truceless
BR 'truːsləs
AM 'trusləs

trucial
BR 'truːʃl
AM 'truʃəl

Trucial States
BR ,truːʃl 'steɪts
AM 'truʃəl ,steɪts

truck
BR trʌk, -s, -ɪŋ, -t
AM trək, -s, -ɪŋ, -t

truckage
BR 'trʌkɪdʒ
AM 'trəkɪdʒ

trucker
BR 'trʌkə(r), -z
AM 'trəkər, -z

truckie
BR 'trʌk|i, -ɪz
AM 'trəki, -z

truckle
BR 'trʌk|l, -lz, -lɪŋ \-lɪŋ,
-ld
AM 'trək|əl, -əlz, -(ə)lɪŋ,
-əld

truckler
BR 'trʌklə(r),
'trʌklə(r), -z
AM 'trək(ə)lər, -z

truckload
BR 'trʌkləʊd, -z
AM 'trək,loʊd, -z

truculence
BR 'trʌkjʊləns,
'trʌkjʊlns
AM 'trəkjələns

truculency
BR 'trʌkjʊlənsi,
'trʌkjʊlnsi
AM 'trəkjələnsi

truculent
BR 'trʌkjʊlənt,
'trʌkjʊlnt
AM 'trəkjələnt

truculently
BR 'trʌkjʊləntli
'trʌkjʊlntli
AM 'trəkjələn(t)li

Trudeau
BR 'truːdəʊ
AM tru'doʊ

trudge
BR trʌdʒ, -ɪz, -ɪŋ, -d
AM trədʒ, -əz, -ɪŋ, -d

trudgen
BR 'trʌdʒ(ə)n
AM 'trədʒən

trudger
BR 'trʌdʒə(r), -z
AM 'trədʒər, -z

Trudgill
BR 'trʌdgɪl
AM 'trəd,gɪl

Trudi
BR 'truːdi
AM 'trudi

Trudy
BR 'truːdi
AM 'trudi

true
BR truː, -z, -ɪŋ, -d, -ə(r),
-ɪst
AM tru, -z, -ɪŋ, -d, -ər,
-əst

true-blue
BR ,truː'bluː, -z
AM 'tru'blu, -z

trueish
BR 'truːɪʃ
AM 'truɪʃ

true-life
BR ,truː'lʌɪf
AM 'tru'laɪf

truelove
BR 'truːlʌv, ,truː'lʌv, -z
AM 'tru'ləv, -z

Trueman
BR 'truːmən
AM 'trumən

trueness
BR 'truːnəs
AM 'trunəs

Truffaut
BR 'trʊfəʊ, 'truːfəʊ
AM trʊ'foʊ, 'trufoʊ

truffle
BR 'trʌfl, -z
AM 'trəfəl, -z

trug
BR trʌg, -z
AM trəg, -z

truism
BR 'truːɪz(ə)m, -z
AM 'tru,ɪzəm, -z

truistic
BR truː'ɪstɪk
AM tru'ɪstɪk

Trujillo
BR truː'hiːjəʊ
AM tru'hijoʊ

Truk
BR trʌk
AM trək

trull
BR trʌl, -z
AM trəl, -z

truly
BR 'truːli
AM 'truli

Truman
BR 'truːmən
AM 'trumən

Trumbull
BR 'trʌmbl
AM 'trəmbəl

trumeau
BR 'truːməʊ, -z
AM 'tru'moʊ, -z

trumeaux
BR 'truːməʊ(z)

AM tru'moʊ

trump
BR trʌm|p, -ps, -pɪŋ, -(p)t
AM trəm|p, -(p)s, -pɪŋ, -(p)t

trumped-up
BR ˌtrʌm(p)t'ʌp
AM ˌtrəm(p)t'əp

trumpery
BR 'trʌmp(ə)r|i, -ɪz
AM 'trəmp(ə)ri, -z

trumpet
BR 'trʌmp|ɪt, -ɪts, -ɪtɪŋ, -ɪtɪd
AM 'trəmpə|t, -ts, -dɪŋ, -dəd

trumpeter
BR 'trʌmpɪtə(r), -z
AM 'trəmpədər, -z

trumpeting
BR 'trʌmpɪtɪŋ, -z
AM 'trəmpədɪŋ, -z

trumpetless
BR 'trʌmpɪtlɪs
AM 'trəmpətləs

truncal
BR 'trʌŋkl
AM 'trəŋkəl

truncate
BR trʌŋ'keɪt, -s, -ɪŋ, -ɪd
AM 'trəŋˌkeɪ|t, -ts, -dɪŋ, -dɪd

truncately
BR trʌŋ'keɪtli
AM 'trəŋˌkeɪtli

truncation
BR trʌŋ'keɪʃn, -z
AM ˌtrəŋ'keɪʃən, -z

truncheon
BR 'trʌn(t)ʃ(ə)n, -z
AM 'trən(t)ʃən, -z

trundle
BR 'trʌnd|l, -lz, -lɪŋ\-lɪŋ, -ld
AM 'trən|dəl, -dəlz, -(d)(ə)lɪŋ, -dəld

trunk
BR trʌŋk, -s
AM trəŋk, -s

trunkful
BR 'trʌŋkfʊl, -z
AM 'trəŋkˌfʊl, -z

trunking
BR 'trʌŋkɪŋ, -z
AM 'trəŋkɪŋ, -z

trunkless
BR 'trʌŋkləs
AM 'trəŋkləs

trunklike
BR 'trʌŋklʌɪk
AM 'trəŋkˌlaɪk

trunnel
BR 'trʌnl, -z, -d
AM 'trənəl, -z, -d

trunnion
BR 'trʌnjən, -z

AM 'trənjən, -z

Truro
BR 'trʊərəʊ
AM 'trʊˌroʊ

Truscott
BR 'trʌskɒt, 'trʌskət
AM 'trəsˌkɑt

truss
BR trʌs, -ɪz, -ɪŋ, -t
AM trəs, -əz, -ɪŋ, -t

trusser
BR 'trʌsə(r), -z
AM 'trəsər, -z

trust
BR trʌst, -s, -ɪŋ, -ɪd
AM trəst, -s, -ɪŋ, -əd

trustable
BR 'trʌstəbl
AM 'trəstəbəl

trustbuster
BR 'trʌs(t)ˌbʌstə(r), -z
AM 'trəs(t)ˌbəstər, -z

trustbusting
BR 'trʌs(t)ˌbʌstɪŋ
AM 'trəs(t)ˌbəstɪŋ

trustee
BR trʌ'stiː, trʌs'tiː, -z
AM trə'sti, -z

trusteeship
BR trʌ'stiːʃɪp, trʌs'tiːʃɪp, -s
AM trə'stiʃɪp, -s

truster
BR 'trʌstə(r), -z
AM 'trəstər, -z

trustful
BR 'trʌs(t)f(ʊ)l
AM 'trəs(t)fəl

trustfully
BR 'trʌs(t)fʊli, 'trʌs(t)fli
AM 'trəs(t)fəli

trustfulness
BR 'trʌstf(ʊ)lnəs
AM 'trəs(t)fəlnəs

trustie
BR 'trʌst|i, -ɪz
AM 'trəsti, -ɪz

trustily
BR 'trʌstɪli
AM 'trəstəli

trustiness
BR 'trʌstɪnɪs
AM 'trəstɪnɪs

trusting
BR 'trʌstɪŋ
AM 'trəstɪŋ

trustingly
BR 'trʌstɪŋli
AM 'trəstɪŋli

trustingness
BR 'trʌstɪŋnɪs
AM 'trəstɪŋnɪs

trustworthily
BR 'trʌs(t)ˌwəːðɪli
AM 'trəs(t)ˌwərðəli

trustworthiness
BR 'trʌs(t)ˌwəːðɪnɪs
AM 'trəs(t)ˌwərðinɪs

trustworthy
BR 'trʌs(t)ˌwəːði
AM 'trəs(t)ˌwərði

trusty
BR 'trʌst|i, -ɪz, -ɪə(r), -ɪɪst
AM 'trəsti, -z, -ər, -ɪst

truth
BR truː|θ, -ðz\-θs
AM truː|θ, -ðz\-θs

truthful
BR 'truːθf(ʊ)l
AM 'truːθfəl

truthfully
BR 'truːθfʊli, 'truːθfli
AM 'truːθfəli

truthfulness
BR 'truːθf(ʊ)lnəs
AM 'truːθfəlnəs

truthless
BR 'truːθləs
AM 'truːθləs

try
BR trʌɪ, -z, -ɪŋ, -d
AM traɪ, -z, -ɪŋ, -d

Tryfan
BR 'trɪvn
AM 'trɪvən
WE 'trʌvan

tryingly
BR 'trʌɪɪŋli
AM 'traɪɪŋli

trypanosome
BR 'trɪpənəsəʊm, 'trɪpnəsəʊm, trɪ'pænəsəʊm, -z
AM trə'pænəˌsoʊm, 'trɪpənəˌsoʊm, -z

trypanosomiasis
BR ˌtrɪpənə(ʊ)sə'mʌɪəsɪs, ˌtrɪpnə(ʊ)sə'mʌɪəsɪs, trɪˌpænə(ʊ)sə'mʌɪəsɪs
AM trəˌpænəsoʊ'maɪəsɪs

trypsin
BR 'trɪpsɪn
AM 'trɪpsɪn

trypsinogen
BR trɪp'sɪnədʒ(ə)n
AM trɪp'sɪnədʒən, trɪp'sɪnəˌdʒɛn

tryptic
BR 'trɪptɪk
AM 'trɪptɪk

tryptophan
BR 'trɪptəfan
AM 'trɪptəˌfæn

trysail
BR 'trʌɪsl, 'trʌɪseɪl, -z
AM 'traɪsəl, 'traɪˌseɪl, -z

tryst
BR trɪst, -s, -ɪŋ, -ɪd
AM trɪst, -s, -ɪŋ, -ɪd

tryster
BR 'trɪstə(r), -z
AM 'trɪstər, -z

tsar
BR zɑː(r), tsɑː(r), -z
AM zɑr, tsɑr, -z

tsardom
BR 'zɑːdəm, 'tsɑːdəm, -z
AM 'zɑrdəm, 'tsɑrdəm, -z

tsarevich
BR 'zɑːrəvɪtʃ, 'tsɑːrəvɪtʃ, -ɪz
AM 'zɑrəˌvɪtʃ, 'tsɑrəˌvɪtʃ, -ɪz

tsarevitch
BR 'zɑːrəvɪtʃ, 'tsɑːrəvɪtʃ, -ɪz
AM 'zɑrəˌvɪtʃ, 'tsɑrəˌvɪtʃ, -ɪz

tsarevna
BR zɑː'rɛvnə(r), tsɑː'rɛvnə(r), 'zɑːrəvnə(r), 'tsɑːrəvnə(r), -z
AM 'zɑrəvnə, 'tsɑrəvnə, -z

tsarina
BR zɑː'riːnə(r), tsɑː'riːnə(r), -z
AM zɑ'rinə, tsɑ'rinə, -z

tsarism
BR 'zɑːrɪz(ə)m, 'tsɑːrɪz(ə)m
AM 'zɑˌrɪzəm, 'tsɑˌrɪzəm

tsarist
BR 'zɑːrɪst, 'tsɑːrɪst, -s
AM 'zɑrəst, 'tsɑrəst, -s

tsessebi
BR '(t)sɛsəb|i, tsɛ'seɪb|i, -ɪz
AM '(t)sɛsəbi, (t)sɛ'seɪbi, -z

tsetse
BR '(t)sɛtsi
AM '(t)sitsi, '(t)sɛtsi

T-shirt
BR 'tiːʃəːt, -s
AM 'tiˌʃərt, -s

Tsinan
BR ˌtsiː'nan
AM ˌtsi'næn

Tsinghai
BR ˌtsɪŋ'hʌɪ
AM ˌtsɪŋ'haɪ

Tsitsikamma
BR ˌ(t)sɪtsɪ'kamə(r)
AM ˌ(t)sɪtsi'kɑmə

tsk
BR ǀ
AM ǀ

T-square
BR 'tiːskwɛː(r), -z
AM 'tiˌskwɛ(ə)r, -z

tsunami
BR (t)sʊ'nɑːm|i, -ɪz

AM (t)suːˈnɑmi, -z

Tsushima
BR (t)sʊˈʃiːmə(r)
AM (t)sʊˈʃimə

Tswana
BR ˈtswɑːnə(r)
AM ˈtswɑnə

TT
BR ˌtiːˈtiː, -z
AM ˌtiˈti, -z

t-test
BR ˈtiːtɛst, -s
AM ˈtiˌtɛst, -s

Tuareg
BR ˈtwɑːrɛg, -z
AM ˈtwɑˌrɛg, -z

tuatara
BR ˌtuːəˈtɑːrə(r), -z
AM ˌtuəˈtɑrə, -z

tub
BR tʌb, -z
AM təb, -z

tuba
BR ˈtjuːbə(r),
ˈtʃuːbə(r), -z
AM ˈt(j)ubə, -z

tubal
BR ˈtjuːbl, ˈtʃuːbl
AM ˈt(j)ubəl

tubbable
BR ˈtʌbəbl
AM ˈtəbəbəl

tubbiness
BR ˈtʌbɪnɪs
AM ˈtəbɪnɪs

tubbish
BR ˈtʌbɪʃ
AM ˈtəbɪʃ

tubby
BR ˈtʌb|i, -ɪə(r), -ɪɪst
AM ˈtəbi, -ər, -ɪɪst

tubbyish
BR ˈtʌbɪɪʃ
AM ˈtəbiɪʃ

tube
BR tjuːb, tʃuːb, -z
AM t(j)ub, -z

tubectomy
BR tjʊˈbɛktəm|i,
tʃʊˈbɛktəm|i, -ɪz
AM t(j)uˈbɛktəmi, -z

tubeless
BR ˈtjuːbləs, ˈtʃuːbləs
AM ˈt(j)ubləs

tubelike
BR ˈtjuːblaɪk,
ˈtʃuːblaɪk
AM ˈt(j)ubˌlaɪk

tuber
BR ˈtjuːbə(r),
ˈtʃuːbə(r), -z
AM ˈt(j)ubər, -z

tubercle
BR ˈtjuːbəkl, ˈtʃuːbəkl,
-z
AM ˈt(j)ubərkəl, -z

tubercular
BR t(j)ʉˈbəːkjʉlə(r),
tʃʉˈbəːkjʉlə(r)
AM təˈbəːkjələr,
t(j)uˈbərkjələr

tuberculate
BR t(j)ʉˈbəːkjʉlət,
tʃʉˈbəːkjʉlət
AM təˈbəːkjə.leɪt,
t(j)uˈbərkjə.leɪt,
təˈbərkjələt,
t(j)uˈbərkjələt

tuberculation
BR t(j)ʉˌbəːkjʉˈleɪʃn,
tʃʉˌbəːkjʉˈleɪʃn
AM təˌbərkjəˈleɪʃən,
t(j)uˌbərkjəˈleɪʃən

tuberculin
BR t(j)ʉˈbəːkjʉlɪn,
tʃʉˈbəːkjʉlɪn
AM təˈbərkjələn,
t(j)uˈbərkjələn

**tuberculin-
tested**
BR t(j)ʉˌbəːkjʉlɪn-
ˈtɛstɪd,
tʃʉˌbəːkjʉlɪnˈtɛstɪd
AM təˈbərkjələnˌtɛstəd,
t(j)uˈbərkjələnˌtɛstəd

tuberculosis
BR t(j)ʉˌbəːkjʉˈləʊsɪs,
tʃʉˌbəːkjʉˈləʊsɪs
AM təˌbərkjəˈloʊsəs,
t(j)uˌbərkjəˈloʊsəs

tuberculous
BR t(j)ʉˈbəːkjʉləs,
tʃʉˈbəːkjʉləs
AM təˈbərkjələs,
t(j)uˈbərkjələs

tuberose
BR ˈtjuːbərəʊz,
ˈtʃuːbərəʊz, -ɪz
AM ˈt(j)ubəˌroʊz,
ˈt(j)ubəˌroʊz, -əz

tuberosity
BR ˌtjuːbəˈrɒsɪti,
ˈtʃuːbəˈrɒsɪti
AM ˌt(j)ubəˈrɑsədi

tuberous
BR ˈtjuːb(ə)rəs,
ˈtʃuːb(ə)rəs
AM ˈt(j)ubərəs

tube worm
BR ˈtjuːb wəːm,
ˈtʃuːb +, -z
AM ˈt(j)ub ˌwərm, -z

tubful
BR ˈtʌbfʊl, -z
AM ˈtəbˌfʊl, -z

tubicolous
BR tjʉˈbɪkələs,
tʃʉˈbɪkələs
AM t(j)uˈbɪkələs

tubicorn
BR ˈtjuːbɪkɔːn,
ˈtʃuːbɪkɔːn, -z
AM ˈt(j)ubəˌkɔ(ə)rn, -z

tubifex
BR ˈtjuːbɪfɛks,
ˈtʃuːbɪfɛks
AM ˈt(j)ubəˌfɛks

tubiform
BR ˈtjuːbɪfɔːm,
ˈtʃuːbɪfɔːm
AM ˈt(j)ubəˌfɔ(ə)rm

tubilingual
BR ˌtjuːbɪˈlɪŋgw(ə)l,
ˌtʃuːbɪˈlɪŋgw(ə)l
AM tubɪˈlɪŋgwəl

tubing
BR ˈtjuːbɪŋ, ˈtʃuːbɪŋ
AM ˈt(j)ubɪŋ

Tubman
BR ˈtʌbmən
AM ˈtəbmən

tub-sized
BR ˈtʌbsaɪzd
AM ˈtəbˌsaɪzd

tubular
BR ˈtjuːbjʉlə(r),
ˈtʃuːbjʉlə(r)
AM ˈt(j)ubjələr

tubule
BR ˈtjuːbjuːl,
ˈtʃuːbjuːl, -z
AM ˈt(j)uˌbjul, -z

tubulous
BR ˈtjuːbjʉləs,
ˈtʃuːbjʉləs
AM ˈt(j)ubjələs

tuck
BR tʌk, -s, -ɪŋ, -t
AM tək, -s, -ɪŋ, -t

tuckahoe
BR ˈtʌkəhəʊ, -z
AM ˈtəkəˌhoʊ, -z

tuckbox
BR ˈtʌkbɒks, -ɪz
AM ˈtəkˌbaks, -əz

tucker
BR ˈtʌkə(r), -z, -d
AM ˈtəkər, -z, -d

tuckerbag
BR ˈtʌkəbag, -z
AM ˈtəkərˌbag, -z

tucket
BR ˈtʌkɪt, -s
AM ˈtəkət, -s

tuckpoint
BR ˈtʌkpɔɪnt, -s
AM ˈtəkˌpɔɪnt, -s

tuckshop
BR ˈtʌkʃɒp, -s
AM ˈtəkˌʃap, -s

Tucson
BR ˈtuːsɒn
AM ˈtuˌsɑn

Tudor
BR ˈtjuːdə(r),
ˈtʃuːdə(r)
AM ˈt(j)udər

Tudorbethan
BR ˌtjuːdəˈbiːθn,
ˌtʃuːdəˈbiːθn
AM ˌt(j)udərˈbiθən

Tudoresque
BR ˌtjuːdərˈɛsk,
ˌtʃuːdərˈɛsk
AM ˌt(j)udərˈrɛsk

Tuesday
BR ˈtjuːzd|eɪ, ˈtʃuːzd|eɪ,
ˈtjuːzd|i, ˈtʃuːzd|i, -eɪz\-ɪz
AM ˈt(j)uzˌdeɪ,
ˈt(j)uzdi, -z

tufa
BR ˈtjuːfə(r), ˈtʃuːfə(r)
AM ˈt(j)ufə

tufaceous
BR tjʊˈfeɪʃəs,
tʃʊˈfeɪʃəs
AM t(j)uˈfeɪʃəs

tuff
BR tʌf
AM təf

tuffaceous
BR tʌˈfeɪʃəs
AM ˌtəˈfeɪʃəs

tuffet
BR ˈtʌfɪt, -s
AM ˈtəfət, -s

Tuffnell
BR ˈtʌfnl
AM ˈtəfnəl, ˈtəfˌnɛl

Tufnell
BR ˈtʌfnl
AM ˈtəfnəl, ˈtəfˌnɛl

tuft
BR tʌft, -s, -ɪd
AM təft, -s, -əd

tuftiness
BR ˈtʌftɪnɪs
AM ˈtəftɪnɪs

tufty
BR ˈtʌfti
AM ˈtəfti

tug
BR tʌg, -z, -ɪŋ, -d
AM təg, -z, -ɪŋ, -d

tugboat
BR ˈtʌgbəʊt, -s
AM ˈtəgˌbout, -s

Tugendhat
BR ˈtuːg(ə)nhɑːt
AM ˈtugən,(h)æt

tugger
BR ˈtʌgə(r), -z
AM ˈtəgər, -z

tug-of-love
BR ˌtʌgəvˈlʌv
AM ˈtəgə(v)ˈləv

tug-of-war
BR ˌtʌgə(v)ˈwɔː(r), -z
AM ˈtəgə(v)ˈwɔ(ə)r, -z

tugrik
BR ˈtuːgriːk, -s
AM ˈtuˌgrik, -s

tui
BR ˈtuːˌi, -ɪz
AM ˈtui, -z

Tuileries
BR ˈtwiːləri, ˈtwiːlərɪz
AM ˈtwiləri(z)

tuition
BR tjuːˈɪʃn, tʃuːˈɪʃn
AM t(j)uˈɪʃən

tuitional
BR tjuːˈɪʃn(ə)l,
tjuːˈɪʃən(ə)l,
tʃuːˈɪʃn(ə)l,
tʃuːˈɪʃən(ə)l
AM t(j)uˈɪʃ(ə)nəl

tuitionary
BR tjuːˈɪʃn(ə)ri,
tʃuːˈɪʃn(ə)ri
AM t(j)uˈɪʃnˌeri

Tula
BR tuːlə(r)
AM ˈtulə

tularaemia
BR ˌt(j)uːləˈriːmiə(r)
AM ˌt(j)uləˈrimiə

tularaemic
BR ˌt(j)uːləˈriːmɪk
AM ˌt(j)uləˈrimɪk

tularemia
BR ˌt(j)uːləˈriːmiə(r)
AM ˌt(j)uləˈrimiə

tularemic
BR ˌt(j)uːləˈriːmɪk
AM ˌt(j)uləˈrimɪk

tulchan
BR ˈtʌlk(ə)n, ˈtʌlx(ə)n,
-z
AM ˈtəlkən, -z

tulip
BR ˈtjuːlɪp, ˈtʃuːlɪp, -s
AM ˈt(j)uləp, -s

tulipwood
BR ˈtjuːlɪpwʊd,
ˈtʃuːlɪpwʊd, -z
AM ˈt(j)uləpˌwʊd, -z

Tull
BR tʌl
AM təl

Tullamore
BR ˈtʌləmɔː(r)
AM ˈtələˌmɔ(ə)r

tulle
BR tjuːl, tʃuːl
AM tul

Tulloch
BR ˈtʌləx, ˈtʌlək
AM ˈtələk

Tully
BR ˈtʌli
AM ˈtəli

Tulsa
BR ˈtʌlsə(r)
AM ˈtəlsə

Tulse Hill
BR ˌtʌls ˈhɪl
AM ˈtəls ˈhɪl

tum
BR tʌm, -z
AM təm, -z

tumble
BR ˈtʌmb|l, -lz,
-lɪŋ \ -lɪŋ, -ld
AM ˈtəmbəl, -əlz,
-(ə)lɪŋ, -əld

tumbledown
BR ˈtʌmbldaʊn
AM ˈtəmbəlˌdaʊn

tumble-drier
BR ˌtʌmblˈdrʌɪə(r), -z
AM ˈtəmbəlˌdraɪər, -z

tumble-dry
BR ˌtʌmblˈdrʌɪ, -z, -ɪŋ,
-d
AM ˈtəmbəlˌdraɪ, -z, -ɪŋ,
-d

tumble-dryer
BR ˌtʌmblˈdrʌɪə(r), -z
AM ˈtəmbəlˌdraɪər, -z

tumbler
BR ˈtʌmblə(r), -z
AM ˈtəmb(ə)lər, -z

tumblerful
BR ˈtʌmbləfʊl, -z
AM ˈtəmblərˌfʊl, -z

tumbleweed
BR ˈtʌmblwiːd, -z
AM ˈtəmbəlˌwid, -z

tumbrel
BR ˈtʌmbr(ɪ)l, -z
AM ˈtəmbrəl, -z

tumbril
BR ˈtʌmbr(ɪ)l, -z
AM ˈtəmbrəl, -z

tumefacient
BR ˌtjuːmɪˈfeɪʃ(ə)nt,
ˌtʃuːmɪˈfeɪʃ(ə)nt
AM ˌt(j)uməˈfeɪʃənt

tumefaction
BR ˌtjuːmɪˈfakʃn,
ˌtʃuːmɪˈfakʃn
AM ˌt(j)uməˈfækʃən

tumefy
BR ˈtjuːmɪfʌɪ,
ˈtʃuːmɪfʌɪ, -z, -ɪŋ, -d
AM ˈt(j)uməˌfaɪ, -z, -ɪŋ,
-d

tumescence
BR tjuːˈmɛsns,
tjʊˈmɛsns,
tʃuːˈmɛsns,
tʃʊˈmɛsns
AM t(j)uˈmɛsəns

tumescent
BR tjuːˈmɛsnt,
tjʊˈmɛsnt,
tʃuːˈmɛsnt, tʃʊˈmɛsnt
AM t(j)uˈmɛsənt

tumescently
BR tjuːˈmɛsntli,
tjʊˈmɛsntli,
tʃuːˈmɛsntli,
tʃʊˈmɛsntli
AM t(j)uˈmɛsn(t)li

tumid
BR ˈtjuːmɪd, ˈtʃuːmɪd
AM ˈt(j)uməd

tumidity
BR tjuːˈmɪdɪti,
tjʊˈmɪdɪti,
tʃuːˈmɪdɪti,
tʃʊˈmɪdɪti
AM t(j)uˈmɪdɪdi

tumidly
BR ˈtjuːmɪdli,
ˈtʃuːmɪdli

tumidness
BR ˈtjuːmɪdnɪs,
ˈtʃuːmɪdnɪs
AM ˈt(j)umədnəs

tummy
BR ˈtʌm|i, -iz
AM ˈtəmi, -z

tumor
BR ˈtjuːmə(r),
ˈtʃuːmə(r), -z, -əs
AM ˈt(j)umər, -z, -əs

tumorous
BR ˈtjuːm(ə)rəs,
ˈtʃuːm(ə)rəs
AM ˈt(j)umərəs

tumour
BR ˈtjuːmə(r),
ˈtʃuːmə(r), -z, -əs
AM ˈt(j)umər, -z, -əs

tump
BR tʌmp, -s
AM təmp, -s

tumtum
BR ˈtʌmtʌm, -z
AM ˈtəmˌtəm, -z

tumular
BR ˈtjuːmjʊlə(r),
ˈtʃuːmjʊlə(r)
AM ˈt(j)umjələr

tumuli
BR ˈtjuːmjʊlʌɪ,
ˈtʃuːmjʊlʌɪ
AM ˈt(j)umjəˌlai

tumult
BR ˈtjuːmʌlt,
ˈtʃuːmʌlt, -s
AM ˈt(j)uˌmʌlt, -s

tumultuary
BR tjʊˈmʌltjʊəri,
tʃʊˈmʌltʃʊəri
AM t(j)uməlˌtʃʊɛri

tumultuous
BR tjʊˈmʌltjʊəs,
tʃʊˈmʌltʃʊəs
AM t(j)uˈməltʃ(əw)əs,
təˈməltʃ(əw)əs

tumultuously
BR tjʊˈmʌltjʊəsli,
tʃʊˈmʌltʃʊəsli
AM t(j)uˈməltʃ(əw)əsli,
təˈməltʃ(əw)əsli

tumultuousness
BR tjʊˈmʌltjʊəsnəs,
tʃʊˈmʌltʃʊəsnəs
AM t(j)uˈməltʃ(əw)əs-
nəs,
təˈməltʃ(əw)əsnəs

tumulus
BR ˈtjuːmjʊləs,
ˈtʃuːmjʊləs, -ɪz
AM ˈt(j)umjələs, -əz

tun
BR tʌn, -z
AM tən, -z

tuna
BR ˈtjuːnə(r),
ˈtʃuːnə(r), -z
AM ˈtunə, -z

tunable
BR ˈtjuːnəbl, ˈtʃuːnəbl
AM ˈt(j)unəbəl

Tunbridge Wells
BR ˌtʌnbrɪdʒ ˈwɛlz
AM ˈtənˌbrɪdʒ ˈwɛlz,
ˈtəmˌbrɪdʒ +

tundish
BR ˈtʌndɪʃ, -ɪz
AM ˈtənˌdɪʃ, -ɪz

tundra
BR ˈtʌndrə(r)
AM ˈtəndrə

tune
BR tjuːn, tʃuːn, -z, -ɪŋ,
-d
AM t(j)un, -z, -ɪŋ, -d

tuneable
BR ˈtjuːnəbl, ˈtʃuːnəbl
AM ˈt(j)unəbəl

tuneful
BR ˈtjuːnf(ʊ)l,
ˈtʃuːnf(ʊ)l
AM ˈt(j)unfəl

tunefully
BR ˈtjuːnfʊli, ˈtjuːnfli,
ˈtʃuːnfʊli, ˈtʃuːnfli
AM ˈt(j)unfəli

tunefulness
BR ˈtjuːnf(ʊ)lnəs,
ˈtʃuːnf(ʊ)lnəs
AM ˈt(j)unfəlnəs

tuneless
BR ˈtjuːnləs, ˈtʃuːnləs
AM ˈt(j)unləs

tunelessly
BR ˈtjuːnləsli,
ˈtʃuːnləsli
AM ˈt(j)unləsli

tunelessness
BR ˈtjuːnləsnəs,
ˈtʃuːnləsnəs
AM ˈt(j)unləsnəs

tuner
BR ˈtjuːnə(r),
ˈtʃuːnə(r), -z
AM ˈt(j)unər, -z

tung
BR tʌŋ, -z
AM təŋ, -z

tungstate
BR ˈtʌŋsteɪt, -s
AM ˈtəŋˌsteɪt, -s

tungsten
BR ˈtʌŋstən
AM ˈtəŋstən

tungstic
BR ˈtʌŋstɪk
AM ˈtəŋstɪk

tungstite
BR ˈtʌŋstʌɪt
AM ˈtəŋstaɪt

Tungus
BR 'tʊŋgʊs, tʊŋ'guːz,
-ɪz
AM 'tʌŋgəs, 'tʊŋ,gʊs,
-əz

Tungusic
BR tʊŋ'gʊsɪk,
tʊŋ'guːzɪk
AM tʌŋ'gʊsɪk,
tʊŋ'gʊsɪk

tunic
BR 'tjuːnɪk, 'tʃuːnɪk, -s
AM 't(j)uːnɪk, -s

tunica
BR 'tjuːnɪkə(r),
'tʃuːnɪkə(r)
AM 't(j)unəkə

tunicae
BR 'tjuːnɪkiː, 'tʃuːnɪkiː
AM 't(j)unəki,
't(j)unəˌkaɪ,
't(j)unəsi, 't(j)unəˌsaɪ

tunicate
BR 'tjuːnɪkeɪt,
'tʃuːnɪkeɪt, -s, -ɪd
AM 't(j)unəˌkeɪt, -ts,
-dɪŋ, -dɪd

tunicle
BR 'tjuːnɪkl, 'tʃuːnɪkl,
-z
AM 't(j)unəkəl, -z

tuning
BR 'tjuːnɪŋ, 'tʃuːnɪŋ, -z
AM 't(j)unɪŋ, -z

Tunis
BR 'tjuːnɪs, 'tʃuːnɪs
AM 'tunəs

Tunisia
BR tjʊ'nɪzɪə(r),
tʃʊ'nɪzɪə(r)
AM tu'niʒə

Tunisian
BR tjʊ'nɪzɪən,
tʃʊ'nɪzɪən, -z
AM tu'niʒən, -z

tunnel
BR 'tʌn|l, -lz, -lɪŋ, -ld
AM 'tʌnəl, -z, -ɪŋ, -d

tunneler
BR 'tʌnlə(r), -z
AM 'tʌnlər, -z

tunneller
BR 'tʌnlə(r), -z
AM 'tʌnlər, -z

tunnel vision
BR ,tʌnl 'vɪʒn
AM 'tʌnəl ,vɪʒn

Tunney
BR 'tʌni
AM 'tʌni

Tunnicliff
BR 'tʌnɪklɪf
AM 'tʌnəˌklɪf

Tunnicliffe
BR 'tʌnɪklɪf
AM 'tʌnəˌklɪf

tunny
BR 'tʌn|i, -ɪz

AM 'təni, -z
Tuohy
BR 'tuːi
AM 'tui

tup
BR tʌp, -s, -ɪŋ, -t
AM təp, -s, -ɪŋ, -t

Tupamaro
BR ,t(j)uːpə'mɑːrəʊ,
,t(j)uːpə'marəʊ, -z
AM ,tupə'mɑ,roʊ, -z

tupelo
BR 'tjuːpələʊ,
'tʃuːpələʊ, -z
AM 't(j)upəˌloʊ, -z

Tupi
BR 'tuːp|i, -ɪz
AM 'tu,pi, -z

tuppence
BR 'tʌp(ə)ns
AM 'təpəns

tuppenny
BR 'tʌp(ə)ni, 'tʌpn̩i
AM 'təpəni

**tuppenny-
ha'penny**
BR 'tʌp(ə)nɪ'heɪp(ə)ni,
'tʌpn̩i'heɪpn̩i
AM 'təpəni'heɪpəni

Tupperware®
BR 'tʌpəwɛː(r)
AM 'təpər,wɛ(ə)r

tuque
BR tjuːk, tʃuːk, -s
AM t(j)uk, -s

tu quoque
BR ,t(j)uː 'kwəʊkw|i,
-ɪz
AM 't(j)u 'kwoʊkwi, -z

turaco
BR 'tʊərəkəʊ, -z
AM 't(j)ʊrə,koʊ, -z

Turandot
BR 't(j)ʊərəndʊt,
't(j)ʊərn̩dʊt
AM 't(j)ʊrən,doʊ

Turanian
BR tjʊ'reɪmɪən,
tʃʊ'reɪmɪən, -z
AM t(j)ʊ'reɪnɪən,
tə'reɪnɪən, -z

turban
BR 'təːb(ə)n, -z, -d
AM 'tərbən, -z, -d

turbary
BR 'təːb(ə)r|i, -ɪz
AM 'tərb(ə)ri, -z

turbellarian
BR ,təːbə'lɛːrɪən, -z
AM ,tərbə'lɛrɪən, -z

turbid
BR 'təːbɪd
AM 'tərbəd

turbidity
BR təː'bɪdɪti
AM tər'bɪdɪdi

turbidly
BR 'təːbɪdli
AM 'tərbədli

turbidness
BR 'təːbɪdnɪs
AM 'tərbɪdnɪs

turbinal
BR 'təːbɪnl, 'təːbn̩l
AM 'tərbənəl

turbinate
BR 'təːbɪnət, 'təːbn̩ət,
'təːbɪneɪt
AM 'tərbənət,
'tərbə,neɪt

turbination
BR ,təːbɪ'neɪʃn
AM ,tərbə'neɪʃən

turbine
BR 'təːbʌɪn, 'təːbɪn, -z
AM 'tərbən, 'tər,baɪn,
-z

turbit
BR 'təːbɪt, -s
AM 'tərbət, -s

turbo
BR 'təːbəʊ, -z
AM 'tərboʊ, -z

turbocharge
BR 'təːbə(ʊ)tʃɑːdʒ, -ɪz,
-ɪŋ, -d
AM 'tərboʊ,tʃɑrdʒ, -əz,
-ɪŋ, -d

turbocharger
BR 'təːbə(ʊ),tʃɑːdʒə(r),
-z
AM 'tərboʊ,tʃɑrdʒər, -z

turbocharging
BR 'təːbə(ʊ),tʃɑːdʒɪŋ
AM 'tərboʊ,tʃɑrdʒɪŋ

turbo-diesel
BR ,təːbəʊ'diːzl, -z
AM 'tərboʊ'dizəl, -z

turbofan
BR 'təːbəʊfan, -z
AM 'tərboʊ,fæn, -z

turbojet
BR 'təːbəʊdʒet, -s
AM 'tərboʊ,dʒɛt, -s

turboprop
BR 'təːbəʊprɒp, -s
AM 'tərboʊ,prap, -s

turboshaft
BR 'təːbəʊʃɑːft,
'təːbəʊʃaft, -s
AM 'tərboʊ,ʃæft, -s

turbosupercharger
BR ,təːbəʊ'suːpəˌtʃɑː-
dʒə(r), -z
AM ,tərboʊ'supər,tʃɑr-
dʒər, -z

turbot
BR 'təːbət, -s
AM 'tərbət, -s

turbulence
BR 'təːbjʊləns,
'təːbjəlns
AM 'tərbjələns

turbulent
BR 'təːbjʊlənt,
'təːbjəlnt
AM 'tərbjələnt

turbulently
BR 'təːbjʊləntli,
'təːbjəlntli
AM 'tərbjələn(t)li

Turco
BR 'təːkəʊ, -z
AM 'tərkoʊ, -z

Turcoman
BR 'təːkəmən,
'təːkəman,
'təːkəmɑːn, -z
AM 'tərkəmən, -z

Turcophile
BR 'təːkə(ʊ)fʌɪl, -z
AM 'tərkə,faɪl, -z

Turcophobe
BR 'təːkə(ʊ)fəʊb, -z
AM 'tərkə,foʊb, -z

turd
BR təːd, -z
AM tərd, -z

turdoid
BR 'təːdɔɪd
AM 'tər,dɔɪd

tureen
BR t(j)ʊ'riːn, tʃʊ'riːn,
-z
AM tə'rin, t(j)ʊ'rin, -z

turf
BR təːf, -s, -ɪŋ, -t
AM tərf, -s, -ɪŋ, -t

turfman
BR 'təːfmən
AM 'tərfmən

turfmen
BR 'təːfmən
AM 'tərfmən

turfy
BR 'təːfi
AM 'tərfi

Turgenev
BR tʊə'geɪnjɛf,
tə:'geɪnjɛf
AM tʊr'geɪˌnjɛf

turgescence
BR təː'dʒɛsns
AM 'tər'dʒɛsəns

turgescent
BR təː'dʒɛsnt
AM tər'dʒɛsənt

turgid
BR 'təːdʒɪd
AM 'tərdʒəd

turgidescence
BR ,təːdʒɪ'dɛsns
AM ,tərdʒə'dɛsəns

turgidescent
BR ,təːdʒɪ'dɛsnt
AM ,tərdʒə'dɛsənt

turgidity
BR təː'dʒɪdɪti
AM tər'dʒɪdɪdi

turgidly
BR 'tɜːdʒɪdli
AM 'tɜrdʒədli

turgidness
BR 'tɜːdʒɪdnɪs
AM 'tɜrdʒɪdnɪs

turgor
BR 'tɜːgə(r)
AM 'tɜrgər

Turin
BR tjʊ'rɪn, tjʊə'rɪn,
tʃʊ'rɪn, tʃʊə'rɪn
AM 't(j)ʊrən

Turing
BR 'tjʊərɪŋ, 'tʃʊərɪŋ
AM 't(j)ʊrɪŋ

turion
BR 't(j)ʊərɪən,
'tʃʊərɪən, -z
AM 't(j)ʊrɪən,
't(j)ʊriˌan, -z

Turk
BR tɜːk, -s
AM tɜrk, -s

Turkana
BR tɜː'kɑːnə(r)
AM tɜr'kɑnə

Turkestan
BR ˌtɜːkɪ'stɑːn,
ˌtɜːkɪ'stan
AM 'tɜrkəˌstæn

turkey
BR 'tɜːk|i, -ɪz
AM 'tɜrki, -z

turkeycock
BR 'tɜːkɪkɒk, -s
AM 'tɜrkiˌkɑk, -s

Turki
BR 'tɜːk|i, -ɪz
AM 'tɜrki, -z

Turkic
BR 'tɜːkɪk
AM 'tɜrkɪk

Turkish
BR 'tɜːkɪʃ
AM 'tɜrkɪʃ

Turkistan
BR ˌtɜːkɪ'stɑːn,
ˌtɜːkɪ'stan
AM 'tɜrkəˌstæn

Turkmenistan
BR tɜːkˌmɛnɪ'stɑːn,
tɜːkˌmɛnɪ'stan
AM tɜrkˈmɛnəˌstæn

Turkoman
BR 'tɜːkəmən,
'tɜːkəman,
'tɜːkəmɑːn, -z
AM 'tɜrkəmən, -z

Turks and Caicos Islands
BR ˌtɜːks (ə)n(d)
'keɪkɒs ˌʌɪlən(d)z
AM 'tɜrks ən 'keɪkəs
'aɪlən(d)z

Turku
BR 'tʊəkuː
AM 'tʊrˌku

turmeric
BR 'tɜːm(ə)rɪk
AM 'tɜrmərɪk

turmoil
BR 'tɜːmɔɪl, -z
AM 'tɜrˌmɔɪl, -z

turn
BR tɜːn, -z, -ɪŋ, -d
AM tɜrn, -z, -ɪŋ, -d

turnabout
BR 'tɜːnəbaʊt, -s
AM 'tɜrnəˌbaʊt, -s

turnaround
BR 'tɜːnəraʊnd, -z
AM 'tɜrnəˌraʊnd, -z

turnback
BR 'tɜːnbak, -s
AM 'tɜrnˌbæk, -s

Turnberry
BR 'tɜːnb(ə)ri
AM 'tɜrnˌberi

turnbuckle
BR 'tɜːnˌbʌkl, -z
AM 'tɜrnˌbəkəl, -z

Turnbull
BR 'tɜːnbʊl
AM 'tɜrnbəl

turncoat
BR 'tɜːnkəʊt, -s
AM 'tɜrnˌkoʊt, -s

turncock
BR 'tɜːnkɒk, -s
AM 'tɜrnˌkɑk, -s

turndown
BR 'tɜːndaʊn, -z
AM 'tɜrnˌdaʊn, -z

turner
BR 'tɜːnə(r), -z
AM 'tɜrnər, -z

turnery
BR 'tɜːn(ə)ri, -ɪz
AM 'tɜrnəri, -z

turning
BR 'tɜːnɪŋ, -z
AM 'tɜrnɪŋ, -z

turnip
BR 'tɜːnɪp, -s
AM 'tɜrnəp, -s

turnipy
BR 'tɜːnɪpi
AM 'tɜrnəpi

turnkey
BR 'tɜːnkiː, -z
AM 'tɜrnˌki, -z

turnout
BR 'tɜːnaʊt, -s
AM 'tɜrnˌaʊt, -s

turnover
BR 'tɜːnˌəʊvə(r), -z
AM 'tɜrnˌoʊvər, -z

turnpike
BR 'tɜːnpʌɪk, -s
AM 'tɜrnˌpaɪk, -s

turnround
BR 'tɜːnraʊnd, -z
AM 'tɜrnˌraʊnd, -z

turnsick
BR 'tɜːnsɪk
AM 'tɜrnˌsɪk

turnside
BR 'tɜːnsʌɪd
AM 'tɜrnˌsaɪd

turnsole
BR 'tɜːnsəʊl, -z
AM 'tɜrnˌsoʊl, -z

turnspike
BR 'tɜːnspʌɪk, -s
AM 'tɜrnˌspaɪk, -s

turnspit
BR 'tɜːnspɪt, -s
AM 'tɜrnˌspɪt, -s

turnstile
BR 'tɜːnstʌɪl, -z
AM 'tɜrnˌstaɪl, -z

turnstone
BR 'tɜːnstəʊn, -z
AM 'tɜrnˌstoʊn, -z

turntable
BR 'tɜːnˌteɪbl, -z
AM 'tɜrnˌteɪbəl, -z

turnup
BR 'tɜːnʌp, -s
AM 'tɜrnˌəp, -s

turpentine
BR 'tɜːp(ɪ)ntʌɪn
AM 'tɜrpənˌtaɪn

turpeth
BR 'tɜːpəθ, -s
AM 'tɜrpəθ

Turpin
BR 'tɜːpɪn
AM 'tɜrpən

turpitude
BR 'tɜːpɪtjuːd,
'tɜːpɪtʃuːd
AM 'tɜrpəˌt(j)ud

turps
BR tɜːps
AM tɜrps

turquoise
BR 'tɜːkwɔɪz, 'tɜːkwɑːz
AM 'tɜrˌk(w)ɔɪz

turret
BR 'tʌrɪt, -s, -ɪd
AM 'tɜrə|t, -ts, -dəd

turtle
BR 'tɜːtl, -z
AM 'tɜrdəl, -z

turtledove
BR 'tɜːtldʌv, -z
AM 'tɜrdlˌdəv, -z

turtleneck
BR 'tɜːtlnɛk, -s
AM 'tɜrdlˌnɛk, -s

turtleshell
BR 'tɜːtlʃɛl
AM 'tɜrdlˌʃɛl

Turton
BR 'tɜːtn
AM 'tɜrtn

turves
BR tɜːvz
AM tɜrvz

Turvey
BR 'tɜːvi
AM 'tɜrvi

Tuscan
BR 'tʌsk(ə)n, -z
AM 'təskən, -z

Tuscany
BR 'tʌskəni
AM 'təskəni

Tuscarora
BR ˌtʌskə'rɔːrə(r)
AM ˌtəskə'rɔrə

tush
BR tʌʃ, -ɪz
AM təʃ, tʊʃ, -əz

tusk
BR tʌsk, -s, -t
AM təsk, -s, -t

tusker
BR 'tʌskə(r), -z
AM 'təskər, -z

tusky
BR 'tʌski
AM 'təski

tussah
BR 'tʌsə(r)
AM 'təsə

Tussaud's
BR tʊ'sɔːdz, tʊ'səʊdz,
'tuːsɔːdz, 'tuːsəʊdz
AM tʊ'souz

tusser
BR 'tʌsə(r)
AM 'təsər

tussive
BR 'tʌsɪv
AM 'təsɪv

tussle
BR tʌs|l, -lz, -lɪŋ\-lɪŋ,
-ld
AM 'təs|əl, -əlz, -(ə)lɪŋ,
-əld

tussock
BR 'tʌsək, -s
AM 'təsək, -s

tussocky
BR 'tʌsəki
AM 'təsəki

tussore
BR 'tʌsə(r), 'tʌsɔː(r)
AM 'tə‚sɔ(ə)r

tut[1]
interjection
BR ǀ, tʌt
AM tət

tut[2]
noun, verb
BR tʌt, -s, -ɪŋ, -ɪd
AM tə|t, -ts, -dɪŋ, -dəd

Tutankhamen
BR ˌtuːt(ə)n'kɑːmən,
ˌtuːtəŋ'kɑːmən
AM ˌtuˌtæŋ'kɑmən,
ˌtətn'kɑmən

Tutankhamun
BR ˌtuːt(ə)n'kɑːmən,
ˌtuːtəŋ'kɑːmən,
ˌtuːtəŋkə'muːn

AM ˌtuˌtæŋˈkɑmən,
ˌtətnˈkɑmən

tutee
BR ˌtjuːˈtiː, ˌtʃuːˈtiː, -z
AM t(j)uˈti, -z

tutelage
BR ˈtjuːtɪlɪdʒ,
ˈtjuːtlɪdʒ, ˈtʃuːtɪlɪdʒ,
ˈtʃuːtlɪdʒ
AM ˈt(j)uːdlɪdʒ

tutelar
BR ˈtjuːtɪlə(r),
ˈtjuːtlə(r),
ˈtʃuːtɪlə(r), ˈtʃuːtlə(r)
AM ˈt(j)uːdlər

tutelary
BR ˈtjuːtɪləri,
ˈtjuːtləri, ˈtʃuːtɪləri,
ˈtʃuːtləri
AM ˈt(j)uːdlˌeri

tutenag
BR ˈtuːtɪnag
AM ˈtuːdəˌnæg

Tutin
BR ˈtjuːtɪn, ˈtʃuːtɪn
AM ˈt(j)uːdən

tutor
BR ˈtjuːtʃə(r),
ˈtʃuːtʃə(r), -əz, -(ə)rɪŋ,
-əd
AM ˈt(j)uːdər, -z, -ɪŋ, -d

tutorage
BR ˈtjuːt(ə)rɪdʒ,
ˈtʃuːt(ə)rɪdʒ
AM ˈt(j)uːdərɪdʒ

tutoress
BR ˈtjuːt(ə)rɪs,
ˈtʃuːt(ə)rɪs, -ɪz
AM ˈt(j)uːdərəs,
ˈt(j)uːdəˌres, -əz

tutorial
BR tjuːˈtɔːriəl,
tjəˈtɔːriəl, tʃuːˈtɔːriəl,
tʃəˈtɔːriəl, -z
AM t(j)uˈtɔriəl, -z

tutorially
BR tjuːˈtɔːriəli,
tjəˈtɔːriəli,
tʃuːˈtɔːriəli,
tʃəˈtɔːriəli
AM t(j)uˈtɔriəli

tutorship
BR ˈtjuːtəʃɪp,
ˈtʃuːtəʃɪp, -s
AM ˈt(j)uːdərˌʃɪp, -s

tutsan
BR ˈtʌtsən, -z
AM ˈtətsən, -z

Tutsi
BR ˈtʊtsi, ˈtuːtsi
AM ˈtutsi

tutti
BR ˈtʊti, ˈtuːti
AM ˈtudi

tutti-frutti
BR ˌtuːtɪˈfruːt‖i, -ɪz
AM ˈtudiˈfrudi, -z

Tuttle
BR ˈtʌtl
AM ˈtədəl

tut-tut
BR ˌtʌtˈtʌt, -s, -ɪŋ, -ɪd
AM ˌtətˈtəlt, -ts, -dɪŋ,
-dəd

tutty
BR ˈtʌti
AM ˈtədi

tutu
BR ˈtuːtuː, -z
AM ˈtuˌtu, -z

Tuva
BR ˈtuːvə(r)
AM ˈtuvə
RUS tuˈva

Tuvalu
BR tʊˈvɑːluː
AM təˈvalu

Tuvaluan
BR tʊˈvɑːlʊən, -z
AM təˈvaluən,
təˈvaləwən, -z

tu-whit tu-whoo
BR tʊˌwɪt tʊˈwuː, -z
AM tuˈ(h)wɪt təˈ(h)wu,
-z

tux
BR tʌks, -ɪz
AM təks, -ɪz

tuxedo
BR tʌkˈsiːdəʊ, -z
AM təkˈsidoʊ, -z

tuyère
BR ˈtuːjɛː(r),
twiːˈjɛː(r), -z
twiˈjɛ(ə)r,
twiˈjɛ(ə)r, -z

Twa
BR twɑː(r), -z
AM twɑ, -z

twaddle
BR ˈtwɒdl
AM ˈtwadəl

twaddler
BR ˈtwɒdlə(r), -z
AM ˈtwad(ə)lər, -z

twaddly
BR ˈtwɒdl‖i
AM ˈtwadl‖i, ˈtwadli

twain
BR tweɪn
AM tweɪn

twang
BR twaŋ, -z, -ɪŋ, -d
AM twæŋ, -z, -ɪŋ, -d

twangle
BR ˈtwaŋg‖l, -lz,
-l̩ŋ\-lɪŋ, -ld
AM ˈtwæŋgəl, -əlz,
-(ə)lɪŋ, -əld

twangy
BR ˈtwaŋi
AM ˈtwæŋi

Twankey
BR ˈtwaŋki
AM ˈtwæŋki

Twanky
BR ˈtwaŋki
AM ˈtwæŋki

'twas
BR twɒz, twəz
AM twəz

twat
BR twɒt, twat, -s
AM twɑt, -s

twayblade
BR ˈtweɪbleɪd, -z
AM ˈtweɪˌbleɪd, -z

tweak
BR twiːk, -s, -ɪŋ, -t
AM twik, -s, -ɪŋ, -t

twee
BR twiː
AM twi

tweed
BR twiːd, -z
AM twid, -z

Tweeddale
BR ˈtwiːddeɪl
AM ˈtwi(d)ˌdeɪl

tweedily
BR ˈtwiːdɪli
AM ˈtwidɪli

tweediness
BR ˈtwiːdɪnɪs
AM ˈtwidɪnɪs

Tweedledee
BR ˌtwiːdlˈdiː
AM ˈtwidlˈdi

Tweedledum
BR ˌtwiːdlˈdʌm
AM ˈtwidlˈdəm

Tweedsmuir
BR ˈtwiːdzmjʊə(r),
ˈtwiːdzmjɔː(r)
AM ˈtwidzˌmjʊ(ə)r

tweedy
BR ˈtwiːdi
AM ˈtwidi

tweely
BR ˈtwiːli
AM ˈtwili

'tween
BR twiːn
AM twin

'tween-decks
BR ˈtwiːndɛks
AM ˈtwinˌdɛks

tweeness
BR ˈtwiːnɪs
AM ˈtwinɪs

tweeny
BR ˈtwiːn‖i, -ɪz
AM ˈtwini, -z

tweet
BR twiːt, -s, -ɪŋ, -ɪd
AM twi‖t, -ts, -dɪŋ, -dɪd

tweeter
BR ˈtwiːtə(r), -z
AM ˈtwidər, -z

tweezer
BR ˈtwiːzə(r), -z, -ɪŋ, -d
AM ˈtwizər, -z, -ɪŋ, -d

twelfth
BR twɛlfθ, -s
AM twɛlf(θ), -s

Twelfth Day
BR ˌtwɛlfθ ˈdeɪ
AM ˈtwɛlf(θ) ˈdeɪ

twelfthly
BR ˈtwɛlfθli
AM ˈtwɛlf(θ)li, ˈtwɛlθli

Twelfth Night
BR ˌtwɛlfθ ˈnaɪt
AM ˈtwɛlf(θ) ˈnaɪt

twelve
BR twɛlv
AM twɛlv

twelvefold
BR ˈtwɛlvfəʊld
AM ˈtwɛl(v)ˌfoʊld

twelvemo
BR ˈtwɛlvməʊ
AM ˈtwɛlvˌmoʊ

twelvemonth
BR ˈtwɛlvmʌnθ, -s
AM ˈtwɛlvˌmənθ, -s

twentieth
BR ˈtwɛntɪɪθ, -s
AM ˈtwɛn(t)iɪθ, -s

twenty
BR ˈtwɛnt‖i, -ɪz
AM ˈtwɛn(t)i, -z

twenty-first
BR ˌtwɛntɪˈfəːst, -s
AM ˈtwɛn(t)iˈfərst, -s

twentyfold
BR ˈtwɛntɪfəʊld
AM ˈtwɛn(t)iˌfoʊld

twenty-fourmo
BR ˌtwɛntɪˈfɔːməʊ
AM ˌtwɛn(t)iˈfɔrˌmoʊ

twentysomething
BR ˈtwɛntɪˌsʌmθɪŋ, -z
AM ˈtwɛn(t)iˌsəmθɪŋ,
-z

twenty-twenty
BR ˌtwɛntɪˈtwɛnti
AM ˌtwɛn(t)iˈtwɛn(t)i

'twere¹
strong form
BR twɜː(r)
AM twər

'twere²
weak form
BR twə(r)
AM twər

twerp
BR twɜːp, -s
AM twərp, -s

Twi
BR twiː, -z
AM twi, -z

twibill
BR ˈtwaɪbɪl, -z
AM ˈtwaɪˌbɪl, ˈtwaɪbəl,
-z

twice
BR twaɪs
AM twaɪs

twicer
BR ˈtwʌɪsə(r), -z
AM ˈtwaɪsər, -z

Twickenham
BR ˈtwɪkənəm,
ˈtwɪknəm
AM ˈtwɪkənəm

twiddle
BR ˈtwɪd|l, -lz, -lɪŋ\-lɪŋ,
-ld
AM ˈtwɪd|əl, -əlz,
-(ə)lɪŋ, -əld

twiddler
BR ˈtwɪdlə(r),
ˈtwɪdlə(r), -z
AM ˈtwɪd(ə)lər, -z

twiddly
BR ˈtwɪdli, ˈtwɪdli
AM ˈtwɪdli, ˈtwɪdli

twig
BR twɪg, -z, -ɪŋ, -d
AM twɪg, -z, -ɪŋ, -d

twiggy
BR ˈtwɪgi
AM ˈtwɪgi

twilight
BR ˈtwʌɪlʌɪt
AM ˈtwaɪˌlaɪt

twilit
BR ˈtwʌɪlɪt
AM ˈtwaɪˌlɪt

twill
BR twɪl, -d
AM twɪl, -d

'twill
BR twɪl
AM twɪl

twin
BR twɪn, -z, -ɪŋ, -d
AM twɪn, -z, -ɪŋ, -d

twine
BR twʌɪn, -z, -ɪŋ, -d
AM twaɪn, -z, -ɪŋ, -d

twiner
BR ˈtwʌɪnə(r), -z
AM ˈtwaɪnər, -z

twinge
BR twɪn(d)ʒ, -ɪz, -ɪŋ, -d
AM twɪndʒ, -ɪz, -ɪŋ, -d

twi-night
BR ˈtwʌɪnʌɪt
AM ˈtwaɪˌnaɪt

Twining
BR ˈtwʌɪnɪŋ
AM ˈtwaɪnɪŋ

twink
BR twɪŋk, -s
AM twɪŋk, -s

twinkle
BR ˈtwɪŋk|l, -lz,
-lɪŋ\-lɪŋ, -ld
AM ˈtwɪŋk|əl, -əlz,
-(ə)lɪŋ, -əld

twinkler
BR ˈtwɪŋklə(r),
ˈtwɪŋkˌlə(r), -z
AM ˈtwɪŋk(ə)lər, -z

twinkly
BR ˈtwɪŋkli, ˈtwɪŋkˌli
AM ˈtwɪŋk(ə)li

twinning
BR ˈtwɪnɪŋ, -z
AM ˈtwɪnɪŋ, -z

twin-screw
BR ˌtwɪnˈskruː
AM ˌtwɪnˈskruː

twinset
BR ˈtwɪnsɛt, -s
AM ˈtwɪnˌsɛt, -s

twin-size
BR ˈtwɪnsʌɪz
AM ˈtwɪnˌsaɪz

twintub
BR ˈtwɪntʌb, -z
AM ˈtwɪnˌtəb, -z

twirl
BR twɜːl, -z, -ɪŋ, -d
AM twɜrl, -z, -ɪŋ, -d

twirler
BR ˈtwɜːlə(r), -z
AM ˈtwɜrlər, -z

twirly
BR ˈtwɜːli
AM ˈtwɜrli

twirp
BR twɜːp, -s
AM twɜrp, -s

twist
BR twɪst, -s, -ɪd
AM twɪst, -s, -ɪŋ, -ɪd

twistable
BR ˈtwɪstəbl
AM ˈtwɪstəbəl

twister
BR ˈtwɪstə(r), -z
AM ˈtwɪstər, -z

twistily
BR ˈtwɪstɪli
AM ˈtwɪstɪli

twistiness
BR ˈtwɪstɪnɪs
AM ˈtwɪstɪnɪs

twisting
BR ˈtwɪstɪŋ, -z
AM ˈtwɪstɪŋ, -z

twisty
BR ˈtwɪst|i, -ɪə(r), -ɪɪst
AM ˈtwɪsti, -ər, -ɪst

twit
BR twɪt, -s, -ɪŋ, -ɪd
AM twɪ|t, -ts, -dɪŋ, -dɪd

twitch
BR twɪtʃ, -ɪz, -ɪŋ, -t
AM twɪtʃ, -ɪz, -ɪŋ, -t

twitcher
BR ˈtwɪtʃə(r), -z
AM ˈtwɪtʃər, -z

twitchily
BR ˈtwɪtʃɪli
AM ˈtwɪtʃɪli

twitchiness
BR ˈtwɪtʃɪnɪs
AM ˈtwɪtʃɪnɪs

twitchy
BR ˈtwɪtʃ|i, -ɪə(r), -ɪɪst
AM ˈtwɪtʃi, -ər, -ɪst

twite
BR twʌɪt, -s
AM twaɪt, -s

twitter
BR ˈtwɪtə(r), -əz,
-(ə)rɪŋ, -əd
AM ˈtwɪdər, -z, -ɪŋ, -d

twitterer
BR ˈtwɪt(ə)rə(r), -z
AM ˈtwɪd(ə)rər, -z

twittery
BR ˈtwɪt(ə)ri
AM ˈtwɪdəri

twittish
BR ˈtwɪtɪʃ
AM ˈtwɪdɪʃ

'twixt
BR twɪkst
AM twɪkst

twizzle
BR ˈtwɪz|l, -lz, -lɪŋ\-lɪŋ,
-ld
AM ˈtwɪz|əl, -əlz,
-(ə)lɪŋ, -əld

two
BR tuː
AM tu

two-a-penny
BR ˌtuːəˈpɛni
AM ˌtuəˈpɛni

two-bit
BR ˈtuːbɪt
AM ˈtuˌbɪt

two-by-four
BR ˌtuːbʌɪˈfɔː(r), -z
AM ˌtuːbaɪˌfɔ(ə)r, -z

two-dimensional
BR ˌtuːdʌɪˈmɛnʃn(ə)l,
ˌtuːdʌɪˈmɛnʃən(ə)l,
ˌtuːdɪˈmɛnʃn(ə)l,
ˌtuːdɪˈmɛnʃən(ə)l
AM ˌtudəˈmɛn(t)ʃ(ə)nəl,
ˌtudaɪˈmɛn(t)ʃ(ə)nəl

twofold
BR ˈtuːfəʊld
AM ˈtuˌfoʊld

Twohy
BR ˈtuːi
AM ˈtui

Twomey
BR ˈtuːmi
AM ˈtumi

twoness
BR ˈtuːnəs
AM ˈtunəs

twopence
BR ˈtʌp(ə)ns
AM ˈtəpəns

twopenny
BR ˈtʌpni, ˈtʌpni
AM ˈtəpəni

twopenny-halfpenny
BR ˌtʌpnɪˈheɪpni,
ˌtʌpnɪˈheɪpni
AM ˈtəpəniˈheɪpəni

twopennyworth
BR ˈtuːˈpɛnəθ,
ˈtʌp(ə)nɪwəːθ,
ˈtʌpnɪwəːθ,
ˈtʌp(ə)nɪwəθ,
ˈtʌpnɪwəθ
AM ˈtəpəniˌwərθ

two-piece¹
adjective
BR ˌtuːˈpiːs
AM ˈtuˌpis

two-piece²
noun
BR ˈtuːpiːs, -ɪz
AM ˈtuˌpis, -ɪz

two-seater
BR ˌtuːˈsiːtə(r), -z
AM ˌtuˈsidər, -z

twosome
BR ˈtuːs(ə)m, -z
AM ˈtusəm, -z

two-timer
BR ˈtuːˌtʌɪmə(r),
ˌtuːˈtʌɪmə(r), -z
AM ˈtuˌtaɪmər, -z

two-tone
BR ˈtuːtəʊn
AM ˈtuˌtoʊn

'twould¹
it would, strong
BR twʊd
AM twʊd

'twould²
it would, weak
BR twəd
AM twəd

two-up
BR ˌtuːˈʌp
AM ˌtuˈəp

two-way
BR ˈtuːˈweɪ
AM ˈtuˌweɪ

two-wheeler
BR ˌtuːˈwiːlə(r), -z
AM ˈtuˈ(h)wilər, -z

twyer
BR ˈtwʌɪə(r), -z
AM ˈtwaɪər, -z

Twyford
BR ˈtwʌɪfəd
AM ˈtwaɪfərd

Tyburn
BR ˈtʌɪb(ə)n, ˈtʌɪbəːn
AM ˈtaɪbərn

Tyche
BR ˈtʌɪki
AM ˈtaɪki

tychism
BR ˈtʌɪkɪz(ə)m
AM ˈtaɪˌkɪzəm

tychist
BR ˈtʌɪkɪst, -s
AM ˈtaɪkɪst, -s

Tycho
BR ˈtaɪkəʊ
AM ˈtaɪkoʊ

Tychonian
BR tʌɪˈkəʊnɪən, -z
AM taɪˈkoʊnɪən, -z

Tychonic
BR tʌɪˈkɒnɪk
AM taɪˈkɑnɪk

tycoon
BR tʌɪˈkuːn, -z
AM taɪˈkun, -z

Tye
BR tʌɪ
AM taɪ

tying
BR ˈtʌɪɪŋ
AM ˈtaɪɪŋ

tyke
BR tʌɪk, -s
AM taɪk, -s

Tyldesley
BR ˈtɪl(d)zli
AM ˈtɪl(d)zli

Tyler
BR ˈtʌɪlə(r)
AM ˈtaɪlər

tylopod
BR ˈtʌɪləpɒd, -z
AM ˈtaɪlə,pɑd, -z

tylopodous
BR tʌɪˈlɒpədəs
AM taɪˈlɑpədəs

tympan
BR ˈtɪmpən, -z
AM ˈtɪmpən, -z

tympana
BR ˈtɪmpənə(r)
AM ˈtɪmpənə

tympani
BR ˈtɪmpəni
AM ˈtɪmpəni

tympanic
BR tɪmˈpanɪk
AM tɪmˈpænɪk

tympanist
BR ˈtɪmpənɪst, -s
AM ˈtɪmpənəst, -s

tympanites
BR ˌtɪmpəˈnʌɪtiːz
AM ˌtɪmpəˈnaɪdiz

tympanitic
BR ˌtɪmpəˈnɪtɪk
AM ˌtɪmpəˈnɪdɪk

tympanitis
BR ˌtɪmpəˈnʌɪtɪs
AM ˌtɪmpəˈnaɪdɪs

tympanum
BR ˈtɪmpənəm, -z
AM ˈtɪmpənəm, -z

Tynan
BR ˈtʌɪnən
AM ˈtaɪnən

Tyndale
BR ˈtɪndl
AM ˈtɪndl

Tyndall
BR ˈtɪndl
AM ˈtɪndl

Tyne
BR tʌɪn
AM taɪn

Tyne and Wear
BR ˌtʌɪn ən(d) ˈwɪə(r)
AM ˈtaɪn ən ˈwɪ(ə)r

Tynemouth
BR ˈtʌɪnmaʊθ
AM ˈtaɪn,maʊθ

Tyneside
BR ˈtʌɪnsʌɪd
AM ˈtaɪn,saɪd

Tynesider
BR ˈtʌɪn,sʌɪdə(r), -z
AM ˈtaɪn,saɪdər, -z

Tynwald
BR ˈtɪnw(ə)ld, ˈtʌɪnw(ə)ld
AM ˈtɪnwəld, ˈtaɪnwəld

typal
BR ˈtʌɪpl
AM ˈtaɪpəl

type
BR tʌɪp, -s, -ɪŋ, -t
AM taɪp, -s, -ɪŋ, -t

typebar
BR ˈtʌɪpbɑː(r), -z
AM ˈtaɪp,bɑr, -z

typecast
BR ˈtʌɪpkɑːst, ˈtʌɪpkast, -s, -ɪŋ
AM ˈtaɪp,kæst, -s, -ɪŋ

typeface
BR ˈtʌɪpfeɪs, -ɪz
AM ˈtaɪp,feɪs, -ɪz

typefounder
BR ˈtʌɪp,faʊndə(r), -z
AM ˈtaɪp,faʊndər, -z

typescript
BR ˈtʌɪpskrɪpt, -s
AM ˈtaɪp,skrɪpt, -s

typeset
BR ˈtʌɪpsɛt, -s, -ɪŋ
AM ˈtaɪp,sɛ|t, -ts, -dɪŋ

typesetter
BR ˈtʌɪp,sɛtə(r), -z
AM ˈtaɪp,sɛdər, -z

typesetting
BR ˈtʌɪp,sɛtɪŋ
AM ˈtaɪp,sɛdɪŋ

typewriter
BR ˈtʌɪp,rʌɪtə(r), -z
AM ˈtaɪp,raɪdər, -z

typewriting
BR ˈtʌɪp,rʌɪtɪŋ
AM ˈtaɪp,raɪdɪŋ

typewritten
BR ˈtʌɪp,rɪtn
AM ˈtaɪp,rɪtn

typhlitic
BR tɪfˈlɪtɪk
AM tɪfˈlɪdɪk

typhlitis
BR tɪfˈlʌɪtɪs

typhoid
BR ˈtʌɪfɔɪd
AM ˈtaɪ,fɔɪd

typhoidal
BR tʌɪˈfɔɪdl
AM taɪˈfɔɪdəl

typhonic
BR tʌɪˈfɒnɪk
AM taɪˈfɑnɪk

Typhoo®
BR ˌtʌɪˈfuː
AM ˌtaɪˈfu

typhoon
BR tʌɪˈfuːn, -z
AM taɪˈfun, -z

typhous
BR ˈtʌɪfəs
AM ˈtaɪfəs

typhus
BR ˈtʌɪfəs
AM ˈtaɪfəs

typical
BR ˈtɪpɪkl
AM ˈtɪpɪkəl

typicality
BR ˌtɪpɪˈkalɪti
AM ˌtɪpəˈkælədi

typically
BR ˈtɪpɪkli
AM ˈtɪpɪk(ə)li

typification
BR ˌtɪpɪfɪˈkeɪʃn, -z
AM ˌtɪpəfəˈkeɪʃən, -z

typifier
BR ˈtɪpɪfʌɪə(r), -z
AM ˈtɪpə,faɪər, -z

typify
BR ˈtɪpɪfʌɪ, -z, -ɪŋ, -d
AM ˈtɪpə,faɪ, -z, -ɪŋ, -d

typist
BR ˈtʌɪpɪst, -s
AM ˈtaɪpɪst, -s

typo
BR ˈtʌɪpəʊ, -z
AM ˈtaɪ,poʊ, -z

typographer
BR tʌɪˈpɒɡrəfə(r), -z
AM taɪˈpɑɡrəfər, -z

typographic
BR ˌtʌɪpəˈɡrafɪk
AM ˌtaɪpəˈɡræfɪk

typographical
BR ˌtʌɪpəˈɡrafɪkl
AM ˌtaɪpəˈɡræfəkəl

typographically
BR ˌtʌɪpəˈɡrafɪkli
AM ˌtaɪpəˈɡræfək(ə)li

typography
BR tʌɪˈpɒɡrəfi
AM taɪˈpɑɡrəfi

typological
BR ˌtʌɪpəˈlɒdʒɪkl
AM ˌtaɪpəˈlɑdʒəkəl

typologist
BR tʌɪˈpɒlədʒɪst, -s
AM taɪˈpɑlədʒəst, -s

typology
BR tʌɪˈpɒlədʒi
AM taɪˈpɑlədʒi

typonym
BR ˈtʌɪpənɪm, -z
AM ˈtaɪpə,nɪm, -z

Tyr
BR tɪə(r), tjʊə(r)
AM tɪ(ə)r

tyramine
BR ˈtʌɪrəmiːn, ˈtɪrəmiːn
AM ˈtaɪrə,min

tyrannical
BR tɪˈranɪkl, tʌɪˈranɪkl
AM təˈrænəkəl

tyrannically
BR tɪˈranɪkli, tʌɪˈranɪkli
AM təˈrænək(ə)li

tyrannicidal
BR tɪ,ranɪˈsʌɪdl, tʌɪ,ranɪˈsʌɪdl
AM tə,rænəˈsaɪdəl

tyrannicide
BR tɪˈranɪsʌɪd, tʌɪˈranɪsʌɪd, -z
AM təˈrænə,saɪd, -z

tyrannise
BR ˈtɪrənʌɪz, ˈtɪrn̩ʌɪz, -ɪz, -ɪŋ, -d
AM ˈtɪrə,naɪz, -ɪz, -ɪŋ, -d

tyrannize
BR ˈtɪrənʌɪz, ˈtɪrn̩ʌɪz, -ɪz, -ɪŋ, -d
AM ˈtɪrə,naɪz, -ɪz, -ɪŋ, -d

tyrannosaur
BR tɪˈranəsɔː(r), tʌɪˈranəsɔː(r), -z
AM təˈrænə,sɔ(ə)r, -z

tyrannosauri
BR tɪ,ranəˈsɔːrʌɪ, tʌɪ,ranəˈsɔːrʌɪ
AM tə,rænəˈsɔ,raɪ

tyrannosaurus
BR tɪ,ranəˈsɔːrəs, tʌɪ,ranəˈsɔːrəs, -ɪz
AM tə,rænəˈsɔrəs, -əz

Tyrannosaurus Rex
BR tɪ,ranəˌsɔːrəs ˈrɛks, tʌɪ,ranəˌsɔːrəs +, -ɪz
AM tə,rænəˈsɔrəs ˈrɛks, -əz

tyrannous
BR ˈtɪrənəs, ˈtɪrn̩əs
AM ˈtɪrənəs

tyrannously
BR ˈtɪrənəsli, ˈtɪrn̩əsli
AM ˈtɪrənəsli

tyranny
BR ˈtɪrən|i, ˈtɪrn̩|i, -ɪz
AM ˈtɪrəni, -z

tyrant
BR ˈtʌɪrənt, ˈtʌɪrn̩t, -s

tyre
AM 'taɪərənt, -s

tyre
BR 'taɪə(r), -z
AM 'taɪ(ə)r, -z

tyremark
BR 'taɪəmɑːk, -s
AM 'taɪ(ə)r,mɑrk, -s

Tyrer
BR 'taɪrə(r)
AM 'taɪrər

Tyrian
BR 'tɪriən
AM 'tɪriən

tyro
BR 'taɪrəʊ, -z
AM 'taɪˌroʊ, -z

Tyrol
BR 'tɪrəl, 'tɪrl, tɪ'rəʊl
AM 'tɪrəl

Tyrolean
BR ˌtɪrə'liːən,
tɪ'rəʊliən, -z
AM tə'roʊliən, -z

Tyrone[1]
forename
BR 'taɪrəʊn, taɪ'rəʊn
AM taɪ'roʊn

Tyrone[2]
Northern Ireland
BR tɪ'rəʊn
AM tə'roʊn

tyrosine
BR 'taɪrə(ʊ)siːn
AM 'taɪrəˌsin

tyrothricin
BR ˌtaɪrə(ʊ)'θraɪsɪn
AM ˌtaɪrə'θraɪsɪn

Tyrrell
BR 'tɪrəl, 'tɪrl̩
AM 'tɪrəl

Tyrrhene
BR tɪ'riːn, -z
AM tə'rin, -z

Tyrrhenian
BR tɪ'riːniən, -z
AM tə'riniən, -z

Tyson
BR 'taɪsn
AM 'taɪsən

Tywyn
BR 'taʊɪn
AM 'taʊən

Tyzack
BR 'taɪzak, 'tɪzak
AM 'taɪzæk, 'tɪzæk

tzar
BR zɑː(r), tsɑː(r), -z
AM zɑr, tsɑr, -z

tzarevitch
BR 'zɑːrəvɪtʃ,

'tsɑːrəvɪtʃ, -ɪz
AM 'zɑrəˌvɪtʃ,
'tsɑrəˌvɪtʃ, -ɪz

tzarina
BR zɑː'riːnə(r),
tsɑː'riːnə(r), -z
AM zɑ'rinə, tsɑ'rinə, -z

tzarist
BR 'zɑːrɪst, 'tsɑːrɪst, -s
AM 'zɑrəst, 'tsɑrəst, -s

tzatziki
BR (t)sat'siːki
AM (t)sɑt'siki

tzetze
BR 't(s)ɛtsi
AM '(t)sitsi,
'(t)sɛtsi

tzigane
BR (t)sɪ'gɑːn, -z
AM (t)sɪ'gɑn, -z

Uu

u
BR juː, -z
AM juː, -z

U-2
BR juː'tuː, -z
AM 'juː'tu, -z

UAW
BR juː'eɪ'dʌbljuː
AM ˌjuːˌeɪ'dəbəlˌju

Ubaid
BR uː'beɪd, uː'baɪd
AM u'beɪd, u'baɪd

Ubange
BR juː'baŋgi
AM ju'bæŋgi

U-bend
BR 'juːbɛnd, -z
AM 'juːˌbɛnd, -z

Übermensch
BR 'uːbəmɛnʃ
AM 'ubərˌmɛn(t)ʃ

Übermenschen
BR 'uːbəmɛnʃn
AM 'ubərˌmɛn(t)ʃən

UB40
BR juːbiː'fɔːti
AM ˌjuːˌbi'fɔrdi

ubiety
BR juː'baɪɪti, jə'baɪɪti
AM ju'baɪədi

ubiquitarian
BR juːˌbɪkwɪ'tɛːrɪən,
jəˌbɪkwɪ'tɛːrɪən, -z
AM juˌbɪkwɪ'tɛrɪən, -z

ubiquitarianism
BR juːˌbɪkwɪ'tɛːrɪən-
ɪz(ə)m,
jəˌbɪkwɪ'tɛːrɪənɪz(ə)m
AM juˌbɪkwɪ'tɛrɪəˌnɪz-
əm

ubiquitous
BR juː'bɪkwɪtəs,
jə'bɪkwɪtəs
AM ju'bɪkwədəs

ubiquitously
BR juː'bɪkwɪtəsli,
jə'bɪkwɪtəsli
AM ju'bɪkwədəsli

ubiquitousness
BR juː'bɪkwɪtəsnəs,
jə'bɪkwɪtəsnəs
AM ju'bɪkwədəsnəs

ubiquity
BR juː'bɪkwɪti,
jə'bɪkwɪti
AM ju'bɪkwɪdi

U-boat
BR 'juːbəʊt, -s
AM 'juːboʊt, -s

U-bolt
BR 'juːbəʊlt, -s

AM 'juːboʊlt, -s

UCATT
BR 'juːkat
AM 'juːˌkæt

UCCA
BR 'ʌkə(r), juːsiːsiː'eɪ
AM ˌjuːˌsiˌsi'eɪ

Uccello
BR uː'tʃɛləʊ
AM u'tʃɛloʊ

Uckfield
BR 'ʌkfiːld
AM 'ək,fild

UCLA
BR juːsɪɛl'eɪ
AM ˌjuːˌsiˌɛl'eɪ

udal
BR 'juːdl, -z
AM 'judəl, -z

Udall
BR 'juːdl, 'juːdɔːl
AM 'juːˌdol, 'juːˌdɑl

udaller
BR 'juːdlə(r), -z
AM 'judlər, -z

udalman
BR 'juːdlmən
AM 'judlmən

udalmen
BR 'juːdlmən
AM 'judlmən

udder
BR 'ʌdə(r), -z, -d
AM 'ədər, -z, -d

UDI
BR 'juːdɪ'ʌɪ
AM ˌjuːˌdi'aɪ

Udmurtia
BR ʊd'mʊəʃə(r)
AM ʊd'mʊrʃə
RUS ud'murtʲijə

udometer
BR juː'dɒmɪtə(r),
jə'dɒmɪtə(r), -z
AM ju'damədər, -z

UEFA
BR juː'eɪfə(r)
AM ju'(w)ɛfə

uey
BR 'juːˌi, -ɪz
AM 'jui, -z

Uffizi
BR (j)ʊ'fɪtsi, (j)ʊ'fiːtsi
AM ju'fitsi

UFO
BR 'juːfəʊ, ˌjuːɛf'əʊ, -z
AM ˌjuːˌɛf'oʊ, -z

ufologist
BR juː'fɒlədʒɪst, -s
AM ju'falədʒəst, -s

ufology
BR juː'fɒlədʒi
AM ju'falədʒi

Uganda
BR juː'gandə(r),
jə'gandə(r)
AM ju'gændə

Ugandan
BR juː'gandən,
jə'gandən, -z
AM ju'gændən, -z

Ugaritic
adjective and noun
BR ˌuːgə'rɪtɪk
AM ˌugə'rɪdɪk

ugh!
BR ə(h), ʌx, ʊɸ
AM əg

ugli
BR 'ʌgli, -ɪz
AM 'ʌgli, -z

uglification
BR ˌʌglɪfɪ'keɪʃn
AM ˌəgləfə'keɪʃən

ugli fruit
BR 'ʌgli fruːt
AM 'əgli ˌfrut

uglify
BR 'ʌglɪfʌɪ, -z, -ɪŋ, -d
AM 'əgləˌfaɪ, -z, -ɪŋ, -d

uglily
BR 'ʌglɪli
AM 'əgləli

ugliness
BR 'ʌglɪnɪs
AM 'əglɪnɪs

ugly
BR 'ʌgli, -ɪə(r), -ɪɪst
AM 'əgli, -ər, -ɪst

Ugrian
BR '(j)uːgrɪən, -z
AM '(j)ugriən, -z

Ugric
BR '(j)uːgrɪk, -s
AM '(j)ugrɪk, -s

UHF
BR ˌjuːeɪtʃ'ɛf
AM ˌjuːˌeɪtʃ'ɛf

uh-huh
BR ə'hə(r), ʌ'hʌ(r)
AM ə'hə

uhlan
BR (j)uː'lɑːn, (j)ʊ'lɑːn,
-z
AM u'lɑn, '(j)ulən, -z

UHT
BR ˌjuːeɪtʃ'tiː
AM ˌjuːˌeɪtʃ'ti

Uighur
BR 'wiːgʊə(r), -z
AM 'wiˌgʊ(ə)r, -z

Uigur
BR 'wiːgʊə(r), -z
AM 'wiˌgʊ(ə)r, -z

Uist
BR 'juːɪst, -s
AM 'juɪst, -s

uitlander
BR 'eɪtˌlandə(r),
'ɔɪtˌlandə(r), -z
AM 'eɪtˌlændər, -z

ujamaa
BR ˌʊdʒa'mɑː(r)
AM ˌudʒə'mɑ

Ujjain
BR uː'dʒeɪn
AM u'dʒeɪn

UK
BR juː'keɪ
AM 'juː'keɪ

ukase
BR juː'keɪz, juː'keɪs, -ɪz
AM ju'keɪs, -ɪz

ukelele
BR ˌjuːkə'leɪlˌi, -ɪz
AM ˌjukə'leɪli, -z

ukiyo-e
BR uː'kɪjəʊ'jeɪ
AM ˌukijoʊ'jeɪ

Ukraine
BR juː'kreɪn, jə'kreɪn
AM ju'kreɪn, ˌju'kreɪn
RUS ukra'inə

Ukrainian
BR juː'kreɪnɪən,
jə'kreɪnɪən, -z
AM ju'kreɪnɪən, -z

ukulele
BR ˌjuːkə'leɪlˌi, -ɪz
AM ˌjukə'leɪli, -z

ulan
BR (j)uː'lɑːn, (j)ʊ'lɑːn,
-z
AM u'lɑn, '(j)ulən, -z

Ulan Bator
BR ʊˌlan ba'tɔː(r)
AM ʊˌlan ˌba'tɔ(ə)r

Ulanova
BR jʊ'lanəvə(r)
AM jʊ'lanəvə
RUS u'lanəvə

ulcer
BR 'ʌlsə(r), -z, -d
AM 'əlsər, -z, -d

ulcerable
BR 'ʌls(ə)rəbl
AM 'əlsərəbəl

ulcerate
BR 'ʌlsəreɪt, -s, -ɪŋ, -ɪd
AM 'əlsəˌreɪ|t, -ts, -dɪŋ,
-dɪd

ulceration
BR ˌʌlsə'reɪʃn
AM ˌəlsə'reɪʃən

ulcerative
BR 'ʌls(ə)rətɪv
AM 'əlsərədɪv,
'əlsəˌreɪdɪv

ulcerous
BR 'ʌls(ə)rəs
AM 'əls(ə)rəs

ulema
BR 'uːliːmə(r),
'uːliːmɑː(r),
ˌuːliː'mɑː(r), -z
AM 'uləˌmɑ, -z

Ulfilas
BR 'ʊlfilas
AM 'ʊlfiˌlas

uliginose
BR juː'lɪdʒɪnəʊs,
jə'lɪdʒɪnəʊs

AM juˈlɪdʒəˌnoʊs,
juˈlɪdʒəˌnoʊz

uliginous
BR juːˈlɪdʒɪnəs,
jəˈlɪdʒɪnəs
AM juˈlɪdʒənəs

ullage
BR ˈʌlɪdʒ
AM ˈəlɪdʒ

Ullapool
BR ˈʌləpuːl
AM ˈələˌpul

Ullman
BR ˈʊlmən, ˈʌlmən
AM ˈəlmən, ˈʊlmən

Ullmann
BR ˈʊlmən, ˈʌlmən
AM ˈəlmən, ˈʊlmən

Ulm
BR ʊlm
AM ʊlm

ulna
BR ˈʌlnə(r), -z
AM ˈəlnə, -z

ulnae
BR ˈʌlniː
AM ˈəlˌni, ˈəlˌnaɪ

ulnar
BR ˈʌlnə(r)
AM ˈəlnər

ulotrichan
BR juːˈlɒtrɪk(ə)n,
jəˈlɒtrɪk(ə)n, -z
AM juˈlɑtrəkən, -z

ulotrichous
BR juːˈlɒtrɪkəs,
jəˈlɒtrɪkəs
AM juˈlɑtrəkəs

Ulpian
BR ˈʌlpiən
AM ˈəlpiən

Ulster
BR ˈʌlstə(r), -z
AM ˈəlstər, -z

Ulsterman
BR ˈʌlstəmən
AM ˈəlstərmən

Ulstermen
BR ˈʌlstəmən
AM ˈəlstərmən

Ulsterwoman
BR ˈʌlstəˌwʊmən
AM ˈəlstərˌwʊmən

Ulsterwomen
BR ˈʌlstəˌwɪmɪn
AM ˈəlstərˌwɪmɪn

ult
BR ʌlt
AM əlt

ulterior
BR ʌlˈtɪərɪə(r)
AM əlˈtɪriər

ulteriorly
BR ʌlˈtɪərɪəli
AM əlˈtɪriərli

ultima
BR ˈʌltɪmə(r)

AM ˈəltəmə

ultimacy
BR ˈʌltɪməsi
AM ˈəltəməsi

ultimata
BR ˌʌltɪˈmeɪtə(r)
AM ˌəltəˈmeɪdə

ultimate
BR ˈʌltɪmət
AM ˈəltəmət

ultimately
BR ˈʌltɪmətli
AM ˈəltəmətli

ultimateness
BR ˈʌltɪmətnəs
AM ˈəltəmətnəs

ultimatum
BR ˌʌltɪˈmeɪtəm, -z
AM ˌəltəˈmeɪdəm, -z

ultimo
BR ˈʌltɪməʊ
AM ˈəltəˌmoʊ

ultimogeniture
BR ˌʌltɪməʊˈdʒenɪtʃə(r),
-z
AM ˌəltəˌmoʊˈdʒenə-
ˌtʃʊ(ə)r,
ˈəltəˌmoʊˈdʒenətʃər,
-z

ultra
BR ˈʌltrə(r), -z
AM ˈʌltrə, -z

ultracentrifuge
BR ˌʌltrəˈsentrɪfjuː(d)ʒ,
-ɪz
AM ˌəltrəˈsentrəˌfjudʒ,
-əz

ultradian
BR ʌlˈtreɪdɪən
AM ˌʌltrəˈdiən

ultraism
BR ˈʌltraɪz(ə)m
AM ˈəltrəˌɪzəm

ultramarine
BR ˌʌltrəməˈriːn
AM ˌəltrəməˈrin

ultramicroscope
BR ˌʌltrəˈmaɪkrəskəʊp,
-s
AM ˌəltrəˈmaɪkrəˌskoup,
-s

ultramicroscopic
BR ˌʌltrəˌmaɪkrəˈskɒp-
ɪk
AM ˌəltrəˌmaɪkrəˈskɑp-
ɪk

ultramontane
BR ˌʌltrəˈmɒnteɪn
AM ˌəltrəˈmɑnˌteɪn

ultramontanism
BR ˌʌltrəˈmɒntənɪz(ə)m
AM ˌəltrəˈmɑn(t)əˌnɪz-
əm

ultramontanist
BR ˌʌltrəˈmɒntənɪst, -s
AM ˌəltrəˈmɑn(t)ənəst,
-s

ultramundane
BR ˌʌltrəˈmʌndeɪn
AM ˌəltrəˌmənˌdeɪn

ultrasonic
BR ˌʌltrəˈsɒnɪk, -s
AM ˌəltrəˈsɑnɪk, -s

ultrasonically
BR ˌʌltrəˈsɒnɪkli
AM ˌəltrəˈsɑnək(ə)li

ultrasound
BR ˈʌltrəsaʊnd
AM ˈəltrəˌsaʊnd

ultrastructure
BR ˈʌltrəˌstrʌktʃə(r),
-z
AM ˈəltrəˌstrək(t)ʃər,
-z

Ultrasuede®
BR ˈʌltrəˌsweɪd
AM ˈəltrəˌsweɪd

ultraviolet
BR ˌʌltrəˈvaɪələt
AM ˌəltrəˈvaɪələt

ultra vires
BR ˌʌltrə ˈvaɪriːz,
+ ˈviːreɪz
AM ˌəltrə ˈvaɪriz

ululant
BR ˈjuː(l)jʊlənt,
ˈʌljʊlənt
AM ˈju(l)jələnt,
ˈəljələnt

ululate
BR ˈjuː(l)jʊleɪt,
ˈʌljʊlert, -s, -ɪŋ, -ɪd
AM ˈju(l)jəˌleɪ|t,
ˈəljəˌleɪ|t, -ts, -dɪŋ, -dɪd

ululation
BR ˌjuː(l)jəˈleɪʃn,
ˌʌljəˈleɪʃn, -z
AM ˌju(l)jəˈleɪʃən,
ˈəljəˈleɪʃən, -z

Ulverston
BR ˈʌlvəst(ə)n
AM ˈəlvərstən

Ulysses
BR ˈjuːlɪsiːz
AM juˈlɪsiz

um
BR (ə)m, ʌm
AM (ə)m

umbel
BR ˈʌmbl, -z
AM ˈəmbəl, -z

umbellar
BR ʌmˈbɛlə(r)
AM ˈəmbələr

umbellate
BR ˈʌmbələt,
ˈʌmbəleɪt
AM ˈəmbələt,
ˈəmbəˌleɪt

umbellifer
BR ʌmˈbɛlɪfə(r), -z
AM əmˈbɛləfər, -z

umbelliferae
BR ˌʌmbəˈlɪfəriː

umbelliferi
AM ˌəmbəˈlɪfəri,
ˌəmbəˈlɪfəˌraɪ

umbelliferous
BR ˌʌmbəˈlɪf(ə)rəs
AM ˌəmbəˈlɪf(ə)rəs

umbellule
BR ʌmˈbɛljuːl, -z
AM ˈəmbəlˌjul,
əmˈbɛljul, -z

umber
BR ˈʌmbə(r), -z
AM ˈəmbər, -z

umbilical
BR ʌmˈbɪlɪkl,
ˌʌmbɪˈlaɪkl
AM əmˈbɪləkəl

umbilically
BR ʌmˈbɪlɪkli
AM əmˈbɪlɪk(ə)li

umbilicate
BR ʌmˈbɪlɪkət,
ʌmˈbɪlɪkert
AM əmˈbɪləkət,
ˌəmbɪləˌkeɪt

umbilicus
BR ʌmˈbɪlɪkəs, -ɪz
AM ˌəmˈbɪlɪkəs, -əz

umble
BR ˈʌmbl, -z
AM ˈəmbəl, -z

umbo
BR ˈʌmbəʊ, -z
AM ˈəmboʊ, -z

umbonal
BR ʌmˈbəʊnl
AM əmˈboʊnəl

umbonate
BR ˈʌmbənət,
ˈʌmbəneɪt
AM ˈəmbənət,
ˈəmbəˌneɪt

umbones
BR ʌmˈbəʊniːz
AM ˌəmˈboʊniz

umbra
BR ˈʌmbrə(r), -z
AM ˈəmbrə, -z

umbrage
BR ˈʌmbrɪdʒ
AM ˈəmbrɪdʒ

umbrageous
BR ʌmˈbrɪdʒəs
AM ˌəmˈbrɪdʒəs

umbral
BR ˈʌmbr(ə)l
AM ˈəmbrəl

umbrella
BR ʌmˈbrɛlə(r), -z
AM ˌəmˈbrɛlə, -z

umbrella-like
BR ʌmˈbrɛləˌlaɪk
AM ˌəmˈbrɛləˌlaɪk

umbrette
BR ʌmˈbrɛt, -s
AM ˌəmˈbrɛt, -s

Umbria
BR ˈʌmbrɪə(r)

AM ˈʌmbrɪə

Umbrian
BR ˈʌmbrɪən, -z
AM ˈʌmbrɪən, -z

Umbriel
BR ˈʌmbrɪəl
AM ˈʌmbrɪəl

umbriferous
BR ʌmˈbrɪf(ə)rəs
AM əmˈbrɪf(ə)rəs

umiak
BR ˈuːmɪak, -s
AM ˈumiˌæk, -s

umlaut
BR ˈʊmlaʊt, -s
AM ˈʊmˌlaʊt, -s

ump
BR ʌmp, -s
AM əmp, -s

umph
BR ʌmf, ʊmf, hm
AM umf, ʊmf, əmf

umpirage
BR ˈʌmpʌɪrɪdʒ
AM ˈəmˌpaɪrɪdʒ

umpire
BR ˈʌmpʌɪə(r), -z, -ɪŋ, -d
AM ˈəmˌpaɪ(ə)r, -z, -ɪŋ, -d

umpireship
BR ˈʌmpʌɪəʃɪp, -s
AM ˈəmˌpaɪ(ə)rˌʃɪp, -s

umpteen
BR ˌʌm(p)ˈtiːn
AM ˌəm(p)ˈtin

umpteenth
BR ˌʌm(p)ˈtiːnθ
AM ˌəm(p)ˈtinθ

umpty
BR ˈʌm(p)ti
AM ˈəm(p)ti

UN
BR ˌjuːˈɛn
AM ˌjuˈɛn

'un
BR ən
AM ən

Una
BR ˈjuːnə(r)
AM ˈ(j)unə

unabashed
BR ˌʌnəˈbaʃt
AM ˌənəˈbæʃt

unabashedly
BR ˌʌnəˈbaʃɪdli
AM ˌənəˈbæʃədli

unabated
BR ˌʌnəˈbeɪtɪd
AM ˌənəˈbeɪdɪd

unabatedly
BR ˌʌnəˈbeɪtɪdli
AM ˌənəˈbeɪdɪdli

unable
BR ʌnˈeɪbl
AM ənˈeɪbəl

unabridged
BR ˌʌnəˈbrɪdʒd
AM ˌənəˈbrɪdʒd

unabsorbed
BR ˌʌnəbˈzɔːbd
AM ˌənəbˈzɔː(ə)rbd

unacademic
BR ˌʌnakəˈdɛmɪk
AM ˌənˌækəˈdɛmɪk

unaccented
BR ˌʌnakˈsɛntɪd
AM ˌənˈækˌsɛn(t)əd

unacceptability
BR ˌʌnəkˌsɛptəˈbɪlɪti
AM ˌənəkˌsɛptəˈbɪlɪdi

unacceptable
BR ˌʌnəkˈsɛptəbl
AM ˌənəkˈsɛptəbəl

unacceptableness
BR ˌʌnəkˈsɛptəblnəs
AM ˌənəkˈsɛptəbəlnəs

unacceptably
BR ˌʌnəkˈsɛptəbli
AM ˌənəkˈsɛptəbli

unaccepted
BR ˌʌnəkˈsɛptɪd
AM ˌənəkˈsɛptəd

unacclaimed
BR ˌʌnəˈkleɪmd
AM ˌənəˈkleɪmd

unacclimatized
BR ˌʌnəˈklʌɪmətʌɪzd
AM ˌənəˈklaɪməˌtaɪzd

unaccommodated
BR ˌʌnəˈkɒmədeɪtɪd
AM ˌənəˈkɑməˌdeɪdɪd

unaccommodating
BR ˌʌnəˈkɒmədeɪtɪŋ
AM ˌənəˈkɑməˌdeɪdɪŋ

unaccompanied
BR ˌʌnəˈkʌmp(ə)nɪd
AM ˌənəˈkəmpənɪd

unaccomplished
BR ˌʌnəˈkʌmplɪʃt
AM ˌənəˈkəmplɪʃt

unaccountability
BR ˌʌnəˌkaʊntəˈbɪlɪti
AM ˌənəˌkaʊn(t)əˈbɪlɪdi

unaccountable
BR ˌʌnəˈkaʊntəbl
AM ˌənəˈkaʊn(t)əbəl

unaccountable-ness
BR ˌʌnəˈkaʊntəblnəs
AM ˌənəˈkaʊn(t)əbəlnəs

unaccountably
BR ˌʌnəˈkaʊntəbli
AM ˌənəˈkaʊn(t)əbli

unaccounted
BR ˌʌnəˈkaʊntɪd
AM ˌənəˈkaʊn(t)əd

unaccustomed
BR ˌʌnəˈkʌstəmd
AM ˌənəˈkəstəmd

unaccustomedly
BR ˌʌnəˈkʌstəmdli
AM ˌənəˈkəstəmdli

unachievable
BR ˌʌnəˈtʃiːvəbl
AM ˌənəˈtʃivəbəl

unacknowledged
BR ˌʌnəkˈnɒlɪdʒd
AM ˌənəkˈnɑlɪdʒd

unacquainted
BR ˌʌnəˈkweɪntɪd
AM ˌənəˈkweɪn(t)ɪd

unadaptable
BR ˌʌnəˈdaptəbl
AM ˌənəˈdæptəbəl

unadapted
BR ˌʌnəˈdaptɪd
AM ˌənəˈdæptəd

unaddressed
BR ˌʌnəˈdrɛst
AM ˌənəˈdrɛst

unadjacent
BR ˌʌnəˈdʒeɪsnt
AM ˌənəˈdʒeɪsənt

unadjusted
BR ˌʌnəˈdʒʌstɪd
AM ˌənəˈdʒəstəd

unadmitted
BR ˌʌnədˈmɪtɪd
AM ˌənədˈmɪdɪd

unadopted
BR ˌʌnəˈdɒptɪd
AM ˌənəˈdɑpted

unadorned
BR ˌʌnəˈdɔːnd
AM ˌənəˈdɔ(ə)rnd

unadulterated
BR ˌʌnəˈdʌltəreɪtɪd
AM ˌənəˈdəltəˌreɪdɪd

unadventurous
BR ˌʌnədˈvɛntʃ(ə)rəs
AM ˌənədˈvɛntʃ(ə)rəs

unadventurously
BR ˌʌnədˈvɛntʃ(ə)rəsli
AM ˌənədˈvɛntʃ(ə)rəsli

unadvertised
BR ʌnˈadvətʌɪzd
AM ənˈædvərˌtaɪzd

unadvisable
BR ˌʌnədˈvʌɪzəbl
AM ˌənədˈvaɪzəbəl

unadvised
BR ˌʌnədˈvʌɪzd
AM ˌənədˈvaɪzd

unadvisedly
BR ˌʌnədˈvʌɪzɪdli
AM ˌənədˈvaɪzɪdli

unadvisedness
BR ˌʌnədˈvʌɪzɪdnɪs
AM ˌənədˈvaɪzɪdnɪs

unaesthetic
BR ˌʌniːsˈθɛtɪk, ˌʌnɪsˈθɛtɪk
AM ˌənəˈsˈθɛdɪk

unaffected
BR ˌʌnəˈfɛktɪd
AM ˌənəˈfɛktəd

unaffectedly
BR ˌʌnəˈfɛktɪdli
AM ˌənəˈfɛktədli

unaffectedness
BR ˌʌnəˈfɛktɪdnɪs
AM ˌənəˈfɛktədnəs

unaffectionate
BR ˌʌnəˈfɛkʃnət, ˌʌnəˈfɛkʃənət
AM ˌənəˈfɛkʃənət

unaffiliated
BR ˌʌnəˈfɪlɪeɪtɪd
AM ˌənəˈfɪliˌeɪdɪd

unaffordable
BR ˌʌnəˈfɔːdəbl
AM ˌənəˈfɔrdəbəl

unafraid
BR ˌʌnəˈfreɪd
AM ˌənəˈfreɪd

unaggressive
BR ˌʌnəˈgrɛsɪv
AM ˌənəˈgrɛsɪv

unaided
BR (ˌ)ʌnˈeɪdɪd
AM ənˈeɪdɪd

unalarmed
BR ˌʌnəˈlɑːmd
AM ˌənəˈlɑrmd

unalienable
BR (ˌ)ʌnˈeɪlɪənəbl
AM ənˈeɪlɪənəbəl, ˌənˈeɪljənəbəl

unalienably
BR (ˌ)ʌnˈeɪlɪənəbli
AM ənˈeɪlɪənəbli, ˌənˈeɪljənəbli

unalienated
BR (ˌ)ʌnˈeɪlɪəneɪtɪd
AM ənˈeɪliəˌneɪdɪd, ˌənˈeɪljəˌneɪdɪd

unaligned
BR ˌʌnəˈlʌɪnd
AM ˌənəˈlaɪnd

unalike
BR ˌʌnəˈlʌɪk
AM ˌənəˈlaɪk

unalive
BR ˌʌnəˈlʌɪv
AM ˌənəˈlaɪv

unalleviated
BR ˌʌnəˈliːvɪeɪtɪd
AM ˌənəˈliviˌeɪdɪd

unallied
BR ˌʌnəˈlʌɪd
AM ˌənəˈlaɪd

unallocated
BR (ˌ)ʌnˈaləkeɪtɪd
AM ənˈæləˌkeɪdɪd

unallotted
BR ˌʌnəˈlɒtɪd
AM ˌənəˈlɑdəd

unallowable
BR ˌʌnəˈlaʊəbl
AM ˌənəˈlaʊəbəl

unalloyed
BR ˌʌnəˈlɔɪd
AM ˌənəˈlɔɪd

unalterable
BR (ˌ)ʌnˈɔːlt(ə)rəbl, (ˌ)ʌnˈɒlt(ə)rəbl

unalterableness
BR (,)ʌnˈɔːlt(ə)rəblnəs,
(,)ʌnˈɒlt(ə)rəblnəs
AM ˌənˈɔːlt(ə)rəbəlnəs,
ˌənˈɑlt(ə)rəbəlnəs

unalterably
BR (,)ʌnˈɔːlt(ə)rəbli,
(,)ʌnˈɒlt(ə)rəbli
AM ˌənˈɔːlt(ə)rəbli,
ˌənˈɑlt(ə)rəbli

unaltered
BR (,)ʌnˈɔːltəd,
(,)ʌnˈɒltəd
AM ˌənˈɔːltərd,
ˌənˈɑltərd

unaltering
BR (,)ʌnˈɔːlt(ə)rɪŋ,
(,)ʌnˈɒlt(ə)rɪŋ
AM ˌənˈɔːlt(ə)rɪŋ,
ˌənˈɑlt(ə)rɪŋ

unamazed
BR ˌʌnəˈmeɪzd
AM ˌənəˈmeɪzd

unambiguity
BR ˌʌnæmbɪˈgjuːti
AM ˌənˌæmbəˈgjuədi

unambiguous
BR ˌʌnæmˈbɪgjuəs
AM ˌənæmˈbɪgjəwəs

unambiguously
BR ˌʌnæmˈbɪgjuəsli
AM ˌənæmˈbɪgjəwəsli

unambitious
BR ˌʌnæmˈbɪʃəs
AM ˌənæmˈbɪʃəs

unambitiously
BR ˌʌnæmˈbɪʃəsli
AM ˌənæmˈbɪʃəsli

unambitiousness
BR ˌʌnæmˈbɪʃəsnəs
AM ˌənæmˈbɪʃəsnəs

unambivalent
BR ˌʌnæmˈbɪvələnt,
ˌʌnæmˈbɪvəln̩t,
ˌʌnæmˈbɪvl̩(ə)nt
AM ˌənæmˈbɪv(ə)lənt

unambivalently
BR ˌʌnæmˈbɪvələntli,
ˌʌnæmˈbɪvəln̩tli,
ˌʌnæmˈbɪvl̩(ə)ntli
AM ˌənæmˈbɪvələn(t)li

unamenable
BR ˌʌnəˈmiːnəbl̩
AM ˌənəˈmiːnəbəl

unamended
BR ˌʌnəˈmendɪd
AM ˌənəˈmendəd

un-American
BR ˌʌnəˈmerɪk(ə)n
AM ˌənəˈmerəkən

un-Americanism
BR ˌʌnəˈmerɪkənɪz(ə)m,
ˌʌnəˈmerɪkn̩ɪz(ə)m
AM ˌənəˈmerəkəˌnɪzəm

unamiable
BR (,)ʌnˈeɪmiəbl̩

unamiable
BR (,)ʌnˈeɪmiəbəl

unamplified
BR (,)ʌnˈæmplɪfaɪd
AM ˌənˈæmpləˌfaɪd

unamused
BR ˌʌnəˈmjuːzd
AM ˌənəˈmjuzd

unamusing
BR ˌʌnəˈmjuːzɪŋ
AM ˌənəˈmjuzɪŋ

unanalysable
BR (,)ʌnˈænəlaɪzəbl̩,
(,)ʌnˈænl̩aɪzəbl̩
AM ˌənˈænəˌlaɪzəbəl

unanalysed
BR (,)ʌnˈænəlaɪzd,
(,)ʌnˈænl̩aɪzd
AM ˌənˈænəˌlaɪzd

unaneled
BR ˌʌnəˈniːld
AM ˌənəˈnild

unanimity
BR ˌjuːnəˈnɪmɪti
AM ˌjunəˈnɪmɪdi

unanimous
BR juːˈnænɪməs,
jəˈnænɪməs
AM juˈnænəməs

unanimously
BR juːˈnænɪməsli,
jəˈnænɪməsli
AM juˈnænəməsli

unanimousness
BR juːˈnænɪməsnəs,
jəˈnænɪməsnəs
AM juˈnænəməsnəs

unannounced
BR ˌʌnəˈnaʊnst
AM ˌənəˈnaʊnst

unanswerable
BR (,)ʌnˈɑːns(ə)rəbl̩,
(,)ʌnˈɑns(ə)rəbl̩
AM ˌənˈæns(ə)rəbəl

**unanswerable-
ness**
BR (,)ʌnˈɑːns(ə)rəblnəs,
(,)ʌnˈɑns(ə)rəblnəs
AM ˌənˈæns(ə)rəbəlnəs

unanswerably
BR (,)ʌnˈɑːns(ə)rəbli,
(,)ʌnˈɑns(ə)rəbli
AM ˌənˈæns(ə)rəbli

unanswered
BR (,)ʌnˈɑːnsəd,
(,)ʌnˈɑnsəd
AM ˌənˈænsərd

unanticipated
BR ˌʌnænˈtɪsɪpeɪtɪd
AM ˌənˌænˈtɪsəˌpeɪtɪd

unapologetic
BR ˌʌnəˌpɒləˈdʒetɪk
AM ˌənəˌpɑləˈdʒedɪk

unapologetically
BR ˌʌnəˌpɒləˈdʒetɪkli
AM ˌənəˌpɑləˈdʒedək-
(ə)li

unapostolic
BR ˌʌnəpəˈstɒlɪk

unapostolic
AM ˌənəpəˈstɑlɪk

unapparent
BR ˌʌnəˈparənt,
ˌʌnəˈparn̩t
AM ˌənəˈperənt

unappealable
BR ˌʌnəˈpiːləbl̩
AM ˌənəˈpiləbəl

unappealing
BR ˌʌnəˈpiːlɪŋ
AM ˌənəˈpilɪŋ

unappealingly
BR ˌʌnəˈpiːlɪŋli
AM ˌənəˈpilɪŋli

unappeasable
BR ˌʌnəˈpiːzəbl̩
AM ˌənəˈpizəbəl

unappeased
BR ˌʌnəˈpiːzd
AM ˌənəˈpizd

unappetising
BR (,)ʌnˈæpɪtaɪzɪŋ
AM ˌənˈæpəˌtaɪzɪŋ

unappetisingly
BR (,)ʌnˈæpɪtaɪzɪŋli
AM ˌənˈæpəˌtaɪzɪŋli

unappetizing
BR (,)ʌnˈæpɪtaɪzɪŋ
AM ˌənˈæpəˌtaɪzɪŋ

unappetizingly
BR (,)ʌnˈæpɪtaɪzɪŋli
AM ˌənˈæpəˌtaɪzɪŋli

unapplied
BR ˌʌnəˈplaɪd
AM ˌənəˈplaɪd

unappreciable
BR ˌʌnəˈpriːʃ(ɪ)əbl̩
AM ˌənəˈpriːʃ(i)əbəl

unappreciated
BR ˌʌnəˈpriːʃieɪtɪd
AM ˌənəˈpriːʃiˌeɪdɪd

unappreciative
BR ˌʌnəˈpriːʃ(ɪ)ətɪv,
ˌʌnəˈpriːsɪətɪv
AM ˌənəˈpriːʃ(i)ədɪv

unapprehended
BR ˌʌnəprɪˈhendɪd
AM ˌənˌæprəˈhendəd

unapproachability
BR ˌʌnəˌprəʊtʃəˈbɪlɪti
AM ˌənəˌproʊtʃəˈbɪlɪdi

unapproachable
BR ˌʌnəˈprəʊtʃəbl̩
AM ˌənəˈproʊtʃəbəl

**unapproachable-
ness**
BR ˌʌnəˈprəʊtʃəblnəs
AM ˌənəˈproʊtʃəbəlnəs

unapproachably
BR ˌʌnəˈprəʊtʃəbli
AM ˌənəˈproʊtʃəbli

unappropriated
BR ˌʌnəˈprəʊprieɪtɪd
AM ˌənəˈproʊpriˌeɪdɪd

unapproved
BR ˌʌnəˈpruːvd
AM ˌənəˈpruvd

unapt
BR (,)ʌnˈapt
AM ˌənˈæpt

unaptly
BR (,)ʌnˈaptli
AM ˌənˈæp(t)li

unaptness
BR (,)ʌnˈap(t)nəs
AM ˌənˈæp(t)nəs

unarguable
BR (,)ʌnˈɑːgjuəbl̩
AM ˌənˈɑrgjəwəbəl

unarguably
BR (,)ʌnˈɑːgjuəbli
AM ˌənˈɑrgjəwəbli

unargued
BR (,)ʌnˈɑːgjuːd
AM ˌənˈɑrgjud

unarm
BR (,)ʌnˈɑːm, -z, -ɪŋ, -d
AM ˌənˈɑrm, -z, -ɪŋ, -d

unarmed
BR (,)ʌnˈɑːmd
AM ˌənˈɑrmd

unarresting
BR ˌʌnəˈrestɪŋ
AM ˌənəˈrestɪŋ

unarrestingly
BR ˌʌnəˈrestɪŋli
AM ˌənəˈrestɪŋli

unarticulated
BR ˌʌnɑːˈtɪkjəleɪtɪd
AM ˌənˌɑrˈtɪkjəˌleɪdɪd

unartistic
BR ˌʌnɑːˈtɪstɪk
AM ˌənɑrˈtɪstɪk

unartistically
BR ˌʌnɑːˈtɪstɪkli
AM ˌənɑrˈtɪstɪk(ə)li

unary
BR ˈjuːnəri
AM ˈjunəri

unascertainable
BR ˌʌnəsəˈteɪnəbl̩
AM ˌənˌæsərˈteɪnəbəl

unascertainably
BR ˌʌnəsəˈteɪnəbli
AM ˌənˌæsərˈteɪnəbli

unascertained
BR ˌʌnəsəˈteɪnd
AM ˌənˌæsərˈteɪnd

unashamed
BR ˌʌnəˈʃeɪmd
AM ˌənəˈʃeɪmd

unashamedly
BR ˌʌnəˈʃeɪm(ɪ)dli
AM ˌənəˈʃeɪm(ɪ)dli

unashamedness
BR ˌʌnəˈʃeɪm(ɪ)dnɪs
AM ˌənəˈʃeɪm(ɪd)nɪs

unasked
BR (,)ʌnˈɑːskt,
(,)ʌnˈaskt
AM ˌənˈæs(k)t

unasked-for
BR (,)ʌnˈɑːsktfɔː(r),
(,)ʌnˈasktfɔː(r)

AM ˌənˈæs(k)tˌfɔ(ə)r

unassailability
BR ˌʌnəˌseɪləˈbɪlɪti
AM ˌənəˌseɪləˈbɪlɪdi

unassailable
BR ˌʌnəˈseɪləbl
AM ˌənəˈseɪləbəl

unassailableness
BR ˌʌnəˈseɪləblnəs
AM ˌənəˈseɪləbəlnəs

unassailably
BR ˌʌnəˈseɪləbli
AM ˌənəˈseɪləbli

unassertive
BR ˌʌnəˈsəːtɪv
AM ˌənəˈsərdɪv

unassertively
BR ˌʌnəˈsəːtɪvli
AM ˌənəˈsərdɪvli

unassertiveness
BR ˌʌnəˈsəːtɪvnɪs
AM ˌənəˈsərdɪvnɪs

unassignable
BR ˌʌnəˈsaɪnəbl
AM ˌənəˈsaɪnəbəl

unassigned
BR ˌʌnəˈsaɪnd
AM ˌənəˈsaɪnd

unassimilable
BR ˌʌnəˈsɪmɪləbl
AM ˌənəˈsɪmələbəl

unassimilated
BR ˌʌnəˈsɪmɪleɪtɪd
AM ˌənəˈsɪmələˌleɪdɪd

unassisted
BR ˌʌnəˈsɪstɪd
AM ˌənəˈsɪstɪd

unassociated
BR ˌʌnəˈsəʊʃieɪtɪd,
ˌʌnəˈsəʊsieɪtɪd
AM ˌənəˈsoʊʃiˌeɪdɪd,
ˌənəˈsoʊsiˌeɪdɪd

unassuageable
BR ˌʌnəˈsweɪdʒəbl
AM ˌənəˈsweɪdʒəbəl

unassuaged
BR ˌʌnəˈʃweɪdʒd
AM ˌənəˈsweɪdʒd

unassuming
BR ˌʌnəˈsjuːmɪŋ
AM ˌənəˈs(j)umɪŋ

unassumingly
BR ˌʌnəˈsjuːmɪŋli
AM ˌənəˈs(j)umɪŋli

unassumingness
BR ˌʌnəˈsjuːmɪŋnɪs
AM ˌənəˈs(j)umɪŋnɪs

unatoned
BR ˌʌnəˈtəʊnd
AM ˌənəˈtoʊnd

unattached
BR ˌʌnəˈtatʃt
AM ˌənəˈtætʃt

unattackable
BR ˌʌnəˈtakəbl
AM ˌənəˈtækəbəl

unattainable
BR ˌʌnəˈteɪnəbl
AM ˌənəˈteɪnəbəl

unattainableness
BR ˌʌnəˈteɪnəblnəs
AM ˌənəˈteɪnəbəlnəs

unattainably
BR ˌʌnəˈteɪnəbli
AM ˌənəˈteɪnəbli

unattained
BR ˌʌnəˈteɪnd
AM ˌənəˈteɪnd

unattempted
BR ˌʌnəˈtem(p)tɪd
AM ˌənəˈtem(p)təd

unattended
BR ˌʌnəˈtendɪd
AM ˌənəˈtendəd

unattested
BR ˌʌnəˈtestɪd
AM ˌənəˈtestəd

unattractive
BR ˌʌnəˈtraktɪv
AM ˌənəˈtræktɪv

unattractively
BR ˌʌnəˈtraktɪvli
AM ˌənəˈtræktɪvli

unattractiveness
BR ˌʌnəˈtraktɪvnɪs
AM ˌənəˈtræktɪvnɪs

unattributable
BR ˌʌnəˈtrɪbjʊtəbl
AM ˌənəˈtrɪbjədəbəl

unattributably
BR ˌʌnəˈtrɪbjʊtəbli
AM ˌənəˈtrɪbjədəbli

unattributed
BR ˌʌnəˈtrɪbjʊtɪd
AM ˌənəˈtrɪbjədəd

unau
BR ˈjuːnɔː(r), -z
AM ˈjuːnaʊ, -z

unaudited
BR (ˌ)ʌnˈɔːdɪtɪd
AM ˌənˈɔdədəd,
ˌənˈɑdədəd

unauthentic
BR ˌʌnɔːˈθentɪk
AM ˌənɔˈθen(t)ɪk,
ˌənɑˈθen(t)ɪk

unauthentically
BR ˌʌnɔːˈθentɪkli
AM ˌənɔˈθen(t)ək(ə)li,
ˌənɑˈθen(t)ək(ə)li

unauthenticated
BR ˌʌnɔːˈθentɪkeɪtɪd
AM ˌənɔˈθen(t)əˌkeɪdɪd,
ˌənɑˈθen(t)əˌkeɪdɪd

unauthorised
BR (ˌ)ʌnˈɔːθərʌɪzd
AM ˌənˈɔθəˌraɪzd,
ˌənˈɑθəˌraɪzd

unauthorized
BR (ˌ)ʌnˈɔːθərʌɪzd
AM ˌənˈɔθəˌraɪzd,
ˌənˈɑθəˌraɪzd

unavailability
BR ˌʌnəˌveɪləˈbɪlɪti
AM ˌənəˌveɪləˈbɪlɪdi

unavailable
BR ˌʌnəˈveɪləbl
AM ˌənəˈveɪləbəl

unavailableness
BR ˌʌnəˈveɪləblnəs
AM ˌənəˈveɪləbəlnəs

unavailing
BR ˌʌnəˈveɪlɪŋ
AM ˌənəˈveɪlɪŋ

unavailingly
BR ˌʌnəˈveɪlɪŋli
AM ˌənəˈveɪlɪŋli

unavenged
BR ˌʌnəˈven(d)ʒd
AM ˌənəˈvendʒd

unavoidability
BR ˌʌnəˌvɔɪdəˈbɪlɪti
AM ˌənəˌvɔɪdəˈbɪlɪdi

unavoidable
BR ˌʌnəˈvɔɪdəbl
AM ˌənəˈvɔɪdəbəl

unavoidableness
BR ˌʌnəˈvɔɪdəblnəs
AM ˌənəˈvɔɪdəbəlnəs

unavoidably
BR ˌʌnəˈvɔɪdəbli
AM ˌənəˈvɔɪdəbli

unavowed
BR ˌʌnəˈvaʊd
AM ˌənəˈvaʊd

unawakened
BR ˌʌnəˈweɪk(ə)nd
AM ˌənəˈweɪkənd

unaware
BR ˌʌnəˈwεː(r), -z
AM ˌənəˈwε(ə)r, -z

unawareness
BR ˌʌnəˈwεːnəs
AM ˌənəˈwεrnəs

unawares
BR ˌʌnəˈwεːz
AM ˌənəˈwε(ə)rz

unawed
BR (ˌ)ʌnˈɔːd
AM ˌənˈɔd, ˌənˈɑd

unbackable
BR ˌʌnˈbakəbl
AM ˌənˈbækəbəl

unbacked
BR (ˌ)ʌnˈbakt
AM ˌənˈbækt

unbaked
BR (ˌ)ʌnˈbeɪkt
AM ˌənˈbeɪkt

unbalance
BR (ˌ)ʌnˈbaləns,
(ˌ)ʌnˈbalns, -ɪz, -ɪŋ, -t
AM ˌənˈbæləns, -əz, -ɪŋ,
-t

unban
BR (ˌ)ʌnˈban, -z, -ɪŋ, -d
AM ˌənˈbæn, -z, -ɪŋ, -d

unbaptised
BR ˌʌnbapˈtʌɪzd

AM ˌənˈbæpˌtaɪzd

unbaptized
BR ˌʌnbapˈtʌɪzd
AM ˌənˈbæpˌtaɪzd

unbar
BR ˌʌnˈbɑː(r), -z, -ɪŋ, -d
AM ˌənˈbɑr, -z, -ɪŋ, -d

unbearable
BR (ˌ)ʌnˈbεːrəbl
AM ˌənˈbεrəbəl

unbearableness
BR (ˌ)ʌnˈbεːrəblnəs
AM ˌənˈbεrəbəlnəs

unbearably
BR (ˌ)ʌnˈbεːrəbli
AM ˌənˈbεrəbli

unbeatable
BR (ˌ)ʌnˈbiːtəbl
AM ˌənˈbidəbəl

unbeatably
BR (ˌ)ʌnˈbiːtəbli
AM ˌənˈbidəbli

unbeaten
BR (ˌ)ʌnˈbiːtn
AM ˌənˈbitn

unbeautiful
BR (ˌ)ʌnˈbjuːtɪf(ʊ)l
AM ˌənˈbjudəfəl

unbeautifully
BR (ˌ)ʌnˈbjuːtɪfəli,
(ˌ)ʌnˈbjuːtɪfli
AM ˌənˈbjudəf(ə)li

unbecoming
BR ˌʌnbɪˈkʌmɪŋ
AM ˌənbəˈkəmɪŋ

unbecomingly
BR ˌʌnbɪˈkʌmɪŋli
AM ˌənbəˈkəmɪŋli

unbecomingness
BR ˌʌnbɪˈkʌmɪŋnɪs
AM ˌənbəˈkəmɪŋnɪs

unbefitting
BR ˌʌnbɪˈfɪtɪŋ
AM ˌənbəˈfɪdɪŋ

unbefittingly
BR ˌʌnbɪˈfɪtɪŋli
AM ˌənbəˈfɪdɪŋli

unbefittingness
BR ˌʌnbɪˈfɪtɪŋnɪs
AM ˌənbəˈfɪdɪŋnɪs

unbefriended
BR ˌʌnbɪˈfrendɪd
AM ˌənbəˈfrendəd

unbegotten
BR ˌʌnbɪˈgɒtn
AM ˌənbəˈgɑtn

unbeholden
BR ˌʌnbɪˈhəʊldn
AM ˌənbəˈhoʊldən

unbeknown
BR ˌʌnbɪˈnəʊn
AM ˌənbəˈnoʊn

unbeknownst
BR ˌʌnbɪˈnəʊnst
AM ˌənbəˈnoʊnst

unbelief
BR ˌʌnbɪˈliːf

AM ˌənbəˈlif

unbelievability
BR ˌʌnbɪˌliːvəˈbɪlɪti
AM ˌənbəˌliːvəˈbɪlɪdi

unbelievable
BR ˌʌnbɪˈliːvəbl
AM ˌənbəˈliːvəbəl

unbelievableness
BR ˌʌnbɪˈliːvəblnəs
AM ˌənbəˈliːvəbəlnəs

unbelievably
BR ˌʌnbɪˈliːvəbli
AM ˌənbəˈliːvəbli

unbelieved
BR ˌʌnbɪˈliːvd
AM ˌənbəˈliːvd

unbeliever
BR ˌʌnbɪˈliːvə(r), -z
AM ˌənbəˈliːvər, -z

unbelieving
BR ˌʌnbɪˈliːvɪŋ
AM ˌənbəˈliːvɪŋ

unbelievingly
BR ˌʌnbɪˈliːvɪŋli
AM ˌənbəˈliːvɪŋli

unbelievingness
BR ˌʌnbɪˈliːvɪŋnɪs
AM ˌənbəˈliːvɪŋnɪs

unbeloved
BR ˌʌnbɪˈlʌvɪd
AM ˌənbəˈləv(ə)d

unbelt
BR ˌʌnˈbelt, -s, -ɪŋ, -ɪd
AM ˌənˈbelt, -s, -ɪŋ, -əd

unbend
BR ˌʌnˈbend, -z, -ɪŋ
AM ˌənˈbend, -z, -ɪŋ

unbendingly
BR ˌʌnˈbendɪŋli
AM ˌənˈbendɪŋli

unbendingness
BR ˌʌnˈbendɪŋnɪs
AM ˌənˈbendɪŋnɪs

unbent
BR ˌʌnˈbent
AM ˌənˈbent

unbiased
BR ˌʌnˈbaɪəst
AM ˌənˈbaɪəst

unbiblical
BR ˌʌnˈbɪblɪkl
AM ˌənˈbɪbləkəl

unbiddable
BR ˌʌnˈbɪdəbl
AM ˌənˈbɪdəbəl

unbidden
BR ˌʌnˈbɪdn
AM ˌənˈbɪdən

unbind
BR ˌʌnˈbaɪnd, -z, -ɪŋ
AM ˌənˈbaɪnd, -z, -ɪŋ

unbirthday
BR ˌʌnˈbəːθdeɪ, -z
AM ˌənˈbərθˌdeɪ, -z

unbleached
BR ˌʌnˈbliːtʃt
AM ˌənˈbliːtʃt

unblemished
BR (ˌ)ʌnˈblemɪʃt
AM ˌənˈblemɪʃt

unblended
BR ˌʌnˈblendɪd
AM ˌənˈblendəd

unblessed
BR ˌʌnˈblest
AM ˌənˈblest

unblest
BR ˌʌnˈblest
AM ˌənˈblest

unblinking
BR ˌʌnˈblɪŋkɪŋ
AM ˌənˈblɪŋkɪŋ

unblinkingly
BR ˌʌnˈblɪŋkɪŋli
AM ˌənˈblɪŋkɪŋli

unblock
BR ˌʌnˈblɒk, -s, -ɪŋ, -t
AM ˌənˈblɑk, -s, -ɪŋ, -t

unbloody
BR ˌʌnˈblʌdi
AM ˌənˈblədi

unblown
BR ˌʌnˈbləʊn
AM ˌənˈbloʊn

unblushing
BR ˌʌnˈblʌʃɪŋ
AM ˌənˈbləʃɪŋ

unblushingly
BR ˌʌnˈblʌʃɪŋli
AM ˌənˈbləʃɪŋli

unbolt
BR ˌʌnˈbəʊlt, -s, -ɪŋ, -ɪd
AM ˌənˈboʊlt, -s, -ɪŋ, -əd

unbonnet
BR ˌʌnˈbɒn|ɪt, -s, -ɪtɪŋ, -ɪtɪd
AM ˌənˈbɑnə|t, -ts, -dɪŋ, -dəd

unbookish
BR (ˌ)ʌnˈbʊkɪʃ
AM ˌənˈbʊkɪʃ

unboot
BR ˌʌnˈbuːt, -s, -ɪŋ, -ɪd
AM ˌənˈbuʃt, -ts, -dɪŋ, -dəd

unborn
BR ˌʌnˈbɔːn
AM ˌənˈbɔ(ə)rn

unbosom
BR ˌʌnˈbʊz|(ə)m, -(ə)mz, -əmɪŋ\-mɪŋ, -(ə)md
AM ˌənˈbʊzəm, -z, -ɪŋ, -d

unbothered
BR (ˌ)ʌnˈbʊðəd
AM ˌənˈbɑðərd

unbound
BR ˌʌnˈbaʊnd
AM ˌənˈbaʊnd

unbounded
BR (ˌ)ʌnˈbaʊndɪd
AM ˌənˈbaʊn(d)əd

unboundedly
BR (ˌ)ʌnˈbaʊndɪdli

AM ˌənˈbaʊn(d)ədli

unboundedness
BR (ˌ)ʌnˈbaʊndɪdnɪs
AM ˌənˈbaʊn(d)ədnəs

unbowed
BR ˌʌnˈbaʊd
AM ˌənˈbaʊd

unbrace
BR ˌʌnˈbreɪs, -ɪz, -ɪŋ, -t
AM ˌənˈbreɪs, -ɪz, -ɪŋ, -t

unbranded
BR (ˌ)ʌnˈbrandɪd
AM ˌənˈbrændəd

unbreachable
BR (ˌ)ʌnˈbriːtʃəbl
AM ˌənˈbritʃəbəl

unbreakable
BR (ˌ)ʌnˈbreɪkəbl
AM ˌənˈbreɪkəbəl

unbreakably
BR (ˌ)ʌnˈbreɪkəbli
AM ˌənˈbreɪkəbli

unbreathable
BR (ˌ)ʌnˈbriːðəbl
AM ˌənˈbriðəbəl

unbribable
BR (ˌ)ʌnˈbraɪbəbl
AM ˌənˈbraɪbəbəl

unbridgeable
BR (ˌ)ʌnˈbrɪdʒəbl
AM ˌənˈbrɪdʒəbəl

unbridle
BR (ˌ)ʌnˈbraɪd|l, -lz, -lɪŋ\-lɪŋ, -ld
AM ˌənˈbraɪd|əl, -əlz, -(ə)lɪŋ, -əld

un-British
BR ˌʌnˈbrɪtɪʃ
AM ˌənˈbrɪdɪʃ

unbroken
BR (ˌ)ʌnˈbrəʊk(ə)n
AM ˌənˈbroʊkən

unbrokenly
BR (ˌ)ʌnˈbrəʊk(ə)nli
AM ˌənˈbroʊkənli

unbrokenness
BR (ˌ)ʌnˈbrəʊk(ə)nnəs
AM ˌənˈbroʊkə(n)nəs

unbrotherly
BR (ˌ)ʌnˈbrʌðəli
AM ˌənˈbrəðərli

unbruised
BR ˌʌnˈbruːzd
AM ˌənˈbruzd

unbrushed
BR ˌʌnˈbrʌʃt
AM ˌənˈbrəʃt

unbuckle
BR (ˌ)ʌnˈbʌk|l, -lz, -lɪŋ\-lɪŋ, -ld
AM ˌənˈbək|əl, -əlz, -(ə)lɪŋ, -əld

unbuild
BR ˌʌnˈbɪld, -z, -ɪŋ
AM ˌənˈbɪld, -z, -ɪŋ

unbuilt
BR (ˌ)ʌnˈbɪlt

AM ˌənˈbɪlt

unbundle
BR (ˌ)ʌnˈbʌnd|l, -lz, -lɪŋ\-lɪŋ, -ld
AM ˌənˈbən|dəl, -dəlz, -(d)(ə)lɪŋ, -dəld

unbundler
BR (ˌ)ʌnˈbʌndlə(r), ˌʌnˈbʌndlə(r), -z
AM ˌənˈbən(d)lər, -z

unburden
BR (ˌ)ʌnˈbəːd|n, -nz, -nɪŋ\-nɪŋ, -nd
AM ˌənˈbərdən, -z, -ɪŋ, -d

unburied
BR (ˌ)ʌnˈberɪd
AM ˌənˈberɪd

unburned
BR (ˌ)ʌnˈbəːnd
AM ˌənˈbərnd

unburnt
BR (ˌ)ʌnˈbəːnt
AM ˌənˈbərnt

unbury
BR (ˌ)ʌnˈbeːr|i, -ɪz, -ɪɪŋ, -ɪd
AM ˌənˈberi, -z, -ɪŋ, -d

unbusinesslike
BR (ˌ)ʌnˈbɪznɪslaɪk
AM ˌənˈbɪznɪsˌlaɪk

unbutton
BR ˌʌnˈbʌtn, -z, -ɪŋ, -d
AM ˌənˈbətn, -z, -ɪŋ, -d

uncage
BR ˌʌnˈkeɪdʒ, ˌʌŋˈkeɪdʒ, -ɪz, -ɪŋ, -d
AM ˌənˈkeɪdʒ, -ɪz, -ɪŋ, -d

uncalculated
BR (ˌ)ʌnˈkalkjʊleɪtɪd, (ˌ)ʌŋˈkalkjʊleɪtɪd
AM ˌənˈkælkjəˌleɪdɪd

uncalculating
BR (ˌ)ʌnˈkalkjʊleɪtɪŋ, (ˌ)ʌŋˈkalkjʊleɪtɪŋ
AM ˈənkælkjəˌleɪdɪŋ

uncalled
BR (ˌ)ʌnˈkɔːld, (ˌ)ʌŋˈkɔːld
AM ˌənˈkɔld, ˌənˈkɑld

uncalled-for
BR (ˌ)ʌnˈkɔːldfɔː(r), (ˌ)ʌŋˈkɔːldfɔː(r)
AM ˌənˈkɔldˌfɔ(ə)r, ˌənˈkɑldˌfɔ(ə)r

uncandid
BR (ˌ)ʌnˈkandɪd, (ˌ)ʌŋˈkandɪd
AM ˌənˈkændəd

uncannily
BR ʌnˈkanɪli, ʌŋˈkanɪli
AM ˌənˈkæneli

uncanniness
BR ʌnˈkanɪnɪs, ʌŋˈkanɪnɪs
AM ˌənˈkænɪnɪs

uncanny
BR ʌn'kæn‖i, ʌŋ'kæn‖i,
-ɪə(r), -ɪɪst
AM ‚ən'kæni, -ər, -ɪst

uncanonical
BR ‚ʌnkə'nɒnɪkl,
‚ʌŋkə'nɒnɪkl
AM ‚ənkə'nɑnəkəl

uncanonically
BR ‚ʌnkə'nɒnɪkli,
‚ʌŋkə'nɒnɪkli
AM ‚ənkə'nɑnək(ə)li

uncap
BR ‚ʌn'kap, ‚ʌŋ'kap, -s,
-ɪŋ, -t
AM ‚ən'kæp, -s, -ɪŋ, -t

uncared-for
BR (‚)ʌn'keːdfɔː(r),
(‚)ʌŋ'keːdfɔː(r)
AM ‚ən'kerd‚fɔ(ə)r

uncaring
BR (‚)ʌn'keːrɪŋ,
(‚)ʌŋ'keːrɪŋ
AM ‚ən'kerɪŋ

uncaringly
BR (‚)ʌn'keːrɪŋli,
(‚)ʌŋ'keːrɪŋli
AM ‚ən'kerɪŋli

uncarpeted
BR (‚)ʌn'kɑːpɪtɪd,
(‚)ʌŋ'kɑːpɪtɪd
AM ‚ən'kɑrpədəd

uncase
BR ‚ʌn'keɪs, ‚ʌŋ'keɪs,
-ɪz, -ɪŋ, -t
AM ‚ən'keɪs, -ɪz, -ɪŋ, -t

uncashed
BR ‚ʌn'kaʃt,
(‚)ʌŋ'kaʃt
AM ‚ən'kæʃt

uncatchable
BR (‚)ʌn'katʃəbl,
(‚)ʌŋ'katʃəbl
AM ‚ən'kɛtʃəbəl

uncategorisable
BR ‚ʌn'katɪɡərʌɪzəbl,
‚ʌŋ'katɪɡərʌɪzəbl
AM ‚ən'kædəɡə‚raɪzəbəl

uncategorizable
BR ‚ʌn'katɪɡərʌɪzəbl,
‚ʌŋ'katɪɡərʌɪzəbl
AM ‚ən'kædəɡə‚raɪzəbəl

uncaught
BR (‚)ʌn'kɔːt, (‚)ʌŋ'kɔːt
AM ‚ən'kɔt, ‚ən'kɑt

uncaused
BR (‚)ʌn'kɔːzd,
(‚)ʌŋ'kɔːzd
AM ‚ən'kɔzd, ‚ən'kɑzd

unceasing
BR (‚)ʌn'siːsɪŋ
AM ‚ən'sisɪŋ

unceasingly
BR (‚)ʌn'siːsɪŋli
AM ‚ən'sisɪŋli

uncelebrated
BR (‚)ʌn'sɛlɪbreɪtɪd
AM ‚ən'sɛlə‚breɪdɪd

uncensored
BR (‚)ʌn'sɛnsəd
AM ‚ən'sɛnsərd

uncensured
BR (‚)ʌn'sɛnʃəd
AM ‚ən'sɛn(t)ʃərd

unceremonious
BR ‚ʌnsɛrɪ'məʊnɪəs
AM ‚ənserə'moʊnɪəs

unceremoniously
BR ‚ʌnsɛrɪ'məʊnɪəsli
AM ‚ənserə'moʊnɪəsli

unceremonious-ness
BR ‚ʌnsɛrɪ'məʊnɪəsnəs
AM ‚ənserə'moʊnɪəsnəs

uncertain
BR (‚)ʌn'sɜːtn
AM ‚ən'sɜrtn

uncertainly
BR (‚)ʌn'sɜːtnli
AM ‚ən'sɜrtnli

uncertainty
BR (‚)ʌn'sɜːtnt‖i, -ɪz
AM ‚ən'sɜrtn(t)i, -z

uncertificated
BR ‚ʌnsə'tɪfɪkeɪtɪd
AM ‚ənsər'tɪfə‚keɪrdɪd

uncertified
BR (‚)ʌn'sɜːtɪfʌɪd
AM ‚ən'sɜrdə‚faɪd

unchain
BR ‚ʌn'tʃeɪn, -z, -ɪŋ, -d
AM ‚ən'tʃeɪn, -z, -ɪŋ, -d

unchallengeable
BR (‚)ʌn'tʃalɪn(d)ʒəbl
AM ‚ən'tʃæləndʒəbəl

unchallengeably
BR (‚)ʌn'tʃalɪn(d)ʒəbli
AM ‚ən'tʃæləndʒəbli

unchallenged
BR (‚)ʌn'tʃalɪn(d)ʒd
AM ‚ən'tʃæləndʒd

unchallenging
BR (‚)ʌn'tʃalɪn(d)ʒɪŋ
AM ‚ən'tʃæləndʒɪŋ

unchangeability
BR ‚ʌntʃeɪn(d)ʒə'bɪlɪti
AM ‚ən‚tʃeɪndʒə'bɪlɪdi

unchangeable
BR (‚)ʌn'tʃeɪn(d)ʒəbl
AM ‚ən'tʃeɪndʒəbəl

unchangeable-ness
BR (‚)ʌn'tʃeɪn(d)ʒəbl-nəs
AM ‚ən'tʃeɪndʒəbəlnəs

unchangeably
BR (‚)ʌn'tʃeɪn(d)ʒəbli
AM ‚ən'tʃeɪndʒəbli

unchanged
BR (‚)ʌn'tʃeɪn(d)ʒd
AM ‚ən'tʃeɪndʒd

unchanging
BR (‚)ʌn'tʃeɪn(d)ʒɪŋ
AM ‚ən'tʃeɪndʒɪŋ

unchangingly
BR (‚)ʌn'tʃeɪn(d)ʒɪŋli
AM ‚ən'tʃeɪndʒɪŋli

unchangingness
BR (‚)ʌn'tʃeɪn(d)ʒɪŋnɪs
AM ‚ən'tʃeɪndʒɪŋnɪs

unchaperoned
BR (‚)ʌn'ʃapərəʊnd
AM ‚ən'ʃæpə‚roʊnd

uncharacteristic
BR ‚ʌnkarəktə'rɪstɪk,
‚ʌŋkarəktə'rɪstɪk
AM ‚ən‚kerəktə'rɪstɪk

uncharacteristic-ally
BR ‚ʌnkarəktə'rɪstɪkli,
‚ʌŋkarəktə'rɪstɪkli
AM ‚ən‚kerəktə'rɪstɪk-(ə)li

uncharged
BR ‚ʌn'tʃɑːdʒd
AM ‚ən'tʃɑrdʒd

uncharismatic
BR ‚ʌnkarɪz'matɪk,
‚ʌŋkarɪz'matɪk
AM ‚ən‚kerəz'mædɪk

uncharitable
BR (‚)ʌn'tʃarɪtəbl
AM ‚ən'tʃɛrədəbəl

uncharitableness
BR (‚)ʌn'tʃarɪtəblnəs
AM ‚ən'tʃɛrədəbəlnəs

uncharitably
BR (‚)ʌn'tʃarɪtəbli
AM ‚ən'tʃɛrədəbli

uncharming
BR ‚ʌn'tʃɑːmɪŋ
AM ‚ən'tʃɑrmɪŋ

uncharted
BR ‚ʌn'tʃɑːtɪd
AM ‚ən'tʃɑrdəd

unchartered
BR ‚ʌn'tʃɑːtəd
AM ‚ən'tʃɑrdərd

unchaste
BR ‚ʌn'tʃeɪst
AM ‚ən'tʃeɪst

unchastely
BR ‚ʌn'tʃeɪs(t)li
AM ‚ən'tʃeɪs(t)li

unchastened
BR (‚)ʌn'tʃeɪsnd
AM ‚ən'tʃeɪsnd

unchasteness
BR ‚ʌn'tʃeɪstnɪs
AM ‚ən'tʃeɪs(t)nɪs

unchastity
BR ‚ʌn'tʃastɪti
AM ‚ən'tʃæstədi

unchecked
BR ‚ʌn'tʃɛkt
AM ‚ən'tʃɛkt

unchivalrous
BR (‚)ʌn'ʃɪvlrəs
AM ‚ən'ʃɪvəlrəs

unchivalrously
BR (‚)ʌn'ʃɪvlrəsli

AM ‚ən'ʃɪvəlrəsli

unchosen
BR (‚)ʌn'tʃəʊzn
AM ‚ən'tʃoʊzn

unchristian
BR (‚)ʌn'krɪstʃ(ə)n
AM ‚ən'krɪstʃən

unchristianly
BR (‚)ʌn'krɪstʃ(ə)nli
AM ‚ən'krɪstʃənli

unchurch
BR ‚ʌn'tʃɜːtʃ, -ɪz, -ɪŋ, -t
AM ‚ən'tʃɜrtʃ, -əz, -ɪŋ, -t

unci
BR 'ʌnsʌɪ
AM 'ən‚saɪ

uncial
BR 'ʌnsɪəl, 'ʌnʃl, -z
AM 'ən(t)sɪəl, 'əntʃəl,
-z

unciform
BR 'ʌnsɪfɔːm
AM 'ənsə‚fɔ(ə)rm

uncinate
BR 'ʌnsɪnət, 'ʌnsn̩ət,
'ʌnsɪneɪt
AM 'ənsənət,
'ənsə‚neɪt

uncircumcised
BR ‚ʌn'sɜː‚kəmsʌɪzd
AM ‚ən'sɜrkəm‚saɪzd

uncircumcision
BR ‚ʌnsɜː'kəm'sɪʒn
AM ‚ən‚sɜrkəm'sɪʒən

uncircumscribed
BR ‚ʌn'sɜː‚kəmskrʌɪbd
AM ‚ən'sɜrkəm‚skraɪbd

uncivil
BR ‚ʌn'sɪvl
AM ‚ən'sɪvəl

uncivilised
BR (‚)ʌn'sɪvɪlʌɪzd,
(‚)ʌn'sɪvlʌɪzd
AM ‚ən'sɪvə‚laɪzd

uncivilized
BR (‚)ʌn'sɪvɪlʌɪzd,
(‚)ʌn'sɪvlʌɪzd
AM ‚ən'sɪvə‚laɪzd

uncivilly
BR ‚ʌn'sɪvɪli
AM ‚ən'sɪvəli

unclad
BR ‚ʌn'klad, ‚ʌŋ'klad
AM ‚ən'klæd

unclaimed
BR ‚ʌn'kleɪmd,
‚ʌŋ'kleɪmd
AM ‚ən'kleɪmd

unclasp
BR ‚ʌn'klɑːsp,
‚ʌn'klasp, ‚ʌŋ'klɑːsp,
‚ʌŋ'klasp, -s, -ɪŋ, -t
AM ‚ən'klæsp, -s, -ɪŋ, -t

unclassifiable
BR (‚)ʌn'klasɪfʌɪəbl,
(‚)ʌŋ'klasɪfʌɪəbl
AM ‚ən‚klæsə'faɪəbəl

unclassified
BR (ˌ)ʌnˈklasɪfʌɪd,
(ˌ)ʌŋˈklasɪfʌɪd
AM ˌənˈklæsəˌfaɪd

uncle
BR ˈʌŋkl, -z
AM ˈəŋkəl, -z

unclean
BR (ˌ)ʌnˈkliːn,
(ˌ)ʌŋˈkliːn, -d
AM ˌənˈklin, -d

uncleanliness
BR (ˌ)ʌnˈklɛnlɪnɪs,
(ˌ)ʌŋˈklɛnlɪnɪs
AM ˌənˈklɛnlɪnɪs

uncleanly[1]
adjective
BR (ˌ)ʌnˈklɛnli,
(ˌ)ʌŋˈklɛnli
AM ˌənˈklɛnli

uncleanly[2]
adverb
BR (ˌ)ʌnˈkliːnli,
(ˌ)ʌŋˈkliːnli
AM ˌənˈklinli

uncleanness
BR (ˌ)ʌnˈkliːnnɪs,
(ˌ)ʌŋˈkliːnnɪs
AM ˌənˈklin(n)ɪs

uncleansed
BR (ˌ)ʌnˈklɛnzd,
(ˌ)ʌŋˈklɛnzd
AM ˌənˈklɛnzd

unclear
BR ˌʌnˈklɪə(r),
ˌʌŋˈklɪə(r), -d
AM ˌənˈklɪ(ə)r, -d

unclearly
BR ˌʌnˈklɪəli, ˌʌŋˈklɪəli
AM ˌənˈklɪrli

unclearness
BR ˌʌnˈklɪənəs,
ˌʌŋˈklɪənəs
AM ˌənˈklɪrnəs

uncle-in-law
BR ˈʌŋklɪnˌlɔː(r)
AM ˈəŋkələnˌlɔ,
ˈəŋkələnˌlɑ

unclench
BR ˌʌnˈklɛn(t)ʃ,
ˌʌŋˈklɛn(t)ʃ, -ɪz, -ɪŋ, -t
AM ˌənˈklɛn(t)ʃ, -əz, -ɪŋ,
-t

Uncle Sam
BR ˌʌŋkl ˈsam
AM ˌəŋkəl ˈsæm

uncles-in-law
BR ˈʌŋklzɪnˌlɔː(r), -z
AM ˈəŋkəlzənˌlɔ,
ˈəŋkəlzənˌlɑ

Uncle Tom
BR ˌʌŋkl ˈtɒm, -z
AM ˌəŋkəl ˈtɑm, -z

unclimbable
BR ˌʌnˈklʌɪməbl,
ˌʌŋˈklʌɪməbl
AM ˌənˈklaɪməbəl

unclimbed
BR ˌʌnˈklʌɪmd,
ˌʌŋˈklʌɪmd
AM ˌənˈklaɪmd

unclinch
BR ˌʌnˈklɪn(t)ʃ,
ˌʌŋˈklɪn(t)ʃ, -ɪz, -ɪŋ, -t
AM ˌənˈklɪn(t)ʃ, -ɪz, -ɪŋ,
-t

unclip
BR ˌʌnˈklɪp, ˌʌŋˈklɪp, -s,
-ɪŋ, -t
AM ˌənˈklɪp, -s, -ɪŋ, -t

uncloak
BR ˌʌnˈkləʊk,
ˌʌŋˈkləʊk, -s, -ɪŋ, -t
AM ˌənˈkloʊk, -s, -ɪŋ, -t

unclog
BR ˌʌnˈklɒg, ˌʌŋˈklɒg,
-z, -ɪŋ, -d
AM ˌənˈklɑg, -z, -ɪŋ, -d

unclose
BR ˌʌnˈkləʊz,
ˌʌŋˈkləʊz, -ɪz, -ɪŋ, -d
AM ˌənˈkloʊz, -ɪz, -ɪŋ, -d

unclothe
BR ˌʌnˈkləʊð,
ˌʌŋˈkləʊð, -z, -ɪŋ, -d
AM ˌənˈkloʊð, -z, -ɪŋ, -d

unclouded
BR (ˌ)ʌnˈklaʊdɪd,
(ˌ)ʌŋˈklaʊdɪd
AM ˌənˈklaʊdəd

uncluttered
BR (ˌ)ʌnˈklʌtəd,
(ˌ)ʌŋˈklʌtəd
AM ˌənˈklədərd

unco
BR ˈʌŋkəʊ, -z
AM ˈəŋkoʊ, -z

uncoded
BR (ˌ)ʌnˈkəʊdɪd,
(ˌ)ʌŋˈkəʊdɪd
AM ˌənˈkoʊdəd

uncoil
BR ˌʌnˈkɔɪl, ˌʌŋˈkɔɪl, -z,
-ɪŋ, -d
AM ˌənˈkɔɪl, -z, -ɪŋ, -d

uncollected
BR ˌʌnkəˈlɛktɪd,
ˌʌŋkəˈlɛktɪd
AM ˌənkəˈlɛktəd

uncolored
BR (ˌ)ʌnˈkʌləd,
(ˌ)ʌŋˈkʌləd
AM ˌənˈkələrd

uncoloured
BR (ˌ)ʌnˈkʌləd,
(ˌ)ʌŋˈkʌləd
AM ˌənˈkələrd

uncombed
BR (ˌ)ʌnˈkəʊmd,
(ˌ)ʌŋˈkəʊmd
AM ˌənˈkoʊmd

uncome-at-able
BR ˌʌnkʌmˈatəbl,
ˌʌŋkʌmˈatəbl
AM ˌənˌkəmˈædəbəl

uncomely
BR ˌʌnˈkʌmli,
ˌʌŋˈkʌmli
AM ˌənˈkəmli

uncomfortable
BR ʌnˈkʌmf(ə)təbl,
ʌŋˈkʌmf(ə)təbl
AM ˌənˈkəmfərdəbəl,
ˌənˈkəmftərbəl

**uncomfortable-
ness**
BR ʌnˈkʌmf(ə)təblnəs,
ʌŋˈkʌmf(ə)təblnəs
AM ˌənˈkəmfərdəbəl-
nəs,
ˌənˈkəmftərbəlnəs

uncomfortably
BR ʌnˈkʌmf(ə)təbli,
ʌŋˈkʌmf(ə)təbli
AM ˌənˈkəmfərdəbli,
ˌənˈkəmftərbli

uncomforted
BR ˌʌnˈkʌmfətɪd,
ˌʌŋˈkʌmfətɪd
AM ˌənˈkəmfərdəd

uncommercial
BR ˌʌnkəˈmɜːʃl,
ˌʌŋkəˈmɜːʃl
AM ˌənkəˈmərʃəl

uncommercially
BR ˌʌnkəˈmɜːʃli,
ˌʌnkəˈmɜːʃəli,
ˌʌŋkəˈmɜːʃli,
ˌʌŋkəˈmɜːʃəli
AM ˌənkəˈmərʃəli

uncommissioned
BR ˌʌnkəˈmɪʃnd,
ˌʌŋkəˈmɪʃnd
AM ˌənkəˈmɪʃənd

uncommitted
BR ˌʌnkəˈmɪtɪd,
ˌʌŋkəˈmɪtɪd
AM ˌənkəˈmɪdɪd

uncommon
BR (ˌ)ʌnˈkɒmən,
(ˌ)ʌŋˈkɒmən
AM ˌənˈkamən

uncommonly
BR (ˌ)ʌnˈkɒmənli,
(ˌ)ʌŋˈkɒmənli
AM ˌənˈkamənli

uncommonness
BR (ˌ)ʌnˈkɒmənnəs,
(ˌ)ʌŋˈkɒmənnəs
AM ˌənˈkamə(n)nəs

uncommunicable
BR ˌʌnkəˈmjuːnɪkəbl,
ˌʌŋkəˈmjuːnɪkəbl
AM ˌənkəˈmjunəkəbəl

uncommunicated
BR ˌʌnkəˈmjuːnɪkeɪtɪd,
ˌʌŋkəˈmjuːnɪkeɪtɪd
AM ˌənkəˈmjunəˌkeɪdɪd

uncommunicative
BR ˌʌnkəˈmjuːnɪkətɪv,
ˌʌŋkəˈmjuːnɪkətɪv
AM ˌənkəˈmjunəˌkeɪdɪv,
ˌənkəˈmjunəkədɪv

**uncommunica-
tively**
BR ˌʌnkəˈmjuːnɪkətɪvli,
ˌʌŋkəˈmjuːnɪkətɪvli
AM ˌənkəˈmjunəˌkeɪ-
dɪvli,
ˌənkəˈmjunəkədɪvli

uncommunicativeness
BR ˌʌnkəˈmjuːnɪkətɪvnɪs,
ˌʌŋkəˈmjuːnɪkətɪvnɪs
AM ˌənkəˈmjunəˌkeɪdɪvnɪs,
ˌənkəˈmjunəkədɪvnɪs

uncompanionable
BR ˌʌnkəmˈpanɪənəbl,
ˌʌŋkəmˈpanɪənəbl
AM ˌənkəmˈpænjənəbəl

uncompensated
BR ˌʌnˈkʌmp(ɛ)nseɪtɪd,
ˌʌŋˈkʌmp(ɛ)nseɪtɪd
AM ˌənˈkampənˌseɪdɪd

uncompetitive
BR ˌʌnkəmˈpɛtɪtɪv,
ˌʌŋkəmˈpɛtɪtɪv
AM ˌənkəmˈpɛdədɪv

uncompetitiveness
BR ˌʌnkəmˈpɛtɪtɪvnɪs,
ˌʌŋkəmˈpɛtɪtɪvnɪs
AM ˌənkəmˈpɛdədɪvnɪs

uncomplaining
BR ˌʌnkəmˈpleɪnɪŋ,
ˌʌŋkəmˈpleɪnɪŋ
AM ˌənkəmˈpleɪnɪŋ

uncomplainingly
BR ˌʌnkəmˈpleɪnɪŋli,
ˌʌŋkəmˈpleɪnɪŋli
AM ˌənkəmˈpleɪnɪŋli

uncompleted
BR ˌʌnkəmˈpliːtɪd,
ˌʌŋkəmˈpliːtɪd
AM ˌənkəmˈplidɪd

uncomplicated
BR ˌʌnˈkɒmplɪkeɪtɪd,
ˌʌŋˈkɒmplɪkeɪtɪd
AM ˌənˈkampləˌkeɪdɪd

uncomplimentary
BR ˌʌnkɒmplɪˈmɛnt(ə)ri,
ˌʌŋkɒmplɪˈmɛnt(ə)ri
AM ˌənˌkampləˈmɛn(t)əri

uncompounded
BR ˌʌnkəmˈpaʊndɪd,
ˌʌŋkəmˈpaʊndɪd
AM ˌənkəmˈpaʊndəd

uncomprehended
BR ˌʌnkɒmprɪˈhɛndɪd,
ˌʌŋkɒmprɪˈhɛndɪd
AM ˌənˌkamprəˈhɛndəd

uncomprehending
BR ˌʌnkɒmprɪˈhɛndɪŋ,
ˌʌŋkɒmprɪˈhɛndɪŋ
AM ˌənˌkamprəˈhɛndɪŋ

uncomprehendingly
BR ˌʌnkɒmprɪˈhɛndɪŋli,
ˌʌŋkɒmprɪˈhɛndɪŋli
AM ˌənˌkamprəˈhɛndɪŋli

uncomprehension
BR ˌʌnkɒmprɪˈhɛnʃn,
ˌʌŋkɒmprɪˈhɛnʃn
AM ˌənˌkamprəˈhɛn(t)ʃən

uncompromising
BR ʌn'kɒmprəmʌɪzɪŋ,
ʌŋ'kɒmprəmʌɪzɪŋ
AM ʌn'kɑmprə,maɪzɪŋ

uncompromisingly
BR ʌn'kɒmprəmʌɪzɪŋli,
ʌŋ'kɒmprəmʌɪzɪŋli
AM ʌn'kɑmprə,maɪzɪŋ-li

uncompromising-ness
BR ʌn'kɒmprəmʌɪzɪŋ-nɪs,
ʌŋ'kɒmprəmʌɪzɪŋnɪs
AM ʌn'kɑmprə,maɪzɪŋ-nɪs

unconcealed
BR ʌnkən'si:ld,
ʌŋkən'si:ld
AM ənkən'sild

unconcern
BR ʌnkən'sə:n,
ʌŋkən'sə:n, -d
AM ənkən'sərn, -d

unconcernedly
BR ʌnkən'sə:nɪdli,
ʌŋkən'sə:nɪdli
AM ənkən'sərnədli

unconcluded
BR ʌnkən'klu:dɪd,
ʌŋkən'klu:dɪd
AM ənkən'kludəd

unconditional
BR ʌnkən'dɪʃn̩(ə)l,
ʌnkən'dɪʃən(ə)l,
ʌŋkən'dɪʃn̩(ə)l,
ʌŋkən'dɪʃən(ə)l
AM ənkən'dɪʃ(ə)nəl

unconditionality
BR ʌnkən,dɪʃə'nalɪti,
ʌŋkən,dɪʃə'nalɪti
AM ənkən,dɪʃə'næledi

unconditionally
BR ʌnkən'dɪʃn̩əli,
ʌnkən'dɪʃ(ə)nəli,
ʌŋkən'dɪʃn̩əli,
ʌŋkən'dɪʃ(ə)nəli
AM ənkən'dɪʃ(ə)nəli

unconditioned
BR ʌnkən'dɪʃnd,
ʌŋkən'dɪʃnd
AM ənkən'dɪʃənd

unconfident
BR ʌn'kɒnfɪdnt,
ʌŋ'kɒnfɪdnt
AM ən'kɑnfədənt

unconfined
BR ʌnkən'fʌɪnd,
ʌŋkən'fʌɪnd
AM ənkən'faɪnd

unconfirmed
BR ʌnkən'fə:md,
ʌŋkən'fə:md
AM ənkən'fərmd

unconformable
BR ʌnkən'fɔ:məbl,
ʌn'kɒnʃ(ə)nəbl,
ʌŋkən'fɔ:məbl
AM ənkən'fɔrməbəl

unconformable-ness
BR ʌnkən'fɔ:məblnəs,
ʌŋkən'fɔ:məblnəs
AM ənkən'fɔrməbəlnəs

unconformably
BR ʌnkən'fɔ:məbli,
ʌŋkən'fɔ:məbli
AM ənkən'fɔrməbli

unconformity
BR ʌnkən'fɔ:mɪti,
ʌŋkən'fɔ:mɪti
AM ənkən'fɔrmədi

uncongenial
BR ʌnkən'dʒi:nɪəl,
ʌŋkən'dʒi:nɪəl
AM ənkən'dʒiniəl,
ənkən'dʒinjəl

uncongenially
BR ʌnkən'dʒi:nɪəli,
ʌŋkən'dʒi:nɪəli
AM ənkən'dʒiniəli,
ənkən'dʒinjəli

uncongested
BR ʌnkən'dʒɛstɪd,
ʌŋkən'dʒɛstɪd
AM ənkən'dʒɛstəd

unconjecturable
BR ʌnkən'dʒɛktʃ(ə)r-əbl,
ʌŋkən'dʒɛktʃ(ə)rəbl
AM ənkən'dʒɛk(t)ʃ(ə)-rəbəl

unconnected
BR ʌnkə'nɛktɪd,
ʌŋkə'nɛktɪd
AM ənkə'nɛktəd

unconnectedly
BR ʌnkə'nɛktɪdli,
ʌŋkə'nɛktɪdli
AM ənkə'nɛktədli

unconnectedness
BR ʌnkə'nɛktɪdnɪs,
ʌŋkə'nɛktɪdnɪs
AM ənkə'nɛktədnəs

unconquerable
BR ʌn'kɒŋk(ə)rəbl,
ʌŋ'kɒŋk(ə)rəbl
AM ən'kɑŋk(ə)rəbəl

unconquerable-ness
BR ʌn'kɒŋk(ə)rəblnəs,
ʌŋ'kɒŋk(ə)rəblnəs
AM ən'kɑŋk(ə)rəbəl-nəs

unconquerably
BR ʌn'kɒŋk(ə)rəbli,
ʌŋ'kɒŋk(ə)rəbli
AM ən'kɑŋk(ə)rəbli

unconquered
BR ʌn'kɒŋkəd,
ʌŋ'kɒŋkəd
AM ən'kɑŋkərd

unconscionable
BR ʌn'kɒnʃn̩əbl,
ʌn'kɒnʃ(ə)nəbl,
ʌŋ'kɒnʃn̩əbl,
ʌŋ'kɒnʃ(ə)nəbl

unconscionable-ness
BR ʌn'kɒnʃn̩əblnəs,
ʌn'kɒnʃ(ə)nəblnəs,
ʌŋ'kɒnʃn̩əblnəs,
ʌŋ'kɒnʃ(ə)nəblnəs
AM ən'kɑnʃ(ə)nəbəl-nəs

unconscionably
BR ʌn'kɒnʃn̩əbli,
ʌn'kɒnʃ(ə)nəbli,
ʌŋ'kɒnʃn̩əbli,
ʌŋ'kɒnʃ(ə)nəbli
AM ən'kɑnʃ(ə)nəbli

unconscious
BR ʌn'kɒnʃəs,
ʌŋ'kɒnʃəs
AM ən'kɑnʃəs

unconsciously
BR ʌn'kɒnʃəsli,
ʌŋ'kɒnʃəsli
AM ən'kɑnʃəsli

unconsciousness
BR ʌn'kɒnʃəsnəs,
ʌŋ'kɒnʃəsnəs
AM ən'kɑnʃəsnəs

unconsecrated
BR (,)ʌn'kɒnsɪkreɪtɪd,
(,)ʌŋ'kɒnsɪkreɪtɪd
AM ən'kɑnsə,kreɪdɪd

unconsenting
BR ʌnkən'sɛntɪŋ,
ʌŋkən'sɛntɪŋ
AM ənkən'sɛn(t)ɪŋ

unconsidered
BR ʌnkən'sɪdəd,
ʌŋkən'sɪdəd
AM ənkən'sɪdərd

unconsolable
BR ʌnkən'səʊləbl,
ʌŋkən'səʊləbl
AM ənkən'soʊləbəl

unconsolably
BR ʌnkən'səʊləbli,
ʌŋkən'səʊləbli
AM ənkən'soʊləbli

unconsolidated
BR ʌnkən'sɒlɪdeɪtɪd,
ʌŋkən'sɒlɪdeɪtɪd
AM ənkən'sɑlə,deɪdɪd

unconstitutional
BR ʌnkɒnstɪ'tju:ʃn̩(ə)l,
ʌnkɒnstɪ'tʃu:ʃn̩(ə)l,
ʌŋkɒnstɪ'tju:ʃn̩(ə)l,
ʌŋkɒnstɪ'tʃu:ʃn̩(ə)l
AM ən,kɑnstə't(j)uʃ(ə)-nəl

unconstitution-ality
BR ʌnkɒnstɪ,tju:ʃə-'nalɪti,
ʌnkɒnstɪ,tʃu:ʃə'nalɪti,
ʌŋkɒnstɪ,tju:ʃə'nalɪti,
ʌŋkɒnstɪ,tʃu:ʃə'nalɪti
AM ən,kɑnstə,t(j)uʃə-'næledi

unconstitutionally
BR ʌnkɒnstɪ'tju:ʃn̩əli,
ʌnkɒnstɪ'tʃu:ʃ(ə)nəli,
ʌnkɒnstɪ't'tʃu:ʃn̩əli,
ʌnkɒnstɪ'tʃu:ʃ(ə)nəli,
ʌŋkɒnstɪ'tju:ʃn̩əli,
ʌŋkɒnstɪ'tʃu:ʃ(ə)nəli,
ʌŋkɒnstɪ'tʃu:ʃn̩əli,
ʌŋkɒnstɪ'tʃu:ʃ(ə)nəli
AM ən,kɑnstə't(j)uʃ(ə)-nəli

unconstrained
BR ʌnkən'streɪnd,
ʌŋkən'streɪnd
AM ənkən'streɪnd

unconstrainedly
BR ʌnkən'streɪnɪdli,
ʌŋkən'streɪnɪdli
AM ənkən'streɪnɪdli

unconstraint
BR ʌnkən'streɪnt,
ʌŋkən'streɪnt
AM ənkən'streɪnt

unconstricted
BR ʌnkən'strɪktɪd,
ʌŋkən'strɪktɪd
AM ənkən'strɪktɪd

unconstructive
BR ʌnkən'strʌktɪv,
ʌŋkən'strʌktɪv
AM ənkən'strʌktɪv

unconsulted
BR ʌnkən'sʌltɪd,
ʌŋkən'sʌltɪd
AM ənkən'səltəd

unconsumed
BR ʌnkən'sju:md,
ʌŋkən'sju:md
AM ənkən's(j)umd

unconsummated
BR ʌn'kɒnsjʊmeɪtɪd,
ʌŋ'kɒnsjʊmeɪtɪd
AM ən'kɑns(j)ə,meɪdɪd

uncontactable
BR ʌn'kɒntaktəbl,
ʌŋ'kɒntaktəbl
AM ən'kɑn,tæktəbəl

uncontainable
BR ʌnkən'teɪnəbl,
ʌŋkən'teɪnəbl
AM ənkən'teɪnəbəl

uncontaminated
BR ʌnkən'tamɪneɪtɪd,
ʌŋkən'tamɪneɪtɪd
AM ənkən'tæmə,neɪdɪd

uncontentious
BR ʌnkən'tɛnʃəs,
ʌŋkən'tɛnʃəs
AM ənkən'tɛn(t)ʃəs

uncontentiously
BR ʌnkən'tɛnʃəsli,
ʌŋkən'tɛnʃəsli
AM ənkən'tɛn(t)ʃəsli

uncontested
BR ʌnkən'tɛstɪd,
ʌŋkən'tɛstɪd
AM ənkən'tɛstəd

uncontestedly
BR ˌʌŋkənˈtɛstɪdli,
ˌʌŋkənˈtɛstɪdli
AM ˌənkənˈtɛstədli

uncontradicted
BR ˌʌŋkɒntrəˈdɪktɪd,
ˌʌŋkɒntrəˈdɪktɪd
AM ˌənkɑntrəˈdɪktɪd

uncontrived
BR ˌʌŋkənˈtrʌɪvd,
ˌʌŋkənˈtrʌɪvd
AM ˌənkənˈtraɪvd

uncontrollable
BR ˌʌŋkənˈtrəʊləbl̩,
ˌʌŋkənˈtrəʊləbl̩
AM ˌənkənˈtroʊləbəl

uncontrollable-ness
BR ˌʌŋkənˈtrəʊləblnəs,
ˌʌŋkənˈtrəʊləblnəs
AM ˌənkənˈtroʊləbəl-nəs

uncontrollably
BR ˌʌŋkənˈtrəʊləbli,
ˌʌŋkənˈtrəʊləbli
AM ˌənkənˈtroʊləbli

uncontrolled
BR ˌʌŋkənˈtrəʊld,
ˌʌŋkənˈtrəʊld
AM ˌənkənˈtroʊld

uncontrolledly
BR ˌʌŋkənˈtrəʊlɪdli,
ˌʌŋkənˈtrəʊlɪdli
AM ˌənkənˈtroʊlədli

uncontroversial
BR ˌʌŋkɒntrəˈvɜːʃl̩,
ˌʌŋkɒntrəˈvɜːʃl̩
AM ˌənˌkɑntrəˈvɜrʃəl,
ˌənˌkɑntrəˈvɜrsiəl

uncontroversially
BR ˌʌŋkɒntrəˈvɜːʃli,
ˌʌŋkɒntrəˈvɜːʃəli,
ˌʌŋkɒntrəˈvɜːʃli,
ˌʌŋkɒntrəˈvɜːʃəli
AM ˌənˌkɑntrəˈvɜrʃəli,
ˌənˌkɑntrəˈvɜrsiəli

uncontroverted
BR ˌʌŋkɒntrəˈvɜːtɪd,
ˌʌŋkɒntrəvɜːtɪd,
ˌʌŋkɒntrəˈvɜːtɪd,
ˌʌŋkɒntrəvɜːtɪd
AM ˌənˌkɑntrəˈvɜrdəd

uncontrovertible
BR ˌʌŋkɒntrəˈvɜːtɪbl̩,
ˌʌŋkɒntrəˈvɜːtɪbl̩
AM ˌənˌkɑntrəˈvɜrdəbəl

unconventional
BR ˌʌŋkənˈvɛnʃn̩(ə)l,
ˌʌŋkənˈvɛnʃən(ə)l,
ˌʌŋkənˈvɛnʃn̩(ə)l,
ˌʌŋkənˈvɛnʃən(ə)l
AM ˌənkənˈvɛn(t)ʃ(ə)-nəl

unconventional-ism
BR ˌʌŋkənˈvɛnʃnəl-ɪz(ə)m,
ˌʌŋkənˈvɛnʃ(ə)nəl-ɪz(ə)m,

ˌʌŋkənˈvɛnʃnəlɪz(ə)m,
ˌʌŋkənˈvɛnʃ(ə)nəl-ɪz(ə)m
AM ˌənkənˈvɛn(t)ʃənl-ˌɪzəm,
ˌənkənˈvɛn(t)ʃnəˌlɪzəm

unconventionality
BR ˌʌŋkənˌvɛnʃəˈnalɪti,
ˌʌŋkənˌvɛnʃəˈnalɪti
AM ˌənkənˌvɛn(t)ʃə-ˈnælədi

unconventionally
BR ˌʌŋkənˈvɛnʃnəli,
ˌʌŋkənˈvɛnʃ(ə)nəli,
ˌʌŋkənˈvɛnʃnəli,
ˌʌŋkənˈvɛnʃ(ə)nəli
AM ˌənkənˈvɛn(t)ʃ(ə)-nəli

unconverted
BR ˌʌŋkənˈvɜːtɪd,
ˌʌŋkənˈvɜːtɪd
AM ˌənkənˈvɜrdəd

unconvertible
BR ˌʌŋkənˈvɜːtɪbl̩,
ˌʌŋkənˈvɜːtɪbl̩
AM ˌənkənˈvɜrdəbəl

unconvicted
BR ˌʌŋkənˈvɪktɪd,
ˌʌŋkənˈvɪktɪd
AM ˌənkənˈvɪktɪd

unconvinced
BR ˌʌŋkənˈvɪnst,
ˌʌŋkənˈvɪnst
AM ˌənkənˈvɪnst

unconvincing
BR ˌʌŋkənˈvɪnsɪŋ,
ˌʌŋkənˈvɪnsɪŋ
AM ˌənkənˈvɪnsɪŋ

unconvincingly
BR ˌʌŋkənˈvɪnsɪŋli,
ˌʌŋkənˈvɪnsɪŋli
AM ˌənkənˈvɪnsɪŋli

uncooked
BR ˌʌnˈkʊkt, ˌʌŋˈkʊkt
AM ˌənˈkʊkt

uncool
BR ˌʌnˈkuːl, ˌʌŋˈkuːl
AM ˈənˈkul

uncooperative
BR ˌʌŋkəʊˈɒp(ə)rətɪv
AM ˌənkoʊˈɑp(ə)rədɪv

uncooperatively
BR ˌʌŋkəʊˈɒp(ə)rətɪvli,
ˌʌŋkəʊˈɒp(ə)rətɪvli
AM ˌənkoʊˈɑp(ə)rədɪvli

uncooperative-ness
BR ˌʌŋkəʊˈɒp(ə)rətɪv-nɪs,
ˌʌŋkəʊˈɒp(ə)rətɪvnɪs
AM ˌənkoʊˈɑp(ə)rədɪv-nɪs

uncoordinated
BR ˌʌŋkəʊˈɔːdɪneɪtɪd,
ˌʌŋkəʊˈɔːdɪneɪtɪd
AM ˌənkoʊˈɔrdəˌneɪdɪd,
ˌənkoʊˈɔrdn̩ˌeɪdɪd

uncopiable
BR ˌʌnˈkɒpɪəbl̩,
ˌʌŋˈkɒpɪəbl
AM ˌənˈkɑpɪəbəl

uncord
BR ˌʌnˈkɔːd, ˌʌŋˈkɔːd,
-z, -ɪŋ, -ɪd
AM ˌənˈkɔ(ə)rd, -z, -ɪŋ,
-əd

uncordial
BR ˌʌnˈkɔːdɪəl,
ˌʌŋˈkɔːdɪəl
AM ˌənˈkɔrdʒəl

uncork
BR ˌʌnˈkɔːk, ˌʌŋˈkɔːk,
-s, -ɪŋ, -t
AM ˌənˈkɔ(ə)rk, -s, -ɪŋ,
-t

uncorrected
BR ˌʌnkəˈrɛktɪd,
ˌʌŋkəˈrɛktɪd
AM ˌənkəˈrɛktɪd

uncorrelated
BR ˌʌnˈkɒrɪleɪtɪd,
ˌʌŋˈkɒrɪleɪtɪd
AM ˌənˈkɔrəˌleɪdɪd

uncorroborated
BR ˌʌnkəˈrɒbəreɪtɪd,
ˌʌŋkəˈrɒbəreɪtɪd
AM ˌənkəˈrɑbəˌreɪdɪd

uncorrupted
BR ˌʌnkəˈrʌptɪd,
ˌʌŋkəˈrʌptɪd
AM ˌənkəˈrəptəd

uncorseted
BR ˌʌnˈkɔːsɪtɪd,
ˌʌŋˈkɔːsɪtɪd
AM ˌənˈkɔrsədəd

uncountability
BR ˌʌnkaʊntəˈbɪlɪti,
ˌʌŋkaʊntəˈbɪlɪti
AM ˌənkaʊn(t)əˈbɪlɪdi

uncountable
BR ˌʌnˈkaʊntəbl̩,
ˌʌŋˈkaʊntəbl
AM ˌənˈkaʊn(t)əbəl

uncountably
BR ˌʌnˈkaʊntəbli,
ˌʌŋˈkaʊntəbli
AM ˌənˈkaʊn(t)əbli

uncounted
BR (ˌ)ʌnˈkaʊntɪd,
(ˌ)ʌŋˈkaʊntɪd
AM ˌənˈkaʊn(t)əd

uncouple
BR ˌʌnˈkʌpl̩, ˌʌŋˈkʌpl̩,
-z, -]ɪŋ\-lɪŋ, -ld
AM ˌənˈkəpl̩əl, -əlz,
-(ə)lɪŋ, -əld

uncourtly
BR ˌʌnˈkɔːtli, ˌʌŋˈkɔːtli
AM ˌənˈkɔrtli

uncouth
BR ˌʌnˈkuːθ, ˌʌŋˈkuːθ
AM ˌənˈkuθ

uncouthly
BR ˌʌnˈkuːθli, ˌʌŋˈkuːθli
AM ˌənˈkuθli

uncouthness
BR ˌʌnˈkuːθnəs,
ˌʌŋˈkuːθnəs
AM ˌənˈkuθnəs

uncovenanted
BR ˌʌnˈkʌvənəntɪd,
ˌʌŋˈkʌvn̩əntɪd,
ˌʌŋˈkʌvənəntɪd,
ˌʌŋˈkʌvn̩əntɪd
AM ˌənˈkəv(ə)nən(t)əd

uncover
BR (ˌ)ʌnˈkʌv|ə(r),
(ˌ)ʌŋˈkʌv|ə(r), -əz,
-(ə)rɪŋ, -əd
AM ˌənˈkəvjər, -ərz,
-(ə)rɪŋ, -ərd

uncrackable
BR ˌʌnˈkrakəbl̩,
(ˌ)ʌŋˈkrakəbl
AM ˌənˈkrækəbəl

uncracked
BR ˌʌnˈkrakt,
ˌʌŋˈkrakt
AM ˌənˈkrækt

uncreased
BR (ˌ)ʌnˈkriːst,
(ˌ)ʌŋˈkriːst
AM ˌənˈkrist

uncreate
BR ˌʌnkrɪˈeɪt,
ˌʌŋkrɪˈeɪt, -s, -ɪŋ, -ɪd
AM ˌənˌkriˈeɪ|t, -ts, -dɪŋ,
-dɪd

uncreative
BR ˌʌnkrɪˈeɪtɪv,
ˌʌŋkrɪˈeɪtɪv
AM ˌənˌkriˈeɪdɪv

uncredited
BR (ˌ)ʌnˈkrɛdɪtɪd,
(ˌ)ʌŋˈkrɛdɪtɪd
AM ˌənˈkrɛdədəd

uncritical
BR (ˌ)ʌnˈkrɪtɪkl̩,
(ˌ)ʌŋˈkrɪtɪkl
AM ˌənˈkrɪdəkəl

uncritically
BR (ˌ)ʌnˈkrɪtɪkli,
(ˌ)ʌŋˈkrɪtɪkli
AM ˌənˈkrɪdək(ə)li

uncropped
BR ˌʌnˈkrɒpt,
ˌʌŋˈkrɒpt
AM ˌənˈkrɑpt

uncross
BR ˌʌnˈkrɒs, ˌʌŋˈkrɒs,
-ɪz, -ɪŋ, -t
AM ˌənˈkrɔs, ˌənˈkrɑs,
-əz, -ɪŋ, -t

uncrossable
BR ˌʌnˈkrɒsəbl̩,
ˌʌŋˈkrɒsəbl
AM ˌənˈkrɔsəbəl,
ˌənˈkrɑsəbəl

uncrowded
BR (ˌ)ʌnˈkraʊdɪd,
(ˌ)ʌŋˈkraʊdɪd
AM ˌənˈkraʊdəd

uncrown
BR ˌʌnˈkraʊn,
ˌʌŋˈkraʊn, -z, -ɪŋ, -d
AM ˌən'kraʊn, -z, -ɪŋ, -d

uncrumpled
BR (ˌ)ʌnˈkrʌmpld,
(ˌ)ʌŋˈkrʌmpld
AM ˌən'krʌmpəld

uncrushable
BR (ˌ)ʌnˈkrʌʃəbl,
(ˌ)ʌŋˈkrʌʃəbl
AM ˌən'krʌʃəbəl

uncrushed
BR (ˌ)ʌnˈkrʌʃt,
(ˌ)ʌŋˈkrʌʃt
AM ˌən'krʌʃt

UNCTAD
BR ˈʌŋktad
AM 'əŋkˌtæd

unction
BR ˈʌŋ(k)ʃn, -z
AM 'əŋkʃən, -z

unctuous
BR ˈʌŋ(k)tjʊəs,
ʌŋ(k)tʃʊəs
AM 'əŋ(k)tʃ(əw)əs

unctuously
BR ˈʌŋ(k)tjʊəsli,
ʌŋ(k)tʃʊəsli
AM 'əŋ(k)tʃ(əw)əsli

unctuousness
BR ˈʌŋ(k)tjʊəsnəs,
ʌŋ(k)tʃʊəsnəs
AM 'əŋ(k)tʃ(əw)əsnəs

unculled
BR ˌʌnˈkʌld, ˌʌŋˈkʌld
AM ˌən'kəld

uncultivated
BR (ˌ)ʌnˈkʌltɪveɪtɪd,
(ˌ)ʌŋˈkʌltɪveɪtɪd
AM ˌən'kəltə,veɪtɪd

uncultured
BR (ˌ)ʌnˈkʌltʃəd,
(ˌ)ʌŋˈkʌltʃəd
AM ˌən'kəltʃərd

uncurb
BR ˌʌnˈkɜːb, ˌʌŋˈkɜːb,
-z, -ɪŋ, -d
AM ˌən'kərb, -z, -ɪŋ, -d

uncured
BR ˌʌnˈkjʊəd,
ˌʌŋˈkjʊəd, ˌʌnˈkjɔːd,
ˌʌŋˈkjɔːd
AM ˌən'kjʊ(ə)rd

uncurl
BR ˌʌnˈkɜːl, ˌʌŋˈkɜːl, -z,
-ɪŋ, -d
AM ˌən'kərl, -z, -ɪŋ, -d

uncurtailed
BR ˌʌnkəˈteɪld,
ˌʌŋkəˈteɪld
AM ˌənkər'teɪld

uncurtained
BR ˌʌnˈkɜːtɪnd,
ˌʌŋˈkɜːtɪnd
AM ˌən'kərtnd

uncus
BR ˈʌŋkəs

AM 'əŋkəs

uncustomed
BR ˌʌnˈkʌstəmd,
ˌʌŋˈkʌstəmd
AM ˌən'kəstəmd

uncut
BR ˌʌnˈkʌt, ˌʌŋˈkʌt
AM 'ən'kət

undamaged
BR ˌʌnˈdamɪdʒd
AM ˌən'dæmɪdʒd

undamped
BR ˌʌnˈdam(p)t
AM ˌən'dæm(p)t

undated
BR ˌʌnˈdeɪtɪd
AM ˌən'deɪdɪd

undaunted
BR (ˌ)ʌnˈdɔːntɪd
AM ˌən'dɔn(t)əd,
ˌən'dan(t)əd

undauntedly
BR (ˌ)ʌnˈdɔːntɪdli
AM ˌən'dɔn(t)ədli,
ˌən'dan(t)ədli

undauntedness
BR (ˌ)ʌnˈdɔːntɪdnɪs
AM ˌən'dɔn(t)ədnəs,
ˌən'dan(t)ədnəs

undead
BR ˌʌnˈdɛd
AM ˌən'dɛd

undealt
BR ˌʌnˈdɛlt
AM ˌən'dɛlt

undecagon
BR ʌnˈdɛkəg(ə)n,
ʌnˈdɛkəgɒn, -z
AM ˌən'dɛkə,gan, -z

undeceive
BR ˌʌndɪ'siːv, -z, -ɪŋ, -d
AM ˌəndə'siv, ˌəndi'siv,
-z, -ɪŋ, -d

undecidability
BR ˌʌndɪˌsaɪdə'bɪlɪti
AM ˌəndə,saɪdə'bɪlɪdi,
ˌəndi,saɪdə'bɪlɪdi

undecidable
BR ˌʌndɪ'saɪdəbl
AM ˌəndə'saɪdəbəl,
ˌəndi'saɪdəbəl

undecided
BR ˌʌndɪ'saɪdɪd
AM ˌəndə'saɪdɪd,
ˌəndi'saɪdɪd

undecidedly
BR ˌʌndɪ'saɪdɪdli
AM ˌəndə'saɪdɪdli,
ˌəndi'saɪdɪdli

undecidedness
BR ˌʌndɪ'saɪdɪdnɪs
AM ˌəndə'saɪdɪdnɪs,
ˌəndi'saɪdɪdnɪs

undecipherable
BR ˌʌndɪ'saɪf(ə)rəbl
AM ˌəndə'saɪf(ə)rəbəl,
ˌəndi'saɪf(ə)rəbəl

undeciphered
BR ˌʌndɪ'saɪfəd,
AM ˌəndə'saɪfərd,
ˌəndi'saɪfərd

undeclared
BR ˌʌndɪ'klɛːd
AM ˌəndə'klɛ(ə)rd,
ˌəndi'klɛ(ə)rd

undecodable
BR ˌʌndɪ'kəʊdəbl
AM ˌəndə'koʊdəbəl,
ˌəndi'koʊdəbəl

undecorated
BR ˌʌnˈdɛkəreɪtɪd
AM ˌən'dɛkə,reɪdɪd

undefeated
BR ˌʌndɪ'fiːtɪd
AM ˌəndə'fidɪd,
ˌəndi'fidɪd

undefended
BR ˌʌndɪ'fɛndɪd
AM ˌəndə'fɛndəd,
ˌəndi'fɛndəd

undefiled
BR ˌʌndɪ'fʌɪld
AM ˌəndə'faɪld,
ˌəndi'faɪld

undefinable
BR ˌʌndɪ'fʌɪnəbl
AM ˌəndə'faɪnəbəl,
ˌəndi'faɪnəbəl

undefinably
BR ˌʌndɪ'fʌɪnəbli
AM ˌəndə'faɪnəbli,
ˌəndi'faɪnəbli

undefined
BR ˌʌndɪ'fʌɪnd
AM ˌəndə'faɪnd,
ˌəndi'faɪnd

undeflected
BR ˌʌndɪ'flɛktɪd
AM ˌəndə'flɛktəd,
ˌəndi'flɛktəd

undeformed
BR ˌʌndɪ'fɔːmd
AM ˌəndə'fɔ(ə)rmd,
ˌəndi'fɔ(ə)rmd

undelivered
BR ˌʌndɪ'lɪvəd
AM ˌəndə'lɪvərd,
ˌəndi'lɪvərd

undemanding
BR ˌʌndɪ'mɑːndɪŋ,
ˌʌndɪ'mandɪŋ
AM ˌəndə'mændɪŋ,
ˌəndi'mændɪŋ

undemandingness
BR ˌʌndɪ'mɑːndɪŋnɪs,
ˌʌndɪ'mandɪŋnɪs
AM ˌəndə'mændɪŋnɪs,
ˌəndi'mændɪŋnɪs

undemocratic
BR ˌʌndɛmə'kratɪk
AM ˌən,dɛmə'krædɪk

undemocratically
BR ˌʌndɛmə'kratɪkli
AM ˌən,dɛmə'krædək-
(ə)li

undemonstrable
BR ˌʌndɪ'mɒnstrəbl,
(ˌ)ʌn'dɛmənstrəbl
AM ˌəndə'manstrəbəl,
ˌəndi'manstrəbəl

undemonstrated
BR (ˌ)ʌn'dɛmənstreɪtɪd
AM ˌən'dɛmən,streɪdɪd

undemonstrative
BR ˌʌndɪ'mɒnstrətɪv
AM ˌəndə'manstrədɪv,
ˌəndi'manstrədɪv

undemonstratively
BR ˌʌndɪ'mɒnstrətɪvli
AM ˌəndə'manstrədɪvli,
ˌəndi'manstrədɪvli

**undemonstrative-
ness**
BR ˌʌndɪ'mɒnstrətɪvnɪs
AM ˌəndə'manstrədɪv-
nɪs,
ˌəndi'manstrədɪvnɪs

undeniable
BR ˌʌndɪ'nʌɪəbl
AM ˌəndə'naɪəbəl,
ˌəndi'naɪəbəl

undeniableness
BR ˌʌndɪ'nʌɪəblnəs
AM ˌəndə'naɪəbəlnəs,
ˌəndi'naɪəbəlnəs

undeniably
BR ˌʌndɪ'nʌɪəbli
AM ˌəndə'naɪəbli,
ˌəndi'naɪəbli

undenied
BR ˌʌndɪ'nʌɪd
AM ˌəndə'naɪd,
ˌəndi'naɪd

undenominational
BR ˌʌndɪ,nɒmɪ'neɪʃn(ə)l,
ˌʌndɪ,nɒmɪ'neɪʃən(ə)l
AM ˌəndə,namə'neɪʃ(ə)nəl,
ˌəndi,namə'neɪʃ(ə)nəl

undented
BR (ˌ)ʌn'dɛntɪd
AM ˌən'dɛn(t)əd

undependable
BR ˌʌndɪ'pɛndəbl
AM ˌəndə'pɛndəbəl,
ˌəndi'pɛndəbəl

under
BR 'ʌndə(r)
AM 'əndər

underachieve
BR ˌʌnd(ə)rə'tʃiːv, -z,
-ɪŋ, -d
AM ˌəndərə'tʃiv, -z, -ɪŋ,
-d

underachievement
BR ˌʌnd(ə)rə'tʃiːvm(ə)nt
AM ˌəndərə'tʃivmənt

underachiever
BR ˌʌnd(ə)rə'tʃiːvə(r),
-z
AM ˌəndərə'tʃivər, -z

underact
BR ˌʌndər'akt, -s, -ɪŋ,
-ɪd

AM ˌəndər'æk|(t), -(t)s,
-tɪŋ, -təd
under-age
BR ˌʌndər'eɪdʒ
AM ˈəndər'eɪdʒ
underappreciated
BR ˌʌnd(ə)rə'priːʃeɪtɪd
AM ˌəndərə'priʃiˌeɪdɪd
underarm
BR ˈʌndərɑːm
AM ˈəndərˌɑrm
underbelly
BR ˈʌndəˌbeli
AM ˈəndərˌbeli
underbid
BR ˌʌndə'bɪd, -z, -ɪŋ
AM ˌəndər'bɪd, -z, -ɪŋ
underbidder
BR ˌʌndə'bɪdə(r), -z
AM ˈəndər'bɪdər, -z
underblanket
BR ˈʌndəˌblaŋkɪt, -s
AM ˈəndərˌblæŋkət, -s
underbody
BR ˈʌndəˌbɒd|i, -ɪz
AM ˈəndərˌbɑdi, -z
underbred
BR ˌʌndə'brɛd
AM ˌəndər'brɛd
underbrush
BR ˈʌndəbrʌʃ
AM ˈəndərˌbrəʃ
undercapacity
BR ˌʌndəkə'pasɪti
AM ˈəndərkə'pæsədi
undercapitalised
BR ˌʌndə'kapɪtəlʌɪzd,
ˌʌndə'kapɪtʃlʌɪzd
AM ˈəndər'kæpədlˌaɪzd
undercapitalized
BR ˌʌndə'kapɪtəlʌɪzd,
ˌʌndə'kapɪtʃlʌɪzd
AM ˈəndər'kæpədlˌaɪzd
undercarriage
BR ˈʌndəˌkarɪdʒ
AM ˈəndərˌkɛrɪdʒ
undercart
BR ˈʌndəkɑːt, -s
AM ˈəndərˌkɑrt, -s
undercharge
BR ˌʌndə'tʃɑːdʒ, -ɪz,
-ɪŋ, -d
AM ˈəndər'tʃɑrdʒ, -əz,
-ɪŋ, -d
underclass
BR ˈʌndəklɑːs,
ˈʌndəklas, -ɪz
AM ˈəndərˌklæs, -əz
underclay
BR ˈʌndəkleɪ
AM ˈəndərˌkleɪ
undercliff
BR ˈʌndəklɪf, -s
AM ˈəndərˌklɪf, -s
underclothes
BR ˈʌndəkləʊ(ð)z
AM ˈəndərˌkloʊ(ð)z

underclothing
BR ˈʌndəˌkləʊðɪŋ
AM ˈəndərˌkloʊðɪŋ
undercoat
BR ˈʌndəkəʊt, -s, -ɪŋ,
-ɪd
AM ˈəndərˌkoʊ|t, -ts,
-dɪŋ, -dəd
underconsumption
BR ˌʌndəkən'sʌm(p)ʃn
AM ˈəndərkən'səmpʃən
**underconsump-
tionist**
BR ˌʌndəkən'sʌm(p)-
ʃnɪst,
ˌʌndəkən'sʌm(p)ʃənˌɪst,
-s
AM ˈəndərkən'səmp-
ʃənəst, -s
undercook
BR ˌʌndə'kʊk, -s, -ɪŋ, -t
AM ˈəndərˌkʊk, -s, -ɪŋ, -t
undercover
BR ˌʌndə'kʌvə(r)
AM ˈəndər'kəvər
undercroft
BR ˈʌndəkrɒft, -s
AM ˈəndərˌkrɔft,
ˈəndərˌkraft, -s
undercurrent
BR ˈʌndəˌkʌrənt,
ˈʌndəˌkʌrn̩t, -s
AM ˈəndərˌkərənt, -s
undercut¹
noun
BR ˈʌndəkʌt, -s
AM ˈəndərˌkət, -s
undercut²
verb
BR ˌʌndə'kʌt, -s, -ɪŋ
AM ˈəndər'kə|t, -ts, -dɪŋ
underdeveloped
BR ˌʌndədɪ'vɛləpt
AM ˈəndərdə'vɛləpt,
ˌəndərdi'vɛləpt
underdevelopment
BR ˌʌndədɪ'vɛləpm(ə)nt
AM ˈəndərdə'vɛləpmənt,
ˌəndərdi'vɛləpmənt
underdid
BR ˌʌndə'dɪd
AM ˈəndər'dɪd
underdo
BR ˌʌndə'duː, -ɪŋ
AM ˈəndər'duː, -ɪŋ
underdoes
BR ˌʌndə'dʌz
AM ˈəndər'dəz
underdog
BR ˈʌndədɒg, -z
AM ˈəndərˌdɔg,
ˈəndərˌdɑg, -z
underdone
BR ˌʌndə'dʌn
AM ˈəndər'dən
underdrainage
BR ˌʌndə'dreɪnɪdʒ
AM ˈəndər'dreɪnɪdʒ

underdrawers
plural noun
BR ˈʌndədrɔːz
AM ˈəndərˌdrɔ(ə)rz
underdrawing
BR ˈʌndəˌdrɔː(r)ɪŋ
AM ˈəndərˌdrɔɪŋ
underdress
BR ˌʌndə'drɛs, -ɪz, -ɪŋ,
-t
AM ˈəndər'drɛs, -əz, -ɪŋ,
-t
undereducated
BR ˌʌndər'ɛdjʊkeɪtɪd,
ˌʌndər'ɛdʒʊkeɪtɪd
AM ˈəndər'ɛdʒə,keɪdɪd
underemphases
BR ˌʌndər'ɛmfəsiːz
AM ˈəndər'ɛmfə,siz
underemphasis
BR ˌʌndər'ɛmfəsɪs
AM ˈəndər'ɛmfəsəs
underemphasise
BR ˌʌndər'ɛmfəsʌɪz,
-ɪz, -ɪŋ, -d
AM ˈəndər'ɛmfə,saɪz,
-ɪz, -ɪŋ, -d
underemphasize
BR ˌʌndər'ɛmfəsʌɪz,
-ɪz, -ɪŋ, -d
AM ˈəndər'ɛmfə,saɪz,
-ɪz, -ɪŋ, -d
underemployed
BR ˌʌnd(ə)rɪm'plɔɪd
AM ˈəndərɛm'plɔɪd,
ˌəndərəm'plɔɪd,
ˌəndərɪm'plɔɪd
underemployment
BR ˌʌnd(ə)rɪm'plɔɪ-
m(ə)nt
AM ˈəndərɛm'plɔɪmənt,
ˌəndərəm'plɔɪmənt,
ˌəndərɪm'plɔɪmənt
underequipped
BR ˌʌnd(ə)rɪ'kwɪpt
AM ˈəndərə'kwɪpt,
ˌəndər,i'kwɪpt
underestimate¹
noun
BR ˌʌndər'ɛstɪmət, -s
AM ˈəndər'ɛstəmət, -s
underestimate²
verb
BR ˌʌndər'ɛstɪmeɪt, -s,
-ɪŋ, -ɪd
AM ˈəndər'ɛstə,meɪ|t,
-ts, -dɪŋ, -dɪd
underestimation
BR ˌʌndər,ɛstɪ'meɪʃn
AM ˈəndər,ɛstə'meɪʃən
underexploited
BR ˌʌnd(ə)rɪks'plɔɪtɪd
AM ˈəndərək'splɔɪdɪd
underexpose
BR ˌʌnd(ə)rɪk'spəʊz,
-ɪz, -ɪŋ, -d
AM ˈəndərək'spoʊz,
-əz, -ɪŋ, -d

underexposure
BR ˌʌnd(ə)rɪk'spəʊʒə(r),
-z
AM ˈəndərək'spoʊʒər,
-z
underfed
BR ˌʌndə'fɛd
AM ˈəndər'fɛd
underfelt
BR ˈʌndəfɛlt
AM ˈəndərˌfɛlt
underfinanced
BR ˌʌndəfʌɪ'nanst,
ˌʌndəfɪ'nanst
AM ˈəndər'faɪ,nænst,
ˌəndərfə'nænst
underfinancing
BR ˌʌndəfʌɪ'nansɪŋ,
ˌʌndəfɪ'nansɪŋ
AM ˈəndər'faɪ,nænsɪŋ,
ˌəndərfə'nænsɪŋ
under-fives
BR ˌʌndə'fʌɪvz,
ˈʌndəfʌɪvz
AM ˈəndərˌfaɪvz
underfloor
BR ˌʌndə'flɔː(r)
AM ˈəndərˌflɔ(ə)r
underflooring
BR ˈʌndəˌflɔːrɪŋ
AM ˈəndərˌflɔrɪŋ
underflow
BR ˈʌndəfləʊ, -z
AM ˈəndərˌfloʊ, -z
underfoot
BR ˌʌndə'fʊt
AM ˈəndər'fʊt
underframe
BR ˈʌndəfreɪm, -z
AM ˈəndərˌfreɪm, -z
underfunded
BR ˌʌndə'fʌndɪd
AM ˈəndər'fəndəd
underfunding
BR ˌʌndə'fʌndɪŋ
AM ˈəndər'fəndɪŋ
underfur
BR ˈʌndəfəː(r)
AM ˈəndərˌfər
under-gardener
BR ˈʌndəˌgɑːdnə(r), -z
AM ˈəndərˌgɑrdnər,
ˈəndərˌgɑrdnər, -z
undergarment
BR ˈʌndəˌgɑːm(ə)nt, -s
AM ˈəndərˌgɑrmənt, -s
undergird
BR ˌʌndə'gəːd, -z, -ɪŋ,
-ɪd
AM ˈəndər'gərd, -z, -ɪŋ,
-əd
underglaze
BR ˈʌndəgleɪz
AM ˈəndərˌgleɪz
undergo
BR ˌʌndə'gəʊ, -z, -ɪŋ
AM ˈəndər'goʊ, -z, -ɪŋ

undergone
BR ˌʌndəˈɡɒn
AM ˌəndərˈɡɔːn,
ˌəndərˈɡɑːn

undergrad
BR ˈʌndəɡræd,
ˌʌndəˈɡræd, -z
AM ˈəndərˌɡræd, -z

undergraduate
BR ˌʌndəˈɡrædʒuət,
ˌʌndəˈɡrædjuət, -s
AM ˌəndərˈɡrædʒəwət,
-s

underground¹
adjective
BR ˌʌndəˈɡraʊnd,
ˈʌndəɡraʊnd
AM ˈəndə(r)ˌɡraʊnd

underground²
adverb
BR ˌʌndəˈɡraʊnd,
ˈʌndəɡraʊnd
AM ˌəndərˈɡraʊnd

underground³
noun
BR ˈʌndəɡraʊnd
AM ˈəndərˌɡraʊnd

undergrowth
BR ˈʌndəɡrəʊθ
AM ˈəndərˌɡroʊθ

underhand
BR ˌʌndəˈhænd
AM ˈəndərˌ(h)ænd

underhanded
BR ˌʌndəˈhændɪd
AM ˌəndərˈhæn(d)əd

underhandedly
BR ˌʌndəˈhændɪdli
AM ˌəndərˈhæn(d)ədli

underhandedness
BR ˌʌndəˈhændɪdnɪs
AM ˌəndərˈhæn(d)ədnəs

underheated
BR ˌʌndəˈhiːtɪd
AM ˌəndərˈhidɪd

Underhill
BR ˈʌndəhɪl
AM ˈəndərˌ(h)ɪl

underhung
BR ˌʌndəˈhʌŋ
AM ˈəndərˈhəŋ

underlain
BR ˌʌndəˈleɪn
AM ˌəndərˈleɪn

underlay¹
noun
BR ˈʌndəleɪ, -z
AM ˈəndərˌleɪ, -z

underlay²
verb
BR ˌʌndəˈleɪ, -z, -ɪŋ
AM ˌəndərˈleɪ, -z, -ɪŋ, -d

underlease¹
noun
BR ˈʌndəliːs, -ɪz
AM ˈəndərˌlis, -ɪz

underlease²
verb
BR ˌʌndəˈliːs, -ɪz, -ɪŋ, -t
AM ˌəndərˈlis, -ɪz, -ɪŋ, -t

underlet
BR ˌʌndəˈlɛt, -s, -ɪŋ
AM ˌəndərˈlɛ|t, -ts, -dɪŋ

underlie
BR ˌʌndəˈlaɪ, -z, -ɪŋ
AM ˌəndərˈlaɪ, -z, -ɪŋ

underline¹
noun
BR ˈʌndəlaɪn, -z
AM ˈəndərˌlaɪn, -z

underline²
verb
BR ˌʌndəˈlaɪn, -z, -ɪŋ, -d
AM ˌəndərˈlaɪn, -z, -ɪŋ, -d

underlinen
BR ˈʌndəˌlɪnɪn
AM ˈəndərˌlɪnɪn

underling
BR ˈʌndəlɪŋ, -z
AM ˈəndərlɪŋ, -z

underlip
BR ˈʌndəlɪp, -s
AM ˈəndərˌlɪp, -s

underlit
BR ˌʌndəˈlɪt
AM ˌəndərˈlɪt

under-manager
BR ˈʌndəˌmanɪdʒə(r), -z
AM ˈəndərˌmænədʒər, -z

undermanned
BR ˌʌndəˈmand
AM ˌəndərˈmænd

undermanning
BR ˌʌndəˈmanɪŋ
AM ˌəndərˈmænɪŋ

undermentioned
BR ˌʌndəˈmɛnʃnd
AM ˌəndərˈmɛn(t)ʃənd

undermine
BR ˌʌndəˈmaɪn, -z, -ɪŋ, -d
AM ˌəndərˈmaɪn, -z, -ɪŋ, -d

underminer
BR ˌʌndəˈmaɪnə(r), -z
AM ˈəndərˌmaɪnər, -z

underminingly
BR ˌʌndəˈmaɪnɪŋli
AM ˌəndərˈmaɪnɪŋli

undermost
BR ˈʌndəməʊst
AM ˈəndərˌmoʊst

underneath
BR ˌʌndəˈniːθ
AM ˌəndərˈniθ

undernourished
BR ˌʌndəˈnʌrɪʃt
AM ˌəndərˈnɜrɪʃt

undernourishment
BR ˌʌndəˈnʌrɪʃm(ə)nt

underlease²
AM ˌəndərˈnɜrɪʃmənt,
ˌəndərˈnʊrɪʃmənt

under-occupancy
BR ˌʌndərˈɒkjʊp(ə)nsi
AM ˌəndərˈɑkjəpənsi

under-occupy
BR ˌʌndərˈɒkjʊpaɪ, -z, -ɪŋ, -d
AM ˌəndərˈɑkjəˌpaɪ, -z, -ɪŋ, -d

underpaid
BR ˌʌndəˈpeɪd
AM ˌəndərˈpeɪd

underpainting
BR ˌʌndəˌpeɪntɪŋ
AM ˌəndərˌpeɪn(t)ɪŋ

underpants
BR ˈʌndəpan(t)s
AM ˈəndərˌpæn(t)s

underpart
BR ˈʌndəpɑːt, -s
AM ˈəndərˌpɑrt, -s

underpass
BR ˈʌndəpɑːs, ˈʌndəpas, -ɪz
AM ˈəndərˌpæs, -əz

underpay
BR ˌʌndəˈpeɪ, -z, -ɪŋ, -d
AM ˌəndərˈpeɪ, -z, -ɪŋ, -d

underpayment
BR ˌʌndəˈpeɪm(ə)nt, -s
AM ˌəndərˈpeɪmənt, -s

underperform
BR ˌʌndəpəˈfɔːm, -z, -ɪŋ, -d
AM ˌəndərpərˈfɔ(ə)rm, -z, -ɪŋ, -d

underperformance
BR ˌʌndəpəˈfɔːməns
AM ˌəndərpərˈfɔrməns

underpin
BR ˌʌndəˈpɪn, -z, -ɪŋ, -d
AM ˌəndərˈpɪn, -z, -ɪŋ, -d

underpinning
BR ˌʌndəˈpɪnɪŋ, ˈʌndəˌpɪnɪŋ, -z
AM ˈəndərˌpɪnɪŋ, -z

underplant
BR ˌʌndəˈplɑːnt, ˌʌndəˈplant, -s, -ɪŋ, -ɪd
AM ˌəndərˈplæn|t, -ts, -(t)ɪŋ, -(t)əd

underplay
verb
BR ˌʌndəˈpleɪ, -z, -ɪŋ, -d
AM ˌəndərˈpleɪ, -z, -ɪŋ, -d

underplot
BR ˈʌndəplɒt, -s
AM ˈəndərˌplɑt, -s

underpopulated
BR ˌʌndəˈpɒpjəleɪtɪd
AM ˌəndərˈpɑpjəˌleɪdɪd

underpowered
BR ˌʌndəˈpaʊəd
AM ˌəndərˈpaʊərd

under-prepared
BR ˌʌndəprɪˈpeːd
AM ˌəndərprəˈpɛ(ə)rd

underprice
BR ˌʌndəˈpraɪs, -ɪz, -ɪŋ, -t
AM ˌəndərˈpraɪs, -ɪz, -ɪŋ, -t

underpriced
BR ˌʌndəˈpraɪst
AM ˌəndərˈpraɪst

underprivileged
BR ˌʌndəˈprɪvɪlɪdʒd
AM ˌəndərˈprɪvɪlɪdʒd

underproduction
BR ˌʌndəprəˈdʌkʃn
AM ˌəndərprəˈdəkʃən

underproof
BR ˌʌndəˈpruːf
AM ˌəndərˈpruf

underprop
BR ˌʌndəˈprɒp, -s, -ɪŋ, -t
AM ˌəndərˈprɑp, -s, -ɪŋ, -t

under-provision
BR ˌʌndəprəˈvɪʒn
AM ˌəndərprəˈvɪʒən

underquote
BR ˌʌndəˈkwəʊt, -s, -ɪŋ, -ɪd
AM ˌəndərˈkwoʊ|t, -ts, -dɪŋ, -dəd

underrate
BR ˌʌndəˈreɪt, -s, -ɪŋ, -ɪd
AM ˌəndə(r)ˈreɪ|t, -ts, -dɪŋ, -dɪd

under-rehearsed
BR ˌʌndərɪˈhɜːst
AM ˌəndə(r)rəˈhɜrst

under-report
BR ˌʌndərɪˈpɔːt, -s, -ɪŋ, -ɪd
AM ˌəndə(r)rəˈpɔ(ə)rt, -ts, -ˈpɔrdɪŋ, -ˈpɔrdəd

under-represented
BR ˌʌndəˌreprɪˈzentɪd
AM ˌəndə(r)ˌreprəˈzɛn(t)əd

under-resourced
BR ˌʌndərɪˈsɔːst
AM ˌəndə(r)ˈriˌsɔ(ə)rst, ˌəndə(r)rəˈsɔ(ə)rst

underripe
BR ˌʌndəˈrʌɪp
AM ˌəndə(r)ˈraɪp

underscore¹
noun
BR ˈʌndəskɔː(r), -z
AM ˈəndərˌskɔ(ə)r, -z

underscore²
verb
BR ˌʌndəˈskɔː(r), -z, -ɪŋ, -d
AM ˌəndərˈskɔ(ə)r, -z, -ɪŋ, -d

undersea
BR ˌʌndəˈsiː
AM ˌəndərˈsi

underseal¹
noun
BR ˈʌndəsiːl
AM ˈəndərˌsil

underseal²
verb
BR ˈʌndəˈsiːl, -z, -ɪŋ, -d
AM ˈʌndərˌsil, -z, -ɪŋ, -d

undersecretary
BR ˈʌndəˈsɛktrɪt(ə)r|i,
ˌʌndəˈsɛkrɪtər|i, -iz
AM ˈəndərˈsekrəˌtɛri,
-z

undersell
BR ˌʌndəˈsɛl, -z, -ɪŋ
AM ˈəndərˈsɛl, -z, -ɪŋ

underset
BR ˌʌndəˈsɛt, -s, -ɪŋ
AM ˈəndərˈsɛt, -ts, -dɪŋ

undersexed
BR ˌʌndəˈsɛkst
AM ˈəndərˈsɛkst

undersheet
BR ˈʌndəʃiːt, -s
AM ˈəndərˌʃit, -s

under-sheriff
BR ˌʌndəˌʃɛrɪf, -s
AM ˈəndərˌʃɛrəf, -s

undershirt
BR ˈʌndəʃɜːt, -s
AM ˈəndərˌʃɜrt, -s

undershoot
BR ˌʌndəˈʃuːt, -s, -ɪŋ
AM ˈəndərˈʃuːt, -ts, -dɪŋ

undershorts
BR ˈʌndəʃɔːts
AM ˈəndərˌʃɔ(ə)rts

undershot
BR ˌʌndəˈʃɒt
AM ˈəndərˈʃɑt

undershrub
BR ˈʌndəʃrʌb, -z
AM ˈəndərˌʃrəb, -z

underside
BR ˈʌndəsʌɪd, -z
AM ˈəndərˌsaid, -z

undersign
BR ˌʌndəˈsʌɪn, -z, -ɪŋ, -d
AM ˈəndərˈsain, -z, -ɪŋ, -d

undersigned
noun
BR ˌʌndəˈsʌɪnd,
ˈʌndəsʌɪnd
AM ˈəndərˌsaind

undersize
BR ˌʌndəˈsʌɪz
AM ˈəndərˈsaiz

undersized
BR ˌʌndəˈsʌɪzd
AM ˈəndərˈsaizd

underskirt
BR ˈʌndəskɜːt, -s
AM ˈəndərˌskɜrt, -s

underslung
BR ˌʌndəˈslʌŋ
AM ˈəndərˌslʌŋ

undersold
BR ˌʌndəˈsəʊld
AM ˈəndərˈsoʊld

undersow
BR ˌʌndəˈsəʊ, -z, -ɪŋ
AM ˈəndərˈsoʊ, -z, -ɪŋ

undersown
BR ˌʌndəˈsəʊn
AM ˈəndərˈsoʊn

underspend
BR ˌʌndəˈspɛnd, -z, -ɪŋ
AM ˈəndərˈspɛnd, -z,
-ɪŋ

underspent
BR ˌʌndəˈspɛnt
AM ˈəndərˈspɛnt

understaffed
BR ˌʌndəˈstɑːft,
ˌʌndəˈstaft
AM ˈəndərˈstæft

understaffing
BR ˌʌndəˈstɑːfɪŋ,
ˌʌndəˈstafɪŋ
AM ˈəndərˈstæfɪŋ

understairs
BR ˌʌndəˈstɛːz
AM ˈəndərˈstɛrz

understand
BR ˌʌndəˈstand, -z, -ɪŋ
AM ˈəndərˈstæn|d,
-(d)z, -dɪŋ

understandability
BR ˌʌndəˌstandəˈbɪlɪti
AM ˈəndərˌstændəˈbɪlɪdi

understandable
BR ˌʌndəˈstandəbl
AM ˈəndərˈstændəbəl

understandably
BR ˌʌndəˈstandəbli
AM ˈəndərˈstændəbli

understander
BR ˌʌndəˈstandə(r), -z
AM ˈəndərˈstændər, -z

understanding
BR ˌʌndəˈstandɪŋ, -z
AM ˈəndərˈstændɪŋ, -z

understandingly
BR ˌʌndəˈstandɪŋli
AM ˈəndərˈstændɪŋli

understate
BR ˌʌndəˈsteɪt, -s, -ɪŋ,
-ɪd
AM ˈəndərˈsteɪ|t, -ts,
-dɪŋ, -dɪd

understatement
BR ˌʌndəˈsteɪtm(ə)nt,
ˈʌndəˌsteɪtm(ə)nt, -s
AM ˈəndərˈsteɪtmənt,
-s

understater
BR ˌʌndəˈsteɪtə(r), -z
AM ˈəndərˈsteɪdər, -z

understeer¹
noun
BR ˈʌndəstɪə(r)
AM ˈəndərˌstɪ(ə)r

understeer²
verb
BR ˌʌndəˈstɪə(r), -z, -ɪŋ,
-d
AM ˈəndərˈstɪ(ə)r, -z,
-ɪŋ, -d

understood
BR ˌʌndəˈstʊd
AM ˈəndərˈstʊd

understorey
BR ˈʌndəˌstɔːr|i, -iz
AM ˈəndərˌstɔri, -z

understrapper
BR ˈʌndəˌstrapə(r), -z
AM ˈəndərˌstræpər, -z

under-strength
BR ˌʌndəˈstrɛŋ(k)θ
AM ˈəndərˈstrɛŋθ

understudy
BR ˈʌndəˌstʌd|i, -iz,
-ɪŋ, -ɪd
AM ˈəndərˌstədi, -z, -ɪŋ,
-d

undersubscribed
BR ˌʌndəsəbˈskrʌɪbd
AM ˈəndərsəbˈskraibd

undersurface
BR ˈʌndəˌsəːfɪs, -ɪz
AM ˈəndərˌsərfəs, -əz

undertake
BR ˌʌndəˈteɪk, -s, -ɪŋ
AM ˈəndərˈteɪk, -s, -ɪŋ

undertaker¹
*person who arranges
funerals*
BR ˈʌndəˌteɪkə(r), -z
AM ˈəndərˌteɪkər, -z

undertaker²
*person who
undertakes
something*
BR ˌʌndəˈteɪkə(r), -z
AM ˈəndərˈteɪkər, -z

undertaking¹
*arranging of
funerals*
BR ˈʌndəˌteɪkɪŋ
AM ˈəndərˌteɪkɪŋ

undertaking²
something to be done
BR ˌʌndəˈteɪkɪŋ,
ˈʌndəˌteɪkɪŋ, -z
AM ˈəndərˈteɪkɪŋ, -z

undertenancy
BR ˈʌndəˌtɛnəns|i,
ˈʌndəˌtɛnəns|i, -iz
AM ˈəndərˌtɛnənsi, -z

undertenant
BR ˈʌndəˌtɛnənt,
ˈʌndəˌtɛnənt, -s
AM ˈəndərˌtɛnənt, -s

**under-the-
counter**
BR ˌʌndəðəˈkaʊntə(r)
AM ˈəndərðəˈkaʊn(t)ər

underthings
BR ˈʌndəθɪŋz
AM ˈəndərˌθɪŋz

undertint
BR ˈʌndətɪnt, -s
AM ˈəndərˌtɪnt, -s

undertone
BR ˈʌndətəʊn, -z
AM ˈəndərˌtoʊn, -z

undertook
BR ˌʌndəˈtʊk
AM ˈəndərˈtʊk

undertow
BR ˈʌndətəʊ, -z
AM ˈəndərˌtoʊ, -z

undertrained
BR ˌʌndəˈtreɪnd
AM ˈəndərˈtreɪnd

undertrick
BR ˈʌndətrɪk, -s
AM ˈəndərˌtrɪk, -s

under-use
BR ˌʌndəˈjuːz, -ɪz, -ɪŋ, -d
AM ˈəndərˈjuz, -əz, -ɪŋ,
-d

underused
BR ˌʌndəˈjuːzd
AM ˈəndərˈjuzd

under-utilisation
BR ˌʌndəˌjuːtɪlʌɪˈzeɪʃn,
ˌʌndəˌjuːtlʌɪˈzeɪʃn
AM ˈəndərˌjudləˈzeɪʃən,
ˈəndərˌjudlʌɪˈzeɪʃən

under-utilise
BR ˌʌndəˈjuːtɪlʌɪz,
ˌʌndəˈjuːtlʌɪz, -ɪz, -ɪŋ,
-d
AM ˈəndərˈjudlˌaɪz, -ɪz,
-ɪŋ, -d

under-utilization
BR ˌʌndəˌjuːtɪlʌɪˈzeɪʃn,
ˌʌndəˌjuːtlʌɪˈzeɪʃn
AM ˈəndərˌjudləˈzeɪʃən,
ˈəndərˌjudlʌɪˈzeɪʃən

under-utilize
BR ˌʌndəˈjuːtɪlʌɪz,
ˌʌndəˈjuːtlʌɪz, -ɪz, -ɪŋ,
-d
AM ˈəndərˈjudlˌaɪz, -ɪz,
-ɪŋ, -d

undervaluation
BR ˌʌndəˌvaljuˈeɪʃn, -z
AM ˈəndərˌvæljəˈweɪʃən,
-z

undervalue
BR ˌʌndəˈvalju|ː, -uːz,
-ʊɪŋ, -uːd
AM ˈəndərˈvæl|ju, -juz,
-jəwɪŋ, -jud

undervest
BR ˈʌndəvɛst, -s
AM ˈəndərˌvɛst, -s

underwater
BR ˌʌndəˈwɔːtə(r)
AM ˈəndərˈwɔdər,
ˈəndərˈwɑdər

underwear
BR ˈʌndəwɛː(r)
AM ˈəndərˌwɛ(ə)r

underweight
BR ˌʌndəˈweɪt

AM ˌəndər'weɪt

underwent
BR ˌʌndə'wɛnt
AM ˌəndər'wɛnt

underwhelm
BR ˌʌndə'wɛlm, -z, -ɪŋ, -d
AM ˌəndər'(h)wɛlm, -z, -ɪŋ, -d

underwing
BR 'ʌndəwɪŋ, -z
AM 'əndər,wɪŋ, -z

underwire
BR 'ʌndə,wʌɪə(r), -z
AM 'əndər,waɪ(ə)r, -z

underwired
BR 'ʌndəwʌɪəd
AM 'əndər,waɪ(ə)rd

underwood
BR 'ʌndəwʊd, -z
AM 'əndər,wʊd, -z

underwork
BR 'ʌndəwəːk, -s, -ɪŋ, -t
AM 'əndər'wərk, -s, -ɪŋ, -t

underworld
BR 'ʌndəwəːld
AM 'əndər,wərld

underwrite
BR ˌʌndə'rʌɪt, 'ʌndərʌɪt, -s, -ɪŋ
AM ˌəndə(r)'raɪ|t, -ts, -dɪŋ

underwriter
BR 'ʌndə,rʌɪtə(r), -z
AM 'əndə(r),raɪdər, -z

underwritten
BR ˌʌndə'rɪtn, 'ʌndə,rɪtn
AM ˌəndə(r)'rɪtn

undescended
BR ˌʌndɪ'sɛndəd
AM ˌəndə'sɛndəd, ˌəndi'sɛndəd

undescribed
BR ˌʌndɪ'skrʌɪbd
AM ˌəndə'skraɪbd, ˌəndi'skraɪbd

undeserved
BR ˌʌndɪ'zəːvd
AM ˌəndə'zərvd, ˌəndi'zərvd

undeservedly
BR ˌʌndɪ'zəːvɪdli
AM ˌəndə'zərvədli, ˌəndi'zərvədli

undeservedness
BR ˌʌndɪ'zəːvɪdnɪs
AM ˌəndə'zərvədnəs, ˌəndi'zərvədnəs

undeserving
BR ˌʌndɪ'zəːvɪŋ
AM ˌəndə'zərvɪŋ, ˌəndi'zərvɪŋ

undeservingly
BR ˌʌndɪ'zəːvɪŋli
AM ˌəndə'zərvɪŋli, ˌəndi'zərvɪŋli

undesignated
BR (ˌ)ʌn'dɛzɪgneɪtɪd
AM ˌən'dɛzɪg,neɪdɪd

undesigned
BR ˌʌndɪ'zʌɪnd
AM ˌəndə'zaɪnd, ˌəndi'zaɪnd

undesignedly
BR ˌʌndɪ'zʌɪnɪdli
AM ˌəndə'zaɪnɪdli, ˌəndi'zaɪnɪdli

undesirability
BR ˌʌndɪ,zʌɪərə'bɪlɪti
AM ˌəndə,zaɪ(ə)rə'bɪlɪdi, ˌəndi,zaɪ(ə)rə'bɪlɪdi

undesirable
BR ˌʌndɪ'zʌɪərəbl
AM ˌəndə'zaɪ(ə)rəbəl, ˌəndi'zaɪ(ə)rəbəl

undesirableness
BR ˌʌndɪ'zʌɪərəblnəs
AM ˌəndə'zaɪ(ə)rəbəlnəs, ˌəndi'zaɪ(ə)rəbəlnəs

undesirably
BR ˌʌndɪ'zʌɪərəbli
AM ˌəndə'zaɪ(ə)rəbli, ˌəndi'zaɪ(ə)rəbli

undesired
BR ˌʌndɪ'zʌɪəd
AM ˌəndə'zaɪ(ə)rd, ˌəndi'zaɪ(ə)rd

undesirous
BR ˌʌndɪ'zʌɪərəs
AM ˌəndə'zaɪ(ə)rəs

undetectability
BR ˌʌndɪ,tɛktə'bɪlɪti
AM ˌəndə,tɛktə'bɪlɪdi, ˌəndi,tɛktə'bɪlɪdi

undetectable
BR ˌʌndɪ'tɛktəbl
AM ˌəndə'tɛktəbəl, ˌəndi'tɛktəbəl

undetectably
BR ˌʌndɪ'tɛktəbli
AM ˌəndə'tɛktəbli, ˌəndi'tɛktəbli

undetected
BR ˌʌndɪ'tɛktɪd
AM ˌəndə'tɛktəd, ˌəndi'tɛktəd

undetermined
BR ˌʌndɪ'təːmɪnd
AM ˌəndə'tərmənd, ˌəndi'tərmənd

undeterred
BR ˌʌndɪ'təːd
AM ˌəndə'tərd, ˌəndi'tərd

undeveloped
BR ˌʌndɪ'vɛləpt
AM ˌəndə'vɛləpt, ˌəndi'vɛləpt

undeviating
BR (ˌ)ʌn'diːvɪeɪtɪŋ
AM ˌən'divi,eɪdɪŋ

undeviatingly
BR (ˌ)ʌn'diːvɪeɪtɪŋli
AM ˌən'divi,eɪdɪŋli

undiagnosed
BR (ˌ)ʌn'dʌɪəgnəʊzd, ˌʌndʌɪəg'nəʊzd
AM ˌən,daɪəg'noʊzd

undid
BR ʌn'dɪd
AM ˌən'dɪd

undies
BR 'ʌndɪz
AM 'əndiz

undifferentiated
BR ˌʌndɪfə'rɛnʃɪeɪtɪd
AM ˌən,dɪfə'rɛnʃi,eɪdɪd

undigested
BR ˌʌndʌɪ'dʒɛstɪd, ˌʌndɪ'dʒɛstɪd
AM ˌəndə'dʒɛstəd, ˌəndaɪ'dʒɛstəd

undignified
BR (ˌ)ʌn'dɪgnɪfʌɪd
AM ˌən'dɪgnə,faɪd

undiluted
BR ˌʌndʌɪ'l(j)uːtɪd, ˌʌndɪ'l(j)uːtɪd
AM ˌəndə'ludəd, ˌəndi'ludəd

undiminished
BR ˌʌndɪ'mɪnɪʃt
AM ˌəndə'mɪnɪʃt, ˌəndi'mɪnɪʃt

undimmed
BR (ˌ)ʌn'dɪmd
AM ˌən'dɪmd

undine
BR 'ʌndiːn, -z
AM 'ən,din, -z

undiplomatic
BR ˌʌndɪplə'matɪk
AM ˌən,dɪplə'mædɪk

undiplomatically
BR ˌʌndɪplə'matɪkli
AM ˌən,dɪplə'mædək(ə)li

undirected
BR ˌʌndɪ'rɛktɪd, ˌʌndʌɪ'rɛktɪd
AM ˌəndə'rɛktəd, ˌən,daɪ'rɛktəd

undiscerning
BR ˌʌndɪ'səːnɪŋ
AM ˌəndɪ'sərnɪŋ

undischarged
BR ˌʌndɪs'tʃɑːdʒd
AM ˌəndɪs'tʃɑrdʒd

undiscipline
BR ʌn'dɪsɪplɪn, -d
AM ˌən'dɪsəplən, -d

undisclosed
BR ˌʌndɪs'kləʊzd
AM ˌəndə'skloʊzd

undiscouraged
BR ˌʌndɪs'kʌrɪdʒd, ˌʌndɪ'skʌrɪdʒd
AM ˌəndə'skərədʒd

undiscoverable
BR ˌʌndɪ'skʌv(ə)rəbl
AM ˌəndə'skʌv(ə)rəbəl

undiscoverably
BR ˌʌndɪ'skʌv(ə)rəbli

AM ˌəndə'skʌv(ə)rəbli

undiscovered
BR ˌʌndɪ'skʌvəd
AM ˌəndə'skəvərd

undiscriminating
BR ˌʌndɪ'skrɪmɪneɪtɪŋ
AM ˌəndə'skrɪmə,neɪdɪŋ

undiscussed
BR ˌʌndɪ'skʌst
AM ˌəndə'skəst

undisguised
BR ˌʌndɪs'gʌɪzd
AM ˌəndɪs'gaɪzd

undisguisedly
BR ˌʌndɪs'gʌɪzɪdli
AM ˌəndɪs'gaɪzədli

undismayed
BR ˌʌndɪs'meɪd
AM ˌəndɪs'meɪd

undisposed
BR ˌʌndɪ'spəʊzd
AM ˌəndə'spoʊzd

undisputed
BR ˌʌndɪ'spjuːtɪd
AM ˌəndə'spjudəd

undissolved
BR ˌʌndɪ'zɒlvd
AM ˌəndə'zalvd

undistinguishable
BR ˌʌndɪ'stɪŋgwɪʃəbl
AM ˌəndə'stɪŋgwɪʃəbəl

undistinguished
BR ˌʌndɪ'stɪŋgwɪʃt
AM ˌəndə'stɪŋgwɪʃt

undistorted
BR ˌʌndɪ'stɔːtɪd
AM ˌəndə'stɔrdəd

undistracted
BR ˌʌndɪ'straktɪd
AM ˌəndə'stræktəd

undistributed
BR ˌʌndɪ'strɪbjʊtɪd
AM ˌəndə'strɪbjədəd

undisturbed
BR ˌʌndɪ'stəːbd
AM ˌəndə'stərbd

undivided
BR ˌʌndɪ'vʌɪdɪd
AM ˌəndə'vaɪdɪd

undivulged
BR ˌʌndʌɪ'vʌldʒd, ˌʌndɪ'vʌldʒd
AM ˌəndə'vəldʒd, ˌən,daɪ'vəldʒd

undo
BR (ˌ)ʌn'd|uː, -ʌz, -uːɪŋ
AM ˌən'd|u, -əz, -uɪŋ

undock
BR (ˌ)ʌn'dɒk, -s, -ɪŋ, -t
AM ˌən'dak, -s, -ɪŋ, -t

undocumented
BR (ˌ)ʌn'dɒkjʊməntɪd
AM ˌən'dakjə,mɛn(t)əd

undogmatic
BR ˌʌndɒg'matɪk
AM ˌən,dɒg'mædɪk, ˌən,dag'mædɪk

undomesticated
BR ˌʌndəˈmestɪkeɪtɪd
AM ˌəndəˈmestəˌkeɪdɪd

undone
BR (ˌ)ʌnˈdʌn
AM ˌənˈdən

undoubtable
BR ʌnˈdaʊtəbl
AM ˌənˈdaʊdəbəl

undoubtably
BR ʌnˈdaʊtəbli
AM ˌənˈdaʊdəbli

undoubted
BR ʌnˈdaʊtɪd
AM ˌənˈdaʊdəd

undoubtedly
BR ʌnˈdaʊtɪdli
AM ˌənˈdaʊdədli

undoubting
BR ʌnˈdaʊtɪŋ
AM ˌənˈdaʊdɪŋ

undrained
BR (ˌ)ʌnˈdreɪnd
AM ˌənˈdreɪnd

undramatic
BR ˌʌndrəˈmatɪk
AM ˌəndrəˈmædɪk

undraped
BR (ˌ)ʌnˈdreɪpt
AM ˌənˈdreɪpt

undreamed
BR (ˌ)ʌnˈdriːmd
AM ˌənˈdrimd

undreamed-of
BR (ˌ)ʌnˈdriːmdɒv
AM ˌənˈdrimdəv

undreamt
BR (ˌ)ʌnˈdrem(p)t
AM ˌənˈdremt

undreamt-of
BR (ˌ)ʌnˈdrem(p)tɒv
AM ˌənˈdremtəv

undress
BR (ˌ)ʌnˈdres, -ɪz, -ɪŋ, -t
AM ˌənˈdres, -əz, -ɪŋ, -t

undrinkable
BR (ˌ)ʌnˈdrɪŋkəbl
AM ˌənˈdrɪŋkəbəl

undrivable
BR (ˌ)ʌnˈdrʌɪvəbl
AM ˌənˈdraɪvəbəl

undriveable
BR (ˌ)ʌnˈdrʌɪvəbl
AM ˌənˈdraɪvəbəl

UNDRO
BR ˈʌndrəʊ
AM ˈən,droʊ

undue
BR ʌnˈdjuː, ˌʌnˈdʒuː
AM ˌənˈd(j)u

undulant
BR ˈʌndjʊlənt, ˈʌndʒʊlənt
AM ˈəndʒələnt, ˈəndjələnt

undulate
BR ˈʌndjʊleɪt, ˈʌndʒʊleɪt, -s, -ɪŋ, -ɪd
AM ˈəndʒəˌleɪt, ˈəndjəˌleɪt, -ts, -dɪŋ, -dɪd

undulately
BR ˈʌndjʊlətli, ˈʌndʒʊlətli
AM ˈəndʒələtli, ˈəndjələtli

undulation
BR ˌʌndjʊˈleɪʃn, ˌʌndʒʊˈleɪʃn, -z
AM ˌəndʒəˈleɪʃən, ˌəndjəˈleɪʃən, -z

undulatory
BR ˈʌndjʊlət(ə)ri, ˈʌndʒʊlət(ə)ri, ˌʌndjʊˈleɪt(ə)ri, ˌʌndʒʊˈleɪt(ə)ri
AM ˈəndʒələˌtɔri, ˈəndjələˌtɔri

unduly
BR (ˌ)ʌnˈdjuːli, (ˌ)ʌnˈdʒuːli
AM ˌənˈd(j)uli

undutiful
BR (ˌ)ʌnˈdjuːtɪf(ʊ)l, (ˌ)ʌnˈdʒuːtɪf(ʊ)l
AM ˌənˈd(j)udəfəl

undutifully
BR (ˌ)ʌnˈdjuːtɪfʊli, (ˌ)ʌnˈdjuːtɪfli, (ˌ)ʌnˈdʒuːtɪfʊli, (ˌ)ʌnˈdʒuːtɪfli
AM ˌənˈd(j)udəf(ə)li

undutifulness
BR (ˌ)ʌnˈdjuːtɪf(ʊ)lnəs, (ˌ)ʌnˈdʒuːtɪf(ʊ)lnəs
AM ˌənˈd(j)udəfəlnəs

undy
BR ˈʌndˌi, -ɪz
AM ˈəndˌi, -iz

undyed
BR (ˌ)ʌnˈdʌɪd
AM ˌənˈdaɪd

undying
BR (ˌ)ʌnˈdʌɪɪŋ
AM ˌənˈdaɪɪŋ

undyingly
BR (ˌ)ʌnˈdʌɪɪŋli
AM ˌənˈdaɪŋli

undynamic
BR ˌʌndʌɪˈnamɪk
AM ˌən,daɪˈnæmɪk

unearned
BR (ˌ)ʌnˈɜːnd
AM ˌənˈɚnd

unearth
BR (ˌ)ʌnˈɜːθ, -s, -ɪŋ, -t
AM ˌənˈɚθ, -s, -ɪŋ, -t

unearthliness
BR (ˌ)ʌnˈɜːθlɪnɪs
AM ˌənˈɚθlinɪs

unearthly
BR ʌnˈɜːθli
AM ˌənˈɚθli

unease
BR ʌnˈiːz
AM ˌənˈiz

uneasily
BR ʌnˈiːzɪli
AM ˌənˈizɪli

uneasiness
BR ʌnˈiːzɪnɪs
AM ˌənˈizɪnɪs

uneasy
BR ʌnˈiːz|i, -ɪə(r), -ɪɪst
AM ˌənˈizi, -ər, -ɪst

uneatable
BR (ˌ)ʌnˈiːtəbl
AM ˌənˈidəbəl

uneatableness
BR (ˌ)ʌnˈiːtəblnəs
AM ˌənˈidəbəlnəs

uneaten
BR (ˌ)ʌnˈiːtn
AM ˌənˈitn

uneconomic
BR ˌʌniːkəˈnɒmɪk, ˌʌnɛkəˈnɒmɪk
AM ˌənikəˈnamɪk, ˌənɛkəˈnamɪk

uneconomical
BR ˌʌniːkəˈnɒmɪkl, ˌʌnɛkəˈnɒmɪkl
AM ˌənikəˈnaməkəl, ˌənɛkəˈnaməkəl

uneconomically
BR ˌʌniːkəˈnɒmɪkli, ˌʌnɛkəˈnɒmɪkli
AM ˌənikəˈnamək(ə)li, ˌənɛkəˈnamək(ə)li

unedifying
BR ʌnˈɛdɪfʌɪɪŋ
AM ˌənˈɛdəˌfaɪɪŋ

unedifyingly
BR ʌnˈɛdɪfʌɪɪŋli
AM ˌənˈɛdəˌfaɪɪŋli

unedited
BR ʌnˈɛdɪtɪd
AM ˌənˈɛdədəd

uneducable
BR (ˌ)ʌnˈɛdjʊkəbl, (ˌ)ʌnˈɛdʒʊkəbl
AM ˌənˈɛdʒəkəbəl

uneducated
BR (ˌ)ʌnˈɛdjʊkeɪtɪd, (ˌ)ʌnˈɛdʒʊkeɪtɪd
AM ˌənˈɛdʒəˌkeɪdɪd

unelectable
BR ˌʌnɪˈlɛktəbl
AM ˌənəˈlɛktəbəl

unelected
BR ˌʌnɪˈlɛktɪd
AM ˌənəˈlɛktəd

unembarrassed
BR ˌʌnɪmˈbarəst
AM ˌənəmˈberəst

unembellished
BR ˌʌnɪmˈbelɪʃt
AM ˌənəmˈbelɪʃt

unembittered
BR ˌʌnɪmˈbɪtəd
AM ˌənəmˈbɪdərd

unembroidered
BR ˌʌnɪmˈbrɔɪdəd
AM ˌənəmˈbrɔɪdərd

unemotional
BR ˌʌnɪˈməʊʃn̩əl, ˌʌnɪˈməʊʃən(ə)l
AM ˌənəˈmoʊʃ(ə)nəl, ˌəniˈmoʊʃ(ə)nəl

unemotionally
BR ˌʌnɪˈməʊʃn̩əli, ˌʌnɪˈməʊʃn̩li, ˌʌnɪˈməʊʃənli, ˌʌnɪˈməʊʃ(ə)nəli
AM ˌənəˈmoʊʃ(ə)nəli, ˌən,ɪˈmoʊʃ(ə)nəli

unemphatic
BR ˌʌnɪmˈfatɪk, ˌʌnɛmˈfatɪk
AM ˌənəmˈfædɪk

unemphatically
BR ˌʌnɪmˈfatɪkli, ˌʌnɛmˈfatɪkli
AM ˌənəmˈfædək(ə)li

unemployability
BR ˌʌnɪm,plɔɪəˈbɪlɪti, ˌʌnɛm,plɔɪəˈbɪlɪti
AM ˌənəmplɔɪəˈbɪlɪdi

unemployable
BR ˌʌnɪmˈplɔɪəbl, ˌʌnɛmˈplɔɪəbl
AM ˌənəmˈplɔɪəbəl

unemployed
BR ˌʌnɪmˈplɔɪd, ˌʌnɛmˈplɔɪd
AM ˌənəmˈplɔɪd

unemployment
BR ˌʌnɪmˈplɔɪm(ə)nt, ˌʌnɛmˈplɔɪm(ə)nt
AM ˌənəmˈplɔɪmənt

unemptied
BR (ˌ)ʌnˈem(p)tɪd
AM ˌənˈɛm(p)tɪd

unenclosed
BR ˌʌnɪnˈkləʊzd, ˌʌnɛnˈkləʊzd
AM ˌənənˈklouzd

unencumbered
BR ˌʌnɪnˈkʌmbəd, ˌʌnɛnˈkʌmbəd
AM ˌənənˈkəmbərd

unendearing
BR ˌʌnɪnˈdɪərɪŋ, ˌʌnɛnˈdɪərɪŋ
AM ˌənənˈdɪrɪŋ

unending
BR ʌnˈɛndɪŋ
AM ˌənˈɛndɪŋ

unendingly
BR ʌnˈɛndɪŋli
AM ˌənˈɛndɪŋli

unendingness
BR ʌnˈɛndɪŋnɪs
AM ˌənˈɛndɪŋnɪs

unendowed
BR ˌʌnɪnˈdaʊd, ˌʌnɛnˈdaʊd
AM ˌənənˈdaʊd

unendurable
BR ˌʌnɪnˈdjʊərəbl,
ˌʌnɪnˈdʒʊərəbl,
ˌʌnɪnˈdjɔːrəbl,
ˌʌnɪnˈdʒɔːrəbl
AM ˌənənˈd(j)ʊrəbəl
unendurably
BR ˌʌnɪnˈdjʊərəbli,
ˌʌnɪnˈdʒʊərəbli,
ˌʌnɪnˈdjɔːrəbli,
ˌʌnɪnˈdʒɔːrəbli
AM ˌənənˈd(j)ʊrəbli
unenforceable
BR ˌʌnɪnˈfɔːsəbl,
ˌʌnɛnˈfɔːsəbl
AM ˌənənˈfɔrsəbəl
unenforced
BR ˌʌnɪnˈfɔːst,
ˌʌnɛnˈfɔːst
AM ˌənənˈfɔ(ə)rst
unengaged
BR ˌʌnɪnˈɡeɪdʒd,
ˌʌnɛnˈɡeɪdʒd
AM ˌənənˈɡeɪdʒd
un-English
BR ˌʌnˈɪŋɡlɪʃ
AM ˌənˈɪŋ(ɡ)lɪʃ
unenjoyable
BR ˌʌnɪnˈdʒɔɪəbl,
ˌʌnɛnˈdʒɔɪəbl
AM ˌənənˈdʒɔɪəbəl
unenlightened
BR ˌʌnɪnˈlaɪtnd,
ˌʌnɛnˈlaɪtnd
AM ˌənənˈlaɪtnd
unenlightening
BR ˌʌnɪnˈlaɪtn̩ɪŋ,
ˌʌnɛnˈlaɪtn̩ɪŋ
AM ˌənənˈlaɪtn̩ɪŋ
unenterprising
BR ʌnˈɛntəprʌɪzɪŋ
AM ˌənˈɛn(t)ərˌpraɪzɪŋ
unenthusiastic
BR ˌʌnɪnˌθjuːzɪˈastɪk,
ˌʌnɛnˌθjuːzɪˈastɪk
AM ˌənənˌθ(j)uziˈæstɪk
unenthusiastically
BR ˌʌnɪnˌθjuːzɪˈastɪkli,
ˌʌnɛnˌθjuːzɪˈastɪkli
AM ˌənənˌθ(j)uziˈæstək-
(ə)li
unenviable
BR (ˌ)ʌnˈɛnvɪəbl
AM ˌənˈɛnviəbəl
unenviably
BR (ˌ)ʌnˈɛnvɪəbli
AM ˌənˈɛnviəbli
unenvied
BR (ˌ)ʌnˈɛnvɪd
AM ˌənˈɛnvɪd
unenvironmental
BR ˌʌnɪnˌvʌɪrənˈmɛntl,
ˌʌnɪnˌvʌɪrn̩ˈmɛntl,
ˌʌnɛnˌvʌɪrənˈmɛntl,
ˌʌnɛnˌvʌɪrn̩ˈmɛntl
AM ˌənənˌvaɪrən-
ˈmɛn(t)l,
ˌənənˌvaɪ(ə)rnˈmɛn(t)l,

ˌənɛnˌvaɪrənˈmɛn(t)l,
ˌənɛnˌvaɪ(ə)rnˈmɛn(t)l
UNEP
BR ˈjuːnɛp
AM ˈjunɛp
unequable
BR (ˌ)ʌnˈɛkwəbl
AM ˌənˈɛkwəbəl
unequal
BR (ˌ)ʌnˈiːkw(ə)l, -z, -d
AM ˌənˈikwəl, -z, -d
unequalise
BR (ˌ)ʌnˈiːkwəlʌɪz, -ɪz,
-ɪŋ, -d
AM ˌənˈikwəˌlaɪz, -ɪz,
-ɪŋ, -d
unequalize
BR (ˌ)ʌnˈiːkwəlʌɪz, -ɪz,
-ɪŋ, -d
AM ˌənˈikwəˌlaɪz, -ɪz,
-ɪŋ, -d
unequally
BR (ˌ)ʌnˈiːkwəli,
(ˌ)ʌnˈiːkwl̩i
AM ˌənˈikwəli
unequalness
BR (ˌ)ʌnˈiːkw(ə)lnəs
AM ˌənˈikwəlnəs
unequipped
BR ˌʌnɪˈkwɪpt
AM ˌənəˈkwɪpt
unequitable
BR (ˌ)ʌnˈɛkwɪtəbl
AM ˌənˈɛkwədəbl
unequitably
BR (ˌ)ʌnˈɛkwɪtəbli
AM ˌənˈɛkwədəbli
unequivocal
BR ˌʌnɪˈkwɪvəkl
AM ˌənəˈkwɪvəkəl
unequivocally
BR ˌʌnɪˈkwɪvəkli
AM ˌənəˈkwɪvək(ə)li
unequivocalness
BR ˌʌnɪˈkwɪvəklnəs
AM ˌənəˈkwɪvəkəlnəs
unerring
BR (ˌ)ʌnˈɜːrɪŋ
AM ˌənˈɛrɪŋ
unerringly
BR (ˌ)ʌnˈɜːrɪŋli
AM ˌənˈɛrɪŋli
unerringness
BR (ˌ)ʌnˈɜːrɪŋnɪs
AM ˌənˈɛrɪŋnɪs
unescapable
BR ˌʌnɪˈskeɪpəbl
AM ˌənəˈskeɪpəbəl
UNESCO
BR juːˈnɛskəʊ,
jəˈnɛskəʊ
AM juˈnɛskoʊ
unescorted
BR ˌʌnɪˈskɔːtɪd
AM ˌənəˈskɔrdəd,
ˌənˈɛskɔrdəd

unessential
BR ˌʌnɪˈsɛnʃl
AM ˌənəˈsɛn(t)ʃəl
unestablished
BR ˌʌnɪˈstablɪʃt
AM ˌənəˈstæblɪʃt
unethical
BR (ˌ)ʌnˈɛθɪkl
AM ˌənˈɛθəkəl
unethically
BR (ˌ)ʌnˈɛθɪkli
AM ˌənˈɛθək(ə)li
uneven
BR (ˌ)ʌnˈiːvn
AM ˌənˈivən
unevenly
BR (ˌ)ʌnˈiːvnli
AM ˌənˈivənli
unevenness
BR (ˌ)ʌnˈiːvn̩nəs
AM ˌənˈivə(n)nəs
uneventful
BR ˌʌnɪˈvɛntf(ʊ)l
AM ˌənəˈvɛn(t)fəl
uneventfully
BR ˌʌnɪˈvɛntfəli,
ˌʌnɪˈvɛntfl̩i
AM ˌənəˈvɛn(t)fəli
uneventfulness
BR ˌʌnɪˈvɛntf(ʊ)lnəs
AM ˌənəˈvɛn(t)fəlnəs
unexacting
BR ˌʌnɪɡˈzaktɪŋ,
ˌʌnɛɡˈzaktɪŋ
AM ˌənəɡˈzæktɪŋ
unexamined
BR ˌʌnɪɡˈzamɪnd,
ˌʌnɛɡˈzamɪnd
AM ˌənəɡˈzæmənd
unexampled
BR ˌʌnɪɡˈzɑːmpld,
ˌʌnɪɡˈzampld,
ˌʌnɛɡˈzɑːmpld,
ˌʌnɛɡˈzampld
AM ˌənəɡˈzæmpəld
unexcavated
BR (ˌ)ʌnˈɛkskəveɪtɪd
AM ˌənˈɛkskəˌveɪdɪd
unexceptionable
BR ˌʌnɪkˈsɛpʃnəbl,
ˌʌnɪkˈsɛpʃ(ə)nəbl,
ˌʌnɛkˈsɛpʃn̩əbl,
ˌʌnɛkˈsɛpʃ(ə)nəbl
AM ˌənəkˈsɛpʃ(ə)nəbəl
**unexceptionable-
ness**
BR ˌʌnɪkˈsɛpʃn̩əblnəs,
ˌʌnɪkˈsɛpʃ(ə)nəblnəs,
ˌʌnɛkˈsɛpʃn̩əblnəs,
ˌʌnɛkˈsɛpʃ(ə)nəblnəs
AM ˌənəkˈsɛpʃ(ə)nəbəl-
nəs
unexceptionably
BR ˌʌnɪkˈsɛpʃn̩əbli,
ˌʌnɪkˈsɛpʃ(ə)nəbli,
ˌʌnɛkˈsɛpʃn̩əbli,
ˌʌnɛkˈsɛpʃ(ə)nəbli

unexceptional
BR ˌʌnɪkˈsɛpʃn(ə)l,
ˌʌnɪkˈsɛpʃən(ə)l,
ˌʌnɛkˈsɛpʃn(ə)l,
ˌʌnɛkˈsɛpʃən(ə)l
AM ˌənəkˈsɛpʃ(ə)nəl
unexceptionally
BR ˌʌnɪkˈsɛpʃnəli,
ˌʌnɪkˈsɛpʃ(ə)nəli,
ˌʌnɛkˈsɛpʃn̩əli,
ˌʌnɛkˈsɛpʃ(ə)nəli
AM ˌənəkˈsɛpʃ(ə)nəli
unexcitability
BR ˌʌnɪkˌsʌɪtəˈbɪlɪti,
ˌʌnɛkˌsʌɪtəˈbɪlɪti
AM ˌənəkˌsaɪdəˈbɪlɪdi
unexcitable
BR ˌʌnɪkˈsʌɪtəbl,
ˌʌnɛkˈsʌɪtəbl
AM ˌənəkˈsaɪdəbəl
unexciting
BR ˌʌnɪkˈsʌɪtɪŋ,
ˌʌnɛkˈsʌɪtɪŋ
AM ˌənəkˈsaɪdɪŋ
unexclusive
BR ˌʌnɪkˈskluːsɪv,
ˌʌnɛkˈskluːsɪv
AM ˌənəkˈsklusɪv
unexecuted
BR (ˌ)ʌnˈɛksɪkjuːtɪd
AM ˌənˈɛksəˌkjudəd
unexhausted
BR ˌʌnɪɡˈzɔːstɪd,
ˌʌnɛɡˈzɔːstɪd
AM ˌənəɡˈzɔstəd,
ˌənəɡˈzʊstəd
unexpected
BR ˌʌnɪkˈspɛktɪd,
ˌʌnɛkˈspɛktɪd
AM ˌənəkˈspɛktəd
unexpectedly
BR ˌʌnɪkˈspɛktɪdli,
ˌʌnɛkˈspɛktɪdli
AM ˌənəkˈspɛktədli
unexpectedness
BR ˌʌnɪkˈspɛktɪdnɪs,
ˌʌnɛkˈspɛktɪdnɪs
AM ˌənəkˈspɛktədnəs
unexpiated
BR (ˌ)ʌnˈɛkspɪeɪtɪd
AM ˌənˈɛkspiˌeɪdɪd
unexpired
BR ˌʌnɪkˈspʌɪəd,
ˌʌnɛkˈspʌɪəd
AM ˌənəkˈspaɪ(ə)rd
unexplainable
BR ˌʌnɪkˈspleɪnəbl,
ˌʌnɛkˈspleɪnəbl
AM ˌənəkˈspleɪnəbəl
unexplainably
BR ˌʌnɪkˈspleɪnəbli,
ˌʌnɛkˈspleɪnəbli
AM ˌənəkˈspleɪnəbli
unexplained
BR ˌʌnɪkˈspleɪnd,
ˌʌnɛkˈspleɪnd
AM ˌənəkˈspleɪnd

unexploded
BR ˌʌnɪkˈspləʊdɪd, ˌʌnɛkˈspləʊdɪd
AM ˌʌnɛkˈsploʊdəd

unexploited
BR ˌʌnɪkˈsplɔɪtɪd, ˌʌnɛkˈsplɔɪtɪd
AM ˌʌnɛkˈsplɔɪdɪd

unexplored
BR ˌʌnɪkˈsplɔːd, ˌʌnɛkˈsplɔːd
AM ˌʌnəkˈsplɔ(ə)rd

unexportable
BR ˌʌnɪkˈspɔːtəbl, ˌʌnɛkˈspɔːtəbl
AM ˌʌnˈɛkspɔrdəbəl, ˌənəkˈspɔrdəbəl

unexposed
BR ˌʌnɪkˈspəʊzd, ˌʌnɛkˈspəʊzd
AM ˌənəkˈspoʊzd

unexpressed
BR ˌʌnɪkˈsprɛst, ˌʌnɛkˈsprɛst
AM ˌənəkˈsprɛst

unexpressible
BR ˌʌnɪkˈsprɛsɪbl, ˌʌnɛkˈsprɛsɪbl
AM ˌənəkˈsprɛsəbəl

unexpressibly
BR ˌʌnɪkˈsprɛsɪbli, ˌʌnɛkˈsprɛsɪbli
AM ˌənəkˈsprɛsəbli

unexpressive
BR ˌʌnɪkˈsprɛsɪv, ˌʌnɛkˈsprɛsɪv
AM ˌənəkˈsprɛsɪv

unexpurgated
BR ˌʌnˈɛkspəɡeɪtɪd
AM ˌənˈɛkspərˌɡeɪdɪd

unfaceable
BR ʌnˈfeɪsəbl
AM ˌənˈfeɪsəbəl

unfaded
BR (ˌ)ʌnˈfeɪdɪd
AM ˌənˈfeɪdɪd

unfading
BR (ˌ)ʌnˈfeɪdɪŋ
AM ˌənˈfeɪdɪŋ

unfadingly
BR (ˌ)ʌnˈfeɪdɪŋli
AM ˌənˈfeɪdɪŋli

unfailing
BR ʌnˈfeɪlɪŋ
AM ˌənˈfeɪlɪŋ

unfailingly
BR ʌnˈfeɪlɪŋli
AM ˌənˈfeɪlɪŋli

unfailingness
BR ʌnˈfeɪlɪŋnɪs
AM ˌənˈfeɪlɪŋnɪs

unfair
BR (ˌ)ʌnˈfɛː(r)
AM ˌənˈfɛ(ə)r

unfairly
BR (ˌ)ʌnˈfɛːli
AM ˌənˈfɛrli

unfairness
BR (ˌ)ʌnˈfɛːnəs
AM ˌənˈfɛrnəs

unfaithful
BR (ˌ)ʌnˈfeɪθ(ʊ)l
AM ˌənˈfeɪθfəl

unfaithfully
BR (ˌ)ʌnˈfeɪθʊli, (ˌ)ʌnˈfeɪθfli
AM ˌənˈfeɪθfəli

unfaithfulness
BR (ˌ)ʌnˈfeɪθ(ʊ)lnəs
AM ˌənˈfeɪθfəlnəs

unfaltering
BR (ˌ)ʌnˈfɔːlt(ə)rɪŋ, (ˌ)ʌnˈfɒlt(ə)rɪŋ
AM ˌənˈfɔːlt(ə)rɪŋ, ˌənˈfɑlt(ə)rɪŋ

unfalteringly
BR (ˌ)ʌnˈfɔːlt(ə)rɪŋli, (ˌ)ʌnˈfɒlt(ə)rɪŋli
AM ˌənˈfɔːlt(ə)rɪŋli, ˌənˈfɑlt(ə)rɪŋli

unfamiliar
BR ˌʌnfəˈmɪlɪə(r)
AM ˌənfəˈmɪljər, ˌənfəˈmɪlɪər

unfamiliarity
BR ˌʌnfəˌmɪlɪˈarɪti
AM ˌənfəˌmɪlˈjɛrədi, ˌənfəˌmɪlɪˈɛrədi

unfancied
BR (ˌ)ʌnˈfansɪd
AM ˌənˈfænsɪd

unfashionable
BR (ˌ)ʌnˈfaʃ(ə)nəbl, (ˌ)ʌnˈfaʃnəbl
AM ˌənˈfæʃ(ə)nəbəl

unfashionableness
BR (ˌ)ʌnˈfaʃ(ə)nəblnəs, (ˌ)ʌnˈfaʃnəblnəs
AM ˌənˈfæʃ(ə)nəbəlnəs

unfashionably
BR (ˌ)ʌnˈfaʃ(ə)nəbli, (ˌ)ʌnˈfaʃnəbli
AM ˌənˈfæʃ(ə)nəbli

unfashioned
BR (ˌ)ʌnˈfaʃnd
AM ˌənˈfæʃənd

unfasten
BR (ˌ)ʌnˈfɑːs|n, (ˌ)ʌnˈfas|n, -nz, -nɪŋ \-nɪŋ, -nd
AM ˌənˈfæsn, -z, -ɪŋ, -d

unfathered
BR (ˌ)ʌnˈfɑːðəd
AM ˌənˈfɑðərd

unfatherliness
BR (ˌ)ʌnˈfɑːðəlɪnɪs
AM ˌənˈfɑðərlɪnɪs

unfatherly
BR (ˌ)ʌnˈfɑːðəli
AM ˌənˈfɑðərli

unfathomable
BR ʌnˈfaðəməbl, ʌnˈfaðməbl
AM ˌənˈfæθ(ə)məbəl

unfathomableness
BR ʌnˈfaðəməblnəs, ʌnˈfaðməblnəs
AM ˌənˈfæθ(ə)məbəlnəs

unfathomably
BR ʌnˈfaðəməbli, ʌnˈfaðməbli
AM ˌənˈfæθ(ə)məbli

unfathomed
BR (ˌ)ʌnˈfað(ə)md
AM ˌənˈfæðəmd

unfavorable
BR (ˌ)ʌnˈfeɪv(ə)rəbl
AM ˌənˈfeɪv(ə)r(ə)bəl

unfavorableness
BR (ˌ)ʌnˈfeɪv(ə)rəblnəs
AM ˌənˈfeɪv(ə)r(ə)bəlnəs

unfavorably
BR (ˌ)ʌnˈfeɪv(ə)rəbli
AM ˌənˈfeɪv(ə)r(ə)bli

unfavorite
BR (ˌ)ʌnˈfeɪv(ə)rɪt
AM ˌənˈfeɪv(ə)rɪt

unfavourable
BR (ˌ)ʌnˈfeɪv(ə)rəbl
AM ˌənˈfeɪv(ə)r(ə)bəl

unfavourableness
BR (ˌ)ʌnˈfeɪv(ə)rəblnəs
AM ˌənˈfeɪv(ə)r(ə)bəlnəs

unfavourably
BR (ˌ)ʌnˈfeɪv(ə)rəbli
AM ˌənˈfeɪv(ə)r(ə)bli

unfavourite
BR (ˌ)ʌnˈfeɪv(ə)rɪt
AM ˌənˈfeɪv(ə)rɪt

unfazed
BR (ˌ)ʌnˈfeɪzd
AM ˌənˈfeɪzd

unfeasibility
BR ʌnˌfiːzɪˈbɪlɪti
AM ˌənfizɪˈbɪlɪdi

unfeasible
BR (ˌ)ʌnˈfiːzɪbl
AM ˌənˈfizəbəl

unfeasibly
BR (ˌ)ʌnˈfiːzɪbli
AM ˌənˈfizəbli

unfed
BR ʌnˈfɛd
AM ˌənˈfɛd

unfeeling
BR ʌnˈfiːlɪŋ
AM ˌənˈfilɪŋ

unfeelingly
BR ʌnˈfiːlɪŋli
AM ˌənˈfilɪŋli

unfeelingness
BR ʌnˈfiːlɪŋnɪs
AM ˌənˈfilɪŋnɪs

unfeigned
BR (ˌ)ʌnˈfeɪnd
AM ˌənˈfeɪnd

unfeignedly
BR ʌnˈfeɪnɪdli
AM ˌənˈfeɪnɪdli

unfelt
BR (ˌ)ʌnˈfɛlt
AM ˌənˈfɛlt

unfeminine
BR ˌʌnˈfɛmɪnɪn
AM ˌənˈfɛmənən

unfemininity
BR ˌʌnfɛmɪˈnɪnɪti
AM ˌənˌfɛməˈnɪnɪdi

unfenced
BR ʌnˈfɛnst
AM ˌənˈfɛnst

unfermented
BR ˌʌnfəˈmɛntɪd
AM ˌənfərˈmɛn(t)əd

unfertilised
BR ʌnˈfɜːtɪlaɪzd, ˌʌnˈfɜːtˌlaɪzd
AM ˌənˈfɜrdlˌaɪzd

unfertilized
BR ʌnˈfɜːtɪlaɪzd, ˌʌnˈfɜːtˌlaɪzd
AM ˌənˈfɜrdlˌaɪzd

unfetter
BR ʌnˈfɛt|ə(r), -əz, -(ə)rɪŋ, -əd
AM ˌənˈfɛdər, -z, -ɪŋ, -d

unfilial
BR ʌnˈfɪlɪəl
AM ˌənˈfɪlɪəl

unfilially
BR ʌnˈfɪlɪəli
AM ˌənˈfɪlɪəli, ˌənˈfɪljəli

unfilled
BR (ˌ)ʌnˈfɪld
AM ˌənˈfɪld

unfiltered
BR ʌnˈfɪltəd
AM ˌənˈfɪltərd

unfinancial
BR ˌʌnfʌɪˈnanʃl, ˌʌnfɪˈnanʃl
AM ˌənˌfaɪˈnæn(t)ʃəl, ˌənfəˈnæn(t)ʃəl

unfinished
BR (ˌ)ʌnˈfɪnɪʃt
AM ˌənˈfɪnɪʃt

unfit
BR (ˌ)ʌnˈfɪt, -s, -ɪŋ, -ɪd
AM ˌənˈfɪ|t, -ts, -dɪŋ, -dɪd

unfitly
BR (ˌ)ʌnˈfɪtli
AM ˌənˈfɪtli

unfitness
BR (ˌ)ʌnˈfɪtnɪs
AM ˌənˈfɪtnɪs

unfitted
BR (ˌ)ʌnˈfɪtɪd
AM ˌənˈfɪdɪd

unfitting
BR (ˌ)ʌnˈfɪtɪŋ
AM ˌənˈfɪdɪŋ

unfittingly
BR (ˌ)ʌnˈfɪtɪŋli
AM ˌənˈfɪdɪŋli

unfix
BR ʌnˈfɪks, -ɪz, -ɪŋ, -t
AM ˌənˈfɪks, -ɪz, -ɪŋ, -t

unflagging
BR (,)ʌnˈflagɪŋ
AM ˌənˈflægɪŋ
unflaggingly
BR (,)ʌnˈflagɪŋli
AM ˌənˈflægɪŋli
unflappability
BR ˌʌnflapəˈbɪlɪti
AM ˌənˌflæpəˈbɪlɪdi
unflappable
BR (,)ʌnˈflapəbl
AM ˌənˈflæpəbəl
unflappably
BR (,)ʌnˈflapəbli
AM ˌənˈflæpəbli
unflattering
BR (,)ʌnˈflat(ə)rɪŋ
AM ˌənˈflædərɪŋ
unflatteringly
BR (,)ʌnˈflat(ə)rɪŋli
AM ˌənˈflædərɪŋli
unflavored
BR ˌʌnˈfleɪvəd
AM ˌənˈfleɪvərd
unflavoured
BR ˌʌnˈfleɪvəd
AM ˌənˈfleɪvərd
unfledged
BR (,)ʌnˈflɛdʒd
AM ˌənˈflɛdʒd
unfleshed
BR ˌʌnˈflɛʃt
AM ˌənˈflɛʃt
unflexed
BR ˌʌnˈflɛkst
AM ˌənˈflɛkst
unflickering
BR (,)ʌnˈflɪk(ə)rɪŋ
AM ˌənˈflɪk(ə)rɪŋ
unflinching
BR (,)ʌnˈflɪn(t)ʃɪŋ
AM ˌənˈflɪn(t)ʃɪŋ
unflinchingly
BR (,)ʌnˈflɪn(t)ʃɪŋli
AM ˌənˈflɪn(t)ʃɪŋli
unflurried
BR (,)ʌnˈflʌrɪd
AM ˌənˈflərid
unflustered
BR (,)ʌnˈflʌstəd
AM ˌənˈfləstərd
unfocused
BR (,)ʌnˈfəʊkəst
AM ˌənˈfoʊkəst
unfocussed
BR (,)ʌnˈfəʊkəst
AM ˌənˈfoʊkəst
unfold
BR (,)ʌnˈfəʊld, -z, -ɪŋ,
-ɪd
AM ˌənˈfoʊld, -z, -ɪŋ, -əd
unfoldment
BR ˌʌnˈfəʊldm(ə)nt
AM ˌənˈfoʊldmənt
unforced
BR (,)ʌnˈfɔːst
AM ˌənˈfɔ(ə)rst

unforcedly
BR ʌnˈfɔːsɪdli
AM ˌənˈforsədli
unfordable
BR (,)ʌnˈfɔːdəbl
AM ˌənˈfordəbəl
unforecast
BR (,)ʌnˈfɔːkɑːst,
(,)ʌnˈfɔːkast
AM ˌənˈfor,kæst
unforeseeable
BR ˌʌnfɔːˈsiːəbl,
ˌʌnfəˈsiːəbl
AM ˌənˌfɔrˈsiəbəl,
ˌənfərˈsiəbəl
unforeseen
BR ˌʌnfɔːˈsiːn,
ˌʌnfəˈsiːn
AM ˌənˌfɔrˈsin,
ˌənfərˈsin
unforetold
BR ˌʌnfɔːˈtəʊld,
ˌʌnfəˈtəʊld
AM ˌənˌfɔrˈtoʊld,
ˌənfərˈtoʊld
unforgettable
BR ˌʌnfəˈgɛtəbl
AM ˌənfərˈgɛdəbəl
unforgettably
BR ˌʌnfəˈgɛtəbli
AM ˌənfərˈgɛdəbli
unforgivable
BR ˌʌnfəˈgɪvəbl
AM ˌənfərˈgɪvəbəl
unforgivably
BR ˌʌnfəˈgɪvəbli
AM ˌənfərˈgɪvəbli
unforgiveable
BR ˌʌnfəˈgɪvəbl
AM ˌənfərˈgɪvəbəl
unforgiveably
BR ˌʌnfəˈgɪvəbli
AM ˌənfərˈgɪvəbli
unforgiven
BR ˌʌnfəˈgɪvn
AM ˌənfərˈgɪvən
unforgiving
BR ˌʌnfəˈgɪvɪŋ
AM ˌənfərˈgɪvɪŋ
unforgivingly
BR ˌʌnfəˈgɪvɪŋli
AM ˌənfərˈgɪvɪŋli
unforgivingness
BR ˌʌnfəˈgɪvɪŋnɪs
AM ˌənfərˈgɪvɪŋnɪs
unforgotten
BR ˌʌnfəˈgɒtn
AM ˌənfərˈgɑtn
unformed
BR ˌʌnˈfɔːmd
AM ˌənˈfɔ(ə)rmd
unformulated
BR (,)ʌnˈfɔːmjʊleɪtɪd
AM ˌənˈfɔrmjəˌleɪdɪd
unforthcoming
BR ˌʌnfɔːθˈkʌmɪŋ
AM ˌənfɔrθˈkəmɪŋ

unfortified
BR ˌʌnˈfɔːtɪfʌɪd
AM ˌənˈfordəˌfaɪd
unfortunate
BR ʌnˈfɔːtʃnət,
ʌnˈfɔːtʃ(ə)nət,
ʌnˈfɔːtjʊnət
AM ˌənˈfɔrtʃ(ə)nət
unfortunately
BR ʌnˈfɔːtʃnətli,
ʌnˈfɔːtʃ(ə)nətli,
ʌnˈfɔːtjʊnətli
AM ˌənˈfɔrtʃ(ə)nətli
unfounded
BR (,)ʌnˈfaʊndɪd
AM ˌənˈfaʊndəd
unfoundedly
BR (,)ʌnˈfaʊndɪdli
AM ˌənˈfaʊndədli
unfoundedness
BR (,)ʌnˈfaʊndɪdnɪs
AM ˌənˈfaʊndədnəs
unframed
BR ˌʌnˈfreɪmd
AM ˌənˈfreɪmd
unfree
BR ˌʌnˈfriː
AM ˌənˈfri
unfreedom
BR ˌʌnˈfriːdəm
AM ˌənˈfridəm
unfreeze
BR ˌʌnˈfriːz, -ɪz, -ɪŋ
AM ˌənˈfriz, -ɪz, -ɪŋ
unfrequented
BR ˌʌnfrɪˈkwɛntɪd,
ˌʌnfriːˈkwɛntɪd
AM ˌənfriˈkwɛn(t)əd,
ˌənˈfriˌkwɛn(t)əd
unfriended
BR ˌʌnˈfrɛndɪd
AM ˌənˈfrɛndəd
unfriendliness
BR (,)ʌnˈfrɛn(d)lɪnɪs
AM ˌənˈfrɛn(d)lɪnɪs
unfriendly
BR (,)ʌnˈfrɛn(d)li
AM ˌənˈfrɛn(d)li
unfrightening
BR ˌʌnˈfrʌɪtnɪŋ,
ˌʌnˈfrʌɪtnɪŋ
AM ˌənˈfraɪtnɪŋ,
ˌənˈfraɪtnɪŋ
unfrock
BR ˌʌnˈfrɒk, -s, -ɪŋ, -t
AM ˌənˈfrɑk, -s, -ɪŋ, -t
unfroze
BR ˌʌnˈfrəʊz
AM ˌənˈfroʊz
unfrozen
BR ˌʌnˈfrəʊzn
AM ˌənˈfroʊzən
unfruitful
BR (,)ʌnˈfruːtf(ʊ)l
AM ˌənˈfrutfəl
unfruitfully
BR (,)ʌnˈfruːtfʊli,
(,)ʌnˈfruːtfli

AM ˌənˈfrutfəli
unfruitfulness
BR (,)ʌnˈfruːtf(ʊ)lnəs
AM ˌənˈfrutfəlnəs
unfuddled
BR ˌʌnˈfʌdld
AM ˌənˈfədld
unfulfillable
BR ˌʌnfʊlˈfɪləbl
AM ˌənfʊ(l)ˈfɪləbəl
unfulfilled
BR ˌʌnfʊlˈfɪld
AM ˌənfʊ(l)ˈfɪld
unfulfilling
BR ˌʌnfʊlˈfɪlɪŋ
AM ˌənfʊ(l)ˈfɪlɪŋ
unfunded
BR (,)ʌnˈfʌndɪd
AM ˌənˈfəndəd
unfunnily
BR ˌʌnˈfʌnɪli
AM ˌənˈfənəli
unfunniness
BR ˌʌnˈfʌnɪnɪs
AM ˌənˈfənɪnɪs
unfunny
BR ˌʌnˈfʌni
AM ˌənˈfəni
unfurl
BR ˌʌnˈfɜːl, -z, -ɪŋ, -d
AM ˌənˈfərl, -z, -ɪŋ, -d
unfurnished
BR (,)ʌnˈfɜːnɪʃt
AM ˌənˈfərnɪʃt
unfussily
BR ˌʌnˈfʌsɪli
AM ˌənˈfəsəli
unfussy
BR ˌʌnˈfʌsi
AM ˌənˈfəsi
ungainliness
BR (,)ʌnˈgeɪnlɪnɪs,
(,)ʌŋˈgeɪnlɪnɪs
AM ˌənˈgeɪnlɪnɪs
ungainly
BR (,)ʌnˈgeɪnli,
(,)ʌŋˈgeɪnli
AM ˌənˈgeɪnli
ungallant
BR (,)ʌnˈgalənt,
(,)ʌnˈgalnt,
(,)ʌŋˈgalənt,
(,)ʌŋˈgalnt
AM ˌənˈgælənt
ungallantly
BR (,)ʌnˈgaləntli,
(,)ʌnˈgalntli,
(,)ʌŋˈgaləntli,
(,)ʌŋˈgalntli
AM ˌənˈgælən(t)li
ungenerous
BR (,)ʌnˈdʒɛn(ə)rəs
AM ˌənˈdʒɛn(ə)rəs
ungenerously
BR (,)ʌnˈdʒɛn(ə)rəsli
AM ˌənˈdʒɛn(ə)rəsli

ungenerousness
BR (,)ʌn'dʒɛn(ə)rəsnəs
AM ,ən'dʒɛn(ə)rəsnəs

ungenial
BR ,ʌn'dʒiːniəl
AM ,ən'dʒiniəl

ungentle
BR ,ʌn'dʒɛntl
AM ,ən'dʒɛn(t)əl

ungentlemanliness
BR ,ʌn'dʒɛntlmənlɪnɪs
AM ,ən'dʒɛn(t)lmənlɪnɪs

ungentlemanly
BR ,ʌn'dʒɛntlmənli
AM ,ən'dʒɛn(t)lmənli

ungentleness
BR ,ʌn'dʒɛntlnəs
AM ,ən'dʒɛn(t)lnəs

ungently
BR ,ʌn'dʒɛntli
AM ,ən'dʒɛn(t)li

un-get-at-able
BR ,ʌnget'atəbl,
,ʌnget'atəbl
AM ,ən,ged'ædəbəl

ungifted
BR ,ʌn'gɪftɪd,
,ʌn'gɪftɪd
AM ,ən'gɪftɪd

ungilded
BR ,ʌn'gɪldɪd,
,ʌn'gɪldɪd
AM ,ən'gɪldɪd

ungird
BR ,ʌn'gəːd, ,ʌn'gəːd,
-z, -ɪŋ, -ɪd
AM ,ən'gərd, -z, -ɪŋ, -əd

unglamorous
BR ,ʌn'glam(ə)rəs,
,ʌn'glam(ə)rəs
AM ,ən'glæm(ə)rəs

unglazed
BR ,ʌn'gleɪzd,
,ʌn'gleɪzd
AM ,ən'gleɪzd

ungloved
BR ,ʌn'glʌvd,
,ʌn'glʌvd
AM ,ən'gləvd

unglued
BR ,ʌn'gluːd, ,ʌn'gluːd
AM ,ən'glud

ungodliness
BR (,)ʌn'gɒdlɪnɪs,
(,)ʌn'gɒdlɪnɪs
AM ,ən'gɑdlɪnɪs

ungodly
BR (,)ʌn'gɒdli,
(,)ʌn'gɒdli
AM ,ən'gɑdli

ungovernability
BR ,ʌngʌv(ə)nə'bɪlɪti,
,ʌngʌvnə'bɪlɪti,
ʌn,gʌv(ə)nə'bɪlɪti,
ʌn,gʌvnə'bɪlɪti,
,ʌngʌv(ə)nə'bɪlɪti,
,ʌngʌvnə'bɪlɪti,

ʌn,gʌv(ə)nə'bɪlɪti,
ʌn,gʌvnə'bɪlɪti
AM ,ən,gəvərnə'bɪlɪdi

ungovernable
BR (,)ʌn'gʌv(ə)nəbl,
(,)ʌn'gʌvnəbl,
(,)ʌŋ'gʌv(ə)nəbl,
(,)ʌŋ'gʌvnəbl
AM ,ən'gəvərnəbəl

ungovernably
BR (,)ʌn'gʌv(ə)nəbli,
(,)ʌn'gʌvnəbli,
(,)ʌŋ'gʌv(ə)nəbli,
(,)ʌŋ'gʌvnəbli
AM ,ən'gəvərnəbli

ungoverned
BR (,)ʌn'gʌvnd,
(,)ʌŋ'gʌvnd
AM ,ən'gəvərnd

ungraceful
BR (,)ʌn'greɪsf(ʊ)l,
(,)ʌŋ'greɪsf(ʊ)l
AM ,ən'greɪsfəl

ungracefully
BR (,)ʌn'greɪsfʊli,
(,)ʌŋ'greɪsfʊli,
(,)ʌŋ'greɪsfli
AM ,ən'greɪsfəli

ungracefulness
BR (,)ʌn'greɪsf(ʊ)lnəs,
(,)ʌŋ'greɪsf(ʊ)lnəs
AM ,ən'greɪsfəlnəs

ungracious
BR (,)ʌn'greɪʃəs,
(,)ʌŋ'greɪʃəs
AM ,ən'greɪʃəs

ungraciously
BR (,)ʌn'greɪʃəsli,
(,)ʌŋ'greɪʃəsli
AM ,ən'greɪʃəsli

ungraciousness
BR (,)ʌn'greɪʃəsnəs,
(,)ʌŋ'greɪʃəsnəs
AM ,ən'greɪʃəsnəs

ungrammatical
BR ,ʌngrə'matɪkl,
,ʌngrə'matɪkl
AM ,əngrə'mædəkəl

ungrammaticality
BR ,ʌngrə,matɪ'kalɪti,
,ʌngrə,matɪ'kalɪti
AM ,əngrə,mædə'kælədi

ungrammatically
BR ,ʌngrə'matɪkli,
,ʌngrə'matɪkli
AM ,əngrə'mædək(ə)li

**ungrammatical-
ness**
BR ,ʌngrə'matɪklnəs,
,ʌngrə'matɪklnəs
AM ,əngrə'mædəkəlnəs

ungraspable
BR (,)ʌn'grɑːspəbl,
(,)ʌn'graspəbl,
(,)ʌŋ'grɑːspəbl,
(,)ʌŋ'graspəbl
AM ,ən'græspəbəl

ungrateful
BR (,)ʌn'greɪtf(ʊ)l,
(,)ʌŋ'greɪtf(ʊ)l
AM ,ən'greɪtfəl

ungratefully
BR (,)ʌn'greɪtfʊli,
(,)ʌn'greɪtfli,
(,)ʌŋ'greɪtfʊli,
(,)ʌŋ'greɪtfli
AM ,ən'greɪtfəli

ungratefulness
BR (,)ʌn'greɪtf(ʊ)lnəs,
(,)ʌŋ'greɪtf(ʊ)lnəs
AM ,ən'greɪtfəlnəs

ungreen
BR ,ʌn'griːn, ,ʌŋ'griːn
AM ,ən'grin

ungrounded
BR (,)ʌn'graʊndɪd,
(,)ʌŋ'graʊndɪd
AM ,ən'graʊndəd

ungrudging
BR (,)ʌn'grʌdʒɪŋ,
(,)ʌŋ'grʌdʒɪŋ
AM ,ən'grədʒɪŋ

ungrudgingly
BR (,)ʌn'grʌdʒɪŋli,
(,)ʌŋ'grʌdʒɪŋli
AM ,ən'grədʒɪŋli

ungual
BR ,ʌŋgw(ə)l, ,ʌŋgjʊəl
AM ,əŋgwəl

unguard
BR (,)ʌn'gɑːd,
(,)ʌŋ'gɑːd, -z, -ɪŋ, -ɪd
AM ,ən'gɑrd, -z, -ɪŋ, -əd

unguardedly
BR (,)ʌn'gɑːdɪdli,
(,)ʌŋ'gɑːdɪdli
AM ,ən'gɑrdədli

unguardedness
BR (,)ʌn'gɑːdɪdnɪs,
(,)ʌŋ'gɑːdɪdnɪs
AM ,ən'gɑrdədnəs

unguent
BR ,ʌŋgwənt,
,ʌŋgjʊənt, -s
AM ,əŋgwənt, -s

unguessable
BR (,)ʌn'gɛsəbl,
(,)ʌŋ'gɛsəbl
AM ,ən'gɛsəbəl

unguiculate
BR ,ʌn'gwɪkjʊlət,
,ʌŋ'gwɪkjʊlət
AM ,ən'gwɪkjə,leɪt,
,ən'gwɪkjələt

unguided
BR (,)ʌn'gʌɪdɪd,
(,)ʌŋ'gʌɪdɪd
AM ,ən'gaɪdɪd

unguis
BR ,ʌŋgwɪs, -ɪz
AM ,əŋgwɪs, -ɪz

ungula
BR ,ʌŋgjʊlə(r)
AM ,əŋgjələ

ungulae
BR ,ʌŋgjʊliː
AM ,əŋgjəli, ,əŋgjə,laɪ

ungulate
BR ,ʌŋgjʊlət,
,ʌŋgjʊleɪt, -s
AM ,əŋgjələt,
,əŋgjə,leɪt, -s

ungum
BR ,ʌn'gʌm, ,ʌŋ'gʌm,
-z, -ɪŋ, -d
AM ,ən'gəm, -z, -ɪŋ, -d

unhallowed
BR (,)ʌn'haləʊd
AM ,ən'hæloʊd

unhampered
BR (,)ʌn'hampəd
AM ,ən'hæmpərd

unhand
BR ,ʌn'hand, -z, -ɪŋ, -ɪd
AM ,ən'hænd, -z, -ɪŋ,
-əd

unhandily
BR (,)ʌn'handɪli
AM ,ən'hændəli

unhandiness
BR (,)ʌn'handɪnɪs
AM ,ən'hændinɪs

unhandsome
BR ,ʌn'han(d)s(ə)m
AM ,ən'hæn(d)səm

unhandy
BR ,ʌn'handi
AM ,ən'hændi

unhang
BR ,ʌn'haŋ, -z, -ɪŋ
AM ,ən'hæŋ, -z, -ɪŋ

unhappily
BR (,)ʌn'hapɪli
AM ,ən'hæpəli

unhappiness
BR (,)ʌn'hapɪnɪs
AM ,ən'hæpinɪs

unhappy
BR (,)ʌn'hapi
AM ,ən'hæpi

unharbour
BR ,ʌn'hɑːbə(r), -z, -ɪŋ,
-d
AM ,ən'hɑrbər, -z, -ɪŋ,
-d

unharmed
BR (,)ʌn'hɑːmd
AM ,ən'hɑrmd

unharmful
BR (,)ʌn'hɑːmf(ʊ)l
AM ,ən'hɑrmfəl

unharmonious
BR ,ʌnhɑː'məʊniəs
AM ,ənhɑr'moʊniəs

unharness
BR (,)ʌn'hɑːnɪs, -ɪz, -ɪŋ,
-t
AM ,ən'hɑrnəs, -əz, -ɪŋ,
-t

unharvested
BR ,ʌn'hɑːvɪstɪd
AM ,ən'hɑrvəstəd

unhasp
BR ʌnˈhɑːsp, ʌnˈhasp, -s, -ɪŋ, -t
AM ˌənˈhæsp, -s, -ɪŋ, -t

unhatched
BR ʌnˈhatʃt
AM ˌənˈhætʃt

UNHCR
BR ˌjuːɛnˌeɪtʃˈsiːˈɑː(r)
AM ˌjuɛnˌeɪtʃˈsiːˈɑr

unhealed
BR ˌʌnˈhiːld
AM ˌənˈhild

unhealthful
BR (ˌ)ʌnˈhɛlθf(ʊ)l
AM ˌənˈhɛlθfəl

unhealthfulness
BR (ˌ)ʌnˈhɛlθf(ʊ)lnəs
AM ˌənˈhɛlθfəlnəs

unhealthily
BR (ˌ)ʌnˈhɛlθɪli
AM ˌənˈhɛlθəli

unhealthiness
BR (ˌ)ʌnˈhɛlθɪnɪs
AM ˌənˈhɛlθinɪs

unhealthy
BR (ˌ)ʌnˈhɛlθ|i, -ɪə(r), -ɪɪst
AM ˌənˈhɛlθi, -ər, -ɪst

unheard
BR (ˌ)ʌnˈhəːd
AM ˌənˈhərd

unheard-of
BR (ˌ)ʌnˈhəːdɒv
AM ˌənˈhərdəv

unhearing
BR (ˌ)ʌnˈhɪərɪŋ
AM ˌənˈhɪrɪŋ

unheated
BR (ˌ)ʌnˈhiːtɪd
AM ˌənˈhidɪd

unhedged
BR ˌʌnˈhɛdʒd
AM ˌənˈhɛdʒd

unheeded
BR (ˌ)ʌnˈhiːdɪd
AM ˌənˈhidɪd

unheedful
BR (ˌ)ʌnˈhiːdf(ʊ)l
AM ˌənˈhidfəl

unheeding
BR (ˌ)ʌnˈhiːdɪŋ
AM ˌənˈhidɪŋ

unheedingly
BR (ˌ)ʌnˈhiːdɪŋli
AM ˌənˈhidɪŋli

unhelpful
BR ʌnˈhɛlpf(ʊ)l
AM ˌənˈhɛlpfəl

unhelpfully
BR ʌnˈhɛlpfəli, ʌnˈhɛlpfʃi
AM ˌənˈhɛlpfəli

unhelpfulness
BR ʌnˈhɛlpf(ʊ)lnəs
AM ˌənˈhɛlpfəlnəs

unheralded
BR (ˌ)ʌnˈhɛrəldɪd, (ˌ)ʌnˈhɛrldɪd
AM ˌənˈhɛrəldəd

unheroic
BR ˌʌnhɪˈrəʊɪk
AM ˌənhəˈrəʊɪk

unheroically
BR ˌʌnhɪˈrəʊɪkli
AM ˌənhəˈrəʊək(ə)li

unhesitating
BR ʌnˈhɛzɪteɪtɪŋ
AM ˌənˈhɛzəˌteɪdɪŋ

unhesitatingly
BR ʌnˈhɛzɪteɪtɪŋli
AM ˌənˈhɛzəˌteɪdɪŋli

unhesitatingness
BR ʌnˈhɛzɪteɪtɪŋnɪs
AM ˌənˈhɛzəˌteɪdɪŋnɪs

unhidden
BR ʌnˈhɪdn
AM ˌənˈhɪdən

unhindered
BR ʌnˈhɪndəd
AM ˌənˈhɪndərd

unhinge
BR (ˌ)ʌnˈhɪm(d)ʒ, -ɪz, -ɪŋ, -d
AM ˌənˈhɪndʒ, -ɪz, -ɪŋ, -d

unhip
BR ʌnˈhɪp
AM ˈənˈhɪp

unhistoric
BR ˌʌnhɪˈstɒrɪk
AM ˌən(h)ɪˈstɔrɪk

unhistorical
BR ˌʌnhɪˈstɒrɪkl
AM ˌən(h)ɪˈstɔrəkəl

unhistorically
BR ˌʌnhɪˈstɒrɪkli
AM ˌən(h)ɪˈstɔrək(ə)li

unhitch
BR (ˌ)ʌnˈhɪtʃ, -ɪz, -ɪŋ, -t
AM ˌənˈhɪtʃ, -ɪz, -ɪŋ, -t

unholiness
BR (ˌ)ʌnˈhəʊlnɪs
AM ˌənˈhoulinɪs

unholy
BR (ˌ)ʌnˈhəʊli
AM ˌənˈhouli

unhonored
BR (ˌ)ʌnˈɒnəd
AM ˌənˈɑnərd

unhonoured
BR (ˌ)ʌnˈɒnəd
AM ˌənˈɑnərd

unhooded
BR (ˌ)ʌnˈhʊdɪd
AM ˌənˈhʊdəd

unhook
BR (ˌ)ʌnˈhʊk, -s, -ɪŋ, -t
AM ˌənˈhʊk, -s, -ɪŋ, -t

unhoped
BR (ˌ)ʌnˈhəʊpt
AM ˌənˈhoupt

unhoped-for
BR (ˌ)ʌnˈhəʊptfɔː(r)

AM ˌənˈhoup(t)ˌfɔ(ə)r

unhopeful
BR (ˌ)ʌnˈhəʊpf(ʊ)l
AM ˌənˈhoupfəl

unhorse
BR (ˌ)ʌnˈhɔːs, -ɪz, -ɪŋ, -t
AM ˌənˈhɔ(ə)rs, -əz, -ɪŋ, -t

unhouse
BR (ˌ)ʌnˈhaʊz, -ɪz, -ɪŋ, -d
AM ˌənˈhaʊz, -əz, -ɪŋ, -d

unhuman
BR ʌnˈhjuːmən
AM ˌənˈ(h)jumən

unhung
BR ʌnˈhʌŋ
AM ˌənˈhəŋ

unhurried
BR (ˌ)ʌnˈhʌrɪd
AM ˌənˈhərid

unhurriedly
BR (ˌ)ʌnˈhʌrɪdli
AM ˌənˈhəridli

unhurrying
BR (ˌ)ʌnˈhʌrɪɪŋ
AM ˌənˈhəriɪŋ

unhurt
BR (ˌ)ʌnˈhəːt
AM ˌənˈhərt

unhusk
BR ʌnˈhʌsk, -s, -ɪŋ, -t
AM ˌənˈhəsk, -s, -ɪŋ, -t

unhygienic
BR ˌʌnhaɪˈdʒiːnɪk
AM ˌənhaɪˈdʒinɪk, ˌənhaɪˈdʒɛnɪk

unhygienically
BR ˌʌnhaɪˈdʒiːnɪkli
AM ˌənhaɪˈdʒɛnək(ə)li, ˌənhaɪˈdʒinək(ə)li

unhyphenated
BR (ˌ)ʌnˈhaɪfɪneɪtɪd
AM ˌənˈhaɪfəˌneɪdɪd

uni
BR ˈjuːn|i, -ɪz
AM ˈjuni, -z

Uniat
BR ˈjuːnɪat
AM ˈjuniˌæt, ˈjuniˌɪt, ˈjuniˌeɪt

Uniate
BR ˈjuːnɪət, ˈjuːnɪeɪt, -s
AM ˈjuniˌæt, ˈjuniˌɪt, ˈjuniˌeɪt, -s

uniaxial
BR ˌjuːnɪˈaksɪəl
AM ˌjuniˈæksɪəl

uniaxially
BR ˌjuːnɪˈaksɪəli
AM ˌjuniˈæksɪəli

unicameral
BR ˌjuːnɪˈkam(ə)rəl, ˌjuːnɪˈkam(ə)rl̩
AM ˌjunəˈkæm(ə)rəl

UNICEF
BR ˈjuːnɪsɛf

AM ˈjunəˌsɛf

unicellular
BR ˌjuːnɪˈsɛljələ(r)
AM ˌjunəˈsɛljələr

unicolor
BR ˌjuːnɪˈkʌlə(r), -d
AM ˈjunəˌkələr, -d

unicolour
BR ˌjuːnɪˈkʌlə(r), -d
AM ˈjunəˌkələr, -d

unicorn
BR ˈjuːnɪkɔːn, -z
AM ˈjunəˌkɔ(ə)rn, -z

unicuspid
BR ˌjuːnɪˈkʌspɪd, -z
AM ˌjunəˈkəspəd, -z

unicycle
BR ˈjuːnɪˌsʌɪkl, -z
AM ˈjunəˌsaɪkəl, -z

unicyclist
BR ˈjuːnɪˌsʌɪklɪst, -s
AM ˈjunəˌsaɪklɪst, -s

unidea'd
BR ˌʌnʌɪˈdɪəd
AM ˌənaɪˈdiəd

unideal
BR ˌʌnʌɪˈdɪəl, ˌʌnʌɪˈdiːəl
AM ˌənaɪˈdiəl

unidentifiable
BR ˌʌnʌɪˈdɛntɪfʌɪəbl
AM ˌənaɪˈdɛn(t)əˌfaɪəbəl

unidentified
BR ˌʌnʌɪˈdɛntɪfʌɪd
AM ˌənaɪˈdɛn(t)əˌfaɪd

unidimensional
BR ˌjuːnɪdʌɪˈmɛnʃn(ə)l, ˌjuːnɪdʌɪˈmɛnʃən(ə)l, ˌjuːnɪdɪˈmɛnʃn(ə)l, ˌjuːnɪdɪˈmɛnʃən(ə)l
AM ˌjunədəˈmen(t)ʃ(ə)nəl

unidiomatic
BR ˌʌnɪdɪəˈmatɪk
AM ˌənɪdiəˈmædɪk

unidirectional
BR ˌjuːnɪdʌɪˈrɛkʃn(ə)l, ˌjuːnɪdʌɪˈrɛkʃən(ə)l, ˌjuːnɪdɪˈrɛkʃn(ə)l, ˌjuːnɪdɪˈrɛkʃən(ə)l
AM ˌjunədəˈrɛkʃ(ə)nəl, ˌjunədaɪˈrɛkʃ(ə)nəl

unidirectionality
BR ˌjuːnɪdʌɪˌrɛkʃəˈnalɪti, ˌjuːnɪdɪˌrɛkʃəˈnalɪti
AM ˌjunədəˌrɛkʃəˈnælədi, ˌjunədaɪˌrɛkʃəˈnælədi

unidirectionally
BR ˌjuːnɪdʌɪˈrɛkʃnəli, ˌjuːnɪdʌɪˈrɛkʃn̩li, ˌjuːnɪdʌɪˈrɛkʃ(ə)nəli, ˌjuːnɪdɪˈrɛkʃnəli, ˌjuːnɪdɪˈrɛkʃn̩li, ˌjuːnɪdɪˈrɛkʃən̩li, ˌjuːnɪdɪˈrɛkʃ(ə)nəli
AM ˌjunədəˈrɛkʃ(ə)nəli, ˌjunədaɪˈrɛkʃ(ə)nəli

UNIDO
BR ˈjuːnɪdəʊ
AM ˈjunəˌdoʊ

unifiable
BR ˈjuːnɪfʌɪəbl
AM ˌjunəˈfaɪəbəl

unification
BR ˌjuːnɪfɪˈkeɪʃn
AM ˌjunəfəˈkeɪʃən

unificatory
BR ˌjuːnɪfɪˈkeɪt(ə)ri, ˌjuːnɪˈfɪkət(ə)ri
AM ˌjunəˈfɪkəˌtɔri

unifier
BR ˈjuːnɪfʌɪə(r), -z
AM ˈjunəˌfaɪər, -z

uniflow
BR ˈjuːnɪfləʊ
AM ˈjunəˌfloʊ

uniform
BR ˈjuːnɪfɔːm, -z
AM ˈjunəˌfɔ(ə)rm, -z

uniformitarian
BR ˌjuːnɪˌfɔːmɪˈtɛːrɪən, -z
AM ˌjunəˌfɔrməˈtɛriən, -z

uniformitarianism
BR ˌjuːnɪˌfɔːmɪˈtɛːrɪənɪz(ə)m
AM ˌjunəˌfɔrməˈtɛriənˌnɪzəm

uniformity
BR ˌjuːnɪˈfɔːmɪti
AM ˌjunəˈfɔrmədi

uniformly
BR ˈjuːnɪfɔːmli
AM ˈjunəˌfɔrmli

unify
BR ˈjuːnɪfʌɪ, -z, -ɪŋ, -d
AM ˈjunəˌfaɪ, -z, -ɪŋ, -d

Unigate®
BR ˈjuːnɪgeɪt
AM ˈjunəˌgeɪt

unilateral
BR ˌjuːnɪˈlat(ə)rəl, ˌjuːnɪˈlat(ə)rl̩
AM ˌjunəˈlædərəl

unilateralism
BR ˌjuːnɪˈlat(ə)rəlɪz(ə)m, ˌjuːnɪˈlat(ə)rl̩ɪz(ə)m
AM ˌjunəˈlædərəˌlɪzəm

unilateralist
BR ˌjuːnɪˈlat(ə)rəlɪst, ˌjuːnɪˈlat(ə)rl̩ɪst, -s
AM ˌjunəˈlædərələst, -s

unilaterally
BR ˌjuːnɪˈlat(ə)rəli, ˌjuːnɪˈlat(ə)rl̩i
AM ˌjunəˈlædərəli

Unilever®
BR ˈjuːnɪˌliːvə(r)
AM ˈjunəˌlivər

unilingual
BR ˌjuːnɪˈlɪŋgw(ə)l
AM ˌjunəˈlɪŋgwəl

unilingually
BR ˌjuːnɪˈlɪŋgwəli, ˌjuːnɪˈlɪŋgwl̩i
AM ˌjunəˈlɪŋgwəli

uniliteral
BR ˌjuːnɪˈlɪt(ə)rəl, ˌjuːnɪˈlɪt(ə)rl̩
AM ˌjunəˈlɪdərəl

unilluminated
BR ˌʌnɪˈl(j)uːmɪneɪtɪd
AM ˌʌnəˈluməˌneɪdɪd

unilluminating
BR ˌʌnɪˈl(j)uːmɪneɪtɪŋ
AM ˌʌnəˈluməˌneɪdɪŋ

unillustrated
BR (ˌ)ʌnˈɪləstreɪtɪd
AM ˌʌnˈɪləˌstreɪdɪd

unilocular
BR ˌjuːnɪˈlɒkjələ(r)
AM ˌjunəˈlakjələr

unimaginable
BR ˌʌnɪˈmadʒɪnəbl, ˌʌnɪˈmadʒn̩əbl
AM ˌʌnəˈmædʒ(ə)nəbəl

unimaginably
BR ˌʌnɪˈmadʒɪnəbli, ˌʌnɪˈmadʒn̩əbli
AM ˌʌnəˈmædʒ(ə)nəbli

unimaginative
BR ˌʌnɪˈmadʒɪnətɪv, ˌʌnɪˈmadʒn̩ətɪv
AM ˌʌnəˈmædʒ(ə)nədɪv

unimaginatively
BR ˌʌnɪˈmadʒɪnətɪvli, ˌʌnɪˈmadʒn̩ətɪvli
AM ˌʌnəˈmædʒ(ə)nədɪvli

unimaginativeness
BR ˌʌnɪˈmadʒɪnətɪvnɪs, ˌʌnɪˈmadʒn̩ətɪvnɪs
AM ˌʌnəˈmædʒ(ə)nədɪvnɪs

unimagined
BR ˌʌnɪˈmadʒ(ɪ)nd
AM ˌʌnəˈmædʒənd

unimpaired
BR ˌʌnɪmˈpɛːd
AM ˌʌnəmˈpɛ(ə)rd

unimparted
BR ˌʌnɪmˈpɑːtɪd
AM ˌʌnəmˈpɑrdəd

unimpassioned
BR ˌʌnɪmˈpaʃnd
AM ˌʌnəmˈpæʃənd

unimpeachable
BR ˌʌnɪmˈpiːtʃəbl
AM ˌʌnəmˈpitʃəbəl

unimpeachably
BR ˌʌnɪmˈpiːtʃəbli
AM ˌʌnəmˈpitʃəbli

unimpeded
BR ˌʌnɪmˈpiːdɪd
AM ˌʌnəmˈpidɪd

unimpededly
BR ˌʌnɪmˈpiːdɪdli
AM ˌʌnəmˈpidɪdli

unimportance
BR ˌʌnɪmˈpɔːt(ə)ns

AM ˌʌnəmˈpɔrtns

unimportant
BR ˌʌnɪmˈpɔːt(ə)nt
AM ˌʌnəmˈpɔrtnt

unimposing
BR ˌʌnɪmˈpəʊzɪŋ
AM ˌʌnəmˈpoʊzɪŋ

unimposingly
BR ˌʌnɪmˈpəʊzɪŋli
AM ˌʌnəmˈpoʊzɪŋli

unimpressed
BR ˌʌnɪmˈprest
AM ˌʌnəmˈprest

unimpressionable
BR ˌʌnɪmˈpreʃ(ə)nəbl, ˌʌnɪmˈpreʃn̩əbl
AM ˌʌnəmˈpreʃ(ə)nəbəl

unimpressive
BR ˌʌnɪmˈpresɪv
AM ˌʌnəmˈpresɪv

unimpressively
BR ˌʌnɪmˈpresɪvli
AM ˌʌnəmˈpresɪvli

unimpressiveness
BR ˌʌnɪmˈpresɪvnɪs
AM ˌʌnəmˈpresɪvnɪs

unimproved
BR ˌʌnɪmˈpruːvd
AM ˌʌnəmˈpruvd

unimpugned
BR ˌʌnɪmˈpjuːnd
AM ˌʌnəmˈpjund

unincorporated
BR ˌʌnɪnˈkɔːpəreɪtɪd
AM ˌʌnənˈkɔrpəˌreɪdɪd, ˌʌnɪŋˈkɔrpəˌreɪdɪd

unindexed
BR ˌʌnˈɪndɛkst
AM ˌʌnˈɪnˌdɛkst

uninfected
BR ˌʌnɪnˈfɛktɪd
AM ˌʌnənˈfɛktəd

uninflamed
BR ˌʌnɪnˈfleɪmd
AM ˌʌnənˈfleɪmd

uninflammable
BR ˌʌnɪnˈflaməbl
AM ˌʌnənˈflæməbəl

uninflected
BR ˌʌnɪnˈflɛktɪd
AM ˌʌnənˈflɛktəd

uninfluenced
BR (ˌ)ʌnˈɪnfluənst
AM ˌʌnˈɪnˌfluənst

uninfluential
BR ˌʌnɪnfluˈɛnʃl
AM ˌʌnənˌfluˈɛn(t)ʃəl

uninformative
BR ˌʌnɪnˈfɔːmətɪv
AM ˌʌnənˈfɔrmədɪv

uninformed
BR ˌʌnɪnˈfɔːmd
AM ˌʌnənˈfɔ(ə)rmd

uninhabitable
BR ˌʌnɪnˈhabɪtəbl
AM ˌʌnənˈhæbədəbəl

uninhabitableness
BR ˌʌnɪnˈhabɪtəblnəs
AM ˌʌnənˈhæbədəbəlnəs

uninhabited
BR ˌʌnɪnˈhabɪtɪd
AM ˌʌnənˈhæbədəd

uninhibited
BR ˌʌnɪnˈhɪbɪtɪd
AM ˌʌnənˈhɪbɪdɪd

uninhibitedly
BR ˌʌnɪnˈhɪbɪtɪdli
AM ˌʌnənˈhɪbɪdɪdli

uninhibitedness
BR ˌʌnɪnˈhɪbɪtɪdnɪs
AM ˌʌnənˈhɪbɪdɪdnɪs

uninitiated
BR ˌʌnɪˈnɪʃieɪtɪd
AM ˌʌnəˈnɪʃiˌeɪdɪd

uninjured
BR (ˌ)ʌnˈɪn(d)ʒəd
AM ˌʌnˈɪndʒərd

uninspired
BR ˌʌnɪnˈspʌɪəd
AM ˌʌnənˈspaɪ(ə)rd

uninspiring
BR ˌʌnɪnˈspʌɪərɪŋ
AM ˌʌnənˈspaɪ(ə)rɪŋ

uninspiringly
BR ˌʌnɪnˈspʌɪərɪŋli
AM ˌʌnənˈspaɪ(ə)rɪŋli

uninstructed
BR ˌʌnɪnˈstrʌktɪd
AM ˌʌnənˈstrəktəd

uninsulated
BR (ˌ)ʌnˈɪnsjəleɪtɪd
AM ˌʌnˈɪns(j)əˌleɪdɪd

uninsurable
BR ˌʌnɪnˈʃʊərəbl, ˌʌnɪnˈʃɔːrəbl
AM ˌʌnənˈʃʊrəbəl

uninsured
BR ˌʌnɪnˈʃʊəd, ˌʌnɪnˈʃɔːd
AM ˌʌnənˈʃʊ(ə)rd

unintegrated
BR (ˌ)ʌnˈɪntɪgreɪtɪd
AM ˌʌnˈɪn(t)əˌgreɪdɪd

unintellectual
BR ˌʌnɪntɪˈlɛktʃʊəl, ˌʌnɪntɪˈlɛktʃ(ʊ)l, ˌʌnɪntɪˈlɛktjʊəl, ˌʌnɪntɪˈlɛktjəl
AM ˌʌnˌɪn(t)əˈlɛk(t)ʃ(əw)əl

unintelligent
BR ˌʌnɪnˈtɛlɪdʒ(ə)nt
AM ˌʌnənˈtɛlədʒənt

unintelligently
BR ˌʌnɪnˈtɛlɪdʒ(ə)ntli
AM ˌʌnənˈtɛlədʒən(t)li

unintelligibility
BR ˌʌnɪnˌtɛlɪdʒɪˈbɪlɪti
AM ˌʌnənˌtɛlədʒəˈbɪlɪdi

unintelligible
BR ˌʌnɪnˈtɛlɪdʒɪbl
AM ˌʌnənˈtɛlədʒəbəl

unintelligibleness
BR ˌʌnɪnˈtɛlɪdʒɪblnəs
AM ˌənənˈtɛlədʒəbəlnəs

unintelligibly
BR ˌʌnɪnˈtɛlɪdʒɪbli
AM ˌənənˈtɛlədʒəbli

unintended
BR ˌʌnɪnˈtɛndɪd
AM ˌənənˈtɛndəd

unintentional
BR ˌʌnɪnˈtɛnʃn̩(ə)l,
ˌʌnɪnˈtɛnʃən(ə)l
AM ˌənənˈtɛn(t)ʃ(ə)nəl

unintentionally
BR ˌʌnɪnˈtɛnʃn̩əli,
ˌʌnɪnˈtɛnʃn̩li,
ˌʌnɪnˈtɛnʃənli,
ˌʌnɪnˈtɛnʃ(ə)nəli
AM ˌənənˈtɛn(t)ʃ(ə)nəli

uninterested
BR (ˌ)ʌnˈɪntrɪstɪd,
(ˌ)ʌnˈɪnt(ə)rɛstɪd
AM ˌənˈɪntrəstəd,
ˌənˈɪn(t)ərəstəd,
ˌənˈɪn(t)əˌrɛstəd

uninterestedly
BR (ˌ)ʌnˈɪntrɪstɪdli,
(ˌ)ʌnˈɪnt(ə)rɛstɪdli
AM ˌənˈɪntrəstədli,
ˌənˈɪn(t)ərəstədli,
ˌənˈɪn(t)əˌrɛstədli

uninterestedness
BR (ˌ)ʌnˈɪntrɪstɪdnɪs,
(ˌ)ʌnˈɪnt(ə)rɛstɪdnɪs
AM ˌənˈɪntrəstədnəs,
ˌənˈɪn(t)ərəstədnəs,
ˌənˈɪn(t)əˌrɛstədnəs

uninteresting
BR (ˌ)ʌnˈɪntrɪstɪŋ,
(ˌ)ʌnˈɪnt(ə)rɛstɪŋ
AM ˌənˈɪntrəstɪŋ,
ˌənˈɪn(t)ərəstɪŋ,
ˌənˈɪn(t)əˌrɛstɪŋ

uninterestingly
BR (ˌ)ʌnˈɪntrɪstɪŋli,
(ˌ)ʌnˈɪnt(ə)rɛstɪŋli
AM ˌənˈɪntrəstɪŋli,
ˌənˈɪn(t)ərəstɪŋli,
ˌənˈɪn(t)əˌrɛstɪŋli

uninterestingness
BR (ˌ)ʌnˈɪntrɪstɪŋnɪs,
(ˌ)ʌnˈɪnt(ə)rɛstɪŋnɪs
AM ˌənˈɪntrəstɪŋnɪs,
ˌənˈɪn(t)ərəstɪŋnɪs,
ˌənˈɪn(t)əˌrɛstɪŋnɪs

uninterpretable
BR ˌʌnɪnˈtəːprɪtəbl
AM ˌənənˈtərprədəbəl

uninterpreted
BR ˌʌnɪnˈtəːprɪtɪd
AM ˌənənˈtərprədəd

uninterrupted
BR ˌʌnɪntəˈrʌptɪd
AM ˌənˌɪn(t)əˈrəptəd

uninterruptedly
BR ˌʌnɪntəˈrʌptɪdli
AM ˌənˌɪn(t)əˈrəptədli

uninterruptedness
BR ˌʌnɪntəˈrʌptɪdnɪs
AM ˌənˌɪn(t)əˈrəptədnəs

uninterruptible
BR ˌʌnɪntəˈrʌptɪbl
AM ˌənˌɪn(t)əˈrəptəbəl

unintimidated
BR ˌʌnɪnˈtɪmɪdeɪtɪd
AM ˌənənˈtɪməˌdeɪdɪd

uninucleate
BR ˌjuːnɪˈnjuːkliːeɪt
AM ˌjuːnəˈn(j)ukliːt

uninvented
BR ˌʌnɪnˈvɛntɪd
AM ˌənənˈven(t)əd

uninventive
BR ˌʌnɪnˈvɛntɪv
AM ˌənənˈven(t)ɪv

uninventively
BR ˌʌnɪnˈvɛntɪvli
AM ˌənənˈven(t)ɪvli

uninventiveness
BR ˌʌnɪnˈvɛntɪvnɪs
AM ˌənənˈven(t)ɪvnɪs

uninvested
BR ˌʌnɪnˈvɛstɪd
AM ˌənənˈvestəd

uninvestigated
BR ˌʌnɪnˈvɛstɪgeɪtɪd
AM ˌənənˈvestəˌgeɪdɪd

uninvited
BR ˌʌnɪnˈvʌɪtɪd
AM ˌənənˈvaɪdɪd

uninvitedly
BR ˌʌnɪnˈvʌɪtɪdli
AM ˌənənˈvaɪdɪdli

uninviting
BR ˌʌnɪnˈvʌɪtɪŋ
AM ˌənənˈvaɪdɪŋ

uninvitingly
BR ˌʌnɪnˈvʌɪtɪŋli
AM ˌənənˈvaɪdɪŋli

uninvoked
BR ˌʌnɪnˈvəʊkt
AM ˌənənˈvoʊkt

uninvolved
BR ˌʌnɪnˈvɒlvd
AM ˌənənˈvalvd

union
BR ˈjuːnɪən, -z
AM ˈjunjən, -z

union-bashing
BR ˈjuːnɪənˌbaʃɪŋ
AM ˈjunjənˌbæʃɪŋ

unionisation
BR ˌjuːnɪənʌɪˈzeɪʃn
AM ˌjunjənəˈzeɪʃən,
ˌjunjəˌnaɪˈzeɪʃən

unionise
BR ˈjuːnɪənʌɪz, -ɪz, -ɪŋ,
-d
AM ˈjunjəˌnaɪz, -ɪz, -ɪŋ,
-d

un-ionised
BR ˌʌnˈʌɪənʌɪzd
AM ˌənˈaɪəˌnaɪzd

unionism
BR ˈjuːnɪənɪz(ə)m
AM ˈjunjəˌnɪzəm

unionist
BR ˈjuːnɪənɪst, -s
AM ˈjunjənəst, -s

unionistic
BR ˌjuːnɪəˈnɪstɪk
AM ˌjunjəˈnɪstɪk

unionization
BR ˌjuːnɪənʌɪˈzeɪʃn
AM ˌjunjənəˈzeɪʃən,
ˌjunjəˌnaɪˈzeɪʃən

unionize
BR ˈjuːnɪənʌɪz, -ɪz, -ɪŋ,
-d
AM ˈjunjəˌnaɪz, -ɪz, -ɪŋ,
-d

un-ionized
BR ˌʌnˈʌɪənʌɪzd
AM ˌənˈaɪəˌnaɪzd

Union Jack
BR ˌjuːnɪən ˈdʒak, -s
AM ˌjunjən ˈdʒæk, -s

uniparous
BR juːˈnɪp(ə)rəs
AM juˈnɪp(ə)rəs

Unipart
BR ˈjuːnɪpɑːt
AM ˈjunəˌpɑrt

unipartite
BR ˌjuːnɪˈpɑːtʌɪt
AM ˌjunəˈpɑrˌtaɪt

uniped
BR ˈjuːnɪpɛd, -z
AM ˈjunəˌpɛd, -z

unipersonal
BR ˌjuːnɪˈpəːsn̩(ə)l
AM ˌjunəˈpərs(ə)nəl

uniplanar
BR ˌjuːnɪˈpleɪnə(r)
AM ˌjunəˈpleɪnər

unipod
BR ˈjuːnɪpɒd, -z
AM ˈjunəˌpad, -z

unipolar
BR ˌjuːnɪˈpəʊlə(r)
AM ˌjunəˈpoʊlər

unipolarity
BR ˌjuːnɪpə(ʊ)ˈlarɪti
AM ˌjunəpəˈlɛrədi,
ˌjunəˌpoʊˈlɛrədi

unique
BR juːˈniːk, jʊˈniːk
AM juˈnik

uniquely
BR juːˈniːkli, jʊˈniːkli
AM juˈnikli

uniqueness
BR juːˈniːknɪs,
jʊˈniːknɪs
AM juˈniknɪs

unironed
BR (ˌ)ʌnˈʌɪənd
AM ˌənˈaɪ(ə)rnd

Uniroyal®
BR ˈjuːnɪˌrɔɪəl

uniserial
BR ˌjuːnɪˈsɪərɪəl
AM ˌjunɪˈsɪriəl

unisex
BR ˈjuːnɪsɛks
AM ˈjunəˌsɛks

unisexual
BR ˌjuːnɪˈsɛkʃʊəl,
juːnɪˈsɛkʃ(ʊ)əl,
juːnɪˈsɛksjʊ(ə)l
AM ˌjunəˈsɛkʃ(əw)əl

unisexuality
BR ˌjuːnɪˌsɛkʃʊˈalɪti,
juːnɪˌsɛksjʊˈalɪti
AM ˌjunəˌsɛkʃəˈwælədi

unisexually
BR ˌjuːnɪˈsɛkʃʊəli,
juːnɪˈsɛkʃʊli,
juːnɪˈsɛkʃli,
juːnɪˈsɛksjʊ(ə)li
AM ˌjunəˈsɛkʃ(əw)əli

UNISON
BR ˈjuːnɪs(ə)n,
ˈjuːnɪz(ə)n
AM ˈjunəs(ə)n,
ˈjunəz(ə)n

unison
BR ˈjuːnɪs(ə)n,
ˈjuːnɪz(ə)n
AM ˈjunəs(ə)n,
ˈjunəz(ə)n

unisonant
BR juːˈnɪsənənt,
juːˈnɪsnənt,
jəˈnɪsənənt,
jəˈnɪsnənt
AM juˈnɪsənənt

unisonous
BR juːˈnɪsənəs,
juːˈnɪsnəs, jəˈnɪsənəs,
jəˈnɪsnəs
AM juˈnɪsənəs

unissued
BR (ˌ)ʌnˈɪʃ(j)uːd,
(ˌ)ʌnˈɪsjuːd
AM ˌənˈɪʃ(j)ud

unit
BR ˈjuːnɪt, -s
AM ˈjunət, -s

UNITA
BR juːˈniːtə(r),
jəˈniːtə(r)
AM juˈnidɑ

UNITAR
BR juːˈniːtɑː(r),
jəˈniːtɑː(r),
ˈjuːnɪtɑː(r)
AM ˈjunəˌtɑr

Unitarian
BR ˌjuːnɪˈtɛːrɪən, -z
AM ˌjunəˈteriən, -z

Unitarianism
BR ˌjuːnɪˈtɛːrɪənɪz(ə)m
AM ˌjunəˈteriəˌnɪzəm

unitarily
BR ˈjuːnɪt(ə)rɪli
AM ˈjunəˌtɛrəli

unitarity
BR ˈjuːnɪˈtarɪti
AM ˈjunəˈtɛrədi

unitary
BR ˈjuːnɪt(ə)ri
AM ˈjunəˌtɛri

unite
BR juːˈnaɪt, jəˈnaɪt, -s, -ɪŋ, -ɪd
AM juˈnaɪ|t, -ts, -dɪŋ, -dɪd

unitedly
BR juːˈnaɪtɪdli, jəˈnaɪtɪdli
AM juˈnaɪdɪdli

United Nations
BR jʊˌnaɪtɪd ˈneɪʃnz
AM juˌnaɪdɪd ˈneɪʃənz

United States
BR jʊˌnaɪtɪd ˈsteɪts
AM juˌnaɪdɪd ˈsteɪts

unitholder
BR ˈjuːnɪtˌhəʊldə(r), -z
AM ˈjunətˌ(h)oʊldər, -z

unitive
BR ˈjuːnɪtɪv
AM ˈjunədɪv

unitively
BR ˈjuːnɪtɪvli
AM ˈjunədɪvli

unitize
BR ˈjuːnɪtaɪz, -ɪz, -ɪŋ, -d
AM ˈjunəˌtaɪz, -ɪz, -ɪŋ, -d

unit-linked
BR ˈjuːnɪtˈlɪŋ(k)t
AM ˈjunətˌlɪŋkt

unit trust
BR ˈjuːnɪt ˈtrʌst, -s
AM ˈjunə(t) ˈtrəst, -s

unity
BR ˈjuːnɪt|i, -ɪz
AM ˈjunədi, -z

Univac
BR ˈjuːnɪvak
AM ˈjunəˌvæk

univalent
BR ˈjuːnɪˈveɪlənt, juːnɪˈveɪlnt, -s
AM ˈjunəˈveɪlənt, -s

univalve
BR ˈjuːnɪvalv, -z
AM ˈjunəˌvælv, -z

universal
BR ˈjuːnɪˈvəːsl
AM ˈjunəˈvərsəl

universalisability
BR ˈjuːnɪvəːsələʌɪzəˈbɪlɪti, juːnɪvəːslʌɪzəˈbɪlɪti
AM ˈjunəˌvərsəˌlaɪzəˈbɪlɪdi

universalisation
BR ˈjuːnɪvəːsəlʌɪˈzeɪʃn, juːnɪvəːslʌɪˈzeɪʃn
AM ˈjunəˌvərsələˈzeɪʃən, ˌjunəˌvərsəˌlaɪˈzeɪʃən

universalise
BR ˈjuːnɪˈvəːsəlʌɪz, juːnɪˈvəːslʌɪz, -ɪz, -ɪŋ, -d
AM ˈjunəˈvərsəˌlaɪz, -ɪz, -ɪŋ, -d

universalism
BR ˈjuːnɪˈvəːsəlɪz(ə)m, juːnɪˈvəːslɪz(ə)m
AM ˈjunəˈvərsəˌlɪzəm

universalist
BR ˈjuːnɪˈvəːsəlɪst, juːnɪˈvəːslɪst, -s
AM ˈjunəˈvərsələst, -s

universalistic
BR ˈjuːnɪˌvəːsəˈlɪstɪk, juːnɪˌvəːslˈɪstɪk
AM ˈjunəˌvərsəˈlɪstɪk

universality
BR ˈjuːnɪvəːˈsalɪti
AM ˈjunəvərˈsælədi

universalizability
BR ˈjuːnɪvəːsələʌɪzəˈbɪlɪti, juːnɪvəːslʌɪzəˈbɪlɪti
AM ˈjunəˌvərsəˌlaɪzəˈbɪlɪdi

universalization
BR ˈjuːnɪvəːsəlʌɪˈzeɪʃn, juːnɪvəːslʌɪˈzeɪʃn
AM ˈjunəˌvərsələˈzeɪʃən, ˌjunəˌvərsəˌlaɪˈzeɪʃən

universalize
BR ˈjuːnɪˈvəːsəlʌɪz, juːnɪˈvəːslʌɪz, -ɪz, -ɪŋ, -d
AM ˈjunəˈvərsəˌlaɪz, -ɪz, -ɪŋ, -d

universally
BR ˈjuːnɪˈvəːsl̩i, juːnɪˈvəːsəli
AM ˈjunəˈvərsəli

universe
BR ˈjuːnɪvəːs, -ɪz
AM ˈjunəvərs, -əz

university
BR ˈjuːnɪˈvəːsɪt|i, -ɪz
AM ˈjunəˈvərsədi, -z

univocal
BR ˈjuːnɪˈvəʊkl
AM ˈjunəˈvoʊkəl

univocality
BR ˈjuːnɪvəʊˈkalɪti
AM ˈjunəˌvooˈkælədi

univocally
BR ˈjuːnɪˈvəʊkl̩i, juːnɪˈvəʊkəli
AM ˈjunəˈvoʊkəli

UNIX®
BR ˈjuːnɪks
AM ˈjunɪks

unjaundiced
BR ˌʌnˈdʒɔːndɪst
AM ˌənˈdʒɔːndəst, ˌənˈdʒɑndəst

unjoin
BR ˌʌnˈdʒɔɪn, -z, -ɪŋ, -d
AM ˌənˈdʒɔɪn, -z, -ɪŋ, -d

unjoint
BR ˌʌnˈdʒɔɪnt, -s, -ɪŋ, -ɪd
AM ˌənˈdʒɔɪn|t, -ts, -(t)ɪŋ, -(t)ɪd

unjust
BR ˌʌnˈdʒʌst
AM ˌənˈdʒəst

unjustifiable
BR ˌ(ˌ)ʌnˈdʒʌstɪfʌɪəbl, ˌʌndʒʌstɪˈfʌɪəbl
AM ˌənˈdʒəstəˈfaɪəbəl

unjustifiably
BR ˌ(ˌ)ʌnˈdʒʌstɪfʌɪəbli, ˌʌndʒʌstɪˈfʌɪəbli
AM ˌən,dʒəstəˈfaɪəbli

unjustified
BR ˌ(ˌ)ʌnˈdʒʌstɪfʌɪd
AM ˌənˈdʒəstəˌfaɪd

unjustly
BR ˌʌnˈdʒʌstli
AM ˌənˈdʒəs(t)li

unjustness
BR ˌʌnˈdʒʌs(t)nəs
AM ˌənˈdʒəs(t)nəs

unkempt
BR ˌʌnˈkɛm(p)t
AM ˌənˈkɛm(p)t

unkemptly
BR ˌʌnˈkɛm(p)tli
AM ˌənˈkɛm(p)tli

unkemptness
BR ˌʌnˈkɛm(p)tnəs
AM ˌənˈkɛm(p)tnəs

unkept
BR ˌʌnˈkɛpt
AM ˌənˈkɛpt

unkillable
BR ˌʌnˈkɪləbl
AM ˌənˈkɪləbəl

unkind
BR ˌʌnˈkʌɪnd, -ə(r), -ɪst
AM ˌənˈkaɪnd, -ər, -ɪst

unkindly
BR ˌʌnˈkʌɪndli
AM ˌənˈkaɪn(d)li

unkindness
BR ˌʌnˈkʌɪn(d)nɪs
AM ˌənˈkaɪn(d)nɪs

unking
BR ˌʌnˈkɪŋ, -z, -ɪŋ, -d
AM ˌənˈkɪŋ, -z, -ɪŋ, -d

unkink
BR ˌʌnˈkɪŋ|k, -ks, -kɪŋ, -(k)t
AM ˌənˈkɪŋ|k, -ks, -kɪŋ, -(k)t

unkissed
BR ˌʌnˈkɪst
AM ˌənˈkɪst

unknit
BR ˌʌnˈnɪt, -s, -ɪŋ, -ɪd
AM ˌənˈnɪ|t, -ts, -dɪŋ, -dɪd

unknot
BR ˌʌnˈnɒt, -s, -ɪŋ, -ɪd
AM ˌənˈnɑ|t, -ts, -dɪŋ, -dəd

unknowable
BR ˌ(ˌ)ʌnˈnəʊəbl
AM ˌənˈnoʊəbəl

unknowing
BR ˌ(ˌ)ʌnˈnəʊɪŋ
AM ˌənˈnoʊɪŋ

unknowingly
BR ˌ(ˌ)ʌnˈnəʊɪŋli
AM ˌənˈnoʊɪŋli

unknowingness
BR ˌ(ˌ)ʌnˈnəʊɪŋnɪs
AM ˌənˈnoʊɪŋnɪs

unknown
BR ˌ(ˌ)ʌnˈnəʊn
AM ˌənˈnoʊn

unknownness
BR ˌ(ˌ)ʌnˈnəʊnnəs
AM ˌənˈnoʊ(n)nəs

unlabelled
BR ˌʌnˈleɪbld
AM ˌənˈleɪbəld

unlaboured
BR ˌʌnˈleɪbəd
AM ˌənˈleɪbərd

unlace
BR ˌʌnˈleɪs, -ɪz, -ɪŋ, -t
AM ˌənˈleɪs, -ɪz, -ɪŋ, -t

unlade
BR ˌʌnˈleɪd, -z, -ɪŋ, -ɪd
AM ˌənˈleɪd, -z, -ɪŋ, -ɪd

unladen
BR ˌʌnˈleɪdn
AM ˌənˈleɪdn

unladylike
BR ˌʌnˈleɪdɪlʌɪk
AM ˌənˈleɪdiˌlaɪk

unlaid
BR ˌʌnˈleɪd
AM ˌənˈleɪd

unlamented
BR ˌʌnləˈmɛntɪd
AM ˌənləˈmɛn(t)əd

unlash
BR ˌʌnˈlaʃ, -ɪz, -ɪŋ, -t
AM ˌənˈlæʃ, -əz, -ɪŋ, -t

unlatch
BR ˌʌnˈlatʃ, -ɪz, -ɪŋ, -t
AM ˌənˈlætʃ, -əz, -ɪŋ, -t

unlawful
BR ˌ(ˌ)ʌnˈlɔːf(ʊ)l
AM ˌənˈlɔfəl, ˌənˈlɑfəl

unlawfully
BR ˌ(ˌ)ʌnˈlɔːfəli, ˌ(ˌ)ʌnˈlɔːfli
AM ˌənˈlɔfəli, ˌənˈlɑfəli

unlawfulness
BR ˌ(ˌ)ʌnˈlɔːf(ʊ)lnəs
AM ˌənˈlɔfəlnəs, ˌənˈlɑfəlnəs

unlay
BR ˌʌnˈleɪ, -z, -ɪŋ
AM ˌənˈleɪ, -z, -ɪŋ

unleaded
BR ˌʌnˈlɛdɪd
AM ˌənˈlɛdəd

unlearn
BR ˌʌnˈləːn, -z, -ɪŋ, -t

AM ˌən'lɜrn, -z, -ɪŋ, -t

unlearned
adjective
BR ˌʌn'lɜːnɪd
AM ˌən'lɜrn(ə)d

unlearnedly
BR ˌʌn'lɜːnɪdli
AM ˌən'lɜrnədli

unlearnedness
BR ˌʌn'lɜːnɪdnɪs
AM ˌən'lɜrnədnəs

unleash
BR (ˌ)ʌn'liːʃ, -ɪz, -ɪŋ, -t
AM ˌən'liːʃ, -ɪz, -ɪŋ, -t

unleavened
BR ˌʌn'lɛvnd
AM ˌən'lɛvənd

unless
BR (ə)n'lɛs, ʌn'lɛs
AM ən'lɛs

unlet
BR ˌʌn'lɛt
AM ˌən'lɛt

unlettered
BR ˌʌn'lɛtəd
AM ˌən'lɛdərd

unliberated
BR ˌʌn'lɪbəreɪtɪd
AM ˌən'lɪbəˌreɪdɪd

unlicensed
BR (ˌ)ʌn'laɪsnst
AM ˌən'laɪsənst

unlighted
BR ˌʌn'laɪtɪd
AM ˌən'laɪdɪd

unlikable
BR (ˌ)ʌn'laɪkəbl
AM ˌən'laɪkəbəl

unlike
BR (ˌ)ʌn'laɪk
AM ˌən'laɪk

unlikeable
BR (ˌ)ʌn'laɪkəbl
AM ˌən'laɪkəbəl

unlikelihood
BR (ˌ)ʌn'laɪklɪhʊd
AM ˌən'laɪkliˌhʊd

unlikeliness
BR (ˌ)ʌn'laɪklɪnɪs
AM ˌən'laɪklinɪs

unlikely
BR (ˌ)ʌn'laɪkli
AM ˌən'laɪkli

unlikeness
BR (ˌ)ʌn'laɪknɪs
AM ˌən'laɪknɪs

unlimited
BR ʌn'lɪmɪtɪd
AM ˌən'lɪmɪdɪd

unlimitedly
BR ʌn'lɪmɪtɪdli
AM ˌən'lɪmɪdɪdli

unlimitedness
BR ʌn'lɪmɪtɪdnɪs
AM ˌən'lɪmɪdɪdnɪs

unlined
BR (ˌ)ʌn'laɪnd

AM ˌən'laɪnd

unlink
BR ˌʌn'lɪŋ|k, -ks, -kɪŋ, -(k)t
AM ˌən'lɪŋ|k, -ks, -kɪŋ, -(k)t

unliquidated
BR ˌʌn'lɪkwɪdeɪtɪd
AM ˌən'lɪkwəˌdeɪdɪd

unlisted
BR (ˌ)ʌn'lɪstɪd
AM ˌən'lɪstɪd

unlistenable
BR ˌʌn'lɪsnəbl
AM ˌən'lɪsnəbəl, ˌən'lɪsnəbəl

unlit
BR ˌʌn'lɪt
AM ˌən'lɪt

unliterary
BR ˌʌn'lɪt(ə)rəri
AM ˌən'lɪtrəri, ˌən'lɪdəˌrɛri

unlivable
BR ˌʌn'lɪvəbl
AM ˌən'lɪvəbəl

unlived-in
BR (ˌ)ʌn'lɪvdɪn
AM ˌən'lɪv.dɪn

unload
BR (ˌ)ʌn'ləʊd, -z, -ɪŋ, -ɪd
AM ˌən'loʊd, -z, -ɪŋ, -əd

unloader
BR (ˌ)ʌn'ləʊdə(r), -z
AM ˌən'loʊdər, -z

unlocatable
BR ˌʌnlə(ʊ)'keɪtəbl
AM ˌən'loʊ'keɪdəbəl

unlocated
BR ˌʌnlə(ʊ)'keɪtɪd
AM ˌən'loʊˌkeɪdɪd

unlock
BR (ˌ)ʌn'lɒk, -s, -ɪŋ, -t
AM ˌən'lɑk, -s, -ɪŋ, -t

unlooked
BR (ˌ)ʌn'lʊkt
AM ˌən'lʊkt

unlooked-for
BR (ˌ)ʌn'lʊktfɔː(r)
AM ˌən'lʊktˌfɔ(ə)r

unloose
BR (ˌ)ʌn'luːs, -ɪz, -ɪŋ, -t
AM ˌən'lus, -əz, -ɪŋ, -t

unloosen
BR (ˌ)ʌn'luːs|n, -nz, -nɪŋ \-nɪŋ, -nd
AM ˌən'lusən, -z, -ɪŋ, -d

unlovable
BR (ˌ)ʌn'lʌvəbl
AM ˌən'lʌvəbəl

unloveable
BR (ˌ)ʌn'lʌvəbl
AM ˌən'lʌvəbəl

unloved
BR (ˌ)ʌn'lʌvd
AM ˌən'lʌvd

unloveliness
BR (ˌ)ʌn'lʌvlɪnɪs
AM ˌən'lʌvlinɪs

unlovely
BR (ˌ)ʌn'lʌvli
AM ˌən'lʌvli

unloving
BR (ˌ)ʌn'lʌvɪŋ
AM ˌən'lʌvɪŋ

unlovingly
BR (ˌ)ʌn'lʌvɪŋli
AM ˌən'lʌvɪŋli

unlovingness
BR (ˌ)ʌn'lʌvɪŋnɪs
AM ˌən'lʌvɪŋnɪs

unluckily
BR (ˌ)ʌn'lʌkɪli
AM ˌən'lʌkəli

unluckiness
BR (ˌ)ʌn'lʌkɪnɪs
AM ˌən'lʌkinɪs

unlucky
BR (ˌ)ʌn'lʌk|i, -ɪə(r), -ɪɪst
AM ˌən'lʌki, -ər, -ɪst

unmade
BR ˌʌn'meɪd
AM ˌən'meɪd

unmaidenly
BR ˌʌn'meɪdnli
AM ˌən'meɪdnli

unmake
BR ˌʌn'meɪk, -s, -ɪŋ
AM ˌən'meɪk, -s, -ɪŋ

unmalleable
BR ˌʌn'malɪəbl
AM ˌən'mælɪəbəl, ˌən'mæl(j)əbəl

unman
BR ˌʌn'man, -z, -ɪŋ, -d
AM ˌən'mæn, -z, -ɪŋ, -d

unmanageable
BR (ˌ)ʌn'manɪdʒəbl
AM ˌən'mænədʒəbəl

unmanageableness
BR (ˌ)ʌn'manɪdʒəblnəs
AM ˌən'mænədʒəbəlnəs

unmanageably
BR (ˌ)ʌn'manɪdʒəbli
AM ˌən'mænədʒəbli

unmanaged
BR (ˌ)ʌn'manɪdʒd
AM ˌən'mænədʒd

unmaneuvrable
BR ˌʌnmə'nuːv(ə)rəbl
AM ˌənmə'n(j)uv(ə)rəbəl

unmanliness
BR (ˌ)ʌn'manlɪnɪs
AM ˌən'mænlinɪs

unmanly
BR (ˌ)ʌn'manli
AM ˌən'mænli

unmanned
BR ˌʌn'mand
AM ˌən'mænd

unmannered
BR ˌʌn'manəd
AM ˌən'mænərd

unmannerliness
BR ˌʌn'manəlɪnɪs
AM ˌən'mænərlinɪs

unmannerly
BR ˌʌn'manəli
AM ˌən'mænərli

unmanoeuvrable
BR ˌʌnmə'nuːv(ə)rəbl
AM ˌənmə'n(j)uv(ə)rəbəl

unmanured
BR ˌʌnmə'njʊəd, ˌʌnmə'njɔːd
AM ˌənmə'n(j)ʊ(ə)rd

unmapped
BR ˌʌn'mapt
AM ˌən'mæpt

unmarked
BR ˌʌn'mɑːkt
AM ˌən'mɑrkt

unmarkedness
BR ˌʌn'mɑːkɪdnɪs
AM ˌən'mɑrkədnəs

unmarketable
BR ˌʌn'mɑːkɪtəbl
AM ˌən'mɑrkədəbəl

unmarred
BR ˌʌn'mɑːd
AM ˌən'mɑrd

unmarriageable
BR ˌʌn'marɪdʒəbl
AM ˌən'mɛrədʒəbəl

unmarried
BR ˌʌn'marɪd
AM ˌən'mɛrɪd

unmasculine
BR ˌʌn'maskjʊlɪn
AM ˌən'mæskjələn

unmask
BR ˌʌn'mɑːsk, ˌʌn'mask, -s, -ɪŋ, -t
AM ˌən'mæsk, -s, -ɪŋ, -t

unmasker
BR ˌʌn'mɑːskə(r), ˌʌn'maskə(r), -z
AM ˌən'mæskər, -z

unmatchable
BR ˌʌn'matʃəbl
AM ˌən'mætʃəbəl

unmatchably
BR ˌʌn'matʃəbli
AM ˌən'mætʃəbli

unmatched
BR ˌʌn'matʃt
AM ˌən'mætʃt

unmated
BR ˌʌn'meɪtɪd
AM ˌən'meɪdɪd

unmatured
BR ˌʌnmə'tʃʊəd, ˌʌnmə'tjʊəd, ˌʌnmə'tʃɔːd, ˌʌnmə'tjɔːd
AM ˌənmə'tʃərd, ˌənmə'tʃʊ(ə)rd

unmeaning
BR (ˌ)ʌnˈmiːnɪŋ
AM ˌənˈminɪŋ

unmeaningly
BR (ˌ)ʌnˈmiːnɪŋli
AM ˌənˈminɪŋli

unmeaningness
BR (ˌ)ʌnˈmiːnɪŋnɪs
AM ˌənˈminɪŋnɪs

unmeant
BR ˌʌnˈmɛnt
AM ˌənˈmɛnt

unmeasurable
BR (ˌ)ʌnˈmɛʒ(ə)rəbl
AM ˌənˈmɛʒ(ə)rəbəl,
ˌənˈmɛʒərbəl

unmeasurably
BR (ˌ)ʌnˈmɛʒ(ə)rəbli
AM ˌənˈmɛʒ(ə)rəbli,
ˌənˈmɛʒərbli

unmeasured
BR (ˌ)ʌnˈmɛʒəd
AM ˌənˈmɛʒərd

unmediated
BR ˌʌnˈmiːdɪeɪtɪd
AM ˌənˈmidiˌeɪdɪd

unmelodious
BR ˌʌnmɪˈləʊdɪəs
AM ˌənməˈloʊdiəs

unmelodiously
BR ˌʌnmɪˈləʊdɪəsli
AM ˌənməˈloʊdiəsli

unmelted
BR ˌʌnˈmɛltɪd
AM ˌənˈmɛltəd

unmemorable
BR ˌʌnˈmɛm(ə)rəbl
AM ˌənˈmɛm(ə)rəbəl,
ˌənˈmɛmərbəl

unmemorably
BR ˌʌnˈmɛm(ə)rəbli
AM ˌənˈmɛm(ə)rəbli,
ˌənˈmɛmərbli

unmended
BR ˌʌnˈmɛndɪd
AM ˌənˈmɛndəd

unmentionability
BR ʌnˌmɛnʃnəˈbɪlɪti,
ʌnˌmɛnʃ(ə)nəˈbɪlɪti
AM ˌənˈmɛn(t)ʃ(ə)nə-
ˈbɪlɪdi

unmentionable
BR ʌnˈmɛnʃnəbl,
ʌnˈmɛnʃ(ə)nəbl, -z
AM ˌənˈmɛn(t)ʃ(ə)nəbəl,
-z

**unmentionable-
ness**
BR ʌnˈmɛnʃnəblnəs,
ʌnˈmɛnʃ(ə)nəblnəs
AM ˌənˈmɛn(t)ʃ(ə)nə-
bəlnəs

unmentionably
BR ʌnˈmɛnʃnəbli,
ʌnˈmɛnʃ(ə)nəbli
AM ˌənˈmɛn(t)ʃ(ə)nəbli

unmentioned
BR ʌnˈmɛnʃnd
AM ˌənˈmɛn(t)ʃənd

unmerchantable
BR ʌnˈməːtʃ(ə)ntəbl
AM ˌənˈmərtʃən(t)əbəl

unmerciful
BR ʌnˈməːsɪf(ʊ)l
AM ˌənˈmərsəfəl

unmercifully
BR ʌnˈməːsɪfʊli,
ʌnˈməːsɪfli
AM ˌənˈmərsəf(ə)li

unmercifulness
BR ʌnˈməːsɪf(ʊ)lnəs
AM ˌənˈmərsəfəlnəs

unmerited
BR (ˌ)ʌnˈmɛrɪtɪd
AM ˌənˈmɛrədəd

unmeritorious
BR ˌʌnmɛrɪˈtɔːrɪəs
AM ˌənˌmɛrəˈtɔriəs

unmet
BR ˌʌnˈmɛt
AM ˌənˈmɛt

unmetalled
BR ʌnˈmɛtld
AM ˌənˈmɛdld

unmethodical
BR ˌʌnmɪˈθɒdɪkl
AM ˌənməˈθɑdəkəl

unmethodically
BR ˌʌnmɪˈθɒdɪkli
AM ˌənməˈθɑdək(ə)li

unmetrical
BR ʌnˈmɛtrɪkl
AM ˌənˈmɛtrəkəl

unmilitary
BR ʌnˈmɪlɪt(ə)ri
AM ˌənˈmɪləˌtɛri

unmindful
BR (ˌ)ʌnˈmʌɪn(d)f(ʊ)l
AM ˌənˈmaɪndfəl

unmindfully
BR (ˌ)ʌnˈmʌɪn(d)fʊli,
(ˌ)ʌnˈmʌɪn(d)fli
AM ˌənˈmaɪn(d)fəli

unmindfulness
BR (ˌ)ʌnˈmʌɪn(d)f(ʊ)l-
nəs
AM ˌənˈmaɪn(d)fəlnəs

unmingled
BR ʌnˈmɪŋgld
AM ˌənˈmɪŋgəld

unmissable
BR ʌnˈmɪsəbl
AM ˌənˈmɪsəbəl

unmistakability
BR ˌʌnmɪˌsteɪkəˈbɪlɪti
AM ˌənməˌsteɪkəˈbɪlɪdi

unmistakable
BR ˌʌnmɪˈsteɪkəbl
AM ˌənməˈsteɪkəbəl

unmistakableness
BR ˌʌnmɪˈsteɪkəblnəs
AM ˌənməˈsteɪkəbəlnəs

unmistakably
BR ˌʌnmɪˈsteɪkəbli
AM ˌənməˈsteɪkəbli

unmistakeability
BR ˌʌnmɪˌsteɪkəˈbɪlɪti
AM ˌənməˌsteɪkəˈbɪlɪdi

unmistakeable
BR ˌʌnmɪˈsteɪkəbl
AM ˌənməˈsteɪkəbəl

**unmistakeable-
ness**
BR ˌʌnmɪˈsteɪkəblnəs
AM ˌənməˈsteɪkəbəlnəs

unmistakeably
BR ˌʌnmɪˈsteɪkəbli
AM ˌənməˈsteɪkəbli

unmistaken
BR ˌʌnmɪˈsteɪk(ə)n
AM ˌənməˈsteɪkən

unmitigated
BR ʌnˈmɪtɪgeɪtɪd
AM ˌənˈmɪdəˌgeɪdɪd

unmitigatedly
BR ʌnˈmɪtɪgeɪtɪdli
AM ˌənˈmɪdəˌgeɪdɪdli

unmixed
BR ˌʌnˈmɪkst
AM ˌənˈmɪkst

unmodernised
BR ˌʌnˈmɒdənʌɪzd
AM ˌənˈmɑdərˌnaɪzd

unmodernized
BR ˌʌnˈmɒdənʌɪzd
AM ˌənˈmɑdərˌnaɪzd

unmodified
BR (ˌ)ʌnˈmɒdɪfʌɪd
AM ˌənˈmɑdəˌfaɪd

unmodulated
BR (ˌ)ʌnˈmɒdjʊleɪtɪd,
(ˌ)ʌnˈmɒdʒʊleɪtɪd
AM ˌənˈmɑdʒəˌleɪdɪd

unmolested
BR ˌʌnməˈlɛstɪd
AM ˌənməˈlɛstəd

unmoor
BR ˌʌnˈmʊə(r),
ˌʌnˈmɔː(r), -z, -ɪŋ, -d
AM ˌənˈmʊ(ə)r, -(ə)rz,
-rɪŋ, -(ə)rd

unmoral
BR ˌʌnˈmɒrəl,
ˌʌnˈmɒrl̩
AM ˌənˈmɔrəl

unmorality
BR ˌʌnməˈralɪti
AM ˌənməˈrælədi

unmorally
BR ˌʌnˈmɒrəli,
ˌʌnˈmɒrl̩i
AM ˌənˈmɔrəli

unmotherly
BR ˌʌnˈmʌðəli
AM ˌənˈməðərli

unmotivated
BR ˌʌnˈməʊtɪveɪtɪd
AM ˌənˈmoʊdəˌveɪdɪd

unmounted
BR ˌʌnˈmaʊntɪd
AM ˌənˈmaʊn(t)əd

unmourned
BR ˌʌnˈmɔːnd
AM ˌənˈmɔrnd

unmovable
BR (ˌ)ʌnˈmuːvəbl
AM ˌənˈmuvəbəl

unmoveable
BR (ˌ)ʌnˈmuːvəbl
AM ˌənˈmuvəbəl

unmoved
BR (ˌ)ʌnˈmuːvd
AM ˌənˈmuvd

unmoving
BR (ˌ)ʌnˈmuːvɪŋ
AM ˌənˈmuvɪŋ

unmown
BR ˌʌnˈməʊn
AM ˌənˈmoʊn

unmuffle
BR ˌʌnˈmʌfl̩, -lz,
-lɪŋ \ -lɪŋ, -ld
AM ˌənˈməfləl, -əlz,
-(ə)lɪŋ, -əld

unmurmuring
BR ˌʌnˈməːm(ə)rɪŋ
AM ˌənˈmərmərɪŋ

unmurmuringly
BR ˌʌnˈməːm(ə)rɪŋli
AM ˌənˈmərmərɪŋli

unmusical
BR ˌʌnˈmjuːzɪkl
AM ˌənˈmjuzəkəl

unmusicality
BR ˌʌnmjuːzɪˈkalɪti
AM ˌənˌmjuzəˈkælədi

unmusically
BR ˌʌnˈmjuːzɪkli
AM ˌənˈmjuzək(ə)li

unmusicalness
BR ˌʌnˈmjuːzɪklnɪs
AM ˌənˈmjuzəkəlnəs

unmutilated
BR ˌʌnˈmjuːtɪleɪtɪd
AM ˌənˈmjudəleɪdɪd

unmuzzle
BR ˌʌnˈmʌzl̩, -lz,
-lɪŋ \ -lɪŋ, -ld
AM ˌənˈməzləl, -əlz,
-(ə)lɪŋ, -əld

unnail
BR ˌʌnˈneɪl, -z, -ɪŋ, -d
AM ˌənˈneɪl, -z, -ɪŋ, -d

unnameable
BR ˌʌnˈneɪməbl
AM ˌənˈneɪməbəl

unnamed
BR ˌʌnˈneɪmd
AM ˌə(n)ˈneɪmd

unnational
BR ˌʌnˈnaʃn(ə)l,
ʌnˌˈnaʃən(ə)l
AM ˌənˈnæʃ(ə)nəl

unnatural
BR (ˌ)ʌnˈnatʃ(ə)rəl,
(ˌ)ʌnˈnatʃ(ə)rl̩
AM ˌənˈnætʃ(ə)rəl

unnaturally
BR (,)ʌn'natʃ(ə)rəli,
(,)ʌn'natʃ(ə)rʲli
AM -ən'nætʃ(ə)rəli

unnaturalness
BR (,)ʌn'natʃ(ə)rəlnəs,
(,)ʌn'natʃ(ə)rʲlnəs
AM -ən'ætʃ(ə)rəlnəs

unnavigability
BR ʌn,navɪgə'bɪlɪti
AM -ən,nævəgə'bɪlɪdi

unnavigable
BR ʌn'navɪgəbl
AM -ən'nævəgəbəl

unnecessarily
BR (,)ʌn'nɛsɪs(ə)rʲli,
,ʌnnɛsɪ'sɛrʲli
AM -ən'nɛsə'sɛrəli

unnecessariness
BR (,)ʌn'nɛsɪs(ə)rɪnɪs
AM -ən'nɛsə,sɛrinɪs

unnecessary
BR (,)ʌn'nɛsɪs(ə)ri,
,ʌn'nɛsɪsɛri
AM -ən'nɛsə,sɛri

unneeded
BR ʌn'niːdɪd
AM -ən'nidɪd

unneighborliness
BR ʌn'neɪbəlnɪs
AM -ən'neɪbərlinɪs

unneighborly
BR ʌn'neɪbəli
AM -ən'neɪbərli

unneighbourliness
BR ʌn'neɪbəlnɪs
AM -ən'neɪbərlinɪs

unneighbourly
BR ʌn'neɪbəli
AM -ən'neɪbərli

unnerve
BR ʌn'nəːv, -z, -ɪŋ, -d
AM -ən'nərv, -z, -ɪŋ, -d

unnervingly
BR ʌn'nəːvɪŋli
AM -ən'nərvɪŋli

unnoticeable
BR (,)ʌn'nəʊtɪsəbl
AM -ən'noʊdəsəbəl

unnoticeably
BR (,)ʌn'nəʊtɪsəbli
AM -ən'noʊdəsəbli

unnoticed
BR (,)ʌn'nəʊtɪst
AM -ən'noʊdəst

UNNRA
BR ʌnrə(r)
AM -ʌnrə

unnumbered
BR ʌn'nʌmbəd
AM -ən'nəmbərd

UNO
BR 'juːnəʊ
AM 'juː,noʊ

Uno
card game
BR 'uːnəʊ

AM 'uːnoʊ

uno
number
BR 'uːnəʊ
AM 'uːnoʊ

unobjectionable
BR ,ʌnəb'dʒɛkʃnəbl,
,ʌnəb'dʒɛkʃ(ə)nəbl
AM -ənəb'dʒɛkʃ(ə)nəbəl

**unobjectionable-
ness**
BR ,ʌnəb'dʒɛkʃnəblnəs,
,ʌnəb'dʒɛkʃ(ə)nəblnəs
AM -ənəb'dʒɛkʃ(ə)nə-
bəlnəs

unobjectionably
BR ,ʌnəb'dʒɛkʃnəbli,
,ʌnəb'dʒɛkʃ(ə)nəbli
AM -ənəb'dʒɛkʃ(ə)nəbli

unobliging
BR ,ʌnə'blʌɪdʒɪŋ
AM -ənə'blaɪdʒɪŋ

unobscured
BR ,ʌnəb'skjʊəd,
,ʌnəb'skjɔːd
AM -ənəb'skjʊ(ə)rd

unobservable
BR ,ʌnəb'zəːvəbl
AM -ənəb'zərvəbəl

unobservant
BR ,ʌnəb'zəːv(ə)nt
AM -ənəb'zərvənt

unobservantly
BR ,ʌnəb'zəːv(ə)ntli
AM -ənəb'zərvən(t)li

unobserved
BR ,ʌnəb'zəːvd
AM -ənəb'zərvd

unobservedly
BR ,ʌnəb'zəːvɪdli
AM -ənəb'zərvədli

unobstructed
BR ,ʌnəb'strʌktɪd
AM -ənəb'straktəd

unobtainable
BR ,ʌnəb'teɪnəbl
AM -ənəb'teɪnəbəl

unobtainably
BR ,ʌnəb'teɪnəbli
AM -ənəb'teɪnəbli

unobtrusive
BR ,ʌnəb'truːsɪv
AM -ənəb'trusɪv

unobtrusively
BR ,ʌnəb'truːsɪvli
AM -ənəb'trusɪvli

unobtrusiveness
BR ,ʌnəb'truːsɪvnɪs
AM -ənəb'trusɪvnɪs

unoccupancy
BR (,)ʌn'ɒkjʊp(ə)nsi
AM -ən'akjəpənsi

unoccupied
BR (,)ʌn'ɒkjʊpʌɪd
AM -ən'akjə,paɪd

unoffended
BR ,ʌnə'fɛndɪd

AM -ənə'fɛndəd

unoffending
BR ,ʌnə'fɛndɪŋ
AM -ənə'fɛndɪŋ

unofficial
BR ,ʌnə'fɪʃl
AM -ənə'fɪʃəl

unofficially
BR ,ʌnə'fɪʃʲli,
,ʌnə'fɪʃʲli
AM -ənə'fɪʃəli

unoiled
BR ʌn'ɔɪld
AM -ən'ɔɪld

unopenable
BR ʌn'əʊp(ə)nəbl,
ʌn'əʊpnəbl
AM -ən'oʊp(ə)nəbəl

unopened
BR ʌn'əʊpnd
AM -ən'oʊpənd

unopposed
BR ,ʌnə'pəʊzd
AM -ənə'poʊzd

unordained
BR ,ʌnɔː'deɪnd
AM -ənɔr'deɪnd

unordered
BR ʌn'ɔːdəd
AM -ən'ɔrdərd

unordinary
BR ʌn'ɔːdɪn(ə)ri,
,ʌn'ɔːdn̩(ə)ri
AM -ən'ɔrdn̩,ɛri

unorganised
BR (,)ʌn'ɔːgənʌɪzd,
(,)ʌn'ɔːgn̩ʌɪzd
AM -ən'ɔrgə,naɪzd

unorganized
BR (,)ʌn'ɔːgənʌɪzd,
(,)ʌn'ɔːgn̩ʌɪzd
AM -ən'ɔrgə,naɪzd

unoriginal
BR ,ʌnə'rɪdʒɪnl
AM -ənə'rɪdʒ(ə)nəl

unoriginality
BR ,ʌnə,rɪdʒɪ'nalɪti
AM -ənə,rɪdʒə'nælədi

unoriginally
BR ,ʌnə'rɪdʒɪnl̩i,
,ʌnə'rɪdʒɪnəli
AM -ənə'rɪdʒ(ə)nəli

unornamental
BR ,ʌnɔːnə'mɛntl
AM -ən,ɔrnə'mɛn(t)l

unornamented
BR ʌn'ɔːnəmɛntɪd
AM -ən'ɔrnə,mɛn(t)əd

unorthodox
BR (,)ʌn'ɔːθədɒks
AM -ən'ɔrθə,daks

unorthodoxly
BR (,)ʌn'ɔːθədɒksli
AM -ən'ɔrθə,daksli

unorthodoxy
BR (,)ʌn'ɔːθədɒksi
AM -ən'ɔrθə,daksi

unostentatious
BR ,ʌnɒstɛn'teɪʃəs,
,ʌnɒst(ə)n'teɪʃəs
AM -ən,ast(ə)n'teɪʃəs

unostentatiously
BR ,ʌnɒstɛn'teɪʃəsli,
,ʌnɒst(ə)n'teɪʃəsli
AM -ən,ast(ə)n'teɪʃəsli

**unostentatious-
ness**
BR ,ʌnɒstɛn'teɪʃəsnəs,
,ʌnɒst(ə)n'teɪʃəs-
nəs
AM -ən,ast(ə)n'teɪʃəs-
nəs

unowned
BR ʌn'əʊnd
AM -ən'oʊnd

unoxidised
BR ʌn'ɒksɪdʌɪzd
AM -ən'aksə,daɪzd

unoxidized
BR ʌn'ɒksɪdʌɪzd
AM -ən'aksə,daɪzd

unpack
BR ʌn'pak, -s, -ɪŋ, -t
AM -ən'pæk, -s, -ɪŋ, -t

unpacker
BR ʌn'pakə(r), -z
AM -ən'pækər, -z

unpadded
BR ʌn'padɪd
AM -ən'pædəd

unpaged
BR ʌn'peɪdʒd
AM -ən'peɪdʒd

unpaginated
BR ʌn'padʒɪneɪtɪd
AM -ən'pædʒə,neɪdɪd

unpaid
BR ʌn'peɪd
AM -ən'peɪd

unpainted
BR ʌn'peɪntɪd
AM -ən'peɪn(t)ɪd

unpaired
BR ʌn'pɛːd
AM -ən'pɛ(ə)rd

unpalatability
BR ʌnpalətə'bɪlɪti
AM -ən,pælədə'bɪlɪdi

unpalatable
BR (,)ʌn'palətəbl
AM -ən'pælədəbəl

unpalatableness
BR (,)ʌn'palətəblnəs
AM -ən'pælədəbəlnəs

unpalatably
BR (,)ʌn'palətəbli
AM -ən'pælədəbli

unparalleled
BR (,)ʌn'parəlɛld
AM -ən'pɛrə,lɛld

unpardonable
BR (,)ʌn'pɑːdn̩əbl,
(,)ʌn'pɑːd(ə)nəbl
AM -ən'pardn̩əbəl

unpardonableness
BR (ˌ)ʌnˈpɑːdnəblnəs,
(ˌ)ʌnˈpɑːd(ə)nəblnəs
AM ˌənˈpɑrdnəbəlnəs

unpardonably
BR (ˌ)ʌnˈpɑːdnəbli,
(ˌ)ʌnˈpɑːd(ə)nəbli
AM ˌənˈpɑrdnəbli

unparliamentary
BR ˌʌnpɑːləˈmɛnt(ə)ri
AM ˌənˌpɑrl(j)əˈmen-
(t)əri

unpasteurised
BR (ˌ)ʌnˈpɑːst(ʃ)ərʌɪzd,
(ˌ)ʌnˈpɑst(ʃ)ərʌɪzd,
(ˌ)ʌnˈpɑːstjərʌɪzd,
(ˌ)ʌnˈpɑstjərʌɪzd
AM ˌənˈpæstʃəˌraɪzd,
ˌənˈpætʃəˌraɪzd,
ˌənˈpæstəˌraɪzd

unpasteurized
BR (ˌ)ʌnˈpɑːst(ʃ)ərʌɪzd,
(ˌ)ʌnˈpɑst(ʃ)ərʌɪzd,
(ˌ)ʌnˈpɑːstjərʌɪzd,
(ˌ)ʌnˈpɑstjərʌɪzd
AM ˌənˈpæstʃəˌraɪzd,
ˌənˈpætʃəˌraɪzd,
ˌənˈpæstəˌraɪzd

unpatented
BR ˌʌnˈpat(ə)ntɪd,
ˌʌnˈpeɪt(ə)ntɪd
AM ˌənˈpætn(t)əd

unpatriotic
BR ˌʌnpatrɪˈɒtɪk,
ˌʌnpeɪtrɪˈɒtɪk
AM ˌənˌpeɪtriˈɑdɪk

unpatriotically
BR ˌʌnpatrɪˈɒtɪkli,
ˌʌnpeɪtrɪˈɒtɪkli
AM ˌənˌpeɪtriˈɑdək(ə)li

unpatronising
BR ˌʌnˈpatrənʌɪzɪŋ
AM ˌənˈpeɪtrəˌnaɪzɪŋ,
ˌənˈpætrəˌnaɪzɪŋ

unpatronizing
BR ˌʌnˈpatrənʌɪzɪŋ
AM ˌənˈpeɪtrəˌnaɪzɪŋ,
ˌənˈpætrəˌnaɪzɪŋ

unpatterned
BR ˌʌnˈpat(ə)nd
AM ˌənˈpædərnd

unpaved
BR ˌʌnˈpeɪvd
AM ˌənˈpeɪvd

unpeaceful
BR ˌʌnˈpiːsf(ʊ)l
AM ˌənˈpisfəl

unpeeled
BR ˌʌnˈpiːld
AM ˌənˈpild

unpeg
BR ˌʌnˈpɛg, -z, -ɪŋ, -d
AM ˌənˈpɛg, -z, -ɪŋ, -d

unpenalised
BR ˌʌnˈpiːnəlʌɪzd,
ˌʌnˈpiːnɭʌɪzd
AM ˌənˈpɛnlˌaɪzd,
ˌənˈpinlˌaɪzd

unpenalized
BR ˌʌnˈpiːnəlʌɪzd,
ˌʌnˈpiːnɭʌɪzd
AM ˌənˈpɛnlˌaɪzd,
ˌənˈpinlˌaɪzd

unpeople
BR ˌʌnˈpiːpl, -z, -ɪŋ, -d
AM ˌənˈpipəl, -z, -ɪŋ, -d

unperceived
BR ˌʌnpəˈsiːvd
AM ˌənpərˈsivd

unperceptive
BR ˌʌnpəˈsɛptɪv
AM ˌənpərˈsɛptɪv

unperceptively
BR ˌʌnpəˈsɛptɪvli
AM ˌənpərˈsɛptɪvli

unperceptiveness
BR ˌʌnpəˈsɛptɪvnɪs
AM ˌənpərˈsɛptɪvnɪs

unperfected
BR ˌʌnpəˈfɛktɪd
AM ˌənpərˈfɛktəd

unperforated
BR (ˌ)ʌnˈpəːfəreɪtɪd
AM ˌənˈpərfəˌreɪdɪd

unperformed
BR ˌʌnpəˈfɔːmd
AM ˌənpərˈfɔrmd

unperfumed
BR ˌʌnˈpəːfjuːmd
AM ˌənˈpərˌfjumd,
ˌənpərˈfjumd

unperson
BR ˌʌnˈpəːsn, -z
AM ˈənˈpərsən, -z

unpersuadable
BR ˌʌnpəˈsweɪdəbl
AM ˌənpərˈsweɪdəbəl

unpersuaded
BR ˌʌnpəˈsweɪdɪd
AM ˌənpərˈsweɪdɪd

unpersuasive
BR ˌʌnpəˈsweɪsɪv
AM ˌənpərˈsweɪsɪv

unpersuasively
BR ˌʌnpəˈsweɪsɪvli
AM ˌənpərˈsweɪsɪvli

unperturbed
BR ˌʌnpəˈtəːbd
AM ˌənpərˈtərbd

unperturbedly
BR ˌʌnpəˈtəːbɪdli
AM ˌənpərˈtərbədli

unphased
BR ˌʌnˈfeɪzd
AM ˌənˈfeɪzd

unphilosophic
BR ˌʌnfɪləˈsɒfɪk
AM ˌənˌfɪləˈsɑfɪk

unphilosophical
BR ˌʌnfɪləˈsɒfɪkl
AM ˌənˌfɪləˈsɑfəkəl

unphilosophically
BR ˌʌnfɪləˈsɒfɪkli
AM ˌənˌfɪləˈsɑfək(ə)li

unphysiological
BR ˌʌnfɪzɪəˈlɒdʒɪkl
AM ˌənˌfɪzɪəˈlɑdʒəkəl

unphysiologically
BR ˌʌnfɪzɪəˈlɒdʒɪkli
AM ˌənˌfɪzɪəˈlɑdʒək(ə)li

unpick
BR ˌʌnˈpɪk, -s, -ɪŋ, -t
AM ˌʌnˈpɪk, -s, -ɪŋ, -t

unpicturesque
BR ˌʌnpɪktʃəˈrɛsk
AM ˌənˌpɪk(t)ʃəˈrɛsk

unpierced
BR ˌʌnˈpɪəst
AM ˌənˈpɪ(ə)rst

unpin
BR ˌʌnˈpɪn, -z, -ɪŋ, -d
AM ˌʌnˈpɪn, -z, -ɪŋ, -d

unpitied
BR ˌʌnˈpɪtɪd
AM ˌənˈpɪdɪd

unpitying
BR ˌʌnˈpɪtɪɪŋ
AM ˌənˈpɪdiɪŋ

unpityingly
BR ˌʌnˈpɪtɪɪŋli
AM ˌənˈpɪdiɪŋli

unplaceable
BR ˌʌnˈpleɪsəbl
AM ˌənˈpleɪsəbəl

unplaced
BR ˌʌnˈpleɪst
AM ˌənˈpleɪst

unplait
BR ˌʌnˈplat, -s, -ɪŋ, -ɪd
AM ˌənˈplæ|t, -ts, -dɪŋ,
-dəd

unplanned
BR ˌʌnˈpland
AM ˈənˈplænd

unplanted
BR ˌʌnˈplɑːntɪd,
ˌʌnˈplantɪd
AM ˌənˈplæn(t)əd

unplastered
BR ˌʌnˈplɑːstəd,
ˌʌnˈplastəd
AM ˌənˈplæstərd

unplasticised
BR ˌʌnˈplastɪsʌɪzd
AM ˌənˈplæstəˌsaɪzd

unplasticized
BR ˌʌnˈplastɪsʌɪzd
AM ˌənˈplæstəˌsaɪzd

unplausible
BR ˌʌnˈplɔːzɪbl
AM ˌənˈplɔzəbəl,
ˌənˈplɑzəbəl

unplayable
BR (ˌ)ʌnˈpleɪəbl
AM ˌənˈpleɪəbəl

unplayably
BR (ˌ)ʌnˈpleɪəbli
AM ˌənˈpleɪəbli

unplayed
BR (ˌ)ʌnˈpleɪd
AM ˌənˈpleɪd

unpleasant
BR ˌʌnˈplɛznt
AM ˌənˈplɛznt

unpleasantly
BR ˌʌnˈplɛzntli
AM ˌənˈplɛzn(t)li

unpleasantness
BR ˌʌnˈplɛzntnəs
AM ˌənˈplɛzn(t)nəs

unpleasantry
BR (ˌ)ʌnˈplɛzntr|i, -ɪz
AM ˌənˈplɛzntri, -z

unpleasing
BR (ˌ)ʌnˈpliːzɪŋ
AM ˌənˈplizɪŋ

unpleasingly
BR ˌʌnˈpliːzɪŋli
AM ˌənˈplizɪŋli

unpleasurable
BR (ˌ)ʌnˈplɛʒ(ə)rəbl
AM ˌənˈplɛʒ(ə)r(ə)bəl

unpledged
BR ˌʌnˈplɛdʒd
AM ˌənˈplɛdʒd

unploughed
BR ˌʌnˈplaʊd
AM ˌənˈplaʊd

unplowed
BR ˌʌnˈplaʊd
AM ˌənˈplaʊd

unplucked
BR ˌʌnˈplʌkt
AM ˌənˈpləkt

unplug
BR ˌʌnˈplʌg, -z, -ɪŋ, -d
AM ˌənˈpləg, -z, -ɪŋ, -d

unplumbable
BR ˌʌnˈplʌməbl
AM ˌənˈpləməbəl

unplumbed
BR ˌʌnˈplʌmd
AM ˌənˈpləmd

unpoetic
BR ˌʌnpəʊˈɛtɪk
AM ˌənpoʊˈɛdɪk

unpoetical
BR ˌʌnpəʊˈɛtɪkl
AM ˌənpoʊˈɛdɪkəl

unpoetically
BR ˌʌnpəʊˈɛtɪkli
AM ˌənpoʊˈɛdək(ə)li

unpoeticalness
BR ˌʌnpəʊˈɛtɪklnəs
AM ˌənpoʊˈɛdɪkəlnəs

unpointed
BR ˌʌnˈpɔɪntɪd
AM ˌənˈpɔɪn(t)ɪd

unpolarised
BR ˌʌnˈpəʊlərʌɪzd
AM ˌənˈpoʊləˌraɪzd

unpolarized
BR ˌʌnˈpəʊlərʌɪzd
AM ˌənˈpoʊləˌraɪzd

unpolished
BR ˌʌnˈpɒlɪʃt
AM ˌənˈpɑlɪʃt

unpolitic
BR ʌnˈpɒlɪtɪk
AM ˌənˈpɑːlədɪk

unpolitical
BR ˌʌnpəˈlɪtɪkl
AM ˌʌnpəˈlɪdɪkəl

unpolitically
BR ˌʌnpəˈlɪtɪkli
AM ˌʌnpəˈlɪdɪk(ə)li

unpolled
BR ʌnˈpəʊld
AM ˌənˈpoʊld

unpollinated
BR ʌnˈpɒlɪneɪtɪd
AM ˌənˈpɑːləˌneɪdɪd

unpolluted
BR ˌʌnpəˈl(j)uːtɪd
AM ˌʌnpəˈluːdəd

unpompous
BR ʌnˈpɒmpəs
AM ˌənˈpɑːmpəs

unpopular
BR (ˌ)ʌnˈpɒpjʊlə(r)
AM ˌənˈpɑːpjələr

unpopularity
BR ˌʌnpɒpjʊˈlarɪti
AM ˌənpɑːpjəˈlɛrədi

unpopularly
BR (ˌ)ʌnˈpɒpjʊləli
AM ˌənˈpɑːpjələrli

unpopulated
BR ʌnˈpɒpjʊleɪtɪd
AM ˌənˈpɑːpjəˌleɪdɪd

unposed
BR ʌnˈpəʊzd
AM ˌənˈpoʊzd

unpossessed
BR ˌʌnpəˈzɛst
AM ˌənpəˈzɛst

unposted
BR ʌnˈpəʊstɪd
AM ˌənˈpoʊstəd

unpowered
BR ʌnˈpaʊəd
AM ˌənˈpaʊərd

unpractical
BR (ˌ)ʌnˈpraktɪkl
AM ˌənˈpræktəkəl

unpracticality
BR ˌʌnpraktɪˈkalɪti
AM ˌənˌpræktəˈkælədi

unpractically
BR (ˌ)ʌnˈpraktɪkli
AM ˌənˈpræktək(ə)li

unpractised
BR (ˌ)ʌnˈpraktɪst
AM ˌənˈpræktəst

unprecedented
BR (ˌ)ʌnˈprɛsɪdentɪd,
(ˌ)ʌnˈprɛsɪd(ə)ntɪd
AM ˌənˈprɛsədən(t)əd

unprecedentedly
BR (ˌ)ʌnˈprɛsɪdentɪdli,
(ˌ)ʌnˈprɛsɪd(ə)ntɪdli
AM ˌənˈprɛsədən(t)ədli

unpredictability
BR ˌʌnprɪˌdɪktəˈbɪlɪti

AM ˌənprəˌdɪktəˈbɪlɪdi

unpredictable
BR ˌʌnprɪˈdɪktəbl
AM ˌənprəˈdɪktəbəl

unpredictableness
BR ˌʌnprɪˈdɪktəblnəs
AM ˌənprəˈdɪktəbəlnəs

unpredictably
BR ˌʌnprɪˈdɪktəbli
AM ˌənprəˈdɪktəbli

unpredicted
BR ˌʌnprɪˈdɪktɪd
AM ˌənprəˈdɪktɪd

unprejudiced
BR (ˌ)ʌnˈprɛdʒʊdɪst
AM ˌənˈprɛdʒədəst

unpremeditated
BR ˌʌnprɪˈmɛdɪteɪtɪd
AM ˌənprəˈmɛdəˌteɪdɪd,
ˌənpriˈmɛdəˌteɪdɪd

unpremeditatedly
BR ˌʌnprɪˈmɛdɪteɪtɪdli
AM ˌənprəˈmɛdəˌteɪdɪd-
li, ˌənpriˈmɛdəˌteɪd-
ɪdli

unprepared
BR ˌʌnprɪˈpɛːd
AM ˌənprəˈpɛ(ə)rd

unpreparedly
BR ˌʌnprɪˈpɛːrɪdli
AM ˌənprəˈpɛr(ə)dli

unpreparedness
BR ˌʌnprɪˈpɛːrɪdnɪs
AM ˌənprəˈpɛr(ə)dnəs

unprepossessing
BR ˌʌnpriːpəˈzɛsɪŋ
AM ˌənpriːpəˈzɛsɪŋ

unprescribed
BR ˌʌnprɪˈskrʌɪbd
AM ˌənprəˈskraɪbd

unpresentable
BR ˌʌnprɪˈzɛntəbl
AM ˌənprəˈzɛn(t)əbəl

unpressed
BR ʌnˈprɛst
AM ˌənˈprɛst

unpressurised
BR ʌnˈprɛʃərʌɪzd
AM ˌənˈprɛʃəˌraɪzd

unpressurized
BR ʌnˈprɛʃərʌɪzd
AM ˌənˈprɛʃəˌraɪzd

unpresuming
BR ˌʌnprɪˈzjuːmɪŋ
AM ˌənprəˈz(j)umɪŋ

unpresumptuous
BR ˌʌnprɪˈzʌm(p)tʃʊəs,
ˌʌnprɪˈzʌm(p)tjʊəs
AM ˌənprɪˈzəm(p)(t)ʃ-
(əw)əs,
ˌənprəˈzəm(p)(t)ʃ-
(əw)əs

unpretending
BR ˌʌnprɪˈtɛndɪŋ
AM ˌənprəˈtɛndɪŋ

unpretendingly
BR ˌʌnprɪˈtɛndɪŋli

AM ˌənprəˈtɛndɪŋli

unpretendingness
BR ˌʌnprɪˈtɛndɪŋnɪs
AM ˌənprəˈtɛndɪŋnɪs

unpretentious
BR ˌʌnprɪˈtɛnʃəs
AM ˌənprəˈten(t)ʃəs

unpretentiously
BR ˌʌnprɪˈtɛnʃəsli
AM ˌənprəˈten(t)ʃəsli

unpretentiousness
BR ˌʌnprɪˈtɛnʃəsnəs
AM ˌənprəˈten(t)ʃəsnəs

unpreventable
BR ˌʌnprɪˈvɛntəbl
AM ˌənprəˈven(t)əbəl

unpriced
BR ʌnˈprʌɪst
AM ˌənˈpraɪst

unprimed
BR ʌnˈprʌɪmd
AM ˌənˈpraɪmd

unprincipled
BR (ˌ)ʌnˈprɪnsɪpld
AM ˌənˈprɪnsəpəld

unprincipledness
BR (ˌ)ʌnˈprɪnsɪpldnəs
AM ˌənˈprɪnsəpəldnəs

unprintable
BR (ˌ)ʌnˈprɪntəbl
AM ˌənˈprɪn(t)əbəl

unprintably
BR (ˌ)ʌnˈprɪntəbli
AM ˌənˈprɪn(t)əbli

unprinted
BR (ˌ)ʌnˈprɪntɪd
AM ˌənˈprɪn(t)ɪd

unprivileged
BR (ˌ)ʌnˈprɪv(ɪ)lɪdʒd,
(ˌ)ʌnˈprɪvlɪdʒd
AM ˌənˈprɪv(ə)lɪdʒd

unproblematic
BR ˌʌnprɒbləˈmatɪk
AM ˌənˌprɑːbləˈmædɪk

unproblematically
BR ˌʌnprɒbləˈmatɪkli
AM ˌənˌprɑːbləˈmædək-
(ə)li

unprocessed
BR ʌnˈprəʊsɛst
AM ˌənˈprɑːˌsɛst

unproclaimed
BR ˌʌnprəˈkleɪmd
AM ˌənprəˈkleɪmd,
ˌənˌproʊˈkleɪmd

unprocurable
BR ˌʌnprəˈkjʊərəbl,
ˌʌnprəˈkjʊːrəbl
AM ˌənprəˈkjurəbəl

unproductive
BR ˌʌnprəˈdʌktɪv
AM ˌənprəˈdʌktɪv

unproductively
BR ˌʌnprəˈdʌktɪvli
AM ˌənprəˈdʌktɪvli

unproductiveness
BR ˌʌnprəˈdʌktɪvnɪs

AM ˌənprəˈdæktɪvnɪs

unprofessional
BR ˌʌnprəˈfɛʃn(ə)l,
ˌʌnprəˈfɛʃən(ə)l
AM ˌənprəˈfɛʃ(ə)nəl

unprofessionalism
BR ˌʌnprəˈfɛʃnəlɪz(ə)m,
ˌʌnprəˈfɛʃn‍lɪz(ə)m,
ˌʌnprəˈfɛʃənlɪz(ə)m,
ˌʌnprəˈfɛʃ(ə)nəlɪz(ə)m
AM ˌənprəˈfɛʃənlˌɪzəm,
ˌənprəˈfɛʃnəˌlɪzəm

unprofessionally
BR ˌʌnprəˈfɛʃnəli,
ˌʌnprəˈfɛʃn‍li,
ˌʌnprəˈfɛʃənli,
ˌʌnprəˈfɛʃ(ə)nəli
AM ˌənprəˈfɛʃ(ə)nəli

unprofitable
BR (ˌ)ʌnˈprɒfɪtəbl
AM ˌənˈprɑːfədəbəl

unprofitableness
BR (ˌ)ʌnˈprɒfɪtəblnəs
AM ˌənˈprɑːfədəbəlnəs

unprofitably
BR (ˌ)ʌnˈprɒfɪtəbli
AM ˌənˈprɑːfədəbli

unprogressive
BR ˌʌnprəˈgrɛsɪv
AM ˌənprəˈgrɛsɪv,
ˌənproʊˈgrɛsɪv

unprohibited
BR ˌʌnprəˈhɪbɪtɪd
AM ˌənproʊˈhɪbɪdɪd

unpromising
BR (ˌ)ʌnˈprɒmɪsɪŋ
AM ˌənˈprɑːməsɪŋ

unpromisingly
BR (ˌ)ʌnˈprɒmɪsɪŋli
AM ˌənˈprɑːməsɪŋli

unprompted
BR (ˌ)ʌnˈprɒm(p)tɪd
AM ˌənˈprɑːm(p)təd

unpronounceable
BR ˌʌnprəˈnaʊnsəbl
AM ˌənprəˈnaʊnsəbəl

unpronounceably
BR ˌʌnprəˈnaʊnsəbli
AM ˌənprəˈnaʊnsəbli

unpropertied
BR ʌnˈprɒpətɪd
AM ˌənˈprɑːpərdid

unprophetic
BR ˌʌnprəˈfɛtɪk
AM ˌənprəˈfɛdɪk

unpropitious
BR ˌʌnprəˈpɪʃəs
AM ˌənprəˈpɪʃəs

unpropitiously
BR ˌʌnprəˈpɪʃəsli
AM ˌənprəˈpɪʃəsli

unpropitiousness
BR ˌʌnprəˈpɪʃəsnəs
AM ˌənprəˈpɪʃəsnəs

unprosperous
BR ˌʌnˈprɒsp(ə)rəs
AM ˌənˈprɑːsp(ə)rəs

unprosperously
BR ˌʌnˈprɒsp(ə)rəsli
AM ˌənˈprɑːsp(ə)rəsli

unprotected
BR ˌʌnprəˈtektɪd
AM ˌənprəˈtektəd

unprotectedness
BR ˌʌnprəˈtektɪdnɪs
AM ˌənprəˈtektədnəs

unprotesting
BR ˌʌnprəˈtestɪŋ
AM ˌənprəˈtestɪŋ,
ˌənprouˈtestɪŋ

unprotestingly
BR ˌʌnprəˈtestɪŋli
AM ˌənprəˈtestɪŋli,
ˌən‚prouˈtestɪŋli

unprovability
BR ˌʌnpruːvəˈbɪlɪti
AM ˌənˌpruːvəˈbɪlɪdi

unprovable
BR ˌʌnˈpruːvəbl
AM ˌənˈpruːvəbəl

unprovableness
BR ˌʌnˈpruːvəblnəs
AM ˌənˈpruːvəbəlnəs

unproved
BR ˌʌnˈpruːvd
AM ˌənˈpruːvd

unproven
BR ˌʌnˈpruːvn
AM ˌənˈpruːvn

unprovided
BR ˌʌnprəˈvʌɪdɪd
AM ˌənprəˈvaɪdɪd

unprovocative
BR ˌʌnprəˈvɒkətɪv
AM ˌənprəˈvɑkədɪv

unprovoked
BR ˌʌnprəˈvəʊkt
AM ˌənprəˈvoʊkt

unpruned
BR ˌʌnˈpruːnd
AM ˌənˈprund

unpublicised
BR ˌʌnˈpʌblɪsʌɪzd
AM ˌənˈpəbləˌsaɪzd

unpublicized
BR ˌʌnˈpʌblɪsʌɪzd
AM ˌənˈpəbləˌsaɪzd

unpublishable
BR ˌʌnˈpʌblɪʃəbl
AM ˌənˈpəbləʃəbəl

unpublished
BR ˌʌnˈpʌblɪʃt
AM ˌənˈpəblɪʃt

unpunctual
BR ˌʌnˈpʌŋ(k)tʃʊəl,
(ˌ)ʌnˈpʌŋ(k)tʃ(ʊ)l,
(ˌ)ʌnˈpʌŋ(k)tjʊl
AM ˌənˈpəŋ(k)(t)ʃ(əw)-
əl

unpunctuality
BR ˌʌnpʌŋ(k)tʃʊˈalɪti,
ˌʌnpʌŋ(k)tjʊˈalɪti
AM ˌənˌpəŋ(k)(t)ʃəˈwæl-
ədi

unpunctually
BR (ˌ)ʌnˈpʌŋ(k)tʃʊəli,
(ˌ)ʌnˈpʌŋ(k)tʃəli,
(ˌ)ʌnˈpʌŋ(k)tʃli,
(ˌ)ʌnˈpʌŋ(k)tjʊli
AM ˌənˈpəŋ(k)(t)ʃ(əw)-
əli

unpunctuated
BR (ˌ)ʌnˈpʌŋ(k)tʃʊeɪtɪd,
(ˌ)ʌnˈpʌŋ(k)tjʊeɪtɪd
AM ˌənˈpəŋ(k)(t)ʃə-
ˌweɪtɪd

unpunishable
BR (ˌ)ʌnˈpʌnɪʃəbl
AM ˌənˈpənəʃəbəl

unpunished
BR (ˌ)ʌnˈpʌnɪʃt
AM ˌənˈpənɪʃt

unpurified
BR (ˌ)ʌnˈpjʊərɪfʌɪd,
(ˌ)ʌnˈpjɔːrɪfʌɪd
AM ˌənˈpjʊrəˌfaɪd

unputdownable
BR ˌʌnpʊtˈdaʊnəbl
AM ˌənˌpʊtˈdaʊnəbəl

unqualified
BR ˌʌnˈkwɒlɪfʌɪd,
ˌʌŋˈkwɒlɪfʌɪd
AM ˌənˈkwɒləˌfaɪd,
ˌənˈkwɑləˌfaɪd

unquantifiable
BR (ˌ)ʌnˈkwɒntɪfʌɪəbl,
(ˌ)ʌŋˈkwɒntɪfʌɪəbl
AM ˌənˈkwɒn(t)əˈfaɪəbəl

unquantified
BR (ˌ)ʌnˈkwɒntɪfʌɪd,
(ˌ)ʌŋˈkwɒntɪfʌɪd
AM ˌənˈkwɒn(t)əˌfaɪd

unquenchable
BR (ˌ)ʌnˈkwɛn(t)ʃəbl,
(ˌ)ʌŋˈkwɛn(t)ʃəbl
AM ˌənˈkwɛn(t)ʃəbəl

unquenchably
BR (ˌ)ʌnˈkwɛn(t)ʃəbli,
(ˌ)ʌŋˈkwɛn(t)ʃəbli
AM ˌənˈkwɛn(t)ʃəbli

unquenched
BR ˌʌnˈkwɛn(t)ʃt,
ˌʌŋˈkwɛn(t)ʃt
AM ˌənˈkwɛn(t)ʃt

unquestionability
BR (ˌ)ʌnˌkwɛstʃənəˈbɪl-
ɪti,
(ˌ)ʌŋˌkwɛstʃŋəˈbɪlɪti
AM ˌənˈkwɛstʃənəˈbɪl-
ɪdi,
ˌənˈkwɛstʃənəˈbɪlɪdi

unquestionable
BR (ˌ)ʌnˈkwɛstʃənəbl,
(ˌ)ʌnˈkwɛstʃŋəbl,
(ˌ)ʌŋˈkwɛstʃənəbl,
(ˌ)ʌŋˈkwɛstʃŋəbl
AM ˌənˈkwɛstʃənəbəl,
ˌənˈkwɛstʃənəbəl

**unquestionable-
ness**
BR (ˌ)ʌnˈkwɛstʃənəbl-
nəs,

unquestionably
(ˌ)ʌnˈkwɛstʃŋəblnəs,
(ˌ)ʌŋˈkwɛstʃənəblnəs,
(ˌ)ʌŋˈkwɛstʃŋəblnəs
AM ˌənˈkwɛstʃənəbəl-
nəs,
ˌənˈkwɛstʃənəbəlnəs

unquestionably
BR (ˌ)ʌnˈkwɛstʃənəbli,
(ˌ)ʌnˈkwɛstʃŋəbli,
(ˌ)ʌŋˈkwɛstʃənəbli,
(ˌ)ʌŋˈkwɛstʃŋəbli
AM ˌənˈkwɛstʃənəbli,
ˌənˈkwɛstʃənəbli

unquestioned
BR (ˌ)ʌnˈkwɛstʃ(ə)nd,
(ˌ)ʌnˈkwɛstʃ(ə)nd
AM ˌənˈkwɛstʃənd,
ˌənˈkwɛstʃənd

unquestioning
BR (ˌ)ʌnˈkwɛstʃənɪŋ,
(ˌ)ʌnˈkwɛstʃŋɪŋ,
(ˌ)ʌŋˈkwɛstʃənɪŋ,
(ˌ)ʌŋˈkwɛstʃŋɪŋ
AM ˌənˈkwɛstʃənɪŋ,
ˌənˈkwɛstʃənɪŋ

unquestioningly
BR (ˌ)ʌnˈkwɛstʃənɪŋli,
(ˌ)ʌnˈkwɛstʃŋɪŋli,
(ˌ)ʌŋˈkwɛstʃənɪŋli,
(ˌ)ʌŋˈkwɛstʃŋɪŋli
AM ˌənˈkwɛstʃənɪŋli,
ˌənˈkwɛstʃənɪŋli

unquiet
BR ˌʌnˈkwʌɪət,
ˌʌŋˈkwʌɪət
AM ˌənˈkwaɪət

unquietly
BR ˌʌnˈkwʌɪətli,
ˌʌŋˈkwʌɪətli
AM ˌənˈkwaɪətli

unquietness
BR ˌʌnˈkwʌɪətnəs,
ˌʌŋˈkwʌɪətnəs
AM ˌənˈkwaɪətnəs

unquotable
BR ˌʌnˈkwəʊtəbl,
ˌʌŋˈkwəʊtəbl
AM ˌənˈkwoʊdəbəl

unquote
BR ˌʌnˈkwəʊt,
ˌʌŋˈkwəʊt
AM ˌənˈkwoʊt

unransomed
BR ˌʌnˈransəmd
AM ˌənˈrænsəmd

unrated
BR ˌʌnˈreɪtɪd
AM ˌənˈreɪdɪd

unratified
BR ˌʌnˈratɪfʌɪd
AM ˌənˈrædəˌfaɪd

unrationed
BR ˌʌnˈraʃnd
AM ˌənˈræʃənd,
ˌənˈreɪʃənd

unravel
BR (ˌ)ʌnˈrav|l, -lz,
-|ɪŋ \-(ə)lɪŋ, -ld

unreally
(ˌ)ʌnˈkwɛstʃŋəblnəs,
(ˌ)ʌŋˈkwɛstʃənəblnəs,
(ˌ)ʌŋˈkwɛstʃŋəblnəs
AM ˌənˈkwɛstʃənəbəl-
nəs,
ˌənˈkwɛstʃənəbəlnəs

unreachable
BR (ˌ)ʌnˈriːtʃəbl
AM ˌənˈritʃəbəl

unreachableness
BR (ˌ)ʌnˈriːtʃəblnəs
AM ˌənˈritʃəbəlnəs

unreachably
BR (ˌ)ʌnˈriːtʃəbli
AM ˌənˈritʃəbli

unreached
BR (ˌ)ʌnˈriːtʃt
AM ˌənˈritʃt

unreactive
BR ˌʌnrɪˈaktɪv
AM ˌənriˈæktɪv

unread
BR ˌʌnˈrɛd
AM ˌənˈrɛd

unreadability
BR ˌʌnˌriːdəˈbɪlɪti
AM ˌənˌridəˈbɪlɪdi

unreadable
BR (ˌ)ʌnˈriːdəbl
AM ˌənˈridəbəl

unreadably
BR (ˌ)ʌnˈriːdəbli
AM ˌənˈridəbli

unreadily
BR (ˌ)ʌnˈrɛdɪli
AM ˌənˈrɛdəli

unreadiness
BR (ˌ)ʌnˈrɛdɪnɪs
AM ˌənˈrɛdinɪs

unready
BR ˌʌnˈrɛdi
AM ˌənˈrɛdi

unreal
BR (ˌ)ʌnˈrɪəl
AM ˌənˈri(ə)l

unrealisable
BR (ˌ)ʌnˈrɪəlʌɪzəbl
AM ˌənˈriəˌlaɪzəbəl

unrealised
BR (ˌ)ʌnˈrɪəlʌɪzd
AM ˌənˈriəˌlaɪzd

unrealism
BR (ˌ)ʌnˈrɪəlɪz(ə)m
AM ˌənˈriəˌlɪzəm

unrealistic
BR ˌʌnrɪəˈlɪstɪk
AM ˌənˌriəˈlɪstɪk

unrealistically
BR ˌʌnrɪəˈlɪstɪkli
AM ˌənˌriəˈlɪstɪk(ə)li

unreality
BR ˌʌnrɪˈalɪti
AM ˌənriˈælədi

unrealizable
BR (ˌ)ʌnˈrɪəlʌɪzəbl
AM ˌənˈriəˌlaɪzəbəl

unrealized
BR (ˌ)ʌnˈrɪəlʌɪzd
AM ˌənˈriəˌlaɪzd

unreally
BR ˌʌnˈrɪəli

AM ˌʌnˈriəli

unreason
BR ˌʌnˈriːzn, -d
AM ˌʌnˈrizn, -d

unreasonable
BR (ˌ)ʌnˈriːznəbl,
(ˌ)ʌnˈriːz(ə)nəbl
AM ˌʌnˈriznəbəl,
ˌʌnˈriznəbəl

unreasonableness
BR (ˌ)ʌnˈriːznəblnəs,
(ˌ)ʌnˈriːz(ə)nəblnəs
AM ˌʌnˈriznəbəlnəs,
ˌʌnˈriznəbəlnəs

unreasonably
BR (ˌ)ʌnˈriːznəbli,
(ˌ)ʌnˈriːz(ə)nəbli
AM ˌʌnˈriznəbli,
ˌʌnˈriznəbli

unreasoning
BR (ˌ)ʌnˈriːznɪŋ,
(ˌ)ʌnˈriːz(ə)nɪŋ
AM ˌʌnˈriznɪŋ,
ˌʌnˈriznɪŋ

unreasoningly
BR (ˌ)ʌnˈriːznɪŋli,
(ˌ)ʌnˈriːz(ə)nɪŋli
AM ˌʌnˈriznɪŋli,
ˌʌnˈriznɪŋli

unrebelliousness
BR ˌʌnrɪˈbeliəsnəs
AM ˌʌnrəˈbeljəsnəs,
ˌʌnrəˈbeliəsnəs,
ˌʌnriˈbeljəsnəs,
ˌʌnriˈbeliəsnəs

unreceptive
BR ˌʌnrɪˈseptɪv
AM ˌʌnrəˈseptɪv,
ˌʌnriˈseptɪv

unreciprocated
BR ˌʌnrɪˈsɪprəkeɪtɪd
AM ˌʌnrəˈsɪprəˌkeɪdɪd,
ˌʌnriˈsɪprəˌkeɪdɪd

unreckoned
BR ˌʌnˈrek(ə)nd
AM ˌʌnˈrekənd

unreclaimed
BR ˌʌnrɪˈkleɪmd
AM ˌʌnrəˈkleɪmd,
ˌʌnriˈkleɪmd

unrecognisable
BR (ˌ)ʌnˈrekəgnʌɪzəbl,
ˌʌnrekəgˈnʌɪzəbl
AM ˌʌnˌrekəgˈnaɪzəbəl

unrecognisable-ness
BR ˌʌnˈrekəgnʌɪzəbl-nəs,
ˌʌnrekəgˈnʌɪzəblnəs
AM ˌʌnˌrekəgˈnaɪzəbəl-nəs

unrecognisably
BR ˌʌnˈrekəgnʌɪzəbli,
ˌʌnrekəgˈnʌɪzəbli
AM ˌʌnˌrekəgˈnaɪzəbli

unrecognised
BR ˌʌnˈrekəgnʌɪzd
AM ˌʌnˈrekəgˌnaɪzd

unrecognizable
BR (ˌ)ʌnˈrekəgnʌɪzəbl,
ˌʌnrekəgˈnʌɪzəbl
AM ˌʌnˌrekəgˈnaɪzəbəl

unrecognizable-ness
BR ˌʌnˈrekəgnʌɪzəblnəs,
ˌʌnrekəgˈnʌɪzəblnəs
AM ˌʌnˌrekəgˈnaɪzəbəl-nəs

unrecognizably
BR ˌʌnˈrekəgnʌɪzəbli,
ˌʌnrekəgˈnʌɪzəbli
AM ˌʌnˌrekəgˈnaɪzəbli

unrecognized
BR ˌʌnˈrekəgnʌɪzd
AM ˌʌnˈrekəgˌnaɪzd

unrecompensed
BR ˌʌnˈrekəmpenst
AM ˌʌnˈrekəmˌpenst

unreconcilable
BR ˌʌnˈrek(ə)nsʌɪləbl,
ˌʌnrek(ə)nˈsʌɪləbl
AM ˌʌnˌrekənˈsaɪləbəl

unreconciled
BR ˌʌnˈrekənsʌɪld,
ˌʌnˈrek(ə)nsʌɪld
AM ˌʌnˈrekənˌsaɪld

unreconstructed
BR ˌʌnriːkənˈstrʌktɪd
AM ˌʌnˌrikənˈstrʌktəd

unrecordable
BR ˌʌnrɪˈkɔːdəbl
AM ˌʌnrəˈkɔrdəbəl,
ˌʌnriˈkɔrdəbəl

unrecorded
BR ˌʌnrɪˈkɔːdɪd
AM ˌʌnrəˈkɔrdəd,
ˌʌnriˈkɔrdəd

unrecovered
BR ˌʌnrɪˈkʌvəd
AM ˌʌnrəˈkəvərd,
ˌʌnriˈkəvərd

unrectified
BR ˌʌnˈrektɪfʌɪd
AM ˌʌnˈrektəˌfaɪd

unredeemable
BR ˌʌnrɪˈdiːməbl
AM ˌʌnrəˈdiməbəl,
ˌʌnriˈdiməbəl

unredeemably
BR ˌʌnrɪˈdiːməbli
AM ˌʌnrəˈdiməbli,
ˌʌnriˈdiməbli

unredeemed
BR ˌʌnrɪˈdiːmd
AM ˌʌnrəˈdimd,
ˌʌnriˈdimd

unredressed
BR ˌʌnrɪˈdrest
AM ˌʌnrəˈdrest,
ˌʌnriˈdrest

unreel
BR ˌʌnˈriːl, -z, -ɪŋ, -d
AM ˌʌnˈril, -z, -ɪŋ, -d

unrefined
BR ˌʌnrɪˈfʌɪnd

AM ˌʌnrəˈfaɪnd,
ˌʌnriˈfaɪnd

unreflected
BR ˌʌnrɪˈflektɪd
AM ˌʌnrəˈflektəd,
ˌʌnriˈflektəd

unreflecting
BR ˌʌnrɪˈflektɪŋ
AM ˌʌnrəˈflektɪŋ,
ˌʌnriˈflektɪŋ

unreflectingly
BR ˌʌnrɪˈflektɪŋli
AM ˌʌnrəˈflektɪŋli,
ˌʌnriˈflektɪŋli

unreflectingness
BR ˌʌnrɪˈflektɪŋnɪs
AM ˌʌnrəˈflektɪŋnɪs,
ˌʌnriˈflektɪŋnɪs

unreflective
BR ˌʌnrɪˈflektɪv
AM ˌʌnrəˈflektɪv,
ˌʌnriˈflektɪv

unreformed
BR ˌʌnrɪˈfɔːmd
AM ˌʌnrəˈfɔ(ə)rmd,
ˌʌnriˈfɔ(ə)rmd

unrefreshed
BR ˌʌnrɪˈfreʃt
AM ˌʌnrəˈfreʃt,
ˌʌnriˈfreʃt

unrefuted
BR ˌʌnrɪˈfjuːtɪd
AM ˌʌnrəˈfjudəd,
ˌʌnriˈfjudəd

unregarded
BR ˌʌnrɪˈgɑːdɪd
AM ˌʌnrəˈgɑrdəd,
ˌʌnriˈgɑrdəd

unregeneracy
BR ˌʌnrɪˈdʒen(ə)rəsi
AM ˌʌnrəˈdʒenərəsi,
ˌʌnriˈdʒenərəsi

unregenerate
BR ˌʌnrɪˈdʒen(ə)rət
AM ˌʌnrəˈdʒenərət,
ˌʌnriˈdʒenərət

unregenerately
BR ˌʌnrɪˈdʒen(ə)rətli
AM ˌʌnrəˈdʒenərətli,
ˌʌnriˈdʒenərətli

unregimented
BR (ˌ)ʌnˈredʒɪmentɪd
AM ˌʌnˈredʒəˌmen(t)əd

unregistered
BR (ˌ)ʌnˈredʒɪstəd
AM ˌʌnˈredʒəstərd

unregretted
BR ˌʌnrɪˈgretɪd
AM ˌʌnrəˈgredəd,
ˌʌnriˈgredəd

unregulated
BR (ˌ)ʌnˈregjʊleɪtɪd
AM ˌʌnˈregjəˌleɪdɪd

unrehearsed
BR ˌʌnrɪˈhəːst
AM ˌʌnrəˈhərst,
ˌʌnriˈhərst

unrein
BR ˌʌnˈreɪn, -z, -ɪŋ, -d
AM ˌʌnˈreɪn, -z, -ɪŋ, -d

unreinforced
BR ˌʌnriːɪnˈfɔːst
AM ˌʌnriːɪnˈfɔ(ə)rst

unrelated
BR ˌʌnrɪˈleɪtɪd
AM ˌʌnrəˈleɪdɪd,
ˌʌnriˈleɪdɪd

unrelatedly
BR ˌʌnrɪˈleɪtɪdli
AM ˌʌnrəˈleɪdɪdli,
ˌʌnriˈleɪdɪdli

unrelatedness
BR ˌʌnrɪˈleɪtɪdnɪs
AM ˌʌnrəˈleɪdɪdnɪs,
ˌʌnriˈleɪdɪdnɪs

unrelaxed
BR ˌʌnrɪˈlakst
AM ˌʌnrəˈlækst,
ˌʌnriˈlækst

unreleased
BR ˌʌnrɪˈliːst
AM ˌʌnrəˈlist, ˌʌnriˈlist

unrelenting
BR ˌʌnrɪˈlentɪŋ
AM ˌʌnrəˈlen(t)ɪŋ,
ˌʌnriˈlen(t)ɪŋ

unrelentingly
BR ˌʌnrɪˈlentɪŋli
AM ˌʌnrəˈlen(t)ɪŋli,
ˌʌnriˈlen(t)ɪŋli

unrelentingness
BR ˌʌnrɪˈlentɪŋnɪs
AM ˌʌnrəˈlen(t)ɪŋnɪs,
ˌʌnriˈlen(t)ɪŋnɪs

unreliability
BR ˌʌnrɪˌlʌɪəˈbɪlɪti
AM ˌʌnrəˌlaɪəˈbɪlɪdi,
ˌʌnriˌlaɪəˈbɪlɪdi

unreliable
BR ˌʌnrɪˈlʌɪəbl
AM ˌʌnrəˈlaɪəbəl,
ˌʌnriˈlaɪəbəl

unreliableness
BR ˌʌnrɪˈlʌɪəblnəs
AM ˌʌnrəˈlaɪəbəlnəs,
ˌʌnriˈlaɪəbəlnəs

unreliably
BR ˌʌnrɪˈlʌɪəbli
AM ˌʌnrəˈlaɪəbli,
ˌʌnriˈlaɪəbli

unrelieved
BR ˌʌnrɪˈliːvd
AM ˌʌnrəˈlivd,
ˌʌnriˈlivd

unrelievedly
BR ˌʌnrɪˈliːvɪdli
AM ˌʌnrəˈlivɪdli,
ˌʌnriˈlivɪdli

unreligious
BR ˌʌnrɪˈlɪdʒəs
AM ˌʌnrəˈlɪdʒəs,
ˌʌnriˈlɪdʒəs

unremarkable
BR ˌʌnrɪˈmɑːkəbl

unremarkably
AM ˌənrəˈmɑrkəbəl,
ˌənriˈmɑrkəbəl

unremarkably
BR ˌʌnrɪˈmɑːkəbli
AM ˌənrəˈmɑrkəbli,
ˌənriˈmɑrkəbli

unremarked
BR ˌʌnrɪˈmɑːkt
AM ˌənrəˈmɑrkt,
ˌənriˈmɑrkt

unremembered
BR ˌʌnrɪˈmɛmbəd
AM ˌənrəˈmɛmbərd,
ˌənriˈmɛmbərd

unremitting
BR ˌʌnrɪˈmɪtɪŋ
AM ˌənrəˈmɪdɪŋ,
ˌənriˈmɪdɪŋ

unremittingly
BR ˌʌnrɪˈmɪtɪŋli
AM ˌənrəˈmɪdɪŋli,
ˌənriˈmɪdɪŋli

unremittingness
BR ˌʌnrɪˈmɪtɪŋnɪs
AM ˌənrəˈmɪdɪŋnɪs,
ˌənriˈmɪdɪŋnɪs

unremorseful
BR ˌʌnrɪˈmɔːsf(ʊ)l
AM ˌənrəˈmɔrsfəl,
ˌənriˈmɔrsfəl

unremorsefully
BR ˌʌnrɪˈmɔːsfʊli,
ˌʌnrɪˈmɔːsfli
AM ˌənrəˈmɔrsfəli,
ˌənrəˈmɔrsfəli

unremovable
BR ˌʌnrɪˈmuːvəbl
AM ˌənrəˈmuvəbəl,
ˌənriˈmuvəbəl

unremunerative
BR ˌʌnrɪˈmjuːn(ə)rətɪv
AM ˌənrəˈmjun(ə)rədɪv,
ˌənriˈmjun(ə)rədɪv

unremuneratively
BR ˌʌnrɪˈmjuːn(ə)rətɪv-
li
AM ˌənrəˈmjun(ə)rədɪv-
li,
ˌənriˈmjun(ə)rədɪvli

**unremunerative-
ness**
BR ˌʌnrɪˈmjuːn(ə)rətɪv-
nɪs
AM ˌənrəˈmjun(ə)rədɪv-
nɪs,
ˌənriˈmjun(ə)rədɪvnɪs

unrenewable
BR ˌʌnrɪˈnjuːəbl
AM ˌənrəˈn(j)uəbəl,
ˌənriˈn(j)uəbəl

unrenewed
BR ˌʌnrɪˈnjuːd
AM ˌənrəˈn(j)ud,
ˌənriˈn(j)ud

unrenounced
BR ˌʌnrɪˈnaʊnst
AM ˌənrəˈnaʊnst,
ˌənriˈnaʊnst

unrepairable
BR ˌʌnrɪˈpɛːrəbl
AM ˌənrəˈpɛrəbəl,
ˌənriˈpɛrəbəl

unrepaired
BR ˌʌnrɪˈpɛːd
AM ˌənrəˈpɛ(ə)rd,
ˌənriˈpɛ(ə)rd

unrepealed
BR ˌʌnrɪˈpiːld
AM ˌənrəˈpild,
ˌənriˈpild

unrepeatability
BR ˌʌnrɪˌpiːtəˈbɪlɪti
AM ˌənrəˌpidəˈbɪlɪdi,
ˌənriˌpidəˈbɪlɪdi

unrepeatable
BR ˌʌnrɪˈpiːtəbl
AM ˌənrəˈpidəbəl,
ˌənriˈpidəbəl

unrepeatably
BR ˌʌnrɪˈpiːtəbli
AM ˌənrəˈpidəbli,
ˌənriˈpidəbli

unrepeated
BR ˌʌnrɪˈpiːtɪd
AM ˌənrəˈpidɪd,
ˌənriˈpidɪd

unrepentant
BR ˌʌnrɪˈpɛntənt
AM ˌənrəˈpɛn(t)ənt,
ˌənriˈpɛn(t)ənt

unrepentantly
BR ˌʌnrɪˈpɛntəntli
AM ˌənrəˈpɛn(t)ən(t)li,
ˌənriˈpɛn(t)ən(t)li

unrepented
BR ˌʌnrɪˈpɛntɪd
AM ˌənrəˈpɛn(t)əd,
ˌənriˈpɛn(t)əd

unreported
BR ˌʌnrəˈpɔːtɪd
AM ˌənrəˈpɔrdəd,
ˌənrəˈpɔrdəd

unrepresentative
BR ˌʌnˌrɛprɪˈzɛntətɪv
AM ˌənˌrɛprəˈzɛn(t)ədɪv

**unrepresentative-
ly**
BR ˌʌnˌrɛprɪˈzɛntətɪvli
AM ˌənˌrɛprəˈzɛn(t)ədɪv-
li

**unrepresentative-
ness**
BR ˌʌnˌrɛprɪˈzɛntətɪvnɪs
AM ˌənˌrɛprəˈzɛn(t)ədɪv-
nɪs

unrepresented
BR ˌʌnˌrɛprɪˈzɛntɪd,
ˌʌnˈrɛprɪzɛntɪd
AM ˌənˌrɛprəˈzɛn(t)əd

unreproved
BR ˌʌnrɪˈpruːvd
AM ˌənrəˈpruvd,
ˌənriˈpruvd

unrequested
BR ˌʌnrɪˈkwɛstɪd

AM ˌənrəˈkwɛstəd,
ˌənriˈkwɛstəd

unrequited
BR ˌʌnrɪˈkwʌɪtɪd
AM ˌənrəˈkwaɪdɪd,
ˌənriˈkwaɪdɪd

unrequitedly
BR ˌʌnrɪˈkwʌɪtɪdli
AM ˌənrəˈkwaɪdɪdli,
ˌənriˈkwaɪdɪdli

unrequitedness
BR ˌʌnrɪˈkwʌɪtɪdnɪs
AM ˌənrəˈkwaɪdɪdnɪs,
ˌənriˈkwaɪdɪdnɪs

unresearched
BR ˌʌnrɪˈsəːtʃt
AM ˌənrəˈsərtʃt,
ˌənriˈsərtʃt

unreserve
BR ˌʌnrɪˈzəːv, -d
AM ˌənrəˈzərv,
ˌənrəˈzərv, -d

unreservedly
BR ˌʌnrɪˈzəːvɪdli
AM ˌənrəˈzərvədli,
ˌənriˈzərvədli

unreservedness
BR ˌʌnrɪˈzəːvɪdnɪs
AM ˌənrəˈzərvədnəs,
ˌənriˈzərvədnəs

unresisted
BR ˌʌnrɪˈzɪstɪd
AM ˌənrəˈzɪstɪd,
ˌənriˈzɪstɪd

unresistedly
BR ˌʌnrɪˈzɪstɪdli
AM ˌənrəˈzɪstɪdli,
ˌənriˈzɪstɪdli

unresisting
BR ˌʌnrɪˈzɪstɪŋ
AM ˌənrəˈzɪstɪŋ,
ˌənriˈzɪstɪŋ

unresistingly
BR ˌʌnrɪˈzɪstɪŋli
AM ˌənrəˈzɪstɪŋli,
ˌənriˈzɪstɪŋli

unresistingness
BR ˌʌnrɪˈzɪstɪŋnɪs
AM ˌənrəˈzɪstɪŋnɪs,
ˌənriˈzɪstɪŋnɪs

unresolvable
BR ˌʌnrɪˈzɒlvəbl
AM ˌənrəˈzɒlvəbəl,
ˌənrəˈzalvəbəl,
ˌənriˈzɒlvəbəl,
ˌənriˈzalvəbəl

unresolved
BR ˌʌnrɪˈzɒlvd
AM ˌənrəˈzɒlvd,
ˌənrəˈzalvd,
ˌənriˈzɒlvd,
ˌənriˈzalvd

unresolvedly
BR ˌʌnrɪˈzɒlvɪdli
AM ˌənrəˈzɒlvədli,
ˌənrəˈzalvədli,
ˌənriˈzɒlvədli,
ˌənriˈzalvədli

unresolvedness
BR ˌʌnrɪˈzɒlvɪdnɪs
AM ˌənrəˈzɒlvədnəs,
ˌənrəˈzalvədnəs,
ˌənriˈzɒlvədnəs,
ˌənriˈzalvədnəs

unresponsive
BR ˌʌnrɪˈspɒnsɪv
AM ˌənrəˈspansɪv,
ˌənriˈspansɪv

unresponsively
BR ˌʌnrɪˈspɒnsɪvli
AM ˌənrəˈspansɪvli,
ˌənriˈspansɪvli

unresponsiveness
BR ˌʌnrɪˈspɒnsɪvnɪs
AM ˌənrəˈspansɪvnɪs,
ˌənriˈspansɪvnɪs

unrest
BR (ˌ)ʌnˈrɛst
AM ˌənˈrɛst

unrested
BR ˌʌnˈrɛstɪd
AM ˌənˈrɛstəd

unrestful
BR ˌʌnˈrɛs(t)f(ʊ)l
AM ˌənˈrɛs(t)fəl

unrestfully
BR ˌʌnˈrɛstfʊli,
ˌʌnˈrɛstfli
AM ˌənˈrɛs(t)fəli

unrestfulness
BR ˌʌnˈrɛs(t)f(ʊ)lnəs
AM ˌənˈrɛs(t)fəlnəs

unresting
BR ˌʌnˈrɛstɪŋ
AM ˌənˈrɛstɪŋ

unrestingly
BR ˌʌnˈrɛstɪŋli
AM ˌənˈrɛstɪŋli

unrestored
BR ˌʌnrɪˈstɔːd
AM ˌənrəˈstɔ(ə)rd,
ˌənriˈstɔ(ə)rd

unrestrainable
BR ˌʌnrɪˈstreɪnəbl
AM ˌənrəˈstreɪnəbəl,
ˌənriˈstreɪnəbəl

unrestrained
BR ˌʌnrɪˈstreɪnd
AM ˌənrəˈstreɪnd,
ˌənriˈstreɪnd

unrestrainedly
BR ˌʌnrɪˈstreɪnɪdli
AM ˌənrəˈstreɪnɪdli,
ˌənriˈstreɪnɪdli

unrestrainedness
BR ˌʌnrɪˈstreɪnɪdnɪs
AM ˌənrəˈstreɪnɪdnɪs,
ˌənriˈstreɪnɪdnɪs

unrestraint
BR ˌʌnrɪˈstreɪnt
AM ˌənrəˈstreɪnt,
ˌənriˈstreɪnt

unrestricted
BR ˌʌnrɪˈstrɪktɪd
AM ˌənrəˈstrɪktɪd,
ˌənriˈstrɪktɪd

unrestrictedly
BR ˌʌnrɪˈstrɪktɪdli
AM ˌənrəˈstrɪktɪdli,
ˌənriˈstrɪktɪdli

unrestrictedness
BR ˌʌnrɪˈstrɪktɪdnɪs
AM ˌənrəˈstrɪktɪdnɪs,
ˌənriˈstrɪktɪdnɪs

unretentive
BR ˌʌnrɪˈtentɪv
AM ˌənrəˈten(t)ɪv,
ˌənriˈten(t)ɪv

unretentively
BR ˌʌnrɪˈtentɪvli
AM ˌənrəˈten(t)ɪvli,
ˌənriˈten(t)ɪvli

unretentiveness
BR ˌʌnrɪˈtentɪvnɪs
AM ˌənrəˈten(t)ɪvnɪs,
ˌənriˈten(t)ɪvnɪs

unreturned
BR ˌʌnrɪˈtəːnd
AM ˌənrəˈtərnd,
ˌənriˈtərnd

unrevealed
BR ˌʌnrɪˈviːld
AM ˌənrəˈvild,
ˌənriˈvild

unrevealing
BR ˌʌnrɪˈviːlɪŋ
AM ˌənrəˈvilɪŋ,
ˌənriˈvilɪŋ

unreversed
BR ˌʌnrɪˈvəːst
AM ˌənrəˈvərst,
ˌənriˈvərst

unrevised
BR ˌʌnrɪˈvaɪzd
AM ˌənrəˈvaɪzd,
ˌənriˈvaɪzd

unrevoked
BR ˌʌnrɪˈvəʊkt
AM ˌənrəˈvoʊkt,
ˌənriˈvoʊkt

unrevolutionary
BR ˌʌnˌrevəˈl(j)uːʃn(ə)ri
AM ˌənˈrevəˌl(j)uʃəˌneri

unrewarded
BR ˌʌnrɪˈwɔːdɪd
AM ˌənrəˈwɔrdəd,
ˌənriˈwɔrdəd

unrewarding
BR ˌʌnrɪˈwɔːdɪŋ
AM ˌənrəˈwɔrdɪŋ,
ˌənriˈwɔrdɪŋ

unrewardingly
BR ˌʌnrɪˈwɔːdɪŋli
AM ˌənrəˈwɔrdɪŋli,
ˌənriˈwɔrdɪŋli

unrhymed
BR ˌʌnˈraɪmd
AM ˌənˈraɪmd

unrhythmical
BR ˌʌnˈrɪðmɪkl
AM ˌənˈrɪðmɪkəl

unrhythmically
BR ˌʌnˈrɪðmɪkli
AM ˌənˈrɪðmɪk(ə)li

unridable
BR (ˌ)ʌnˈraɪdəbl
AM ˌənˈraɪdəbəl

unridden
BR ˌʌnˈrɪdn
AM ˌənˈrɪdən

unriddle
BR ˌʌnˈrɪd|l, -lz,
-|ɪŋ \-lŋ, -ld
AM ˌənˈrɪd|əl, -əlz,
-(ə)lŋ, -əld

unriddler
BR ˌʌnˈrɪdlə(r),
ˌʌnˈrɪdlə(r), -z
AM ˌənˈrɪd(ə)lər, -z

unrideable
BR (ˌ)ʌnˈraɪdəbl
AM ˌənˈraɪdəbəl

unrig
BR ˌʌnˈrɪg, -z, -ɪŋ, -d
AM ˌənˈrɪg, -z, -ɪŋ, -d

unrighteous
BR (ˌ)ʌnˈraɪtʃəs
AM ˌənˈraɪtʃəs

unrighteously
BR (ˌ)ʌnˈraɪtʃəsli
AM ˌənˈraɪtʃəsli

unrighteousness
BR (ˌ)ʌnˈraɪtʃəsnəs
AM ˌənˈraɪtʃəsnəs

unrip
BR ˌʌnˈrɪp, -s, -ɪŋ, -t
AM ˌənˈrɪp, -s, -ɪŋ, -t

unripe
BR (ˌ)ʌnˈraɪp
AM ˌənˈraɪp

unripened
BR (ˌ)ʌnˈraɪpnd
AM ˌənˈraɪpənd

unripeness
BR (ˌ)ʌnˈraɪpnɪs
AM ˌənˈraɪpnɪs

unrisen
BR ˌʌnˈrɪzn
AM ˌənˈrɪzn

unrivalled
BR (ˌ)ʌnˈraɪvld
AM ˌənˈraɪvəld

unrivet
BR ˌʌnˈrɪv|ɪt, -ɪts, -ɪtɪŋ,
-ɪtɪd
AM ˌənˈrɪv|ɪt, -ts, -dɪŋ,
-dɪd

unroasted
BR (ˌ)ʌnˈrəʊstɪd
AM ˌənˈroʊstəd

unrobe
BR (ˌ)ʌnˈrəʊb, -z, -ɪŋ, -d
AM ˌənˈroʊb, -z, -ɪŋ, -d

unroll
BR (ˌ)ʌnˈrəʊl, -z, -ɪŋ, -d
AM ˌənˈroʊl, -z, -ɪŋ, -d

unromantic
BR ˌʌnrə(ʊ)ˈmæntɪk
AM ˌənrəˈmæn(t)ɪk,
ˌənroʊˈmæn(t)ɪk

unromantically
BR ˌʌnrə(ʊ)ˈmæntɪkli
AM ˌənrəˈmæn(t)ək(ə)li,
ˌənroʊˈmæn(t)ək(ə)li

unroof
BR ˌʌnˈruːf, ˌʌnˈrʊf, -s,
-ɪŋ, -t
AM ˌənˈruf, ˌənˈrʊf, -s,
-ɪŋ, -t

unroot
BR ˌʌnˈruːt, -s, -ɪŋ, -ɪd
AM ˌənˈrut, ˌənˈrʊt, -ts,
-dɪŋ, -dəd

unrope
BR ˌʌnˈrəʊp, -s, -ɪŋ, -t
AM ˌənˈroʊp, -s, -ɪŋ, -t

unrounded
BR ˌʌnˈraʊndɪd
AM ˌənˈraʊndəd

unrove
BR ˌʌnˈrəʊv
AM ˌənˈroʊv

unroyal
BR ˌʌnˈrɔɪəl
AM ˌənˈrɔɪəl

UNRRA
BR ˈʌnrə(r)
AM ˈənrə

unruffled
BR (ˌ)ʌnˈrʌfld
AM ˌənˈrəfəld

unruled
BR ˌʌnˈruːld
AM ˌənˈruld

unruliness
BR ˌʌnˈruːlɪnɪs
AM ˌənˈrulɪnɪs

unruly
BR ˌʌnˈruːli
AM ˌənˈruli

UNRWA
BR ˈʌnrə(r)
AM ˈənrə

unsackable
BR (ˌ)ʌnˈsakəbl
AM ˌənˈsækəbəl

unsaddle
BR (ˌ)ʌnˈsad|l, -lz,
-|ɪŋ \-lŋ, -ld
AM ˌənˈsæd|əl, -əlz,
-(ə)lŋ, -əld

unsafe
BR (ˌ)ʌnˈseɪf
AM ˌənˈseɪf

unsafely
BR (ˌ)ʌnˈseɪfli
AM ˌənˈseɪfli

unsafeness
BR (ˌ)ʌnˈseɪfnɪs
AM ˌənˈseɪfnɪs

unsaid
BR (ˌ)ʌnˈsed
AM ˌənˈsed

unsalability
BR ˌʌnˌseɪləˈbɪlɪti,
ˌʌnseɪləˈbɪlɪti
AM ˌənˌseɪləˈbɪlɪdi

unsalable
BR (ˌ)ʌnˈseɪləbl
AM ˌənˈseɪləbəl

unsalableness
BR (ˌ)ʌnˈseɪləblnəs
AM ˌənˈseɪləbəlnəs

unsalaried
BR ˌʌnˈsalərɪd
AM ˌənˈsælərɪd

unsaleability
BR ˌʌnˌseɪləˈbɪlɪti,
ˌʌnseɪləˈbɪlɪti
AM ˌənˌseɪləˈbɪlɪdi

unsaleable
BR (ˌ)ʌnˈseɪləbl
AM ˌənˈseɪləbəl

unsaleableness
BR (ˌ)ʌnˈseɪləblnəs
AM ˌənˈseɪləbəlnəs

unsalted
BR ˌʌnˈsɔːltɪd,
ˌʌnˈsɒltɪd
AM ˌənˈsɔltəd,
ˌənˈsɑltəd

unsalubrious
BR ˌʌnsəˈl(j)uːbrɪəs
AM ˌənsəˈl(j)ubrɪəs

unsalvageable
BR ˌʌnˈsalvɪdʒəbl
AM ˌənˈsælvədʒəbəl

unsanctified
BR ˌʌnˈsaŋ(k)tɪfʌɪd
AM ˌənˈsæŋ(k)təˌfaɪd

unsanctioned
BR ˌʌnˈsaŋ(k)ʃnd
AM ˌənˈsæŋkʃənd

unsanitary
BR ˌʌnˈsanɪt(ə)ri
AM ˌənˈsænəˌteri

unsatisfactorily
BR ˌʌnsatɪsˈfakt(ə)rɪli
AM ˌənˌsædəsˈfæktərəli

unsatisfactoriness
BR ˌʌnsatɪsˈfakt(ə)rɪnɪs
AM ˌənˌsædəsˈfæktəri-
nɪs

unsatisfactory
BR ˌʌnsatɪsˈfakt(ə)ri
AM ˌənsædəsˈfæktəri

unsatisfied
BR (ˌ)ʌnˈsatɪsfʌɪd
AM ˌənˈsædəsˌfaɪd

unsatisfiedness
BR (ˌ)ʌnˈsatɪsfʌɪdnɪs
AM ˌənˈsædəsˌfaɪdnɪs

unsatisfying
BR (ˌ)ʌnˈsatɪsfʌɪɪŋ
AM ˌənˈsædəsˌfaɪɪŋ

unsatisfyingly
BR (ˌ)ʌnˈsatɪsfʌɪɪŋli
AM ˌənˈsædəsˌfaɪɪŋli

unsaturated
BR (ˌ)ʌnˈsatʃəreɪtɪd,
(ˌ)ʌnˈsatjəreɪtɪd
AM ˌənˈsætʃəˌreɪdɪd

unsaturation
BR ˌʌnsatʃəˈreɪʃn,
ˌʌnsatjʊˈreɪʃn
AM ˌʌnˌsætʃəˈreɪʃən

unsaved
BR ˌʌnˈseɪvd
AM ˌənˈseɪvd

unsavorily
BR (ˌ)ʌnˈseɪv(ə)rɪli
AM ˌənˈseɪv(ə)rəli

unsavoriness
BR (ˌ)ʌnˈseɪv(ə)rɪnɪs
AM ˌənˈseɪv(ə)rɪnɪs

unsavory
BR (ˌ)ʌnˈseɪv(ə)ri
AM ˌənˈseɪv(ə)ri

unsavourily
BR (ˌ)ʌnˈseɪv(ə)rɪli
AM ˌənˈseɪv(ə)rəli

unsavouriness
BR (ˌ)ʌnˈseɪv(ə)rɪnɪs
AM ˌənˈseɪv(ə)rɪnɪs

unsavoury
BR (ˌ)ʌnˈseɪv(ə)ri
AM ˌənˈseɪv(ə)ri

unsay
BR ˌʌnˈs|eɪ, -ɛz, -eɪɪŋ,
-ɛd
AM ˌənˈs|eɪ, -ɛz, -eɪɪŋ,
-ɛd

unsayable
BR ˌʌnˈseɪəbl
AM ˌənˈseɪəbəl

unscalable
BR ˌʌnˈskeɪləbl
AM ˌənˈskeɪləbəl

unscaleable
BR ˌʌnˈskeɪləbl
AM ˌənˈskeɪləbəl

unscaled
BR ˌʌnˈskeɪld
AM ˌənˈskeɪld

unscarred
BR ˌʌnˈskɑːd
AM ˌənˈskɑrd

unscathed
BR (ˌ)ʌnˈskeɪðd
AM ˌənˈskeɪðd

unscented
BR ˌʌnˈsɛntɪd
AM ˌənˈsɛn(t)əd

unscheduled
BR ˌʌnˈʃɛdjʊld,
ˌʌnˈʃɛdjuːld,
ˌʌnˈskɛdʒʊld,
ˌʌnˈʃɛdʒʊld,
ˌʌnˈskɛdʒʊld,
ˌʌnˈskɛdjuːld
AM ˌənˈskɛdʒəld,
ˌənˈskɛˌdʒʊld

unscholarliness
BR ˌʌnˈskɒləlɪnɪs
AM ˌənˈskɑlərlɪnɪs

unscholarly
BR ˌʌnˈskɒləli
AM ˌənˈskɑlərli

unschooled
BR ˌʌnˈskuːld

AM ˌənˈskuld
unscientific
BR ˌʌnsʌɪənˈtɪfɪk
AM ˌənsaɪənˈtɪfɪk

unscientifically
BR ˌʌnsʌɪənˈtɪfɪkli
AM ˌənsaɪənˈtɪfɪk(ə)li

unscramble
BR (ˌ)ʌnˈskrambl̩, -lz,
-l̩ŋ \ -lŋ, -ld
AM ˌənˈskræmbəl,
-əlz, -(ə)lŋ, -əld

unscrambler
BR (ˌ)ʌnˈskramblə(r),
(ˌ)ʌnˈskramblə(r), -z
AM ˌənˈskræmb(ə)lər,
-z

unscratched
BR (ˌ)ʌnˈskratʃt
AM ˌənˈskrætʃt

unscreened
BR ˌʌnˈskriːnd
AM ˌənˈskrind

unscrew
BR ˌʌnˈskruː, -z, -ɪŋ, -d
AM ˌənˈskru, -z, -ɪŋ, -d

unscripted
BR ˌʌnˈskrɪptɪd
AM ˌənˈskrɪptɪd

unscriptural
BR ˌʌnˈskrɪptʃ(ə)rəl,
ˌʌnˈskrɪptʃ(ə)r]
AM ˌənˈskrɪptʃərəl,
ˌənˈskrɪptʃ(ə)rəl

unscripturally
BR ˌʌnˈskrɪptʃ(ə)rəli,
ˌʌnˈskrɪptʃ(ə)r]i
AM ˌənˈskrɪptʃərəli,
ˌənˈskrɪptʃ(ə)rəli

unscrupulous
BR (ˌ)ʌnˈskruːpjʊləs
AM ˌənˈskrupjələs

unscrupulously
BR (ˌ)ʌnˈskruːpjʊləsli
AM ˌənˈskrupjələsli

**unscrupulous-
ness**
BR (ˌ)ʌnˈskruːpjʊləs-
nəs
AM ˌənˈskrupjələsnəs

unseal
BR ˌʌnˈsiːl, -z, -ɪŋ, -d
AM ˌənˈsil, -z, -ɪŋ, -d

unsealed
BR ˌʌnˈsiːld
AM ˌənˈsild

unsearchable
BR (ˌ)ʌnˈsəːtʃəbl
AM ˌənˈsərtʃəbəl

**unsearchable-
ness**
BR (ˌ)ʌnˈsəːtʃəblnəs
AM ˌənˈsərtʃəbəlnəs

unsearchably
BR (ˌ)ʌnˈsəːtʃəbli
AM ˌənˈsərtʃəbli

unsearched
BR ˌʌnˈsəːtʃt

AM ˌənˈsərtʃt
unseasonable
BR (ˌ)ʌnˈsiːznəbl,
(ˌ)ʌnˈsiːz(ə)nəbl
AM ˌənˈsiznəbəl,
ˌənˈsiznəbəl

**unseasonable-
ness**
BR (ˌ)ʌnˈsiːznəblnəs,
(ˌ)ʌnˈsiːz(ə)nəblnəs
AM ˌənˈsiznəbəlnəs,
ˌənˈsiznəbəlnəs

unseasonably
BR (ˌ)ʌnˈsiːznəbli,
(ˌ)ʌnˈsiːz(ə)nəbli
AM ˌənˈsiznəbli,
ˌənˈsiznəbli

unseasoned
BR ˌʌnˈsiːznd
AM ˌənˈsiznd

unseat
BR ˌʌnˈsiːt, -s, -ɪŋ, -ɪd
AM ˌənˈsi|t, -ts, -dɪŋ,
-dɪd

unseaworthiness
BR (ˌ)ʌnˈsiːˌwəːðɪnɪs
AM ˌənˈsiˌwərðɪnɪs

unseaworthy
BR (ˌ)ʌnˈsiːˌwəːði
AM ˌənˈsiˌwərði

unseconded
BR ˌʌnˈsɛk(ə)ndɪd
AM ˌənˈsɛkəndəd

unsectarian
BR ˌʌnsɛkˈtɛːrɪən
AM ˌənˌsɛkˈtɛrɪən

unsecured
BR ˌʌnsɪˈkjʊəd,
ˌʌnsɪˈkjɔːd
AM ˌənsəˈkjʊ(ə)rd

unseeable
BR ˌʌnˈsiːəbl
AM ˌənˈsiəbəl

unseeded
BR ˌʌnˈsiːdɪd
AM ˌənˈsidɪd

unseeing
BR ˌʌnˈsiːɪŋ
AM ˌənˈsiɪŋ

unseeingly
BR ˌʌnˈsiːɪŋli
AM ˌənˈsiɪŋli

unseemliness
BR ˌʌnˈsiːmlɪnɪs
AM ˌənˈsimlɪnɪs

unseemly
BR ˌʌnˈsiːmli
AM ˌənˈsimli

unseen
BR ˌʌnˈsiːn, -z
AM ˌənˈsin, -z

unsegregated
BR ˌʌnˈsɛgrɪgeɪtɪd
AM ˌənˈsɛgrəˌgeɪdɪd

unselect
BR ˌʌnsɪˈlɛkt
AM ˌənsəˈlɛk(t)

unselected
BR ˌʌnsɪˈlɛktɪd
AM ˌənsəˈlɛktəd

unselective
BR ˌʌnsɪˈlɛktɪv
AM ˌənsəˈlɛktɪv

unselfconscious
BR ˌʌnsɛlfˈkɒnʃəs
AM ˌənˌsɛlfˈkɑnʃəs

unselfconsciously
BR ˌʌnsɛlfˈkɒnʃəsli
AM ˌənˌsɛlfˈkɑnʃəsli

**unselfconscious-
ness**
BR ˌʌnsɛlfˈkɒnʃəsnəs
AM ˌənˌsɛlfˈkɑnʃəsnəs

unselfish
BR (ˌ)ʌnˈsɛlfɪʃ
AM ˌənˈsɛlfɪʃ

unselfishly
BR (ˌ)ʌnˈsɛlfɪʃli
AM ˌənˈsɛlfɪʃli

unselfishness
BR (ˌ)ʌnˈsɛlfɪʃnɪs
AM ˌənˈsɛlfɪʃnɪs

unsellable
BR ˌʌnˈsɛləbl
AM ˌənˈsɛləbəl

unsensational
BR ˌʌnsɛnˈseɪʃn(ə)l,
ˌʌnsɛnˈseɪʃən(ə)l
AM ˌənsɛnˈseɪʃ(ə)nəl

unsensationally
BR ˌʌnsɛnˈseɪʃnəli,
ˌʌnsɛnˈseɪʃn̩li,
ˌʌnsɛnˈseɪʃənl̩i,
ˌʌnsɛnˈseɪʃ(ə)nəli
AM ˌənsɛnˈseɪʃ(ə)nəli

unsensitive
BR (ˌ)ʌnˈsɛnsɪtɪv
AM ˌənˈsɛnsədɪv

unsensitively
BR (ˌ)ʌnˈsɛnsɪtɪvli
AM ˌənˈsɛnsədɪvli

unsent
BR ˌʌnˈsɛnt
AM ˌənˈsɛnt

unsentimental
BR ˌʌnsɛntɪˈmɛntl
AM ˌənˌsɛn(t)əˈmɛn(t)l

unsentimentality
BR ˌʌnsɛntɪmɛnˈtalɪti,
ˌʌnsɛntɪmənˈtalɪti
AM ˈʌnˌsɛn(t)əˌmɛn-
ˈtælədi,
ˈənˌsɛn(t)əmənˈtælədi

unsentimentally
BR ˌʌnsɛntɪˈmɛntl̩i
AM ˌənˌsɛn(t)əˈmɛn(t)li

unseparated
BR (ˌ)ʌnˈsɛpəreɪtɪd
AM ˌənˈsɛpəˌreɪdɪd

unserious
BR ˌʌnˈsɪərɪəs
AM ˌənˈsɪrɪəs

unserviceability
BR ˌʌnˌsəːˈvɪsəˈbɪlɪti
AM ˌənˌsərvəsəˈbɪlɪdi

unserviceable
BR (ˌ)ʌnˈsɜːvɪsəbl
AM ˌənˈsɜrvəsəbəl

unset
BR ʌnˈsɛt
AM ˌənˈsɛt

unsettle
BR (ˌ)ʌnˈsɛt|l, -lz,
-|ɪŋ\-lɪŋ, -ld
AM ˌənˈsɛ|dəl, -dlz,
-dlɪŋ\-tlɪŋ, -dld

unsettledness
BR (ˌ)ʌnˈsɛtldnəs
AM ˌənˈsɛdldnəs

unsettlement
BR (ˌ)ʌnˈsɛtlm(ə)nt
AM ˌənˈsɛdlmənt

unsevered
BR ʌnˈsɛvəd
AM ˌənˈsɛvərd

unsewn
BR (ˌ)ʌnˈsəʊn
AM ˌənˈsoʊn

unsex
BR (ˌ)ʌnˈsɛks, -ɪz, -ɪŋ, -t
AM ˌənˈsɛks, -əz, -ɪŋ, -t

unsexy
BR ʌnˈsɛksi
AM ˌənˈsɛksi

unshackle
BR (ˌ)ʌnˈʃak|l, -lz,
-|ɪŋ\-lɪŋ, -ld
AM ˌənˈʃæk|əl, -əlz,
-(ə)lɪŋ, -əld

unshaded
BR ʌnˈʃeɪdɪd
AM ˌənˈʃeɪdɪd

unshakability
BR ʌnˌʃeɪkəˈbɪlɪti,
ˌʌnʃeɪkəˈbɪlɪti
AM ˌənˌʃeɪkəˈbɪlɪdi

unshakable
BR ʌnˈʃeɪkəbl
AM ˌənˈʃeɪkəbəl

unshakably
BR ʌnˈʃeɪkəbli
AM ˌənˈʃeɪkəbli

unshakeability
BR ʌnˌʃeɪkəˈbɪlɪti,
ˌʌnʃeɪkəˈbɪlɪti
AM ˌənˌʃeɪkəˈbɪlɪdi

unshakeable
BR ʌnˈʃeɪkəbl
AM ˌənˈʃeɪkəbəl

unshakeably
BR ʌnˈʃeɪkəbli
AM ˌənˈʃeɪkəbli

unshaken
BR (ˌ)ʌnˈʃeɪk(ə)n
AM ˌənˈʃeɪkən

unshakenly
BR (ˌ)ʌnˈʃeɪk(ə)nli
AM ˌənˈʃeɪkənli

unshapeliness
BR (ˌ)ʌnˈʃeɪplɪnɪs
AM ˌənˈʃeɪplɪnɪs

unshapely
BR (ˌ)ʌnˈʃeɪpli
AM ˌənˈʃeɪpli

unshared
BR ʌnˈʃɛːd
AM ˌənˈʃɛ(ə)rd

unsharp
BR ʌnˈʃɑːp
AM ˌənˈʃɑrp

unsharpened
BR (ˌ)ʌnˈʃɑːpnd
AM ˌənˈʃɑrpənd

unsharpness
BR ʌnˈʃɑːpnəs
AM ˌənˈʃɑrpnəs

unshaved
BR ʌnˈʃeɪvd
AM ˌənˈʃeɪvd

unshaven
BR ʌnˈʃeɪvn
AM ˌənˈʃeɪvən

unsheathe
BR (ˌ)ʌnˈʃiː|ð,
(ˌ)ʌnˈʃiː|θ, -ðz\-θs,
-ðɪŋ\-θɪŋ, -ðd\-θt
AM ˌənˈʃið, -z, -ɪŋ, -d

unshed
BR ʌnˈʃɛd
AM ˌənˈʃɛd

unshell
BR ʌnˈʃɛl, -z, -ɪŋ, -d
AM ˌənˈʃɛl, -z, -ɪŋ, -d

unsheltered
BR ʌnˈʃɛltəd
AM ˌənˈʃɛltərd

unshielded
BR ʌnˈʃiːldɪd
AM ˌənˈʃildɪd

unshiftable
BR ʌnˈʃɪftəbl
AM ˌənˈʃɪftəbəl

unshifted
BR ʌnˈʃɪftɪd
AM ˌənˈʃɪftɪd

unship
BR ʌnˈʃɪp, -s, -ɪŋ, -t
AM ˌənˈʃɪp, -s, -ɪŋ, -t

unshockability
BR ʌnˌʃɒkəˈbɪlɪti,
ˌʌnʃɒkəˈbɪlɪti
AM ˌənˌʃɑkəˈbɪlɪdi

unshockable
BR ʌnˈʃɒkəbl
AM ˌənˈʃɑkəbəl

unshockably
BR ʌnˈʃɒkəbli
AM ˌənˈʃɑkəbli

unshod
BR ʌnˈʃɒd
AM ˌənˈʃɑd

unshorn
BR ʌnˈʃɔːn
AM ˌənˈʃɔ(ə)rn

unshrinkability
BR ʌnˌʃrɪŋkəˈbɪlɪti,
ˌʌnʃrɪŋkəˈbɪlɪti
AM ˌənˌʃrɪŋkəˈbɪlɪdi

unshrinkable
BR (ˌ)ʌnˈʃrɪŋkəbl
AM ˌənˈʃrɪŋkəbəl

unshrinking
BR ʌnˈʃrɪŋkɪŋ
AM ˌənˈʃrɪŋkɪŋ

unshrinkingly
BR ʌnˈʃrɪŋkɪŋli
AM ˌənˈʃrɪŋkɪŋli

unshriven
BR ʌnˈʃrɪvn
AM ˌənˈʃrɪvən

unshut
BR ʌnˈʃʌt
AM ˌənˈʃət

unshuttered
BR ʌnˈʃʌtəd
AM ˌənˈʃədərd

unsighted
BR (ˌ)ʌnˈsaɪtɪd
AM ˌənˈsaɪdɪd

unsightliness
BR ʌnˈsaɪtlɪnɪs
AM ˌənˈsaɪtlɪnɪs

unsightly
BR ʌnˈsaɪtl|i, -ɪə(r),
-ɪst
AM ˌənˈsaɪtli, -ər, -ɪst

unsigned
BR ʌnˈsaɪnd
AM ˌənˈsaɪnd

unsignposted
BR ʌnˈsaɪnpəʊstɪd
AM ˌənˈsaɪnˌpoʊstəd

unsilenced
BR ʌnˈsaɪlənst
AM ˌənˈsaɪlənst

unsimplified
BR (ˌ)ʌnˈsɪmplɪfaɪd
AM ˌənˈsɪmpləˌfaɪd

unsinkability
BR ʌnˌsɪŋkəˈbɪlɪti,
ˌʌnsɪŋkəˈbɪlɪti
AM ˌənˌsɪŋkəˈbɪlɪdi

unsinkable
BR (ˌ)ʌnˈsɪŋkəbl
AM ˌənˈsɪŋkəbəl

unsized
BR ʌnˈsaɪzd
AM ˌənˈsaɪzd

unskilful
BR (ˌ)ʌnˈskɪlf(ʊ)l
AM ˌənˈskɪlfəl

unskilfully
BR (ˌ)ʌnˈskɪlfʊli,
(ˌ)ʌnˈskɪlfli
AM ˌənˈskɪlfəli

unskilfulness
BR (ˌ)ʌnˈskɪlf(ʊ)lnəs
AM ˌənˈskɪlfəlnəs

unskilled
BR ʌnˈskɪld
AM ˌənˈskɪld

unskimmed
BR ʌnˈskɪmd
AM ˌənˈskɪmd

unslakeable
BR (ˌ)ʌnˈsleɪkəbl
AM ˌənˈsleɪkəbəl

unslaked
BR ʌnˈsleɪkt
AM ˌənˈsleɪkt

unsleeping
BR (ˌ)ʌnˈsliːpɪŋ
AM ˌənˈslipɪŋ

unsleepingly
BR ʌnˈsliːpɪŋli
AM ˌənˈslipɪŋli

unsliced
BR ʌnˈslaɪst
AM ˌənˈslaɪst

unsling
BR ʌnˈslɪŋ, -z, -ɪŋ
AM ˌənˈslɪŋ, -z, -ɪŋ

unslung
BR ʌnˈslʌŋ
AM ˌənˈsləŋ

unsmiling
BR (ˌ)ʌnˈsmaɪlɪŋ
AM ˌənˈsmaɪlɪŋ

unsmilingly
BR (ˌ)ʌnˈsmaɪlɪŋli
AM ˌənˈsmaɪlɪŋli

unsmilingness
BR (ˌ)ʌnˈsmaɪlɪŋnɪs
AM ˌənˈsmaɪlɪŋnɪs

unsmoked
BR ʌnˈsməʊkt
AM ˌənˈsmoʊkt

unsmoothed
BR ʌnˈsmuːð
AM ˌənˈsmuð

unsnarl
BR ʌnˈsnɑːl, -z, -ɪŋ, -d
AM ˌənˈsnɑrl, -z, -ɪŋ, -d

unsoaked
BR ʌnˈsəʊkt
AM ˌənˈsoʊkt

unsociability
BR ʌnˌsəʊʃəˈbɪlɪti,
ˌʌnsəʊʃəˈbɪlɪti
AM ˌənsoʊʃəˈbɪlɪdi

unsociable
BR (ˌ)ʌnˈsəʊʃəbl
AM ˌənˈsoʊʃəbəl

unsociableness
BR (ˌ)ʌnˈsəʊʃəblnəs
AM ˌənˈsoʊʃəbəlnəs

unsociably
BR (ˌ)ʌnˈsəʊʃəbli
AM ˌənˈsoʊʃəbli

unsocial
BR ʌnˈsəʊʃl
AM ˌənˈsoʊʃəl

unsocialist
BR ʌnˈsəʊʃlɪst,
ʌnˈsəʊʃəlɪst, -s
AM ˌənˈsoʊʃələst, -s

unsocially
BR ʌnˈsəʊʃli,
ʌnˈsəʊʃəli
AM ˌənˈsoʊʃəli

unsoftened
BR ˌʌn'sɒfnd
AM ˌən'sɔfənd,
ˌən'sɑfənd
unsoiled
BR ˌʌn'sɔɪld
AM ˌən'sɔɪld
unsold
BR ˌʌn'səʊld
AM ˌən'soʊld
unsolder
BR ˌʌn'sɒld|ə(r),
ˌʌn'səʊld|ə(r), -əz,
-(ə)rɪŋ, -əd
AM ˌən'sɑdər, -z, -ɪŋ, -d
unsoldierly
BR ˌʌn'səʊldʒəli
AM ˌən'soʊldʒərli
unsolicited
BR ˌʌnsə'lɪsɪtɪd
AM ˌənsə'lɪsɪdɪd
unsolicitedly
BR ˌʌnsə'lɪsɪtɪdli
AM ˌənsə'lɪsɪdɪdli
unsolvability
BR ʌnˌsɒlvə'bɪlɪti,
ˌʌnsɒlvə'bɪlɪti
AM ˌʌnˌsɑlvə'bɪlɪdi
unsolvable
BR ˌʌn'sɒlvəbl
AM ˌən'sɑlvəbəl
unsolvableness
BR ˌʌn'sɒlvəblnəs
AM ˌən'sɑlvəbəlnəs
unsolved
BR ˌʌn'sɒlvd
AM ˌən'sɑlvd
unsophisticated
BR ˌʌnsə'fɪstɪkeɪtɪd
AM ˌənsə'fɪstə,keɪdɪd
unsophisticatedly
BR ˌʌnsə'fɪstɪkeɪtɪdli
AM ˌənsə'fɪstə,keɪdɪdli
**unsophisticated-
ness**
BR ˌʌnsə'fɪstɪkeɪtɪdnɪs
AM ˌənsə'fɪstə,keɪdɪdnɪs
unsophistication
BR ˌʌnsə,fɪstɪ'keɪʃn
AM ˌənsə,fɪstə'keɪʃən
unsorted
BR ˌʌn'sɔːtɪd
AM ˌən'sɔrdəd
unsought
BR ˌʌn'sɔːt
AM ˌən'sɔt, ˌʌn'sɑt
unsound
BR ˌʌn'saʊnd
AM ˌən'saʊnd
unsounded
BR ˌʌn'saʊndɪd
AM ˌən'saʊndəd
unsoundly
BR ˌʌn'saʊndli
AM ˌən'saʊndli
unsoundness
BR ˌʌn'saʊn(d)nəs

AM ˌən'saʊn(d)nəs
unsoured
BR ˌʌn'saʊəd
AM ˌən'saʊ(ə)rd
unsown
BR ˌʌn'səʊn
AM ˌən'soʊn
unsparing
BR ˌʌn'speərɪŋ
AM ˌən'sperɪŋ
unsparingly
BR ˌʌn'speərɪŋli
AM ˌən'sperɪŋli
unsparingness
BR ˌʌn'speərɪŋnɪs
AM ˌən'sperɪŋnɪs
unspeakable
BR ˌʌn'spiːkəbl
AM ˌən'spikəbəl
unspeakableness
BR ˌʌn'spiːkəblnəs
AM ˌən'spikəbəlnəs
unspeakably
BR ˌʌn'spiːkəbli
AM ˌən'spikəbli
unspeaking
BR (ˌ)ʌn'spiːkɪŋ
AM ˌən'spikɪŋ
unspecial
BR ˌʌn'speʃl
AM ˌən'speʃəl
unspecialised
BR (ˌ)ʌn'speʃəlʌɪzd,
(ˌ)ʌn'speʃˌlʌɪzd
AM ˌən'speʃə,laɪzd
unspecialized
BR (ˌ)ʌn'speʃəlʌɪzd,
(ˌ)ʌn'speʃˌlʌɪzd
AM ˌən'speʃə,laɪzd
unspecific
BR ˌʌnspɪ'sɪfɪk
AM ˌənspə'sɪfɪk
unspecified
BR (ˌ)ʌn'spesɪfʌɪd
AM ˌən'spesə,faɪd
unspectacular
BR ˌʌnspɛk'takjələ(r)
AM ˌən,spɛk'tækjələr
unspectacularly
BR ˌʌnspɛk'takjələli
AM ˌən,spɛk'tækjələrli
unspent
BR ˌʌn'spɛnt
AM ˌən'spɛnt
unspilled
BR ˌʌn'spɪld
AM ˌən'spɪld
unspilt
BR ˌʌn'spɪlt
AM ˌən'spɪlt
unspiritual
BR ˌʌn'spɪrɪtʃʊəl,
ˌʌn'spɪrɪtʃ(ʉ)l,
ˌʌn'spɪrɪtjʊəl,
ˌʌn'spɪrɪtjəl
AM ˌən'spɪrɪtʃ(əwə)l

unspirituality
BR ˌʌnspɪrɪtʃʊ'alɪti,
ˌʌnspɪrɪtjʊ'alɪti
AM ˌən,spɪrɪtʃ(ə)'wæl-
ədi
unspiritually
BR ˌʌn'spɪrɪtʃʊəli,
ˌʌn'spɪrɪtʃəli,
ˌʌn'spɪrɪtʃli
AM ˌən'spɪrɪtʃ(əw)əli
unspiritualness
BR ˌʌn'spɪrɪtʃʊəlnəs,
ˌʌn'spɪrɪtʃ(ʉ)nəs
AM ˌən'spɪrɪtʃ(əw)əl-
nəs
unspoiled
BR ˌʌn'spɔɪld,
ˌʌn'spɔɪlt
AM ˌən'spɔɪld
unspoilt
BR ˌʌn'spɔɪlt
AM ˌən'spɔɪlt
unspoken
BR (ˌ)ʌn'spəʊk(ə)n
AM ˌən'spoʊkən
unsponsored
BR ˌʌn'spɒnsəd
AM ˌən'spɑnsərd
unsporting
BR ˌʌn'spɔːtɪŋ
AM ˌən'spɔrdɪŋ
unsportingly
BR (ˌ)ʌn'spɔːtɪŋli
AM ˌən'spɔrdɪŋli
unsportingness
BR (ˌ)ʌn'spɔːtɪŋnɪs
AM ˌən'spɔrdɪŋnɪs
unsportsmanlike
BR (ˌ)ʌn'spɔːtsmənlʌɪk
AM ˌən'spɔrtsmən,laɪk
unspotted
BR ˌʌn'spɒtɪd
AM ˌən'spɑdəd
unsprayed
BR ˌʌn'spreɪd
AM ˌən'spreɪd
unsprung
BR ˌʌn'sprʌŋ
AM ˌən'sprəŋ
Unst
BR ʌnst
AM ənst
unstable
BR (ˌ)ʌn'steɪbl
AM ˌən'steɪbəl
unstableness
BR (ˌ)ʌn'steɪblnəs
AM ˌən'steɪbəlnəs
unstably
BR (ˌ)ʌn'steɪbli
AM ˌən'steɪb(ə)li
unstaffed
BR ˌʌn'stɑːft, ˌʌn'staft
AM ˌən'stæft
unstained
BR ˌʌn'steɪnd
AM ˌən'steɪnd

unstall
BR ˌʌn'stɔːl, -z, -ɪŋ, -d
AM ˌən'stɔl, ˌən'stɑl, -z,
-ɪŋ, -d
unstamped
BR ˌʌn'stam(p)t
AM ˌən'stæm(p)t
unstandardised
BR ˌʌn'standədʌɪzd
AM ˌən'stændər,daɪzd
unstandardized
BR ˌʌn'standədʌɪzd
AM ˌən'stændər,daɪzd
unstarched
BR ˌʌn'stɑːtʃt
AM ˌən'stɑrtʃt
unstatable
BR ˌʌn'steɪtəbl
AM ˌən'steɪdəbəl
unstated
BR ˌʌn'steɪtɪd
AM ˌən'steɪdɪd
unstatesmanlike
BR (ˌ)ʌn'steɪtsmənlʌɪk
AM ˌən'steɪtsmən,laɪk
unstatutable
BR ˌʌn'statʃuːtəbl,
ˌʌn'statjuːtəbl
AM ˌən'stætʃudəbəl,
ˌən'stætʃədəbəl
unstatutably
BR ˌʌn'statʃuːtəbli,
ˌʌn'statjuːtəbli
AM ˌən'stætʃudəbli,
ˌən'stætʃədəbli
unsteadfast
BR ˌʌn'stɛdfɑːst,
ˌʌn'stɛdfast
AM ˌən'stɛd,fæst
unsteadfastly
BR ˌʌn'stɛdfɑːstli,
ˌʌn'stɛdfastli
AM ˌən'stɛd,fæst(l)i
unsteadfastness
BR ˌʌn'stɛdfɑːs(t)nəs,
ˌʌn'stɛdfas(t)nəs
AM ˌən'stɛd,fæs(t)nəs
unsteadily
BR (ˌ)ʌn'stɛdɪli
AM ˌən'stɛdəli
unsteadiness
BR (ˌ)ʌn'stɛdɪnɪs
AM ˌən'stɛdinɪs
unsteady
BR (ˌ)ʌn'stɛdi
AM ˌən'stɛdi
unsterile
BR ˌʌn'stɛrʌɪl
AM ˌən'stɛrəl
unsterilely
BR ˌʌn'stɛrʌɪlli
AM ˌən'stɛrə(l)li
unsterilised
BR (ˌ)ʌn'stɛrɪlʌɪzd
AM ˌən'stɛrə,laɪzd
unsterilized
BR (ˌ)ʌn'stɛrɪlʌɪzd
AM ˌən'stɛrə,laɪzd

unstick
BR ˌʌnˈstɪk, -s, -ɪŋ
AM ˌənˈstɪk, -s, -ɪŋ
unstifled
BR ˌʌnˈstaɪfld
AM ˌənˈstaɪfəld
unstimulated
BR ˌʌnˈstɪmjʊleɪtɪd
AM ˌənˈstɪmjəˌleɪdɪd
unstimulating
BR ˌʌnˈstɪmjʊleɪtɪŋ
AM ˌənˈstɪmjəˌleɪdɪŋ
unstinted
BR ˌʌnˈstɪntɪd
AM ˌənˈstɪn(t)ɪd
unstintedly
BR ʌnˈstɪntɪdli
AM ˌənˈstɪn(t)ɪdli
unstinting
BR ʌnˈstɪntɪŋ
AM ˌənˈstɪn(t)ɪŋ
unstintingly
BR ʌnˈstɪntɪŋli
AM ˌənˈstɪn(t)ɪŋli
unstirred
BR ˌʌnˈstɜːd
AM ˌənˈstərd
unstitch
BR ˌʌnˈstɪtʃ, -ɪz, -ɪŋ, -t
AM ˌənˈstɪtʃ, -ɪz, -ɪŋ, -t
unstocked
BR (ˌ)ʌnˈstɒkt
AM ˌənˈstɑkt
unstockinged
BR ˌʌnˈstɒkɪŋd
AM ˌənˈstɑkɪŋd
unstop
BR ˌʌnˈstɒp, -s, -ɪŋ, -t
AM ˌənˈstɑp, -s, -ɪŋ, -t
unstoppability
BR ˌʌnˌstɒpəˈbɪlɪti,
ˌʌnstɒpəˈbɪlɪti
AM ˌənˌstɑpəˈbɪlɪdi
unstoppable
BR (ˌ)ʌnˈstɒpəbl
AM ˌənˈstɑpəbəl
unstoppably
BR (ˌ)ʌnˈstɒpəbli
AM ˌənˈstɑpəbli
unstopper
BR (ˌ)ʌnˈstɒp|ə(r), -əz,
-(ə)rɪŋ, -əd
AM ˌənˈstɑpər, -z, -ɪŋ, -d
unstrained
BR ˌʌnˈstreɪnd
AM ˌənˈstreɪnd
unstrap
BR ˌʌnˈstræp, -s, -ɪŋ, -t
AM ˌənˈstræp, -s, -ɪŋ, -t
unstratified
BR (ˌ)ʌnˈstrætɪfaɪd
AM ˌənˈstrædəˌfaɪd
unstreamed
BR ˌʌnˈstriːmd
AM ˌənˈstrimd
unstreamlined
BR (ˌ)ʌnˈstriːmlaɪnd

AM ˌənˈstrimˌlaɪnd
unstrengthened
BR ˌʌnˈstreŋ(k)θnd
AM ˌənˈstreŋ(k)θənd
unstressed
BR ˌʌnˈstrest
AM ˌənˈstrest
unstretched
BR ˌʌnˈstretʃt
AM ˌənˈstretʃt
unstring
BR ˌʌnˈstrɪŋ, -z, -ɪŋ
AM ˌənˈstrɪŋ, -z, -ɪŋ
unstripped
BR ˌʌnˈstrɪpt
AM ˌənˈstrɪpt
unstructured
BR (ˌ)ʌnˈstrʌktʃəd
AM ˌənˈstrək(t)ʃərd
unstrung
BR ˌʌnˈstrʌŋ
AM ˌənˈstrəŋ
unstuck
BR ˌʌnˈstʌk
AM ˌənˈstək
unstudied
BR ˌʌnˈstʌdɪd
AM ˌənˈstədɪd
unstudiedly
BR ˌʌnˈstʌdɪdli
AM ˌənˈstədidli
unstuffed
BR ˌʌnˈstʌft
AM ˌənˈstəft
unstuffy
BR ˌʌnˈstʌfi
AM ˌənˈstəfi
unstylish
BR ˌʌnˈstaɪlɪʃ
AM ˌənˈstaɪlɪʃ
unsubdued
BR ˌʌnsəbˈdjuːd,
ˌʌnsəbˈdʒuːd
AM ˌənsəbˈd(j)ud
unsubjugated
BR ˌʌnˈsʌbdʒʊgeɪtɪd
AM ˌənˈsəbdʒəˌgeɪtɪd
unsubscribed
BR ˌʌnsəbˈskraɪbd
AM ˌənsəbˈskraɪbd
unsubsidised
BR ˌʌnˈsʌbsɪdaɪzd
AM ˌənˈsəbsəˌdaɪzd
unsubsidized
BR ˌʌnˈsʌbsɪdaɪzd
AM ˌənˈsəbsəˌdaɪzd
unsubstantial
BR ˌʌnsəbˈstanʃl
AM ˌənsəbˈstæn(t)ʃəl
unsubstantiality
BR ˌʌnsəbˌstanʃɪˈalɪti
AM ˌənsəbˌstæn(t)ʃiˈæl ədi
unsubstantially
BR ˌʌnsəbˈstanʃli,
ˌʌnsəbˈstanʃəli
AM ˌənsəbˈstæn(t)ʃəli

unsubstantiated
BR ˌʌnsəbˈstanʃɪeɪtɪd
AM ˌənsəbˈstæn(t)ʃiˌeɪdɪd
unsubtle
BR ˌʌnˈsʌtl
AM ˌənˈsədəl
unsubtly
BR ˌʌnˈsʌtli
AM ˌənˈsəd(ə)li
unsuccess
BR ˌʌnsəkˈses
AM ˌənsəkˈses
unsuccessful
BR ˌʌnsəkˈsesf(ʊ)l
AM ˌənsəkˈsesfəl
unsuccessfully
BR ˌʌnsəkˈsesfʊli,
ˌʌnsəkˈsesfli
AM ˌənsəkˈsesfəli
unsuccessfulness
BR ˌʌnsəkˈsesf(ʊ)lnəs
AM ˌənsəkˈsesfəlnəs
unsugared
BR ˌʌnˈʃʊgəd
AM ˌənˈʃʊgərd
unsuggestive
BR ˌʌnsəˈdʒestɪv
AM ˌənsə(g)ˈdʒestɪv
unsuitability
BR ˌʌnˌs(j)uːtəˈbɪlɪti,
ˌʌns(j)uːtəˈbɪlɪti
AM ˌənsudəˈbɪlɪdi
unsuitable
BR (ˌ)ʌnˈs(j)uːtəbl
AM ˌənˈsudəbəl
unsuitableness
BR (ˌ)ʌnˈs(j)uːtəblnəs
AM ˌənˈsudəbəlnəs
unsuitably
BR (ˌ)ʌnˈs(j)uːtəbli
AM ˌənˈsudəbli
unsuited
BR (ˌ)ʌnˈs(j)uːtɪd
AM ˌənˈsudəd
unsullied
BR ˌʌnˈsʌlɪd
AM ˌənˈsəlid
unsummoned
BR ˌʌnˈsʌmənd
AM ˌənˈsəmənd
unsung
BR ˌʌnˈsʌŋ
AM ˌənˈsəŋ
unsupervised
BR ˌʌnˈs(j)uːpəvaɪzd
AM ˌənˈsupərˌvaɪzd
unsupplied
BR ˌʌnsəˈplʌɪd
AM ˌənsəˈplaɪd
unsupportable
BR ˌʌnsəˈpɔːtəbl
AM ˌənsəˈpɔrdəbəl
unsupportably
BR ˌʌnsəˈpɔːtəbli
AM ˌənsəˈpɔrdəbli

unsupported
BR ˌʌnsəˈpɔːtɪd
AM ˌənsəˈpɔrdəd
unsupportedly
BR ˌʌnsəˈpɔːtɪdli
AM ˌənsəˈpɔrdədli
unsupportive
BR ˌʌnsəˈpɔːtɪv
AM ˌənsəˈpɔrdɪv
unsuppressed
BR ˌʌnsəˈprest
AM ˌənsəˈprest
unsure
BR ˌʌnˈʃʊə(r),
ˌʌnˈʃɔː(r)
AM ˌənˈʃʊ(ə)r
unsurely
BR ˌʌnˈʃʊəli, ˌʌnˈʃɔːli
AM ˌənˈʃʊrli
unsureness
BR ˌʌnˈʃʊənəs,
ˌʌnˈʃɔːnəs
AM ˌənˈʃʊrnəs
unsurfaced
BR ˌʌnˈsɜːfɪst
AM ˌənˈsɜrfəst
unsurmountable
BR ˌʌnsəˈmaʊntəbl
AM ˌənsərˈmaʊn(t)əbəl
unsurpassable
BR ˌʌnsəˈpɑːsəbl,
ˌʌnsəˈpasəbl
AM ˌənsərˈpæsəbəl
unsurpassably
BR ˌʌnsəˈpɑːsəbli,
ˌʌnsəˈpasəbli
AM ˌənsərˈpæsəbli
unsurpassed
BR ˌʌnsəˈpɑːst,
ˌʌnsəˈpast
AM ˌənsərˈpæst
unsurprised
BR ˌʌnsəˈpraɪzd
AM ˌənsə(r)ˈpraɪzd
unsurprising
BR ˌʌnsəˈpraɪzɪŋ
AM ˌənsə(r)ˈpraɪzɪŋ
unsurprisingly
BR ˌʌnsəˈpraɪzɪŋli
AM ˌənsə(r)ˈpraɪzɪŋli
unsurveyed
BR ˌʌnsəˈveɪd
AM ˌənsərˈveɪd
unsurvivable
BR ˌʌnsəˈvaɪvəbl
AM ˌənsərˈvaɪvəbəl
unsusceptibility
BR ˌʌnsəˌseptɪˈbɪlɪti
AM ˌənsəˌseptəˈbɪlɪdi
unsusceptible
BR ˌʌnsəˈseptɪbl
AM ˌənsəˈseptəbəl
unsuspected
BR ˌʌnsəˈspektɪd
AM ˌənsəˈspektəd
unsuspectedly
BR ˌʌnsəˈspektɪdli

AM ˌənsəˈspɛktədli
unsuspecting
BR ˌʌnsəˈspɛktɪŋ
AM ˌənsəˈspɛktɪŋ
unsuspectingly
BR ˌʌnsəˈspɛktɪŋli
AM ˌənsəˈspɛktɪŋli
unsuspectingness
BR ˌʌnsəˈspɛktɪŋnɪs
AM ˌənsəˈspɛktɪŋnɪs
unsuspicious
BR ˌʌnsəˈspɪʃəs
AM ˌənsəˈspɪʃəs
unsuspiciously
BR ˌʌnsəˈspɪʃəsli
AM ˌənsəˈspɪʃəsli
unsuspiciousness
BR ˌʌnsəˈspɪʃəsnəs
AM ˌənsəˈspɪʃəsnəs
unsustainable
BR ˌʌnsəˈsteɪnəbl
AM ˌənsəˈsteɪnəbəl
unsustainably
BR ˌʌnsəˈsteɪnəbli
AM ˌənsəˈsteɪnəbli
unsustained
BR ˌʌnsəˈsteɪnd
AM ˌənsəˈsteɪnd
unswallowed
BR ˌʌnˈswɒləʊd
AM ˌʌnˈswɑːloʊd
unswathe
BR ˌʌnˈsweɪð, -z, -ɪŋ, -d
AM ˌənˈsweɪð, -z, -ɪŋ, -d
unswayed
BR ˌʌnˈsweɪd
AM ˌənˈsweɪd
unsweetened
BR ˌʌnˈswiːtnd
AM ˌənˈswiːtnd
unswept
BR ˌʌnˈswɛpt
AM ˌənˈswɛpt
unswerving
BR (ˌ)ʌnˈswɜːvɪŋ
AM ˌənˈswɜːvɪŋ
unswervingly
BR (ˌ)ʌnˈswɜːvɪŋli
AM ˌənˈswɜːvɪŋli
unsworn
BR ˌʌnˈswɔːn
AM ˌənˈswɔː(ə)rn
Unsworth
BR ˈʌnzwɜːθ, ˈʌnzwəθ
AM ˈənzˌwɜrθ
unsymmetrical
BR ˌʌnsɪˈmɛtrɪkl
AM ˌənsəˈmɛtrəkəl
unsymmetrically
BR ˌʌnsɪˈmɛtrɪkli
AM ˌənsəˈmɛtrək(ə)li
unsympathetic
BR ˌʌnsɪmpəˈθɛtɪk
AM ˌənsɪmpəˈθɛdɪk
unsympathetic-
ally
BR ˌʌnsɪmpəˈθɛtɪkli

AM ˌənˌsɪmpəˈθɛdək-
(ə)li
unsystematic
BR ˌʌnsɪstɪˈmætɪk
AM ˌənˌsɪstəˈmædɪk
unsystematically
BR ˌʌnsɪstɪˈmætɪkli
AM ˌənˌsɪstəˈmædək-
(ə)li
untack
BR ˌʌnˈtak, -s, -ɪŋ, -t
AM ˌənˈtæk, -s, -ɪŋ, -t
untainted
BR (ˌ)ʌnˈteɪntɪd
AM ˌənˈteɪn(t)ɪd
untaken
BR ˌʌnˈteɪk(ə)n
AM ˌənˈteɪkən
untalented
BR (ˌ)ʌnˈtaləntɪd
AM ˌənˈtæləntəd
untamable
BR ˌʌnˈteɪməbl
AM ˌənˈteɪməbəl
untameable
BR ˌʌnˈteɪməbl
AM ˌənˈteɪməbəl
untamed
BR ˌʌnˈteɪmd
AM ˌənˈteɪmd
untangle
BR (ˌ)ʌnˈtaŋg|l, -lz,
-lɪŋ \-l̩ɪŋ, -ld
AM ˌənˈtæŋg|əl, -əlz,
-(ə)lɪŋ, -əld
untanned
BR ˌʌnˈtand
AM ˌənˈtænd
untapped
BR ˌʌnˈtapt
AM ˌənˈtæpt
untarnished
BR (ˌ)ʌnˈtɑːnɪʃt
AM ˌənˈtɑrnɪʃt
untasted
BR ˌʌnˈteɪstɪd
AM ˌənˈteɪstɪd
untaught
BR ˌʌnˈtɔːt
AM ˌənˈtɔt, ˌənˈtɑt
untaxed
BR ˌʌnˈtakst
AM ˌənˈtækst
unteach
BR ˌʌnˈtiːtʃ, -ɪz, -ɪŋ
AM ˌənˈtitʃ, -ɪz, -ɪŋ
unteachable
BR (ˌ)ʌnˈtiːtʃəbl
AM ˌənˈtitʃəbəl
untearable
BR ˌʌnˈtɛːrəbl
AM ˌənˈtɛrəbəl
untechnical
BR ˌʌnˈtɛknɪkl
AM ˌənˈtɛknəkəl
untechnically
BR ˌʌnˈtɛknɪkli

AM ˌənˈtɛknək(ə)li
untempered
BR ˌʌnˈtɛmpəd
AM ˌənˈtɛmpərd
untempted
BR ˌʌnˈtɛm(p)tɪd
AM ˌənˈtɛm(p)təd
untenability
BR ˌʌnˌtɛnəˈbɪlɪti,
ˌʌntɛnəˈbɪlɪti
AM ˌənˌtɛnəˈbɪlɪdi
untenable
BR (ˌ)ʌnˈtɛnəbl
AM ˌənˈtɛnəbəl
untenableness
BR (ˌ)ʌnˈtɛnəblnəs
AM ˌənˈtɛnəbəlnəs
untenably
BR (ˌ)ʌnˈtɛnəbli
AM ˌənˈtɛnəbli
untenanted
BR ˌʌnˈtɛnəntɪd
AM ˌənˈtɛnən(t)əd
untended
BR ˌʌnˈtɛndɪd
AM ˌənˈtɛndəd
untenured
BR ˌʌnˈtɛnjəd
AM ˌənˈtɛnjərd
Untermensch
BR ˈʊntəmɛnʃ
AM ˈʊntərˌmɛn(t)ʃ
Untermenschen
BR ˈʊntəˌmɛnʃn
AM ˈʊntərˌmɛn(t)ʃn
untestable
BR ˌʌnˈtɛstəbl
AM ˌənˈtɛstəbəl
untested
BR ˌʌnˈtɛstɪd
AM ˌənˈtɛstəd
untether
BR ˌʌnˈtɛð|ə(r), -əz,
-(ə)rɪŋ, -əd
AM ˌənˈtɛðər, -z, -ɪŋ, -d
Unthank
BR ˈʌnθaŋk
AM ˌənˌθæŋk
unthanked
BR ˌʌnˈθaŋ(k)t
AM ˌənˈθæŋ(k)t
unthankful
BR (ˌ)ʌnˈθaŋkf(ʊ)l
AM ˌənˈθæŋkfəl
unthankfully
BR (ˌ)ʌnˈθaŋkfʊli,
(ˌ)ʌnˈθaŋkfli
AM ˌənˈθæŋkfəli
unthankfulness
BR (ˌ)ʌnˈθaŋkf(ʊ)lnəs
AM ˌənˈθæŋkfəlnəs
unthatched
BR ˌʌnˈθatʃt
AM ˌənˈθætʃt
untheological
BR ˌʌnθɪəˈlɒdʒɪkl
AM ˌənˌθiəˈlɑdʒəkəl

AM ˌənˈtɛknək(ə)li
untheoretical
BR ˌʌnθɪəˈrɛtɪkl
AM ˌənˌθiəˈrɛdəkəl
untheorised
BR ˌʌnˈθɪərʌɪzd
AM ˌənˈθiəˌraɪzd
untheorized
BR ˌʌnˈθɪərʌɪzd
AM ˌənˈθiəˌraɪzd
unthickened
BR ˌʌnˈθɪknd
AM ˌənˈθɪkənd
unthink
BR ˌʌnˈθɪŋk, -s, -ɪŋ
AM ˌənˈθɪŋk, -s, -ɪŋ
unthinkability
BR ˌʌnˌθɪŋkəˈbɪlɪti,
ˌʌnθɪŋkəˈbɪlɪti
AM ˌənˌθɪŋkəˈbɪlɪdi
unthinkable
BR ˌʌnˈθɪŋkəbl
AM ˌənˈθɪŋkəbəl
unthinkableness
BR ˌʌnˈθɪŋkəblnəs
AM ˌənˈθɪŋkəbəlnəs
unthinkably
BR ˌʌnˈθɪŋkəbli
AM ˌənˈθɪŋkəbli
unthinking
BR (ˌ)ʌnˈθɪŋkɪŋ
AM ˌənˈθɪŋkɪŋ
unthinkingly
BR (ˌ)ʌnˈθɪŋkɪŋli
AM ˌənˈθɪŋkɪŋli
unthinkingness
BR (ˌ)ʌnˈθɪŋkɪŋnɪs
AM ˌənˈθɪŋkɪŋnɪs
unthought
BR ˌʌnˈθɔːt
AM ˌənˈθɔt, ˌənˈθɑt
unthoughtful
BR (ˌ)ʌnˈθɔːtf(ʊ)l
AM ˌənˈθɔtfəl,
ˌənˈθɑtfəl
unthoughtfully
BR (ˌ)ʌnˈθɔːtfʊli,
(ˌ)ʌnˈθɔːtfli
AM ˌənˈθɔtfəli,
ˌənˈθɑtfəli
unthoughtfulness
BR (ˌ)ʌnˈθɔːtf(ʊ)lnəs
AM ˌənˈθɔtfəlnəs,
ˌənˈθɑtfəlnəs
unthought-of
BR ˌʌnˈθɔːtɒv, ˌʌnˈθɔːtəv
AM ˌənˈθɔdəv,
ˌənˈθɑdəv
unthought-out
BR ˌʌnθɔːˈtaʊt
AM ˌənˌθɔˈdaʊt,
ˌənˌθɑˈdaʊt
unthread
BR ˌʌnˈθrɛd, -z, -ɪŋ, -ɪd
AM ˌənˈθrɛd, -z, -ɪŋ, -əd
unthreatened
BR ˌʌnˈθrɛtnd
AM ˌənˈθrɛtnd

unthreatening
BR ˌʌnˈθretnɪŋ,
ˌʌnˈθretnɪŋ
AM ˌənˈθretnɪŋ,
ˌənˈθretnɪŋ

unthreshed
BR ˌʌnˈθreʃt
AM ˌənˈθreʃt

unthriftily
BR (ˌ)ʌnˈθrɪftɪli
AM ˌənˈθrɪftɪli

unthriftiness
BR (ˌ)ʌnˈθrɪftɪnɪs
AM ˌənˈθrɪftɪnɪs

unthrifty
BR (ˌ)ʌnˈθrɪfti
AM ˌənˈθrɪfti

unthrone
BR ˌʌnˈθrəʊn, -z, -ɪŋ, -d
AM ˌənˈθroʊn, -z, -ɪŋ, -d

untidily
BR (ˌ)ʌnˈtaɪdɪli
AM ˌənˈtaɪdɪli

untidiness
BR (ˌ)ʌnˈtaɪdɪnɪs
AM ˌənˈtaɪdɪnɪs

untidy
BR (ˌ)ʌnˈtaɪd|i, -ɪz, -ɪɪŋ,
-ɪd, -ɪə(r), -ɪɪst
AM ˌənˈtaɪdi, -z, -ɪŋ, -d,
-ər, -ɪst

untie
BR ˌʌnˈtaɪ, -z, -ɪŋ, -d
AM ˌənˈtaɪ, -z, -ɪŋ, -d

until
BR (ə)nˈtɪl, (ˌ)ʌnˈtɪl
AM ˌənˈtɪl, ənˈtɪl

untilled
BR ˌʌnˈtɪld
AM ˌənˈtɪld

untimed
BR ˌʌnˈtaɪmd
AM ˌənˈtaɪmd

untimeliness
BR (ˌ)ʌnˈtaɪmlɪnɪs
AM ˌənˈtaɪmlɪnɪs

untimely
BR (ˌ)ʌnˈtaɪmli
AM ˌənˈtaɪmli

untinged
BR ˌʌnˈtɪn(d)ʒd
AM ˌənˈtɪndʒd

untipped
BR ˌʌnˈtɪpt
AM ˌənˈtɪpt

untired
BR (ˌ)ʌnˈtaɪəd
AM ˌənˈtaɪ(ə)rd

untiring
BR ˌʌnˈtaɪərɪŋ
AM ˌənˈtaɪ(ə)rɪŋ

untiringly
BR ˌʌnˈtaɪərɪŋli
AM ˌənˈtaɪ(ə)rɪŋli

untitled
BR ˌʌnˈtaɪtld
AM ˌənˈtaɪdld

unto
BR ˈʌntʊ, ˈʌntuː, ˈʌntə
AM ˈəntə, ˈəntu

untoasted
BR ˌʌnˈtəʊstɪd
AM ˌənˈtoʊstəd

untold
BR (ˌ)ʌnˈtəʊld
AM ˌənˈtoʊld

untouchability
BR ˌʌnˌtʌtʃəˈbɪlɪti,
ˌʌntʌtʃəˈbɪlɪti
AM ˌənˌtʌtʃəˈbɪlɪdi

untouchable
BR (ˌ)ʌnˈtʌtʃəbl, -z
AM ˌənˈtʌtʃəbəl, -z

untouchableness
BR ˌʌnˈtʌtʃəblnəs
AM ˌənˈtʌtʃəbəlnəs

untouched
BR (ˌ)ʌnˈtʌtʃt
AM ˌənˈtʌtʃt

untoward
BR ˌʌntəˈwɔːd
AM ˌənˌtoˈ(ə)rd

untowardly
BR ˌʌntəˈwɔːdli
AM ˌənˈtɔrdli

untowardness
BR ˌʌntəˈwɔːdnəs
AM ˌənˈtɔrdnəs

untraceable
BR ˌʌnˈtreɪsəbl
AM ˌənˈtreɪsəbəl

untraceably
BR ˌʌnˈtreɪsəbli
AM ˌənˈtreɪsəbli

untraced
BR ˌʌnˈtreɪst
AM ˌənˈtreɪst

untracked
BR ˌʌnˈtrakt
AM ˌənˈtrækt

untraditional
BR ˌʌntrəˈdɪʃŋ(ə)l,
ˌʌntrəˈdɪʃən(ə)l
AM ˌəntrəˈdɪʃ(ə)nəl

untrainable
BR ˌʌnˈtreɪnəbl
AM ˌənˈtreɪnəbəl

untrained
BR (ˌ)ʌnˈtreɪnd
AM ˌənˈtreɪnd

untrammeled
BR (ˌ)ʌnˈtramld
AM ˌənˈtræməld

untrammelled
BR (ˌ)ʌnˈtramld
AM ˌənˈtræməld

untrampled
BR ˌʌnˈtrampld
AM ˌənˈtræmpəld

untransferable
BR ˌʌntransˈfəːrəbl,
ˌʌntrɑːnsˈfəːrəbl,
ˌʌntranzˈfəːrəbl,
ˌʌntrɑːnzˈfəːrəbl,

(ˌ)ʌnˈtransf(ə)rəbl,
(ˌ)ʌnˈtrɑːnsf(ə)rəbl,
(ˌ)ʌnˈtranzf(ə)rəbl,
(ˌ)ʌnˈtrɑːnzf(ə)rəbl
AM ˌənˈtræn(t)sf(ə)r-
əbəl,
ˌənˈtræn(t)sfərbəl,
ˌənˌtræn(t)sˈfərəbəl

untransformed
BR ˌʌntransˈfɔːmd,
ˌʌntrɑːnsˈfɔːmd,
ˌʌntranzˈfɔːmd,
ˌʌntrɑːnzˈfɔːmd
AM ˌənˈtræn(t)sˈfɔrmd

untranslatability
BR ˌʌntransˌleɪtəˈbɪlɪti,
ˌʌntrɑːnsˌleɪtəˈbɪlɪti,
ˌʌntranzˌleɪtəˈbɪlɪti,
ˌʌntrɑːnzˌleɪtəˈbɪlɪti
AM ˌənˌtræn(t)sˌleɪdə-
ˈbɪlɪdi,
ˌənˌtrænzˌleɪdəˈbɪlɪdi

untranslatable
BR ˌʌntransˈleɪtəbl,
ˌʌntrɑːnsˈleɪtəbl,
ˌʌntranzˈleɪtəbl,
ˌʌntrɑːnzˈleɪtəbl
AM ˌənˈtræn(t)sˈleɪd-
əbəl,
ˌənˈtrænzˌleɪdəbəl,
ˌənˈtræn(t)sˈleɪdəbəl,
ˌənˈtrænzˈleɪdəbəl

untranslatably
BR ˌʌntransˈleɪtəbli,
ˌʌntrɑːnsˈleɪtəbli,
ˌʌntranzˈleɪtəbli,
ˌʌntrɑːnzˈleɪtəbli
AM ˌənˈtræn(t)sˈleɪd-
əbli,
ˌənˌtrænzˈleɪdəbli

untranslated
BR ˌʌntransˈleɪtɪd,
ˌʌntrɑːnsˈleɪtɪd,
ˌʌntranzˈleɪtɪd,
ˌʌntrɑːnzˈleɪtɪd
AM ˌənˈtræn(t)sˈleɪdɪd,
ˌənˈtrænzˌleɪdɪd

untransmitted
BR ˌʌntranzˈmɪtɪd,
ˌʌntrɑːnzˈmɪtɪd,
ˌʌntransˈmɪtɪd,
ˌʌntrɑːnzˈmɪtɪd
AM ˌənˈtrænzˈmɪdɪd,
ˌəntræn(t)sˈmɪdɪd,
ˌənˈtrænzˌmɪdɪd,
ˌənˈtræn(t)sˌmɪdɪd

untransportable
BR ˌʌntranˈspɔːtəbl,
ˌʌntrɑːnˈspɔːtəbl
AM ˌənˌtræn(t)sˈpɔrd-
əbəl,
ˌənˌtrænzˈpɔrdəbəl

untravelled
BR (ˌ)ʌnˈtravld
AM ˌənˈtrævəld

untreatable
BR (ˌ)ʌnˈtriːtəbl
AM ˌənˈtridəbəl

untreated
BR ˌʌnˈtriːtɪd
AM ˌənˈtridɪd

untrendy
BR ˌʌnˈtrendi
AM ˌənˈtrendi

untried
BR ˌʌnˈtrʌɪd
AM ˌənˈtraɪd

untrimmed
BR ˌʌnˈtrɪmd
AM ˌənˈtrɪmd

untrodden
BR ˌʌnˈtrɒdn
AM ˌənˈtrɑdən

untroubled
BR (ˌ)ʌnˈtrʌbld
AM ˌənˈtrəbəld

untrue
BR ˌʌnˈtruː
AM ˌənˈtru

untruly
BR ˌʌnˈtruːli
AM ˌənˈtruli

untruss
BR ˌʌnˈtrʌs, -ɪz, -ɪŋ, -t
AM ˌənˈtrəs, -əz, -ɪŋ, -t

untrusting
BR ˌʌnˈtrʌstɪŋ
AM ˌənˈtrəstɪŋ

untrustworthily
BR (ˌ)ʌnˈtrʌs(t)wəːðɪli
AM ˌənˈtrəs(t)ˌwərðəli

untrustworthiness
BR (ˌ)ʌnˈtrʌs(t)wəːðɪnɪs
AM ˌənˈtrəs(t)ˌwərðinɪs

untrustworthy
BR (ˌ)ʌnˈtrʌs(t)wəːði
AM ˌənˈtrəs(t)ˌwərði

untruth
BR (ˌ)ʌnˈtruː|θ, -ðz\-θs
AM ˌənˈtru|θ, -ðz\-θs

untruthful
BR (ˌ)ʌnˈtruː|θf(ʊ)l
AM ˌənˈtruθfəl

untruthfully
BR (ˌ)ʌnˈtruː|θfʊli,
(ˌ)ʌnˈtruː|θfli
AM ˌənˈtruθfəli

untruthfulness
BR (ˌ)ʌnˈtruː|θf(ʊ)lnəs
AM ˌənˈtruθfəlnəs

untuck
BR ˌʌnˈtak, -s, -ɪŋ, -t
AM ˌənˈtək, -s, -ɪŋ, -t

untunable
BR ˌʌnˈtjuːnəbl,
ˌʌnˈtʃuːnəbl
AM ˌənˈt(j)unəbəl

untuned
BR ˌʌnˈtjuːnd,
ˌʌnˈtʃuːnd
AM ˌənˈt(j)und

untuneful
BR ˌʌnˈtjuːnf(ʊ)l,
ˌʌnˈtʃuːnf(ʊ)l
AM ˌənˈt(j)unfəl

untunefully
BR ˌʌnˈtjuːnfʊli,
ˌʌnˈtjuːnfᵊli,
ˌʌnˈtʃuːnfʊli,
ˌʌnˈtʃuːnfᵊli
AM ˌənˈt(j)uːnfᵊli

untunefulness
BR ˌʌnˈtjuːnf(ʊ)lnəs,
ˌʌnˈtʃuːnf(ʊ)lnəs
AM ˌənˈt(j)uːnfᵊlnəs

unturned
BR ˌʌnˈtɜːnd
AM ˌənˈtɜrnd

untutored
BR ˌʌnˈtjuːtəd,
ˌʌnˈtʃuːtəd
AM ˌənˈt(j)uːdərd

untwine
BR (ˌ)ʌnˈtwaɪn, -z, -ɪŋ,
-d
AM ˌənˈtwaɪn, -z, -ɪŋ, -d

untwist
BR (ˌ)ʌnˈtwɪst, -s, -ɪŋ,
-ɪd
AM ˌənˈtwɪst, -s, -ɪŋ, -ɪd

untying
BR (ˌ)ʌnˈtaɪɪŋ
AM ˌənˈtaɪɪŋ

untypical
BR ˌʌnˈtɪpɪkl̩
AM ˌənˈtɪpɪkəl

untypically
BR ˌʌnˈtɪpɪkli
AM ˌənˈtɪpək(ə)li

unusable
BR (ˌ)ʌnˈjuːzəbl̩
AM ˌənˈjuːzəbəl

unuseable
BR (ˌ)ʌnˈjuːzəbl̩
AM ˌənˈjuːzəbəl

unused¹
not made use of
BR (ˌ)ʌnˈjuːzd
AM ˌənˈjuːzd

unused²
unaccustomed
BR (ˌ)ʌnˈjuːst
AM ˌənˈjuːst

unusual
BR (ˌ)ʌnˈjuːʒʊəl,
(ˌ)ʌnˈjuːʒ(ʉ)l
AM ˌənˈjuːʒ(əw)əl

unusually
BR (ˌ)ʌnˈjuːʒʊəli,
(ˌ)ʌnˈjuːʒʉli,
(ˌ)ʌnˈjuːʒl̩i
AM ˌənˈjuːʒ(əw)əli

unusualness
BR (ˌ)ʌnˈjuːʒʊəlnəs,
(ˌ)ʌnˈjuːʒ(ʉ)lnəs
AM ˌənˈjuːʒ(əw)əlnəs

unutterable
BR ʌnˈʌt(ə)rəbl̩
AM ˌənˈədərəbəl

unutterableness
BR ʌnˈʌt(ə)rəblnəs
AM ˌənˈədərəbəlnəs

unutterably
BR ʌnˈʌt(ə)rəbli
AM ˌənˈədərəbli

unuttered
BR ʌnˈʌtəd
AM ˌənˈədərd

unvaccinated
BR ʌnˈvaksɪneɪtɪd
AM ˌənˈvæksə͵neɪdɪd

unvalued
BR ʌnˈvaljuːd
AM ˌənˈvæljud

unvandalised
BR ʌnˈvandl̩ʌɪzd,
ˌʌnˈvandəlʌɪzd
AM ˌənˈvændl̩͵aɪzd

unvandalized
BR ʌnˈvandl̩ʌɪzd,
ˌʌnˈvandəlʌɪzd
AM ˌənˈvændl̩͵aɪzd

unvanquished
BR ʌnˈvaŋkwɪʃt
AM ˌənˈvæŋkwɪʃt

unvaried
BR ʌnˈvɛːrɪd
AM ˌənˈverɪd

unvarnished
BR (ˌ)ʌnˈvɑːnɪʃt
AM ˌənˈvɑrnɪʃt

unvarying
BR ʌnˈvɛːrɪɪŋ
AM ˌənˈverɪɪŋ

unvaryingly
BR ʌnˈvɛːrɪɪŋli
AM ˌənˈverɪɪŋli

unvaryingness
BR ʌnˈvɛːrɪɪŋnɪs
AM ˌənˈverɪɪŋnɪs

unveil
BR (ˌ)ʌnˈveɪl, -z, -ɪŋ, -d
AM ˌənˈveɪl, -z, -ɪŋ, -d

unvented
BR ʌnˈventɪd
AM ˌənˈven(t)əd

unventilated
BR (ˌ)ʌnˈventɪleɪtɪd
AM ˌənˈven(t)ə͵leɪdɪd

unverifiable
BR (ˌ)ʌnˈverɪfʌɪəbl̩
AM ˌənˌverəˈfaɪəbəl

unverified
BR (ˌ)ʌnˈverɪfʌɪd
AM ˌənˈverəˌfaɪd

unversed
BR (ˌ)ʌnˈvɜːst
AM ˌənˈvɜrst

unviability
BR ˌʌnˌvʌɪəˈbɪlɪti
AM ˌənˌvaɪəˈbɪlɪdi

unviable
BR ʌnˈvʌɪəbl̩
AM ˌənˈvaɪəbəl

unviolated
BR ˌʌnˈvʌɪəleɪtɪd
AM ˌənˈvaɪə͵leɪdɪd

unvisited
BR (ˌ)ʌnˈvɪzɪtɪd
AM ˌənˈvɪzɪdɪd

unvitiated
BR (ˌ)ʌnˈvɪʃɪeɪtɪd
AM ˌənˈvɪʃiˌeɪdɪd

unvoiced
BR (ˌ)ʌnˈvɔɪst
AM ˌənˈvɔɪst

unwaged
BR ʌnˈweɪdʒd
AM ˌənˈweɪdʒd

unwakened
BR ʌnˈweɪk(ə)nd
AM ˌənˈweɪkənd

unwalled
BR ʌnˈwɔːld
AM ˌənˈwɔld, ˌənˈwald

unwanted
BR (ˌ)ʌnˈwɒntɪd
AM ˌənˈwɑn(t)əd

unwarily
BR ʌnˈwɛːrɪli
AM ˌənˈwɛrəli

unwariness
BR ʌnˈwɛːrɪnɪs
AM ˌənˈwɛrɪnɪs

unwarlike
BR ʌnˈwɔːlʌɪk
AM ˌənˈwɔrˌlaɪk

unwarmed
BR ʌnˈwɔːmd
AM ˌənˈwɔ(ə)rmd

unwarned
BR ʌnˈwɔːnd
AM ˌənˈwɔ(ə)rnd

unwarrantable
BR ʌnˈwɒrəntəbl̩,
ʌnˈwɒrn̩təbl
AM ˌənˈwɔrən(t)əbəl

**unwarrantable-
ness**
BR ʌnˈwɒrəntəblnəs,
ʌnˈwɒrn̩təblnəs
AM ˌənˈwɔrən(t)əbəl-
nəs

unwarrantably
BR ʌnˈwɒrəntəbli,
ʌnˈwɒrn̩təbli
AM ˌənˈwɔrən(t)əbli

unwarranted
BR ʌnˈwɒrəntɪd,
ʌnˈwɒrn̩tɪd
AM ˌənˈwɔrən(t)əd

unwary
BR (ˌ)ʌnˈwɛːri
AM ˌənˈwɛri

unwashed
BR ʌnˈwɒʃt
AM ˌənˈwɔʃt, ˌənˈwɑʃt

unwatchable
BR ʌnˈwɒtʃəbl
AM ˌənˈwɑtʃəbəl

unwatched
BR ʌnˈwɒtʃt
AM ˌənˈwɑtʃt

unwatchful
BR ʌnˈwɒtʃf(ʊ)l
AM ˌənˈwɑtʃfəl

unwatered
BR ʌnˈwɔːtəd
AM ˌənˈwɔdərd,
ˌənˈwadərd

unwavering
BR ʌnˈweɪv(ə)rɪŋ
AM ˌənˈweɪv(ə)rɪŋ

unwaveringly
BR ʌnˈweɪv(ə)rɪŋli
AM ˌənˈweɪv(ə)rɪŋli

unwaxed
BR ʌnˈwakst
AM ˌənˈwækst

unweakened
BR (ˌ)ʌnˈwiːk(ə)nd
AM ˌənˈwikənd

unweaned
BR ʌnˈwiːnd
AM ˌənˈwind

unwearable
BR (ˌ)ʌnˈwɛːrəbl
AM ˌənˈwɛrəbəl

unwearied
BR ʌnˈwɪərɪd
AM ˌənˈwɪrid

unweariedly
BR ʌnˈwɪərɪdli
AM ˌənˈwɪridli

unweariedness
BR ʌnˈwɪərɪdnɪs
AM ˌənˈwɪridnɪs

unweary
BR ʌnˈwɪəri
AM ˌənˈwɪri

unwearying
BR ʌnˈwɪərɪɪŋ
AM ˌənˈwɪrɪɪŋ

unwearyingly
BR ʌnˈwɪərɪɪŋli
AM ˌənˈwɪrɪɪŋli

unwed
BR ʌnˈwɛd
AM ˌənˈwed

unwedded
BR ʌnˈwɛdɪd
AM ˌənˈweded

unweddedness
BR (ˌ)ʌnˈwɛdɪdnɪs
AM ˌənˈwedədnəs

unweeded
BR ʌnˈwiːdɪd
AM ˌənˈwidɪd

unweighed
BR ʌnˈweɪd
AM ˌənˈweɪd

unweight
BR ʌnˈweɪt, -s, -ɪŋ, -ɪd
AM ˌənˈweɪt, -ts, -dɪŋ,
-dɪd

unwelcome
BR (ˌ)ʌnˈwɛlkəm, -ɪŋ,
-d
AM ˌənˈwɛlkəm, -ɪŋ, -d

unwelcomely
BR (ˌ)ʌnˈwɛlkəmli
AM ˌənˈwɛlkəmli

unwelcomeness
BR (ˌ)ʌnˈwelkəmnəs
AM ˌənˈwelkəmnəs

unwell
BR (ˌ)ʌnˈwel
AM ˌənˈwel

unwept
BR ˌʌnˈwept
AM ˌənˈwept

unwetted
BR ˌʌnˈwetɪd
AM ˌənˈweḑəd

unwhipped
BR ˌʌnˈwɪpt
AM ˌʌnˈ(h)wɪpt

unwhitened
BR ˌʌnˈwaɪtnd
AM ˌənˈ(h)waɪtnd

unwholesome
BR (ˌ)ʌnˈhəʊls(ə)m
AM ˌənˈhoʊlsəm

unwholesomely
BR (ˌ)ʌnˈhəʊls(ə)mli
AM ˌənˈhoʊlsəmli

unwholesomeness
BR (ˌ)ʌnˈhəʊls(ə)mnəs
AM ˌənˈhoʊlsəmnəs

unwieldily
BR ʌnˈwiːldɪli
AM ˌənˈwiː(ə)ldɪli

unwieldiness
BR ʌnˈwiːldɪnɪs
AM ˌənˈwiː(ə)ldɪnɪs

unwieldy
BR ʌnˈwiːldi
AM ˌənˈwiː(ə)ldi

unwilled
BR ˌʌnˈwɪld
AM ˌənˈwɪld

unwilling
BR ˌʌnˈwɪlɪŋ
AM ˌənˈwɪlɪŋ

unwillingly
BR ˌʌnˈwɪlɪŋli
AM ˌənˈwɪlɪŋli

unwillingness
BR ʌnˈwɪlɪŋnɪs
AM ˌənˈwɪlɪŋnɪs

Unwin
BR ˈʌnwɪn
AM ˈənwən

unwind
BR (ˌ)ʌnˈwaɪnd, -z, -ɪŋ
AM ˌənˈwaɪnd, -z, -ɪŋ

unwinking
BR ˌʌnˈwɪŋkɪŋ
AM ˌənˈwɪŋkɪŋ

unwinkingly
BR ˌʌnˈwɪŋkɪŋli
AM ˌənˈwɪŋkɪŋli

unwinnable
BR ˌʌnˈwɪnəbl
AM ˌənˈwɪnəbəl

unwiped
BR ˌʌnˈwaɪpt
AM ˌənˈwaɪpt

unwired
BR ˌʌnˈwaɪəd
AM ˌʌnˈwaɪ(ə)rd

unwisdom
BR ˌʌnˈwɪzdəm
AM ˌənˈwɪzdəm

unwise
BR (ˌ)ʌnˈwaɪz
AM ˌənˈwaɪz

unwisely
BR (ˌ)ʌnˈwaɪzli
AM ˌənˈwaɪzli

unwish
BR ˌʌnˈwɪʃ, -ɪz, -ɪŋ, -t
AM ˌʌnˈwɪʃ, -ɪz, -ɪŋ, -t

unwithered
BR ˌʌnˈwɪðəd
AM ˌənˈwɪðərd

unwitnessed
BR ˌʌnˈwɪtnɪst
AM ˌənˈwɪtnɪst

unwitting
BR (ˌ)ʌnˈwɪtɪŋ
AM ˌənˈwɪdɪŋ

unwittingly
BR ʌnˈwɪtɪŋli
AM ˌənˈwɪdɪŋli

unwittingness
BR ʌnˈwɪtɪŋnɪs
AM ˌənˈwɪdɪŋnɪs

unwomanliness
BR (ˌ)ʌnˈwʊmənlɪnɪs
AM ˌənˈwʊmənlɪnɪs

unwomanly
BR (ˌ)ʌnˈwʊmənli
AM ˌənˈwʊmənli

unwonted
BR ˌʌnˈwəʊntɪd,
ʌnˈwɒntɪd
AM ˌənˈwoʊn(t)əd,
ˌənˈwɒn(t)əd,
ˌənˈwɑn(t)əd

unwontedly
BR ʌnˈwəʊntɪdli,
ʌnˈwɒntɪdli
AM ˌənˈwoʊn(t)ədli,
ˌənˈwɒn(t)ədli,
ˌənˈwɑn(t)ədli

unwontedness
BR ʌnˈwəʊntɪdnɪs,
ʌnˈwɒntɪdnɪs
AM ˌənˈwoʊn(t)ədnɪs,
ˌənˈwɒn(t)ədnəs,
ˌənˈwɑn(t)ədnəs

unwooded
BR ˌʌnˈwʊdɪd
AM ˌənˈwʊdəd

unworkability
BR ʌnˌwəːkəˈbɪlɪti,
ˌʌnwəːkəˈbɪlɪti
AM ˌənˌwɜrkəˈbɪlɪdi

unworkable
BR (ˌ)ʌnˈwəːkəbl
AM ˌənˈwɜrkəbəl

unworkableness
BR (ˌ)ʌnˈwəːkəblnəs
AM ˌənˈwɜrkəbəlnəs

unworkably
BR (ˌ)ʌnˈwəːkəbli
AM ˌənˈwɜrkəbli

unworked
BR ˌʌnˈwəːkt
AM ˌənˈwɜrkt

unworkmanlike
BR ˌʌnˈwəːkmənlaɪk
AM ˌənˈwɜrkmənˌlaɪk

unworldliness
BR (ˌ)ʌnˈwəːldlɪnɪs
AM ˌənˈwɜrldlɪnɪs

unworldly
BR (ˌ)ʌnˈwəːldli
AM ˌənˈwɜrldli

unworn
BR ˌʌnˈwɔːn
AM ˌənˈwɔː(ə)rn

unworried
BR ˌʌnˈwʌrɪd
AM ˌənˈwɜrid

unworshipped
BR ˌʌnˈwəːʃɪpt
AM ˌənˈwɜrʃɪpt

unworthily
BR (ˌ)ʌnˈwəːðɪli
AM ˌənˈwɜrðəli

unworthiness
BR (ˌ)ʌnˈwəːðɪnɪs
AM ˌənˈwɜrðɪnɪs

unworthy
BR (ˌ)ʌnˈwəːði
AM ˌənˈwɜrði

unwound
BR ˌʌnˈwaʊnd
AM ˌənˈwaʊnd

unwounded
BR ˌʌnˈwuːndɪd
AM ˌənˈwundəd

unwoven
BR ˌʌnˈwəʊvn
AM ˌənˈwoʊvən

unwrap
BR (ˌ)ʌnˈrap, -s, -ɪŋ, -t
AM ˌənˈræp, -s, -ɪŋ, -t

unwrinkled
BR ˌʌnˈrɪŋkld
AM ˌənˈrɪŋkəld

unwritable
BR ˌʌnˈraɪtəbl
AM ˌənˈraɪdəbəl

unwritten
BR ˌʌnˈrɪtn
AM ˌənˈrɪtn

unwrought
BR ˌʌnˈrɔːt
AM ˌənˈrɒt, ˌənˈrɑt

unwrung
BR ˌʌnˈrʌŋ
AM ˌənˈrəŋ

unyielding
BR (ˌ)ʌnˈjiːldɪŋ
AM ˌənˈjildɪŋ

unyieldingly
BR (ˌ)ʌnˈjiːldɪŋli
AM ˌənˈjildɪŋli

unyieldingness
BR (ˌ)ʌnˈjiːldɪŋnɪs
AM ˌənˈjildɪŋnɪs

unyoke
BR (ˌ)ʌnˈjəʊk, -s, -ɪŋ, -t
AM ˌənˈjoʊk, -s, -ɪŋ, -t

unzip
BR ˌʌnˈzɪp, -s, -ɪŋ, -t
AM ˌənˈzɪp, -s, -ɪŋ, -t

up
BR ʌp
AM əp

up-anchor
BR ˈʌpˈaŋkə(r), -əz,
-(ə)rɪŋ, -əd
AM ˈəpˈæŋkər, -z, -ɪŋ, -d

up-and-coming
BR ˌʌp(ə)n(d)ˈkʌmɪŋ
AM ˌəpənˈkəmɪŋ

up-and-over
BR ˌʌp(ə)n(d)ˈəʊvə(r)
AM ˌəpənˈoʊvər

up and running
BR ˌʌp (ə)n(d) ˈrʌnɪŋ
AM ˌəp ən ˈrənɪŋ

up-and-under
BR ˌʌp(ə)n(d)ˈʌndə(r),
-z
AM ˌəpənˈəndər, -z

up-and-up
BR ˌʌp(ə)n(d)ˈʌp
AM ˌəpənˈəp

Upanishad
BR (j)uːˈpanɪʃad,
(j)ʊˈpanɪʃad, -z
AM (j)ʊˈpænəˌʃæd, -z

upas
BR ˈjuːpəs, -ɪz
AM ˈjupəs, -əz

upas tree
BR ˈjuːpəs triː, -z
AM ˈjupəs ˌtri, -z

upbeat
BR ˈʌpbiːt, -s
AM ˈəpˈbit, -s

upbraid
BR ˈʌpˈbreɪd, -z, -ɪŋ, -ɪd
AM ˌəpˈbreɪd, -z, -ɪŋ, -ɪd

upbraiding
BR ˈʌpˈbreɪdɪŋ, -z
AM ˌəpˈbreɪdɪŋ, -z

upbringing
BR ˈʌpˌbrɪŋɪŋ
AM ˈəpˌbrɪŋɪŋ

upbuild
BR ˈʌpˈbɪld
AM ˌəpˈbɪld

upbuilt
BR ˈʌpˈbɪlt
AM ˌəpˈbɪlt

UPC
BR ˌjuːpiːˈsiː
AM ˌjuˌpiˈsi

upcast
BR ˈʌpkɑːst, ˈʌpkast, -s,
-ɪŋ
AM ˈəpˌkæst, -s, -ɪŋ

upchuck
BR ˌʌpˈtʃʌk, -s, -ɪŋ, -t
AM ˈʌpˌtʃʌk, -s, -ɪŋ, -t

upcoming
BR ˌʌpˈkʌmɪŋ
AM ˈʌpˌkʌmɪŋ

upcountry
BR ˌʌpˈkʌntri
AM ˈʌpˌkʌntri

upcurrent
BR ˈʌpˌkʌrənt,
ˈʌpˌkʌrn̩t, -s
AM ˈʌpˌkɜːrənt, -s

update¹
noun
BR ˈʌpdeɪt, -s
AM ˈʌpˌdeɪt, -s

update²
verb
BR ˌʌpˈdeɪt, -s, -ɪŋ, -ɪd
AM ˌʌpˈdeɪt, -ts, -dɪŋ,
-dɪd

updater
BR ˌʌpˈdeɪtə(r), -z
AM ˌʌpˈdeɪdər, -z

Updike
BR ˈʌpdaɪk
AM ˈʌpˌdaɪk

updraft
BR ˈʌpdrɑːft, ˈʌpdraft,
-s
AM ˈʌpˌdræft, -s

updraught
BR ˈʌpdrɑːft, ˈʌpdraft,
-s
AM ˈʌpˌdræft, -s

upend
BR ʌpˈɛnd, -z, -ɪŋ, -ɪd
AM ˌʌpˈɛnd, -z, -ɪŋ, -əd

upfield
BR ˈʌpfiːld
AM ˈʌpˌfild

upflow
BR ˈʌpfləʊ, -z
AM ˈʌpˌfloʊ, -z

upfold
BR ˈʌpfəʊld, -z
AM ˈʌpˌfoʊld, -z

up-front
BR ˌʌpˈfrʌnt
AM ˌʌpˈfrʌnt

upgrade¹
noun
BR ˈʌpgreɪd, -z
AM ˈʌpˌgreɪd, -z

upgrade²
verb
BR ˌʌpˈgreɪd, -z, -ɪŋ, -ɪd
AM ˌʌpˈgreɪd, -z, -ɪŋ, -ɪd

upgradeable
BR ˌʌpˈgreɪdəbl
AM ˌʌpˈgreɪdəbəl

upgrader
BR ˌʌpˈgreɪdə(r), -z
AM ˌʌpˈgreɪdər, -z

upgrowth
BR ˈʌpgrəʊθ, -s
AM ˈʌpˌgroʊθ, -s

uphaul
BR ˌʌpˈhɔːl, -z
AM ˌʌpˈhɔl, ˌʌpˈhɑl, -z

upheaval
BR ʌpˈhiːvl̩, -z
AM ʌpˈhivəl, -z

upheave
BR ʌpˈhiːv, -z, -ɪŋ, -d
AM ʌpˈhiv, -z, -ɪŋ, -d

upheld
BR ʌpˈhɛld
AM ˌʌpˈhɛld

uphill
BR ˌʌpˈhɪl
AM ˈʌpˈhɪl

uphold
BR ʌpˈhəʊld, -z, -ɪŋ
AM ˌʌpˈhoʊld, -z, -ɪŋ

upholder
BR ʌpˈhəʊldə(r), -z
AM ˌʌpˈhoʊldər, -z

upholster
BR ʌpˈhəʊlstə(r), -əz,
-(ə)rɪŋ, -əd
AM ˌʌpˈ(h)oʊlstər,
-ərz, -(ə)rɪŋ, -ərd

upholsterer
BR ʌpˈhəʊlst(ə)rə(r),
-z
AM ˌʌpˈ(h)oʊlst(ə)rər,
-z

upholstery
BR ʌpˈhəʊlst(ə)ri
AM ˌʌpˈ(h)oʊlst(ə)ri

UPI
BR ˌjuːpiːˈaɪ
AM ˌjuˌpiˈaɪ

Upjohn
BR ˈʌpdʒɒn
AM ˈʌpdʒɑn

upkeep
BR ˈʌpkiːp
AM ˈʌpˌkip

upland
BR ˈʌplənd, -z
AM ˈʌplənd, -z

uplift¹
noun
BR ˈʌplɪft
AM ˈʌpˌlɪft

uplift²
verb
BR ʌpˈlɪft, -s, -ɪŋ, -ɪd
AM ˈʌpˈlɪft, -s, -ɪŋ, -ɪd

uplifter
BR ʌpˈlɪftə(r), -z
AM ˈʌpˈlɪftər, -z

uplighter
BR ˈʌpˌlaɪtə(r), -z
AM ˈʌpˌlaɪdər, -z

upload
BR ˌʌpˈləʊd, -z, -ɪŋ, -ɪd
AM ˌʌpˈloʊd, -z, -ɪŋ, -əd

uplying
BR ˌʌpˈlaɪɪŋ
AM ˈʌpˈlaɪɪŋ

upmarket
BR ˌʌpˈmɑːkɪt
AM ˌʌpˈmarkət

upmost
BR ˈʌpməʊst
AM ˈʌpˌmoʊst

upon
BR əˈpɒn
AM əˈpɑn

upper
BR ˈʌpə(r)
AM ˈʌpər

uppercase
BR ˌʌpəˈkeɪs
AM ˌʌpərˈkeɪs

upper-class
BR ˌʌpəˈklɑːs,
ˌʌpəˈklas
AM ˌʌpərˈklæs

upperclassman
BR ˌʌpəˈklɑːsmən,
ˌʌpəˈklasmən
AM ˌʌpərˈklæsmən

upperclassmen
BR ˌʌpəˈklɑːsmən,
ˌʌpəˈklasmən
AM ˌʌpərˈklæsmən

uppercut
BR ˈʌpəkʌt, -s
AM ˈʌpərˌkət, -s

uppermost
BR ˈʌpəməʊst
AM ˈʌpərˌmoʊst

Upper Volta
BR ˌʌpə ˈvɒltə(r)
AM ˌʌpər ˈvɑltə,
ˌʌpər ˈvoʊltə

Uppingham
BR ˈʌpɪŋəm
AM ˈʌpɪŋəm

uppish
BR ˈʌpɪʃ
AM ˈʌpɪʃ

uppishly
BR ˈʌpɪʃli
AM ˈʌpɪʃli

uppishness
BR ˈʌpɪʃnɪs
AM ˈʌpɪʃnɪs

uppity
BR ˈʌpɪti
AM ˈʌpədi

Uppsala
BR ʊpˈsɑːlə(r),
ʌpˈsɑːlə(r),
ˈʊpsɑːlə(r),
ˈʌpsɑːlə(r)
AM ˈʊpsɑlə
SW ˈapsɑːla

upraise
BR ˌʌpˈreɪz, -ɪz, -ɪŋ, -d
AM ˌʌpˈreɪz, -ɪz, -ɪŋ, -d

uprate
BR ˌʌpˈreɪt, -s, -ɪŋ, -ɪd
AM ˌʌpˈreɪt, -ts, -dɪŋ,
-dɪd

uprating
BR ˌʌpˈreɪtɪŋ, -z

AM ˌʌpˈreɪdɪŋ, -z

upright
BR ˈʌpraɪt, -s
AM ˈʌpˌraɪt, -s

uprightly
BR ˈʌpraɪtli
AM ˈʌpˌraɪtli

uprightness
BR ˈʌpraɪtnɪs
AM ˈʌpˌraɪtnɪs

uprise
verb
BR ˌʌpˈraɪz, -z, -ɪŋ
AM ˌʌpˈraɪz, -z, -ɪŋ

uprisen
BR ˌʌpˈrɪzn
AM ˌʌpˈrɪzn

uprising
BR ˈʌpraɪzɪŋ, -z
AM ˈʌpˌraɪzɪŋ, -z

upriver
BR ˌʌpˈrɪvə(r)
AM ˈʌpˈrɪvər

uproar
BR ˈʌprɔː(r), -z
AM ˈʌpˌrɔ(ə)r, -z

uproarious
BR ˌʌpˈrɔːriəs
AM ˌʌpˈrɔriəs

uproariously
BR ˌʌpˈrɔːriəsli
AM ˌʌpˈrɔriəsli

uproariousness
BR ˌʌpˈrɔːriəsnəs
AM ˌʌpˈrɔriəsnəs

uproot
BR ˌʌpˈruːt, -s, -ɪŋ, -ɪd
AM ˌʌpˈrut, -ts, -dɪŋ,
-dəd

uprooter
BR ˌʌpˈruːtə(r), -z
AM ˌʌpˈrudər, -z

uprose
BR ˌʌpˈrəʊz
AM ˌʌpˈroʊz

uprush
BR ˈʌprʌʃ, -ɪz
AM ˈʌpˌrəʃ, -əz

ups-a-daisy
BR ˌʌpsəˈdeɪzi
AM ˈʌpsəˈdeɪsi,
ˈʌpsiˈdeɪsi

upscale
BR ˌʌpˈskeɪl
AM ˈʌpˈskeɪl

upset¹
adjective
BR ˌʌpˈsɛt
AM ˈʌpˈsɛt

upset²
noun
BR ˈʌpsɛt, -s
AM ˈʌpsət, -s

upset³
verb
BR ʌpˈsɛt, -s, -ɪŋ
AM ˌʌpˈsɛt, -ts, -dɪŋ

upsetter
BR ʌpˈsɛtə(r), -z
AM ˌəpˈsɛdər, -z

upsettingly
BR ʌpˈsɛtɪŋli
AM ˌəpˈsɛdɪŋli

upshift
BR ʌpˈʃɪft, ʌpˈʃɪft, -s,
-ɪŋ, -ɪd
AM ˌəpˌʃɪft, -s, -ɪŋ, -ɪd

upshot
BR ʌpˈʃɒt
AM ˌəpˌʃɑt

upside-down
BR ʌpˈsʌɪ(d)ˈdaʊn
AM ˌəpˌsaɪ(d)ˈdaʊn

upsides
adverb
BR ʌpsʌɪdz
AM ˌəpˌsaɪdz

upsilon
BR (j)uːpˈsʌɪlən,
ˈjuːpsɪlən, ʊpˈsʌɪlən,
-z
AM ˈəpsəˌlɑn,
ˈ(j)ʊpsəˌlɑn, -z

upstage
BR ʌpˈsteɪdʒ, -ɪz, -ɪŋ, -d
AM ˌəpˈsteɪdʒ, -ɪz, -ɪŋ, -d

upstager
BR ʌpˈsteɪdʒə(r), -z
AM ˌəpˈsteɪdʒər, -z

upstair
adjective
BR ʌpˈstɛː(r)
AM ˌəpˈstɛ(ə)r

upstairs
BR ʌpˈstɛːz
AM ˌəpˈstɛ(ə)rz

upstanding
BR (ˌ)ʌpˈstandɪŋ
AM ˌəpˈstændɪŋ

upstart
BR ʌpstɑːt, -s
AM ˌəpˌstɑrt, -s

upstate
BR ʌpˈsteɪt
AM ˌəpˌsteɪt

upstater
BR ʌpˈsteɪtə(r), -z
AM ˌəpˈsteɪdər, -z

upstream
BR ʌpˈstriːm
AM ˌəpˈstrim

upstretched
BR ʌpˈstrɛtʃt
AM ˌəpˈstrɛtʃt

upstroke
BR ʌpstrəʊk, -s
AM ˌəpˌstroʊk, -s

upsurge
BR ʌpsəːdʒ, -ɪz
AM ˌəpˌsərdʒ, -əz

upswept
BR ʌpˈswɛpt
AM ˌəpˌswɛpt

upswing
BR ˈʌpswɪŋ, -z
AM ˈəpˌswɪŋ, -z

upsy-daisy
BR ˌʌpsɪˈdeɪzi
AM ˌəpsɪˈdeɪzi,
ˈəpsəˌdeɪzi

uptake
BR ˈʌpteɪk
AM ˈəpˌteɪk

up-tempo
BR ˌʌpˈtɛmpəʊ
AM ˌəpˈtɛmpoʊ

upthrow
BR ˈʌpθrəʊ, -z
AM ˈəpˌθroʊ, -z

upthrust
BR ˈʌpθrʌst, -s
AM ˈəpˌθrəst, -s

uptight
BR ʌpˈtʌɪt, ˈʌptʌɪt
AM ˌəpˈtaɪt

uptilt
BR ʌpˈtɪlt, -s, -ɪŋ, -ɪd
AM ˌəpˌtɪlt, -s, -ɪŋ, -ɪd

uptime
BR ˈʌptʌɪm
AM ˈəpˌtaɪm

up-to-date
BR ʌptəˈdeɪt
AM ˌəptəˈdeɪt

Upton
BR ˈʌpt(ə)n
AM ˈəptən

up-to-the-minute
BR ʌptəðəˈmɪnɪt
AM ˌəptəðəˈmɪnɪt

uptown
BR ʌpˈtaʊn
AM ˌəpˈtaʊn

uptowner
BR ʌpˈtaʊnə(r), -z
AM ˌəpˈtaʊnər, -z

upturn
BR ˈʌptəːn, -z
AM ˈəpˌtərn, -z

upturned
BR ʌpˈtəːnd
AM ˌəpˈtərnd

upward
BR ˈʌpwəd, -z
AM ˈəpwərd, -z

upwardly
BR ˈʌpwədli
AM ˈəpwərdli

upwarp
BR ˈʌpwɔːp, -s
AM ˈəpˌwɔ(ə)rp, -s

upwell
BR ʌpˈwɛl, -z, -ɪŋ, -d
AM ˌəpˈwɛl, -z, -ɪŋ, -d

upwelling
BR ʌpˈwɛlɪŋ
AM ˈəpˈwɛlɪŋ

upwind
BR ʌpˈwɪnd
AM ˌəpˈwɪnd

Ur
BR əː(r)
AM ər

uracil
BR ˈjʊərəsɪl, ˈjɔːrəsɪl
AM ˈjʊrəˌsɪl

uraei
BR jʊˈriːʌɪ
AM jʊˈriˌaɪ

uraemia
BR jʊˈriːmɪə(r)
AM jʊˈrimiə

uraemic
BR jʊˈriːmɪk
AM jʊˈrimɪk

uraeus
BR jʊˈriːəs
AM jʊˈriəs

Ural
BR ˈjʊərəl, ˈjʊərl̩,
ˈjɔːrəl, ˈjɔːrl̩, -z
AM ˈjʊrəl, -z

Ural-Altaic
BR ˌjʊərəlalˈteɪɪk,
ˌjʊərl̩alˈteɪɪk,
ˌjɔːrəlalˈteɪɪk,
ˌjɔːrl̩alˈteɪɪk, -s
AM ˌjʊrəlˌælˈteɪɪk, -s

Uralic
BR jʊˈralɪk, -s
AM jʊˈrælɪk, -s

Urania
BR jʊˈreɪnɪə(r)
AM jʊˈreɪniə

uranic
BR jʊˈranɪk
AM jʊˈrænɪk

uranism
BR ˈjʊərəˌnɪz(ə)m,
ˈjʊərˌnɪz(ə)m,
ˈjɔːrəˌnɪz(ə)m,
ˈjɔːrˌnɪz(ə)m
AM ˈjʊrəˌnɪzəm

uranium
BR jʊˈreɪnɪəm
AM jʊˈreɪniəm,
juˈreɪniəm

uranographer
BR ˌjʊərəˈnɒɡrəfə(r),
ˌjɔːrəˈnɒɡrəfə(r), -z
AM ˌjʊrəˈnɑɡrəfər, -z

uranographic
BR ˌjʊərənəˈɡrafɪk,
ˌjɔːrənəˈɡrafk
AM ˌjʊrənəˈɡræfɪk

uranography
BR ˌjʊərəˈnɒɡrəfi,
ˌjɔːrəˈnɒɡrəfi
AM ˌjʊrəˈnɑɡrəfi

uranometry
BR ˌjʊərəˈnɒmɪtri,
ˌjɔːrəˈnɒmɪtri
AM ˌjʊrəˈnɑmətri

uranous
BR ˈjʊərənəs, ˈjɔːrənəs
AM ˈjʊrənəs, jʊˈreɪnəs

Uranus
BR ˈjʊərənəs, ˈjʊərˌnəs,
ˈjɔːrənəs, ˈjɔːrˌnəs,
jʊˈreɪnəs
AM ˈjʊrənəs, jʊˈreɪnəs

urate
BR ˈjʊəreɪt, ˈjɔːreɪt, -s
AM ˈjʊˌreɪt, -s

urban
BR əːˈb(ə)n
AM ˈərbən

urbane
BR əːˈbeɪn
AM ərˈbeɪn

urbanely
BR əːˈbeɪnli
AM ərˈbeɪnli

urbaneness
BR ˈʌpˈbeɪnnɪs
AM ərˈbeɪ(n)nɪs

urbanisation
BR ˌəːbənʌɪˈzeɪʃn,
ˌəːbʌɪˈzeɪʃn
AM ˌərbənəˈzeɪʃən,
ˌərbəˌnaɪˈzeɪʃən

urbanise
BR ˈəːbənʌɪz, ˈəːbʌɪz,
-ɪz, -ɪŋ, -d
AM ˈərbəˌnaɪz, -ɪz, -ɪŋ,
-d

urbanism
BR ˈəːbənɪz(ə)m,
ˈəːbˌɪz(ə)m
AM ˈərbəˌnɪzəm

urbanist
BR ˈəːbənɪst, ˈəːbˌɪst, -s
AM ˈərbənəst, -s

urbanite
BR ˈəːbənʌɪt, ˈəːbˌɪt,
-s
AM ˈərbəˌnaɪt, -s

urbanity
BR əːˈbanɪti
AM ərˈbænədi

urbanization
BR ˌəːbənʌɪˈzeɪʃn,
ˌəːbʌɪˈzeɪʃn
AM ˌərbənəˈzeɪʃən,
ˌərbəˌnaɪˈzeɪʃən

urbanize
BR ˈəːbənʌɪz, ˈəːbʌɪz,
-ɪz, -ɪŋ, -d
AM ˈərbəˌnaɪz, -ɪz, -ɪŋ,
-d

urceolate
BR ˈəːsɪələt, ˈəːsɪəleɪt
AM ˈərˌsɪələt,
ˈərˈsɪəˌleɪt

urchin
BR ˈəːtʃɪn, -z
AM ˈərtʃən, -z

Urdu
BR ˈʊəduː, ˈəːduː
AM ˈʊrdu, ˈərdu

Ure
BR ˈjʊə(r)
AM ˈjʊ(ə)r

urea
BR jʊəˈriːə(r)
AM jʊˈriə

urea-
formaldehyde
BR jʊəˌriːˈɔːfəːˈmaldɪhaɪd
AM jʊˌriəˌfɔrˈmældə-
ˌhaɪd

ureal
BR jʊəˈriːəl
AM jʊˈriəl

uremia
BR jʊəˈriːmɪə(r)
AM jʊˈrimiə

uremic
BR jʊəˈriːmɪk
AM jʊˈrimɪk

ureter
BR jʊəˈriːtə(r),
ˈjʊərɪtə(r), -z
AM ˈjʊrədər, -z

ureteral
BR jʊəˈriːt(ə)rəl,
jʊˈriːt(ə)rl̩
AM jʊˈridərəl

ureteric
BR jʊərɪˈtɛrɪk,
jʊˈriːt(ə)rɪk,
ˌjɔːrɪˈtɛrɪk
AM jʊrəˈtɛrɪk

ureteritis
BR jʊəˌriːtəˈrʌɪtɪs,
ˌjʊərɪtəˈrʌɪtɪs,
ˌjɔːrɪtəˈrʌɪtɪs
AM jʊrədəˈraɪdɪs

ureterotomy
BR jʊəˌriːtəˈrɒtəm|i, -ɪz
AM jʊrədəˈrɑdəmi, -z

urethane
BR ˈjʊərɪθeɪn,
ˈjɔːrɪθeɪn
AM ˈjʊrəˌθeɪn

urethra
BR jʊəˈriːθrə(r), -z
AM jʊˈriθrə, -z

urethral
BR jʊəˈriːθrəl, jʊˈriːθrl̩
AM jʊˈriθrəl

urethritis
BR ˌjʊərɪˈθrʌɪtɪs,
ˌjɔːrɪˈθrʌɪtɪs
AM ˌjʊrəˈθraɪdɪs

urethrotomy
BR ˌjʊərɪˈθrɒtəm|i,
ˌjɔːrɪˈθrɒtəm|i, -ɪz
AM jʊrəˈθrɑdəmi, -z

Urey
BR ˈjʊəri
AM ˈ(j)ʊri

Urga
BR ˈəːɡə(r)
AM ˈərɡə

urge
BR əːdʒ, -ɪz, -ɪŋ, -d
AM ərdʒ, -əz, -ɪŋ, -d

urgency
BR ˈəːdʒ(ə)nsi
AM ˈərdʒənsi

urgent
BR ˈəːdʒ(ə)nt
AM ˈərdʒənt

urgently
BR ˈəːdʒ(ə)ntli
AM ˈərdʒən(t)li

urger
BR ˈəːdʒə(r), -z
AM ˈərdʒər, -z

urging
BR ˈəːdʒɪŋ, -z
AM ˈərdʒɪŋ, -z

Uriah
BR jʊəˈrʌɪə(r)
AM jʊˈraɪə

uric
BR ˈjʊərɪk, ˈjɔːrɪk
AM ˈjʊrɪk

Uriel
BR ˈjʊərɪəl, ˈjɔːrɪəl
AM ˈjʊriəl, ˈjʊriˌɛl

urim
BR ˈjʊərɪm, ˈjɔːrɪm
AM ˈ(j)ʊrəm

urinal
BR jʊəˈrʌɪnl̩, ˈjʊərɪnl̩,
ˈjɔːrɪnl̩, -z
AM ˈjʊrənəl, -z

urinalyses
BR ˌjʊərɪˈnalɪsiːz,
ˌjɔːrɪˈnalɪsiːz
AM jʊrəˈnælɪˌsiz

urinalysis
BR ˌjʊərɪˈnalɪsɪs,
ˌjɔːrɪˈnalɪsɪs
AM jʊrəˈnæləsəs

urinary
BR ˈjʊərɪn(ə)ri,
ˈjɔːrɪn(ə)ri
AM ˈjʊrəˌnɛri

urinate
BR ˈjʊərɪneɪt,
ˈjɔːrɪneɪt, -s, -ɪŋ, -ɪd
AM ˈjʊrəˌneɪ|t, -ts, -dɪŋ,
-dɪd

urination
BR ˌjʊərɪˈneɪʃn̩,
ˌjɔːrɪˈneɪʃn̩
AM jʊrəˈneɪʃən

urine
BR ˈjʊərɪn, ˈjɔːrɪn
AM ˈjʊrən

urinous
BR ˈjʊərɪnəs, ˈjɔːrɪnəs
AM ˈjʊrənəs

Urmston
BR ˈəːmst(ə)n
AM ˈərmstən

urn
BR əːn, -z
AM ərn, -z

urnfield
BR ˈəːnfiːld, -z
AM ˈərnˌfild, -z

urnful
BR ˈəːnfʊl, -z
AM ˈərnˌfʊl, -z

urochord
BR ˈjʊərə(ʊ)kɔːd,
ˈjɔːrə(ʊ)kɔːd, -z
AM ˈjʊrəˌkɔ(ə)rd, -z

urodele
BR ˈjʊərə(ʊ)diːl,
ˈjɔːrə(ʊ)diːl, -z
AM ˈjʊrəˌdil, -z

urogenital
BR ˌjʊərə(ʊ)ˈdʒɛnɪtl̩,
ˌjɔːrə(ʊ)ˈdʒɛnɪtl̩
AM jʊroʊˈdʒɛnədl̩,
ˈjʊrəˈdʒɛnədl̩

urolithiasis
BR ˌjʊərə(ʊ)lɪˈθʌɪəsɪs,
ˌjɔːrə(ʊ)lɪˈθʌɪəsɪs
AM jʊrələˈθaɪəsəs

urologic
BR ˌjʊərəˈlɒdʒɪk,
ˌjɔːrəˈlɒdʒɪk
AM jʊrəˈlɑdʒɪk

urologist
BR jʊˈrɒlədʒɪst, -s
AM jʊˈrɑlədʒəst, -s

urology
BR jʊˈrɒlədʒi
AM jʊˈrɑlədʒi

uropygium
BR ˌjʊərəˈpɪdʒɪəm,
ˌjɔːrəˈpɪdʒɪəm, -z
AM jʊrəˈpɪdʒiəm, -z

uroscopy
BR jʊˈrɒskəpi
AM jʊˈraskəpi

Urquhart
BR ˈəːkət
AM ˈərkət

Ursa
BR ˈəːsə(r)
AM ˈərsə

Ursa Major
BR ˌəːsə ˈmeɪdʒə(r)
AM ˌərsə ˈmeɪdʒər

Ursa Minor
BR ˌəːsə ˈmʌɪnə(r)
AM ˌərsə ˈmaɪnər

ursine
BR ˈəːsʌɪn
AM ˈərˌsɪn

Ursula
BR ˈəːsjʊlə(r)
AM ˈərsələ

Ursuline
BR ˈəːsjʊlʌɪn, -z
AM ˈərsələn, ˈərsəˌlin,
ˈərsəˌlaɪn, -z

urticaria
BR ˌəːtɪˈkɛːrɪə(r)
AM ˌərdəˈkɛriə

urticate
BR ˈəːtɪkeɪt, -s, -ɪŋ, -ɪd
AM ˈərdəˌkeɪ|t, -ts, -dɪŋ,
-dɪd

urtication
BR ˌəːtɪˈkeɪʃn̩
AM ˌərdəˈkeɪʃən

Uruguay
BR ˈjʊərəɡwʌɪ,
ˈjɔːrəɡwʌɪ
AM ˈ(j)ʊrəˌgwaɪ
SP uruˈɣwaj

Uruguayan
BR ˌjʊərəˈgwʌɪən,
ˌjɔːrəˈgwʌɪən, -z
AM ˈ(j)ʊrəˈgwaɪən, -z

Uruk
BR ˈʊrʊk
AM ˈʊrʊk

Urwin
BR ˈəːwɪn
AM ˈərwən

US
BR ˌjuːˈɛs
AM ˌjuˈɛs

us¹
strong form
BR ʌs
AM əs

us²
weak form
BR əs, s
AM əs

USA
BR ˌjuːˌɛsˈeɪ
AM ˌjuˌɛsˈeɪ

usability
BR ˌjuːzəˈbɪlɪti
AM juzəˈbɪlɪdi

usable
BR ˈjuːzəbl̩
AM ˈjuzəbəl

usableness
BR ˈjuːzəblnəs
AM ˈjuzəbəlnəs

usage
BR ˈjuːs|ɪdʒ, ˈjuːz|ɪdʒ,
-ɪdʒɪz
AM ˈjusɪdʒ, ˈjuzɪdʒ, -ɪz

usance
BR ˈjuːzns
AM ˈjuzəns

Usborne
BR ˈʌzbɔːn
AM ˈəzˌbɔ(ə)rn

USDAW
BR ˈʌzdɔː(r)
AM ˈəzˌdɔ

use¹
noun
BR juːs, -ɪz
AM jus, -əz

use²
verb, make use of
BR juːz, -ɪz, -ɪŋ, -d
AM juz, -əz, -ɪŋ, -d

useability
BR ˌjuːzəˈbɪlɪti
AM ˌjuzəˈbɪlɪdi

useable
BR ˈjuːzəbl̩
AM ˈjuzəbəl

useableness
BR ˈjuːzəblnəs
AM ˈjuzəbəlnəs

used[1]
adjective, accustomed
BR juːst
AM just

used[2]
adjective, not new,
past tense of verb
'use'
BR juːzd
AM juzd

usedn't
BR ˈjuːsnt
AM ˈjusnt

useful
BR ˈjuːsf(ʊ)l
AM ˈjusfəl

usefully
BR ˈjuːsfəli, ˈjuːsfli
AM ˈjusfəli

usefulness
BR ˈjuːsf(ʊ)lnəs
AM ˈjusfəlnəs

useless
BR ˈjuːsləs
AM ˈjusləs

uselessly
BR ˈjuːsləsli
AM ˈjusləsli

uselessness
BR ˈjuːsləsnəs
AM ˈjusləsnəs

usen't
BR ˈjuːsnt
AM ˈjusnt

user
BR ˈjuːzə(r), -z
AM ˈjuzər, -z

user-friendliness
BR ˌjuːzəˈfrɛn(d)lɪnɪs
AM ˌjuzərˈfrɛn(d)linɪs

user-friendly
BR ˌjuːzəˈfrɛn(d)li
AM ˌjuzərˈfrɛn(d)li

ushabti
BR uːˈʃabt|i, -ɪz
AM (j)uˈʃæbti, -z

Ushant
BR ˈʌʃnt
AM ˈəʃənt

U-shaped
BR ˈjuːʃeɪpt
AM ˈjuˌʃeɪpt

usher
BR ˈʌʃə(r), -əz, -(ə)rɪŋ, -əd
AM ˈəʃər, -ərz, -(ə)rɪŋ, -ərd

usherette
BR ˌʌʃəˈrɛt, -s
AM ˈəʃəˌrɛt, -s

ushership
BR ˈʌʃəʃɪp, -s
AM ˈəʃərˌʃɪp, -s

USIA
BR ˌjuːɛsaɪˈeɪ
AM ˌjuˌɛsˌaɪˈeɪ

Usk
BR ʌsk
AM əsk

USMC
BR ˌjuːɛsɛmˈsiː
AM ˌjuˌɛsˌɛmˈsi

USO
BR ˌjuːɛsˈəʊ
AM ˌjuˌɛsˈoʊ

USP
BR ˌjuːɛsˈpiː
AM ˌjuˌɛsˈpi

USPS
BR ˌjuːɛsˌpiːˈɛs
AM ˌjuˌɛsˌpiˈɛs

usquebaugh
BR ˈʌskwɪbɔː(r)
AM ˈəskwəˌbɔ, ˈəskwəˌba

USS
BR ˌjuːɛsˈɛs
AM ˌjuˌɛsˈɛs

USSR
BR ˌjuːɛsɛsˈɑː(r)
AM ˌjuˌɛsˌɛsˈar

Ustashe
BR ʊˈstɑːʃi
AM ʊˈstaʃi

Ustinov
BR ˈjuːstɪnɒf, ˈjuːstɪnɒv
AM ˈjustəˌnɔf, ˈjustəˌnɔv, ˈjustəˌnaf, ˈjustəˌnav
RUS uˈstʲinəf

usual
BR ˈjuːʒʊəl, ˈjuːʒ(ʊ)l
AM ˈjuʒ(əw)əl

usually
BR ˈjuːʒʊəli, ˈjuːʒʊli, ˈjuːʒli
AM ˈjuʒ(əw)əli

usualness
BR ˈjuːʒʊəlnəs, ˈjuːʒ(ʊ)lnəs
AM ˈjuʒ(əw)əlnəs

usucaption
BR ˌjuːsjʊˈkapʃn, ˌjuːzjʊˈkapʃn
AM ˌjuzəˈkæpʃən, ˌjusəˈkæpʃən

usufruct
BR ˈjuːsjʊfrʌkt, ˈjuːzjʊfrʌkt, -s
AM ˈjuzəˌfrək|(t), ˈjusəˌfrək|(t), -(t)s

usufructuary
BR ˌjuːsjʊˈfrʌktjʊəri, ˌjuːzjʊˈfrʌktjʊəri, ˌjuːsjʊˈfrʌktʃ(ʊ)əri, ˌjuːzjʊˈfrʌktʃ(ʊ)əri, -ɪz
AM ˌjuzəˈfrək(t)ʃəˌwɛri, ˌjusəˈfrək(t)ʃəˌwɛri, -z

usurer
BR ˈjuːʒ(ə)rə(r), -z
AM ˈjuʒərər, -z

usurious
BR juːˈzjʊəriəs, juːˈzjɔːriəs, juːˈʒʊəriəs, juːˈʒɔːriəs
AM juˈʒʊriəs

usuriously
BR juːˈzjʊəriəsli, juːˈzjɔːriəsli, juːˈʒʊəriəsli, juːˈʒɔːriəsli
AM juˈʒʊriəsli

usuriousness
BR juːˈzjʊəriəsnəs, juːˈzjɔːriəsnəs, juːˈʒʊəriəsnəs, juːˈʒɔːriəsnəs, juːˈʒɔːriəsnəs
AM juˈʒʊriəsnəs

usurp
BR juːˈzɜːp, jʊˈzɜːp, -s, -ɪŋ, -t
AM juˈsɜrp, -s, -ɪŋ, -t

usurpation
BR ˌjuːzɜːˈpeɪʃn
AM ˌjusərˈpeɪʃən

usurper
BR juːˈzɜːpə(r), jʊˈzɜːpə(r), -z
AM juˈsɜrpər, -z

usury
BR ˈjuːʒ(ə)ri
AM ˈjuʒ(ə)ri

Utah
BR ˈjuːtɔː(r), ˈjuːtɑː(r)
AM ˈjuˌtɔ, ˈjuˌta

Ute
BR juːt, -s
AM jut, -s

utensil
BR juːˈtɛns(ɪ)l, jʊˈtɛns(ɪ)l, -z
AM juˈtɛnsəl, -z

uteri
BR ˈjuːtərʌɪ
AM ˈjudəˌraɪ

uterine
BR ˈjuːtərʌɪn
AM ˈjudərən, ˈjudəˌraɪn

uteritis
BR ˌjuːtəˈrʌɪtɪs
AM ˌjudəˈraɪdɪs

uterus
BR ˈjuːt(ə)rəs, -ɪz
AM ˈjudərəs, -əz

utile
BR ˈjuːtʌɪl
AM ˈjudl, ˈjuˌtaɪl

utilisable
BR ˈjuːtɪlʌɪzəbl, ˈjuːtlʌɪzəbl
AM ˈjudlˌaɪzəbəl

utilisation
BR ˌjuːtɪlʌɪˈzeɪʃn, ˌjuːtlʌɪˈzeɪʃn
AM ˌjudləˈzeɪʃən, ˌjudlˌaɪˈzeɪʃən

utilise
BR ˈjuːtɪlʌɪz, ˈjuːtlʌɪz, -ɪz, -ɪŋ, -d
AM ˈjudlˌaɪz, -ɪz, -ɪŋ, -d

utiliser
BR ˈjuːtɪlʌɪzə(r), ˈjuːtlʌɪzə(r), -z
AM ˈjudlˌaɪzər, -z

utilitarian
BR juˌtɪlɪˈtɛːriən, juːˌtɪlɪˈtɛːriən, jəˌtɪlɪˈtɛːriən, -z
AM juˌtɪləˈtɛriən, -z

utilitarianism
BR juˌtɪlɪˈtɛːriənɪz(ə)m, juːˌtɪlɪˈtɛːriənɪz(ə)m, jəˌtɪlɪˈtɛːriənɪz(ə)m
AM juˌtɪləˈtɛriəˌnɪzəm

utility
BR juːˈtɪlɪt|i, jəˈtɪlɪt|i, -ɪz
AM juˈtɪlɪdi, -z

utilizable
BR ˈjuːtɪlʌɪzəbl, ˈjuːtlʌɪzəbl
AM ˈjudlˈaɪzəbəl

utilization
BR ˌjuːtɪlʌɪˈzeɪʃn, ˌjuːtlʌɪˈzeɪʃn
AM ˌjudləˈzeɪʃən, ˌjudlˌaɪˈzeɪʃən

utilize
BR ˈjuːtɪlʌɪz, ˈjuːtlʌɪz, -ɪz, -ɪŋ, -d
AM ˈjudlˌaɪz, -ɪz, -ɪŋ, -d

utilizer
BR ˈjuːtɪlʌɪzə(r), ˈjuːtlʌɪzə(r), -z
AM ˈjudlˌaɪzər, -z

Utley
BR ˈʌtli
AM ˈətli

utmost
BR ˈʌtməʊst
AM ˈətˌmoʊst

utopia
BR juːˈtəʊpɪə(r), jəˈtəʊpɪə(r), -z
AM juˈtoʊpiə, -z

Utopian
BR juːˈtəʊpɪən, jəˈtəʊpɪən, -z
AM juˈtoʊpiən, -z

utopianism
BR juːˈtəʊpɪənɪz(ə)m, jəˈtəʊpɪənɪz(ə)m
AM juˈtoʊpiəˌnɪzəm

Utrecht
BR juːˈtrɛkt, juːˈtrɛxt
AM ˈjuˌtrɛk(t)

utricle
BR ˈjuːtrɪkl, -z
AM ˈjutrəkəl, -z

utricular
BR jəˈtrɪkjʊlə(r)
AM jəˈtrɪkjələr, juˈtrɪkjələr

Utrillo
BR ju'trɪləʊ
AM ʊ'triːoʊ, juː'trɪloʊ
FR ytʀijo

Utsire
BR ʊt'sɪərə(r)
AM ʊt'sɪrə

Uttar Pradesh
BR ˌʊtə prɑ'deʃ
AM ˌʊtər prɑ'deʃ

utter
BR 'ʌtə(r), -əz- -(ə)rɪŋ,
-əd
AM 'ədər, -z, -ɪŋ, d-

utterable
BR 'ʌt(ə)rəbl
AM 'ədərəbəl

utterance
BR 'ʌt(ə)rəns,
'ʌt(ə)rn̩s, -ɪz
AM 'ədərəns, -əz

utterer
BR 'ʌt(ə)rə(r), -z
AM 'ədərər, -z

utterly
BR 'ʌtəli
AM 'ədərli

uttermost
BR 'ʌtəməʊst
AM 'ədərˌmoʊst

utterness
BR 'ʌtənəs
AM 'ədərnəs

Uttley
BR 'ʌtli
AM 'ətli

Uttoxeter
BR jʊ'tɒksɪtə(r)
AM juː'tɑksədər

U-turn
BR 'juːtəːn, -z
AM 'juːˌtɜːrn, -z

uvea
BR 'juːviə(r), -z
AM 'juːviə, -z

uvula
BR 'juːvjʊlə(r), -z
AM 'juːvjələ, -z

uvulae
BR 'juːvjʊliː

AM 'juvjəli, 'juvjəˌlaɪ

uvular
BR 'juːvjʊlə(r)
AM 'juvjələr

UWIST
BR 'juːwɪst
AM 'juwɪst

Uxbridge
BR 'ʌksbrɪdʒ
AM 'əksˌbrɪdʒ

uxorial
BR ʌk'sɔːriəl
AM ək'zɔriəl, ək'sɔriəl

uxoricidal
BR ʌkˌsɔːrɪ'saɪdl
AM əkˌzɔrə'saɪdəl,
əkˌsɔrə'saɪdəl

uxoricide
BR ʌk'sɔːrɪˌsaɪd, -z
AM ək'zɔrəˌsaɪd,
ək'sɔrəˌsaɪd, -z

uxorious
BR ʌk'sɔːriəs

AM ˌək'sɔriəs,
ˌək'zɔriəs

uxoriously
BR ʌk'sɔːriəsli
AM ˌək'sɔriəsli,
ˌək'zɔriəsli

uxoriousness
BR ʌk'sɔːriəsnəs
AM ˌək'sɔriəsnəs,
ˌək'zɔriəsnəs

Uzbek
BR 'ʊzbɛk, 'ʌzbɛk, -s
AM 'ʊz,bɛk, 'əz,bɛk, -s

Uzbekistan
BR ʊzˌbɛkɪ'stɑːn,
ʌzˌbɛkɪ'stɑːn,
ʊzˌbɛkɪ'stan,
ʌzˌbɛkɪ'stan
AM ʊz'bɛkəˌstæn,
əz'bɛkəˌstæn

Uzi®
BR 'uːzi|i, -ɪz
AM 'uzi, -z

Vv

v¹
BR viː, -z
AM vi, -z

v²
versus
BR 'vəːsəs, viː
AM 'vərsəs, vi

Vaal
BR vɑːl
AM vɑl

Vaasa
BR 'vɑːsə(r)
AM 'vɑsə, 'vɑˌsɑ

vac
BR vak, -s, -ɪŋ, -t
AM væk, -s, -ɪŋ, -t

vacancy
BR 'veɪk(ə)ns|i, -ɪz
AM 'veɪkənsi, -z

vacant
BR 'veɪk(ə)nt
AM 'veɪkənt

vacantly
BR 'veɪk(ə)ntli
AM 'veɪkən(t)li

vacatable
BR və'keɪtəbl,
veɪ'keɪtəbl
AM 'veɪˌkeɪdəbəl

vacate
BR və'keɪt, veɪ'keɪt, -s,
-ɪŋ, -ɪd
AM 'veɪˌkeɪ|t, -ts, -dɪŋ,
-dɪd

vacation
BR və'keɪʃn,
veɪ'keɪʃn, -z, -ɪŋ, -d
AM veɪ'keɪʃən,
və'keɪʃən, -z, -ɪŋ, -d

vacationer
BR və'keɪʃn̩ə(r),
veɪ'keɪʃn̩ə(r), -z
AM veɪ'keɪʃənər,
və'keɪʃənər, -z

vacationist
BR və'keɪʃn̩ɪst,
veɪ'keɪʃn̩ɪst, -s
AM veɪ'keɪʃənəst,
və'keɪʃənəst, -s

vaccinal
BR 'vaksɪnl
AM 'væksənəl

vaccinate
BR 'vaksɪneɪt, -s, -ɪŋ,
-ɪd
AM 'væksəˌneɪ|t, -ts,
-dɪŋ, -dɪd

vaccination
BR ˌvaksɪ'neɪʃn, -z
AM ˌvæksə'neɪʃən, -z

vaccinator
BR 'vaksɪneɪtə(r), -z
AM 'væksəˌneɪdər, -z

vaccine
BR 'vaksiːn, -z
AM væk'sin, -z

vaccinia
BR vak'sɪnɪə(r)
AM væk'sɪnɪə

vacillate
BR 'vasɪleɪt, -s, -ɪŋ, -ɪd
AM 'væsəˌleɪ|t, -ts, -dɪŋ,
-dɪd

vacillation
BR ˌvasɪ'leɪʃn
AM ˌvæsə'leɪʃən

vacillator
BR 'vasɪleɪtə(r), -z
AM 'væsəˌleɪdər, -z

vacua
BR 'vakjuə(r)
AM 'vækjəwə

vacuity
BR və'kjuːɪt|i,
va'kjuːɪt|i, -ɪz
AM væ'kjuədi,
və'kjuədi, -z

vacuolar
BR 'vakjuələ(r)
AM ˌvækju'oʊlər,
'vækjələr

vacuolation
BR ˌvakjuə'leɪʃn, -z
AM ˌvækjə'leɪʃən, -z

vacuole
BR 'vakjuəʊl, -z
AM 'vækjuˌoʊl, -z

vacuous
BR 'vakjuəs
AM 'vækjəwəs

vacuously
BR 'vakjuəsli
AM 'vækjəwəsli

vacuousness
BR 'vakjuəsnəs
AM 'vækjəwəsnəs

vacuum
BR 'vakjuːm, -z, -ɪŋ, -d
AM 'vækˌjum, -z, -ɪŋ, -d

vade mecum
BR ˌvɑːdɪ 'meɪkəm,
ˌveɪdɪ +, + 'miːkəm, -z
AM ˌveɪdɪ 'mikəm,
ˌvɑdɪ +, -z

Vaduz
BR va'duːz, və'duːz
AM və'duz

vag
BR vag, -z, -ɪŋ, -d
AM væg, -z, -ɪŋ, -d

vagabond
BR 'vagəbɒnd, -z
AM 'vægəˌbɑnd, -z

vagabondage
BR 'vagəbɒndɪdʒ
AM 'vægəˌbɑndɪdʒ

vagal
BR 'veɪgl
AM 'veɪgəl

vagarious
BR və'gɛːrɪəs
AM və'gɛrɪəs,
veɪ'gɛrɪəs

vagary
BR 'veɪg(ə)r|i, -ɪz
AM 'veɪgəri, -z

vagi
BR 'veɪdʒʌɪ, 'veɪgʌɪ
AM 'veɪˌgaɪ, 'veɪˌdʒaɪ

vagina
BR və'dʒʌɪnə(r), -z
AM və'dʒaɪnə, -z

vaginal
BR və'dʒʌɪnl
AM 'vædʒənəl

vaginally
BR və'dʒʌɪnl̩i
AM 'vædʒ(ə)nəli

vaginismus
BR ˌvadʒɪ'nɪzməs
AM ˌvædʒə'nɪzməs

vaginitis
BR ˌvadʒɪ'nʌɪtɪs
AM ˌvædʒə'naɪdɪs

vagotomy
BR veɪ'gɒtəm|i, -ɪz
AM veɪ'gɑdəmi, -z

vagrancy
BR 'veɪgr(ə)nsi
AM 'veɪgrənsi

vagrant
BR 'veɪgr(ə)nt, -s
AM 'veɪgrənt, -s

vagrantly
BR 'veɪgr(ə)ntli
AM 'veɪgrən(t)li

vague
BR veɪg, -ə(r), -ɪst
AM veɪg, -ər, -ɪst

vaguely
BR 'veɪgli
AM 'veɪgli

vagueness
BR 'veɪgnɪs
AM 'veɪgnɪs

vaguish
BR 'veɪgɪʃ
AM 'veɪgɪʃ

vagus
BR 'veɪgəs
AM 'veɪgəs

vail
BR veɪl, -z, -ɪŋ, -d
AM veɪl, -z, -ɪŋ, -d

vain
BR veɪn, -ə(r), -ɪst
AM veɪn, -ər, -ɪst

vainglorious
BR (ˌ)veɪn'glɔːrɪəs
AM ˌveɪn'glɔrɪəs

vaingloriously
BR (ˌ)veɪn'glɔːrɪəsli
AM ˌveɪn'glɔrɪəsli

vaingloriousness
BR (ˌ)veɪn'glɔːrɪəsnəs
AM ˌveɪn'glɔrɪəsnəs

vainglory
BR (ˌ)veɪn'glɔːri
AM 'veɪnˌglɔri

vainly
BR 'veɪnli
AM 'veɪnli

vainness
BR 'veɪnnɪs
AM 'veɪ(n)nɪs

vair
BR vɛː(r)
AM vɛ(ə)r

Vaishnava
BR 'vʌɪʃnəvə(r), -z
AM 'vɪʃnəvə, -z

Vaisya
BR 'vʌɪsjə(r),
'vʌɪʃjə(r), -z
AM 'vaɪsjə, -z

Vaizey
BR 'veɪzi
AM 'veɪzi

Val
BR val
AM væl

Valais
BR va'lɛ
AM vɑ'lɛ

valance
BR 'valəns, 'valn̩s, -ɪz
AM 'væləns, -əz

valanced
BR 'valənst, 'valn̩st
AM 'vælənst

Valda
BR 'valdə(r)
AM 'vɑldə

Valdemar
BR 'valdɪmɑː(r)
AM 'vɑldəˌmɑr

Valderma
BR val'dəːmə(r)
AM 'vɑldəmə

Valdez
BR val'diːz
AM vɑl'dɛz, vɑl'diz

vale
BR veɪl, -z
AM veɪl, -z

valediction
BR ˌvalɪ'dɪkʃn, -z
AM ˌvælə'dɪkʃən, -z

valedictorian
BR ˌvalɪdɪk'tɔːrɪən, -z
AM ˌvælədɪk'tɔriən, -z

valedictory
BR ˌvalɪ'dɪkt(ə)ri
AM ˌvælə'dɪkt(ə)ri

valence
BR 'veɪləns, 'veɪln̩s, -ɪz
AM 'veɪləns, -əz

valencia
BR və'lɛnsɪə(r), -z

AM vəˈlɛn(t)sɪə, vəˈlɛntʃɪə, -z

Valencian
BR vəˈlɛnsɪən
AM vəˈlɛn(t)siən, vəˈlɛn(t)ʃ(i)ən
SP baˈlenθja, baˈlensja

Valenciennes
BR ˌvalənsɪˈɛn, ˌvaln̩sɪˈɛn
AM ˌvælənsiˈɛn

valency
BR ˈveɪləns|i, ˈveɪln̩s|i, -ɪz
AM ˈveɪlənsi, -z

valentine
BR ˈvaləntʌɪn, ˈvaln̩tʌɪn, -z
AM ˈvælənˌtaɪn, -z

Valentinian
BR ˌvalənˈtɪnɪən, ˌvaln̩ˈtɪnɪən
AM ˌvælənˈtɪnɪən

Valentino
BR ˌvalənˈtiːnəʊ, ˌvaln̩ˈtiːnəʊ
AM ˌvælənˈtinoʊ

Valera
BR vəˈlɛːrə(r), vəˈlɪərə(r)
AM vəˈlɛrə

valerate
BR ˈvaləreɪt, -s
AM ˈvæləˌreɪt, -s

valerian
BR vəˈlɪərɪən, vəˈlɛːrɪən, -z
AM vəˈlɪrɪən, vəˈlɛrɪən, -z

valeric
BR vəˈlɪərɪk, vəˈlɛːrɪk, vəˈlɛrɪk
AM vəˈlɛrɪk

Valerie
BR ˈval(ə)ri
AM ˈvæl(ə)ri

Valéry
BR ˈvaləri
AM ˈvæləri

valet¹
noun
BR ˈval|ɪt, ˈval|eɪ, -ɪts\-eɪz
AM væˈl|eɪ, ˈvælə|t, -ts\-eɪz

valet²
verb
BR ˈvalɪt, -s, -ɪŋ, -ɪd
AM ˈvælə|t, -ts, -dɪŋ, -dəd

valeta
BR vəˈliːtə(r), -z
AM vəˈlidə, -z

valetudinarian
BR ˌvalɪˌtjuːdɪˈnɛːrɪən, ˌvalɪˌtʃuːdɪˈnɛːrɪən, -z

AM ˌvælə.t(j)udnˈɛrɪən, -z

valetudinarianism
BR ˌvalɪˌtjuːdɪˈnɛːrɪən-ɪz(ə)m, ˌvalɪˌtʃuːdɪˈnɛːrɪən-ɪz(ə)m
AM ˌvælə.t(j)udnˈɛrɪə-ˌnɪzəm

valetudinary
BR ˌvalɪˈtjuːdɪn(ə)ri, ˌvalɪˈtʃuːdɪn(ə)ri
AM ˌvælə.t(j)udnˌɛri

valgus
BR ˈvalgəs
AM ˈvælgəs

Valhalla
BR valˈhalə(r)
AM vælˈhælə, valˈhɑlə

valiant
BR ˈvalɪənt
AM ˈvæljənt

valiantly
BR ˈvalɪəntli
AM ˈvæljən(t)li

valid
BR ˈvalɪd
AM ˈvæləd

validate
BR ˈvalɪdeɪt, -s, -ɪŋ, -ɪd
AM ˈvæləˌdeɪ|t, -ts, -dɪŋ, -dɪd

validation
BR ˌvalɪˈdeɪʃn
AM ˌvæləˈdeɪʃən

validity
BR vəˈlɪdɪti
AM vəˈlɪdɪdi

validly
BR ˈvalɪdli
AM ˈvælədli

validness
BR ˈvalɪdnɪs
AM ˈvælədnəs

valine
BR ˈveɪliːn
AM ˈvæ.lin, ˈveɪ.lin

valise
BR vəˈliːz, -ɪz
AM vəˈlis, -ɪz

valium
BR ˈvalɪəm
AM ˈvælɪəm

Valkyrie
BR ˈvalkɪr|i, -ɪz
AM vælˈkɪri, ˈvælˌkɪri, -z

Vallance
BR ˈvaləns, ˈvaln̩s
AM ˈvæləns

Vallans
BR ˈvaləns, ˈvaln̩s
AM ˈvæləns

Valle Crucis
BR ˌvalɪ ˈkruːsɪs
AM ˌvæli ˈkrusəs

vallecula
BR vəˈlɛkjʊlə(r), vaˈlɛkjʊlə(r)
AM vəˈlɛkjələ

valleculae
BR vəˈlɛkjʊliː, vaˈlɛkjʊliː
AM vəˈlɛkjəli, vəˈlɛkjəˌlaɪ

vallecular
BR vəˈlɛkjʊlə(r), vaˈlɛkjʊlə(r)
AM vəˈlɛkjələr

valleculate
BR vəˈlɛkjʊleɪt, vaˈlɛkjʊleɪt
AM vəˈlɛkjəˌleɪt

Valletta
BR vəˈlɛtə(r)
AM vəˈlɛdə

valley
BR ˈval|i, -ɪz
AM ˈvæli, -z

vallum
BR ˈvaləm
AM ˈvæləm

Valois
BR ˈvalwɑː(r)
AM ˈvælˈwɑ, ˈvɛlwɑ

Valona
BR vəˈləʊnə(r)
AM vəˈloʊnə

valonia
BR vəˈləʊnɪə(r)
AM vəˈloʊnɪə

valor
BR ˈvalə(r)
AM ˈvælər

valorem
BR vəˈlɔːrɛm, vəˈlɔːrəm
AM vəˈlorəm

valorisation
BR ˌval(ə)rʌɪˈzeɪʃn
AM ˌvælərəˈzeɪʃən, ˌvæləˌraɪˈzeɪʃən

valorise
BR ˈvalərʌɪz, -ɪz, -ɪŋ, -d
AM ˈvæləˌraɪz, -ɪz, -ɪŋ, -d

valorization
BR ˌval(ə)rʌɪˈzeɪʃn
AM ˌvælərəˈzeɪʃən, ˌvæləˌraɪˈzeɪʃən

valorize
BR ˈvalərʌɪz, -ɪz, -ɪŋ, -d
AM ˈvæləˌraɪz, -ɪz, -ɪŋ, -d

valorous
BR ˈval(ə)rəs
AM ˈvælərəs

valorously
BR ˈval(ə)rəsli
AM ˈvælərəsli

valour
BR ˈvalə(r)
AM ˈvælər

Valparaiso
BR ˌvalpəˈrʌɪzəʊ
AM ˌvælpəˈraɪˌzoʊ, ˌvælpəˈreɪˌzoʊ
SP ˌbalparaˈiso

valproic
BR valˈprəʊɪk
AM vælˈproʊɪk

valse
BR vɑːls, vals, vɔːls, -ɪz
AM vɑls, -əz

valuable
BR ˈvaljʊbl, ˈvaljʊəbl, -z
AM ˈvælj(əw)əbəl, -z

valuably
BR ˈvaljʊbli, ˈvaljʊəbli
AM ˈvælj(əw)əbli

valuate
BR ˈvaljʊeɪt, -s, -ɪŋ, -ɪd
AM ˈvæljəˌweɪ|t, -ts, -dɪŋ, -dɪd

valuation
BR ˌvaljʊˈeɪʃn, -z
AM ˌvæljəˈweɪʃən, -z

valuator
BR ˈvaljʊeɪtə(r), -z
AM ˈvæljəˌweɪdər, -z

value
BR ˈvaljuː, -z, -ɪŋ, -d
AM ˈvælju, -z, -əwɪŋ, -d

valueless
BR ˈvaljʊləs, ˈvaljuːləs
AM ˈvæljuləs

valuelessness
BR ˈvaljʊləsnəs, ˈvaljuːləsnəs
AM ˈvæljuləsnəs

valuer
BR ˈvaljʊə(r), -z
AM ˈvæljuər, -z

valuta
BR vəˈl(j)uːtə(r)
AM vəˈludə

valvate
BR ˈvalveɪt
AM ˈvælˌveɪt

valve
BR valv, -z, -d
AM vælv, -z, -d

valveless
BR ˈvalvləs
AM ˈvælvləs

valvular
BR ˈvalvjʊlə(r)
AM ˈvælvjələr

valvule
BR ˈvalvjuːl, -z
AM ˈvælvˌjul, -z

valvulitis
BR ˌvalvjʊˈlʌɪtɪs
AM ˌvælvjəˈlaɪdɪs

vambrace
BR ˈvambreɪs, -ɪz
AM ˈvæmˌbreɪs, -ɪz

vamoose
BR və'muːs, va'muːs,
-ɪz, -ɪŋ, -t
AM væ'muːs, və'mus,
-əz, -ɪŋ, -t

vamp
BR væmp, -ps, -pɪŋ,
-(p)t
AM væmp, -s, -ɪŋ, -t

vampire
BR 'væmpʌɪə(r), -z
AM 'væm,paɪ(ə)r, -z

vampiric
BR vam'pɪrɪk
AM væm'pɪrɪk

vampirism
BR 'væmpʌɪərɪz(ə)m
AM 'væmpaɪ(ə),rɪzəm

vampish
BR 'væmpɪʃ
AM 'væmpɪʃ

vamplate
BR 'væmpleɪt, -s
AM 'væm,pleɪt, -s

vampy
BR 'væmp|i, -ɪə(r), -ɪɪst
AM 'væmpi, -ər, -ɪɪst

van
BR van, -z
AM væn, -z

vanadate
BR 'vanədeɪt, -s
AM 'vænə,deɪt, -s

vanadic
BR və'nadɪk,
və'neɪdɪk,
AM və'neɪdɪk,
və'nædɪk

vanadium
BR və'neɪdɪəm
AM və'neɪdɪəm

vanadous
BR 'vanədəs
AM və'nædəs,
'vænədəs

Van Allen
BR van 'alən
AM væn 'ælən

Vanbrugh
BR 'vanbrə(r)
AM 'vænbrə

Van Buren
BR van 'bjʊərən,
+ 'bjʊərn̩, + 'bjɔːrən,
+ 'bjɔːrŋ
AM væn 'bjʊrən

Vance
BR vans, vaːns
AM væns

Vancouver
BR van'kuːvə(r),
vaŋ'kuːvə(r)
AM væn'kuvər

Vanda
BR 'vandə(r)
AM 'vɑndə

vandal
BR 'vandl, -z

AM 'vændəl, -z

Vandalic
BR van'dalɪk
AM væn'dælɪk

vandalise
BR 'vandəlʌɪz,
'vandlʌɪz, -ɪz, -ɪŋ, -d
AM 'vændl,aɪz, -ɪz, -ɪŋ,
-d

vandalism
BR 'vandəlɪz(ə)m,
'vandlɪz(ə)m
AM 'vændl,ɪzəm

vandalistic
BR ,vandə'lɪstɪk,
,vandl'ɪstɪk
AM ,vændə'lɪstɪk

vandalistically
BR ,vandə'lɪstɪkli,
,vandl'ɪstɪkli
AM ,vændə'lɪstək(ə)li

vandalize
BR 'vandəlʌɪz,
'vandlʌɪz, -ɪz, -ɪŋ, -d
AM 'vændl,aɪz, -ɪz, -ɪŋ,
-d

Van de Graaff
BR ,van də 'grɑːf,
+ 'graf
AM ,væn də 'graf

Vandenberg
BR 'vandənbəːg
AM 'vændən,bərg

Vanden Plas
BR ,vandən 'plas,
+ 'plɑːs
AM ,vændən 'plas

Vanderbilt
BR 'vandəbɪlt
AM 'vændər,bɪlt

Van der Post
BR ,van də 'pɒst,
+ 'pəʊst
AM ,væn dər 'poʊst

Van Der Rohe
BR ,van də 'rəʊə(r)
AM ,væn də(r) 'roʊə

van de Velde
BR ,van də 'vɛldə(r)
AM ,væn də 'vɛldə

**Van Diemen's
Land**
BR ,van 'diːmənz land
AM ,væn 'dimənz
,lænd

Van Dyck
BR van 'dʌɪk
AM ,væn 'daɪk

vandyke
BR van'dʌɪk, -s
AM ,væn'daɪk, -s

vane
BR veɪn, -z, -d
AM veɪn, -z, -d

vaneless
BR 'veɪnlɪs
AM 'veɪnlɪs

Vanessa
BR və'nɛsə(r)
AM və'nɛsə

van Eyck
BR van 'ʌɪk
AM ,væn 'aɪk

vang
BR vaŋ, -z
AM væŋ, -z

van Gogh
BR van 'gɒf, vaŋ +,
+ 'gɒx, -s
AM ,væn 'goʊ, -s
DU van 'xɔx

vanguard
BR 'vangɑːd, 'vaŋgɑːd,
-z
AM 'væn,gɑrd, -z

vanilla
BR və'nɪlə(r), -z
AM və'nɪlə, -z

vanillin
BR və'nɪlɪn, 'vanɪlɪn,
'vanlɪn
AM və'nɪlɪn, 'vænələn

vanish
BR 'van|ɪʃ, -ɪʃɪz, -ɪʃɪŋ,
-ɪʃt
AM 'vænɪʃ, -ɪz, -ɪŋ, -t

vanitory
BR 'vanɪt(ə)ri
AM 'vænə,tɔri

vanity
BR 'vanɪt|i, -ɪz
AM 'vænədi, -z

vanload
BR 'vanləʊd, -z
AM 'væn,loʊd, -z

vanquish
BR 'vaŋkw|ɪʃ, -ɪʃɪz,
-ɪʃɪŋ, -ɪʃt
AM 'væŋkwɪʃ, -ɪz, -ɪŋ, -t

vanquishable
BR 'vaŋkwɪʃəbl
AM 'væŋkwəʃəbəl

vanquisher
BR 'vaŋkwɪʃə(r), -z
AM 'væŋkwɪʃər, -z

Vansittart
BR van'sɪtət
AM ,væn'sɪdərt

vantage
BR 'vaːntɪdʒ, 'vantɪdʒ
AM 'væn(t)ɪdʒ

vantagepoint
BR 'vaːntɪdʒpɔɪnt,
'vantɪdʒpɔɪnt, -s
AM 'væn(t)ɪdʒ,pɔɪnt, -s

Vanuatu
BR ,vanʊˈɑːtuː,
,vanʊˈatuː
AM ,vanʊˈɑdu

Vanya
BR 'vɑːnjə(r),
'vanjə(r)
AM 'vɑnjə

vapid
BR 'vapɪd

AM 'væpəd

vapidity
BR va'pɪdɪti, və'pɪdɪti
AM və'pɪdɪdi

vapidly
BR 'vapɪdli
AM 'væpədli

vapidness
BR 'vapɪdnɪs
AM 'væpədnəs

vapor
BR 'veɪp|ə(r), -əz,
-(ə)rɪŋ, -əd
AM 'veɪpər, -z, -ɪŋ, -d

vaporer
BR 'veɪp(ə)rə(r), -z
AM 'veɪpərər, -z

vaporetti
BR ,vapə'rɛti
AM ,veɪpə'rɛdi

vaporetto
BR ,vapə'rɛtəʊ, -z
AM ,veɪpə'rɛdoʊ, -z

vaporific
BR ,veɪpə'rɪfɪk
AM ,veɪpə'rɪfɪk

vaporiform
BR 'veɪp(ə)rɪfɔːm
AM veɪ'pərə,fɔ(ə)rm

vaporimeter
BR ,veɪpə'rɪmɪtə(r), -z
AM ,veɪpə'rɪmɪdər, -z

vaporisable
BR 'veɪp(ə)rʌɪzəbl
AM 'veɪpə,raɪzəbəl

vaporisation
BR ,veɪp(ə)rʌɪ'zeɪʃn
AM ,veɪpərə'zeɪʃən,
,veɪpə,raɪ'zeɪʃən

vaporise
BR 'veɪpərʌɪz, -ɪz, -ɪŋ,
-d
AM 'veɪpə,raɪz, -ɪz, -ɪŋ,
-d

vaporiser
BR 'veɪp(ə)rʌɪzə(r), -z
AM 'veɪpə,raɪzər, -z

vaporish
BR 'veɪp(ə)rɪʃ
AM 'veɪpərɪʃ

vaporizable
BR 'veɪp(ə)rʌɪzəbl
AM 'veɪpə,raɪzəbəl

vaporization
BR ,veɪp(ə)rʌɪ'zeɪʃn
AM ,veɪpərə'zeɪʃən,
,veɪpə,raɪ'zeɪʃən

vaporize
BR 'veɪpərʌɪz, -ɪz, -ɪŋ,
-d
AM 'veɪpə,raɪz, -ɪz, -ɪŋ,
-d

vaporizer
BR 'veɪp(ə)rʌɪzə(r), -z
AM 'veɪpə,raɪzər, -z

vaporous
BR 'veɪp(ə)rəs

vaporously
AM ˈveɪp(ə)rəs
vaporously
BR ˈveɪp(ə)rəsli
AM ˈveɪp(ə)rəsli
vaporousness
BR ˈveɪp(ə)rəsnəs
AM ˈveɪp(ə)rəsnəs
vapory
BR ˈveɪp(ə)ri
AM ˈveɪp(ə)ri
vapour
BR veɪp|ə(r), -əz,
-(ə)rɪŋ, -əd
AM ˈveɪpər, -z, -ɪŋ, -d
vapour-check
BR ˈveɪpətʃek
AM ˈveɪpərˌtʃek
vapourer
BR ˈveɪp(ə)rə(r)
AM ˈveɪp(ə)rər
vapourish
BR ˈveɪp(ə)rɪʃ
AM ˈveɪp(ə)rɪʃ
vapoury
BR ˈveɪp(ə)ri
AM ˈveɪp(ə)ri
vaquero
BR vəˈkɛːrəʊ,
vaˈkɛːrəʊ, -z
AM vɑˈkeroʊ, -z
varactor
BR vəˈraktə(r), -z
AM vɛˌræktər, -z
Varah
BR ˈvɑːrə(r)
AM ˈvɑːrə
Varangian
BR vəˈran(d)ʒɪən, -z
AM vəˈrandʒɪən, -z
Vardon
BR ˈvɑːdn
AM ˈvɑːrdən
varec
BR ˈvarɛk
AM ˈvɛrək
Varèse
BR vəˈrɛz
AM vəˈreɪz, vəˈrɛz
Vargas
BR ˈvɑːgas, ˈvɑːgəs
AM ˈvɑːrgəs
varia
BR ˈvɛːrɪə(r)
AM ˈvɛrɪə
variability
BR ˌvɛːrɪəˈbɪlɪti
AM ˌvɛrɪəˈbɪlɪdi
variable
BR ˈvɛːrɪəbl, -z
AM ˈvɛrɪəbəl, -z
variableness
BR ˈvɛːrɪəblnəs
AM ˈvɛrɪəbəlnəs
variably
BR ˈvɛːrɪəbli
AM ˈvɛrɪəbli

variance
BR ˈvɛːrɪəns
AM ˈvɛrɪəns
variant
BR ˈvɛːrɪənt, -s
AM ˈvɛrɪənt, -s
variate
BR ˈvɛːrɪət, ˈvɛːrɪeɪt, -s
AM ˈvɛrɪət, -s
variation
BR ˌvɛːrɪˈeɪʃn, -z
AM ˌvɛriˈeɪʃən, -z
variational
BR ˌvɛːrɪˈeɪʃ(ə)l,
ˌvɛːrɪˈeɪʃən(ə)l
AM ˌvɛriˈeɪʃ(ə)nəl
variationally
BR ˌvɛːrɪˈeɪʃnəli,
ˌvɛːrɪˈeɪʃn̩li,
ˌvɛːrɪˈeɪʃənli,
ˌvɛːrɪˈeɪʃ(ə)nəli
AM ˌvɛriˈeɪʃ(ə)nəli
variationist
BR ˌvɛːrɪˈeɪʃn̩ɪst,
ˌvɛːrɪˈeɪʃənɪst, -s
AM ˌvɛrɪˈeɪʃənəst, -s
varicella
BR ˌvarɪˈsɛlə(r)
AM ˌvɛrəˈsɛlə
varices
BR ˈvarɪsiːz, ˈvɛːrɪsiːz
AM ˈvɛrəˌsiz
varicocele
BR ˈvarɪkə(ʊ)siːl, -z
AM ˈvɛrəkoʊˌsil, -z
varicolored
BR ˌvɛːrɪˈkʌləd
AM ˈvɛriˌkələrd
varicoloured
BR ˌvɛːrɪˈkʌləd
AM ˈvɛriˌkələrd
varicose
BR ˈvarɪkə(ʊ)s
AM ˈvɛrəˌkoʊs,
ˈvɛrəˌkoʊz
varicosed
BR ˈvarɪkə(ʊ)st,
ˈvarɪkəʊzd
AM ˈvɛrəˌkoʊst,
ˈvɛrəˌkoʊzd
varicosity
BR ˌvarɪˈkɒsɪt|i, -ɪz
AM ˌvɛrəˈkɑsədi, -z
varied
BR ˈvɛːrɪd
AM ˈvɛrɪd
variedly
BR ˈvɛːrɪdli
AM ˈvɛrɪdli
variegate
BR ˈvɛːrɪəgeɪt, -s, -ɪŋ,
-ɪd
AM ˈvɛr(i)əˌgeɪt, -ts,
-dɪŋ, -dɪd
variegation
BR ˌvɛːrɪəˈgeɪʃn, -z
AM ˌvɛr(i)əˈgeɪʃən, -z

varietal
BR vəˈrʌɪtl
AM vəˈraɪədl
varietally
BR vəˈrʌɪtʃli,
vəˈrʌɪtʃəli
AM vəˈraɪədli
varietist
BR vəˈrʌɪtɪst, -s
AM vəˈraɪədəst, -s
variety
BR vəˈrʌɪt|i, -ɪz
AM vəˈraɪədi, -z
varifocal
BR ˌvɛːrɪˈfəʊkl, -z
AM ˌvɛriˈfoʊkəl, -z
variform
BR ˈvɛːrɪfɔːm
AM ˈvɛrəˌfɔ(ə)rm
variola
BR vəˈrʌɪələ(r)
AM vəˈraɪələ,
ˌvɛriˈoʊlə
variolar
BR vəˈrʌɪələ(r)
AM vəˈrɪələr
variolate
BR ˈvɛːrɪəleɪt
AM ˈvɛrɪəˌleɪt
variole
BR ˈvɛːrɪəʊl, -z
AM ˈvɛriˌoʊl, -z
variolite
BR ˈvɛːrɪəlʌɪt, -s
AM ˈvɛriəˌlaɪt, -s
variolitic
BR ˌvɛːrɪəˈlɪtɪk
AM ˌvɛriəˈlɪdɪk
varioloid
BR ˈvɛːrɪələɪd, -z
AM ˈvɛriəˌlɔɪd, -z
variolous
BR ˈvɛːrɪələs
AM ˈvɛriələs
variometer
BR ˌvɛːrɪˈɒmɪtə(r), -z
AM ˌvɛriˈɑmədər, -z
variorum
BR ˌvɛːrɪˈɔːrəm
AM ˌvɛriˈɔrəm
various
BR ˈvɛːrɪəs
AM ˈvɛriəs
variously
BR ˈvɛːrɪəsli
AM ˈvɛriəsli
variousness
BR ˈvɛːrɪəsnəs
AM ˈvɛriəsnəs
varistor
BR (ˌ)vɛːˈrɪstə(r),
vəˈrɪstə(r), -z
AM vəˈrɪstər, -z
varix
BR ˈvɛːrɪks
AM ˈvɛrɪks

varlet
BR ˈvɑːlɪt, -s
AM ˈvɑrlət, -s
varletry
BR ˈvɑːlɪtri
AM ˈvɑrlətri
Varley
BR ˈvɑːli
AM ˈvɑrli
varmint
BR ˈvɑːmɪnt, -s
AM ˈvɑrmənt, -s
varna
BR ˈvɑːnə(r), -z
AM ˈvɑrnə, -z
Varney
BR ˈvɑːni
AM ˈvɑrni
varnish
BR ˈvɑːn|ɪʃ, -ɪʃɪz, -ɪʃɪŋ,
-ɪʃt
AM ˈvɑrnɪʃ, -ɪz, -ɪŋ, -t
varnisher
BR ˈvɑːnɪʃə(r), -z
AM ˈvɑrnɪʃər, -z
Varro
BR ˈvarəʊ
AM ˈvɛroʊ
varsity
BR ˈvɑːsɪt|i, -ɪz
AM ˈvɑrsədi, -z
Varsovian
BR vɑːˈsəʊvɪən, -z
AM vɑrˈsoʊvɪən, -z
varsoviana
BR vɑːˌsəʊvɪˈɑːnə(r), -z
AM vɑrˌsoʊvɪˈɑnə, -z
varsovienne
BR vɑːˌsəʊvɪˈɛn, -z
AM vɑrˌsoʊvɪˈɛn, -z
varus
BR ˈvɛːrəs, -ɪz
AM ˈvɛrəs, -əz
varve
BR vɑːv, -z, -d
AM vɑrv, -z, -d
vary
BR ˈvɛːr|i, -ɪz, -ɪɪŋ, -ɪd
AM ˈvɛri, -z, -ɪŋ, -d
varyingly
BR ˈvɛːrɪɪŋli
AM ˈvɛrɪɪŋli
vas
BR vas
AM væs, væz
vasa deferentia
BR ˌvasə
ˌdɛfəˈrɛnʃ(ɪ)ə(r)
AM ˌvæsə
ˌdɛfəˈrɛn(t)ʃ(i)ə
vasal
BR ˈveɪsl, ˈveɪzl
AM ˈveɪsəl, ˈveɪzəl
Vasari
BR vəˈsɑːri
AM vəˈsɑri

Vasco da Gama
BR ˌvaskəʊ də
'gɑːmə(r)
AM ˌvæskoʊ də 'gɑmə,
ˌvaskoʊ də 'gɑmə

vascula
BR 'vaskjʊlə(r)
AM 'væskjələ

vascular
BR 'vaskjʊlə(r)
AM 'væskjələr

vascularise
BR 'vaskjʊlərʌɪz, -ɪz,
-ɪŋ, -d
AM 'væskjələˌraɪz, -ɪz,
-ɪŋ, -d

vascularity
BR ˌvaskjʊ'larɪti
AM ˌvæskjə'lɛrədi

vascularize
BR 'vaskjʊlərʌɪz, -ɪz,
-ɪŋ, -d
AM 'væskjələˌraɪz, -ɪz,
-ɪŋ, -d

vascularly
BR 'vaskjʊləli
AM 'væskjələrli

vasculum
BR 'vaskjʊləm
AM 'væskjələm

vas deferens
BR ˌvas 'dɛfərɛnz
AM ˌvæs 'dɛfərənz,
ˌvæs 'dɛfəˌrɛnz, ˌvæz
'dɛfərənz, ˌvæz
'dɛfəˌrɛnz

vase
BR vɑːz, -ɪz
AM veɪs, veɪz, vɑz, -ɪz

vasectomise
BR və'sɛktəmʌɪz, -ɪz,
-ɪŋ, -d
AM və'sɛktəˌmaɪz, -ɪz,
-ɪŋ, -d

vasectomize
BR və'sɛktəmʌɪz, -ɪz,
-ɪŋ, -d
AM və'sɛktəˌmaɪz, -ɪz,
-ɪŋ, -d

vasectomy
BR və'sɛktəm|i, -ɪz
AM və'sɛktəmi, -z

vaseful
BR 'vɑːzfʊl, -z
AM 'veɪsˌfʊl, 'veɪzˌfʊl,
vɑzˌfʊl, -z

vaseline®
BR 'vasɪliːn, 'vasˌliːn,
ˌvasɪ'liːn, ˌvasl'iːn, -z,
-ɪŋ, -d
AM ˌvæsə'lin, -z, -ɪŋ, -d

vasiform
BR 'veɪzɪfɔːm
AM 'veɪsəˌfɔː(ə)rm,
'veɪzəˌfɔː(ə)rm,
'væsəˌfɔː(ə)rm,
'væzəˌfɔː(ə)rm

vasoactive
BR ˌveɪzəʊ'aktɪv
AM ˌveɪzoʊ'æktɪv

vasoconstriction
BR ˌveɪzəʊkən'strɪkʃn
AM ˌveɪzoʊkən'strɪkʃən

vasoconstrictive
BR ˌveɪzəʊkən'strɪktɪv
AM ˌveɪzoʊkən'strɪktɪv

vasoconstrictor
BR ˌveɪzəʊkən'strɪk-
tə(r), -z
AM ˌveɪzoʊkən'strɪk-
tər, -z

vasodilating
BR ˌveɪzəʊdʌɪ'leɪtɪŋ
AM ˌveɪzoʊˌdaɪˌleɪdɪŋ

vasodilation
BR ˌveɪzəʊdʌɪ'leɪʃn
AM ˌveɪzoʊˌdaɪ'leɪʃən

vasodilator
BR ˌveɪzəʊdʌɪ'leɪtə(r),
-z
AM ˌveɪzoʊ'daɪˌleɪdər,
-z

vasomotor
BR ˌveɪzəʊ'məʊtə(r)
AM ˌveɪzoʊ'moʊdər

vasopressin
BR ˌveɪzəʊ'prɛsɪn
AM ˌveɪzoʊ'prɛsən

Vásquez
BR 'vaskwɛz
AM ˌvæs'k(w)ɛz,
'væsˌk(w)ɛz
SP 'baskeθ, 'baskes

vassal
BR 'vasl, -z
AM 'væsəl, -z

vassalage
BR 'vaslɪdʒ
AM 'væsəlɪdʒ

vast
BR vɑːst, vast, -ə(r),
-ɪst
AM væst, -ər, -əst

vastation
BR va'steɪʃn
AM vɑ'steɪʃn

vastitude
BR 'vɑːstɪtjuːd,
'vɑːstɪtʃuːd,
'vastɪtjuːd,
'vastɪtʃuːd
AM 'væstəˌt(j)ud

vastly
BR 'vɑːs(t)li, 'vas(t)li
AM 'væs(t)li

vastness
BR 'vɑːs(t)nəs,
'vas(t)nəs, -ɪz
AM 'væs(t)nəs, -əz

VAT
BR ˌviːeɪ'tiː, vat
AM ˌviˌeɪ'ti, væt

vat
BR vat, -s
AM væt, -s

Vatersay
BR 'vatəseɪ
AM 'vædərˌseɪ

VAT-free
BR ˌvat'friː
AM ˌvæt'fri

vatful
BR 'vatfʊl, -z
AM 'vætˌfʊl, -z

vatic
BR 'vatɪk
AM 'vædɪk

Vatican
BR 'vatɪk(ə)n
AM 'vædəkən

Vatican City
BR ˌvatɪk(ə)n 'sɪti
AM ˌvædəkən 'sɪdi

Vaticanism
BR 'vatɪkənɪz(ə)m,
'vatɪkˌnɪz(ə)m
AM 'vædəkəˌnɪzəm

Vaticanist
BR 'vatɪkənɪst,
'vatɪkˌnɪst, -s
AM 'vædəkənəst, -s

vaticinal
BR va'tɪsɪnl, və'tɪsɪnl,
va'tɪsn̩l, və'tɪsn̩l
AM və'tɪsɪnəl

vaticinate
BR va'tɪsɪneɪt,
və'tɪsɪneɪt, va'tɪsn̩eɪt,
və'tɪsn̩eɪt, -s, -ɪŋ, -ɪd
AM və'tɪsn̩ˌeɪ|t, -ts, -dɪŋ,
-dɪd

vaticination
BR vəˌtɪsɪ'neɪʃn, -z
AM vəˌtɪsn̩'eɪʃən, -z

vaticinator
BR və'tɪsɪneɪtə(r),
və'tɪsɪneɪtə(r), -z
AM və'tɪsəˌneɪdər, -z

vaticinatory
BR və'tɪsɪnət(ə)ri,
və'tɪsn̩ət(ə)ri
AM və'tɪsn̩əˌtɔri

VAT-registered
BR vat'rɛdʒɪstəd
AM 'vætˌrɛdʒɪstərd

Vättern
BR 'vatəːn
AM 'vɛdərn
SW 'vɛtɛn

vaudeville
BR 'vɔːd(ə)vɪl,
'vəʊd(ə)vɪl
AM 'vɔd(ə)ˌvɪl,
'vɔd(ə)vəl,
'vɑd(ə)ˌvɪl, 'vɑd(ə)vəl

vaudevillian
BR ˌvɔːd(ɪ)'vɪliən,
ˌvəʊd(ɪ)'vɪliən, -z
AM ˌvɔd(ə)'vɪljən,
ˌvɑd(ə)'vɪljən,
ˌvɔd(ə)'vɪliən,
ˌvɑd(ə)'vɪliən, -z

Vaudois
BR 'vɔːdwɑː(r),
'vəʊdwɑː(r), -z
AM vɔ'dwɑ, 'vɔdwɑ, -z

Vaughan
BR vɔːn
AM vɔn, vɑn

Vaughan Williams
BR ˌvɔːn 'wɪliəmz
AM ˌvɔn 'wɪljəmz,
ˌvɑn +, + 'wɪliəmz

Vaughn
BR vɔːn
AM vɔn, vɑn

vault
BR vɔːlt, vɒlt, -s, -ɪŋ, -ɪd
AM vɔlt, vɑlt, -s, -ɪŋ, -əd

vaulter
BR 'vɔːltə(r), 'vɒltə(r),
-z
AM 'vɔltər, 'vɑltər, -z

vaunt
BR vɔːnt, -s, -ɪŋ, -ɪd
AM vɔn|t, vɑn|t, -ts,
-(t)ɪŋ, -(t)əd

vaunter
BR 'vɔːntə(r), -z
AM 'vɔn(t)ər,
'vɑn(t)ər, -z

vauntingly
BR 'vɔːntɪŋli
AM 'vɔn(t)ɪŋli,
'vɑn(t)ɪŋli

Vaux
BR vɔːks, vɒks, vəʊ
AM vɔks, vɑks

Vauxhall
BR 'vɒks(h)ɔːl, -z
AM 'vɔks,(h)ɔl,
'vɑks,(h)ɑl, -z

vavasor
BR 'vavəsɔː(r),
'vavəsʊə(r),
'vavəsə(r), -z
AM 'vavəˌsɔ(ə)r, -z

vavasory
BR 'vavəs(ə)r|i, -ɪz
AM 'vavəˌsɔri, -z

vavasour
BR 'vavəsɔː(r),
'vavəsʊə(r),
'vavəsə(r), -z
AM 'vavəˌsɔ(ə)r, -z

Vavasseur
BR ˌvavə'sə:(r)
AM ˌvavə'sər

veal
BR viːl
AM vil

Veale
BR viːl
AM vil

vealy
BR 'viːli
AM 'vili

Veblen
BR 'vɛblən

AM 'vɛblən, 'veɪblən

vector
BR 'vɛktə(r), -z
AM 'vɛktər, -z

vectorial
BR vɛk'tɔːrɪəl
AM vɛk'tɔriəl

vectorisation
BR ˌvɛkt(ə)rʌɪ'zeɪʃn
AM ˌvɛktərə'zeɪʃən,
ˌvɛktəˌraɪ'zeɪʃən

vectorise
BR 'vɛktərʌɪz, -ɪz, -ɪŋ,
-d
AM 'vɛktəˌraɪz, -ɪz, -ɪŋ,
-d

vectorization
BR ˌvɛkt(ə)rʌɪ'zeɪʃn
AM ˌvɛktərə'zeɪʃən,
ˌvɛktəˌraɪ'zeɪʃən

vectorize
BR 'vɛktərʌɪz, -ɪz, -ɪŋ,
-d
AM 'vɛktəˌraɪz, -ɪz, -ɪŋ,
-d

Veda
BR 'veɪdə(r), 'viːdə(r),
-z
AM 'veɪdə, 'vidə, -z

Vedanta
BR vɪ'dɑːntə(r),
vɛ'dɑːntə(r),
vɪ'dantə(r),
vɛ'dantə(r)
AM və'dɑn(t)ə

Vedantic
BR vɪ'dɑːntɪk,
vɛ'dɑntɪk, vɪ'dantɪk,
vɛ'dantɪk
AM və'dɑn(t)ɪk

Vedantist
BR vɪ'dɑːntɪst,
vɛ'dɑːntɪst,
vɪ'dantɪst, vɛ'dantɪst,
-s
AM və'dɑn(t)əst, -s

Vedda
BR 'vɛdə(r), -z
AM 'vɛdə, -z

vedette
BR vɪ'dɛt, -s
AM və'dɛt, -s

Vedic
BR 'veɪdɪk, 'viːdɪk
AM 'veɪdɪk, 'vidɪk

vee
BR viː, -z
AM vi, -z

veep
BR viːp, -s
AM vip, -s

veer
BR vɪə(r), -z, -ɪŋ, -d
AM vɪ(ə)r, -z, -ɪŋ, -d

veg
BR vɛdʒ, -ɪz
AM vɛdʒ, -əz

Vega
BR 'viːgə(r), 'veɪgə(r)
AM 'veɪgə

vegan
BR 'viːg(ə)n, -z
AM 'vigən, 'veɪgən, -z

veganism
BR 'viːgənɪz(ə)m,
'viːgnɪz(ə)m
AM 'vigənˌɪzəm,
'veɪgənˌɪzəm

Vegeburger
BR 'vɛdʒɪˌbəːgə(r), -z
AM 'vɛdʒiˌbərgər, -z

Vegemite®
BR 'vɛdʒɪmʌɪt
AM 'vɛdʒəˌmaɪt

vegetable
BR 'vɛdʒ(ɪ)təbl, -z
AM 'vɛdʒtəbəl,
'vɛdʒədəbəl, -z

vegetal
BR 'vɛdʒɪtl
AM 'vɛdʒədl

vegetarian
BR ˌvɛdʒɪ'tɛːrɪən, -z
AM ˌvɛdʒə'tɛriən, -z

vegetarianism
BR ˌvɛdʒɪ'tɛːrɪənɪz(ə)m
AM ˌvɛdʒə'tɛriəˌnɪzəm

vegetate
BR 'vɛdʒɪteɪt, -s, -ɪŋ, -ɪd
AM 'vɛdʒəˌteɪt, -ts,
-dɪŋ, -dɪd

vegetation
BR ˌvɛdʒɪ'teɪʃn
AM ˌvɛdʒə'teɪʃən

vegetational
BR ˌvɛdʒɪ'teɪʃn(ə)l,
ˌvɛdʒɪ'teɪʃən(ə)l
AM ˌvɛdʒə'teɪʃ(ə)nəl

vegetative
BR 'vɛdʒɪtətɪv
AM 'vɛdʒəˌteɪdɪv

vegetatively
BR 'vɛdʒɪtətɪvli
AM 'vɛdʒəˌteɪdɪvli

vegetativeness
BR 'vɛdʒɪtətɪvnɪs
AM 'vɛdʒəˌteɪdɪvnɪs

veggie
BR 'vɛdʒi, -ɪz
AM 'vɛdʒi, -z

vegie
BR 'vɛdʒi, -ɪz
AM 'vɛdʒi, -z

vehemence
BR 'viːɪm(ə)ns
AM 'vi(h)əməns

vehement
BR 'viːɪm(ə)nt
AM 'vi(h)əmənt

vehemently
BR 'viːɪm(ə)ntli
AM 'vi(h)əmən(t)li

vehicle
BR 'viːɪkl, -z

AM 'viˌhɪkəl, 'viəkəl, -z

vehicular
BR vɪ'hɪkjələ(r),
viːˈhɪkjələ(r)
AM vɪ'hɪkjələr

veil
BR veɪl, -z, -ɪŋ, -d
AM veɪl, -z, -ɪŋ, -d

veiling
BR 'veɪlɪŋ, -z
AM 'veɪlɪŋ, -z

veilless
BR 'veɪllɪs
AM 'veɪ(l)lɪs

vein
BR veɪn, -z, -ɪŋ, -d
AM veɪn, -z, -ɪŋ, -d

veinless
BR 'veɪnlɪs
AM 'veɪnləs

veinlet
BR 'veɪnlɪt, -s
AM 'veɪnlɪt, -s

veinlike
BR 'veɪnlʌɪk
AM 'veɪnˌlaɪk

veinstone
BR 'veɪnstəʊn
AM 'veɪnˌstoʊn

veiny
BR 'veɪnli, -ɪə(r), -ɪɪst
AM 'veɪni, -ər, -ɪst

vela
BR 'viːlə(r)
AM 'vilə

velamen
BR 'veɪleɪmən
AM və'leɪmən

velamina
BR vɪ'lamɪnə(r)
AM və'læmənə

velar
BR 'viːlə(r), -z
AM 'vilər, -z

velarization
BR ˌviːl(ə)rʌɪ'zeɪʃn, -z
AM ˌvilərə'zeɪʃən,
ˌvilərˌraɪ'zeɪʃən, -z

velarize
BR 'viːlərʌɪz, -ɪz, -ɪŋ, -d
AM 'viləˌraɪz, -ɪz, -ɪŋ, -d

Velásquez
BR vɪ'laskwɪz,
vɛ'laskwɪz,
vɪ'laskwɛz,
vɛ'laskwɛz
AM və'lasˌk(w)ɛz,
və'lazˌk(w)ɛz
SP be'laskeθ,
be'laskes

Velázquez
BR vɪ'laskwɪz,
vɛ'laskwɪz,
vɪ'laskwɛz,
vɛ'laskwɛz
AM və'lasˌk(w)ɛz,
və'lazˌk(w)ɛz

SP be'laθkeθ,
be'laskes

velcro
BR 'vɛlkrəʊ, -d
AM 'vɛlˌkroʊ, -d

veld
BR vɛlt, fɛlt, -s
AM vɛlt, -s

veldskoen
BR 'fɛltˌsku:n,
'vɛltˌsku:n, -z
AM 'vɛltˌskun, -z

veldt
BR vɛlt, fɛlt, -s
AM vɛlt, -s

veleta
BR vɪ'liːtə(r), -z
AM və'lidə, -z

velic
BR 'viːlɪk
AM 'vilɪk

velitation
BR ˌvɛlɪ'teɪʃn, -z
AM ˌvɛlə'teɪʃən, -z

velleity
BR vɛ'liːɪti, və'liːɪti
AM və'lidi, vɛ'lidi

vellum
BR 'vɛləm
AM 'vɛləm

Velma
BR 'vɛlmə(r)
AM 'vɛlmə

velocimeter
BR ˌvɛlə'sɪmɪtə(r), -z
AM ˌvɛlə'sɪmɪdər, -z

velocipede
BR vɪ'lɒsɪpiːd, -z
AM və'lɑsəˌpid, -z

velocipedist
BR vɪ'lɒsɪpiːdɪst, -s
AM və'lɑsəˌpidɪst, -s

velociraptor
BR və'lɒsɪraptə(r), -z
AM və'lɑsəˌræptər, -z

velocity
BR vɪ'lɒsɪtli, -ɪz
AM və'lɑsədi, -z

velodrome
BR 'vɛlədrəʊm, -z
AM 'vɛləˌdroʊm, -z

velour
BR və'lʊə(r), vɛ'lʊə(r),
və'lɔː(r), vɛ'lɔː(r), -z
AM və'lʊ(ə)r, -z

velours
BR və'lʊə(r), vɛ'lʊə(r),
və'lɔː(r), vɛ'lɔː(r), -z
AM və'lʊ(ə)r, -z

velouté
BR və'luːteɪ, -z
AM vəˌlu'teɪ, -z

velum
BR 'viːləm, -z
AM 'viləm, -z

velutinous
BR vɪˈl(j)uːtɪnəs,
vɛˈl(j)uːtɪnəs
AM vəˈlutnəs

velvet
BR ˈvɛlvɪt, -s
AM ˈvɛlvət, -s

velveted
BR ˈvɛlvɪtɪd
AM ˈvɛlvədəd

velveteen
BR ˌvɛlvɪˈtiːn,
ˈvɛlvɪtiːn, -z
AM ˈvɛlvəˌtiːn, -z

velvety
BR ˈvɛlvɪti
AM ˈvɛlvədi

vena
BR ˈviːnə(r)
AM ˈvinə

Venables
BR ˈvɛnəblz
AM ˈvɛnəbəlz

vena cava
BR ˌviːnə ˈkeɪvə(r)
AM ˌvinə ˈkavə, ˌvinə
ˈkeɪvə

venae
BR ˈviːniː
AM ˈvini, ˈviˌnaɪ

venae cavae
BR ˌviːniː ˈkeɪviː
AM ˌvini ˈkavi, ˌvini
ˈkeɪvi, ˌvini ˈkɑˌvaɪ,
ˌvini ˈkeɪˌvaɪ

venal
BR ˈviːnl
AM ˈvinəl

venality
BR viːˈnalɪti, vɪˈnalɪti
AM viˈnælədi,
vəˈnælədi

venally
BR ˈviːnli, ˈviːnəli
AM ˈvinəli

venation
BR vɪˈneɪʃn
AM vɪˈneɪʃən

venational
BR viːˈneɪʃn(ə)l,
viːˈneɪʃən(ə)l,
vɪˈneɪʃn(ə)l,
vɪˈneɪʃən(ə)l
AM vɪˈneɪʃ(ə)nəl

vend
BR vɛnd, -z, -ɪŋ, -ɪd
AM vɛnd, -z, -ɪŋ, -əd

Venda
BR ˈvɛndə(r), -z
AM ˈvɛndə, -z

vendace
BR ˈvɛndɪs, ˈvɛndeɪs
AM ˈvɛndəs

Vendée
BR ˈvɒdeɪ
AM vɑnˈdeɪ

vendee
BR ˌvɛnˈdiː, -z

AM ˌvɛnˈdi, -z

vender
BR ˈvɛndə(r), -z
AM ˈvɛndər, -z

vendetta
BR vɛnˈdɛtə(r), -z
AM vɛnˈdɛdə, -z

vendeuse
BR vɒ̃ˈdəːz, -ɪz
AM vɑnˈdʊz, -əz

vendible
BR ˈvɛndɪbl, -z
AM ˈvɛndəbəl, -z

vendor
BR ˈvɛndɔː(r),
ˈvɛndə(r), -z
AM ˈvɛndər, -z

vendue
BR vɛnˈdjuː, -z
AM vɛnˈd(j)u, -z

veneer
BR vɪˈnɪə(r), -z, -ɪŋ, -d
AM vəˈnɪ(ə)r, -z, -ɪŋ, -d

venepuncture
BR ˈvɛnɪˌpʌŋ(k)tʃə(r),
ˈviːnɪˌpʌŋ(k)tʃə(r), -z
AM ˈvinəˌpəŋ(kt)ʃər, -z

venerability
BR ˌvɛn(ə)rəˈbɪlɪti
AM ˌvɛn(ə)rəˈbɪlɪdi

venerable
BR ˈvɛn(ə)rəbl
AM ˈvɛnər(ə)bəl,
ˈvɛnrəbəl

venerableness
BR ˈvɛn(ə)rəblnəs
AM ˈvɛnər(ə)bəlnəs,
ˈvɛnrəbəlnəs

venerably
BR ˈvɛn(ə)rəbli
AM ˈvɛnər(ə)bli,
ˈvɛnrəbli

venerate
BR ˈvɛnəreɪt, -s, -ɪŋ, -ɪd
AM ˈvɛnəˌreɪ|t, -ts, -dɪŋ,
-dɪd

veneration
BR ˌvɛnəˈreɪʃn
AM ˌvɛnəˈreɪʃən

venerator
BR ˈvɛnəreɪtə(r), -z
AM ˈvɛnəˌreɪdər, -z

venereal
BR vɪˈnɪərɪəl
AM vəˈnɪrɪəl

venereally
BR vɪˈnɪərɪəli
AM vəˈnɪrɪəli

venereological
BR vɪˌnɪərɪəˈlɒdʒɪkl
AM vəˌnɪriəˈlɑdʒəkəl

venereologist
BR vɪˌnɪərɪˈɒlədʒɪst, -s
AM vəˌnɪriˈɑlədʒəst, -s

venereology
BR vɪˌnɪərɪˈɒlədʒi
AM vəˌnɪriˈɑlədʒi

venery
BR ˈvɛn(ə)ri, ˈviːn(ə)ri
AM ˈvɛnəri

venesection
BR ˈvɛnɪˌsɛkʃn,
ˌviːnɪˈsɛkʃn, -z
AM ˈvinəˌsɛkʃən, -z

Venetia
BR vɪˈniːʃə(r)
AM vəˈniʃə

venetian
BR vɪˈniːʃn, -z, -d
AM vəˈniʃən, -z, -d

Veneto
BR vɪˈniːtəʊ
AM vəˈnɛdoʊ

Venezuela
BR ˌvɛnɪˈzweɪlə(r)
AM ˌvɛnəz(ə)ˈweɪlə
SP beneˈθwela,
beneˈswela

Venezuelan
BR ˌvɛnɪˈzweɪlən, -z
AM ˌvɛnəz(ə)ˈweɪlən,
-z

vengeance
BR ˈvɛn(d)ʒ(ə)nz
AM ˈvɛndʒəns

vengeful
BR ˈvɛn(d)ʒf(ʊ)l
AM ˈvɛndʒfəl

vengefully
BR ˈvɛn(d)ʒfʊli,
ˈvɛn(d)ʒfli
AM ˈvɛndʒfəli

vengefulness
BR ˈvɛn(d)ʒf(ʊ)lnəs
AM ˈvɛndʒfəlnəs

venial
BR ˈviːnɪəl
AM ˈvinɪəl, ˈvinjəl

veniality
BR ˌviːnɪˈalɪti
AM ˌvini ˈælədi

venially
BR ˈviːnɪəli
AM ˈvinɪəli, ˈvinjəli

venialness
BR ˈviːnɪəlnəs
AM ˈvinɪəlnəs,
ˈvinjəlnəs

Venice
BR ˈvɛnɪs
AM ˈvɛnəs

venipuncture
BR ˈvɛnɪˌpʌŋ(k)tʃə(r),
ˈviːnɪˌpʌŋ(k)tʃə(r), -z
AM ˈvinəˌpəŋ(kt)ʃər, -z

venisection
BR ˈvɛnɪˈsɛkʃn,
ˌviːnɪˈsɛkʃn, -z
AM ˈvinəˌsɛkʃən, -z

venison
BR ˈvɛnɪsn, ˈvɛnɪzn
AM ˈvɛnəsən, ˈvɛnəzn

Venite
BR vɪˈnaɪt|i, ˈviːniːt|i,
-ɪz

venery
BR vəˈnaɪdi, vəˈnidi, -z

Venn diagram
BR ˈvɛn ˌdaɪəgram, -z
AM ˈvɛn ˈdaɪəˌgræm, -z

Venner
BR ˈvɛnə(r)
AM ˈvɛnər

venom
BR ˈvɛnəm, -d
AM ˈvɛnəm, -d

venomous
BR ˈvɛnəməs
AM ˈvɛnəməs

venomously
BR ˈvɛnəməsli
AM ˈvɛnəməsli

venomousness
BR ˈvɛnəməsnəs
AM ˈvɛnəməsnəs

venose
BR ˈviːnəʊs
AM ˈviˌnoʊs, ˈviˌnoʊz

venosity
BR vɪˈnɒsɪti
AM vəˈnɑsədi,
vɪˈnɑsədi

venous
BR ˈviːnəs
AM ˈvinəs

venously
BR ˈviːnəsli
AM ˈvinəsli

vent
BR vɛnt, -s, -ɪŋ, -ɪd
AM vɛn|t, -ts, -(t)ɪŋ,
-(t)əd

ventage
BR ˈvɛnt|ɪdʒ, -ɪdʒɪz
AM ˈvɛn(t)ɪdʒ, -ɪz

Vent-Axia®
BR ˌvɛntˈaksɪə(r)
AM ˈvɛnˈtæksɪə

vent-hole
BR ˈvɛnthəʊl, -z
AM ˈvɛnt,(h)oʊl, -z

ventiduct
BR ˈvɛntɪdʌkt, -s
AM ˈvɛn(t)əˌdək|(t),
-(t)s

ventifact
BR ˈvɛntɪfakt, -s
AM ˈvɛn(t)əˌfæk|(t),
-(t)s

ventil
BR ˈvɛntɪl, -z
AM ˈvɛn(t)l, -z

ventilate
BR ˈvɛntɪleɪt, -s, -ɪŋ, -ɪd
AM ˈvɛn(t)əˌleɪ|t, -ts,
-dɪŋ, -dɪd

ventilation
BR ˌvɛntɪˈleɪʃn
AM ˌvɛn(t)əˈleɪʃən

ventilative
BR ˈvɛntɪleɪtɪv
AM ˈvɛn(t)əˌleɪdɪv

ventilator
BR ˈvɛntɪleɪtə(r), -z
AM ˈvɛn(t)əˌleɪdər, -z

ventless
BR ˈvɛntləs
AM ˈvɛn(t)ləs

Ventnor
BR ˈvɛntnə(r)
AM ˈvɛntnər

Ventolin®
BR ˈvɛntə(ʊ)lɪn
AM ˈvɛn(t)ələn

ventouse
BR ˈvɛntuːs, -ɪz
AM ˈvɛnˌtus, -əz

ventral
BR ˈvɛntr(ə)l
AM ˈvɛntrəl

ventrally
BR ˈvɛntrəli, ˈvɛntr|i
AM ˈvɛntrəli

ventre à terre
BR ˌvɒtr(ə) a ˈtɛː(r)
AM ˌvɑntrə ɑ ˈtɛ(ə)r

ventricle
BR ˈvɛntrɪkl, -z
AM ˈvɛntrəkəl, -z

ventricose
BR ˈvɛntrɪkəʊs
AM ˈvɛntrəˌkoʊs, ˈvɛntrəˌkoʊz

ventricular
BR vɛnˈtrɪkjʊlə(r)
AM vɛnˈtrɪkjələr

ventriloquial
BR ˌvɛntrɪˈləʊkwɪəl
AM ˌvɛntrəˈloʊkwɪəl

ventriloquially
BR ˌvɛntrɪˈləʊkwɪəli
AM ˌvɛntrəˈloʊkwɪəli

ventriloquise
BR vɛnˈtrɪləkwʌɪz, -ɪz, -ɪŋ, -d
AM vɛnˈtrɪləˌkwaɪz, -ɪz, -ɪŋ, -d

ventriloquism
BR vɛnˈtrɪləkwɪz(ə)m
AM vɛnˈtrɪləˌkwɪzəm

ventriloquist
BR vɛnˈtrɪləkwɪst, -s
AM vɛnˈtrɪləkwəst, -s

ventriloquistic
BR vɛnˌtrɪləˈkwɪstɪk
AM vɛnˌtrɪləˈkwɪstɪk

ventriloquize
BR vɛnˈtrɪləkwʌɪz, -ɪz, -ɪŋ, -d
AM vɛnˈtrɪləˌkwaɪz, -ɪz, -ɪŋ, -d

ventriloquous
BR vɛnˈtrɪləkwəs
AM vɛnˈtrɪləkwəs

ventriloquy
BR vɛnˈtrɪləkwi
AM vɛnˈtrɪləkwi

venture
BR ˈvɛn(t)ʃ|ə(r), -əz, -(ə)rɪŋ, -əd
AM ˈvɛn(t)ʃər, -z, -ɪŋ, -d

venturer
BR ˈvɛn(t)ʃ(ə)rə(r), -z
AM ˈvɛn(t)ʃərər, -z

venturesome
BR ˈvɛn(t)ʃəs(ə)m
AM ˈvɛn(t)ʃərsəm

venturesomely
BR ˈvɛn(t)ʃəs(ə)mli
AM ˈvɛn(t)ʃərsəmli

venturesomeness
BR ˈvɛn(t)ʃəs(ə)mnəs
AM ˈvɛn(t)ʃərsəmnəs

venturi
BR vɛnˈtjʊər|i, vɛnˈtʃʊər|i, -ɪz
AM vɛnˈt(ʃ)ʊri, -z

venturous
BR ˈvɛn(t)ʃ(ə)rəs
AM ˈvɛn(t)ʃ(ə)rəs

venturously
BR ˈvɛn(t)ʃ(ə)rəsli
AM ˈvɛn(t)ʃ(ə)rəsli

venturousness
BR ˈvɛn(t)ʃ(ə)rəsnəs
AM ˈvɛn(t)ʃ(ə)rəsnəs

venue
BR ˈvɛnjuː, -z
AM ˈvɛnˌju, -z

venule
BR ˈvɛnjuːl, ˈvɪnjuːl, -z
AM ˈvɛnˌjul, -z

Venus
BR ˈviːnəs
AM ˈvinəs

Venusian
BR vɪˈnjuːzɪən, vɪˈnjuːsɪən, -z
AM vəˈn(j)uʃən, vəˈn(j)uʃ(i)ən, -z

Vera
BR ˈvɪərə(r)
AM ˈvɛrə, ˈvɪrə

veracious
BR vɪˈreɪʃəs
AM vəˈreɪʃəs

veraciously
BR vɪˈreɪʃəsli
AM vəˈreɪʃəsli

veraciousness
BR vɪˈreɪʃəsnəs
AM vəˈreɪʃəsnəs

veracity
BR vɪˈrasɪti
AM vəˈræsədi

Veracruz
BR ˌvɪərəˈkruːz, ˌvɛrəˈkruːz, ˌvɛːrəˈkruːz
AM ˌvɛrəˈkruz
SP ˌberaˈkruθ, ˌberaˈkrus

veranda
BR vəˈrandə(r), -z, -d
AM vəˈrændə, -z, -d

verandah
BR vəˈrandə(r), -z
AM vəˈrændə, -z

veratrine
BR ˈvɛrətriːn, ˈvɛrətrɪn
AM ˈvɛrəˌtrin, ˈvɛrətrən

verb
BR vəːb, -z
AM vərb, -z

verbal
BR ˈvəːbl
AM ˈvərbəl

verbalisable
BR ˈvəːbəlʌɪzəbl, ˈvəːblʌɪzəbl
AM ˈvərbəˌlaɪzəbəl

verbalisation
BR ˌvəːbəlʌɪˈzeɪʃn, ˌvəːblʌɪˈzeɪʃn, -z
AM ˈvərbələˈzeɪʃən, ˌvərbəˌlaɪˈzeɪʃən, -z

verbalise
BR ˈvəːbəlʌɪz, ˈvəːblʌɪz, -ɪz, -ɪŋ, -d
AM ˈvərbəˌlaɪz, -ɪz, -ɪŋ, -d

verbaliser
BR ˈvəːbəlʌɪzə(r), ˈvəːblʌɪzə(r), -z
AM ˈvərbəˌlaɪzər, -z

verbalism
BR ˈvəːbəlɪz(ə)m, ˈvəːblɪz(ə)m
AM ˈvərbəˌlɪzəm

verbalist
BR ˈvəːbəlɪst, ˈvəːblɪst, -s
AM ˈvərbələst, -s

verbalistic
BR ˌvəːbəˈlɪstɪk, ˌvəːblˈɪstɪk
AM ˌvərbəˈlɪstɪk

verbalizable
BR ˈvəːbəlʌɪzəbl, ˈvəːblʌɪzəbl
AM ˈvərbəˌlaɪzəbəl

verbalization
BR ˌvəːbəlʌɪˈzeɪʃn, ˌvəːblʌɪˈzeɪʃn, -z
AM ˌvərbələˈzeɪʃən, ˌvərbəˌlaɪˈzeɪʃən, -z

verbalize
BR ˈvəːbəlʌɪz, ˈvəːblʌɪz, -ɪz, -ɪŋ, -d
AM ˈvərbəˌlaɪz, -ɪz, -ɪŋ, -d

verbalizer
BR ˈvəːbəlʌɪzə(r), ˈvəːblʌɪzə(r), -z
AM ˈvərbəˌlaɪzər, -z

verbally
BR ˈvəːbli, ˈvəːbəli
AM ˈvərbəli

verbatim
BR vəːˈbeɪtɪm, vəˈbeɪtɪm

verandah
BR vəˈrandə(r), -z
AM vəˈrændə, -z

verbena
BR vəːˈbiːnə(r), vəˈbiːnə(r), -z
AM vərˈbinə, -z

verbiage
BR ˈvəːbɪɪdʒ
AM ˈvərbiɪdʒ

verbose
BR vəːˈbəʊs, vəˈbəʊs
AM vərˈboʊs

verbosely
BR vəːˈbəʊsli, vəˈbəʊsli
AM vərˈboʊsli

verboseness
BR vəːˈbəʊsnəs, vəˈbəʊsnəs
AM vərˈboʊsnəs

verbosity
BR vəːˈbɒsɪti, vəˈbɒsɪti
AM vərˈbɑsədi

verboten
BR fəˈbəʊtn, vəˈbəʊtn, fɛːˈbɔːtn
AM fərˈboʊtn

verb. sap.
BR ˌvəːb ˈsap
AM ˌvərb ˈsæp

Vercingetorix
BR ˌvəːsɪnˈgɛt(ə)rɪks, ˌvəːsɪnˈdʒɛt(ə)rɪks
AM ˌvərsɪnˈgɛdərɪks, ˌvərsɪnˈdʒɛdərɪks

verd
BR vəːd
AM vərd

verdancy
BR ˈvəːdnsi
AM ˈvərdnsi

verdant
BR ˈvəːdnt
AM ˈvərdnt

verd-antique
BR ˌvəːdanˈtiːk
AM ˌvərˌdænˈtik

verdantly
BR ˈvəːdntli
AM ˈvərdn(t)li

verdelho
BR vəːˈdɛljuː, vəːˈdɛljəʊ
AM vərˈdɛljoʊ

verderer
BR ˈvəːd(ə)rə(r), -z
AM ˈvərdərər, -z

Verdi
BR ˈvɛːdi
AM ˈvɛrdi

Verdian
BR ˈvɛːdɪən, -z
AM ˈvɛrdiən, -z

verdict
BR ˈvəːdɪkt, -s
AM ˈvərdɪk|(t), -(t)s

verdigris
BR ˈvəːdɪɡriː(s)

AM 'vɜːdəˌgris

verditer
BR 'vɜːdɪtə(r)
AM 'vɜːdədər

Verdun
BR vɜː'dʌn
AM vər'dən, 'vɜːdn
FR vɛʁdœ̃

verdure
BR 'vɜːdʒə(r),
'vɜːdjə(r), -d
AM 'vɜːdʒər, -d

verdurous
BR 'vɜːdʒ(ə)rəs,
'vɜːdjərəs
AM 'vɜːdʒərəs

Vere
BR vɪə(r)
AM vɪ(ə)r

Vereeniging
BR vɪ'riːnɪɡɪŋ
AM və'rinɪɡɪŋ
AFK fər'iənəxəŋ

verge
BR vɜːdʒ, -ɪz, -ɪŋ, -d
AM vɜːdʒ, -əz, -ɪŋ, -d

vergence
BR 'vɜːdʒ(ə)ns
AM 'vɜːdʒəns

verger
BR 'vɜːdʒə(r), -z
AM 'vɜːdʒər, -z

vergership
BR 'vɜːdʒəʃɪp, -s
AM 'vɜːdʒərˌʃɪp, -s

Vergil
BR 'vɜːdʒ(ɪ)l
AM 'vɜːdʒəl

Vergilian
BR vɜː'dʒɪlɪən
AM vər'dʒɪljən,
vər'dʒɪlɪən

verglas
BR 'vɛːɡlɑː(r)
AM 'vɛːrɡlɑ(s)

veridical
BR vɪ'rɪdɪkl
AM və'rɪdəkəl

veridicality
BR vɪˌrɪdɪ'kalɪti
AM vəˌrɪdə'kælədi

veridically
BR vɪ'rɪdɪkli
AM və'rɪdɪk(ə)li

veriest
BR 'vɛrɪɪst
AM 'vɛrɪɪst

verifiable
BR 'vɛrɪfʌɪəbl
AM 'vɛrəˌfaɪəbəl

verifiably
BR 'vɛrɪfʌɪəbli
AM 'vɛrəˌfaɪəbli

verification
BR ˌvɛrɪfɪ'keɪʃn
AM ˌvɛrəfə'keɪʃən

verifier
BR 'vɛrɪfʌɪə(r)
AM 'vɛrəˌfaɪər

verify
BR 'vɛrɪfʌɪ, -z, -ɪŋ, -d
AM 'vɛrəˌfaɪ, -z, -ɪŋ, -d

verily
BR 'vɛrɪli
AM 'vɛrəli

verisimilar
BR ˌvɛrɪ'sɪmɪlə(r),
ˌvɛrɪ'sɪmlə(r)
AM ˌvɛrə'sɪmələr

verisimilitude
BR ˌvɛrɪsɪ'mɪlɪtjuːd,
ˌvɛrɪsɪ'mɪlɪtʃuːd
AM ˌvɛrəsə'mɪləˌt(j)ud

verism
BR 'vɛrɪz(ə)m
AM 'vɛrɪzəm

verismo
BR vɛ'rɪzməʊ, -z
AM və'rɪzmoʊ,
vɛ'rɪzmoʊ, -z

verist
BR 'vɛrɪst, -s
AM 'vɛrəst, -s

veristic
BR vɛ'rɪstɪk
AM və'rɪstɪk

veritable
BR 'vɛrɪtəbl
AM 'vɛrədəbəl

veritably
BR 'vɛrɪtəbli
AM 'vɛrədəbli

verity
BR 'vɛrɪt|i, -ɪz
AM 'vɛrədi, -z

verjuice
BR 'vɜːdʒuːs
AM 'vɜːdʒəs

verkrampte
BR fə'kram(p)tə(r), -z
AM fər'krɑm(p)tə, -z

Verlaine
BR və'leɪn, vɛː'leɪn
AM vər'leɪn

verligte
BR fə'lɪktə(r), -z
AM vər'lɪktə, -z

Vermeer
BR və'mɪə(r),
vɜː'mɪə(r)
AM vər'mɪ(ə)r
DU vər'meːr

vermeil
BR 'vɜːmeɪl, 'vɜːmɪl
AM 'vɜːrmɪl, 'vɜːrˌmeɪl,
vər'meɪl

vermian
BR 'vɜːmɪən
AM 'vɜːrmɪən

vermicelli
BR ˌvɜːmɪ'sɛli,
ˌvɜːmɪ'tʃɛli
AM ˌvɜːrmə'tʃɛli,
ˌvɜːrmə'sɛli

vermicide
BR 'vɜːmɪsʌɪd, -z
AM 'vɜːrməˌsaɪd, -z

vermicular
BR və(ː)'mɪkjələ(r)
AM vər'mɪkjələr

vermiculate
BR və(ː)'mɪkjʊleɪt
AM vər'mɪkjəˌleɪt

vermiculation
BR və(ː)'mɪkjʊ'leɪʃn
AM vərˌmɪkjə'leɪʃən,
-z

vermiculite
BR və(ː)'mɪkjʊlʌɪt,
və'mɪkjʊlʌɪt
AM vər'mɪkjəˌlaɪt

vermiform
BR 'vɜːmɪfɔːm
AM 'vɜːrməˌfɔ(ə)rm

vermifuge
BR 'vɜːmɪfjuː(d)ʒ, -ɪz
AM 'vɜːrməˌfjudʒ, -ɪz

vermilion
BR və'mɪlɪən
AM vər'mɪljən,
vər'mɪlɪən

vermin
BR 'vɜːmɪn
AM 'vɜːrmən

verminate
BR 'vɜːmɪneɪt, -s, -ɪŋ,
-ɪd
AM 'vɜːrməˌneɪt, -ts,
-dɪŋ, -dɪd

vermination
BR ˌvɜːmɪ'neɪʃn
AM ˌvɜːrmə'neɪʃən

verminous
BR 'vɜːmɪnəs
AM 'vɜːrmənəs

verminously
BR 'vɜːmɪnəsli
AM 'vɜːrmənəsli

verminousness
BR 'vɜːmɪnəsnəs
AM 'vɜːrmənəsnəs

vermivorous
BR və(ː)'mɪv(ə)rəs
AM vər'mɪv(ə)rəs

Vermont
BR və'mɒnt, vəː'mɒnt
AM vər'mɑnt

vermouth
BR 'vɜːməθ, və(ː)'muːθ
AM vər'muθ

vernacular
BR və'nakjələ(r), -z
AM vər'nækjələr, -z

vernacularise
BR və'nakjʊlərʌɪz, -ɪz,
-ɪŋ, -d
AM vər'nækjələˌraɪz,
-ɪz, -ɪŋ, -d

vernacularism
BR və'nakjʊlərɪz(ə)m,
-z

AM vər'nækjələˌrɪzəm,
-z

vernacularity
BR vəˌnakjʊ'larɪti
AM vərˌnækjə'lɛrədi

vernacularize
BR və'nakjʊlərʌɪz, -ɪz,
-ɪŋ, -d
AM vər'nækjələˌraɪz,
-ɪz, -ɪŋ, -d

vernacularly
BR və'nakjʊləli
AM vər'nækjələrli

vernal
BR 'vɜːnl
AM 'vɜːrnəl

vernalisation
BR ˌvɜːnəlʌɪ'zeɪʃn,
ˌvɜːnlʌɪ'zeɪʃn
AM ˌvɜːrnlə'zeɪʃən,
ˌvɜːrnlaɪ'zeɪʃən

vernalise
BR 'vɜːnəlʌɪz,
'vɜːnlʌɪz, -ɪz, -ɪŋ, -d
AM 'vɜːrnlˌaɪz, -ɪz, -ɪŋ, -d

vernalization
BR ˌvɜːnəlʌɪ'zeɪʃn,
ˌvɜːnlʌɪ'zeɪʃn
AM ˌvɜːrnlə'zeɪʃən,
ˌvɜːrnlaɪ'zeɪʃən

vernalize
BR 'vɜːnəlʌɪz,
'vɜːnlʌɪz, -ɪz, -ɪŋ, -d
AM 'vɜːrnlˌaɪz, -ɪz, -ɪŋ, -d

vernally
BR 'vɜːnli, 'vɜːnəli
AM 'vɜːrnl̩i, 'vɜːrnəli

vernation
BR vəː'neɪʃn
AM vər'neɪʃən

Verne
BR vɜːn
AM vɜːrn

Verner
BR 'vɜːnə(r), 'vɛːnə(r)
AM 'vɜːrnər

Verney
BR 'vɜːni
AM 'vɜːrni

vernicle
BR 'vɜːnɪkl, -z
AM 'vɜːrnəkəl, -z

vernier
BR 'vɜːnɪə(r), -z
AM 'vɜːrnɪər, -z

vernissage
BR ˌvɛːnɪ'sɑːʒ
AM ˌvɜːrni'sɑʒ

vernix
BR 'vɜːnɪks
AM 'vɜːrnɪks

Vernon
BR 'vɜːnən
AM 'vɜːrnən

Verny
BR 'vɜːni
AM 'vɜːrni

Verona
BR vɪˈrəʊnə(r)
AM vəˈroʊnə

veronal
BR ˈverənl, ˈvern̩l
AM ˈverə,nɔl, ˈverənl,
ˈverə,nɑl, ˈverənəl

Veronese
BR ˌverəˈneɪzi
AM ˌverəˈneɪzi

veronica
BR vɪˈrɒnɪkə(r), -z
AM vəˈrɑnəkə, -z

veronique
BR ˌverəˈniːk
AM ˌverəˈnik

Verrazano
BR ˌverəˈzɑːnəʊ
AM ˌverəˈzɑnoʊ

verruca
BR vɪˈruːkə(r),
veˈruːkə(r), -z
AM vəˈrukə, -z

verrucae
BR vɪˈruːkiː, vɪˈruːsiː,
veˈruːkiː, veˈruːsi
AM vəˈruki, vəˈruˌkaɪ

verrucose
BR ˌverəˈkəʊs,
vɪˈruːkəʊs,
veˈruːkəʊs
AM ˈver(j)əˌkoʊs,
ˈver(j)əˌkoʊz

verrucous
BR vɪˈruːkəs,
veˈruːkəs, ˈverəkəs
AM vəˈrukəs, veˈrukəs

versa
BR ˈvɜːsə(r)
AM ˈvɜrsə

Versailles
BR veːˈsaɪ, vəˈsaɪ
AM vərˈsaɪ

versant
BR ˈvɜːsnt, -s
AM ˈvɜrsənt, -s

versatile
BR ˈvɜːsətʌɪl
AM ˈvɜrsədl

versatilely
BR ˈvɜːsətʌɪlli
AM ˈvɜrsədli

versatility
BR ˌvɜːsəˈtɪlɪti
AM ˌvɜrsəˈtɪlɪdi

verse
BR vɜːs, -ɪz, -t
AM vɜrs, -əz, -t

verselet
BR ˈvɜːslɪt, -s
AM ˈvɜrslət, -s

verset
BR ˈvɜːsɪt, -s
AM ˈvɜrsət, -s

versicle
BR ˈvɜːsɪkl, -z
AM ˈvɜrsəkəl, -z

versicolored
BR ˌvɜːsɪˈkʌləd
AM ˈvɜrsəˌkələrd

versicoloured
BR ˌvɜːsɪˈkʌləd
AM ˈvɜrsəˌkələrd

versicular
BR və(ː)ˈsɪkjələ(r)
AM vərˈsɪkjələr

versification
BR ˌvɜːsɪfɪˈkeɪʃn
AM ˌvɜrsəfəˈkeɪʃən

versifier
BR ˈvɜːsɪfʌɪə(r), -z
AM ˈvɜrsəˌfaɪər, -z

versify
BR ˈvɜːsɪfʌɪ, -z, -ɪŋ, -d
AM ˈvɜrsəˌfaɪ, -z, -ɪŋ, -d

versin
BR ˈvɜːsɪn, -z
AM ˈvɜrˌsaɪn, -z

versine
BR ˈvɜːsaɪn, -z
AM ˈvɜrˌsaɪn, -z

version
BR ˈvɜːʃn, -z
AM ˈvɜrʒən, -z

versional
BR ˈvɜːʃn(ə)l,
ˈvɜːʃən(ə)l, ˈvɜːʒn(ə)l,
ˈvɜːʒən(ə)l
AM ˈvɜrʒ(ə)nəl

vers libre
BR ˌveː ˈliːbr(ər)
AM ˌvɜr ˈlibrə

verso
BR ˈvɜːsəʊ
AM ˈvɜrsoʊ

verst
BR ˈvɜːst, -s
AM vɜrst, -s

versus
BR ˈvɜːsəs
AM ˈvɜrsəs

vert
BR vɜːt
AM vɜrt

vertebra
BR ˈvɜːtɪbrə(r)
AM ˈvɜrdəbrə

vertebrae
BR ˈvɜːtɪbreɪ, ˈvɜːtɪbriː
AM ˈvɜrdəˌbreɪ

vertebral
BR ˈvɜːtɪbr(ə)l
AM ˈvɜrdəbrəl,
vərˈtibrəl

vertebrally
BR ˈvɜːtɪbrl̩i,
ˈvɜːtɪbrəli
AM ˈvɜrdəbrəli,
vərˈtibrəli

vertebrate
BR ˈvɜːtɪbrət,
ˈvɜːtɪbreɪt, -s
AM ˈvɜrdəbrət,
ˈvɜrdəˌbreɪt, -s

vertebration
BR ˌvɜːtɪˈbreɪʃn
AM ˌvɜrdəˈbreɪʃən

vertex
BR ˈvɜːteks, -ɪz
AM ˈvɜrˌteks, -əz

vertical
BR ˈvɜːtɪkl
AM ˈvɜrdəkəl

verticalise
BR ˈvɜːtɪklʌɪz, -ɪz, -ɪŋ, -d
AM ˈvɜrdəkəˌlaɪz, -ɪz, -ɪŋ, -d

verticality
BR ˌvɜːtɪˈkalɪti
AM ˌvɜrdəˈkælədi

verticalize
BR ˈvɜːtɪklʌɪz, -ɪz, -ɪŋ, -d
AM ˈvɜrdəkəˌlaɪz, -ɪz, -ɪŋ, -d

vertically
BR ˈvɜːtɪkli, ˈvɜːtɪkl̩i
AM ˈvɜrdək(ə)li

vertices
BR ˈvɜːtɪsiːz
AM ˈvɜrdəˌsiz

verticil
BR ˈvɜːtɪsɪl, -z
AM ˈvɜrdəˌsɪl, -z

verticillate
BR ˈvɜːtɪsɪlət,
vəˈtɪsl̩ət, ˌvɜːtɪˈsɪlət
AM ˈvɜrdəˈsɪlət,
vərdəˈsɪleɪt

vertiginous
BR vɜːˈtɪdʒɪnəs,
vəˈtɪdʒnəs
AM vərˈtɪdʒənəs

vertiginously
BR vɜːˈtɪdʒɪnəsli,
vəˈtɪgnəsli
AM vərˈtɪdʒənəsli

vertigo
BR ˈvɜːtɪgəʊ
AM ˈvɜrdəgoʊ

vertu
BR vɜːˈtuː
AM vərˈtu

Verulamium
BR ˌver(j)əˈleɪmɪəm,
ˌver(j)əˈleɪmɪəm

vervain
BR ˈvɜːveɪn, -z
AM ˈvɜrˌveɪn, -z

verve
BR vɜːv
AM vɜrv

vervet
BR ˈvɜːvɪt, -s
AM ˈvɜrvət, -s

Verwoerd
BR fəˈvʊət
AM fərˈvʊ(ə)rt

very
BR ˈveri
AM ˈveri

Very light
BR ˈvɪəri ˌlaɪt, ˈveri +, -s
AM ˈviri ˌlaɪt, ˈveri +, -s

Very pistol
BR ˈvɪəri ˌpɪstl, ˈveri +, -z
AM ˈviri ˌpɪstl, ˈveri +, -z

Vesalius
BR vɪˈseɪlɪəs
AM vəˈseɪlɪəs

Vesey
BR ˈviːzi
AM ˈvizi

vesica
BR ˈvesɪkə(r), ˈviːsɪkə(r), vɪˈsaɪkə(r), -z
AM vəˈsikə, vəˈsaɪkə, ˈvesəkə, -z

vesical
BR ˈvesɪkl, ˈviːsɪkl, vɪˈsaɪkl
AM ˈvesəkəl

vesicant
BR ˈvesɪk(ə)nt, ˈviːsɪk(ə)nt, vɪˈsaɪk(ə)nt, -s
AM ˈvesəkənt, -s

vesicate
BR ˈvesɪkeɪt, -s, -ɪŋ, -ɪd
AM ˈvesəˌkeɪt, -ts, -dɪŋ, -dɪd

vesication
BR ˌvesɪˈkeɪʃn, -z
AM ˌvesəˈkeɪʃən, -z

vesicatory
BR ˈvesɪkət(ə)ri
AM ˈvesəkəˌtori, vəˈsɪkəˌtori

vesicle
BR ˈvesɪkl, -z
AM ˈvesəkəl, -z

vesicular
BR vɪˈsɪkjələ(r)
AM vəˈsɪkjələr

vesicularly
BR vɪˈsɪkjələli
AM vəˈsɪkjələrli

vesiculate
BR vɪˈsɪkjələt, vɪˈsɪkjəleɪt
AM vəˈsɪkjəˌleɪt, vəˈsɪkjələt

vesiculation
BR vɪˌsɪkjəˈleɪʃn, -z
AM vəˌsɪkjəˈleɪʃən, -z

Vespa®
BR ˈvespə(r), -z
AM ˈvespə, -z

Vespasian
BR vesˈpeɪʒn, vesˈpeɪzɪən
AM vəˈspeɪʒ(i)ən, vəˈspeɪzɪən

vesper
BR ˈvespə(r), -z

AM ˈvespər, -z

vespertilionid
BR ˌvespətɪlrˈɒnɪd
AM ˌvespərˌtɪliˈɑnɪd

vespertine
BR ˈvespətʌɪm
AM ˈvespərˌtin,
ˈvespərˌtaɪn

vespiary
BR ˈvespɪərˌi, -ɪz
AM ˈvespiˌɛri, -z

vespine
BR ˈvespʌɪm
AM ˈvɛˌspaɪn, ˈvespən

Vespucci
BR vɪˈspuːtʃi,
vɛˈspuːtʃi
AM vəˈsputʃi,
vɛˈsputʃi

vessel
BR ˈvesl, -z
AM ˈvesəl, -z

vest
BR vest, -s, -ɪŋ, -ɪd
AM vest, -s, -ɪŋ, -əd

vesta
BR ˈvestə(r), -z
AM ˈvestə, -z

vestal
BR ˈvestl, -z
AM ˈvestl, -z

vestee
BR ˌveˈstiː, -z
AM ˌvesˈti, -z

vestiary
BR ˈvestɪərˌi, -ɪz
AM ˈvestiˌɛri, -z

vestibular
BR veˈstɪbjələ(r)
AM vəˈstɪbjələr,
veˈstɪbjələr

vestibule
BR ˈvestɪbjuːl, -z
AM ˈvestəˌbjul, -z

vestige
BR ˈvestɪdʒ, -ɪdʒɪz
AM ˈvestɪdʒ, -ɪz

vestigial
BR veˈstɪdʒɪəl,
vəˈstɪdʒɪəl,
veˈstɪdʒ(ə)l,
vəˈstɪdʒ(ə)l
AM veˈstɪdʒ(i)əl

vestigially
BR veˈstɪdʒɪəli,
vəˈstɪdʒɪəli,
veˈstɪdʒəli,
vəˈstɪdʒəli, veˈstɪdʒli,
vəˈstɪdʒli
AM veˈstɪdʒ(i)əli

vestiture
BR ˈvestɪtʃə(r), -z
AM ˈvestɪtʃər,
ˈvestəˌtʃʊ(ə)r, -z

vestment
BR ˈves(t)m(ə)nt, -s
AM ˈves(t)mənt, -s

vestral
BR ˈvestr(ə)l
AM ˈvestrəl

vestry
BR ˈvestrˌi, -ɪz
AM ˈvestri, -z

vestryman
BR ˈvestrɪmən
AM ˈvestrimən

vestrymen
BR ˈvestrɪmən
AM ˈvestrɪmən

vesture
BR ˈvestʃə(r), -z
AM ˈvestʃər, -z

Vesuvian
BR vɪˈsjuːvɪən
AM vəˈsuviən

Vesuvius
BR vɪˈsjuːvɪəs
AM vəˈsuviəs

vet
BR vet, -s, -ɪŋ, -ɪd
AM veɪt, -ts, -dɪŋ, -dəd

vetch
BR vetʃ, -ɪz
AM vetʃ, -əz

vetchling
BR ˈvetʃlɪŋ, -z
AM ˈvetʃlɪŋ, -z

vetchy
BR ˈvetʃi
AM ˈvetʃi

veteran
BR ˈvet(ə)rən,
ˈvet(ə)rn̩, -z
AM ˈvedərən, ˈvetrən,
-z

veterinarian
BR ˌvet(ə)rɪˈnɛːrɪən, -z
AM ˌvedərəˈnɛrɪən,
ˌvetrəˈnɛrɪən, -z

veterinary
BR ˈvet(ə)rɪn(ə)ri
AM ˈvedərəˌnɛri,
ˈvetrəˌnɛri

vetiver
BR ˈvetɪvə(r)
AM ˈvedəvər

veto
BR ˈviːtəʊ, -z, -ɪŋ, -d
AM ˈvidoʊ, ˈviˌtoʊ, -z,
-ɪŋ, -d

vetoer
BR ˈviːtəʊə(r), -z
AM ˈvidoʊər, ˈviˌtoʊər,
-z

vex
BR veks, -ɪz, -ɪŋ, -t
AM veks, -əz, -ɪŋ, -t

vexation
BR vekˈseɪʃn, -z
AM vekˈseɪʃən, -z

vexatious
BR vekˈseɪʃəs
AM vekˈseɪʃəs

vexatiously
BR vekˈseɪʃəsli
AM vekˈseɪʃəsli

vexatiousness
BR vekˈseɪʃəsnəs
AM vekˈseɪʃəsnəs

vexedly
BR ˈveksɪdli
AM ˈveksədli

vexer
BR ˈveksə(r), -z
AM ˈveksər, -z

vexilla
BR vekˈsɪlə(r)
AM vekˈsɪlə

vexillological
BR ˌveksɪləˈlɒdʒɪkl
AM ˌveksələˈlɑdʒəkəl

vexillologist
BR ˌveksɪˈlɒlədʒɪst, -s
AM ˌveksəˈlɑlədʒəst, -s

vexillology
BR ˌveksɪˈlɒlədʒi
AM ˌveksəˈlɑlədʒi

vexillum
BR vekˈsɪləm
AM vekˈsɪləm

vexingly
BR ˈveksɪŋli
AM ˈveksɪŋli

Vi
BR vʌɪ
AM vaɪ

via
BR ˈvʌɪə(r)
AM ˈviə, ˈvaɪə

viability
BR ˌvʌɪəˈbɪlɪti
AM ˌvaɪəˈbɪlɪdi

viable
BR ˈvʌɪəbl
AM ˈvaɪəbəl

viably
BR ˈvʌɪəbli
AM ˈvaɪəbli

Via Dolorosa
BR ˌviːə ˌdʊləˈrəʊsə(r)
AM ˌviə doʊlərˈoʊsə

viaduct
BR ˈvʌɪədʌkt, -s
AM ˈvaɪəˌdək(t), -(t)s

Viagra
BR vʌɪˈagrə(r)
AM vaɪˈægrə

vial
BR ˈvʌɪəl, -z
AM ˈvaɪ(ə)l, -z

vialful
BR ˈvʌɪəlfʊl, -z
AM ˈvaɪ(ə)lˌfʊl, -z

via media
BR ˌvʌɪə ˈmiːdɪə(r),
ˌviːə +, + ˈmedɪə(r),
+ ˈmeɪdɪə(r)
AM ˈviə ˈmidiə, ˈvaɪə +,
+ ˈmeɪdiə

viand
BR ˈvʌɪənd, -z
AM ˈvaɪən|d, -(d)z

viatica
BR vʌɪˈatɪkə(r),
vɪˈatɪkə(r)
AM vaɪˈædəkə

viaticum
BR vʌɪˈatɪkəm,
vɪˈatɪkəm, -z
AM vaɪˈædəkəm, -z

vibes
BR vʌɪbz
AM vaɪbz

vibist
BR ˈvʌɪbɪst, -s
AM ˈvaɪbɪst, -s

vibracula
BR vʌɪˈbrakjələ(r)
AM vaɪˈbrækjələ

vibracular
BR vʌɪˈbrakjələ(r)
AM vaɪˈbrækjələr

vibraculum
BR vʌɪˈbrakjələm
AM vaɪˈbrækjələm

Vibram®
BR ˈvʌɪbram,
ˈvʌɪbrəm
AM ˈvaɪˌbræm

vibrancy
BR ˈvʌɪbr(ə)nsi
AM ˈvaɪbrənsi

vibrant
BR ˈvʌɪbr(ə)nt
AM ˈvaɪbrənt

vibrantly
BR ˈvʌɪbr(ə)ntli
AM ˈvaɪbrən(t)li

vibraphone
BR ˈvʌɪbrəfəʊn, -z
AM ˈvaɪbrəˌfoʊn, -z

vibraphonist
BR ˈvʌɪbrəfəʊnɪst, -s
AM ˈvaɪbrəˌfoʊnəst, -s

vibrate
BR vʌɪˈbreɪt, -s, -ɪŋ, -ɪd
AM ˈvaɪˌbreɪt, -ts, -dɪŋ,
-dɪd

vibratile
BR ˈvʌɪbrətʌɪl
AM ˈvaɪbrədl,
ˈvaɪbrəˌtaɪl

vibration
BR vʌɪˈbreɪʃn, -z
AM vaɪˈbreɪʃən, -z

vibrational
BR vʌɪˈbreɪʃn̩(ə)l,
vʌɪˈbreɪʃən(ə)l
AM vaɪˈbreɪʃ(ə)nəl

vibrative
BR ˈvʌɪbrətɪv
AM ˈvaɪbrədɪv

vibrato
BR vɪˈbrɑːtəʊ, -z
AM vəˈbrɑdoʊ, -z

vibrator
BR vʌɪˈbreɪtə(r), -z
AM ˈvaɪˌbreɪdər, -z

vibratory
BR ˈvʌɪbrət(ə)ri,
vʌɪˈbreɪt(ə)ri
AM ˈvaɪbrəˌtɔri

vibrio
BR ˈvɪbrɪəʊ, -z
AM ˈvɪbrioʊ, -z

vibrissae
BR vʌɪˈbrɪsiː
AM vaɪˈbrɪsi,
vaɪˈbrɪˌsaɪ

viburnum
BR vʌɪˈbəːnəm
AM vaɪˈbərnəm

Vic
BR vɪk
AM vɪk

vicar
BR ˈvɪkə(r), -z
AM ˈvɪkər, -z

vicarage
BR ˈvɪk(ə)r|ɪdʒ, -ɪdʒɪz
AM ˈvɪk(ə)rɪdʒ, -ɪz

vicarial
BR vɪˈkɛːrɪəl,
vʌɪˈkɛːrɪəl
AM vaɪˈkɛriəl,
vəˈkɛriəl

vicariate
BR vɪˈkɛːrɪət,
vʌɪˈkɛːrɪət, -s
AM vəˈkɛriət,
vaɪˈkɛriət,
vaɪˈkɛriˌeɪt,
vəˈkɛriˌeɪt, -s

vicarious
BR vɪˈkɛːrɪəs,
vʌɪˈkɛːrɪəs
AM vəˈkɛriəs,
vaɪˈkɛriəs

vicariously
BR vɪˈkɛːrɪəsli,
vʌɪˈkɛːrɪəsli
AM vəˈkɛriəsli,
vaɪˈkɛriəsli

vicariousness
BR vɪˈkɛːrɪəsnəs,
vʌɪˈkɛːrɪəsnəs
AM vəˈkɛriəsnəs,
vaɪˈkɛriəsnəs

vicarship
BR ˈvɪkəʃɪp, -s
AM ˈvɪkərˌʃɪp, -s

vice¹
noun
BR vʌɪs, -ɪz
AM vaɪs, -ɪz

vice²
preposition
BR ˈvʌɪsi, ˈvʌɪsɪ
AM ˈvaɪs(ə), ˈvaɪs(i)

viceless
BR ˈvʌɪslɪs
AM ˈvaɪslɪs

vicelike
BR ˈvʌɪslʌɪk
AM ˈvaɪsˌlaɪk

vicennial
BR vʌɪˈsenɪəl
AM vaɪˈsenɪəl

viceregal
BR ˌvʌɪsˈriːgl
AM ˌvaɪsˈrigəl

viceregally
BR ˌvʌɪsˈriːgli,
ˌvʌɪsˈriːgəli
AM ˌvaɪsˈrigəli

vicereine
BR ˌvʌɪsˈreɪn,
ˈvʌɪsreɪn, -z
AM ˈvaɪsˌreɪn, -z

viceroy
BR ˈvʌɪsrɔɪ, -z
AM ˈvaɪsˌrɔɪ, -z

viceroyal
BR ˌvʌɪsˈrɔɪ(ə)l
AM ˌvaɪsˈrɔɪəl

viceroyalty
BR ˌvʌɪsˈrɔɪ(ə)lti
AM ˌvaɪsˈrɔɪəlti

viceroyship
BR ˈvʌɪsrɔɪʃɪp, -s
AM ˈvaɪsˌrɔɪˌʃɪp, -s

vicesimal
BR vʌɪˈsesɪml
AM vaɪˈsesɪml

vice versa
BR ˌvʌɪs(ɪ) ˈvəːsə(r)
AM ˈvaɪs(ə) ˈvərsə,
ˈvaɪs(i) +

Vichy
BR ˈviːʃi
AM ˈviːʃi

vichyssoise
BR ˌviːʃɪˈswɑːz
AM ˌviːʃiˈswaz,
ˈviːʃiˈswaz

vicinage
BR ˈvɪsɪn|ɪdʒ, -ɪdʒɪz
AM ˈvɪsn̩ɪdʒ, -ɪz

vicinal
BR ˈvɪsɪnl, ˈvɪsn̩l
AM ˈvɪsənəl

vicinity
BR vɪˈsɪnɪti
AM vəˈsɪnɪdi, -z

vicious
BR ˈvɪʃəs
AM ˈvɪʃəs

viciously
BR ˈvɪʃəsli
AM ˈvɪʃəsli

viciousness
BR ˈvɪʃəsnəs
AM ˈvɪʃəsnəs

vicissitude
BR vɪˈsɪsɪtjuːd,
vɪˈsɪsɪtʃuːd,
vʌɪˈsɪsɪtjuːd,
vʌɪˈsɪsɪtʃuːd, -z
AM vəˈsɪsəˌt(j)ud, -z

vicissitudinous
BR vɪˌsɪsɪˈtjuːdɪnəs,
vɪˌsɪsɪˈtʃuːdɪnəs,
vʌɪˌsɪsɪˈtjuːdɪnəs,
vʌɪˌsɪsɪˈtʃuːdɪnəs
AM vəˌsɪsəˈt(j)udənəs

Vick
BR vɪk
AM vɪk

Vickers
BR ˈvɪkəz
AM ˈvɪkərz

Vickery
BR ˈvɪk(ə)ri
AM ˈvɪk(ə)ri

Vicki
BR ˈvɪki
AM ˈvɪki

Vickie
BR ˈvɪki
AM ˈvɪki

Vicksburg
BR ˈvɪksbəːg
AM ˈvɪksˌbərg

Vicky
BR ˈvɪki
AM ˈvɪki

Vico
BR ˈvɪkəʊ
AM ˈvikoʊ

vicomte
BR viːˈkɒ̃t, ˈviːkɒmt
AM ˈvaɪˌkɒnt

vicomtesse
BR ˌviːkɒ̃ˈtes,
ˌviːkɒnˈtes
AM ˈvaɪˌkaʊn(t)əs

victim
BR ˈvɪktɪm, -z
AM ˈvɪktɪm, -z

victimhood
BR ˈvɪktɪmhʊd
AM ˈvɪktɪm,(h)ʊd

victimisation
BR ˌvɪktɪmʌɪˈzeɪʃn
AM ˌvɪktəməˈzeɪʃən,
ˌvɪktəˌmaɪˈzeɪʃən

victimise
BR ˈvɪktɪmʌɪz, -ɪz, -ɪŋ, -d
AM ˈvɪktəˌmaɪz, -ɪz, -ɪŋ, -d

victimiser
BR ˈvɪktɪmʌɪzə(r), -z
AM ˈvɪktəˌmaɪzər, -z

victimization
BR ˌvɪktɪmʌɪˈzeɪʃn
AM ˌvɪktəməˈzeɪʃən,
ˌvɪktəˌmaɪˈzeɪʃən

victimize
BR ˈvɪktɪmʌɪz, -ɪz, -ɪŋ, -d
AM ˈvɪktəˌmaɪz, -ɪz, -ɪŋ, -d

victimizer
BR ˈvɪktɪmʌɪzə(r), -z
AM ˈvɪktəˌmaɪzər, -z

victimless
BR ˈvɪktɪmlɪs
AM ˈvɪktɪmlɪs

victimology
BR ˌvɪktɪˈmɒlədʒ|i, -ɪz
AM ˌvɪktəˈmɑlədʒi, -z

victor
BR ˈvɪktə(r), -z
AM ˈvɪktər, -z

victoria
BR vɪkˈtɔːrɪə(r), -z
AM vɪkˈtɔriə, -z

Victorian
BR vɪkˈtɔːrɪən, -z
AM vɪkˈtɔriən, -z

Victoriana
BR vɪkˌtɔːrɪˈɑːnə(r)
AM vɪkˌtɔriˈɑnə

Victorianism
BR vɪkˈtɔːrɪənɪz(ə)m,
-z
AM vɪkˈtɔriəˌnɪzəm, -z

victorious
BR vɪkˈtɔːrɪəs
AM vɪkˈtɔriəs

victoriously
BR vɪkˈtɔːrɪəsli
AM vɪkˈtɔriəsli

victoriousness
BR vɪkˈtɔːrɪəsnəs
AM vɪkˈtɔriəsnəs

victory
BR ˈvɪkt(ə)r|i, -ɪz
AM ˈvɪkt(ə)ri, -z

Victrola®
BR vɪkˈtrəʊlə(r)
AM vɪkˈtroʊlə

victual
BR ˈvɪtl̩, -z, -ɪŋ, -d
AM ˈvɪdl̩, -z, -ɪŋ, -d

victualler
BR ˈvɪtlə(r), -z
AM ˈvɪdlər, -z

victualless
BR ˈvɪtl̩lɪs
AM ˈvɪdl̩(l)ɪs

vicuna
BR vɪˈk(j)uːn(j)ə(r),
vʌɪˈk(j)uːn(j)ə(r), -z
AM vaɪˈk(j)unə,
vəˈk(j)unə, -z

vicuña
BR vɪˈk(j)uːn(j)ə(r),
vʌɪˈk(j)uːn(j)ə(r), -z
AM vaɪˈk(j)unə,
vəˈk(j)unə, -z

vid
video
BR vɪd, -z
AM vɪd, -z

Vidal
BR vɪˈdɑːl
AM vəˈdɑl

vide
BR ˈvʌɪdi, ˈvɪdi, ˈviːdi,
ˈvɪdeɪ, ˈviːdeɪ
AM ˈvidi, ˈvideɪ

videlicet
BR vɪˈdiːlɪsɛt,
vɪˈdiːlɪkɛt, vɪˈdeɪlɪsɛt,
vɪˈdeɪlɪkɛt, vɪˈdɛlɪsɛt,
vɪˈdɛlɪkɛt
AM vəˈdɛləˌsɛt,
vəˈdɛləsət,
vəˈdeɪləˌkɛt

video
BR ˈvɪdɪəʊ, -z, -ɪŋ, -d
AM ˈvɪdioʊ, -z, -ɪŋ, -d

videocassette
BR ˈvɪdɪəʊkəˌsɛt, -s
AM ˈvɪdioʊkəˈsɛt, -s

videoconferencing
BR ˌvɪdɪəʊˈkɒnf(ə)rən-
sɪŋ,
ˌvɪdɪəʊˈkɒnf(ə)rn̩sɪŋ
AM ˌvɪdioʊˈkɑnf(ə)rən-
sɪŋ

videodisc
BR ˈvɪdɪəʊdɪsk, -s
AM ˈvɪdioʊˌdɪsk, -s

videodisk
BR ˈvɪdɪəʊdɪsk, -s
AM ˈvɪdioʊˌdɪsk, -s

video nasty
BR ˌvɪdɪəʊ ˈnɑːstǀi, +
ˈnastǀi, -ɪz
AM ˌvɪdioʊ ˈnæsti, -z

videophile
BR ˈvɪdɪə(ʊ)fʌɪl, -z
AM ˈvɪdiəˌfaɪl, -z

videophone
BR ˈvɪdɪə(ʊ)fəʊn, -z
AM ˈvɪdioʊˌfoʊn, -z

videorecorder
BR ˈvɪdɪəʊrɪˌkɔːdə(r),
-z
AM ˈvɪdioʊrəˈkɔrdər,
-z

videorecording
BR ˈvɪdɪəʊrɪˌkɔːdɪŋ, -z
AM ˈvɪdioʊrəˈkɔrdɪŋ,
-z

videotape
BR ˈvɪdɪə(ʊ)teɪp, -s, -ɪŋ,
-t
AM ˈvɪdioʊˌteɪp, -s, -ɪŋ,
-t

videotex
BR ˈvɪdɪə(ʊ)tɛks
AM ˈvɪdioʊˌtɛks

videotext
BR ˈvɪdɪə(ʊ)tɛkst
AM ˈvɪdioʊˌtɛkst

vidimus
BR ˈvʌɪdɪməs, -ɪz
AM ˈvɪdɪməs,
ˈvaɪdɪməs, -əz

vie
BR vʌɪ, -z, -ɪŋ, -d
AM vaɪ, -z, -ɪŋ, -d

vielle
BR vɪˈɛl, -z
AM viˈɛl, -z

Vienna
BR vɪˈɛnə(r)

AM ˌviˈɛnə

Viennese
BR ˌviːəˈniːz
AM ˌviəˈniz

Vientiane
BR vjɛnˈtjɑːn,
vɪˌɛntɪˈɑːn
AM vjɛnˈtjɑn,
vɪˌɛntɪˈɑn

Vietcong
BR ˌvjɛtˈkɒŋ, vɪˌɛtˈkɒŋ
AM viˈɛtˈkɒŋ, ˈvjɛtˈkɒŋ,
viˈɛtˈkɑŋ, ˈvjɛtˈkɑŋ

Vietminh
BR ˌvjɛtˈmɪn, vɪˌɛtˈmɪn
AM viˈɛtˈmɪn,
ˈvjɛtˈmɪn

Vietnam
BR ˌvjɛtˈnam,
vɪˌɛtˈnam
AM viˈɛtˈnam,
vjɛtˈnam, viˈɛtˈnæm,
vjɛtˈnæm

Vietnamese
BR ˌvjɛtnəˈmiːz,
vɪˌɛtnəˈmiːz
AM vɪˌɛtnəˈmiz,
ˌvjɛtnəˈmiz

vieux jeu
BR vjə ˈʒə
AM vjə ˈʒə

view
BR vjuː, -z, -ɪŋ, -d
AM vju, -z, -ɪŋ, -d

viewable
BR ˈvjuːəbl
AM ˈvjuəbəl

viewdata
BR ˈvjuːˌdeɪtə(r),
ˈvjuːˌdɑːtə(r)
AM ˈvjuˌdædə,
ˈvjuˌdeɪdə

viewer
BR ˈvjuːə(r), -z
AM ˈvjuər, -z

viewership
BR ˈvjuːəʃɪp
AM ˈvjuərˌʃɪp

viewfinder
BR ˈvjuːˌfʌɪndə(r), -z
AM ˈvjuˌfaɪndər, -z

viewgraph
BR ˈvjuːˌgrɑːf,
ˈvjuːˌgraf, -s
AM ˈvjuˌgræf, -s

viewing
BR ˈvjuːwɪŋ, -z
AM ˈvjuwɪŋ, -z

viewless
BR ˈvjuːləs
AM ˈvjuləs

viewpoint
BR ˈvjuːpɔɪnt, -s
AM ˈvjuˌpɔɪnt, -s

viewport
BR ˈvjuːpɔːt, -s
AM ˈvjuˌpɔ(ə)rt, -s

viewscreen
BR ˈvjuːskriːn, -z
AM ˈvjuˌskrin, -z

vigesimal
BR vʌɪˈdʒɛsɪml
AM vaɪˈdʒɛsəml

vigesimally
BR vʌɪˈdʒɛsɪml̩i,
vʌɪˈdʒɛsəməli
AM vaɪˈdʒɛsəmli

vigil
BR ˈvɪdʒ(ɪ)l, -z
AM ˈvɪdʒɪl, -z

vigilance
BR ˈvɪdʒɪləns,
ˈvɪdʒɪlns, ˈvɪdʒl̩(ə)ns
AM ˈvɪdʒələns

vigilant
BR ˈvɪdʒɪlənt, ˈvɪdʒɪln̩t,
ˈvɪdʒl̩(ə)nt
AM ˈvɪdʒələnt

vigilante
BR ˌvɪdʒɪˈlantǀi, -ɪz
AM ˌvɪdʒəˈlæn(t)i, -z

vigilantism
BR ˌvɪdʒɪˈlantɪz(ə)m
AM ˌvɪdʒəˈlæn(t)(i)-
ˌɪzəm

vigilantly
BR ˈvɪdʒɪləntli,
ˈvɪdʒɪln̩tli,
ˈvɪdʒl̩(ə)ntli
AM ˈvɪdʒələn(t)li

vigneron
BR ˈviːnjərɒn, -z
AM ˌvɪnjəˈrɒn,
ˌvɪnjəˈroʊn, -z

vignette
BR viːˈnjɛt, vɪˈnjɛt, -s
AM vɪnˈjɛt, -s

vignetter
BR viːˈnjɛtə(r),
vɪˈnjɛtə(r), -z
AM vɪnˈjɛdər, -z

vignettist
BR viːˈnjɛtɪst,
vɪˈnjɛtɪst, -s
AM vɪnˈjɛdəst, -s

Vignola
BR vɪˈnjəʊlə(r)
AM vɪnˈjoʊlə

Vigo
BR ˈviːɡəʊ
AM ˈviɡoʊ

vigor
BR ˈvɪɡə(r)
AM ˈvɪɡər

vigorish
BR ˈvɪɡ(ə)rɪʃ
AM ˈvɪɡərɪʃ

vigorless
BR ˈvɪɡələs
AM ˈvɪɡərləs

vigoro
BR ˈvɪɡ(ə)rəʊ
AM ˈvɪɡəˌroʊ

vigorous
BR ˈvɪɡ(ə)rəs

AM ˈvɪɡ(ə)rəs

vigorously
BR ˈvɪɡ(ə)rəsli
AM ˈvɪɡ(ə)rəsli

vigorousness
BR ˈvɪɡ(ə)rəsnəs
AM ˈvɪɡ(ə)rəsnəs

vigour
BR ˈvɪɡə(r)
AM ˈvɪɡər

vigourless
BR ˈvɪɡələs
AM ˈvɪɡərləs

vihara
BR vɪˈhɑːrə(r), -z
AM vəˈhɑrə, -z

vihuela
BR vɪˈ(h)weɪlə(r), -z
AM vɪˈ(h)weɪlə, -z

Viking
BR ˈvʌɪkɪŋ, -z
AM ˈvaɪkɪŋ, -z

Vikki
BR ˈvɪki
AM ˈvɪki

Vila
BR ˈviːlə(r)
AM ˈvilə

vilayet
BR vɪˈlɑːjɛt, -s
AM ˌvɪləˈjɛt, -s

vile
BR vʌɪl, -ə(r), -ɪst
AM vaɪl, -ər, -ɪst

Vileda
BR vʌɪˈliːdə(r)
AM vaɪˈlidə

vilely
BR ˈvʌɪlli
AM ˈvaɪl(l)li

vileness
BR ˈvʌɪlnɪs
AM ˈvaɪlnɪs

vilification
BR ˌvɪlɪfɪˈkeɪʃn
AM ˌvɪləfəˈkeɪʃən

vilifier
BR ˈvɪlɪfʌɪə(r), -z
AM ˈvɪləˌfaɪər, -z

vilify
BR ˈvɪlɪfʌɪ, -z, -ɪŋ, -d
AM ˈvɪləˌfaɪ, -z, -ɪŋ, -d

vill
BR vɪl, -z
AM vɪl, -z

Villa
Pancho
BR vɪˈlɑː(r), vɪˈjɑː(r)
AM ˈvɪjə
SP ˈbija

villa
BR ˈvɪlə(r), -z
AM ˈvɪlə, -z

village
BR ˈvɪlǀɪdʒ, -ɪdʒɪz
AM ˈvɪlɪdʒ, -ɪz

villager
BR 'vɪlɪdʒə(r), -z
AM 'vɪlɪdʒər, -z

villagey
BR 'vɪlɪdʒi
AM 'vɪlɪdʒi

villagisation
BR ˌvɪlɪdʒʌɪ'zeɪʃn
AM ˌvɪlɪdʒə'zeɪʃən,
ˌvɪlɪˌdʒaɪ'zeɪʃən

villagization
BR ˌvɪlɪdʒʌɪ'zeɪʃn
AM ˌvɪlɪdʒə'zeɪʃən,
ˌvɪlɪˌdʒaɪ'zeɪʃən

villain
BR 'vɪlən, -z
AM 'vɪlən, -z

villainess
BR 'vɪlənɪs, -ɪz
AM 'vɪlənəs, -əz

villainous
BR 'vɪlənəs
AM 'vɪlənəs

villainously
BR 'vɪlənəsli
AM 'vɪlənəsli

villainousness
BR 'vɪlənəsnəs
AM 'vɪlənəsnəs

villainy
BR 'vɪlən|i, -ɪz
AM 'vɪləni, -z

Villa-Lobos
BR ˌvɪlə'lɒbɒs,
ˌvɪlə'ləʊbɒs
AM ˌvɪlə'loʊˌboʊs

villanella
BR ˌvɪlə'nɛlə(r), -z
AM ˌvɪlə'nɛlə, -z

villanelle
BR ˌvɪlə'nɛl, -z
AM ˌvɪlə'nɛl, -z

villeggiatura
BR vɪˌledʒ(ɪ)ə't(j)ʊə-
rə(r)
AM vəˌledʒə'tʊrə

villeggiature
BR vɪˌledʒ(ɪ)ə't(j)ʊəreɪ
AM vəˌledʒə'tʊreɪ

villein
BR 'vɪlɪn, 'vɪleɪn, -z
AM 'vɪlɪn, və'leɪn, -z

villeinage
BR 'vɪlɪnɪdʒ
AM 'vɪlɪnɪdʒ,
və'leɪnɪdʒ

villenage
BR 'vɪlɪnɪdʒ
AM 'vɪlɪnɪdʒ,
və'leɪnɪdʒ

villi
BR 'vɪlʌɪ
AM 'vi:ˌlaɪ, 'vɪli

villiform
BR 'vɪlɪfɔːm
AM 'vɪlɪˌfɔ(ə)rm

Villon
BR vi:'jɒ̃

AM vi'joʊn

villose
BR 'vɪləʊs
AM 'vɪˌloʊs, 'vɪˌloʊz

villosity
BR vɪ'lɒsɪt|i, -ɪz
AM və'lɑsədi, -z

villous
BR 'vɪləs
AM 'vɪləs

villously
BR 'vɪləsli
AM 'vɪləsli

villus
BR 'vɪləs
AM 'vɪləs

Vilnius
BR 'vɪlnɪəs
AM 'vɪlnɪəs

vim
BR vɪm
AM vɪm

vimineous
BR vɪ'mɪnɪəs
AM və'mɪnɪəs

vin
BR vã, van
AM væn

vina
BR 'vi:nə(r), -z
AM 'vinə, -z

vinaceous
BR vʌɪ'neɪʃəs,
vɪ'neɪʃəs
AM və'neɪʃəs,
vaɪ'neɪʃəs

vinaigrette
BR ˌvɪnɪ'grɛt, -s
AM ˌvɪnə'grɛt, -s

vinca
BR 'vɪŋkə(r), -z
AM 'vɪŋkə, -z

Vince
BR vɪns
AM vɪns

Vincent
BR 'vɪns(ə)nt
AM 'vɪnsənt

Vinci
BR 'vɪn(t)ʃi
AM 'vɪn(t)ʃi

vincibility
BR ˌvɪnsɪ'bɪlɪti
AM ˌvɪnsə'bɪlɪdi

vincible
BR 'vɪnsɪbl
AM 'vɪnsəbəl

vincula
BR 'vɪŋkjʉlə(r)
AM 'vɪŋkjələ

vinculum
BR 'vɪŋkjʉləm, -z
AM 'vɪŋkjələm, -z

vindaloo
BR ˌvɪndə'luː, -z
AM ˌvɪndə'lu, -z

vindicability
BR ˌvɪndɪkə'bɪlɪti
AM ˌvɪndəkə'bɪlɪdi

vindicable
BR 'vɪndɪkəbl
AM 'vɪndəkəbəl

vindicate
BR 'vɪndɪkeɪt, -s, -ɪŋ,
-ɪd
AM 'vɪndəˌkeɪ|t, -ts,
-dɪŋ, -dɪd

vindication
BR ˌvɪndɪ'keɪʃn
AM ˌvɪndə'keɪʃən

vindicative
BR vɪn'dɪkətɪv,
'vɪndɪkeɪtɪv
AM vɪn'dɪkədɪv,
'vɪndəˌkeɪdɪv

vindicator
BR 'vɪndɪkeɪtə(r), -z
AM 'vɪndəˌkeɪdər, -z

vindicatory
BR vɪn'dɪkət(ə)ri,
'vɪndɪkeɪt(ə)ri
AM 'vɪndəkəˌtɔri

vindictive
BR vɪn'dɪktɪv
AM vin'dɪktɪv

vindictively
BR vɪn'dɪktɪvli
AM vin'dɪktɪvli

vindictiveness
BR vɪn'dɪktɪvnɪs
AM vin'dɪktɪvnɪs

vine
BR vʌɪn, -z
AM vaɪn, -z

vine-dresser
BR 'vʌɪnˌdrɛsə(r), -z
AM 'vaɪnˌdrɛsər, -z

vine-dressing
BR 'vʌɪnˌdrɛsɪŋ
AM 'vaɪnˌdrɛsɪŋ

vinegar
BR 'vɪnɪgə(r), -d
AM 'vɪnəgər, -d

vinegarish
BR 'vɪnɪg(ə)rɪʃ
AM 'vɪnəg(ə)rɪʃ

vinegary
BR 'vɪnɪg(ə)ri
AM 'vɪnəg(ə)ri

Viner
BR 'vʌɪnə(r)
AM 'vaɪnər

vinery
BR 'vʌɪn(ə)r|i, -ɪz
AM 'vaɪnəri, -z

vinestock
BR 'vʌɪnstɒk, -s
AM 'vaɪnˌstɑk, -s

vineyard
BR 'vɪnjəd, 'vɪnjɑːd, -z
AM 'vɪnjərd, -z

vingt-et-un
BR ˌvãteɪ'ə:ŋ,
ˌvanteɪ'ə:ŋ,
ˌvanteɪ'ə:n
AM 'vænteɪ'ən

vinho verde
BR ˌviːnəʊ 'vəːd|i, -ɪz
AM 'vɪnjoʊ 'vərdi, -z

vinicultural
BR ˌvɪnɪ'kʌltʃ(ə)rəl,
ˌvɪnɪ'kʌltʃ(ə)rl
AM ˌvɪnə'kəltʃ(ə)rəl

viniculture
BR 'vɪnɪˌkʌltʃə(r)
AM 'vɪnəˌkəltʃər

viniculturist
BR ˌvɪnɪ'kʌltʃ(ə)rɪst,
-s
AM ˌvɪnə'kəltʃ(ə)rəst,
-s

vinification
BR ˌvɪnɪfɪ'keɪʃn
AM ˌvɪnəfə'keɪʃən

vinify
BR 'vɪnɪfʌɪ, -z, -ɪŋ, -d
AM 'vɪnəˌfaɪ, -z, -ɪŋ, -d

vining
BR 'vʌɪnɪŋ
AM 'vaɪnɪŋ

Vinland
BR 'vɪnlənd, 'vɪnland
AM 'vɪnlənd

Vinney
BR 'vɪni
AM 'vɪni

Vinnitsa
BR 'vɪnɪtsə(r)
AM 'vɪnətsə

vino
BR 'viːnəʊ, -z
AM 'vinoʊ, -z

vin ordinaire
BR ˌvã ˌɔːdɪ'nɛː(r),
ˌvan +, -z
AM 'væn ˌɔrdɪ'nɛ(ə)r,
-z

vinosity
BR vʌɪ'nɒsɪti,
vɪ'nɒsɪti
AM və'nɑsədi

vinous
BR 'vʌɪnəs
AM 'vaɪnəs

vin rosé
BR ˌvã 'rəʊzeɪ, ˌvan +,
-z
AM 'væn roʊ'zeɪ, -z

vint
BR vɪnt, -s, -ɪŋ, -ɪd
AM vɪn|t, -ts, -(t)ɪŋ,
-(t)ɪd

vintage
BR 'vɪnt|ɪdʒ, -ɪdʒɪz
AM 'vɪn(t)ɪdʒ, -ɪz

vintager
BR 'vɪntɪdʒə(r), -z
AM 'vɪn(t)ɪdʒər, -z

vintner
BR 'vɪntnə(r), -z
AM 'vɪntnər, -z

viny
BR 'vaɪn|i, -ɪə(r), -ɪɪst
AM 'vaɪni, -ər, -ɪst

vinyl
BR 'vaɪn(ɪ)l
AM 'vaɪnl

viol
BR 'vaɪəl, -z
AM 'vaɪ(ə)l, -z

Viola
BR 'vaɪələ(r), 'vɪələ(r), vaɪ'əʊlə(r)
AM vi'oʊlə

viola¹
flower
BR 'vaɪələ(r), 'vɪələ(r), vaɪ'əʊlə(r), -z
AM vaɪ'oʊlə, 'vaɪələ, -z

viola²
musical instrument
BR vɪ'əʊlə(r), -z
AM vi'oʊlə, -z

violable
BR 'vaɪələbl
AM 'vaɪələbəl

violaceous
BR ˌvaɪə'leɪʃəs
AM ˌvaɪə'leɪʃəs

violate
BR 'vaɪəleɪt, -s, -ɪŋ, -ɪd-
AM 'vaɪəˌlaɪt, -ts, -dɪŋ, -dɪd

violation
BR ˌvaɪə'leɪʃn, -z
AM ˌvaɪə'leɪʃən, -z

violator
BR 'vaɪəleɪtə(r), -z
AM 'vaɪəˌleɪdər, -z

violence
BR 'vaɪələns, 'vaɪəlŋs
AM 'vaɪ(ə)ləns

violent
BR 'vaɪələnt, 'vaɪəlŋt
AM 'vaɪ(ə)lənt

violently
BR 'vaɪələntli, 'vaɪəlŋtli
AM 'vaɪ(ə)lən(t)li

violet
BR 'vaɪələt, -s
AM 'vaɪ(ə)lət, -s

violin
BR ˌvaɪə'lɪn, -z
AM ˌvaɪə'lɪn, -z

violinist
BR ˌvaɪə'lɪnɪst, -s
AM ˌvaɪə'lɪnɪst, -s

violist
BR 'vaɪəlɪst, -s
AM vi'oʊləst, -s

violoncellist
BR ˌvaɪələn'tʃɛlɪst, -s
AM ˌvaɪələn'tʃɛləst, -s

violoncello
BR ˌvaɪələn'tʃɛləʊ, -z
AM ˌvaɪələn'tʃɛloʊ, -z

violone
BR 'vaɪələʊn, 'viːələʊn, ˌviːə'ləʊneɪ, -z
AM ˌviə'loʊˌneɪ, -z

VIP
BR ˌviːaɪ'piː, -z
AM ˌviˌaɪ'pi, -z

viper
BR 'vaɪpə(r), -z
AM 'vaɪpər, -z

viperiform
BR 'vaɪp(ə)rɪfɔːm
AM 'vaɪpərəˌfɔ(ə)rm

viperine
BR 'vaɪpərʌɪn
AM 'vaɪpərən, 'vaɪpəˌraɪn

viperish
BR 'vaɪp(ə)rɪʃ
AM 'vaɪpərɪʃ

viper-like
BR 'vaɪpəlʌɪk
AM 'vaɪpərˌlaɪk

viperous
BR 'vaɪp(ə)rəs
AM 'vaɪp(ə)rəs

virago
BR vɪ'rɑːgəʊ, -z
AM və'rɑgoʊ, -z

viral
BR 'vaɪrəl, 'vaɪrl
AM 'vaɪrəl

virally
BR 'vaɪrl̩i, 'vaɪrəli
AM 'vaɪrəli

virelay
BR 'vɪrɪleɪ, -z
AM 'vɪrəˌleɪ, -z

virement
BR 'vaɪəm(ə)nt, 'vɪəmɒ̃, -s
AM 'vɪrmɑn, -s

vireo
BR 'vɪriəʊ, -z
AM 'vɪrioʊ, -z

vires
BR 'vaɪriːz
AM 'vaɪˌriz

virescence
BR vɪ'rɛsns, vaɪ'rɛsns
AM və'rɛsns, vaɪ'rɛsəns

virescent
BR vɪ'rɛsnt, vaɪ'rɛsnt
AM və'rɛsnt, vaɪ'rɛsənt

virgate
BR 'vɜːgət, 'vɜːgeɪt, -s
AM 'vɜrgət, 'vɜrˌgeɪt, -s

virger
BR 'vɜːdʒə(r), -z
AM 'vɜrdʒər, -z

Virgil
BR 'vɜːdʒ(ɪ)l
AM 'vɜrdʒəl

Virgilian
BR və'dʒɪliən
AM vər'dʒɪljən, vər'dʒɪliən

virgin
BR 'vɜːdʒɪn, -z
AM 'vɜrdʒən, -z

virginal
BR 'vɜːdʒɪnl, -z
AM 'vɜrdʒənəl, -z

virginalist
BR 'vɜːdʒɪnlɪst, -s
AM 'vɜrdʒənləst, -s

virginally
BR 'vɜːdʒɪnli
AM 'vɜrdʒ(ə)nəli

virginhood
BR 'vɜːdʒɪnhʊd
AM 'vɜrdʒən,(h)ʊd

Virginia
BR və'dʒɪnɪə(r)
AM vər'dʒɪnjə

Virginian
BR və'dʒɪnɪən, -z
AM vər'dʒɪnjən, -z

virginibus puerisque
BR vəˌgɪnɪbəs p(j)ʊə'rɪskwi, vəˌdʒɪnɪbəs
AM vərˌdʒɪnəbəs p(j)ʊə'rɪsˌkwi

Virgin Islands
BR 'vɜːdʒɪn ˌʌɪlən(d)z
AM 'vɜrdʒən ˌaɪlən(d)z

virginity
BR və'dʒɪnɪti, və:'dʒɪnɪti
AM vər'dʒɪnɪdi

Virgo
BR 'vɜːgəʊ, -z
AM 'vɜrgoʊ, -z

Virgoan
BR 'vɜːgəʊən, -z
AM 'vɜrgoʊən, -z

virgule
BR 'vɜːgjuːl, -z
AM 'vɜrˌgjul, -z

viridescence
BR ˌvɪrɪ'dɛsns
AM ˌvɪrə'dɛsəns

viridescent
BR ˌvɪrɪ'dɛsnt
AM ˌvɪrə'dɛsənt

viridian
BR vɪ'rɪdɪən
AM və'rɪdiən

viridity
BR vɪ'rɪdɪti
AM və'rɪdɪdi

virile
BR 'vɪrʌɪl
AM 'vɪrəl

virilism
BR 'vɪrɪlɪz(ə)m
AM 'vɪrəˌlɪzəm

virility
BR vɪ'rɪlɪti
AM və'rɪlɪdi

viroid
BR 'vaɪrɔɪd, 'vɪrɔɪd, -z
AM 'vaɪˌrɔɪd, -z

Virol
BR 'vaɪrɒl
AM 'vaɪˌrɔl, 'vaɪˌrɑl

virological
BR ˌvaɪ(ə)rə'lɒdʒɪkl
AM ˌvaɪrə'lɑdʒəkəl

virologically
BR ˌvaɪ(ə)rə'lɒdʒɪkli
AM ˌvaɪrə'lɑdʒək(ə)li

virologist
BR vaɪ'rɒlədʒɪst, -s
AM vaɪ'rɑlədʒəst, -s

virology
BR vaɪ'rɒlədʒi
AM vaɪ'rɑlədʒi

virtu
BR vɜː'tuː
AM ˌvɜr'tu

virtual
BR 'vɜːtʃʊəl, 'vɜːtʃ(ʊ)l, 'vɜːtjʊəl, 'vɜːtjəl
AM 'vɜrtʃ(əw)əl

virtuality
BR ˌvɜːtʃʊ'alɪti, ˌvɜːtjʊ'alɪti
AM ˌvɜrtʃə'wælədi

virtually
BR 'vɜːtʃʊəli, 'vɜːtʃʊli, 'vɜːtʃli, 'vɜːtjʊəli, 'vɜːtjəli
AM 'vɜrtʃ(əw)əli

virtue
BR 'vɜːtʃuː, 'vɜːtjuː, -z
AM 'vɜrtʃu, -z

virtueless
BR 'vɜːtʃuːləs, 'vɜːtjuːləs
AM 'vɜrtʃuləs

virtuosic
BR ˌvɜːtʃʊ'ɒsɪk, ˌvɜːtjʊ'ɒsɪk
AM ˌvɜrtʃə'wɑsɪk

virtuosity
BR ˌvɜːtʃʊ'ɒsɪti, ˌvɜːtjʊ'ɒsɪti
AM ˌvɜrtʃə'wɑsədi

virtuoso
BR ˌvɜːtʃʊ'əʊzəʊ, ˌvɜːtʃʊ'əʊsəʊ, ˌvɜːtjʊ'əʊzəʊ, ˌvɜːtjʊ'əʊsəʊ, -z
AM ˌvɜrtʃə'woʊsoʊ, ˌvɜrtʃə'woʊzoʊ, -z

virtuosoship
BR ˌvɜːtʃʊ'əʊzəʊʃɪp, ˌvɜːtʃʊ'əʊsəʊʃɪp, ˌvɜːtjʊ'əʊzəʊʃɪp, ˌvɜːtjʊ'əʊsəʊʃɪp

virtuous
AM ˌvɜːtʃəˈwoʊsoʊˌʃɪp,
ˌvɜːtʃəˈwoʊzoʊˌʃɪp

virtuous
BR ˈvɜːtʃʊəs, ˈvɜːtjʊəs
AM ˈvɜːtʃ(əw)əs

virtuously
BR ˈvɜːtʃʊəs,
ˈvɜːtjʊəsli
AM ˈvɜːtʃ(əw)əsli

virtuousness
BR ˈvɜːtʃʊəsnəs,
ˈvɜːtjʊəsnəs
AM ˈvɜːtʃ(əw)əsnəs

virulence
BR ˈvɪr(j)ʊləns,
ˈvɪr(j)ʊlns
AM ˈvɪr(j)ələns

virulent
BR ˈvɪr(j)ʊlənt,
ˈvɪr(j)ʊlņt
AM ˈvɪr(j)ələnt

virulently
BR ˈvɪr(j)ʊləntli,
ˈvɪr(j)ʊlņtli
AM ˈvɪr(j)ələn(t)li

virus
BR ˈvaɪrəs, -ɪz
AM ˈvaɪrəs, -əz

vis
BR vɪs
AM vɪs

visa
BR ˈviːzə(r), -z
AM ˈviːzə, -z

visage
BR ˈvɪz|ɪdʒ, -ɪdʒɪz,
-ɪdʒd
AM ˈvɪzɪdʒ, -ɪz, -ɪdʒd

vis-à-vis
BR ˌviːzɑːˈviː, ˌviːzəˈviː
AM ˌviːzəˈvi

Visby
BR ˈvɪzbi
AM ˈvɪzbi

viscacha
BR vɪˈskɑːtʃə(r),
vɪˈskatʃə(r), -z
AM vɪˈskatʃə, -z

viscera
BR ˈvɪs(ə)rə(r)
AM ˈvɪsərə

visceral
BR ˈvɪs(ə)rəl, ˈvɪs(ə)rļ
AM ˈvɪs(ə)rəl

viscerally
BR ˈvɪs(ə)rəli,
ˈvɪs(ə)rļi
AM ˈvɪs(ə)rəli

viscerotonic
BR ˌvɪs(ə)rəˈtɒnɪk
AM ˌvɪsərəˈtɑnɪk

viscid
BR ˈvɪsɪd
AM ˈvɪsɪd

viscidity
BR vɪˈsɪdɪti
AM vəˈsɪdɪdi

viscometer
BR vɪsˈkɒmɪtə(r),
vɪˈskɒmɪtə(r), -z
AM vəˈskamədər, -z

viscometric
BR ˌvɪskəˈmɛtrɪk
AM ˌvɪskəˈmɛtrɪk

viscometrically
BR ˌvɪskəˈmɛtrɪkli
AM ˌvɪskəˈmɛtrək(ə)li

viscometry
BR vɪsˈkɒmɪtri,
vɪˈskɒmɪtri
AM vəˈskamətri

Visconti
BR vɪˈskɒnti
AM vəˈskɑn(t)i

viscose
BR ˈvɪskəʊs, ˈvɪskəʊz
AM ˈvɪskoʊs, ˈvɪskoʊz

viscosimeter
BR ˌvɪskəˈsɪmɪtə(r), -z
AM ˌvɪskəˈsɪmɪdər, -z

viscosity
BR vɪˈskɒsɪti
AM ˌvɪsˈkɑsədi

viscount
BR ˈvaɪkaʊnt, -s
AM ˈvaɪˌkaʊnt, -s

viscountcy
BR ˈvaɪkaʊn(t)s|i, -iz
AM ˈvaɪˌkaʊn(t)si, -z

viscountess
BR ˈvaɪkaʊntɪs,
ˈvaɪkaʊntes, -ɪz
AM ˈvaɪˌkaʊn(t)əs, -əz

viscountship
BR ˈvaɪkaʊntʃɪp, -s
AM ˈvaɪˌkaʊntˌʃɪp, -s

viscounty
BR ˈvaɪkaʊn(t)|i, -iz
AM ˈvaɪˌkaʊn(t)i, -z

viscous
BR ˈvɪskəs
AM ˈvɪskəs

viscously
BR ˈvɪskəsli
AM ˈvɪskəsli

viscousness
BR ˈvɪskəsnəs
AM ˈvɪskəsnəs

viscus
BR ˈvɪskəs
AM ˈvɪskəs

vise
BR vʌɪs, -ɪz
AM vaɪs, vaɪz, -ɪz

Vishnu
BR ˈvɪʃnuː
AM ˈvɪʃnu

Vishnuism
BR ˈvɪʃnuːɪz(ə)m,
ˈvɪʃnʊɪz(ə)m
AM ˈvɪʃnuˌɪzəm,
ˈvɪʃnəˌwɪzəm

Vishnuite
BR ˈvɪʃnuːʌɪt,
ˈvɪʃnʊʌɪt, -s
AM ˈvɪʃnuˌaɪt,
ˈvɪʃnəˌwaɪt, -s

visibility
BR ˌvɪzɪˈbɪlɪti
AM ˌvɪzəˈbɪlɪdi

visible
BR ˈvɪzɪbl
AM ˈvɪzəbəl

visibleness
BR ˈvɪzɪblnɪs
AM ˈvɪzəbəlnəs

visibly
BR ˈvɪzɪbli
AM ˈvɪzəbli

VisiCalc
BR ˈvɪzɪkalk
AM ˈvɪzɪˌkælk

Visigoth
BR ˈvɪzɪgɒθ, -s
AM ˈvɪzɪˌgɑθ, ˈvɪzɪˌgɑθ,
-s

Visigothic
BR ˌvɪzɪˈgɒθɪk
AM ˌvɪzɪˈgɑθɪk,
ˌvɪzɪˈgɑθɪk

vision
BR ˈvɪʒn, -z
AM ˈvɪʒən, -z

visional
BR ˈvɪʒn(ə)l, ˈvɪʒən(ə)l
AM ˈvɪʒ(ə)nəl

visionariness
BR ˈvɪʒņ(ə)rɪnɪs
AM ˈvɪʒəˌnɛrinɪs

visionary
BR ˈvɪʒņ(ə)r|i, -iz
AM ˈvɪʒəˌnɛri, -z

visionist
BR ˈvɪʒņɪst, ˈvɪʒənɪst, -s
AM ˈvɪʒənəst, -s

visionless
BR ˈvɪʒnləs
AM ˈvɪʒənləs

visit
BR ˈvɪz|ɪt, -ɪts, -ɪtɪŋ,
-ɪtɪd
AM ˈvɪzɪ|t, -ts, -dɪŋ, -dɪd

visitable
BR ˈvɪzɪtəbl
AM ˈvɪzɪdəbəl

visitant
BR ˈvɪzɪt(ə)nt, -s
AM ˈvɪzətnt, -s

visitation
BR ˌvɪzɪˈteɪ∫n, -z
AM ˌvɪzəˈteɪʃən, -z

visitatorial
BR ˌvɪzɪtəˈtɔːriəl
AM ˌvɪzədəˈtɔːriəl

visiting
BR ˈvɪzɪtɪŋ, -z
AM ˈvɪzɪdɪŋ, -z

visitor
BR ˈvɪzɪtə(r), -z

visitorial
BR ˌvɪzɪˈtɔːriəl
AM ˌvɪzəˈtɔːriəl

visna
BR ˈvɪznə(r)
AM ˈvɪznə

visor
BR ˈvaɪzə(r), -z, -d
AM ˈvaɪzər, -z, -d

visorless
BR ˈvaɪzələs
AM ˈvaɪzərləs

vista
BR ˈvɪstə(r), -z, -d
AM ˈvɪstə, -z, -d

Vistula
BR ˈvɪstjələ(r),
ˈvɪstʃələ(r)
AM ˈvɪstʃələ

visual
BR ˈvɪʒʊ(ə)l, ˈvɪzjʊ(ə)l,
ˈvɪʒ(ʊ)l, ˈvɪzj(ʊ)l
AM ˈvɪʒ(ə)wəl, ˈvɪʒəl

visualisable
BR ˈvɪʒjʊlʌɪzəbl,
ˈvɪʒjʊəlʌɪzəbl,
ˈvɪzjʊlʌɪzəbl,
ˈvɪzjʊəlʌɪzəbl
AM ˈvɪʒ(ə)wəˌlaɪzəbəl,
ˈvɪʒəˌlaɪzəbəl

visualisation
BR ˌvɪʒjʊlʌɪˈzeɪʃn,
ˌvɪzjʊlʌɪˈzeɪʃn
AM ˌvɪʒələˈzeɪʃən,
ˌvɪʒ(ə)wələˈzeɪʃən,
ˌvɪʒəˌlaɪˈzeɪʃən,
ˌvɪʒ(ə)wəˌlaɪˈzeɪʃən

visualise
BR ˈvɪʒjʊlʌɪz,
ˈvɪʒjʊəlʌɪz, ˈvɪzjʊlʌɪz,
ˈvɪzjʊəlʌɪz, -ɪz, -ɪŋ, -d
AM ˈvɪʒ(ə)wəˌlaɪz,
ˈvɪʒəˌlaɪz, -ɪz, -ɪŋ, -d

visuality
BR ˌvɪʒjʊˈalɪti,
ˌvɪzjʊˈalɪti
AM ˌvɪʒəˈwælədi

visualizable
BR ˈvɪʒjʊlʌɪzəbl,
ˈvɪʒjʊəlʌɪzəbl,
ˈvɪzjʊlʌɪzəbl,
ˈvɪzjʊəlʌɪzəbl
AM ˈvɪʒ(ə)wəˌlaɪzəbəl,
ˈvɪʒəˌlaɪzəbəl

visualization
BR ˌvɪʒjʊlʌɪˈzeɪʃn,
ˌvɪzjʊlʌɪˈzeɪʃn
AM ˌvɪʒələˈzeɪʃən,
ˌvɪʒ(ə)wələˈzeɪʃən,
ˌvɪʒəˌlaɪˈzeɪʃən,
ˌvɪʒ(ə)wəˌlaɪˈzeɪʃən

visualize
BR ˈvɪʒjʊlʌɪz,
ˈvɪʒjʊəlʌɪz, ˈvɪzjʊlʌɪz,
ˈvɪzjʊəlʌɪz, -ɪz, -ɪŋ, -d
AM ˈvɪʒ(ə)wəˌlaɪz,
ˈvɪʒəˌlaɪz, -ɪz, -ɪŋ, -d

visually
BR ˈvɪʒ(j)ʊəli,
ˈvɪʒ(j)ᵿli, ˈvɪzjʊəli,
ˈvɪzjᵿli
AM ˈvɪʒ(ə)wəli, ˈvɪʒəli

vita
BR ˈviːtə(r), ˈvaɪtə(r),
-z
AM ˈvidə, -z

vitae
BR ˈviːtʌɪ
AM ˈvidi, ˈviˌtaɪ

vital
BR ˈvaɪtl, -z
AM ˈvaɪdl, -z

vitalisation
BR ˌvaɪtəlʌɪˈzeɪʃn,
ˌvaɪtl̩ʌɪˈzeɪʃn
AM ˌvaɪdlə̩ˈzeɪʃən,
ˌvaɪdlˌaɪˈzeɪʃən

vitalise
BR ˈvaɪtəlʌɪz,
ˈvaɪtl̩ʌɪz, -ɪz, -ɪŋ, -d
AM ˈvaɪdlˌaɪz, -ɪz, -ɪŋ, -d

vitalism
BR ˈvaɪtəlɪz(ə)m,
ˈvaɪtl̩ɪz(ə)m
AM ˈvaɪdl̩ɪzəm

vitalist
BR ˈvaɪtəlɪst, ˈvaɪtl̩ɪst,
-s
AM ˈvaɪdl̩ɪst, -s

vitalistic
BR ˌvaɪtəˈlɪstɪk,
ˌvaɪtl̩ˈɪstɪk
AM ˈvaɪdl̩ˈɪstɪk

vitality
BR vaɪˈtaliti
AM vaɪˈtælədi

vitalization
BR ˌvaɪtəlʌɪˈzeɪʃn,
ˌvaɪtl̩ʌɪˈzeɪʃn
AM ˌvaɪdlə̩ˈzeɪʃən,
ˌvaɪdlˌaɪˈzeɪʃən

vitalize
BR ˈvaɪtəlʌɪz,
ˈvaɪtl̩ʌɪz, -ɪz, -ɪŋ, -d
AM ˈvaɪdl̩ˌaɪz, -ɪz, -ɪŋ, -d

vitally
BR ˈvaɪtəli, ˈvaɪtl̩i
AM ˈvaɪdl̩i

vitamin
BR ˈvɪtəmɪn,
ˈvʌɪtəmɪn, -z
AM ˈvaɪdəmən, -z

vitaminise
BR ˈvɪtəmɪnʌɪz,
ˈvʌɪtəmɪnʌɪz, -ɪz, -ɪŋ,
-d
AM ˈvaɪdəməˌnaɪz, -ɪz,
-ɪŋ, -d

vitaminize
BR ˈvɪtəmɪnʌɪz,
ˈvʌɪtəmɪnʌɪz, -ɪz, -ɪŋ,
-d
AM ˈvaɪdəməˌnaɪz, -ɪz,
-ɪŋ, -d

VitBe®
BR ˈvɪtbi
AM ˈvɪtbi

Vitebsk
BR vɪˈtɛbsk
AM vɪˈtɛbsk
RUS ˈvʲitʲipsk

vitellary
BR ˈvɪtl̩(ə)ri,
vɪˈtɛl(ə)ri,
vʌɪˈtɛl(ə)ri
AM vəˈtɛləri, ˈvaɪdl̩ˌɛri,
ˈvɪdlˌɛri, vaɪˈtɛləri

vitelli
BR vɪˈtɛlʌɪ, vʌɪˈtɛlʌɪ
AM vəˈtɛˌlaɪ, vaɪˈtɛˌlaɪ

vitellin
BR vɪˈtɛlɪn, vʌɪˈtɛlɪn
AM vəˈtɛlən, vaɪˈtɛlən

vitelline
BR vɪˈtɛlʌɪn,
vʌɪˈtɛlʌɪn, vɪˈtɛlɪn,
vʌɪˈtɛlɪn
AM vəˈtɛlən, vaɪˈtɛlən,
vaɪˈtɛlin, vəˈtɛlin,
vaɪˈtɛˌlaɪn, vəˈtɛˌlaɪn

Vitellius
BR vɪˈtɛliəs
AM vəˈtɛliəs

vitellus
BR vɪˈtɛləs, vʌɪˈtɛləs
AM vəˈtɛləs, vaɪˈtɛləs

vitiate
BR ˈvɪʃɪeɪt, -s, -ɪŋ, -ɪd
AM ˈvɪʃiˌeɪ|t, -ts, -dɪŋ,
-dɪd

vitiation
BR ˌvɪʃɪˈeɪʃn
AM ˌvɪʃiˈeɪʃən

vitiator
BR ˈvɪʃɪeɪtə(r), -z
AM ˈvɪʃiˌeɪdər, -z

viticultural
BR ˌvɪtɪˈkʌltʃ(ə)rəl,
ˌvɪtɪˈkʌltʃ(ə)rl̩
AM ˈvɪdəˌkəltʃ(ə)rəl

viticulturally
BR ˌvɪtɪˈkʌltʃ(ə)rəli,
ˌvɪtɪˈkʌltʃ(ə)rl̩i
AM ˈvɪdəˈkəltʃərəli

viticulture
BR ˈvɪtɪˌkʌltʃə(r)
AM ˈvɪdəˌkəltʃər

viticulturist
BR ˌvɪtɪˈkʌltʃ(ə)rɪst, -s
AM ˈvɪdəˌkəltʃ(ə)rəst,
-s

Viti Levu
BR ˌvɪtɪ ˈleɪvuː, + ˈlɛvuː
AM ˌvidi ˈlɛˌvu

vitiligo
BR ˌvɪtɪˈlʌɪgəʊ
AM ˌvɪdɪˈlaɪgoʊ

Vitoria
BR vɪˈtɔːrɪə(r)
AM vəˈtɔriə

Vitosha
BR vɪˈtəʊʃə(r)

AM vəˈtoʊʃə

vitreous
BR ˈvɪtrɪəs
AM ˈvɪtriəs

vitreousness
BR ˈvɪtrɪəsnəs
AM ˈvɪtriəsnəs

vitrescence
BR vɪˈtrɛsns
AM vəˈtrɛsəns

vitrescent
BR vɪˈtrɛsnt
AM vəˈtrɛsənt

vitrifaction
BR ˌvɪtrɪˈfakʃn
AM ˌvɪtrəˈfækʃən

vitrifiable
BR ˈvɪtrɪfʌɪəbl,
ˌvɪtrɪˈfʌɪəbl
AM ˈvɪtrəˌfaɪəbəl

vitrification
BR ˌvɪtrɪfɪˈkeɪʃn
AM ˌvɪtrəfəˈkeɪʃən

vitriform
BR ˈvɪtrɪfɔːm
AM ˈvɪtrəˌfɔ(ə)rm

vitrify
BR ˈvɪtrɪfʌɪ, -z, -ɪŋ, -d
AM ˈvɪtrəˌfaɪ, -z, -ɪŋ, -d

vitriol
BR ˈvɪtrɪəl, ˈvɪtrɪɒl
AM ˈvɪtriəl

vitriolic
BR ˌvɪtrɪˈɒlɪk
AM ˌvɪtriˈɑlɪk

vitro
BR ˈviːtrəʊ
AM ˈvɪˌtroʊ

Vitruvian
BR vɪˈtruːvɪən
AM vəˈtruviən

Vitruvius
BR vɪˈtruːvɪəs
AM vəˈtruviəs

vitta
BR ˈvɪtə(r)
AM ˈvɪdə

vittae
BR ˈvɪtiː
AM ˈvidi, ˈvɪˌtaɪ

vittate
BR ˈvɪteɪt
AM ˈvɪˌteɪt

vituperate
BR vɪˈtjuːpəreɪt,
vʌɪˈtjuːpəreɪt,
vɪˈtʃuːpəreɪt,
vʌɪˈtʃuːpəreɪt, -s, -ɪŋ,
-ɪd
AM vəˈt(j)upəˌreɪ|t,
vaɪˈt(j)upəˌreɪt, -ts,
-dɪŋ, -dɪd

vituperation
BR vɪˌtjuːpəˈreɪʃn,
vʌɪˌtjuːpəˈreɪʃn,
vɪˌtʃuːpəˈreɪʃn,
vʌɪˌtʃuːpəˈreɪʃn,

AM vəˌt(j)upəˈreɪʃən,
vaɪˌt(j)upəˈreɪʃən

vituperative
BR vɪˈtjuːp(ə)rətɪv,
vʌɪˈtjuːp(ə)rətɪv,
vɪˈtʃuːp(ə)rətɪv,
vʌɪˈtʃuːp(ə)rətɪv
AM vəˈt(j)upəˌreɪdɪv,
vaɪˈt(j)upəˌreɪdɪv,
vaɪˈt(j)up(ə)rədɪv,
vəˈt(j)up(ə)rədɪv

vituperatively
BR vɪˈtjuːp(ə)rətɪvli,
vʌɪˈtjuːp(ə)rətɪvli,
vɪˈtʃuːp(ə)rətɪvli,
vʌɪˈtʃuːp(ə)rətɪvli
AM vəˈt(j)upəˌreɪdɪvli,
vaɪˈt(j)upəˌreɪdɪvli,
vaɪˈt(j)up(ə)rədɪvli,
vəˈt(j)up(ə)rədɪvli

vituperator
BR vɪˈtjuːpəreɪtə(r),
vʌɪˈtjuːpəreɪtə(r),
vɪˈtʃuːpəreɪtə(r),
vʌɪˈtʃuːpəreɪtə(r), -z
AM vəˈt(j)upəˌreɪdər,
vaɪˈt(j)upəˌreɪdər, -z

Vitus
BR ˈvʌɪtəs
AM ˈvaɪdəs

Viv
BR vɪv
AM vɪv

vival¹
interjection
BR ˈviːvə(r)
AM ˈvivə

viva²
spoken examination
BR ˈvʌɪvə(r), -z
AM ˈvaɪvə, -z

vivace
BR vɪˈvɑːtʃi, vɪˈvɑːtʃeɪ
AM viˈvɑˌtʃei, viˈvɑˌtʃi

vivacious
BR vɪˈveɪʃəs
AM vəˈveɪʃəs

vivaciously
BR vɪˈveɪʃəsli
AM vəˈveɪʃəsli

vivaciousness
BR vɪˈveɪʃəsnəs
AM vəˈveɪʃəsnəs

vivacity
BR vɪˈvasɪti
AM vəˈvæsədi

Vivaldi
BR vɪˈvaldi
AM vəˈvɑldi

vivaria
BR vʌɪˈveːrɪə(r),
vɪˈvɛːrɪə(r)
AM vaɪˈvɛriə, vaɪˈvɛriə

vivarium
BR vʌɪˈveːrɪəm,
vɪˈvɛːrɪəm, -z
AM vəˈvɛriəm,
vaɪˈvɛriəm, -z

vivat
BR 'vʌɪvat
AM 'viˌvæt, 'vaɪˌvæt

viva-voce
BR ˌvʌɪvə'vəʊtʃ|i,
ˌviːvə'vəʊtʃi,
ˌvʌɪvə'vəʊs|i,
ˌviːvə'vəʊs|i, -ɪz, -ɪŋ,
-ɪd
AM ˌvivə'voʊtʃeɪ,
ˌvaɪvə 'voʊsi, -z, -ɪŋ, -t

vivax
BR 'vʌɪvaks
AM 'vaɪˌvæks

viverrid
BR vɪ'vɛrɪd, vʌɪ'vɛrɪd,
-z
AM vaɪ'vɛrəd,
və'vɛrəd, -z

viverrine
BR vɪ'vɛrʌɪn,
vʌɪ'vɛrʌɪn
AM vaɪ'vɛrən,
və'vɛrən, vaɪ'vɛˌraɪn,
və'vɛˌraɪn

vivers
BR 'vʌɪvəz
AM 'vaɪvərz

Vivian
BR 'vɪvɪən
AM 'vɪvɪən

vivid
BR 'vɪvɪd
AM 'vɪvɪd

vividly
BR 'vɪvɪdli
AM 'vɪvɪdli

vividness
BR 'vɪvɪdnɪs
AM 'vɪvɪdnɪs

Vivien
BR 'vɪvɪən
AM 'vɪvɪən

Vivienne
BR 'vɪvɪən, ˌvɪvɪ'ɛn
AM vɪvi'ɛn

vivification
BR ˌvɪvɪfɪ'keɪʃn
AM ˌvɪvəfə'keɪʃən

vivify
BR 'vɪvɪfʌɪ, -z, -ɪŋ, -d
AM 'vɪvəˌfaɪ, -z, -ɪŋ, -d

viviparity
BR ˌvɪvɪ'parɪti
AM ˌvɪvə'pɛrədi

viviparous
BR vɪ'vɪp(ə)rəs,
vʌɪ'vɪp(ə)rəs
AM və'vɪp(ə)rəs

viviparously
BR vɪ'vɪp(ə)rəsli,
vʌɪ'vɪp(ə)rəsli
AM və'vɪp(ə)rəsli

viviparousness
BR vɪ'vɪp(ə)rəsnəs,
vʌɪ'vɪp(ə)rəsnəs
AM və'vɪp(ə)rəsnəs

vivisect
BR 'vɪvɪsɛkt, -s, -ɪŋ, -ɪd
AM 'vɪvəˌsɛk|(t), -(t)s,
-tɪŋ, -təd

vivisection
BR ˌvɪvɪ'sɛkʃn,
'vɪvɪsɛkʃn
AM 'vɪvəˌsɛkʃən

vivisectional
BR ˌvɪvɪ'sɛkʃn(ə)l,
ˌvɪvɪ'sɛkʃən(ə)l
AM ˌvɪvə'sɛkʃ(ə)nəl

vivisectionist
BR ˌvɪvɪ'sɛkʃnɪst,
ˌvɪvɪ'sɛkʃənɪst, -s
AM ˌvɪvə'sɛkʃ(ə)nəst,
-s

vivisector
BR 'vɪvɪsɛktə(r), -z
AM 'vɪvəˌsɛktər, -z

vivo
BR 'viːvəʊ
AM 'viˌvoʊ

vixen
BR 'vɪks(ə)n, -z
AM 'vɪksən, -z

vixenish
BR 'vɪksənɪʃ, 'vɪksnɪʃ
AM 'vɪksənɪʃ

vixenly
BR 'vɪks(ə)nli
AM 'vɪksənli

Viyella®
BR 'vʌɪ'ɛlə(r)
AM ˌvaɪ'ɛlə

viz
BR VIZ
AM VIZ

vizard
BR 'vɪzəd, -z
AM 'vɪzərd, -z

vizcacha
BR vɪ'skɑːtʃə(r),
vɪz'kɑːtʃə(r),
vɪ'skatʃə(r),
vɪz'katʃə(r), -z
AM və'skatʃə, -z

vizier
BR vɪ'zɪə(r), 'vɪzɪə(r),
-z
AM və'zɪ(ə)r, -z

vizierate
BR vɪ'zɪərət, 'vɪzɪərət,
vɪ'zɪəreɪt, 'vɪzɪəreɪt,
-s
AM və'zɪrət, və'zɪˌreɪt,
-s

vizierial
BR vɪ'zɪərɪəl
AM və'zɪrɪəl

viziership
BR vɪ'zɪəʃɪp, 'vɪzɪəʃɪp,
-s
AM və'zɪrˌʃɪp, -s

vizor
BR 'vʌɪzə(r), -z
AM 'vaɪzər, -z

Vlach
BR vlɑːk, -s
AM vlɑk, vlæk, -s

Vlad
BR vlad
AM vlæd

Vladimir
BR 'vladɪmɪə(r)
AM 'vlædəˌmɪ(ə)r
RUS vla'dʲimʲir

Vladivostok
BR ˌvladɪ'vɒstɒk
AM ˌvlædə'vɑstɑk
RUS vlədʲiva'stok

vlei
BR fleɪ, vlʌɪ, -z
AM fleɪ, vleɪ, -z

Vlissingen
BR 'vlɪsɪŋən
AM 'vlɪsɪŋən

Vlorë
BR 'vlɔːrə(r)
AM 'vlɔrə

Vltava
BR 'v(ə)ltəvə(r)
AM 'vəldəvə

V-neck
BR 'viːˌnɛk, ˌviːˈnɛk, -s,
-t
AM 'viˌnɛk, -s, -t

vocab
BR 'vəʊkab, -z
AM 'voʊˌkæb, -z

vocable
BR 'vəʊkəbl, -z
AM 'voʊkəbəl, -z

vocabulary
BR və(ʊ)'kabjʊlər|i,
-ɪz
AM voʊ'kabjəˌlɛri,
və'kabjəˌlɛri, -z

vocal
BR 'vəʊkl
AM 'voʊkəl

vocalese
BR ˌvəʊkə'liːz,
ˌvəʊkl'iːz
AM voʊkəl'iz

vocalic
BR və(ʊ)'kalɪk
AM voʊ'kælɪk,
və'kælɪk

vocalisation
BR ˌvəʊkəlʌɪ'zeɪʃn,
ˌvəʊkl'ʌɪ'zeɪʃn, -z
AM ˌvoʊkələ'zeɪʃən,
ˌvoʊkəˌlaɪ'zeɪʃən, -z

vocalise
BR 'vəʊkəlʌɪz,
'vəʊklʌɪz, -ɪz, -ɪŋ, -d
AM 'voʊkəˌlaɪz, -ɪz, -ɪŋ,
-d

vocaliser
BR 'vəʊkəlʌɪzə(r),
'vəʊklʌɪzə(r), -z
AM 'voʊkəˌlaɪzər, -z

vocalism
BR 'vəʊkəlɪz(ə)m,
'vəʊklɪz(ə)m, -z
AM 'voʊkəˌlɪzəm, -z

vocalist
BR 'vəʊkəlɪst,
vəʊklɪst, -s
AM 'voʊkələst, -s

vocality
BR və(ʊ)'kalɪti
AM voʊ'kæledi

vocalization
BR ˌvəʊkəlʌɪ'zeɪʃn,
ˌvəʊklʌɪ'zeɪʃn, -z
AM ˌvoʊkələ'zeɪʃən,
ˌvoʊkəˌlaɪ'zeɪʃən, -z

vocalize
BR 'vəʊkəlʌɪz,
'vəʊklʌɪz, -ɪz, -ɪŋ, -d
AM 'voʊkəˌlaɪz, -ɪz, -ɪŋ,
-d

vocalizer
BR 'vəʊkəlʌɪzə(r),
'vəʊklʌɪzə(r), -z
AM 'voʊkəˌlaɪzər, -z

vocally
BR 'vəʊkli, 'vəʊkəli
AM 'voʊk(ə)li

vocation
BR və(ʊ)'keɪʃn, -z
AM voʊ'keɪʃən, -z

vocational
BR və(ʊ)'keɪʃn(ə)l,
və(ʊ)'keɪʃən(ə)l
AM voʊ'keɪʃ(ə)nəl

vocationalise
BR və(ʊ)'keɪʃnəlʌɪz,
və(ʊ)'keɪʃn̩lʌɪz,
və(ʊ)'keɪʃ(ə)nəlʌɪz,
-ɪz, -ɪŋ, -d
AM voʊ'keɪʃ(ə)nəˌlaɪz,
-ɪz, -ɪŋ, -d

vocationalism
BR və(ʊ)'keɪʃnəlɪz(ə)m,
və(ʊ)'keɪʃn̩lɪz(ə)m,
və(ʊ)'keɪʃ(ə)n|ɪz(ə)m,
və(ʊ)'keɪʃ(ə)nəlɪz(ə)m
AM voʊ'keɪʃ(ə)nəˌlɪzəm

vocationalize
BR və(ʊ)'keɪʃnəlʌɪz,
və(ʊ)'keɪʃn̩lʌɪz,
və(ʊ)'keɪʃən|lʌɪz,
və(ʊ)'keɪʃ(ə)nəlʌɪz,
-ɪz, -ɪŋ, -d
AM voʊ'keɪʃ(ə)nəˌlaɪz,
-ɪz, -ɪŋ, -d

vocationally
BR və(ʊ)'keɪʃnəli,
və(ʊ)'keɪʃn̩li,
və(ʊ)'keɪʃənli,
və(ʊ)'keɪʃ(ə)nəli
AM voʊ'keɪʃ(ə)nəli

vocative
BR 'vɒkətɪv, -z
AM 'vɑkədɪv, -z

Voce
BR vəʊs

AM voʊs

vociferance
BR və(ʊ)ˈsɪf(ə)rəns,
və(ʊ)ˈsɪf(ə)rn̩s
AM vəˈsɪfərəns

vociferant
BR və(ʊ)ˈsɪf(ə)rənt,
və(ʊ)ˈsɪf(ə)rn̩t, -s
AM vəˈsɪfərənt, -s

vociferate
BR və(ʊ)ˈsɪfəreɪt, -s,
-ɪŋ, -ɪd
AM vəˈsɪfəˌreɪ|t, -ts,
-dɪŋ, -dɪd

vociferation
BR və(ʊ)ˌsɪfəˈreɪʃn, -z
AM vəˌsɪfəˈreɪʃən, -z

vociferator
BR və(ʊ)ˈsɪfəreɪtə(r),
-z
AM vəˈsɪfəˌreɪdər, -z

vociferous
BR və(ʊ)ˈsɪf(ə)rəs
AM vəˈsɪfərəs

vociferously
BR və(ʊ)ˈsɪf(ə)rəsli
AM vəˈsɪfərəsli

vociferousness
BR və(ʊ)ˈsɪf(ə)rəsnəs
AM vəˈsɪfərəsnəs

vocoder
BR ˌvəʊˈkəʊdə(r), -z
AM ˈvoʊˌkoʊdər, -z

vocoid
BR ˈvəʊkɔɪd, -z
AM ˈvoʊˌkɔɪd, -z

Vodaphone®
BR ˈvəʊdəfəʊn
AM ˈvoʊdəˌfoʊn

vodka
BR ˈvɒdkə(r), -z
AM ˈvɑdkə, -z

vodun
BR ˈvəʊduːn
AM ˈvoʊdun

voe
BR vəʊ, -z
AM voʊ, -z

Vogel
BR ˈvəʊgl
AM ˈvoʊgəl

vogue
BR vəʊg, -z
AM voʊg, -z

voguish
BR ˈvəʊgɪʃ
AM ˈvoʊgɪʃ

voguishness
BR ˈvəʊgɪʃnɪs
AM ˈvoʊgɪʃnəs

voice
BR vɔɪs, -ɪz, -ɪŋ, -t
AM vɔɪs, -ɪz, -ɪŋ, -t

voiceful
BR ˈvɔɪsf(ʊ)l
AM ˈvɔɪsfəl

voiceless
BR ˈvɔɪslɪs
AM ˈvɔɪslɪs

voicelessly
BR ˈvɔɪslɪsli
AM ˈvɔɪslɪsli

voicelessness
BR ˈvɔɪslɪsnɪs
AM ˈvɔɪslɪsnɪs

voiceprint
BR ˈvɔɪsprɪnt, -s
AM ˈvɔɪsˌprɪnt, -s

voicer
BR ˈvɔɪsə(r), -z
AM ˈvɔɪsər, -z

voicing
BR ˈvɔɪsɪŋ, -z
AM ˈvɔɪsɪŋ, -z

void
BR vɔɪd, -z, -ɪŋ, -ɪd
AM vɔɪd, -z, -ɪŋ, -ɪd

voidable
BR ˈvɔɪdəbl
AM ˈvɔɪdəbəl

voidance
BR ˈvɔɪdns
AM ˈvɔɪdəns

voidness
BR ˈvɔɪdnɪs
AM ˈvɔɪdnɪs

voilà
BR vwʌˈlɑː(r),
vwʌˈlɑ(r)
AM vwɑˈlɑ

voile
BR vɔɪl, vwɑːl
AM vɔɪl

vol
BR vɒl, -z
AM vɑl, -z

vol.
BR vɒl, -z
AM vɑl, -z

volant
BR ˈvəʊlənt
AM ˈvoʊlənt

Volapük
BR ˈvɒləpʊk,
ˈvɒləpuːk, ˈvəʊləpʊk,
ˈvəʊləpuːk
AM ˈvoʊləˌpʊk,
ˈvɒləˌpʊk

volar
BR ˈvəʊlə(r)
AM ˈvoʊlər

volatile¹
adjective
BR ˈvɒlətʌɪl
AM ˈvɑlədl̩

volatile²
in 'sal volatile'
BR vəˈlatɪli, vəˈlatl̩i
AM vəˈladli

volatileness
BR ˈvɒlətʌɪlnɪs
AM ˈvɑlədlnəs

volatilisable
BR vəˈlatɪlˌʌɪzəbl,
ˈvɒlətɪlˌʌɪzəbl
AM ˈvɑlədl̩ˌaɪzəbəl

volatilisation
BR vəˌlatɪlʌɪˈzeɪʃn,
ˌvɒlətɪlʌɪˈzeɪʃn
AM ˌvɑlədləˈzeɪʃən,
ˌvɑlədl̩ˌaɪˈzeɪʃən

volatilise
BR vəˈlatɪlʌɪz,
ˈvɒlətɪlʌɪz, -ɪz, -ɪŋ, -d
AM ˈvɑlədlˌaɪz, -ɪz, -ɪŋ,
-d

volatility
BR ˌvɒləˈtɪlɪti
AM ˌvɑləˈtɪlɪdi

volatilizable
BR vəˈlatɪlʌɪzəbl,
ˈvɒlətɪlʌɪzəbl
AM ˈvɑlədl̩ˌaɪzəbəl

volatilization
BR vəˌlatɪlʌɪˈzeɪʃn,
ˌvɒlətɪlʌɪˈzeɪʃn
AM ˌvɑlədləˈzeɪʃən,
ˌvɑlədl̩ˌaɪˈzeɪʃən

volatilize
BR vəˈlatɪlʌɪz,
ˈvɒlətɪlʌɪz, -ɪz, -ɪŋ, -d
AM ˈvɑlədlˌaɪz, -ɪz, -ɪŋ,
-d

vol-au-vent
BR ˈvɒləvɒ̃, -z
AM ˈvɒləˈvan, -z

volcanic
BR vɒlˈkanɪk
AM vɒlˈkænɪk,
vɑlˈkænɪk

volcanically
BR vɒlˈkanɪkli
AM vɒlˈkænək(ə)li,
vɑlˈkænək(ə)li

volcanicity
BR ˌvɒlkəˈnɪsɪti
AM ˌvɑlkəˈnɪsɪdi,
ˌvɑlkəˈnɪsɪdi

volcanism
BR ˈvɒlkənɪz(ə)m
AM ˈvɑlkəˌnɪzəm,
ˈvɑlkəˌnɪzəm

volcano
BR vɒlˈkeɪnəʊ, -z
AM vɒlˈkeɪnoʊ,
vɑlˈkeɪnoʊ, -z

volcanological
BR ˌvɒlkənəˈlɒdʒɪkl,
ˌvɒlkn̩əˈlɒdʒɪkl
AM ˌvɑlkænlˈadʒəkəl,
ˌvɑlkænlˈadʒəkəl

volcanologist
BR ˌvɒlkəˈnɒlədʒɪst, -s
AM ˌvɑlkəˈnɑlədʒəst,
ˌvɑlkəˈnɑlədʒəst, -s

volcanology
BR ˌvɒlkəˈnɒlədʒi
AM ˌvɒlkəˈnɑlədʒi,
ˌvɑlkəˈnɑlədʒi

vole
BR vəʊl, -z
AM voʊl, -z

volet
BR ˈvɒleɪ, -z
AM voʊˈleɪ, -z

Volga
BR ˈvɒlgə(r)
AM ˈvoʊlgə

Volgograd
BR ˈvɒlgəgrad
AM ˈvoʊlgəˌgræd
RUS valgaˈgrat

volitant
BR ˈvɒlɪt(ə)nt
AM ˈvɑlədənt, ˈvɑlətnt

volition
BR vəˈlɪʃn
AM voʊˈlɪʃən, vəˈlɪʃən

volitional
BR vəˈlɪʃn̩l,
vəˈlɪʃ(ə)n(ə)l
AM voʊˈlɪʃ(ə)nəl,
vəˈlɪʃ(ə)nəl

volitionally
BR vəˈlɪʃn̩əli, vəˈlɪʃn̩li,
vəˈlɪʃənl̩i,
vəˈlɪʃ(ə)nəli
AM vəˈlɪʃ(ə)nəli,
voʊˈlɪʃ(ə)nəli

volitive
BR ˈvɒlɪtɪv
AM ˈvɑlədɪv

Volk¹
German 'people'
BR fɒlk, vɒlk
AM fɔ(l)k, foʊ(l)k

Volk²
surname
BR vɒlk
AM voʊk

Völkerwanderung
BR ˈfəːlkəˌvaːndərʊŋ
AM ˈfɑlkə(r)ˌvandəˌrʊŋ

Völkerwanderungen
BR ˈfəːlkəˌvaːndərʊŋən
AM ˈfɑlkə(r)ˌvandəˌrʊŋən

völkisch
BR ˈfəːlkɪʃ
AM ˈfəlkɪʃ

Volkswagen®
BR ˈvɒlks,wag(ə)n,
ˈfɒlks,vaːg(ə)n, -z
AM ˈvoʊ(l)ks,wægən,
ˈvoʊ(l)ks,wagən, -z

volley
BR ˈvɒl|i, -ɪz, -ɪɪŋ, -ɪd
AM ˈvɑli, -z, -ɪŋ, -d

volleyball
BR ˈvɒlibɔːl
AM ˈvɑli,bɔl, ˈvɑli,bɑl

volleyer
BR ˈvɒlɪə(r), -z
AM ˈvɑliər, -z

Vólos
BR ˈvəʊlɒs
AM ˈvoʊ,lɑs, ˈvoʊ,las
GR ˈvɔlɔs

volplane
BR ˈvɒlpleɪn, -z, -ɪŋ, -d
AM ˈvɑlˌpleɪn, -z, -ɪŋ, -d

Volpone
BR vɒlˈpəʊni
AM vɔlˈpoʊni, voʊlˈpoʊni

Volscian
BR ˈvɒlskɪən, -z
AM ˈvɑlʃən, -z

Volski
BR ˈvɒlski, ˈvɒlskiː
AM ˈvɔlski, ˈvɑlski

volt
BR vəʊlt, vɒlt, -s
AM voʊlt, -s

Volta¹
African lake and river
BR ˈvɒltə(r)
AM ˈvoʊltə

Volta²
physicist
BR ˈvəʊltə(r), ˈvɒltə(r)
AM ˈvoʊltə

volta
BR ˈvɒltə(r), -z
AM ˈvoʊltə, -z

voltage
BR ˈvəʊltˌɪdʒ, ˈvɒltˌɪdʒ, -ɪdʒɪz
AM ˈvoʊltɪdʒ, -ɪz

voltaic
BR vɒlˈteɪɪk
AM vɑlˈteɪɪk, voʊlˈteɪɪk

Voltaire
BR vɒlˈtɛː(r), ˈvɒltɛː(r)
AM vɔlˈtɛ(ə)r, vɑlˈtɛ(ə)r

voltameter
BR vɒlˈtamɪtə(r), -z
AM voʊlˈtæmədər, -z

volte
BR vɒlt, vəʊlt, -s
AM vɑlt(ə), ˈvoʊlt(ə), -z

volte-face
BR ˌvɒltˈfɑːs, ˌvɒltˈfas, -ɪz
AM ˌvɑlt(ə)ˈfas, ˌvoʊlt(ə)ˈfas, -əz

voltmeter
BR ˈvəʊltˌmiːtə(r), ˈvɒltˌmiːtə(r), -z
AM ˈvoʊltˌmidər, -z

volubility
BR ˌvɒljʊˈbɪlɪti
AM ˌvɑljəˈbɪlɪdi

voluble
BR ˈvɒljʊbl
AM ˈvɑljəbəl

volubleness
BR ˈvɒljʊblnəs
AM ˈvɑljəbəlnəs

volubly
BR ˈvɒljʊbli
AM ˈvɑljəbli

volume
BR ˈvɒljuːm, -z, -d
AM ˈvɑlˌjum, ˈvɑljəm, -z, -d

volumetric
BR ˌvɒljʊˈmetrɪk
AM ˌvɑljəˈmetrɪk

volumetrical
BR ˌvɒljʊˈmetrɪkl
AM ˌvɑljəˈmetrəkəl

volumetrically
BR ˌvɒljʊˈmetrɪkli
AM ˌvɑljəˈmetrək(ə)li

voluminosity
BR vəˌl(j)uːmɪˈnɒsɪti
AM vəˌl(j)uːməˈnɑsədi

voluminous
BR vəˈl(j)uːmɪnəs
AM vəˈl(j)uːmənəs

voluminously
BR vəˈl(j)uːmɪnəsli
AM vəˈl(j)uːmənəsli

voluminousness
BR vəˈl(j)uːmɪnəsnəs
AM vəˈl(j)uːmənəsnəs

voluntarily
BR ˈvɒləntrɪli, ˈvɒlntrɪli
AM ˌvɑlənˈterəli

voluntariness
BR ˈvɒləntrɪnɪs, ˈvɒlntrɪnɪs
AM ˌvɑlənˈterɪnɪs

voluntarism
BR ˈvɒlənt(ə)rɪz(ə)m, ˈvɒlnt(ə)rɪz(ə)m
AM ˈvɑlən(t)əˌrɪzəm

voluntarist
BR ˈvɒlənt(ə)rɪst, ˈvɒlnt(ə)rɪst
AM ˈvɑlən(t)ərəst

voluntary
BR ˈvɒlənt(ə)rˌi, ˈvɒlnt(ə)rˌi, -ɪz
AM ˈvɑlənˌteri, -z

voluntary-aided
BR ˌvɒlənt(ə)rɪˈeɪdɪd, ˌvɒlnt(ə)rɪˈeɪdɪd
AM ˌvɑlənˌteriˈeɪdɪd

voluntaryism
BR ˈvɒlənt(ə)rɪɪz(ə)m, ˈvɒlnt(ə)rɪɪz(ə)m
AM ˌvɑlənˌteriˌɪzəm

voluntaryist
BR ˈvɒlənt(ə)rɪɪst, ˈvɒlnt(ə)rɪɪst, -s
AM ˌvɑlənˌteriɪst, -s

volunteer
BR ˌvɒlənˈtɪə(r), ˌvɒlnˈtɪə(r), -z, -ɪŋ, -d
AM ˌvɑlənˈtɪ(ə)r, -z, -ɪŋ, -d

volunteerism
BR ˌvɒlənˈtɪərɪz(ə)m, ˌvɒlnˈtɪərɪz(ə)m
AM ˌvɑlənˈtɪ(ə)ˌrɪzəm

voluptuary
BR vəˈlʌptʃʊərˌi, vəˈlʌptʃ(ʊ)rˌi, vəˈlʌptjʊərˌi, vəˈlʌptjərˌi, -ɪz
AM vəˈləp(t)ʃəˌweri, -z

voluptuous
BR vəˈlʌptʃʊəs, vəˈlʌptjʊəs
AM vəˈləp(t)ʃ(əw)əs

voluptuously
BR vəˈlʌptʃʊəsli, vəˈlʌptjʊəsli
AM vəˈləp(t)ʃ(əw)əsli

voluptuousness
BR vəˈlʌptʃʊəsnəs, vəˈlʌptjʊəsnəs
AM vəˈləp(t)ʃ(əw)əsnəs

volute
BR vəˈl(j)uːt, -s, -ɪd
AM vəˈl(j)uːlt, -ts, -dəd

voluted
BR vəˈl(j)uːtɪd
AM vəˈl(j)udəd

volution
BR vəˈl(j)uːʃn, -z
AM vəˈluʃən, -z

Volvo®
BR ˈvɒlvəʊ, -z
AM ˈvɑlˌvoʊ, ˈvɑlˌvoʊ, -z

volvox
BR ˈvɒlvɒks
AM ˈvɑlˌvɑks

vomer
BR ˈvəʊmə(r), -z
AM ˈvoʊmər, -z

vomit
BR ˈvɒmˌɪt, -ɪts, -ɪtɪŋ, -ɪtɪd
AM ˈvɑməˌlt, -ts, -dɪŋ, -dəd

vomiter
BR ˈvɒmɪtə(r), -z
AM ˈvɑmədər, -z

vomitoria
BR ˌvɒmɪˈtɔːrɪə(r)
AM ˌvɑməˈtɔrɪə

vomitorium
BR ˌvɒmɪˈtɔːrɪəm
AM ˌvɑməˈtɔrɪəm

vomitory
BR ˈvɒmɪt(ə)rˌi, -ɪz
AM ˈvɑməˌtori, -z

vomitus
BR ˈvɒmɪtəs
AM ˈvɑmədəs

von
BR vɒn, fɒn
AM vɑn

Vonnegut
BR ˈvɒnɪgʌt
AM ˈvɑnəgət

voodoo
BR ˈvuːduː
AM ˈvuˌdu

voodooism
BR ˈvuːduːɪz(ə)m
AM ˈvuˌduˌɪzəm

voodooist
BR ˈvuːduːɪst, -s
AM ˈvuˌduəst, -s

Voortrekker
BR ˈfʊəˌtrekə(r), ˈvʊəˌtrekə(r), ˈfɔːˌtrekə(r), ˈvɔːˌtrekə(r)
AM ˈfʊrˌtrekər, ˈfɔrˌtrekər, ˈvʊrˌtrekər, ˈvɔrˌtrekər

Vopo
BR ˈfəʊpəʊ, -z
AM ˈvoʊˌpoʊ, -z

voracious
BR vəˈreɪʃəs
AM vəˈreɪʃəs

voraciously
BR vəˈreɪʃəsli
AM vəˈreɪʃəsli

voraciousness
BR vəˈreɪʃəsnəs
AM vəˈreɪʃəsnəs

voracity
BR vəˈrasɪti
AM vəˈræsədi

Vorarlberg
BR ˈfɔːrɑːlbəːg
AM ˈfɔrˌɑrlˌbərg

Vorster
BR ˈvɔːstə(r)
AM ˈvɔrstər

vortex
BR ˈvɔːteks, -ɪz
AM ˈvɔrˌteks, -əz

vortex ring
BR ˈvɔːteks rɪŋ, -z
AM ˈvɔrˌteks ˌrɪŋ, -z

vortical
BR ˈvɔːtɪkl
AM ˈvɔrdəkəl

vortically
BR ˈvɔːtɪkli
AM ˈvɔrdək(ə)li

vorticella
BR ˌvɔːtɪˈselə(r), -z
AM ˌvɔrdəˈselə, -z

vortices
BR ˈvɔːtɪsiːz
AM ˈvɔrdəˌsiz

vorticism
BR ˈvɔːtɪsɪz(ə)m
AM ˈvɔrdəˌsɪzəm

vorticist
BR ˈvɔːtɪsɪst, -s
AM ˈvɔrdəsəst, -s

vorticity
BR vɔːˈtɪsɪti
AM vɔrˈtɪsɪdi

vorticose
BR ˈvɔːtɪkəʊs, ˌvɔːtɪˈkəʊs
AM ˈvɔrdəˌkoʊs, ˈvɔrdəˌkoʊz

vorticular
BR vɔːˈtɪkjələ(r)
AM vɔrˈtɪkjələr

Vortigern
BR 'vɔːtɪgəːn,
'vɔːtɪg(ə)n,
'vɔːtɪdʒəːn,
'vɔːtɪdʒ(ə)n
AM 'vɔrdə,gərn

Vosburgh
BR 'vɒsb(ə)rə(r)
AM 'vɑs,bərə

Vosene
BR 'vəʊziːn
AM 'voʊ,zin

Vosges
BR vəʊʒ
AM voʊʒ

Voss
BR vɒs
AM vɔs, vɑs

Vostok
BR 'vɒstɒk
AM 'vɑ,stɑk

votable
BR 'vəʊtəbl
AM 'voʊdəbəl

votaress
BR 'vəʊt(ə)rɪs,
'vəʊtəres, -ɪz
AM 'voʊdərəs, -əz

votarist
BR 'vəʊt(ə)rɪst, -s
AM 'voʊdərəst, -s

votary
BR 'vəʊt(ə)r|i, -iz
AM 'voʊdəri, -z

vote
BR vəʊt, -s, -ɪŋ, -ɪd
AM voʊ|t, -ts, -dɪŋ, -dəd

voteless
BR 'vəʊtləs
AM 'voʊtləs

voter
BR 'vəʊtə(r), -z
AM 'voʊdər, -z

voting machine
BR 'vəʊtɪŋ məˌʃiːn, -z
AM 'voʊdɪŋ məˌʃin, -z

voting paper
BR 'vəʊtɪŋ ˌpeɪpə(r), -z
AM 'voʊdɪŋ ˌpeɪpər, -z

votive
BR 'vəʊtɪv
AM 'voʊdɪv

vouch
BR vaʊtʃ, -ɪz, -ɪŋ, -t
AM vaʊtʃ, -əz, -ɪŋ, -t

voucher
BR 'vaʊtʃə(r), -z
AM 'vaʊtʃər, -z

vouchsafe
BR (ˌ)vaʊtʃ'seɪf, -s, -ɪŋ,
-t
AM vaʊtʃ'seɪf,
'vaʊtʃ,seɪf, -s, -ɪŋ, -t

voussoir
BR 'vuː'swɑː(r), -z
AM vu'swɑr, -z

Vouvray
BR 'vuːvreɪ, -z
AM vu'vreɪ, -z

vow
BR vaʊ, -z, -ɪŋ, -d
AM vaʊ, -z, -ɪŋ, -d

vowel
BR 'vaʊəl, vaʊl, -z, -d
AM 'vaʊ(ə)l, -z, -d

vowelise
BR 'vaʊ(ə)laɪz, -ɪz, -ɪŋ,
-d
AM 'vaʊə,laɪz, -ɪz, -ɪŋ, -d

vowelize
BR 'vaʊ(ə)laɪz, -ɪz, -ɪŋ,
-d
AM 'vaʊə,laɪz, -ɪz, -ɪŋ, -d

vowelless
BR 'vaʊ(ə)ləs
AM 'vaʊ(ə)(l)ləs

vowelly
BR 'vaʊ(ə)lli
AM 'vaʊ(ə)li

vowel-point
BR 'vaʊ(ə)lpɔɪnt, -s
AM 'vaʊ(ə)l,pɔɪnt, -s

Vowles
BR vəʊlz, vaʊlz
AM voʊlz, vaʊlz

vox angelica
BR ˌvɒks an'dʒɛlɪkə(r)
AM ˌvaks æn'dʒɛlɪkə

vox humana
BR ˌvɒks
hjuː'mɑːnə(r)
AM ˌvaks (h)ju'mɑnə

vox pop
BR ˌvɒks 'pɒp, -s
AM ˌvaks 'pap, -s

vox populi
BR ˌvɒks 'pɒpjʊliː,
+ 'pɒpjʊlaɪ
AM ˌvaks 'pɑpjə,laɪ

voyage
BR 'vɔɪ(ɪ)dʒ, vɔɪdʒ, -ɪz,
-ɪŋ, -d
AM 'vɔɪ(ɪ)dʒ, -ɪz, -ɪŋ, -d

voyageable
BR 'vɔɪ(ɪ)dʒəbl
AM 'vɔɪ(ɪ)dʒəbəl

voyager
BR 'vɔɪ(ɪ)dʒə(r), -z
AM 'vɔɪ(ɪ)dʒər, -z

voyageur
BR ˌvwɑːjə'ʒəː(r), -z
AM ˌvwɑjə'ʒɛ(ə)r, -z

voyeur
BR (ˌ)vɔɪ'jəː(r),
(ˌ)vwɑː'jəː(r),
(ˌ)vwʌɪ'jəː(r), -z
AM vɔɪ'jər, -z

voyeurism
BR 'vɔɪjərɪz(ə)m,
(ˌ)vɔɪ'(j)əːrɪz(ə)m,
(ˌ)vwʌɪ'(j)əːrɪz(ə)m,
(ˌ)vwɑː'jəːrɪz(ə)m
AM 'vɔɪjə,rɪzəm

voyeuristic
BR ˌvɔɪə'rɪstɪk,
ˌvwʌɪə'rɪstɪk,
ˌvwɑːjə'rɪstɪk
AM ˌvɔɪjə'rɪstɪk

voyeuristically
BR ˌvɔɪə'rɪstɪkli,
ˌvwʌɪə'rɪstɪkli,
ˌvwɑːjə'rɪstɪkli
AM ˌvɔɪjə'rɪstək(ə)li

vraic
BR vreɪk
AM vreɪk

vroom
BR vruːm, -z, -ɪŋ, -d
AM vrum, -z, -ɪŋ, -d

vs
BR 'vəːsəs
AM 'vərsəs

V-sign
BR 'viːsaɪn, -z
AM 'vi,saɪn, -z

V/STOL
BR 'viːstɒl
AM 'vi,stɑl

VTOL
BR 'viːtɒl
AM 'vi,tɑl

vug
BR vʌg, -z
AM vəg, vʊg, -z

vuggy
BR 'vʌgi
AM 'vəgi, 'vʊgi

vugular
BR 'vʌgjələ(r)
AM 'vəgjələr, 'vʊgjələr

Vulcan
BR 'vʌlkən
AM 'vəlkən

Vulcanian
BR vʌl'keɪnɪən, -z
AM vəl'keɪnɪən, -z

vulcanic
BR vʌl'kanɪk
AM vəl'kænɪk

vulcanisable
BR 'vʌlkənaɪzəbl
AM 'vəlkə,naɪzəbəl

vulcanisation
BR ˌvʌlkənaɪ'zeɪʃn
AM ˌvəlkənə'zeɪʃən,
ˌvəlkə,naɪ'zeɪʃən

vulcanise
BR 'vʌlkənaɪz, -ɪz, -ɪŋ,
-d
AM 'vəlkə,naɪz, -ɪz, -ɪŋ,
-d

vulcaniser
BR 'vʌlkənaɪzə(r), -z
AM 'vəlkə,naɪzər, -z

vulcanism
BR 'vʌlkənɪz(ə)m
AM 'vəlkə,nɪzəm

Vulcanist
BR 'vʌlkənɪst, -s
AM 'vəlkənəst, -s

vulcanite
BR 'vʌlkənʌɪt
AM 'vəlkə,naɪt

vulcanizable
BR 'vʌlkənaɪzəbl
AM 'vəlkə,naɪzəbəl

vulcanization
BR ˌvʌlkənaɪ'zeɪʃn
AM ˌvəlkənə'zeɪʃən,
ˌvəlkə,naɪ'zeɪʃən

vulcanize
BR 'vʌlkənaɪz, -ɪz, -ɪŋ,
-d
AM 'vəlkə,naɪz, -ɪz, -ɪŋ,
-d

vulcanizer
BR 'vʌlkənaɪzə(r), -z
AM 'vəlkə,naɪzər, -z

vulcanological
BR ˌvʌlkənə'lɒdʒɪkl,
ˌvʌlknə'lɒdʒɪkl
AM ˌvəlkənə'lɑdʒəkəl

vulcanologist
BR ˌvʌlkə'nɒlədʒɪst, -s
AM ˌvəlkə'nɑlədʒəst, -s

vulcanology
BR ˌvʌlkə'nɒlədʒi
AM ˌvəlkə'nɑlədʒi

vulgar
BR 'vʌlgə(r)
AM 'vəlgər

vulgarian
BR vʌl'gɛːrɪən, -z
AM vəl'gɛriən, -z

vulgarisation
BR ˌvʌlg(ə)rʌɪ'zeɪʃn
AM ˌvəlgərə'zeɪʃən,
ˌvəlgə,raɪ'zeɪʃən

vulgarise
BR 'vʌlgərʌɪz, -ɪz, -ɪŋ,
-d
AM 'vəlgə,raɪz, -ɪz, -ɪŋ,
-d

vulgarism
BR 'vʌlgərɪz(ə)m, -z
AM 'vəlgə,rɪzəm, -z

vulgarity
BR vʌl'garɪt|i, -ɪz
AM vəl'gɛrədi, -z

vulgarization
BR ˌvʌlg(ə)rʌɪ'zeɪʃn
AM ˌvəlgərə'zeɪʃən,
ˌvəlgə,raɪ'zeɪʃən

vulgarize
BR 'vʌlgərʌɪz, -ɪz, -ɪŋ,
-d
AM 'vəlgə,raɪz, -ɪz, -ɪŋ,
-d

vulgarly
BR 'vʌlgəli
AM 'vəlgərli

vulgate
BR 'vʌlgeɪt, 'vʌlgət
AM 'vəl,geɪt

vulnerability
BR ˌvʌln(ə)rə'bɪlɪti
AM ˌvəln(ə)rə'bɪlɪdi

vulnerable
BR 'vʌln(ə)rəbl
AM 'vəlnər(ə)bəl

vulnerableness
BR 'vʌln(ə)rəblnəs
AM 'vəlnər(ə)bəlnəs

vulnerably
BR 'vʌln(ə)rəbli
AM 'vəlnər(ə)bli

vulnerary
BR 'vʌln(ə)rər|i, -ɪz
AM 'vəlnə͵reri, -z

vulpine
BR 'vʌlpʌɪn
AM 'vəl͵paɪn

vulture
BR 'vʌltʃə(r), -z
AM 'vəltʃər, -z

vulturine
BR 'vʌltʃərʌɪn
AM 'vəltʃərən

vulturish
BR 'vʌltʃ(ə)rɪʃ
AM 'vəltʃ(ə)rɪʃ

vulturous
BR 'vʌltʃ(ə)rəs
AM 'vəltʃ(ə)rəs

vulva
BR 'vʌlvə(r), -z
AM 'vəlvə, -z

vulval
BR 'vʌlvl
AM 'vəlvəl

vulvar
BR 'vʌlvə(r)
AM 'vəlvər

vulvitis
BR vʌl'vaɪtɪs
AM vəl'vaɪdɪs

vying
BR 'vaɪɪŋ
AM 'vaɪɪŋ

Vyrnwy
BR 'vəːnwi
AM 'vərnwi
WE 'vʌrnwi

Vyvyan
BR 'vɪvɪən
AM 'vɪvɪən

Ww

w
BR 'dʌblju:, -z
AM 'dəbəl.ju, -z

WAAF
BR waf, -s
AM wæf, -s

Waal
BR vɑːl
AM vɑl

Wabash
BR 'wɔːbæʃ
AM 'wɔ.bæʃ, 'wɑ.bæʃ

WAC
BR wak, -s
AM wæk, -s

Wace
BR weɪs
AM wɑs, weɪs

wack
BR wak
AM wæk

wacke
BR 'wakə(r), -z
AM 'wækə, -z

wackily
BR 'wakɪli
AM 'wækəli

wackiness
BR 'wakɪnɪs
AM 'wækɪnɪs

wacko
BR 'wakəʊ, -z
AM 'wækoʊ, -z

wacky
BR 'wak|i, -ɪə(r), -ɪɪst
AM 'wæki, -ər, -ɪst

Waco
BR 'weɪkəʊ
AM 'weɪkoʊ

wad
BR wɒd, -z
AM wɑd, -z

wadable
BR 'weɪdəbl
AM 'weɪdəbəl

Waddell
BR wɒ'dɛl, wə'dɛl
AM wɑ'del

wadding
BR 'wɒdɪŋ
AM 'wadɪŋ

Waddington
BR 'wɒdɪŋt(ə)n
AM 'wadɪŋtən

waddle
BR 'wɒd|l, -lz, -lɪŋ \ -lɪŋ, -ld
AM 'wad|əl, -əlz, -(ə)lɪŋ, -əld

waddler
BR 'wɒdlə(r), 'wɒdlə(r), -z
AM 'wad(ə)lər, -z

waddy
BR 'wɒd|i, -ɪz
AM 'wadi, -z

wade
BR weɪd, -z, -ɪŋ, -ɪd
AM weɪd, -z, -ɪŋ, -ɪd

wadeable
BR 'weɪdəbl
AM 'weɪdəbəl

Wadebridge
BR 'weɪdbrɪdʒ
AM 'weɪd.brɪdʒ

Wade-Giles
BR ˌweɪd'dʒʌɪlz
AM ˌweɪd'dʒaɪlz

wader
BR 'weɪdə(r), -z
AM 'weɪdər, -z

wadge
BR wɒdʒ, -ɪz
AM wadʒ, -əz

Wadham
BR 'wɒdəm
AM 'wadəm

wadi
BR 'wɒd|i, -ɪz
AM 'wadi, -z

Wadi Halfa
BR ˌwɒdɪ 'halfə(r)
AM 'wadi 'halfə

Wadsworth
BR 'wɒdzwəθ, 'wɒdzwə:θ
AM 'wads.wərθ

wady
BR 'wɒd|i, -ɪz
AM 'wadi, -z

WAF
BR waf, -s
AM wæf, -s

wafer
BR 'weɪfə(r), -z
AM 'weɪfər, -z

wafery
BR 'weɪf(ə)ri
AM 'weɪf(ə)ri

Waffen SS
BR ˌvɑːf(ə)n ˌɛs'ɛs, ˌvaf(ə)n +
AM 'vɑfən ˌɛs'ɛs

waffle
BR 'wɒf|l, -lz, -lɪŋ \ -lɪŋ, -ld
AM 'wɑf|əl, -əlz, -(ə)lɪŋ, -əld

waffler
BR 'wɒflə(r), 'wɒflə(r), -z
AM 'wɑf(ə)lər, -z

waffly
BR 'wɒf|i, 'wɒfli
AM 'wɑf(ə)li

waft
BR wɑːft, wɒft, waft, -s, -ɪŋ, -ɪd
AM wɑft, -s, -ɪŋ, -əd

wag
BR wag, -z, -ɪŋ, -d
AM wæg, -z, -ɪŋ, -d

wage
BR weɪdʒ, -ɪz, -ɪŋ, -d
AM weɪdʒ, -ɪz, -ɪŋ, -d

wager
BR 'weɪdʒ|ə(r), -əz, -(ə)rɪŋ, -əd
AM 'weɪdʒər, -z, -ɪŋ, -d

Wagga Wagga
BR ˌwɒgə 'wɒgə(r)
AM 'wagə 'wagə

waggery
BR 'wag(ə)r|i, -ɪz
AM 'wægəri, -z

waggish
BR 'wagɪʃ
AM 'wægɪʃ

waggishly
BR 'wagɪʃli
AM 'wægɪʃli

waggishness
BR 'wagɪʃnɪs
AM 'wægɪʃnɪs

waggle
BR 'wag|l, -lz, -lɪŋ \ -lɪŋ, -ld
AM 'wæg|əl, -əlz, -(ə)lɪŋ, -əld

waggly
BR 'wag|i, 'wagli
AM 'wæg(ə)li

waggon
BR 'wag(ə)n, -z
AM 'wægən, -z

waggoner
BR 'wagənə(r), 'wagnə(r)
AM 'wægənər

waggonette
BR ˌwagə'nɛt, -s
AM ˌwægə'nɛt, -s

waggonful
BR 'wag(ə)nfʊl
AM 'wægən.fʊl

waggonload
BR 'wagənləʊd, -z
AM 'wægən.loʊd, -z

Wagnall
BR 'wagnl
AM 'wægnəl

Wagner¹
English surname
BR 'wagnə(r)
AM 'wægnər

Wagner²
German surname
BR 'vɑːgnə(r)
AM 'vagnər

Wagnerian
BR vɑːg'nɪərɪən, -z
AM vag'nɛrɪən, -z

wagon
BR 'wag(ə)n, -z
AM 'wægən, -z

wagoner
BR 'wagənə(r), 'wagnə(r), -z
AM 'wægənər, -z

wagonette
BR ˌwagə'nɛt, -s
AM ˌwægə'nɛt, -s

wagonful
BR 'wag(ə)nfʊl, -z
AM 'wægən.fʊl, -z

wagon-lit
BR ˌvagɒ'liː, ˌvagɒn'liː, -z
AM 'vagɒn.li, -z

wagonload
BR 'wag(ə)nləʊd, -z
AM 'wægən.loʊd, -z

wagtail
BR 'wagteɪl, -z
AM 'wæg.teɪl, -z

Wahabi
BR wə'hɑːb|i, wɑː'hɑːb|i, -ɪz
AM wə'habi, wa'habi, -z

Wahhabi
BR wə'hɑːb|i, wɑː'hɑːb|i, -ɪz
AM wə'habi, wa'habi, -z

wahine
BR wɑː'hiːn|i, -ɪz
AM wɑ'hini, -z

wahoo
BR ˌwɑː'huː, wə'huː, -z
AM 'wa'hu, -z

Wahran
BR wɑː'rɑːn
AM wa'ran

wah-wah
BR 'wɑːwɑː(r)
AM 'wa'wa

waif
BR weɪf, -s
AM weɪf, -s

waifish
BR 'weɪfɪʃ
AM 'weɪfɪʃ

waif-like
BR 'weɪflʌɪk
AM 'weɪf.laɪk

Waikato
BR wʌɪ'kɑːtəʊ
AM 'waɪ.kadoʊ

Waikiki
BR ˌwʌɪkɪ'kiː, 'wʌɪkɪkiː
AM ˌwaɪki'ki

wail
BR weɪl, -z, -ɪŋ, -d
AM weɪl, -z, -ɪŋ, -d

wailer
BR 'weɪlə(r), -z
AM 'weɪlər, -z

wailful
BR 'weɪlf(ʊ)l
AM 'weɪlfəl

wailing
BR 'weɪlɪŋ, -z
AM 'weɪlɪŋ, -z

wailingly
BR 'weɪlɪŋli
AM 'weɪlɪŋli

wain
BR weɪn, -z
AM weɪn, -z

Waine
BR weɪn
AM weɪn

Wainfleet
BR 'weɪnfliːt
AM 'weɪn,flit

wainscot
BR 'weɪnskət,
'weɪnskɒt, -s, -ɪŋ
AM 'weɪn,skoʊt
'weɪnskə|t,
'weɪn,skɑ|t, -ts, -dɪŋ

wainwright
BR 'weɪnrʌɪt, -s
AM 'weɪnraɪt, -s

waist
BR weɪst, -s, -ɪd
AM weɪst, -s, -ɪd

waistband
BR 'weɪs(t)band, -z
AM 'weɪs(t),bænd, -z

waist-cloth
BR 'weɪs(t)klɒ|θ,
-θs\-ðz
AM 'weɪs(t),klɑ|θ,
'weɪs(t),klɑ|θ, -θs\-ðz

waistcoat
BR 'weɪs(t)kəʊt, -s
AM 'weɪs(t),koʊt, -s

waisted
BR 'weɪstɪd
AM 'weɪstɪd

waistless
BR 'weɪstlɪs
AM 'weɪs(t)lɪs

waistline
BR 'weɪs(t)lʌɪn, -z
AM 'weɪs(t),laɪn, -z

wait
BR weɪt, -s, -ɪŋ, -ɪd
AM weɪ|t, -ts, -dɪŋ, -dɪd

Waite
BR weɪt
AM weɪt

waiter
BR 'weɪtə(r), -z
AM 'weɪdər, -z

Waites
BR weɪts
AM weɪts

waitress
BR 'weɪtrɪs, -ɪz, -ɪŋ
AM 'weɪtrɪs, -ɪz, -ɪŋ

Waitrose
BR 'weɪtrəʊz

AM 'weɪt,roʊz

waive
BR weɪv, -z, -ɪŋ, -d
AM weɪv, -z, -ɪŋ, -d

waiver
BR 'weɪvə(r), -z
AM 'weɪvər, -z

wake
BR weɪk, -s, -ɪŋ, -t
AM weɪk, -s, -ɪŋ, -t

Wakefield
BR 'weɪkfiːld
AM 'weɪk,fild

wakeful
BR 'weɪkf(ʊ)l
AM 'weɪkfəl

wakefully
BR 'weɪkfʊli, 'weɪkf‚li
AM 'weɪkfəli

wakefulness
BR 'weɪkf(ʊ)lnəs
AM 'weɪkfəlnəs

Wakelin
BR 'weɪklɪn
AM 'weɪklɪn

waken
BR 'weɪk|(ə)n, -(ə)nz,
-nɪŋ\-(ə)nɪŋ, -(ə)nd
AM 'weɪk|ən, -ənz,
-(ə)nɪŋ, -ənd

waker
BR 'weɪkə(r), -z
AM 'weɪkər, -z

wake-robin
BR 'weɪk,rɒbɪn, -z
AM 'weɪk,rɑbən, -z

wakey-wakey
BR ,weɪkɪ'weɪkɪ
AM ,weɪki'weɪki

Walach
BR 'wɒlək
AM 'wɑlək

Walachia
BR wɒ'leɪkɪə(r),
wə'leɪkɪə(r)
AM wɑ'leɪkiə,
wə'leɪkiən

Walachian
BR wɒ'leɪkɪən,
wə'leɪkɪən, -z
AM wɑ'leɪkiən,
wə'leɪkiən, -z

Walbrook
BR 'wɔːlbrʊk,
'wɒlbrʊk
AM 'wɔl,brʊk,
'wɑl,brʊk

Walcot
BR 'wɔːlkət, 'wɔːlkɒt,
'wɒlkət, 'wɒlkɒt
AM 'wɔl,kɑt, 'wɑl,kɑt

Walcott
BR 'wɔːlkət, 'wɔːlkɒt,
'wɒlkət, 'wɒlkɒt
AM 'wɔl,kɑt, 'wɑl,kɑt

Waldegrave
BR 'wɔːld(ɪ)greɪv,
'wɒld(ɪ)greɪv,
'wɔːlgreɪv
AM 'wɔl,greɪv,
'wɑl,greɪv

Waldemar
BR 'valdɪmɑː(r),
'wɔːldɪmɑː(r)
AM 'wɔldə,mɑr,
'wɑldə,mɑr

Walden
BR 'wɔːld(ə)n,
'wɒld(ə)n
AM 'wɔldən, 'wɑldən

Waldenses
BR wɔːl'dɛnsiːz,
wɒl'dɛnsiːz
AM wɔl'dɛnsiz,
wɑl'dɛnsiz

Waldensian
BR wɔːl'dɛnsɪən,
wɒl'dɛnsɪən, -z
AM wɔl'dɛnsiən,
wɑl'dɛnsiən, -z

Waldheim
BR 'vɑːldhʌɪm,
'valdhʌɪm
AM 'vɑld,(h)aɪm,
'wɔld,(h)aɪm

Waldo
BR 'wɔːldəʊ, 'wɒldəʊ
AM 'wɔl,doʊ, 'wɑl,doʊ

Waldorf
BR 'wɔːldɔːf, 'wɒldɔːf
AM 'wɔl,dɔ(ə)rf,
'wɑl,dɔ(ə)rf

Waldron
BR 'wɔːldr(ə)n,
'wɒldr(ə)n
AM 'wɔldrən, 'wɑldrən

wale
BR weɪl, -z, -ɪŋ, -d
AM weɪl, -z, -ɪŋ, -d

Wales
BR weɪlz
AM weɪlz

Waley
BR 'weɪli
AM 'weɪli

Walford
BR 'wɔːlfəd, 'wɒlfəd
AM 'wɔlfərd, 'wɑlfərd

Walian
BR 'weɪlɪən, -z
AM 'weɪljən, 'weɪliən,
-z

walk
BR wɔːk, -s, -ɪŋ, -t
AM wɔk, wɑk, -s, -ɪŋ, -t

walkable
BR 'wɔːkəbl
AM 'wɔkəbəl,
'wɑkəbəl

walkabout
BR 'wɔːkəbaʊt, -s
AM 'wɔkə,baʊt,
'wɑkə,baʊt, -s

walkathon
BR 'wɔːkəθɒn, -z
AM 'wɔkə,θɑn,
'wɑkə,θɑn, -z

walkaway
BR 'wɔːkəweɪ,
AM 'wɔkə,weɪ,
'wɑkə,weɪ, -z

Walkden
BR 'wɔːkdən
AM 'wɔkdən, 'wɑkdən

walker
BR 'wɔːkə(r), -z
AM 'wɔkər, 'wɑkər, -z

walkies
BR 'wɔːkɪz
AM 'wɔkiz, 'wɑkiz

walkie-talkie
BR ,wɔːkɪ'tɔːk|i, -ɪz
AM ,wɔki'tɔki,
,wɑki'tɑki, -z

walk-in
BR 'wɔːkɪn, -z
AM 'wɔk,ɪn, 'wɑk,ɪn, -z

Walkman®
BR 'wɔːkmən, -z
AM 'wɔk,mæn,
'wɔkmən, 'wɑk,mæn,
'wɑkmən, -z

walk-on
BR 'wɔːkɒn, -z
AM 'wɔk,ɔn, 'wɑk,ɑn, -z

walkout
BR 'wɔːkaʊt, -s
AM 'wɔk,aʊt, 'wɑk,aʊt,
-s

walkover
BR 'wɔːk,əʊvə(r), -z
AM 'wɔk,oʊvər,
'wɑk,oʊvər, -z

walk-through
BR 'wɔːkθruː, -z
AM 'wɔk,θru, 'wɑk,θru,
-z

walkup
BR 'wɔːkʌp, -s
AM 'wɔk,əp, 'wɑk,əp, -s

walkway
BR 'wɔːkweɪ, -z
AM 'wɔk,weɪ,
'wɑk,weɪ, -z

wall
BR wɔːl, -z, -ɪŋ, -d
AM wɔl, wɑl, -z, -ɪŋ, -d

walla
BR 'wɒlə(r), -z
AM 'wɑlə, -z

wallaby
BR 'wɒləb|i, -ɪz
AM 'wɑləbi, -z

Wallace
BR 'wɒlɪs
AM 'wɔləs, 'wɑləs

Wallachia
BR wɒ'leɪkɪə(r),
wə'leɪkɪə(r)
AM wɑ'leɪkiə,
wə'leɪkiə

Wallachian
BR wɒˈleɪkɪən,
wəˈleɪkɪən, -z
AM wɑˈleɪkɪən,
wəˈleɪkɪən, -z

wallah
BR ˈwɒlə(r), -z
AM ˈwɑlə, -z

wallaroo
BR ˌwɒləˈruː, -z
AM ˌwɑləˈruː, ˌwɑləˈruː,
-z

Wallasey
BR ˈwɒləsi
AM ˈwɒləsi, ˈwɑləsi

wallchart
BR ˈwɔːltʃɑːt, -s
AM ˈwɔlˌtʃɑrt,
ˈwɑlˌtʃɑrt, -s

wallcovering
BR ˈwɔːlˌkʌv(ə)rɪŋ, -z
AM ˈwɔlˌkʌv(ə)rɪŋ,
ˈwɑlˌkʌv(ə)rɪŋ, -z

Wallenberg
BR ˈwɒlənbɜːg,
ˈwɒlnbɜːg
AM ˈwɑlənˌbɜrg,
ˈvɑlənˌbɜrg

Waller
BR ˈwɒlə(r)
AM ˈwɔlər, ˈwɑlər

wallet
BR ˈwɒlɪt, -s
AM ˈwɑlət, ˈwɔlət, -s

wall-eye
BR ˈwɔːlˌaɪ, -z
AM ˈwɔlˌaɪ, ˈwɑlˌaɪ, -z

wall-eyed
BR ˌwɔːlˈaɪd
AM ˈwɔlˌaɪd, ˈwɑlˌaɪd

wallflower
BR ˈwɔːlˌflaʊə(r), -z
AM ˈwɔlˌflaʊər,
ˈwɑlˌflaʊər, -z

wall-hung
BR ˌwɔːlˈhʌŋ
AM ˈwɔlˌ(h)əŋ,
ˈwɑlˌ(h)əŋ

Wallingford
BR ˈwɒlɪŋfəd
AM ˈwɒlɪŋfərd,
ˈwɑlɪŋfərd

Wallis
BR ˈwɒlɪs
AM ˈwɒləs, ˈwɑləs

wall-less
BR ˈwɔːlləs
AM ˈwɔ(l)ləs, ˈwɑ(l)ləs

Wallonia
BR wɒˈləʊnɪə(r)
AM wəˈloʊniə,
wɒˈloʊniə, wɑˈloʊniə

Walloon
BR wɒˈluːn, wəˈluːn, -z
AM wɑˈlun, wəˈlun, -z

wallop
BR ˈwɒləp, -s, -ɪŋ, -t
AM ˈwɑləp, -s, -ɪŋ, -t

walloper
BR ˈwɒləpə(r), -z
AM ˈwɑləpər, -z

wallow
BR ˈwɒləʊ, -z, -ɪŋ, -d
AM ˈwɑloʊ, -z, -ɪŋ, -d

wallower
BR ˈwɒləʊə(r), -z
AM ˈwɑləwər, -z

wallpaper
BR ˈwɔːlˌpeɪp|ə(r), -əz,
-(ə)rɪŋ, -əd
AM ˈwɔlˌpeɪp|ər,
ˈwɑlˌpeɪp|ər, -ərz,
-(ə)rɪŋ, -ərd

wallplanner
BR ˈwɔːlˌplɑnə(r), -z
AM ˈwɔlˌplænər,
ˈwɑlˌplænər, -z

Walls
BR wɔːlz
AM wɔlz, wɑlz

wally
BR ˈwɒl|i, -ɪz
AM ˈwɔli, ˈwɑli, -z

Walmesley
BR ˈwɔːmzli
AM ˈwɔmzli, ˈwɑmzli

Walmsley
BR ˈwɔːmzli
AM ˈwɔmzli, ˈwɑmzli

walnut
BR ˈwɔːlnʌt, -s
AM ˈwɔlˌnət, ˈwɑlˌnət,
-s

Walpamur
BR ˈwɔːlpəmjʊə(r),
ˈwɒlpəmjʊə(r)
AM ˈwɔlpəˌmjʊ(ə)r,
ˈwɑlpəˌmjʊ(ə)r

Walpole
BR ˈwɔːlpəʊl, ˈwɒlpəʊl
AM ˈwɔlˌpoʊl,
ˈwɑlˌpoʊl

Walpurgis
BR vælˈpɜːgɪs,
vælˈpɜːgɪs,
vɑːlˈpɜːgɪs,
vɑːlˈpʊəgɪs
AM vælˈpʊrgəs

walrus
BR ˈwɔːlrəs, ˈwɔːlrʌs,
ˈwɒlrəs, ˈwɒlrʌs, -ɪz
AM ˈwɔlrəs, ˈwɑlrəs,
-əz

Walsall
BR ˈwɔːls(ɔː)l,
ˈwɒls(ɔː)l, ˈwɔːsl
AM ˈwɔlˌsɔl, ˈwɑlˌsɑl

Walsh
BR wɔːlʃ, wɒlʃ
AM wɔlʃ, wɑlʃ

Walsham
BR ˈwɔːlʃəm, ˈwɒlʃəm
AM ˈwɔlʃəm, ˈwɑlʃəm

Walsingham[1]
place in UK
BR ˈwɔːlzɪŋəm,
ˈwɒlzɪŋəm
AM ˈwɔlzɪŋəm,
ˈwɑlzɪŋəm

Walsingham[2]
surname
BR ˈwɔːlsɪŋəm,
ˈwɒlsɪŋəm
AM ˈwɔlzɪŋəm,
ˈwɑlzɪŋəm

Walter
BR ˈwɔːltə(r), ˈwɒltə(r)
AM ˈwɔltər, ˈwɑltər

Walters
BR ˈwɔːltəz, ˈwɒltəz
AM ˈwɔltərz, ˈwɑltərz

Waltham
BR ˈwɔːlθəm, ˈwɒlθəm
AM ˈwɔlθəm, ˈwɑlθəm

Walthamstow
BR ˈwɔːlθəmstəʊ,
ˈwɒlθəmstəʊ
AM ˈwɔlθəmˌstoʊ,
ˈwɑlθəmˌstoʊ

Walton
BR ˈwɔːlt(ə)n,
ˈwɒlt(ə)n
AM ˈwɔltən, ˈwɑltən

waltz
BR wɔːl(t)s, wɒl(t)s,
-ɪz, -ɪŋ, -t
AM wɔl(t)s, wɑl(t)s,
-əz, -ɪŋ, -t

waltzer
BR ˈwɔːl(t)sə(r),
ˈwɒl(t)sə(r), -z
AM ˈwɔl(t)sər,
ˈwɑl(t)sər, -z

Walvis Bay
BR ˌwɔːlvɪs ˈbeɪ
AM ˈwɔlvəs ˈbeɪ,
ˌwɑlvəs ˈbeɪ

Walworth
BR ˈwɔːlwəθ, ˈwɔːlwəθ,
ˈwɒlwəθ, ˈwɒlwəθ
AM ˈwɔlˌwərθ,
ˈwɑlˌwərθ

wampum
BR ˈwɒmpəm
AM ˈwɑmpəm

WAN
wide area network
BR wɑn
AM wæn

wan
pale
BR wɒn, -ə(r), -ɪst
AM wɑn, -ər, -ɪst

Wanamaker
BR ˈwɒnəmeɪkə(r)
AM ˈwɑnəˌmeɪkər

wand
BR wɒnd, -z
AM wɑnd, -z

Wanda
BR ˈwɒndə(r)

AM ˈwɑndə

wander
BR ˈwɒnd|ə(r), -əz,
-(ə)rɪŋ, -əd
AM ˈwɑnd|ər, -ərz,
-(ə)rɪŋ, -ərd

wanderer
BR ˈwɒnd(ə)rə(r), -z
AM ˈwɑnd(ə)rər, -z

wandering
BR ˈwɒnd(ə)rɪŋ, -z
AM ˈwɑnd(ə)rɪŋ, -z

wanderlust
BR ˈwɒndəlʌst
AM ˈwɑndərˌləst

wanderoo
BR ˌwɒndəˈruː, -z
AM ˌwɑndəˈru, -z

wandoo
BR ˈwɒnˈduː, -z
AM ˈwɑnˈdu, -z

Wandsworth
BR ˈwɒn(d)zwəθ,
ˈwɒn(d)zwɑːθ
AM ˈwɑn(d)zˌwərθ

wane
BR weɪn, -z, -ɪŋ, -d
AM weɪn, -z, -ɪŋ, -d

waney
BR ˈweɪni
AM ˈweɪni

wang
BR waŋ, -z, -ɪŋ, -d
AM wæŋ, -z, -ɪŋ, -d

Wanganui
BR ˌwaŋəˈnuːi
AM ˌwaŋəˈnui

wangle
BR ˈwaŋgl̩, -lz,
-lɪŋ\-lɪŋ, -ld
AM ˈwæŋgl̩əl, -əlz,
-(ə)lɪŋ, -əld

wangler
BR ˈwaŋglə(r),
ˈwaŋglə(r), -z
AM ˈwæŋ(ə)lər, -z

wank
BR waŋ|k, -ks, -kɪŋ,
-(k)t
AM wæŋ|k, -ks, -kɪŋ,
-(k)t

Wankel
BR ˈwaŋkl
AM ˈwæŋkəl

wanker
BR ˈwaŋkə(r), -z
AM ˈwæŋkər, -z

Wankie
BR ˈwaŋki
AM ˈwæŋki

wanky
BR ˈwaŋki
AM ˈwæŋki

wanly
BR ˈwɒnli
AM ˈwɑnli

wanna
want to
BR 'wɒnə(r)
AM 'wɑnə

wannabe
BR 'wɒnəbiː, -z
AM 'wɒnəbi, -z

wanness
BR 'wɒnnəs
AM 'wɑ(n)nəs

Wanstead
BR 'wɒnstɪd, 'wɒnstəd
AM 'wɑn,stɛd

want
BR wɒnt, -s, -ɪŋ, -ɪd-
AM wɑn|t, -ts, -(t)ɪŋ,
-(t)əd

Wantage
BR 'wɒntɪdʒ
AM 'wɑn(t)ɪdʒ

wanter
BR 'wɒntə(r), -z
AM 'wɑn(t)ər, -z

wanton
BR 'wɒntən, -z
AM 'wɑn(t)ən, -z

wantonly
BR 'wɒntənli
AM 'wɑn(t)nli

wantonness
BR 'wɒntənnəs
AM 'wɑn(t)nnəs,
'wɑnt(n)nəs

wapentake
BR 'wɒp(ə)nteɪk,
'wæp(ə)nteɪk, -s
AM 'wæpən,teɪk,
'wɑpən,teɪk, -s

wapiti
BR 'wɒpɪt|i, -ɪz
AM 'wɑpədi, -z

Wapping
BR 'wɒpɪŋ
AM 'wɑpɪŋ

war
BR wɔː(r), -z, -ɪŋ, -d
AM wɔ(ə)r, -z, -ɪŋ, -d

waratah
BR 'wɒrətɑː(r), -z
AM 'wɔrətɑ, -z

warb
BR wɔːb, -z
AM wɔ(ə)rb, -z

Warbeck
BR 'wɔːbɛk
AM 'wɔr,bɛk

warble
BR 'wɔːb|l, -lz,
-lɪŋ\-lɪŋ, -ld
AM 'wɔrbəl, -əlz,
-(ə)lɪŋ, -əld

warbler
BR 'wɔːblə(r), -z
AM 'wɔrb(ə)lər, -z

Warboys
BR 'wɔːbɔɪz
AM 'wɔr,bɔɪz

Warburg
BR 'wɔːbɜːg
AM 'wɔr,bɜrg

Warburton
BR 'wɔːbət(ə)n,
'wɔː,bɜːtn
AM 'wɔr,bɜrtən

warby
BR 'wɔːbi
AM 'wɔrbi

ward
BR wɔːd, -z, -ɪŋ, -d-
AM wɔ(ə)rd, -z, -ɪŋ, -əd

Wardell
BR wɔː'dɛl
AM ,wɔr'dɛl

warden
BR 'wɔːdn, -z
AM 'wɔrdən, -z

wardenship
BR 'wɔːdnʃɪp, -s
AM 'wɔrdn,ʃɪp, -s

warder
BR 'wɔːdə(r), -z
AM 'wɔrdər, -z

Wardle
BR 'wɔːdl
AM 'wɔrdəl

Wardour
BR 'wɔːdə(r),
'wɔːdɔː(r)
AM 'wɔr,dɔ(ə)r

wardress
BR 'wɔːdrɪs, -ɪz
AM 'wɔrdrəs, -əz

wardrobe
BR 'wɔːdrəʊb, -z
AM 'wɔr,droʊb, -z

wardroom
BR 'wɔːdruːm,
'wɔːdrʊm, -z
AM 'wɔrd,rum,
'wɔrd,rʊm, -z

wardship
BR 'wɔːdʃɪp, -s
AM 'wɔrd,ʃɪp, -s

ware
BR 'wɛː(r), -z
AM 'wɛ(ə)r, -z

Wareham
BR 'wɛːrəm, 'wɛːrm
AM 'wɛrəm

warehouse
BR 'wɛːhaʊ|s, -zɪz, -zɪŋ,
-zd
AM 'wɛr,(h)aʊ|s, -zəz,
-zɪŋ, -zd

warehouseman
BR 'wɛːhaʊsmən
AM 'wɛr,(h)aʊsmən

warehousemen
BR 'wɛːhaʊsmən
AM 'wɛr,(h)aʊsmən

Wareing
BR 'wɛːrɪŋ
AM 'wɛrɪŋ

warfare
BR 'wɔːfɛː(r)
AM 'wɔr,fɛ(ə)r

warfarin
BR 'wɔːf(ə)rɪn
AM 'wɔrfərən

Wargrave
BR 'wɔːgreɪv
AM 'wɔr,greɪv

warhead
BR 'wɔːhɛd, -z
AM 'wɔr,(h)ɛd, -z

Warhol
BR 'wɔːhəʊl, 'wɔːhɒl
AM 'wɔr,(h)ɔl,
'wɔr,(h)ɑl

warhorse
BR 'wɔːhɔːs, -ɪz
AM 'wɔr,(h)ɔ(ə)rs, -əz

warily
BR 'wɛːrɪli
AM 'wɛrəli

wariness
BR 'wɛːrɪnɪs
AM 'wɛrɪnɪs

Waring
BR 'wɛːrɪŋ
AM 'wɛrɪŋ

Warkworth
BR 'wɔːkwəθ,
'wɔːkwəθ
AM 'wɔrk,wərθ

Warley
BR 'wɔːli
AM 'wɔrli

warlike
BR 'wɔːlaɪk
AM 'wɔr,laɪk

warlock
BR 'wɔːlɒk, -s
AM 'wɔr,lɑk, -s

warlord
BR 'wɔːlɔːd, -z
AM 'wɔr,lɔ(ə)rd, -z

warm
BR wɔːm, -z, -ɪŋ, -d,
-ə(r), -ɪst
AM 'wɔ(ə)rm, -z, -ɪŋ, -d,
-ər, -əst

warm-blooded
BR ,wɔːm'blʌdɪd
AM ,wɔrm'blədəd

**warm-
bloodedness**
BR ,wɔːm'blʌdɪdnɪs
AM ,wɔrm'blədədnəs

warmed-over
BR ,wɔːmd'əʊvə(r)
AM ,wɔrmd'oʊvər

warmed-up
BR ,wɔːmd'ʌp
AM ,wɔrmd'əp

warmer
BR 'wɔːmə(r), -z
AM 'wɔrmər, -z

warm-hearted
BR ,wɔːm'hɑːtɪd

AM 'wɔrm,hɑrdəd

warm-heartedly
BR ,wɔːm'hɑːtɪdli
AM 'wɔrm,hɑrdədli

**warm-
heartedness**
BR ,wɔːm'hɑːtɪdnɪs
AM 'wɔrm,hɑrdədnəs

Warminster
BR 'wɔːmɪnstə(r)
AM 'wɔr,mɪnstər

warmish
BR 'wɔːmɪʃ
AM 'wɔrmɪʃ

warmly
BR 'wɔːmli
AM 'wɔrmli

warmness
BR 'wɔːmnəs
AM 'wɔrmnəs

warmonger
BR 'wɔː,mʌŋglə(r), -əz,
-ərɪŋ
AM 'wɔr,mʌŋgər,
'wɔr,mɑŋgər, -z, -ɪŋ

warmth
BR wɔːmθ
AM 'wɔrmθ

warm-up
BR 'wɔːmʌp, -s
AM 'wɔrməp, -s

warn
BR wɔːn, -z, -ɪŋ, -d
AM wɔ(ə)rn, -z, -ɪŋ, -d

warner
BR 'wɔːnə(r), -z
AM 'wɔrnər, -z

warning
BR 'wɔːnɪŋ, -z
AM 'wɔrnɪŋ, -z

warningly
BR 'wɔːnɪŋli
AM 'wɔrnɪŋli

Warnock
BR 'wɔːnɒk
AM 'wɔrnək

warp
BR wɔːp, -s, -ɪŋ, -t
AM wɔ(ə)rp, -s, -ɪŋ, -t

warpage
BR 'wɔːpɪdʒ
AM 'wɔrpɪdʒ

warpaint
BR 'wɔːpeɪnt
AM 'wɔr,peɪnt

warpath
BR 'wɔːpɑːθ, 'wɔːpæθ
AM 'wɔr,pæθ

warper
BR 'wɔːpə(r), -z
AM 'wɔrpər, -z

warplane
BR 'wɔːpleɪn, -z
AM 'wɔr,pleɪn, -z

warragal
BR 'wɒrəgl, -z
AM 'wɔrəgəl, -z

warrant
BR ˈwɒrənt, ˈwɒrnt, -s,
-ɪŋ, -ɪd
AM ˈwɔːrən|t, -ts, -(t)ɪŋ,
-(t)əd

warrantable
BR ˈwɒrəntəbl,
ˈwɒrntəbl
AM ˈwɔːrən(t)əbəl

warrantableness
BR ˈwɒrəntəblnəs,
ˈwɒrntəblnəs
AM ˈwɔːrən(t)əbəlnəs

warrantably
BR ˈwɒrəntəbli,
ˈwɒrntəbli
AM ˈwɔːrən(t)əbli

warrantee
BR ˌwɒrənˈtiː,
ˌwɒrn̩ˈtiː, -z
AM ˌwɔːrənˈti, -z

warranter
BR ˈwɒrəntə(r),
ˈwɒrntə(r), -z
AM ˈwɔːrən(t)ər, -z

warrantor
BR ˌwɒrənˈtɔː(r),
ˌwɒrn̩ˈtɔː(r),
ˈwɒrəntɔː(r),
ˈwɒrntɔː(r), -z
AM ˈwɔːrən(t)ər, -z

warranty
BR ˈwɒrənt|i, ˈwɒrnt|i,
-ɪz
AM ˈwɔːrən(t)i, -z

warren
BR ˈwɒrən, ˈwɒrn̩, -z
AM ˈwɔːrən, -z

Warrender
BR ˈwɒrɪndə(r)
AM ˈwɔːrəndər

warrener
BR ˈwɒrənə(r),
ˈwɒrn̩ə(r), -z
AM ˈwɔːrənər, -z

warrigal
BR ˈwɒrɪgl, -z
AM ˈwɔːrəgəl, -z

Warrington
BR ˈwɒrɪŋt(ə)n
AM ˈwɔːrɪŋtən

warrior
BR ˈwɒrɪə(r), -z
AM ˈwɔːrɪər, -z

Warsaw
BR ˈwɔːsɔː(r)
AM ˈwɔːrˌsɔ

warship
BR ˈwɔːˌʃɪp, -s
AM ˈwɔːrˌʃɪp, -s

Warsop
BR ˈwɔːsɒp
AM ˈwɔːrsəp

Warspite
BR ˈwɔːspaɪt
AM ˈwɔːrˌspaɪt

wart
BR wɔːt, -s
AM wɔ(ə)rt, -s

Wartburg
BR ˈwɔːtbɜːg, ˈvɑːtbɜːg
AM ˈwɔːrtˌbɜrg

warthog
BR ˈwɔːthɒg, -z
AM ˈwɔːrtˌ(h)ɑg,
ˈwɑrtˌ(h)ɑg, -z

wartime
BR ˈwɔːtʌɪm
AM ˈwɔːrˌtaɪm

Warton
BR ˈwɔːtn
AM ˈwɔːrtən

wartorn
BR ˈwɔːtɔːn
AM ˈwɔːrˌtɔ(ə)rn

warty
BR ˈwɔːt|i, -ɪə(r), -ɪst
AM ˈwɔːrdi, -ər, -ɪst

Warwick[1]
in UK, place and surname
BR ˈwɒrɪk
AM ˈwɔːr(w)ɪk

Warwick[2]
in US, place and surname
BR ˈwɔːwɪk
AM ˈwɔːr(w)ɪk

Warwickshire
BR ˈwɒrɪkʃ(ɪ)ə(r)
AM ˈwɔːr(w)əkˌʃɪ(ə)r

warworn
BR ˈwɔːwɔːn
AM ˈwɔːrˌwɔ(ə)rn

wary
BR ˈwɛːr|i(1)ə(r), -ɪə(r), -ɪst
AM ˈwɛri, -ər, -ɪst

was[1]
strong form
BR wɒz
AM wəz

was[2]
weak form
BR wəz
AM wəz

Wasatch
BR ˈwɔːsatʃ
AM ˈwɔˌsætʃ, ˈwɑˌsætʃ

wash
BR wɒʃ, -ɪz, -ɪŋ, -t
AM wɔːʃ, wɑʃ, -əz, -ɪŋ, -t

washability
BR ˌwɒʃəˈbɪlɪti
AM ˌwɔːʃəˈbɪlɪdi,
ˌwɑʃəˈbɪlɪdi

washable
BR ˈwɒʃəbl
AM ˈwɔːʃəbəl, ˈwɑʃəbəl

wash-and-wear
BR ˌwɒʃ(ə)n(d)ˈwɛː(r)
AM ˌwɔʃənˈwɛ(ə)r,
ˌwɑʃənˈwɛ(ə)r

washbag
BR ˈwɒʃbag, -z
AM ˈwɔʃˌbæg,
ˈwɑʃˌbæg, -z

washbasin
BR ˈwɒʃbeɪsn, -z
AM ˈwɔʃˌbeɪsn,
ˈwɑʃˌbeɪsn, -z

washboard
BR ˈwɒʃbɔːd, -z
AM ˈwɔʃˌbɔ(ə)rd,
ˈwɑʃˌbɔ(ə)rd, -z

Washbourn
BR ˈwɒʃbɔːn
AM ˈwɔʃˌbɔ(ə)rn,
ˈwɑʃˌbɔ(ə)rn

Washbourne
BR ˈwɒʃbɔːn
AM ˈwɔʃˌbɔ(ə)rn,
ˈwɑʃˌbɔ(ə)rn

washbowl
BR ˈwɒʃbəʊl, -z
AM ˈwɔʃˌboʊl,
ˈwɑʃˌboʊl, -z

Washbrook
BR ˈwɒʃbrʊk
AM ˈwɔʃˌbrʊk,
ˈwɑʃˌbrʊk

Washburn
BR ˈwɒʃbɜːn
AM ˈwɔʃˌbɜrn,
ˈwɑʃˌbɜrn

washcloth
BR ˈwɒʃklɒθ, -θs \-ðz
AM ˈwɔʃˌklɔθ,
ˈwɑʃˌklɑ|θ, -θs \-ðz

washday
BR ˈwɒʃdeɪ, -z
AM ˈwɔʃˌdeɪ, ˈwɑʃˌdeɪ, -z

washed out
BR ˌwɒʃt ˈaʊt
AM ˌwɔʃt ˈaʊt, ˈwɑʃt +

washed up
BR ˌwɒʃt ˈʌp
AM ˌwɔʃt ˈəp, ˈwɑʃt +

washer
BR ˈwɒʃə(r), -z
AM ˈwɔʃər, ˈwɑʃər, -z

washer/dryer
BR ˈwɒʃəˈdrʌɪə(r), -z
AM ˈwɔʃərˈdraɪər,
ˈwɑʃərˈdraɪər, -z

washerman
BR ˈwɒʃəmən
AM ˈwɔʃərmən,
ˈwɑʃərmən

washermen
BR ˈwɒʃəmən
AM ˈwɔʃərmən,
ˈwɑʃərmən

washerwoman
BR ˈwɒʃəˌwʊmən
AM ˈwɔʃərˌwʊmən,
ˈwɑʃərˌwʊmən

washerwomen
BR ˈwɒʃəˌwɪmɪn
AM ˈwɔʃərˌwɪmɪn,
ˈwɑʃərˌwɪmɪn

washery
BR ˈwɒʃ(ə)r|i, -ɪz
AM ˈwɔʃəri, ˈwɑʃəri, -z

washeteria
BR ˌwɒʃəˈtɪərɪə(r), -z
AM ˈwɔʃəˈtɪriə,
ˌwɑʃəˈtɪ(ə)riə, -z

wash-hand basin
BR ˈwɒʃhan(d)ˌbeɪsn,
-z
AM ˈwɔʃˌ(h)ænd
ˌbeɪsn,
ˈwɑʃˌ(h)ænd +, -z

washhouse
BR ˈwɒʃhaʊ|s, -zɪz
AM ˈwɔʃˌ(h)aʊ|s,
ˈwɑʃˌ(h)aʊ|s, -zəz

Washington
BR ˈwɒʃɪŋt(ə)n
AM ˈwɔʃɪŋtən,
ˈwɑʃɪŋtən

Washingtonian
BR ˌwɒʃɪŋˈtəʊnɪən
AM ˌwɔʃɪŋˈtoʊnɪən,
ˌwɑʃɪŋˈtoʊnɪən

washing-up
BR ˌwɒʃɪŋˈʌp
AM ˌwɔʃɪŋˈəp,
ˌwɑʃɪŋˈəp

washland
BR ˈwɒʃland, -z
AM ˈwɔʃˌlænd,
ˈwɑʃˌlænd, -z

washout
BR ˈwɒʃaʊt, -s
AM ˈwɔʃˌaʊt, ˈwɑʃˌaʊt,
-s

washroom
BR ˈwɒʃruːm,
ˈwɒʃrʊm, -z
AM ˈwɔʃˌrum,
ˈwɔʃˌrʊm, ˈwɑʃˌrum,
ˈwɑʃˌrʊm, -z

washstand
BR ˈwɒʃstand, -z
AM ˈwɔʃˌstænd,
ˈwɑʃˌstænd, -z

washtub
BR ˈwɒʃtʌb, -z
AM ˈwɔʃˌtəb, ˈwɑʃˌtəb,
-z

wash-up
BR ˈwɒʃʌp
AM ˈwɔʃˌəp, ˈwɑʃˌəp

wash/wipe
BR ˈwɒʃˈwʌɪp
AM ˈwɔʃˈwaɪp,
ˈwɑʃˈwaɪp

washy
BR ˈwɒʃ|i, -ɪə(r), -ɪst
AM ˈwɔʃi, ˈwɑʃi, -ər, -ɪst

wasn't
BR ˈwɒznt
AM ˈwəznt

WASP
BR ˈwɒsp, -s
AM ˈwɑsp, -s

wasp
BR ˈwɒsp, -s
AM ˈwɑsp, -s

waspie
BR ˈwɒspi, -ız
AM ˈwɑspi, -z

waspish
BR ˈwɒspıʃ
AM ˈwɑspıʃ

waspishly
BR ˈwɒspıʃli
AM ˈwɑspıʃli

waspishness
BR ˈwɒspıʃnıs
AM ˈwɑspıʃnıs

wasplike
BR ˈwɒsplʌık
AM ˈwɑspˌlaık

waspy
BR ˈwɒspi
AM ˈwɑspi

wassail
BR ˈwɒseıl, ˈwɒsl̩, -z, -ıŋ
AM ˈwɑˌseıl, ˈwɑsəl, -z, -ıŋ

wassail-bowl
BR ˈwɒseılbəʊl, ˈwɒslbəʊl, -z
AM ˈwɑˌseılˌbəʊl, ˈwɑsəlˌbəʊl, -z

wassail-cup
BR ˈwɒseılkʌp, ˈwɒslkʌp, -s
AM ˈwɑˌseılˌkəp, ˈwɑsəlˌkəp, -s

wassailer
BR ˈwɒseılə(r), ˈwɒslə(r), -z
AM ˈwɑˌseılər, ˈwɑsələr, -z

wast¹
strong form
BR wɒst
AM wɔst, wɑst

wast²
weak form
BR wəst
AM wəst

wastable
BR ˈweıstəbl
AM ˈweıstəbəl

wastage
BR ˈweıstıdʒ
AM ˈweıstıdʒ

waste
BR weıst, -s, -ıŋ, -ıd
AM weıst, -s, -ıŋ, -ıd

wastebasket
BR ˈweıs(t)ˌbɑːskıt, ˈweıs(t)ˌbaskıt, -s
AM ˈweıs(t)ˌbæskət, -s

wasteful
BR ˈweıstf(ʊ)l
AM ˈweıs(t)fəl

wastefully
BR ˈweıstfʊli, ˈweıstfli
AM ˈweıs(t)fəli

wastefulness
BR ˈweıstf(ʊ)lnəs
AM ˈweıs(t)fəlnəs

wasteland
BR ˈweıs(t)land, -z
AM ˈweıs(t)ˌlænd, -z

wasteless
BR ˈweıstlıs
AM ˈweıs(t)lıs

waster
BR ˈweıstə(r), -z
AM ˈweıstər, -z

wastrel
BR ˈweıstr(ə)l, -z
AM ˈweıstrəl, ˈwɑstrəl, -z

Wastwater
BR ˈwɒst,wɔːtə(r)
AM ˈwɑs(t),wɔdər, ˈwɑs(t),wɑdər

Wat
BR wɒt
AM wɑt

watch
BR wɒtʃ, -ız, -ıŋ, -t
AM wɑtʃ, -əz, -ıŋ, -t

watchable
BR ˈwɒtʃəbl
AM ˈwɑtʃəbəl

watchband
BR ˈwɒtʃband, -z
AM ˈwɑtʃˌbænd, -z

watchcase
BR ˈwɒtʃkeıs, -ız
AM ˈwɑtʃˌkeıs, -ız

watchchain
BR ˈwɒtʃtʃeın, -z
AM ˈwɑtʃˌtʃeın, -z

watchdog
BR ˈwɒtʃdɒg, -z
AM ˈwɑtʃˌdɑg, -z

watcher
BR ˈwɒtʃə(r), -z
AM ˈwɑtʃər, -z

Watchet
BR ˈwɒtʃıt
AM ˈwɑtʃət

watchfire
BR ˈwɒtʃˌfʌıə(r), -z
AM ˈwɑtʃˌfaı(ə)r, -z

watchful
BR ˈwɒtʃf(ʊ)l
AM ˈwɑtʃfəl

watchfully
BR ˈwɒtʃfʊli, ˈwɒtʃfli
AM ˈwɑtʃfəli

watchfulness
BR ˈwɒtʃf(ʊ)lnəs
AM ˈwɑtʃfəlnəs

watch-glass
BR ˈwɒtʃglɑːs, ˈwɒtʃglas, -ız
AM ˈwɑtʃˌglæs, -əz

watchkeeper
BR ˈwɒtʃˌkiːpə(r), -z
AM ˈwɑtʃˌkipər, -z

watchmaker
BR ˈwɒtʃˌmeıkə(r), -z
AM ˈwɑtʃˌmeıkər, -z

watchmaking
BR ˈwɒtʃˌmeıkıŋ
AM ˈwɑtʃˌmeıkıŋ

watchman
BR ˈwɒtʃmən
AM ˈwɑtʃmən

watchmen
BR ˈwɒtʃmən
AM ˈwɑtʃmən

watchnight
BR ˈwɒtʃnʌıt
AM ˈwɑtʃˌnaıt

watchspring
BR ˈwɒtʃsprıŋ, -z
AM ˈwɑtʃˌ(s)prıŋ, -z

watchstrap
BR ˈwɒtʃstrap, -s
AM ˈwɑtʃˌ(s)træp, -s

watchtower
BR ˈwɒtʃˌtaʊə(r), -z
AM ˈwɑtʃˌtaʊər, -z

watchword
BR ˈwɒtʃwəːd, -z
AM ˈwɑtʃˌwərd, -z

Watendlath
BR wɒˈtɛndləθ
AM wɑˈtɛn(d)ləθ

water
BR ˈwɔːt|ə(r), -əz, -(ə)rıŋ, -əd
AM ˈwɔdər, ˈwɑdər, -z, -ıŋ, -d

waterbed
BR ˈwɔːtəbɛd, -z
AM ˈwɔdərˌbɛd, ˈwɑdərˌbɛd, -z

waterbird
BR ˈwɔːtəbəːd, -z
AM ˈwɔdərˌbərd, ˈwɑdərˌbərd, -z

waterborne
BR ˈwɔːtəbɔːn
AM ˈwɔdərˌbɔ(ə)rn, ˈwɑdərˌbɔ(ə)rn

waterbrash
BR ˈwɔːtəbraʃ
AM ˈwɔdərˌbræʃ, ˈwɑdərˌbræʃ

watercolor
BR ˈwɔːtəˌkʌlə(r), -z
AM ˈwɔdərˌkələr, ˈwɑdərˌkələr, -z

watercolorist
BR ˈwɔːtəˌkʌl(ə)rıst, -s
AM ˈwɔdərˌkələrəst, ˈwɑdərˌkələrəst, -s

watercolour
BR ˈwɔːtəˌkʌlə(r), -z
AM ˈwɔdərˌkələr, ˈwɑdərˌkələr, -z

watercolourist
BR ˈwɔːtəˌkʌl(ə)rıst, -s

watercourse
BR ˈwɔːtəkɔːs, -ız
AM ˈwɔdərˌkɔ(ə)rs, ˈwɑdərˌkɔ(ə)rs, -əz

watercraft
BR ˈwɔːtəkrɑːft, ˈwɔːtəkraft, -s
AM ˈwɔdərˌkræft, ˈwɑdərˌkræft, -s

watercress
BR ˈwɔːtəkrɛs
AM ˈwɔdərˌkrɛs, ˈwɑdərˌkrɛs

waterer
BR ˈwɔːt(ə)rə(r), -z
AM ˈwɔdərər, ˈwɑdərər, -z

waterfall
BR ˈwɔːtəfɔːl, -z
AM ˈwɔdərˌfɔl, ˈwɑdərˌfɑl, -z

Waterford
BR ˈwɔːtəfəd
AM ˈwɔdərfərd, ˈwɑdərfərd

waterfowl
BR ˈwɔːtəfaʊl
AM ˈwɔdərˌfaʊl, ˈwɑdərˌfaʊl

waterfront
BR ˈwɔːtəfrʌnt, -s
AM ˈwɔdərˌfrənt, ˈwɑdərˌfrənt, -s

watergate
BR ˈwɔːtəgeıt, -s
AM ˈwɔdərˌgeıt, ˈwɑdərˌgeıt, -s

waterhole
BR ˈwɔːtəhəʊl, -z
AM ˈwɔdərˌ(h)oʊl, ˈwɑdərˌ(h)oʊl, -z

Waterhouse
BR ˈwɔːtəhaʊs
AM ˈwɔdərˌ(h)aʊs, ˈwɑdərˌ(h)aʊs

wateriness
BR ˈwɔːt(ə)rınıs
AM ˈwɔdərınıs, ˈwɑdərınıs

watering
BR ˈwɔːt(ə)rıŋ, -z
AM ˈwɔdərıŋ, ˈwɑdərıŋ, -z

waterless
BR ˈwɔːtələs
AM ˈwɔdərləs, ˈwɑdərləs

waterline
BR ˈwɔːtəlʌın, -z
AM ˈwɔdərˌlaın, ˈwɑdərˌlaın, -z

waterlogged
BR ˈwɔːtəlɒgd
AM ˈwɔdərˌlɒgd, ˈwɑdərˌlɒgd

Waterloo
BR ˌwɔːtəˈluː
AM ˈwɔdərˌlu,
ˈwɑdərˌlu

waterman
BR ˈwɔːtəmən
AM ˈwɔdərmən,
ˈwɑdərmən

watermark
BR ˈwɔːtəmɑːk, -s
AM ˈwɔdərˌmɑrk,
ˈwɑdərˌmɑrk, -s

watermelon
BR ˈwɔːtəˌmɛlən, -z
AM ˈwɔdərˌmɛlən,
ˈwɑdərˌmɛlən, -z

watermen
BR ˈwɔːtəmən
AM ˈwɔdərmən,
ˈwɑdərmən

watermill
BR ˈwɔːtəmɪl, -z
AM ˈwɔdərˌmɪl,
ˈwɑdərˌmɪl, -z

waterpower
BR ˈwɔːtəˌpaʊə(r)
AM ˈwɔdərˌpaʊər,
ˈwɑdərˌpaʊər

waterproof
BR ˈwɔːtəpruːf, -s, -ɪŋ, -t
AM ˈwɔdərˌpruf,
ˈwɑdərˌpruf, -s, -ɪŋ, -t

waterproofer
BR ˈwɔːtəpruːfə(r), -z
AM ˈwɔdərˌprufər,
ˈwɑdərˌprufər, -z

waterproofness
BR ˈwɔːtəpruːfnəs
AM ˈwɔdərˌprufnəs,
ˈwɑdərˌprufnəs

water-repellant
BR ˌwɔːtərɪˈpɛlənt,
ˌwɔːtərɪˈpɛlnt,
ˈwɔːtərɪˌpɛlənt,
ˈwɔːtərɪˌpɛlnt
AM ˈwɔdə(r)rəˌpɛlənt,
ˈwɑdə(r)rəˌpɛlənt

water-repellency
BR ˌwɔːtərɪˈpɛlənsi,
ˌwɔːtərɪˈpɛlnsi,
ˈwɔːtərɪˌpɛlənsi,
ˈwɔːtərɪˌpɛlnsi
AM ˈwɔdə(r)rəˌpɛlənsi,
ˈwɑdə(r)rəˌpɛlənsi

water-repellent
BR ˌwɔːtərɪˈpɛlənt,
ˌwɔːtərɪˈpɛlnt,
ˈwɔːtərɪˌpɛlənt,
ˈwɔːtərɪˌpɛlnt
AM ˈwɔdə(r)rəˌpɛlənt,
ˈwɑdə(r)rəˌpɛlənt

water-resistance
BR ˌwɔːtərɪˈzɪst(ə)ns,
ˈwɔːtərɪˌzɪst(ə)ns
AM ˈwɔdə(r)rəˌzɪstəns,
ˈwɑdə(r)rəˌzɪstəns

water-resistant
BR ˌwɔːtərɪˈzɪst(ə)nt,
ˈwɔːtərɪˌzɪst(ə)nt
AM ˈwɔdə(r)rəˌzɪstənt,
ˈwɑdə(r)rəˌzɪstənt

Waters
BR ˈwɔːtəz
AM ˈwɔdərz, ˈwɑdərz

watershed
BR ˈwɔːtəˌʃɛd, -z
AM ˈwɔdərˌʃɛd,
ˈwɑdərˌʃɛd, -z

waterside
BR ˈwɔːtəsaɪd
AM ˈwɔdərˌsaɪd,
ˈwɑdərˌsaɪd

water-soluble
BR ˈwɔːtəˈsɒljəbl
AM ˈwɔdərˌsɑl(j)əbəl,
ˈwɑdərˌsɑl(j)əbəl

Waterson
BR ˈwɔːtəs(ə)n
AM ˈwɔdərsən,
ˈwɑdərsən

watersport
BR ˈwɔːtəspɔːt, -s
AM ˈwɔdərˌspɔ(ə)rt,
ˈwɑdərˌspɔ(ə)rt, -s

waterspout
BR ˈwɔːtəspaʊt, -s
AM ˈwɔdərˌspaʊt,
ˈwɑdərˌspaʊt, -s

watertight
BR ˈwɔːtətaɪt
AM ˈwɔdərˌtaɪt,
ˈwɑdərˌtaɪt

waterway
BR ˈwɔːtəweɪ, -z
AM ˈwɔdərˌweɪ,
ˈwɑdərˌweɪ, -z

waterweed
BR ˈwɔːtəwiːd, -z
AM ˈwɔdərˌwid,
ˈwɑdərˌwid, -z

waterwheel
BR ˈwɔːtəwiːl, -z
AM ˈwɔdərˌ(h)wil,
ˈwɑdərˌ(h)wil, -z

waterwings
BR ˈwɔːtəwɪŋz
AM ˈwɔdərˌwɪŋz,
ˈwɑdərˌwɪŋz

waterworks
BR ˈwɔːtəwɜːks
AM ˈwɔdərˌwɜrks,
ˈwɑdərˌwɜrks

watery
BR ˈwɔːt(ə)ri
AM ˈwɔdəri, ˈwɑdəri

Wates
BR weɪts
AM weɪts

Watford
BR ˈwɒtfəd
AM ˈwɑtfərd

Wath
BR wɒθ
AM wɑθ

Watkin
BR ˈwɒtkɪn
AM ˈwatkən

Watkins
BR ˈwɒtkɪnz
AM ˈwatkənz

Watkinson
BR ˈwɒtkɪns(ə)n
AM ˈwatkənsən

Watling Street
BR ˈwɒtlɪŋ striːt
AM ˈwatlɪŋ ˌstrit

Watney
BR ˈwɒtni
AM ˈwatni

WATS line
BR ˈwɒts lʌɪn
AM ˈwats ˌlaɪn

Watson
BR ˈwɒtsn
AM ˈwatsən

watsonia
BR wɒtˈsəʊnɪə(r), -z
AM watˈsoʊniə, -z

Watson-Watt
BR ˌwɒtsnˈwɒt
AM ˌwatsənˈwat

Watt
BR wɒt
AM wat

watt
BR wɒt, -s
AM wat, -s

wattage
BR ˈwɒtɪdʒ
AM ˈwadɪdʒ

Watteau
BR ˈwɒtəʊ
AM waˈtoʊ

watt-hour
BR ˌwɒtˈaʊə(r), -z
AM ˌwadˌaʊər, -z

wattle
BR ˈwɒtl, -z, -d
AM ˈwadəl, -z, -d

wattlebird
BR ˈwɒtlbəːd, -z
AM ˈwadlˌbərd, -z

wattmeter
BR ˈwɒtˌmiːtə(r), -z
AM ˈwatˌmidər, -z

Watts
BR wɒts
AM wats

Watusi
BR wəˈtuːsli,
wɑːˈtuːsli, -ɪz
AM waˈtusi, -z

Watutsi
BR wəˈtʊtsi, wɑːˈtʊtsi
AM waˈtutsi

Waugh
BR wɔː(r)
AM wɔ

waul
BR wɔːl, -z, -ɪŋ, -d
AM wɔl, wal, -z, -ɪŋ, -d

wave
BR weɪv, -z, -ɪŋ, -d
AM weɪv, -z, -ɪŋ, -d

waveband
BR ˈweɪvband, -z
AM ˈweɪvˌbænd, -z

waveform
BR ˈweɪvfɔːm
AM ˈweɪvˌfɔ(ə)rm

wavefront
BR ˈweɪvfrʌnt, -s
AM ˈweɪvˌfrʌnt, -s

waveguide
BR ˈweɪvɡʌɪd, -z
AM ˈweɪvˌɡaɪd, -z

wavelength
BR ˈweɪvlɛŋ(k)θ, -s
AM ˌweɪvˌlɛŋ(k)θ, -s

waveless
BR ˈweɪvlɪs
AM ˈweɪvlɪs

wavelet
BR ˈweɪvlɪt, -s
AM ˈweɪvlɪt, -s

wavelike
BR ˈweɪvlaɪk
AM ˈweɪvˌlaɪk

waver
BR ˈweɪvlə(r), -əz,
-(ə)rɪŋ, -əd
AM ˈweɪvlər, -ərz,
-(ə)rɪŋ, -ərd

waverer
BR ˈweɪv(ə)rə(r), -z
AM ˈweɪv(ə)rər, -z

waveringly
BR ˈweɪv(ə)rɪŋli
AM ˈweɪv(ə)rɪŋli

wavery
BR ˈweɪv(ə)ri
AM ˈweɪv(ə)ri

wavetop
BR ˈweɪvtɒp, -s
AM ˈweɪvˌtap, -s

wavily
BR ˈweɪvɪli
AM ˈweɪvɪli

waviness
BR ˈweɪvɪnɪs
AM ˈweɪvɪnɪs

wavy
BR ˈweɪv|i, -ɪə(r), -ɪɪst
AM ˈweɪvi, -ər, -ɪst

wa-wa
BR ˈwɑːwɑː(r), -z
AM ˈwɑˌwɑ, -z

wawl
BR wɔːl, -z, -ɪŋ, -d
AM wɔl, wal, -z, -ɪŋ, -d

wax
BR waks, -ɪz, -ɪŋ, -t
AM wæks, -əz, -ɪŋ, -t

waxberry
BR ˈwaksb(ə)r|i, -ɪz
AM ˈwæksˌbɛri, -z

waxbill
BR ˈwaksbɪl, -z

AM ˈwæksˌbɪl, -z

waxcloth
BR ˈwaksklɒ|θ, -θs\-ðz
AM ˈwæksˌklɒ|θ,
ˈwæksˌklɑ|θ, -θs\-ðz

waxen
BR ˈwaksn
AM ˈwæksən

waxer
BR ˈwaksə(r), -z
AM ˈwæksər, -z

waxily
BR ˈwaksɪli
AM ˈwæksəli

waxiness
BR ˈwaksɪnɪs
AM ˈwæksinɪs

waxing
BR ˈwaksɪŋ, -z
AM ˈwæksɪŋ, -z

wax-light
BR ˈwakslʌɪt, -s
AM ˈwæksˌlaɪt, -s

wax-like
BR ˈwakslʌɪk
AM ˈwæksˌlaɪk

waxplant
BR ˈwaksplɑːnt,
ˈwaksplant, -s
AM ˈwæksˌplænt, -s

waxwing
BR ˈwakswɪŋ, -z
AM ˈwæksˌwɪŋ, -z

waxwork
BR ˈwakswəːk, -s
AM ˈwæksˌwərk, -s

waxy
BR ˈwaks|i, -ɪə(r), -ɪɪst
AM ˈwæksi, -ər, -ɪst

way
BR weɪ, -z
AM weɪ, -z

wayback
BR ˈweɪbak
AM ˈweɪˌbæk

waybill
BR ˈweɪbɪl, -z
AM ˈweɪˌbɪl, -z

waybread
BR ˈweɪbrɛd, -z
AM ˈweɪˌbrɛd, -z

wayfarer
BR ˈweɪˌfɛːrə(r), -z
AM ˈweɪˌfɛrər, -z

wayfaring
BR ˈweɪfɛːrɪŋ
AM ˈweɪˌfɛrɪŋ

Wayland
BR ˈweɪlənd
AM ˈweɪlənd

waylay
BR ˌweɪˈleɪ, -z, -ɪŋ, -d
AM ˌweɪˌleɪ, -z, -ɪŋ, -d

waylayer
BR ˌweɪˈleɪə(r), -z
AM ˌweɪˌleɪər, -z

wayleave
BR ˈweɪliːv, -z
AM ˈweɪˌliv, -z

waymark
BR ˈweɪmɑːk, -s, -ɪŋ, -t
AM ˈweɪˌmɑrk, -s, -ɪŋ, -t

waymarker
BR ˈweɪˌmɑːkə(r), -z
AM ˈweɪˌmɑrkər, -z

Wayne
BR weɪn
AM weɪn

way-out
BR ˌweɪˈaʊt
AM ˌweɪˈaʊt

waypoint
BR ˈweɪpɔɪnt, -s
AM ˈweɪˌpɔɪnt, -s

wayside
BR ˈweɪsʌɪd
AM ˈweɪˌsaɪd

wayward
BR ˈweɪwəd
AM ˈweɪwərd

waywardly
BR ˈweɪwədli
AM ˈweɪwərdli

waywardness
BR ˈweɪwədnəs
AM ˈweɪwərdnəs

way-worn
BR ˈweɪwɔːn
AM ˈweɪˌwɔ(ə)rn

wayzgoose
BR ˈweɪzguːs, -ɪz
AM ˈweɪzˌgus, -əz

wazzock
BR ˈwazək, -s
AM ˈwɑzək, -s

WC
BR ˌdʌblju:ˈsi:, -z
AM ˌdəbəlju'si, -z

we¹
strong form
BR wi:
AM wi

we²
weak form
BR wɪ
AM wɪ

weak
BR wi:k, -ə(r), -ɪɪst
AM wik, -ər, -ɪst

weaken
BR ˈwiːk|(ə)n, -(ə)nz,
-nɪŋ\-(ə)nɪŋ, -(ə)nd
AM ˈwik|ən, -ənz,
-(ə)nɪŋ, -ənd

weakener
BR ˈwiːk(ə)nə(r),
ˈwiːkn̩ə(r), -z
AM ˈwik(ə)nər, -z

weakfish
BR ˈwiːkfɪʃ, -ɪz
AM ˈwikˌfɪʃ, -ɪz

weakish
BR ˈwiːkɪʃ

AM ˈwikɪʃ

weak-kneed
BR ˌwiːkˈniːd
AM ˌwikˈnid

weakliness
BR ˈwiːklɪnɪs
AM ˈwiklɪnɪs

weakling
BR ˈwiːklɪŋ, -z
AM ˈwiklɪŋ, -z

weakly
BR ˈwiːkl|i, -ɪə(r), -ɪɪst
AM ˈwikli, -ər, -ɪst

weakness
BR ˈwiːknɪs, -ɪz
AM ˈwiknɪs, -ɪz

weak-willed
BR ˌwiːkˈwɪld
AM ˌwikˈwɪld

weal
BR wi:l, -z
AM wil, -z

weald
BR wi:ld, -z
AM wild, -z

wealden
BR ˈwiːld(ə)n
AM ˈwildən

Wealdstone
BR ˈwiːl(d)stəʊn
AM ˈwil(d)ˌstoʊn

wealth
BR wɛlθ, -s
AM wɛlθ, -s

wealthily
BR ˈwɛlθɪli
AM ˈwɛlθəli

wealthiness
BR ˈwɛlθɪnɪs
AM ˈwɛlθinɪs

wealthy
BR ˈwɛlθ|i, -ɪə(r), -ɪɪst
AM ˈwɛlθi, -ər, -ɪst

wean
BR wiːn, -z, -ɪŋ, -d
AM win, -z, -ɪŋ, -d

weaner
BR ˈwiːnə(r), -z
AM ˈwinər, -z

weanling
BR ˈwiːnlɪŋ, -z
AM ˈwinlɪŋ, -z

weapon
BR ˈwɛp(ə)n, -z, -d
AM ˈwɛpən, -z, -d

weaponless
BR ˈwɛp(ə)nləs
AM ˈwɛpənləs

weaponry
BR ˈwɛp(ə)nri
AM ˈwɛpənri

Wear
river etc
BR wɪə(r)
AM wɪ(ə)r

wear
BR wɛː(r), -z, -ɪŋ

AM ˈwikɪʃ

AM wɛ(ə)r, -z, -ɪŋ

wearability
BR ˌwɛːrəˈbɪlɪti
AM ˌwɛrəˈbɪlɪdi

wearable
BR ˈwɛːrəbl
AM ˈwɛrəbəl

wear-and-tear
BR ˌwɛːrən(d)ˈtɛː(r),
ˌwɛːrn̩(d)ˈtɛː(r)
AM ˈwɛrən'tɛ(ə)r

wearer
BR ˈwɛːrə(r), -z
AM ˈwɛrər, -z

weariless
BR ˈwɪərɪlɪs
AM ˈwɪrilɪs

wearily
BR ˈwɪərɪli
AM ˈwɪrɪli

weariness
BR ˈwɪərɪnɪs
AM ˈwɪrinɪs

wearing
BR ˈwɛːrɪŋ
AM ˈwɛrɪŋ

wearingly
BR ˈwɛːrɪŋli
AM ˈwɛrɪŋli

wearisome
BR ˈwɪərɪs(ə)m
AM ˈwɪrisəm

wearisomely
BR ˈwɪərɪs(ə)mli
AM ˈwɪrisəmli

wearisomeness
BR ˈwɪərɪs(ə)mnəs
AM ˈwɪrisəmnəs

Wearmouth
BR ˈwɪəmaʊθ
AM ˈwɪrˌmaʊθ,
ˈwɪrməθ

Wearside
BR ˈwɪəsʌɪd
AM ˈwɪrˌsaɪd

weary
BR ˈwɪər|i, -ɪz, -ɪɪŋ, -ɪd,
-ɪə(r), -ɪɪst
AM ˈwɪri, -z, -ɪŋ, -d, -ər,
-ɪst

wearyingly
BR ˈwɪərɪɪŋli
AM ˈwɪrɪɪŋli

weasel
BR ˈwiːzl, -z
AM ˈwizəl, -z

weaselly
BR ˈwiːzli
AM ˈwiz(ə)li

weather
BR ˈwɛðə(r), -əz,
-(ə)rɪŋ, -əd
AM ˈwɛðər, -ərz,
-(ə)rɪŋ, -ərd

Weatherall
BR ˈwɛð(ə)rɔːl,
ˈwɛð(ə)rl̩

weatherbeaten
AM ˈweðərˌɔl,
ˈweðərˌɑl
BR ˈweðəˌbiːtn
AM ˈweðərˌbitn

weatherboard
BR ˈweðəbɔːd, -z, -ɪŋ
AM ˈweðərˌbɔ(ə)rd, -z, -ɪŋ

weatherbound
BR ˈweðəbaʊnd
AM ˈweðərˌbaʊnd

weathercock
BR ˈweðəkɒk, -s
AM ˈweðərˌkɑk, -s

weather eye
BR ˈweðər ˈʌɪ, ˈweðər ʌɪ
AM ˈweðər ˌaɪ

weathergirl
BR ˈweðəgɜːl, -z
AM ˈweðərˌgɜrl, -z

weatherglass
BR ˈweðəglɑːs, ˈweðəglas, -ɪz
AM ˈweðərˌglæs, -əz

Weatherhead
BR ˈweðəhɛd
AM ˈweðərˌ(h)ɛd

weatherize
BR ˈweðərʌɪz, -ɪz, -ɪŋ, -d
AM ˈweðəˌraɪz, -ɪz, -ɪŋ, -d

weatherliness
BR ˈweðəlɪnɪs
AM ˈweðərlɪnɪs

weatherly
BR ˈweðəli
AM ˈweðərli

weatherman
BR ˈweðəman
AM ˈweðərˌmæn

weathermen
BR ˈweðəmen
AM ˈweðərˌmen

weathermost
BR ˈweðəməʊst
AM ˈweðərˌmoʊst

weatherproof
BR ˈweðəpruːf, -s, -ɪŋ, -t
AM ˈweðərˌpruf, -s, -ɪŋ, -t

weatherstrip
BR ˈweðəstrɪp, -s, -ɪŋ, -t
AM ˈweðərˌstrɪp, -s, -ɪŋ, -t

weathertight
BR ˈweðətʌɪt
AM ˈweðərˌtaɪt

weathervane
BR ˈweðəveɪn, -z
AM ˈweðərˌveɪn, -z

weatherworn
BR ˈweðəwɔːn
AM ˈweðərˌwɔ(ə)rn

weave
BR wiːv, -z, -ɪŋ

AM wiːv, -z, -ɪŋ

weaver
BR ˈwiːvə(r), -z
AM ˈwiːvər, -z

weaverbird
BR ˈwiːvəbɜːd, -z
AM ˈwiːvərˌbɜrd, -z

weaving
BR ˈwiːvɪŋ, -z
AM ˈwiːvɪŋ, -z

web
BR web, -z, -ɪŋ, -d
AM web, -z, -ɪŋ, -d

Webb
BR web
AM web

Webber
BR ˈwebə(r)
AM ˈwebər

webby
BR ˈwebi
AM ˈwebi

Weber[1]
composer, physicist
BR ˈveɪbə(r)
AM ˈveɪbər

Weber[2]
English surname
BR ˈwebə(r), ˈwiːbə(r), ˈweɪbə(r)
AM ˈwebər

weber
BR ˈveɪbə(r), -z
AM ˈwebər, -z

web-footed
BR ˌwebˈfʊtɪd
AM ˌwebˈfʊdəd

Webley®
BR ˈwebli
AM ˈwebli

Webster
BR ˈwebstə(r)
AM ˈwebstər

web-toed
BR ˌwebˈtəʊd
AM ˌwebˈtoʊd

wed
BR wed, -z, -ɪŋ, -ɪd
AM wed, -z, -ɪŋ, -əd

we'd
BR wiːd
AM wid

Weddell
BR ˈwedl
AM ˈwedəl

wedding
BR ˈwedɪŋ, -z
AM ˈwedɪŋ, -z

Wedekind
BR ˈweɪdəkɪnd
AM ˈweɪdəˌkɪnd

wedge
BR wedʒ, -ɪz, -ɪŋ, -d
AM wedʒ, -əz, -ɪŋ, -d

wedgelike
BR ˈwedʒlʌɪk
AM ˈwedʒˌlaɪk

wedge-shaped
BR ˈwedʒˌʃeɪpt, ˌwedʒˈʃeɪpt
AM ˈwedʒˌʃeɪpt

wedgewise
BR ˈwedʒwʌɪz
AM ˈwedʒˌwaɪz

Wedgewood
BR ˈwedʒwʊd
AM ˈwedʒˌwʊd

wedgie
BR ˈwedʒi, -ɪz
AM ˈwedʒi, -z

Wedgwood
BR ˈwedʒwʊd
AM ˈwedʒˌwʊd

wedlock
BR ˈwedlɒk
AM ˈwedˌlɑk

Wednesbury
BR ˈwenzb(ə)ri
AM ˈwenzˌberi

Wednesday
BR ˈwenzdˌeɪ, ˈwenzdˌi, -eɪz\-ɪz
AM ˈwenzˌdeɪ, ˈwenzdi, -z

Wednesfield
BR ˈwenzfiːld
AM ˈwenzˌfild

wee
BR wiː, -z, -ɪŋ, -d
AM wi, -z, -ɪŋ, -d

weed
BR wiːd, -z, -ɪŋ, -ɪd
AM wid, -z, -ɪŋ, -ɪd

weeder
BR ˈwiːdə(r), -z
AM ˈwidər, -z

weediness
BR ˈwiːdɪnɪs
AM ˈwidɪnɪs

weedkiller
BR ˈwiːdˌkɪlə(r), -z
AM ˈwidˌkɪlər, -z

weedless
BR ˈwiːdlɪs
AM ˈwidlɪs

Weedon
BR ˈwiːdn
AM ˈwidən

weedy
BR ˈwiːdˌi, -ɪə(r), -ɪɪst
AM ˈwidi, -ər, -ɪst

Wee Free
BR ˌwiː ˈfriː, -z
AM ˌwi ˈfri, -z

week
BR wiːk, -s
AM wik, -s

weekday
BR ˈwiːkdeɪ, -z
AM ˈwikˌdeɪ, -z

weekend
BR ˌwiːkˈend, ˈwiːkend, -z
AM ˈwɪkˌend, -z

weekender
BR ˌwiːkˈendə(r), -z
AM ˈwikˌendər, -z

Weekes
BR wiːks
AM wiks

Weekley
BR ˈwiːkli
AM ˈwikli

week-long
BR ˈwiːklɒŋ, ˌwiːkˈlɒŋ
AM ˈwikˌlɔŋ, ˈwikˌlɑŋ

weekly
BR ˈwiːklˌi, -ɪz
AM ˈwikli, -z

weeknight
BR ˈwiːkˌnʌɪt, -s
AM ˈwikˌnaɪt, -s

Weeks
BR wiːks
AM wiks

ween
BR wiːn, -z, -ɪŋ, -d
AM win, -z, -ɪŋ, -d

weenie
BR ˈwiːnˌi, -ɪz
AM ˈwini, -z

weeny
BR ˈwiːnˌi, -ɪz, -ɪə(r), -ɪɪst
AM ˈwini, -z, -ər, -ɪst

weeny-bopper
BR ˈwiːnɪˌbɒpə(r), -z
AM ˈwiniˌbɑpər, -z

weep
BR wiːp, -s, -ɪŋ
AM wip, -s, -ɪŋ

weeper
BR ˈwiːpə(r), -z
AM ˈwipər, -z

weepie
BR ˈwiːpˌi, -ɪz
AM ˈwipi, -z

weepily
BR ˈwiːpˌɪli
AM ˈwipɪli

weepiness
BR ˈwiːpɪnɪs
AM ˈwipɪnɪs

weepingly
BR ˈwiːpɪŋli
AM ˈwipɪŋli

weepy
BR ˈwiːpˌi, -ɪz, -ɪə(r), -ɪɪst
AM ˈwipi, -z, -ər, -ɪst

Weetabix®
BR ˈwiːtəbɪks
AM ˈwidəˌbɪks

weever
BR ˈwiːvə(r), -z
AM ˈwivər, -z

weevil
BR ˈwiːv(ɪ)l, -z
AM ˈwivəl, -z

weevily
BR ˈwiːvɪli, ˈwiːvˌli

AM 'wɪvɪli

weewee
BR 'wiːwiː, -z, -ɪŋ, -d
AM 'wi͟ˌwi, -z, -ɪŋ, -d

weft
BR wɛft
AM wɛft

Wehrmacht
BR 'veːˈmɑːkt,
'veːmɑːxt
AM 'vɜːˌmɑkt

Wei
BR weɪ
AM weɪ

Weidenfeld
BR 'vaɪdnfɛlt
AM 'waɪdənˌfɛld,
'vaɪdənˌfɛld

weigh
BR weɪ, -z, -ɪŋ, -d
AM weɪ, -z, -ɪŋ, -d

weighable
BR 'weɪəbl
AM 'weɪəbəl

weighbridge
BR 'weɪbrɪdʒ, -ɪz
AM 'weɪˌbrɪdʒ, -ɪz

Weighell
BR wiːl, 'weɪəl, weɪl
AM 'weɪəl

weigher
BR 'weɪə(r), -z
AM 'weɪər, -z

weigh-in
BR 'weɪɪn, -z
AM 'weɪˌɪn, -z

weight
BR weɪt, -s, -ɪŋ, -ɪd
AM weɪt, -ts, -dɪŋ, -dɪd

weightily
BR 'weɪtɪli
AM 'weɪdɪli

weightiness
BR 'weɪtɪnɪs
AM 'weɪdɪnɪs

weighting
BR 'weɪtɪŋ, -z
AM 'weɪdɪŋ, -z

weightless
BR 'weɪtlɪs
AM 'weɪtlɪs

weightlessly
BR 'weɪtlɪsli
AM 'weɪtlɪsli

weightlessness
BR 'weɪtlɪsnɪs
AM 'weɪtlɪsnɪs

weightlifter
BR 'weɪtˌlɪftə(r), -z
AM 'weɪtˌlɪftər, -z

weightlifting
BR 'weɪtˌlɪftɪŋ
AM 'weɪtˌlɪftɪŋ

weight loss
BR 'weɪt lɒs
AM 'weɪt ˌlɒs, 'weɪt ˌlɑs

Weightwatchers®
BR 'weɪtˌwɒtʃəz
AM 'weɪtˌwɑtʃərz

weighty
BR 'weɪt|i, -iə(r), -iɪst
AM 'weɪdi, -ər, -ɪst

Weil
BR vaɪl, wiːl
AM vaɪl, waɪl

Weill
BR vaɪl, wiːl
AM vaɪl, waɪl

Weimar
BR 'vaɪmɑː(r)
AM 'vaɪˌmɑr

Weimaraner
BR 'vaɪmərɑːnə(r),
'waɪmərɑːnə(r),
ˌvaɪmə'rɑːnə(r),
ˌwaɪmə'rɑːnə(r), -z
AM 'waɪməˌrɑnər, -z

Weinberger
BR 'waɪnbəːgə(r)
AM 'waɪnˌbɜrgər

Weiner
BR 'vaɪnə(r)
AM 'waɪnər

Weinstock
BR 'waɪnstɒk
AM 'waɪnˌstɑk

weir
BR wɪə(r), -z
AM wɪ(ə)r, -z

weird
BR wɪəd, -ə(r), -ɪst
AM wɪ(ə)rd, -ər, -ɪst

weirdie
BR 'wɪəd|i, -ɪz
AM 'wɪrdi, -z

weirdly
BR 'wɪədli
AM 'wɪrdli

weirdness
BR 'wɪədnəs
AM 'wɪrdnəs

weirdo
BR 'wɪədəʊ, -z
AM 'wɪrdoʊ, -z

Weismann
BR 'vaɪsmən
AM 'waɪsmən

Weismannism
BR 'vaɪsmənɪz(ə)m
AM 'waɪsməˌnɪzəm

Weiss
BR vaɪs, weɪs
AM waɪs, vaɪs

Weissmuller
BR 'waɪsˌmʊlə(r)
AM 'waɪsˌmʊlər

Weizmann
BR 'vaɪtsmən
AM 'vaɪtsmən

weka
BR 'wɛkə(r), -z
AM 'wɛkə, -z

welch
BR wɛl(t)ʃ, -ɪz, -ɪŋ, -t
AM wɛl(t)ʃ, -əz, -ɪŋ, -t

welcome
BR 'wɛlkəm, -z, -ɪŋ, -d
AM 'wɛlkəm, -z, -ɪŋ, -d

welcomely
BR 'wɛlkəmli
AM 'wɛlkəmli

welcomeness
BR 'wɛlkəmnəs
AM 'wɛlkəmnəs

welcomer
BR 'wɛlkəmə(r), -z
AM 'wɛlkəmər, -z

welcomingly
BR 'wɛlkəmɪŋli
AM 'wɛlkəmɪŋli

weld
BR wɛld, -z, -ɪŋ, -ɪd
AM wɛld, -z, -ɪŋ, -əd

weldability
BR ˌwɛldə'bɪlɪti
AM ˌwɛldə'bɪlɪdi

weldable
BR 'wɛldəbl
AM 'wɛldəbəl

welder
BR 'wɛldə(r), -z
AM 'wɛldər, -z

Weldon
BR 'wɛld(ə)n
AM 'wɛldən

welfare
BR 'wɛlfɛː(r)
AM 'wɛlˌfɛ(ə)r

welfare state
BR ˌwɛlfɛː 'steɪt, -s
AM 'wɛlfɛr ˌsteɪt, -s

welfarism
BR 'wɛlfərɪz(ə)m,
'wɛlfɛːrɪz(ə)m
AM 'wɛlˌfɛrˌɪzəm

welfarist
BR 'wɛlfərɪst,
'wɛlfɛːrɪst, -s
AM 'wɛlˌfɛrəst, -s

Welford
BR 'wɛlfəd
AM 'wɛlfərd

welkin
BR 'wɛlkɪn
AM 'wɛlkən

well
BR wɛl, -z, -ɪŋ, -d
AM wɛl, -z, -ɪŋ, -d

we'll[1]
strong form
BR wiːl
AM wiːl

we'll[2]
weak form
BR wɪl
AM wəl

Welland
BR 'wɛlənd
AM 'wɛlənd

wellbeing
BR 'wɛlbiːɪŋ
AM 'wɛlˌbiːɪŋ

Wellbeloved
BR 'wɛlbɪlʌvd
AM 'wɛlbəˌlʌvd

Wellcome
BR 'wɛlkəm
AM 'wɛlkəm

well deck
BR 'wɛl dɛk, -s
AM 'wɛl ˌdɛk, -s

well-dressing
BR 'wɛlˌdrɛsɪŋ, -z
AM 'wɛlˌdrɛsɪŋ, -z

Weller
BR 'wɛlə(r)
AM 'wɛlər

Welles
BR wɛlz
AM 'wɛlz

Wellesbourne
BR 'wɛlzbɔːn
AM 'wɛlzˌbɔ(ə)rn

Wellesley
BR 'wɛlzli
AM 'wɛlzli

wellhead
BR 'wɛlhɛd, -z
AM 'wɛlˌ(h)ɛd, -z

wellie
BR 'wɛl|i, -ɪz
AM 'wɛli, -z

Wellingborough
BR 'wɛlɪŋb(ə)rə(r)
AM 'wɛlɪŋˌbərə

wellington
BR 'wɛlɪŋt(ə)n, -z
AM 'wɛlɪŋtən, -z

wellness
BR 'wɛlnəs
AM 'wɛlnəs

Wells
BR wɛlz
AM wɛlz

wellspring
BR 'wɛlsprɪŋ, -z
AM 'wɛlˌsprɪŋ, -z

well-to-do
BR ˌwɛltə'duː
AM 'wɛldə'du

well-wisher
BR 'wɛlˌwɪʃə(r), -z
AM 'wɛlˌwɪʃər, -z

welly
BR 'wɛl|i, -ɪz
AM 'wɛli, -z

welsh
BR wɛlʃ, -ɪz, -ɪŋ, -t
AM wɛlʃ, -əz, -ɪŋ, -t

welsher
BR 'wɛlʃə(r), -z
AM 'wɛlʃər, -z

Welshman
BR 'wɛlʃmən
AM 'wɛlʃmən

Welshmen
BR ˈwelʃmən
AM ˈwelʃmən

Welshness
BR ˈwelʃnəs
AM ˈwelʃnəs

Welshpool
BR ˈwelʃpuːl
AM ˈwelʃˌpul

welsh rarebit
BR ˌwelʃ ˈreːbɪt
+ ˈrabɪt
AM ˌwelʃ ˈreːˌbɪt

Welshwoman
BR ˈwelʃˌwʊmən
AM ˈwelʃˌwʊmən

Welshwomen
BR ˈwelʃˌwɪmɪn
AM ˈwelʃˌwɪmɪn

welt
BR welt, -s, -ɪŋ, -ɪd
AM welt, -s, -ɪŋ, -əd

Weltanschauung
BR ˈveltanˌʃaʊʊŋ,
ˈvelt(ə)nˌʃaʊʊŋ
AM ˈvelt'anˌʃaʊʊŋ

**Weltanschauung-
en**
BR ˈveltanˌʃaʊʊŋən,
ˈvelt(ə)nˌʃaʊʊŋən
AM ˈvelt'anˌʃaʊʊŋən

welter
BR ˈwelt|ə(r), -əz,
-(ə)rɪŋ, -əd
AM ˈwelt|ər, -ərz,
-(ə)rɪŋ, -ərd

welterweight
BR ˈweltəweit, -s
AM ˈweltərˌweit, -s

Weltschmerz
BR ˈveltˌʃmɑːts
AM ˈveltˌʃmɑrts

Welty
BR ˈwelti
AM ˈwelti

Welwyn
BR ˈwelɪn
AM ˈwelwən

Wem
BR wem
AM wem

Wembley
BR ˈwembli
AM ˈwembli

Wemyss
BR wiːmz
AM wimz

wen
BR wen, -z
AM wen, -z

Wenceslas
BR ˈwensɪsləs,
ˈwensɪslas
AM ˈwensəsˌlas

wench
BR wen(t)ʃ, -ɪz, -ɪŋ, -t
AM wen(t)ʃ, -əz, -ɪŋ, -t

wencher
BR ˈwen(t)ʃə(r), -z
AM ˈwen(t)ʃər, -z

wend
BR wend, -z, -ɪŋ, -ɪd
AM wend, -z, -ɪŋ, -əd

Wenda
BR ˈwendə(r)
AM ˈwendə

Wendell
BR ˈwendl
AM ˈwendəl, ˌwenˈdel

Wendic
BR ˈwendɪk
AM ˈwendɪk

Wendish
BR ˈwendɪʃ
AM ˈwendɪʃ

Wendover
BR ˈwendəʊvə(r)
AM ˈwenˌdoʊvər

Wendy
BR ˈwendi
AM ˈwendi

Wenham
BR ˈwenəm
AM ˈwenəm

Wenlock Edge
BR ˌwenlɒk ˈedʒ
AM ˌwenlak ˈedʒ

Wensleydale
BR ˈwenzlɪdeɪl, -z
AM ˈwenzliˌdeɪl, -z

Wensum
BR ˈwensəm, ˈwensm̩
AM ˈwensəm

went
BR went
AM went

wentletrap
BR ˈwentltrap, -s
AM ˈwen(t)lˌtræp, -s

Wentworth
BR ˈwentw(ə)θ
AM ˈwentˌwərθ

Wenvoe
BR ˈwenvəʊ
AM ˈwenvoʊ

Weobley
BR ˈwebli
AM ˈwebli

wept
BR wept
AM wept

were
BR wəː(r)
AM wər

we're[1]
strong form
BR wɪə(r)
AM wɪ(ə)r

we're[2]
weak form
BR wə(r)
AM wər

weren't
BR wəːnt

AM wər(ə)nt

werewolf
BR ˈweːwʊlf, ˈwɪəwʊlf
AM ˈwerˌwʊlf

werewolves
BR ˈweːwʊlvz,
ˈwɪəwʊlvz
AM ˈwerˌwʊlvz

wergeld
BR ˈwəːgeld, ˈweːgeld,
ˈwɪəgeld
AM ˈwerˌgeld, ˈwɪrˌgeld

wergild
BR ˈwəːgɪld, ˈweːgɪld,
ˈwɪəgɪld
AM ˈwerˌgɪld, ˈwɪrˌgɪld

Werner
BR ˈwəːnə(r), ˈvəːnə(r)
AM ˈwərnər, ˈvərnər

wert[1]
strong form
BR wəːt
AM wərt

wert[2]
weak form
BR wət
AM wərt

Weser
BR ˈveɪzə(r)
AM ˈweɪzər, ˈweɪsər

Wesker
BR ˈweskə(r)
AM ˈweskər

Wesley
BR ˈwezli, ˈwesli
AM ˈwezli, ˈwesli

Wesleyan
BR ˈwezliən, ˈwesliən,
-z
AM ˈwesliən, ˈwezliən,
-z

Wesleyanism
BR ˈwezliənɪz(ə)m,
ˈwesliənɪz(ə)m
AM ˈwesliəˌnɪzəm,
ˈwezliəˌnɪzəm

Wessex
BR ˈwesɪks
AM ˈwesəks

Wesson
BR ˈwesn
AM ˈwesən

west
BR west
AM west

westabout
BR ˈwestəbaʊt
AM ˈwestəbaʊt

westbound
BR ˈwes(t)baʊnd
AM ˈwes(t)ˌbaʊnd

West Bromwich
BR ˌwes(t) ˈbrɒmɪdʒ
AM ˈwes(t)
ˈbrɑm(w)ɪtʃ

Westbury
BR ˈwes(t)b(ə)ri
AM ˈwes(t)ˌberi

Westclox
BR ˈwes(t)klɒks
AM ˈwes(t)ˌklɑks

Westcott
BR ˈwes(t)kət,
ˈwes(t)kɒt
AM ˈwes(t)ˌkɑt,
ˈwes(t)kət

West Country
BR ˈwes(t) ˌkʌntri
AM ˈwes(t) ˌkəntri

**West
Countryman**
BR ˈwes(t) ˌkʌntrimən
AM ˈwes(t) ˌkəntrimən

**West
Countrymen**
BR ˌwes(t) ˈkʌntrimən
AM ˈwes(t) ˌkəntrimən

wester
BR ˈwestə(r), -əz,
-(ə)rɪŋ, -əd
AM ˈwestər, -z, -ɪŋ, -d

Westerham
BR ˈwest(ə)rəm,
ˈwest(ə)rm̩
AM ˈwestərəm

westerly
BR ˈwestəl|i, -ɪz
AM ˈwestərli, -z

western
BR ˈwest(ə)n, -z
AM ˈwestərn, -z

westerner
BR ˈwestənə(r),
ˈwestnə(r), -z
AM ˈwestərnər, -z

westernisation
BR ˌwestənʌɪˈzeɪʃn,
ˌwestnʌɪˈzeɪʃn
AM ˌwestərnəˈzeɪʃən,
ˌwestərˌnʌɪˈzeɪʃən

westernise
BR ˈwestənʌɪz,
ˈwestnʌɪz, -ɪz, -ɪŋ, -d
AM ˈwestərˌnʌɪz, -ɪz,
-ɪŋ, -d

westerniser
BR ˈwestənʌɪzə(r),
ˈwestnʌɪzə(r), -z
AM ˈwestərˌnʌɪzər, -z

westernization
BR ˌwestənʌɪˈzeɪʃn,
ˌwestnʌɪˈzeɪʃn
AM ˌwestərnəˈzeɪʃən,
ˌwestərˌnʌɪˈzeɪʃən

westernize
BR ˈwestənʌɪz,
ˈwestnʌɪz, -ɪz, -ɪŋ, -d
AM ˈwestərˌnʌɪz, -ɪz,
-ɪŋ, -d

westernizer
BR ˈwestənʌɪzə(r),
ˈwestnʌɪzə(r), -z
AM ˈwestərˌnʌɪzər, -z

westernmost
BR ˈwestənməʊst,
ˈwestnməʊst

AM 'wɛstərnˌmoʊst

Westfield
BR 'wɛs(t)fiːld
AM 'wɛs(t)ˌfild

Westgate
BR 'wɛs(t)geɪt
AM 'wɛs(t)ˌgeɪt

westing
BR 'wɛstɪŋ, -z
AM 'wɛstɪŋ, -z

Westinghouse
BR 'wɛstɪŋhaʊs
AM 'wɛstɪŋˌ(h)aʊs

Westland
BR 'wɛs(t)lənd
AM 'wɛs(t)lənd

Westmeath
BR ˌwɛs(t)'miːθ
AM ˌwɛs(t)'miθ

Westminster
BR 'wɛs(t)mɪnstə(r),
ˌwɛs(t)'mɪnstə(r)
AM ˌwɛs(t)'mɪnstər

Westmorland[1]
*in Kansas and
Pennsylvania, USA*
BR ˌwɛs(t)'mɔːlənd
AM ˌwɛs(t)'mɔrlənd

Westmorland[2]
*in UK and in
Virginia, USA*
BR 'wɛs(t)mələnd
AM 'wɛs(t)mərlənd

Westmorland[3]
surname
BR 'wɛs(t)ˌmɔːlənd
AM ˌwɛs(t)'mɔrlənd

west-northwest[1]
BR ˌwɛs(t)nɔːθ'wɛst
AM ˌwɛs(t)ˌnɔrθ'wɛst

west-northwest[2]
nautical use
BR ˌwɛs(t)nɔː'wɛst
AM ˌwɛs(t)ˌnɔr'wɛst

Weston
BR 'wɛst(ə)n
AM 'wɛstən

**Weston-super-
Mare**
BR ˌwɛst(ə)nˌs(j)uːpə-
'mɛː(r)
AM ˌwɛstənˌs(j)upər-
'mɛ(ə)r

Westphalia
BR wɛs(t)'feɪlɪə(r)
AM ˌwɛs(t)'feɪljə,
ˌwɛs(t)'feɪlɪə

Westphalian
BR wɛs(t)'feɪlɪən, -z
AM ˌwɛs(t)'feɪljən,
ˌwɛs(t)'feɪlɪən, -z

west-southwest[1]
BR ˌwɛs(t)saʊθ'wɛst
AM ˌwɛs(t)ˌsaʊθ'wɛst

west-southwest[2]
nautical use
BR ˌwɛs(t)saʊ'wɛst
AM ˌwɛs(t)ˌsaʊ'wɛst

westward
BR 'wɛstwəd, -z
AM 'wɛs(t)wərd, -z

westwardly
BR 'wɛstwədli
AM 'wɛs(t)wərdli

Westwood
BR 'wɛs(t)wʊd
AM 'wɛs(t)ˌwʊd

wet
BR wɛt, -s, -ɪŋ, -ɪd, -ə(r),
-ɪst
AM wɛ|t, -ts, -dɪŋ, -dɪd,
-dər, -dəst

wet-and-dry
BR ˌwɛt(ə)n(d)'drʌɪ
AM ˌwɛdən'draɪ,
ˌwɛtn'draɪ

wetback
BR 'wɛtbak, -s
AM 'wɛtˌbæk, -s

wether
BR 'wɛðə(r), -z
AM 'wɛðər, -z

Wetherall
BR 'wɛð(ə)rɔːl,
'wɛð(ə)rl̩
AM 'wɛðərˌɔl,
'wɛðərˌɑl

Wetherby
BR 'wɛðəbi
AM 'wɛðərbi

wetland
BR 'wɛtland, 'wɛtlənd,
-z
AM 'wɛtˌlænd,
'wɛtlənd, -z

wetlook
BR 'wɛtlʊk
AM 'wɛtˌlʊk

wetly
BR 'wɛtli
AM 'wɛtli

wetness
BR 'wɛtnəs
AM 'wɛtnəs

wet-nurse
BR 'wɛtnəːs, -ɪz, -ɪŋ, -t
AM 'wɛtˌnərs, -əz, -ɪŋ, -t

wetsuit
BR 'wɛts(j)uːt, -s
AM 'wɛtˌsut, -s

wettable
BR 'wɛtəbl̩
AM 'wɛdəbəl

wetting
BR 'wɛtɪŋ, -z
AM 'wɛdɪŋ, -z

wettish
BR 'wɛtɪʃ
AM 'wɛdɪʃ

wetware
BR 'wɛtwɛː(r)
AM 'wɛtˌwɛ(ə)r

wet-weather
BR ˌwɛt'wɛðə(r)
AM ˌwɛtˌwɛðər

we've[1]
strong form
BR wiːv
AM wiv

we've[2]
weak form
BR wɪv
AM wɪv

Wexford
BR 'wɛksfəd
AM 'wɛksfərd

wey
BR weɪ, -z
AM weɪ, -z

Weybridge
BR 'weɪbrɪdʒ
AM 'weɪˌbrɪdʒ

Weymouth
BR 'weɪməθ
AM 'weɪməθ

whack
BR wak, -s, -ɪŋ, -t
AM (h)wæk, -s, -ɪŋ, -t

whacker
BR 'wakə(r), -z
AM '(h)wækər, -z

whacking
BR 'wakɪŋ, -z
AM '(h)wækɪŋ, -z

whacko
BR ˌwak'əʊ
AM 'wækoʊ

whacky
BR 'waki
AM 'wæki

whale
BR weɪl, -z, -ɪŋ
AM (h)weɪl, -z, -ɪŋ

whaleback
BR 'weɪlbak, -s
AM '(h)weɪlˌbæk, -s

whaleboat
BR 'weɪlbəʊt, -s
AM '(h)weɪlˌboʊt, -s

whalebone
BR 'weɪlbəʊn
AM '(h)weɪlˌboʊn

whale-oil
BR 'weɪlɔɪl
AM '(h)weɪlˌɔɪl

whaler
BR 'weɪlə(r), -z
AM '(h)weɪlər, -z

whale-watching
BR 'weɪlˌwɒtʃɪŋ
AM '(h)weɪlˌwatʃɪŋ

Whaley
BR 'weɪli
AM '(h)weɪli

whaling-master
BR 'weɪlɪŋˌmɑːstə(r),
'weɪlɪŋˌmastə(r), -z
AM '(h)weɪlɪŋˌmæstər,
-z

Whalley
BR 'wɒli, 'wɔːli, 'weɪli

AM '(h)weɪli, '(h)wɔli,
'(h)wɑli

Whalley Range
BR ˌwɒli 'reɪn(d)ʒ
AM '(h)wɒli ˌreɪndʒ,
'(h)wɑli ˌreɪndʒ

wham
BR wam
AM (h)wæm

whammy
BR 'wam|i, -ɪz
AM '(h)wæmi, -z

whang
BR waŋ, -z
AM (h)wæŋ, -z

Whangarei
BR ˌwaŋə'reɪ
AM ˌ(h)wɑŋə'reɪ

whangee
BR ˌwaŋ'(g)iː, -z
AM (h)wæŋ'gi, -z

whap
BR wɒp
AM (h)wæp

whare
BR 'wɒr|i, -ɪz
AM '(h)wɑˌreɪ, -z

wharf
BR wɔːf
AM (h)wɔ(ə)rf

wharfage
BR wɔːfɪdʒ
AM '(h)wɔrfɪdʒ

Wharfe
BR wɔːf
AM (h)wɔ(ə)rf

Wharfedale
BR 'wɔːfdeɪl
AM '(h)wɔrfˌdeɪl

wharfie
BR 'wɔːf|i, -ɪz
AM '(h)wɔrfi, -z

wharfinger
BR 'wɔːfɪn(d)ʒə(r), -z
AM '(h)wɔrfəndʒər, -z

Wharton
BR 'wɔːtn
AM '(h)wɔrtən

wharves
BR wɔːvz
AM (h)wɔ(ə)rvz

what
BR wɒt
AM (h)wət

whate'er
BR wɒt'ɛː(r), wət'ɛː(r)
AM (h)wət'ɛ(ə)r

whatever
BR wɒt'ɛvə(r),
wət'ɛvə(r)
AM (h)wət'ɛvər,
'(h)wədɛvər

Whatmough
BR 'wɒtməʊ, 'wɒtmʌf
AM '(h)wətmoʊ

whatnot
BR 'wɒtnɒt, -s

AM '(h)wət,nɑt, -s

what's-her-name
BR 'wɒtsəneɪm
AM '(h)wətsər,neɪm

what's-his-name
BR 'wɒtsɪzneɪm
AM '(h)wətsɪz,neɪm

whatsit
BR 'wɒtsɪt, -s
AM '(h)wətsɪt, -s

what's it
BR 'wɒts ɪt, -s
AM '(h)wəts ɪt, -s

what's-its-name
BR 'wɒtsɪtsneɪm
AM '(h)wətsɪts,neɪm

whatsoe'er
BR ,wɒtsəʊ'ɛː(r)
AM ,(h)wətsoʊ'ɛ(ə)r

whatsoever
BR ,wɒtsəʊ'ɛvə(r)
AM ,(h)wətsoʊ'ɛvər

what-you-may-call-it
BR 'wɒtʃəmə,kɔːlɪt, 'wɒdʒəmə,kɔːlɪt
AM '(h)wɑtʃəmə,kɔlɪt, '(h)wɑtʃəmə,kɑlɪt

whaup
BR wɔːp, -s
AM '(h)wɑp, -s

wheal
BR wiːl, -z, -ɪŋ, -d
AM '(h)wil, -z, -ɪŋ, -d

wheat
BR wiːt
AM '(h)wit

wheat cake
BR 'wiːt keɪk, -s
AM '(h)wit ,keɪk, -s

Wheatcroft
BR 'wiːtkrɒft
AM '(h)wit,krɔft, '(h)wit,krɑft

wheatear
BR 'wiːtɪə(r), -z
AM 'wid,ɪ(ə)r, -z

wheaten
BR 'wiːtn
AM '(h)witn

wheatgerm
BR 'wiːtdʒəːm
AM '(h)wit,dʒərm

wheatgrass
BR 'wiːtɡrɑːs, 'wiːtɡras
AM '(h)wit,ɡræs

Wheathampstead
BR 'wiːt(ə)mstəd, 'wiːt(ə)mstɪd, 'wetəmstɛd, 'wetəmstɪd
AM '(h)widəm,stɛd, '(h)wedəm,stɛd

Wheatley
BR 'wiːtli
AM '(h)witli

wheatmeal
BR 'wiːtmiːl
AM '(h)wit,mil

wheatsheaf
BR 'wiːtʃiːf
AM '(h)wit,ʃif

wheatsheaves
BR 'wiːtʃiːvz
AM '(h)wit,ʃivz

Wheatstone
BR 'wiːtstəʊn
AM '(h)wit,stoʊn

whee
BR wiː
AM (h)wi

wheedle
BR 'wiːd|l, -lz, -lɪŋ\-lɪŋ, -ld
AM '(h)wid|əl, -əlz, -(ə)lɪŋ, -əld

wheedler
BR 'wiːd|ə(r), 'wiːdlə(r), -z
AM '(h)wid(ə)lər, -z

wheedlingly
BR 'wiːd|lɪŋli, 'wiːdlɪŋli
AM '(h)widlɪŋli

wheel
BR wiːl, -z, -ɪŋ, -d
AM '(h)wil, -z, -ɪŋ, -d

wheelbarrow
BR 'wiːl,barəʊ, -z
AM '(h)wil,bɛroʊ, -z

wheelbase
BR 'wiːlbeɪs, -ɪz
AM '(h)wil,beɪs, -ɪz

wheelchair
BR 'wiːltʃɛː(r), -z
AM '(h)wil,tʃɛ(ə)r, -z

wheel-clamp
BR 'wiːlklam|p, -ps, -pɪŋ, -(p)t
AM '(h)wil,klæm|p, -(p)s, -pɪŋ, -(p)t

wheeler
BR 'wiːlə(r), -z
AM '(h)wilər, -z

wheeler-dealer
BR ,wiːlə'diːlə(r), -z
AM ,(h)wilər'dilər, -z

wheeler-dealing
BR ,wiːlə'diːlɪŋ
AM ,(h)wilɪŋ'dilɪŋ

wheelhouse
BR 'wiːlhaʊ|s, -zɪz
AM '(h)wil,(h)aʊ|s, -zəz

wheelie
BR 'wiːl|i, -ɪz
AM '(h)wili, -z

wheeling
BR 'wiːlɪŋ, -z
AM '(h)wilɪŋ, -z

wheelless
BR 'wiːlɪs
AM '(h)wi(l)lɪs

wheelman
BR 'wiːlman
AM '(h)wil,mæn

wheelmen
BR 'wiːlmɛn
AM '(h)wil,mɛn

wheelright
BR 'wiːlrʌɪt, -s
AM '(h)wil,raɪt, -s

wheelslip
BR 'wiːlslɪp
AM '(h)wil,slɪp

wheelsman
BR 'wiːlzmən
AM '(h)wilzmən

wheelsmen
BR 'wiːlzmən
AM '(h)wilzmən

wheelspin
BR 'wiːlspɪn
AM '(h)wil,spɪn

wheelwright
BR 'wiːlrʌɪt, -s
AM '(h)wil,raɪt, -s

Wheen
BR wiːn
AM (h)win

wheeze
BR wiːz, -ɪz, -ɪŋ, -d
AM (h)wiz, -ɪz, -ɪŋ, -d

wheezer
BR 'wiːzə(r), -z
AM '(h)wizər, -z

wheezily
BR 'wiːzɪli
AM '(h)wizɪli

wheeziness
BR 'wiːzɪnɪs
AM '(h)wizinɪs

wheezingly
BR 'wiːzɪŋli
AM '(h)wizɪŋli

wheezy
BR 'wiːz|i, -ɪə(r), -ɪɪst
AM '(h)wizi, -ər, -ɪst

Whelan
BR 'wiːlən
AM '(h)weɪlən, '(h)wilən

whelk
BR wɛlk, -s
AM '(h)wɛlk, -s

whelp
BR wɛlp, -s
AM '(h)wɛlp, -s

when
BR wɛn
AM (h)wɛn

whence
BR wɛns
AM '(h)wɛns

whencesoever
BR ,wɛns(s)əʊ'ɛvə(r)
AM '(h)wɛn(s)soʊ'ɛvər

whene'er
BR wə'nɛː(r), wɛ'nɛː(r)

AM (h)wə'nɛ(ə)r, (h)wɛ'nɛ(ə)r

whenever
BR wə'nɛvə(r), wɛ'nɛvə(r)
AM (h)wə'nɛvər, (h)wɛ'nɛvər

whensoe'er
BR ,wɛnsəʊ'ɛː(r)
AM '(h)wɛnsoʊ'ɛ(ə)r

whensoever
BR ,wɛnsəʊ'ɛvə(r)
AM ,(h)wɛnsoʊ'ɛvər

where
BR wɛː(r)
AM (h)wɛ(ə)r

whereabouts¹
adverb
BR ,wɛːrə'baʊts, 'wɛːrəbaʊts
AM ,(h)wɛrə'baʊts

whereabouts²
noun
BR 'wɛːrəbaʊts
AM '(h)wɛrə,baʊts

whereafter
BR wər'ɑːftə(r), wɛːr'ɑːftə(r), wɛr'ɑːftə(r), wər'ɑftə(r), wɛːr'ɑftə(r), wər'ɑftə(r)
AM (h)wə'ræftər, (h)wɛ'ræftər

whereas
BR wər'az, wɛːr'az, wɛr'az
AM (h)wə'ræz, (h)wɛ'ræz

whereat
BR wər'at, wɛːr'at, wɛr'at
AM (h)wə'ræt, (h)wɛ'ræt

whereby
BR wɛː'bʌɪ
AM (h)wɛr'baɪ

where'er
BR wɛːr'ɛː(r)
AM (h)wɛr'ɛ(ə)r

wherefore
BR 'wɛːfɔː(r), -z
AM '(h)wɛr,fɔ(ə)r, -z

wherefrom
BR wɛː'frɒm
AM ,(h)wɛr'frəm

wherein
BR wər'ɪn, wɛː'rɪn, wɛr'ɪn
AM (h)wɛ'rɪn

whereof
BR wər'ɒv, wɛːr'ɒv, wɛr'ɒv
AM (h)wɛ'rɒv, (h)wɛ'rɑv

whereon
BR wər'ɒn, wɛː'rɒn, wɛr'ɒn

AM (h)wɛˈrɑːn

wheresoe'er
BR ˌwɛːsəʊˈɛː(r)
AM ˌ(h)wɛrsoʊˈɛ(ə)r

wheresoever
BR ˌwɛːsəʊˈɛvə(r)
AM ˌ(h)wɛrsoʊˈɛvər

whereto
BR wɛːˈtuː
AM (h)wɛrˈto

whereupon
BR ˌwɛːrəˈpɒn
AM ˌ(h)wɛrəˈpɑn

wherever
BR wərˈɛvə(r),
wɛːrˈɛvə(r),
wɛrˈɛvə(r)
AM (h)wəˈrɛvər,
(h)wɛˈrɛvər

wherewith
BR wɛːˈwɪð
AM (h)wɛrˈwɪð,
(h)wɛrˈwɪθ

wherewithal[1]
adverb
BR ˌwɛːwɪˈðɔːl,
ˈwɛːwɪðɔːl
AM ˈ(h)wɛrwəˌðɔl,
ˈ(h)wɛrwəˌθɔl,
ˈ(h)wɛrwəˌðɑl,
ˈ(h)wɛrwəˌθɑl

wherewithal[2]
noun
BR ˈwɛːwɪðɔːl
AM ˈ(h)wɛrwəˌðɔl,
ˈ(h)wɛrwəˌθɔl,
ˈ(h)wɛrwəˌðɑl,
ˈ(h)wɛrwəˌθɑl

Whernside
BR ˈwəːnsʌɪd
AM ˈ(h)wərnˌsaɪd

wherry
BR ˈwɛr|i, -ɪz
AM ˈ(h)wɛri, -z

wherryman
BR ˈwɛrɪmən
AM ˈ(h)wɛrɪmən

wherrymen
BR ˈwɛrɪmən
AM ˈ(h)wɛrɪmən

whet
BR wɛt, -s, -ɪŋ, -ɪd
AM ˈ(h)wɛt, -s, -ɪŋ, -əd

whether
BR ˈwɛðə(r)
AM ˈ(h)wɛðər

whetstone
BR ˈwɛtstəʊn, -z
AM ˈ(h)wɛtˌstoʊn, -z

whetter
BR ˈwɛtə(r), -z
AM ˈ(h)wɛdər, -z

whew
BR h(w)juː
AM h(w)ju

Whewell
BR ˈhjuː(ə)l
AM ˈhju(ə)l

whey
BR weɪ
AM (h)weɪ

which
BR wɪtʃ
AM (h)wɪtʃ

whichever
BR wɪtʃˈɛvə(r)
AM ˌ(h)wɪˈtʃɛvər

whichsoever
BR ˌwɪtʃsəʊˈɛvə(r)
AM ˈ(h)wɪtʃsoʊˈɛvər

whicker
BR ˈwɪk|ə(r), -əz,
-(ə)rɪŋ, -əd
AM ˈ(h)wɪkər, -z, -ɪŋ, -d

whidah
BR ˈwɪdə(r), -z
AM ˈ(h)wɪdə, -z

whiff
BR wɪf, -s, -ɪŋ, -t
AM ˈ(h)wɪf, -s, -ɪŋ, -t

whiffiness
BR ˈwɪfɪnɪs
AM ˈwɪfɪnɪs

whiffle
BR ˈwɪf|l, -lz, -]ɪŋ \-lɪŋ,
-ld
AM ˈ(h)wɪfəl, -əlz,
-(ə)lɪŋ, -əld

whiffler
BR ˈwɪf|ə(r), ˈwɪflə(r),
-z
AM ˈ(h)wɪf(ə)lər, -z

whiffletree
BR ˈwɪfltriː, -z
AM ˈ(h)wɪfəlˌtri, -z

whiffy
BR ˈwɪf|i, -ɪə(r), -ɪɪst
AM ˈ(h)wɪfi, -ər, -ɪst

Whig
BR wɪg, -z
AM (h)wɪg, -z

whiggery
BR ˈwɪg(ə)ri
AM ˈ(h)wɪgəri

whiggish
BR ˈwɪgɪʃ
AM ˈ(h)wɪgɪʃ

whiggishness
BR ˈwɪgɪʃnɪs
AM ˈ(h)wɪgɪʃnɪs

whiggism
BR ˈwɪgɪz(ə)m
AM ˈ(h)wɪgˌɪzəm

while
BR wʌɪl, -z, -ɪŋ, -d
AM waɪl, -z, -ɪŋ, -d

whilom
BR ˈwʌɪləm
AM ˈ(h)waɪləm

whilst
BR wʌɪlst
AM (h)waɪlst

whim
BR wɪm, -z
AM (h)wɪm, -z

whimbrel
BR ˈwɪmbr(ə)l, -z
AM ˈ(h)wɪmbrəl, -z

whimper
BR ˈwɪmp|ə(r), -əz,
-(ə)rɪŋ, -əd
AM ˈ(h)wɪmp|ər, -ərz,
-(ə)rɪŋ, -ərd

whimperer
BR ˈwɪmp(ə)rə(r), -z
AM ˈ(h)wɪmp(ə)rər, -z

whimpering
BR ˈwɪmp(ə)rɪŋ, -z
AM ˈ(h)wɪmp(ə)rɪŋ, -z

whimperingly
BR ˈwɪmp(ə)rɪŋli
AM ˈ(h)wɪmp(ə)rɪŋli

whimsey
BR ˈwɪmz|i, -ɪz
AM ˈ(h)wɪmzi, -z

whimsical
BR ˈwɪmzɪkl
AM ˈ(h)wɪmzɪkəl

whimsicality
BR ˌwɪmzɪˈkalɪti
AM ˌ(h)wɪmzəˈkælədi

whimsically
BR ˈwɪmzɪkli
AM ˈ(h)wɪmzɪk(ə)li

whimsicalness
BR ˈwɪmzɪklnəs
AM ˈ(h)wɪmzɪkəlnəs

whimsy
BR ˈwɪmz|i, -ɪz
AM ˈ(h)wɪmzi, -z

whim-wham
BR ˈwɪmwam, -z
AM ˈ(h)wɪm,(h)wæm,
-z

whin
BR wɪn
AM (h)wɪn

whinchat
BR ˈwɪntʃat, -s
AM ˈ(h)wɪnˌtʃæt, -s

whine
BR wʌɪn, -z, -ɪŋ, -d
AM waɪn, -z, -ɪŋ, -d

whiner
BR ˈwʌɪnə(r), -z
AM ˈ(h)waɪnər, -z

whinge
BR wɪn(d)ʒ, -ɪz, -ɪŋ, -d
AM (h)wɪndʒ, -ɪz, -ɪŋ, -d

whingeingly
BR ˈwɪn(d)ʒɪŋli
AM ˈ(h)wɪndʒɪŋli

whinger
BR ˈwɪn(d)ʒə(r), -z
AM ˈ(h)wɪndʒər, -z

whingey
BR ˈwɪn(d)ʒi
AM ˈ(h)wɪndʒi

whingingly
BR ˈwɪn(d)ʒɪŋli
AM ˈ(h)wɪndʒɪŋli

whingy
BR ˈwɪn(d)ʒi
AM ˈ(h)wɪndʒi

whiningly
BR ˈwʌɪnɪŋli
AM ˈ(h)waɪnɪŋli

whinny
BR wɪn|i, -ɪz, -ɪɪŋ, -ɪd
AM ˈ(h)wɪni, -z, -ɪŋ, -d

whinsill
BR ˈwɪnsɪl, -z
AM ˈ(h)wɪnˌsɪl, -z

whinstone
BR ˈwɪnstəʊn
AM ˈ(h)wɪnˌstoʊn

whiny
BR ˈwʌɪn|i, -ɪə(r), -ɪɪst
AM ˈ(h)waɪni, -ər, -ɪst

whip
BR wɪp, -s, -ɪŋ, -t
AM ˈ(h)wɪp, -s, -ɪŋ, -t

whipcord
BR ˈwɪpkɔːd
AM ˈ(h)wɪpˌkɔ(ə)rd

whipcracking
BR ˈwɪpˌkrakɪŋ
AM ˈ(h)wɪpˌkrækɪŋ

whip hand
BR ˌwɪp ˈhand
AM ˈ(h)wɪp ˌ(h)ænd

whiplash
BR ˈwɪplaʃ
AM ˈ(h)wɪpˌlaʃ

whipless
BR ˈwɪplɪs
AM ˈ(h)wɪplɪs

whipper
BR ˈwɪpə(r), -z
AM ˈ(h)wɪpər, -z

whipper-in
BR ˌwɪpərˈɪn
AM ˈ(h)wɪpəˈrɪn

whippers-in
BR ˌwɪpəzˈɪn
AM ˈ(h)wɪpərzˈɪn

whippersnapper
BR ˈwɪpəˌsnapə(r), -z
AM ˈ(h)wɪpərˌsnæpər,
-z

whippet
BR ˈwɪpɪt, -s
AM ˈ(h)wɪpɪt, -s

whippiness
BR ˈwɪpɪnɪs
AM ˈ(h)wɪpɪnɪs

whipping
BR ˈwɪpɪŋ, -z
AM ˈ(h)wɪpɪŋ, -z

whippletree
BR ˈwɪpltriː, -z
AM ˈ(h)wɪpəlˌtri, -z

whippoorwill
BR ˈwɪpəwɪl, -z
AM ˈ(h)wɪpərˌwɪl, -z

whippy
BR ˈwɪpi
AM ˈ(h)wɪpi

whip-round
BR ˈwɪpraʊnd, -z
AM ˈ(h)wɪpˌraʊnd, -z
whipsaw
BR ˈwɪpsɔː(r), -z
AM ˈ(h)wɪpˌsɔː,
ˈ(h)wɪpˌsɑː, -z
Whipsnade
BR ˈwɪpsneɪd
AM ˈ(h)wɪpˌsneɪd
whipster
BR ˈwɪpstə(r), -z
AM ˈ(h)wɪpstər, -z
whipstock
BR ˈwɪpstɒk, -s
AM ˈ(h)wɪpˌstɑk, -s
whipworm
BR ˈwɪpwɜːm, -z
AM ˈ(h)wɪpˌwɜrm, -z
whir
BR wɜː(r), -z, -ɪŋ, -d
AM ˈ(h)wɜr, -z, -ɪŋ, -d
whirl
BR wɜːl, -z, -ɪŋ, -d
AM ˈ(h)wɜrl, -z, -ɪŋ, -d
whirler
BR ˈwɜːlə(r), -z
AM ˈ(h)wɜrlər, -z
whirligig
BR ˈwɜːlɪgɪg, -z
AM ˈ(h)wɜrliˌgɪg, -z
whirlingly
BR ˈwɜːlɪŋli
AM ˈ(h)wɜrlɪŋli
whirlpool
BR ˈwɜːlpuːl, -z
AM ˈ(h)wɜrlˌpul, -z
whirlwind
BR ˈwɜːlwɪnd, -z
AM ˈ(h)wɜrlˌwɪnd, -z
whirlybird
BR ˈwɜːlɪbɜːd, -z
AM ˈ(h)wɜrliˌbɜrd, -z
whirr
BR wɜː(r), -z, -ɪŋ, -d
AM ˈ(h)wɜr, -z, -ɪŋ, -d
whisht
BR (h)wɪʃt
AM ˈ(h)wɪʃt
whisk
BR wɪsk, -s, -ɪŋ, -t
AM ˈ(h)wɪsk, -s, -ɪŋ, -t
Whiskas®
BR ˈwɪskəz
AM ˈ(h)wɪskəz
whiskbroom
BR ˈwɪs(k)bruːm, -z
AM ˈ(h)wɪs(k)ˌbrum,
ˈ(h)wɪs(k)ˌbrʊm, -z
whisker
BR ˈwɪskə(r), -z, -d
AM ˈ(h)wɪskər, -z, -d
whiskery
BR ˈwɪsk(ə)ri
AM ˈ(h)wɪskəri
whiskey
BR ˈwɪskli, -ɪz

AM ˈ(h)wɪski, -z
whisky
BR ˈwɪskli, -ɪz
AM ˈ(h)wɪski, -z
whisper
BR ˈwɪsp|ə(r), -əz,
-(ə)rɪŋ, -əd
AM ˈ(h)wɪsp|ər, -ərz,
-(ə)rɪŋ, -ərd
whisperer
BR ˈwɪsp(ə)rə(r), -z
AM ˈ(h)wɪsp(ə)rər, -z
whispering
BR ˈwɪsp(ə)rɪŋ, -z
AM ˈ(h)wɪsp(ə)rɪŋ, -z
whist
BR wɪst
AM ˈ(h)wɪst
whistle
BR ˈwɪs|l, -lz, -lɪŋ \-lɪŋ, -ld
AM ˈ(h)wɪs|əl, -əlz, -(ə)lɪŋ, -əld
whistler
BR ˈwɪslə(r), ˈwɪslə(r), -z
AM ˈ(h)wɪs(ə)lər, -z
Whistlerian
BR wɪˈslɪəriən
AM (h)wɪˈslɪriən
whistle-stop
BR ˈwɪslstɒp
AM ˈ(h)wɪsəlˌstɑp
whit
BR wɪt
AM ˈ(h)wɪt
Whitaker
BR ˈwɪtəkə(r)
AM ˈ(h)wɪdəkər
Whitbread
BR ˈwɪtbrɛd
AM ˈ(h)wɪtˌbrɛd
Whitby
BR ˈwɪtbi
AM ˈ(h)wɪtbi
Whitchurch
BR ˈwɪttʃɜːtʃ
AM ˈ(h)wɪt(t)ʃɜrtʃ
Whitcut
BR ˈwɪtkʌt
AM ˈ(h)wɪtkət
Whitcutt
BR ˈwɪtkʌt
AM ˈ(h)wɪtkət
white
BR wʌɪt, -s, -ɪŋ, -ə(r), -ɪst
AM ˈ(h)waɪ|t, -ts, -dɪŋ, -dər, -dəst
whitebait
BR ˈwʌɪtbeɪt
AM ˈ(h)waɪtˌbeɪt
whitebeam
BR ˈwʌɪtbiːm, -z
AM ˈ(h)waɪtˌbim, -z
whiteboard
BR ˈwʌɪtbɔːd, -z

AM ˈ(h)waɪtˌbɔ(ə)rd, -z
whitecap
BR ˈwʌɪtkap, -s
AM ˈ(h)waɪtˌkæp, -s
Whitechapel
BR ˈwʌɪtˌtʃapl
AM ˈ(h)waɪtˌtʃæpəl
white-collar
BR ˌwʌɪtˈkɒlə(r)
AM ˌ(h)waɪtˈkələr
whitecurrant
BR ˈwʌɪtˌkʌrənt, ˈwʌɪtˌkʌrnt, -s
AM ˈ(h)waɪtˌkərənt, -s
whited sepulchre
BR ˌwʌɪtɪd ˈsɛp(ə)lkə(r), -z
AM ˌ(h)waɪdɪd ˈsɛpəlkər, -z
white-eye
BR ˈwʌɪtʌɪ, -z
AM ˈ(h)waɪdˌaɪ, -z
whiteface
BR ˈwʌɪtfeɪs, -ɪz
AM ˈ(h)waɪtˌfeɪs, -ɪz
whitefaced
BR ˌwʌɪtˈfeɪst
AM ˈ(h)waɪtˌfeɪst
Whitefield
BR ˈwʌɪtfiːld, ˈwɪtfiːld
AM ˈ(h)waɪtˌfild
whitefish
BR ˈwʌɪtfɪʃ
AM ˈ(h)waɪtˌfɪʃ
whitefly
BR ˈwʌɪtflʌɪ, -z
AM ˈ(h)waɪtˌflaɪ, -z
Whitefriars
BR ˈwʌɪtˌfrʌɪəz
AM ˈ(h)waɪtˌfraɪərz
Whitehall
BR ˈwʌɪthɔːl, ˌwʌɪtˈhɔːl
AM ˈ(h)waɪtˌ(h)ɔl, ˈ(h)waɪtˌ(h)ɑl
Whitehaven
BR ˈwʌɪtˌheɪvn
AM ˈ(h)waɪtˌ(h)eɪvən
whitehead
BR ˈwʌɪthɛd, -z
AM ˈ(h)waɪtˌ(h)ɛd, ˈ(h)waɪtˌ(h)ɛd, -z
Whitehorn
BR ˈwʌɪthɔːn
AM ˈ(h)waɪtˌ(h)ɔ(ə)rn
Whitehorse
BR ˈwʌɪthɔːs
AM ˈ(h)waɪtˌ(h)ɔ(ə)rs
Whitehouse
BR ˈwʌɪthaʊs
AM ˈ(h)waɪtˌ(h)aʊs
White House
BR ˈwʌɪt haʊs
AM ˈ(h)waɪt ˌ(h)aʊs
Whitelaw
BR ˈwʌɪtlɔː(r)

AM ˈ(h)waɪtˌlɔ, ˈ(h)waɪtˌlɑ
Whiteley
BR ˈwʌɪtli
AM ˈ(h)waɪtli
whitely
BR ˈwʌɪtli
AM ˈ(h)waɪtli
white man
BR ˈwʌɪt man
AM ˈ(h)waɪt ˌmæn
white men
BR ˈwʌɪt mɛn
AM ˈ(h)waɪt ˌmɛn
whiten
BR ˈwʌɪt|n, -nz, -nɪŋ \-nɪŋ, -nd
AM ˈ(h)waɪtn, -z, -ɪŋ, -d
whitener
BR ˈwʌɪtnə(r), ˈwʌɪtnə(r), -z
AM ˈ(h)waɪtnər, -z
whiteness
BR ˈwʌɪtnɪs
AM ˈ(h)waɪtnɪs
white-out
BR ˈwʌɪtaʊt, -s
AM ˈ(h)waɪtˌaʊt, -s
whitesmith
BR ˈwʌɪtsmɪθ, -s
AM ˈ(h)waɪtˌsmɪθ, -s
white-tail
BR ˈwʌɪtteɪl, -z, -d
AM ˈ(h)waɪtˌteɪl, -z, -d
whitethorn
BR ˈwʌɪtθɔːn, -z
AM ˈ(h)waɪtˌθɔ(ə)rn, -z
whitethroat
BR ˈwʌɪtθrəʊt, -s
AM ˈ(h)waɪtˌθroʊt, -s
whitewall
BR ˈwʌɪtwɔːl, -z
AM ˈ(h)waɪtˌwɔl, ˈ(h)waɪtˌwɑl, -z
whitewash
BR ˈwʌɪtwɒʃ, -ɪz, -ɪŋ, -t
AM ˈ(h)waɪtˌwɔʃ, ˈ(h)waɪtˌwɑʃ, -əz, -ɪŋ, -t
whitewasher
BR ˈwʌɪtwɒʃə(r), -z
AM ˈ(h)waɪtˌwɔʃər, ˈ(h)waɪtˌwɑʃər, -z
Whitewater
BR ˈwʌɪtˌwɔːtə(r)
AM ˈ(h)waɪtˌwɔdər, ˈ(h)waɪtˌwɑdər
whitewood
BR ˈwʌɪtwʊd
AM ˈ(h)waɪtˌwʊd
whitey
BR ˈwʌɪt|i, -ɪz
AM ˈ(h)waɪdi, -z
Whitfield
BR ˈwɪtfiːld
AM ˈ(h)wɪtˌfild

Whitgift
BR ˈwɪtgɪft
AM ˈ(h)wɪtˌgɪft

whither
BR ˈwɪðə(r)
AM ˈ(h)wɪðər

whithersoever
BR ˌwɪðəsəʊˈevə(r)
AM ˌ(h)wɪðərsoʊˈevər

whitherward
BR ˈwɪðəwəd
AM ˈ(h)wɪðərwərd

whiting
BR ˈwʌɪtɪŋ
AM ˈ(h)waɪdɪŋ

whitish
BR ˈwʌɪtɪʃ
AM ˈ(h)waɪdɪʃ

Whitlam
BR ˈwɪtləm
AM ˈ(h)wɪtləm

whitleather
BR ˈwɪtˌleðə(r)
AM ˈ(h)wɪtˌleðər

Whitley
BR ˈwɪtli
AM ˈ(h)wɪtli

Whitlock
BR ˈwɪtlɒk
AM ˈ(h)wɪtˌlɑk

whitlow
BR ˈwɪtləʊ
AM ˈ(h)wɪtˌloʊ, -z

Whitman
BR ˈwɪtmən
AM ˈ(h)wɪtmən

Whitmore
BR ˈwɪtmɔː(r)
AM ˈ(h)wɪtˌmɔ(ə)r

Whitney
BR ˈwɪtni
AM ˈ(h)wɪtni

Whitstable
BR ˈwɪtstəbl
AM ˈ(h)wɪtstəbəl

Whitsun
BR ˈwɪtsn, -z
AM ˈ(h)wɪtsən, -z

Whit Sunday
BR ˌwɪt ˈsʌndˌeɪ, +
ˈsʌndˌi, -eɪz\-ɪz
AM ˌ(h)wɪt ˈsənˌdeɪ, +
ˈsəndi, -z

Whitsuntide
BR ˈwɪtsntˌaɪd, -z
AM ˈ(h)wɪtsənˌtaɪd, -z

Whittaker
BR ˈwɪtəkə(r)
AM ˈ(h)wɪdəkər

Whittier
BR ˈwɪtɪə(r)
AM ˈ(h)wɪdiər

Whittington
BR ˈwɪtɪŋt(ə)n

AM ˈ(h)wɪdɪŋtən

whittle
BR ˈwɪt|l, -lz, -lɪŋ \-lm̩,
-ld
AM ˈ(h)wɪdəl, -z, -ɪŋ, -d

Whitty
BR ˈwɪti
AM ˈ(h)wɪdi

Whitworth
BR ˈwɪtwəːθ, ˈwɪtwəθ
AM ˈ(h)wɪtˌwərθ

whity
BR ˈwʌɪt|i, -ɪz
AM ˈ(h)waɪdi, -z

whiz
BR wɪz, -ɪz, -ɪŋ, -d
AM (h)wɪz, -ɪz, -ɪŋ, -d

whiz-bang
BR ˈwɪzbaŋ, -z
AM ˈ(h)wɪzˌbæŋ, -z

whizkid
BR ˈwɪzkɪd, -z
AM ˈ(h)wɪzˌkɪd, -z

whizz
BR wɪz, -ɪz, -ɪŋ, -d
AM (h)wɪz, -ɪz, -ɪŋ, -d

whizzbang
BR ˈwɪzbaŋ, -z
AM ˈ(h)wɪzˌbæŋ, -z

whizzer
BR ˈwɪzə(r), -z
AM ˈ(h)wɪzər, -z

whizz-kid
BR ˈwɪzkɪd, -z
AM ˈ(h)wɪzˌkɪd, -z

whizzo
BR ˈwɪzəʊ
AM ˈ(h)wɪˌzoʊ

WHO
BR ˌdʌbljuˌertʃˈəʊ
AM ˌdəbəljuˌeɪtʃˈoʊ

who
BR huː
AM hu

whoa!
BR wəʊ
AM (h)woʊ

who'd[1]
strong form, who
had, who would
BR huːd
AM hud

who'd[2]
weak form, who had,
who would
BR hʊd
AM hʊd

whodunit
BR ˌhuːˈdʌnɪt, -s
AM huˈdənət, -s

whodunnit
BR ˌhuːˈdʌnɪt, -s
AM huˈdənət, -s

whoe'er
BR huːˈɛː(r), hʊˈɛː(r)
AM huˈɛ(ə)r

whoever
BR huːˈevə(r),
hʊˈevə(r)
AM huˈevər

whole
BR həʊl
AM hoʊl

wholefood
BR ˈhəʊlfuːd, -z
AM ˈhoʊlˌfud, -z

wholegrain
BR ˈhəʊlgreɪn, -z
AM ˈhoʊlˌgreɪn, -z

wholehearted
BR ˌhəʊlˈhɑːtɪd
AM ˈhoʊlˈhɑrdəd

wholeheartedly
BR ˌhəʊlˈhɑːtɪdli
AM ˈhoʊlˈhɑrdədli

wholeheartedness
BR ˌhəʊlˈhɑːtɪdnɪs
AM ˈhoʊlˈhɑrdədnəs

**whole-life
insurance**
BR ˌhəʊllʌɪf
ɪnˈʃʊərəns,
+ ɪnˈʃʊərn̩s,
+ ɪnˈʃɔːrəns,
+ ɪnˈʃɔːrn̩s
AM ˈhoʊlˈlaɪf
ɪnˈʃʊrəns

wholely
BR ˈhəʊlli
AM ˈhoʊ(l)li

wholemeal
BR ˈhəʊlmiːl
AM ˈhoʊlˌmil

wholeness
BR ˈhəʊlnəs
AM ˈhoʊlnəs

wholesale
BR ˈhəʊlseɪl
AM ˈhoʊlˌseɪl

wholesaler
BR ˈhəʊlseɪlə(r), -z
AM ˈhoʊlˌseɪlər, -z

wholesome
BR ˈhəʊls(ə)m
AM ˈhoʊlsəm

wholesomely
BR ˈhəʊls(ə)mli
AM ˈhoʊlsəmli

wholesomeness
BR ˈhəʊls(ə)mnəs
AM ˈhoʊlsəmnəs

whole-time
BR ˈhəʊltʌɪm
AM ˈhoʊlˌtaɪm

wholewheat
BR ˈhəʊlwiːt
AM ˈhoʊlˈwit

wholism
BR ˈhəʊlɪz(ə)m
AM ˈhoʊlˌɪzəm

wholly
BR ˈhəʊlli
AM ˈhoʊ(l)li

whom[1]
strong form
BR huːm
AM hum

whom[2]
weak form
BR hʊm
AM hʊm

whomever
BR huːmˈevə(r)
AM humˈevər

whomp
BR wɒmp, -s
AM (h)wɒmp,
(h)wɑmp, -s

whomso
BR ˈhuːmsəʊ
AM ˈhumsoʊ

whomsoever
BR ˌhuːmsəʊˈevə(r)
AM ˌhumsoʊˈevər

whoop
BR wuːp, huːp, -s, -ɪŋ, -t
AM (h)wup, hup, -s, -ɪŋ,
-t

whoopee[1]
interjection
BR wʊˈpiː
AM ˈ(h)wuˈpi

whoopee[2]
noun
BR ˈwʊpiː
AM ˈ(h)wupi

whooper
BR ˈwuːpə(r),
ˈhuːpə(r), -z
AM ˈ(h)wupər, ˈhupər,
-z

whooping cough
BR ˈhuːpɪŋ kɒf
AM ˈhupɪŋ ˌkɔf, + ˌkɑf

whoopla
BR ˈhuːplɑː(r)
AM ˈh(w)upˌlɑ

whoops
BR wʊps, wuːps
AM (h)wups, (h)wʊps

whoosh
BR wʊʃ, wuːʃ, -ɪz, -ɪŋ, -t
AM wuʃ, (h)wʊʃ, -ɪz,
-ɪŋ, -t

whop
BR wɒp, -s, -ɪŋ, -t
AM (h)wɑp, -s, -ɪŋ, -t

whopper
BR ˈwɒpə(r), -z
AM ˈ(h)wɑpər, -z

whore
BR hɔː(r), -z, -ɪŋ, -d
AM hɔ(ə)r, -z, -ɪŋ, -d

who're
BR ˈhuːə(r), hʊə(r)
AM ˈhuər, ˈhʊ(ə)r

whoredom
BR ˈhɔːdəm
AM ˈhɔrdəm

whorehouse
BR ˈhɔːhaʊ|s, -zɪz

AM ˈhɔr‚(h)aʊ|s, -zəz

whoremaster
BR ˈhɔː‚mɑːstə(r),
ˈhɔː‚mɑstə(r), -z
AM ˈhɔr‚mæstər, -z

whoremonger
BR ˈhɔː‚mʌŋgə(r), -z
AM ˈhɔr‚mʌŋgər,
ˈhɔr‚mɒŋgər, -z

whorer
BR ˈhɔːrə(r), -z
AM ˈhɔrər, -z

whoreson
BR ˈhɔːsn
AM ˈhɔrsən

Whorf
BR wɔːf
AM (h)wɔ(ə)rf

whorish
BR ˈhɔːrɪʃ
AM ˈhɔrɪʃ

whorishly
BR ˈhɔːrɪʃli
AM ˈhɔrɪʃli

whorishness
BR ˈhɔːrɪʃnɪs
AM ˈhɔrɪʃnɪs

whorl
BR wəːl, -z, -d
AM (h)wɔ(ə)rl, -z, -d

whortleberry
BR ˈwəːtl‚bɛr|i,
ˈwəːtlb(ə)r|i, -ɪz
AM ˈ(h)wərdl‚bɛri, -z

who's
BR huːz
AM huz

whose
BR huːz
AM huz

whosesoever
BR ‚huːzsəʊˈevə(r)
AM ‚huz‚soʊˈevər

whoso
BR ˈhuːsəʊ
AM ˈhu‚soʊ

whosoever
BR ‚huːsəʊˈevə(r),
ˈhuːsəʊevə(r)
AM ‚husoʊˈevər

Who's Who
BR ‚huːz ˈhuː, -z
AM ‚huzˈhu, -z

who've
BR huːv
AM huv

whump
BR wʌmp, -s, -ɪŋ, -t
AM (h)wəmp, -s, -ɪŋ, -t

why
BR wʌɪ
AM (h)waɪ

Whyalla
BR wʌɪˈalə(r)
AM (h)waɪˈælə

whydah
BR ˈwɪdə(r), -z

AM ˈ(h)wɪdə, -z

Whymper
BR ˈwɪmpə(r)
AM ˈ(h)wɪmpər

Whyte
BR wʌɪt
AM (h)waɪt

Whythorne
BR ˈwʌɪthɔːn
AM ˈ(h)waɪt‚(h)ɔ(ə)rn

wibbly-wobbly
BR ‚wɪbliˈwɒbli
AM ˈwɪbliˈwɑbli

Wibsey
BR ˈwɪbsi, ˈwɪbzi
AM ˈwɪbsi, ˈwɪbzi

Wicca
BR ˈwɪkə(r)
AM ˈwɪkə

Wiccan
BR ˈwɪk(ə)n
AM ˈwɪkən

Wichita
BR ˈwɪtʃɪtɑː(r)
AM ˈwɪtʃə‚tɑ

Wichnor
BR ˈwɪtʃnɔː(r),
ˈwɪtʃnə(r)
AM ˈwɪtʃnər

wick
BR wɪk, -s
AM wɪk, -s

wicked
BR ˈwɪk|ɪd, -ɪdɪst
AM ˈwɪkɪd, -ɪst

wickedly
BR ˈwɪkɪdli
AM ˈwɪkɪdli

wickedness
BR ˈwɪkɪdnɪs
AM ˈwɪkɪdnɪs

Wicken
BR ˈwɪk(ɪ)n
AM ˈwɪkən

wicker
BR ˈwɪkə(r)
AM ˈwɪkər

wickerwork
BR ˈwɪkəwəːk
AM ˈwɪkər‚wərk

wicket
BR ˈwɪkɪt, -s
AM ˈwɪkɪt, -s

wicketkeeper
BR ˈwɪkɪt‚kiːpə(r), -z
AM ˈwɪkɪt‚kipər, -z

wicketkeeping
BR ˈwɪkɪt‚kiːpɪŋ
AM ˈwɪkɪt‚kipɪŋ

wicket-taker
BR ˈwɪkɪt‚teɪkə(r), -z
AM ˈwɪkɪt‚teɪkər, -z

wicket-taking
BR ˈwɪkɪt‚teɪkɪŋ
AM ˈwɪkɪt‚teɪkɪŋ

Wickham
BR ˈwɪkəm

AM ˈwɪkəm

wickiup
BR ˈwɪkɪʌp, -s
AM ˈwɪki‚əp, -s

Wicklow
BR ˈwɪkləʊ
AM ˈwɪkloʊ

Wicks
BR wɪks
AM wɪks

Widdecombe
BR ˈwɪdɪkəm
AM ˈwɪdəkəm

widdershins
BR ˈwɪdəʃɪnz
AM ˈwɪdərˌʃɪnz

Widdicombe
BR ˈwɪdɪkəm
AM ˈwɪdəkəm

Widdowson
BR ˈwɪdə(ʊ)sn
AM ˈwɪdəsən

wide
BR wʌɪd, -ə(r), -ɪst
AM waɪd, -ər, -ɪst

wide-angle
BR ‚wʌɪdˈaŋgl
AM ˈwaɪdˈæŋgəl

wideawake
BR ‚wʌɪdəˈweɪk, -s
AM ˈwaɪdəˈweɪk, -s

Widecombe
BR ˈwɪdɪkəm
AM ˈwɪdəkəm

widely
BR ˈwʌɪdli
AM ˈwaɪdli

widemouth
BR ˈwʌɪdmaʊθ
AM ˈwaɪdˌmaʊθ

widemouthed
BR ‚wʌɪdˈmaʊðd,
‚wʌɪdˈmaʊθt
AM ˈwaɪdˌmaʊθ(t)

widen
BR ˈwʌɪd|n, -nz,
-nɪŋ\-nɪŋ, -nd
AM ˈwaɪdən, -z, -ɪŋ, -d

widener
BR ˈwʌɪdnə(r),
ˈwʌɪdnə(r), -z
AM ˈwaɪdnər,
ˈwaɪdnər, -z

wideness
BR ˈwʌɪdnɪs
AM ˈwaɪdnɪs

widening
BR ˈwʌɪdnɪŋ, ˈwʌɪdnɪŋ,
-z
AM ˈwaɪdnɪŋ,
ˈwaɪdnɪŋ, -z

widespread
BR ˈwʌɪdsprɛd,
‚wʌɪdˈspred
AM ˈwaɪdˈsprɛd

widgeon
BR ˈwɪdʒ(ɪ)n, -z

AM ˈwɪdʒən, -z

widget
BR ˈwɪdʒɪt, -s
AM ˈwɪdʒɪt, -s

widgie
BR ˈwɪdʒ|i, -ɪz
AM ˈwɪdʒi, -z

widish
BR ˈwʌɪdɪʃ
AM ˈwaɪdɪʃ

Widlake
BR ˈwɪdleɪk
AM ˈwɪd‚leɪk

Widmark
BR ˈwɪdmɑːk
AM ˈwɪd‚mɑrk

Widnes
BR ˈwɪdnɪs
AM ˈwɪdnəs

widow
BR ˈwɪdəʊ, -z, -ɪŋ, -d
AM ˈwɪdoʊ, -z, -ɪŋ, -d

widow-bird
BR ˈwɪdəʊbəːd, -z
AM ˈwɪdoʊ‚bərd, -z

widower
BR ˈwɪdəʊə(r), -z
AM ˈwɪdoʊər, -z

widowhood
BR ˈwɪdəʊhʊd
AM ˈwɪdoʊ‚(h)ʊd

widow-maker
BR ˈwɪdə(ʊ)‚meɪkə(r),
-z
AM ˈwɪdoʊ‚meɪkər, -z

width
BR wɪdθ, wɪtθ, -s
AM wɪdθ, -s

widthways
BR ˈwɪdθweɪz,
ˈwɪtθweɪz
AM ˈwɪ(d)θ‚weɪz,
ˈwɪð‚weɪz

widthwise
BR ˈwɪdθwʌɪz,
ˈwɪtθwʌɪz
AM ˈwɪ(d)θ‚waɪz,
ˈwɪð‚waɪz

Wieland
BR ˈwiːlənd
AM ˈwilənd

wield
BR wiːld, -z, -ɪŋ, -ɪd
AM wild, -z, -ɪŋ, -ɪd

wielder
BR ˈwiːldə(r), -z
AM ˈwildər, -z

wieldy
BR ˈwiːldi
AM ˈwildi

wiener
BR ˈwiːnə(r), -z
AM ˈwinər, -z

Wiener schnitzel
BR ‚wiːnə ˈʃnɪtsl
AM ‚winər ˈʃnɪtsəl

wienie
BR 'wiːnʲi, -ɪz
AM 'wini, -z

Wiesbaden
BR 'viːs,baːdn
AM 'wisbɑdən,
'visbɑdən

Wiesel
BR 'viːsl
AM 'visəl

Wiesenthal
BR 'viːzntɑːl
AM 'wizən,tɑl,
'wizən,θɑl

wife
BR wʌɪf
AM waɪf

wifehood
BR 'wʌɪfhʊd
AM 'waɪf,(h)ʊd

wifeless
BR 'wʌɪflɪs
AM 'waɪflɪs

wifelike
BR 'wʌɪflʌɪk
AM 'waɪf,laɪk

wifeliness
BR 'wʌɪflɪnɪs
AM 'waɪflɪnɪs

wifely
BR 'wʌɪfli
AM 'waɪfli

wife-swapping
BR 'wʌɪf,swɒpɪŋ
AM 'waɪf,swɑpɪŋ

wifish
BR 'wʌɪfɪʃ
AM 'waɪfɪʃ

wig
BR wɪg, -z, -d
AM wɪg, -z, -d

Wigan
BR 'wɪg(ə)n
AM 'wɪgən

wigeon
BR 'wɪdʒ(ɪ)n, -z
AM 'wɪdʒən, -z

Wiggin
BR 'wɪgɪn
AM 'wɪgɪn

wigging
BR 'wɪgɪŋ, -z
AM 'wɪgɪŋ, -z

Wiggins
BR 'wɪgɪnz
AM 'wɪgɪnz

wiggle
BR 'wɪgl̩, -lz, -lɪŋ\-l̩ɪŋ,
-ld
AM 'wɪgǀəl, -əlz, -(ə)lɪŋ,
-əld

wiggler
BR 'wɪglə(r),
'wɪglə(r), -z
AM 'wɪg(ə)lər, -z

Wigglesworth
BR 'wɪglzwəːθ,
'wɪglzwəθ
AM 'wɪgəlz,wərθ

wiggly
BR 'wɪgl̩i, 'wɪgli
AM 'wɪg(ə)li

wight
BR wʌɪt, -s
AM waɪt, -s

Wigley
BR 'wɪgli
AM 'wɪgli

Wigmore
BR 'wɪgmɔː(r)
AM 'wɪg,mɔ(ə)r

Wigram
BR 'wɪgrəm
AM 'wɪgrəm

Wigton
BR 'wɪgt(ə)n
AM 'wɪgtən

Wigtownshire
BR 'wɪgt(ə)nʃ(ɪ)ə(r)
AM 'wɪgtənʃɪ(ə)r

wigwag
BR 'wɪgwag, -z, -ɪŋ, -d
AM 'wɪg,wæg, -z, -ɪŋ, -d

wigwam
BR 'wɪgwam, -z
AM 'wɪ,gwɑm, -z

Wilberforce
BR 'wɪlbəfɔːs
AM 'wɪlbər,fɔ(ə)rs

Wilbert
BR 'wɪlbət
AM 'wɪlbərt

Wilbraham
BR 'wɪlbrəhəm,
'wɪlbrəm
AM 'wɪlbrəm,
'wɪlbrə,hæm

Wilbur
BR 'wɪlbə(r)
AM 'wɪlbər

Wilby
BR 'wɪlbi
AM 'wɪlbi

wilco
BR 'wɪlkəʊ
AM 'wɪlkoʊ

Wilcock
BR 'wɪlkɒk
AM 'wɪl,kɑk

Wilcocks
BR 'wɪlkɒks
AM 'wɪl,kɑks

Wilcox
BR 'wɪlkɒks
AM 'wɪl,kɑks

Wilcoxon
BR 'wɪlkɒksn
AM 'wɪl,kɑksən

wild
BR wʌɪld, -z, -ə(r), -ɪst
AM waɪld, -z, -ər, -ɪst

Wildblood
BR 'wʌɪl(d)blʌd
AM 'waɪl(d),blʊd

wild card
BR 'wʌɪl(d) kɑːd, -z
AM 'waɪl(d) ,kɑrd, -z

wildcat
BR 'wʌɪl(d)kat
AM 'waɪl(d),kæt

Wilde
BR wʌɪld
AM waɪld

wildebeest
BR 'wɪldɪbiːst, -s
AM 'wɪldə,bist, -s

Wildenstein
BR 'wɪld(ə)nstʌɪn
AM 'wɪldən,staɪn

Wilder
BR 'wʌɪldə(r)
AM 'waɪldər

wilder
bewilder
BR 'wɪldǀə(r), -əz,
-(ə)rɪŋ, -əd
AM 'wɪldər, -z, -ɪŋ, -d

wilderness
BR 'wɪldənəs, -ɪz
AM 'wɪldərnəs, -əz

wild-eyed
BR ,wʌɪld'ʌɪd
AM ,waɪld,aɪd

wildfire
BR 'wʌɪl(d)fʌɪə(r)
AM 'waɪl(d),faɪ(ə)r

wildfowl
BR 'wʌɪl(d)faʊl
AM 'waɪl(d),faʊl

wildfowler
BR 'wʌɪl(d)faʊlə(r), -z
AM 'waɪl(d),faʊlər, -z

wildfowling
BR 'wʌɪl(d)faʊlɪŋ
AM 'waɪl(d),faʊlɪŋ

**wild-goose
chase**
BR ,wʌɪl(d)'guːs tʃeɪs,
-ɪz
AM ,waɪl(d)'gus ,tʃeɪs,
-ɪz

wilding
BR 'wʌɪldɪŋ, -z
AM 'waɪldɪŋ, -z

wildish
BR 'wʌɪldɪʃ
AM 'waɪldɪʃ

wildlife
BR 'wʌɪl(d)lʌɪf
AM 'waɪl(d),laɪf

wildly
BR 'wʌɪldli
AM 'waɪl(d)li

wildness
BR 'wʌɪldnɪs
AM 'waɪl(d)nɪs

wildwood
BR 'wʌɪldwʊd, -z

Willa
BR 'wʌɪl(d),wʊd, -z

wile
BR wʌɪl, -z, -ɪŋ, -d
AM waɪl, -z, -ɪŋ, -d

Wiley
BR 'wʌɪli
AM 'waɪli

Wilf
BR wɪlf
AM wɪlf

Wilford
BR 'wɪlfəd
AM 'wɪlfərd

Wilfred
BR 'wɪlfrɪd
AM 'wɪlfrɪd

Wilfrid
BR 'wɪlfrɪd
AM 'wɪlfrɪd

wilful
BR 'wɪlf(ʊ)l
AM 'wɪlfəl

wilfully
BR 'wɪlfʊli, 'wɪlfl̩i
AM 'wɪlfəli

wilfulness
BR 'wɪlf(ʊ)lnəs
AM 'wɪlfəlnəs

wilga
BR 'wɪlgə(r), -z
AM 'wɪlgə, -z

Wilhelmina
BR ,wɪlhɛl'miːnə(r),
,wɪlhəl'miːnə(r)
AM ,wɪlɛl'minə

Wilhelmshaven
BR 'wɪlhɛlmz,hɑːvn,
'wɪlhɛlmz,hɑːfn
AM ,wɪl,(h)ɛlmz,hɑvən

wilily
BR 'wʌɪlɪli
AM 'waɪlɪli

wiliness
BR 'wʌɪlɪnɪs
AM 'waɪlinɪs

Wilkerson
BR 'wɪlkəs(ə)n
AM 'wɪlkərsən

Wilkes
BR wɪlks
AM wɪlks

Wilkie
BR 'wɪlki
AM 'wɪlki

Wilkins
BR 'wɪlkɪnz
AM 'wɪlkɪnz

Wilkinson
BR 'wɪlkɪns(ə)n
AM 'wɪlkɪnsən

will
BR wɪl, -z, -ɪŋ, -d
AM wɪl, -z, -ɪŋ, -d

Willa
BR 'wɪlə(r)
AM 'wɪlə

Willard
BR ˈwɪlɑːd
AM ˈwɪlərd

Willcock
BR ˈwɪlkɒk
AM ˈwɪlˌkɑk

Willcocks
BR ˈwɪlkɒks
AM ˈwɪlˌkɑks

Willcox
BR ˈwɪlkɒks
AM ˈwɪlˌkɑks

Willemstadt
BR ˈwɪləmstat
AM ˈwɪləmˌstat,
ˈwɪləmˌʃtat

Willenhall
BR ˈwɪlənhɔːl
AM ˈwɪlən,(h)ɔl,
ˈwɪlən,(h)ɑl

willer
BR ˈwɪlə(r), -z
AM ˈwɪlər, -z

Willesden
BR ˈwɪlzdən
AM ˈwɪlzdən

willet
BR ˈwɪlɪt, -s
AM ˈwɪlɪt, -s

Willetts
BR ˈwɪlɪts
AM ˈwɪlɪts

Willey
BR ˈwɪli
AM ˈwɪli

willful
BR ˈwɪlf(ʊ)l
AM ˈwɪlfəl

willfully
BR ˈwɪlfəli, ˈwɪlfli
AM ˈwɪlfəli

willfulness
BR ˈwɪlf(ʊ)lnəs
AM ˈwɪlfəlnəs

William
BR ˈwɪljəm
AM ˈwɪljəm, ˈwɪliəm

Williams
BR ˈwɪljəmz
AM ˈwɪljəmz, ˈwɪliəmz

Williamsburg
BR ˈwɪljəmzbɜːg
AM ˈwɪljəmzˌbɜrg,
ˈwɪliəmzˌbɜrg

Williamson
BR ˈwɪljəms(ə)n
AM ˈwɪljəmsən,
ˈwɪliəmsən

willie
BR ˈwɪli, -ɪz
AM ˈwɪli, -z

willing
BR ˈwɪlɪŋ
AM ˈwɪlɪŋ

willingly
BR ˈwɪlɪŋli
AM ˈwɪlɪŋli

willingness
BR ˈwɪlɪŋnɪs
AM ˈwɪlɪŋnɪs

Willis
BR ˈwɪlɪs
AM ˈwɪlɪs

will-less
BR ˈwɪllɪs
AM ˈwɪ(l)lɪs

Willmott
BR ˈwɪlmɒt
AM ˈwɪlˌmɑt

will-o'-the-wisp
BR ˌwɪləðəˈwɪsp, -s
AM ˌwɪləðəˈwɪsp, -s

Willoughby
BR ˈwɪləbi
AM ˈwɪləbi

willow
BR ˈwɪləʊ, -z
AM ˈwɪloʊ, -z

willowherb
BR ˈwɪləʊhɜːb
AM ˈwɪloʊˌɜrb

willowy
BR ˈwɪləʊi
AM ˈwɪloʊi

willpower
BR ˈwɪlˌpaʊə(r)
AM ˈwɪlˌpaʊər

Wills
BR wɪlz
AM wɪlz

willy
BR ˈwɪli, -ɪz
AM ˈwɪli, -z

willy-nilly
BR ˌwɪliˈnɪli
AM ˌwɪliˈnɪli

willy-willy
BR ˈwɪliˌwɪli, -ɪz
AM ˈwɪliˈwɪli, -z

Wilma
BR ˈwɪlmə(r)
AM ˈwɪlmə

Wilmcote
BR ˈwɪlmkəʊt
AM ˈwɪlmˌkoʊt

Wilmer
BR ˈwɪlmə(r)
AM ˈwɪlmər

Wilmington
BR ˈwɪlmɪŋt(ə)n
AM ˈwɪlmɪŋtən

Wilmot
BR ˈwɪlmɒt
AM ˈwɪlˌmɑt

Wilmott
BR ˈwɪlmɒt
AM ˈwɪlˌmɑt

Wilmslow
BR ˈwɪlmzləʊ
AM ˈwɪlmzloʊ

Wilsher
BR ˈwɪlʃə(r)
AM ˈwɪlʃər

Wilson
BR ˈwɪlsn
AM ˈwɪlsən

Wilsonian
BR wɪlˈsəʊniən
AM wɪlˈsoʊniən

wilt
BR wɪlt, -s, -ɪŋ, -ɪd
AM wɪlt, -s, -ɪŋ, -ɪd

Wilton
BR ˈwɪltn, -z
AM ˈwɪltən, -z

Wilts.
BR wɪlts
AM wɪlts

Wiltshire
BR ˈwɪltʃ(ɪ)ə(r)
AM ˈwɪltʃɪ(ə)r

wily
BR ˈwaɪli, -iə(r), -ɪɪst
AM ˈwaɪli, -ər, -ɪst

wimble
BR ˈwɪmbl, -z
AM ˈwɪmbəl, -z

Wimbledon
BR ˈwɪmbld(ə)n
AM ˈwɪmbəldən

Wimborne
BR ˈwɪmbɔːn
AM ˈwɪmˌbɔ(ə)rn

Wimbourne
BR ˈwɪmbɔːn
AM ˈwɪmˌbɔ(ə)rn

Wimbush
BR ˈwɪmbʊʃ
AM ˈwɪmbəʃ

Wimoweh
BR ˈwɪməweɪ
AM ˈwɪməˌweɪ

wimp
BR wɪmp, -s
AM wɪmp, -s

wimpish
BR ˈwɪmpɪʃ
AM ˈwɪmpɪʃ

wimpishly
BR ˈwɪmpɪʃli
AM ˈwɪmpɪʃli

wimpishness
BR ˈwɪmpɪʃnɪs
AM ˈwɪmpɪʃnɪs

wimple
BR ˈwɪmpl, -z
AM ˈwɪmpəl, -z

Wimpole
BR ˈwɪmpəʊl
AM ˈwɪmˌpoʊl

wimpy
BR ˈwɪmpi, -iə(r), -ɪɪst
AM ˈwɪmpi, -ər, -ɪst

win
BR wɪn, -z, -ɪŋ
AM wɪn, -z, -ɪŋ

Winalot®
BR ˈwɪnəlɒt
AM ˈwɪnəˌlɑt

Wincanton
BR wɪnˈkantən
AM wɪnˈkæn(t)ən

Wincarnis
BR wɪnˈkɑːnɪs
AM wɪnˈkɑrnəs

wince
BR wɪns, -ɪz, -ɪŋ, -t
AM wɪns, -ɪz, -ɪŋ, -t

wincer
BR ˈwɪnsə(r), -z
AM ˈwɪnsər, -z

wincey
BR ˈwɪnsˌi, -ɪz
AM ˈwɪnsi, -z

winceyette
BR ˌwɪnsiˈɛt
AM ˌwɪnsiˈɛt

winch¹
BR wɪn(t)ʃ, -ɪz, -ɪŋ, -t
AM wɪn(t)ʃ, -ɪz, -ɪŋ, -t

winch²
BR wɪn(t)ʃ, -ɪz, -ɪŋ, -t
AM wɪn(t)ʃ, -ɪz, -ɪŋ, -t

Winchelsea
BR ˈwɪn(t)ʃlsiː
AM ˈwɪn(t)ʃəlˌsi

wincher
BR ˈwɪn(t)ʃə(r), -z
AM ˈwɪn(t)ʃər, -z

winchester
BR ˈwɪntʃɪstə(r),
ˈwɪntʃestə(r), -z
AM ˈwɪnˌtʃestər, -z

Winchmore
BR ˈwɪn(t)ʃmɔː(r)
AM ˈwɪn(t)ʃˌmɔ(ə)r

wincingly
BR ˈwɪnsɪŋli
AM ˈwɪnsɪŋli

Winckelmann
BR ˈwɪŋklman
AM ˈwɪŋkəlmən

wind¹
verb make breathless,
noun air
BR wɪnd, -z, -ɪŋ, -ɪd
AM wɪnd, -z, -ɪŋ, -ɪd

wind²
verb turn, blow
BR waɪnd, -z, -ɪŋ
AM waɪnd, -z, -ɪŋ

windage
BR ˈwɪndˌɪdʒ, -ɪdʒɪz
AM ˈwɪndɪdʒ, -ɪz

Windaus
BR ˈvɪndaʊs
AM ˈvɪndaʊs

windbag
BR ˈwɪn(d)bag, -z
AM ˈwɪn(d)ˌbæg, -z

windblown
BR ˈwɪn(d)bləʊn
AM ˈwɪn(d)ˌbloʊn

windbound
BR ˈwɪn(d)baʊnd
AM ˈwɪn(d)ˌbaʊnd

windbreak
BR ˈwɪn(d)breɪk, -s
AM ˈwɪn(d)ˌbreɪk, -s

Windbreaker®
BR ˈwɪn(d)ˌbreɪkə(r), -z
AM ˈwɪn(d)ˌbreɪkər, -z

windburn
BR ˈwɪn(d)bɜːn, -d
AM ˈwɪn(d)ˌbɜrn, -d

windcheater
BR ˈwɪn(d)ˌtʃiːtə(r), -z
AM ˈwɪn(d)ˌtʃidər, -z

windchill
BR ˈwɪn(d)tʃɪl
AM ˈwɪn(d)tʃɪl

windcone
BR ˈwɪn(d)kəʊn, -z
AM ˈwɪn(d)ˌkoʊn, -z

wind-down
BR ˈwʌɪn(d)daʊn, -z
AM ˈwʌɪn(d)ˌdaʊn, -z

winder
BR ˈwʌɪndə(r), -z
AM ˈwʌɪndər, -z

Windermere
BR ˈwɪndəmɪə(r)
AM ˈwɪndərˌmɪ(ə)r

windfall
BR ˈwɪn(d)fɔːl, -z
AM ˈwɪn(d)ˌfɔl,
ˈwɪn(d)ˌfɑl, -z

windfarm
BR ˈwɪn(d)fɑːm, -z
AM ˈwɪn(d)fɑrm, -z

windflower
BR ˈwɪn(d)ˌflaʊə(r), -z
AM ˈwɪn(d)ˌflaʊər, -z

Windhoek
BR ˈwɪndhʊk,
ˈvɪnthʊk
AM ˈwɪn(d)ˌ(h)ʊk

windhover
BR ˈwɪndˌhʊvə(r), -z
AM ˈwɪn(d)ˌ(h)əvər, -z

windily
BR ˈwɪndɨli
AM ˈwɪndɨli

windiness
BR ˈwɪndɪnɪs
AM ˈwɪndɪnɪs

windjammer
BR ˈwɪn(d)ˌdʒamə(r),
-z
AM ˈwɪn(d)ˌdʒæmər, -z

windlass
BR ˈwɪndləs, -ɪz
AM ˈwɪn(d)ləs, -əz

Windlesham
BR ˈwɪndlʃ(ə)m
AM ˈwɪndlˌʃəm

windless
BR ˈwɪndlɪs
AM ˈwɪn(d)lɪs

windlestraw
BR ˈwɪndlstrɔː(r), -z

AM ˈwɪndlˌstrɔ,
ˈwɪndlˌstrɑ, -z

windmill
BR ˈwɪn(d)mɪl, -z
AM ˈwɪn(d)ˌmɪl, -z

Windolene®
BR ˈwɪndə(ʊ)liːn
AM ˈwɪndəˌlin

window
BR ˈwɪndəʊ, -z, -ɪŋ, -d
AM ˈwɪndoʊ, -z, -ɪŋ, -d

windowless
BR ˈwɪndə(ʊ)ləs
AM ˈwɪndoʊləs

windowpane
BR ˈwɪndə(ʊ)peɪn, -z
AM ˈwɪndoʊˌpeɪn, -z

windowseat
BR ˈwɪndə(ʊ)siːt, -s
AM ˈwɪndoʊˌsit, -s

window-shop
BR ˈwɪndəʊˌʃɒp, -s, -ɪŋ,
-t
AM ˈwɪndoʊˌʃɑp, -s, -ɪŋ,
-t

window-shopper
BR ˈwɪndəʊˌʃɒpə(r), -z
AM ˈwɪndoʊˌʃɑpər, -z

windowsill
BR ˈwɪndə(ʊ)sɪl, -z
AM ˈwɪndoʊˌsɪl, -z

windpipe
BR ˈwɪn(d)pʌɪp, -s
AM ˈwɪn(d)ˌpaɪp, -s

windproof
BR ˈwɪn(d)pruːf
AM ˈwɪn(d)ˌprʊf

windrow
BR ˈwɪn(d)rəʊ, -z
AM ˈwɪn(d)ˌroʊ, -z

Windrush
BR ˈwɪndrʌʃ
AM ˈwɪn(d)ˌrəʃ

windsail
BR ˈwɪn(d)sl,
ˈwɪn(d)seɪl
AM ˈwɪn(d)ˌseɪl,
ˈwɪn(d)səl

Windscale
BR ˈwɪn(d)skeɪl
AM ˈwɪn(d)ˌskeɪl

windscreen
BR ˈwɪn(d)skriːn, -z
AM ˈwɪn(d)ˌskrin, -z

windshield
BR ˈwɪn(d)ʃiːld, -z
AM ˈwɪn(d)ˌʃild, -z

windsock
BR ˈwɪn(d)sɒk, -s
AM ˈwɪn(d)ˌsɑk, -s

Windsor
BR ˈwɪnzə(r)
AM ˈwɪnzər

windstorm
BR ˈwɪn(d)stɔːm, -z
AM ˈwɪn(d)ˌstɔ(ə)rm,
-z

windsurf
BR ˈwɪn(d)sɜːf, -s, -ɪŋ, -t
AM ˈwɪn(d)ˌsɜrf, -s, -ɪŋ,
-t

windsurfer
BR ˈwɪn(d)ˌsɜːfə(r), -z
AM ˈwɪn(d)ˌsɜrfər, -z

windswept
BR ˈwɪn(d)swept
AM ˈwɪn(d)ˌswɛpt

wind-up
BR ˈwʌɪndʌp, -s
AM ˈwaɪndəp, -s

windward
BR ˈwɪndwəd
AM ˈwɪn(d)wərd

windy
BR ˈwɪnd|i, -ɪə(r), -ɪst
AM ˈwɪndi, -ər, -ɪst

wine
BR ˈwʌɪn, -z, -ɪŋ, -d
AM ˈwaɪn, -z, -ɪŋ, -d

wineberry
BR ˈwʌɪnb(ə)r|i, -ɪz
AM ˈwaɪnˌbɛri, -z

winebibber
BR ˈwʌɪnˌbɪbə(r), -z
AM ˈwaɪnˌbɪbər, -z

winebibbing
BR ˈwʌɪnˌbɪbɪŋ
AM ˈwaɪnˌbɪbɪŋ

wineglass
BR ˈwʌɪnglɑːs,
ˈwʌɪnglas, -ɪz
AM ˈwaɪnˌglæs, -ɪz

wineglassful
BR ˈwʌɪnglɑːsfʊl,
ˈwʌɪnglasfʊl, -z
AM ˈwaɪnˌglæsˌfʊl, -z

winegrower
BR ˈwʌɪnˌgrəʊə(r), -z
AM ˈwaɪnˌgroʊər, -z

wineless
BR ˈwʌɪnlɪs
AM ˈwaɪnlɪs

winemaker
BR ˈwʌɪnˌmeɪkə(r), -z
AM ˈwaɪnˌmeɪkər, -z

winemaking
BR ˈwʌɪnˌmeɪkɪŋ
AM ˈwaɪnˌmeɪkɪŋ

winepress
BR ˈwʌɪnpres, -ɪz
AM ˈwaɪnˌpres, -əz

winery
BR ˈwʌɪn(ə)r|i, -ɪz
AM ˈwaɪn(ə)ri, -z

wineskin
BR ˈwʌɪnskɪn, -z
AM ˈwaɪnˌskɪn, -z

Winfield
BR ˈwɪnfiːld
AM ˈwɪnˌfild

Winford
BR ˈwɪnfəd
AM ˈwɪnfərd

Winfred
BR ˈwɪnfrɪd
AM ˈwɪnˌfrɛd

Winfrith
BR ˈwɪnfrɪθ
AM ˈwɪnˌfrɪθ

wing
BR ˈwɪŋ, -z, -ɪŋ, -d
AM ˈwɪŋ, -z, -ɪŋ, -d

Wingate
BR ˈwɪŋgeɪt, ˈwɪŋgeɪt
AM ˈwɪnˌgeɪt

wingback
BR ˈwɪŋbak, -s
AM ˈwɪŋˌbæk, -s

wingding
BR ˈwɪŋdɪŋ, -z
AM ˈwɪŋˌdɪŋ, -z

winge
BR ˈwɪn(d)ʒ, -ɪz, -ɪŋ, -d
AM ˈ(h)wɪndʒ, -ɪz, -ɪŋ, -d

winged[1]
with wings
BR ˈwɪŋd
AM ˈwɪŋd

winged[2]
*with wings, old poetic
form*
BR ˈwɪŋɨd
AM ˈwɪŋɨd

winger[1]
complainer
BR ˈwɪn(d)ʒə(r), -z
AM ˈwɪndʒər, -z

winger[2]
player etc
BR ˈwɪŋə(r), -z
AM ˈwɪŋər, -z

Wingfield
BR ˈwɪŋfiːld
AM ˈwɪŋˌfild

wing forward
BR ˈwɪŋ ˈfɔːwəd, -z
AM ˈwɪŋ ˈfɔrwərd, -z

wing-half
BR ˈwɪŋˈhɑːf, -s
AM ˈwɪŋˌ(h)æf, -s

wingless
BR ˈwɪŋlɪs
AM ˈwɪŋlɪs

winglet
BR ˈwɪŋlɪt, -s
AM ˈwɪŋlɪt, -s

winglike
BR ˈwɪŋlʌɪk
AM ˈwɪŋˌlaɪk

wingman
BR ˈwɪŋman
AM ˈwɪŋˌmæn

wingmen
BR ˈwɪŋmen
AM ˈwɪŋˌmɛn

wingnut
BR ˈwɪŋnʌt, -s
AM ˈwɪŋˌnət, -s

wingover
BR ˈwɪŋˌəʊvə(r), -z

AM 'wɪŋˌoʊvər, -z
wingspan
 BR 'wɪŋspæn, -z
 AM 'wɪŋˌspæn, -z
wingspread
 BR 'wɪŋsprɛd
 AM 'wɪŋˌsprɛd
wingtip
 BR 'wɪŋtɪp, -s
 AM 'wɪŋˌtɪp, -s
Winifred
 BR 'wɪnɪfrɪd
 AM 'wɪnɪfrəd
wink
 BR wɪŋ|k, -ks, -kɪŋ,
 -(k)t
 AM wɪŋ|k, -ks, -kɪŋ,
 -(k)t
winker
 BR 'wɪŋkə(r), -z
 AM 'wɪŋkər, -z
winkle
 BR 'wɪŋk|l̩, -lz,
 -l̩ɪŋ \-lɪŋ, -ld
 AM 'wɪŋkəl, -əlz,
 -(ə)lɪŋ, -əld
winklehawk
 BR 'wɪŋklhɔːk, -s
 AM 'wɪŋkəl̩(h)ɑk,
 'wɪŋkəl̩(h)ɑk, -s
winkler
 BR 'wɪŋklə(r),
 'wɪŋklə(r), -z
 AM 'wɪŋk(ə)lər, -z
winless
 BR 'wɪnlɪs
 AM 'wɪnlɪs
winnable
 BR 'wɪnəbl̩
 AM 'wɪnəbəl
Winnebago
 BR ˌwɪnɪ'beɪgəʊ, -z
 AM ˌwɪnə'beɪgoʊ, -z
winner
 BR 'wɪnə(r), -z
 AM 'wɪnər, -z
Winnie
 BR 'wɪni
 AM 'wɪni
Winnie-the-Pooh
 BR ˌwɪnɪðə'puː
 AM ˌwɪnɪðə'pu
winning
 BR 'wɪnɪŋ, -z, -ɪst
 AM 'wɪnɪŋ, -z, -ɪst
winningly
 BR 'wɪnɪŋli
 AM 'wɪnɪŋli
winningness
 BR 'wɪnɪŋnɪs
 AM 'wɪnɪŋnɪs
Winnipeg
 BR 'wɪnɪpeg
 AM 'wɪnəˌpeg
winnow
 BR 'wɪnəʊ, -z, -ɪŋ, -d
 AM 'wɪnoʊ, -z, -ɪŋ, -d

winnower
 BR 'wɪnəʊə(r), -z
 AM 'wɪnəwər, -z
wino
 BR 'waɪnəʊ, -z
 AM 'waɪˌnoʊ, -z
Winona
 BR wɪ'nəʊnə(r)
 AM wɪ'noʊnə,
 waɪ'noʊnə
Winifred
 BR 'wɪnɪfrɪd
 AM 'wɪnɪfrəd
Winslow
 BR 'wɪnzləʊ
 AM 'wɪnzloʊ
winsome
 BR 'wɪns(ə)m
 AM 'wɪnsəm
winsomely
 BR 'wɪns(ə)mli
 AM 'wɪnsəmli
winsomeness
 BR 'wɪns(ə)mnəs
 AM 'wɪnsəmnəs
Winstanley
 BR wɪn'stænli,
 'wɪnst(ə)nli
 AM 'wɪnstənli,
 wɪn'stænli
Winston
 BR 'wɪnst(ə)n
 AM 'wɪnstən
winter
 BR 'wɪntə(r), -əz,
 -(ə)rɪŋ, -əd
 AM 'wɪn|t(ər, -(t)ərz,
 -(t)ərɪŋ \-trɪŋ, -(t)ərd
Winterbotham
 BR 'wɪntəˌbɒtəm
 AM 'wɪn|t(ər,badəm
Winterbottom
 BR 'wɪntəˌbɒtəm
 AM 'wɪn|t(ər,badəm
Winterbourn
 BR 'wɪntəbɔːn
 AM 'wɪn|t(ər,bɔ(ə)rn
Winterbourne
 BR 'wɪntəbɔːn
 AM 'wɪn|t(ər,bɔ(ə)rn
winterer
 BR 'wɪnt(ə)rə(r), -z
 AM 'wɪn|t(ərər,
 'wɪntrər, -z
wintergreen
 BR 'wɪntəgriːn
 AM 'wɪn|t(ər,grin
winterisation
 BR ˌwɪnt(ə)rʌɪ'zeɪʃn
 AM ˌwɪn|t(ərə'zeɪʃən,
 ˌwɪn|t(ə)raɪ'zeɪʃən,
 ˌwɪntrə'zeɪʃən
winterise
 BR 'wɪntərʌɪz, -ɪz, -ɪŋ,
 -d
 AM 'wɪn|t(ər,aɪz, -ɪz,
 -ɪŋ, -d
winterization
 BR ˌwɪnt(ə)rʌɪ'zeɪʃn

AM ˌwɪn|t(ə)rə'zeɪʃən,
 ˌwɪn|t(ə)raɪ'zeɪʃən,
 ˌwɪntrə'zeɪʃən
winterize
 BR 'wɪntərʌɪz, -ɪz, -ɪŋ,
 -d
 AM 'wɪn|t(ər,aɪz, -ɪz,
 -ɪŋ, -d
winterless
 BR 'wɪntələs
 AM 'wɪn|t(ərləs
winterly
 BR 'wɪntəli
 AM 'wɪn|t(ərli
Winters
 BR 'wɪntəz
 AM 'wɪn|t(ərz
wintertime
 BR 'wɪntətʌɪm
 AM 'wɪn|t(ər,taɪm
Winterton
 BR 'wɪntət(ə)n
 AM 'wɪn|t(ərtən
wintery
 BR 'wɪnt(ə)ri
 AM 'wɪntri, 'wɪnəri
Winthrop
 BR 'wɪnθrɒp, 'wɪnθrəp
 AM 'wɪnθrəp
Winton
 BR 'wɪntən
 AM 'wɪn|t(ə)n
Wintour
 BR 'wɪntə(r)
 AM 'wɪn|t(ər
wintrily
 BR 'wɪntrɪli
 AM 'wɪntrɪli
wintriness
 BR 'wɪntrɪnɪs
 AM 'wɪntrɪnɪs
wintry
 BR 'wɪntri
 AM 'wɪntri
winy
 BR 'wʌɪn|i, -ɪə(r), -ɪɪst
 AM 'waɪni, -ər, -ɪst
wipe
 BR wʌɪp, -s, -ɪŋ, -t
 AM waɪp, -s, -ɪŋ, -t
wipeable
 BR 'wʌɪpəbl̩
 AM 'waɪpəbəl
wipeout
 BR 'wʌɪpaʊt, -s
 AM 'waɪp,aʊt, -s
wiper
 BR 'wʌɪpə(r), -z
 AM 'waɪpər, -z
WIPO
 BR 'wʌɪpəʊ
 AM 'waɪˌpoʊ
wire
 BR 'wʌɪə(r), -z, -ɪŋ, -d
 AM 'waɪ(ə)r, -z, -ɪŋ, -d
wiredraw
 BR 'wʌɪədrɔː(r), -z, -ɪŋ

AM ˌwaɪ(ə)r,drɔ,
 'waɪ(ə)r,drɑ, -z, -ɪŋ
wiredrawn
 BR 'wʌɪədrɔːn
 AM 'waɪ(ə)r,drɒn,
 'waɪ(ə)r,drɑn
wiredrew
 BR 'wʌɪədruː
 AM 'waɪ(ə)r,dru
wireless
 BR 'wʌɪələs, -ɪz
 AM 'waɪ(ə)rləs, -əz
wireman
 BR 'wʌɪəmən
 AM 'waɪ(ə)r,mæn
wiremen
 BR 'wʌɪəmɛn
 AM 'waɪ(ə)r,mɛn
wirepuller
 BR 'wʌɪə,pʊlə(r), -z
 AM 'waɪ(ə)r,pʊlər, -z
wirepulling
 BR 'wʌɪə,pʊlɪŋ
 AM 'waɪ(ə)r,pʊlɪŋ
wirer
 BR 'wʌɪərə(r), -z
 AM 'waɪ(ə)rər, -z
wireworm
 BR 'wʌɪəwəːm, -z
 AM 'waɪ(ə)r,wərm, -z
wirily
 BR 'wʌɪərɪli
 AM 'waɪrɪli
wiriness
 BR 'wʌɪərɪnɪs
 AM 'waɪrɪnɪs
wiring
 BR 'wʌɪərɪŋ
 AM 'waɪ(ə)rɪŋ
Wirksworth
 BR 'wəːkswəθ,
 'wəːkswəːθ
 AM 'wərks,wərθ
Wirral
 BR 'wɪrəl, 'wɪrl̩
 AM 'wɪrəl
wiry
 BR 'wʌɪər|i, -ɪə(r), -ɪɪst
 AM 'waɪ(ə)ri, -ər, -ɪst
Wisbech
 BR 'wɪzbiːtʃ
 AM 'wɪz,bitʃ
Wisconsin
 BR wɪ'skɒnsɪn
 AM wə'skɑnsən
Wisden
 BR 'wɪzd(ə)n
 AM 'wɪzdən
wisdom
 BR 'wɪzdəm
 AM 'wɪzdəm
wise
 BR wʌɪz, -ə(r), -ɪst
 AM waɪz, -ər, -ɪst
wiseacre
 BR 'wʌɪz,eɪkə(r), -z
 AM 'waɪz,eɪkər, -z

wiseass
BR 'wʌɪzas, -ɪz
AM 'waɪˌzæs, -ɪz

wisecrack
BR 'wʌɪzkrak, -s, -ɪŋ, -t
AM 'waɪzˌkræk, -s, -ɪŋ, -t

wisecracker
BR 'wʌɪzˌkrakə(r), -z
AM 'waɪzˌkrækər, -z

wisely
BR 'wʌɪzli
AM 'waɪzli

Wiseman
BR 'wʌɪzmən
AM 'waɪzmən

wisenheimer
BR 'wʌɪz(ə)nˌhʌɪmə(r), -z
AM 'waɪzənˌ(h)aɪmər, -z

wisent
BR 'viːzent, 'viːz(ə)nt, 'wiːzent, 'wiːz(ə)nt, -s
AM 'viˌzent, 'wiˌzent, -s

wish
BR wɪʃ, -ɪz, -ɪŋ, -t
AM wɪʃ, -ɪz, -ɪŋ, -t

Wishart
BR 'wɪʃət
AM 'wɪʃərt

Wishaw
BR 'wɪʃɔː(r)
AM 'wɪˌʃɔ, 'wɪˌʃɑ

wishbone
BR 'wɪʃbəʊn, -z
AM 'wɪʃˌboʊn, -z

wisher
BR 'wɪʃə(r), -z
AM 'wɪʃər, -z

wishful
BR 'wɪʃf(ʊ)l
AM 'wɪʃfəl

wish-fulfilling
BR 'wɪʃfʊlˌfɪlɪŋ
AM 'wɪʃfə(l)ˌfɪlɪŋ

wish-fulfillment
BR 'wɪʃfʊlˌfɪlm(ə)nt
AM 'wɪʃfə(l)ˌfɪlmənt

wish-fulfilment
BR 'wɪʃfʊlˌfɪlm(ə)nt
AM 'wɪʃfə(l)ˌfɪlmənt

wishfully
BR 'wɪʃfʊli, 'wɪʃfli
AM 'wɪʃfʊli

wishfulness
BR 'wɪʃf(ʊ)lnəs
AM 'wɪʃfəlnəs

wishing-well
BR 'wɪʃɪŋwɛl, -z
AM 'wɪʃɪŋˌwɛl, -z

wish-list
BR 'wɪʃlɪst, -s
AM 'wɪʃˌlɪst, -s

wish-wash
BR 'wɪʃwɒʃ, -ɪz

AM 'wɪʃˌwɒʃ, 'wɪʃˌwɑʃ, -əz

wishy-washy
BR 'wɪʃiˌwɒʃi, ˌwɪʃi'wɒʃi
AM 'wɪʃiˌwɒʃi, 'wɪʃiˌwɑʃi

Wisley
BR 'wɪzli
AM 'wɪzli

wisp
BR wɪsp, -s
AM wɪsp, -s

Wispa®
BR 'wɪspə(r)
AM 'wɪspə

wispily
BR 'wɪspɪli
AM 'wɪspɪli

wispiness
BR 'wɪspɪnɪs
AM 'wɪspɪnɪs

wispy
BR 'wɪspi
AM 'wɪspi

wist
BR wɪst
AM wɪst

wistaria
BR wɪˈstɪərɪə(r)
AM wəˈstɪriə, wəˈstɛriə

wisteria
BR wɪˈstɪərɪə(r)
AM wəˈstɪriə

wistful
BR wɪs(t)f(ʊ)l
AM 'wɪs(t)fəl

wistfully
BR 'wɪs(t)fʊli, 'wɪs(t)fli
AM 'wɪs(t)fəli

wistfulness
BR 'wɪs(t)f(ʊ)lnəs
AM 'wɪs(t)fəlnəs

Wiston
BR 'wɪst(ə)n, 'wɪsn
AM 'wɪstən

wit
BR wɪt, -s
AM wɪt, -s

witan
BR 'wɪtan
AM 'wɪˌtɑn

witch
BR wɪtʃ, -ɪz, -ɪŋ
AM wɪtʃ, -ɪz, -ɪŋ

witchcraft
BR 'wɪtʃkrɑːft, 'wɪtʃkraft
AM ˌwɪtʃˈkræft

witchdoctor
BR 'wɪtʃˌdɒktə(r), -z
AM 'wɪtʃˌdɑktər, -z

witchelm
BR 'wɪtʃɛlm, -z
AM 'wɪtʃˌɛlm, -z

witchery
BR 'wɪtʃ(ə)ri
AM 'wɪtʃəri

witchetty
BR 'wɪtʃɪtli, -ɪz
AM 'wɪtʃɪdi, -z

witch hazel
BR 'wɪtʃ ˌheɪzl, -z
AM 'wɪtʃ ˌ(h)eɪzəl, -z

witch-hunt
BR 'wɪtʃhʌnt, -s
AM 'wɪtʃˌ(h)ənt, -s

witchlike
BR 'wɪtʃlʌɪk
AM 'wɪtʃˌlaɪk

witenagemot
BR 'wɪtnəjəˌməʊt, 'wɪtnəjəˌməʊt, 'wɪtnəgɪˌməʊt, 'wɪtnəgɪˌməʊt, -s
AM 'wɪtnəgəˌmoʊt, -s

with
BR wɪð
AM wɪð, wɪθ

withal
BR wɪðˈɔːl
AM wəˈðɔl, wəˈθɔl, wəˈðal, wəˈθal

Witham
BR 'wɪð(ə)m
AM 'wɪðəm

withdraw
BR wɪðˈdrɔː(r), wɪθˈdrɔː(r), -z, -ɪŋ
AM wɪðˈdrɔ, wɪθˈdrɔ, wɪðˈdrɑ, wɪθˈdrɑ, -z, -ɪŋ

withdrawal
BR wɪðˈdrɔː(r)əl, wɪðˈdrɔː(r)l, wɪθˈdrɔː(r)əl, wɪθˈdrɔː(r)l, -z
AM wɪðˈdrɔ(ə)l, wɪθˈdrɔ(ə)l, wɪðˈdrɑ(ə)l, wɪθˈdrɑ(ə)l, -z

withdrawer
BR wɪðˈdrɔː(r)ə(r), wɪθˈdrɔː(r)ə(r), -z
AM wɪðˈdrɔ(w)ər, wɪθˈdrɔ(w)ər, wɪðˈdrɑ(w)ər, wɪθˈdrɑ(w)ər, -z

withdrawn
BR wɪðˈdrɔːn, wɪθˈdrɔːn
AM wɪðˈdrɔn, wɪθˈdrɔn, wɪðˈdrɑn, wɪθˈdrɑn

withdrew
BR wɪðˈdruː, wɪθˈdruː
AM wɪðˈdru, wɪθˈdru

withe
BR wɪθ, wɪð, wʌɪð, wɪθs\wɪðz\wʌɪðz
AM wɪ|θ, wɪ|ð, -θs\-ðz

wither
BR 'wɪðə(r), -əz, -(ə)rɪŋ, -əd
AM 'wɪð|ər, -ərz, -(ə)rɪŋ, -ərd

witheringly
BR 'wɪð(ə)rɪŋli
AM 'wɪðərɪŋli

Withernsea
BR 'wɪðnsi:
AM 'wɪðərnˌsi

withers
BR 'wɪðəz
AM 'wɪðərz

withershins
BR 'wɪðəʃɪnz
AM 'wɪðərˌʃɪnz

withheld
BR wɪðˈhɛld, wɪθˈhɛld
AM wɪθˈ(h)ɛld, wɪðˈ(h)ɛld

withhold
BR wɪðˈhəʊld, wɪθˈhəʊld, -z, -ɪŋ
AM wɪθˈ(h)oʊld, wɪðˈ(h)oʊld, -z, -ɪŋ

withholder
BR wɪðˈhəʊldə(r), wɪθˈhəʊldə(r), -z
AM wɪθˈ(h)oʊldər, wɪðˈ(h)oʊldər, -z

within
BR wɪðˈɪn
AM wəˈðɪn, wəˈθɪn

Withington
BR 'wɪðɪŋt(ə)n
AM 'wɪðɪŋtən, 'wɪθɪŋtən

with-it
BR 'wɪðɪt
AM 'wɪðɪt, 'wɪθɪt

without
BR wɪðˈaʊt
AM wəˈðaʊt, wəˈθaʊt

with-profits
BR wɪðˈprɒfɪts
AM wɪθˈprɑfəts, wɪðˈprɑfəts

withstand
BR wɪðˈstand
AM wɪθˈstænd, wɪðˈstænd, -z, -ɪŋ

withstander
BR wɪðˈstandə(r), wɪθˈstandə(r), -z
AM wɪθˈstændər, wɪðˈstændər, -z

withstood
BR wɪðˈstʊd, wɪθˈstʊd
AM wɪθˈstʊd, wɪðˈstʊd

withy
BR 'wɪði, -ɪz
AM 'wɪði, 'wɪθi, -z

witless
BR 'wɪtlɪs
AM 'wɪtlɪs

witlessly
BR ˈwɪtlɪsli
AM ˈwɪtlɪsli

witlessness
BR ˈwɪtlɪsnɪs
AM ˈwɪtlɪsnɪs

Witley
BR ˈwɪtli
AM ˈwɪtli

witling
BR ˈwɪtlɪŋ, -z
AM ˈwɪtlɪŋ, -z

witloof
BR ˈwɪtluːf
AM ˈwɪtˌluf

witness
BR ˈwɪtnɪs, -ɪz, -ɪŋ, -t
AM ˈwɪtnɪs, -ɪz, -ɪŋ, -t

Witney
BR ˈwɪtni
AM ˈwɪtni

Witt
BR wɪt
AM wɪt

Wittenberg
BR ˈwɪtnbɜːg
AM ˈwɪtnˌbɜrg

witter
BR ˈwɪt|ə(r), -əz,
-(ə)rɪŋ, -əd
AM ˈwɪd|ər, -z, -ɪŋ, -d

witterer
BR ˈwɪt(ə)rə(r), -z
AM ˈwɪdərər, -z

wittering
BR ˈwɪt(ə)rɪŋ, -z
AM ˈwɪdərɪŋ, -z

Wittgenstein
BR ˈvɪtg(ə)nstʌɪn,
ˈvɪtg(ə)nʃtʌɪn
AM ˈvɪtgənˌstaɪn,
ˈvɪtgənˌʃtaɪn

witticism
BR ˈwɪtɪsɪz(ə)m, -z
AM ˈwɪdəˌsɪzəm, -z

wittily
BR ˈwɪtɪli
AM ˈwɪdɪli

wittiness
BR ˈwɪtɪnɪs
AM ˈwɪdɪnɪs

witting
BR ˈwɪtɪŋ
AM ˈwɪdɪŋ

wittingly
BR ˈwɪtɪŋli
AM ˈwɪdɪŋli

Witton
BR ˈwɪtn
AM ˈwɪtn

witty
BR ˈwɪt|i, -ɪə(r), -ɪɪst
AM ˈwɪdi, -ər, -ɪst

Witwatersrand
BR wɪtˈwɔːtəzrand
AM ˌwɪtˈwɔdərzˌrænd,
ˌwɪtˈwadərzˌrænd

AFK vətˈvɑːtərsˌrant

wive
BR wʌɪv, -z, -ɪŋ, -d
AM waɪv, -z, -ɪŋ, -d

Wiveliscombe
BR ˈwɪvəlɪskəm,
ˈwɪlskəm
AM ˈwɪvələskəm

Wivelsfield
BR ˈwɪvlzfiːld
AM ˈwɪvəlzˌfild

Wivenhoe
BR ˈwɪvnhəʊ
AM ˈwɪvənˌhoʊ

wivern
BR ˈwʌɪv(ə:)n, -z
AM ˈwaɪvərn, -z

wives
BR wʌɪvz
AM waɪvz

wiz
BR wɪz
AM wɪz

wizard
BR ˈwɪzəd, -z
AM ˈwɪzərd, -z

wizardly
BR ˈwɪzədli
AM ˈwɪzərdli

wizardry
BR ˈwɪzədri
AM ˈwɪzərdri

wizened
BR ˈwɪznd
AM ˈwɪzənd, ˈwaɪzənd

wizzo
BR ˈwɪzəʊ, wɪˈzəʊ
AM ˈwɪzoʊ

wo
BR wəʊ
AM woʊ

woad
BR wəʊd
AM woʊd

wobbegong
BR ˈwɒbɪgɒŋ, -z
AM ˈwabəˌgɒŋ,
ˈwabəˌgaŋ, -z

wobble
BR ˈwɒb|l, -lz, -lɪŋ\-lɪŋ,
-ld
AM ˈwabəl, -əlz, -(ə)lɪŋ,
-əld

wobble-board
BR ˈwɒblbɔːd, -z
AM ˈwabəlˌbɔ(ə)rd, -z

wobbler
BR ˈwɒblə(r),
ˈwɒblə(r), -z
AM ˈwab(ə)lər, -z

wobbliness
BR ˈwɒb|lɪnɪs,
ˈwɒblɪnɪs
AM ˈwab(ə)linɪs

wobbly
BR ˈwɒbl̩i, wɒbl̩i,
-ɪə(r), -ɪɪst

AM ˈwɒb(ə)li, -ər, -ɪst

Wobegon
BR ˈwəʊbɪgɒn
AM ˈwoʊbəˌgɒn,
ˈwoʊbəˌgan

Woburn
BR ˈwəʊbəːn,
ˈwəʊb(ə)n, ˈwuːbəːn,
ˈwuːb(ə)n
AM woʊˌbərn

Wodehouse
BR ˈwʊdhaʊs
AM ˈwʊd,(h)aʊs

Woden
BR ˈwəʊdn
AM ˈwoʊdən

wodge
BR wɒdʒ, -ɪz
AM wadʒ, -əz

woe
BR wəʊ, -z
AM woʊ, -z

woebegone
BR ˈwəʊbɪgɒn
AM ˈwoʊbəˌgɒn,
ˈwoʊbəˌgan

woeful
BR ˈwəʊf(ʊ)l
AM ˈwoʊfəl

woefully
BR ˈwəʊfʊli, ˈwəʊfl̩i
AM ˈwoʊfəli

woefulness
BR ˈwəʊf(ʊ)lnəs
AM ˈwoʊfəlnəs

wog
BR wɒg, -z
AM wag, -z

Wogan
BR ˈwəʊg(ə)n
AM ˈwoʊgən

woggle
BR ˈwɒgl, -z
AM ˈwagəl, -z

wok
BR wɒk, -s
AM wak, -s

woke
BR wəʊk
AM woʊk

woken
BR ˈwəʊk(ə)n
AM ˈwoʊkən

Woking
BR ˈwəʊkɪŋ
AM ˈwoʊkɪŋ

Wokingham
BR ˈwəʊkɪŋəm
AM ˈwoʊkɪŋəm

wold
BR wəʊld, -z
AM woʊld, -z

Wolf¹
English name
BR wʊlf
AM wʊlf

Wolf²
German name
BR vɒlf
AM vɔlf

wolf
BR wʊlf, -s, -ɪŋ, -t
AM wʊlf, -s, -ɪŋ, -t

wolfcub
BR ˈwʊlfkʌb, -z
AM ˈwʊlfˌkəb, -z

Wolfe
BR wʊlf
AM wʊlf

Wolfenden
BR ˈwʊlfndən
AM ˈwʊlfəndən

Wolff
BR wʊlf
AM wʊlf

Wolfgang
BR ˈwʊlfgaŋ
AM ˈwʊlfˌgæŋ

wolfhound
BR ˈwʊlfhaʊnd, -z
AM ˈwʊlf,(h)aʊnd, -z

wolfish
BR ˈwʊlfɪʃ
AM ˈwʊlfɪʃ

wolfishly
BR ˈwʊlfɪʃli
AM ˈwʊlfɪʃli

wolfishness
BR ˈwʊlfɪʃnɪs
AM ˈwʊlfɪʃnɪs

Wolfit
BR ˈwʊlfɪt
AM ˈwʊlfət

wolf-like
BR ˈwʊlflʌɪk
AM ˈwʊlfˌlaɪk

wolf-man
BR ˈwʊlfman
AM ˈwʊlfˌmæn

wolf-men
BR ˈwʊlfmɛn
AM ˈwʊlfˌmɛn

wolfram
BR ˈwʊlfrəm
AM ˈwʊlfrəm

wolframite
BR ˈwʊlfrəmʌɪt
AM ˈwʊlfrəˌmaɪt

wolfsbane
BR ˈwʊlfsbeɪn
AM ˈwʊlfsˌbeɪn

wolfskin
BR ˈwʊlfskɪn, -z
AM ˈwʊlfˌskɪn, -z

wolf's-milk
BR ˈwʊlfsmɪlk
AM ˈwʊlfsˌmɪlk

Wolfson
BR ˈwʊlfsn
AM ˈwʊlfsən

Wollaston
BR ˈwʊləst(ə)n
AM ˈwʊləstən

Wollongong
BR 'wʊləŋɒŋ,
'wʊləŋɒŋ
AM 'wʊləŋɔŋ,
'wʊləŋɑŋ

Wollstonecraft
BR 'wʊlstnkrɑːft,
'wʊlstnkraft
AM 'wʊlstən,kræft

Wolof
BR 'wɒlɒf
AM 'woʊ,lɑf

Wolseley
BR 'wʊlzli
AM 'wʊlzli

Wolsey
BR 'wʊlzi
AM 'wʊlzi

Wolsingham
BR 'wʊlzɪŋəm
AM 'wʊlzɪŋəm

Wolstenholme
BR 'wʊlst(ə)nhəʊm
AM 'wʊlstən,(h)oʊm

Wolverhampton
BR ,wʊlvə'ham(p)t(ə)n
AM 'wʊlvər,(h)æm(p)-
tən

wolverine
BR 'wʊlvəriːn, -z
AM ,wʊlvə'riːn, -z

Wolverton
BR 'wʊlvət(ə)n
AM 'wʊlvərtən

wolves
BR wʊlvz
AM wʊlvz

woman
BR 'wʊmən
AM 'wʊmən

womanhood
BR 'wʊmənhʊd
AM 'wʊmən,(h)ʊd

womanise
BR 'wʊmənʌɪz, -ɪz, -ɪŋ,
-d
AM 'wʊmə,naɪz, -ɪz, -ɪŋ,
-d

womaniser
BR 'wʊmənʌɪzə(r), -z
AM 'wʊmə,naɪzər, -z

womanish
BR 'wʊmənɪʃ
AM 'wʊmənɪʃ

womanishly
BR 'wʊmənɪʃli
AM 'wʊmənɪʃli

womanishness
BR 'wʊmənɪʃnɪs
AM 'wʊmənɪʃnɪs

womanize
BR 'wʊmənʌɪz, -ɪz, -ɪŋ,
-d
AM 'wʊmə,naɪz, -ɪz, -ɪŋ,
-d

womanizer
BR 'wʊmənʌɪzə(r), -z
AM 'wʊmə,naɪzər, -z

womankind
BR 'wʊmənkʌɪnd
AM 'wʊmən,kaɪnd

womanless
BR 'wʊmənləs
AM 'wʊmənləs

womanlike
BR 'wʊmənlʌɪk
AM 'wʊmən,laɪk

womanliness
BR 'wʊmənlɪnɪs
AM 'wʊmənlɪnɪs

womanly
BR 'wʊmənli
AM 'wʊmənli

womb
BR wuːm, -z
AM wuːm, -z

wombat
BR 'wɒmbat, -s
AM 'wɑm,bæt, -s

womb-like
BR 'wuːmlʌɪk
AM 'wum,laɪk

Wombwell
BR 'wʊmw(ɛ)l,
'wuːmw(ɛ)l
AM 'wʊm,wɛl

women
BR 'wɪmɪn
AM 'wɪmɪn

womenfolk
BR 'wɪmɪnfəʊk
AM 'wɪmɪn,foʊk

womenkind
BR 'wɪmɪnkʌɪnd
AM 'wɪmɪn,kaɪnd

women's lib
BR ,wɪmɪnz 'lɪb
AM ,wɪmɪnz 'lɪb

women's libber
BR ,wɪmɪnz 'lɪbə(r), -z
AM ,wɪmɪnz 'lɪbər, -z

womenswear
BR 'wɪmɪnzwɛː(r)
AM 'wɪmɪnz,wɛ(ə)r

won[1]
BR wʌn
AM wən

won[2]
currency
BR wɒn
AM wɑn

wonder
BR 'wʌnd|ə(r), -əz,
-(ə)rɪŋ, -əd
AM 'wʌnd|ər, -ərz,
-(ə)rɪŋ, -ərd

wonderer
BR 'wʌnd(ə)rə(r), -z
AM 'wʌnd(ə)rər, -z

wonderful
BR 'wʌndəf(ʊ)l
AM 'wʌndərfəl

wonderfully
BR 'wʌndəfʊli,
'wʌndəfli

AM 'wʌndərf(ə)li

wonderfulness
BR 'wʌndəf(ʊ)lnəs
AM 'wʌndərfəlnəs

wondering
BR 'wʌnd(ə)rɪŋ, -z
AM 'wʌnd(ə)rɪŋ, -z

wonderingly
BR 'wʌnd(ə)rɪŋli
AM 'wʌnd(ə)rɪŋli

wonderland
BR 'wʌndəland
AM 'wʌndər,lænd

wonderment
BR 'wʌndəm(ə)nt
AM 'wʌndərmənt

wondrous
BR 'wʌndrəs
AM 'wʌndrəs

wondrously
BR 'wʌndrəsli
AM 'wʌndrəsli

wondrousness
BR 'wʌndrəsnəs
AM 'wʌndrəsnəs

Wong
BR wɒŋ
AM wɔŋ, wɑŋ

wonkily
BR 'wɒŋkɪli
AM 'wɑŋkəli

wonkiness
BR 'wɒŋkɪnɪs
AM 'wɑŋkɪnɪs

wonky
BR 'wɒŋk|i, -ɪə(r), -ɪɪst
AM 'wɑŋki, -ər, -ɪst

wont
BR wəʊnt, wɒnt
AM woʊnt, woʊnt, wɑnt

won't
BR wəʊnt
AM woʊnt

wonted
BR 'wəʊntɪd, 'wɒntɪd
AM 'wɑn(t)əd,
'woʊn(t)əd, 'wɑn(t)əd

wonton
BR ,wɒn'tɒn, -z
AM ,wɑn,tɑn, -z

woo
BR wuː, -z, -ɪŋ, -d
AM wu, -z, -ɪŋ, -d

wooable
BR 'wuːəbl
AM 'wuəbəl

wood
BR wʊd, -z
AM wʊd, -z

Woodall
BR 'wʊdɔːl
AM 'wʊd,ɔl, 'wʊd,ɑl

Woodard
BR 'wʊdɑːd
AM 'wʊdərd

woodbind
BR 'wʊdbʌɪnd, -z

woodbine
BR 'wʊdbʌɪn, -z
AM 'wʊd,baɪn, -z

woodblock
BR 'wʊdblɒk, -s
AM 'wʊd,blɑk, -s

Woodbridge
BR 'wʊdbrɪdʒ
AM 'wʊd,brɪdʒ

woodcarver
BR 'wʊd,kɑːvə(r), -z
AM 'wʊd,kɑrvər, -z

woodcarving
BR 'wʊd,kɑːvɪŋ, -z
AM 'wʊd,kɑrvɪŋ, -z

woodchip
BR 'wʊdtʃɪp, -s
AM 'wʊd,tʃɪp, -s

woodchopper
BR 'wʊd,tʃɒpə(r), -z
AM 'wʊd,tʃɑpər, -z

woodchuck
BR 'wʊdtʃʌk, -s
AM 'wʊd,tʃək, -s

woodcock
BR 'wʊdkɒk, -s
AM 'wʊd,kak, -s

woodcraft
BR 'wʊdkrɑːft,
'wʊdkraft
AM 'wʊd,kræft

woodcut
BR 'wʊdkʌt, -s
AM 'wʊd,kət, -s

woodcutter
BR 'wʊd,kʌtə(r), -z
AM 'wʊd,kədər, -z

woodcutting
BR 'wʊd,kʌtɪŋ
AM 'wʊd,kədɪŋ

wooded
BR 'wʊdɪd
AM 'wʊdəd

wooden
BR 'wʊdn
AM 'wʊdən

woodenhead
BR 'wʊdnhɛd, -z
AM 'wʊdn,(h)ɛd, -z

woodenheaded
BR ,wʊdn'hɛdɪd
AM 'wʊdn'hɛdəd

**wooden-
headedness**
BR ,wʊdn'hɛdɪdnɪs
AM 'wʊdn'hɛdədnəs

woodenly
BR 'wʊdnli
AM 'wʊdnli

woodenness
BR 'wʊdnnəs
AM 'wʊdn(n)əs

Woodford
BR 'wʊdfəd
AM 'wʊdfərd

woodgrouse
BR 'wʊdgraʊs
AM 'wʊd,graʊs

Woodhall
BR 'wʊdhɔ:l
AM 'wʊd,(h)ɔl,
'wʊd,(h)əl

Woodhead
BR 'wʊdhɛd
AM 'wʊd,(h)ɛd

Woodhouse
BR 'wʊdhaʊs
AM 'wʊd,(h)aʊs

woodiness
BR 'wʊdɪnɪs
AM 'wʊdinɪs

woodland
BR 'wʊdlənd, -z
AM 'wʊdlənd, -z

woodlander
BR 'wʊdləndə(r), -z
AM 'wʊdləndər, -z

woodlark
BR 'wʊdlɑ:k, -s
AM 'wʊd,lɑrk, -s

Woodlesford
BR 'wʊdlzfəd
AM 'wʊdəlzfərd

woodless
BR 'wʊdləs
AM 'wʊdləs

Woodley
BR 'wʊdli
AM 'wʊdli

woodlice
BR 'wʊdlʌɪs
AM 'wʊd,laɪs

woodlot
BR 'wʊdlɒt, -s
AM 'wʊd,lɑt, -s

woodlouse
BR 'wʊdlaʊs
AM 'wʊd,laʊs

woodman
BR 'wʊdmən
AM 'wʊdmən

woodmen
BR 'wʊdmən
AM 'wʊdmən

woodnote
BR 'wʊdnəʊt, -s
AM 'wʊd,noʊt, -s

woodpecker
BR 'wʊd,pɛkə(r), -z
AM 'wʊd,pɛkər, -z

woodpie
BR 'wʊdpʌɪ, -z
AM 'wʊd,paɪ, -z

woodpigeon
BR 'wʊd,pɪdʒ(ɪ)n, -z
AM 'wʊd,pɪdʒən, -z

woodpile
BR 'wʊdpʌɪl, -z
AM 'wʊd,paɪl, -z

Woodrow
BR 'wʊdrəʊ
AM 'wʊdroʊ

woodruff
BR 'wʊdrʌf, -s
AM 'wʊdrəf, -s

woodrush
BR 'wʊdrʌʃ, -ɪz
AM 'wʊd,rəʃ, -əz

Woods
BR wʊdz
AM wʊdz

woodscrew
BR 'wʊdskru:, -z
AM 'wʊd,skru, -z

woodshed
BR 'wʊdʃɛd, -z
AM 'wʊd,ʃɛd, -z

woodsman
BR 'wʊdzmən
AM 'wʊdzmən

woodsmen
BR 'wʊdzmən
AM 'wʊdzmən

woodsmoke
BR 'wʊdsməʊk
AM 'wʊd,smoʊk

Woodstock
BR 'wʊdstɒk
AM 'wʊd,stɑk

woodsy
BR 'wʊdzji, -iə(r), -ɪɪst
AM 'wʊdzi, -ər, -ɪst

woodturner
BR 'wʊd,tɜːnə(r), -z
AM 'wʊd,tɜrnər, -z

woodturning
BR 'wʊd,tɜːnɪŋ
AM 'wʊd,tɜrnɪŋ

Woodward
BR 'wʊdwəd
AM 'wʊdwərd

woodwasp
BR 'wʊdwɒsp, -s
AM 'wʊd,wɑsp, -s

woodwind
BR 'wʊdwɪnd
AM 'wʊd,wɪnd

woodwork
BR 'wʊdwɜːk
AM 'wʊd,wɜrk

woodworker
BR 'wʊd,wɜːkə(r), -z
AM 'wʊd,wɜrkər, -z

woodworking
BR 'wʊd,wɜːkɪŋ
AM 'wʊd,wɜrkɪŋ

woodworm
BR 'wʊdwɜːm
AM 'wʊd,wɜrm

woody
BR 'wʊdji, -iə(r), -ɪɪst
AM 'wʊdi, -ər, -ɪst

woodyard
BR 'wʊdjɑːd, -z
AM 'wʊd,jɑrd, -z

wooer
BR 'wu:ə(r), -z
AM 'wuər, -z

woof[1]
dog's bark
BR wʊf
AM wʊf, wuf

woof[2]
weaving
BR wu:f, -s
AM wʊf, wuf, -s

woofer
BR 'wu:fə(r), 'wʊfə(r), -z
AM 'wʊfər, -z

Woofferton
BR 'wʊfət(ə)n
AM 'wʊfərtən

Wookey
BR 'wʊki
AM 'wʊki

wool
BR wʊl, -z
AM wʊl, -z

Woolacombe
BR 'wʊləkəm
AM 'wʊləkəm

Woolard
BR 'wʊlɑːd
AM 'wʊlərd

Wooldridge
BR 'wʊldrɪdʒ
AM 'wʊl,rɪdʒ

woolen
BR 'wʊlən, -z
AM 'wʊlən, -z

Wooler
BR 'wʊlə(r)
AM 'wʊlər

Woolf
BR wʊlf
AM wʊlf

woolgathering
BR 'wʊl,gað(ə)rɪŋ
AM 'wʊl,gæð(ə)rɪŋ

Woollard
BR 'wʊlɑːd
AM 'wʊlərd

woollen
BR 'wʊlən, -z
AM 'wʊlən, -z

Woolley
BR 'wʊli
AM 'wʊli

wool-like
BR 'wʊllʌɪk
AM 'wʊl,laɪk

woolliness
BR 'wʊlɪnɪs
AM 'wʊlinɪs

woolly
BR 'wʊlji, -ɪz, -iə(r), -ɪɪst
AM 'wʊli, -z, -ər, -ɪst

woolly-bear
BR 'wʊlibɛː(r), -z
AM 'wʊli,bɛ(ə)r, -z

woolly-headed
BR ˌwʊli'hɛdɪd
AM ˌwʊli'hɛdəd

woolpack
BR 'wʊlpak, -s
AM 'wʊl,pæk, -s

woolsack
BR 'wʊlsak, -s
AM 'wʊl,sæk, -s

woolsey
BR 'wʊlzi
AM 'wʊlzi

woolshed
BR 'wʊlʃɛd, -z
AM 'wʊl,ʃɛd, -z

Woolwich
BR 'wʊlɪdʒ, 'wʊlɪtʃ
AM 'wʊl,wɪtʃ

Woolworth
BR 'wʊlwəθ, 'wʊlwəːθ, -s
AM 'wʊl,wərθ, -s

woomera
BR 'wʊm(ə)rə(r), 'wu:m(ə)rə(r), -z
AM 'wumərə, -z

woops
BR wʊps
AM wʊps, wups

woosh
BR wʊʃ, -ɪz, -ɪŋ, -t
AM wʊʃ, -əz, -ɪŋ, -t

Woosnam
BR 'wu:znəm
AM 'wuznəm

Wooster
BR 'wʊstə(r), 'wu:stə(r)
AM 'wʊstər, 'wustər

Wooten
BR 'wʊtn
AM 'wʊtn

Wootton
BR 'wʊtn
AM 'wʊtn

woozily
BR 'wu:zɪli
AM 'wuzəli

wooziness
BR 'wu:zɪnɪs
AM 'wuzinɪs

woozy
BR 'wu:zji, -iə(r), -ɪɪst
AM 'wuzi, -ər, -ɪst

wop
BR wɒp, -s
AM wɑp, -s

Worcester
BR 'wʊstə(r)
AM 'wʊstər

Worcestershire
BR 'wʊstəʃ(ɪ)ə(r)
AM 'wʊstərʃɪ(ə)r

word
BR wɜːd, -z, -ɪŋ, -ɪd
AM wərd, -z, -ɪŋ, -əd

wordage
BR 'wɜːdɪdʒ
AM 'wərdɪdʒ

wordbook
BR ˈwɜːdbʊk, -s
AM ˈwɝdˌbʊk, -s

wordfinder
BR ˈwɜːdˌfaɪndə(r), -z
AM ˈwɝdˌfaɪndər, -z

word for word
BR ˌwɜːd fə ˈwɜːd
AM ˌwɝd fər ˈwɝd

wordily
BR ˈwɜːdɪli
AM ˈwɝdəli

wordiness
BR ˈwɜːdɪnɪs
AM ˈwɝdɪnɪs

wording
BR ˈwɜːdɪŋ, -z
AM ˈwɝdɪŋ, -z

wordless
BR ˈwɜːdləs
AM ˈwɝdləs

wordlessly
BR ˈwɜːdləsli
AM ˈwɝdləsli

wordlessness
BR ˈwɜːdləsnəs
AM ˈwɝdləsnəs

word-perfect
BR ˌwɜːdˈpɜːfɪkt
AM ˈwɝdˌpɝfək(t)

wordplay
BR ˈwɜːdpleɪ
AM ˈwɝdˌpleɪ

wordsearch
BR ˈwɜːdsɜːtʃ, -ɪz
AM ˈwɝdˌsɝtʃ, -əz

wordsmith
BR ˈwɜːdsmɪθ, -s
AM ˈwɝdˌsmɪθ, -s

WordStar
BR ˈwɜːdstɑː(r)
AM ˈwɝdˌstɑr

Wordsworth
BR ˈwɜːdzwəθ,
ˈwɜːdzwɜːθ
AM ˈwɝdzˌwɝθ

Wordsworthian
BR ˌwɜːdzˈwɜːðiən
AM ˌwɝdzˈwɝðiən

wordy
BR ˈwɜːdli, -ɪə(r), -ɪɪst
AM ˈwɝdi, -ər, -ɪst

wore
BR wɔː(r)
AM wɔ(ə)r

work
BR wɜːk, -s, -ɪŋ, -t
AM wɝk, -s, -ɪŋ, -t

workability
BR ˌwɜːkəˈbɪlɪti
AM ˌwɝkəˈbɪlɪdi

workable
BR ˈwɜːkəbl
AM ˈwɝkəbəl

workableness
BR ˈwɜːkəblnəs
AM ˈwɝkəbəlnəs

workably
BR ˈwɜːkəbli
AM ˈwɝkəbli

workaday
BR ˈwɜːkədeɪ
AM ˈwɝkəˌdeɪ

workaholic
BR ˌwɜːkəˈhɒlɪk, -s
AM ˌwɝkəˈhɒlɪk,
ˈwɝkəˈhɑlɪk, -s

workbasket
BR ˈwɜːkˌbɑːskɪt,
ˈwɜːkˌbaskɪt, -s
AM ˈwɝkˌbæskət, -s

workbench
BR ˈwɜːkbɛn(t)ʃ, -ɪz
AM ˈwɝkˌbɛn(t)ʃ, -əz

workboat
BR ˈwɜːkbəʊt, -s
AM ˈwɝkˌbout, -s

workbook
BR ˈwɜːkbʊk, -s
AM ˈwɝkˌbʊk, -s

workbox
BR ˈwɜːkbɒks, -ɪz
AM ˈwɝkˌbaks, -əz

workday
BR ˈwɜːkdeɪ, -z
AM ˈwɝkˌdeɪ, -z

worker
BR ˈwɜːkə(r), -z
AM ˈwɝkər, -z

workfare
BR ˈwɜːkfɛː(r)
AM ˈwɝkˌfɛ(ə)r

workforce
BR ˈwɜːkfɔːs
AM ˈwɝkˌfɔ(ə)rs

workhorse
BR ˈwɜːkhɔːs, -ɪz
AM ˈwɝkˌ(h)ɔ(ə)rs, -əz

workhouse
BR ˈwɜːkhaʊs, -zɪz
AM ˈwɝkˌ(h)aʊs, -zəz

working
BR ˈwɜːkɪŋ, -z
AM ˈwɝkɪŋ, -z

Workington
BR ˈwɜːkɪŋt(ə)n
AM ˈwɝkɪŋtən

workless
BR ˈwɜːkləs
AM ˈwɝkləs

workload
BR ˈwɜːkləʊd, -z
AM ˈwɝkˌloud, -z

workman
BR ˈwɜːkmən
AM ˈwɝkmən

workmanlike
BR ˈwɜːkmənlaɪk
AM ˈwɝkmənˌlaɪk

workmanship
BR ˈwɜːkmənʃɪp
AM ˈwɝkmənˌʃɪp

workmate
BR ˈwɜːkmeɪt, -s

workmen
BR ˈwɜːkmən
AM ˈwɝkmən

workout
BR ˈwɜːkaʊt, -s
AM ˈwɝkˌaʊt, -s

workpeople
BR ˈwɜːkˌpiːpl
AM ˈwɝkˌpipəl

workpiece
BR ˈwɜːkpiːs, -ɪz
AM ˈwɝkˌpis, -ɪz

workplace
BR ˈwɜːkpleɪs, -ɪz
AM ˈwɝkˌpleɪs, -ɪz

workroom
BR ˈwɜːkruːm,
ˈwɜːkrʊm, -z
AM ˈwɝkˌrum,
ˈwɝkˌrʊm, -z

worksharing
BR ˈwɜːkˌʃɛːrɪŋ
AM ˈwɝkˌʃɛrɪŋ

worksheet
BR ˈwɜːkʃiːt, -s
AM ˈwɝkˌʃit, -s

workshop
BR ˈwɜːkʃɒp, -s
AM ˈwɝkˌʃap, -s

workshy
BR ˈwɜːkʃaɪ
AM ˈwɝkˌʃaɪ

worksite
BR ˈwɜːksaɪt, -s
AM ˈwɝkˌsaɪt, -s

Worksop
BR ˈwɜːksɒp
AM ˈwɝkˌsap

workspace
BR ˈwɜːkspeɪs, -ɪz
AM ˈwɝkˌspeɪs, -ɪz

workstation
BR ˈwɜːkˌsteɪʃn, -z
AM ˈwɝkˌsteɪʃən, -z

worktop
BR ˈwɜːktɒp, -s
AM ˈwɝkˌtap, -s

work-to-rule
BR ˌwɜːktəˈruːl, -z
AM ˈwɝktəˈrul, -z

workwear
BR ˈwɜːkwɛː(r)
AM ˈwɝkˌwɛ(ə)r

workweek
BR ˈwɜːkwiːk, -s
AM ˈwɝkˌwik, -s

workwoman
BR ˈwɜːkˌwʊmən
AM ˈwɝkˌwʊmən

workwomen
BR ˈwɜːkˌwɪmɪn
AM ˈwɝkˌwɪmɪn

world
BR ˈwɜːld, -z
AM wɝ(ə)ld, -z

World Cup
BR ˈwɜːl(d) kʌp
AM ˌwɝr(ə)l(d) ˈkəp

worlde
BR ˈwɜːld(i)
AM wɝr(ə)ld(i)

worldliness
BR ˈwɜːldlɪnɪs
AM ˈwɝr(ə)l(d)linɪs

worldling
BR ˈwɜːldlɪŋ, -z
AM ˈwɝr(ə)l(d)lɪŋ, -z

worldly
BR ˈwɜːldli, -ɪə(r), -ɪɪst
AM ˈwɝr(ə)l(d)li, -ər,
-ɪst

worldview
BR ˈwɜːldˈvjuː, -z
AM ˌwɝr(ə)l(d)ˈvju, -z

worldwide
BR ˌwɜːl(d)ˈwaɪd
AM ˌwɝr(ə)l(d)ˈwaɪd

worm
BR wɜːm, -z, -ɪŋ, -d
AM wɝm, -z, -ɪŋ, -d

Wormald
BR ˈwɜːmld
AM ˈwɝməld

worm-cast
BR ˈwɜːmkɑːst,
ˈwɜːmkast, -s
AM ˈwɝmˌkæst, -s

wormer
BR ˈwɜːmə(r), -z
AM ˈwɝmər, -z

wormhole
BR ˈwɜːmhəʊl, -z
AM ˈwɝmˌ(h)oul, -z

worminess
BR ˈwɜːmɪnɪs
AM ˈwɝmɪnɪs

wormlike
BR ˈwɜːmlaɪk
AM ˈwɝmˌlaɪk

Wormold
BR ˈwɜːməʊld,
ˈwɜːmld
AM ˈwɝməld,
ˈwɝˌmould

Worms
BR wɜːmz, vɔːmz
AM wɝmz
GER vɔrmz

wormseed
BR ˈwɜːmsiːd, -z
AM ˈwɝmˌsid, -z

wormwood
BR ˈwɜːmwʊd
AM ˈwɝmˌwʊd

wormy
BR ˈwɜːmli, -ɪə(r), -ɪɪst
AM ˈwɝmi, -ər, -ɪst

worn
BR wɔːn
AM wɔ(ə)rn

Worrall
BR ˈwɒrəl, ˈwɒrl̩

AM 'wɔːəl
worriedly
 BR 'wʌrɪdli
 AM 'wəridli
worrier
 BR 'wʌrɪə(r), -z
 AM 'wəriər, -z
worriment
 BR 'wʌrɪm(ə)nt
 AM 'wərimənt
worrisome
 BR 'wʌrɪs(ə)m
 AM 'wəri,səm
worrisomely
 BR 'wʌrɪs(ə)mli
 AM 'wəri,səmli
worrit
 BR 'wʌr|ɪt, -ɪts, -ɪtɪŋ,
 -ɪtɪd
 AM 'wərə|t, -ts, -dɪŋ,
 -dəd
worry
 BR 'wʌr|i, -ɪz, -ɪɪŋ, -ɪd
 AM 'wəri, -z, -ɪŋ, -d
worryingly
 BR 'wʌrɪɪŋli
 AM 'wəriɪŋli
worrywart
 BR 'wʌrɪwɔːt, -s
 AM 'wəri,wɔ(ə)rt, -s
worse
 BR wəːs
 AM wərs
worsen
 BR 'wəːs|n, -nz,
 -nɪŋ \-nɪŋ, -nd
 AM 'wərsən, -z, -ɪŋ, -d
worship
 BR 'wəː|ʃɪp, -ɪps, -ɪpɪŋ,
 -ɪpt
 AM 'wərʃəp, -s, -ɪŋ, -t
worshipable
 BR 'wəːʃɪpəbl
 AM 'wərʃəpəbəl
worshiper
 BR 'wəːʃɪpə(r), -z
 AM 'wərʃəpər, -z
worshipful
 BR 'wəːʃɪpf(ʊ)l
 AM 'wərʃəpfəl
worshipfully
 BR 'wəːʃɪpfʊli,
 'wəːʃɪpfli
 AM 'wərʃɪpf(ə)li
worshipfulness
 BR 'wəːʃɪpf(ʊ)lnəs
 AM 'wərʃɪpfəlnəs
worshipper
 BR 'wəːʃɪpə(r), -z
 AM 'wərʃəpər, -z
Worsley
 BR 'wəːsli, 'wəːzli
 AM 'wərzli
Worsnip
 BR 'wəːsnɪp
 AM 'wərsnəp

worst
 BR wəːst
 AM wərst
worsted¹
 noun
 BR 'wʊstɪd
 AM 'wʊstəd, 'wərstəd
worsted²
 past tense, adjective,
 from 'worse'
 BR 'wəːstɪd
 AM 'wərstəd
Worsthorne
 BR 'wəːsθɔːn
 AM 'wərs,θɔ(ə)rn
wort
 BR wəːt, -s
 AM wərt, wɔ(ə)rt, -s
worth
 BR wəːθ
 AM wərθ
worthily
 BR 'wəːðɪli
 AM 'wərðəli
worthiness
 BR 'wəːðɪnɪs
 AM 'wərðinɪs
Worthing
 BR 'wəːðɪŋ
 AM 'wərðɪŋ
Worthington
 BR 'wəːðɪŋt(ə)n
 AM 'wərðɪŋtən
worthless
 BR 'wəːθləs
 AM 'wərθləs
worthlessly
 BR 'wəːθləsli
 AM 'wərθləsli
worthlessness
 BR 'wəːθləsnəs
 AM 'wərθləsnəs
worthwhile
 BR ,wəːθ'wʌɪl
 AM ,wərθ,(h)waɪl
worthwhileness
 BR ,wəːθ'wʌɪlnɪs
 AM ,wərθ,(h)waɪlnɪs
worthy
 BR 'wəːð|i, -ɪz, -ɪə(r),
 -ɪɪst
 AM 'wərði, -z, -ər, -ɪst
Wortley
 BR 'wəːtli
 AM 'wərtli
wot
 BR wɒt
 AM wɑt
wotcha
 BR 'wɒtʃə(r)
 AM 'wɑtʃə
wotcher
 BR 'wɒtʃə(r)
 AM 'wɑtʃər
Wotton
 BR 'wʊtn, 'wɒtn
 AM 'wɑtn

would¹
 strong form
 BR wʊd
 AM wʊd
would²
 weak form
 BR wəd, (ə)d
 AM wəd, (ə)d
would-be
 BR 'wʊdbiː, 'wʊdbɪ
 AM 'wʊd,bi
wouldn't
 BR 'wʊdnt
 AM 'wʊdnt
wouldst
 BR wʊdst, wʊtst
 AM wʊdst, wʊtst
wound¹
 injury, injure
 BR wuːnd, -z, -ɪŋ, -ɪd
 AM wund, -z, -ɪŋ, -ɪd
wound²
 past tense, adjective,
 from wind
 BR waʊnd
 AM waʊnd
Wounded Knee
 BR ,wuːndɪd 'niː
 AM ,wundəd 'ni
woundedness
 BR 'wuːndɪdnɪs
 AM 'wundədnəs
wounding
 BR 'wuːndɪŋ, -z
 AM 'wundɪŋ, -z
woundingly
 BR 'wuːndɪŋli
 AM 'wundɪŋli
woundless
 BR 'wuːndləs
 AM 'wun(d)ləs
woundwort
 BR 'wuːndwəːt, -s
 AM 'wund,wərt,
 'wund,wɔ(ə)rt, -s
wove
 BR wəʊv
 AM woʊv
woven
 BR 'wəʊvn
 AM 'woʊvən
wow
 BR waʊ, -z, -ɪŋ, -d
 AM waʊ, -z, -ɪŋ, -d
wowser
 BR 'waʊzə(r), -z
 AM 'waʊzər, -z
WRAC
 BR rak, -s
 AM ræk, -s
wrack
 BR rak, -s
 AM ræk, -s
WRAF
 BR raf, -s
 AM ræf, -s

wraggle-taggle
 BR ,ragl'tagl
 AM 'rægəl,tægəl
wraith
 BR reɪθ, -s
 AM reɪθ, -s
wraithlike
 BR 'reɪθlʌɪk
 AM 'reɪθ,laɪk
Wrangel
 BR 'rangl
 AM 'ræŋgəl
wrangle
 BR 'raŋg|l, -lz,
 -lɪŋ \-lɪŋ, -ld
 AM 'ræŋg|əl, -əlz,
 -(ə)lɪŋ, -əld
wrangler
 BR 'raŋglə(r), -z
 AM 'ræŋg(ə)lər, -z
wrangling
 BR 'raŋglɪŋ, 'raŋglɪŋ,
 -z
 AM 'ræŋg(ə)lɪŋ, -z
wrap
 BR rap, -s, -ɪŋ, -t
 AM ræp, -s, -ɪŋ, -t
wraparound
 BR 'rapəraʊnd
 AM 'ræpə,raʊnd
wrappage
 BR 'rapɪdʒ
 AM 'ræpɪdʒ
wrapper
 BR 'rapə(r), -z
 AM 'ræpər, -z
wrapping
 BR 'rapɪŋ, -z
 AM 'ræpɪŋ, -z
wraparound
 BR 'rapraʊnd, -z
 AM 'ræp,raʊnd, -z
wrasse
 BR ras, -ɪz
 AM ræs, -əz
wrath
 BR rɒθ
 AM ræθ
wrathful
 BR 'rɒθf(ʊ)l
 AM 'ræθfəl
wrathfully
 BR 'rɒθfʊli, 'rɒθfli
 AM 'ræθfəli
wrathfulness
 BR 'rɒθf(ʊ)lnəs
 AM 'ræθfəlnəs
wrathy
 BR 'rɒθi
 AM 'ræθi
Wray
 BR reɪ
 AM reɪ
wreak
 BR riːk, -s, -ɪŋ, -t
 AM rik, -s, -ɪŋ, -t

wreaker
BR ˈriːkə(r), -z
AM ˈriːkər, -z

wreath
BR riː|θ, -ðz\-θs
AM riː|θ, -ðz\-θs

wreathe
BR riːð, -z, -ɪŋ, -d
AM rið, -z, -ɪŋ, -d

wreck
BR rɛk, -s, -ɪŋ, -t
AM rɛk, -s, -ɪŋ, -t

wreckage
BR ˈrɛkɪdʒ
AM ˈrɛkɪdʒ

wrecker
BR ˈrɛkə(r), -z
AM ˈrɛkər, -z

Wrekin
BR ˈriːkɪn
AM ˈrikɪn

wren
BR rɛn, -z
AM rɛn, -z

wrench
BR rɛn(t)ʃ, -ɪz, -ɪŋ, -t
AM rɛn(t)ʃ, -əz, -ɪŋ, -t

wrentit
BR ˈrɛntɪt, -s
AM ˈrɛn,tɪt, -s

wrest
BR rɛst, -s, -ɪŋ, -ɪd
AM rɛst, -s, -ɪŋ, -əd

wrest-block
BR ˈrɛs(t)blɒk, -s
AM ˈrɛs(t),blɑk, -s

wrestle
BR ˈrɛs|l, -lz, -lɪŋ\-lɪŋ, -ld
AM ˈrɛsəl, -əlz, -(ə)lɪŋ, -əld

wrestler
BR ˈrɛslə(r), ˈrɛslə(r), -z
AM ˈrɛs(ə)lər, -z

wrestling
BR ˈrɛslɪŋ, ˈrɛslɪŋ, -z
AM ˈrɛs(ə)lɪŋ, -z

wrest-pin
BR ˈrɛs(t)pɪn, -z
AM ˈrɛs(t),pɪn, -z

wretch
BR rɛtʃ, -ɪz
AM rɛtʃ, -əz

wretched
BR ˈrɛtʃɪd
AM ˈrɛtʃəd

wretchedly
BR ˈrɛtʃɪdli
AM ˈrɛtʃədli

wretchedness
BR ˈrɛtʃɪdnɪs
AM ˈrɛtʃədnəs

Wrexham
BR ˈrɛks(ə)m
AM ˈrɛksəm

wrick
BR rɪk, -s, -ɪŋ, -t
AM rɪk, -s, -ɪŋ, -t

wriggle
BR ˈrɪg|l, -lz, -lɪŋ\-lɪŋ, -ld
AM ˈrɪgəl, -əlz, -(ə)lɪŋ, -əld

wriggler
BR ˈrɪglə(r), ˈrɪglə(r), -z
AM ˈrɪg(ə)lər, -z

wriggly
BR ˈrɪgli, ˈrɪg|li, -ɪə(r), -ɪɪst
AM ˈrɪg(ə)li, -ər, -ɪst

wright
BR rʌɪt, -s
AM raɪt, -s

Wrighton
BR ˈrʌɪtn
AM ˈraɪtn

Wrigley
BR ˈrɪgli
AM ˈrɪgli

wrily
BR ˈrʌɪli
AM ˈraɪli

wring
BR rɪŋ, -z, -ɪŋ
AM rɪŋ, -z, -ɪŋ

wringer
BR ˈrɪŋə(r), -z
AM ˈrɪŋgər, -z

wrinkle
BR ˈrɪŋk|l, -lz, -lɪŋ\-lɪŋ, -ld
AM ˈrɪŋkəl, -əlz, -(ə)lɪŋ, -əld

wrinkliness
BR ˈrɪŋklɪnɪs
AM ˈrɪŋk(ə)linɪs

wrinkly
BR ˈrɪŋk|li, -ɪz
AM ˈrɪŋk(ə)li, -z

wrist
BR rɪst, -s
AM rɪst, -s

wristband
BR ˈrɪs(t)band, -z
AM ˈrɪs(t),bænd, -z

wristlet
BR ˈrɪs(t)lɪt, -s
AM ˈrɪs(t)lət, -s

wristwatch
BR ˈrɪs(t)wɒtʃ, -ɪz
AM ˈrɪs(t),watʃ, -əz

wristy
BR ˈrɪsti
AM ˈrɪsti

writ
BR rɪt, -s
AM rɪt, -s

writable
BR ˈrʌɪtəbl
AM ˈraɪdəbəl

write
BR rʌɪt, -s, -ɪŋ
AM raɪt, -ts, -dɪŋ

writer
BR ˈrʌɪtə(r), -z
AM ˈraɪdər, -z

writerly
BR ˈrʌɪtəli
AM ˈraɪdərli

writhe
BR rʌɪð, -z, -ɪŋ, -d
AM raɪð, -z, -ɪŋ, -d

writhing
BR ˈrʌɪðɪŋ, -z
AM ˈraɪðɪŋ, -z

writing
BR ˈrʌɪtɪŋ, -z
AM ˈraɪdɪŋ, -z

written
BR ˈrɪtn
AM ˈrɪtn

WRNS
BR rɛnz
AM rɛnz

Wrocław
BR ˈvrɒtslɑːv, ˈvrɒtslav
AM ˈ(v)rɔ(t)slɑf, ˈ(v)rɑ(t)slav
POL ˈvrɒtswav

wrong
BR rɒŋ, -z, -ɪŋ, -d
AM rɔŋ, rɑŋ, -z, -ɪŋ, -d

wrongdoer
BR ˈrɒŋ,duːə(r), -z
AM ˈrɔŋ,duər, ˈraŋ,duər, -z

wrongdoing
BR ˈrɒŋ,duːɪŋ, ˌrɒŋˈduːɪŋ
AM ˈrɔŋ,duɪŋ, ˈraŋ,duɪŋ

wronger
BR ˈrɒŋə(r), -z
AM ˈrɔŋgər, ˈraŋgər, -z

wrong-foot
BR ˌrɒŋˈfʊt, -s, -ɪŋ, -ɪd
AM ˌrɔŋˈfʊt, ˌraŋˈfʊt, -ts, -dɪŋ, -dəd

wrong-footed
BR ˌrɒŋˈfʊtɪd
AM ˌrɔŋˈfʊdəd, ˌraŋˈfʊdəd

wrongful
BR ˈrɒŋf(ʊ)l
AM ˈrɔŋfəl, ˈraŋfəl

wrongfully
BR ˈrɒŋfʊli, ˈrɒŋfli
AM ˈrɔŋfəli, ˈraŋfəli

wrongfulness
BR ˈrɒŋf(ʊ)lnəs
AM ˈrɔŋfəlnəs, ˈraŋfəlnəs

wrong-headed
BR ˌrɒŋˈhɛdɪd
AM ˌrɒŋˈhɛdəd, ˌraŋˈhɛdəd

wrong-headedly
BR ˌrɒŋˈhɛdɪdli
AM ˌrɔŋˈhɛdədli, ˌraŋˈhɛdədli

wrong-headedness
BR ˌrɒŋˈhɛdɪdnɪs
AM ˌrɔŋˈhɛdədnəs, ˌraŋˈhɛdədnəs

wrongly
BR ˈrɒŋli
AM ˈrɔŋli, ˈraŋli

wrongness
BR ˈrɒŋnəs
AM ˈrɔŋnəs, ˈraŋnəs

wrong'un
BR ˈrɒŋən, -z
AM ˈrɔŋən, ˈraŋən, -z

wrote
BR rəʊt
AM roʊt

wroth
BR rəʊθ, rɒθ
AM rɔθ, rɑθ

wrought
BR rɔːt
AM rɔt, rɑt

wrought-iron
BR ˌrɔːtˈʌɪən
AM ˌrɔtˈaɪ(ə)rn, ˌrɑtˈaɪ(ə)rn

Wroxeter
BR ˈrɒksɪtə(r)
AM ˈraksədər

Wroxham
BR ˈrɒks(ə)m
AM ˈraksəm

wrung
BR rʌŋ, -z
AM rəŋ, -z

WRVS
BR ˌdʌbljuːaːviːˈɛs
AM ˌdəbəljuˌarˌviˈɛs

wry
BR rʌɪ, -ə(r), -ɪst
AM raɪ, -ər, -ɪst

wrybill
BR ˈrʌɪbɪl, -z
AM ˈraɪˌbɪl, -z

wryly
BR ˈrʌɪli
AM ˈraɪli

wry-mouth
BR ˈrʌɪmaʊθ, -s
AM ˈraɪˌmaʊθ, -s

wry-mouthed
BR ˌrʌɪˈmaʊðd, ˌrʌɪˈmaʊθt
AM ˌraɪˌmaʊθt

wryneck
BR ˈrʌɪnɛk, -s
AM ˈraɪˌnɛk, -s

wryness
BR ˈrʌɪnɪs
AM ˈraɪnɪs

Wu
BR wuː

AM wu

Wuhan
BR ˌwuːˈhan
AM ˈwuˈhæn

Wulfila
BR ˈwʊlfɪlə(r)
AM ˈwʊlfələ

Wulfrun
BR ˈwʊlfrən, ˈwʊlfrn̩
AM ˈwʊlˌrən

Wulstan
BR ˈwʊlst(ə)n
AM ˈwʊlstən

wunderkind
BR ˈwʊndəkɪnd, -z
AM ˈwʊndərˌkɪnd, -z

Wuppertal
BR ˈvʊpətɑːl, ˈwʊpətɑːl
AM ˈwʊpərˌtɑl, ˈvupərˌtɑl

Wurlitzer®
BR ˈwəːlɪtsə(r), -z
AM ˈwərˌlɪtsər, -z

wurst
BR wəːst, wʊəst, vʊəst
AM wərst, wʊ(ə)rst

Württemberg
BR ˈvəːtəmbəːg, ˈwəːtəmbəːg
AM ˈwərtəmˌbərg, ˈvərtəmˌbərg
GER ˈvʏrtmbɛrk

Würzburg
BR ˈvəːtsbəːg, ˈwəːtsbəːg
AM ˈwərtsˌbərg, ˈvərtsˌbərg

GER ˈvʏrtsbʊrk

wu-wei
BR ˌwuːˈwei
AM ˈwuˈwei

Wyandot
BR ˈwʌɪəndɒt
AM ˈwaɪənˌdɑt

Wyandotte
BR ˈwʌɪəndɒt
AM ˈwaɪənˌdɑt

Wyatt
BR ˈwʌɪət
AM ˈwaɪət

wych alder
BR ˈwɪtʃ ˌɔːldə(r), + ˌɒldə(r), -z
AM ˈwɪtʃ ˌɔldər, ˈwɪtʃ ˌɑldər, -z

wychelm
BR ˈwɪtʃɛlm, -z
AM ˈwɪˌtʃɛlm, -z

Wycherley
BR ˈwɪtʃəli
AM ˈwɪtʃərli

wych-hazel
BR ˈwɪtʃˌheɪzl, -z
AM ˈwɪtʃˌ(h)eɪzəl, -z

Wychwood
BR ˈwɪtʃwʊd
AM ˈwɪtʃˌwʊd

Wyclif
BR ˈwɪklɪf
AM ˈwɪklɪf

Wycliffe
BR ˈwɪklɪf
AM ˈwɪklɪf

Wycombe
BR ˈwɪkəm

AM ˈwɪkəm

Wye
BR wʌɪ
AM waɪ

Wyke
BR wʌɪk
AM waɪk

Wykehamist
BR ˈwɪkəmɪst, -s
AM ˈwɪkəməst, -s

Wyld
BR wʌɪld
AM waɪld

Wylde
BR wʌɪld
AM waɪld

Wylfa
BR ˈwɪlvə(r)
AM ˈwɪlfə

Wylie
BR ˈwʌɪli
AM ˈwaɪli

Wyllie
BR ˈwʌɪli
AM ˈwaɪli

Wylye
BR ˈwʌɪli
AM ˈwaɪli

Wyman
BR ˈwʌɪmən
AM ˈwaɪmən

Wymondham[1]
Leicestershire, UK
BR ˈwʌɪməndəm
AM ˈwaɪməndem

Wymondham[2]
Norfolk, UK
BR ˈwɪməndəm, ˈwɪndəm

AM ˈwɪməndəm, ˈwɪndəm

Wyn
BR wɪn
AM wɪn

wynd
BR wʌɪnd, -z
AM waɪnd, -z

Wyndham
BR ˈwɪndəm
AM ˈwɪndəm

Wynford
BR ˈwɪnfəd
AM ˈwɪnfərd

Wynn
BR wɪn
AM wɪn

Wynne
BR wɪn
AM wɪn

Wyoming
BR wʌɪˈəʊmɪŋ
AM waɪˈoʊmɪŋ

Wyre
BR ˈwʌɪə(r)
AM ˈwaɪ(ə)r

WYSIWYG
BR ˈwɪziwɪg
AM ˈwɪziˌwɪg

Wystan
BR ˈwɪst(ə)n
AM ˈwɪstən

Wythenshawe
BR ˈwɪðnʃɔː(r)
AM ˈwɪðənˌʃɔ

wyvern
BR ˈwʌɪvəːn, ˈwʌɪvn̩, -z
AM ˈwaɪvərn, -z

Xx

x
BR ɛks, -ɪz
AM ɛks, -əz

Xanadu
BR 'zænədu:
AM 'zænə,du

xanthate
BR 'zanθeɪt, -s
AM 'zæn,θeɪt, -s

Xanthe
BR 'zanθi
AM 'zænθi

xanthic
BR 'zanθɪk
AM 'zænθɪk

xanthine
BR 'zanθi:n
AM 'zænθin, 'zænθən

Xanthippe
BR zan'θɪpi, zan'tɪpi
AM zæn'θɪpi, zæn'tɪpi

xanthoma
BR zan'θəʊmə(r), -z
AM zæn'θoʊmə, -z

xanthomata
BR zan'θəʊmətə(r), -z
AM zæn'θoʊmədə, -z

xanthophyll
BR 'zanθə(ʊ)fɪl
AM 'zænθə,fɪl

Xantippe
BR zan'tɪpi
AM zæn'tɪpi

Xavier
BR 'zeɪvɪə(r), 'zavɪə(r)
AM 'zeɪvɪər, 'zeɪvjər

x-axes
BR 'ɛks,aksi:z
AM 'ɛks,æksiz

x-axis
BR 'ɛks,aksɪs
AM 'ɛks,æksəs

xebec
BR 'zi:bɛk, 'zeɪbɛk, -s
AM 'zi,bɛk, -s

xenia
BR 'zi:nɪə(r), 'zɛnɪə(r)
AM 'ziniə

Xenix
BR 'zi:nɪks
AM 'ziniks

xenogamous
BR zɛ'nɒgəməs,
zi:'nɒgəməs,
zɪ'nɒgəməs
AM zə'nagəməs

xenogamy
BR zɛ'nɒgəmi,
zi:'nɒgəmi,
zɪ'nɒgəmi
AM zə'nagəmi

xenograft
BR 'zɛnə(ʊ)grɑ:ft,
'zɛnə(ʊ)graft, -s
AM 'zɛnə,græft, -s

xenolith
BR 'zɛnəlɪθ, -s
AM 'zɛnə,lɪθ, -s

xenon
BR 'zi:nɒn, 'zɛnɒn
AM 'zi,nɑn

Xenophanes
BR 'zɛnɒfəni:z,
zɪ'nɒfəni:z
AM zə'nɑfə,niz

xenophile
BR 'zɛnəfʌɪl, -z
AM 'zinə,faɪl,
'zɛnə,faɪl, -z

xenophobe
BR 'zɛnəfəʊb, -z
AM 'zinə,foʊb,
'zɛnə,foʊb, -z

xenophobia
BR ,zɛnə'fəʊbɪə(r)
AM ,zinə'foʊbiə,
,zɛnə'foʊbiə

xenophobic
BR ,zɛnə'fəʊbɪk
AM ,zinə'foʊbɪk,
,zɛnə'foʊbɪk

Xenophon
BR 'zɛnəfɒn
AM 'zɛnə,fan

xenotropic
BR ,zɛnə(ʊ)'trɒpɪk,
,zɛnə(ʊ)'trəʊpɪk
AM ,zinə'trapɪk

xeranthemum
BR zɪ'ranθɪməm, -z
AM zə'rænθəməm, -z

xeric
BR 'zɪərɪk
AM 'zɛrɪk

xeroderma
BR ,zɪərə(ʊ)'də:mə(r)
AM ,zɪrə'dərmə

xerograph
BR 'zɪərə(ʊ)grɑ:f,
'zɪərə(ʊ)graf, -s
AM 'zɪrə,græf, -s

xerographic
BR ,zɪərə(ʊ)'grafɪk
AM ,zɪrə'græfɪk

xerographically
BR ,zɪərə(ʊ)'grafɪkli
AM ,zɪrə'græfək(ə)li

xerography
BR zɪə'rɒgrəfi,
zɛ'rɒgrəfi, zɪ'rɒgrəfi
AM zɪr'agrəfi

xerophile
BR 'zɪərə(ʊ)fʌɪl, -z

AM 'zɪrə,faɪl, -z

xerophilous
BR zɪə'rɒfɪləs,
zɛ'rɒfɪləs, zɪ'rɒfɪləs
AM zə'rafələs

xerophyte
BR 'zɪərə(ʊ)fʌɪt, -s
AM 'zɪrə,faɪt, -s

xerox
BR 'zɪərɒks, 'zɛrɒks,
-ɪz, -ɪŋ, -t
AM 'zi,raks, 'zɪ,raks,
-əz, -ɪŋ, -t

Xerxes
BR 'zə:ksi:z
AM 'zər,ksiz

Xhosa
BR 'kɔ:sə(r), 'kəʊsə(r),
'kɔ:zə(r), 'kəʊzə(r)
AM 'koʊsə, 'kɔsə, 'kasə

xi
BR (k)sʌɪ, (g)zʌɪ, -z
AM zaɪ, ksaɪ, -z

Xian
BR ʃan
AM ʃæn

Ximenes
BR 'zɪmɪni:z
AM 'zɪmɪniz

Xingtai
BR ,ʃɪŋ'tʌɪ
AM 'ʃɪŋ'taɪ

Xining
BR ,ʃi:'nɪŋ
AM 'ʃɪ'nɪŋ

Xinjiang
BR ,ʃɪn'dʒ(ɪ)aŋ
AM 'ʃɪn'dʒæŋ

Xiphias
BR 'zɪfɪəs
AM 'zɪfiəs

xiphisterna
BR zɪfɪ'stə:nə(r)
AM ,zɪfə'stərnə

xiphisternum
BR ,zɪfɪ'stə:nəm, -z
AM ,zɪfə'stərnəm, -z

xiphoid
BR 'zɪfɔɪd
AM 'zaɪ,fɔɪd, 'zɪ,fɔɪd

Xizang
BR ,ʃi:'zaŋ
AM 'ʃɪ'zæŋ

Xmas
BR 'krɪsməs, 'ɛksməs,
-ɪz
AM 'krɪsməs, 'ɛksməs,
-əz

xoana
BR 'zəʊənə(r)
AM 'zoʊənə

xoanon
BR 'zəʊənɒn
AM 'zoʊə,nɑn

X-rated
BR ,ɛks'reɪtɪd
AM ,ɛks'reɪdɪd

X-ray
BR 'ɛksreɪ, -z, -ɪŋ, -d
AM 'ɛks,reɪ, -z, -ɪŋ, -d

Xuzhou
BR ,ʃu:'dʒəʊ
AM 'ʃu'dʒoʊ

xylem
BR 'zʌɪləm
AM 'zaɪləm

xylene
BR 'zʌɪli:n
AM 'zaɪ,lin

xylocarp
BR 'zʌɪlə(ʊ)kɑ:p, -s
AM 'zaɪlə,karp, -s

xylocarpous
BR ,zʌɪlə(ʊ)'kɑ:pəs
AM ,zaɪlə'karpəs

xylograph
BR 'zʌɪləgrɑ:f,
'zʌɪləgraf, -s
AM 'zaɪlə,græf, -s

xylographer
BR zʌɪ'lɒgrəfə(r), -z
AM zaɪ'lagrəfər, -z

xylography
BR zʌɪ'lɒgrəfi
AM ,zaɪ'lagrəfi

xylonite
BR 'zʌɪlənʌɪt
AM 'zaɪlə,naɪt

xylophagous
BR zʌɪ'lɒfəgəs
AM zaɪ'lafəgəs

xylophone
BR 'zʌɪləfəʊn, -z
AM 'zaɪlə,foʊn, -z

xylophonic
BR ,zʌɪlə'fɒnɪk
AM ,zaɪlə'fanɪk

xylophonist
BR zʌɪ'lɒfənɪst,
zʌɪ'lɒfnɪst,
'zʌɪləfəʊnɪst, -s
AM 'zaɪlə,foʊnəst, -s

xylose
BR 'zʌɪləʊz, 'zʌɪləʊs
AM 'zaɪ,loʊs, 'zaɪ,loʊz

xysti
BR 'zɪstʌɪ
AM 'zɪs,taɪ

xystus
BR 'zɪstəs
AM 'zɪstəs

Yy

y
BR wʌɪ, -z
AM waɪ, -z

yabber
BR 'jæblə(r), -əz,
-(ə)rɪŋ, -əd
AM 'jæbər, -z, -ɪŋ, -d

yabbie
BR 'jæb|i, -ɪz
AM 'jæbi, -z

yabby
BR 'jæb|i, -ɪz
AM 'jæbi, -z

yacht
BR jɒt, -s, -ɪŋ
AM jɑt, -s, -ɪŋ

yachtie
BR 'jɒt|i, -ɪz
AM 'jɑdi, -z

yachtsman
BR 'jɒtsmən
AM 'jɑtsmən

yachtsmen
BR 'jɒtsmən
AM 'jɑtsmən

yachtswoman
BR 'jɒts,wʊmən
AM 'jɑts,wʊmən

yachtswomen
BR 'jɒts,wɪmɪn
AM 'jɑts,wɪmɪn

yack
BR jak, -s, -ɪŋ, -t
AM jæk, -s, -ɪŋ, -t

yacka
BR 'jakə(r)
AM 'jækə

yacker
BR 'jakə(r)
AM 'jækər

yackety-yack
BR jakətɪ'jak
AM 'jækədi'jæk

yadda-yadda
BR 'jadəjadə
AM 'jɑdə'jɑdə

yaffle
BR 'jafl, -z
AM 'jæfəl, -z

Yafo
BR 'jɑːfəʊ
AM 'jɑfoʊ

YAG
BR jag
AM jæg

yager
BR 'jeɪgə(r), -z
AM 'jeɪgər, -z

Yagi antenna
BR 'jɑːgɪ ən,tɛnə(r), -z
AM 'jɑgi ən'tɛnə, -z

yah
BR jɑː(r)
AM jɑ

yahoo
BR jɑː'huː, jə'huː, -z
AM 'jɑ,hu, -z

Yahveh
BR 'jɑːveɪ
AM 'jɑ,veɪ

Yahvist
BR 'jɑːvɪst, -s
AM 'jɑvəst, -s

Yahweh
BR 'jɑːweɪ
AM 'jɑ,weɪ

Yahwist
BR 'jɑːwɪst, -s
AM 'jɑwəst, -s

yak
BR jak, -s
AM jæk, -s

Yakima
BR 'jakɪmə(r)
AM 'jækəmə

yakka
BR 'jakə(r)
AM 'jækə

yakker
BR 'jakə(r), -z
AM 'jækər, -z

Yakut
BR jɑ'kʊt, -s
AM jæ'kʊt, -s

Yakutia
BR jɑ'kʊtɪə(r)
AM jæ'kuʃə

Yakutsk
BR jə'kʊtsk, jɑ'kʊtsk,
jɑː'kʊtsk
AM jə'kʊ(t)sk,
jæ'kʊ(t)sk

yakuza
BR jɑː'kuːzə(r),
jə'kuːzə(r)
AM jɑ'kuzə

Yale
BR jeɪl
AM jeɪl

Yalta
BR 'jaltə(r), 'jʊltə(r),
'jɔːltə(r)
AM 'jɑltə

Yalu
BR 'jaluː
AM 'jɑ,lu

yam
BR jam, -z
AM jæm, -z

Yama
BR 'jɑːmə(r)
AM 'jɑmə

Yamaha
BR 'jamɑhɑː(r), -z
AM 'jɑmə,hɑ, -z

Yamamoto
BR jamə'məʊtəʊ
AM jɑmə'moʊdoʊ

yammer
BR 'jam|ə(r), -əz,
-(ə)rɪŋ, -əd
AM 'jæmər, -z, -ɪŋ, -d

Yamoussoukro
BR jamʊ'suːkrəʊ
AM jɑmə'su,kroʊ

Yancheng
BR ,jan'tʃɛŋ
AM ,jæn'tʃɛŋ

yandy
BR 'jand|i, -ɪz, -ɪŋ, -d
AM 'jændi, -z, -ɪŋ, -d

yang
BR jaŋ
AM jæŋ

Yangshao
BR ,jaŋ'ʃaʊ
AM 'jæŋk'ʃaʊ

Yangtse
BR 'jaŋ(k)tsi, 'jaŋsi
AM 'jaŋk'(t)si

Yangtze
BR 'jaŋ(k)tsi, 'jaŋsi
AM 'jaŋk'(t)si

yank
BR jaŋ|k, -ks, -kɪŋ, -(k)t
AM 'jæŋ|k, -ks, -kɪŋ,
-(k)t

Yankee
BR 'jaŋk|i, -ɪz
AM 'jæŋki, -z

Yankee Doodle
BR ,jaŋkɪ 'duːdl
AM 'jæŋki 'dudəl

Yanomami
BR ,janə'mɑːmi
AM ,janə'mami

Yantai
BR ,jan'tʌɪ
AM ,jæn'taɪ

yantra
BR 'jantrə(r), -z
AM 'jæntrə, -z

Yaoundé
BR jɑː'ʊndeɪ,
jaʊ'ʊndeɪ
AM ,jaʊn'deɪ

yap
BR jap, -s, -ɪŋ, -t
AM jæp, -s, -ɪŋ, -t

yapok
BR jə'pɒk, -s
AM jə'pɑk, -s

yapp
BR jap, -s
AM jæp, -s

yapper
BR 'japə(r), -z
AM 'jæpər, -z

yappy
BR 'jap|i, -ɪə(r), -ɪɪst
AM 'jæpi, -ər, -ɪst

yarborough
BR 'jɑːb(ə)rə(r), -z
AM 'jɑr,b(ə)rə, -z

yard
BR jɑːd, -z
AM jɑrd, -z

yardage
BR 'jɑːdɪdʒ
AM 'jɑrdɪdʒ

yardarm
BR 'jɑːdɑːm, -z
AM 'jɑrd,ɑrm, -z

yardbird
BR 'jɑːdbɜːd, -z
AM 'jɑrd,bɜrd, -z

Yardie
BR 'jɑːd|i, -ɪz
AM 'jɑrdi, -z

Yardley
BR 'jɑːdli
AM 'jɑrdli

yardline
BR 'jɑːdlʌɪn, -z
AM 'jɑrd,laɪn, -z

yardman
BR 'jɑːdman
BR 'jɑːdmən
AM 'jɑrd,mæn, -z

yardmaster
BR 'jɑːdmɑːstə(r),
'jɑːdmɑstə(r)
AM 'jɑrd,mæstər, -z

yardmen
BR 'jɑːdmɛn
AM 'jɑrd,mɛn

yardstick
BR 'jɑːdstɪk, -s
AM 'jɑrd,stɪk, -s

Yarm
BR 'jɑːm
AM 'jɑrm

Yarmouth
BR 'jɑːməθ
AM 'jɑrməθ

yarmulka
BR 'jɑːm(ʊ)lkə(r), -z
AM 'jɑməlkə, -z

yarmulke
BR 'jɑːm(ʊ)lkə(r), -z
AM 'jɑməlkə, -z

yarn
BR 'jɑːn, -z, -ɪŋ, -d
AM jɑrn, -z, -ɪŋ, -d

yarran
BR 'jarən, -z
AM 'jɛrən, -z

yarrow
BR 'jarəʊ, -z
AM 'jæroʊ, -z

Yarwood
BR 'jɑːwʊd
AM 'jɑr,wʊd

yashmak
BR 'jaʃmak, -s
AM jɑʃ'mɑk,
'jæʃ,mæk, -s

Yasmin
BR jazmɪn, 'jasmɪn
AM 'jæzmən

yataghan
BR 'jatəg(ə)n, -z

AM ˈjædəgən,
ˈjædəˌgæn, -z

Yates
BR jeɪts
AM jeɪts

yatter
BR ˈjatǀə(r), -əz, -(ə)rɪŋ,
-əd
AM ˈjædər, -z, -ɪŋ, -d

yaupon
BR ˈjɔːpɒn
AM ˈjɔˌpɒn, ˈjɑˌpɑn

yaw
BR jɔː(r), -z, -ɪŋ, -d
AM jɔ, jɑ, -z, -ɪŋ, -d

yawl
BR jɔːl, -z
AM jɔl, jɑl, -z

yawn
BR jɔːn, -z, -ɪŋ, -d
AM jɔn, jɑn, -z, -ɪŋ, -d

yawner
BR ˈjɔːnə(r), -z
AM ˈjɔnər, ˈjɑnər, -z

yawningly
BR ˈjɔːnɪŋli
AM ˈjɔnɪŋli, ˈjɑnɪŋli

yawp
BR jɔːp, -s, -ɪŋ, -t
AM jɔp, jɑp, -s, -ɪŋ, -t

yawper
BR ˈjɔːpə(r), -z
AM ˈjɔpər, ˈjɑpər, -z

yaws
BR jɔːz
AM jɔz, jɑz

y-axes
BR ˈwʌɪˌaksiːz
AM ˈwaɪˌæksiz

y-axis
BR ˈwʌɪˌaksɪs
AM ˈwaɪˌæksəs

Yayoi
BR ˈjɑːjɔɪ
AM ˈjɑˌjɔɪ

yclept
BR ɪˈklɛpt
AM ɪˈklɛpt

ye
BR jiː
AM ji

yea
BR jeɪ
AM jeɪ

Yeadon¹
placename, UK
BR ˈjiːdn
AM ˈjidən

Yeadon²
placename, USA
BR ˈjeɪdn
AM ˈjeɪdən

Yeadon³
surname
BR ˈjiːdn, ˈjɛdn, ˈjeɪdn
AM ˈjidən, ˈjeɪdən

Yeadon⁴
placename, US
BR ˈjeɪdn
AM ˈjeɪdən

yeah
BR jɛː(r), jɛ(r)
AM jɛ(ə), jæ(ə)

yean
BR jiːn, -z, -ɪŋ, -d
AM jin, -z, -ɪŋ, -d

yeanling
BR ˈjiːnlɪŋ, -z
AM ˈjinlɪŋ, -z

year
BR jɪə(r), jəː(r), -z
AM jɪ(ə)r, -z

yearbook
BR ˈjɪəbʊk, ˈjəːbʊk, -s
AM ˈjɪrˌbʊk, -s

yearling
BR ˈjɪəlɪŋ, ˈjəːlɪŋ, -z
AM ˈjɪrlɪŋ, -z

yearlong
BR ˌjɪəˈlɒŋ, ˌjəːˈlɒŋ
AM ˈjɪrˌlɔŋ, ˈjɪrˌlɑŋ

yearly
BR ˈjɪəli, ˈjəːli
AM ˈjɪrli

yearn
BR jəːn, -z, -ɪŋ, -d
AM jərn, -z, -ɪŋ, -d

yearner
BR ˈjəːnə(r), -z
AM ˈjərnər, -z

yearning
BR ˈjəːnɪŋ, -z
AM ˈjərnɪŋ, -z

yearningly
BR ˈjəːnɪŋli
AM ˈjərnɪŋli

yeast
BR jiːst
AM jist

yeastily
BR ˈjiːstɪli
AM ˈjistɪli

yeastiness
BR ˈjiːstɪnɪs
AM ˈjistɪnɪs

yeastless
BR ˈjiːstlɪs
AM ˈjis(t)lɪs

yeastlike
BR ˈjiːstlʌɪk
AM ˈjis(t)ˌlaɪk

yeasty
BR ˈjiːsti
AM ˈjisti

Yeates
BR jeɪts
AM jeɪts

Yeats
BR jeɪts

AM jeɪts

Yeatsian
BR ˈjeɪtsɪən
AM ˈjeɪtsiən

yecch
BR jɛk, jɛx
AM jək, jɛk

yech
BR jɛk, jɛx
AM jək, jɛk

yegg
BR jɛg, -z
AM jɛg, -z

Yehudi
BR jɪˈhuːdi, jɛˈhuːdi
AM jəˈhudi

Yekaterinburg
BR jɪˈkat(ə)rɪnbəːg
AM jəˈkætrənˌbərg
RUS jikətʲirʲinʲburk

yell
BR jɛl, -z, -ɪŋ, -d
AM jɛl, -z, -ɪŋ, -d

Yelland
BR ˈjɛlənd
AM ˈjɛlənd

yellow
BR ˈjɛləʊ, -z, -ɪŋ, -d,
-ə(r), -ɪst
AM ˈjɛlˌoʊ, -oʊz, -əwɪŋ,
-oʊd, -əwər, -əwəst

yellowback
BR ˈjɛlə(ʊ)bak, -s
AM ˈjɛloʊˌbæk, -s

yellow-bellied
BR ˌjɛlə(ʊ)ˈbɛlɪd
AM ˌjɛloʊˈbɛlid

yellow-belly
BR ˈjɛlə(ʊ)ˌbɛlǀi, -ɪz
AM ˈjɛloʊˌbɛli, -z

yellow-bill
BR ˈjɛlə(ʊ)bɪl
AM ˈjɛloʊˌbɪl

yellow fever
BR ˈjɛləʊ ˌfiːvə(r),
ˌjɛləʊ ˈfiːvə(r)
AM ˈjɛloʊ ˈfivər

yellowfin
BR ˈjɛlə(ʊ)fɪn, -z
AM ˈjɛloʊˌfɪn, -z

yellowhammer
BR ˈjɛlə(ʊ)ˌhamə(r), -z
AM ˈjɛloʊˌhæmər, -z

yellowish
BR ˈjɛləʊɪʃ
AM ˈjɛləwɪʃ

Yellowknife
BR ˈjɛlə(ʊ)nʌɪf
AM ˈjɛloʊˌnaɪf

yellowlegs
BR ˈjɛlə(ʊ)lɛgz
AM ˈjɛloʊˌlɛgz

yellowness
BR ˈjɛlə(ʊ)nəs
AM ˈjɛloʊnəs

Yellowstone
BR ˈjɛlə(ʊ)stəʊn

AM ˈjɛloʊˌstoʊn

yellowy
BR ˈjɛləʊi
AM ˈjɛləwi

yelp
BR jɛlp, -s, -ɪŋ, -t
AM jɛlp, -s, -ɪŋ, -t

yelper
BR ˈjɛlpə(r), -z
AM ˈjɛlpər, -z

Yeltsin
BR ˈjɛltsɪn
AM ˈjɛltsən

Yelverton
BR ˈjɛlvət(ə)n
AM ˈjɛlvərtən

Yemen
BR ˈjɛmən
AM ˈjɛmən

Yemeni
BR ˈjɛmənǀi, -ɪz
AM ˈjɛməni, -z

yen
BR jɛn, -z
AM jɛn, -z

Yen-cheng
BR ˌjɛnˈtʃɛŋ
AM ˌjɛnˈtʃɛŋ

Yenisey
BR ˌjɛnɪˈseɪ
AM ˌjɛniˈseɪ

yeoman
BR ˈjəʊmən
AM ˈjoʊmən

yeomanly
BR ˈjəʊmənli
AM ˈjoʊmənli

yeomanry
BR ˈjəʊmənri
AM ˈjoʊmənri

Yeomans
BR ˈjəʊmənz
AM ˈjoʊmənz

yeomen
BR ˈjəʊmən
AM ˈjoʊmən

Yeovil
BR ˈjəʊv(ɪ)l
AM ˈjoʊvəl

yep
BR jɛp
AM jɛp

yerba buena
BR jəːbə ˈbweɪnə(r)
AM jərbə ˈbweɪnə

yerba maté
BR ˌjəːbə ˈmateɪ,
+ ˈmɑːteɪ
AM jərbə ˈmɑˌteɪ

Yerevan
BR ˌjɛrəˈvan
AM ˌjɛrəˈvɑn

Yerkes
BR ˈjəːkɪz
AM ˈjərkiz

yes
BR jɛs
AM jɛs

yeshiva
BR jəˈʃiːvə(r), -z
AM jəˈʃivə, jəˈʃɪvə, -z

yesterday
BR ˈjɛstədeɪ, ˈjɛstədi, -eɪz\-ɪz
AM ˈjɛstərˌdeɪ, ˈjɛstərdi, -z

yestereve
BR ˈjɛstəriːv
AM ˈjɛstərˌiv

yestermorn
BR ˈjɛstəmɔːn
AM ˈjɛstərˌmɔ(ə)rn

yesternight
BR ˈjɛstənʌɪt
AM ˈjɛstərˌnaɪt

yesteryear
BR ˈjɛstəjɪə(r), ˈjɛstəjəː
AM ˈjɛstərˌjɪ(ə)r

yet
BR jɛt
AM jɛt

yeti
BR ˈjɛtˌi, -ɪz
AM ˈjɛdi, ˈjeɪdi, -z

Yevtushenko
BR ˌjɛvtəˈʃɛŋkəʊ
AM ˌjɛvtəˈʃɛŋˌkoʊ
RUS jiftuˈʃenkə

yew
BR juː, -z
AM ju, -z

Y-fronts®
BR ˈwʌɪfrʌnts
AM ˈwaɪˌfrʌn(t)s

Ygdrasil
BR ˈɪgdrəsɪl
AM ˈɪgdrəsəl

Yggdrasil
BR ˈɪgdrəsɪl
AM ˈɪgdrəsəl

yid
BR jɪd, -z
AM jɪd, -z

Yiddish
BR ˈjɪdɪʃ
AM ˈjɪdɪʃ

Yiddisher
BR ˈjɪdɪʃə(r), -z
AM ˈjɪdɪʃər, -z

Yiddishism
BR ˈjɪdɪʃɪz(ə)m, -z
AM ˈjɪdəˌʃɪzəm, -z

yield
BR jiːld, -z, -ɪŋ, -ɪd
AM jild, -z, -ɪŋ, -ɪd

yielder
BR ˈjiːldə(r), -z
AM ˈjildər, -z

yielding
BR ˈjiːldɪŋ
AM ˈjildɪŋ

yieldingly
BR ˈjiːldɪŋli
AM ˈjildɪŋli

yieldingness
BR ˈjiːldɪŋnɪs
AM ˈjildɪŋnɪs

yikes
BR jʌɪks
AM jaɪks

yin
BR jɪn
AM jɪn

Yinchuan
BR ˌjɪnˈtʃwaːn
AM ˌjɪnˈtʃwɑn

yip
BR jɪp, -s, -ɪŋ, -t
AM jɪp, -s, -ɪŋ, -t

yippee
BR jɪˈpiː
AM ˈjɪpi, jɪˈpi

ylang-ylang
BR ˌiːlaŋˈiːlaŋ, -z
AM ˌiːlɑŋˈilɑŋ, -z

YMCA
BR ˌwʌɪɛmsiːˈeɪ
AM ˌwaɪˌɛmˌsiˈeɪ

Ymir
BR ˈɪmɪə(r)
AM ˈiːˌmɪ(ə)r

Ynys
BR ˈʌnɪs
AM ˈɪnɪs

Ynys-ddu
BR ˌʌnɪsˈðiː, ˌʌnɪsˈdi:
AM ˌɪnɪsˈði

Ynysybwl
BR ˌʌnɪsəˈbʊl
AM ˌɪnɪsˈbʊl

yo
BR jəʊ
AM joʊ

yob
BR jɒb, -z
AM jɑb, -z

yobbish
BR ˈjɒbɪʃ
AM ˈjɑbɪʃ

yobbishly
BR ˈjɒbɪʃli
AM ˈjɑbɪʃli

yobbishness
BR ˈjɒbɪʃnɪs
AM ˈjɑbɪʃnɪs

yobbo
BR ˈjɒbəʊ, -z
AM ˈjɑboʊ, -z

yobo
BR ˈjɒbəʊ, -z
AM ˈjɑboʊ, -z

yod
BR jɒd, -z
AM jɑd, -z

yodel
BR ˈjəʊdl̩, -lz, -lɪŋ\-lɪŋ, -ld

BR ˈjəʊdl̩əl, -əlz, -(ə)lɪŋ, -əld

yodeler
BR ˈjəʊdlə(r), ˈjəʊdlə(r), -z
AM ˈjoʊdlər, ˈjoʊdlər, -z

yodeller
BR ˈjəʊdlə(r), ˈjəʊdlə(r), -z
AM ˈjoʊdlər, ˈjoʊdlər, -z

Yoder
BR ˈjəʊdə(r)
AM ˈjoʊdər

yoga
BR ˈjəʊgə(r)
AM ˈjoʊgə

yogh
BR jɒg, -z
AM joʊg, -z

yoghourt
BR ˈjɒgət, -s
AM ˈjoʊgərt, -s

yoghurt
BR ˈjɒgət, -s
AM ˈjoʊgərt, -s

yogi
BR ˈjəʊgˌi, -ɪz
AM ˈjoʊgi, -z

yogic
BR ˈjəʊgɪk
AM ˈjoʊgɪk

yogism
BR ˈjəʊgɪz(ə)m
AM ˈjoʊˌgɪzəm

yogurt
BR ˈjɒgət, -s
AM ˈjoʊgərt, -s

yo-heave-ho
BR ˌjəʊhiːvˈhəʊ
AM ˌjoʊˌhivˈhoʊ

yohimbe
BR jə(ʊ)ˈhɪmbeɪ
AM joʊˈhɪmbeɪ

yohimbine
BR jə(ʊ)ˈhɪmbiːn
AM joʊˈhɪmbin

yo-ho
BR jəʊˈhəʊ
AM joʊˈhoʊ

yo-ho-ho
BR ˌjəʊhəʊˈhəʊ
AM ˌjoʊˌhoʊˈhoʊ

yoicks
BR jɔɪks
AM jɔɪks

yoke
BR jəʊk, -s, -ɪŋ, -t
AM joʊk, -s, -ɪŋ, -t

yokel
BR ˈjəʊkl̩, -z
AM ˈjoʊkəl, -z

Yokohama
BR ˌjəʊkəˈhaːmə(r)
AM ˌjoʊkəˈhɑmə

yokozuna
BR ˌjəʊkəˈzuːnə(r)
AM ˌjoʊkəˈzunə

Yolanda
BR jə(ʊ)ˈlandə(r)
AM joʊˈlændə

yolk
BR jəʊk, -s, -t
AM joʊk, -s, -t

yolkless
BR ˈjəʊkləs
AM ˈjoʊkləs

yolky
BR ˈjəʊki
AM ˈjoʊki

Yom Kippur
BR jɒm kɪˈpʊə(r), + kɪˈpɔː(r), + ˈkɪpə(r)
AM jɒm ˈkɪpər, jɒm kɪˈpʊ(ə)r, jɑm ˈkɪpər, ˈjɑm kɪˈpʊ(ə)r

yomp
BR jɒmp, -(p)s, -pɪŋ, -(p)t
AM jɑmp, -ps, -pɪŋ, -(p)t

yon
BR jɒn
AM jɑn

yond
BR jɒnd
AM jɑnd

yonder
BR ˈjɒndə(r)
AM ˈjɑndər

Yonge
BR jʌŋ
AM jəŋ

yoni
BR ˈjəʊni
AM ˈjoʊni

Yonkers
BR ˈjɒŋkəz
AM ˈjɑŋkərz

yonks
BR jɒŋks
AM jɑŋks

yoof
youth
BR juːf
AM juf

yoo-hoo
BR ˈjuːhuː, juːˈhuː
AM ˈjuˌhu

yore
BR jɔː(r)
AM jɔ(ə)r

Yorick
BR ˈjɒrɪk
AM ˈjɔrək

york¹
BR jɔːk, -s, -ɪŋ, -t
AM jɔ(ə)rk, -s, -ɪŋ, -t

york²
BR jɔːk, -s, -ɪŋ, -t

AM jɔ(ə)rk, -s, -ɪŋ, -t

Yorke
BR jɔːk
AM jɔ(ə)rk

yorker
BR 'jɔːkə(r), -z
AM 'jɔrkər, -z

Yorkist
BR 'jɔːkɪst, -s
AM 'jɔrkəst, -s

Yorkshire
BR 'jɔːkʃ(ɪ)ə(r)
AM 'jɔrkʃɪ(ə)r

Yorkshireman
BR 'jɔːkʃəmən
AM 'jɔrkʃɪrmən

Yorkshiremen
BR 'jɔːkʃəmən
AM 'jɔrkʃɪrmən

Yorkshirewoman
BR 'jɔːkʃə,wʊmən
AM 'jɔrkʃɪr,wʊmən

Yorkshirewomen
BR 'jɔːkʃə,wɪmɪn
AM 'jɔrkʃɪr,wɪmɪn

Yorktown
BR 'jɔːktaʊn
AM 'jɔrk,taʊn

Yoruba
BR 'jɒrʊbə(r)
AM 'jɔrəbə

Yosemite
BR jə(ʊ)'sɛmɪti
AM joʊ'sɛmədi

you[1]
strong form
BR juː
AM ju

you[2]
weak form
BR jə
AM jə

you-all
BR ,juː'ɔːl, jɔːl
AM 'ju,ɔl, jɔl

you'd
BR juːd
AM jud

Youel
BR 'juː(ə)l
AM 'ju(ə)l

Youell
BR 'juːəl, juːl
AM 'ju(ə)l

Youens
BR 'juːɪnz
AM 'juənz

you-know-what
BR ,juːnəʊ'wɒt, -s
AM ,ju,noʊ'(h)wɑt, -s

you-know-who
BR ,juːnəʊ'huː
AM ,ju,noʊ'hu

you'll
BR juːl
AM jul

young
BR jʌŋ, -gə(r), -gɪst
AM jəŋ, -ər, -əst

Younger
BR 'jʌŋgə(r)
AM 'jəŋgər

Younghusband
BR 'jʌŋ,hʌzb(ə)nd
AM 'jəŋ,(h)əzbənd

youngish
BR 'jʌŋɪʃ
AM 'jəŋɪʃ

youngling
BR 'jʌŋlɪŋ, -z
AM 'jəŋlɪŋ, -z

youngster
BR 'jʌŋ(k)stə(r), -z
AM 'jəŋztər,
'jəŋ(k)stər, -z

Youngstown
BR 'jʌŋztaʊn
AM 'jəŋz,taʊn

younker
BR 'jʌŋkə(r), -z
AM 'jəŋkər, -z

your[1]
strong form
BR jɔː(r), jʊə(r)
AM jɔ(ə)r, jʊ(ə)r

your[2]
weak form
BR jə(r)
AM jər

you're
BR jʊə(r)
AM jʊ(ə)r, jɔ(ə)r, jər

yours
BR jɔːz, jʊəz
AM jɔ(ə)rz, jʊ(ə)rz, jərz

yourself
BR jɔː'sɛlf, jʊə'sɛlf, jə'sɛlf
AM jɔr'sɛlf, jʊr'sɛlf, jər'sɛlf

yourselves
BR jɔː'sɛlvz, jʊə'sɛlvz, jə'sɛlvz
AM jɔr'sɛlvz, jʊr'sɛlvz, jər'sɛlvz

youse
BR juːz
AM juz

youth
BR juː|θ, -ðz
AM ju|θ, -θs\-ðz

youthful
BR 'juːθf(ʊ)l
AM 'juθfəl

youthfully
BR 'juːθfəli, 'juːθfli
AM 'juθfəli

youthfulness
BR 'juːθf(ʊ)lnəs
AM 'juθfəlnəs

youth hostel
BR 'juːθ ,hɒst|l, -lz,

-lɪŋ\-əlɪŋ, -ld
AM 'juθ ,(h)ɑstl, -z, -ɪŋ, -d

youth hosteller
BR 'juːθ ,hɒstlə(r), + ,hɒstələ(r), -z
AM 'juθ ,(h)ɑs(t)lər, + ,(h)əstələr, -z

you've[1]
strong form
BR juːv
AM juv

you've[2]
weak form
BR jəv
AM jəv

yowl
BR jaʊl, -z, -ɪŋ, -d
AM jaʊl, -z, -ɪŋ, -d

yo-yo®
BR 'jəʊjəʊ, -z, -ɪŋ, -d
AM 'joʊjoʊ, -z, -ɪŋ, -d

Ypres
BR 'iː,pr(ər)
AM 'iprə

Ystalyfera
BR ,ʌstələ'vɛrə(r), ,ʌstlə'vɛrə(r)
AM ,ɪstələ'vɛrə
WE ,ʌstala'verə

Ystrad
BR 'ʌstrəd
AM 'ɪstrəd

Ystradgynlais
BR ,ʌstrə(d)'gʌnlʌɪs
AM ,ɪstrə'gɪn,laɪs

Ystwyth
BR 'ʌstwɪθ
AM 'ɪstwɪθ

ytterbium
BR ɪ'tɜːbɪəm
AM ɪ'tɜrbiəm

yttrium
BR 'ɪtrɪəm
AM 'ɪtriəm

yuan
BR juː'ɑːn, juː'an
AM 'ju'ɑn

Yucatán
BR jʊkə'taːn, jʊkə'tan
AM jukə'tæn, 'jukə'tɑn

yucca
BR 'jʌkə(r), -z
AM 'jəkə, -z

yuck
BR jʌk
AM jək

yuckiness
BR 'jʌkɪnɪs
AM 'jəkinɪs

yucky
BR 'jʌk|i, -ɪə(r), -ɪɪst
AM 'jəki, -ər, -ɪst

Yudkin
BR 'juːdkɪn

AM 'judkən

Yugo
BR 'juːgəʊ
AM 'ju,goʊ

Yugoslav
BR 'juːgə(ʊ)slaːv, -z
AM 'jugoʊ,slɑv, 'jugə,slɑv, -z

Yugoslavia
BR ,juːgə(ʊ)'slɑːvɪə(r)
AM ,jugoʊ'slɑviə, ,jugə'slɑviə

Yugoslavian
BR ,juːgə(ʊ)'slɑːvɪən, -z
AM ,jugoʊ'slɑviən, ,jugə'slɑviən, -z

Yuit
BR 'juːɪt, -s
AM 'juət, -s

yuk
BR jʌk
AM jək

yukkiness
BR 'jʌkɪnɪs
AM 'jəkinɪs

yukky
BR 'jʌk|i, -ɪə(r), -ɪɪst
AM 'jəki, -ər, -ɪst

Yukon
BR 'juːkɒn
AM 'ju,kɑn

yule
BR juːl
AM jul

yule log
BR 'juːl lɒg, -z
AM 'jul ,lɔg, 'jul ,lɑg, -z

Yuletide
BR 'juːltʌɪd
AM 'jul,taɪd

yum
BR jʌm
AM jəm

yummy
BR 'jʌm|i, -ɪə(r), -ɪɪst
AM 'jəmi, -ər, -ɪst

yum-yum
BR ,jʌm'jʌm
AM ,jəm'jəm

Yunnan
BR juː'nan
AM ju'næn

yup
BR jʌp, -s
AM jəp, -s

Yupik
BR 'juːpɪk
AM 'ju,pɪk

yuppie
BR 'jʌp|i, -ɪz
AM 'jəpi, -z

yuppiedom
BR 'jʌpɪdəm
AM 'jəpi,dəm

yuppification
BR ˌjʌpɪfɪˈkeɪʃn
AM ˌjəpəfəˈkeɪʃən

yuppify
BR ˈjʌpɪfʌɪ, -z, -ɪŋ, -d
AM ˈjəpəˌfaɪ, -z, -ɪŋ, -d

yuppy
BR ˈjʌp|i, -ɪz
AM ˈjəpi, -z

yurt
BR jəːt, -s
AM jərt, -s

Yves
BR iːv
AM iːv(z)

Yvette
BR ɪˈvɛt
AM ɪˈvɛt

Yvonne
BR ɪˈvɒn
AM ɪˈvɒn, ɪˈvɑn

YWCA
BR ˌwʌɪˌdʌbljuˌsiːˈeɪ
AM ˌwaɪˌdəbəljuˌsiˈeɪ

Zz

z
BR zɛd, -z
AM zi, -z

zabaglione
BR ˌzɑblˈjəʊni,
ˌzɑbælˈjəʊni
AM ˌzɑbəlˈjoʊni

Zacatecas
BR ˌzækəˈteɪkəs
AM ˌzɑkəˈteɪkəs

Zacchaeus
BR zəˈkiːəs
AM zəˈkijəs

Zachariah
BR ˌzækəˈrʌɪə(r)
AM zækəˈraɪə

Zachary
BR ˈzæk(ə)ri
AM ˈzæk(ə)ri

Zack
BR zæk
AM zæk

Zadok
BR ˈzeɪdɒk
AM ˈzeɪˌdɑk

zaffer
BR ˈzæfə(r)
AM ˈzæfər

zaffre
BR ˈzæfə(r)
AM ˈzæfər

zag
BR zæg, -z
AM zæg, -z

Zagazig
BR ˈzægəzɪg
AM ˈzægəˌzɪg

Zagreb
BR ˈzɑːgrɛb
AM ˈzɑˌgrɛb

zaibatsu
BR zʌɪˈbatsuː
AM zaɪˈbatsu

Zaïre
BR (ˌ)zʌɪˈɪə(r),
(ˌ)zɑːˈɪə(r)
AM zɑɪˈɪ(ə)r

Zaïrean
BR zʌɪˈɪərɪən,
zɑːˈɪərɪən, -z
AM zaɪˈɪrɪən, -z

Zairian
BR zʌɪˈɪərɪən,
zɑːˈɪərɪən, -z
AM zaɪˈɪrɪən, -z

zakat
BR zəˈkɑːt
AM zɑˈkɑt

Zakopane
BR ˌzækəˈpɑːni

Zambesi
BR zæmˈbiːzi
AM zæmˈbizi

Zambezi
BR zæmˈbiːzi
AM zæmˈbizi

Zambia
BR ˈzæmbɪə(r)
AM ˈzæmbɪə

Zambian
BR ˈzæmbɪən, -z
AM ˈzæmbɪən, -z

Zamboanga
BR ˌzæmbəʊˈæŋgə(r)
AM ˌzæmboʊˈæŋgə

Zamboni
BR zæmˈbəʊni
AM ˌzæmˈboʊni

zamindar
BR zəˈmiːndɑː(r), -z
AM ˈzæmənˌdɑr, -z

zander
BR ˈzændə(r), -z
AM ˈzændər, -z

Zandra
BR ˈzɑːndrə(r),
ˈzandrə(r)
AM ˈzændrə

Zane
BR zeɪn
AM zeɪn

zanily
BR ˈzeɪnɪli
AM ˈzeɪnɪli

zaniness
BR ˈzeɪnɪnɪs
AM ˈzeɪnɪnɪs

Zanskar
BR ˈzanskɑː(r)
AM ˈzænˌskar

Zanskari
BR zanˈskɑːr|i, -ɪz
AM zænˈskɑri,
zænˈskɛri, -z

Zante
BR ˈzanti
AM ˈzæn(t)i

ZANU
BR ˈzɑːnuː, ˈzanuː
AM ˈzæˌnu

Zanuck
BR ˈzanək
AM ˈzænək

zany
BR ˈzeɪn|i, -ɪə(r), -ɪɪst
AM ˈzeɪni, -ər, -ɪst

Zanzibar
BR ˈzanzɪbɑː(r),
ˌzanzɪˈbɑː(r)
AM ˈzænzəˌbar

Zanzibari
BR ˌzanzɪˈbɑːr|i, -ɪz
AM ˌzænzəˈbari, -z

Zaozhuang
BR ˌzaʊˈʒwaŋ
AM ˈzaʊˈʒwaŋ

zap
BR zap, -s, -ɪŋ, -t
AM zæp, -s, -ɪŋ, -t

Zapata
BR zəˈpɑːtə(r)
AM zəˈpɑdə

zapateado
BR ˌzɑːpətiˈɑːdəʊ,
zɑˌpætiˈɑːdəʊ, -z
AM ˌzɑpədiˈɑdoʊ, -z

Zapotec
BR ˈzapətɛk, ˈzɑːpətɛk, -s
AM ˈzɑpəˌtɛk, -s

Zappa
BR ˈzapə(r)
AM ˈzæpə

zappy
BR ˈzap|i, -ɪə(r), -ɪɪst
AM ˈzæpi, -ər, -ɪst

ZAPU
BR ˈzɑːpuː, ˈzapuː
AM ˈzæˌpu

Zaqaziq
BR ˈzakəzɪk
AM ˈzɑkəˌzɪk

Zara
BR ˈzɑːrə(r)
AM ˈzɑrə

Zaragoza
BR ˌzarəˈgɒsə(r)
AM ˌzarəˈgosə,
ˌzarəˈgasə
SP θaraˈɣoθa,
saraˈɣosa

Zarathustra
BR ˌzarəˈθuːstrə(r)
AM ˌzɛrəˈθustrə

Zarathustrian
BR ˌzarəˈθuːstrɪən, -z
AM ˌzɛrəˈθustrɪən, -z

zareba
BR zəˈriːbə(r), -z
AM zəˈribə, -z

Zaria
BR ˈzɑːrɪə(r)
AM ˈzɑrɪə

zariba
BR zəˈriːbə(r), -z
AM zəˈribə, -z

Zarqa
BR ˈzɑːkə(r)
AM ˈzɑrkə

zarzuela
BR zɑːˈzweɪlə(r), -z
AM zɑrˈzweɪlə, -z

zax
BR zaks, -ɪz
AM zæks, -əz

z-axes
BR ˈzɛdˌaksiːz
AM ˈziˌæksiz

z-axis
BR ˈzɛdˌaksɪs

Zaozhuang
AM ˈziˌæksɪs

zazen
BR zɑːˈzɛn
AM zɑˈzɛn

Z-bend
BR ˈzɛdbɛnd, -z
AM ˈziˌbɛnd, -z

zeal
BR ziːl
AM zil

Zealand
BR ˈziːlənd
AM ˈzilənd

zealot
BR ˈzɛlət, -s
AM ˈzɛlət, -s

zealotry
BR ˈzɛlətri
AM ˈzɛlətri

zealous
BR ˈzɛləs
AM ˈzɛləs

zealously
BR ˈzɛləsli
AM ˈzɛləsli

zealousness
BR ˈzɛləsnəs
AM ˈzɛləsnəs

zebec
BR ˈziːbɛk, -s
AM ˈziˌbɛk, -s

zebeck
BR ˈziːbɛk, -s
AM ˈziˌbɛk, -s

Zebedee
BR ˈzɛbɪdi
AM ˈzɛbəˌdi

zebra
BR ˈzɛbrə(r), ˈziːbrə(r), -z
AM ˈzibrə, -z

zebrine
BR ˈzɛbrʌɪn, ˈziːbrʌɪn
AM ˈziˌbraɪn, ˈzibrən

zebu
BR ˈziːb(j)uː, -z
AM ˈziˌb(j)u, -z

Zebulon
BR ˈzɛbjʊlən,
zeˈbjuːlən
AM ˈzɛbjələn,
ˈzɛbjəˌlan

Zech.
BR zɛk
AM zɛk

Zechariah
BR ˌzɛkəˈrʌɪə(r)
AM ˌzɛkəˈraɪə

zed
BR zɛd, -z
AM zɛd, -z

Zedekiah
BR ˌzɛdɪˈkʌɪə(r)
AM ˌzɛdəˈkaɪə

zedoary
BR ˈzɛdəʊər|i, -ɪz
AM ˈzɛdoʊˌər|i, -z

zee
BR ziː, -z
AM zi, -z

Zeebrugge
BR ˌzeɪˈbrʊɡə(r),
ˌziːˈbrʊɡə(r),
ˈzeɪˌbrʊɡə(r),
ˈziːˌbrʊɡə(r)
AM ˈziˌbrʊɡə
FL ˈzeːbrəxə

Zeeland
BR ˈziːlənd
AM ˈziːlənd
DU ˈzeːlɑnt

Zeffirelli
BR ˌzɛfɪˈrɛli
AM ˌzɛfəˈrɛli

zein
BR ˈziːɪn
AM ˈziɪn

Zeiss
BR zʌɪs
AM zaɪs

Zeitgeist
BR ˈzʌɪtɡʌɪst
AM ˈzaɪtˌɡaɪst

zek
BR zɛk, -s
AM zɛk, -s

Zelda
BR ˈzɛldə(r)
AM ˈzɛldə

Zelotes
BR zɪˈləʊtiːz, zɛˈləʊtiːz
AM zəˈloʊdiz

zemindar
BR zəˈmiːndɑː(r), -z
AM ˈzɛmənˌdɑr, -z

zemstvo
BR ˈzɛmstvəʊ, -z
AM ˈzɛmstvoʊ, -z
RUS ˈzʲemstvə

Zen
BR zɛn
AM zɛn

Zena
BR ˈziːnə(r)
AM ˈzinə

zenana
BR zɪˈnɑːnə(r), -z
AM zəˈnɑnə, -z

Zend
BR zɛnd, -z
AM zɛnd, -z

Zend-Avesta
BR ˌzɛndəˈvɛstə(r)
AM ˌzɛndəˈvɛstə

Zener diode
BR ˌziːnə ˈdʌɪəʊd,
ˌzenə +, -z
AM ˈzinər ˌdaɪoʊd, -z

Zenist
BR ˈzɛnɪst, -s
AM ˈzɛnɪst, -s

zenith
BR ˈzɛnɪθ, ˈziːnɪθ, -s
AM ˈzinɪθ, -s

zenithal
BR ˈzɛnɪθl, ˈziːnɪθl
AM ˈzinɪθəl

Zeno
BR ˈziːnəʊ
AM ˈzinoʊ

Zenobia
BR zɪˈnəʊbɪə(r)
AM zəˈnoʊbiə

zeolite
BR ˈziːəlʌɪt, -s
AM ˈziəˌlaɪt, -s

zeolitic
BR ˌziːəˈlɪtɪk
AM ˌziəˈlɪdɪk

Zephaniah
BR ˌzɛfəˈnʌɪə(r)
AM ˌzɛfəˈnaɪə

zephyr
BR ˈzɛfə(r), -z
AM ˈzɛfər, -z

Zephyrus
BR ˈzɛf(ɪ)rəs
AM ˈzɛf(ə)rəs

zeppelin
BR ˈzɛpəlɪn, ˈzɛpl̩ɪn, -z
AM ˈzɛp(ə)lən, -z

Zermatt
BR ˈzəːmat
AM ˈzərmɑt

zero
BR ˈzɪərəʊ, -z, -ɪŋ, -d
AM ˈzɪroʊ, ˈzɪroʊ, -z, -ɪŋ, -d

zeroth
BR ˈzɪərəʊθ
AM ˈzɪroʊθ, ˈzɪroʊθ

zest
BR zɛst
AM zɛst

zester
BR ˈzɛstə(r), -z
AM ˈzɛstər, -z

zestful
BR ˈzɛs(t)f(ʊ)l
AM ˈzɛs(t)fəl

zestfully
BR ˈzɛs(t)fʊli,
ˈzɛs(t)fli
AM ˈzɛs(t)fəli

zestfulness
BR ˈzɛs(t)f(ʊ)lnəs
AM ˈzɛs(t)fəlnəs

zestiness
BR ˈzɛstɪnɪs
AM ˈzɛstɪnɪs

zesty
BR ˈzɛst|i, -ɪə(r), -ɪɪst
AM ˈzɛsti, -ər, -ɪst

zeta
BR ˈziːtə(r)
AM ˈzeɪdə

zetetic
BR zɪˈtɛtɪk
AM zəˈtɛdɪk

Zetland
BR ˈzɛtlənd

AM ˈzɛtlənd

zeugma
BR ˈz(j)uːɡmə(r)
AM ˈzugmə

zeugmatic
BR z(j)uːɡˈmatɪk
AM zuɡˈmædɪk

Zeus
BR z(j)uːs
AM zus

Zeuxis
BR ˈz(j)uːksɪs
AM ˈz(j)uksəs

Zhang
BR dʒaŋ
AM dʒæŋ

Zhanjiang
BR ˌʒanˈdʒ(ɪ)aŋ
AM ˈʒænˈdʒæŋ

Zhdanov
BR ˈʒdɑːnɒv, ˈʒdanɒv
AM ˈʒdɑˌnɔv, ˈʒdɑˌnɑv

Zhengzhou
BR ˌʒɛŋˈʒəʊ
AM ˈʒɛŋˈʒu

Zhenjiang
BR ˌʒɛnˈdʒ(ɪ)aŋ
AM ˈʒɛnˈdʒ(i)æŋ

Zhivago
BR ʒɪˈvɑːɡəʊ
AM ˌʒɪˈvɑɡoʊ

zho
BR zəʊ, -z
AM zoʊ, -z

Zhongshan
BR ˌʒɒŋˈʃan
AM ˈʒɔŋˈʃæn, ˈʒɑŋˈʃæn

Zhou
BR dʒəʊ
AM dʒoʊ

Zhukov
BR ˈʒuːkɒv, ˈʒuːkɒf
AM ˈʒukɔv, ˈʒukɔf,
ˈʒukɑv, ˈʒukɑf

Zia
BR ˈzɪə(r)
AM ˈziə

zibet
BR ˈzɪbɪt, -s
AM ˈzɪbɪt, -s

zibeth
BR ˈzɪbɪθ, -s
AM ˈzɪbɪθ, -s

Ziegfeld
BR ˈziːɡfɛld
AM ˈziɡˌfɛld

Ziegler
BR ˈziːɡlə(r)
AM ˈziɡlər, ˈzɪɡlər

ziff
BR zɪf, -s
AM zɪf, -s

ziggurat
BR ˈzɪɡʊrat, -s
AM ˈzɪɡəˌræt, -s

zigzag
BR ˈzɪɡzaɡ, -z, -ɪŋ, -d

AM ˈzɪɡˌzæɡ, -z, -ɪŋ, -d

zilch
BR zɪltʃ
AM zɪltʃ

zillah
BR ˈzɪlə(r), -z
AM ˈzɪlə, -z

zillion
BR ˈzɪljən, -z
AM ˈzɪljən, -z

zillionth
BR ˈzɪljənθ, -s
AM ˈzɪljənθ, -s

Zimbabwe
BR zɪmˈbɑːbwi,
zɪmˈbabwi,
zɪmˈbɑːbweɪ,
zɪmˈbabweɪ
AM zɪmˈbɑbˌweɪ

Zimbabwean
BR zɪmˈbɑːbwɪən,
zɪmˈbabwɪən,
zɪmˈbɑːbweɪən,
zɪmˈbabweɪən, -z
AM zɪmˈbɑbˌweɪən, -z

zimmer
BR ˈzɪmə(r), -z
AM ˈzɪmər, -z

Zimmerman
BR ˈzɪməmən
AM ˈzɪmərmən

zinc
BR zɪŋk
AM zɪŋk

zinco
BR ˈzɪŋkəʊ, -z, -ɪŋ, -d
AM ˈzɪŋkoʊ, -z, -ɪŋ, -d

zincograph
BR ˈzɪŋkəɡrɑːf,
ˈzɪŋkəɡraf, -s
AM ˈzɪŋkəˌɡræf, -s

zincography
BR zɪŋˈkɒɡrəfi
AM zɪŋˈkɑɡrəfi

zincotype
BR ˈzɪŋkətʌɪp, -s
AM ˈzɪŋkəˌtaɪp, -s

zincy
BR ˈzɪŋki
AM ˈzɪŋki

zinfandel
BR ˈzɪnf(ə)ndɛl,
ˌzɪnf(ə)nˈdɛl, -z
AM ˈzɪnfənˌdɛl, -z

zing
BR zɪŋ
AM zɪŋ

zingari
BR ˈ(d)zɪŋɡəriː
AM ˈ(d)zɪŋ(ɡ)əri

zingaro
BR ˈ(d)zɪŋɡərəʊ
AM ˈ(d)zɪŋ(ɡ)əˌroʊ

zinger
BR ˈzɪŋə(r), -z
AM ˈzɪŋər, -z

zingy
BR 'zɪŋ|i, -iə(r), -ɪɪst
AM 'zɪŋi, -ɪr, -ɪst

Zinjanthropus
BR zɪn'dʒanθrəpəs
AM zɪn'dʒanθrəpəs

zinnia
BR 'zɪnɪə(r), -z
AM 'zɪnɪə, -z

Zion
BR 'zʌɪən
AM 'zaɪən

Zionism
BR 'zʌɪənɪz(ə)m
AM 'zaɪə,nɪzəm

Zionist
BR 'zʌɪənɪst, -s
AM 'zaɪənəst, -s

zip
BR zɪp, -s, -ɪŋ, -t
AM zɪp, -s, -ɪŋ, -t

zip-code
BR 'zɪpkəʊd, -z
AM 'zɪp,kʊʊd, -z

zip-fastener
BR ,zɪp'fɑ:sṇə(r),
,zɪp'fɑ:snə(r),
,zɪp'fasnə(r),
,zɪp'fasnə(r), -z
AM 'zɪp,fæsn̩ər, -z

zip-lock
BR 'zɪplɒk
AM 'zɪp,lak

zip-on
BR 'zɪpɒn, -z
AM 'zɪp,ɑn, -z

zipper
BR 'zɪpə(r), -z, -ɪŋ, -d
AM 'zɪpər, -z, -ɪŋ, -d

zippily
BR 'zɪpɪli
AM 'zɪpɪli

zippiness
BR 'zɪpɪnɪs
AM 'zɪpɪnɪs

zippy
BR 'zɪp|i, -iə(r), -ɪɪst
AM 'zɪpi, -ər, -ɪst

zip-up
BR 'zɪpʌp, -s
AM 'zɪpəp, -s

zircon
BR 'zə:kɒn
AM 'zər,kɑn

zirconia
BR zə:'kəʊnɪə(r)
AM zər'koʊnɪə

zirconium
BR zə:'kəʊnɪəm
AM zər'koʊnɪəm

zit
BR zɪt, -s
AM zɪt, -s

zither
BR 'zɪðə(r), -z
AM 'zɪðər, 'zɪθər, -z

zitherist
BR 'zɪð(ə)rɪst, -s
AM 'zɪðərəst, 'zɪθərəst, -s

zizz
BR zɪz
AM zɪz

złoty
BR 'zlɒt|i, -ɪz
AM 'zlɒdi, 'zlɑdi, -z
POL 'zwɒti

zodiac
BR 'zəʊdɪak
AM 'zoʊdi,æk, -s

zodiacal
BR zə(ʊ)'dʌɪəkl
AM zoʊ'daɪəkl

Zoë
BR 'zəʊi
AM 'zoʊi

zoetrope
BR 'zəʊɪtrəʊp
AM 'zoʊə,troʊp

Zoffany
BR 'zɒfəni, 'zɒfṇi
AM 'zɒfəni, 'zɑfəni

Zog
BR zɒg
AM zɑg

zoic
BR 'zəʊɪk
AM 'zoʊɪk

zoisite
BR 'zɔɪsʌɪt
AM 'zɔɪ,saɪt

Zola
BR 'zəʊlə(r)
AM 'zoʊlə, ,zoʊ'lɑ

zollverein
BR 'tsɒlfərʌɪn,
'zɒlfərʌɪn, -z
AM 'tsɔlfə,raɪn,
'zɔlfə,raɪn, -z

Zomba
BR 'zɒmbə(r)
AM 'zɑmbə

zombi
BR 'zɒmb|i, -ɪz
AM 'zɑmbi, -z

zombie
BR 'zɒmb|i, -ɪz
AM 'zɑmbi, -z

zonal
BR 'zəʊnl
AM 'zoʊnəl

zonally
BR 'zəʊnli
AM 'zoʊnəli

zonary
BR 'zəʊn(ə)ri
AM 'zoʊnəri

zonate
BR 'zəʊneɪt
AM 'zoʊ,neɪt

zonation
BR zəʊ'neɪʃn, -z
AM zoʊ'neɪʃən, -z

zonda
BR 'zɒndə(r), -z
AM 'zɑndə, 'zandə, -z

zone
BR zəʊn, -z, -ɪŋ, -d
AM zoʊn, -z, -ɪŋ, -d

zonk
BR zɒŋ|k, -ks, -kɪŋ, -(k)t
AM zɒŋ|k, zɑŋ|k, -ks, -kɪŋ, -(k)t

Zonta
BR 'zɒntə(r)
AM 'zɑn(t)ə

Zontian
BR 'zɒntɪən
AM 'zɑn(t)iən

zoo
BR zu:, -z
AM zu, -z

zoogeographic
BR ,zu:ə(ʊ),dʒi:ə'grafɪk,
,zəʊə(ʊ),dʒi:ə'grafɪk,
,zu:dʒɪə'grafɪk
AM ,zuə,dʒɪə'græfɪk,
'zoʊə,dʒɪə'græfɪk

zoogeographical
BR ,zu:ə(ʊ),dʒi:ə'grafɪkl,
,zəʊə(ʊ),dʒi:ə'grafɪkl
AM ,zuə,dʒɪə'græfəkəl,
'zoʊə,dʒɪə'græfəkəl

zoogeographically
BR ,zu:ə(ʊ),dʒi:ə'grafɪkli,
,zəʊə(ʊ),dʒi:ə'grafɪkli,
,zu:dʒɪə'grafɪkli
AM ,zuə,dʒɪə'græfək(ə)li,
'zoʊə,dʒɪə'græfək(ə)li

zoogeography
BR ,zu:ə(ʊ)dʒɪ'ɒgrəfi,
,zəʊə(ʊ)dʒɪ'ɒgrəfi,
,zu:dʒɪ'ɒgrəfi,
,zu:əʊ'dʒɒgrəfi,
,zəʊəʊ'dʒɒgrəfi,
,zu:'dʒɒgrəfi
AM ,zuə,dʒɪ'ɑgrəfi,
'zoʊə,dʒɪ'ɑgrəfi

zoography
BR zu:'ɒgrəfi,
zəʊ'ɒgrəfi
AM zu'ɑgrəfi,
zoʊ'ɑgrəfi

zooid
BR 'zu:ɔɪd, 'zəʊɔɪd,
'zu:ɪd, -z
AM 'zu,ɔɪd, 'zoʊ,ɔɪd, -z

zooidal
BR zu:'ɔɪdl, zəʊ'ɔɪdl,
'zu:ɪdl
AM ,zu'ɔɪdəl, ,zoʊ'ɔɪdəl

zookeeper
BR 'zu:,ki:pə(r), -z
AM 'zu,kipər, -z

zoolatry
BR zu:'ɒlətri,
zəʊ'ɒlətri

zoolatri
AM zu'ɑlətri,
zoʊ'ɑlətri

zoological
BR ,zu:ə'lɒdʒɪkl,
,zəʊə'lɒdʒɪkl
AM ,zuə'ladʒəkəl,
,zoʊə'ladʒəkəl

zoologically
BR ,zu:ə'lɒdʒɪkli,
,zəʊə'lɒdʒɪkli
AM ,zuə'ladʒək(ə)li,
,zoʊə'ladʒək(ə)li

zoologist
BR zu:'ɒlədʒɪst,
zəʊ'ɒlədʒɪst, -s
AM zu'ɑlədʒəst,
zoʊ'ɑlədʒəst, -s

zoology
BR zu:'ɒlədʒi,
zəʊ'ɒlədʒi
AM zu'ɑlədʒi,
zoʊ'ɑlədʒi

zoom
BR zu:m, -z, -ɪŋ, -d
AM zum, -z, -ɪŋ, -d

zoomancy
BR 'zu:ə,mansi,
'zəʊə,mansi
AM 'zuə,mænsi,
'zoʊə,mænsi

zoometry
BR zu:'ɒmɪtri,
zəʊ'ɒmɪtri
AM zu'ɑmətri,
zoʊ'ɑmətri

zoom lens
BR ,zu:m 'lenz, 'zu:m
lenz, -ɪz
AM 'zum 'lenz, -əz

zoomorphic
BR ,zu:ə(ʊ)'mɔ:fɪk,
,zəʊə(ʊ)'mɔ:fɪk,
zu:'mɔ:fɪk
AM ,zu(ə)'mɔrfɪk,
,zoʊ(ə)'mɔrfɪk

zoomorphism
BR ,zu:ə(ʊ)'mɔ:fɪz(ə)m,
,zəʊə(ʊ)'mɔ:fɪz(ə)m
AM ,zu(ə)'mɔr,fɪzəm,
,zoʊ(ə)'mɔr,fɪzəm

zoonoses
BR ,zu:ə'nəʊsi:z,
,zəʊə'nəʊsi:z,
zu:'nəʊsi:z
AM ,zu'noʊsiz,
zoʊ'noʊsiz

zoonosis
BR ,zu:ə'nəʊsɪs,
,zəʊə'nəʊsɪs,
zu:'nəʊsɪs
AM ,zu'noʊsəs,
zoʊ'noʊsəs

zoophyte
BR 'zu:əfʌɪt, 'zəʊəfʌɪt,
'zu:fʌɪt, -s
AM 'zu(ə),faɪt,
'zoʊ(ə),faɪt, -s

zoophytic
BR ˌzuːəˈfɪtɪk,
ˌzəʊəˈfɪtɪk, zuːˈfɪtɪk
AM ˌzuəˈfɪdɪk,
ˌzoʊəˈfɪdɪk

zooplankton
BR ˈzuːə(ʊ)ˌplaŋ(k)tən,
ˈzəʊə(ʊ)ˌplaŋ(k)tən,
ˈzuːˌplaŋ(k)tən
AM ˈzuəˌplæŋktən,
ˈzoʊəˌplæŋktən

zoospore
BR ˈzuːə(ʊ)spɔː(r),
ˈzəʊə(ʊ)spɔː(r),
ˈzuːˌspɔː(r), -z
AM ˈzuəˌspɔː(ə)r,
ˈzoʊəˌspɔː(ə)r, -z

zoosporic
BR ˌzuːə(ʊ)ˈspɔːrɪk,
ˌzəʊə(ʊ)ˈspɔːrɪk,
zuːˈspɔːrɪk
AM ˌzuəˈspɔrɪk,
ˌzoʊəˈspɔrɪk

zootomy
BR zuːˈɒtəmi,
zəʊˈɒtəmi
AM zuˈɑdəmi,
zoʊˈɑdəmi

zoot suit
BR ˈzuːt suːt, -s
AM ˈzut ˌsut, -s

Zora
BR ˈzɔːrə(r)
AM ˈzɔrə

Zorah
BR ˈzɔːrə(r)
AM ˈzɔrə

zorbing
BR ˈzɔːbɪŋ
AM ˈzɔrbɪŋ

zori
BR ˈzɔːr|i, ˈzɒr|i, -ɪz
AM ˈzɔri, -z

zoril
BR ˈzɒrɪl, -z
AM ˈzɔrəl, -z

zorilla
BR zɒˈrɪlə(r),
zəˈrɪlə(r), -z
AM zəˈrɪlə, -z

Zoroaster
BR ˌzɒrəʊˈastə(r),
ˈzɒrəʊastə(r)
AM ˌzɔroʊˈæstər

Zoroastrian
BR ˌzɒrəʊˈastrɪən, -z
AM ˌzɔroʊˈæstrɪən, -z

Zoroastrianism
BR ˌzɒrəʊˈastrɪənɪz(ə)m
AM ˌzɔroʊˈæstrɪəˌnɪzəm

zoster
BR ˈzɒstə(r)
AM ˈzɑstər

Zouave
BR zuːˈɑːv, ˈzuːɑːv,
zwɑːv, -z
AM ʒuˈɑv, ʒwɑv, -z

zouk
BR zuːk
AM zuk

zounds
BR zaʊndz, zuːndz
AM zaʊndz

Zsa Zsa
BR ˈʒɑː ˈʒɑː
AM ˈʒɑ ˌʒɑ

Z score
BR ˈzed skɔː(r), -z
AM ˈzi ˌskɔ(ə)r, -z

Zubes
BR z(j)uːbz
AM z(j)ubz

zucchetto
BR tsʊˈkɛtəʊ, zʊˈkɛtəʊ,
-z
AM (t)suˈkɛdoʊ,
zuˈkɛdoʊ, -z

zucchini
BR zʊˈkiːn|i, -ɪz
AM zuˈkini, -z

Zuckerman
BR ˈzʊkəmən
AM ˈzʌkərmən

zugzwang
BR ˈzuːgzwaŋ,
ˈzʌgzwaŋ,
ˈtsʊktsvɑːŋ, -z
AM ˈzəgˌzwæŋ,
ˈtsugˌtsvæŋ, -z

Zuider Zee
BR ˌzʌɪdə ˈziː
AM ˌzaɪdər ˈzi

Zuleika
BR zuːˈleɪkə(r),
zuːˈlʌɪkə(r),
zuːˈliːkə(r)
AM zuˈlaɪkə, zuˈlikə

Zulu
BR ˈzuːluː, -z
AM ˈzulu, -z

Zululand
BR ˈzuːluːland,
ˈzuːlʊland
AM ˈzuluˌlænd

Zürich
BR ˈz(j)ʊərɪk
AM ˈzurɪk
GER ˈtsyːrɪç

zwieback
BR ˈzwiːbak, ˈtsviːbak,
ˈtsviːbaːk, -s
AM ˈswiˌbæk, -s

Zwingli
BR ˈzwɪŋgli
AM ˈswɪŋli

Zwinglian
BR ˈzwɪŋglɪən, -z
AM ˈ(t)swɪŋlɪən, -z

zwitterion
BR ˈzwɪtərˌʌɪən,
ˈtsvɪtərˌʌɪən, -z
AM ˈ(t)swɪdərˌaɪən, -z

Zwolle
BR ˈzwɒlə(r)
AM ˈzwɒlə, ˈzwɑlə
DU ˈzvɒlə

Zworykin
BR ˈzwɔːrɪkɪn
AM ˈzwɔrəkən

zydeco
BR ˈzʌɪdɪkəʊ
AM ˈzaɪdəˌkoʊ

zygodactyl
BR ˌzʌɪɡə(ʊ)ˈdakt(ɪ)l,
ˌzɪɡə(ʊ)ˈdakt(ɪ)l, -z
AM ˌzaɪɡoʊˈdæktl, -z

zygodactylous
BR ˌzʌɪɡə(ʊ)ˈdaktɪləs,
ˌzɪɡə(ʊ)ˈdaktɪləs
AM ˌzaɪɡoʊˈdæktʃləs

zygoma
BR zʌɪˈɡəʊmə(r),
zɪˈɡəʊmə(r), -z
AM zaɪˈɡoʊmə, -z

zygomata
BR zʌɪˈɡəʊmətə(r),
zɪˈɡəʊmətə(r)
AM zaɪˈɡoʊmədə

zygomatic
BR ˌzʌɪɡə(ʊ)ˈmatɪk,
ˌzɪɡə(ʊ)ˈmatɪk
AM ˌzaɪɡəˈmædɪk

zygomorphic
BR ˌzʌɪɡə(ʊ)ˈmɔːfɪk,
ˌzɪɡə(ʊ)ˈmɔːfɪk
AM ˌzaɪɡəˈmɔrfɪk

zygomorphous
BR ˌzʌɪɡəˈmɔːfəs,
ˌzɪɡəˈmɔːfəs
AM ˌzaɪɡəˈmɔrfəs

zygosis
BR zʌɪˈɡəʊsɪs,
zɪˈɡəʊsɪs
AM zaɪˈɡoʊsəs

zygospore
BR ˈzʌɪɡə(ʊ)spɔː(r),
ˈzɪɡə(ʊ)spɔː(r), -z
AM ˈzaɪɡəˌspɔ(ə)r, -z

zygote
BR ˈzʌɪɡəʊt, -s
AM ˈzaɪˌɡoʊt, -s

zygotene
BR ˈzʌɪɡətiːn, ˈzɪɡətiːn
AM ˈzaɪɡəˌtin

zygotic
BR zʌɪˈɡɒtɪk
AM zaɪˈɡɑdɪk

zygotically
BR zʌɪˈɡɒtɪkli,
zɪˈɡɒtɪkli
AM zaɪˈɡɑdək(ə)li

zymase
BR ˈzʌɪmeɪs, ˈzʌɪmeɪz
AM ˈzaɪˌmeɪs, ˈzaɪˌmeɪz

zymological
BR ˌzʌɪməˈlɒdʒɪkl
AM ˌzaɪməˈlɑdʒəkəl

zymologist
BR zʌɪˈmɒlədʒɪst, -s
AM zaɪˈmɑlədʒəst, -s

zymology
BR zʌɪˈmɒlədʒi
AM zaɪˈmɑlədʒi

zymosis
BR zʌɪˈməʊsɪs
AM zaɪˈmoʊsəs

zymotic
BR zʌɪˈmɒtɪk
AM zaɪˈmɑdɪk

zymotically
BR zʌɪˈmɒtɪkli
AM zaɪˈmɑdək(ə)li

zymurgy
BR ˈzʌɪˌməːdʒi
AM ˈzaɪˌmərdʒi

zzz
BR zː
AM z